ABBREVIATIONS OF PERIODICALS INDEXED

Motor B—Motor Boating
Motor T—Motor Trend
Mus Q—Musical Quarterly

N Y Times Mag—New York Times Magazine
*Nat Geog—National Geographic Magazine
Nat Parks—National Parks Magazine
Nat R—National Review (44p issue only, pub. in alternate weeks)
Nat Wildlife—National Wildlife
Nation—Nation
Nations Bsns—Nation's Business
*Natur Hist—Natural History
Negro Hist Bul—Negro History Bulletin
New Repub—New Republic
New Yorker—New Yorker
*Newsweek—Newsweek

Opera N—Opera News
Org Gard & Farm—Organic Gardening & Farming
Outdoor Life—Outdoor Life

PTA Mag—PTA Magazine
Parents Mag—Parents' Magazine & Better Family Living
Parks & Rec—Parks & Recreation
Phys Today—Physics Today
Plays—Plays
Poetry—Poetry
Pop Electr—Popular Electronics
Pop Gard—Popular Gardening & Living Outdoors
    Incorporated in Field & Stream My '69
*Pop Mech—Popular Mechanics
Pop Phot—Popular Photography
Pop Sci—Popular Science Monthly
Pub W—Publishers' Weekly

R Pop Astron—Review of Popular Astronomy
Radio-Electr—Radio-Electronics
Ramp Mag—Ramparts Magazine
*Read Digest—Reader's Digest
Redbook—Redbook

Sat Eve Post—Saturday Evening Post
    Discontinued publication F 8 '69
*Sat R—Saturday Review

Sch & Soc—School and Society
Sch Arts—School Arts
Schol Teach—Scholastic Teacher
    Bound in Senior Scholastic
Schol Teach Sec Teach Sup—Scholastic Teacher Secondary Teachers' Supplement
School Library Journal. See Library Journal
*Sci Am—Scientific American
Sci & Cit—Scientist and Citizen
    Continued as Environment Ja '69
Sci Digest—Science Digest
Sci N—Science News
Science—Science
Sea Front—Sea Frontiers
*Seventeen—Seventeen
Sky & Tel—Sky and Telescope
Space World—Space World
*Sports Illus—Sports Illustrated
Sr Schol—Senior Scholastic (Teacher edition)
Suc Farm—Successful Farming (Midwest edition)
Sunset—Sunset (Central edition)

Time—Time
Todays Ed—Today's Education
*Todays Health—Today's Health
Trans-Action—Trans-Action
Travel—Travel
Travel & Camera—Travel & Camera
    Formerly U.S. Camera & Travel

UN Mo Chron—UN Monthly Chronicle
UNESCO Courier—UNESCO Courier
U S Camera—U.S. Camera & Travel
    Continued as Travel & Camera F '69
U S News—U.S. News & World Report

Vital Speeches—Vital Speeches of the Day
Vogue—Vogue

Weatherwise—Weatherwise
Wilson Lib Bul—Wilson Library Bulletin
*Writer—Writer
Writers Digest—Writer's Digest

Yachting—Yachting
Yale R—Yale Review

* Available for blind and other physically handicapped readers on talking books, in braille, or on magnetic tape. For information address Division for the Blind and Physically Handicapped, Library of Congress, Washington, D.C. 20542

KEY TO ABBREVIATIONS

+	continued on later pages of same issue		jr	junior
			jt auth	joint author
abp	archbishop			
abr	abridged		ltd	limited
Ag	August			
Ap	April		m	monthly
arch	architect		Mr	March
assn	association		My	May
Aut	Autumn			
av	avenue		N	November
			no	number
bart	baronet			
bibliog	bibliography		O	October
bibliog f	bibliographical footnotes			
			por	portrait
bi-m	bimonthly		pseud	pseudonym
bi-w	biweekly		pt	part
bldg	building		pub	published, publisher, publishing
bp	bishop			
			q	quarterly
co	company			
comp	compiled, compiler		rev	revised
cond	condensed			
cont	continued		S	September
corp	corporation		semi-m	semimonthly
			soc	society
D	December		Spr	Spring
dept	department		sq	square
			sr	senior
ed	edited, edition, editor		st	street
			Sum	Summer
F	February		sup	supplement
			supt	superintendent
Hon	Honorable			
			tr	translated, translation, translator
il	illustrated, illustration, illustrator			
inc	incorporated		v	volume
introd	introduction, introductory			
			w	weekly
Ja	January		Wint	Winter
Je	June			
Jl	July		yr	year

Sample entry: CAMPING
Cast loose all cares. E. S. Gardner. il Motor B 123:267+ Ja '69

Explanation: An illustrated article on the subject CAMPING entitled "Cast loose all cares," by E. S. Gardner, will be found in volume 123 of Motor Boating, page 267 (continued on later pages of the same issue) the January 1969 number

Readers' Guide to
Periodical Literature

MARCH 1969 — FEBRUARY 1970

READERS' GUIDE TO
PERIODICAL LITERATURE

Cumulated Volumes

READERS' GUIDE TO PERIODICAL LITERATURE

An Author and Subject Index

MARCH 1969 — FEBRUARY 1970

Edited by
ZADA LIMERICK

Assistant Editor
LINDA LACK HOY

Indexers
ANN F. DIETZ
ANNE W. FURNESS
LOVISA J. JENKINS
MURIEL M. PHILLIPS
BERTA PISCIOTTANO

REFERENCE ROOM

qAI
3
R2
69/70

A26972

THE H. W. WILSON COMPANY
NEW YORK   1970

ST. PAUL PUBLIC LIBRARY

PRINTED IN THE UNITED STATES OF AMERICA

International Standard Book Number 0-8242-0428-x

Library of Congress Catalog Card No. (6-8232)

ST. PAUL PUBLIC LIBRARY

ACKNOWLEDGMENTS

In addition to the staff members whose names appear on the title page we wish to acknowledge the contributions of Lois B. Levine and Virginia Turrell who indexed for this volume.

Z. L.

ABBREVIATIONS OF PERIODICALS INDEXED

March 1969 — February 1970

FOR FULL INFORMATION, CONSULT PAGES IX-XII

ALA Bul—ALA Bulletin
Aging—Aging
Am Artist—American Artist
Am City—American City
Am Ed—American Education
Am For—American Forests
*Am Heritage—American Heritage
Am Hist R—American Historical Review
Am Home—American Home
Am Imago—American Imago
Am Rec G—American Record Guide
Am Scholar—American Scholar
Am West—American West
America—America
Américas—Américas
Ann Am Acad—Annals of the American Academy of Political and Social Science
Antiques—Antiques
Arch Forum—Architectural Forum
Arch Rec—Architectural Record
Art in Am—Art in America
Art N—Art News
*Atlan—Atlantic
Audubon—Audubon
Aviation W—Aviation Week & Space Technology

Bet Hom & Gard—Better Homes and Gardens
Bsns W—Business Week
Bul Atom Sci—Bulletin of the Atomic Scientists

Camp Mag—Camping Magazine
Cath World—Catholic World
Ceram Mo—Ceramics Monthly
*Changing T—Changing Times
Chem—Chemistry
Chr Cent—Christian Century
Chr Today—Christianity Today
Clear House—Clearing House
Commentary—Commentary
Commonweal—Commonweal
Cong Digest—Congressional Digest
Cons—Conservationist (Albany)
*Consumer Bul—Consumer Bulletin
*Consumer Rep—Consumer Reports
Craft Horiz—Craft Horizons
Cur—Current
Cur Hist—Current History

Dance Mag—Dance Magazine
Dept State Bul—Department of State Bulletin
Design—Design
Duns R—Dun's Review

*Ebony—Ebony
Ed Digest—Education Digest
Electr World—Electronics World
Engl J—English Journal
Environ—Environment
     Formerly Scientist and Citizen
Esquire—Esquire

*Farm J—Farm Journal (Central edition)
Field & S—Field & Stream
     Incorporating Popular Gardening and Living Outdoors My '69
Film Q—Film Quarterly
Flying—Flying
Focus—Focus
*For Affairs—Foreign Affairs
Forbes—Forbes
Fortune—Fortune

*Good H—Good Housekeeping

* Har Yrs—Harvest Years
Harp Baz—Harper's Bazaar
*Harper—Harper's Magazine
Harvard Bsns R—Harvard Business Review
*Hi Fi—High Fidelity incorporating Musical America
Hobbies—Hobbies
*Holiday—Holiday
Home Gard—Home Garden & Flower Grower
*Horizon—Horizon
Horn Bk—Horn Book Magazine
Horticulture—Horticulture
Hot Rod—Hot Rod
House & Gard—House & Garden incorporating Living for Young Homemakers
House B—House Beautiful

Int Concil—International Conciliation

*Ladies Home J—Ladies' Home Journal
Library J—Library Journal
     Includes School Library Journal
Life—Life
Liv Wildn—Living Wilderness
*Look—Look

McCalls—McCall's
Mech Illus—Mechanix Illustrated
Ment Hy—Mental Hygiene
Mlle—Mademoiselle
Mo Labor R—Monthly Labor Review
Mod Phot—Modern Photography

Motor B—Motor Boating
Motor T—Motor Trend
Mus Q—Musical Quarterly

N Y Times Mag—New York Times Magazine
*Nat Geog—National Geographic Magazine
Nat Parks—National Parks Magazine
Nat R—National Review (44p issue only, pub. in alternate weeks)
Nat Wildlife—National Wildlife
Nation—Nation
Nations Bsns—Nation's Business
*Natur Hist—Natural History
Negro Hist Bul—Negro History Bulletin
New Repub—New Republic
New Yorker—New Yorker
*Newsweek—Newsweek

Opera N—Opera News
Org Gard & Farm—Organic Gardening & Farming
Outdoor Life—Outdoor Life

PTA Mag—PTA Magazine
Parents Mag—Parents' Magazine & Better Family Living
Parks & Rec—Parks & Recreation
Phys Today—Physics Today
Plays—Plays
Poetry—Poetry
Pop Electr—Popular Electronics
Pop Gard—Popular Gardening & Living Outdoor
　　　Incorporated in Field & Stream My '69
*Pop Mech—Popular Mechanics
Pop Phot—Popular Photography
Pop Sci—Popular Science Monthly
Pub W—Publishers' Weekly

R Pop Astron—Review of Popular Astronomy
Radio-Electr—Radio-Electronics
Ramp Mag—Ramparts Magazine
*Read Digest—Reader's Digest
Redbook—Redbook

Sat Eve Post—Saturday Evening Post
　　　Discontinued publication F 8 '69
*Sat R—Saturday Review

Sch & Soc—School and Society
Sch Arts—School Arts
Schol Teach—Scholastic Teacher
　　　Bound in Senior Scholastic
Schol Teach Sec Teach Sup—Scholastic Teacher Secondary Teachers' Supplement
School Library Journal. See Library Journal
*Sci Am—Scientific American
Sci & Cit—Scientist and Citizen
　　　Continued as Environment Ja '69
Sci Digest—Science Digest
Sci N—Science News
Science—Science
Sea Front—Sea Frontiers
*Seventeen—Seventeen
Sky & Tel—Sky and Telescope
Space World—Space World
*Sports Illus—Sports Illustrated
Sr Schol—Senior Scholastic (Teacher edition)
Suc Farm—Successful Farming (Midwest edition)
Sunset—Sunset (Central edition)

Time—Time
Todays Ed—Today's Education
*Todays Health—Today's Health
Trans-Action—Trans-Action
Travel—Travel
Travel & Camera—Travel & Camera
　　　Formerly U.S. Camera & Travel

UN Mo Chron—UN Monthly Chronicle
UNESCO Courier—UNESCO Courier
U S Camera—U.S. Camera & Travel
　　　Continued as Travel & Camera F '69
U S News—U.S. News & World Report

Vital Speeches—Vital Speeches of the Day
Vogue—Vogue

Weatherwise—Weatherwise
Wilson Lib Bul—Wilson Library Bulletin
*Writer—Writer
Writers Digest—Writer's Digest

Yachting—Yachting
Yale R—Yale Review

* Available for blind and other physically handicapped readers on talking books, in braille, or on magnetic tape. For information address Division for the Blind and Physically Handicapped, Library of Congress, Washington, D.C. 20542

LIST OF PERIODICALS INDEXED

All data as of latest issue received

ALA Bulletin—available only to members. m (bi-m Jl-Ag) American Library Association, 50 E Huron St, Chicago 60611

Aging—$2. m Aging, Superintendent of Documents, U.S. Government Printing Office, Washington, D.C. 20402

America—$10. w (bi-w Jl, Ag and year-end issue) America Press, 106 W 56th St, New York 10019

The American Academy of Political and Social Science Annals—$12. free to members. bi-m American Academy of Political and Social Science, 3937 Chestnut St, Philadelphia 19104

American Artist—$10. m (Ag-Je) American Artist, 2160 Patterson St, Cincinnati, Ohio 45214

The American City—$10. m Berkshire Common, Pittsfield, Mass. 01201

American Education—$7. m (bi-m Je, Ag) American Education, Superintendent of Documents, U.S. Government Printing Office, Washington, D.C. 20402

American Forests—$6. m American Forestry Association, 919 17th St, NW, Washington, D.C. 20006

*American Heritage—$20. bi-m American Heritage, 383 W Center St, Marion, Ohio 43302

The American Historical Review—$20. free to members of the American Historical Association, 5 times a yr (O, D, F, Ap, Je) American Historical Association, 400 A St, SE, Washington, D.C. 20003

The American Home—$4. m (bi-m Ja,Jl) The American Home, Flushing, New York 11357

American Imago—$10. q Wayne State Univ. Press, 5980 Cass Av, Detroit, Mich. 48202

The American Record Guide—$4.50. m American Record Guide, P.O. Box 319, Radio City Station, New York 10019

The American Scholar—$5. q United Chapters of Phi Beta Kappa, 1811 Q St, NW, Washington, D.C. 20009

The American West—$9. bi-m American West Pub. Co, 577 College Av, Palo Alto, Calif. 94306

Américas—$5. m Pan American Union, Washington, D.C. 20006

Antiques—$14. m Straight Enterprises, Inc, 551 5th Av, New York 10017

The Architectural Forum—$12. m (bi-m Ja, Jl) The Architectural Forum, 111 W 57th St, New York 10019

Architectural Record—$6.60. m (semi-m My) Architectural Record, P.O. Box 430, Hightstown, N.J. 08520

Art in America—$15. bi-m Art in America, 115 Tenth St, Des Moines, Ia. 50301

Art News—$13. m (S-Je) Art News, 444 Madison Av, New York 10022

*The Atlantic—$9.50. m Atlantic, 125 Garden St, Marion, Ohio 43302

Audubon—$8.50. bi-m National Audubon Society, 1130 5th Av, New York 10028

Aviation Week & Space Technology—$15. w Aviation Week, P.O. Box 430, Hightstown, N.J. 08520

Better Homes and Gardens—$4. m Better Homes and Gardens, 1716 Locust St, Des Moines, Ia. 50303

Bulletin of the Atomic Scientists—$8.50. m (S-Je) Bulletin of the Atomic Scientists, 935 E 60th St, Chicago 60637

Business Week—$10. w Business Week, P.O. Box 430, Hightstown, N.J. 08520

Camping Magazine—$7.50. free to members of the American Camping Association, m (Ja-Je, bi-m S-D) Camping Magazine, 5 Mountain Av, N Plainfield, N.J. 07060

The Catholic World—$8. m Catholic World, 404 Sette Drive, Paramus, N.J. 07652

Ceramics Monthly—$6. m (S-Je) Ceramics Monthly, P.O. Box 4548, Columbus, Ohio 43212

*Changing Times—$6. m Changing Times, The Kiplinger Magazine, Editors Park, Md. 20782

Chemistry—$4. m (bi-m Jl-Ag) American Chemical Society, 1155 16th St, NW, Washington, D.C. 20036

The Christian Century—$8.50. w Christian Century Foundation, 407 S Dearborn St, Chicago 60605

Christianity Today—$6. fortn. Christianity Today, 1014 Washington Building, Washington, D.C. 20005

The Clearing House—$5. m (S-My) The Clearing House, 205 Lexington Av, Sweet Springs, Missouri 65351

Commentary—$10. m American Jewish Committee, 165 E 56th St, New York 10022

Commonweal—$12. w (bi-w year-end issue, mid-Jl-mid-S) Commonweal Pub. Co, Inc, 232 Madison Av, New York 10016

Congressional Digest—$12.50. m (bi-m Je, Ag) Congressional Digest Corp, 3231 P St, NW, Washington, D.C. 20007

Conservationist (Albany)—$2. bi-m New York State Conservation Department, State Campus, Albany, N.Y. 12226

*Consumer Bulletin—$8. m Consumers' Research, Inc, Washington, N.J. 07882

*Consumer Reports—$6. m Consumers Union of U.S, Inc, 256 Washington St, Mount Vernon, N.Y. 10550

Craft Horizons—$10. bi-m American Craftsmen's Council, 44 W 53d St, New York 10019

Current—$10. m (except Jl) Current, Plainfield, Vermont 05667

Current History—$8.50. m Current History, Inc, 1822 Ludlow St, Philadelphia 19103

Dance Magazine—$9. m Dance Magazine, 268 W 47th St, New York 10036

The Department of State Bulletin—$16. w Department of State Bulletin, Superintendent of Documents, U.S. Government Printing Office, Washington, D.C. 20402

Design—$4.50. bi-m (S-Je) Design Magazine, 1100 Waterway Blvd, Indianapolis, Ind. 46202

Dun's Review—$7. m Dun & Bradstreet Pub. Corp, P.O. Box 3088, Grand Central Station, New York 10017

*Ebony—$6. m Johnson Pub. Co, Inc, 1820 S Michigan Av, Chicago 60616

The Education Digest—$6. m (S-My) Prakken Publications, Inc, 416 Longshore Drive, Ann Arbor, Michigan 48107

Electronics World—$7. m Electronics World, Portland Pl, Boulder, Colo. 80301

English Journal—$10. m (S-My) National Council of Teachers of English, 508 S Sixth St, Champaign, Illinois 61820

Environment—$8.50. 10 issues a yr Environment, 438 N Skinker Blvd, St Louis, Missouri 63130

Esquire—$7.50. m Esquire, Portland Pl, Boulder, Colo. 80301

*Farm Journal (Central edition)—$2. m Farm Journal, Inc, 230 W Washington Sq, Philadelphia 19105

Field & Stream—$5. m Holt, Rinehart and Winston, Inc, 383 Madison Av, New York 10017
 Incorporating Popular Gardening & Living Outdoors My '69

Film Quarterly—$4. q University of California Press, Berkeley, Calif. 94720

Flying—$7. m Flying, Portland Pl, Boulder, Colo. 80301

Focus—$3. m (S-Je) American Geographical Society, Broadway at 156th St, New York 10032

Forbes—$9.50. semi-m Forbes, 60 Fifth Av, New York 10011

*Foreign Affairs—$8. q Council on Foreign Relations, Inc, 58 E 68th St, New York 10021

Fortune—$14. m (semi-m My, Ag) Fortune, 541 N Fairbanks Court, Chicago 60611

*Good Housekeeping—$5. m Good Housekeeping, Box 517, New York 10019

Harper's Bazaar—$7. m Harper's Bazaar, P.O. Box 552, New York 10019

*Harper's Magazine—$8.50. m Harper's Magazine, 381 W Center St, Marion, Ohio 43302

Harvard Business Review—$12. bi-m Harvard Business Review, 108 10th Av, Des Moines, Ia. 50305

*Harvest Years—$5. m Harvest Years, 104 E 40th St, New York 10016

*High Fidelity incorporating Musical America—$12. m High Fidelity, 2160 Patterson St, Cincinnati, Ohio 45214

Hobbies—$5. m Lightner Pub. Corp, 1006 S Michigan Av, Chicago 60605

*Holiday—$7. m Holiday, 1255 Portland Pl, Boulder, Colo. 80302

Home Garden & Flower Grower—$7. m Home Garden, Portland Pl, Boulder, Colo. 80302

*Horizon—$20. q Horizon, 379 W Center St, Marion, Ohio 43302

The Horn Book Magazine—$6. bi-m Horn Book, Inc, 585 Boylston St, Boston 02116

Horticulture—$6. m Horticulture, 300 Massachusetts Av, Boston 02115

Hot Rod—$5. m Petersen Pub. Co, 8490 Sunset Blvd, Los Angeles 90069

House & Garden incorporating Living for Young Homemakers—$7. m House & Garden, Box 2202, Boulder, Colo. 80302

House Beautiful—$7. m House Beautiful, P.O. Box 560, New York 10019

International Conciliation—$2.75. 5 times a yr (S, N, Ja, Mr, My) Carnegie Endowment for International Peace, 345 E 46th St, New York 10017

*Ladies Home Journal—$4. m Ladies' Home Journal, Flushing, New York 11357

Library Journal—$12. semi-m (m Jl-Ag) R. R. Bowker Co, 1180 Avenue of the Americas, New York 10036

Life—$10. w (except one issue at the beginning and one issue at the year end) Life, 541 N Fairbanks Court, Chicago 60611

The Living Wilderness—$7.50. q The Wilderness Society, 729 15th St, NW, Washington, D.C. 20005

*Look—$5. bi-w Look, Box 857, Des Moines, Ia. 50304

McCall's—$3.95. m McCall's, McCall St, Dayton, Ohio 45401

Mademoiselle—$6. m Mademoiselle, P.O. Box 2204, Boulder, Colo. 80302

Mechanix Illustrated—$4. m Fawcett Publications, Inc, Fawcett Pl, Greenwich, Conn. 06830

Mental Hygiene—$10. q National Association for Mental Health, 10 Columbus Circle, New York 10019

Modern Photography—$7. m Modern Photography, 2160 Patterson St, Cincinnati, Ohio 45214

Monthly Labor Review—$9. m Superintendent of Documents, U.S. Government Printing Office, Washington, D.C. 20402

Motor Boating—$7. m Motor Boating, P.O. Box 544, New York 10019

Motor Trend—$5. m Petersen Pub. Co, 8490 Sunset Blvd, Los Angeles 90069

The Musical Quarterly—$9. q G. Schirmer, Inc, 609 Fifth Av, New York 10017

The Nation—$10. w (bi-w Jl, first bi-w period in Ag, last bi-w period in D) Nation Associates, Inc, 333 6th Av, New York 10014

*National Geographic Magazine—$9. m The Secretary, National Geographic Society, Washington, D.C. 20036

National Parks Magazine—$8. m National Parks Association, 1701 18th St, NW, Washington, D.C. 20009

National Review—$12. bi-w (44p issue) National Review, 150 E 35th St, New York 10016

National Wildlife—$5. bi-m National Wildlife Federation, 1412 16th St, Washington, D.C. 20036

Nation's Business—$26.75. (3 yrs) m Chamber of Commerce of the U.S, 1615 H St, NW, Washington, D.C. 20006

*Natural History—$7. m (bi-m Je-S) American Museum of Natural History, Central Park W at 79th St, New York 10024

The Negro History Bulletin—$3.50. m (O-My) Association for the Study of Negro Life and History, Inc, 1538 9th St, NW, Washington, D.C. 20001

The New Republic—$12. w (48 issues a yr) New Republic, 381 W Center St, Marion, Ohio 43302

The New York Times Magazine—$39. w (complete Sunday ed; not sold separately) New York Times, Times Bldg, 229 W 43d St, New York 10036

The New Yorker—$10. w New Yorker Magazine, Inc, 25 W 43d St, New York 10036

*Newsweek—$12. w Newsweek, 117 E 3d St, Dayton, Ohio 45402

Opera News—$8. w (27 issues S 6-Je 13) The Metropolitan Opera Guild, Inc, 1865 Broadway, New York 10023

Organic Gardening and Farming—$5.85. m Rodale Press, Inc, 33 E Minor St, Emmaus, Pa. 18049

Outdoor Life—$5. m Outdoor Life, Boulder, Colo. 80302

The PTA Magazine—$2.50. m (S-Je) The PTA Magazine, 700 N Rush St, Chicago 60611

Parents' Magazine & Better Family Living—$5. m Parents' Magazine, Bergenfield, N.J. 07621

Parks & Recreation—$7.50. m National Recreation and Park Association, 1700 Pennsylvania Av, NW, Washington, D.C. 20006

Physics Today—$7. m American Institute of Physics, Inc, 335 E 45th St, New York 10017

Plays—$8. m (O-My) Plays, Inc, 8 Arlington St, Boston 02116

Poetry—$12. m (bi-m Ap-My) Modern Poetry Association, 1018 N State St, Chicago 60610

Popular Electronics—$6. m Popular Electronics, Portland Pl, Boulder, Colo. 80302

Popular Gardening & Living Outdoors—$2. q Holt, Rinehart & Winston, Inc, 383 Madison Av, New York 10017
    Incorporated in Field & Stream My '69

*Popular Mechanics—$5. m Popular Mechanics, Box 646, New York 10019

Popular Photography—$7. m Popular Photography, Portland Pi, Boulder, Colo. 80302

Popular Science Monthly—$5. m Popular Science, Boulder, Colo. 80302

Publisher's Weekly—$16.50. w (bi-w year-end issue) R. R. Bowker Co, 1180 Avenue of the Americas, New York 10036

Radio-Electronics—$6. m Radio-Electronics, Boulder, Colo. 80302

Ramparts Magazine—$8.50. m Ramparts Magazine, P.O. Box 452, San Francisco, Calif. 94101

*Reader's Digest—$3.97. m Reader's Digest Association, Inc, Pleasantville, N.Y. 10570
    Enlarged type available from Xerox Corp, P.O. Box 3300, Grand Central Station, New York, N.Y. $4.50 a month or $25.65 for six months

Redbook—$3.95. m Redbook, McCall St, Dayton, Ohio 45401

The Review of Popular Astronomy—$4. bi-m Sky Map Publications, Inc, 111 S Meramec, St. Louis, Missouri 63105

The Saturday Evening Post—$8. 26 issues per year The Saturday Evening Post, Independence Sq, Philadelphia 19105
    Discontinued publication F 8 '69

*Saturday Review—$9. w Saturday Review, Inc, 380 Madison Av, New York 10017

Scholastic Teacher Secondary Teachers' Supplement—$5. m (S-My) Scholastic Magazines, 902 Sylvan Av, Englewood Cliffs, N.J. 07632

School & Society—$9.50. m (O-My) Society for the Advancement of Education, Inc, 1860 Broadway, New York 10023

School Arts—$7. m (S-Je) School Arts, Printers Bldg, Worcester, Mass. 01608

School Library Journal. See Library Journal

Science—$12. w American Association for the Advancement of Science, 1515 Massachusetts Av, NW, Washington, D.C. 20005

Science Digest—$5. m Science Digest, Box 654, New York 10019

Science News—$7.50. w Science Service Inc, 1719 N St, NW, Washington, D.C. 20036

*Scientific American—$10. m Scientific American, 415 Madison Av, New York 10017

Scientist and Citizen—$6. 10 issues a yr Scientist and Citizen, 438 N Skinker Blvd, St. Louis, Missouri 63130
    Continued as Environment Ja '69

Sea Frontiers—$6. bi-m International Oceanographic Foundation, 10 Rickenbacker Causeway, Virginia Key, Miami, Florida 33149

Senior Scholastic (Teacher edition)—$5. w (S-My) Senior Scholastic, 902 Sylvan Av, Englewood Cliffs, N.J. 07632

*Seventeen—$6. m Seventeen, Radnor, Pa. 19088

Sky and Telescope—$7. m Sky Pub. Corp, 49-50-51 Bay State Road, Cambridge, Mass. 02138

Space World—$7. m Space World, Amherst, Wisconsin 54406

*Sports Illustrated—$10. w (except one issue at year end) Sports Illustrated, 541 N Fairbanks Court, Chicago 60611

Successful Farming (Midwest edition)—$2. m (semi-m F, Mr, bi-m Je-Jl, N-D) Successful Farming, 1716 Locust St, Des Moines, Ia. 50303

Sunset (Central edition)—$3.95. in Calif, Ore, Wash, Idaho, Ariz, Nev, Utah, Hawaii, Alaska. $5 in other states m Sunset Magazine, Menlo Park, Calif. 94025

Time—$12. w Time, 541 N Fairbanks Court, Chicago 60611

Today's Education—available only to members. m (S-My) National Education Association of the United States, 1201 16th St, NW, Washington, D.C. 20036

*Today's Health—$5. m Today's Health, 535 N Dearborn St, Chicago 60610

Trans-Action—$8.50. m (bi-m Jl-Ag) Transaction, Box A, Rutgers—The State University, New Brunswick, N.J. 08903

Travel—$7.50. m Travel, Travel Bldg, Floral Park, N.Y. 11001

Travel & Camera—$7.50. m Travel & Camera, Box 562, Des Moines, Ia. 50302
Formerly U.S. Camera & Travel

UN Monthly Chronicle—$7. m (except in Ag) United Nations Publications, Room 1059, New York 10017

The UNESCO Courier—$5. m (bi-m Ag-S) UNESCO Pub. Center, Box 433, New York 10016

U.S. Camera & Travel—$7. m U.S. Camera & Travel, Box 562, Des Moines, Ia. 50302
Continued as Travel & Camera F '69

U.S. News & World Report—$12. w U.S. News & World Report, 435 Parker Av, Dayton, Ohio 45401

Vital Speeches of the Day—$10. semi-m City News Pub. Co, Inc, Box 606, Southold, N.Y. 11971

Vogue—$10. semi-m (m My-Jl, D) Vogue, Box 2201, Boulder, Colo. 80302

Weatherwise—$5. bi-m American Meteorological Society, 45 Beacon St, Boston, Mass. 02108

Wilson Library Bulletin—$7. m (S-Je) The H. W. Wilson Co, 950 University Av, Bronx, N.Y. 10452

*The Writer—$6. m The Writer, Inc, 8 Arlington St, Boston 02116

Writer's Digest—$4. m Writer's Digest, 22 E 12th St, Cincinnati, Ohio 45210

Yachting—$7. m Yachting Pub. Corp, 50 W 44th St, New York 10036

The Yale Review—$5. q Yale Review, 28 Hillhouse Av, New Haven, Conn. 06520

* Available for blind and other physically handicapped readers on talking books, in braille, or on magnetic tape. For information address Division for the Blind and Physically Handicapped, Library of Congress, Washington, D.C. 20542

POLICY STATEMENT

Selection of the magazines indexed in the READERS' GUIDE TO PERIODICAL LITERATURE is made by the subscribers to the Index. This is done only at intervals of several years by means of voting lists supervised by the Committee on Wilson Indexes, appointed by the Reference Services Division of the American Library Association. In casting their votes the subscribers are governed by the general policy statement which they first endorsed in 1953 and reaffirmed in 1960 and 1967. This statement reads as follows: "THE READERS' GUIDE will continue to index U.S. periodicals of broad, general and popular character. It will also aim to provide a well-balanced selection of U.S. popular, non-technical magazines representing all the important scientific, technical and subject fields." In addition the subscribers are asked to cast their votes carefully and objectively, with primary emphasis on the reference value of the periodicals upon which they are voting. They are also urged to give serious consideration to the maintenance of a good subject balance so that no important field will be overlooked and none will be too heavily indexed.

SUGGESTIONS FOR THE USE OF THE READERS' GUIDE TO PERIODICAL LITERATURE

Arrangement

Authors and subjects are arranged in one alphabet. Under authors and subjects, titles are arranged also in alphabetical order by the first word, initial articles being disregarded. Under personal names titles *by* author precede those *about* him. Subdivisions of a subject are arranged alphabetically under the subject. Geographical subheads follow the other subdivisions in a separate alphabet.

Cross References

See references are made from various forms of personal names and subject headings to the most generally accepted forms appearing in the first issue, after made, and thereafter in but one quarterly issue, until the annual volume. They are also made from titles of dramas, operas, and stories to names of authors and composers.

See also references are made from a subject to related subjects under which additional material may be found.

Dramas

Dramas are indexed under the dramatist's name with a *see* reference from the title of the drama; titles are also listed under the heading—Dramas—Criticisms, plots, etc.—Single works.

Fiction

Novels and short stories are indexed under the author's name with a *see* reference from the title to the author. Subject entries are made for selected types of fiction, e.g. Historical fiction; Christmas stories; etc.

Moving Pictures

Moving picture plays are indexed only under the headings Moving picture plays—Criticisms, plots, etc.—Single works, or Moving pictures—Documentary films—Criticisms, plots, etc. No title references are made.

Musical comedies, revues, etc.

Musical comedies, revues, etc. are indexed under the heading Musical comedies, revues, etc.—Criticisms, plots, etc. with a *see* reference from the title of the work.

Operas, Operettas

Operas, Operettas are indexed under the composer's name with a *see* reference from the title of the opera or operetta; titles are also listed under the headings Operas—Criticisms, plots, etc., or Operettas—Criticisms, plots, etc.

Sample entry: CAMPING
Cast loose all cares. E. S. Gardner. il Motor B 123:267+ Ja '69

Explanation: An illustrated article on the subject CAMPING entitled "Cast loose all cares," by E. S. Gardner, will be found in volume 123 of Motor Boating, page 267 (continued on later pages of the same issue) the January 1969 number

KEY TO ABBREVIATIONS

+	continued on later pages of same issue
abp	archbishop
abr	abridged
Ag	August
Ap	April
arch	architect
assn	association
Aut	Autumn
av	avenue
bart	baronet
bibliog	bibliography
bibliog f	bibliographical footnotes
bi-m	bimonthly
bi-w	biweekly
bldg	building
bp	bishop
co	company
comp	compiled, compiler
cond	condensed
cont	continued
corp	corporation
D	December
dept	department
ed	edited, edition, editor
F	February
Hon	Honorable
il	illustrated, illustration, illustrator
inc	incorporated
introd	introduction, introductory
Ja	January
Je	June
Jl	July
jr	junior
jt auth	joint author
ltd	limited
m	monthly
Mr	March
My	May
N	November
no	number
O	October
por	portrait
pseud	pseudonym
pt	part
pub	published, publisher, publishing
q	quarterly
rev	revised
S	September
semi-m	semimonthly
soc	society
Spr	Spring
sq	square
sr	senior
st	street
Sum	Summer
sup	supplement
sup	superintendent
tr	translated, translation, translator
v	volume
w	weekly
Wint	Winter
yr	year

READERS' GUIDE TO
PERIODICAL LITERATURE

March 1969 — February 1970

ABOLITIONISTS
Means and ends in American abolitionism, by A. S. Kraditor. Review Nation 208:214-15 F 17 '69. E. Magdol
Voice of dissent: John Jay Chapman and the great wickedness. L. M. Sims. bibliog Negro Hist Bul 32:12-13 Mr '69

ABORTION
Abortion. C. Tietze and S. Lewit. il Sci Am 220:21-7 bibliog(p 138) Ja '69
Abortion: a painful lesson for Britain. il Time 93:48 Mr 7 '69
Abortion decision. by D. Granfield. Review America 120:653 My 31 '69. R. F. Drinan
Abortion for whom? New Repub 161:12 O 25 '69
Abortion law developments. America 120:518-19 My 3 '69
Abortion laws and the courts. America 121:515 N 29 '69
Abortionist rhetoric. America 120:639 My 31 '69
Abortions for all? Newsweek 73:104 Mr 17 '69
Birth control now, country by country. il US News 66:49-52 Mr 17 '69
Canada debates abortion and homosexuality. J. C. Fleck. Chr Cent 86:354-8 Mr 12 '69
Child; his birth without permission; excerpt from Ethical issues in medicine. R. E. Hall; reply with rejoinder. V. R. Dillon. Sat R 52:59-60 Mr 1 '69
Clergy and abortions; Michigan clergy for problem pregnancy counseling. il Time 94:82 N 28 '69
Father as non-parent. D. W. Louisell and C. Carroll. il Cath World 210:108-10 D '69
Fundamental right. Sci Am 221:56-7 N '69
Growing battle over abortion reform. A. Q. Maisel. Read Digest 94:152-4+ Je '69
Guideline on abortion. Time 94:66 S 19 '69
Hearing: demonstration by women when Joint legislative committee on the problems of public health convened. New Yorker 45:28-9 F 22 '69
Humanizing the abortion debate. J. J. Diamond. America 121:36-9 Jl 19 '69
King of the abortionists; clinic operated by R. D. Spencer. il Newsweek 73:92 F 17 '69
Legal abortions: a pregnant question. Chr Today 14:43 N 21 '69
Liberal abortion laws. F. J. Ayd, jr. America 120:130-2 F 1 '69
One small gain; Washington, D.C. decision. Nation 209:589 D 1 '69
Open city for abortion. Time 94:65 N 21 '69
Il Papa and the pill; birth control and abortion in Italy. L. J. Berry. Commonweal 90:44-6 Mr 28 '69; Reply. J. Rettie. 90:183 Ap 25 '69
Pliny's pheromonic abortifacients. H. McCully. Science 165:236-7 Jl 18 '69
Professor Williams on abortion. America 120:320 Mr 22 '69
Public policy and abortion laws. America 120:239-40 Mr 1 '69; Reply. J. G. Milhaven. 120:317 Mr 22 '69
Right of abortion. H. Pilpel. Atlan 223:69-71 Je '69
Sophists will play; decision of California supreme court. W. F. Buckley, jr. Nat R 21:1182 N 18 '69
Step toward legal abortions. U S News 67:12 N 24 '69
TLC for miscarriages. Newsweek 73:67 Ja 27 '69
Triumph of irrelevance: New York reform bill defeated. Nation 208:588-9 My 12 '69

ABOUSSOUAN, Camille
Avicenna; reprint. UNESCO Courier 22:38 Ag '69

ABPLANALP, Robert
Spitmouth puffers in the living room. R. H. Boyle. il por Sports Illus 31:28-30+ D 8 '69

ABRAHAM, the patriarch
Abraham's faith and ours today. H. K. Stothard. Chr Today 14:8-10 D 19 '69

ABRAHAM, George
Bulbs for winter beauty. Horticulture 46:20-3 N '68
Everbearers, raspberries that laugh at cold. Org Gard & Farm 16:44-5 Mr '69

ABRAHAM, Gerald
Personal history. Sat R 52:51-2 N 15 '69

ABRAHAMS, Sidney C.
Crystals. por Phys Today 22:30-7 Ag '69

ABRAM, Morris Berthold
Eleven days at Brandeis, as seen from the president's chair. por N Y Times Mag p28-9+ F 16 '69
War of the words; interview, ed. by P. Brinkley-Rogers. Newsweek 73:68-9 Ja 27 '69

about

Black power play; report from Brandeis. D. Brudnoy. Nat R 21:66 Ja 28 '69
Doves v. hawks on campus. D. Brudnoy. Nat R 21:172-4 F 25 '69

ABRAMS, Creighton Williams, 1914-
Close-up: one day they will go it alone. C. Leinster. il pors Life 66:38-40+ Ap 25 '69
General Abrams deserves a better war. K. P. Buckley. il pors N Y Times Mag p34-5+ O 5 '69

ABRAMS, Frank Whittemore
Frank Abrams way. L. L. L. Golden. Sat R 52:86 N 8 '69

ABRAMSON, Martin
(comp) Christmas that meant the most to me. Good H 169:74-5+ D '69
How to score higher on college boards. Seventeen 28:132-3+ N '69

ABRAMSON, Ruth N.
Israel dances. Sr Schol 94:Schol Teach 12-13 Ap 25 '69

ABRASIVE wheels. See Grinding wheels

ABRASIVES
GE's gem-hard grit; Borazon II. Bsns W p49 Jl 5 '69
What you should know about choosing and using abrasives. J. P. Schenley. il Pop Mech 131:186-8+ Ap '69
See also
Sandpaper

ABRUS precatorius. See Crabs eye vine

ABSCISSION (botany)
See also
Defoliation

ABSENTEEISM
Absentee executive; AWOLism. il Newsweek 74:104-6 N 17 '69
Case of the alcoholic absentee. J. W. Kelley. il Harvard Bsns R 47:14-16+ My '69

ABSHIRE, David M.
Problems of disengagement; address, November 13, 1969. Vital Speeches 36:190-2 Ja 1 '70

ABSOLUTE zero
Lab bench; Charles' law: estimating absolute zero. M. Spritzer and J. Markham. il Chem 42:24-5 S '69

ABSOLUTION
What of priestly absolution? J. R. Mantey. Chr Today 13:12+ Ja 31 '69

ABSORPTION (physiology)
25-Hydroxycholecalciferol: stimulation of bone resorption in tissue culture. C. L. Trummel and others. bibliog il Science 163:1450-1 Mr 28 '69
Uptake of isolated chloroplasts by mammalian cells. M. M. K. Nass. bibliog il Science 165:1128-31 S 12 '69

ABSTRACT art. See Art, Abstract

ABSTRACT expressionism
Art; show at Museum of modern art. L. Alloway. Nation 208:837-8 Je 30 '69
Color it Berkowitz; exhibition at Corcoran gallery, Washington, D.C. S. Burton. il Art N 68:32-3+ Mr '69
Five states of mind. P. Pavia. il Art N 68:23-5+ My '69
Halfway house; between representationalism and formal geometry. il Time 94:50-1 Ag 1 '69
New ancestors; show at Manhattan's Museum of modern art. il Time 93:60-5 Je 27 '69

ABSTRACT films. See Moving pictures—Abstract films

ABSTRACT photography. See Photography, Artistic

ABSURD, Theater of the. See Theater, Experimental

ABU DHABI
Blooming desert. C. O. Hodge. il Bul Atom Sci 25:32-3 N '69

ABU SIMBEL, Temples of
Abu Simbel's ancient temples reborn. G. Gerster. il Nat Geog 135:724-44 My '69

ABU ZABI. See Abu Dhabi

ABUNDANCES of elements. See Chemical elements

ABUSE. See Invective

ACACIAS
Golden acacias. F. Kaltenbach. Horticulture 47:20 F '69

ACADEMIA republicii socialiste România. See Academy of the socialist republic of Romania

ACADEMIC achievement. See Student achievements

ACADEMIC degrees. See Degrees, Academic

ACADEMIC freedom
Academic freedom again; firing of Communist professor at UCLA. Nat R 21:1103 N 4 '69
Academic freedom and tenure, by L. Joughlin. Review
  Bul Atom Sci 25:46-7 Ap '69. T. Dinell
Academic freedom and the Christian college. G. F. Kreyche. Chr Cent 86:1217-20 S 24 '69
Academic freedom and the educational task. H. B. Kuhn. Chr Today 13:5-8 Ap 25; 16-18 My 9 '69
Academic freedom and the Third Reich, can it happen here? L. L. Beall. Clear House 43: 483-7 Ap '69
Case of Angela the red; firing of militant black professor at UCLA. Time 94:64 O 17 '69
Communist and the governor. A. S. Kaufman. New Repub 162:21-4 Ja 3 '70
Faculty fights back. Newsweek 73:78-9 Mr 3 '69
Inqui 67: some reflections on the Lyndian heresy. H. A. Patin. bibliog f Sch & Soc 97:98-100 F '69
New assault on academic freedom. W. W. Brickman. Sch & Soc 97:268 Sum '69; Same abr. Ed Digest 35:40-1 N '69
Obsolete neutrality of higher education. N. Shimahara. bibliog f Sch & Soc 97:18-20 Ja '69
On hiring Communists; California superior court decision on case of A. Davis. il Sat R 52:64-5 D 20 '69
Real crisis on the campus; interview. S. Hook. il U S News 66:40-4 My 19 '69; Excerpts. Read Digest 95:41-5 Ag '69
St John's: four years after. J. A. Scimecca. Commonweal 91:326-7 D 12 '69
Student demands and academic freedom. A. M. Bickel. New Repub 161:15-16 S 20 '69
Whither higher education? A look at the state college. G. M. Schurr. Chr Cent 86:373-7 Mr 19 '69
  See also
Colleges and universities—Administration
Colleges and universities—Political control
Propaganda in the schools
Tennessee evolution controversy
ACADEMIC performance. See Student achievements
ACADEMIC tenure. See College professors and instructors—Tenure
ACADEMIC town, Siberia. See Akademgorodok, Siberia
ACADEMY awards (moving pictures)
From Oscars to boredom, or is there any noticeable difference? C. Barnes. Holiday 45:8+ My '69
Grand illusion. il Time 93:83 Ap 25 '69
How about an Oscar for 'Oliver!'? R. Schickel. Life 66:16 Ap 4 '69
ACADEMY of motion picture arts and sciences
  See also
Academy awards (moving pictures)
ACADEMY of parish clergy
Academy of parish clergy founded. Chr Cent 86:704 My 21 '69
ACADEMY of sciences of the USSR
Getting out the cast iron. Sci N 95:548 Je 7 '69
ACADEMY of television arts and sciences
Emmys of irony. Time 93:65 Je 20 '69
Short rap with the moonmen: the Emmy awards. J. Leonard. Life 67:12 Jl 18 '69
ACADEMY of the socialist republic of Romania
Romania: academy links basic science to current needs. A. Jamison. Science 166:853-5 N 14 '69
ACADIANS in Louisiana
Waning echo in Cajun country. D. Snell. Life 66:18B Mr 14 '69
ACANTHASTER planci. See Starfishes
ACANTHUS
  See also
Ruellias
ACAPULCO, Mexico
Duel in the Acapulco sun. D. Butwin. Sat R 52:34+ My 3 '69
ACCELERATION
Secular accelerations of the earth and moon. R. R. Newton. bibliog il Science 166:825-31 N 14 '69
ACCELERATION of particles. See Particles (nuclear physics)—Acceleration
ACCELERATORS (electrons, etc)
Big machine, by R. Jungk. Review
  Bul Atom Sci 25:34-5 Mr '69. M. S. Livingston
CERN storage rings in two years: experimenters are making plans. il Phys Today 22:62-3 Jl '69
Cry from the South; heavy-ion accelerators. Sci N 96:349-50 O 18 '69

Delay and growing despair; CERN's accelerator. Sci N 96:593-4 D 27 '69
Electron, cloud to produce highly stripped heavy ions. G. B. Lubkin. il Phys Today 22:58-9 My '69
Going along for the ride; electron ring accelerator. D. E. Thomsen. il Sci N 96:35-7 Jl 12 '69
Internationalizing Batavia; proposed Canadian partnership. Sci N 95:305 Mr 29 '69
Navy accelerator goes begging. Sci N 96:130-1 Ag 16 '69
One more for the 300 GeV; French participation. N. Hardy. il Sci N 96:486 N 22 '69
PPA proposes heavy-ion improvement program to AEC. Phys Today 22:59 O '69
Planning for the giant; National accelerator laboratory. il Sci N 96:128 Ag 16 '69
Probing the depths of the nucleus; meson factories. D. E. Thomsen. il Sci N 96:332-3 O 11 '69
Radlab adds another physics first; element 104 identified and ERA under development. il Bsns W p64-6+ Ap 19 '69
Science and man: breaking new ground at Batavia. E. L. Goldwasser. il Bul Atom Sci 25:7-10 O '69
Tokamak. Sci Am 221:51-2 D '69
Trillion-volt accelerator; electron-ring. Sci Am 221:48-9 O '69
Weisskopf panel reports on high-energy physics in next decade. il Phys Today 22:65+ O '69
ACCELERATORS, incorporated
They may have built the better mouse trap; ion implantation accelerator. Bsns W p30 N 29 '69
ACCELEROMETERS
Geee meter, a dyno on your dash. P. Estrada. il Hot Rod 22:96-7 F '69
ACCESS to books in libraries. See Open and closed shelves
ACCESSORIES, Household. See Household furnishings
ACCESSORIES, Photographic. See Photography—Apparatus and supplies
ACCIDENT litigation. See Actions and defenses
ACCIDENTAL war. See Atomic weapons—Accidents
ACCIDENTS
Bad case of common sense. M. Grove. il Good H 169:36+ Ag '69
Do aging and accidents go together? Todays Health 47:84 Mr '69
Social benefit versus technological risk; adaptation of address, November 1968. C. Starr. bibliog il Science 165:1232-8 S 19 '69
Turning points; accident in the afternoon; a child's face cut by paring knife. M. Yusko. McCalls 96:14+ F '69
What to do when emergencies occur on a vacation. il Good H 169:142-3 Ag '69
  See also
Burns and scalds
Collisions at sea
Explosions
First aid in illness and injury
Traffic accidents
Traumatism
  also subhead Accidents under various subjects, e.g. Aviation—Accidents

Prevention
Are you heading for a fall? M. Michaelson. il Todays Health 47:52-5+ O '69
Predictable hazards of childhood. I. M. Rabasca. il Todays Health 48:53-5+ Ja '70
  See also
Aviation—Safety devices and measures
Safety education

Psychological aspects
Are you accident-prone? S. L. Englebardt. Read Digest 95:127-30 S '69
ACCIDENTS, industrial
  See also
Disability—Measurement
Industrial safety
ACCOMPANIMENT, Music. See Musical accompaniment
ACCORDION playing
Accordion to taste. il Time 94:61 Ag 22 '69
ACCOUNTABILITY. See Responsibility
ACCOUNTANTS
  See also
Spacek, L.
ACCOUNTING
  See also
Airlines—Accounting
Billing
Controllership
Corporations—Accounting

ACCOUNTING, Household. See Domestic finance

ACCOUNTING principles board. See American institute of certified public accountants

ACCREDITATION, College. See Colleges and universities—Accreditation

ACCREDITATION of library schools. See Library schools and education

ACCULTURATION
See also
Indians of South America—Acculturation

ACCUMULATORS, Heat. See Heat regenerators

ACE, Goodman
Top of my head. See issues of Saturday review

ACETOXYCYLOHEXIMIDE
Memory in the Japanese quail: effects of puromycin and acetoxycycloheximide. S. J. Mayor. bibliog Science 166:1165-7 N 28 '69

ACETYLCHOLINE
Acetylcholine action: biochemical aspects. J. Durell and others. bibliog il Science 165:862-6 Ag 29 '69
Acetylcholine facilitation, atropine block of synaptic excitation of cortical neurons. R. Spehlmann. bibliog il Science 165:404-5 Jl 25 '69
Acetylcholine receptor: covalent attachment of depolarizing groups at the active site. I. Silman and A. Karlin. bibliog il Science 164:1420-1 Je 20 '69
Acetylcholine: release from neural tissue and identification by pyrolysis-gas chromatography. D. E. Schmidt and others. bibliog il Science 165:1370-1 S 26 '69

ACETYLSALICYLIC acid. See Aspirin

ACEVEDO, Guillermo
Guillermo Acevedo: draughtsman. F. Whitaker. il Am Artist 33:26-31+ S '69

ACHATINA fulica. See Snails

ACHESON, Dean Gooderham
Dean Acheson's version of Robert Kennedy's version of the Cuban missile affair. Esquire 71:76-7+ F '69
Greatness of Harry Truman. Esquire 72:124-7+ S '69
Memories of Joe McCarthy; excerpts from Present at the creation. Harper 239:113+ O '69
Witch hunt against military? A warning; excerpts from statement, June 11, 1969. por U S News 66:16 Je 23 '69

about
Anti-anti-ABM. por Time 93:29-30 Je 6 '69
Authors & editors. B. A. Bannon. por Pub W 195:25-7 Je 30 '69
Weighty Acheson. A. Campbell. New Repub 161:23-4 N 1 '69

ACHIEVEMENT motivation. See Motivation (education)

ACHIEVEMENT tests
Prospects for evaluation of learning. R. L. Ebel. Ed Digest 34:22-5 Mr '69

ACHIEVEMENTS, Student. See Student achievements

ACIDS
Dilute solutions of strong acids: the effect of water on ph. P. H. Mogul and J. S. Schmuckler. bibliog il Chem 42:14-17 O '69
See also names of acids, e.g. Succinic acid

ACIDS, Fatty
Cola and cholesterol. A. J. Snider. il Sci Digest 65:74 Mr '69
Mycoplasma membrane lipids: variations in fatty acid composition. R. N. McElhaney and M. E. Tourtellotte. bibliog il Science 164:433-4 Ap 25 '69
Rats enriched with odd-carbon fatty acids: maintenance of liver glycogen during starvation. T. B. VanItallie and A. K. Khachadurian. bibliog il Science 165:811-13 Ag 22 '69
See also
Prostaglandins

ACK, Marvin
Increasing responsibilities of the schools. por Sci Digest 65:61-3 Mr '69

ACKERLEY, Joe Randolph
Painful, witty oddity. S. Kauffmann. New Repub 160:26-8 Mr 29 '69

ACKERMAN, Ann W.
Reading for pleasure and profit. Engl J 58:1042-4 O '69

ACKERMAN, Martin Sol
Ackerman looks beyond the Post. por Bsns W p26+ Ja 18 '69
Curtis affair. por Newsweek 73:86+ F 17 '69
I am Marty Ackerman. . ; excerpts from Decline and fall. O. Friedrich. il por Harper 239:92-100+ D '69
Perfect wants a better image. por Bsns W p 100+ Je 28 '69

ACKERMAN, Nathan W.
Divorce and alienation in modern society; address, October 20, 1966. bibliog Ment Hy 53:118-26 Ja '69

ACKLAND, Len E. See Porter, D. G. jt. auth.

ACNE
What to do about acne. L. W. Sauer. il PTA Mag 64:29-30 N '69

ACOMYS. See Spiny mice

ACOSTA, Mary J.
Ah! Sunflower. Design 70:36 mid-Wint '69
Aluminum foil figures. Design 70:23 Sum '69
Op art can be simple. Design 70:16-18 mid-Wint '69
Tonality, white to black. Design 70:33-5 Spr '69

ACOUSTICAL holography. See Holography

ACOUSTICS. See Music—Acoustics and physics; Sound

ACOUSTICS, Architectural
Of orchestras and echoes. E. Greenfield. Hi Fi 19:MA27+ Je '69
Sound-absorptive shell improves arena hearing conditions. il Arch Rec 146:138 D '69
Structure suits architecture that suits acoustics; Blossom music center. il Arch Rec 145:191-6 Je '69
Use your room to enhance your stereo. E. F. McIntyre. il Hi Fi 19:50-5 S '69

ACOUSTICS and physics. See Music—Acoustics and physics

ACQUISITIONS, Corporate. See Corporate acquisitions

ACQUISITIONS, School library. See School libraries—Acquisitions

ACRASIALES. See Slime molds, Cellular

ACRASIN
Adenosine-3',5'-phosphate; identification as acrasin in a species of cellular slime mold. D. S. Barkley. bibliog il Science 165:1133-4 S 12 '69

ACROBATS and acrobatism
After tragedy: a new age of Flying Wallendas. M. Smith. il Life 66:58-60 My 30 '69
Onward and upward with the arts; research for biography of J. Cocteau. F. Steegmuller. il New Yorker 45:130-4+ S 27 '69

ACRONYMS
Inside acronyms. B. H. Gehman. Esquire 72:64+ S '69

ACROPOLIS; drama. See Grotowski, J.

ACRYLICS. See Plastics

ACTING
Alec McCowen; interview. A. McCowen. New Yorker 44:22-4 Ja 25 '69
Bring 'em back alive; key to revivals. P. Tavernia. il Opera N 33:8-11 F 1 '69
Faa-bu-lous long run of Gordon and Kanin. S. Lydon. il N Y Times Mag p64-5+ O 5 '69
High-level acting. R. Gilman. New Repub 160:32-4 Ja 25 '69
Hollywood scene; ed. by E. Miller. P. Clark. il Seventeen 28:130+ Ag '69
I've come to conquer you! ed. by E. Miller. M. York. il Seventeen 28:168-9+ Ap '69
Mark this man! ed. by E. Miller. M. McDowell. Seventeen 28:88-9+ Jl '69
More than a chip off the old block; ed. by E. Miller. M. Douglas. Seventeen 28:330-1+ Ag '69
New name, a new life; ed. by E. Miller. K. Darby. il Seventeen 28:116-17+ Je '69
On my own at last! ed. by E. Miller. P. Franklin. Seventeen 28:96-7+ Ja '69
Raquel Raquel; interview. ed. by J. Hamilton. R. Welch. il Look 33:78-82+ Ap 15 '69
Real like you; ed. by E. Miller. il J. Shimkus. il Seventeen 28:156-7+ My '69
Something to talk about; J. Grotowski. L. Lerman. il Mlle 68:210-11 Mr '69
Sweet singing man; ed. by E. Miller. G. Campbell. il Seventeen 28:148-9+ Mr '69
Towards a poor theatre, revolutionary. J. Gruen. Vogue 153:132 F 1 '69
V for Voight; ed by E. Miller. J. Voight. il Seventeen 28:148-9+ S '69
See also
Gesture

ACTINOMYCIN
Actinomycin binding to DNA: inability of a DNA containing guanine to bind actinomycin D. R. D. Wells. bibliog il Science 165:75-6 Jl 4 '69
Actinomycin D: uptake by sea urchin eggs and embryos. M. M. Thaler and others. bibliog il Science 164:832-4 My 16 '69; Reply. C. A. Villee and P. R. Gross. 166:402 O 17 '69
Chromatin and histones: binding of tritiated actinomycin D to heterochromatin in mealy bugs. L. Berlowitz and others. bibliog il Science 164:1527-9 Je 27 '69

ACTINOMYCOSIS
Fungus diseases that fool the doctors. J. D. Wassersug. Sci Digest 66:83 Ag '69
ACTION for progress for the Americas
Gringo manifesto. J. Bishop and M. Elmer. Commonweal 91:334-7 D 12 '69
New theme: Action for progress; address, October 31, 1969; with introduction. R. M. Nixon. il U S News 67:104-7 N 10 '69; Same. Dept State Bul 61:409-14 N 17 '69; Same abr. with title Action for progress. Vital Speeches 36:70-3 N 15 '69
ACTION group for the defense of civil rights in the U.S.S.R. See Civil rights—Russia
ACTION in art
Introducing motion. S. D. Hochman. il Sch Arts 69:12-13 S '69
See also
Mobiles
ACTION potentials. See Electrophysiology
ACTIONS and defenses
Australia sues two firms over P3B accident. Aviation W 91:18 Ag 25 '69
Avenging father; battle for justice for Germany's 3,000 thalidomide children. A. Levy. il Good H 168:50+ Ap '69
Dial V for vengeance; class action suit against Michigan Bell telephone co. Newsweek 75:51+ Ja 5 '70
Giving the consumer class; consumer class actions. D. Sanford. New Repub 161:15-17 Jl 26 '69
Leasco sues Maxwell, who denounces Ross meeting. Pub W 196:63 N 17 '69
See also
Injunctions
Libel and slander

History
Most celebrated dog case ever tried in Johnson County, Missouri, or the world; Old Drum trial, 1869; C. Burden vs. L. Hornsby. G. Carson. il Natur Hist 78:6-8+ D '69
ACTIVATED charcoal filters. See Cigarette filters
ACTIVATED sludge. See Sewage disposal—Activated sludge method
ACTIVATION analysis. See Radioactivation analysis
ACTIVITIES, Student. See Student activities
ACTIVITIES committee on new directions. See American library association—Committee on new directions
ACTIVITY centers for the aged. See Recreation for the aged
ACTON, John Emerich Edward Dalberg Acton, 1st baron
Lord Acton and his times, by D. Mathew. Review
America 120:310+ Mr 15 '69. M. Adelman, Jr
ACTOR, P. and others
Resistance to metronidazole by trichomonas foetus in hamsters infected intravaginally. bibliog Science 164:439-40 Ap 25 '69
ACTORS and actresses
Say hello to the Dirty half dozen. Sierra Bandit, the American playground and all the superstars of the new theatre. A. Warhol. il Esquire 71:144-7 My '69
Xanadu, class of '52, revisited; Black mountain college, N.C. il Esquire 71:150-1 My '69
See also
Acting
Moving picture actors and actresses
Negro actors and actresses
Television broadcasting—Performers
ACUITY, Visual. See Sight
ADAM, Stephen F.
Hot-carrier diodes. por Electr World 82:46-8 Jl '69
ADAM, Theo
Adam returns. E. Davidson. por Opera N 33:29 Mr 1 '69
ADAMO, Ralph
For the assassins; poem. Am Scholar 38:401 Sum '69
ADAMO, S. J.
Press. See issues of America
ADAMOVICH, Boris, and others
Water in space travel. Space World F-6-66:8-9 Je '69
ADAMS, Alice
Gift of grass; story. New Yorker 45:58-62 N 8 '69
ADAMS, Ansel
Ansel Adams & the national parks; photographs. Am West 6:17-23, 41-8, 65-72 S '69
Eliot Porter, master of nature's color. Mod Phot 33:92+ O '69
Free man in a free country. Am West 6:40-7 N '69

about
Ansel Adams: a Pacific portfolio. M. Hollis. il por Travel & Camera 32:66-71 Ag '69
Ansel Adams, brilliant recorder of nature's magnificence. N. Newhall. il Mod Phot 33:66-71+ S '69
Famed photographer to conduct workshop. W. Lane. il Travel 131:77 Ap '69
ADAMS, Arverna
Sharecropper is me, the small farmer is me, the domestic is me. por Wilson Lib Bul 44:58-63 S '69
ADAMS, Brooks
Brooks Adams I knew. W. S. Harris. Yale R 59:50-70 O '69
ADAMS, Charles Francis, 1807-1886
Apprenticeship of Charles Francis Adams. P. Shaw. Am Scholar 38:312+ Spr '69
ADAMS, Eldred V.
Give your garden tractor a lift. Pop Sci 194:136-7+ Je '69
ADAMS, Elizabeth
In defense of shyness. Parents Mag 44:56-7+ Mr '69
ADAMS, Fred
Effect of leeway. Yachting 125:63+ My '69
ADAMS, Harriet S. See Keene, C. pseud.
ADAMS, Henry
Success of Henry Adams. P. Shaw. Yale R 59:71-8 O '69
ADAMS, James Luther
Blessed are the powerful; address, 1968. Chr Cent 86:838-41 Je 18 '69
ADAMS, John
Americanization of history. H. S. Commager. Sat R 52:24-5+ N 1 '69
ADAMS, John B. See McCord, T. B. jt. auth.
ADAMS, Joseph
Build your own boat trailer. Mech Illus 65:81-4+ Mr '69
ADAMS, Kipling
Amateur scientist. Sci Am 221:132-3 D '69
ADAMS, Molly
Great Swamp of New Jersey; photographs. Audubon 71:29-36 Mr '69
ADAMS, Phoebe Lou
Short reviews: books. See issues of Atlantic
ADAMS, Sherman
Society of useful men: Ayres and his crowd; summary of address. por Am For 75:40-3+ Mr '69
ADAMSON, Joy
Born free star is saved from freedom. il Life 67:47-8 N 28 '69
ADAPTATION (biology)
Crabs move ashore. M. Gruber and J. Shoup. il Sea Front 15:364-75 N '69
Human adaptation to high altitude. P. T. Baker. bibliog il Science 163:1149-56 Mr 14 '69
Human biological adaptability; excerpt from Evolution of man. G. W. Lasker. bibliog Science 166:1480-6 D 19 '69
See also
Ecology
Evolution
Man—Influence of environment
ADAPTATION; drama. See May, E.
ADAPTATION, Social. See Adjustment, Social
ADAPTIVE control systems
Ultimate in automation. G. J. Berkwitt. il Duns R 93:61-2+ Ja '69
ADCOCK, Betty
Limit; poem. Nation 209:638 D 8 '69
ADCOCK, Joe
Philadelphia street players. Nation 209:611-12 D 1 '69
ADDICOTT, W. O.
Tertiary climatic change in the marginal northeastern Pacific Ocean. bibliog Science 165:583-6 Ag 8 '69
ADDICTS, Drug. See Narcotic addicts
ADDIS ABABA
Well traveled camera. H. Keppler. il Mod Phot 33:150-1+ Ap '69
ADDITION
How fast can computers add? S. Winograd; reply with rejoinder. B. Belzer. Sci Am 220:8+ Ja '69
ADDITIONS, House. See Houses, Remodeled
ADDITIVES. See Gasoline—Additives; Lubrication and lubricants—Additives
ADDITIVES, Food. See Food additives
ADDONIZIO, Hugh Joseph
City under indictment. il Time 94:10 D 26 '69
Crackdown in New Jersey. por Time 94:17 D 19 '69
Jersey bounce. il Newsweek 74:27 D 22 '69
Mayor in the dock. il por Newsweek 74:21-2 D 29 '69

ADDRESSOGRAPH-multigraph corporation
  Taking on Xerox with a fast copier; AMCD,
  copier-duplicator. il Bsns W p78+ Ap 26
  '69
ADE, Ginny
  Redbook guide to family camping. Redbook
  134:35-42 N '69
ADELA. See Atlantic community development
  group for Latin America
ADELMAN, George
  Ask the men who know. por Library J 94:
  1413-15 Ap 1 '69
ADELMAN, Maurice, Jr
  Biography. America 120:542-5 My 3 '69
  [Book review] America 120:310+ Mr 15 '69
ADELSEN, Charles E.
  Bosphorus. Travel 132:28-33+ S '69
  House on the golden horn. Opera N 34:22-3 O
  11 '69
ADELSON, Alan M.
  Please don't steal the atomic bomb. Esquire
  71:130-3+ My '69
ADELSON, Charles E.
  Lake Manyas: a Turkish park for birds. Nat
  Parks 43:25-7 Ap '69
ADEN. See Southern Yemen
ADENOSINE monophosphate
  Adenosine 3',5'-monophosphate-dependent pro-
  tein kinase from brain. E. Miyamoto and
  others. bibliog il Science 165:63-5 Jl 4 '69
  Adenosine-3',5'-phosphate: identification as
  acrasin in a species of cellular slime mold.
  D. S. Barkley. bibliog il Science 165:1133-4
  S 12 '69
  Cyclic adenosine monophosphate: possible
  mediator for norepinephrine effects on
  cerebellar purkinje cells. G. R. Siggins and
  others. bibliog il Science 165:1018-20 S 5 '69
  Cyclic adenosine monophosphate: stimulation
  of melatonin and serotonin synthesis in cul-
  tured rat pineals. H. M. Shein and R. J.
  Wurtman. bibliog il Science 166:519-20 O 24
  '69
  Hormones in social amoebae and mammals.
  J. T. Bonner. il Sci Am 220:78-84+ Je '69
  Thyroid-stimulating hormone and prostaglan-
  din E₁ stimulation of cyclic 3',5'-adenosine
  monophosphate in thyroid slices. T. Kaneko
  and others. bibliog il Science 163:1062-3 Mr 7
  '69
ADENOSINE phosphates
    See also
  Acrasin
ADENOSINE triphosphatase
  Adenosine triphosphatase and myopathy. G.
  A. Klassen and R. Blostein. bibliog il Sci-
  ence 163:492-3 Ja 31 '69
  Adenosine triphosphatase sensitive to DDT
  in synapses of rat brain. F. Matsumura
  and K. C. Patil. bibliog il Science 166:121-2
  O 3 '69
  Renal concentrating mechanism: possible
  role for sodium-potassium activated
  adenosine triphosphatase. M. Martinez-
  Maldonado and others. bibliog il Science
  165:807-8 Ag 22 '69
ADENOSINE triphosphate
  Micelle formation between 5-hydroxytryp-
  tamine and adenosine triphosphate in
  platelet storage organelles. K. H. Berneis
  and others. bibliog il Science 165:913-14
  Ag 29 '69
ADER, Robert
  Early experiences accelerate maturation of the
  24-hour adrenocortical rhythm. bibliog Sci-
  ence 163:1225-6 Mr 14 '69
ADEY, W. R. and others
  Biosatellite III: preliminary findings. Science
  166:492-3 O 24 '69
ADHESIVES
  Aerosol tissue adhesive. Chem 42:24 F '69
  What's new in glue? Scotch super strength
  adhesive. C. Conley. il Field & S 74:105 D '69
    See also
  Glue
ADIE, W. A. C.
  China's second liberation in perspective. Bul
  Atom Sci 25:12-16+ F '69
ADIPOSE tissues
  Brown adipose cells: spontaneous mobiliza-
  tion of endogenously synthesized lipid. A.
  Angel. bibliog il Science 163:288-90 Ja 17 '69
  Obesity starts in childhood. il Sci Digest 65:
  59-60 My '69
  Vitellogenic blood protein synthesis by in-
  sect fat body. M. L. Pan and others. bib-
  liog il Science 165:393-4 Jl 25 '69
ADIRONDACK MOUNTAINS
  Adirondacks; with paintings. Am Heritage
  20:44-63+ Ag '69
  All is not well at Baker. H. Fosburgh. il Am
  For 75:32-4 Mr '69
  Decline of the Adirondack painters. W. K.
  Verner. Cons 23:17+ Ap '69
  Discoverer of the Hudson's source. M. Mac-
  Kenzie. il Cons 23:28-31 F '69

ADIRONDACK park. See New York (state)—
  Parks and reserves
ADISESHIAH, Malcolm S.
  Gandhi on students and politics. UNESCO
  Courier 22:28-31 O '69
ADJECTIVES
  Adjectival idea. V. Sneider. Writers Digest
  49:42-7 Ag '69
ADJUSTMENT (biology) See Adaptation (bio-
  logy)
ADJUSTMENT, Economic
    See also
  Job satisfaction
ADJUSTMENT, Social
  Child and society: excerpt from Children and
  adolescents. T. Alexander. Sch & Soc 97:
  241-7 Ap '69
  First four hours of camp. W. Shalinsky and
  J. Witkovsky. il Camp Mag 41:16-17 Je '69
  Growing away from home. D. A. Sugarman
  and R. Hochstein. il Seventeen 27:132-3+
  N '68
  Growing up the hard way. Seventeen 28:90-1
  Ja '69
  Pre-Copernican views of the city. G. Rand.
  il Arch Forum 131:76-81 S '69
  Violence and man's struggle to adapt. M. F.
  Gilula and D. N. Daniels. bibliog Science
  164:396-405 Ap 25 '69; Discussion. 164:1465-6
  Je 27 '69
  You can banish Christmas blues. N. V.
  Peale. Har Yrs 9:32 D '69
    See also
  Aged—Adjustment problems
  College students—Adjustment
  Individual and society
  Maturity
  Normality
  School children—Adjustment
  Security and insecurity (psychology)
ADKINS, Arthur
  Inequities between suburban and urban
  schools. Ed Digest 34:50-1 F '69
ADLER, Bill
  Dear baby-sitter. Good H 168:122-3 Mr '69
ADLER, Dick
  New partner for Dan Rowan, the werewolf
  Life 66:54-60 My 23 '69
ADLER, J. E. M. and Salisbury, J. W.
  Behavior of water in vacuum: implications for
  lunar rivers. Science 164:589 My 2 '69
ADLER, Julius
  Chemoreceptors in bacteria. bibliog Science
  166:1588-97 D 26 '69
ADLER, Kraig
  Extraoptic phase shifting of circadian loco-
  motor rhythm in salamanders. bibliog Sci-
  ence 164:1290-2 Je 13 '69
ADLER, Mortimer Jerome
  New Annals of America. H. J. Sievers.
  America 120:491 Ap 26 '69
ADLER, Peter Herman
  Cruel medium. por Opera N 33:8-11 Je 14
  '69
  Music: the silent stepchild. Sat R 52:22-5+
  Ap 26 '69
ADLER, Renata
  Letter from Biafra. New Yorker 45:47-8+
  O 4 '69
ADLER, Selig
  Prelude to genocide. New Repub 160:25-6 F 15
  '69
ADLER shoe shops, incorporated
  Men's shoes go on the boutique kick. il
  Bsns W p54 Ja 3 '70
ADMINISTRATION, Public. See Public admin-
  istration
ADMINISTRATION of justice. See Justice, Ad-
  ministration of
ADMINISTRATIVE communication. See Com-
  munication in management
ADMINISTRATIVE efficiency. See Efficiency,
  Administrative
ADMINISTRATIVE law
    See also
  Government liability
ADMINISTRATIVE remedies
    See also
  Ombudsman
ADMINISTRATIVE responsibility
    See also
  Government liability
ADMINISTRATORS, College. See College offi-
  cials
ADMINISTRATORS, Government. See Public
  officers
ADMIRAL'S cup race. See Yacht racing
ADMISSION of territories to statehood. See
  States (United States)

ADMIXTURES, Concrete. See Concrete—Chemistry

ADOLESCENCE
Adolescent stage: it's for real. R. Kramer. il N Y Times Mag p 116+ D 7 '69
Fiery vehemence of youth; with study-discussion program, by C. Smallenburg and H. Smallenburg. P. Marin. bibliog PTA Mag 63:15-17, 35 Je '69
Growing away from home. D. A. Sugarman and R. Hochstein. il Seventeen 27:132-3+ N '68
Growing up the hard way. Seventeen 28:90-1 Ja '69
New stage of American man, almost endless adolescence. B. M. Berger. il N Y Times Mag p32-3+ N 2 '69; Discussion. p 142 N 23: 38+ N 30 '69
Research with adolescents sheds new light on early lesbianism. Sci N 96:45 Jl 19 '69
Too little too late. il Good H 169:12+ O '69
See also
Boys
Girls
Puberty
Youth

Anecdotes, facetiae, satire, etc.
Day my son grew a foot. L. Johnson. il Good H 168:34+ Je '69

Psychology
Crushes; what should you do about them? with marginal comments. S. Berman; R. Gibson. Todays Ed 58:12-16 D '69

ADOLESCENT drinking. See Liquor problem—United States

ADOLESCENT literature. See Young adults literature

ADOLESCENTS. See Boys; Girls; Youth

ADOLESCENTS and drugs. See Narcotics and youth

ADOLFO
Big A. il Time 94:70 Jl 18 '69

ADOPTED children. See Children, Adopted

ADOPTION
Adopting a child is easier now. il Changing T 23:21-3 Ap '69
Adopting black babies. il Newsweek 74:70 N 3 '69
Adopting deprived children. Sci Digest 66:55 D '69
At the Foundling, the child is everything. T. M. Gannon. il America 121:331-3 O 18 '69; Reply. J. Werner. 121:575 D 13 '69
Child market; Metromedia stations hawk unwanted children. il Newsweek 73:70 Je 16 '69
Magic of mother love. C. Remsberg and B. Remsberg. il Good H 169:74-5+ Ag '69
More questions and answers about adoption. L. W. Sauer. il PTA Mag 64:15-16 O '69
Perspective on adoption. F. Infausto. bibliog f Ann Am Acad 383:1-12 My '69
Should a single person adopt a child? GH poll. il Good H 169:12+ Ag '69
We do not cry; blind woman's adoption of blind child. V. Franklin. il Redbook 132: 98-9+ Ap '69
We're the lucky ones! child of mixed racial background. B. Dolliver. il Good H 169:90-1+ D '69
What adoptive parents need to know. M. A. Wessel. il Parents Mag 44:38-9+ D '69
See also
Foster home care

ADRENAL glands
Endocrine control of adrenal progesterone secretion in the ovariectomized rat. J. A. Resko. bibliog il Science 164:70-1 Ap 4 '69
See also
ACTH
Adrenalin

ADRENALIN
Epinephrine metabolism in mammalian brain after intravenous and intraventricular administration. A. M. Steinman and others. bibliog Science 165:616-17 Ag 8 '69

ADRENOCORTICOTROPHIC hormone. See ACTH

ADRIA; story. See Vivante, A.

ADRIANA Lecouvreur; opera. See Cilea, F.

ADRIANI, John
Adriani affair. il por Newsweek 74:55 S 8 '69

ADRIATIC SEA islands. See Islands of the Adriatic Sea

ADSORPTION
Adsorption of alkyl trimethy lammonium chlorides at a porous glass-potassium chloride solution interface. L. S. Hersh. bibliog il Science 164:179-81 Ap 11 '69

Potassium ion: is the bulk of intracelluar K^+ adsorbed? G. N. Ling and F. W. Cope. bibliog il Science 163:1335-6 Mr 21 '69

ADULT education
Chautauqua: an experience in adult education. D. E. Weischadle. Ed Digest 34:47-9 Ja '69
Deeper understanding of children. V. F. Banks. Todays Ed 58:31-2 F '69
Got some time? Try a new thing. il Changing T 23:42 F '69
Open university: Britain's new venture in higher education. D. S. Greenberg. Science 165:881-2 Ag 29 '69
Small college program for adults; Brooklyn college. il Sch & Soc 97:208-10 Ap '69
They're learning to be students again; New York university's School of continuing education and extension services. il Am Ed 5:14-19 N '69
Thirty million adults go to school. J. E. Welden. il Am Ed 5:11-13 N '69
Wanted: retirees to teach. il Har Yrs 9:6-10 Ag '69
See also
Aged—Education
Cooper union for the advancement of science and art
Education of prisoners
Education of women
Employees—Training
Illiteracy
Self culture
United States—Air force—Education

Library participation
Noon-hour talks for adults; Enoch Pratt free library. J. A. McCrossan. ALA Bul 63: 1244-5 O '69

ADULT reading. See Books and reading

ADULT toys. See Toys

ADULT-youth relationship. See Youth-adult relationship

ADULTERATIONS
In vino various; fake wine in Italy. Newsweek 73:54 My 26 '69
Wine into water; selling adulterated brew in Italy. il Time 93:40 My 30 '69

ADULTERY
Changing standards; discussing adultery at the annual meeting of the American psychiatric association. Time 93:52 My 16 '69
Incidence of adultery. Chr Today 13:35-6 S 12 '69
News and views; greater crime for women than for men? J. Deedy. Commonweal 89: 630 F 21 '69

ADULTS camps. See Camps

ADVENT
Advent of good news. Chr Cent 86:1537 D 3 '69

ADVENTISTS, Seventh day. See Seventh day Adventists

ADVENTURE stories
Write me an adventure novel. B. Cassiday. Writer 82:11-14 Mr '69

ADVENTURE tours. See Travel

ADVENTURE travel. See Travel

ADVENTURES in movement (organization) See Dance therapy

ADVERTISEMENTS. See Advertising

ADVERTISEMENTS, Personal. See Newspapers—Personal advertisements

ADVERTISING
Everyone's gone to the moon; ads featuring Apollo 11 mission. il Newsweek 74:69-70 Ag 4 '69
Five myths of consumership. D. Smythe. il Nation 208:82-4 Ja 20 '69
How Miss Rheingold died; advertising for a Negro market. il Newsweek 73:60 Mr 31 '69
Madison avenue; ad which became famous. J. Caples. Sat R 52:57-8 F 8 '69
Memo to tomorrow's Madison avenue; excerpts from With all its faults. F. M. Cone. Sat R 52:71-4 O 11 '69
News behind the ads. See issues of Changing times
No man ought to advertise; excerpt from The humbugs of the world. P. T. Barnum. il Am Heritage 21:120 D '69
Not modest, because . . ; ad for Warner-Lambert's Pristeen, vaginal spray deodorant. il Time 93:78 F 21 '69
Selling the smell; micro fragrance advertisement. il Time 95:67 Ja 12 '70
'Tis the season; early Christmas shopping promotions. Chr Cent 86:1629 D 17 '69
See also
Animals in advertising
Bank advertising
Moving picture photography in advertising

ADVERTISING—See also—*Continued*
Newspapers—Advertising policy
Photography in advertising
Radio advertising
Religious advertising
Television advertising
   also subhead Advertising under various
subjects, e.g. Cigarettes—Advertising

Anecdotes, facetiae, satire, etc.
Whither advertising? J. Noonan. il Cath
World 209:126-8 Je '69

Bibliography
Books in communications. S. W. Little. See
issues of Saturday review

Costs
Madison avenue; $1,000 a word. J. Caples.
Sat R 52:126-7 Mr 8 '69

Psychological aspects
Antidisestablishmentarianism. G. Lees. Hi Fi
19:102 Ag '69
Getting them to church; best-read magazine
ads of 1968. A. Cooper. il Newsweek 74:113
O 6 '69

Social aspects
Fighting the propaganda; a war at home;
address. A. E. Meyerhoff. Vital Speeches
35:469-73 My 15 '69
Old-fashioned values that lead to profits.
Bsns W p54-5 Ja 3 '70

Testimonials
Hot pitchmen in the selling game: athletes'
endorsements. F. Deford. il Sports Illus
31:110-12+ N 17 '69
Madison avenue takes moon trip; claiming
a piece of the action. Bsns W p36 Jl 19 '69
Name game. Forbes 104:30-2 Ag 15 '69

Japan
Demons of Dentsu. il Newsweek 73:75 Mr 24 '69
ADVERTISING, Classified
If you need a director, try placing a want ad.
il Bsns W p72+ Ja 18 '69
ADVERTISING, Pictorial. See Posters
ADVERTISING, Political
   See also
Television in politics
ADVERTISING, Public service
Army may be hazardous to your health; San
Francisco peace groups plan anti-recruit-
ment ads. P. Barnes. New Repub 161:13-14
D 20 '69
SR's seventeenth annual advertising awards.
R. L. Tobin. il Sat R 52:75-80 Ap 12 '69
ADVERTISING agencies
Ad accounts turn nomad. il Bsns W p61 Ag
30 '69
Admen thrive by thinking small; new agencies.
il Bsns W p66-7+ My 17 '69
Advertising agency; the challenge of find-
ing and using; address, April 17, 1969.
R. C. Christian. Vital Speeches 35:696-9 S
1 '69
Advertising's creative explosion. il News-
week 74:62-6+ Ag 18 '69
Black man in the gray flannel suit; Negro
advertising agencies. il Time 93:76 Je 27
'69
Copycats. il Time 94:73 Jl 11 '69
Demons of Dentsu. il Newsweek 73:75 Mr 24 '69
Madison avenue; $1,000 a word. J. Caples.
Sat R 52:126-7 Mr 8 '69
Musical chairs; shifting of accounts. W.
Weir. Sat R 52:74 D 13 '69
Thyme (rhymes with time) S. Freberg's
agency. il Newsweek 73:70 Mr 31 '69
What a tough kid with *fegataccio* can do on
Madison avenue. C. Sopkin. il N Y Times
Mag p32-4+ Ja 26 '69
   See also names of advertising agencies,
e.g. Foote, Cone and Belding, incorporated

Consolidations and mergers
Agencies merge on global scale: Chicago's
Leo Burnett co to acquire London press
exchange, ltd. Bsns W p42 My 17 '69
Burnett branches out: two units of the Lon-
don press exchange to be acquired. il
Newsweek 73:102 My 26 '69

Securities
Ad leader joins trend; J. Walter Thompson
going public. Bsns W p28 Ap 5 '69
Marketing Madison avenue. Time 93:90 Ap 11
'69

Time buyers
See Advertising mediums—Purchasing
ADVERTISING art
Art for ad's sake; Art directors club awards.
M. R. Weiss. il Sat R 52:54-5 Je 14 '69

ADVERTISING campaigns
Advertising's creative explosion. il News-
week 74:62-6+ Ag 18 '69
ADVERTISING characters
Ban the Bandito? il Newsweek 74:82+ D 22
'69
Legend of Smokey Bear. M. Hardy. il Nat
Parks 43:18-20 Ja '69
ADVERTISING mediums

Comics (books, strips, etc)
Admen try the comics. il Bsns W p 104 S 20
'69

Newspapers
Films; accepting advertising for X films.
S. Kauffmann. New Repub 161:39-40 S 6
'69

Periodicals
Playboy puts a glint in the admen's eyes. il
Bsns W p 142-4+ Je 28 '69

Purchasing
Ad men confront independent media services.
Bsns W p 124 N 29 '69
Broadcasting's hidden power: the TV-radio
reps. J. Tebbel. Sat R 52:68-9 D 13 '69
Middlemen put squeeze on admen; media
buying services. il Bsns W p80-1+ O 18 '69
ADVERTISING men
Poet doubles as an adman; L. E. Sissman.
Bsns W p 153-4 S 20 '69
ADVERTISING models. See Models (persons)
ADVERTISING research
Getting them to church; best-read magazine
ads of 1968. A. Cooper. il Newsweek 74:113
O 6 '69
   See also
Nielsen, A. C. company
ADVERTISING signs. See Signs and sign-
boards
ADVICE
How to sift advice. Nations Bsns 57:47 My
'69
Mini-maxims for my godson. A. Gordon.
Read Digest 95:135-8 Ag '69
Some advice on advice; or Take it from me.
R. Armour. il Parents Mag 44:44-5 Jl '69
ADVICE columns. See Newspapers—Advice
columns
ADVISORY commission on civil disorders. See
United States—National advisory commis-
sion on civil disorders
ADVISORY commissions. See United States—
Federal commissions
ADVISORY council on executive organization.
See United States—Advisory council on ex-
ecutive organization
ADVOCATE (newspaper) See Catholic press
ADZES
It's the ultimate whacker? il Sunset 142:208
Je '69
AEGEAN ISLANDS
Present charm and ancient past. H. Stephens.
il Yachting 125:50-1+ My '69
Some still unspoiled islands in the Greek sun.
D. Beal. il Holiday 46:46-7+ Ag '69
AEGOPODIUM. See Goutweed
AEKEN, Hieronymus van. See Bosch, H.
AERATION of grain. See Grain aeration
AERCAB (integrated aircrew escape/rescue
system capability) See Airplanes—Escape
devices
AERIAL cableways. See Cableways
AERIAL gunnery
   See also
Fire control (aerial gunnery)
AERIAL mapping. See Mapping, Aerial
AERIAL photography. See Photography, Aerial
AERIAL reconnaissance
Gamble goes on; intelligence gathering by
EC-121. Time 93:23 My 16 '69
Nixon warns North Korea: U.S. flights will
be protected; text of news conference,
April 18, 1969. R. M. Nixon. U S News 66:
72-5 Ap 28 '69
Protection money. il Newsweek 73:50+ My 5
'69
Spy business as usual for U.S. spook fleet;
navy's task force 71 in Sea of Japan. il
Bsns W p54+ Ap 26 '69
Surveillance; how it gets done. il Bsns W
p69-70 Jl 12 '69
Why spy? Nation 208:523-4 Ap 28 '69
Why spy planes are necessary. U S News 66:
27 Ap 28 '69
   See also
EC-121 incident, 1969
AERIAL reconnaissance cameras. See Cameras
AERIAL warfare. See European war, 1914-
1918—Aerial operations

AERO Commander division. See North American Rockwell corporation

AERO commuter
Aero commuter and Cable merge air taxi operations in California. Aviation W 90:41 Mr 31 '69

AEROBATIC airplanes. See Airplanes, Aerobatic

AEROBATICS. See Aviation—Stunt flying

AEROCARS. See Airplanes, Light—Automobile combinations

AERODYNAMICS
See also
Birds—Flight

AERODYNAMICS, Supersonic
Hypersonic studies get new focus. M. L. Yaffee. il Aviation W 91:34-5 D 22 '69

AEROFLOT (airline) See Airlines—Russia

AERONAUTIC engineers. See Aviation engineers

AERONAUTIC instruments
New products. See issues of Flying
Newest navcom; Edo-aire 771/772. il Flying 85:22+ Jl '69
Safe flight's SC-100; angle of attack speed control indicator. R. B. Weeghman. il Flying 84:84 Ap '69
What's your angle? angle-of-attack instruments. J. Gilbert. il Flying 84:82-3 Ap '69
See also
Airplanes—Instrument boards
Altimeters
Automatic pilot (airplanes)
Detectors, Infrared
Inertial guidance systems
Proximity warning indicators

Display systems
Helmet-mounted display interest revives. B. Miller. il Aviation W 90:71+ F 24 '69
Norden expands attitude indicator trials. K. J. Stein. il Aviation W 90:76-7+ Ja 27 '69
Sperry developing electronic ADI. B. Miller. il Aviation W 91:103-4+ Ag 18 '69

AERONAUTIC laboratories
See also
Cornell aeronautical laboratory, incorporated

AERONAUTIC meteorology. See Meteorology, Aeronautic

AERONAUTIC museums
See also
Smithsonian institution—National air and space museum

AERONAUTIC research
NASA, Transportation dept. plan study on civil aviation research. K. Johnsen. Aviation W 90:22 My 19 '69
Nixon sets aeronautic research timetable. K. Johnsen. Aviation W 91:29 S 22 '69
See also
Airborne instrument laboratory

AERONAUTICS
See also
Aviation
Balloon ascensions

History
Flier's journal. G. C. Kenney. il Am Heritage 21:46-57 D '69
Jenny. J. Gilbert. il Flying 84:52-5 Mr '69
See also
Smithsonian institution—National air and space museum

Laws and regulations
See Aviation—Laws and regulations

Safety devices and measures
See Aviation—Safety devices and measures

AERONAUTICS, Commercial
Challenges mark opening of 1970s. il Aviation W 91:14-15 mid-D '69
Clouded issue. A. H. Sypher. Nations Bsns 57:31-2 Ap '69
Coming: the twelve-hour world. il Nations Bsns 57:32-5 Ag '69
See also
Air travel
Airlines

Finance
Jam-up; the Nixon bill. il Newsweek 73:66 Je 30 '69

International aspects
See Aviation—International aspects

Alaska
Big airlift to the North Slope. F. A. Tinker. il Pop Mech 132:94-7+ N '69
Sightseeing by plane in Alaska. Sunset 143:34-5 O '69

Arctic Regions
See also
Aeronautics, Commercial—Alaska

Europe, Western
Case of who-builds-what; European airbus. il Sci N 95:327-8 Ap 5 '69

France
French to stress civil aircraft projects. E. H. Kolcum. Aviation W 91:23-4 D 1 '69

Great Britain
See also
Airlines—Great Britain

Latin America
Economic slowdown cuts growth in South America air traffic. il Aviation W 91:80 O 20 '69

Russia
Soviets expand airports, airways. Aviation W 91:32 D 1 '69

United States
Washington scene; unhappy landings: the mess in civil aviation. W. Hines. il Bul Atom Sci 25:37-40 My '69
See also
Airlines—United States
Airplane industry and trade—United States

AERONAUTICS, Military
See also
Airplanes, Military

Denmark
Denmark unifying top military command. W. L. Wetmore. il Aviation W 90:55-7+ Mr 31 '69

Europe, Western
Consortium fate linked to MRCA project. il Aviation W 90:108-9+ Je 2 '69
Fighter modernization top western goal. il Aviation W 90:186-8+ Je 2 '69

Israel
See also
Israeli-Arab war, 1967- —Aerial operations

Italy
See also
Airplanes, Military—Italy

Norway
Norwegian defense posture gives key role to air force. W. C. Wetmore. il Aviation W 90:40-1+ Mr 17 '69

Sweden
See also
Sweden—Air force

United States
See also
Air bases

AEROSOLS
Aerosol tissue adhesive. Chem 42:24 F '69
Atmospheric aerosols. R. O. McCaldin and others. bibliog il Science 166:381-2 O 17 '69
Gain on sprays; FDA investigation findings. J. Deedy. Commonweal 91:90 O 24 '69
Inhaling aerosol propellant. Todays Health 47:78 Ap '69
Lecithin aerosols generated ultrasonically above 25°C. E. W. Merrill and others. bibliog Science 164:1167-8 Je 6 '69
Mace for the masses. J. A. Page. Commonweal 90:141-3 Ap 18 '69
Mace in the face; frightening data revealed by Senate subcommittee hearings. J. Deedy. Commonweal 90:402 Je 27 '69

AEROSPACE industries
Special report: the 1970s: challenge in the marketplace; symposium, with editorial comment. il Aviation W 90:53, 84-9+ Je 2 '69
See also
Airplane industry and trade

Consolidations and mergers
Aerospace companies face antitrust inquiry in House. Aviation W 90:21 F 24 '69
French detail merger plan; Sud aviation, Nord-aviation and SEREB. Aviation W 91:18 O 13 '69

Directories
Marketing directory section. Aviation W 91:25+ mid-D '69

Employees
Apollo cuts trigger slump at Cape. Aviation W 91:63-4+ D 8 '69
Business flow spurs workforce changes. Aviation W 91:26-7 Jl 7 '69

AEROSPACE industries—Employees—*Cont.*
Sunnyvale: prunes to missiles. il Newsweek 73:77 Je 9 '69
Work force at KSC being cut to meet Saturn 5 launch rate. Aviation W 91:72 S 15 '69
  See also
International association of machinists and aerospace workers

Finance

Aerospace sales dip decreasing. Aviation W 92:24 Ja 5 '70
Boeing net seen slipping again this year. S. P. Siciliano. Aviation W 90:21 Mr 3 '69
Engine delay for 747 cuts Rohr profits. Aviation W 91:94 D 8 '69
Litton sales top $2 billion, set record for year. Aviation W 91:119 S 15 '69
More companies in aerospace report 1968 sales, profit gains. il Aviation W 90:94 Mr 31 '69
Nine-month sales dip reported by three major aerospace firms. Aviation W 91:31 N 17 '69
747 development costs push down Boeing's profits. Aviation W 90:30 My 5 '69
Several firms show gains in profits, sales. il Aviation W 91:121 Ag 11 '69
United aircraft deliveries slip in quarter; profit up. Aviation W 90:36 My 12 '69
United aircraft six-month net, sales decline. Aviation W 91:28 Ag 18 '69

International aspects

Courage to compete; excerpts from address. D. J. Haughton. Aviation W 90:21 Ap 14 '69
Paris air show underscores intense race for worldwide aerospace export markets; with editorial comment. C. Brownlow. il Aviation W 90:11, 24-8 Je 9 '69

Oceanographic activities

Pie in the sky (oceans division) wet-space industry. il Forbes 104:36+ Jl 15 '69

Pollution control activities

Pollution control market emerging. M. L. Yaffee. Aviation W 91:63+ Ag 18 '69

Europe, Western

Czech invasion bares NATO's atrophy. E. H. Kolcum. il Aviation W 90:81+ Mr 10 '69
Status of major U.S. European defense, aerospace programs. Aviation W 90:34-8 Mr 10 '69

France

France reorganizing aerospace industry. D. E. Fink. Aviation W 90:18-19 Mr 3 '69
Timing on eased Israel embargo awaited. D. E. Fink. Aviation W 91:22-3 Jl 21 '69
Varying effects on aerospace expected in franc devaluation. D. E. Fink. Aviation W 91:26 Ag 18 '69

Great Britain

Fund vise tightens on British aerospace. H. J. Coleman. il Aviation W 90:61+ Mr 10 '69
  See also
Society of British aerospace companies

Russia

Soviet defense outlays show continued increase. il Aviation W 90:71+ Mr 10 '69

United States

Aerospace layoffs hardly hurt. il Bsns W p92 Jl 19 '69
After Apollo, what? Newsweek 74:70 Ag 4 '69
Apollo's builders start closing the lines. il Bsns W p76-7 My 17 '69
Emerging pattern; Nixon administration policies affecting the aerospace industry. R. Hotz. Aviation W 90:17 My 12 '69
Evaluation register aimed for wider use. Aviation W 90:64+ Ja 27 '69
Failures in forecasting aircraft, missiles & space flight trends. Harvard Bsns R 47:74 S '69
Industrial impact of Apollo. F. A. Long. il Bul Atom Sci 25:70-3 S '69
Industry eyes housing field warily. W. H. Gregory. Aviation W 91:113+ S 15 '69
Industry is flying at low altitude. il Bsns W p29-30 S 6 '69
It takes 350,000 people to put three on the moon. A. Hamilton. il Sci Digest 65:22-6 Mr '69
New aerospace products. See issues of Aviation week & space technology
Outlook for 1970. R. Hotz. Aviation W 92:11 Ja 12 '70

Price of arms control; with editorial comment. il Bsns W p64-5+, 148 Jl 12 '69
Ready to design the new hardware. il Bsns W p51-2 S 13 '69
Status of major U.S. European defense, aerospace programs. Aviation W 90:34-8 Mr 10 '69
Transition period to spur new policies, technology for aerospace. R. Hotz. Aviation W 90:32-3 Mr 10 '69
Trouble in the marketplace. R. Hotz. Aviation W 90:11 F 17 '69
U.S. aerospace export decline foreseen. C. Brownlow. il Aviation W 90:104-6 Je 2 '69
Workhorse satellites. I. Geller. il Duns R 93: 67-8+ F '69
  See also
Government investigations—Aerospace industries
Lockheed aircraft corporation

AEROSPACE industries association of America, incorporated
AIA seeks new crashworthiness criteria. Aviation W 90:34 My 19 '69

AEROSPACE medical association
Aerospace medicine. Sci N 95:505 My 24 '69

AEROSPACE telemetry. See Space telemetry

AEROSPACE workers. See Aerospace industries—Employees

AESCHYLUS
Oresteia; adaptation. See Lewin, J. House of Atreus
Prometheus bound; adaptation. See Lowell, R.
  about
Forethinker updated; Robert Lowell's version of Prometheus bound. J. Chadwick. Sat R 52:30 My 3 '69

AESTHETICS
Christianity and aesthetics: conflict or correlation? V. R. Mollenkott. Chr Today 13: 6-9 My 9 '69
Five states of mind. P. Pavia. il Art N 68:23-5+ My '69
Hogarth and the ladies. I. Smith. il Horticulture 47:22-3 O '69
New aesthetics of sex: ugly is beautiful. il Esquire 72:172-7 D '69
State of taste. R. Lynes. Art in Am 57:121 My; 23 S; 47 N '69
State of taste: time, place and circumstance. R. Lynes. Art in Am 57:121 My '69
  See also
Art—Philosophy
Color
Form (art)
Music—Philosophy and aesthetics

AFFECTION. See Friendship; Love

AFFILIATE artists, incorporated
Affiliate artists, a success story. C. L. Osborne. il Hi Fi 19:MA18-19 D '69

AFFIRMING flame of Ardith Manners; story. See Hochstein, R.

AFGHANISTAN
  See also
Air travel—Afghanistan
Americans in Afghanistan
Hindu Kush
Hotels, taverns, etc.—Afghanistan

Description and travel

Adventures in Afghanland. D. Butwin. il Sat R 52:44+ O 25; 49-50+ N 1 '69

History

  See also
Kushan empire

Social life and customs

Memoirs of Afghanistan. P. Chesler. Mlle 69: 154-60 Je '69

AFGHANS (coverlets)
Knit an afghan in the gypsy spirit. il Good H 169:132+ S '69

AFLATOXIN. See Fungi

AFRICA
Africa: a symposium. D. Carney; A. A. Mazrui. il Bul Atom Sci 25:11-19 N '69
Nations of Africa; symposium. bibliog f Cur Hist 56:257-97+ My '69
  See also
Agriculture—Africa
Arts and crafts—Africa
Botswana
Communism—Africa
Economic assistance in Africa
Education—Africa
Hunting—Africa
Kilimanjaro
Negroes in Africa
Public health—Africa
Zoology—Africa

AFRICA—*Continued*

Bibliography

Studies on Africa. W. A. E. Skurnik. Cur Hist 56:300-4+ My '69

Civilization

Rediscovery of Africa; reprint. B. Davidson. il UNESCO Courier 22:66-7 Ag '69

Colonization

See also
Back-to-Africa movements

Discovery and exploration

Doctor Livingstone presumes. B. Farwell. il Horiz 11:104-11 Sum '69

Economic conditions

Economic development. D. Carney. Bul Atom Sci 25:11-15 N '69
Economic development in Africa today. R. L. West. bibliog f Cur Hist 56:263-8+ My '69
Economics & Africa: out in the cold? Sr Schol 94:18-19 Ja 31 '69
Progress: Africa's untold story. E. B. Thompson. il Ebony 24:74-6+ Je '69
See also
United Nations—Economic commission for Africa

Economic policy

Africa's problems; the other side of the story. E. B. Thompson. il Ebony 24:116-18+ Jl '69

History

Africa in history, by B. Davidson. Review
Sat R il 52:51-2+ Mr 22 '69. C. Miller

Bibliography

Articles and other books received; comp. by D. E. Gardinier. See issues of American historical review

Languages

See also
Swahili language

Nationalism

Africa on the eve of tomorrow. A. A. Mazrui. Bul Atom Sci 25:15-19 N '69
Africa's problems; the other side of the story. E. B. Thompson. il Ebony 24:116-18+ Jl '69

Native races

Difficult choice; conflict between tribalism and nationalism. P. Webb. il Newsweek 74:52-3 N 3 '69
Original affluent society; the Bushmen. il Time 94:55 Jl 25 '69
See also
Kenya—Native races
Negroes in Africa

Politics

Africa: continent of change; address, December 5, 1968. J. Palmer. 2d. Dept State Bul 59:696-702 D 30 '68
Africa on the eve of tomorrow. A. A. Mazrui. Bul Atom Sci 25:15-19 N '69
Africa's problems; the other side of the story. E. B. Thompson. il Ebony 24:117-18+ Jl '69
Are there any conservative Africans? G. Comte. Nat R 21:491+ My 20 '69
Last words from a murdered African leader: the American Negro cannot look to Africa for an escape. T. Mboya. il N Y Times Mag p30+ Jl 13 '69
Progress: Africa's untold story. E. B. Thompson. il Ebony 24:74-6+ Je '69
Rising star, rising crescent; militant Islam. R. W. Howe. New Repub 161:6-7 D 6 '69
Tanzania; stability and change in Africa; address, October 2, 1969. J. K. Nyerere. Vital Speeches 36:48-53 N 1 '69
Tshombe and Mboya. Chr Cent 86:942 Jl 16 '69
See also
Organization of African unity
Pan-Africanism

Religious institutions and affairs

Rising star, rising crescent; militant Islam. R. W. Howe. New Repub 161:6-7 D 6 '69
See also
Catholic church in Africa
Christians in Africa

Union (proposed)

Progress toward African unity. V. McKay. Cur Hist 56:257-62+ My '69

AFRICA, CENTRAL
See also
Chad
Congo (Democratic Republic)

AFRICA, EAST
See also
East African Federation (proposed)
Hunting—Africa, East

Description and travel

Elephants have the right of way! O. Gately. il Har Yrs 9:19-23 Ag '69

Politics

East African experience. K. W. Grundy and F. Fulton. bibliog f Cur Hist 56:275-81 My '69

AFRICA, NORTH
See also
Libya
Morocco
Niger
Tunisia

Politics

Politics and Islam in North Africa. W. H. Lewis. Cur Hist 56:136-40+ Mr '69

AFRICA, SOUTH

Foreign relations

Future of southern white Africa. D. J. Murray. bibliog f Cur Hist 56:269-74+ My '69

AFRICA, SOUTHEAST
See also
Swaziland

AFRICA, SOUTHERN
See also
Botswana
Guerrillas—Africa, Southern
United Nations—Africa, Southern
United Nations educational and training program for southern Africans

Economic relations

Apartheid's empire. I. Robertson. il Nation 208:596-7+ My 12 '69

Politics

Future of southern white Africa. D. J. Murray. bibliog f Cur Hist 56:269-74+ My '69
War in southern Africa. R. W. Howe. il For Affairs 48:150-65 O '69

Race problems

Apartheid's empire. I. Robertson. il Nation 208:596-7+ My 12 '69
Future of southern white Africa. D. J. Murray. bibliog f Cur Hist 56:269-74+ My '69
Here we go again; American journalists denounce white governments. Nat R 21:994+ O 7 '69
Southern Africa: a smuggled account from a guerrilla fighter. il Ramp Mag 8:8+ O '69

AFRICA, SUB-SAHARAN
Bend of the Niger River. M. Mangus. il Natur Hist 78:26-37 Ja '69
Islam in Sub-Saharan Africa. T. Y. Ismael. bibliog f il Cur Hist 56:146-50+ Mr '69

AFRICA, WEST
See also
Angola
Equatorial Guinea
Niger River
Sierra Leone

AFRICA evangelical conference. See Religious conferences

AFRICAN antelopes. See Antelopes

AFRICAN art. See Art, African

AFRICAN art objects. See Art objects, African

AFRICAN cookery. See Cookery, African

AFRICAN dance company of Ghana. See Dancing, African

AFRICAN dancing. See Dancing, African

AFRICAN languages
Vernacular languages in changing Africa; reprint. P. Diagne. il UNESCO Courier 22:30-1 Ag '69

AFRICAN Methodist Episcopal church
Daniel A. Payne and the A.M.E. general conference of 1888: a display of contrasts. C. Killian. bibliog por Negro Hist Bul 32:11-14 N '69

AFRICAN mice. See Rats

AFRICAN snails. See Snails

AFRICAN studies
Doctor Sunday comes to town; a Biafran teacher in the U.S. L. Rich. il Am Ed 5:20-3 My '69

AFRICAN trio; drama. See Winther, B.

AFRICAN violets
African violets under fluorescent lights. L. H. St Lawrence. Horticulture 47:37+ O '69
Latest news of African violets. C. C. Calkins. il Home Gard 56:64-5 Ap '69
New miniature African violets. H. Van Zele. il Horticulture 46:18-19+ Ag '68
No secrets to African violets. A. Tinari. il Org Gard & Farm 16:66-9 N '69
AFRICANA publishing corporation. See International university booksellers, incorporated
AFRICANUS, pseud.
Nkrumah's gone; Ghana's agony remains. Commonweal 90:136 Ap 18 '69
AFRIFA, Akwasi Amankwa
Chairman bows out. Newsweek 73:58 Ap 14 '69
Reformer removed. Time 93:39 Ap 11 '69
AFRO-AMERICAN culture. See Negroes—Culture
AFRO-AMERICAN dance ensemble
Philadelphia company finds its feet. D. Webster. il Dance Mag 43:62-4 Jl '69
AFRO-AMERICAN students. See Negro students
AFRO-AMERICAN studies
Achieving educational equality; stemming the black brain drain. V. Harding. Cur 105:37-40 Mr '69
Black dimension in curriculum. il Sch & Soc 97:83 F '69
Black history, or black mythology? P. Chew. il Am Heritage 20:4-9+ Ag '69
Black is...for credit. il Newsweek 74:102-3 O 20 '69
Black mood on campus; symposium. il Newsweek 73:53-9 F 10 '69
Black moods on the campus. Life 66:32 Ja 31 '69
Black studies; a top Negro's view; excerpts from address, August 28, 1969. A. F. Brimmer. U S News 67:12 S 8 '69
Black studies: an intellectual crisis; address. J. W. Blassingame. Am Scholar 38:548-61 Aut '69
Black studies at Harvard; personal reflections concerning recent events. H. Rosovsky. Am Scholar 38:562-72 Aut '69
Black studies curricula: University of California, Berkeley. Negro Hist Bul 32:6 My '69
Black-studies programs. Chr Today 13:25 Mr 14 '69
Black studies programs. Ed Digest 34:60 Ap '69
Black studies; San Francisco state courses. M. Mauk. New Repub 160:12-13 Mr 15 '69
Black studies studied; American council on education report. America 120:698 Je 21 '69
Black studies: the real issue. J. Hatch. Nation 208:755-8 Je 16 '69; Excerpts. Cur 109:33-8 Ag '69
Black studies thing. E. Dunbar. il N Y Times Mag p25-7+ Ap 6 '69
Black studies: trouble ahead. E. D. Genovese. Atlan 223:37-41 Je '69; Same abr. with title Black studies: legitimacy versus propaganda. Cur 109:39-42 Ag '69
Black studies Vatican; workshop on the black world at the Institute of the black world, Atlanta. il Newsweek 74:38 Ag 11 '69
Black studies: yes or no? America 120:578-9 My 17 '69
Boosting black studies; Ford foundation grants. B. B. Stretch. Sat R 52:58 Jl 19 '69
Calming the furor? Harvard university program. il Sr Schol 94:14-15 F 7 '69
Case for black studies. D. E. Pentony. Atlan 223:81-2+ Ap '69
College beset by black revolutionaries; Federal city college, Washington, D.C. il U S News 66:38-40 My 12 '69
Dilemma of black studies; Time essay. il Time 93:39-40 My 2 '69
Exclude whites? No, says top Negro educator. U S News 66:18 Je 2 '69
Fair Harvard. Newsweek 73:56 F 3 '69
Federal city college, Washington, D.C; offering Black studies program. Negro Hist Bul 32:5 My '69
Ghetto and gown: the birth of black studies. R. A. Fischer. Cur Hist 57:290-4+ N '69
Ivy league boost for black studies. U S News 66:10 F 3 '69
Putting "soul" into history. America 120:557 My 10 '69
Puzzled about Afro-American culture? il U S News 66:52-4 F 24 '69
Standards for Black studies: Society for religion in higher education meeting at Wells college. Chr Cent 86:1153 S 10 '69

Story of Swahili, an in language. il U S News 66:82 Mr 31 '69
Summer institutes in Afro-American studies. Sr Schol 94:Schol Teach 20 F 28 '69
Under federal fire: black studies. U S News 66:13 Mr 17 '69
Yale's new Afro-American studies program. Sch & Soc 97:206-7 Ap '69
AFRO-AMERICAN week. See Negro history week
AFTER images
Size adaptation: a new aftereffect. C. Blakemore and P. Sutton. bibliog il Science 166:245-7 O 10 '69
Visual motion perception: experimental modification. R. H. Masland. bibliog il Science 165:819-21 Ag 22 '69
See also
Eidetic imagery
AFTER-shave lotions. See Cosmetics for men
AFTER the night; story. See Stetson. N.
AFTERIMAGES. See After images
AFTERMATH; story. See Henderson, R.
AFTERNOON newspapers. See Newspapers
AGA Khan IV
Sardinia; the Aga Khan's hideaway; with photographs by E. Sarsini. Life 67:44-8 Ag 22 '69
AGE
Animal ages; life-spans and relative ages of man and other animals. D. P. Willoughby. il Natur Hist 78:56-9 D '69
Are you older than you think? Adult growth examination. il Sci Digest 66:20-1 Ag '69
See also
Age groups
Aging
Middle age
Old age
AGE (animals)
Animal ages; life-spans and relative ages of man and other animals. D. P. Willoughby. il Natur Hist 78:56-9 D '69
Only trees and tortoises live longer than people. D. Gunston. il Sci Digest 66:47-51 Ag '69
AGE (plants)
Only trees and tortoises live longer than people. D. Gunston. il Sci Digest 66:47-51 Ag '69
AGE, Voting. See Suffrage; Suffrage—United States
AGE and employment
Gray power; discrimination because of age. C. W. Phillips. America 120:132-3 F 1 '69
In Tucson, TOCER means jobs to 4,047 seniors in period of eleven years. Aging 173:15 Mr '69
Instant jobs for instant people; with report by M. L. Crum. il Har Yrs 9:6-10 N '69
Job bureau begun with OAA is funded locally. Aging 180:17 O '69
New source of help. Suc Farm 67:A2 N '69
Seniors succeed as teacher aides in Florida high schools project. Aging 171:9-10 Ja '69
Vermont finds older library aides boon in 4-county, 2,500-mile area. Aging 173:9 Mr '69
Wanted: retirees to teach. il Har Yrs 9:6-10 Ag '69
AGE determination of animals. See Animals—Age determination
AGE for marrying. See Marriage
AGE groups
Is age a dating problem? questions and answers. A. Wood. Seventeen 28:176+ Mr '69
See also
Youth-adult relationship
AGED
Among the aged. D. Rabinowitz. Commentary 47:61-6 Mr '69
Old love-patters not in vogue. Sci Digest 66:59 Ag '69
Prescription: one puppy; pets for the aged. Sci Digest 66:35 N '69
They are stealing things from me. J. Weinberg. Forbes 103:29 Ja 15 '69
See also
Aging
Christmas gifts for the aged
Gerontology
Old age
Old age assistance
Retirement
Retirement income
Senior citizens month
United States—Aging, Administration on

AGED—*Continued*

Adjustment problems

Are emotional problems necessary? symposium. il Har Yrs 9:34-7 O '69
Looking at retirement problems. N. V. Peale. Har Yrs 9:30-1 Je '69
Pets and old age. B. M. Levinson. bibliog Ment Hy 53:364-8 Jl '69
Psychologic rehabilitation for the normal elderly. T. Hickey. bibliog Ment Hy 53:369-74 Jl '69
Road back. B. Bergoff. Har Yrs 9:36-7 Jl '69
World scientists analyze aging. H. Alpert. il Har Yrs 9:33-5 D '69

Bibliography

Publications. See issues of Aging

Camps

See Camps

Care and hygiene

Doctor, I have a question; questions and answers. M. A. Hinrichs. See issues of Harvest years
Guided exercise big boon to older people. Aging 173:10-11 Mr '69
I'm the most geriatric of them all, community placement of geriatric patients. J. K. Thompson. bibliog Ment Hy 53:375-80 Jl '69
Life care housing; interview, ed. by W. P. Dumont. J. Frush, jr. il Har Yrs 9:6-13 D '69
Manpower needs in the field of aging. C. Tibbitts. Aging 173:3-5 Mr '69
NCSC has biggest convention; backs broader aging programs. Aging 178:13 Ag '69
New definition of protective services for aged is proposed. Aging 171:10-11 Ja '69
News of federal agencies. See issues of Aging
Older people are helped by families but home care programs needed also; report of a research and demonstration project. Aging 180:14 O '69
Poor health not result, but cause, of retirement, Missouri study finds. Aging 173:11-12 Mr '69
State budgets scanty on aging funds, official says. Aging 170:27 D '68
Treasure for grandma. G. O'Hara. il Redbook 133:14+ Je '69
See also
Aged—Housing
Aged—Medical care
Jewish association for services for the aging
Nursing homes
Physical education for the aged

Clothing and dress

Fashions for flattery. V. Jaxon. il Har Yrs 9:42-4 O '69

Economic conditions

Plight of retired people: second-class living standard; text of study made for the U.S. Senate's Special committee on aging. U S News 67:62-3 S 8 '69
Study spotlights plight of aged; findings of Senate's special committee on aging. U S News 66:67 Ap 28 '69
What did you say? with editorial comment. I. Ladimer. Har Yrs 9:2, 38-43+ Ag '69

Education

Six colleges give free tuition to aging; data sought on others. Aging 172:12 F '69
Time for learning. il Har Yrs 9:46-8 Je '69

Employment

See Age and employment

Federal aid

See Old age assistance

Health

See Aged—Care and hygiene

Housing

HUD housing awards. il Aging 172:10-11 F '69
Life care housing; interview, ed. by W. P. Dumont. J. Frush, jr. il Har Yrs 9:6-13 D '69
Ohio's golden age villages provide for independent living. il Aging 172:6-8 F '69
Resources for elderly included in 1968 housing act. Aging 172:9+ F '69

Medical care

Doctor, I have a question; questions and answers. M. A. Hinrichs. See issues of Harvest years

Nutrition

Eat your way to better health; with questions and answers. K. Anderson; K. Hillyard. il Har Yrs 9:6-18 F '69
Martin testifies on nutrition needs of aging. J. B. Martin. Aging 180:12-13 O '69
New AoA nutrition program funded for nation's capital. Aging 176:12 Je '69

Recreation

See Recreation for the aged

Rehabilitation

I'm the most geriatric of them all, community placement of geriatric patients. J. K. Thompson. bibliog Ment Hy 53:375-80 Jl '69
Psychologic rehabilitation for the normal elderly. T. Hickey. bibliog Ment Hy 53:369-74 Jl '69
Who cares for the aged? R. E. Burger. il Sat R 52:14-17 Ja 25 '69; Discussion. 52:35 F 15 '69

Statistics

Facts about older Americans. il Aging 175:12-13 My '69

Transportation

Older persons getting lower transit fares in NYC, San Francisco. Aging 176:16 Je '69
AGED, Homes for the. See Old age homes
AGED as consumers. See Consumers
AGEE, Hugh
Adolescent initiation: a thematic study in the secondary school; address, November 1968. Engl J 58:1021-4 O '69
AGEE, James
Appreciating Agee. A. Cooper. por Newsweek 73:86+ Ap 7 '69
[Book reviews] V. A. Kramer. Commonweal 90:211+ My 2 '69
Comment. T. Cassity; D. Jackson Poetry 114:409-12 S '69
Literary horizons. G. Hicks. Sat R 52:26 Mr 1 '69
AGENCIES, Advertising. See Advertising agencies
AGENCIES, Employment. See Employment agencies
AGENCIES, Regulatory. See Independent regulatory commissions
AGENCIES, Travel. See Travel agencies
AGENCY for international development. See United States—Agency for international development
AGENCY for technological development (proposed) See United States—Agency for technological development (proposed)
AGENTS. See Athletes agents; Literary agents; Purchasing agents; Real estate agents
AGENTS, Talent. See Theatrical agencies
AGGEN, Erich A. Jr
Beyond the moon. Space World F-5-65:38-9 My '69
Guest editorial. Space World F-5-65:4 My '69
AGGER, Donald G.
Reassessing the travel deficit. Sat R 52:38 Ja 25 '69
AGGLUTININS
Isopentenyladenosine stimulates and inhibits mitosis of human lymphocytes treated with phytohemagglutinin. R. C. Gallo and others. bibliog il Science 165:400-2 Jl 25 '69
AGGRESSION (international law)
Trouble spots in the world; as Laird sees them; excerpts from testimony. Senate foreign relations committee, July 15, 1969. M. R. Laird. U S News 67:8 Jl 28 '69
U.N. legal committee discusses the question of defining aggression; statements, November 19 and 25, 1968. J. S. Cooper. Dept State Bul 59:664-72 D 23 '68
See also
United Nations—Special committee on the question of defining aggression
AGGRESSIVENESS (psychology)
Art of family fighting. G. R. Bach and P. Wyden. il N Y Times Mag p61-2+ Ja 26 '69
Notes on aggression. J. Thompson. Commentary 47:63-6 Ap '69
Pretend he's your sister; advice at aggression clinic for overprivileged boys. B. Gilbert. il Sports Illus 30:58-62+ F 17 '69
Science and violence; adaptation of address, October 14, 1969. E. Rabinowitch. Bul Atom Sci 25:2-4+ D '69
Violence and aggression; symposium. il Todays Ed 58:29-40 S '69
See also
Violence

AGHA Khan IV. See Aga Khan IV
AGING
Aging, the disease with a cure. B. Frisch. il
Sci Digest 65:32-6 F '69
Do aging and accidents go together? Todays
Health 47:84 Mr '69
How to handle problems of aging. T. Irwin.
il Todays Health 47:28-31+ Jl '69
Slow aging. Sci Am 220:50+ Mr '69
What every middle-aged man should know.
Bsns W p89-90 Ag 30 '69
World scientists analyze aging. H. Alpert.
il Har Yrs 9:33-5 D '69
    See also
Age
    Anecdotes, facetiae, satire, etc.
. . . 20, 21, 73 and counting. R. Gordon. Vogue
154:174-5+ N 1 '69
You've come a long way, fella. il Esquire 72:
158-9 N '69
AGING, Administration on. See United States
—Aging, Administration on
AGING, Conferences on
Ann Arbor conference focuses on problems
of older consumer. il Aging 178:5-10+ Ag
'69
Conference calendar. See issues of Aging
Conference studies priorities allotted to
youth and age. il Aging 180:8+ O '69
Experts from thirty-six countries attend ger-
ontology congress. il Aging 180:5 O '69
OAA bill delay tragic, Cohen tells state ex-
ecutives on aging; urges action in 1969. il
Aging 170:3-5 D '68
Welcome to delegates to the International
congress of gerontology. J. B. Martin.
Aging 178:3 Ag '69
What do we need as consumers? University
of Michigan's Conference on aging discus-
ses the aging consumer. C. Rice. il Har
Yrs 9:46-8 S '69
World scientists analyze aging; Internation-
al congress of gerontology. H. Alpert. il
Har Yrs 9:33-5 D '69
AGNELLI, Giovanni, 1921-
Agnelli gets a horse. il Time 94:72 Jl 4 '69
Il boom transforms Italy. por Read Digest 94:
195-8+ Ap '69
Donna Marella and the avvocato; with in-
trod. T. Capote. il por Vogue 153:204-9
Ap 1 '69
Man who changed the A in Fiat. E. Seidler.
il por Motor T 21:98-9 Ap '69
AGNELLI, Marella (Caracciolo di Castagneto)
Donna Marella and the avvocato; with in-
trod. T. Capote. il pors Vogue 153:204-9
Ap 1 '69
AGNES Murphy, Sister. See Murphy, A.
AGNEW, Spiro Theodore
Agnew: is a college degree necessary? ex-
cerpts from address, December 10, 1969. U S
News 67:14 D 22 '69
Agnew's language, and the storm it's caus-
ing; interview with introduction. pors U S
News 67:19-20 N 17 '69
Agnew's ten commandments of protest; ex-
cerpts from remarks, December 3, 1969. por
U S News 67:14 D 15 '69
Look inside the Nixon administration; inter-
view. pors U S News 67:32-8 O 6 '69
Newspaper monopoly; address, November 20,
1969. Vital Speeches 36:133-6 D 15 '69;
Excerpts. U S News 67:12 D 1 '69
Quotations from the Vice President. por
Newsweek 74:39 N 17 '69
Spiro Agnew explains himself. por Life 67:34-
5 N 28 '69
Spiro speaks; excerpts from interview, ed. by
S. Alsop. Newsweek 74:110 N 3 '69
Television news coverage; address, Novem-
ber 13, 1969. Vital Speeches 36:98-101 D 1 '69;
Excerpts. por U S News 67:10 N 24 '69

about

Administration v. the critics. il por Time 94:
19-20 N 28 '69
Agnew ascendant. por Time 93:14 Mr 28 '69
Agnew demands equal time. il por Time 94:
18-19+ N 21 '69
Agnew finds a role. il pors Newsweek 74:38+
N 17 '69
Agnew on TV. W. F. Buckley, jr. Nat R 21:
1235 D 2 '69
Agnew: other voices, other views. H. J.
Sievers. America 121:579 D 13 '69
Agnew unleashed. il por Time 94:12 O 31 '69
Agnew vs. the Sun. il Newsweek 74:46 D 29
'69
Agnew: what to expect, and what he's really
like. por U S News 66:14-15 Ja 27 '69
Agnew's complaint: the trouble with TV. il
por Newsweek 74:88-90+ N 24 '69
Balancing act. il por Newsweek 74:35 S 29 '69

Beat the press, round two. il por Newsweek
74:25-6 D 1 '69
Curt words for the Veep. Newsweek 73:42+
Je 30 '69
Dick loves Ted; reaction on attacks on the
Viet Nam Moratorium. Time 94:22+ N 7 '69
Does Agnew tell it straight? L. Bernstein.
Newsweek 74:90-1 N 24 '69
First 100 days of Spiro Agnew. Life 66:32B
My 2 '69
For God so loves Spiro Agnew that he made
him Vice-President. G. Wills. por Esquire
71:57-61+ F '69
Freedom to cheer. Nation 209:586-7 D 1 '69
Government vs. press. K. Crawford. Newsweek
74:33 D 1 '69
Letter from Washington. R. H. Rovere. New
Yorker 45:165-9 N 29 '69
Making of a veep. il por Newsweek 73:27-8
Mr 10 '69
Mirror of the news and big brother. R. L.
Tobin. Sat R 52:59-60 D 13 '69
Mr Agnew and the demonstrators; Agnew
comes through. W. F. Buckley, jr. Nat R
21:1182-3 N 18 '69
Mob and the media. Nat R 21:1204 D 2 '69
Mouth that roared. por Newsweek 74:26 N 3 '69
New kind of vice president? il pors U S News
66:32-4 Mr 17 '69
Notes and comment; attacks on television
and newspapers. New Yorker 45:51-3 D 6
'69
Now listen to this. New Repub 161:9 N 29 '69
Old Agnew we knew. G. W. Johnson. New
Repub 161:13-14 N 29 '69
Operation Spiro. Nat R 21:1255-6 D 16 '69
Press faces its critics. Life 67:46 D 5 '69
Public regulation and the news media. J.
McLaughlin. America 121:586-9 D 13 '69
Role of Agnew. W. F. Buckley, jr. Nat R 21:
1286 D 16 '69
Some sober second thoughts on Vice Presi-
dent Agnew. F. W. Friendly. Sat R 52:61-2+
D 13 '69
Spiro Agnew: the king's taster. il pors Time
94:17-22 N 14 '69
Spiro Agnew's mission. J. Osborne. por New
Repub 161:17-20 N 15 '69
Spiro and middle America. Nation 209:492 N 10
'69
Spiro the veep. J. Osborne. New Repub 160:
10-12 Mr 1 '69
Spoofing Spiro. Time 94:78 D 5 '69
Statement of policy. Chr Cent 86:1565 D 3 '69
Storm over Agnew. F. S. Meyer. Nat R 21:
1220 D 2 '69
TRB from Washington. New Repub 161:6
N 1 '69
TRB from Washington; President Nixon's al-
ternate voice. New Repub 161:8 N 15 '69
Tale of two speeches. P. Steinfels. Common-
weal 91:272 N 28 '69
Television and Vice President Agnew. Amer-
ica 121:519 N 29 '69
Threat from Spiro. Commonweal 91:293-4 D
5 '69
Threat to the climate for free opinion. C. B.
Grannis. Pub W 196:29 N 24 '69
Tip of the iceberg. R. L. Shayon. Sat R 52:
24 N 29 '69
Weekly Agnew special. Time 94:62+ N 28 '69
Welcome, Spiro Agnew. B. Hennessy. New
Repub 161:13-14 D 13 '69

    Anecdotes, facetiae, satire, etc.
Report from the future. Commonweal 91:239
N 21 '69
Scram gets green light; Spiro Agnew to rise
at Marshgrass. T. Meehan. New Yorker 44:
32-3 F 15 '69
    Visit to Asia
Agnew abroad: selling the Nixon doctrine.
il pors U S News 68:4 Ja 12 '70
First look at Asia. il Time 95:11 Ja 12 '70
Getting to know you. il por Newsweek 75:
20 Ja 19 '70
Low profile. il pors Newsweek 75:16-17 Ja 12
'70
On tour. il por Time 95:19 Ja 5 '70
Orient express. il por Newsweek 75:13 Ja 5
'70
Programmed diplomacy. il por Time 95:17 Ja
19 '70
AGNEW family
Spiro, won't you please come home? B.
Angelo. il Time 94:21 N 14 '69
AGREEMENTS, International. See Treaties
AGREEMENTS, Trade. See Trade agreements

AGRICULTURAL administration
Current effect of the American aid program; with questions and answers. W. S. Gaud. Ann Am Acad 384:73-84 Jl '69

See also
Production, Agricultural
Surplus products, Agricultural

Canada
Trouble in the prairies; policy towards wheat farmers. il Newsweek 74:50 Ag 4 '69

Europe, Western
Europe builds a milk bomb. Farm J 93:D24 Ap '69

Latin America
Agrarian reform in Latin America. F. M. Foland. For Affairs 48:97-112 O '69

Peru
Startling innovation: more drastic Agrarian reform law; evaluation. E. A. Watlington. Chr Cent 86:1074 Ag 13 '69

United States
Are we headed for a big new land retirement program? with editorial comment. C. W. Gifford. Farm J 93:65+, 114 Ap '69
Death for a sacred cow? farm subsidy program. Newsweek 73:33 Je 9 '68
Farmer in the till; policies on federal payments and food programs. J. A. Schnittker. Atlan 224:43-5 Ag '69; Excerpts. Cur 110:32-7 S '69
Government and agriculture in the '70s. F. Bailey, jr. il Suc Farm 67:42-3 F '69
Hardin listens in. O. Bay and G. Lorang. il Farm J 93:16-16A+ Je '69
How do you want your farm credit system run? with editorial comment. C. W. Gifford. Farm J 93:28-9, 74 S '69
How not to help farmers. Farm J 93:70 My '69
Last minute report straight from Washington. See issues of Farm journal
Lifting farm policy out of its rut. E. K. Faltermayer. il Fortune 79:121+ My 15 '69
New farm plan for '71. C. W. Gifford. Farm J 93:19+ S '69
Once the headlines vanished; Paul Findley and payments to larger growers. Nation 209:429 O 27 '69
Politics of hunger. J. A. Hamilton. il Sat R 52:18-21+ Je 21 '69
Reading the subsidies. R. G. Sherrill. Nation 209:561-6 N 24 '69
Shifts ahead in farm policy. W. E. Swegle. Suc Farm 67:20 Ja '69
Should we limit government payments per farm? pro and con discussion. P. Findley; W. R. Poage. il Farm J 93:15+ Jl '69
Sweet smell of subsidy; Findley-Conte amendment. Nation 208:749 Je 16 '69
TRB from Washington; price-support payments. New Repub 161:4 Jl 5 '69
Too much of a good thing? how to grow less food. il Nations Bsns 57:40-2+ S '69
Tractor march on Washington? B. Coffman. il Farm J 93:26 Ag '69
What new farm plans next? with editorial comment. C. W. Gifford. Farm J 93:23+, 102 Mr '69

See also
Surplus products, Agricultural

AGRICULTURAL airplanes. See Airplanes in agriculture

AGRICULTURAL and technical college of North Carolina, Greensboro, N.C.
Changing Greensboro; black protest. il Time 93:22 My 30 '69
Siege of Greensboro. il Newsweek 73:38 Je 2 '69

AGRICULTURAL chemical records. See Farm records

AGRICULTURAL chemicals
Gambling with nature; usages of pesticides and herbicides. Commonweal 89:512-13 Ja 24 '69
Hints for mixing farm chemicals. C. E. Sommers. il Suc Farm 67:66-7 F '69
How's your chemical I.Q? Suc Farm 67:76 F '69
We've got them on the run. R. Rodale. Org Gard & Farm 16:25-7 N '69

See also
Herbicides
Weeds—Chemical control

Residues
What to do about chemical carryover. C. E. Sommers. il Suc Farm 67:24-5 D '69

AGRICULTURAL chemistry
See also
Soil fertility

AGRICULTURAL credit
See also
Farm finance

AGRICULTURAL economics. See Agriculture—Economic aspects

AGRICULTURAL experiment stations
More and better corn. V. E. Green, jr. il Américas 21:42-5 N '69
See also
Agricultural research

AGRICULTURAL forecasts
Agriculture, the ten years ahead. R. Krumme. il Suc Farm 67:28-9 Ja '69
Big challenge ahead in crops. C. E. Sommers. il Suc Farm 67:34-5 Jl '69
Farmcast. See issues of Farm journal

AGRICULTURAL innovations
Green revolution: cornucopia, or Pandora's box? C. R. Wharton, jr. For Affairs 47:464-76 Ap '69

AGRICULTURAL labor. See Farm labor

AGRICULTURAL machinery
Machinery ideas for tillage and planting. P. B. Jones and G. Earle. il Suc Farm 67:28-9 D '69
Machinery management guide; symposium. il Suc Farm 67:45-50+ Ja '69
Machinery parade; photographs. See issues of Farm journal
What's new. P. B. Jones. See issues of Successful farming
See also
Cultivators
Fertilizer spreaders
Grain handling
Planters (farm machines)
Plows
Spraying apparatus
Tractors

Depreciation
See Depreciation

Maintenance and repair
Get ready for spring work. P. B. Jones. il Suc Farm 67:38-9 Mr '69
Grease stretches machinery life. Suc Farm 67:55 Ja '69

Prices
He defends today's machinery prices; interview, ed. by J. Carlson. W. Stone. Farm J 93:52J Mr '69

Safety devices and measures
Proof: safety does pay; slow moving vehicle emblems on farm machinery traveling public roads. Suc Farm 67:94 Mr '69

AGRICULTURAL machinery industry and trade

Finance
Thin harvest; sales and earnings. il Forbes 103:48 Je 1 '69

AGRICULTURAL mechanization. See Farm mechanization

AGRICULTURAL pests
See also
Insects, Injurious and beneficial
also names of agricultural pests, e.g. Nematodes; *also* subhead Diseases and pests under names of crops, e.g. Corn—Diseases and pests

AGRICULTURAL production. See Production, Agricultural

AGRICULTURAL research
Agricultural development in Africa; adaptation of address, April 1968. A. L. Mabogunie. Bul Atom Sci 25:21-3+ Ap '69
Agricultural sciences (cont) Sci N 95:284 Mr 22 '69
See also
Botanical research
Dairy research
Plant breeding
Purdue university, Lafayette, Ind.—Laboratory for agricultural remote sensing

AGRICULTURAL research service. See United States—Agricultural research service

AGRICULTURAL schools
See also
Pan American agricultural school

AGRICULTURAL societies
See also
American farm bureau federation
United grain farmers of America

AGRICULTURAL subsidies. See Agricultural administration—United States

AGRICULTURAL surplus products. See Surplus products, Agricultural

AGRICULTURAL tractors. See Tractors

AGRICULTURAL workers. See Farm labor

AGRICULTURE
What's new: Washington. See issues of Successful farming
See also
Crops
Food and agriculture organization of the United Nations
Food supply
Greenhouses
Livestock
Threshing
also headings beginning Agricultural, Farm, Soil

Awards, prizes, etc.
Tiniest farm in America; award for superior agricultural achievement. L. Riotte. il Org Gard & Farm 16:24-7 Je '69

Economic aspects
Agriculture trends 1969: too much and too little? il Sr Schol 94:9 Ja 31 '69
Color the cattle green. il Fortune 80:26+ S '69
Farm business. See issues of Farm journal
Farm of the future; address, July 11, 1969. J. P. Campbell. Vital Speeches 35:636-9 Ag 1 '69
Farmcast. See issues of Farm journal
Know what it costs to grow corn, soybeans. G. Grooms. Suc Farm 67:A4 N '69
Let's stop tax-dodge farming! R. Krumme. Suc Farm 67:39+ F '69
Midyear outlook: for crops, prices and money. C. W. Gifford. Farm J 93:17+ Ag '69
1970 farm outlook. R. Krumme and R. Reiman. il Suc Farm 67:8-9 D '69
Rich get richer. B. J. Culliton. il Sci N 95: 335-7 Ap 5 '69
What's new: money management. R. Krumme. See issues of Successful farming
See also
Production, Agricultural
Wheat trade

Federal aid
See Agricultural administration—United States

Periodicals
See also
Successful farming (periodical)

Africa
Agricultural development in Africa; adaptation of address, April 1968. A. L. Mabogunje. Bul Atom Sci 25:21-3+ Ap '69

Asia
Green revolution; cornucopia, or Pandora's box? C. R. Wharton, jr. For Affairs 47: 464-76 Ap '69
Rich get richer. B. J. Culliton. il Sci N 95: 335-7 Ap 5 '69

Colombia
Story of Antonio Arango: soil erosion in Colombia; reprint. G. Nannetti. UNESCO Courier 22:6-7 Ag '69

Cuba
Report; Cuba. E. Rothschild. Atlan 223:14+ Mr '69

Great Britain
Akenfield: portrait of an English village. by R. Blythe. Review
Atlan 224:110-12 S '69. Y. Blumenfeld
England's cruel earth; excerpt from Akenfield: portrait of an English village. R. Blythe. Harper 238:46-52+ Ap '69

India
India pushes its green revolution; fourth five year plan. il Bsns W p 104+ My 31 '69
Rich get richer. B. J. Culliton. il Sci N 95: 335-7 Ap 5 '69
Unknown saint of India: V. Ferrer, with photographs by C. Rentmeester. Life 66: 36-44 F 28 '69

Long Island, N.Y.
Annals of agriculture; land around East Hampton and Amagansett. M. Hunt. New Yorker 45:57-8+ N 1 '69

Mexico
A.F.S.C. teams aid Mexican farmers. F. U. Ross. il Chr Cent 86:1624-6 D 17 '69

Russia
USSR resources for agriculture. C. D. Harris. bibliog il Focus 20:1-7 D '69

Scotland
Profiles; Colonsay: the island of the crofter and the laird. J. McPhee. il New Yorker 45:69-70+ D 6 '69

Southern states
Farming on the Blue Ridge parkway. S. H. Evison. il Nat Parks 43:18-20 O '69

Taiwan
How to develop the developing nations. il Newsweek 73:43-4 F 3 '69

Tunisia
See also
Irrigation—Tunisia

Turkey
Villager's role in a half-century of change. J. Kolars. bibliog il Focus 19:8-11 Ap '69

Underdeveloped areas
Feeding the hungry; Indicative world plan of the FAO. R. Critchfield. New Repub 161: 16-19 O 25 '69
How to develop the developing nations. il Newsweek 73:43-4 F 3 '69
U.S. agribusiness shows the way; American companies putting agricultural and marketing skills to work in poor lands. il Bsns W p52-6+ Ja 18 '69

United States
Blueprint for farming in the '70s. il Suc Farm 67:27-9 Ja; 42-3 F; 36-7 Mr; 32-3 Ap; 28-9+ My; 24-5 Je; 34-5 Jl '69
Farmcast. See issues of Farm journal
Last minutes report straight from Washington. See issues of Farm journal
What's new: Washington. See issues of Successful farming
Where are the great leaders? D. Hanson. Suc Farm 67:18 Ap '69
Where food prices are headed; interview. C. M. Hardin. il U S News 67:69-72 O 27 '69
Will we run out of farmers? D. Hanson. Suc Farm 67:16 Je '69; Reply. S. Johnson. 67: 16+ Ag '69
Worries of a Nebraska farmer and a Missouri biologist. J. Olds. Org Gard & Farm 16:66-70 D '69
See also
Agricultural administration—United States
Agriculture—Economic aspects
County agents
United States—Agriculture, Department of

AGRICULTURE, Prehistoric
See also
Grain—History

AGRICULTURE and state. See Agricultural administration

AGUALLO, Thomaline
Celebration; story. Seventeen 28:138-9 N '69
World's mirror; story. Seventeen 28:120-1 O '69

AGUIRRE, Emiliano
Evolutionary history of the elephant. bibliog Science 164:1366-76 Je 20 '69

AH, wilderness! drama. See O'Neill. E. G.

AHLBRANDT, Laird Kleine-. See Kleine-Ahlbrandt, L.

AHLERS, Arvel
Cash-in on your photographs. Pop Phot 64: 75-7+ Mr '69

AHLERS, Eleanor, and Sypert, Mary
Case for decentralization. bibliog pors Library J 94:4207-10 N 15 '69

AHMAD, Aijaz
Law & order in Pakistan. Nation 208:455-8 Ap 14 '69

AHMAD, Eqbal
How we look to the third world. Nation 208: 265-9 Mr 3 '69

AHRENS, J. F. See Miller. P. M. jt. auth.

AICHI, Kiichi
Japan's legacy and destiny of change. For Affairs 48:21-38 O '69

AICHINGER, Ilse
Where I live; story, tr. by A. Weinreich. Vogue 153:259+ My '69

AID-to-education award. See American city (periodical)

AID to families with dependent children (program) See Child welfare—United States

AIDA; opera. See Verdi. G.

AIDES, Psychiatric. See Hospitals, Psychiatric —Staff

AIDES, Teachers. See Teachers aides

AIDS in teaching. See Teaching—Aids and devices

AIGNER, Lucien
(ed) See Mills. J. Five sales in one year to Reader's digest

AIKEN, Conrad
One thing and another; interview, ed. by J. K. Hutchens. por Sat R 52:24-5 D 20 '69

AIKEN, D. E.
Photoperiod, endocrinology and the crustacean molt cycle. bibliog Science 164:149-55 Ap 11 '69

AIKEN, Michael
Community power and community mobilization; excerpts from The structure of community power: readings. bibliog f Ann Am Acad 385:76-88 S '69

AIKEN, Scott
Cincinnati airs world affairs. Am Ed 5:24-6 My '69

AIKMAN, Alexander B. See Mattick, H. W. jt. auth.

AILEY, Alvin, American dance theatre. See Alvin Ailey American dance theater

AIMÉE, Anouk
African idyll. pors Harp Baz 102:184-7 Ap '69

AIMS in education. See Education—Aims and objectives

AINSWORTH, Norma
How to create live characters in a juvenile short story. Writers Digest 49:36-9+ D '69

AINSWORTH, Robert Andrew, 1910-
Code for judges. por Time 93:61 Je 20 '69

AIR
See also
Fog

Analysis
Antarctic atmospheric chemistry: preliminary exploration. W. H. Fischer and others. bibliog il Science 164:66-7 Ap 4 '69

AIR Alpes. See Airlines—France

AIR bases
Attention: Mr Fulbright; defense treaty and use of Taiwan for Vietnam operations. New Repub 160:6-7 My 10 '69
Bare-base test spurs debate on funding. D. A. Brown. il Aviation W 91:30-1 N 17 '69
Master of air defense; J. J. Kelly, head of unit at Saglek Bay, Labrador. il Ebony 24:124-6+ O '69
Now: more bomber bases in America. il U S News 67:49 Ag 4 '69
USAF to test bare-base concept. C. Brownlow. Aviation W 91:16-17 O 6 '69
USAFE studies Wheelus pullout. Aviation W 91:110 N 17 '69

AIR buses. See Airplanes, Jet propelled

AIR California (airline)
Merger could reshape California market. N. S. Himmel. Aviation W 92:42+ Ja 12 '70

AIR cargo containers. See Containers for shipping

AIR cargo planes. See Airplanes, Freight

AIR cargo thefts. See Stealing

AIR conditioning
How to air condition your home with well water. E. F. Luscinskas. il Pop Sci 195:126-30+ Jl '69
Sum of comfort: central air conditioning. House & Gard 136:58+ N '69
What the systems approach means to air conditioning. R. E. Fischer and F. J. Walsh. il Arch Rec 145:197-204 Ap; 146. 151-8 Ag; 165-72 N '69
See also subhead Air conditioning under various subjects. e.g. Airplanes—Air conditioning

AIR conditioning equipment
Basic air-conditioning components and packages. il Arch Rec 146:156-7 Ag '69
Considering an air conditioner? Sunset 143:78-9 Ag '69
Fixing up an older home. il Bet Hom & Gard 47:38 My '69
Hot and cold running air; energy separator for air conditioning and heating. A. P. Armagnac. il Pop Sci 195:60-1 Jl '69
Let's cool it; what's new in the field of room air conditioners? il Consumer Bul 52:7-12 Jl '69

Installation
Air conditioner in a fireplace? H. R. Pfister. il Pop Sci 195:38 Jl '69

Maintenance and repair
Keeping the cool in your room air conditioner. E. Powell. il Pop Sci 195:153-9+ Ag '69

AIR conditioning industry and trade

Finance
Wait until next year! air-conditioner market is growing. il Forbes 103:74-5 Ap 15 '69

AIR currents. See Winds

AIR cushion vehicles
Air car comes in a kit. J. Capotosto. il Mech Illus 65:68-9+ My '69

Air cushion vehicle. G. R. Boling. il Sea Front 15:376-9 N '69
Boats that fly: the Hovercraft and Hydroskimmer. F. T. Moss. il Yachting 125:112-14+ Ja '69
Can hovercraft lick its jinx? il Bsns W p 111 Ja 10 '70
Coming: streamliners without wheels. J. A. Volpe. il Pop Sci 195:51-5+ D '69
Contract for air cushion ship expected by Bell in December. Aviation W 91:55 O 13 '69
Flying ships: how they're working. il U S News 67:13 Jl 14 '69
Flying the English Channel: altitude 7 feet. J. A. Maxtone-Graham. il Pop Mech 131:102-5+ Ja '69
High speed on a blast. Bsns W p48 Ap 5 '69
Leading international ground effect machines; specifications (cont) Aviation W 90:174 Mr 10 '69
New life for Hovercraft. il Time 95:39 Ja 19 '70
Now: air-cushion vehicle you can buy. C. E. Nerpel. il Pop Sci 194:59-61 Ja '69
Surface effect ship contracts awarded. il Aviation W 90:22 F 3 '69
Trains without wheels. E. Gross. il Sci N 95:358-60 Ap 12 '69
Up, up (a couple of inches or so) and away; Cushionflight-240. il Esquire 72:94-5 Jl '69
Volpe assesses potential of air cushion vehicle. Aviation W 90:56 My 5 '69
Will Britannia rule the waves, on air? A. C. Book. il Sea Front 15:30-3 Ja '69

AIR filters
New filters eliminate auditorium odors. Am City 84:20 Ja '69
Right way to replace furnace filters. il Pop Mech 132:173 D '69
Ultimate indoor comfort. J. H. Ingersoll. il House B 111:88-9+ F '69

AIR force association
At play with the military-industrial complex: Air force association and Army association meetings. P. Dickson and R. Skole. Esquire 73:66B+ Ja '70

AIR force bases. See Air bases

AIR force systems command. See United States —Air force—Systems command

AIR freight service
Air forwarding authority granted to truckers again. J. W. Carter. Aviation W 90:27 Ap 28 '69
Airfreight volume grows, yield slumps. J. Carter. il Aviation W 90:197-8+ Mr 10 '69
Big airlift to the North Slope. F. A. Tinker. il Pop Mech 132:94-7+ N '69
CAB study underscores trunks' dominance of air cargo market. Aviation W 91:52 Jl 21 '69
Cargo diverted by dock strike clogs N.Y. airfreight terminals. J. W. Carter. Aviation W 90:30 F 10 '69
Computerization urged to ease airfreight paperwork backlog. Aviation W 90:39 My 12 '69
Customs plan bypasses JFK jam. J. W. Carter. Aviation W 91:28-9 Jl '69
Lockheed mass cargo system. D. A. Brown. il Aviation W 91:24-6 D 22 '69; 92:30-2 Ja 12 '70 (to be cont)
Textile firm considering buying own air freighters. R. G. O'Lone. Aviation W 90:42+ Ap 21 '69
See also
Flying Tiger line, incorporated

Rates
Airlines consider increased tariff bids. L. Doty. Aviation W 90:36 My 5 '69
Revised IATA cargo rates to favor bulk containers. Aviation W 90:29 My 19 '69

Statistics
Growth in North Atlantic air cargo and mail, first six months of 1969 over 1968; table. Aviation W 91:70 O 20 '69
Growth in U.S. airline mail and cargo: tables. Aviation W 90:34 Ap 7 '69
North Atlantic air cargo and mail data, first six months of 1969; tables. Aviation W 91:40-1 N 10 '69

AIR freight terminals. See Airport buildings

AIR Glaciers. See Airlines—Switzerland

AIR houses. See Domes

AIR-India International. See Airlines—India

AIR Intelligence. See Military intelligence

AIR ions. See Ions

AIR layering of plants. See Plant propagation

AIR traffic control—*Continued*
Radar replacement studies for control of air traffic. Aviation W 90:28 Mr 31 '69
Tangled mess in aviation; with editorial comment. Bsns W p52-4+, 100 Ag 9 '69
Target is 1980. E. Gross. il Sci N 95:531-3 My 31 '69
Traffic control draws emphasis in congressional safety hearings. D. C. Winston. Aviation W 90:20 F 10 '69
Warning issued on traffic control. P. J. Klass. Aviation W 91:37-9 S 15 '69
Washington advisory. D. H. Scott. Flying 84:30-1+ My '69
　　See also
Airports—Traffic control
Radar in aviation

AIR traffic controllers (persons)
Air controller hiring postponed by FAA. Aviation W 90:19 Ap 21 '69
Air controllers plead sickness; staging a slowdown. U S News 66:65 Je 30 '69
Air traffic cop; on the hottest spot in Aviation; Kennedy international airport. R. Lindsey. il N Y Times Mag p28-9+ S 14 '69
Airport/airways legislation due for decisive votes in September. Aviation W 91:58 Ag 11 '69
FAA to revise air controller programs. D. A. Brown. Aviation W 91:24-5 Ag 18 '69
Flying toward more air traffic jams; caused by air traffic controllers tactics. Bsns W p33-4 Jl 26 '69
Jam-up. il Newsweek 73:66 Je 30 '69
Senate unit hears warning by controllers. D. C. Winston. Aviation W 90:28-9 Je 30 '69
Traffic cop of the sky. C. Peet. il Pop Mech 130:104-7+ D '68
U.S. court ruling upholds FAA in transfer of air controllers. Aviation W 91:27 N 10 '69
Wide absenteeism of controllers at FAA posts slows air traffic. Aviation W 90:32 Je 23 '69
　　See also
Professional air traffic controllers organization
Supervisory air traffic controllers organization

Training
What does it take to be a controller? il Bsns W p54 Ag 9 '69

AIR transport agreements. See Aviation—International aspects

AIR transport association of America
ATA offers new system for air traffic control. Aviation W 91:37 Ag 11 '69
ATA unit divided on equipment for retrieving disabled jets. Aviation W 91:32 S 29 '69
Looking for a traffic cop in the sky. il Bsns W p76-7+ N 29 '69
No holds; ATA recommendations for modernizing air traffic control system. R. B. Parke. Flying 85:33 Jl '69

AIR travel
Changes in air travel; both good and bad. il U S News 67:58-60 S 29 '69
Confessions of an air traveler. W. A. Rusher. il Nat R 21:650-1 Jl 1 '69
Future of air travel; a special issue; symposium. il Holiday 46:28-67+ Jl '69
Jumbo-jet service; set now for '69. U S News 66:14 F 24 '69
Passenger comfort; letter. W. Botstiber; discussion. Aviation W 90:94 Ja 20 '69
Pleasures of a birdman. W. F. Rickenbacker. il Nat R 21:84 Ja 28 '69
Travel notes; what the next ten years will bring. R. Joseph. Esquire 73:58-9 Ja '70
　　See also
Aeronautics, Commercial
Airlines
Private flying

Anecdotes, facetiae, satire, etc.
And we hope you'll fly with us again; drawings by T. Ungerer. Holiday 46:96 Jl '69

Economic aspects
Air travel bargains. N. D. Ford. il Har Yrs 9:6-15+ Je '69

Physiological aspects
See Aviation—Physiological aspects

Taxation
Airlines prepare for tough fight on New Jersey passenger tax. Aviation W 91:36 D 15 '69
New Jersey considers tax on Newark air passengers. Aviation W 90:30 Mr 31 '69

Afghanistan
Adventures in Afghanland; the flying bazaar. D. Butwin. Sat R 52:44+ O 25 '69

Europe, Western
Economic clouds dim European airline traffic outlook for 1969. il Aviation W 90:217-18 Mr 10 '69

Germany (Federal Republic)
Allies fight over Berlin; joint service of BEA and Air France. il Bsns W p 148 Je 21 '69

Latin America
Tourism in South America. M. B. Mármol. il Américas 21:49-53 N '69

Middle East
El Al thrives despite Arab fire. il Bsns W p34+ Mr 1 '69

United States
Down, down and away; Grand Canyon sightseeing. L. Barry. il Pop Phot 64:14+ Mr '69
New dazzle to travel, U.S.A. D. Messinesi. Vogue 153:102-3 F 1 '69
Nixon's ideas for improving air travel. il U S News 66:44 Je 30 '69
On flying more and enjoying it less. Time essay. il Time 93:84-5 Ap 18 '69

AIR travel clubs
To the Super bowl with a flying country club; Sky roamer society. R. Blount, jr. Sports Illus 30:42+ Ja 27 '69
Travel notes; community flying clubs. R. Joseph. Esquire 71:48+ Ja '69

AIR turbulence. See Atmospheric turbulence

AIR West, incorporated
Air West seeks end to Idaho Piper route. Aviation W 91:37 N 17 '69
Examiner backs Hughes-Air West pact. Aviation W 90:29 Ap 21 '69
Hughes seeks Air West revisions. Aviation W 91:26 N 3 '69
Losses, CAB terms imperil Hughes' Air West purchase. Aviation W 91:32 Ag 18 '69

AIRBORNE instruments laboratory
Sweden picks microwave ILS for Viggen. il Aviation W 90:64-6 F 3 '69

AIRBORNE searchlights. See Searchlights

AIRBUSES. See Airplanes, Jet propelled

AIRCRAFT
　　See also
Balloons
Gliders (aeronautics)

AIRCRAFT carriers
Before the colors fade; captain of the Franklin; interview, ed. by D. Davidson. L. E. Gehres. il Am Heritage 20:60-3+ Ap '69
Korean assignment strains carrier force. C. Brownlow. Aviation W 90:18 Ap 28 '69
Navy prepares fight for carriers. C. Brownlow. Aviation W 91:16-17 Ag 25 '69

Fires and fire protection
Back to Pearl Harbor; U.S.S. Enterprise fire. il Time 93:14-15 Ja 24 '69
Fire at sea; Enterprise fire. il Newsweek 73: 29-30 Ja 27 '69

AIRCRAFT carriers, Atomic powered
Go ahead for nuclear carrier. U S News 67: 11 S 22 '69

AIRCRAFT shows. See Aviation—Exhibitions

AIRD, Catherine, pseud.
Detective novel. Writer 82:11-14 Ag '69

AIRDOMES. See Domes

AIRFOILS
　　See also
Flaps, Airplane

AIRFREIGHT. See Air freight service

AIRGLOW
Airglow and star photographs in the daytime from a rocket. D. C. Evans and L. Dunkelman. bibliog il Science 164:1391-3 Je 20 '69

AIRHOUSES. See Domes

AIRLINE hostesses. See Airlines—Hostesses

AIRLINE magazines. See Periodicals for airline passengers

AIRLINE mechanics. See Airplane mechanics

AIRLINE mergers. See Airlines—Consolidations and mergers

AIRLINES
Airlines will make it easier to fly. il Nations Bsns 57:42-4+ Mr '69
U.S. route policy irks Europeans. L. Doty. Aviation W 90:42 Ap 14 '69
　　See also
Air travel
　　also names of airlines, e.g. Pan American World airways

AIRLINES—*Continued*

Accounting
Quick depreciation grows among trunks. W. H. Gregory. il Aviation W 90:28-9 Ap 28 '69

Advertising
Airline promotions featuring happiness. R. F. Coburn. Aviation W 90:49 Ap 14 '69
Bunny club airline; BOAC's The beautiful singles of London tour. il Time 94:58+ S 26 '69
Canceled date; BOAC's promotion. il Newsweek 74:86 S 29 '69
Miami carriers launching traffic promotions early. R. H. Kahn. il Aviation W 91:29-30 N 3 '69

Automation
Automated baggage system tested for use by airlines. E. J. Bulban. il Aviation W 91:150-1+ O 20 '69

Communication systems
FAA, airlines weigh Pacific satcom. P. J Klass. Aviation W 91:199-200+ O 20 '69

Consolidations and mergers
Aero commuter and Cable merge air taxi operations in California. Aviation W 90:41 Mr 31 '69
Airline merger guidelines readied. H. D. Watkins. Aviation W 91:27-8 D 22 '69
Bill to prevent takeovers of airlines seen passing. L. Doty. Aviation W 90:28 Ap 7 '69
Difficulties beset local service mergers. R. G. O'Lone. Aviation W 90:27-9 Mr 17 '69
Mating season for big birds; Northwest-Northeast combination. Time 94:86+ N 21 '69
Merger movement in the airline industry. il Fortune 81:37-8+ Ja '70
New flight plan for the airlines. G. Burck. il Fortune 79:98-101+ Ap '69
New trunkline merger talks open. L. Doty. Aviation W 91:25 Ag 25 '69
1970s industry pattern emerging; Northwest-Northeast merger. L. Doty. Aviation W 91:33-4 N 17 '69
Northeast meets Northwest. il Newsweek 74:73 N 24 '69
Routes that lead to merger. il Bsns W p33 Jl 26 '69
See also
Local service airlines—Consolidations and mergers

Cooperation
Pooling runs into cost, revenue share snags. R. F. Coburn. Aviation W 91:204-5+ O 20 '69
SAS-Aeroflot transasian pact to influence future authority. Aviation W 91:36-7 N 17 '69

Cost of operation
Four/three-engine turbojet/fan aircraft operation costs, first half, 1969; tables. Aviation W 91:48 S 29 '69
Two-engine turbojet/turbofan aircraft operating costs, first half, 1969; tables. Aviation W 91:49 S 29 '69

Costs
High cost of flying. P. Fiori. il Holiday 46:63 Jl '69

Credit cards
See Credit cards

Employees
See also
Airlines—Hostesses
Airlines—Wages and hours

Equipment and supplies
CSA faces reliance on Soviet aircraft. E. H. Kolcum. il Aviation W 91:111 O 20 '69
737 eases smoothly into Lufthansa fleet. R. F. Coburn. il Aviation W 91:36-7 S 29 '69
See also
Airports—Equipment

Fares
Air fare war revs up: plan to cut group rates sets off dispute with nonskeds and agents. il Bsns W p44+ Ap 5 '69
Airlines consider increased tariff bids. L. Doty.   Aviation W 90:36 My 5 '69
Airlines gird to match Alitalia cuts. Aviation W 91:30-1 S 29 '69
Al's fare; Alitalia's plan. Newsweek 74:98 S 29 '69
April target set for new Atlantic fares. Aviation W 91:196 O 20 '69
Atlantic tariff imbroglio persists. R. F. Coburn. Aviation W 91:24-5 O 13 '69

Bargain season. Time 94:94+ N 7 '69
Bargains, if you are flying east. Sunset 142:50 My '69
Basic revisions to fares sought. il Aviation W 91:36-7 Ag 11 '69
Can airlines digest Alitalia rate recipe? il Bsns W p30-1 S 27 '69
CAB orders further youth fares hearings. Aviation W 91:30 S 1 '69
CAB proposes conditions on new IATA tour fare. Aviation W 91:31 Jl 7 '69
CAB to weigh fare formula advisability. H. D. Watkins. Aviation W 91:29 Ag 25 '69
CAB, trunks facing fare clash. H. D. Watkins. Aviation W 91:31 D 8 '69
CAB weighs contract bulk fare extension. H. D. Watkins. Aviation W 91:27-8 N 3 '69
Climax nears in domestic fare imbroglio. H. D. Watkins. Aviation W 92:28-9 Ja 12 '70
Competition, fares cloud Hawaii outlook. H. D. Watkins. Aviation W 91:38-9+ Ag 11 '69
Congressmen plan to oppose fare increases. Aviation W 91:32 Ag 18 '69
Economic squeeze intensifies scrutiny of airline fares. H. D. Watkins. il Aviation W 90:208-9+ Mr 10 '69
End to the price war? Newsweek 74:86 O 13 '69
Fare increase tied to interline changes. H. D. Watkins. Aviation W 91:36-7 S 22 '69
Fare increases may face new challenges. H. D. Watkins. Aviation W 91:31 O 6 '69
Fare surcharge for Concorde is probable; all first-class, 112-seat layout planned. il Aviation W 90:156-8+ Je 2 '69
Fight for lower fares. Time 94:90 O 10 '69
Fly the thrifty skies. K. C. Tessendorf. House B 111:76-7 S '69
Flying with student power; cut-rate fares. il Time 93:97 My 23 '69
Formula found for fare increase. H. D. Watkins. il Aviation W 90:25-7 Ja 27 '69
Hawaii fare-cut drive gains momentum. H. D. Watkins. Aviation W 91:31 Ag 18 '69
How to stretch your air fare dollar. D. Gollan. Travel & Camera 32:38+ N '69
IATA establishes two-phase fare schedule. E. H. Kolcum. Aviation W 90:47 Ap 14 '69
IATA slates North European fare raise. Aviation W 90:31-2 Mr 17 '69
JAL files excursion tariffs for Pacific. Aviation W 91:28 S 1 '69
Lower excursion fares may end Atlantic open price competition. R. F. Coburn. Aviation W 91:34 N 10 '69
New fares for new planes? il Bsns W p 100+ N 15 '69
New interline fare split formula urged. H. D. Watkins. Aviation W 91:29-30 S 1 '69
Non-trunks bid to attach other goals to fare rise. H. D. Watkins. Aviation W 91:26 S 8 '69
North Atlantic carriers set fare priorities. Aviation W 91:28 O 27 '69
Two-year Atlantic fare package set after lengthy IATA talks. Aviation W 90:32 F 10 '69
See also
Local service airlines—Federal aid

Federal aid
See also
Local service airlines—Federal aid

Finance
Airline income and expense; tables. See issues of Aviation week & space technology
Airline profits are flying lower. Bsns W p25 Ag 2 '69
Airlines fear $1.2-billion loss in five years. Aviation W 90:34 Je 23 '69
Bailing out the airlines. Duns R 94:88 D '69
Ballad of the diminishing dollar. R. Burkhardt. il Holiday 46:62-3+ Jl '69
Champagne on a beer budget; Continental's loss of transpacific routes. il Forbes 104:61-2 S 15 '69
Changing habits cloud forecasts. L. Doty. Aviation W 91:29-30 Ag 18 '69
Higher air fares? Newsweek 73:83 My 12 '69
Increases in airline operating revenues; tables. Aviation W 90:51 My 5 '69
Lower United air lines net follows industry pattern. Aviation W 90:39 Mr 17 '69
Marketing push, cost cutback cited in Braniff profit climb. Aviation W 90:34 F 17 '69
Mayday in the market. il Time 94:67 Ag 1 '69
New flight plan for the airlines. G. Burck. il Fortune 79:98-101+ Ap '69
Quarter net of Northwest Orient slumps. il Aviation W 90:40 My 12 '69
Strike cuts American net; Delta counters tide. il Aviation W 90:37 My 5 '69
Strike reflected in weak first quarter. Aviation W 90:31 Ap 28 '69

AIRLINES—Finance—*Continued*
Supplementals' 1968 revenues, expenses; tables. Aviation W 90:42 Je 9 '69
Trunks' third quarter results show lackluster profit gains. il Aviation W 91:28 N 3 '69
U.S. airline assets and liabilities; tables (cont) Aviation W 90:58 My 5; 91:47 S 29 '69
U.S. airline increases in operating revenues, first six months, 1969 over 1968; tables. Aviation W 91:39 S 8 '69
U.S. airline operating revenues and expenses for year 1968; tables. Aviation W 90:52-3 My 5 '69
U.S. airline revenues & expenses; tables (title varies) Aviation W 91:34 S 8; 28 N 3 '69
See also
Airlines—Accounting
Airlines—Cost of operation
Airlines—Securities

Food service

Great airlines food race. N. Gittelson. McCalls 96:95+ My '69
Lockheed improves L-1011 meal process. G. S. Hunter. il Aviation W 90:55-7 Ja 20 '69

Freight service

See Air freight service; Airplanes, Freight

Hostesses

Look what you started, Ellen Church. il Holiday 46:58-9 Jl '69
Question of style; United air lines fires Negro over Afro hair-do. il Newsweek 74:104 O 6 '69

Hotel operations

Ballad of the diminishing dollar. R. Burkhardt. il Holiday 46:62-3+ Jl '69

International services

Concorde route study nears completion. H. J. Coleman. il Aviation W 90:34+ Mr 17 '69
Global route explosion; symposium with editorial comment. Aviation W 91:21, 27-41+ O 20 '69
Moscow-New York air link; how it's getting along. il U S News 67:14 N 10 '69
New authority to Moscow urged. Aviation W 90:43 My 12 '69
New transsiberian awards seen. Aviation W 92:24 Ja 12 '70
New York-Moscow traffic gains expected. J. W. Carter. Aviation W 90:41+ My 12 '69
Outdated policies slowing route changes. L. Doty. Aviation W 90:130+ Je 2 '69
SST will develop global route pattern. il Aviation W 92:45-50 Ja 5 '70
United States and Greece modify air transport services agreement; Department announcement, with text of note exchanges, December 20, 1968. Dept State Bul 60:70-3 Ja 20 '69
Whatever happened to New York-Moscow air link. il U S News 66:16 Ap 14 '69

Europe, Western

Modern air expands Berlin tour flights. E .H. Kolcum. il Aviation W 91:45-6 Ag 4 '69

European-African

African route fight forms. Aviation W 91:33 O 6 '69

European-Asiatic

JAL to inaugurate flights beyond Moscow. C. Brownlow. Aviation W 91:36 N 17 '69

Great Circle route

Japan wins Great Circle Tokyo-New York routing. L. Doty. Aviation W 91:25-6 O 13 '69

Latin America

Outlook for Latin America traffic clouded by events. Aviation W 91:28 Jl 14 '69

Transatlantic

Atlantic site for first supersonic service. il Aviation W 91:29 O 20 '69
Czechs to use IL-62s on New York route. Aviation W 90:46 My 5 '69
Lower excursion fares may end Atlantic open price competition. R. F. Coburn. Aviation W 91:34 N 10 '69
New U.S.-Europe service pattern forged H. D. Watkins. Aviation W 91:59+ O 20 '69

Transpacific

Air routes; Nixon reverses Johnson. U S News 66:12 F 3 '69
Airlines press South Pacific bids. L. Doty. Aviation W 90:26-7 My 19 '69
American goes west. Newsweek 74:75 Ag 4 '69

Australia seeks mid-U.S. routes. Aviation W 91:41 Ag 11 '69
Bilateral, pilot talks block start of American service in Pacific. Aviation W 91:33 D 15 '69
Champagne on a beer budget; Continental's loss of transpacific routes. il Forbes 104:61-2 S 15 '69
Chicanery, cronyism, or sour grapes? Nixon cancels new transpacific-route awards. il Newsweek 73:69-70 F 3 '69
Crossing the lonely latitudes. N. Morgan. il Sat R 52:46-7+ S 13 '69
Final word on Pacific air routes. U S News 66:12 Ap 21 '69
Flying Tiger inaugurates Pacific service. il Aviation W 91:39+ S 22 '69
Flying to Expo: four routes. D. Gollan. Travel & Camera 32:105 O '69
Japan presses Pacific demands. L. Doty. Aviation W 90:24-5 F 17 '69
New transpacific service started as problems delay some airlines. Aviation W 91:33 Ag 4 '69
Nixon move clouds Pacific case. L. Doty. Aviation W 90:24-6 Ap 21 '69
Nixon rejection increases confusion in Pacific case. L. Doty. il Aviation W 91:25-6 Jl 14 '69
Northwest to contest decision in Pacific Islands route case. Aviation W 91:34 Ag 25 '69
Pacific air battle roars on; Nixon to review Johnson's route decision. Bsns W p26 F 1 '69
Pacific case seen facing courts; with editorial comment. H. D. Watkins. Aviation W 90:11, 26-8 F 3 '69
Pacific solutions. Time 93:86 Ap 18 '69
Storm over the Pacific; R. Nixon to recall the matter. Time 93:62 Ja 31 '69
Traffic soars on new transpacific route. il Aviation W 91:85+ O 20 '69
Trans-Pacific air route tangle. D. Sanford. New Repub 160:16-18 F 15 '69
Transpacific case finally settled. L. Doty. Aviation W 91:45 Jl 28 '69
Transpacific decision. Newsweek 73:84 Ap 21 '69
U.S. route policy irks Europeans. L. Doty. Aviation W 90:42 Ap 14 '69
Where will everybody be going soon? The Pacific, that's where. H. Greig. il Holiday 46:64-5 Jl '69

Luggage handling

Automated baggage system tested for use by airlines. E. J. Bulban. il Aviation W 91:150-1+ O 20 '69

Management

Heads you lose, tails you lose; Eastern famous for bad service. il Forbes 103:33-4 Ap 15 '69

Non-scheduled operations

Air transport opens remote alpine areas; Air Glaciers and Air Alpes. D. E. Fink. il Aviation W 90:85+ Ja 20 '69
Airlines join to fight illegal charters. J. W. Carter. Aviation W 91:41-2+ Ag 4 '69
CAB authorizations boost supplementals. Aviation W 90:207 Mr 10 '69
Charter battle threatens traditional roles. L. Doty. Aviation W 91:37 D 15 '69
Conflict over supplemental role deepens. H. D. Watkins. Aviation W 91:47-9 N 24 '69
Inclusive tours register uneven progress. H. D. Watkins. Aviation W 90:26-7 Mr 3 '69
Supplementals seek charter shifts. R. S. Kahn. Aviation W 91:33 Jl 7 '69
Tour surge lures European flag carriers. R. F. Coburn. il Aviation W 91:27-9+ S 8 '69
Travel notes; supplemental airlines operate inclusive tour charters. R. Joseph. Esquire 71:46+ Mr '69
See also
Overseas national airways

Passenger service

Airlines prepare for introduction of 747. J. P. Woolsey. il Aviation W 91:36-41+ O 20 '69
Helping the handicapped travel by air. M. McEachern. il Todays Health 47:66-8+ Mr '69
Hi fi in the sky? R. Angus. il Hi Fi 19:62-5 F '69
Lost luggage? Why not anticipate. . . Sunset 142:71 Ap '69
Mohawk discards variety flight series. Aviation W 90:32 F 3 '69
Multiplexed seat units designed for 747. B. Miller. il Aviation W 90:81-2+ F 17 '69

AIRLINES—Passenger service—*Continued*
Multiplexing audio entertainment for the Boeing superjet. J. W. Partridge. il Electr World 82:40-1+ S '69
Passenger comfort; letter. W. Botstiber; discussion. Aviation W 90:94 Ja 20 '69
Preview of the giant jet; 747. R. Burkhardt. il Travel & Camera 32:76-8+ D '69
Western acts to bolster Hawaii service. N. S. Himmel. Aviation W 91:43+ N 24 '69
See also
Periodicals for airline passengers

Passenger traffic
See Airlines—Traffic

Pooled operations
See Airlines—Cooperation

Public relations
Airline promotions featuring happiness. R. F. Coburn. Aviation W 90:49 Ap 14 '69
Carriers urged to act on social problems. R. G. O'Lone. Aviation W 91:53-5 Ag 11 '69
That million-dollar smile. il Time 93:104 Je 6 '69
Why Northwest puts on the ritz. il Bsns W p30-2 Jl 5 '69
See also
Periodicals for airline passengers

Purchasing
End of tax credit could curtail aircraft purchases. Aviation W 90:30 Ap 28 '69

Rates
See Air freight service—Rates; Airlines—Fares

Regulations
See Aviation—Laws and regulations

Reservation systems
Aeroflot hit by slippages in computer development; siren-1 system. il Aviation W 90:32 Mr 31 '69
Moscow speeds ticket handling. il Aviation W 90:60 My 12 '69
SAS uses new data processing system. Aviation W 90:41-2 Je 9 '69

Safety devices and measures
See Aviation—Safety devices and measures

Securities
Watch the moneymen! views of M. Siebert. A. Hershman. Duns R 94:79-80 D '69

Shuttle service
Houston shuttle weighs expansion. il Aviation W 91:88+ N 10 '69

Statistics
Airline traffic; tables. See occasional issues of Aviation week & space technology
Growth in North Atlantic traffic and service, first six months of 1969 over 1968; table. Aviation W 91:59 O 20 '69
Growth in U.S. air passengers; tables. Aviation W 91:40 Ag 4 '69
Growth in U.S. airline passenger traffic; table. Aviation W 90:39 Mr 24 '69
Increases in boardings by U.S. carriers; tables. Aviation W 91:39 N 3 '69
1968 U.S. air, sea passengers; tables. Aviation W 91:42 Ag 4 '69
Passenger boardings by U.S. carriers; tables. Aviation W 91:89-90 O 20 '69
Three/four-engine turbojet/fan load factors; tables. Aviation W 91:57 S 22 '69
Trunkline load factors; tables. Aviation W 90:37 My 12; 46 Je 9; 32 Je 16; 91:24 Jl 14; 29 Ag 18; 41 S 15;24 O 13; 34 N 17; 30 D 15 '69; 92:29 Ja 12 '70
Turbojet/turbofan Aircraft 1968 scheduled traffic statistics; tables. Aviation W 90:104-5 Ap 14 '69
Turbojet/Turbofan aircraft 1968 traffic; tables. Aviation W 90:51+ Ap 7 '69
Turboprop aircraft 1968 operations and traffic statistics; tables. Aviation W 90:40-1 Ap 21 '69
Turboprop load factors in scheduled service; tables. Aviation W 91:55 S 22 '69
Two-engine turbojet/fan load factors; tables. Aviation W 91:58 S 22 '69
U.S. airline operations and traffic, 1968; table. Aviation W 90:30-1 Mr 3 '69
U.S. airline scheduled service load factors; table. Aviation W 91:33 S 1 '69
U.S. airline scheduled service traffic growth; tables. Aviation W 91:43 Ag 25 '69

Taxation
State tax bids pose new threat to beleaguered airline finances. Aviation W 91:34 D 1 '69

Tickets
See also
Computers—Ticket selling applications

Traffic
Airlines watch Metroliner traffic. R. F. Coburn. Aviation W 90:26-7 Mr 31 '69
Changes in air travel: both good and bad. il U S News 67:58-60 S 29 '69
Executive airlines reports Florida traffic expansion. J. W. Carter. Aviation W 90:44 Ap 14 '69
Melting yield dims Atlantic outlook. J. W. Carter. Aviation W 90:26-7 Je 23 '69
New routes challenge old concepts. L. Doty. Aviation W 91:27-8 O 20 '69
New seasonal fluctuations cloud reasons for slow traffic growth. Aviation W 92:29 Ja 12 '70
N.Y.-Miami competition intensifies. R. F. Coburn. il Aviation W 90:24-5 F 10 '69
1968 air passengers between the United States, and other countries by flag of carrier; tables. Aviation W 91:32-3 Jl 21 '69
Non-aviation elements cloud traffic rise. L. Doty. il Aviation W 90:137-9+ Mr 10 '69
North Atlantic air passengers, load factors, first six months of 1969; tables. Aviation W 91:40-1 N 3 '69
Sluggish traffic laid to global upheavals. Aviation W 90:47 Je 16 '69
Summer air jam expected despite peak-hour quotas. Aviation W 90:29 My 26 '69
Summer traffic trims 1970 forecasts. H. D. Watkins. Aviation W 91:41 S 15 '69
Traffic growth shows soft spots. J. W. Carter. Aviation W 91:24-5 Jl 14 '69
Traffic soars on new transpacific route. il Aviation W 91:85+ O 20 '69
Wide absenteeism of controllers at FAA posts slows air traffic. Aviation W 90:32 Je 23 '69

Wages and hours
Airline wage rise gains momentum. J. W. Carter. Aviation W 90:35 My 5 '69

Canada
Canada draws area guidelines for its regional, trunk airlines. D. A. Brown. Aviation W 91:28 S 1 '69
Canada's regional airlines seen taking greater role. D. A. Brown. Aviation W 90:26-7 Ap 21 '69
Nordair jet schedules cross Arctic Circle. D. A. Brown. il Aviation W 90:39-41+ Ap 7 '69

Czechoslovakia
CSA faces reliance on Soviet aircraft. E. H. Kolcum. il Aviation W 91:111 O 20 '69
Czechs to use IL-62s on New York route. Aviation W 90:46 My 5 '69

Europe, Western
Economic clouds dim European airline traffic outlook for 1969. il Aviation W 90:217-18 Mr 10 '69
European carriers try long-term leasing. R. F. Coburn. Aviation W 91:32-3 D 15 '69
European carriers weighing airbus plans. R. F. Coburn. Aviation W 91:41 Ag 18 '69
European group orders 36 DC-10s; KSSU consortium. Aviation W 90:31-2 Je 16 '69
Pooling runs into cost, revenue share snags. R. F. Coburn. Aviation W 91:204-5+ O 20 '69
Tour surge lures European flag carriers. R. F. Coburn. il Aviation W 91:27-9+ S 8 '69

Finland
Finnish salute to summer. D. Butwin. il Sat R 52:36-7 Jl 26 '69

France
Air transport opens remote alpine areas; Air Glaciers and Air Alpes. D. E. Fink. il Aviation W 90:85+ Ja 20 '69

Germany (Federal Republic)
737 eases smoothly into Lufthansa fleeet. R. F. Coburn. il Aviation W 91:36-7 S 29 '69

Great Britain
British airlines face sweeping changes; proposed British civil aviation authority. H. J. Coleman. Aviation W 91:40-1 N 17 '69
U.K. urged to unify control over state-owned airlines. Aviation W 90:48 My 12 '69
See also
British overseas airways corporation

Hawaii
Flight overscheduling in Hawaii charged. Aviation W 91:36 N 24 '69

AIRLINES—*Continued*

India

New authority to Moscow urged; Air-India. Aviation W 90:43 My 12 '69

Israel

Commandos strike again; attack on El Al plane in Zurich. il Newsweek 73:36 Mr 3 '69

El Al returning to schedule after Arab attack at Zurich. D. E. Fink. Aviation W 90:29-30 F 24 '69

El Al thrives despite Arab fire. il Bsns W p34+ Mr 1 '69

Terror in two cities; Arab terrorists attack El Al plane at Zurich. il Time 93:30+ F 28 '69

U.S. calls for international action to safeguard civilian aviation; Department statements; with text of Ambassador Yost's letter, February 19, 1969. C. W. Yost. Dept State Bul 60:197-8 Mr 10 '69

Italy

Airlines gird to match Alitalia cuts. Aviation W 91:30-1 S 29 '69

Alitalia begins image change campaign. il Aviation W 91:43 N 17 '69

Can airlines digest Alitalia rate recipe? il Bsns W p30-1 S 27 '69

Japan

JAL to inaugurate flights beyond Moscow. C. Brownlow. Aviation W 91:36 N 17 '69

Japan wins Great Circle Tokyo-New York routing. L. Doty. Aviation W 91:25-6 O 13 '69

Transpacific decision hardens JAL stand for gains in U.S. Aviation W 90:27 My 19 '69

Lebanon

Gold in the ashes. Time 93:65 Ja 31 '69

Peru

U.S. rift cools airline expansion in Peru. R. G. O'Lone. il Aviation W 90:31-2 F 24 '69

Puerto Rico

Caribair asks service cut as fiscal problems mount. Aviation W 91:197 O 20 '59

Russia

Aeroflot expands service to Mideast, Africa points. Aviation W 90:25 Mr 3 '69

Aeroflot hit by slippages in computer development. il Aviation W 90:32 Mr 31 '69

Aeroflot to seek alternate global routes. D. C. Winston. il Aviation W 91:112-13+ O 20 '69

Scandinavia

See also
Scandinavian airlines system

Switzerland

Air transport opens remote alpine areas; Air Glaciers and Air Alpes. D. E. Fink. il Aviation W 90:85+ Ja 20 '69

United States

Pacific air battle roars on; Nixon to review Johnson's route decision. Bsns W p26 F 1 '69

Solving airline problems; excerpts from address, December 1969. M. Sadler. Aviation W 91:11 D 15 '69

Tangled mess in aviation; with editorial comment. Bsns W p52-4+, 100 Ag 9 '69

Trans-Pacific air route tangle. D. Sanford. New Repub 160:16-18 F 15 '69

Winter of discontent; fare increases and airport restrictions. Newsweek 73:79+ Ja 27 '69

See also
Air transport association of America
Local service airlines
Strikes—United States—Airlines
    also names of airlines, e.g. Ozark air lines

Routes

Airlines propose major changes in New England route alignment. Aviation W 91:48 Ag 25 '69

Bumpy flight for Nixon bill; plans for airways and airport development. Bsns W p46 Je 21 '69

Competition, fares cloud Hawaii outlook. H. D. Watkins. Aviation W 91:38-9+ Ag 11 '69

Los Angeles Northeast route open. il Aviation W 91:30 O 6 '69

New nonstop authority awarded for Gulf states-Midwest points. Aviation W 90:40 My 12 '69

Pan Am reduces frequencies on West Coast-Hawaii routes. Aviation W 91:30 O 27 '69

Pan Am to cut San Juan trips. Aviation W 91:26 N 10 '69

Regional makes it to the big town; direct service between Midwest and Washington and New York. il Bsns W p 102+ Ap 26 '69

Southern cases spur competition. L. Doty. Aviation W 91:32-3 Ag 4 '69

Three carriers prepare for Hawaii flights. N. S. Himmel. Aviation W 90:54 Ap 14 '69

United gears for industry shifts. H. D. Watkins. il Aviation W 91:29-31 D 15 '69

AIRLINES, Supplemental. See Airlines—Nonscheduled operations

AIRPLANE accident investigation. See Aviation—Accident investigation

AIRPLANE accidents, Liability for. See Liability (law)

AIRPLANE brakes. See Brakes, Airplane

AIRPLANE buying. See Airplanes—Purchasing

AIRPLANE cabins

Boeing proposes new 727,707 interior. R. G. O'Lone. il Aviation W 90:32-3 Ap 28 '69

DC-10, L-1011 cabin design contrasted. il Aviation W 91:28-9 N 10 '69

Economy, first-class interior of 747 shown. il Aviation W 91:35 Jl 7 '69

Fare surcharge for Concorde is probable; all first-class, 112-seat layout planned. il Aviation W 90:156-8+ Je 2 '69

Mercure interior details shown in mockup. il Aviation W 90:30-1 Je 30 '69

Air conditioning

See Airplanes—Air conditioning

Pressurization

See Airplanes—Pressurization

AIRPLANE canopies

Test set for frangible glass canopy. M. L. Yaffee. il Aviation W 91:57+ Ag 25 '69

AIRPLANE carriers. See Aircraft carriers

AIRPLANE cockpits

Follow me through; danger in the right seat. R. Blodget. Flying 85:41 Ag '69

AIRPLANE collisions. See Aviation—Accidents

AIRPLANE crews

Third man in 737 cockpit costing United $5 million. N. S. Himmel. Aviation W 90:32 Mr 17 '69

Three-man 737 crew continued to 1970. N. S. Himmel. Aviation W 90:34 Mr 3 '69

Training

FAA proposes changes in crew training. Aviation W 90:43 Ap 14 '69

747 crew training plans ready. Aviation W 91:43 O 20 '69

AIRPLANE dealers. See Airplane industry and trade

AIRPLANE ducts. See Ducts

AIRPLANE engines

Back to basics. P. Garrison. il Flying 85:56-9 D '69

See also
Avco corporation—Lycoming division
Gas turbines, Aircraft
Jet airplane engines

Design

Aircraft engine revolution. R. Blodget. il Flying 84:66-72 F '69

Exhaust

See also
Jet airplane engines—Exhaust

Failures

Why engines stop. R. L. Collins. Flying 85:70-1 D '69

Specifications

U.S. reciprocating engines (cont) Aviation W 90:156-7 Mr 10 '69

Starting devices

See also
Jet airplane engines—Starting devices

Throttle

Prop and throttle, the power levers. P. Garrison. il Flying 85:56-9 D '69

AIRPLANE fares. See Airlines—Fares

AIRPLANE hijacking

Airlines, government accelerate efforts at hijacking prevention. Aviation W 90:33 Ja 27 '69

Anatomy of a skyjacker. il Time 94:67-8+ D 5 '69

AIRPLANE hijacking—*Continued*

Anti-hijacking system being used by TWA. il Aviation W 91:32 D 22 '69

Committee hears introductory statement on air hijacking. UN Mo Chron 6:104-5 D '69

Death to hijackers: Ethiopian gambit. Newsweek 74:50 D 22 '69

Department reviews problem of aircraft hijacking and proposals for international action; statement, February 5, 1969. F. E. Loy. Dept State Bul 60:212-15 Mr 10 '69

FAA to initiate passenger search. Aviation W 90:27 Mr 3 '69

Halting hijackers: how one system is working out. il U S News 67:14 N 17 '69

Havana hop: hassle over hijacking. Sr Schol 94:17-18 Mr 7 '69

High and the mighty: California to Rome hijacking. il Newsweek 74:42+ N 10 '69

Hijack detector tested by FAA. Aviation W 91:53 S 22 '69

Hi Jack, hi Fidel! New Repub 160:11 Ja 25 '69

Hijacked to Cuba: hijacker's wife tells why he did it; with report by S. McBee. il Life 66:22D-29 Ap 18 '69

Hijacking in the skies: 48 planes this year; so far. U S News 67:50 S 22 '69

Holding pattern. Newsweek 73:34+ F 17 '69

ICAO notified of U.S. ratification of Tokyo convention. Dept State Bul 61:275 S 22 '69

IFALPA mounts anti-hijack drive. il Aviation W 91:22-4 S 8 '69

IFALPA pushing to thrust hijack issue before U.N; with editorial comment. H. J. Coleman. Aviation W 91:21, 39-40 S 15 '69

IFALPA theatens strike in push against hijackings. Aviation W 90:31 Mr 31 '69

Is there any answer to plane hijackers? il U S News 67:34-5 O 20 '69

More on hijacking. R. Hotz. Aviation W 91:11 N 10 '69

My plea to Castro for return of my child. J. Washington. il Ebony 24:66-8+ O '69

Pilot's story of a hijacking: pandemonium in the cockpit; testimony before the House interstate and foreign commerce committee. J. G. Brown. il U S News 66:36 F 24 '69

Piracy above, politics below: Polish LOT airliner forced to West Berlin. Time 94:30+ O 31 '69

Puzzle of the plane hijackers. il U S News 66:10 F 10 '69

Return of the native. il Time 94:30+ N 14 '69

6,900-mile skyjack. il Time 94:29 N 7 '69

Skyjacking: what causes it, and a way to end it. il U S News 66:68-9 F 17 '69

Take this plane to Havana! I. Ross. Read Digest 94:113-17 My '69

This is your captain: TWA plane hijacked by Palestinian commandos. il Newsweek 74:37-8 S 8 '69

To catch a thief. il Time 93:26 F 14 '69

Unions take aim at skyjackers: Conference of transportation trades proposal. U S News 66:75 F 24 '69

U.S. calls upon Syria to release all passengers of hijacked plane; statements, August 29 and 30, 1969. W. P. Rogers. Dept State Bul 61:245-6 S 15 '69

U.S. to ask denial of asylum to hijackers. Aviation W 90:27-8 F 10 '69

Up, up and ole? Newsweek 73:34-5 F 3 '69

What can be done about skyjacking? il Time 93:19-20 Ja 31 '69

Wing and a prayer: hijacking foiled by prayer. A. Taft. Chr Today 13:45 F 28 '69

World law and the hijackers. K. M. Ruppenthal. Nation 208:144-6 F 3 '69

Anecdotes, facetiae, satire, etc.

Havana survival kit. il Esquire 71:139-41 Je '69

Is it safe to fly? Hmmmm. R. Serling. il Holiday 46:54-5 Jl '69

AIRPLANE industry and trade

Foreign accent. J. Fricker. See issues of Flying

See also

Helicopter industry and trade

Advertising

Consortium readies A-300B sales drive. E. H. Kolcum. il Aviation W 91:33-4 N 3 '69

Consolidations and mergers

Struggle looming over control of Piper. S. P. Siliciano. Aviation W 90:23 F 3 '69

Directories

List of Discover flying dealers. Flying 84:19-23+ Je '69

Marketing directory section. Aviation W 91:25+ mid-D '69

Federal aid

Appropriations unit SST hearing spurs clash among senators. Aviation W 91:32 D 1 '69

Competition key to House units approving SST prototype funds. Aviation W 91:37 N 17 '69

House votes $96 million SST funding. K. Johnsen. Aviation W 91:38 N 24 '69

Finance

Access limits seen cutting aircraft buys. Aviation W 91:17 O 27 '69

Boeing 6-month net, sales dip. Aviation W 91:28 Ag 4 '69

C.I.T.-type operation for the world: proposed Private export finance corp. il Forbes 103:25 F 1 '69

Handley Page unions seeking British aid to protect jobs. Aviation W 91:96-7 Ag 25 '69

Van Dusen net, sales hit peaks. il Aviation W 90:98 My 26 '69

International aspects

Germany, France sign airbus pact. R. F. Coburn. Aviation W 90:33 Je 9 '69

How U.S. stole Paris air show. il U S News 66:14-15 Je 16 '69

Special report: the 1970s: challenge in the marketplace; symposium, with editorial comment. il Aviation W 90:53, 84-9+ Je 2 '69

Statistics

U.S. business, utility aircraft shipments; tables. See occasional issues of Aviation week

Czechoslovakia

Czech industry seeks western ties. E. H. Kolcum. il Aviation W 91:55-7+ O 6 '69

Europe, Western

Firm schedule set for MRCA program. E. H. Kolcum. Aviation W 90:31-2 Je 9 '69

Foreign accent. J. Fricker. Flying 84:34+ Je; 85:16-17+ N '69

Foreign accent; minijet marathon. il Flying 84:14+ Mr '69

Merging over the border: Holland's Fokker and West Germany's Vereinigte flugtechnische werke. Bsns W p38 My 17 '69

VFW, Fokker form equal partnership. Aviation W 90:24 My 19 '69

France

Embargo dims French aerospace outlook. D. E. Fink. Aviation W 90:21-2 Ja 27 '69

French aim to improve engines for export. M. L. Yaffee. il Aviation W 90:270-1+ Je 2 '69

French driving for more export sales. Aviation W 90:355 Je 2 '69

Germany (Federal Republic)

F-4 becomes West German election issue. Aviation W 91:28-9 S 29 '69

Germans pushing engine development. il Aviation W 90:262-3+ Je 2 '69

Wheels and wings for Germany: return of Willy Messerschmitt. il Fortune 80:171 Ag 15 '69

Great Britain

U.K. aircraft industry productivity lags. H. J. Coleman. il Aviation W 91:23-4 N 3 '69

See also

Beagle aircraft, limited

British aircraft corporation

Handley Page, limited

Rolls-Royce, limited

Italy

Charter to modify Yak-40 to attract West. Aviation W 91:33 O 6 '69

Fiat climbing out of slump in production. E. H. Kolcum. il Aviation W 90:60-1 Mr 3 '69

Japan

Japan spurs Asian aviation surge. C. Brownlow. il Aviation W 92:56-7+ Ja 12 '70

Russia

Soviets strive to bolster export program. D. C. Winston. Aviation W 90:29-30 Je 9 '69

United States

Industry fighting slide in economy. Aviation W 91:17 mid-D '69

Race for a superjet: can U.S. catch up? il U S News 66:38-9 Mr 17 '69

747: into a new air age; with report by J. Lubenow. il Newsweek 74:95+ O 27 '69

AIRPLANE industry and trade—United States
    —Continued
Strong competition marks business aircraft
    market. D. A. Brown. Aviation W 91:27-8
    S 29 '69
U.S. industry regains military export sales
    responsibility. il Aviation W 90:126-7 Je 2
    '69
    See also names of airplane manufacturing
    companies, e.g. Beech aircraft corporation
        Yugoslavia
Yugoslavia seeks to gain exports to West. H.
    J. Coleman. il Aviation W 90:207-9+ Je 2 '69
AIRPLANE insurance. See Insurance, Aviation
AIRPLANE lease and rental services. See Air-
    planes—Leasing and renting
AIRPLANE lifting equipment. See Airports—
    Equipment
AIRPLANE markings
American gives its transports new markings.
    il Aviation W 90:31 My 26 '69
AIRPLANE mechanics (persons)
Up, up and away with wages. il Time 93:
    89-90 Ap 11 '69
AIRPLANE models
Model hydroplane skims the water. R. L.
    Clough, jr. il Pop Sci 194:140-3 My '69
AIRPLANE parts
    See also
Southwest airmotive company
        Manufacture
Component production begins for L-1011. il
    Aviation W 91:48-50 O 20 '69
        Testing
Capacitance probes in industrial instrumenta-
    tion. R. A. Shiver. il Electr World 81:42-3+
    My '69
Krypton flaw detection system designed. il
    Aviation W 90:85 Je 9 '69
AIRPLANE propellers
Prop and throttle, the power levers. P. Gar-
    rison. il Flying 85:56-9 D '69
Propeller research gains emphasis. M. L.
    Yaffee. il Aviation W 91:56-7+ N 24 '69
USAF contract for V/STOL propeller set.
    Aviation W 91:58 S 29 '69
AIRPLANE racing
Comeback of the National air races; Reno,
    Nev. T. Bacon. il Pop Sci 195:88-91 S '69
Ferry flight; for London daily mail trans-
    atlantic air race. S. Wilkinson. il Fly-
    ing 84:44-8+ Ap '69
From the tower; London Daily mail trans-
    atlantic air race. il Flying 85:4+ Jl '69
Great air race; London Daily mail trans-
    atlantic racing. il Ebony 24:80-2+ Jl '69
Harrier demonstrates capability for VTOL
    city center operation in transatlantic race.
    il Aviation W 90:28-30 My 12 '69
Races wild. D. Berliner and J. Gilbert. il Fly-
    ing 85:58-67 Ag '69
Suburbia's Angels cool it in the run for
    pylons; Reno's national air races. W. John-
    son. il Sports Illus 31:56-7 O 6 '69
Susi queue to London; Daily mail trans-
    atlantic air race; with editorial comment.
    B. Ottum. il Sports Illus 30:6. 90-4+ Je
    9 '69
Uncommon men; transatlantic air race spon-
    sored by the London Daily mail. il Time
    93:63-4 My 23 '69
Up and away; top U.S. air races; National
    championship air races. il Travel 131:22 My
    '69
AIRPLANE seats. See Airplanes—Seats
AIRPLANE selling. See Airplane industry and
    and trade
AIRPLANE tires. See Tires, Airplane
AIRPLANE travel. See Air travel
AIRPLANE wings
New design for transonic wing to be tested
    on modified F-8. W. C. Wetmore. il Avia-
    tion W 90:22-3 F 17 '69
Superwing. Sci Am 221:95 S '69
Upside-down wing. il Time 93:66 F 21 '69
    See also
Flaps, Airplane
AIRPLANES
Up, up and more on the way. J. R. Roberson.
    il Holiday 46:36-7+ Jl '69
    See also
Aviation
Salvage (airplanes)
Seaplanes
        Anchorage
    See Airplanes—Mooring
    Automobile combinations
    See Airplanes, Light—Automobile com-
    binations

        Bird collisions
    See Aviation—Bird hazards
        Brakes
    See Brakes, Airplane
        Cabins
    See Airplane cabins
        Canopies
    See Airplane canopies
        Chartering
Charter flights: what to check. Good H 169:
    147 Jl '69
Comparison of North Atlantic charter activ-
    ity, first six months of 1969 over 1968; table.
    Aviation W 91:66 O 20 '69
Sightseeing by plane in Alaska. Sunset 143:
    34-5 O '69
        Cockpits
    See Airplane cockpits
        Collectors and collecting
    See also
Smithsonian institution—National air and
    space museum
        Control
American amasses STOL navaid data. K. J.
    Stein. il Aviation W 90:81+ My 26 '69
    See also
Automatic pilot (airplanes)
        Corrosion
    See Corrosion and anticorrosives
        Cost of operation
Four/three-engine turbojet/fan aircraft op-
    eration costs, first half, 1969; tables. Avia-
    tion W 91:48 S 29 '69
1968 hourly costs of turboprop transports;
    tables. Aviation W 90:70-1 My 12 '69
Turboprop 1968 per-mile costs; tables. Avia-
    tion W 90:69 My 12 '69
Two-engine turbojet/turbofan aircraft oper-
    ating costs, first half, 1969; tables. Avia-
    tion W 91:49 S 29 '69
        Crews
    See Airplane crews
        Design
    See also
Airplane cabins
Airplanes, Freight—Design
Airplanes, Military—Design
Helicopters—Design
        Electric equipment
Safety check; electrical failure. J. Gilbert.
    Flying 84:81 Ap '69
        Electronic equipment
Interest rising in voice warnings. G. Hunter.
    il Aviation W 90:68-71+ Mr 3 '69
New avionic products. See occasional issues
    of Aviation week & space technology
Resistance to complexity rises. Aviation W
    91:16-17 Mid-D '69
    See also
Automatic pilot (airplanes)
Computers—Aeronautic applications
        Engines
    See Airplane engines
        Equipment
New products. See issues of Flying
        Escape devices
Hot seat to bring 'em back alive; jet-powered
    ejection seat. K. V. Brown. il Pop Mech
    132:90-3+ S '69
Inflatable slide chosen for 747. Aviation W
    90:73 F 3 '69
Navy may evaluate flying ejection seats;
    Aercab system. Aviation W 90:29 Ap 14
    '69
747 surpasses FAA evacuation standards. R.
    G. O'Lone. il Aviation W 91:33 D 1 '69
USAF studies ejection seat flight system. il
    Aviation W 90:39 F 17 '69
        Fires and fire protection
Fire suppression system tested. il Aviation W
    90:93-4+ Ap 14 '69
        Flaps
    See Flaps, Airplane
        Fuel tank gages
Simmonds develops L-1011 fuel probe. Avia-
    tion W 90:74 Mr 3 '69

AIRPLANES—*Continued*

Fueling
See Airplanes—Refueling

Fuselage
DC-10 fuselage section delivery lags. il Aviation W 91:25 D 15 '69

History
See Aeronautics—History

Hydraulic equipment
Portable aircraft hydraulic tester built. il Aviation W 90:85-6 My 12 '69

Ice protection
Limitations. T. J. Slaybaugh. Flying 84:94+ My '69
What harm can a little ice do? J. M. Donahoe. Flying 84:76-7 F '69

Inspection
Do it yourself; annual inspection. A. Trammell. il Flying 84:26-7 Ap '69
Do it yourself; preflight checks. A. Trammell. il Flying 85:96-7 Jl '69
Too many cooks. M. I. Gaston. Flying 85:82 D '69
Wayward wheel. B. Rhode. Flying 84:86-7 Ap '69

Instrument boards
New panel nears USAF test; all-electroluminescent instrument panel. il Aviation W 90: 99 My 5 '69

Instrument flying
See Aviation—Instrument flying

Instruments
See Aeronautic instruments

Insurance
See Insurance, Aviation

Landing
British test C-band hyperbolic ILS; correlation protected instrument landing system. P. J. Klass. il Aviation W 91:75+ Jl 21 '69
Diamonds on the runway. R. Blodget. il Flying 85:70-1 Ag '69
FAA to test modular landing aid system. P. J. Klass. il Aviation W 90:61-2+ Mr 24 '69
FAA using new glide path monitor. P. J. Klass. il Aviation W 91:67+ D 15 '69
Fine art of landing. R. L. Collins. Flying 85: 68-9+ Ag '69
Follow me through; glide-path control. R. Blodget. Flying 84:16-17 F '69
Follow me through: nosewheels, crosswinds and ground loops. R. Blodget. Flying 84: 36-7 My '69
Follow me through: pattern problem. R. Blodget. Flying 85:112-13 S '69
Follow me through; slow to approach speed. R. Blodget. Flying 85:18 D '69
New ILS sought for civil, military roles. P. J. Klass. il Aviation W 90:63-5 F 10 '69
New radar landing technique explored. P. J. Klass. Aviation W 90:32 My 19 '69
Norden expands attitude indicator trials. K. J. Stein. il Aviation W 90:76-7+ Ja 27 '69
Norway designs new landing aid; Hermes blind landing system. W. C. Wetmore. il Aviation W 90:67+ Ap 28 '69
Scanning-beam technique selected for landing aid. Aviation W 91:26 O 13 '69
Sweden picks microwave ILS for Viggen. il Aviation W 90:64-6 F 3 '69
What's your angle? angle-of-attack instruments. J. Gilbert. il Flying 84:82-3 Ap '69
See also
Airplanes—Radar equipment
Airplanes, Jet propelled—Landing
Automatic pilot (airplanes)

Landing gear
This gadget won't let you land wheels-up. N. Aubuchon. il Pop Sci 195:60-3+ Ag '69

Landing on carriers
See Airplanes, Military—Landing on carriers

Leasing and renting
European carriers try long-term leasing. R. F. Coburn. Aviation W 91:32-3 D 15 '69

Loading
See Loading and unloading

Maintenance and repair
See also
Airplanes—Inspection
Airplanes, Military—Maintenance and repair

Manufacture
Build this new four-place cabin plane for $3500. K. V. Brown. il Pop Mech 131:112-17+ My '69
Incredible Volksplane; Volkswagen engine powered plane. il Mech Illus 65:72-7 S '69
See also
Airplanes, Jet propelled—Manufacture
Airplanes, Supersonic—Manufacture
Helicopters—Manufacture

Marketing
Aero Commander adopts new sales plan; franchise financing. D. A. Brown. il Aviation W 90:68-9+ F 3 '69
Special report: the 1970s: challenge in the marketplace; symposium, with editorial comment. il Aviation W 90:53, 84-9+ Je 2 '69

Markings
See Airplane markings

Materials
Tough featherweight plays hard to get; boron filament. il Bsns W p38 N 15 '69
See also
Airplanes, Jet propelled—Materials
Gas turbines, Aircraft—Materials

Mooring
Do it yourself; tiedown technique. il Flying 84:24-5 Mr '69

Noise
Aircraft noise study set for city centers, suburbs. Aviation W 90:27 Ja 27 '69
Airport council finds noise rule inadequate. Aviation W 91:38 N 24 '69
FAA to act on 747 noise requirements. R. G. O'Lone. il Aviation W 91:35-6 D 8 '69
Growing problem of airplane noise, what is being done. il Good H 168:155-7 F '69
Muffling the jet. Time 94:59 N 21 '69
New aircraft noise requirements detailed. il Aviation W 91:35 N 17 '69
Noise a key in DC-10 pod design. C. M. Plattner. il Aviation W 90:64-6+ Je 16 '69
Quieter turbofans could hit cost snag. M. L. Yaffee. Aviation W 91:31+ O 27 '69
SST noise critical to airport compatibility. il Aviation W 92:83-4 Ja 5 '70
STOL future keyed to noise limitations. Aviation W 90:46+ F 24 '69
STOL noise standards spur interest in propeller design. Aviation W 90:87 Je 16 '69
See also
Helicopters—Noise

Operation
See Airplanes—Piloting

Parts
See Airplane parts

Performance
Business jet flying quality studied. D. A. Brown. il Aviation W 91:79+ O 27 '69

Photographs
Two Concordes in flying display at Paris. Aviation W 90:16-23 Je 16 '69

Piloting
Case of the vanishing checkpoint. B. Carlisle. Flying 84:86+ Je '69
Fly right. R. B. Parke. Flying 84:30 F '69
Follow me through; danger in the right seat. R. Blodget. Flying 85:41 Ag '69
Gone flying again. W. F. Rickenbacker. Nat R 21:1171 N 18 '69
I learned about flying from that. See issues of Flying
Sniff; reasoning under pressure in emergencies. P. Garrison. Flying 85:88-9 Ag '69
When VFR goes IFR. R. L. Collins. Flying 84:38-40 F '69
Your first flight on the fabulous 747. B. Kocivar. il Pop Sci 195:76-9 D '69

Pneumatic equipment
DC-10 cabin air unit design evolves. il Aviation W 90:78-9+ Mr 31 '69

Power supply
Airborne MHD generator studied. M. L. Yaffee. il Aviation W 90:51-2 Ja 20 '69

Pressurization
DC-10 cabin air unit design evolves. il Aviation W 90:78-9+ Mr 31 '69

AIRPLANES—*Continued*

Private ownership

Sleek new private planes from across the seas. B. Kocivar. il Pop Sci 195:88-91+ O '69

See also
Airplanes in business
Private flying

Propellers

See Airplane propellers

Purchasing

Buying tips from a professional scrooge. R. B. Weeghman. Flying 84:49+ My '69
Which airplane should you buy? il Flying 85:70-5 O '69

Racing

See Airplane racing

Radar equipment

Lockheed tests landing monitor for L-1011. il Aviation W 91:42-3 D 22 '69

Radio equipment

See Radio apparatus on aircraft

Refueling

SAE fuel truck standards set for giant jets. Aviation W 91:189 O 20 '69

Rocket propulsion

See Rocket propulsion

Safety devices and measures

AIA seeks new crashworthiness criteria. Aviation W 90:34 My 19 '69
Answer at last to collisions in the sky? W. R. Young. il Read Digest 95:106-10 Jl '69
Avoiding collisions; demonstration of CAS. il Time 94:72 O 3 '69
Collision avoidance test slated by navy. Aviation W 91:68-9 N 24 '69
Interest rising in voice warnings. G. Hunter. il Aviation W 90:68-71+ Mr 3 '69
Looking for a traffic cop in the sky; anti-collision devices. il Bsns W p76-7+ N 29 '69
See also
Airplanes—Escape devices
Aviation—Safety devices and measures
Safety belts

Seats

Board, airlines scrutinize jets' six-abreast seating. J. P. Woolsey. Aviation W 92:34 Ja 12 '70
Sabena tests contoured seat for 747. il Aviation W 91:46 N 3 '69

Specifications

Eastern drafts STOL criteria from Northeast corridor tests. Aviation W 90:30 F 3 '69
Leading international aircraft (cont) Aviation W 90:179-82 Mr 10 '69
Leading turbine-powered business aircraft (cont) Aviation W 90:153 Mr 10 '69
USSR military and civil aircraft (cont) Aviation W 90:145 Mr 10 '69
U.S. agricultural aircraft. Aviation W 90:154 Mr 10 '69
U.S. and Canadian STOL aircraft. Aviation W 90:154 Mr 10 '69
U.S. and Canadian VTOL aircraft. Aviation W 90:157 Mr 10 '69
U.S. business, personal and utility aircraft (cont) Aviation W 90:155 Mr 10 '69
U.S. commercial transports (cont) Aviation W 90:149 Mr 10 '69
U.S. military aircraft (cont) Aviation W 90:137-8 Mr 10 '69

Speed

See also
Airplanes, Supersonic
Aviation records

Spinning

Accidental spin. R. L. Collins. il Flying 85:49-52+ Jl '69
Follow me through; spin training. R. Blodget. il Flying 84:20-1 Ap '69
What about the Twin Comanche? R. L. Collins. il Flying 84:46-50 Mr '69

Stability and stabilizers

NASA testing variable-stability PA-30. C. M. Plattner. il Aviation W 90:84+ F 24 '69

Stalling

What about the twin Comanche? R. L. Collins. il Flying 84:46-50 Mr '69

Standards

See also
Airplanes, Jet propelled—Standards
Airplanes, Light—Standards

Take-off

Safety check; abort, abort. S. Wilkinson. il Flying 85:18-19+ S '69

Testing

NASA plans to evaluate nine aircraft. Aviation W 90:39 Ap 7 '69
See also
Airplanes, Military—Testing
Airplanes, Military transport—Testing
Society of experimental test pilots

Weight

Experts struggled to control 2707 weight. R. G. O'Lone. Aviation W 90:79-80+ My 19 '69

Wings

See Airplane wings

AIRPLANES, Aerobatic

150 goes aerobatic. A. Trammell. il Flying 85:56-8 O '69

AIRPLANES, Amphibious

Amphibian design stresses reduced drag. B. K. Thomas, jr. il Aviation W 91:111-13 N 17 '69
CL-215 proves rugged, dependable in water bomber role. D. A. Brown. il Aviation W 91:64-5+ S 22 '69

AIRPLANES, Business

Aerostar 601. R. Blodget. il Flying 84:82-3 F '69
Beech sets sales targets, adds new models. E. J. Bulban. il Aviation W 91:78-9+ D 15 '69
Bizjets. A. Trammell. il Flying 85:52-5 O '69
Business jet export growth accelerating. D. A. Brown. il Aviation W 90:350-2 Je 2 '69
Business model of T-11 nears initial flight. il Aviation W 90:82-3 Mr 3 '69
Cessna model 500 makes initial flight. il Aviation W 91:28 S 22 '69
Cessna shows new line for utility market. il Aviation W 90:79-80 Mr 17 '69
Foreign accent; minijet marathon. il Flying 84:14+ My '69
HS-125 paves way for Beech expansion. E. J. Bulban. Aviation W 92:21-2 Ja 5 '70
Navajo. J. Fricker. il Flying 84:36-41 Mr '69
Piston aircraft unit sales drop causes concern. Aviation W 90:239-40 Mr 10 '69
Stretched MU-2 turboprop to be produced by Mooney. il Aviation W 90:80 Mr 3 '69
Transonic business jet to fly in 1970; Swearingen SA-28T. il Aviation W 90:18 Ap 7 '69
Turbine fleet size expected to mushroom in next decade. E. J. Bulban. il Aviation W 90:234-8 Mr 10 '69
Two new business jets planned. Aviation W 91:26 D 15 '69
Where business planes have their day; Reading, Pa. air show. il Bsns W p 116-18 Je 14 '69
See also
Airplanes in business
Helicopters, Business

Design

Beech seeks airline viewpoints for advanced commuter aircraft. Aviation W 90:80 Mr 17 '69
Cessna girds for sluggish market. E. J. Bulban. il Aviation W 91:46-7+ D 22 '69
Design changes detailed on Cessna 500 jet prototype. il Aviation W 91:74-5 S 29 '69
General aviation scores at Paris. D. E. Fink. il Aviation W 90:82-4+ Je 23 '69
Lockheed considers three-engine JetStar. Aviation W 91:24 S 29 '69
Progress report; Handley Page Jetstream. A. Trammell. il Flying 84:50-3 F '69
Three business aircraft models unveiled. E. J. Bulban. il Aviation W 91:25-7 S 29 '69
Turbofan commuter aircraft held feasible. D. A. Brown. il Aviation W 90:83+ F 10 '69

Performance

See Airplanes—Performance

Specifications

See Airplanes—Specifications

Testing

Esquire Shrike. R. B. Weeghman. il Flying 85:38-43 D '69
Pilot report:
  Gates Learjet model 25. E. M. Miller. il Flying 84:32-7 F '69
  Grumman Gulfstream II. E. M. Miller. il Flying 85:44-51 O '69

AIRPLANES, Convertible

Convertible cargo DC-10s ordered by two carriers. C. M. Plattner. Aviation W 90:25 Je 23 '69

AIRPLANES, Experimental
Taps for the X-15. il Newsweek 73:16 Je 2 '69

See also
Experimental aircraft association

Photographs
Mirage G sweeps wings during slow roll. Aviation W 90:54-5 Je 23 '69

AIRPLANES, Freight
Make way for tomorrow. il Forbes 104:40 O 15 '69
Modified An-24 cargo version has larger loading ramp. il Aviation W 90:68-9 Je 30 '69
Skyvan. J. Gilbert. il Flying 85:74-8 N '69

See also
Air freight service
Airplanes, Convertible
Airplanes, Military transport

Design
CL-44 modified to airlift L-1011 pods. il Aviation W 91:40-1 D 15 '69
Stretched Hercules will carry RB.211 engines to California. Aviation W 91:26 D 22 '69

Manufacture
Lockheed C-5 moves through production. il Aviation W 91:41-9 Jl 21 '69

AIRPLANES, Government
Magic carpet of presidents. H. Sidey. il Life 67:2 Ag 1 '69
Weekend pilot; air force one. F. K. Smith. Flying 85:80 N '69

AIRPLANES, Jet propelled
Boeing 747: first of a great new breed. J. F. Pearson. il Pop Mech 132:104-11+ D '69
Case of who-builds-what; European airbus. il Sci N 95:327-8 Ap 5 '69
Consortium readies A-300B sales drive E. H. Kolcum. il Aviation W 91:33-4 N 3 '69
Cost sharing proposed for A-300B airbus. il Aviation W 90:165+ Je 2 '69
European carriers weighing airbus plans. R. F. Coburn. Aviation W 91:41 Ag 18 '69
Extended-range L-1011 offered. Aviation W 91:31 Ag 4 '69
France, Germany push A-300B program. E. H. Kolcum. Aviation W 90:30 Ap 21 '69
Giant takes off; Boeing 747 jets. il Time 93:81 F 21 '69
Jumbo-jet service: set now for '69. U S News 66:14 F 24 '69
Lockheed plans new transports. Aviation W 90:26-7 Ap 28 '69
McDonnell Douglas' billion-dollar gamble. il Forbes 104:28-34 Ag 1 '69
Modified JT9D tested on stand. Aviation W 91:34 N 17 '69
New commuter line transport studied by PAC. Aviation W 91:77+ O 13 '69
New jet are: the jumbos are coming. il U S News 67:13 S 8 '69
Preview of the giant jet; 747. R. Burkhardt. il Travel & Camera 32:76-8+ D '69
Preview of travel in the giant jets; Boeing 747. il U S News 67:62 D 15 '69
Race for giant jet market intensifies as backlogs dwindle on present-generation aircraft. il Aviation W 90:220-1 Mr 10 '69
Ready or not, here comes jumbo; Boeing 747. il Time 95:52-6 Ja 19 '70
747 delivery delay to vary with airlines. Aviation W 91:35 S 22 '69
747: into a new air age; with report by J. Lubenow. il Newsweek 74:95+ O 27 '69
Snow, cold delay first flight of Boeing 747 as orders rise. il Aviation W 90:29 F 3 '69
Spa in the sky; Boeing's 400-passenger 747. il Travel & Camera 32:40+ F '69
Study finds problems in wide-body jets. Aviation W 91:28-9 D 1 '69
Superjet: Boeing 747; interview. New Yorker 45:24-6 Ag 9 '69
U.S. commuter market attracts imports. R. F. Coburn. il Aviation W 90:184 Je 2 '69
What delayed the jumbo jets. il Bsns W p94 6+ N 15 '69
Will it be the soaring seventies? H. Sutton and D. Butwin. il Sat R 53:31-4 Ja 3 '70

Cost
$160 million in U.K. funding seen necessary for BAC 311. Aviation W 90:30 F 24 '69

Cost of operation
1968 hourly costs, three and four engine turbojet/turbofan transports; tables. Aviation W 90:54-5 My 12 '69
Three and four turbofan/turbojet transport, 1968 per-mile costs; tables. Aviation W 90:53 My 12 '69

Twin engine jet 1968 per-mile costs; tables. Aviation W 90:56-7 My 12 '69
Twin turbofan/turbojet engine transports, 1968 hourly costs; tables. Aviation W 90:56-7 My 12 '69

Design
Advanced transport development spurred. il Aviation W 91:30-2 O 20 '69
Boeing designs aircraft to challenge airbuses. C. M. Plattner. il Aviation W 90:26-9 F 24 '69
Boeing modifies 737 for operations from short airfields. C. M. Plattner. il Aviation W 90:40-1+ My 19 '69
Boeing to deliver improved 737 soon. il Aviation W 90:28-9 Mr 3 '69
Business, growth Yak-40s planned. D. C. Winston. il Aviation W 91:96-7+ Jl 21 '69
European group orders 36 DC-10s; KSSU consortium. Aviation W 90:31-2 Je 16 '69
Europeans boost commuter airliner size. il Aviation W 90:171+ Je 2 '69
FAA to act on 747 noise requirements. R. G. O'Lone. il Aviation W 91:35-6 D 8 '69
L-1011 version aimed at European order. C. M. Plattner. il Aviation W 91:55-6 N 17 '69
737 will undergo braking, lift changes. C. M. Plattner. il Aviation W 91:40-1+ O 27 '69
Trouble with jumbo. il Time 94:84 S 26 '69
Tu-154 design advances Soviet transport technology. W. H. Gregory. il Aviation W 91:54-7+ Jl 7 '69
Yak-40 spearheading Soviet export drive. il Aviation W 90:64-6 Je 2 '69

Electronic equipment
Boeing adds attitude sensors to 747, plans buyers meeting. Aviation W 91:30 Ag 18 '69
Multiplexed seat units designed for 747. B. Miller. il Aviation W 90:81-2+ F 17 '69
Multiplexing audio entertainment for the Boeing superjet. J. W. Partridge. il Electr World 82:40-1+ S '69
Norden expands attitude indicator trials. K. J. Stein. il Aviation W 90:76-7+ Ja 27 '69

Equipment
Automatic cockpit checklist studied by KSSU for DC-10s. Aviation W 91:29 O 13 '69
Lockheed improves L-1011 meal process. G. S. Hunter. il Aviation W 90:55-7 Ja 20 '69

Landing
Super-radar; Lockheed's independent landing monitor. il Newsweek 75:44 Ja 5 '70

Manufacture
First DC-10 fuselages enter production. il Aviation W 91:55-7 O 20 '69
Jetstream production rate accelerating. il Aviation W 90:348-9 Je 2 '69
L-1011 fuselage assembly on schedule. il Aviation W 91:25 S 8 '69
Manufacturing pace accelerates for 747. il Aviation W 90:39-44+ Ap 28 '69

Materials
Carbon composite program gains. W. S. Hieronymus. il Aviation W 91:51+ Ag 18 '69
Noise a key in DC-10 pod design. C. M. Plattner. il Aviation W 90:64-6+ Je 16 '69

Noise
See Airplanes—Noise

Parts
See Airplane parts

Radar equipment
See Airplanes—Radar equipment

Seats
See Airplanes—Seats

Standards
Boeing pushes 747 certification program. C. M. Plattner. il Aviation W 90:30-1 F 17 '69
747 surpasses FAA evacuation standards. R. G. O'Lone. il Aviation W 91:33 D 1 '69
747 type certification tests completed; FAA review awaited. R. G. O'Lone. Aviation W 91:30 D 22 '69

Testing
Boeing 747 begins flight testing phase. il Aviation W 90:26-9 F 17 '69
Boeing 747 flies at Mach 0.983. Aviation W 90:31 Ap 28 '69
Problems beset 747 as delivery nears. R. G. O'Lone. il Aviation W 91:24-7 S 1 '69

Used airplanes
See Airplanes, Used

AIRPLANES, Military—Europe, Western—
Continued
Multi-role fighter design accord reached. E.
H. Kolcum. Aviation W 90:23-4 Ap 7 '69
NATO credibility keyed to new aircraft. il
Aviation W 90:116-18 Je 2 '69
Problems loom for multi-national fighter. E.
H. Kolcum. Aviation W 90:27-8 My 5 '69

Germany (Federal Republic)
Learning to handle the flying coffin: F-104G
Starfighter. Time 94:35 O 24 '69

Great Britain
Why marines want to buy British; they need
short take-off jets. il Bsns W D 128 Je 7
'69

Italy
Italian air force reaffirms MRCA need. R.
F. Coburn. Aviation W 91:23-4 D 15 '69

Japan
Nihon plans to roll out C-1 in 1970. il Aviation
W 90:46-7 Ja 27 '69

Russia
Russian V/STOL fighter details shown. il
Aviation W 90:32-3 Ap 14 '69
Soviets show new STOL fighter details. il
Aviation W 90:20-1 Ap 7 '69
USSR military and civil aircraft (cont) Aviation
W 90:145 Mr 10 '69

Sweden
How to build an instant air force; use of
Swedish single-engine aircraft. MFI-9B in
Nigeria. il Time 93:38 Je 6 '69
Two MFI-9B growth versions designed. il
Aviation W 90:61 F 3 '69
Viggen avionics will perform varied roles. il
Aviation W 90:226-7+ Je 2 '69

Switzerland
Swiss seek new aircraft offset contract. Aviation
W 90:225 Je 2 '69

United States
Air force hopes for approval of F-15 buy to
total 700. il Aviation W 92:18-19 Ja 5 '70
Arms costs escalate; Congress and Pentagon
at loggerheads. il Bsns W p42+ Ja 25 '69
Competitors scramble to replace old fighter;
air force contract sought by McDonnell
Douglas, North American, and Fairchild
Hiller. il Bsns W p 110+ My 17 '69
Dogfight over the F-15. il Bsns W p96-8 D
20 '69
F-111: a pilot's verdict. R. B. Weeghman.
il Flying 84:80-5 My '69
Fifteen-year AMSA operational life forecast.
C. Brownlow. Aviation W 90:20-1 Ap 21
'69
First AMSA flight scheduled by air force
for April, 1973. Aviation W 90:17 Mr 31 '69
Gamble goes on; intelligence gathering by
EC-121. Time 93:23 My 16 '69
High flying in the Pentagon; campaigns for
new aircraft. A. Hamilton. New Repub 160:
16-18 My 31 '69
House unit to hear USAF reasons for Wren
choice. Aviation W 90:17 Mr 17 '69
In the works, new U.S. fighter: the F-15.
il U S News 68:6 Ja 5 '70
Major AMSA funding approved. C. Brownlow.
Aviation W 90:16-17 Mr 17 '69
New bomber runs into old flak; proposed
bomber AMSA. il Bsns W p43-4 My 3 '69
New muscle for navy's air arm: the F-14A.
il Bsns W p58+ F 1 '69
New ups and downs for the F-111. Bsns W
p56+ S 20 '69
Northrop plans F-5-21 as export fighter.
C. M. Plattner. il Aviation W 90:42+ Mr
3 '69
OV-10A export sales drive pushed. C. Brownlow.
il Aviation W 91:67+ N 17 '69
People vs. the F-111. J. Fricker. il Flying
84:64-72+ My '69
Pre-emptive strike; airborne systems unaffected
by budget cuts. il Newsweek 74:22B
S 1 '69
S-3 program to test contracting concept. il
Aviation W 91:34 Ag 11 '69
Secret ways of a speedy blackbird; SR-71.
il Time 93:51 Ap 11 '69
Spy planes; what they do and why; EC-121
incident. il Time 93:17 Ap 25 '69
Superiority in the '70s; forthcoming F-15
fighter. il Time 95:49 Ja 5 '70
They're putting the old birds back into battle;
converting World war II bombers.
N. Sklarewitz. il Pop Mech 131:92-4 Ja '69
Thunderbirds probe F-4E potential. C. M.
Plattner. il Aviation W 91:36-9+ S 1 '69

20001: aerospace odyssey; XB-70. il Newsweek
73:30 F 17 '69
U for utility: U-2s. il Newsweek 73:20 F 17 '69
USAF, navy press tactical fighter work. il
Aviation W 90:47+ M 10 '69
USAF to seek additional B-1A funds for 1971.
Aviation W 91:31 S 22 '69
Varieties of elint: the EC-121. il Newsweek
73:30 Ap 28 '69
See also
EC-121 incident. 1969

Yugoslavia
Yugoslavia seeks to gain exports to West.
H. J. Coleman. il Aviation W 90:207-9+
Je 2 '69

AIRPLANES, Military. Theft of
Flight of Sergeant Meyer. Time 93:23 My 30
'69
I've got trouble; case of P. A. Meyer in
England. il Newsweek 73:50+ Je 2 '69
Russians bungle attempt to steal Mirage.
Aviation W 91:23 O 13 '69

AIRPLANES, Military transport
Austria puts Skyvan into military service.
il Aviation W 91:51 S 29 '69
Biggest airplane ever built; C-5A Galaxy.
J. Goodrum. il Pop Sci 194:98-100 My '69
C-5 cut seen influencing foreign policy.
D. C. Winston. Aviation W 91:33 N 24 '69
C-5As with wing modifications planned for
September delivery. Aviation W 91:13 D 22
'69
How C-5A cutback will hurt Lockheed. il
Bsns W p41-2 N 22 '69
In service; the biggest plane yet; C-5A. U S
News 67:7 D 29 '69
Major shift expected in C-5A delivery date.
B. K. Thomas. il Aviation W 90:40-1 Mr 3
'69
Overruns on C-5A costs face intensified
scrutiny. D. C. Winston. Aviation W 90:
26-7 My 26 '69
Polishing the brass; criticism of price of
C-5A transport plane. il Time 93:25-6 My 9
'69
Propagandizing the C-5A. Commonweal 91:
60 O 17 '69
Senate renews attack on C-5A requests. D.
C. Winston. il Aviation W 91:18-19 S 8 '69
Skyvan offered for Vietnam military role.
Aviation W 90:22 Ap 21 '69
Talks started on C-5 contract revisions. D.
C. Winston. Aviation W 91:29-30 Ag 4 '69
USAF, Lockheed diverge over C-5A terms.
Aviation W 90:20 Je 23 '69
USAF team studies C-5 cost overruns. C.
Brownlow. Aviation W 90:24 My 12 '69
What price the C-5A? il Newsweek 73:80+
My 12 '69

Testing
C-5A amasses 687 hr. in flight program. il
Aviation W 91:59-63 S 8 '69

AIRPLANES, Private. See Airplanes—Private
ownership

AIRPLANES, Remodeled
Charter to modify Yak-40 to attract West.
Aviation W 91:33 O 6 '69
Foreign accent; Vampire fighter becomes a
bizjet. J. Fricker. il Flying 84:24-5 My '69
P-51; everybody's favorite airplane. S. Wilkinson.
il Flying 84:54-8 F '69
They're putting the old birds back into battle;
converting World war II bombers. N.
Sklarewitz. il Pop Mech 131:92-4 Ja '69

AIRPLANES, Research. See Airplanes, Experimental

AIRPLANES, Restored
Great-antiques pilot report:
The de Havilland Tiger Moth. J. Gilbert.
il Flying 85:46-51 N '69

AIRPLANES, Short take-off and landing
American amasses STOL navaid data. K. J.
Stein. il Aviation W 90:81+ My 26 '69
Czechs launch Turbolet sales campaign. D. E.
Fink. il Aviation W 91:29-32 Jl 14 '69
New Waco STOL Minerva has real get-upand-go.
N. Aubuchon. il Pop Sci 195:60-3+
D '69
STOL future keyed to noise limitations. Aviation
W 90:46+ F 24 '69
STOL-mods myth. A. Trammell. il Flying
84:54-6+ Ap '69
Turboprop Courier begins flight testing. il
Aviation W 91:74 Jl 7 '69

Design
Broad market expected for DHC-7. D. A.
Brown. il Aviation W 91:40-1+ S 8 '69

Specifications
See Airplanes—Specifications

AIRPLANES, Supersonic

Airlines appear to be diverging in degrees of support for SST. H. D. Watkins. Aviation W 90:25 F 17 '69

Belated entry. Time 93:86 Mr 28 '69

Boeing, General electric study boomless transonic transport. Aviation W 91:29 D 22 '69

Coming: the twelve-hour world. il Nations Bsns 57:32-5 Ag '69

Concorde officials study plan for subsonic overland flights. il Aviation W 91:34 O 13 '69

Concorde route study nears completion. H. J. Coleman. il Aviation W 90:34+ Mr 17 '69

Concorde: the costs are rising, but so are prospects for success. D. S. Greenberg. il Science 165:374-7 Jl 25 '69

Concorde's moment of truth. il Fortune 79:128-9+ Mr '69

Concordes star in flying display at Paris. W. H. Gregory. il Aviation W 90:39-42+ Je 23 '69

Critics' sound barrier may slow the SST. il Bsns W p39 Mr 22 '69

Down on its uppers. Sci N 95:473-4 My 17 '69

Fare surcharge for Concorde is probable; all first-class, 112-seat layout planned. il Aviation W 90:156-8+ Je 2 '69

Faster! Faster! go-ahead on American SST program. G. Lardner. New Repub 161:9-11 O 18 '69

Go. but wait, again. Sci N 95:329-30 Ap 5 '69

Less noise; interagency review of Supersonic transport program. New Repub 160:10 Mr 8 '69

Lockheed studies mach 1.15 SST. Aviation W 91:31 Jl 21 '69

Lower ceiling on hopes for SST; for lack of money. Bsns W p29-30 My 31 '69

Moving at last. Sci N 96:265 S 27 '69

Never mind the experts; SST ad hoc review committee report. Nation 209:620 D 8 '69

Pressure grows to delay SST prototype. H. D. Watkins. Aviation W 90:29-30 Mr 31 '69

Race for a superjet: can U.S. catch up? il U S News 66:38-9 Mr 17 '69

Race for the SST; with report on the Concorde test flight by M. Mok. il Life 66:28-31 Mr 14 '69

Ramming through the SST. Nation 209:364 O 13 '69

SST faces congressional hurdle; with editorial comment. H. D. Watkins. il Aviation W 91:11, 16-18 S 29 '69

SST funding bid left to Nixon. H. D. Watkins. Aviation W 90:30-1 Ja 20 '69

SST: riding a technological tiger. il Time 94:91-2 O 3 '69

SST study committee formation slowed. H. D. Watkins. Aviation W 90:29-30 F 10 '69

SST study yields negative view. H. D. Watkins. Aviation W 90:29 Mr 24 '69

Soviet SST shows its face: Tu-144. il Bsns W p35 My 24 '69

Special report: U.S. supersonic transport program; symposium. with editorial comment. il Aviation W 92:11. 26-31+ Ja 5 '70

Statecraft and the SST; need for an SST nondeployment and nonproliferation treaty. A. W. Smith. Nat Parks 43:2 D '69

Three hours to Europe, a go ahead for supersonic jet. il U S News 67:10 O 6 '69

Up, up and more on the way. J. R. Roberson. il Holiday 46:36-7+ Jl '69

Volpe seen backing SST prototype work. H. D. Watkins. Aviation W 90:30 Mr 17 '69

Will it be the soaring seventies? faster than sound. H. Sutton and D. Butwin. Sat R 53:73+ Ja 3 '70

Wind and temperature effects on supersonic aircraft operations. N. B. Guttman and H. L. Crutcher. bibliog il Weatherwise 21:220-6 D '68

World's first giant jet: Boeing 747. A. Bester. il Holiday 46:28-35+ Jl '69

See also
Sonic boom

Control

U.S. firm studies Concorde guidance. Aviation W 90:75 Mr 17 '69

Cost

Concorde costs estimate rises. Aviation W 91:27-8 Jl 14 '69

Financing poses unprecedented challenge. il Aviation W 92:61-3+ Ja 5 '70

House votes $96 million SST funding. K. Johnsen. Aviation W 91:38 N 24 '69

Market outlook hinges on Concorde sales. il Aviation W 92:51-3+ Ja 5 '70

Novel financing proposed for SST. Bsns W p64 My 3 '69

SST gets clearance for a late takeoff. il Bsns W p29-30 S 27 '69

Design

Can passengers take the punishment of supersonic flight? il Sci Digest 65:62-7 Ap '69

Inlets posed YF-12 design hurdle. C. M. Plattner. il Aviation W 91:65+ Ag 11 '69

Supersonic family evolving at Boeing. W. H. Gregory. il Aviation W 92:29-31+ Ja 5 '70

SST keyed to current airline operations. J. P. Woolsey. il Aviation W 92:38-9+ Ja 5 '70

Tu-144 heading for 1972 service start. R. G. O'Lone. il Aviation W 91:26-8 Ag 25 '69

Engines

See Jet airplane engines

Fuel

See Jet airplane engines—Fuel

Manufacture

Concorde production study pushed. H. J. Coleman. il Aviation W 92:65+ Ja 12 '70

Noise

See Airplanes—Noise

Photographs

First Concorde supersonic transport flies. Aviation W 90:283-5 Mr 10 '69

Testing

Airline pilots flight test Concorde. H. J. Coleman. il Aviation W 91:35 N 24 '69

British Concorde in 22-min. first flight. H. J. Coleman. Aviation W 90:45 Ap 14 '69

British Concorde lifts off on first flight. il Aviation W 90:32-4 Ap 21 '69

Concorde enters flight test phase. D. E. Fink. il Aviation W 90:287+ Mr 10 '69

Concorde moving into supersonic testing. H. J. Coleman. il Aviation W 91:30-2 Ag 25 '69

Concorde 002 in third flight. Aviation W 90:39 My 5 '69

Early flight tests will decide fate of Anglo-French Concorde. H. J. Coleman. Aviation W 90:28-9 F 3 '69

Flight of the fast bird; Concorde maiden flight. il Time 93:87-8 Mr 14 '69

Weight

See Airplanes—Weight

AIRPLANES, Tank. See Tank airplanes

AIRPLANES, Theft of

See also
Airplanes, Military, Theft of

AIRPLANES, Training

British, Italians sign agreements for joint development of trainers. Aviation W 91:120 Ag 11 '69

Cessna's learn-to-fly airplanes. A. Trammell. il Flying 84:57-9 Mr '69

Consortium trainer proposals due Jan. 2. Aviation W 91:21 D 22 '69

Harrier trainer phased into production. il Aviation W 90:54-5 Ap 7 '69

Japan moves to produce Mach 1.6 trainer. il Aviation W 91:20-2 Ag 25 '69

Pilot report: North American T-6. R. B. Weeghman. il Flying 84:60-5 Je '69

AIRPLANES, Used

Eight great buys in used airplanes. J. Gilbert. il Flying 84:44-9 My '69

Poor little rich kid. R. Bach. il Flying 85:35+ Ag '69

Used short-body jet market sought. D. A. Brown. il Aviation 91:73-4+ O 13 '69

Marketing

Used short-body jet market sought. D. A. Brown. il Aviation W 91:73-4+ O 13 '69

Purchasing

Fly your own plane, for no more than a new car. T. Hook. il Pop Sci 195:58-61+ Je '69

Testing

Used-plane pilot report: Globe Swift. S. Wilkinson. il Flying 85:64-9 N '69

AIRPLANES, Vertical take-off and landing

Bitter about VTOL: German government has dropped support. T. Shoemaker. Sci N 95:562 Je 7 '69

British firms vie for civil VTOL design. il Aviation W 90:345+ Je 2 '69

Canadian forces to test tilt-wing VTOL. il Aviation W 90:98 Ap 14 '69

Harrier demonstrates capability for VTOL city center operation in transatlantic race. il Aviation W 90:28-30 My 12 '69

Russian V/STOL fighter details shown. il Aviation W 90:32-3 Ap 14 '69

AIRPLANES, Vertical take-off and landing—
Continued
Third-level V/STOL pushed. Aviation W 91:41 D 15 '69
VFW developing 90-seat tilt-wing VTOL. il Aviation W 91:67 Jl 21 '69
VTOL operations; help for metropolitan problems. W. A. Kuhrt. Aviation W 91:102 N 10 '69
Why marines want to buy British; they need short take-off jets. il Bsns W ᴅ 128 Je 7 '69

Design
Eastern asks V/STOL design proposals. K. J. Stein. Aviation W 91:34 Ag 18 '69
Germans emphasize V/STOL transports. E. H. Kolcum. il Aviation W 91:43+ D 8 '69

Specifications
See Airplanes—Specifications

Testing
Canadian forces program CL-84 testing. W. H. Gregory. Aviation W 90:19-20 Je 30 '69
Navy seeking extended joint X-22 testing. Aviation W 91:58 N 3 '69

AIRPLANES in agriculture
U.S. agricultural aircraft (cont) Aviation W 90:154 Mr 10 '69

AIRPLANES in business
Business relies more on own aircraft. D. A. Brown. il Aviation W 90:225-8 Mr 10 '69
Editorial. R. B. Parke. il Flying 85:34 O '69
See also
Airplanes. Business
National business aircraft association

AIRPLANES in church work
Fruitful shakedown for evangel craft. Chr Today 14:38 N 21 '69

AIRPLANES in fire protection
CL-215 proves rugged, dependable in water bomber role. D. A. Brown. il Aviation W 91:64-5+ S 22 '69
First wings over the forest. H. Clepper. il Am For 75:24-7 +Je: 20-3+ Jl '69

AIRPLANES in fish culture. See Fish culture

AIRPLANES in fishing. See Airplanes in hunting and fishing

AIRPLANES in forest fire protection. See Forest fire patrol. Aerial

AIRPLANES in hunting and fishing
Take the high road to Alaska. G. Laycock. il Field & S 74:50-3+ My '69

AIRPLANES in missionary work. See Airplanes in church work

AIRPLANES in newspaper service
Japanese air force. il Time 93:82 My 2 '69

AIRPLANES in rescue work
See also
Helicopters in rescue work

AIRPLANES in weather control
See also
Helicopters in weather control

AIRPORT adventure; drama. See Murray, J.

AIRPORT buildings
American seeks advanced modular loading dock design. W. H. Gregory. il Aviation W 91:26-30 O 6 '69
Lufthansa planning JFK cargo facility. Aviation W 90:32 F 10 '69
Orly to get special 747 passenger areas. il Aviation W 90:40-1 F 10 '69
Soft landing in Houston. J. M. Dixon. il Arch Forum 131:60-9 S '69

AIRPORT management. See Airports—Management

AIRPORT operations council international
Airport council asks user tax, aviation planning commission. Aviation W 90:31 F 3 '69

AIRPORT thefts. See Stealing

AIRPORTS
Airports; when will the ground catch up with the sky? W. Burrows. il Holiday 46:48-51+ Jl '69
See also subhead Airports under names of cities, e.g. Los Angeles—Airports

Buildings
See Airport buildings

Design
Airport planning and design; address, October 22, 1969. M. Sadler. Vital Speeches 36:124-8 D 1 '69
Metroport tied to developing STOL system. Aviation W 91:54 S 8 '69

Equipment
ATA unit divided on equipment for retrieving disabled jets. Aviation W 91:32 S 29 '69
Airlines prepare for introduction of 747. J. P. Woolsey. il Aviation W 91:36-41+ O 20 '69
Decision on 747 loading system awaited. R. S. Kahn. il Aviation W 91:49-50 N 17 '69

Europeans join to market 747 equipment. R. F. Coburn. il Aviation W 91:36-7+ Jl 7 '69
Giant jets spur ground equipment boom. N. Himmel. il Aviation W 91:169+ O 20 '69
Loading devices designed for giant jets. N. S. Himmel. il Aviation W 91:51+ Jl 28 '69
New generation of ground units services 747. il Aviation W 90:28-30 Je 23 '69
Pan American checks ground equipment with 747 at New York; photographs. Aviation W 91:32-4 D 8 '69
Pan Am testing mobile loading system for 747. il Aviation W 90:43+ Je 9 '69
See also
Airports—Safety devices and measures

Federal aid
Short-term airport funding voted. D. C. Winston. Aviation W 91:25-6 N 3 '69

Finance
Airport crisis. il Flying 85:58-61+ Jl '69
Broader airport bill introduced. Aviation W 91:27 N 10 '69
Committee sets tax threshold at 6,000 lb. Aviation W 91:29 O 13 '69
FAA criticized on safety, traffic control. Aviation W 91:34 D 15 '69
House unit votes user taxes on aircraft. D. C. Winston. Aviation W 91:22 O 6 '69
Move over; joint ATA-AOPA position on airport improvement. R. B. Parke. il Flying 85:42 Ag '69
Municipal bond problems pose obstacles to airport funding. N. S. Himmel. Aviation W 91:56+ N 17 '69
Nixon user tax plan drops trust fund. D. C. Winston. Aviation W 90:21-2 My 19 '69
Nixon user tax program could face court testing. D. C. Winston. Aviation W 91:33-4 S 22 '69
Presenting the airport bill; major overhaul job of the nation's airports. il Forbes 103:30-1 Mr 1 '69
Short-term airport funding voted. D. C. Winston. Aviation W 91:25-6 N 3 '69
Trust fund plan hits opposition. D. C. Winston. Aviation W 90:26-7 Ap 7 '69
Up in the air. M. Friedman. Newsweek 74:63 Jl 28 '69
User tax boost marks air facilities plan. D. C. Winston. Aviation W 90:31-2 Je 23 '69

Lighting
Finds light faults in one hour instead of seven; using electronic locator at Bradley international airport, Windsor Locks, Conn. il Am City 84:118-19 Ap '69
New guide for airport parking area lighting. il Am City 84:134 Ap '69

Location
Airports at sea. il Time 93:61 My 30 '69
Study reports offshore airports technically feasible, more costly. Aviation W 91:41 N 17 '69

Management
Up in the air. M. Friedman. Newsweek 74:63 Jl 28 '69
See also
Airport operations council international

Marking
Diamonds on the runway. R. Blodget. il Flying 85:70-1 Ag '69

Planning
Airport planning and design; address, October 22, 1969. M. Sadler. Vital Speeches 36:124-8 D 1 '69
Paris airport system plans are drafted. Aviation W 91:147+ O 20 '69
Target is 1980. E. Gross. il Sci N 95:531-3 My 31 '59
Will it be the soaring seventies? survey of plans and accomplishments to meet the jumbos. H. Sutton and D. Butwin. il Sat R 53:34-8+ Ja 3 '70
See also
Airports—Location

Runways
Finds light faults in one hour instead of seven; using electronic locator at Bradley international airport, Windsor Locks, Conn. il Am City 84:118-19 Ap '69
See also
Airports—Marking
Airports—Surfaces

Safety devices and measures
Pop-up arresting cable tested. il Aviation W 90:67 Ap 21 '69
See also
Radar in aviation

AIRPORTS—*Continued*

Stores

Guide to jet-age bazaars. il Time 93:30+ My 30 '69

Surfaces

Pavements tested for giant transports. J. W. Carter. il Aviation W 90:84-5 Mr 31 '69

Traffic

Another season of stacking up. Bsns W p21-2 Jl 5 '69

As traffic jams the airways; government figures show congested and unsafe conditions. U S News 67:4-5 Jl 28 '69

Cost of restrictions; excerpts from address. S. G. Tipton. Aviation W 90:11 F 10 '69

Day in the life of an airport. J. N. Miller. il Read Digest 94:146-50 F '69

Flying toward more air traffic jams; caused by air traffic controllers tactics. Bsns W p33-4 Jl 26 '69

NBAA suit seeks stay of access limits. Aviation W 90:83 Ja 27 '69

Paris delays laid to lack of controllers. congestion. D. E. Fink. Aviation W 91:139+ O 20 '69

Traffic control

Crosswinds over congested airports; new FAA rule. Bsns W p31 O 4 '69

FAA eases limitations on airport access. D. A. Brown. Aviation W 90:22 Mr 3 '69

FAA proposes new control system. J. P. Woolsey. il Aviation W 91:24-5 O 6 '69

FAA seeks extension of landing quotas. Aviation W 91:34 N 24 '69

On top; reservations system. R. L. Collins. Flying 85:12-14 Ag '69

Quota system for landings. Time 93:103 Je 6 '69

Radar failure delays traffic after launch. Aviation W 91:31 Jl 21 '69

Super beacon concepts emerging; intermittent positive control concept. P. J. Klass. il Aviation W 91:75+ D 8 '69

Taped lines keep airport traffic moving; Washington national airport. C. R. Melugin, jr. il Am City 84:146 F '69

Target is 1980. E. Gross. il Sci N 95:531-3 My 31 '69

Visibility

Airline warm fog dispersal program. W. G. Osmun. il Weatherwise 22:48-53+ Ap '69

Clearing ground fog with helicopters. V. G. Plank. il Weatherwise 22:91-8+ Je '69

California

Diamonds on the runway. R. Blodget. il Flying 85:70-1 Ag '69

See also
Los Angeles—Airports

Canada

See also
Montreal—Airports

Connecticut

Finds light faults in one hour instead of seven; using electronic locator at Bradley international airport, Windsor Locks. il Am City 84:118-19 Ap '69

Florida

Coalition forms to fight Florida jetport. Nat Parks 43:28 My '69

Conservationists press Florida jetport issue. Nat Parks 43:20 Je '69

Everglades jetport: Academy prepares a model. M. Mueller. il Science 166:202-3 O 10 '69

Everglades jetport; appeal to prevent airport. M. Nadel. Liv Wildn 32:2 Aut '68

Foes of Everglades airport gaining; studies started. B. K. Thomas. Aviation W 91:42 S 15 '69

Jetport and the Everglades; life or runaway? il Liv Wildn 33:13-20 Spr '69

Jetport or Everglades park? The Leopold report; summary .L. B. Leopold. il Audubon 71:151-3 N '69

Jets v. Everglades. il Time 94:42-3 Ag 22 '69

Jets vs. the call of the wild. il Bsns W p76-7 Ag 30 '69

Last chance to save the Everglades. J. D. McDonald. il Life 67:58-61+ S 5 '69

Leopold report: Everglades jetport; with editorial comment. L. B. Leopold. Nat Parks 43:10, 11-13 N '69

More trouble for Everglades. il Sci N 96:296-7 O 4 '69

Progress menaces the Everglades. il Nat Parks 43:8-15 Jl '69

Superjetport or Everglades Park? P. Brooks. il Audubon 71:4-11 Jl '69

See also
Tampa, Fla.—Airports

France

See also
Paris—Airports

Great Britain

Lag in jetport program spurs British to emphasize Gatwick. Aviation W 91:37 S 29 '69

Hawaii

See also
Honolulu—Airports

New Hampshire

Safety check; airplane and the mountain, Lebanon approach. R. L. Collins. Flying 85:22-3 Ag '69

Texas

See also
Dallas—Airports

United States

Airport changes urged in report. Aviation W 91:33 S 29 '69

Airport crisis. il Flying 85:58-61+ Jl '69

Bumpy flight for Nixon bill: plan for airways and airport development. Bsns W p46 Je 21 '69

Folly in Florida; project to build jetport in the Everglades A. W. Smith. Nat Parks 43:2+ Ja '69

Presenting the airport bill; major overhaul job of the nation's airports. il Forbes 103: 30-1 Mr 1 '69

Tangled mess in aviation; with editorial comment. Bsns W p52-4+, 100 Ag 9 '69

See also subhead Airports under names of cities, e.g. New York (city)—Airports

AIRSHIPS

Go-go slow; Goodyear blimps, Mayflower and Columbia. C. Phinizy. il Sports Illus 30:68-70+ Mr 17 '69

AIRSPACE (international law)

Ratification of air crimes convention seen. D. C. Winston. Aviation W 90:41 My 5 '69

AIRWAYS

Routes that lead to merger. il Bsns W p33 Jl 26 '69

See also
Airlines—International services
Airlines—United States—Routes

See also
Traffic control

See also
Air traffic control

AIRWORTHINESS directives. See Aviation—Laws and regulations

AISLAN, Eduardo Ritter. See Ritter Aislán, E.

AIX-EN-PROVENCE festival. See Music festivals—France

AJMONE-MARSAN, Barbara

I don't want to live through a man. por Redbook 133:13+ Ag '69

AKADEMGORODOK, Siberia

Akademgorodok; Academic town. T. Shabad. il Focus 19:9-12 F '69

Matter meets antimatter in Akademgorodok; Nuclear physics institute. G. B. Lubkin. il Phys Today 22:62-6 Ag '69

AKERS, Charles K. See Parsons, D. F. jt. auth.

AKERS, Georgia

What's cooking? Org Gard & Farm 16:77-8 Jl '69

AKESON, W. R. and others

Sweetclover-weevil feeding deterrent B: isolation and identification. bibliog Science 163:293-4 Ja 17 '69

AKHMADULINA, Bella

Different smile. A. Hollo. Nation 209:666-7 D 15 '69

AKHMATOVA, Anna Andreevna

Different smile. A. Hollo. Nation 209:666-7 D 15 '69

AKIN, R. M. jr

Sport fisherman; interview. ed. by F. Moss. Yachting 125:80 Ja '69

AKRON, Ohio

Housing

This is the housing that Jack built. il Bsns W p89 S 13 '69

Labor and laboring classes

Hopes and fears of blue-collar youth. P. M. Swerdloff. il Fortune 79:148-50+ Ja '69

Recreation

Tire town U.S.A. M. E. Fay. il Parks & Rec 4:24-5 Jl '69

Al AKSA mosque. See Jerusalem—Mosques

AKURI Indians. See Indians of South America—Surinam

AKWEI, Richard Maximilian
Occasion; interview. New Yorker 45:27-8 Ap 5 '69

ALABAMA
Description and travel
Alabama's mountain lakes. J. Goodrum. il Travel 131:40-3+ Je '69

Race problems
See also
Birmingham, Ala.—Negroes

Social conditions
U.S. journal: Gees Bend, Ala. groundbreaking of sewing center of Freedom quilting bee. C. Trillin. New Yorker 45:102+ Mr 22 '69

ALABAMA International motor speedway. See Speedways

ALAMEDA, Calif.
Housing
Disciplined variety creates interest on a flat site for a townhouse complex. il Arch Rec 146:190-1 S '69

ALAMO, San Antonio, Tex.
Remember the Alamo, please. G. Cartwright. il Life 66:62-4 Ap 25 '69

ALAN Wood steel company. See Wood, Alan, steel company

ALARM guns. See Firearms

ALARM pheromones. See Pheromones

ALARMS
See also
Burglar alarms
Electric alarms
Fire alarms

ALARMS, Automobile. See Automobiles—Electronic equipment

ALASKA
Arctic walk; walking trip from Brooks Range to Barter Island. J. P. Milton. il Natur Hist 78:44-53 My '69
Northern adventure, a winter tour into Arctic Alaska. Sunset 142:28 F '69
Now that you own Alaska, friends, what are you going to do with it? A. Barry. il Esquire 71:119-25 Ap '69
Ted's troubles in the tundra; investigating condition of Alaskan natives. il Time 93:22-3 Ap 18 '69
What Alaska offers young marrieds. T. Lowell, jr. McCalls 96:99-100 Ap '69
See also
Aeronautics, Commercial—Alaska
Christmas—Alaska
Conservation of resources—Alaska
Earthquakes—Alaska
Eskimos
Fishing—Alaska
Forests and forestry—Alaska
Geology—Alaska
Hunting—Alaska
Klondike
Land tenure—Alaska
Landscape protection—Alaska
Medical relief work—Alaska
Mines and mineral resources—Alaska
Natural resources—Alaska
Negroes—Alaska
Nome
Petroleum—Alaska
Petroleum industry and trade—Alaska
Stikine River
Tourist trade—Alaska
Water pollution—Alaska
Wilderness areas—Alaska
Wildlife conservation—Alaska

Antiquities
See Eskimos—Antiquities

Climate
Water pollution in Alaska: present and future. F. B. Lotspeich. bibliog il Science 166:1239-45 D 5 '69

Description and travel
Arctic Alaska circle tour. il Bet Hom & Gard 47:117 F '69
Facts about the last frontier. il U S News 66:84-5 F 24 '69
Great northwest cruise. C. West. il Motor B 123:142-6 Ja '69
Harding's Alaskan dream; excerpt from The shadow of Blooming Grove. F. Russell. il Sat R 52:63-4 Mr 8 '69
Travel notes. R. Joseph. Esquire 71:20+ Ap '69

Economic conditions
Alaska: bonanza for blacks? il Ebony 25:123-6+ N '69
Alaska's $50-billion boom. il Forbes 104:30-3+ N 15 '69
Facts about the last frontier. il U S News 66:84-5 F 24 '69
How big is Alaska? G. Laycock. il Audubon 71:66-70+ Mr '69
Nomad in Alaska's outback. T. J. Abercrombie. il Nat Geog 135:540-67 Ap '69

Economic policy
When a state gets a 900-million windfall; oil fortune. il U S News 67:68 S 22 '69

Exploration
Ultimate confrontation. R. Cantwell. il Sports Illus 30:66-70+ Mr 24 '69

Fish and game, Department of
Another shakeup in Alaska. B. East. il Outdoor Life 144:4+ O '69
New status for Alaska's rainbow trout. H. M. Hershberger. Field & S 74:112 Je '69

ALASKA airlines
Travel notes. R. Joseph. Esquire 71:20+ Ap '69

ALASKA forest fire. See Forest fires

ALASKA. University
University of Alaska: academe's outpost in the subarctic. L. J. Carter. il Science 166:353-8 O 17 '69

ALBACORE fishing
Run for the blue water; longfin tuna fishing. D. Holm. il Outdoor Life 144:52-5+ N '69

ALBANIA
Red China in Europe. D. Bligh. America 120:280-1 Mr 8 '69

Politics and government
Albanian demonology. A. Tuckerman. Nation 208:566-7 My 5 '69

ALBANY, N.Y.
City planning
Mister Rockefeller builds his dream house. W. D. Gardner. il Ramp Mag 8:36-9 S '69

ALBANY, N.Y. diocese. See Catholic church—Dioceses

ALBEE, Edward
Medium is the absurd; address, November 1968. L. Mussoff. Engl J 58:566-70+ Ap '69
Tiny Alice. Criticism
America 121:342 O 18 '69
Nat R 21:1334 D 30 '69
Nation 209:451 O 27 '69
New Repub 161:22+ N 1 '69
New Yorker 45:85-6 O 11 '69
Newsweek 74:125 O 13 '69
Sat R 52:20 O 18 '69
Time il 94:72 O 17 '69

ALBERSTADT, Milton
Dress rehearsal. Space World F-8-68:32-3 Ag '69

ALBERT, D. J. and Storlien, L. H.
Hyperphagia in rats with cuts between the ventromedial and lateral hypothalamus. bibliog Science 165:599-600 Ag 8 '69

ALBERT, Daniel M. and others
Neoplastic transformation in vitro of hamster lens epithelium by simian virus 40. bibliog Science 164:1077-8 My 30 '69

ALBERT, Eugen d'
Music to my ears. I. Kolodin. Sat R 52:53+ Ap 26 '69

ALBERT, Lee
Doing something relevant. il Time 93:27-8 My 9 '69

ALBERT LEA, Minn.
Secret of prosperity. il Nations Bsns 57:46-8+ Je '69

ALBERT Parvin foundation. See Parvin foundation

ALBERT Schweitzer hospital. See Hospitals—Gabon

ALBERTA
See also
Edmonton

ALBERTS, Ian
Has success spoiled FM? Hi Fi 19:61-3 N '69

ALBIN, Wyo.
Tiny town telephone fire report. M. D. Anderson. il Am City 84:136-7 Ag '69

ALBINOS and albinism
Hopi Indians, inbreeding, and albinism. C. M. Woolf and F. C. Dukepoo. bibliog il Science 164:30-7 Ap 4 '69
Horizontal ghost. E. Mason. il Outdoor Life 144:76+ Ag '69

ALBION, Neb.
Paving cures dust and drainage ills. J. Lough. il Am City 84:97-8 Jl '69

ALBRECHT, Milton C.
Novel reflections. Trans-Action 6:54-5 O '69

ALBRECHT, P. and Ourisson, G.
Triterpene alcohol isolation from oil shale. bibliog Science 163:1192 Mr 14 '69

ALBRIGHT, Alton P.
Sheridan grapes for Christmas. por Org Gard & Farm 16:75 D '69

ALBRIGHT, Archie Earl, 1920-
Street gets a pro manager. por Bsns W p93 Ag 16 '69

ALBRIGHT, Arnita W.
Wind sculptures. Sch Arts 69:12-15 O '69

ALBRIGHT, George C.
Sunset to remember. por Outdoor Life 143: 70-1+ F '69

ALBRIGHT, Horace Marden
Harding, Coolidge, and the lady who lost her dress. Am West 6:25-32 S '69
Scenic tribute to Stephen Mather; address, April 17, 1969. por Nat Parks 43:12-14 Je '69

ALBRIGHT, Horace M, training center. See United States—National park service

ALBROOK, Robert C.
Frustrations of the acquired executive. Fortune 80:152-6+ N '69
One thing sure, parenthood today is no bore! Fortune 79:92-3+ Ja '69
Those boxed-in, left-out vice presidents. Fortune 79:104-7+ My 1 '69
Why there's so much incompetence in business. Fortune 79:203+ Mr '69

ALBUMINS
Lactose synthetase: progesterone inhibition of the induction of α-lactalbumin. R. W. Turkington and R. L. Hill. bibliog il Science 163:1458-60 Mr 28 '69
See also
Blood—Proteins
Egg white

ALBUMS
See also
Photographic albums

ALCAN. See Aluminum company of Canada

ALCATRAZ, (island)
New flag over Alcatraz. il Time 95:20 Ja 5 '70
Siege of the Rock; Lamar Hunt plan. il Newsweek 74:81 O 27 '69
Tribal rock; group of Indians claim Alcatraz. il Newsweek 74:52 D 8 '69

ALCHEMY
Catalog of alchemy: a problem in design. il Pub W 195:74+ Ap 7 '69

ALCINDOR, Lewis
My story; ed. by J. Olsen. pors Sports Illus 31:82-8+ O 27; 34-40+ N 3; 35-8+ N 10 '69
about
Beaten once but far from out. J. Jares. il por Sports Illus 30:28-30+ Mr 17 '69
Big Lew against the big men. il por Life 67: 40-3 N 14 '69
Big man among men. il Time 94:24 D 26 '69
Bleak house. Newsweek 73:98 Ap 14 '69
Coming-out party for Lew and Connie. T. Maule. il por Sports Illus 31:26-7 O 6 '69
Now he gets to shoot. P. Putnam. il Sports Illus 30:56-63 F 24 '69
Two big men. il por Newsweek 74:108 N 3 '69
Voodoo might help. J. Jares. il por Sports Illus 30:18-21 Mr 24 '69
Week he finally got rid of the yoke. C. Kirkpatrick. por Sports Illus 30:18-19 Mr 31 '69
With a flourish of trumpets; photographs; with accounts by J. Jares and C. Kirkpatrick. pors Sports Illus 30:14-19 Mr 31 '69

ALCO standard corporation
Conglomerate chief on a fast track; T. Veale. 2d. il Bsns W p 154+ Je 7 '69

ALCOHOL
Physiological effects
Alcohol and amitriptyline effects on skills related to driving behavior. A. A. Landauer and others. bibliog il Science 163: 1467-8 Mr 28 '69
Alcohol and recall: state-dependent effects in man. D. W. Goodwin and others. bibliog il Science 163:1358-60 Mr 21 '69
Alcohol; man and science; address, July 13, 1969. M. A. Block. Vital Speeches 35:720-5 S 15 '69
Comparison of the effects of marihuana and alcohol on simulated driving performance. A. Crancer, jr. and others. bibliog il Science 164:851-4 My 16 '69; Discussion. 166: 640 O 31 '69
See also
Drinking and traffic accidents

ALCOHOL dehydrogenases. See Dehydrogenases

ALCOHOL education. See Temperance—Study and teaching

ALCOHOL in the body
Alcohol metabolism: role of microsomal oxidation in vivo. T. R. Tephly and others. bibliog il Science 166:627-8 O 31 '69

ALCOHOL tripping; story. See Mitchell, D.

ALCOHOLIC drinks. See Liquors

ALCOHOLICS
Of drunkards and junkies. Trans-Action 6:5-6 Jl '69
Passive protesters; inhabitants of skid row. il Time 93:62 F 28 '69
Problem-child of alcoholism. il Sci N 95:279 Mr 22 '69
Reaching the unmotivated patient. A. J. R. Koumans. Ment Hy 53:298-300 Ap '69

Rehabilitation
Legal commitment and hospital behavior: recalcitrance of tuberculous alcoholics; address, May 10, 1967. E. Rubington. bibliog Ment Hy 53:41-53 Ja '69
See also
Synanon foundation, incorporated

ALCOHOLISM
Case of the alcoholic absentee. J. W. Kelley. il Harvard Bsns R 47:14-16+ My '69
Long-winded lady; drunk middle-aged woman in Time square. New Yorker 45:18-19 Ja 10 '70
See also
Liquor problem

Research
Relatives as informants in mental health research. C. A. Bentinck and others. bibliog Ment Hy 53:446-50 Jl '69

Study and teaching
See Temperance—Study and teaching

Therapy
Business and the compulsive drinker. A. Hamilton. Read Digest 95:25-6+ N '69

ALCOHOLS
Fatty alcohols (normal and isoprenoid) in sediments. J. Sever and P. L. Parker. bibliog il Science 164:1052-4 My 30 '69
Phenethyl alcohol and tryptophol: autoantibiotics produced by the fungus Candida albicans. B. T. Lingappa and others. bibliog il Science 163:192-4 Ja 10 '69
Triterpene alcohol isolation from oil shale. P. Albrecht and G. Ourisson. bibliog il Science 163:1192 Mr 14 '69
See also
Glycols
Polyols

ALDACTONE. See Spironolactone

ALDERMAN, Elinor R.
Hamelot; drama. Plays 29:11-19 Ja '70

ALDERSON, George
Another look at Glen Canyon. Am For 75: 6-7+ Mr '69
Lava beds: a wilderness in sight. il Liv Wildn 33:21-3 Spr '69
Logan Canyon: standards for destruction. Nat Parks 43:18-20 N '69

ALDERTON, Gordon, and Snell, Neva
Bacterial spores: chemical sensitization to heat. bibliog Science 163:1212-13 Mr 14 '69

ALDO Garzanti. See Publishers and publishing —Italy

ALDRICH, Herbert
Especially for children (cont) Negro Hist Bul 31:14-15 D '68; 32:13-14 Ja '69

ALDRICH, Larry
Young lyrical painters. Art in Am 57:104-13 N '69
about
Collector: Larry Aldrich. J. Russell. il pors Art in Am 57:56-65 Ja '69

ALDRICH, Robert S.
Let's bring back 1909! Sat R 52:10 S 13 '69

ALDRIDGE, Alan
Making fun of themselves. il pors Vogue 153:124-5 Je '69

ALDRIDGE, Ira Frederick
To Madam Engel; Angel guardian; poems. Negro Hist Bul 32:25-6 N '69
about
African trajedian in golden Prague. J. J. Napier and S. B. Winters. bibliog por Negro Hist Bul 32:23-6 N '69

ALDRIDGE, John W.
In the country of the young. Harper 239:56-64 O; 93-4+ N '69

ALDRIDGE, Leslie
Algonquin's sedate sitting room. Holiday 45:110-11 Ap '69
7,000,000 American women take the pill. Very soon now, it will be your turn. Esquire 71:92-3+ Ja '69

ALDRIN, Edwin E. 1930-
Lunar dust smelled just like gunpowder. por Life 67:25-7 Ag 22 '69
Man walks on another world. il Nat Geog 136:738-49 D '69
Space exploration; address, September 16, 1969. Vital Speeches 35:741 O 1 '69
What it's like for man on the moon. U S News 67:25 Ag 4 '69

about

Apollo 11's team: the three who will carry the flag. por U S News 67:33 Jl 21 '69
Astronauts detail lunar flight experience; with editorial comment. Z. Strickland. il por Aviation W 91:11, 18-20 Ag 18 '69
Buzz Aldrin has the best scientific mind we have sent into space. G. Farmer. il pors Life 67:22-5 Jl 4 '69
Crew: men apart. il por Time 94:27-30 Jl 18 '69
Homage to the men from the moon. il pors Time 94:8-11 Ag 22 '69
Men for the moon. il por Newsweek 74:72-3 Jl 21 '69
They were there. il Newsweek 74:73 Ag 25 '69
Two for the moon. il por Sci Digest 65:32-3 Ap '69
We love you. il pors Newsweek 74:20B-23 Ag 25 '69
See also
Space flight to the moon—Manned flights—Armstrong-Aldrin-Collins flight. 1969

ALDRIN
Insect metabolism of photoaldrin and photodieldrin. M. A. Q. Khan and others. bibliog il Science 164:318-19 Ap 18 '69

ALEMAGNA group. See Italy—Industries

ALENIKOFF, Frances
Dance & media; Cubiculo theatre. J. Dowlin. Dance Mag 43:32 Mr '69

ALEUTIAN abyssal plain. See Ocean bottom

ALEUTIAN Canada geese. See Geese, Wild

ALEUTIAN ISLANDS
See also
Amchitka Island

ALEXANDER the Great, king of Macedonia
Alexander's ascent to greatness on a ladder of gore. L. Casson. Sat R 52:61-2 N 29 '69

ALEXANDER, Abner
Dignity in the court. E. K. Shanahan. New Repub 160:12 F 1 '69

ALEXANDER, Archibald S.
Cost of world armaments; with biographical sketch. Sci Am 221:14, 21-7 bibliog(p 148) O '69

ALEXANDER, G. D.
Buck ranger. Nat Parks 43:21-3 O '69

ALEXANDER, James, jr
Urban esthetics can be functional. Am City 84:79-81 D '69

ALEXANDER, Lincoln
Canada's black member of Parliament. il pors Ebony 24:132-4+ Ap '69

ALEXANDER, Lloyd
Newbery award acceptance; address, June 24, 1969. Horn Bk 45:378-81 Ag '69
Where the novel went. Sat R 52:62 Mr 22 '69

about

Lloyd Alexander: Newbery winner. A. Durell. il Library J 94:2066-8 My 15 '69
Newbery-Caldecott secret, not a secret any more. il por Pub W 195:129-30 F 17 '69
Who's Lloyd Alexander? A. Durell. il por Horn Bk 45:332-4 Ag '69

ALEXANDER, Melanie
On the boards. W. Como. por Dance Mag 43:20 O '69

ALEXANDER, Shana
Feminine eye. por McCalls 97:7 D '69; 8 Ja '70

about

Feminine eye. por Time 93:78 Ap 25 '69
Lady at the top. por Newsweek 73:88 Ap 28 '69

ALEXANDER, Sidney
Is I Tatti the keeper of the flame? Holiday 46:36-7+ S '69

ALEXANDER, Theron
Child and society; excerpt from Children and adolescents. Sch & Soc 97:241-7 Ap '69

ALEXANDER, Tom
Computers can't solve everything. Fortune 80:126-9+ O '69
Science rediscovers gravity. Fortune 80:100-4+ D '69

Secret of the spreading ocean floors. Fortune 79:112-17+ F '69
Unexpected payoff of Project Apollo. Fortune 80:114-17+ Jl '69

ALEXANDER, William
(tr) See Sanesi, R. Nothing new at Kindu

ALEXANDRIA, Egypt
Justine; behind the novels and the motion picture. L. Durrell. il Holiday 45:74-7 Ap '69

ALEXANDRIA, Va.
Stores
Capital headliner; F. Welch's boutique. il Newsweek 73:104+ My 19 '69

ALEXIS, Brother
Revolution by Brother Alexis. W. A. McWhirter. il pors Life 66:67-8+ Ja 31 '69

ALFALFA
How to make alfalfa your big-money crop. D. Hagen. il Farm J 93:52C-52D Ap '69

ALFONTE, James M.
New crop for Winston-Salem. Opera N 33:6-7 F 1 '69

ALFRED P. Sloan school of management. See Massachusetts institute of technology, Cambridge—Alfred P. Sloan school of management

ALFREY, Elsie V.
Destroy tent caterpillars before they hatch. Org Gard & Farm 16:74-5 Ja '69
Is moon-planting a lot of green cheese? Org Gard & Farm 16:70-3 My '69

ALFRINK, Bernardus Johannes, cardinal
Alfrink of Utrecht, legate from Utopia. F. Franck. Commonweal 90:460-1 Jl 25 '69

ALFVÉN, Hannes, and Arrhenius, G.
Two alternatives for the history of the moon. bibliog Science 165:11-17 Jl 4 '69
—and Elvius, Aina
Antimatter, quasi-stellar objects, and the evolution of galaxies. bibliog Science 164:911-17 My 23 '69

ALGAE
Algae live without light. E. J. F. Wood. il Sea Front 15:278-83 S '69
Cellulosic wall component produced by the Golgi apparatus of pleurochrysis scherffelii. R. M. Brown and others. bibliog il Science 166:894-6 N 14 '69
Cytophaga that kills or lyses algae. J. R. Stewart and R. M. Brown, jr. bibliog il Science 164:1523-4 Je 27 '69
French have word for it; *maladie verte.* il Sci Digest 66:47-8 D '69
Gas vacuole development in a blue-green alga. J. R. Waaland and D. Branton. bibliog il Science 163:1339-41 Mr 21 '69
Green plants that live without cellulose. R. D. Preston. il Chem 42:24-6 Ja '69
Hydrocarbons of blue-green algae: geochemical significance. K. Winters and others. bibliog il Science 163:467-8 Ja 31 '69
Nitrogen fixation by gloeocapsa. J. T. Wyatt and J. K. G. Silvey. bibliog il Science 165:908-9 Ag 29 '69
Saving the cave paintings; Lascaux cave being treated for *maladie verte.* il Time 94:74 S 19 '69
See also
Diatoms
Euglena

ALGAE, Effect of light on
Cytochrome a₃ destruction by light. B. Epel and W. L. Butler. bibliog il Science 166:621-2 O 31 '69

ALGAE, Fossil
Algal stromatolites: deepwater forms in the Devonian of Western Australia. P. E. Playford and A. E. Cockbain. bibliog il Science 165:1008-10 S 5 '69
Arrival of nitosis; oldest eucaryotic cells known. Sci Am 221:49-50 Ag '69
Precambrian columnar stromatolites in Australia: morphological and stratigraphic analysis. M. F. Glaessner and others. bibliog il Science 164:1056-8 My 30 '69

ALGAE as food
Algae, three times as nourishing as steak. il UNESCO Courier 22:11 Mr '69

ALGARVE, Portugal
Beating the crowds to the Algarve. A. Chamberlin. Vogue 153:70+ F 1 '69

ALGEBRA, Boolean
Boolean algebra. Venn diagrams and the propositional calculus. M. Gardner. il Sci Am 220:110-13 F '69

ALGEO, John
Linguistics: where do we go from here? Engl J 58:102-12 Ja '69

ALGERIA
See also
Investments, Foreign (in Algeria)

ALGERIA—*Continued*

Defenses

North African arms race. A. Smith. Atlan 223:20+ F '69

Foreign relations

Would-be leader of Arab militants. R. W. Howe. New Repub 160:11-12 F 15 '69

ALGERIAN revolutionists. See Revolutionists, Algerian

ALGONQUIN hotel. See New York (city)—Hotels, restaurants, etc.

ALGREN, Nelson
Decline & fall of Dingdong-Daddyland; story. Commentary 48:69-76 S '69

ALI, Muhammad. See Clay, C.

ALI, Tariq
Young and angry talent. M. C. Shefftz. Nation 208:720-4 Je 9 '69

ALIBIS. See Excuses

ALICE Tully Hall. See Lincoln Center for the performing arts, New York—Juilliard school

ALIENATION (social psychology)
Divorce and alienation in modern society; address, October 20, 1966. N. W. Ackerman. bibliog Ment Hy 53:118-26 Ja '69
New reformation. P. Goodman. il N Y Times Mag p32-3+ S 14 '69; Discussion. p 16+ O 19; Same abr. with title Living through a new reformation. Cur 112:4-9 N '69
Sound of a different drummer. Trans-Action 6:8+ O '69

ALIENATION, Social. See Alienation (social psychology)

ALIENS, Deportation of. See Deportation

ALIMONY
Alimony. M. Ploscowe. bibliog f Ann Am Acad 383:13-22 My '69

ALINSKY, Saul David
John L: something of a man. Nation 208:827-8 Je 30 '69

about

Agitator zeroes in on the suburbanites. il pors Bsns W p44-6 F 8 '69

ALIOTO, Joseph Lawrence
California weather breeder. M. Harris. il Nation 208:110-13 Ja 27 '69
Mayor v. the magazine. il por Time 94:49 S 19 '69
Say it ain't so, Joe. Newsweek 74:29 S 15 '69
Two strikes on Alioto. Time 95:20 Ja 5 '70
Web that links San Francisco's Mayor Alioto and the Mafia. R. Carlson and L. Brisson. il pors Look 33:17-21 S 23 '69

ALISON, Jean, pseud.
Afterflash! ed. by V. Whitman. Read Digest 95:81-5 D '69

ALITALIA (airline) See Airlines—Italy

ALKALI bees. See Bees

ALKALINE phosphatase. See Phosphatases

ALKALOIDS
Induction in vitro of microtubular crystals by vinca alkaloids. K. G. Bensch and others. bibliog il Science 165:495-6 Ag 1 '69
See also
Berberine
Colchicine
Vinblastine

ALKANES. See Hydrocarbons

ALKYL trimethylammonium chlorides. See Ammonium chlorides

ALL-America cities
All-America cities for 1968. Am City 84:28 My '69
1968 All America cities. A. Wolff. il Look 33:96-100 Ap 15 '69

ALL-America football team. See Football players

ALL America selections. See Plants—All America selections

ALL fools day. See April fools day

ALL-terrain vehicle. See Motor vehicles, Amphibious

ALL the days of love and courage; story. See Buck, P. S.

ALL-weather carrier landing system. See Airplanes, Military—Landing on carriers

ALL year schools. See School year

ALLAN, Donald
Central park's fountain café. Travel & Camera 32:52 S '69

ALLAN, Skip
Douzes francaises. Yachting 125:88-9+ Ja '69
Match race infighting. Yachting 125:49+ F '69

ALLANTOINASE. See Enzymes

ALLARD, Gilles O. and Hurst, V. J.
Brazil-Gabon geologic link supports continental drift. bibliog il Science 163:528-32 F 7 '69

ALLBROOK, Robert C.
Europe's lush market for advice, American preferred. Fortune 80:128-31+ Jl '69

ALLEGHENY commuter service
Where others get in pilot's seat. il Bsns W p90+ Mr 1 '69

ALLEGHANY corporation
What next? acquisition of Jones motor co. Forbes 103:218 My 15 '69

ALLEGHENY reservoir project. See Dams

ALLEGORY (art) See Symbolism in art

ALLEGRA'S child; story. See Letton, J.

ALLEGRO, John Marco
Reporter at large; Dead Sea scrolls scholar. E. Wilson. New Yorker 45:45-6+ Mr 29 '69

ALLELOMORPHISM
Complementation analysis on virus-fused Chinese hamster cells with nutritional markers. F. T. Kao and others. bibliog il Science 164:312-14 Ap 18 '69
Gene dosage at the lactate dehydrogenase b locus in triploid and diploid teiid lizards. W. B. Neaves and P. S. Gerald. bibliog il Science 164:557-9 My 2 '69

ALLEN, Arthur T. and Seaberg, D. I.
Teaching literature to children. Ed Digest 34:39-41 Mr '69

ALLEN, Asa Alonso
Brother A. A. Allen on the gospel trail: he feels, he heals, & he turns you on with God. W. Hedgepeth. il pors Look 33:23-31 O 7 '69
Getting back double from God. il por Time 93:64+ Mr 7 '69

ALLEN, Betty
Lively arts; interview. ed. by R. Hemming. pors Sr Schol 94:21-2 My 2 '69

about

Recordings. M. Mayer. Esquire 72:32+ N '69

ALLEN, Brandt
Time sharing takes off. Harvard Bsns R 47:128-36 Mr '69

ALLEN, Carole H.
Hatfield hams and the CB McCoys. Pop Electr 30:73-5+ F '69

ALLEN, D. A. and Ney, E. P.
Lunar thermal anomalies: infrared observations. bibliog Science 164:419-21 Ap 25 '69

ALLEN, Denzil R.
Incident at Van Duong; excerpts from 5 by 7. J. Shepherd. il Look 33:26-8+ Ag 12 '69

ALLEN, Durward L.
Too many strangers. Nat Parks 43:12-17 Ag '69

ALLEN, Dwight W.
Curriculum for the 80's; address, 1968. Sr Schol 93:Schol Teach 13+ Ja 10 '69
—and Wagschal, Peter
New look in credentialing. Clear House 44:137-40 N '69

ALLEN, Elizabeth
Pink pagoda; story. Seventeen 28:124-5+ O '69
Wrong road; story. Seventeen 28:142-3 F '69

ALLEN, George and Unwin, limited
Allen and Unwin: what happens now? H. R. Lottman. il Pub W 195:20-2 My 5 '69

ALLEN, George M.
Excerpt from testimony before House committee on ways and means, February 21, 1969. Cong Digest 48:159 My '69

ALLEN, Howard W. See Clubb, J. M. jt. auth.

ALLEN, Ivan, 1911-
Allen of Atlanta; interview. ed. by F. Powledge. por(p69) Harper 239:79-83 N '69

ALLEN, James Edward, 1911-
Crisis in city schools; interview. por U S News 66:30-4 Je 30 '69
Education and the renaissance of state government; adaptation of address, January 9, 1968. Sch & Soc 97:148-51 Mr '69
National commitment to early childhood education. por Parents Mag 44:34 O '69
Right to read; address, October 3, 1969. Vital Speeches 36:42-4 N 1 '69
Right to read: target for the 1970's PTA Mag 64:6-8 D '69
Special dimension to our responsibility. por Todays Ed 58:73 S '69
Target for the 70's: the right to read; excerpts from testimony, October 1969. por Am Ed 5:2-4 D '69
Two warnings to state and local school officials. por U S News 67:65 S 22 '69

ALLEN, James Edward—*Continued*

about

Allen gets top U.S. education post. Library J 94:1271-2 Mr 15 '69

Committed to integration. por Sr Schol 94: Schol Teach 4 F 28 '69

Cool man in a hot seat. R. H. De Lone. il por Sat R 52:67-9+ S 20 '69

Education: Nixon nominates a schoolman as commissioner. J. Walsh. por Science 163: 912-15 F 28 '69

Exercise of authority. por Time 93:59 F 14 '69

Key job for a backer of integration. por U S News 66:17 F 17 '69

Meet James E. Allen, jr. il por Todays Ed 58:41 Ap '69

Right and ability to read. C. B. Grannis. Pub W 196:40 O 13 '69

Second time around. por Newsweek 73:71 F 17 '69

U.S. education chief sees moon shot for education. S. Wagner. Pub W 196:24-5 Ag 11 '69

ALLEN, Jay
Forty carats; adaptation. See Barillet, P. and Grédy, J. P.

ALLEN, John M. See Visentin, L. P. jt. auth.

ALLEN, Larry
How car stereos work. Radio-Electr 40:61-3+ Jl '69

How to use triggered scopes. Radio-Electr 40: 33-7 Ag '69

ALLEN, Linda
(ed) The look you like; questions and answers. See issues of Today's health

ALLEN, Louis L.
Making capitalism work in the ghettos. Harvard Bsns R 47:83-92 My '69

ALLEN, Paul M.
Student evaluation dilemma. Todays Ed 58: 48-50 F '69

ALLEN, Richie
Let's everybody boo Rich Allen! D. Wolf. il pors Life 67:50-2+ Ag 22 '69

Who's on first? Second? Third? M. Mulvoy. por Sports Illus 31:48-9 Jl 14 '69

ALLEN, Robert V.
(comp) Articles and other books received; Soviet Union. See issues of American historical review

ALLEN, Sallie D.
Native American heathers. il Horticulture 47: 24-5 F '69

ALLEN, Steve
Happy Jack fish hatchery papers; letters. Esquire 73:73-7+ Ja '69

ALLEN, Woody
Conversation with Woody Allen; ed. by A. Bester. por Holiday 45:70-1+ My '69

How Bogart made me the superb lover I am today. pors Life 66:64-7 Mr 21 '69

Metterling lists. New Yorker 45:34-5 My 10 '69

My philosophy. New Yorker 45:25-6 D 27 '69

Walking with Woody Allen; ed. by L. Tornabene. pors McCalls 96:44+ Je '69

about

Play it again, Sam. Criticism
America 120:434 Ap 5 '69
Commonweal 90:438 Jl 11 '69
Nation 208:282-3 Mr 3 '69
New Yorker 45:89 F 22 '69
Sat R 52:45 Mr 1 '69
Time il por 93:42 F 21 '69
Vogue 153:150 Ap 1 '69

ALLEN-Bradley company
Demonstrating again at Allen-Bradley. il Bsns W p44 Ag 16 '69

ALLEN university, Columbia, S.C.
Build up rather than tear down. il U S News 66:36-7 My 26 '69

ALLENDALE school. See Private schools

ALLENDE meteorite. See Meteorites

ALLENDOERFER, Carl B.
Dilemma in geometry. Ed Digest 34:40-3 My '69

ALLER, Lawrence H.
Planetary nebulae. Sky & Tel 37:282-6, 348-52; 38:12-18, 82-5, 152-5, 227-9, 306-9, 377-9; 39:15-18 My '69-Ja '70 (to be cont)

ALLERGENS
Allergenic component of a liverwort: a sesquiterpene lactone. H. Knoche and others. bibliog il Science 166:239-40 O 10 '69

Wheeze machine tracks down allergies. R. Gannon. il Pop Sci 194:82-3+ My '69

ALLERGIC encephalomyelitis. See Encephalomyelitis

ALLERGY
Christmas tree allergy? il Sci Digest 66:55-6 D '69

Leukotactic factor produced by sensitized lymphocytes. P. A. Ward and others. bibliog il Science 163:1079-81 Mr 7 '69

Medical sciences. Sci N 95:427 My 3 '69

Stinging insects, armed and dangerous. R. Wolkomir. il Todays Health 47:48-9+ Je '69

When the next bug bites, it may not be love. A. Lake. il Seventeen 28:174-5+ Ap '69

Your allergies: what doctors know and may do right now. A. Talmey. Vogue 154:122-3 Ag 15 '69

See also
Food allergy

ALLEY theater, Houston. See Houston, Tex.—Theater

ALLIANCE for labor action
ALA: new voice of labor; conference. B. J. Widick. il Nation 208:758-60 Je 16 '69

ALA picks Atlanta as a starter. il Bsns W p78 S 13 '69

Challenge for AFL-CIO? U S News 66:64 Mr 3 '69

Labor chafes at Nixon pace. Bsns W p34 My 24 '69

Labor dissidents set strategy. U S News 66: 74 Je 2 '69

Meany-Reuther showdown, with unity the likely loser. Bsns W p34-5 Ag 30 '69

Odd couple. il Newsweek 73:87 Je 9 '69

Reuther's grand alliance: meaning to business and labor. il U S News 66:70-1 Je 9 '69

Tough new team gets on the road; teamsters and UAW join forces. il Bsns W p76-7 My 31 '69

UAW-teamsters launch Alliance. America 120: 680 Je 14 '69

ALLIANCE for progress
Alliance anniversary appraisal. Américas 21: 42-3 Ag '69

Alliance for or against progress? J. B. Sheerin. Cath World 208:242-3 Mr '69

Alliance for progress and the O.A.S. H. J. Sievers. America 120:723 Je 28 '69

Building from the ground up; excerpts from interview, ed. by E. Peer. S. M. Linowitz. Newsweek 73:54 Ap 14 '69

Lack of progress? summary of address, April 1969. R. M. Nixon. Sr Schol 94:20 My 2 '69

Latin America puts itself on trial; Inter-American committee on the Alliance for progress. il Bsns W p 146+ Ja 25 '69

Matter of priorities. Commonweal 90:221-2 My 9 '69

Perspectives on Latin America; address, September 9, 1969. W. Morse. Vital Speeches 36:86-90 N 15 '69

View North and South; excerpts from Today show interview. G. Plaza. il Américas 21: 44 Ag '69

Whatever happened to the Alliance for progress? il U S News 67:8 N 3 '69

ALLIANCES
Are our military alliances meaningful? G. S. McGovern. Ann Am Acad 384:14-20 Jl '69

See also
NATO

ALLIED bank international. See New York (city)—Banks

ALLIED chemical corporation
Allied chemical: a long rough road back. il Forbes 103:205-8 My 15 '69

How Allied chemical breaks with its past. il Bsns W p80-2+ Ap 5 '69

ALLIED invasion, June 6, 1944. See World war 1939-1945—Campaigns and battles—Western

ALLIGATORS
Preferred centripetal conduction of dendritic spikes in alligator Purkinje cells. R. Llinás and others. bibliog il Science 163: 184-7 Ja 10 '68

See you later, alligator: poaching in Florida. M. Kane. il Sports Illus 31:38-40+ S 29 '69

Ugly alligator. il Sci Digest 65:34 Je '69

See also
Crocodiles

ALLILUEVA, Svetlana. See Stalina, S. I.

ALLINE, Emile
Build this one-man golf cart. Pop Mech 131: 176-9 Je '69

ALLIS-Chalmers manufacturing company
Battle for Allis-Chalmers; White consolidated seeking control. Bsns W p92 Mr 8 '69

Bit of rouge for Allis-Chalmers. H. B. Meyers. Fortune 79:234+ My 15 '69

Classic defense. il Forbes 104:21-3 Ag 1 '69

From the frying pan into the . . ; home appliance business. il Forbes 104:65-6 N 15 '69

ALLIS-Chalmers manufacturing company—*Cont.*
It's no tea party at Allis. il Bsns W p54+
N 15 '69
Will White unload its stake in Allis? FTC op-
position to merger. Bsns W p31-2 Jl 26 '69
ALLISON, John M.
Creating stability out of revolution. Sat R
52:52 My 10 '69
ALLIUMS
Perennial onions for yields every year. R.
Tirrell. il Org Gard & Farm 16:33-5 D '69
ALLOGRAPH corporation
Allograph holds first stockholders meeting.
Pub W 196:36 Jl 28 '69
ALLON, Yigal
Israeli view; excerpts from remarks, ed. by
M. Levin. por Time 95:22 Ja 5 '70

about

Invitation to a coup. il por Newsweek 74:60+
O 27 '69
Yigal Allon has supporters, Moshe Dayan has
disciples. J. Feron. il pors N Y Times Mag
p30-1+ Ap 27 '69
ALLONBY, Charles
Happiness: organic gardening's bumper crop.
Org Gard & Farm 16:33-5 S '69
You have to improve it. Org Gard & Farm
16:58-9 D '69
ALLOTT, Gordon
Excerpt from address, August 8, 1969. Cong
Digest 48:296+ D '69
ALLOWANCES, Family. See Family allowances
ALLOWAY, Lawrence
Art. See issues of Nation
ALLOYS
Superplastic metals. H. W. Hayden and
others. il Sci Am 220:28-35 bibliog(p 148)
Mr '69
ALLREAD, Joe
Jr. stock science lesson. J. Dianna. il Hot
Rod 22:54-7 S '69
ALLRICH, Theodore C.
Truk. por Travel 132:48-51 D '69
ALLT, W. R. and others
Nicotine hydrogen tartrate: effect on essen-
tial fatty acid deficiency in mature pigs.
bibliog Science 163:391 Ja 24 '69
ALMANACS
See also
World almanac and book of facts
ALMASY, Paul
Three-dimensional history class in Hungary.
il UNESCO Courier 22:31 N '69
ALMEIDA, Alphonse
Duty-free lunch periods. Todays Ed 58:80-1
Mr '69
ALMONDS, Flowering. See Flowering almonds
ALMOST any Friday; story. See Robinson, B.
ALPER, Chester A. and others
Human C'3: evidence for the liver as the
primary site of synthesis. bibliog Science
163:286-8 Ja 17 '69
ALPEROVITZ, Gar
Community economic self-help. Cur 107:27-31
My '69
ALPERS, Antony
News from New Zealand. Opera N 33:26-8
Ap 5 '69
ALPERT, Arthur
TV game. New Repub 161:17-21 O 18 '69
ALPERT, Helen
World scientists analyze aging. Har Yrs 9:33-5
D '69
ALPERT, Herb
Herb Alpert: everybody's music maker; in-
terview. pors Am Home 72:86-7+ O '69
ALPERT, Hollis
Fellini at work. Sat R 52:14-17 Jl 12 '69
SR goes to the movies. See issues of
Saturday review
ALPERT, Richard
Founding fathers of LSD. pors Newsweek 73:
26 Ap 21 '69
ALPHA kappa; drama. See Paradis, M. B.
ALPHA particles. See Alpha rays
ALPHA rays
Alpha-particle emissivity of the moon: an ob-
served upper limit. R. S. Yeh and J. A. Van
Allen. bibliog il Science 166:370-2 O 17 '69
Alpha-recoil tracks in mica; registration ef-
ficiency. S. Katcoff. il Science 166:382-4 O
17 '69
Particle track enhancement in cellulose ni-
trate by application of an electric field. H.
Crannell and others. bibliog il Science 166:
606-7 O 31 '69
ALPHA₁-globulin. See Blood—Proteins
ALPHABET
See also
Lettering
ALPHANUMERIC readout tubes. See Vacuum
tubes

ALPINE climbing. See Mountaineering
ALPINE flora
Alpine summer. B. Ratcliffe. il Audubon 71:
44-51 Jl '69
See also
Plants, Rock garden
ALROY, Gil Carl
Prospect of war in the Middle East. Com-
mentary 47:53-9 Mr '69
ALSBERG, Libby Smith
Herbs in salad. Horticulture 46:33+ Ag '68
ALSEP (Apollo lunar surface experiments
package) See Moon—Exploration—Equip-
ment
ALSOP, Joseph
Profiles; K. Z. Lorenz. New Yorker 45:39-42+
Mr 8 '69
Vietcong is losing its grip. Read Digest 95:
53-61 D '69
ALSOP, Stewart
[Column on public affairs] See issues of
Newsweek
Small thoughts. por Newsweek 74:112 Jl 21
'69
ALSPAUGH, John W.
Utilization of computing and data process-
ing in education. bibliog Clear House 43:
455-7 Ap '69
ALSTON, Walter Emmons
Some kids make a sad man happy. W.
Leggett. il Sports Illus 30:28-30+ My 19 '69
ALT, Herschel
Toward a technology of child care for chil-
dren in residence. bibliog Ment Hy 53:564-
74 O '69
ALTBACH, Philip G.
India's continuing language problem. Sch
& Soc 97:107-18 F '69
ALTER, Robert
Fiction. Sat R 52:33+ N 1 '69
In the community (cont) Commentary 47:55-9
F; 59-66 Je; 48:86-93 S '69
ALTERNATORS. See Electric generators, Al-
ternating current
ALTIMETERS
Altimeter uses constant beat frequency. P. J.
Klass. il Aviation W 90:80-2 Je 9 '69
ALTITUDE, Influence of
Human adaptation to high altitude. P. T.
Baker. bibliog il Science 163:1149-56 Mr 14
'69
ALTOMARE, Alvaro
Build this handsome bookcase desk. Pop Mech
132:164-7 Ag '69
ALTSHULER, Alan
Politics of full employment. Trans-Action
6:43-7 My '69
ALUM, Manuel
Brief biography. S. Goodman. pors Dance Mag
43:66-7 Mr '69
ALUMINIUM limited (of Canada) See Alu-
minum company of Canada
ALUMINUM
Featherweight champion of metals. O. A.
Battista. il Chem 42:14-15 Mr '69

Marketing

How Alcoa sweetens its success; new selling strategy il Bsns W p38-40+ Ja 18 '69

Prices

Aluminum frets over another big glut. il
Bsns W p28-9 N 29 '69
Nonferrous metals join price parade. Bsns W
p21-2 Ag 9 '69
Sparks fly in aluminum war; giants clash
over price boosts. Bsns W p49 My 10 '69
Where the price spiral gets that extra twist.
il Bsns W p 18-19 Ap 5 '69
ALUMINUM, Powdered
Aluminum gets a run in the powder derby.
il Bsns W p 152 My 10 '69
ALUMINUM, Structural
Aluminum columns in glass walls carry both
roof loads and wind loads. il Arch Rec 145:
167 F '69
Insulated aluminum covers sheathe John
Hancock building. il Arch Rec 145:168-70
Mr '69
ALUMINUM boats. See Boats—Materials
ALUMINUM cans
See also
Beverage containers

Manufacture

See Cans—Manufacture
ALUMINUM company of America
Aluminum gets a run in the powder derby.
il Bsns W p 152 My 10 '69
How Alcoa sweetens its success; new sell-
ing strategy. il Bsns W p38-40+ Ja 18 '69
ALUMINUM company of Canada
Defensive standoff. Forbes 103:59 F 15 '69
ALUMINUM containers. See Containers
ALUMINUM fences. See Fences

ALUMINUM foil
Aluminum foil figures. M. J. Acosta. il
Design 70:23 Sum '69
ALUMINUM foil mulch. See Mulching
ALUMINUM foil sculpture. See Metal sculpture
ALUMINUM industry and trade
See also
Kaiser aluminum and chemical corporation

Norway
Harvey's battle in the fjords. B. Caplan. il
Duns R 94:91+ S '69

United States
Aluminum frets over another big glut. il
Bsns W p28-9 N 29 '69
Sparks fly in aluminum war; giants clash
over price boosts. Bsns W p49 My 10 '69
See also
Harvey aluminum, incorporated
Reynolds metals company
ALUMINUM plants
House plant you should know. P. F. Frese.
il Hom Gard 56:62 Je '69
ALUMINUM scrap. See Scrap metal
ALUMINUM sculpture. See Metal sculpture
ALUMNI. See College graduates
ALUMNI funds. See Colleges and universities—
Gifts, legacies, etc.
ALVARADO, Juan Velasco. See Velasco
Alvarado, J.
ALVAREZ, A.
Operation: poem. Mlle 68:116 F '69
ALVAREZ, Luis Echeverria. See Echeverria
Alvarez, L.
ALVAREZ, Luis W.
Recent developments in particle physics;
Nobel lecture, January 1969. bibliog por Sci-
ence 165:1071-91 S 12 '69
ALVAREZ, Walter Clement
Medicine's Mark Twain. F. G. Loyd. il pors
Todays Health 47:52-5 My '69
ALVES, Márcio Moreira
Coup that never was. Commonweal 91:277-
8 N 28 '69
Wrong man, wrong time, wrong mission.
Commonweal 90:407-9 Je 27 '69
ALVES, Rubem
Rubem Alves: hopeful radical. H. Cox. por
Chr Cent 86:1417-19 N 5 '69
ALVEZ DE SOUZA, Wladimir
Past splendor of Pelourinho. Américas 21:2-8
S '69
ALVIN Ailey American dance theater
Alvin Ailey American dance theater; Billy
Rose theatre. M. Marks. Dance Mag 43:92
Mr '69
Alvin Ailey American dance theater, Brooklyn
academy of music. T. Borek. Dance Mag
43:35 Je '69
Ballet in black. H. Saal. il Newsweek 73:76
F 10 '69
Festival in Brooklyn. W. Terry. il Sat R 52:
49 D 13 '69
Musical events; program at the Brooklyn
academy of music. W. Sargeant. New
Yorker 45:200 D 6 '69
ALWIN Nikolais dance company. See Dance
companies
ALWOOD, Richard C. See Eidt, M. B. jt. auth.
ALWORTH, Lance
Lance Alworth: Charger goes groovy. G.
Astor. il pors Look 33:91-2+ D 2 '69
ALZEN, Ria
Bei Ria. il por Time 93:38 My 23 '69
AMACHER, Peter, and others
Preventing obsolescence of scientific reviews:
an updated-review project. Science 165:1029-
30 S 5 '69
AMADON, Dean
Gotham's birds; with biographical sketch. por
Natur Hist 78:6, 48-55 Ap '69
AMAGANSETT, N.Y.
Annals of agriculture. M. Hunt. New Yorker
45:57-8+ N 1 '69
AMAKER, Norman C.
1950's: racial equality and the law. bibliog f
Cur Hist 57:275-80+ N '69
AMALGAMATED clothing workers of America
Case to watch; ACWA vs. four Chicago news-
papers. Nation 209:332-3 O 6 '69
AMALGAMATED meat cutters and butcher
workmen of North America
Fighting over the cost of cutting meat.
Bsns W p74+ N 22 '69
AMALRIC, Andrei
Apocalyptic view of Russia's future. il por
Time 94:31 D 19 '69
Letter to Anatoly Kuznetsov. Time 94:49
D 5 '69

AMANITAS. See Mushrooms
AMANN, R. See Davies, R. W. jt. auth.
AMANTADINE hydrochloride
Amantadine for Parkinsonism. Sci N 95:550
Je 7 '69
Amantadine vs. Hong Kong flu. Sci N 95:613-
14 Je 28 '69
Drugs v. vaccines. il Time 93:57 Je 27 '69
AMARILLO, Tex.
Rapid transit
Extracars update a city transit system. E. B.
Fair. il Am City 84:136 Ap '69
AMARYLLIS
It's easy to grow an amaryllis. A. R. Giordan.
il Org Gard & Farm 16:84-5 N '69
AMATEUR art. See Art, Amateur
AMATEUR astronomers. See Astronomers, Ama-
teur
AMATEUR athletic union of the United States
PTA meeting is tougher; D. Brown, Na-
tional AAU women's cross-country cham-
pionship winner. S. Myslenski. il Sports
Illus 31:69-70 D 8 '69
Some dashing dolls debut in Daytona;
women's national AAU championship. A.
Verschoth. il Sports Illus 31:20-3 Jl 14 '69
AMATEUR builders. See Building—Study and
teaching
AMATEUR golf. See Golf
AMATEUR photographers. See Photographers
AMATEUR radio operators. See Radio operators,
Amateur
AMATEUR tennis. See Tennis
AMATEUR theatricals
How to arrange for an amateur play produc-
tion. McCalls 96:58 Ap '69
AMATEURISM (sports)
No goody two-shoes; Olympic athletes paid
by German firms of Adidas and Puma to
wear their track shoes. J. Underwood. il
Sports Illus 30:14-23 Mr 10 '69
Sport: a philosophic inquiry, by P. Weiss.
Review
Nat R 21:1071 O 21 '69. J. C. Smith
AMAYA, Mario
Flesh and filigree. Art N 68:24-7+ D '69
AMAZON dolphins. See Dolphins (mammals)
AMAZON jungle. See Rain forests
AMAZON RIVER
Funny thing happened on the way to the
jungle. S. Turner. il Sr Schol 94:Schol Teach
18-19 Ap 11 '69
Getting the Amazon right. V. S. Pritchett. il
Holiday 46:42-5 Ag '69
Steamer down the Amazon. il Bet Hom &
Gard 47:117-18 F '69
AMAZON VALLEY
See also
Birds—Amazon Valley
AMAZONAS, Brazil
Taming the jungle for profit. il Bsns W
p 162-3 S 13 '69
AMAZONIA. See Amazonas, Brazil
AMBASSADORS
American uniques in France; the Shrivers;
with photographs by H. Clarke. il Vogue
153:160-7 My '69
AMBER
Amber: a botanical inquiry. J. H. Langen-
heim. bibliog il Science 163:1157-69 Mr 14
'69
AMBERFISH fishing
Monsters of hurricane hole; yellowtails or
amberjacks. G. P. Fones. il Field & S 74:48-
9+ Jl '69
AMBERJACK fishing. See Amberfish fishing
AMBLYOPSIDAE. See Cave fishes
AMBOINESE
Pride and prejudice; Netherlands. il News-
week 74:62 N 17 '69
AMBROSE, Stephen E.
Fateful friendship. Am Heritage 20:40-1+
Ap '69
AMBULANCES
Ambulances inadequate, says study group.
Todays Health 47:72 Je '69
AMBUSHES and surprises
See also
Snipers
AMCHITKA ISLAND
Earthquakes and nuclear tests; playing the
odds on Amchitka. L. J. Carter. il Science
165:773-6 Ag 22 '69
Faultless? il Newsweek 74:100 O 13 '69
AMEBAS
Amoebic meningoencephalitis: a new amoeba
isolate. L Červa and others. bibliog Science
163:575-6 F 7 '69

AMEBAS—*Continued*

Culture media

Amoebic meningoencephalitis: axenic culture of naegleria. L. Cerva. Science 163:576 F 7 '69

AMEBIASIS

Amoebic meningoencephalitis: a new amoeba isolate. L. Cerva and others. bibliog Science 163:575-6 F 7 '69

AMERADA Hess corporation

Leon Hess never plays it safe. A. M. Louis. il Fortune 81:104-7+ Ja '70

AMERADA-Hess merger. See Petroleum industry and trade—Consolidations and mergers

AMERADA petroleum corporation. See Amerada Hess corporation

AMERICA, Richard F. Jr

What do you people want? Harvard Bsns R 47:103-12 Mr '69

AMERICA

Our America. G. de Zéndegui. il Américas 21: 30-5 N '69

See also

United States

Antiquities

See also

Mayas

Discovery and exploration

Pathfinder of the Papagueria. R. L. Ives. il Américas 21:13-20 S; 14-21 O '69

AMERICA (periodical)

Of many things; America's identity and support. D. R. Campion. America 120:inside cover Ap 19 '69

Reflections on a sixtieth birthday; editorial comment. America 120:458-9 Ap 19 '69

60th anniversary; America associates. il America 120:506-7 Ap 26 '69

AMERICA (yacht)

1851 re-enacted. E. F. Haylock. il Motor B 123:110+ Ap '69

AMERICA in literature

Children's books; the pageant that is America. R. Gagliardo. il PTA Mag 63:32-3 Mr '69

AMERICAN academy in Rome

Academy that overlooks Rome. R. Lynes. Harper 238:28+ My '69

AMERICAN academy of orthopedic surgeons

Orthopedics. Sci N 95:115 F 1 '69

AMERICAN academy of pediatrics

Following up on Head Start; Dr Mendelsohn's resignation. New Repub 160:12-13 Ap 12 '69

AMERICAN academy of theology (proposed)

American academy of theology. Chr Cent 86: 395 Mr 26 '69

AMERICAN accordionists' association

Accordion to taste. il Time 94:61 Ag 22 '69

AMERICAN-AFRO studies. See Afro-American studies

AMERICAN airlines, incorporated

American amasses STOL navaid data. K. J. Stein. il Aviation W 90:81+ My 26 '69

American gives its transports new markings. il Aviation W 90:31 My 26 '69

American plans self-service ticketer test. B. M. Elson. Aviation W 91:81-2+ N 10 '69

American seeks advanced modular loading dock design. W. H. Gregory. il Aviation W 91:26-30 O 6 '69

American's loss in strike set at $2.7 million daily. Aviation W 90:29 Mr 17 '69

Bilateral, pilot talks block start of American service in Pacific. Aviation W 91:33 D 15 '69

Strike cuts American net; Delta counters tide. il Aviation W 90:37 My 5 '69

Who's happy? il Forbes 104:73-4 N 15 '69

AMERICAN alumni council

New alumni council president. Sch & Soc 97: 350 O '69

AMERICAN antelopes. See Pronghorns

AMERICAN anthropological association

In and out of the field. A. Meyer. il Natur Hist 78:6 F '69

AMERICAN antiquarian society, Worcester, Mass.

Portraits owned by the American antiquarian society. L. Dresser. il Antiques 96:717-27 N '69

AMERICAN arbitration association

How companies stay out of the courtroom. S. H. Lieberstein. il Duns R 94:64-6+ S '69

New center for dispute settlement; Center for dispute settlement. S. C. Jackson. Mo Labor R 92:10 Ja '69

AMERICAN art. See Art, American

AMERICAN artichokes. See Jerusalem artichokes

AMERICAN artist (periodical)

Magazine is people. N. Kent. Am Artist 33: 5 Ja '69

AMERICAN assembly

States and the urban crisis. America 121:447 N 15 '69

AMERICAN association for the advancement of science

AAAS meetings: a progress report. W. G. Berl. Science 163:767 F 21 '69

AAAS officers, committees, and representatives for 1969. Science 163:835-8 F 21 '69

Worried scientists. Time 95:29 Ja 12 '70

Meetings, 1968

AAAS council meeting, 1968. D. Wolfle. Science 163:832-4 F 21 '69

Meetings, 1969

AAAS annual meeting; December 26-31, 1969. il Science 166:1035-67 N 21 '69

AAAS Boston meeting: dissenters fined a forum. J. K. Glassman. Science 167:36-8 Je 2 '70

AAAS; report of papers. Sci N 97:10-11 Ja 3 '70

Dissent, dissension at AAAS. il Sci N 97:5-6 Ja 3 '70

Out of the ivory tower. W. G. Berl. Science 166:1553-6 D 19 '69

Perspectives on the promise of the present. W. G. Berl. Science 165:1150-5 S 12 '69

Preliminary program AAAS annual meeting, Boston, Massachusetts, 26-31 December 1969. il Science 165:719-25 Ag 15 '69

Program, AAAS annual meeting, Boston, Massachusetts, December 26-31, 1969. Science 166:261-73 O 10 '69

Science and society; convention in Boston. Nation 210:3-4 Ja 12 '70

Committee on science in the promotion of human welfare

Secrecy and dissemination in science and technology. bibliog Science 163:787-90 F 21 '69

AMERICAN association of evangelical students

Setback for evangelical students. M. Bock. Chr Today 13:44 Je 6 '69

AMERICAN association of junior colleges

See also

National council of independent junior colleges

AMERICAN association of library schools. See Association of American library schools

AMERICAN association of nurserymen

Oldest bank cited for landscaping; Citizens and Southern national bank of South Carolina, Charleston. Home Gard 56:21 N '69

AMERICAN association of physics teachers

AAPT-APS meeting returns to New York. J. P. Wiley, jr. il Phys Today 22:57-9 Ja '69

Dissidents force a vote on 1970 Chicago meeting. Phys Today 22:85+ Ap '69

See also

Commission on college physics

AMERICAN association of school administrators

AASA academy for school executives. S. J. Knezevich. il Am Ed 5:25-6 F '69

Meeting, 1969. W. D. Boutwell and others. Sr Schol 94:Schol Teach 3 Mr 21 '69

News made at the AASA convention. W. D. Boutwell. PTA Mag 63:11-13 Ap '69

AMERICAN association of school librarians

AASL: a search for identity. E. Geller. il Library J 94:3139-42 S 15 '69

AASL invites comments on school library bill of rights. Library J 94:1288 Mr 15 '69

AASL program at ALA annual conference. ALA Bul 63:1139-42 S '69

Crossroads 1970; address, June 1969. J. Rowell. il Library J 94:4575-7 D 15 '69

Outstanding innovation: joint AASL-DAVI standards for school media programs. L. O. Vinson. il ALA Bul 63:235-7 F '69

Raps and routines. L. Mesiano. il Library J 94:3147-8 S 15 '69

Strategies and ploys: reactions to AASL-DAVI standards for school media programs. W. Meierhenry. bibliog il Library J 94: 1728-30 Ap 15 '69

Summer scoop; highlights of the meetings of the three youth divisions. E. Geller and L. Mesiano. Library J 94:2755 Ag '69

AMERICAN association of university presses. See Association of American university presses

AMERICAN association of university professors

Academic freedom and tenure, by L. Joughlin. Review

Bul Atom Sci 25:46-7 Ap '69. T. Dinell

AMERICAN association of variable star observers

Scientific highlights from the AAVSO spring meeting. M. E. Baldwin. il Sky & Tel 38:89 Ag '69

AMERICAN association of women ministers
  Reverend ladies: collars and curls. J. Rohler.
    Chr Today 13:34 Ag 22 '69
  Women ministers celebrate jubilee. M. P.
    Harrington. Chr Cent 86:1295-6 O 8 '69
AMERICAN astronomical society
  American astronomers report; highlights of
    some papers. See issues of Sky and tele-
    scope
  Astronomy. Sci N 95:382 Ap 19 '69
AMERICAN authors. See Authors, American
AMERICAN bakeries company
  Name of the game. Forbes 104:23 D 1 '69
AMERICAN ballads. See Ballads, American
AMERICAN ballet company
  American ballet company? D. Hering. il Dance
    Mag 43:34-6+ D '69
  Brooklyn bow. W. Terry. Sat R 52:40 N 8 '69
  Dance grows in Brooklyn. H. Saal. il
    Newsweek 74:91 N 3 '69
  New company is born. W. Terry. il Sat R
    52:62-3 N 15 '69
  Two for the season. il Time 94:71-2 N 7 '69
AMERICAN ballet theatre
  ABT at BAM. D. Hering; M. Marks; J. An-
    derson. il Dance Mag 43:30-2+ F '69
  Brooklyn, maybe? W. Terry. Sat R 52:46 D
    27 '69
  Giselle on film, with Fracci and Bruhn. M.
    Harriton. il Dance Mag 43:24-7 D '69
  Musical events; program at the Brooklyn
    academy of music. W. Sargeant. New York-
    er 45:108 D 20 '69
  World of dance; ballet in Brooklyn. W. Terry.
    il Sat R 53:77 Ja 3 '70
AMERICAN bankers association
  Crawling toward new flexibility; creating spe-
    cial drawing rights (SDRs) in IMF. Bsns
    W p38-9 Je 21 '69
    See also
  Committee on uniform security identification
    procedures
AMERICAN Baptist convention. See Baptists
  in the United States
AMERICAN bar association
  Conglomerates speak out; ABA symposium.
    il Bsns W p94+ N 1 '69
  Consumer's impotent friend in Washington.
    Time 94:83 S 26 '69
  Highly visible Chief; W. Burger at conven-
    tion. Time 94:58 Ag 22 '69
  Investigating the FTC. New Repub 160:7-8
    My 3 '69
  Jury of his club mates; Haynsworth and
    the bar. P. Owens. Nation 209:462-4 N
    3 '69
  Regulation, Nixon style. il Newsweek 74:85-6
    S 29 '69
AMERICAN basketball association
  ABA competition will be stimulating but the
    quality is second best. F. Deford. il Sports
    Illus 31:34-5 O 27 '69
  Bleak house; reaction to L. Alcindor depar-
    ture. Newsweek 73:98 Ap 14 '69
  Tossing bombs into the hoops; ABA vs NBA.
    G. Ronberg. il Sports Illus 31:30-2+ S 22
    '69
AMERICAN battle flags. See Flags—United
  States
AMERICAN beef packers, incorporated
  Youngest giant. Fortune 79:293 My 15 '69
AMERICAN bishops' conference. See National
  conference of Catholic bishops
AMERICAN book publishers council
  ABPC annual meeting: federal funds, man-
    power and markets are reviewed; highlights
    of panel discussions. il Pub W 195:25-30 Je
    9 '69
  ABPC 1968 sales survey: industry-wide total
    over $2½-billion; with tables. Pub W
    196:25-7 D 8 '69
  ABPC seminar: minority manpower in pub-
    lishing. Pub W 195:34-6 F 3 '69
  ABPC votes clearinghouse for minority man-
    power. Pub W 195:37-8 My 19 '69
  Govt. vs. publisher; report of seminar spon-
    sored by the Technical, scientific and medi-
    cal book publishers group. Pub W 196:20-3
    D 1 '69
  1968 in review. Pub W 195:41-2 Mr 10 '69
      Religious publishers group
  Booksellers view the changing market for re-
    ligious books; report of meeting. Pub W 196:
    35-6 D 29 '69
  RPG annual meeting: revolution in churches:
    effect on publishing; summary of panel dis-
    cussions. Pub W 195:50-1 Je 16 '69
  RPG forum: religious publishers and media
    review each other; summary of addresses.
    Pub W 195:69-71 Ja 27 '69
  Trouble in book city; with editorial comment.
    R. L. Love. Chr Today 13:23, 47 Je 6 '69

AMERICAN booksellers association
  ABA convention; training, inventory and the
    publishers are top topics. il Pub W 195:26-
    33 Je 23 '69
  Children's books discussed at the ABA con-
    vention; highlights of panel discussion. il
    Pub W 195:43-5 Je 16 '69
  Is it all fair at ABA regionals? il Pub W 196:
    34-6 O 13 '69
  1968 in review. Pub W 195:42-4 Mr 10 '69
  Plea for books and reason opens ABA conven-
    tion. Pub W 195:42 Je 9 '69
  Topics of ABA busines: growth, manpower,
    censorship. il Pub W 195:46-9 Je 16 '69
  Trade winds; authors at convention. J. Beatty,
    jr. Sat R 52:12+ Ja 21 '69
AMERICAN bowling congress. See Bowling
AMERICAN broadcasting companies
  That long, lively pursuit of A.B.C. C. J.
    Loomis. il Fortune 79:130-4+ Mr '69
AMERICAN businessmen. See Businessmen
AMERICAN businessmen, Hall of fame for.
  See Michigan. University, Ann Arbor—Busi-
  ness hall of fame (proposed)
AMERICAN camping association
  Accounting to ACA members. E. F. Schmidt.
    Camp Mag 41:5 My '69
  New look for the standards program; ACA
    National standards committee. J. J. Kirk.
    Camp Mag 41:6 Mr '69
  New National ACA officers elected. il Camp
    Mag 41:9 Mr '69
  News of the month. See issues of Camping
    magazine
AMERICAN can company
  Separate ways. Forbes 104:68 N 15 '69
AMERICAN Catholic philosophical association
  Catholic philosopher. R. J. Gerber. Common-
    weal 90:105-6+ Ap 11 '69
AMERICAN Catholicism. See Catholic church
  in the United States
AMERICAN Catholics. See Catholics in the
  United States
AMERICAN cement corporation
  War is over at American cement. il Bsns W
    p29 Ag 2 '69
AMERICAN chemical society
  Environment: ACS report is practical anti-
    pollution guide. P. M. Boffey. Science 165:
    1104-7 S 12 '69
AMERICAN children. See Children—United
  States
AMERICAN Chinese. See Chinese Americans
AMERICAN city (periodical)
  As we start our 60th year. Am City 84:8
    Ja '69
  Congressmen, editorial writers praise winning
    cities; American city magazine merit-
    award. il Am City 84:109+ My '69
  Microfilm sales of American city magazine
    jumps. il Am City 84:30 My '69
  1968 merit award winners. il Am City 84:
    71-4 Ja '69
  Notre Dame student wins the American city
    Aid-to-education award. Am City 84:116 N
    '69
  Our 60th anniversary issue. Am City 84:8
    O '69
AMERICAN civil liberties union
  Breaking ranks and breaking dissenters. S. V.
    Roberts. Commonweal 91:397-8 Ja 9 '70
  Happy Jack fish hatchery papers; letters. S.
    Allen and D. Trumbo. Esquire 73:73-7+ Ja
    '70
  Profiles: C. Morgan, jr. F. Powledge. New
    Yorker 45:63-4 O 25 '69
AMERICAN clock and watch museum. See Bris-
  tol, Conn.—Galleries and museums
AMERICAN college testing program
  Lowdown on those college entrance tests;
    CEEB and ACT. il Changing T 23:37-40
    S '69
AMERICAN college theatre festival. See Drama
  festivals
AMERICAN Communist party. See Communist
  party (United States)
AMERICAN conservatism. See Conservatism
AMERICAN conservatory theater
  ACT in New York; San Francisco's American
    conservatory theatre. J. Kroll. il News-
    week 74:125 O 13 '69
  Blood and honeysuckle; production of Glory!
    Hallelujah! J. Kroll. il Newsweek 73:123
    Je 9 '69
  Re: ACT. H. Hewes. Sat R 52:20 Jl 5 '69
  Theater paprika; production of E. Albee's
    Tiny Alice. H. Hewes. Sat R 52:20 O 18
    '69
  Theatre; productions in New York. H. Clur-
    man. Nation 209:451-2 O 27 '69

AMERICAN conservatory theater—*Continued*
Theater; productions in New York. S. Kauff-
mann. New Repub 161:22+ N 1 '69
Theatre; William Ball's production of Chek-
hov's The three sisters. H. Clurman. Nation
209:486 N 3 '69
AMERICAN cookery. See Cookery, American
AMERICAN council of Christian churches
ACCC: no longer doing its founder's will.
D. Tinder. Chr Today 14:41 N 21 '69
ACCC on the move. Chr Today 13:34 My 23
'69
Counter-counter ecumaniac; removal of C.
McIntire from executive committee. Chr
Cent 86:1475 N 19 '69
Doctor McIntire's magic touch. il Time 94:
81 N 14 '69
AMERICAN council on education
ACE study on campus unrest: questions for
behavioral scientists; with statement by ad-
visory committee. J. Walsh; J. Coburn.
Science 165:157-61 Jl 11 '69; Discussion.
165:1206-7; 166:945 S 19, N 21 '69
Dealing with disruption; special committee on
campus disruption. Sch & Soc 97:341 O '69
Declaration on campus unrest; excerpt from
statement. Cur 108:8-11 Je '69
Indignation and a wrist slap. Sci N 95:425-6
My 3 '69
AMERICAN crafts council
Focus on Albuquerque; ACC's sixth national
conference. A. R. Meisel. il Craft Horiz 29:
46-9 S '69
AMERICAN craftsmen's council
Quarter century of arts & crafts. D. Preiss.
il Am Artist 33:28-34 F '69
AMERICAN cyanamid company
Cyanamid: we've come out of our shell.
R. Levy. il Duns R 93:36-40 My '69
AMERICAN dance festival. See Dance festivals
AMERICAN dance symposium. See Dance con-
ferences
AMERICAN depositary receipts. See Banks
and banking—Securities handling
AMERICAN documentation institute. See
American society for information science
AMERICAN drama
See also
Theatre—United States
AMERICAN economic assistance. See Economic
assistance, American
AMERICAN economic association
Stirrings from the new left. Time 95:66 Ja 12
'70
AMERICAN education (periodical)
From the editor. Am Ed 5:inside cover D '69
AMERICAN educational publishers institute
AEPI annual meeting: publishers study edu-
cation's turmoil, trouble and growth; high-
lights of panel discussions. il Pub W 195:
34-8 Je 9 '69
Erratic winds of change: AEPI-NEA's joint
dilemma; report of meeting. il Pub W 196:
30-2 D 29 '69
1968 in review. Pub W 195:42 Mr 10 '69
Science foundation's role analyzed for AEPI
group. Pub W 195:40-1 Ap 21 '69
AMERICAN educational research association
Researchers speak; AERA annual meeting.
W. D. Boutwell. Sr Schol 94:Schol Teach
12+ Mr 14 '69
AMERICAN elm. See Elm
AMERICAN Episcopal church
New Episcopal splinter. J. L. Adams. Chr
Today 13:49 Ap 11 '69
AMERICAN express cards. See Credit cards
AMERICAN express company
Disaster can be good for you. Forbes 103:
18-19 F 1 '69
License to print money. il Time 94:94 N
7 '69
AMERICAN farm bureau federation
Reaping the subsidies. R. G. Sherrill. Nation
209:565-6 N 24 '69
True religion at the farm bureau. Chr Cent
86:363 Mr 19 '69
AMERICAN federation of information process-
ing societies
Does the jumping Joint make any sense?
fall and spring Joint computer confer-
ences. il Bsns W p 100-1 N 29 '69
AMERICAN federation of labor and Congress
of industrial organizations
AFL-CIO as paid propagandist: agent Meany;
funneling AID funds into overseas in-
stitutes. R. Dudman. New Repub 160:13-16
My 3 '69
AFL-CIO weathers the loss; withdrawal of
UAW from federation. Bsns W p77 My 31
'69
AFL-CIO's internal disputes plan. D. L. Cole.
Mo Labor R 92:12-15 S '69
Alienated rank and file. A. Bilik. Nation
209:527-30 N 17 '69

Blue-collar war of words heats up; 40,000-
word white paper details the events leading
to the UAW's disaffiliation from the AFL-
CIO. il Bsns W p76+ Ap 12 '69
Challenge for AFL-CIO? U S News 66:64 Mr
3 '69
Federation steps up its attack on GE. il
Bsns W p38-9 N 22 '69
Feuding over jobless pay; proposed changes
sent to Congress by President Nixon.
Bsns W p47-8 Jl 12 '69
God bless and goodby; position on tax re-
form. Nation 208:718 Je 9 '69
Heir apparent? Newsweek 73:92 My 26 '69
Is AFL-CIO ready for the 1970s? il Bsns W
p 136+ O 11 '69
Isolation of George Meany. B. J. Widick.
Nation 209:398-9 O 20 '69
Labor and foreign policy. R. Radosh. Nation
209:208-11 S 8 '69
Labor dissidents set strategy; Alliance for
labor action. U S News 66:74 Je 2 '69
Labor maps 1969 goals; higher hourly wage
and full employment. Bsns W p36 Mr 1 '69
Labor shoots the breeze; Atlantic City con-
vention. J. Hill. Commonweal 91:176 N
7 '69
Meany & Reuther: labor's main bout. B. J.
Widick. Nation 208:601-2 My 12 '69
Meany-Reuther showdown, with unity the
likely loser. Bsns W p34-5 Ag 30 '69
Meany, Romney: troubled start. U S News
66:64 F 3 '69
Mr Meany replies to Sen Fulbright; AID pay-
ments to AIFLD. B. L. Masse. America
121:111 Ag 30 '69
Nixon-Meany: an odd couple. J. Hill. Com-
monweal 90:537+ S 5 '69
No hardening of arteries in AFL-CIO. B. L.
Masse. America 121:409 N 8 '69
One big union for the blue Meanys. J. Hill.
Commonweal 90:37-8 Mr 28 '69
Stop the world; labor's establishment. J. Hill.
Commonweal 90:5-6 Mr 21 '69
Unions and Nixon: harmony at the start. il
U S News 66:62-3 Mr 3 '69
Walter Reuther's gamble; contesting Meany's
status quo. J. Hill. Commonweal 90:261-3
My 16 '69
What White House and unions are telling
each other. il U S News 66:65-6 Ap 28 '69
Why union leaders look for troubles in the
'70s. il U S News 67:85-6 O 20 '69

    Industrial union department
IUD builds up its war chest. Bsns W p66 O 4
'69
    United farm workers organizing
        committee
For a vote in the vineyards. America 121:
482 N 22 '69
Four-year strike, two-year boycott: show-
down. il U S News 67:83-4 Jl 14 '69
Grapes of wrath. J. R. Coyne, jr. Nat R
21:639 Jl 1 '69
Labor in the vineyard: the boycott and the
NLRA. R. B. Taylor. il Nation 208:591-3
My 12 '69
Letter from Delano. C. Chávez. Chr Cent
86:539-40 Ap 23 '69; Discussion. 86:110-11,
1115-16 Je 11, Ag 27 '69
Non violence still works: UFWOC during
California grape pickers strike; interview.
C. Chavez. il Look 33:52+ Ap 1 '69; Reply.
C. G. Adamy. 33:6+ Je 10 '69
Pentagon scabs. Ramp Mag 7:12+ N 30 '68
Poisons, profits and politics; cases of death
and severe illness due to pesticide poison-
ing in Calif. R. Harmer. Nation 209:134-7
Ag 25 '69
Profiles; C. Chavez. P. Matthiessen. New
Yorker 45:42-4+ Je 21; 43-4+ Je 28 '69
Rights for farm workers. America 120:492-3
Ap 26 '69
AMERICAN federation of musicians
Bargaining in major symphony orchestras. L.
E. Lunden. bibliog Mo Labor R 92:15-19 Jl
'69
Deficits bring sour note to world of music.
il Bsns W p77-8 Jl 12 '69
AMERICAN federation of teachers
Is an NEA-AFT merger imminent? R. Dew-
ing. Ed Digest 35:35-7 N '69
Teacher union's rising power; fewer strikes
ahead? il U S News 67:56-7 S 1 '69
AMERICAN fiction
See also
Negro fiction

AMERICAN field service
  President Nixon meets with foreign exchange
    students; remarks, July 22, 1969. R. M.
    Nixon. Dept State Bul 61:111-13 Ag 11 '69
AMERICAN film institute
  Take 1 scene 1; sites selected for AFI grants.
    Sr Schol 94:Schol Teach 7 F 7 '69
AMERICAN flag. See Flags—United States
AMERICAN folk art. See Folk art
AMERICAN folk music. See Folk music, Amer-
  ican
AMERICAN football league
  Curse of the endless playoff; affliction of pro
    hockey, basketball, and baseball, now,
    spreading to pro football. T. Maule. il
    Sports Illus 30:18-21 Ap 7 '69
  They'd rather switch; Cleveland, Baltimore
    and Pittsburgh move to AFL. T. Maule. il
    Sports Illus 30:20-3 My 26 '69
  Three for the money. il Newsweek 73:108
    My 26 '69
AMERICAN forces Vietnam radio-television
  network
  Shape up or. . .; censorship of news. Newsweek
    75:41 Ja 12 '70
  Time for a change? newcasters and censor-
    ship issue. Newsweek 75:27 Ja 19 '70
  Where there is no napalm; censorship of
    news to American forces in Vietnam. il
    Newsweek 74:77 O 20 '69
AMERICAN forestry association
  AFA annual meeting awards. il Am For
    75:8-9+ N '69
  AFA eyes on Colorado; AFA's public lands con-
    ference, September 21-24, 1969. Am For 75:
    28-9+ Jl '69
  AFA people; photographs. W. E. Towell.
    Am For 75:31+ D '69
  Destiny of conservation depends on truth.
    J. B. Craig. Am For 75:11 N '69
  Grazing lands must be restored; reprint.
    J. B. Craig. Am For 75:6-7 Ja '69
  Meet your AFA members. W. E. Towell. il Am
    For 75:35+ F '69
  Public lands conference called. il Am For
    75:10-11 Ap '69
  Rights or privileges? address. P. E. Terzick.
    il Am For 75:28-30+ D '69
AMERICAN freedom from hunger foundation
  They walk to feed the hungry: Walks for de-
    velopment. C. Remsberg and B. Rems-
    berg. il Good H 169:82-3+ S '69
AMERICAN Friends service committee
  A.F.S.C. report indicts federal food pro-
    grams. Chr Cent 86:1573 D 10 '69
  A.F.S.C. teams aid Mexican farmers. F. U.
    Ross. il Chr Cent 86:1624-6 D 17 '69
AMERICAN furniture. See Furniture, American
AMERICAN general insurance company
  Going up by going down. il Forbes 104:50 N
    15 '69
AMERICAN geographical society
  Travel plans: annual dinner. New Yorker 45:
    17-18 Ja 10 '70
AMERICAN geophysical union
  AGU. Sci N 95:454 My 10 '69
  Publication savings and shortcuts; letter. S. F.
    Singer. Science 166:43-4 O 3 '69
AMERICAN glass. See Glassware
AMERICAN heart association
  Should your family's diet be changed to
    prevent heart attacks? Good H 168:185-7
    My '69
AMERICAN heritage (periodical)
  Anniversary. O. Jensen. il Am Heritage 21:3
    D '69
AMERICAN heritage dictionary of the English
  language. See English language—Dictio-
  naries
AMERICAN heritage publishing company
  American heritage press launches its first
    list. Pub W 195:113-14 Je 2 '69
  Money: a big word in lexicography. il Bsns
    W p54+ F 8 '69
AMERICAN historical association
  Hassle of historians. J. Gilbert. Nation 208:
    77-9 Ja 20 '69
  Return to the fold; debate on Vietnam policy.
    il Newsweek 75:42 Ja 12 '70
AMERICAN hospital of Paris. See Paris— Hos-
  pitals
AMERICAN hot rod association national races.
  See Automobile racing
AMERICAN humor. See Humor, American
AMERICAN illustrators. See Illustrators
AMERICAN imperialism. See Imperialism
AMERICAN income life insurance company
  Insurance pitch with a union label. Bsns W
    p88 Mr 29 '69
AMERICAN independent party. See Political
  parties—United States
AMERICAN Indians. See Indians

AMERICAN institute for foreign study
  American students abroad: we really got a
    cultural shock; interviews, ed. by R. Hemm-
    ing. il Sr Schol 94:12-13 Mr 14 '69
    See also
  Travel study courses
AMERICAN institute for free labor development
  Fulbright vs. Meany; AID subsidy hearings.
    K. Crawford. Newsweek 74:29 Ag 18 '69
  Mr Meany replies to Sen Fulbright; AID pay-
    ments. B. L. Masse. America 121:111 Ag 30
    '69
AMERICAN institute of aeronautics and as-
  tronautics
  Urban use of systems analysis stressed. R.
    S. Kahn. Aviation W 90:103-4 My 12 '69
AMERICAN institute of architects
  A.I.A. takes three giant steps in the right
    direction. W. F. Wagner, jr. Arch Rec
    146:9 N '69
  Announcing the 1969-1970 Western home
    awards. il Sunset 142:96-7 F '69
  Students win support of A.I.A. in Chicago;
    sweeping changes proposed in professional
    ethics. il Arch Rec 146:35 Ag '69
AMERICAN institute of biological sciences
  Biological science. Sci N 96:163 Ag 30 '69
AMERICAN institute of certified public ac-
  countants
  Accountants turn tougher; rule-making Ac-
    counting principles board. il Bsns W p 124-
    5+ O 18 '69
AMERICAN institute of physics
  AIP, APS adopt new policies for unsupported
    publishing. Phys Today 22:69 F '69
  AIP in 1968: expansion and experimentation.
    J. P. Wiley, jr. il Phys Today 22:43-50 Je
    '69
  New information program for AIP. A. Hersch-
    man and others. il Phys Today 22:29-32 D '69
AMERICAN institute of planners
  Perspective into the future. E. Contini. Sat
    R 52:35-8 F 22 '69
AMERICAN intellectuals. See Intellectuals
AMERICAN international racing (organization)
  See Automobile racing
AMERICAN investments abroad. See Invest-
  ments, Foreign
AMERICAN iron and steel institute
  Design-in-steel awards. il Am City 84:90-1
    Je '69
AMERICAN Jewish committee
  AJC survey finds errors and prejudice in
    textbooks. Library J 94:3122+ S 15 '69
AMERICAN Jews in Israel. See Americans in
  Israel
AMERICAN language. See English language
AMERICAN legion
  Bunny bop. C. Amory. il Holiday 46:20+ D
    '69
AMERICAN liberalism. See Liberalism
AMERICAN libraries abroad
  Library colonialism; letter to the editor. S.
    L. Jackson. Library J 94:2537 Jl '69
    See also
  American library in Paris
AMERICAN library association
  ALA: advancing the reach. R. H. McDonough.
    Wilson Lib Bul 43:858-9 My '69
  ALA award winners; 1969. il ALA Bul 63:
    1169-76 S '69
  ALA awards and scholarships for 1970. Wil-
    son Lib Bul 44:379-81 D '69; Same. Li-
    brary J 94:4472+, 4572-3 D 15 '69
  ALA awards, citations, scholarships and
    grants. Wilson Lib Bul 44:84 S '69
  ALA growth, or proliferation. R. N. Sheridan.
    ALA Bul 63:204-6 F '69
  ALA 1969 election results. Wilson Lib Bul 44:
    90 S '69
  ALA president, 1975; letter to the editor.
    J. F. Carroll. Library J 94:4466-7 D 15 '69
  Awards and citations ALA, 1969. il Library
    J 94:2756-7 Ag '69
  Election results announced. ALA Bul 63:
    963-4 Jl '69
  Know your ALA. ALA Bul 63:211-19, 377-85,
    503-11 F-Ap '69
  Libraries and the need for understanding;
    address, June 27, 1969. W. S. Dix. ALA Bul
    63:965-71 Jl '69
  Memo to members. W. S. Dix. ALA Bul
    63:900-1 Jl '69
  New ALA officers. il Library J 94:2718+ Ag
    '69
  Nominating committee reports. ALA Bul 63:
    1507 D '69
  Organizational information 69/70. il ALA Bul
    63:1334-469 N '69
  State of the association message; excerpts.
    January 1969. R. H. McDonough. il ALA
    Bul 63:334-8 Mr '69
  Tax reform. G. Krettek and E. D. Cooke.
    ALA Bul 63:1240-1 O '69

AMERICAN library association—*Continued*
Use of the ALA name (cont) ALA Bul 63:
386-7 Mr '69
Young librarians challenge relevancy of ALA;
annual conference. il Pub W 196:16-17 Ag
11 '69
  See also
American association of school librarians

Meetings

Case for ALA regional annual conferences.
E. M. Oboler. il ALA Bul 63:1099-101 S '69
Members ask: questions and answers. ALA
Bul 63:1211-14 O '69

Anecdotes, facetiae, satire, etc.

A!L!A! A!L!A! Here we go! Rah! Rah! Rah!
Conventions past. C. E. Werkley. il Library
J 94:2421-4 Je 15 '69
Kansas City hop; or, How Novia sprained
her ankle at ALA and found her footing;
short play. S. Olofson. il ALA Bul 63:817-
26 Je '69

Meetings, 1969

ALA conference roundup. Library J 94:1832,
2392+ My 1, Je 15 '69
ALA conference roundup; symposium. il Li-
brary J 94:2709, 2727-57+ Ag '69
ALA midwinter: a random sampling. Wilson
Lib Bul 43:595-6 Mr '69
ALAiad: or, A tale of two conferences: with
photographs. Wilson Lib Bul 44:80-95 S '69
Assignation of a profession by the sea as
it will be performed by the membership
of ALA at Atlantic City, June 22-28, 1969.
ALA Bul 63:624-7 My '69
Atlantic City conference: great show in
two parts and a cast of thousands. il
ALA Bul 63:915-53+ Jl '69
Crisis in red and black; 1969 ALA conference.
E. Geller. il Library J 94:3134-8 S 15 '69
Highlights of annual conference, June 22-28,
1969. il ALA Bul 63:1137-60 S '69
Highlights of midwinter meeting January
26-February 1, 1969. ALA Bul 63:483-500 Ap
'69
Midwinter meeting 1969: the search for ALA;
or, a short trip down the rabbit hole. il
ALA Bul 63:325-47 Mr '69
Midwinter 1969. E. Geller. il Library J 94:
1303-5 Mr 15 '69
On the program at ALA: youth meetings.
Library J 94:2046 My 15 '69
Overdue; members from the Congress for
change at ALA convention. L. Lynch. il
Wilson Lib Bul 44:326-7 N '69; Reply. T. L.
Vince. 44:502-4 Ja '70
Programming the ALA program. J. Berry.
Library J 94:2379 Je 15 '69; Reply. D.
Cohen. 94:3585 O 15 '69
Raps and routines; 1969 ALA conference. L.
Mesiano. il Library J 94:3143-8 S 15 '69
Tentative program of the 88th annual ALA
conference. ALA Bul 63:629-60 My '69
Thousand voices; summary of answers to
questionnaire in conference kit. P. Mag-
geroli. ALA Bul 63:1270-3 O '69
Wait 'til Atlantic City; ALA's midwinter
mood. J. Berry and S. Havens. il Library J
94:1104-11 Mr 15 '69

Meetings, 1970

ALA midwinter meeting. ALA Bul 63:1609-11
D '69
1970 ALA midwinter meeting; Chicago,
Illinois, January 18-24. ALA Bul 63:1162-3
S '69
"No" action: midwinter meeting in Chicago;
letter to the editor. M. B. Goodman. ALA
Bul 63:1219-20 O '69
Overdue: thoughts for ALA midwinter. E.
Smith. Wilson Lib Bul 44:458-9 D '69

Adult services division

ALA cites 1968's notable books. Pub W 195:
133 F 17 '68; Same. Library J 94:927+
Mr 1 '69; ALA Bul 63:373-5 Mr '69
Book talk in Chicago. G. R. Shields. ALA
Bul 63:1017-18 Jl '69
Notable nominations. ALA Bul 63:1178, 1293,
1614-15 S-O, D '69

Children's services division

1968 children's books for international in-
terest. Todays Ed 58:76-9 N '69
Notable children's books 1968. il ALA Bul
63:467-70 Ap '69; Same. Library J 94:2036+
My 15 '69
Raps and routines; 1969 ALA conference. L.
Mesiano. il Library J 94:3143-5 S 15 '69
Summer scoop; highlights of the meetings
of the three youth divisions. E. Geller and
L. Mesiano. Library J 94:2755 Ag '69

Committee on new directions

Dix-mix committee meets on ALA changes.
il Library J 94:4081 N 15 '69

Constitution and bylaws committee

ALA constitution and bylaws committee
report. ALA Bul 63:618-22 My '69

Council

Atlantic City conference. il ALA Bul 63:936-
53+ Jl '69
Midwinter meeting 1969; Council I, and
Council II. il ALA Bul 63:334-45 Mr '69
Overdue: a truly modest proposal: bringing
their young members into more active roles.
W. D. Laird, jr. Wilson Lib Bul 43:669+
Mr '69
Platform proposal: letter to the editor. J.
Forsman and T. Raley. ALA Bul 63:1217-
18 O '69
Washington D.C. group urges ALA changes;
with editorial comment. Library J 94:3383,
3392 O 1 '69

Finance

Treasurer's report (cont) il ALA Bul 63:1602-
8 D '69

Headquarters

From out of a desk drawer: the beginnings of
ALA headquarters. V. F. Massman. bibliog
ALA Bul 63:475-81 Ap '69

Intellectual freedom committee

IFC action proposal. J. Berry. il Library J
94:2752-4 Ag '69
Intellectual freedom's program of action.
ALA Bul 63:1205 O '69

Library administration division

Editor's choice; policy and procedure regarding tenure investigations by the board
of directors of the Library administration
division of the American library association. ALA Bul 63:1223-4 O '69
Library employment of minority group personnel. R. R. Frame and J. F. Anderson.
il ALA Bul 63:985-7 Jl '69

Library education division

New technician standards released by LED.
Library J 94:1830 My 1 '69

Library technology program

Evaluating the evaluators. M. L. Bob. Library J 94:1416 Ap 1 '69; Reply with rejoinder. F. F. Carhart, jr. 94:2705-6 Ag '69
Ltp news. ALA Bul 63:1611 D '69
LTP news (cont) M. E. Weissman. ALA Bul
63:274, 394, 520, 662, 1181, 1295 F-My, S-O
'69
Note regarding library technology reports: a
criticism; letter to the editor; with reply.
H. Elstein. ALA Bul 63:703-4 Je '69

Membership

ALA and collective bargaining. L. W. S.
Auld; reply. D. Moulton. ALA Bul 63:431
Ap '69
ALA dues structure: background to a recom-
mendation. S. L. Wallace. ALA Bul 63:
614-15 My '69
ALA membership statistics. ALA Bul 63:466
Ap '69
ALAiad; or, A tale of two conferences. il
Wilson Lib Bul 44:80-91 S '69
Atlantic City conference. il ALA Bul 63:937-
53+ Jl '69
Due(s) ALAver twist: I want some more.
Wilson Lib Bul 43:1014+ Je '69
Flat rate dues; letter to the editor. F. Gior-
dano. ALA Bul 63:893-4 Jl '69
HUG for membership: Heads of units group
in headquarters staff. ALA Bul 63:1208-9
O '69
High cost of membership; symposium. Li-
brary J 94:2411-14 Je 15 '69
Members ask; questions and answers. ALA
Bul 63:1211-14, 1508-9 O, D '69
New constituency: Congress for change. J.
Berry. il Library J 94:2727-39 Ag '69; Dis-
cussion. 94:3941-3 N 1 '69
Open hearings: midwinter meeting; Member-
ship committee's subcommittee to Study
the ALA dues structure (SALADS) J.
Berry and S. Havens. Library J 94:1109-10
Mr 15 '69
Overdue; a truly modest proposal: bringing
their young members into more active
role. W. D. Laird, jr. Wilson Lib Bul
43:669+ Mr '69
Overdue professional pursuits: ALA a library
or a librarians' association? R. P. Haro.
Wilson Lib Bul 43:561+ F '69

AMERICAN opera society—*Continued*
Musical events:
Bellini's La straniera. W. Sargeant. New
Yorker 45:131 Ap 5 '69
Eugène d'Albert's Tiefland. W. Sargeant.
New Yorker 45:164+ Ap 19 '69
Giacomo Meyerbeer's Les Huguenots. W.
Sargeant. New Yorker 45:134+ My 24
'69
Report: New York; concert performance of
Bellini's La Straniera. J. W. Freeman.
Opera N 33:24 My 17 '69
Report: New York; concert version of Meyer-
beer's Huguenots. F. Merkling. Opera N
33:22 Je 14 '69
AMERICAN overseas libraries. See American
libraries abroad
AMERICAN painting. See Painting, American
AMERICAN petrofina, incorporated
Not so dumb. Forbes 104:54-5 Jl 15 '69
AMERICAN philosophy. See Philosophy, Amer-
ican
AMERICAN photocopy equipment company
Turning a company around; interview. C. L.
Rautbord. il Nations Bsns 57:62-3+ Je '69
AMERICAN physical society
AAPT-APS meeting returns to New York.
J. P. Wiley, jr. il Phys Today 22:57-9 Ja
'69
AIP, APS adopt new policies for unsupported
publishing. Phys Today 22:69 F '69
Dissidents force a vote on 1970 Chicago
meeting. Phys Today 22:85+ Ap '69
Other space is available; letter with reply by
W. W. Havens, jr. J. Orear. il Phys Today
22:9+ My '69
Science and defense. Sci N 95:185 F 22 '69
Strike of the physicists. Newsweek 73:98 F
17 '69
AMERICAN poetry
Alone with America, by R. Howard. Review
New Repub 161:24-6 D 20 '69. H. Kramer
Benét's John Brown's body: for study. P. J.
Sheehan. Engl J 58:219-25 F '69
Lyrics, heroic and otherwise. R. D. Spector.
Sat R 52:33-5 Mr 15 '69
Poetry: combatting society with surrealism.
Time 93:72-73A+ Ja 24 '69
Spot check: some observations on poetry in
America. J. Claman. il Harp Baz 102:122K
F '69
Undergraduate poems; comp. by J. Moffitt.
America 120:404-5 Ap 5 '69
Voice of the poet: oracular, eerie, daring.
D. Jaffe. Sat R 52:28-9+ S 6 '69
See also
Negro poetry
AMERICAN poets. See Poets, American
AMERICAN portraits. See Portraits, American
AMERICAN pottery. See Pottery, American
AMERICAN power boat association
APBA action report. J. D. Paris. See issues
of Motor boating
More power to you. M. Crook. See issues
of Yachting
AMERICAN propaganda. See Propaganda
AMERICAN psychological association
Psychologists: searching for social relevance
at APA meeting. B. Nelson. il Science 165:
1101-4 S 12 '69
Relevance in Washington. Sci N 96:177-8 S
6 '69
AMERICAN public opinion. See Public opinion
—United States
AMERICAN radiator and standard sanitary
corporation
Radiator maker starts to swing. under Presi-
dent Eberle. il Bsns W p86-7 My 3 '69
AMERICAN record guide (periodical)
From the editor: 35th anniversary. J. Lyons.
Am Rec G 35:679-80+ My '69
AMERICAN rehabilitation foundation
Helping the handicapped travel by air. M.
McEachern. il Todays Health 47:66-8+ Mr
'69
AMERICAN research and development cor-
poration
Very special affair. Forbes 104:42 O 15 '69
AMERICAN scientific affiliation
Target: social neglect. Chr Today 13:44 S
26 '69
AMERICAN scientists. See Scientists, Amer-
ican
AMERICAN sculpture. See Sculpture, American
AMERICAN Shakespeare festival theatre and
academy, Stratford, Conn.
Fresh revivals; production of Henry V. H.
Hewes Sat R 52:10+ Je 13 '69
Tapestry of violence; unorthodox production
of Henry V. il Time 93:80 Je 13 '69
Theatre: production of Henry V. B. Gill. il
New Yorker 45:178 N 22 '69

AMERICAN smelting and refining company
White Cloud peaks; a time for decision. D.
B. Clement. il Am For 75:28-31+ S '69
AMERICAN society for African culture
CIA as an equal opportunity employer. D.
Schechter and others. il Ramp Mag 7:26-33
Je '69
AMERICAN society for engineering education
ASEE-Ford foundation residencies program.
Sch & Soc 97:10 Ja '69
AMERICAN society for information science
Shared time, on line: ASIS meeting. W. R.
Eshelman. Wilson Lib Bul 44:240+ N '69
AMERICAN society for the prevention of cru-
elty to animals
Animal kingdom ball: fund-raising dinner
dance. A. Meyer. il Natur Hist 78:10+ Ap
'69
AMERICAN society of travel agents
Tyro traveler: who needs a travel agent?
Travel 132:26 Ag '69
AMERICAN society of university composers
Current chronicle: Summer institute in com-
positional studies. J. E. Ivey. Mus Q
55:87-91 Ja '69
AMERICAN sociological association
See also
Association for Asian studies
AMERICAN songs. See Ballads, American;
Songs, American
AMERICAN soybean association
Can we save our export markets? L. Palmer.
il Farm J 93:20-1+ S '69
AMERICAN statistical association
ASA conference papers; symposium. il Mo
Labor R 92:43-61 N '69
Forecasters who don't share the fears. Bsns W
p24 Ag 23 '69
AMERICAN stock exchange
Paperwork mess goes into a think tank. Bsns
W p 126+ F 22 '69
AMERICAN students in Cuba. See Foreign
students in Cuba
AMERICAN students in foreign countries
Marching to a different tourist beat. il Sat
R 52:64+ F 15 '69
Thirty thousand innocents abroad. W. Roberts.
il Sat R 52:61-2+ F 15 '69
See also
Foreign study
AMERICAN students in Germany; American
students in Russia; etc. See Foreign stu-
dents in Germany; Foreign students in Rus-
sia; etc.
AMERICAN studies
America watching; new kind of specialist in
the Soviet Union. Time 93:24 F 7 '69
AMERICAN sugar company
Not so sweet. Forbes 104:66 S 15 '69
AMERICAN symphony orchestra
Musical events; concert in Carnegie Hall.
W. Sargeant. New Yorker 45:171-2 O 18
'69
Musical events; performance of Bruckner's
Fifth symphony in Carnegie Hall. W.
Sargeant. New Yorker 45:100+ Mr 8 '69
Musical events; performance of Copland's
Music for a great city in Carnegie Hall. W.
Sargeant. New Yorker 45:109 Mr 22 '69
Musical events; program conducted by Sir W.
Walton of his own works. W. Sargeant.
New Yorker 44:106 F 8 '69
Yankee Doodle dandy. il Newsweek 74:130
O 20 '69
AMERICAN teachers in foreign countries
Our Mrs Brooks; Fulbright exchange teach-
er in England. P. Pine. il Am Ed 5:9-10
My '69
AMERICAN technical assistance. See Technical
assistance, American
AMERICAN telephone and telegraph company
AT&T and Comsat tangle over cables. Bsns
W p 14-15 Ja 3 '70
AT&T calls for indefinite delay in domestic
satcom inception. K. Johnsen. Aviation W
92:20 Ja 5 '70
AT&T, Comsat oppose GE on domestic Sat-
com plan. K. Johnsen. Aviation W 90:21
Ap 21 '69
Dial-A-Bomb: AT&T and the ABM. J. Goul-
den and M. Singer. il Ramp Mag 8:29-35+
N '69
FCC launches cable-satellite investigation to
establish policy. K. Johnsen. Aviation W
91:23 D 8 '69
Giants will stay that way. Bsns W p70 S 6
'69
Great telephone snarl. W. A. McWhirter. il
Life 67:86-86D+ D 5 '69
Indiscretions of Ma Bell; with editorial com-
ment. J. C. Goulden. Nation 209:333, 346-9
O 6 '69
Ma Bell rental agency. W. P. Rokes. il Na-
tion 208:820-3 Je 30 '69

AMERICAN telephone and telegraph company
—*Continued*
Making a job more than a job. il Bsns W
p88-9 Ap 19 '69
Mother Bell's migraine; pay phones put out
of commission by vandals and thieves.
Time 93:92 F 28 '69
Over the phone: good news; lower charges
on interstate calls. U S News 67:18 N 17
'69
Round AT&T lost; FCC's approval of MCI to
carry voices and data. il Bsns W p68+ S
6 '69
Strictly modern ma. il Newsweek 74:56-7 Ag
11 '69
Whole new market; data communications. il
Forbes 104:43-4 Jl 1 '69
Why you hear a busy signal at AT&T. il Bsns
W p40-1+ D 27 '69
　See also
Government investigations—American tele-
phone and telegraph company
AMERICAN tobacco company
Smoke signals; dropping the New York
times. il Newsweek 74:66 S 15 '69
AMERICAN tourists. See Travelers
AMERICAN tradition. See Tradition
AMERICAN university, Washington, D.C.
University contractors cut ties with CRESS,
HumRRO, army's two main centers of
social, behavioral research. J. Coburn.
Science 164:1039-41 My 30 '69
AMERICAN visitors in Liberia; American visi-
tors in Rumania; etc. See Foreign visitors
in Liberia; Foreign visitors in Rumania; etc.
AMERICAN water works association
AWWA officers to assume duties in May. il
Am City 84:14 Ap '69
What waterworks men want. Am City 84:8
My '69
AMERICAN wines. See Wine
AMERICAN women. See Women—United States
AMERICAN writers. See Authors, American
AMERICAN youth hostels. See Youth hostels
AMERICANISM
Day I knew I belonged to the flag. D. D.
Eisenhower. il Read Digest 94:93 Mr '69
Decalcomania over the American flag. il Life
67:32-3 Jl 18 '69
High-flying flags. il Newsweek 73:78 Je 30
'69
Notes and comment. New Yorker 44:25 Ja
18 '69
Who is America? What are we all about?
excerpt from address. H. Donovan. il For-
tune 79:83-4+ Ap '69
AMERICANISMS (speech)
　See also
Slang
AMERICANS
Forgotten American. P. Schrag. il Harper
239:27-34 Ag '69
Growing up in America; symposium. il Mlle
68:206-9+ Ap '69
How one middle-class family gets along in
New York; Flushing, Queens. R. Rogin. il
N Y Times Mag p32-4+ Ag 17 '69; Discus-
sion. p 12+ S 7 '69
Interval between. J. E. Hoover. Chr Today
14:3-5 D 19 '69
Interview with Norman Mailer; ed. by O.
Fallaci. N. Mailer. il Writers Digest 49:40-
7+ D '69
Man and woman of the year: the middle
Americans. il Time 95:10-17 Ja 5 '70
Moon and middle America. il Time 94:10-11
Ag 1 '69
Revolt of the middle class; with interview
with H. H. Humphrey. il U S News 67:
52-8 N 24 '69
Spiro and middle America. Nation 209:492
N 10 '69
Time to remember forgotten America; Time
essay. il Time 94:42-3 Ag 8 '69
Troubled American: a special report on the
white majority; with reports by K. Fleming
and R. M. Scammon. il Newsweek 74:28-52+
O 6 '69; Same abr. Read Digest 95:94-9
D '69
　See also
Californians
Easterners
United States
AMERICANS; drama. See De Grazia. E.
AMERICANS abroad. See Americans in foreign
countries
AMERICANS for democratic action
Plight of the U. S. liberals; signs that an era
is ending. il U S News 67:38-41 Jl 14 '69

AMERICANS in Afghanistan
Memoirs of Afghanistan. P. Chesler. Mlle 69:
154-60 Je '69
AMERICANS in Africa
Into the wilderness; group from Chicago's
Alpha Beta Israel center. J. Barnes. il
Newsweek 73:52 Ja 27 '69
AMERICANS in England
American artist works abroad. B. Mac-
Donald. il Am Artist 33:31-6+ O '69
　See also
United States—Armed forces—Forces in Great
Britain
AMERICANS in Europe
American as indentured servant; working in
a continental household as an au pair. L.
Arking. Mlle 69:211+ My '69
Another way of living, by J. Bainbridge. Re-
view
Travel & Camera 32:32-3 Ap '69. L. Hadley
Are they overpaid overseas? American busi-
nessmen working abroad. il Time 94:93 S
19 '69
U.S. moneymen: no innocence abroad. J.
Ross-Skinner. il Duns R 93:48-9+ My '69
　See also
United States—Armed forces—Forces in
Europe
AMERICANS in foreign countries
Another way of living. J. Bainbridge. McCalls
96:157-60 Ap '69
New multinational managers. W. M. Reddig,
jr. il Sat R 52:35-6+ N 22 '69
What children learn from living in distant
lands. B. Harrison. Redbook 132:95+ Ap '69
Who makes ends meet in Milan? comparative
costs of U.S. executives in key cities. il
Bsns W p58+ Ap 19 '69
　See also
American teachers in foreign countries
United States—Armed forces—Forces in for-
eign countries

Employment
President Nixon orders reduction in U.S. per-
sonnel abroad; July 9. 1969. Dept State Bul
61:92 Ag 4 '69
AMERICANS in Israel
Promised land. il Newsweek 74:58+ O 27 '69
AMERICANS in Japan
Eddychan. E. Hahn. New Yorker 44:33-9
Ja 18 '69
AMERICANS in Laos
Laos is at war, but Vientiane yawns. W. War-
ren. il N Y Times Mag p 12-13+ Ja 4 '70
AMERICANS in literature
Children's books; the pageant that is Ameri-
ca. R. Gagliardo. il PTA Mag 63:32-3 Mr '69
AMERICANS in Russia
Bringing down thunderbolts; Russia expels
Washington post's correspondent. Time
93:37-8 My 30 '69
AMERICANS in Scotland
Profiles; Colonsay: the island of the crofter
and the laird. J. McPhee. il New Yorker
45:69-70+ D 6; 61-2+ D 13 '69
AMERICANS in Sweden
Ministry to G.I.s in Sweden. R. J. Neuhaus.
Chr Cent 86:378-80+ Mr 19 '69; Reply.
K. H. Brevik. 86:684 My 14 '69
AMERICANS in Thailand
　See also
United States—Armed forces—Forces in Thai-
land
AMERICANS in Vietnam
For profiteers, what a lovely war; Vietnam-
ese and American do a flourishing business
in corruption. F. McCulloch. il Life 67:46-
8+ Ag 1 '69
　See also
United States—Army—Forces in Vietnam
AMERICANS united for separation of church
and state
NEA. POAU and tax exemptions. America
120:662 Je 7 '69
AMÉRICAS (periodical)
Américas celebrates its twentieth anni-
versary. G. de Zéndegui. Américas 21:1 F
'69
AMERICA'S cup race. See Yacht racing
AMES, Felicia
Living with a dog, and loving it. Parents
Mag 44:50-1+ F '69
AMES, Louise Bates
Children and divorce: what the teacher can
do. Ed Digest 35:19-21 N '69
AMES, Morgan, and others
Lighter side. See issues of High fidelity in-
corporating Musical America
AMES, Thomas Robert
Independent living for the mentally handi-
capped: a program for young adults. Ment
Hy 53:641-2 O '69

AMPHIBIOUS airplanes. See Airplanes, Amphibious

AMPHIBIOUS motor vehicles. See Motor vehicles, Amphibious

AMPLIFIERS
Build a FET stick; R.F. amplifier experiment. A. Trauffer. il Pop Electr 31:57-8 D '69
Build the FET preamp. D. Meyer. il Pop Electr 20:27-33 My '69
Equipment report; Heathkit AA-15 stereo amplifier. R. Free. il Radio-Electr 40:89 Je '69
Excellent preamplifier kit: Dynakit. il Consumer Rep 34:356-7 Jl '69
Experiment with 15-watt IC powerhouse. J. Ashe. il Radio-Electr 40:33-5 S '69
Experiment with ten emitter-coupled circuits. R. L. Petrowsky. il Radio-Electr 40:37-40 Mr '69
50-watt booster amplifier. J. Jaques. il Radio-Electr 40:55-6 My '69
IC stereo preamplifier. P. B. Jarrett. il Pop Electr 30:52-4 Mr '69
JFETS. R. Clifton. il Radio-Electr 40:55-7 Je '69
Living with Dynakits. I. Berger. Sat R 52:77 Ap 26 '69
No-hands amplifier for your telephone. W. Salm. il Pop Mech 131:144-7 Ja '69
125 watts per channel stereo amplifier. K. F. Buegel. il Radio-Electr 40:41-4+ Ap '69
Recipe for an IC preamp. J. Teeling. il Radio-Electr 40:44-5+ Jl '69
Stereo IC preamp. K. Buegel. il Radio-Electr 40:45-7 My '69
Ten-watt PA amplifier. E. Francis. il Pop Electr 31:55-60 N '69
Tigers that roar. D. Meyer. il Pop Electr 31:51-3 Jl '69
200-watt stereo amp. F. S. Kamp and J. C. Sondermeyer. il Radio-Electr 40:71-3 O '69
Use the PA-222 in audio circuits. J. Ashe. il Radio-Electr 40:54-6 F '69
What does an op amp do? quiz. J. Seginski. il Pop Electr 31:50+ O '69
See also
Man amplifiers
Masers
Musical instruments, Electronic—Equipment

Testing
Hi-fi product report:
Eico model 3150 stereo amplifier. il Electr World 82:16+ S '69
J. B. Lansing SE400S stereo power amplifier. il Electr World 81:22+ F '69
Kenwood KA-6000 stereo amplifier. il Electr World 81:22+ Mr '69
Sony TA-2000 stereo preamplifier. il Electr World 81:76-7 My '69

AMPUTEES
Rehabilitation
For amputees, the Boston arm. L. Galton. Read Digest 94:151-4 F '69

AMRAM, David
Music. Vogue 153:98 Ja 15 '69; 155:78 Ja 15 '70

about
Musical events: Twelfth night, New York première in Hunter college playhouse. W. Sargeant. New Yorker 45:120-1 My 3 '69
Twelfth night. Criticism
Sat R 52:39 My 10 '69

AMSAC. See American society for African culture

AMSTERDAM, Netherlands
Clubs
Hash in Holland: the Dutch find it easier to let traffic flourish; youth clubs as drug centers. D. S. Greenberg. Science 165:476-8 Ag 1 '69

Description
Amsterdam. J. Hughes. il Travel & Camera 32:52-3+ Mr '69
Young and in Amsterdam. D. Butwin. il Sat R 52:45-6 Ap 5 '69

Historic houses, etc.
House of silence: Anne Frank museum. H. Frankel. Holiday 46:16+ S '69

Music
Report: Amsterdam; operatic productions. J. Mindszenthy. il Opera N 33:1-2 My 15 '69

Religious institutions and affairs
Priests, prostitutes, and the dead God: a meditation; a visitor in Amsterdam. R. E. Warren. il Cath World 208:261-3 Mr '69
See also
Catholic church in the Netherlands

AMSTERDAM news, New York. See Negro press

AMTEL, incorporated
Roy Little's latest Textron? J. Ottmar. Forbes 103:33-4 My 1 '69

AMUSEMENT parks
Disney unwraps its newest extravaganza; Walt Disney world experimental prototype community of tomorrow. il Bsns W p32+ My 3 '69
Magic kingdom is on the way: Walt Disney world, Orlando, Fla. F. Somers. Redbook 133:141 Ag '69
See also
Disneyland park, Anaheim, Calif.

Equipment
See also
Ferris wheels

AMUSEMENTS
Ordeal of fun. F. Trippett. il Look 33:24-34 Jl 29 '69; Same abr. with title Unending quest for fun. Read Digest 95:62-4 D '69
Tuned in, spaced out. il Harp Baz 103:137 Ja '70
See also
Camping—Activities
Games
Hobbies
Mathematical recreations
Recreation

AMY Loveman national award
Eighth Amy Loveman award. D. Dempsey. Sat R 52:28 Jl 12 '69

ANABAPTISTS
See also
Mennonites

ANABLE, Anthony, jr
Marinas, marinas, and... Motor B 123:238-41 Ja '69

ANACONDA copper mining company
Clamor over Chilean copper. il Time 93:75 Je 27 '69
Copper giant learns the hard way. il Bsns W p 17 Jl 5 '69

ANAGNOSTOPOULOS family. See Agnew family

ANAHEIM, Calif.
Sweepers get parks cleaner in less time. il Am City 84:14 S '69
See also
Disneyland park

ANALGESIA
Surgery in the rat during electrical analgesia induced by focal brain stimulation. D. V. Reynolds. bibliog il Science 164:444-5 Ap 25 '69

ANALOG computers. See Computers—Analog computers

ANAPHYLATOXIN. See Toxins and antitoxins

ANARCHISM and anarchists
Anarchists (who are with us again) J. W. Burrow. il Horizon 11:32-43 Sum '69
See also
Terrorism

ANARCHISTS. See Anarchism and anarchists

ANASAZI culture. See Pueblo Indians

ANASTASIOW, Nicholas
Educational relevance and Jensen's conclusions. Ed Digest 35:34-7 D '69

ANATOL, A. pseud. See Kuznetsov, A. V.

ANATOLIA. See Asia Minor

ANATOMICAL models
Electronic ear can identify spoken words. B. Miller. il Aviation W 90:89+ My 12 '69
Inside look at man; Hall of the biology of man. il Todays Health 47:12-13 Mr '69

ANATOMY, Artistic
See also
Human figure in photography

ANATOMY, Comparative
Man is no swinger. il Sci Digest 65:74-5 My '69
See also
Jaws (animals)

ANCHOR Hocking glass corporation
It's a question of technical skill. il Forbes 103:41 Mr 1 '69

ANCHOR lines. See Rope

ANCHORAGE, Alaska
Rochester progress; Anchorage partnership. il Am City 84:112+ N '69

ANCHORS
Anchor you shoot from a gun. J. Joseph. il Mech Illus 65:123 N '69
Anchors and anchoring. J. A. Emmett. il Outdoor Life 144:168-72 O '69
Explosive anchor really holds ships fast. il Pop Sci 195:182 Ag '69

ANCIENT coins. See Coins, Ancient

ANDEAN Indians. See Indians of South America—Bolivia

ANDECHS, Bavaria
Monks' brew; made in Andechs, Germany.
W. H. Nelson. il Holiday 45:58-9+ Je '69
ANDERS, Edward, and Heymann, Dieter
Elements 112 to 119: were they present in
meteorites? bibliog Science 164:821-3 My
16 '69
ANDERS, William A.
Astronauts as photographers. M. Edelson. il
Travel & Camera 32:80-3 Ap '69
See also
Space flight to the moon—Manned flights—
Borman-Lovell-Anders flight, 1968
ANDERSEN, Hans Christian
Emperor's nightingale; dramatization. See
Winther, B.
ANDERSON, A. E. Jr, and others
Selective venting of cigarette smoke in
dichotomous ducts and preserved human
bronchi. bibliog Science 162:668-9; 163:1227
N 8 '68, Mr 14 '69
ANDERSON, Albert D.
Dust in the lower atmosphere of Venus.
bibliog Science 163:275-6 Ja 17 '69
ANDERSON, Art. See Stoner, D. jt. auth.
ANDERSON, Benedict R. O'G.
Indonesia's uncertain future. bibliog f Cur
Hist 57:355-60 D '69
ANDERSON, Charles A.
Changes of change; address, February 17,
1969. Vital Speeches 35:360-3 Ap 1 '69
How to manage brainpower; excerpts from
address, August 1969. Science 165:1106 S 12
'69
ANDERSON, Charles B.
(tr) See Ramseger, G. New European book-
store
ANDERSON, Charles H. Jr. See Halliday, W.
R. jt. auth.
ANDERSON, Clayton and company
Cotton is still king. il Forbes 104:74 S 15 '69
ANDERSON, Dewey
Big Sur: where the forest meets the sea.
Nat Parks 43:4-12 O '69
Looking ahead in California's coast red-
woods. Nat Parks 43:4-8 Ag '69
ANDERSON, Diane. See Joyner, C. jt. auth.
ANDERSON, Donald Jack
Hell on hares. Field & S 74:30-1+ D '69
Last of Boone's breed. Field & S 73:64-5+
Mr '69
ANDERSON, Duwayne M. and others
Bentonite debris flows in northern Alaska.
bibliog Science 164:173-4 Ap 11 '69
ANDERSON, Fred
Who will decide who is to live? New Repub
160:9-10 Ap 19 '69
ANDERSON, Gordon A.
Newly identified clausula-motets in the Las
Huelgas manuscript. bibliog f Mus Q 55:228-
45 Ap '69
ANDERSON, Helen J.
Picture lady program: seven years old and
still going strong! Sch Arts 69:36-7 S '69
ANDERSON, Herbert L.
Day the atomic age was born; ed. by J. D.
Ratcliff. Read Digest 94:129-33 Mr '69
ANDERSON, Jack
Ferment and controversy. Dance Mag 43:46-
55 Ag '69
ANDERSON, Jack (poet)
Hair; poem. Nation 209:482 N 3 '69
North; poem. Nation 208:644 My 19 '69
ANDERSON, Jack, 1922-
Aggressive inheritor. il por Time 94:82 S 12
'69
Columnist and Kennedy. por Newsweek 74:75
Ag 25 '69
ANDERSON, James P.
Who shall teach children art? Sch Arts 69:
24-5 N '69
ANDERSON, Jean H.
Stars of very large proper motion. Sky &
Tel 38:76-8 Ag '69
ANDERSON, John Bayard
House: the Anderson switch. P. Duke. New
Repub 160:22-4 F 1 '69
ANDERSON, John M. and Peterson, M. R.
DDT: sublethal effects on brook trout ner-
vous system. bibliog Science 164:440-1 Ap
25 '69
ANDERSON, John R. and Ayala, S. C.
Trypanosome transmitted by plebotomus;
first report from the Americas. bibliog Sci-
ence 161:1023-5; 165:1380-1 S 6 '68, S 26
'69
ANDERSON, Jon
Child within him; poem. Poetry 114:23-4 Ap
'69
Of government; Next president; Mouths of
the poor; Robots, the city of Paradise; poems. Poetry 115:154-9 D '69
Parachutist; poem. New Yorker 45:36 Mr 22
'69

ANDERSON, Jourdon
To my old master; excerpt from The freed-
men's book. L. M. Child. Negro Hist Bul
32:15 Ja '69
ANDERSON, Keith M.
Ethnographic analogy and archeological in-
terpretation. bibliog Science 163:133-8 Ja
10 '69
ANDERSON, Kemmer
Cross fire; poem. Chr Cent 86:205 F 12 '69
ANDERSON, Kenneth N.
Eat your way to better health. Har Yrs 9:
6-13 F '69
How to stay warm. Field & S 74:53+ N '69
Mechanics of medicine: new tools for mend-
ing hearts. Pop Mech 131:120-3 My '69
ANDERSON, LaVere
Forgotten Lincoln. Read Digest 94:172-4+ F
'69
ANDERSON, Lee F. See Becker, J. M. jt.
auth.
ANDERSON, Leonard H.
IC lab power supply. Radio-Electr 40:49-53
Ag; 62-3+ S '69
ANDERSON, Lindsay
Current cinema. P. Kael. New Yorker 45:152+
Mr 15 '69
ANDERSON, Luther A.
Bag your buck on a crossing. Field & S 74:
46-7+ O '69
ANDERSON, Mary Lou
Christmas specials. PTA Mag 64:23 D '69
ANDERSON, Norman G.
Computer interfaced fast analyzers. bibliog
Science 166:317-24 O 17 '69
ANDERSON, Patrick
Only power Kissinger has is the confidence
of the President. N Y Times Mag p 10-
11+ Je 1 '69; Same abr. with title My
only power is the confidence of the Presi-
dent. Read Digest 95:161-5 O '69
ANDERSON, Paul
Paul Anderson can lift eight of you. J. F.
Ryan. il por Esquire 72:69-71+ Jl '69
World's strongest man. C. Trillin. New Yorker
44:38-40+ F 1 '69
ANDERSON, Richard M.
Anguish in the defense industry. Harvard
Bsns R 47:162-4+ N '69
Handling risk in defense contracting. Har-
vard Bsns R 47:90-8 Jl '69
ANDERSON, Robert
Future space flights; address, September 26,
1969. Vital Speeches 36:175-8 Ja 1 '70
ANDERSON, Robert V.
Pioneers and panthers. bibliog Cons 23:6-7 Je
'69
ANDERSON, Sherwood
Growing up in Winesburg. por Newsweek 74:
82-3 Ag 25 '69
Personal history. B. Weber. por Sat R 52:
38-9 Ag 23 '69
ANDERSON, Stephen S.
East Europe: the politics of recovery. Cur
Hist 57:207-13+ O '69
Yugoslavia: the diplomacy of balance. bibliog
f Cur Hist 56:212-17+ Ap '69
ANDERSON, Steve
Electronic golf range. Parks & Rec 4:45+
S '69
ANDERSON, Susan
Nation's Christmas tree. Parks & Rec 3:10-
13+ D '68
ANDERSON, Thelma
$11 plant-starter. Org Gard & Farm 16:86-8
D '69
ANDERSON, Thomas P.
Great fútbol war. Commonweal 90:479-80 Ag
8 '69
ANDERSON, W. E.
Put new life in your trophies. Outdoor Life
143:78-80+ F '69
ANDERSON, William C.
Two ton albatross; story. Good H 168:105-
12 Ap '69
ANDERTON, Craig
For your guitar, a compression sustainer.
Pop Electr 30:63-4+ My '69
ANDES MOUNTAINS
Andean delight: Nahuel Huapi National Park.
L. Zalamea. Travel 132:75 S '69
ANDRADE, Jorge Carrera. See Carrera An-
drade, J.
ANDREEVA, Tamara
Bells of San Luis Obispo. Américas 21:12-14
Ag '69
ANDREOTTI, Dante
Friendly fuzz. A. A. Rosenfeld. il Nation
208:503-7 Ap 21 '69
ANDREWS, Ed
Future of camping. por Camp Mag 41:5 Ja '69
ANDREWS, Gloria
In my opinion. por Seventeen 28:248 My '69
ANDREWS, Henry John
In private service. por Vogue 153:151-3 F 15
'69

ANDREWS, Hope
Living with antiques. Antiques 96:559-66 O '69
ANDREWS, James F.
Circulation and weather of 1968. Weatherwise 22:4-11 F '69
ANDREWS, Julie
Sweet Julie. H. Lawrenson. por Esquire 71: 62-4+ Ja '69
ANDREWS, Katherine A.
New concepts in composition. Engl J 58:96-101 Ja '69
ANDREWS, Kenneth R.
Toward professionalism in business management. bibliog f Harvard Bsns R 47:49-60 Mr '69
ANDREWS, Lewis M.
Making a million under thirty. Nation 208: 315-17 Mr 10 '69
ANDREWS, Martin H.
Open question. Nat R 21:338 Ap 8 '69
ANDREWS, Siri
Bertha Mahony Miller and Horn book publications. Horn Bk 45:566-9 O '69
ANDROGENESIS
Androgenesis conditioned by a mutation in maize. J. L. Kermicle. bibliog il Science 166: 1422-4 D 12 '69
ANDROGENS
Androgen accumulation and binding to macromolecules in seminal vesicles: inhibition by cyproterone. J. M. Stern and A. J. Eisenfeld. bibliog il Science 166:233-5 O 10 '69
    See also
    Methandrostenolone
ANDROID fiction. See Science fiction
ANDROIDS. See Automatons
ANDRON, Philip
Convenience foods? Paper service? Camp Mag 41:18-19 Je '69
ANDROUET, Pierre
Pierre Androuet: insatiable with cheese and snails. N. Lyon. Vogue 154:131 N 1 '69
ANDRUS, Ethel Percy, gerontology center. See Southern California university, Los Angeles—Ethel Percy Andrus gerontology center
ANDUJAR, Claudia
In the shadow of the mountain: photographs; with biographical sketch. por Natur Hist 78:4, 28-33 F '69
Tchikrin; photographs. Natur Hist 78:50-9+ O '69
ANECDOTES
    See also subhead Anecdotes, facetiae, satire, etc. under various subjects, e.g. Words, New—Anecdotes, facetiae, satire, etc.
ANECDOTES, Musical. See Music—Anecdotes, facetiae, satire, etc.
ANEMIA
Vitamin-related anemias; report of meeting. F. Weber and R. E. Olson. Science 164: 1311-12 Je 13 '69
    See also
    Leukemia
ANESHANSLEY, Daniel J. and others
Biochemistry at 100°C: explosive secretory discharge of bombardier beetles (brachinus) bibliog Science 165:61-3 Jl 4 '69; Same abr. with title Ingenuities of nature. Sat R 52: 48 Ap 2 '69
ANESTHESIA
    See also
    Analgesia
    Anesthetics
ANESTHETICS
Local anesthetics: significance of hydrogen bonding in mechanism of action. M. Sax and J. Pletcher. bibliog il Science 166:1546-8 D 19 '69
    See also
    Halothane
    Novocaine
    Pentothal sodium
ANEURYSMS
Magnetism in medical treatment. il Chem 42: 21-3 Mr '69
ANGEL, Aubie
Brown adipose cells: spontaneous mobilization of endogenously synthesized lipid. bibliog Science 163:288-90 Ja 17 '69
ANGEL, Klaus
Parent and child. N Y Times Mag p 170+ N 30 '69
ANGELES, Victoria de los
Many pleasures of the Spanish zarzuela. P. L. Miller. il por Am Rec G 35:536-7 Mr '69
Songs of Andalusia in the middle ages and renaissance. J. W. Barker. por Am Rec G 35:362-3 Ja '69
ANGELINO, Marie
Three California craftsmen. Am Artist 33:45-53+ S '69

ANGELL, Roger
Ainmosni. New Yorker 45:32-4 My 31 '69
How they brought the bad news from Ghent (N.Y.) to Aix (Kans.) New Yorker 45:24-7 Ja 3 '70
Life in these now United States. New Yorker 45:34-6 Mr 15 '69
Sporting scene (cont) New Yorker 45:70-80 Ag 9; 145-52+ N 1 '69
Your horoscope. New Yorker 45:33 Mr 29 '69
ANGELOCH, Robert
Outdoor sketching in miniature. Am Artist 33:48-9 Je '69
ANGELS
Men and angels, by T. Ward. Review
    Time il 94:54 D 26 '69
ANGEL'S trumpets. See Daturas
ANGER
Anger in children; excerpt. G. V. Sheviakov. Todays Ed 58:37 S '69
We just want to help you: a note on anger in adolescent group therapy. J. G. May and W. Main. Ment Hy 53:638-40 O '69
    See also
    Temper
ANGERMANN, Gerhard
More bad news for smokers. Read Digest 94:93-4 F '69
ÄNGGARD, Erik, and others
Prostaglandins: enzymatic analysis. bibliog Science 163:479-80 Ja 31 '69
ANGINA pectoris. See Heart—Diseases
ANGIOKERATOMA
Glycolipid and mucopolysaccharide abnormality in fibroblasts of Fabry's disease. R. Matalon and others. bibliog il Science 164: 1522-3 Je 27 '69
ANGKOR, Cambodia
Angkor Wat; place of great splendor; excerpts from Once around lightly. R. St John. il Travel & Camera 32:72-7 Jl '69
ANGLE, Lucy
It takes integrity to model and be yourself. por Seventeen 28:95+ Ja '69
ANGLICAN church. See Church of England
ANGLICAN church of Canada. See Church of England in Canada
ANGLING. See Fishing
ANGOLA
Angola: report from Hanoi II; with editorial comment. D. Barnett. il Ramp Mag 7:49-54 Ap '69
Eight years after the terror. D. L. Niddrie. il Nat R 21:1064-5+ O 21 '69
Report: Portuguese Africa. S. Meisler. Atlan 223:14+ Ja '69
ANGST, Ernst
Liberal's lexicon; excerpts from So you want to be a liberal? Nat R 21:1177 N 18 '69
ANGUILLA (island)
Anguilla caper. A. Lejeune. Nat R 21:386 Ap 22 '69
Better late; Lord Caradon's role. Newsweek 73:50 Ap 14 '69
Britain's Bay of Piglets. il Time 93:28+ Mr 28 '69
British take isle. il Sr Schol 94:15-17 Ap 11 '69
Invaded Anguilla: island of trouble in a strategic sea. il U S News 66:8+ Mr 31 '69
Lion that meowed. il Newsweek 73:40+ Mr 31 '69
Mini-war in the least of the Lesser Antilles; with battle reports from the front and home front by B. Bruns and J. Newcombe. il Life 66:55-6 Mr 28 '69
Oh, what a lovely 'oliday; British occupation. il Newsweek 73:44 Ap 7 '69
ANGUISH, Mental. See Suffering
ANGUS, Robert
Notes from our correspondents. Hi Fi 19: 24-5 My '69
Scrutable Orient. Hi Fi 19:63-5 O '69
Video topics (cont) Hi Fi 19:36 F '69
ANHEUSER-Busch, incorporated
Williamsburg's new flavor; brewery project. Time 94:93 S 26 '69
ANHYDROUS ammonia. See Ammonia
ANIMAL behavior. See Animals—Habits and behavior
ANIMAL bites
R for insect and animal bites. G. M. Knox. Bet Hom & Gard 47:91-2 Jl '69
ANIMAL cages. See Cages
ANIMAL calling
Truth about calling elk. L. Bowman. il Field & S 74:74-5+ Ag '69
ANIMAL collecting. See Animals—Collection

ANIMAL communication
Animal languages; excerpts from Signals in the animal world. D. Burkhardt and others. il Todays Ed 58:34-6+ O '69
Animal talk. F. L. Remington. il Mech Illus 65:76+ F '69
Chimp human chit-chat. il Sci Digest 65:73-4 F '69
Discourse with an ape. Sci Am 220:50 Ja '69
Many voices of life. J. C. George. il Nat Wildlife 7:34-7 Je '69; Same abr. with title Surprising signals in the wild. Read Digest 94:163-4+ Je '69
Messages of vertebrate communication; adaptation of address, December 28, 1967. W. J. Smith. bibliog Science 165:145-50 Jl 11 '69
Secrets of the animal world. R. Petrow. il Pop Mech 132:84-7+ S '69
Surprising signals in the wild; excerpts. J. George. il Read Digest 94:163-4+ Je '69
Teaching sign language to a chimpanzee. R. A. Gardner and B. T. Gardner. bibliog il Science 165:664-72 Ag 15 '69
See also
Animal sounds
Insect communication
Sound production by animals
ANIMAL courtship. See Courtship of animals
ANIMAL evolution. See Evolution
ANIMAL experimentation
Animal experimentation by high school students; letter. F. B. Orlans. Science 163:128-9 Ja 10 '69
Is your food safe? Dispute over testing; with interview with U. Saffiotti. il U S News 67:44-7 D 15 '69
See also
Laboratory animals
Stimulation (physiology)
ANIMAL extinction. See Animals, Extinct
ANIMAL husbandry. See Livestock
ANIMAL intelligence
Creative monkeys of Koshima. B. O'Connell. il Sci Digest 65:80-2 Ap '69
Music hath charms; experiments with albino rats. il Time 93:62 My 30 '69
See also
Animal learning
Maze tests
ANIMAL introduction
Bobwhite for western New York? S. B. Robeson. il Cons 24:8-9 D '69
Indigens and immigrants; plants and animals in the New York city region. A. B. Klots. il Natur Hist 78:38-45 Ap '69
Tale of a snail; giant African land snail introduced into Miami. il Time 94:51 O 17 '69
ANIMAL kingdom. See Zoology
ANIMAL language. See Animal communication; Sound production by animals
ANIMAL learning
Maternal influence in learning by observation in kittens. P. Chesler. bibliog il Science 166:901-3 N 14 '69
Olfactory stimuli and the pseudo-extinction effect. E. A. Wasserman and D. D. Jensen. bibliog il Science 166:1307-9 D 5 '69
Stimulus generalization as a function of discrimination learning with and without errors. J. Lyons. il Science 163:490-1 Ja 31 '69
ANIMAL locomotion
Agile mollusc. A. D. Ansell. il Sea Front 15:180-4 My '69
See also
Walking
ANIMAL lore
Imaginary beings; tr. by N. T. Di Giovanni. J. L. Borges and M. Guerrero. New Yorker 45:39-46 O 4 '69
See also
Bestiaries
Unicorns
ANIMAL pets. See Pets
ANIMAL populations
Estimating the number of animals: a rapid method for unidentified individuals. W. R. Hanson; reply with rejoinder. J. T. Enright and J. H. Wormuth. il Science 165:824-5 Ag 22 '69
Green sea turtles; a discrete simulation of density-dependent population regulation. H. R. Bustard and K. P. Tognetti. bibliog il Science 163:939-41 F 28 '69
Population explosion; question of cottontails. il Cons 23:29 Je '69
Wildlife population cycles. P. M. Kelsey. il Cons 24:32 O '69
See also
Animal tagging
Bird populations
Insect populations

ANIMAL pottery
Creatures made from collapsed pots. J. Kozlowski. il Ceram Mo 17:16-19 O '69
ANIMAL psychology. See Animal intelligence
ANIMAL sculpture
Art as an antidote for the boredom of retirement. J. B. How. il Am Artist 33:30-1+ N '69
Camel as art; exhibit at Whitney museum. il Time 93:70 Ap 4 '69
ANIMAL shows. See Animals—Training
ANIMAL sonar. See Sonar
ANIMAL sounds
Dialects in elephant seals. B. J. Le Boeuf and R. S. Peterson. bibliog il Science 166:1654-6 D 26 '69
Songs of an August night. K. W. Moseley. il Nat Wildlife 7:32-4 Ag '69
See also
Insect sounds
ANIMAL tagging
Deer trapping and tagging. W. T. Hesselton. il Cons 23:14-17 F '69
Ear-tagging moose. F. Dickie. il Am For 75:28-9+ Ap '69
Stalking the mountain lion, to save him. M. G. Hornocker. il Nat Geog 136:638-55 N '69
See also
Fish tagging
ANIMAL temperature. See Temperature, Animal and human
ANIMAL toys. See Toys
ANIMAL training. See Animals—Training
ANIMAL trials and punishment. See Animals, Prosecution and punishment of
ANIMAL waste as fuel. See Fuel
ANIMALS
How good a zoologist are you? quiz. J. Daugherty and M. Daugherty. il Sci Digest 66:78-80 Ag '69
See also
Age (animals)
Herbivora
Nature
Pets
Photography of animals
Wildlife
also names of animals, e.g. Camels

Accidents and hazards
See also
Automobile driving—Animal hazards
Deer—Collisions with snowmobiles

Age
See Age (animals)

Age determination
How to age your deer. P. M. Kelsey. il Cons 24:48-9+ O '69

Anecdotes, facetiae, satire, etc.
Anthropomorphizers are coming! R. Starnes. Field & S 74:22+ S '69

Breeding
See Breeding

Capture
Consumption of wildlife by man; reprint. W. G. Conway. il Parks & Rec 4:20-6+ F '69
See also
International animal exchange, incorporated

Collection
What Noah left behind. J. Goméz-Sicre. il Américas 21:32-7 O '69

Courtship
See Courtship of animals

Economic value
See Zoology, Economic

Feet
See Foot (animals)

Food and feeding
Gulp! egg-eating snake. il Natur Hist 78:42-3 Je '69
Winter feeding. P. M. Kelsey. Cons 24:33 O '69
See also
Food chains (ecology)

Habits and behavior
Big animals sleep best. Sci Digest 66:37 S '69
Fire Smokey? il Sr Schol 94:18 F 14 '69
Genetic aspects of learning and memory in mice. D. Bovet and others. bibliog il Science 163:139-49 Ja 10 '69; Reply with rejoinder. K. R. Henry and others. 165:1148 S 12 '69

ANIMALS—Habits and behavior—*Continued*
Has Smokey Bear outlived his usefulness?
public perception of and attitude towards
wild animals. E. G. Bowman; discussion.
Am For 75:2-3+ Ja; 2 F '69
Multimedia zoo: night becomes day for noc-
turnal animals; Bronx zoo. J. S. Margolies.
il Arch Forum 130:86-91 Je '69
Must we have zoos? Yes, but. . . D. Morris.
Read Digest 94:195-200 Mr '69
Object-carrying by rats: an approach to the
behavior produced by brain stimulation.
A. G. Phillips and others. bibliog il Sci-
ence 166:903-5 N 14 '69
Plastic animals fool real ones in Africa. il
Life 66:69-71 My 2 '69
Profiles; K. Z. Lorenz, Austrian zoologist,
specializing in ethology. J. Alsop. New
Yorker 45:39-42+ Mr 8 '69
Queuing behavior of spiny lobsters. W. Herrn-
kind. bibliog il Science 164:1425-7 Je 20 '69
Secrets of the animal world. R. Petrow. il
Pop Mech 132:84-7+ S '69
Strange world of night creatures. B. Ford.
il Sci Digest 66:38-42 O '69
T. C. Schneirla and animal behavior. E.
Tobach. il Natur Hist 78:52-7 Ja '69
Uncus and amygdala lesions: effects on so-
cial behavior in the free-ranging rhesus
monkey. D. Dicks and others. bibliog il
Science 165:69-71 Jl 4 '69
See also
Animal intelligence
Birds—Habits and behavior
Courtship of animals
Hibernation
Sex behavior

Intelligence
See Animal intelligence

Jaws
See Jaws (animals)

Language
See Animal communication

Migration
Queuing behavior of spiny lobsters. W. Herrn-
kind. bibliog il Science 164:1425-7 Je 20 '69
'69
See also
Animal tagging

Photographs
Cougar! Cougar! Nat Wildlife 7:14-15 Ap
'69
Huh. . .what hot tin roof? leopard in a tree.
J. Carrick. Outdoor Life 143:72-3+ Mr '69
See also
Photography of animals

Poetry
See also
Deer—Poetry

Protection
See also
American society for the prevention of cru-
elty to animals
Game protection

Protective equipment
See Defense mechanisms (biology)

Sight
See Sight (animals)

Sleep
See Animals—Habits and behavior

Stories
See also
Wolves—Stories

Training
Learning in fish with transplanted brain
tissue. D. E. Bresler and M. E. Bitterman.
bibliog il Science 163:590-2 F 7 '69
Man who makes pets of gorillas. D. Both-
well and D. Coleman. il Sci Digest 65:26-
31 F '69
What psychological conditioning can do for
animals; Farmyard theatre. B. Ford. il Sci
Digest 66:76-81 N '69
See also
Elephants—Training
Horse training

Transportation
Moving day for sea otters. G. Laycock. il
Audubon 71:58-62+ Ja '69

Treatment
Henry Bergh: founder of the ASPCA. C. W.
Ferguson. il PTA Mag 63:9-11 My '69
Parting shots: mad dogs, horses and English-
men; with photographs. Life 67:66A-68 D
19 '69

Thrill killers: Superior national forest; with
editorial comment. G. Lazan. il Am For
75:6-7+, 11 My '69
See also
Animal experimentation
Animals in advertising
ANIMALS, Aquatic. See Marine fauna
ANIMALS, Cruelty to. See Animals—Treat-
ment
ANIMALS, Domestication of. See Domestica-
tion
ANIMALS, Effect of light on. See Light—
Physiological effects
ANIMALS, Effect of radiation on. See Radia-
tion—Physiological effects
ANIMALS, Extinct
Great dinosaur disaster. D. Cohen. il Sci
Digest 65:45-52 Mr '69
See also
Dinosaurs
ANIMALS, Food habits of. See Animals—Food
and feeding
ANIMALS, Geographic distribution of. See
Geographical distribution of animals and
plants
ANIMALS, Germfree. See Germfree life
ANIMALS, Infancy of
Communal nursing in mice: influence of
multiple mothers on the growth of the
young. A. Sayler and M. Salmon. bibliog
il Science 164:1309-10 Je 13 '69
Small fry; names for young animals. H.
Borland. il Audubon 71:13-15 My '69
See also
Birds, Infancy of
ANIMALS, Injurious and beneficial. See Zool-
ogy, Economic
ANIMALS, Mythical
See also
Animal lore
Dragons
Unicorns
ANIMALS, Performing. See Animals—Training
ANIMALS, Predatory
See also
Predation (zoology)
Trapping
ANIMALS, Prehistoric. See Animals, Extinct
ANIMALS, Prosecution and punishment of
Most celebrated dog case ever tried in John-
son County, Missouri, or the world; Old
Drum trial, 1869; C. Burden vs. L. Hornsby.
G. Carson. il Natur Hist 78:6-8+ D '69
ANIMALS, Respiration of. See Respiration
ANIMALS, Training of. See Animals—Training
ANIMALS, Water requirements of. See Water
requirements of animals
ANIMALS in advertising
Lion's share: a union for the animals. News-
week 74:53 Ag 25 '69
ANIMALS in art
See also
Animal pottery
Animal sculpture
Design, Decorative—Animal forms
ANIMALS in captivity. See Menageries; Zo-
ological gardens
ANIMALS in fiction. See Animals in literature
ANIMALS in literature
Will the real Peter Rabbit please stand up?
letter to the editor. J. Hurwitz. Library J
94:1687-8 Ap 15 '69
See also
Bestiaries
ANIMALS in moving pictures
Cats: first International cat film festival, or,
Intercat '69. New Yorker 45:19-20 Ja 3 '69
ANIMALS in opera
Animals in opera. R. Kerr. il Opera N 33:6-7
F 22 '69
ANIMATED cartoons. See Moving pictures—
Animated cartoons
ANIMUS; ballet. See Ballets—Criticisms
ANISFIELD-Wolf awards
SR's 1969 Anisfield-Wolf awards. S. W.
Little. Sat R 52:23 My 24 '69
ANKER, Dorothy. See Bowman, B. jt. auth.
ANKRUM, Janet. See Miller, M. jt. auth.
ANN ARBOR, Mich.

Housing
Something new in student strikes; rent strike
by University of Michigan studenst. D.
Zwerdling. New Repub 160:13 My 31 '69
Tenants' revolt in Ann Arbor. N. C. Mills.
Commonweal 91:294-5 D 5 '69
ANNA Galina's théâtre d'art du ballet. See
Ballet—France

ANNALS of America (publication)
New Annals of America. H. J. Sievers. Amer-
ica 120:491 Ap 26 '69
Twenty-five issues programmed for retrieval.
D. J. Boorstin. Sat R 52:25-7+ Ag 9 '69
ANNAPOLIS, Md.
Annapolis has it all. B. Schill and B. Schill.
il Yachting 125:69+ My '69
ANNAPOLIS naval academy. See United
States naval academy. Annapolis
ANNE, princess of Great Britain
Coming of age. por Newsweek 73:66 Mr 17 '69
ANNE ARUNDEL COUNTY, Md.

Historic houses, etc.
Living with antiques; Tulip Hill, the Mary-
land home of Mr and Mrs Lewis R. An-
drews. H. Andrews. il Antiques 96:559-66
O '69
ANNE Frank museum. See Amsterdam, Nether-
lands—Historic houses, etc.
ANNEALING
See also
Steel—Heat treatment
ANNELIDS
Honeycomb worm; sabellaria worm of the
bristleworm family. D. P. Wilson. il Sea
Front 15:322-9 N '69
See also
Nervous system—Annelids
ANNENBERG, Walter H.
Knight in Philadelphia. il por Newsweek 74:
98 N 10 '69
Letting go of a legacy. Time 94:88 N 7 '69
Making haste slowly. il por Time 93:15 Mr
21 '69
Trials of Walter Annenberg. W. F. Buckley,
jr. Nat R 21:870-1 Ag 26 '69
ANNETTE Walters, Sister. See Walters, A.
ANNIVERSARIES
See also
Fourth of July
ANNIVERSARY gifts. See Gifts
ANNUAL meetings, Stockholders. See Stock-
holders meetings
ANNUAL reports, corporate. See Corporation
reports
ANNUALS (plants)
Annual flowers 1969. il Horticulture 47:30-3
Ja '69
Annuals for edgings. V. Howie. il Horticul-
ture 47:30-3+ My '69
For summer splendor; annuals in containers.
H. Mason. il Bet Hom & Gard 47:74-7 Mr
'69
Winter-spring flowers you plant in the fall.
il Sunset 143:174-6 S '69
ANNUITIES
Tax-deferred annuity program. Todays Ed
58:50 Ap '69
See also
Insurance. Life
ANNULMENT of marriage. See Marriage—An-
nulment
ANNUNZIO, Gabriele d'
Italian heroines. A. Arbasino. il Vogue 153:
202+ Ap 1 '69
ANOMALOUS water. See Water
ANORTHOSITE
Anorthosite belts, continental drift, and the
anorthosite event. N. Herz. bibliog il Sci-
ence 164:944-7 My 23 '69
ANOTHER mother for peace (organization)
See Women and peace
ANOUILH, Jean
Ardèle. Criticism
Sat R 52:40 My 10 '69
Cher Antoine. Criticism
New Yorker 45:196+ N 29 '69
Time por 94:57 N 14 '69
ANOXEMIA
Carbon monoxide-induced arterial hypox-
emia. J. S. Brody and R. F. Coburn. bibliog
il Science 164:1297-8 Je 13 '69
Hypobaric hypoxia; effects on early develop-
ment of tryptophan oxygenase in neonatal
rats. R. P. Francesconi and M. Mager. bib-
liog il Science 166:1412-13 D 12 '69
Mental retardation due to germinal matrix
infarction. A. Towbin. bibliog il Science 164:
156-61 Ap 11 '69
ANRIG, Gregory R.
Decentralization controversy. Am Ed 5:2-3
F '69; Same abr. Ed Digest 34:1-3 My '69
Trouble in the high schools. Am Ed 5:2-4 O
'69
ANSELL, Alan D.
Agile mollusc; with biographical sketch. por
Sea Front 15:180-4, 190-1 My '69
ANSERMET, Ernest
Ansermet's own valedictory. R. Lawrence. il
por Sat R 52:50 D 27 '69

Ernest Ansermet, November 11, 1883-February
20, 1969. W. Sargeant. por Opera N 33:29
Ap 5 '69
Music's debt to Ernest Ansermet; the great
Swiss conductor. A. Haddy and T. Heinitz.
por Sat R 52:55+ Mr 29 '69
ANSHEN, Melvin
Management of ideas. Harvard Bsns R 47:99-
107 Jl '69
ANSONIA, Conn.

Public works
Ansonia's public works complex. L. Hale
and W. La Rovera. il Am City 84:101-3
Jl; 94-6 Ag '69
ANTARCTIC exploration
Antarctica, international land of science; re-
print. G. Wendt. il UNESCO Courier 22:
14-15 Ag '69
ANTARCTIC REGIONS
Antarctic research, a prelude to space re-
search; adaptation of address, September
18, 1968. E. Stuhlinger. Space World F-5-
65:5-11 My '69
Prelude to space research; Antarctic research
program; excerpt from address, September
1968. E. Stuhlinger. Bul Atom Sci 25:24-7
Mr '69
Prospects for international cooperation on
the moon; the Antarctic analogy. P. M.
Smith. il Bul Atom Sci 25:36-40 S '69
Watching seals at Turtle Rock. C. Ray and
M. A. DeCamp. il Natur Hist 78:26-35 Mr
'69
See also
Antarctic exploration
Geology—Antarctic Regions
Ice—Polar Regions
Oceanographic research—Antarctic Regions
Paleontology—Antarctic Regions
Soils—Antarctic Regions
ANTEATERS
Little package, big kick; numbats. il Sci
Digest 66:89 O '69
ANTELOPE hunting
Short order antelope. L. Miracle. il Outdoor
Life 144:62-3+ O '69
See also
Pronghorn hunting
ANTELOPES
Antelope of East Africa; with photographs
by J. Dominis and editorial comment by
R. Graves. Life 67:5, 74-85 D 5 '69
Eland and the oryx. C. R. Taylor. il Sci Am
220:88-95 Ja '69
ANTELOPES, American. See Pronghorns
ANTENNA rotators. See Television antennas
—Rotators
ANTENNAS (electronics)
In the news; multi frequency ground antenna
for research and comunications satellite
applications. il Space World F-6-66:44-5 Je
'69
See also
Radio antennas
Television antennas
ANTHERIDIOGENS. See Hormones, Plant
ANTHOLOGIES
Making of anthologies. W. Cole. Writers
Digest 49:48-52 Mr '69
Range of voices. B. B. Stretch. Sat R 52:70-1
Mr 15 '69
This is my best; ed. by W. Burnett. Review
Sat R 52:41 F 15 '69. D. Dempsey
ANTHONY, Charles
How to soup up low-quality speakers. Radio-
Electr 40:62-3 Mr '69
ANTHONY, Daniel S.
Handwriting analysis. Mech Illus 65:58-60+
D '69
ANTHONY, M. V.
Environmental contamination; address, Feb-
ruary 1, 1969. Vital Speeches 35:434-8 My
1 '69
ANTHRACENE
See also
Naphthacene
ANTHRACNOSE
Anthracnose in sycamores. R. Dallmer. il
Horticulture 47:22+ Je '69
ANTHROP, Donald F.
Environmental noise pollution; a new threat
to sanity. Bul Atom Sci 25:11-16 My '69
ANTHROPOGEOGRAPHY
New geography; Central place theory. P. R.
Gould. il Harper 238:91-2+ Mr '69; Reply.
R. E. Crist. 239:6+ Jl '69
See also
Man—Migrations
ANTHROPOLOGISTS
See also
Leakey, R.
Mead, M.

ANTHROPOLOGY
Public policy and behavioral science; excerpt from testimony before the U.S. Senate foreign relations committee. June 20, 1969. M. Mead. Bul Atom Sci 25:8-10 D '69
Rousseau, father of anthropology; summary of address, reprint. C. Lévi-Strauss. il UNESCO Courier 22:61-3 Ag '69
  See also
Culture
Evolution
Language and languages
Man
Man—Migrations
Man, Prehistoric
Society, Primitive
Somatology

ANTHROPOLOGY, Psychological. See Psychological anthropology

ANTHROPONOSES. See Communicable diseases in animals

ANTI-AMERICANISM. See United States—Foreign opinion

ANTI-BALLISTIC missile system. See Guided missiles—Defenses

ANTIBIOTIC feed supplements
Penicillin by the pound. M. E. Duffy. bibliog il Environ 11:14-21 O '69
Will we lose the use of antibiotics? J. Herrick. Suc Farm 67:36 Ag '69

ANTIBIOTICS
Animal antibiotic attack; British plan to restrict use in food animals. D. Fishlock. il Sci N 97:26 Ja 3 '70
Antibiotics alter methotrexate metabolism and excretion. D. S. Zaharko and others. bibliog il Science 166:887-8 N 14 '69
Antibiotics in court; Panalba case. Sci N 96:6 Jl 5 '69
Drug against a virus: rifampicin. H. Gillon. il Sci N 96:414 N 1 '69
FDA and Panalba: a conflict of commercial, therapeutic goals? M. Mintz. Science 165:875-81 Ag 29 '69; Reply. R. T. Parfet, jr. bibliog 166:1354 D 12 '69
FDA vs. the boss: Panalba case. il Sci N 95:523 My 31 '69
Infection structures from rust urediospores: effect of RNA and protein synthesis inhibitors. L. D. Dunkle and others. bibliog il Science 163:481-2 Ja 31 '69
Penicillin by the pound; agricultural uses. M. E. Duffy. bibliog il Environ 11:14-21 O '69
Peptide antibiotics. M. Bodanszky and D. Perlman. bibliog il Science 163:352-8 Ja 24 '69
Phosphonomycin, a new antibiotic produced by strains of streptomyces. D. Hendlin and others. bibliog il Science 166:122-3 O 3 '69
Phosphonomycin: structure and synthesis. B. G. Christensen and others. bibliog il Science 166:123-5 O 3 '69
Ribosomal protein conferring sensitivity to the antibiotic spectinomycin in escherichia coli. A. Bollen and others. bibliog il Science 165:85-6 Jl 4 '69
Ventricular arrhythmias related to antibiotic usage in dogs. T. J. Regan and others. bibliog il Science 165:509-10 Ag 1 '69
  See also
Actinomycin
Bacteria—Resistance and sensitivity
Chloramphenicol
Colicines
Fusidic acid
Neomycin
Puromycin
Streptomycin
Tetracyclines

ANTICOAGULANTS
  See also
Warfarin

ANTI-COLLISION systems. See Airplanes—Safety devices and measures

ANTI-COMMUNIST measures in the United States. See Communism—United States—Anti-Communist measures; United States—Foreign relations—Anti-Communist measures

ANTI-COMMUNIST movements

Asia, Southeastern
Some dilemmas of counterinsurgency. G. K. Tanham and D. J. Duncanson. For Affairs 48:113-22 O '69

Thailand
What are we doing in Thailand? Z. B. Grant. New Repub 160:19-21 My 24 '69

ANTI-COMMUNIST propaganda. See Propaganda

ANTI-CRIME legislation. See Crime prevention

ANTI-DEFAMATION league. See B'nai b'rith—Anti-defamation league

ANTIDEPRESSANTS
  See also
Amitriptyline
Desipramine

ANTI-DEPRESSION measures. See United States—Economic policy

ANTI-DISCRIMINATION laws. See Race discrimination

ANTI-EVOLUTION controversy. See Tennessee evolution controversy

ANTI-EVOLUTION legislation. See Evolution—Laws and legislation

ANTIFERROMAGNETISM. See Magnetism

ANTIFLU drug. See Amantadine hydrochloride

ANTIFOULING paint. See Paint, Protective

ANTIFREEZE solutions
Secret of those new anti-leak anti-freezes. R. C. Sickler. il Pop Sci 195:70-1 N '69
Winterize your home on wheels. B. F. Samuels. il Pop Sci 195:170-3+ O '69

ANTIGENS and antibodies
Antibodies to polynucleotides: distribution in human serums. D. Koffler and others. bibliog il Science 166:1648-9 D 26 '69
Antigenic streptococcal components in acute glomerulonephritis. G. Treser and others. bibliog il Science 163:676-7 F 14 '69
Antigenicity: some molecular aspects. M. Sela. bibliog il Science 166:1365-74 D 12 '69
Antigens on the cell; role of immune system in growth and control of human cancers. B. J. Culliton. il Sci N 95:457-9 My 10 '69
Duplicate plating of immune cell products: analysis of globulin class secretion by single cells. B. Merchant and Z. Brahmi. bibliog il Science 167:69-72 Ja 2 '70
Elution of glomerular bound antibodies in experimental streptococcal glomerulonephritis. L. H. Lindberg and K. L. Vosti. bibliog il Science 166:1032-3 N 21 '69
Feline leukemia virus: occurrence of viral antigen in the tissues of cats with lymphosarcoma and other diseases. W. D. Hardy, jr. and others. bibliog il Science 166:1019-21 N 21 '69
Inv(1) allotype: effect of immunoglobulin G heavy chain subtype on its expression. A. G. Steinberg and I. Rostenberg. bibliog il Science 164:1072-3 My 30 '69
Leukemia-associated antigens in the mixed leukocyte culture test. M. L. Bach and others. bibliog il Science 166:1520-2 D 19 '69
Localization of antigenic determinants in the polypeptide chains of collagen. D. Michaeli and others. bibliog il Science 166:1522-4 D 19 '69
Macrophage ribonucleoprotein: nature of the antigenic fragment. A. A. Gottlieb. bibliog il Science 165:592-4 Ag 8 '69
Mammary tumor virus antigen: sensitive immunoassay. L. R. Sibal and others. bibliog il Science 164:76-8 Ap 4 '69
Molecular heterogeneity of human lymphoid (HL-A) alloantigens. D. L. Mann and others. bibliog il Science 163:1460-2 Mr 28 '69
Protein-bacteriophage conjugates: application in detection of antibodies and antigens. J. Haimovich and M. Sela. bibliog il Science 164:1279-80 Je 13 '69
Receptor site for a bacterial virus. R. Losick and P. W. Robbins. il Sci Am 221:120-4 bibliog(p 166) N '69
Tadpole antibodies against frog hemoglobin and their effect on development. G. M. Maniatis and others. bibliog il Science 165:67-9 Jl 4 '69
Transplantation antigens. B. D. Kahan and R. A. Reisfeld. bibliog Science 164:514-21 My 2 '69
Tumor-specific antigens detected by inhibition of macrophage migration. B. S. Kronman and others. il Science 165:296-7 Jl 18 '69
  See also
Antiserum
Autoimmune diseases
Complement fixation
Complements (immunity)
Gamma globulins
Globulinemia

ANTI-GRAVITATION. See Gravitation

ANTIGUA (Island)
Antigua. I. Stanger. il Harp Baz 102:106+ F '69

ANTIGUA, Guatemala

Architecture
Architecture of Antigua Guatemala 1543-1773, by V. L. Annis. Review
  Américas il 21:36-9 Ag '69. F. L. Phelps

ANTIHEMORRHAGIC vitamin. See Vitamins—
Vitamin K

ANTI-IMPERIALISM. See Imperialism

ANTI-INFLATION measures. See Inflation
(finance)

ANTI-INTELLECTUALISM. See Intellectuals

ANTILLES. See West Indies

ANTI-LOCUST research center. See Grasshoppers—Control

ANTIMATTER. See Matter; Matter, Interstellar

ANTIMETABOLITES
See also
Acetoxycycloheximide

ANTIMILITARISM. See Militarism

ANTIMISSILE defense system. See Guided
missiles—Defenses

ANTI-NEGRO prejudice. See Race prejudice

ANTIOCH college, Yellow Springs, Ohio
Exclude whites? No, says top Negro educator. U S News 66:18 Je 2 '69

ANTIOCH review
Poetry; from the editorial desk. J. Jerome.
Writers Digest 49:26-9+ Ap '69

ANTIOXIDANTS
Reticulocytosis in response to dietary antio-
xidants. B. T. March and others. bibliog
il Science 164:1398-400 Je 20 '69
See also
Ethoxyquin

ANTI-PARTICLES.   See Particles (nuclear
physics)

ANTIPERSONNEL weapons. See Weapons

ANTI-POVERTY program, 1964-
Antipoverty programs. W. D. Boutwell. PTA
Mag 63:33-4 My '69
Antipoverty war under fire again. il U S
News 66:37-41 Je 30 '69
Blaming Ophelia for not playing Hamlet;
Community action program. D. Yankelovich.
il Fortune 79:197-8+ Ap '69
Disadvantaged. L. A. Candeub. Sat R 52:60-2
O 25 '69
Evaluating the war on poverty; symposium,
ed. by L. A. Ferman. bibliog f il Ann Am
Acad 385:1-156 S '69
Great society's poor law, by S. A. Levitan.
Review
Commentary 48:99-101+ O '69. B. B.
Seligman
Nation 209:228-9 S 8 '69 G. Brager
Maximum feasible misunderstanding, by D.
P. Moynihan. Review
Cath World 210:127-8 D '69. D. O'Shea
Commentary 47:87+ My '69. S. Thernstrom
New Repub 160:23-4 F 22 '69. F. Pierce
New Yorker 45:143-6+ Je 7 '69. N. Bliven
Science 164:663-5 My 9 '69. H. W. Riecken
New look for the war on poverty. U S News
66:10 Mr 3 '69
Politics of anti-poverty; commitment to com-
munity action. R. H. Davidson. il Nation
208:233-7 F 24 '69
The poor, the power structure and the pole-
micist. H. Wolman. Commonweal 90:267-9
My 16 '69
Poverty audit; study of the Office of eco-
nomic opportunity and its anti-poverty
programs. New Repub 160:7 Mr 29 '69
Poverty: in search of the best weapons. Bsns
W p 114 Je 21 '69
Poverty, politics and social studies. J. P.
Fitzpatrick. America 120:558-61 My 10 '69
Voting rights or wrongs; House votes for
extension. il Newsweek 74:20 D 22 '69
War and poverty. Sci N 95:232-3 Mr 8 '69
Waste in poverty war; an official appraisal;
General accounting office report. il U S
News 66:58 Mr 31 '69
See also
Chicago—Anti-poverty program
Kentucky—Anti-poverty program
Public welfare—United States
Roanoke, Va.—Anti-poverty program
Washington, D.C.—Anti-poverty program

ANTI-PRIVACY. See Privacy, Right of

ANTIQUE airplanes. See Aeronautics—History

ANTIQUE automobile museums. See Automobile
museums

ANTIQUE automobiles

Collectors and collecting
See Automobiles—Collectors and collecting

ANTIQUE dealers
Antique dealers as educators. L. F. Reals.
Hobbies 74:98EE Je '69

ANTIQUE dolls. See Dolls

ANTIQUE jewelry. See Jewelry

ANTIQUES
Antiques are for everybody. il Am Home 72:
39 Ja '69
Antiques: questions and answers. L. A.
Boger. See issues of House & garden in-
corporating Living for young homemakers
Antiques set the stage for historical novels.
K. Dulgar. il Hobbies 74:98V-98W+ Jl '69
Boudinot furnishings in the Art museum of
Princeton university. H. Backlin-Landman.
il Antiques 96:366-71 S '69
Clues and footnotes; ed. by W. D. Garrett. il
Antiques 96:808+ D '69
Living with antiques:
Blakeford, in Queen Anne's County. E. A.
W. Miles. il Antiques 95:526-31 Ap '69
Camden, New Jersey, residence of Mr and
Mrs Joseph Wiederspohn. L. H. Solis-
Cohen. il Antiques 95:832-7 Je '69
Cogswell's Grant, the Essex County home
of Mr and Mrs Bertram K. Little. A.
Winchester. il Antiques 95:242-51 F '69
Connecticut home of Mary Allis. W. D.
Garrett. il Antiques 96:754-62 N '69
Massachusetts home of Mr & Mrs Cham-
berlain. N. G. Chamberlain and S.
Chamberlain. il Antiques 95:696-701 My
'69
Millwood: the Mercer County, Kentucky,
residence of Mr and Mrs Robert Mc-
Alfee Brewer. il Antiques 96:82-7 Jl '69
New York apartment of Mr and Mrs Leon
Levy. M. D. Schwartz. il Antiques 96:
376-81 S '69
Tulip Hill, the Maryland home of Mr
and Mrs Lewis R. Andrews. H. Andrews.
il Antiques 96:559-66 O '69
Widehall in Chestertown, Kent County.
E. Gaines. il Antiques 95:532-7 Ap '69
Wye house, in Talbot County. E. Gaines.
il Antiques 95:520-5 Ap '69
So you've been looking at antiques. Chang-
ing T 23:23-4 My '69
See also
Art objects
Chairs
Clocks
Collectors and collecting
Music boxes
Bibliography
Books about antiques. R. Davidson. See issues
of Antiques
Museum publications. Antiques 95:410+ Mr
'69
Exhibitions
Calendar of shows. See issues of Antiques
Current and coming. E. P. Birk. See issues
of Antiques

ANTIQUES, Reproductions of
Masterpiece furniture made in America;
from England's stately Woburn abbey. il
House B 111:144-7 My '69

ANTIQUES, Theft of
Château gang; excerpt from The discriminating thief. D. Leitch. il Horizon 11:114-
20 Spr '69

ANTIQUES dealers. See Antique dealers

ANTIQUITIES. See Archeology

ANTIQUITIES, Forgery of. See Forgery of
works of art

ANTIQUITY of man. See Man—Origin and antiquity

ANTI-SEMITISM
A.D.L. finds anti-Semitism on rise in New
York schools. Chr Cent 86:175 F 5 '69
Anti-Semitism persists in Italian and Spanish
religious textbooks. Chr Cent 83:1035 Ag 6
'69
Black anti-Semitism. J. Leo. Commonweal
89:618-20 F 14 '69; Discussion. 89:695+; 90:
3+ Mr 7, 21 '69
Black revolution & the Jewish question. E.
Raab; discussion. Commentary 47:6+ Ap
'69
Blacks, Jews & the intellectuals. N. Glazer.
Commentary 47:33-9 Ap '69; Discussion.
48:4+ Jl '69
Hatred abuilding; destruction of places of
worship and education. Chr Today 13:25
F 14 '69
How free the air? increasing anti-Semitism
among New York's militant black com-
munity. il Newsweek 73:25-6 F 10 '69
Inflating the threat of black anti-semitism.
J. Featherstone. New Repub 160:14-15 Mr 8
'69
Judaism and Christian education: the Stro-
ber report. Chr Cent 86:1410 N 5 '69; Dis-
cussion. 86:1583 D 10 '69
Mayor Lindsay and the Jewish community.
W. F. Buckley, jr. Nat R 21:88 Ja 28 '69
Memoirs of an anti-Semite. G. Von Rezzori.
New Yorker 45:42-52+ Ap 26 '69

ANTI-SEMITISM—*Continued*
Myth of black anti-Semitism. J. B. Sheerin. Cath World 209:50-1 My '69; Reply. A. Gilbert. 209:196 Ag '69
New approach to Judaism; excerpts from Anti-Semitism and the Christian mind. A. T. Davies. Cath World 210:74-7 N '69
Old vice. Nation 209:461 N 3 '69
Postscript to Babi Yar; sentence of B. Kochubiyevsky. il Time 94:40+ O 10 '69
Soviet Jewry today. M. Friedberg. Commentary 48:45-7 Ag '69
Unredeemed, by R. I. Rubin. Review Sat R 52:29-30 Ag 2 '69. E. Goldhagen
   See also
Jews—Political and social conditions

ANTISERUM
Antigenic changes in lymph-node cells after administration of antiserum to thymus cells. M. Schlesinger and I. Yron. bibliog il Science 164:1412-13 Je 20 '69
Human leukocyte antigenic specificity HL-A3: frequency of occurrence. D. B. Amos and E. Yunis. bibliog il Science 165:300-2 Jl 18 '69
Protective effect of antilymphocyte serum on mice infected with plasmodium berghei. J. N. Sheagren and A. P. Monaco. bibliog il Science 164:1423-5 Je 20 '69

ANTI-SLAVERY movement. See Slavery— United States

ANTI-SMOG devices. See Automobile engines —Exhaust

ANTI-SMOKING devices. See Smoking

ANTI-STRIKE legislation. See Labor laws and legislation; Labor laws and legislation— United States

ANTI-SUBMARINE warfare
Antisubmarine warfare; defense against the elusive nuclear submarine. R. Zimmerman. il Pop Mech 132:114-19+ S '69

ANTI-SUBMARINE warfare airplanes. See Airplanes, Military

ANTI-SUBVERSIVE laws. See Subversive activities

ANTITHROMBIN III. See Blood—Proteins

ANTITRUST division. See United States— Justice, Department of—Antitrust division

ANTITRUST legislation. See Trusts, Industrial —Law

ANTITRYPSIN. See Serum

ANTI-VIETNAM demonstrations. See Vietnamese war, 1957- —Protests, demonstrations, etc. against

ANTIVIRAL proteins. See Interferon

ANTLERS
Antler development. P. M. Kelly. il Cons 23:31 Je '69
Horns and antlers. W. Modell. il Sci Am 220:114-22 bibliog (p 146) Ap '69

ANTONINUS, Brother
All there was was a man, struggling. R. L. Stanger. por Chr Cent 86:1247-9 O 1 '69

ANTONIONI, Michelangelo
Antonioni discovers America. P. Bosworth. il por Holiday 45:64-5+ Mr '69
Antonioni: from super 8 to panavision. H. V. Fondiller. por Pop Phot 65:112-13 S '69
Antonioni's America. J. Hamilton. il pors Look 33:36-40 N 18 '69

ANTS
Ant alarm pheromone activity: correlation with molecular shape by scanning computer. J. E. Amoore and others. bibliog il Science 165:1266-9 S 19 '69
Homing in the ant cataglyphis bicolor. R Wehner and R. Menzel. bibliog il Science 164:192-4 Ap 11 '69
Host finding by odor in the myrmecophilic beetle atemeles pubicollis bris. (staphylinidae) B. Hölldobler. bibliog il Science 166:757-8 N 7 '69
Lore of the ant. W. L. Brown, jr. il Audubon 71:86+ Ja '69
Of ants and men; reprint. J. Gray. il UNESCO Courier 22:46-7 Ag '69
   See also
Termites

ANTWERP
       Harbor
At mouth of Rhine: a new megalopolis. il U S News 66:58-9 Je 23 '69

ANUSZKIEWICZ, Richard
Checker game. Art in Am 57:76 N '69

ANXIETY
Anger in children; excerpt. G. V. Sheviakov. Todays Ed 58:37 S '69
Antidote for anxiety. Chr Today 13:28 Mr 28 '69
   See also
Fear

ANXIETY neurosis. See Neuroses

ANYONE will do; story. See Rule, J.

ANZUS council
ANZUS council holds 19th meeting at Canberra; text of the communique, August 8, 1969. Dept State Bul 61:186-8 S 1 '69
Asia's self-defense plan: a hedge against U.S. pullout. il U S News 66:80-1 Mr 10 '69

AORTA
Polyol pathway in aorta: regulation by hormones. R. S. Clements, jr. and others. bibliog il Science 166:1007-8 N 21 '69

APACHE Indian reservation. See Indians of North America—Reservations

APACHE Indians
Arizona's Apacheland. T. B. Lesure. il Travel 131:71-3 My '69
   See also
Montezuma, C.

APACHE national forest, Ariz. See National forests

APAREJOS. See Pack transportation

APARTHEID. See South Africa—Race problems

APARTMENT building research. See Building research

APARTMENT decoration. See House decoration

APARTMENT houses
Has UN Plaza nosed out the Dakota and the Beresford in New York's celebrity race? G. Sheehy. il Holiday 46:58-61+ S '69
Kafka's castle; Barcelona. P. Hodgkinson. il Arch Forum 131:35-41 N '69
Lake Point Tower: the first skyscraper with an undulating glass wall; Chicago's new high-rise. il Arch Rec 146:123-30 O '69
Self-contained community in Bayonne, France combines high- and low-rise apartment houses. il Arch Rec 146:108-12 Ag '69
   See also
Row houses

   Condominium plan ownership
Condominiums are here to stay. il Bet Hom & Gard 47:110 S '69
Gold coast booms again: Florida high-rise condominiums under construction. il Bsns W p 144+ Jl 12 '69
Six families make identical space unique. il House & Gard 135:126-31 Ap '69

   Cooperative ownership
   See also
Apartment houses—Condominium plan ownership

   Designs and plans
Urban housing: a comprehensive approach to quality; plans for New York city. il Arch Rec 145:97-118 Ja '69

   Garden apartments
Building types study. Arch Rec 146:183-97 S '69
Clustered in a garden; Heritage apartments, Simsbury, Conn. il Am Home 72:82-3 N '69
Florida minivillage. il Arch Forum 130:92-5 Ja '69
Privacy in a crowd; Lakeridge view apartments, Bellevue, Wash. il Am Home 72:84-5 N '69

APARTMENT houses, Remodeled
Silos for singles. Time 94:95 S 19 '69

APARTMENT in the attic; story. See Hildesheimer, W.

APARTMENTS
Best of two worlds; Van Day Truex apartment in Manhattan and house in south of France. B. Plumb. il N Y Times Mag p32-3 Ag 31 '69
Box becomes a home. V. D. Hahn and A. C. Borg. il Am Home 72:60-1 Ap '69
Comfort, rich color, and the things we love. il House & Gard 136:42-7 Jl '69
Designer's domain; Paris apartment of Marc Bohan. B. Plumb. il N Y Times Mag p48-9 Je 29 '69
Elegance in a one-room *pied-à-terre*. E. Kinard. il House B 111:78-9 Ag '69
11x22' small but sky-high in effect; attic space expands small apartment. V. D. Hahn and A. C. Borg. il Am Home 72:58-9 Ap '69
Elite meet; Fred Mueller's Manhattan penthouse. B. Plumb. il N Y Times Mag p44-5 D 21 '69
Flirty thirties; emphasis on white. B. Plumb. il N Y Times Mag p46-7 Ag 3 '69
How to judge the new apartments and townhouses. J. H. Ingersoll. House B 111:48+ S '69
I love the sunny colors and wide open spaces of my new apartment. il House & Gard 136:58-61 Jl; 58-61 Ag '69

APARTMENTS—*Continued*
Imagination divides space: equivalent of four rooms; model room created by David Hicks. il House & Gard 135:56-7 F '69
Instant apartment. B. Plumb. il N Y Times Mag p 114-15 S 7 '69
Jane Holzer, the lion-hearted in her New York apartment. il Vogue 154:210-17 N 1 '69
Livability lives here; designed by B. Baldwin. B. Plumb. il N Y Times Mag p 118-19 O 5 '69
Lively beat of young New Yorkers. il House B 111:38-9 Jl '69
Living big in mini-digs. il Mlle 69:173+ S '69
Living with antiques; the New York apartment of Mr and Mrs Leon Levy. M. D. Schwartz. il Antiques 96:376-81 S '69
Living with color: bright flashes in cool settings. il House & Gard 136:120-9 S '69
Long, lean apartment full of surprises. il Am Home 72:64-5 Ap '69
Off the beaten track: adventure-filled apartment of the Marquesa de Portago. il Vogue 153:118-21 Ap 15 '69
Open-and-shut case; remodeled apartment, Washington, D.C. B. Plumb. il N Y Times Mag p64-5 Ag 24 '69
Perfectly ordinary, extra-special, way-out, wild and wonderful one-room apartment. il Redbook 132:74-7+ Ja '69
Room for more; every room a double or triple role. B. Plumb. il N Y Times Mag p82-3 My 25 '69
Rush to apartments. il U S News 67:46-8 D 8 '69
Space tricks in an attic. V. D. Hahn and A. C. Borg. il Am Home 72:62-3 Ap '69
Le style Pauline; Paris apartment. V. Lawford. il Vogue 153:150-3 Je '69
Young chic for the old sheik's lair. il House B 111:40-2 Jl '69
Yves St Laurent: his very special world. il McCalls 97:64-7 Ja '70
APARTMENTS, Remodeled
Designer virtuoso; renovation of New York apartment. il House B 111:124-9 O '69
APATITE
Aluminum-rich apatite. D. J. Fisher and D. McConnell. bibliog il Science 164:551-3 My 2 '69
Atherosclerotic plaque: X-ray diffraction investigation. M. Spector and others. bibliog Science 165:711 Ag 15 '69
See also
Hydroxyapatite
APECO. See American photocopy equipment company
APES
Knuckle-walking and the problem of human origins. R. H. Tuttle. bibliog il Science 166: 953-61 N 21 '69
See also
Chimpanzees
Gorillas
Orangutans
Primates
APGAR, Virginia
How a mother protects her infant from infectious diseases. Redbook 133:46 Ag '69
Questions & answers on German measles. PTA Mag 63:12-13 My '69
APHIDS. See Plant lice
APHORISMS and apothegms
Poor woman's almanac. B. Pfizer. Ladies Home J 86:16 S; 24 O; 22 N '69
APHRODISIACS
Love for sale. Newsweek 74:106-7 N 10 '69
Plain man's guide to aphrodisia. J. E. Cox. il Holiday 46:22-3 O '69
Sex drug: p-chlorophenylalanine. Newsweek 75:57 Ja 5 '70
Supermarket for Eros; fast growing retail business in West Germany. il Time 93:90 My 2 '69
APICULTURE. See Bee culture
APLODONTIA rufa. See Mountain beavers
APLYSIA. See Sea hares
APOCALYPSIS cum figuris; drama. See Grotowski, J.
APOCALYPTIC thought
Apocalyptic social change. W. B. Abernethy. Chr Cent 86:343-4 Mr 12 '69; Reply. C. E. Fager. 86:1249-51 O 1 '69; Rejoinder. 86:1488+ N 19 '69
APOLLINAIRE, Guillaume, pseud.
Apollinaire! the perfect romantic. L. Simpson. il pors N Y Times Mag p26-7+ Ja 19 '69
Letter from Paris: exhibition at the Bibliotheque nationale. Genêt. New Yorker 45: 181-2+ D 13 '69
APOLLO 8 flight. See Space flight to the moon —Manned flights—Borman-Lovell-Anders flight, 1968

APOLLO 9 flight. See Space flight—Manned flights—McDivitt-Scott-Schweickart flight, 1969
APOLLO 10 flight. See Space flight to the moon—Manned flights—Stafford-Cernan-Young flight, 1969
APOLLO 11 flight. See Space flight to the moon—Manned flights—Armstrong-Aldrin-Collins flight, 1969
APOLLO 12 flight. See Space flight to the moon—Manned flights—Conrad-Bean-Gordon flight, 1969 (proposed)
APOLLO 13 flight. See Space flight to the moon—Manned flights—Lovell-Haise-Mattingly flight, 1970 (proposed)
APOLLO flight training. See Astronauts—Training
APOLLO lunar module. See Space vehicles—Landing systems—Moon
APOLLO lunar surface experiments package. See Moon—Exploration—Equipment
APOLLO project. See Space flight to the moon
APOLLOS (space vehicles) See Space vehicles
APOSTASY
Termites in the house of God. Chr Today 13: 20 My 23 '69
See also
Heresy
APOSTOLIC authority. See Church—Authority
APPALACHIAN MOUNTAINS
Wild boar of the Appalachians. H. L. Lawrence. il Natur Hist 78:46-7 O '69
See also
Great Smoky Mountains
APPALACHIAN REGION
Appalachia is where my heart is. S. Brashear. il Seventeen 28:86-7+ Jl '69
Appalachia: 1914. R. M. Ketchum. il Am Heritage 20:26-41+ F '69
Appalachia: who's helping whom? M. Rzeczkowski. il Cath World 210:155-8 Ja '70
Corporate fiefdom; poverty and the dole in Appalachia. H. M. Caudill. Commonweal 89:523-5 Ja 24 '69
George's Branch, Ky; Rado Combs, former miner and his family. W. Hedgepeth. il Look 33:25-33 Mr 4 '69
See also
Arts and crafts—Appalachian Region
Education—Appalachian Region
Geology—Appalachian Region

History

Appalachia: 1914. R. M. Ketchum. il Am Heritage 20:26-41+ F '69

Recovery program, 1965

Appalachian economy; excerpts from address, September 25, 1968. J. W. Fleming. 2d. il Parks & Rec 4:21-3+ Ja '69
APPALACHIAN trail
Birds along the Appalachian trail. E. R. Brown. il Cons 23:2-4 F '69
APPALACHIAN volunteers. See Volunteers in service to America
APPARATUS for the blind. See Blind, Apparatus for the
APPARENT movement. See Optical illusions
APPARITIONS
See also
Jesus Christ—Apparitions and miracles (modern)
Spiritualism
APPEL, Fredric C.
Coming revolution in transportation. Nat Geog 136:301-41 S '69
APPETITE
See also
Hyperphagia
APPETITE, Abnormal. See Pica (pathology)
APPETIZERS
Fast and fancy holiday party snacks. il Bet Hom & Gard 47:71-2 D '69
Fruit and dips! with recipes. il Seventeen 28:334-5+ Ag '69
Great Greek appetizers; with recipes. E. Alston. il Look 33:82-3 Mr 18 '69
Hot appetizers, right off the grill. il Sunset 142:92-3 My '69
Little filled pancakes as appetizers. il Sunset 142:150 F '69
Pride of Provence; *brandade de morue.* C. Claiborne. il N Y Times Mag p 136 O 26 '69
APPLE cider. See Cider
APPLE juice
See also
Cider
APPLE orchards. See Apple trees
APPLE RIVER
Action on the Apple. J. Engh. il Travel 131: 55-9 My '69

APPLE trees
Get started growing apples. A. P. Thomson. il Org Gard & Farm 16:48-52 N '69
APPLEBAUM, Max H.
Channel separation nomogram. Radio-Electr 40:73 N '69
APPLEBY, Thomas
Experiment with gravity. Pop Electr 32:66 Ja '70
APPLEGATE, Beth M.
Thunderheads; poem. Horn Bk 45:377 Ag '69
APPLEGATE, Jimmie R.
Why don't pupils talk in class discussions? Clear House 44:78-81 O '69
APPLES
Apples. F. A. Cochran. il Horticulture 48:36-7 Ja '70
Apples of yesteryear. C. L. Davenport. il Horticulture 46:16-17+ O '68
Number one apple? Golden Delicious. il Sunset 142:74-7 F '69
See also
Cookery—Fruit
APPLETON, Jon
Current chronicle. Mus Q 55:112-14 Ja '69
APPLETON, Wis.
We beat business disruption. F. H. Keuler. il Am City 84:91-3 Ag '69
APPLEY, Lawrence A.
Executives who will score in the '80's; interview. por Nations Bsns 57:80-3 Je '69
APPLEYARD, J. A.
Catholic university; again. America 121:224-6 S 27 '69
APPLIANCE warranties. See Warranty
APPLICATIONS for positions
First step to successful professionalism: a portfolio that sells you and your work. J. Scully. Mod Phot 33:14+ O '69
See also
Interviewing
APPLIED art. See Arts and crafts
APPLIED mathematics. See Mathematics
APPORTIONMENT (election law)
New shake-up of voting districts? il U S News 66:39-40 Ap 21 '69
Political power in the '70s: gains to South and West. il U S News 66:52-3 Ap 7 '69
Slide rule for legislators; Supreme court handing down series of one-man, one-vote decisions. Time 93:77 Ap 18 '69
APPRAISAL of public schools. See Evaluation (education)
APPRECIATION of art. See Art—Appreciation
APPRENTICES
See also
Employees—Training
APRIL fools day
April fools' day delights. Q. Crewe. Vogue 153:156+ Ap 1 '69
APRONS
Give your own version of the French chef's apron. il Sunset 143:68-9 D '69
APPROXIMATE computation
Estimating proportions in petrographic mixing equations by least-squares approximation. W. B. Bryan and others. bibliog il Science 163:926-7 F 28 '69
See also
Numerical analysis
APTE, Stu
Sex and the sailfish. Field & S 73:72-3+ Ap '69
APTER, Harold
Iberia & the Magreb. Travel & Camera 32:40, 49-53+ Ap '69
APTHEKER, Herbert
Du Bois as historian. bibliog Negro Hist Bul 32:6-16 Ap '69

about

Bryn Mawr tells it not quite like it is. Nat R 21:580-1 Je 17 '69
APTITUDE tests
Prospects for evaluation of learning. R. L. Ebel. Ed Digest 34:22-5 Mr '69
Why so many students are unhappy. D. Lawrence. U S News 67:84 Jl 21 '69
AQUACULTURE. See Fish culture
AQUAMANILIA. See Pitchers
AQUANAUTS
See also
Cannon, B. L.
AQUARIUM heaters. See Water heaters
AQUARIUMS
Spitmouth puffers in the living room; Precision valve plans to manufacture saltwater aquarium. R. H. Boyle. il Sports Illus 31:28-30+ D 8 '69
AQUARIUS (ski boat) See Motor boats
AQUASCOOTERS. See Motor boats
AQUATIC animals. See Marine fauna

AQUATIC birds. See Water birds
AQUATIC fungi. See Fungi, Aquatic
AQUATIC life. See Fresh water biology
AQUATIC plants
Aquatic weeds. L. G. Holm and others. bibliog il Science 166:699-709 N 7 '69
See also
Duckweeds
Water chestnut
Water lilies
AQUATIC shows
Pre-season promenade. Motor B 123:53+ Ap '69
AQUATIC sports
Action on the Apple. J. Engh. il Travel 131: 55-9 My '69
Watersports. F. Rohr. jr. See issues of Motor boating
See also
Boats and boating
Surf riding
Swimming
Water skis and skiing
Yachts and yachting
ARAB-Israeli war, 1967. See Israeli-Arab war, 1967-
ARAB-Jewish relations. See Jewish-Arab relations
ARAB league. See Arab states
ARAB refugees. See Refugees, Arab
ARAB states
Arab world; with report by M. J. Kubic. il Newsweek 74:49-50+ S 29 '69
Confusion at the summit; Rabat summit of Moslem nations. il Time 94:32+ O 3 '69
Summit in Rabat. il Time 94:17 D 26 '69
See also
France—Foreign relations—Arab states
Guerrillas—Arab states
Jewish-Arab relations
Jews in Arab states
Research—Arab states
Student demonstrations—Arab states
United Arab Republic

Foreign relations

Both sides take a hard look; mini-summit in Cairo. il Newsweek 74:39 S 15 '69
Cry for a holy war; reactions to the Al Aksa mosque fire. Newsweek 74:37 S 8 '69
With the Arab commandos; no peace for Israel; a campaign of terror. J. Law. il U S News 66:60-2 F 24 '69

Israel

Great power responsibilities. Commonweal 89:487-8 Ja 17 '69

Israeli occupation, 1967-

Invitation to a coup. il Newsweek 74:60+ O 27 '69
Israel: the shape of things to come? il Newsweek 74:42 Ag 18 '69
Vicious circle. S. Alsop. Newsweek 73:130 Ap 21 '69
See also
Jordan—Israeli occupation, 1967-

Nationalism

Fedayeen; new factor in the Middle East. J. B. Sheerin. Cath World 210:146-7 Ja '70
Islam and the West in the Middle East. G. Lenczowski. bibliog f Cur Hist 56:129-35+ Mr '69

Politics

Can the Arabs make peace? New Repub 160: 6 Mr 22 '69
Middle East: no closer to unity. il Time 94:32 S 12 '69
ARAB students
Rebels without hope. Newsweek 74:27-8 Jl 7 '69
ARAB terrorists. See Terrorism
ARABIA

Antiquities

Rise and fall of Arabia Felix. G. W. Van Beek. il Sci Am 221:36-46 bibliog(p 152) D '69

History

Rise and fall of Arabia Felix. G. W. Van Beek. il Sci Am 221:36-46 bibliog(p 152) D '69
ARABIC civilization. See Civilization, Arabic
ARABIC cookery. See Cookery, Arabic
ARABS
See also
Moors (people)

ARABS in Israel
Crossroads of Jerusalem. H. Krosney. Nation 208:134-8 F 3 '69
Jews and Arabs live side by side, but not together, no man's land remains in Jerusalem. A. Rubinstein. il N Y Times Mag p30-1+ My 11 '69
Lamb between two wolves. il Time 95:27 Ja 5 '70
ARACHNIDS, Fossil
Oldest known terrestrial arachnids. L. Størmer. bibliog il Science 164:1276-7 Je 13 '69
ARAFAT, Mohammed
Calling the tune; with report by M. J. Kubic. il por Newsweek 74:47 N 10 '69
Children of the storm: the Arab commandos. il por Newsweek 74:37-8+ D 22 '69
Lebanon: along the Arafat trail. il por Time 94:30+ N 7 '69
ARAFAT, Yasser. See Arafat, M.
ARAGONITE
Methane-derived marine carbonates of pleistocene age. J. C. Hathaway and E. T. Degens. bibliog il Science 165:690-2 Ag 15 '69
ARAKI, Minol
Contemporary career: design detective. il por Design 70:28-30 mid-Wint '69
ARALIACEAE
See also
Tetraplasandra
ARALIAS
See also
Fatsias
ARAN ISLANDS
Windswept Irish edge of Europe. R. Harrity. il Look 33:56-68 Mr 18 '69
ARARAT, MOUNT
Wood on Mount Ararat intrigues explorers. il Chr Today 13:48 S 12 '69
ARBASINO, Alberto
Italian heroines. Vogue 153:202+ Ap 1 '69
ARBATOV, Georgii A.
Letter from Moscow. por Newsweek 74:36 Jl 21 '69
about
America watching. por Time 93:25 F 7 '69
ARBITRAGE
Arcane art of arbitrage. il Bsns W p 138+ N 22 '69
Feast for the arbitrageurs. W. Robertson. il Fortune 79:165-6 F '69
ARBITRATION, Commercial
How companies stay out of the courtroom. S. H. Lieberstein. il Duns R 94:64-6+ S '69
ARBITRATION, Industrial
Collective bargaining and community disputes. T. W. Kheel. Mo Labor R 92:3-8 Ja '69
Strike strategy of Mr Shultz: magic and a bit of luck. il U S News 67:56-7 Jl 7 '69
Why arbitrators reinstate discharged employees. M. Stone. il Mo Labor R 92:47-50 O '69
Why not compulsory arbitration? America. 121:520 N 29 '69
See also
Collective bargaining
Industrial relations
Labor courts
United States
Arbitration and the Labor board. B. Samoff. bibliog Mo Labor R 92:54-6 My '69
Taking the grief out of grievances; voluntary arbitration wins favor with management and unions. il Bsns W p78+ Mr 8 '69
See also
United States—Federal mediation and conciliation service
ARBITRATION, International
Challenge of Rhodesia. R. Zacklin. bibliog f il Int Council 575:5-72 N '69
Inviting an era of negotiation. il Life 66:32 Ja 31 '69
See also
Disarmament
International court of arbitration, The Hague
League of Nations
Peace
ARBITRATION, Judicial. See Procedure (law)
ARBITRATION association, American. See American arbitration association
ARBORETUMS
See also
Bernheim forest landscape arboretum, Kentucky
Harvard university—Arnold arboretum
Washington, D.C.—National arboretum
ARBORS
Hideaway garden arbor for $25. G. Arnold. il Org Gard & Farm 16:72-3 Ap '69
Place in the shade. E. Kondonellis. il Am Home 72:62-3 Je '69

ARBORVITAE
American Arborvitae. C. E. Lewis. Horticulture 48:43-4 Ja '70
ARBUS, Diane
Tokyo Rose is home. il Esquire 71:168-9 My '69
about
Arbus, does she cater to the peeping Tom within us? M. Mann. Pop Phot 65:25-6+ D '69
ARBUTHNOT, May (Hill)
Obituary
Library J 94:4198 N 15 '69. D. Broderick
ARC welders. See Welders
ARCEO, Sergio Méndez, bp. See Méndez Arceo, S.
ARCHAEOLOGY. See Archeology
ARCHEOLOGICAL research. See Archeology—Methodology
ARCHEOLOGY
Archaeology; the truth of human behavior; address, September 3, 1969. J. B. Pritchard. Vital Speeches 35:754-6 O 1 '69
Dig. K. E. Meyer. il Esquire 71:94-5+ F '69
Selected aspects of archaeology, 1964-1968. C. C. Lamberg-Karlovsky. bibliog f Ann Am Acad 379:132-50 S '68
See also
Anthropology
Bible—Antiquities
Cave drawings and paintings
Dwellings, Prehistoric
Excavations (archeology)
Indians of North America—Antiquities
Man—Origin and antiquity
Man, Prehistoric
Petroglyphs
Stone age
Methodology
Archeology in the Soviet Union. C. S. Chard. bibliog Science 163:774-9 F 21 '69
Fauna of Çatal Hüyük: evidence for early cattle domestication in Anatolia. D. Perkins, jr. bibliog il Science 164:177-9 Ap 11 '69
Hoabinhian: a pebble-tool complex with early plant associations in southeast Asia. C. F. Gorman. bibliog il Science 163:671-3 F 14 '69
Infrared scanning images: an archeological application. G. G. Schaber and G. J. Gumerman. bibliog il Science 164:712-13 My 9 '69
Obsidian hydration rate for the Klamath basin of California and Oregon. L. Johnson, jr. bibliog il Science 165:1354-6 S 26 '69
Paleomagnetism & archeomagnetism. D. E. Lancaster. il Electr World 82:23-6+ S '69
Stone tools and human behavior. S. R. Binford and L. R. Binford. il Sci Am 220:70-2+ bibliog(p 146) Ap '69
X-ray fluorescence spectrography: use in field archeology. J. D. Frierman and others. Science 164:588 My 2 '69
See also
Radiocarbon dating
Study and teaching
Students underground. J. Marks. il Mlle 70: 150-1+ D '69
ARCHEOLOGY, Submarine
Adventures in the sponge trade; excerpt from Shipwrecks and archaeology: the unharvested sea. P. Throckmorton. Atlan 224:96-103 S '69
Ancient shipwreck yields new facts; and a strange cargo; marble coffins found in the Gulf of Taranto. P. Throckmorton. il Nat Geog 135:282-300 F '69
Ruins under the sea. G. F. Bass. il Holiday 46:25+ Ag '69
ARCHER, George
Archer grabs the giveaway Masters; with account by D. Jenkins. il por Sports Illus 30:24-9 Ap 1 '69
Archer makes his bow. il por Time 93:56 Ap 25 '69
New master. il por Newsweek 73:110-11 Ap 28 '69
Sporting scene. H. W. Wind. New Yorker 45: 129-32+ My 3 '69
ARCHER, James A.
Your own private OWL. Pop Electr 30:51-3+ Je '69
ARCHERY
Add action to your archery program. B. Wadsworth. il Camp Mag 41:14-15 F '69
Future of archery. G. H. Gillelan. il Outdoor Life 143:104-7+ F '69
Hardy boy and his bow and arrow. H. Weiskopf. il Sports Illus 31:20-2+ Ag 11 '69
Hit where you aim. G. H. Gillelan. il Outdoor Life 144:90+ Ag '69

ARCHERY—*Continued*
Just call him the man with the golden aim; H. Ward. H. Weiskopf. il Sports Illus 31:42-3 S 1 '69
Offbeat archery. G. H. Gillelan. il Outdoor Life 143:144-6 My '69
See also
Hunting with bow and arrow

Competition
World archery championship. G. H. Gillelan. il Outdoor Life 144:24+ N '69

Equipment
Bowhunter's checklist. G. H. Gillelan. il Outdoor Life 144:34+ O '69
What's new in archery. G. H. Gillelan. il Outdoor Life 143:158+ Ap '69
See also
Bow and arrow

ARCHES NATIONAL MONUMENT
How to save our national parks; excerpt from Desert solitaire: a season in the wilderness. E. Abbey. il Field & S 73:74-5+ Mr '69

ARCHITECTS
Archiworks, collapsible cities: visionary concepts of rebelling young architects. J. Gruen. Vogue 154:64 N 15 '69
Practice abroad: a rewarding study in comprehensive frustrations. R. S. McMillan. il Arch Rec 145:88-9 My '69
Role of the artist in contributing elements of grandeur to our physical environment. il Sch Arts 68:21-9 Mr '69
See also
American institute of architects
Architecture as a profession
Women as architects
also names of architects, e.g. Wright, F. L.

Fees
Delayed fees: curse of the funding process. Arch Rec 145:83-4 Ap '69

Licenses and registration
Case for specialized registration. P. B. Farrell, jr. Arch Forum 130:50-1 Mr '69
N.C.A.R.B. pushes toward new exam bases. Arch Rec 146:67 Ag; 83-4 S '69

Training
See Architectural education

ARCHITECTS, Landscape. See Landscape gardening

ARCHITECTS, Professional ethics for
Students win support of A.I.A. in Chicago; sweeping changes proposed in professional ethics. il Arch Rec 146:35 Ag '69

ARCHITECTS offices. See Offices

ARCHITECTURAL acoustics. See Acoustics, Architectural

ARCHITECTURAL decoration. See Decoration and ornament, Architectural

ARCHITECTURAL drawing
Urban individualist. il Arch Forum 130:52-5 Mr '69
Study and teaching
Bring architecture home. A. Sauther. il Sch Arts 68:14-15 Mr '69

ARCHITECTURAL education
Internship: bridge to future practice. il Arch Rec 146:86-7 O '69
Making of non-architects. S. Moholy-Nagy Arch Rec 145:149-52 O '69
N.C.A.R.B. pushes toward new exam bases. Arch Rec 146:67 Ag; 83-4 S '69
See also
Bauhaus
Frank Lloyd Wright school of architecture

ARCHITECTURAL firms
Practice. See issues of Architectural record
Some thoughts on starting your own office. E. R. Flansburgh. il Arch Rec 145:149-60 Ap '69
See also
Hellmuth, Obata and Kassabaum (firm)
Urban design development group, incorporated

ARCHITECTURAL league of New York
Worst art show. il Life 67:81-2 D 12 '69

ARCHITECTURAL lighting. See Lighting, Architectural and decorative

ARCHITECTURAL models
Fountain scale model serves as an engineering design tool. R. Chaix. il Arch Rec 145:165-7 Mr '69
Spacious living in a heap. il Life 67:102-5 D 5 '69
See also
Models of cities, towns, etc.

ARCHITECTURAL photography. See Photography of buildings and structures

ARCHITECTURAL record (periodical)
First look at the award-winners for 1969 Record houses. il Arch Rec 145:40-3 Ap '69

ARCHITECTURAL schools. See Architectural education

ARCHITECTURAL space. See Space (architecture)

ARCHITECTURE
Architectural business. See issues of Architectural record
Buildings in the news. See issues of Architectural record
Focus, monthly review of notable buildings. See issues of Architectural forum
Forum, monthly review of events and notable buildings. See issues of Architectural forum
On the scene (cont) C. Barnes. Holiday 45:10+ F: 12+ Mr: 12+ Ap: 8+ My: 8+ Je: 46:8+ Jl '69
See also
Acoustics, Architectural
Architects
Bank buildings
Capitols
Church architecture
City halls
City planning
College architecture
Environmental engineering (buildings)
Follies (architecture)
Glass construction
Hillside architecture
Hotels, taverns, etc.
Industrial buildings
Laboratories—Architecture
Library architecture
Moving picture theaters
Museums—Architecture
Opera houses
Park buildings
Pavilions
Police stations
Printing offices
Public buildings
Recreation buildings
School buildings
Spires
Theater buildings

Awards, prizes, etc.
First look at the award-winners for 1969 Record houses. il Arch Rec 145:40-3 Ap '69

Bibliography
Books. See issues of Architectural forum

Caricatures and cartoons
Kindergarten chats. R. Hedman. Arch Forum 130:52-3 Ap '69

Conservation and restoration
Bank with a past in its future: Bank of California. J. M. Fitch. il Arch Forum 130:68-75 My '69
Group action in preservation; Historic sites federation of Tennessee. S. Benedict. il Antiques 95:388-9 Mr '69
Philadelphia story; Society hill. K. Chapin. il Am Home 72:58-61+ D '69
Preservation in Europe. 1969. il Antiques 95:842-6; 96:88-90, 214-17, 406-8, 592-4, 918-20 Je-O. D '69
Saving a stone prayer; York minster. F. C. Livingston. il Sci N 95:263-9 Mr 15 '69
What's cooking in the preservation kettle? reprint. H. D. Bullock. Hobbies 74:98FF Jl '69
See also
Laws, Calif.
Newport, R.I.—Historic houses, etc.

Bibliography
Historic preservation: a basic reference shelf. Antiques 96:116 Jl '69

Designs and plans
See also
Architectural drawing

Details
See also
Cupolas

History
Bravura in Brooklyn. C. Robinson. il Arch Forum 131:42-7 N '69
2001 B.C. to 2001 Centre avenue. E. Kaufmann, jr. il Arch Forum 131:54-7 O '69

International aspects
Practice abroad: a rewarding study in comprehensive frustrations. R. S. McMillan. il Arch Rec 145:88-9 My '69

ARCHITECTURE—*Continued*

Philosophy

Architecture through improvisation? S. Moholy-Nagy. il Arch Forum 131:40-7 S '69

Bauhaus, by H. M. Wingler. Review
New Repub 161:28-31 O 11 '69. P. Jacobsohn

Issues in architecture. See issues of Architectural record

2001 B.C. to 2001 Centre avenue. E. Kaufmann, jr. il Arch Forum 131:54-7 O '69

Social aspects

Architecture in the cause of people: yesterday, today and tomorrow. W. W. Caudill. Arch Rec 145:127-30 Ja '69

Study and teaching

Architectural design in the classroom. T. Thatcher. il Sch Arts 68:7 Mr '69

Cry of the peacock. F. Megarity. il House B 111:72+ Ap '69

See also
Architectural education

Australia

See also
Sydney, Australia—Architecture

Belgium

See also
Brussels—Architecture

Connecticut

New solutions from old problems. C. Knight, 3d. il Arch Forum 131:58-65 O '69

England

Duke of Wellington's search for a palace. E. Longford. il Horizon 11:106-13 Spr '69

Europe, Western

New European bookstore; tr. by C. B. Anderson. G. Ramseger. il Pub W 195:19-22 My 26 '69

France

See also
Architecture. Domestic—France

Germany (Federal Republic)

Building fast, but well. il Fortune 79:92-7 Ap '69

Last work of Walter Gropius. il Arch Rec 146:131-50 S '69

Walter Gropius, 1883-1969; Fagus shoe last factory and administration building in Alfeld-an-der-Leine. il Arch Forum 131:34-9 S '69

Guatemala

See also
Antigua, Guatemala—Architecture

India

See also
Temples—India

Indiana

See also
Columbus. Ind.—Architecture

Italy

See also
Architecture. Domestic—Italy
Naples—Architecture
Venice—Architecture

Japan

Japan's Crystal palace; prefabricated Nagashima tropical garden. il Arch Forum 130:76-83 My '69

Massachusetts

After the Boston city hall. il Arch Forum 130:54-7 Ja '69

Mexico

See also
Mexico (city)—Architecture

Netherlands

Modern museum piece; hunting lodge, called St Hubert's. B. Plumb. il N Y Times Mag p94-5 S 14 '69

See also
Dronten, Netherlands—Architecture

New York (state)

See also
Brooklyn—Architecture

Russia

See also
Churches—Russia

Spain

See also
Barcelona—Architecture

United States

Another step towards a national policy on architecture. D. P. Moynihan. Arch Rec 145:10 Je '69

Architecture. P. F. Norton. il Antiques 96:373 S '69

Buildings in the news. See issues of Architectural record

Essence of architecture is space; interview. P. Rudolph. House & Gard 136:26+ N '69

Franzen unifies an architecture of fragments into good places for people; five new projects by U. Franzen. il Arch Rec 145:113-32 F '69

Mies; his eloquent legacy: purity of structure. J. De Long. House B 111:132-5 N '69

Spot check: some observations on architecture in America. J. Claman. il Harp Baz 102:122T-122W F '69

ARCHITECTURE, American

Model for the frontier; Shaker architecture. Hancock. Mass. il Time 94:54-5 Jl 4 '69

ARCHITECTURE, Baroque

Salzburg: baroque jewel in central Europe. A. Werner. il Am Artist 33:46-51 Ap '69

ARCHITECTURE, Domestic

Architect speaks his mind: greatest advance in 200 years; the nail; interview. C. Moore. House & Gard 136:30+ O '69

Architecture without fingerprints; interviews with twenty architects. ed. by P. L. Levin House B 111:96-7+ S '69

Can you have the house you want? il Parents Mag 44:92-5 Mr '69

People come to architects to improve the quality of their lives; interview. R. Meier. House & Gard 136:12+ D '69

Promising step forward in assembly-line housing; single-family townhouses. J. Reedy. il Bet Hom & Gard 47:52+ F '69

Seven smart, affordable houses. N. Seney and S. Mead. il Bet Hom & Gard 47:55-61 F '69

See also
Apartment houses
Architects
Bathrooms
Buildings, Round
City houses
Courtyards
Dining rooms
Fireplaces
Garages
Hillside architecture
House decoration
Houses, Prefabricated
Houses, Remodeled
Housing
Landscape gardening
Laundries
Row houses
Stone houses
Summer homes
Vacation houses

Conservation and restoration

See Architecture—Conservation and restoration

Designs and plans

Cube house vs. the squares; Arlington, Va. neighbors' court action. J. Neary. il Life 67:83-4+ N 14 '69

Eight good houses that you can afford. N. Seney. il Bet Hom & Gard 47:78-85+ Mr '69

Glowing house of glass and cedar. Long Island. E. Sverbeyeff. il House B 111:91-5 S '69

Hallmark house for 1969. il House & Gard 136:54-63 Ag '69

Homes mothers want most. il Parents Mag 44:72-5 Ap; 66-9+ Je '69

House that sets us free. E. Saltzman and R. Saltzman. il House & Gard 136:78-87 D '69

House with a great new slant. N. Seney. il Bet Hom & Gard 47:76-81 Ap '69

How to obtain low-cost second home designs. H. D. Mack. il Mech Illus 65:93-5 Mr '69

Ideas in houses (cont) il Life 66:70-2 F 21; 80-2+ Mr 21; 86-8+ Ap 11; 90-2+ My 9; 68-70+ Je 20; 67-56-61 Ag 1 '69

New kind of total house. il Bet Hom & Gard 47:74-9 S '69

P/M encourages young homemakers to speak out for better housing. R. Charles. il Parents Mag 44:104-7+ S '69

Plan provides privacy, flexibility, and variety. il House & Gard 135:48-9+ Ja '69

Record houses of 1969. il Arch Rec 145:25-86 mid-My '69

We built this house for $7500. R. R. Hunt. il Pop Mech 132:126-33+ N '69

ARCHITECTURE, Domestic—Designs and plans
—*Continued*
Well-built, well-kept house. J. H. Ingersoll.
  See issues of House beautiful
See also
Architectural drawing
Blueprints

Arizona

Carefree concept. il Art in Am 57:114-17 N
  '69

Bequia (island)

Moonhole, where time stands still. P. A. Jenkins. il House B 111:38-43+ Ag '69

British Columbia

House of terraces on a rocky hill. il Arch
  Rec 145:141-6 Ja '69

California

By the ocean: narrow house with double
  decks: Mr and Mrs Charles W. Fay's
  week-end house at Aptos Beach. il House
  & Gard 135:84-7 Je '69
California house in trimly handsome post-
  and-beam style. il Arch Rec 145:143-6 Mr '69
California, leader in housing design. A. C.
  Borg. il Am Home 72:60-3 Ja '69
Cross-shaped house gives privacy, space
  and views. il Arch Rec 146:131-4 Jl '69
Family united in a house divided. il House
  & Gard 135:136-41+ Ap '69
Giant window in the woods: vacation and
  weekend retreat. il Sunset 142:80-2 F '69
Here is a look at the new townhouses. il
  Sunset 143:102-7 N '69
Homes mothers want most; San Diego. il
  Parents Mag 44:72-3 Ap '69
House spectacular. il House & Gard 135:100-
  9 My '69
Living in a garden: a quiet house built for
  two; home of Mr & Mrs Ted Factor. il
  House & Gard 136:130-7 S '69
McElrath house, Santa Cruz. il Arch Rec 145:
  46-7 mid-My '69
New privacy. il Sunset 142:72-9 Ap '69
Spanish style house wins award; built by M.
  Ozer. il Parents Mag 44:88-91 O '69

Canada

Privacy for a vigorous house built on a drop-
  away city lot. J. H. Ingersoll. il House B
  111:112-15 S '69

Caribbean Region

An odd grotto for a Caribbean getaway. il
  Life 66:70-2 F 21 '69
Island bonanza; homes in the Virgin Islands.
  il House & Gard 135:92-7 Ja '69

Colorado

American action; the ski life in Colorado. il
  Vogue 153:220-9 F 1 '69
At home on a private plaza. il Life 66:68-70+
  Je 20 '69

Connecticut

All line and light. B. Plumb. il N Y Times
  Mag p 126-7 N 23 '69
As natural as all outdoors: cedar-shingled
  house on different levels. B. Plumb. il N Y
  Times Mag p28-9 Jl 6 '69
Beautiful detailing enhances a very special
  house. il Arch Rec 145:177-80 Ap '69
Carrousel house; R. T. Foster's revolving
  house in Wilton. J. Peter. il Look 33:32-4 My
  27 '69
From a rustic stable: a stylish country
  place: John Scoville's home. il House B
  111:66-72 Je '69
Goldberg house, Manchester. il Arch Rec 145:
  40-3 mid-My '69
House that runs by itself. il House & Gard
  136:54-7 Jl '69
Nine rooms in search of a view: R. Foster's
  revolving house. il House & Gard 135:64-9
  F '69
Traverso house, Westbrook. il Arch Rec 145:
  44-5 mid-My '69
Warren Platner house. il Arch Rec 146:98-9
  D '69

England

Bright new look of old England; J. Bannen-
  berg's house on Carlyle Square. il House B
  111:108-11 S '69
First aid for a crumbling English farmhouse.
  B. Plumb. il N Y Times Mag p54-5 Jl 13
  '69

Finland

Lesson from the Finns. S. Wrede. Am Home
  72:118-19 S '69

Fire Island

Treehouse of cubes at the water's edge. E.
  Sverbeyeff. il House B 111:62-5 Jl '69

Florida

Weinberger house, Miami. il Arch Rec 145:38-
  9 mid-My '69

France

Best of two worlds; Van Day Truex apart-
  ment in Manhattan and house in south of
  France. B. Plumb. il N Y Times Mag p32-3
  Ag 31 '69
Cherchez l'espace; remodeling of dilapidated
  farm buildings. B. Plumb. il N Y Times
  Mag p 44-5 Jl 27 '69
Choice of past; home of the François Hé-
  bert-Stevens. V. Lawford. il Vogue 154:244-
  9+ O 1 '69
How to enjoy a vacation house an ocean
  away; excerpts from A farmhouse in Prov-
  ence. M. R. Henry. il House & Gard 135:
  72-3+ Je '69
Romantic summers in a walled town; David
  Hicks family in south of France. il House
  & Gard 135:74-7 Je '69

Georgia

Bold angles; hillside house built for J. Walker.
  Dalton. Ga. F. Heard. il House B 111:102-5
  S '69
Gruber house, Atlanta. il Arch Rec 145:52-3
  mid-My '69

Illinois

Architect's own; I. W. Colburn's house. Lake
  Forest. il House & Gard 135:94-101+ Mr '69
Complete house and lot. il Am Home 72:56-61
  Mr '69

Iowa

Weitz house, Des Moines. il Arch Rec 145:32-
  3 mid-My '69

Ireland

Atrium house in Ireland. il Arch Forum 130:
  46-9 Mr '69

Italy

From an ancient Florentine farm, a contemporary pavilion; a house of Theodore Waddell on Tuscany hilltop. E. Kinard. il House
  B 111:76-81 Je '69

Long Island, N.Y.

Arcs and bridges, the breakaway feeling. E.
  Sverbeyeff. il House B 111:70-3 Ag '69
Canal house. L. Grundy. il House B 111:58-
  61 Jl '69
De Vido house, East Hampton. il Arch Rec
  145:84-6 mid-My '69
Glowing house of glass and cedar. E. Sver-
  beyeff. il House B 111:91-5 S '69
Gorman house, Amagansett. il Arch Rec 145:
  54-7 mid-My '69
Hoffman house. East Hampton. il Arch Rec
  145:76-9 mid-My '69
Imagination achieves privacy behind glass
  walls. il House & Gard 135:58-63+ F '69
Imagination gives an individual stamp; house
  of Mr and Mrs Saul Steinberg. il House &
  Gard 135:44-9 F '69
Nine suntraps on one beach house; Fire Is-
  land Pines. il Home & Gard 135:68-71 Je
  '69
On the dunes; inventive house in three parts;
  Dr and Mrs Louis Langman's weekend
  house. il Home & Gard 135:88-93+ Je '69
When a weekend is the object: retreat for
  Ruth Emmet, in East Hampton. L. Grundy.
  il House B 111:56-7 F '69

Louisiana

Braselman house. New Orleans. il Arch Rec
  145:58-61 mid-My '69
Homes mothers want most; New Orleans. il
  Parents Mag 44:68-9+ Je '69
Revival of a southern showpiece; New Or-
  leans house. il Life 67:56-61 Ag 1 '69

Maine

Adventure in the Maine woods; level changes
  to make life-size playhouse. il Life 66:80-2+
  Mr 21 '69
Handsome country estate is designed for
  expansion. il Arch Rec 145:173-6 Ap '69

Maryland

House of our time, latticed with light. il
  House & Gard 136:118-23+ O '69
Miller house. Owings Mills. il Arch Rec 145:
  82-3 mid-My '69
Under one roof; personal space for three
  generations. il House & Gard 135:112-19
  Ap '69

Massachusetts

Instant nostalgia in a barn house. il Life
  67:136-9 O 10 '69
Lam house, Cotuit. il Arch Rec 145:30-1 mid-
  My '69
New England house in the woods. il Arch Rec
  146:131-4 Ag '69

ARCHITECTURE,   Domestic—Massachusetts—
    Continued
Snug harbor; Nantucket home of V. Kagan.
    R. Reif. il N Y Times Mag p94-6 N 9 '69
Storybook house: Wayland. il House B 111:
    98-101 S '69
Where the sand meets the sea. il House B 111:
    54-7 Jl '69
Young house to grow in: designed by Victor
    Cromie for his own family in Cambridge.
    E. Sverbeyeff. il House B 111:52-5 F '69

Michigan
Home for art for W. H. Ferry. Grosse Pointe,
    Mich. J. De Long. il House B 111:86-90 S
    '69

Missouri
Homes mothers want most; St Louis. il Pa-
    rents Mag 44:66-7 Je '69

New England
From an abandoned mill, an 18th-century
    treasure house. il House B 111:72-5 Je '69

New York (state)
Dream house in the country; weekend re-
    treat of Col and Mrs Roger Brunschwig in
    Old Chatham. il House & Gard 135:78-83
    Je '69
Fitzpatrick house, Yorktown. il Arch Rec 145:
    62-5 mid-My '69
French translation; 19th-century grist mill in
    Columbia County. R. Reif. il N Y Times
    Mag p54-6+ Je 22 '69
Giant size screen. il Am Home 72:56-9 Je '69
Glasswork that looks ahead to the seventies;
    Katonah, N.Y. J. De Long. il House B 111:
    130-5 O '69
House reflects a sprawling knoll; residence in
    Pound Ridge, N.Y. il Arch Rec 145:118-19
    F '69
In a rural schoolhouse, an ambience of pro-
    vincial France; house in Brewster. il House
    B 111:82-4 Je '69
    See also
Architecture, Domestic—Fire Island
Architecture, Domestic—Long Island, N.Y.

Ohio
Hisaka house. il Arch Forum 131:86-9 Jl '69

Oklahoma
Homes mothers want most; Tulsa. il Par-
    ents Mag 44:74-5 Ap '69

Ontario
Island escape. J. H. Ingersoll. il House B 111:
    66-7 Jl '69

Pennsylvania
Indoor-outdoor fieldstone in the Pennsylva-
    nia farmlands. il Life 66:86-8+ Ap 11 '69

Rhode Island
Homey and zooey; white clapboard farm-
    house above Narragansett Bay. L. Ham-
    mel. il N Y Times Mag p 114-15 O 12 '69

Switzerland
Chalet: contemporary slant. il House B 111:
    76-9 D '69
Terraced house on an alpine lake. il Arch
    Forum 131:52-9 D '69

Tennessee
Estate living on a small lot: one-story house
    for John Millard, jr. of Memphis. F. Heard.
    il House B 111:46-51 F '69
Markell house, Memphis. il Arch Rec 145:66-9
    mid-My '69

Texas
1969 house of ideas. il House & Gard 135:
    46-71+ Ja '69
Romantic totality, past and present. F.
    Heard and J. DeLong. il House B 111:96-
    102 Mr '69
Texas Victorian. T. Webb. il Art in Am 57:
    96-9 Jl '69

United States
These houses set a style standard for the
    seventies. il Bet Hom & Gard 47:80-7 S '69
Today, tomorrow, yesterday. il Am Home 72:
    63-73+ S '69
Whatever happened to the new building ideas
    of a few years back? il Bet Hom & Gard
    47:62-3+ S '69

Vermont
Dunbar house, Winhall. il Arch Rec 145:34-7
    mid-My '69
Roughing it in style; weekend house in
    Vermont. B. Plumb. il N Y Times Mag
    p60-1 F 2 '69
Space frame: Peter Berman structure. il Arch
    Forum 129:50-7 D '68

Virginia
Cube house vs. the squares. J. Neary. il Life
    67:83-4+ N 14 '69

Washington, D.C.
Art museum designed for living; home of
    Mr and Mrs David Lloyd Kreeger. R.
    Fitzgerald. il House B 111:58-65 F '69
Clean sweep in an old Victorian. il House
    B 111:144-7 N '69
Gallery house. B. Plumb. il N Y Times Mag
    p82-3 S 21 '69
Truly stately home; Kreeger residence. il
    Arch Rec 146:88-91 D '69

Washington (state)
Meilleur house, Bellevue. il Arch Rec 145:74-
    5 mid-My '69
On an island: glass enclosed living center;
    James G. Scripps family at mouth of Puget
    Sound. il House & Gard 135:94-7 Je '69

Western states
    See also
Western home awards
ARCHITECTURE, Ecclesiastical. See Church
    architecture
ARCHITECTURE, Gothic
    See also
Cathedrals
ARCHITECTURE, Hillside. See Hillside archi-
    tecture
ARCHITECTURE, Latin American
Architecture of Antigua Guatemala 1543-1773,
    by V. L. Annis. Review
    Américas il 21:36-9 Ag '69. F. L. Phelps
ARCHITECTURE, Maya
Mystifying Maya. K. Kuh. il Sat R 52:11-17
    Je 28 '69
ARCHITECTURE, Medieval
Life and death of Bruges. R. McMullen. il
    Horizon 11:74-91 Sum '69
ARCHITECTURE, Modern
Idea-giver; W. A. Gropius. il Time 94:49-50
    Jl 18 '69
Mies the master. D. L. Shirey. il Newsweek
    74:74-5 S 1 '69
Mies van der Rohe: disciplinarian for a con-
    fused age. il Time 94:46-7 Ag 29 '69
    See also
Bauhaus
ARCHITECTURE, Persian
Taliesin in Teheran; palace planned for Prin-
    cess Shams Pahlavi. W. W. Peters. il Art in
    Am 57:44-51 Jl '69
ARCHITECTURE, School. See School build-
    ings
ARCHITECTURE, Victorian
Texas Victorian. T. Webb. il Art in Am 57:96-9
    Jl '69
ARCHITECTURE and climate
Weinberger house, Miami, Florida. il Arch
    Rec 145:38-9 mid-My '69
ARCHITECTURE as a profession
Reports of the profession's death are greatly
    exaggerated. W. F. Wagner, jr. Arch Rec
    146:9-10 Jl '69
ARCHITECTURE follies. See Follies (architec-
    ture)
ARCHIVES
    See also
Oral history
Records, Preservation of

Germany
Secrets of the Nazi archives. D. Kahn. Atlan
    223:50-6 My '69

United States
Availability of Negro source material in
    Philadelphia. Negro Hist Bul 32:17 Mr '69
Department's records for 1939-41 now open
    to researchers. Dept State Bul 60:543 Je
    23 '69
    See also
Dwight David Eisenhower library, Abilene,
    Kan.
Presidential libraries
United States—National archives
ARCINIEGAS, Germán
Mosquito that stang. Américas 21:22-31 O
    '69
ARCTANDER, Erik H.
Are motorcycle safety helmets good enough?
    Pop Sci 194:122-4+ F '69
Join the out-of-season campers. Pop Sci
    195:140-2 S '69
What we're learning about electric cars. por
    Pop Sci 194:106-9+ Ja '69
ARCTIC exploration
Mystery in the Arctic; Hall's expedition and
    death. D. Jackson. il Life 66:66B-67+ Ap
    25 '69
South to Spitsbergen; British Trans-Arctic
    expedition. il Newsweek 73:49 Ap 21 '69

ARCTIC OCEAN
Thermal stratification in the Arctic Ocean.
V. T. Neal and others. bibliog il Science
166:373-4 O 17 '69
ARCTIC REGIONS
Hands across the ice; sovereignty in the
Arctic. R. F. Neill. Commonweal 91:302-3
D 5 '69
See also
Airlines—International services—Great Circle
route
Alaska
Antarctic Regions
Aviation—Arctic Regions
Geology—Arctic Regions
Greenland
Ice—Polar Regions
North Pole
Northwest Passage
Petroleum—Arctic Regions
Shipping—Arctic Regions
Yukon

Climate

Can the Pacific warm the Arctic? E. M.
Gushchenkov. Bul Atom Sci 25:49 My '69
Terrestrial microclimate; amelioration at
high latitudes. P. S. Corbet. bibliog il Sci-
ence 166:865-6 N 14 '69
ARCTIC sculpins. See Fishes
ARCTOSTAPHYLOS. See Bearberries
ARDÈLE; drama. See Anouilh, J.
ARDENNES, Battle of the, 1944-1945
Bitter woods, by J. S. D. Eisenhower. Review
Nat R 21:182-3 F 25 '69. G. F. Eliot
Hitler's last great gamble. il Time 94:36 D 19
'69
ARDERY, Philip P. Jr
Art. Nat R 21:240-1 Mr 11 '69
Going to the fair. Nat R 21:908+ S 9 '69
Upon a time in Woodstock. Nat R 21:908+
S 9 '69; Same abr. with title Woodstock
scene revisited. Cur 111:54-5 O '69
ARDOIN, John
DCO: good news. Hi Fi 19:MA27+ F '69
(ed) See Rescigno, N. Traditionalist
ARDREY, Dan
How to do Europe by train. Travel & Came-
ra 32:13-14 Jl '69
ARDREY, Robert
Tiger about to stir up a mare's nest. Life 66:
9+ Je 20 '69
about
African genesis and Lord of the flies: two
studies of the beastie within. R. Lederer
and P. H. Beattie. Engl J 58:1316-21+ D '69
AREA navigation. See Navigation, Aerial
AREA studies
Sinews of empire. D. Horowitz. il Ramp Mag
8:32-42 O '69
See also
African studies
American studies
Oriental studies
ARECIBO ionospheric observatory. See Astro-
nomical observatories—Puerto Rico
AREHART, Joan Lynn
Caring for a premature baby. Parents Mag
44:42-3+ Je '69
Oceanic drug chest. Sea Front 15:98-107 Mr
'69
ARENAS
See also
New York (city)—Madison Square Garden
ARENAS, Sports. See Stadiums
ARES, Charles E.
Excerpt from statement submitted to Sub-
committee on constitutional rights, Janu-
ary 1969. Cong Digest 48:123+ Ap '69
ARF; drama. See Greenburg, D.
ARGALI hunting
Breakfast at midnight. J. R. Mellon. il Out-
door Life 144:60-3+ Jl '69
ARGENTINA
See also
Andes Mountains
Arts and crafts—Argentina
Geology—Argentina
Investments, Foreign (in Argentina)
Periodicals—Argentina
Railroads and state—Argentina
Strikes—Argentina

Description and travel

Beyond Buenos Aires: Argentina's coastal
playground. A. Colbin. il Travel 132:71-3
N '69

Economic conditions

Argentina steps up its tempo. il Bsns W
p56-7+ My 17 '69

Politics and government

Freedom curtailed in Argentina. J. M. Swomley, jr. Chr Cent 86:1230-1 S 24 '69
Siege of Copolletti. Time 94:38 O 3 '69

Religious institutions
and affairs

See also
Methodist church in Argentina

Riots

End to tranquillity. Time 93:44+ Je 6 '69
Rocky way. il Newsweek 73:65 Je 9 '69
ARGENTINE poetry

Translations into English

Ars poetica; tr. by W. S. Merwin. J. L.
Borges. Harp Baz 102:238 Mr '69
Daybreak; tr. by N. T. di Giovanni. J. L.
Borges. New Yorker 45:133 My 24 '69
Embarking on the study of Anglo-Saxon
grammar; tr. by A. Reid. J. L. Borges.
Harp Baz 102:238 Mr '69
Heraclitus; poem; tr. by N. T. Di Giovanni.
J. L. Borges. New Yorker 45:34 Ag 9 '69
How the mountains talk; poem; tr. by S.
Blackwell. L. Lugones. il Américas 21:18
Ja '69
Isidoro Acevedo; tr. by N. T. Di Giovanni.
J. L. Borges. New Yorker 45:60 N 8 '69
Return without returning. J. Villaverde.
Américas 21:42-3 Jl '69
Six poems: Keeper of the books; June 1968;
Cambridge; Invocation to Joyce; In praise
of darkness; Plain things; tr. by N. T. Di
Giovanni. J. L. Borges. New Yorker 45:
52-3 D 13 '69
To a Saxon poet; tr. by N. T. di Giovanni.
J. L. Borges. New Yorker 44:40 F 8 '69
Unending gift; tr. by N. T. Di Giovanni. J.
L. Borges. Harp Baz 102:238 Mr '69
ARGON
Viscosity of argon at high temperatures. R.
A. Dawe and E. B. Smith. bibliog il Sci-
ence 163:675-6 F 14 '69
ARGONNE national laboratory
Redirecting a national lab. Sci N 96:112 Ag 9
'69
ARGUELLO, Frank B.
We created our own data-processing division.
por Am City 84:155-6 S '69
ARGUS, M. K.
My friend, the terrorist. Sat R 52:26 My 24 '69
ARGUS, incorporated
Try selling red ink; GT&E trying to get rid
of 42 per cent Argus stock. Forbes 103:69
Ap 15 '69
ARGUS research corporation
Wall Street's wizards of odds; securities an-
alysts climbing from file room to councils of
power. il Bsns W p 122-4+ Mr 15 '69
ARGYLL COUNTY, Scotland
See also
Colonsay (island)
ARIADNE auf Naxos; opera. See Strauss, R.
ARIAS, Arnulfo
Exit Panama's lesser evil. Ramp Mag 7:16+
N 30 '68
ARIAS
See also
Phonograph records—Arias
ARID regions
See also
Desert vegetation
Deserts
Irrigation
ARIKARA Indians
Arikara Indian ceramics. L. A. Brown. il
Ceram Mo 17:16-19 Mr '69
ARISTOCRACY
See also
Great Britain—Peerage
ARISTOTLE
Classics revisited. K. Rexroth. Sat R 52:28+
F 22 '69
ARITHMETIC
Study and teaching
Learning at home with Dial-a-drill; New
York city program. il (p 1) Sr Schol 94:
Schol Teach 4 Ap 18 '69
ARITHMETIC, Mental
Decibels without logs. W. G. Miller. Electr
World 82:71 S '69
ARIZONA
See also
Architecture, Domestic—Arizona
Canyon De Chelly National Monument
Chiricahua National Monument
Education—Arizona
Fishing—Arizona

ARIZONA—See also—*Continued*
  Glen Canyon
  Grand Canyon
  Hunting—Arizona
  Montezuma Castle National Monument
  Wilderness areas—Arizona

Description and travel
Arizona, nature's gaudiest paintpot. F. Drake
  and K. Drake. il Read Digest 94:146-53 Mr
  '69
Arizona's Apacheland. T. B. Lesure. il Trav-
  el 131:71-3 My '69
Letter from cowboy and Canyon country. P.
  Devlin. Vogue 153:50+ Mr 1 '69

History
Arizona vanquished; life on a military fron-
  tier. R. M. Utley. il Am West 6:16-21 N '69
ARIZONA state university, Tempe
  Odd one for the Sun Devils; third collegiate
  championship. P. Carry. Sports Illus 30:
  48-9 Je 30 '69
  Undersea world of Jonah and Thetis; Exotic
  environments laboratory. J. Matthews. il
  Sci Digest 66:66-70 N '69
ARKANSAS
  Growing up in the Arkansas Delta. C. Cloar.
  il Esquire 71:128-31 Je '69
  See also
  Buffalo River
  Fishing—Arkansas
  Prisons—Arkansas
  Radioactive fallout—Arkansas
ARKIN, Alan
  Trade winds. C. Amory. Sat R 52:8+ S 6 '69
ARKING, Linda
  American as indentured servant. Mlle 69:211+
  My '69
ARKVILLE press
  Publishing scene. D. Dempsey. Sat R 52:39
  Ap 12 '69
ARLEN, Michael J.
  Least passive viewer. S. W. Little. Sat R
  52:128-9 Mr 8 '69
  Old fear of Gould and the new criticism of
  Arlen. R. Burgheim. Harper 239:98-100 Ag
  '69
ARLES, James E.
  County government. Parks & Rec 4:30-2+ Ag
  '69
ARLINGTON COUNTY, Va.
  Evaluate the present and chart the future.
  B. W. Johnson. il Am City 84:75-7 Ag '69
ARMAGNAC, Alden P.
  Condon report on UFO's, should you believe
  it? Pop Sci 194:72-6 Ap '69
  World's biggest atom-power plant. Pop Sci
  195:94-7+ S '69
ARMAMENT industries. See Munitions indus-
  tries
ARMAMENTS
  Let's internationalize defense marketing. R. E.
  McGarrah. Harvard Bsns R 47:146-55 My '69
  See also
  Airplanes, Military—Armaments
  Armed forces
  Disarmament
  Tanks, Military

Cost
Cost of world armaments. A. S. Alexander.
  il Sci Am 221:21-7 bibliog(p 148) O '69
Cost of world armaments. il UNESCO Courier
  23:13-15 Ja '70
New SIPRI yearbook of armaments, disarma-
  ment documents the direction, pace of the
  arms race. D. S. Greenberg. Science 166:
  1124-5 N 28 '69
ARMBRUSTER, Carl J.
  Trends to intercommunion. America 121:455-6
  N 15 '69
ARMCO steel corporation
  Armco is opening a door for the young. il
  Nations Bsns 57:16 D '69
  Bill Verity's Monday afternoon club. S. Blick-
  stein. il Duns R 93:33-5 My '69
  Diversify to beat the take-over; Armco
  steel's strategy. il Bsns W p 168-9 O 11
  '69
ARMED forces

Appropriations and expenditures
Cost of world armaments. A. S. Alexander.
  il Sci Am 221:21-7 bibliog(p 148) O '69
To arms! world outlays for wars. New Repub
  160:8 F 22 '69
ARMED services committee. See United States
  —Congress—House of representatives—
  Armed services, Committee on; United
  States—Congress—Senate—Armed services,
  Committee on

ARMELAGOS, George J.
  Disease in ancient Nubia. bibliog Science
  163:255-9 Ja 17 '69
ARMENIAN cookery. See Cookery, Armenian
ARMIES
  Old rule that doesn't work; military power.
  S. Alsop. Newsweek 73:120 My 12 '69
ARMISTICE day. See Veterans day
ARMITAGE, Evelyn E.
  Mushrooms, an unexpected organic dividend.
  Org Gard & Farm 16:100-2+ F '69
ARMOIRES. See Chests
ARMORIES
  Rediscovery: a Tiffany room; Seventh regi-
  ment and armory, New York city. E. Rob-
  inson. il Art in Am 57:72-7 Jl '69
  See also
  Military museums
ARMOUR, Richard
  Bookseller's garden of verses. Pub W 195:126
  Je 2 '69
  Born too soon; poem. Todays Ed 58:28 N
  '69
  How about humor? Writer 82:24-6 Je '69
  Some advice on advice; or, Take it from me.
  Parents Mag 44:44-5 Jl '69
ARMOUR and company
  Evolution of private manpower planning in
  Armour's plant closings. J. L. Stern. bib-
  liog il Mo Labor R 92:21-8 D '69
  Greyhound makes a run for Armour. Bsns
  W p 19 F 1 '69
  Greyhound winning race for Armour. Bsns
  W p 170 O 18 '69
  Helping workers locate jobs following a
  plant shutdown. J. C. Ullman. bibliog Mo
  Labor R 92:35-40 Ap '69
  High-stakes game. Newsweek 74:70+ Jl 7
  '69
  Over a barrel? General Host wins control of
  Armour. Forbes 103:44 Mr 15 '69
  Packing up at Armour; acquisition by Gen-
  eral host. Bsns W p27 Mr 3 '69
  Pistell packer? anti-merger maneuver. News-
  week 73:83-4 Ap 14 '69
  Prince, the General and the Greyhound.
  Time 93:94 My 9 '69
  You can't lose 'em all. il Forbes 104:25-6 N 15
  '69
ARMS, Artificial. See Artificial limbs
ARMS, Coats of. See Heraldry
ARMS control. See Disarmament
ARMS control and disarmament agency. See
  United States—Arms control and disarma-
  ment agency
ARMS control legislation. See Firearms—Laws
  and regulations
ARMS limitation talks. See Strategic arms
  limitation talks
ARMS sales. See Purchasing, Military
ARMSTRONG, Bill
  Big red, something new in street mainten-
  ance. Am City 84:90-1 N '69
ARMSTRONG, Herbert W.
  Colleges re-educate for Christ's return. A. B.
  Haines. Chr Cent 86:264 F 19 '69
ARMSTRONG, James, bp
—and Conyers, John, jr
  Vietnam: sojourn and sequel. pors Chr Cent
  86:1307-9 O 15 '69
        about
  New York radio station bans church pro-
  gram. Chr Cent 86:1132 S 3 '69
ARMSTRONG, Kathy Lees
  Growing tricks with plastic sheeting. Org
  Gard & Farm 16:40-2 Je '69
ARMSTRONG, Kenneth
  John Wesley college; disengaging the Haza-
  renes. H. H. Ward. Chr Today 14:39 N 21
  '69
ARMSTRONG, Lois Dickert
  Los Angeles. See issues of Art news
ARMSTRONG, Marion
  Apostate; poem. Chr Cent 86:801 Je 11 '69
  Movies (title varies) Chr Cent 86:186, 258, 323,
  420-1, 452+, 521-2, 686-7, 815, 905, 960, 1225-
  6, 1253-4, 1352, 1423-4, 1587-8; 87:22+ F 5,
  19, Mr 5, 26-Ap 2, 16, My 14, Je 11, Jl 2,
  16, S 24-O 1, 22, N 5, D 10 '69, Ja 7 '70
ARMSTRONG, Neil A.
  Armstrong recalls moon landing details; ex-
  cerpts from address. Aviation W 91:20-2
  O 13 '69
  Man walks on another world. il por Nat
  Geog 136:738-49 D '69
  Moon had been awaiting us a long time. por
  Life 67:24-5 Ag 22 '69
  Space exploration; address. September 16,
  1969. Vital Speeches 35:742 O 1 '69
  What it's like for man on the moon. U S
  News 67:25 Ag 4 '69

ARMSTRONG, Neil A.—*Continued*

about

Apollo 11's team: the three who will carry the flag. por U S News 67:33 Jl 21 '69
Astronauts detail lunar flight experience; with editorial comment. Z. Strickland. il por Aviation W 91:11, 18-20 Ag 18 '69
Crew: men apart. il por Time 94:27-30 Jl 18 '69
From Texas to tranquillity. il por Newsweek 73:63 Je 30 '69
Homage to the men from the moon. il pors Time 94:8-11 Ag 22 '69
Men for the moon. il por Newsweek 74:72 Jl 21 '69
Le mot juste for the moon. W. H. Honan. Esquire 72:53-6+ Jl '69
Neil Armstrong refuses to waste any heartbeats. D. J. Hamblin. il pors Life 67:18-21 Jl 4 '69
Series of lunar landings simulated. Z. Strickland. il Aviation W 90:55-9 Je 30 '69
They were there. il Newsweek 74:73 Ag 25 '69
Two for the moon. il por Sci Digest 65:32-3 Ap '69
We love you. il pors Newsweek 74:20B-23 Ag 25 '69
See also
Space flight to the moon—Manned flights—Armstrong-Aldrin-Collins flight, 1969

ARMSTRONG, O. K.
Free China gives Africa a helping hand. Read Digest 95:183-4+ N '69
Should churches be allowed to do business tax-free? Read Digest 94:84-8 Mr '69

ARMSTRONG, Richard
Labor 1970: angry, aggressive, acquisitive. Fortune 80:94-7+ O '69
McGeorge Bundy confronts the teachers. N Y Times Mag p25-7+ Ap 20 '69
Military-industrial complex, Russian style. Fortune 80:34-7+ Ag 1 '69

ARMSTRONG, Robert L.
Research in name only. Clear House 43:298-300 Ja '69

ARMSTRONG-JONES, Antony Charles Robert, 1st earl of Snowdon. See Snowdon, A. C. R. A.-J.

ARMSTRONG cork company
New house for Armstrong cork. R. Levy. il Duns R 94:41-4+ N '69
People have to live somewhere. Forbes 104:22-3 Jl 15 '69

ARMY, International. See International police

ARMY air force. See United States—Air force, Army

ARMY chaplains. See Chaplains, Military

ARMY engineers. See United States—Army—Corps of engineers

ARMY football. See Football

ARMY investigations. See Government investigations

ARMY-McCarthy controversy, 1954. See McCarthy- Army controversy, 1954

ARMY reserves. See United States—Army—Reserves

ARMY service clubs. See Clubs

ARNASON, H. H.
Motherwell: the window and the wall. Art N 68:48-52+ Sum '69

ARNDT, Linda A.
Teaching the writing of poetry. Sr Schol 94: Schol Teach 16-17 F 14 '69

ARNESON, George Stephen
Pro at Vendo. por Duns R 93:72+ My '69

ARNETT, Edward M.
Chemical information test station. por Chem 42:16-18 Mr '69

ARNETT, Peter
ARVN: prospects for the army of South Vietnam. Cur Hist 57:333-8 D '69
National liberation front. Cur Hist 56:82-7+ F '69

ARNEZ, Nancy L.
Racial understanding through literature. bibliog f Engl J 58:56-61 Ja '69

ARNO, Stephen F.
Glaciers in the American West; with biographical sketch. por Natur Hist 78:4, 84-9 F '69
Interpreting the rattlesnake. il Nat Parks 43:15-17 D '69

ARNOLD, Grace
Hideaway garden arbor for $25. Org Gard & Farm 16:72-3 Ap '69

ARNOLD, Martin
There is no rest for Roy Wilkins. N Y Times Mag p40-1+ S 28 '69

ARNOLD, Matthew
Hebraism & Hellenism now. M. Himmelfarb. Commentary 48:50-7 Jl '69

ARNOLD, Oren
Apache doctor who sparked a new era for Indians. Todays Health 47:30-3+ O '69

ARNOLD, Rus
Answers; questions and answers. See issues of Travel & Camera
Look before you shoot! Writers Digest 49:54-7 My '69
Photo answers; questions and answers. por Travel & Camera 32:88-9 Ap; 96-7 My; 96-7 Je '69
Photojournalism. See every other issue of Writer's digest

ARNOLD, Walter
[Book review] Commonweal 90:180-2 Ap 25 '69
Punishment and guilt. Cath World 208:276-7 Mr '69

ARNOLD arboretum. See Harvard university

ARNOLDO Mondadori editore. See Publishers and publishing—Italy

ARNSTEIN, Felix G.
Mantle of Palestrina. Opera N 34:20-1 D 13 '69

ARNSTEIN, Flora J.
Sea horses; poem. Nation 208:345 Mr 17 '69
Sea horses; poem. Nation 209:122 Ag 11 '69

ARNSTEIN, Helene S.
Parent and child. N Y Times Mag p 101-3 F 23 '69

AROMATIC plants
Aromatherapy; could there be more to perfume than meets the nose? il Vogue 153:198-9+ My '69

ARON, Raymond
Already de Gaulle has largely disappeared; interview. por U S News 66:26-9 My 12 '69
If American will crumbles; interview. por U S News 67:43 D 1 '69

ARONOW, Don
Master of those mad racers. J. Kirshenbaum. il por Sports Illus 31:50-2+ N 17 '69

ARONOWITZ, Alfred G.
Wisdom of their years; the Beatles. Life 66:12 Ja 31 '69

AROVA, Sonia
Norway; interview, ed. by O. Maynard. pors Dance Mag 43:41-3+ My '69

ARP, Halton
On the origin of arms in spiral galaxies. il Sky & Tel 38:385-7 D '69

ARP, Hans
Art world; retrospective exhibition at Guggenheim. H. Rosenberg. New Yorker 45:91-2+ Je 21 '69

ARP, Jean. See Arp, Hans

ARP, Leon J.
Breath of life. Newsweek 73:68 Je 9 '69

ARPIN, Jean V.
Contract snowfighting. por Am City 84:98-9 D '69

ARRABAL, Fernando
Le jardin des delices. Criticism
New Yorker 45:200+ N 29 '69

ARRANGEMENT of flowers. See Flowers, Arrangement of

ARRANGEMENT of furniture. See Furniture, Arrangement of

ARREST
Bail for the rich, jail for the poor. H. Subin. Nation 208:363-6 Mr 24 '69
Dragnet arrests: Court says no. U S News 66:12 My 5 '69
Jail before trial. A. S. Goldstein. New Repub 160:15-18 Mr 8 '69
Nightmare for the innocent in a California jail. J. P. Ritter, jr. il Life 67:51-2+ Ag 15 '69
What to do when you're arrested. L. David. il Mech Illus 65:45-7+ N '69
See also
Bail
United Nations—Committee on the right of everyone to be free from arbitrary arrest, detention, and exile

ARREST of judgment
Sisson's complaint. Wyzanski's ploy. I. Silver. Commonweal 90:385-9 Je 20 '69

ARRHENIUS, G. See Alfvén, H. jt. auth.

ARROWHEADS
What's up front? broadhead arrows. G. H Gillelan. il Outdoor Life 144:28+ S '69

ARROWS. See Bow and arrow

ARSENIC
Arsenic. D. Sabine Chem 42:20 Ap '69

ARSENIC poisoning
Murder at Thank God Bay; early Arctic explorer's death solved by neutron activation analysis. Sci Am 220:52 Mr '69

ARSON
See also
Trials (arson)

ART

Jacob Landau on art, etc. J. Landau. il
  Ramp Mag 8:20 O '69
On the scene. C. Barnes. See issues of Holi-
  day to August 1969
    See also
Action in art
Advertising art
Aesthetics
Artists
Arts and crafts
Black and white (art)
Childrens art
Composition (art)
Drawing
Drawings
Electronics in art
Expressionism (art)
Form (art)
Frescoes
Glass painting and staining
Graffiti
Graphic arts
Grotesque in art
Impressionism (art)
Landscape painting
Light in art
Mannerism (art)
Mural painting and decoration
Nature in art
Negroes in art
Nude in art
Pen drawing
Performing arts
Photography, Artistic
Plastics as an art form
Pottery
Realism in art
Sculpture
Sex in art
Space flight in art
Surrealism (art)
Symbolism in art
Windows in art
Women in art
Youth in art

Appreciation

Cultural commercialism. G. Phillips. Art N
  68:29+ S '69
Enrichment through informal art appreciation
  with related art activity. L. J. Bell. il Sch
  Arts 69:10-11 S '69
Have we lost our marbles? K. H. Laramee. il
  Sch Arts 69:36-7 N '69
Louvre comes to the classroom. J. F. Bryson.
  il Sch Arts 68:38-9 F '69
Picture lady program: seven years old and
  still going strong! mothers presenting repro-
  ductions of masterpieces. H. J. Anderson. il
  Sch Arts 69:36-7 S '69
Readers' choice. il Art in Am 57:26-7 S; 51 N
  '69
    See also
Art criticism

Awards

Awards and honors   (cont) il Design 70:37
  mid-Wint; 37 Spr; 37 Sum '69
Manhattan woman sixty-seven is chosen '69
  Golden age painter in NY show. il Aging
  180:15 O '69

Bibliography

Art books. L. Alloway. Nation 209:704-7 D 22
  '69
Book review section. See issues of Design
Book reviews. See issues of American artist:
  School arts
Kate's writings; a selected bibliography;
  comp. by J. M. Edelstein. K. Steinitz. il
  Wilson Lib Bul 44:529-34 Ja '70
Museum publications. Antiques 95:410+ Mr '69
    See also
Art literature

Collections

See Art—Galleries and museums

Collectors and collecting

Collecting originals on a shoestring. N. R.
  Piene. House & Gard 136:80-1+ O '69
Collector: Henry P. McIlhenny. A. Pryce-
  Jones. il Art in Am 57:94-103 N '69
    See also
Art—Private collections
Art as an investment

Competitions

1969 Scholastic art awards. il Sr Schol 94:
  18-19 My 9 '69
    See also
Childrens art—Competitions

Conservation and restoration

New science of art conservation: reprint. H.
  J. Plenderleith. il UNESCO Courier 22:56-
  7+ Ag '69

Copyright

See Copyright—Art

Courses of study

See Art—Study and teaching

Criticism

See Art criticism

Dictionaries and encyclopedias

McGraw-Hill dictionary of art. ed. by B. S.
  Myers. Review
    America 121:204 S 20 '69. C. J. McNaspy

Education

See Art education

Exhibitions

American artist travelogue. il Am Artist 33:
  35-42 Ap '69
Art; annual exhibition of contemporary
  American art at the Whitney museum. L.
  Alloway. Nation 210:29-30 Ja 12 '70
Art; Paintings from the photo at the River-
  side museum. L. Alloway. Nation 209:741-2
  D 29 '69
Art; Plastic presence at the Jewish museum.
  L. Alloway. Nation 209:646 D 8 '69
Art; R. Doty's exhibition at the Whitney mu-
  seum. L. Alloway. Nation 209:483+ N 3 '69
Art; surrealist exhibitions. L. Alloway. Na-
  tion 209:357 O 6 '69
Art world (cont) H. Rosenberg. New Yorker
  44:86+ Ja 25; 45:107-8+ F 22; 110+ Mr
  21; 136+ Ap 19; 118+ My 17; 91-2+ Je
  21; 102+ S 27; 167-70+ N 8; 171-2+ D
  6 '69
Artists and Mr Daley. T. B. Hess. Art N
  67:29 N '68
Bauhaus is alive and well in soup plates and
  skyscrapers. J. R. Mellow. il N Y Times
  Mag p34-5+ S 14 '69
Big big show; the cost of competitive ex-
  hibitions. N. Kent. Am Artist 33:5 D '69
Boston is here, now. J. Koethe. il Art N
  68:30-3+ S '69
Bulletin board. See issues of American artist
Coming soon, art exhibits. See issues of
  Design
Current and coming. E. P. Birk. See issues
  of Antiques
Emphasis. B. Diamonstein. Harp Baz 103:
  200+ N '69
Exhibition at San Diego; Old Town galleries.
  N. Kent. il Am Artist 33:36-44+ S '69
Feel it; Museum of contemporary crafts ex-
  hibition explores anti-visual experience. I.
  Horovitz. il Craft Horiz 29:14-15+ Mr '69
Flesh and filigree; exhibition at Toronto
  museum. M. Amaya. il Art N 68:24-7+ D
  '69
Foreign exchange; Biennale of illustrations
  Bratislava. J. Donovan. il Sat R 52:61-2 N
  8 '69
From the brink, something grand; Metro-
  politan museum centennial exhibition, New
  York painting and sculpture: 1940-1970. il
  Time 94:78-81 O 24 '69
Fun city festival; exhibition of modern
  American painting and sculpture at the
  Metropolitan museum. T. B. Hess. Art N
  68:23 D '69
Goings on about town. See issues of New
  Yorker
Hooked on bigness; Metropolitan museum's
  centennial exhibition, New York painting
  and sculpture: 1940-1970. K. Kuh. Sat R 52:
  69-70 N 22 '69
Horror show; Human concern/Personal tor-
  ment at the Whitney museum. D. L. Shirey.
  il Newsweek 74:107 N 3 '69
How to attend an opening; Manhattan gal-
  leries. il Time 93:75 F 14 '69
In pursuit of antiquity; exhibition of Wang
  Hui's works. K. Kuh. il Sat R 52:60-2
  O 4 '69
In the worst of taste. D. L. Shirey. il News-
  week 74:125 N 10 '69
Inheritor and activator; traveling exhibition
  of works by L. Moholy-Nagy. K. Kuh. il
  Sat R 52:38-40 Jl 26 '69
Modern masters amid the old; New York
  painting and sculpture. 1940-1970 at the
  Met. D. Bourdon. il Life 67:12 O 24 '69
Museum calendar. See issues of American
  artist
New York gallery notes. G. Glueck. See
  issues of Art in America

ART—Exhibitions—*Continued*

19th-century franc revalued; exhibition at the Minneapolis institute of arts. R. Rosenblum. il Art N 68:26-31+ Sum '69

Pervasive excitement for the eye and mind; display of N. Rockefeller's holdings at three Manhattan museums. il Time 93:88-93 My 16 '69

Pop reappraised; exhibition Hayward gallery, London. J. Russell. il Art in Am 57:78-89 Jl '69

Portal to illumination: exhibit at Museum of art, Rhode Island school of design, of Romanesque and early Gothic stone sculptures. il Time 93:64 My 30 '69

Rembrandt, the unrealistic realist. K. Kuh. il Sat R 53:46-8 Ja 10 '70

Reviews and previews. See issues of Art news

Rocky as collector; exhibiting in three New York museums. il Newsweek 73:88 My 26 '69

Santa Barbara's weekend art show. il Sunset 142:34 Je '69

Television as art, inevitable; exhibition at the Howard Wise gallery. B. Rose. Vogue 154:36 Ag 15 '69

Thirty years of the New York school; exhibition. New York painting and sculpture: 1940-1970 to open Metropolitan museum's centennial celebrations. H. Kramer. il N Y Times p28-31+ O 12 '69

Tour of a long spiral; exhibition season in Europe. H. Judson. il Time 94:30-3 D 26 '69

Variety of high traditions; exhibitions from Europe, Asia and Peru. R. Berenson. il Nat R 21:33-4 Ja 14 '69

Where and when to exhibit. See issues of Art news

Worst art show: annual members' show at the Architectural league of New York. il Life 67:81-2 D 12 '69

Young lyrical painters; lyrical abstraction of this art season. L. Aldrich. il Art in Am 57:104-13 N '69

See also
Exhibitions, Traveling
Metropolitan museum of art, New York
Museum of modern art, New York
Whitney museum of American art, New York
also subhead Exhibitions under various subjects, e.g. Bronzes—Exhibitions

Anecdotes, facetiae, satire, etc.

Notes from an exhibition. J. Stevenson. il New Yorker 45:32-3 Mr 22 '69

Galleries and museums

Art museum in today's society. S. E. Lee. Art N 68:27+ Ap '69

Museum accessions. R. Davidson. See issues of Antiques

Museums of New York state. il Am Artist 33:8 Ja '69

See also
Harvard university—Fogg museum
Minneapolis institute of arts

Architecture
See Museums—Architecture

Work with children

Going to school in an art museum. il Sunset 143:100-1 O '69

Philosophy

Art as intersecting fields of energy. J. Unterecker. Sat R 52:27-9+ Je 14 '69

Artworks and packages, by H. Rosenberg. Review
  Nation 209:544-5 N 17 '69. L. Alloway

Bauhaus, by H. M. Wingler. Review
  New Repub 161:28-31 O 11 '69. P. Jacobsohn

Heritage. N. Kent. Am Artist 33:5 N '69

Neuestern's ultimate non-act; interview, ed. by K. Kundry. O. Neuestern. il Art N 68:54-6+ S '69

On doing-one's-thing. W. Goodman. Am Scholar 38:240-7 Spr '69

Poets, prophets, and potters. D. Rutherford. bibliog Ceram Mo 17:31 N '69

Sweet mystery of life. A. Goldin. il Art N 68:46-51+ My '69

See also
Aesthetics

Prices

See also
Art as an investment

Private collections

Agnelli time-space: the past turned forward in Turin. il Vogue 153:210-11 Ap 1 '69

Apotheosis of an art addict. il Harp Baz 102:118-19 Ja '69

As I see it; interview, ed. by W. Welch and S. Fogelson. P. Pollen. il Forbes 103:50+ Ap 15 '69

Collector: Joseph H. Hirshhorn. J. Jacobs. il Art in Am 57:56-71 Jl '69

Collector: Larry Aldrich. J. Russell. il Art in Am 57:56-65 Ja '69

Collector: Paul Bernat; rare collection of Chinese porcelain. A. Pryce-Jones. il Art in Am 57:68-75 S '69

Collectors: Edgar and Bernice Chrysler Garbisch. M. Black. il Art in Am 57:48-59 My '69

Collectors: Paul and Ruth Tishman. R. Sieber. il Art in Am 57:50-61 Mr '69

Decisive art collection: Tremaine collection. G. Baro. il Vogue 153:132-41+ F 15 '69

Geneva Khmer; the collection of Tan Phuoc Nguyen. H. La Farge. il Art N 68:53+ Sum '69

German genre paintings from the Von Schleinitz collection. T. Atkinson. il Antiques 96:712-16 N '69

Lively arts; interview, ed. by E. Sparn. P. Guggenheim. Sr Schol 94:15 My 9 '69

Nelson Rockefeller collection. A. Saarinen. il McCalls 96:26-7 Ja '69

Nelson Rockefeller's collections; primitive art (African, Oceanic and pre-Columbian) exhibitions. T. S. Hess. Art N 68:25 Sum '69

Paintings descending a ramp; Peggy Guggenheim collection at Uncle Solomon's museum. G. Glueck. il N Y Times Mag p36-8+ Ja 19 '69

Peggy Guggenheim's art comes to America. H. Ehrlich. il Look 33:34-7 F 4 '69

Peggy's back in town; collection of P. Guggenheim at the Guggenheim. D. L. Shirey. il Newsweek 73:70-3 Ja 27 '69

Pervasive excitement for the eye and mind; display of N. Rockefeller's holdings at three Manhattan museums. il Time 93:88-93 My 16 '69

Rocky as a collector; collections on display at Metropolitan museum. Museum of modern art and at Museum of primitive art. J. R. Mellow. il N Y Times Mag p34-6+ My 18 '69

Rocky as collector; exhibiting in three New York museums. il Newsweek 73:88 My 26 '69

Taste of the Guggenheims. B. Rose. Vogue 153:152 Ap 1 '69

Windfall for Texas; Michener collection. E. Freed. il Art in Am 57:78-85 N '69

See also
Art in the home
Pierpont Morgan library

Psychology

Manifest and the latent content of two paintings by Hieronymus Bosch. E. Fromm. bibliog il Am Imago 26:145-66 Sum '69

See also
Art therapy

Scholarships and fellowships

Competitions, scholarships. See issues of Art news

Social aspects
See Art and society

Study and teaching

Art for black students; a change in objectives. C. Lawrence. il Sch Arts 68:18-21 F '69

Case for curriculum in the arts. S. Liby. il Sch Arts 69:8-9 S '69

Clipboard. V. G. Timmons. See issues of School arts

Group pictures, group organization. V. R. Jackson. il Design 70:4-7 mid-Wint '69

Loss of reason and a lack of structure. A. W. Beck. il Sch Arts 69:24-5 O '69

Students and teachers. N. Kent. Am Artist 33:5 Mr '69

Teachers need to do their thing too! in-service projects or workshops. D. O. Williams. il Sch Arts 69:18-21 S '69

Teaching of art as social revolution. V. Lanier. Ed Digest 34-42-5 Ap '69

See also
Art—Appreciation
Art education
Art teachers
Color
Design—Study and teaching
Drawing—Study and teaching
Painting—Study and teaching

Materials

Acrylics in the classroom. J. T. Brandstadter. il Sch Arts 68:28-9 Ap '69

Design experiments with natural materials. R. Moore. il Sch Arts 68:16-17 Mr '69

Fold and dip. M. Foster. Sch Arts 69:22-4 Ja '70

ART—Study and teaching—Materials—*Cont.*
Glue-tempera relief. H. M. Stahl. il Sch Arts 69:12-13 N '69
Op art can be simple. M. J. Acosta. il Design 70:16-18 mid-Wint '69
Painting with developer. P. Greenberg and M. Greenberg. il Sch Arts 68:30-1 My '69
Stones come of age. J. F. Warwick and A. Smith. il Sch Arts 68:30-1 Mr '69
Stretching and enclosing space; use of styrofoam packing material. Mrs C. Noel. il Sch Arts 69:34 S '69
　See also
Arts and crafts—Study and teaching—Materials
Papier-mâché
Sculpture—Study and teaching—Materials

Projects
Ah! Sunflower. M. J. Acosta. il Design 70:36 mid-Wint '69
Art motivation for ghetto children. J. Comins. il Sch Arts 69:6-7 O '69
Art students design computer; areas of school curricula in Kennett consolidated school. Kennett Square, Pa. S. Pursel. il Sch Arts '68:6-7 Je '69
Let's focus on the group. J. Kranser. il Sch Arts 68:8 Mr '69
Our moon discoveries. R. Sherin. il Sch Arts 69:38-40 D '69
Stained glass reflects today's spirit. C. Young. il Sch Arts 68:8 Ap '68
Tonality, white to black. M. Acosta. il Design 70:33-5 Spr '69
Total art experience for third graders. C. Bowles. il Sch Arts 68:37-8 Ap '69
　See also
Collage
Enamel and enameling
Mobiles
Mosaics
Mural painting and decoration
Paper work

Technique
Materials of art versus the art of materials. H. Aach. il Craft Horiz 29:37-8 Jl '69

Themes
Beholden to no one; farm people Wyeth painted. G. Logsdon. il Farm J 93:28-9+ Mr '69
Getting in the mood; to create a Halloween painting. J. Williamson. il Sch Arts 69:54 O '69
Motherwell: the window and the wall; Open series. H. H. Arnason. il Art N 68:48-52+ Sum '69
Statements in paint; works of art that deal with other works of art. il Time 93:68-71 F 28 '69
Stream of consciousness drawing. E. J. Dorsey. il Design 70:25-7 mid-Wint '69
Where do we come from? What are we? Where are we going? Gauguin's greatest painting. J. Jacobs. il Horizon 11:52-65 Sum '69
　See also
California in art
European war in art
Florida in art
Israel in art
Music in art
South America in art
Violence in art
West in art
Windows in art
Women in art

Therapeutic use
See Art therapy

Africa
　See also
Arts and crafts—Africa

Belgium
　See also
Art, Flemish

California
California's cultural nugget; symposium, with introd. by N. Kent. il Am Artist 33:5, 24-32+ S '69

Canada
　See also
London, Ontario—Art

Cuba
Agit pop art of Cuba. D. Stermer. il Ramp Mag 7:32-7 D 14 '68

Europe
Tour of a long spiral; exhibition season. H. Judson. il Time 94:30-3 D 26 '69

Europe, Western
American artist travelogue: Europe. il Am Artist 33:42 Ap '69

Ireland
Art in Ireland. A. Werner. il Am Artist 33:28-33+ D '69

Italy
Rome. M. Gendel. il Art N 68:8 Sum '69
　See also
Genoa—Art
Painting, Italian

Japan
History
1,600-year memory in a nation's art. il Fortune 80:103-9 Ag 1 '69

Mexico
My art speaks for both my peoples. E. Catlett il Ebony 25:94-6+ Ja '70

New York (state)
Museums of New York state. Am Artist 33:8 Ja '69

Russia
Visual vs. aural in Russia. C. J. McNaspy. America 120:371-2 Mr 29 '69

United States
American artist travelogue; events. il Am Artist 33:36-42 Ap '69
Cultural commercialism. G. Phillips. Art N 68:29+ S '69
　See also
Art, American
Painting, American

ART, Abstract
Art world; B. Newman's stripe paintings. H. Rosenberg. New Yorker 45:136+ Ap 19 '69
Painting at the degree zero. J. Harithas. il Art N 67:52-3+ N '68
Young lyrical painters; lyrical abstraction of this art season. L. Aldrich. il Art in Am 57:104-13 N '69
　See also
Abstract expressionism

ART, African
African arts for the school. J. F. Povey. il Sch Arts 69:30-1 Ja '70
　See also
Arts and crafts—Africa

ART, Amateur
Art as an antidote for the boredom of retirement. J. B. How. il Am Artist 33:30-1+ N '69

ART, American
Art: New York painting and sculpture, 1940-1970; exhibition at Metropolitan museum of art. L. Alloway. Nation 209:582 N 24 '69
Art world: New American painting at Museum of modern art. H. Rosenberg. New Yorker 45:102+ S 27 '69
Artists on a houseboat. M. L. Norwood. il Am Artist 33:20-7 Ap '69
Hooked on bigness; Metropolitan museum's centennial exhibition, New York painting and sculpture: 1940-1970. K. Kuh. Sat R 52:69-70 N 22 '69
Rembrandt and American art. C. J. McNaspy America 121:370 O 25 '69
Super-show; New York painting and sculpture, 1940-1970 show at New York's Metropolitan museum. D. L. Shirey. il Newsweek 74:80-4 O 20 '69
Thirty years of the New York school; exhibition. New York painting and sculpture: 1940-1970 to open Metropolitan museum's centennial celebrations. H. Kramer. il N Y Times Mag p28-31+ O 12 '69
　See also
Art, Negro (American)
Arts and crafts—United States
Painting, American
Sculpture, American
Whitney museum of American art, New York

ART, Ancient
　See also
Art, Greek

ART, Applied. See Arts and crafts

ART, Asian
Perilous pilgrimage: Himalayan art. il Time 93:72-4 F 14 '69
Unknown treasures of Himalayan art. M. Singh. il UNESCO Courier 22:14-25+ F '69
　See also
Art, Kushan

ART, Baroque
　See also
Architecture, Baroque
Painting, Baroque

ART, Buddhist
  See also
  Art, Tibetan
ART, Cambodian. See Art, Khmer
ART, Celtic
  See also
  Art, Irish
ART, Commercial
  Interview for an art job. il Design 70:28-31+
  Sum '69
  See also
  Advertising art
  Design, Industrial
  Illustration of books and periodicals
  Push pin studios
ART, Dominican (of Dominican Republic)
  Dominican art; a growing tree. R. Squirru.
  il Américas 21:32-7 Ja '69
ART, Dutch
  What makes Dutch art Dutch. K. Kuh. il
  Sat R 52:42-4 F 1 '69
  See also
  Painting, Dutch
ART, Flemish
  Life and death of Bruges. R. McMullen. il
  Horizon 11:74-91 Sum '69
ART, French
  Paris; Centre national d'art contemporain.
  M. Conil-Lacoste. Art N 68:42 My '69
  See also
  Dadaism
  Painting, French
ART, German
  See also
  Painting, German
ART, Graphic. See Graphic arts
ART, Greek
  Age of Homer; exhibition at University of
  Pennsylvania museum, Philadelphia, traces
  evolution of Greek art. P. P. Betancourt. il
  Art N 68:32-3+ D '69
  Greece, gods, and art, by A. Liberman. Re-
  view
    Travel & Camera 32:62-3+ Mr '69. M.
    Wright
ART, Indian (East Indian)
  Treasure from the Orient; Los Angeles
  County museum of art acquires Heerama-
  neck Indian collection. il Time 93:70 Mr 14
  '69
ART, Influence of. See Art therapy
ART, Irish
  Art in Ireland. A. Werner. il Am Artist 33:28-
  33+ D '69
ART, Italian
  See also
  Painting, Italian
ART, Japanese
  Hour of the ox; burning of Sanjo palace
  in Heiji war as turning point in history. E.
  O. Reischauer. il Horizon 11:12-25 Wint '69
  See also
  Sculpture, Japanese
ART, Khmer
  Cambodian canons; Khmer art at Asia house.
  E. C. Baker. il Art N 68:28-31+ D '69
ART, Kushan
  Great civilization of the Kushans. B. Gafurov.
  il UNESCO Courier 22:4-13 F '69
ART, Latin American
  Hemisphere art. See issues of Américas
  Latin American art. New England setting;
  the Nancy Sayles Day collection of modern
  Latin American art. J. H. Kay. il Américas
  21:19-27 Ap '69
ART, Modern
  Advanced; environment: Feel it at the Mu-
  seum of contemporary crafts. New Yorker
  44:28-9 F 15 '69
  Art and words; current exhibits of contem-
  porary painting and sculpture in New
  York. H. Rosenberg. New Yorker 45:110+
  Mr 21 '69
  Art; pop art season. L. Alloway. Nation 209:
  261-2 S 15 '69
  Art; presence of earth sculpture at this
  moment ramified by political situation. M.
  Kozloff. Nation 208:347-8 Mr 17 '69
  Art: R. Doty's exhibition at the Whitney
  museum. L. Alloway. Nation 209:483+ N 3
  '69
  Art world; pop art: Lichtenstein, Oldenburg
  and other artists. H. Rosenberg. New
  Yorker 45:167-70+ N 8 '69
  Denials, affirmations, and art. K. Kuh. il Sat
  R 52:41-2 My 31 '69
  Disposable art; the plastic man L. Levine.
  D. Bourdon. il Life 67:62-7 Ag 22 '69
  Down to earth; earthworks at Cornell uni-
  versity's Andrew Dickson White museum
  of art. H. Junker. il Newsweek 73:101 Mr
  24 '69
  Emperor's new bikini; boundaries of non-art.
  H. Kramer. il Art in Am 57:48-55 Ja '69

Ferment and controversy; new look in dance
  and the arts keeps changing its sights. J.
  Anderson. il Dance Mag 43:46-55 Ag '69
High priest of danger; artist of minimal art,
  optional art and earthworks. il Time 93:54
  My 2 '69
Idea as art; anti-object art. H. Junker. il
  Newsweek 74:81 Ag 11 '69
Impossible art; what it is. D. L. Shirey. il
  Art in Am 57:32-47 My '69
Impossible art; why it is. T. M. Messer. il
  Art in Am 57:30-1 My '69
Lively arts; interview, ed. by E. Sparn. P.
  Guggenheim. Sr Schol 94:15 My 9 '69
Mark of Max is everywhere. il Life 67:34-9
  S 5 '69
More art than money. il Vogue 154:160-1 Ag 1
  '69
No biz like art biz. il Newsweek 74:97 S 22
  '69
Painting is alive and well; exhibit at the
  Tibor de Nagy gallery. B. Rose. Vogue
  154:122 N 1 '69
Paper money made into art you can bank on.
  il Life 67:51-2+ S 19 '69
Peggy Guggenheim's art comes to America.
  H. Ehrlich. il Look 33:34-7 F 4 '69
Planned coincidence; mingling elements
  from different domains. D. Ashton. il Art
  in Am 57:36-47 S '69
Polymorphism, mystic crackpot. J. Gruen.
  Vogue 153:38 Ap 15 '69
Pop reappraised; exhibition Haywood gallery,
  London. J. Russell. il Art in Am 57:78-89
  Jl '69
Process and protest, grate on the senses. B.
  Rose. Vogue 154:54 Jl '69
Scuba sculpture. W. Johnson. il Art N 68:
  52-3+ N '69
Sea works, creative explorations. J. Gruen.
  Vogue 154:64 S 15 '69
Spiritual in art; static works that appear
  to change. B. Rose. Vogue 155:76 Ja 1 '70
Surf realism; it's hard to tell a painting from
  a photograph. il Life 66:44-9 Je 27 '69
Sweet mystery of life. A. Goldin. il Art N
  68:46-51+ My '69
Television as art, inevitable; TV as a cre-
  ative medium exhibition. B. Rose. Vogue
  154:36 Ag 15 '69
TV: the next medium. J. S. Margolies. il
  Art in Am 57:48-55 S '69
Thirty years of the New York school; exhibition, New York painting and sculpture:
  1940-1970 to open Metropolitan museum's
  centennial celebrations. H. Kramer. il N Y
  Times Mag p28-31+ O 12 '69
Three Austrians and the New Jersey turnpike; Laurids, Zamp, and Pinter. I. Hor-
  ovitz. il Craft Horiz 29:10-13+ Ja '69
Time on their hands; works of young artists
  at the Whitney and the Guggenheim mu-
  seums. S. Burton. il Art N 68:40-3 Sum '69
To see, to feel; brave new whorls of color.
  il Time 93:64-5 My 30 '69
View from Hill and Main; environmental art
  of J. Turrell. Newsweek 74:111 O 27 '69
What on earth! D. Bourdon. il Life 66:80-3+
  Ap 25 '69
Wrap-in Down Under; first natural landscape
  to be wrapped. il Time 94:56 N 14 '69
  See also
  Abstract expressionism
  Dadaism
ART, Negro
  See also
  Negroes in art
ART, Negro (American)
  And so it is... H. Ghent. il Sch Arts 68:21-6
  Ap '69
  Primitive art of Clementine Hunter. S. Morris.
  il Ebony 24:144-8 My '69
  You see, this is the way it is! M. W. Brown.
  il Sch Arts 68:30-3 Ap '69
  See also
  Tanner, H. O.
ART, Oriental
  See also
  Art, Japanese
  Pottery, Oriental

        Bibliography
  Are art books not books? R. Edwards. il Sat
  R 52:37-9+ D 6 '69
ART, Pre-Columbian
  Touch of the primitive. B. Plumb. il N Y
  Times Mag p84-5 O 19 '69
  See also
  Sculpture, Pre-Columbian

ART, Primitive
Art of Oceania, Africa, and the Americas, from the Museum of primitive art in New York, exhibit at the Metropolitan museum of art. H. Aaach. il Craft Horiz 29:40-5 S '69
Collectors: Paul and Ruth Tishman. R. Sieber. il Art in Am 57:50-61 Mr '69
Just whose art is primitive? Museum of primitive art collection at the Metropolitan. R. Phelps. il Life 67:8 Ag 8 '69
  See also
Art, Pre-Columbian
Cave drawings and paintings
Petroglyphs
ART, Religious. See Christian art and symbolism
ART, Romantic. See Romanticism
ART, Spanish
  See also
Prado museum, Madrid
ART, Tibetan
Adamantine way; exhibition of Tibetan pictures and sculptures. C. Von Wiegand. il Art N 68:38-41+ Ap '69
Art of Tibet; exhibition at Asia House, New York. D. I. Shirey. il Newsweek 73:91-2 Ap 28 '69
ART, Victorian
Aesthetic movement, by E. Aslin. Review Sat R il 52:32+ N 29 '69. F. Schulze
ART and children. See Children and art
ART and communism. See Communism and art
ART and hallucinogenic drugs. See Hallucinogenic drugs and art
ART and industry
Artists use an industrial palette; Art & technology program. il Bsns W p96-7+ N 8 '69
One man's vision, many men's skills; portfolio. Fortune 80:102-5 O '69
  See also
Advertising art
Art, Commercial
Business in the arts award
Design, Industrial
ART and libraries. See Libraries and art
ART and mental illness
Art and sanity; case of M. Barnes of east London. Newsweek 73:96 +My 19 '69
ART and morals
Perils of puritanism. C. J. McNaspy. il America 120:175-6 F 8 '69
  See also
Nude in art
Theater—Moral and religious aspects
ART and music
  See also
Music in art
ART and nature. See Nature (aesthetics)
ART and photography
Art; Paintings from the photo at the Riverside museum. L. Alloway. Nation 209:741-2 D 29 '69
Artistic frauds, embalmed pictures. N. Rothschild. Pop Phot 65:36+ D '69
Portraiture enlargement. A. W. Sande. il Design 70:24-6 Spr '69
Seeing pictures. J. Scully. Mod Phot 33:10+ Ag '69
Super realism; it's hard to tell a painting from a photograph. il Life 66:44-9 Je 27 '69
Terrible tempered Dr Emerson; excerpts from Naturalistic photography, ed. by D. Vestal. P. H. Emerson. il Pop Phot 64:102-3+ My '69
  See also
Photography, Artistic
ART and politics
Art and politics, can't eat art. N. Rorem. Vogue 154:92+ D '69
Art; presence of earth sculpture at this moment ramified by political situation. M. Kozloff. Nation 208:347-8 Mr 17 '69
How to make politics from art, and vice versa; an open letter to the chairman of the National endowment for the arts. R. Lynes. Harper 239:21-4 Ag '69
Political revolution & current art. B. Rose. Vogue 153:207 Ja 15 '69
  See also
White House festival of the arts, 1965
ART and religion
Fine arts; The rosary-in-art. C. J. McNaspy. America 120:632-4 My 24 '69
ART and science
Forms of nature. A. Feininger. il UNESCO Courier 22:18-19 Mr '69
Poetry; how and why; science and poetry. J. Jerome. Writers Digest 49:26+ Jl '69
Reflections on leaving America for good. R. Huelsenbeck. Am Scholar 39:80-5 Wint '69
Science as art. B. Stegeman. Bul Atom Sci 25:27-30 Ap '69

Where art and science meet; story of mural describing development of science at the Polytechnic institute of Brooklyn. E. Keller. il Chem 42:17-20 D '69
  See also
Art and technology
ART and society
Art museum in today's society. S. E. Lee. Art N 68:27+ Ap '69
Artists as social reformers; Boston art scene. J. H. Kay. il Art in Am 57:44-7 Ja '69
Duality of the artist; relation of the artist to the community? R. Henri. Am Artist 32: 5 N '68
Fun and art; values of discovery and the pure fun of art. C. J. McNaspy. America 120:548 My 3 '69
Late notes on camp plus Papa Hemingway. C. Barnes. Holiday 45:8+ Je '69
Necessity of art; excerpt from The arts and man. H. Read. Sat R 52:24-7 D 6 '69
Response to crisis in American art. D. Ashton. il Art in Am 57:24-35 Ja '69
Teaching of art as social revolution. V. Lanier. Ed Digest 34:42-5 Ap '69
Three Austrians and the New Jersey turnpike; Laurids, Zamp, and Pinter. I. Horovitz. il Craft Horiz 29:10-13+ Ja '69
You see, this is the way it is! M. W. Brown. il Sch Arts 68:30-3 Ap '69
ART and state
Can museums survive tax reform? T. B. Hess. Art N 68:27 O '69
Government and art; letter to the editor. B. Lauritzen; A. Earnest. Art in Am 57:108 Jl '69
  See also
State encouragement of science, literature, and art
United States—National foundation on the arts and the humanities
ART and technology
Art and technology in California. F. Tuten. Vogue 153:36 Ap 15 '69
Art as machine; Cybernetic serendipity exhibit at Corcoran gallery of art, Washington, D.C. D. L. Shirey. il Newsweek 74:81 Ag 11 '69
Artists use an industrial palette; Art & technology program. il Bsns W p96-7+ N 8 '69
Problem of art in a technological age. J. Reboli; reply. T. C. Ley. Cath World 209: 148 Jl '69
ART appreciation. See Art—Appreciation
ART as a profession
New breeds in art. K. Kuh. Sat R 52:48-9 Ap 26 '69
ART as an investment
As I see it; interview, ed. by W. Welch and S. Fogelson. P. Pollen. il Forbes 103:50+ Ap 15 '69
Buying art as an investment. N. R. Piene. House & Gard 136:68+ N '69
  See also
Art investment companies
ART books. See Art literature
ART centers
  See also
Walker art center, Minneapolis
ART classes. See Art—Study and teaching
ART collecting. See Art—Collectors and collecting
ART collectors. See Art—Collectors and collecting
ART competitions. See Art—Competitions
ART criticism
Art of time, by M. Kirby. Review Dance Mag 43:25-7+ S '69. J. Anderson
  See also
Art—Appreciation
ART critics
Letter from Paris; exhibition on C. Baudelaire as art critic. Genêt. New Yorker 45: 131-2 Mr 22 '69
People are talking about: C. Greenberg, masterly art critic. Vogue 153:166-7 Mr 1 '69
ART dealers
Art; artists; discontent about presentations in galleries. L. Alloway. Nation 208:444+ Ap 7 '69
Care and feeding of the artist. M. A. Guitar. il Mlle 70:166-7+ N '69
No biz like art biz. il Newsweek 74:97 S 22 '69
Two housewives run a gallery; Bermen-Medalie art gallery, Newtonville, Mass. J. Kuh. il Ladies Home J 89:31 Mr '69
  See also
Sotheby and company
ART directors club
Art for ad's sake. M. R. Weiss. il Sat R 52: 54-5 Je 14 '69

ARTIFICIAL insemination, Human—*Continued*
Birth without sex. D. M. Rorvik. il Esquire 71:110 Ap '69
Man's participatory evolution: living in a biological revolution. R. M. Davidson. Cur 105: 4-10 Mr '69

ARTIFICIAL intelligence
Cells that learn electronically. S. V. Jones. Sci Digest 65:53 Mr '69

ARTIFICIAL islands
Urban expansion takes to the water. W. McQuade. il Fortune 80:131-5+ S '69

ARTIFICIAL kidneys. See Kidneys, Artificial

ARTIFICIAL lakes. See Lakes, Artificial

ARTIFICIAL light gardening
African violets under fluorescent lights. L. H. St Lawrence. Horticulture 47:37+ O '69
Light-work way to an indoor garden. R. C. Davids. il Read Digest 94:120-3 Mr '69
Make your own sunshine for indoor plants. J. Kramer. il Home Gard 56:31 O '69
Seedlings in my cellar; Fluorescent light gardening. C. B. Lees. il Horticulture 47:38-9 Mr '69

ARTIFICIAL lightning. See Lightning, Artificial

ARTIFICIAL limbs
Amazing Boston arm. A. S. Freese. il Pop Mech 131:102-6+ Mr '69
For amputees, the Boston arm. L. Galton. Read Digest 94:151-4 F '69
For Tron, gifts and a new leg. il Life 67:85-6 D 12 '69
Helping hand; electronic arm. il Newsweek 73:58 F 24 '69

ARTIFICIAL lungs. See Lungs, Artificial

ARTIFICIAL organs. See Prosthesis

ARTIFICIAL pacemaker (heart). See Pacemaker, Artificial (heart)

ARTIFICIAL placenta. See Placenta, Artificial

ARTIFICIAL respirator. See Respiratory apparatus

ARTIFICIAL sapphires. See Sapphires, Artificial

ARTIFICIAL satellites
NASA considers satellite network. P. J. Klass. il Aviation W 91:58-9+ O 13 '69
Satellite report; tables. See issues of Space world
Workhorse satellites. I. Geller. il Duns R 93:67-8+ F '69
See also
Space stations

Astronomical applications
Another successful OSO. R. N. Watts, jr. il Sky & Tel 33:230 O '69
Deflating NASA's universe; examining data transmitted from second Orbiting astronomical observatory. Time 94:28 D 26 '69
Earth's broadcasting atmosphere. il Sci N 95:423-4 My 3 '69
Far-ultraviolet solar observatory. R. N. Watts, jr. il Sky & Tel 38:390-1 D '69
Music of the spheres; radio signals detected by Explorer 38. Newsweek 73:75 My 5 '69
On a clear day; OAO-2. Newsweek 74:77 D 15 '69
One more in the line; OSO-5. il Sci N 95: 137 F 8 '69
OAO-A2, high-accuracy stellar observatory. il Space World F-3-63:4-10 Mr '69
OGO measurements successful. Space World G-1-73:44 Ja '70
Orbiting solar observatory. il Space World F-4-64:6-10 Ap; F-11-71:42-6 N '69
OSO 5 is operative. R. N. Watts, jr. Sky & Tel 37:164 Mr '69
Out from under; large space telescopes. D. E. Thomsen. il Sci N 96:505 N 29 '69
Pioneer 6: measurement of transient Faraday rotation phenomena observed during solar occultation. G. S. Levy and others. bibliog il Science 166:596-8 O 31 '69
Riddle from Andromeda; OAO-II results. il Sci N 95:349-50 Ap 12 '69
Soft X-ray observations from OSO-4. J. L. Culhane and others. il Sky & Tel 37:287+ My '69
Some early results from Celescope. R. N. Watts, jr. il Sky & Tel 37:280-1 My '69
Space astronomy; AAAS symposium, December 28, 1969. M. D. Papagiannis. il Science 166:775-6 N 7 '69
Star trackers in fourth month of successful operation. il Space World F-8-68:20 Ag '69
Superior conjunction of Pioneer 6. R. M. Goldstein. il Science 166:598-601 O 31 '69
Two-year life expected for OAO satellite. Aviation W 90:33 My 12 '69
Ultraviolet astronomy. L. Goldberg. il Sci Am 220:92-102 bibliog(p 144) Je '69
Ultraviolet photometry from a spacecraft. A. D. Code and others. il Sky & Tel 38:290-3 N '69

Communications applications
See Communications satellites

Electronic equipment
Satellite to evaluate L-band navaid. P. J. Klass. il Aviation 90:63+ Je 23 '69

Launching
Second try to launch Nimbus B scheduled by NASA for Apr. 10. W. J. Normyle. Aviation W 90:19 Ap 7 '69

Manufacture
See Space vehicles—Manufacture

Meteorological applications
Accomplishments of Nimbus II. il Space World F-7-67:40-1 Jl '69
Atmospheric temperature: successful test of remote probing. D. Q. Wark and D. T. Hilleary. bibliog il Science 165:1256-8 S 19 '69
Calling the long shots on weather; Nimbus III. il Bsns W p46+ My 3 '69
Catching the weather coming; GARP global weatherwatch system. K. Frazier. il Sci N 96:185-7 S 6 '69
ESSA VHF weather radio stations. il Weatherwise 22:157 Ag '69
From above: Camille; ESSA 9 tracking Camille across Southeast and catches Debbie in Atlantic. il Weatherwise 22:209 O '69
Global data collection system gets initial tryout with Nimbus-III. il Space World F-8-68:18-19 Ag '69
How television works from space: APT system. il Space World F-3-63:41-6 Mr '69
Interferometer experiment on Nimbus 3: preliminary results. R. Hanel and B. Conrath. il Science 165:1258-60 S 19 '69
Nimbus 3 soundings exceed expectations. W. C. Wetmore. il Aviation W 90:32-3 My 5 '69
Satellite observations of the earth's radiation budget. T. H. Vonder Haar and V. E. Suomi. bibliog il Science 163:667-9 F 14 '69
Satellite weather forecasting. B. O'Connell. bibliog il Sci Digest 65:43-8+ My '69
Satellites gave warning of Midwest floods. P. T. White. il Nat Geog 136:574-92 O '69
Second try to launch Nimbus B scheduled by NASA for Apr. 10. W. J. Normyle. Aviation W 90:19 Ap 7 '69
Sounding from above. K. Frazier. il Sci N 96:509-11 N 29 '69
Third Nimbus weather satellite. R. N. Watts, jr. il Sky & Tel 37:365 Je '69
Weather satellites; II. A. W. Johnson. il Sci Am 220:52-68 Ja '69

Military applications
Military satellites gain vital data. P. J. Klass. il Aviation W 91:55-61 S 15 '69
Sky spies: nobody has a secret anymore; reconnaissance satellites. E. Clark. il Newsweek 73:62-4 Ap 21 '69
Space control: how the U.S. watches the Russians. il U S News 67:32-3 N 24 '69
See also
Ballistic missile early warning system

Navigational applications
Satellite to evaluate L-band navaid. P. J. Klass. il Aviation 90:63+ Je 23 '69

Power supply
See Space vehicles—Power supply

Propulsion systems
See Space vehicles—Propulsion systems

Stability and stabilizers
See Space vehicles—Stability and stabilizers

Use in research
Earth resources satellite: finally off the ground? L. J. Carter. Science 163:796-8 F 21 '69; Discussion. 164:494, 1009 My 2, My 30 '69
Exploring the earth from space: ERTS satellite. il Bsns W p 151-2 N 8 '69
IMP-G experiments near full operation. Aviation W 90:18 Je 30 '69
Magnetospheric wind. J. W. Freeman, jr. bibliog il Science 163:1061-2 Mr 7 '69
New space policy may stress earth uses. W. C. Wetmore. il Aviation W 90:113-14+ Mr 10 '69
Prospecting from space; earth resources satellite program. il Space World F-6-66: 14-25 Je '69

ARTIFICIAL satellites—Use in research—
Continued
Resource satellite effort spurred. W. S.
Hieronymus. il Aviation W 91:79+ N 17 '69
West Germans' gas cloud study; electrical
fields in space. il Space World F-6-66:12-13
Je '69
See also
Biosatellite program
ARTIFICIAL satellites, European
Fourth ESRO satellite. il Space World G-1-73:
18-19 Ja '70
ARTIFICIAL satellites, French
French plan commercial satellite system;
Dioscures project. E. H. Kolcum. Aviation
W 91:31 N 24 '69
ARTIFICIAL satellites, German
German satellite launch. il Space World G-1-
73:42-3 Ja '70
ARTIFICIAL satellites, Japanese
Space satellite ambitions. S. Griffin. Sci N
96:288 S 27 '69
ARTIFICIAL satellites, Russian
See also
Space probes, Russian
ARTIFICIAL sweeteners. See Sugar substitutes
ARTIFICIAL teeth. See Teeth, Artificial
ARTIFICIAL textile fibers. See Textile fibers,
Synthetic
ARTIFICIAL turf. See Turf, Artificial
ARTISANS
Last artisans; photographs. G. Frazier.
Esquire 72:57-64 Jl '69
ARTISTIC ability. See Creation (literary, artis-
tic, etc)
ARTISTIC photography. See Photography,
Artistic
ARTISTS
Indignant eye, by R. E. Shikes. Review
Nation 209:482 N 3 '69. E. Bendiner
Let's make artists rich. F. Whitaker. Am
Artist 33:3 Je '69
Masters in the art news. See Issues of Art
news
Work in progress. il Esquire 72:210-7 D '69
See also
Architects
Cartoonists
Illustrators
Potters
Scientists as artists

Political activities
Artists and Mr Daley. T. B. Hess. Art N 67:
29 N '68

ARTISTS, American
Artist signed post cards. B. Finnegan. il
Hobbies 74:125 Ap; 124-5+ My; 124-5 Je;
158-9 S '69
Boston is here, now. J. Koethe. il Art N
68:30-3+ S '69
Response to crisis in American art. D. Ash-
ton. il Art in Am 57:24-35 Ja '69
See also
Bearden. R.
Bollinger, B.
Bradford, W.
Evans. M.
Fechin. N.
Grooms. R.
Hutchinson, P.
Levine. L.
Morris, L.
Neuestern. O.
Oppenheim, D.
Ossorio, A.
Painting, American
Paris, H.
Paulson, C.
Russell, C. M.
Saul, P.
Schwartz, D.
Sculpture, American
Smithson. R.
ARTISTS, British
See also
Paolozzi. E.
ARTISTS, Canadian
New work from Montreal. B. Lord. il Art in
Am 57:99-101 My '69
Three young Canadians. B. Lord. il Art in Am
57:87-9 Ja '69
ARTISTS, Costa Rican
See also
Amighetti Ruiz, F.
ARTISTS, Czech
Talk of the town; plight of the artist under
communism. New Yorker 45:35 S 13 '69
See also
Kolár, J.
ARTISTS, English
See also
Hogarth, W.

ARTISTS, French
See also
Arp, H.
ARTISTS, Greek
See also
Samaras. L.
ARTISTS, Hungarian
See also
Moholy-Nagy. L.
ARTISTS, Norwegian
See also
Munch. E.
ARTISTS, Peruvian
See also
Acevedo, G.
ARTISTS, Puerto Rican
Contemporary Puerto Rican artists. il Sch
Arts 69:26-7 O '69
ARTISTS as authors
Dubuffet as a writer. J. Russell. il Art in Am
57:86-9 My '69
ARTISTS games. See Games
ARTISTS materials
Art mart. See issues of American artist
Barry Le Va and the non-descript distri-
bution. L. Rosing. il Art N 68:52-3 S '69
Bollinger phenomenon. H. Rosenstein. il Art
N 68:48-51+ S '69
Bottle cap model maker. R. Wolfe. il Design
70:4-7 Spr '69
Clipboard. V. G. Timmons. See issues of
School arts
Culinary print. R. Broner. il Craft Horiz 29:
52-3 My '69
Materials of art versus the art of materials.
H. Aach. il Craft Horiz 29:37-8 Jl '69
1969 buyers' guide. Sch Arts 68:57-62 F '69
Old hat no more; use of wooden hat blocks.
il Time 94:47-8 D 19 '69
Ralph Mayer's technical question & answer
page. R. Mayer. See issues of American
artist
What's new, where to buy it. See issues of
Design
See also
Aluminum foil
Plastics as art material
ARTLEY, A. Steri
Developmental reading in the 60's. Ed Digest
34:38-41 Ap '69
ARTMAN, J. O.
Meet the elite. Am For 75:32-4+ Ja '69
The ARTS
Arts. C. J. McNaspy. America 122:20-1 Ja 10
'70
Arts and man; symposium. il UNESCO
Courier 22:4-36 My '69
Necessity of art; excerpt from The arts and
man. H. Read. Sat R 52:24-7 D 6 '69
See also
Religion and the arts
Sex in the arts
Television broadcasting and the arts

Study and teaching
Dorothy Maynor; director of Harlem school
of the arts. C. W. Ferguson. il PTA Mag
64:10-12 N '69
No-fail subject; the arts; with study-discus-
sion program, by E. Harris and D. Harris.
M. Sherman. bibliog il PTA Mag 64:20-2+,
34-5 D '69
War in the classroom; mass media vs. educa-
tion. L. Penfield. il Schol Teach Sec Teach
Sup p 14-15+ S 22 '69
Where all the arts are lively; New Jersey.
E. L. Raichle. il PTA Mag 63:27-8 Je '69
See also
California institute of the arts
ARTS, Graphic. See Graphic arts
ARTS and crafts
Crafts. K. Chattopadhyay. il UNESCO Cou-
rier 22:15-17+ My '69
Decorator crafts. M. Garrity. il Bet Hom &
Gard 47:88-91 Mr '69
Fourteen kits to help children say: I made it
myself. J. H. Ingersoll. il House B 111:94-6
D '69
Travel talk about crafts; symposium. il Craft
Horiz 29:48-9 My '69
See also
Batik
Block printing
Bookbinding
Collage
Decoration and ornament
Design. Decorative
Enamel and enameling
Folk art
Handicraft

ARTS and crafts—See also—*Continued*
Leather work
Needlework
Pottery
Silversmithing
Stencil work
Weaving
Woodworking

Bibliography

Book review section. See issues of Design
Books (cont) il Craft Horiz 29:8-9 Ja; 6 Jl;
8 S; 12-13 N '69
Resource materials: books; filmstrips, films,
slides, loops. V. G. Timmons. Sch Arts 69:
32-3 Ja '70
Seven new crafts books. Am Home 72:79 Ap
'69

Exhibitions

Art of Oceania, Africa, and the Americas,
from the Museum of primitive art in New
York; exhibit at the Metropolitan museum
of art. H. Aach. il Craft Horiz 29:40-5 S '69
British artist craftsmen. R. Carr. il Craft
Horiz 29:24-7+ S '69
Calendar; Where to show. See issues of
Craft horizons
Dimensions 1969; exhibition at the Royal On-
tario museum. D. Piper. il Craft Horiz 29:
28-31+ S '69
Exhibitions. See issues of Craft horizons
Objects: USA; the Johnson collection of con-
temporary crafts. R. H. Simmons. il Craft
Horiz 29:24-51+ N '69
Senior citizens exhibit arts and crafts at
Brooklyn museum's Community gallery. il
Aging 180:16 O '69
Stuttgart: international handcraft. K. W.
Keith. il Craft Horiz 29:20-3 S '69
Young Americans 1969. A. T. New. il Craft
Horiz 29:8-15+ Jl '69
Young craftsmen; exhibition at New York's
Museum of contemporary crafts. il House
B 111:22-3 Jl '69

Study and teaching

Crafts program gets whoops from the hollows;
eastern Kentucky. B. T. Balke. il Am Ed
5:25-6 Je '69
Creative craft program in the summer camp.
E. A. Mills. il Sch Arts 68:34-5 My '69
Kinetic art: art-science project. P. Holter. il
Sch Arts 68:26-7 My '69
Sharing the wealth; in-service course. D. M.
Ritchie. il Sch Arts 69:32-3 S '69
To study crafts this summer; Directory of
craft courses. Sunset 142:32 Ap '69
Travel and study directory: lists of schools
and colleges in the U.S.A. and abroad (cont)
il Craft Horiz 29:27-46 My '69
   See also
Embroidery—Study and teaching

Materials

Arts & crafts supplies, sources and books.
Am Artist 33:22-7 F '69
Originality in opalescence: styrofoam egg
cartons. E. E. Welch. il Design 70:16-18
Sum '69

Africa

Art of African pulleys. F. N'Diaye. il
UNESCO Courier 22:18-24 My '69
Travelogue. M. M. Patch. il Craft Horiz 29:
32-9+ S '69 (to be cont)

Appalachian Region

Rebirth in the hollers. P. Deutschman. il
Travel & Camera 32:62-7 S '69

Argentina

Argentine folk arts; excerpts from address.
A. E. Abeledo. il Américas 21:34-9 My '69

Brazil

Popular imagery from north-east Brazil. il
UNESCO Courier 22:34-5 My '69

California

Three California craftsmen. M. Angelino. il
Am Artist 33:45-53+ S '69

Canada

Dimensions 1969; exhibition at the Royal Ontario museum. D. Piper. il Craft Horiz 29:
28-31+ S '69

China

Chinese pipes for tobacco and opium. C. E.
Kennedy. il Antiques 95:408-9 Mr '69

Great Britain

British artist craftsmen; exhibition at Smithsonian institution. R. Carr. il Craft Horiz
29:24-7+ S '69

Peru

Mastercraftsmen of Peru. il Design 70:24-7
Sum '69

Russia

Utensils as works of art. V. Fabritskiĭ and
I. Shmelyov. il UNESCO Courier 22:25-7
My '69

Turkey

Handcraft in Turkey. B. Kadish. il Craft Horiz
29:50-1 My '69

United States

Arts in America: the nineteenth century; ex-
cerpts. W. D. Garrett and others. il An-
tiques 96:372-5 S '69
Crafting their own world. il Newsweek 74:
62-7 Jl 21 '69
Crafts program gets whoops from the hollows;
eastern Kentucky. B. T. Balke. il Am Ed
5:25-6 Je '69
Little red schoolhouse reopens; craft shop. R.
Peterson. Har Yrs 9:18 Je '69
Objects: USA; the Johnson collection of con-
temporary crafts. R. H. Simmons. il Craft
Horiz 29:24-51+ N '69
Shopping for mountain crafts in North Caro-
lina. il Bet Hom & Gard 47:148 My '69
   See also
American crafts council
Museum of contemporary crafts, New York
ARTS and crafts, Indian. See Indians of North
America—Industries
ARTS and crafts trade. See Art trade
The ARTS and industry
Trend; patronage of the arts by big busi-
ness. New Yorker 45:46-7 D 13 '69
ARTS and television. See Television broadcast-
ing and the arts
ARTS departments. See Colleges and univer-
sities—Departments of the arts
ARTS education. See The Arts—Study and
teaching
ARTSAY, Aida Favia-. See Favia-Artsay, A.
ARTSIMOVICH, Lev Andreevich
Artsimovich talks about controlled-fusion re-
search; ed. by J. L. Tuck and G. B. Lub-
kin. pors Phys Todays 22:54-7 Je '69
ARYA, H. C. See Tiwari, M. M. jt. auth.
ARZHAK, Nikolai, pseud. See Daniel, Y.
ASARCO. See American smelting and refining
company
ASBELL, Bernard
Does Robert Finch have soul? N Y Times
Mag p28-9+ Ap 6 '69
Pat Moynihan: too much! And too little!
N Y Times Mag p44-5+ N 2 '69
Teachers without tempers. Redbook 132:44+
Ja '69
ASBESTOS roofing. See Roofing
ASBESTOS workers
Asbestos; environmental hazards, adaptation
of address, December 28, 1968. I. J. Selikoff.
bibliog il Environ 11:2-7 Mr '69
ASBESTOSIS. See Lungs—Dust diseases
ASBILLE, Bob
Fishing. Sports Illus 31:94+ S 15 '69
High jinks in the alley, cats. Sports Illus
30:26-7 Mr 17 '69
ASBURY, Barbara. See Galvin, H. R. jt. auth.
ASCARIS lumbricoides. See Nematodes
ASCENSION day
Day to remember. C. G. Fry. Chr Today 13:
3-5 My 9 '69
ASCORBIC acid. See Vitamins—Vitamin C
ASERLIND, LeRoy, and McCarthy, J. J.
IMC network. Ed Digest 34:35-8 Mr '69
ASEXUAL reproduction. See Reproduction,
Asexual
ASH, K. Owen
Ascorbic acid: cofactor in rabbit olfactory
preparations. bibliog Science 165:901-2 Ag
29 '69
ASH, Roy Lawrence
New anatomy of world business; address,
November 13, 1969. Vital Speeches 36:154-7
D 15 '69
   about
Cleaning up the maze in Washington. il por
Bsns W p163-4 Je 21 '69
ASH, Plant. See Plant ash
ASHANIN, Charles B.
Open letter to the Union of Soviet writers.
Chr Cent 86:1617-18 D 17 '69
ASHBERY, John
Clouds; poem. Harper 239:44 D '69
Saul Steinberg: the stamp of genius. Art N
68:45+ N '69

ASHBERY, John—*Continued*
Sortes Vergilianae; For John Clare; It was raining in the capital; Outing; poems. Poetry 114:1-9 Ap '69
(tr) See Dali, S. De Kooning's 300,000,000th birthday
ASHBROOK, Joseph
Astronomical scrapbook. See issues of Sky and telescope
ASHBY, Neal
How to know when you're sick. Todays Health 47:36-9 My '69
ASHCOM, Benjamin M. and Beren, R. S.
Inductive unit on historiography. Ed Digest 34:47-9 F '69
ASHCROFT, N. W.
Liquid metals; with biographical sketch. Sci Am 221:16, 72-82 bibliog(p 140) Jl '69
ASHE, Arthur, 1943-
Profiles. J. McPhee. por New Yorker 45:45-8+ Je 7; 44-8+ Je 14 '69
ASHE, James
ABC's of circuit breadboarding. Radio-Electr 40:62-3+ N '69
Experiment with digital readouts. Radio-Electr 40:46-8 Ag '69
Experiment with 15-watt IC powerhouse. Radio-Electr 40:33-5 S '69
Simplest antenna bridge. Pop Electr 30:66-7 Ap '69
Use the PA-222 in audio circuits. Radio-Electr 40:54-6 F '69
ASHER, Robert E.
Foreign aid: the postwar record and targets for the 1970's; excerpts from A forward look at foreign aid. bibliog f Mo Labor R 92:23-30 N '69
ASHES
Air pollutant cleans a lake; fly ash. Am City 84:30 Ja '69
ASHEVILLE, N.C.

Description
Climate fit for a weathermen. D. Butwin. il Sat R 52:32+ My 31 '69
ASHKENAZY, Vladimir
Music to my ears; Carnegie Hall. I. Kolodin. Sat R 52:52 Ap 5 '69
ASHLAND oil and refining company
First-class crap game. il Forbes 104:41 Ag 1 '69
ASHLEY, Paul
Router rides a track. Pop Sci 194:156+ Je '69
ASHMEAD, Lawrence P.
Specialized needs at Doubleday: mystery-suspense and science fiction. Writer 82:23-4 My '69
ASHMORE, Harry S.
Our fractured politics. Cur 113:14-21 D '69
ASHTON, Dore
Planned coincidence. Art in Am 57:36-47 S '69
Response to crisis in American art. Art in Am 57:24-35 Ja '69
ASHTON, Sir Frederick
In the English style. il por Time 93:68 My 2 '69
Royal enigma. H. Saal. il Newsweek 73:117 My 5 '69
ASIA
Myth of Asia. by J. M. Steadman. Review Sat R 52:36 O 11 '69. J. M. Allison
New world of Asia. G. Thomson. For Affairs 48:123-38 O '69
See also
Agriculture—Asia
Australia—Foreign relations—Asia
Book industries and trade—Asia
East and West
Education—Asia
Hindu Kush
Missions—Asia
Mongolia
Transportation—Asia
United Nations—Economic commission for Asia and the Far East
United States—Foreign relations—Asia
World war, 1939-1945—Asia

Defenses
New defense line in Asia? with interview with Park Chung Hee. il U S News 67:21-5 Ag 25 '69

Economic conditions
Economics & Asia; no. 1 problem: survival. Sr Schol 94:18 Ja 31 '69

History
Bibliography
Articles and other books received; comp. by C. Hobbs. See issues of American historical review

Moral conditions
Beyond the blue horizon. il Time 94:34 O 17 '69

Politics
Asia and America at the crossroads: with questions and answers. K. T. Young. Ann Am Acad 384:53-65 Jl '69
Look at Asian regionalism; address, October 20, 1969. M. Green. Dept State Bul 61:445-8 N 24 '69
See also
Balance of power

Religious institutions and affairs
See also
Christians in Asia
Pentecostal churches in Asia

Social life and customs
Beyond the blue horizon. il Time 94:34 O 17 '69
ASIA, CENTRAL
Antiquities
Great civilization of the Kushans. B. Gafurov. il UNESCO Courier 22:4-13 F '69

History
See also
Kushan empire
ASIA, SOUTHEASTERN
Southeast Asia; symposium. bibliog f il Cur Hist 57:321-69 D '69
Vietnam and southeast Asia; symposium. bibliog f il Cur Hist 56:65-109+ F '69
See also
Airplanes, Military—Asia, Southeastern
Anti-Communist movements—Asia, Southeastern
Asia, Southern
Communism—Asia, Southeastern
Guerrillas—Asia, Southeastern
Investments, Foreign (in Southeast Asia)
Petroleum—Asia, Southeastern
United States—Foreign relations—Asia, Southeastern

Antiquities
Hoabinhian: a pebble-tool complex with early plant associations in southeast Asia. C. F. Gorman. bibliog il Science 163:671-3 F 14 '69

Bibliography
On southeast Asia. R. Peritz. Cur Hist 56: 106-8+ F '69

Defenses
Address before the National press club, Canberra, Australia, August 8, 1969. W. P. Rogers. Dept State Bul 61:178-81 S 1 '69
Asia's self-defense plan: a hedge against U.S. pullout. il U S News 66:80-1 Mr 10 '69
Seven Asian and Pacific nations examine security situation in Asia; text of communique. Dept State Bul 60:481-3 Je 9 '69
U.S. defense in the nuclear age. B. K. Gordon. bibliog f Cur Hist 57:100-4+ Ag '69
When war ends, U.S. role in Asia. il U S News 66:34-6 Ap 14 '69
Why the Philippines are drifting away from U.S; interview, ed. by K. M. Chrysler. F. E. Marcos. U S News 66:80-1 Mr 31 '69
See also
Southeast Asia treaty organization

Economic conditions
Asia's emerging industrial revolution. il Bsns W p60-1 D 13 '69
Southeast Asia builds for the post-Vietnam age. L. Kraar. il Fortune 80:76-80+ Ag 15 '69
Viet-Nam in the perspective of East Asia: address, April 21, 1969. W. P. Rogers. Dept State Bul 60:397-400 My 12 '69

Foreign relations
China and southeast Asia. S. C. Y. Pan. bibliog f Cur Hist 57:164-7+ S '69
Future of the US military presence. A. Campbell. New Repub 160:14-17 Ap 5 '69
Toward a new balance in Asia: an Australian view. B. Grant. For Affairs 47:711-20 Jl '69

Politics
Asia. V. S. Kearney. America 122:14-16 Ja 10 '70
Future of the US military presence. A. Campbell. New Repub 160:14-17 Ap 5 '69
Those sanctuaries; Laos and Cambodia. il Time 93:34+ Ap 25 '69

Religious institutions and affairs
See also
Buddha and Buddhism

ASIA, SOUTHERN
See also
Asia, Southeastern

Economic conditions
Asian drama: an inquiry into the poverty of nations. by G. Myrdal. Review
Sci Am 221:128+ Jl '69. P. C. Mahalanobis
Asian drama. by G. Myrdal. Review
New Yorker 44:116-18+ F 15 '69. N. Bliven

Social conditions
Asian drama. by G. Myrdal. Review
New Yorker 44:116-18+ F 15 '69. N. Bliven

ASIA MINOR
Antiquities
Fauna of Çatal Hüyük: evidence for early cattle domestication in Anatolia. D. Perkins, jr. bibliog il Science 164:177-9 Ap 11 '69

ASIAN art. See Art, Asian

ASIAN Christians. See Christians in Asia

ASIAN studies. See Oriental studies

ASIANS
Never the twain shall; Singapore Open golf championship. E. Shrake. il Sports Illus 30: 66-77 Je 16 '69

ASIANS in Africa
See also
Asians in Kenya

ASIANS in Kenya
Kenya's Asian outcasts. S. Meisler. il Nation 209:173-6 S 1 '69

ASIATIC diseases. See Communicable diseases

ASIATIC-European airline services. See Airlines —International services—European-Asiatic

ASIMINA triloba. See Papaws

ASIMOV, Isaac
Isaac Asimov explains. See issues of Science digest
Moon could answer the riddle of life. N Y Times Mag p 12-15+ Jl 13 '69; Same with title Why we must explore the moon. Sci Digest 66:8-17 O '69
Outer space, wet space. Seventeen 29:82-3+ Ja '70
Speed limit 186,300 m.p.s. Holiday 46:40-1+ Jl '69
We came in peace for all mankind, special view of Christmas Redbook 134:151 D '69

about
Asimov's hundred. P. Nathan. Pub W 196: 270 Ag 25 '69

ASINOF, Eliot
Crazy Fatso, the putting fool, may now be the world's best golfer. N Y Times Mag p32-3+ Ap 6 '69
Turbulent century of swat. Life 66:28 Je 6 '69
Why Rocket is better than the best. N Y Times Mag p58-9+ N 30 '69

ASKENASY, Alexander R.
American and British mental health workers look at rehabilitation. Ment Hy 53:466-71 Jl '69

ASKEW, Richard Burton Marlowe
Basin stand in England and America. Antiques 95:258-63 F '69

ASLAN, Anna
Real truth behind the youth pill. E. Ubell. il McCalls 96:14+ Ag '69

ASLIN, Elizabeth
Art style in furniture; excerpt from The aesthetic movement. Antiques 96:578-81 O '69

ASOLO state theater company. See Sarasota, Fla.—Ringling center

ASPARAGINASE
Crystalline L-asparaginase from escherichia coli B. P. P. K. Ho and others. bibliog il Science 165:510-12 Ag 1 '69

ASPARAGUS
$5 for asparagus, $1 for hay. J. Ingersoll, jr. il Org Gard & Farm 16:97-9 Mr '69
Two vegetables for a permanent patch. M. G. Benzinger. il Org Gard & Farm 16:46-7 Je '69

ASPEN
Trembling poplar. W. Radcliffe. il Horticulture 47:16-18+ F '69

ASPEN international design conference. See International design conference

ASPHYXIA
Brain damage by asphyxia at birth. W. F. Windle. il Sci Am 221:76-84 O '69

ASPIC
Dandy chicken in aspic; with recipe by E. Graves. il Life 67:56-7+ Ag 8 '69

ASPINALL, Wayne Norviel
Keynote on the public lands. pors Am For 75:12-15+ N '69

ASPIRIN
Aspirin: its effect on platelet glycolysis and release of adenosine diphosphate. J. C. G. Doery and others. bibliog il Science 165:65-7 Jl 4 '69
Aspirin, safe drug or common danger? Consumer Bul 52:25-6 Mr '69

ASQUITH, Lady Cynthia Mary Evelyn (Charteris)
Modern beauty. A. Cooper. por Newsweek 73: 124+ Mr 17 '69

ASSASSIN; drama. See Boyd, J.

ASSASSINATION
Anarchists (who are with us again) J. W. Burrow. il Horizon 11:32-43 Sum '69
Assassination in the Middle East. C. Leiden. il Trans-Action 6:20-3 My '69
Assassins: rising danger in America; statement by National commission on the causes and prevention of violence. U S News 67: 15 N 10 '69
Black arts in a free society. N. Cousins. Sat R 52:26 O 18 '69
Social psychopathology of political assassination. S. J. Slomich and R. E. Kantor. Bul Atom Sci 25:9-12 Mr '69
See also
Kennedy, J. F.—Assassination
Mboya, T. J.—Assassination
Presidents—United States—Assassination

ASSASSINS
Whatever happened to the assassins of Kennedy and King? il U S News 67:10 Ag 18 '69

ASSATEAGUE ISLAND NATIONAL SEASHORE
Assateague effort grows. Nat Parks 43:20-1 Je '69
Assateague Island: with editorial comment. J. V. Morris. bibliog il Nat Parks 43:2, 15-20 F '69
Rebuff on Assateague. Nat Parks 43:21-2 Jl '69

ASSAULT and battery
Assault at Chicago. Newsweek 73:70-1 My 19 '69
Mugger's tale. G. B. Porter. il Newsweek 73: 63+ My 19 '69
See also
Trials (assault and battery)

ASSEMBLAGE. See Collage; Sculpture

ASSEMBLIES of God. See Church of God

ASSESSMENT
As taxes go up, protests grow; increased assessments. U S News 67:83 Jl 28 '69
How to appraise your personal belongings. McCalls 96:56 Ap '69

ASSESSMENT of public schools. See Evaluation (education)

ASSETS, Liquid. See Liquidity (economics)

ASSIGNMENTS, Teaching. See Teaching assignments

ASSISTANCE in emergencies
Shortage of Samaritans; plight of New York city patrolman Alfredo Rivera. Newsweek 74:71-2 O 20 '69
Subway samaritan; experiments conducted by Columbia students. Time 95:44 Ja 19 '70
Why people don't help. il Time 94:66 Jl 18 '69

ASSISTANT teachers. See Teachers aides

ASSOCIATE reformed Presbyterian church
Evangelism in the ARPC. A. H. Matthews. Chr Today 13:37 Jl 18 '69

ASSOCIATED church press (organization)
Award for the Century; at A.C.P.'s annual convention. Chr Cent 86:767 Je 4 '69
Of many things: first joint convention of the Catholic press association and the Associated church press. D. R. Campion. America 120:inside cover Je 7 '69

ASSOCIATED general contractors of America
Contractors try strike insurance; employer weapon to counter labor's collective bargaining. Bsns W p56 Ap 5 '69

ASSOCIATED spring corporation
To the rescue! il Forbes 103:215-16 My 15 '69

ASSOCIATION (biology) See Symbiosis

ASSOCIATION for Asian studies
Vietnam on their minds. Newsweek 73:74 Ap 14 '69

ASSOCIATION for supervision and curriculum development
Meeting, 1969. D. L. Burleson. Sr Schol 94: Schol Teach 6 Ap 18 '69

ASSOCIATION for the study of Negro life and history
54th anniversary convention in Birmingham. Negro Hist Bul 32:4-5 N '69
Negro history week; ASNLH branches celebrate. Negro Hist Bul 32:21-2 Ap '69

ASSOCIATION for the study of Negro life and history—*Continued*
Our 53rd anniversary convention at the New York Hilton. il Negro Hist Bul 31:4-5 D '68
Pictures from our 53rd anniversary convention. il Negro Hist Bul 32:22 F '69
ASSOCIATION of American dance companies
Pit to hiss in; report on the third annual national conference of the Association of American dance companies. M. Marks. Dance Mag 43:85-6 Jl '69
ASSOCIATION of American library schools
Anti-Chicago resolution aired at AALS. Library J 94:927 Mr 1 '69
ASSOCIATION of American university presses
AAUP: annual meeting. il Pub W 196:22-35 Jl 28; 22-8. 56-8+ Ag 4 '69
1968 in review. Pub W 195:42 Mr 10 '69
University presses examine the new technology. Pub W 195:23-7 My 26 '69
See also
National council on the arts selection (program)
ASSOCIATION of American university presses annual book show. See Book exhibits
ASSOCIATION of classroom teachers. See National education association—Association of classroom teachers
ASSOCIATION of college and research libraries
See also
Choice (periodical)
ASSOCIATION of public television producers
Producers organize. C. Horman. Nation 208: 634-6 My 19 '69
ASSOCIATION of student governments
Nixon meets students. J. Osborne. New Republic 161:9-10 O 4 '69
Quiet majority; other side of campus revolt. il U S News 66:34-7 My 26 '69
ASSOCIATION of the United States army
At play with the military-industrial complex; Air force association and Army association meetings. P. Dickson and R. Skole. Esquire 73:66B+ Ja '70
ASSOCIATIONS, institutions, etc.
See also
Corporations
Groups (sociology)
Professional associations
ASTAIRE, Fred
Dancing on TV. W. Terry. il pors Sat R 52:42-3 Mr 1 '69
ASTARTE; ballet. See Ballets—Criticisms
ASTEROIDS
Asteroid, Icarus. Chem 42:24 Mr '69
Hektor scrutinized. Sky & Tel 38:300 N '69
JPL radar indicates Icarus tiny, very rough. il R Pop Astron 63:32 F '69
Minor planet geographos. Sky & Tel 38:79 Ag '69
Minor planet 324 Bamberga. il Sky & Tel 38: 131 Ag '69
Minor planets from comets? Sky & Tel 38: 302 N '69
Nature of Icarus. il Sky & Tel 37:93-4 F '69
Observing the asteroids. F. Pilcher. il R Pop Astron 63:14-16 F; 16-17 Mr; 22-3 My '69
Unusual asteroid needs observations; 531 Zerlina. F. Pilcher. R Pop Astron 63:12 Mr '69
ASTERS
China aster show come summer. il Sunset 142: 254 My '69
In bloom from now to November; Michaelmas daisies. il Sunset 143:132 Ag '69
ASTHMA
Electric fog to smother asthma; electro-aerosol therapy. T. W. Hill. il Sci Digest 65:74-7 Ap '69
Wheeze machine tracks down allergies. R. Gannon. il Pop Sci 194:82-3+ My '69
ASTIN, Alexander W.
Folklore of selectivity; excerpt from The campus and the racial crisis. Sat R 52:57-8+ D 20 '69
Total view of campus unrest. Science 166: 195 N 21 '69
about
ACE study on campus unrest; questions for behavioral scientists. J. Walsh; J. Coburn. Science 165:157-61 Jl 11 '69
ASTIN, Allen V.
Scientific community and international cooperation; address, April 8, 1969. Dept State Bul 61:32-7 Jl 14 '69
about
National bureau of standards prepares for the 1970's. il por Science 165:867-74 Ag 29 '69
ASTONISHMENT. See Wonder
ASTOR, Brooke (Russell)
Mrs Vincent Astor, woman with the wit for giving. il por Vogue 153:178-9 My '69

ASTOR, Mary
What it was like to kiss Clark Gable. Read Digest 94:49-53 Je '69
ASTRODOME, Houston. See Stadiums
ASTROLOGERS
Astrologers. J. H. Plumb. il Horizon 11:102-3 Sum '69
Black astrologers predict the future. E. B. Thompson. il Ebony 24:62-4+ Ap '69
ASTROLOGY
Astrologers. J. H. Plumb. il Horizon 11:102-3 Sum '69
Astrologers as useful marriage counselors. L. Sechrest and J. H. Bryan; reply. A. S. La Vey. Trans-Action 6:63-4 F '69
Astrology: fad and phenomenon il Time 93: 47-8+ Mr 21 '69
Astrology: fun, fraud or key-hole to the future? I. Taves. il Look 33:96-8+ My 13 '69
Black astrologers predict the future. E. B. Thompson. il Ebony 24:62-4+ Ap '69
Can the stars foretell? F. L. Remington. Mech Illus 65:32+ F '69
Eye on the sky. X. Pové. See issues of Harper's bazaar
Horoscope. M. E. Crummere. Vogue 154:55 Ag 1; 28-9 Ag 15; 356 S 1; 70 S 15; 165 O 1, 67 O 15; 133 N 1; 69 N 15; 149 D '69; 155: 87 Ja 1; 83 Ja 15 '70
Horoscope for April. S. Hairston. il Ebony 24:70 Ap '69
Horoscopes. S. Leek. Ladies Home J 86: 53-4 N '69
Horoscopes: his and hers. M. Woodruff. See issues of McCall's
Now it can be foretold. A. Bayer. il Life 67: 70B+ S 26 '69
Of planets and personalities. X. Pové. il House B 111:S2-11 Ap '69
Of thee I Ching. E. Janeway. Atlan 224:155-8 N '69
Opera and the stars. F. Stevenson and D. Brown. il Opera N 34:14-16 Ja 17 '70
President Nixon's horoscope. il Time 93:54-5 Mr 21 '69
Providence? Or age of Aquarius? H. B. Kuhn. Chr Today 13:39 Je 20 '69
Signs are right for astrology. T. Buckley. il Read Digest 94:237-8+ My '69
Under the spell of the zodiac. M. Graubard. il Natur Hist 78:10-12+ My '69
Universe of ready-made characters; zodiac signs of literary characters. W. J. Watkins. Writers Digest 49:38-9 Ag '69
What the stars really say. J. Brothers. Good H 168:65-7 Ap '69
What's the mutter with astrology? J. Rohler. il Chr Today 14:42 N 21 '69
Your birth sign. il House B 111:S24 Ap '69
See also
Computers—Astrological applications

Anecdotes, facetiae, satire, etc.
Your horoscope. R. Angell. New Yorker 45: 33 Mr 29 '69
Periodicals
New interest in astrology. B. Donchess. il Writers Digest 49:36-7+ Ag '69
ASTROM, Sverker C.
United Nations trust fund for South Africa. UN Mo Chron 6:43-7 F '69
ASTRONAUTICS. See Space flight
ASTRONAUTS
Agreement on rescue and return of astronauts enters into force; White House announcement, December 3, 1968. Dept State Bul 59:652 D 23 '68
Apollo 11 astronauts: recognition of religion? il Chr Today 13:31 Jl 18 '69
Everybody's happy but Esquire. R. P. Crossley. Pop Mech 132:48 N '69
Homage to the men from the moon; honoring in New York, Chicago and Los Angeles. il Time 94:8-11 Ag 22 '69
In Paris a successful link-up of spacemen, fueled by vodka. M. Mok. il Life 66:30-1 Je 13 '69
Man inside the spacesuit. il Newsweek 73: 56-7 Mr 3 '69
Matter of overtime; Apollo-earth time equation. il Time 93:42 Mr 7 '69
Le mot juste for the moon; consideration of what the first man on the moon might say; with suggestions by well known men and women. W. H. Honan. Esquire 72:53-6+ Jl '69
New breed. R. Starnes. Field & S 74:6+ D '69
On courage in the lunar age; Time essay. Time 94:19 Jl 25 '69
Psychology of astronauts; excerpt from A fire on the moon. N. Mailer. il Life 67:50-60+ N 14 '69

ASTRONAUTS—*Continued*
Science gets a chance; scientist-astronauts in Apollo program. J. Eberhart. il Sci N 96: 355-6 O 18 '69
Ten years that led to Apollo 11; thirty-two Life covers. R. Graves. il Life 67:3 Jl 25 '69
Today's astronauts; new breed of cosmic explorer. il U S News 67:34-5 Jl 21 '69
Whatever happened to the original seven astronauts. il U S News 67:16 Jl 21 '69

See also
Aldrin, E. E. jr
Armstrong, N. A.
Cernan, G.
Collins, M.
Eliseev, A.
Khrumov, E.
Schmitt, H. H.
Shatalov, V.
Shepard, A. B. jr
Space flight—Manned flights
Space flight to the moon—Manned flights
Stafford, T.
Volynov, B.
Young, J.

Clothing
Advanced space suits developed by Litton. C. M. Plattner. il Aviation W 90:71-3+ Ap 14 '69
How to dress for a walk on the moon. il Chem 42:23 D '69
Improved suit proposed for lunar wear. W. C. Wetmore. il Aviation W 90:51+ Mr 3 '69
In the news; extravehicular visor assembly. il Space World F-7-67:48 Jl '69
Mobility unhindered by bulky space suit. W. C. Wetmore. Aviation W 91:34-6 Jl 28 '69
Suits that sell for $100,000; Apollo space-suits. il Bsns W p 103-4 Jl 19 '69

Food
See Space flight—Food problems

Health and hygiene
Journey to the moon; what health hazards? R. Nessen. il Todays Health 47:16-21 Jl '69
Mission health problems minor. Aviation W 90:53-4 Je 9 '69

Training
Geologists prime Apollo crew for landing, exploration. W. J. Normyle. il Aviation W 91:80-1+ Jl 14 '69
Lunar surface crew simulates mission tasks. il Aviation W 90:20-3 Ap 28 '69
Moon-earth broadcast antenna erected in simulation of lunar surface mission tasks. il Aviation W 90:-81 My 5 '69
Moon landing training aided by computer. il Aviation W 91:95 Ag 11 '69
Rigorous training precedes moon liftoff. Z. Strickland. il Aviation W 91:59+ Jl 14 '69
Series of lunar landings simulated; lunar landing training vehicle. Z. Strickland. il Aviation W 90:55-9 Je 30 '69
To the moon; man's most daring voyage. I. Wolfert. il Read Digest 95:45-50 Jl '69

ASTRONAUTS families
Apollo 9 album. il Life 66:26+ Mr 28 '69
Apollo 9 families. il Life 66:24-5 F 28 '69
Apollo 10; Apollo 11; crews with their families; photographs. R. Morse. pors Life 66:44-51 My 16 '69
Crew: men apart. il Time 94:27-30 Jl 18 '69
Moon people. L. Tornabene. McCalls 96:60-1 Ag '69
Moonshoot; watching it all at home, the three astronauts' families coaxed them on. il Life 67:28-31 Ag 1 '69

ASTRONOMERS
See also
Herschel, J.
Pond, J.
Shapley, H.

ASTRONOMERS, Amateur
Amateur astronomers. See issues of Sky and telescope
Amateurs in action. See issues of Review of popular astronomy
Clubs for amateur star-gazers. il Mech Illus 65:106-7 Ag '69
Gleanings for ATM's; ed. by R. E. Cox. See issues of Sky and telescope

ASTRONOMICAL clocks
Astronomical clock of Jens Olsen. Danish astro-mechanic. O. Hagans. il Hobbies 74: 48-9+ Ap; 48-9+ My '69
World clock; astronomical, chronological, symbolical. O. R. Hagans. il Hobbies 74:48-9+ Mr '69

ASTRONOMICAL conferences
Highlights from the Denver convention; Nationwide amateur astronomers convention. W. E. Shawcross. il Sky & Tel 38:240-2 O '69
Highlights from the San Diego convention. il Sky & Tel 38:294-8 N '69
Report from Rome; X-rays and gamma rays. G. S. Mumford. il Sky & Tel 38:96-8 Ag '69
Vienna planetarium conference. G. Lovi. il Sky & Tel 38:236-9 O '69

ASTRONOMICAL instruments
Gnomon, brightly-painted wand, will land on moon with first man. il Space World F-7-67:10 Jl '69
Homebuilt machine for scanning plates; blink comparator. H. Vehrenberg. il Sky & Tel 38:186+ S '69
See also
Chronograph
Prisms
Telescope

ASTRONOMICAL league
Eclipse survey for the Astronomical league. R. C. Maag. il Sky & Tel 39: 28-30 Ja '70

ASTRONOMICAL observatories
Arcadia observatory, a sliding-roof construction. R. Maag. il R Pop Astron 63:24-6 F '69
Harrisburg observatory. J. A. Betz. il R Pop Astron 63:27-30 My '69
Inexpensive slide-off roof observatory. W. D. Williams, jr. il Sky & Tel 38:49-50 Jl '69
New Mexico's sunspot. J. Peterson. il Travel 132:48-9 Ag '69
New solar observatory in California; Aerospace corporation's San Fernando observatory. E. B. Mayfield and others. il Sky & Tel 37:208-13 Ap '69
Photo album of Kitt Peak's 158-inch telescope building. il Sky & Tel 38:284-9 N '69
Small domed observatory. M. D. Scott. il Sky & Tel 38:119-20 Ag '69

Chile
European southern observatory dedicated in Chile. B. E. Westerlund. il Sky & Tel 37: 340-7 Je '69

Czechoslovakia
Public observatories in Czechoslovakia. il R Pop Astron 63:4-6 My '69

Puerto Rico
They listen to the language of the universe. I. Wolfert. Read Digest 94:95-9 F '69
Visit to Arecibo finds a telescope seeking improvement. R. H. Ellis. il Phys Today 22:65+ Ap '69

ASTRONOMICAL photography
Amateur scientist; color photographs of the night sky are made by refrigerating the film. J. R. Bruman. il Sci Am 221:124-9 Ag '69
Astrophotography without a drive. R. Dickinson. il R Pop Astron 63:31-2 My '69
Cooled-emulsion photography without a vacuum. J. D. Wiseman. jr. bibliog il Sky & Tel 37:118-21 F '69
Image-tube photography. J. R. Hansen. il R Pop Astron 63:28-32 F '69
Photography with a 10-inch reflector. G. LeGendre. il Sky & Tel 38:194-7 S '69
See also
Television in astronomy

ASTRONOMICAL photometry. See Photometry, Astronomical

ASTRONOMICAL research
Science rediscovers gravity. T. Alexander. il Fortune 80:100-4+ D '69
See also
Artificial satellites—Astronomical applications
Astrophysics

Federal aid
Astronomy; tight budget gains stranglehold on radio facilities. R. W. Holcomb. il Science 166:984-6 N 21 '69

ASTRONOMICAL societies
Clubs for amateur star-gazers. il Mech Illus 65:106-7 Ag '69
See also names of astronomical societies. e.g. International astronomical union

ASTRONOMICAL spectroscopy
Composition of Saturn's rings. il Sky & Tel 39:14 Ja '70
Planetary spectroscopy with the 107-inch telescope. R. G. Tull. il Sky & Tel 38:156-60 S '69
See also
Stars—Spectra

ASTRONOMY
Astronomy (cont) Sci N 95:118, 240, 382;
  96:9, 351, 375, 406, 425, 577 F 1, Mr 8, Ap 19,
  Jl 5, O 18-N 8, D 20 '69
Astronomy. J. Stokley. See fourth issue of
  each month of Science news
Diamonds in the sky. J. A. Moore. bibliog
  il Har Yrs 9:6-11 Ap '69
How good are you as an astronomer? quiz. J.
  Daugherty and M. Daugherty. il Sci Digest
  66:68-70 O '69

  See also
Astrology
Astronomical research
Astrophysics
Computers—Astronomical applications
Constellations
Cosmogony
Eclipses, Solar
Galactic systems
Life on other planets
Magellanic clouds
Meteors
Milky way
Nautical astronomy
Nebulae
Occultations
Orbits
Quasars
Radar in astronomy
Radio astronomy
Satellites
Solar system
Television in astronomy
Universe
Zodiac

          Bibliography
Book reviews. See issues of Review of popular astronomy
Books and the sky. See issues of Sky and
  telescope

        Charts, diagrams, etc.
Evening sky map for [month] See issues of
  Review of popular astronomy
Sky reporter. J. P. Wiley, jr. See issues of
  Natural history
Stars for [the month] See issues of Sky and
  telescope

            History
John Pond: sixth astronomer Royal. J. Ash-
  brook. bibliog il Sky & Tel 38:224-5 O '69
Search for Vulcan. R. G. Hodgson. R Pop
  Astron 63:10-12 Mr; 10-11 My '69

       International aspects
East-West baseline; Soviet and U.S. astron-
  omers cooperate on small sources. D. E.
  Thomsen. il Sci N 96:437 N 8 '69

          Observations
Locating the Messier objects (cont) W. J.
  Busler. il R Pop Astron 63:21 Mr '69
  See also
Planets—Observations
Sun—Observations

        Study and teaching
Conference on laboratory exercises. S. S.
  Ross. il Sky & Tel 38:304-5 N '69
  See also
Planetariums

          Tables, etc.
Events of 1970 in the Graphic time table.
  Sky & Tel 39:35-7 Ja '70
ASTRONOMY, Indian
Their relics remain in the Americas; ex-
  cerpts from Flights into yesterday. L.
  Deuel. il Sat R 53:105-8 Ja 10 '70
ASTRONOMY, Japanese
History of Japanese astronomy, Chinese back-
  ground and western impact. by S. Naka-
  yama. Review
  Bul Atom Sci 25:38+ D '69. J. J. Saku-
  rai
ASTRONOMY, Maya
Five Mayan eclipses in thirteen years. H. E.
  Harber. il Sky & Tel 37:72-4 F '69
ASTRONOMY, Oriental
  See also
Astronomy, Japanese
ASTRONOMY, Prehistoric
  See also
Astronomy, Indian
ASTROPHYSICS
Astronomical evidence for nucleosynthesis in
  stars. G. Wallerstein. bibliog il Science 162:
  625-31 N 8 '68; Correction. 163:622 F 14 '69
Astrophysics of cosmic rays. V. L. Ginzburg.
  il Sci Am 220:50-63 bibliog (p 132) F '69
Infrared astrophysics. F. J. Low. bibliog il
  Science 164:501-5 My 2 '69

Progress in astronomy summarized for New
  York state section. R. L. Pompi. il Phys
  Today 22:89+ Je '69
Radioisotopes and the history of nucleosyn-
  thesis in the galaxy. C. M. Hohenberg. bib-
  liog il Science 166:212-15 O 10 '69
Vast spectrum of cosmic vibrations; cyma-
  tics. H. Jenny. il UNESCO Courier 22:29-
  30 D '69
  See also
Astronomical spectroscopy
Stars—Evolution
ASTURIAS, Miguel Ángel
Epic of Tropbanana. E. Capouya. Nation 208:
  213 F 17 '69
Square bananas. L. Segal. New Repub 160:
  24+ F 22 '69
ASTWOOD, Henry K.
Why sales executives fail. J. J. Tarrant. il
  Nations Bsns 57:100-2 S '69
ASWAN HIGH DAM
Dam U.S. wouldn't build: a big success for
  Russia. J. Law. il U S News 67:66-7 D
  29 '69
Sadd al 'Ali. J. S. Haupert. il Focus 19:9-11
  Mr '69
ASYLUM, Right of
Sanctuary. J. G. Dunne. Sat Eve Post 242:
  16 F 8 '69
Sanctuary at the Pacific Crossroads. F. Riley.
  Chr Cent 86:1526+ N 26 '69
Sanctuary in Evanston: Methodist churches
  accommodate Weathermen. Newsweek 74:
  73+ O 27 '69
U.S. to ask denial of asylum to hijackers.
  Aviation W 90:27-8 F 10 '69
AT Auntie Lou's: story. See Amft. M. J.
AT the falls at nine; story. See Clark. E.
AT the Tolstoy museum; story. See Barthelme,
  D.
ATACAMA DESERT
Garuma, gull of the desert; grey gull. G. M.
  Moffett, jr. il Sea Front 15:330-8 N '69
ATAHUALLPA
When civilizations collide. il Sr Schol 95:
  4-5 O 6 '69
ATCHESON, Richard
Encounter in Berlin. Holiday 45:22+ Ap '69
Encounter in London. Holiday 46:10-11 Ag '69
Encounter in Nairobi. Holiday 46:14-17 O '69
Montana is the message. Holiday 45:56-9+
  My '69
South Africa: it could have been Arcadia.
  Holiday 46:32-3+ N '69
ATCHISON, David Rice
David R. Atchison, president of the United
  States. C. Clemens. Hobbies 74:108 Jl '69
ATGET, Eugène
Atget, the little man who influenced a gen-
  eration of photographers. D. Vestal. il por
  Pop Phot 64:86-91+ F '69
ATHEISM
God in exile, by C. Fabro. Review
  Chr Cent 86:844-5 Je 18 '69. R. E. Koenig
Intimidated Christians. A. Lunn; discussion.
  Nat R 21:206+ Mr 11 '69
Non-existence of God: antitheism from
  Hegel to Dumèry. by H. R. Burkle. Review
  Chr Cent 86:1551 D 3 '69. J. C. Logan
Symposium in Rome: is unbelief believable?
  H. Cox. Commonweal 90:159-60 Ap 25 '69
Thomas Paine: to do good is my religion.
  Sr Schol 93:15 Ja 10 '69
ATHENAGORAS I, patriarch
Orthodox patriarch honored in ecumenical
  celebration. Chr Cent 86:247 F 19 '69
ATHENS, Greece
            Antiquities
Gift of wonder; Tower of the winds. Sci Am
  220:46 F '69

        Hotels, restaurants, etc.
Dionysos restaurant, Athens. M. Woodward.
  il Travel 132:71 D '69
ATHERAN, Robert A.
Shortcut to inventory control. Pub W 195:62-4
  My 19 '69
ATHEROSCLEROSIS. See Arteriosclerosis
ATHETOSIS. See Movement disorders
ATHLETES
All-America all the way; E. M. Vandeweghe
  family of Los Angeles. R. F. Jones. il
  Sports Illus 30:82-6+ My 26 '69
Desperate coach. J. Underwood. il Sports
  Illus 31:66-8+ Ag 25; 20-7 S 1; 28-32+ S
  8 '69
No goody two-shoes; Olympic athletes paid
  by German firms of Adidas and Puma to
  wear their track shoes. J. Underwood. il
  Sports Illus 30:14-23 Mr 10 '69
Rebels any way you cut it; bearded athletes.
  il Sports Illus 30:26-7 My 19 '69

ATHLETES—*Continued*
Social life of the long-distance runner. J.
 Casey. il Sports Illus 30:104-6+ Ap 14 '69
There were no greener pastures; pictorial re-
 view of sport in the '60s. Sports Illus 31:
 38-79 D 22 '69
Top three by a long shot; University of
 Kansas three mighty shotputters. J. Jares.
 il Sports Illus 30:78+ My 5 '69
 See also
Amateurism (sports)
Baseball players
Basketball players
Fellowship of Christian athletes
Football players
Negro athletes

Health and hygiene
Doc Kerlan: Rx for athletes. A. Wright. il
 Sports Illus 31:72-4+ N 24 '69

Salaries
Hero's off-season payoff; T. Seaver, the av-
 erage that really counts is Dow Jones;
 with report by W. Zinsser. il Life 67:38-41
 N 7 '69
 See also
Baseball players—Salaries, pensions, etc.
Football players—Salaries, pensions, etc.

Training
 See also
Basketball players—Training
ATHLETES, Resignation of

Anecdotes, facetiae, satire, etc.
Quitting is the name of any game. F. Deford.
 il Sports Illus 30:20-1 Je 30 '69
ATHLETES, Women. See Women as athletes
ATHLETES agents
All-star agent is a high scorer; C. Barnes.
 Bsns W p 153 S 20 '69
Playing the money game; agents represent-
 ing professional athletes. il Time 93:94
 Mr 21 '69
ATHLETES as sports announcers. See Tele-
 vision broadcasting—Sports
ATHLETIC fields
Garage roof doubles as turfed playfield. il
 Arch Rec 145:168-9 Ap '69
ATHLETIC goods industry. See Sporting goods
 industry
ATHLETICS
 See also
Athletes
College athletics
Fencing
Football
Gymnastics
Rowing
Running
School athletics
Sports
Track athletics
Wrestling
ATHLETICS for girls and women. See Sports
 for women
ATHOS, MOUNT
Walk through the 13th century. J. L. Herlihy.
 Commonweal 91:279-81 N 28 '69
ATKIN, John
Boatkeeper looks at his boat. Motor B 123:
 50-1+ Mr '69
Designs. Yachting 125:78-82 Mr '69
ATKINS, Anselm
(comp) Forty-four theses. Commonweal 91:
 208-9 N 14 '69
From chaos to Toronto I. Commonweal 91:
 149-55 O 31 '69
ATKINS, George
Token-dispensing parking meters. Am City
 84:125-6 Je '69
ATKINS, Ollie
White House photographers. J. Neubauer. il
 por Pop Phot 65:108-11+ D '69
ATKINS, Susan
Checkbook journalism. il por Newsweek 74:
 45-6 D 29 '69
ATKINSON, Andrews O.
Regional data-processing center. Am City 84:
 91-2+ Jl '69
ATKINSON, Tracy
German genre paintings from the Von
 Schleinitz collection. Antiques 96:712-16 N
 '69
ATLANTA
Discover Atlanta, by D. Lockerman and P.
 LaHatte. Review
 Atlan 224:94-6 Ag '69. S. Bingham

Architecture
Atlanta. il Arch Forum 130:42-51 Ap '69

Banks
Georgia cracker's crackerjack bank; Citizens
 & southern national bank of Georgia. R.
 Loving. jr. il Fortune 80:134-7+ N '69

City planning
Atlanta. il Arch Forum 130:42-51 Ap '69

Description
Atlanta. R. Bongartz. il Holiday 46:80-1+
 O '69
Atlanta, pacesetter city of the South. W. S.
 Ellis. il Nat Geog 135:246-81 F '69
Editor's report: resurgent Atlanta. M. M.
 Davis. il Travel 132:67-9 Ag '69

Education
All-year year; new four-quarter plan for year-
 round schooling. Time 94:64+ Ag 15 '69
Getting to know you day; experiences of B.
 Phillips. il Newsweek 74:69 S 15 '69
Year-round school, report on the latest test.
 il U S News 67:32-4 Ag 18 '69
 See also
Spelman college

Elections
In the mayor's seat. il Newsweek 74:39 N 3
 '69
Racial pincers of Atlanta politics. il Bsns W
 p 104 O 4 '69
Southern vote without a race tag. U S News
 67:14 O 20 '69
Vote of confidence; mayoral election. il Newsweek 74:44+ O 20 '69

Historic houses, etc.
Now it's underground tourism; restoration of
 subterranean shops. L. Barry. il Pop Phot
 64:44+ Je '69

Housing
Unbusted blocks. il Newsweek 74:55 D 1 '69

Labor and laboring classes
ALA picks Atlanta as a starter. il Bsns
 W p78 S 13 '69

Memorial arts center
Atlanta: progress in the arts. E. P. Birk. il
 Antiques 96:476+ O '69
Atlanta's culture for all seasons. R. Lynes. il
 Harper 238:23-4+ F '69
Culture shock; financial troubles. il News-
 week 73:94-5 Ja 27 '69
High cost of culture; ballet, opera and dra-
 matic repertory folding. Time 93:59 Ja 24
 '69

Music
Report: Atlanta; production of the magic
 flute by Atlanta chamber opera society.
 C. White. Opera N 33:31 Mr 15 '69

Police
Great hippie hunt. il Time 94:22-3 O 10 '69

Politics and government
Allen of Atlanta; interview, ed. by F. Pow-
 ledge. I. Allen, jr. il Harper 239:79-83 N '69
 See also
Atlanta—Elections

Recreation
Guitar babies; crash course for disadvantaged
 children. Newsweek 74:76+ Jl 28 '69

Social life and customs
Single life: Atlanta. il Mlle 69:133+ S '69
ATLANTA (periodical)
Battle of Atlanta. Time 95:49 Ja 12 '69
ATLANTA ballet
Beautiful gesture. D. Hering. il Dance Mag
 43:46-9 Ja '69
First repertory program reviewed. G. Beis-
 wanger. il Dance Mag 43:49-50 Ja '69
ATLANTA Braves (baseball) See Baseball
 clubs
ATLANTA civic ballet. See Atlanta ballet
ATLANTA Falcons (football club) See Foot-
 ball clubs
ATLANTA 500. See Automobile racing
ATLANTA Hawks (basketball team) See Bas-
 ketball teams
ATLANTA legal aid society. See Legal aid
 societies
ATLANTA memorial arts center. See Atlanta—
 Memorial arts center
ATLANTA zoo. See Zoological gardens
ATLANTIC alliance. See Nato
ATLANTIC cables. See Cables, Submarine

ATLANTIC CITY
Atlantic City; photographs. G. Gardner. Travel & Camera 32:94-8 Jl '69
Place of the month. C. Brossard. il Holiday 46:90-1+ S '69

Description

Beaches, boardwalks and beauties; past and present. il Library J 94:2419-20 Je 15 '69

Hotels, restaurants, etc.

Snow cones and frankfurters. B. Pearce and S. Pearce. il Library J 94:2415-18 Je 15 '69

ATLANTIC community
New Europe: what Nixon will find. J. Fromm. U S News 66:24 Mr 3 '69
Toward a new partnership with Europe. G. C. McGhee. Sat R 52:16-18 Mr 8 '69

ATLANTIC community development group for Latin America
ADELA: capital idea for Latin America. S. Seegers. Read Digest 94:154-6+ Mr '69

ATLANTIC flights. See Aviation—Transatlantic flights

ATLANTIC OCEAN
Asking for trouble; departure for southern waters via the offshore route. B. Robinson. il Yachting 126:60-1+ Ag '69
Carbonate sediments: oriented lithified samples from the North Atlantic. G. A. Bartlett and R. G. Greggs. bibliog il Science 166:740-1 N 7 '69
See also
Biscay, Bay of
Gulf Stream
North Sea
Radioactive fallout—Atlantic Ocean
Sargasso Sea

ATLANTIC salmon. See Salmon

ATLANTIC states
East is East and West is second, or is it? A. Hano. il N Y Times Mag p32-3+ Mr 16 '69
See also
Hunting—Atlantic states

Description and travel

Eventide on the East coast. E. Newmark. il Yachting 126:68-70+ O '69
Way south. W. R. Juettner. il Motor B 124:52-5+ O '69

ATLANTIC village plan. See Brooklyn—Housing

ATLANTIC world port, incorporated
Machiasport gets two new bidders: battle over building a refinery at Machiasport, Me. Bsns W p20 Jl 5 '69

ATLAS, James
Celebration; poem. Poetry 115:26-9 O '69
Chronicle of younger poets. Poetry 113:428-33 Mr '69
Dream songs: to terrify & comfort. Poetry 115:43-6 O '69
Roethke's Boswell. Poetry 114:327-30 Ag '69
Way of all loss; excerpt; poem. Poetry 113:317 F '69

ATLASES
Best route from Aa to Zywiec; Rand McNally's new international atlas. W. Zinsser. il Life 67:14 D 5 '69
Modern ideas for new atlas: Rand McNally's international atlas. il Pub W 195:66-72+ My 5 '69
Rand-McNally and EB copublish atlas. Library J 94:3594+ O 15 '69
See also
Publishers and publishing—Atlases

ATLEE, Frank
What ever happened to Atwater Kent? Pop Electr 31:53-5+ Jl '69

ATMOSPHERE
Carbon monoxide: residence time in the atmosphere. B. Weinstock. bibliog il Science 166:224-5 O 10 '69
Imbalance of nature. C. J. Roy. il Todays Ed 58:26-8+ Ja '69
Wind from Dugway: death of sheep near Proving ground, testing poisonous agents. V. Brodine and others. il Environ 11:2-9+ Ja '69
See also
Winds

ATMOSPHERE, Upper
Earth's broadcasting atmosphere. il Sci N 95:423-4 My 3 '69
Magnetospheric wind. J. W. Freeman, jr. bibliog il Science 163:1061-2 Mr 7 '69
Nitric acid in the upper atmosphere. Sky & Tel 38:388 D '69
See also
Atmospheric temperature

ATMOSPHERIC aerosols. See Aerosols
ATMOSPHERIC dust. See Dust

ATMOSPHERIC electricity
Electricity and rain. J. D. Sartor. bibliog il Phys Today 22:45-51 Ag '69
See also
Auroras

ATMOSPHERIC humidity. See Humidity
ATMOSPHERIC ions. See Ions
ATMOSPHERIC nucleation
Cloud condensation nuclei from a simulated forest fire. P. V. Hobbs and L. F. Radke. bibliog il Science 163:279-80 Ja 17 '69

ATMOSPHERIC pollution. See Air pollution
ATMOSPHERIC research
Atmospheric absorption anomalies in the ultraviolet near an altitude of fifty kilometers. A. J. Krueger. bibliog il Science 166:998-1000 N 21 '69
In pursuit of atmospheres. R. D. Cadle and W. O. Roberts. il Chem 42:7-11 Ja '69
See also
Artificial satellites—Use in research
Polar research
United States—National oceanic and atmospheric agency (proposed)

ATMOSPHERIC temperature
Atmosphere and the ocean. R. W. Stewart. il Sci Am 221:76-86 bibliog(p284) S '69
Atmospheric temperature: successful test of remote probing. D. Q. Wark and D. T. Hilleary. bibliog il Science 165:1256-8 S 19 '69

ATMOSPHERIC turbulence
Who will bell the invisible CAT? F. A. Tinker. il Pop Mech 132:94-7+ Ag '69
See also
Winds

ATOMIC age
Day the atomic age was born; ed. by J. D. Ratcliff. Read Digest 94:129-33 Mr '69
International atom, a new appraisal, the past and the promise; address, January 29, 1969. G. T. Seaborg. Dept State Bul 60:173-84, 199-211 Mr 3-10 '69

ATOMIC and space development authority. See New York (state)—Atomic and space development authority

ATOMIC blasting
Australian plans gang agley. Sci N 95:352 Ap 12 '69
Blasting a nuclear haven: proposed harbor at Cape Keraudren, Australia. il Sci N 95:159-60 F 15 '69
Boom! Project Rulison. Newsweek 74:76 S 22 '69
Going deep for gas; Project Rulison. Sci N 96:236 S 20 '69
Is this blast necessary? Project Rulison, Colorado. Time 94:39 Ag 29 '69
Nuclear explosions: can they really be made into useful tools? Operation Plowshare achievements. G. T. Seaborg. Sci Digest 65:7-13 Je '69
Nuclear perseverance. W. A. Scholes. il Sci N 96:408-9 N 1 '69
Once more for the money. il Sci N 95:376 Ap 19 '69
Plowing a nuclear furrow. E. A. Martell. bibliog il Environ 11:2-10+ Ap '69
Six questions for Australians: proposal to use nuclear explosives to dig a harbor. il Environ 11:16-19 Ap '69
U.S. U.S.S.R. conclude technical talks on peaceful uses of nuclear explosions; joint communique. Dept State Bul 60:401 My 12 '69
Unsnug harbor; Australian Plowshare harbor still a possibility. V. Brodine. il Environ 11:34-6 My '69

Protests, demonstrations, etc, against

Bombs away; Rulison and Gasbuggy projects. il Newsweek 74:106-7 S 15 '69
Pollution foes seek to defuze nuclear test. Bsns W p 18-19 Ag 30 '69

ATOMIC bomb shelters
Helping managers head for the hills; corporate survival centers. il Bsns W p37 D 27 '69
Safe City: apartment living inside a mountain. B. Ford. il Sci Digest 66:16-19 Ag '69
Where are they now? fallout-shelters. il Newsweek 74:10 Ag 25 '69

ATOMIC bombs
Death in life: a statement. R. J. Lifton. Bul Atom Sci 25:39 Je '69
See also
Hydrogen bombs

History

Whatever happened to cities that built the A-bombs? U S News 67:13 S 8 '69

ATOMIC bombs—*Continued*

Manufacture

Bombs and bombast; Atomic energy commission releases data on nuclear weapons. J. Deedy. Commonweal 90:450 Jl 25 '69

Do-it-yourself A-bombs. T. M. Conrad. il Commonweal 90:455-7 Jl 25 '69

Please don't steal the atomic bomb. A. M. **Adelson.** il Esquire 71:130-3+ My '69

Physiological effects

See Radioactivity—Physiological effects

Testing

Eighth big blast: Chinese H-bomb. Sr Schol 94:16 Ja 17 '69

Look, no earthquake. W. Zinsser. il Life 67: 4 N 14 '69

Upgrading a test-ban safeguard; readiness for atmospheric testing. il Sci N 95:447 My 10 '69

See also
Radioactive fallout

Testing, Detection of

Underground test detector. Sci N 97:7-8 Ja 3 '69

Testing, Underground

About 355 of those things have exploded in Nevada. G. Hill. il N Y Times Mag p6-7+ Jl 27 '69; Reply. S. Novick. p23 Ag 17 '69

Aftershocks below, uncertainty above: Amchitka thermonuclear test. il Sci N 96:322-3 O 11 '69

Amchitka and international regulation. E. B. Skolnikoff. Science 166:315 O 17 '69

Can AEC defuse Hughes? Bsns W p 19-20 Ap 5 '69

Earthquakes and nuclear tests: playing the odds on Amchitka. L. J. Carter. il Science 165:773-6 Ag 22 '69; Reply with rejoinder. G. Davidson. 166:688+ N 7 '69

Faultless? il Newsweek 74:100 O 13 '69

Have bombs, will travel. il Bsns W p 166 S 20 '69

H-bombs for earthquakes. Time 94:82+ O 17 '69

News and views; relations between underground nuclear explosions and earthquakes. J. Deedy. Commonweal 89:486 Ja 17 '69

Odds on the croupier; Howard Hughes questions AEC plans. Nation 208:453 Ap 14 '69

Planned; biggest underground atom tests yet. il U S News 66:12 Ap 21 '69

Secrets, secrets; report on possibility of earthquakes. Nation 209:397-8 O 20 '69

Seismic activity and faulting associated with a large underground nuclear explosion. R. M. Hamilton and others. bibliog il Science 166:601-4 O 31 '69

Shaking up Las Vegas. Sci & Cit 10:264-5 D '68

Smooth going for atomic test. U S News 67:10 O 13 '69

Underground nuclear explosions and the control of earthquakes. C. Emiliani and others. bibliog il Science 165:1255-6 S 19 '69

U.S. proposes world wide seismic investigation of underground nuclear explosions; statement with text of resolutions, December 5 and 20, 1968. W. C. Foster. Dept State Bul 60:53-64 Ja 20 '69

Who says it's safe? Nation 208:556-7 My 5 '69

ATOMIC cities. See Cities and towns—United States

ATOMIC clocks

Slowdown at sunrise. il Time 95:41 Ja 19 '70

ATOMIC energy. See Atomic power

ATOMIC energy commission. See United States—Atomic energy commission

ATOMIC fuels. See Nuclear fuels

ATOMIC industries. See Atomic power industry

ATOMIC nuclei

Fuzzy shell. Sci Am 221:52 Jl '69

Lifetime of compound nucleus is measured by crystal blocking. G. B. Lubkin. Phys Today 22:67 Jl '69

Nuclear models; adaptation of address. October 5, 1968. D. R. **Inglis.** bibliog il Phys Today 22:29-40 Je '69

Nudging the nucleus; Argonne's superconducting internal conversion electron spectrometer. D. E. Thomsen. il Sci N 95:147+ F 8 '69

Size and shape of atomic nuclei. M. Baranger and R. A. Sorensen. il Sci Am 221:58-64+ Ag '69

Fusion

See Nuclear fusion

Spin

See Nuclear spin

ATOMIC physics. See Nuclear physics

ATOMIC power

See also
Nuclear fusion
Nuclear reactors

Economic aspects

Bombs for peace; EG&G to drill for gas and oil and dig ditches by atomic explosives. il Forbes 104:71-2 S 15 '69

Coal industry; atomic power. address, January 21, 1969. B. O'Brien. Vital Speeches 35: 379-84 Ap 1 '69

General conference of the International atomic energy agency holds 13th session at Vienna; statement, September 24, 1969. G. T. Seaborg. Dept State Bul 61:329-33 O 20 '69

Getting science to pay off. F. C. Livingstone. il Sci N 96:224 S 13 '69

International atom, a new appraisal, the past and the promise; address, January 29, 1969. G. T. Seaborg. Dept State Bul 60: 173-84, 199-211 Mr 3-10 '69

Once more for the money. il Sci N **95:376** Ap 19 '69

See also
Atomic blasting
Atomic power industry
Atomic power plants
Nuclear reactors
Ships, Atomic powered

Exhibitions

Atom at ease. P. Mygatt. il Travel 132:68-70 N '69

Industrial aspects

See Atomic power—Economic aspects

International aspects

Amchitka and international regulation. E. B. Skolnikoff. Science 166:315 O 17 '69

International atom, a new appraisal, the past and the promise: address, January 29, 1969. G. T. Seaborg. Dept State Bul 60:173-84, 199-211 Mr 3-10 '69

Nuclear power plays form chain reaction. Bsns W p39-40 N 22 '69

See also
Euratom
International atomic energy agency

Medical applications

See Radiology, Medical

Social aspects

Social impact of a nuplex: advantages of nuclear-powered, industrial complexes. R. L. Meier. il Bul Atom Sci 25:16-21 Mr '69

Australia

Atom Down Under. W. A. Scholes. Sci N 96: 168 Ag 30 '69

Nuclear perseverance. W. A. Scholes. il Sci N 96:408-9 N 1 '69

Canada

Fortune for a plant that can't produce. il Bsns W p58-9 D 13 '69

China (People's Republic)

China's nuclear option. M. B. Yahuda. il Bul Atom Sci 25:72-7 F '69

Europe, Eastern

Nuclear power in Europe at the crossroads. J. G. Polach. il Bul Atom Sci 25:15-18+ O '69

Europe, Western

European notes: quids pro quo. D. S. Greenberg. Science 165:267 Jl 18 '69

Nuclear power in Europe at the crossroads. J. G. Polach. il Bul Atom Sci 25:15-18+ O '69

Great Britain

Getting science to pay off. F. C. Livingstone. il Sci N 96:224 S 13 '69

India

Possibility of successful nuplex for India's Thar Desert. R. D. Sharma. Bul Atom Sci 25:31 N '69

Toward breeder reactors. S. K. **Ghaswala.** il Sci N 95:603 Je 21 '69

Israel

Israel and the nuclear non-proliferation treaty. G. H. Quester. il Bul Atom Sci 25:7-9+ Je '69

ATOMIC power—*Continued*

Japan

Steel and nucleonics. S. Griffin. Sci N 95:318 Mr 29 '69

Underdeveloped areas

Nuclear technology, weapons, and the third world. C. Zoppo. bibliog f Ann Am Acad 386:113-25 N '69

United States

See Atomic power

ATOMIC power industry

IAEA seeks better ways to detect nuclear-material diversion. J. P. Wiley. il Phys Today 22:69-70 Ag '69

Nuclear double-check; IAEA inspection of nuclear reprocessing plant facilities. il Bsns W p84 Je 28 '69

Nuclear power plays form chain reaction. Bsns W p39-40 N 22 '69

Nuclear safeguards: the US program. W. A. Higinbotham. bibliog il Phys Today 22:40-4 N '69

Social impact of a nuplex; advantages of nuclear-powered, industrial complexes. R. L. Meier. il Bul Atom Sci 25:16-21 Mr '69

ATOMIC power plants

AEC goes public on nuclear safety. il Bsns W p52 S 20 '69

Atom Down Under. W. A. Scholes. Sci N 96:168 Ag 30 '69

Atomic power in industry: a slump now, but . . . il U S News 67:54-5 Jl 7 '69

Cooling it in Minnesota; report of Minnesota committee for environmental information on benefits and risks of nuclear reactors. il Environ 11:21-5 Mr '69

Desalted seawater for agriculture: is it economic? M. Clawson and others. bibliog Science 164:1141-8 Je 6 '69; Discussion. 165:850-1 Ag 29 '69

Dilemmas of power il Time 94:38 Ag 29 '69

Early bird; Commonwealth Edison. il Forbes 104:38 S 15 '69

Energy for man and environmental protection. P. Sporn. Science 166:555 O 31 '69; Discussion. 166:1459-60+ D 19 '69

Fortune for a plant that can't produce; Canada's heavy water plant. il Bsns W p58-9 D 13 '69

France buries its pride. Time 94:96+ N 23 '69

GE's nuclear giant warms up; Oyster Creek plant. Toms River, N.J. Bsns W p46 My 17 '69

Myth of omnipotence; hidden costs of nuclear power. B. Commoner. il Environ 11: 8-13+ Mr '69

Myth of the peaceful atom. R. Curtis and E. Hogan. il Natur Hist 78:6-8+ Mr '69; Discussion. 78:6+ My '69

Nukes are in hot water; thermal pollution caused by hot-water from nuclear plants. R. H. Boyle. il Sports Illus 30:24-8 Ja 20 '69

Overselling a dream. Sci N 96:113-14 Ag 9 '69

Peaceful atom: friend or foe? il Time 95:42-3 Ja 19 '70

Radioactive pollution: Minnesota finds AEC standards too lax. P. M. Boffey. Science 163:1043-4+ Mr 7 '69

Sluggish atom; delays in construction. Newsweek 73:81-2 Je 23 '69

Standardization will aid nuclear energy growth. il Am City 84:75 Jl '69

Thermal pollution: a threat to Cayuga's waters? L. J. Carter; discussion. Science 163:517-18 F 7 '69

Those atomic power plants; excerpts from letters. W. D. Burden; H. Forster. Liv Wildn 33:28-30 Spr '69

War over the peaceful atom; radioactive and thermal hazards. il Life 67:26B-33 S 12 '69

Who gets last radioactive word? Minnesota vs Atomic energy commission. Bsns W p28 My 31 '69

Why utilities can't meet demand. il Bsns W p53+ N 29 '69

World's biggest atom-power plant; Browns ferry nuclear plant. A. P. Armagnac. il Pop Sci 195:94-7+ S '69

See also

Nuclear reactors

Accidents and injuries

Aftermath of a fire; plutonium fire at Rocky Flats. il Sci N 96:496 N 29 '69

Incident at Rocky Flats; fire at Dow chemical. Nation 208:781 Je 23 '69

Location

Mile from Times square; adaptation of address, December 2, 1968. S. Novick. bibliog f il Environ 11:10-15+ Ja '69

ATOMIC powered aircraft carriers. See Aircraft carriers, Atomic powered

ATOMIC powered ships. See Ships, Atomic powered

ATOMIC powered submarine boats. See Submarine boats, Atomic powered

ATOMIC powered warships. See Warships, Atomic powered

ATOMIC radiation. See Radioactivity

ATOMIC research

See also

Accelerators (electrons, etc)

American nuclear society

China (People's Republic)

ABM, China, and the arms race. H. A. Bethe. il Bul Atom Sci 25:41-4 My '69

China's nuclear option. M. B. Yahuda. il Bul Atom Sci 25:72-7 F '69

Europe, Western

Lack of scientific planning in Europe; adaptation of address, December 1968. J. Guéron. Bul Atom Sci 25:10-14+ O '69

See also

Euratom

European organization for nuclear research

Great Britain

See also

Great Britain—Atomic energy authority

Japan

Atoms for everybody? diffusion technique mastered. Newsweek 73:88-9 Ap 14 '69

Russia

Fusion power; optimism and a Tokamak gap at Dubna. R. W. Holcomb. Science 166:363-4 O 17 '69

Russia's H-bomb tamers. il Bsns W p 176+ S 20 '69

Tokamak. Sci Am 221:51-2 D '69

Triumph for Tokamak. Newsweek 74:70 N 10 '69

ATOMIC research laboratories

Government labs; Britain's Harwell finds new role in industrial work. D. S. Greenberg. Science 163:1041-3 Mr 7 '69

See also

Argonne national laboratory

California, University—Lawrence radiation laboratories

ATOMIC submarines. See Submarine boats, Atomic powered

ATOMIC warfare

See also

Atomic bombs

Civil defense

Emergency communication systems

Defenses

ABM and the MAD strategy. J. Raser. Ramp Mag 8:36-7 N '69

Can President Nixon stop the arms race? J. K. Javits. Sat R 52:14-16+ Mr 1 '69

See also

United States—Defenses

Psychological aspects

Failure of fail-safe. J. R. Raser. il Trans-Action 6:11-19 Ja '69

ATOMIC warfare and society

What's bothering the students? excerpts from address, March 4, 1969. G. Wald. Chem 42:1+ My '69

ATOMIC waste. See Radioactive waste disposal

ATOMIC weapons

Arms control: the critical moment; U.S. to discuss possible limits on nuclear weapons with the Soviet Union. Time 93:13-15 Je 27 '69

In Helsinki, a step ahead: Meanwhile, the nuclear race speeds up. il U S News 68:5 Ja 5 '70

Luv that bomb; NATO nuclear arsenal. J. Deedy. Commonweal 90:402 Je 27 '69

Missiles and bombers. il Sci N 95:184-5 F 22 '69

Weapons culture, by R. E. Lapp. Review Environ il 11:30-1 N '69. C. Hohenemser

Accidents

Bombs, bombs everywhere. Nation 209:588-9 D 1 '69

Failure of fail-safe. J. R. Raser. il Trans-Action 6:11-19 Ja '69

ATOMIC weapons—Accidents—*Continued*
Nuclear accidents and the ABM. J. Larus.
Sat R 52:10-13 My 31 '69
Shh! let's tell the Russians; how J. F. Kennedy decided to make the Russians aware of our permissive-action link system. E. Klein and R. Littell. il Newsweek 73:46-7 My 5 '69

International control
Action on the NPT. T. Shoemaker. il Sci N 96:386 O 25 '69
All smiles. il Newsweek 73:39 Mr 31 '69
Ambassador Smith presents U.S. views on seabed proposal at Eighteen-nation disarmament conference; statement, March 25, 1969. G. Smith. Dept State Bul 60:333-7 Ap 21 '69
America's high stakes in nuclear treaty. il U S News 66:32-3 Mr 10 '69
Another nuclear treaty ahead? il U S News 66:12 Mr 31 '69
Assembly adopts seven resolutions; with text of resolutions. UN Mo Chron 6:46-55 Ja '69
Backing a bit from the brink; nonproliferation treaty signed by U.S. and Russia. il Newsweek 74:43+ D 8 '69
Battle inside the Kremlin. V. Zorza. Look 33:93-7+ Mr 18 '69
Can President Nixon stop the arms race? J. K. Javits. Sat R 52:14-16+ Mr 1 '69
Department emphasizes the importance of the nuclear nonproliferation treaty; statement, February 18, 1969. W. P. Rogers. Dept State Bul 60:189-90 Mr 10 '69
Does technology determine policy? R. Scott. Cur 109:45 Ag '69
Doves and hawks; new clash. il U S News 66:8 Mr 17 '69
Great nonproliferation hoax. W. H. Chamberlain. Nat R 21:229-30 Mr 11 '69
High government source; excerpts from news conference, ed. by F. Taddeo. E. Dirksen. Sr Schol 94:12-13 F 28 '69
Improving the atmosphere; ratification of nonproliferation treaty. il Time 94:44+ D 5 '69
Israel and the nuclear non-proliferation treaty. G. H. Quester. il Bul Atom Sci 25:7-9+ Je '69
Letter from Washington; nuclear-non-proliferation treaty. R. H. Rovere. New Yorker 45:115-16+ Mr 22 '69
NPT: movement toward a viable world; ratification by the U.S. Senate of the nuclear non-proliferation treaty. E. Rabinowitch. Bul Atom Sci 25:48 Ap '69
Nonproliferation for whom? Nat R 21:105 F 11 '69
Nonproliferation treaty: another step. Time 93:14 Mr 21 '69
Non-proliferation treaty on Japan. R. Imai. il Bul Atom Sci 25:2-7 My '69
Non-proliferation: two views. B. Pilkington; P. Steinfels. Commonweal 89:721-3 Mr 14 '69
Nuclear logic. Commonweal 90:35-6 Mr 28 '69
Nuclear safeguards: the IAEA program. B. W. Sharpe. il Phys Today 22:33-7 N '69
Nuclear safeguards, the peaceful atom, and the IAEA. L. Scheinman. bibliog f il Int Concil 572:5-64 Mr '69
Nuclear technology, weapons, and the third world. C. Zoppo. bibliog f Ann Am Acad 386:113-25 N '69
Nuclear treaty: step toward peace, or a Soviet trick? il U S News 66:10-11 Mr 24 '69
Nuclear weapons; treaty on nonproliferation; address, January 20, 1969. B. Goldwater. Vital Speeches 35:262-3 F 15 '69
Pleasant reading, for a change; signing of the nonproliferation treaty. Nation 209: 652 D 15 '69
President Nixon urges Senate action on nuclear nonproliferation treaty; message to the Senate, February 5, 1969. R. M. Nixon. Dept State Bul 60:162 F 24 '69
Prospects for arms control. W. C. Foster. For Affairs 47:413-21 Ap '69
Role of world law in arms control. S. C. Yuter. Bul Atom Sci 25:23-5 O '69
To guard the guards. J. Burnham. Nat R 21:583 Je 17 '69
U.S. receives U.K. ratification of nonproliferation treaty; statement, November 27, 1968. W. C. Foster. Dept State Bul 59:679 D 23 '68
U.S. views on nuclear weapon material cutoff agreement and verification of comprehensive nuclear test ban; statement, April 8, 1969. A. S. Fisher. Dept State Bul 60: 409-13 My 12 '69

What prospects for arms talks? M. Woollacott. Cur 109:43-5 Ag '69
See also
Ocean bottom—International aspects

Manufacture
Plutonium fire raises questions; investigation after fire at weapons plant, Rocky Flats, Colo. il Sci N 96:25 Jl 12 '69

Safety devices and measures
Shh! let's tell the Russians; how J. F. Kennedy decided to make the Russians aware of our permissive-action link system. E. Klein and R. Littell. il Newsweek 73:46-7 My 5 '69

Testing
China's nuclear option. M. B. Yahuda. il Bul Atom Sci 25:72-7 F '69
Is China's bomb on target? il Bsns W p 108 S 6 '69

ATOMIC weapons and disarmament
Arms talks. New Repub 160:9-10 F 8 '69
Chances for an end to the arms race. il U S News 66:32-3 F 3 '69
Controlling the arms race; ABM debate; symposium. Cur 106:3-21 Ap '69
Generation in search of a future; address, March 4, 1969. G. Wald. Vital Speeches 35: 410-13 Ap 15 '69; Same with title Our business is with life. Redbook 133:68+ Ag '69; Excerpts New Yorker 45:29-31 Mr 22 '69
George Wald: the man, the speech. R. Todd. il N Y Times Mag p28-9+ Ag 17 '69
Hopeful words on arms control. Time 93:14 Ja 31 '69
Kicking the weapons habit. Chr Cent 86:893 Jl 2 '69
Limiting strategic technology: the need for national self-restraint. L. S. Rodberg. Bul Atom Sci 25:36-8 N '69
Nixon and the weapons talks. H. Brandon. Sat R 52:9-10+ Jl 5 '69
Nixon says yes to arms talks; with report by L. Norman. il Newsweek 73:28-9 Je 23 '69
Price of arms control; with editorial comment. il Bsns W p64-5+. 148 Jl 12 '69
Soviet intrigue? reprint. D. Lawrence. U S News 66:100 Mr 24 '69
Start on strategic stabilization. D. G. Brennan. Bul Atom Sci 25:35-6 Ja '69
Stop, look, talk. New Repub 160:7 Ap 19 '69
Two Dutch treats and the arms race. A. Geyer. Chr Cent 86:1272-3 O 8 '69
U.S. positions at Eighteen-nation disarmament conference outlined by President Nixon; text of letter, March 15, 1969. R. M. Nixon. Dept State Bul 60:289-90 Ap 7 '69
U.S. proposes world wide seismic investigation of underground nuclear explosions; statement with text of resolutions, December 5 and 20, 1968. W. C. Foster. Dept State Bul 60:58-64 Ja 20 '69
Vicious acronyms. R. E. Lapp. il New Repub 160:15-19 Je 21 '69
Where superpowers stand in arms race; Institute for strategic studies report. il U S News 67:56 S 22 '69
See also
Strategic arms limitation talks

ATOMIC weights
Theodore William Richards and the atomic weight problem: adaptation of address, December 27, 1968. A. J. Ihde. il Science 164:647-51 My 9 '69

ATOMS
How good are you as a chemist? J. Daugherty and M. Daugherty. il Sci Digest 66:88-90 S '69
See also
Atomic nuclei
Atomic weights
Matter
Neutrons
Nuclear physics
Nucleons

Space arrangement
See Stereochemistry

ATOMS for peace awards
Atoms for peace awards; address, May 14, 1969. R. E. Marshak. Science 164:1496-8 Je 27 '69

ATOMS for peace program. See Atomic power—Economic aspects

ATONALITY. See Tonality

ATROPINE
Acetylcholine facilitation, atropine block of synaptic excitation of cortical neurons. R. Spehlmann. bibliog il Science 165:404-5 Jl 25 '69

ATTACHED houses. See Row houses

ATTACHES, Scientific. See United States—Foreign service

ATTACHMENT and garnishment
Winners and losers: garnishment & bankruptcy in Wisconsin; excerpts from Debtors in court. H. Jacob. il Trans-Action 6:24-32 My '69

ATTACK on Pearl Harbor, 1941. See Pearl Harbor, Attack on, 1941

ATTENTION
Are you listening, teacher? E. Caldwell. Todays Ed 58:33-4 Ja '69
Art of listening to children; with group-discussion program. Y. Postelle. il Parents Mag 44:58-9+, 76 Ap '69
Attention as a concept in neurophysiology; report of meeting. C. R. Evans and T. B. Mulholland. Science 163:495-6 Ja 31 '69
Attention reduction and suppressed direct-current potentials in the human brain. J. J. Tecce and N. M. Scheff. bibliog il Science 164:331-3 Ap 18 '69
Attention shifts in a maintained discrimination. D. S. Blough. bibliog il Science 166: 125-6 O 3 '69
Healing touch of attention. D. E. Smith. Read Digest 94:175-6+ Ap '69
Listen to what you can't hear. N. B. Sigband. il Nations Bsns 57:70-2 Je '69
Look, listen, learn! M. Van Hoosan. Todays Ed 58:51 F '69
See also
Vigilance (psychology)

ATTICS
How I remodeled a problem attic. H. Wicks. il Pop Sci 194:124-5+ Je '69
Space tricks in an attic. V. D. Hahn and A. C. Borg il Am Home 72:62-3 Ap '69
Treasure in the attic. il Am Home 72:64-5 My '69

ATTITUDE director indicator. See Aeronautic instruments—Display systems

ATTITUDES
Applying pressure and changing attitudes. C. A. Kiesler. Todays Ed 58:66-7 Mr '69
Dialogue across the gap. J. J. Evoy. America 120:356-9 Mr 29 '69
Divisive tendencies within NEA affiliates. K. H. Ostrander. bibliog f Sch & Soc 97:116-18 F '69
Hopes and fears of blue-collar youth; report from Akron. P. M. Swerdloff. il Fortune 79:148-50+ Ja '69
Old order is becoming old hat. il Bsns W p 120-2+ D 6 '69
Our President, Appalachian style; children's political attitudes. Trans-Action 6:6 F '69
People who know how; excerpts from Brave enough for life. B. W. Overstreet. il PTA Mag 63:24-5 Mr '69
Self-fulfilling prophecy, a key to success. J. K. Lagemann. Read Digest 94:80-3 F '69
Special kind of rebellion. D. Seligman. il Fortune 79:66-9+ Ja '69
They want to know; survey of school children. R. Kramer. il N Y Times Mag p 107+ S 7 '69
Under twenty-one. S. Reice. McCalls 97:76+ Ja '70
Under twenty-one: how I would change the world at Christmastime. S. Reice. il McCalls 97:42+ D '69
Voices from abroad. Seventeen 29:88-9+ Ja '70
See also
Moral attitudes
Political attitudes
Public opinion
Value (psychology)

ATTITUDES, Professional. See Professionalism

ATTORNEY, Power of. See Power of attorney

ATTORNEY General (United States) See United States—Justice, Department of

ATTORNEYS. See Lawyers

ATTORNEYS general
See also
Public prosecutors

ATTRACTING of birds. See Birds, Attracting of

ATWATER, Sandra
Hope of the Hudson. Cons 23:15-16 Je '69

ATWELL, Willis W.
Atwell appointed deputy commissioner. il por Aging 178:4 Ag '69

ATWOOD, Margaret
For archeologists; Dream; bluejay or archeopteryx; Three desk objects; Carrying food home in winter; Projected slide of an unknown soldier; poems. Poetry 114:34-9 Ap '69
Night in the Royal Ontario museum; poem. Atlan 223:92 Ja '69

AUBERGE de l'Ill, Illhaeusern, Alsace. See Restaurants—France

AUBREY, James Thomas, 1918-
Again the smiling cobra. por Newsweek 74: 84-5 N 3 '69
James Aubrey makes comeback in movies. por Bsns W p40 O 25 '69
Return of smiling Jim. por Time 94:80 O 31 '69
Teaching MGM's lion new tricks. por Bsns W p44 Ja 3 '70

AUBUCHON, Norbert
Flying the Yankee; first sport plane built like an airliner. Pop Sci 195:72-5+ Jl '69
New Waco STOL Minerva has real get-up-and-go. Pop Sci 195:60-3+ D '69
This gadget won't let you land wheels-up. Pop Sci 195:60-3+ Ag '69

AUBUSSON rugs. See Rugs and carpets

AUCHINCLOSS, Louis
Cathedral builder; story. McCalls 96:88-9+ My '69

AUCTION; story. See Brautigan, R.

AUCTIONEERS. See Auctions

AUCTIONS
For art's sake; Camelot auction. H. Saal. Newsweek 74:133 N 24 '69
Fun and profit at a country auction. E. Kinard. il House B 111:60+ Je '69
U.S. journal: Atlantic City galleries selling other merchandise as warmup for diamonds. C. Trillin. New Yorker 45:104+ Je 14 '69
Vying for vintages; first vintage-wine auction in the U.S. il Newsweek 73:90 Je 9 '69
See also
Art sales
Book sales
Nation-wide auto auction. limited

Anecdotes, facetiae, satire, etc.
What on earth did you bid on that for? A. Fettig. Farm J 93:30C Je '69

AUDEN, Wystan Hugh
Art of healing; poem. New Yorker 45:38 S 27 '69
Books (cont) New Yorker 45:128+ F 22 '69
Doggerel by a senior citizen; poem. Poetry 115:185-6 D '69
Horatians; poem. New Yorker 45:44 My 24 '69
In defense of the tall story. New Yorker 45:205-6+ N 29 '69
Moon landing; poem. New Yorker 45:38 S 6 '69
Mosaic for Marianne Moore; poem. Wilson Lib Bul 43:624-5 Mr '69
Natural linguistics; poem. Harper 239:86 O '69
New Year greeting; poem. Sci Am 221:134 D '69
about
Auden's poetry, by J. Replogle. Review Sat R 52:55 Je 21 '69. R. D. Spector
Christianity and art. H. Bloom. New Repub 160:25-8 Ap 5 '69
Comment. M. L. Rosenthal. Poetry 114:126-9 My '69
Conversation with W. H. Auden. pors Holiday 45:56-7+ Je '69
Holding to schedule with W. H. Auden. J. Bradshaw. il por Esquire 73:136-9+ Ja '70

AUDIBLE noise override. See Sound—Apparatus

AUDIENCE participation. See Audiences

AUDIENCES
Building better music audiences. B. R. Purrington. Clear House 43:497-9 Ap '69
Kill the first night, kill it dead. C. Barnes. Holiday 45:10+ F '69
Not to be missed; you don't just sit there, you participate. G. Trotta. il Harp Baz 102: 220-1 Mr '69
Trash, art, and the movies. P. Kael. il Harper 238:65-8+ F '69; Discussion. 238:6 Ap '69

AUDIO amplifiers. See Amplifiers

AUDIO equalization curves. See Frequency standards

AUDIO equipment. See Sound—Apparatus

AUDIO fairs
Capital show in the capital city; high fidelity show. il Hi Fi 19:39-40 My '69
Hi-fi at L.A: the sunshine show. I. Berger. Sat R 52:68+ O 25 '69
Stereo shows, a tale of three cities: San Francisco, Toronto, and Paramus, N.J. il Hi Fi 19:42+ F '69

AUDIO generators. See Signal generators

AUDIO mixers. See Sound—Apparatus

AUDIO-visual aids
A-V happening. D. Molner. il Sr Schol 94:
Schol Teach 14-15 F 7 '69
Audiovisual guide; comp. by G. Sporich and
M. Moore. Library J 94:4231-2+ N 15 '69
Audiovisual guide; comp. by L. Mesiano
(cont) Library J 94:1741-2+ Ap 15 '69
Joint media standards published: Standards
for school media programs. Wilson Lib Bul
43:825 My '69
Media for mediacy. M. Ronan. Sr Schol 94:
Schol Teach 22 F 7 '69
Mr Ed: the talking bus; Gunnison, Colo. J. R.
Raine. il Sr Schol 94:Schol Teach 13 Ja 17
'69
New audiovisual products. D. Molner. il Sr
Schol 94:Schol Teach 10+ Ja 17 '69
New educational materials. See occasional
issues of Scholastic teacher
Resource materials: books, filmstrips, films,
slides, loops. V. G. Timmons. Sch Arts 69:
32-3 Ja '70
Screenings: media mix. D. A. Durfee. Li-
brary J 94:3160. 3805 S 15. O 15 '69
Screenings: media mix. Library J 94:3160 S
15 '69
See also
Education market
Film strips
Instructional materials centers
Libraries and audio-visual materials
Magnetic recorders and recording—Education-
al application
Pictures in education
Teaching machines

Bibliography
Selected bibliography of A-V media in library
literature, 1958-69. T. Eason. il Wilson Lib
Bul 44:312-19 N '69

Indexes
Bowker to publish NICEM media indexes.
Pub W 195:64 Ap 28 '69

Statistics
Educational A/V spending down slightly in
1967. Library J 94:256 Ja 15 '69
AUDIO-visual instruction
Audio-graphic network aids rural high
schools. R. F. Campbell. Clear House 44:
157-60 N '69
A-V happening. D. Molar. il Sr Schol 94:
Schol Teach 14-15 F 7 '69
Communications-arts teams; Broward Coun-
ty, Fla. G. Marsh. il Todays Ed 58:39-41
D '69
Lab-carts are rolling; Enfield, Conn. pro-
gram. F. S. Gross. il Schol Teach Sec
Teach Sup p 14-15+ O 6 '69
Mediacy: what it can do for you. W. D.
Boutwell. Sr Schol 94:Schol Teach 2 F 7 '69
Psychedelic multimedia happening; Gunn se-
nior high, Palo Alto, Calif. R. M. Glenden-
ing. il Sr Schol 94:Schol Teach 18-19 Ap
18 '69
See how they learn! symposium. il Todays Ed
58:15-30 F '69
War in the classroom: mass media vs. educa-
tion. L. Penfield. il Schol Teach Sec Teach
Sup p 14-15+ S 22 '69
See also
Computers—Educational applications
Educational media personnel
Libraries and audio-visual materials
Moving pictures in education
National education association—Department of
audio-visual instruction
AUDIO-visual materials, Cataloging of. See Cat-
aloging
AUDIO-visual specialists. See Educational me-
dia personnel
AUDITING
See also
Tax auditing
United States—General accounting office
AUDITIONS. See Dancing—Auditions
AUDITORIUMS
New filters eliminate auditorium odors; use
in Mobile's municipal auditorium and thea-
ter. Am City 84:20 Ja '69
See also
Concert halls
AUDITORY perception. See Sound perception
AUDUBON, John James
Wanted: a lost Audubon watercolor. N. Kent.
il Am Artist 33:58-9 Je '69
AUDUBON, John Woodhouse
Jornada del muerto. F. Egan. bibliog il Am
West 6:12-19+ Jl '69
AUDUBON medal
Fairfield Osborn; Audubon medalist, 1968.
Audubon 71:57 Ja '69

AUDUBON nature camps
John H. Baker, the Audubon years. C. W.
Buchheister and R. T. Peterson. Audubon
71:83-5 N '69
AUER, Lucijan, and Thanos, Harry
One-1C radio. Radio-Electr 40:49-51 N '69
AUERBACH, Alfred
Relevance of Jean-Michel Frank. House B
111:144-7 O '69
AUERBACH, Arnold. See Auerbach. R.
AUERBACH, Arnold M.
Best of Times, the worst of Times. Sat R
52:8+ O 11 '69
AUERBACH, Red
Two guys on a Boston hot seat. F. Deford. il
por Sports Illus 31:22-5 N 3 '69
AUERBACH, Pollak and Richardson, Incor-
porated
Lady analyst takes charge. Bsns W p 100+
Mr 8 '69
AUG, Stephen M.
Rules are changing. Nations Bsns 57:76-8+
O '69
AUGERS
Make holes in the ground with an electric
drill? New augers do it. R. P. Stevenson.
il Pop Sci 195:152+ Ag '69
AUGUST, Ronald
Algiers verdict. Time 93:23 Je 20 '69
License to kill? Newsweek 73:32+ Je 23 '69
AUGUSTA, Ga.
Clubs
Place of the month; Augusta; world's most
famous golf classic. il Holiday 45:106-7
Ap '69
AUGUSTA national golf club course. See Golf
courses
AUGUSTA opera company
Report: production of Rossini's Barber of
Seville. H. Blumenfeld. Opera N 34:26 D
13 '69
AUKEMA, Richard L.
Oshkosh: black student revolt in microcosm.
Chr Cent 86:219-21 F 12 '69
AUKS
Little auk! Little auk! excerpt from In de-
fense of nature. J. Hay. il Audubon 71:
13-15 Ja '69
AUL, Henry B.
Late-blooming perennials. Horticulture 47:20-
1+ Ag '69
AUMENTE, Jerome
Urban design with soul. Arch Forum 131:144-
5 D '69
AUMENTO, F.
Diorites from the mid-Atlantic ridge at 45°N.
bibliog Science 165:1112-13 S 12 '69
AURORA, Ill. public library
Carnegie facelift job for Aurora, Illinois.
il Library J 94:4388-9 D 1 '69
AURORAS
Colorful March aurora. il Sky & Tel 37:276-9
My '69
Generation of an artificial aurora. W. N.
Hess. il Science 164:1512-13 Je 27 '69
Widely seen September aurora. il Sky & Tel
38:431 D '69
AUSTIN, James M.
Educational monograph series of the AMS.
Weatherwise 22:132-3 Ag '69
AUSTIN, John C.
Ceramics. Antiques 95:112-20 Ja '69
AUSTIN, Richard
Victory for reason. por Time 94:24 S 19 '69
AUSTIN, Tex.
Instant help. il Am City 84:50 D '69
LBJ's land grab. il Newsweek 74:39 N 10 '69

Lighting
New street lighting helps fulfill a pledge. il
Am City 84:144 O '69

Rapid transit
Shuttle bus proves popular and permanent.
R. M. Tinstman. il Am City 84:110 D '69

Sanitary affairs
Colorful litter boxes. C. Barkley. il Am City
84:52 D '69
AUSTRALASIA
See also
Paleontology—Australasia
AUSTRALIA
See also
Atomic power—Australia
Elections—Australia
Fisheries—Australia
Great Barrier Reef
Harbors—Australia
Immigrants in Australia
Investments, Foreign (in Australia)
Iron mines and mining—Australia
Libraries—Australia
Mines and mineral resources—Australia

AUSTRALIA—See also—*Continued*
Opera—Australia
Paleontology—Australia
Private schools—Australia
Skis and skiing—Australia
Tasmania

Defenses

Mr Gorton's Australia: a country in search of a role. R. Terrill. New Repub 160:14-17 My 10 '69

Foreign relations

Mr Gorton's Australia: a country in search of a role. R. Terrill. New Repub 160:14-17 My 10 '69

Asia

Toward a new balance in Asia: an Australian view. B. Grant. For Affairs 47:711-20 Jl '69

United States

Exchange of toasts; May 6, 1969. R. M. Nixon; J. G. Gordon. Nat R 21:472+ My 20 '69
Prime Minister Gorton of Australia visits Washington, exchange of toasts; with remarks, May 6, 7, 1969. R. M. Nixon; J. G. Gorton. Dept State Bul 60:436-9 My 26 '69

Politics and government

World around us. R. Mathias. Chr Cent 86: 1360-2 O 22 '69

Religious institutions and affairs

Denominations and government policy. R. Mathias. Chr Cent 86:1433-4 N 5 '69
World around us (cont) Chr Cent 86:162-4, 196, 722-4, 1099-100 Ja 29-F 5, My 21, Ag 20 '69
See also
Methodist church in Australia

Social conditions

Reports: Australia. A. Koestler. Atlan 223: 12+ Je '69
AUSTRALIA, New Zealand, and United States treaty council. See Anzus council
AUSTRALIA and the United States
See also
United States—Foreign opinion—Australian
AUSTRALIAN duckbill. See Platypuses
AUSTRALIAN pottery. See Pottery, Australian
AUSTRALOPITHECUS africanus. See Man, Prehistoric
AUSTRIA
See also
Ballet—Austria
Burgenland
Gardens—Austria
Hotels, taverns, etc.—Austria
Jews in Austria
Salzburg
Shopping and shoppers—Austria
Skis and skiing—Austria
Tourist trade—Austria
Trials—Austria
Tyrol
Vienna

Description and travel

Austria: baroque bonanza. M. Gough. il House B 111:54+ Mr '69

History
Bibliography

Articles and other books received; comp. by A. H. Price. See issues of American historical review

Industries

Only filling orders; manufacturers of Nazi insignia. il Newsweek 74:107-8 O 6 '69
AUSTRIAN pastry. See Pastry
AUTHORITY
Decline of authority. M. Smith. Ed Digest 35:5-7 O '69
I was only following orders; question of following orders to perform inhuman actions. Trans-Action 6:7-8 My '69
AUTHORITY (religion)
See also
Popes—Infallibility
AUTHORS
Authors & editors. See issues of Publishers' weekly
Explorers of inner space. D. M. Murray. Engl J 58:908-11 S '69
Role of the writer in a troubled world. I. Stone. Writer 82:18-21 Ap '69
Selling your first article. D. C. Gleasner. Writers Digest 49:51-3 My '69
Who writes for LJ? A second look. E. Moon. il Library J 94:1101-3 Mr 15 '69
Writer and social security. L. Boggess. il Writers Digest 49:56-9+ D '69

You meet such interesting people; diary of a free-lancer. C. Schwalberg. U S Camera 32: 64-5+ Ja '69
See also
Artists as authors
Authorship
Book and author luncheons
Librarians as authors
Literary agents
PEN club
Poets
Prisoners as authors
Publishers and publishing
Royalties
Self employed
Teachers as authors
Women as authors
    also classes of writers, e.g. Dramatists, Historians, Novelists, etc.

Homes and haunts
See Literary landmarks

Psychology

Without prospect or retrospect. L. Conger. Writer 82:7-8 My '69
AUTHORS, American
Our accurately honored authors; Center of editions of American authors. J. Childs. il Library J 94:722-4 F 15 '69
This is my best; ed. by W. Burnett. Review Sat R 52:41 F 15 '69. D. Dempsey
Writer between generations. D. T. Bazelon. Commentary 47:43-54 F '69
Writers of Santa Fe. A. Gregg. il Writers Digest 49:54-9 Ap '69
See also
Agee, J.
Ardrey, R.
Clemens, S. L.
Dos Passos, J.
Fast, H.
Gardner, L.
Halsell, G.
Hawkes, J.
Hawthorne, N.
Hecker, I. T.
Hoffer, E.
Hughes, L.
Jones, J.
London, J.
Mailer, N.
Melville, H.
Mencken, H. L.
Miller, H.
Negro authors
O'Connor, F.
Poets, American
Roth, P.
Scarry, R.
Stafford, J.
Steinbeck, J.
Taylor, P.
Thoreau, H. D.
Van Doren, M.
Vidal, G.
Warren, R. P.
West, J.
Wolfe, T. K.
AUTHORS, Argentine
See also
Lugones, L.
AUTHORS, Australian
See also
Chauncy, N.
AUTHORS, British. See Authors, English
AUTHORS, Colombian
See also
García Márquez, G.
AUTHORS, Czech
European literary scene; Czech writers; intention to write on despite censorship. R. J. Clements. Sat R 52:27 F 1 '69
See also
Benes, J.
Kafka, F.
AUTHORS, English
Rise and fall of the man of letters, by J. Gross. Review
    Time il 94:98+ S 19 '69
See also
Ackerley, J. R.
Amis, K.
Christie, A.
Compton-Burnett, I.
Eliot, G. pseud.
Francis, D.
Fuller, T.
Galsworthy, J.
Lehmann, J.
Orwell, G. pseud.
Rolfe, F. W.

AUTOMOBILE drivers—*Continued*

Licenses

Rap 'n 'pinion; testing programs. M. Jones. Motor T 21:18 D '69

Psychology

Driving under the influence of emotion. S. A. Franzmeier. il Todays Health 47:40-1+ O '69

No rallentare for Rocco; the Italian motorist. J. Ferris. Sat R 52:2 Je 28 '69

Testing

Incentive plan for good drivers. D. E. Feyk. Travel 132:73-4 D '69

News on wheels; road-e-o! road-e-o! Jay-cee safe driving auto road-e-o. M. Spiegel. il Sr Schol 93:24 Ja 10 '69

Rap 'n 'pinion; testing programs. M. Jones. Motor T 21:18 D '69

What close calls do to you and your driving. J. G. Busse and W. S. Bacon. il Pop Sci 194:98-101 Mr '69

See also
Automobile racing drivers—Testing

AUTOMOBILE driving

Boondock driving; back-road travel. C. B. Colby. il Outdoor Life 144:106+ S '69

Defensive driving; what is it? il Good H 169:142-3 Jl '69

Drivin' with Dan; questions and answers. D. Gurney. See issues of Popular mechanics

How to survive freeway on/off ramps. D. L. Gregg. il Bet Hom & Gard 47:50-1+ Jl '69

Safe-driving tips from driving schools. McCalls 96:54 Ap '69

Skillful driver:
If your gas pedal sticks. il Pop Sci 195:48 N '69
If your headlights quit. il Pop Sci 195:147 D '69
If your hood flies open. il Pop Sci 195:64 O '69

Ten tips for winter driving; ed. by C. W. Casewit. G. R. Carrel. Read Digest 94:33-4 F '69

Tips from Detroit on breaking in a new car. il Changing T 23:23-4 N '69

Trends in travel. V. L. Oertle. See issues of Motor trend

See also
Automobile drivers
Automobile touring

Animal hazards

Highway mortality of squirrels. Cons 23:40 Je '69

Competitions

News on wheels; road-e-o! road-e-o! Jaycee safe driving auto road-e-o. M. Spiegel. il Sr Schol 93:24 Ja 10 '69

On the scene; car rallies. il Seventeen 28:170-1 Ap '69

Laws and regulations

See Automobile laws and regulations

Safety devices and measures

How to buck a blizzard. E. D. Fales. jr. il Pop Mech 131:96-9+ F '69

In defense of the automobile. L. Levine. il Motor T 21:48-51 Ap '69

Snow driving. D. McCluggage. il Travel & Camera 32:56-7+ D '69

Snowstorms

See Automobile driving—Storm hazards

Storm hazards

How to buck a blizzard. E. D. Fales. jr. il Pop Mech 131:96-9+ F '69

Study and teaching

Does driver education save lives? A. Lake. McCalls 97:153+ N '69

Driver education that's different; Janesville, Wis. N. Gesteland. il Todays Ed 58:60-1 S '69

Driver training: does it really do any good? J. N. Bell. il Pop Mech 131:93-7+ Ap '69

Fallacy of the untrained driver. G. Driessen. Ed Digest 35:43-5 O '69

Learn to drive defensively. il Todays Health 47:14-15 F '69

Schools for *scandale*; France. Newsweek 74:119A O 20 '69

Six ways to help your teenager become a better driver. A. Scott. Parents Mag 44:52-3 F '69

France

Schools for *scandale*. Newsweek 74:119A O 20 '69

AUTOMOBILE driving and drinking. See Drinking and traffic accidents

AUTOMOBILE engines

Achtung! It's the 411. J. Thawley. il Hot Rod 22:38-40 S '69

All-American mill. B. Lang. il Hot Rod 22:88-90 N '69

Big engines and little cars; Can-Am 1969. S. Kelly. il Hot Rod 22:54-6 Ag '69

Crower power-times two. J. Thawley. il Hot Rod 22:94-6 Ag '69

Daring Wankel Mercedes. K. Ludvigsen. il Motor T 21:42-4+ O '69

Dutch on the road to a pollution-free engine; Stirling engine. il Bsns W p52-3 Ja 10 '70

Dyno tunes in a kit. B. Neumann. il Hot Rod 22:84-6 Ja '69

Experimentally speaking. J. Dianna. il Hot Rod 22:58-9 Jl '69

Ford's big small-block. J. Thawley. il Hot Rod 22:40-2 Ja '69

Ford's boss 429 & Kalitta. B. Lang. il Hot Rod 22:34-5 Je '69

Forty three-hp VW bolt-on. J. Thawley. il Hot Rod 22:100-1 N '69

French piston engine has no crankshaft; Turbomotor. D. Scott. il Pop Sci 194:68-71+ My '69

Good rods never die. B. Lang. il Hot Rod 22:110-11 F '69

Hark! Detroit mid-engine sports cars are coming. K. Ludvigsen. il Motor T 21:62-7+ D '69

Head surgery. J. Thawley. il Hot Rod 22:148-9 O '69

Headline news; Gurney-Eagle cylinder heads. B. Lang. il Hot Rod 22:74-5 Jl '69

Hot engines for seventy. A. Shuman; B. Sanders. il Motor T 21:62-73 N '69

How far can we go with the piston engine? R. Huntington. il Pop Mech 131:95-9+ Ja '69

Incredible Volksplane; Volkswagen engine powered plane. il Mech Illus 65:72-7 S '69

Jr. stock science lesson. J. Dianna. il Hot Rod 22:54-7 S '69

Just look what Plymouth's up to now; 318 engine for Indy. E. Dahlquist. il Motor T 21:76-9 Jl '69

Mach one up for Ford. S. Kelly. il Hot Rod 22:40-2 My '69

Mercedes spins out an engine for the future; rotating pistons. D. Jenkinson. il Sports Illus 31:38-40+ S 15 '69

Mighty Sampson lives! J. Thawley. il Hot Rod 22:60-2 Je '69

Mighty tough horse; Mustang. J. Thawley. il Hot Rod 22:34-6 F '69

Mod fittings; compact hydropneumatic fittings. B. Lang. il Hot Rod 22:76 Jl '69

MoPar manipulatin'. J. Dianna. il Hot Rod 22:62-3 S '69

MoPar manipulatin'; Chrysler 340. J. Dianna. il Hot Rod 22:38-40 Ag; 62-3 S '69

Muscle for big-block Fords. S. Kelly. il Hot Rod 22:70-2 Ag '69

Noiseless, nontoxic steam engine. E. Cox. New Repub 160:12-14 Je 28 '69

On turbines, Indy, and Andy; interview, ed. by S. Kelly. A. Granatelli. il Hot Rod 22:48-50 Mr '69

Opening up the rat's nest; 454-cubic-inch Chevrolet engine. S. Kelly. il Hot Rod 22:46-7 O '69

Poncho's tunnel port four-oh-oh! J. Dianna. il Hot Rod 22:36-8 My '69

Rebirth of the Corvair; powerplant for buggies. il Hot Rod 22:70-2 Jl '69

Sensational new Mercedes has triple-rotor Wankel engine. J. P. Norbye. il Pop Sci 195:73-7 O '69

Simple addition. J. Dianna. il Hot Rod 22:58-60 D '69

Steam dream; STP/PRC steam engine design. Hot Rod 22:120 Jl '69

Surprise! It's a six! J. Thawley. il Hot Rod 22:94-5 Ap '69

Swap for a skyrolet. E. Rickman. il Hot Rod 22:90-1 Ja '69

10-second trip; interview. T. Langdon. il Motor T 21:39-40+ O '69

VW varoom. D. Wells. il Motor T 21:70-2+ S: 124-5+ O '69

Wankel, here to stay? R. Brock. il Hot Rod 22:40-3 D '69

AUTOMOBILE engines—*Continued*
Webster's wing-ding Ford. J. Thawley. il
  Hot Rod 22:59-61 N '69

See also
Automobiles—Cams
Cranks and crankshafts
Cylinders (engines, etc)
Diesel engines, Automotive
Gas turbines, Automotive
Indicators for gas and oil engines
Manifolds
Pistons
Snowmobile engines

Air supply
Airflow facts; interview, ed. by J. Dianna.
  G. Burrell; D. Cordell. il Hot Rod 22:48-50
  N '69
Big breather. B. Lang. il Hot Rod 22:48-9
  Jl '69
Do de air do de deed? J. Thawley. il Hot
  Rod 22:94 S '69
Flow-er-power. J. McFarland. il Hot Rod 22:
  76-8 My '69
Jetting with know-how; air density meter.
  J. Dianna. il Hot Rod 22:106-7 F '69

Choke
R for automatic chokes. T. Tappett. il
  Mech Illus 65:90-2+ Mr '69

Cooling
Coolant recovery system proven. E. Dahl-
  quist. il Motor T 21:80 D '69
Exit, old faithful; coolant recovery system.
  E. Rickman. il Hot Rod 22:76 Ap '69
Hot tips on engine cooling. M. Schultz. il
  Pop Mech 132:138-41 Ag '69
Little tank works big wonders; Coolant re-
  covery system. J. P. Norbye. il Pop Sci
  194:56 Mr '69
Make your own coolant-recovery system.
  C. J. Baker. il Pop Sci 195:192 O '69

Design
Amazing radial engine in Pontiac's minicar. J. Dunne. il Pop Sci 194:63-5+ Ap '69
Exciting new rotary engine is piston-pow-
  ered. D. Scott. il Pop Sci 195:45-9 D '69
Olds Can-Am 455. J. Dianna. il Hot Rod
  22:60-1 Jl '69

Exhaust
Air pollution and the roadside. F. A. Wood.
  il Horticulture 46:36-8+ D '68
Auto men gasp in the smog. il Bsns W p76+
  N 1 '69
Cars and air pollution. L. Fermi. il Bul Atom
  Sci 25:35-7 O '69
Ford's better idea. Time 94:51 D 19 '69
Globe is circled with a girdle of filth; inter-
  view. L. J. Fuller. il Forbes 104:55-7 D 15
  '69
Green light for the smogless car. J. Lear.
  il Sat R 52:81-6 D 6 '69
Hold your nose. New Repub 161:10 Ag 2 '69
Mr Clean of the engine world; positive crank-
  case ventilation. S. Kelly. il Hot Rod 22:
  96-7 Ja '69
New gas fuels pollution fight; new additive
  that eliminates pollutants from exhaust.
  Bsns W p 19 D 20 '69
Pain in the exhaust; anti-smog systems
  under fire. Newsweek 74:78-9 Jl 14 '69
Smog at the bar. il Newsweek 74:67 N 10 '69
Smog over auto accord; auto makers vs.
  Justice dept. Bsns W p28 Ja 18 '69
Smog suit settled out of court. Sr Schol 95:13
  O 6 '69
Toward a cleaner car. Time 94:51 O 17 '69
Whys, wise, and Y's of headers; questions
  and answers. J. Thawley. il Hot Rod 22:
  60-3 O '69

Fuel
See also
Gasoline

Fuel feeding
Eight-holer for go. B. Lang. il Hot Rod 22:
  85 S '69
Fuel injection tries a comeback. il Bsns W
  p54 Ja 10 '70
Some fuelish thoughts. E. Rickman. il Hot
  Rod 22:48-9 D '69
Ya gotta have a system. M. Strong. il Mo-
  tor T 21:84+ D '69

Heaters
Warm starts for cold cars. T. Tappett. il
  Mech Illus 65:90-2+ D '69

Ignition
Add electronic ignition to your car. B. C.
  Goldberg and R. G. Wilkins. il Radio-Electr
  40:32-4 Ap '69

High-Q inductive electronic ignition system.
  H. I. Keroes. il Electr World 82:32-4+ Jl
  '69
How to check distributor vacuum advance.
  M. Schultz. il Pop Mech 131:152-5+ My '69
How to replace your car's ignition wiring.
  M. Schultz. il Pop Mech 131:134-7 Ja '69
Isn't that the limiter? ARE limiter and dwell
  stretcher. J. McFarland. il Hot Rod 22:46
  S '69
Ten clues to hidden ignition troubles. M.
  Schultz. il Pop Mech 132:182-5 S '69
See also
Spark plugs

Lubrication
See Automobiles—Lubrication

Maintenance and repair
Color tuning. il Hot Rod 22:159 Mr '69
How to stop a dieseling engine. M. Schultz.
  il Pop Mech 132:154-7 O '69
Removing broken studs. J. Brenner. il Hot
  Rod 22:85 D '69
Shop talk. J. McFarland. See issues of Hot
  rod
Under-hood jobs any man can do. D. L.
  Gregg. il Bet Hom & Gard 47:38-9+ O '69

Mounting
Keep your heads. B. Lang. il Hot Rod 22:
  116 Mr '69

Mufflers
Auto men gasp in the smog; new muffler to
  reduce NOx pollution. il Bsns W p76+ N 1
  '69

Radiators
Taking care of your car's radiator. T. Tappett. il Mech Illus 65:105-7+ N '69

Starting
See Automobiles—Starting

Superchargers
Air-lock blower. B. Lang. il Hot Rod 22:92-3
  Ja '69

Testing
Build your own tune-up meter. B. C. Snow.
  il Mech Illus 65:108-11+ O '69

Valves
Keep your heads. B. Lang. il Hot Rod 22:
  116 Mr '69
Rocker arm roundup. B. Lang. il Hot Rod
  22:110-11 My '69
Seat 'um quick and accurately; valve seat
  checker. J. Dianna. il Hot Rod 22:88 Mr '69
AUTOMOBILE equipment. See Automobiles—
  Equipment
AUTOMOBILE exhibitions. See Automobiles—
  Exhibitions
AUTOMOBILE factories
Smog suit settled out of court. Sr Schol 95:13
  O 6 '69
See also
Automobile industry and trade

Employees
Black rage on the auto lines. il Time 93:89
  Ap 11 '69
Detroit shows the way with hard-core job-
  less. il Bsns W p32-5 F 1 '69
Hard-core blacks and the shiny auto; lay-
  off problems. R. Dietsch. New Repub 160:
  10 Mr 1 '69
Job makes the man; Detroit's inner city hir-
  ing program. il Nations Bsns 57:34-6+ Je '69
See also
Automobile industry and trade—Wages and
  hours
AUTOMOBILE financing. See Automobiles—
  Purchasing
AUTOMOBILE gages. See Gages
AUTOMOBILE headlights. See Automobiles—
  Lighting
AUTOMOBILE industry and trade
U.S. cars in Europe. E. Seidler. il Motor T
  21:46-7 Ap '69
See also
Automobile factories

Advertising
Detroit's cloudy spring. il Bsns W p48-9
  My 10 '69
FTC is reading the auto ads. Bsns W p27-8
  My 31 '69
Pick on your own size. Newsweek 73:86 Ap
  28 '69
Viewpoint. L. Levine. Motor T 21:8 F '69

Employees
See Automobile factories—Employees

AUTOMOBILE industry and trade—*Continued*

Finance

From first to last; profits of automobile, tire and auto parts industries. il Forbes 104:57-8 N 1 '69

International aspects

Mexican auto swindle; foreign plants and low-paced machinery. L. Fenster. il Nation 208:693-7 Je 2 '69

Public relations

Will the callbacks dent Detroit? il Bsns W p36 Mr 8 '69

Quality control

New try at getting the bugs out of new cars. il Changing T 23:43-4 My '69

Study and teaching

Labor with love: General motors and Chrysler institutes. J. G. Schmidt. il Motor T 21:98-100+ My '69

Used cars

The used car lot, where else but Sunset Strip? Rolls-Royces of the 1930s and other vintage gems for sale. B. Sanders. il Motor T 21:32-3 Jl '69

See also
Nation-wide auto auction, limited

Wages and hours

GM workers say Roche is wrong. U S News 66-88 My 12 '69

Europe, Western

Ford's better idea scores in Europe. Bsns W p66 D 20 '69
Overseas report. E. Seidler. See issues of Motor trend

Germany (Federal Republic)

Beetle's brothers; NSU motorenwerke to merge with Volkswagen subsidiary, Auto union. il Time 93:96+ My 9 '69
Beetle's spider web; Volkswagen's expansion kick. il Newsweek 74:81-2 Jl 21 '69
Doctor Kurt Lotz *vorstandsvorsitzender* of Volkswagen. E. Seidler. il Motor T 21:18+ Ag '69
Mercedes spins out an engine for the future; rotating pistons. D. Jenkinson. il Sports Illus 31:38-40+ S 15 '69
There's a gap in every market; Bayerische motoren werke. il Forbes 103:35 Ap 15 '69
Wheels and wings for Germany; BMW's tame racehorses. Fortune 80:171 Ag 15 '69

Great Britain

Britain's autos get ready to compete. il Bsns W p92-3+ Je 21 '69
Strike crisis for British autos. U S News 67:85 N 10 '69

See also
Ford motor company, limited, Dagenham, England
Rolls-Royce, limited
Rootes motors, incorporated

Italy

Agnelli gets a horse; Ferrari-Fiat merger. il Time 94:72 Jl 4 '69
Ferrari's co-driver: Fiat. il Newsweek 74:77-8 Jl 7 '69
Milestones on the Bertone trail. G. Borgeson. il Motor T 21:38-40 My '69
Turin. E. Seidler. il Motor T 21:62-6 Mr '69
When will we have factory service centers like these? Fiat's company-run service centers. B. Hartford. il Pop Mech 132:98-101 Jl '69

Japan

Chrysler's trade: Valiant for Colt; joint venture with Mitsubishi heavy industries. il Bsns W p37 Je 7 '69
Is Chrysler's sun rising in Japanese deal? collaboration with Mitsubishi heavy industries. Bsns W p37 My 24 '69
Japanese safety issue; recall of defective cars sold in the U.S. Time 93:76+ Je 27 '69
Recall generation. il Newsweek 73:72+ Je 30 '69
Shift to high gear. Time 93:89-90 My 2 '69
Tokyo. M. Holmes. il Motor T 21:62+ Mr '69
Tremor in Japan's trade wall: Chrysler-Mitsubishi deal causes unexpected furor. Bsns W p98 Je 21 '69
Wave of callbacks worries Japan. Bsns W p50 Je 28 '69
World's fastest-growing auto company; Toyota. W. S. Rukeyser. il Fortune 80:76-81+ D '69

Latin America

Latin millstone. L. Fenster. Nation 209:525-6 N 17 '69

Mexico

Caramba! a Mexican Borgward? L. E. Sabal. il Pop Mech 130:124-7 D '68
Mexican auto swindle; foreign plants and low-paced machinery. L. Fenster. il Nation 208:693-7 Je 2 '69

Russia

Iron curtain gold rush. E. Seidler. Motor T 21:68 Je '69
Motoring in Russia. P Davis. Mech Illus 65:38+ S '69

Spain

Chrysler tune sours partner; Eduardo Barreiros walks out on U.S. partner. Bsns W p34 My 31 '69
Conflict of cultures. Time 93:100 Je 13 '69

Sweden

Saab's new model. il Duns R 93:97-8+ My '69

United States

Auto boom? How dealers see it. il U S News 66:81 F 24 '69
Auto sales: compacts are big again. il U S News 67:37 Jl 14 '69
Bargain season. il Time 94:69-70 Ag 22 '69
Biggest recall. Newsweek 73:79-80 Mr 10 '69
Billion-dollar trip to the wilds; recreational vehicle business. il Bsns W p34-5 D 13 '69
Can Detroit break the Beetle's grip? il Bsns W p28-9 Ja 10 '70
Compacts run with Maverick. il Bsns W p44 Jl 12 '69
Confidence sets style for '70 model debuts. il Bsns W p48-9 S 13 '69
Detroit guns into 1969 at a snappy new pace. il Bsns W p34-5 Mr 15 '69
Detroit is watching stockpiles; inventories high and sales down. il Bsns W p35-6 Ap 12 '69
Detroit listening post. B. Kilpatrick. See issues of Popular mechanics
Detroit races to meet challenge of imports. il Bsns W p 104-6+ Mr 29 '69
Detroit sizes up the drop in sales. il Bsns W p60-1 D 6 '69
Detroit's answer to the beetle. il U S News 66:8 Mr 3 '69
Detroit's reluctant ride into smallsville; to counter import boom. W. S. Rukeyser. il Fortune 79:110-13+ Mr '69
Detroit's road is foggy. il Bsns W p25-7 F 8 '69
Foreign-car boom: who is gaining. il U S News 67:45 Jl 28 '69
Future of the automobile: interview. J. M. Roche. il U S News 66:64-71 F 10 '69
How consumer spending for automobiles creates jobs. R. E. Dempsey and D. F. Schmude. bibliog f il Mo Labor R 92:33-6 Mr '69
How the '70 cars are selling. il U S News 67:69-70 D 1 '69
Inside Detroit. See issues of Motor trend
Muscle-car market. il Time 93:110 My 16 '69
1969's scorecard. il Newsweek 74:71+ Ag 18 '69
No-show slowdown. Bsns W p37 Je 7 '69
Poor parts? report by the National highway safety bureau. Newsweek 74:86 N 24 '69
Pray for Iacocca's baby. W. A. McWhirter. il Life 66:68-72 Ap 11 '69
Public selects its transportation; address, January 15, 1969. S. E. Knudsen. Vital Speeches 35:279-82 F 15 '69
Reasonable doubt; recall of 4.9 million cars and trucks. Nation 208:325 Mr 17 '69
Record recall. il Time 93:23 Mr 7 '69
Report on productivity increases in the auto industry. C. Myslicki. il Mo Labor R 92:37-9 Mr '69
Ring out the old, gear up the new. il Bsns W p26-7 Ag 2 '69
Signs of a slowdown in '69 auto production. il U S News 66:6 F 10 '69
Slowdown time. Time 94:95 N 28 '69
Slower pace for the Bug. il U S News 67:82-3 O 13 '69
Smog at the bar. il Newsweek 74:67 N 10 '69
Smog over auto accord; auto makers vs. Justice dept. Bsns W p28+ Ja 18 '69
Softening sales? Newsweek 74:78+ D 1 '69
Three-car families and a boom in extras. il U S News 66:80 Ap 7 '69
Utopia; essay contest. Motor T 21:68+ Ap '69
When nearly 5 million cars are recalled; General motors inspection of four-barrel carburetors. U S News 66:14 Mr 17 '69

AUTOMOBILE industry and trade—United States—*Continued*
Why auto makers worry as new model year begins. il U S News 67:54-6 Ag 25 '69
Why Detroit is wary of the 1970s; with editorial comment. il Bsns W p 110-12+, 188 S 20 '69
Will the callbacks dent Detroit? il Bsns W p36 Mr 8 '69
Word now in car recalls: fix them all. U S News 66:14 Mr 31 '69
   See also
Automobile dealers
Automobiles—Prices
Government investigations—Automobile industry and trade
Strikes—United States—Automobile industry and trade
   also names of automobile manufacturing companies, e.g. Ford motor company

Uruguay
Uruguay says olé to cars of yesterday. B. Forbis. il Sports Illus 30:44-8 F 10 '69
AUTOMOBILE inspection. See Automobiles—Inspection
AUTOMOBILE insurance. See Insurance, Automobile
AUTOMOBILE laws and regulations
Auto makers build a straw man; safety certification label and the car identification number. il Consumer Rep 34:236-7 My '69
What to do after an accident. D. Green. il Mech Illus 65:61-3+ Ag '69
Who's fit to drive? G. Town. il Har Yrs 9:19-21 Mr '69
Why Detroit is wary of the 1970s; with editorial comment. il Bsns W p 110-12+, 188 S 20 '69
   See also
Automobiles—Inspection
Insurance, Automobile
Traffic accidents
Traffic accidents—Cases
Traffic regulations
Traffic violations
AUTOMOBILE lighting. See Automobiles—Lighting
AUTOMOBILE mechanics (persons)
[Gus Wilson's model garage] M. Bunn. See issues of Popular science monthly to June 1969
   See also
Pink, E.
Webster, M.
AUTOMOBILE models
Fords illustrated car. D. Wells. il Motor T 21:108-10 O '69
Racing
Build slot-car Win detector. W. T. Lemen. il Pop Electr 30:41-5 My '69
Radio control
Build this R/C gasser. L. E. Sabal. il Pop Mech 130:158-61+ D '68
AUTOMOBILE museums
Turin's magnificent Museo dell' automobile; Carlo Biscaretti di Raffia. G. Borgeson. il Motor T 21:52-5 My '69
AUTOMOBILE oil filters. See Oil filters
AUTOMOBILE ownership
   See also
Automobiles—Purchasing
Automobiles—Selling
AUTOMOBILE painting. See Automobiles—Painting
AUTOMOBILE parking
Eight ways to get more off-street parking. G. K. Geerlings. il Pop Mech 131:148-51 Mr '69
Meter revenue builds parking garages: Decatur. Ill. J. W. Loftus. il Am City 84:142 F '69
No more mud for Sooner sports fans; parking area in Oklahoma City. il Am City 84:76-7 D '69
   See also
Garages
Garages, Municipal
Parking meters
AUTOMOBILE parts
Fords illustrated car. D. Wells. il Motor T 21:108-10 O '69
From first to last; profits of automobile, tire and auto parts industries. il Forbes 104:57-8 N 1 '69
Going thing wants you! Ford's new drag club program. il Hot Rod 22:123 My '69
Ground grabber; bolt-on traction bars for street/strip combo. J. Dianna. il Hot Rod 22:91 O '69

Inside a digger; AA/Fuel dragster. D. Scott. il Hot Rod 22:88-91 D '69
Muscle for big-block Fords. S. Kelly. il Hot Rod 22:70-2 Ag '69
Muscle parts; interview. D. Eames. il Motor T 21:68-70 Ag '69
Poor parts? report by the National highway safety bureau. Newsweek 74:86 N 24 '69
Product trends. il Motor T 21:104-7 F; 98:101 Mr; 116-20 Ap; 118+ My; 116-20 Je '69
Super-duty trick stuff. B. Lang. il Hot Rod 22:72-4 Ap '69
289 Ford+stock parts=294 hp. J. Thawley. il Hot Rod 22:42-4 O '69
   See also
Borg-Warner corporation
AUTOMOBILE racing
AHRA show of shows; summer nationals. D. Evans. il Hot Rod 22:84-6 N '69
AHRA's best-yet winter meet. J. Thawley. il Hot Rod 22:62-4 Ap '69
All-pro carnival; Orange County international raceway. B. Lang. il Hot Rod 22:44-6 Mr '69
Another great Scot races in; J. Stewart. K. Chapin. Sports Illus 30:50-1 Je 30 '69
Atlanta 500. W. Clark. il Motor T 21:90-2 Jl '69
Bakershogan. J. Thawley. il Hot Rod 22:84-5 My '69
Belated anniversary party; Bonneville's national speed trials. E. Rickman. il Hot Rod 22:44-7+ Ja '69
Big Dallas drags; NHRA's springnationals. B. Lang. il Hot Rod 22:44-7 Ag '69
Big engines and little cars; Can-Am 1969. S. Kelly. il Hot Rod 22:54-6 Ag '69
Brotherhood; street drag racing in L.A. il Newsweek 74:51 S 15 '69
Bruce and Denny show. il Motor T 21:100 D '69
Bug-in II. B. Sanders. il Motor T 21:32-4 Je '69
Can Chrysler put the crunch on Cale? Daytona preview. B. Kilpatrick. il Pop Mech 131:87-90+ F '69
Cornering the market; Can-Am series. il Newsweek 74:129 S 29 '69
Day for Henry and Georges; Ford won from Porsche at Le Mans. K. Chapin. il Sports Illus 30:58+ Je 23 '69
La dolce Indy; triumph Italian style by Mario Andretti. K. Chapin. il Sports Illus 30:24-9 Je 9 '69
Don't say woman driver when you talk about Pat Carlsson. K. Prentiss. Holiday 46:64-5 S '69
End of an Indy jinx. il Newsweek 73:97 Je 9 '69
Engine grinder; Sicily's Targa Florio. Newsweek 73:77 My 19 '69
Episode in racing; Motor State 500. S. Kelly. il Hot Rod 22:48-9 S '69
Ford lights the fuse at Firecracker 400. L. Laye. il Motor T 21:78-81 S '69
Fun racing; Inland empire racing association. S. Kelly. il Hot Rod 22:114 Jl '69
Gentlemen, start your engines! the Indianapolis 500. J. Sanders. il Read Digest 94:124-8 My '69
Hail to king Jackie! Italian Grand prix. R. F. Jones. il Sports Illus 31:22-7 S 22 '69
Hot rod's 1968 top ten. B. Lang. il Hot Rod 22:58-9 Mr '69
In the warm California sun. J. Dianna and B. Lang. il Hot Rod 22:44-7 Je '69
Instant replay. J. Lamm. il Motor T 21:78-9 D '69
Italian campaign; Indianapolis 500. E. Dahlquist. il Motor T 21:54-7 Ag '69
Italian 500; Indianapolis Memorial day classic; with editorial comment. J. Dianna. il Hot Rod 22:8, 34-7 Ag '69
James Garner's new act. D. Wells. il Motor T 21:74-6 Je '69
Life among the drag racers. B. Surface. il N Y Times Mag p36-8+ My 25 '69
Masten Gregory lives! K. Purdy. il Esquire 71:65-9+ Ja '69
Mickey Thompson, perpetual motion. B. Lang. il Hot Rod 22:50-2 Jl '69
Mission Bell 250. J. Dianna. il Hot Rod 22:94-6 D '69
MT 500: the rain and Richard. E. Dahlquist. il Motor T 21:76-7 Ap '69
Motor trend interview. W. Parks. il Motor T 21:101-2+ O '69
Motor trend profile: R. Penske, the organizer. R. Penske. il Motor T 21:32+ D '69
NHRA's '69 Winternationals. B. Lang and J. Dianna. il Hot Rod 22:32-6 Ap '69
News on wheels; highest mark in his class: M. Coletti, dragracer. M. Spiegel. il Sr Schol 94:32 My 2 '69
1968: the year of Cale Yarborough. S. Kelly. il Hot Rod 22:54-6 Ja '69

AUTOMOBILE racing—*Continued*

OK digs at Pa; NHRA Division I world championship drag races. B. Lang. il Hot Rod 22:66-7 S '69

On Tulsa turf. J. Dianna and J. McFarland. il Hot Rod 22:36-8 Ja '69

On turbines. Indy, and Andy; interview, ed. by S. Kelly. A. Granatelli. il Hot Rod 22:48-50 Mr '69

100 miles of pay-dirt. S. Kelly. il Hot Rod 22:94-5 Ja '69

Oval trackers in England. R. Smith. il Hot Rod 22:142-3 Ag '69

Pitfalls in Daytona. il Newsweek 73:74 F 17 '69

Poem of a run by Ford and Ferrari; Ford GT-40 wins at Sebring. R. F. Jones. il Sports Illus 30:24-5 Mr 31 '69

Rain check on speed at Indy. K. Chapin. il Sports Illus 30:28-9 My 26 '69

Rex Maze 300. E. Dahlquist. il Motor T 21:80-3 Mr '69

Road racing's big big league; Can-Am racing series. D. Gurney. il Pop Mech 131:77-9+ Je '69

Roddin' at random. See issues of Hot rod

Roundy-round corner. S. Kelly. See issues of Hot rod

Ruler of the road. il Time 94:53 Ag 1 '69

Salt was fine in '69; SCTA's 21st Bonneville meet. E. Rickman. il Hot Rod 22:30-3 N '69

Serenity on the edge of disaster; ed. by G. S. Brown. G. Hill. il Sports Illus 30:40+ Mr 10 '69

Shocker at Daytona. R. F. Jones. il Sports Illus 30:16-19 F 10 '69

Show & go. See issues of Hot rod

Sixteen-day stock car race. S. Kelly. il Hot Rod 22:44-6 Ap '69

Smothers brothers racing team. J. W. Wright. il Pop Sci 194:80-3 Ja '69

Some sweet theft at Daytona; stock-car racing. K. Chapin. Sports Illus 30:50 Mr 3 '69

Something for everybody. S. Kelly. il Hot Rod 22:92-4 F '69

Sox & Martin. B. Lang. il Hot Rod 22:52-4 F '69

Stardust in your eyes; Stardust national open drag championship. J. Dianna. il Hot Rod 22:46-7 My '69

Super stock showdown; NHRA style. D. Wells. il Motor T 21:48-53 N '69

Talladega's troubled baptism. L. Laye. il Motor T 21:34-6 N '69

Talladega's troubled Sunday. S. Kelly. il Hot Rod 22:44-6 D '69

1320 smorgasbord; Scandinavian international drag meet. K. Gustafson. il Hot Rod 22:78 N '69

Those wonderful brothers Wood. B. Kilpatrick. il Pop Mech 131:118-21+ Ja '69

Together, man! NHRA's 15th annual nationals. B. Lang. il Hot Rod 22:42-6 N '69

Up in Michigan. il Motor T 21:72-4 Ag '69

Up the down track; Wilkesboro. S. Kelly. il Hot Rod 22:102-4 Jl '69

Up, up and away; Pikes Peak auto hill climb. R. Brock. il Hot Rod 22:58-60 S '69

Vees at Nurburgring. R. Brock. il Hot Rod 22:64-6 O '69

Winter dreams; Daytona speed week. E. Dahlquist. il Motor T 21:90-6 My '69

Wizards of the wild wheels; Ford in bigtime stock-car racing. C. Phinizy. il Sports Illus 31:30-2+ Jl 14 '69

World 600. L. Laye. il Motor T 21:64-6 Ag '69

Yak with Ak; interview, ed. by J. Dianna. il Hot Rod 22:50-2 Ap '69

Yankee bread for an Austrian; United States Grand prix. R. F. Jones. il Sports Illus 31:78-81 O 13 '69

Yarborough fare; winner of fourth straight at Daytona. S. Kelly. il Hot Rod 22:58-61 My '69

You gotta have heart; Model T Fords. F. Taylor. il Motor T 21:40-1 S '69

See also
Midget automobile racing
Motor vehicle racing
Speedways

Accidents and injuries

Publisher's memo; clutch explosion. R. Brock. Hot Rod 22:6 N '69

Economic aspects

Getting on the right track. il Bsns W p70-1 Ag 30 '69

Motor trend interview. L. H. LoPatin. il Motor T 21:87-8+ S '69

Wizard of Ozzie; auto racing sponsorship. C. Pendergast. il Motor T 21:26-8 N '69

History

Grandest Grand prix; French Grand prix of 1914. L. W. Steinwedel. il Motor T 21:52-4+ S '69

Nürburgring; circa 1956. L. Levine. il Motor T 21:24-7 Mr '69

Rules

NHRA teardown. J. Dianna. il Hot Rod 22:72-4 Je '69

Safety devices and measures

Rap 'n 'pinion. F. Wylie. Motor T 21:18+ N '69

Study and teaching

How we turned Paul Newman into a winning driver. B. Bondurant. il Pop Sci 194:50-3 Je '69

AUTOMOBILE racing drivers

Life among the drag racers. B. Surface. il N Y Times Mag p36-8+ My 25 '69

You can go as fast as your mind lets you; speed lover Sam Posey. C. Coe. il Life 66:48-50+ My 23 '69

See also
Durham, M.
Professional drivers association
Yarbrough, L. R.

Testing

You can be replaced by a machine; use of a telemetry van. J. G. Schmidt. il Motor T 21:41-3 F '69

AUTOMOBILE radiators. See Automobile engines—Radiators

AUTOMOBILE rallies. See Automobile driving—Competitions

AUTOMOBILE ramps. See Ramps

AUTOMOBILE renting. See Automobiles—Leasing and renting

AUTOMOBILE research

Computer on wheels promises perfect handling in future cars; GM Variable-response vehicle. J. Dunne. il Pop Sci 195:76-9 Ag '69

Will it be the soaring seventies? H. Sutton and D. Butwin. Sat R 53:51-2+ Ja 3 '70

See also
Automobiles, Experimental

AUTOMOBILE seats. See Automobiles—Seats

AUTOMOBILE service stations

Automatic doctors for autos; diagnostic centers. il Bsns W p78-81 Ag 30 '69

Automobile diagnostic centers. il Consumer Bul 52:7-8 D '69

C-6 trans tricks; Winter's transmission service, York, Pa. B. Lang. il Hot Rod 22:38-40 N '69

Familiar faces in new places; Sears high-performance program. il Hot Rod 22:132-3 D '69

Going into business; gas stations. il Changing T 23:35-8 F '69

Viewpoint; auto repair business. L. Levine. Motor T 21:8 Mr '69

When will we have factory service centers like these? Fiat's company-run service centers. B. Hartford. il Pop Mech 132:98-101 Jl '69

Where to have the car fixed. il Changing T 23:13-14 F '69

Your outrageous car-repair bills, what can be done about them? interview, ed. by H. Shuldiner. P. A. Hart. il Pop Sci 194:62-5+ Je '69

AUTOMOBILE shows. See Automobiles—Exhibitions

AUTOMOBILE speedways. See Speedways

AUTOMOBILE stealing. See Automobiles, Theft of

AUTOMOBILE styling. See Automobiles—Design

AUTOMOBILE thefts. See Automobiles, Theft of

AUTOMOBILE tires. See Tires, Automobile

AUTOMOBILE tools. See Tools

AUTOMOBILE touring

Before you drive into high country. Sunset 143:22 Ag '69

Cooking on six cylinders. H. W. Riggs. il Travel 132:65-7 O '69

Notes for nomads. See issues of Travel

Vacation driving special. D. L. Gregg. Bet Hom & Gard 47:22+ Je '69

Woman driver; vacations on wheels; rent or buy a recreational vehicle. il McCalls 96:38 Je '69

Economic aspects

How to save money when you travel. L. David. il Mech Illus 65:48-50+ Ap '69

AUTOMOBILE touring—*Continued*

Europe, Western

Seeing Europe by car. il Changing T 23:15-18 Mr '69

Mexico

Winter sunshine at bargain rates. N. D. Ford. bibliog il Har Yrs 9:12-15 O '69

New York (state)

Small journey from New York. R. McKenney. il Travel & Camera 32:54-5+ Ap '69

United States

On the road this summer. il Changing T 23: 20-4 Jl '69

Overland cruising. H. M. Rizer. il Motor B 123:64-5+ Je '69

Teen travel talk; driving know-how for girls on a car trip. il Seventeen 28:32 Ap '69

Winter sunshine at bargain rates. N. D. Ford. il Har Yrs 9:6-12 bibliog(p 15) O '69

AUTOMOBILE touring with children. See Travel with children

AUTOMOBILE touring with dogs. See Travel with pets

AUTOMOBILE towing. See Towing

AUTOMOBILE traffic. See Road traffic

AUTOMOBILE trailer camps
   See also
Mobile home parks

AUTOMOBILE trailer hitches. See Automobiles —Equipment

AUTOMOBILE trailers
Forty ways to test a camper before you buy it. V. L. Oertle. il Pop Mech 132:79+ Jl '69
Practically speaking. V. Jaxon. Har Yrs 9: 42-3 Mr '69
Questions we're asked about recreational vehicles. D. L. Gregg. il Bet Hom & Gard 47:74-5+ Ap '69
This land is your land; national park camping with travel trailer. S. Haft. il Sr Schol 94:Schol Teach 16-17 Ap 11 '69
Tyro trailerite. M. Miller. il Travel 131:64-70 My '69
We built this tent trailer for $250. J. L. Bennett. il Pop Mech 131:164-8 F '69
Wheels for sportsmen. J. Gartner. il Field & S 73:45-59 Mr '69
Your 1969 guide to camping on wheels. il Pop Sci 194:163-72+ My '69
   See also
Automobile boat trailers
Mobile homes

Equipment

How to enjoy all the comforts of home on wheels. E. F. Lindsley. il Pop Sci 194:182+ My '69

AUTOMOBILE trips. See Automobile touring

AUTOMOBILE trucks. See Motor trucks

AUTOMOBILE warranty. See Warranty

AUTOMOBILE wheels. See Automobiles— Wheels

AUTOMOBILE wiring. See Automobiles—Electric wiring

AUTOMOBILE workers. See Automobile factories—Employees

AUTOMOBILES
Arrival of the fittest. B. Sanders. il Motor T 21:80-6 Ap '69
Autos 1969. il Consumer Rep 34:172-222 Ap '69
Beep-beep-beep! Road Runner. E. Dahlquist. il Motor T 21:35-7 F '69
Buick; another bag of better cars. il Motor T 21:84-7 O '69
Buying a 1970 car now? Some word of advice. Consumer Rep 34:603 O '69
Capri: Ford's new select-a-car. J. G. Schmidt. il Motor T 21:72 My '69
Car that captured 4000 people its first day; Thunderbird. il Motor T 21:56-7 N '69
Cars in your family. D. L. Gregg. See issues of Better homes and gardens
Checker marathon. il Consumer Rep 34:404-6 Jl '69
Chevy's Monte Carlo tackles the T-Bird. il Pop Sci 195:104-5 O '69
CR's reports on full-size cars. il Consumer Bul 52:17-23 My '69
Daring Wankel Mercedes. K. Ludvigsen. il Motor T 21:42-4+ O '69
Eliminator; Mercury's 69 supercar. il Hot Rod 22:82-3 Ja '69
Ford's going things. il Motor T 21:48-50 S '69
Ford's hot sheet. B. Sanders. il Motor T 21:46-50 O '69

Ford's Maverick. E. Dahlquist. il Motor T 21:28-30 My '69
Ford's new Maverick; Mustang man rides again. L. Iacocca. A. Rothenberg. il Look 33:69+ Ap 15 '69
Future of the automobile; interview. J. M. Roche. il U S News 66:64-71 F 10 '69
GTO; 1970 super car extraordinary. B. Sanders. il Motor T 21:56-62+ S '69
Great breakaway conspiracy; Pontiac Transam. E. Dahlquist. il Motor T 21:52-4 Je '69
Hairiest Oldsmobile. E. Dahlquist. il Motor T 21:30-1 Je '69
Here come the 1970 cars. Changing T 23:6 S '69
Here come the '70s. R. W. Irvin. il Motor T 21:26-31 Jl '69
Here comes McCahill, with the Judge! T. McCahill. il Mech Illus 65:72-4+ Ap '69
Hornet with a stinger. B. Sanders. il Motor T 21:28-31 S '69
Judge holds court. B. Sanders. il Motor T 21: 104-5 My '69
Last Corvair. Time 93:97-8 My 23 '69
Loser lovers; Edsel making a comeback. Time 94:24 Ag 15 '69
Luxury, Detroit style. K. Prentiss. il Holiday 46:82-7+ O '69
Luxury with a flair. Thunderbird, Marauder X-100, Riviera, Grand Prix, Toronado. B. Sanders. il Motor T 21:74-85 F '69
Mark III revisited. B. Sanders. il Motor T 21:66 Jl '69
Maverick revisited; views of Ford executives. il Motor T 21:58-60+ Ag '69
Maverick V-8-on the loose. il Motor T 21: 44:5 Ag '69
Medium-priced full-sized V8s: Pontiac Executive, Buick LeSabre, Chrysler Newport, Mercury Monterey, and Oldsmobile Delta 88. il Consumer Rep 34:152-9 Mr '69
Mercury's giant streep scene. B. Sanders. il Motor T 21:64-9 S '69
Mighty tough horse: Mustang. J. Thawley. il Hot Rod 22:34-6 F '69
Muscle-car market. il Time 93:110 My 16 '69
Muscle car with luxury: Hurst/Olds. S. Kelly. il Hot Rod 22:66-7 Jl '69
Nine 1969 intermediate-size cars. il Consumer Bul 52:17-29 Ap '69
1969 cars. il Changing T 22:20-6 D '68
1970 cars. J. P. Norbye and J. Dunne. il Pop Sci 195:110-21 O '69
1970 Lincoln Continental. B. Sanders. il Motor T 21:46-8+ Ag '69
Personal business; new models hit the showrooms. Bsns W p 135-6 S 13 '69
Plymouth performance surprises for '70. il Motor T 21:50-2 Ag '69
Plymouth's beat goes on! B. Sanders. il Motor T 21:42-7 S '69
Pontiac; another Indian uprising. il Motor T 21:58-60 O '69
PM owners report:
   AMC Ambassador. B. Hartford. il Pop Mech 132:102-5 Jl '69
   American motors AMX. B. Hartford. il Pop Mech 131:140-3 F '69
   Buick Le Sabre. B. Hartford. il Pop Mech 131:102-5 My '69
   Cadillac Eldorado. B. Hartford. il Pop Mech 132:122-5 Jl '69
   Chevrolet Impala. B. Hartford. il Pop Mech 132:98-101 Ag '69
   Chrysler New Yorker. B. Hartford. il Pop Mech 131:122-5 Je '69
   Dodge Coronet. B. Hartford. il Pop Mech 131:118-21 Mr '69
   Ford Maverick. B. Hartford. il Pop Mech 132:88-91 D '69
   Ford XL. B. Hartford. il Pop Mech 131: 140-3 Ap '69
   Mercury Montego. B. Hartford. il Pop Mech 131:98-101 Je '69
   Oldsmobile Delta 88. B. Hartford. il Pop Mech 132:116-19 Ag '69
   Plymouth Valiant. B. Hartford. il Pop Mech 132:96-9 S '69
   Pontiac Grand prix. B. Kilpatrick. il Pop Mech 131:102-5 Ap '69
Preview of the 1970 cars. D. MacDonald. il Mech Illus 65:39-41+ Jl '69
Preview; the '70 cars. il U S News 66:64-7 My 12 '69
Quiet revolution; Cadillac. il Motor T 21:90-2 O '69
Rambler is dead, long live the Hornet. il Pop Sci 195:106-7 O '69
Scat pack; Challenger. B. Sanders. il Motor T 21:32-7 S '69
Seventy Chevrolets. E. Dahlquist. il Motor T 21:34-8 O '69
Show stoppers. E. Dahlquist. il Motor T 21: 66 Ap '69

AUTOMOBILES—Design—*Continued*
Why your car looks the way it does. M. Lamm. il Pop Mech 131:88-91+ Ja '69
Young and sporty. il McCalls 97:94-9+ O '69
See also
Automobiles—Bodies
Automobiles—Safety devices and measures

Doors
How to adjust car doors. T. Tappett. il Mech Illus 65:74-6+ My '69

Driving
See Automobile driving

Electric equipment
What to do with a balky electric clock. T. Tappett il Mech Illus 65:102-4+ S '69

Electric wiring
Your car's wiring system and what you can do about it. T. Tappett. il Mech Illus 65:82-4+ Ag '69

Electronic equipment
Add-on headlight alarms. il Mech Illus 65:74-5+ D '69
Advances in automotive electronics. F. W. Holder. il Radio-Electr 40:47-51 Ap '69
Build a low-water warning for your windshield washer. J. Stogel. il Pop Sci 194:156-7 Ja '69
Build the Time Out; turns off car lights. J. Stayton. il Pop Electr 32:52-3+ Ja '70
Dipstick oil-level indicator you can make. G. J. Whalen and R. F. Graf. il Pop Sci 194:116-19 Je '69
Isn't that the limiter? ARE limiter and dwell stretcher. J. McFarland. il Hot Rod 22:46 S '69

Equipment
Car mirror that may get in the way. il Consumer Rep 34:56-7 F '69
Car-top luggage carrier. il Mech Illus 65:114-15 F '69
Car-toppers and carriers: easiest way to boating fun. C. R. Meyer. il Pop Sci 194:100-3 Je '69
Handles & cranks. B. Lang. il Hot Rod 22:114 My '69
How safe are add-on auto accessories? D. L. Gregg. il Bet Hom & Gard 47:12+ Ag '69
New cars: the more they're loaded, the better they sell. il U S News 67:98-9 D 15 '69
Options: which are worth buying? (cont) Consumer Rep 34:196-8 Ap '69
Product trends. il Motor T 21:104-7 F; 98-101 Mr; 116-20 Ap; 118+ My; 116-20 Je '69
Snow driving. D. McCluggage. il Travel & Camera 32:56-7+ D '69
Those handy car-top luggage carriers. il Changing T 23:20-1 Jl '69
Trailer hitches: tips to keep you out of trouble. V. L. Oertle. il Pop Mech 132:134-7 Jl '69
Trailer tripper; trailer towing packages. B. Sanders. il Motor T 21:42-4 My '69
What's new. See issues of Hot rod
When radiators were regal; hood-ornament art. M. Lamm. il Pop Mech 131:110-11 Ja '69
Wide awake sleeper, The Z/28. S. Kelly. il Hot Rod 22:32-4 Ja '69
Woman driver; take me along. il McCalls 96:30 Jl '69
See also
Automobiles—Protection against theft
Automobiles—Safety devices and measures
Odometers

Exhaust
See Automobile engines—Exhaust

Exhibitions
Automobiles: International automobile show in Coliseum. New Yorker 45:31-2 Ap 19 '69
Beautiful; International automobile show in Germany. E. Dahlquist. il Motor T 21:88-90 D '69
Brazil's industry on show; sixth automobile show in Sao Paulo. L. Ludvigsen. il Motor T 21:28-31 Ap '69
East meets West. M. Holmes; E. Seidler. il Motor T 21:62-6 Mr '69
High hope on wheels for imports; debut of Ford's Maverick at New York's International auto show. il Bsns W p34-5 Ap 12 '69
News on wheels; automotive show 'n' tell. M. Spiegel. il Sr Schol 94:24 F 14 '69
Show & go. See issues of Hot rod
Who wants economy cars? Geneva auto show. E. Seidler. il Motor T 21:48-51 Je '69

Four wheel drive
K5 Blazer: Chevy's new off-road four-wheel-drive car. J. W. Wright. il Pop Sci 194:65-7 My '69
Norbye-Dunne report; new four-wheel-drive cars go almost anywhere, and fast. J. P. Norbye and J. Dunne. il Pop Sci 194:112-17 My '69

Frames
See also
Smith, A. O. corporation

Fuel systems
See Automobile engines—Fuel feeding

Gages
See Gages

Gaskets
See Gaskets

Gearing
Borg-Warner's wonder box; overdrive unit. E. Rickman. il Hot Rod 22:44-5 S '69
Bustproof three-speeds! J. Dianna. il Hot Rod 22:98-100 Ap '69
Cam gear drive kits. B. Lang. il Hot Rod 22:86-7 D '69
Geee meter, a dyno on your dash. P. Estrada. il Hot Rod 22:96-7 F '69
See also
Automobiles—Transmission

History
Buick boom. M. Lamm. il Motor T 21:98-100 Je '69
Hudsons that might have been. M. Lamm. il Motor T 21:84-6 Mr '69
If Cord had survived. M. Lamm. il Motor T 21:38-9 F '69
Motorandom. A. G. Michaelian. See issues of Motor trend
Rare La Salle roadster. F. Taylor. il Motor T 21:63-9 Jl '69
So what else is new? J. Bentley. il Pop Mech 131:114-19+ F '69
See also
Automobile museums

Ignition
See Automobile engines—Ignition

Inspection
Private vehicle inspection; operates as an arm of the municipal garage, Cincinnati. T. J. Frey. il Am City 84:112-13 Ap '69

Insurance
See Insurance, Automobile

Laws and regulations
See Automobile laws and regulations

Leasing and renting
Automobile leasing. Todays Ed 58:10 Mr '69
Rent-a-car roars ahead. il Bsns W p84-6+ N 1 '69
Seeing Europe by car. il Changing T 23:15-18 Mr '69
See also
Hertz corporation

Lighting
Brighter days. il Motor T 21:30 D '69
Broadside protection; sidelights. E. Rickman. il Hot Rod 22:110 Jl '69
Improved headlights the law won't let you have. J. P. Norbye. il Pop Sci 195:56-9 Ag '69
Light 'er up; legalized use of European-style lights. B. Lang. il Hot Rod 22:48 Ag '69
New long-reach headlights have automatic antidazzle shutter. il Pop Sci 194:56 F '69
Swinging headlights. K. Ludvigsen. il Motor T 21:38-9+ S '69
Through the night, brightly. E. Dahlquist. il Motor T 21:34-6 Ap '69
Update your car with marker lights. il Mech Illus 65:106-7 F '69
See also
Automobiles—Signal lights

Lubrication
Baffling solution; VW's oil. J. Thawley. il Hot Rod 22:82 O '69
Big profits in little cans; growing market for oil additives. il Time 94:70-1 Ag 8 '69
Dry sump oiler for the VW. J. Thawley. il Hot Rod 22:108-9 Mr '69
How to read an oil can. M. Schultz. il Pop Mech 132:134-7+ N '69
How to set up your own lube shop. M. Schultz. il Pop Mech 131:154-7 Ap '69
Pump kits for deep pans. B. Lang. il Hot Rod 22:126 Mr '69

AUTOMOBILES—*Continued*

Maintenance and repair

Action at the front. S. Kelly. il Hot Rod 22: 80-1 My '69

Behind the high cost of auto repairs. R. K. Bennett. Read Digest 95:57-62 S '69

Car care: prevacation car check. T. Tappett. il Mech Illus 65:71-3+ Je '69

Dollars and dents. Sr Schol 93:18-19 Ja 10 '69

Four safety tips for auto work. C. E. Cohn. il Radio-Electr 40:48 Je '69

Frequency-of-repair records: 1963 to 1968 models. il Consumer Rep 34:212-17 Ap '69

Hints from the model garage. See issues of Popular science monthly to May 1969

How to get a good body job. B. Kilpatrick. il Pop Mech 130:79-82+ D '68

How to store your car. T. Tappett. il Mech Illus 65:108-10+ F '69

Saturday mechanic. M. Schultz. See issues of Popular mechanics

Say, Smokey; questions and answers. S. Yunick. See issues of Popular science monthly

Shop talk. J. McFarland. See issues of Hot rod

Taking care of your car. il Pop Sci 195:180 N '69

Taking care of your car. J. Davis. il Pop Sci 195:170-1 D '69

Why it's getting harder to have your auto repaired. il U S News 66:59-60 Ja 27 '69

Woman driver. McCalls 96:60 Ap '69

See also
Automobile mechanics (persons)
Automobile service stations

Manufacture

Caramba! a Mexican Borgward? L. E. Sabal. il Pop Mech 130:124-7 D '68

Where auto defects come from. il Time 93: 83 Mr 28 '69

See also
Automobile factories
Automobile industry and trade
Automobile parts
Automobiles, Racing—Manufacture

Materials

People who drive in glass cars. E. Zubryn. il Motor T 21:50 F '69

Rundown on rubber. M. Schultz. il Pop Mech 131:142-5 Je '69

Painting

Prepping for perfection; using epoxy paint. J. Dianna. il Hot Rod 22:140-2 O '69

Parking

See Automobile parking

Prices

Detroit's cloudy spring. il Bsns W p48-9 My 10 '69

Do auto prices mean what they say? il Bsns W p60-1+ S 6 '69

Double trouble for auto prices. Bsns W p45 Jl 12 '69

FTC is reading the auto ads. Bsns W p27-8 My 31 '69

Full-sized, low-priced cars. Consumer Rep 34: 206-9 Ap '69

Higher stickers. Newsweek 74:90+ S 22 '69

Road looks clear for auto price hike. il Bsns W p46 S 20 '69

What price power? B. Kilpatrick. il Pop Mech 131:120-3 Ap '69

Protection against theft

Make your car tougher to steal. il Changing T 23:21-3 O '69

Popular science anti-car-theft device competition. il Pop Sci 195:68-71 Jl; 66-7 Ag; 82-5+ S; 92-5+ O; 80-3 N '69

Purchasing

Art of buying a new car. Consumer Rep 34: 175-6 Ap '69

Four ways to buy and sell your family's two cars. D. L. Gregg. Bet Hom & Gard 47:66-7 F '69

Honest dishonesty. L. Levine. il Motor T 21:67-9 F '69

How to save money when you finance a car; excerpts from How to save money when you buy and drive your car. M. E. Dowd. il Pop Mech 130:94-8+ D '68

They're off to an uncertain start. il Bsns W p39-40 O 11 '69

Radio equipment

Computer gives directions as you drive; ERGS system. J. Dunne. il Pop Sci 194: 102-3 My '69

Rating

Medium-priced ful-sized V8s: Pontiac Executive, Buick LeSabre, Chrysler Newport, Mercury Monterey, and Oldsmobile Delta 88. il Consumer Rep 34:156-9 Mr '69

Performance ratings on the 1969 cars. il Changing T 23:5 Mr '69

Ratings of the 1969 U.S. cars. Consumer Rep 34:199 Ap '69

Repairing

See Automobiles—Maintenance and repair

Safety devices and measures

Air bags: next in auto safety? il U S News 67:11 Jl 14 '69

Air bags: will they help you survive fatal car crashes? J. P. Norbye and J. Dunne. il Pop Sci 195:88-92 N '69

Automotive safety features are saving lives. D. L. Gregg. il Bet Hom & Gard 47:4 N '69

Blow-ups for SEMA. E. Rickman. il Hot Rod 22:94 Je '69

Collision cushion. D. Wells. il Motor T 21: 62-3+ O '69

Expensive lesson. il Time 93:66 My 23 '69

How safe are add-on auto accessories? D. L. Gregg. il Bet Hom & Gard 47:12+ Ag '69

How safe are the '70 cars? A. Rosenthal. il Todays Health 47:34-9+ O '69

How to crashproof your car. T. McCahill. il Mech Illus 65:52-4+ Je '69

More safety, cleaner exhaust, and better repairability in the '70 cars. J. P. Norbye and J. Dunne. il Pop Sci 195:96-9+ O '69

New safety device pressures Detroit; air bag. il Bsns W p45 Jl 12 '69

Pillow talk; federal safety bureau's hearings on safety cushions. il Newsweek 74:71-2 S 8 '69

Safety is a high-back seat. E. Rickman. il Hot Rod 22:118-19 N '69

Safety: the reluctant dragon. il Consumer Rep 34:182-5 Ap '69

Sand and balloons. Time 93:66 My 2 '69

What's new from Detroit in 1970? R. Huntington. il Consumer Bul 52:16-22 O '69

Why Detroit is wary of the 1970s; with editorial comment. il Bsns W p 110-12+, 188 S 20 '69

Your car is probably unsafe. il Motor T 21: 14 My '69

See also
Automobile driving—Safety devices and measures
Automobiles—Bumpers
Automobiles—Testing
Automobiles, Foreign—Safety devices and measures
Brakes. Automobile—Control
Safety belts

Scrapping

See Automobiles—Wrecking

Seats

Safety is a high-back seat. E. Rickman. il Hot Rod 22:118-19 N '69

Selling

Four ways to buy and sell your family's two cars. D. L. Gregg. Bet Hom & Gard 47: 66-7 F '69

Service stations

See Automobile service stations

Shock absorbers

Good put-on. J. Dianna. il Hot Rod 22:112 D '69

In shocking amounts. J. Dianna. il Hot Rod 22:60-1 Mr '69

Shows

See Automobiles—Exhibitions

Signal lights

1-2-3 sequential turn signal. J. Nunley. il Radio-Electr 40:38-40 Ap '69

Skidding

See also
Pavements—Slipperiness

Social aspects

Race for (automobile) space; adaptation of address, April 17, 1969. E. Corning, 2d. Bul Atom Sci 25:15-16 D '69

Specifications

CR's reports on full-size cars. il Consumer Bul 52:18-19 My '69

Facts and figures on the '70 cars. il Pop Sci 195:100-3 O '69

Guide to mechanical specifications; table (cont) il Consumer Rep 34:186-9 Ap '69

AUTOMOBILES—Specifications—*Continued*
Important characteristics, specifications, and test data, 1969 intermediate and compact automobiles. Consumer Bul 52:22-3 Ap '69
Important characteristics, specifications, and test data, 1969 semi-sport automobiles. Consumers Bul 52:18-20 Je '69

Speed

Rallye 'round the 1204; Simca. il Motor T 21:54+ O '69
Trans AM 303. il Motor T 21:61 O '69

Springs and suspension

ABCs of chassis frames and suspensions. R. W. Temple. il Pop Mech 132:128-33 S '69
Action at the front. S. Kelly. il Hot Rod 22:80-1 My '69
Beef a steer; trick-steel tie rods. J. Thawley. il Hot Rod 22:93 Ag '69
How to check ball joints. M. Schultz. il Pop Mech 132:132-5 D '69
New twist in rod suspension. B. Lang. il Hot Rod 22:92-3 Je '69
Rock & roll control; making AMC cars handle better for Trans-Am. S. Kelly. il Hot Rod 22:110-11 N '69
Spring boosters. E. Rickman. il Hot Rod 22:110 Mr '69
Swingin' rears for early rods. B. Lang. il Hot Rod 22:98-9 Mr '69

Stability and stabilizers

Rock & roll control; making AMC cars handle better for Trans-Am. S. Kelly. il Hot Rod 22:110-11 N '69
Spoiler sport. E. Rickman. il Hot Rod 22:100 S '69
'Vette set spoiler. B. Lang. il Hot Rod 22:110 D '69

Starting

How to get your car started in cold weather. R. Day. il Pop Sci 194:149-53 Ja '69
Moving a stalled vehicle. D. L. Gregg. Bet Hom & Gard 47:6 N '69
Warm starts for cold cars. T. Tappett. il Mech Illus 65:90-2+ D '69

Steering gear

Un-invention of the steering-wheel. K. Ludvigsen. il Motor T 21:90-3 F '69

Storage

How to store your car. T. Tappett. il Mech Illus 65:108-10+ F '69

Tape equipment

How car stereos work. L. Allen. il Radio-Electr 40:61-3+ Jl '69

Testing

Bleep, bleep, the Union/Pure oil trails are over; this is a recording. L. Levine. il Motor T 21:52-4 Ap '69
Coronet, Satellite, Fairlane, Montego, Rebel, Chevelle, Cutlass. il Consumer Rep 34:78-87 F '69
Driving the silver bullet; Mercedes C111. E. Dahlquist. il Motor T 21:38-9 N '69
Five specialty cars; Mercury Cougar, Ford Mustang, Chevrolet Camaro, American Motors AMX, Pontiac Grand Prix. il Consumer Rep 34:317-25 Je '69
Golden age of the dinosaurs; road test of the Chrysler New Yorker, Oldsmobile 98 and Mercury Marquis Brougham. B. Sanders. il Motor T 21:80-8 Jl '69
Hot Rod road test:
Brute force; Dodge. S. Kelly. il Hot Rod 22:36-8 D '69
Trans-Am Firebird. S. Kelly. il Hot Rod 22:40-2 Mr '69
How CU buys and tests its cars. il Consumer Rep 34:190-1 Ap '69
Mister muscle of 1970; Buick's new GS 455. S. Kelly. il Hot Rod 22:34-6 N '69
News on wheels; Pure oil performance trials. M. Spiegel. il Sr Schol 94:24 Mr 7 '69
Norbye-Dunne report:
Full-size family cars; biggest bargain for your buck? J. P. Norbye and J. Dunne. il Pop Sci 194:70-5 F '69
Just how sporty are this year's sporty cars? J. P. Norbye and J. Dunne. il Pop Sci 194:72-7 Ja '69
Road tests:
AMX, a matter of detail. E. Dahlquist. il Motor T 21:74-5+ D '69
Challenger. B. Sanders. il Motor T 21:40-2 N '69
Chevy Nova, Rambler, Dodge Dart, Ford Falcon perform for '69. B. Sanders. il Motor T 21:80-9 My '69

Date with three strippers; Chevelle SS 454, Torino Cobra and the Road Runner 440 6-bbl. A. B. Shuman. il Motor T 21:36-40+ D '69
Five car stud; Camero RS/SS350, Firebird 350, Cougar XR-7 351, Mustang Mach I 351, Javelin SST 343. B. Saunders. il Motor T 21:68-79 Mr '69
Six semi-sport cars; Camaro, Charger, Cougar, Firebird, Javelin, and Mustang. il Consumer Bul 52:15-23 Je '69
They're big in Pasadena. B. Sanders. il Motor T 21:84-92 Je '69
Three for the road; Chevy's Monte Carlo tangling with the Grand Prix and Thunderbird. B. Sanders. il Motor T 21:74-8+ N '69
Tom McCahill gives the Mercury Marquis an extended test. T. McCahill. il Mech Illus 65:50-2+ Mr '69
Tom McCahill revisits the Toronado. T. McCahill. il Mech Illus 65:47-9+ Je '69
Tom McCahill tests:
Chrysler Newport. T. McCahill. il Mech Illus 65:65-7+ Mr '69
Ford's 1970 Maverick. T. McCahill. il Mech Illus 65:64-6 My '69
Mercury Cyclone GT. T. McCahill. il Mech Illus 65:63-5+ S '69
1970 Chevrolet. T. McCahill. il Mech Illus 65:63-5+ N '69
1970 Dodge Challenger. T. McCahill. il Mech Illus 65:50-2 S '69
Olds' youngestmobile. T. McCahill. il Mech Illus 65:56-8+ F '69
Restyled Ambassador. T. McCahill. il Mech Illus 65:77-9+ F '69
Thunderbird. T. McCahill. il Mech Illus 65:53-5 Ap '69
Thunderbird. T. McCahill. il Mech Illus 65:47-9 D '69
World's greatest sedan! T. McCahill. il Mech Illus 65:49-51+ My '69
Track-testing Dodge's new pony car. P. Goldsmith. il Pop Mech 132:96-9+ D '69
Up with the rebel machine. B. Sanders. il Motor T 21:80-1 N '69

Tires

See Tires, Automobile

Towing

See Towing

Traction

Ground grabber; bolt-on traction bars for street/strip combo. J. Dianna. il Hot Rod 22:91 O '69
How to install chemical chains on your car. C. J. Baker. il Pop Sci 195:143+ D '69
New police car has power and antiskid on all four wheels. D. Scott. il Pop Sci 195:76-9 N '69
Twice the traction for your next car? four-wheel-drive for road cars. K. Ludvigsen. il Motor T 21:34-7 Jl '69

Trailers

See Automobile trailers

Transmission

Automatic dyno. J. Thawley. il Hot Rod 22:32-5 D '69
C-6 trans tricks. B. Lang. il Hot Rod 22:38-40 N '69
Close-ratio hydro. J. Dianna. il Hot Rod 22:66-8 Ag '69
Gearless transmission from GM. P. Weissler. il Mech Illus 65:44-6+ D '69
Help support your local C-6! B. Lang. il Hot Rod 22:88-9 F '69
Hone-O-Drive. E. Rickman. il Hot Rod 22:106 My '69
New overdrive unit fits auto-transmission cars. J. Dunne. il Pop Sci 195:74-5 Ag '69
Putting the power into Powerglide. J. Dianna. il Hot Rod 22:48-50 Ja '69
Revolution's here; automatic racing transmission. E. Dahlquist. il Motor T 21:42-3+ D '69
Slick tricks for four-speeds. E. Rickman. il Hot Rod 22:123-5 O '69
Toughening AM's automatic. B. Lang. il Hot Rod 22:104-5 My '69
Troubleshooting an automatic transmission. T. Tappett. il Mech Illus 65:92-4+ O '69
See also
Automobiles—Gearing

Warranty

See Warranty

AUTOMOBILES, Foreign—*Continued*

Design

All-new VW. J. C. Jones. il Newsweek 74: 98B O 20 '69

Planned obsolescence for Europe. E. Seidler. il Motor T 21:24+ Ag '69

History

Classics at Crystal palace; photographs of early English cars. C. W. Maydole. Motor T 21:58-9 Ap '69

Volkswagen, 1938-1969. E. Dahlquist. il Motor T 21:44 F '69

Marketing

Detroit races to meet challenge of imports. il Bsns W p 104-6+ Mr 29 '69

Volkswagen mounts a new invasion of U.S. il Bsns W p26 F 8 '69
See also
Volkswagen of America, incorporated

Safety devices and measures

Japanese safety issue; recall of defective cars sold in the U.S. Time 93:76+ Je 27 '69

Take the Fiat 850 sedan to the dealer. Consumer Rep 34:356 Jl '69

Specifications

Specifications and test data. Consumer Bul 52:13 S '69

Testing

Limité, économe, faclité; Simca 1204 GLS. E. Dahlquist. il Motor T 21:58-60 Jl '69

MI tests:
New big Beetle. G. Wilkins. il Mech Illus 65:46-7+ Ap '69

Norbye-Dunne report:
Those small GT coupes. J. P. Norbye and J. Dunne. il Pop Sci 195:88-93 Jl '69

$3,000 roadsters. J. P. Norbye and J. Dunne. il Pop Sci 195:96-100 Ag '69

Road tests:
Made in Japan by Mazda. B. Sanders. il Motor T 21:44-5+ D '69

Road tests of the Volvo 164. il Consumer Rep 34:592-5 O '69

Subaru 360, not acceptable; Japanese minicar. il Consumer Rep 34:220-2 Ap '69

Three imported sedans; Fiat 124; Renault 10 and Volvo 144. il Consumer Bul 52:8-13 S '69

Tom McCahill tests:
Cars of Sweden; Saab 99 and Volvo 164. Mech Illus 65:43-7+ Ag '69

Four most exciting new imports. T. Mc-Cahill. il Mech Illus 65:46-53+ Jl '69

AUTOMOBILES, Military
See also
Motor trucks, Military

AUTOMOBILES, Police

New police car has power and antiskid on all four wheels. D. Scott. il Pop Sci 195:76-9 N '69

Small police cars, big results; Mamaroneck, N.Y. J. Geary. il Am City 84:68 F '69
See also
Motor vehicles, Police

Lighting

New lights increase police efficiency; Dearborn, Mich. O. L. Hubbard. il Am City 84:34 Ag '69

AUTOMOBILES, Racing

Argentina's amazing TC racers. K. Ludvigsen. il Motor T 21:72-5 Ap '69

Baddest of the bad; T. Beebe and J. Mulligan. J. Thawley. il Hot Rod 22:64-6 My '69

Belated anniversary party; Bonneville's national speed trials. E. Rickman. il Hot Rod 22:44-7+ Ja '69

Big engines and little cars; Can-Am 1969. S. Kelly. il Hot Rod 22:54-6 Ag '69

Can Chrysler put the crunch on Cale? Daytona preview. B. Kilpatrick. il Pop Mech 131:87-90+ F '69

Day for Henry and Georges; Ford won from Porsche at Le Mans. K. Chapin. il Sports Illus 30:58+ Je 23 '69

Ferrari-Porsche showdown. il Motor T 21:70 My '69

Inconclusive Charlotte. L. Laye. il Motor T 21:70-2 D '69

Indy crop forecast. E. Rickman. il Hot Rod 22:48-50 My '69

Indy preview; 1969. il Motor T 21:94-6 Je '69

Inside a digger; AA/Fuel dragster. D. Scott. il Hot Rod 22:88-91 D '69

Italian campaign; Indianapolis 500. E. Dahlquist. il Motor T 21:54-7 Ag '69

Keeping the pace. il Motor T 21:33+ Ag '69

King Cobra is the name. il Motor T 21:51-3 O '69

Let there be steam. B. Ottum. il Sports Illus 30:50-6 F 3 '69

Like bounding gazelles. S. Murray. il Motor T 21:62-3 Ag '69

Mission Bell 250. J. Dianna. il Hot Rod 22:94-6 D '69

MT looks at super stockers. Motor T 21:96+ S '69

Muscle cars. A. Bester. il Holiday 45:72-5 F '69

NHRA teardown. J. Dianna. il Hot Rod 22: 72-4 Je '69

NHRA's '69 Winternationals. B. Lang and J. Dianna. il Hot Rod 22:32-6 Ap '69

Old Poison Ivy goes jr. stock scratchin. B. Lang. il Hot Rod 22:50-1 F '69

On Tulsa turf. J. Dianna and J. McFarland. il Hot Rod 22:36-8 Ja '69

Poem of a run by Ford and Ferrari; Ford GT-40 wins at Sebring. R. F. Jones. il Sports Illus 30:24-5 Mr 31 '69

Rex Maze 300. E. Dahlquist. il Motor T 21:80-3 Mr '69

Rock & roll control; making AMC cars handle better for Trans-Am. S. Kelly. il Hot Rod 22:110-11 N '69

Roddin' at random. See issues of Hot rod

Salt was fine in '69; SCTA's 21st Bonneville meet. E. Rickman. il Hot Rod 22:30-3 N '69

Sixteen-day stock car race. S. Kelly. il Hot Rod 22:44-6 Ap '69

Something for everybody. S. Kelly. il Hot Rod 22:92-4 F '69

Stocks & funnies. J. Dianna. il Hot Rod 22: 48-50 O '69

Strickler Trick. J. Dianna. il Hot Rod 22: 68-70 Mr '69

Strip preppin' the Z/28. J. Dianna. il Hot Rod 22:52-3 My '69

2,000-hp. car poised for new speed-record try; Ford autolite special. J. Wright. il Pop Sci 195:90-1+ Ag '69

Vees at Nurburgring. R. Brock. il Hot Rod 22:64-6 O '69

Versatile racer. A. Hall. il Hot Rod 22: 55-7 Mr '69

Will the Eagles scream again? B. Kilpatrick. il Pop Mech 131:132-5+ My '69

Winter dreams; Daytona speed week. E. Dahlquist. il Motor T 21:90-6 My '69

You may need four-wheel drive to win at Indy this year. J. W. Wright and D. Phipps. il Pop Sci 194:84-7 My '69
See also
Karts (midget cars)

Design

Strange story of the man who shook Indy. L. Levine. il Mech Illus 65:43-5+ My '69

Equipment

It's about time; Digitimer produced by Automotive research associates for race cars. B. Lang. il Hot Rod 22:106-7 D '69

Strictly for stocks. J. Dianna. See issues of Hot rod

Manufacture

Race maker; John Holman. S. Kelly. il Hot Rod 22:74-6 Ag '69

Safety devices and measures

Can this car make race driving safe? il Pop Sci 195:42 Jl '69

Rubber-flavored lifesaver; rollbars. J. Dianna. il Hot Rod 22:90 S '69

Super safety for the competition car. G. Borgeson. il Motor T 21:50-2 Jl '69

Springs and suspension
See Automobiles—Springs and suspension

Transmission
See Automobiles—Transmission

AUTOMOBILES, Remodeled

Backyarding the 396 Chevy . . . rat now. J. Dianna. il Hot Rod 22:46-8 F '69

Better-built mover; Buick's GS400. S. Kelly. il Hot Rod 22:36-8 Je '69

From out of the past. M. Lamm. il Hot Rod 22:52-3 Ja '69

It's a Chevrostang! J. Thawley. il Hot Rod 22:92-3 S '69

Lightweights; kit-car craze. J. Thawley. il Hot Rod 22:34-8 Mr '69

New one-piece body turns bug into a beauty. L. E. Sabal. il Pop Mech 132:156-61 Jl '69

Old Poison Ivy goes jr. stock scratchin. B. Lang. il Hot Rod 22:50-1 F '69

Simple addition. J. Dianna. il Hot Rod 22:58-60 D '69

Super-duty trick stuff. B. Lang. il Hot Rod 22:72-4 Ap '69

AUTOMOBILES, Remodeled—*Continued*
Surprise! It's a six! J. Thawley. il Hot Rod 22:94-5 Ap '69
289 + MGB, sum fun. B. Lang. il Hot Rod 22:60-2 F '69
VW varoom. D. Wells. il Motor T 21:70-2+ S; 124-5+ O '69
VW's take gas. J. Dianna. il Hot Rod 22:40-2 Jl '69

AUTOMOBILES, Second-hand. See Automobiles, Used

AUTOMOBILES, Steam
Bill Lear's steam car. M. Lamm. il Pop Mech 131:128-31+ Ap '69
Blowing the steam dream; interview. ed. by J. Zmuda. W. J. Besler. il Motor T 21:44-6+ N '69
Doctored Stanley, we presume? Lear's steam car. il Time 93:74 Ap 11 '69
GM takes the wraps off its steam cars. J. P. Norbye and J. Dunne. il Pop Sci 195: 84-5 Jl '69
Green light for the smogless car. J. Lear. il Sat R 52:81-6 D 6 '69
Is the steam car ready for a comeback? K. Prentiss. il Holiday 46:46-7 N '69
Lear's steam dream: a reality? D. Wells. il Motor T 21:26-9 Je '69
Let there be steam. B. Ottum. ill Sports Illus 30:50-6 F 3 '69
Modern steam cars are really on the way. D. Francis. il Pop Sci 194:45-9+ Je '69
Stanley's dream makes a comeback. E. Gross. il Sci N 96:247-9 S 20 '69
Steam cars: jet tycoon, others, espouse the cause. A. Jamison. il Science 163:370-4 Ja 24 '69
Steam cars try to get back in the running. il Bsns W p 130-2 Mr 29 '69
Tempest over a teapot. T. Aaronson. il Environ 11:22-7 O '69

AUTOMOBILES, Theft of
Heist a minute. L. Raskin. il Nation 208:434-6 Ap 7 '69
Midnight auto parts. il Newsweek 74:120+ O 27 '69
Will your car be stolen next? B. Surface. Read Digest 95:157-8+ D '69
See also
Automobiles—Protection against theft

AUTOMOBILES, Used
Close look at used car buying. D. L. Gregg. il Bet Hom & Gard 47:44+ My '69
Great odometer raid. il Consumer Rep 34: 250-3 My '69
Used cars. M. Lamm. See issues of Motor trend
See also
Automobile industry and trade—Used cars
Automobiles—Wrecking

AUTOMOTIVE diesel engines. See Diesel engines, Automotive

AUTOMOTIVE gas turbines. See Gas turbines, Automotive

AUTOMOTIVE mathematics. See Mathematics—Formulae

AUTOMOTIVE research. See Automobile research

AUTONETICS division. See North American Rockwell corporation

AUTONOMIC nervous system. See Nervous system

AUTOPILOTS. See Automatic pilot (airplanes)

AUTOPSY
What autopsies show. P. Gwynne. il Newsweek 74:88 S 15 69

AUTORADIOGRAPHY
Adrenal cholesterol: localization by electron-microscope autoradiography. H. L. Moses and others. bibliog il Science 163:1203-5 Mr 14 '69
Cell population kinetics: a modified interpretation of the graph of labeled mitoses. A. I. Hamilton. bibliog il Science 164:952-4 My 23 '69
Cell wall protein in plants: autoradiographic evidence. D. Sadava and M. J. Chrispeels. bibliog il Science 165:299-300 Jl 18 '69
Direct pathway to the brain. M. R. Kare and others. bibliog il Science 163:952-3 F 28 '69
Electron microscopic radioautography; identification of origin of synaptic terminals in normal nervous tissue. A. Hendrickson. bibliog il Science 165:194-6 Jl 11 '69
High-resolution autoradiography of intracellular plutonium. A. Lindenbaum and M. H. Smoler. bibliog il Science 165:192-4 Jl 11 '69
Intracranial drug implants: an autoradiographic analysis of diffusion. S. P. Grossman and W. E. Stumpf. bibliog il Science 166:1410-12 D 12 '69

LSD: autoradiographic study on the placental transfer and tissue distribution in mice. J. E. Idänpään-Heikkilä and J. C. Schoolar. bibliog il Science 164:1295-7 Je 13 '69
Nerve endings: rapid appearance of labeled protein shown by electron microscope radioautography. B. Droz and S. H. Barondes. bibliog il Science 165:1131-3 S 12 '69
Too much noise in the autoradiogram? W. E. Stumpf. bibliog Science 163:958-9 F 28 '69

AUTUMN
Autumn: a celebration. H. Borland. il Audubon 71:18-36 S '69
Autumn's acres; Great Smokies' Balsam Range. M. B. Mellinger. il Nat Parks 43:12-13 Ja '69
When fall begins. J. Mills. il Read Digest 95:79-81 O '69

AUTUMN; story. See Beauchamp, L.

AUTUMN crocuses
Bulbs for autumn. B. Miles. il Horticulture 46:36-7+ Ag '68

AUTUMN leaves. See Leaves

AUTUMN music festival, Naples. See Music festivals—Italy

AUXINS
Ethylene: a factor in defoliation induced by auxins. M. Hallaway and D. J. Osborne. bibliog il Science 163:1067-8 Mr 7 '69
See also
Indolebutyric acid

AVAKIAN, Aram
If people don't love this film, they'll hate it. Life 67:66+ N 7 '69

AVALLONE, Michael
Letter to a still unkown author. Writer 82: 21-2+ F '69

AVALON BAY. See Santa Catalina Island—Harbor

AVANT-Garde (periodical)
On borrowed time. Newsweek 73:92 Je 23 '69

AVANT-garde films. See Moving pictures, Experimental

AVANT-garde music. See Music

AVANT-garde theater. See Theater, Experimental

AVCO corporation

Lycoming division
Aircraft engine revolution. R. Blodget. il Flying 84:66-72 F '69

AVEBURY, England
Stonehenge. Travel & Camera 32:42-5+ Mr '69

AVEDON, Richard
Twiggy. il McCalls 96:86-7 Mr '69

AVENA. See Oats

AVERAGES, Stock. See Stocks—Price indexes and averages

AVERILL, James R.
Good grief. Sci Am 220:52 Ap '69

AVERILL, Lloyd J.
Ecology of discontent. Chr Cent 86:835-8 Je 18 '69

AVERY, Earle
Pops wants to win his own golden anniversary present. W. F. Reed, jr. por Sports Illus 30:64-5 Je 16 '69

AVERY, Milton
Motivated by love; exhibition at Washington's National collection of fine arts. D. L. Shirey. il por Newsweek 74:58 D 29 '69

AVERY, Paul
Training for Song My. Nation 209:716 D 29 '69

AVERY, Thomas L.
Pheromone-induced changes in the acidophil concentration of mouse pituitary glands. bibliog Science 164:423-4 Ap 25 '69

AVIARIES
Life with birds il Sunset 143:62-71, 113 S '69

AVIATION
Foreign accent. J. Fricker. See issues of Flying
See also
Air travel
Airlines
Airplane racing
Airplanes—Piloting
Balloon ascensions
Gliding and soaring
Private flying

Accident investigation
One seat cushion and cause of accident. il Chem 42:23-5 Jl '69
Systems safety approach urged in crash analysis. Aviation W 90:38 My 12 '69

Accidents
AH-56 wreckage studied for cause of crash in sea. Aviation W 90:23 Mr 24 '69
Aircraft collisions in 1968 follow pattern. Aviation W 91:107+ Ag 11 '69

AVIATION—Physiological aspects—*Continued*
Jetlag: walk, do not rush, and easy on the
martinis. il Holiday 46:60-1 Jl '69
Time-zone effects. P. V. Siegel and others.
bibliog il Science 164:1249-55 Je 13 '69
See also
Aerospace medical association

Psychological aspects
My island in the sky; open cockpit of a
Bücker Jungmann. E. K. Gann. il Flying
84:68-71 Ap '69
Not her cup of tea. R. Peterson. il Flying
84:56-9 Je '69

Public relations
Discover flying. R. B. Parke. il Flying 84:36
Ap '69
See also
Airlines—Public relations

Rain hazards
See Aviation—Storm hazards

Records
See Aviation records

Safety devices and measures
Data exchange on safety urged. Aviation W
90:100-2 Je 16 '69
Diversity marks air safety proposals. P. J.
Klass. Aviation W 91:38-9 N 17 '69
FAA group urges twenty safety proposals.
D. A. Brown. Aviation W 91:103+ Ag 11 '69
General aviation safety concern increases. il
Aviation W 90:83-4 Mr 17 '69
Growing worries about safety in the air
lanes. il U S News 67:12 S 22 '69
Is it safe to fly? Some say no; nine famous
landlubbers. il Holiday 46:52-3 Jl '69
It doesn't matter where you sit, by F. Mc-
Clement. Review
Sat R 52:35-6 Je 28 '69. C. A. Zraket
NTSB finds aviation safety rates improve.
Aviation W 90:30-1 Ap 14 '69
On top; R. Nader's investigation of general
aviation. R. L. Collins. Flying 85:24+ N '69
Six ways to make the going really great. B.
Kocivar. il Holiday 46:42-7 Jl '69
Yes, it is safe to fly, but is it safe to crash?
R. Nader. il Holiday 46:56-7+ Jl '69
See also
Airplanes—Safety devices and measures
Proximity warning indicators
Radio beacons

Snowstorm hazards
See Aviation—Storm hazards

Speed records
See Aviation records

Storm hazards
Follow me through; flying in rain. R. Blod-
get. Flying 85:26-7 O '69
Samaritan. E. Gillette. il Flying 85:80 N '69
Snow clogs Northwest traffic. Aviation W 90:
26 F 10 '69
Snow overwhelms airports at N.Y.; 6,000
stranded. Aviation W 90:31-2 F 17 '69
Sucker trap. T. J. Berry. Flying 84:70-1 Mr
'69
When VFR goes IFR. R. L. Collins. Flying
84:38-40 F '69

Stunt flying
Blue Angels enlarge repertoire in shift to
F-4J aircraft. C. M. Plattner. il Aviation
W 90:102-3+ My 5 '69
My wildest airplane ride. R. Gannon. il Pop
Sci 194:82-5+ F '69
Precision flying displayed at Paris show.
il Aviation W 90:52-3 Je 23 '69
Thunderbirds probe F-4E potential. C. M.
Plattner. il Aviation W 91:36-9+ S 1 '69

Transatlantic flights
Ferry flight; for London daily mail transatlantic air race. S. Wilkinson. il Flying
84:44-8+ Ap '69
First to fly the Atlantic; American naval
airmen in Navy Curtiss or NC flying
boats. B. A. Weisberger. il Am Heritage
20:16-21+ Je '69
See also
Airlines—International services—Transatlantic

Transcontinental flights
Across the US in a new Cherokee 140B. J.
Gilbert. il Flying 84:42-3+ F '69

Transoceanic flights
See also
Aviation—Transatlantic flights

Transpacific flights
Wind waves and stars; exploratory flight
from Chile to Easter Island and Tahiti; ed.
by L. Zalamea. R. Pairoa. il Américas 21:
2-11 Ap '69
See also
Airlines—International services—Transpacific

Winter flying
Big airlift to the North Slope. F. A. Tinker.
il Pop Mech 132:94-7+ N '69
Richard Bach. R. Bach. il Flying 85:10-12 D
'69
See also
Aviation—Storm hazards

Arctic Regions
Nordair jet schedules cross Arctic Circle. D.
A. Brown. il Aviation W 90:39-41+ Ap 7 '69

Cuba
Comanche C. Cuba si. S. Wilkinson. il Flying 85:32-9 S '69

Great Britain
Stone-age aviation. J. Fricker. Flying 85:104
S '69

Hawaii
When Hawaii calls. R. Blodget. il Flying
85:63-5 S '69

Ireland
Irish air. D. D. C. Pochin Mould. il Flying
84:50-1+ My '69

Jamaica
Man who made his dreams come true: R.
Mantel of Jamaica air taxi ltd. J. Gilbert.
il Flying 85:88-92 Jl '69

South Africa
South Africa seeking own air capability. L.
Doty. il Aviation W 90:35-7 Mr 3 '69

United States
Airways jam; threat to private flying. il
U S News 67:42-3 D 29 '69
Nixon policy on aviation emerges. L. Doty.
il Aviation W 90:28-9 My 26 '69
See also
Airlines—United States
Airports—United States

AVIATION, Commercial. See Aeronautics,
Commercial

AVIATION associations
Aerospace calendar. See issues of Aviation
week & space technology
Calendar. See issues of Flying
See also names of aviation associations,
e.g. Radio technical commission for aeronautics

AVIATION clubs
Club scene. S. Wilkinson. See issues of Flying
to September 1969
See also
Air travel clubs

AVIATION education
Follow me through; book learning has limits.
R. Blodget. il Flying 84:20-1 Mr '69

AVIATION engineers

Salaries, allowances, etc.
Question of salaries; letters to the editor.
Aviation W 91:110 Jl 14; 118 Ag 4 '69

AVIATION instructors. See Air pilots—Training

AVIATION instruments. See Aeronautic instruments

AVIATION insurance. See Insurance, Aviation

AVIATION lobby. See Lobbying

AVIATION records
Electrical failure halts record attempt. Aviation W 91:74-5 N 24 '69
Fastest prop in the world. R. L. Emerson. il
Pop Mech 132:94-5 D '69
If at first you don't succeed..; attempt to
fly a light twin over both poles. J. Gilbert.
il Flying 85:90-5 D '69
Piston speed record claimed; challenges
mark set in 1939. Aviation W 91:18 Ag 25
'69
Run for a record; world's propeller-driven
speed record. D. Greenamyer. Aviation W
91:110 Jl 14 '69

AVIATION research. See Aeronautic research

AVIATION week and space technology (peri-
odical)
Message from the publisher. R. A. Hubley.
Aviation W 92:5 Ja 12 '70

AVIATION workers
　　See also
Airplane mechanics
AVICENNA
　Avicenna; reprint. C. Aboussouan. UNESCO
　　Courier 22:38 Ag '69
AVIGNON
　　　　Architecture
　Avignon: the surroundings of the Palace of
　　the popes. J. L. Taupin. il Antiques 96:
　　409-11 S '69
AVIOLI, Louis V. and others
　Intestinal calcium absorption: nature of de-
　　fect in chronic renal disease. bibliog Science
　　166:1154-6 N 28 '69
AVIONICS industry. See Electronic apparatus
　industry and trade
AVITAL, Samuel
　Avital: Anne Wilson dance co, the Cubiculo.
　　J. Anderson. Dance Mag 43:32 My '69
AVNERY, Uri
　Clever idea that does more harm than good.
　　Life 66:8 F 21 '69
AVNET, incorporated
　Shattered dream. Forbes 104:71 O 15 '69
AVNI, M.
　Photography is my very life. Hattersley.
　　il Pop Phot 64:108+ Je '69
AVOCADOS. See Cookery—Fruit
AVOCATIONS
　　See also
Hobbies
AVORN, Jerry L.
　Columbia: to be a revolutionary or not to
　　be? Look 33:13-14 My 13 '69
AVSIUK, Grigorii Aleksandrovich, and Kotlia-
　kov, V. M.
　Glaciers on the move. UNESCO Courier 22:
　　16-21+ Je '69
AWARENESS house. See Narcotic addicts—
　Rehabilitation
AWE. See Wonder
AWNINGS
　How to buy and care for the new fabric
　　awnings & umbrellas. il Good H 168:142+
　　Je '69
AXAM, John A.
　Philadelphia: the Reader development pro-
　　gram. Wilson Lib Bul 43:894-7 My '69
AXELBANK, Albert
　Short fuse in Japan. Nation 208:141-3 F 3 '69
AXELRAD, Nancy
　Jobscope: for the science-minded. Mlle 69:
　　218 My '69
　They give other people's parties. Mlle 69:
　　180-1+ O '69
AXELROD, David. See Martin, M. A. jt. auth.
AXELROD, Julius. See Molinoff, P. jt. auth.
AXES
　　See also
Adzes
AXIOMATIC field theory. See Quantum field
　theory
AXIOMS
　Isaac Asimov explains: truth in Gödel's proof.
　　I. Asimov. Sci Digest 65:86+ F '69
AXLES
　　See also
Automobiles—Axles
AXONAL dystrophy. See Nervous system—
　Diseases
AXTHELM, Pete
　Trot, trot, trot. Travel & Camera 32:62-7 My
　　'69
AYALA, Stephen C. See Anderson, J. R. jt.
　auth.
AYD, Frank J. jr
　Liberal abortion laws. America 120:130-2 F 1
　　'69
AYERS, Nancy
　Forming a nature corps for action. Cons
　　24:2-5 O '69
AYROUT, Henri Habib
　Henri Ayrout Egypt's loss and ours. C. J
　　McNaspy. America 120:494 Ap 26 '69
AYRTON, Michael
　Knossos in the Catskills. il Time 94:48 Ag 15
　　'69
AYUB KHAN, Mohammad
　Developing society: address. December 1, 1968.
　　Vital Speeches 35:200-2 Ja 15 '69
　　　　about
　Abdication, Asian style. il por Newsweek 73:
　　35-6 Mr 3 '69
　Army takes over Pakistan. por Time 93:32
　　Ap 4 '69
　Ayub calls it quits. il Sr Schol 94:23 Mr 28 '69
　Ayub's strategic retreat. il Time 93:29-30 F
　　21 '69
　Not by bread alone. il por Newsweek 73:
　　43 F 10 '69

Pakistan: new leader, same troubles. il por
　U S News 66:54 Ap 7 '69
Pakistan: why Ayub quit. il por Newsweek
　73:38-9 Ap 7 '69
Pakistan's Ayub steps down. il por Time 93:
　29-30 F 28 '69
Precarious task. il por Time 93:36 Mr 28 '69
AYURVEDIC medicine. See Medicine, Hindu
AZALEAS
　Beautiful and useful? il Sunset 142:186-7 F '69
　For rhododendron-azalea keepers, or paper
　　experts. il Sunset 143:176 D '69
　Here's how to move an azalea or rhododen-
　　dron. il Sunset 142:190-1 F '69
　Problems people have with azaleas and
　　rhododendrons; questions and answers. il
　　Sunset 143:248+ O '69
AZCARRAGA, Emilio
　Rivals challenge Mexican TV czar. il por Bsns
　　W p50-2 Mr 15 '69
AZMITIA, Efrain C. jr, and McEwen, B. S.
　Corticosterone regulation of tryptopahn hy-
　　droxylase in midbrain of the rat. bibliog
　　Science 166:1274-6 D 5 '69
AZODRIN. See Insecticides
AZOTOBACTER
　Azotobacter cysts: reactivation by white light
　　after inactivation by ultraviolet radiation.
　　G. R. Vela and J. W. Peterson. bibliog il
　　Science 166:1296-7 D 5 '69
AZTEC music. See Aztecs—Music
AZTECS
　　　　Music
　Music in Aztec & Inca territory, by R. Steven-
　　son. Review
　　Mus Q 55:115-20 Ja '69. G. Béhague
AZURIN
　Azurin: X-ray data for crystals from pseu-
　　domonas denitrificans. G. Strahs. bibliog
　　Science 165:60-1 Jl 4 '69

B

BAAS. See British association for the ad-
　vancement of science
BART (Bay area rapid transit) See San Fran-
　cisco—Rapid transit
BCA-Esquire awards
　Honor to those who honor the arts. A. Ging-
　　rich. Esquire 72:6 Jl '69
BCDS. See Black cultural development society
BEU (Black economic union) See Cooperative
　associations
B. F. Goodrich company. See Goodrich, B. F,
　company
BGA. See Better government association
BIA. See United States—Indian affairs, Bu-
　reau of
BIS. See Bank for international settlements
BMI. See Book manufacturers' institute
BMW (automobile) See Automobiles, Foreign
BOAC. See British overseas airways corporation
BOR. See United States—Outdoor recreation,
　Bureau of
BP oil corporation. See British petroleum
　company
BSC. See British steel corporation
BAALBEK festival. See Music festivals—Le-
　banon
BAB, Herbert J. G.
　Gut issues of urban financing. Am City 84:
　　67-9 Jl '69
BABA, Meher. See Meher Baba
BABA, Sai. See Sai Baba
BABA Ram Dass. See Alpert, R.
BABBIDGE, Homer D. jr
　Who owns New York. Science 164:658-60 My
　　9 '69
BABBITT, Milton
　Music; Relata II. D. Hamilton. Nation 208:218
　　F 17 '69
　Musical events; performance of Relata II by
　　New York philharmonic. W. Sargeant. New
　　Yorker 44:80 Ja 25 '69
BABCOCK and Wilcox company
　Boilermaker loses its steam. Bsns W p62+
　　O 25 '69
　Great nuclear fizzle at old B.&W; pressure
　　vessels for nuclear power plants. H. B.
　　Meyers. il Fortune 80:123-5+ N '69
　Pressure; B&W's production problems with
　　nuclear reactor boilers. il Forbes 104:26-7
　　O 1 '69

BABCOX, Peter
Meet the women of the revolution. 1969. N Y Times Mag p34-5+ F 9 '69
BABEL', Isaak Emmanuilovich
Isaac Babel talks about writing; excerpts from Years of hope. by K. G. Paustovskii. Nation 208:406-7 Mr 31 '69

about

Arithmetic of silence. L. Epstein. Nation 209: 119-21 Ag 11 '69
High-assay find in the Babel gold mine. R. Phelps. Life 67:10 Jl 18 '69
Poignant polarity. C. Leviant. por Sat R 52: 25-7 Jl 12 '69
Tower of Babel. G. Wolff. por Newsweek 74: 89+ Jl 14 '69
BABEL CANYON model. See Architectural models
BABIAN, Haig
Can taxes do more than raise revenue? Sat R 52:30-2+ Mr 22 '69
BABIES. See Infants
BABY animals. See Animals, Infancy of
BABY care. See Infants—Care and hygiene
BABY cribs. See Cribs (beds)
BABY foods. See Infants food
BABY incubators. See Infants, Premature
BABY sitter; story. See Willis, S.
BABY sitters
Baby sitters money can't buy; neighborhood co-op. Y. Postelle. il Parents Mag 44:56-7+ Ag '69
Good emergency mothers are GEMS. F. G. Loyd. il Todays Health 47:12-13+ S '69
How to coddle and keep a babysitter. S. Essary. il Parents Mag 44:40-1 D '69

Anecdotes, facetiae, satire, etc.

Dear baby-sitter; last-minute instructions. B. Adler. il Good H 168:122-3 Mr '69
BACCALAUREATE addresses
Auguration at graduation; topic of student unrest and its meaning in relation to society. Chr Cent 86:857 Je 18 '69
Stamp out commencement speakers! W. E. Davis. Ed Digest 35:32-4 N '69
Youth: the jeremiads of June. il Time 93: 16-17 Je 13 '69
BACCALONI, Salvatore
Historical records. A. Favia-Artsay. por Hobbies 74:35-6 N '69
BACCHAE; drama. See Euripides
BACH, Dirk
Stamp collection of Dirk Bach. Ramp Mag 7: 42-3 N 30 '68
BACH, George R.
—and Wyden, Peter
Parent and child. N Y Times Mag p61-2+ Ja 26 '69
Six fights you won't want to miss; excerpts from The intimate enemy. Ladies Home J 86:64+ F '69

about

Marathon therapy is a psychological pressure cooker. K. Lamott. il N Y Times Mag p28-9+ Jl 13 '69
BACH, Johann Sebastian
Bach by the book. R. Jacobson. Sat R 52:53 Jl 26 '69
Bach's B minor mass, does the concentus musicus' authenticity make musical sense? C. F. Gilmore; P. H. Lang. il Hi Fi 19:76-8 Jl '69
Bach's last keyboard works. D. Hamilton. il Hi Fi 19:74-5 Ag '69
Bargain-priced Christmas oratorio. P. L. Miller. Am Rec G 36:171 N '69
Charles Rosen's Bach on the piano. il Am Rec G 35:939 Je '69
Critic answers his critics. P. H. Lang. Hi Fi 19:22 N '69
Dancing Bach. R. Tureck. Dance Mag 43:49-50 O '69
Editorial. P. H. Lang. Mus Q 55:545-58 O '69
From Bach to Bach. R. Jacobson. Sat R 52: 79-80 O 25 '69
Indispensable album. M. N. Kanny. Am Rec G 36:36 S '69
Interpretation of Bach: the role of dance; the Metropolitan museum of art. J. Armstrong. Dance Mag 43:78 D '69
Johann Sebastian Bach: the culmination of an era, by K. Geiringer. Review
Mus Q 55:120-5 Ja '69. J. F. Ohl
No violinist does unaccompanied Bach quite like Henryk Szeryng. M. Sherwin. Hi Fi 19: 86 Mr '69
One of the outstanding Bach releases of the year. Am Rec G 36:114 O '69

Records:
Cantatas no. 56, 82. Opera N 34:36 Ja 10 '70
Christmas oratorio. Opera N 34:30 D 20 '69
Mass in B minor. Opera N 33:35 F 1 '69
Mass in B minor. Opera N 34:34 Ja 17 '70
St Matthew passion. Opera N 34:28 O 11 '69
Switched-on Bach story. I. Berger. il Sat R 52:45-7+ Ja 25 '69
Synthesizing Johann S. Bach. R. Freedman. Life 66:12 Ja 24 '69
Szeryng, Ricci, and Bach. B. Schwarz. Sat R 52:53+ My 31 '69
Well-tempura'd Bach; New sound from the Japanese Bach scene. A. Frankenstein. Hi Fi 19:88 O '69
Wiedrigkeit and *verdriesslichkeit* in Mühlhausen. H. Serwer. bibliog f Mus Q 55:20-30 Ja '69
BACH, Marilyn L. and others
Leukemia-associated antigens in the mixed leukocyte culture test. bibliog Science 166: 1520-2 D 19 '69
BACH, Richard
Helmet and goggles (cont) Flying 84:26-7 F '69
Richard Bach (cont) Flying 84:32-3 Ap; 32-3 Je; 85:35+ Ag; 92-3 O; 14 N; 10-12 D '69
BACHARACH, Burt
Popular records. D. Watt. New Yorker 44: 84-6 Ja 18 '69
BACHELER, Jack
Tallest, fastest and buggiest. R. Blount, jr. il pors Sports Illus 30:58-9+ Je 16 '69
BACHELORS. See Single men
BACHELORS III (bar) See Bars and barrooms
BACIU, Stefan
Amighetti: engraver. Américas 21:10-15 F '69
BACK
See also
Backache
BACK pay. See Wage payment plans
BACK-to-Africa movements
Into the wilderness: group from Chicago's Alpha Beta Israel center. J. Barnes. il Newsweek 73:52 Ja 27 '69
J. Albert Thorne, back-to-Africanist. R. G. Weisbord. bibliog il Negro Hist Bul 32:14-16 Mr '69
Mboya's rebuttal. T. Mboya. il Ebony 24:90-1+ Ag '69
BACK to Methuselah; drama. See Shaw, G. B.
BACKACHE
Solving the mystery of old-fashioned backache. G. M. Knox. Bet Hom & Gard 47:48+ Ap '69
BACKFLOW connections (plumbing) See Water distribution
BACKGROUND in fiction. See Fiction—Technique
BACKLIN-LANDMAN, Hedy
Boudinot furnishings in the Art museum of Princeton university. Antiques 96:366-71 S '69
BACKPACKING. See Walking
BACKSTER, Cleve
Electronics and the living plant. L. G. Lawrence. bibliog il Electr World 82:25-8 O '69
Man who reads nature's secret signals. T. Bacon. il por Nat Wildlife 7:4-8 F '69
BACKUS, Richard H. See Lineaweaver, T. H. 3d, jt. auth.
BACKWARD areas. See Underdeveloped areas
BACKWARD children. See Mentally handicapped children
BACON, Dorothy
She hears music and there's someone there. Life 67:48E-48F Ag 8 '69
BACON, Edmund Norwood
Urban process: planning with and for the community; reprint. Arch Rec 145:129-34 My '69
BACON, Martha
Tantrums and unicorns. Atlan 224:148+ D '69
BACON, Thorn
Comeback of the National air races. Pop Sci 195:88-91 S '69
Contact lenses anyone can wear. Pop Sci 194: 84-6+ Ja '69
Man who reads nature's secret signals. Nat Wildlife 7:4-8 F '69
Polybag, the any-weather sleeping bag. Pop Sci 195:134-5 Ag '69
—See Jenkinson. M. jt. auth.
BACON, W. Stevenson
Science newsfront. See issues of Popular science monthly to December 1969
Thunderbolt machine tests tomorrow's power lines. Pop Sci 195:82-5+ O '69

BACON, W. Stevenson—*Continued*
Why they turned off Niagara's American Falls. Pop Sci 195:84-5+ Ag '69
World's tallest chimney. Pop Sci 195:66-7 D '69
—See Busse. J. G. jt. auth.

BACON
Bacon; brands rated. Il Consumer Rep 34: 510-13 S '69

BACONE junior college, Muskogee, Okla.
No givers for these Indians. P. Carry. Il Sports Illus 30:62+ Je 2 '69

BACTERIA
Bacterial cell wall. N. Sharon. Il Sci Am 220:92-8 My '69
Chemoreceptors in bacteria. J. Adler. bibliog il Science 166:1588-97 D 26 '69
See also
Azotobacter
Escherichia coli
Micrococcus
Microorganisms
Mutation (bacteria)
Mycobacterium
Myxobacteria
Pseudomonas
Vibrio

Growth
See Growth (bacteria)

Metabolism
Regulation of branched biosynthetic pathways in bacteria. P. Datta. bibliog il Science 165:556-62 Ag 8 '69

Resistance and sensitivity
Kasugamycin resistance: 30S ribosomal mutation with an unusual location on the escherichia coli chromosome. P. F. Sparling. bibliog il Science 167:56-8 Ja 2 '70

Respiration
Extraparticulate chain interaction between different electron transport particles. E. Bogin and others. bibliog il Science 165: 1364-7 S 26 '69

BACTERIA, Effect of antibiotics on. See Bacteria—Resistance and sensitivity

BACTERIA, Effect of light on. See Light—Physiological effects

BACTERIA, Effect of temperature on. See Temperature—Physiological effects

BACTERIA, Marine
Macromolecular subunits in the walls of marine nitrifying bacteria. S. W. Watson and C. C. Remsen. bibliog il Science 163: 685-6 F 14 '69

BACTERIA, Nitrifying
Macromolecular subunits in the walls of marine nitrifying bacteria. S. W. Watson and C. C. Remsen. bibliog il Science 163: 685-6 F 14 '69

BACTERIA, Nitrogen fixing
See also
Rhizobium

BACTERIA, Pathogenic
See also
Pasteurella pestis
Pneumococci

BACTERIA, Photosynthetic
Energy flux and membrane synthesis in photosynthetic bacteria. G. A. Sojka and others. bibliog il Science 166:113-15 O 3 '69

BACTERIAL growth. See Growth (bacteria)

BACTERIAL oxidation. See Oxidation, Physiological

BACTERIAL spores
Bacterial spores: chemical sensitization to heat. G. Alderton and N. Snell. bibliog il Science 163:1212-13 My 14 '69

BACTERIAL viruses. See Bacteriophages

BACTERIOLOGICAL warfare. See Biological warfare

BACTERIOLOGY
See also
Bacteriolysis

BACTERIOLYSIS
Cytophaga that kills or lyses algae. J. R. Stewart and R. M. Brown, jr. bibliog il Science 164:1523-4 Je 27 '69
See also
Lysozyme

BACTERIOPHAGES
Cytosine to thymine transitions from decay of cytosine-5-^{3}H in bacteriophage S13. F. Funk and S. Person. bibliog il Science 166:1629-31 D 26 '69
Genetic coding: oligonucleotide coding for first six amino acid residues of the coat protein of R17 bacteriophage. W. E. Robinson and others. bibliog il Science 166: 1291-3 D 5 '69

Mapping of deletions and substitutions in heteroduplex DNA molecules of bacteriophage lambda by electron microscopy. B. C. Westmoreland and others. bibliog il Science 163: 1343-8 Mr 21 '69
Multiplicity reactivation as a test for recombination function. R. J. Huskey. bibliog il Science 164:319-20 Ap 18 '69
1969 Nobel prize for physiology or medicine. G. Stent. Science 166:479-81 O 24 '69
Protein-bacteriophage conjugates: application in detection of antibodies and antigens. J. Haimovich and M. Sela. bibliog il Science 164:1279-80 Je 13 '69
Receptor site for a bacterial virus. R. Losick and P. W. Robbins. il Sci Am 221:120-4 bibliog(p 166) N '69
Self-assembly of Qβ and MS2 phage particles: possible function of initiation complexes. P. P. Hung and others. bibliog il Science 166:1638-40 D 26 '69
Short fragments from both complementary strands in the newly replicated DNA of bacteriophage SPP-1. M. Polsinelli and others. bibliog il Science 166:243-5 O 10 '69

BAD ISCHL, Austria
Emperor's pastry shop; Zauner of Bad Ischl. J. Friedberg. il Travel & Camera 32:60-1+ Jl '69

BAD taste. See Vulgarity

BADEN-Württemberg state theater ballet. See Stuttgart ballet

BADGER, Anthony
Gaucho acquires a wind vane. il Yachting 126:64+ Jl '69

BADGER, Nanci
Exploring the Galapagos. il Yachting 126: 64-6+ O '69

BADHAM, Michael
Stitch in time. Motor B 123:70-1+ Mr '69

BADISCHE anilin and soda-fabrik. See Chemical industries—Germany (Federal Republic)

BAER, Walter E.
Arbitrating the discharge and discipline of union officials. bibliog Mo Labor R 92:39-45 S '69

BAEZ, Joan
Song for a small voyager. pors McCalls 97: 44-5 Ja '70
about
Garden gathering. New Yorker 45:22-3 Ag 23 '69
Summer's gain, autumn's loss. R. L. Shayon. Sat R 52:55 Ag 23 '69
Swinging, singing, sloganry. S. Potter. por Am Rec G 35:507-8 F '69
Thumbs down, thumbs up. C. E. Fager. Chr Cent 86:1320 O 15 '69

BAFFA, John J. and Bartilucci, Nicholas
How to dispose of bulky wastes. Am City 84: 64-6+ N '69

BAGG, Terry R.
Sunburst, icones florarum sanctorumque; Musical offering; Perigee; poems. Poetry 114:234-7 Jl '69

BAGGAGE. See Luggage

BAGLEY, Elizabeth B.
Bittersweet charity. Chr Cent 86:1313 O 15 '69

BAGLEY, Wayne
Sketches from the Med. Yachting 126:59-61+ D '69

BAGPIPES
Rufus Harley's black bag. il Ebony 24:101-2+ Jl '69

BAGS
See also
Handbags

BAGS under the eyes. See Eyelids

BAHAMA ISLANDS
Walker Cay. W. R. Juettner. il Motor B 124:58-9 D '69
See also
Fishing—Bahama Islands
Grand Bahama Island
Nassau, Bahama Islands
Taxation—Bahama Islands
Tourist trade—Bahama Islands

History
Bahamas. J. H. Bounds. bibliog il Focus 19:1-7 My '69

Industries
Bahamas. J. H. Bounds. bibliog il Focus 19: 1-7 My '69

BAHCALL, John N.
Neutrinos from the sun; with biographical sketch. Sci Am 221:16, 28-37 bibliog (p 140) Jl '69

BAHIA. See Salvador, Brazil

BAHR, Jerome
Non-professional teachers enliven the subject matter. Clear House 43:494-6 Ap '69
BAHREIN
Bahrain. D. W. Marston. il Travel 132:61-7 N '69
BAIL
Bail for the rich, jail for the poor. H. Subin. Nation 208:363-6 Mr 24 '69
Crime war: the Nixon team's model plan; District of Columbia. il U S News 67:8 Jl 21 '69
Crimes while on bail; the hunt for a remedy. il U S News 66:42 F 17 '69
Jail before trial. A. S. Goldstein. New Repub 160:15-18 Mr 8 '69
Legal quackery in D.C. M. L. Wulf. Commonweal 89:668-9 F 28 '69
Presumption of guilt? legal experts discuss pretrial detention. Newsweek 74:67-8 N 10 '69
Preventive detention. il Time 93:76 F 14 '69
Preventive detention, corrective or corruptive? pro and con discussion. Sr Schol 94:10-11 Ap 11 '69
Reasonable man; wiretapping, pretrial detention & civil rights; address, August 13, 1969. J. N. Mitchell. Vital Speeches 35:678-81 S 1 '69
This month's feature: Congress and federal bail reform. Cong Digest 48:98-128 Ap '69
BAILEY, Anthony
Noise is a slow agent of death. N Y Times Mag p46-7+ N 23 '69
BAILEY, Charles W. and Wright, Frank
Defense establishment. Look 33:17-24+ Ag 26 '69
BAILEY, David
Style of the '60s. il por Time 94:81 D 12 '69
BAILEY, Francis Lee
For the defense. Newsweek 74:93 O 6 '69
BAILEY, Frederick Augustus Washington. See Douglass, F.
BAILEY, Frederick Marshman
Bold exploits of spy photographer. G. P. Hunt. por Life 66:3 Mr 21 '69
BAILEY, George R. See Breedlove, C. H. jr. jt. auth.
BAILEY, John M. Jr, and Schubart, Henry, Jr
One billion dollar subsidy for slums. Arch Forum 131:56-7 Jl; 10+ N '69
BAILEY, Lloyd W.
Time for reforms? Nixon's faithless elector. Sr Schol 94:22-3 Ja 31 '69
BAILEY, Pearl
To be or not to be nude. Cur 109:18-19 Ag '69
BAILEY, Peter
Black theater. Ebony 24:126-8+ Ag '69
Importance of being black. Newsweek 73:102-3 F 24 '69
Urban league conducts a guided tour. Ebony 24:48-50+ S '69
BAILEY, Richard W.
Build ANOD, an audible noise override. Radio-Electr 40:58 Ag '69
BAILEY, Roger
Susan and the elders. por Newsweek 73:37 Je 23 '69
BAILEY, Susan
Susan and the elders. por Newsweek 73:37 Je 23 '69
BAILEY, Susan R.
Sparkling surfaces. Sch Arts 69:11 Ja '70
BAILEY, William O.
Ahead: a new system of auto insurance? interview. por U S News 66:54-6 Ap 28 '69
BAILEY, go home; drama. See Cable, H.
BAIN, Helen
NEA president-elect. il por Sch & Soc 97:349-50 O '69
BAINBRIDGE, John
Another way of living; excerpt. McCalls 96:157-60 Ap '69
BAINBRIDGE ISLAND
What to do about roadside mess? Let children clean up after parents. il Sunset 142:104-5 My '69
BAIRD, Joseph Armstrong, Jr
California's pictorial letter sheets; excerpts. Antiques 96:412-17 S '69
BAIRD, William
Perils of the pill. A. Goldberg. Ramp Mag 7:45-6+ My '69
BAIT
Crash course in bugology; mayflies. A. I. Alexander, 3d. il Field & S 74:80 My '69
Eels take the prizes. G. Heinold. il Outdoor Life 144:54-5+ Ag '69
Live-lining saves the day. G. Heinold. il Outdoor Life 144:116-18 S '69
Pork rind and bluegill. T. Nixon. il Field & S 74:64-5+ Je '69

Recipe for winter bait; wax moth bait. W. L. Gojmerac; J. W. Slominski. il Field & S 74:50-1 D '69
See also
Crickets
Earthworms
Fishing lures, flies, etc.
BAJA CALIFORNIA. See California, Lower
BAKER, Augusta
Guidelines for black books: an open letter to juvenile editors; adaptation of address, May 8, 1969. por Pub W 196:131-3 Jl 14 '69
BAKER, Betty Jean
You're going to hear from her. G. Lees. Hi Fi 19:132 D '69
BAKER, Carlos
Egg man's daughter. New Repub 161:30+ Ag 23 '69
Ernest Hemingway: living, loving, dying; excerpt from Ernest Hemingway: a life story. Atlan 223:45-67 Ja; 91-5+ F '69
about
Authors & editors. R. H. Smith. por Pub W 195:15-17 Mr 31 '69
BAKER, Clyde J.
How to install chemical chains on your car. Pop Sci 195:143+ D '69
Make your own coolant-recovery system. Pop Sci 195:192 O '69
BAKER, Elizabeth C.
Barnett Newman in a new light. Art N 67:38-41+ F '69
Cambodian canons. Art N 68:28-31+ D '69
Secret life of John Chamberlain. Art N 68:48-51+ Ap '69
BAKER, Elliott
Penny wars; dramatization of novel. Criticism New Yorker 45:137 O 25 '69
BAKER, Erwin George
Bake. D. Wells. Motor T 21:94-5+ O '69
BAKER, Evelyn
Mums don't need good weather. Org Gard & Farm 16:74-5 N '69
BAKER, F. W. G.
Boost for IBP; letter. Science 164:245 Ap 18 '69
BAKER, Frank, and others
Changing mental hospital, its perceived image and contact with the community. bibliog Ment Hy 53:237-44 Ap '69
BAKER, H.
(tr) See Molière, J. B. P. Miser
BAKER, Howard D. See Lansford, T. G. jt. auth.
BAKER, Howard Henry, 1925-
Excerpt from address, March 24, 1969. Cong Digest 48:234+ O '69
BAKER, James Chamberlain, bp
Bishop Baker. F. T. Trotter. Chr Cent 86:1340 O 22 '69
Priest's tribute. J. A. O'Brien. Chr Cent 86:1549 D 3 '69
BAKER, John Hopkinson
John H. Baker, the Audubon years. por C. W. Buchheister and R. T. Peterson. Audubon 71:83-5 N '69
BAKER, John K. and Schaffer, R. H.
Making staff consulting more effective. Harvard Bsns R 47:62-71 Ja '69
BAKER, Joseph E.
Landmark case. il por Newsweek 73:73 Je 9 '69
BAKER, Paul T.
Human adaptation to high altitude. bibliog Science 163:1149-56 Mr 14 '69
BAKER, Robert Gene
New light on how Bobby Baker rose to riches? por U S News 67:8 Jl 28 '69
BAKER, Russell
Conglomeration of Newt Ogilvy. Life 66:4 Ap 18 '69
Don't ask me, I only live here. Life 67:32-7 Jl 25 '69
Excellence of Welby Stitch jr. Life 66:24 Mr 21 '69
Good things that undone poor Gum. Life 67:16B Ag 15 '69
Land of the powerful nostrils. Arch Forum 131:90 N '69
Wanted: new heads for old ivy. Life 66:28B My 23 '69
We're rotten. Laura. Rotten to the core. Life 66:18D F 21 '69
Who is the man in the White House? Look 33:92+ D 16 '69
BAKER, Samm Sinclair
Nonfiction, three to one. Writer 82:19-20+ Ja '69
about
Lock that up in your Funk & Wagnalls. R. L. Shayon. Sat R 52:48-9 N 22 '69

BAKER, Willis M.
Reminiscing about the TVA. por Am For 75:
30-1+ My '69
BAKER and Taylor company
Baker & Taylor expands in Somerville, New
Jersey. Pub W 195:26 My 5 '69
BAKERS and bakeries
If you're starved for real old-fashioned bread,
there's a little man in Paris. D. Muscatine.
il Holiday 46:74-5 S '69
    See also
American bakeries company
National biscuit company
BAKERS ISLAND
Reports. K. Spivack. Atlan 224:22-3 Ag '69
BAKERSFIELD fuel and gas championship.
See Automobile racing
BAKING
    See also
Bakers and bakeries
Bread
Cake
Coffee cake
Pastry
Pie
BALAGUER, Joaquin
Good house; address, January 27, 1969. Vital
Speeches 35:327-9 Mr 15 '69

    about
Inflaming the inflammable. il por Time 93:39
Mr 7 '69
BALAKIAN, Anna
Program to remake human understanding.
Sat R 52:19-21 My 31 '69
BALAKIREV, Milii Alekseevich
Balakirev, by E. Garden. Review
Am Rec pors 35:578-82 Mr '69. J. Ringo
Two by Balakirev. M. N. Kanny. Am Rec
G 35:556 Mr '69

BALANCE of nature. See Ecology
BALANCE of payments
American share in the stream of interna-
tional payments; with questions and an-
swers. R. V. Roosa. Ann Am Acad 384:21-34
Jl '69
Balance of payments is still a worry. il Bsns
W p34 N 22 '69
Big problem is still inflation. il Newsweek
73:90+ My 26 '69
Bit of cheer for Mr Wilson. il Bsns W p54+
S 20 '69
Booming economy drains off the surplus. il
Bsns W p26+ Ap 5 '69
Changing policy of trade deficit. U S News
66:73 Ap 14 '69
Declining balance. Fortune 79:32+ Ap '69
Financing the world empire. M. Hudson.
Commonweal 91:243-5 N 21 '69
Government, business, and the balance of
payments; address, March 26, 1969. J. J.
Powers, jr. Vital Speeches 35:430-4 My 1 '69
Hard choices for the embattled dollar. R. N.
Gardner. il Sat R 52:46+ N 22 '69
How safe is the dollar now? il U S News 67:
19-21 S 1 '69
Indelicate balance. il Fortune 80:40+ N '69
Market fever zigzags down; foreign exchange
markets taking a breather. il Bsns W p25-7
Ag 23 '69
Payments gap yawns wider. Bsns W p34
My 17 '69
Uncompetitive U.S. Time 94:69 Ag 22 '69
U.S. balance of payments; statement, April
4, 1969. R. M. Nixon. Dept State Bul 60:
403-4 My 12 '69
Why deficits stir world tension. il Bsns W
p88 F 22 '69
    See also
Balance of trade
BALANCE of power
Can U.S. quit as world policeman? interview,
ed. by J. Fromm. A. Buchan. U S News
66:48-51 F 17 '69
Dynamics of the arms race. G. W. Rathjens.
il Sci Am 220:15-25 biblog(p 146) Ap '69
Price of power for U.S. il U S News 66:29-31
F 3 '69
Russia's new target; Asia. il U S News 67:
32-4 Ag 11 '69
Strike three and out. J. Burnham. Nat R 21:
531+ Je 3 '69
To guard the guards. J. Burnham. Nat R
21:583 Je 17 '69
U.S. invented the imbalance of power. J. P.
Davies. il N Y Times Mag p50-1+ D 7 '69
Vicious acronyms. R. E. Lapp. il New Repub
160:15-19 Je 21 '69
World power and population. C. Clark. il
Nat R 21:481-4 My 20 '69
    See also
Great powers
Hegemony
World politics

BALANCE of trade
Britain clamps down harder. il Bsns W p42+
Ap 19 '69
Help on the way for U.S. exporters. il Bsns
W p33-4 N 22 '69
Is U.S. being squeezed out of world markets?
interview. M. H. Stans. il U S News 67:
56-9 S 8 '69
World trade and investment; address, March
10, 1969. R. A. Peterson. Vital Speeches 35:
413-16 Ap 15 '69
    See also
Balance of payments
BALANCED diet. See Diet
BALANCHINE, George
Balanchine+girls=ballet. R. Kotlowitz. il
Holiday 45:54-7+ Mr '69
Return to Monte Carlo. il por Newsweek
73:93 Je 30 '69
Russian heaven. H. Saal. il por Newsweek
73:102 Ap 14 '69
BALAND, Timothy
Fun in words. Nation 208:547 Ap 28 '69
BALD eagles. See Eagles
BALDERSTON, C. Canby
Fiscal and monetary policy. bibliog f Ann Am
Acad 379:78-82 S '68
BALDNESS
Personal business; hair transplants and weav-
ing, hair styling, and hairpieces. Bsns W
p89-90 Ap 5 '69
BALDWIN, Clifford G.
Hark, the hounds. Outdoor Life 143:66-19+ Mr
'69
BALDWIN, Hanson Weightman
NATO: an alliance in search of a future.
Read Digest 94:161-2+ Ap '69
BALDWIN, James
Sweet Lorraine. Esquire 72:139-40 N '69
BALDWIN, Malcolm F.
Snowmobile and environmental quality. Liv
Wildn 32:14-17 Wint '68
BALDWIN, Nancy H.
Changing the base on a wheel-thrown
pot. Ceram Mo 17:20-2 N '69
BALDWIN, Roger
Norman Thomas: a memoir. por Sat R 52:
41-2 Ap 12 '69
BALDWIN, William
Decorator speaks his mind. House & Gard
136:12-13+ O; 12-13+ N; 10-11 D '69
Good taste has no price tag. House & Gard
135:38+ My '69
Logic of the eye. House & Gard 135:72+ Ap
'69
Sterility of perfection. House & Gard 135:38-
9 Je '69
BALEARIC ISLANDS
    See also
Iviza (island)
BALES, Carol
Slum in winter, the street and the park; pho-
tographs. Trans-Action 60:20-1 F '69
BALES, William
Project for the farthest-out college. J. Ander-
son. il por Dance Mag 43:45-6+ F '69
BALESTI, Sandra
On the boards. W. Como. por Dance Mag
43:20 Jl '69
BALI
Bali. R. Crawford and K. Crawford. il Travel
132:42-5 O '69
Bali by the back roads. D. K. Grosvenor
and G. M. Grosvenor. il Nat Geog 136:
656-97 N '69
Bali hi. T. Gerst. il Travel & Camera 32:
52-3+ My '69
Hello Bali; with photographs by C. Rent-
meester and account. by M. Leatherbee.
Life 66:42-56 Ja 31 '69
On the road to Bali. T. Fox. Commonweal
90:556-7 S 19 '69
BALIN, Robert P.
[Electronics quiz] See issues of Popular elec-
tronics to September, 1969
LCR circuits quiz. Electr World 82:99+ N '69
BALINESE dancing. See Dancing, Balinese
BALINT, Nicholas G.
(comp) As others see us. See issues of Satur-
day review
(comp) Letters to the world's editors. See
issues of Saturday review
BALKE, Betty T.
Crafts programs gets whoops from the hol-
lows. Am Ed 5:25-6 Je '69
BALL, George W.
Slogans and realities. For Affairs 47:623-41
Jl '69
We should de-escalate the importance of
Vietnam. por N Y Times Mag p6-7+ D 21
'69
BALL, Hilary
Portrait of Hilary; with editorial comment by
R. Graves. pors Life 67:1, 97-101 N 7 '69

BALL, Howard T.
County's responsibilities for recreation. Parks
& Rec 3:35-6+ O '68
BALL, John
Johnny get your gun; novel. Good H 169:73-5
S '69
BALL, Robert
Foreign aid for Wall Street. Fortune 80:125+
Ag 15 '69
BALL, Robert M.
Is medicare worth the price? interview. por
U S News 67:48-51 Jl 21 '69
BALL, William B.
Hidden bonus to education. Parents Mag 44:
66-7+ Mr '69
BALL joints. See Joints (engineering)
BALL point pens. See Fountain pens
BALLAD of Baby Doe; opera. See Moore, D. S.
BALLADS
See also
Phonograph records—Folk music
BALLADS, American
Collector's choice; Border affair. A. E. Fife.
il Am West 6:26-7 Mr '69
Songs of the pioneers. J. M. Park. il Améri-
cas 21:21-8 My '69
BALLARD, Florence
Former Supreme talks a little. il pors Ebony
24:83-6+ F '69
BALLERINAS. See Dancers
BALLET
Hot ballet with a freezing finale. il Life 66:
30-1 Ap 4 '69
Looking at the dance; excerpts. E. Denby.
il Dance Mag 43:51-9 Ja '69
Presstime news. See issues of Dance maga-
zine
Reviews. See issues of Dance magazine
Why shouldn't parents say, sure, I'll let
my son become a dancer. E. Villella. il Life
66:58 Je 6 '69
See also
Choreography
Moving pictures—Dance films
Television broadcasting—Dancing

Bibliography

Books in print; comp. by R. Fentress. il Dance
Mag 43:51-8 Mr '69

Competitions

Contest in Moscow; international ballet com-
petition. W. Terry. il Sat R 52:39-40 Ag 9 '69
USSR's first International ballet competition.
B. Dean; J. Barker. il Dance Mag 43:26-8+
Ag '69; Discussion. 43:26 Ag; 23+ O '69

History

Making of The three-cornered hat; excerpts
from memoirs; symposium. il Dance Mag
43:34-8+ S '69
Sleeping beauty; history of her perambu-
lations. J. Anderson. il Dance Mag 43:37-
9+ Je '69

Study and teaching

American teacher in Leningrad; month at
the Kirov's Vaganova choreographic tech-
nicum. J. Anderson. il Dance Mag 43:24-7
Ja '69
Flamboyant maestro; a portrait of Hector
Zaraspe. il Dance Mag 43:62-5 O '69
Leon Danielian at the helm; director of
American ballet theatre school. R. Gold. il
Dance Mag 43:60-3 Ag '69
National conference on ballet in higher edu-
cation; a report on the meetings. May 15-
17, 1969. D. McLain. Dance Mag 43:88 Jl '69

Austria

Scandalous and delightful; Viennese children
on tour. F. Crisp. il Dance Mag 43:29-31 Ag
'69

Canada

Les Feux-follets. M. Siegel. il Dance Mag
43:64-7 S '69

Czechoslovakia

See also
Prague ballet

Denmark

See also
Royal Danish ballet

France

France; the ballet world of Anna Galina.
R. Estrada. il Dance Mag 43:64-7 My '69

Germany (Federal Republic)

Dancing master; interview. ed. by J. Boutwell. J. Cranko. il Opera N 34:17-20 O 11
'69

Great Britain

New angles in English dance. il Dance Mag
43:34-5 My '69
See also
Royal academy of dancing
Royal ballet, Great Britain

Israel

Building a new dance in a new country. D.
Sowden. il Dance Mag 43:62-4 Ja '69

Mexico

See also
Ballet folklórico of Mexico

Norway

Norway; interview. ed. by O. Maynard. S.
Arova. il Dance Mag 43:41-3+ My '69

Philippines

Vivacity of Philippine folk ballet. il UNESCO
Courier 22:26-9+ F '69

Russia

Ballet news from the Soviet Union. Y. Suritz.
Dance Mag 43:95 Mr '69
USSR's first International ballet competition.
B. Dean; J. Barker. il Dance Mag 43:26-8+
Ag '69; Discussion. 43:26 Ag; 23+ O '69
See also
Bolshoi ballet
Kirov ballet

Spain

Mariano Parra ballet espanol; Town Hall. M.
Marks. Dance Mag 43:90+ My '69

Sweden

Sweden: theatre child; Niklas Ek. M. Kats.
il Dance Mag 43:49-50 My '69
Swedish ballet triumph; summer festival. W.
Terry. il Sat R 52:22-3+ Jl 5 '69

United States

Spot check: some observations on the dance
in America. J. Claman. il Harp Baz 102:
122P-122Q F '69
BALLET, Photography of. See Photography
of dancing
BALLET center of Buffalo. See Dance schools
BALLET companies
See also
American ballet company
American ballet theatre
Atlanta ballet
Ballet russe de Monte Carlo
Boston ballet company
City center Joffrey ballet
Harkness ballet
National ballet
New York city ballet
Royal ballet, Great Britain
BALLET costume. See Costume, Theatrical
BALLET dancers. See Dancers
BALLET design. See Theater—Stage scenery
BALLET festivals. See Dance festivals
BALLET folklórico of Mexico
Ballet folklorico; City center. J. Dowlin. Dance
Mag 43:90 My '69
Folk ballet; high-class hybrids. il Time 93:80
Ap 4 '69
Viva Amalia y Mexico! W. Terry. il Sat R
52:60 Ap 12 '69
BALLET music
Introduction to music for the choreographer.
R. G. Long. il Dance Mag 43:63-5 F '69
BALLET notation. See Dance notation
BALLET russe de Monte Carlo
Return to Monte Carlo. il Newsweek 73:93
Je 30 '69
BALLET theatre. See American ballet theatre
BALLETS
Back to fundamentals; New York city bal-
let's world première of Robbins' Dances at
a gathering. il Time 93:67 My 30 '69
Making of The three-cornered hat; excerpts
from memoirs; symposium. il Dance Mag
43:34-8+ S '69
Scandalous and delightful; Viennese children
on tour. F. Crisp. il Dance Mag 43:29-31 Ag
'69
World of dance. W. Terry. il Sat R 52:69-71
Mr 22 '69

Choreographies

See Choreography

Criticisms

Animus
Dance Mag 43:29 My '69
Astarte
Dance Mag 43:29+ My '69

BALLETS—Criticisms—*Continued*
  Les biches
    Sat R 52:39 S 6 '69
  Brahms quintet
    Sat R il 53:77 Ja 3 '70
  Brahms variations
    Sat R 52:39 S 6 '69
  Coppelia
    Dance Mag il 43:30-2+ F '69
  Cortege burlesque
    Newsweek il 74:91 N 3 '69
  Dances at a gathering
    Life il 67:49 O 3 '69
    New Yorker 45:96 My 31 '69
    Newsweek il 73:103 Je 2 '69
    Sat R il 52:41-2 Jl 26 '69
  Enigma variations
    Newsweek il 73:117 My 5 '69
    Sat R 52:42 My 24 '69
  Facade
    Dance Mag 43:29 My '69
  Fantasies
    Dance Mag 43:86+ Ap '69
    New Yorker 44:95 F 15 '69
  Giselle
    Dance Mag 43:24-7 D '69
    Sat R il 52:54 Ag 23 '69
  Metastaseis & Pithoprakta
    New Yorker 44:96 F 15 '69
  Moments
    Dance Mag 43:36+ Mr '69
  Pas de deux: la source
    Dance Mag 43:85 Ap '69
  Peer Gynt
    Dance Mag 43:29+ S '69
  Pelléas and Mélisande
    Sat R 52:38 My 31 '69
  Peter and the wolf
    Dance Mag 43:36+ Je '69
    Sat R 52:51-2 Ap 19 '69
  Poppet
    Dance Mag 43:85 D '69
    Sat R 52:40 N 8 '69
  Prince Igor
    Dance Mag 43:26 My '69
  Rakhel Kafri's interview
    Dance Mag 43:87 Jl '69
  Romeo and Juliet
    New Yorker 45:138 My 17 '69
    Sat R 52:45 Je 7 '69
    Sat R il 52:57 O 25 '69
  Sleeping beauty
    New Yorker 45:124+ My 10 '69
  Stages and reflections
    Dance Mag il 43:34+ Mr '69
  Swan lake
    New Yorker 45:124 My 10 '69
    Sat R 52:42 Jl 26 '69
  La sylphide
    Sat R il 52:46 N 1 '69
  Taming of the shrew
    Sat R il 52:44-5 Je 7 '69
  Tchaikovsky suite
    Dance Mag 43:85-6 Ap '69
    New Yorker 44:95 F 15 '69
  Three-cornered hat
    Dance Mag 43:85 D '69
    Dance Mag il 43:37-8 N '69
    New Yorker 45:148 O 25 '69
    Sat R 52:65+ O 18 '69
  Wax
    Dance Mag 43:76 Jl '69
  William Tell variations
    Dance Mag 43:29 My '69

Production and direction
  See Dance production
BALLIETT, Whitney
  Jazz (cont) New Yorker 45:167-8+ Mr 15;
    139-40+ My 17; 98+ My 31 '69
  Musical events (cont) New Yorker 45:76-7
    Je 28; 73-4+ Jl 19 '69
  Our far-flung correspondents. New Yorker 45:
    175-6+ O 18 '69
BALLINGER, Charles O.
  Glassware patents by Charles Ballinger. A. G.
    Peterson. il Hobbies 74:98DD-98EE Je '69
BALLISTIC missile early warning system
  DOD accelerates plan to deploy early warn-
    ing satellite system. Aviation W 92:18
    Ja 12 '70
BALLISTIC photometers. See Photometers
BALLOON ascensions
  Winds aloft; learning to fly a hot air bal-
    loon. K. Connes. Flying 85:132 O '69
BALLOON astronomy. See Balloons—Use in
  research
BALLOON racing
  Lift up your balloon unto the hills; Interna-
    tional high alpine ballooning week. il
    Esquire 71:82-7 Mr '69

BALLOONS
  Sailing the waveless sea. G. Kirschenbaum.
    il Travel & Camera 32:56-63 Ap '69
  Up, up and away! il Mech illus 65:40-1 Ag '69
    See also
  Balloon ascensions

Use in research
  Space astronomy; AAAS symposium, De-
    cember 28, 1969. M. D. Papagiannis. il Sci-
    ence 166:775-6 N 7 '69
    See also
  Balloons, Meteorological
BALLOONS, Meteorological
  Superpressure balloon flights in the tropical
    stratosphere. V. E. Lally and others. bib-
    liog il Science 166:738-9 N 7 '69
BALLS
    See also
  Bowling balls
  Golf balls
BALLS (parties)
  Ball game; charity dances, dinners, and
    shows collect millions. il Bsns W p44+ My
    17 '69
  Biography of a charity ball. T. Meehan. il
    N Y Times Mag p 12-13+ Je 1 '69
  Viennese opera ball celebrating the hundreth
    anniversary of Vienna state opera. il Opera
    N 33:14-16 Ap 12 '69
BALM in Gilead; story. See Fremantle, A.
BALMORAL castle. See Castles
BALTIMORE
  City: requiem for the Block. il Time 93:16-17
    Mr 28 '69

City planning
  Baltimore breaks out of its shell. il Bsns
    W p56-8+ F 15 '69
  Biggest snarl on city highways. il Bsns W
    p 144+ O 18 '69
  Charles center. J. M. Dixon. il Arch Forum
    130:48-57 My '69
  How S.O.M. took on the Baltimore road gang.
    J. Bailey. il Arch Forum 130:40-5 Mr '69

Crime
  Cage of fear; crime in Baltimore; with report
    by J. Rosenthal. il Life 67:16-23 Jl 11 '69

Description
  Personal business. Bsns W p 148 O 11 '69

Education
  Early school admissions; a Baltimore best
    seller. A. C. Harding. il Todays Ed 58:57-8+
    N '69

Housing
  Spotlight on blockbusting. T. M. Gannon.
    America 120:563-4 My 10 '69

Libraries
    See also
  Enoch Pratt free library

Music
    See also
  Baltimore civic opera company
  Chamber opera society of Baltimore

Recreation
  Unique recreationist: J. McCraw is blind but
    far from handicapped. D. Samuels. il Parks
    & Rec 4:35+ Jl '69
  Weaving as a creative art; Recreation de-
    partment program. V. M. West. il Parks &
    Rec 3:41-2+ O '68
BALTIMORE civic opera company
  Report: performance of Otello. M.
    DeSchauensee. Opera N 34:40 D 27 '69
BALTIMORE Orioles (baseball). See Baseball
  clubs
BALTIMORE sun
  Agnew vs. the Sun. il Newsweek 74:46 D 29
    '69
  Letters from an American mother; hoax by
    Holger A. Koppel. E. Lund. il Am Heri-
    tage 21:44-5 D '69
BALTO (dog) See Eskimo dogs
BAMBOO
  Making bamboo handles. C. C. Miller. il
    Ceram Mo 17:28-9 O '69
BANANA melon. See Melon
BANANAS, Joe. See Bonanno, J.
BAND instruments
  Face to face with a one-man band. D. Muro.
    Seventeen 28:133 F '69
BAND music
  Russian horn bands. R. Ricks. bibliog f il
    Mus Q 55:364-71 Jl '69
BANDEIRA, Fagundes
  Brazil: subverting the universities. New
    Repub 161:17-19 N 8 '69

BANDITS. See Brigands and robbers

BANDS (music)
Big little band in Toronto. R. Gehman. il Sat R 52:46-7 F 8 '69
Booker T. and the M.G.'s. P. Garland. il Ebony 24:92-4+ Ap '69
Down to old Dixie and back; The band. il Time 95:42-6 Ja 12 '70
Jazz at the White House; Modern jazz quartet at state dinner. S. Dance. il Sat R 52:73+ N 15 '69
Jazz; so-called world's greatest jazz band. W. Balliett. New Yorker 45:139-40+ My 17 '69
Musical events; C. Mingus' appearances at Village Vanguard. W. Balliett. New Yorker 45:76-7 Je 28 '69
Notes and comment; D. Ellington at the Rainbow grill. New Yorker 45:23 Ag 9 '69
Teen scene; boys in the bands. il Seventeen 28:132-3 F '69
Where are they now? Charlie Spivak and his band. il Newsweek 75:10 Ja 12 '70
See also
Band music
Rock 'n' roll groups

BANDS, College
University of Minnesota band returns from tour of Soviet Union; excerpts from remarks, May 23, 1969. R. M. Nixon; A. F. Dobrynin. Dept State Bul 60:540-2 Je 23 '69

BANGKOK
Description
Bangkok revisited. A. Waugh. Nat R 21:242+ Mr 11 '69

BANGOR Punta corporation
Piper proves elusive prize. il Bsns W p62+ Ag 16 '69

BANISTER, John R.
Overdue. por Wilson Lib Bul 44:561+ Ja '70

BANISTER, Judith
English provincial silver in a London collection. Antiques 96:106-13 Jl '69

BANJO
Cadwell's banjo; interview. P. Cadwell. New Yorker 45:39-41 Ap 12 '69

BANK, Stanley
Literary hero for adolescents; the adolescent; adaptation of address, September 1968. Engl J 58:1013-20 O '69

BANK advertising
Enticers, 1970; tempting new depositors with free gifts. E. Kendall. Vogue 155:119+ Ja 15 '70
Premium race. Newsweek 75:50 Ja 5 '70

BANK buildings
Architectural interiors for banks with divergent problems; Banco do Brasil and American bank and trust company, New York. il Arch Rec 146:113-20 Ag '69
Bank with a past in its future; Bank of California. J. M. Fitch. il Arch Forum 130: 68-75 My '69
Evolution of a special form to meet its program; First national bank of Chicago. il Arch Rec 145:192-6 Ap '69
Federal reserve in suspense; new head office, Minneapolis. il Arch Forum 130:100-5 Ja '69
Sculptured precast tower paces downtown redevelopment; Virginia national bank. il Arch Rec 146:141-4 O '69

BANK checks. See Checks

BANK consolidations and mergers
Alabama's battling bankers; aborted Central-State national merger. Bsns W p60 Ag 2 '69

BANK credit. See Credit

BANK credit cards. See Credit cards

BANK deposits
Interest
Burns's problem; what to do about regulation Q. Bsns W p78 N 15 '69

BANK employees
See also
Strikes—United States—Bank employees

BANK failures
Carefree collapse; Texas. Time 94:89-90 S 12 '69

BANK for international settlements
Reports; Basel. D. Cook. Atlan 224:14-15+ Jl '69
Tough talk on paper gold. Bsns W p43 Je 14 '69
Weathering the storm. Newsweek 73:99+ My 26 '69

BANK holding companies
Bankers in a cross fire; attempted takeover of Chemical bank by Leasco data processing equipment corp. il Fortune 79:43-4 Ap '69
Banks' paper route is coming to stop. Bsns W p35-6 N 8 '69

Banks win point in holding campaign. Bsns W p 15 Jl 5 '69
Block that loophole. il Newsweek 73:60 Ap 7 '69
Brace of blockbusters; antitrust suit against First national city corp. of New York. Newsweek 73:84+ Je 23 '69
Case for the one-bank holding company. S. Rose. il Fortune 79:162-5+ My 15 '69
Going shopping at your bank; how it soon may work. il U S News 66:76-7 F 3 '69
Growth-minded banks take fight to Senate; with editorial comment. Bsns W p42+, 164 N 15 '69
Holding action; new proposals for government regulation. Newsweek 73:66+ Mr 3 '69
Line is drawn on banks; Administration bill to regulate one-bank holding companies. Bsns W p42-3 Mr 29 '69
New realities of corporate powers; interview. ed. by G. R. Rosen. A. A. Berle. il Duns R 92:43-5+ D '68
One-bank holding companies; a banker's view. J. R. Bunting, jr. bibliog f il Harvard Bsns R 47:99-106 My '69
One-bank holding companies; the public interest. P. S. Nadler. Harvard Bsns R 47: 107-13 My '69
Plug for bank loophole; one-bank holding companies. Bsns W p28 F 15 '69
What company can banks keep? Bsns W p37 Je 21 '69
Youth movement stirs the banks; one-bank holding company. il Bsns W p 120-2+ Je 14 '69
See also
Wachovia corporation

BANK loans. See Loans, Bank

BANK notes
See also
Paper money

BANK of America national trust and savings association
And now the cashomat; cash dispenser. il Time 94:91 O 10 '69
New boss for the biggest. il Time 94:50 D 26 '69
Under the wire; passing the big Eastern banks internationally. il Forbes 103:61-2 Je 15 '69

BANK of China
Defying red China; actions by Singapore. Newsweek 73:102+ My 26 '69

BANK of London and South America
Yanqui bankers feel competition's bite il Bsns W p50-1 D 27 '69

BANK rates. See Interest

BANK robberies. See Robberies and assaults

BANKAMERICARDS. See Credit cards

BANKERS
See also
American bankers association
Bleichröder, G. von

BANKHEAD, Tallulah
Unforgettable Tallulah. A. Loos. por Read Digest 95:130-4 Jl '69

BANKING law
Alabama's bankers fall out on branching; Central bank of Birmingham tackles grandfather clause in 1911 law. il Bsns W p92+ My 17 '69
Alabama's battling bankers. Bsns W p60 Ag 2 '69
Beirut bank reform pays dividends; stringent controls following Intra bank scandal. il Bsns W p54 Mr 15 '69
Finance outlook; Fed buys trouble with Regulation Q. Bsns W p 130 Ja 18 '69
Line is drawn on banks; Administration bill to regulate one-bank holding companies. Bsns W p42-3 Mr 29 '69
What company can banks keep? Bsns W p37 Je 21 '69
See also
Banks and banking—Regulation

BANKRUPTCY
Winners and losers; garnishment & bankruptcy in Wisconsin; excerpts from Debtors in court. H. Jacob. il Trans-Action 6: 24-32 My '69

BANKS, Ernie
Ageless Ernie, keeper of a dream. il pors Ebony 24:136-8 Je '69
Mr Cub. il por Time 93:52 My 30 '69
Tale of two men and one city. M. Kram. il pors Sports Illus 31:78-80+ S 29 '69

BANKS, Lacy J.
Vikings' front four. Ebony 25:83-6+ Ja '70

BANKS, Virginia F.
Deeper understanding of children. Todays Ed 58:31-2 F '69

BANKS, Coin
Old mechanical banks. F. H. Griffith. See issues of Hobbies

BANKS, Negro. See Banks and banking—United States

BANKS and banking
Fifty largest commercial banks outside the U.S. il Fortune 80:112-14 Ag 15 '69
See also
Consumer credit
Credit
Discount
Foreign exchange
Interest
Loans, Bank
Mortgage banks
Safe deposit boxes
Savings and loan associations

Advertising
See Bank advertising

Anecdotes, facetiae, satire, etc.
End of a beautiful friendship with my friendly bank. B. Pfizer. McCalls 96:92-3 Mr '69

Branch banking
Alabama's bankers fall out on branching; Central bank of Birmingham tackles grandfather clause in 1911 law. il Bsns W p92+ My 17 '69

Checking accounts
Banks go psychedelic to lure customers; scrambling for demand deposits. il Bsns W p78+ Je 21 '69
Check up on your checkbook (and your bank) checking account records. il Changing T 23:13-14 Mr '69
Free checking accounts; services to seniors. F. C. Weed. Har Yrs 9:22-3 O '69

Credit service
See also
Banks and banking—Freight payment plan

Finance
Bank profits boom, small business pines. il Newsweek 75:69-70 Ja 19 '70
Big banks turn a big quarter. Bsns W p43 Jl 12 '69
Profit squeeze spreads to banks. Bsns W p50 O 11 '69
Tougher slogging ahead? il Forbes 104:28-9 Ag 15 '69

Freight payment plan
Freight shippers enter the checkless society; Chase Manhattan bank's Computer oriented freight remittance system. Bsns W p33 My 31 '69

Holding companies
See Bank holding companies

International aspects
Under the wire; passing the big Eastern banks internationally. il Forbes 103:61-2 Je 15 '69

Protection
Transfer: Wellington fund securities moved from First Pennsylvania banking & trust co, Philadelphia, to State street bank & trust co, Boston. New Yorker 45:23-7 Jl 12 '69

Public relations
Georgia's cracker's crackerjack bank; Citizens & southern national bank of Georgia. R. Loving, jr. il Fortune 80:134-7+ N '69

Regulation
Banks get FCC static on radio-TV stocks. Bsns W p41 Je 7 '69
Case for the one-bank holding company. S. Rose. il Fortune 79:162-5+ My 15 '69
Growth-minded banks take fight to Senate; with editorial comment. Bsns W p42+, 164 N 15 '69
Next place to tighten; possible new move to control bank credit. il Bsns W p45-6 Je 28 '69
Will the Fed lose its bank jobs? Bsns W p 144 S 20 '69

Safety devices and measures
Outdoing Bonnie and Clyde; Bank protection act, requires minimal precautions. il Time 93:92 F 14 '69

Securities
Booming banks. Duns R 93:123-5 My '69

Securities handling
Easy way to buy stock in foreign firms; American depositary receipts. il Changing T 23:46 Mr '69

Importing the action in foreign securities; American depositary receipts. il Bsns W p90+ F 8 '69

Service
One-bank holding companies: the public interest. P. S. Nadler. Harvard Bsns R 47: 107-13 My '69

Trust departments
New realities of corporate power; interview, ed. by G. R. Rosen. A. A. Berle. il Duns R 92:43-5+ D '68

California
See also
Bank of America national trust and savings association

Canada
Taking out the starch from Canada's banks. il Bsns W p92-4+ Ag 23 '69

China (People's Republic)
See also
Bank of China

Germany (Federal Republic)
Germany's banks flex muscles; function as investment bankers, underwriting issues of securities, and as stockbrokers. il Bsns W p96-8 My 24 '69

Great Britain
See also
Bank of London and South America

Lebanon
Beirut bank reform pays dividends; stringent controls following Intra bank scandal. il Bsns W p54 Mr 15 '69

Mexico
See also
Finance—Mexico

Switzerland
Brothers to Dillinger; House banking and currency committee looking into secret accounts. Newsweek 74:90+ D 15 '69
Nobody here but us foreigners? money smugglers. il Forbes 103:24-7 My 1 '69
Stocks the Swiss banks don't like. J. Ross-Skinner. il Duns R 92:23-5 D '68
Swiss gnomes start to swing. il Bsns W p 120 N 8 '69

United States
Assets for the ghetto; Negro-owned and operated banks. il Time 93:89 F 28 '69
Divergent directions of bank profits. il Fortune 80:33-4 Ag 1 '69
Fifty largest commercial banks. Fortune 79: 190-1 My 15 '69
Some banks now offer concessions to seniors, but number is unknown. Aging 170:19 D '68
Whole new groove in banking. J. Poindexter. il Duns R 93:38-41 Ap '69
See also
American bankers association
Bank failures
Banking law
Money—United States
United States—Federal reserve board
  also subhead Banks under names of cities, e.g. New York (city)—Banks

BANKS and banking, Cooperative
See also
Credit unions

BANKS and banking, International
Bankers team up to go abroad; Allied bank international. il Bsns W p88-9+ N 8 '69
See also
Bank for international settlements
International bank for reconstruction and development

BANNED books. See Prohibited books

BANNERS. See Flags

BANNON, Anthony
Writing and selling to city magazines. Writer 82:24-6 S '69

BANTA, Merle
Making money on leisure time. il pors Bsns W p62-4+ Ja 18 '69

BANTAM books, incorporated
Extra! instant books. il Newsweek 73:98-9 Mr 31 '69

BANZHAF, John F. 3d
Power of the press, and of television. R. L. Tobin. il Sat R 52:47-8 Je 14 '69

BAPTISM
Baptism and liturgical integrity; R. H. Bolton. il Chr Cent 86:369-72 Mr 19 '69; Discussion. 86:846-8, 1109-13 Je 18, Ag 27 '69

BAPTISTS
See also
Mennonites
BAPTISTS in the United States
American Baptists in annual session. R. G.
Middleton. Chr Cent 86:822-4 Je 11 '69
Baptists and church taxation. America 121:
373 N 1 '69
Baptists face issues, in living color; American Baptist convention. E. Plowman. Chr
Today 13:41 Je 6 '69
Battle of the book; Southern Baptist liberals
challenge fundamentalist literature. Newsweek 73:96-7 My 5 '69
Black Baptist sees red in reparations manifesto; National Baptist convention, USA,
inc. Chr Today 14:46-7 O 10 '69
Black concern in the Baptist general conference. Chr Today 13:37 Ag 1 '69
Catholics, Southern Baptists in dialogue. R.
Ryland. Chr Cent 86:816-17 Je 11 '69
Southern Baptist tunes: the fall conventions.
J. Rohler. Chr Today 14:32 D 19 '69
Southern Baptists and the Bible. Chr Today
13:34 Ap 25 '69
Southern Baptists: authority and autonomy.
Chr Today 13:23 Jl 4 '69
Southern Baptists avert showdown. R. L.
Love. Chr Today 13:33-4 Jl 4 '69
Southern Baptists hold firm course; annual
meeting. D. Stepp. Chr Cent 86:961-2 Jl 16
'69
Southern Baptists preach: the day of judgment is about to come. B. Surface. Il N Y
Times Mag p30-2+ Ag 24 '69; Reply. F. A.
Sharp. p22+ S 14 '69
Southern Baptists try self-analysis. A. P.
Klausler. Chr Cent 86:660-1 My 7 '69
That old-time religion; non-progress report
on Southern Baptists. B. W. Eggler. New
Repub 161:15-17 O 11 '69
Two racial firsts for Southern Baptists. Chr
Cent 86:705 My 21 '69
Valley Forge; summer of discontent. E. E.
Plowman. Chr Today 13:50 S 12 '69
BAR-ILLAN, David
Drop-in night at the Electric circus. Sat R
52:72-3 N 15 '69
BARACH, Philip G.
U.S. shoe: diversification dropout. il por
Bsns W p52-3 S 6 '69
BARANGER, Michel, and Sorensen, R. A.
Size and shape of atomic nuclei; with biographical sketches. Sci Am 221:12, 58-64+
Ag '69
BARBADOS
Maddox: House of Messel; with photograph
by Snowdon. P. Devlin. Vogue 153:194-201
Mr 1 '69
Description and travel
Barbados. A. Bower. il Harp Baz 102:82+
Ap '69
Where to go. S. Lord. Harp Baz 102:167 My
'69
**BARBADOS oceanographic and meteorological
experiment.** See Weather research
BARBARIE, Thomas J.
Case of the cautious Communists. Nat R 21:
389+ Ap 22 '69
BARBEAU, André, and others
Renin-aldosterone system in Parkinson's
disease. bibliog Science 165:291-2 Jl 18 '69
BARBECUE cookery
Barbecues with new zing! il Good H 169:
88-103 Ag '69
Barbecuing. H. McCully. il House B 111:82-
3+ Ag '69
Cold-weather barbecuing. il Bet Hom & Gard
47:30 N '69
For the novice at grilling. Sunset 142:165
My '69
Pork cuts for the barbecue. Sunset 143:130
Jl '69
Two bargain charcoal cuts. il Sunset 143:161-2
S '69
Equipment
Along the barbecue beat. N. Craig. il House
B 111:84-5 Ag '69
Australians have different ideas about barbecuing; two-prong skewers. il Sunset 142:
136-8 Je '69
Working tools for the barbecue chef. E.
Kinard. il House B 111:2+ Ag '69
BARBECUE grills
Barbecue grills. il Consumer Bul 52:25-9 Jl
'69
Convert your outdoor grill to gas. R. J.
Tuers. il Pop Mech 131:166-7 Ap '69
Indoor cookout. il McCalls 96:98-9+ F '69
BARBECUE skewers. See Barbecue cookery—
Equipment

BARBER, James David
President's analyst. summary of address.
por Time 94:58 S 12 '69
—and Mayhew, D. R.
From the streets to the polls. New Repub
161:9-11 D 6 '69
BARBER, Miller
Mister X. the mainstay of the tour. M. Mulvoy. il por Sports Illus 30:52 Mr 3 '69
BARBER, Red
Can baseball be saved? Read Digest 94:155-8+
Ap '69
BARBER, Samuel
Records:
Arias and songs. Opera N 33:34 Ap 19 '69
BARBER of Seville; opera. See Rossini, G.
BARBER shop models See Models and modelmaking
BARBERA, Joseph
Men behind Dastardly & Muttley. J. Culhane.
il por N Y Times Mag p50-1+ N 23 '69
BARBETTE
Onward and upward with the arts. F. Steegmuller. il New Yorker 45:130-4+ S 27 '69
BARBIE dolls. See Dolls
Il BARBIERE di Siviglia; opera. See Rossini,
G.
BARBIROLLI, Sir John
Sir John; interview, ed. by B. Fischer-Williams. por Opera N 34:16 D 6 '69
BARBITURATES
Amphetamines and barbiturates: the up and
down drugs; questions and answers. il Todays Ed 58:42-4 Mr '69
Auditory habituation and barbiturate-induced neural activity. W. R. Webster. bibliog il Science 164:970-1 My 23 '69
BARBOUR, Ian G.
On to Mars? Chr Cent 86:1478-80 N 19 '69
BARBWIRE theater. See Theater—United
States
BARCELONA
Architecture
Kafka's castle. P. Hodgkinson. il Arch Forum
131:35-41 N '69
BARCHRIS construction corporation
What the BarChris directors did (not enough)
Fortune 79:151 My 15 '69
BARCLAY, Charlotte
I've always gone where fate led me. Dance
Mag 43:34-7+ Ja '69
BARD, Bernard
College students: why they drop out. Ed Digest 34:18-21 Mr '69
Mentally unfit teachers. Ladies Home J 86:
80-1+ F '69
Why our schools are failing. Parents Mag
44:53-5+ S '69
BARD, C. R, incorporated
What the doctor ordered. S. Margetts. Duns
R 94:87-8 N '69
BARDACH, Eugene
Lawmaking in Washington. Trans-Action 6:
57-9 O '69
BARDACH, John E.
Aquaculture. bibliog Science 161:1098-106 S
13 '68; Correction. 163:493 Ja 31 '69
BARDACKE, F.
Who owns the park? Ramp Mag 8:8 Ag '69
BARDEEN, John
Advances in superconductivity; adaptation of
address. February 1969. bibliog por Phys
Today 22:40-6 O '69
BARDOT, Brigitte
Brigitte Bardot, Coco Chanel and me. B. Rollin. Look 33:13-14 Ap 1 '69
BAREA, Ilsa
One hundred years of the opera on the Ring,
1869-1969. Sat R 52:45-7 My 31 '69
BARELA, Patrocinio
Saint-maker from Taos. M. T. Crews. il pors
Américas 21:33-7 Mr '69
BARENBOIM, Daniel
Barenboim and Beethoven. E. Greenfield. por
Hi Fi 19:28 N '69
Triangle: Daniel and Jacqueline Barenboim
and the cello. M. Cleave. il pors N Y Times
Mag p50-1+ Mr 16 '69
BARGE ships. See Freight vessels
BARGES
Build a fun barge. M. E. Daniels. il Mech
Illus 65:70-3+ My '69
Transportation
Barges that cross the ocean. il Time 94:94+
S 12 '69
BARHAM, E. G. and others
Microvolt electric signals from fishes and
the environment. bibliog Science 164:965-8
My 23 '69

BARILLET, Pierre, and Grédy, J. P.
Forty carats; adapted by J. Allen. Criticism
America 120:148 F 1 '69
Life 66:10 F 14 '69
Nation 208:125 Ja 27 '69
Vogue 153:54 F 15 '69
BARING-GOULD, William S.
Limericks are jovial things; excerpts from
The lure of the limerick. Read Digest 94:
84-5 F '69
BARISCH, Sylvia, and Johnides, Theodora
National register looks at manpower. por
Phys Today 22:48-52 O '69
BARITE
Coesite from the Richat dome, Mauritania: a
misidentification. R. F. Fudali. bibliog il
Science 166:228-30 O 10 '69
BARIUM sulfate
See also
Barite
BARK
Recognizing woody plants in winter. E. H.
Ketchledge. il Cons 24:20-7+ O '69
BARK beetles. See Beetles
BARKÉ, Harvey E.
Lawn weeds and their cures. Horticulture
47:20-1+ Jl '69
BARKER, B. Devereux, 3d
Deep water racing. See issues of Yachting
Designs. il Yachting 125:80-1 Je '69
BARKER, Elliott S.
Cougar the hard way. Field & S 74:70-1+
My '69
BARKER, Eric
Accident; poem. Nation 209:516 N 10 '69
BARKER, Jerry W.
You don't need sports to build physical fitness.
Camp Mag 41:22-3 My '69
BARKER, Jonn
USSR's first International ballet competition.
Dance Mag 43:28+ Ag '69
BARKER, John W.
Couperin, mostly, by Marlowe and others.
Am Rec G 36:10-11 S '69
Reissue of Alexander's feast, plus first
editions of two other oratorios by George
Frideric Handel: Thedora & Joshua. Am
Rec G 36:108-12 O '69
BARKER, Lewellys F. See Shulman, N. R. jt.
auth.
BARKEY, Patrick
Office landscape: a new concept for library
planners. Library J 94:4358-9 D 1 '69
BARKIN, Elaine
Reviews of books. Mus Q 55:125-31 Ja '69
BARKLEY, David S.
Adenosine-3',5'-phosphate: identification as
acrasin in a species of cellular slime mold.
bibliog Science 165:1133-4 S 12 '69
BARKSDALE, A. W.
Sexual hormones of achlya and other fungi.
bibliog Science 166:831-7 N 14 '69
BARLETT, Donald L. See Sheridan, T. jt.
auth.
BARLEV, Halm
Talk with General Barley; interview, ed. by
M. Elkins. por Newsweek 74:52 N 24 '69
BARLOW, Anna Marie
Glory! Hallelujah! Criticism
Newsweek il 73:123 Je 9 '69
BARLOW, Dorothy P.
Hippy birthday; poem. McCalls 96:141 Mr '69
BARN houses. See Houses, Prefabricated
BARN owls. See Owls
BARNACLES
Current-voltage relations during illumination:
photoreceptor membrane of a barnacle. H.
M. Brown and others. bibliog il Science
166:240-3 O 10 '69
Rate of intracellular diffusion as measured
in barnacle muscle. W. H. Bunch and G.
Kallsen. bibliog il Science 164:1178-9 Je 6
'69
BARNARD, Christiaan Neethling
Dr Barnard: a sense of the future. P. Nathan.
Pub W 196:38 Ag 4 '69
Why Blaiberg died. Time 94:34 Ag 29 '69
—and Pepper, C. B.
Christiaan Barnard: one life; excerpt. pors
McCalls 97:144-52 O; 127-34 N '69
BARNARD, Harry
Playing the game. Nation 208:89-90 Ja 20 '69
BARNARD, Henry
Early educational journalists in America. C.
L. Hall. Ed Digest 35:44-5 N '69
BARNARD college, New York
Because I am black. D. L. Perry. Sat R 52:73
Je 21 '69
BARNES, Ben F.
Sweepstakes of the '70s: five entries. il por
Newsweek 73:27-8 F 24 '69
BARNES, Charles M. jr
All-star agent is a high scorer. por Bsns W
p 153 S 20 '69

BARNES, Clive
On the scene. See issues of Holiday to August
1969
about
Overachiever. il por Time 93:98+ Ap 11 '69
BARNES, Djuna
Quarry; poem. New Yorker 45:53 D 27 '69
BARNES, Edward Larrabee
Barnes completes the first stage of Emma
Willard expansion. il Arch Rec 145:163-70
Je '69
BARNES, Mary
Art and sanity. por Newsweek 73:96+ My
19 '69
BARNES, N. Spencer
Frankenstein argument against peacekeeping.
Bul Atom Sci 25:16-18 My '69
BARNES, Peter
Army and the First amendment. New Repub
160:13-14 My 24 '69
Army may be hazardous to your health. New
Repub 161:13-14 D 20 '69
Carpetbagger draft boards. Nation 209:195 S
8 '69
Presidio mutiny. New Repub 161:21-5 Jl 5
'69
BARNES, Peter (playwright)
Ruling class. Criticism
Atlan 224:99-100 Ag '69
BARNES, Wallace
To the rescue! il por Forbes 103:215-16 My
15 '69
BARNESBORO, Pa.
Token-dispensing parking meters. G. Atkins.
il Am City 84:125-6 Je '69
BARNET, Richard J.
Pentagon product. New Repub 160:20-2 F 8 '69
BARNETT, Audrey
Cell division: a second circadian clock system
in paramecium multimicronucleatum. bib-
liog Science 164:1417-19 Je 20 '69
BARNETT, Correlli
Guerrilla warfare. Horizon 11:4-11 Wint '69
BARNETT, Donald
Angola; report from Hanoi II. Ramp Mag
7:49-54 Ap '69
BARNETT, Michael P.
Late news. por Wilson Lib Bul 43:595+ Mr
'69
BARNETT, Norman L.
Beyond market segmentation. bibliog f Har-
vard Bsns R 47:152-4+ Ja '69
BARNETT, Robert E.
Thirty-four deaths; and 376 confirmed cases
of encephalitis. por Am City 84:127-8 F '69
BARNETT, Robert Warren
Japan's economic dynamism and our com-
mon interests in East Asia; excerpts from
address, March 18, 1969. Dept State Bul 60:
447-50 My 26 '69
BARNETT Frummer in urban crisis; story.
See Trillin, C.
BARNS and stables
Building a baby barn. M. L. Champie. il Org
Gard & Farm 16:73-6 O '69
Pay for an indoor lot in three years? il Farm
J 93:30D Je '69
Slick new setup that cuts chore time.
J. R. Borcherding. il Suc Farm 67:D4 O '69
Stable in the desert is crowded with ideas
for other stable planners. il Sunset 142:
110+ F '69
These horses have a loafing shed. il Sunset
143:94 Jl '69
Toughen calves in the cold? Or pamper them
with comfort? D. Hagen; N. Reeder. il
Farm J 93:D12-13+ F '69

Equipment
Rescue dairy cows from stress. J. R. Borcherding. il Suc Farm 67:62-3 O '69

Floors
Try putting calves on slats. J. R. Borcherding. il Suc Farm 67:D2 O '69

Lighting
More time for management; mechanization.
D. K. O'Brien. il Farm J 93:B12-13+ S '69

Maintenance and repair
Barn that cleans itself. il Farm J 93:D12 Ap
'69

Ventilation
Ventilation is a must in cold weather. G. L.
Earle. Suc Farm 67:T4 O '69

Windows
His stable has plastic windows. il Sunset
143:158 O '69
BARNUM, John Lee
Design of a light meter & exposure calcu-
lator. Electr World 81:52-4+ My '69

BARNUM, Phineas Taylor
No man ought to advertise; excerpt from The humbugs of the world. Am Heritage 21:120 D '69

BARO, Gene
Decisive art collection. Vogue 153:132-41+ F 15 '69

BARON, Robert Alex
Crusader for quiet. por Time 94:85 D 5 '69

BARONDES, Samuel H. See Droz, B.; Dutton. G. R. jt. auths.

BARONE, Anthony. See Malins, D. C. jt. auth.

BAROQUE architecture. See Architecture, Baroque

BAROQUE music. See Music, Baroque

BAROQUE painting. See Painting, Baroque

BARR, Browne
Pop sermons. Chr Cent 86:1190-2 S 17 '69

BARR, Donald
Parents' guide to the age of revolt. McCalls 97:73+ O '69

BARR, E. L. Jr. See Sanderson, R. K. jt. auth.

BARR, Joseph Moran
One mayor's story of the mess in cities; excerpts from remarks. por U S News 66:57-9 Ap 21 '69

BARR, Joseph Walker
Tax reform: the time is now. Sat R 52:22-5 Mr 22 '69

BARR, Stringfellow
Why students revolt. Ed Digest 34:4-5 My '69

BARRACKS; drama. See Leonard, H.

BARRACLOUGH, Geoffrey
Storms of the 70s. Nation 210:6-8 Ja 12 '70

BARRACLOUGH, W. E. and others
Shallow scattering layer in the subarctic Pacific Ocean: detection by high-frequency echo sounder. bibliog Science 166:611-13 O 31 '69

BARRACO MÁRMOL, Mario
Darien. Américas 21:23-31 Jl '69

BARRAGÁN, Luis
Architecture in Mexico. N. Silver. Nation 209: 123-5 Ag 11 '69

BARRAULT, Jean Louis
French side of it. il por Yachting 125:66-8+ F '69

BARRAULT, Jean Michel
Rabelais. Criticism
America 121:616-17 D 29 '69

BARREIROS RODRÍGUEZ, Eduardo
Conflict of cultures. por Time 93:100 Je 13 '69

BARRETT, B. L.
Well brought up girl; excerpt from Love in Atlantis. Redbook 133:155-77 Je '69

BARRETT, Charles S.
Crystallography with protons. por(p32) Phys Today 22:33 Ag '69

BARRETT, Edward L. Jr
Excerpt from statement submitted to Subcommittee on constitutional rights, January 1969. Cong Digest 48:119+ Ap '69

BARRETT, George West, bp
Bishop Barrett resigns. Chr Cent 86:1541 D 3 '69

BARRETT, Peter
Africa stares back. Field & S 74:42-7+ D '69
Suddenly, you are fishing in Italy. pors Outdoor Life 143:72-5+ F '69

BARRETT, Rona
Close up! TV snoop; gossip about celebrities. J. Barthel. il pors Life 66:41-2+ Mr 21 '69

BARRETT, Sweet Emma
Local legend. L. Lerman. il por Mlle 68:150-1 F '69

BARRIENTOS ORTUÑO, René
Barrientos, the man who captured Che. R. C. Hirschfield. Commonweal 89:609-10 F 14 '69; Reply with rejoinder. J. W. Knudson. 90: 155+ Ap 25 '69
Charmed life ended. M. Arias. Chr Cent 86: 849-50 Je 18 '69
Death of a caudillo. J. L. Klaiber. America 120:589-91 My 17 '69
Mourning the pilot. Newsweek 73:55 My 12 '69
Not a bird, not a plane but Barrientos. il por Time 93:31 F 7 '69
One crash too many. il Time 93:47 My 9 '69
U.S. extends condolences on death of President Barrientos of Bolivia: texts of messages. R. M. Nixon; W. P. Rogers. Dept State Bul 60:423-4 My 19 '69

BARRINGERITE. See Phosphides

BARRIS, Chuck
King of TV gamesmanship. J. Barthel. il pors Life 67:116B-116D+ O 10 '69

BARRO COLORADO ISLAND
Traveler's choice. K. B. Peavy. Travel 132: 5 D '69

BARRONS, Keith C.
Some ecological benefits of woody plant control with herbicides. bibliog Science 165: 465-8 Ag 1 '69

BARRUS, Gabby
Pre-hunt scouting: key to filling your license. por Field & S 74:52-3+ Ag '69

BARRY, Anne
Now that you own Alaska, friends, what are you going to do with it? Esquire 71:119-25 Ap '69

BARRY, Iris
Film library and how it grew. Film Q 22:19-27 Sum '69

BARRY, James J.
Consumer services for older Americans; address, May 24, 1969. Vital Speeches 35: 649-52 Ag 15 '69

BARRY, Joseph Amber
1848 again? Horizon 11:66-83 Spr '69
New life, a new love; Audrey Hepburn at forty. McCalls 96:56-7+ Jl '69
On French leave with de Gaulle. Sat R 52:66+ Mr 8 '69
Sophia Loren's baby: the doctor who made it possible. McCalls 96:124-5+ Ap '69

BARRY, Les
Travel. See issues of Popular photography
Traveler's camera. Pop Phot 65:66+ Jl '69

BARRY, Thomas
Importance of being Mr James Brown. Look 33:56-62 F 18 '69; Same abr. with title Soul brother no. 1. Read Digest 94:131-4 My '69

BARRY, William H. See Carnay, L. D. jt. auth.

BARRYMAINE, Norman
End of the ordeal. Time 94:59-60+ O 24 '69

BARS, Snack. See Snack bars

BARS and barrooms
Algonquin's sedate sitting room. L. Aldridge. il Holiday 45:110-11 Ap '69
Downey's, the poor actor's Sardi's. A. Bester. il Holiday 46:90-2 N '69
Enrico's of San Francisco. A. Karlen il Holiday 45:90+ Mr '69
Hangouts. P. Hamill. Mlle 70:151+ N '69
How to get a great drink at a great bar. R. A. De Groot. il Esquire 71:108-11 Ja '69
Last night at Joe's place: Bachelors III. R. Reed. il Esquire 72:106+ O '69
Manhattan's Hibernian haunts. D. Butwin. il Sat R 52:66+ N 22 '69
Polo lounge; Beverly Hills Oasis. J. Smith. il Holiday 46:58+ Ag '69
Pubbing and clubbing. Sat R 52:74-6 F 15 '69
San Francisco's Buena Vista. H. Caen. il Holiday 46:84-6 D '69
Steady drinkers at Toots Shor. P. Maas. il Holiday 45:73+ Je '69
Wrigley bar; Chicago's friendly neighborhood martini hangout. I. Kupcinet. il Holiday 45:18+ My '69

History
Nevada's thirsty legacy; Rhyolite, Nev. F. Taylor. il Travel & Camera 32:32 D '69

BARS and barrooms, Miniature
Deadwood, S.D. history made into miniature. S. A. Parvin. il Hobbies 74:148 D '69

BARS for the home
Bar full of bright ideas. il Pop Mech 131: 130-1 F '69
Shipshape bar. R. Capotosto. il Mech Illus 65:68-70 D '69

BARSCHALL, Henry H.
Three decades of fast-neutron experiments; adaptation of address. bibliog por Phys Today 22:54-9 Ag '69

BARTEL, Constance
Beauty at home. See issues of American home
Spa in your bath. Am Home 72:38 S '69

BARTEL, Robert J.
Campus tensions and evangelical response. Chr Today 13:12-15 Je 6 '69

BARTEL, Roy A. and Coppedge, F. L.
Why teach? bibliog f Clear House 44:238-41 D '69

BARTELL, George
George Bartell: California illustrator. F. Whitaker. il por Am Artist 33:64-9+ Mr '69

BARTH, C. A. and others
Mariner 6: ultraviolet spectrum of Mars upper atmosphere. bibliog Science 165:1004-5 S 5 '69

BARTH, John
Help; a stereophonic narrative for authorial voice. Esquire 72:108-9 S '69

BARTH, Karl
  Farewell in Basel. J. R. Nelson. Commonweal
    89:526-7 Ja 24 '69
  Karl Barth. P. S. Minear. New Repub 160:
    12-13 F 1 '69
  Karl Barth, 1886-1968: his place in history.
    K. Runia. Chr Today 14:6-9 D 5 '69
  Karl Barth; symposium. por Chr Cent 86:402-
    15 Mr 26 '69
  Obituary notice erratum. W. Herberg. Nat
    R 21:64 Ja 28 '69
BARTHA, Richard
  Pesticide interaction creates hybrid residue.
    bibliog Science 166:1299-300 D 5 '69
BARTHEL, Joan
  Anybody need 683 dancers? Life 67:61-2+ D
    5 '69
  Close up! Rona Barrett. TV snoop. Life 66:
    41-2+ Mr 21 '69
  King of TV gamesmanship. Life 67:116B-
    116D+ O 10 '69
  Panic in TV censorship. Life 67:51-4 Ag 1 '69
  Requiem for Peyton Place. Life 66:47-50 Ap
    25 '69
  Survivor on TV: Lana. Life 67:78-80+ S 26
    '69
  (ed) See Bloom, C. Rod Steiger and Claire
    Bloom, no happy ending?
  (ed) See Steiger, R. Rod Steiger and Claire
    Bloom, no happy ending?
BARTHELME, Donald
  And now let's hear it for the Ed Sullivan
    show! Esquire 71:126-7+ Ap '69
  At the Tolstoy museum; story. New Yorker
    45:32-7 My 24 '69
  City life; story. New Yorker 44:31-2 Ja 18;
    45:32-7 Je 21 '69
  On angels; story. New Yorker 45:29 Ag 9 '69
  Paraguay. New Yorker 45:32-4 S 6 '69
  Views of my father weeping; story. New
    Yorker 45:56-60 D 6 '69
BARTHELMES, Wes
  Too bad. Mr Nobel Laureate. Commonweal
    91:245-7 N 21 '69
BARTILUCCI, Nicholas. See Baffa, J. J. jt.
    auth.
BARTIMOLE, Roldo
  Bad day in Cleveland. Nation 209:41-5+ Jl
    14 '69
BARTLESVILLE, Okla.
  Big red, something new in street mainte-
    nance. B. Armstrong. il Am City 84:90-1 N
    '69
BARTLETT, Alexandra S. and others
  Fossil maize from Panama. bibliog Science
    165:389-90 Jl 25 '69
BARTLETT, Dewey Follett
  Oklahoma's salesman-governor. por Bsns W
    p 152+ O 11 '69
BARTLETT, Grant A. and Greggs, R. G.
  Carbonate sediments: oriented lithified sam-
    ples from the North Atlantic. bibliog Sci-
    ence 166:740-1 N 7 '69
BARTLETT, Phyllis
  Chez Mlle. See issues of Mademoiselle
BARTLETT, Richard A.
  West is getting lonely again. Read Digest
    95:46-50 Ag '69
  Will anyone come here for pleasure? Am
    West 6:10-16 S '69
BARTLEY, Edward J.
  Now, while there's time. Read Digest 95:101-
    4 D '69
BARTLEY, S. Howard
  What do you mean, tired? Todays Ed 58:40-1
    F '69
BARTNICKI-GARCIA, S. and Lippman, Eleanor
  Fungal morphogenesis: cell wall construction
    in mucor rouxii. bibliog Science 165:302-4
    Jl 18 '69
BARTON, Derek Harold Richard
  Nobel laureates in economics, chemistry, and
    physics. E. L. Eliel. por Science 166:718-20
    N 7 '69
  Nobel prizes. por Sci N 96:421-2 N 8 '69
BARTON, Peter
  Little Tri and power; poems. Sat R 52:17
    Jl 26 '69
BARTOS, Milan
  Special missions and the United Nations. UN
    Mo Chron 6:89-95 N '69
BARTOW, Fla.
  Brighter sports lights at less cost. il Am
    City 84:34 D '69
BARUCH, Ruth-Marion
  Black Panthers photographic essay. M. Mann.
    il Pop Phot 64:82-3+ My '69
BARVIE, Myrta
  On the boards. W. Como. por Dance Mag
    43:20 D '69
BARZEL, Ann
  Looking at television. See issues of Dance
    magazine

BARZUN, Jacques
  [Book review] America 120:416+ Ap 5 '69
  Book, the bibliographer and the absence of
    mind. Am Scholar 39:138+ Wint '69
  New librarian to the rescue; address, April
    1969. por Library J 94:3963-5 N 1 '69
  Tomorrow's university, back to the middle
    ages? Sat R 52:23-5+ N 15 '69
BASALT
  Basalt rock, an untapped mineral supply. J.
    I. Rodale. Org Gard & Farm 16:81-3 Je '69
  Dredged trachyte and basalt from Kodiak
    seamount and the adjacent Aleutian Trench,
    Alaska. R. B. Forbes and C. M. Hoskin. il
    Science 166:502-4 O 24 '69
  Fissure basalts and ocean-floor spreading on
    the East Pacific rise. E. Bonatti; reply
    with rejoinder. R. P. Herzen. bibliog il
    Science 166:1181-3 N 28 '69
  Magnetic polarity of pillow basalts from
    Reykjanes ridge. J. De Boer and others.
    bibliog il Science 166:996-8 N 21 '69
  Shock and thermal metamorphism of basalt
    by nuclear explosion, Nevada test site.
    O. B. James. bibliog il Science 166:1615-20
    D 26 '69
BASCIO, Patrick
  Need for revolution. Cath World 209:207-9
    Ag '69
BASCOM, Willard
  Technology and the ocean; with biographical
    sketch. Sci Am 221:46+, 198-204+ S '69
BASEBALL
  Bonanza in Red Springs; minor league owner
    M. Boykin. P. Carry. il Sports Illus 31:42+
    Jl 28 '69
  Marianne Moore, baseball fan. J. Durso. Sat
    R 52:51-2 Jl 12 '69
  Odd one for the Sun Devils; Arizona state's
    third collegiate championship. P. Carry.
    Sports Illus 30:48-9 Je 30 '69
  Trigonometric outfielding. Sci Am 220:49 Ja
    '69
  Whole new ball game. P. Axthelm. Newsweek
    74:104-5 O 20 '69
    See also
  Baseball clubs
  Little leagues
  Pitching (baseball)
  World series (baseball)

            Accidents and injuries
  Conig's comeback. il Time 93:84-5 Ap 11 '69
  Now playing in right field; Boston's T. Co-
    nigliaro. M. Mulvoy. il Sports Illus 30:26-8+
    Ap 7 '69

            Anecdotes, facetiae,
                satire, etc.
  Order in the ball park! J. R. McDermott. il
    Life 66:83-4 Mr 7 '69

            Bibliography
  Books for young people. Z. Sutherland. Sat
    R 52:38 Je 28 '69

            History
  Baseball's Johnny Appleseed. H. Peterson. il
    Sports Illus 30:56-64+ Ap 14 '69
  Maybe what baseball needs is a Henry Da-
    vid Thoreau. M. Harris. il N Y Times
    Mag p66-7+ My 4 '69
  Turbulent century of swat. E. Asinof. Life 66:
    28 Je 6 '69

            Organization and administration
  Baseball needs a new pitch. R. Smith. il
    Look 33:74+ F 18 '69
  Big leagues select a fan; B. Kuhn, new com-
    missioner of baseball. W. Leggett. Sports
    Illus 30:16-17 F 17 '69

            Rules
  Maybe what baseball needs is a Henry Da-
    vid Thoreau. M. Harris. il N Y Times
    Mag p66-7+ My 4 '69
  R: a DH factor for baseball ills; permanent
    pinch-hitter to bat for the pitcher. W.
    Leggett. il Sports Illus 31:16-17 Ag 11 '69

            Study and teaching
  Johnny Sain teaches the power of positive
    pitching. B. Surface. il N Y Times Mag
    p48-9+ Ap 20 '69

            Canada
  Vive les Expos! il Newsweek 73:110 Ap 28 '69

            Japan
  Let's hear it for boru! Inter-City baseball
    tournament at Tokyo's Korakuen stadium.
    W. Leggett. il Sports Illus 31:30-5 Jl 21 '69
BASEBALL accidents. See Baseball—Acci-
    dents and injuries

BASEBALL clubs

American league short shots. H. L. Masin. il Sr Schol 94:22 Ap 18 '69

Annual baseball roundup. il Ebony 24:136-40+ Je '69

Atlanta on edge. Newsweek 74:129-30 S 29 '69

Atlanta tranquillity base here; P. Niekro. R. Blount, jr. il Sports Illus 31:46-9 Ag 4 '69

Au jeu! Montreal Expos vs. St Louis Cardinals. il Time 93:56 Ap 25 '69

Baseball à la Franglais; Montreal les Expos? M. Richler. il Holiday 46:54-6 Ag '69

Baseball booms again. M. Mulvoy. il Sports Illus 31:12-17 Ag 4 '69

Baseball strikes out. C. McCarthy. New Repub 160:8-9 Ap 19 '69

Baseball's week. H. Weiskopf. See issues of Sports illustrated published during baseball season

Baseball's wild West; contenders for the National league western title. il Newsweek 74:61 S 8 '69

Best arm in baseball; M. Moore and New York Yankees. M. Burke il Wilson Lib Bul 43:622-3 Mr '69

Big blasts from a toy cannon; Astros' Jim Wynn. M. Mulvoy. il Sports Illus 30:76+ Je 9 '69

Big zinger from Binger; J. Bench, catcher for Cincinnati Reds. R. Blount, jr. il Sports Illus 30:26-8+ Mr 31 '69

Black athlete in the golden age of sports; an old man makes baseball history; Cleveland Indians signing S. Paige. A. S. Young. il Ebony 24:122-4+ Mr '69

Black athlete in the golden age of sports; integration of American league by Cleveland Indians. A. S. Young il Ebony 24:66-8+ F '69

Bottom part of the lineup; compleat utility man, C. Ruiz of the Reds. G. Ronberg. il Sports Illus 31:30-2+ Ag 25 '69

Bring back the real Mets! New York Mets in pennant race. L. Shecter. il N Y Times Mag p66-7+ S 7 '69

Can baseball be saved? R. Barber. Read Digest 94:155-8+ Ap '69

Cardinals are coming tra la tra la. W. Leggett. il Sports Illus 31:14-17 S 1 '69

Deck is shuffled; Red Schoendienst's Cardinals in the cellar. M. Mulvoy. il Sports Illus 30:20-3 My 5 '69

Departure of big D; Drysdale of the Los Angeles Dodgers. Time 94:59 Ag 22 '69

Diamond-bright art form. J. Wright. il Sports Illus 30:32-4+ Je 23 '69

Fence-busters; Oakland's R. Jackson and Washington's F. Howard. il Time 94:48 Jl 25 '69

Flying high; Baltimore Orioles. il Time 94: 45-6 Jl 11 '69

Fraternal Twins. il Time 94:59+ Ag 15 '69

Golden days that sustain the dream; illustrations by M. Ramus; with account by W. Leggett. Sports Illus 30:34-9 Mr 10 '69

Goodbye, Leo; Mets-Cubs game. New Yorker 45:33-4 S 20 '69

Guess who's coming up now! pitcher-rich, power-poor New York Mets. R. Blount, jr. il Sports Illus 30:48+ Je 23 '69

Hawk; excerpt. K. Harrelson and A. Hirshberg. il Sports Illus 31:54-64+ Jl 14; 22-8 Jl 21 '69

Home run king Reggie Jackson. il Ebony 24:92-4+ O '69

Ideal team in Harm's way; Orioles vs Twins in American league playoffs. W. Leggett. il Sports Illus 31:20-3 O 6 '69

In Chicago the left field bleacher bums are chanting: abeebee! Ungowa! Cub powuh! H. Higdon. il N Y Times Mag p28-9+ Ag 24 '69

Jam-up of talent at third; seven new men at baseball's hottest base. W. Leggett. il Sports Illus 30:26-31 Ap 28 '69

Just plain fun; all-star game. Newsweek 74:66 Ag 4 '69

KC is back with a vengeance; Kansas City Royals, most successful expansion club. M. Mulvoy. il Sports Illus 30:75-6+ My 26 '69

Keeping up with Jones; victories of New York Mets. il Time 93:57 Je 13 '69

Kids' crusade in Boston; young New Englanders in Fenway park. W. Leggett. il Sports Illus 30:36-8+ Je 16 '69

Knockdown time in the wild, wild West; Giants and Braves. M. Mulvoy. il Sports Illus 31:24-6+ S 29 '69

Leading man; wondrous Willie; batting first in San Francisco lineup. R. Blount, jr. il Sports Illus 30:32-4 Ap 21 '69

Leo's bums rap for the Cubs; Chicago's North side pennant contender. R. H. Boyle. il Sports Illus 30:14-19 Je 30 '69

Let's everybody boo Rich Allen! D. Wolf. il pors Life 67:50-2+ Ag 22 '69

Let's go Mets, and they do. il Newsweek 74:88-9 Jl 21 '69

Little love, and a few punches, make a team; Minnesota Twins. M. Cope. il Life 67:79-80+ S 19 '69

Little team that can; New York Mets. il Time 94:49-52+ S 5 '69

Long and short of Leo and me; the Chicago Cubs in New York. B. Farrell. Life 67:4 Jl 25 '69

Mad scramble East and West; National league's close pennant race. P. Carry. il Sports Illus 31:22-3 S 8 '69

Magnificent Mets il Newsweek 74:70 S 22 '69

Maris and the Babe, move over! R. Jackson of Oakland Athletics. M. Mulvoy. il Sports Illus 31:22-5 Jl 7 '69

Maybe it's time to break up the Mets; pursuit of championship. W. Leggett. il Sports Illus 31:28-9 S 22 '69

Maybe what baseball needs is a Henry David Thoreau. M. Harris. il N Y Times Mag p66-7+ My 4 '69

Mickey Mantle's decision; Look diary of the great Yankee; ed. by G. Astor. M. Mantle. il Look 33:28-32+ Mr 18 '69

Mr Cub. il Time 93:52 My 30 '69

Mrs Payson and her lovable Mets. D. Dempsey. Read Digest 94:201-2+ Je '69

Name is Carter—er, Cater; Oakland's first baseman. R. Blount, jr. Sports Illus 30:65-6 My 19 '69

National league sport shots. H. L. Masin. il Sr Schol 94:23 Ap 25 '69

New deal for an old sport; major league baseball playoffs. il Sports Illus 31:26-9 O 13 '69

Newest Senator in town; T. Williams as Washington Senators manager. J. Underwood. il Sports Illus 30:20-1 F 24 '69

Notes and comment; rejoicing in New York over Mets victory. New Yorker 45:47 O 25 '69

One hundred and one; beginning the second century of professional baseball. W. Leggett. il Sports Illus 30:44-7 Ap 14 '69

Pitching, and an omen favors the Mets; Mets vs the Braves in National league playoffs. il Sports Illus 31:23-5 O 6 '69

Pursuit of Willie and Clyde; San Francisco Giants in pennant race. M. Mulvoy. il Sports Illus 31:22-5 S 15 '69

Return of the kid; Washington Senators. il Newsweek 73:77 Mr 17 '69

Return to myth; New York Mets. Time 94: 62-3 O 17 '69

Scouting reports; assessments of all twenty-four big-league teams; symposium. il Sports Illus 30:79-86+ Ap 14 '69

September song; Amazing New York Mets. il Newsweek 74:70 O 13 '69

Solid brass ad; New York Mets cash in on success. il Newsweek 74:69 N 3 '69

Some kids make a sad man happy; Dodger manager W. Alston. il Sports Illus 30:28-30+ My 19 '69

Splendid splinter swings again; T. Williams, manager of the Washington Senators. G. Astor. il Look 33:88-90+ Ap 29 '69

Sporting scene. R. Angell. New Yorker 45: 70-80 Ag 9 '69

Sporting scene; World series; New York Mets vs. Baltimore Orioles. R. Angell. New Yorker 45:145-52+ N 1 '69

Tale of two men and one city; Chicago Cubs. M. Kram. il Sports Illus 31:78-80+ S 29 '69

Teaching them Ted's way; Washington Senators. J. Underwood. il Sports Illus 30:18-23 Mr 17 '69

Torrid time for the Twins. R. Blount, jr. il Sports Illus 31:16-19 Jl 14 '69

Vacuum meets New York's team of destiny; Orioles vs Mets. M. Mulvoy. il Sports Illus 31:42-4+ O 20 '69

Vive les Expos! il Newsweek 73:110 Ap 28 '69

West in a birdbath; Orioles defeat Minnesota and Oakland. W. Leggett. il Sports Illus 30: 18-23 Je 2 '69

What really happened when a very nice team from Atlanta encountered a force known as the New York Mets; with cartoons by M. Gerberg and photographs by J. Olson. il Life 67:42-5 O 17 '69

Where the majors find new (and old) stars; Florida instructional league. W. Leggett. il Sports Illus 31:86+ D 1 '69

BASEBALL clubs—*Continued*
Who woulda thunk it? Mets lunge for the pennant. P. O'Neil. il Life 67:34B-41 S 26 '69
Who's on first? Second? Third? R. Allen-less Phillies. M. Mulvoy. il Sports Illus 31:48-9 Jl 14 '69
See also
World series (baseball)

History
Colorful century. Sports Illus 30:46-7 Ap 14 '69
BASEBALL fans
Baseball booms again. M. Mulvoy. il Sports Illus 31:12-17 Ag 4 '69
Best arm in baseball; M. Moore and New York Yankees. M. Burke. il Wilson Lib Bul 43:622-3 Mr '69
Bring back the real Mets! New York Mets in pennant race. L. Shecter. il N Y Times Mag p66-7+ S 7 '69
Confessions of a retarded Tiger. B. Gilbert. il Sports Illus 30:72-6+ Je 2 '69
Festive lose-in at Montreal. il Sports Illus 31:24-5 S 8 '69
Goodbye, Leo; Mets-Cubs game chant. New Yorker 45:33-4 S 20 '69
In Chicago the left field bleacher bums are chanting: abeebee! Ungowa! Cub powuh! H. Higdon. il N Y Times Mag p28-9+ Ag 24 '69
Kids' crusade in Boston; young New Englanders in Fenway park. W. Leggett. il Sports Illus 30:36-8+ Je 16 '69
Leo's bums rap for the Cubs; Chicago's North side pennant contender. R. H. Boyle. il Sports Illus 30:14-19 Je 30 '69
Maybe what baseball needs is a Henry David Thoreau. M. Harris. il N Y Times Mag p66-7+ My 4 '69
Notes and comment; rejoicing in New York over Mets victory. New Yorker 45:47 O 25 '69
World series with Marianne Moore; reprint. G. Plimpton. il Wilson Lib Bul 43:626-33 Mr '69
BASEBALL fields
From mountain to molehill: the pitching mound. W. Leggett. il Sports Illus 30:22-3 Mr 24 '69
BASEBALL hall of fame. See National baseball hall of fame and museum
BASEBALL managers
High flight for an Oriole; F. Robinson may become the majors' first Negro pilot. W. Leggett. il Sports Illus 30:38-9 F 3 '69
Two managers and two teams; Martin at Minnesota. Bauer at Oakland. Sports Illus 30:82-3 Ap 14 '69
See also
Durocher, L.
McGraw, J. J.
Martin, B.
Stengel, C.
Williams, T.
BASEBALL pitching

Study and teaching
See Baseball—Study and teaching
BASEBALL players
American league short shots. H. L. Masin. il Sr Schol 94:22 Au 18 '69
Baseball's wild West: contenders for the National league western title. il Newsweek 74:61 S 8 '69
Big zinger from Binger; J. Bench, catcher for Cincinnati Reds. R. Blount, jr. il Sports Illus 30:26-8+ Mr 31 '69
Black athlete in the golden age of sports; stereotypes, prejudices, other unfunny hilarities. A. S. Young. il Ebony 24:118+ Je '69
Cardinals are coming tra la tra la. W. Leggett. il Sports Illus 31:14-17 S 1 '69
Confessions of a retarded Tiger. B. Gilbert. il Sports Illus 30:72-6+ Je 2 '69
Deck is shuffled; Red Schoendienst's Cardinals in the cellar. M. Mulvoy. il Sports Illus 30:20-3 My 5 '69
Diamond-bright art form. J. Wright. il Sports Illus 30:32-4+ Je 23 '69
Fable for our time; Amazin' Mets. il Time 94:43 O 24 '69
Flood tide; reserve clause to be challenged. Newsweek 75:45 Ja 12 '70
Golden days that sustain the dream; illustrations by M. Ramus; with account by W. Leggett. Sports Illus 30:34-9 Mr 10 '69
Guess who's coming up now! pitcher-rich, power-poor New York Mets. R. Blount, jr. il Sports Illus 30:48+ Je 23 '69
Have the hitters really gone? debate. J. Brosnan; F. Robinson; J. Sain. il Look 33:84+ My 13 '69

Hawk; excerpt. K. Harrelson and A. Hirshberg. il Sports Illus 31:54-64+ Jl 14; 22-8 Jl 21 '69
Here come the hitters, maybe. M. Mulvoy. il Sports Illus 30:20-1 My 12 '69
Jam-up of talent at third; seven new men at baseball's hottest base. W. Leggett. il Sports Illus 30:26-31 Ag 28 '69
Just call them plain folk heroes; New York Mets. il Sports Illus 31:40-4+ O 20 '69
Let's go Mets, and they do. il Newsweek 74:88-9 Jl 21 '69
Little team that can; New York Mets. il Time 94:49-52+ S 5 '69
Mad scramble East and West; National league's close pennant race. P. Carry. il Sports Illus 31:22-3 S 8 '69
Maybe it's time to break up the Mets: pursuit of championship. W. Leggett. il Sports Illus 31:28-9 S 22 '69
Most likely to succeed. H. L. Masin. Sr Schol 94:26 Mr 28 '69
National league short shots. H. L. Masin. il Sr Schol 94:23 Ap 25 '69
Never pumpkins again; New York Mets. W. Leggett. il Sports Illus 31:14-21 O 27 '69
New Mets go bump in the light of day; defeat of the Cubs in Wrigley field. M. Mulvoy. il Sports Illus 31:8-11 Jl 28 '69
One hundred and one; beginning the second century of professional baseball. W. Leggett. il Sports Illus 30:44-7 Ap 14 '69
Phoenixes of the world, arise! Pacific coast league. P. Carry. il Sports Illus 31:46-9 Ag 18 '69
Pitching, and an omen favors the Mets; Mets vs the Braves in National league playoffs. il Sports Illus 31:23-5 O 6 '69
Play ball! Newsweek 73:83 Mr 10 '69
R: a DH factor for baseball ills; permanent pinch-hitter to bat for the pitcher. W. Leggett. il Sports Illus 31:16-17 Ag 11 '69
Restoring the balance. Time 94:53 Ag 1 '69
Return to myth; New York Mets. Time 94: 62-3 O 17 '69
Scouting reports: assessments of all twenty-four big-league teams; symposium. il Sports Illus 30:79-86+ Ap 14 '69
Some kids make a sad man happy; Dodger manager W. Alston. W. Leggett. il Sports Illus 30:28-30+ My 19 '69
Sporting scene. R. Angell. New Yorker 45: 70-80 Ag 9 '69
Sporting scene: World series: New York Mets vs. Baltimore Orioles. R. Angell. New Yorker 45:145-52+ N 1 '69
Where the majors find new (and old) stars; Florida instructional league. W. Leggett. il Sports Illus 31:86+ D 1 '69
Who woulda thunk it? Mets lunge for the pennant. P. O'Neil. il Life 67:34B-41 S 26 '69
See also
National baseball hall of fame and museum
also names of baseball players, e.g. T. Conigliaro

Pensions
See Baseball players—Salaries, pensions, etc.

Photographs
Iron men. il Sports Illus 30:48-55 Ap 14 '69

Salaries, pensions, etc.
Baseball needs a new pitch. R. Smith. il Look 33:74+ F 18 '69
Baseball: players win demands. U S News 66:96 Mr 10 '69
Game deserves the best; M. Miller as executive director of Baseball players association. R. Roberts. Sports Illus 30:46-7 F 24 '69
One strike? How many out? U S News 66: 75 F 17 '69
Strike one; spring training boycott. Time 93: 79 F 28 '69

BASEBALL players association. See Major league baseball players association
BASEBALL rules. See Baseball—Rules
BASEBALL scouting
Scouting reports; assessments of all twenty-four big-league teams; symposium. il Sports Illus 30:79-86+ Ap 14 '69
BASEBALL teams. See Baseball clubs
BASEBALL umpires. See Umpires (sports)
BASEMENTS and cellars
Finish your basement like a pro. J. Gaynor and H. Wicks. il Pop Mech 132:154-7 D '69
Two basements into racket rooms for children. il House & Gard 135:126-7 My '69
See also
Dampness in buildings
BASES, Air. See Air bases

BASES, Guided missile. See Guided missile bases

BASES, Military. See Military bases

BASHFULNESS
Shyness is ruining my life! questions and answers. A. Wood. Seventeen 28:108+ Jl '69

BASHLINE, L. James
All-around dog? Field & S 74:178-80+ O '69
Keystone coho. Field & S 73:54-5+ Ap '69
No. 1 deer spot in the U.S? Field & S 74:54-5+ S '69
Throw darts for winter trout. Field & S 74:112-14+ D '69
Trout by the bottleful. Field & S 73:70-1+ Mr '69

BASIDIOMYCETES
Schizophyllum commune: gene controlling induced haploid fruiting. T. J. Leonard and J. R. Raper. bibliog il Science 165:190 Jl 11 '69

BASIDIOMYCETES, Fossil. See Fungi, Fossil

BASIE, Count
Basie. B. Korall. il por Sat R 52:82-3 N 29 '69

BASIE, William. See Basie, C.

BASILISKS
Basilisk walks on water. il Life 67:88-90 D 12 '69

BASIN stands. See Stands (furniture)

BASKET making
Corn shucks can make attractive baskets. M. C. Fuller. il Camp Mag 41:22 F '69

BASKET of apples; story. See Faessler, S.

BASKETBALL
Beaten once but far from out; UCLA favored to win third national championship. J. Jares. il Sports Illus 30:28-30+ Mr 17 '69
Big man among men. il Time 94:24 D 26 '69
College basketball. S. Treadwell. Sports Illus 32:44 Ja 5 '70
E—Rupption in wildcat country; Kentucky Wildcats. C. Kirkpatrick. il Sports Illus 31:22-5 D 22 '69
I finally got the point; basketball on an aircraft carrier. E. Bowen. il Sports Illus 30:60-2+ F 10 '69
I want to put on a show; ed. by C. Kirkpatrick. P. Maravich. il Sports Illus 31:39-42+ D 1 '69
Lamar may be little, but it sure isn't minor; Lamar Tech of Beaumont. P. F. Putnam. il Sports Illus 30:40+ F 3 '69
New Mr Bones has a winner; St John's coach L. Carnesecca. il Sports Illus 30:48-9 Ja 27 '69
Old pros, like the Celtics; Kentucky Wesleyan team. W. F. Reed, jr. il Sports Illus 30:62+ Mr 24 '69
On top with no place to go; Tom Gola's La-Salle Explorers, east's leading team. C. Kirkpatrick. il Sports Illus 30:22-4+ F 17 '69
Pete and Press Maravich; life with father on the court; Louisiana state university's basketball team. C. Coe. il Life 66:30-2+ F 7 '69
Roughhouse in the big ten; Illinois not eligible for the NCAA tournament. il Sports Illus 30:20-3 Ja 20 '69
Skeletons and snakes and a scramble for first; Missouri Valley conference. C. Kirkpatrick. il Sports Illus 30:48-9 Mr 3 '69
Unexpected star forward; University of Havana. R. Erlich. Ramp Mag 7:60-1 N 30 '68
Voodoo might help; quarterfinal rounds of National collegiate basketball championship. J. Jares. il Sports Illus 30:18-21 Mr 24 '69
With a flourish of trumpets; photographs; with accounts by J. Jares and C. Kirkpatrick. Sports Illus 30:14-19 Mr 31 '69
Wolfpack waged psychological warfare; University of New Mexico vs. New Mexico state. C. Kirkpatrick. il Sports Illus 30:54-6 F 10 '69
    See also
American basketball association
National basketball association

BASKETBALL coaches. See Coaches (athletics)

BASKETBALL fixes. See Bribery

BASKETBALL players
All America basketball. I. R. McVay. il Look 33:79-80+ Ap 1 '69
Anyone for *pallacanestro?* Americans playing for industrial teams and sports clubs in Europe. il Time 93:79-80 F 28 '69
Big big men cash in on league war; black players. il Ebony 25:164-6+ D '69
Bradley effect. il Newsweek 75:64 Ja 19 '70
Dazzling Knicks. il Newsweek 74:64-6+ D 15 '69
Les girls in Des Moines; photographs by B. Peterson; with account by R. M. Mechem. Sports Illus 30:34-9 F 17 '69

Long "e" has the last laugh; Weber state athletes. C. Kirkpatrick. il Sports Illus 30:58+ Mr 10 '69
1969 All-American H.S. basketball squad. H. L. Masin. il Sr Schol 94:26 My 9 '69
Old pros, like the Celtics; Kentucky Wesleyan team. W. F. Reed, jr. il Sports Illus 30:62+ Mr 24 '69
Overdue winner in New York: the Knicks. J. Kirshenbaum. il Sports Illus 31:16-21 D 8 '69
Pete and Press Maravich. C. Coe. il Life 66:30-2+ F 7 '69
Skeletons and snakes and a scramble for first; Missouri Valley conference. C. Kirkpatrick. il Sports Illus 30:48-9 Mr 3 '69
Stardust on a spree. H. Kanovitz. il Sports Illus 31:34-9 D 1 '69
Up, up and away go Artis and new J.U. J. Jares. il Sports Illus 32:18-21 Ja 5 '70
    See also names of basketball players, e.g. L. Alcindor

Photographs
With a flourish of trumpets; photographs; with accounts by J. Jares and C. Kirkpatrick. Sports Illus 30:14-19 Mr 31 '69

Recruiting
See Basketball scouting

Retirement
I'm not involved anymore; with editorial comment. W. F. Russell. il Sports Illus 31:6, 18-19 Ag 4 '69

Training
Sporting scene; UCLA basketball coach, J. R. Wooden. H. W. Wind. New Yorker 45: 93-6+ Mr 22 '69

BASKETBALL scouting
Scouting reports on the top twenty teams. Sports Illus 31:48-52+ D 1 '69

BASKETBALL teams
Aesthetics of basketball; without me the Knicks wouldn't exist. J. Baumbach. il Esquire 73:140-6 Ja '70
And that old Celtics wheel rolls again; Boston goes into finals against Los Angeles. F. Deford. il Sports Illus 30:24-5 Ap 28 '69
At the end, it was up to the two big men underneath; New York's W. Reed and Boston's B. Russell. F. Deford. il Sports Illus 30:66+ Ap 21 '69
Boston's old, old pros; championship. il Newsweek 73:77 My 19 '69
Brave words from a Hawk and a Warrior. A. Wright. Sports Illus 30:26-8+ Mr 24 '69
Comebacks all over; Boston Celtics in semifinals of NBA playoffs against New York Knicks. F. Deford. il Sports Illus 30:28-31 Ap 14 '69
Coming-out party for Lew and Connie; exhibition game; Bucks against Phoenix Suns. T. Maule. il Sports Illus 31:26-7 O 6 '69
Dazzling Knicks. il Newsweek 74:64-6+ D 15 '69
Don't beat them, absorb them; merger of ABA and NBA. F. Deford. il Sports Illus 31:44-5 Ag 18 '69
Four for the bundle; Baltimore, Philadelphia, New York and Boston in race for NBA stakes. J. Jares. il Sports Illus 30:14-19 F 24 '69
Knickerbocker holiday. Time 94:79 D 5 '69
Last drop in the bucket; Celtics and Lakers in the seventh game. F. Deford. il Sports Illus 30:22-4+ My 12 '69
New knack of the Knicks; New York Knickerbockers. il Newsweek 73:82-3 F 24 '69
New York intangibles; New York Knickerbockers. Time 93:50 F 21 '69
Now he gets to shoot; W. Pavalon's plan to get Alcindor and big sport for Milwaukee. P. Putnam. il Sports Illus 30:56-63 F 24 '69
On top, but in trouble; Los Angeles Lakers. F. Deford. il Sports Illus 30:10-13 Ja 27 '69
Overdue winner in New York: the Knicks. J. Kirshenbaum. il Sports Illus 31:16-21 D 8 '69
Power game in the city; San Francisco Warriors. A. Wright. il Sports Illus 31:36-9 N 17 '69
Red-hot Knicks. Newsweek 74:73 N 10 '69
Rescued from disaster by the hard-to-love giant; Los Angeles Lakers in semifinals of the NBA playoffs. T. Maule. il Sports Illus 30:32-3 Ap 14 '69
Solid hit in the funny league; Indiana Pacers in ABA playoffs against Kentucky Colonels. W. F. Reed, jr. il Sports Illus 30:60-2 Ap 28 '69
Sweety Cakes runs the Sonics; coach of the Seattle SuperSonics. F. Deford. il Sports Illus 31:42-4+ N 24 '69

BASKETBALL teams—*Continued*
Two guys on a Boston hot seat; Celtics. Auerbach and Heinsohn. F. Deford. il Sports Illus 31:22-5 N 3 '69

See also
American basketball association
National basketball association

BASKETBALL tournaments
Big game, basketball with a halo; Aiken, S.C. E.M. Fuller. il Parks & Rec 3:13-14+ N '68
Festival of hula and hoops; Hawaii's Rainbow classic. C. Kirkpatrick. Sports Illus 32:55 Ja 12 '70
Nobody waits on this Lefty; Davidson Wildcats in NCAA playoffs. M. Cope. il Sports Illus 30:28-30+ Mr 10 '69
Vintage Litwack spoiled the grand exit; Owls from Philadelphia take the NIT from Boston college. W. F. Reed, jr. il Sports Illus 30:50-1 Mr 31 '69
Voodoo might help; quarterfinal rounds of National collegiate basketball championship. J. Jares. il Sports Illus 30:18-21 Mr 24 '69
With a flourish of trumpets; photographs; with accounts by J. Jares and C. Kirkpatrick. Sports Illus 30:14-19 Mr 31 '69

BASKETRY. See Basket making

BASKETS
Wonderful world of baskets. il House & Gard 136:168-9 N '69

See also
Waste baskets

BASKETT, George
O'Brien: I want to kill a nigger. A. Goldberg and G. Marine. il por Ramp Mag 8:10-18 Jl '69

BASOLO, Fred. See Crumbliss, A. L. jt. auth.

BASQUE cookery. See Cookery, Basque

BASS, Doris
Can this marriage be saved? por Library J 94:3023-7 S 15 '69

BASS, George F.
Ruins under the sea. Holiday 46:25+ Ag '69

BASS, Jack
Hospital strike. New Repub 160:8 Je 7 '69

BASS, John
Rembrandt, Vermeer, Hals, you name it, Bass says he's got it. il por Life 67:44-5 O 24 '69

BASS, Lawrence W. See Price, W. J. jt. auth.

BASS
Bigmouths tell all; home aquarium. T. McNally. il Outdoor Life 144:64-7+ N '69

See also
Cookery—Fish

BASS anglers sportsman society, Arkansas. See Sports clubs

BASS art museum. See Miami, Fla.—Galleries and museums

BASS fishing
Assateague; great fishing-camping combo. P. McLain. il Field & S 74:68-9+ My '69
Ballard's bass boom. E. A. Bauer. il Outdoor Life 143:68-71+ Ap '69
Bass like wildfire. J. Brang. il Outdoor Life 143:58-9+ Mr '69
Bass man in steelhead country. S. Fagerstrom. il Outdoor Life 143:94-6+ Ap '69
Can anyone catch a new record bass? C. Nansen. il Field & S 73:42-3+ F '69
Fishing the thick stuff. C. F. Waterman. il Field & S 73:58-9+ F '69
Fly fishing in a forest; Toledo Bend Lake, Tex. B. W. Dalrymple. il Outdoor Life 144:64-7+ O '69
Good fishing at Lake Powell. il Sunset 143:74 O '69
Jigging for bass, east Tennessee style. S. Sutton. il Field & S 74:58-9+ Je '69
Jumping with bass. H. Bradshaw. il Outdoor Life 144:48-51+ Ag '69
Lake of bragging fish. P. Curtis. il Field & S 74:44-5+ Jl '69
Lunker-busting on the level. J. A. Brang. il Field & S 74:12-14+ Jl '69
Lunkers of the Roanoke. B. Cochran. il Outdoor Life 143:80-2+ Mr '69
More fish to fry; fishing Dardanelle Lake. C. Elliott. il Outdoor Life 144:66-7+ S '69
New way for surf stripers; kite fishing. J. Samson. il Field & S 74:22+ Je '69
Strategy for smallmouths T. McNally. il Outdoor Life 143:56-9+ My '69
Stripers down south. G. Laycock. il Field & S 73:54-5+ F '69
Stripers in the Big Red. C. C. Niehuis. il Field & S 73:68-9+ Ap '69

Swim a jig for summer bass. C. B. Pfeiffer. il Outdoor Life 144:44-5+ Jl '69

Toledo Bend: big new bass lake. L. A. Wilke. il Field & S 74:148-9+ Je '69
Who says propellers are obsolete? L. Green. il Field & S 74:54-5+ Je '69

BASSETT, William W.
When a priest leaves the ministry. America 120:242-5 Mr 1 '69

BASSINE, Charles C.
Spartans' new game plan. Forbes 104:56 O 15 '69

BASTARDY. See Illegitimacy

BASTOGNE, Battle of, 1944-1945. See Ardennes, Battle of the, 1944-1945

BASU, Jyoti
As Bengal goes. . . E. Behr. il por Newsweek 73:55 Ap 21 '69

BATCHELLDER, Robin
Whimsical creatures. Sch Arts 69:28 O '69

BATEMAN, Mildred Mitchell-. See Mitchell-Bateman, M.

BATEMAN, Ruth Conrad
Creams and custards. House & Gard 136:143-5+ O '69

BATES, Alan
Among the best. D. Platt. il pors Harp Baz 102:118-19 Mr '69

BATES, Devon A. See Good, T. L. jt. auth.

BATES, Ernest W. Jr
Of course we soften our water. Am City 84:108+ Ap '69

BATES, Frederick L.
Impact of automation on society. Bul Atom Sci 25:4-6 Je '69

BATES, Scott
Classical halcyon; poem. New Repub 162:32 Ja 10 '70
Fable of the retiring candle; poem. New Repub 161:36 N 29 '69

BATES, Ted, and company
Annals of television. T. Whiteside. New Yorker 45:47-50+ S 27 '69

BATESVILLE, Miss.

Education

Freedom of choice; suspending federal aid to southern districts. il Newsweek 73:31 F 17 '69

BATH rooms. See Bathrooms

BATH tubs. See Bathtubs

BATHING. See Baths

BATHING beaches. See Beaches

BATHING suits
Peekaboo. il Newsweek 73:86 Je 2 '69
Sand, surf and new swimwear; photographs by Jay Maisel; with account by Jule Campbell. Sports Illus 32:34-42 Ja 12 '70
Swimsuit know-how. il Seventeen 28:38 Jl '69

BATHROOM fixtures
Bath is a place that can use ideas. il Sunset 142:92-9 Ap '69
Great new designs and plans for bathrooms. il House & Gard 136:130-7 O '69
Super bath. S. Lindsay and L. Bohlig. il House B 111:73-9 Mr '69
Vertical assets for the vertical bath. S. Lindsay. il House B 111:116-21 S '69

See also
Toilets

Manufacture

See also
Plumbing fixture manufacturers association

BATHROOM furnishings. See Household furnishings

BATHROOMS
Bath is a place that can use ideas. il Sunset 142:92-9 Ap '69
Bathrooms and dressing rooms, a pampering center. il House & Gard 135:56-7 Ja '69
Extra bathroom in a package. il Bet Hom & Gard 47:42 My '69
Family bathroom planned for children. il Parents Mag 44:78-81 Ja '69
Fast way to modernize your bathroom. J. R. Connor. il Mech Illus 65:95-7+ S '69
For remodelers: a bath unit that comes in pieces. il Pop Sci 195:153 N '69
Great new designs and plans for bathrooms. il House & Gard 136:130-7 O '69
Innovative bath. S. Lindsay. il House B 111:110-13+ Je '69
It's a better bathroom and it's about time. il Bet Hom & Gard 47:22+ S '69
Mini bath & laundry. B. Duggan. il Mech Illus 65:90-3 Ag '69
New order of the bath. B. Plumb. il N Y Times Mag p66-7 Ja 26 '69
Now bathrooms can offer more. N. Seney. il Bet Hom & Gard 47:58-9 Jl '69
Small wonders. il Redbook 133:113-15+ O '69
Super bath. S. Lindsay and L. Bohlig. il House B 111:73-9 Mr '69

BATHROOMS—*Continued*
Two built-ins for the bath. A. Lees. il Pop Sci 194:146-8+ Ap '69
Vertical assets for the vertical bath. S. Lindsay. il House B 111:116-21 S '69

BATHS
Art of the bath. il Redbook 132:86-7+ F '69
Bath. P. Van Wagenen. il Parents Mag 44:42 S '69
The bath; Mrs Theodoracopulos and her mirrored bathroom. il Vogue 154:180-5 O 1 '69
Best of all possible baths. il Mlle 70:116-17 D '69
Daily bath: a few medical facts that may surprise you. G. M. Knox. Bet Hom & Gard 47:34-5+ Mr '69
Heavenly bath. il Seventeen 28:148-9 N '69
Spa in your bath. C. Bartel. il Am Home 72:38 S '69
Unhurried splendor of the Japanese bath. F. Robertson. il Holiday 46:88-9+ O '69

BATHS, Finnish. See Sauna

BATHS, Sawdust
Sawdust bath for health; Japanese treatment. il Mech Illus 65:70 O '69

BATHTUBS
Beauty and the bath. S. Lindsay. il House B 111:16+ Je '69
Rub-a-double-tub. il Time 95:39 Ja 19 '70

BATIE, Jean
(ed) See Chase, D. Forms for dance

BATIK
Batik as a painting technique. A. C. Webb. il Sch Arts 68:6-8 My '69
Discovering: color magic. B. Farmer. il Sch Arts 69:12-13 Ja '70

BATISSE, Michel
Can we keep our planet habitable? UNESCO Courier 22:4-5 Ja '69
World's growing water shortage: reprint. UNESCO Courier 22:58-9 Ag '69

BATON ROUGE, La.

Industries
Big shakedown in Baton Rouge. A. J. Reichley. il Fortune 80:96-9+ Ag 1 '69

BATRA, Suzanne W. T. and Bohart, G. E.
Alkali bees: response of adults to pathogenic fungi in brood cells. bibliog Science 165:607 Ag 8 '69

BATS
America's rarest mammal. D. Esterla and P. Esterla. il Nat Wildlife 7:14-18 Ag '69
Interpubic ligament: elasticity in pregnant free-tailed bat. E. S. Crelin. il Science 164:81 Ap 4 '69
Testicular lactate dehydrogenase isozyme; cyclic appearance in bats. A. Blanco and others. bibliog il Science 164:835-6 My 16 '69

Diseases and pests
Macronyssid mites in oral mucosa of long-nosed bats: occurrence and associated pathology. C. J. Phillips and others. bibliog il Science 165:1368-9 S 26 '69

BATSHEVA dance company. See Dancing, Israeli

BATTELLE, Kenneth. See Kenneth

BATTELLE, Phyllis
Reshaping nature: the history of the brassiere. Ladies Home J 86:80+ O '69
Sky-high cost of hotel weddings. McCalls 96:54+ Je '69

BATTELLE Northwest laboratories, Richland, Wash.
Imagery and symbol in research: the laboratory as a place to think. il Arch Rec 146:142-5 Ag '69

BATTEN, James K.
Why the Pentagon pays homage to John Cornelius Stennis. N Y Times Mag p44-5+ N 23 '69

BATTERED child syndrome. See Cruelty to children

BATTERS, Baseball. See Baseball players

BATTERY chargers. See Storage battery chargers

BATTERY charging. See Electric batteries—Charging

BATTERY park city (proposed) See New York (city)—Battery park city (proposed)

BATTING records. See Sports records

BATTIST, Sondra
Mural is ... Sch Arts 68:24-5 My '69

BATTISTA, O. A.
Chromium, the metal that glitters. por Chem 42:19-20 Ja '69
Copper, a metal known to ancient man. por Chem 42:6-7 S '69

Featherweight champion of metals. Chem 42:14-15 Mr '69
Titanium the Cinderella of metals. por Chem 42:13-15 My '69

BATTISTINI, Lawrence H.
Sino-American detente? Cur 104:55-64 F '69

BATTISTINI, Mattia
From a rich heritage: the art of baritone Mattia Battistini. C. L. Osborne. por Hi Fi 19:63-4 Ap '69

BATTLE fatigue. See Neuroses

BATTLE flags, American. See Flags—United States

BATTLE of the bulge. See Ardennes, Battle of the, 1944-1945

BATTLEFIELDS
Europe twenty-five years later: special veterans tours arranged by Galaxy tours of Chicago. G. Bush. il Bet Hom & Gard 47:34-8+ N '69

BATTLES, Edith
Light touch. Todays Ed 58:45 My '69

BATTLESHIPS. See Warships

BATTS, Herman M.
New and brighter lighting era. Am City 84:136+ F '69

BAUCHILLON, Emily
Composting for tired people. Org Gard & Farm 16:41-2 Ja '69

BAUDELAIRE, Charles Pierre
Letter from Paris; exhibition as art critic. Genêt. New Yorker 45:131-2 Mr 22 '69

BAUER, Erwin A.
Alaska: unfinished pleasure. Outdoor Life 143:62-5+ My '69
Ballard's bass boom. pors Outdoor Life 143:68-71+ Ap '69
Big boom for old ruff. Outdoor Life 144:48-9+ D '69
Fall vacation. Outdoor Life 144:56-9+ Ag: 62-5+ S '69
Home where the buffalo roam. Outdoor Life 144:56-9+ Ag '69
It really isn't rabbit hunting without hounds. Outdoor Life 144:58-61+ N '69
We plugged the ocean. por Outdoor Life 144:76-9+ O '69

BAUER, George
World beyond the classroom. Clear House 43:371-2 F '69

BAUER, Hank
Two managers and two teams. Sports Illus 30:82-3 Ap 14 '69

BAUER, J. A.
Computer-designed PC boards. por Electr World 82:47-9 O '69

BAUER, John P.
Alan Wood affair: a tale of intrigue. il por Bsns W p94-6+ Jl 12 '69

BAUER, W. W.
Folk remedies: part wisdom, part hokum; excerpts from Potions, remedies, and old wives' tales. Todays Health 48:6+ Ja '70

BAUGH, Sammy
Life for two tough Texans. M. Cope. il pors Sports Illus 31:84-8+ O 20 '69

BAUGHER, William L. and Campbell, T. C.
Gossypol detoxication by fungi. bibliog Science 164:1526-7 Je 27 '69

BAUGHMAN, Milo
Designer shapes space. House & Gard 135:120-5 Ap '69

BAUHAUS
Bauhaus. J. F. McCullogh. il Pub W 196:23-9 S 1 '69
Bauhaus, by H. M. Wingler. Review
New Repub 161:28-31 O 11 '69. P. Jacobsohn
Bauhaus is alive and well in soup plates and skyscrapers. J. R. Mellow. il N Y Times Mag p34-5+ S 14 '69
Idea-giver: W. A. Gropius. il Time 94:49-50 Jl 18 '69
Letter from Paris: art exhibition in Musée national d'art moderne and the Musée municipal d'art moderne. Genêt. New Yorker 45:145-8 Ap 19 '69
Mies and the closing of the Bauhaus. R. Stern. Nation 209:290 S 22 '69

BAULING, Fay. See Neisser, E. G. jt. auth.

BAUM, Gregory
New ecclesiology. Commonweal 91:123-8 O 31 '69
Papacy. Cath World 209:64-6 My '69
Suenens crying in the wilderness. Cath World 210:103-7 D '69

BAUMBACH, Jonathan
Aesthetics of basketball. Esquire 73:140-6 Ja '70

BAUMHOLTZ, Joyce A.
(ed) Books to come (cont) Library J 94:1353-85 Mr 15 '69
(comp) Children's paperbacks (cont) Library J 94:324-6, 2135-8 Ja 15, My 15 '69

BAUR, Ernst W. and Schorr, R. T.
Genetic polymorphism of tetrazolium oxidase in dogs. bibliog Science 166:1524-5 D 19 '69
BAUR, John Ireland Howe
Rediscovery: Van Dearing Perrine. Art in Am 57:76-9 Ja '69
BAUTZER, Gregson
Lawyer of the big deals. pors Bsns W p56+ N 8 '69
BAVARIA

Education

See Education—Germany (Federal Republic)
BAVARIAN motor works. See Automobile industry and trade—Germany (Federal Republic)
BAVIER, Robert Newton, 1918-
From the cockpit. See issues of Yachting
BAWDEN, Nina
Inside Uriah Heep. Writer 82:9-11 My '69
BAXTER, Mrs C. B.
Victorian rooms in miniature; interview, ed. by S. A. Parvin. Hobbies 74:148+ O '69
BAXTER, William F.
Nixon's antitrust policy. New Repub 161:13-16 Ag 9 '69
BAY, Christian
Academic citizenship in a time of campus revolt. Trans-Action 6:4+ Ja '69
BAY area rapid transit. See San Francisco—Rapid transit
BAY OF BISCAY. See Biscay, Bay of
BAY OF PIGS invasion. See Cuba—History—Invasion, 1961
BAYBERRY candles. See Candles
BAYER, Ann
Eye of the needle; story. Mlle 69:204-6 O '69
Now it can be foretold. por Life 67:70B+ S 26 '69
BAYERISCHE motoren werke. See Automobile industry and trade—Germany (Federal Republic)
BAYLISS, William H.
Management by CSROEPM. bibliog Harvard Bsns R 47:85-9 Mr '69
BAYLOR, Julius A.
Punch card pros. il pors Ebony 24:113-14+ Ap '69
BAYONNE, France

Architecture

Self-contained community in Bayonne, France combines high- and low-rise apartment houses. il Arch Rec 146:108-12 Ag '69
BAYREUTH festival
Report: Bayreuth; new production of Fliegende Holländer. J. H. Sutcliffe. il Opera N 34:25-6 S 20 '69
BAYREUTH festspielhaus
Master's apprentices; Friedelind Wagner's Bayreuth master class tackled Aida. J. Rockwell. il Opera N 34:6-7 Ja 10 '70
el-BAZ, Farouk
Lunar igneous intrusions. bibliog Science 167:49-50 Ja 2 '70
BAZELI, Frank P.
Organization and training of paraprofessionals. bibliog Clear House 44:206-9 D '69
BAZELON, David T.
Writer between generations. Commentary 47: 43-54 F '69
BEACH, E. B.
Pola-testers. Pop Electr 31:59-61+ S '69
BEACH architecture
At water's edge: come-join-us houses. il House & Gard 135:84-97+ Je '69
Clustered apartments make unusual, and successful, group on Oregon beach. il Arch Rec 146:186-7 S '69
Gorman house, Amagansett, New York. il Arch Rec 145:54-7 mid-My '69
Moonhole, where time stands still. P. A. Jenkins. il House B 111:38-43+ Ag '69
Nine suntraps on one beach house; Fire Island Pines, Long Island, N.Y. il House & Gard 135:68-71 Je '69
Slash of cypress. E. Sverbeyeff. il House B 111:138-41 N '69
Summer by the water: four sites, four houses. il House B 111:54-67 Jl '69.
BEACH erosion
See also
Shore protection
BEACH plants. See Seashore vegetation
BEACH umbrellas. See Umbrellas
BEACHES
Beyond Buenos Aires: Argentina's coastal playground. A. Colbin. il Travel 132:71-3 N '69
Who owns the beaches? il Time 94:43 Ag 29 '69

BEACHPHONES. See Life saving equipment
BEACONS
See also
Lighthouses
Radio beacons
BEACONS, Radar. See Radar in aviation
BEACONSFIELD, Benjamin Disraeli, 1st earl of
Two risings against the liberals. R. Kirk. Nat R 21:1170 N 18 '69
BEAD necklaces. See Necklaces
BEADED curtains. See Curtains and draperies
BEADLE, George W.
George Beadle talks about the new genetics. C. B. Hicks. il por Todays Health 47:44-7+ Jl '69
BEADS
Worryworryworry; the Greeks have a cure for it. E. Kulukundis. il Holiday 45:32+ Ap '69
BEAGLE, Charles W.
Maintenance savings finance street paving. Am City 84:80-1+ Mr '69
BEAGLE aircraft, limited
Beagle ready to recall 100 Pup aircraft. Aviation W 91:85+ O 27 '69
BEAGLE expedition, 1831-1836
Annals of discovery. A. Moorehead. il New Yorker 45:31-4+ Ag 30; 41-4+ S 6 '69
Darwin and the Beagle, by A. Moorehead. Review
Atlan 224:164-6 N '69. E. Weeks
Newsweek 74:122-3 O 20 '69. R. A. Sokolov
In the wake of Darwin's Beagle. A. Villiers. il Nat Geog 136:449-95 O '69
BEAGLES (dogs)
It really isn't rabbit hunting without hounds. E. A. Bauer. il Outdoor Life 144:58-61+ N '69
What's good beagle work? D. M. Duffey. il Outdoor Life 144:122-14+ Ag '69
BEAL, Doone
Some still unspoiled islands in the Greek sun. Holiday 46:46-7+ Ag '69
BEAL, Jack
Unphotography. il por Time 93:80-1 Ap 11 '69
BEALE, Betty
Greatest snobs are men; interview, ed. by deR. McQuade. pors Life 66:31+ F 28 '69
BEALL, Lewis L.
Academic freedom and the Third reich. Clear House 43:483-7 Ap '69
BEALS, Edward W.
Vegetational change along altitudinal gradients. bibliog Science 165:981-5 S 5 '69
BEAMS, Jesse Wakefield
Beams retires at Virginia but only to go on working. R. H. Ellis. pors Phys Today 22: 97-8 Ag '69
BEAMS. See Girders
BEAN, Alan L.
Apollo 12, by the crew. por Life 67:33+ D 19 '69
Moonwalk: the sky was never as black as here. U S News 67:30 D 1 '69

about

Blithe spirits in space. por Time 94:30 N 21 '69
To the moon with a light touch. por Newsweek 74:90 N 17 '69
See also
Space flight to the moon—Manned flights—Conrad-Bean-Gordon flight, 1969
BEAN bags. See Beanbags
BEANBAGS
Bean bag frog is good at poses. il Sunset 142:148 Ap '69
BEANS
Broadwalk for the beans. N. H. Berlin. il Org Gard & Farm 16:35 Jl '69
Scarlet runners, a heroic harvest. il Sunset 142:228+ Mr '69
See also
Cookery—Vegetables
Lima beans
BEAR, Fred Bernard
Of Bear, bow & buck. R. Kennedy. il por Time 94:61 N 14 '69
BEAR, Marjorie Warvelle
Herbs for permanence. Horticulture 47:26-7+ S '69
BEAR claws. See Pastry
BEAR hunting
Bear by the ear. B. Cochran. il Outdoor Life 144:72-5+ N '69
Bear that wouldn't quit; ed. by B. East. M. Reynolds. il Outdoor Life 143:66-7+ My '69
Bears I have known. B. Cheff. il Outdoor Life 143:48-51+ F '69
Big track: Ottawa national forest. C. T. Johnson. il Outdoor Life 144:68-9+ Jl '69

BEAR hunting—*Continued*
Green Mountain bear chase. D. Knight. il
Outdoor Life 144:72-5+ O '69
Icy expedition; polar bear hunting, Spitz-
bergen islands. il Travel 131:19 Ap '69
Last grizzly in Shasta. E. Weigart. il Field
& S 74:60-1+ Je '69
Mark of the grizzly. R. V. Broadbent. il
Outdoor Life 144:68-71+ Ag '69
Spring bear hunt. J. W. Valentine. il Outdoor
Life 143:78-9+ Mr '69
BEARBERRIES
Attractive native; manzanita. W. Radcliffe.
Horticulture 47:12 N '69
If the going is rough, manzanita. il Sunset
143:240+ N '69
BEARD, Butch
Beard that's the greatest! H. L. Masin. por
Sr Schol 94:28-9 Mr 7 '69
BEARD, James A.
Glasses to use in many ways. House & Gard
135:165 Ap '69
House & garden cook book (cont) House &
Gard 135:157-9+ Ap '69
BEARD, Peter Hill
Twelve strokes of the cane. il por Newsweek
74:47 D 1 '69
BEARDED irises. See Irises
BEARDEN, Romare
Romare Bearden. H. Ghent. il por Sch Arts
68:22-3 Ap '69
BEARDSLEY, Aubrey Vincent
Black and white: a portrait of Aubrey
Beardsley, by B. Brophy. Review
Art in Am 57:57 N '69. J. Jacobs
BEARDSLEY, Grant L. Jr
New Atlantic tuna fishery; with biographical
sketch. por Sea Front 15:152-9. 191 My '69
BEARDWOOD, Roger
Doctors of the corporate ego. Fortune 79:108-
10+ My 1 '69
Melville draws a bead on the $50-billion
fashion market. Fortune 80:110-14+ D '69
Reveille sounds for the hoteliers. Fortune
80:110-15+ S '69
Sophistication comes to the tax havens. For-
tune 79:94-7+ F '69
BEARINGS (machinery)
Kaman designs ball bearing replacement;
ceramic-faced sliding bearings. il Avia-
tion W 91:76-7+ Ag 18 '69
BEARS
Emperor of the floes. G. Ott. il Nat Wildlife
7:42-7 F '69
Getting along with grizzlies. J. S. Crawford.
il Outdoor Life 144:45-7+ N; 44-7+ D '69
Grizzlies must go? attacks on national park
visitors. il Sci Digest 66:45 O '69
Grizzlies, the magnificent menace. J. George.
il Read Digest 95:117-21 Jl '69
Grizzly bear in the national parks. E. G.
Bowman. il Am For 75:16-18+ Jl; 16-18+
Ag '69
In defense of the grizzly. R. Caras. il Audu-
bon 71:52-5 My '69; Reply. G. B. Moment.
71:108-12 S '69
Night of the grizzlies; condensation. J. Ol-
sen. il Sports Illus 30:38-44+ My 12; 44-8+
My 19; 36-8+ My 26 '69
Polar bear. S. Christoph. il Nat Parks 43:9-11
Ag '69
To the aid of the defenseless grizzly. Nat
Parks 43:22 D '69
BEARS, Photography. See Photography of
animals
BEASLEY, Joseph Diehl
Louisiana's quiet revolution in family plan-
ning. A. Gordon. il por Todays Health
48:38-41+ Ja '70
BEASLEY, Thomas M. and Held, E. E.
Nickel-63 in marine and terrestrial biota.
soil, and sediment. bibliog Science 164:
1161-3 Je 6 '69
BEASON, Eugene
Getting started in gem cutting. Mech Illus
65:114-16+ O '69
BEATLES
Apple corps four. C. E. Fager. Chr Cent 86:
386-8 Mr 19 '69
Beatles: Abbey Road. E. Sander. il pors Sat
R 52:69 O 25 '69
Beatles besieged; Allen Klein to manage en-
terprises. il Time 93:78 My 30 '69
Beatles: cheerful coherence. il Time 94:57 O
3 '69
Beatles illustrated lyrics, ed. by A. Aldridge.
Review
New Repub 161:25-6 N 8 '69. R. Whitte-
more
Beatles in the web. pors Newsweek 74:130-1
O 20 '69
Beatles' ninety-minute bore, and the Rolling
Stones' Beggars banquet. J. Gabree. il pors
Hi Fi 19:84-5 Mr '69

Great rock conspiracy. P. A. Luce. Nat R
21:959+ S 23 '69
Records: rock, etc. E. Willis. New Yorker
44:55-6+ F 1 '69
Wisdom of their years. A. G. Aronowitz.
Life 66:12 Ja 31 '69
Worm in the apple. il Newsweek 73:84+ My
12 '69
Would you want your sister to marry a
Beatle? S. Lydon. Ramp Mag 7:65-6+ N
30 '68
Bibliography
Up from Liverpool. H. Gould. Commentary
47:79-83 Ap '69
BEATNIKS
See also
Hippies
BEATON, Cecil
Shooting the plums; show at the Museum of
the city of New York. D. I. Shirey. il News-
week 73:118 My 12 '69
BEATTIE, Paul Hamilton. See Lederer, R. jt.
auth.
BEATTY, Barbara R. See Miller, O. L. jr. jt.
auth.
BEATTY, Jerome, Jr
Sunfish. Holiday 45:62-3+ Je '69
Trade winds. See issues of Saturday review
BEATTY, Joseph
Poems (after the Japanese) Commonweal
91:47 O 10 '69
BEATTY, Talley
Talley Beatty dance co; NY city center. J.
Anderson. Dance Mag 43:33-4 Jl '69
BEAUBIER, Edward W.
Experiences with differentiated staffing. To-
days Ed 58:56-7 Mr '69
BEAUCHAMP, Louise
Autumn; story. Seventeen 29:80-1 Ja '70
BEAUDIN, Bruce D.
Excerpt from testimony before Subcommit-
tee on constitutional rights, January 21.
1969. Cong Digest 48:113+ Ap '69
BEAUFORT COUNTY, S.C.
Underdeveloped country. il Time 93:25 F 28
'69
BEAUJON, Paul, pseud. See Warde, B. L. B.
BEAUMONT, Lynn
Charting the wide Pacific; Fiji to the Philip-
pines. Sat R 52:48 S 13 '69
BEAUTIFUL, The. See Aesthetics
BEAUTIFUL one is here! story. See Bradbury,
R.
BEAUTIFYING of cities. See Municipal im-
provement
BEAUTY. See Aesthetics
BEAUTY, Personal
Beauty at home. C. Bartel. See issues of
American home
Beauty bulletin. See issues of Vogue
Beauty checkout. See issues of Vogue
Beauty markers, 1970. il McCalls 97:62-3 Ja
'70
Beauty month of May. il Seventeen 28:144-5
My '69
Beauty of it. il Redbook 134:66-7+ Ja '70
Beauty problems you may have too, and
new ways to solve them. il Seventeen
29:70-1 Ja '70
Beauty question box; questions and answers.
McCalls 96:64 Mr; 76 Ap; 54 My; 40 Je '69
Beauty safari; Mona Grant and Margie Lind-
say on a tour of Manhattan. il Seventeen
28:144-5 Mr '69
Dear beauty editor. See issues of Seventeen
Dear beauty editors: questions and answers
(cont of) Beauty question box; questions
and answers. See issues of McCall's
Electrifying beauty. il Redbook 132:78-80+
Ja '69
Facial flip-ups: the new feminine logic. Vogue
153:116 Je '69
Focus on summertime beauty. il Good H 169:
76-7 Jl '69
Good looks & good health. R. Warfield.
See issues of House & garden incorporat-
ing Living for young homemakers
The look you like; questions and answers; ed.
by L. Allen. See issues of Today's health
Non-stop beauty. Harp Baz 103:122 Ja '70
Plot a pretty angle or curve; face shape. il
Seventeen 28:156-9 Ap '69
Round-the-clock beauty on a time budget.
il Good H 168:148-9 Mr '69
She's fifteen and fabulous; M. F. Boles. il
Seventeen 28:150-1 My '69
Spas: the healthy way to weekend. il Mlle
69:88-9 Jl '69
Stay young and beautiful. N. Heineman. See
issues of Parents' magazine & better
family living
Summer and you. il Vogue 153:105+ Je '69

BEAUTY, Personal—*Continued*
Teachers' dress and grooming. A. C. Harding. Todays Ed 58:46-7 Ja '69
Things to come in beauty. Harp Baz 103:91 Ja '70
Thirty-five pick-up tricks. il Mlle 68:136-9 F '69
Three beauty make-overs that will last. il Redbook 133:102-7+ O '69
Three faces of beauty; three generations, the Powerses have a message for you, ed. by S. Harney. il Ladies Home J 86:88-9+ Mr '69
Twelve ways to give yourself the best beauty care. il Good H 169:276-8 O '69
Twenty-five ways to feel better, look better. il Vogue 155:100-3 Ja 15 '70
Your own private mini-spa. il House & Gard 135:37+ Ja '69
See also
Baths
Exercise
Hair
Hairdressing
Hand
Make-up
Manicuring

Anecdotes, facetiae, satire, etc.
How well you look! E. Sheppard. Harp Baz 102:168-9 Ag '69

Terminology
Vogue's own beauty dictionary. il Vogue 153:196-9+ F 1; 172-7+ Mr 1 '69
BEAUTY contests
Atlantic City; site of the Miss America pageant. C. Brossard. il Holiday 46:90-1+ S '69
Face to face with Miss Black America. S. Williams. Seventeen 28:151 Mr '69
There she is, Miss America. P. Ryan. il Sports Illus 31:70-2+ O 6 '69
BEAUTY culture
Charm is her business. N. Bowden. il Farm J 93:84-5 Mr '69
BEAUVOIR, Simone de
More on the second sex. D. Littlejohn. New Repub 160:27-8 Mr 8 '69
BEAVERS, Allen L. Jr
Use computers in my camp? Never! address. Camp Mag 41:10-11 F '69
BEAVERS, Fred
One-armed high-wire artist. F. Taylor. il pors Pop Mech 131:138-9 Ap '69
BEBOUT, Sheila
Traveler's choice. Travel 131:16 Je '69
BECAUSE of the waters of the flood; story. See Helprin, M. H.
BECHARA, Antonio
Contemporary Puerto Rican artists. Sch Arts 69:27 O '69
BECHER, Bernhard
Beauty in the awful. il Time 94:68+ S 5 '69
—and Becher, Hilla
Mineheads; photographs. Arch Forum 129: 68-73 D '68
BECHER, Hilla. See Becher. B. jt. auth.
BECHER, Ulrich
European literary scene. R. J. Clements. Sat R 52:23 Ag 2 '69
BECHILL, William D.
Older Americans act; three years from the beginning. Aging 171:3-4 Ja '69
BECHUANALAND. See Botswana
BECK, Albert W.
Children's art; a case against contests. Sch Arts 69:18-19 N '69
Loss of reason and a lack of structure. Sch Arts 69:24-5 O '69
BECK, Evelyn Torton
(tr) See Singer, I. B. Key
BECK, James F.
Try a modified business education program. Todays Ed 58:69 N '69
BECK, Joan
Christmas without crises? Are you kidding? Todays Health 47:28-31+ D '69
BECK, Julian
Theater of ignorance. R. Gilman. Atlan 224: 35-42 Jl '69
BECK, Toni
Call them exercises if you must; excerpts from Fashion your figure. Harp Baz 102: 200 O '69
BECKER, Ernest
Evaded question; science and human nature. Commonweal 89:638-42+; 90:34 F 21, Ap 4 '69
BECKER, Harold K.
Do police helicopters justify their cost? Am City 84:70-1 N '69

BECKER, Herman F.
Ancestral American forests. Am For 75:12-15+ Mr '69
Some living plant fossils. Am For 75:12-15+ Jl '69
BECKER, James M. and Anderson, L. F.
Riders on the earth together. Am Ed 5:2-4 My '69
BECKER, Jim
Look what's happened to Honolulu! Nat Geog 136:500-31 O '69
BECKER, Russell J.
Can seminaries break out? Chr Cent 86:585-6+ Ap 23 '69
BECKET, James
Greece: the rack and the bomb. Nation 209: 6-7 Jl 7 '69
BECKETT, Samuel
Come and go; a dramaticule for John Calder. Harp Baz 102:136-7 Ag '69
Samuel Beckett talks about Beckett; interview, ed. by J. Gruen. por Vogue 154:210-11 D '69

about
Beckett wins a Nobel prize. il pors Life 67: 93-4 N 7 '69
Kyrie eleison without God. por Time 94:55 O 31 '69
Samuel Beckett. T. Bishop. por Sat R 52: 26-7+ N 15 '69
Samuel Beckett wins Nobel literature prize. por Pub W 196:29-30 N 3 '69
73,000 gallons of chicken soup. K. Nyren. Library J 94:4327 D 1 '69
These were the hours, by N. Cunard. Review
New Yorker 45:207-8 N 15 '69. Genêt
View from the wasteland. por Newsweek 74:54 N 3 '69
BECKHAM, Barry
Listen to the black graduate. you might learn something. Esquire 72:98+ S '69
BECKMAN Instruments, Incorporated
Long-distance runner. il Forbes 104:46+ S 1 '69
BECKWOURTH, James Pierson
Black man in the American West. D. T. Schoenberger. bibliog il por Negro Hist Bul 32:7-11 Mr '69
BED linens. See Linen, Household
BED-sitting rooms. See Bedrooms
BEDARD, William D. and others
Western pine beetle: field response to its sex pheromone and a synergistic host terpene. myrcene. bibliog Science 164:1284-5 Je 13 '69
BEDDING
See also
Blankets
Coverlets
Sheets
BEDE, James
Build this new four-place cabin plane for $3500. K. V. Brown. il Pop Mech 131:112-17+ My '69
Electrical failure halts record attempt. Aviation W 91:74-5 N 24 '69
BEDELL, Eugenia
Least Antilles. Motor B 124:60-1+ N '69
BEDFORD, Sybille
Authors & editors. Pub W 195:18 Ap 7 '69
BEDFORD-Stuyvesant restoration corporation, Brooklyn
Super block. New Yorker 45:48-9 N 22 '69
BEDIENT, Calvin
To be a salvation. Nation 208:120 Ja 27 '69
BEDROOM furnishings. See Household furnishings
BEDROOM furniture
Inside story on buying bedroom furniture. il Good H 169:122-8+ S '69
BEDROOMS
Adults only retreat. il Bet Hom & Gard 47: 68-9 O '69
Corner your talent. il Seventeen 28:322-3+ Ag '69
Country-look nooks. il Seventeen 28:180-3 Ap '69
Design for living; scratch pad. P. Bartlett. il Mlle 69:194-5 Ag '69
Parents' suite, a private personal world. il House & Gard 135:54-5 Ja '69
Room service. il Seventeen 28:168-9 My '69
Small wonders; the master bedroom. il Redbook 133:102-5+ S '69
Space to spare. il Seventeen 28:160-3 Mr '69
Three designs for the bedroom-plus. il House B 111:118-21 O '69
Twenty-four hour bedroom. il House & Gard 135:72-9 F '69
Where did the bedroom go? E. Kirk. House B 111:38+ Je '69

BEDS
Headboard with cabinet-tables. il Sunset 143:96 S '69
Here and now; midsummer pickup for the bedroom doldrums; new headboards. T. Bowman. il House B 111:80-1 Ag '69
Moving beddo; Japanese beds. il Time 94:78 D 12 '69
These bunk beds just go away. il Sunset 142:116 F '69
See also
Cribs (beds)
Mattresses

BEDSPREADS. See Coverlets

BEDTIME tale; story. See Kaufman, L.

BEE-balm. See Horsemint

BEE culture
Varied fare of the honeybee. R. A. Morse. il Natur Hist 78:58-65 Je '69

BEE hunts. See Bees

BEE stings. See Insect bites and stings

BEE trees. See Bees

BEEBE, Lynne C.
Unanimous decision; story. Todays Ed 58:35-6 Ja '69

BEEBE, Tim
Baddest of the bad. J. Thawley. il pors Hot Rod 22:64-6 My '69

BEECH aircraft corporation
Beech, Cessna sales hit peak in fiscal year. Aviation W 91:55 N 24 '69
Beech sales hit six-month peak. Aviation W 90:101 Ap 28 '69
Beech seeks airline viewpoints for advanced commuter aircraft. Aviation W 90:80 Mr 17 '69
Beech sets sales targets, adds new models. E. J. Bulban. il Aviation W 91:78-9+ D 15 '69
Beech's first-quarter volume soars; record year expected. Aviation W 90:24 Ja 27 '69
HS-125 paves way for Beech expansion. E. J. Bulban. Aviation W 92:21-2 Ja 5 '70

BEECHER, Henry K.
Human studies. bibliog Science 164:1256-8 Je 13 '69

BEEF
See also
Cookery—Meat

Prices
See Meat—Prices

BEEF grading. See Meat—Grading and standardization

BEEF imports. See Import quotas

BEEF industry. See Meat industry and trade

BEEKEEPING. See Bee culture

BEELER, George W. jr. See Reuter, H. jt. auth.

BEER, C. G.
Laughing gull chicks: recognition of their parents' voices. bibliog Science 166:1030-2 N 21 '69

BEER
Beer. Consumer Bul 52:24+ Mr '69
Beers. il Consumer Rep 34:474-7 Ag '69
Monks' brew; made in Andechs, Germany. W. H. Nelson. il Holiday 45:58-9+ Je '69
See also
Blatz brewing company
Brewing industries
Rheingold breweries, incorporated

BEERMAN, Miriam
Beyond nightmare. il Time 93:74+ Je 13 '69

BEES
Alkali bees: response of adults to pathogenic fungi in brood cells. S. W. T. Batra and G. E. Bohart. bibliog il Science 165:607 Ag 8 '69
Are honeybees deficient in phosphomannose isomerase? S. A. Saunders and others. bibliog il Science 164:858-9 My 16 '69
Biologically active compounds in orchid fragrances. C. H. Dodson and others. bibliog il Science 164:1243-9 Je 13 '69
Brood care in halictine bees. G. Knerer. bibliog il Science 164:429-30 Ap 25 '69
Dance versus smell. J. Chamblin. il Sci N 95:383 Ap 19 '69
Honey bee recruitment to food sources: olfaction or language? A. M. Wenner and others. bibliog il Science 164:84-6 Ap 4 '69; Reply. R. Dawkins. 165:751 Ag 22 '69
Sex control by bees: a voluntary act of egg fertilization during oviposition. H. S. Gerber and E. C. Klostermeyer. bibliog il Science 167:82-4 Ja 2 '70
Tapping a bee tree. R. A. Morse. il Cons 23:10-11 F '69
See also
Bee culture

Anecdotes, facetiae, satire, etc.
Uncle Perk's bee tree. C. Ford. il Field & S 74:8+ Ag '69

BEES, Spelling. See Spelling—Competitions

BEESWAX
Tapping a bee tree. R. A. Morse. il Cons 23:10-11 F '69

BEETHOVEN, Ludwig van
Anyone for Furtwangler's 1942 Beethoven Ninth in stereo? D. Hamilton. il Hi Fi 19:68 Ap '69
Beethoven, by G. R. Marek. Review
New Yorker 45:51 D 27 '69. W. Sargeant
Early Beethoven by Blumental. M. Kanny. Am Rec G 36:16-17 S '69
Gospel of Beethoven as Szell is his prophet; performance of Ninth symphony. I. Kolodin. Sat R 52:62-3 N 29 '69
His 200th anniversary celebration is starting the Beethoven revolution; excerpts from Lives of the great composers. H. C. Schonberg. il pors N Y Times Mag p32-3+ O 19 '69; Discussion. p36+ N 9 '69
Late Beethoven subtly nuanced. R. P. Morgan. Hi Fi 19:78 Ag '69
Records:
Mass in C. Opera N 33:33 F 22 '69
Yale quartet's triumphant Beethoven: an opus 127 from Cardinal. M. Kanny. il Am Rec G 36:100-1 O '69

Anecdotes, facetiae, satire, etc.
Beethoven new-born. E. T. Cone. Am Scholar 38:389-400 Sum '69

BEETLES
Biochemistry at 100°C: explosive secretory discharge of bombardier beetles (brachinus) D. J. Aneshansley and others. bibliog il Science 165:61-3 Jl 4 '69; Same abr. with title Ingenuities of nature. Sat R 52:48 Ag 2 '69
Freezing tolerance in an adult insect. L. K. Miller. bibliog il Science 166:105-6 O 3 '69
Host findings by odor in the myrmecophilic beetle atemeles pubicollis bris. (staphylinidae) B. Hölldobler. bibliog il Science 166:757-8 N 7 '69
Hot beetle. bombardier. Sci Am 221:102 S '69
Masking of the aggregation pheromone in dendroctonus pseudotsugae hopk. J. A. Rudinsky. bibliog il Science 166:884-5 N 14 '69
Maxillary mycangium in the mountain pine beetle. H. S. Whitney and S. H. Farris. bibliog il Science 167:54-5 Ja 2 '70
Mimicry of hymenoptera by beetles with unconventional flight. R. E. Silberglied and T. Eisner. il Science 163:486-8 Ja 31 '69
Pheromone response in pine bark beetles: influence of host volatiles. G. B. Pitman. bibliog Science 166:905-6 N 14 '69
Sex attractant of female dermestid beetle trogoderma inclusum le conte. J. O. Rodin and others. bibliog il Science 165:904-5 Ag 29 '69
Sharpshooters of the insect world; bombardier beetle. il Chem 42:6-7 N '69
Synthetic juvenile hormone: induction of sex pheromone production in ips confusus. J. H. Borden and others. bibliog il Science 166:1626-7 D 26 '69
Western pine beetle: field response to its sex pheromone and a synergistic host terpene. myrcene. W. D Bedard and others. bibliog il Science 164:1284-5 Je 13 '69
See also
Deathwatch beetles
Japanese beetles
Sweet clover weevils
Water beetles

BEETON, Isabella Mary (Mayson)
World's greatest cookery book. E. Marlowe. il por Am Home 72:40+ D '69

BEFORE a girl marries; story. See Kaufman, L.

BEGGING and beggars
Panhandling 1969 style. America 121:347 O 25 '69
Young beggars; panhandling in Manhattan. il Newsweek 74:49 Ag 25 '69

BEGGS, James M.
Never mind the experts. Nation 209:620 D 8 '69

BEGLEITER, H. and Platz, A.
Evoked potentials: modifications by classical conditioning. bibliog Science 166:769-71 N 7 '69

BEGONIAS
Fascinating begonias. R. P. Merry. il Horticulture 47:26-9 Je '69
His are beginner's begonias. il Sunset 142:228 Ap '69

BEGUIA (island)
  See also
  Architecture, Domestic—Beguia (island)
BEHAGUE, Gerard
  Reviews of books. Mus Q 55:115-20 Ja '69
BEHAVIOR. See Etiquette; Manners and customs
BEHAVIOR (psychology)
  Air piracy: they want a moment of power and glory. S. McBee. il Life 66:26-7 Ap 18 '69
  Behavior patterns of scientists; address, December 1968. R. K. Merton. Am Scholar 38:197-225 Spr '69
  Brain control: tomorrow's curse or blessing? J. Reinert. Il Sci Digest 66:14-19 N '69
  Crime and mental illness: some problems in defining and labeling deviant behavior. S. A. Shah. bibliog Ment Hy 53:21-33 Ja '69
  Evaded question. science and human nature. E. Becker. il Commonweal 89:638-42+ F 21 '69; Reply with rejoinder. J. R. Pleasants. Commonweal 90:59+ Ap 4 '69
  Man, one of evolution's mistakes? adaptation of address, September 1969. A. Koestler. il N Y Times Mag p28-9+ O 19 '69; Discussion. p 14 N 9; 52+ N 23 '69
  Man talk; oh, would you like to swing with a star? D. Newman and R. Benton. il Mlle 68:118 Ap '69
  Man's silent signals; nonverbal vocabulary of gestures and expressions. il Time 93:86 Je 13 '69
  On permanent commitment. R. J. Westley. America 120:612-17 My 24 '69; Discussion. 121:1 Jl 5 '69
  Proof of Parkinson. Time 94:66 Jl 18 '69
  Time of the fugitive; religious man: from ritual to self-discovery. C. A. Weber. Commonweal 90:137-40 Ap 18 '69; Reply. M. L. Farrell. 90:221+ My 9 '69
  Why people don't help in a crisis. J. M. Darley and B. Latané. Read Digest 94:65-9 My '69
  See also
  Man
  Motivation (psychology)
BEHAVIOR, Group. See Groups (sociology)
BEHAVIOR of animals. See Animals—Habits and behavior
BEHAVIOR problems (children) See Problem children
BEHAVIOR therapy. See Psychotherapy
BEHAVIORAL sciences
  Behavioral sciences. See issues of Science news
  Behavioral sciences and the medical school; report of meeting. J. H. U. Brown. Science 163:964-7 F 28 '69
  Behavioral science or electioneering? excerpt from study by a National academy of sciences panel. Sat R 52:65-7 N 1 '69
  Public policy and behavioral science; excerpt from testimony before the U.S. Senate foreign relations committee, June 20, 1969. M. Mead. Bul Atom Sci 25:8-10 D '69
  Science takes a closer look at man. L. Lessing. il Fortune 81:112-14+ Ja '70
BEHME, Bob
  September of the humpback. Field & S 74:140-2 S '69
  Those amazing A.T.V.'s. Field & S 74:48-51+ Ag '69
BEHRENS, Herbert R.
  Private stock exchange? por Forbes 103:70+ Mr 15 '69
BEHRENS, John C.
  Freelance job idea: political ghostwriting. Writers Digest 49:48-50+ N '69
BEHRENS, Richard
  Ash glazes for Cone 6. Ceram Mo 17:31 Ja '69
  Cone 6 stoneware. Ceram Mo 17:32-3 Mr '69
  Crackle glazes. Ceram Mo 17:23+ O '69
  Oven and range-top clay bodies and glazes. Ceram Mo 17:27+ S '69
  Raku glazes. Ceram Mo 17:29 N '69
  Testing clay bodies. Ceram Mo 17:26-7 My '69
BEHRING, Kenneth E.
  Trial run for instant housing. il Bsns W p 111-12 O 11 '69
BEHRMAN, Daniel
  Don Quixote of the radio; reprint. UNESCO Courier 22:73-4+ Ag '69
  New world of the oceans; excerpt. UNESCO Courier 22:4-15 Je '69
BEICHMAN, Arnold
  Will teacher be the new drop-out? bibliog f N Y Times Mag p48-9+ D 7 '69
BEIDERBECKE, Bix
  Few corrections concerning Bix Beiderbecke. R. Dickerson. Esquire 71:72+ Ap '69
BEIDERBECKE, Leon Bismarck. See Beiderbecke, B.

BEIDLEMAN, Richard G.
  David Douglas in pursuit of plants. Horticulture 47:30-1+ F '69
BEINEMAN, Karen Sue
  Rainy day murders. il por Time 94:19 Ag 8 '69
BEIRUT
                    Banks
  See Banks and banking—Lebanon
            Hotels, restaurants, etc.
  Beirut p.m. D. Holden. il Holiday 45:60-1+ Je '69
BEISWANGER, George
  First repertory program reviewed. Dance Mag 43:49-50 Ja '69
BEJERANO, N. Roth-. See Roth-Bejerano, N.
BELAFONTE, Harry
  Belafonte plays angel on and off the screen. il pors Ebony 24:76-8+ O '69
  Making of The angel Levine. R. Kotlowitz. Harper 239:98-100 Jl '69
BELAÚNDE TERRY, Fernando
  New junta, but same old Peru. Ramp Mag 7:18+ N 30 '68
BELDING Heminway company
  Thread of prosperity. S. Margetts. Duns R 94:77-8+ S '69
BELEY, Gene
  At home with Andy Williams. Parents Mag 44:50-2 Jl '69
BELFAST
                    Parades
  Belfast: in glorious remembrance; Orangemen's parade. C. McWilliams. Nation 209:137-8 Ag 25 '69
                    Riots
  Backlash in Belfast. il Newsweek 74:54+ O 27 '69
BELFORD, Barbara
  Bermuda: the timeless island. Travel & Camera 32:78-81 S '69
  Cruise ships. Travel & Camera 32:64-5 N '69
  Italy's five lands. Travel 131:46-9 F '69
  Queen Elizabeth 2. Travel & Camera 32:35+ Jl '69
  Restorations West. Travel 132:56-60 N '69
BELGIAN CONGO. See Congo (Democratic Republic)
BELGIAN cookery. See Cookery, Belgian
BELGIUM
      See also
  Booksellers and bookselling—Belgium
  Bruges
  Brussels
  Colleges and universities—Belgium
  Mining industry and finance—Belgium
  Protestant churches—Belgium
            Description and travel
  Oh to be in Belgium. N. S. Hazelton. Nat R 21:599 Je 17 '69
            Foreign relations
  Consular convention with Belgium transmitted to the Senate; message, October 8, 1969. R. M. Nixon. Dept State Bul 61:424 N 17 '69
            Historic houses, etc.
  See also
  Louvain, Belgium—Historic houses, etc.
            History
              Bibliography
  Articles and other books received; comp. by P. H. Laurent. See issues of American historical review
            Industries
  Belgium's muscle-bound giant; Société générale. P. Siekman. il Fortune 79:98-103+ F '69
  Empain: the durable dynasty. il Fortune 80:191 Ag 15 '69
      See also
  Brussels—Industries
BELÍAEV, Pavel Ivanovich
      See also
  Space flight—Manned flights—Belíaev-Leonov flight, 1965
BELIEF in God. See Faith
BELIEVE in me; story. See Cave, H.
BELIKOV, Vasilii. See Nesmeíanov, A. N. jt. auth.
BELITT, Ben
  On quaking bog; poem. New Yorker 45:34 Ja 3 '69
BELIVEAU, Jean
  Grand Jean a mighty man is he. G. Ronberg. il pors Sports Illus 30:24-7 My 5 '69

BELKNAP, Bill
Shooting the Canyon. Travel & Camera 32:
46-7 Je '69
BELL, Alexander Graham
Father Bell. por Forbes 103:33 Ja 15 '69
BELL, Alexander Melville
Father Bell. por Forbes 103:33 Ja 15 '69
BELL, Arthur
Richard Scarry's best Switzerland ever. Pub
W 196:41-2 O 20 '69
BELL, Arthur H.
Brats and bayonets: the rhetorics of the
Children's campaign. bibliog f Engl J 58:
1038-41 O '69
BELL, Charles G.
Litany of women; poem. Poetry 114:298 Ag
'69
BELL, Daniel
Social change in education and the change
in educational concepts; excerpt from Ap-
proaches to education for character, ed. by
C. H. Faust and J. Feingold. Sch & Soc 97:
322-6 Sum '69
BELL, Eugene. See MacKintosh, F. R. jt. auth.
BELL, George A. See Crihfield, B. jt. auth.
BELL, James G. See Hansen, E. jt. auth.
BELL, Joseph N.
Driver training: does it really do any good?
Pop Mech 131:93-7+ Ap '69
How to get along with a college freshman.
Todays Health 47:56-7+ My '69
Why the revolt against sex education? Good
H 169:92-3+ N '69
BELL, L. Nelson
Supernatural and miraculous. Chr Today 13:
30-1 F 28 '69
BELL, Larry J.
Enrichment through informal art apprecia-
tion with related art activity. Sch Arts 69:
10-11 S '69
BELL, Marvin
In memory of H. G. Grand (5-10¢ to $1.00)
poem. New Yorker 45:36 Je 21 '69
Ring; Escape into you; Drifting; More going
for walks; On the death of a great critic;
Toward certain divorce; Present; Students;
poems. Poetry 113:302-9 F '69
To the sky; poem. Poetry 115:109 N '69
BELL, Rod
Choosing a digital display. Electr World 81:
25-9 F '69
BELL, Stanley E. and others
Students as tutors. Clear House 44:242-4 D
'69
BELL, Vic
How to repair VTR's. Radio-Electr 40:79-83
Je '69
BELL of Dolores; drama. See Campbell, C.
BELL telephone laboratories
Magnetic tug toward the future; work on
memory devices. il Bsns W p78-9 Ag 9 '69
Operation survival; systems that will survive
almost any catastrophe. J. W. Foss and
R. W. Mayo. il Electr World 82:41-3 Ag '69
BELLAK, Richard
Montessori in Guatemala. il Sat R 52:47-9 Ag
16 '69
BELLEVUE, Wash.

Housing

High density, low-rents for young families
in complex on wooded hill. il Arch Rec
146:194-5 S '69
**BELLEVUE hospital, New York. See New York
(city)—Bellevue hospital**
BELLFLOWERS. See Codonanthe crassifolia
BELLI, James A. and Shelton, Merijean
Potentially lethal radiation damage; repair by
mammalian cells in culture. bibliog Science
165:490-2 Ag 1 '69
BELLINGHAM family
Bellingham coat-of-arms. H. K. Eilers. il
Hobbies 74:114 Je '69
BELLINI, Vincenzo
Bellini, by L. Orrey. Review
Am Rec G por 36:227-8 N '69. R. W.
Gutman
Opera N 34:30-1 O 11 '69. R. A. Tuggle
La Callas of yore, iridescence and marble.
P. L. Miller. Am Rec G 36:106 O '69
Music to my ears; concert performance of
La straniera. I. Kolondin. Sat R 52:67 Ap
12 '69
Report: New York: concert performance of
La straniera. J. W. Freeman Opera N 33:
24 My 17 '69
BELLONI, Manuel
Leopoldo Lugones. Américas 21:15-17+ Ja '69

BELLOTTO, Bernardo
Canaletto's paintings helped rebuild shat-
tered Warsaw, reprint. J. Hryniewiecki. il
UNESCO Courier 22:48-9 Ag '69
BELLOW, Saul
Mr Sammler's planet; novel. Atlan 224:95-
150 N; 99-142 D '69

about

From Cohn to Herzog. M. J. Hoffman. Yale
R 58:342-58 Mr '69
Odyssey of Saul Bellow. A. Bezanker. Yale
R 58:359-71 Mr '69
BELLS
Bells of San Luis Obispo. T. Andreeva. il
Américas 21:12-14 Ag '69
Cire-perdue bells. L. E. Springer. il Hob-
bies 74:49+ D '69
BELLUZZI, James D. and Grossman, S. P.
Avoidance learning: long-lasting deficits af-
ter temporal lobe seizure. bibliog Science
166:1435-7 D 12 '69
BELLY dance. See Dancing, Moroccan
BELMONT, Michael de Levisson
American stocks, British style; interview.
Duns R 93:40-1+ Ja '69
BELMONT, Calif.

Housing

Luxury apartments with emphasis on spa-
cious units and individual privacy. il Arch
Rec 146:188-9 S '69
BELMONT market. See Brooklyn—Markets
BELMONT stakes. See Horse racing
BELMONTE, Robert M.
Voluntary joint public bidding. por Am City
84:162+ O '69
BELOFF, Nora
Professor Bismarck goes to Washington.
Atlan 224:77-82+ D '69
BELOGORODSKAĬA, Irina
Flowers for Irina. Time 93:36+ F 28 '69
BELOIT, Wis.
New idea is the ovals. R. G. Miller and S.
J. Goldschmidt. il Am City 84:101-2+ Je
'69

Music

Affiliate artists, a success story. C. L. Osborne. il Hi Fi 19:MA18-19 D '69
BELOIT college, Beloit, Wis.

Libraries

Two in one; letter to the editor. H. V. Deale.
ALA Bul 63:149 F '69
BELOPERONE guttata. See Shrimp plants
BELORUSSIA
Fifty years of Byelorussia. il UNESCO Cou-
rier 22:36-7 F '69
BELOUS, Leon Philip
Guideline on abortion. por Time 94:66 S 19 '69
BELOUS, Robert
Elf of the Alpine. il Audubon 71:52-7 N '69
BELSON, James A.
Excerpt from statement submitted to Sub-
committee on constitutional rights, January
30, 1969. Cong Digest 48:118+ Ap '69
BELT, Byron
Records. Chr Cent 86:421 Mr 26 '69
BELT, Elmer
Joy of Kate Steinitz. por Wilson Lib Bul
44:514-17 Ja '70
BELT, Forest H.
Hot, new multiband portables tune in al-
most anything. Pop Mech 132:46+ Jl '69
How to get better sound from your TV set.
Pop Mech 132:148-51+ S '69
How to have TV in every room in the house.
Pop Mech 132:126-9+ Ag '69
Improve your stereo sound. Am Home 72: 72+
Jl '69
New TV front-ends. Electr World 82:47-50
S '69
Radio & television news. See issues of Elec-
tronics world
TV chroma circuit alignment. Electr World
81:48-51 F '69
BELT, Louise M.
At last! a lawn we're proud of! Org Gard &
Farm 16:80-1 Ag '69
BELT sanders. See Sanding machines
BELTING
Tighten your belt. E. H. Nabb. il Yachting
125:108-9+ Ja '69
BELTON, Michael J. S. and Hunten, D. M.
Spectrographic detection of topographic fea-
tures on Mars. bibliog Science 166:225-7 O
10 '69
BELTRAN, Enrique
Forestry and the public domain; address. por
Am For 75:36-7+ D '69 (to be cont)

BELTRÁN, Enrique—*Continued*
about
Enrique Beltran receives Fernow awards. il pors Am For 75:8-9+ N '69
BELTS
Newest twist in belts; yarn belts. il Redbook 134:118-19+ D '69
BELTS, Safety. See Safety belts
BELTZ, John
John Beltz the new doctor Oldsmobile: interview, ed. by R. Brock. pors Motor T 21:62-4 Jl '69
BELUGA. See Griddle cakes
BEMBO, Pietro, cardinal
Pietro Bembo and the literary origins of the Italian madrigal. D. T. Mace. bibliog f il Mus Q 55:65-86 Ja '69
BEN, Philip
Absent presence of General de Gaulle. New Repub 161:12-13 O 11 '69
Arabs are not ready to make peace. New Repub 160:15-17 Mr 15 '69
Cairo says no and so does Moscow. New Repub 161:11-12 Jl 26 '69
Close ranks, the Chinese are coming! New Repub 161:18-19 S 20 '69
Paying the price for survival. New Repub 161:10-11 O 4 '69
Rich Richard's red Rumanians. New Repub 161:8-10 Ag 9 '69
Why's the President going to Bucharest? New Repub 161:16-17 Jl 12 '69
BEN-ARI, Uri
Generals mean business. il por Time 94:103 O 17 '69
BEN-NATAN, Asher
Undiplomatic diversions. Newsweek 74:30+ Jl 7 '69
BEN SALAH, Ahmed
Widening ripples. E. Behr. Newsweek 74: 46+ S 22 '69
BEN Franklin plays cupid; drama. See Nicholson, M. A.
BENACERRAF, Baruj. See Pierce, C. W. jt. auth.
BENCH, Johnny
Big zinger from Binger. R. Blount, jr. il pors Sports Illus 30:26-8+ Mr 31 '69
BENCHLEY, Nathaniel
Great Salt Lake, Mormons, purple mountains. Utah. Holiday 46:38-9+ Ag '69
BENCHLEY, Peter
I know what I'm doing here, I think. pors Holiday 46:18-21+ Ag '69
Rose garden rubbish and other glorious compositions. Life 66:60B-60D+ My 23 '69
BEND, Ore.
Hotels, restaurants, etc.
Sunriver: relaxed and natural down-home vernacular in Oregon. il Arch Rec 146:132-4 D '69
BENDETSEN, Karl Robin
Plywood-Champion: after the merger. S. Blickstein. il por Duns R 94:52-5 O '69
BENDINER, Elmer
Scholarly cop watching. Nation 208:515-18 Ap 21 '69
Troubadour of revolution. Nation 208:832-3 Je 30 '69
BENDITT, Earl P. See Page, R. C. jt. auth.
BENDIX, Dorothy
Teaching the concept of intellectual freedom: the state of the art; address, January 14, 1967. bibliog ALA Bul 63:351-62 Mr '69
BENDIX corporation
Miracles take longer. Forbes 104:22-3 S 1 '69
BENEDETTI-PICHLER, Anton Alexander
Benedetti-Pichler: the father of American microchemistry. D. B. Sabine. il por Chem 42:12-15 Je '69
BENEDICT, Sarah
Group action in preservation. Antiques 95: 388-9 Mr '69
BENEDIKT, Michael
Four psalms. Poetry 115:97-100 N '69
Water; Money; Sky; poems. Poetry 113:383-6 Mr '69
about
Box: plastic poetry; the Cubiculo. J. Anderson. Dance Mag 43:93 My '69
Critic of the month. L. Lieberman. Poetry 114:50-1 Ap '69
Fun in words. T. Baland. Nation 208:547 Ap 28 '69
BENEFICIAL finance company
See also
Benevest, incorporated
BENEFICIAL finance company of New York
Backslider; no. two to old rival Household finance. il Forbes 103:38 Mr 1 '69

BENELLI, Giovanni, abp
Pope's powerful no. 2. il por Time 93:63-4 Mr 14 '69
BENES, Jan
Authors & editors. B. A. Bannon. por Pub W 196:13-15 N 24 '69
BENESH, Rudolf
Choreology. R. Holden. il Opera N 33:8-12 Ap 19 '69
BENÉT, Stephen Vincent
Benét's John Brown's body: for study. P. J. Sheehan. Engl J 58:219-25 F '69
BENEVEST, incorporated
Luring clients with on-the-spot tax refunds. il Bsns W p80 D 20 '69
BENGALS (football club) See Football clubs
BENGNER, Lutz H.
Electronic loadbank, tests power supplies dynamically. Electr World 81:44-5+ Je '69
BENGTSON, Phil
Death by inches: Green Bay Packers 1968 season; excerpt from Jerry Kramer's farewell to football; ed. by D. Schaap. J. Kramer. il Sports Illus 31:50-9 Ag 4 '69
BEN HET, Seige of. See Vietnamese war, 1957 —Campaigns and battles
BENJAMIN, Annette Francis
Health in the home. See issues of American home
BENJAMIN, Curtis G.
Developing book industries of Asia. por Pub W 195:17-19 My 5 '69
BENJAMIN, Fred
Fred Benjamin dance company, Clark center for the performing arts. M. Marks. Dance Mag 43:84 Ja '69
BENJAMIN, Harry
Background. Sat R 52:72 O 4 '69
BENJAMIN, Joel
Joel Benjamin & dancers; the Cubiculo. J. Anderson. Dance Mag 43:76 Ag '69
BENJAMIN, Kathleen
Intimacy; poem. Seventeen 28:210 Ag '69
BENJAMIN, Richard
Dick Benjamin and Paula Prentiss: to love, honor, and analyze. M. W. Lear. il por Redbook 134:54-5+ Ja '70
Trade winds. C. Amory. Sat R 52:8 Jl 26 '69
BENJAMIN, Walter
Illuminations, ed. by H. Arendt. Review Commonweal 90:525-7 Ag 22 '69. M. Roloff
On Walter Benjamin. R. Alter. bibliog f Commentary 48:86-93 S '69
Thinking poetically. V. Lange. Atlan 223:138-41 Mr '69
BENJAMIN, William B. and Goodman, R. M.
Phosphorylation of dipteran chromosomes and rat liver nuclei. bibliog Science 166:629-31 O 31 '69
BENNETT, Benjamin K.
For H.K; Alcaics; poems. Poetry 115:41 O '69
BENNETT, Charles Edward
American seapower, 1969; address, May 13, 1969. Vital Speeches 35:550-3 Jl 1 '69
BENNETT, Edward L. and others
Rat brain: effects of environmental enrichment on wet and dry weights. bibliog Science 163:825-6 F 21 '69
BENNETT, Gudrun S. and Edelman, G. M.
Amino acid incorporation into rat brain proteins during spreading cortical depression. bibliog Science 163:393-5 Ja 24 '69
BENNETT, Hank
Short-wave listening. See issues of Popular electronics
BENNETT, I. See Thompson, T. E. jt. auth.
BENNETT, James L.
We built this tent trailer for $250. Pop Mech 131:164-8 F '69
BENNETT, Lerone, jr
Birth of black America. por Ebony 24:31-4+ Je: 25:31-4+ N '69
Of time, space and revolution. por Ebony 24: 31-4+ Ag '69
Rise of black power; excerpt from Before the Mayflower. Ebony 24:36-41+ F '69
BENNETT, Paul A.
Paul Bennett, private press keepsake. il Pub W 195:72-4 Ap 7 '69
Typophiles and a keepsake. F. Johnson. il pors Am Artist 33:66-9+ My '69
BENNETT, Ralph Kinney
Behind the high cost of auto repairs. Read Digest 95:57-62 S '69
BENNETT, Virginia D. C. and others
Experimental course in sex education for teachers. bibliog Ment Hy 53:625-31 O '69
BENNETT, Wallace Foster
Excerpt from address, August 11, 1969. Cong Digest 48:296 D '69
BENNETT, William M.
Bennett's revenge. por Newsweek 73:71-2 Je 30 '69

BENNETTE, Guy
San Francisco: down these meaningful
streets. bibliog por Wilson Lib Bul 43:872-5
My '69
BENNINGTON college, Bennington, Vt.
At Bennington the boys are the coeds. T.
Meehan. il N Y Times Mag p 12-13+ D 21
'69
BENNIS, Warren G.
Post-bureaucratic leadership. bibliog por
Trans-Action 6:44-51+ Jl '69; Excerpts. Cur
110:42-9 S '69
    about
Of many things; conception of leadership in
the church. D. R. Campion. America 120:
374 Ap 5 '69
BENOIT, Milton J.
Kids, crime and conservation. Cons 23:18-20+
Ap '69
BENREY, Ronald M.
Are electric watches really better? Pop Sci
195:130-3 Ag '69
Colorimeter you can build. Pop Sci 195:163-
6+ N '69
Electronic-flash light meter you can build.
Pop Sci 194:112-15 Mr '69
Great new locks, bad news for burglars. Pop
Sci 195:170-3+ S '69
I learned to fly without leaving the ground,
and so can you. Pop Sci 194:92-5+ Mr '69
I learned to ski electronically! Pop Sci 195:
136-8 D '69
Magic box tells you when one more is too
many. Pop Sci 194:102-5 Ap '69
Measure the speed of a bullet with this elec-
tronic stopwatch. Pop Sci 195:144-6+ Jl '69
Solder in a steel-wool blanket. Pop Sci 194:
214-15 Mr '69
BENS, John H.
If it isn't boring, it isn't education. Engl J
58:418-22 Mr '69
BENSCH, Klaus G. and others
Induction in vitro of microtubular crystals
by vinca alkaloids. bibliog Science 165:495-6
Ag 1 '69
BENSON, George A.
Psychoanalytic notes on the disavowal of
priestly authority. Chr Cent 86:738-41 My
28 '69
BENSON, Lee
Irrepressible world revolt; excerpt from The
irresponsible style in American politics. New
Repub 160:17-22 Ja 18; 32-3 F 22 '69
BENTHOS
Down into the sea in ships. R. S. Dietz and
R. F. Dill. il Sea Front 15:2-9 Ja '69
Ecology of the deep-sea benthos. H. L.
Sanders and R. R. Hessler. bibliog il Sci-
ence 163:1419-24 Mr 28 '69; Reply with re-
joinder. A. H. Clarke. 166:1033-4 N 21 '69
BENTINCK, Catherine A. and others
Relatives as informants in mental health re-
search. bibliog Ment Hy 53:446-50 Jl '69
BENTLEY, Beth
Morning fog; poem. Nation 209:292 S 22 '69
BENTLEY, Eric
Dialogue with Robert Brustein. New Re-
pub 160:12-13 My 17 '69
Naked American. New Repub 161:31-4 Ag 16
'69; Same abr. with title Changing sexual
mores; why the naked American on stage?
Cur 111:60-4 O '69
Theater. New Repub 161:31-4 Ag 9 '69
Theatre of interpretations. Nation 209:148-
9+ Ag 25 '69
(tr) See Biermann, W. Ballads by Wolf
Biermann
BENTLEY, Helen Delich
Lady skipper for the merchant fleet. il por
Bsns W p74-5 S 20 '69
BENTLEY, John
So what else is new? Pop Mech 131:114-19+
F '69
BENTLEY, Walter Owen
Man who made Bentleys. J. McCaughey. il
pors Pop Mech 132:260 O '69
BENTON, Robert. See Newman, D. jt. auth.
BENTON, Thomas Hart
Tom Benton at eighty, still at war with
bores and boobs. W. A. McWhirter. il
pors Life 67:64-6+ O 3 '69
BENTON, Ill.
Coal mining. T. Goldwasser. Atlan 224:28+
N '69
BENTONITE
Bentonite debris flows in northern Alaska.
D. M. Anderson and others. bibliog il
Science 164:173-4 Ap 11 '69
BENTZ, W. Kenneth, and others
Perceptions of mental illness among people
in a rural area. bibliog Ment Hy 53:459-65
Jl '69

BENVENUTI, Nino
Nino's hook stopped a Roman riot. M. Kram.
il pors Sports Illus 31:24-7 D 1 '69
BENZEDRINE. See Amphetamines
BENZENE
Benzene complexes with copper(II)montmor-
illonite. H. E. Doner and M. M. Mortland.
bibliog il Science 166:1406-7 D 12 '69
Crystal structure of benzene II at 25 kilobars.
C. J. Piermarini and others. bibliog il Sci-
ence 165:1250-5 19 '69
BENZINGER, Maude G.
Two vegetables for a permanent patch. Org
Gard & Farm 16:46-7 Je '69
BENZOPYRENE
Sarcoma-producing cell lines derived from
clones transformed in vitro by benzo
[a]pyrene. J. A. DiPaolo and others. bib-
liog il Science 165:917-18 Ag 29 '69
BENZPYRENE. See Benzopyrene
BERANEK, Leo L.
Acoustics. bibliog por Phys Today 22:47-53
N '69
BERBERINE
Berberine: complex with DNA. A. K. Krey
and F. E. Hahn. bibliog il Science 166:
755-7 N 7 '69
BERDAEV, Nikolai Aleksandrovich
Berdyaev: philosopher of hope. C. S. Calian.
Chr Cent 86:924-6 Jl 9 '69
BEREAVEMENT
Dual role of comforter and bereaved; re-
actions of medical personnel to the dying
child and his parents. E. Wallace and B. D.
Townes. bibliog Ment Hy 53:327-32 Jl '69
Good grief. Sci Am 220:52 Ap '69
Message of the kite. D. R. Stewart. il Read
Digest 95:122-5 Jl '69
BERELSON, Bernard
Beyond family planning. bibliog Science 163:
533-43 F 7 '69
BEREN, Ralph S. See Ashcom, B. M. jt. auth.
BERENSON, Bernard
Is I Tatti the keeper of the flame? S. Alex-
ander. il Holiday 46:36-7+ S '69
BERENSON, Conrad. See Dash, J. F. jt. auth.
BERENSON, Ruth
Art. Nat R 21:395-6 Ap 22 '69
Harlem on everybody's mind. Nat R 21:125 F
11 '69
How modern the Modern museum? Nat R 21:
656-8 Jl 1 '69
Metropolitan: worst foot forward. Nat R
21:1281-3 D 16 '69
Return to an older America. Nat R 21:813-
15 Ag 12 '69
This year's Christmas thing; toys as art.
Nat R 21:1272+ D 16 '69
Variety of high traditions. Nat R 21:33-4
Ja 14 '69
BERENSTAIN, Janice. See Berenstain, S. jt.
auth.
BERENSTAIN, Stanley, and Berenstain, Janice
It's all in the family. See issues of McCall's
BERESFORD, Aveline
Traveler's choice. Travel 132:24 Jl '69
BERG, Alban
Buchner and Berg. G. Weales. Commonweal
90:265 My 16 '69
Frau Berg; interview, ed. by J. H. Sutcliffe.
H. Berg. il por Opera N 33:12-13 Ap 12 '69
Loners. S. Jenkins, jr. Opera N 33:24-5 Ap 5
'69
Man who feels. J. W. Freeman. Opera N 33:
24-6 Ap 12 '69
Wozzeck. Criticism
    Commonweal 90:265 My 16 '69
    New Yorker 45:174+ Ap 12 '69
    Opera N 33:17-20 Ap 12 '69
    Opera N 33:24-6 Ap 12 '69
    Sat R 52:52-3 Ap 19 '69
    Sat R il 52:61-2 My 17 '69
BERG, Helene
Frau Berg; interview, ed. by J. H. Sutcliffe.
por Opera N 33:12-13 Ap 12 '69
BERG, Ivar
Rich man's qualifications for poor man's
jobs. por Trans-Action 6:45-50 Mr '69
BERG, Norman A.
What's different about conglomerate man-
agement? bibliog f Harvard Bsns R 47:112-
20 N '69
BERG, Roland H.
Call for help from Vietnam. il por Look
33:24-30+ D 16 '69
Heart-saver squad. Look 33:26-9 F 4 '69
No more heart attacks. Look 33:30-2 F 4 '69;
Same abr. with title Heart attacks can be
prevented! Read Digest 94:76-81 Ap '69
Warning: steer clear of THC. Look 33:46
Ap 15 '69
(ed) See Gwinup, G. The one sensible way
to diet

BERG, Stephen
Dreaming with a friend; poem. New Yorker 45:40 Mr 15 '69
Holes; poem. New Yorker 44:34 F 1 '69
BERGAMOT. See Horsemint
BERGEN, Candice
Little women. il Esquire 71:136-7+ My '69
BERGEN, Norway
Bergen: Fjordland hub. J. H. Winchester. il Travel 131:42-6 Mr '69
BERGEN COUNTY, N.J.
Mobile multi-purpose unit. il Am City 84:80 F '69
BERGEN international festival. See Music festivals—Norway
BERGER, Barry D. See Stein, L. jt. auth.
BERGER, Bennett M.
New stage of American man, almost endless adolescence. N Y Times Mag p32-3+ N 2 '69
BERGER, Ivan
First 100 feet are the hardest. Pop Phot 64: 112+ Ap '69
Four-channel sound is here, sort of. Sat R 52:77 N 29 '69
Hi-Fi at L.A: the sunshine show. Sat R 52:68+ O 25 '69
Living with Dynakits. Sat R 52:77 Ap 26 '69
Mild fun and games with video tape. Sat R 52:57 D 27 '69
More tape recorders I have known and loved. Sat R 52:49 Ag 30 '69
Stereo: the myth of the experts' equipment. Sat R 52:49 Mr 15 '69
Switched-on Bach story. Sat R 52:45-7+ Ja 25 '69
Tape recorders I have known and loved Sat R 52:57-8 Je 28 '69
Tape today. Sat R 52:49-55 S 27 '69
BERGER, Rainer, and Libby, W. F.
Equilibration of atmospheric carbon dioxide with sea water; possible enzymatic control of the rate. bibliog Science 164:1395-7 Je 20 '69
BERGER, Thomas
Controversy: the Arthur Bader show; story. Esquire 71:90-3 Mr '69
BERGERON, David M.
Arthur Miller's The crucible and Nathaniel Hawthorne: some parallels. Engl J 58:47-55 Ja '69
BERGERY, Bettina
Diane de Poitiers. Vogue 154:178-9+ O 1 '69
BERGETHON, K. Roald
Learning from the young; excerpts from address, November, 1968. por Sch & Soc 97: 140 Mr '69
BERGGREN, Dwain
Survivor of Pinkville; poem. Chr Cent 86: 1572 D 10 '69
BERGH, Henry
Henry Bergh. C. W. Ferguson. il por PTA Mag 63:9-11 My '69
BERGMAN, Ingmar
Bergman's Shame and Sartre's stare. R. E. Lauder. il Cath World 209:247-50 S '69
Ingmar Bergman at fifty. J. Cantor. Atlan 223:150+ Mr '69
BERGMAN, Ingrid
Ingrid Bergman: the new happiness in her life. M. Davidson. por Good H 168:82-3+ My '69
BERGMAN, Lewis
Reading the tea leaves: what will happen in 1970. N Y Times Mag p8-10+ D 28 '69
BERGOFF, Beatrice
Road back. Har Yrs 9:36-7 Jl '69
BERGQUIST, Laura
Gore Vidal: the elegant white knife. Look 33:73-8 Jl 29 '69
BERGSTEIN, Eleanor
I'll be happy happy; story. Redbook 134:62-3 Ja '70
BERIIA, Lavrentii Pavlovich
Beria's pleasure dome. il por Newsweek 75: 45 Ja 19 '70
BERIO, Luciano
Magic theater of Luciano Berio. D. Henahan. por Hi Fi 19:71-2 Ag '69
World of Luciano Berio. I. Kolodin. por Sat R 52:73 N 29 '69
BERKELEY, Busby
Return of Busby Berkeley. W. Murray. il pors N Y Times Mag p26-7+ Mr 2 '69
BERKELEY, Calif.
Those little wars. Nation 208:715-16 Je 9 '69

Education

Berkeley story: commitment to integration. S. G. Streshinsky. il Parents Mag 44:48-51+ My '69
School where little kids teach the teachers; Far West laboratory for educational research and development. il Parents Mag 44:70-2 S '69

Parks and playgrounds

Battle of Berkeley. Nat R 21:578-9 Je 17 '69
Battle of Berkeley. il Newsweek 73:35-6+ Je 2 '69
Dialectics of confrontation. R. Scheer. il Ramp Mag 8:42-9+ Ag '69
Flower power; People's park issue. il Newsweek 73:92 Je 9 '69
Occupied Berkeley. il Time 93:22-3 My 30 '69
People, the police and the park. J. A. Coleman. America 120:668-71 Je 7 '69
People's park. il Newsweek 73:39-40 My 26 '69
People's park: a history in pictures, comp. by D. Stermer. il Ramp Mag 8:34-40 Ag '69
People's park, 270' x 450' of confrontation. W. Griffith. il N Y Times Mag p5-7+ Je 29 '69
People's park; what's in store. U S News 67:5 Jl 7 '69
Positively the last word on the People's park. J. R. Coyne, jr. il Nat R 21:1003-5+ O 7 '69
Regents v. guerrilla base. Nat R 21:683-4 Jl 15 '69
Street people; taking over a park. il Time 93:27 My 23 '69
Terror in a teapot. F. Berry and others. il Nation 208:784-8 Je 23 '69
Who owns the park? F. Bardacke. Ramp Mag 8:8 Ag '69

Police

Editor's choice; Berkeley, May 1969: general conditions. il ALA Bul 63:897-9 Jl '69
Pacifying California; search and destroy operation against the People's park. C. Horman. Commonweal 90:356-7 Je 13 '69

Riots

Battle of Berkeley. R. Scheer and others. il Ramp Mag 8:41-59 Ag '69
BERKELEY campus. See California, University—Berkeley campus
BERKELEY SPRINGS, W.Va.
Very first resort: George Washington bathed here. T. L. Christie. Sat R 52:58 Mr 8 '69
BERKES, Ross N.
World war II in Asia. bibliog f Cur Hist 57: 71-6+ Ag '69
BERKLEY, George E.
How the police work. New Repub 161:15-18 Ag 2 '69
Myth of war profiteering. New Repub 161:15-18 D 20 '69
BERKLEY, William R.
How young can talent get? il por Bsns W p74+ Ag 23 '69
Up, up, up, up. por Forbes 103:52 Ja 15 '69
BERKOWITZ, Leon
Color it Berkowitz; exhibition at Corcoran gallery, Washington, D.C. S. Burton. il Art N 68:32-3+ Mr '69
BERKSHIRE symphonic festival
Mozart miracle at Tanglewood. G. Movshon. il Hi Fi 19:MA20-1 O '69
Tanglewood. M. Zwerin. il Holiday 45:54-5+ Je '69
To be, or not to be? BU helps; Young artists program. C. Stinson. il Hi Fi 19: MA22-3 O '69
BERKSON, Bill
Clearing the air; Shady grove; poems. Poetry 114:99-101 My '69
Comment. Poetry 114:251-65 Jl '69
BERL, Kathe
Combining enamels and plastics. Ceram Mo 17:23 My: 18 Je: 31 O '69
Enameled masks. Ceram Mo 17:22 F '69
BERL, Walter G.
Perspectives on the promise of the present. Science 165:1150 S 12 '69
BERLAND, Theodore
But is it really sinus trouble? Todays Health 47:34-7 Mr '69
Nobel prize: supreme sanction, or silly ceremony? Todays Health 47:24-7+ D '69
Periodontal disease: hidden threat to grown-ups' teeth. Todays Health 47:28-30 Ag '69
BERLE, Adolf Augustus, 1895-
New realities of corporate power; interview, ed. by G. R. Rosen. pors Duns R 92:43-5+ D '68
BERLE, Milton
Berle, Benson, Bleeck. P. Nathan. Pub W 196:46 O 13 '69
BERLIN, Sir Isaiah
Vico, one of the boldest innovators in the history of human thought. N Y Times Mag p76-7+ N 23 '69
BERLIN, Newton H.
Boardwalk for the beans. Org Gard & Farm 16:35 Jl '69
Raising strawberry plants from runners. Org Gard & Farm 16:51 F '69

BERLIN, Richard D.
Purines: active transport by isolated choroid
plexus. bibliog Science 163:1194-5 Mr 14 '69
BERLIN
Berlin: a tale of two cities. J. Gunther. il
Read Digest 95:106-11 O '69

Description
Berlin: German glamour city. P. Lindberg.
il Bet Hom & Gard 47:69 Je '69

History

Allied occupation, 1945-
See also
Berlin air lift

Russian blockade, 1948-1949
See also
Berlin air lift
BERLIN (East Berlin)

Description
Berlin: on both sides of the wall. H. Sochurek. il Nat Geog 137:1-47 Ja '70

Music
Report: East Berlin; performance of Aida.
J. H. Sutcliffe. il Opera N 33:26-7 My 17 '69
Report: East Berlin; production of Dmitri
Shostakovich's The nose. J. H. Sutcliffe.
il Opera N 33:28 Ap 12 '69
Report: East Berlin; production of Proko-
fiev's Love for three oranges. J. H. Sut-
cliffe. Opera N 33:30 Mr 1 '69
Report: production of Flowers of Hiroshima
by Jean Kurt Forest. J. H. Sutcliffe. il
Opera N 34:28 D 20 '69
Report: production of Richard Strauss'
Daphne at East Berlin's Staatsoper. J. H.
Sutcliffe. Opera N 34:26 N 22 '69
Report: productions by the visiting Bolshoi
theater. J. H. Sutcliffe. il Opera N 34:25-6
D 6 '69
Triumph of Felsenstein's La Traviata;
Komische oper. G. R. Marek. Hi Fi 19:
MA28-9+ F '69

Theater
Ghost of Brecht; productions by Berliner
ensemble. J. P. O'Donnell. Atlan 223:110-
13 Ja '69
BERLIN (West Berlin)
Berlin jitters again. il Newsweek 73:39 F 24
'69
Nixon lands on Willy Brandt's special island;
interview. ed. by R. Meryman. W. Brandt.
il Life 66:28-9 Mr 7 '69
Once more, trouble in Berlin. il Time 93:22-3
F 21 '69
Same wall, new mood. C. W. Wiley. il Nat R
21:282-3 Mr 25 '69

Description
Berlin: on both sides of the wall. H. Sochurek. il Nat Geog 137:1-47 Ja '70
Encounter in Berlin. R. Atcheson. il Holiday
45:22+ Ap '69

Economic conditions
Background on Berlin. C. Wilpert. Commonweal 89:698-9 Mr 7 '69
Durable Berlin prospers again. il U S News
67:43 S 8 '69

Hospitals
See also
Berlin university—Hospital

Music
Blacher premiere; Karajan competition. P.
Moor. il Hi Fi 19:MA21+ D '69
Current chronicle; *Internationale woche für
experimentelle musik.* J. Appleton. Mus Q
55:112-14 Ja '69
Report: Berlin; production of Verdi's Simon
Boccanegra. J. H. Sutcliffe. Opera N 33:30
Mr 29 '69
Report: performance of Janácek's The excur-
sions of Mr Broucek. J. H. Sutcliffe. il
Opera N 34:25 N 1 '69

Sanitary affairs
Garbage crisis. il Newsweek 73:60-1 Je 23 '69
BERLIN air lift
Before the colors fade: Berlin airlift com-
mander; interview. ed. by C. V. Glines.
W. H. Tunner. il Am Heritage 20:44-5+
O '69
BERLIN question, 1945-
Background on Berlin. C. Wilpert. Com-
monweal 89:698-9 Mr 7 '69
Berlin weathers another crisis, but—. il U S
News 66:31 Mr 17 '69

City on the spot. il Sr Schol 94:15 Mr 21 '69
Crisis that wasn't. Time 93:38+ Mr 14 '69
Hour we have waited for. il Newsweek 73:
57-8 Mr 17 69
Isolating the island city. il Newsweek 73:41
Mr 10 '69
Nixon lands on Willy Brandt's special island;
interview. ed. by R. Meryman. W. Brandt.
il Life 66:28-9 Mr 7 '69
Soviet charges concerning Berlin rejected by
U.S, U.K, and France; tripartite statement
with White House announcement. Dept
State Bul 60:248 Mr 24 '69
Sticky situation; travel permits not issued to
delegates traveling to West Berlin for pres-
idential election. Nation 208:228-9 F 24 '69
U.S, U.K, and France reaffirm right of access
to Berlin; text of a tripartite statement,
February 10, 1969. Dept State Bul 60:186
Mr 3 '69
West Berlin; bracing for a crisis. il Time 93:
30-1 Mr 7 '69
Why Communists get tough over Berlin. il U S
News 66:25-6 Mr 3 '69
See also
Berlin wall, 1961-
BERLIN university

Hospital
Berlin university hospital: international de-
sign for optimum form and function. il
Arch Rec 146:134-40 O '69
BERLIN wall, 1961-
View of the Wall from the East. H. J.
Sievers. America 120:294 Mr 15 '69
BERLINER, Don, and Gilbert, James
Races wild. Flying 85:58-67 Ag '69
BERLINER, Robert William
NIH policymaker. B. J. Culliton. il pors Sci
N 95:263-4 Mr 15 '69
BERLINER ensemble. See Berlin (East Ber-
lin)—Theater
BERLINGUER, Enrico
Bottom's up. por Time 93:34 F 28 '69
BERLIOZ, Hector
Berlioz and the realm of the imaginary; tr.
by D. Noakes. P. Boulez. il por Hi Fi
19:42-6 Mr '69
Berlioz on records. B. Jacobson. il Hi Fi
19:56-60+ Mr '69
Berlioz projects to celebrate a centenary. R.
Gelatt. Hi Fi 19:22+ Mr '69
Berlioz-sur-Seine; pictorial essay. R. McMul-
len. Hi Fi 19:47-54 Mr '69
Berlioz Troyens for the record; Royal
opera's production and recording. T. Hei-
nitz. Sat R 52:70 N 29 '69
Berlioz's songs. A. E. F. Dickinson. bibliog f
il Mus Q 55:329-43 Jl '69
Big sound from Berlioz. D. Hamilton. il Hi
Fi 19:94-5 D '69
Colin Davis' Romeo and Juliet, as near
perfect as possible. B. Jacobson. Hi Fi 19:
81 Mr '69
L'enfance du Christ, Martinon's best buy
Berlioz. J. W. Barker. Am Rec G 36:166
N '69
On the 100th anniversary of his death, Berlioz
still sounds new. H. C. Schonberg. il pors
N Y Times Mag p24-5+ Mr 9 '69
Other side; Berlioz by Davis. T. Heinitz.
Sat R 52:54 Jl 26 '69
Other side; Berlioz in the Strand. T.
Heinitz. Sat R 52:47 Ag 30 '69
Ozawa on Berlioz. I. Kolodin. Sat R 52:41-2
Mr 1 '69
Personal history. G. Abraham. por Sat R
52:51-2 N 15 '69
Records:
Roméo and Juliette. Opera N 33:30 Je 14
'69
Star-crossed Hector and his Harriet. R.
Freedman. Life 66:14 My 30 '69
Stokowski continues to invade new territories.
R. D. Darrell; H. Goldsmith. Hi Fi 19:75
Jl '69
Together at last, the Fantastique and its
sequel. J. W. Barker. il por Am Rec G 35:
370-2 Ja '69
Trojans. C. Davis. il Hi Fi 19:61-3 Mr '69
Two albums from Philips: Haydn and Berlioz
by Colin Davis. J. W. Barker. il Am Rec
G 35:936-8 Je '69
Unusual sound. S. L. Fogel. il Opera N 34:
14-16 S 20 '69
BERLITZ, Charles Frambach
How to insult everyone regardless of race,
color, creed, or national origin. Horizon
11:120 Wint '69
BERLOWITZ, Laurence, and others
Chromatin and histones: binding of tritiated
actinomycin D to heterochromatin in mealy
bugs. bibliog Science 164:1527-9 Je 27 '69

BERMAN, Frances
Two housewives run a gallery. J. Kuh. por Ladies Home J 86:31 Mr '69
BERMAN, Sidney
Crushes. Todays Ed 58:13-15 D '69
BERMES, Dorothea
Our ten money-making raspberry bushes. Org Gard & Farm 16:70-1 S '69
BERMUDA
Bermuda: the timeless island. B. Belford. il Travel & Camera 32:78-81 S '69
See also
Shopping and shoppers—Bermuda

Description and travel
Swinging Bermuda? D. Butwin. il Sat R 52: 33-4 Ag 30 '69

Hotels, restaurants, etc.
Terrace room, Hamilton, Bermuda. M. Woodward. il Travel 132:16 S '69
BERNAL, Joe J.
I am Mexican-American. Todays Ed 58:51-2 My '69
BERNARD, Tomás Diego, 1919-
Indian's birthright. Américas 21:2-8 Jl '69
BERNARD family
Bernard coat-of-arms. H. K. Eilers. il Hobbies 74:146-7+ N '69
BERNART de Ventadorn
Era-m cosselhatz, senhor; poem, tr. by J. F. Nims. Sat R 52:52 S 20 '69
BERNAT, Paul, collection. See Art—Private collections
BERNAYS, Minna
Freudian affair. por Time 95:41 Ja 12 '70
BERNE, Daniel
Silent Sam; interview. New Yorker 45:45-6 D 13 '69
BERNEIS, K. H. and others
Micelle formation between 5-hydroxytryptamine and adenosine triphosphate in platelet storage organelles. bibliog Science 165: 913-14 Ag 29 '69
BERNHAGEN, Lillian
Sex education that parents approve; interview, ed. by M. Longwell. por Farm J 93: 57-8 S '69
BERNHARD, Arnold
Money-changers in the temple. por Forbes 104:78+ O 1 '69
BERNHARDT, Michael
Story of a soldier who refused to fire at Songmy. J. Lelyveld. il por N Y Times Mag p32-3+ D 14 '69
BERNHEIM, Isaac W.
Arboretum, a place for trees? F. H. Bunce. il Parks & Rec 4:71-2 S '69
BERNHEIM forest landscape arboretum, Kentucky
Arboretum, a place for trees? F. H. Bunce. il Parks & Rec 4:71-2 S '69
Bernheim forest landscape arboretum. F. H. Bunce. il Horticulture 47:22-3 Jl '69
BERNHEIMER, Martin
Escape, but something missing. Hi Fi 19: MA23 Ag '69
BERNIER, Rosamond
Au revoir les Halles. Travel & Camera 32:54-5 My '69
BERNINI, Giovanni Lorenzo
Bernini. S. De Grmont. il Horizon 11:34-47 Spr '69
BERNSON, Marcella
In my opinion. por Seventeen 28:254 Ap '69
BERNSTEIN, Burton
Letter from Israel. New Yorker 45:133-40+ N 29 '69
BERNSTEIN, Emil O. and Jones, C. B.
Skin replication procedure for the scanning electron microscope. bibliog Science 166: 252-3 O 10 '69
BERNSTEIN, Jeremy
Books (cont) New Yorker 44:80 F 1; 45:141-2+ My 10 '69
Profiles: A. C. Clarke. New Yorker 45:40-2+ Ag 9 '69
BERNSTEIN, Leonard
Bernstein on Wagner. I. Kolodin. Sat R 52: 41+ Mr 15 '69
I've done what I was supposed to do. T. Thompson. il pors Life 66:53-4+ F 21 '69
Laureate's farewell. il por Time 93:52 My 23 '69
Lebe wohl. New Yorker 45:30-1 My 24 '69
Music to my ears. I. Kolodin. Sat R 52:39 My 31 '69
Musical events; Third symphony by New York philharmonic, farewell appearance as conductor. W. Sargeant. New Yorker 45: 137 My 24 '69

Private world of Leonard Bernstein, by J. Gruen. Review
Am Rec G il 35:862-4 My '69. G. Fox
BERNSTEIN, Merton C.
Should welfare mothers work? America 120: 704-6 Je 21 '69
BERNSTEIN, Victor H.
Five million children with part-time mothers and nowhere to go. Redbook 134:86+ N '69
When the home makes the best hospital for a child. Redbook 133:91+ S '69
BERRELLEZ, Robert
Dope control; reprint. U S News 67:108 O 20 '69
BERREMAN, Gerald D.
Academic colonialism: not so innocent abroad. Nation 209:505-8 N 10 '69
BERREUR, P. and Fraenkel, G.
Puparium formation in flies: contraction to puparium induced by ecdysone. bibliog Science 164:1182-3 Je '69
BERRI, Claude
Rights and permissions. P. Nathan. Pub W 195:45 Mr 24 '69
BERRIAULT, Gina
Cove; story. Esquire 71:81-2 Ja '69
BERRIES
Instant fruit and berries; dwarf varieties. P. E. Mahan. il Org Gard & Farm 16:86-7 N '69
Their business is the berries! M. C. Goldman. il Org Gard & Farm 16:28-32 My '69
See also
Spraying and dusting
also names of berries, e.g. Raspberries
BERRIGAN, Daniel
Bishop & the ghosts of Filetto. Commonweal 91:39-42 O 10 '69

about
Case of the jail-bound Jesuit. J. Roddy. por Look 33:63-5 Ap 15 '69
Catholic rebels at the summit: the Bernadette-Berrigan encounter. J. Roddy. por Look 33:81 O 7 '69
Comment. R. Cohen. Poetry 115:194-5 D '69
Word for Dan. J. Deedy. Commonweal 91: 90 O 24 '69
BERRIGAN, Philip
Berrigan, Darst et al. J. Deedy. Commonweal 91:236 N 21 '69
BERRIGAN, Ted
I like to (B)eat people up. A. Hoyem. Poetry 113:426 Mr '69
BERROCAL, Miguel Ortiz
Take apart and look again. il por Time 93: 78 My 23 '69
BERRY, Charles Alden
Risks facing man in space; interview. por U S News 67:58-60 N 17 '69

about
Still a mystery. B. J. Culliton. il por Sci N 96:61-3 Jl 19 '69
BERRY, Chuck
Chuck Berry. M. Lydon. pors Ramp Mag 8: 47-56 D '69
BERRY, Edward J.
Sucker trap. Flying 84:70-1 Mr '69
BERRY, Frederick, and others
Terror in a teapot. Nation 208:784-8 Je 23 '69
BERRY, James R.
Alone in a body counter. Pop Mech 131:80-3+ Je '69
Famous marques of the famous makers. Mech Illus 65:50-2+ D '69
Here come the strange-change products! Mech Illus 65:56-8+ Ap '69
High-pressure medicine. Pop Mech 130:99-103 D '68
Man's first day on the moon. Pop Mech 132:84-7+ Jl '69
They smash things, and get paid for it! Mech Illus 65:53-5+ F '69
BERRY, Ken
Ken Berry on TV. V. H. Swisher. il pors Dance Mag 43:22-4 Jl '69
BERRY, Leonard J.
According to Pasolini. Commonweal 89:706-7 Mr 7 '69
Crisis within a crisis. Commonweal 89:491-2 Ja 17 '69
No Vatican Oscar for Teorema. Commonweal 90:292-3 My 23 '69
Il Papa and the pill. Commonweal 90:44-6 Mr 28 '69
Screen. Commonweal 91:103 O 24 '69
Strung out and gassed at Fort Dix. Commonweal 91:173-4 N 7 '69

BERRY, Michael
Ins and outs of islands. Sat R 52:40+ Je 7
'69
New kick in the Italian boot. Sat R 52:48-50
Ag 23 '69
Yes, the Orient hasn't changed. Sat R 52:
70+ S 13 '69
BERRY, R. W.
Ribonucleic acid metabolism of a single neu-
ron: correlation with electrical activity.
bibliog Science 166:1021-3 N 21 '69
BERRY, W. T. jr
Good today, but we can make it better to-
morrow. por Farm J 93:22-3+ My '69
BERRY, Wendell
Books that look out, books that look in. W.
Stafford. Poetry 113:421-2 Mr '69
BERRY-eating birds. See Birds, Injurious and
beneficial
BERRYMAN, John
Berryman: without impudence and vanity. M.
Goldman. Nation 208:245-6 F 24 '69
Book industry presents the 20th National
book awards; with excerpts from accep-
tance address. il por Pub W 195:28 Mr 24
'69
Dream songs: to terrify & comfort. J. Atlas.
Poetry 115:43-6 O '69
BERSANI, Leo
Blue blood and his women. New Repub 160:
22+ F 8 '69
BERTILLON system
Origin of modern criminology. il Chem 42:
8-11 Jl '69
BERTOLINO, Jack J.
Membership-negotiator relationship. Todays
Ed 58:55-6 Ja '69
BERTOLINO, James
Notes for an elegy; Seasonal poem; Under
Mayan sun; poems. Poetry 114:383-5 S '69
BERTONE, Nuccio
Milestones on the Bertone trail. G. Borgeson.
il por Motor T 21:38-40 My '69
BERUBE, Maurice R.
Black power and the learning process. Com-
monweal 90:98-101 Ap 11 '69
[Book review] Commonweal 90:122-4 Ap 11
'69
Head Start to nowhere. Commonweal 90:311-
13 My 30 '69
Jensen's complaint. Commonweal 91:42-4 O
10 '69
Unschooling of New York's children. Com-
monweal 89:103-5. 658-9 O 25 '68. F 21 '69
BERZON, Marsha L.
What the blacks found out. Nation 208:
793-5 Je 23 '69
BESANT, Lloyd
Rodman experience with dropouts. Todays
Ed 58:52-4 F '69; Same abr. Ed Digest 34:
35-7 Ap '69
BESLER, William J.
Blowing the steam dream; interview, ed. by
J. Zmuda. pors Motor T 21:44-6+ N '69
BESRET, Bernard
Downfall of Dom Besret. il por Time 94:81
N 14 '69
BESS, Donovan
Menace of the Barbie dolls. Ramp Mag 7:
25-8 Ja 25 '69
Total freedom and beyond. Nation 209:311-
15 S 29 '69
BESSIE, Okla.
Reverse osmosis water for Bessie. il Am City
84:60 S '69
BEST. Georgie
Pop goes Georgie. il por Newsweek 73:83 F 24
'69
BEST, J. B. and Noel, J.
Complex synaptic configurations in plana-
rian brain. bibliog Science 164:1070-1 My
30 '69
—and others
Fissioning in planarians: control by the brain.
bibliog Science 164:565-6 My 2 '69
BEST, Richard
National artists. F. Merkling. Opera N 34:25
S 6 '69
BEST books. See Books and reading—Best
books
BEST dressed women. See Clothing and dress
BEST friends; drama. See MacLellan, E. and
Schroll, C. V.
BEST play awards. See New York drama critics
circle
BEST sellers
Best sellers. See issues of Publishers' weekly
Case history of a best seller; The Peter
principle. il Pub W 196:16-17 D 15 '69
Hardcover best sellers of 1968 in the U.S.
book trade. A. P. Hackett il Pub W 195:
30-2 Mr 10 '69

Journal's preview of best sellers. il Ladies
Home J 86:96-7+ S '69
Paperback best sellers of the year 1968. il
Pub W 195:33-6 Mr 10 '69
BEST things in life; story. See Mauermann,
M. A.
BEST year; drama. See Hark, M. and Mc-
Queen, N.
BESTER, Alfred
Bloomsday in Dublin. Holiday 45:40-5 Je '69
Downey's, the poor actor's Sardi's. Holiday 46:
90-2 N '69
Leonard in the Lyons den. Holiday 45:44-7+
Mr '69
Muscle cars. Holiday 45:72-5 F '69
Sun. Holiday 45:38-9+ Je '69
World's first giant jet. Holiday 46:28-35+
Jl '69
(ed) See Allen, W. Conversation with Woody
Allen
(ed) See Stout, R. Conversation with Rex
Stout
BESTIARIES
Book of imaginary beings, by J. L. Borges.
Review
Time il 95:56+ Ja 5 '70
BETA-manganous orthogermanate. See German-
ates
BETANCOURT, Philip P.
Age of Homer. Art N 68:32-3+ D '69
BETHE, Hans Albrecht
ABM, China and the arms race. Bul Atom Sci
25:41-4 My '69
Hard point vs. city defense. Bul Atom Sci
25:25-6 Je '69
BETHEL, James S.
Future of multiple use; address. por Am For
75:32-4+ D '69
BETHEL rock festival. See Music festivals—
New York (state)
BETHESDA, Md.
Education
Reaching in; Bethesda school's experiment
in free-form education. D. Leff. Seven-
teen 29:84-5+ Ja '70
BETHLEHEM steel corporation
Doctor Bethlehem's new steel formula. Bsns
W p39 N 15 '69
BETTELHEIM, Bruno
Dialogue with mothers. See occasional issues
of Ladies' home journal
Parent and child. N Y Times Mag p 125+
Ap 13 '69
Psychoanalysis and education. Ed Digest 35:
38-42 O '69
Student revolt; statement before the House
special subcommittee on education. March
20, 1969. Vital Speeches 35:405-10 Ap 15
'69; Excerpts. por U S News 66:61-3 Ap 7
'69
Too many misfits in college; excerpts from
statement to the House special subcom-
mittee on education, March 20, 1969. por
U S News 66:61-3 Ap 7 '69

about

Bruno Bettelheim is Dr No. D. Dempsey.
il pors N Y Times Mag p22-3+ Ja 11 '70
Confused parents, confused kids. por Time
94:58 S 5 '69
BETTER government association
BGA is coming! il Newsweek 74:59 S 22 '69
BETTING. See Gambling
BETTIS, Moody C. and Roberts, R. E.
Mental health manpower dilemma. bibliog
Ment Hy 53:163-75 Ap '69
BETULA papyrifera. See Birch
BETZ, John A.
Harrisburg observatory. R Pop Astron 63:27-
30 My '69
BEUTLER, Ernest
Glutathione reductase: stimulation in nor-
mal subjects by riboflavin supplementa-
tion. bibliog Science 165:613-15 Ag 8 '69
BEUVE-MÉRY, Hubert
As Le Monde turns. il por Time 94:36 D 26
'69
BEVERAGE containers
Bulb-shaped bottle is new weapon for glass;
glass-and-plastic container. il Bsns W
p 152+ Ap 19 '69
Can plastic bottles squeeze into market? il
Bsns W p81 N 8 '69
Soda-pop game: throwaway pennies. il Con-
sumer Rep 34:88-9 F '69
BEVERAGE glasses. See Drinking vessels
BEVERAGE industry. See Soft drink industry
BEVERAGES
After the last run; exotic drinks. J. T. Elson.
il Travel & Camera 32:58-63 D '69
Artificially sweetened drinks, potentials for
harm. Consumer Bul 52:31 N '69

BEVERAGES—*Continued*
Children make their own; ice cream soda. il Sunset 143:126 Jl '69
Cola and cholesterol. A. J. Snider. il Sci Digest 65:74 Mr '69
Do high protein drinks threaten milk? F. E. Breth. il Farm J 93:D7+ Ap '69
Gastronomy recalled; with recipes. M. F. K. Fisher. New Yorker 45:140-6+ Ap 26 '69
Gay quenchers. S. Lord. Harp Baz 102:90-1 Je '69
Hot buttered and aromatic. il Sunset 143:141 D '69
Hot drinks of winter. S. Spitzer. il Holiday 46:40+ D '69
How fruity are fruit drinks? il Good H 168:161 F '69
New drink in town: Gatorade. L. Sanders. il Mech Illus 65:32+ N '69
Picnic drinks. P. S. Brown. il House & Gard 135:100+ Je '69
  See also
Beer
Cider
Coffee
Liquors
Punch (beverage)
Soft drink industry
Tea
Wine

Advertising
7-Up bids for youth with a negative pitch. il Bsns W p48-9 F 15 '69

BEVERIDGE, Lowell P.
Church music: pop or pro? Chr Today 13:6-8 Mr 14 '69

BEVERLY HILLS, Calif.

Hotels, restaurants, etc.
America's unique hotels; Beverly Wilshire, California luxury. R. Carson. il Holiday 46:56-7+ S '69
Love letter from Beverly Hills. B. Rollin. il Look 33:10 Ag 12 '69

BEYER, John
New museum for the West. Am West 6:34-9 N '69

BEYER, William
Children and wind; poem. Horn Bk 45:440 Ag '69

BEYLE, Marie Henri
Of Stendhal. W. Fowlie. Commonweal 90:208-9 My 2 '69

BEYOND mutiny; drama. See Peterson, M. N.

BEZANKER, Abraham
Odyssey of Saul Bellow. Yale R 58:359-71 Mr '69
Three generations. Nation 208:800-1 Je 23 '69

BEZAZIAN, Paul D. See Leviton, T. S. jt. auth.

BHASHANI, Abdul Hamid
Prophet of violence. il por Time 93:39 Ap 18 '69

BHUMIBOL Adulyadej, king of Thailand
Siam by-the-sea. P. Simms. il pors Sat R 52:86-8 Mr 8 '69

BHUTTO, Zulfikar Ali
Law & order in Pakistan. A. Ahmad. il Nation 208:455-8 Ap 14 '69

BIAFRA
Biafra. W. Hedgepeth. il Look 33:22-8 Ap 1 '69
Biafra and the American conscience. C. E. Goodell. il Sat R 52:24-7+ Ap 12 '69
Last stand? Time 95:33 Ja 19 '70
Letter from Biafra. R. Adler. il New Yorker 45:47-8+ O 4 '69
My summer vacation in Biafra. H. Gold. il Harper 239:63-8 N '69
Report on Biafra; interview. C. Goodell. New Yorker 45:37-8 Ap 12 '69
  See also
Food relief—Biafra
Medical relief work—Biafra
Nigeria—Civil war. 1967-
Nutrition problems—Biafra
Prisoners—Biafra

BIAFRAN refugees. See Refugees, Biafran

BIAFRAN teachers in the United States. See Foreign teachers in the United States

BIALOGUSKI, Michael
Dreaming the possible dream. il por Time 93:53+ My 9 '69

BIANCHI, Eugene C.
Resistance in the church. Commonweal 90:257-60, 398-9 My 16, Je 20 '69

BIANCO, Vito
Here's why I join. Todays Ed 58:67 My '69

BIAS-belt tires. See Tires, Automobile

BIBER, Heinrich Ignaz Franz von
Epiphany cantata by Bibre. J. W. Barker. Am Rec G 36:173-4 N '69
Third and best recording of Biber's Rosary sonatas. D. W. Moore. por Am Rec G 35:374-7 Ja '69

BIBLE, Alan
Legislation to halt air cargo theft studied. Aviation W 90:34 Je 30 '69
Senate tracks business thieves. por Bsns W p 100 My 31 '69

BIBLE
Biblenaper; theft and recovery of Widener library's Gutenberg Bible. Newsweek 74:24 S 1 '69
Teaching the Bible as literature. T. S. Warshaw. Engl J 58:571-6 Ap '69
  See also
Nudity in the Bible
Religion and science
Sex in the Bible

Antiquities
Hazor's hidden resource. il Time 93:78+ My 16 '69
Stones, scripts, and scholars. E. M. Yamauchi. Chr Today 13:8-10+ F 14 '69

Bibliography
Books on the Bible: 1969. D. Stanley. America 121:563-4+ D 6 '69
Fall Bibles and related books. il Pub W 196:56-60 S 22 '69
Spring Bibles and related books. il Pub W 195:65-8 Ja 27 '69

Biography
Age of strong man Samson; excerpt from Hamlet's mill: an essay on myth and the frame of time. G. De Santillana and H. Von Dechend. il Sat R 53:103-5 Ja 10 '70

Collectors and collecting
Walton's London polyglot Bible. P. W. Schmidtchen. il Hobbies 74:104-5+ Je '69

Criticism, interpretation, etc.
Southern Baptists and the Bible. Chr Today 13:34 Ap 25 '69
  See also
Bible—Hermeneutics

Distribution
See Bible—Publication and distribution

Hermeneutics
Presence of Christ: a contemporary view. J. A. Hill. Chr Today 13:5-8 Je 20 '69

History of biblical events
Reason, history, and Biblical authenticity. P. E. Hughes. Chr Today 13:3-7 S 12 '69

Illustrations
See Bible—Pictorial illustrations

Inspiration
See Revelation

Interpretation
See Bible—Criticism, interpretation, etc.

Literary character
Bible as culture. il Time 94:80+ O 3 '69
Christian approach to literature. L. Ryken. Chr Today 14:10-12 D 5 '69

Medicine, hygiene, etc.
Strange facts about the Bible; excerpts. W. Garrison. il Todays Health 47:64-5 S; 12-13 O '69

Pictorial illustrations
Inspired drawings of Lajos Szalay. N. Kent. il Am Artist 33:66-71+ D '69

Publication and distribution
Book for all seasons. Chr Today 14:26-7 N 21 '69
  See also
Bible societies

Reading
What the Bible says to me. B. Graham. Read Digest 94:83-7 My '69

Study
See Bible study

Translations
See Bible—Versions

BIBLE—*Continued*

Versions

Bible: the talk of Yugoslavia; Serbo-Croatian translation. T. Cosmades. Chr Today 13:34 F 14 '69

Compleat NEB; New English Bible translation. Chr Today 14:37 N 21 '69

Ignorant preachers; increased use of RSV Bible. A. DeVries. Chr Today 14:8-10 Ja 2 '70

New Arabic common Bible. A. Isteero. Chr Cent 86:298+ F 26 '69

Old Testament

Biblical legends. D. Daiches. Commentary 48:80-3 O '69

Bibliography

Bonanza in Old Testament studies. J. B. Payne. Chr Today 13:9-12 F 28 '69

Manuscripts

See also
Dead Sea scrolls

Psalms

Psalms for reading and recitation, by A. Neame. Review
Chr Cent 87:20 Ja 7 '70. C. Northcott

Song of Solomon

Classics revisited: Song of songs. K. Rexroth. Sat R 52:16 Ap 26 '69

New Testament

Jesus of history and Christian faith. D. T. Rowlingson; discussion. Chr Cent 86:121-2 Ja 22 '69

Bibliography

Brighter outlook in the New Testament field. R. P. Martin. il Chr Today 13:6-8 F 28 '69

Versions

Biblical scholarship: thirty years closer to Jesus. D. Baker. Chr Today 14:46-7 D 5 '69

Gospels

Biblical scholarship: thirty years closer to Jesus. D. Baker. Chr Today 14:46-7 D 5 '69

In clearer light: the four gospels. V. P. McCorry. America 121:inside back cover Jl 5 '69

Madness, comfort and love. J. P. Crossley, jr. Chr Cent 86:1542-6 D 3 '69

See also
Jesus Christ—Miracles
Jesus Christ—Teachings

John

John and miracle. V. P. McCorry. America 121:311-12 O 11 '69

BIBLE as literature. See Bible—Literary character

BIBLE characters. See Bible—Biography

BIBLE colleges
Colleges re-educate for Christ's return: Ambassador colleges supported by Radio church of God. A. B. Haines. Chr Cent 86:264 F 19 '69
Evangelical education; Catholic campuses purchased by evangelical schools. Chr Today 14:45 O 24 '69

BIBLE in literature
Realistic approach to biblical literature. A. C. Capps. Engl J 58:230-5 F '69
Teaching the Bible as literature. T. S. Warshaw. Engl J 58:571-6 Ap '69

BIBLE schools. See Bible colleges

BIBLE societies
Bible societies of the Americas meet: Oaxtepec, Mexico. M. Arias. Chr Cent 86:128-9 Ja 22 '69

BIBLE study
Bible reader: an interfaith interpretation. Review
Time il 94:80 O 3 '69
Criteria for curricula. E. L. Hayes. Chr Today 13:42-3 F 28 '69
Error through ignorance. L. N. Bell. Chr Today 13:18-19 My 23 '69
For lack of knowledge. J. M. Hopkins. Chr Today 13:10-11 Je 6 '69
No ban on Bible study. W. D. Boutwell. PTA Mag 63:14 F '69
Question for rabbis, pastors, and teachers. M. R. Wilson. Chr Today 13:5-7 F 14 '69
See also
Bible colleges
Sunday school lessons

BIBLICAL archeology. See Bible—Antiquities

BIBLICAL seminary in New York. See New York theological seminary

BIBLIOGRAPHY
See also
Reading lists
also subhead Bibliography under various subjects. e.g. Graphic arts—Bibliography

BIBLIOGRAPHY, National

Italy

Italian national bibliography. Sch & Soc 97:74+ F '69

BIBLIOTHERAPY
Why does that man stare at me? N. T. Samet. Library J 94:156-7 Ja 15 '69
See also
Libraries, Hospital

BICH, Marcel, baron
Bich the ballpoint king. Fortune 80:122 Ag 15 '69
King of the ballpoints. il Newsweek 74:77-8 Jl 14 '69
$2 million berth to Newport. C. Mitchell. il por Sports Illus 31:28-30+ N 24 '69

Les BICHES; ballet. See Ballets—Criticisms

BICKEL, Alexander M.
Close of the Warren era. New Repub 161:13-16 Jl 12 '69
Does it stand up? New Repub 161:13-15 N 1 '69
How to beat crime. New Repub 161:10-12 Ag 23 '69
Is electoral reform the answer? bibliog f Commentary 46:41-51 D '68; 47:30 Mr '69
Mr Justice Fortas. New Repub 160:9-10 My 17 '69
Pornography & the Courts. Commentary 46:97-8+ N '68; 47:20 F '69
Student demands and academic freedom. New Repub 161:15-16 S 20 '69
Wait a minute! Popular election of future presidents. New Repub 160:11-13 My 10 '69

BICKEL, Lennard
Battle for the reef. Sci N 96:218-20 S 13 '69

BICYCLE brakes. See Brakes, Bicycle

BICYCLE camping. See Camping

BICYCLE racks
Three-way bike stand. E. H. Gustafson. il Pop Sci 195:139 D '69

BICYCLE trips. See Cycling trips

BICYCLES
Bicycle built for you. R. Teeger. il Har Yrs 9:6-12 Mr '69
For a really wild bike ride, build PM's Ground Hugger. D. Carey and R. Q. Riley. il Pop Mech 131:192-4 Ap '69
It's an electric bicycle! il Mech Illus 65:58+ Mr '69
Those wild new bikes. G. Emory. il Pop Mech 132:150-5+ Jl '69
See also
Cycling

BICYCLING. See Cycling

BIDDING, Competitive. See Building—Contracts and specifications; Municipal contracts

BIDDISCOMBE, John S.
Day campers enjoy water skiing. Camp Mag 41:30 My '69

BIEDER, Joan
Beauty: the TV specials. il pors Mlle 68:180+ Mr '69

BIEL, Heinz H.
Stock analysis. See issues of Forbes

BIELBY, Carl
Clergy and abortions. il por Time 94:82 N 28 '69

BIELEFELD, Germany

Galleries and museums

Impressive museum; Richard Kaselowsky musuem. il Arch Rec 146:94-5 D '69

BIENEN, Henry
Ideology for Africa. For Affairs 47:545-59 Ap '69

BIENNALE of illustrations, Bratislava. See Art—Exhibitions

BIENVENU, Millard J.
Parent and child. N Y Times Mag p87+ S 14 '69

BIER, Justus
Fond recollections of Kate Steinitz. Wilson Lib Bul 44:518-19 Ja '70

BIERI, J. G. and others
Survival of germfree rats without vitamin A. Science 163:574-5 F 7 '69

BIERMANN, Wolf
Ballads by Wolf Biermann; Song of the worst thing; Hanns Eisler, or the anatomy of a sphere; Comrades, which of us wouldn't be against war; Devastating side effect of the Vietnam war; tr. by E. Bentley. Nation 208:440 Ap 7 '69

about
Poet in the collective. D. Kleinbard. Nation 208:438+ Ap 7 '69

BIERWAGEN, Walter J.
Excerpt from testimony before Housing and urban affairs subcommittee, October 15, 1969. Cong Digest 48:307+ D '69
BIG business. See Corporations; Trusts, Industrial
BIG SUR, Calif.
Big Sur: where the forest meets the sea. D. Anderson. il Nat Parks 43:4-12 O '69
BIG Thicket. See Forests and forestry—Texas
BIG trees. See Sequoia, Giant
BIGGS, Ronald Arthur
Paradise lost. il por Time 94:34 O 31 '69
BIGHORN hunting. See Mountain sheep hunting
BIGNELL, Edward E.
Recreation enrichment classes. Parks & Rec 3:43 O '68
BIGOTRY. See Toleration
BIKINI
Reclaiming the world's most H-bombed area. il U S News 67:98-101 O 13 '69
BILANIUK, Olexa-Myron, and Sudarshan, E. C. G.
Particles beyond the light barrier. bibliog pors Phys Today 22:43-51 My '69; Discussion. 22:50-2 D '69
BILATERAL air agreements. See Aviation—International aspects
BILDERBACK, Carolyn
Fragments and observations; Judson memorial church. J. Anderson. Dance Mag 43:84 Ap '69
BILHARZIASIS. See Schistosomiasis
BILIK, Al
Alienated rank and file. Nation 209:527-30 N 17 '69
BILINGUAL instruction
Projects under the new Bilingual education program. il Am Ed 5:26-7 O '69
BILL; story. See Powers, J. F.
BILL of rights (United States)   See United States—Constitution—Bill of rights
BILL Saunders shoots the works; story. See Erfert, E. L.
BILLARD, Jules B.
Macao clings to the bamboo curtain. Nat Geog 135:520-39 Ap '69
Okinawa: the island without a country. Nat Geog 136:422-48 S '69
BILLBERGIA nutans. See Queen's tears
BILLBOARDS
How to remove billboards. il Time 94:72 O 31 '69
Letting Lady Bird down. Nation 209:236 S 15 '69
Must we put up with billboards? D. P. Watson. il Horticulture 47:16-17+ N '69
BILLFISH fishing. See Sailfish fishing
BILLING
Computerized billing collects 98 per cent of the taxes: Milwaukee, Wis. J. J. Krueger. il Am City 84:115+ Ag '69
Great snafu. il Newsweek 74:79-80 S 15 '69
Wanna bet, MasterCharge? J. Middlebrook. New Repub 161:17-18 S 20 '69
When the computer fouls up your charge account. il Changing T 23:7-10 S '69
BILLINGS, Elden E.
Interwar years. bibliog f Cur Hist 57:8-12+ Jl '69
BILLINGS, William
Continental harmony of William Billings. A. Frankenstein. Hi Fi 19:79 S '69
BILLINGS, Mont.
No downtown gloom. W. E. Fraser. il Am City 84:132+ Ap '69
BILLINGS hospital. See Chicago. University —Billings hospital
BILLINSKY, John M.
Freudian affair. Time 95:41 Ja 12 '70
BILLS (legislation) See Legislation
BILLY; musical comedy. See Musical comedies, revues, etc.—Criticisms, plots, etc.
BILLY Budd; drama. See Hall, A.
BILOXI, Miss.
Modern luminaires with an historic look. il Am City 84:118 Ja '69

BILSKI, Catherine
Exciting new products. See issues of Popular mechanics
BINARY number system. See Numeration
BINARY stars. See Stars, Double
BINDER, Alan B.
Martian craters: comparison of statistical counts. bibliog Science 164:297-9 Ap 18 '69
BINDER, David
Willy Brandt's wanderjahre are finished. N Y Times Mag p34-5+ N 30 '69
BINDER, Henry
Coffee break; poem. Chr Cent 86:707 My 21 '69
BINDING (books) See Bookbinding
BINFORD, Lewis R. See Binford, S. R. jt. auth.
BINFORD, Sally R. and Binford, L. R.
Stone tools and human behavior; with biographical sketches. Sci Am 220:12, 70-2+ bibliog(p 146) Ap '69
BING, Rudolf
Met as museum. H. Green. Commonweal 90: 206-7 My 2 '69
Musical events. W. Sargeant. New Yorker 45:174+ Ap 12 '69
Singing is believing. por Time 94:67 D 12 '69
BING Crosby tournament. See Golf—Tournaments
BINGHAM, Don
Bonaire is for loafing. Travel 132:57-60 D '69
BINGHAM, Jonathan B.
Can military spending be controlled? For Affairs 48:51-66 O '69
BINGHAM, June
Before the colors fade: Alice Roosevelt Longworth. Am Heritage 20:42-3+ F '69
Ethel Kennedy, a capacity for life. Redbook 133:86-7+ S '69
Your privacy. House & Gard 136:116-17 O '69
BINGHAM, Sam
Nation of Schweiks. Atlan 223:119-21 F '69
BINGHAMTON, N.Y.

Music
See also
Tri-Cities opera
BINKLEY, Kenneth M.
Checkpoint. See issues of Flying
BINNS, James Hazlett
Citizenship with a shrug; address, December 3, 1968. Vital Speeches 35:207-10 Ja 15 '69

about
New house for Armstrong cork. R. Levy. il por Duns R 94:41-4+ N '69
BINOCULARS. See Field glasses
BIOCHEMISTRY
Life sciences. See occasional issues of Science news
Will the science brain bank go conglomerate? biochemical research activities of P. Handler. J. Lear. il Sat R 52:37-44 Jl 5 '69
See also
Biosynthesis
Chemoreceptivity
Lactic acid
BIOCRYSTALLOGRAPHY. See Crystallography
BIOGRAPHIES
See also
Publishers and publishing—Biographies
BIOGRAPHY
Biographer and his hero; excerpt from The craft and the calling. C. D. Bowen. Am Heritage 20:16-17 D '68
Electronic diary; tape recorder technique of D. Schaap. P. D. Zimmerman. il Newsweek 73:88+ F 3 '69
Plotting the biography; excerpts from Biography: the craft and the calling. C. D. Bowen. Writer 82:16-18 F '69

Anecdotes, facetiae, satire, etc.
Metterling lists. W. Allen. New Yorker 45: 34-5 My 10 '69

Bibliography
Biography. M. Adelman, jr. America 120:542-5 My 3 '69
Men of arts and letters. Sr Schol 94:Schol Teach 18-19 My 2 '69
Men who shaped history. il Sr Schol 94: Schol Teach 22-4 My 2 '69
People: famous and interesting; paperback books. il Sr Schol 94:Schol Teach 24-5 Ja 31 '69
Stories of great Americans. il Schol Teach Sec Teach Sup p28+ S 22 '69

BIOLOGICAL and chemical weapons. See Chemical and biological weapons

BIOLOGICAL apparatus and supplies
See also
Computers—Biological applications

BIOLOGICAL assay
Mammary tumor virus antigen: sensitive immunoassay. L. R. Sibal and others. bibliog il Science 164:76-8 Ap 4 '69
Radiation leukemia virus: quantitative tissue culture assay. P. J. Fischinger and T. E. O'Connor. bibliog il Science 165:306-9 Jl 18 '69
L-Tyrosine-3,5-³H assay for tyrosinase development in skin of newborn hamsters. S. H. Pomerantz. bibliog il Science 164:838-9 My 16 '69

BIOLOGICAL balance. See Ecology

BIOLOGICAL chemistry. See Biochemistry

BIOLOGICAL clocks. See Periodicity

BIOLOGICAL control of insects. See Insects, Injurious and beneficial—Biological control

BIOLOGICAL control systems
Information and control processes in living systems: report of meeting. L. R. Troncale and D. M. Ramsey-Klee. Science 166:132+ O 3 '69
See also
Insects, Injurious and beneficial—Biological control

BIOLOGICAL cycles. See Periodicity

BIOLOGICAL physics
See also
Biological control systems
Molecular biology

BIOLOGICAL research
Living nature and the knowledge gap. P. A. Weiss. Sat R 52:19-22+ N 29 '69
Man's participatory evolution: living in a biological revolution. R. M. Davidson. Cur 105:4-10 Mr '69
On living in a biological revolution. D. Fleming. il Atlan 223:64-70 F '69; Discussion. 223:46-50 Mr '69; Same with title Mood of the new revolutionaries. Cur 105:10-19 Mr '69
See also
Animal experimentation
Biotelemetry
Brain
Ecological research
Fishery research
Genetic research
Germfree life
International biological program

Federal aid
Wrong place to cut: funds slashed for biological and medical research. Nation 209:362-3 O 13 '69

BIOLOGICAL societies
See also
American institute of biological sciences

BIOLOGICAL specimens

Collection and preservation
See also
Tissues—Preservation

BIOLOGICAL surveys
Biological warfare: is the Smithsonian really a cover? NBC's charge aired on First Tuesday. P. M. Boffey. il Science 163:791-6 F 21 '69

BIOLOGICAL telemetry. See Biotelemetry

BIOLOGICAL transport
Axonal transport of proteins in experimental neuropathies. D. E. Pleasure and others. bibliog il Science 166:524-5 O 24 '69
Binding of alkali metal ions by cyclic polyethers: significance in ion transport processes. R. M. Izatt and others. bibliog il Science 164:443-4 Ap 25 '69
Do trehalose and trehalase function in renal glucose transport? E. Van Handel. bibliog il Science 163:1075-6 Mr 7 '69
Fast transport system of materials in mammalian nerve fibers. S. Ochs and others. bibliog il Science 163:686-7 F 14 '69
25-Hydroxycholecalciferol; direct effect on calcium transport. E. B. Olson and H. F. DeLuca. bibliog il Science 165:405-7 Jl 25 '69

Ionic mobility in muscle cells. M. J. Kushmerick and R. J. Podolsky. bibliog il Science 166:1297-8 D 5 '69
Maturation of renal organic acid transport: substrate stimulation by penicillin. G. H. Hirsch and J. B. Hook. bibliog il Science 165:909-10 Ag 29 '69
Pulmonary gas transport time: larynx to alveolus. W. W. Wagner, jr. and others. bibliog il Science 163:1210-11 Mr 14 '69; Reply with rejoinder. F. H. Shair. 165:823-4 Ag 22 '69
Purines: active transport by isolated choroid plexus R. D. Berlin. bibliog il Science 163:1194-5 Mr 14 '69
Toad urinary bladder: intercellular spaces. D. R. DiBona and M. M. Civan. bibliog il Science 165:503-4 Ag 1 '69
See also
Blood-brain barrier
Diffusion
Osmosis
Secretion

BIOLOGICAL warfare
Biological warfare: is the Smithsonian really a cover? NBC's charge aired on First Tuesday. P. M. Boffey. il Science 163:791-6 F 21 '69
Breath of death: the dilemma of chemical and biological warfare. il Sr Schol 94:3-6+ F 7 '69
CBW. ed. by S. Rose. Review
Sat R 52:29-31+ Ap 26 '69. E. B. Skolnikoff
Dare we develop biological weapons? S. M. Hersh. il N Y Times Mag p28-9+ S 28 '69; Reply. P. O'Dwyer. p42 N 2 '69
Germs, anyone? Commonweal 90:475-6 Ag 8 '69
Poison for peace. R. D. McCarthy. Commonweal 90:335-7 Je 6 '69
Tracking CBW. il Sci N 95:470-1 My 17 '69
See also
Chemical and biological weapons

Bibliography
Deadly weapons. S. Novick. Commentary 47:85-9 Je '69

BIOLOGISTS
See also
Lysenko, T. D.

BIOLOGY
Hierarchical structures; report of symposium at the Douglas advanced research laboratories, Huntington Beach, Calif. T. Page. il Science 163:1228-30 Mr 14 '69
Life sciences. See occasional issues of Science news
Living nature and the knowledge gap. P. A. Weiss. Sat R 52:19-22+ N 29 '69
Modern biology: a terrifying power. S. E. Luria. il Nation 209:406-9 O 20 '69
Tropical biology; symposium on Amazonian biology. Sci N 95:165 F 15 '69
See also
Adaptation (biology)
American institute of biological sciences
Cell division (biology)
Clones (biology)
Death (biology)
Ecology
Evolution
Fertilization (biology)
Growth
Marine biology
Morphogenesis
Mutation (biology)
Phylogeny
Polymorphism (biology)
Psychobiology
Regeneration (biology)
Reproduction
Sex (biology)
Space biology

Classification
Controversial taxonomy of fossil hominids. E. L. Simons and others. bibliog Science 166:258-9 O 10 '69
New concepts of kingdoms of organisms. R. H. Whittaker. bibliog il Science 163:150-60 Ja 10 '69; Reply with rejoinder. L. S. Olive. 164:857 My 16 69

Field work
Wilderness biological station; two State university of New York units combine summer study in the Adirondacks. N. Drahos. il Cons 23:18-20 F '69

BIOLOGY—*Continued*
Study and teaching
It takes brains to learn from forty-six black mice. J. Margolskee. il Seventeen 28:94+ Ja '69
On teaching biology in a biological revolution. S. E. Luria. Sci Am 220:131-2+ Mr '69
Wilderness biological station; two State university of New York units combine summer study in the Adirondacks. N. Drahos. il Cons 23:18-20 F '69

BIOLUMINESCENCE
Burning of the sea; bioluminescent bays. R. G. Johnsson. il Parks & Rec 4:31-3 Je '69
Cypridina bioluminescence: light-emitting oxyluciferin-luciferase complex. O. Shimomura and others. bibliog il Science 164:1299-300 Je 13 '69
Luminescent systems in apogonid fishes from the Philippines. Y. Haneda and others. bibliog il Science 165:188-90 Jl 11 '69
See also
Fireflies

BIOMEDICAL engineering
Biomedical engineering: new lifesaving science. J. Lentz. il Todays Health 47:20-3+ F '69
Biomedical engineers stress need for rapport with MD's. Electr World 81:72 Ap '69
Medical engineers: doctors/designers for tomorrow's people. A. S. Freese. bibliog il Sci Digest 66:46-8+ S '69

BIOMEDICAL research. See Medical research

BIONICS
See also
Human information processing
Man amplifiers

BIOSATELLITE program
Biosat curtailment retards zero-g study. Aviation W 91:19-20 Jl 14 '69
Biosatellite III: preliminary findings. W. R. Adey and others. Science 166:492-3 O 24 '69
Bioscience programs in space. O. E. Reynolds. il Space World F-9-69:4-15 S '69
In the news; monkey in space. Space World F-7-67:49-50 Jl '69
Latest biosatellite. R. N. Watts, jr. il Sky & Tel 38:80-1 Ag '69
More vertebrates in space; report of meeting. Sci N 96:77 Jl 26 '69
Sad end to Biosat 3. il Sci N 96:46 Jl 19 '69
Thirty-day zero-g mission set for monkey. Z. Strickland. il Aviation W 90:70+ My 5 '69
To fill the gaps in space medicine. il Sci N 95:569-70 Je 14 '69
Zero gravity's deadly effects. il Sci N 96:393-4 N 1 '69

BIOSYNTHESIS
Biosynthesis of oligosaccharides and polysaccharides in plants. W. Z. Hassid. bibliog il Science 165:137-44 Jl 11 '69
Computer-assisted design of complex organic syntheses. E. J. Corey and W. T. Wipke. bibliog il Science 166:178-92 O 10 '69
Enzyme synthesis in synchronous cultures. J. M. Mitchison. bibliog il Science 165:657-63 Ag 15 '69
Phenylalanine and tyrosine synthesis under primitive earth conditions. N. Friedmann and S. L. Miller. bibliog il Science 166:766-7 N 7 '69
Photochemical reactions and the chemical evolution of purines and nicotinamide derivatives. J. P. Ferris and others. bibliog il Science 166:765-6 N 7 '69
Polypeptide chain elongation in protein biosynthesis. F. Lipmann. bibliog il Science 164:1024-31 My 30 '69
Regulation of branched biosynthetic pathways in bacteria. P. Datta. bibliog il Science 165:556-62 Ag 8 '69
Ribonucleic acid biosynthesis in adult and infant rat brain in vitro. T. Itoh and J. H. Quastel. bibliog il Science 164:79-80 Ap 4 '69

BIOTELEMETRY
Outer space helps man. V. Parin. il Space World F-10-70:38-9 O '69

BIOTITE
Orientation of the dipole moments of hydroxyl groups in oxidized and unoxidized biotite. A. S. R. Juo and J. L. White. bibliog il Science 165:804-5 Ag 22 '69

BIPHENYL compounds. See Diphenyl compounds

BIRCH, Alison Wyrley
Blessed be the foster grandparent. Read Digest 95:21-4 N '69

BIRCH, Hal
Vortex mower promises a revolution in grass cutting. Pop Sci 195:86-7+ O '69

BIRCH, John, society. See John Birch society
BIRCH
Betula papyrifera. C. E. Lewis. Horticulture 47:48-9 S '69
BIRD, Arthur D.
How to plan for the pedestrian. Am City 84:76-7+ Jl '69
BIRD, J. F. and Mowbray, G. H.
Visual transient phenomenon: its polarity and a paradox. bibliog Science 165:588-9 Ag 8 '69
BIRD attracting. See Birds, Attracting of
BIRD baths, etc.
See what comes to pass when sculptors create birdbaths. il Home Gard 56:30 Ag '69
BIRD calling
Championship goose calling. H. Bradshaw and V. Bradshaw. il Field & S 74:140-1 N '69
BIRD calls. See Birds—Song
BIRD dogs
Dogs. D. M. Duffey. See issues of Outdoor life
How close, and how? G. B. Evans. il Field & S 74:152-4+ S '69
How to keep a grouse dog close. H. G. Tapply. il Field & S 74:74 N '69
See also
Pointers (dogs)
Setters
Training
See Dogs—Training
BIRD feeders. See Feeders (birds)
BIRD flight. See Birds—Flight
BIRD gardens
Maxi-plantings for the birds. H. G. Lendle. il Org Gard & Farm 16:53-4 N '69
BIRD houses
Birds are particular. il Sunset 142:222-3 Mr '69
It's a high-rise birdhouse. il Sunset 142:137 Ap '69
Making bird homes for the garden. J. Plewes. il Org Gard & Farm 16:82-4 Ja '69
Purple martinsville. G. Schneider. il Am For 75:36-7+ F '69
Put your fence posts to work! R. Van Vorse. il Org Gard & Farm 16:74-6 Jl '69
BIRD migration. See Birds—Migration
BIRD PARADISE NATIONAL PARK, Turkey. See Manyas, Lake
BIRD photography. See Photography of birds
BIRD populations
Why the long grouse season? R. B. Colson. il Cons 24:9+ O '69
BIRD prints. See Birds in art
BIRD refuges. See Bird sanctuaries
BIRD sanctuaries
Lake Manyas: a Turkish park for birds. C. E. Adelson. il Nat Parks 43:25-7 Ap '69
Waterfowl on the wane? M. Frome. Field & S 74:34+ Ag '69
Where have all the pelicans gone? G. Laycock. il Audubon 71:10-17 S '69
BIRD songs. See Birds—Song
BIRD study
Bird watching, an abiding avocation. R. C. Murphy. il Natur Hist 78:80+ Ap '69
Birding through the year. E. M. Woodford. 48:24-5+ Ja '70
Birdwatching, the accommodating sport. B. Miles. il Pop Gard 20:34-7+ Spr '69
Multimedia zoo: an artificial thunderstorm for the birds: Bronx zoo. J. S. Margolies. il Arch Forum 130:90-1 Je '69
Our local correspondents; Central park bird walk. E. Kinkead. New Yorker 45:58+ Ag 2 '69
Where the birds are. M. Gough. House B 111:104+ My '69
Winging it through Russia. D. Thomas. il Sports Illus 31:42-7 S 8 '69
See also
Audubon nature camps
BIRD watching. See Bird study
BIRDBATHS. See Bird baths, etc.
BIRDHOUSES. See Bird houses
BIRDS
L-Ascorbic acid synthesis in birds: phylogenetic trend. C. R. Chaudhuri and I. B. Chatterjee. bibliog il Science 164:435-6 Ap 25 '69
Birds are coming back. E. M. Woodford. il Horticulture 47:40-1+ Mr '69
See also
Aviaries
Color of birds
Water birds
also names of birds, e.g. Mockingbirds

BIRDS—*Continued*

Accidents and hazards
See also
Aviation—Bird hazards

Bibliography
Bird watching, an abiding avocation. R. C. Murphy. il Natur Hist 78:80+ Ap '69

Care
Mr Tweedy; condensation. A. M. Schilling. Read Digest 94:277-87+ My '69

Caricatures and cartoons
What's in a name? B. Roos. Audubon 71:46-7 Mr '69

Collisions with airplanes
See Aviation—Bird hazards

Color
See Color of birds

Diseases and pests
See also
Botulism

Flight
Birds that fly nowhere. D. Seaver. il Sci Digest 65:19-21 Ap '69
Energetics of bird flight. V. A. Tucker. il Sci Am 220:70-6+ My '69

Food and feeding
Guests in my garden. V. Withee. il Horticulture 47:32+ Ag '69
Hackettstown is for the birds; Panther Valley, N.J. M. A. Guitar. il Am Home 72:12+ S '69
Outdoor tree with Christmas edibles for the birds. il Sunset 143:173 D '69
Short fracas at a carcass; activities of the bald eagle; photographs; with introduction. C. Scott and J. Swedberg. Audubon 71:16-19 Mr '69
Sunflower seeds. il Home Gard 56:39 Je '69
See also
Bird gardens
Food chains (ecology)

Habits and behavior
Cardinal in the mirror. J. Stuart. il Am For 75:8+ Je '69
Messages of vertebrate communication; adaptation of address. December 28, 1967. W. J. Smith. bibliog Science 165:145-50 Jl 11 '69
Punishment by response-contingent withdrawal of an imprinted stimulus. H. S. Hoffman and others. bibliog il Science 163: 702-4 F 14 '69
See also
Birds—Food and feeding
Courtship of birds
Instinct

Memory
See Memory

Migration
Are duck laws outdated? J. O. Cartier. il Outdoor Life 143:45-7+ F '69
Bird migration; influence of physiological state upon celestial orientation. S. T. Emlen. bibliog il Science 165:716-18 Ag 15 '69
Birds migrate by the stars. il Sci Digest 66: 43-4 O '69
Mystery of migration. M. J. Walker. il Am For 75:32-5+ N '69
See also
Orientation

Nests
See Nests

Orientation
See Orientation

Photographs
Feather's in full bloom. T. Daniel. Nat Wildlife 7:12-13 Ap '69
Inside a hornbill's walled-up nest. J. Root and A. Root. Nat Geog 136:846-55 D '69
Wings. Audubon 71:56-65 My '69

Protection
See also
Bird sanctuaries
Birds of prey—Protection

Sanctuaries
See Bird sanctuaries

Song
Bird vocalizations; ed. by R. A. Hinde. Review
Science 167:39-41 Ja 2 '70. W. J. Smith

Hearing, single-unit analysis, and vocalizations in songbirds. M. Konishi. bibliog il Science 166:1178-81 N 28 '69
How birds sing. C. H. Greenewalt. il Sci Am 221:126-34+ N '69
Music in the garden. M. D. Hodgins. il Horticulture 47:38-9 Je '69
Teaching songbirds how to sing. B. Ford. il Sci Digest 66:20-5 Jl '69

Species
See Species

Stories
Mr Tweedy; condensation. A. M. Schilling. Read Digest 94:277-87+ My '69

Study
See Bird study

Africa
See also
Flamingos

Amazon Valley
Speciation in Amazonian forest birds. J. Haffer. bibliog il Science 165:131-7 Jl 11 '69

Great Lakes Region
Inland sea gulls. G. S. Smith. il Sea Front 15:12-20 Ja '69
See also
Birds—Amazon Valley

Latin America
See also
Birds—Amazon Valley

Laysan
Leeward Islands. R. Northshield. il Natur Hist 78:60-7 O '69

New York (state)
Birds along the Appalachian trail. E. R. Brown. il Cons 23:2-4 F '69
Bobwhite for western New York? S. B. Robeson. il Cons 24:8-9 D '69
Gotham's birds. D. Amadon. il Natur Hist 78:48-55 Ap '69

Texas
Golden-cheeked warbler; threatened bird of the cedar brakes. W. M. Pulich. il Nat Parks 43:10-12 Mr '69

Trinidad (island)
Bird of darkness. J. Lindblad. il Natur Hist 78:80-4 F '69

BIRDS, Attracting of
Ways to attract birds with plants. il Good H 168:206 Ap '69

BIRDS, Color of. *See* Color of birds

BIRDS, Effect of solar radiation on
Bird energetics; effects of artificial radiation. S. Lustick. bibliog il Science 163:387-90 Ja 24 '69

BIRDS, Extinct
Last parakeet; Carolina parakeet. G. Laycock. il Audubon 71:20-5 Mr '69

BIRDS, Fossil
See also
Penguins, Fossil

BIRDS, Infancy of
How an instinct is learned. J. P. Hailman. il Sci Am 221:98-106 bibliog(p 152) D '69
Laughing gull chicks; recognition of their parents' voices. C. G. Beer. bibliog il Science 166:1030-2 N 21 '69

BIRDS, Injurious and beneficial
Boysenberries, without the birds. G. L'Allemand. il Org Gard & Farm 16:50 Ap '69

BIRDS eggs
See also
Egg shells

BIRDS eggs, Fossil. *See* Eggs, Fossil

BIRDS in art
Roger Peterson's whooping cranes. il Audubon 71:80-2 N '69
Stunning birds of Fen Lansdowne. D. MacDonald. il Read Digest 95:147-52 Ag '69
Wanted: a lost Audubon watercolor. N. Kent. il Am Artist 33:58-9 Je '69
See also
Design, Decorative—Animal forms

BIRDS nests. *See* Nests

BIRDS of prey
See also
Condors
Eagles

Protection
Laws and education and the birds of prey. il Audubon 71:4 Ja '69

BIRDS of the air; story. *See* Frame, J.

BIRDWATCHING. *See* Bird study

BIRGE, E. A. and Kurland, C. G.
Altered ribosomal protein in streptomycin-dependent escherichia coli. bibliog Science 166:1282-4 D 5 '69
—and others
Structural determinant of a ribosomal protein: K locus. bibliog Science 164:1285-6 Je 13 '69
BIRK, Eileen P.
Current and coming. See issues of Antiques
Fine art in decoration. Antiques 95:830-1 Je '69
BIRKIN, Jane
Baby Jane. por Newsweek 75:61 Ja 5 '70
BIRKMAIER, Emma M. and Lange, D. L.
Static in the language lab; what about the Pennsylvania studies? Todays Ed 58:49+ O '69
BIRKS, Tony
Anthony Hepburn. Craft Horiz 29:34-6 Jl '69
BIRLEY, Rheda Vava Mary (Pike) lady
Lady Birley: fish soup for the roses. N. Lyon. Vogue 154:163 O 1 '69
BIRMINGHAM, Stephen
Fairfield County; New York's best address. Holiday 45:58-63+ Ap '69
Good, good life of the Alpine set. McCalls 97:46-7+ Ja '70
Poor little Palm Beach. Esquire 73:112-20+ Ja '70
Rugged art of social climbing. Vogue 153:190-1+ My '69
BIRMINGHAM, William
Crisis or kairos? Commonweal 91:210-14 N 14 '69
BIRMINGHAM, Ala.

Cemeteries

Integration in death; burial of Private Bill Terry. Chr Cent 87:37 Ja 14 '70
No bells for Bill. G. Shockley. Chr Cent 86:1508 N 26 '69

Negroes

Can Birmingham break with its past? civic leaders launch reforms and open communications between whites and blacks. il Bsns W p 140-2+ Mr 15 '69
Change in Birmingham. il Newsweek 74:79-80 D 8 '69

Politics and government

Change in Birmingham. il Newsweek 74:79-80 D 8 '69
BIRMINGHAM, Mich.

Housing

Town that voted yes for justice. M. A. Rodgers. Good H 168:67+ F '69
BIRMINGHAM-Southern college, Birmingham, Ala.
Avant-garde arena. il Travel 131:22 F '69
Teaching machine for drama. il Arch Forum 130:78-83 Ap '69
BIRNBAUM, Henry. See Lowenthal, J. jt. auth.
BIRNBAUM, Hubert C.
Color print services; how good are they? U S Camera 32:54-5+ Ja '69
BIRNBAUM, Max
Sense about sensitivity training. Sat R 52:82-3+ N 15 '69
BIRNBAUM, Norman
From vulgar Marxism to crude psychological determinism. Commonweal 90:238+ My 9 '69
BIRNIE, William A. H.
Jules Verne's trip to the moon. Read Digest 95:112-14 O '69
Notre-Dame of Paris. Read Digest 95:184-6+ Ag '69
BIRNN, Roland
U.S. Coast guard auxiliary. See issues of Yachting
BIRREN, James E.
Prospects for gerontology: psychology. Aging 180:7 O '69
BIRSTEIN, Ann
Liz Taylor and Richard Burton. Vogue 153:100-1+ F 15 '69
Movies. See occasional issues of Vogue
BIRTH. See Childbirth
BIRTH control
Beyond family planning. B. Berelson. bibliog il Science 163:533-43 F 7 '69; Discussion. 164:129-30 Ap 11 '69
Birth control now, country by country. il U S News 66:49-52 Mr 17 '69
Blacks cry genocide; opposition to the Planned parenthood association programs. R. Z. Hallow. Nation 208:535-7 Ap 28 '69
Doctor Guttmacher is the evangelist of birth control. D. Dempsey. il N Y Times Mag p32-3+ F 9 '69; Discussion. p 14+ Mr 16 '69

Excessive population growth; address. May 1, 1969. R. S. McNamara. Vital Speeches 35:500-5 Je 1 '69
Family-planning campaign; the Louisiana story. il U S News 67:55-7 Jl 28 '69
How to succeed at family planning; excerpts from Birth control and love. A. F. Guttmacher. il Parents Mag 44:54-5+ Ja '69
Louisiana's quiet revolution in family planning. A. Gordon. il Todays Health 48:38-41+ Ja '70
More studies and more people. D. Sanford. New Repub 160:14-15 My 24 '69
National plan for curbing births; proposals of President Nixon. U S News 67:4 Jl 28 '69
Perils of the pill; campaign by W. Baird. A. Goldberg. Ramp Mag 7:45-6+ My '69
Population crisis: rising concern at home. L. J. Carter. Science 166:722-6 N 7 '69
Population policy for Americans: is the government being misled? J. Blake. bibliog il Science 164:522-9 My 2 '69; Discussion. 165:121-2+, 367-73, 1203-4 Jl 11, 25, S 19 '69
Report on family planning programme in Pakistan; India. UN Mo Chron 6:47-8 Je '69
Rhythm method of birth control; Georgetown university study. America 120:663 Je 7; Reply. A. E. Hellegers. 121-51 Ag 2 '69
Should we teach about birth control in high school sex education? H. S. Hoyman. Ed Digest 34:20-3 F '69
See also
Abortion
Contraceptives

Religious aspects

American Catholic marriages and the church. A. V. Krebs, jr. Cath World 208:225-9 F '69
Catholic case for contraception; ed. by D. Callahan. Review
America 120:627-8 My 24 '69. R. A. McCormick
Cath World 210:42-3 O '69. P. Marx
Catholics and the population explosion. Trans-Action 6:8+ Je '69
Humanae vitae: reactions and consequences. J. A. O'Brien. Chr Cent 86:288-9 F 26 '69
Love and the pill; study of encyclical, Humanae vitae initiated and approved by bishops of Austria. Newsweek 73:84 Mr 10 '69
Muckraking contraception. W. Hinckle. il Ramp Mag 7:150+ Ja 25 '69
Vatican speaks out; about series of newspaper articles on Humanae vitae. J. A. O'Brien. il Chr Cent 86:1580-2 D 10 '69
What's heroic about continence? ed. by D. Curran. Cath World 209:21-3 Ap '69

Study and teaching

Should birth control be taught? H. S. Hoyman. Ed Digest 35:28-30 D '69

India

Ford condom in India's future; US-backed program. Z. B. Grant. New Repub 161:14-16 S 6 '69

Italy

Il Papa and the pill. L. J. Berry. Commonweal 90:44-6 Mr 28 '69; Reply. J. Rettie. 90:183 Ap 25 '69

Latin America

They'd rather decide for themselves. E. K. Culhane. America 120:621-3 My 24 '69

South Africa

Family planning in South Africa. America 120:638 My 31 '69

Underdeveloped areas

AID's family planning strategy; letter. R. T. Ravenholt. Science 163:124+ Ja 10 '69
Birth control for economic development. S. Enke. bibliog il Science 164:798-802 My 16 '69
Population threat; excerpts from address. May 1969. R. S. McNamara. il Todays Ed 58:20-3 D '69

United States

See Birth control
BIRTH defects. See Deformities
BIRTH order
Birth order, what it means to your children. T. Irwin. Todays Health 47:26-7+ O '69
See also
Children, First-born

BIRTH rate
See also
Birth control
Population, Increase of
India
See also
Birth control—India
Russia
Needed, mother heroines. Newsweek 74:33 S 1 '69
United States
Anabaptist explosion; adaptation of Pockets of high fertility in the United States. W. F. Pratt. il Natur Hist 78:8-10+ F '69
Birth rate levels out, bigger baby crops ahead. il U S News 66:80 F 3 '69
BIRTHDAY cake. See Cake
BIRTHDAY parties. See Childrens parties
BISBEE, Charles
Challenge yourself to success. Nations Bsns 57:94 N '69
BISCAY, BAY OF
Age of the Bay of Biscay: evidence from seismic profiles and bottom samples. E. J. W. Jones and J. I. Ewing. bibliog il Science 166:102-5 O 3 '69
BISCAYNE BAY
New Key for the white house. M. Wright. il Travel & Camera 32:64-7 Ap '69
BISCUIT company, National. See National biscuit company
BISHKO, C. J.
(comp) Articles and other books received; Spain and Portugal. See issues of American historical review
BISHOP, Beata
Queen's Scottish summer. Sat R 52:73-4+ Mr 8 '69
BISHOP, Elizabeth
Minor poet with major fund of love. C. Elliott. Life 67:13 Jl 4 '69
BISHOP, Sir Henry Rowley
Unholy Bishop. R. Rushmore. por Opera N 34:6-7 D 20 '69
BISHOP, Jim
Clear the road for Nancy! Read Digest 95: 37-40 Ag '69
Philosopher and the school girl. Read Digest 95:132-4 O '69
Romance, Honolulu style. Read Digest 95: 136-40 D '69
BISHOP, Joey
Battle of the talk shows. il por Newsweek 74:42-4+ S 1 '69
BISHOP, Jordan
Papal infallibility and all that. Commonweal 90:481-4 Ag 8 '69
—and Elmer, Michael
Gringo manifesto. Commonweal 91:334-7 D 12 '69
BISHOP, Joseph W. Jr
Privacy vs. protection, the bugged society. N Y Times Mag p30-1+ Je 8; 28 Je 29; 29 Jl 20 '69
Warren court is not likely to be overruled. N Y Times Mag p31-3+ S 7 '69
BISHOP, Lee R.
Low-noise receiver performance measurements. Electr World 81:38-9+ Mr '69
BISHOP, Morris
Constant and the King of Siam. Horizon 11: 58-9 Wint '69
End of the Iroquois. Am Heritage 20:28-33+ O '69
Great Oneida love-in. Am Heritage 20:14-17+ F '69
Louis Philippe in America. Am Heritage 20: 42-5+ Ap '69
Lower depths of higher education. Am Heritage 21:26-31+ D '69
So to speak. Horizon 11:44-7 Sum '69
BISHOP, Thomas
Movies. Vogue 155:80 Ja 1 '70
Samuel Beckett. Sat R 52:26-7+ N 15 '69
BISHOP Hill, Ill.
Prairie dream recaptured; utopian Swedish colony. D. G. Lowe. il Am Heritage 20: 14-23+ O '69
BISHOPS
Conflict at Chur; meetings of European bishops and priests; with editorial comment. M. von Galli. America 121:52, 68-70 Ag 2 '69
North American bishops meet. America 120: 516 My 3 '69
Shannon affair. Commonweal 90:380 Je 20 '69
See also
Catholic church—Dioceses
National conference of Catholic bishops
Popes—Primacy
Synod of bishops, 1969

Installation
See Catholic church—Clergy—Installation
Selection
On the problem of selecting bishops. America 121:287 O 11 '69
BISHOP'S weed. See Goutweed
BISMARCK, Otto, fürst von
Gold and iron: the collaboration and friendship of Gerson Bleichröder and Otto von Bismarck. F. Stern. bibliog f Am Hist R 75:37-46 O '69
BISWELL, Harold Hubert. See Weaver, H. jt. auth.
BITENSKY, Reuben
Social action, the therapy of poor folk. Ment Hy 53:503-8 O '69
BITO, Laszlo Z.
Blood-brain barrier: evidence for active cation transport between blood and the extracellular fluid of brain. bibliog Science 165: 81-3 Jl 4 '69
BITTERMAN, M. E. See Bresler, D. E. jt. auth.
BITTNER, John R.
News media; address, October 4, 1969. Vital Speeches 36:139-41 D 15 '69
BIVALVES. See Mollusks
BIXLER, Richard C.
Vocational live-in. Am Ed 5:7-9 Mr '69
BIZARRE, incorporated
Mephisto in Hollywood; LPs under direction of F. Zappa. il Time 94:46+ O 31 '69
BIZET, Georges
Carmen. Criticism
Opera N 33:24-5 Mr 15 '69
Opera N il 33:17-20 Mr 15 '69
BLACHFORD, B. W.
SCS frequency calibrator. Pop Electr 31:53-4 D '69
BLACK, Eli M.
How United fruit was plucked. il por Bsns W p 122-4 F 22 '69
BLACK, Jonathan
Street academies: one step off the sidewalk. Sat R 52:88-9+ N 15 '69
BLACK, Mary
Collectors: Edgar and Bernice Chrysler Garbisch. Art in Am 57:48-59 My '69
Gansevoort limner. Antiques 96:738-44 N '69
Wooden parade. Am Heritage 21:34-43 D '69
BLACK, Patricia, and Black, Ralph
Screenings: 16mm. Library J 94:4587-8 D 15 '69
BLACK, Ralph. See Black, P. jt. auth.
BLACK, Shirley (Temple) See Temple, S.
BLACK, W. Joseph
Farsighted study and some blind spots. Arch Forum 129:44-9 D '68
BLACK and Brown trading stamp company. See Trading stamps
BLACK and Decker manufacturing company
A. G. Decker of Black & Decker; interview. A. G. Decker, jr. il Nations Bsns 57:64-9 D '69
Black & Decker. il Forbes 104:38 Ag 15 '69
BLACK and white (art)
Drawings of Malcolm Cameron. M. Cameron. il Am Artist 33:50-5+ Je '69
BLACK-and-white transparencies. See Transparencies
BLACK bear hunting. See Bear hunting
BLACK capitalism
Black business, bleak business. G. Eckstein. Nation 209:243-5 S 15 '69
Black capitalism; a disappointing start. il Time 94:71 Ag 15 '69
Black capitalism, by T. L. Cross. Review America 121:170 S 13 '69. A. Cook
Black capitalism has a hollow ring. il Bsns W p51+ Ag 30 '69
Black capitalism, it offers little, says a top Negro. A. F. Brimmer. U S News 68:9 Ja 12 '70
Black capitalism: prospects and problems; symposium. il Sat R 52.15-29+ Ag 23 '69
Blacks debate black capitalism. Bsns W p38 Ja 10 '70
Bridge to nowhere? views of A. Brimmer. Newsweek 75:59 Ja 12 '70
Capitalist slow down. S. Cotton. New Repub 161:15-16 S 27 '69
Chicago's leaders bankroll the blacks. Bsns W p56 S 13 '69
Into the big leagues; black capitalism is progressing. il Time 94:70 Jl 25 '69
Is black capitalism a mistake? Time 95:66-7 Ja 12 '70
On black capitalism. W. F. Buckley, jr. Nat R 21:298-9 Mr 25 '69

BLACKBURN, Paul—*Continued*

about

Comment. B. Berkson. Poetry 114:257-9 Jl '69
Comment. M. L. Rosenthal. Poetry 114:129-30 My '69

BLACKBURN, Sara
Taxi! New Yorker 44:102-4 F 8 '69

BLACKETT, Patrick Maynard Stuart
Ever-widening gap. Bul Atom Sci 25:23-5 My '69

BLACKFORD, Charles M.
Offshore passages on D.R. Motor B 123:54-5+ F '69

BLACKIE, Margery Grace
Queen's homeopath. por Newsweek 73:67 F 3 '69

BLACKLISTING
See also
Boycott

BLACKLISTING of scientists
Blacklisting lingers on; blacklisted scientists. Life 67:46 N 7 '69
Blacklists and loyalty oaths. Sci N 97:36-7 Ja 10 '70
Blacklist's backlash; HEW's security practices. Newsweek 74:71 N 3 '69
Ending the blacklist; HEW action. Newsweek 75:61 Ja 12 '70
Too bad, Mr Nobel Laureate. W. Barthelmes. Commonweal 91:245-7 N 21 '69

BLACKMAN, Samuel G.
Gospel according to Blackman. por Sat R 52:45-6+ Ag 9 '69

BLACKMON, Rosemary
What hypnosis can do for you. Vogue 153:136-7+ Ja 15 '69

BLACKSTONE Rangers. See Gangs

BLACKWELL, Alice Stone
(tr) See Lugones, L. How the mountains talk

BLACKWOOD, Easley
Meet Mr Four no trump. C. H. Goren. il McCalls 96:64+ Ap '69

BLACKWOOD, Linda
Teenagers and the law. Schol Teach Sec Teach Sup p 18-19+ S 22 '69

BLADEN, Ronald
Artist speaks: Ronald Bladen; interview, ed. by C. Robins. Art in Am 57:76-81 S '69

BLADES. Saw. See Saws

BLAGONRAVOV, Anatolii Arkadievich
Flights to other planets are becoming a realistic fact; interview, ed. by IU. Kanin. Space World F-10-70:27-9 O '69
—and Zaitsev, IUrii
Progress in science and cosmonautics. Space World F-2-62:4-5 F '69

BLAIBERG, Philip
Borrowed time ends. Sci N 96:147 Ag 23 '69
Reassessing transplants. il por Newsweek 74:73 S 1 '69
Why Blaiberg died. por Time 94:34 Ag 29 '69

BLAINE, Graham, jr
Décor and the psyche. House B 111:46+ Ap '69

BLAINE, James B.
Bookbinding, from craft to industry; excerpts from address, November 1969. Pub W 196:56 D 1 '69

BLAIR, Clay Drewry, 1925–
Peripatetic reviewer. E. Weeks. Atlan 224:106 Jl '69

BLAIR, Eric. See Orwell, G. pseud.

BLAIR, Frank
Extremism; address, June 8, 1969. Vital Speeches 35:598-601 Jl 15 '69

BLAIR, Gerry
Two guides and the no-peek sheep. Field & S 74:54-5+ Ag '69

BLAIR, Streeter
Late starter. il por Time 93:80-3 Mr 21 '69

BLAIR, W. L. See Levy, S. jt. auth.

BLAIR, Wes
Harvest trout. Field & S 74:136-8+ Ag '69

BLAIR, Wren
Won't somebody please get me out of here? G. Ronberg. por Sports Illus 31:81-2+ D 1 '69

BLAKE, Ernie
Passionate skier. J. Egan. il Sat R 52:42-4 D 27 '69

BLAKE, Fay
Library-college movement: dying of old age at thirty; a personal view. Wilson Lib Bul 44:557-60 Ja '70

BLAKE, George
Irish 'who' in a British whodunit. M. Mok. il por Life 66:59-62 Ja 24 '69

BLAKE, J. Herman
Black nationalism. bibliog f Ann Am Acad 382:15-25 Mr '69

BLAKE, James
Widow, bereft; story. Esquire 73:96-102 Ja '70

BLAKE, Judith
Population policy for Americans: is the government being misled? bibliog Science 164:522-9; 165:1203-4 My 2, S 19 '69

BLAKE, N. M. and others
Lactate dehydrogenase electrophoretic variant in a New Guinea highland population. bibliog Science 163:701-2 F 14 '69

BLAKE, Peter
Tomorrow's city is alive and well and has been going full blast all over the world except possibly here. Mlle 68:120-1+ F '69
Vincent Ponte: a new kind of urban designer. Art in Am 57:62-7 S '69

BLAKE, Ran
New music of political protest. M. Cuscuna. Sat R 52:55-6 D 13 '69

BLAKE, Richard A.
Facing a new priesthood. Cath World 209:67-70 My '69

BLAKE, Robert R.
Grid puts executives on the griddle. il por Bsns W p 158-60 O 18 '69

BLAKE, William
Blake and tradition, by K. Raine. Review
Nation il 209:700-1 D 22 '69. J. Bronowski
William Blake and nonviolence. J. Sutherland. Nation 208:542-4 Ap 28 '69

BLAKEFORD (historic house). See Queen Annes County, Md.—Historic houses, etc.

BLAKELEY, Godfrey
Ischia. Harp Baz 102:59+ Je '69

BLAKEMORE, Colin, and Sutton, Peter
Size adaptation: a new aftereffect. bibliog Science 166:245-7 O 10 '69

BLAKESLEE, Alton L.
Today's health news. See issues of Today's health

BLANCH, Lesley
Sea gull from the wings. Vogue 153:216-17+ Ap 1 '69

BLANCHARD, William H.
His own special blend. Nation 208:609-10 My 12 '69

BLANCO, Antonio, and others
Testicular lactate dehydrogenase isozyme: cyclic appearance in bats. bibliog Science 164:835-6 My 16 '69

BLAND diets. See Diet in disease

BLANK, Joseph P.
And not to yield; condensation. Read Digest 94:221-4+ Je '69
Six long, long months. Read Digest 95:97-101 N '69

BLANKETS
New blankets. Good H 19:186 N '69

BLANKFORT, Jeffrey
Our town: the war comes home to Beallsville, Ohio. il Ramp Mag 8:39-46 Jl '69

BLANKSHINE, Robert
Brief biography. S. Goodman. pors Dance Mag 43:60-1 Ja '69

BLASI BRAMBILLA, Alberto
Three marías. Américas 21:35-9 Jl '69

BLASINGAME, Ralph, jr
Signposts to disaster; or, Road to Utopia? address, November 8, 1968. bibliog por Library J 94:715-18 F 15 '69

BLASPHEMY
Damning blasphemy; violation of Maryland's 320-year-old law. il Time 93:72 My 16 '69
Taking names in vain; Italy's anti-blasphemy campaign. Newsweek 73:111A+ My 26 '69
See also
Swearing

BLASS, Bill
Close-up: man who made the Scarsdale Mafia suit; interview, ed. by H. Carlton. pors Life 66:67-8+ Je 13 '69

BLASSINGAME, John W.
Black studies: an intellectual crisis; address. Am Scholar 38:548-61 Aut '69

BLAST cleaning. See Sand blast

BLASTING
Blasting rock with water; hydrotechnology research. il Bsns W p 130 Jl 19 '69
See also
Atomic blasting

BLASTOCLADIA. See Phycomyces

BLASTOMYCOSIS
Fungus diseases that fool the doctors. J. D. Wassersug. Sci Digest 66:83-4 Ag '69

BLATCHFORD, Joseph H.
New broom. S. Ungar. il por Newsweek 73:56+ Je 2 '69
Uncivil war afflicts the Peace corps; confronting the Pentagon in Micronesia. P. Stern. New Repub 161:14-16 Ag 23 '69

BLATZ, Hanson
Are there hidden radiation hazards in your home? Pop Sci 194:90-3 My '69
BLATZ brewing company
Blatz is beautiful to rival bidders. Bsns W p32 Jl 26 '69
BLAUKOPF, Kurt
Notes from our correspondents (cont) Hi Fi 19:18 Ap '69
BLAUSTEIN, Arthur
536 characters in search of a legislative program. Harper 238:28+ Mr '69
BLEACHES. See Bleaching materials
BLEACHING (photography) See Photography— Retouching
BLEACHING materials
Bleachmakers slug back; challenge of enzyme detergents. il Bsns W p 146 S 13 '69
Laundry bleaches. Consumer Rep 34:534-6 S '69
BLEEDING. See Hemorrhage
BLEICHRÖDER, Gershon von
Gold and iron: the collaboration and friendship of Gerson Bleichröder and Otto von Bismarck. F. Stern. bibliog f Am Hist R 75: 37-46 O '69
BLEIL, Gordon B.
Safety and survival at sea. il Yachting 125: 78-9+ My '69
BLENDERS, Electric. See Electric apparatus and appliances, Domestic
BLENHEIM palace. See Palaces
BLENKINSOPP, Joseph
Language of the tribe. Commonweal 90:505-8 Ag 22 '69
BLENNIES
Sexual pheromone in some fishes of the genus hypsoblennius gill. G. S. Losey, jr. bibliog il Science 163:181-3 Ja 10 '69
BLEPHAROPLASTY. See Surgery, Plastic
BLESSITT, Arthur O.
Preacher in the mud: rapping for Christ. A. Taft. Chr Today 14:34 D 19 '69
BLICKSTEIN, Edward
More than a clown. Hi Fi 19:59-62 Jl '69
BLIGH, David
Red China in Europe. America 120:280-1 Mr 8 '69
BLIMPS. See Airships
BLIND, Mathilde
(tr) See Hugo, V. M. Victor Hugo on the burning of a library. juin 1871
BLIND
Blind men are made; survey on service groups. il Time 93:69-70 My 23 '69
Trade winds; concerning Robert A. Scott's The making of blind men. J. Beatty, jr. Sat R 52:10+ Ap 26 '69
We do not cry; blind woman's adoption of blind child. V. Franklin. il Redbook 132:98-9+ Ap '69
Whose eyes are closed? A. Wood. Seventeen 27:126+ D '68
See also
Recording for the blind, incorporated
Sports for the blind

Employment
Key people; blind people test flavorings and fragrances. K. B. Pomeroy. il Am For 75:30-1 Ag '69

Recreation
See Recreation for the blind

Rehabilitation
Bright faith. B. Falconer. il Good H 168:88-91 My '69

BLIND, Apparatus for the
Reading aid for the blind; optical-tactile converter. J. S. Brugler and W. T. Young. il Electr World 82:48-50+ N '69
Replacing Braille? Linvill's Opticon. il Time 94:52+ S 19 '69
Seeing-eye backpack; tactile vision substitution system. il Newsweek 74:108 N 24 '69
Seeing with the skin of the back; new electronic system. il Life 67:59-60 D 19 '69
Shall we have seeing aids for the blind? D. R. Zimmerman. il Todays Health 47: 21-3+ D '69
BLIND, Nature trails for the. See Trails
BLIND, Periodicals for the
Now: Today's health for the blind. il Todays Health 47:58 Ag '69
BLIND fishes. See Cave fishes
BLIND river dolphins. See Dolphins (mammals)
BLINDNESS
Blind man's buff; case of Gypsy Joe Harris. M. Kram. il Sports Illus 30:68-72+ Mr 10 '69

Blindness; handicap, or characteristic? address, July 3, 1969. K. Jernigan. Vital Speeches 36:10-14 O 15 '69
Milk and blindness in Brazil. G. E. Bunce. Natur Hist 78:52-5 F '69
See also
Eye banks
BLINDS, Duck. See Duck blinds
BLINK comparators. See Comparators
BLINKING lights. See Electric lamps. Flashing
BLINTZES. See Griddle cakes
BLINZINGER, K. and others
Poliovirus crystals within the endoplasmic reticulum of endothelial and mononuclear cells in the monkey spinal cord. bibliog Science 163:1336-7 Mr 21 '69
BLISS, Ray Charles
His own man. Newsweek 73:27 Mr 3 '69
Sic transit Bliss. il por Time 93:26 F 28 '69
BLIVEN, Naomi
Books (cont) New Yorker 44:116-18+ F 15 '69
BLIZZARDS. See Snowstorms
BLOCH, Donald, and Blum, Sam
Unwed couples: do they live happily ever after? Redbook 132:90-1+ Ap '69
BLOCK, Allan
Letter from Genoa; poem. New Repub 160: 28 Mr 1 '69
BLOCK, Bette
Land of the free; drama. Plays 29:21-32 Ja '70
BLOCK, H. & R, Incorporated
Little man's friend. il Newsweek 73:71-2 F 10 '69
BLOCK, Jean Libman
Accident that saved five lives. Good H 169: 60+ N '69
BLOCK, Marvin A.
Alcohol; address, July 13, 1969. Vital Speeches 35:720-5 S 15 '69
BLOCK, Victor
Best of Maine. il Todays Health 47:34-7+ Jl '69
Hosteling, the family way. Parents Mag 44: 46-7+ Jl '69
What's happened to the American dream? Parents Mag 44:40-1+ Je '69
When a secret is better than a patent. Pop Mech 132:110-12+ N '69
BLOCK ISLAND
Small boat to Block Island. C. R. Meyer. il Yachting 126:72-3+ Jl '69
BLOCK ISLAND race week. See Regattas
BLOCK printing
Gesso cut for printmaking. P. Kelly and A. Sarvis. il Sch Arts 69:8-11 D '69
Polystyrene prints. W. O'Malley. il Sch Arts 69:20-3 D '69
See also
Linoleum block printing
Textile printing
BLOCKS. See Pulleys
BLODGET, Robert
Follow me through. See issues of Flying
BLOND hair. See Hair
BLONDEL, Maurice
Total commitment: Blondel's L'action. by J. M. Somerville. Review
Commonweal 90:373-4 Je 13 '69. T. Berry
BLONDELL, Douglas L.
Love those diesels! Yachting 126:64-5+ S '69
BLOOD
See also
Erythropoiesis

Circulation
Amateur scientist; flow of blood, weather vanes, telescope mirrors and the conductivity of insulators. C. L. Stong. il Sci Am 221:134-5 O '69
Traube-Hering waves in the pulmonary circulation of the dog. J. P. Szidon and others. bibliog il Science 164:75-6 Ap 4 '69
See also
Blood-brain barrier

Circulation, Disorders of
See also
Hypotension

Coagulation
Hepatic influence on splenic synthesis and release of coagulation activities. W. J. Dodds. bibliog il Science 166:882-3 N 14 '69
New test for blood clots. A. J. Snider. Sci Digest 66:53 D '69
Onions against clots. il Time 93:52 Mr 28 '69
Vitamin K, savior of bleeding babies. W. Garrison. il Todays Health 47:42-3+ S '69
See also
Embolism

BLOOD—*Continued*

Collection and preservation

Answer to our blood shortage. R. K. Massie. Read Digest 95:199-200+ O '69

Blood brothers. il Newsweek 74:80-3 S 29 '69

See also
Blood banks

Color and coloring matter

See Blood—Pigments

Corpuscles and platelets

Aspirin: its effect on platelet glycolysis and release of adenosine diphosphate. J. C. G. Doery and others. bibliog il Science 165:65-7 Jl 4 '69

Deformation of red blood cells in capillaries. R. Skalak and P. I. Brånemark. bibliog il Science 164:717-19 My 9 '69

Micelle formation between 5-hydroxytrypta-mine and adenosine triphosphate in plate-let storage organellas. K. H. Berneis and others. bibliog il Science 165:913-14 Ag 29 '69

Serine requirement in leukemic and normal blood cells. J. D. Regan and others. bibliog il Science 163:1452-3 Mr 28 '69

Thrombin-induced release of calcium from blood platelets. E. H. Mürer. bibliog il Science 166:623 O 31 '69

See also
Erythrocytes
Leukocytes

Dialysis

See Kidneys, Artificial

Diseases

Getting to the core of blood diseases; trans-planting bone marrow. il Bsns W p92+ Ja 18 '69

Reticulocytosis in response to dietary anti-oxidants. B. E. March and others. bibliog il Science 164:1398-400 Je 20 '69

See also
Anemia
Leukemia

Freezing

Freezing resistance in some Antarctic fishes. A. L. DeVries and D. E. Wohlschlag. bib-liog il Science 163:1073-5 Mr 7 '69

Irradiation

Rays of hope; extracorporeal blood irradia-tors. Newsweek 73:88 Je 23 '69

Oxygen content

Oxygen-hemoglobulin dissociation curves: ef-fect of inherited enzyme defects of the red cell. M. Delivoria-Papadopoulos and others. bibliog il Science 165:601-2 Ag 8 '60

Pigments

Green blood pigment in lizards; skinks. A. E. Greer and G. Raizes. bibliog Science 166:392 O 17 '69

See also
Hemoglobin

Plasma

Plasma saluretic activity: its nature nad re-lation to oxytocin analogs. E. Sedláková and others. bibliog il Science 164:580-2 My 2 '69

Pressure

See Blood pressure

Proteins

Analyzing an antibody; gamma globulin molecule. il Time 93:93 Ap 25 '69

Antigen combining activity associated with immunoglobulin D. G. J. Gleich and others. bibliog il Science 165:606 Ag 8 '69

Antithrombin III: protection against death after injection of thromboplastin. L. T. Mann, jr. and others. bibliog il Science 166:517-18 O 24 '69

Deciphering a giant; gamma globulin ana-lyzed. Sci N 95:401-2 Ap 26 '69

Human serum inhibitor of C'1 esterase: identity with α₂-neuraminoglycoprotein. J. Pensky and H. G. Schwick. bibliog il Sci-ence 163:698-9 F 14 '69

Immunoglobulins, G, A, and M determined in single cells from human tonsil. D. Gitlin and T. Sasaki. bibliog il Science 164:1532-4 Je 27 '69

Inv(1) allotype effect of immunoglobulin G heavy chain subtype on its expression. A. G. Steinberg and I. Rostenberg. bibliog il Science 164:1072-3 My 30 '69

Limited periods of gene expression in im-munoglobulin-synthesizing cells. D. N. Buell and J. L. Fahey. bibliog il Science 164:1524-5 Je 27 '69

New light on immunity; gamma globulin structure determined. il Newsweek 73:69-70 Ap 28 '69

Physical and chemical studies on cerulopla-smin: crystallization of desialized human ceruloplasmin asialoceruloplasmin. A. G. Morell and others. bibliog il Science 166: 1293-4 D 5 '69

Preferential synthesis of ferritin and albumin by different populations of liver polysomes. S. J. Hicks and others. bibliog il Science 164: 584-5 My 2 '69

Venom neutralization by rattlesnake serum albumin. W. C. Clark and H. K. Voris. bibliog il Science 164:1462-4 Je 20 '69

Vitellogenic blood protein synthesis by insect fat body. M. L. Pan and others. bibliog il Science 165:393-4 Jl 25 '69

See also
Cytochromes

Transfusion

White corpuscle transfusion: newly perfected continuous flow cell separator. N. Hardy. Sci N 96:88 Jl 26 '69

Viscosity

Fluid drop-like transition of erythrocytes un-der shear. H. Schmid-Schönbein and R. Wells. bibliog il Science 165:288-91 Jl 18 '69

BLOOD banks
How safe is your blood bank? il Good H 169:139-41 Ag '69

BLOOD-brain barrier
Blood-brain barrier: evidence for active cation transport between blood and the extra-cellular fluid of brain. L. Z. Bito. bibliog il Science 165:81-3 Jl 4 '69

BLOOD cells. See Blood—Corpuscles and platelets

BLOOD clotting. See Blood—Coagulation

BLOOD donors
See also
Blood—Collection and preservation

BLOOD groups
Blood of the pharaohs. Sci Am 221:55 D '69

Genetic drift in an Italian population. L. L. Cavalli-Sforza. il Sci Am 221:30-7 Ag '69

Glycosphingolipids with Lewis blood group activity: uptake by human erythrocytes. D. M. Marcus and L. E. Cass. bibliog il Sci-ence 164:553-5 My 2 '69

Hageman factor (factor XII) deficiency in marine mammals. A. J. Robinson and oth-ers. bibliog il Science 166:1420-2 D 12 '69

Hepatic influence on splenic synthesis and release of coagulation activities. W. J. Dodds. bibliog il Science 166:882-3 N 14 '69

MN blood-group locus; data concerning the possible chromosomal location. J. German and others; reply. L. Weitkamp. Science 164:1187 Je 6 '69

BLOOD letting; story. See Gerald, J. B.

BLOOD plasma. See Blood—Plasma

BLOOD pressure
Adrenergic blood pressure responses in the shark. S. L. Schwartz and J. F. Borzelleca. bibliog il Science 163:395-7 Ja 24 '69

Effects of feedback and reinforcement on the control of human systolic blood pres-sure. D. Shapiro and others. bibliog il Sci-ence 163:588-90 F 7 '69

Traube-Hering waves in the pulmonary cir-culation of the dog. J. P. Szidon and others. bibliog il Science 164:75-6 Ap 4 '69

See also
Hypertension

BLOOD sugar
Hypoglycemia, the disease that makes women tired. B. O'Connell. il Sci Digest 65: 40-4 Mr '69

Sweet poison. W. Endicott. Harp Baz 102: 224-5+ O '69

BLOOD types. See Blood groups

BLOOD vessels
See also
Aorta
Capillaries

Diseases

See also
Aneurysms

BLOOM, Claire
Rod Steiger and Claire Bloom, no happy ending? interview; ed. by J. Barthel. por Redbook 133:98-9+ Jl '69

BLOOM, F. E. and others
Lesions of central norepinephrine terminals with 6-OH-dopamine: biochemistry and fine structure. bibliog Science 166:1284-6 D 5 '69

BLOOM, Harold
Christianity and art. New Repub 160:25-8 Ap 5 '69
Internalization of quest romance. Yale R 58:526-36 Je '69

BLOOM, Justin L. See Seaborg, G. T. jt. auth.

BLOOMFIELD, Arthur I.
Recent trends in international economics. bibliog f Ann Am Acad 386:148-67 N '69

BLOOMFIELD, Howard V.
Quandary on the campgrounds. Am For 75:4-7+ Jl '69
Slow death for DDT? Am For 75:16-19+ N '69
Snowmobiles; boon or bane? Am For 75:4-5+ My '69

BLOOMINGDALE, Alfred S.
Shuffling cards at Diners' club. por Bsns W p20 D 27 '69

BLOOMINGTON, Minn.

Education
Swinging with mini-projects. E. Cain and A. St. Pierre. il Am Ed 5:5-8 D '69

BLOSSOM music center. See Cleveland—Blossom center

BLOSTEIN, Rhoda. See Klassen, G. A. jt. auth.

BLOUGH, Donald S.
Attention shifts in a maintained discrimination. bibliog Science 166:125-6 O 3 '69

BLOUGH, Glenn O.
Firsthand science experiences. Ed Digest 34:38-9 F '69

BLOUGH, Herbert A. See Tiffany, J. M. jt. auth.

BLOUGH, Roger M.
Roger's roundtable. por Time 94:58 Ag 29 '69

BLOUNT, Nathan S.
Summary of investigations relating to the English language arts in secondary education: 1968. bibliog Engl J 58:735-47 My '69
—See Searles, J. R. jt. ed.

BLOUNT, Roy, Jr
Baseball. Sports Illus 30:65-6 My 19; 48+ Je 23; 31:46-9 Ag 4 '69
Golf. Sports Illus 31:54-5 Ag 25 '69
Hey, that's Missouri and Oklahoma out there! Sports Illus 31:46-7 N 3 '69
Pro football. Sports Illus 31:40-1 S 1 '69
Tennis (cont) Sports Illus 31:99-100 S 15 '69
Track and field (title varies) Sports Illus 30:58-9+ Je 16 '69
Travel. Sports Illus 30:42+ Ja 27 '69
Yes! Bert is in, with go power. Sports Illus 30:34-6+ Mr 3 '69

BLOUNT, Winton Malcolm
Can the mails be managed? interview, ed. by G. R. Rosen. por Duns R 94:14-17 S '69
Case for postal reform. pors Nations Bsns 57:52-4 S '69
Postmaster General Blount; interview. New Yorker 45:49-51 O 18 '69
What's wrong with the mails; interview. pors US News 66:40-4 Mr 31 '69

about
No. 1 mailman: can he deliver? por U S News 66:14 Mr 3 '69
Postal reform riles Congress. por Bsns W p33 My 24 '69

BLOWERS, Snow. See Snow blowers, throwers, etc.

BLOY, Myron B. Jr
Counter curriculum. Commonweal 91:8-12 O 3 '69
Culture and counter-culture. Commonweal 89:493-6 Ja 17 '69

BLUE Angels. See Aviation—Stunt flying

BLUE collar workers. See Labor and laboring classes

BLUE crabs. See Crabs

BLUE cross hospital service. See Insurance, Hospitalization

BLUE-eyed grass
Yellow-eyed grass in the shade; sisyrinchium californicum. il Sunset 143:222 N '69

BLUE quail shooting. See Quail shooting

BLUE RIDGE MOUNTAINS
See also
Shenandoah National Park

BLUE RIDGE parkway. See Express highways—Southern states

BLUEBERRIES
Plant worth propagating, the lowbush blueberry. D. A. Abdalla. il Org Gard & Farm 16:38-9 Je '69

BLUEFIN tuna fishing. See Tuna fishing

BLUEFISH fishing
Wire for the blues; Long Island Sound. A. Glowka. il Field & S 74:56-7+ Jl '69

BLUEPRINTS
Why you need a decorator before you build. W. Baldwin. House & Gard 136:10-11 D '69

BLUES. See Depression, Mental

BLUES (hockey team) See Hockey teams

BLUES (songs, etc)
Black 'n blues. R. V. Weinstein. il Negro Hist Bul 32:13-15 My '69
It's hard to fake the true blues; Johnny Winter. A. Goldman. Life 67:8 Jl 4 '69
Local legend; Sweet Emma Barrett. L. Lerman. il Mlle 68:150-1 F '69
Rebirth of the blues. il Newsweek 73:82-5 My 26 '69
Rock-and-rollers latch on to the blues. G. Lees. House & Gard 136:90+ O '69
Story of the blues, by P. Oliver. Review Sat R 52:53 D 13 '69. S. Dance
Winter blues. T. Barry. il Look 33:80-4+ Jl 29 '69
See also
Phonograph records—Blues (songs, etc)

BLUESTONE, Barbara Z. and Ericksen, S. C.
Teacher-made test. Ed Digest 35:22-5 O '69

BLUHDORN, Charles G.
Some glitter is gone at Gulf & Western. il pors Bsns W p34-5+ Jl 5 '69

BLUHM, Norman
Perennial Bluhms. K. G. Kline. il Art N 68:34-7 Ap '69
Rice and hamburger; show at Washington's Corcoran gallery. por Newsweek 73:91 Ap 28 '69

BLUM, Eric
Far-out flexible surfboard, the wave of the future? ed. by E. Blum. Pop Sci 195:92-5 Ag '69

BLUM, Nancy Phelps
A. Phelps' inn at North Colebrook. Antiques 95:404-7 Mr '69

BLUM, Sam
Perfect parent. McCalls 96:51+ Ag '69
Sophia Loren and Carlo Ponti talk about their new baby. Redbook 133:80-1+ My '69
What would really make you happy? Redbook 132:49+ Ja '69
Why it's hard to love your parents. Redbook 133:84-5+ My '69
—See Bloch, D. jt. auth.

BLUM, Virgil C.
Tax funds for nonpublic education. America 121:227-30 S 27 '69

BLUME, Robert M.
Psychiatric patients returned to military duty. bibliog Ment Hy 53:438-42 Jl '69

BLUMENFELD, Harold
Battle of Baby Doe. Opera N 33:8+ Mr 8 '69

BLUMENFELD, Yorick
London show. Atlan 224:99-101 Ag '69
Scenario society. Nation 208:788-91 Je 23 '69

BLUMENTHAL, Dick
Patriot in the basement. H. Sidey. por Life 66:4 Mr 28 '69

BLUMENTHAL, Irving J. See Singer, R. G. jt. auth.

BLUMHARDT, Christoph
Wait and hasten. Chr Cent 86:1011 Jl 30 '69; Discussion. 86:1170+ S 10 '69
Who are these Blumhardt characters anyhow? V. Eller. por Chr Cent 86:1274-8 O 8 '69

BLUMHARDT, Johann Christoph
Who are these Blumhardt characters anyhow? V. Eller. por Chr Cent 86:1274-8 O 8 '69

BLUMROSEN, Alfred W.
Job seniority and discrimination; excerpt from Discrimination in the union and on the job. Mo Labor R 92:52-3 Mr '69

BLUNDERS
Grab bag of gaucheries. Chr Cent 86:1029 Jl 30 '69

BLY, Robert
Ants; poem. Nation 208:739 Je 9 '69
Private gardens, cloisters, silent women; introd. to Forty poems of Juan Ramón Jiménez. Nation 209:17 Jl 7 '69
(tr) See Jiménez, J. R. Full consciousness; Oceans; Lumber wagons; Dawns of moguer; Road; Dawn outside the city walls

BLY, Steven W.
Across state lines. por Parks & Rec 4:41+ F '69

BLYTHE, Ronald
England's cruel earth; excerpt from Akenfield: portrait of an English village. Harper 238:46-52+ Ap '69

BOATS—*Continued*

Gages
See Gages

Heating and ventilation
Heating your boat. E. Crimmin; Y. K. Adam. il Motor B 124:62-5+ N '69

Hulls
See Hulls (naval architecture)

Leasing and renting
Boat chartering; interview, ed. by J. Smith and R. Smith. J. T. Westcott. 3d. il Travel 131:28-33+ Je '69
On Puget Sound, charter boats. Sunset 142: 41 My '69
Want to rent a boat? Here's where it's done. G. E. Miller. Motor B 123:116+ My '69
You can keep it small; renting boats by the day, at Great Exuma. il Yachting 126:62-3+ N '69
See also
Canoes—Leasing and renting

Maintenance and repair
Beat the opening-day gun. J. A. Emmett. il Outdoor Life 143:38+ Mr '69
Boatkeeper See issues of Motor boating
Boatkeeper looks at his boat. J. Atkin. il Motor B 123:50-1+ Mr '69
Corrosion and infestation. E. A. Zadig. il Motor B 123:56-9+ F '69
Improving your boat. J. A. Emmett. il Outdoor Life 144:20+ D '69
Minimum program for readying your boat's machinery. C. Miller. il Motor B 123:80+ Ap '69
Pay her a mid-winter visit. C. Miller. il Motor B 123:50-2 F '69
Preventive maintenance. R. C. Eiseman. il Yachting 126:70-1+ Ag '69
Seaworthy stickums and fillers for fitting out. F. M. Paulson. il Field & S 73:150-1+ Ap '69
Short cuts to fitting out. B. McKeown. il Mech Illus 65:67+ My '69
TLC. P. Smyth See issues of Motor boating
What do you know about..; symposium. il Yachting 125:70-86+ Ap '69
Winter projects for your boat. T. Bottomley. Motor B 124:84 D '69
You still have time to make these major improvements. C. Miller. il Motor B 123:68-9 Mr '69

Bibliography
Sources of maintenance information. E. Horan. Yachting 125:70-1+ Ap '69

Materials
Advantages of aluminum. F. M. Paulson. il Field & S 74:122-5 N '69
Care and maintenance of aluminum boats. C. W. Leveau. il Motor B 123:77+ Ap '69
Linking the transoceanic cultures; a study of reed boats. T. Heyerdahl. il Sci N 95: 534-7 My 31 '69
Maintenance with new products. W. Robberson. Yachting 125:70-1+ Ap '69
Modern marine materials. E. A. Zadig. il Motor B 123:72-3+ Mr '69
Seagoing sidewalks: ferro-cement boats. J. Duffet. il Motor B 124:68-9+ N '69
Showroom shine for your fiberglass boat. P. Smyth. il Motor B 123:76 Ap '69
Touring a fiberglass plant. T. Cobb. il Yachting 125:63-5+ Ap '69
What can go wrong with fiberglass hulls? W. Cloud. il Pop Sci 194:102-5+ Mr '69
What do you know about... N. Feige. il Yachting 125:80-1+ Ap '69
What do you know about ferro cement. J. Smith. il Yachting 125:84-6+ Ap '69
Wood-grained fiberglass. T. Bottomley. il Motor B 123:74-5+ Mr '69
Your next boat may be ferro-cement. R. Day. il Pop Sci 195:110-13+ S '69
See also
Houseboats—Materials
Yachts—Materials

Names
Boat name contest. il Motor B 123:66-7 F '69

Painting
Finishing touches. il Motor B 123:218+ Ja '69
Painting wooden hulls. P. Smyth. il Motor B 123:74-5+ Ap '69
What do you know about varnishing. N. Levy. il Yachting 125:82+ Ap '69

Propellers
See Propellers

Purchasing
Your new boat; how to buy, equip & enjoy her; symposium. il Motor B 123:94-127 Ja '69
See also
Boat ownership

Renting
See Boats—Leasing and renting

Sanitation
Clean look at dirty water. B. McKeon. il Mech Illus 65:66+ Ag '69
Lawmen vs boatmen; New York pollution ruling. P. Smyth. Motor B 123:59 Ap '69
See also
Boats—Toilet facilities

Speed
See also
Sailboats—Speed

Stability and stabilizers
Balancing act. J. A. Emmett. il Outdoor Life 143:32+ My '69

Storage
Build an easy-loading boat cradle. R. Sprint. il Pop Sci 194:168-9 Ap '69
Disappearing boat garage. il Sunset 142:113 My '69
How to get your boat ready for winter. il Bet Hom & Gard 47:34 O '69
Winter boat storage. J. A. Emmett. il Outdoor Life 144:34+ N '69
See also
Yachts—Storage

Testing
How much torture can your boat take? W. Cloud. il Pop Mech 131:146-50+ Ap '69

Toilet facilities
Plan a head. V. L. Oertle. il Pop Mech 130: 140-4 D '68

Towing
Towing beats rowing. W. S. Kals. il Pop Mech 131:174-7 Mr '69

Transportation
Portable boats. J. A. Emmett. il Outdoor Life 143:26+ F '69
Two boats on top? il Sunset 142:152 My '69
See also
Automobile boat trailers

Water supply
Fresh water from the sea; seagoing distillation plants. C. F. Kelley. il Yachting 126: 72-3+ D '69
Water, water, everywhere . . . J. D. Williamson. il Motor B 124:58-9+ O '69

BOATS, Fire. See Fireboats
BOATS, Folding. See Boats and boating
BOATS, Ice. See Ice boats and ice boating
BOATS, Remodeled
See also
Yachts, Remodeled
BOATS, Size of. See Boats—Size
BOATS, Used
Character boat, what is it? G. Hogan. il Motor B 123:173-5 My '69
How to spot a used-boat bargain. B. McKeown. il Mech Illus 65:66+ S '69
Used boats. il Motor B 123:126-7 Ja '69
See also
Yachts, Used

BOATS and boating
Bahamas bearings. J. McClish. See issues of Motor boating
Boat showcase. See issues of Motor boating
Boating. J. A. Emmett. See issues of Outdoor life
Boating. F. M. Paulson. See issues of Field & stream
Boating '69. il Pop Mech 131:168-83 Mr '69
Boatkeeper. See issues of Motor boating
Boats and boating. B. McKeown. See issues of Mechanix illustrated
Boats for restricted waters; gasoline motors banned. J. A. Emmett. il Outdoor Life 144: 86-8+ Jl '69
Boats you can carry in bags; folding boats. il Changing T 23:15-16 My '69
Calendar of coming events; comp. by R. B. Smith. See issues of Motor boating
Chesapeake log. W. B. Matthews, jr. See issues of Motor boating
Common questions & answers. P. Smyth. il Motor B 123:121-3 Ja '69
Down to the sea in anything. il Sports Illus 30:40-57 Je 2 '69

BOATS and boating—*Continued*
From the cockpit. B. Bavier. See issues of Yachting
How to be an old salt in a new boat; a condensed course in seamanship. L. Hilts. il Todays Health 47:20-5 Je '69
How to get started in boating for $1,000 or less. J. Roe. il Pop Sci 194:118-21 My '69
Inflation hits the waterfront. B. McKeown. il Mech Illus 65:83+ Jl '69
Joys of life afloat. il Newsweek 74:58-63 Ag 4 '69
Last of the coracle makers. il Mech Illus 65:151 O '69
Motor boating USA. See issues of Motor boating
New boats. See issues of Yachting
New on the waterfront; boating accessories. F. M. Paulson. il Field & S 73:132-3+ Mr '69
News from yachting centers. See issues of Yachting
1968, it was great. il Motor B 123:29-40 Ja '69
Northwest gales. E. Crimmin. See issues of Motor boating
Now! Enjoy boating all winter. B. Weis. il Mech Illus 65:96-7+ N '69
Preview of the 1970 boats. B. McKeown. il Mech Illus 65:64-6+ D '69
Rafting the rapids; boom in white-water boating. il Newsweek 74:87 Jl 21 '69
Southward ho. J. Wilson. See issues of Motor boating
Special report: southern yachting; symposium. bibliog il Yachting 126:50-66+ N '69
TLC. P. Smyth. See issues of Motor boating boating
Their thing in the spring; white water boating on McKenzie River. il Sports Illus 30:38-43 Mr 24 '69
Westward ho. B. Ruskauff. See issues of Motor boating
What do you know about. . ; symposium. il Yachting 125:70-86+ Ap '69
What's new. See issues of Motor boating
Where the rapids run gently; rafting voyage on Jamaica's Rio Grande. F. Rohr, jr. il Motor B 124:72-3 S '69
Which boat for your family? J. A. Emmett. il Outdoor Life 144:30-3 Ag '69
Who needs rudders? St Lawrence skiffs controlled without them. A. C. Ettinger. il Yachting 126:70-1+ N '69
Wildest boat trip in the world. R. P. Crossley. il Pop Mech 131:122-6+ Mr '69
Yachting eyes a boat. See issues of Yachting
Your new boat; how to buy, equip & enjoy her; symposium. il Motor B 123:94-127 Ja '69

See also
Barges
Canoes and canoeing
Catamarans
Children in boating
Cookery, Marine
Fishing boats
Houseboats
Ice boats and ice boating
Ice breaking vessels
Kayaks
Marinas
Motor boats
Navigation
Regattas
River trips
Rowing
Sailboats
Sailing
Trimarans
United States—Coast guard—Boats
United States power squadrons, incorporated
Yacht clubs
Yachts and yachting

Accidents
Disaster on Lake Michigan. R. Starnes. Field & S 73:12-14+ Ap '69
Sea fight with time and a tempest. D. Kearns. il Motor B 123:95-7+ Ap '69
See also
Fishing—Accidents and injuries
Yachts and yachting—Accidents

Anecdotes, facetiae, satire, etc.
Dad, can I have the boat tonight? four teen-agers cruise to their high school prom. B. Schoenfield. il Motor B 123:72-3 Je '69
For the love of Grace. B. K. Tytus. il Motor B 123:80-1+ Mr '69

Bibliography
Book notes and reviews; ed. by K. Aamodt. See issues of Yachting
Book shelf. T. Gibbs. See issues of Motor boating
Yachtings' publications. Yachting 125:229 Mr '69

Laws and regulations
Disaster on Lake Michigan. R. Starnes. Field & S 73:12-14+ Ap '69
Lawmen vs boatmen; New York pollution ruling. P. Smyth. Motor B 123:59 Ap '69
Pleasure boating; next target for the rule-makers. R. Starnes. Field & S 74:24+ Ag '69
Problem boating. F. M. Paulson. il Field & S 73:122-5+ F '69
Summary of state laws governing watercraft waste disposal. Motor B 123:270-1 Ja '69
Washington report. W. T. Stone. See issues of Yachting

Lightning hazards
Thunderbolts at sea. D. Whitehead. Motor B 124:124-5+ S '69
See also
Lightning protection
Yachts and yachting—Lightning hazards

Safety devices and measures
Boating's dozen deadly sins. A. Gonzalez. il Mech Illus 65:56-7+ Ag '69
Built-in buoyancy saves lives. C. R. Meyer. il Pop Sci 194:114-16+ Ja '69
Electronic gear for safer boating. F. M. Paulson. il Field & S 74:126-30 S '69
Fast way to make a boat unsinkable. B. Kasha. il Mech Illus 65:64-5+ Je '69
How to be an old salt in a new boat. L. Hilts. il Todays Health 47:20-5 Je '69
How to survive in rough water. C. R. Meyer. il Pop Sci 194:110-13+ F '69
It's floatable, unflippable, even when flooded. J. Roe. il Pop Sci 194:106-8 Mr '69
Pleasure boating; next target for the rule-makers. R. Starnes. Field & S 74:24+ Ag '69
Safety and survival at sea; safety harnesses. G. B. Bleil. il Yachting 125:78-9+ My '69
Yachting interviews: Rear Admiral William J. Morrison. W. T. Stone. il Yachting 125:67+ Mr '69
See also
Life preservers
Life-saving equipment

Study and teaching
Call USCGA, free public instruction courses. Motor B 124:29+ Ag '69
We took the power squadron course. J. R. Whiting. il Motor B 124:154 Ag '69

Terminology
Anecdotes, facetiae, satire, etc.
Glossary of crew terms. Yachting 126:208 D '69

BOATWRIGHT, Purvis James, jr
All right with Boatwright. C. Kirkpatrick. por Sports Illus 30:56-7 Je 16 '69
BOATYARDS. See Shipyards
BOAZ, Ruth L.
Dilemma of statistics for public libraries. por ALA Bul 63:1572-5 D '69
BOB, Murray L.
Evaluating the evaluators. Library J 94:1416, 2705-6 Ap 1, Ag '69
BOB whites. See Quails
BOBCAT hunting
Fat cat. C. Ormond. il Outdoor Life 143:62-3+ F '69
Judie's cat. J. R. Higley. il Outdoor Life 144:58-9+ S '69
BOBELE, Rebecca
On the boards. W. Como. por Dance Mag 43:22 N '69
BOBWHITE shooting. See Quail shooting
BOBWHITES. See Quails
BOCCA, Geoffrey
Exciting adventures in bad eating. Esquire 71:80+ My '69
BOCK, Frederick
Tomato juice; Snow and ice; poems. Poetry 115:106-7 N '69
BODANSZKY, M. and Perlman, D.
Peptide antibiotics. bibliog Science 163:352-3 Ja 24 '69
BODE, Carl
Confusion; poem. New Repub 161:28 Ag 23 '69
BODET, Jaime Torres. See Torres Bodet, J.

BODGER, Joan
Mrs Bodger resigns. Wilson Lib Bul 44:275 N '69
Mother Goose: is the old girl relevant? bibliog por Wilson Lib Bul 44:402-8 D '69

about

Joan Bodger incident; statement; October 1969, ed. by G. R. Shields. R. Parker. ALA Bul 63:1561-3 D '69
Missouri library commission defended by Ralph Parker. Library J 94:4082 N 15 '69
Missouri quicksand: an in-depth survey. W. R. Eshelman. Wilson Lib Bul 44:266-8 N '69
Ray of light in Missouri. Wilson Lib Bul 44:498 Ja '70

BODIE, Calif. See Abandoned towns
BODINE, Lillian Lewis
Tray decorations. Horticulture 47:26-7 N '69
BODLEIAN library. See Oxford. University
—Bodleian library
BODY, Human
Limits of celebration. Chr Cent 86:1213 S 24 '69
New man; scientists suggestions for alteration. il Newsweek 75:44-5 Ja 5 '70
Too little too late. il Good H 169:12+ O '69
Worlds within us; with photographs by L. Nilsson. Life 68:40-56 Ja 9 '70

Anecdotes, facetiae, satire, etc.

Redesign your body: what changes would you make? B. Ford. il Sci Digest 66:20-3 N '69
You've come a long way, fella. il Esquire 72:158-9 N '69

BODY age. See Age
BODY counters. See Counters (electrons, ions, etc)
BODY fluids
See also
Edema
Perspiration
Urine
BODY image
Your body image: what it tells about you; reprint. R. M. Kurtz. il Sci Digest 66:52-5 Ag '69
BODY movements. See Movement, Psychology of
BODY odors. See Odors
BODY paint. See Indians of South America—Costume and adornment
BODY parts, Artificial. See Prosthesis
BODY temperature. See Temperature, Animal and human
BODY water. See Water in the body
BODY weight. See Weight (physiology)
BOEGLY, W. J. Jr, and Griffith, W. L.
Utility tunnels enhance urban renewal areas. bibliog Am City 84:101-3 F '69
BOEHM, George A. W.
Unsung trailblazer to the moon. Read Digest 94:134-8 Je '69
BOEING company
Boeing buying gear to build prototype. il Aviation W 92:86-8 Ja 5 '70
Boeing moving toward decision to launch 767 project by spring. Aviation W 91:27-8 S 1 '69
Boeing net seen slipping again this year. S. P. Siciliano. Aviation W 90:21 Mr 3 '69
Boeing network cuts Apollo work costs. W. C. Wetmore. il Aviation W 90:43-4+ F 10 '69
Boeing picking Canadian site to produce glass-fiber parts. Aviation W 91:25 Jl 21 '69
Boeing proposes tanker version of 747. Aviation W 91:35 Ag 11 '69
Boeing sees tourism growth as spur to European 720 sales. Aviation W 91:34 O 27 '69
Boeing 6-month net, sales dip. Aviation W 91:28 Ag 4 '69
Boeing transport activities reorganized under Stamper. Aviation W 90:39 My 5 '69
Boeing wins lunar rover award; vehicles to have 58-mi. range. il Aviation W 91:20-1 N 3 '69
747 development costs push down Boeing's profits. Aviation W 90:30 My 5 '69
747: into a new air age; with report by J. Lubenow. il Newsweek 74:95+ O 27 '69
TIEing the loose ends in Apollo program; technical integration and evaluation. il Bsns W p 128-9 My 24 '69
World's first giant jet: Boeing 747. A. Bester. il Holiday 46:28-35+ Jl '69

BOESCHENSTEIN, Harold
General and the genius. il por Forbes 104:48+ O 15 '69
BOESEL, David, and others
White institutions & black rage. Trans-Action 6:24-31 Mr '69
BOETHIUS, d 524
Boethius, the last of the Romans. P. W. Schmidtchen. il Hobbies 74:104-5+ Jl '69
BOETSCH, Jacques
(ed) See Dayan, M. We must not return to the old map
BOG vegetation
We call them frog plants. il Sunset 142:279 Ap '69
BOGACZ, Victor J.
My railroad-tie terrace garden. Org Gard & Farm 16:46-7 Ag '69
BOGAN, Louise
Balance exactly struck. H. Carruth. Poetry 114:330-1 Ag '69
BOGER, Louise Ade
Antiques: questions & answers. See issues of House & garden incorporating Living for young homemakers
BOGGESS, Louise
Writer and social security. Writers Digest 49:56-9+ D '69
BOGGS, Hale
Hostage for tax reform. por Time 94:16 Ag 1 '69
Nixon's deal for the tax surcharge. il Newsweek 73:75-6 Je 23 '69
BOGGS, Horatio Marion
Family pottery. J. Roberts. il por Ceram Mo 17:28-9 Je '69
BOGIN, Eitan, and others
Extraparticulate chain interaction between different electron transport particles. bibliog Science 165:1364-7 S 26 '69
BOGLE, Donald E.
Black and proud behind bars. Ebony 24:64-6+ Ag '69
Richie Havens: coffee house favorite becomes college crowd's folk rock star. Ebony 24:101-2+ My '69
BOGLE, John Clifton
Buy stocks now. R. Brady. il por Duns R 94:119-20 S '69
BOGS
See also
Peat bogs
BOHART, G. E. See Batra, S. W. T. jt. auth.
BOHEMIANISM
See also
Hippies
BOHLEN, Charles Eustis
Chip and Tommy. il por Newsweek 73:28-9 Ja 27 '69
BOHLEN UND HALBACH, Arndt Krupp von. See Krupp von Bohlen und Halbach, A.
BÖHM, Karl
The Strauss I know. por Opera N 33:14-16 Mr 8 '69
BOICE, James Montgomery
Barnhouse and Boice. Chr Today 13:41 Ja 31 '69
BOIKO, Claire
Johnny question-mark; drama. Plays 29:1-16, 38 N '69
Little red hen; drama. Plays 28:69-75 Mr '69
Long table; drama. Plays 29:89-95 N '69
May basket fantasia; drama. Plays 28:36-40, 68 My '69
Next stop, spring! drama. Plays 28:53-8 Mr '69
Take me to your marshal; drama. Plays 29:45-51 Ja '70
Wild rabbit chase; drama. Plays 28:35-43 Ap '69

BOILERMAKERS
See also
Babcock and Wilcox company
BOILING water reactors. See Nuclear reactors
BOISE, Idaho

Newspapers

Independence in Idaho; policy of Intermountain observer. il Time 93:72 My 23 '69
BOISE Cascade corporation
Behold the bridegroom. Forbes 103:41-2 Mr 15 '69
Bob Hansberger shows how to grow without becoming a conglomerate; interview, ed. by J. McDonald. R. V. Hansberger. il Fortune 80:134-8+ O '69
State of mind. Newsweek 74:63 S 1 '69
When publishers feud over newsprint; West Tacoma newsprint co. merger. Bsns W p39 O 25 '69

BOITO, Arrigo
  Mefistofele. Criticism
    Dance Mag il 43:32+ N '69
    Hi Fi il 19:MA10-11 D '69
    Nation 209:388-9 O 13 '69
    New Yorker 45:116-18 O 4 '69
    Newsweek 74:132 O 6 '69
    Sat R 52:52 O 11 '69
    Time 94:57-8 O 3 '69
  Records:
    Mefistofele (prologue) Opera N 34:42 D
     27 '69

BOK, Bart J.
  Spiral structure of our galaxy. Sky & Tel 38:
   392-5; 39:21-5 D '69-Ja '70

BOLAND, Thomas Aloysius, abp
  Bold voice. S. J. Adamo. America 120:204
   F 15 '69

BOLAS
  Three marias. A. Blasi Brambilla. il Américas 21:35-9 Jl '69

BOLDUC, David
  Three young Canadians. B. Lord. il Art in
   Am 57:88-9 Ja '69

BOLES, Alan
  Black homeowning. New Repub 161:7-9 D 13
   '69
  Upstarts in the ivy. Nation 208:429-32 Ap 7 '69

BOLES, Mary Frances
  She's fifteen and fabulous. il pors Seventeen
   28:150-1 My '69

BOLES, Paul Darcy
  Holiday rider; story. Seventeen 27:96-7 D '68
  Miss Rose; story. Seventeen 28:326-7 Ag '69
  Today is my sister's wedding; story. Good H
   169:110-11 O '69

BOLEY, Okla.
  New change for a black town. il Bsns W
   p96-7 Ag 9 '69

BOLIN, T. D. See Davis, A. E. jt. auth.

BOLING, Gerald R.
  Air cushion vehicle. Sea Front 15:376-9 N '69

BOLIVAR, Simón
  Angostura. A. U. Pietri. il por Américas
   21:2-6 My '69

BOLIVIA
    See also
  Government ownership—Bolivia
  Indians of South America—Bolivia
  Investments, Foreign (in Bolivia)
  Petroleum industry and trade—Bolivia
  Santa Cruz

    Description and travel
  Bolivia; view from the Altiplano; ed. by G.
   de Zéndegui. il Américas 21:2-9 F '69

    Expropriation policy
  New arrangement; nationalization of U.S.-
   owned Gulf oil co. Newsweek 74:53-4 N 3
   '69

    Politics and government
  Barrientos, the man who captured Che. R. C.
   Hirschfeld. Commonweal 89:609-10 F 14 '69;
   Reply with rejoinder. J. W. Knudson. 90:
   155+ Ap 25 '69
  Changeover. M. Arias. Chr Cent 86:1428+
   N 5 '69
  Coup in Bolivia; General Ovando's takeover.
   New Repub 161:7-8 O 18 '69
  Coup to the left. Newsweek 74:90-1 O 6 '69
  Death of a caudillo. J. L. Klaiber. America
   120:589-91 My 17 '69
  Exporting Perunismo. il Time 94:38 O 3 '69
  Mourning the pilot. Newsweek 73:55 My 12
   '69
  Not a bird, not a plane but Barrientos. il
   por Time 93:31 F 7 '69
  One crash too many; sudden death of presi-
   dent leaves government in confusion. il
   Time 93:47 My 9 '69
  Uneasy calm in Bolivia. New Repub 160:8
   My 17 '69

    Religious institutions and affairs
  World around us (cont) Chr Cent 86:849-50
   Je 18 '69

BOLIVIAN Indians. See Indians of South America—Bolivia

BOLKHOVITINOV, N. N.
  Study of United States history in the Soviet
   Union; excerpts from address, tr. by M.
   Pundeff. bibliog f Am Hist R 74:1221-42 Ap
   '69

BOLL weevils
  Sex pheromones produced by male boll weevil: isolation, identification, and synthesis.
   J. H. Tumlinson and others. bibliog il Science 166:1010-12 N 21 '69

BOLLAS, Barclay M.
  Newspaper mastheads. Hobbies 74:159 N '69

BOLLEN, A. and others
  Ribosomal protein conferring sensitivity to
   the antibiotic spectinomycin in escherichia
   coli. bibliog Science 165:85-6 Jl 4 '69

BOLLES family
  Bolles coat-of-arms. H. K. Eilers. il Hobbies
   74:114-15+ Ap '69

BOLLINGER, Bill
  Bollinger phenomenon. H. Rosenstein. por Art
   N 68:48-51+ S '69

BOLSA. See Bank of London and South America

BOLSHOI ballet
  USSR; the Bolshoi's new hit. il Dance Mag
   43:60-2 My '69
  World of dance; appearance in Helsinki festival. W. Terry. il Sat R 52:32 Je 21 '69

BOLT, John R.
  Lissamphibian origins: possible protolissamphibian from the lower Permian of Oklahoma. bibliog Science 166:888-91 N 14 '69

BOLT, Richard H. and others
  Identification of a speaker by speech spectrograms. bibliog Science 166:338-43 O 17 '69

BOLTON, Robert H.
  Baptism and liturgical integrity. Chr Cent
   86:369-72 Mr 19 '69

BOMB shelters. See Atomic bomb shelters

BOMBARDIER beetles. See Beetles

BOMBAY
    Riots
  Fires of hatred. il Time 93:26+ F 21 '69

BOMBECK, Erma
  Me and the miniskirt. Good H 169:58+ S '69
  Up the wall. Good H 169:12+ N '69

BOMBINGS, Terrorist. See Terrorism

BOMBS
    See also
  Hydrogen bombs

BOMEX (Barbados oceanographic and meteorological experiment) See Weather research

BOMPIANI, Valentino
  Bompiani: the personal touch. H. R. Lottman. il por Pub W 195:42-4 F 10 '69

BOMSER, Jill
  Mind-blowing barn. por House B 111:30-7
   Jl '69

BONAFEDE, Dom
  Reports: Brazil. Atlan 223:14+ Ap '69
  Washington backs the pooh bahs. Nation
   208:663-6 My 26 '69

BONAIRE (island)
  Bonaire is for loafing. D. Bingham. il
   Travel 132:57-60 D '69

BONANNO, Joseph
  Portrait of an obsolete mobster. por Time
   94:27 Ag 22 '69

BONAPARTE, Napoleon. See Napoleon I,
  emperor of the French

BONATTI, Enrico
  Fissure basalts and ocean-floor spreading on
   the East Pacific rise. bibliog Science 161:
   886-8; 166:1132-3 Ag 30 '68, N 28 '69

BOND, Edward
  Early morning. Criticism
    Atlan 224:100 Ag '69
  Narrow road to the Deep North. Criticism
    Atlan 224:100 Ag '69
    Newsweek 74:135 N 24 '69
    Sat R 52:14-15 D 13 '69
    Time 94:71 N 28 '69

BOND, Harold
  Adam: Rodin; poem. New Repub 161:30 S
   27 '69
  Stone: poem. New Repub 161:27 Jl 5 '69

BOND, Horace Julian. See Bond, J.

BOND, Howard E. and others
  Microsome-associated DNA. bibliog Science
   165:705-6 Ag 15 '69

BOND, Julian
  Students are an oppressed class; interview,
   ed. by J. Romer. pors Mlle 68:166-7+ F
   '69
  Surprising talk between a black leader and
   a top segregationist; ed. by B. Cohn and
   S. Ball, jr. pors N Y Times Mag p34-5+ Ap
   27 '69
    about
  Harris on Bond. R. Harris. N Y Times Mag
   p 114 Ap 27 '69
  Julian Bond. D. Llorens. il pors Ebony 24:
   58-62+ My '69
  Julian Bond. por Negro Hist Bul 31:21-2 D '68
  Sweepstakes of the '70s; five entries. il por
   Newsweek 73:27-8 F 24 '69

BOND, Marshall
  To the Klondike with a big dog who met
   Jack London; excerpts from Gold hunter,
   ed. with commentary by M. Bond, jr. Am
   West 6:44-8 Ja '69

BOND, Marshall, jr
  (ed) See Bond, M. To the Klondike with a
   big dog who met Jack London

BOND, Thomas G. See Samp, R. R. jt. auth.
BOND, William H.
Other books. Pub W 195:76 Mr 3 '69
BONDED fabrics. See Textile fabrics. Laminated
BONDED oil company
Ads are kooky, and they sell. il Bsns W p50 F 15 '69
BONDI, Inge
Ernst Haas, creative force in contemporary color. Mod Phot 33:62-7+ Jl '69
BONDS, Bobby
Highlight. por Sports Illus 31:75 S 8 '69
BONDS
Clouds lift, a little. il Bsns W p 124 Ap 19 '69
How to invest in stocks and bonds. R. Krumme. il Suc Farm 67:46-7 Ag '69
Investing in bonds, what you can get now. il U S News 66:73-5 Je 30 '69
More and more people are buying bonds. il Changing T 23:25-9 Jl '69
More interest in bonds. il Fortune 80:207+ N '69
Playing the turn in corporate bonds. A. Hershman. il Duns R 94:47-5+ Ag '69
Tight money chokes the Eurobond market. Bsns W p75 Je 28 '69
With stocks in trouble, what about bonds? il U S News 66:102-4 Mr 10 '69
See also
Municipal bonds
State bonds

Marketing
Are interest rates about to turn down? il U S News 66:90-1 My 5 '69
Wall Street: a time for bonds? C. Morgello. il Newsweek 73:78 Mr 10 '69

Rating
Depressed bonds for high yields. E. Merillat. il Har Yrs 9:24-5 My '69
BONDS, Convertible
Convertible bonds: the parachute that failed to open; with table. il Forbes 104:30-1 S 15 '69
One way to hedge bets. C. Morgello. il Newsweek 73:89 Ap 21 '69
BONDS, Government
Adjustable bonds; purchasing-power bonds. H. C. Wallich. Newsweek 74:86 N 24 '69
Better deal for buyers of savings bonds. il U S News 67:81-2 Jl 21 '69
Billion in bond issues, but taxpayers' revolt is still on. il U S News 67:120-2 N 17 '69
Bond prices: down again. U S News 66:87-8 Je 2 '69
Disarray in the market; trouble hits U.S. Treasury. il U S News 66:100-1 F 17 '69
Now a stir over savings bonds. il U S News 66:76-8 Mr 3 '69
Personal business. Bsns W p 121 Ja 18 '69
Savings bonds earning powers lag compared with other investments. Har Yrs 9:4 My '69
Stake in the system; national urban bonds; address, May 28, 1969. A. E. Gershen. Vital Speeches 35:763-5 O 1 '69
Time for government bonds? C. A. Connell, jr. il Duns 94:41-2+ Jl '69
Treasury tugs at bond rate lid. Bsns W p34 My 17 '69
What owners of savings bonds need to know now. il U S News 68:60-1 Ja 12 '70
See also
Municipal bonds
State bonds
BONDS, Revenue
Money squeeze forces municipals to adapt. il Bsns W p68+ Ap 12 '69
BONDURANT, Bob
How we turned Paul Newman into a winning driver. pors Pop Sci 194:50-3 Je '69
BONE, Harold R.
Watch out for the friendly arrangement. Am City 84:104 F '69
BONE, Robert
Negro literature in the secondary school: problems and perspectives; address, November 1968. Engl J 58:510-15 Ap '69
BONE
Calcified tissues; report of meeting. B. E. C. Nordin and F. G. E. Pautard. Science 164: 466-9 Ap 25 '69
Elastic coefficients of animal bone. S. B. Lang. bibliog il Science 165:287-8 Jl 18 '69
BONE, Artificial
Ceramic to replace bone. il Chem 42:19-20 S '69
Replacing bones with pottery. Sci Digest 66:57 Ag '69
BONE marrow. See Marrow
BONEFISH fishing
Challenge of thin water. J. Brooks. il Outdoor Life 143:82-3+ F '69

BONERS. See Blunders
BONES
See also
Leg
Skeleton
BONES, Fossil. See Paleontology
BONEY, F. N.
Dilemma for parochial schools. America 121: 161 S 13 '69
BONFANTE, Jordan
Oil in the Arctic. Life 66:28-9 F 14 '69
Out go the beloved saints. Life 66:47 My 23 '69
Town in trouble; plague of drugs among kids in California. Life 66:48-54+ Mr 21 '69
BONGARTZ, Roy
Atlanta. Holiday 46:80-1+ O '69
Chicano rebellion. Nation 208:271-4 Mr 3 '69
Pacific Northwest 164 years after Lewis and Clark. Holiday 45:48-51+ My '69
BONGIORNO, James
ULD sine wave generator. Pop Electr 31:55-61 O '69
BONHAM, Roger D.
Clyde Singer: Ohio painter. Am Artist 33:58-67 F '69
Parliament of owls. Ceram Mo 17:23-5 Ja '69
BONHOEFFER, Dietrich
Life and death of Dietrich Bonhoeffer, by M. Bosanquet. Review
New Repub 160:30-1 My 24 '69. J. Finn
BONI, Charles
Obituary
Pub W 195:36 Mr 3 '69
BONINSEGNA, Celestina
Enigma of Boninsegna. M. De Schauensee. por Opera N 33:12-13 F 15 '69
BONITO fishing
Double take on bonito; Redondo Harbor. L. Green; J. R. Gregg. il Field & S 73:50-3 F '69
BONK, James
Point Lobos; poem. Commonweal 91:303 D 5 '69
BONN, Hans
Hans Bonn on aggressive sailing. Yachting 125:38-9+ Je '69 (to be cont)
BONN, Myrtle
High on teaching. Am Ed 5:5-7 N '69
BONN

City planning
Bonn builds itself up into a capital city. il Bsns W p 140-1+ Ja 25 '69

Hotels, restaurants, etc.
Bei Ria; Weinhaus Maternus in the Bonn suburb of Bad Godesberg. il Time 93:38 My 23 '69
BONNER, John Tyler
Hormones in social amoebae and mammals; with biographical sketch. Sci Am 220:14, 78-84+ Je '69
Size of life; with biographical sketch. por Natur Hist 78:6, 40-5 Ja '69
BONNER, Nellie J.
O.K: Vachel Lindsay. Engl J 58:1338-40 D '69
BONNETS. Doll. See Doll clothes
BONNEVILLE national races. See Automobile racing
BONNEY, Orrin H.
Big Thicket: biological crossroads of North America; excerpt from The biological crossroads of North America. Liv Wildn 33:19-21 Sum '69
BONNIN and Morris pottery. See Pottery, American
BONONCINI, Giovanni
Festival of baroque operas: Graun's Montezuma and Bononcini's Griselda. P. L. Miller. por Am Rec G 35:366-7 Ja '69
Giovanni Bononcini: Griselda (excerpts) P. H. Lang. Mus Q 55:276-8 Ap '69
BONSAI. See Trees, Dwarf
BONSAI pots. See Flower pots
BONTECOU, Lee
Lee Bontecou, a powerful American sculptor. il por Vogue 153:194-5 My '69
BOOBIES (birds) See Gannets
BOOHER, Edward E.
Not whether but how the book will survive; address. por Pub W 195:39-41 Je 9 '69
BOOK, Albert C.
Will Britannia rule the waves, on air? Sea Front 15:30-3 Ja '69
BOOK advertising. See Books—Advertising
BOOK and author luncheons
Washington author luncheons celebrate 25th anniversary. S. Wagner. Pub W 196:24-5 D 1 '69

BOOK auctions. See Book sales

BOOK awards. See Literary prizes

BOOK awards, National. See National book awards

BOOK binding. See Bookbinding

BOOK buying, Personal. See Libraries, Private

BOOK buying for school libraries. See School libraries—Acquisitions

BOOK censorship. See Censorship

BOOK clerks. See Booksellers and bookselling —Employees

BOOK clubs
AEP starts book club for young readers; American education publications paperback elementary school program. Library J 94: 4194-5 N 15 '69
Rights and permissions; summary of address. H. Reich. il Pub W 196:24-5 Ag 4 '69
When a child, a book & a teacher get together; Scholastic Lucky book club. il Sr Schol 94:Schol Teach 16 Ja 31 '69
See also
Book of the month club

BOOK collecting
Booksellers and collectors: a dealer's apprenticeship; excerpts from Dukedom large enough. D. Randall. Pub W 196:35-8 Jl 21 '69
Eighth Amy Loveman award. D. Dempsey. Sat R 52:28 Jl 12 '69
Playing the bookmarket. F. Pollak. il Library J 94:2890-1 S 1 '69
See also
Book rarities
Libraries, Private

BOOK covers
Binding specifications and cover treatments. S. Salter. Pub W 196:72 O 6 '69
Book jackets tested in the bookstore. il Pub W 196:61 S 1 '69
Cover materials; excerpts from address, November 1969. R. Harper. Pub W 196:53 D 1 '69
Pocket's art director tells goals for covers. il Pub W 195:70 Ap 7 '69

BOOK decoration. See Book ornamentation

BOOK design
Catalog of alchemy: a problem in design. il Pub W 195:74+ Ap 7 '69
Designer's corner. S. Salter. See first issue of each month of Publishers' weekly to December 1, 1969
New England book show; vigorous evaluation. il Pub W 195:68-70 Mr 3 '69
Notes on redesign. S. Salter. Pub W 196:75 Ag 4 '69
Production and design notes on The complete pelican Shakespeare. H. Schmoller. il Pub W 196:62+ O 6 '69
Random thoughts about book design 1968-69; address, April 23, 1969. R. Stinehour. il Pub W 195:90+ My 5 '69

BOOK exhibits
AIGA fifty books show: what has changed! C. F. Zahn. il Pub W 195:80-3+ Je 9 '69
Children's book show at Israel museum calls for participation. I. Soifer. il Pub W 195: 66 Ap 7 '69
European scene; Internationale buchausstellung in Berlin. H. R. Lottman. Pub W 196: 15 D 15 '69
Exhibit report; an estimate of importance; books on Negro life and history. F. Cohn. il Negro Hist Bul 31:6-7 D '68
Fifth annual AAUP show: not very adventurous? il Pub W 195:72-4+ Je 9 '69
International exhibits in marketing scholarly books; summary of remarks at AAUP session, June 24, 1969. il Pub W 196:26-7 Ag 4 '69
Midwestern and southern book competition choices. Pub W 195:94-5 Mr 3 '69
New England book show; vigorous evaluation. il Pub W 195:68-70+ Mr 3 '69
Rounce & Coffin members choose western books. il Pub W 196:76-8 Jl 7 '69
20th annual Chicago book clinic show. il Pub W 195:90-2 Je 9 '69
Western publishers hold a book design show. il Pub W 197:67 Ja 5 '70
See also
Book fairs
Library exhibits

BOOK fairs
Book fair in Nice challenges Frankfurt. H. R. Lottman. il Pub W 196:30-4 Jl 21 '69
Brussels' first international book fair. H. R. Lottman. il Pub W 195:35-6 Ap 21 '69
Frankfurt notes: 1969. il Pub W 196:24-7 N 10 '69
Is it all fair at ABA regionals? il Pub W 196:34-6 O 13 '69
It's still the land of the book. P. E. Lapide. Chr Cent 86:1383-4 O 29 '69

Jerusalem book fair: coming of age in 1969. I. Soifer. il Pub W 195:25-9 My 12 '69
Law-and-order at Frankfurt; letter. R. Bechtle. Pub W 196:29-30 Ag 18 '69

BOOK illustration. See Illustration of books and periodicals

BOOK imports. See Books—Importation

BOOK industries and trade
Bookmaking. See issues of Publishers' weekly
See also
Book fairs
Books—Prices
Printing industry
Publishers and publishing
Strikes—United States—Book industries and trade

Employees
Franklin U.S. a plan to enlist talent, provide training; adaptation of address. April 10, 1969. C. F. Bound. Pub W 195:32-4 Ap 21 '69

Heraldry
See Heraldry

Law
But can you do that? H. F. Pilpel and K. P. Norwick. See occasional issues of Publishers' weekly

Asia
Developing book industries of Asia. C. G. Benjamin. il Pub W 195:17-19 My 5 '69

Latin America
Book hunter's advice; letter to editor. S. Miller. Américas 21:47 Je '69

Spain
See also
Publishers and publishing—Spain

United States
ABPC annual meeting: federal funds, manpower and markets are reviewed; highlights of panel discussions. il Pub W 195:25-30 Je 9 '69
Discounts and shipping costs. C. B. Grannis. Pub W 195:135 F 17 '69; Reply. J. Mashman. 195:17-18 Ap 5 '69
Publishing scene; remainder trade. D. Dempsey. Sat R 52:33 D 13 '69
See also
Book manufacturers' institute
Publishers and publishing—United States

BOOK jackets. See Book covers

BOOK jobbers
Holland depository for U.S. books relocates. il Pub W 195:53 Mr 10 '69
See also
Baker and Taylor company
Book people (firm)

BOOK lending, Library. See Libraries—Circulation, loans, etc.

BOOK lists. See Books and reading—Best books; Childrens literature—Bibliography; Reading lists

BOOK making (betting)
Betting the point spread, how the bookies beat the odds; football betting. il Newsweek 74:59 S 15 '69

BOOK manufacturers' institute
Annual meeting. il Pub W 196:44+ D 1; 19-24 D 8 '69
Increasing need for book industry information. C. B. Grannis. Pub W 196:33 D 8 '69
1968 in review. Pub W 195:44 Mr 10 '69

BOOK numbers
Progress report on SBN in Britain. D. Whitaker. Pub W 195:72-3 Ja 27 '69

BOOK-of-the-month club
Harry Scherman, 1887-1969. J. K. Hutchens. Sat R 52:23 N 29 '69
See also
Amy Loveman national award

BOOK orders, School library. See School libraries—Acquisitions

BOOK ornamentation
Ancient art of fore-edge painting. V. E. Dutter. il Am Artist 33:56-7+ Ja '69
Uses of gold in the graphic and decorative arts; address. H. L. Hunter. Pub W 195: 76+ My 5 '69

BOOK paper. See Paper

BOOK people (firm)
Book people: a West coast paperback wholesaler. P. Johnson, jr. il Pub W 195:44-6 Je 23 '69

BOOK plates. See Bookplates

BOOK prices. See Books—Prices

BOOK prizes. See Literary prizes

BOOK processing in libraries. See Libraries—Technical processes

BOOK rarities
Books. P. W. Schmidtchen. See issues of Hobbies
  See also
Booksellers and bookselling—Book rarities

Facsimiles

Fine Italian hands; facsimile writing manuals published by Nattali & Maurice of London. P. Standard. il Pub W 195:92-3+ F 3 '69
Our accurately honored authors; Center of editions of American authors. J. Childs. il Library J 94:722-4 F 15 '69
Publishing color facsimiles of rare manuscripts and books; Eugrammia press. H. L. Hunter. il Pub W 196:92-3 Jl 7 '69

BOOK reports
Novel ways with book reports. I. M. Decker. Sr Schol 94:Schol Teach 20 My 2 '69

BOOK reviewers. See Critics

BOOK reviews
In search of critics; religious books. il Newsweek 73:90 Mr 24 '69
RPG forum; religious publishers and media review each other; summary of addresses. Pub W 195:69-71 Ja 27 '69
Reviewing stand; children's literature. Z. Sutherland. Sat R 52:26 Ag 16 '69
  See also
Choice (periodical)
Literary criticism

BOOK sales
Book sale at Cabra; castle in Ireland. W. Ready. il ALA Bul 63:989-91 Jl '69
Leary's auction exceeds all expectations. Pub W 195:86-7 Ja 27 '69

BOOK selection
Can this marriage be saved? materials selection policy of the Brooklyn public library. D. Bass. Library J 94:3023-7 S 15 '69; Reply. J. C. Pine. 94:4321-2 D 1 '69
Challenging the censor: some responsibilities of the English department; address, November, 1968. K. L. Donelson. bibliog Engl J 58:869-76 S '69
  See also
Books and reading—Best books
School libraries—Book selection

BOOK series. See Series, Book

BOOK shelves. See Bookcases

BOOK therapy. See Bibliotherapy

BOOK titles. See Titles of books, stories, etc.

BOOK trade. See Book industries and trade; Publishers and publishing

BOOK week
Author editor "Be in" marks Ocean Hill book week. il Library J 94:4569 D 15 '69
50th anniversary of Children's book week. il Pub W 196:138-6 Jl 14 '69
Fifty years of children's book week: fifty years of independent American children's book publishing. S. C. Silberberg and J. Donovan. il Horn Bk 45:702-11 D '69
Selection for Catholic book week. Commonweal 89:677-82+ F 28 '69

BOOK wholesalers. See Book jobbers

BOOKBINDING
Bloop-de-bloop bindings; library prebinds; letter to the editor. Library J 94:4183 N 15 '69
Bookbinding from craft to industry; excerpts from address, November 1969. J. B. Blaine. Pub W 196:56 D 1 '69
Bookbindings decorating to order. il Vogue 153:119 Mr 1 '69
California case #69 C 1096; letter to the editor. F. G. Bennett. ALA Bul 63:1511 D '69
Librarians for and against paperbacks: the buckram syndrome. Pub W 195:27-8 Mr 3 '69
Practical notes about binding; summary of address at AAUP meeting, June 24, 1969. C. Rheault. il Pub W 196:57-8 Ag 4 '69
  See also
Book covers
Horowitz, A, and son

Materials

Spotlight on binding: elephant hide and patterned papers. il Pub W 195:95-6 Je 9 '69

Study and teaching

Your own thing. il Seventeen 28:236 Ag '69

BOOKCASES
Book walls. il Sunset 142:126-7 Ap '69
Build this handsome bookcase desk. A. Altomare. il Pop Mech 132:164-7 Ag '69
Easy-to-make displays for paperbacks. W. D. Boutwell. il Sr Schol 94:Schol Teach 22-3 Ja 31 '69
Gentle tyranny of books. R. Lynes. il House B 111:142-3 My '69

How to find more space for books. il House B 111:56+ My '69
Instant freestanding shelves. A. R. Johnson. il Pop Mech 132:164-5 Jl '69

BOOKER, Hylan
Black designer is tops in London style house. il pors Ebony 24:157-8+ S '69

BOOKER, Marion
Pink is from mama. por Redbook 133:12+ O '69

BOOKLETS. See Pamphlets

BOOKMAKING (betting) See Book making (betting)

BOOKMOBILES
Bookmobile goes in Brooklyn. I. E. Moran. il Library J 94:4487-9 D 15 '69
Chicago: the public library reaches out. A. Ladenson. il Wilson Lib Bul 43:875-81 My '69
Penntap: Carnegie library of Pittsburgh's mobile service to industry. D. R. Pfoutz. il Library J 94:1589-91 Ap 15 '69
Statewide outreach: desert booktrails to the Indians; New Mexico state library. W. H. Farrington. il Wilson Lib Bul 43:864-71 My '69

BOOKPLATES
Bookplates for literacy: a Unesco project. il ALA Bul 63:835 Je '69

BOOKS
  See also
Books and reading
Royalties
Titles of books, stories, etc.

Advertising

Birth of a new book promotion idea; tapes on cassettes produced by Video Books. il Pub W 196:31-2 D 1 '69
Case history of a best seller. il Pub W 196: 16-17 D 15 '69
Content of book ads debated in letters. H. F. Pilpel and K. P. Norwick. Pub W 195:31 My 26 '69
Doubleday signals new era in advertising. il Pub W 195:257-8 Ja 20 '69
Fall highspots, October-December books. il Pub W 196:205-35 Ag 25 '69
Firm producing full-color commercials for books. Pub W 196:41 S 29 '69
January books. il Pub W 196:27-34 O 27 '69
Lock that up in your Funk & Wagnalls; controversy surrounding S. S. Baker's The permissible lie. R. L. Shayon. Sat R 52:48-9 N 22 '69
On the fringe; publishing party honoring The homosexual handbook. H. Frankel. Sat R 52:30 Je 14 '69
September books; choices of publishers for major promotion. il Pub W 195:65-81 Je 2 '69
Spring highspots, 275 leading books. il Pub W 195:189-220 Ja 20 '69
Summer books: June-August campaigns. il Pub W 195:41-61 Ap 28 '69
Television advertising for the small bookstore. L. Boyle. il Pub W 196:59-60 Jl 7 '69
  See also
Book reviews

Classification

See Classification

Collectors and collecting

See Book collecting

Conservation and restoration

  See also
Paper—Preservation

Exhibitions

See Book exhibits

Importation

Free worldwide flow of books urged. Sch & Soc 97:376 O '69

Mutilation, defacement, etc.

Abuse of books, and then there are toys; letter to editor. M. Cannon. ALA Bul 63: 1053-4 S '69

Out of print books

  See also
Booksellers and bookselling—Out of print books

Photographic reproduction and projection

  See also
Microforms

BOOKS—*Continued*

Prices

California case #69 C 1096; letter to the editor. F. G. Bennett. ALA Bul 63:1511 D '69
Publishing scene. D. Dempsey. Sat R 52:32 Mr 15 '69

See also
Discount, Trade

Reprints

Xerox withdraws Mother Goose; with editorial comment. Library J 94:2031, 2034 My 15 '69

See also
Publishers and publishing—Reprints

Reprints, Unauthorized

See Copyright—Unauthorized reprints

Translations

See Translations and translating
BOOKS, Censorship of. See Censorship
BOOKS, Filmed. See Film adaptations
BOOKS, Illustration of. See Illustration of books and periodicals
BOOKS, Prohibited. See Prohibited books
BOOKS, Rare. See Book rarities
BOOKS, Secondhand
See also
Booksellers and bookselling—Secondhand books
BOOKS and reading
Architectonics of the mind. D. Melcher. il Library J 94:3785-8 O 15 '69
Books. M. Muggeridge. See issues of Esquire
Books and culture; a reevaluation; address, June 22, 1968. J. M. Thompson. ALA Bul 63:603-9 My '69
Books and transplants. N. Cousins. Sat R 52:18 Jl 5 '69
Books in the field; with editorial comment. R. G. Lillard; D. Polacheck; D. C. Dickinson. bibliog il Wilson Lib Bul 44:157-87 O '69
Electronic vs. linear. J. McLaughlin. America 120:634+ My 24 '69
General adult books: a look at the future; report of two-day meeting in Chicago, sponsored by the American library association, American book publishers council and the National book committee. Pub W 195:22-4 My 12 '69
Gentle tyranny of books. R. Lynes. il House B 111:142-3 My '69
Life book review. See issues of Life
Lobotomy and the future of the book: general adult books and reading in America, two-day conference. Wilson Lib Bul 43:931-2 Je '69
Not whether but how the book will survive; address. E. E. Booher. il Pub W 195:39-41 Je 9 '69
Other people's bookshelves. L. Conger. Writer 82:9-10 Ag '69
Peripatetic reviewer. E. Weeks. See issues of Atlantic
Perspective; guide for the insomniac's reading. J. H. Plumb. Sat R 52:23 Jl 26 '69
The scene; ed. by E. Farrell and L. Ruth. Engl J 58:756-61 My '69
Too much teaching; too little reading. R. E. Martin. Ed Digest 35:38-40 S '69
Two books with soul: for defiant ones. A. A. Shockley. Engl J 58:396-8 Mr '69

See also
Best sellers
Biography
Book selection
Childrens literature
Childrens reading
College students—Reading
Fiction
High school students—Reading
Immoral literature and pictures
Libraries
Libraries, Private
Libraries and readers
Literary criticism
Literature
National book committee
Picture books
Reading—Special groups of readers—Young militants
Reference books
Supplementary reading
Young adults reading
also Religious literature; Scientific literature; etc.

Best books

ALA cites 1968's notable books. Pub W 195:133 F 17 '69; Same Library J 94:927+ Mr 1 '69; ALA Bul 63:373-5 Mr '69

America's survey of notable fall books (cont)
America 121:527+ N 29 '69
America's survey of notable spring books. America 120:535-6+ My 3 '69
Book review; ed. by M. Cooley and others. See issues of Library journal to April 15, 1969
Book review; ed. by J. Serebnick and others. See issues of Library journal
Books; critics' choices for Christmas (cont) Commonweal 91:311-19 D 5 '69
Books they loved; childhood reading of famous people. L. B. J. Robb. il McCalls 96:28+ Ja '69
Musical bookshelf for the Christmas shopper. R. Jacobson. Sat R 52:52-3 D 13 '69
New fall books. M. M. Dorcy. America 121:235-8 S 27 '69
1969, a rich year for the novel; comp. by G. Wolff. il Newsweek 74:97-8+ D 22 '69
Notable nominations. ALA Bul 63:1178, 1293, 1614-15 S-O, D '69
On the fringe; for Christmas giving. H. Frankel. Sat R 52:45 N 29 '69
Power of the word; comp. by K. L. Woodward. il Newsweek 74:47 D 29 '69
Recommended recent books from the university presses. Am Scholar 38:500 Sum '69
SR's checklist of books for Christmas. Sat R 52:40+ N 29 '69

See also
Best sellers
Reading lists

Bibliography

Affluent tomes for the times; comp. by R. A. Sokolov. il Newsweek 74:98-100 D 15 '69
Books by Nation contributors. Nation 209:708-10 D 22 '69
Books to come; ed. by J. Donathan and J. Fletcher. Library J 94:3481-576 O 1 '69
Books to come; ed. by J. Putnam (cont) Library J 94:587-684, 2262-86+ F 1, Je 1 '69
Fall and winter books. Changing T 23:24-33 O '69
Fall highspots, October-December books. il Pub W 196:205-35 Ag 25 '69
January books. il Pub W 196:27-34 O 27 '69
Journal's preview of best sellers. il Ladies Home J 86:96-7+ S '69
New Yorker lists at this season some books by its contributors published during the year (cont) New Yorker 45:194-5 N 29 '69
Notable. New Repub 161:37-40 N 29 '69
October-December previews. il Pub W 195:83-104 Je 2 '69
On the books. J. Herbert. House & Gard 136:58+ S '69
One week: the literary overflow. il Time 94:108-10 O 24 '69
Rich Christmas sampling. il Time 94:108-10 D 5 '69
Short reviews: books. P. Adams. See issues of Atlantic
Something for everybody. S. Paul. Nation 209:672-3 D 15 '69
Spring highspots, 275 leading books. il Pub W 195:189-220 Ja 20 '69
Spring previews 1970: January through June. il Pub W 196:236-47 Ag 25 '69
Summer previews; June through September. il Pub W 195:221-33 Ja 20 '69
This week. See issues of Christian century
Time listings. See issues of Time
Weekly record. See issues of Publishers' weekly

International aspects

See also
Operation bookshelf

Reading aloud

Choral reading and the English teacher. M. E. Stassen. Engl J 58:436-9 Mr '69
Living Latin and Greek; informal monthly reading sessions in Austin, Tex. Sch & Soc 97:199 Ap '69
Slow readers can enjoy oral reading. E. Schwartz. Ed Digest 34:36-7 Ja '69

Study and teaching

See Literature—Study and teaching

United States

See Books and reading
BOOKS and reading for young adults. See Young adults literature
BOOKS as gifts
Books for holiday giving. D. J. Soria. Hi Fi 19:MA6-7 D '69
Our Christmas gift choices. Chr Cent 86:1554-5 D 3 '69

See also
Operation bookshelf

BOOKS for children. See Childrens literature
BOOKS for girls. See Childrens literature
BOOKS for the sick
    See also
Libraries. Hospital
BOOKS of instruction. See Instruction manuals
BOOKS-on-file (firm)
Name the book, we'll find it. Pub W 196:55-6 D 29 '69
BOOKS USA, incorporated. See Freedom house/Books USA
BOOKSELLERS and bookselling
    See also
Books—Advertising
Books—Prices
College bookstores
Department stores—Book departments
Publishers and publishing

Art literature

Selling art books in a suburban store. M. B. Tarshish. il Pub W 195:77-8 Ap 28 '69

Book rarities

Booksellers and collectors: a dealer's apprenticeship; excerpts from Dukedom large enough. D. Randall. Pub W 196:35-8 Jl 21 '69

Childrens literature

Bookshop-lined street gets a handsome new addition; Heffers children's bookshop, Cambridge. il Pub W 195:53-4 Ap 21 '69
Children's book centre: devoted to more than selling. il Pub W 195:46-8 Mr 17 '69
Children's books discussed at the ABA convention; highlights of panel discussion. il Pub W 195:43-5 Je 16 '69
Once you have found her never let her go; or, Who sells children's books. L. Russ. Pub W 196:38 Ag 18 '69
Wise bookshop owners don't pussyfoot around; Owl and the pussycat bookshop, Lexington, Ky. K. Weisbuch. il Pub W 196:31-2 Ag 11 '69

Cookbooks

Cooking up something special for the professional; Radio City book store. Pub W 196:51-2 S 15 '69

Employees

Book clerk's view of things. M. J. O'Hanlon. Pub W 195:54-5 Ap 21 '69

Finance

Bookselling and the dollar squeeze. G. R. Smith. Pub W 195:41-2 My 5 '69

International aspects

Shop the Common market calls its own; European bookshop in Brussels. H. R. Lottman. il Pub W 195:55-7 Je 9 '69

Medical literature

Johns Hopkins bookshop comes of age. N. J. Lange. il Pub W 196:73-4 N 17 '69

Nature literature

Building a nature and sports section. M. O'Hanlon. Pub W 196:39-40 Ag 4 '69

Order processing

Solution to the special order problem. M. G. Hurtig. Pub W 196:271-2+ Ag 25 '69

Out of print books

Gettysburg retailer focuses on out-of-print books. E. Oliver. il Pub W 196:48-9 Jl 21 '69
    See also
Books-on-file (firm)

Paperback books

Paperback bookshop ups volume to $150,000 in five years; Main court book fair, White Plains. M. B. Tarshish. il Pub W 195:43-4 Mr 24 '69
Scribner's reassesses its position in paperbacks. Pub W 195:47-8 Mr 31 '69
Selling and promoting paperbacks; highlights of panel discussion at annual meeting of AAUP. H. R. Kessell; M. Abel; J. N. Rountree. il Pub W 196:35 Jl 28 '69

Poetry

Bookseller's garden of verses. R. Armour. Pub W 195:126 Je 2 '69

Publicity

    See also
Book and author luncheons
Show windows

Religious literature

Bookshop planned around social involvement; The Search ecumenical shop and home for girls. Elyria. T. H. Peters. il Pub W 195:44-6 Mr 3 '69
What is a religious bookstore? H. Jones. il Pub W 196:75-7 S 22 '69

Returns policy

Communications breakdown: publishers and booksellers. Pub W 195:29-30 Mr 17 '69

Secondhand books

Fourth avenue book trade. M. B. Tarshish. il Pub W 196:52-5 O 20; 50-3 O 27; 40-3 N 3 '69
My two weeks in the book business. J. Goyer. il Har Yrs 9:14-15 D '69
Second-hand diamonds. L. Conger. Writer 82:7-8 D '69
    See also
Booksellers and bookselling—Out of print books

Stock

Accentuate the positive with EDP. P. M. Welsh. il Pub W 196:37-9 D 8 '69
Shortcut to inventory control. R. A. Atheran. Pub W 195:62-4 My 19 '69
Stock control is more than counting. M. J. Goodman. il Pub W 196:155-7 Jl 14; 49-50 Jl 21 '69
Successful inventory control; panel discussion. il Pub W 195:27 Je 23 '69

Study and teaching

Booksellers' school a success; with editorial comment. il Pub W 195:25-7, 36 Ap 7 '69

Textbooks

This textbook thing. R. W. Vanderhoef. Pub W 197:47-8 Ja 5 '70

Toy departments

New winning streak for adult games; Brentano's fun & games shop. il Bsns W p33-4 N 29 '69

Belgium

Shop the Common market calls its own; European bookshop in Brussels. H. R. Lottman. il Pub W 195:55-7 Je 9 '69

California

Brentano's unveils new San Francisco shop. Pub W 196:46 Jl 28 '69
Japanese bookseller attempts to bridge two cultures; Kinokuniya bookstore in San Francisco. il Pub W 196:34-5 N 24 '69

Canada

    See also
Canadian booksellers association

Colorado

Chinook celebrates a birthday and an expansion. J. Noyes. Pub W 196:52-3 S 15 '69

England

Bookshop-lined street gets a handsome new addition; Heffers children's bookshop, Cambridge. il Pub W 195:53-4 Ap 21 '69

Europe, Western

New European bookstore; tr. by C. B. Anderson. G. Ramseger. il Pub W 195:19-22 My 26 '69

Great Britain

As it looks in Britain: finding the book buyer of the '70s. W. G. Graham. Pub W 195:39-40 F 3 '69
Children's book centre: devoted to more than selling. il Pub W 195:46-8 Mr 17 '69
    See also
Booksellers and bookselling—England

Ireland

Book sale at Cabra. W. Ready. il ALA Bul 63:989-91 Jl '69

Italy

Rizzoli: it happens to be an industry. H. R. Lottman. il Pub W 197:39-42 Ja 5 '70

Kentucky

Wise bookshop owners don't pussyfoot around; Owl and the pussycat bookshop, Lexington, Ky. K. Weisbuch. il Pub W 196:31-2 Ag 11 '69

Maine

Television advertising for the small bookstore; Jones book shop, Portland. L. Boyle. il Pub W 196:59-60 Jl 7 '69

BOOKSELLERS and bookselling—*Continued*

Massachusetts

From barber to bookman; Book shop of Beverly Farms. E. Oliver. il Pub W 196:50-1 S 29 '69

Goodspeed's: the Yankee bookseller from Boston. M. B. Tarshish. il Pub W 195:54-6 Je 30 '69

Harvard square's own Mandrake. M. B. Tarshish. il Pub W 196:30-1 Ag 11 '69

Minnesota

Handcrafted construction, antiques, mark Gold door; bookshop in Hibbings. il Pub W 195:46-7 Mr 3 '69

New York (state)

Brentano's N.Y. employees return, but picket CCM. Pub W 196:37-8 O 13 '69

Brentano's returns to White Plains. M. B. Tarshish. il Pub W 195:45-6 Ap 7 '69

Change of ownership and emphasis bring immediate results; Herder bookshop, now Perrain book store. il Pub W 196:45-6 Jl 28 '69

Cooking up something special for the professional; Radio City book store. Pub W 196:51-2 S 15 '69

Employees go on strike at Brentano's, N.Y. Pub W 196:45 S 15 '69

Fourth avenue book trade. M. B. Tarshish. il Pub W 196:52-5 O 20; 50-3 O 27; 40-3 N 3 '69

Frances Steloff, L.H.D; visits to Gotham book mart. New Yorker 45:23-6 Ag 16 '69

Larousse opens Fifth avenue store. il Pub W 196:54-5 D 29 '69

New winning streak for adult games; Brentano's fun & games shop. il Bsns W p33-4 N 29 '69

On the fringe; bookstores in Greenwich Village. H. Frankel. Sat R 52:29 Mr 8 '69

Only real live bookstore in New York; Gotham book mart. D. Dempsey. Holiday 46:8+ N '69

Paperback bookshop ups volume to $150,000 in five years; Main court book fair, White Plains. M. B. Tarshish. il Pub W 195:43-4 Mr 24 '69

Scribner's reassesses its position in paperbacks. Pub W 195:47-8 Mr 31 '69

Selling art books in a suburban store. M. B. Tarshish. il Pub W 195:77-8 Ap 28 '69

Ohio

Bookshop planned around social involvement; The Search ecumenical shop and home for girls. Elyria. T. H. Peters. il Pub W 195:44-6 Mr 3 '69

Oregon

What is a religious bookstore? Interfaith service center, Portland. H. Jones. il Pub W 196:75-7 S 22 '69

Pennsylvania

Gettysburg retailer focuses on out-of-print books. E. Oliver. il Pub W 196:48-9 Jl 21 '69

Leary's auction exceeds all expectations. Pub W 195:86-7 Ja 27 '69

United States

Bookstores are never sinning? N. McCaffrey. Pub W 196:16 Ag 4 '69

Bookstores as outlets for university press books; excerpts from addresses, June 22, 1969; with editorial comment. F. W. Boardman, jr; G. R. Smith; J. N. Rountree. il Pub W 196:26-31, 39 Jl 28 '69

1968: a year of tragedy and dramatic economic upsurge; Book openings continue two-year decline. Pub W 195:61-3 Mr 10 '69

Opinionated man. G. R. Smith. Pub W 196:45-6 S 8; 47-8 O 13; 39-41 N 10; 27-8 D 15 '69

Retailing. See issues of Publishers' weekly

U.S. bookselling; a European critique. Pub W 197:58 Ja 5 '70

Where do you stand on employee benefits? Pub W 195:84-5+ Ap 14 '69

Who's who among the travelers: publishers' salesmen. Pub W 195:77-94 Mr 10 '69

See also

American booksellers association

Christian booksellers association

College bookstores

Virgin Islands

Jeltrups' books, St Croix's booksellers. E. Oliver. il Pub W 195:41 My 12 '69

BOOKSHELVES. See Bookcases

BOOKSTANDS. See Bookcases

BOOKSTORE windows. See Show windows

BOOKSTORES. See College bookstores

BOOKSTORES, Secondhand. See Booksellers and bookselling—Secondhand books

BOOLEAN algebra. See Algebra, Boolean

BOONDOGGLING

Big boondoggle at Lordstown; with editorial comment. D. Sider. il Fortune 80:85-6, 106-9+ S '69

BOONE, Pat

Cross and the switchblade: boon for the cinema. Chr Today 14:52-3 O 10 '69

BOONE, Richard

Issue is priorities. Cur 113:40-1 D '69

BOONVILLE, Calif.

Harpin' boont in Boonville. T. Tyler. il Time 93:20-1 F 7 '69

Woolgrowers gather in Boonville on July 27. il Sunset 143:32-3 Jl '69

BOORSTIN, Daniel J.

American academics; address, June 1, 1969. Vital Speeches 36:21-4 O 15 '69

BOOT makers. See Shoemakers

BOOTH, Paul

Students and workers. Ramp Mag 8:19-20 S '69

BOOTH, Philip

Crows; Bolt; Chekhov; poems. Poetry 113:242-5 Ja '69

BOOTH, Stanley

Rebirth of the blues: soul. Sat Eve Post 242:26-31+ F 8 '69

BOOZ, Allen and Hamilton, incorporated

Booz, Allen tells rich inside story. Bsns W p22-3 D 20 '69

BOPF, Della

High-diving grandma. Har Yrs 9:43 Je '69

BORAZON. See Boron nitrides

BORCHERDING, James R.

What's new. See issues of Successful farming

BORDAZ, Jacques

Flint flaking in Turkey; with biographical sketch. por Natur Hist 78:4, 73-7 F '69

about

Knappers of Cakmak. Sci Am 220:51-2 Ap '69

BORDEAUX festival. See Music festivals—France

BORDEN, John H. and others

Synthetic juvenile hormone: induction of sex pheromone production in ips confusus. bibliog Science 166:1626-7 D 26 '69

BORDEN incorporated

Easier said than done. il Forbes 104:98 N 15 '69

BOREDOM

Business of boredom. L. Woodrum. Chr Today 13:11 Ja 31 '69

Should you quit your job? R. Bugg. il Todays Health 47:26-9+ My '69

BOREK, Tom

Preview of a ballet costume and design exhibit. Dance Mag 43:47-62 F '69

BORERS (insects) See European corn borers

BORES (tidal phenomena)

Ebb and flow. F. G. W. Smith. il Sea Front 15:86-96 Mr '69

BORG-Warner corporation

Just like yesterday; auto-parts business. Forbes 104:28-9 N 15 '69

BORGES, Jorge Luis

Ars poetica; poem, tr. by W. S. Merwin. Harp Baz 102:238 Mr '69

Borges on Borges; interview, ed. by R. Stern. Am Scholar 38:452-8 Sum '69

Daybreak; poem, tr. by N. T. Di Giovanni. New Yorker 45:133 My 24 '69

Embarking on the study of Anglo-Saxon grammar; poem, tr. by A. Reid. Harp Baz 102:238 Mr '69

Fragment; poem, tr. by N. T. Di Giovanni. New Yorker 45:42 S 6 '69

Heraclitus; poem, tr. by N. T. Di Giovanni. New Yorker 45:34 Ag 9 '69

Isidoro Acevedo; poem, tr. by N. T. Di Giovanni. New Yorker 45:60 N 8 '69

Labyrinth; poem; tr. by J. Updike. Atlan 223:72 Ap '69

Six poems: Keeper of the books; June 1968; Cambridge; Invocation to Joyce: In praise of darkness; Plain things; tr. by N. T. Di Giovanni. New Yorker 45:52-3 D 13 '69

To a Saxon poet; poem, tr. by N. T. Di Giovanni. New Yorker 44:40 F 8 '69

Unending gift; poem, tr. by N. T. Di Giovanni. Harp Baz 102:238 Mr '69

—and Guerrero, Margarita

Imaginary beings; tr. by N. T. Di Giovanni. New Yorker 45:39-46 O 4 '69

BORGES, Jorge Luis and Guerrero, Margarita
—*Continued*
about
Conversations with Jorge Luis Borge, by
R. Burgin. Review
Sat R 52:25-6+ Je 7 '69. S. Rodman
BORGESON, Griffith
Milestones on the Bertone trail. Motor T 21:
38-40 My '69
Super safety for the competition car. Mo-
tor T 21:50-2 Jl '69
Turin's magnificent Museo dell' automobile.
Motor T 21:52-5 My '69
BORING machinery. See Drilling and boring
machinery
BORISOV, P. M.
Can we control the Arctic climate? Bul
Atom Sci 25:43-8 Mr '69
BORJA, Olympio
Trust Territory of the Pacific Islands;
statements, June 6 and 13, 1969. Dept State
Bul 61:227-9, 232-3 S 8 '69
BORK, Robert H.
Antitrust in dubious battle. Fortune 80:103-
5+ S '69
BORLAND, Hal
Autumn: a celebration. Audubon 71:18-36 S
'69
May baskets. Audubon 71:inside cover My
'69
Salamanders. Audubon 71:inside cover Mr '69
Skulk of foxes, etc. Audubon 71:46-7 Ja '69
Small fry. Audubon 71:13-15 My '69
Spider webs. Audubon 71:inside cover Jl '69
Woodies. Audubon 71:inside cover Ja '69
about
Dispatches from the unpaved world. J. C.
Devlin. Natur Hist 78:70-2 My '69
Vacation meditations. M. Bush. Am For 75:
34 Jl '69
BORMAN, Frank
Sounds of the space age; with phonograph
record. por Nat Geog 136:750 D '69
See also
Space flight to the moon—Manned flights—
Borman-Lovell-Anders flight, 1968
BORN, Max
Passionate physicist. por Time 95:41 Ja 19
'70
BORN, Roscoe E.
Headline hunting in the consumer's name.
Consumer Bul 52:24-6 Je '69
BORNEO
Native races
Got ark: need Boston whaler; progress re-
port on W. Sargent's project to save the
Dyaks. Nat R 21:893 S 9 '69
Needed: an ark; Operation Dyak, project to
aid head-hunters. Nat R 21:581-2 Je 17 '69
BORNS, H. W. Jr, and Hall, B. A.
Mawson tillite in Antarctica: preliminary re-
port of a volcanic deposit of Jurassic age.
bibliog Science 166:870-2 N 14 '69
BORODIN, Aleksandr Porfir'evich
Doctor Borodin's formula. F. Rizzo. il por
Opera N 33:12-13 Mr 1 '69
Prince Igor. Criticism
New Yorker 45:98 Mr 8 '69
Newsweek il 73:114 Mr 17 '69
Sat R 52:40 Mr 15 '69
BORODIN quartet. See String quartets
BORON
Boron modifications produced in an induc-
tion-coupled argon plasma. D. B. Sullenger
and others. bibliog il Science 163:935-7 F
28 '69
Boron shortage causing program delays.
Aviation W 91:53 N 3 '69
Tough featherweight plays hard to get. il
Bsns W p38 N 15 '69
BORON nitrides
GE's gem-hard grit; Borazon II. Bsns W p49
Jl 5 '69
BORONIA
You grow it for its fragrance; brown boronia.
il Sunset 142:200 F '69
BOROS, Julius
Putting it on the line. il pors Esquire 71:
143-5 Ap '69
BOROVETS, Bulgaria
Borovets: Bulgaria's year-round resort. J. E.
Lynge. il Travel 131:60-1 Mr '69
BORROFF, Edith
Current chronicle. Mus Q 55:396-401 Jl '69
BORROWING
Neighborly borrowing: is it cricket? Good H
168:165 Je '69
BORROWING of money. See Credit; Debt
BORROWMAN, Barbara
Seeds in watermelons, who needs them?
Org Gard & Farm 16:51-3 Ap '69

BORST, Lyle B.
Megalithic plan underlying Canterbury ca-
thedral. bibliog Science 163:567-70: 166:
774 F 7, N 7 '69
BORTIN, Mortimer M. and Saltzstein, E. C.
Graft versus host inhibition: fetal liver and
thymus cells to minimize secondary dis-
ease. bibliog Science 164.316-18 Ap 18 '69
BORTLE, John
On the brightness of comets. R Pop Astron
63:10-13 F '69
BORTON, Terry
Teaching for personal growth: an introduction
to new materials. bibliog Ment Hy 53:594-9
O '69
BORZELLECA, Joseph F. See Schwartz, S. L.
jt. auth.
BOSC, Robert
Gaullism with de Gaulle. America 121:13-15
Jl 5 '69
U.S. Catholicism revisited. America 121:389-
91 N 1 '69
BOSCH, Hieronymus
Manifest and the latent content of two paint-
ings by Hieronymus Bosch. E. Fromm. bib-
liog il Am Imago 26:145-66 Sum '69
BOSCH, Juan
Dominican Republic revisited. E. von
Kuehnelt-Leddihn. Nat R 21:324 Ap 8 '69
BOSKIN, Joseph
Revolt of the urban ghettos, 1964-1967. bib-
liog f Ann Am Acad 382:1-14 Mr '69
—and Rosenstone, R. A.
(eds) Protest in the sixties. bibliog f Ann
Am Acad 382:1-144 Mr '69
BOSMANN, H. Bruce, and Martin, S. S.
Mitochondrial autonomy: incorporation of
monosaccharides into glycoprotein by iso-
lated mitochondria. bibliog Science 164:190-2
Ap 11 '69
BOSOM. See Breast
BOSOM exercise. See Exercise
BOSPORUS
Bosphorus. C. E. Adelsen. il Travel 132:28-
33+ S '69
BOSS rule
Political machine. W. V. Shannon; T. J.
Fleming. il Am Heritage 20:26-48 Je '69
BOSSONE, Richard M.
Remedial program. Clear House 43:364-7 F
'69
BOSTON
Hippies get Boston up tight. il Bsns W p 142-
3 My 17 '69
Art
Artists as social reformers. J. H. Kay. il Art
in Am 57:44-7 Ja '69
Boston is here, now. J. Koethe. Art N 68:
30-3+ S '69
Bookstores
See Booksellers and bookselling—Massa-
chusetts
Churches
Arlington street scene. il Newsweek 74:120-1
S 22 '69
City hall
Airy fortress. il Time 93:60 F 21 '69
Boston's city hall; with account by S.
Moholy-Nagy. il Arch Forum 130:38-53 Ja
'69
New Boston city hall. M. F. Schmertz. il
Arch Rec 145:133-44 F '69
New horizons. il Newsweek 73:36 F 24 '69
You can fight city hall. D. L. Shirey. il
Newsweek 74:93 Jl 7 '69
Climate
Hundred years of Boston snowstorms. D.
M. Ludlum. Weatherwise 22:72-5 Ap '69
Description
Back to the hub. W. Sullivan. il Sat R 52:
43-5 D 20 '69
Let's travel: capes, bays, and college boys.
B. Gillman. il Mlle 69:48-50+ Jl '69
Traveler's guide. J. O. Killens. bibliog il
Redbook 133:55-62 Jl '69
Docks
Issues that threaten life of ports; the future
of Boston's port. U S News 66:70 Mr 31 '69
Education
Bulls & bears in Boston; North Dorchester
McCormack middle school. A. J. Owens.
il Sr Schol 94:Schol Teach 14 Ap 18 '69
Tension: a tool for reform; types of decen-
tralizing ventures. G. B. Thomas. il Sat R
52:50-2+ Jl 19 '69
Festivals
See Festivals—Massachusetts

BOSTON—*Continued*

Galleries and museums
See also
Boston museum of fine arts
Museum of science

Gardens
In Boston: getting the most from a small space. il Home Gard 56:42-3 Jl '69

Hotels, restaurants, etc.
America's unique hotels; Boston Ritz. G. Cotler. il Holiday 45:84-7+ Ap '69
Dunfey touch; acquisition of Parker house. il Newsweek 73:84+ Ap 14 '69

Housing
BURP and make money; urban housing rehabilitation venture. E. Goldston. bibliog il Harvard Bsns R 47:84-99 S '69

Music
Report. Boston; production of Donizetti's Lucia di Lammermoor. M. Harris. il Opera N 33:30 Mr 15 '69
See also
Boston symphony orchestra
Opera company of Boston

History
Big boom in Boston; National peace jubilee, 1869. R. Jarman. il Am Heritage 20:46-51+ O '69

Negroes
Promises, promises; broken pledges by Businessmen. il Newsweek 74:37 Ag 11 '69

Neurosciences research program
See Neurosciences research program. Boston

Newspapers
Dissent in Boston; unfavorable reviews of the Boston symphony. Nation 209:653-4 D 15 '69
Radical voice: Old mole. il Time 93:55 Ap 18 '69

Police
On the vice beat. B. McCabe. Atlan 223:122-6 Mr '69

Publishers and publishing
See Publishers and publishing—Massachusetts

Schools
See Boston—Education

Social life and customs
Single life: Boston. il Mlle 69:136-7+ S '69

Social work
View from VISTA; Bonney Smith and Carla Bryson. il Newsweek 74:50+ D 1 '69

Stores
Boston supershoppers; Filene's automatic bargain basement. il Time 94:27 D 26 '69

Theater
Bond in Boston; production of Narrow road to the deep north by the Charles playhouse. J. Kroll. Newsweek 74:135 N 24 '69
Japanese puzzle; Charles playhouse production of Narrow road to the deep north. H. Hewes. Sat R 52:14-15 D 13 '69

Water supply
Ecology of a reservoir; Quabbin reservoir, Mass. P. A. Erickson and J. T. Reynolds. il Natur Hist 78:48-53 N '69

BOSTON and Maine railroad
So it's crummy. So what? Forbes 103:32-3 Je 15 '69

BOSTON arm. See Artificial limbs

BOSTON ballet company
Boston ballet company; Loeb drama center, Harvard university. S. Smoliar. Dance Mag 43:90+ Mr '69
Boston ballet company; Orpheum theatre. S. Smoliar. Dance Mag 43:88 My; 80 Jl '69

BOSTON Bruins (hockey team) See Hockey teams

BOSTON Celtics (basketball team) See Basketball teams

BOSTON childrens medical center. See Children—Hospitals

BOSTON college
Phasing out Mary Daly. M. Malec. Commonweal 90:61-2 Ap 4 '69

BOSTON marathon. See Running

BOSTON museum of fine arts
Boston museum of fine arts, 1870-1970; with colorplates. W. Eisenhart. il Art N 68:34-47+ S '69
Yankee dinner for a royal collection; Boston Forsyth Wickes collection. French and English 18th-century antiques. E. Alston. il Look 33:68-72 F 18 '69

BOSTON museum of science. See Museum of science, Boston

BOSTON Red Sox (baseball) See Baseball clubs

BOSTON symphony orchestra
Boston symphony; end of the Leinsdorf era. G. Movshon. il Hi Fi 19:MA12-13 N '69
Dissent in Boston; unfavorable reviews. Nation 209:653-4 D 15 '69
Music; concert performance of Ariadne auf Naxos. D. Hamilton. Nation 208:413-14 Mr 31 '69
Music to my ears; Thomas for Steinberg. I. Kolodin. Sat R 52:44+ N 8 '69
Musical events:
M. T. Thomas as a substitute for W. Steinberg. W. Sargeant. New Yorker 45:163 N 1 '69
Rise and decline of the Boston symphony. A. Chasins. il McCalls 96:34+ Mr '69
See also
Berkshire symphonic festival

BOSTON university
Scientific report, the effects of marijuana on human beings; research by Boston university school of medicine. N. E. Zinberg and A. T. Weil. il N Y Times Mag p28-9+ My 11 '69; Discussion. p22+ Je 8 '69
To be, or not to be? BU helps; Young artists program. C. Stinson. il Hi Fi 19:MA22-3 O '69

BOSTON urban rehabilitation program. See Boston—Housing

BOSTWICK, Henry, jr
Industrial park; what it is, and isn't. Nations Bsns 57:72-5 S '69

BOSWORTH, Patricia
Antonioni discovers America. Holiday 45:64-5+ Mr '69
Marrakech. Holiday 46:44-7+ D '69

BOTANICAL chemistry
See also
Enzymes, Plant
Photosynthesis

BOTANICAL exploration
David Douglas in pursuit of plants. R. G. Beidleman. Horticulture 47:30-1+ F '69
F. Kingdon-Ward, plant hunter extraordinary. D. S. Manks. il Horticulture 46:20-1+ O '68
Mutis in New Granada; iconographic collection of regional flora. N. López Pellón. il Américas 21:29-33 F '69
Plant hunting in Formosa. J. L. Creech. il Horticulture 47:34-5+ Ap '69

BOTANICAL gardens
Rancho Santa Ana botanic garden. L. W. Lenz. il Horticulture 47:32-3 N '69
See also
Harvard university—Arnold arboretum
Missouri botanical garden
Phipps conservatory. Pittsburgh

BOTANICAL research
Electronics and the living plant. L. G. Lawrence. bibliog il Electr World 82:25-8 O '69
Man who reads nature's secret signals. T. Bacon. il Nat Wildlife 7:4-8 F '69
1969, breakthrough in plant science. M. C. Goldman. il Org Gard & Farm 16:33-7 Ja '69
See also
Plant breeding

BOTANICAL societies
See also
Horticultural societies

BOTANICAL specimens. See Plants—Collection and preservation

BOTANISTS
See also
Plée, A.

BOTANY
What do you know about botany? quiz. J. Daugherty and M. Daugherty. il Sci Digest 66:82-3+ N '69
See also
Alpine flora
Bark
Biology
Buds
Cave fauna and flora
Genetics (botany)
Nature study

BOTANY—See also—*Continued*
  Paleobotany
  Polymorphism (botany)
  Seedlings
  Shrubs
  Trees

Anatomy
Pistillate papaya flower: a morphological anomaly. W. B. Storey. bibliog il Science 163:401-5 Ja 24 '69

Classification
See also
Botany—Nomenclature

Ecology
See also
Forest ecology
Plant introduction
Plant succession
Vegetation

Nomenclature
Glossary of some ancient Chinese plant names. P. T. Ho. bibliog f Am Hist R 75:34-6 O '69
How to read a botanical name. Sunset 142: 260 Ap '69

Physiology
See also
Photosynthesis
Plants—Translocation
Spiral growth and movement

Structure
See Botany—Anatomy

California
California's wild flowers from seed. J. Broughton. il Horticulture 47:38-9 S '69

Ecuador
Ecuador's edible jewels. M. B. Pomeroy. il Américas 21:33-7 Ap '69

Hawaii
Hawaii first; 201 champion big trees. L. C. Littlecott. il Am For 75:12-15+ F '69
Native trees of Hawaii. E. L. Little, jr. il Am For 75:16-17+ F '69

Islands of the Pacific
Flower of tetraplasandra gymnocarpa hypogyny with epigynous ancestry. R. H. Eyde and C. C. Tseng. bibliog il Science 166:506-8 O 24 '69

North America
Landscaping with natives from the Plains and the Rockies. G. W. Kelly. il Horticulture 46:28-33 D '68

Philippines
Gardens of the Philippines. R. H. Smiley. il Horticulture 46ff:34-5+ S '68

South Africa
South Africa, the botanical adventure of a lifetime. P. S. Parr. il Home Gard 56:34-6 Je '69
South Africa's flowers. W. J. Tijmens. il Horticulture 47:22-3+ D '69

Taiwan
Plant hunting in Formosa. J. L. Creech. il Horticulture 47:34-5+ Ap '69

BOTANY prints. See Prints

BOTHWELL, Dick, and Coleman, David
  Man who makes pets of gorillas. Sci Digest 65:26-31 F '69

BOTHWELL, Frank Edgar
  Is the ICBM obsolete? Bul Atom Sci 25:21-2 O '69

BOTOS, Bob
  Digital RTL frequency counter. Radio-Electr 40:23-6 Ag; 52-3+ S '69

BOTSWANA
  Botswana; problems & potential; address, September 1969. S. Khama. Vital Speeches 36:121-4 D 1 '69
    See also
  Education—Botswana
  Kalahari Desert
  Natural resources—Botswana

Economic conditions
External politico-economic problems. D. B. Knight. bibliog il Focus 20:9-12 N '69

Foreign relations
External politico-economic problems. D. B. Knight. bibliog il Focus 20:9-12 N '69

Native races
Eating Christmas in the Kalhari; Tswana-Herero custom of slaughtering an ox for bushmen neighbors. R. B. Lee. Natur Hist 78:14+ D '69

Victorian fashions at the edge of the Kalahari; traditional costume of Herero women. F. L. Lambrecht and D. Lambrecht. il Natur Hist 78:48-51 Mr '69

BOTT, Thomas L. and Brock, T. D.
  Bacterial growth rates above 90°C in Yellowstone hot springs. Science 164:1411-12 Je 20 '69

BOTTEL, Helen
  No cure like love. Har Yrs 9:35-7 My '69

BOTTING, Tom
  (tr) See Kazakova, R. Pattering rain set runlets flowing

BOTTLE feeding. See Infants—Nutrition

BOTTLES
  Can plastic bottles squeeze into market? il Bsns W p81 N 8 '69
  Pleasures of the extravagant bottle. W. Clifford. House B 111:98-100 F '69
    See also
  Beverage containers

BOTTLES, Miniature
  Bottled art; scenes painted inside by K. Wagener. B. Notts. il Design 70:20-2 Sum '69

BOTTLING Industry
    See also
  Coca-Cola bottling company of Los Angeles

BOTULISM
  Lethal haven; threat to ducks at Tulare Lake. Newsweek 74:59 S 8 '69

BOTWIN, Carol
  Parent and child. N Y Times Mag p73+ Ja 11 '70

BOUCHER, Virginia P.
  Have you tried a municipal reference library? Am City 84:118-19 F '69

BOUCHET, Edward Alexander
  Edward A. Bouchet, Ph.D. il pors Negro Hist Bul 31:11 D '68

BOUGAINVILLEA
  It does anything you ask. il Sunset 142:258 My '69

BOUILLABAISSE. See Chowder

BOULAT, Pierre
  Stavros Niarchos; the other Greek; photographs. Life 66:58-65 Mr 28 '69

BOULDER, Colo.
Libraries
Have you tried a municipal reference library? V. P. Boucher. il Am City 84:118-19 F '69

BOULER, André
  Rembrandt and American art. C. J. McNaspy. America 121:370 O 25 '69

BOULEZ, Pierre
  Berlioz and the realm of the imaginary; tr. by D. Noakes. Hi Fi 19:42-6 Mr '69
  Conversations with Pierre Boulez; interview, ed. by R. Gelatt. Harper 238:96-100 Je '69

about
Boulez at Blossom. B. Murray. il por Hi Fi 19:MA26-7 O '69
Boulez in top form. I. Kolodin. Sat R 52: 51 Ja 25 '69
Conductors at work. E. Greenfield. il por Hi Fi 19:14+ S '69
Don't try to hum along with Pierre Boulez. S. De Gramont. por Esquire 71:102-5+ F '69
Letter from Paris; conducting of BBC orchestra at the Palais de Cahillot. Genêt. New Yorker 45:127-8 My 24 '69
Music. D. Hamilton. Nation 209:325-6 S 29 '69
Music; Philharmonic series and Hunter college performances. D. Hamilton. Nation 208:549-50 Ap 28 '69
Music to my ears; appearances with the New York philharmonic. I. Kolodin. Sat R 52:51 Ap 5 '69
Music to my ears; final program with New York philharmonic orchestra. I. Kolodin. Sat R 52:52-3 Ap 19 '69
Music to my ears; third program with the New York Philharmonic orchestra. I. Kolodin. Sat R 52:61+ Ap 12 '69
Musician of the month. M. Bernheimer. Hi Fi 19:MA4 Ap '69
Partisan pied piper. il por Time 93:52 Je 20 '69
Philharmonic chooses. por Newsweek 73:61-2 Je 23 '69
Recordings. M. Mayer. Esquire 71:52+ Je '69
Revolutionary. H. Saal. pors Newsweek 73:96 Mr 24 '69

BOULOGNE, Charles Damien
  Reassessing transplants. il por Newsweek 74:73 S 1 '69

BOULTON, Laura Craytor
  Americans not everyone knows. C. W. Ferguson. PTA Mag 63:16-18 Ja '69

BOULWARE, Lemuel Ricketts
Boulware writes on Boulwarism. por Bsns W p24+ Ag 30 '69
BOULWARISM in collective bargaining. See Collective bargaining
BOUMEDIENNE, Houari
Would-be leader of Arab militants. R. W. Howe. New Repub 160:11-12 F 15 '69
BOUND, Charles F.
Franklin U.S. a plan to enlist talent, provide training; adaptation of address, April 10, 1969. Pub W 195:32-4 Ap 21 '69
BOUNDARIES
See also subhead Boundaries under names of countries, states, etc. e.g. Russia— Boundaries
BOUNDS, John H.
Bahamas. bibliog Focus 19:1-7 My '69
BOUQUETS, Dried. See Flowers, Dried
BOURBON whiskey. See Whiskey
BOURDEAUX, Michael
Valya and Vadim struggle for religious faith. America 121:614-16 D 20 '69
BOURDET, Claude
Alexander Werth; obituary. Nation 208:358 Mr 24 '69
France without father. Nation 208:589-90 My 12 '69
French referendum. Nation 208:526-9 Ap 28 '69

about

Claude Bourdet. Nation 208:388 Mr 31 '69
BOURDON, David
Andy Warhol's exhibition. Art N 68:44-5+ O '69
Disposable art; plastic man. Life 67:62-7 Ag 22 '69
Life art review. Life 67:12 O 24 '69
What on earth! Life 66:80-3+ Ap 25 '69
BOURGEOIS, Louise
Fabric of construction; interview. Craft Horiz 28:30-5 Mr '69
BOURGOIGNIE, Jacques, and others
Cyclic guanosine monophosphate: effects on short-circuit current and water permeability. bibliog Science 165:1362-3 S 26 '69
BOURGUIBA, Habib ben Ali
Bourguiba: wise voice of the Arab world. D. Reed. por Read Digest 94:175-6+ Je '69
BOURKE, George
From tip to top in Florida. See issues of Travel
BOURKE, Sean Alphonsus
Irish 'who' in a British whodunit. M. Mok. il pors Life 66:59-62 Ja 24 '69
BOURKE-WHITE, Margaret
Incredible will of creativity. R. Graves. por Life 66:3 Je 27 '69
BOURLAND, D. David, jr
Un-isness of is. il Time 93:69 My 23 '69
BOURRET, J. A. and others
Fungal endogenous rhythms expressed by spiral figures. bibliog Science 166:763-4 N 7 '69
BOUSSOIS-Souchon-Neuvesel-Saint-Gobain merger. See Business consolidations and mergers—France
BOUTILIER, Joy
Joy Boutilier dance company, Henry street playhouse. A. J. Fortney. Dance Mag 43:80-1 Ja '69
BOUTOS. See Dolphins (mammals)
BOUTWELL, Jane
Guild at work. Opera N 33:26-9 Mr 8; 26-9 Mr 15; 26-9 Mr 29; 20-3 My 17; 18-20 Je 14 '69
(ed) See Cranko, J. Dancing master
BOUTWELL, William D.
Happenings in education. See issues of PTA magazine
Is there a college in his future? PTA Mag 63:10-12 bibliog(p34) Je '69
Our obsolescent leisure-time education. PTA Mag 64:12-14 bibliog(p36) O '69; Same abr. Ed Digest 35:25-7 D '69
BOUVIER family
Bouviers, by J. H. Davis. Review
New Repub 160:27-8 Ap 12 '69. G. W. Johnson
Sat R 52:46 Ap 12 '69. P. L. Meras
Time il 93:114+ My 16 '69
Bouviers; excerpts. J. H. Davis. il pors Ladies Home J 86:123-30 F; 90-3+ Mr '69
BOVASSO, Julie
Gloria and Esperanza. Criticism
Sat R 52:54 Ap 19 '69
Moon dreamers. Criticism
New Yorker 45:58 D 20 '69
BOVET, Daniel, and others
Genetic aspects of learning and memory in mice. bibliog Science 163:139-49; 165:1148 Ja 10, S 12 '69
BOVINE mastitis. See Mastitis

BOW and arrow
Look what's happened to bows and arrows; computer design and the use of new materials. N. Carlisle. il Pop Mech 132:120-3 S '69
See also
Archery
BOW hunting. See Hunting with bow and arrow
BOWDITCH, Nathaniel
Bowditch. W. S. Kals. il por Motor B 123:136-7+ Ja '69
BOWEN, Catherine Drinker
Biographer and his hero; excerpt from The craft and the calling. Am Heritage 20:16-17 D '68
Plotting the biography; excerpt from Biography: the craft and the calling. Writer 82:16-18 F '69
BOWEN, Elizabeth
New ways of the future. Am Home 72:69-71 O '69
BOWEN, Ezra
Hero in a sneak box. Sports Illus 31:46-50+ S 1 '69
I finally got the point. Sports Illus 30:60-2+ F 10 '69
BOWEN, Howard R.
New era for higher education; address, March 4, 1969. Vital Speeches 35:373-9 Ap 1 '69
BOWEN, John
Lost state of Franklin. Travel 131:47-9+ Mr '69
BOWEN, John, 1924-
Little boxes. Criticism
Nation 209:703 D 22 '69
New Yorker 45:116 D 13 '69
BOWEN, Vaughan T. and others
Strontium-90: concentrations in surface waters of the Atlantic Ocean. bibliog Science 164:825-7 My 16 '69
BOWER, Anthony
Barbados. Harp Baz 102:82+ Ap '69
BOWERING, George
Adonai; poem. Nation 209:416 O 20 '69
On Quadra Island; Passport doves; poems. Poetry 114:78-9 My '69
BOWERS, Faubion
Music. Vogue 153:106 Mr 1 '69
Opera primer: who paints the scenery? Opera N 33:26-9 F 8 '69
Sixty-year-old controversy flares up again; Koussevitzky-Scriabin scandal. Hi Fi 19:55+ Je '69
BOWERS, Gerald W.
Fisherman's paradise on workingman's budget. Outdoor Life 144:64-7+ Jl '69
BOWERS, William S.
Juvenile hormone: activity of aromatic terpenoid ethers. bibliog Science 164:323-5 Ap 18 '69
BOWERS. See Arbors
BOWFISHING. See Fishing with bow and arrow
BOWKER, R. R, company
See also
Carey-Thomas award
BOWL football games. See Football
BOWLEGS. See Leg
BOWLER (hat) See Hats
BOWLES, Cherri
Total art experience for third graders. Sch Arts 68:37-8 Ap '69
BOWLES, Chester
America's next rendezvous with destiny. Sat R 52:17-19+ S 6 '69
BOWLES, Paul
Scenes; poems. Harp Baz 102:114-15+ Ja '69
BOWLEY, Clinton J. and others
Sunglint patterns: unusual dark patches. bibliog Science 165:1360-2 S 26 '69
BOWLING
Breakthrough for the Kiddie Korps at Akron; Firestone tournament. K. Chapin. Sports Illus 30:100-2 Ap 14 '69
High jinks in the alley, cats: investigating Des Moines's bowling establishments. B. Asbille. il Sports Illus 30:26-7 Mr 17 '69
BOWLING alleys
High jinks in the alley, cats; investigating Des Moines's bowling establishments. B. Asbille. il Sports Illus 30:26-7 Mr 17 '69
See also
BarChris construction corporation

Equipment and supplies
Laxative that didn't work; corporate write-offs. Forbes 104:55-6 O 15 '69
BOWLING balls
Rolling out a new bowling ball. il Pop Sci 194-90-1 F '69

BOWLING GREEN state university. See Ohio.
State university, Bowling Green
BOWMAN Barbara, and Anker, Dorothy
Score early reading. PTA Mag 64:6-8 bib-
liog(p35) N '69
—See Piers, M. W. jt. auth.
BOWMAN, Barbara Allen
Excerpt from testimony before Subcommit-
tee on constitutional rights, January 30,
1969. Cong Digest 48:115+ Ap '69
BOWMAN, Barbara H. and others
Oyster ciliary inhibition by cystic fibrosis
factor. bibliog Science 164:325-6 Ap 18 '69
BOWMAN, Eldon G.
Grizzly bear in the national parks. Am For
75:16-18+ Jl; 16-18+ Ag '69
BOWMAN, Jean G.
Green-thumb luck. Org Gard & Farm 16:32-5
Ag '69
Spring comes early with potted bulbs. Org
Gard & Farm 16:98-100 N '69
BOWMAN, Les
Truth about calling elk. Field S 74:74-5+
Ag '69
BOWMAN, M. Bruce
Circle, triangle, rectangle. Design 70:35 Sum
'69
BOWMAN'S HILL state wildflower preserve.
See Pennsylvania—Parks and reserves
BOWSER, Hallowell
Books are not expendable. Sat R 52:22 Je 7
'69
One every minute. Sat R 52:16 My 31 '69
BOWYER, Richard
Church and Farmington no. 9. Chr Cent 86:
161-2 Ja 29 '69
BOX cameras. See Cameras
BOX lunches. See Lunches
BOXER, Arthur D.
Camps and the new morality; address, 1969.
Camp Mag 41:15+ S '69
BOXERS
In the corner for kicks. Dr F. Pacheco. M.
Kram. il Sports Illus 30:34-8 Je 2 '69
Unconquerable Muhammad Ali. H. J. Mas-
saquoi. il Ebony 24:16x-70+ Ap '69
See also names of boxers, e.g. E. Charles
BOXES, cases, etc.
Passion for boxes. J. T. Butler. il House B
111:98+ My '69
See also
Eyeglass cases
Laundry boxes, kits, etc.
BOXES, Toy. See Toys—Storage
BOXING
Boxing's great white hoopla; T. Brenner.
J. Kirshenbaum. il Sports Illus 31:48-50+
Jl 21 '69
Brawler at the threshold; Jerry Quarry vs
Joe Frazier. M. Kram. il Sports Illus 30:
28-30+ Je 16 '69
Fighting marine they named MacArthur;
twenty-two consecutive knockouts. M.
Kane. il Sports Illus 32:46-7 Ja 5 '70
Flaunt it and you may lose it; J. Quarry
vs J. Frazier. M. Kram. il Sports Illus 31:
26-9 Jl 7 '69
Frankie the banger gets bombed; DePaula-
Foster fight. M. Kane. il Sports Illus 30:
46-7 F 3 '69
Frazier's quarry; Frazier-Quarry fight. il
Newsweek 74:84 Jl 7 '69
Hungry Bobby Foster. il Ebony 24:124-6+
S '69
Jose settles an old account; Griffith-Napoles
fight. J. Kirshenbaum. il Sports Illus 31:40-1
O 27 '69
Knock-out by a brain-in; light heavyweight
E. Spence. P. Putnam. il Sports Illus 30:
42-4 Mr 3 '69
Nino's hook stopped a Roman riot; L. Rod-
riguez-N. Benvenuti fight. M. Kram. il
Sports Illus 31:24-7 D 1 '69
Ruben wilts a Rose; championship bantam-
weight fight. J. Tobin. il Sports Illus 31:
10-13 S 1 '69
Super fight; Ali v. Marciano. il Time 95:59
Ja 19 '70
Winner, and still (partial) champ; Frazier-
Quarry fight. il Time 94:36 Jl 4 '69

Laws and regulations

Blind man's buff; case of Gypsy Joe Harris.
M. Kram. il Sports Illus 30:68-72+ Mr 10
'69

Photographs

Art of Ali; with account by M. Kane. il
Sports Illus 30:48-57 My 5 '69
BOY on the straight-back chair; drama. See
Tavel, R.

BOY scouts
Building to serve; theme of the 1969 Boy
scout jamboree. J. Colgate. il Parks & Rec
4:38-9+ O '69
Meet today's scouts. T. Irwin. il Parents Mag
44:64-5+ O '69
BOYAN, A. Stephen, Jr
Democrats confront 1970. Nation 209:600-2 D
1 '69
BOYCOTT
Arabs step up Israeli boycott. Bsns W p80+
Ag 23 '69
Boycott of GE goods may prolong strike.
Bsns W p32-3 N 29 '69
Clergy and the grape strike; Delano verdict.
M. Day. America 121:114-17 Ag 30 '69
Consumer revolt; meat boycotts. il News-
week 74:74+ S 15 '69
Don't eat grapes along with me. W. F.
Buckley, jr. Nat R 21:715 Jl 15 '69
Four-year strike, two-year boycott; show-
down. il U S News 67:83-4 Jl 14 '69
Grape boycott still in force. America 120:291-
2 Mr 15 '69
Labor in the vineyard; the boycott and the
NLRA. R. B. Taylor. il Nation 208:591-3
My 12 '69
Letter from Delano. C. Chávez. Chr Cent 86:
539-40 Ap 23 '69; Discussion. 86:110-11,
1115-16 Je 11, Ag 27 '69
Obstinacy of Bill Schanen; advertisers with-
drawal from newspapers. J. Pekkanen.
Life 67:59 S 26 '69
Pentagon scabs. Ramp Mag 7:12+ N 30 '68
Profiles; C. Chávez. P. Matthiessen. New
Yorker 45:42-4+ Je 21; 43-4+ Je 28 '69
Rights for farm workers. America 120:492-3
Ap 26 '69
Strike to boycott to what? GE case. Nat R
21:1256 D 16 '69
What the blacks found out; boycott by Mar-
shall County negroes. M. L. Berzon. Na-
tion 208:793-5 Je 23 '69
Wrath of grapes. il Time 93:24 My 16 '69
Year of turmoil and decision; Olympic boy-
cott; ed. by J. Olsen. L. Alcindor. il Sports
Illus 31:35-8+ N 10 '69
BOYCOTTS, School. See School boycotts
BOYD, Alan Stephenson
Working for a different Johnson. il por Time
93:63-4 Ja 31 '69
BOYD, Andrew
Coming winter of discontent. Nation 209:566-
9 N 24 '69
BOYD, Joe Dan
Backyard crop brings in $15,000. Farm J
93:77 Ap '69
BOYD, John
Assassin. Criticism
Nation 209:579-80 N 24 '69
BOYD, M. F.
Pin money conversion. Library J 94:4228
N 15 '69
BOYD, Malcolm
Interview with Malcolm Boyd; ed. by P. Gran-
field. por Cath World 208:208-13 F '69
BOYD, Robin
Australia square. Arch Forum 130:26-35 Ap
'69
BOYD, William, and others
Other city; excerpts. pors Ebony 24:90-1+
Jl '69
BOYD, William B.
Post modern youth; address, November 18,
1968. Vital Speeches 35:246-50 F 1 '69
BOYER, Calvin J. See Heineke, C. D. jt. auth
BOYER, J. S.
Free-energy transfer in plants. bibliog Sci-
ence 163:1219-20 Mr 14 '69
BOYER, L. L. Jr
How to keep down noise levels in computer
facilities. bibliog Arch Rec 145:165-6 My
'69
BOYER, Samuel H. and others
Hemoglobins A and A₂ in New World
primates: comparative variation and its
evolutionary implications. bibliog Science
166:1428-31 D 12 '69
BOYER, Susan
Private model for public schools. Sat R 52:
99 F 15 '69
BOYKIN, Arsene O.
Student activism drama; roles for the princi-
pal. bibliog Clear House 44:145-8 N '69
BOYKIN, Matt
Bonanza in Red Springs. P. Carry. il por
Sports Illus 31:42+ Jl 28 '69
BOYLE, James Ambrose
Kennedy's time of trial. il por Newsweek
74:19-20 S 8 '69
Men who may decide Kennedy's fate. por
U S News 67:18 S 15 '69

BOYLE, Leo
Television advertising for the small bookstore. por Pub W 196:59-60 Jl 7 '69
BOYLE, Marjorie O'Rourke
Toward a theology of garbage. Commonweal 90:200-1 My 2 '69
BOYLE, Robert H.
Fishing. Sports Illus 31:66+ O 20 '69
Uncrowned king of caviar; excerpt from The Hudson River, a natural and unnatural history. Sports Illus 31:70-6+ N 3 '69
BOYLE, Tony. See Boyle, W. A.
BOYLE, William Anthony
Coal mining. A. B. Hume. Atlan 224:22+ N '69
In the wake of John L. Lewis. J. Hill. Commonweal 90:430-1 Jl 11 '69
John L. wins again. Newsweek 74:76+ D 22 '69
Lewis heir faces revolt. il por Bsns W p110+ N 15 '69
Mine-union battle: just beginning? por U S News 67:79 D 22 '69
Mine workers: can they survive reform? por Bsns W p32 D 20 '69
Mine workers' revolt. il por Newsweek 73: 74 Je 16 '69
Miners play rough. E. Cox. New Repub 161: 13-14 Ag 2 '69
Shades of John L. il por Newsweek 74:83-4+ D 15 '69
Underground revolt. por Time 93:92 Ap 18 '69
UMW battle heats up. il por Bsns W p51 My 10 '69
BOYLON, Francis Oscar
Catching up with the times. Forbes 104:43 Jl 15 '69
BOYS
Great date debate; panel discussion by seven girls. Seventeen 28:332-3+ Ag '69
How to write to a boy. il Seventeen 28:102-5+ Je '69
In my opinion; boys should cry too! C. Hrdlicka. Seventeen 28:202 O '69
Rate your date. A. L. Doenecke. Seventeen 28:152-3 My '69
State of the boy, 1969; findings of study by Daniel Offer. R. Kramer. il N Y Times Mag p97+ Mr 30 '69; Discussion. p 14+ Ap 27 '69
Telephone tactics; or, Every boy is a telephone operator. D. Rustin. il Seventeen 28:14+ Ag '69
Young living; questions and answers. A. Wood. See issues of Seventeen
    See also
Little leagues
School children
BOYS clubs of America, incorporated
America's Boy of the year. il Ebony 24:70-2+ Jl '69
BOYS haircuts. See Haircutting
BOYS rooms. See Childrens rooms
BOYS schools. See Private schools
BOYSENBERRIES
Boysenberries, without the birds. G. L'Allemand. il Org Gard & Farm 16:50 Ap '69
BOZELL, L. Brent
Is conservatism dead? Nat R 21:317 Ap 8 '69
BRA. See Brassieres
BRABYN, Howard
Race between education & catastrophe. UNESCO Courier 23:11-13 Ja '70
BRACE, William F. See Byerlee, J. D. jt. auth.
BRACELET; story. See Simon, M. L.
BRACELETS. Medic-alert. See Identification tags, bracelets, etc.
BRACEROS. See Migrant labor
BRACKEN, Peg
Middle age: for adults only; excerpts from I didn't come here to argue. Read Digest 95: 86-8 D '69
Peg Bracken's 108 original sins; excerpts from I didn't come here to argue. McCalls 96:74-5+ S '69
Why you should make your kids miserable. Redbook 133:69+ Ag '69
BRACKMAN, Arnold C.
Indonesia: another Communist disaster. bibliog f Cur Hist 56:156-60+ Mr '69
BRACKMAN, Jacob
Films. See issues of Esquire
BRADBURY, Ray
Beautiful one is here! story. McCalls 96:62-3 Ag '69
BRADDOCK, Clayton
Where standard English seems foreign, and is taught as if it were. Ed Digest 34:52-3 Ap '69

BRADEN, Thomas W.
Columnists; Washington's third pair. il por Time 94:68 Ag 15 '69
BRADERMAN, Eugene M.
Contributions of foreign investment to national development. Dept State Bul 61: 359-62 O 27 '69
BRADFORD, Albert. See Evans, D. M. jt. auth.
BRADFORD, Ernle
Democracy's fortress: unsinkable Malta. Nat Geog 135:852-79 Je '69
BRADFORD, Jean
How to get alone with your husband. Read Digest 94:71-4 My '69
BRADFORD, M. E.
Leaven in a heavy lump. Nat R 21:393-4 Ap 22 '69
BRADFORD, William
Bradford paintings in New England. E. P. Birk. il Antiques 96:864 D '69
BRADLEY, Gene E.
Trade: rift of reason. Nations Bsns 57:96-9 S '69
BRADLEY, Harold B.
Designing for change: problems of planned innovation in corrections. bibliog f Ann Am Acad 381:89-98 Ja '69
BRADLEY, Isabel K.
Playing fields of Ware. Todays Ed 58:24-6 My '69
BRADLEY, Omar Nelson
Organizing with confidence; interview. pors Nations Bsns 57.42-3+ Ap '69
    about
Tunes of glory. il por Time 93:20 Je 13 '69
BRADLEY, Sam
Serpent Mound; Uncle Satyr; poems. Poetry 115:14-15 O '69
BRADLEY, Thomas
Bitter victory. il por Time 93:28-9 Je 6 '69
Black ballot power. il por Newsweek 73:36 Ap 14 '69
Bradley challenge. il por Time 93:26 My 23 '69
Mayor Yorty's big upset. il por Newsweek 73:31-2 Je 9 '69
Negro mayor for Los Angeles? por U S News 66:12 Ap 14 '69
Round one for Bradley. Nation 208:485 Ap 21 '69
Sad Sam. il por Time 93:28 Ap 11 '69
That new black magic. il por Newsweek 73: 40+ My 26 '69
Victory for a specter. P. Kerby. Nation 208: 749-50 Je 16 '69
What Yorty's victory shows about the mood in Los Angeles. por U S News 66:36 Je 9 '69
BRADLEY, Valerie Jo
First black man to survive heart transplant. Ebony 24:82-4+ My '69
BRADSHAW, George
Florida surprises. Vogue 153:184-5+ Ja 15 '69
Lustrous binge. Vogue 155:178+ Ja 1 '70
Travel. Vogue 153:100+ Ja 15 '69
BRADSHAW, Glenn R.
Are juried exhibitions worth saving? Am Artist 33:56-7+ F '69
Jackson's prairie. Am Artist 33:60-5 My '69
BRADSHAW, Hank
Georgia is helping America learn to fish. Field & S 73:10-13 F '69
Jumping with bass. Outdoor Life 144:48-51 Ag '69
Madness for muskies. Field & S 73:66-7+ Mr '69
To find a quail. Field & S 74:34-5+ D '69
—and Bradshaw, Vera
Championship goose calling. Field & S 74: 140-1 N '69
Eight ways to hop up a snowmobile engine. Pop Mech 131:138-41 Ja '69
Exploring Idaho. il Todays Health 47:34-7+ Je '69
Now you can see tornadoes on TV. Pop Mech 131:93-6+ Mr '69
BRADSHAW, Jon
Holding to schedule with W. H. Auden. Esquire 73:136-9+ Ja '70
BRADSHAW, Lillian (Moore)
New ALA officer. S. G. Whitten. por ALA Bul 63:1166-8 S '69
BRADSHAW, Vera. See Bradshaw, H. jt. auth.
BRADSHER, Henry S.
Tibet struggles to survive. For Affairs 47: 750-62 Jl '69
BRADWAY, John S.
(ed) Progress in family law. bibliog f Ann Am Acad 383:1-158 My '69

BRAKES, Airplane
USAF, Proxmire A-7 brake views diverge. K. Johnsen. Aviation W 91:75 Ag 18 '69
BRAKES, Automobile
Behold, disc binders! B. Lang. il Hot Rod 22:98-9 S '69
Brakes for your car; special report. R. Day. il Pop Sci 194:117-32 Mr '69
Brakes to make panic stops safer; no-skid, no-lock brakes. il Changing T 23:13-15 Ap '69
Give yourself a brake. B. Lang. il Hot Rod 22:98-9 Ja '69
Light hubs & heavy stoppers; aluminum conversion kits. B. Lang. il Hot Rod 22:42-3 Ap '69
Stop V-dubs! J. Thawley. il Hot Rod 22: 92-3 D '69
Super stoppers. K. Ludvigsen. il Motor T 21:36-9 Je '69
What you should know about trailer brakes. V. L. Oertle. il Pop Sci 195:111-13 Jl '69

Control
Control that roll! demand for Hurst's Line/loc. J. Dianna. il Hot Rod 22:70 F '69

Maintenance and repair
Taking care of the dual brake system. T. Tappett. il Mech Illus 65:75-7+ Ap '69
BRAKES, Bicycle
Braking peculiarity of some Raleigh bikes; pedal-operated coaster brakes. il Consumer Rep 34:560 O '69
BRAKES, Motorcycle
Brake job for your motor bike. il Mech Illus 65:112-13 F '69
BRAMBILLA, Alberto Blasi. See Blasi Brambilla, A.
BRAMHAM, Kenneth
Marina expansion in the Med. Yachting 126: 58+ D '69
BRAMMER, J. D. and White, R. H.
Vitamin A deficiency; effect on mosquito eye ultrastructure. bibliog Science 163:821-3 F 21 '69
BRANAN, Karen
Set of attitudes. Sat R 52:67 Ap 19 '69
BRANCH, C. H. Hardin
Patient must prescribe for the physician. bibliog Ment Hy 53:403-9 Jl '69
BRANCH, Hilda S. Rollman-. See Rollman-Branch, H. S.
BRANCH, William McKinley
Alabama Branch. New Repub 161:10 S 6 '69
BRANCH banking. See Banks and banking—Branch banking
BRANCH factories
New plants dot the black slums. il Bsns W p 100+ Mr 22 '69
BRANCH libraries. See Libraries—Branches and stations
BRANCH weaving. See Weaving
BRANCUSI, Constantin
Brancusi: master of reductions. il por Time 94:88-9 O 17 '69
Essence of things; display at New York's Guggenheim museum. D. L. Shirey. il por Newsweek 74:137 D 8 '69
Is Brancusi still relevant? exhibition at the Philadelphia museum. J. Tancock. il Art N 68:40-3+ O '69
BRAND, Sister Marian Frances
Antihero; poem. Chr Cent 86:255 F 19 '69
Requiem for a nun-gardener; poem. Chr Cent 86:510 Ap 16 '69
Soliloquy in a poetry seminar; poem. Engl J 58:1060 O '69
BRAND, Mary
Sundials. Ceram Mo 17:18-19 My '69
BRAND, Stewart
Missal for mammals. il por Time 94:74+ N 21 '69
BRANDEIS university, Waltham, Mass.
Angry and alone together. K. G. Gross. Nation 208:207-10 F 17 '69
Black power play; report from Brandeis. D. Brudnoy. Nat R 21:66 Ja 28 '69
Blacks at Brandeis. M. Rosenthal and others. Commonweal 89:727-30 Mr 14 '69; Reply. E. Witten. 90:131+ Ap 18 '69
Brandeis: how a liberal university reacts to a black take-over. B. Nelson. Science 163:1431-4 Mr 28 '69
Doves v. hawks on campus. D. Brudnoy. Nat R 21:172-4 F 25 '69
Eleven days at Brandeis, as seen from the president's chair. M. B. Abram. il N Y Times Mag p28-9+ F 16 '69; Discussion. p97-8 Mr 9; 12+ Mr 16; 119 Mr 30 '69

Theater; productions by the performing arts department. H. Hewes. Sat R 52:24 Je 7 '69
War of the words; interview, ed. by P. Brinkley-Rogers. M. Abram. Newsweek 73: 68-9 Ja 27 '69
BRANDES, Norman S.
Group psychotherapy in the treatment of emotional disturbance. bibliog Ment Hy 53: 105-9 Ja '69
Influence of the emotionally disturbed teacher on schoolchildren. Ment Hy 53:606-10 O '69
BRANDES, Therese J.
Fan; interview. New Yorker 45:21-3 Ag 2 '69
BRANDIES, Monica
Vegetables by the boxful. Org Gard & Farm 16:100-1 Ja '69
BRANDON, Henry
(ed) See Lippmann, W. Talk with Walter Lippmann, at eighty, about this minor dark age
Robert McNamara's new sense of mission. N Y Times Mag p40-1+ N 9 '69
State of affairs. See issues of Saturday review
BRANDSTADTER, Judith T.
Acrylics in the classroom. Sch Arts 68:28-9 Ap '69
BRANDT, Bill
Gallery; photographs. Life 67:8-11 O 10 '69
about
Brandt's Britain. M. R. Weiss. il Sat R 52:52-3 O 25 '69
BRANDT, Edwin H.
Moving finger rites. Esquire 72:253-6+ D '69
BRANDT, Karl
How to avoid making our planet unlivable; address, August 15, 1969. Vital Speeches 35:712-15 S 15 '69
BRANDT, Larry G.
Spinners: an articulation of the curriculum. Engl J 58:1064-70 O '69
BRANDT, Richard M.
Durham education improvement program. Todays Ed 58:62-4 F '69
BRANDT, Willy
New Germany of Willy Brandt; interview, ed. by B. Cate. por Time 94:36 N 14 '69
Nixon lands on Willy Brandt's special island; interview, ed. by R. Meryman. por Life 66:28-9 Mr 7 '69
North Atlantic council celebrates the 20th anniversary of the signing of the North Atlantic treaty; opening remarks, April 10, 1969. Dept State Bul 60:350 Ap 28 '69
West Germany; address, October 28, 1969. Vital Speeches 36:105-14 D 1 '69
about
After twenty-five years. New Repub 161:9-10 N 8 '69
Brandt and the bogeyman. W. S. Schlamm. por Nat R 21:1061-2 O 21 '69
Brandt era begins. Newsweek 74:59 N 10 '69
Brandt on the threshold. il por Newsweek 74:46-7 O 13 '69
Demolishing a shibboleth. por Time 93:31 Ap 25 '69
Germany on a new path, which way will it lead? il por U S News 67:20+ O 13 '69
Germany's changing role; interview, ed. by R. Haeger. por U S News 67:28-32 D 29 '69
Getting together in Europe. Time 94:34+ N 14 '69
New team. Newsweek 74:46+ N 3 '69
Once an outcast, now on top; portrait of a chancellor. por U S News 67:12-13 N 3 '69
Open house on the Rhine. il por Time 94:24+ O 31 '69
President Nixon congratulates Chancellor Brandt of Germany; text of letter, October 21, 1969. R. M. Nixon. Dept State Bul 61: 415 N 17 '69
West Germany; outcasts at the helm. il pors Time 94:24-6+ O 10 '69
West Germany's decision for the 70's. il por Time 94:24 O 3 '69
Willy Brandt looks ahead. J. A. Morris, jr. Nation 209:363-4 O 13 '69
Willy Brandt's wanderjahre are finished. D. Binder. il pors N Y Times Mag p34-5+ N 30 '69
Willy vs. Walter. Newsweek 75:24 Ja 5 '70
BRANDT, Yanna Kroyt
What doctors now know about your unborn baby. Redbook 132:69-71+ F '69
BRANDWEIN, Larry. See Lubin, M. jt. auth.
BRANDY, Orville L. and others
Alaskan upper miocene marine glacial deposits and the turborotalia pachyderma datum plane. bibliog Science 166:607-9 O 31 '69

BRANDYWINE CREEK
Brandywine basin; defeat of an almost perfect plan. P. Thompson. il Science 163: 1180-2 Mr '69; Reply. G. E. Willeke. 164:769 My 16 '69

BRANEMARK, P. I. See Skalak, R. jt. auth.

BRANG, James A.
Bass like wildfire. por Outdoor Life 143:58-9+ Mr '69
Lunker-busting on the level. Field & S 74:12-14+ Jl '69

BRANIFF international airways
Braniff monorail system at Dallas to begin soon. N. S. Himmel. Aviation W 90:85 Mr 31 '69
Economic slowdown cuts growth in South America air traffic. il Aviation W 91:80 O 20 '69
Marketing push, cost cutback cited in Braniff profit climb. Aviation W 90:34 F 17 '69
Tomorrow's air terminal, today. H. Apter. il Travel & Camera 32:33-4 Mr '69

BRANSCOMB, Lewis M.
McElroy proposed to head NSF; Branscomb, Bureau of standards. P. M. Boffey. por Science 164:1504-6 Je 27 '69
National bureau of standards prepares for the 1970's. il por Science 165:864-74 Ag 29 '69
Spate of science appointments. por Sci N 96:5-6 Jl 5 '69

BRANSON, Roy E.
Time to meet the evangelicals? Chr Cent 86: 1640-3 D 24 '69

BRANT, Rosemary
Flow within; poem. Ment Hy 53:409 Jl '69

BRANT. See Geese. Wild

BRANTON, Daniel. See Waaland, J. R. jt. auth.

BRASH, Edward
Airmail; poem. Poetry 114:11 Ap '69

BRASHEAR, Sher
Appalachia is where my heart is. por Seventeen 28:86-7+ Jl '69

BRASS polishes. See Polishing materials

BRASSAÏ
Brassai comes to America; interview. ed. by J. Deschin. por Pop Phot 64:20+ Mr '69
Brassai's Paris; interview. pors Travel & Camera 32:72-5+ Mr '69

BRASSIERES
Big letdown; anti-bra movement. il Newsweek 74:49-50 S 1 '69
Reshaping nature: the history of the brassiere. P. Battelle. il Ladies Home J 86: 80+ O '69
Wither the bra. C. Lindsay. il McCalls 97:90-1+ N '69

BRASSINE, Phillip C.
Transistor curve tracer. Radio-Electr 40:33-6+ D '69

BRASWELL, Joseph
Designer virtuoso. il House B 111:124-9 O '69

BRATHWAITE, Edward
Critic of the month. L. Lieberman. Poetry 114:56-7 Ap '69

BRATISLAVA biennale. See Art—Exhibitions

BRAUDE, Michael
Am I my brother's salesman? poem. Chr Cent 86:1412 N 5 '69

BRAUDY, Leo
Newsreel: a report. Film Q 22:48-51 Wint '68

BRAUDY, Susan
As Arlo Guthrie sees it . . . kids are groovy. Adults aren't. N Y Times Mag p56-7+ Ap 27 '69
How honorable are honorary degrees? McCalls 96:86+ Je '69

BRAUER, Earle W.
Sun and you; excerpts from Your skin and hair. Vogue 153:111+ Je '69

BRAUER, Erich
Beyond the nightmare. il por Time 93:76-7 Je 13 '69

BRAUN, Henry
Shed; poem. Poetry 115:31-2 O '69

BRAUN, Saul
Cop as social scientist. N Y Times Mag p40-7+ Ag 24 '69
Going the rounds with a Dow recruiter. N Y Times Mag p27-9+ Ap 13 '69

BRAUN, Toby
Rockets; poem. Seventeen 28:210 Ag '69

BRAUTIGAN, Richard
Auction; story. Vogue 155:179 Ja 1 '70
Weather in San Francisco; story. Vogue 154: 126 O 1 '69
Wood; poem. Poetry 115:30 O '69

about
Energy and whimsy. A. H. Norman. il por Newsweek 74:53C+ D 29 '69

BRAVERMAN, Miriam
In touch; connecting the library's resources to the ghetto. por Wilson Lib Bul 43:854-7 My '69

BRAVERY. See Courage

BRAVES (baseball) See Baseball clubs

BRAYBROOKE, David
Marcuse's merits. Trans-Action 6:51-4 O '69

BRAYBROOKE, Neville
Up from antiquity. Sat R 52:34+ Mr 1 '69

BRAYMAN, Harold H.
Really beautiful stuff. Sci Digest 65:70-2 My '69

BRAZELTON, T. Berry
Infants and mothers: differences in development; excerpts; with biographical sketch. por Redbook 133:38, 85-7+ O '69
Second month of life: reaching out; excerpts from Infants and mothers: differences in development. Redbook 134:75+ D '69
Third month: the baby is a person; excerpts from Infants and mothers: differences in development. Redbook 134:52-3+ Ja '70
When infants come home; excerpts from Infants and mothers: differences in development. Redbook 134:82-3+ N '69

BRAZIL
See also
Amazon River
Amazonas
Arts and crafts—Brazil
Colleges and universities—Brazil
Elections—Brazil
Fishing—Brazil
Foreign visitors in Brazil
Geology—Brazil
Government, Resistance to—Brazil
Guerrillas—Brazil
Housing—Brazil
Investments, Foreign (in Brazil)
Newspapers—Brazil
Ouro Preto
Salvador
São Paulo
Textbooks—Brazil
World war, 1939-1945—Brazil

Commerce
See also
Brazil—Industries

Commercial treaties and agreements
U.S. and Brazil sign agreement on soluble coffee: Department announcement with exchange of notes. Dept State Bul 60:455 My 26 '69

Economic conditions
For Rio's market, it's still carnival. Bsns W p36+ S 6 '69
Measurement of modernism, by J. A. Kahl. Review
Américas 21:41-2 Ja '69. F. D. McCann, jr
When inflation gets out of hand; the story of Brazil. il U S News 67:83-4 D 22 '69

Foreign relations
Washington backs the pooh bahs. D. Bonafede. Nation 208:663-6 My 26 '69

History
Ouro Preto, gold, art and revolution in Brazil. D. Bestal. il Travel & Camera 32: 72-9 Ag '69

Industries
Taming the jungle for profit. il Bsns W p 162-3 S 13 '69

Native races
See Indians of South America—Brazil

Politics and government
Brazil: repression and resistance. Chr Cent 86:1413 N 5 '69
Brazilian storm warning. F. B. Kent. Nation 208:178-9 F 10 '69
Brazil's bishops criticize junta. America 121: 250 O 4 '69
Camouflaging the braid. Time 94:39 S 12 '69
Cold blood in Brazil; Anti-Communist hunt commando. T. E. Quigley. Commonweal 90: 452-3 Jl 25 '69
Dictatorial rule. Sr Schol 94:14 Ja 17 '69
Generals' choice. il Newsweek 74:64 O 20 '69
News you won't find in Brazil's newspapers. B. Lando. il New Repub 161:11-12 Ag 2 '69
No cheers for the heroes; fifth anniversary of army's revolution. il Time 93:36 Ap 11 '69
Report from Brazil: what the left is saying. J. Yglesias. il N Y Times Mag p52-3+ D 7 '69
Reports. D. Bonafede. Atlan 223:14+ Ap '69

BRAZIL—Politics and government—*Continued*
Too bad; military troika takes over. News-
week 74:44-5 S 15 '69
You can take Brazil out of Portugal, but—.
H. Estenssoro. Commonweal 91:5-6 O 3 '69
See also
Elections—Brazil

Religious institutions and affairs
World around us (cont) Chr Cent 86:1179-80
S 10 '69
See also
Catholic church in Brazil

Social life and customs
Annual vibrations; carnaval. il Time 93:36+
F 14 '69
Soccer: opium of the Brazilian people. J. Le-
ver. il Trans-Action 7:36-43 D '69
BRAZILIAN students
Better than riots; volunteers in Amazonia.
il Time 93:42+ Mr 21 '69
BREA, LA. See La Brea, Los Angeles
BREACH of contract
Into the breach: twelve students at Columbia
charged university trustees with breach of
contract. Nat R 21:61-2 Ja 28 '69
BREAD
Apricots flavor this coffee bread. il Sunset
142:156 Ap '69
Bake the bread. il Am Home 72:96+ O '69
Bread you bake. D. Eby. il Bet Hom & Gard
47:80-5+ O '69
Brioche, queen among breads. J. A. Beard.
il House & Gard 135:133+ My '69
Coffee with a Swedish twist. il Sunset 142:
180 Mr '69
Come to my bread buffet. N. B. Nichols. il
Farm J 93:80 Mr '69
Eat; French nut bread and Portuguese *broa*.
M. Cantwell. Mlle 68:62+ F '69
Fast yeast breads and rolls. il Bet Hom &
Gard 47:99-100+ Ap '69
For Easter morning, a coffee cake duckling.
il Sunset 142:180-1 Ap '69
Fresh from the oven. il Redbook 133:116-17+
O '69
It's thin, flat, quick, foldable; lefse. il Sunset
143:153-4 D '69
Mmm, mmm! Smell that homemade bread!
il Farm J 93:76-9 Mr '69
Our beautiful Christmas breads. il Sunset 143:
54-5 D '69
Picnic loaves and pastries. L. Seibert. il
House & Gard 135:101-3+ Je '69
Sour rye with a hearty flavor. il Sunset 143:
225 O '69
Sourdough bread for sportsmen. C. Massey.
il Field & S 74:40-1+ D '69
Three flours are its secret. il Sunset 142:142
F '69
Treasury of breads. J. Hewitt. il N Y Times
Mag p95-6 Mr 16 '69
Treat for Easter Sunday; Jeweled egg in
emerald nest. il Farm J 93:96-7 Ap '69
Whole wheat joins with sourdough. il Sunset
142:170 Ap '69
See also
Bakers and bakeries
Coffee cake
Muffins

BREAKFAST foods. See Cereal foods
BREAKFASTS
Bacon roll and other lively breakfast ideas
that can be made in a trice. il McCalls
96:124-5+ Mr '69
Better breakfast ideas. il Bet Hom & Gard
47:114 Mr; 100 Je; 124 S; 120 O; 118 N '69
Mourning meal; British breakfast. Time 95:37
Ja 5 '70
Regional breakfasts. il Ebony 24:160+ Ap
'69
Starting the day in high style. C. Claiborne.
il N Y Times Mag p 104-6 D 14 '69
Tray decorations. L. L. Bodine. il Horti-
culture 47:26-7 N '69
See also
Brunches
BREAST
The bosom; symposium. il Ladies Home J
86:78-83+ O '69
New young body, new bosom. il Vogue 155:
140-1+ Ja 1 '70
Surgery
Healthier bosom: all the latest medical &
surgical news. J. Ramsey. il Ladies Home
J 86:82+ O '69
Overcoming problems after breast surgery:
mastectomy. Good H 169:183 S '69
Still a woman; breast-cancer surgery. W. S.
Ross. Read Digest 94:165-6+ Mr '69

BREAST amputation. See Breast—Surgery
BREAST cancer. See Cancer
BREAST feeding
How to have a healthy baby. L. W. Sauer.
il PTA Mag 63:29-30 Mr '69
Return to breast-feeding? il Newsweek 75:
62-3 Ja 12 '70
BREATHING. See Respiration
BREATHING apparatus. See Respiratory appa-
ratus
BREAUX, Elwyn E. and Perry, T. D.
Inman E. Page outstanding educator. Negro
Hist Bul 32:8-12 My '69
BRECHER, Edward M.
We are all our mothers' daughters; what sex
research reveals about unhappy wives; ex-
cerpts from The sex researchers. Redbook
134:71+ N '69
BRECHT, Bertolt
Ghost of Brecht. J. P. O'Connell. Atlan 223:
110-13 Ja '69
Resistible rise of Arturo Ui. Criticism
Commonweal 89:528 Ja 24 '69
BRECKENFELD, Gurney
Letter from the publisher. J. R. Shepley.
il por Time 93:17 Ap 4 '69
BREEDER reactors. See Nuclear reactors
BREEDING
If you want to raise pedigreed animals.
Good H 168:157 F '69
See also
Cattle breeding
Eugenics
Genetics
Horse breeding
Swine breeding
BREEDLOVE, C. H. Jr
Determination of acetic acid in vinegar using
gravimetric titrimetry. por Chem 42:24-5
My '69
—and Bailey, G. R.
Demonstrating Faradays laws. pors Chem 42:
26-7 F '69
BREEDS of cattle. See Cattle—Breeds
BREELING, James L.
Are we snacking our way to malnutrition?
Todays Health 48:48-50+ Ja '70
Marketing protein for the world's poor. To-
days Health 47:42-5+ F '69
BREHAN, marquise de, fl 1786
Washington miniature. R. Davidson. il An-
tiques 96:318+ S '69
BREINER, Leon
Verdicts of history; take the hatred away,
and you have nothing left; O. and G.
Sweet in white neighborhood. T. J. Flem-
ing. il Am Heritage 20:74-80+ D '68
BREMER, John
A curriculum, a vigor, a local abstraction.
Ed Digest 35:13-16 S '69
Experiment: Philadelphia's school without
walls. Life 66:40-2 My 16 '69
BREMME, Wolfgang
Great margin maul. Duns R 94:90+ S '69
BREMNER, R. M.
Plastic sewer liner. Am City 84:98-101 S '69
BRENNAN, Donald George
Argument for ABM. Cur 106:10-14 Ap '69
Case for missile defense. bibliog f For Affairs
47:433-48 Ap '69
Start on strategic stabilization. Bul Atom Sci
25:35-6 Ja '69
BRENNAN, John
Gould theory. Nat R 21:802+ Ag 12 '69
Where are you Fr O'Brien? Where are you,
Fr Fitzgerald? Nat R 21:231+ Mr 11 '69
BRENNAN, Joseph Gerard
Morals or literature: the abstractive fallacy.
Engl J 58:226-9 F '69
BRENNAN, William Joseph, 3d
Mob scene in Jersey. W. Schechner. Com-
monweal 89:514-15 Ja 24 '69
BRENNER, Joe
Removing broken studs. Hot Rod 22:85 D '69
BRENNER, Michael J.
France's new defense strategy and the At-
lantic puzzle. Bul Atom Sci 25:4-7 N '69
BRENNER, Teddy
Boxing's great white hoopla. J. Kirshen-
baum. il pors Sports Illus 31:48-50+ Jl 21
'69
BRENT, Stephen
Divvying up Alaska. New Repub 161:11-13 D
13 '69
BRENTANO'S bookstores (New York) See
Booksellers and bookselling—New York
(state)
BRERETON, Nina
I hurt! I hurt! I hurt! Seventeen 28:144-5+
F '69
BRESLER, David E. and Bitterman, M. E.
Learning in fish with transplanted brain
tissue. bibliog Science 163:590-2 F 7 '69

BRESLER, E. H. and Wendt, R. P.
Diffusive and convective flow across membranes: irreversible thermodynamic approach. bibliog Science 163:944-5; 166:1438 F 28, D 12 '69

BRESLER, Robert J.
Wilmington: occupied city. Commonweal 89: 513-14 Ja 24 '69

BRESLIN, Jimmy
Column right, column left. il por Newsweek 73:58 Mr 3 '69
Joining a bigger league. il Time 93:76 F 28 '69
Literary ticket for the 51st state. R. Woodley. il por Life 66:71-2 My 30 '69
Odd couple. il por Newsweek 73:37-8 My 12 '69
Year of New York. Time 93:98 Ap 11 '69

BRESNAHAN, James F.
White racism. America 120:278-80 Mr 8 '69

BRESSON, Henri Cartier-. See Cartier-Bresson, H.

BRETH, Fred E.
Do high protein drinks threaten milk? Farm J 93:D7+ Ap '69

BRETHREN, Church of the. See Church of the Brethren

BRETON, André
Program to remake human understanding. A. Balakian. Sat R 52:19-21 My 31 '69

BRETTON WOODS conference. See United Nations monetary and financial conference

BREUER, Marcel
Breuer two. il Arch Forum 130:35 My '69

BREUGHEL, Peeter. See Brueghel, P.

BREWER, Gene C.
Plywood-Champion: after the merger. S. Blickstein. il Duns R 94:52-5 O '69
Why top executives fall out. por Bsns W p60 Mr 29 '69

BREWER, James
Gandhi's South African settlement. Chr Cent 86:950+ Jl 16 '69

BREWER, Jo
How to attract butterflies. Horticulture 47: 24-5+ Jl '69

BREWER family
Brewer coat-of-arms. H. K. Eilers. il Hobbies 74:114-15 My '69

BREWING industries
Keeping your head in the beer business. il Bsns W p 138:40+ S 13 '69
   See also
Anheuser-Busch, incorporated
Coors, Adolph, company
Heileman, G, brewing company
Miller brewing company
Rheingold breweries, incorporated

BREWSTER, Kingman, 1919–
Admission of women to Yale college; address, November 14, 1968. Sch & Soc 97:162-4 Mr '69
   about
Antidote for cynicism; excerpt from address, September 1969. por Time 94:47 S 26 '69
Scenario. Nation 208:588 My 12 '69
Seven-year itch. Newsweek 74:101 O 6 '69
Yale revisited. S. Alsop. Newsweek 73:120 My 19 '69

BREZHNEV, Leonid Il'ich
For greater unity of communism; address, June 7, 1969. Vital Speeches 35:573-92 Jl 15 '69
Our internationalist duty; address, October 28, 1969. Vital Speeches 36:101-5 D 1 '69
   about
B and K: maintaining the status quo. il por Newsweek 74:45-6 O 27 '69
Brezhnev: man to watch in the Kremlin. il por U S News 67:68-9 D 8 '69
Brezhnev sets the clock back. H. Kamm. il N Y Times Mag p 14-15+ Ag 10 '69; Discussion. p 12+ Ag 24 '69

BREZONIK, Patrick L. and Harper, C. L.
Nitrogen fixation in some anoxic lacustrine environments. bibliog Science 164:1277-9 Je 13 '69

BRIBERY
Big shakedown in Baton Rouge. A. J. Reichley. il Fortune 80:96-9+ Ag 1 '69
$1 million end to an unjust exile. D. Wolf. il Life 66:67 Je 27 '69
Unjust exile of a superstar; case of C. Hawkins. D. Wolf. il Life 66:52-52B+ My 16 '69
   See also
Politics, Corruption in

BRICK driveways. See Driveways

BRICK walks. See Walks (paths)

BRICKER, John William
Where are they now? il pors Newsweek 74: 18 D 15 '69

BRICKER amendment. See United States—Treaties

BRICKLIN, Mark
New, new, self-improved me! Read Digest 94:123-5 F '69

BRICKMAN, William W.
Books for educators. Sch & Soc 97:301-2+, 501-2+ Sum, D '69
New assault on academic freedom. Sch & Soc 97:268 Sum '69; Same abr. Ed Digest 35:40-1 N '69
Newer clichés in education. Ed Digest 34: 32-3 F '69

BRICKS
Building blocks for adults; bricks make patterns. il Mech Illus 65:62 D '69

BRIDES
   See also
Weddings

BRIDGE (game)
Almost anonymous partner; V. Mitchell. C. Goren. il Sports Illus 30:58-9 My 12 '69
Bridge. A. Truscott. See issues of New York times magazine
Call it a signal victory. C. Goren. il Sports Illus 30:68-9 Je 2 '69
Four youthful new kings. C. Goren. il Sports Illus 30:96-7 Ap 14 '69
Goren's Christmas quiz. C. Goren. il Sports Illus 31:80-2+ D 22 '69
Lean on your defense; contract bridge. C. Goren. il Sports Illus 31:100+ N 17 '69
Little computer that teaches you bridge: Bridgeveryone. P. Wahl. il Pop Sci 195: 170 N '69
Mystic Wei of the East. C. Goren. il Sports Illus 31:46-7 Jl 21 '69
South had a golden rule. C. Goren. il Sports Illus 30:44+ Je 30 '69

BRIDGE fishing. See Fishing

BRIDGE players
Bidding like a Roman Blue with Benito; E. Kaplan. C. Goren. il Sports Illus 30:54 Mr 31 '69
Chalk one up for youth. C. Goren. il Sports Illus 31:58-9 O 6 '69
Four youthful new kings. C. Goren. il Sports Illus 30:96-7 Ap 14 '69
Girls bid it right. C. Goren. il Sports Illus 31:68-9 N 3 '69
Goodby to a perfect partner; H. Sobel. C. Goren. il Sports Illus 31:96 S 22 '69
Picking the champions a bit ahead of time. C. Goren. il Sports Illus 31:79-80 O 27 '69
Two lame ducks in the Bowl; World bridge team championship. C. Goren. il Sports Illus 30:63-4 My 5 '69
Win or lose in any position. C. Goren. Il Sports Illus 30:86-7 Je 9 '69
   See also
Blackwood, E.

BRIDGE to Killybog fair; drama. See Watts, F. B.

BRIDGE tournaments
Aussie squeeze on the Chinese; Far Eastern bridge championship. C. Goren. Sports Illus 30:58 F 10 '69
Corn's aces prove they're really pros. C. Goren. Sports Illus 31:104+ S 15 '69
Prof ducks a trap. C. Goren. il Sports Illus 30:66-7 Mr 17 '69
Solution to a silly slam. C. Goren. il Sports Illus 30:55 F 24 '69
Two lame ducks in the Bowl; World bridge team championship. C. Goren. il Sports Illus 30:63-4 My 5 '69

BRIDGER, James
Old Gabe of Her Majesty's English life guards. M. Goosman. il Am West 6:14-15 N '69

BRIDGER, Wagner. See Golden, M. jt. auth.

BRIDGER national forest, Wyo. See National forests

BRIDGES, Bill
Brave words from a Hawk and a Warrior. A. Wright. por Sports Illus 30:26-8+ Mr 24 '69

BRIDGES, Douglas W.
Computerized management; or, Jungle administration. Parks & Rec 4:37-8+ D '69

BRIDGES
   See also
Chesapeake Bay bridge-tunnel
Hudson River bridges
   also subhead Bridges under names of cities, e.g. London—Bridges

   Accidents
Death of a bridge by vibration; 1940 collapse of Tacoma bridge. il UNESCO Courier 22: 31 D '69

   Floors
Bridge deck overlay gains stability with asbestos fibers; George Washington bridge. il Am City 34:37-9 F '69

BRIDGES—*Continued*

Materials

Aluminum pedestrian bridge a first; Pontiac, Mich. J. Koren. il Am City 84:49 F '69

Safety devices and measures

Water-filled cells stop traffic crashes; water bumpers on New York's George Washington and Verrazano bridges. il Am City 84: 102 N '69

BRIDGES, Foot

Aluminum pedestrian bridge a first. J. Koren. il Am City 84:49 F '69

Up, up and away: bridge over highway in Wyoming, Mich. il Am City 84:54 Je '69

BRIDGES, Pedestrian. See Bridges, Foot

BRIDGMAN, Betty

Lady political ghost speaks up. Writers Digest 49:51 N '69

BRIEHL, Daniel

Air pollution. America 120:580-2 My 17 '69

BRIEN, Alan

Sex: the new status symbol. Mlle 69:62+ Jl '69

BRIER, Herbert S.

Amateur radio. Pop Electr 30:87+ Mr '69

BRIER, Warren J.

Newspaper feature market. Writer 82:27-9 Je '69

BRIGANDS and robbers

Paradise lost; lives of bandits who robbed Glasgow-to-London royal mail train. il Time 94:34 O 31 '69

See also

Outlaws

Thugs

BRIGGEMAN, Jane

Christian faith and beauty: congenial terms. por Chr Today 14:52 O 10 '69

BRIGHAM, Morton R.

Proposed St Joe wilderness. Liv Wildn 33:15-18 Sum '69

BRIGHAM Young university, Provo, Utah

Are we bandwagoneers? reasons against changing to LC at Brigham Young university library. M. E. Lamson. bibliog ALA Bul 63:1278-9 O '69

Trouble in Happy Valley. il Newsweek 74: 102-3 D 1 '69

BRIGHT children. See Children, Gifted

BRIGHTON festival. See Music festivals—England

BRILLEMAN, Edna Lane

Why the yacht broker. Motor B 123:127 Ja '69

BRILLIANT, Alan

Searching for signs; poem. Poetry 114:362-3 S '69

BRIMACOMBE, Gerald

Siege of water; photographs. Life 66:53-9 Ap 25 '69

BRIMBERG, Robert

Lucrative lunch. il por Newsweek 73:79-80 Je 2 '69

BRIMBERG and company

Lucrative lunch. il Newsweek 73:79-80 Je 2 '69

BRIMM, Claude Edward

Gospel of BRIMM. il por Newsweek 74:98+ D 8 '69

BRIMM, R. P.

Course electives. Clear House 43:417-20 Mr '69

BRIMMER, Andrew Felton

Black capitalism, it offers little, says a top Negro. por U S News 68:9 Ja 12 '70

Black revolution and the economic future of Negroes in the United States; excerpts from address, June 8, 1969. Am Scholar 38:629-43 Aut '69

Black studies; a top Negro's view: excerpts from address, August 28, 1969. por U S News 67:12 S 8 '69

Profit versus pride: the trouble with black capitalism. Nations Bsns 57:78-9 My '69

about

Blacks debate black capitalism. por Bsns W p38 Ja 10 '70

Bridge to nowhere? por Newsweek 75:59 Ja 12 '70

BRINHART, Betty

Florida sunshine and papaya. Org Gard & Farm 16:62-4 D '69

Greenhouse that pays for itself in one season. Org Gard & Farm 16:80-1 Ja '69

Increasing hyacinth bulbs. Horticulture 47: 16-17+ My '69

Madonna lily. Org Gard & Farm 16:42-3 Ag '69

Storing cannas. Horticulture 47:24+ O '69

Tulips by the hundreds. Org Gard & Farm 16: 52-5 S '69

BRINKLEY, David

Mr Brinkley goes to New York. pors Time 93:82+ Mr 14 '69

BRINNIN, John Malcolm

Middle age: a Chinese restaurant; poem. New Yorker 45:58 N 22 '69

BRIOCHE. See Bread

BRISCO, Milo M.

Jamieson and Brisco of Jersey Standard. por Fortune 80:39 O '69

BRISCOE, Cecil D.

Reading program. Clear House 43:373-7 F '69

BRISKIN, Jacqueline

How will I know? story. Seventeen 28:178-9 Ap '69

BRISSETT, Donald T.

Operation raincheck. Weatherwise 22:64-7 Ap '69

BRISSON, Lance. See Carlson. R. jt. auth.

BRISTER, Bob

How to rattle whitetails and muleys! il Field & S 74:28-9+ D '69

BRISTLECONE pine. See Pine

BRISTLEWORMS. See Annelids

BRISTOL, Conn.

Total-cost bidding saves in the long run. K. W. Gordon. il Am City 84:104+ Ag '69

Galleries and museums

Clock watching, 19th-century style; interview, ed. by S. Nerenberg. il House B 111:50-1 Ag '69

BRISTOL, Va. and Tenn.

Most complex city. Am City 84:78 Ja '69

BRITAIN, Battle of. See World war, 1939-1945

—Great Britain

BRITANNICA atlas. See Atlases

BRITISH

See also

English

BRITISH aircraft corporation

BAC names Davies technical director. Aviation W 91:70 Ag 18 '69

BRITISH-American tobacco company

Bold bet of British-American tobacco; cosmetics venture. J. Ross-Skinner. il Duns R 94:32-3+ Jl '69

BRITISH association for the advancement of science

British AAS: counterattack on gloom about science and man. D. S. Greenberg. Science 165:1239-40 S 19 '69

BRITISH coins. See Coins

BRITISH COLUMBIA

See also

Architecture, Domestic—British Columbia

Gardening—British Columbia

Stikine River

Vancouver

Vancouver Island

Description and travel

Notes from the century before, by E. Hoagland. Review

Commentary 48:107-8+ S '69. M. B. Lowry

Up B.C. 101, along the sunshine coast. il Sunset 143:24-5 Ag '69

Politics and government

Provincial election with a long reach; key issue, free enterprise vs. Marxist socialism. Bsns W p31 Ag 23 '69

BRITISH Commonwealth. See Commonwealth of nations

BRITISH cookery. See Cookery, English

BRITISH council of churches

British churches set new goals for international development. Chr Cent 86:1445 N 12 '69

BRITISH East India company. See East India company

BRITISH economic assistance. See Economic assistance, British

BRITISH empire. See Commonwealth of nations

BRITISH Ford. See Ford motor company, limited, Dagenham, England

BRITISH gipsies. See Gipsies in England

BRITISH humor. See Humor, English

BRITISH illustrators. See Illustrators

BRITISH Labor party. See Labor party (Great Britain)

BRITISH money. See Money—Great Britain

BRITISH national trust. See National trust for places of historic interest or natural beauty

BRITISH Open golf tournament. See Golf—Tournaments

BRITISH overseas airways corporation
  BOAC earnings climb for year despite strike.
    Aviation W 91:48 Ag 25 '69
  Bunny club airline; BOAC's The beautiful
    singles of London tour. il Time 94:58+ S
    26 '69
  Canceled date. il Newsweek 74:86 S 29 '69
  Pilots strike grounds BOAC. Aviation W 90:
    29 Ap 7 '69
BRITISH petroleum company
  Affair of state. Newsweek 74:98B+ O 20 '69
  Blocking the British; disputed merger be-
    tween BP and Sohio. il Time 94:98 O 17 '69
  British are coming. il Newsweek 73:84 Ap 21
    '69
  British petroleum gets Sohio visa. Bsns W
    p38 N 22 '69
  BP strikes again; Sohio merger plans. il
    Newsweek 73:84 Je 16 '69
  BP's new boy has welcome mat yanked; BP-
    Sohio merger. Bsns W p48 O 11 '69
  Britons strike oil in Ohio. il Bsns W p40-1
    Je 7 '69
  Jersey, Texaco, Gulf, meet BP. il Forbes
    103:32+ Ap 1 '69
BRITISH portraits. See Portraits, British
BRITISH royal ballet. See Royal ballet, Great
    Britain
BRITISH sculptors. See Sculptors, British
BRITISH society for social responsibility in
    science
  Britain: scientists form new group to pro-
    mote social responsibility. D. S. Greenberg.
    Science 164:931-3 My 23 '69
BRITISH steel corporation
  Competitive twist for steel; Lord Melchett
    of Landford to run the steel industry.
    Bsns W p40 +Jl 19 '69
  Ingots round his neck. Fortune 80:186 Ag 15
    '69
BRITISH tournament and tattoo. See Great
    Britain—Army—Scottish regiments
BRITISH united airways
  African route fight forms. Aviation W 91:33
    O 6 '69
BRITISH VIRGIN ISLANDS
  Going places, finding things in the Virgin
    Islands. J. Wilson. il House & Gard 135:
    26+ F '69
  We had them to ourselves; cruising the Vir-
    gins in the early '30s. D. Puleston. il Yacht-
    ing 126:64-5+ N '69
BRITTAIN, W. Christie
  Discovering New Brunswick. Travel 131:40-
    3+ Ap '69
BRITTAN, Samuel
  Britain's economists; confused and confus-
    ing self-contradictory irresponsible, igno-
    rant. Fortune 79:183-4 Ja '69; Correction.
    79:67 Ap '69
BRITTANY
  Brittany: revolution in a cemetery. M. Main-
    waring. Nation 208:229-33 F 24 '69
  Occupying power. il Newsweek 73:49 F 3 '69
BRITTEN, Benjamin
  No ivory tower; interview. por Opera N
    33:8-11 Ap 5 '69
                    about
  Britten. by P. M. Young. Review
    Am Rec G 35:435-7 Ja '69. J. Diether
  Britten premiere and a mad King George.
    E. Greenfield. Hi Fi 19:MA26-7 Ag '69
  Britten's unchanged aesthetic. D. Hamilton.
    Hi Fi 19:90 N '69
  Loners. S. Jenkins, jr. Opera N 33:24-5 Ap
    5 '69
  Operas of Benjamin Britten, by P. Howard.
    Review
    Am Rec G por 36:70-2 S '69. J. Diether
  Peter Grimes. Criticism
    Opera N il 33:17-20 Ap 5 '69
BRITTEN, Roy J. and Davidson, E. H.
  Gene regulation for higher cells: a theory.
    bibliog Science 165:349-57 Jl 25 '69
BRITTON, Wright
  Sailing Iceland's rugged coasts. por Nat
    Geog 136:228-65 Ag '69
BROADBENT, Robert V.
  Mark of the grizzly. Outdoor Life 144:68-71+
    Ag '69
BROADCASTING (periodical)
  Nicholas Johnson vs. Broadcasting. R. L.
    Shayon. Sat R 52:82+ Ap 12 '69
BROADHEADS. See Arrowheads
BROADS, The. See Norfolk Broads, England
BROADWAY. See New York (city)—Streets
BROADWAY, New York (theater district) See
    New York (city)—Theater
BROCADE
  Brocaded embellishment in textiles; exhibition
    at the Los Angeles County museum of art.
    E. Birk. il Antiques 95:8 Ja '69

BROCCOLI
  Bigger, better, and earlier; broccoli. L. Ri-
    otte. il Org Gard & Farm 16:40-2 D '69
BROCHETTERIA (restaurant) See New York
    (city)—Hotels, restaurants, etc.
BROCHURES. See Pamphlets
BROCINER, Victor
  Loudspeakers, can we measure what we
    hear? Electr World 81:25-9+ Mr '69
BROCK, Alice
  Alice's cookbook. il por Time 94:67 O 24 '69
  Alice's; family of folk song fame becomes
    a movie. J. Stickney. il pors Life 66:43-5+
    Mr 28 '69
  Alice's restaurant's children. il Newsweek 74:
    101-4+ S 29 '69
BROCK, Lou
  Highlight. por Sports Illus 31:60 Jl 28 '69
BROCK, Paul
  Jokes the old masters used to play. Sci Di-
    gest 65:12-17 My '69
  Saga of the Sargasso. Motor B 123:195-7 Ap
    '69
  Twelve ways you can learn to predict the
    weather. Sci Digest 66:23-7 D '69
BROCK, Peggy Ann
  (ed) See Keyes, F. P. Exclusive interview
    with Frances Parkinson Keyes
BROCK, Ray
  (ed) See Beltz, J. John Beltz the new doctor
    Oldsmobile
                    about
  Alice's; family of folk song fame becomes
    a movie. J. Stickney. il por Life 66:43-5+
    Mr 28 '69
BROCK, Robert E.
  Metal boxes built to size. Electr World 81:
    84 Mr '69
  Use the wired board technique. Radio-Electr
    40:23-6 Mr '69
BROCK, Stanley E.
  Cat that kills with a single spring. Read
    Digest 94:152-4+ My '69
  Jungle challenge. Outdoor Life 143:64-7+ Ap
    '69
BROCK, Thomas D. See Bott, T. L. jt. auth.
BROCKELBANK, William John
  Family desertion problem across state lines.
    bibliog f Ann Am Acad 383:23-33 My '69
BROCKI, A. C.
  New literature for inner-city students. Engl
    J 58:1151-61 N '69
BROCKMAN, John
  Underground. J. Gruen. Vogue 153:138 My '69
BROCKTON, Mass.
  Park site lends serendipity to new art mu-
    seum; Fuller memorial. il Arch Rec 145:
    188-90 Je '69
    Education
  Keeping up; new high school. B. B. Stretch.
    Sat R 52:58-9 Jl 19 '69
BROCKWAY, James
  Pathway to the sea; poem. Harp Baz 102:
    261 Mr '69
BROD, Pearl
  Middle school in practice. Clear House 43:
    530-2 My '69
BRODBELT, Samuel
  Teacher professionalization: its determina-
    tion and achievement. bibliog f Sch & Soc
    97:151-2 Mr '69
BRODER, David S.
  Permanent minority? New Repub 160:15-19
    F 1 '69
BRODERICK, Dorothy
  People; M. H. Arbuthnot. Library J 94:4198 N
    15 '69
BRODERICK, Edwin B. bp
  Albany stows its first throne. D. Grumbach.
    Commonweal 90:333-4 Je 6 '69
BRODEUR, A. E. See Fruchtl, G. F. jt. auth.
BRODIE, Arnold F. See Krishna Murti, C. R.
    jt. auth.
BRODIE, Fawn M.
  He burned the Constitution. New Repub 160:
    31-2+ F 15 '69
BRODIE, Henry
  Seventh annual review of the long-term cot-
    ton textile arrangement; statement. Octo-
    ber 8, 1969. Dept State Bul 61:404-7 N 10 '69
BRODIE, Rima
  Rima Brodie dance company; 92nd street Y.
    D. Hering. Dance Mag 43:81+ Ap '69
BRODIN, Nils Eric
  Letter from Scandinavia. Nat R 21:73+ Ja
    28 '69

BRODINE, Virginia
Secret weapons; with excerpts from testimony. bibliog Environ 11:12-26 Je '69
Unsnug harbor. Environ 11:34-6 My '69
—and others
Wind from Dugway. pors Environ 11:2-9+ Ja '69

BRODKEY, Harold
Hofstedt and Jean, and others; story. New Yorker 44:26-36 Ja 25 '69
Shooting range; story. New Yorker 45:46-54 S 13 '69

BRODSKY, Louis Daniel
God grant us the strength each and every day; poem. Camp Mag 41:47 Mr '69

BRODSKY, Mimi
Dance department with the aloha spirit. Dance Mag 43:62-5 D '69

BRODY, Jerome S. and Coburn, R. F.
Carbon monoxide-induced arterial hypoxemia. bibliog Science 164:1297-8 Je 13 '69

BROECKER, W. L.
Japanese photography today. Travel & Camera 32:72-85 O '69

BROEMEL, Carl
Cover; The sugar hut. il Am Artist 33:6 F '69

BROGAN, Colm
Letter from London. Nat R 21:232 Mr 11 '69

BROGAN, Sir Denis William
How it looks from the colonies. Esquire 72: 26+ O; 48+ D '69; 73:32+ Ja '70
Kennedy dynasty: an appraisal. Esquire 72: 162-3+ N '69

BROKE, Sir Philip Bowes Vere
Great sea battle; excerpts from Broke and The Shannon. P. Padfield. il por Am Heritage 20:29-65 D '68

BROKEN homes
Can a mother play a father's role? B. Spock. Redbook 133:46+ My '69
Children and divorce: what the teacher can do. L. B. Ames. Ed Digest 35:19-21 N '69

BROKERS
Are brokers squeezing out small investors? refusing to accept small buy and sell orders. il Changing T 23:38 My '69
Brokers feel the bear's claws. il Bsns W p 130+ S 20 '69
Brokers go on the offensive. il Bsns W p 102+ N 1 '69
How to rise from the fails; Executive securities corp. goes public. il Bsns W p 108 Je 28 '69
Let your broker hold your stocks? il Changing T 23:28 Ag '69
Local scouts hunt for talented stocks; acting as the eyes and ears for institutional investors. il Bsns W p 128+ My 17 '69
Prescribing a cure for paper mess; management consultants to Wall Street. il Bsns W p 122-3 Ap 19 '69
Pulling in its horns. Newsweek 74:58+ Ag 25 '69
Step nearer public ownership. il Bsns W p 106+ S 27 '69
Street goes public. C. Morgello. il Newsweek 74:68 Jl 28 '69
Wall Street's empty prosperity. il Fortune 79:39 Mr '69
See also
Auerbach, Pollack and Richardson, incorporated
Brimberg and company
Donaldson, Lufkin and Jenrette, incorporated
McDonnell and company
Merrill Lynch, Pierce, Fenner and Smith, incorporated
Oppenheimer fund, incorporated
Salomon brothers and Hutzler (firm)
Stock exchange

Commissions
Blood in the Street. il Newsweek 75:53-4 Ja 5 '70
Commissions. H. C. Wallich. Newsweek 74: 65 S 1 '69
Commissions: they may stay fixed. Bsns W p88 Ja 10 '70
Stock salesmen's cut may be on the block. Bsns W p41 D 13 '69
They're tearing up Wall Street. C. J. Loomis. il Fortune 80:88-91+ Ag 1 '69

Consolidations and mergers
Odd-lot firms set to merge. Bsns W p81 Ag 9 '69

BROKERS, Yacht. See Yacht brokers
BROMBERG, Walter, and George, Gerald
Can TV crime shows prevent violence? Todays Health 47:88+ My '69

BROMELIADS. See Pineapples
BROMILEY, Geoffrey W.
Historical works overshadow dogmatics. Chr Today 13:3-5 F 28 '69

BROMLEY, Albert W.
A. W. Bromley, former conservationist editor, retires from post as head of Conservation education unit. por Cons 24:35 D '69

BROMWELL, Pat
Better homes and gardens family discovers the Caribbean; interview, ed. by P. Plawin. por Bet Hom & Gard 47:153-8 O '69

BROMWELL, Ron
Better homes and gardens family discovers the Caribbean; interview, ed. by P. Plawin. pors Bet Hom & Gard 47:153-8 O '69

BRONER, Robert
Culinary print. Craft Horiz 29:52-3 My '69

BRONFENBRENNER, Martin
Japanese howdunit. por Trans-Action 6:32-6 Ja '69

BRONFMAN, Edgar Miles
Dash of bitters for a Bronfman. por Bsns W p60 N 8 '69

BRONK, Detlev Wulf
Will the science brain bank go conglomerate? J. Lear. il por Sat R 52:41-4 Jl 5 '69

BRONOWSKI, Jacob
Protest, past and present; address, June 1969. Am Scholar 38:535-46 Aut '69
Science as a humanistic discipline. Bul Atom Sci 24:33-8 O '68; 25:50 My '69
What we can't know; excerpt from The environment of change. Sat R 52:44-5 Jl 5 '69

BRONSON, William
Nome. Am West 6:20-31 Jl '69

BRONX, N.Y.
Homecoming; interview. C. Reiner. New Yorker 45:47-9 D 13 '69

Housing
See New York (city)—Housing

Synagogues
Disappearing world of a New York Jew. C. Mangel. il Look 33:66+ F 4 '69

BRONX zoo. See New York zoological park
BRONZES
French bronzes. R. Davidson. il Antiques 96:316+ S '69

Exhibitions
Five stages of Shang; Shang and Han bronze vessels at Asia house. W. Watson. il Art N 67:42-7+ N '68
Mini-monuments; French bronzes of the 17th and 18th centuries. H. Landais. bibliog il Art N 67:30-3+ N '68

BROOK Farm
Thoreau and Hecker: freemen, friends, mystics. M. W. Hess. Cath World 209:265-7 S '69

BROOK trout fishing. See Trout fishing
BROOKE, Edward William
National security; address, October 6, 1969. Vital Speeches 36:44-7 N 1 '69

about
Brooke says no. Sr Schol 94:23-4 F 28 '69

BROOKE, Gerald
Gambit accepted. il por Newsweek 74:47 Ag 4 '69

BROOKE, Rupert
Letters of Rupert Brooke; ed. by G. Keynes. Review
Commonweal 90:81-2 Ap 4 '69. M. Magalaner

BROOKHOUSE, Christopher
Witch; poem. Atlan 224:74 Ag '69

BROOKINGS institution
Advice to the new boys; report. A. Howard. New Repub 160:29-30 F 1 '69

BROOKINS, Milton, Jr
Return of the phantom. il por Newsweek 74: 24 Jl 14 '69

BROOKLINE, Mass.
Adding to the legend; J.F.K. birthplace. il Time 93:30 Je 6 '69

BROOKLYN
Architecture
Bravura in Brooklyn. C. Robinson. il Arch Forum 131:42-7 N '69

City planning
Student power in urban design. B. Thorne. il Arch Forum 131:74-7 N '69

Education
Author editor "Be in" marks Ocean Hill book week. il Library J 94:4569 D 15 '69
Battle for urban schools. W. Roberts. Ed Digest 34:4-7 Ja '69

BROOKLYN—Education—*Continued*
Due process, the real issue; Ocean Hill-Brownsville district; letter to the editor. R. Z. Sellers. Library J 94:123 Ja 15 '69; Reply. K Weibel and others. 94:1397-8 Ap 1 '69
New York school crisis; Brownsville-Ocean Hill controversy. M. J. Goldbloom; discussion. Commentary 47:22+ Ap '69
War for city schools; today, New York, tomorrow everywhere; community control. I. Mothner. il Look 33:42-4+ My 13 '69

Housing
Master builder's plan; R. Moses' Atlantic village plan. il Newsweek 73:64 My 12 '69
See also
Bedford-Stuyvesant restoration corporation, Brooklyn

Markets
Student power in urban design. B. Thorne. il Arch Forum 131:74-7 N '69

Music
See also
Brooklyn academy of music

Poetry
Poems and images: three from Brooklyn. W. Whitman; H. Crane; A. Kazin. il Travel & Camera 32:57-9 S '69

Politics and government
See New York (city)—Politics and government

BROOKLYN academy of music
Bravos in Brooklyn; performances by Guild's education department. Q. Eaton. il Opera N 33:6-7 Ap 12 '69
Dance grows in Brooklyn. H. Saal. il Newsweek 74:91 N 3 '69

BROOKLYN college
Small college program for adults. il Sch & Soc 97:208-10 Ap '69

Library
Unusual library of radical literature at Brooklyn college. il Sch & Soc 97:72-3 F '69

BROOKLYN polytechnic institute. See Polytechnic institute, Brooklyn

BROOKLYN public library
Bookmobile goes in Brooklyn. I. E. Moran. il Library J 94:4487-9 D 15 '69
Can this marriage be saved? materials selection policy. D. Bass. il Library J 94:3023-7 S 15 '69; Reply. J. C. Pine. 94:4321-2 D 1 '69
Negotiating a collective bargaining agreement, the union perspective. M. Lubin and L. Brandwein. il ALA Bul 63:973-9 Jl '69
New dimension in library administration; negotiating a union contract. R. Lewis and M. F. Payson. il ALA Bul 63:455-64 Ap '69

BROOKS, Angie E.
Human rights day, 10 December 1969; message. UN Mo Chron 6:i-iii D '69
United Nations day 24 October 1969; message. UN Mo Chron 6:i-ii O '69

about
Angie Brooks; UN's madame president. il pors Ebony 25:27-30+ Ja '70
Everybody's Miss Brooks. por Time 94:27 S 26 '69
Leading lady. il por Newsweek 74:62 S 29 '69

BROOKS, Charlotte
Our Mrs Brooks. P. Pine. il Am Ed 5:9-10 My '69

BROOKS, Colleen
Open and shut. New Yorker 45:34-5 Jl 5 '69

BROOKS, Dori
Hearty winter fare with a welcome change of pace. Home Gard 56:52 F '69
Pleasures of June's table: crispy peas, asparagus and blushing strawberries. Home Gard 56:44 Je '69
Ripe time to pickle and preserve. Home Gard 56:45 S '69
Salad bowl. Home Gard 56:71 Ap '69
Sweets & sauerbraten, and a salad surprise. Home Gard 56:60 Mr '69

BROOKS, Doyle K.
Mercury, up high Down Under. R Pop Astron 63:13-15 Mr '69

BROOKS, Edward M.
Weather prospects for next March's total eclipse. Sky & Tel 38:7-11 Jl '69

BROOKS, Gwendolyn
Henry Rago; poem. Poetry 115:95-6 N '69

about
Books that look out, books that look in. W. Stafford. Poetry 113:424 Mr '69

BROOKS, Joe
Fishing. See issues of Outdoor life
Fishing in New Zealand. Outdoor Life 144: 69-3+ D '69
Fishing in Yugoslavia. por Outdoor Life 144: 42-5+ S '69

BROOKS, John
Annals of finance (cont) New Yorker 45:74-82 Ag 23; 107-26 S 13 '69
Millionaire & the midget; excerpts from Once in golconda: a true drama of Wall Street, 1920-1938. Am Heritage 20:34-5 O '69
Reporter at large. New Yorker 45:97-8+ Ap 26 '69

BROOKS, Patricia
Make mine teppanyaki. Sat R 52:62+ S 13 '69

BROOKS, Patricia K.
Manila's new cultural center. Art in Am 57: 140-2 N '69

BROOKS, Paul
Superjetport, or Everglades Park? Audubon 71:4-11 Jl '69

BROOKS, Robert R. R.
Can India make it? Sat R 52:12-16 Ag 9 '69

BROOKS, Roger
Twins who found each other; excerpts. B. Lindeman. il pors Good H 169:107-9+ O '69

BROOKS, Thomas R.
Metamorphosis in S.D.S. the new left is showing its age. N Y Times Mag p 14-15+ Je 15 '69
Reports: Newark. Atlan 224:4+ Ag '69
Strategist without a movement. N Y Times Mag p24-5+ F 16: 117+ Mr 30 '69

BROOKS RANGE wilderness area. See Wilderness areas—Alaska

BROSIO, Manlio
North Atlantic council celebrates the 20th anniversary of the signing of the North Atlantic treaty; opening remarks, April 10, 1969. Dept State Bul 60:350-1 Ap 28 '69

BROSNAN, Jim
Have the hitters really gone? debate. Look 33:84+ My 13 '69

BROSSARD, Chandler
Harvard square. Holiday 45:50-1+ Mr '69
Place of the month. Holiday 46:90-1+ S '69
Rittenhouse square from riches to rags. Holiday 45:78-9+ Ap '69
Riviera of the American West. Holiday 46: 50-3+ Ag '69
Santa Fe, our last unspoiled city? Holiday 45:64-7+ My '69

BROTHELS. See Prostitution

BROTHERHOOD of locomotive firemen and enginemen. See United transportation union

BROTHERHOOD of man
Building of an outlook. B. W. Overstreet. PTA Mag 63:20-1 Je '69
Organization is not the essence of community; excerpts from address, August 1969. I. M. Sussman. il Cath World 210:114-18 D '69

Bibliography
Books for brotherhood. il Commonweal 89: 643-7 F 21 '69

BROTHERHOOD of teamsters. See International brotherhood of teamsters, chauffeurs, warehousemen and helpers of America

BROTHERS, Joyce
On being a woman. See issues of Good housekeeping

BROTHERS and sisters. See Siblings

BROTMAN, Herman B.
65+ incomes well under those of younger groups. Aging 173:13-14 Mr '69

BROUDY, Harry S.
Can we define good teaching? Ed Digest 35:20-3 S '69

BROUGHTON, Jacqueline
California's wild flowers from seed. Horticulture 47:38-9 S '69

BROUGHTON, T. Robert S.
(comp) Articles and other books received; ancient. See issues of American historical review

BROWARD COUNTY, Fla.

Education
Communications-arts teams. G. Marsh. il Todays Ed 58:39-41 D '69

BROWER, Brock
Incident at the Dyke bridge. Life 67:16B-25 Ag 1 '69

BROWER, David Ross
Brower power awaits the verdict. H. Peterson. por Sports Illus 30:36-8+ Ap 14 '69
Fratricide in the Sierra club. R. A. Jones. Nation 208:567-70 My 5 '69
Mom vs. apple pie. il por Newsweek 73:25 F 10 '69

BROWER, Lincoln Pierson
Ecological chemistry; with biographical sketch. Sci Am 220:12, 22-9 F '69
BROWN, Alan
Great triangle cruise. Yachting 126:68-9+ D '69
BROWN, Betty B.
Daffodils are a family affair. Home Gard 56:60-1 S '69
BROWN, Bill
Of Brown and Penland. J. Williams. il Craft Horiz 29:47 My '69
BROWN, Carol. See Tatko, D. jt. auth.
BROWN, Charles H.
How to get a bill through Congress. Todays Ed 58:30-1 Mr '69
BROWN, Chelsea
Living, breathing picture gallery. il pors Ebony 24:54-6+ Ap '69
BROWN, Clarence
Paronomasia and I'll tell you no lies. New Repub 160:30-2 Mr 1 '69
Pushkin boom. Atlan 223:107-8 Ja '69
Slightly to the right of the czar. New Repub 160:25-7 Ap 19 '69
BROWN, Claude
Two books with soul: for defiant ones. A. A. Shockley. Engl J 58:396-8 Mr '69
BROWN, Clayton E.
Death waited in white; ed. by B. East. Outdoor Life 144:58-9+ D '69
BROWN, Courtney C.
New world symphony; excerpt from World business: promise and problems. Sat R 52: 56 N 22 '69
BROWN, Davitt. See Stevenson, F. jt. auth.
BROWN, Denise Scott, and Venturi, Robert
Bicentennial commemoration 1976. Arch Forum 131:66-9 O '69
BROWN, Dennis A.
Art of bedding. Horticulture 47:25-6+ O '69
BROWN, Doris
PTA meeting is tougher. S. Myslenski. il por Sports Illus 31:69-70 D 8 '69
BROWN, Dorothy Foster
Button collecting. See issues of Hobbies
BROWN, Dorothy S.
Thesis and theme in Uncle Tom's cabin bibliog f Engl J 58:1330-4+ D '69
BROWN, Earle
Sculpture in sound. il por Time 93:48-9 Ja 24 '69
BROWN, Edmund Gerald Pat
Man who beat Nixon. il pors Newsweek 73:11 Ja 27 '69
No dice for braceros.W. Turner. Ramp Mag 7:37-40 Ja 25 '69
BROWN, Eugene R.
Birds along the Appalachian trail. Cons 23: 2-4 F '69
BROWN, Francis
Reviewing for The New York times book review. Writer 82:21 N '69
BROWN, Frederick
(tr) See Ponge, F. Taking sides with things
BROWN, Gwilym S.
Golf. Sports Illus 31:67-8 S 29 '69
Track and field (title varies) Sports Illus 31:44-5 Ag 4 '69
Winter sports. Sports Illus 30:50-1 F 17 '69
(ed) See Hill, G. Serenity on the edge of disaster
BROWN, H. Douglas
Gems and minerals. See issues of Hobbies
BROWN, H. Mack, and others
Current-voltage relations during illumination: photoreceptor membrane of a barnacle. bibliog Science 166:240-3 O 10 '69
BROWN, H. Rap
Dukes up. J. Eisen. New Repub 160:36+ Je 14 '69
BROWN, Harold
Security through limitations. For Affairs 47: 422-32 Ap '69
BROWN, Harold O. J.
Christianity: the durable establishment. Chr Today 13:3-5 Ja 31 '69
Rome and reformation today. Chr Today 14: 3-5 O 24 '69
Struggle for the German church. Nat R 21: 334-7+ Ap 8 '69
Theology of trust. Chr Today 13:3-5 Ap 11 '69
BROWN, Harry
This labyrinthine garden; Caveat everywhere; Flesh is allowed its disasters; poems. Poetry 114:322-6 Ag '69
True and lamentable account of my generation of New Englanders; poem. Sat R 52:18 Je 14 '69
BROWN, Herbert M.
Intercamp sports. Camp Mag 41:33 Ja '69
BROWN, J. H. U. and Dickson, J. F. 3d
Instrumentation and the delivery of health services. bibliog Science 166:334-8 O 17 '69

BROWN, James
Cultivated catfish; Gold platter franchises. il por Newsweek 74:66 S 8 '69
Importance of being Mr James Brown. T. Barry. il Look 33:56-62 F 18 '69; Same abr. with title Soul brother no. 1. Read Digest 94:131-4 My '69
Soul stamps. il por Time 94:74 Jl 11 '69
BROWN, James G.
Pilot's story of a hijacking: pandemonium in the cockpit. por U S News 66:36 F 24 '69
BROWN, James W.
Promise of the new media standards. Sr Schol 94:Schol Teach 34-5 Ja 17 '69
BROWN, Jimmy
Close-up: he likes to keep you psyched. R. Woodley. il pors Life 66:69-72+ My 23 '69
BROWN, John, 1800-1859
To wash this land in blood. . . S. B. Oates. por Am West 6:36-41 Jl; 24-7+ N '69
BROWN, John Carter
Change at the National gallery. por Time 93:70 My 9 '69
BROWN, John Mason
Gentle dynamo. por Newsweek 73:105-6 Mr 31 '69
Obituary
Sat R por 52:18-19 Mr 29 '69. N. Cousins
BROWN, Joseph
Jazz variation; poem. America 121:166 S 13 '69
BROWN, Ken
Only in Iceland! Travel 131:44-9+ My '69
BROWN, Kevin V.
Build this new four-place cabin plane for $3500. Pop Mech 131:112-17+ My '69
ELF: how we'll broadcast with mystery radio waves. Pop Sci 195:104-7+ S '69
Hot seat to bring 'em back alive. Pop Mech 132:90-3+ S '69
BROWN, Lionel A.
Arikara Indian ceramics. Ceram Mo 17:16-19 Mr '69
BROWN, Lloyd L.
Fomented conflict. Nation 208:179-81 F 10 '69
BROWN, Margery W.
You see, this is the way it is! Sch Arts 68:30-3 Ap '69
BROWN, Michael E.
Condemnation and persecution of hippies. bibliog por Trans-Action 6:33-46 S '69; Excerpts. Cur 112:9-13 N '69
BROWN, Norman B. See Huff. W. H. jt. auth.
BROWN, Pat. See Brown, E. G. P.
BROWN, Paul, and others
Virus of the 1918 influenza pandemic era: new evidence about its antigenic character. bibliog Science 166:117-19 O 3 '69
BROWN, Paul, 1909?-
No clink and no clank in Cincy. P. F. Putnam. il por Sports Illus 31:26-7 S 15 '69
BROWN, Peter A. G.
Exhibition of folk art. Antiques 95:252-7 F '69
Recent acquisitions at the Abby Aldrich Rockefeller folk art collection. Antiques 96:734-5 N '69
BROWN, Peter J.
Cooperative purchasing pays. Am City 84:88+ D '69
BROWN, Philip S.
Alcohol. House & Gard 135:132+ My '69
Escalopes, a meal in minutes. House & Gard 135:121-4+ Mr '69
Picnic drinks. House & Gard 135:100+ Je '69
What is your liquor I.Q? House & Gard 135: 92+ F '69
BROWN, R. Malcolm, Jr, and others
Cellulosic wall component produced by the Golgi apparatus of pleurochrysis scherffelii. bibliog Science 166:894-6 N 14 '69
BROWN, Robert McAfee
Karl Barth on election. Chr Cent 86:405-7 Mr 26 '69
Moon shot afterthoughts. Cur 111:11-12 O '69
Robert McAfee Brown on reform. Commonweal 91:215-16 N 14 '69
BROWN, Rosellen
Going on thirty; poem. Nation 209:354 O 6 '69
BROWN, Rosemary
She hears music and there's someone there. D. Bacon. il pors Life 67:48E-48F Ag 8 '69
BROWN, Royal S.
Shostakovich's symphonies. Hi Fi 19:43-7+ Ap '69
Strings and electronics pack an emotional wallop. Hi Fi 19:104 O '69
BROWN, Sam, Jr
America and the world; a new fix? A. Schlesinger, jr. Vogue 153:184-5+ F 1 '69
Politics of peanut butter. A. R. Dolan. il Nat R 21:492+ My 20 '69

BRUHN, Erik
　Beyond technique. W. Terry. il pors Sat R 52:
　　56-7 F 22 '69
　Dance magazine award, 1968. por Dance Mag
　　43:36+ Ap '69
　Report on Dance magazine award reception.
　　il pors Dance Mag 43:44-6 Jl '69
　Swedish ballet triumph. W. Terry. il Sat R
　　52:22-3+ Jl 5 '69

BRUINS (hockey team) See Hockey teams

BRUISES
　First aid. C. J. Potthoff. Todays Health 47:
　　74 My '69

BRUMAN, J. R.
　Amateur scientist. Sci Am 221:124-9 Ag '69

BRUMBY, Colin
　Touring in the Outback. Opera N 34:13 Ja
　　10 '70

BRUMEL, Valeri
　You can't keep a good high jumper down. J.
　　Schecter. il pors Sports Illus 31:72+ O 20 '69

BRUMMELL, O. B.
　Drunkenness, incest, murder, and rape,
　　fa-la-la la. Hi Fi 19:48-9 My '69

BRUMMET, R. L. and others
　Human resource myopia. Mo Labor R 92:29-30
　　Ja '69

BRUMSTED, Harlan B. See Wilkins, B. T. jt.
　auth.

BRUNCHES
　Christmas brunch, champagne and country
　　ham. il Am Home 72:52-3+ D '69

BRUNELLE, Al
　Rollin Crampton, modest master. Art N 68:
　　52-5 My '69

BRUNER, Jerome S.
　Intelligent infant. il por Time 93:56 Mr 28 '69
　Teaching man to children. il por Time 95:
　　50 Ja 19 '70

BRUNER, Louise
　Glass workshop. Am Artist 33:48-53+ F '69

BRUNGARDT, Theresa S.
　South Pacific adventure. Parks & Rec 4:48-
　　53+ Je '69

BRUNIG, Walter
　Make your grounds care-free! Mech Illus
　　65:78-9 My '69

BRUNNER, Karl
　Will tight money drop interest rates? il Bsns
　　W p 146+ Ap 19 '69

BRUNOT, James
　To my mother; poem. Nation 209:292 S 22 '69

BRUNS, Bill
　Instant-minister racket. Life 67:67-8+ N 14
　　'69

BRUNTON, Frank L.
　Squire of poodle patch. Am For 75:37+ Ap
　　'69

BRUSHES
　Brushes, useful, whimsical. il Sunset 143:97
　　D '69
　Personal-use report: new auto-mechanic's
　　brush has other uses. E. F. Lindsley. il Pop
　　Sci 194:138 Je '69
　　See also
　Paint brushes

BRUSSELS
　　　　　　Architecture
　Quartier des arts in Brussels. J. Tordeur. il
　　Antiques 96:595-7 O '69
　　　　Hotels, restaurants, etc.
　Restaurant Chantraine. M. Woodward. Travel
　　132:24 Jl '69
　　　　　　Industries
　Brussels: the executive city. J. Lambert. il
　　Duns R 93:48-51 Mr '69
　　　　　　　Music
　Report: Brussels; production of Arabella. L.
　　Mueller. Opera N 33:28 My 17 '69
　Report: Brussels; Purcell's Dido and Aeneas
　　and Berio's Laborintus II. L. Mueller. Opera
　　N 33:33 F 8 '69
　Report: production of Lohengrin. L. Mueller.
　　Opera N 34:39 D 27 '69

BRUSSELS international book fair. See Book
　fairs

BRUSSELS sprouts
　Brussels sprouts stretch the vegetable sea-
　　son. W. Masson. il Org Gard & Farm 16:
　　60 Mr '69

BRUSSELS university. See Colleges and uni-
　versities—Belgium

BRUSTEIN, Robert
　Whose university? The case for professional-
　　ism. New Repub 160:16-18 Ap 26; 13-14 My
　　17; 31+ My 24 '69; Same. Cur 108:19-24 Je
　　'69
　　　　　　　about
　Yale school of drama: winter of their dis-
　　content? E. Lester. il Holiday 46:50-1+ S
　　'69

BRUTALITY. See Cruelty

BRY, Ed
　Oxbow. il Audubon 71:27 My '69

BRY, Michael E.
　Gallery snooping. Mod Phot 33:36+ Mr '69

BRYAN, Harrison
　American automation updated. D. Fielding.
　　bibliog il Library J 94:2881-5 S 1 '69

BRYAN, J. 3d
　Colosseum. Holiday 46:70-1+ D '69
　I slaughter myself twice daily. Holiday 45:
　　16-17 My '69
　Quiet, please, while I murmur a witticism.
　　Holiday 46:14-15 S '69
　Rome's international peacock alley. Holiday
　　45:80-1+ Ap '69

BRYAN, L. W.
　Hawaii first. L. C. Littlecott. il pors Am
　　For 75:12-15+ F '69

BRYAN, W. B. and others
　Estimating proportions in petrographic mix-
　　ing equations by least-squares approxima-
　　tion. bibliog Science 163:926-7 F 28 '69

BRYAN, William Jennings
　William Jennings Bryan, by P. E. Coletta.
　　Review
　　Sat R 52:31-2 Ag 9 '69. M. L. Colt

BRYANT, Betty
　It doesn't have to taste like liver! Todays
　　Health 48:60-3 Ja '70

BRYANT, Edward
　Rediscovery: John Storrs. Art in Am 57:66-71
　　My '69

BRYANT, J. Kenneth, jr
　Counselor's number-one job: setting the
　　tone of camp; address. Camp Mag 41:10
　　Ap '69

BRYANT, Mrs Kendall Stebbins. See Pace, P.
　pseud.

BRYANT, Lynwood
　Rudolf Diesel and his rational engine; with
　　biographical sketch. Sci Am 221:12, 108-17
　　bibliog(p 136) Ag '69

BRYANT park. See New York (city)—Parks
　and playgrounds

BRYN MAWR college, Bryn Mawr, Pa.
　Bryn Mawr tells it not quite like it is; H.
　　Aptheker to head program of black studies.
　　Nat R 21:580-1 Je 17 '69
　Musical events; Donald Swann's Perelandra.
　　W. Sargeant. New Yorker 45:196+ D 6 '69

BRYOPHYTES
　　See also
　Liverworts

BRYSON, Jack F.
　Louvre comes to the classroom. Sch Arts
　　68:38-9 F '69

BRZEZINSKI, Zbigniew
　Detente in the '70s. New Repub 162:17-18
　　Ja 3 '70
　Great escape. New Repub 160:32 F 8 '69
　　　　　　　about
　Robots and rebels. A. P. Mendel; reply with
　　rejoinder. Z. Brzezinski. New Repub 160:
　　32+ F 8 '69

BUBBLE birth. See Childbirth

BUBBLE chambers
　Planning for the giant; National accelerator
　　laboratory. il Sci N 96:128 Ag 16 '69
　Recent developments in particle physics;
　　Nobel lecture, January 1969. L. W. Alvarez.
　　bibliog il Science 165:1071-91 S 12 '69

BUBBLES
　Doctor Grosse and his wonderful bubble ma-
　　chine. F. Harvey. il Pop Sci 195:60-3 N '69
　Slumping structures caused by organically
　　derived gases in sediments. J. N. Monroe.
　　bibliog il Science 164:1394-5 Je 20 '69

BUBBLES, Soap. See Soap bubbles and films

BUBER, Martin
　Jewish view of redemption. C. R. Shaffer.
　　Commonweal 90:512-15 Ag 22 '69; Discussion
　　90:574-5 S 19 '69
　Promise of Buber, by L. D. Streiker. Review
　　Chr Cent 86:1586-7 D 10 '69. D. W. Stump

BUCHAN, Alastair
　Can U.S. quit as world policeman? interview,
　　ed. by J. Fromm. por U S News 66:48-51 F
　　17 '69

BUCHAN, Perdita
　Winter in the spare-parts yard; story. New
　　Yorker 45:38-44 Mr 22 '69

BUCHANAN, Chester L.
　Strange devices that found the sunken sub
　　Scorpion; ed. by H. Shuldiner. por Pop Sci
　　194:66-71+ Ap '69

BUCHANAN, Doris
　Ah, the Irish, they're super! Yachting 126:
　　195-6 S '69
　Racing initiation. il Yachting 125:115+ Ja '69

BUCHANAN, Ernest T. 3d
Reluctant swimmer. Camp Mag 41:14-15 Je '69

BUCHANAN, Frederick S.
Secular schoolmen and Amish aims; excerpts from The old paths: a study of the Amish response to public schooling in Ohio. Sch & Soc 97:104-5 F '69

BUCHANAN, Thomas G.
Largest underwater treasure hunt. Sea Front 15:21-9 Ja '69

BUCHAREST
Theater
Theatre. H. Clurman. Nation 209:90-2 Jl 28 '69

BUCHER, J. F.
Our grapes grow best on fir trees. Org Gard & Farm 16:59-61 F '69

BUCHER, Lloyd Mark
Bucher vs. who? W. F. Buckley, jr. Nat R 21: 141 F 11 '69; Reply. 21:365+ Ap 22 '69
Dilemmas of duty. il pors Life 66:14F-23 F 7 '69
End of the affair. il por Newsweek 73:34-5 My 19 '69
How fellow officers view the case of Commander Bucher. il U S News 66:34 F 10 '69
I never surrendered. il por Newsweek 73:27 Mr 24 '69
In the matter of Lloyd Mark Bucher. B. Weinraub. il pors N Y Times Mag p25-7+ My 11 '69
Is Bucher to blame? New Repub 160:11-12 F 8 '69
Message from the Pueblo. Nation 208:620 My 19 '69
Proud men of the Pueblo. il Read Digest 94: 54-61 Je '69
Pueblo: an odyssey of anguish replayed. il por Time 93:14-16 Ja 31 '69
Pueblo: don't give up the ship, ever? il pors Newsweek 73:24-8+ F 3 '69
Pueblo surrender: who made the mistakes? il por U S News 66:58-9 F 24 '69
Rose Bucher and the ordeal of the Pueblo; ed. by D. Hellyer and S. North. R. Bucher. il por McCalls 96:72-5+ My '69
Strange tale of the Pueblo. por U S News 66: 50-1 F 3 '69

BUCHER, Rose
Rose Bucher and the ordeal of the Pueblo; ed. by D. Hellyer and S. North. pors McCalls 96:72-5+ My '69

BUCHHEISTER, Carl W. and Peterson, R. T.
John H. Baker, the Audubon years. Audubon 71:83-5 N '69

BÜCHNER, Georg
Buchner and Berg. G. Weales. Commonweal 90:264-5 My 16 '69
Wozzeck. Criticism
Commonweal 90:264 My 16 '69
Sat R il 52:24 My 17 '69

BUCHSBAUM, Walter H.
Will there be, an electronic mail service? Electr World 82:30-2+ Ag '69

BUCHTEL, Henry A.
Visual form discrimination on the basis of relative distribution of light. bibliog Science 164:857-8 My 16 '69

BUCHWALD, Art
Eyed from the eyrie; excerpts from The establishment is alive and well in Washington and Have I ever lied to you? Read Digest 95:153-6 N '69
How I grew a mustache and found happiness. pors Ladies Home J 86:74 Mr '69
Institute for utter frustration. por Travel & Camera 32:58-9 Je '69
One giant step for supermankind. McCalls 97:116 Ja '70

BUCK, Pearl (Sydenstricker)
All the days of love and courage; story Good H 169:72-3 D '69
about
Crumbling foundation. il por Time 94:60 Jl 25 '69
Pearl S. Buck: a biography, by T. F. Harris. Review
Cath World 210:138-9 D '69. P. J. Fleming

BUCK, William C.
Nil disprandum. M. Teague and Z. Cowan. il por Am Heritage 20:18-25 F '69

BUCKEYE. See Horse chestnut

BUCKINGHAM, Nash
Gone are the honkers. Outdoor Life 143:78-9+ My '69

BUCKLAND, Lawrence
Producing a $4 million book. il Pub W 196: 56-8 S 1 '69

BUCKLER, Ernest
Seven crows a secret; excerpts from Ox bells and fireflies. Read Digest 94:64-8 F '69

Son's discovery; excerpts from Ox bells and fireflies. Read Digest 95:127-30 N '69

BUCKLEY, Charles E.
Decorative arts in the City art museum of St Louis. Antiques 96:76-81 Jl '69

BUCKLEY, Fergus Reid
Delectations. Nat R 21:1067+ O 21 '69
Letter from Madrid. Nat R 21:904-6+ S 9 '69

BUCKLEY, Jack
An ancient woman. Opera N 34:8-13 D 13 '69

BUCKLEY, James T.
Reforming the university. Cath World 208: 235-6 F '69

BUCKLEY, Kevin P.
General Abrams deserves a better war. N Y Times Mag p34-5+ O 5 '69
No one can be sure what Thieu is thinking. N Y Times Mag p28-9+ Mr 2 '69

BUCKLEY, Louis F.
[Book review] America 120:257-8 Mr 1 '69

BUCKLEY, Marylou
Still life: poem. America 120:134 F 1 '69

BUCKLEY, Priscilla L.
Delectations. Nat R 21:449-50 My 6 '69
Seeing it like Mailer does. Nat R 21:129-30 F 11 '69

BUCKLEY, Richard
Posthumous stardom for a once and future lord. A. Goldman. por Life 67:13 D 19 '69

BUCKLEY, Tom
All they talk about is sex, sex, sex. N Y Times Mag p28-9+ Ap 20 '69
Answering November's big question: what is a Mario Procaccino? N Y Times Mag p7-9+ Ag 10 '69
ARVN is bigger and better, but—. N Y Times Mag p34-5+ O 12 '69
It looks like a Martian, it will land our men on the moon. N Y Times Mag p32-5+ F 23 '69
NASA's Tom Paine, is this a job for a prudent man? N Y Times Mag p34-8+ Je 8 '69
Signs are right for astrology. Read Digest 94:237-8+ My '69
Wagner tries a quiet comeback. N Y Times Mag p7+ Je 15 '69
What life's like in Vietcong territory. N Y Times Mag p48-9+ N 23 '69

BUCKLEY, William Frank, 1925-
Nixon after six months. por(p27) N Y Times Mag p4 Jl 20 '69
Notes & asides. See issues of National review
Old man in the back of the room. Nat R 21:287-8 Mr 25 '69
On experiencing Gore Vidal. Esquire 72:108-13+ Ag '69
On the right. See issues of National review
Toward an imperfect understanding of the Namath affair. Esquire 72:113+ O '69
Why Galbraith-hating is an impossible activity. Life 67:12 O 17 '69

about
Distasteful encounter with William F. Buckley jr. G. Vidal. Esquire 72:140-3+ S '69
Wasted talent; Buckley-Vidal vendetta. por Time 94:49 Ag 22 '69

BUCKMAN, Peter
Ireland's niggers; with interview with B. Devlin. Ramp Mag 8:19-22 Jl '69

BUCKMANN, Carol A. See Shields, J. T. jt. auth.

BUCKOW, Ed
Exotics: new threat to U.S. waters. Field & S 74:16+ My '69

BUCKS COUNTY, Pa.
U.S. journal: buying and selling along Route 1. C. Trillin. New Yorker 45:169-75 N 15 '69

BUCKWALTER, Len
Amazing paint-on heating element. Mech Illus 65:51-3+ Ag '69
CB radio to the rescue. Pop Sci 195:166-8+ D '69
1970 color TV: the picture is brighter than ever. Pop Sci 195:142-5+ O '69
Tape your own TV shows. Pop Mech 131:108-12+ Ap '69
Thrills in taking a flight test. pors Pop Sci 195:138-40+ N '69
What's new in 5-watt CB gear. Radio-Electr 40:48-51 My '69
World's smallest color TV. Pop Mech 130: 118-21+ D '68

BUDAPEST
Historic houses, etc.
Historic quarter of Buda. M. Horler. il Antiques 96:918-20 D '69

BUDAPEST—*Continued*

Music

Report: world premiere of Crime and punishment. D. Stevens. il Opera N 34:39 D 27 '69

BUDDHA and Buddhism
Concept of grace in Jodo Shin Buddhism. H. Hashimoto. Chr Cent 86:318-19 Mr 5 '69
Spread of Buddhist culture; reprint. A. De Silva. il UNESCO Courier 22:22-5 Ag '69
  See also
Soka Gakkai (sect)

BUDGE, Hamer Harold
Budge for the SEC. por Newsweek 73:66 Mr 3 '69
Consensus man heads the SEC. por Bsns W p68 Mr 1 '69
Democrats lean on Budge. il por Bsns W p80 Ag 9 '69
New chairman of SEC; how tough will he be? il por US News 66:13 Mr 10 '69
Tough to nudge Judge Budge. por Time 94:69-70 Ag 8 '69

BUDGET

France

French science: austerity drive ends rapid budget growth. D. S. Greenberg. Science 163:266-7 Ja 17 '69

Great Britain

Britain clamps down harder. il Bsns W p42+ Ap 19 '69
Harold's hope. il Newsweek 73:51+ Ap 28 '69

Russia

See also
Russia—Appropriations and expenditures
Russia—Armed forces—Appropriations and expenditures

United States

Administration: beginning to begin; Nixon presenting domestic program. Time 93:18-19 Ap 25 '69
Administration's money troubles. il Newsweek 74:99-100 N 17 '69
Budget: a five-year look. U S News 66:88 Je 16 '69
Budget makers face first 1971 worries. il Bsns W p45-6 S 13 '69
Budget of the United States government fiscal year 1970; excerpts. L. B. Johnson. Dept State Bul 60:95-100 F 3 '69
Budget surplus that got away; with editorial comment. il Bsns W p 15-16, 96 Ag 30 '69
Budgeting for federal responsibilities. C. J. Zwick. Ann Am Acad 379:13-21 S '68
Down and down some more. Sci N 95:399-400 Ap 26 '69
Enough brake? Newsweek 73:60+ Ap 7 '69
Fan dance; post-war budget. Nation 209:236-7 S 15 '69
Federal budget and expenditure control. E. F. Rinta. Ann Am Acad 379:22-30 S '68
Federal spending cuts now in the works. il U S News 66:94-6 Ap 28 '69
Growth and peace dividend. America 121:182-3 S 20 '69
Happier days in sight for Nixon's budget. il U S News 67:65-6 S 1 '69
Medicine ball budget. R. Hotz. Aviation W 90:11 Ja 20 '69
Mr Nixon's priorities. New Repub 160:5-6 Ap 26 '69
Nixon inherits budget that faces reality; with editorial comment. il Bsns W p 18-19, 132 Ja 18 '69
Nixon, the Negro and the budget. il Time 93:19-20 Ap 18 '69
Nixon unsheathes his budget sword. il Bsns W p22-3 Ag 2 '69
Nixon's new direction. il Newsweek 73:32+ Ap 28 '69
1.9-billion-dollar surprise in budget. U S News 67:67 Ag 11 '69
$192.9-billion budget that got away. il Bsns W p 11 Ja 3 '70
Science lets out a yell for money; new federal budget calls for curtailing R&D spending plans. il Bsns W p86-7 Ja 25 '69
Slim pickings for research. il Sci N 95:87-91 Ja 25 '69
Spending up, surplus down. il Fortune 80:24+ D '69
TRB from Washington: big fault. New Repub 160:4 My 3 '69
Tax bill could handcuff budget; with editorial comment. il Bsns W p 12-13, 84 D 27 '69
Tax exemptions, the artful dodge. H. Aaron. Trans-Action 6:4-6 Mr '69
Tight budget of $195 billion. il Newsweek 73:77-9 Ja 27 '69

200-billion budget? Why it seems near. U S News 67:78 N 24 '69
200-billion-dollar budget; the problems Nixon faces. il U S News 67:85-7 D 1 '69
Viet Nam peace and the budget. M. L. Weidenbaum. Nations Bsns 57:78 Ag '69
What dividend? post-Vietnam finances. Newsweek 74:28 S 8 '69
Where 198 billions will come from and go. il U S News 66:78-81 Ja 27 '69
Where to cut spending. Bsns W p 16 F 1 '69
Where we go beyond the moon; NASA's budget under attack. il Bsns W p98-9 Jl 19 '69
Will budget inhibit Nixon's slowdown? il Bsns W p35-6 N 15 '69
  See also
Taxation—United States
United States—Appropriations and expenditures

BUDGET, Business
It's high season for the budgeters. il Bsns W p36-7 N 22 '69

BUDGET, Household
Family money management; ed. by P. Lindberg. See issues of Better homes and gardens
How to keep from drowning in debt. il Changing T 23:7-10 F '69; Same abr. with title Way to keep your debts under control. Read Digest 94:88-91 My '69
Measuring retired couples' living costs in urban areas; with tables. M. H. Hawes. bibliog f Mo Labor R 92:3-16 N '69
New BLS budgets provide yardsticks for measuring family living costs; with tables. J. C. Brackett. bibliog Mo Labor R 92:3-16 Ap '69
Pregnancy I couldn't face. il Good H 169:12+ S '69
Tips on building a financial reserve. D. Green. Mech Illus 65.64-5+ O '69
What's happened to the family budget? S. Grafton. il McCalls 96:42+ S '69
When the problem is money; questions and answers. A. Wood. Seventeen 28:160+ N '69

BUDGET, Personal
Moneywise-senior sessions held in Massachusetts and Hawaii. il Aging 178:11 Ag '69
  See also
Finance, Personal

BUDGET, School. See School finance

BUDGETS, Library. See Libraries—Finance

BUDKER, Andrei
Matter meets antimatter in Akademgordok. G. H. Lubin. il pors Phys Today 22:62-6 Ag '69

BUDS
Recognizing woody plants in winter. E. H. Ketchledge. il Cons 24:20-7+ O '69

BUDZKO, Delia B. and Müller-Eberhard, H. J.
Anaphylatoxin release from the third component of human complement by hydroxylamine. bibliog Science 165:506-7 Ag 1 '69

BUECHNER, Frederick
Comfort for a sorrowing mother. Chr Cent 86:309 Mr 5 '69
Despair in the final hour. Chr Cent 86:340 Mr 12 '69
Finality and completion. Chr Cent 86:396 Mr 26 '69
Forgiveness for failed saints. Chr Cent 86:244 F 19 '69
[Meditations] Chr Cent 86:244, 276, 309, 340, 364, 396, 436 F 19-Ap 2 '69
Promise of paradise. Chr Cent 86:276 F 26 '69
Thirst for fulfillment. Chr Cent 86:364 Mr 19 '69

BUECHNER, Robert D.
Bird's eye view can help park officials. Parks & Rec 3:27-8+ N '68
Consultants, guidelines for selection. por Parks & Rec 4:54+ S '69

BUEGEL, Kenneth F.
Last-word, IC stereo tuner. Radio-Electr 40:36-40 Je '69
125 watts per channel stereo amplifier. Radio-Electr 40:41-4+ Ap '69
Stereo IC preamp. Radio-Electr 40:45-7 My '69

BUEHLER, Alfred G.
Cost of democracy. Ann Am Acad 379:1-12 S '68
(ed) Financing democracy. bibliog f Ann Am Acad 379:1-131 S '68

BUEHR, Karl Albert
My most unforgettable character. K. B. Granger. il Read Digest 94:88-92 Ap '69

BUELL, Donald N. and Fahey, J. L.
Limited periods of gene expression in immunoglobulin-synthesizing cells. bibliog Science 164:1524-5 Je 27 '69

BUILDING industry—*Continued*

Hope deferred; Operation Breakthrough. Newsweek 74:49 D 29 '69

Housing shortage goes criticial. L. A. Mayer. il Fortune 80:86-9+ D '69

Industrialized housing; can it happen here? J. M. Dixon. il Arch Forum 131:100-8 Jl '69

Is a breakthrough near in housing? il Bsns W p80-2+ S 13 '69

Mass-produced housing? G. Romney's plan. Commonweal 90:332 Je 6 '69

Money, and housing; interview, ed. by G. R. Rosen. P. Martin. Duns R 94:12-15 Ag '69

Patching up construction woes. Bsns W p98+ S 20 '69

Rising construction costs and anti-inflation policies; a report on western Europe. E. J. Howenstine. il Mo Labor R 92:3-10 Je '69

Seasonality in construction; a continuing problem. J. L. Russell and M. J. Pilot. bibliog il Mo Labor R 92:3-8 D '69

Ten problems the building industry must face up to. Bet Hom & Gard 47:6+ S '69

Trying to tackle industry troubles; CIF. Bsns W p33 My 31 '69

What building slump means. U S News 67:30-1 Ag 18 '69

Why is the building industry like the rebellious students? W. F. Wagner, jr. Arch Rec 146:9-10 O '69

Why Nixon ordered construction cutback. U S News 67:15 S 15 '69

See also
Associated general contractors of America
Brown and Root, incorporated
Building—Statistics
Construction for progress, incorporated
Contractors
Houses, Prefabricated
Kaufman and Broad building company
Uris buildings corporation

Employees

Building pickets to spread? U S News 67:79 S 8 '69

Jobs in building for Negroes: agencies split on rules. il U S News 67:91-2 N 24 '69

Justice in the building trades; Pittsburgh churchmen proposals. America 121:256 O 4 '69

Negro rights: Mr Nixon vs. labor Congress repeals rider to Philadelphia plan. il Newsweek 75:49-50 Ja 5 '70

Overtime plum lures craftsmen. U S News 66:73 Je 9 '69

Philadelphia plan in trouble. U S News 67:71-2 O 6 '69

Plan to spur minority hiring. U S News 67:57-8 Jl 7 '69

Reducing skill shortages in construction. E. Weinberg. bibliog f il Mo Labor R 92:3-9 F '69

Showdown on Negro jobs in the building trades. il U S News 67:95-7 S 29 '69

Soul power drive for jobs expands. il Bsns W p22+ Ag 30 '69

Union Six pack springs a leak; St Louis alliance of cement masons, carpenters, hoist engineers, and laborers. Bsns W p30-1 Ag 23 '69

U.S. looks into building-job fight. U S News 67:100-1 S 22 '69

Finance

Manhattan's office building binge. E. Carruth. il Fortune 80:114-17+ O '69

New area feels the pinch; slowdown in commercial building. il Bsns W p 176 O 11 '69

Painful fashion of facelifting homes; tight money pinches. il Bsns W p29 Ag 23 '69

Labor conditions

Big shakedown in Baton Rouge. A. J. Reichley. il Fortune 80:96-9+ Ag 1 '69

Wages and hours

Big boondoggle at Lordstown; with editorial comment. D. Sider. il Fortune 80:85-6, 106-9+ S '69

Building trades push for more. Bsns W p90 My 10 '69

Construction labor: problems, and partial solution. W. H. Edgerton. Arch Rec 146:71 Jl '69

High-paying blue collar jobs and how to get one. L. David. il Mech Illus 65:31-3+ D '69

Industry's plan to halt soaring costs of building. il U S News 67:85-6 Ag 11 '69

More pressure to curb wage costs in building. il U S News 66:73-5 My 5 '69

Wage differentials in the building trades. A. Rose. il Mo Labor R 92:14-17 O '69

Wages of building zoom; overtime and record contract settlements jump industry costs. il Bsns W p89-90 Jl 19 '69

Russia

Russia faces up to the realities of construction industry in reorganizing its approach to producing housing. J. Winkler. il Arch Rec 146:169-72 O '69

BUILDING laws and regulations

Exploring restrictive building practices; excerpt from report, Building the American city. Mo Labor R 92:31-9 Jl '69

See also
Zoning law

BUILDING lots. See Building sites

BUILDING machinery industry and trade

See also
Clark equipment company

BUILDING machinery operators

Facts on a big-pay job. A. Markovich. il Mech Illus 65:71-3+ O '69

BUILDING materials

Building components. See issues of Architectural record

Building industry needs a new approach to product design! Bet Hom & Gard 47:60 S '69

Crazy things they'll use to build your new house. A. S. Freese. il Sci Digest 65:42-8+ F '69

A few important things are happening in materials and systems. il Bet Hom & Gard 47:28+ S '69

Ideas to build on. J. H. Ingersoll. See issues of House beautiful

New building products you should know about. il Pop Mech 132:170-1 S; 174-7 D '69

Product reports. See issues of Architectural record

Tools for the housing revolution. il Bsns W p 106+ S 13 '69

See also
Aluminum, Structural
Bricks
Plastics in building
Plywood
Roofing
Siding (building)

BUILDING materials industry

Supermarket for builders; Wickers centers. S. Margetts. il Duns R 94:85-6+ S '69

Suppliers feel building pinch. il Bsns W p33-4 N 1 '69

See also
Fibreboard corporation
Flintkote company
Johns-Manville
National gypsum company
Plywood industry
United States plywood-Champion papers, incorporated

BUILDING movement. See Strains and stresses

BUILDING research

Construction equipment shakes. R. H. Ferahian and W. D. Hurst. bibliog il Am City 84:102-6 S '69

See also
Housing research

BUILDING sites

Coping with the high price of land. il Am Home 72:49-60 Mr '69

Cross-shaped house gives privacy, space and views. il Arch Rec 146:131-4 Jl '69

Florida minivillage: Fort Lauderdale, Fla. il Arch Forum 130:92-5 Ja '69

Franzen unifies an architecture of fragments into good places for people; five new projects by U. Franzen. il Arch Rec 145:113-32 F '69

Garages on city streets. il Arch Rec 145:165-72 Ap '69

Giant size screen. il Am Home 72:56-9 Je '69

Gruber house, Atlanta, Georgia. il Arch Rec 145:52-3 mid-My '69

McElrath house, Santa Cruz, California. il Arch Rec 145:46-7 mid-My '69

New England house in the woods: Dover, Mass. il Arch Rec 146:131-4 Ag '69

New privacy. il Sunset 142:72-9 Ap '69

Proper land planning, will we learn how at last? il Bet Hom & Gard 47:56+ S '69

Sites and program generate a new school shape. il Arch Rec 145:135-40 My '69

Terraced house on an alpine lake. il Arch Forum 131:52-9 D '69

See also
Hillside architecture

BUILDING trades. See Building industry

BUILDING trades unions

Backlash builds on black demands. il Bsns W p31-2 S 27 '69

Black Monday and White Friday. il Newsweek 74:105-7 O 6 '69

Crusade against the craft unions. A. Plonsett. il Ebony 25:33-6+ D '69

BULLITT, Orville H.
Sybarite; interview. New Yorker 45:19-21 Jl 5 '69

BULLOCK, Helen Duprey
What's cooking in the preservation kettle? reprint. Hobbies 74:98FF Jl '69

BULLOCK'S-Magnin company
See also
Magnin, I. and company

BULLS
Case against castration; with editorial comment. il Suc Farm 67:25, 26-7 S '69
How eight top ranchers buy herd bulls. C. Peterson, jr. il Farm J 93:52 Ap '69

BULOVA watch company
Humming with Henshel. R. Levy. il Duns R 93:68-70 Mr '69
Organizing with confidence; interview. O. N. Bradley. il Nations Bsns 57:42-3+ Ap '69

BULPITT, Stan
Money for your old leaves! Org Gard & Farm 16:42-5 S '69

BULTMANN, Rudolf Karl
Rudolf Bultmann in Catholic thought, ed. by T. O'Meara and D. Weisser. Review
Cath World 209:273-4 S '69. J. E. Bruns
Commonweal 90:179-80 Ap 25 '69. W. A. Scott

BUMPER shock mount system. See Automobiles—Safety devices and measures

BUMPER stickers. See Labels

BUMPERS, Automobile. See Automobiles—Bumpers

BUMPERS, Boat. See Boats—Equipment

BUMPING RIVER
Up the Bumping is a pleasure. Sunset 142:77 My '69

BUNCE, Frank H.
Arboretum, a place for trees? Parks & Rec 4:71-2 S '69
Bernheim forest landscape arboretum. Horticulture 47:22-3 Jl '69

BUNCE, G. Edwin
Milk and blindness in Brazil. Natur Hist 78:52-5 F '69

BUNCH, Wilton H. and Kallsen, Gene
Rate of intracellular diffusion as measured in barnacle muscle. bibliog Science 164:1178-9 Je 6 '69

BUNCHE, Ralph Johnson
My most unforgettable character. Read Digest 95:45-9 S '69

BUNDLING
Pillow talk; Society to bring back bundling. Chr Today 14:36 O 10 '69

BUNDY, McGeorge
How to wind down the nuclear arms race. N Y Times Mag p46-7+ N 16 '69
To cap the volcano. For Affairs 48:1-20 O '69; Excerpts. Cur 113:46-53 D '69

about
McGeorge Bundy confronts the teachers. R. Armstrong. il pors N Y Times Mag p25-7+ Ap 20 '69; Discussion. p 118 My 25 '69
Very expensive education of McGeorge Bundy. D. Halberstam. il pors Harper 239:21-41 Jl '69

BUNI, Andrew
[Book review] America 120:172 F 8 '69

BUNK beds. See Beds

BUNKER, Ellsworth
Close look at progress inside Vietnam; interview, ed. by W. S. Merick. por U S News 67:46-9+ N 17 '69

BUNKER-Ramo corporation
Perils of little orphan Bunker-Ramo. il Forbes 103:45 My 1 '69

BUNKS. See Beds

BUNN, Martin
[Gus Wilson's model garage] See issues of Popular science monthly to June 1969

BUNNELL, Peter C.
Photographs as sculpture and prints. Art in Am 57:56-61 S '69

BUNTING, John R. Jr
One-bank holding companies; a banker's view. bibliog f Harvard Bsns R 47:99-106 My '69

BUÑUEL, Luis
Current cinema. P. Kael. New Yorker 44:109-12+ F 15 '69

BUNZEL, John H.
Arrogant minority victimized the college. Look 33:62+ My 27 '69
War of the flea at San Francisco state. N Y Times Mag p28-9+ N 9; 44+ D 7 '69
What's happening to democracy? Sat R 52:28-9 My 17 '69

BUONONCINI, Giovanni. See Bononcini, G.

BUOYANCY
Buoyancy and solar spin-down. J. L. Modisette and J. E. Novotny. bibliog il Science 166:872-4 N 14 '69
Buoyancy control in the freshwater turtle, pseudemys scripta elegans. D. C. Jackson. bibliog il Science 166:1649-51 D 26 '69.
Fast way to make a boat unsinkable. B. Kasha. il Mech Illus 65:64-5+ Je '69
Glyceryl ether metabolism; regulation of buoyancy in dogfish squalus scanthias. D. C. Malins and A. Barone. bibliog il Science 167:79-80 Ja 2 '60

BUOYANCY apparatus. See Sailboats—Safety devices and measures

BUOYS
How to navigate around buoys. E. H. Moore. il Cons 23:48-inside back cover Ap '69

BURANT, Ralph J.
[Book review] America 120:113-15 Ja 25 '69

BURBANK, Calif.
Lights add esthetics to a mall. il Am City 84:128 Je '69

Lighting
Burbank banks on good lighting. R. Foy. il Am City 84:122+ Ag '69

BURCH, Dean
Activist at the FCC? por Time 94:22 N 21 '69
New chief for the FCC. por Time 94:75-6 S 5 '69
Strange new man at the FCC. il por Forbes 104:26-7 N 15 '69
Two nominees to a key agency. por U S News 67:23 S 29 '69

BURCH, Lyndon Walkup
To the moon via a cellar. il por Bsns W p 140 Je 14 '69

BURCHAM, Lester Arthur
Up from stock boy. por Bsns W p75 D 27 '69

BURCHINAL, David Arthur
Burchinal incident. Nation 208:323-4 Mr 17 '69

BURCK, Charles G.
New products of tomorrow; a 1975 sampler. Fortune 79:161+ My 15 '69
Riches under the earth's crust. Fortune 80:92-101 Ag 15 '69
Student activists; free-form revolutionaries. Fortune 79:108-11+ Ja '69

BURCK, Gilbert
Merger movement rides high. Fortune 79:78-82+ F '69
New flight plan for the airlines. Fortune 79:98-101+ Ap '69
Railroads are running scared. Fortune 79:122-5+ Je '69

about
Editor's desk. L. Banks. por Fortune 79:95 Je '69

BURDEN, Amanda
Amanda Burden. por Vogue 153:154-5 My '69

BURDEN, William Douglas
Those atomic power plants; excerpts from letter. Liv Wildn 33:28-9 Spr '69

BURDMAN, Milton
Realism in community-based correctional services. bibliog f Ann Am Acad 381:71-80 Ja '69

BUREAU international des poids et mesures. See International bureau of weights and measures

BUREAU of Indian affairs. See United States—Indian affairs, Bureau of

BUREAU of intelligence and research. See United States—State, Department of—Intelligence and research, Bureau of

BUREAU of labor statistics. See United States—Labor statistics, Bureau of

BUREAU of land management. See United States—Land management, Bureau of

BUREAU of outdoor recreation. See United States—Outdoor recreation, Bureau of

BUREAUCRACY
Big brother is dead too; about conformity. K. Melvin. Nat R 21:116-18 F 11 '69; Discussion. 21:180, 338 F 25, Ap 8 '69
Big government; is it out of hand? il U S News 66:28-30 Mr 24 '69
Call to revolt. S. Alsop. Newsweek 74:108 D 22 '69
Post-bureaucratic leadership. W. G. Bennis. bibliog il Trans-Action 6:44-51+ Jl '69; Excerpts. Cur 110:42-9 S '69
Proliferation of bureaucracy. P. H. Abelson. Science 163:883 F 28 '69
Vietnam: are there any lessons? T. M. Conrad. Commonweal 90:78-80 Ap 4 '69

BURG, David
Mikhail Dyomin was a successful writer in Soviet Russia. Yet he defected. Why? N Y Times Mag p34-5+ Ap 13 '69

BURGENLAND
Burgenland bonus. R. Deardorff. il Travel 132:60-2 Jl '69
BURGER, Robert E.
Who cares for the aged? Sat R 52:14-17 Ja 25 '69
BURGER, Warren Earl
Judge Burger's philosophy on justice in U.S. a key speech; excerpts, May 1967; reprint. por U S News 66:82-5 Je 2 '69; Same abr. with title Rights and wrongs of U.S. justice. Read Digest 95:84-8 Ag '69

about

Air of approval; Senate judiciary committee appearance. il por Newsweek 73:29 Je 16 '69
Beginning of the Burger era. Time 94:57 O 10 '69
Burger court. I. Silver. Commonweal 90:585-8 S 26 '69
Burger vs. FCC. R. L. Shayon. Sat R 52:40 Jl 26 '69
Burgher from Minnesota. il Time 93:17 My 30 '69
Changing of the guard. il por Newsweek 73: 28-9 Je 2 '69
Chief justice. New Repub 160:7 My 31 '69
Chief Justice Burger asks: If it doesn't make good sense, how can it make good law? J. Duscha. il por N Y Times Mag p30-1+ O 5 '69
Chief justice calls for reforms. por U S News 67:9 Ag 18 '69
Ccurt. old and new. R. Shogan. por Newsweek 73:46+ Je 30 '69
Court reform: Burger's role. por U S News 67:14 Jl 14 '69
Highly visible Chief. por Time 94:58 Ag 22 '69
Hope for Warren Burger? Chr Cent 86:800 Je 11 '69
How Mr Nixon made his choice. il U S News 66:33 Je 2 '69
In the footsteps of Marshall and Taney. H. J. Sievers. America 121:317 O 18 '69
Integration now. por Time 94:19-20 N 7 '69
Judge Burger: champion of law and order. il por U S News 66:32 Je 2 '69
Legacy of the Warren court. il por Time 94: 62-3 Jl 4 '69
Most important nomination that a president makes. il pors Life 66:40-1 My 30 '69
New era for Supreme court. il pors U S News 66:30-2 Je 2 '69
Nixon's Court choice. Bsns W p38 My 24 '69
Outside handler. Nation 208:749 Je 16 '69
Professional for the High court. il por Time 93:16+ My 30 '69
Quick decision. por Newsweek 73:30 Je 23 '69
Some heretical views. Time 93:21 Je 20 '69
Supreme court: no friends need apply. Life 66:44 Je '69
Warren court vs. Congress. il por U S News 66:23-4 Je 30 '69
BURGESS, Anthony, pseud.
Letter from Europe. Am Scholar 38:297-9, 684-6 Spr. Aut '69
Our bedfellow, the Marquis de Sade. Horizon 11:104-9 Wint '69
Seen any good Galsworthy lately? N Y Times Mag p57+ N 16 '69
Woman and women. Vogue 154:194+ O 1 '69
BURGESS, Howard F.
Make your own ion chamber. Pop Electr 31: 31-5 N '69
Strange power of air ions. Pop Electr 31: 29-30+ N '69
BURGESS, John Melville, bp
Bishop Burgess of Massachusetts. il pors Ebony 24:54-6+ O '69
BURGESS, Roger D. and Hults, M. E.
Shadow-band experiment. Sky & Tel 38:95 Ag '69
BURGESS, Thomas K.
Old and new design philosophies used in library automation. por ALA Bul 63:1265-7 O '69
BURGHEIM, Richard
Old fear of Gould and the new criticism of Arlen. Harper 239:98-101 Ag '69
BURGIN, Bryan E.
Hunting accidents decline in 1968. Cons 23: 32-3 Ap '69
BURGLAR alarms
Build low-cost touch alarm. R. F. Graf. il Pop Electr 30:92-3 F '69
Build the homesteader. D. Meyer. il Pop Electr 31:71-3+ O '69
Burglar deterrents. il Consumer Bul 52:29-31 F '69
Electronic watchdog in a can. R. F. Graf and G. J. Whalen. il Pop Sci 195:182+ N '69
How to put in an alarm system. il Bet Hom & Gard 47:58+ N '69

Intruder alarms. L. Steckler. il Radio-Electr 40:33-6 Jl '69
Protecting your home from burglars. Bsns W p 142 O 18 '69
To scare a thief. J. A. Morris. Read Digest 95:183-4+ S '69
What you should know about home burglar alarms. S. J. Howard. il Pop Mech 132:156-8 N '69
BURGLARY and burglars
Behind the scenes with the big-city burglar. N. Pileggi. il Read Digest 94:101-5 Mr '69
Suddenly it happens to you; there is a noise in the night. McCalls 96:52+ Je '69
BURGLARY insurance. See Insurance, Burglary
BURGLARY protection
Burglars beware. S. N. Scherer. il Har Yrs 9: 46-8 Ag '69
How to foil the burglar. M. Cousins. il House B 111:72-3+ F '69
New weapons to protect you against crime; SBA report. il Nations Bsns 57:90-1+ Ap '69
BURGUNDER, Rose
Cemetery: Litchfield County; poem. Harper 238:26 F '69
Pages from a Tashkent diary. Vogue 154:240+ S 1 '69
BURGUNDY (wine) See Wine
BURIAL
   See also
Cemeteries
BURIAL mounds. See Mounds and mound builders
BURIAL rites. See Funeral rites and ceremonies
BURIĆ, Lubomir. See Zicha, B. jt. auth.
BURIED treasure. See Treasure trove
BURKE, Bernard F.
Long-baseline interferometry. bibliog por Phys Today 22:54-63 Jl '69
BURKE, Frank
Trans-Caribbean delivery. Yachting 126:61+ N '69
BURKE, Hubert D.
Wilderness engenders new management traditions. Liv Wildn 33:9-13 Sum '69
BURKE, John Gordon
Encino press: one man's tribute to the Southwest. por Pub W 195:96-7 My 5 '69
BURKE, Kenneth
Eye-crossing, from Brooklyn to Manhattan; poem. Nation 208:700-4 Je 2 '69
Her will; poem. New Repub 161:28 Jl 5 '69
Modernism so far is but peanuts; poem. New Repub 161:30 N 8 '69
Serious business of comedy. New Repub 160:23-4+ Mr 15 '69
Toward the perfectly poisonous. New Repub 160:28-30 My 31 '69
BURKE, Michael
Best arm in baseball. por Wilson Lib Bul 43: 622-3 Mr '69
BURKE, Tom
Do not smoke Skippy peanut butter. Esquire 72:129-32+ O '69
Goldie rush. McCalls 97:81+ O '69
New homosexuality. Esquire 72:178-9+ D '69
(ed) See Fonda, J. Conversation with Jane Fonda
BURKETT, Lowell A.
Access to a future. Am Ed 5:2-3 Mr '69
BURKHARDT, Dietrich, and others
Animal languages; excerpts from Signals in the animal world. Todays Ed 58:34-6+ O '69
BURKHARDT, Robert
Ballad of the diminishing dollar. Holiday 46: 62-3+ Jl '69
Preview of the giant jet; 747. Travel & Camera 32:76-8+ D '69
Washington memo. Travel & Camera 32:10 Je; 18 Ag '69
BURKS, George F. See Sullivan, J. D. jt. auth.
BURLAGE, John D. and Hendley, H. R.
Now: hands off landings on a carrier. Pop Mech 132:96-9+ O '69
BURLESON, Charlotte
Honey thieves; drama. Plays 28:71-3 Ap '69
See Wee the octopus; drama. Plays 28:84-6 Mr '69
BURLESON, Derek L.
Convention exhibit notes; NCTE. Sr Schol 93:Schol Teach 8 Ja 10 '69
BURLESQUE. See Vaudeville
BURLINGTON industries, incorporated
Textile firm considering buying own air freighters. R. G. O'Lone. Aviation W 90: 42+ Ap 21 '69
   See also
Erwin mills, incorporated

BURMA

Politics and government

Another left turn. il Time 94:42 N 28 '69

Don't eat the animals. M. Parker. il Newsweek 73:47 Mr 10 '69

Religious institutions and affairs

See also

Christians in Burma

BURMAH oil company. See Petroleum industry and trade—Great Britain

BURMAN, Ben Lucien

Canada's fabulous Yukon. Read Digest 94:
194-6+ F '69

BURNETT, Clinton Brown

Company of the old school. il Forbes 103:18-19
F 1 '69

BURNETT, Dame Ivy Compton-. See Compton-
Burnett, I.

BURNETT, Warren Edsel

Warren Burnett: Texas lawyer. L. L. King. il
pors Harper 239:66-7+ Jl '69

BURNFORD, Sheila

Indian dog. Atlan 224:85-8 Ag '69

BURNHAM, James

Letter from Brussels. Nat R 21:21 Ja 14 '69

Open question. Nat R 21:222 Mr 11 '69

Third world war. See issues of National review

Travels with Melrose. Nat R 21:1210-11, 1269-
71 D 2; D 16 '69

Twilight of de Gaulle. Nat R 21:114-15 F 11
'69

Whose national interest? por Nat R 21:442-3
My 6 '69

BURNHAM, Sophy

Twelve rebels of the student right. N Y
Times Mag p32-3+ Mr 9; 112+ Mr 30 '69

BURNHAM, Walter Dean

End of American party politics. bibliog por
Trans-Action 7:12-22 D '69

BURNS, Arthur

Repetitive ramp generator. Electr World 82:87
O '69

BURNS, Arthur Frank

Arthur Burns on easier credit, business in
'70; excerpts from the hearings held by
the Senate committee on banking and currency. por U S News 68:56-9 Ja 12 '70

As I see it; interview. pors Forbes 103:68-9
Mr 15 '69

Nation's biggest danger; interview. pors U S
News 67:60-5 Jl 14 '69

about

Adviser who may stand closest to Nixon.
pors Bsns W p62-6 Mr 1 '69

At Nixon's right hand. por Bsns W p 15 F 1
'69

Burns: the devil's advocate. R. B. Semple, jr.
il por(p9) N Y Times Mag p45+ Ag 3 '69

Burns kind of liberal conservatism. M.
Viorst. il por N Y Times Mag p30-1+ N
9 '69

Discipline and order but an open image. J.
Osborne. New Repub 160:11-13 F 22 '69

How Burns will change the Fed. il por Bsns
W p 102-4+ O 25 '69

Minister without portfolio. por Time 93:16 F 7
'69

Mr Nixon has a friend at the Fed. il por
Newsweek 74:88+ O 27 '69

New key man in battle on how to tune economy: what next? por U S News 67:16 O 27
'69

Nixon's new maestro of money. por Time 94:
89-90 O 24 '69

No. 1 on White House staff, how he'll advise
Nixon. por U S News 66:15 F 3 '69

TRB from Washington. New Repub 160:4 Mr
1 '69

What Burns said that sparked a market
rally. por U S News 67:8 D 29 '69

Where Arthur sits. Fortune 80:62 D '69

BURNS, Catherine

Flowering of a late bloomer. J. Howard.
il pors Life 67:82-8 N 21 '69

BURNS, Hugh M.

Un-un-American activities. Nation 208:134
F 3 '69

BURNS, Jean Harker

Greatest Halloween prank of them all. Read
Digest 95:157-60 O '69

BURNS, Julie

(ed) See Durrell, L. Art is very curative,
you purge yourself by putting down

BURNS, R. O. See Hatfield, G. W. jt. auth.

BURNS, Robert

Burns's poems. H. Carruth. Poetry 114:191-3
Je '69

Classics revisited. K. Rexroth. Sat R 52:56 Ap
12 '69

BURNS, Robert Grant

Nutria; Storm warning; Field problem and
midnight convoy; poems. Poetry 114:165-9
Je '69

BURNS and scalds

Six long, long months; treatment at the
Burn unit at University of Michigan medical center. J P. Blank. Read Digest 95:97-
101 N '69

BURNSIDE, Irene Mortenson

Clock called conscience; poem. Ment Hy 53:
414 Jl '69

Sensory stimulation: an adjunct to group
work with the disabled aged. bibliog Ment
Hy 53:381-8 Jl '69

BURPEE, Edith

Bright faith. B. Falconer. il pors Good H
168:88-91 My '69

BURPEE, W. Atlee, company

Keeping the bloom on a flower business. il
Bsns W p94-5 Ap 12 '69

BURRELL, Gilbert

Airflow facts; interview, ed. by J. Dianna.
Hot Rod 22:48-50 N '69

BURRIDGE, Gaston

Collectors of centuries. Américas 21:31-6 Je
'69

BURRILL, Roger H.

Volunteer-powered recreation for geriatric
patients. Ment Hy 53:389-92 Jl '69

BURROUGHS, Edgar Rice

Me Tarzan, you Jane. D. Sharp. por Read
Digest 95:111-14 S '69

BURROUGHS, John

Are small 110-v.a.c. arc welders really any
good? Pop Mech 131:182-6+ Je '69

Build this box-leg power-tool stand. Pop
Mech 131:178-9 Ja '69

Circular saw: a worksaver for all workshops.
Pop Mech 131:188-91 F '69

Here's a dovetailing device that's really different. Pop Mech 132:170-2 Ag '69

How to choose and use small vernier calipers. Pop Mech 131:192-5 My '69

How to mount grinding wheels with epoxy.
Pop Mech 132:184-6 Jl '69

How to power-whet cutting edges. Pop Sci
194:140-1 Je '69

What's new for polishing and buffing. Pop
Mech 132:188-91 S '69

Woodturning fun for beginners. Pop Mech
132:196-9 N '69

BURROUGHS, William Seward

Last words of Dutch Schultz; scenario. Atlan
223:72-6+ Je '69

BURROW, J. W.

Anarchists. Horizon 11:32-43 Sum '69

Many faces of Karl Marx. Horizon 11:52-7
Wint '69

BURROWS, Larry

Vietnam: a degree of disillusion. il por Life
67:66-75 S 19 '69

BURROWS, William

Airports. Holiday 46:48-51+ Jl '69

BURSITIS

Strain, pain, is it bursitis? R. R. Keaton. il
Har Yrs 9:45 S '69

BURSTYN, Harold L.

Tradition and understanding: the sciences
and the humanities; adaptation of address,
April 1968. bibliog Sch & Soc 97:419-24 N
'69

BURTLE, Gerry Lynn

Mystery of the gumdrop dragon; drama, reprint from May 1960 issue. Plays 28:51-62,
68 My '69

BURTON, Hester

Writing of historical novels; excerpt from
address, August 1968. Horn Bk 45:271-7
Je '69

BURTON, Maurice

Seals in peril; with biographical sketch. por
Sea Front 15:160-9, 191 My '69

BURTON, Philip

Ever green was his valley. Sat R 52:35 Ap
26 '69

about

Elder Burton. M. Croyden. il por Sat R 52:
51 My 10 '69

BURTON, Richard

Who cares about Wales? I care. por Look
33:74-7 Je 24 '69

about

Liz Taylor and Richard Burton; what it's
like to be walking investments. A. Birstein. Vogue 153:100-1+ F 15 '69

BURTON, Scott

Color it Berkowitz. Art N 68:32-3+ Mr '69

Time on their hands. Art N 68:40-3 Sum '69

BURTON, Virginia Lee

Obituary

Horn Bk 45:110 F '69. L. Kingman

BURTON, Walter E.
Add a rest to your lathe. Pop Mech 131:200-3+ Mr '69
Dent puller from pipe parts. Pop Mech 132:198-9 O '69
Don't play taps for broken taps. Pop Mech 131:200-2 Ap '69
Filing on a lathe. Pop Mech 130:174-7 D '68
How to plane on a lathe. Pop Mech 132:194-7+ O '69
How to put holes of any shape into metal. Pop Sci 194:123+ Je '69
Make a king-size toolpost for hefty turning bits. Pop Mech 131:194-6 F '69
Make this back holder and use upside-down tool bits. Pop Mech 132:180-4+ Ag '69
Model this 24-pounder. Pop Mech 131:134-9+ F '69
New wood planer attachment for your Unimat lathe. Pop Mech 130:179-81 D '68
Turning rings on a lathe. Pop Mech 131:186-90 Ja '69

BUS drivers. See Motor bus drivers

BUS lines. See Motor bus lines

BUS-wagons. See Station wagons

BUSACK, Stephen D.
Spotted salamander. Cons 23:8-9 F '69

BUSCH, Niven
Palm Beach; the rarest resort of them all. por Holiday 45:38-45 F '69

BUSCH, Noel F.
Guide lines to Temple Fielding. Travel 131:69-72 Mr '69
Mountains that blow their tops. Read Digest 95:127-32 Ag '69

BUSCHER, John B. See Denny, T. J. jt. auth.

BUSECK, Peter R.
Phosphide from meteorites: barringerite, a new iron-nickel mineral. bibliog Science 165:169-71 Jl 11 '69

BUSES, Motor. See Motor buses

BUSH, Josef
De Sade illustrated; adaptation of Philosophy in the bedroom, by D. A. F. de Sade.
Criticism
New Yorker 45:114 My 24 '69
Newsweek il 73:101 Je 2 '69

BUSH, Monroe
Benton MacKaye in review. Am For 75:11 Mr '69
Reading about resources. See issues of American forests

BUSH anemone. See Carpenteria californica

BUSH germander. See Germander

BUSHMEN. See Africa—Native races; Botswana—Native races

BUSHNELL, Horace
Revolution within an evolution. R. R. Winkelmann. Chr Cent 86:1577-80 D 10 '69

BUSHONG, Barbara
And in conclusion; poem. Engl J 58:1056 O '69

BUSIA, Kofi Abrefa
Friday's child. por Time 94:39 S 12 '69

BUSINESS
Semantics for the swinging executive. S. Sauerhaft. il Duns R 93:42-3 Ap '69
See also
Chamber of commerce of the United States of America
Christmas business
Corporations
Entrepreneurs
Free enterprise
Ideas in business
Monopolies
Occupations
Retail trade
Stock exchange

Bibliography
Books to come; ed. by J. Donathan and J. Fletcher. Library J 94:4052-6 N 1 '69
Books to come; ed. by J. Putnam (cont) Library J 94:1055-63, 2667-70 Mr 1, Jl '69
Business books of 1968; comp. by D. Stoeckle. il Library J 94:956-9 Mr 1 '69
Check list of 1969 business books. Sat R 53:83 Ja 10 '70
Is that fact? paperback fact books. S. Mechanic. il Library J 94:960-1 Mr 1 '69
Some business high spots April-July. il Pub W 195:57-63 Ap 14; 196:55-60 N 17 '69

Exhibitions
See Exhibitions

Foreign expansion
American business abroad; symposium. il Sat R 52:31-6+ N 22 '69
Brussels: the executive city. J. Lambert. il Duns R 93:48-51 Mr '69

Chemical industry pushes into hostile country. J. Davenport. il Fortune 79:108-15+ Ap '69
Survival of the European headquarters. F. N. Parks. Harvard Bsns R 47:79-84 Mr '69
Where in the world should we put that plant? manufacturing operations in foreign countries. R. B. Stobaugh, jr. bibliog f il Harvard Bsns R 47:129-36 Ja '69
See also
Corporations—Foreign subsidiaries

Information services
See Information services

International aspects
How business took the news; devaluation of the franc. Bsns W p85+ Ag 16 '69
International business. See issues of Dun's review
New anatomy of world business; address, November 13, 1969. R. L. Ash. Vital Speeches 36:154-7 D 15 '69
Now it's the Europeans versus I.B.M. P. Siekman. il Fortune 80:86-91+ Ag 15 '69

Periodicals
Gatsby lives; new student magazine at Princeton: Business today. A. R. Dolan. Nat R 21:648 Jl 1 '69
See also
Nation's business (periodical)

Political aspects
Attorney at war. D. Welsh and D. Horowitz. il Ramp Mag 7:132-4+ Ja 25 '69
Big business in German politics: four studies. bibliog f Am Hist R 75:37-78 O '69
Building Lyndon Johnson. D. Welsh. il Ramp Mag 7:104-14 Ja 25 '69
Learning political processes. L. L. L. Golden. Sat R 52:88+ Ap 12 '69
Lucrative lunch. il Newsweek 73:79-80 Je 2 '69
What businessmen did on protest day. il Bsns W p40-1 O 18 '69
When companies find giving isn't blessed; political contributions. Bsns W p31-2 N 8 '69

Public relations
Business responds to consumerism; with editorial comment. il Bsns W p94-6+. 132 S 6 '69
Frank Abrams way. L. L. L. Golden. Sat R 52:86 N 8 '69
Meeting the challenge of communication; address, June 2, 1969. R. C. Rockefeller. Vital Speeches 35:716-18 S 15 '69
See also
Business and the press

Small business
See Small business

Social aspects
After Vietnam: can industry manufacture social solutions? J. M. Gavin. Sat R 52:21-2 My 24 '69
Agitator zeroes in on the suburbanites; school to train alienated executives. il Bsns W p44-6 F 8 '69
Are model cities the business of business? il Nations Bsns 57:42-4+ F '69
BURP and make money; urban housing rehabilitation venture. E. Goldston. bibliog il Harvard Bsns R 47:84-99 S '69
Business and youth; with editorial comment. A. Gingrich. Esquire 72:6+, 73+ O '69
Business has a war to win; excerpts from address, December 5, 1968. J. I. Miller. Harvard Bsns R 47:4-6+ Mr '69
Business in a doghouse. P. A. Samuelson. Newsweek 73:85 Ja 27 '69
Businessmen and their responsibilities to a changing society; address, April 23, 1969. G. Hammond. Vital Speeches 35:595-8 Jl 15 '69
Corporation within the community; address, January 27, 1969. M. F. Cohen. Vital Speeches 35:270-3 F 15 '69
Crime; a businessman's challenge; address, April 28, 1969. R. L. Gelb. Vital Speeches 35:639-40 Ag 1 '69
Crime; the community and the corporation; address, July 28, 1969. M. R. Wilkey. Vital Speeches 35:718-20 S 15 '69
Equitable puts premium on social role. il Bsns W p68-9 N 29 '69
Hidden revolution; the profit motive, a social force; address, June 5, 1969. H. Ford, 2d. Vital Speeches 35:566-8 Jl 1 '69
How private is business nowadays? B. L. Masse. America 121:551 D 6 '69

BUSINESS—Social aspects—*Continued*
International financial challenges; address, October 16, 1969. D. Rockefeller. Vital Speeches 36:83-6 N 15 '69
Next: rose-chip stocks? Forbes 104:100+ N 15 '69
Nixon's prime goals. T. Trussell. Nations Bsns 57:7-8 Ap '69
Positive action; the middle managers; address, October 3, 1968. R. W. Goldfarb. Vital Speeches 35:315-18 Mr 1 '69
Sail with the winds of change. L. I. Wood. il Nations Bsns 57:58-62 D '69
Take a modest step; address, April 1969. G. Gabetti. Vital Speeches 35:533-5 Je 15 '69
Telling it as it really is. B. L. Masse. America 120:389 Ap 5 '69
Toward professionalism in business management. K. R. Andrews. bibliog f il Harvard Bsns R 47:49-60 Mr '69
U.S. troubles: a business view. U S News 66:18 My 5 '69
U.S. versus Latin America: business & culture. S. M. Davis. bibliog f Harvard Bsns R 47:88-98 N '69
War that business must win; with editorial comment. il Bsns W p63-74, 136 N 1 '69
Where bosses are told off, and like it; Forums for economic and political discussion, sponsored by the National chamber foundation. il Nations Bsns 57:62-5 Jl '69
Winning over indifferent youth. P. O. Gaddis. Harvard Bsns R 47:154-6+ Jl '69
See also
Business and race problems
Unemployment—Relief measures

Terminology
Semantics for the swinging executive. S. Sauerhaft. il Duns R 93:42-3 Ap '69
BUSINESS, Roadside. See Roadside business
BUSINESS administration. See Business management and organization
BUSINESS airplanes. See Airplanes, Business
BUSINESS and alcoholism. See Alcoholism
BUSINESS and art. See Art and industry
BUSINESS and education
Armco is opening a door for the young. il Nations Bsns 57:16 D '69
Business and campus unrest; vocational training; address. January 16, 1969. E. H. Wasson. Vital Speeches 35:335-8 Mr 15 '69
Closed corporation: American universities in crisis, by J. Ridgeway. Review
Ramp Mag 7:63-4 Ap '69. S. Weissman
Columbia and the closed corporation. N. Von Hoffman. Commonweal 89:566-9 Ja 31 '69
Corporate search for soul: role of corporate urban affairs departments. J. Poindexter. il Duns R 94:36-9 Ag '69
Courage and confusion in choosing a career; Time essay. Time 93:42-3 My 30 '69
Education, servant of industry. P. Krich. Sch & Soc 97:280-1 Sum '69
Guaranteed learning; Dorsett education systems incentive contract. Sat R 52:85 O 18 '69
Holding the line; corporate aid to education. L. L. L. Golden. Sat R 52:73 D 13 '69
Industry and education. B. Nelson. Ed Digest 34:46-7 Mr '69
Industry: New partner in education. S. Holzman. il Sr Schol 94:Schol Teach 10-11 Mr 21 '69
Lockheed sells first educational program. R. G. O'Lone. il Aviation W 90:121+ Ap 14 '69
Reading, writing, and profit; Dorsett education systems incentive contract. Bsns W p 104 O 4 '69
Schools get 3Rs from business. Bsns W p68 Ag 2 '69
Technology, not teachers; audiovisual teaching machine in Texarkana schools. il Sr Schol 95:Schol Teach 1 O 27 '69
Universities: industry links raise conflict of interest issue; questioning relation of petroleum engineering professors to oil industry. J. Walsh. Science 164:411-12 Ap 25 '69; Reply. J. J. Schanz, jr. 164:1466 Je 27 '69
See also
Business education
College students and business
Education market
BUSINESS and government. See Industry and state
BUSINESS and professional women
Action: a beauty investment. B. Wysor. il Harp Baz 102:158-61 Ag '69
See also
Women as executives

BUSINESS and race problems
Business and black capitalism. J. Chamberlain. Nat R 21:742-4 Jl 29 '69
Business picks up the urban challenge. A. T. Demaree. il Fortune 79:102-4+ Ap '69; Reply. R. Taggart. 3d. 79:56 My 1 '69
Corporate search for soul: role of corporate urban affairs departments. J. Poindexter. il Duns R 94:36-9 Ag '69
Limits of black capitalism. F. D. Sturdivant. bibliog f il Harvard Bsns R 47:122-8 Ja '69
Promises, promises; broken pledges by businessmen: Boston and New York. il Newsweek 74:37 Ag 11 '69
Race, jobs, and cities; what business can do. J. R. Lowe; reply. E. L. Stoll. Sat R 52:32-3 F 22 '69
War that business must win; with editorial comment. il Bsns W p63-74, 136 N 1 '69
Why whitey is failing in the cities. R. W. Goldfarb. Read Digest 95:139-44 O '69
See also
National alliance of businessmen
BUSINESS and religion
Billy's apostles; U.S. business establishment behind New York crusade. il Newsweek 73:65 Je 23 '69
BUSINESS and state. See Industry and state
BUSINESS and the community. See Business—Social aspects
BUSINESS and the press
Fourth estate: smoothing press relations. Bsns W p99-100 Ja 10 '70
BUSINESS arbitration. See Arbitration, Commercial
BUSINESS budgets. See Budget, Business
BUSINESS charts
See also
Business management and organization—Charts, graphs, etc.
BUSINESS committee for the arts (BCA) See Business in the arts award
BUSINESS communication. See Communication in management
BUSINESS conditions
And the boom goes on. il Nations Bsns 57:34-7 Ap '69
Arthur Burns on easier credit, business in 70; excerpts from the hearings held by the Senate committee on banking and currency. A. F. Burns. U S News 68:56-9 Ja 12 '70
Big debate about a business slowdown in U.S. il U S News 67:40-1 S 15 '69
Business and finance. See issues of Newsweek
Business outlook. See issues of Business week
Business roundup. S. S. Parker and others. See issues of Fortune
Business trend now. il U S News 66:32-3 My 12 '69
Cities where business is best. il U S News 66:56-9 Ap 14 '69
Credit crunch: who is hurt. il U S News 66:60-1 Je 16 '69
Executives waken to slowdown; with editorial comment. il Bsns W p23-4, 148 O 4 '69
First signs of a business lag. il U S News 66:100 Mr 17 '69
Plus & minus; business activity of the week. See issues of U S news & World report
Project Own; address, December 4, 1968. H. J. Samuels. Vital Speeches 35:250-3 F 1 '69
Recession coming? Opinions of the experts now. il U S News 67:89-91 O 6 '69
Reformer stirs French business; M. Demonque's reformist ideas. il Bsns W p 122+ Ap 26 '69
Signs of a business slowdown. il U S News 66:23-4 Je 9 '69
Spotlight on business. See issues of Newsweek
Those order books are staying filled. il Bsns W p34-5 N 15 '69
Trend of American business. See issues of U S News & World report
What bankers see ahead now. U S News 67:91-4 O 13 '69
Where business is good; city-by-city survey. il U S News 67:92-5 O 6 '69
Why recession will be avoided; interview. P. W. McCracken. U S News 68:52-5 Ja 12 '70
Word from businessmen: boom cooling. U S News 66:69 My 19 '69
See also
Business cycles
Business depression
Inflation (finance)
Investments

BUSINESS conferences

How to be a better meeting chairman. G. M. Prince. il Harvard Bsns R 47:98-108 Ja '69

Where bosses are told off, and like it; Forums for economic and political discussion, sponsored by the National chamber foundation. il Nations Bsns 57:62-5 Jl '69

See also
International industrial conference

BUSINESS consolidations and mergers

After the merger, what next? acquisition's aftermath. il Bsns W p50-2 Ap 26 '69

Antitrust problems that Nixon inherits. il U S News 66:96-7 F 17 '69

Antitrusters lose a round; acquisition of Hartford fire insurance co. by ITT approved. Time 94:80 O 31 '69

Attacking the giants; planned merger of International telephone & telegraph with Hartford fire insurance co. Time 94:72+ Jl 4 '69

Bankrolling new brainpower; USM-IRA deal. Bsns W p20-1 Jl 5 '69

Better than the savings bank; merger of Lykes with Youngstown. il Forbes 103:30-1 Ap 1 '69

Bid and lost; conglomerates losing investor confidence. Time 95:52 Ja 5 '70

Big trucker acquires steamship company; Consolidated freightways acquires Pacific Far East line. Bsns W p52 Ap 26 '69

Brokers feel the bear's claws. il Bsns W p 130+ S 20 '69

Business mergers, what's right, what's wrong; interview. W. F. Rockwell, jr. il U S News 66:70-3 My 19 '69

Control postmerger change. F. W. Searby. Harvard Bsns R 47:4-6+ S '69

Day after the wedding night; Foremost dairies and McKesson & Robbins. il Forbes 103:203-4 My 15 '69

Feast for the arbitrageurs. W. Robertson. il Fortune 79:165-6 F '69

Financial realities of mergers; excerpts from address, March 28, 1969. J. S. R. Shad. il Harvard Bsns R 47:133-46 N '69

Finding buyers for the bad buys. il Bsns W p49-51 S 13 '69

Frustrations of the acquired executive. R. C. Albrook. il Fortune 80:152-6+ N '69

How a lonely company can find happiness. Nations Bsns 57:103 S '69

How United fruit was plucked. il Bsns W p 122-4 F 22 '69

Is the merger fever really cooling off? antitrusters talk tough about mergers. il Bsns W p35-7 Je 21 '69

Kiss and tell on romantic Wall Street. S. Sauerhaft. il Duns R 93:26-9 F '69

Latest turn in attack on mergers. il U S News 66:53 Ap 28 '69

Leasco's noisy battle for a British publisher; Leasco-Pergamon press proposed merger. il Bsns W p30-2 S 6 '69

Lykes-Youngstown merger nears. Bsns W p 106 F 15 '69

McLaren talks about conglomerates; crackdown on mergers. Bsns W p38 Mr 15 '69

Merger as an inflation hedge; Engelhard industries merge with Minerals & chemicals Phillipp. il Forbes 103:65 Je 15 '69

Merger boom: who owns what? R. Dietsch. New Repub 160:14-16 F 22 '69

Merger movement rides high. G. Burck. il Fortune 79:78-82+ F '69

Merger tide runs higher; popularity of tender offers also increased. Bsns W p44 Ap 12 '69

Merger wave keeps rolling. Bsns W p44 Mr 22 '69

Mergers under scrutiny; excerpts from Managerial analysis in marketing. L. W. Stern. bibliog il Harvard Bsns R 47:18-20+ Jl '69

Mills squints at conglomerates; warns them on debt-for-equity mergers. Bsns W p30 Mr 8 '69

Old formula, new Field. Time 93:92+ Ap 11 '69

Setback for McLaren; acquisition of Hartford fire insurance co. and Grinnell corp. by ITT, approved. Newsweek 74:78 N 3 '69

Storm over conglomerates: latest plans for curbs; hearing by the House ways and means committee. il U S News 66:86-8 Mr 24 '69

To expand, sell the company; Rochester-Pauley petroleum merger. il Bsns W p 168+ O 18 '69

United fruit's shotgun marriage. S. H. Brown. il Fortune 79:132+ Ap '69

War on mergers escalates. il Bsns W p36-7 Ap 19 '69

Ward's joins the now generation; merger with Container corp. il Bsns W p84-6+ Mr 22 '69

What did you say the company's name was (is)? il Forbes 103:31-2 Ap 15 '69

Whittaker aims to redesign its merger plans. Aviation W 90:86-7 Mr 31 '69

See also
Bank consolidations and mergers
Conglomerate corporations
Corporate acquisitions
Diversification in industry
Monopolies
also subhead Consolidations and mergers under various subjects, e.g. Advertising agencies—Consolidations and mergers

Directories

His book steers merger hunters; Hudson's corporate mergers. il Bsns W p98+ F 8 '69

Europe, Western

Agfa-Gevaert, model merger? il Bsns W p62-3 Jl 5 '69

Merging over the border; Holland's Fokker and West Gemany's Vereinigte flugtechnische werke. Bsns W p38 My 17 '69

VFW, Fokker form equal partnership. Aviation W 90:24 My 19 '69

France

L'affaire Saint-Gobain; Boussois-Souchon-Neuvesel offer to buy 30 per cent of stock. il Newsweek 73:77 F 3 '69

Great glass battle; Saint-Gobain beat takeover attempt by Boussois Souchon Neuvesel. Time 93:77-8 F 7 '69

Marriage of French cousins. il Fortune 80:118 Ag 15 '69

Great Britain

Two old foes may make up; proposed ICI-Courtaulds merger. Bsns W p30 Ja 10 '70

Japan

Bigger is better; Yawata iron & steel and Fuji iron & steel merger. il Time 93:88+ Mr 14 '69

Japan forges a colossus in steel; merger of Yawata and Fuji. il Bsns W p92-4+ Ap 5 '69

BUSINESS consultants

Business healers, by H. Higdon. Review Bsns W p70 D 20 '69

Companies tune to a new oracle; economic consultants. il Bsns W p 116-18 S 13 '69

Europe's lush market for advice. American preferred. R. C. Allbrook. il Fortune 80:128-31+ Jl '69

Hatchet man for deadwood operations; J. Lobb. Bsns W p80 S 6 '69

Making staff consulting more effective. J. K. Baker and R. H. Schaffer. Harvard Bsns R 47:62-71 Ja '69

Prescribing a cure for paper mess; management consultants to Wall Street. il Bsns W p 122-3 Ap 19 '69

Rush in on to get into consulting. Bsns W p 157 O 18 '69

See also
Booz, Allen and Hamilton, incorporated
Lippincott and Margulies, incorporated
Little, Arthur D, incorporated

BUSINESS council

Who speaks for business? G. R. Rosen. il Duns R 94:45-7+ N '69

BUSINESS cycles

Business cycle in a changing world, by A. F. Burns. Review
Duns R 94:7 D '69. R. Lekachman
New Repub 161:28-9 O 18 '69. A. Campbell

BUSINESS depression

Closer to avoiding recession; third annual survey by the McGraw-Hill economics dept. il Bsns W p88-9 My 24 '69

Daddy, what's a recession? il Changing T 23:45-7 N '69

Debate mounts on recession. U S News 67:78-80 O 20 '69

Is recession a cure now? U S News 66:23-5 Ap 7 '69

Is recession on the way? As top economists see it. il U S News 67:17-19 Ag 4 '69

Is the recession coming? with editorial comment. G. R. Rosen. il Duns R 94:60-1+, 146 O '69

New bears growl recession. Bsns W p26-7 Jl 26 '69

Recession ahead? what the odds are. il U S News 67:21-2 N 3 '69

Recession danger, how real? il U S News 66:31-3 F 17 '69

Recession fears; wild gyrations of financial opinion in the press. P. A. Samuelson. Newsweek 74:65 Ag 25 '69

BUSINESS depression— *Continued*
Rising risk of recession. il Time 94:66-70+
D 19 '69
TRB from Washington: bad? That's good.
New Repub 162:6 Ja 10 '70
See also
Business conditions

BUSINESS districts
Charles center; Baltimore. J. M. Dixon. il
Arch Forum 130:48-57 My '69
Enclosed air-conditioned downtown; Rockville. Md. il Am City 84:86 Je '69
How to plan business districts. A. Cooperstock. il Am City 84:121-2 Ap '69
How to plan for the pedestrian; Cincinnati,
Ohio. A. D. Bird. il Am City 84:76-7+ Jl '69
New street scene: Minneapolis pedestrian
mall. il Arch Forum 130:74-81 Ja '69
Revitalizing downtown shopping centers. L.
Douglass. il Arch Rec 146:136-7 Jl '69
Two cities built malls that bring new vitality
to Main Street; Montevideo Minn, and
Danville, Ill. G. M. Chamberlain. il Am City
84:78+ N '69

BUSINESS education
Geneva's international training ground; Centre d'etudes industrielles. A. McGregor.
Duns R 93:58 Ja '69
Making it in the learning trade. Bsns W p74+
S 6 '69
Try a modified business education program.
J. F. Beck. Todays Ed 58:69 N '69
See also
Distributive education
Executives—Training
Texas. University—Austin campus—College of
business administration

India
Teaching business success; course held at
India's Small industries extension training
institute in Hyderabad. il Time 93:64 Ap
25 '69

BUSINESS enterprises, New
Closing a military base need not be a tragedy.
J. B. Coffey, jr. il Nations Bsns 57:84-5 S
'69
Corporate growth through venture management. M. Hanan. il Harvard Bsns R 47:
43-61 Ja '69
How the high-fliers take off. il Bsns W p 112-
14+ N 22 '69
They gamble on new technology; risk management by New business resources. il
Bsns W p 128+ N 1 '69

BUSINESS entertaining
Absolutely free; Elvis Presley's opening performance. M. Hentoff. Harper 239:28+ N '69
Film fest's best jests; week-long jamboree
at King's Inn, Grand Bahama Island, given
by Warner brothers. H. V. Fondiller. il Pop
Phot 65:118+ O '69
Reporter at large; four day celebration of
Brown brothers Harriman & co. hundred-
and-fiftieth anniversary. J. Brooks. New
Yorker 45:97-8+ Ap 26 '69

BUSINESS ethics
See also
Competition, Unfair
Medical ethics
Trade secrets

BUSINESS expansion. See Industrial expansion

BUSINESS expenses. See Expense accounts
(business)

BUSINESS failures
Business failures. R. Wyant. See issues of
Dun's review
See also
Bankruptcy

BUSINESS flying. See Airplanes in business

BUSINESS forecasting
And the boom goes on. il Nations Bsns 57:
34-7 Ap '69
Are technological upheavals inevitable? M.
W. Hunter, 2d. il Harvard Bsns R 47:73-83
S '69
Business: a look ahead. See issues of Nation's business
Business barrels toward a trillion dollar to-
morrow. il Nations Bsns 57:28-31 N '69
Business men's expectations (cont) il Duns R
93:113 Mr; 94:131 S; 87 D '69
Business predictions for 1969: mixed optimism. Arch Rec 145:69 Ja '69
Business slowdown coming? interview. P. W.
McCracken. il U S News 66:44-8 Ap 28 '69
Business trends 1969: a trillion dollar economy. il Sr Schol 94:7 Ja 31 '69
Businessmen's expectations (cont) il Duns R
93:113 Mr: 94:131 S '69
Forecasters who don't share the fears; American statistical assn. Bsns W p24 Ag 23 '69
How businessmen view the coming year. il
Bsns W p 112-14+ Ja 10 '70

In the new year, what business can expect.
il U S News 68:18-20 Ja 5 '70
Key executives' forecast: when business will
turn up; with editorial comment. il Nations Bsns 57:5-6, 44-9 O '69
Latest official word on business outlook. il
U S News 66:80 Mr 3 '69
Next year's biggest challenge; Dun's presidents' panel sees trouble ahead. G. R.
Rosen. Duns R 92:36-7 D '68
Official look ahead at business. il U S News
66:52 Mr 10 '69
Probes of the technological future. H. Q.
North and D. L. Pyke. il Harvard Bsns R
47:68-82 My '69
Recession fears; wild gyrations of financial
opinion in the press. P. A. Samuelson.
Newsweek 74:65 Ag 25 '69
Signs businessmen should watch. K. H. Militzer. Nations Bsns 57:73 Je '69
Top executives forecast; profits point higher
for '69. il Nations Bsns 57:28-31 Ja '69
Trend of American business. See issues of
U S news & World report
What bankers see ahead now. U S News 67:
91-4 O 13 '69
What's ahead for business now. il U S News
67:17-19 Jl 7 '69
See also
Forecasts (economics)

BUSINESS hall of fame. See Michigan. University. Ann Arbor—Business hall of fame
(proposed)

BUSINESS helicopters. See Helicopters in business

BUSINESS hours
Turn to Sunday shopping. il U S News 68:7
Ja 5 '70
See also
Hours of labor

BUSINESS in the arts award
Business and the arts: some progress to be
reported. A. Gingrich. Esquire 73:8+ Ja '70
BCA-Esquire third annual business in the
arts awards. Esquire 72:128-9 Jl '69
Ever-widening circle of business and the arts.
A. Gingrich. Esquire 71:6+ Ja '69
Honor to those who honor the arts. A.
Gingrich. Esquire 72:6 Jl '69

BUSINESS information service. See Information
services

BUSINESS journals. See Business—Periodicals;
Trade journals

BUSINESS libraries. See Libraries, Business

BUSINESS literature
See also
Business—Bibliography

BUSINESS magazines. See Business—Periodicals

BUSINESS management and organization
Addition to the lexicon of management;
hierarchiology. Bsns W p 134 F 22 '69
After the acquisition: continuing challenge.
C. M. Leighton and G. R. Tod. bibliog f
il Harvard Bsns R 47:90-102 Mr '69
Allied chemical: a long rough road back. il
Forbes 103:205-8 My 15 '69
Books & ideas: management's need for another kind of thinking. W. S. Rukeyser.
Fortune 80:211-12 S '69
Closed loop; management's tightening grip.
G. J. Berkwitt. il Duns R 92:38-40 D '68
Control postmerger change. F. W. Searby.
Harvard Bsns R 47:4-6+ S '69
Corporate growth through internal spin-outs.
M. Hanan. il Harvard Bsns R 47:55-66 N
'69
Corporate growth through venture management. M. Hanan. il Harvard Bsns R 47:
43-61 Ja '69
Corporation within the community; address,
January 27, 1969. M. F. Cohen. Vital
Speeches 35:270-3 F 15 '69
Do profit centers really work? G. J. Berkwitt. il Duns R 93:29-31+ My '69
Dry rot: the most elusive enemy. G. J. Berkwitt. il Duns R 94:57-9 O '69
Executive trends. See issues of Nation's business
Generals mean business; recruiting civilian
executives from the brass in Israel. il Time
94:103 O 17 '69
Glossary of incompetence; Peter principle
of hierarchies. Time 93:58 Mr 28 '69
How Allied chemical breaks with its past.
il Bsns W p80-2+ Ap 5 '69
How to delegate. J. G. Mason. il Nations
Bsns 57:60-1+ O '69
How to fend off a take-over. Fortune 79:83+
F '69
How to keep on target. H. O. Golightly. il
Nations Bsns 57:75-7 My '69

BUTANO state park. See California—Parks and reserves
BUTCHER, Jeanne Malcolm
All Greek? Engl J 58:1335-7 D '69
BUTLER, Clifford C.
Graduate student. bibliog por Phys Today 22:39-42 Mr '69
BUTLER, George D.
Survey of retired recreation and park professionals. Parks & Rec 4:21-5+ Je '69
BUTLER, Harry
Australia's embarrassing egg. Sci Digest 65:70-3 Mr '69
BUTLER, Jerry
Jerry Butler: history's hottest iceman. il pors Ebony 25:64-6+ D '69
BUTLER, Joseph T.
Decorative arts. Antiques 96:375 S '69
Passion for boxes. House B 111:98+ My '69
—See Gerry, R. jt. auth.
BUTLER, Michael
Hippie, hairy heir. I. Mothner. il pors Look 33:46-51 Ag 12 '69
Man who gave us Hair. J. Greenfeld. il pors Life 66:50B-50D+ Je 27 '69
BUTLER, Patrick
How to start a library with nothing. por Library J 95:44-5 Ja 1 '70
Would you spend $2.98 for a college education? Sat R 52:23 Ap 12 '69
BUTLER, Thomas Marius Joseph
Gray ghost wins again. J. Stewart-Gordon. Read Digest 95:229-34 Jl '69
BUTLER, Warren L. See Epel, B. jt. auth.
BUTLER, Willis P.
Cuba's revolutionary medicine. Ramp Mag 7:6+ My '69
BUTLER university, Indianapolis
Romantic revival; Butler's second annual festival of romantic music. il Time 93:85 My 30 '69
BUTLER'S festival of romantic music. See Music festivals—Indiana
BUTOR, Michel
Library; story. Harp Baz 102:124 Ap '69
BUTT, Ronald
Speaking for themselves; letter to the Times. Nat R 21:372 Ap 22 '69
BUTTER, Charles M. and others
Orality, preference behavior, and reinforcement value of nonfood object in monkeys with orbital frontal lesions. bibliog Science 164:1306-7 Je 13 '69
BUTTER
Butter is beautiful. il Sunset 142:179 Mr '69
BUTTERFLIES
How to attract butterflies. J. Brewer. il Horticulture 47:24-5+ Jl '69
Sex pheromone of the queen butterfly: biology. T. E. Pliske and T. Eisner. bibliog il Science 164:1170-2 Je 6 '69
Sex pheromone of the queen butterfly: chemistry. J. Meinwald and others. bibliog il Science 164:1174-5 Je 6 '69
Sex pheromone of the queen butterfly: electroantennogram responses. D. Schneider and U. Seibt. bibliog il Science 164:1173-4 Je 6 '69
See also
Lepidoptera
BUTTERFLIES are free; drama. See Gershe, L.
BUTTERS, Nelson, and Pandya, Deepak
Retention of delayed-alternation: effect of selective lesions of sulcus principalis. bibliog Science 165:1271-3 S 19 '69
BUTTERWORTH, F. M.
Lipids of drosophila: a newly detected lipid in the male. bibliog Science 163:1356-7 Mr 21 '69
BUTTON fastener. See Sewing equipment
BUTTONEER. See Sewing equipment
BUTTONS
Button collecting. D. F. Brown. See issues of Hobbies
Grand army of the Republic; G.A.R. buttons. D. F. Brown. il Hobbies 74:50-1 My '69
Lacy glass buttons. D. F. Brown. il Hobbies 74:50-1 Ap '69
Some button history. D. T. Harrell. Hobbies 74:129 D '69
BUTWELL, Richard
Growing involvement in Asia: 1960-1968. bibliog f Cur Hist 57:88-92+ Ag '69
Many-sided politics of South Vietnam. bibliog f Cur Hist 56:71-6+ F '69
Thailand after Vietnam. bibliog f Cur Hist 57:339-43+ D '69
BUTWIN, David W.
Booked for travel. See issues of Saturday review
BUYING. See Shopping and shoppers

BUYING motives. See Market research
BUYNAK, Michael F.
Business side of your camp should be run like a business! Camp Mag 41:8-10 N '69
BUYUKMIHCI, Hope Sawyer
Organic gardeners in the wilds. Org Gard & Farm 16:56-8 F '69
BUZICK, William Alonson, 1920-
Coup at Consolidated. Newsweek 74:49+ D 29 '69
BUZZARDS, Turkey. See Turkey buzzards
BUZZARDS BAY, Mass.
Bay and the Sound; excerpts. J. Parkinson, jr. il Motor B 123:57-63 Je '69
Cleveland on the Cape. T. L. Christie. il Sat R 52:56+ Mr 8 '69
BUZZATI-TRAVERSO, Adriano A.
Italy: first Ph.D. program stalled by new and old politics. D. S. Greenberg. por Science 163:1306-8 Mr 21 '69
BUZZI, Ruth
Girls from L-I. por Newsweek 73:62 Ja 27 '69
BWAYE, Malam Adi. See Malam Adi Bwaye
BY-elections. See Elections—Great Britain
BYELORUSSIA. See Belorussia
BYERLEE, James D. and Brace, W. F.
High-pressure mechanical instability in rocks. bibliog Science 164:713-15 My 9 '69
BYERS, A. M, and company
Wrought iron on scrap heap. il Bsns W p 18 Ja 3 '70
BYERS, Walter
Out of right field. por Newsweek 75:35 Ja 5 '70
BYLINSKY, Gene
Biochemical clues to mental illness. Fortune 80:124-7+ Jl '69
Bringing the laser down to earth. Fortune 80:126-9+ S '69
Improving on nature to vanquish hunger. Fortune 79:126-31+ Ap '69
Penetrating the secrets of the planets. Fortune 80:138-43 N '69
BYNDER, Herbert
How doctors choose a doctor. Time 94:46-7 Ag 15 '69
BYRD, Elizabeth
Rewards of a gracious heart. Read Digest 94:106-8 Je '69
BYRD, Harry Flood, 1914-
Excerpt from debate, October 9, 1968. Cong Digest 48:56+ F '69
BYRD, Max
Nero Wolfe's brand of beer. Nation 208:251-2 F 24 '69
BYRD, Robert Carlyle
Excerpt from statement, February 4, 1969. Cong Digest 48:104+ Ap '69
BYRD, William
Some aspects of word treatment in the music of William Byrd. W. Gray. bibliog f Mus Q 55:45-64 Ja '69
BYRNES, James Francis
Where are they now? il pors Newsweek 74:28 N 17 '69
BYRNES, Robert F.
American scholars in Russia soon learn about the K.G.B. N Y Times Mag p84-5+ N 16 '69
BYROM, Fletcher Lauman
Hang loose; address, June 16, 1969. Vital Speeches 35:604-8 Jl 15 '69
Top executive's advice: hang loose. Duns R 94:51-3+ S '69
BYRON, George Gordon Noël Byron, 6th baron
Byron, the Don Juan, plus Shakespeare & Jonson. P. W. Schmidtchen. por Hobbies 74:104-5+ My '69
Lady and the lion. L. Kronenberger. Atlan 223:93+ Ja '69
BYRON, William J.
American pastor and social change. America 120:246-9 Mr 1 '69
BYZANTINE rite. See Catholic church—Byzantine rite

C

C-5A (airplane) See Airplanes, Military transport
CAB. See United States—Civil aeronautics board
CAINS (carrier aircraft inertial navigation system) See Inertial guidance systems
CAIP. See Catholic association for international peace
CAL. See Cornell aeronautical laboratory, incorporated

CAM (cybernetic anthropomorphous machine)
See Man amplifiers
CAPEI. See Central American program of economic integration
CAS (collision avoidance systems) See Airplanes
—Safety devices and measures
CAT (clear air turbulence) See Atmospheric turbulence
CATV system
Boost for CATV. Newsweek 73:88 Je 9 '69
Cable TV leaps into the big time. il Bsns W p 100-3+ N 22 '69
Cable TV, the hottest thing in television. H. Manchester. Read Digest 94:19-20+ Je '69
CATV: a perfect picture, and more channels, too. H. Fantel. il Pop Sci 194:68-70+ Ja '69
CATV projects a new ad picture. il Bsns W p 140+ Jl 12 '69
Confusion in TV land: fee, free, or what? CATV? il Sr Schol 94:14-15 F 14 '69
Designing a receiver for cable-TV. J. Frye. il Electr World 81:50+ Je '69
Getting the signals straight on CATV. Bsns W p42 Je 7 '69
More wraps off CATV. R. H. Smith. Pub W 196:33 N 3 '69
Signals: one, two, three; new FCC order. R. L. Shayon. Sat R 52:75 D 6 '69
CATV system and copyright. See Copyright—Broadcasting rights
CB radio. See Citizens radio service
CBA. See Christian booksellers association
CBS. See Columbia broadcasting system
CBW research. See Chemical and biological weapons
CCC. See Commercial credit company
CCD. See Confraternity of Christian doctrine
CCM. See Crowell Collier and Macmillan, incorporated
CCNY. See New York (city). City university of New York—City college
CCP. See Commission on college physics
CDC. See Community development corporations; Control data corporation
CDU (Christian democratic union) See Political parties—Germany (Federal Republic)
CEA. See United States—Council of economic advisers
CED. See Committee for economic development
CERN (Conseil européen pour la recherche nucléaire) See European organization for nuclear research
C. H. Masland and sons. See Masland, C. H, and sons
CIA. See United States—Central intelligence agency
CICOP (Catholic Inter-American cooperation program) See Religious conferences
CIF. See Construction industry foundation
CITEL (Inter-American telecommunications commission) See Inter-American economic and social council
CLA. See California library association
CLR. See Council on library resources, incorporated
CNA financial corporation
Insurance giants move into funds. il Bsns W p 114-16+ Mr 15 '69
Keep 'em guessing; CNA as a holding company. Forbes 104:58 O 15 '69
COCU. See Consultation on church union
COM (computer output microfilming) See Computers—Input-output equipment
COMES. See European community of writers
COPE (consortium of publishers for employment) See Socially handicapped—Employment
CORE. See Congress of racial equality
COS. See Central opera service
COSPAR. See International council of scientific unions—Committee on space research
CPA. See Catholic press association
CPB. See Corporation for public broadcasting
CP-ILS (correlation protected instrument landing system) See Airplanes—Landing
CPM (critical path method) See Critical path analysis
CRIA. See Committee to rescue Italian art
CRLA (California rural legal assistance) See Legal aid
CRT. See Cathode ray tubes
CSD. See American library association—Children's services division
CSO. See Industrial areas foundation—Community service organization

CTIP (Compagnia tecnica industrie petroli) See Petroleum industry and trade—Italy
CU. See Consumers union of United States
CUNY. See New York (city). City university of New York
CUSIP. See Committee on uniform security identification procedures
CWSA. See Campus worker-student alliance (organization)
CAB drivers. See Taxicab drivers
CABALLÉ, Montserrat
Many pleasures of the Spanish zarzuela. P. L. Miller. il por Am Rec G 35:536-7 Mr '69
CABARETS
Neutral DMZ; political cabaret. P. Velde. Commonweal 89:529-30 Ja 24 '69
Tokyo P.M. G. Cotler. il Holiday 46:52-5+ S '69
See also
Night clubs
CABBAGE moths. See Cabbages—Diseases and pests
CABBAGES
Cabbages in your garden. C. L. Fessenden. il Org Gard & Farm 16:39-41 Mr '69
See also
Brussels sprouts
Cookery—Vegetables

Diseases and pests
Mini-tent keeps cabbage moths away. H. W. Kortz. il Org Gard & Farm 16:104-5 Ja '69
CABINET (United States) See United States—Cabinet
CABINET committee on voluntary action. See United States—Cabinet committee on voluntary action
CABINET officers
Decision makers. il Parks & Rec 4:6 My '69
Flavor of the new; with colored photographs. Time 93:12-13 Ja 24 '69
Innovator, some administrators, some homework, and some hopes. W. F. Wagner, jr. Arch Rec 145:9 Ja '69
Key men around Nixon: who's calling the signals. il U S News 66:70-3 My 12 '69
Members of new Cabinet tell where they stand; answers to questions at confirmation hearings. il U S News 66:43-4 Ja 27 '69
Mr Rogers and Mr Finch; key men on the Nixon team. il Life 66:16B-23 Ja 24 '69
New Cabinet. Sr Schol 94:14-15 Ja 17 '69
Washington now: who's in, who's out of power. pors U S News 66:26-9 Ja 27 '69
See also
United States—Cabinet

Appointment, qualifications, tenure, etc.
Conservationist; W. J. Hickel as Secretary of the interior. New Repub 160:9 Ja 25 '69
Interior's Walter Hickel: frontier figure in a Cabinet hot seat. U S News 66:14 F 3 '69
Packard dilemma. Nation 208:66-7 Ja 20 '69
Pass for Mitchell. J. Osborne. New Repub 160:13 Ja 25 '69
CABINET officers wives
Interesting women. il McCalls 96:112-13 Ap '69
Wives listen in on the Cabinet. il U S News 66:16 Ap 28 '69
CABINET system
See also
France—Cabinet
Spain—Cabinet
CABINETMAKERS
See also
Chippendale, T.
CABINETS (furniture)
Build a swivel-top projection cabinet. T. W. Cotton. il Pop Sci 194:146-9 Je '69
Build this colonial cabinet-top desk. P. K. Snook. il Pop Mech 131:132-3 F '69
Build this storage into your pool table. il Pop Mech 131:154-7 Ja '69
New shape of sound. il House & Gard 136:88-9 D '69
See also
Kitchen cabinets
CABINS
Want a summer house? prefab the parts this winter. D. Norton. il Pop Sci 194:158-63 Ja '69
Way-out fun house for your vacation lot. K. Isaacs. il Pop Sci 195:131-5+ Jl '69
CABLE, Harold
Bailey, go home; drama. Plays 28:27-38 Mr '69
Reform of Sterling Silverheart; drama. Plays 29:27-37 N '69
Reluctant Columbus; drama. Plays 29:1-13 O '69

CABLE, Mary
Main street of America; excerpt from The avenue of the presidents; with a portfolio of illustrations. Am Heritage 20:44-53+ F '69

CABLE television. See CATV system

CABLES
See also
Rochester corporation

CABLES, Submarine
Cable talk; cable from Green Hill, R. I. to San Fernando, Spain. il Sea Front 15:97 Mr '69
Comsat, cable owners clash over traffic. K. Johnsen. Aviation W 90:19-20 F 10 '69
FCC launches cable-satellite investigation to establish policy. K. Johnsen. Aviation W 91:23 D 8 '69

CABLEWAYS
One-armed high-wire artist; maintenance man on Mt San Jacinto tramway. F. Taylor il Pop Mech 131:138-9 Ap '69

CABOT, Paul Codman
Warning: it may be later than you think. pors Forbes 103:65+ F 15 '69

CABRILLO BEACH. See San Pedro, Calif.

CACAO
Diseases and pests
Consequence of insecticides; pests follow the chemicals in the cocoa of Malaysia. G. R. Conway. il Natur Hist 78:46-51 F '69

CACCIA, David A.
Acres of diamonds? Org Gard & Farm 16:54-5 O '69
Cranberry harvest; photographs; with biographical sketch. por Natur Hist 78:6, 54-7 N '69
Homemade sundial. Org Gard & Farm 16:74-6 Je '69
Regulating humidity in the home. Org Gard & Farm 16:112-16 F '69

CACEK, Terry
Hill country antelope. Field & S 74:48-9+ S '69

CACHE national forest, Utah. See National forests

CACTUS
Cacti, ideal indoor plants. L. Cutak. il Horticulture 46:36-7+ N '68
How to succeed with Christmas cactus. il Bet Hom & Gard 47:158 N '69
How to succeed with Christmas cactus. B. Brinhart. il Home Gard 56:52-3 D '69
See also
Peyote

CADAVERS
Bodies for education; letter. J. W. Miller. Sci N 95:545-6 Je 7 '69
Let the dead help the living; proposed uniform anatomical gift act. R. S. Fisher. Todays Health 47:38+ Ap '69
Making transplants easier; legislation based on Uniform anatomical gift act. Time 93:61+ 25 '69

CADDELL, Foster
Foster Caddell: painter & teacher. N. Kent. il pors Am Artist 32:36-42+ D '68

CADDICK, J. W.
Ring for flowers. Horticulture 47:18 My '69

CADDIS flies
Amazing caddis-fly. N. Smith. il Nat Wildlife 7:31 Ag '69

CADE, James Robert
Battle bubbles over Gatorade profits. Bsns W p33 S 6 '69

CADE, Robert
New drink in town. L. Sanders. il Mech Illus 65:32+ N '69

CADE, Toni
Children who get cheated. Redbook 134:64-5+ Ja '70

CADELL, Elizabeth
Third surprise; excerpt from The past tense of love; novel. Redbook 133:167-89 Jl '69

CADET corps organizations. See Youth associations

CADIEUX, Charles L.
Cruising in a marine zoo. Yachting 126:60-1+ S '69
Outboard on Vancouver Island. Yachting 125:50-1+ Je '69

CADLE, Richard D. and Roberts, W. O.
In pursuit of atmospheres. pors Chem 42:7-11 Ja '69

CADMIUM poisoning
Soft water and heart disease; worldwide puzzle. Sci N 95:471 My 17 '69

CADMIUM sulfide
Lab bench; effect of temperature on light absorption by crystalline cadmium sulfide. J. A. Isenberg. il Chem 42:26-8 Je '69; Correction. 42:32 Jl '69

CADWALADER, Alfred
Vacationing with organic foods. Org Gard & Farm 16:38-40 Jl '69
We are doing for ourselves. Org Gard & Farm 16:40-1 Ja '69

CADWELL, Paul
Cadwell's banjo; interview. New Yorker 45:39-41 Ap 12 '69

CAEN, Herb
San Francisco's Buena Vista. Holiday 46:84-6 D '69

CAESAR salad. See Salads

CAETANO, Marcello
Cracks in the facade. Newsweek 74:53-4 O 27 '69
In a minor key. P. S. Cook. por Newsweek 73:48+ Je 2 '69
New style of tyranny. L. Jenkins. Nation 209:532-4 N 17 '69
Premier and prodigal; Mozambique visit. Newsweek 73:59-60 Ap '69
Shades of Salazar. il por Time 94:30 O 31 '69
Smooth shift of gears. P. Witonski. Nat R 21:851 Ag 26 '69

CAFE curtains. See Curtains and draperies

CAFETERIAS
See also
New York (city)—Hotels, restaurants, etc.

CAFFÉ Greco. See Rome (city)—Hotels, restaurants, etc.

CAGE, John
Of dice and din. Time 93:85-6 My 30 '69

CAGE; drama. See Cluchey, R.

CAGES
Two-story house for rats. il Sunset 142:132+ Mr '69

CAHAN, Abraham
Downtown Jews, by R. Sanders. Review
Nation 210:24-6 Ja 12 '70. M. T. Gilmore
Sat R 53:40 Ja 10 '70. Y. Jacobs

CAHIER, Bernard
Peugeot 504. Motor T 21:52 F '69

CAHIER, Philippe
Vienna convention on diplomatic relations. bibliog f por(backcover) Int Concil 571:5-40 Ja '69

CAHILL, Thomas
Friendly fuzz. A. A. Rosenfeld. il Nation 208:503-7 Ap 21 '69

CAHILL, William Thomas
1969 elections showed a movement to republicanism; interview. por U S News 67:39 N 17 '69

CAHN, Robert
Making economic aid effective. Cur 104:41-5 F '69

CAIMANS. See Alligators

CAIN, Edwin, and St Pierre, Anne
Swinging with mini-projects. Am Ed 5:5-8 D '69

CAIN, Margret
In my opinion. por Seventeen 28:160 Jl '69

CAIN, Seymour
Semper fidelis: the ethic of the warrior. Chr Cent 86:677-81 My 14 '69

CAIRNS, E. J. and Shimotake, H.
High-temperature batteries. bibliog Science 164:1347-55 Je 20 '69

CAIRO
In Cairo: threats of war but business better than usual. il U S News 67:39-40 Jl 7 '69
1,000th (happy?) birthday; Cairo's blue period. A. Carthew. il N Y Times Mag p6+ Ag 17 '69; Reply. M. Cohen. p4 Ag 31 '69

CAIRO, Ill.
Cairo: love it or leave it. W. Willoughby. il Chr Today 14:46 O 24 '69
Eyeless in Cairo. il Newsweek 74:47 S 29 '69
Flood of hate rises in Cairo. il Bsns W p48-9 Jl 12 '69
Trouble in Cairo. Newsweek 73:41 My 5 '69

Negroes
Black and poor in Cairo. R. Middeke. Commonweal 90:453-4 Jl 25 '69
Racial pallor of Cairo. G. L. Heath. Nation 209:692-5 D 22 '69
War in Little Egypt. Time 94:23 S 26 '69

CAJUNS. See Acadians in Louisiana

CAKE
A la mode, move over! il Bet Hom & Gard 47:66-7 Ag '69
And to each a Christmas log. il Sunset 143:131 D '69
Angel bright, silver white; Christmas tree cake. il Seventeen 27:124-5+ D '68
Bride makes walnut-raisin cake. il McCalls 97:42 N '69
Cakes with pour-on icings. E. W. Manning. il Farm J 93:82 Mr '69

CAKE—*Continued*
Fabulous featherweights: three cakes in one. M. Happel. il Ladies Home J 86:114-15+ S '69
Fast and fancy cakes, all kinds. il Bet Hom & Gard 47:109-10 S '69
For champagne tastes; sponge roll. C. Claiborne. il N Y Times Mag p67-8+ Ap 6 '69
From layer cake, a grand torte. il Sunset 142:131 F '69
Glistening savarin, fruit's good companion. il Sunset 143:88 Ag '69
Good grief, it's a birthday; party with recipes from the Peanuts cookbook. M. Happel. il Ladies Home J 86:122-3+ O '69
Handle with care; French chocolate cake. J. Hewitt. il N Y Times Mag p 120 S 7 '69
It's a cake that's soggy. il Sunset 142:140 F '69
It's good looking and it's easy: self-frosted one-layer cake il Sunset 142:167 Ap '69
My cake won! E. W. Manning. il Farm J 93:32-3+ Jl '69
Peaches and cream, and rum baba. il Sunset 143:104 Ag '69
Three really nutty cakes. il Sunset 142:124-5 F '69
Very special pies and cakes. il Bet Hom & Gard 47:85-96 My '69
We baked our Christmas tree cakes in kitchen funnels; fruitcake. il Sunset 143:144-5 D '69
You are the originator, but it's a package cake mix that saves you. il Sunset 142:206 My '69

See also
Cheesecake
Coffee cake
Pastry

CAKE decorations. See Icings

CALABRIA, Italy
New kick in the Italian boot. M. Berry. il Sat R 52:48-50 Ag 23 '69

CALABRIAN company
AID raises weeds in Thailand corn deal; government's Extended risk guarantee program. il Bsns W p78-9 Mr 22 '69

CALAM, John
New books. See issues of Saturday review

CALAMAR, Gloria
Gloria Calamar has affinity for her subject; with biographical sketch. il por Am Artist 33:52-3+ Ap '69

CALARTS. See California institute of the arts

CALAS, Nicolas
Large glass. Art in Am 57:34-5 Jl '69

CALCIFICATION
Diphosphonates inhibit formation of calcium phosphate crystals in vitro and pathological calcification in vivo. M. D. Francis and others. bibliog il Science 165:1264-6 S 19 '69
See also
Bone

CALCITE
Methane-derived marine carbonates of pleistocene age. J. C. Hathaway and E. T. Degens. bibliog il Science 165:690-2 Ag 15 '69

CALCITONIN
Thyrocalcitonin: evidence for physiological function T. K. Gray and P. L. Munson. bibliog il Science 166:512-13 O 24 '69

CALCIUM
See also
Plants, Effect of calcium on

CALCIUM carbonate
See also
Calcite

CALCIUM compounds
See also
Hydroxyapatite

CALCIUM in the body
Calcium current and activation of contraction in ventricular myocardial fibers. H. Reuter and G. W. Beeler, jr. bibliog il Science 163:399-401 Ja 24 '69
Calcium uptake by isolated sarcoplasmic reticulum treated with dithiothreitol. W. Van Der Kloot. bibliog il Science 164:1294 Je 13 '69
Intestinal calcium absorption: nature of defect in chronic renal disease. L. V. Avioli and others. bibliog il Science 166:1154-6 N 28 '69
Regenerative calcium release within muscle cells. L. E. Ford and R. J. Podolsky. bibliog il Science 167:58-9 Ja 2 '70
See also
Calcification
Hypercalcemia

CALCULATING charts. See Charts, Calculating

CALCULI
Amino acid uptake by kidney and jejunal tissue from dogs with cystine stones. P. G. Holtzapple and others. bibliog il Science 166:1525-7 D 19 '69

CALCULI, Urinary
Are kidney stones really stones? Todays Health 47:67-8 Ag '69

CALCUTTA
Social conditions
If you think America has slums—. il U S News 66:64-5 Je 23 '69
Theater
Left theatre in India. J. V. Hatch. Nation 208:804-6 Je 23 '69

CALCUTTA pools. See Gambling

CALDECOTT medal
Caldecott award acceptance; address, June 24, 1969. U. Shulevitz. il Horn Bk 45:385-8 Ag '69
Here are the winners! R. Gagliardo. PTA Mag 63:32-3 Ap '69
Newbery-Caldecott secret, not a secret any more. il Pub W 195:129-30 F 17 '69
Newbery-Caldecott winners announced at ALA midwinter. Library J 94:1280+ Mr 15 '69
Uri Shulevitz: Caldecott winner. M. Di Capua. il Library J 94:2068-9 My 15 '69

CALDER, Alexander
Calder's international monuments; interview, ed. by R. Osborn. por Art in Am 57:32-49 Mr '69

CALDER, Peter Ritchie, baron Ritchie-Calder. See Ritchie-Calder. P. R. C.

CALDERA, Rafael
Man of el cambio. il Time 93:30 My 2 '69

CALDERÓN DE LA BARCA, Pedro
Constant prince; adaptation. See Grotowski, J.

CALDERONE, Mary Steichen
Doctor Mary Steichen Calderone, sex educator. il por Vogue 153:180 My '69

CALDWELL, David K. See Caldwell, M. C. jt. auth.

CALDWELL, Douglas R. and others
Sensors in the deep sea. bibliog por Phys Today 22:34-42 Jl '69

CALDWELL, Edson
Are you listening, teacher? Todays Ed 58:33-4 Ja '69

CALDWELL, George W.
Winners! Consumer challenge essays. por Har Yrs 9:16-17 Jl '69

CALDWELL, Gilbert H.
Black folk in white churches. Chr Cent 86:209-11 F 12 '69

CALDWELL, Melba C. and Caldwell, D. K.
Ugly dolphin; with biographical sketches. Sea Front 15:308-14, 318, 349-55 S-N '69

CALDWELL, Turner
Making optical flats with simple equipment. R Pop Astron 63:26-32 Mr '69

CALENDAR
See also
Indians of South America—Calendar

CALENDULAS
Plant these now for color later. il Sunset 143:190 S '69

CALF scours. See Calves—Diseases and pests

CALFPASTURE RIVER
Marble Valley controversy. R. Lyle, jr. il Nat Parks 43:14-17 N '69

CALHOUN, Mary
Tracking down elves in folklore. Horn Bk 45:278-82 Je '69

CALIAN, Carnegie Samuel
Berdyaev: philosopher of hope. Chr Cent 86:924-6 Jl 9 '69

CALIBRATION
Calibrate for peak-to-peak volts. J. Darr. il Radio-Electr 40:17+ Ap '69

CALIBRATORS
Low-cost d.c.-voltage calibrator. L. H. Garner. il Electr World 82:42 S '69
Low-cost precious scope & V.T.V.M. calibrator. G. H. Lehmann. il Electr World 81:80-2 Mr '69
SCS frequency calibrator. B. W. Blachford. il Pop Electr 31:53-4 D '69

CALICO, Calif. See Abandoned towns

CALIFORNIA
Doomsday in the Golden state. il Time 93:59 Ap 11 '69
Warning! California will fall into the ocean in April! S. V. Roberts. il N Y Times Mag p 12+ Ap 6 '69
See also
Airports—California
Architecture, Domestic—California
Art—California
Arts and crafts—California

CALIFORNIA—See also—*Continued*
  Booksellers and bookselling—California
  Botany—California
  Camping—California
  Central Valley
  Colleges and universities—California
  Colleges and universities, State—California
  Conservation of resources—California
  Contra Costa County
  Crime and criminals—California
  Death Valley
  Divorce—California
  Ecology—California
  Education—California
  Festivals—California
  Fishing—California
  Geology—California
  Gunther Island
  Hunting—California
  Justice, Administration of—California
  Kings Canyon National Park
  Lakes—California
  Lava Beds National Monument
  Law—California
  Laws, Calif.
  Libraries—California
  Music festivals—California
  National parks and reserves—California
  Paleontology—California
  Police—California
  Politics, Corruption in—California
  Prisons—California
  Recreation areas—California
  Redwood National Park
  Roads—California
  Sacramento River
  Sacramento-San Joaquin Delta
  San Francisco Bay
  San Francisco Bay Region
  Sequoia National Park
  Tahoe, Lake
  Trials—California
  Water supply—California
  Wilderness areas—California
  Wildlife sanctuaries—California
  Yosemite National Park
  Yosemite Valley

Description and travel
Away from the crowds, in Klamath country. il Sunset 142:28+ Ag '69
California: a state of excitement. il Time 94: 60-6 N 7 '69
Journey to California. N. Cousins. Sat R 52: 20-1 Mr 1 '69
Only in spots have we tamed the California coast. M. F. K. Fisher. il Holiday 46:40-5+ N '69

Foreign population
See also
Chinese in the United States

Historic houses, etc.
At the Ide Adobe you step back into the 19th century. il Sunset 143:76 O '69
See also
Sacramento, Calif.—Historic houses, etc.

History
Twilight of the Californios. F. Egan. il Am West 6.34-42 Mr '69
See also
California—Missions

Bibliography
Great year for California history. il Sunset 142:66 Mr '69

Missions
Bells of San Luis Obispo. T. Andreeva. il Américas 21:12-14 Ag '69
End of a mission? bicentennial celebration of Mission San Diego de Alcalá. D. Butwin. il Sat R 52:52+ F 22 '69
Pathfinder of the Papagueria. R. L. Ives. il Américas 21:13-20 S; 14-21 O '69
Visiting with California's memories. L. Payne. il Todays Health 47:42-7+ D '69

Parks and reserves
Back road adventure in the redwoods; Prairie Creek redwoods state park. il Sunset 143:45-6+ S '69
Butano's now open to hikers and campers. il Sunset 143:3 O '69
California parks welcome horsemen. Sunset 142:59 Je '69
Hearst gardens; San Simeon state historical monument. G. Taloumis. il Horticulture 46:40-3 D '68
New park in the Valley of the moon. il Sunset 143:62+ O '69
San Diego: to celebrate a 200th anniversary, a spirited fiesta in Old Town. il Sunset 143:66-9 Jl '69

What this footbridge offers is an invitation to walk in the redwoods; Nickerson ranch trail through Jedediah Smith redwoods state park. il Sunset 143:50 N '69
See also
Disneyland park, Anaheim

Politics and government
California: the rending of the veil. M. Frady. il Harper 239:57-73 D '69
California weather breeder. M. Harris. il Nation 208:110-13 Ja 27 '69
Democrats confront 1970. P. Kerby. Nation 209:594-5 D 1 '69
Goldwater and son; Barry jr. elected for Congress. il Time 93:29 My 9 '69
New tribune for California? W. Wingfield. Chr Cent 86:724+ My 21 '69
See also
Politics, Corruption in—California

Recreation
See Recreation—United States

Social life and customs
California: a state of excitement. il Time 94: 60-6 N 7 '69
Few hazards of the good life. K. Lamott. Horizon 11:26-9 Spr '69

Theaters
See Theater—United States
CALIFORNIA, GULF OF
Cruising in a marine zoo; Gulf of Cortez. C. L. Cadieux. il Yachting 126:60-1+ S '69
Next Mediterranean Sea. R. Joseph. il Esquire 71:152-3+ Je '69
CALIFORNIA, LOWER
Bottom of Baja. il Sunset 142:76-85 Mr '69
Down into Baja; a photographic journey. E. S. Gardner. il Travel & Camera 32:80-3 Ag '69
Next Mediterranean Sea. R. Joseph. il Esquire 71:152-3+ Je '69
Pathfinder of the Papagueria. R. L. Ives. il Américas 21:13-20 S; 14-21 O '69
CALIFORNIA big trees. See Sequoia, Giant
CALIFORNIA buckeye. See Horse chestnut
CALIFORNIA cookery. See Cookery, American
CALIFORNIA cup series. See Yacht racing
CALIFORNIA earthquakes. See Earthquakes—United States
CALIFORNIA forest fire. See Forest fires
CALIFORNIA grape pickers strike. See Strikes—United States—Farm labor
CALIFORNIA gray whales. See Whales
CALIFORNIA in art
California's pictorial letter sheets; excerpts. J. A. Baird, jr. il Antiques 96:412-17 S '69
Exhibition at San Diego; Old Town galleries. N. Kent. il Am Artist 33:36-44+ S '69
Herbert Ryman: California painter. B. Howell. il Am Artist 33:66-71 Ap '69
Regional art in Oakland. P. Selz; P. Mills. il Art in Am 57:108-9 S '69
CALIFORNIA institute of technology, Pasadena
Drugs & the Caltech student; excerpts, with editorial comment. il Chem 42:4, 8-18 N '69
See also
Jet propulsion laboratory
CALIFORNIA institute of the arts
Music to my ears; Calarts at Valencia. I. Kolodin. Sat R 52:45 S 6 '69
West coast report. P. Selz; H. J. Seldis. il Art in Am 57:107-9 Mr '69
CALIFORNIA library association
California library association resolution on sanctions against the California state colleges. ALA Bul 63:1205-7 O '69
California L.A. takes lead in social responsibility; meeting. Library J 93:4599+ D 15 '68; Correction 94:696 F 15 '69
Oh, California! seventy-first annual conference. W. R. Eshelman. Wilson Lib Bul 44: 493-4 Ja '70
Paid leave during strike urged by California L.A; Berkeley campus of the University of California. Library J 94:1404+ Ap 1 '69; Discussion. 94:2175 Je 1 '69
Quiet revolution; CLA sanctions against state colleges. R. D. Galloway. il ALA Bul 63:1257-61 O '69
CALIFORNIA national guard. See United States—National guard
CALIFORNIA rural legal assistance program. See Legal aid

CALIFORNIANS
Almost ancestors, the first Californians, by T. Kroeber and R. F. Heizer. Review
  Américas 21:41-3 F '69. F. L. Phelps
Californians: a new in group in Washington. il U S News 66:80-1 My 5 '69
Long-winded lady; visitor to New York. New Yorker 45:16-19 Jl 19 '69

CALIGUIRI, Lawrence A. and Tamm, Igor
Membranous structures associated with translation and transcription of poliovirus RNA. bibliog Science 166:885-6 N 14 '69

CALIGURI, Joseph P.
College student drug abuse. bibliog f Clear House 44:50-3 S '69

CALIPERS
How to choose and use small vernier calipers. J. Burroughs. il Pop Mech 131:192-5 My '69

CALISCH, Richard W.
So you want to be a real teacher? Todays Ed 58:49-51 N '69

CALISHER, Hortense
Interview with Hortense Calisher; ed. by R. Newquist; reprint. por Writers Digest 49: 58-60+ Mr '69
'30s. Mlle 69:169+ My '69

about
Authors & editors. B. A Bannon. por Pub W 195:19-20 Ap 21 '69

CALISTHENICS. See Gymnastics

CALITRI, Charles J.
Everybody wants in. Sat R 52:83 My 17 '69

CALKING compounds. See Caulking compounds

CALKINS, Frank
Simple streamers for impatient anglers. Field & S 74:78-9+ My '69

CALL it love; story. See Litvinov, I.

CALLAGHAN, Brian
Social studies: the flexible content approach. Clear House 43:368-70 F '69

CALLAGHAN, James
Rigor mortis. il por Newsweek 73:53-4 My 26 '69

CALLAHAN, Daniel
Choking on pious goodies. Commonweal 91: 128-9 O 31 '69

CALLAHAN, Dorothy M.
Is Title I worthwhile? Sr Schol 94:School Teach 17 My 2 '69

CALLAHAN, Harry
Try this short photo course. J. Dreyfuss. il Mod Phot 33:92-7 Je '69
Who is Callahan? D. Vestal. il Travel & Camera 32:68-72+ My '69

CALLAN, Edward
Song of sorrow and thanksgiving. Sat R 52:31-2+ N 8 '69

CALLAS, Maria
An ancient woman. J. Buckley. il pors Opera N 34:8-13 D 13 '69
Art of la Divina. P. L. Miller. Am Rec G 36: 102-3 O '69
La Callas of yore, iridescence and marble. P. L. Miller. Am Rec G 36:106 O '69
Will Maria Callas sing again? R. Gelatt. McCalls 96:90-1 Mr '69

CALLENDER, Eugene S.
Will there ever be a housing boom? interview. por Forbes 104:72+ O 15 '69

CALLENDER, James Thomson
President again; reprint from Recorder, Richmond, September 1, 1802. Negro Hist Bul 32:20-1 N '69

about
Thomas Jefferson and James Thomson Callender: the myth of Black Sally. J. W. Knudson. Negro Hist Bul 32:15-19 bibliog(p22) N '69

CALLEY, William Laws, Jr
Atrocity reports: the aftermath. il por U S News 67:4 D 8 '69
Average American boy? por Time 94:25 D 5 '69
Calley case. por Newsweek 74:40+ N 24 '69
Can Calley get a fair trial? il Time 94:22 D 26 '69
Fair trial vs. free press. Newsweek 74:71-2 D 15 '69
Fallout from Song My. il por Newsweek 74: 40-1 D 15 '69
Killings at Song My; with report by L. Norman. il por Newsweek 74:33-4+ D 8 '69
My Lai massacre. il por Time 94:17-19 N 28 '69
Probing the massacre probe. por Time 94: 16-17 D 12 '69
Song My; a U.S. atrocity? il por Newsweek 74:35-7 D 1 '69

CALLIGRAPHERS
  See also
  Carpi, U. da

CALLIGRAPHY
Art of written forms, by D. M. Anderson. Review
  Pub W il 196:70-2+ Ag 4 '69. P. Standard
Colorful calligraphy: projects at the Corcoran school of art in Washington. R. Foster. il Am Artist 33:83-7+ Mr '69

CALLIGRAPHY, Korean. See Korean language—Writing

CALLING, Animal. See Animal calling

CALLISON, Charles H.
National outlook. See issues of Audubon

CALLISTO (satellite). See Satellites

CALLOW, Philip
Blame me on civilization. Vogue 154:318+ S 1 '69

CALOCHORTUS. See Mariposa lilies

CALORIES, Food. See Diet

CALTECH. See California institute of technology, Pasadena

CALVES
  Care
Toughen calves in the cold? Or pamper them with comfort? D. Hagen; N. Reeder. il Farm J 93:D12-13+ F '69

  Diseases and pests
New hope in the battle against calf scours. O. Bay. il Farm J 93:26 My '69

  Feeding
Feed club calves like commercials, and win. R. C. Black. il Farm J 93:B12+ Mr '69

  Hormone fattening
Implant young beef calves; stilbestrol implant. Suc Farm 67:62 Ap '69

CALVINO, Italo
Night driver; story tr. by W. Weaver. Mlle 69:174-5 S '69

CALZONE. See Cookery, Italian

CAM RANH BAY. See Camranh Bay

CAMARA, Helder Pessôa, abp
From dichotomy to integration. por Chr Cent 86:1574-7 D 10 '69

  about
Cooling Helder Camara. Commonweal 90:554 S 19 '69
Solidarity with the dispossessed. R. Shaull. Chr Cent 86:1421-2 N 5 '69

CAMBODIA
Report. J. Hughes. Atlan 223:4+ F '69
  See also
  Communism—Cambodia
  United States—Foreign relations—Cambodia

  Antiquities
  See also
  Angkor, Cambodia

  Foreign relations
Balancing as usual; to resume U.S. relations. il Newsweek 74:33-4 S 1 '69
Beyond Vietnam borders: war moves, a peace step. il U S News 66:8 Ap 28 '69
Cambodia: growing problem for U.S. military men. il U S News 66:28 Ap 7 '69
Cambodia, growing trouble spot. il U S News 67:31 Ag 11 '69
Cambodia's strategy of survival. D. Chandler. bibliog f Cur Hist 57:344-8+ D '69
Mending fences. Newsweek 73:46-7 Ap 28 '69

  Politics and government
Balancing as usual. il Newsweek 74:33-4 S 1 '69
Rebellion or subversion in Cambodia? M. Leifer. bibliog f Cur Hist 56:88-93+ F '69
Sihanouk: prince on a tightrope. N. Turner. Read Digest 94:177-82 My '69

CAMBODIAN art. See Art, Khmer

CAMBRELENG, Robert W.
Case of the nettlesome nepot. Harvard Bsns R 47:14-16+ Mr '69

CAMBRIAN period. See Paleontology—Cambrian

CAMBRIDGE, Godfrey
Godfrey Cambridge turns white. E. Dunbar. il pors Look 33:57+ D 30 '69

CAMBRIDGE, Mass.
Harvard square. C. Brossard. il Holiday 45: 50-1+ Mr '69
  Education
Fishing around; Trout fishing in America, inc. Newsweek 74:55 S 1 '69
  See also
  Schools, Experimental

CAMBRIDGE, Mass.—*Continued*

Historic houses, etc.

Concord and Cambridge confidential. W. Sullivan. il Sat R 52:40-1 S 27 '69

Police

Harvard and the police. W. F. Buckley, jr. Nat R 21:454-5 My 6 '69

CAMDEN, N.J.

Historic houses, etc.

Living with antiques; Camden, New Jersey, residence of Mr and Mrs Joseph Wiederspohn. L. H. Solis-Cohen. il Antiques 95: 832-7 Je '69

CAMELLIA exhibits. See Flower exhibits

CAMELS

Camels and elands: at home on the range? Sr Schol 94:15 Ja 17 '69

Three worlds of the camel. W. Jonathan. il Sat R 52:70-1 Ap 5 '69

CAMERA buying. See Cameras—Purchasing

CAMERA lenses. See Lenses, Photographic

CAMERA shutters

IC electronics for shutterbugs. J. R. Free. il Radio-Electr 40:39-42 F '69

What's your camera's TP? time parallax. N. Goldberg. il Pop Phot 64:56+ F '69

CAMERA tripods

How to make a better tripod than you can buy. N. Fried. il Pop Sci 194:159-63+ F '69

Pocket a tripod for low-light shots. C. W. Kennedy. il Pop Phot 65:48+ D '69

CAMERAS

Alpa 10d. W. J. Frazier. il Travel & Camera 32:151-2 F '69

Are you as good as that box camera? N. Rothschild. il Pop Phot 65:73-5+ O '69

Bargain-priced rangefinder camera: photography's liveliest corpse. N. Rothschild. il Pop Phot 64:76-7+ Ap '69

Behind the scenes. See issues of Modern photography

Camera collector; folding roll film cameras. J. Schneider. il Mod Phot 33:83-5 O '69

Camera guide (title varies) il Travel & Camera 32:13-14+ F; 15-17 Mr; 19-20 Ap; 27-8 My; 27-8 Je '69

Camera news. See issues of Travel & Camera

Camera-on-a-card; Kodak Instamatic 44. il Bsns W p84 Je 14 '69

Coat-pocket compact 35s. L. Drukker. il Pop Phot 65:82-4+ Ag '69

Confessions of a camera snob. N. Goldberg. il Pop Phot 65:58+ Ag '69

Expo '69: not much but something. il Mod Phot 33:56-61 S '69

First look. See issues of Popular photography

Fujica compact deluxe. W. J. Frazier. il Travel & Camera 32:77-8 Mr '69

Giant 35-mm add-on. N. Goldberg. il Pop Phot 65:76-7+ Ag '69

How Hasselblad shot the moon. il Bsns W p26 Jl 26 '69

Instant-load autoexposure cameras. il Consumer Rep 34:428-33 Ag '69

Instructions are for experts. B. Schwalberg. il Pop Phot 64:82-3+ F '69

It really happened; Photo expo 69 June 7-15 N.Y. coliseum. il Pop Phot 65:76-7+ S '69

It's back to the big negative. N. Goldberg. il Pop Phot 65:64+ O '69

Konica Autoreflex T. H. Zucker. il Pop Phot 65:102 Ag '69

Kookie kamera: Ideal's answer to Polaroid? H. Keppler. il Mod Phot 33:74-5 Mr '69

Kookie Kamera makes three-minute prints. S. Nathan. il Pop Phot 64:58 Ap '69

Lab reports. See issues of Popular photography

Large camera. A. Feininger. See issues of Modern photography

Minox goes automatic; Minox ultraminiature camera. H. Keppler. il Mod Phot 33:14 Jl '69

New camera does double duty. W. Lane. il Travel 132:77 D '69

New Kodak with instant think. C. Conley. il Field & S 74:103 Jl '69

New products. See issues of Travel & camera

No expo for Expo 69. L. Drukker. il Pop Phot 65:98-9+ Jl '69

Now: shoot underwater photos for under $20. C. B. Hicks and D. L. Hicks. il Pop Mech 131:107-10+ Je '69

Photokina '68. T. Morton; M. Edelson; J. Hughes. il U S Camera 32:42-51 Ja '69

Pocket cameras for sportsmen. F. McKinley. il Outdoor Life 144:36-9+ D '69

Probing the depths. R. Kinne. il Travel & Camera 32:96+ D '69

Simon says; Hasselblad. S. Nathan. Mod Phot 33:144-5+ Mr '69

Simple camera solves tough problem; aerial reconnaissance. N. Goldberg. il Pop Phot 65:58+ N '69

T&C tests. See issues of Travel & camera

35mm for all subjects? No! ed. by M. A. Matzkin. B. Davidson; A. Newman; C. Weston. il Mod Phot 33:88-93 N '69

35; why I prefer it for color. N. Rothschild. il Pop Phot 65:85-93 Ag '69

Those inexpensive cameras are good. N. Goldberg. il Pop Phot 65:62+ S '69

$20 scope camera. D. E. Coy. il Radio-Electr 40:52-4 Ap '69

Ultra-wide 6x9 of uncertain ancestry. S. Nathan. il Pop Phot 64:30 My '69

Weight watcher's guide; an ideal hiker's camera? K. Poli. il Pop Phot 65:86-7+ Jl '69

What's your camera's TP? time parallax. N. Goldberg. il Pop Phot 64:56+ F '69

Why our astronauts can't make good pictures; problem with type of Hasselblad used. S. Nathan. il Pop Phot 65:71-5+ Ag '69

See also

Fairchild camera and instrument corporation
Moving picture cameras
Polaroid corporation
Polaroid Land cameras
Single-lens reflex cameras
Television cameras
Twin-lens cameras
View finders

Care

Camera troubles in winter? Pro tells you what to do. J. Rychetnik. Mod Phot 33: 142+ Ap '69

Collectors and collecting

Camera collector. J. Schneider. il Mod Phot 33:83-5 O; 124+ N '69

How far have we gone (cont) H. Keppler. il Mod Phot 33:130+ F '69

Electronic control

See Photography—Electronic equipment

Loading

Instant-load autoexposure cameras. il Consumer Rep 34:428-33 Ag '69

Maintenance and repair

Keppler on the SLR. H. Keppler. il Mod Phot 33:18+ Mr '69

Where for repairs? See issues of Modern photography

Manufacture

Quality is a way of life; visit to the Leica plant in Wetzlar, Germany. N. Goldberg. il Pop Phot 64:16+ Mr '69

Purchasing

Do your camera-shopping early, and wisely! L. Drukker. il Pop Phot 65:88-9+ D '69

Keppler on the SLR; how long should cameras last? H. Keppler. Mod Phot 33:60+ Je '69

Should you buy a camera abroad? W. Lane. il Travel 131:26 My '69

That 21-jewel, 24-karat, 35-mm camera in the sky. W. Hanson. il Pop Phot 65:80-1+ Ag '69

Testing

Modern tests. See issues of Modern photography

Some improve with torture. N. Goldberg. il Pop Phot 64:60+ Ap '69

CAMERAS, Used

How to buy or swap a used camera. N. Rothschild. il Pop Phot 64:69-71 Je '69

Used camera buying guide; comp. by D. Gatto. il Mod Phot 33:91-106 My; 99-113 Ap '69

CAMERMAN, Arthur, and Jensen, L. H.

2-p-Toluidinyl-6-naphthalene sulfonate: relation of structure to fluorescence properties in different media. bibliog Science 165:493-5 Ag 1 '69

CAMERON, Eleanor

Art of Elizabeth Enright. Horn Bk 45:641-51 D '69 (to be cont)

The owl service: a study. bibliog por Wilson Lib Bul 44:425-33 D '69

CAMERON, J. M.

U.S. campus war through English eyes. Commonweal 90:404-5 Je 27 '69

CAMERON, John

GI's long last month in Vietnam. J. Saar. il pors Life 67:51-4 Ag 8 '69

CAMERON, Juan
Case for cutting defense spending. Fortune 80:68–73+ Ag 1 '69
Demands for cuts in the defense budget have led to a fundamental change in our global strategy. Fortune 80:43+ D '69
It's open season on conglomerates, and established business couldn't be happier. Fortune 79:43-4 My 1 '69
Political pro at the Pentagon. Fortune 79:116-19+ Ap '69
Report from Washington. Fortune 79:47+ F '69
Threatening weather in South America. Fortune 80:98-101+ O '69

CAMERON, Kenneth
Papp. Criticism
New Yorker 45:122-3 My 10 '69

CAMERON, Malcolm
Drawings of Malcolm Cameron. il por Am Artist 33:50-5+ Ja '69

CAMERON, Ralph Henry
Man who owned Grand Canyon. D. H. Strong. il Am West 6:33-40 S '69

CAMERON machine press. See Printing presses

CAMEROON REPUBLIC

Native races

Kirdis of Cameroon; with photographs by I. Penn. M. R. Henry. Vogue 154:174-81+ D '69

CAMINO real; drama. See Williams, T.

CAMMETT, John M.
Variations on a theme by Marx. Nation 208: 733-5 Je 9 '69

CAMP activities. See Camping—Activities

CAMP administration. See Camps—Administration

CAMP cookery
Camp chef. C. B. Colby. See issues of Outdoor life
Convenience foods? Paper service? P. Andron. il Camp Mag 41:18-19 Je '69
Early menu planning helps your food buying. Camp Mag 41:16-17 F '69
Food outlook for 1969. R. G. Murphy. il Camp Mag 41:13+ Ap '69
How to save on camp food bills. R. Hodgson. il Camp Mag 41:20+ Mr '69
Kitchen labor problems eased by use of convenience foods; San Francisco Bay Girl scout camps. il Camp Mag 41:24-5 Ja '69
Plan for kitchen success. H. P. Rung. il Camp Mag 41:10-12 S '69
Solving camp food storage problems. E. Rose. Camp Mag 41:14 My '69
See also
Cookery, Outdoor

CAMP counselors
Camp counselor, me? T. Kerr. Camp Mag 41:22 Ap '69
Counselor's number-one job: setting the tone of camp; address. J. K. Bryant, jr. Camp Mag 41:10 Ap '69
First four hours of camp. W. Shalinsky and J. Witkovsky. il Camp Mag 41:16-17 Je '69
Guidelines for better CIT training. S. H. Webb. il Camp Mag 41:26-8 My '69
How to help your campers overcome their fears. M. Miller. il Camp Mag 41:20+ Je '69
Measuring counselors' needs aids success prediction in camps for the handicapped. R. F. Kingsley and C. H. Hargis. Camp Mag 41: 20 S '69; Correction. 41:30 N '69
Pre-camp counselor training programs can be as different as day and night. L. La Roque; R. B. Wasserman. il Camp Mag 41:8-9+ Ap '69
Reluctant swimmer. E. T. Buchanan, 3d. il Camp Mag 41:14-15 Je '69
Stop, look, and listen, if you want to be heard; address. A. Van Krevelen. il Camp Mag 41:17-18 Mr '69
Today's counselors are different; address. A. Fried. il Camp Mag 41:8-9 F '69
What counselors get from camping. M. G. Pena and L. C. Pedicord. il Camp Mag 41: 11-12 Ap '69
What kind of staff training helps both staff and campers attain best personal growth? Camp Becket in Mass. D. Shellenberger. il Camp Mag 41:12-14 Mr '69

Recruiting

Better interviewing can mean better staff. P. Moon. Camp Mag 41:17 Ja '69

CAMP discipline
Camps and the new morality; address, 1969. A. D. Boxer. Camp Mag 41:15+ S '69
Don't use food as punishment! D. B. Hunter. il Camp Mag 41:18 N '69

Our commitment is to diversification of campers; Blueberry Cove, Me. A. Goldsmith and R. Hellerson. il Camp Mag 41: 19+ Mr '69
We need to try harder; inner-city children need active recruitment. J. H. Ramey. il Camp Mag 41:12+ F '69

CAMP equipment. See Camping—Outfits, supplies, etc.

CAMP kitchens
Plan for kitchen success. H. P. Rung. il Camp Mag 41:10-12 S '69

CAMP lanterns, Electric. See Electric lanterns

CAMP management. See Camps—Administration

CAMP Pendleton prison. See United States—Marine corps—Prisons

CAMP sanitation
Facts and fallacies in camp sanitation. E. S. Temple. Camp Mag 41:28-9 Ja '69

CAMP sites, facilities, etc.
Camp acreage dwindling? Convert croplands. R. P. Church. il Camp Mag 41:16 Ap '69
Dynamic camp design aids creative arts program; Usdan arts center day camp, N.Y. M. Melamed. il Camp Mag 41:8-9 S '69
Make a year-end check up of your camp facilities. J. H. Salomon. Camp Mag 41:11-12 N '69
Multi-purpose building solves our space problems; Camp Kippewa for girls, Winthrop, Me. M. Silverman. Camp Mag 41:18 F '69
Must our campgrounds be outdoor slums? M. Frome. Read Digest 95:169-70+ S '69
Rules of the road and campsite tips. V. L. Oertle. il Pop Sci 194:176+ My '69
Ten top camping sites. P. Czura. il Todays Health 47:42-7 My '69
We moved a farmhouse and saved on building costs; Alford Lake camp, Maine. Mrs A. McMullan. il Camp Mag 41:26 Ja '69
Your campsites are waiting. H. Shuldiner. il Pop Sci 195:136-9 Jl '69

CAMP stoves
Camp stoves. il Consumer Rep 34:338-43 Je '69

CAMP water supply
Facts and fallacies in camp sanitation. E. S. Temple. Camp Mag 41:28-9 Ja '69

CAMPAIGN funds
Can a poor man get to be president? S. Alsop. Newsweek 73:136 Mr 17 '69
Financing better elections; excerpt from report of the Research and policy committee of the Committee of economic development. Cur 104:35-40 F '69
Nixon's dog. G. Wills. il Esquire 72:91-5+ Ag '69
Political peonage; Seafarers' international union contributions. Nation 208:68-9 Ja 20 '69
When companies find giving isn't blessed; political contributions. Bsns W p31-2 N 8 '69

CAMPAIGN ghost writing. See Authorship—Collaboration

CAMPAIGN issues
Next election: what party chairmen see as big campaign issues. R. C. B. Morton; F. R. Harris. Nations Bsns 57:36-7 N '69
Promises that Nixon has made; excerpts from campaign proposals. R. M. Nixon. il U S News 66:50-2 Mr 3 '69
Vote that went against Nixon. U S News 67: 16 O 13 '69
What the voters want; environment issue in elections. Time 94:55 N 14 '69

CAMPAIGNS, Money raising. See Fund raising

CAMPAIGNS, Political. See Political campaigns

CAMPAIGNS, Presidential. See Presidential campaigns

CAMPANELLA, Roy
Black athlete in the golden age of sports; the saga of Campy. A. S. Young. il pors Ebony 24:100-2+ Ap '69

CAMPANULARIA flexuosa. See Hydromedusa

CAMPBELL, Alan K.
Inequities of school finance. Ed Digest 34: 10-13 Ap '69

CAMPBELL, Alex
Divided they stand. New Repub 160:15-19 Mr 22 '69
Future of the US military presence. New Repub 160:14-17 Ap 5 '69
Home of the China-watchers. New Repub 160:11-13 My 3 '69
Indonesia: the greatest prize. New Repub 160:17-20 Ap 19 '69
Lawless and corrupt Philippines. New Repub 160:15-17 My 17 '69
Motorboats, monarchy and private enterprise. New Repub 160:13-15 Mr 29 '69

CAMPBELL, Alex—*Continued*
South Korea and the US. New Repub 160:
9-11 Je 7 '69
Sun up in Asia. New Repub 161:16-18 Jl 5
'69
Taiwan's future under Chiang. jr. New Repub
160:14-15 My 31 '69
Why Singapore might make it. New Repub
160:13-15 Ap 26 '69
Why we're returning Okinawa to Japan. New
Repub 160:11-13 Je 14 '69
CAMPBELL, Andrew
Last great air war; paintings. Esquire 72:
75-83 Ag '69
CAMPBELL, Astry
New fashion doll. C. H. Fawcett. il Hobbies
74:46-7 O '69
CAMPBELL, Byron A. and others
Ontogeny of adrenergic arousal and cholin-
ergic inhibitory mechanisms in the rat.
bibliog Science 166:635-7 O 31 '69
CAMPBELL, Camilia
Bell of Dolores; drama. Plays 28:75-86 Ap
'69
CAMPBELL, Charles
Low-cost recreation centers. Parks & Rec 3:
16-17 N '68
CAMPBELL, Ernest
How to pick a church; interview, ed. by T.
Shea. Read Digest 94:62-4 Je '69
CAMPBELL, Frederick L. and others
Law and order in public parks. il Parks &
Rec 3:28-31+ D '68
CAMPBELL, Gladys
How to keep your glads glad. Org Gard &
Farm 16:50-1 Mr '69
CAMPBELL, Glen
Sweet singing man; ed. by E. Miller. pors
Seventeen 28:148-9+ Mr '69

about

Hip hick. il por Time 93:73 Ja 31 '69
CAMPBELL, Howard W. See Hartline, P. H.
jt. auth.
CAMPBELL, J. Phil, 1917-
Farm of the future; address, July 11, 1969.
Vital Speeches 35:636-9 Ag 1 '69

about

New under-secretary of agriculture. por Farm
J 93:52U Mr '69
CAMPBELL, Josephine E.
St Patrick's eve; drama. Plays 28:39-44 Mr
'69
CAMPBELL, Jule
Sporting look (cont) Sports Illus 30:64-5 Ap
21; 31:56-61 Ag 25 '69
CAMPBELL, Lawrence
Ah, sweet mystery of gerontion. Art N 67:
38-41+ N '68
City rises. Art N 68:42-4+ N '69
Crash of symbols. Art N 68:42-3+ Mr '69
In the mist of life. Art N 67:42-3+ F '69
Well-tempered color-wheel. Art N 68:42-3+
Ap '69
CAMPBELL, Malcolm J. and others
Moon: two new mascon basins. bibliog Sci-
ence 164:1273-5 Je 13 '69
CAMPBELL, Mary E.
How to lose a job by an eyelash; interview.
Mlle 68:162-3 Mr '69
CAMPBELL, Philip M.
Spin-orbit resonance of the inner planets.
bibliog Science 165:930 Ag 29 '69
CAMPBELL, Richard D.
Special workshop for the gifted. Todays Ed
58:32-3 D '69
CAMPBELL, Roald F.
Teaching and teachers, today and tomorrow;
excerpts from Schools and the challenge of
innovation. Ed Digest 35:12-15 N '69
CAMPBELL, Robert F.
Audio-graphic network aids rural high
schools. Clear House 44:157-60 N '69
CAMPBELL, T. Colin. See Baugher, W. L.
jt. auth.
CAMPBELL, Wesley Glenn
Cold-war scholarship. P. S. Stern. il Nation
209:176-80 S 1 '69
CAMPERS and coaches, Truck
Boat tops off my camper. R. Chapellier and
D. Rasmussen. il Pop Sci 194:120-2+ Je
'69
Camper vans: what they're good for, what
they cost, how to pick them. H. E. Dark.
il Changing T 23:37-40 Je '69
Forty ways to test a camper before you buy
it. V. L. Oertle. il Pop Mech 132:77-9+ Jl
'69
Homelike conveniences to make camping
easier. il Good H 168:204-5 Ap '69
Land yacht's day has come. il Sunset 142:78-
85 My '69

Luxury camping. B. Thomas. il Travel 132:
44-7 S '69
New camp rigs for '69. D. Fales. il Pop Mech
131:138-41 My '69
Notes for nomads. See issues of Travel
Pickup camper you can build. M. D. Werten-
berger. il Mech Illus 65:96-9+ Mr '69
Questions we're asked about recreational ve-
hicles. D. L. Gregg. il Bet Hom & Gard
47:74-5+ Ap '69
Saving a small town; bringing industry to
Forest City, Ia. il Time 94:90 S 19 '69
Summer special for campers. W. Davis. il
Mech Illus 65:52-5+ My '69
Trucks highballing in sales growth. il Bsns W
p 160+ Ja 25 '69
Wheels for sportsmen. J. Gartner. il Field
& S 73:45-59 Mr '69
Win raves with a redwood camper. R. M.
Engelbrecht. il Pop Sci 194:162-4+ Mr '69
Winterize your home on wheels. B. F. Sam-
uels. il Pop Sci 195:170-3+ O '69
You can live it up at 70 m.p.h; Dodge motor
home. il Pop Sci 194:164-5+ Je '69
Your 1969 guide to camping on wheels. il
Pop Sci 194:163-72+ My '69

Equipment

How to enjoy all the comforts of home on
wheels. E. F. Lindsley. il Pop Sci 194:182+
My '69

Storage

Right way to winterize your camper. V. L.
Oertle. il Pop Mech 132:116-19+ N '69

Testing

MI tests:
Plush motor home. V. L. Oertle. il Mech
Illus 65:58-9+ Ag '69
PM tests:
Ford's new $4800 motor home. A. Mark-
ovich. il Pop Mech 131:116-19+ Je '69
Rugged new camper, a controversial new
park. V. L. Oertle. il Pop Mech 131:124-
7+ My '69

CAMPING
Best of two worlds. boat camping. il Motor B
123:118-19 Ja '69
Camping. C. B. Colby. See issues of Outdoor
life
Camping catches up with the times; spe-
cialized camps for youth. il Bsns W p 120
Ag 16 '69
Cast loose all cares. E. S. Gardner. il Motor B
123:267+ Ja '69
Conquering Minnesota's wilderness by snow-
mobile. D. Fales. il Pop Mech 132:150-3
D '69
Cruise your way to camping pleasure. N.
Phillips. il Pop Gard 20:2-5+ Spr '69
Grandma's gone to camp! day camp program
in Seattle. A. Lovell and A. Ransford. il
Parks & Rec 3:15 N '68
Join the out-of-season campers. E. H. Arctan-
der. il Pop Sci 195:140-2 S '69
Kid camping. P. McManus. il Field & S
73:68-9+ Mr '69
Make your next camp-out by boat. N. Phil-
lips. il Pop Mech 131:178-80 My '69
Overland cruising. H. M. Rizer. il Motor B
123:64-5+ Je '69
Quandary on the campgrounds. H. Bloom-
field. il Am For 75:4-7+ Jl '69
Redbook guide to family camping. G. Ade. il
Redbook 134:35-42 N '69
Secrets of camping. W. T. McKeown. il Travel
& Camera 32:57+ Je '69
Snowmobile camping. C. B. Colby. il Out-
door Life 144:12+ N '69
Storage ideas for campers; tips for tenters.
il Bet Hom & Gard 47:94-5 Je '69
Summer special for campers. W. Davis. il
Mech Illus 65:52-5+ My '69
Try bicycle-camping. C. B. Colby. il Out-
door Life 143:18+ Mr '69
Wife in the wilderness. E. Durbin. il To-
days Health 47:32-3+ Jl '69
Woman driver; vacations on wheels; rent or
buy a recreational vehicle. il McCalls 96:
38 Je '69
See also
American camping association
Boy scouts
Camp sites, facilities, etc.
Guides
Outdoor life
Wilderness survival

Activities

Add action to your archery program. B.
Wadsworth. il Camp Mag 41:14-15 F '69
Flicker ball: new program idea. W. Farley. il
Camp Mag 41:18 Ja '69

CAMPING—Activities—*Continued*
Intercamp sports. H. M. Brown. Camp Mag 41:33 Ja '69
New ideas stimulate your camp programs. M. C. Fuller; J. Leitman; P. M. Kelly. il Camp Mag 41:22-3 F '69
Twenty-four tested ideas to spark your camp program. Camp Mag 41:12+ Je '69
You don't need sports to build physical fitness. J. W. Barker. il Camp Mag 41:22-3 My '69

Bibliography
Books [in review]. See issues of Camping magazine

Economic aspects
See Camps—Finance

Educational aspects
Outward bound adventures; showing outdoors to teenagers from the ghettos. W. C. Dillinger. il Nat Wildlife 7:12-16 Je '69
Use a planned progression of camping experiences to achieve your goals; Incarnation camp, Conn. R. C. Gundersen. il Camp Mag 41:48-9 Mr '69
See also
Nature study

Health aspects
You don't need sports to build physical fitness. J. W. Barker. il Camp Mag 41:22-3 My '69

Insurance aspects
Comprehensive liability insurance. J. M. Farrow and B. M. Pinney. Camp Mag 41:24-5 My '69
What risks should you insure? Camp Mag 41:13-15 Ja '69

Outfits, supplies, etc.
Air mattresses. il Consumer Rep 34:275-7 My '69
Camping is great in the winter, too. il Changing T 23:17-18 N '69
Equipment for rent when you go camping. McCalls 96:56 Ap '69
How to save a camping trip. C. B. Colby. il Outdoor Life 144:18+ Ag '69
New gear means new cheer for backpackers. E. P. Haddon. il Pop Mech 131:132-5 Ap '69
New items for '69. C. B. Colby. il Outdoor Life 143:16+ My '69
Secrets of camping. W. T. McKeown. il Travel & Camera 32:57+ Je '69
Snowmobile camping. C. B. Colby. il Outdoor Life 144:12+ N '69
Summer special for campers. W. Davis. il Mech Illus 65:52-5+ My '69
Tent heaters. il Consumer Rep 34:537-40 S '69
What's new? (title varies) See issues of Camping magazine
Wheels for sportsmen. J. Gartner. il Field & S 73:45-59 Mr '69
You can't top a tarp. C. B. Colby. il Outdoor Life 144:12+ D '69
Your guide to camping gear. il Bet Hom & Gard 47:10+ Je '69
Your 1969 buying guide. Camp Mag 41:22-6+ Mr '69
Your 1969 guide to camping on wheels. il Pop Sci 194:163-72+ My '69
See also
Camp stoves
Sleeping bags
Tents

Periodicals
See also
Camping magazine

Religious life and activities
Youth speaks a new language at camp worship services; with poem by L. D. Brodsky. S. A. Brown. il Camp Mag 41:46-7 Mr '69

Safety devices and measures
Don't be a missing camper. C. B. Colby. il Outdoor Life 144:12+ Jl '69
Reluctant swimmer. E. T. Buchanan. 3d. il Camp Mag 41:14-15 Je '69
To summon help, press the button; alarm system for campers in the Hamilton County park district, Ohio. J. A. Rollman. il Am City 84:16 Jl '69
Your riding program; keeping it as safe as your waterfront. D. D. Hirn. Camp Mag 41:31 My '69

Study and teaching
Guidelines for better CIT training; counselor-in-training programs. S. H. Webb. il Camp Mag 41:26-8 My '69

Pre-camp counselor training programs can be as different as day and night. L. La Roque; R. B. Wasserman. il Camp Mag 41:8-9+ Ap '69

California
Kitchen labor problems eased by use of convenience foods; San Francisco Bay Girl scout camps. il Camp Mag 41:24-5 Ja '69
Winter camping in the redwoods. il Sunset 142:41 F '69

Connecticut
Use a planned progression of camping experiences to achieve your goals; Incarnation camp. R. C. Gundersen. il Camp Mag 41:48-9 Mr '69

Florida
Tropical camping in Florida's Tampa Bay. G. Ade. il Redbook 134:37 N '69

Ireland
Through Ireland by tinker wagon. N. Ickeringill. il Travel & Camera 32:35-6 Ap '69

Maine
Multi-purpose building solves our space problems; Camp Kippewa for girls, Winthrop. M. Silverman. Camp Mag 41:18 F '69
Our commitment is to diversification of campers; Blueberry Cove. A. Goldsmith and R. Hellerson. il Camp Mag 41:19+ Mr '69
Visual aids spark tripping calendar; Camp Pinecliffe. T. A. Jambro. Camp Mag 41:21 F '69

Massachusetts
What kind of staff training helps both staff and campers attain best personal growth? Camp Becket. D. Shellenberger. il Camp Mag 41:12-14 Mr '69

Missouri
EMR campers gain from regular camp; Camp Hawthorn. H. M. Lainoff. il Camp Mag 41:24-5 F '69

New Hampshire
How one camp operates its successful counselor training program; Camp Naticook. R. B. Wasserman. il Camp Mag 41:9+ Ap '69

New Mexico
100-mile campground. B. W. Dalrymple. il Field & S 74:42-3+ Jl '69

New York (state)
Dynamic camp design aids creative arts program; Usdan arts center day camp. M. Melamed. il Camp Mag 41:8-9 S '69
Should camp cabins be inter-aged and co-ed? experiments at Camp Thoreau. K. Rodman. il Camp Mag 41:14-15 Ap '69

Pennsylvania
Camping the wild way; rural Pennsylvania. E. Gibbons. il Nat Wildlife 7:34-8 Ap '69
Have a fling in Pennsylvania's Laurel highlands. G. Ade. il Redbook 134:41 N '69
How to use your camp all year long; YMCA of Philadelphia. E. S. Smith, jr. il Camp Mag 41:16-17 N '69

Rhode Island
Handling S.S. in camp; Separation sydrome or homesickness at Boy Scout camp Yawgoog. E. Ohlsen. Camp Mag 41:16 My '69

United States
Future of camping. E. Andrews. Camp Mag 41:5 Ja '69
This land is your land; national park camping with an automobile travel trailer. S. Haft. il Sr Schol 94:Schol Teach 16-17 Ap 11 '69
Why not take to the woods this summer. B. Thomas. il Parents Mag 44:60-1+ Ap '69
See also
Sierra club

Wisconsin
Luxury camping. B. Thomas. il Travel 132:44-7 S '69
Vacation in Wisconsin's scenic Black River country. G. Ade. il Redbook 134:39 N '69
CAMPING, Cost of. See Camps—Finance
CAMPING, Value of
Camping and self-concept. F. Raymond. il Camp Mag 41:18 My '69
Camping can be unique; address, 1969. J. J. Kirk. Camp Mag 41:8-11 Je '69
Camping's third dimension. B. J. Silva and B. Jackson. il Camp Mag 41:12+ Ja '69

CAMPING, Value of—*Continued*
Generation gap: fact or fiction? F. M. Washburn. Camp Mag 41:4 N '69
Oasis for youth. E. F. Schmidt. Camp Mag 41:4 S '69
Some goals for the seventies. I. Cowle. il Camp Mag 41:10-11 Ja '69
Use a planned progression of camping experiences to achieve your goals; Incarnation camp, Conn. R. C. Gundersen. il Camp Mag 41:48-9 Mr '69

CAMPING equipment. See Camping—Outfits, supplies, etc.

CAMPING for the handicapped. See Camps for the handicapped

CAMPING magazine
Anniversary present. H. Galloway. Camp Mag 41:26 S '69
Editor's view. H. Galloway. Camp Mag 41: 37 Ap '69

CAMPING outfits. See Camping—Outfits, supplies, etc

CAMPING shelters. See Shelters

CAMPION, Donald R.
Catholic colleges face up to change. America 121:590-2 D 13 '69
Unfinished business. America 122:26-7 Ja 10 '70
—See Haughey, J. C. jt. auth.

CAMPOS, C. Victor
Speakers, present and future. por Hi Fi 19: 49-53 Je '69

CAMPS
Build this super camp for less than $1500. il Pop Mech 131:174-5 Ap '69
Can of worms: opposition to summer day camp sports program administered by the National collegiate athletic association. Parks & Rec 4:23 My '69
Christian camps: unique opportunity; Christian camping international convention. R. L. Love. Chr Today 14:36+ D 5 '69
Day campers enjoy water skiing; Fair acres day camp, Cape Cod, Mass. J. S. Biddiscombe. il Camp Mag 41:30 My '69
Dynamic camp design aids creative arts program; Usdan arts center day camp, N.Y. M. Melamed. il Camp Mag 41:8-9 S '69
Kids, crime and conservation; youth forestry camps. M. J. Benoit. il Cons 23:18-20+ Ap '69
Recreation in flux; needs and aims; addresses, November 2, 1968. C. G. Fuller; J. W. Monroe. il Am For 75:20-3+ Ag '69
Summer day art center; Usdan center for the performing arts. il Arch Forum 131: 56-61 N '69
Town where every kid can go to camp; Milford, Conn. community day camp. M. Strumpf. il Parents Mag 44:42-3+ Jl '69
Two experts view camping for older adults. M. M. Glascock and E. A. Scholer. Camp Mag 41:15-16 Mr '69
Walking high in Yosemite; High Sierra camps. il Sunset 142:56+ F '69
See also
Audubon nature camps
Camp sites, facilities, etc.
Camping

Activities
See Camping—Activities

Administration
Business side of your camp should be run like a business! M. F. Buynak. il Camp Mag 41:8-10 N '69
Choice. F. M. Washburn. Camp Mag 41:5 F '69
It is rather exciting. N. E. Wieters. il Camp Mag 41:5 Ap '69
Secret to achieving your camp goals. B. R. Horn. il Camp Mag 41:13+ N '69
Some goals for the seventies. I. Cowle. il Camp Mag 41:10-11 Ja '69
Stop, look, and listen, if you want to be heard; address. A. Van Krevelen. il Camp Mag 41:17-18 Mr '69
Today's counselors are different; address. A. Fried. il Camp Mag 41:8-9 F '69
Two modern challenges for every camp director; conserving human resources: disadvantaged groups, and physically or mentally handicapped children. P. M. Ford. Camp Mag 41:18-19 S '69
Two modern challenges for every camp director: saving natural resources, serving human resources. P. M. Ford. il Camp Mag 41:12-13 My '69
Use computers in my camp? Never! address. A. L. Beavers, jr. il Camp Mag 41:10-11 F '69
We get close to staff concerns; Wel-met camps, N.Y. R. Salmon. Camp Mag 41:24 Ap '69

What kind of staff training helps both staff and campers attain best personal growth? Camp Becket in Mass. D. Shellenberger. il Camp Mag 41:12-14 Mr '69

Counselors
See Camp counselors

Finance
Business side of your camp should be run like a business! M. F. Buynak. il Camp Mag 41:8-10 N '69
Costs of camping. il Camp Mag 41:8-11 My '69
What price camping? C. B. Colby. il Outdoor Life 144:16+ O '69

Public relations
More time tested enrollment ideas. H. H. Cohen. Camp Mag 41:23 Ja '69
We need to try harder; inner-city children need active recruitment. J. H. Ramey. il Camp Mag 41:12+ F '69
What can we do about the camp drop out? H. Loren. il Camp Mag 41:14+ N '69

Standards
New look for the standards program; ACA National standards committee. J. J. Kirk. Camp Mag 41:6 Mr '69
Parents who plan to send a child to camp this summer. Todays Health 47:77-8 Ap '69

Statistics
Future of camping. E. Andrews. Camp Mag 41:5 Ja '69

Sweden
Politics of sex; Falcon organization and the Lake Vätter scandal. Newsweek 74:32-3 S 1 '69

CAMPS for the aged. See Camps

CAMPS for the handicapped
EMR campers gain from regular camp; Camp Hawthorn, Mo. H. M. Lainoff. il Camp Mag 41:24-5 F '69
Measuring counselors' needs aids success prediction in camps for the handicapped. R. F. Kingsley and C. H. Hargis. Camp Mag 41:20 S '69; Correction. 41:30 N '69
Two modern challenges for every camp director; conserving human resources: disadvantaged groups, and physically or mentally handicapped children. P. M. Ford. Camp Mag 41:18-19 S '69

CAMPUS CITY, Chicago. See Illinois. University —Chicago campus

CAMPUS crusade for Christ (organization)
New face of Campus crusade. A. B. Haines. Chr Cent 86:1650-1 D 24 '69

CAMPUS life. See Student life

CAMPUS ombudsman. See Ombudsman

CAMPUS planning
Benjamin Thompson designs the space between and the space within for Amherst college's music building. M. F. Schmertz. il Arch Rec 145:119-26 Ja '69
Building types study. il Arch Rec 145:145-60 My '69
Teachers college master building program. il Sch & Soc 97:200-1 Ap '69
Trent university. il Arch Rec 146:151-62 S '69
University of East Anglia. il Arch Rec 146: 99-110 Jl '69
See also
College architecture

CAMPUS worker-student alliance (organization)
Long and the short. Newsweek 75:43 Ja 12 '70

CAMRANH BAY
Shock for a symbol; Cam Ranh raid. il Time 94:31 Ag 15 '69

CAMS
See also
Automobiles—Cams

CAN labels. See Labels

CANAAN, Conn.
Lawrence tavern in Canaan. J. A. Lyles. il Antiques 95:400-3 Mr '69

CANADA
See also
Agricultural administration—Canada
Airlines—Canada
Architecture, Domestic—Canada
Arts and crafts—Canada
Atomic power—Canada
Ballet—Canada
Banks and banking—Canada
Church unity—Canada
Colleges and universities—Canada
Electric power—Canada

CANADA—See also—*Continued*
Fishing—Canada
Flood prevention and control—Canada
Frontier and pioneer life—Canada
Government employees—Canada
Helicopter industry and trade—Canada
Hunting—Canada
Insurance, Unemployment—Canada
Investments, Foreign (in Canada)
Justice, Administration of—Canada
Libraries—Canada
Mining industry and finance—Canada
National parks and reserves—Canada
Northwest, Canadian
Northwest Territories
Nuns' Island
Phonograph record industry—Canada
Railroads—Canada
Restaurants—Canada
Roads—Canada
Science—Canada
Skis and skiing—Canada
Strikes—Canada
Student demonstrations—Canada
Taxation
Trade unions—Canada
Waterways—Canada
Wilderness areas—Canada
Yukon

Boundaries
See also
International joint commission (United States and Canada)

Defenses
See also
North American air defense command

Description and travel
Catch up on Canada; see the states. il Seventeen 28:140-1+ My '69
Great northwest cruise. C. West. il Motor B 123:142-6 Ja '69
Travels with Melrose. J. Burnham. Nat R 21:1210-11 D 2 '69

Economic conditions
Canada's dilemmas. R. Lekachman. Duns R 94:11 O '69
See also
Wages—Canada

Economic policy
Anti-inflation, de-escalation. Nat R 21:947 S 23 '69
Ottawa steps up war on inflation. il Bsns W p21-2 D 27 '69

Economic relations
Latin America
Closer Canadian-Latin American ties. Américas 21:44 Jl '69

United States
Prominent U.S. attorney. Ramp Mag 7:54+ N 30 '68
See also
Joint United States-Canadian committee on trade and economic affairs

Food and drug directorate
Drug test dilemma. F. Poland. il Sci N 96:438 N 8 '69

Foreign population
See also
Dukhobors

Foreign relations
China (People's Republic)
Hello, China; talks about establishing full diplomatic relations. Newsweek 73:47 F 24 '69

United States
Elephant and friends. il Time 93:27 Ap 4 '69
For Canada's Trudeau, fallout from U.S. ABM. U S News 66:15 Mr 31 '69
Hands across the ice; sovereignty in the Arctic. R. F. Neill. Commonweal 91:302-3 D 5 '69
President Nixon and Prime Minister Trudeau of Canada hold talks at Washington; exchange of greetings, toasts, March 24 and 25, 1969, with announcement at news briefing. R. M. Nixon; P. E. Trudeau. Dept State Bul 60:319-24 Ap 14 '69
Silent partner. J. W. Warnock. Commonweal 90.536-9 S 5 '69
Trudeau's ABM doubts. il U S News 66:14 Ap 7 '69
See also
International joint commission (United States and Canada)

Indians
See Indians of North America—Canada

Industries
See also
Mining industry and finance—Canada

National film board
Photographers to a nation. P. S. Prichard. il Américas 21:36-41 S '69

Parliament
Canada's black member of Parliament; lawyer wins election to House of commons. il Ebony 24:132-4+ Ap '69

Politics and government
Political and evangelical Canada. W. Fitch. Chr Today 13:48 F 14 '69
Profiles; P. Trudeau. E. Iglauer. il New Yorker 45:36-42+ Jl 5 '69
Unhappy Pierre. il Newsweek 73:50 F 3 '69
See also
Canada—Parliament

Prime ministers
See also
Trudeau, P. E.

Race problems
See also
Negroes in Canada

Relations (diplomatic)
Catholic church
See Catholic church—Relations (diplomatic)—Canada

Religious institutions and affairs
After four years, a launch; Evangelical fellowship of Canada. J. B. Reynolds. Chr Today 13:41 Mr 28 '69
Political and evangelical Canada. W. Fitch. Chr Today 13:48 F 14 '69
See also
Canadian council of churches
Catholic church in Canada
Church of England in Canada
Presbyterian church in Canada
Saskatchewan—Religious institutions and affairs
United church of Canada

Royal Canadian mounted police
Last patrol; Mounties must get rid of their sled dogs. Newsweek 73:44 Mr 31 '69

Science council
Identifying and moving toward national goals. P. H. Abelson. Science 164:909 My 23 '69

CANADA geese. See Geese, Wild
CANADA'S cup race. See Yacht racing
CANADIAN-American challenge cup series. See Automobile racing
CANADIAN artists. See Artists, Canadian
CANADIAN booksellers association
Canadian booksellers: optimism despite difficulties. il Pub W 195:34-5 Je 30 '69
CANADIAN congress on evangelism. See Religious conferences
CANADIAN council of churches
Canadian church council: will activism pay? L. K. Tarr. Chr Today 14:41 Ja 2 '70
Canadian council of churches reorganizes. D. H. Rayner. Chr Cent 86:131-2 Ja 22 '69
Churches unite for development; Christian conscience and poverty. America 120:724 Je 28 '69
CANADIAN Indians. See Indians of North America—Canada
CANADIAN library association
Newfoundland revisited; annual conference. E. Moon. Library J 94:2562-6 Jl '69
CANADIAN national railways
Canadian national cools on riders. Bsns W p 134 Jl 12 '69
Railroad that cared. Newsweek 74:74 Ag 18 '69
CANADIAN-NORTHWEST. See Northwest, Canadian
CANADIAN NORTHWEST TERRITORIES. See Northwest Territories, Canada
CANADIAN poets. See Poets, Canadian
CANADIAN pottery. See Pottery, Canadian
CANADIAN purple. See Potatoes
CANADIAN students
See also
Student demonstrations—Canada

CANADIANS
  See also
  French Canadians
CANADIENS (hockey team) See Hockey teams
CANAIRIS, Vlassis
  Hope in plaster. il por Time 93:76 Je 6 '69
CANALETTO, 1720-1780. See Bellotto, B.
CANALS
  See also
  Suez Canal

Central America
Central American sea-level canal; possible
  biological effects. I. Rubinoff; discussion.
  Science 162:511-13, 1329; 163:760+ N 1, D 20
  '68; F 21 '69
Interoceanic sea-level canal: effects on the
  fish faunas. R. W. Topp. bibliog Science
  165:1324-7 S 26 '69
New canal: what about bioenvironmental
  research? M. Mueller. Science 163:165-7
  Ja 10 '69
Plowing a nuclear furrow. E. A. Martell. bibliog il Environ 11:2-10+ Ap '69

England
Touring England by narrow boat. il Sunset
  142:42 Ap '69

Florida
Final episode of Florida Canal 111. Audu-
  bon 71:5 Mr '69
  See also
  Cross Florida Barge Canal
CAN-Am racing series. See Automobile racing
CANARIES
  How to get a canary to sing like one. K.
  Sullivan. Redbook 132:82 Ap '69
CANAVAN, James
  Glass medallions of Carl Paulson. Am Artist
  33:22-5 Ag '69
CANAVERAL, CAPE. See Kennedy, Cape
CANBY, Edward Tatnall
  Recording as a medium. Opera N 33:8-11 F
  8 '69
CANBY, Vincent
  Going critical. por Newsweek 73:86-7 Mr 10
  '69
CANCER
  Battle report. M. Clark. il Newsweek 73:127-8
  Ap 14 '69
  Beware that noonday sun; skin damage from
  ultraviolet radiation. A. S. Freese. il Sci
  Digest 65:38-42 Je '69
  Carcinoma of the cervix: deficiency of nexus
  intercellular junctions. N. S. McNutt and
  R. S. Weinstein. bibliog il Science 165:597-9
  Ag 8 '69
  Chemists and cancer. Sci N 95:234 Mr 8 '69
  Circumcision and cancer. J. S. Berkes. Sci
  N 96:4 Jl 5 '69; Reply. A. Ravich. 96:231
  S 20 '69
  Healthier bosom: all the latest medical &
  surgical news. J. Ramsey. il Ladies Home
  J 86:82+ O '69
  Hormonal stimulation of lactose synthetase
  in mammary carcinoma. W. L. McGuire.
  bibliog il Science 165:1013-14 S 5 '69
  Life sciences. Sci N 95:379 Ap 19 '69
  Malignant argyrophilic gastric carcinoids of
  praomys (mastomys) natalensis. K. C. Snell
  and H. L. Stewart. bibliog il Science 163:
  470 Ja 31 '69
  Mammary cancer induction by 7,12-dimethyl-
  benz(a)anthracene: relation to age. T. L.
  Dao. bibliog il Science 165:810-11 Ag 22 '69
  Nuns and breast cancer. il Sci Digest 66:58
  Ag '69
  Still a woman; breast-cancer surgery. W. S.
  Ross. Read Digest 94:165-6+ Mr '69
  When cancer strikes someone in the family.
  G. G. Greer. Bet Hom & Gard 47:50+ My
  '69
  Why me? condensation. W. Gargan. il Good
  H 168:92-5+ Mr '69
  See also
  Cancer research
  Leukemia
  Sarcoma

Causes
Antigens on the cell; role of immune system
  in growth and control of human cancers.
  B. J. Cullition. il Sci N 95:457-9 My 10 '69
Beware that noonday sun; skin damage from
  ultraviolet radiation. A. S. Freese. il Sci
  Digest 65:38-42 Je '69
Cigarettes cause lung cancer. Sci Digest 66:
  56-7 Ag '69
Clue from under the eaves; soya-paste molds
  may cause stomach cancer. il Time 93:81
  My 9 '69

Defective virus a key. B. J. Culliton. il Sci
  N 96:308-9 O 4 '69
Doubts about the pill. il Newsweek 73:118
  My 19 '69
Immunity to cancer? Newsweek 73:76 My 12
  '69
Is intercourse a factor? cancer of the uterus
  triggered by a common virus. Time 94:77
  N 14 '69
  See also
  Cancer research

Diagnosis
Are doctors finding the cause of cervical
  cancer? Good H 168:157-9 Je '69
New check for cancer; sigmoidoscopy. Newsweek 73:78 Ap 21 '69

Therapy
Immune response and cancer therapy. Sci N
  96:422 N 8 '69
  See also
  Leukemia—Therapy
  X rays—Therapeutic applications

Vaccines
Hunt for cancer vaccine closes in; EBV
  implication in wide spectrum of cancers.
  il Bsns W p68+ N 15 '69
CANCER cells
  Battle report: how tumors grow. M. Clark.
  il Newsweek 73:128 Ap 14 '69
  Centrioles of a human cancer: intercellular
  order and intracellular disorder. P. W. Scha-
  fer. bibliog il Science 164:1300-3 Je 13 '69
  Defective virus a key. B. J. Culliton. il Sci
  N 96:308-9 O 4 '69
CANCER inhibiting substances
  Alpha-naphthoflavone: an inhibitor of hy-
  drocarbon cytotoxicity and microsomal hy-
  droxylase. L. Diamond and H. V. Gelboin.
  bibliog il Science 166:1023-5 N 21 '69
  Stronger arm in the arsenal; cytosine ara-
  binoside. il Sci N 96:349 O 18 '69
  See also
  Asparaginase
  Fluorouracil
CANCER producing substances
  Carcinogenesis: physicochemical mechanisms;
  report of meeting. J. H. Weisburger and
  others. Science 165:417-18+ Jl 25 '69
  Chemicals and cancer. P. H. Abelson. Sci-
  ence 166:693 N 7 '69
  Cyclamates banned. il Sci N 96:369-70 O 25
  '69
  Experimental tobacco carcinogenesis. E. L.
  Wynder and D. Hoffmann; reply with re-
  joinder. E. P. Radford and others. Science
  165:312-13 Jl 18 '69
  Mouse leukemia virus activation by chemical
  carcinogens. H. J. Igel and others. bibliog
  il Science 166:1624-6 D 26 '69
  See also
  Benzopyrene
  Dimethylbenzanthracene
  Methylcholanthrene
CANCER research
  Carcinogenesis: physicochemical mechanisms;
  report of meeting J. H. Weisburger and
  others. Science 165:417-18+ Jl 25 '69
  Experimental tobacco carcinogenesis. E. L.
  Wynder and D. Hoffmann; reply with re-
  joinder. E. P. Radford and others. Science
  165:312-13 Jl 18 '69
  Interfering with tumors. Sci Am 221:50 O '69
  Metastasizing mammary carcinomas in rats:
  induction and study of their immunogenic-
  ity. U. Kim. bibliog il Science 167:72-4
  Ja 2 '70
  Pill and cancer; findings of Melamed-Dubrow
  study. il Newsweek 74:59 Ag 11 '69
CANCER tests. See Cancer—Diagnosis
CANDELARIA, Nev. See Abandoned towns
CANDEUB, Isadore
  Pioneer planner with over-all view. por Bsns
  W p74:5 Ag 16 '69
CANDIA, Alfredo Ovando. See Ovando Candia,
  A.
CANDIDA albicans. See Fungi, Pathogenic
CANDIDATES, Political
  Around city hall. A. Logan. New Yorker 45:
  131-2+ S 13 '69
  Poher pulls ahead in France. il Time 93:29-30
  My 23 '69
  Son also rises; Los Angeles and Wisconsin
  congressional contenders. Newsweek 73:43-4
  Ap 14 '69
  See also
  Political campaigns
CANDIDIASIS. See Vaginitis

CANDLES
Candle-making at the beach. il Sunset 142:
104 Je '69
Traditional use of bayberry candles. il Good
H 169:179 D '69

CANDLESTICKS
Custom candlesticks. il Bet Hom & Gard 47:
134 Mr '69
Dating English brass candlesticks. B. Gins-
burg.il Antiques 96:907-11 D '69

CANDOLLEA laricifolia. See Hairtrigger flower

CANDY
All I want for Christmas are those fruit-nut
things; marzipan. il Sunset 143:70-1 D '69
Butterscotch treats. il Bet Hom & Gard 47:
97 Je '69
Gift of brittle sesame toffee. il Sunset 143:157
D '69
Nuts in candy overcoats. il Sunset 143:158
D '69
Please don't eat your present. il Seventeen
27:136-7 N '68

CANE, Melville
Jabberdegook; poem. Am Scholar 39:24 Wint
'69

about

Celebration: the lyric poetry of Melville Cane.
J. Robinson. Am Scholar 38:286-96 Spr '69

CANE weaving
Simple way to cane chair seats. il Sunset
142:94+ Je '69

CANFIELD, Cass
Real and the ideal editor; excerpts from address. por Pub W 195:24-7 Mr 31 '69

about

Publishing scene. D. Dempsey. por Sat R
52:28 Ag 9 '69

CANGEMI, Joseph P.
Disturbed parents: a challenge to the school.
Ed Digest 35:22-4 D '69

CANING. See Cane weaving

CANNABIS. See Marijuana

CANNABIS sativa. See Hemp

CANNAS
Storing cannas. B. Brinhart. il Horticulture
47:24+ O '69

CANNED food
Work wonders with canned puddings. il Ladies
Home J 86:92+ F '69
See also
Fruit, Canned

CANNED food industry

Finance

Drastic measures. il Forbes 104:43-4 D 15 '69

CANNED fruit. See Fruit, Canned

CANNES international film festival
Cannes after the events. R. Gelatt. il Sat R
52:22-3+ Je 21 '69

CANNIBALISM
Fossil evidence of human violence. T. D.
Stewart. il Trans-Action 6:48-53 My '69;
Reply with rejoinder. S. Parker. 6:60-1 O
'69

CANNING and preserving
Ripe time to pickle and preserve. D. Brooks.
il Home Gard 56:45 S '69
What's cooking?
New way to preserve fruit. F. W. Town-
ley. il Org Gard & Farm 16:81-2 N '69
See also
Fruit—Preservation
Jelly, Jam, etc.
Pectins

CANNON, Berry L.
Board of inquiry. Sci N 95:235 Mr 8 '69
Death at 100 fathoms. il por Newsweek 73:56
Mr 3 '69
Death disrupts ocean project. il Sr Schol
94:17 Mr 7 '69
Death in the depths. il por Time 93:59 F 28
'69
Tragedy and delay. il por Sci N 95:210-11
Mr 1 '69
Undersea frontier tests man's resilience. il
Bsns W p96-8 Mr 1 '69

CANNON, Julie
Library reference sources. Writers Digest 49:
46-7 F '69

CANNON, Maureen
Letter to Dylan; poem. Cath World 209:111
Je '69
To a fourteen, growing; poem. McCalls 96:
155 Mr '69

CANNON, Terence
American view of a meeting with Vietnam's
NLF. Ramp Mag 7:56 N 30 '68
—and Erlich, Reese
Oakland seven. Ramp Mag 7:35-7 Ap '69

CANNON models. See Gun models

CANOE racing
Ravaging mountain streams challenge white
water canoeists. B. Thomas. il Pop Gard 20:
12-17 Spr '69; Same abr. with title Whitewater canoe race. Travel 131:50-3+ Mr '69
Whitewater! National whitewater championships. J. B. Robinson. il Motor B 124:80-1+
Ag '69
Wild & wet canoe derby; White water derby,
North Creek, N.Y. il Mech Illus 65:36+ My
'69

CANOE trips
Canoe adventures for rent. F. M. Paulson.
il Field & S 74:126-8+ Je '69
Trailing Lewis and Clark. B. Jensen. il Natur
Hist 78:8-10+ bibliog(p75) Ag '69
See also
Canoes and canoeing

CANOES

Leasing and renting

Canoe adventures for rent. F. M. Paulson.
il Field & S 74:126-8+ Je '69

CANOES and canoeing
How to choose and use a canoe. C. R. Meyer.
il Pop Sci 194:108-11 Ap '69
How to make a good canoe better. R. P.
Stevenson. il Pop Sci 195:149-51 N '69
Mini-this, mini-that, now mini-canoe. C.
Conley. il Field & S 74:143 Je '69
Winter canoeing. B. Thomas. il Travel 132:
28-33 O '69

CANOGA electronics corporation. See Canoga
industries

CANOGA industries
Canoga planning to speed growth. Aviation
W 90:127 Ap 14 '69

CANON law
Ending catch 2222; guidelines for due-pro-
cess procedures. Newsweek 74:58 D 1 '69

CANONIZATION
Furor over forty; canonization of English
martyrs. il Time 95:46 Ja 19 '70
Saints march slowly. il Newsweek 73:73 Ap
28 '69
Updating sainthood. Chr Cent 86:606 Ap 30
'69

CANOPIES, Airplane. See Airplane canopies

CANOPY, Forest crown. See Forest crown
canopy

CANS

Manufacture

Canmakers head off do-it-yourself packers.
il Bsns W p53 S 20 '69
See also
American can company
National can corporation

CANTALOUPE pie. See Pie

CANTATAS
See also
Phonograph records—Cantatas

CANTEEN corporation
McLaren pours it on. Newsweek 73:89-90 My
12 '69
Meals at the Met; the Opera club and Café in
the Metropolitan opera house. Q. Eaton. il
Opera N 33:12-15 Mr 29 '69

CANTER, David S. See Rose, D. jt. auth.

CANTER, Jacob
Our cultural exports: a view of the United
States exchange program; with questions
and answers. Ann Am Acad 384:85-95 Jl '69

CANTERBURY cathedral. See Cathedrals—
England

CANTERBURY tales; musical comedy. See
Musical comedies, revues, etc.—Criticisms,
plots, etc.

CANTLON, John E.
Confrontation or cooperation in the cornfield; reprint. Science 166:1465 D 19 '69

CANTOR, Jay
Ingmar Bergman at fifty. Atlan 223:150+ Mr
'69

CANTWELL, Mary
Boy named Johnny. Mlle 70:162-3+ N '69
Eat. See issues of Mademoiselle

CANTWELL, Robert
Sport was box-office. Sports Illus 31:108-12+
S 15 '69
Ultimate confrontation. Sports Illus 30:66-
70+ Mr 24 '69

CANVAS
See also
Awnings

CANVASBACKS. See Ducks, Wild

CANYON, Calif.
Trouble in paradise. S. Stern. il Ramp Mag
8:22-8 N '69

CANYON DE CHELLY NATIONAL MONU-
MENT
Navajo's canyon of history. il Sunset 143:
52-7 Jl '69
CANYONLANDS NATIONAL PARK
Some thoughts on a hike through Canyon-
lands Park. P. L. Nelson. il Nat Parks 43:
28-31 Ap '69
CANYONS
Escalante Canyon. E. Abbey. il Natur Hist
78:58-63 N '69
Logan Canyon; standards for destruction. G.
Alderson. il Nat Parks 43:18-20 N '69
Wilderness of slickrock. P. Hyde. il Audubon
71:44-9 S '69
See also
Glen Canyon
Grand Canyon
Hells Canyon
CAP (community action programs) See Anti-
poverty program, 1964-
CAP o' rushes; drama. See Feather, J.
CAPA, Robert, award. See Photography,
Journalistic—Awards
CAPACITANCE meters. See Electric meters
CAPE COD
Assignment: seeing between the scenics. J.
Scully. il Mod Phot 33:92-5+ F '69
Cape Cod, best in autumn. E. J. Kahn, jr.
il Travel & Camera 32:75-7 S '69
In the path of the Pilgrims. M. H. Koehler.
il Travel 132:52-7 O '69
Shape of water; excerpts from In defense of
nature. J. Hay. il Audubon 71:16-26 Jl '69
See also
Buzzards Bay, Mass
CAPE COD murders. See Murder
CAPE COD NATIONAL SEASHORE
Bicycle trails of Cape Cod National Seashore.
C. R. Koehler. il Nat Parks 43:16-17 Ja '69
Ribbon of green; the epic of a salt marsh,
its birth, life, death, excerpts from Life
and death of a salt marsh. J. Teal and
M. Teal. il Audubon 71:4-8+ N '69
Visit Cape Cod National Sea-shore this sum-
mer. A. G. Melvin. il Hobbies 74:113 My
'69
CAPE colored people. See Colored people
(South Africa)
CAPE fuchsia
Cape fuchsia. R. D. Pearce. Horticulture 47:
41 Jl '69
CAPE HATTERAS NATIONAL SEASHORE
RECREATION AREA
Lonely Cape Hatteras, besieged by the sea.
W. S. Ellis. il Nat Geog 136:392-421 S '69
CAPE HORN. See Horn, Cape
CAPE KENNEDY. See Kennedy, Cape
CAPE TOWN, Robert Selby Taylor, abp of.
See Taylor, R. S.
CAPELL, Martin D.
Passive mastery of helplessness in games.
bibliog Am Imago 25:309-32 Wint '68
CAPEN, Charles F.
Mars, a dynamic world. C. F. Capen. il R Pop
Astron 63:4-7 F '69
Visual observations of Apollo 8. R Pop
Astron 63:12-13 My '69
—and Capen, V. W.
Planet Mars in 1969. il Sky & Tel 37:190-4 Mr
'69
CAPEN, V. W. See Capen, C. F. jt. auth.
CAPILLARIES
Deformation of red blood cells in capillaries.
R. Skalak and P. I. Branemark. bibliog il
Science 164:717-19 My 9 '69
CAPILLARITY
See also
Brownian movements
CAPITAL
Federal taxation; cost of capital; address,
December 6, 1968. N. B. Ture. Vital Speeches
35:221-4 Ja 15 '69
See also
Corporations—Finance
Liquidity (economics)
Small business—Finance
CAPITAL, Venture
Golden equation of venture capital. il Duns R
94:42-5 S '69
New kind of oil boom; oil venture funds.
il Forbes 104:19-20 Ag 1 '69
Wall Street: in on the ground floor. C. Mor-
gello. il Newsweek 73:70 F 10 '69
CAPITAL development fund. See United Na-
tions—Capital development fund
CAPITAL gains tax. See Income tax—Capi-
tal gains tax
CAPITAL investments
Brakes on investment. il Fortune 79:16+ Je
'69
Business plans to ignore the chill; McGraw-
Hill survey. il Bsns W p27-8 N 8 '69

Capital-goods puzzle. il Fortune 80:20+ D
'69
First look at business in 1970; McGraw-Hill
survey. il Bsns W p 13-14 Ag 30 '69
More capital goes abroad; McGraw-Hill sur-
vey. il Bsns W p38 Ag 9 '69
Shell saves money by spending more. il Bsns
W p56-8+ Mr 8 '69
Spending spree goes on. il Bsns W p34-5 Mr
22 '69
Why companies still bet on expansion. L. A.
Mayer. il Fortune 80:106-9+ Jl '69
Why Nixon wants to wield the ax; repeal of
the 7 per cent tax credit. il Bsns W p 108-
10+ Ap 26 '69
See also
Art as an investment
Industrial expansion
Investment tax credit
CAPITAL punishment
Capital punishment: has it become cruel and
unusual? A. W. Green. il Nat R 21:384-5+
Ap 22 '69
Case that could end capital punishment;
Maxwell v. Bishop. R. Hammer. il N Y
Times Mag p46-7+ O 12 '69
Death row for Robert Kennedy's killer,
but. . . il U S News 66:16 Je 2 '69
Double jeopardy; black and poor; address,
January 12, 1969. F. H. Williams. Vital
Speeches 35:273-7 F 15 '69
End to capital punishment. Life 66:36 Je 20
'69
New debate on death penalty; major issue in
California. U S News 66:13 My 5 '69
No work for the hangman. E. Gertz. Nation
208:101-2 Ja 27 '69
Should capital punishment be revived? GH
poll. il Good H 169:24+ N '69
See also
Hanging
CAPITAL spending. See Capital investments
CAPITALISM
Anti-capitalism in Latin America. America
120:266-7 Mr 8 '69
Memories; concerning J. Schumpeter-P.
Sweezy debate. P. A. Samuelson. News-
week 73:83 Je 2 '69
See also
Black capitalism
Free enterprise
CAPITALISM and communism. See Communism
and democracy
CAPITALISTS and financiers
See also
Entrepreneurs
Rich, The
CAPITOL park, Sacramento. See Sacramento,
Calif.—Parks and reserves
CAPITOLS
Capitol need not be synonymous with dome. il
Arch Rec 145:117-28 My '69
See also subhead Capitol under names of
countries, states, etc. e.g. Hawaii—Capitol
CAPLAN, Basil
Harvey's battle in the fjords. Duns R 94:
91+ S '69
CAPLAN, Gerald
Psychiatrist's casebook (title varies) See is-
sues of McCalls April 1969-
CAPLES, John
Madison avenue: ad which became famous.
Sat R 52:57-8 F 8 '69
Madison avenue: $1,000 a word. Sat R 52:
126-7 Mr 8 '69
CAPLIN, Mortimer M.
Excerpt from testimony before House com-
mittee on ways and means, February
24, 1969. Cong Digest 48:138+ My '69
Time for lower, fairer taxes is now! Read
Digest 95:39-44 S '69
CAPOBIANCO, Tito
Corsaro, Capobianco, and Merrill. D. Hering.
il por Dance Mag 43:28-30 Mr '69
CAPON, Brian
Light, leaves and life. Horticulture 47:30-1+
Jl '69
CAPON, Robert Farrar
Calories are only a demon to be exorcised;
interview, ed. by M. C. Wrenn. pors Life
66:39-40+ Mr 14 '69
Christmas afternoon is forever. por Redbook
134:80-8 D '69
How to become a connoisseur of California
white wines. House & Gard 136:20+ Ag '69
about
Authors & editors. B. A. Bannon. por Pub W
195:30 F 10 '69
Cook for all seasons. il por Time 93:64 Ap
4 '69
Wonderful paradigm. Chr Cent 86:335 Mr 5
'69

CAPONI, Donna
Cool one turned the heat on. C. Kirkpatrick.
Sports Illus 31:54 Jl 7 '69
CAPONIGRO, Paul
Stonehenge; photographs. Travel & Camera
32:42-5+ Mr '69
CAPOTE, Truman
At the sea and in the city. House B 111:93-8
Ap '69
Donna Marella and the avvocato. Vogue 153:
206-9 Ap 1 '69
Greek paragraphs. Travel & Camera 32:46+
My '69
CAPOTOSTO, John
Build this jogger-walker for $30. Pop Mech
131:156-9 Je '69
How to turn a go-cart into a baby Chap-
arral. Mech Illus 65:74-8 Ag '69
Make a lamp on your lathe. Mech Illus 65:
102+ O '69
CAPOTOSTO, Rosario
It's easy now to form your own wrought
iron. Pop Sci 194:196+ Mr '69
CAPOUYA, Emile
Age of allegiance. Sat R 52:29 My 3 '69
Epic of Tropbanana. Nation 208:213 F 17 '69
Fugitive voice speaks out. Sat R 52:25+
Mr 1 '69
CAPP, Al
Is this your university? address, April 27,
1969. Vital Speeches 35:634-6 Ag 1 '69

about

Capp's cuts. il por Time 93:67-8 Ap 11 '69
CAPPS, Alton C.
Realistic approach to biblical literature. Engl
J 58:230-5 F '69
CAPPS, Osal B.
Rural fires; let's control them. Am For 75:
18-19+ Je '69
CAPPUCCILLI, Piero
What's in a name; interview, ed. by E.
Davidson. por Opera N 34:18 N 1 '69
CAPRICCIO; opera. See Strauss, R.
CAPRIO, Mario W.
ABC's of science. Parents Mag 44:54-6+ My
'69
CAPRON, Louis
Florida's emerging Seminoles. Nat Geog 136:
716-34 N '69
CAPSIR, Mercedes
Obituary
Opera N 34:33 S 6 '69
CAPTAIN Kangaroo (television program) See
Television broadcasting—Childrens programs
CAPTAIN'S daughter; story. See Pritchett, V.
S.
CAPTIVE animals. See Zoological gardens
CAPTURE at sea
See also
Privateering
CAPTURE of animals. See Animals—Capture
CAR cookery. See Cookery, Outdoor
CAR operating costs. See Automobiles—Cost
of operation
CAR pool; story. See Oppenheimer, M.
CAR rallies. See Automobile driving—Compe-
titions
CAR-top carriers. See Automobiles—Equipment
CARAMOOR festival orchestra
Report: Waterloo Village, N.J; concert per-
formance of Handel's Semele. S. L. Fogel.
Opera N 34:22 S 20 '69
CARAMOOR festivals. See Music festivals—
New York (state)
CARAS, Roger
In defense of the grizzly. Audubon 71:52-5 My
'69
Lingering of savages. Audubon 71:12-15 Jl
'69
CARAVANS
Through Ireland by tinker wagon. N. Icker-
ingill. il Travel & Camera 32:35-6 Ap '69
CARBERRY, John Joseph, cardinal
Cardinal Carberry taken to task by Lutheran
publication, St Louis Lutheran, and by
Eden theological seminary faculty. Chr
Cent 86:737 My 28 '69
Of many things. D. R. Campion. America 120:
inside cover My 31 '69
CARBINES. See Rifles
CARBON
Carbon: observations on the new allotropic
form. A. G. Whittaker and P. L. Kintner.
bibliog il Science 165:589-91 Ag 8 '69

Isotopes

Man-made carbon-14 in deep Pacific waters:
transport by biological skeletal material.
B. L. K. Somayajulu and others. bibliog
il Science 166:1397-9 D 12 '69
See also
Radiocarbon dating

CARBON compounds
See also
Fluorocarbons
CARBON dioxide
Carbon dioxide: chemical, biological, and
physiological aspects; report of meeting,
August 19-21, 1968. R. E. Forster and J. T.
Edsall. Science 166:410+ O 17 '69
Equilibration of atmospheric carbon dioxide
with sea water; possible enzymatic control
of the rate. R. Berger and W. F. Libby.
bibliog il Science 164:1395-7 Je 20 '69; Reply.
K. V. Krishnamurty. 165:929 Ag 29 '69
Evidence for solid carbon dioxide in the
upper atmosphere of Mars. K. C. Herr and
G. C. Pimentel. il Science 167:47-9 Ja 2 '70
See also
Photosynthesis
CARBON fibers. See Fibers
CARBON monoxide
Carbon monoxide-induced arterial hypoxemia.
J. S. Brody and R. F. Coburn. bibliog il
Science 164:1297-8 Je 13 '69
Carbon monixide: residence time in the at-
mosphere. B. Weinstock. bibliog il Science
166:224-5 O 10 '69
Elusive polluter. J. Bockel. il Sci N 96:480-1
N 22 '69
CARBON tetrachloride
Products containing carbon tetrachloride. To-
days Health 47:77-8 Mr '69
CARBONADOS. See Diamonds, Industrial
CARBONATES
Carbonate sediments: oriented lithified sam-
ples from the North Atlantic. G. A. Bart-
lett and R. G. Greggs. bibliog il Science
166:740-1 N 7 '69
Hydrocalcite ($CaCO_3:H_2O$) and nesquehonite
($MgCO_3:3H_2O$) in carbonate scales. H.
Marschner. bibliog il Science 165:1119-21 S
12 '69; Reply. M. Fleischer. 166:1309 D 5 '69
See also
Dolomite (mineral)
CARBORUNDUM company
Behavioral approach to industrial selling.
J. W. Thompson and W. W. Evans. il Har-
vard Bsns R 47:137-51 Mr '69
CARBOXYLASES
Acetyl coenzyme A carboxylase: filamentous
nature of the animal enzymes. A. K. Klein-
schmidt and others. bibliog il Science 166:
1276-8 D 5 '69
CARBURETORS
Care & feeding of carburetors. T. Tappett.
il Mech Illus 65:70-2+ Jl '69
Carter carb mods. J. Dianna. il Hot Rod
22:86-7 S '69
Carter's cool thermo quad. E. Rickman. il
Hot Rod 22:72-3 Mr '69
Fine-tuning your carburetor. M. Schultz. il
Pop Mech 131:184-7+ Mr '69
Holley's four-hole monster. S. Kelly. il Hot
Rod 22:64-5 Je '69
How it works: the marine carburetor. C.
Miller. il Motor B 123:106+ My '69
Mixer. D. Hill. il Hot Rod 22:40-2 Je '69
Performance from a Rochester Q-jet; ques-
tions and answers. il Motor T 21:84-5
S '69
Put life back in your carburetor. M. Schultz.
il Pop Mech 131:160-3 F '69
Truth about two-barrels. B. Lang. il Hot
Rod 22:50-2 Ag '69
Twin H power. A. B. Shuman. il Motor T
21:60 N '69
CARCINOGENS. See Cancer producing sub-
stances
CARCINOMA cells. See Cancer cells
CARDIAC diseases. See Heart—Diseases
CARDIAC glycosides
Ecological chemistry. L. P. Brower. il Sci Am
220:22-9 F '69
See also
Ouabain
CARDIAC pacers. See Pacemaker, Artificial
(heart)
CARDIAC resuscitation
Fourth doctor. P. F. Eastman. il Todays
Health 47:28-9+ Ap '69
CARDIAC rhythm. See Heart beat
CARDIFF, Wales
Music
Report: production of Falstaff at the Welsh
national opera. F. G. Barker. Opera N 34:
26 D 6 '69
CARDIN, Pierre
Designing man. por Time 93:60-1 Ja 31 '69
CARDINAL stays all winter; story. See Levin,
R.

CARLISLE, Lilian Baker
Pennsylvania German pillowcases. Antiques
95:556-8 Ap '69
CARLISLE, Norman
How to know the lay of the land. Pop Mech
131:130-3+ Je '69
Look what's happened to bows and arrows.
Pop Mech 132:120-3 S '69
Man with a million rockets. Mech Illus 65:64-
5+ Ag '69
Super lab that nobody knows. Pop Mech 131:
124-7+ Ap '69
CARLISLE, Olga
Provence still life. por Holiday 45:26-31+
Je '69
CARLISLE, Thomas John
Grand Canyon; poem. America 121:71 Ag 2 '69
Report; poem. Chr Cent 86:211 F 12 '69
Seismic disturbance; poem. Chr Cent 86:873
Je 25 '69
Unactivated; poem. Chr Cent 86:783 Je 4 '69
CARLISLE and Jacquelin (brokers)
Odd-lot firms set to merge. Bsns W p81 Ag
9 '69
CARLOS, John
Best in the world. il pors Newsweek 73:106+
My 26 '69
I do what I think is right. S. Myslenski. pors
Sports Illus 30:56-8+ Je 9 '69
Way to San Jose. S. Myslenski. il por Sports
Illus 30:10-13 Je 30 '69
CARLOS, Walter
Electric Bach. H. Saal. il Newsweek 73:90
F 3 '69
Switched-on Bach story. I. Berger. il Sat R
52:45-7+ Ja 25 '69
Synthesizing Johann S. Bach. R. Freedman.
Life 66:12 Ja 24 '69
CARLOS Avery management area and game
farm. See Wildlife sanctuaries—Minnesota
CARLSEN, G. Robert
English below the salt: the miscellaneous
crowds and people. Engl J 58:363-7 Mr '69
CARLSEN, Karen L.
Pansies, last in the fall, and first in the
spring. Org Gard & Farm 16:68-9 O '69
Queen's tears, carefree houseplant. Org Gard
& Farm 16:114-15 Ja '69
CARLSON, Barbara W.
Exodus from one's native land. New Repub
160:14-15 Je 28 '69
CARLSON, Burton L.
Abram; poem. Chr Cent 86:476 Ap 9 '69
CARLSON, Carl E.
Weekly and suburban press. Writers Digest
49:60-2 Ap '69
CARLSON, Carolyn
Dance images of now and thensome; Martini-
que theatre. M. Marks. Dance Mag 43:76 Ap
'69
CARLSON, Curtis L.
Czar of Gold bond stamps. il pors Bsns W
p 104+ Ag 23 '69
CARLSON, Katherine
Why mom supports the game. Sports Illus
31:48-51 S 8 '69
CARLSON, Leland H.
(comp) Articles and other books received;
British Commonwealth and Ireland. See is-
sues of American historical review
CARLSON, Richard, and Brisson, Lance
Web that links San Francisco's Mayor Alioto
and the Mafia. Look 33:17-21 S 23 '69
CARLSSON, Pat (Moss)
Don't say woman driver when you talk
about Pat Carlsson. K. Prentiss. por Holi-
day 46:64-5 S '69
CARLYSLE, John
Rhine. Travel & Camera 32:65-7+ Mr '69
CARMACK, Rex
Programmed street cleaning. Am City 84:78-9
Jl '69
CARMELA'S marriage; story. See Ritter
Aislán, E.
CARMEN; opera. See Bizet, G.
CARMICHAEL, Hoagy
Hoagy; interview. ed. by I. Kolodin. B. Free-
man. il pors Sat R 52:43-5+ Je 28 '69
CARMICHAEL, James H. jr
Jumping spiders; with biographical sketch.
por Natur Hist 78:4, 28-35+ O '69
CARMICHAEL, Stokely
Open letter to Stokely Carmichael. E. Cleaver.
il por Ramp Mag 8:31-2 S '69
CARMINES, Alvin
Sing a song of God. il por Newsweek 73:50
Ap 7 '69
CARNABY street. See London—Streets
CARNACINA, Luigi
Great Italian cooking; excerpts. Ladies Home
J 86:90-1+ F '69
CARNAVAL d'hiver de Quebec. See Carnival

CARNAY, Laurence D. and Barry, W. H.
Turbidity, birefringence, and fluorescence
changes in skeletal muscle coincident with
the action potential. bibliog Science 165:608-
9 Ag 8 '69
CARNE, Judy
Girls from L-I. por Newsweek 73:62 Ja 27 '69
CARNEGIE, Andrew
Carnegie libraries: their history and impact
on American public library development.
G. S. Bobinski; reply. H. V. Deale. ALA
Bul 63:149 F '69
CARNEGIE commission on higher education
Civilian G.I. bill? Carnegie commission on
higher education report. Commonweal 89:
545-6 Ja 31 '69
CARNEGIE libraries. See Libraries—United
States
CARNEGIE library of Pittsburgh
Penntap: mobile service to industry. D. R.
Pfoutz. il Library J 94:1589-91 Ap 15 '69
CARNER, JoAnne (Gunderson)
Gundy's victory was no fluke. por Sports
Illus 30:52-3 F 10 '69
CARNESECCA, Lou
New Mr Bones has a winner. C. Kirkpatrick.
il por Sports Illus 30:48-9 Ja 27 '69
CARNEVALI, Francesca, and others
Cytoplasmic DNA from petite colonies of
saccharomyces cerevisiae: a hypothesis on
the nature of the mutation. bibliog Science
163:1331-3 Mr 21 '69
CARNEY, David
Economic development. Bul Atom Sci 25:11-
15 N '69
CARNIVAL
Annual vibrations; Brazilian carnaval. il
Time 93:36+ F 14 '69
Place of the month: Rio de Janeiro: three
days of frenzy make the Rio carnival a
must. il Holiday 45:88-9 F '69
Quebec's lively ice; Carnaval d'hiver de
Quebec. R. Arnold. il U S Camera 32:56-8+
Ja '69
CARNIVALS, Street. See Street carnivals
CARNIVORA
See also
Martens
CAROL, Raymond L.
[Book review] America 120:171-2 F 8 '69
CAROLINA hemlock. See Hemlock
CAROLINA parakeets. See Parrots
CAROLINE ISLANDS
See also
Truk Islands
CAROUSEL inertial navigation system. See
Inertial guidance systems
CAROUSEL models. See Models and model-
making
CARP
See also
Cookery—Fish
CARP fishing
Bownanza. E. A. Bauer. il Outdoor Life 143:
74-7+ Mr '69
Call of the bugle. J. Parry. il Field & S 74:
70-1+ Je '69
CARPENTER, Earl
My painting technique. il por Am Artist 32:
66-71 N '68
CARPENTER, Edwin D.
Pollutants and the roadside. Horticulture 46:
18-19+ O '68
CARPENTER, Elizabeth
Ruffles and flourishes; excerpts. McCalls 97:
76-7+ D '69; 20+ Ja '70
CARPENTER, John Wilson, 1916-
Adequate defense; address, October 4, 1969.
Vital Speeches 36:93-6 N 15 '69
CARPENTER, Rhys
Climate and history; excerpt from Discon-
tinuity in Greek civilization. Horizon 11:
48-57 Spr '69
CARPENTER, Scott
Escape from the deep. por Pop Sci 195:78-81+
S '69
New underwater breathing systems. Pop Sci
195:72-5+ N '69
CARPENTERIA californica
Bush-anemone. L. E. Hoffman. Horticulture
47:50 S '69
CARPENTERS
See also
Strikes—United States—Carpenters
United brotherhood of carpenters and joiners
of America
CARPENTRY
See also
Joints (carpentry)
Woodworking

CARPER, Jean
Defense against gouging. Nation 209:473-5 N 3 '69
Disease prevention, tomorrow's best hope. Todays Health 47:20-3+ Mr '69
Exposing histo, disease in disguise. Todays Health 47:30-1+ My '69
CARPET cleaning. See Rugs and carpets—Care
CARPET mulch. See Mulching
CARPETS. See Rugs and carpets
CARPETS. Outdoor. See Rugs and carpets. Outdoor
CARPI, Ugo da
Fine Italian hands. P. Standard. il Pub W 195:92-3+ F 3 '69
CARR, Archie
Naturalist at large. Natur Hist 78:18+ Mr '69
Thoughts on wilderness preservation and a Central American ethic. Audubon 71:50-5 S '69
CARR, Donald E.
Only the giant car-eater can save us. N Y Times Mag p87+ My 4 '69
CARR, Fred
Fred Carr says: I've had enough. por Bsns W p65 D 6 '69
Fund wizard builds an empire. il por Bsns W p76-8 My 3 '69
You call it speculation; I call it investment. por Forbes 104:56+ S 1 '69
CARR, Gregg. See Hartman, C. W. jt. auth.
CARR, Laurence A. and Moore, K. E.
Norepinephrine: release from brain by d-amphetamine in vivo. bibliog Science 164: 322-3 Ap 18 '69
CARR, Richard
British artist craftsmen. Craft Horiz 29:24-7+ S '69
CARR, Stephen, and Lynch, Kevin
Where learning happens. Ed Digest 35:9-12 S '69
CARREL, Gilbert R.
Ten tips for winter driving; ed. by C. W. Casewit. Read Digest 94:33-4 F '69
CARRERA ANDRADE, Jorge
Royal highway of the Incas; reprint. UNESCO Courier 22:71-3 Ag '69
CARRIAR, Shirley M.
Teaching reading skills in the junior high school. bibliog Engl J 58:1357-61 D '69
CARRICK, James
Huh...what hot tin roof? Outdoor Life 143: 72-3+ Mr '69
CARRICK, Robert W.
Ahab wouldn't know it. Yachting 125:54-5+ My '69
Beat the freeze. Yachting 125:69+ F '69
Brains and the money; excerpts from Defending the America's cup. Yachting 126:62-3+ O '69
CARRIER aircraft inertial navigation system. See Inertial guidance systems
CARRIER corporation
Wait until next year! air-conditioner market is growing. il Forbes 103:74-5 Ap 15 '69
CARRIERS
See also
Transportation
CARRIERS, Aircraft. See Aircraft carriers
CARRIERS, Car-top. See Automobiles—Equipment
CARRIGAN, Casey
Right-way Carrigan flies to a record. G. Ronberg. il por Sports Illus 30:26-8+ Je 23 '69
CARRIUOLO, Christopher W.
New talents test their mettle. por Bsns W p33+ Ja 3 '70
CARROLL, Charles. See Louisell, D. W. jt. auth.
CARROLL, Clay
Highlight. por Sports Illus 31:74 Jl 7 '69
CARROLL, Corky
Doo wa diddie squiggly wigglies: get lost! D. Levin. il por Sports Illus 31:22-3 D 8 '69
CARROLL, Daniel T.
What future for the conglomerate? Harvard Bsns R 47:4-6+ My '69
CARROLL, Diahann
Diahann Carroll presents the Julia dolls. il pors Ebony 24:148-50+ O '69
Diahann Carroll's juggling act. R. Hochstein. il pors Good H 168:38+ My '69
CARROLL, Diane Lee
Jewelry of the nineteenth century. Antiques 96:237-41 Ag '69
CARROLL, Frances Laverne
Library education in West Germany. por Wilson Lib Bul 43:992-6 Je '69
CARROLL, Irwin
Variable-capacitance diodes. por Electr World 82:38-40 Jl '69

CARROLL, James
Beginning bell; poem. Cath World 209:267 S '69
Campus ministry: a new taste of the old salt. Cath World 210:59-61 N '69
Distances; poem. Poetry 114:31-3 Ap '69
CARROLL, James D.
Science and the city: the question of authority. bibliog Science 163:902-11 F 28 '69
CARROLL, Lewis, pseud.
World of fantasy. D. Powills. Hobbies 74: 152-13 D '69
CARROLL, Ronald L.
Simple frequency counter. Electr World 82: 82 Jl '69
CARROLL, Wallace
Murder, mayhem and the mother tongue; address, May 4, 1969. Vital Speeches 35:542-4 Je 15 '69; Same abr. with title Murder and the mother tongue. Read Digest 95:57-9+ O '69
CARROLL, X. William
Theology students rebel. America 120:268-71. 515 Mr 8, My 3 '69
CARROT for a chestnut; story. See Francis, D.
CARROTS
Sweetest carrots ever. I. Grant. Org Gard & Farm 16:37 Ap '69
CARRUTH, Eleanore
Federated department stores: growing pains at forty. Fortune 79:142-7+ Je '69
International paper sees the forest through the trees. Fortune 79:104-9+ Mr '69
Manhattan's office building binge. Fortune 80:114-17+ O '69
CARRUTH, Hayden
Balance exactly struck. Poetry 114:330-1 Ag '69
Islands waited, wait still... Poetry 115:130-2 N '69
CARRY, Peter
Baseball. Sports Illus 31:42+ Jl 28; 46-9 Ag 18 '69
Baseball's week (cont) Sports Illus 30:78-9 Ap 28; 100-1 My 5; 86-7 My 12; 95-6 My 19; 87-8 Je 2; 108-9 Je 9; 80-1 Je 16; 64-5 Je 30; 31:66-7 Jl 14; 56+ Jl 21; 60-1 Jl 28; 62 Ag 4; 60-1 Ag 18; 81-2 Ag 25; 58-9 S 1; 128-9 S 22; 86-7 O 6 '69
Basketball's week (title varies) Sports Illus 30:70-1 F 17; 31:106+ D 22 '69; 32:44-5 Ja 5; 55-6 Ja 12 '70
College baseball. Sports Illus 30:62+ Je 2: 48-9 Je 30 '69
Lacrosse. Sports Illus 30:84-5 My 5 '69
CARS (automobiles) See Automobiles
CARSON, Gerald
Most celebrated dog case ever tried in Johnson County, Missouri, or the world; with biographical sketch. por Natur Hist 78:5, 6-8+ D '69
CARSON, Johnny
Battle of the talk shows. il por Newsweek 74:42-4+ S 1 '69
CARSON, Robert
America's unique hotels: Beverly Wilshire. California luxury. Holiday 46:56-7+ S '69
Outer Hawaiian Islands. Holiday 46:56-61+ O '69
There are still some unspoiled islands. Holiday 46:50-3+ N '69
CARSON, Robert K. See Plummer, W. T. jt. auth.
CARSWELL, George Harrold
Invisible appointments. New Repub 161:11 Jl 12 '69
CARTAGENA, Colombia
Heroic Cartagena. G. Porras Troconis. il Américas 21:21-30 Je '69
CARTER, Albert Howard
Thought; poem. Chr Cent 86:248 F 19 '69
CARTER, Alexander, bp
Pre-synod conversation; interview. ed. by J. C. Haughey. America 121:233-4 S 27 '69
CARTER, Angela
Tokyo: choreography of protest. Nation 209: 476-7 N 3 '69
CARTER, Arthur
Arthur Carter's concept. por Forbes 104:93 S 15 '69
CARTER, Elliott, 1908-
Current chronicle. K. Stone. bibliog f il Mus Q 55:559-72 O '69
CARTER, Gilbert L.
Real England. Travel & Camera 32:50-1+ Mr '69
CARTER, Jane
Psalm of springtime. Farm J 93:60 My '69
CARTER, John Mitchell
Boll weevil six feet long. pors Library J 94:3615-18 O 15 '69

CARTER, Manfred A.
Crystal Christ; Escape; poems. Chr Cent 86: 472, 479 Ap 9 '69
Glass box; poem. Chr Cent 87:6 Ja 7 '70
Golfers; poem. Chr Cent 86:831 Je 18 '69
Men before; poem. Chr Cent 86:1665 D 31 '69
Space; poem. Chr Cent 86:616 Ap 30 '69

CARTHEW, Anthony
Moscow report: . . . the more it remains the same. N Y Times Mag p28-9+ My 18 '69
1,000th (happy?) birthday; Cairo's blue period. N Y Times Mag p6+ Ag 17 '69

CARTIER, John O.
Are duck laws outdated? Outdoor Life 143:75-7+ F '69
Boom in steelhead. Outdoor Life 143:60-3+ Mr '69
Devil's own geese. Outdoor Life 144:82-4+ O '69
Lake trout are back! por Outdoor Life 143:88-9+ Ap '69
Unforgettable hunt. Outdoor Life 143:72-5+ My '69

CARTIER, Warren A.
Pigs of the Cheery Cows. por Outdoor Life 143:54-7+ Mr '69

CARTIER-BRESSON, Henri
Free at last. L. Gross. il por Look 33:58-63 S 23 '69
Land and its people: photographs. Travel & Camera 32:47-50 My '69

CARTIER diamond. See Diamonds

CARTILAGE
Cartilaginous dermal scales in cephalopods. P. Person. bibliog il Science 164:1404-5 Je 20 '69

CARTOGRAPHY
In the centre of the map; reprint. M. G. S. Hodgson. UNESCO Courier 22:54-5 Ag '69
Mapmaking: the gentleman's business. J. Poindexter. il Duns R 94:56-61 N '69

CARTOONISTS
Where are they now? creators of Buck Rogers and Flash Gordon. il Newsweek 74:8 Ag 4 '69

See also
Scarfe, G.
Schulz, C. M.
Stevenson, J.

CARTOONS. See Caricatures and cartoons; Moving pictures—Animated cartoons

CARTRIDGE loaded tape. See Magnetic tape

CARTRIDGES
Changes in shotgun shells. J. O'Connor. il Outdoor Life 143:130-5 Mr '69
Do we need another .25 caliber? W. Page. il Field & S 74:86-8+ Ag '69
Giving guns a shot of iron. F. Graham. Sports Illus 30:68+ My 19 '69
How to reload rifle cartridges. J. A. Schempp. il Cons 23:48-9+ F '69
Late-blooming .22/250. J. O'Connor. il Outdoor Life 144:94+ Jl '69
Selecting the bullet. J. O'Connor. il Outdoor Life 144:86+ O '69
South gate six; Weatherby's newest cartridge. Field & S 73:131-2 F '69
Sweet seventeen. W. Page. il Field & S 74:98-101 Jl '69

CARTS
Build-it-yourself garden cart. il Mech Illus 65:88-9 Ag '69
If you don't have a real goat, the riders can take turns being goat. il Sunset 143:46-7 Ag '69
Junior pickup. il Mech Illus 65:134-5 N '69

See also
Serving carts

CARTS, Motor. See Motor vehicles

CARTWRIGHT, Alexander Joy
Baseball's Johnny Appleseed. H. Peterson. il por Sports Illus 30:56-64+ Ap 14 '69

CARTWRIGHT, Gary
Remember the Alamo, please. Life 66:62-4 Ap 25 '69
Vincification of Sonny Jurgensen. Life 67:48-51 O 24 '69

CARTWRIGHT, Rufus
Ask Rufus. See issues of Mechanix illustrated

CARUBA, Alan
Poetry as merchandise. por Pub W 196:34 D 29 '69

CARUSO, Enrico
Caruso's other line. il por Opera N 34:8-12 Ja 10 '70
about
Enrico Caruso. G. Movshon. Hi Fi 19:77-8 S '69

CARVING (art industries)
From the herds and flocks. G. Norman-Wilcox. il Antiques 96:218-21 Ag '69
See also
Scrimshaw
Wood carving

CARVING (meat, etc)
How to carve a turkey. W. Davis. il Mech Illus 65:60-1 N '69

CARVING knives. See Knives

CARY, Bob
System for deer. Outdoor Life 144:70-1+ N '69

CARY, Joyce
Joyce Cary, by M. Foster. Review America 120:143-4 F 1 '69. J. G. Murray

CARYA ovata. See Hickory

CASADESUS, Robert
Music to my ears; performance of Mozart's D-major concerto. I. Kolodin. Sat R 52:50 D 13 '69

CASALS, Pablo
Musician of the month. A. Matilla. il por Hi Fi 19:MA4+ Je '69
Our far-flung correspondents. B. Taper. New Yorker 45:123-4+ Ap 19 '69

CASALS festival. See Music festivals—Puerto Rico

CASANOVA DE SEINGALT, Giacomo Girolamo
Adventurous life. P. Zweig. Nation 208:183-4 F 10 '69

CASASCO, Juan A.
Slums of hope and despair. Américas 21:13-20 Je '69

CASASCO, Remo R.
Designing your own boat. Yachting 126:42+ D '69

CASCADE RANGE
See also
Crater Lake

CASE, J. I. company
Tenneco makes a case for Case. il Bsns W p 166-8 S 13 '69

CASE, Robert N.
Criteria of excellence: the school library manpower project identifies outstanding school library centers. ALA Bul 63:247-8 F '69

CASE for two detectives; drama. See Murray, J.

CASELESS ammunition. See Ammunition

CASEWIT, Curtis W.
Skier's West. Harp Baz 103:86+ D '69
Thanks, I'll take the chair lift. Holiday 45:62-3+ My '69
(ed) See Carrel, G. R. Ten tips for winter driving

CASEY, Brian
Brittle snow; poem. America 120:307 Mr 15 '69
In those days; poem. America 121:612 D 20 '69
Rabbi; poem. America 121:166 S 13 '69
Swanboats; poem. America 120:531 My 3 '69

CASEY, Genevieve
(ed) Libraries in the therapeutic society. por ALA Bul 63:1085-6, 1280-3, 1554-9 S-O, D '69

CASEY, John
Mandarins in a farther field; story. New Yorker 45:34-42 Je 14 '69
Social life of the long-distance runner. Sports Illus 30:104-6+ Ap 14 '69

CASEY, Susan
Brief biography. S. Goodman. il pors Dance Mag 43:72-3 Ag '69

CASH, Johnny
Boy named Johnny. M. Cantwell. il pors Mlle 70:162-3+ N '69
Cashing in. il por Time 93:94 Je 6 '69
First angry man of country singers. T. Dearmore. il pors N Y Times Mag p32-4+ S 21 '69
Hard-times king of song; with report by J. Frook. il pors Life 67:44-8 N 21 '69
Johnny Cash, something rude showing. R. Goldstein. Vogue 154:46 Ag 15 '69
Restless ballad of Johnny Cash. C. S. Wren. il pors Look 33:68-72+ Ap 29 '69

CASH and carry plan (merchandising) See Cash business

CASH business
Spending cash can be a way to save. il Changing T 23:35 Ag '69

CASH registers
GE builds a robot cashier; TRADAR system. il Bsns W p70 My 10 '69

CASINOS
Buffeted Parvin/Dohrmann prepares for a new game; merger with Denny's restaurants, inc. il Bsns W p 100+ Je 14 '69
Duel of aces in Las Vegas. il Bsns W p49-50 Jl 12 '69
Investors take a chance on chance; stocks of companies with stakes in Las Vegas and Bahamas. il Bsns W p 139-40 Ap 26 '69

CASO, Adolph
Language programs are shortchanging our students! Ed Digest 34:48-9 My '69
CASO, Louis
Save with a single-turn pot. Electr World 81:32 Ap '69
CASPER, Billy
Crazy fatso, the putting fool, may now be the world's best golfer. E. Asinof. il pors N Y Times Mag p32-3+ Ap 6 '69
Has anybody here seen Billy? R. F. Jones. il pors Sports Illus 31:24-6+ Jl 14 '69
Sporting scene. H. W. Wind. New Yorker 45:129-32+ My 3 '69
CASS, Louise E. See Marcus, D. M. jt. auth.
CASSAVETES, John
After Faces, a film to keep the man-child alive; with report by A. Guerin. il pors Life 66:53-6+ My 9 '69
Faces of the husbands. New Yorker 45:32-3 Mr 15 '69
CASSEL, Shelley
Redbook reader Mrs Diedrick S. Cassel: cooking is her hobby. il por Redbook 134:100-3+ N '69
CASSELL, Eric J.
Death & the physician. Commentary 47:73-9 Je '69
CASSELS, Louis
Recovery of the positive; excerpt from address February 26, 1969. Chr Today 13:3-4 Ap 25 '69
CASSERLY, Bernard
One issue: L&O. Commonweal 90:384 Je 20 '69
CASSEROLE cookery
Beef casserole Mexican style. il Sunset 142:176 Ap '69
CASSETTE recorders. See Magnetic recorders and recording, Portable
CASSETTE tape. See Magnetic tape
CASSIAN, George. See Cuthbertson, G. jt. auth.
CASSIDAY, Bruce
Write me an adventure novel. Writer 82:11-14 Mr '69
CASSITY, Turner
Comment. Poetry 114:409-11 S '69
Eva Beatifield; Condemned of Belgrano: Mascots: Pacelli and the ethiop: Plot for a Guianese operetta; poems. Poetry 114:183-90 Je '69
CASSON, Lionel
Alexander's ascent to greatness on a ladder of gore. Sat R 52:27-9+ N 29 '69
Imhotep. Horizon 11:92-101 Sum '69
CASSREINO, John
Flushing and sweeping. Am City 84:80-1 Ap '69
CASTALDO, Joseph
Current chronicle; performance of Flight by Philadelphia musical academy. D. Chittum. il Mus Q 55:95-9 Ja '69
CASTELLUCCI, Vincent. See Manfredi, M. jt. auth.
CASTER, Arthur D.
County-owned, city-managed sewerage system. Am City 84:117-18 Ag '69
CASTIGLIONE, Lawrence. See Dropkin, S. jt. auth.
CASTILE, Spain
Beginnings of the Cortes of León-Castile. J. F. O'Callaghan. bibliog f Am Hist R 74:1503-37 Je '69
Old Castile. F. R. Buckley. il Nat R 21:1067+ O 21 '69
CASTING (fishing)
Accuracy casting. A. J. McClane. il Field & S 74:98-101 D '69
Mini course in spinning. W. Davis. il Mech Illus 65:53-5+ Mr '69
You need bait casting, too. T. Trueblood. il Field & S 74:29-30+ Jl '69
See also
Fly casting
CASTING (founding) See Foundry practice
CASTING (sculpture)
Casting with glass. E. W. Pollman. il Ceram Mo 17:26-7 Ja '69
Sand casting. D. Marchese. il Sch Arts 69:25 Ja 70
Styrofoam sandcasting. J. Hertzke and F. Crump, jr. il Sch Arts 69:16-17 O '69
CASTING, Die. See Die casting
CASTING, Plastics. See Plastics—Molding
CASTING, Precision. See Lost wax process
CASTING reels. See Fishing tackle
CASTLE, Barbara Anne
Mrs Castle's recipe. por Time 93:63 Ja 31 '69
Sweetening for the ladies. por Bsns W p 140 O 11 '69

CASTLE, Wendell
Mike Nevelson: the gender of wood. Craft Horiz 29:16-21 Mr '69
CASTLE COMBE, England
Loveliest village. D. Butwin. Sat R 52:62 O 18 '69
CASTLES
Queen's Scottish summer; holiday at Balmoral castle. B. Bishop. il Sat R 52:73-4+ Mr 8 '69
Surreal Gothic surprise: castle in the English countryside near Stroud. il House B 111:82-3 Ap '69
To reign in Spain. il Newsweek 74:91 S 8 '69
Why not stay in a castle? L. Hadley. Travel & Camera 32:62 Jl '69

Anecdotes, facetiae, satire, etc.
Room and bored; why not rent an Irish castle for a week or two? S. J. Perelman. il Holiday 45:40-1+ Mr '69
CASTRATION
Case against castration; with editorial comment. il Suc Farm 67:25, 26-7 S '69
CASTRO, Alonso
Alonso Castro dance co; La Mama E.T.C. M. Marks. Dance Mag 43:86 Jl '69
CASTRO, Fidel
Castro's Cuba. drums, guns, and the new man. J. Corry. Harper 238:37-45 Ap '69
Cuba ten years after; symposium. bibliog il pors Trans-Action 6:8-47+ Ap '69
Fidel Castro, by H. L. Matthews. Review
Commonweal 90:492 Ag 8 '69. J. Yglesias; Reply. J. F. Thorning. 91:237+ N 21 '69
Nation 208:609-10 My 12 '69. W. H. Blanchard
Newsweek il por 73:109D-110 My 19 '69. A. Cooper
Fidel's tokenism. L. Stearns. Nat R 21:596-7 Je 17 '69
For Castro: tighter Soviet ties as popularity ebbs. il por U S News 67:9 Ag 4 '69
Unexpected star forward. R. Erlich. Ramp Mag 7:60-1 N 30 '68
Visit to Cuba. K. Witker. Vogue 154:92+ O 1 '69
We should start talking with Castro. J. Plank. il N Y Times Mag p28-31+ Mr 30 '69; Same abr. with title Should we talk with Castro? Cur 107:10-17 My '69; Reply. P. D. Bethel. N Y Times Mag p 133 My 11 '69
CASTRO, Raúl Silva. See Silva Castro, R.
CASUALTY insurance. See Insurance, Casualty
CAT scratch disease. See Diseases
CATAGLYPHIS bicolor. See Ants
ÇATAL Hüyük excavations. See Asia Minor—Antiquities
CATALANI, Alfredo
Fritz and Wally. R. Jacobson. Sat R 52:79-80 Ap 26 '69
La Wally, the first stereo edition. P. L. Miller. Am Rec G 35:734+ My '69
Records:
La Wally. Opera N 33:35 Mr 29 '69
CATALOGING
Backlog to frontlog scheme for circulating nonfiction books at the Orange public library. M. H. Scilken. il Library J 94:3014-15 S 15 '69; Reply. R. O. Laythe. 95:13 Ja 1 '70
Bibliographic control of media: the librarian's Excedrin headache. P. S. Grove and H. L. Totten. bibliog f il Wilson Lib Bul 44:299-311 N '69
Now where did I put that Franck Sonata? D. Hamilton. il Hi Fi 19:56-60 S '69
Speed cataloging; prudence and pitfalls; University of Wisconsin. Milwaukee. J. Z. Nitecki. il Library J 94:1417-21 Ap 1 '69
Top priority for cataloging-in-source. J. L. Wheeler. bibliog il Library J 94:3007-13 S 15 '69; Discussion. 94:4074, 4321; 95:13 N 15, D 1 '69, Ja 1 '70
See also
Indexing
Subject headings
CATALOGING, Computerized. See Libraries—Automation
CATALOGS, Library
Dictionary catalog? Ha! letter to the editor. M. Rademacher. ALA Bul 63:707 Je '69
CATALOGS, Mail order
Missal for mammals; Whole earth catalog. il Time 94:74+ N 21 '69
CATALOGS, Seed and plant
Dreams of glory for armchair gardeners. il Changing T 23:11-12 F '69
Keeping the bloom on a flower business; Burpee catalogs. il Bsns W p94-5 Ap 12 '69

CATALOGS, Trade
Tidings, glad and otherwise; Christmas catalogues. R. Lynes. Art in Am 57:47 N '69
CATAMARANS
Cruising on the level. H. Estes. il Yachting 126:66-8+ Ag '69
New breed of racing catamaran. B. Ebsen. il Pop Sci 194:86-9 F '69
New power catamaran. F. T. Moss. il Yachting 125:54-6+ F '69
Ocean racing catamaran. B. Ebsen. il Yachting 125:84+ Ja '69
Poor Russian boy on a hot cat. F. Rohr. il Motor B 123:434-5 Ja '69
CATAPULTS, Toy. See Toys
CATARACT CANYON. See Grand Canyon
CATASTROPHE coverage. See Insurance—Catastrophe coverage
CATE, Curtis
Tale of the purloined saint. Horizon 11:68-79 Wint '69
CATE, Eleanor. See Holck, F. jt. auth.
CATECHISMS
See also
Catholic church—Catechisms
CATECHOLAMINES
Biochemical clues to mental illness. G. Bylinsky. il Fortune 80:124-7+ Jl '69
Contracture and catecholamines in mammalian myocardium. M. Morad. bibliog il Science 166:505-6 O 24 '69
Facilitation of brain self-stimulation by central administration of norepinephrine. C. D. Wise and L. Stein. bibliog il Science 163:299-301 Ja 17 '69
Quantal secretion from adrenal medulla: allor-none release of storage vesicle content. O. H. Viveros and others. bibliog il Science 165:911-13 Ag 29 '69
See also
Adrenalin
Dopamine
Norepinephrine
CATER, Danny
Name is Carter—er, Cater. R. Blount, jr. por Sports Illus 30:65-6 My 19 '69
CATERPILLAR tractor company
Rematch; GM's earthmoving equipment division. il Forbes 104:62+ O 15 '69
CATERPILLAR tractors. See Crawler vehicles
CATERPILLARS
See also
Gipsy moths
Tent caterpillars
CATFISH fishing
Channel cats on a slack line. J. M. Harris. il Field & S 74:84+ Je '69
See also
Bullhead fishing
CATFISHES
Catfish harvest; thriving catfish industry in the South. il Time 93:112 My 16 '69
Exotics: new threat to U.S. waters. E. Buckow. il Field & S 74:16+ My '69
New Florida resident, the walking catfish. C. P. Idyll. il Nat Geog 135:846-51 Je '69
Suffering catfish! clarias batrachus in Florida. Sci Am 220:50 Ja '69
CATHEDRAL builder; story. See Auchincloss, L.
CATHEDRALS
Testing architectural stress with a cathedral made of plastic. il Life 67:95-6+ S 19 '69

England
Megalithic plan underlying Canterbury cathedral. L. B. Borst. bibliog il Science 163:567-70 F 7 '69; Discussion. 164:769-70; 166:772-4 My 16, N 7 '69
Saving a stone prayer: York minster. F. C. Livingstone. il Sci N 95:268-9 Mr 15 '69

France
Legacy from the age of faith: Chartres. K. MacLeish. il Nat Geog 136:856-82 D '69
See also
Paris—Notre Dame (cathedral)

United States
Sad, slow death of a cathedral. D. Grumbach. il Commonweal 90:316-17 My 30 '69
CATHETERS
Magnetism in medical treatment. il Chem 42:21-3 Mr '69
CATHODE ray tubes
Distributed plates improve CRT response. A. H. Pettis. il Electr World 82:28 N '69
CATHOLIC association for international peace
Farewell to CAIP. America 120:609-10 My 24 '69

CATHOLIC authors
See also
O'Connor, F.
CATHOLIC book week. See Book week
CATHOLIC church
Agony of Paul VI. W. F. Buckley, jr. Nat R 21:402-3 Ap 22 '69
Can Catholicism make it? T. F. O'Dea. Chr Cent 86:283-7 F 26 '69
Can the church survive? J. B. Sheerin. Cath World 209:2-3 Ap '69
Cardinal as critic. il Time 94:47 Ag 1 '69
Catholic unity; in the light of Vatican II; excerpts from interview. L. J. Suenens. America 120:611 My 24 '69
Church in the year 2000; Commonweal paper; symposium. Commonweal 91:116-60+ O 31 '69; Reply. W. H. Clark. 91:287+ N 28 '69
Conversation with Karl Rahner; ed. by M. M. Dorcy and J. P. Jurich. K. Rahner. America 120:733-5 Je 28 '69
Crisis or kairos? W. Birmingham. Commonweal 91:210-14 N 14 '69
How not to review anybody's book; distortions of The underground church; cartoons. Cath World 208:222-4 F '69
Is it the same church? by F. J. Sheed. Review America 120:104 Ja 25 '69. C. P. Kindregan
Little and late. Commonweal 90:187-8 My 2 '69
New church? R. Ruether. Commonweal 90:64-6 Ap 4 '69; Discussion. 90:187+ My 2 '69
On making Christianity habitable. K. Rexroth. Commonweal 91:199-202 N 14 '69
Papal infallibility revisited; bishop denies the validity of a key teaching of the church. J. C. Haughey; discussion. America 120:345 Mr 29 '69
Pope's concern; church rebellion. U S News 66:16 Ap 14 '69
Problems of the papacy. Commonweal 90:132-3 Ap 18 '69
Questions & answers; symposium. Commonweal 91:215-18+ N 14 '69
Reconstruction after renewal; discussion. Chr Cent 86:155-6 Ja 29 '69
Reporter at large; Emmaus house, radical Catholic community in East Harlem. F. Du Plessix. New Yorker 44:37-8+ Ja 25 '69
Return of the Protestant principle. M. Daly. Commonweal 90:338-41 Je 6 '69
Right, duty, and dissent. N. J. Rigali. Cath World 208:214-18 F '69
Spectrum of Catholic attitudes, ed. by R. Campbell. Review
Cath World 209:276-7 S '69. K. P. Coyle
Tension is not schism; excerpts from interview. L. Suenens. America 120:152 F 8 '69
When Christians go underground. il U S News 66:42-3 Ap 14 '69
Where did all the spirit go? M. Novak. Commonweal 90:540-2 S 5 '69
Where's the church headed? J. J. McManmon. New Repub 160:16-19 Je 7 '69
Why I remain a Catholic. H. Graef. Cath World 209:77-80 My '69
See also
Canon law
Canonization
Concordats
Ecclesiastical courts
Ecumenical movement
Jesuits
Laity—Catholic church
Lent
Mass
Papacy
Pilgrims and pilgrimages
Popes
Purgatory
Reformation
Religious orders
Rosary
Saints
Synod of bishops
Synod of bishops, 1969
Vatican council, 2d
Women and the church
Worker priests

Authority
See Church—Authority

Byzantine rite
Fight for equal rites; Vatican and the Melkites. Newsweek 73:88 Je 16 '69
Melchite rite controversy; appointment of Melchite bishop for the United States. America 120:721 Je 28 '69; Reply. W. J. Baroody. 121:51 Ag 2 '69

Catechisms
Children of Isolotto; an imaginative new catechism. V. M. Marabelli and L. J. O'Donovan. America 120:706-9 Je 21 '69

CATHOLIC church—*Continued*

Clergy

Badgered bishops; bishops and cardinals meeting in Chur. Switzerland. il Newsweek 74:91 Jl 21 '69

Celibacy, ministry, church, by J. Blenkinsopp. Review
    Commonweal 91:53-5 O 10 '69. M. Daly

Challenge in Chur; symposium to duscuss the crisis in the Roman Catholic priesthood. Time 94:63 Jl 18 '69

Church communication. J. McLaughlin. America 121:173-4 S 13 '69

Church dissent: its rising toll. U S News 66: 18 Je 16 '69

Church without priests? by J. Duquesne. Review
    Commonweal 90:443-4 Jl 11 '69. R. P. McBrien

Major and the brothers; Marist brothers attempt to visit a Fort Dix prisoner. America 120:337 Ap 5 '69

Of many things; conception of leadership in the church. D. R. Campion. America 120: 374 Ap 5 '69

Revolt of the young priests. A. Whitman. McCalls 96:60-1+ Jl '69
    See also
Bishops
Cardinals
Priests

Installation

Albany stows its first throne: installation of a bishop. D. Grumbach. Commonweal 90:333-4 Je 6 '69

Dioceses

Albany stows its first throne: installation of a bishop. D. Grumbach. Commonweal 90:333-4 Je 6 '69

Calvary in Rochester; resignation by F. Sheen. Time 94:51-2 O 24 '69

Long time, no see; titular sees. Newsweek 73: 55 Ja 27 '69

New model from Detroit. Time 93:62 Ap 11 '69

Discipline

Vatican bars priests from Cuernavaca study center. Chr Cent 86:172 F 5 '69
    See also
Congregation for the doctrine of the faith
Dispensations (canon law)
Marriage (canon law)
Obedience (canon law)

Education

Black power and the learning process; learning a lesson from Catholic education. M. R. Berube. Commonweal 90:98-101 Ap 11 '69

Catholic alumni: seven years after. A. M. Greeley. il America 120:96-100 Ja 25 '69; Reply. N. J. Rigali. 120:178 F 15 '69

Catholic education faces its future, by N. G. McCluskey. Review
    America 120:416+ Ap 5 '69. J. Barzun
    Commonweal 90:494-5 Ag 8 '69. R. Hassenger

Catholic education: to be or not to be? M. J. Huth. bibliog f Sch & Soc 97:101-4 F '69

Child support or wall of separation: excerpt from Catholic education faces its future. N. G. McCluskey. Chr Cent 86:775-9 Je 4 '69

Hesburgh's law; the problems of campus secular or Catholic. Commonweal 89:719-20 Mr 14 '69; Reply. W. J. Wilson. 90:151 Ap 18 '69

Right to be educated, ed. by R. F. Drinan. Review
    America 120:227-8 F 22 '69. J. W. Evans

Seminary that won't quit. J. Mahoney. Commonweal 90:478-9 Ag 8 '69; Reply with rejoinder. F. X. Canfield. 90:579+ S 26 '69
    See also
Catholic colleges and universities
Catholic schools
Center of intercultural documentation
National Catholic educational association

Eucharist

Corpus Christi. V. P. McCorry. America 120: 676-inside back cover Je 7 '69

New Eucharistic fast; problem of Eucharistic unity. America 121:240-2 S 27 '69 Discussion. 121:343 O 25 '69

Paul VI and liturgical change; recent instructions on the distribution of holy communion. America 121:84-5 Ag 16 '69

Finance

Bishops and tax reform; U.S. Catholic conference testifying before the House ways and means committee. America 120:442-3 Ap 12 '69

Counting Peter's pence; Institute for religious works. il Time 93:70 Ja 24 '69

Money pinch. Commonweal 91:292 D 5 '69

Government

How Pope reacted to bids for change. il U S News 67:13 N 10 '69

Latest test for Catholic church. il U S News 67:42-3 N 3 '69

Plea to the bishops. P. O'Malley. Commonweal 91:267-8 N 28 '69

Suenens crying in the wilderness. G. Baum. Cath World 210:103-7 D '69
    See also
Catholic church—Dioceses

History

Crisis of the seventeenth century. by H. R. Trevor-Roper. Review
    Commonweal 89:595-6 F 7 '69. J. Ratté
    See also
Catholic church—Dioceses

Infallibility

    See also
Popes—Infallibility

Liturgy and ritual

At last, the new English liturgy. C. J. McNaspy. America 121:554-5 D 6 '69

Books. C. J. McNaspy. America 121:272-4 O 4 '69

Burial liturgy in Detroit. America 121:82 Ag 16 '69

Liturgical translation; Consilium for the implementation of the constitution on the sacred liturgy guidelines. America 120:348 Mr 29 '69

Liturgy and the perils of experience. K. McDonnell. America 121:93-5 Ag 16 '69

News and views; latest decree of the Concilium for the implementation of the constitution on the liturgy. J. Deedy. Commonweal 89:630 F 21 '69

No time to stop; reform of the liturgy. Commonweal 90:275-6 My 23 '69

Papal decree on church ritual. U S News 66:16 My 12 '69

Paul VI and liturgical change; recent instructions on the distribution of Holy communion. America 121:84-5 Ag 16 '69

Responsorial psalm tones for the Mozarabic office, by D. M. Randel. Review
    Mus Q 55:575-80 O '69. R. Steiner

What about the new liturgy? R. J. Ledogar. America 120:408-11 Ap 5 '69
    See also
Liturgical week
Missals

Missions

Cardinal Leger: leper colony at Nyamsong and village of Nsimalen in Cameroon. R. Harrity. il Look 33:37-8+ Jl 29 '69

Making of a saint; Mother Teresa; Superior General of the Missionaries of Charity. C. B. Pepper. il Look 33.34+ Mr 4 '69

One-to-one missions. W. M. O'Neil. America 121:357 O 25 '69

Reports: Peru; Maryknoll fathers on the altiplano. W. S. Just. Atlan 223:14+ My '69

Worker-priests in jurisdictional dispute. A. Woodrow. Commonweal 90:192-3 My 2 '69
    See also
Jesuits—Missions

Modernism

See Modernism

Mozarabic rite

Responsorial psalm tones for the Mozarabic office, by D. M. Randel. Review
    Mus Q 55:575-80 O '69. R. Steiner

Negroes

Black Catholicism; meeting of Black Catholic clergy caucus. J. C. Haughey. America 120:325-7 Mr 22 '69

Office for black Catholics; formation of National office for black Catholics. America 121:516 N 29 '69

Relations

Jews

New approach to Judaism; excerpts from Anti-Semitism and the Christian mind. A. T. Davies. Cath World 210:74-7 N '69

Rome and the Jews; Vatican document urges reconciliation. Newsweek 74:69 D 22 '69

CATHOLIC church in the Philippines
Birth control controversy. C. M. Ferrer. Chr Cent 86:1122-3 Ag 27 '69
CATHOLIC church in the United States
American Catholic exodus, ed. by J. O'Connor. Review
Commonweal 89:506-7 Ja 17 '69. J. W. Groutt
American Catholicism. R. Haughton. Cath World 209:5-6 Ap '69
Bishop Shannon's resignation. America 120: 678 Je 14 '69
Bit by bit: the story of Bishop James P. Shannon's resignation. S. J. Adamo. il America 120:717-18 Je 21 '69
Black Catholicism; meeting of Black Catholic clergy caucus. J. C. Haughey. America 120:325-7 Mr 22 '69
Can the Catholic revolution succeed? T. J. Fleming. il Redbook 133:77+ My '69
Charismatics gain bishops' blessing. Chr Today 14:41-2 Ja 2 '70
Contemporary Catholicism in the United States; ed. by P. Gleason. Review
Cath World 209:226-8 Ag '69. J. T. Ellis
Importance of being Roman Catholic. J. G. Milhaven America. 120:728-31 Je 28 '69; Discussion. 121:79 Ag 16 '69
Of many things; views of Cardinal John Dearden. D. R. Campion. America 121:inside cover N 22 '69
Plea to the bishops. P. O'Malley. Commonweal 91:267-8 N 28 '69
U.S. Catholicism revisited. R. Bosc. America 121:389-91 N 1 '69
USCC advisory council meets. America 120: 323-4 Mr 22 '69
See also
Catholics in the United States

History
Needed: a new history. D. J. O'Brien. America 120:528-30 My 3 '69
CATHOLIC church in the West Indies
Black power and the archbishop; cooperation in Jamaica. America 121:316 O 18 '69
Black power in the Caribbean. J. J. McEleney. America 121:557-8 D 6 '69
CATHOLIC church in Uganda
Uganda awaits the Pope. il Newsweek 74:67 Ag 4 '69
CATHOLIC church in Uruguay
Rightist press against bishops. America 121: 405 N 8 '69
CATHOLIC church in Yugoslavia
Church under Tito. il Newsweek 74:53 S 1 '69
See also
Church and state in Yugoslavia
CATHOLIC clergy conference on the interracial apostolate. See Priests—Associations, institutions, etc.
CATHOLIC college graduates. See College graduates
CATHOLIC colleges and universities
America's 1969 directory of Catholic colleges. America 121:458-60 N 15 '69
Catholic colleges face up to change; conference of Jesuit leaders and students in Denver. D. R. Campion. America 121:590-2 D 13 '69
Catholic colleges in the service of man. J. B. Kelley. Cath World 210:19-21 O '69
Catholic presence. L. M. Orsy. America 120: 396-7 Ap 5 '69; Reply. R. V. Schoder. 120: 602-3 My 24 '69
Catholic university; again. J. A. Appleyard. America 121:224-6 S 27 '69
Changing Catholic college. by A. M. Greeley. Review
Cath World 209:132 Je '69. J. P. Locigno
Conflict in the Catholic colleges. R. Hassenger. bibliog f Ann Am Acad 382:95-108 Mr '69
Hesburgh's law; the problems of campus, secular or Catholic. Commonweal 89:719-20 Mr 14 '69
Law and order on the Catholic campus. J. L. Walsh. Commonweal 90:562-3 S 19 '69
New Christian college? R. Kirk. Nat R 21:441 My 6 '69
Reformation of the Catholic college. R. Hassenger. il Sat R 52:47-9+ Jl 19 '69
Repeat performance? Catholic universities. J. Hitchcock. Commonweal 89:556-9 Ja 31 '69
Rome listens to the universities. N. G. McCluskey. America 121:58-60 Ag 2 '69
Tilton v. Finch. C. M. Whelan. America 121:222-3 S 27 '69
See also
Catholic university of America
Fordham university
Holy Cross college. Worcester. Mass.

Loyola college, Montreal
Notre Dame, Ind. University
Rome (city)—Pontifical Gregorian university
St John's university, Collegeville, Minn.
Woodstock college, Woodstock, Mass.

Curriculum
Theology for undergraduates. W. J. Sullivan. America 121:463-6 N 15 '69

Finance
Catholic colleges: the cost spiral catches up. J. E. Hobson and M. E. Robbins. America 121:634-6 D 27 '69

Italy
Up against the Catholic wall; Catholic university in Milan. H. ten Kortenaar. Commonweal 90:309-10 My 30 '69
CATHOLIC dissenters. See Dissenters, Religious
CATHOLIC education. See Catholic church—Education
CATHOLIC inter-American cooperation program. See Religious conferences
CATHOLIC junior colleges
Catholic junior colleges. America 120:618 My 24 '69
CATHOLIC laymen. See Laity—Catholic church
CATHOLIC library association
See also
Regina award
CATHOLIC literature
See also
Publishers and publishing—Catholic literature

Bibliography
Religion (cont) E. S. Stanton. America 120: 540-2; 121:532-4 My 3, N 29 '69
Reviews of books in the Catholic field. Chr Cent 86:745-50+ My 28 '69
Selection for Catholic book week. Commonweal 89:677-82+ F 28 '69
Suggestions for Lenten reading. America 120: 197-202 F 15 '69
CATHOLIC philosophical association, American. See American Catholic philosophical association
CATHOLIC philosophy. See Philosophy
CATHOLIC poetry society of America
News and views; demise. J. Deedy. Commonweal 90:130 Ap 18 '69
CATHOLIC press
Bishops' poll, the results of their attitudes toward diocesan newspapers. S. J. Adamo. America 122:28 Ja 10 '70
Bold voice: The Advocate of Newark. S. J. Adamo. America 120:203-4 F 15 '69
Catholic press and dissent in the church. America 120:211 F 22 '69
Change, promise and trauma in Catholic publishing. Chr Cent 86:735 My 28 '69
Cool message; traditional policies of the Catholic press. S. J. Adamo. America 120: 117-19 Ja 25 '69
Diocesan bugle. J. Deedy. Commonweal 91: 170 N 7 '69
Diocesan press. A. E. P. Wall. America 120: 220 F 22 '69
Dispirit of St Louis. S. J. Adamo. America 121:508+ N 22 '69; Reply. B. J. Huger. 121: 603 D 20 '69
Elite: Alfred N. Delahaye survey findings. S. J. Adamo. America 121:125 Ag 30 '69
High noon: Oklahoma courier. S. J. Adamo. America 120:370 Mr 29 '69
Murder most foul? the diocesan Catholic press. S. J. Adamo. America 120:287 Mr 8 '69; Reply. D. Zirkel. 120:376 Ap 5 '69
Necrology. J. Deedy. Commonweal 91:236 N 21 '69
New venture; Colorado graphic. S. J. Adamo. America 121:46-7 Jl 19 '69
Pope's bulletin board; L'Osservatore romano. il Time 93:63 Ja 24 '69
Press. S. J. Adamo. See issues of America
Smell of death. S. J. Adamo. America 121:398-9 N 1 '69; Discussion. 121:481 N 22 '69
Squaring the Circle; Twin circle and Our Sunday visitor alliance? S. J. Adamo. America 121:202-3 S 20 '69
See also
America (periodical)
Catholic press association
Catholic review
Catholic worker (periodical)
Commonweal (periodical)
National Catholic reporter
Triumph (periodical)

CATHOLIC press association
Of many things: first joint convention of the Catholic press association and the Associated church press. D. R. Campion. America 120:inside cover Je 7 '69

CATHOLIC programs. See Television broadcasting—Religious programs

CATHOLIC relief services
Catholic relief services. America 120:295-6 Mr 15 '69
  See also
Nigeria—Civil war, 1967-1970—Relief work

CATHOLIC review
Baltimore's Wall. S. J. Adamo. America 120: 568-9 My 10 '69

CATHOLIC schools
Are the Catholic schools dying? interview, ed. by J. Star. J. C. Donohue. il Look 33:105-6+ O 21 '69
Catholic schools. N. G. McCluskey. America 122:22-4 Ja 10 '70
Crisis hits Catholic schools. il U S News 67: 33-4 S 29 '69
Education without school libraries? J. B. Sheerin. Cath World 209:146-7 Jl '69
Mendicant church schools. Sat R 52:66 Ap 19 '69
Missing ingredient in Catholic schools. F. E. Fitzpatrick. America 120:406-7 Ap 5 '69; Reply. J. Lynch. 120:551 My 10 '69
NCEA study a helpful tool. How good are Catholic schools? study. America 120:263 Mr 8 '69
Revolution by Brother Alexis; living theater at Antonian high school, San Antonio. W. A. McWhirter. il Life 66:67-8+ Ja 31 '69
Silliness in sex education. R. Kirk. Nat R 21:1274 D 16 '69
Somebody up there likes Holy Cross high. il Time 94:34 D 26 '69
Teachers' unions in Catholic schools. J. P. Mooney. America 120:301-3 Mr 15 '69; Discussion. 120:437 Ap 12 '69
Will Catholic schools survive? America 120: 460 Ap 19 '69
  See also
Education and state

Desegregation
Dilemma for parochial schools. F. N. Boney. America 121:161 S 13 '69; Reply. C. Francell. 121:249 O 4 '69

Federal aid
Catholic education: mixture of hope and concern. J. Lloyd. Sr Schol 94:Schol Teach 5 My 9 '69
Catholic schools in crisis. America 121:7 Jl 5 '69
Church, state and the courts. G. R. La Noue. Nation 209:656-9 D 15 '69
Diversity in schooling. R. Kirk. Nat R 21:542 Je 3 '69
Tax funds for nonpublic education. V. C. Blum. America 121:227-30 S 27 '69; Reply. W. C. Kessel. 121:404 N 8 '69

Finance
Catholic schools should carry their own burden. C. Grieder. Ed Digest 35:26-7 O '69
Crisis hits Catholic schools. il U S News 67:33-4 S 29 '69
Ecumenism and the school aid issue. J. M. Swomley, jr. Chr Cent 86:780-3 Je 4 '69
Fiscal crisis. il Time 93:42+ Mr 28 '69
Funding Catholic schools: a Canadian way. C. J. Matthews. America 121:231-2 S 27 '69
  See also
Catholic schools—Federal aid

CATHOLIC theologians. See Theologians

CATHOLIC university of America
C.U.A. board of inquiry report; academic propriety of the dissenting theologians action. America 120:489 Ap 26 '69
Rights and wrongs; dissident theologians exonerated. Newsweek 73:81 Ap 21 '69
Vindication at C.U; right of theological dissent. Commonweal 90:155-6 Ap 25 '69

CATHOLIC university of the Sacred Heart, Milan. See Catholic colleges and universities—Italy

CATHOLIC worker (periodical)
Penny a copy, ed. by T. C. Cornell and J. H. Forest. Review
  Commonweal 90:114-16 Ap 11 '69. J. C. Cort

CATHOLIC worker movement
Dorothy Day: a sign of contradiction. S. Vishnewski. Cath World 209:203-6 Ag '69

CATHOLICISM. See Catholic church

CATHOLICS
American Catholic exodus, ed. by J. O'Connor. Review
  Commonweal 89:506-7 Ja 17 '69. J. W. Groutt
Importance of being Roman Catholic. J. G. Milhaven. America 120:728-31 Je 28 '69; Discussion. 121:79 Ag 16 '69
Roman Catholic: visible and invisible; address, October 1969. F. Sontag. America 121:298-301 O 11 '69
Where did all the spirit go? M. Novak. Commonweal 90:540-2 S 5 '69
Why I remain a Catholic. H. Graef. Cath World 209:77-80 My '69

CATHOLICS in Japan
Hidden Christians; adherents of Catholicism that St Francis Xavier brought in 1549 still separated from Rome. il Newsweek 73:112+ Mr 17 '69

CATHOLICS in Northern Ireland
Ireland's niggers; with interview with B. Devlin. P. Buckman. Ramp Mag 8:19-22 Jl '69

CATHOLICS in the United States
American Catholics and social reform, by D. J. O'Brien. Review
  Chr Cent 86:124+ Ja 22 '69. L. C. Rudolph
Catholics, Southern Baptists in dialogue. R. Ryland. Chr Cent 86:816-17 Je 11 '69
Continual reformation at last? S. Cunneen. il Chr Cent 86:670-1 My 14 '69
News and views; Becker survey of Worcester, Mass, diocese. J. Deedy. Commonweal 90: 92 Ap 11 '69
U.S. Catholicism revisited. R. Bosc. America 121:389-91 N 1 '69
  See also
Catholic worker movement

CATHOLICS in Vietnam
Hang down your head, Tom Dooley; Vietnamese Catholics, a pawn of American foreign policy. R. Scheer. il Ramp Mag 7: 15-19 Ja 25 '69

CATLETT, Elizabeth
My art speaks for both my peoples. il pors Ebony 25:94-6+ Ja '70

CATNIP
  See also
Nepetalactone

CATOIR, John T.
Promises in a mixed marriage. America 120: 446-9 Ap 12 '69

CATON, Hiram
Conservative liberalism. Nat R 21:181-2 F 25 '69

CATS
Acute axonal dystrophy caused by flouorocitrate: the role of mitochondrial swelling. H. Koenig. bibliog il Science 164:310-12 18 '69
Athetoid and choreiform hyperkinesias produced by caudate lesions in the cat. S. L. Liles and G. D. Davis. bibliog il Science 164:195-7 Ap 11 '69
Checkup for cats' role in leukemia. Bsns W p65 D 27 '69
Feline attractant, cis,trans-nepetalactone: metabolism in the domestic cat. G. R. Waller and others. bibliog il Science 164:1281-2 Je 13 '69
Feline leukemia virus: occurrence of viral antigen in the tissues of cats with lymphosarcoma and other diseases. W. D. Hardy, jr. and others. bibliog il Science 166:1019-21 N 21 '69
Glycine in the spinal cord of cats with local tetanus rigidity. T. Semba and M. Kano. bibliog il Science 164:571-2 My 2 '69
Neural readout from memory during generalization. E. R. John and others. bibliog il Science 164:1534-6 Je 27 '69
Opponent color cells in the cat lateral geniculate nucleus. A. L. Pearlman and N. W. Daw. bibliog il Science 167:84-6 Ja 2 '70
Relation of pharmacological and behavioral effects of a hallucinogenic amphetamine to distribution in cat brain; DOM or STP. J. E. Idänapään-Heikkilä and others. bibliog il Science 164:1085-7 My 30 '69
Steady potential correlates of positive reinforcement; reward contingent positive variation. T. J. Marczynski and others. bibliog il Science 163:301-4 Ja 17 '69

Anecdotes, facetiae, satire, etc.
Bon voyage, but don't tell the cat. G. Trotta. House B 111:189 O '69

Care
In case of emergency. L. F. Whitney. McCalls 97:44+ N '69
Just how well do you take care of your dog or cat? il Bet Hom & Gard 47:86-7+ Mr '69

CATTON, Bruce
Miracle on Missionary ridge; excerpt from Grant takes command; with introd. by the editors. il Am Heritage 20:60-73 F '69
CATULLI carmina; opera. See Orff, C.
CAUCASIAN rugs. See Rugs and carpets, Oriental
CAUDATE nucleus. See Brain
CAUDILL, Harry Monroe
Corporate fiefdom. Commonweal 89:523-5 Ja 24 '69

about

Loneley war of a good angry man. D. G. McCullough. il por Am Heritage 21:97-113 D '69
CAUDILL, Rebecca
Appalachian heritage; address, November 2, 1968. Horn Bk 45:143-7 Ap '69
CAUDILL, William W.
Architecture in the cause of people: yesterday, today and tomorrow. Arch Rec 145: 127-30 Ja '69
CAULFIELD, Patricia
Flowing grass; photographs. Audubon 71:28-45 Ja '69
CAULKING compounds
All those new caulks. R. Day. il Pop Sci 195: 148-52+ S '69
Caulking compounds. Consumer Bul 52:4 My '69
Caulking compounds. il Consumer Rep 34: 247-9 My '69
Caulking that really sticks and lasts. il Changing T 23:10 N '69
Seaworthy stickums and fillers for fitting out. F. M. Paulson. il Field & S 73:150-2+ Ap '69
CAUTHEN, Kenneth
Case for Christian biopolitics. Chr Cent 86: 1481-3 N 19 '69
CAUTION: a love story (about a certain Duke and Duchess) musical comedy. See Musical comedies, revues, etc.—Criticisms, plots, etc.
CAVAFY, C. P.
Beginning; Remaining; Painted; poems; tr. by S. Spender. por Harp Baz 102:202-3 F '69
CAVAGNARO, David
Oceanic filter, game of chance; with biographical sketch. por Natur Hist 78:4, 52-7 Mr '69
CAVALLERIA rusticana; opera. See Mascagni, P.
CAVALLI, Charles
I retired to the library; interview. ed. by R. Peterson. por Har Yrs 9:41 S '69
CAVALLI, Francesco. See Cavalli, P. F.
CAVALLI, Pier Francesco
From the dawn of opera. H. Weinstock. il Sat R 52:80+ D 6 '69
L'Ormindo. J. W. Barker. il Am Rec G 35: 1024-7 Jl '69
L'Ormindo, a delicious 325-year-old operatic hit. S. T. Sommer. Hi Fi 19:88+ Je '69
Records:
Ormindo. Opera N 33:30 Je 14 '69
Venice 1644 (?), Glyndebourne 1967. H. Weinstock. Sat R 52:57 My 31 '69
CAVALLI-SFORZA, Luigi Luca
Genetic drift in an Italian population; with biographical sketch. Sci Am 221:12, 30-7 Ag '69
CAVALLO, Diana
Sixty-year-old controversy flares up again; Koussevitzky-Scriabin scandal. Hi Fi 19: 54+ Je '69
CAVANAGH, Jerome Patrick
Cavanagh of Detroit; interview. ed. by F. Powledge. por(p69) Harper 239:83-6 N '69

about

Dim day in Detroit. por Newsweek 74:36-7 Jl 7 '69
CAVANAUGH, Arthur
Miss Awful; story. McCalls 96:82-3 Ap '69
CAVANDER, Kenneth
(tr) See Euripides. Bacchae
CAVARADOSSI (operatic character) See Characters in opera
CAVE, Hugh
Believe in me; story. Good H 168:96-7 Mr '69
Forever kind of thing; story. Good H 169:72-3 Ag '69
Search for little Mary; story. Good H 168:73-5 Je '69
CAVE drawings and paintings
Lascaux puzzle. R. McMullen. il Horizon 11: 94-105 Spr '69
Olmec cave paintings: discovery from Guerrero, Mexico. D. C. Grove. bibliog il Science 164:421-3 Ap 25 '69
Saving the cave paintings; Lascaux cave being treated for *maladie verte*. il Time 94:74 S 19 '69

CAVE fauna and flora
Cave environment. T. L. Poulson and W. B. White. bibliog il Science 165:971-81 S 5 '69
CAVE fishes
Cave environment. T. L. Poulson and W. B. White. bibliog il Science 165:971-81 S 5 '69
CAVERLY, Joseph M.
Rochester senior citizens love life. Parks & Rec 4:15+ N '69
CAVES
Caving: exploring underground. il Changing T 23:13-14 Je '69
Exploring the world within. B. Gilbert. il Sports Illus 31:80-4+ N 10 '69
Traveler's choice; Sea lion caves. S. Bebout. Travel 131:16 Je '69
See also
Ice caves
Mammoth Cave National Park
CAVETT, Dick
Cavett's return. il por Time 93:65 Je 20 '69
Does Cavett have it? B. Baer. il pors Look 33:61-5 Jl 15 '69
Happy talker. il por Newsweek 73:65 F 3 '69
CAVIAR
Caviar for the Russians; development of synthetic product. Chem 42:3 D '69
CAWLEY, J. L. and others
Chemical weathering in central Iceland: an analog of pre-Silurian weathering. bibliog Science 165:391-2 Jl 25 '69
CAWS, Peter
Structure of discovery; adaptation of address, December 30, 1967. bibliog Science 166:1375-80 D 12 '69
CAXTON, William, Jr
Portfolio of lithographs by Stow Wengenroth. Am Artist 33:62-7+ N '69
CAYCE, Edgar
Trade winds. J. Beatty, jr. Sat R 52:8 Ag 2 '69
ÇAYÖNÜ excavations. See Turkey—Antiquities
CAYUGA, LAKE
Thermal pollution: a threat to Cayuga's waters? L. J. Carter; discussion. Science 163:517-18 F 7 '69
CAZDEN, Norman
Second note is free. bibliog f Am Rec G 35:1096-7+ Ag '69
CEAUSESCU, Nicolae
How does Rumania do it? with report by A. Tillier. il por Newsweek 74:41-2 Ag 4 '69
Letter from Bucharest. T. Szulc. New Yorker 45:105-6+ S 6 '69
Rumania's red carpet for a U.S. president. il por U S News 67:40-1 Ag 4 '69
Shadow. por Newsweek 74:36 Ag 25 '69
CEBUS monkeys. See Monkeys
CECERE, James G.
Self confidence in art for the elementary teacher. Sch Arts 69:28-9 S '69
CEDAR
Cedars of the Lord; cedar of Lebanon. E. R. Yarham. il Am For 75:24-6+ Ja '69
CEDARBURG, Wis.
Sex education in school; debate splits town in Wisconsin. il Life 67:34-41 S 19 '69
CEDARHURST, N.Y.
Mini-park on private property. il Am City 84: 51 Ap '69
CEILINGS
Fashions in living. il Vogue 154:63 Jl '69
Fixing up an older home. il Bet Hom & Gard 47:20 My '69
CELEBRATION; musical comedy. See Musical comedies, revues. etc.—Criticisms, plots, etc.
CELEBRATION; story. See Aguallo, T.
CELEBRATIONS
Coast to coast, a day for heroes; trio of astronauts. il U S News 67:12 Ag 25 '69
Homage to the men from the moon; honoring the astronauts in New York, Chicago and Los Angeles. il Time 94:8-11 Ag 22 '69
We love you; honoring the Apollo 11 moon voyagers in New York, Chicago and Los Angeles. il Newsweek 74:20B-23 Ag 25 '69
See also
Festivals
CELEBRITIES
Before the colors fade. il Am Heritage 20:42-3+ F; 60-3+ Ap; 22-5+ Je; 42-3+ Ag '69
Celebrity spotlight. E. N. Mintz. See issues of Travel
Girl of the year; J. Holzer. il Newsweek 73:22 My 19 '69
Has UN Plaza nosed out the Dakota and the Beresford in New York's celebrity race? G. Sheehy. il Holiday 46:58-61+ S '69
Here's me. April Sheffield, with James Mason! A. Sheffield. il Esquire 71:136-8+ Je '69

CELEBRITIES—*Continued*

Love letter from Beverly Hills. B. Rollin. il Look 33:10 Ag 12 '69

Man talk; oh, would you like to swing with a star? D. Newman and R. Benton. il Mlle 68:118 Ap '69

Most admired by Americans. il U S News 68:9 Ja 12 '70

People are talking about... il Vogue 153:96-7 F 15 '69

Young zoom: fifty-two doers, goers, thinkers, none over twenty-five. il Vogue 154:120-3+ Ag 1 '69

See also
Great men
Negro celebrities
Women, Famous

Anecdotes, facetiae, satire, etc.

Dream party nightmare. B. Pfizer. il Ladies Home J 86:52+ O '69

Suggested pranks, jokes and put-ons for thirty-nine really fun people. K. McCoy and C. H. Simonds. Nat R 21:575 Je 17 '69

CELESTIAL navigation. See Navigation

CELIAC disease

Is celiac disease a clue to the pathogenesis of schizophrenia? F. C. Dohan. bibliog Ment Hy 53:525-9 O '69

CELIBACY

Africans question celibacy. R. C. Pfaff. America 120:305-6 Mr 15 '69; Discussion. 120:488, 657 Ap 26, Je 7 '69

Cardinal Wright on celibacy; Comment by Fr. Greeley. America 121:128-9 S 6 '69

Celibacy: a Christian option. Chr Today 14: 33 N 7 '69

Celibacy and church structure; letter to the editor. W. L. Santry. America 120:637 My 31 '69

Celibacy and the synod. America 120:556-7 My 10 '69

Celibacy in springtime. Chr Cent 86:669 My 14 '69

Celibacy, no! recommendations of the Dutch pastoral council. Time 95:49 Ja 19 '70

Christian celibacy. T. E. Clarke; M. R. Joyce; R. A. McCormick. America 120:464-74 Ap 19 '69; Discussion. 120:571-2 My 17 '69

Post-marital priesthood; with editorial comment. F. Franck. Commonweal 89:720,724-6 Mr 14 '69

Priests and celibacy. America 121:372 N 1 '69

Quasi-comedy; USCC and the document on priestly celibacy. S. J. Adamo. America 121: 601 D 13 '69

Reflections on priesthood and marriage. G. Grudzen. il Cath World 210:111-13 D '69

Where's the church headed? J. J. McManmon. New Repub 160:16-19 Je 7 '69

Why priests marry. E. B. Fiske. Read Digest 95:105-10 D '69

See also
Marriage of priests

CÉLINE, Louis Ferdinand, pseud. See Destouches, L. F.

CELIS, Pérez

Song to life. C. A. Salatino. Américas 21:42 My '69

CELL division (biology)

Animal cells: noncorrelation of length of G_1 phase with size after mitosis. T. O. Fox and A. B. Pardee. bibliog il Science 167:80-2 Ja 2 '70

Cell division: a second circadian clock system in paramecium multimicronucleatum. A. Barnett. bibliog il Science 164:1417-19 Je 20 '69

Cell population kinetics: a modified interpretation of the graph of labeled mitoses. A. I. Hamilton. bibliog il Science 164:952-4 My 23 '69

Centromeres in human meiotic chromosomes. A. T. L. Chen and A. Falek. bibliog il Science 166:1008-10 N 21 '69

Circadian periodicity of bone marrow mitotic activity and reticulocyte counts in rats and mice. R. H. Clark and D. R. Korst. bibliog il Science 166:236-7 O 10 '69

Circadian rhythm of cell division in euglena: effects of a random illumination regimen. L. N. Edmunds, jr. and R. R. Funch. bibliog il Science 165:500-3 Ag 1 '69

Isopentenyladenosine stimulates and inhibits mitosis of human lymphocytes treated with phytohemagglutinin. R. C. Gallo and others. bibliog il Science 165:400-2 Jl 25 '69

Limited periods of gene expression in immunoglobulin-synthesizing cells. D. N. Buell and J. L. Fahey. bibliog il Science 164: 1524-5 Je 27 '69

Mitotic division in pancreatic beta cells. A. A. Like and W. L. Chick. bibliog il Science 163:941-3 F 28 '69

Potentially lethal radiation damage: repair by mammalian cells in culture. J. A. Belli and M. Shelton. bibliog il Science 165:490-2 Ag 1 '69

Radiosensitivity and rate of cell division: law of Bergonié and Tribondeau. A. H. Haber and B. E. Rothstein. bibliog il Science 163:1338-9 Mr 21 '69

Ribosomal RNA synthesis during cleavage of ascaris lumbricoides eggs. M. S. Kaulenas and others. bibliog il Science 163:1201-3 Mr 14 '69

CELL fusion. See Plasmogamy

CELL membranes. See Membranes (biology)

CELL microfluorometry. See Fluorometric analysis

CELL nuclei

Visualization of nucleolar genes. O. L. Miller, jr. and B. R. Beatty. bibliog il Science 164:955-7 My 23 '69

CELL separator. See Physiological apparatus

CELL spectrophotometers. See Spectrophotometers

CELL wall proteins. See Plant proteins

CELL walls. See Membranes (biology)

CELLARS. See Basements and cellars

CELLARS, Wine. See Wine cellars

CELLER, Emanuel

Excerpt from debate, June 26, 1968. Cong Digest 48:51 F '69

CELLISTS

See also
Du Pré, J.
Rostropovich, M.

CELLS

Automated analysis of cellular change in histological sections; image analysis computer. L. E. Mawdesley-Thomas and P. Healey. bibliog il Science 163:1200 Mr 14 '69

Automatic identification and measurement of cells by computer. S. A. Rosenberg and others. il Science 163:1065-6 Mr 7 '69

Cell death during early morphogenesis: parallels between insect limb and vertebrate limb development. J. M. Whitten. bibliog il Science 163:1456-7 Mr 28 '69

Cell microfluorometry: a method for rapid fluorescence measurement. M. A. Van Dilla and others. bibliog il Science 163:1213-14 Mr 14 '69

Cell sorting: automated separation of mamalian cells as a function of intracellular fluorescence. H. R. Hulett and others. bibliog il Science 166:747-9 N 7 '69

Cytotoxic test automation: a live-dead cell differential counter. M. R. Melamed and others. bibliog il Science 163:285-6 Ja 17 '69

Duplicate plating of immune cell products: analysis of globulin class secretion by single cells. B. Merchant and Z. Brahmi. bibliog il Science 167:69-72 Ja 2 '70

Hybrid somatic cells. B. Ephrussi and M. C. Weiss. il Sci Am 220:26-35 bibliog(p 146) Ap '69

Mapping the genes; man-mouse hybrid cells. il Sci N 96:323-4 O 11 '69

Microtubules in brain homogenates. J. B. Kirkpatrick. bibliog il Science 163:187-8 Ja 10 '70

Somatic cell hybrid between the established human line D98 (presumptive HeLa) and 3T3. Y. Matsuya and H. Green. bibliog il Science 163:697-8 F 14 '69

Some animals have light-sensitive cells which humans do not have. Sci Digest 66:83-4 D '69

See also
Antigens and antibodies
Cancer cells
Centrosomes
Chromatin
Cilia and ciliary motion
Differentiation (biology)
Endoplasmic reticulum
Genes
Germ cells
Golgi apparatus
Lymphoid cells
Macromolecules
Membranes (biology)
Microsomes
Nematocysts
Nerve cells
Peroxisomes
Plant cells and tissues
Regeneration (biology)

Culture

See Tissues—Culture

CELLS—*Continued*

Inclusions

Gas vacuole development in a blue-green alga. J. R. Waaland and D. Branton. bibliog il Science 163:1339-41 Mr 21 '69

Rhapidosomes: absence of a highly 2'-O-methylated RNA component. A. S. Delk and C. A. Dekker. bibliog il Science 166:1646-7 D 26 '69

See also
Lysosomes
Mitochondria

Preservation

See Tissues—Preservation

CELLS, Effect of radiation on. See Radiation—Physiological effécts

CELLULAR differentiation. See Differentiation (biology)

CELLULAR glass. See Glass, Cellular

CELLULAR therapy
Sweet poison. W. Endicott. Harp Baz 102:224-5+ O '69

CELLULOSE
Biosynthesis of oligosaccharides and polysaccharides in plants. W. Z. Hassid bibliog il Science 165:140-1 Jl 11 '69

Cellulose: refutation of a folded-chain structure. R. E. Mark and others. bibliog il Science 164:72-3 Ap 4 '69

See also
Nitrocellulose

CELLULOSE nitrate. See Nitrocellulose

CELORIA, Francis
Archaeology of serendip. bibliog por Library J 94:1846-8 My 1 '69

CELTICS (basketball team) See Basketball teams

CELTS
Conamara man, by S. Ridge. Review
Sat R 52:35-6 Ap 19 '69. W. H. A. Williams

CEMENT
Portland cement: pseudomorphs of original cement grains observed in hardened pastes. R. B. Williamson. bibliog il Science 164:549-51 My 2 '69

CEMENT boats. See Boats—Materials

CEMENT industry and trade
See also
American cement corporation
Lone Star cement corporation

CEMETERIES
Cemetery planting. C. Chowins. il Horticulture 47:26-7+ F '69

Ecumenism in the cemetery. Chr Cent 86 1411-12 N 5 '69

See also
Washington, D.C.—Cemeteries

CEMETERY planting. See Cemeteries

CENCO instruments corporation
Hot stock that came back. Forbes 103:47 My 1 '69

CENOZOIC period. See Geology, Stratigraphic—Cenozoic

CENSORSHIP
Art and responsibility. C. Hughes. Cath World 209:210-12 Ag '69

Book burning. FCC style: anti-smoking ads. M. Friedman. Newsweek 73:86 Je 16 '69

C*ns*r *t w*rk. Newsweek 73:90+ Je 16 '69

Challenging the censor: some responsibilities of the English department: address, November, 1968. K. L. Donelson. bibliog Engl J 58:869-76 S '69

Comstock's complaint. S. Maloff. Commonweal 91:362-3 D 19 '69

Government censorship or freedom of the press? D. Lawrence. U S News 67:84 Ag 4 '69

Great Minnesota compromise. J. Challman. Library J 94:3627 O 15 '69

Hughes, Twain, Child, and Sanger: four who locked horns with the censors; adaptation of addresses. M. Meltzer. il Wilson Lib Bul 44:278-86 N '69

Lock that up in your Funk & Wagnalls; controversy surrounding S. S. Baker's The permissible lie. R. L. Shayon. Sat R 52:48-9 N 22 '69

1968 in review: censorship and books. Pub W 195:40 Mr 10 '69

Obscenity of censorship. Chr Cent 86:830 Je 18 '69; Discussion. 86:1116 Ag 27 '69

Report on censorship trends: highlights of address. A. P. Suits. il Pub W 195:49 Je 16 '69

Sex, shock and sensuality; the lively arts; with accounts by J. Barthel and T. Prideaux. il Life 66:22-35 Ap 4 '69

Teachers are true censors; NCTE convention. Sr Schol 93:School Teach 18 Ja 10 '69

Uproar hits the campus press. J. Star. il Look 33:36+ F 18 '69

What's become of voluntary censorship? D. Lawrence. U S News 67:92 S 8 '69

Where do you draw the line? withdrawal of facsimile Mother Goose for offensive language. C. B. Grannis. Pub W 195:73 Ap 14 '69

Will the real Peter Rabbit please stand up? letter to the editor. J. Hurwitz. Library J 94:1687-8 Ap 15 '69

See also
Dramatic censorship
Freedom of the press
Government and the press
Immoral literature and pictures
Information, Freedom of
Intellectual liberty
Library bill of rights
Moving picture censorship
Obscenity (law)
Postal censorship
Prohibited books

also subhead Censorship under various subjects, e.g. Television broadcasting—Censorship

Czechoslovakia

Cleaning up the press. Newsweek 73:36+ F 10 '69

Repression as regression. Chr Cent 86:1057 Ag 13 '69

Denmark

Pornography: what is permitted is boring. il Time 93:47 Je 6 '69

Ireland

Irish literary censorship. M. Sheehy. Nation 208:833-4+ Je 30 '69

Israel

Israel's image; new Minister of information. il Newsweek 75:59-60 Ja 19 '70

Russia

Open letter to the Union of Soviet writers; expulsion of A. Solzhenitsyn. C. B. Ashanin. Chr Cent 86:1617-18 D 17 '69

Repression as regression. Chr Cent 86:1057 Ag 13 '69

United States

See Censorship

Vietnam (Republic)

Dissident intellectuals: South Viet Nam. il Time 94:41-2 Jl 18 '69

Ominous signs in Saigon: press freedom for foreigners in jeopardy. Time 94:68 Jl 4 '69

CENSUS
See also
United States—Census

CENSUS, Fish. See Fish census

CENSUS bureau (United States) See United States—Census, Bureau of the

CENSUS workers
Hand that rocks the cradle counts it, too. il Nations Bsns 57:103 S '69

CENTENARIANS
Second hundred years. R. R. Jalbert. il Har Yrs 9:40-1 N '69

CENTENNIALS
End of a mission? bicentennial celebration of San Diego. D. Butwin. il Sat R 52:52+ F 22 '69

Happy birthday, San Diego! 200th anniversary celebration. il Am City 84:132+ Jl '69

On the Green and the Colorado a summer-long Powell centennial. il Sunset 142:64 My '69

Pacific railroad centennial: the transcontinental railroad; symposium. il Am West 6:4-32+ My '69

San Diego: to celebrate a 200th anniversary, a spirited fiesta in Old Town. il Sunset 143:66-9 Jl '69

CENTER, Stella Stewart
Obituary
Engl J 58:518 Ap '69

CENTER for advanced visual studies. See Massachusetts institute of technology, Cambridge—Center for advanced visual studies

CENTER for cognitive studies. See Harvard university—Graduate school of education

CENTER for dispute settlement. See American arbitration association

CENTER for Inter-American relations, New York
Studying Latin American affairs; Ford foundation's appropriation for research on Cuba. Sch & Soc 97:213 Ap '69

CENTER for intercultural documentation. See Center of intercultural documentation

CENTER for international affairs, Harvard university. See Harvard university—Center for international affairs

CENTER for shortlived phenomena. See Smithsonian institution

CENTER for the study of democratic institutions, Santa Barbara, Calif.
Anguish on a hilltop. R. H. Sollen. in Nation 209:336-9 O 6 '69
New appointments to Center for the study of democratic institutions. Sch & Soc 97:412+ N '69
Off center? Newsweek 73:76-7 Je 30 '69

CENTER for urban-black studies
Urban-black studies center is launched. E. T. Culver. Chr Cent 86:1004 Jl 23 '69

CENTER for urban education, New York
Hot-line educational service. Sch & Soc 97:11-12+ Ja '69

CENTER of intercultural documentation
Camara and Illich. Commonweal 89:575-6 F 7 '69
Get going, and don't come back; Vatican investigations. Time 93:48+ F 14 '69
Ivan Illich: the Christian as rebel. P. Schrag. il Sat R 52:14-19 Jl 19 '69
Joyful place. il Time 94:48 Ag 29 '69
Life of Ivan Illich. D. Dolan. New Repub 160:18-19 Mr 1 '69
Of many things; Center for intercultural documentation at Cuernavaca, out of bounds to priests and religious. D. R. Campion. America 120:120 F 1 '69
Questions about a questionnaire; controversy over the Cuernavaca center, with text of letter from I. Illich. L. M. Orsy. America 120:185-9 F 15 '69
Vatican bars priests from Cuernavaca study center. Chr Cent 86:172 F 5 '69

CENTERPIECES. See Table decoration

CENTERS for the performing arts
Building types study: architecture for the arts of music, dance and drama. il Arch Rec 146:147 N '69
How cultural is the cultural explosion? H. C. Schonberg. McCalls 96:70+ Jl '69
See also
Atlanta—Memorial arts center
Cleveland—Blossom center
Cultural centers
Lincoln Center for the performing arts, New York
Manila—Philippine cultural center
Milwaukee—Center for the performing arts
Ottawa—National arts center
Urbana, Ill.—Krannert center for the performing arts

Anecdotes, facetiae, satire, etc.
Now, sing Melancholy baby. il Esquire 71:158-9+ My '69

CENTERVILLE, Mass. public library
Trade winds; W. Lippmann's gift of his book collection. J. Beatty, jr. Sat R 52:18+ O 25 '69

CENTO. See Central treaty organization

CENTRAL AMERICA
See also
Canals—Central America
Wilderness areas—Central America

Economic policy
See also
Central American program of economic integration

Maps
Map weaves history with geography. il Nat Geog 137:112-13, sup(folded map) Ja '70

CENTRAL AMERICAN common market. See Central American program of economic integration

CENTRAL AMERICAN program of economic integration
Central American common market: initiative for development: address. April 30, 1969. C. A. Meyer. Dept State Bul 60:421-3 My 19 '69
Triumph for the system; the Central American common market. G. de Zéndegui. Américas 21:1 S '69

CENTRAL conference of American rabbis
Frustrated rabbi. il Newsweek 73:79 Je 30 '69

CENTRAL intelligence agency. See United States—Central intelligence agency

CENTRAL opera service
C.O.S. conference. C. L. Osborne. Opera N 34:25 N 22 '69
Clearing house: the C.O.S. after fifteen years. A. M. Lingg. il Opera N 33:6-7 Mr 22 '69

CENTRAL Pacific railroad
Iron spine; the Union Pacific met the Central Pacific at Promontory. H. Sturgis. il Am Heritage 20:46-57+ Ap '69

Pacific railroad centennial; the transcontinental railroad; symposium. il Am West 6:4-32+ My '69
See also
Golden Spike national historic site

CENTRAL park. See New York (city)—Parks and playgrounds

CENTRAL place theory. See Anthropogeography

CENTRAL treaty organization
CENTO council of ministers meets at Tehran; statement. My 26 and 27, 1969; with text of communique. W. P. Rogers. Dept State Bul 60:501-3 Je 16 '69

CENTRAL VALLEY, Calif.
Desalting California; San Joaquin master drain controversy. F. M. Stead. il Environ 11:2-10 Je '69

CENTRALIA, Wash.
Small computer for a little city. H. Hackett. il Am City 84:114+ Je '69

CENTRE d'etudes industrielles. See Business education

CENTRIFUGATION
Allantoinase: association with amphibian hepatic peroxisomes. L. P. Visentin and J. M. Allen. bibliog il Science 163:1463-4 Mr 28 '69
Animal cells: noncorrelation of length of of G1 phase with size after mitosis. T. O. Fox and A. B. Pardee. bibliog il Science 167:80-2 Ja 2 '70
Cationic protein-bearing granules of polymorphonuclear leukocytes: separation from enzyme-rich granules. H. I. Zeya and J. K. Spitznagel. bibliog il Science 163:1069-71 Mr 7 '69

CENTRIFUGES
Atoms for everybody? technique for producing nuclear energy perfected by a British-Dutch-German consortium. Newsweek 73:89 Ap 14 '69
Britain's toe on the Continent; collaboration on gas centrifuge apparatus for enriching uranium. D. Fishlock. il Sci N 96:566 D 13 '69
Centrifuge to the fore; gas centrifuge for uranium separation. T. Shoemaker. Sci N 95:150 F 8 '69
Politics and uranium; British, Dutch and German commitment to joint development of gas centrifuge. J. Lambert. il Sci N 95:438 My 3 '69
Researchers build huge centrifuge to study weightlessness. M. Steinmann. il Life 66:75+ F 21 '69
U-235 centrifuge. Sci Am 220:52 My '69
Uranium: three European nations plan to build centrifuge plants. D. S. Greenberg. Science 164:53-5 Ap 4 '69

Medical applications
Lead in the head. Sci Digest 65:54-5 Ap '69

CENTRIOLES. See Centrosomes

CENTROMERES. See Chromosomes

CENTROSOMES
Centrioles of a human cancer: intercellular order and intracellular disorder. P. W. Schafer. bibliog il Science 164:1300-3 Je 13 '69

CEPHALOPODS
See also
Squids

CEPHALOSPORIUM lamellaecola. See Fungi

CERACCHI, Giuseppe
Great men of America in Roman guise. U. Desportes. il Antiques 96:72-5 Jl '69

CERAME-VIVAS, Máximo J.
Wreck of the Ocean Eagle; with biographical sketch. Sea Front 15:224-31, 254 Jl '69

CERAMIC animals. See Animal pottery

CERAMIC costume jewelry. See Jewelry

CERAMIC materials
See also
Pyroceram

CERAMIC national exhibition. See Pottery—Exhibitions

CERAMIC necklaces. See Necklaces

CERAMIC sculpture
Hollow-built sculpture. R. F. Eilenberger. il Ceram Mo 17:25-8 Mr '69
Ruth Duckworth. T. W. Collins. il Ceram Mo 17:18-21 S '69
Victor Spinski. F. Kriwanek. il Ceram Mo 17:24-5 O '69
West coast report: California ceramics. P. Selz; B. Richardson. il Art in Am 57:104-5 My '69

CERAMIC tiles. See Tiles

CERAMICS. See Pottery

CERATOCYSTIS ulmi. See Elm—Diseases and pests

CERAVOLO, Joseph
Comment. R. Cohen. Poetry 115:189-92 D '69

CEREAL foods
55 million bowls every single day. il Am Home 72:102-3 S '69
Where have all the cornflakes gone? J. L. O'Neill. Am Home 72:104+ S '69
See also
Cookery—Cereals
Oatmeal
Quaker oats company

CEREALS. See Grain

CEREBRAL cortex
Evolution of neocortex. I. T. Diamond and W. C. Hall. bibliog il Science 164:251-62 Ap 18 '69
Surface areas of the cerebral cortex of mammals determined by stereological methods. H. Elias and D. Schwartz. bibliog il Science 166:111-13 O 3 '69
Two visual systems. G. E. Schneider. bibliog il Science 163:895-902 F 28 '69
Visual form discrimination on the basis of relative distribution of light. H. A. Buchtel; S. S. Winans. bibliog il Science 164:857-8 My 16 '69

CEREBRAL hemorrhage
Cerebrovascular disease: behavioral changes; report of meeting. A. L. Benton. Science 165:314-15 Jl 18 '69
See also
Cerebrovascular disease

CEREBRAL palsied children
Can your little boy come out to play? S. Schwartz. il Parents Mag 44:42-3+ F '69

CEREBROSPINAL fluid
Choroid plexus cerebrospinal fluid production. T. H. Milhorat. bibliog il Science 166:1514-16 D 19 '69
See also
Blood-brain barrier

CEREBROVASCULAR disease
Cerebrovascular disease: behavioral changes; report of meeting. A. L. Benton. Science 165:314-15 Jl 18 '69

CEREMONIES
See also
Rites and ceremonies

CEREMONIES in dark old men; drama. See Elder, L, 3d

CERN (Conseil européan pour la recherche nucléaire) See European organization for nuclear research

CERNAN, Eugene A.
Our happy moon journey. por(p40) Life 66:44-5 Je 20 '69
See also
Space flight to the moon—Manned flights—Stafford-Cernan-Young flight, 1969

CERRO corporation
Copper giant is still waiting at the altar; looking for merger mate. il Bsns W p 102-3 My 31 '69

CERRUTI, James
Netherlands Antilles: Holland in the Caribbean. Nat Geog 137:114-46 Ja '70

CERTIFICATES of merit. See Rewards, prizes, etc.

CERTIFICATION of teachers. See Teachers—Certification

CERULOPLASMIN. See Blood—Proteins

CERUMEN. See Earwax

ČERVA, L.
Amoebic meningoencephalitis: axenic culture of naegleria. Science 163:576 F 7 '69
—and others
Amoebic meningoencephalitis: a sew amoeba isolate. bibliog Science 163:575-6 F 7 '69

CERVICAL cancer. See Cancer

CERVINIA, Italy (resort) See Winter resorts

CERVIX
Uterine cervix; report of North American conference on fertility and sterility. E. S. E. Hafez. Science 164:334-5 Ap 18 '69
What is a cervical erosion? W. R. Lang and P. Feinstein. Redbook 134:31 N '69

CERVO, Nathan A.
Caravan; poem. Poetry 114:371 S '69

CESIUM beam devices. See Time measurements

CESIUM clock. See Time measurements

CESSNA aircraft company
Beech, Cessna sales hit peak in fiscal year. Aviation W 91:55 N 24 '69
Cessna girds for sluggish market. E. J. Bulban. il Aviation W 91:46-7+ D 22 '69
Cessna shows new line for utility market. il Aviation W 90:79-80 Mr 17 '69

CETACEA
Hageman factor (factor XII) deficiency in marine mammals. A. J. Robinson and others. bibliog il Science 166:1420-2 D 12 '69
See also
Dolphins (mammals)

CEYLON
Description and travel
Profiles: A. C. Clarke. J. Bernstein. il New Yorker 45:40-2+ Ag 9 '69

CHABAN-DELMAS, Jacques Pierre Michel
France's new premier. por Time 93:25 Je 27 '69
Touch of independence. il por Newsweek 74:28-9 Jl 7 '69

CHABAUD, André
Unknown opera. S. L. Fogel. il por Opera N 34:8-13 D 6 '69

CHABROWE, Leonard
Existentialist opposition. Commonweal 89:585-7 F 7 '69

CHACON, Abel
Self-help for the single farm worker. G. M. Bergman. Chr Cent 86:1426+ N 5 '69

CHAD
U.S. aircraft to assist in famine relief in Chad; Department statement, Ocotber 9, 1969. Dept State Bul 61:403 N 10 '69
Unnoticed war. A. Jaffe. il Newsweek 74:41 S 15 '69

CHADRON, Neb.
Sex movies? Chadron, Neb. tries gentle persuasion. H. Moffett. il Life 66:52B-52D+ My 30 '69

CHADWICK, John
Forethinker updated. Sat R 52:30 My 3 '69

CHAFFEE, John, Jr
First manpower assessment. Am Ed 5:11-12 F '69

CHAIKIN, Joseph
Serpent. Criticism
Commonweal 90:110-12 Ap 11 '69
Newsweek il 73:128+ My 26 '69

CHAIN letters
Why most chain letters are illegal. Good H 169:141 Jl '69

CHAIN saws. See Saws

CHAIN stores
Christmas every weekday? chain discount toy stores. il Forbes 103:55+ Mr 15 '69
See also
Federated department stores, incorporated
Penney, J. C, company
Seven-Eleven food stores
Wakefern food corporation
Woolworth, F. W. company

CHAINEY, Sullivan E.
Silent evangelist. Chr Today 13:35 Ap 25 '69

CHAIR seats
See also
Cane weaving

CHAIRMEN
How to be a better meeting chairman. G. M. Prince. il Harvard Bsns R 47:98-108 Ja '69

CHAIRS
Anti-casting couch; Eames-Wilder chaise. il Time 95:37 Ja 5 '70
China, Japan, and the Anglo-American chair. R. C. Smith. il Antiques 96:552-8 O '69
Elegant dining: an I table and a set of cube chairs. K. Isaacs. il Pop Sci 195:162-6 O '69
Important chair. T. Bowman. il House B 111:160-1 O '69
Please be seated; exhibition. M. Morrison. il House B 111:90-1 F '69
Pull up a chair. il Seventeen 28:198+ Mr '69
See also
Stools

Exhibitions
Chairs; exhibit at Lever house. New Yorker 45:27-8 S 6 '69

History
American windsor chairs: a style survey. N. A. Goyne. il Antiques 95:538-43 Ap '69

CHAIX, Richard
Fountain scale model serves as an engineering design tool. Arch Rec 145:165-7 Mr '69

CHAKI-SIRCAR, Manjusri
Glimpses of India by Manjusri and her ensemble; McMillan theater. M. Marks. Dance Mag 43:81 D '69

CHALCEDONY
Desert find, a chalcedony rose. il Sunset 142:59 Mr '69

CHALETS. See Architecture, Domestic—Switzerland

CHALL, Jeanne S.
  Beginning reading: where do we go from here? excerpts from Learning to read: the great debate. Todays Ed 58:36-9 F '69
CHALLANS, Mary. See Renault, M. pseud.
CHALLMAN, Jean
  Viewpoint. Library J 94:3627 O 15 '69
CHAMBER music
  Answer is chamber music. C. Wadsworth. Hi Fi 19:MA9+ S '69
  Fresh music from the university laboratory. R. P. Morgan. Hi Fi 19:75-6 Je '69
  Musical events; Music from Marlboro series at Town Hall. W. Sargeant. New Yorker 44:108-9 F 8 '69
    See also
  Phonograph records—Chamber music
  String quartets
CHAMBER music society of Lincoln Center
  Memorable opening for Alice Tully hall. I. Kolodin. Sat R 52:20 S 27 '69
  Music; opening of Alice Tully Hall. D. Hamilton Nation 209:325-6 S 29 '69
CHAMBER of commerce of the United States of America
  How business hopes to change the Nation's labor laws. U S News 66:68-9 Je 16 '69
  Memo from the editor; regional meetings to discuss problems. J. Wooldridge. il Nations Bsns 57:5-6 Ag; 5-6 O '69
  Thinking the unthinkable; interview. J. L. Jones. il Nations Bsns 57:50-7 My '69
  Three prescriptions for urban ills. Nations Bsns 57:49 F '69
  Where bosses are told off, and like it; Forums for economic and political discussion, sponsored by the National chamber foundation. il Nations Bsns 57:62-5 Jl '69
  Who speaks for business? G. R. Rosen. il Duns R 94:45-7+ N '69
CHAMBER opera society of Baltimore
  Report: production of Britten's Rape of Lucretia. F. C. Smith. Opera N 34:27 D 13 '69
CHAMBER orchestras
  Report: Princeton; concert version of Amadigi. H. E. Phillips. Opera N 33:34 Ap 5 '69
CHAMBER theatre. See New York (city)—Theater
CHAMBERLAIN, Charles Ernest
  On lawbreaking congressmen. Chr Today 13:28-9 My 9 '69
CHAMBERLAIN, Gary M.
  Summer work programs. Am City 84:92+ N '69
  Two cities built malls that bring new vitality to Main Street. Am City 84:78+ N '69
—and Chamberlain, Sharon
  Reflections on God in marriage. Cath World 210:11-14 O '69
CHAMBERLAIN, John
  Business and black capitalism. Nat R 21:742-4 Jl 29 '69
CHAMBERLAIN, John, 1927-
  Secret life of John Chamberlain. E. C. Baker. il Art N 68:48-51+ Ap '69
CHAMBERLAIN, Narcissa G. and Chamberlain, Samuel
  Living with antiques: the Massachusetts home of Mr & Mrs Samuel Chamberlain. il Antiques 95:696-701 My '69
CHAMBERLAIN, Neville
  On borrowed time. by L. Mosley. Review Time il por 93:82 Je 27 '69
CHAMBERLAIN, Samuel. See Chamberlain, N. G. jt. auth.
CHAMBERLAIN, Sharon. See Chamberlain, G. jt. auth.
CHAMBERLAIN, Wilt
  On top, in trouble. F. Deford. il pors Sports Illus 30:10-13 Ja 27 '69
  Parting shots. Newsweek 73:67 Ja 2 '69
  Rescued from disaster by the hard-to-love giant. T. Maule. il por Sports Illus 30:32-3 Ap 14 '69
CHAMBERLIN, Anne
  Beating the crowds to the Algarve. Vogue 153:70+ F 1 '69
  Israel onrush. Vogue 154:106-15 Jl '69
  Pierre Elliott Trudeau, prime minister of Canada. Vogue 153:110-11+ Mr 15 '69
  Travel. Vogue 154:158 Jl '69
  What to expect when you're invited to dinner in D.C. McCalls 96:65+ Jl '69
CHAMBERLIN, William Henry
  Great nonproliferation hoax. Nat R 21:229-30 Mr 11 '69
  Obituary
    Nat R 21:1000 O 7 '69
CHAMBERS, Gurney
  Educational essentialism thirty years after. bibliog f Sch & Soc 97:14-16 Ja '69

CHAMBERS, Kathryn I.
  Newer iris. il Horticulture 47:30-1+ Je '69
CHAMBERS, Mary Jane
  Don't launch him he's mine! condensation. Read Digest 95:241-4+ Jl '69
CHAMBERS, S. T.
  What do you know about yacht insurance? Yachting 125:78-9+ Ap; 76-7+ My '69
  What do you know about... Yachting 125:78-9+ Ap '69
CHAMBERS, Whittaker
  Shore of space; statements. November 2, 1957, October 25, 1958. Nat R 21:738 Jl 29 '69
CHAMBERS, Metabolic. See Physiological apparatus
CHAMBERS brothers. See Singers
CHAMBERS of commerce
  Boosters awake, but slowly. il Bsns W p 150 O 18 '69
    See also
  Chamber of commerce of the United States of America
  International chamber of commerce
CHAMNESS, Ed
  Folding method for large slab constructions. Ceram Mo 17:14-17 N '69
CHAMPAGNE
  Vin de rigueur. A. Waugh. il Nat R 21:1275+ D 16 '69
CHAMPIE, Margaret L.
  Building a baby barn. Org Gard & Farm 16:73-6 O '69
  Plant some comfrey. Org Gard & Farm 16:44-5 O '69
CHAMPION paper and fibre company. See United States plywood-Champion papers, incorporated
CHAMPIONS golf club course. Houston. See Golf courses
CHANCE, Britton, Jr
  New look in twelves. Yachting 126:58-9+ Ag '69
CHANDLER, Christopher
  Black Panther killings in Chicago. New Repub 162:21-4 Ja 10 '70
    about
  News and views. J. Deedy. Commonweal 89:606 F 14 '69
CHANDLER, David
  Cambodia's strategy of survival. bibliog f Cur Hist 57:344-8+ D '69
CHANDLER, Edgar Hugh Storer
  Project indignity. Chr Today 13:45 F 28 '69
CHANDRA, G. S. Sharat
  I feel let down; poem. Poetry 113:399 Mr '69
CHANEL, Coco. See Chanel, G.
CHANEL, Gabrielle
  Brigitte Bardot, Coco Chanel and me. B. Rollin. Look 33:13-14 Ap 1 '69
  Chanel always now. F. Rose. Vogue 154:116+ D '69
  Chanel for men. E. Sheppard. il Harp Baz 103:158-9 D '69
  Kate and Coco. H. Saal. il pors Newsweek 74:75-9 N 10 '69
  Real Coco. il pors Life 67:38-45 D 19 '69
  Very expensive Coco. il por Time 94:86-7 N 7 '69
CHANEY, Ed
  DDT threatens you! Nat Wildlife 7:48-9 Ag '69
CHANG, Lit-sen
  Cult of iconoclasm: new menace to the West. Chr Today 13:5-6 Jl 4 '69
CHANG, Parris H.
  China's scientists in the cultural revolution. Bul Atom Sci 25:19-20+ My '69
CHANGE
  America's next rendezvous with destiny. C. Bowles. Sat R 52:17-19+ S 6 '69
  From here to eternity; reprint from September 16, 1957 issue. L. N. Bell. Chr Today 13:18-19 Je 20 '69
    See also
  Social change
  Technological change
CHANGE, Educational. See Educational innovations
CHANGE in personality. See Personality change
CHANGE of life in women. See Menopause
CHANGE of sex
  Maturing science of sex reassignment; transsexualism and sex surgery. H. Benjamin; I. B. Pauly. Sat R 52:72-8 O 4 '69
  Realities of changing sex. A. J. Snider. Sci Digest 66:56 Ag '69
CHANGE of sex surgery. See Generative organs—Surgery
CHANNEL catfish fishing. See Catfish fishing

CHANNEL ISLANDS (English Channel)
See also
Sark
CHANNEL ISLANDS, Calif. See Santa Barbara
Islands, Calif.
CHANNEL ISLANDS NATIONAL PARK (pro-
posed). See National parks and reserves—
United States
CHANSONS. See Songs, French
CHANTS (Gregorian, plain, etc)

History and criticism
Responsorial psalm tones for the Mozarabic
office, by D. M. Randel. Review
Mus Q 55:575-80 O '69. R. Steiner
CHAPARRAL cocks. See Road runners (birds)
CHAPEL HILL, N.C.
Breakthrough in Chapel Hill; Negro elected
mayor. il Time 93:26 My 16 '69
Mayor of Chapel Hill. Newsweek 73:41 My
19 '69
CHAPELLIER, Robert, and Rasmussen, Dana
Boat tops off my camper. por Pop Sci 194:
120-2+ Je '69
CHAPELS
Chapel for Tuskegee by Rudolph. il Arch
Rec 146:117-26 N '69
Spectacular space in a university chapel;
University Methodist chapel for the Wesley
foundation, Florida state university, Tal-
lahassee. il Arch Forum 131:84-5 N '69
CHAPIN, Ansil B.
Caribbean golfing. Travel 132:28-35 N '69
How to attend a writers' conference. Writers
Digest 49:30-2 My '69
CHAPIN, Emerson
Success story in South Korea. For Affairs 47:
560-74 Ap '69
CHAPIN, Katherine Garrison
Death tree; poem. New Repub 161:22 O 25 '69
CHAPIN, Kim
Bowling. Sports Illus 30:100-2 Ap 14 '69
Motor sports (cont) Sports Illus 30:50 Mr
3; 58+ Je 23; 50-1 Je 30 '69
Philadelphia story; Society hill. Am Home
72:58-61+ D '69
Tennis (cont) Sports Illus 31:56-9 Jl 7; 50-2
Jl 14 '69
CHAPIN, Louis
Drama. Chr Cent 86:1646-7 D 24 '69
CHAPLAINS, College. See Colleges and uni-
versities—Religious life
CHAPLAINS, Congressional. See United States
—Congress—Chaplains
CHAPLAINS, Military
Chaplains' role under new scrutiny. W. Wil-
loughby. Chr Today 13:32 Ap 25 '69
Honest to God, or faithful to the Pentagon?
il Time 93:49 My 30 '69
Navy chaplains in Vietnam, by W. M. Moore.
Review
Chr Cent 86:1282 O 8 '69. R. Kern
Optional approach to clerical exemption. D.
E. Messer. Chr Cent 86:921-4 Jl 9 '69
What did you do during the war, father? G.
Zahn. Commonweal 90:195-9 My 2 '69;
Discussion. 90:275+, 403+ My 23, Je 27 '69
CHAPLIN, Charles, 1889-
Quixote with a bowler. il por Time 95:54 Ja
5 '70
CHAPMAN, Colin
Strange story of the man who shook Indy.
L. Levine. il pors Mech Illus 65:43-5+ My
'69
CHAPMAN, John Jay
Voice of dissent: John Jay Chapman and the
great wickedness. L. M. Sims. bibliog por
Negro Hist Bul 32:12-13 Mr '69
CHAPMAN, Richard L.
Congress and science policy: the organiza-
tional dilemma. Bul Atom Sci 25:4-7+ Mr
'69
CHAPMAN, Seville
Significance of Apollo. por Space World
F-9-69:26-7 S '69
CHAPPUIS, Eduardo Dibos. See Dibos Chap-
puis, E.
CHAPULTEPEC park. See Mexico (city)—Parks
and playgrounds
CHARACTER
See also
Individuality
Responsibility
CHARACTER education. See Moral education
CHARACTER reading. See Graphology
CHARACTER sketches
Most unforgettable character I've met. See
issues of Reader's digest
CHARACTERIZATION
Don't dare put me in your play! B. J. Fried-
man. Writer 82:16-18 Je '69

Everybody change places! M. J. Amft. Writer
82:12-13 D '69
How people sound. M. Lee. Writer 82:13-15+
S '69
I loved the way you described Aunt
Mary... E. Hawes. Writer 82:15-16+ Mr
'69
Inside Uriah Heep. N. Bawden. Writer 82:
9-11 My '69
Participant past imperfect. A. B. Malec.
Writer 82:19-21 Ag '69
Six ways to successful confessions. F. K.
Palmer. Writer 82:15-18 My '69
Till (violent) death do us part. G. P. Elliott.
Writer 82:15-16 O '69
CHARACTERS in literature
How to create live characters in a juvenile
short story. N. Ainsworth. il Writers Digest
49:36-9+ D '69
Idea of the hero. S. Schwartz. Engl J 58:82-6
Ja '69
Literary hero for adolescents: the adolescent;
adaptation of address, September 1968. S.
Bank. Engl J 58:1013-20 O '69
La Mancha's man; Massenet's Don Quixote.
W. Starkie. il Opera N 33:14-16 Ap 19 '69
Nation of Schweiks. S. Bingham. Atlan 223:
119-21 F '69
Nero Wolfe of West Thirty-fifth street. by
W. S. Baring-Gould. Review
Nation 208:251-2 F 24 '69. M. Byrd
Pip: a love affair; C. Dickens' Great expecta-
tions. S. Simmons. Engl J 58:416-17 Mr '69
Root and measure of realism; modern stories
for children. V. L. Wolf. il Wilson Lib Bul
44:409-15 D '69
Secret of Nancy Drew, pushing forty and
going strong. A. Prager. il Sat R 52:18-19+
Ja 25 '69
Separate peace: meaning and myth; analyz-
ing Gene Forrester. M. E. Mengeling. Engl
J 58:1322-9 D '69
Stover at the barricades. M. J. Halberstam.
Am Scholar 38:470+ Sum '69
Universe of ready-made characters; zodiac
signs of literary characters. W. J. Watkins.
Writers Digest 49:38-9 Ag '69
See also
Animals in literature
Characterization
Jews in literature

Anecdotes, facetiae, satire, etc.
Books from the wood. H. F. Ellis. New Yorker
44:81-3 Ja 18 '69
CHARACTERS in moving pictures
Dear Benjamin; dissecting Mike Nichols' The
graduate. B. Geller. Engl J 58:423-5 Mr '69
CHARACTERS in opera
Che & Lizzie & Joe & Lola. E. R. Gruenwald.
Opera N 34:6-7 Ja 17 '70
Hero as revolutionary: Puccini's Mario
Cavaradossi. L. Kleine-Ahlbrandt. Opera N
33:24-5 F 15 '69
Holy terror: sacristan in Tosca. J. Ferris.
Opera N 33:6-7 F 15 '69
How old are they? A. M. Lingg. Opera N
33:6-7 Mr 1 '69
Loners; Peter Grimes and Wozzeck. S. Jen-
kins, jr. Opera N 33:24-5 Ap 5 '69
CHARD, Chester S.
Archeology in the Soviet Union. bibliog Sci-
ence 163:774-9 F 21 '69
CHARDIN, Pierre Teilhard de. See Teilhard de
Chardin, P.
CHARGE accounts (retail trade)
Spending cash can be a way to save. il
Changing T 23:35 Ag '69
Turning off the computer's wrath. Consumer
Rep 34:492-3 S '69
CHARGERS (football club) See Football clubs
CHARGERS, Battery. See Storage battery
chargers
CHARISMATIC leadership. See Leadership
CHARITABLE societies
See also
Charities
CHARITIES
Bittersweet charity; duplication of charity
appeals. E. B. Bagley. Chr Cent 86:1313 O
15 '69
Of many things: support for Fr. Roberts
home for the deaf, Suhaile, Lebanon. V. S.
Kearney. America 121:inside cover Jl 19
'69
See also
Foundations, Charitable and educational
Fund raising
Giving
United fund

CHARITY
All things in common. R. Haughton. Cath World 209:197 Ag '69
See also
Humanity
CHARITY balls. See Balls (parties)
CHARLES I, king of Great Britain
Charles I. by C. Hibbert. Review
Nat R 21:80 Ja 28 '69. J. C. Lobdell
CHARLES, prince of Wales
Ascent of Prince Charles. J. Newcombe. il pors Life 66:36-41 Je 27 '69
Bonnie Prince Charles in bush country. Sat R 52:88 Mr 8 '69
Britain's Prince Charles: the apprentice king. il por Time 93:27-8+ Je 27 '69; Same abr. with title Man who will be king. Read Digest 95:131-4 S '69
Charles. L. Gross. por Look 33:66-7 Je 24 '69
Coming of age of Britain's Prince Charles. G. Fisher and H. Fisher. il pors Good H 169:68-9+ Jl '69
How many British birds are fit for a prince? il pors Life 67:58B-62 Ag 8 '69
I, Charles, Prince of Wales. A. Lejeune. Nat R 21:747 Jl 29 '69
Investiture of Great Britain's Prince of Wales. A. C. Fisher, jr. il pors Nat Geog 136:698-715 N '69
Letter to Charles: fellow student writes his views. J. Holmes. Time 93:31 Je 27 '69; Same abr. with title Contemporary speaks. Read Digest 95:133 S '69
Magnificent spectacle for a future king. A. Menen. il pors McCalls 96:58-9+ Je '69
Monarch for the moon age. il pors Newsweek 74:26-31 Jl 14 '69
Now a prince, someday a king; growing role for young Charles. il por U S News 66:10 Je 30 '69
Popular young lad. il por Time 94:32 Jl 11 '69
Prince who'll bust the scene? views of young Britons. il Newsweek 74:30-1 Jl 14 '69
Tune in on life with Charlie. A. Howard. New Repub 161:13 Jl 5 '69
Will the Welsh welch on the prince of Wales? D. Hart-Davis. il por Holiday 45: 16+ Je '69
CHARLES, Ezzard
Most important bout for Ezzard Charles. il pors Ebony 24:102-4+ Mr '69
CHARLES, Robert
What's new for children. See occasional issues of Parents' magazine & better family living
CHARLES Hamilton autographs, incorporated. See Hamilton, Charles, autographs, incorporated
CHARLES' law. See Gases
CHARLES Pfizer and company. See Pfizer, Charles, and company
CHARLESTON, Robert J.
Porcelain as room decoration in eighteenth-century England. Antiques 96:894-9 D '69
CHARLESTON, S.C.

Description
Stir in Hominyland. D. Butwin. il Sat R 52:28+ My 24 '69

Negroes
City: echoes of Memphis. Time 93:23 Ap 25 '69

Sanitary affairs
Refuse as a resource. il Am City 84:115-16 O '69

Street traffic
Charleston to go solid state; installation of new traffic control system. il Am City 84: 35 Ap '69

Strikes
See also
Strikes—United States—Hospital employees
CHARLESTON, W.Va.

City planning
Progress and protest. E. P. Berkeley. il Arch Forum 131:48-55 N '69
CHARLESWORTH, James C.
(ed) America's changing role as a world leader. bibliog f Ann Am Acad 385:1-103 Jl '69
CHARLIE Mitchell, you rat, be kind to my little girl; story. See Cormier, R.
CHARLIER, Roger Henri
Tidal energy; with biographical sketch. por Sea Front 15:339-48, 382 N '69

CHARLOTTE, N. C.

Police
Merchant's hot line on crime. il Am City 84:38 Ja '69
CHARLOTTE and Mecklenburg County, N.C, public library
Mecklenburg County: reaching for the un-reached. H. Galvin. il Wilson Lib Bul 43: 899-900 My '69
CHARLOTTE CREEK DAM (proposed) See Dams
CHARM, Walter B.
Working the Glomar Challenger. il Sea Front 15:258-67 S '69
CHARNEY, George
Communist-Catholic neurosis? Reflections on A long journey. C. A. Weber. Common-weal 90:389-93 Je 20 '69
CHARNEY, Nicolas H.
Synergistic scheme of things. il por Time 93:65+ F 14 '69
CHARRIÈRE, Henri
Letter from Paris. Genêt. New Yorker 45: 200+ N 15 '69
CHARTENER, William H
Dear Virginia; address, June 23, 1969. Vital Speeches 35:645-9 Ag 15 '69
CHARTER airlines. See Airlines—Non-sched-uled operations
CHARTER New York corporation. See New York (city)—Banks
CHARTERING of boats. See Boats—Leasing and renting
CHARTERING of yachts. See Yachts—Char-tering
CHARTRES, France
Legacy from the age of faith: Chartres. K. MacLeish. il Nat Geog 136:856-82 D '69
CHARTRES cathedral. See Cathedrals—France
CHARTS, Calculating
Channel separation nomogram. M. H. Apple-baum. il Radio-Electr 40:73 N '69
CHARTS, Nautical. See Nautical charts
CHARTS, Stock. See Stocks—Price indexes and averages
CHASE, Doris
Forms for dance; interview, ed. by J. Batie. Craft Horiz 29:16-19 Jl '69
CHASE, Edward T.
Super-futurist. New Repub 160:25-6+ Je 21 '69
CHASE, Sherret S.
Anti-famine strategy: genetic engineering for food. Bul Atom Sci 25:2-6 O '69
CHASE; story. See Moravia, A.
CHASE Manhattan bank. See New York (city) —Banks
CHASES, Police. See Police chases
CHASIN, Helen
Andalusia; poem. Poetry 113:387-8 Mr '69
CHASINS, Abram
Rise and decline of the Boston symphony. McCalls 96:34+ Mr '69
CHASSIS, Automobile. See Automobiles—Chas-sis
CHASSIS frame of motorcycles. See Motor-cycles—Frames
CHASTITY belts
Iron belt: reviving art of hand-forging chas-tity belts. Time 93:61 My 30 '69
CHATHAM, Mass.
Monomoy, a day on the island. L. Harrigan. and R. Harrigan. il Liv Wildn 33:24-7 Spr '69
CHATTANOOGA, Battle of the, 1863
Miracle on Missonary ridge; excerpt from Grant takes command; with introd. by the editors. B. Catton. il Am Heritage 20:60-73 F '69
CHATTERJEE, I. B. See Chaudhuri, C. R. jt. auth.
CHATTOPADHYAY, Kamaladevi
Crafts. UNESCO Courier 22:15-17+ My '69
CHAUDHURI, C. Ray, and Chatterjee, I. B.
L-Ascorbic acid synthesis in birds: phylo-genetic trend. bibliog Science 164:435-6 Ap 25 '69
CHAUNCY, Nan
World's end is home for Nan Chauncy. L. Harrington. por Horn Bk 45:441-5 Ag '69
CHAUTAUQUAS
Chautauqua: a nostalgic salute. J. Tebbel; discussion. Sat R 52:52 F 8; 118-19 Mr 8 '69
Chautauqua: an experience in adult educa-tion. D. E. Weischadle. Ed Digest 34:47-9 Ja '69
CHÁVEZ, César
Letter from Delano. Chr Cent 86:539-40 Ap 23 '69
Nonviolence still works; interview. por Look 33:52+ Ap 1 '69

CHÁVEZ, César—*Continued*

about

Breakthrough for *la huelga*. Time 93:13 Je 27 '69
California grape boycott. Trans-Action 6:6 F '69
Don't eat grapes along with me. W. F. Buckley, jr. Nat R 21:715 Jl 15 '69
Grapes of wrath. J. R. Coyne, jr. Nat R 21: 639 Jl 1 '69
Little strike that grew to *la causa*. il pors Time 94:16-21 Jl 4 '69; Same abr. with title Battle of the grapes. Read Digest 95: 88-92 O '69
Profiles. P. Matthiessen. por New Yorker 45:42-4+ Je 21; 43-4+ Je 28 '69
Why grape growers do not render unto Cesar. R. K. Sanderson and E. L. Barr, jr. Chr Cent 86:810-11 Je 11 '69
Wrath of grapes. G. Logsdon. Farm J 93:33+ F '69

CHAYES, Abram
Battle of the ABM. Newsweek 73:36 My 12 '69

CHAZEN, Leonard
Price of free TV. Atlan 223:59-61 Mr '69

CHEI drama. See Raphael, L.

CHEATING
See also
Fraud
CHEATING at cards. See Cardsharping
CHEATING in schoolwork
Cheating: comparison of college bound and non-college bound pupils. F. Schab. Clear House 44:179-81 N '69

CHECK, John F.
Contract signing. Clear House 43:411-12 Mr '69
CHECKING accounts. See Banks and banking—Checking accounts
CHECKMATE; story. See Porter, J.

CHECKS
Banks go psychedelic to lure customers; scrambling for demand deposits. il Bsns W p78+ Je 21 '69
Negotiable art. il Time 93:74-5 Je 27 '69

CHECKUP, Medical. See Physical examinations

CHEEK, James E. jr
Cheek brothers, a new breed of college president. il pors Ebony 24:35-8+ O '69

CHEEK, King V.
Cheek brothers, a new breed of college president. il pors Ebony 24:35-8+ O '69

CHEESE
Cream cheese with rosemary. il Sunset 143: 207 N '69
Pears to begin with. il Sunset 143:48-51 Ag '69
See also
Cookery—Cheese

CHEESE; story. See Warner, S. T.

CHEESECAKE
Cake top makes a moat which you then fill with strawberries. il Sunset 142:142 Mr '69
It's a less wicked cheesecake. il Sunset 143: 194 N '69

CHEEVER, John
Close-up: novelist of suburbia. W. Sheed. il por Life 66:39-40+ Ap 18 '69

CHEFF, Bud
Bears I have known. Outdoor Life 143:48-51+ F '69

CHEFS. See Cooks

CHEFS salad. See Salads

CHEKHOV, Anton Pavlovich
Three sisters. Criticism
America 121:145-6 S 6 '69
Nation 209:486 N 3 '69
New Repub 161:33 N 1 '69
New Yorker 45:149 O 18 '69
Sat R 52:20 Jl 5 '69
Uncle Vanya. Criticism
Nation 209:293 S 22 '69
Sat R 52:20 N 15 '69

CHELMINSKI, Rudolph
Close-up: Tigran Petrosian. Life 66:41-2+ Ap 11 '69

CHEMICAL additives in cattle feed. See Antibiotic feed supplements

CHEMICAL additives in food. See Food additives

CHEMICAL aerosols. See Aerosols

CHEMICAL and biological weapons
Backing a bit from the brink; R. M. Nixon renunciation pledge. il Newsweek 74:43+ D 8 '69
Banning the germs. Time 94:38+ D 5 '69
Biological warfare as national policy; address, August 10, 1969. R. D. McCarthy. Vital Speeches 35:681-3 S 1 '69
Bugs banned. Chr Cent 86:1570 D 10 '69

Chemical-biological warfare: a killing shame. G. Astor. il Look 33:67-8+ D 16 '69
CBW: Nixon initiative on treaty anticipates congressional critics. A. Hamilton. Science 166:1249-50 D 5 '69
CBW: pressures for control build in Congress, international groups. P. M. Boffey. Science 164:1376-8 Je 20 '69
Choice in the making. Sci N 96:373 O 25 '69
Dare we develop biological weapons? S. M. Hersh. il N Y Times Mag p28-9+ S 28 '69; Reply. P. O'Dwyer. p42 N 2 '69
Defense R&D programs lopped; blow to the U.S. offensive chemical and biological warfare program. Sci N 96:47-8 Jl 19 '69
Dilemma of chemical warfare; Time essay. il Time 93:20-1 Je 27 '69
Fiendish vials. N. Cousins. Sat R 52:16-17 Ag 30 '69
Gas and germ weapons: a look inside the arsenal. il U S News 67:28-9 Ag 18 '69
Gaseous and buggy: CBW program. Chr Cent 86:941 Jl 16 '69
Germ warfare and the arms race; President Nixon's decision to renounce use and manufacture. N. Cousins. Sat R 52:26 D 13 '69
Germ warfare: for alma mater, God and country. S. Hersh. il Ramp Mag 8:20-8 D '69
Germs and gas as weapons; congressional hearings. S. M. Hersh. New Repub 160:13-16 Je 7 '69
Ghost of Geneva. A. Tuckerman. Nation 209: 714 D 29 '69
Nobody here but us dead sheep. W. Zinsser. il Life 67:42-3 Ag 22 '69
Out with CBW. Sci N 96:495 N 29 '69
Pleasant reading, for a change. Nation 209: 652 D 15 '69
Poison bullets, for what? Nation 209:589 D 1 '69
Sharp U.S. limit now on any germ or gas warfare. il U S News 67:7 D 8 '69
Silent arsenal; excerpts from United Nations report. Sat R 52:14-17+ S 27 '69
TRB from Washington. New Repub 160:6 Je 21 '69
Terrifying armory the U.S. scraps, and keeps. il Newsweek 74:44 D 8 '69
Toxins are in. J. Deedy. Commonweal 91: 394 Ja 9 '70
U.N: experts' report on CBW supports disarmament effort. E. Langer. Science 165: 163-4 Jl 11 '69
See also
Gases, Asphyxiating and poisonous
Government investigations—Chemical and biological weapons
Tear gas

Testing
How the sheep died in Skull Valley; testing of nerve gas. R. G. Fowler. il Farm J 93: 34B-34D S '69
Wind from Dugway; death of sheep near Proving ground, testing poisonous agents. V. Brodine and others. il Environ 11:2-9+ Ja '69
See also
Gases, Asphyxiating and poisonous—Testing

CHEMICAL apparatus and supplies
Computer interfaced fast analyzers. N. G. Anderson. bibliog il Science 166:317-24 O 17 '69
See also
Glassware, Laboratory

CHEMICAL bank and trust company. See New York (city)—Banks

CHEMICAL bonds
Binding of alkali metal ions by cyclic polyethers: significance in ion transport processes. R. M. Izatt and others. bibliog il Science 164:443-4 Ap 25 '69
Carbon-phosphorus bond in nature. J. S. Kittredge and E. Roberts. bibliog il Science 164:37-42 Ap 4 '69
Electron repulsion theory. W. F. Luder. bibliog il Chem 42:16-19 Je '69
New bond; carbon-phosphorus bond. Sci Am 220:58 Je '69

CHEMICAL deodorants. See Deodorants

CHEMICAL education. See Chemistry—Study and teaching

CHEMICAL elements
Chemical analysis in a wink. Chem 42:22 F '69
Great moments in chemistry; from Thales to Bohr. F. Szabadvary. Chem 42:6-9 D '69
New element? island of stability theory. il Chem 42:21 F '69
Origin of the elements; adaptation of address, September 1968. D. D. Clayton. bibliog il Phys Today 22:28-36 My '69; Reply. S. Silverman. 22:15+ O '69

CHEMISTRY, Analytic
Lab bench. See issues of Chemistry
  See also
Chromatographic analysis
Electrolysis
Fluorometric analysis
Radioactivation analysis
Spectrophotometry
Water—Analysis

Quantitative
  See also
Titration

CHEMISTRY, Legal
Lab bench; some analytical methods used in crime laboratories. S. S. Rogers. bibliog il Chem 42:29-30 Jl '69
Scientific methods of crime investigation. il Chem 42:12-21 Jl '69

CHEMISTRY, Physical and theoretical
  See also
Adsorption
Atomic weights
Atoms
Dissociation
Emulsions
Hydration
Periodic law
Phases (chemistry)
Radiochemistry

CHEMISTS
Chemists and cancer. Sci N 95:234 Mr 8 '69
  See also
Benedetti-Pichler, A. A.
Chemistry—Study and teaching
Hannay, J. B.
Richards, T. W.

CHEMORECEPTIVITY
Chemoreceptors in bacteria. J. Adler. bibliog il Science 166:1588-97 D 26 '69

CHEMOTAXIS. See Chemotropism

CHEMOTROPISM
Chemoreceptors in bacteria. J. Adler. bibliog il Science 166:1588-97 D 26 '69

CHEN, Andrew T. L. and Faiek, Arthur
Centromeres in human meiotic chromosomes. bibliog Science 166:1008-10 N 21 '69

CHEN, John S. and Levi-Montalcini, Rita
Axonal outgrowth and cell migration in vitro from nervous system of cockroach embryos. bibliog Science 166:631-2 O 31 '69

CHEN, Tsu-teh, and others
Subacute sclerosing panencephalitis: propagation of measles virus from brain biopsy in tissue culture. bibliog Science 163:1193-4 Mr 14 '69

CHENEY, Frances Neel
Current reference books. See issues of Wilson library bulletin

CHENG, Peter P.
Taiwan and the two Chinas. bibliog f Cur Hist 57:168-74+ S '69

CHEONG, George S. C.
Education as enterprise in Hong Kong. Sch & Soc 97:395-6+ O '69

CHER Antoine; drama. See Anouilh, J.

CHERINGTON, Paul W.
Tough professor climbs aboard. il pors Bsns W p 100-2+ Ap 19 '69
Transportation dept. role to spur federal conflicts. Aviation W 91:31 S 29 '69

CHERNISS, Ruth
Saint-Lô: the resurrection of a dead city. Sat R 52:11-15+ Jl 5 '69

CHEROKEE, Ia.

Galleries and museums
Sanford museum and planetarium. J. L. Stoutenburgh. il Hobbies 74:126 Je '69

CHEROKEE Indians
Like it really is, how to tell it that way. R. Hattersley. il Pop Phot 65:114-17+ D '69
Renaissance and repression; the Oklahoma Cherokee. A. L. Wahrhaftig and R. K. Thomas. il Trans-Action 6:42-8 F '69

CHERRIES
  See also
Cookery—Fruit

CHERRY, Jim
NEA committee acts on ethics complaint. E. Faulconer and others. Todays Ed 58:34-5+ N '69

CHERRY trees
Purple-leaf chokecherries. P. H. Wright. Horticulture 47:46+ D '69

CHESAPEAKE and Ohio railway-Norfolk and Western merger (proposed) See Railroads —Consolidations and mergers

CHESAPEAKE BAY
Chesapeake Bay sail cruise. il Bet Hom & Gard 47:116 F '69

CHESAPEAKE BAY bridge-tunnel
White elephant on the Bay. il Time 95:70 Ja 12 '70

CHESAREK, Ferdinand Joseph
Trends in the army; address. October 30, 1968. Vital Speeches 35:287-8 F 15 '69

CHESHER, Richard H.
Destruction of Pacific corals by the sea star acanthaster planci. bibliog Science 165:280-3 Jl 18 '69

CHESHIRE, Maxine
Hostesses have become comic figures; interview, ed. by deR. McQuade. pors Life 66:30+ F 28 '69

CHESHIRE cheese (tavern) See London—Hotels, restaurants, etc.

CHESLER, Phyllis
Maternal influence in learning by observation in kittens. bibliog Science 166:901-3 N 14 '69
Memoirs of Afghanistan. Mlle 69:154-60 Je '69

CHESS
Checkmating game. C Amory. Holiday 46:8+ S '69
Chess corner. A. Horowitz. See issues of Saturday review
Tigran and the tiger; world championship contest in Moscow. il Time 93:51-2 Je 27 '69
  See also
Chessmen

CHESS men. See Chessmen

CHESS players
Close-up: Tigran Petrosian, world chess champion. R. Chelminski. il Life 66:41-2+ Ap 11 '69

CHESS sets
Make this handsome chess set for Christmas. B. Fifer and W. Lange. il Pop Mech 132:162-5+ N '69
Woodworker's project, patio chess. il Sunset 142:139 My '69

CHESSBOARDS
Make this handsome chess set for Christmas. B. Fifer and W. Lange. il Pop Mech 132:162-5+ N '69

CHESSMEN
Make this handsome chess set for Christmas. B. Fifer and W. Lange. il Pop Mech 132:162-5+ N '69

CHESSWAS, John
Are there really too many teachers? UNESCO Courier 23:21-3+ Ja '70

CHEST pain. See Pain

CHESTER, Robert, and others
Gap in social work education. bibliog Ment Hy 53:84-9 Ja '69

CHESTER, Pa.

Music
  See also
Suburban opera company

CHESTNUT trees
Progress with chestnuts. R. A. Jaynes. il Horticulture 46:16-17+ D '68

CHESTNUTS
  See also
Cookery—Nuts

CHESTS
Armoires; closets with nothing to hide. il McCalls 96:100-3 Mr '69
Toujours l'armoire. il House B 111:81 F '69

CHETHAM, Charles
Smith college museum of art. Antiques 96:768-75 N '69

CHEVALIER, Lois R.
No, thank you, I'd rather not live twice. Ladies Home J 86:68+ Mr '69
What's new in medicine. See issues of McCall's

CHEVIGNY, Paul
Abuses of police power; excerpt from Police power. Atlan 223:128 Mr '69

CHEVIGNY, Pierre
Authors & editors. B. A. Bannon. por Pub W 195:25-6 F 3 '69

CHEVRETTE, John M.
Roadblocks to adult fitness. Parks & Rec 4:25-7 Ap '69

CHEVROLET motor company. See General motors corporation—Chevrolet division

CHEW, Peter
Black history, or black mythology? Am Heritage 20:4-9+ Ag '69

CHEWING gum
Chewing gum, a big industry. E. Keller. il Chem 42:16-17 S '69

CHEYENNE, Wyo.
Cheyenne media baron stands up to lawmen; R. McCraken vs Justice dept. il Bsns W p 102-3 Ja 25 '69

CHEYENNE (helicopter gunship). See Helicopters—Military applications

CHEYENNE MOUNTAIN zoological park. See Zoological gardens

CHI, Nguyen-huu-. See Nguyen-huu- Chi

CHIANG, Ching-kuo
Taiwan's future under Chiang, jr. A. Campbell. New Repub 160:14-15 My 31 '69
CHIANG, Kai-shek
Communist struggle: address. January 1. 1969. Vital Speeches 35:231-4 F 1 '69
about
Fading dream. il por Newsweek 74:59-60 O 13 '69
Seeking a new image. por Time 93:34+ Ap 18 '69
CHIANTI. See Wine
CHIAPPETTA, Jerry
Even pros have problems. Field & S 73:64-5+ F '69
Hunt those smart barnyard bucks. Field & S 74:108-10+ Jl '69
Once is enough. Field & S 74:46-7+ S '69
CHICAGO
Coming of age in Chicago. J. Epstein. Commentary 48:61-7 D '69

Air attacks
See Chicago—Defenses

Air pollution
Sulfur and Daley: the lawless air. R. Whitehead, jr. Nation 209:503-5 N 10 '69

Anti-poverty program
Antipoverty R&D: Chicago debacle suggests pitfalls facing OEO. J. Walsh. Science 165: 1243-5 S 19 '69

Architecture
Aesthetic stylist for the world; Chicago's skyline. il Bsns W p58-61 Je 21 '69
Lake Point Tower: the first skyscraper with an undulating glass wall. il Arch Rec 146: 123-30 O '69

Art
Chicago (cont) Art N 68:59 Ap '69

Banks
Evolution of a special form to meet its program; First national bank. il Arch Rec 145: 192-6 Ap '69
First's big move; First national bank of Chicago. il Newsweek 73:80 Je 2 '69

Board of trade
See Chicago board of trade

Buildings
Chicago's whopper skyscraper; John Hancock center. J. Downs. il Life 67:51-2 D 12 '69
Profits in vertical city; John Hancock center. il Time 93:74-5 F 7 '69

Churches
Church in a grove of skyscrapers: Seventh church of Christ, Scientist. J. M. Dixon. il Arch Forum 130:42-5 Je '69
Ministers and Weathermen; sheltering the Weathermen. America 121:449 N 15 '69
Moody church's survival plan. W. Hartzell. Chr Today 13:38-40 Mr 14 '69

City planning
Farsighted study and some blind spots; Park-Mall Lawndale study. W. J. Black. il Arch Forum 129:44-9 D '68

Civil defense
See Chicago—Defenses

Courts
Problem is: we have too many rights; picketing of the Democratic convention. S. W. Dry. New Repub 160:11 My 17 '69

Crime
No taste for truth, Senator McClellan? the charges against J. Fry. Chr Cent 86:1271 O 8 '69
See also
Mafia

Defenses
U.S. journal: Lake County, Ill: reactions to future Sentinel anti-ballistic missile system site. C. Trillin. New Yorker 44:100-6 F 15 '69

Description
Exciting cities, a Redbook vacation guide to sight-seeing with children; excerpts from America's exciting cities. A. Schwartz. il Redbook 132:38 Ap '69

Education
How one city teaches sex education and family life. B. A. Hawkins. il PTA Mag 63:24-6 Je '69

Room for miracles; Independent learning center at Chicago's Ray school. L. Wille. il Am Ed 5:7-10 Ag '69
Why the government is threatening to sue Chicago; white resistance to segregation. Time 94:15 Jl 18 '69
See also
Chicago city college
Illinois. University—Chicago campus

Elections
Chicago voters tilt Mayor Daley's machine. R. Whitehead. Commonweal 90:157-8 Ap 15 '69
Daley stumbles. Nation 208:389 Mr 31 '69
Porcupine power; William S. Singer knocks Daley man out of the aldermanic race. Newsweek 73:61 Ap 21 '69

Galleries and museums
See also
Chicago art institute
Chicago natural history museum

Haymarket square riot, 1886
[Harry Golden column] H. Golden. Nation 209:82 Jl 28 '69

Hotels, restaurants, etc.
When you're out at the inn; tips to ensure hotel accommodations. R. C. Strobell. il Parks & Rec 4:26-7+ Ag '69
Wrigley bar. I. Kupcinet. il Holiday 45:18+ My '69

Housing
Black homeowning; Contract buyers league lawsuits for price exploitation. A. Boles. New Repub 161:7-9 D 13 '69
Breach of contract; Contract buyers league revolt. Newsweek 75:56 Ja 19 '70
Chicago's quiet slum revolt. America 121: 350 O 25 '69
Existing without the north shore. il Bsns W p 146 Je 14 '69
Factory-fabricated townhouses. il Am City 84:42 F '69
Landmark ruling: public housing projects. il Newsweek 74:74 Jl 14 '69
Public housing in black and white. H. D. Shapiro. Commonweal 90:253-4 My 16 '69
Roof caves in on Mayor Daley's housing plan. il Bsns W p56-7 Ag 30 '69
Woodlawn gardens. E. P. Berkeley il Arch Forum 131:72-7 Jl '69

John Hancock center
See Chicago—Buildings

Libraries
See also
Chicago public library

Lighting
Chicago maintains its claim to lighting fame. J. V. Fitzpatrick. il Am City 84:116 Ja '69

Music
See also
Chicago symphony orchestra
Lyric opera of Chicago

Negroes
Blacks wrap up slice of action at food chains; Operation Breadbasket's boycott of Chicago A&P stores. il Bsns W p 162-3+ Ap 26 '69
Chicago's leaders bankroll the blacks. Bsns W p56 S 13 '69
Jesse Jackson: heir to Dr King? head of Operation Breadbasket. R. Levine. Harper 238:58-64+ Mr '69
North: hustler, preacher, panther. J. Rodgers. il Newsweek 73:32-3 Je 30 '69
Public housing in black and white. H. D. Shapiro. Commonweal 90:253-4 My 16 '69

Newspapers
Front page revisited; City news bureau of Chicago. il Time 94:44+ Ag 22 '69
Self-criticism in Chicago; reporters as critics of newspapers. il Time 93:71 Mr 21 '69
See also
Chicago today
Chicago tribune

Parks and playgrounds
Chicago park district, it keeps on growing. M. Trais. il Parks & Rec 4:29-30+ Je '69

Police
Beyond the law. New Repub 160:11 Je 28 '69
Black Panther killings in Chicago. C. Chandler. New Repub 162:21-4 Ja 10 '70
Confrontation at the Conrad Hilton; excerpts from the Walker commission report. Rights in conflict. il Trans-Action 6:37-49 Ja '69

CHICAGO—Police—*Continued*
Daley vs. the guerrilla theatre; Chicago indictments. R. Whitehead, jr. Nation 208: 422-3 Ap 7 '69
Dissent and law enforcement; excerpts from report Rights in conflict. D. Walker. Cur 103:33-40 Ja '69
Mabley's martyrs. Time 93:56+ Ap 4 '69
News and views; the one-sided Walker report. J. Deedy. Commonweal 89:606 F 14 '69
Out to get the Panthers. L. F. Palmer, jr. Nation 209:78-82 Jl 28 '69
Police riot? summary of report. Sr Schol 93:13 Ja 10 '69
Shoot it out; police-vs.-Panther. il Newsweek 74:37 D 15 '69
Sticking the pigs; concerning Walker report. J. Jeffries. Nat R 21:236-8 Mr 11 '69
U.S. anti-riot law gets test. Sr Schol 94: 16-17 Ap 18 '69
You'd never believe he was a cop; W. H. Sherrod's career as policeman, preacher, teacher. B. Reynolds. il Ebony 24:106-10+ Jl '69

Politics and government
Defense against Daley: the conspiracy on trial. L. D. Nachman. Nation 208:752-4 Je 16 '69
Democrats confront 1970. D. Rose and D. S. Canter. Nation 209:595-7 D 1 '69
Mayor Daley: solvent but worried. D. Rose and D. S. Canter. Nation 209:169-73 S 1 '69
See also
Chicago—Elections

Poor
One man's fight against hunger in the city. F. G. Loyd. il Todays Health 47:48-53+ D '69

Recreation
Family fun in Chicago. J. Reedy. Bet Hom & Gard 47:47 Mr '69
See also
Chicago—Parks and playgrounds

Riots
Back to Chicago. il Newsweek 74:81 O 6 '69
Back to Chicago. il Time 94:22-3 S 26 '69
Chicago riots: sixteen indictments. U S News 66:11 Mr 31 '69
Collision of absurdities; Conspiracy eight case. Chr Cent 86:1473 N 19 '69
Conspiracy in Chicago; trial of anti-war demonstrators. Nation 209:364-5 O 13 '69
Daley vs. the guerrilla theatre; Chicago indictments. R. Whitehead, jr. Nation 208: 422-3 Ap 7 '69
Disorder in the court; Chicago trial of eight radicals. il Time 94:27-8 N 7 '69
Inside the great pigasus plot; excerpts from Do it! J. Rubin. il Ramp Mag 8:10-12+ D '69
Julius the just; trial of the Chicago eight. Time 94:75 O 24 '69
Mockery of justice? trial of the Chicago eight. il Newsweek 74:41-2 O 27 '69
Place where all America was radicalized. T. Wicker. il N Y Times Mag p26-7+ Ag 24 '69; Reply with rejoinder. E. F. Berman. p58+ O 5 '69
Poor climate for weathermen. il Time 94:24-5 O 17 '69
Risk of mockery; trying eight radicals on anti-conspiracy law. il Time 94:21 O 10 '69
Sticking the pigs; concerning Walker report. J. Jeffries. Nat R 21:236-8 Mr 11 '69
Theater of the conspiracy. P. A. Luce. Nat R 21:1264 D 16 '69
Trial of Chicago eight. W. B. Furlong. il Life 67:28D-31 O 10 '69
U.S. anti-riot law gets test. Sr Schol 94:16-17 Ap 18 '69
Vandals in the mother country. J. Kifner. il N Y Times Mag p 14-16+ Ja 4 '70
See also
Chicago—Haymarket square riot, 1886

Social conditions
Age of Aquarius; a real community; address, October 11, 1969. T. Powell. Vital Speeches 36:90-2 N 15 '69
Anatomy of a Chicago slum; excerpts from The social order of the slum. G. D. Suttles. il Trans-Action 6:16-19+ F '69
See also
Chicago—Poor

Water supply
Watchdog computer keeps tabs on water treatment. il Am City 84:12 N '69

CHICAGO American (newspaper). See Chicago today

CHICAGO art institute
Fine arts; story of a picture; Excavation by de Kooning. K. Kuh. il Sat R 52.38-9 Mr 29 '69
Masterpieces of western textiles. C. C. Mayer. il Antiques 95:264-9 F '69
Some early English silver at the Art institute of Chicago. A. Wardwell. il Antiques 95:818-24 Je '69
CHICAGO Bears (football club) See Football clubs
CHICAGO Black Hawks (hockey team) See Hockey teams
CHICAGO board of trade
Stock futures. Newsweek 73:73+ Mr 3 '69
Using futures, how the market works. F. Bailey, jr. il Suc Farm 67:30-1+ N '69
CHICAGO book clinic annual exhibit. See Book exhibits
CHICAGO city college
Age of Aquarius; a real community; address, October 11, 1969. T. Powell. Vital Speeches 36:90-2 N 15 '69
CHICAGO city news bureau. See News agencies
CHICAGO conspiracy trial. See Trials (conspiracy)
CHICAGO convention, 1968. See National conventions. Democratic
CHICAGO Cubs (baseball). See Baseball clubs
CHICAGO in art
Anybody want to buy Chicago? work of Red Grooms. D. L. Goodrich. il Sat Eve Post 242:36-9 F 8 '69
CHICAGO journalism review
Self-criticism in Chicago; reporters as critics of newspapers. il Time 93:71 Mr 21 '69
CHICAGO lyric opera. See Lyric opera of Chicago
CHICAGO mercantile exchange
Chicago's Merc reaches for no. 1. il Bsns W p 118+ My 24 '69
CHICAGO natural history museum
Chicago's septuagenarian swinger; 75th anniversary exhibit. K. Poli. il Pop Phot 65: 80 N '69
CHICAGO public library
Chicago headed toward 21st century? ALA Bul 63:879 Jl '69
Chicago public library eyes moonlighting. Library J 94:3594 O 15 '69
Chicago: the public library reaches out. A. Ladenson. il Wilson Lib Bul 43:875-81 My '69
Lowell Martin survey blasts Chicago P.L; summary. L. Martin. il Library J 94:1825 My 1 '69
Pied Piper in Chicago; Reading and study center. Z. Sutherland. Sat R 52:36 S 13 '69

Branches
Branch power. F. Field. il Library J 94:3408-10 O 1 '69

CHICAGO symphony orchestra
Solti, at last. R. C. Marsh. Hi Fi 19:MA26+ Ap '69
CHICAGO symphony string quartet. See String quartets
CHICAGO theological seminary. See Chicago. University—Federated theological faculty
CHICAGO today
Tabloid today. il Newsweek 73:69 My 12 '69
CHICAGO tribune
Chicago exclusive; coverage of police raid on Black Panther headquarters. il Newsweek 74:90-1 D 22 '69
CHICAGO. University
Afterthoughts of a prodigy. E. Shorris. Esquire 72:28+ D '69
Assault at Chicago. Newsweek 73:70-1 My 19 '69
Campus spring offensive. Newsweek 73:68-9 Ap 28 '69
Styles of handling student demonstrations. M. Salk. il Bul Atom Sci 25:36-8 Je '69
Who's in charge here? il Newsweek 73:70-1 F 17 '69

Billings hospital
Profound lesson for the living; seminar. L. Wainwright. il Life 67:36-43 N 21 '69

Federated theological faculty
Vanderbilt congress: the Chicago school. W. A. Geier. Chr Cent 86:491-4 Ap 9 '69; Reply. H. W. Hansen. 86:756 My 28 '69

CHICANO students. See Mexican American students
CHICHESTER, Sir Francis Charles
Keeping fit with Sir Francis Chichester. Esquire 71:98-101+ Je '69
CHICHESTER-CLARK, James Dawson
From captain to major. por Newsweek 73: 50+ My 12 '69
Quiet man. por Time 93:42 My 9 '69

CHILDREN
Children of the world; with photographs by
J. Hansen. J. R. Moskin. Look 33:50-5
D 30 '69
See also
Adoption
Birth order
Children and music
Cookery by children
Education of children
Family
Fathers
Mothers
Museums—Work with children
Play
Preschool children
Presidents—United States—Children
Problem children
School children
Siblings
Stepchildren
Stepparents
Television broadcasting and children
Travel with children

Accidents
See Accidents

Adjustment
See Adjustment, Social

Aggressiveness
See Aggressiveness (psychology)

Amusement
See Childrens amusements

Anxiety
See Anxiety

Care and hygiene
Growing pains; questions and answers. See
issues of Today's health
Your child's health. L. W. Sauer. See issues of
PTA magazine
See also
Baby sitters
Child welfare
Children—Diseases—Diagnosis
Children—Nutrition
Infants—Care and hygiene
Parent education
Pediatrics
Public schools—Health service
Thumb sucking

Caricatures and cartoons
Small wonders. R. Marcus. See issues of
Good housekeeping

Charities, protection, etc.
See Child welfare

Clothing and dress
See Clothing and dress—Children

Day care
See Day nurseries; Nursery schools

Development
See Children—Growth and development

Diseases
Poisoning the wells; rising nitrate content
causing increased hazard of methemoglo-
binemia. il Environ 11:16-23+ Ja '69
Your child's health. L. W. Sauer. See issues
of PTA magazine
See also
Celiac disease
Chicken pox
Convulsions
Diphtheria
Pediatrics

Diagnosis
Laboratory tests: how they aid in diagnosing
children's diseases. L. W. Sauer. il PTA
Mag 63:33-4 Ja '69

Education
See Education of children

Employment
See also
Youth—Employment

Etiquette
See Etiquette for children and youth

Food
See Children—Nutrition

Growth and development
Baby on the go. H. W. Jacoby. il Parents
Mag 44:54-5+ Ap '69
Child who won't try; with group-discussion
program. T. P. Millar. il Parents Mag 44:
26, 44-5+ F '69
In the wake of starvation, a wound food can-
not heal. A. H. Moore. il Life 66:52 Ja 24 '69
Malnutrition and learning. M. S. Read. il Am
Ed 5:11-14 D '69
Nurture key to I.Q. P. McBroom. il Sci N
95:243-5 Mr 8 '69
On explaining language. E. H. Lenneberg.
bibliog il Science 164:635-43 My 9 '69; Reply
with rejoinder. P. W. Dixon. 165:1065 S 12
'69
Pampered, neglected child. W. Kempler. To-
days Health 47:46-9 Mr '69
They want to know; survey of school children.
R. Kramer. il N Y Times Mag p 107+ S 7
'69
Too little too late. il Good H 169:12+ O '69
What will that child do next! il Changing T
23:47 Je '69
See also
Adolescence
Child study
Infants—Growth and development

Hospital care
All the ice cream you want. Trans-Action 6:8
S '69
Juvenile journalists find humor in a hos-
pital. J. H. Pollack. il Todays Health 47:12-
13 Ap '69
There are cures for fear, too. P. Feinstein.
il N Y Times Mag p 122+ O 26 '69; Reply.
E. Lazar. p 144 N 23 '69

Hospitals
Adolescent stage: it's for real; adolescent
unit at Boston's children's hospital. R.
Kramer. il N Y Times Mag p 116+ D 7 '69

Institutional care
Managing wake-up behavior in a children's
home. J. K. Whittaker and M. Komives.
bibliog Ment Hy 53:575-84 O '69
They got the feeling that everybody's somebody. M. P. Pfeil. il Am Ed 5:21-4 D '69

Language
Baby learns to talk. G. W. Weinstein. il
Parents Mag 44:66-7+ S '69
How babies learn to talk. D. V. Whipple.
il Parents Mag 44:48-9+ F '69
How babies learn to talk. il Good H 169:200
N '69
In the beginning is the word. G. L. Wyatt.
il N Y Times Mag p99-100+ O 19 '69
On explaining language. E. H. Lenneberg
bibliog il Science 164:635-43 My 9 '69; Reply
with rejoinder. P. W. Dixon. 165:1065 S 12
'69
Respecting the words of kids. W. Martin.
Clear House 43:380-1 F '69
Talk and intelligence; with study discus-
sion-program, ed. by R. Strang. J. W.
Kessler. bibliog il PTA Mag 64:15-17+,
34 S '69

Law
See also
Adoption
Guardian and ward
Illegitimacy
Juvenile courts
Juvenile delinquency
Parent and child (law)

Management and training
Between parent and child. H. Ginott. il Mc-
Calls 96:40+ Mr; 40+ Ap '69
Cheated generation. L. N. Bell. Chr Today
13:29-30 Ag 1 '69
Child who won't try; with group-discussion
program. T. P. Millar. il Parents Mag 44:
26, 44-5+ F '69
Children must learn to fear. B. Bettelheim.
il N Y Times Mag p 125+ Ap 13 '69; Dis-
cussion. p 128+ My 18 '69
Discipline or indulgence? child-rearing in
Korea. M. S. Johnston. il Parents Mag 44:
37-9+ Jl '69
Dramatic measures and laconic language. H.
Ginott. il McCalls 96:40 Jl '69
Family clinic. See issues of Parents' maga-
zine & better family living
Growing pains; questions and answers. See
issues of Today's health
Hippies as parents. W. Hedgepeth. il Look
33:69-74 Jl 15 '69
Holidays and children. H. G. Ginott. McCalls
97:14+ D '69

CHILDREN—Management and training—*Cont.*
How can we ask children to be better than we are? S. Lloyd Redbook 133:56+ Je '69
How to be a better parent; excerpts from Child sense: a pediatrician's guide for today's families. W. E. Homan. Read Digest 95:187-8+ O '69
Look back in wonder; era of permissive parents. R. Kramer. il N Y Times Mag p93-4+ Je 8 '69
Managing wake-up behavior in a children's home. J. K. Whittaker and M. Komives. bibliog Ment Hy 53:575-84 O '69
Mrs Nixon tells how she brought up Tricia and Julie; interview; ed. by T. B. Feldman. P. R. Nixon. il McCalls 96:74-5+ Mr '69
Must brothers (and sisters) fight? interview; ed. by A. Rosenthal. B. Siegel. il Todays Health 48:26-9+ Ja '70
Phasing out mom and dad; permissiveness vs parental authority. R. Kramer. il N Y Times Mag p95+ N 2 '69
Raising children by instinct. B. Spock. Redbook 133:24+ Ag '69
Suburban isolation controversy; Skinner box. S. Strom; Mrs S. Sterman. il Sci Digest 65: 28-30 Je '69
They learn what they live. H. Ginott. McCalls 97:35+ N '69
Toward a technology of child care for children in residence. H. Alt. bibliog Ment Hy 53:564-74 O '69
What every preschooler needs. E. G. Neisser and F. Bauling il Parents Mag 44:49-51+ Ap '69
What makes some children bad? they're suffering from a hidden physical handicap. E. Margolis. il Parents Mag 44:52-3+ My '69
When youngsters cling to babyish ways. R. M. Silberstein and C. Levine. il Parents Mag 44:51-3+ Mr '69
Whining child. B. Spock. Redbook 134:33-4 D '69
Who sets the standards in your house? B. P. McCarthy. il Parents Mag 44:51-3+ O '69
Why children won't go to bed. Good H 168:200 Mr '69
Why you should make your kids miserable. P. Bracken. Redbook 133:69+ Ag '69
  See also
Camp discipline
Child study
Discipline
Honesty
Moral education
Occupations for children
Parent-child relationship
Parent education
Problem children
Quarrels

   Anecdotes, facetiae, satire, etc.
What this generation needs is a rousing chorus of the woodshed blues. H. Domnick. Todays Ed 58:38-9 Ap '69

    Bibliography
Books for parents; comp. by P. Pinson. il Parents Mag 44:42 Ap '69

    History
Housekeeping and childkeeping in the olden days. B. Spock. Redbook 133:44+ O '69

    Nutrition
Hunger problem and how one town is beating it. il U S News 66:53-4 F 10 '69
Malnutrition and learning. M. S. Read. il Am Ed 5:11-14 D '69
Things we ate: or, How did I live this long? H. La Barre. McCalls 96:86+ Je '69
Your health; food facts. C. G. King. il Todays Ed 58:62-3 S '69
  See also
Eating, Psychology of
School lunches

    Photographs
Security is a thumb and a blanket. S. Szasz. Good H 168:74+ Ap '69

    Photography
  See also
Photography of children

  Preparation for medical and dental care
Preparing children for psychologic evaluations. L. W. Mondy. Ment Hy 53:635-7 O '69

    Psychiatry
  See Child psychiatry

    Psychology
  See Child study

    Punishment
  See Children—Management and training

    Religion
  See also
Sunday schools

    Sayings
God is a good friend to have; excerpts, comp. by S. Hample and E. Marshall. il Good H 169:76-7 D '69
What is a father? excerpts. L. P. McGrath and J. Scobey. Good H 168:100-1 Je '69; il Read Digest 95:100-1 S '69
What your child is really saying. M. Tonn. Farm J 93:44 Ag '69

   Social and economic status
  See also
Socially handicapped children
Students—Social and economic status

    Speech
  See Children—Language

    Suicide
  See Suicide

    Surgery
Sex differences in verbal and performance IQ's of children undergoing open-heart surgery. M. P. Honzik and others. bibliog il Science 164:445-7 Ap 25 '69; Reply with rejoinder. A. F. Paolino. 166:259-60 O 10 '69

    Training
  See Children—Management and training

    Israel
Children of the dream, by B. Bettelheim. Review
  New Repub 160:23-6 My 24 '69. J. Featherstone
  Sat R il 52:72-3+ S 20 '69. U. Bronfenbrenner

    Japan
Report on a thousand cranes. B. J. Lifton. il Horn Bk 45:148-52 Ap '69

   Korea (Republic)
Discipline or indulgence? child-rearing in Korea. M. S. Johnston. il Parents Mag 44: 37-9+ Jl '69

   United States
Our President, Appalachian style; children's political attitudes. Trans-Action 6:6 F '69
  See also
Child welfare—United States
Negro children

   Vietnam (Republic)
Forgotten victims of the war in Vietnam. D. E. Ronk. il Parents Mag 44:43-5+ Ag '69
CHILDREN, Adopted
Twins who found each other; excerpt. B. Lindeman. il Good H 169:107-9+ O '69
Unmarried mother for Mike. C. Mangel. il Look 33:54-9 F 4 '69
  See also
Adoption
CHILDREN, Blind. See Blind
CHILDREN, Cost of raising. See Domestic finance
CHILDREN, Cruelty to. See Cruelty to children
CHILDREN, Deaf. See Deaf
CHILDREN, Deformed. See Deformities
CHILDREN, Education of. See Education of children
CHILDREN, Exceptional
  See also
Children, Gifted
Children, Handicapped
Minimal brain dysfunction
Problem children
Special classes and special schools

    Education
IMC network; Instructional materials center network for handicapped children and youth. L. Aserlind and J. J. McCarthy. Ed Digest 34:35-8 Mr '69
CHILDREN, First-born
First, last or middle child: the surprising differences. V. Packard. Read Digest 95: 25+ D '69
CHILDREN, Gifted
American museum's youngest scientist; J. Hurtt. il Ebony 24:86-7+ O '69
Boy who knows too much. N. M. Lobsenz. il Redbook 133:74-5+ Je '69
Child prodigies; M. Grost and Edith Stern. il Newsweek 73:18 Ap 28 '69

CHILDREN, Gifted—Continued

Education

Special workshop for the gifted; Greenwich, Conn. R. D. Campbell. il Todays Ed 58:32-3 D '69

We're wasting the gifted! C. Klinger. Todays Ed 58:86 S '69

CHILDREN, Handicapped

See also
Camps for the handicapped
Deaf
Recreation for the handicapped

Education

Avenging father; battle for justice for Germany's 3,000 thalidomide children. A. Levy. il Good H 168:50+ Ap '69

Pioneering nursery school; one-room nursery school at New York university medical center's Institute of rehabilitation medicine. E. P. Berkeley. il Arch Forum 130: 68-9 Mr '69

Program for handicapped children; British Honduras. il Sch & Soc 97:211-13 Ap '69

Teaching the handicapped child. C. H. Hanson. il Todays Ed 58:46-7 D '69

They're sharing something special; special education programs, Richmond County, Ga. J. S. Park. il Am Ed 5:23-5 Mr '69

Washington report; help for the handicapped. J. Lloyd. Sr Schol 95:Schol Teach 2 O 6 '69
See also
Special classes and special schools

CHILDREN, Illegitimate. See Illegitimacy

CHILDREN, Mentally handicapped. See Mentally handicapped children

CHILDREN, Mentally superior. See Children, Gifted

CHILDREN, Photography of. See Photography of children

CHILDREN, Preschool. See Preschool children

CHILDREN, Problem. See Problem children

CHILDREN, Professional

See also
Children as dancers
Children as models

CHILDREN, Retarded. See Mentally handicapped children

CHILDREN, Sick. See Sick children

CHILDREN, Spoiling of. See Children—Management and training

CHILDREN, Timid. See Timidity

CHILDREN; story. See De Hartog, J.

CHILDREN and art

Art as a language. E. V. Colton. il Sch Arts 69:14-15 S '69

Fun and art; values of discovery and the pure fun of art. C. J. McNaspy. America 120:543 My 3 '69

Showcase of student art; symposium, ed. by G. F. Horn. il Sch Arts 68:5, 8-39 Je '69

Very young in art; kindergarten class having spring art show. M. M. Day. il Sch Arts 69: 30-1 D '69

CHILDREN and death

Seven crows a secret; excerpts from Ox bells and fireflies. E. Buckler. Read Digest 94: 64-8 F '69

CHILDREN and music

How to make music part of your child's world. M. S. Welch. Redbook 132:95+ Ap '69

Touring in the Outback. C. Brumby. Opera N 34:13 Ja 10 '70

What pop music means to kids; with group-discussion program. N. Hentoff. Parents Mag 44:46-7+ My '69
See also
Metropolitan opera guild
Opera—Appreciation

CHILDREN and parents. See Parent-child relationship

CHILDREN and science

ABC's of science. M. W. Caprio. il Parents Mag 44:54-6+ My '69

CHILDREN and television. See Television broadcasting and children

CHILDREN as air pilots

Weekend pilot. F. K. Smith. Flying 85:126 S '69

CHILDREN as artists. See Childrens art

CHILDREN as authors

Other city; excerpts. W. Boyd and others. il Ebony 24:90-1+ Jl '69
See also
Childrens poems (by children)

CHILDREN as dancers

Visit to Konfitürenburg; past and present Nutcracker dancers. W. Terry. il Sat R 53: 28 Ja 10 '70

CHILDREN as journalists. See Childrens newspapers

CHILDREN as models

Child-model racket: what to avoid. il Good H 169:197 N '69

CHILDREN as photographers

Other city; excerpts. W. Boyd and others. il Ebony 24:90-1+ Jl '69

CHILDREN in boating

Junior yachting. See issues of Yachting

Keep your cool with the kids. B. Thaxton. Motor B 123:156+ Ap '69

CHILDREN in literature

See also
Negro children in literature

CHILDREN of Chocolate street; drama. See Kane, E. B.

CHILDREN of composers

Under the shadow; sons of famous composers. R. Jacobson. il Opera N 34:8-12 N 22 '69

CHILDREN of migrant laborers

Education

Children of Mexican-American migrants, aliens in their own homeland. H. Kirby. il Todays Ed 58:44-5 N '69

Regional program for migrant education. F. Lopez. Ed Digest 34:10-12 Ja '69

Rise and shine; Eastern Oregon program. J. Guernsey. il Am Ed 5:20-1 N '69

CHILDREN separated from their fathers. See Broken homes

CHILDRENS amusements

Fun for kids in the cities; ed. by P. Plawin. il Bet Hom & Gard 47:143-6 Ap '69

Secret of having fun. E. J. LeShan. il Read Digest 95:116-20 O '69
See also
Camping activities
Childrens parties
Games
Nature study
Play
Playhouses
Puppets and puppet plays
Story telling
Television broadcasting—Childrens programs

CHILDRENS art

Days of our talented youth. H. La Barre. McCalls 96:89+ S '69

Enrichment through informal art appreciation with related art activity. L. J. Bell. il Sch Arts 69:10-11 S '69

Group pictures, group organization. V. R. Jackson. il Design 70:4-7 mid-Wint '69

Junior McCall's club. See issues of McCall's

School artists. il Sch Arts 69:20-1 Ja '70

Showcase of student art; symposium, ed. by G. F. Horn. il Sch Arts 68:5, 8-39 Je '69

Whale of a time: school trip to Marine world, Redwood City, Calif. il Design 70:19 Sum '69

You see, this is the way it is! M. W. Brown. il Sch Arts 68:30-3 Ap '69
See also
Paper work

Competitions

Children's art: a case against contests. A. W. Beck. il Sch Arts 69:18-19 N '69

Yule gift from poor children; winners of contest on exhibition at the Junior museum of New York's Metropolitan museum of art. il Life 67:62-5 D 19 '69

Exhibitions

Very young in art; kindergarten class having spring art show. il Sch Arts 69:30-1 D '69

Yule gift from poor children; winners of contest on exhibition at the Junior museum of New York's Metropolitan museum of art. il Life 67:62-5 D 19 '69

CHILDRENS attitudes. See Attitudes

CHILDRENS ballets. See Ballets

CHILDRENS book centre, London. See Booksellers and bookselling—Childrens literature

CHILDRENS book clubs. See Book clubs

CHILDRENS book exhibits. See Book exhibits

CHILDRENS book week. See Book week

CHILDRENS books. See Childrens literature

CHILDRENS bookshops. See Booksellers and bookselling—Childrens literature

CHILDRENS bureau. See United States—Childrens bureau

CHILDRENS camps. See Camps

CHILDRENS center, New York. See New York (city)—Welfare, Department of

CHILDRENS clothes. See Clothing and dress
—Children
CHILDRENS courts. See Juvenile courts
CHILDRENS diseases. See Children—Diseases
CHILDRENS exhibitions
    See also
Childrens art—Exhibitions
CHILDRENS fantasies
    Fantasy and reality; children need both;
        with study-discussion program, by R.
        Strang. F. R. Horwich. bibliog il PTA Mag
        64:10-12, 34 D '69
CHILDRENS fears. See Fear
CHILDRENS friends. See Playmates
CHILDRENS furniture. See Furniture, Children
drens
CHILDRENS gardens
    Child gardeners, how to encourage success,
        discourage dropping out. il Sunset 142:200-1
        Je '69
    Children's gardens keep them interested. H.
        G. Wendler. il Horticulture 47:40-2+ Ja '69
    Garden projects and pastimes for children. il
        Home Gard 56:33-40 Jl '69
    Give the kids a garden of their own. R.
        Charles. il Parents Mag 44:77 Ja '69
    Green thumb, junior style. F. Johnson. il Org
        Gard & Farm 16:61 Je '69
    Meet some people who started gardening
        at ages five to sixteen. il Sunset 142:100-2
        Ap '69
    Three teen-age organic gardeners. M. Franz.
        il Org Gard & Farm 16:52-6 D '69
CHILDRENS homes. See Homes, Institutional
CHILDRENS homesickness. See Nostalgia
CHILDRENS hospital, Boston. See Children—
Hospitals
CHILDRENS hospitals. See Children—Hospitals
tals
CHILDRENS literature
    Black perspective in books for children. J.
        Thompson and G. Woodard. bibliog il Wilson Lib Bul 44:416-24 D '69
    Children's literature as a scholarly resource:
        the need for a national plan. J. Fraser.
        bibliog il Library J 94:4490-1 D '69
    Children's NBA. E. Geller. Library J 94:1693
        Ap 15 '69
    How to criticise and revise a juvenile book.
        K. Mason. il Writers Digest 49:52-5+ Ag '69
    How to select magazines and books for children. il Good H 169:184 D '69
    Inheritance of storytelling. L. Conger. Writer
        82:7+ Ja '69
    Little prince, a story for our time. P. Mooney.
        America 121:610-11+ D 20 '69
    NBA to be given for children's literature. Library J 94:250 Ja 15 '69
    Secret of Nancy Drew, pushing forty and going strong. A. Prager. il Sat R 52:18-19+
        Ja 25 '69
    Sense or sensibility; Inter-mountain conference on children's literature. Z. Sutherland.
        Sat R 52:42 Jl 19 '69
    Stevie; realism in a book about black children il Life 67:54-9 Ag 29 '69
    Summer reading for children. Am Home 72:78
        Jl '69
    Trade winds; realism in children's books. J.
        Beatty, jr. il Sat R 52:11 Je 14 '69
    Valid criticism for children's books; symposium, ed. by D. MacCann. bibliog il Wilson Lib Bul 44:394-457 D '69
    Where the novel went. L. Alexander. Sat R
        52:62 Mr 22 '69
    Wonderful world of books. R. H. Viguers. il
        Parents Mag 44:42+ N '69
    See also
Book selection
Book week
Booksellers and bookselling—Childrens literature
Childrens poetry
Childrens reading
Horn book magazine
International board on books for young people
National book award
Negroes in childrens literature
Newbery medal
Paperback books
Publishers and publishing—Childrens literature
Scientific literature for children
William Allen White children's book award

    Bibliography
Best books of the spring; ed. by L. N.
    Gernhardt and others. il Library J 94:2072-3
    My 15 '69

Best books of the year; selected by the
    editors of SLJ book review. L. N. Gerhardt and others. il Library J 94:4580-4 D
    15 '69
Blowing in the wind; books on black history
    and life in America. E. L. Morris. Library
    J 94:1298-300 Mr 15 '69
Bonus books. Z. Sutherland. Sat R 52:53-62
    My 10 '69
Book review. L. N. Gerhardt and others.
    See second issue of each month of Library
    journal
Booklist (title varies) comp. by P. Heins and
    others. See issues of Horn book magazine
Books. J. Stafford. New Yorker 45:191-2+
    D 13 '69
Books for boys and girls. D. E. Leland.
    See issues of Parents' magazine & better
    family living
Books for brotherhood. Commonweal 89:644-
    7 F 21 '69
Books for children. N. O'Gorman. Nation
    209:670-2 D 15 '69
Books for children (title varies) R. Gagliardo.
    See issues of PTA magazine
Books for young people. Z. Sutherland. See
    issues of Saturday review
Books for young westerners. D. Powers. Am
    West 6:49+ Ja '69
Books they loved; childhood reading of famous people. L. B. J. Robb. il McCalls 96:
    28+ Ja '69
Books to come; ed. by J. A. Baumholtz
    (cont) Library J 94:1353-85 Mr 15 '69
Books to come; ed. by E. N. Schwartz. Library J 94:3857-96 O 15 '69
Children, books, and living things; comp.
    by J. Verts. Am For 75:49-50+ D '69
Children's books. See issues of Publishers'
    weekly
Children's books at Christmastime. E. Sheehan. America 121:593-6+ D 13 '69
Children's books forecast. series. il Pub W
    196:167-77 Jl 14 '69
Children's books forecast: series; comp. by
    P. Bragg. il Pub W 195:161-7 F 17 '69
Children's books to remember. il Pub W 195:
    39 Je 30; 196:36-7 S 29 '69
Children's Christmas book list. Chr Cent
    86:1584-5 D 10 '69
Children's paperbacks (cont) Library J 94:
    324-6, 2135-8, 3163-91 Ja 15, My 15, S 15 '69
Exceptional books for children. Harp Baz
    102:192 S '69
Fanfare 1969; the Horn book's honor list;
    books of 1968. Horn Bk 45:554-5 O '69
Fiction fantasia. il Schol Teach Sec Teach
    Sup p 16+ O 6 '69
Juveniles to remember. il Pub W 195:34 Mr
    31 '69
Literary launchings. M. Eble. il Library J
    94:3789-91 O 15 '69
Nature books for a child's summer reading.
    Good H 169:147 Jl '69
1968 children's books of international interest. Todays Ed 58:76-9 N '69
Notable children's books 1968. il ALA Bul
    63:467-70 Ap '69; Same. Library J 94:2036+
    My 15 '69
Select don't settle, some select children's
    books of 1969. L. Russ. Pub W 196:62 N 17
    '69
Selected list of children's books. E. M.
    Graves. il Commonweal 91:252-4+ N 21 '69
Selected list of children's books (cont) L. P.
    Scanlon. il Commonweal 90:294+ My 23 '69
Some leading fall children's books. il Pub W
    196:96-130 Jl 14 '69
Some leading spring children's books. il
    Pub W 195:90-123 F 17 '69
Some 1969 books for and about Negro children. Pub W 197:76 Ja 5 '70
Summer fare for small fry. Chr Cent 86:1020
    Jl 30 '69
Tantrums and unicorns. M. Bacon. Atlan
    224:148+ D '69
Visions of sugarplums; Christmas books. Z.
    Sutherland. Sat R 52:28-9 D 20 '69
When you choose your own; Reading is fundamental booklist for children, program sponsored by the Ford foundation. il Library J
    94:269+ Ja 15 '69
    See also
Reading lists

        Book reviews
    See Book reviews

        Censorship
    See Censorship

        Exhibitions
    See Book exhibits

CHILDRENS literature—*Continued*

History and criticism

Higglety, pigglety, pop! or The man who tried to murder Mother Goose. M. Maxwell. bibliog f Horn Bk 45:392-4 Ag '69

Part played by Boston publishers of 1860-1900 in the field of children's books. H. L. Jones. bibliog il Horn Bk 45:20-8, 153-9, 329-36 F-Je '69

Illustrations

See Illustration of books and periodicals

Technique

Art of Elizabeth Enright. E. Cameron. il Horn Bk 45:641-51 D '69 (to be cont)

Confessions of a leprechaun. B. Turkle. il Pub W 196:133-6 Jl 14 '69

How to create live characters in a juvenile short story. N. Ainsworth. il Writers Digest 49:36-9+ D'69

Last buffalo killed in Tennessee; excerpt from address, 1967. W. O. Steele. il Horn Bk 45:196-9 Ap '69

Persuaded muse; writing for children. Z. Sutherland. Sat R 52:46 F 22 '69

Themes

See Literature—Themes

CHILDRENS literature (by children)
Junior McCall's club. See issues of McCall's

CHILDRENS literature, Influence of
To each his own, book. E. Hautzig. Pub W 195:124-5 F 17 '69

CHILDRENS manners. See Etiquette for children and youth

CHILDRENS music
See also
Composition (music)

CHILDRENS newspapers
Juvenile journalists find humor in a hospital. J. H. Pollack. il Todays Health 47: 12-13 Ap '69

CHILDRENS opera. See Music for children

CHILDRENS opinions
Perfect parent; survey of children's opinions. S. Blum. il McCalls 96:51+ Ag '69

CHILDRENS parties
Good grief, it's a birthday party; with recipes from the Peanuts cookbook. M. Happel. il Ladies Home J 86:122-3+ O '69
Wild party. il Ladies Home J 86:120 O '69

CHILDRENS periodicals
279 editors looking for writers. K. M. Sommers. il Writers Digest 49:48-51+ S '69
See also
Brownies' book (periodical)
St Nicholas (periodical)

Bibliography

Magazines for kids. il Changing T 23:33-4 My '69

CHILDRENS pets. See Pets

CHILDRENS phonograph records. See Phonograph records—Childrens records

CHILDRENS plays
See also
Dramatization in education

Texts

Middle grades; lower grades. See issues of Plays

CHILDRENS poems (by children)
Childhood is a strange book; excerpts from address, 1969. V. Sorensen. il PTA Mag 64:13-15 N '69
Culture begins at home; poems from issues of Foxfire. Sat R 52:59 Jl 19 '69
Horn book league. See issues of Horn book magazine
Junior McCall's club. See issues of McCall's
Poetry by children. L. Clark. Horn Bk 45:15-19 F '69

CHILDRENS poems (for children)
See also
Mother Goose

CHILDRENS poetry
Life ain't been no crystal stair; address, 1968. N. Larrick. il Library J 94:843-5 F 15 '69
Poetry is the natural language of children. N. Larrick. il Parents Mag 44:46-7+ Ag '69
Tune beyond us; the bases of choice. M. C. Livingston. bibliog il Wilson Lib Bul 44: 448-55 D '69
See also
Childrens poems (by children)
Childrens songs

CHILDRENS private libraries. See Libraries, Private

CHILDRENS quarrels. See Quarrels

CHILDRENS reading
Guidelines for black books: an open letter to juvenile editors; adaptation of address, May 8, 1969. A. Baker. Pub W 196:131-3 Jl 14 '69
Reading can be fun everywhere; Reading is fundamental program, sponsored by Ford foundation. K. W. Lumley. il Sr Schol 94: Schol Teach 21 Ja 31 '69
Some notes on fantasy and realism. C. B. Grannis. Pub W 196:143 Jl 14 '69
To each his own, book. E. Hautzig. Pub W 195:124-5 F 17 '69
Too much teaching; too little reading. R. E. Martin. Ed Digest 35:38-40 S '69
Washington, D.C: reading is fun-damental; Ford foundation and Smithsonian institution program. J. Sandler. il Wilson Lib Bul 43:881-5 My '69
What does research in reading reveal: about attitudes toward reading? J. R. Squire. bibliog Engl J 58:523-33 Ap '69
When a child a book & a teacher get together; Scholastic Lucky book club. il Sr Schol 94:Schol Teach 16 Ja 31 '69
When you choose your own; Reading is fundamental booklist for children. program sponsored by the Ford foundation. il Library J 94:269+ Ja 15 '69
See also
Childrens literature
Childrens periodicals
Libraries, Childrens—Projects

CHILDRENS rooms
Children's world, fantasy with common sense. il House & Gard 135:64-7 Ja '69
Color girls bright, color boys bold. H. Brown. il Am Home 72:74-7 N '69
Do a daredevil room. il Seventeen 28:80-1 Ja '69
For toy storage, and for work space. il Sunset 142:112 Mr '69
Room that's great for two active boys. . . and a room that's perfect for study. il Bet Hom & Gard 47:64-5 O '69
Small wonders, a boy's room and a girl's room. il Redbook 133:110-13+ Jl '69
Two basements into racket rooms for children. il House & Gard 135:126-7 My '69
Very special little girl's room. il House B 111:81-5 D '69
Young rooms with verve. il Bet Hom & Gard 47:170 N '69

CHILDRENS sayings. See Children—Sayings

CHILDRENS seat belts. See Safety belts

CHILDREN'S services division, American library association. See American library association—Children's services division

CHILDRENS shoes. See Shoes

CHILDRENS shopping. See Shopping and shoppers

CHILDRENS songs
But what goes after the third line? Little Orphan Annie theme song. R. Gehman. Sat R 52:4 Jl 12 '69
Writing songs for children. K. S. Rieder. Writers Digest 49:56-7+ Je '69
See also
Mother Goose

CHILDRENS squabbles. See Quarrels

CHILDRENS stories
Especially for children (cont) H. Aldrich. il Negro Hist Bul 31:14-15 D '68; 32:13-14 Ja '69
Great wolf and the good woodsman; excerpts. H. Hoover. il Parents Mag 44:44-7 D '69
Unfinished story. See issues of Today's education

Technique

See Childrens literature—Technique

CHILDRENS stories (by children)
Children tell stories, an analysis of fantasy, by E. G. Pitcher and E. Prelinger. Review N Y Times Mag p 132+ N 16 '69. P. Feinstein

CHILDREN'S television workshop. See Television broadcasting—Childrens programs; Television in education

CHILDRENS theater. See Theater, Childrens

CHILDRENS thefts. See Shoplifting

CHILDRENS toilet preparations. See Toilet preparations

CHILDRENS toiletries. See Toilet preparations

CHINA (People's Republic)——*Continued*

Diplomatic and consular service

Diplomatic thaw. Newsweek 73:43-4 F 10 '69

Economic conditions

China's economy: a balance sheet after twenty years. J. S. Prybyla. bibliog f Cur Hist 57:135-41+ S '69

Economic realities and China's political economics. R. F. Dernberger. il Bul Atom Sci 25:34-42 F '69

Economic policy

Economic realities and China's political economics. R. F. Dernberger. il Bul Atom Sci 25:34-42 F '69

Economics of Maoism. J. Gray. il Bul Atom Sci 25:42-51 F '69

New leap. Time 93:23 Mr 21 '69

Economic relations

Red China: world's no. 1 enigma. il U S News 66:52-4 Mr 31 '69

Foreign opinion

Russian

Watching Russia's China watchers; observations of Newsweek's Hong Kong correspondent. S. Liu. il Newsweek 74:51 Jl 21 '69

Foreign relations

Bayonets and bomb shelters. il Time 94:35 D 19 '69

China: a positive policy. W. V. Kennedy. America 121:87-90 Ag 16 '69

China's foreign policy in historical perspective. J. K. Fairbank. For Affairs 47:449-63 Ap '69

Communist China 1969; foreign and domestic policy; address, April 1, 1969. P. Lin. Vital Speeches 35:485-97 Je 1 '69

Global triangle. il Newsweek 74:26-7 D 29 '69

Next foreign minister? Time 94:58+ D 5 '69

Now's time to talk with China. E. Friedman. il Bul Atom Sci 25:10-11+ Je '69

One-man diplomacy? R. Harris. il Bul Atom Sci 25:60-5 F '69

Red China after twenty years of Mao: threat to world peace? il U S News 67:66-8 O 13 '69

Revolutionary hiatus. C. P. Fitzgerald. il Bul Atom Sci 25:53-60 F '69

Shifting great power politics; the end of U S-Soviet hegemony. Cur 108:61-4 Je '69

War scare. Time 94:38 N 28 '69

See also

China (People's Republic)—Boundaries

Albania

Red China in Europe. D. Bligh. America 120:280-1 Mr 8 '69

Asia

China and southeast Asia. S. C. Y. Pan. bibliog f Cur Hist 57:164-7+ S '69

Great Britain

Tit for tat; exchange of prisoners. il Newsweek 74:65 O 27 '69

India

China's relations with India and Pakistan. H. Kapur. bibliog f il Cur Hist 57:156-63 S '69

Japan

China; how does the study of China in the United States compare with that in Japan? H. Yu. Chr Cent 86:1124 Ag 27 '69

Laos

Chinese highwaymen. il Time 94:63 D 5 '69

Nepal

Can a ministate find true happiness in a world dominated by protagonist powers? The Nepal case. L. E. Rose and R. Dial. bibliog f Ann Am Acad 386:89-101 N '69

Pakistan

China's relations with India and Pakistan. H. Kapur. bibliog f il Cur Hist 57:156-63 S '69

Russia

Battle for the backyards. Time 93:38 Ap 4 '69

China's door northward; confrontation between the Soviet Union and Communist China? America 120:443 Ap 12 '69

Chinese blinked. il Time 94:31-2 O 17 '69

Even money; Sino-Soviet battlefield. il Newsweek 73:58-9 Mr 17 '69

Fastest guns in the East? il Sr Schol 94:14 Mr 21 '69

Fraught with grave consequences. il Newsweek 73:44+ Mr 24 '69

If Russia and China fight. il Newsweek 74:35+ Ag 18 '69

Limited war or nuclear holocaust? R. S. Elegant. Cur 112:48-52 N '69

Moscow v. Peking: offensive diplomacy. il Time 93:22 Mr 21 '69

Sino-Soviet tensions and American foreign policy. D. F. Halloran. Cath World 209:151-5 Jl '69

Three-way international sparring match. America 120:154 F 8 '69

Twenty years of Sino-Soviet relations. F. Michael. Cur Hist 57:150-5+ S '69

Urgent question that dominates the Asian heartland today is: will there be war between Russia and China? H. E. Salisbury. il N Y Times Mag p 10-11+ Jl 27 '69

Violence on the Sino-Soviet border. il Time 93:32-3 Mr 14 '69

Why Russia and China prepare for war. il U S News 67:32-4 S 15 '69

See also

Sino-Russian border dispute, 1969-

Underdeveloped areas

Peking's revolutionary strategy in the developing world: the failures of success. T. W Robinson. bibliog f Ann Am Acad 386:64-77 N '69

United States

Back-scratching between Peking and Washington. Chr Cent 86:308 Mr 5 '69

China: on the verge of speaking terms. il Time 94:13 D 26 '69

China spurns U.S. bid; cancellation of talks in Warsaw. Sr Schol 94:18 Mr 7 '69

Crumbling castles; cancellation of talks. Newsweek 73:42 Mr 3 '69

Five principles, a new approach. M. Selk. Bul Atom Sci 25:78 F '69

How we almost went to war with China. A. S. Whiting. il Look 33:76-7+ Ap 29 '69

Most powerful country; most populous country; address, January 1969. J. W. Fulbright. Vital Speeches 35:258-62 F 15 '69

Sino-American detente? L. H. Battistini. Cur 104:55-64 F '69

Three-way international sparring match. America 120:154 F 8 '69

Intellectual life

China; how does the study of China in the United States compare with that in Japan? H. Yu. Chr Cent 86:1124 Ag 27 '69

Politics and government

China. H. Yu. See last issue of each month of Christian century

Chinese communist leadership. K. Y. Hsu. bibliog f Cur Hist 57:129-34+ S '69

Errant army, stubborn peasants. il Time 93:30 F 21 '69

Mao and the new mandate. E. Snow. New Repub 160:17-21 My 10 '69

Mao's health and China's leadership. il Time 94:24 S 26 '69

Most powerful country; most populous country; address, January 1969. J. W. Fulbright. Vital Speeches 35:258-62 F 15 '69

Now's time to talk with China. E. Friedman. il Bul Atom Sci 25:10-11+ Je '69

Peking puzzles; celebration of Communist China's 20th anniversary. Time 94:41 O 10 '69

Red China after twenty years of Mao: threat to world peace? il U S News 67:66-8 O 13 '69

Red China: twenty years after. il Newsweek 74:48-9 O 13 '69

Rethinking U.S. China policy; Time essay. il Time 93:48-9 Je 6 '69

Spirit of Chinese politics, by L. W. Pye. Review

Nat R 21:550-1 Je 3 '69. D. N. Rowe

Summing up; People's liberation army runs China. Newsweek 73:34+ Mr 31 '69

Where China stands now: an introduction. D. Wilson. Bul Atom Sci 25:4-10 F '69

See also

China (People's Republic)—Constitution
Communism—China (People's Republic)
Communist party (China [People's Republic])

Religious institutions and affairs

Locked-in generation. D. Hillis. Chr Today 13:10-11 My 23 '69

Religion in red China. L. La Dany. America 120:282-3 Mr 8 '69

See also

Christians in China

CHINA (People's Republic)—*Continued*

Social conditions

Glimpses of everyday life. il Newsweek 74: 50+ O 13 '69

Red China: world's no. 1 enigma. il U S News 66:52-4 Mr 31 '69

See also

Communism—China (People's Republic)

CHINA (porcelain) See Pottery

CHINA asters. See Asters

CHINA-fir

China-fir. J. V. Watkins. Horticulture 47:18 Ap '69

CHINA trade paintings. See Painting, Chinese

CHINATOWN, New York city. See New York (city)—Chinatown

CHINATOWN, San Francisco. See San Francisco—Chinatown

CHINESE AMERICANS

Americans from Asia: the East came to the West. il Sr Schol 94:12-17 Ap 25 '69

CHINESE atomic bomb test. See Atomic bombs —Testing

CHINESE bronzes. See Bronzes

CHINESE cabbage

Cabbage, Chinese style. W. Masson. il Org Gard & Farm 16:80 Ap '69

Try a self-weeding garden! canopy of soil-shading leaves. J. Krill. il Org Gard & Farm 16:28-9 Jl '69

CHINESE cookery. See Cookery, Chinese

CHINESE enamels. See Enamel and enameling

CHINESE hydrogen bomb. See Hydrogen bombs

CHINESE in Hawaii

Romance Honolulu style; the life of Chinn Ho. J. Bishop. il Read Digest 95:136-40 D '69

CHINESE in the United States

New yellow peril; Chinatown gangs. T. Wolfe. Esquire 72:190-9+ D '69

See also

Chinese Americans

CHINESE-Indian border dispute, 1957-. See Sino-Indian border dispute, 1957-

CHINESE-JAPANESE war, 1937-1945

Aerial operations

See also

Panay (gunboat) incident

CHINESE opera. See Opera, Chinese

CHINESE refugees. See Refugees, Chinese

CHINESE restaurant syndrome. See Food allergy

CHINESE-Russian border disputes. See Sino-Russian border disputes

CHINESE scientists. See Scientists, Chinese

CHINESE studies (Sinology)

Learning about China; three books. O. Schell. Nation 209:58-60 Jl 14 '69

Watching Russia's China watchers; observations of Newsweek's Hong Kong correspondent. S. Liu. il Newsweek 74:51 Jl 21 '69

CHINH, Truong. See Truong Chinh

CHINITZ, Allen. See McDevitt, H. O. jt. auth.

CHINITZ, Wallace

Rotary engines; with biographical sketch. Sci Am 220:12, 90-9 bibliog (p 132) F '69

CHINN, Herman I.

International scientific co-operation. Bul Atom Sci 25:34-5+ N '69

CHINOOK winds. See Winds

CHIO, K. S. and others

Peroxidation of subcellular organelles: formation of lipofuscinlike fluorescent pigments. bibliog Science 166:1535-6 D 19 '69

CHIPMAN, David M. and Sharon, Nathan

Mechanism of lysozyme action. bibliog Science 165:454-65 Ag 1 '69

CHIPPENDALE, Thomas

Clockmaker and cabinetmaker. N. Goodison. il Antiques 95:825-9 Je '69

CHIPPENDALE furniture. See Furniture, English

CHIRICAHUA NATIONAL MONUMENT

Wonderland of giant rocks. il Sunset 143:41 O '69

CHIROPRACTIC

Chiropractic: issues and answers; excerpts from At your own risk; with introd. by J. A. Sabatier, jr. R. L. Smith. il Todays Health 48:64-9 Ja '70

HEW rejects chiropractic. Todays Health 47: 54-5 Ap '69

CHISHOLM, Freddie

Shrimp co-op makes blacks own bosses. il por Ebony 25:106-8+ N '69

CHISHOLM, Shirley A.

As the first black woman congressman herself puts it, this is fighting Shirley Chisholm. il pors N Y Times Mag p32-3+ Ap 13 '69

Congresswoman Shirley Chisholm. por Vogue 153:170-1 My '69

First black woman on Capitol hill. il pors Ebony 24:58-9 F '69

CHISHOLM, William Hardenbergh

Paper and the book; excerpts from address, November 1969. Pub W 196:50+ D 1 '69

CHISSELL, Noble

They danced till they dropped. D. Adler. il por Life 67:60-1 Jl 25 '69

CHITTUM, Donald

Current chronicle. Mus Q 55:91-102, 401-7 Ja, Jl '69

CHIU, Celia C. and others

Oxytocin: crystal data of a seleno analog. bibliog Science 163:925-6 F 28 '69

CHIVALRY

Age of chivalry. Review

Nat Geog il 136:544-51 O '69. M. B. Grosvenor

See also

Courtly love

CHLORAMPHENICOL

Chloramphenicol: effects on mouse myeloma cells in tissue culture. B. K. Hartman and others. bibliog il Science 165:297-8 Jl 18 '69

Chloroplast ribosomes: stereospecificity of inhibition by chloramphenicol. R. J. Ellis. bibliog il Science 163:477-8 Ja 31 '69

CHLOROPHENYLALANINE. See Phenylalanine

CHLOROPHYLL

See also

Chloroplasts

CHLOROPLASTS

Chloroplast replication and growth in tobacco. R. Boasson and W. M. Laetsch. bibliog il Science 166:749-51 N 7 '69

Paramagnetic unit in spinach subchloroplast particles: estimation of size. E. C. Weaver and others. bibliog il Science 165:906-7 Ag 29 '69

Uptake of isolated chloroplasts by mammalian cells. M. M. K. Nass. bibliog il Science 165:1128-31 S 12 '69

CHLORPROMAZINE

Hallucinogen-tranquilizer interaction: its nature. M. F. Halasz and others. bibliog il Science 164:569-71 My 2 '69

Reticular stimulation and chlorpromazine: an animal model for schizophrenic over-arousal. C. Kornetsky and M. Eliasson. bibliog il Science 165:1273-4 S 19 '69

Unexpected adrenergic effect of chlorpromazine: eating elicited by injection into rat hypothalamus. S. F. Leibowitz and N. E. Miller. bibliog il Science 165:609-11 Ag 8 '69

CHO, Philip

Week of song as well as singers. I. Kolodin. Sat R 52:61 N 22 '69

CHOATE, Joseph E.

Facts and figures. Yachting 125:66+ Ja '69

CHOATE school, Wallingford, Conn. See Private schools

CHOCO Indians. See Indians of Central America

CHOCOLATE desserts. See Desserts

CHOCOLATE tarts. See Tarts

CHOCOLATE tree. See Cacao

CHOCTAW Indians

Cerumen types in Choctaw Indians. L. M. Martin and J. F. Jackson. Science 163:677-8 F 14 '69

CHOGHA MISH. See Iran—Antiquities

CHOICE (periodical)

What's your choice? P. M. Doiron. ALA Bul 63:1505 D '69

CHOICE of college. See College. Choice of

CHOICE of occupation. See Occupations; Vocational guidance

CHOKE, Automobile. See Automobile engines —Choke

CHOKECHERRY. See Cherry trees

CHOLERA, Hog. See Hog cholera

CHOLERA toxins. See Toxins and antitoxins

CHOLESTEROL

Adrenal cholesterol: localization by electron-microscope autoradiography. H. L. Moses and others. bibliog il Science 163:1203-5 Mr 14 '69

Breaking down cholesterol. Sci Digest 66:54 D '69

No more heart attacks. R. H. Berg. il Look 33:30-2 F 4 '69

Serum cholesterol reduction by chromium in hypercholesterolemic rats. H. W. Staub and others. bibliog il Science 166:746-7 N 7 '69

CHOLINE
Potential energy fields about nitrogen in choline and ethanolamine; biological function at cellular surfaces. J. E. Zull and A. J. Hopfinger. bibliog il Science 165:512-13 Ag 1 '69
See also
Acetylcholine
Hemicholinium

CHOMSKY, Noam
Books. G. Steiner. New Yorker 45:217-18+ N 15 '69
Intellectual power elite. R. Sklar. Nation 208:373-4 Mr 24 '69
Position of Noam Chomsky. L. Abel. Commentary 47:35-44 My '69; Discussion. 48:9-10+ Ag '69

CHONDRITES. See Meteorites

CHOPIN, Frédéric François
Chopin without tears. F. V. Grunfeld. il por Horizon 11:84-93 Spr '69
Van Cliburn recital; the two Chopin sonatas. C. J. Luten. Am Rec G 35:373 Ja '69

CHOPS. See Cookery—Meat

CHORAL groups and societies
History of the Peerless quartet. J. Walsh. il Hobbies 74:38-40+ D '69
Lively arts; second International university choral festival, at Lincoln Center. R. Hemming. il Sr Schol 94:18 Ap 18 '69

CHORAL music
See also
Phonograph records—Choral music

CHORAL singing
Texas Southern university chorus, best. D. Amram. Vogue 153:98 Ja 15 '69
See also
Choral groups and societies
Phonograph records—Choral singing

CHOREA. See Movement disorders

CHOREOGRAPHY
Choreographer became: me! V. H. Swisher. il Dance Mag 43:39-41 S '69
Choreography of the object. N. J. Loftis. il Craft Horiz 29:10-13+ Mr '69
Dancing Bach. W. Hilton; R. Tureck. il Dance Mag 43:47-51+ O '69
Introduction to music for the choreographer. R. G. Long. il Dance Mag 43:63-5 F '69
Making of a ballet; The eternal idol. W. Terry. il Sat R 52:58-60 N 29 '69
New direction; direction and choreography of Elmer Gantry and other musicals; interview. O. White. New Yorker 45:19-22 D 27 '69
Norman Walker; a romantic poet, a sculptor in space. K. Cunningham. il Dance Mag 43:42-5 D '69
Opera primer; how do you make a dance? S. J. Cohen. il Opera N 33:26-9 F 1 '69
Steps from Stuttgart. W. Terry. il Sat R 52:40+ My 31 '69
See also
Dance notation

CHORES, Childrens. See Occupations for children

CHOROID plexus. See Brain

CHOTINER, Murray M.
His own man. Newsweek 73:27 Mr 3 '69

CHOU, En-lai
Surprise red summit after years of conflict. por U S News 67:11 S 22 '69
When good Communists get together. il por Newsweek 74:43 S 22 '69

CHOW, Ven Te
Room with a built-in deluge. il por Life 66:77-8 Je 6 '69

CHOWDER
Catch of the season; bouillabaisse. C. Claiborne. il N Y Times Mag p52 Ag 3 '69
Cioppino: California bouillabaisse; with recipe. E. Alston. il Look 33:92 Je 24 '69
Eat; soupmaking. M. Cantwell. Mlle 69:94+ My '69
Hearty chowders; with recipes. il Bet Hom & Gard 47:12+ D '69
Soups and chowders; prize tested recipes. il Bet Hom & Gard 47:99-100 F '69
Two great fish soups from the Mediterranean. il Sunset 142:208+ Ap '69

CHOWINS, Christopher
Cemetery planting. Horticulture 47:26-7+ F '69

CHRIS-CRAFT industries, incorporated
Boats are for people. B. Robinson. il Yachting 126:71+ O '69
Piper proves elusive prize. il Bsns W p62+ Ag 16 '69

CHRISPEELS, Maarten J. See Sadava, D. jt. auth.

CHRIST. See Jesus Christ

CHRIST, Henry I.
Self-fulfilling prophecy and the haiku. Engl J 58:1189-91 N '69

CHRISTENING. See Baptism

CHRISTENSEN, B. G. and others
Phosphonomycin: structure and synthesis. bibliog Science 166:123-5 O 3 '69

CHRISTENSEN, Dan
To see, to feel. il Time 93:64-5 Mr 30 '69

CHRISTGAU, Robert
Secular music (cont) Esquire 71:62+ Ap '69

CHRISTIAN, Charlie
Guitar by Charlie Christian. M. Williams. Sat R 52:65 My 17 '69

CHRISTIAN, George Busby, 1873-1951
How Harding saved the Versailles treaty. R. K. Murray. il por Am Heritage 20:66-7+ D '68

CHRISTIAN, Richard Carlton
Advertising agency; address, April 17, 1969. Vital Speeches 35:696-9 S 1 '69

CHRISTIAN and missionary alliance
Bangkok conference loosens the western grip. W. T. Bray and G. E. Roffe. Chr Today 13:51-2 Ap 11 '69
Sounds of the times. D. E. Kucharsky. Chr Today 13:45 Je 6 '69

CHRISTIAN art and symbolism
Art. R. L. Sundbye. Chr Cent 86:186-7 F 5 '69
Christian art in Africa and Asia, by A. Lehmann. Review
Chr Cent 86:1283 O 8 '69. R. Steele
Cuzco's mystical dolls. G. de Zéndegui. il Américas 21:7-12 Je '69
See also
Church architecture
Cross and crosses
Glass painting and staining
Jesus Christ—Art

CHRISTIAN associations. See Young men's Christian association

CHRISTIAN booksellers association
Growth marks 20th session of Christian booksellers. il Pub W 196:61-2 S 22 '69

CHRISTIAN camps. See Camps

CHRISTIAN century (periodical)
Award for the Century; at A.C.P.'s annual convention. Chr Cent 86:767 Je 4 '69
Beyond rhetoric? Letters to the editor regarding blank editorial page. Chr Cent 86:1019 Jl 30 '69
Did we endorse the Black manifesto? Chr Cent 86:894 Jl 2 '69
Ex oriente sex? cover photo on March 5, 1969 issue. Chr Cent 86:495 Ap 9 '69
Good-by to Gothic; discussion. Chr Cent 86:184 F 5 '69

CHRISTIAN century foundation
Announcement; new business manager of the Christian century foundation. Chr Cent 86:365 Mr 19 '69
Invisible hands. A. Geyer. Chr Cent 86:1507 N 26 '69

CHRISTIAN church, Disciples of Christ
Disciples heed minority-group needs. E. E. Plowman. Chr Today 13:56 S 12 '69
Power struggle among Disciples. H. E. Fey. Chr Cent 86:1187-9 S 17 '69; Reply. C. H. Bayer. 86:1402-3 O 29 '69

CHRISTIAN colleges. See Church colleges

CHRISTIAN communication. See Communication (theology)

CHRISTIAN crusade (organization)
Crusaders in Tulsa. America 121:81 Ag 16 '69

CHRISTIAN democrats (Chile). See Political parties—Chile

CHRISTIAN democrats (Germany) See Political parties—Germany (Federal Republic)

CHRISTIAN democrats (Latin America) See Political parties—Latin America

CHRISTIAN education. See Religious education

CHRISTIAN ethics
Answer to corruption. B. Graham. Nations Bsns 57:46-9 S '69
Christian morals. R. McCormick. America 122:5-6 Ja 10 '70
Co-belligerent reconciliation. R. L. Love. Chr Today 14:38 N 21 '69
Ethical theory and moral practice. J. M. Gustafson. Chr Cent 86:1613-17 D 17 '69
Exit for ethicists; with reply. J. G. Milhaven. il Commonweal 91:135-41 O 31 '69
Man has changed; God hasn't. D. Lawrence. U S News 67:76 Jl 7 '69
Ministry of admonition. Chr Today 14:27 D 5 '69
Moral law. R. Haughton. Cath World 208:197-8 F '69
Morals, marriage and youth; discussion at the Dutch council. H. Fleddermann and F. L. Ingram. America 120:194-6 F 15 '69; Reply. H. McKemie. 120:317 Mr 22 '69
Realities. L. N. Bell. Chr Today 14:28+ D 5 '69
Test tube fertilization; the field of genetic research and moral theology. America 120:292 Mr 15 '69

CHRISTIAN ethics—*Continued*
Toward a contemporary Christian moral philosophy. T. A. Wassmer. Cath World 209: 115-20 Je '69; Discussion. 210:4 O '69
Word. V. P. McCorry. See issues of America

See also
Church and social problems
Conscience
Virtues
War and religion

CHRISTIAN humanism. See Humanism

CHRISTIAN life
Being Christian in an affluent society. N. V. Hope. Chr Today 13:7-8 F 14 '69
Christian answers to immaturity. O. S. Walters. Chr Today 13:3-6 My 23 '69
Hole in your head. A. H. Leitch. Chr Today 13:38-9 Ap 25 '69
Instruction by metaphor. V. P. McCorry. America 120:148-inside back cover F 1 '69
It can happen here. L. N. Bell. Chr Today 14:20-1 Ja 2 '70
Joy of family life. B. Graham. il Good H 169:103+ O '69
Light in darkness. L. N. Bell Chr Today 13:29-30 Ja 31 '69
Man in the cutaway suit. L. R. Ward. il Commonweal 90:165-7 Ap 25 '69
New dimensions in Catholic life, by B. J. Cooke. Review
America 120:113-15 Ja 25 '69. R. J. Burant
On being the people of God. L. Morris. Chr Today 14:40 D 19 '69
Religious life and the religious layman. J. O'Connor. Cath World 208:199-204 F '69
Testing for maturity. A. Bustanoby. Chr Today 14:22-3 N 21 '69
Three American illusions; excerpts from address, Novemeber 19, 1969. B. Graham. Chr Today 14:12-14 D 19 '69
When should a Christian weep? J. R. W. Stott. Chr Today 14:3-5 N 7 '69

See also
Christian ethics
Conduct of life
Conversion
Holiness
Piety

CHRISTIAN ministry (periodical)
Christian ministry: a new beginning. Chr Cent 86:733 My 28 '69

CHRISTIAN missions. See Missions

CHRISTIAN movements, Student. See Student Christian movements

CHRISTIAN peace conference, Prague. See Peace conferences

CHRISTIAN psychiatry. See Psychiatry and religion

CHRISTIAN witness. See Witness bearing (Christianity)

CHRISTIAN year
Fracas about saints. C. J. McNaspy. America 120:608 My 24 '69
See also
Advent

CHRISTIANITY
Because Christ arose: the new man. J. F. Miller. Chr Today 13:8-9 S 26 '69
Bridge between two cultures. R. Haughton. Cath World 209:53-4 My '69
Christian faith and secular faiths. L. Paul. Chr Cent 86:477-81 Ap 9 '69
Christianity and aesthetics: conflict or correlation? V. R. Mollenkott. Chr Today 13: 6-9 My 9 '69
Christianity: the durable establishment. H. O. J. Brown. Chr Today 13:3-5 Ja 31 '69
Faith and conviction; excerpt from Faith under challenge. H. Fries. il Cath World 210:119-23 D '69
Growth; the kingdom of heaven. V. P. McCorry. America 121:479-80 N 15 '69
Inclusive but exclusive. Chr Today 13:27 F 28 '69
Interview with Malcolm Boyd; ed. by P. Granfield. M. Boyd. Cath World 208:208-13 F '69
Intimidated Christians. A. Lunn; discussion. Nat R 21:206+ Mr 11 '69
Life's chief discoveries; reminiscences of an octogenarian. J. A. Mackay. Chr Today 14:3-5 Ja 2 '70
Myth of the Judeo-Christian tradition; excerpts. A. A. Cohen. Commentary 48:73-7 N '69
On making Christianity habitable. K. Rexroth. Commonweal 91:199-202 N 14 '69
One true religion. H. K. Stothard. Chr Today 13:8-13 Ag 1 '69
Peripheral Christianity; reprint from June 18, 1964 issue. L. N. Bell. Chr Today 13:30+ S 26 '69
Rational Christianity. E. Trueblood. Chr Today 13:3-5 F 14 '69

Universe and two chairs; excerpt from Death in the city. F. A. Schaeffer. Chr Today 13: 8-11 Ap 25 '69
See also
Apocalyptic thought
Catholic church
Christian ethics
Church
Fundamentalism
God
Jesus Christ—Teachings
Paul, Saint—Teaching
Protestantism
Religion
Religion and science
Theism
Theology

CHRISTIANITY, Primitive. See Church history—Primitive and early church

CHRISTIANITY and communism. See Communism and religion

CHRISTIANITY and culture
Mind to win. C. F. H. Henry. Chr Today 13: 24-5 Ap 11 '69
New heaven and new earth; with reply. A. Gibson. il Commonweal 91:117-23 O 31 '69
Religious cultures, high and low. D. Cutler. il Commonweal 91:156-60 O 31 '69

CHRISTIANITY and democracy. See Religion and democracy

CHRISTIANITY and economics
Bread, not circuses, for the world. J. R. Nelson. Chr Cent 86:438-9 Ap 2 '69

CHRISTIANITY and international affairs. See Church and international relations

CHRISTIANITY and law. See Religion and law

CHRISTIANITY and other religions
Across a deep canyon: the challenge to Christian-Jewish relations. J. T. Pawlikowski. Commonweal 90:313-15+ My 30 '69; Discussion. 90:427+ Jl 11 '69
Black Wasps. Trans-Action 6:8-9 My '69
Christianity's greatest challenge. C. G. Fry. Chr Today 14:9-12 N 7 '69
Christians and Jews: an inconclusive quest for accord. M. E. Marty. Chr Cent 86:206-7 F 12 '69; Reply. S. M. Silver. 86:523-4 Ap 16 '69
Confronting other religions. C. F. H. Henry. Chr Today 13:31 Ag 1 '69
Ex oriente lux? F. Holck and E. Cate. Chr Cent 86:315-18 Mr 5 '69; Discussion. 86:624-5 Ap 30 '69
Jeshua, a basic encounter for young Israelis; with editorial comment. R. C. Dodds. America 121:626, 630-2 D 27 '69
Judaism and Christian education: the Strober report. Chr Cent 86:1410 N 5 '69; Discussion. 86:1583 D 10 '69
Mideast raid reaction mars Christian-Jewish relations. Chr Today 13:36 Ja 31 '69
Possibilities of Christian-Moslem dialogue; excerpts from interview. G. Habib. Chr Cent 86:111 Ja 22 '69
Southern Baptist, Jewish dialogue: a first. Chr Cent 86:1306 O 15 '69
Toward Judah; sermon delivered at Riverside church, New York. C. Marney. Chr Cent 86: 1345-8 O 22 '69

CHRISTIANITY and psychiatry. See Psychiatry and religion

CHRISTIANITY and science. See Religion and science

CHRISTIANITY and social problems. See Church and social problems

CHRISTIANITY and the arts. See Religion and the arts

CHRISTIANITY and the world. See Church and the world

CHRISTIANITY and war. See War and religion

CHRISTIANITY today (periodical)
Who's captive to what? Chr Cent 86:702-3 My 21 '69

CHRISTIANS
Christian and change. J. Hitchcock. Chr Cent 87:7-11 Ja 7 '70
Manners of the Christians. Chr Today 13:27 Ap 11 '69

CHRISTIANS and Jews. See Christianity and other religions

CHRISTIANS in Africa
Another base. Time 95:35 Ja 12 '70
Christianity still on the move. Chr Today 14:30-1 D 19 '69

CHRISTIANS in Asia
Encouraging missionary movement in Asian churches. W. H. Chua. Chr Today 13:9-12 Je 20 '69

CHRISTIANS in Burma
W.C.C. official finds high morale and growth in Burmese churches. Chr Cent 86:673 My 14 '69

CHRISTIANS in China
China. H. Yu. Chr Cent 86:430 Mr 26 '69

CHRISTIANS in Czechoslovakia
Environment of faith. Chr Cent 86:107 Ja 22 '69

CHRISTIANS in eastern Europe
Gospel in east Europe; Pastors' conference in Novi Sad, Yugoslavia. C. F. H. Henry. Chr Today 14:39-40 O 10 '69

CHRISTIANS in Iraq
Iraqi Christians martyred. J. J. van Capelleveen. Chr Today 13:47 S 26 '69

CHRISTIANS in Russia
Russian letter to Gene. J. J. Van Capelleveen. Chr Today 14:47 O 10 '69
Valya and Vadim struggle for religious faith. M. Bourdeaux. America 121:614-16 D 20 '69

CHRISTIE, Agatha
Agatha Christie: the world's most mysterious woman. W. Petschek. il pors McCalls 96:80-1+ F '69

CHRISTIE, Trevor L.
Cleveland on the Cape. Sat R 52:56+ Mr 8 '69

CHRISTIE'S
Rivals. il Newsweek 74:74+ Ag 18 '69

CHRISTINE, Sister
Recipe for a short story. Writer 82:17-21 D '69

CHRISTINE Winkelman, Sister. See Winkelman, C.

CHRISTMAN, Gene
Fences; photographs. Am West 6:33-9 My '69

CHRISTMAS, Louise
To answer a letter. por Sr Schol 94:Schol Teach 28 Ja 17 '69

CHRISTMAS
At Christmas I remember... M. Mead. Redbook 134:66+ D '69
Christmas. X. Pové. Harp Baz 103:100A D '69
Christmas ideas from stories, legends, and songs. E. Craster and D. Eby. il Bet Hom & Gard 47:38-63 D '69
Christmas is a tree. D. Hardie. House & Gard 136:69-70+ D '69
Christmas quarreling in the good old days. P. Steinfels. Commonweal 91:374 D 26 '69
Christmas reminds us to hope. B. L. Masse. America 121:607 D 20 '69
Christmas specials. M. L. Anderson. PTA Mag 64:23 D '69
Christmas survival kit. Mlle 70:94-5+ D '69
Christmas without crises? Are you kidding? J. Beck. il Todays Health 47:28-31+ D '69
If Christmas were only Christmas; reprint. D. Lawrence. U S News 67:68 D 29 '69
In praise of unhung wreaths and love. J. Didion. il Life 67:2B D 19 '69
Ironies of Christmas 1969. America 121:608 D 20 '69
No room at the inn. L. Spigelgass. il Mc Calls 97:96-7+ N '69
On earth peace... il Redbook 134:25 D '69
Story of Christmas. V. L. Edwards il Américas 21:18-27 N '69
Three lights of Christmas. P. B. Price. PTA Mag 64:15 D '69
Time off; Christmas travels. P. O'Higgins. il McCalls 97:48+ D '69
We came in peace for all mankind, special view of Christmas; symposium, ed. by E. Efron. il Redbook 134:76-7+ D '69
When holiday pleasures turn to pressures. A. Wood. Seventeen 28:128 D '69
See also
Advent
Santa Claus

Anecdotes, facetiae, satire, etc.
Over the river and through the woods. D. Shane. Har Yrs 9:29 D '69
Trapp family Christmas. A. B. Heath. il Nat R 21:1317-19 D 30 '69

Alaska
Christmas in Alaska. P. S. Coyne. il Nat R 21:1320-1+ D 30 '69

Great Britain
Yuletide in England. A. V. Pike. il Horticulture 47:28-30 D '69

United States
Carnage and the incarnation. Chr Cent 86:1633 D 24 '69
Christmas afternoon is forever. R. F. Capon. il Redbook 134:80-8 D '69

Christmas at the Nixons'. il Time 94:6-7 D 26 '69
Christmas is something else. L. Clifton. House & Gard 136:70-1+ D '69
Christmas that meant the most to me; memories of celebrated Americans; comp. by M. Abramson. il Good H 169:74-5+ D '69
Garlands for Christmas at Williamsburg. il Home Gard 56:54-5 D '69
Lighting of the Nation's Christmas tree; remarks, December 16, 1968. L. B. Johnson. Dept State Bul 60:3 Ja 6 '69
My Christmas discovery. N. Walter. il Har Yrs 9:18 D '69
Nation's Christmas tree; Washington, D.C. S. Anderson. il Parks & Rec 3:10-13+ D '68

Vietnam (Republic)
Merry Christmas, all authorized personnel? J. Steinbeck, 4th. House & Gard 136:68-9+ D '69

CHRISTMAS breads. See Bread

CHRISTMAS buffet. See Buffet meals

CHRISTMAS business
Christmas trade: the outlook around U.S. il U S News 67:45-6 O 20 '69
Creeping Christmas. il Newsweek 74:80 D 1 '69
Late shoppers eased the pain. Bsns W p21 Ja 3 '70
There's less reason to be jolly. il Bsns W p 14-15 D 27 '69
'Tis the season: early Christmas shopping promotions. Chr Cent 86:1629 D 17 '69
Uncertain ring of Christmas. il Bsns W p59-60 D 6 '69
What Christmas trade shows. il U S News 67:30-2 D 22 '69

CHRISTMAS cactus. See Cactus

CHRISTMAS cake. See Cake

CHRISTMAS candles. See Candles

CHRISTMAS candy. See Candy

CHRISTMAS cards
Bold cutouts for cards. il Sunset 143:89 D '69
Cards, custom-made. il Ladies Home J 86:44+ N '69
Cards for friends; for little fingers: paper-torn Santas and trees. il House B 111:91 D '69
Christmas card designs. il Sch Arts 69:29 D '69
How to make your own linoleum block Christmas cards. il House B 111:30 D '69
Mallinckrodt is coming to town; photographic card ideas. D. B. Eisendrath. il Pop Phot 65:18+ D '69
Putting soul in Christmas. il Bsns W p58 D 20 '69
Seasoned greetings. il Time 94:6 D 26 '69
There is still time if you hurry! the artist's personal card. il Am Artist 33:40-4 D '69
Who sent the first Christmas card? Good H 169:181 D '69

CHRISTMAS carols
Carols for Christmas, 1969. N Y Times Mag p5 D 21 '69

CHRISTMAS cookery
Christmas afternoon is forever. R. F. Capon. il Redbook 134:80-8 D '69
Christmas gifts from the kitchen. il Ebony 25:158+ D '69
Christmas recipes. il Bet Hom & Gard 47:64+ D '69
Eat. M. Cantwell. Mlle 70:14+ D '69
GH's Christmas cookbook; one hundred favorites old and new. il Good H 169:94-123 D '69
Holiday treats to make now; with recipes. il Redbook 134:104+ N '69
In a helpful mood; for holiday tables; with recipes. N. S. Hazelton. Nat R 21:1221+ D 2 '69
Many feasts of Christmas. il McCalls 97:94-103+ D '69
Merry eating and drinking. H. McCully. il House B 111:66-7+ D '69
Special-diet holiday treats. il Good H 169:190+ D '69
Sweet fruits of Christmas. G. Maddox. il Todays Health 47:60-3 D '69
See also
Christmas meals
Christmas suppers
Cookery, Ornamental

CHRISTMAS cookies. See Cookies

CHRISTMAS cribs
On that night; a modern parable of Christmas eve. E. Yates. il Read Digest 95:227-30+ D '69

CHRISTMAS poetry—*Continued*
Two Christmases. B. Via, jr. Chr Today 14:
5 D 19 '69
Written in Advent. E. L. Pierce. Chr Cent 86:
1578 D 10 '69
See also
Christmas carols
Jesus Christ—Poetry

CHRISTMAS presents. See Christmas gifts

CHRISTMAS promise; drama. See Miller, H. L.

CHRISTMAS safety devices and measures. See
Safety devices and measures

CHRISTMAS services. See Church services

CHRISTMAS shopping
Cautious Santas. il Time 94:48 D 26 '69
Christmas shopping abroad in New York. L.
Hadley. il Travel & Camera 32:87-9 D '69
Now's the time for Christmas shopping in
Europe. V. Creed. il Travel 132:62-4+ O '69
Six rules for buying during the holidays.
Good H 169:182 D '69

CHRISTMAS stories
All the days of love and courage. P. S.
Buck. il Good H 169:72-3 D '69
Christmas carol. T. Meehan. il Mlle 70:124+
D '69
Doubly blessed. V. Lee. il Good H 169:78-9
D '69
Gift for the Christ child. C. G. Marsden. il
Américas 21:28-9 N '69
Holiday rider. D. Boles. il Seventeen 27:96-7
D '68
Holly green, the ivy green. M. J. Amft. il
Seventeen 28:112-13+ D '69
Joel of the far hills. M. Garthwaite. Horn
Bk 45:652-8 D '69
Merry Christmas, mother! Merry Christmas,
Barracliff! L. Lewis. il Redbook 134:96-7+
D '69
My secret, your secret. F. J. Soman. il Good
H 169:92-3 D '69
Ring out the new. E. Pearlman. il Seventeen
28:96-7+ D '69

CHRISTMAS stories, Childrens. See Childrens
stories

CHRISTMAS suppers
Chili Christmas supper. il Am Home 72:54-5+
D '69

CHRISTMAS sweets. See Confectionery

CHRISTMAS toys. See Toys

CHRISTMAS tree light control. See Electric
lighting—Control

CHRISTMAS tree lights
Christmas lights keep time to music. G. J.
Whalen and R. F. Graf. il Pop Sci 195:144-6
D '69
Turning on Christmas; history of electric
Christmas-tree lights. il Newsweek 74:8 D
29 '69

CHRISTMAS tree ornaments. See Christmas
decorations

CHRISTMAS trees
Christmas tree. il Horticulture 47:16-17 D
'69
Christmas tree allergy? il Sci Digest 66:55-6
D '69
Christmas tree to trim, and plant in the
garden later. il Home Gard 56:32-3 D '69
Custer's last stand; tree grower's livelihood
threatened by air pollution. Time 94:51 D
19 '69
Get your Christmas tree out alive! M. M.
Gunn. il Org Gard & Farm 16:49 D '69
Little trees with big ideas. M. Mulvey. il
Good H 169:132-3+ D '69
Living trees can come indoors and take it. il
Sunset 143:72-4 D '69
Nation's Christmas tree; Washington, D.C. S.
Anderson. il Parks & Rec 3:10-13+ D '68
Rockefeller Center. Holiday 46:76-7 D '69
Tasseled yarn tree. il Good H 169:146+ D
'69
Traditional in one home; 100 Christmas trees.
W. Reaugh. il Hobbies 74:154-5 D '69
Tree that blooms on Christmas. il House B
111:45-9+ D '69
Tree; tree ornamented with eighteenth-cen-
tury Neapolitan baroque angels, cherubs,
and Nativity figures at Metropolitan mu-
seum. L. H. Howard. New Yorker 45:31-2
D 20 '69

CHRISTMAS wrappings. See Wrapping of packages

CHRISTMAS wreaths
Wheat & walnuts, pine & roses. il Am Home
72:62-3+ D '69
Wreaths for all around the house. M. Mulvey.
il Good H 169:130-1+ D '69

CHRISTO
All package. il por Time 93:60 F 7 '69
Shroud for Sydney's cliffs. il por Life 67:
46-7 N 14 '69

Under wraps. il por Newsweek 73:77 F 10 '69
Wrap-in Down Under. il por Time 94:56 N
14 '69

CHRISTOLOGY. See Jesus Christ

CHRISTOPH, Shawn
Polar bear. Nat Parks 43:9-11 Ag '69

CHRISTOPHE, Henri, king of Haiti
Monuments to Haiti's only king. W. Jeffs.
il por Negro Hist Bul 32:11-13 O '69

CHRISTUS gardens. See Gatlinburg, Tenn.—
Gardens

CHRISTY, George
Dad's last good-bye. Good H 168:89+ Ap '69
Holiday with music. Good H 169:40-2+ D
'69

CHROMATIN
Chromatin and histones: binding of tritiated
actinomycin D, to heterochromatin in mealy
bugs. L. Berlowitz and others. bibliog il
Science 164:1527-9 Je 27 '69

CHROMATOGRAPHIC analysis
Acetylcholine: release from neural tissue and
identification by pyrolysis-gas chromatography. D. E. Schmidt and others. bibliog
il Science 165:1370-1 S 26 '69
Acidic components of Green River shale identified by a gas chromatography-mass spectrometry-computer system. R. C. Murphy
and others. bibliog il Science 165:695-7 Ag 15
'69
Analytic instruments in process control. F.
W. Karasek. il Sci Am 220:112-20 Je '69
Microparticulates: isolation from water and
identification of associated chlorinated
pesticides. R. M. Pfister and others. bibliog il Science 166:878-9 N 14 '69
Separation of type 2 toxins of vibrio cholerae.
A. C. Lewis and B. A. Freeman. bibliog
il Science 165:808-9 Ag 22 '69
Various kinds of chromatography, especial-
ly the thin-layer method. C. L. Stong.
il Sci Am 220:124-8 Mr '69
Wind from Dugway; death of sheep near
Proving ground, testing poisonous agents.
V. Brodine and others. il Environ 11:2-9+
Ja '69

CHROMIUM
Chromium, the metal that glitters. O. A. Battista. il Chem 42:19-20 Ja '69
Serum cholesterol reduction by chromium
in hypercholesterolemic rats. H. W. Staub
and others. bibliog il Science 166:746-7 N
7 '69

CHROMIUM ores
Rhodesian chrome caper. il Bsns W p50-1 Je
28 '69

CHROMOSOMES
Anatomy of violence; findings of Frank R.
Ervin and Lawrence Razavi. il Newsweek
75:60-1 Ja 12 '70
Case of the double male. Newsweek 73:73 My
5 '69
Centromeres in human meiotic chromosomes. A. T. L. Chen and A. Falek. bibliog il Science 166:1008-10 N 21 '69
Chromosomal fragments transmitted through
three generations in oncopeltus (hemipter-
al) L. E. LaChance and M. Degrugillier.
bibliog il Science 166:235-6 O 10 '69
Chromosome number of a small protist: accurate determination. P. B. Moens and
F. O. Perkins. bibliog il Science 166:1289-
91 D 5 '69
Chromosomes and crime. il Chem 42:22 Jl '69
Cytogenetic effects of cyclamates on human
cells in vitro. D. Stone and others. bibliog
il Science 164:568-9 My 2 '69; Discussion.
165:517 Ag 1 '69
Gene regulation for higher cells: a theory;
clue in organization of the genome. R. J.
Britten and E. H. Davidson. bibliog il Science 165:349-57 Jl 25 '69; Reply. C. H. Wad-
ington. 166:639 O 31 '69
Lymphocytoid lines from persons with sex
chromosome anomalies. G. E. Moore and
others. bibliog il Science 163:1453-4 Mr 28
'69
MN blood-group locus: data concerning the
possible chromosomal location. J. German
and others; reply. L. Weitkamp. Science
164:1187 Je 6 '69
Mammalian oocytes: X chromosome activity.
C. J. Epstein. bibliog il Science 163:1078-9
Mr 7 '69
Mole rat spalax: evolutionary significance of
chromosome variation. J. Wahrman and
others. bibliog il Science 164:82-4 Ap 4 '69
Somatic cell hybrid between the established
human line D98 (presumptive HeLa) and
3T3. Y. Matsuya and H. Green. bibliog
Science 163:697-8 F 14 '69
Supermale fish from sex hormones. il Sci
Digest 66:68-9 Jl '69

CHROMOSOMES—*Continued*
XYY chromosome and criminal acts; letter.
K. McWhirter. Science 164:1117 Je 6 '69;
Discussion. 165:442, 967; 166:947-9 Ag 1, S 5,
N 21 '69
See also
Androgenesis
Chromatin
Crossing over (genetics)
Genes
Genetics

CHRONIC, Halka
Tropics: a frontier in meteorology; with biographical sketch. Sea Front 15:288-94, 319
S '69

CHRONICLE, San Francisco. See San Francisco chronicle

CHRONICLE of the nightmare; story. See Findley, T.

CHRONOGRAPH
Photo-chronograph for timing observations.
A. S. Clarke. il Sky & Tel 37:386-8 Je '69

CHRYSANTHEMUMS
Chrysanthemums, springtime in September.
P. Shedesky. il Org Gard & Farm 16:49-51
S '69
Consider the rewards of chrysanthemums from seed. M. Leister. il Home Gard 56:
75 Mr '69
Magic with mums. F. J. Taylor. il Read
Digest 95:170-5 O '69
Mums don't need good weather. E. Baker. il
Org Gard & Farm 16:74-5 N '69

CHRYSLER corporation
Chrysler shrinks its white collars. Bsns W
p41 O 11 '69
Chrysler tune sours partner; Eduardo Barreiros walks out on U.S. partner. Bsns W
p34 My 31 '69
Chrysler's trade; Valiant for Colt; joint venture with Mitsubishi heavy industries. il
Bsns W p37 Je 7 '69
Is Chrysler's sun rising in Japanese deal?
collaboration with Mitsubishi heavy industries. Bsns W p37 My 24 '69
Shake-up at Chrysler. il Newsweek 75:76 Ja
19 '70
Tremor in Japan's trade wall; Chrysler-Mitsubishi deal causes unexpected furor.
Bsns W p98 Je 21 '69
What's good for Chrysler is good for Lynn
Townsend. N. Thimmesch. il Esquire 71:
105-7+ Mr '69
What's the matter with Britain? Ask Chrysler. il Forbes 103:37-8 Je 1 '69
What's wrong at Chrysler. il Bsns W p46-8
Jl 5 '69

Dodge division
Conflict of cultures. Time 93:100 Je 13 '69
CHRYSLER institute. See Automobile industry
and trade—Study and teaching
CHRYSOGONUM. See Golden star
CHRYSOPSIS. See Golden asters
CHUA, Wee-hian
Encouraging missionary movement in Asian
churches. Chr Today 13:9-12 Je 20 '69
CHUCK hunting. See Woodchuck hunting
CHUJOY, Anatole
Obituary
Dance Mag por 43:5 Ap '69
CHUKAR shooting. See Partridge shooting
CHUR, Switzerland
Badgered bishops; bishops and cardinals
meeting. il Newsweek 74:91 Jl 21 '69
Challenge in Chur; symposium to discuss the
crisis in the Roman Catholic priesthood.
Time 94:63 Jl 18 '69
CHURCH, Frank
Excerpt from debate, June 20, 1969. Cong
Digest 48:216+ Ag '69
New conservation; excerpts from address.
por Parks & Rec 4:36-40+ S '69
Two sentinels of the status quo; address,
July 11, 1969. bibliog f Vital Speeches 35:
614-17 Ag 1 '69
Vietnam; address, October 8, 1969. bibliog f
Vital Speeches 36:34-9 N 1 '69
CHURCH, Ronald P.
Camp acreage dwindling? Convert croplands.
Camp Mag 41:16 Ap '69
CHURCH
After much prayerful consideration. . . Chr
Today 14:24-5 D 5 '69
Christian values and a secular future. J.
Hitchcock. America 121:155-9 S 13 '69
Church for today and tomorrow. W. M.
Elliott. Chr Today 13:10-11 Jl 4 '69
Contemporary church: instrument or idol?
W. C. Hobbs. Chr Today 13:7-8 Je 6 '69
Last years of the church, by D. Poling. Review
Cath World 209:84-5 My '69. P. J. Cunningham

New ecclesiology; with reply. G. Baum. il
Commonweal 91:123-9 O 31 '69
New troubles in the churches. il U S News
66:41-4 Ap 14 '69; Same abr. with title Our
troubled churches. Read Digest 95:126-9 Jl
'69
New wine, maybe new wineskins, for the
church. R. Ruether. Chr Cent 86:445-9 Ap
2 '69
Save your clerical collars, boys! R. E.
Wentz. Chr Cent 86:1133-5 S 3 '69
Supernatural and miraculous. L. N. Bell.
Chr Today 13:30-1 F 28 '69
Underground church is nonsense. D. B. Ward.
Look 33:75 O 21 '69
Unrest in the church. L. N. Bell. Chr Today
13:30-1 Ap 11 '69
See also
Catholic church
Mission of the church
Protestantism

Authority
Apostolic authority. H. K. Stothard. Chr
Today 14:12-15 N 7 '69
Catholic unity; in the light of Vatican II;
excerpts from interview. L. J. Suensens.
America 120:611 My 24 '69
Confrontation: curia style. F. X. Murphy.
America 121:91-3 Ag 16 '69
Crisis or *kairos*? W. Birmingham. Commonweal 91:210-14 N 14 '69
Language of the tribe. J. Blenkinsopp. il
Commonweal 90:505-8 Ag 22 '69
Not fathers, but brothers. G. Baum. Chr
Cent 86:607-8 Ap 30 '69
Papacy. G. Baum. Cath World 209:64-6 My
'69
Papal infallibility and all that. J. Bishop.
Commonweal 90:481-4 Ag 8 '69
Pope as Hamlet: the church at the crossroads. J. H. Knox. il Nat R 21:1058-60 O
21 '69
Priests' counter-Synod; meeting of Europe's
reformist Roman Catholic priests. B. Bastien. Chr Today 14:46 N 7 '69
Push for bishop-power. Chr Today 14:32-
3 N 7 '69
Revolt of the young priests. A. Whitman.
McCalls 96:60-1+ Jl '69
Roman Catholic: visible and invisible; address, October 1969. F. Sontag. America
121:298-301 O 11 '69
Rome listens to the universities. N. G. McCluskey. America 121:58-60 Ag 2 '69
Scandal and schism; Pope Paul's messages.
il Newsweek 73:95 Ap 14 '69
Suenens crying in the wilderness. G. Baum.
Cath World 210:103-7 D '69
See also
Popes—Primacy

Mission
See Mission of the church

Purpose
See Mission of the church
CHURCH advertising
Fresh theme for church publicists; educational programs. D. E. Kucharsky. Chr Today
13:20-1 Ag 22 '69

Anecdotes, facetiae, satire, etc.
Revivalism revisited. Chr Cent 86:135 Ja 22 '69
CHURCH and economic problems. See Christianity and economics
CHURCH and education
See also
Catholic schools
Church schools
Public schools and religion
Religious education
CHURCH and international relations
Affective ministries in international affairs.
P. Dietterich. Chr Cent 86:579-81 Ap 23 '69
International dimensions of the seminary.
L. H. DeWolf. Chr Cent 86:545-7 Ap 23 '69
Seminary's ostrich mentality on international
affairs. T. Smith. Chr Cent 86:573-9 Ap 23
'69
CHURCH and labor
Church and the ILO. J. A. Lucal. America
120:644-6 My 31 '69
Clergy and the grape strike; Delano verdict.
M. Day. America 121:114-17 Ag 30 '69
Union dues and don'ts. Chr Today 14:55 N 7
'69
CHURCH and politics
Barth as political thinker. W. Hordern. Chr
Cent 86:411-13 Mr 26 '69
Church and political action. M. Nygren.
Chr Today 13:9-10+ Mr 14 '69

CHURCH and politics—*Continued*
Civil religion; inaugural ceremony. il Newsweek 73:82 F 3 '69
Conflicts in churches: new moves to heal differences. il US News 67:73-5 O 6 '69
Opus Dei: in Spain, a political force. W. E. Greening. Chr Cent 87:27-9 Ja 7 '70
Religion and revolution. M. Harrington. Commonweal 91:203-4 N 14 '69
See also
Church and state

CHURCH and race problems
Black churchmen plan NCC takeover; with editorial comment. E. E. Plowman. Chr Today 14:26, 33 D 5 '69
Burning question that splits our churches. D. J. Hamblin. Read Digest 94:112-16 F '69
Church as petitioner for the public interest; action to protest renewal of license for WLBT-TV in Jackson, Miss. Chr Cent 86: 919 Jl 9 '69
Crash attack on prejudice; suggestions for a parish effort during Lent. M. Hellwig. America 120:193-4 F 15 '69
[Harry Golden column] H. Golden. Nation 208:602-3 My 12 '69
Indian reservations about the church. J. Huffman. Chr Today 13:54-5 S 12 '69
Non-prophet organization; church in the inner city. W. J. Duncan; discussion. Commonweal 89:607+ F 14 '69
Preparation for separation and reparation: the churches' response to racism? demands on the World council of churches. J. R. Nelson. Chr Cent 86:862-5 Je 25 '69
Scranton: a short view, a microcosm. L. D. Mitchell. Cath World 210:7-10 O '69
Segregating grants; Episcopal church. Chr Today 14:51 N 7 '69
Violence justified. Time 93:88+ Je 6 '69
What the black community wants; recommended program of apostolic initiatives. T. M. Gannon. America 121:558-62 D 6 '69
When conservatism is liberalism. G. H. Shriver. Chr Cent 86:1040-1 Ag 6 '69
World council and race: give the black man his own turf! J. R. Nelson. il Cath World 209:256-61 S '69
See also
Catholic schools—Desegregation
Interreligious foundation for community organization

CHURCH and social problems
Accent on man; meeting of faith and order committee of the World council of churches. J. R. Nelson Chr Cent 86:1107 Ag 27 '69
Affective ministries in international affairs. P. Dietterich. Chr Cent 86:579-81 Ap 23 '69
Almoners' dilemma; schism over social action in the Episcopal church. il Newsweek 74:96-7 D 15 '69
American pastor and social change. W. J. Byron. America 120:246-9 Mr 1 '69; Discussion. 120:317-18 Mr 22 '69
Arrested development. Chr Cent 86:765 Je 4 '69
Better way to confront poverty? Chr Today 13:24-6 Ja 31 '69
Black preacher looks at the Black manifesto. R. D. Abernathy. Chr Cent 86:1064-5 Ag 13 '69
Border consultation gets new perspective. R. R. Winkelmann. Chr Cent 86:460-2 Ap 2 '69
Christian and change. J. Hitchcock. Chr Cent 87:7-11 Ja 7 '70
Church and colonialism, by H. P. Câmara. Review
Chr Cent 86:1421-2 N 5 '69. R. Shaull
Church and Farmington no. 9. R. Bowyer. Chr Cent 86:161-2 Ja 29 '69
Church groups in housing. America 121:213 S 27 '69
Churches unite for development. America 120:724 Je 28 '69
Clergy and abortions; Michigan clergy for problem pregnancy counseling. il Time 94: 82 N 28 '69
Conflicts in churches: new moves to heal differences. il US News 67:73-5 O 6 '69
Crime, violence and the local church. L. E. Schaller. Chr Cent 86:641-5 My 7 '69
Cross and sword in Latin America. Chr Today 14:26-7 D 5 '69
Labor day statement; by the Division of urban life of the department of social development, USCC. America+121:113 Ag 30 '69
Last hurrah of Cardinal Patrick Aloysius O'Boyle. M. Hinckle. Ramp Mag 7:28-31 D 14 '68
Michael bit the archbishop; Witness social apostolate program. C. J. McNaspy. America 121:122 Ag 30 '69
On the role of the church in society. B. L. Masse. America 121:215 S 27 '69

Paul VI and violence. P. J. Riga. Cath World 208:251-4 Mr '69
Pauline advice; the apostle's moral directives. V. P. McCorry. America 120:119-20 Ja 25 '69
Priests, prostitutes, and the dead God: a meditation. R. E. Warren. il Cath World 208:261-3 Mr '69
Religion and revolution. M. Harrington. Commonweal 91:203-4 N 14 '69
Roundup, religious agencies and the urban crisis. Chr Cent 86:223-4+ F 12 '69
Sad, slow death of a cathedral. D. Grumbach il Commonweal 90:316-17 My 30 '69
Till we have built Jerusalem. R. F. Smith. Nation 208:829-30 Je 30 '69
Vatican council in perspective; interview, ed. by H. J. Cargas. G. MacEoin. America 121: 289-94 O 11 '69
World around us. See issues of Christian century
Young churchmen eye the seventies; symposium. il Chr Today 14:24-30 Ja 2 '70
See also
Birth control—Religious aspects
Christian ethics
Church and labor
Church and race problems
Church work with migrants
Interreligious foundation for community organization
Social action
Sociology, Christian

CHURCH and state
Americanizing American religious life. S. Poole. America 120:297-300 Mr 15 '69; Discussion. 120:457 Ap 19 '69
Church, state and the courts. G. R. La Noue. Nation 209:656-9 D 15 '69
Historians debate God-and-country theme; Conference on faith and history. R. V. Pierard. Chr Today 14:51-2 N 7 '69
Law, politics and religion. America 121:179 S 20 '69; Reply. M. Berman. 121:404 N 8 '69
Pentagon piety; Character guidance program to eliminate passages with religious connections. Nation 208:325-6 Mr 17 '69
Tarheelers, remember Torcaso, and Iredell! Chr Cent 86:703 My 21 '69
Vs. church-state sloganizing. J. Evanson. Chr Today 13:40 F 14 '69
See also
Americans united for separation of church and state
Catholic schools
Church property
Church schools
Concordats
Public schools and religion

CHURCH and state in Brazil
See also
Catholic church in Brazil

CHURCH and state in Israel
Faith in Israel. H. Fisch. Commentary 47:64-7 F '69

CHURCH and state in Norway
See also
Lutheran church in Norway

CHURCH and state in Paraguay
Indigestion in Paraguay; Stroessner regime criticized by Catholic weekly Comunidad. America 120:347-8 Mr 29 '69

CHURCH and state in Poland
See also
Catholic church in Poland

CHURCH and state in Rumania
Rumania's opening to the churches. G. A. Maloney. America 121:490-3 N 22 '69

CHURCH and state in Spain
Church and state in Spain. J. E. Griffiss, jr. il Chr Cent 86:802-6 Je 11 '69
Council changed all that. J. Ruiz-Gimenez. America 120:127 F 1 '69
See also
Catholic church in Spain

CHURCH and state in Yugoslavia
Renewal in Yugoslavia. M. M. Mestrovic. America 121:488-90 N 22 '69
See also
Catholic church in Yugoslavia

CHURCH and the press
News from Rome; the relationship between the church and the press. Commonweal 91: 326 D 12 '69
Scolding the press; attacks against the news media after the episcopal conference in Washington. S. J. Adamo; discussion. America 120:30, 121 Ja 11, F 1 '69
See also
Vatican and the press

CHURCH and the theater
Irreverent themes invading reverent theaters. T. Tolnay. Chr Cent 86:1519-20 N 26 '69

CHURCH and the world
Being Christian in an affluent society. M. V. Hope. Chr Today 13:7-8 F 14 '69
Christian faith and secular faiths. L. Paul. Chr Cent 86:477-81 Ap 9 '69
Church and the world; excerpts from Theology of the world. J. B. Metz. bibliog f Cath World 208:247-50 Mr '69
Church invasions. Chr Today 13:22 My 23 '69
Confused and confusing. L. N. Bell. Chr Today 13:27-8 Jl 4 '69
Crisis of hope? Pope voices pessimism in Christmas message. Commonweal 89:488-9 Ja 17 '69
Evangelism in a day of revolution. L. Ford. Chr Today 14:6-12 O 24 '69
Missing the yellow submarine; young travelers are not taking their trip with Jesus. C. Hubbard; reply. P. Ritterman. Commonweal 89:601-3 F 7 '69
National council of churches: melancholia in Memphis. D. E. Kucharsky. Chr Today 13:38 F 14 '69
New heaven and new earth; with reply. A. Gibson. il Commonweal 91:117-123 O 31 '69
Not radical enough? excerpts from Christian freedom in a permissive society. J. A. T. Robinson. Chr Cent 86:1446-9 N 12 '69
Sex, church, and culture. J. Hitchcock. Cath World 209:17-20 Ap '69
Sodom and the city of God. T. Howard. Chr Today 13:8-10 Ja 31 '69
Upheaval in the religious arena. R. V. Morris. Sat R 52:64+ My 10 '69
Visibility of the church. T. C. Oden. bibliog Chr Cent 86:613-16 Ap 30 '69

CHURCH architecture
Architecture for mission: designs for action. Chr Cent 86:638-9 My 7 '69
Building for the space age: architectural innovations in church-building. Chr Cent 86:167 Ja 29 '69
Church in a grove of skyscrapers: Seventh church of Christ, Scientist, Chicago. J. M. Dixon. il Arch Forum 130:42-5 Je '69
Revelation from old Russia. il Time 94:74-9 S 12 '69
Symbol and shelter: All Saints Episcopal church, Palo Alto, Calif. il Arch Forum 131:76-9 O '69
Unity temple, Oak Park, Ill. H. Wright. bibliog f il Arch Forum 130:28-37 Je '69
See also
Chapels
National conference on religious architecture
Spires
Synagogues

Conservation and restoration
See Architecture—Conservation and restoration

CHURCH attendance
How to pick a church; interview, ed. by T. Shea. E. Campbell. Read Digest 94:62-4 Je '69
Talking with God. R. Coles. Commonweal 91:330-4 D 12 '69
Vehicular spectacular: Sunday school and church promotion gimmicks. Chr Cent 86:889 Je 25 '69
You can't find God in church anymore; Journal's survey. K. L. Woodward. il Ladies Home J 86:86-7+ Mr '69

CHURCH cadet corps. See Youth associations

CHURCH calendar
See also
Church year

CHURCH camps. See Camps

CHURCH colleges
Academic freedom and the Christian college. G. F. Kreyche. Chr Cent 86:1217-20 S 24 '69
Campus tensions and evangelical response. R. J. Bartel. Chr Today 13:12-15 Je 6 '69
Christian colleges try innovations. Chr Today 13:49-50 S 12 '69
Christian perspective. Q. L. Quade. America 120:392-6 Ap 5 '69
John Wesley college: disengaging the Nazarenes. H. H. Ward. Chr Today 14:39 N 21 '69
See also
McMurry college, Abilene, Tex.
Shelton college, Cape May, N.J.
Stetson university, Deland, Fla.

Federal aid
Tilton v. Finch; validity of grants to church-related colleges. C. M. Whelan. America 121:222-3 S 27 '69

CHURCH committees
Committee folly. D. Edman. Chr Cent 86:1091-2 Ag 20 '69

CHURCH conferences. See Religious conferences

CHURCH cooperation. See Religious cooperation

CHURCH councils. See Councils and synods

CHURCH decoration and ornament
See also
Glass painting and staining

CHURCH entertainments
See also
Recreation in church work

CHURCH finance
[Book reviews] J. J. Graham. Commonweal 89:741-2 Mr 14 '69
Church income: depressing pinch. Chr Today 14:48 O 24 '69
New-style attack on the denominational budget. L. E. Schaller. Chr Cent 86:1515-18 N 26 '69
Should churches be allowed to do business tax-free? O. K. Armstrong. Read Digest 94:84-8 Mr '69
See also
Catholic church—Finance
Church property
Fund raising

CHURCH furniture
Holy cushions and shades; excerpt from liturgy performed at St John's Evangelical Lutheran church in Brooklyn. Chr Cent 86:199 F 5 '69

CHURCH going. See Church attendance

CHURCH government
See also
Catholic church—Government

CHURCH history
Bibliography
Historical works overshadow dogmatics. G. W. Bromiley. Chr Today 13:3-5 F 28 '69

Primitive and early church
Bishops' conferences past and present. D. R. Campion. America 121:327-9 O 18 '69
Constantine, by R. MacMullen. Review Sat R 52:28 D 27 '69. J. H. Plumb
Poor in the early church. J. J. Magee. il America 121:164-5 S 13 '69

CHURCH league basketball games. See Basketball tournaments

CHURCH membership
Let's drop unbiblical rules for church membership. N. L. Geisler. Chr Today 13:17-18 Ja 31 '69
See also
Church statistics

CHURCH music
Church music: pop or pro? L. P. Beveridge. Chr Today 13:6-8 Mr 14 '69
Jazz and the liberation of worship. Chr Cent 86:499 Ap 16 '69
Threnody for sacred music, 1968. R. Thibodeau; discussion. Commonweal 89:487+ Ja 17 '69
See also
Motets
Passion music
Phonograph records—Church music

History
Wiedrigkeit and *verdriesslichkeit* in Mühlhausen; church music of eighteenth century. H. Serwer. bibliog f Mus Q 55:20-30 Ja '69

CHURCH of Christ in the United States
Churches of Christ; orchestrating unity. M. Moss. Chr Today 14:48 N 7 '69

CHURCH of England
Anglicans vote no; failure to reunite Methodist church of Great Britain with Church of England. il Time 94:62 Jl 18 '69
Church of England votes. W. J. O'Rourke. America 121:64-6 Ag 2 '69
Ecumenical saints; new names for inclusion on the church calendar for commemoration in daily services. il Time 93:53 F 14 '69
England's dying churches; country parishes, empty and neglected. il Time 93:75 Mr 28 '69
Latin, litter, limitations, Canterbury convocation. J. D. Douglas. Chr Today 14:40 N 21 '69
Power without glory, by I. Henderson. Review Chr Cent 86:1139 S 3 '69. E. G. Homrighausen
Where defeat is a mandate. J. D. Douglas. Chr Today 13:44 Ag 22 '69
See also
Church unity—Great Britain
Oxford movement

CHURCH of England—*Continued*

Clergy

Gadara then and now; current Anglican-Methodist unity scheme. J. D. Douglas. Chr Today 13:46-7 Mr 14 '69

CHURCH of England in Canada

Ontario; Anglican general synod. J. R. Mutchmor. Chr Cent 86:1258-9 O 1 '69

Redundant request? D. E. Kucharsky. Chr Today 13:48-9 S 12 '69

CHURCH of God

Assemblies of God: fair skies at Dallas. R. E. Friedrich, jr. Chr Today 13:41 S 26 '69

Hark! The herald; Faith center's KHOF-TV; Glendale, Calif. il Newsweek 74:110 N 17 '69

CHURCH of Scotland

Church of Scotland: the 1969 assembly. I. Logan. Chr Cent 86:879-80 Je 25 '69

Colorful convention capers: a man named Paisley. J. D. Douglas. Chr Today 13:34 Je 20 '69

Power without glory, by I. Henderson. Review
    Chr Cent 86:1139 S 3 '69. E. G. Homrighausen

CHURCH of the Brethren

Church of the Brethren in annual gathering. F. E. Bantz. Chr Cent 86:1050-2 Ag 6 '69

CHURCH of the New Jerusalem. See New Jerusalem church

CHURCH property

Church-owned business: stretching religion. Chr Today 13:48-9 F 28 '69

Georgia court again backs congregations. A. H. Matthews. Chr Today 13:42 My 9 '69

Sad, slow death of a cathedral. D. Grumbach. il Commonweal 90:316-17 My 30 '69

Secular courts must avoid doctrinal disputes; ruling on church property in Georgia. Chr Today 13:42+ F 14 '69

Setback in Court for breakaway church groups. U S News 66:11 F 10 '69

Supreme court and ecumenism. America 120:154 F 8 '69

Taxation

Baptists and church taxation. America 121:373 N 1 '69

Church bodies stung by new taxes. J Huffman. Chr Today 13:48 Je 6 '69

Church, state and the courts. G. R. La Noue. Nation 209:656-9 D 15 '69

Church wealth and tax exemptions. C. S. Lowell. Ed Digest 35:17-19 S '69

Churches and tax exemptions. America 120:577 My 17 '69

Court to rule on church taxes. U S News 66:75-6 Je 30 '69

Oral argument on church taxes. America 121:550 D 6 '69

Should churches be taxed? by D. B. Robertson. Review
    Chr Cent 86:519 Ap 16 '69. H. E. Fey

Should churches pay taxes? On issue coming to a head. il U S News 66:92-3 Je 16 '69

Taxing the churches. America 121:132-3 S 6 '69

Those unlevied taxes. Nation 280:619-20 My 19 '69

To tax, or not? suit by F. Walz. il Newsweek 74:57-8 Jl 14 '69

CHURCH-related colleges. See Church colleges

CHURCH-related schools. See Catholic schools; Church schools

CHURCH renewal

Can the Catholic revolution succeed? T. J. Fleming. il Redbook 133:77+ My '69

Cardinals, thirty-five; aggiornamento. O. H. ten Kortenaar. Commonweal 90:277-9 My 23 '69

Coresponsibility in the church, by L. J. Suenens. Review
    Commonweal 89:534-6 Ja 24 '69. D. O. Dugan

New church? R. Ruether. Commonweal 90:64-6 Ap 4 '69; Discussion. 90:187+ My 2 '69

New wine, maybe new wineskins, for the church. R. Ruether. Chr Cent 86:445-9 Ap 2 '69

Patience is all. V. P. McCorry. America 121:436 N 8 '69

Problems of the papacy. Commonweal 90:132-3 Ap 18 '69

Questions & answers; symposium. Commonweal 91:215-18+ N 14 '69

Reconstruction after renewal; discussion. Chr Cent 86:155-6 Ja 29 '69

Resistance in the church. E. C. Bianchi. Commonweal 90:257-60 My 16 '69; Reply with rejoinder. P. Foote. 90:379+ Je 20 '69

Revolution within an evolution. R. R. Winkelmann. Chr Cent 86:1577-80 D 10 '69

Times of refreshing. Chr Today 13:32 S 12 '69

Upheaval in the religious arena. R. V. Morris. Sat R 52:64+ My 10 '69

Visibility of the church. T. C. Oden. bibliog Chr Cent 86:613-16 Ap 30 '69

Where did all the spirit go? M. Novak. Commonweal 90:540-2 S 5 '69

See also
Mission of the church

CHURCH schools

See also
Education and state
Sunday schools
Vacation schools, Religious

Federal aid

Aid to schools; letters to the editor. Chr Cent 86:1066-7 Ag 13 '69

Child support or wall of separation; excerpt from Catholic education faces its future. N. G. McCluskey. Chr Cent 86:775-9 Je 4 '69

Ecumenism and the school aid issue. J. M. Swomley, jr. Chr Cent 86:780-3 Je 4 '69

Hidden bonus to education. W. B. Ball. Parents Mag 44:66-7+ Mr '69

Parochial school crisis fuels state aid debate. W. Willoughby. Chr Today 13:37-8 Mr 28 '69

Public aid, public controls; public assistance to parochial schools. America 120:346 Mr 29 '69

Tax funds for religious education? C. S. Lowell; G. Oosterman. Chr Today 13:6-10+ Mr 28 '69

CHURCH services

On that night; a modern parable of Christmas eve. E. Yates. il Read Digest 95:227-30+ D '69

See also
Church music
Liturgies

Anecdotes, facetiae, satire, etc.

Churchgoing, Washington style; services at the White House. Chr Cent 86:271 F 19 '69

Out from under; underground church kicked upstairs. Chr Cent 86:239 F 12 '69

CHURCH statistics

Church statistics: the slips are showing. W. Willoughby. Chr Today 13:33-4 Mr 14 '69

CHURCH unity

Believers' church, by D. F. Durnbaugh. Review
    Chr Today 13:19-20 F 14 '69. B. L. Shelley

See also
Consultation on church union
Ecumenical movement
Religious cooperation
World council of churches

Canada

Canada and church union. W. Fitch. Chr Today 13:38-9 My 23 '69

Canadian union a disaster area? A. Wice. Chr Today 13:34 My 23 '69

Great Britain

Anglicans vote no; failure to reunite Methodist church of Great Britain with Church of England. il Time 94:62 Jl 18 '69

British unity plan fails. J. D. Douglas. Chr Today 13:38 Ag 1 '69

Church of England votes. W. J. O'Rourke. America 121:64-6 Ag 2 '69

Disunited kingdom; Church of England rejects reunion with Methodists. Newsweek 74:91 Jl 21 '69

Ecumenical calamity? British Methodists and Church of England. Chr Cent 86:969 Jl 23 '69

Gadara then and now; current Anglican-Methodist unity scheme. J. D. Douglas. Chr Today 13:46-7 Mr 14 '69

Where defeat is a mandate. J. D. Douglas. Chr Today 13:44 Ag 22 '69

Italy

Waldensian-Methodist unity. R. W. Zeuner. Chr Cent 86:999-1000 Jl 23 '69

CHURCH work

See also
Airplanes in church work
Church and social problems
Mass media in religion
Pastoral theology
Recreation in church work

CHURCH work with migrants

Discord along the Rio Grande; TCC and Mexican American farm workers. J. C. Evans. il Chr Cent 86:397-400 Mr 26 '69

CHURCH work with the deaf. See Church work with the handicapped
CHURCH work with the handicapped
Silent evangelist; S. E. Chainey's ministry to the deaf. Chr Today 13:35 Ap 25 '69
CHURCH work with youth
Wave of disaster. L. N. Bell. Chr Today 14:37-8 O 10 '69
CHURCH workers
Bridging the manpower gap. K. O. Gangel. Chr Today 13:34-5 S 26 '69
CHURCH year
Out go the beloved saints. J. Bonfante. il Life 66:47 My 23 '69
See also
Ascension day
CHURCHES
See also
Chapels
Church architecture
Computers—Church applications

Public relations
See Church advertising

England
England's dying churches; country parishes, empty and neglected. il Time 93:75 Mr 28 '69

Russia
Miraculous churches of Kizhi; with photographs by A. De Rosnay. P. de Rothschild. Vogue 154:156-61+ D '69
Revelation from old Russia. il Time 94:74-9 S 12 '69

United States
New lives for old churches; photographs by J. Dominis. Life 67:70-4 S 12 '69
See also
Negro militants and churches
also subhead Churches under names of cities, e.g. New York (city)—Churches
CHURCHILL, Creighton
Victorious clarets. Sat R 52:34-5 Ap 19 '69
CHURCHILL, Lady Jennie (Jerome)
Jennie, by R. G. Martin. Review
Newsweek por 73:85-6 F 3 '69. P. D. Zimmerman
CHURCHILL, Judith Chase
How to do more work with less fatigue. Read Digest 95:167-8 N '69
CHURCHILL, Sir Winston Leonard Spencer
Churchill revised, by A. J. P. Taylor and others. Review
Nation 208:637-8 My 19 '69. G. Dangerfield
Last great man: commemorative stamps. D. F. Brown. il pors Hobbies 74:50-1 Je '69
Night Stalin and Churchill divided Europe. J. Lukacs. il pors N Y Times Mag p36-8+ O 5 '69
Winston Churchill's black dog. A. Storr. por Esquire 71:94-9+ Ja '69

Memorials
Monument to an occasion; London church of St Mary, Aldermanbury, resurrected at Westminster college, Fulton, Mo. il Time 93:78-9 My 23 '69
CHURCHILL, Winston Spencer, 1940-
More than a name; grandson of Sir Winston writes articles on the Nigerian war. il por Time 93:56 Ap 4 '69
CHURCHILL FALLS
Task for ecologists around waterfalls in Labrador-Ungava. P. Kallio. bibliog il Science 166:1598-601 D 26 '69
CHURCHILL-Stalin conference, Moscow, 1944.
See World war, 1939-1945—Diplomatic history
CHURKIN, Michael, jr
Paleozoic tectonic history of the Arctic basin north of Alaska. bibliog Science 165: 549-55 Ag 8 '69
CHUTE, B. J.
End of it all. Writer 82:15-18 Ja '69
CHUYEN, Thai-khac-. See Thai-khac-Chuyen
CHWAT, Jacques
TV log. Opera N 34:17-19 D 6 '69
CIARDI, John
Cal Coolidge & the co; poem. Harper 238:62-4 Je '69
Feasts; poem Sat R 52:16-17 Jl 5 '69
Letter to an indolent Norn; poem. Sat R 52:52 O 4 '69
Manner of speaking. See issues of Saturday review
Out of the rathole. Sat R 52:19-23+ S 13 '69
Romancing with our beasts; poem. Sat R 52:36-7 My 22 '69
Shaft; poem. Sat R 52:18-19 Mr 1 '69
CICADAS
Seventeen year locusts: massive infestation predicted for 1970. R. G. Coleman. il Horticulture 48:22-3+ Ja '70

CIDER
Ardent apple. H. Johnson. 135:98+ Ja '69
CIESLAK, Ryszard
Theatre. E. Oliver. New Yorker 45:85-6+ N 29 '69
CIGAR industry
Return of the cigar. P. Maas. il Holiday 45: 42-3+ Mr '69
CIGAR smoking. See Smoking
CIGARETTE filters
Hope for cigarettes; activated charcoal filters trap gas molecules. Fortune 79:34 Ja '69
CIGARETTE labels. See Labels
CIGARETTE smoke
Experimental tobacco carcinogenesis. E. L. Wynder and D. Hoffmann; reply with rejoinder. E. P. Radford and others. Science 165:312-13 Jl 18 '69
Hope for cigarettes; activated charcoal filters trap gas molecules. Fortune 79:34 Ja '69
Now, a new drop in cigarette smoking. il U S News 66:10 Ja 27 '69
Selective venting of cigarette smoke in dichotomous ducts and preserved human bronchi. A. E. Anderson, jr. and others; reply with rejoinder. P. C. Pratt. Science 163:1227 Mr 14 '69
Tobacco smoke toxicity: loss of human oral leukocyte function and fluid-cell metabolism. B. Eichel and H. A. Shahrik. bibliog il Science 166:1424-8 D 12 '69
CIGARETTE smoking. See Smoking
CIGARETTE smoking and youth. See Smoking and youth
CIGARETTES
From beyond the cigarette: notes of a redeemed smoker. J. Hollander. Harper 238: 87-91 Ap '69
On not smoking. W. F. Buckley, jr. Nat R 21:1078-9 O 21 '69
Will cigarettes take to pot? Bsns W p28 S 6 '69
See also
Morris, Philip, incorporated

Advertising
Anti-smoking forces gain ground. M. Mueller. Science 165:569 Ag 8 '69
Book burning, FCC style; anti-smoking ads. M. Friedman. Newsweek 73:86 Je 16 '69
Calling Dr Killjoy; antismoking commercials and How to stop smoking, programs on TV. il Time 93:82+ My 9 '69
Caution: cigarette smoking may be hazardous to health. Trans-Action 6:7-8 Mr '69
Caution: regulators may be hazardous. Bsns W p52 Je 28 '69
Caution: this hearing is hazardous; hearings on the cautionary warning on cigarette packages. il Newsweek 73:82-3+ Ap 28 '69
Cigarette ads, latest action. U S News 66:12 Je 9 '69
Cigarette advertising; House commerce committee hearings. New Repub 160:9 Je 28 '69
Cigarette ban on TV? pro and con discussion. Sr Schol 94:4-5 Mr 14 '69
Cigarette companies would rather fight than switch; showdown coming in cigarette advertising. E. B. Drew. il N Y Times Mag p36-7+ My 4 '69
Cigarette labels and ads. America 120:680 Je 14 '69
Cigarette men agree to snuff out ads. Bsns W p29 Jl 26 '69
Cigarettes and society: a growing dilemma. il Time 93:98-100+ Ap 25 '69
Clearing smoke from the airwaves; ban on TV and radio cigarette commercials looms. il Bsns W p38-9 Ap 5 '69
Countdown for cigarettes. il Newsweek 73: 94 F 17 '69
Curve for Vinegar Bend. W. Willoughby. Chr Today 13:47 F 28 '69
Cyclamates and cigarettes. New Repub 161: 9 N 1 '69
Dike breaks; TV and cigarette advertising. il Time 94:68 Ag 1 '69
Down to the ash; four-year phase-out. Newsweek 74:82+ Jl 21 '69
Government censorship or freedom of the press? D. Lawrence. U S News 67:84 Ag 4 '69
Hazards of legislation. Newsweek 73:66+ Je 30 '69
It's turmoil for cigarette admen. il Bsns W p82-4 D 13 '69
June 30: moment of truth. Sci N 95:574 Je 14 '69
Media line up for share of tobacco dollars. Bsns W p 102 Mr 29 '69
Move to limit cigarette ads. U S News 66:16 F 17 '69

CIGARETTES—Advertising—*Continued*
No smoking on the air? Bsns W p36 F 8 '69
Politics of tobacco. E. Schneier. Nation 209:
274-9 S 22 '69
Rising battle over cigarette advertising. il
Time 93:85 F 14 '69
Showdown in Marlboro country il Consumer
Rep 34:516-21 S '69
Smoke-free wasteland. il Sci N 95:185-6 F 22
'69
Smoke on the air. Nat R 21:842 Ag 26 '69
Smoke rings; broadcasting industry resisting
cancellation of contracts. Newsweek 74:78
Ag 18 '69
Smoke signal. il Newsweek 73:104 Ap 21 '69
Smoking and health: Closing the ring on the
cigarette. L. J. Carter. Science 164:1258-61 Je
13 '69
Switching and fighting; offer to phase out
cigarette commercials by the NAB. R. L.
Shayon. Sat R 52:36 Ag 2 '69
Television and cigarettes: whither fairness?
S. Cupps. Chr Cent 86:1085-7 Ag 20 '69
They will not puff. Time 93:93-4 Mr 14 '69
This month's feature: controversy over ciga-
rette advertising. Cong Digest 48:163-92 Je
'69
Trouble from an old friend; broadcast indus-
try. Time 94:76 Jl 18 '69
Vote against cigarettes. Sci N 96:575 D 20 '69
Waging war on the weed. Chr Today 13:26
F 28 '69
Westinghouse is sure. Nation 208:685 Je 2
'69

Anecdotes, facetiae, satire, etc.
Sterilized puff and the great cancer scare.
J. Keefauver. Nat R 21:1168 N 18 '69
CIGARS
Connoisseur's book of the cigar, by Z. Da-
vidoff. Review
Newsweek il 74:101-2+ N 3 '69. S. K.
Oberbeck

Marketing
Boon from Fidel; rights to international sales
of Havana sales rights given to Swiss cigar
store. il Newsweek 74:79-80 Jl 14 '69
CILEA, Francesco
Adriana Lecouvreur. Criticism
Opera N 33:24-5 Ap 19 '69
Opera N il 33:17-20 Ap 19 '69
CILIA and ciliary motion
Ciliary orientation: controlled by cell mem-
brane or by intracellular fibrils? Y. Naitoh
and R. Eckert. bibliog il Science 166:1633-5
D 26 '69
Critical point drying for scanning electron
microscopic study of ciliary motion. G. A.
Horridge and S. L. Tamm. bibliog il Sci-
ence 163:817-18 F 21 '69
Oyster ciliary inhibition by cystic fibrosis
factor. B. Bowman and others. bibliog
il Science 164:325-6 Ap 18 '69
CILIATA
Colchicine-inhibited cilia regeneration: expla-
nation for lack of effect in tris buffer medium L. Margulis and others. bibliog il Science
164:1177-8 Je 6 '69
Critical point drying for scanning electron
microscopic study of ciliary motion. G. A.
Horridge and S. L. Tamm. bibliog il Sci-
ence 163:817-18 F 21 '69
CINCINNATI
Private vehicle inspection. T. J. Frey. il Am
City 84:112-13 Ap '69
Regional data-processing center. A. O. At-
kinson. il Am City 84:91-2+ Jl '69

Education
Crisis in the high schools; the Life poll; with
report by B. Hooper. L. Harris. il Life 66:
22-35+ My 16 '69

Finance
Purchasing guide for city employees. J. G.
Krieg. il Am City 84:75+ Ja '69
Term purchasing cuts the purchasing cost.
J. G. Krieg. Am City 84:138 Jl '69

Industries
See also
Procter and Gamble company

Music
Home sweet zoo; performing opera in the
city zoo. Time 94:48 Ag 8 '69
Report: Cincinnati, summer opera. W.
Mootz. Opera N 34:26 S 6 '69

Sanitary affairs
County-owned, city-managed sewerage sys-
tem. A. D. Caster. il Am City 84:117-18
Ag '69

Street traffic
How to plan for the pedestrian. A. D. Bird.
il Am City 84:76-7+ Jl '69

Theater
Cincinnati's playhouse in the park; Rob-
ert S. Marx theater. il Arch Rec 145:122-8
Mr '69
CINCINNATI ballet company
Dance, architecture, music. W. Terry. il Sat
R 52:38+ My 10 '69
CINCINNATI Bengals (football club) See
Football clubs
CINCINNATI council on world affairs
Cincinnati airs world affairs. S. Aiken. il
Am Ed 5:24-6 My '69
CINCINNATI Reds (baseball) See Baseball
clubs
CINCINNATI. University

College-conservatory of music
See also
Cincinnati ballet company
CINEMOBILE. See Moving picture studios
CINETHEODOLITE. See Theodolites
CIPHER and telegraph codes
Learn code! (time: 30 minutes) R. Teich-
man. il Field & S 73:144+ Ap '69
CIRCADIAN rhythms. See Periodicity
CIRCLES
Is this tile pattern a new math discovery? A.
Earle. il Pop Sci 195:150-1+ Jl '69
CIRCUIT breakers, Electric. See Electric cir-
cuit breakers
CIRCULAR saws. See Saws
CIRCULATING libraries. See Libraries
CIRCULATION departments in libraries. See
Libraries—Circulation, loans, etc.
CIRCUS
Bread from circuses; Ringling bros.-Barnum
& Bailey circus going public. il Time 93:
75 F 21 '69

History
Circusiana; Circus world museum, Baraboo.
Wis. il Hobbies 74:98DD-98EE Ap '69

Photographs
Portfolio: circus. E. Fenander. Atlan 223:53-
60 Je '69
CIRCUS performers
See also
Acrobats and acrobatism
Clowns
CIRCUS world museum, Baraboo, Wis.
Circusiana. il Hobbies 74:98DD-98EE Ap '69
CIRE-perdue process. See Lost wax process
CISTUS. See Rock roses
CITIBANK. See New York (city)—Banks
CITIES and towns
Economy of cities, by J. Jacobs. Review
Atlan 224:104 Jl '69. E. Weeks
New Repub 160:28-30 Je 7 '69. H. J. Gans
Newsweek 73:63 Je 2 '69 L. S. Martz
Sat R 52:35+ Jl 5 '69. C. W. Griffin, jr
Time il 93:104 Je 13 '69
Pre-Copernican views of the city. G. Rand.
il Arch Forum 131:76-81 S '69
Some essentials of successful urban space.
D. K. Specter. il Arch Rec 145:131-40 Ja
'69
What makes a city great? Time essay. il
Time 94:47-8 N 14 '69
Where learning happens; city of the future
as a school. S. Carr and K. Lynch. Ed
Digest 35:9-12 S '69
See also
Business districts
City and town life
Cleaning of cities, towns, etc.
College towns
Education, Urban
Neighborhoods
New cities and towns
Parks
Slums
Sociology, Urban
Street cleaning
Urbanization
also headings beginning City, Municipal,
Urban

Defenses
See also
Civil defense

Federal aid
See Federal and municipal relations

CITIES and towns—*Continued*

Growth

Census report that set off a furor. U S News 66:11 Ap 28 '69

Fastest-growth cities; latest census estimates. il U S News 66:55-7 Mr 31 '69

Still more changes in central cities. il U S News 66:52 Je 30 '69

Industries

Central cities fight back. K. E. Fry. il Nations Bsns 57:60+ S '69

Location

New geography; Central place theory. P. R. Gould. il Harper 238:91-2+ Mr '69; Reply. R. E. Crist. 239:6+ Jl '69

Planning

See City planning

Sports

See Sports—United States

Taxation

Commuters and city income taxes. J. Friedgut. il Nations Bsns 57:66 O '69

Transportation

See also
Rapid transit

Water supply

See Water supply

Zone system

See Zoning

Canada

See also
New cities and towns
Urban renewal—Canada

Europe

Perspective; concerning the quality and beauty of Paris and London. J. H. Plumb. Sat R 52:40-1 F 22 '69

See also
New cities and towns

Finland

See also
New cities and towns
Tapiola

France

See also
New cities and towns

Great Britain

See also
New cities and towns

Latin America

See also
Urbanization

Spain

History

Beginnings of the Cortes of León-Castile. J. F. O'Callaghan. bibliog f Am Hist R 74: 1503-37 Je '69

United States

As I see it; interview. W. Zeckendorf. Forbes 103:55-6 Mr 1 '69

Big changes in America's small towns; stories of six in Iowa. il U S News 66:58-60 Ap 28 '69

Can anyone run a city? G. Tyler. il Sat R 52:22-5 N 8 '69

Cities outlook. Bsns W p48 Mr 1 '69

Cities: waging a battle for survival. il Newsweek 73:40-2 Mr 17 '69

Countdown for small towns. O. Newman. il Esquire 72:180-7 D '69

Exciting cities, a Redbook vacation guide to sight-seeing with children; excerpts from America's exciting cities. A. Schwartz. il Redbook 132:37-44 Ap '69

Fun for the kids in the cities; ed. by P. Piawin. il Bet Hom & Gard 47:143-6 Ap '69

Jane Jacobs: against urban renewal, for urban life; interview, ed. by L. Kent. J. Jacobs. il N Y Times Mag p34-5+ My 25 '69

Quantitative studies of urban problems; AAAS symposium. December 27, 1969. D. Boodman. il Science 166:407 O 17 '69

Soulless city; excerpts from address. D. P. Moynihan. il Am Heritage 20:4-9+ F '69

Suburbia & the city; flight, fight or apathy; address, October 29, 1969. H. Maier. Vital Speeches 36:184-7 Ja 1 '70

Survey of mayors on ills and remedies. il Nations Bsns 57:38-41 F '69

Urban misconceptions. W. S. Foster. bibliog il Am City 84:73-5+ Je '69

We can afford a better America; with editorial comment. E. K. Faltermayer. il Fortune 79:81-2, 88-91+ Mr '69

We won't end the urban crisis until we end majority rule. H. J. Gans. il N Y Times Mag p 12-15+ Ag 3 '69; Discussion. p6+ Ag 24 '69

What Nixon plans to do. il Newsweek 73:49-50+ Mr 17 '69

Where are they now; atomic cities of Oak Ridge, Richland and Los Alamos. il Newsweek 74:20 O 20 '69

Where the jobs are. Mlle 69:152-7 S '69

See also
Abandoned towns
All-America cities
National cleanest town achievement contest
National league of cities
New cities and towns
United States—Housing and urban development, Department of
Urban renewal

CITIZENS and southern national bank of Georgia. *See* Atlanta—Banks

CITIES and towns, Ruined, extinct, etc.
Lost cities of the Maya. L. Payne. il Todays Health 47:56-9+ F '69

See also
Troy

CITIES and towns, Underground
Safe City: apartment living inside a mountain. B. Ford. il Sci Digest 66:16-19 Ag '69

CITIES in Bezique; drama. *See* Kennedy, A.

CITIZENS band radio. *See* Citizens radio service

CITIZENS committee for peace with freedom in Vietnam
Cut and look, not cut and run; excerpts from report. Nat R 21:1052 O 21 '69

New plan for ending the war. il U S News 67:8 N 10 '69

CITIZENS complaints. *See* Complaints

CITIZENS obligations. *See* Citizenship

CITIZENS radio service
Citizen band radio enlarges police; Des Plaines, Ill. H. H. Behrel. il Am City 84:28 Ap '69

CB radio to the rescue. L. Buckwalter. il Pop Sci 195:166-8+ D '69

Hatfield hams and the CB McCoys. C. H. Allen. il Pop Electr 30:73-5+ F '69

Is CB for your boat? E. Robberson. il Yachting 125:60-1+ F '69

On the citizens band. M. P. Spinello. *See* issues of Popular electronics to May 1969

See also
React (organization)

Equipment

CB troubleshooter's casebook; comp. by A. J. Mueller (cont) il Radio-Electr 40:77 F; 86-7 Je; 85 Ag; 82 O '69

Fix CB fast. A. J. Mueller. il Radio-Electr 41:70-2+ Ja '70

What's new in 5-watt CB gear. L. Buckwalter. il Radio-Electr 40:48-51 My '69

See also
Radio telephone

CITIZENSHIP
Chief political question of our time; reprint. W. Karp and H. R. Shapiro. ALA Bul 63:165-7 F '69

Citizenship with a shrug; address, December 3, 1968. J. H. Binns. Vital Speeches 35:207-10 Ja 15 '69

Dissent and involvement; address, October 18, 1969. J. C. Humes. Vital Speeches 36: 183-4 Ja 1 '70

Government finances and citizen responsibility. A. Parker. bibliog f Ann Am Acad 379:123-31 S '68

See also
Patriotism
Social ethics

CITIZENSHIP, Education for
Citizenship education. K. J. Weimer. bibliog Clear House 43:355-7 F '69

Needed: a revolution in citizenship education; address, March 3, 1969. J. S. Gibson. Vital Speeches 35:473-8 My 15 '69

See also
International education

CITRUS fruit trees. *See* Trees

CITRUS fruits
See also
Oranges

CITY and country
See also
Suburban life

CITY and town life
Flight to the city. il Fortune 79:100-3 Mr '69
Learning to live with fear. il Newsweek 73:
62-3 Mr 24 '69; Same abr. with title Fear in
the streets. Read Digest 85:51-3 Jl '69
Man and nature in the city. B. S. Tindall.
il Parks & Rec 4:39-40+ Ja '69
My year as a snob. L. F. Macgregor. il Red-
book 132:14+ Ap '69
Nice place to visit? il Newsweek 73:43-4+
Mr 17 '69
Small town. G. Lidstrom. Sat R 52:4-5 Jl 5
'69
TRB from Main street. New Repub 160:4
My 24 '69
        See also
Church and social problems
CITY art museum of St Louis. See St Louis
city art museum
CITY center Joffrey ballet
Backstage with the Joffrey ballet in Chicago.
J. Anderson. il Dance Mag 43:43-9 Mr '69
Ballet; Saran wrap paradise. R. Kotlowitz.
il Harper 238:105-7 F '69
City center Joffrey ballet revives Leonide
Massine's Three-cornered hat; New York
city center. D. Hering. il Dance Mag 43:37-8
N '69
City center Joffrey ballet: the Three-cor-
nered hat and the Poppet. D. Hering.
Dance Mag 43:85 D '69
Joffrey enterprises. W. Terry. il Sat R 52:52-
3 Ap 5 '69
Phoenix too frequent? M. Marks. Dance Mag
43:29-30+ My '69
Please pass the Danish; new productions of
Konservatoriet and Facade. W. Terry. il
Sat R 52:69-70 Mr 22 '69
World of dance: production of The poppet.
W. Terry. Sat R 52:40 N 8 '69
World of dance; production of Three-cor-
nered hat. W. Terry. Sat R 52:65+ O 18 '69
CITY college of New York. See New York
(city). City university of New York—City
college
CITY college of San Francisco. See San Fran-
cisco. City college
CITY dumps. See Municipal dumps
CITY elections. See Municipal elections
CITY employees. See Municipal employees
CITY gardens
Plants for city gardens. P. Truex. il Hor-
ticulture 46:38-9+ Ag '68
        See also
Boston—Gardens
Roof gardens
CITY government. See Municipal government
CITY growth. See Cities and towns—Growth
CITY halls
How to design a city hall: Martinsville, Va.
T. B. Noland. il Am City 84:93-4 Ap '69
CITY houses
Contemporary house that moves the emo-
tions; new townhouse in Georgetown. E.
Sverbeyeff. il House B 111:84-9 Ap '69
Flight to the city. il Fortune 79:100-3 Mr '69
Garment house, Brooklyn, New York. il Arch
Rec 145:70-3 mid-My '69
Nine-G cooperative; brownstones in New York
city. il Arch Forum 131:78-81 Jl '69
Remodeling. il Am Home 72:59-71 My '69
Tinkertoy houses; town houses. il Arch
Forum 130:96-9 Ja '69
Total town house. il House & Gard 136:
122-5 N '69
Townhouses, Houston, Texas. il Arch Rec
145:48-51 mid-My '69
Trentman house, Washington, D.C. il Arch Rec
145:26-9 mid-My '69
CITY life. See City and town life
CITY life; story. See Barthelme, D.
CITY magazines. See Periodicals—United
States
CITY managers
How do you define urban success? interview;
ed. by B. Foster. J. C. Johnson. il Am City
84:69-71 D '69
Recent city manager appointments. M. E.
Keane. See issues of American city to July
1969
        See also
International city management association
CITY news bureau of Chicago. See News agen-
cies
CITY noise. See Noise
CITY parks. See Parks

CITY planners
They think cities are for people; women
in the field. J. Steinberg. il Mlle 68:140-2+
F '69
        See also
Candeub, I.
Ponte, V. de P.
CITY planning
Cities to live in: planning versus the in-
evitable; excerpts from Last landscape.
W. H. Whyte. Cur 103:48-58 Ja '69
Deghettoization; choice of the new militancy.
C. Funnyé. Arch Forum 130:74-7 Ap '69
How to design with nature. il Time 94:70-1 O
10 '69
NRPA urban plan. Parks & Rec 4:47-9 N '69
Neon city: proposed bridge to Sicily and re-
lated amenities; project of T. Waddell.
il Arch Forum 130:68-73 Ap '69
1969 to 2019. New Yorker 45:29-31 F 22 '69
Oracles at Delos. Time 94:36+ Ag 8 '69
Park values and the city. D. F. Rettie.
il Nat Parks 43:8-10 F '69
Pioneer planner with over-all view; I. Can-
deub. Bsns W p74-5 Ag 16 '69
Planning semantics need improvement. A.
Z. Guttenberg. Am City 84:134 O '69
Structure of motion in the ctiy. P. Wolf.
il Art in Am 57:66-75 Ja '69
Tomorrow's city is alive and well and has
been going full blast all over the world
except possibly here. P. Blake. Mlle 68:
120-1+ F '69
Two new French towns, by Marcel Breuer
and Robert F. Gatje. il Arch Rec 146:101-
12 Ag '69
Urban expansion takes to the water. W.
McQuade. il Fortune 80:131-5+ S '69
Urban processs planning with and for the
community; reprint. E. N. Bacon. Arch Rec
145:129-34 My '69
We can afford a better America; with edi-
torial comment. E. K. Faltermayer. il For-
tune 79:81-2, 88-91+ Mr '69
What urban design means. R. Warburton.
il Am City 84:110+ My '69
        See also
American institute of planners
Building laws and regulations
Business districts
Cities and towns
Computers—City planning applications
Rural planning
Streets
Streets—Intersections
Suburbs
Urban renewal
Water fronts
        also subhead City planning under names
of cities, e.g. New York (city)—City plan-
ning

Bibliography
Our cities, their wretched present, their
hopeful future. J. Herbert. House & Gard
135:44+ Mr '69

History
City no one knew; the Amoskeag millyard,
Manchester, N.H. R. Langenbach. il Arch
Forum 130:84-91 Ja '69

Study and teaching
Environmental education: from kindergarten
on up. E. P. Berkeley. il Arch Forum 130:
46-53+ Je '69
New gamesmanship; urban games, played for
understanding of urban problems. E. P.
Berkeley. il Arch Forum 129:53-63 D '68

Zone system
        See Zoning
CITY school systems. See Public schools
CITY streets. See Streets
CITY transit. See Rapid transit
CITY university of New York. See New York
(city). City university of New York
CIVAN, M. M. See Dibona, D. R. jt. auth.
CIVIC education. See Citizenship. Education
for
CIVIL aeronautics board. See United States—
Civil aeronautics board
CIVIL defense
        See also
Atomic bomb shelters
Emergency communication systems
Radio in civil defense

Russia
Seven warning signals: a review of Soviet
civil defense. J. L. Gailar. Bul Atom Sci
25:18-22 D '69

CIVIL disobedience. See Government, Resistance to: Lawlessness

CIVIL engineering
 See also
 Piles and pile driving

CIVIL liberties. See Civil rights

CIVIL liberties union, American. See American civil liberties union

CIVIL liberty. See Liberty

CIVIL procedure
 See also
 Attachment and garnishment
 Injunctions
 Jury

CIVIL rights
 Human rights and the Nixon administration.
  T. P. Melady and M. B. Melady. Cath
  World 209:55-8 My '69
 Human rights questions; Assembly acts on
  fourteen resolutions; with text of resolutions. UN Mo Chron 6:124-38 Ja '69
 National conference on continuing action for
  human rights; address, December 4, 1968.
  E. Warren. Dept State Bul 59:686-90 D
  30 '68
 National conference on continuing action for
  human rights; remarks, December 4, 1968.
  L. B. Johnson. Dept State Bul 59:685-6
  D 30 '68
 See also
 Due process of law
 Free speech
 Human rights day and week
 Intellectual liberty
 Natural law
 Privacy Right of
 Right to education
 Trials (civil rights)
 United Nations—Commission on human
  rights
 Universal declaration of human rights
 Woman—Equal rights
  also subhead Civil rights under various
  subjects, e.g. Teachers—Civil rights

Study and teaching

Teaching about human rights. Sch & Soc
 97:233-4 Ap '69

Greece, Modern

Greece: how free? Close-up of a military
 dictatorship. C. S. Foltz, jr. il U S News
 67:60-1 Ag 18 '69
Window dressing; partial restoration. il
 Newsweek 73:52+ Ap 21 '69

Mexico

Law and hair down Mexico way. C. Manne.
 Commonweal 91:36-7 O 10 '69; Reply with
 rejoinder. J. A. Magner. 91:415 Ja 9 '70

Northern Ireland

At the brink in Northern Ireland. J. A.
 Coulter. Cath World 209:164-7 Jl '69
Behind all the turmoil in Northern Ireland—
 il U S News 66:10 My 5 '69
Bernadette on Fifth avenue. T. M. Gannon.
 America 121:137-9 S 6 '69
Case of Ireland. Commonweal 90:579-80 S 26
 '69
Critical election in Ulster. America 120:212
 F 22 '69
For Ireland: spectre of civil war. il U S News
 67:6 Ag 25 '69
Human rights in Ulster. Cath World 210:2 O
 '69
Ireland's niggers; with interview with B.
 Devlin. P. Buckman. Ramp Mag 8:19-22
 Jl '69
Irish ire. Chr Cent 86:1106 Ag 27 '69
Irish power on First avenue. P. Tracy. Commonweal 90:278-9 My 23 '69
Not Conor Cruise O'Brien. A. Lejeune. Nat R
 21:1009 O 7 '69
Price of my soul, by B. Devlin. Review
 Sat R 52:32-3+ N 8 '69. M. Ward
Ulster vote disappointing. America 120:263
 Mr 8 '69

Russia

Filed and forgotten; appeal to UN by intellectuals and citizens. New Repub 161:8
 Jl 26 '69
New Stalinism; Action group for the defense
 of civil rights in the U.S.S.R. America
 121:3 Jl 5 '69

Spain

Exception is the rule. P. Steinfels. Commonweal 89:633-4 F 21 '69

Taiwan

China; arrests and imprisonment of dissident
 intellectuals in Taiwan. H. Yu. Chr Cent
 86:1404 O 29 '69

United States

Civil rights and symbolic language. A. Neier.
 Cur 104:29-34 F '69
Civil rights, the Nixon fiddle. B. Sellers. Nation 209:344-6 O 6 '69
Close-up: blackest white man I know; interview, ed. by R. Busch. W. M. Kunstler. il
 Life 67:50-50D Jl 25 '69
Commitment to the law? America 121:315
 O 18 '69
Defense against Daley: the conspiracy on
 trial; case of the Chicago defendants. L. D.
 Nachman. Nation 208:752-4 Je 16 '69
Federal government and protest. D. Mars.
 bibliog f Ann Am Acad 382:120-30 Mr '69
Few soft words for the rabble-rousers;
 clients of W. M. Kunstler. C. McCarry. il
 Esquire 72:106-8+ Jl '69
Nixon's first test. G. Orfield. Nation 208:79-82
 Ja 20 '69
Nixon's moves in civil rights. il U S News
 66:15 Ap 21 '69
One generation speaks to another; exchange
 of letters. M. Machiz; J. L. Robertson. U S
 News 67:28-31 Jl 7 '69
Protecting civil liberties; psychiatry's role in
 civil commitment cases. A. M. Dershowitz.
 Cur 105:32-6 Mr '69
Road Nixon is taking on civil rights. il U S
 News 67:36-7 Jl 21 '69
What to do when you're arrested. L. David.
 il Mech Illus 65:45-7+ N '69
 See also
 American civil liberties union
 Negroes—Civil rights
 United States—Commission on civil rights
 United States—Constitution—Bill of rights

CIVIL rights commission. See United States—
 Commission on civil rights

CIVIL rights demonstrations
 Answer to poverty; sit-ins, camp-ins and
  sleep-in banned in Washington, D. C.
  Nation 209:4 Jl 7 '69
 Bernadette of the Irish. P. Tracy. Commonweal 90:583-4 S 26 '69
 Bernadette on Fifth avenue; National assn.
  for Irish justice demonstration. T. M.
  Gannon. America 121:137-9 S 6 '69
 Date at the White House. il Newsweek 73:37
  My 26 '69
 Queen is with us; C. S. King's march in
  Charleston. il Newsweek 73:37 My 12 '69
 South Carolina; the movement finally arrives; activities in Beaufort, Charleston,
  Denmark. D. Nolan. Nation 208:654-6 My 26
  '69
 See also
 Negroes—Segregation. Resistance to
 Poor people's march on Washington, 1969

CIVIL rights division. See United States—
 Justice, Department of—Civil rights division

CIVIL rights organizations
 Answer to riots; the Rochester plan; FIGHT
  organization. il U S News 67:58-61 Ag 4 '69
 From civil rights to black liberation; the unsettled 1960's. R. L. Zangrando. Cur Hist
  57:281-6+ N '69
 Scientist with a cause; B. Gifford and FIGHT.
  il Ebony 25:73-6+ D '69
 See also
 Southern Christian leadership conference
 Student national coordinating committee

CIVIL service
 Merit system today; address, October 21, 1968.
  J. W. Macy, jr. Vital Speeches 35:196-200
  Ja 15 '69
 See also
 Bureaucracy
 Patronage, Political

Asia, Southern

Soft states of South Asia: the civil servant
 problem; address, November 14, 1968. K.
 G. Myrdal. Bul Atom Sci 25:7-10 Ap '69

United States

When public servants revolt. A. H. Raskin.
 Cur 103:27-32 Ja '69

CIVIL service pensions
 Pension benefits: higher now for federal
  workers. U S News 67:8 N 3 '69

CIVILIAN conscription. See Service, Compulsory non-military

CIVILIAN defense. See Civil defense

CIVILIAN evacuation. See Evacuation, Civilian

CIVILIAN-military relations. See United States
 —Armed forces—Relations with civilians

CIVILIAN morale. See Morale, National

CIVILIZATION

Civilization process, by D. Ribeiro. Review
Natur Hist il 78:72-3+ Je '69. A. F. C.
Wallace
Evolution on a bad trip; Can man survive
exhibit at American museum of natural
history. W. Sheed. il Life 67:7 Jl 11 '69
Leisure and the masses; address. E. Hoffer.
Parks & Rec 4:31-4+ Mr '69
Proposal to a foundation; question of a com-
mission to study and report on the state
of mankind. N. Cousins. Sat R 52:26 Ap 26
'69
Quote, unquote. UNESCO Courier 22:12-13+
Ag '69
Vertical is to live, horizontal is to die. R. B.
Fuller. Am Scholar 39:27-47 Wint '69
　　See also
Anthropology
Culture
History
Humanism
Inventions
Man—Migrations
Man, Prehistoric
Manners and customs
Popular culture
Social change
Social progress
Social sciences
Society, Primitive
Sociology
Technology and civilization
　　also subhead Civilization under names of
countries, e.g. India—Civilization

　　　　Philosophy

Experiences, by A. Toynbee. Review
Sat R 52:57-8 Je 21 '69. G. Culligan
Future is not what it used to be; excerpt
from address, May 1969. A. L. Sachar. PTA
Mag 64:2-5+ S '69

　　　Preservation of records

Millenial mementos; Time Capsule EXPO '70.
S. Griffin. il Sci N 95:102 Ja 25 '69

　　Anecdotes, facetiae, satire, etc.

Mementos for the moon. Chr Cent 86:937 Jl
9 '69

CIVILIZATION, Ancient
　　See also
Mayas
Science, Ancient

CIVILIZATION, Arabic
Research into contemporary Arab culture.
Sch & Soc 97:376-8 O '69

CIVILIZATION, Christian
　　See also
Christianity and culture

CIVILIZATION, Greco-Roman
Greeks and Romans at their ease. G. Highet.
il Horizon 11:8-11 Spr '69

CIVILIZATION, Greek
　　See also
Hellenism

CIVILIZATION, Medieval
Pursuit of happiness in a villa. I. Origo.
il Horizon 11:14-17 Spr '69

CIVILIZATION, Minoan
Time clock for history. B. C. Heezen. il Sat
R 52:87-90 D 6 '69

CIVILIZATION and science. See Science and
civilization

CIVILIZATION and technology. See Technology
and civilization

CLACKAMAS COUNTY, Ore.
Quick service ditch cleaning; Scoopmobile
with ditch-cleaning attachment. il Am City
84:32 N '69

CLAGUE, Ewan
Why one expert sees no big rise in layoffs
when economy cools; excerpts from report.
por U S News 67:69-70 Ag 4 '69

CLAIBORNE, Craig
Food. See issues of New York times magazine

CLAIMS
　　See also
Insurance—Adjustment of claims

CLAM chowder. See Chowder

CLAMAN, Julian
Spot check; some observations on the state
of the arts in America today. Harp Baz
102:122B-122X F '69

CLAMPITT, Mary O. and Rankin, K. R.
For sound teeth. Parents Mag 44:64-5+ N
'69

CLAMPS
Sliding miter clamp. R. J. DeCristoforo. il
Mech Illus 65:67 D '69

CLAMS
Oxygen consumption and pumping rates in
the hard clam Mercenaria mercenaria: a
direct method. A. Hamwi and H. H. Haskin. bibliog il Science 163:823-4 F 21 '69;
Reply. J. Verduin. 166:1309-10 D 5 '69
Pace of the tides; clam digging in Maine;
excerpt from In defense of nature. J. Hay.
il Audubon 71:26-7 Mr '69

CLANCY, Richard J.
Wax sculpture. Sch Arts 68:28-9 My '69

CLAPPER, Louis S.
Washington report. See issues of National
wildlife
　　　　　about
Clapper named to pollution board. por Nat
Wildlife 7:31 F '69

CLARIAS batrachus. See Catfishes

CLARION music society, incorporated
Musical events; Simone Mayr's Medea in
Corinto at Alice Tully Hall. W. Sargeant.
New Yorker 45:186-8 D 13 '69

CLARK, Alfred, jr, and others
Solar differential rotation and oblateness.
bibliog Science 164:290-1 Ap '68 '69

CLARK, Alvan, and sons company
Clarks and some of their refractors. J.
Ashbrook. il Sky & Tel 37:74-5 F '69

CLARK, Blair
Question is what kind of army? Harper
239:80-3 S '69

CLARK, Blake
America's greatest earthquake. Read Digest
94:110-14 Ap '69
U.S. diplomat no. 1. Read Digest 95:141-5
D '69

CLARK, Brian R. See Rubin, R. T. jt. auth.

CLARK, Colin
World power and population. Nat R 21:481-4
My 20 '69

CLARK, E. D.
Matching resistors to close tolerances. Radio-
Electr 41:43 Ja '70

CLARK, Earl
Sail with the mail! Travel 132:44-7 D '69

CLARK, Eleanor
At the falls at nine; story. Yale R 58:572-7
Je '69

CLARK, Fred
Shock cord: boatman's handiest tiedown.
Mech Illus 65:114-15 S '69

CLARK, Fred C. jr
Impossible dream: England's Island cruising
club. Motor B 124:56-7+ D '69
Work boats for fun. Motor B 124:56-9 S '69

CLARK, George P. and Purcell, Donald
Winds of change in Haitian education. Negro
Hist Bul 32:7-10 O '69

CLARK, Gerald
What happens when the police strike. N Y
Times Mag p45+ N 16 '69

CLARK, Hank
Build this foldaway hobby center. Pop Mech
132:144-7 Ag '69

CLARK, Howard Longstreth
License to print money. il por Time 94:94 N
7 '69

CLARK, James Dawson Chichester-. See Chichester-Clark, J. D.

CLARK, John R.
Heat pollution. Nat Parks 43:4-8 D '69
Thermal pollution and aquatic life; with biographical sketch. Sci Am 220:14, 18-27 bib-
liog(p 148) Mr '69

CLARK, Kenneth Bancroft
Dealing with the urban crisis; excerpts
from Agenda for the Nation. Cur 103:21-3
Ja '69
Efficiency as a prod to social action; ex-
cerpt from address. Mo Labor R 92:54-6
Ag '69
Fifteen years of deliberate speed; excerpt
from Argument. Sat R 52:59-61+ D 20 '69
　　　　　about
Exclude whites? No, says top Negro edu-
cator. U S News 66:18 Je 2 '69

CLARK, Kenneth McKenzie, baron Clark of
Saltwood. See Clark of Saltwood, K. M. C.

CLARK, Leonard
Poetry by children. Horn Bk 45:15-19 F '69

CLARK, Petula
Hollywood scene; ed. by E. Miller. pors
Seventeen 28:130+ Ag '69
　　　　　about
Is Petula Clark another Julie Andrews? A.
Levy. il por Good H 168:88-9+ Mr '69
Petula Clark, Mrs Chips. J. Hamilton. il pors
Look 33:50-3+ O 7 '69

CLARK, Phil
140 million-year-old plant. Horticulture 47:41
S '69
Succulents. Horticulture 47:24-5+ N '69
CLARK, Ramsey
Annals of politics. R. Harris. New Yorker
45:63-4+ N 8; 64-8+ N 15; 61-4+ N 22 '69
CLARK, Ray H. and Korst, D. R.
Circadian periodicity of bone marrow mito-
tic activity and reticulocyte counts in rats
and mice. bibliog Science 166:236-7 O 10 '69
CLARK, Robert
Tempera paintings of Robert Clark. J.
Lovoos. il pors Am Artist 33:60-5+ D '69
CLARK, Roger C.
NCTE/ERIC report on innovation in teaching
English. Engl J 58:949-55 S '69
CLARK, Tom
Greeks; Power of the watchman continually
increases tenfold; Crows; poems. Poetry
114:319-21 Ag '69
Pillow; poem. New Yorker 45:146 S 27 '69
CLARK, Walter
Atlanta 500. Motor T 21:90-2 Jl '69
CLARK, Willard
Era of silent films ended for amateur travel
photographer. Holiday 46:49 O '69
CLARK, William
See also
Lewis and Clark expedition
CLARK, William C. and Voris, H. K.
Venom neutralization by rattlesnake serum
albumin. bibliog Science 164:1402-4 Je 20
'69
CLARK, York
Black man in the American West. D. T.
Schoenberger. bibliog il Negro Hist Bul 32:
7-11 Mr '69
CLARK of Saltwood, Kenneth McKenzie Clark,
baron
Grand tour. il por Newsweek 74:71 D 15 '69
People are talking about... por Vogue 155:
120-1 Ja 15 '70
CLARK equipment company
Two steps forward. il Forbes 104:32-3 N 1
'69
CLARK university, Worcester, Mass.
Architecture through improvisation? S. Mo-
holy-Nagy. il Arch Forum 131:40-7 S '69
CLARKE, Arthur Charles
Apollo & beyond. Look 33:43-9 Jl 15 '69
Beyond the moon: no end. Time 94:31 Jl 18
'69
Challenge of the spaceship; reprint. UNESCO
Courier 22:25-8 Ag '69
Views from earth on the odyssey into space.
Look 33:72+ F 4 '69
about
Arthur Clarke: prophet of the space age. J.
Reddy. por Read Digest 94:134-6+ Ap '69
Profiles. J. Bernstein. por New Yorker 45:
40-2+ Ag 9 '69
CLARKE, Bobby
Philly takes a flyer on a rookie with heart.
G. Ronberg. il por Sports Illus 31:92+ N
17 '69
CLARKE, Gary K.
European zoo marathon. Parks & Rec 4:41-
2 O '69
Upgrading a zoo. por Am City 84:82-4+ N
'69
CLARKE, Henry
American uniques in France: the Shrivers;
photographs. Vogue 153:160-7 My '69
CLARKE, Henry Leland
Reviews of records. Mus Q 55:584-6 O '69
CLARKE, John Clem
Copy cat. D. L. Shirey. il Newsweek 73:105
Je 16 '69
John Clem Clarke transmits a picture. W. S.
Wilson. il por Art N 68:46-7+ Sum '69
CLARKE, Kenneth E.
What can we expect from the Nixon years?
Chr Cent 86:182-3 F 5 '69
CLARKE, Richard
Opportunities; interview. New Yorker 45:15-
16 Jl 19 '69
CLARKE, Ron
This coliseum could have used lions. S.
Myslenski. Sports Illus 31:38 Jl 28 '69
CLARKE, Thomas E.
Celibacy: challenge to tribalism. America 120:
464-7 Ap 19 '69
Theology. America 122:24-5 Ja 10 '70
CLASS actions. See Actions and defenses
CLASS discussions. See Discussion method
(education)
CLASS distinction. See Equality; Social classes
CLASS reunions. See College graduates
CLASS size
See also
Double shifts (public schools)

CLASS struggle. See Social conflict
CLASSEN, J.
First maps of the moon. Sky & Tel 37:82-3
F '69
CLASSES, Special. See Special classes and spe-
cial schools
CLASSICAL education
See also
Humanism
Humanities
CLASSICAL literature
Classics revisited:
Aristotle's poetics. K. Rexroth. Sat R
52:28+ F 22 '69
Goethe. K. Rexroth. Sat R 52:21 Ap 19
'69
Gulliver's travels. K. Rexroth. Sat R 52:
12+ Mr 22 '69
Robert Burns. K. Rexroth. Sat R 52:56
Ap 12 '69
Song of songs. K. Rexroth. Sat R 52:16
Ap 26 '69
Living Latin and Greek; informal monthly
reading sessions in Austin, Tex. Sch & Soc
97:199 Ap '69
CLASSICAL music. See Music
CLASSICISM
See also
Hellenism
CLASSIFICATION
Additions and changes: a study of selected
LC classification schedules. L. Rowell. bib-
liog il Library J 94:3975-7 N 1 '69
Are we bandwagoneers? reasons against
changing to LC at Brigham Young univer-
sity library. M. E. Lamson. bibliog ALA
Bul 63:1278-9 O '69
Dead heads? letter to the editor. A. C. Fos-
kett. Library J 94:1559 Ap 15 '69
See also
Biology—Classification
CLASSIFICATION, Decimal
Let's keep Dewey alive. D. J. Lehnus. il
Wilson Lib Bul 43:552-3 F '69
CLASSIFICATION of movies. See Moving pic-
tures—Classification
CLASSIFIED defense information. See Defense
information, Classified
CLASSROOM films. See Moving pictures in
education
CLASSROOM management
Aggression in the classroom; excerpts from
address. F. Redl. Todays Ed 58:30-2 S '69;
Same abr. Ed Digest 35:5-8 N '69
Benevolent dictator in the inner-city schools.
E. D. Ruth, jr. il Todays Ed 58:60-1 O '69
Check your inquiry-teaching technique. M.
Sugrue and J. A. Sweeney. Todays Ed
58:43-4 My '69
Interaction analysis improves classroom in-
struction. L. F. Psencik. bibliog f Clear
House 43:555-60 My '69
Some tips on classroom management. J.
Spencer. Todays Ed 58:50 D '69
CLASSROOM teachers, Association of. See Na-
tional education association—Association of
classroom teachers
CLASSROOM visitation. See School supervi-
sion and supervisors
CLASSROOMS
Anyplace can be a classroom. il Am Ed 5:
15-9 D '69
CLATHRATE hydrates. See Hydrates
CLAUSEN, Alden Winship
How private is business nowadays. B. L.
Masse. America 121:551 D 6 '69
New boss for the biggest. por Time 94:50
D 26 '69
CLAWSON, Marion, and others
Desalted seawater for agriculture: is it eco-
nomic? bibliog Science 164:1141-8 Je 6 '69
CLAY, Cassius
Art of Ali. M. Kane. il pors Sports Illus
30:48-57 My 5 '69
Confessions of the FBI. Newsweek 73:29-30 Je
16 '69
Knock-down, put-on. J. Morgenstern. il por
Newsweek 74:122+ D 8 '69
Muhammad Ali and the little people. I.
Shaw. il por Esquire 72:121-5+ N '69
Muhammad Ali on campus. C. W. Edwards.
por Cath World 210:69-73 N '69
Return of Muhammad Ali, a/k/a Cassius
Marcellus Clay jr. P. Wood. il pors N Y
Times Mag p32-3+ N 30 '69
Super fight. il por Time 95:59 Ja 19 '70
Unconquerable Muhammad Ali. H. J. Mas-
saquoi. il pors Ebony 24:168-70+ Ap '69
Will Ali fight again? por Newsweek 73:52+
Ap 7 '69
CLAY, William L.
Militant with a knack for wins. il pors Ebony
24:61+ F '69

CLERCQ, E. de. See Ormai, S. jt. auth.
CLERGY
Change of pace for parsons. Chr Cent 86:1101 Ag 20 '69
Instant-minister racket. B. Bruns. il Life 67: 67-8+ N 14 '69
New ministry: bringing God back to life. il Time 94:40-5 D 26 '69
Recharging the peace movement; Washington mobilization of clergy and laymen concerned about Vietnam. R. L. Kuttner. Commonweal 89:669-70 F 28 '69
Save your clerical collars, boys! R. E. Wentz. Chr Cent 86:1133-5 S 3 '69
Theological education 1969; symposium. Chr Cent 86:541-50+ Ap 23 '69
    See also
Academy of parish clergy
Catholic church—Clergy
Chaplains, Military
Church of England—Clergy
Laity
Negro clergy
Parishes
Pastoral theology
Preaching
Priests
Sermons
Theological education
Women as ministers

Anecdotes, facetiae, satire, etc.
Ministerial images. Chr Cent 86:1125 Ag 27 '69
Protocol for campus pastors. Chr Cent 86: 1297 O 8 '69

Education
Hard times for Ph.D.s Chr Cent 86:1658 D 31 '69

Salaries, allowances, etc.
Fair pay for preachers. Chr Today 13:26-7 Mr 14 '69
Low ministerial income induces few to quit, study finds. il Chr Cent 86:1509 N 26 '69
On accepting clergy discounts; psychological implications. W. R. Rogers. Chr Cent 86: 1113-14 Ag 27 '69; Discussion. 86:1285-6 O 8 '69

CLERGY and laymen concerned about Vietnam. See Vietnamese war, 1957- —Protests, demonstrations, etc. against
CLERGY conferences
Badgered bishops; bishops and cardinals meeting in Chur, Switzerland. il News-week 74:91 Jl 21 '69
Challenge in Chur; symposium to discuss the crisis in the Roman Catholic priest-hood. Time 94:63 Jl 18 '69
CLERGY discount. See Discount
CLERGYMENS wives
Minister and his wife. R. M. Smucker. Chr Today 13:3-4 Je 20 '69
Women ministers marry. J. Rohler. il Chr Today 13:41-2 Ja 31 '69
CLESS, Elizabeth L.
Modest proposal for the educating of wo-men. Am Scholar 38:618-27 Aut '69
CLEVELAND, Grover
Cleveland on the Cape. T. L. Christie. il pors Sat R 52:56+ Mr 8 '69
CLEVELAND, Harlan
Road back to internationalism. Atlan 223:57-9 My '69
CLEVELAND, Harold van B.
Common market after de Gaulle. For Affairs 47:697-710 Jl '69
CLEVELAND, J. M.
Plutonium, the lively element. Chem 42:13-16 D '69 (to be cont)
CLEVELAND, Patsy
Head start for Patsy. Am Ed 5:19 O '69
CLEVELAND
Buzzards of Hinckley. B. Thomas. il Nat Wildlife 7:34-5 F '69

Airports
Are trains best way to get to the airport? downtown-to-airport rail connection. il Bsns W p80-1 My 10 '69

Blossom center
Boulez at Blossom. B. Murray. il Hi Fi 19: MA26-7 O '69
Structure suits architecture that suits acoustics. il Arch Rec 145:191-6 Je '69

City planning
Cleveland: Now! C. B. Stokes. il Am City 84: 95-7 S '69
Cleveland's Carl Stokes: making it; Cleveland now program. il Newsweek 73:67-8+ My 26 '69

Education
Advisory teacher program benefits begin-ning teachers; English teacher program. R. J. Goodrich. Clear House 44:12-15 S '69
Warehouse school. T. Kaib. il Todays Ed 58: 58-9 S '69

Elections
Mayor Stokes' West side story. M. D. Daley. Commonweal 91:270-1 N 28 '69
We have overcome; mayoralty results. il Newsweek 74:48 N 17 '69

Libraries
    See also
Cleveland public library

Music
Report: Cleveland; production of Rimsky-Korsakov's Golden cockerel. R. Finn. Opera N 34:23 N 1 '69
    See also
Cleveland orchestra

Negroes
Bad day in Cleveland; Glenville shootings; Civil violence report. R. Bartimole. Na-tion 209:41-5 Jl 14 '69
Black city: a footnote. Trans-Action 6:7 My '69
Name of the beast. Nation 208:292 Mr 10 '69
Sniping a new pattern of violence? T. A. Knopf. bibliog il Trans-Action 6:22-9 Jl '69; Reply with rejoinder. J. R. Corsi and L. H. Masotti. 6:5+ S '69

Parks and playgrounds
Lighting adds thrills to a toboggan chute. O. D. Graham. il Am City 84:124 Ag '69

Police
Bad day in Cleveland; Glenville shootings; Civil violence report. R. Bartimole. Na-tion 209:41-5+ Jl 14 '69

Politics and government
Challenge to Mayor Stokes. D. Henninger. New Repub 161:12-14 Ag 23 '69
Mayor Stokes's troubles. Newsweek 74:42 S 29 '69
Second lap. A. Z. Silver. Nation 208:524 Ap 28 '69
    See also
Cleveland—Elections

Rapid transit
Are trains best way to get to the airport? downtown-to-airport rail connection. il Bsns W p80-1 My 10 '69
Who will pay the bill? direct rapid transit line connecting downtown center to air-port. A. H. Sypher. Nations Bsns 57:19-20 Ja '69
    See also
Cleveland—Parks and playgrounds

Riots
Sniping a new pattern of violence? T. A. Knopf. bibliog il Trans-Action 6:22-9 Jl '69; Reply with rejoinder. J. R. Corsi and L. H. Masotti. 6:5+ S '69

Sanitary affairs
Cities: the price of optimism. il Time 94:41 Ag 1 '69

Social conditions
    See also
Cleveland—Negroes
CLEVELAND Browns (football club) See Football clubs
CLEVELAND Indians (baseball) See Baseball clubs
CLEVELAND Now project. See Cleveland—City planning
CLEVELAND orchestra
Music, political and other; concerts at Car-negie Hall. C. J. McNaspy. America 120: 259-60 Mr 1 '69
Musical events; performance of Mahler's Ninth symphony, conducted by G. Szell. New Yorker 44:94 F 15 '69
CLEVELAND public library
Cleveland: books/jobs and the manpower crisis. M. A. Springman. il Wilson Lib Bul 43:397-9 My '69
Cleveland public library: 1869-1969; with statement by R. M. Nixon and address by H. Donovan. P. Vandemark. il Wilson Lib Bul 43:728-39 Ap '69
New librarian to the rescue; address, April 1969. J. Barzun. il Library J 94:3963-5 N 1 '69
CLEVELAND symphony orchestra. See Cleve-land orchestra

CLEVELAND transit system. See Cleveland—Rapid transit
CLEVER cobbler; drama. See Feather, J.
CLEWORTH, Derek, and Edman, K. A. P.
Laser diffraction studies on single skeletal muscle fibers. bibliog Science 163:296-8 Ja 17 '69
CLIBURN, Van
Van Cliburn recital: the two Chopin sonatas. C. J. Luten. Am Rec G 35:373 Ja '69
CLICHÉS. See English language—Terms and phrases
CLIFF, Edward P.
As I see the forest fire challenge. Am For 75: 20-3+ Je '69
CLIFF ISLAND
Taking an island for granite; student investment in Crotch Island. Bsns W p 125 N 8 '69
CLIFFORD, Clark McAdams
Clifford's call for withdrawal; excerpts from remarks. Newsweek 73:42 Je 30 '69
U.S. posture. Clifford's size-up; excerpts from statement, January 18, 1969. U S News 66:6 Ja 27 '69
Viet Nam reappraisal. For Affairs 47:601-22 Jl '69
War pullout? Clifford's plan; excerpts from remarks. por U S News 66:11 Je 30 '69

about

Attorney at war. D. Welsh and D. Horowitz. il Ramp Mag 7:132-4+ Ja 25 '69
Clifford reviewed. K. Crawford. Newsweek 74:20 Jl 7 '69
Clifford sees U.S. continuing nuclear superiority over Soviets. Aviation W 90:20 Ja 27 '69
Pullout; whose timetable? por Newsweek 73:40+ Je 30 '69
Viet Nam timetable. il por Time 93:12-13 Je 27 '69
CLIFFORD, John
Brief biography. S. Goodman. pors Dance Mag 43:68-9 Je '69
CLIFFORD, William
Cordially yours. House B 111:166+ O '69
It may be offal to some but to others it's sweetbreads, kidney pie and calf's liver. Holiday 46:68-9+ O '69
Little wonder restaurants of New York's Chinatown. il Holiday 45:72:3+ Ap '69
Now it's mug time, summertime or anytime. House B 111:70-1+ Jl '69
Pleasures of the extravagant bottle. House B 111:98-100 F '69
CLIFTON, Linda J.
Two Corys: a sample of inductive teaching. Engl J 58:414-15 Mr '69
CLIFTON, Lucille
Carols for Christmas, 1969: Moon walkers. N Y Times Mag p5 D 21 '69
Christmas is something else. House & Gard 136:70-1+ D '69
Generations; poem. Mlle 70:146 N '69
Magic mama; story. Redbook 134:88-9 N '69
CLIFTON, Ray
JFETS. Radio-Electr 40:55-7 Je '69
MOSFET's. Radio-Electr 40:61-3+ D '69
CLIFTON, N. J.
Pin-point plowing. A. Mazowiecki. il Am City 84:89-90 Ja '69
CLIMACTERIC
See also
Menopause
CLIMATE
Another ice age? Sci Digest 65:39 My '69
Climate and history; excerpt from Discontinuity in Greek civilization. R. Carpenter. il Horizon 11:48-57 Spr '69
Climate and man; AAAS symposium, December 29, 1969. L. J. Battan. il Science 166: 536-7 O 24 '69
Earth's cooling climate. K. Frazier. il Sci N 96:458-9 N 15 '69
Science and the planet earth. il Chem 42: 24-5 D '69
See also
Paleoclimatology
Plants, Effect of climate on
Weather
also subhead Climate under names of continents, countries, cities, etc. e.g. Boston—Climate
CLIMATE and architecture. See Architecture and climate
CLIMATOLOGY. See Climate
CLIMBING plants
Seldom used vines. E. S. Henderson. il Horticulture 47:36-7+ S '69

Tepee, stepladder, shelf, wire, old boards; help to get off the ground. il Sunset 142: 210-11 Je '69
See also
Bougainvillea
Clematis
Ivy
Sweet peas
CLIMO, James
Pass/fail at Longmeadow. Clear House 43: 341-3 F '69
CLINE, Ray Steiner
Our man at State. por Newsweek 74:40 N 10 '69
CLINGERMAN, Polly
Ganesh in the house. Mlle 68:221-2 Mr '69
CLINICAL laboratories. See Medical laboratories
CLINICS. See Health clinics
CLINOPYROXENES. See Pyroxenes
CLINTON, Farley
Movies. Nat R 21:1125-6 N 4 '69
St Christopher, we're on your side. Nat R 21:595+ Je 17 '69
CLINTON, Realto P.
New kind of oil boom. il por Forbes 104:19-20 Ag 1 '69
CLINTON family
Clinton coat-of-arms. H. K. Eilers. il Hobbies 74:146-7+ S '69
CLIO awards. See Television awards
CLOAK, Evelyn Campbell
Glossary of paperweight terms. Antiques 95: 559-63 Ap '69
CLOAR, Carroll
Growing up in the Arkansas Delta. il Esquire 71:128-31 Je '69
CLOCK and watch makers
Arthur Pequegnat clock company. R. Phillip. il Hobbies 74:48-9+ Je '69
See also
Bulova watch company
Cox, J. d 1798
Vulliamy, J.
CLOCKS
Build this Connecticut shelf clock. F. L. Greenwald. il Pop Mech 131:150-3+ Ja '69
Clock watching, 1969. il House B 111:52-3 Ag '69
Clock watching, 19th-century style; interview, ed. by S. Nerenberg. il House B 111-50-1 Ag '69
Gift of wonder; Tower of the winds. Sci Am 220:46 F '69
Gift to Napoleon, a remarkable clock. O. A. Hagans. il Hobbies 74:126-7 S '69
PM's handsome hall clock. W. C. Lammey. il Pop Mech 132:124-9 O; 176-80+ N '69
See also
Astronomical clocks
Atomic clocks
Time measurements

Collectors and collecting

Clock in the boiler strikes two? il Pop Mech 131:98-9 Ap '69

History

Astronomical clock of Jens Olsen, Danish astro-mechanic. O. Hagans. il Hobbies 74: 48-9+ Ap; 48-9+ My '69
Fine clocks of a bygone age. O. R. Hagans. il Hobbies 74:48-9 Jl '69
Great automatic clock, where is it? O. R. Hagans. il Hobbies 74:126 O '69
Two notable clocks: eighteenth-century English pagoda clock at Toledo museum and seventeenth century pendulum clock at Cleveland museum. R. Davidson. il Antiques 95:496+ Ap '69
CLOCKS, Electric
What to do with a balky electric clock. T. Tappett. il Mech Illus 65:102-4+ S '69
CLOCKS, Electronic
IC digital clocks. E. Lord. il Radio-Electr 40:43-6 S '69
$200 IC digital clock. A. B. Plavcan. il Radio-Electr 40:23-6 Ap '69
CLOGS. See Wooden shoes
CLOISONNÉ
Mary Sharp demonstrates cloisonne techniques. P. Rothenberg. il Ceram Mo 17:24-6 N '69
CLOISONNE mosaics. See Mosaics
CLOISTERS. See Convents and nunneries
CLONES (biology)
Cloning: asexual human reproduction? D. M. Rorvik. il Sci Digest 66:6-13 N '69
League of Joe Namaths. D. M. Rorvik. il Esquire 71:112-13 Ap '69
CLOSE the coalhouse door; drama. See Plater, A.

CLOSE-up photography. See Photography, Close-up

CLOSED-end investment companies. See Investment trusts

CLOSED shelves in libraries. See Open and closed shelves

CLOSETS
How to outfit a closet for special jobs; compact work/storage center. il Bet Hom & Gard 47:30+ F '69
See also
Storage in the home

Equipment
Creative closet. etc. il Ladies Home J 86:82+ S '69

CLOTHES closets. See Closets

CLOTHES dryers
Gas and electric clothes dryers. il Consumer Rep 34:523-33 S '69
Laundry dollar, well-spent. N. Craig. il House B 111:86-7+ F '69
1-2-3 guide to buying laundry appliances. S. Schuler. Am Home 72:60+ N '69

Maintenance and repair
Clothes dryer frequency-of-repair records. il Consumer Rep 34:530-3 S '69

Repairing
See Clothes dryers—Maintenance and repair

CLOTHES hampers
Handiest hamper yet. il Mech Illus 65:90-1 F '69

CLOTHES lines. See Clotheslines

CLOTHES washing machines. See Washing machines

CLOTHESLINES
Clotheslines. il Consumer Bul 52:12-14 O '69

CLOTHIER, William
Orbiter refrain. Space World F-9-69:24-5 S '69
Viking exploration of Mars. Space World F-6-66:39-41 Je '69

CLOTHING, Cold weather
Clues and clothing for snow survival. E. P. Haddon. il Pop Mech 132:104-7+ N '69
How to stay warm. K. Anderson. Field & S 74:53+ N '69

CLOTHING, Protective
Rooster tales; safety outfits for boat racing. E. Rickman. il Hot Rod 22:132-3 N '69
Safety clothes for children. Good H 169:203 N '69
See also
Helmets

CLOTHING and dress
After a fashion. il Harp Baz 103:128-31 Ja '70
All-over nothing; stretch suits. il Time 94:67 O 24 '69
Best dressed women. il Ebony 24:174-6+ My '69
Fall grab bag of dos. il Time 94:76-83 S 19 '69
Fashions for the '70s. R. Gernreich. il Life 68:115-18 Ja 9 '70
Four ways to win; how to wear: see-throughs, pants, knits, maxis. il Seventeen 28:318-19 Ag '69
Girls who wear miniskirts; correlation between short skirts and extensive sexual symbolism. Trans-Action 6:9 My '69
Haute couture in paper dresses. P. Greenberg. il Sch Arts 68:29-30 F '69
How to stretch a wardrobe to fit vacation activities. il Good H 169:146 Jl '69
Italianissimo! il Vogue 153:165 Ap 1 '69
Of knees and noise; Knudsen's findings on sound-absorption problems. Chr Cent 86:1443 N 12 '69
Pants show shapely sales figures; biggest boom in women's fashions. il Bsns W p72 My 17 '69
Problems in pants. il Time 93:95 Ap 18 '69
Sense of style. G. Frazier. Esquire 72:191-5 S '69
Skirt trends: mini, midi and maxi. il U S News 67:12 Ag 11 '69
What shall I wear? G. Guinness. Harp Baz 102:142-3 Ap '69
See also
Bathing suits
Brassieres
Clothing industry
Coats
Costume design
Costume designers
Dressmaking
Fashion
Models (persons)
Scarves

Underwear
Veils
Vests
Wedding gowns

Aged
See Aged—Clothing and dress

Anecdotes, facetiae, satire, etc.
Are you slightly rectangular? E. Sheppard. Harp Baz 102:238-9 O '69
Bodies are so boring. E. Sheppard. Harp Baz 102:168 Ap '69
Me and the miniskirt. E. Bombeck. il Good H 169:58+ S '69
Skirting the question, and vice versa. G. Ace. Sat R 52:4 F 8 '69

Care
Space-age clothes care. il Seventeen 28:30 N '69
Winter coats: the fabrics of the season and how to care for them. il Good H 169:214 N '69

Children
Chic 'n' little. il Time 94:88 O 3 '69
Safety clothes for children. Good H 169:203 N '69
Les small fry de Paris. il McCalls 96:68-75 Ag '69

Materials
Try vinyls for sewing and crafts. il Bet Hom & Gard 47:150 +Mr '69

Men
Apparel arts of the Europeans. il Esquire 72:109-16 Jl '69
His bazaar. C. Kriebel. il Harp Baz 103:90-1 D '69; 103:72-3 Ja '70
Male plumage '69. il Read Digest 94:108-11 F '69
Memo on menswear. B. Ullmann. il Good H 169:170 Ag '69
Men in Vogue; those Italians. il Vogue 153:163 Ap 1 '69
Millionaire's sartorial tour of Europe. P. O'Higgins. Harp Baz 102:92-3 Ag '69
Their new bag; handbags for men. il Time 94:58 S 26 '69
See also
Shirts
Sweaters

History
Era of the dandy. L. Ungaro de Fox. il Américas 21:29-33 My '69

Negroes
Fly vines; observatories in Harlem. il Esquire 71:94-5 Mr '69

Prices
Why I don't buy wholesale any more. B. Pfizer. McCalls 96:87+ Je '69

Sports clothes
After 100 years: the classic coat again. J. Campbell. il Sports Illus 31:56-61 Ag 25 '69
Dress cool: clothes for boatmen and boat-women. il Motor B 124:30-3 Jl '69
Golf. C. Price. Esquire 71:44+ Je '69
Italy: splash of color in a sparkling ski setting; Pucci designs; photographs. E. Haas. il Sports Illus 31:60-72 N 17 '69
Jeans with a dash of tonic. J. Campbell. il Sports Illus 30:64-5 Ap 21 '69
Little lace goes a long, long way: T. Tinling tennis clothes. G. S. Brown. il Sports Illus 31:44-7 Jl 7 '69
Polybag caper. U. S. Williams. il Motor B 123:126-7 Je '69
Shiny idea is to stay dry and still soak it to 'em. R. Lieder. il Sports Illus 30:52-3 Je 23 '69

Students
High school fashion fling. il Life 67:40-5 O 10 '69
Schoolboy's dilemma. D. Tierney. Todays Ed 58:79-80 F '69
Teacher opinion poll; student dress and grooming. il Todays Ed 58:63 My '69

Teachers
Teachers' dress and grooming. A. C. Harding. Todays Ed 58:46-7 Ja '69

CLOTHING industry
See also
Garment factories

Wages and hours
Wages in the shirt and nightwear manufacturing industry. R. G. Bryan. il Mo Labor R 92:66-7 N '69

CLOTHING industry—*Continued*

Hong Kong

Custom-tailored Hong Kong suits. Consumer Bul 52:36 Ap '69

United States

Boutique king bounces back. il Bsns W p57 Jl 26 '69

Clothes are the silver lining. il Bsns W p48 S 20 '69

See also

Evan-Picone, incorporated
Genesco, incorporated
International ladies garment workers' union
New York (city)—Industries
Strauss, Levi, and company
Terry manufacturing company
Villager industries

CLOTTING of blood. See Blood—Coagulation

CLOTURE rule. See United States—Congress—Senate—Rules and practice

CLOUD, John M.

Overdue. por Wilson Lib Bul 43:787+ Ap '69

CLOUD, Wallace

Are we changing our weather by accident? Pop Sci 194:74-7+ My '69

From Florida to Cape Cod without moving. Pop Mech 131:128-31 +My '69

Fuel for your outboard. Pop Sci 194:117-19+ F '69

How deep will divers work? Pop Mech 131:92-5+ F '69

Moon bug learns to mate. Pop Mech 131:121-5+ F '69

Ship that digs holes in the sea. Pop Mech 131:108-11+ Mr '69

Ten years in deep space. Pop Mech 131:128-31+ Mr '69

What can go wrong with fiberglass hulls? Pop Sci 194:102-5+ Mr '69

CLOUD chambers

World's largest cloud chamber. Chem 42:23 Je '69

See also

Bubble chambers

CLOUD condensation nuclei. See Atmospheric nucleation

CLOUD physics

See also

Atmospheric nucleation
Precipitation (meteorology)

CLOUD seeding. See Rain making; Weather control

CLOUDS

From above: West coast stratus. il Weatherwise 22:163 Ag '69

Hole-in-cloud; a meteorological whodunit; discussion. il Weatherwise 21:194-5+, 238-45; 22:19+ O, D '68, F '69

Making clouds has a silver lining. il Bsns W p82 D 27 '69

Wind measurements in noctilucent clouds. J. S. Theon and others. bibliog il Science 164:715-16 My 9 '69

CLOUDS, Magellanic. See Magellanic clouds

CLOUGH, Arthur C.

Arthur Clough, lawyer. J. Walsh. Hobbies 74:36+ My '69

CLOUGH, George S.

He helps the managers manage cash. por Bsns W p76 N 15 '69

CLOUGH, Roy L. Jr

Model hydroplane skims the water. Pop Sci 194:140-3 My '69

CLOVE apples, oranges, etc. See Pomanders

CLOVER, Sweet

Sweetclover-weevil feeding deterrent B: isolation and identification. W. R. Akeson and others. bibliog il Science 163:293-4 Ja 17 '69

Diseases and pests

See also

Sweet clover weevils

CLOWNEY, Edmund P.

Lord of the manger. Chr Today 14:3-5 D 5 '69

CLOWNS

Clown Alley; Lubbock, Tex; offers classes in clowning. L. Witcher. il Parks & Rec 4:37+ F '69

Color comes to the circus; arena's first black clown. il Ebony 25:155-8+ N '69

CLUB continental. See Travel clubs

CLUB luncheons. See Luncheons

CLUB Méditerranée. See Vacation villages

CLUB wagons. See Station wagons

CLUBB, Jerome M. and Allen, H. W.

Cities and the election of 1928: partisan realignment? bibliog f Am Hist R 74:1205-20 Ap '69

CLUBHOUSES

Pop scene for profs; Faculty club. D. Gebhard. il Arch Forum 130:78-85 Mr '69

CLUBS

Clubs for unusual hobbies. il Good H 168:158-9 F '69

Everybody in the pool; discrimination in community-owned recreational center, Virginia's Fairfax County. Time 94:23 D 26 '69

50th anniversary for army service clubs. C. H. Reid. il Parks & Rec 4:16-19+ N '69

Getaway game; outing clubs. B. Gillam. il Mlle 68:176-7 F '69

Havens of good living for members only; portfolio. J. Gooding. Fortune 80:126-33 N '69

Join the out-of-season campers. E. H. Arctander. il Pop Sci 95:140-2 S '69

See also

Air travel clubs
Businessmens clubs
Health clubs
Investment clubs
Kiwanis clubs
Political clubs and associations
Railroad clubs
Travel clubs
Womens clubs and societies

also subhead Clubs under names of cities, e.g. Paris—Clubs

CLUBS, Astronomical. See Astronomical societies

CLUBS, School. See Student activities

CLUCHEY, Rick

Cage. Criticism

Newsweek il 75:67 Ja 12 '70

CLUNE, John R.

Overdue. por Wilson Lib Bul 43:905+ My '69

CLURMAN, Harold

Doctor Dapertutto. Nation 209:608-9 D 1 '69

Film festival. Nation 209:389-90, 421-2 O 13-20 '69

French characters. Nation 208:88-9 Ja 20 '69

Salka's incorrigible heart. Nation 208:580 My 5 '69

Theatre. See issues of Nation

CLUSTER housing. See Housing projects—Site planning

CLUTCHES, Automobile. See Automobiles—Clutches

COACHES (athletics)

Country slicker; football coach D. Royal. Time 94:62+ N 14 '69

Crunch for coach Roderick. C. Coe. il Life 66:75+ F 14 '69

Desperate coach. J. Underwood. il Sports Illus 31:66-8+ Ag 25; 20-7 S 1; 28-32+ S 8 '69

Pete and Press Maravich. C. Coe. il Life 66:30-2+ F 7 '69

Sweety Cakes runs the Sonics; coach of the Seattle SuperSonics. F. Deford. il Sports Illus 31:42-4+ N 24 '69

Won't somebody please get me out of here? W. Blair, coach of Minnesota's North Stars. G. Ronberg. Sports Illus 31:81-2+ D 1 '69

See also

Driesell, C.
Glover, F.
Hayes, W. W.
Varnell, L.

COACHES and coaching

See also

Driving

COACHING (basketball) See Basketball players—Training

COAL

Transportation

Canada's superport for superships; Roberts bank. il Bsns W p 120-2 S 27 '69

COAL handling

See also

Coal—Transportation

COAL Industry

United States

Coal bin is running short. il Bsns W p 19-20 Jl 5 '69

Coal industry: atomic power; address, January 21, 1969. B. O'Brien. Vital Speeches 35:379-84 Ap 1 '69

Coalmen do slow burn. il Bsns W p50-1 My 10 '69

Coal's new prosperity can't ease its pains. il Bsns W p64-5+ Ag 23 '69

See also

Coal mines and mining—United States

COAL miners

Black lung; mining as a way of death. R. Coles and H. Huge. New Repub 160:17-21 Ja 25 '69

Black lung rebellion; West Virginia's new compensation law. R. G. Sherrill. il Nation 208:529-35 Ap 28 '69

COAL miners—*Continued*
Coal mining; Benton, Illinois. T. Goldwasser. Atlan 224:28+ N '69
Coalmen do slow burn. il Bsns W p50-1 My 10 '69
Farmington no. 9: will the tragedy be compounded? G. F. Massay. Chr Cent 86:871-4 Je 25 '69
Scandal of death and injury in the mines. B. A. Franklin. il N Y Times Mag p25-7+ Mr 30 '69; Reply with rejoinder. I. A. Given. p60+ My 4 '69
   See also
United mine workers of America

COAL mines and mining
   See also
Coal miners
Mine hoisting

    Accidents and explosions
Scandal of death and injury in the mines. B. A. Franklin. il N Y Times Mag p25-7+ Mr 30 '69; Reply with rejoinder. I. A. Given. p60+ Mr 4 '69
   See also
Coal mines and mining—Safety devices and measures

     Equipment
   See also
Coal mining machinery

   Safety devices and measures
Action after a decade; Federal coal mine safety act. Sci N 96:592 D 27 '69
Approach to mine safety. il Sci N 95:570-1 Je 14 '69
Black lung bills stir dust storm in Congress. Bsns W p32 My 31 '69
Black lung; mining as a way of death. R. Coles and H. Huge. New Repub 160:17-21 Ja 25 '69
Boy who got excited; West Virginia miners on strike to obtain effective mine safety and health legislation. New Repub 160:7 Mr 22 '69
Breaking new ground to make mines safe. il Bsns W p 139-40+ N 8 '69
Breath of change? Sr Schol 94:21-2 Mr 28 '69
Coalmen do slow burn. il Bsns W p50-1 My 10 '69
Coal's new prosperity can't ease its pains. il Bsns W p64-5+ Ag 23 '69
Farmington no. 9: will the tragedy be compounded? G. F. Massay. Chr Cent 86:871-4 Je 25 '69
Mine-safety act breaks precedent. U S News 68:87-8 Ja 12 '70
Pair of bills, a brace of problems. il Sci N 95:278-9 Mr 22 '69; Reply. L. E. Evans. 95:545 Je 7 '69
Scandal of death and injury in the mines. B. A. Franklin. il N Y Times Mag p25-7+ Mr 30 '69; Reply with rejoinder. I. A. Given. p60+ My 4 '69

   Stripping operations
George's Branch, Ky; Rado Combs, former miner and his family. W. Hedgepeth. il Look 33:25-33 Mr 4 '69
Lonely war of a good angry man; H. M. Caudill of eastern Kentucky. D. G. McCullough. il Am Heritage 21:97-113 D '69
Strip mine conservationist; J. F. Hillman. Forbes 104:44 S 15 '69
U.S. journal: Kentucky. C. Trillin. New Yorker 45:33-6 D 27 '69

   United States
Coal mining; Benton, Illinois. T. Goldwasser. Atlan 224:28+ N '69
Corporate fiefdom; poverty in the dole in Appalachia. H. M. Caudill. Commonweal 89:523-5 Ja 24 '69
   See also
Coal industry—United States

COAL mining machinery
Mineheads; photographs of winding gear towers in Europe. B. Becher and H. Becher. il Arch Forum 129:68-73 D '68

COALINGA, Calif.
Desalting Coalinga's water; using reverse-osmosis process. il Am City 84:22 Mr '69

COALITION bargaining. See Collective bargaining, Industry wide

COAN, Hilliard Jerome
Odyssey of Hilliard J. Coan. S. Margetts. por Duns R 94:89-90+ O '69

COAST changes
Florida submergence curve revised: its relation to coastal sedimentation rates. D. W. Scholl and others. bibliog il Science 163:562-4 F 7 '69

COAST guard auxiliary. See United States—Coast guard auxiliary

COASTAL engineering. See Shore protection

COASTAL marshes. See Salt marshes

COASTAL states gas producing company
Wyatt effect. il Forbes 103:34-5 Ja 15 '69

COASTAL waters. See Territorial waters

COASTER brakes. See Brakes, Bicycle

COASTING
Frenzied ride on Placid ice; Olympic bobsled run, Lake Placid, N.Y. B. Ottum. il Sports Illus 30:20-3 Mr 3 '69

COASTS
   See also
Estuaries

   United States
Coastal waters and the Nation; address, February 3, 1969. E. Wenk, jr. Vital Speeches 35:349-52 Mr 15 '69

COATING materials. See Protective coatings

COATS, Reed
Santa Clara: the land of YAP. Wilson Lib Bul 43:901-3 My '69
—See Minudri, R. jt. auth.

COATS
Maxi cover-up. il Life 67:42-5 N 7 '69
Maxi question: is it fad or fashion? il Bsns W p49 S 20 '69
Winter coats: the fabrics of the season and how to care for them. il Good H 169:214 N '69
   See also
Fur coats, wraps, etc.

COATS of arms. See Heraldry

CO-AUTHORSHIP. See Authorship—Collaboration

COBALT compounds
Monomeric cobalt-oxygen complexes. A. L. Crumbliss and F. Basolo. bibliog il Science 164:1168-70 Je 6 '69
Structure of an oxygen-carrying cobalt complex; Bis(3-fluorosalicylaldehyde) ethylenediimine cobalt(II) B. C. Wang and W. P. Schaefer. bibliog il Science 166:1404-6 D 12 '69

COBB, Daniel
Mr Nixon and the Court. Chr Cent 86:1245-7 O 1 '69

COBB, Rick
First report: California's new ice fishing season. Field & S 74:26-7+ D '69
Surf cats launch new rage in sailboat racing. Pop Sci 195:48-9 Ag '69

COBB, Tony
Custom fiberglass yacht. il Yachting 125:118-19+ Ja '69
Touring a fiberglass plant. Yachting 125:63-5+ Ap '69

COBBS, Price M.
How to have a bloodless riot. G. B. Leonard. il pors Look 33:24-8 Je 10 '69

COBURN, Alvin Langdon
Book review. B. Newhall. Pop Phot 64:52+ F '69

COBURN, Ronald F. See Brody, J. S. jt. auth.

COBWEBS. See Spider webs

COCA-COLA bottling company of Los Angeles
Some men are never satisfied. Forbes 104:36 Ag 1 '69

COCA-COLA company
Coke's new image. il Time 94:88+ O 10 '69
Things grow bitter; Coke's Japanese branch. il Newsweek 74:86 O 13 '69

COCCHI, Maurice
Orphans of the universe; poem. Chr Cent 86:773 Je 4 '69

COCCIDIA
Gametogony of eimeria tenella (coccidia) in cell cultures. R. G. Strout and C. A. Ouellette. bibliog il Science 163:695-6 F 14 '69

COCHLEA. See Ear

COCHRAN, Bill
Bear by the ear. Outdoor Life 144:72-5+ N '69
Lunkers of the Roanoke. por Outdoor Life 143:80-2+ Mr '69

COCHRAN, Fred A.
Apples. Horticulture 48:36-7 Ja '70

COCHRAN, George
Autumn skiing in Europe. Travel & Camera 32:14+ O '69

COCHRAN, Leonard
On the continuity of deer, falcons and other things; poem. Poetry 115:110 N '69

COCHRAN, Thomas C.
Economic history old and new. bibliog f Am Hist R 74:1561-72 Je '69

COCHRAN, William
Searching for heroes. por Time 93:53 F 28 '69

COCHRANE, Eric
Incident at Isolotto. Commonweal 91:400-3
Ja 9 '70
COCK-a-doodle dandy; drama. See O'Casey. S.
COCK fighting
Death all day in Kansas. R. Rhodes. il Es-
quire 72:146-9+ N '69
COCKBAIN, Anthony E. See Playford, P. E.
jt. auth.
COCKE, Erle, 1921-
Alan Wood affair: a tale of intrigue. il por
Bsns W p94-6+ Jl 12 '69; Reply. J. P.
Bauer. p5 Ag 2 '69
COCKERHAM, Antoinette
Oldfields incident. por Newsweek 73:65 Je 16
'69
COCKERHAM, Karen
Oldfields incident. por Newsweek 73:65 Je 16
'69
COCKFIGHTING. See Cock fighting
COCKLEBURS
Photoperiod in three xanthium populations
from the tropic of Cancer in Mexico. C.
McMillan. bibliog il Science 165:292-4 Jl 18
'69
COCKPITS. See Boat cockpits
COCKROACHES
Axonal outgrowth and cell migration in vitro
from nervous system of cockroach embryos.
J. S. Chen and R. Levi-Montalcini. bibliog
il Science 166:631-2 O 31 '69
Female specific protein: biosynthesis con-
trolled by corpus allatum in leucophaea
maderae. F. Engelmann. bibliog il Science
165:407-9 Jl 25 '69
Lysozyme retention by cockroach periplaneta
americana L. D. R. A. Wharton. bibliog
il Science 163:183-4 Ja 10 '69
COCKROACHES as carriers of infection
Tips for your home and family; cockroach
indicated as salmonella carrier. Todays
Health 47:78 D '69
COCKS, G. T. and Wilson, A. C.
Immunological detection of single amino acid
substitutions in alkaline phosphatase. bib-
liog Science 164:188-9 Ap 11 '69
COCKTAILS
How to get a great drink at a great bar.
R. A. De Groot. il Esquire 71:108-11 Ja '69
Time-savers for the host; premixed drinks
and mixes. N. Ickeringill. House B 111:47+
Ag '69
COCKTAILS, Fruit. See Appetizers
COCO, James
Adventures of the fat man. il por Time 95:65
Ja 12 '70
COCO; musical comedy. See Musical comedies,
revues, etc.—Criticisms, plots, etc.
COCOA
See also
Cacao
Prices
Case of jitters in cocoa; brisk trading on
New York cocoa exchange. il Bsns W
p 122+ Ja 25 '69
COCTEAU, Jean
French characters. H. Clurman. Nation 208:
88-9 Ja 20 '69
Impersonation of angels: a biography of Jean
Cocteau, by F. Brown. Review
Commonweal 89:622-4 F 14 '69. W. Fowlie
Onward and upward with the arts. F. Steeg-
muller. il New Yorker 45:130-4+ S 27 '69
Report: New York; all-Cocteau program at
Juilliard opera theater. H. E. Phillips.
Opera N 33:23 Je 14 '69
COD, CAPE. See Cape Cod
CODA, Frank
Pointers for designing and specifying perlite
roof decks. Arch Rec 145:175-6 F '69
CODE, A. D. and others
Ultraviolet photometry from a spacecraft.
Sky & Tel 38:290-3 N '69
CODE instruments. See Radio telegraph—Equip-
ment
CODES, Number. See Numbering systems
CODONANTHE crassifolia
For indoor gardeners: a plant with many
charms: bellflower. C. Ferguson. il Home
Gard 56:24 O '69
CODY, Frank E.
50-MHz digital counter. Electr World 81:40-
2+ Mr '69
CODY, Wyo.
See also
Buffalo Bill historical center
COE, Charles
Pete and Press Maravich. Life 66:30-2+
F 7 '69
You can go as fast as your mind lets you.
Life 66:48-50+ My 23 '69

COE, Richard L.
Today's movies. Todays Ed 58:20-2 Mr '69
CO-ED dormitories. See Dormitories
COEDUCATION
Admission of women to the University of
Missouri in 1868. M. M. Meredith and L. P.
Jorgenson. bibliog f il Sch & Soc 97:282-5
Sum '69
Admission of women to Yale college; ad-
dress, November 14, 1968. K. Brewster, jr.
Sch & Soc 97:162-4 Mr '69
At Bennington the boys are the coeds. T.
Meehan. il N Y Times Mag p 12-13+ D 21
'69
Better coed than dead? Read Digest 94:41-
2+ F '69
Boys and girls together. il Newsweek 73:68
Ja 27 '69
Coeducation: the walls are tumbling down! R.
Tunley. il Seventeen 28:114-15+ Je '69
Cracking the cloisters. Time 94:47 S 26 '69
Girl and boy at Yale. il Newsweek 74:63 D
15 '69
Great admissions sweepstakes, how Yale se-
lected her first coeds. J. Lear. il N Y Times
Mag p52-3+ Ap 13 '69
Lady into tiger; girls came to Princeton. il
Life 67:105-6 S 19 '69
Prep schools go coed. B. B. Stretch. il Sat
R 52:80 My 17 '69
214 to 1: coeds at Princeton. J. Steinberg. il
Mlle 68:232-3+ Ap '69
Watch out girls! D. M. Keezer. New Repub
161:30-1 S 6 '69
COELENTERATES
See also
Corals
Embryology—Coelenterates
Hydromedusa
COENZYMES
Acetyl coenzyme A carboxylase: filamentous
nature of the animal enzymes. A. K. Klein-
schmidt and others. bibliog il Science 166:
1276-8 D 5 '69
Glutathione reductase: stimulation in normal
subjects by riboflavin supplementation. E.
Beutler. bibliog il Science 165:613-15 Ag 8
'69
COESITE
Coesite from the Richat dome, Mauritania:
a misidentification. R. F. Fudali. bibliog il
Science 166:228-30 O 10 '69
COEXISTENCE. See World politics, 1945-
COEXISTENCE policy. See United States—
Foreign relations—Russia
COFFEE
Cooking with cool. il Seventeen 28:196 My '69
Prices
Why coffee prices are percolating. il Bsns W
p 124 S 27 '69
COFFEE, Freeze-dried
How good is freeze-dried coffee? Consumer
Rep 34:434-5 Ag '69
COFFEE cake
Chocolate dappled coffee cake. il Sunset 143:
119 Jl '69
Coffee time is cake time. P. Pollock. il Bet
Hom & Gard 47:114 Ap '69
Derek and Alexis make a tasty coffee spiral.
il Sunset 143:148-9 N '69
From one buttery dough, three different coffee
cakes. il Sunset 142:160-1 F '69
COFFEE houses
Best cup of coffee in Rome; la Tazza d'oro.
W. Root. Holiday 46:14+ D '69
COFFEE pots, percolators, etc.
Coffee urns and small coffee-makers. il Con-
sumer Rep 34:240-6 My '69
COFFEE table books. See Picture books
COFFEE tables. See Tables
COFFEE trade
U.S. and Brazil sign agreement on soluble
coffee; Department announcement with ex-
change of notes. Dept State Bul 60:455 My
26 '69
Why coffee prices are percolating. il Bsns W
p 124 S 27 '69
See also
International coffee council
COFFEE urns. See Coffee pots, percolators,
etc.
COFFEY, Babette
(ed) See Lander, T. Toni Lander and Bruce
Marks; on and off stage
(ed) See Marks, B. Toni Lander and Bruce
Marks; on and off stage
COFFEY, James B. jr
Closing a military base need not be a trag-
edy. Nations Bsns 57:84-5 S '69
COFFEY, Warren
Gentleness and a stylish sense of the
ridiculous. Commonweal 90:347-8 Je 6 '69

COFFEYVILLE, Kan.
Computer programs a city's growth. B. J. DeMoss. il Am City 84:100+ D '69
COFFIN, Judy
Casey's walk. Read Digest 95:206-8 S '69
COFFIN, Tristram
Nixon's war in Vietnam. Nation 208:262-4 Mr 3 '69
COFFMAN, Jane
CO and the draft. Library J 94:2059-65 My 15 '69
COFFMAN, R. N.
Build your own earthworm-casting factory. Org Gard & Farm 16:58+ My '69
COGAR corporation
Newcomer bets on hitting the big time. il Bsns W p 112-13 N 22 '69
COGLEY, John
Man of faith, child of doubt. Life 67:62A-64 S 19 '69
COGNITION
Linguistic structure and transposition. M. Cole and others. bibliog il Science 164:90-1 Ap 4 '69
COGSWELL, Coralie
Students need a course in thinking. Todays Ed 58:60 N '69
COGSWELL, Henry D.
Hail to the crystal spring. T. H. Watkins. il por Am West 6:26-7+ Ja '69
COHELAN, Jeffery
Excerpt from debate, June 26, 1968. Cong Digest 48:51+ F '69
COHEN, Abraham
Screenings: 8mm (cont) Library J 94:1309, 1739, 2083, 4589 Mr 15, Ap 15, My 15, D 15 '69
COHEN, Abraham B.
Speaker-matching problems in public address systems. Electr World 82:32-6 O '69
Which P.A. speaker should you use? Electr World 82:50-4+ D '69
You can build these sixteen speaker enclosures. Radio-Electr 40:44-5+ Mr '69
COHEN, Albert
L'art de bien chanter (1666) of Jean Millet. bibliog f Mus Q 55:170-9 Ap '69
COHEN, Arthur Allen
Myth of the Judeo-Christian tradition; excerpts. Commentary 48:73-7 N '69
Rethinking Judaism. New Repub 160:28+ Mr 15 '69
COHEN, Arthur M.
Junior college objectives: reactions and criticisms; excerpts from Dateline '79: heretical concepts for the community college. bibliog Sch & Soc 97:330-3 Sum '69
COHEN, Carl
Democracy and the curriculum. Nation 208: 334-8, 604 Mr 17, My 12 '69
COHEN, Daniel
Dragons: past and present. Sci Digest 66:36-43 D '69
Great dinosaur disaster. Sci Digest 65:45-52 Mr '69
Medieval riddle of bodies in the bog. Sci Digest 65:9-14 F '69
COHEN, David K.
Economics of inequality. Sat R 52:64-5+ Ap 19 '69
Price of community control. Commentary 48:23-32 Jl; 18+ N '69
COHEN, Edwin Samuel
Quiet crusader for a new tax approach. por Bsns W p60+ My 24 '69
COHEN, Helen H.
More time tested enrollment ideas. Camp Mag 41:23 Ja '69
COHEN, Hennig
Why isn't Melville for the masses? Sat R 52:19-21 Ag 16 '69
COHEN, Herbert, and Cohen, Phyllis
Not altogether forgotten electret. Pop Electr 30:70-4+ Mr '69
COHEN, Larry
New audience: from Andy Hardy to Arlo Guthrie. Sat R 52:8-11+ D 27 '69
COHEN, Leonard
Suzanne takes you down; poem. N Y Times Mag p50 Ap 13 '69

about

Curl up & read. C. Ferdinandsen. Seventeen 28:32 My '69
Leonard Cohen: songs sacred and profane; with poems. I. Mothner. il pors Look 33:92-6 Je 10 '69
People are talking about. . . por Vogue 154: 116-17 Ag 1 '69
COHEN, Malcolm S.
Married women in the labor force: an analysis of participation rates. bibliog f Mo Labor R 92:31-5 O '69
Micro data in manpower study. Mo Labor R 92:53-4 Ap '69

COHEN, Manuel Frederick
Corporation within the community; address, January 27, 1969. Vital Speeches 35:270-3 F 15 '69

about

Private citizen Cohen gets down to business. Bsns W p28 My 31 '69
Speculating about Manny Cohen. il por Bsns W p 108+ F 15 '69
COHEN, Marshall
Norman Vincent Peale of the left. Atlan 223:108-10 Je '69
COHEN, Martin
Some dimensions of illiteracy in the U.S: one in fifty or fifty percent? bibliog por Wilson Lib Bul 44:45-8 S '69
COHEN, Mortimer T.
Wise guy. Commentary 47:88+ Mr '69
COHEN, Nathan E.
University and social change; excerpts from Social welfare forum, 1969. bibliog Sch & Soc 97:479-84 D '69
COHEN, Phyllis. See Cohen, H. jt. auth.
COHEN, R. Kelf-. See Kelf-Cohen, R.
COHEN, Richard M.
Antiwar for everyman. New Repub 161:10-11 S 6 '69
Teaching sex in school. New Repub 160:11-12 Je 28 '69
COHEN, Robert
Comment. Poetry 115:189-95 D '69
Law; poem. Poetry 114:179-80 Je '69
COHEN, Robert David
Death; poem. New Yorker 45:118 S 6 '69
COHEN, Selma Jeanne
Opera primer: how do you make a dance? Opera N 33:26-9 F 1 '69
COHEN, Sheldon S.
Improving the tax code; address, December 12, 1968. Vital Speeches 35:267-70 F 15 '69
Warning to taxpayers; interview. pors U S News 66:36-9 F 3 '69
COHEN, Stewart
Ghetto dropout. bibliog Clear House 44:118-22 O '69
COHEN, Vivian. See Stewart, P. B. jt. auth.
COHEN, Wilbur J.
Action line for aging; excerpts from address, October 24, 1968. Aging 170:17 D '68
Property taxes inadequate, new school financing needed; summary of address, November 1968. Sr Schol 93:Schol Teach 5 Ja 10 '69
COHERENT optics. See Optics
COHN, Arthur
Paul Hindemith's kammermusiken. Am Rec G 36:22-3 S '69
COHN, Charles E.
Four safety tips for auto work. Radio-Electr 40:48 Je '69
COHN, Florence
Exhibit report; an estimate of importance. Negro Hist Bul 31:6-7 D '68
COHN, Roy Marcus
One-man Roy Cohn lobby. W. Lambert. il pors Life 67:26-31 S 5 '69
COHO fishing. See Salmon fishing
COHO salmon. See Salmon
COHOCTON, N.Y.
Blower solves both urban and rural problems. il Am City 84:40 Ja '69
COIFFURE. See Hairdressing
COIL pottery. See Pottery
COILS, Electric. See Electric coils
COIN banks. See Banks, Coin
COIN collecting. See Numismatics
COINS
Case of the missing 1849 gold piece. McCalls 96:54 Ap '69
Coin quiz. C. French. See issues of Hobbies
Fantasy Washington coin of Alfred S. Robinson. C. F. French. il Hobbies 73:102 F '69
50¢ mystery. il Sr Schol 94:23 F 28 '69
Heptagonal hex; new British coins. Time 94: 41 N 14 '69
On the way: new Eisenhower dollar. il U S News 67:10 O 27 '69
Our first silver dollar. C. F. French. il Hobbies 74:132 O '69
Teddy Roosevelt's famous $20 gold piece. C. French. il Hobbies 74:102 Mr '69
Where are they now? Kennedy half dollars. il Newsweek 74:26 N 10 '69
See also
Silver as money

Collectors and collecting
See Numismatics

COINS, Ancient
Alexander the Great's famous tetradachm. C.
F. French. il Hobbies 74:102 Ap '69
COKER, W. Rory, and Moore, C. F.
Isobaric analog resonances bibliog pors Phys
Today 22:53–61 Ap '69
COLA beverages. See Beverages
COLAS, Alain
Record passage. il por Yachting 125:58-60+
Ap '69
COLAUTTI, Arturo
Adriana from five to four. R. D. Daniels.
Opera N 33:24-5 Ap 19 '69
COLBIN, Annemarie
Beyond Buenos Aires: Argentina's coastal
playground. Travel 132:71-3 N '69
COLBY, Carroll B.
Camping. See issues of Outdoor life
COLCHICINE
Colchicine-inhibited cilia regeneration: ex-
planation of lack of effect in tris buffer
medium. L. Margulis and others. bibliog il
Science 164:1177-8 Je 6 '69
COLD
See also
Low temperatures

Physiological effects
First aid; exposure to cold. C. J. Potthoff.
Todays Health 48:74 Ja '70
Freezing resistance in some Antarctic fishes.
A. L. DeVries and D. E. Wohlschlag. bib-
liog il Science 163:1073-5 Mr 7 '69
How to stay warm. K. Anderson. Field & S
74:53+ N '69
Tropical reef corals: tolerance of low tem-
peratures on the North Carolina continental
shelf. I. G. MacIntyre and O. H. Pilkey.
bibliog il Science 166:374-5 O 17 '69
See also
Hibernation
Insects, Freezing of
COLD (disease)
Preventing the common cold. T. F. Walsh.
McCalls 96:36+ F '69
What can be done about colds. A. Lake.
Seventeen 28:134-5+ F '69

Vaccines
On the way: vaccines to snuff out sniffles.
R. Bugg. il Todays Health 47:36-7+ D '69
COLD cuts. See Meat
COLD drinks. See Beverages
COLD frames
Fiberglass cold frame. W. C. Leckey. il Pop
Mech 131:164-7+ Mr '69
Get the most use from your cold frame. C.
O. Wisham. il Org Gard & Farm 16:113 Mr '69
Getting the jump on spring. V. Talbot. il
Org Gard & Farm 16:94-6 N '69
Vegetables by the boxful. M. Brandies. il Org
Gard & Farm 16:100-1 Ja '69
See also
Hotbeds
COLD soups. See Soups
COLD war. See Communism and democracy;
World politics, 1945-
COLD war (United States and Russia) See Rus-
sia—Foreign relations—United States; Unit-
ed States—Foreign relations—Russia
COLD weather
See also
Winter
COLD weather. Physiological effect of. See
Temperature—Physiological effects
COLD weather clothing. See Clothing, Cold
weather
COLD weather photography. See Photography
—Cold weather conditions
COLDFRAMES. See Cold frames
COLDS. See Cold (disease)
COLE, Barry
Face to face; poem. Atlan 223:49 F '69
COLE, Bernice
Voices of Harlem. il por Time 95:42 Ja 5
'70
COLE, David L.
AFL-CIO's internal disputes plan. Mo Labor
R 92:12-15 S '69
Devising alternatives to the right to strike.
bibliog Mo Labor R 92:60-2 Jl '69
COLE, Heather A. See Collier, R. J. jt. auth.
COLE, James
Piano lesson; poem. Poetry 114:376-7 S '69
COLE, John N.
Trying to save Maine. il por Time 94:72+
O 31 '69
COLE, Juanita P. and Cole, W. E.
Volunteers helping families of the mentally
ill. bibliog Ment Hy 53:188-95 Ap '69

COLE, Malcolm S.
Sonata-rondo, the formulation of a theoreti-
cal concept in the 18th and 19th centuries.
bibliog f Mus Q 55:180-92 Ap '69
COLE, Michael, and others
Linguistic structure and transposition. bib-
liog Science 164:90-1 Ap 4 '69
COLE, Thomas
American prospects, American skies; exhibi-
tion at Albany institute of history and art.
il Time 93:76-7 Je 6 '69
Art; exhibition at the Smithsonian. L. Allo-
way. Nation 209:158 Ag 25 '69
COLE, W. Edward. See Cole, J. P. jt. auth.
COLE, William
Disease battlers at our borders. Todays
Health 47:48-51+ My '69
Making of anthologies. Writers Digest 49:48-
52 Mr '69
COLE, William Graham
Between the generations: the confidence gap.
Sch & Soc 97:38-9 Ja '69
COLEBROOK, Conn.
A. Phelps' inn at North Colebrook. N. P.
Blum. il Antiques 95:404-7 Mr '69
COLEMAN, A. D.
Land imposes limitations. Pop Phot 65:90-
1+ D '69
COLEMAN, Charles H.
Your chemical thermostat. Sci Digest 65:81-4
My '69
COLEMAN, David. See Bothwell, D. jt. auth.
COLEMAN, Delbert William
Buffeted Parvin/Dohrmann prepares for a
new game. il por Bsns W p 100+ Je 14 '69
COLEMAN, Elliott
Priceless catch. Nation 208:345-6 Mr 17 '69
COLEMAN, Frank
History in houses. Antiques 96:222-7 Ag '69
COLEMAN, James Samuel
Reappraisal of the most controversial educa-
tional document of our time. C. Jencks. il
por N Y Times Mag p 12-13+ Ag 10 '69;
Discussion. p74+ S 14; 12+ O 12 '69
COLEMAN, Jean, and Liesse, Melanie
Spohn. ALA Bul 63:266-7 F '69
COLEMAN, John A.
People, the police and the park. America 120:
668-71 Je 7 '69
COLEMAN, John R.
Danger of legislative over-reaction; summary
of statement. por Sch & Soc 97:341 O '69
COLEMAN, R. H.
Owner's comments. Yachting 125:77+ F '69
COLEMAN, Robert G.
Seventeen year locusts: massive infestation
predicted for 1970. Horticulture 48:22-3+
Ja '70
COLEMAN, Tracey
6,900-mile skyjack. il por Time 94:29 N 7 '69
COLEMAN, William T. Jr
Centennial of the birth of Mahatma Gandhi;
statement. October 2, 1969. Dept State Bul
61:459-60 N 24 '69
COLEOPTERA. See Beetles
COLES, Robert
Books. New Yorker 45:169-70+ Ap 19 '69
Talking with God. Commonweal 91:330-4 D
12 '69
Youthful offenders. New Repub 161:12-14
O 4 '69
—and Huge, Harry
America's starving children. Parents Mag 44:
68-71+ N '69
Black lung. New Repub 160:17-21 Ja 25 '69
Peonage in Florida. New Repub 161:17-21
Jl 26 '69
Thorns on the yellow rose of Texas. New
Repub 16013-17 Ap 19 '69
We need help. New Repub 160:18-21 Mr 8 '69

about
Parents' magazine awards for outstanding
service to children. il por Parents Mag 44:
62 Ja '69
COLETTE, Sidonie Gabrielle
Shackle; excerpts from novel. pors Mlle 69:
110-29 Jl '69
COLETTI, Mark
News on wheels. M. Spiegel. il por Sr Schol
94:32 My 2 '69
COLEUS
Coleus colorful in every season. il Home Gard
56:30 S '69
COLGATE, Jessie
Building to serve: theme of the 1969 Boy
scout jamboree. Parks & Rec 4:38-9+ O
'69
COLGATE, Steve
Piece of cake! Yachting 126:46+ S '69
COLGATE, Stirling A.
Quasistellar objects and Seyfert galaxies;
with biographical sketch. bibliog por Phys
Today 22:27-35 Ja '69

COLGATE-Palmolive corporation
More for Lesch? Colgate far behind Procter & Gamble. Forbes 103:30-1 Mr 1 '69
COLGATE Rochester divinity school
Student revolt hits the seminaries. Chr Today 13:25 Mr 28 '69
COLICINES
Escherichia coli; strains that excrete an inhibitor of colicin B. S. K. Guterman and S. E. Luria. bibliog il Science 164:1414 Je 20 '69
COLIMORE, Benjamin
Paradise now? An essay on the living theater. Cath World 209:30-4 Ap '69
COLITT, Leslie R.
Letter from Germany. Nation 208:283-4 Mr 3 '69
COLLABORATION, Literary. See Authorship—Collaboration
COLLAGE
Art. L. Alloway. Nation 209:419-21 O 20 '69
Collage. T. A. Jambro. il Sch Arts 68:10-11 Mr '69
Collage and collage prints. L. J. Miller. il Sch Arts 69:32-5 D '69
From pen to pastepot; work of J. Kolář. il Time 93:80 Mr 21 '69
Romare Bearden. H. Ghent. il Sch Arts 68: 22-3 Ap '69
Seashell seascapes. B. Skarstedt. il Har Yrs 9:16 Ag '69
COLLAGE posters. See Posters
COLLAGEN
Collagen gels: design for a vitreous replacement. K. H. Stenzel and others. bibliog il Science 164:1282-3 Je 13 '69
Collagen has a discrete family of reactive hydroxylysyl and lysyl side-chain amino groups. R. C. Page and E. P. Benditt. bibliog il Science 163:578-9 F 7 '69
Localization of antigenic determinants in the polypeptide chains of collagen. D. Michaeli and others. bibliog il Science 166:1522-4 D 19 '69
Mechanochemical turbine: a new power cycle. M. V. Sussman and A. Katchalsky. il Science 167:45-7 Ja 2 '70
COLLAMORE, Elizabeth
False starts and distorted vision in April morning. Eng J 58:1186-8 N '69
COLLAPSIBLE boats. See Boats and boating
COLLECTING of accounts
See also
Billing
COLLECTION of strangers; story. See Hitchens, D.
COLLECTIVE bargaining
Better basis for collective bargaining. Bsns W p 148 O 25 '69
Boulware writes on Boulwarism. Bsns W p24+ Ag 30 '69
Building industry: pattern for White House intervention? setting up Construction industry collective bargaining commission. U S News 67:70-1 O 6 '69
Collective bargaining and community disputes. T. W. Kheel. Mo Labor R 92:3-8 Ja '69
Curb on union democracy? the Pike bill on collective bargaining process. America 120: 351 Mr 29 '69
Future of collective bargaining: close look at unions, employers. il U S News 66:91-3 My 26 '69
Labor arbitration: Britain and the U.S. B. Rathbun. Atlan 223:22+ Ja '69
Nixon's men try a lighter touch; less intervention in bargaining disputes. il Bsns W p60+ O 4 '69
No restraint at the bargaining table; with editorial comment. Bsns W p68-70, 84 Ja 3 '70
Shultz policy brings rail pact; model for other disputes? il U S News 67:100-1 D 15 '69
Something has to give; address, June 11, 1969. R. H. Larry. Vital Speeches 35:725-8 S 15 '69
Why the unions will be talking tough; hot spots in 1970 labor bargaining. Bsns W p68 N 8 '69
Year of troubles looms in Canada. il Bsns W p72+ Ja 10 '70
See also
Trade agreements

Automobile industry
Restyling American motors' pact; UAW-AM talks. il Bsns W p42 Ag 23 '69

Electric industries
Can GE's unions exorcise Boulwarism? il Bsns W p73 O 18 '69

Coalition fires opening salvo; demands drafted by AFL-CIO unions for coming negotiations with Westinghouse and GE. il Bsns W p72-3 Mr 15 '69
Costliest GE contract? il Bsns W p 132 Je 28 '69
Crisis bargaining looms in GE talks. Bsns W p62+ O 4 '69
First big test for Nixon's hold-down on wages. il U S News 67:81-2 N 3 '69
GE and unions open wage battle. il Bsns W p96+ Ag 16 '69
General electric; pattern for next year's labor gains? il U S News 67:97-8 O 27 '69
GE talks come to first crunch. Bsns W p48+ O 11 '69
Hopes are flickering for GE settlement. Bsns W p50 O 18 '69
Issue is Boulwarism. B. J. Widick. Nation 209:491 N 10 '69

Farm labor
Labor in the vineyard: the boycott and the NLRA. R. B. Taylor. il Nation 208:591-3 My 12 '69

Farmers
Can a farm group really bargain without telling you what to do? C. W. Gifford. Farm J 93:52G+ Mr '69

Government employees
Collective bargaining in the public sector; excerpts from addresses at Collective bargaining forum, sponsored by Institute of collective bargaining and group relations. bibliog Mo Labor R 92:60-9 Jl '69
FMCS and dispute mediation in the federal government. W. Abner. Mo Labor R 92:27-9 My '69
Public employee bargaining in Europe; excerpt. E. M. Kassalow. Mo Labor R 92: 47-9 Mr '69
Public employee unions and the right to strike. A. M. Ross. bibliog f il Mo Labor R 92:14-18 Mr '69
Work stoppages of government employees. S. C. White. bibliog il Mo Labor R 92:29-34 D '69

Railroads
Rail unions talk whipsaw. Bsns W p33-4 Ag 30 '69
Warning signal on the railroads. Bsns W p65 D 13 '69

Steel industry
Steelworkers crusade in Canada. Bsns W p88 My 10 '69

Trucking industry
Truckers count cost of teamsters demands. Bsns W p21 Ja 3 '70

COLLECTIVE bargaining, Industry wide
Coalition talks in GE's future. Bsns W p52+ Je 14 '69
Coordinated bargaining: some unresolved questions. S. B. Goldberg. Mo Labor R 92:56-8 Ap '69
Multilateral bargaining in the public sector. K. McLennan and M. H. Moskow. Mo Labor R 92:58-60 Ap '69
COLLECTIVE farms
See also
Collective settlements

Russia
Soviet collective farm. W. A. D. Jackson. bibliog il Focus 20:7-12 D '69
COLLECTIVE labor agreements. See Trade agreements
COLLECTIVE nouns. See Nouns
COLLECTIVE settlements
Commune comes to America. il Life 67:16B-23 Jl 18 '69
Communing in Meadville. R. Houriet. Ramp Mag 7:10+ N 30 '68
Great Oneida love-in. M. Bishop. il Am Heritage 20:14-17+ F '69
Life and death of a commune called Oz; a hippie settlement near Meadville, Pa. R. Houriet. il N Y Times Mag p30-1+ F 16 '69; Discussion. p 12+ Mr 9 '69
New back to the land movement. R. Rodale. il Org Gard & Farm 16:21-4 S '69
New communes. H. B. Kuhn. Chr Today 13: 63-4 S 12 '69
Trouble in paradise: off-beat rural community of Canyon, Calif. S. Stern. il Ramp Mag 8:22-8 N '69
Year of the commune. il Newsweek 74:89-90 Ag 18 '69
See also
Bishop Hill, Ill.
Brook Farm

COLLECTIVE settlements—*Continued*

Israel

Can a young wife from Baltimore find fulfillment feeding turkeys on a farm in Israel? T. Morris. il Redbook 132:78-9+ F '69

Children of the dream. by B. Bettelheim. Review
New Repub 160:23-6 My 24 '69. J. Featherstone
Sat R il 52:72-3+ S 20 '69. U. Bronfenbrenner

Israel settling in to stay; soldier farmers of Kallia. M. Levin. il Time 93:33-4 F 28 '69

Kibbutz: a commune that works. il Bsns W p 118-20 S 6 '69

Kibbutzim for the disadvantaged; with excerpts from articles by L. Y. Rabkin and K. Rabkin, and B. Bettelheim. B. R. Metalitz. il Todays Ed 58:17-19 D '69

Scandinavia

Experiments in marriage; group families in Sweden and Denmark. M. Durham. il Life 67:38-48A Ag 15 '69

South Africa

Gandhi's South African settlement. J. Brewer. Chr Cent 86:950+ Jl 16 '69

COLLECTORS and collecting

Americana page. Hobbies 74:100 Ap '69

Antiques' travel guide. See occasional issues of Antiques

Collectors' notes; ed. by E. Gaines. See issues of Antiques

Return of yesterday's artifacts. il Time 93:65 My 2 '69

See also
Book collecting
Bottles
Buttons
Clocks
Collyer brothers
Display of antiques, art objects, etc.
Dolls
   also subhead Collection and preservation or Collectors and collecting under various subjects, e.g. Insects—Collection and preservation

COLLEGE, Choice of

Campus climate and college choice. D. Klein. Seventeen 28:70+ S '69

College & careers. D. Klein. See issues of Seventeen

College confidential, by L. Handel. Review
Sat R 52:89-90 O 18 '69. S. Boyer

How to get into college by really trying. S. Reice. il McCalls 97:52+ N '69

Ivy league guidebook, by A. Tobias and others. Review
Sat R 52:89-90 O 18 '69. S. Boyer

So you want to go to college? il Ebony 24:79-86 S '69

COLLEGE administration See Colleges and universities—Administration

COLLEGE administrators. See College officials

COLLEGE admission. See Colleges and universities—Entrance requirements

COLLEGE alumni. See College graduates

COLLEGE and school drama

Hasty pudding à la Billy Wilson; dancer directing famed Harvard troupe. il Ebony 24:134-6+ Mr '69

Wellesley incident; a case of obscenity, dramatic presentation of The slave at Wellesley senior high. T. J. Cottle. il Sat R 52:67-8+ Mr 15 '69

See also
College theater

Texts

Junior and senior high. See issues of Plays

COLLEGE and school journalism

Culture begins at home; Foxfire magazine. B. B. Stretch. Sat R 52:59 Jl 19 '69

Freedom for the academic press; American alumni council's Statement on professional standards for college publications. J. Cass. Sat R 52:77 N 15 '69

Gatsby lives; new student magazine at Princeton: Business today. A. R. Dolan. Nat R 21:648 Jl 1 '69

How free should the high school press be? E. Einsiedler. il Todays Ed 58:52-4+ S '69

Let them write responsibly; freedom of the press in the high school. R. J. Sullivan. Ed Digest 34:50-1 Ja '69

Letter: Jetstream of Cumberland County high school. J. E. Hodges. il Sch Arts 68:40 F '69

Opposition press on campus. Time 94:48 D 12 '69

Overrated threat; high school underground newspapers. R. J. Sullivan. Ed Digest 35:49-51 N '69

Revolt in the high schools; the way it's going to be. D. Divoky. il Sat R 52:83-4+ F 15 '69; Discussion. 52:56 Mr 15 '69

Scoop on the high school underground press. D. Divoky. il Schol Teach Sec Teach Sup p6-8 O 6 '69

State of high school journalism: above-and underground. il Seventeen 28:142-3+ N '69

Uproar hits the campus press. J. Star. il Look 33:36+ F 18 '69

Upstarts in the ivy. A. Boles. il Nation 208:429-32 Ap 7 '69

See also
United States student press association

COLLEGE and the community. See Colleges and universities—Public relations

COLLEGE aptitude tests. See Aptitude tests

COLLEGE architecture

Academic center at Fredonia. J. Bailey. il Arch Forum 130:36-47 My '69

Benjamin Thompson designs the space between and the space within for Amherst college's music building. M. F. Schmertz. il Arch Rec 145:119-26 Ja '69

Building types study. il Arch Rec 145:145-60 My '69

Campus City continued: SOM's plan for the University of Illinois' Chicago circle campus Architecture and art building. J. M. Dixon. il Arch Forum 129:28-43 D '68

Cooper union addition gives plaza as bonus. il Arch Rec 145:114-17 F '69

Dining halls at human scale. il Arch Rec 145:120-1 F '69

Forty tons of mosaic; Mathematical sciences building, Westwood campus of the University of California. il Am Artist 33:18-21+ Ag '69

Harvard graduate school of design. il Arch Forum 131:62-7 D '69

Lively student center; Houston's Texas southern university. il Arch Rec 146:145-8 O '69

Teachers college master building program. il Sch & Soc 97:200-1 Ap '69

Trent university. il Arch Rec 146:151-62 S '69

University of East Anglia. il Arch Rec 146:99-110 Jl '69

See also
Dormitories

COLLEGE arts departments. See Colleges and universities—Departments of the arts

COLLEGE at Old Westbury. See New York (state). State university—College at Old Westbury

COLLEGE athletes. See Athletes

COLLEGE athletics

Desperate coach. J. Underwood. il Sports Illus 31:66-8+ Ag 25; 20-7 S 1; 28-32+ S 8 '69

Down with the heathen; the cry at Sewanee. H. Peterson. il Sports Illus 30:38-40+ F 24 '69

No givers for these Indians; superior ball club of Bacone junior college. P. Carry. il Sports Illus 30:62+ Je 2 '69

Rat pack; athletic team. il Newsweek 73:111 Ap 28 '69

See also
Football
Lacrosse
National collegiate athletic association
Rowing
Track athletics
Wrestling

COLLEGE attendance. See Colleges and universities—Attendance

COLLEGE bands. See Bands, College

COLLEGE bookstores

Bookstores as outlets for university press books; excerpts from addresses, June 22, 1969; with editorial comment. F. W. Boardman, jr; G. R. Smith; J. N. Rountree. il Pub W 196:26-31, 39 Jl 28 '69

College store's temporary solution to space problem. University of Pennsylvania bookstore. D. Davis. il Pub W 195:47-8 My 26 '69

Cornell university's campus store joins the underground. J. B. Kitching. il Pub W 195:50-2 F 24 '69

Johns Hopkins bookshop comes of age. N. J. Lange. il Pub W 196:73-4 N 17 '69

Ken White: renaissance man of architecture. il Pub W 195:54-6 F 3 '69

Package deal offered by Williams college store. R. R. Renzi. Pub W 195:85-6 Ja 27 '69

Perils of the college establishment. R. H. Smith. Pub W 195:41 My 19 '69

Revolution in campus bookselling. I. Sanderson. il Pub W 196:44-6 O 6 '69

COLLEGE bookstores—*Continued*
Special services key to university store success; West Virginia university book store. il Pub W 195:52-3 F 24 '69
University store gets faculty rapport; University of Massachusetts. B. Wilkes. Pub W 196:51 Ag 18 '69
See also
National association of college stores

COLLEGE buildings. See College architecture

COLLEGE clubs and societies
See also
College fraternities

COLLEGE commencements. See Commencements

COLLEGE consortiums. See Colleges and universities—Cooperation

COLLEGE credits. See Grading and marking (students)

COLLEGE degrees. See Degrees, Academic

COLLEGE dining halls. See Colleges and universities—Dining halls

COLLEGE discipline
Intervisitation. P. Woodring. Sat R 52:68 Ap 12 '69
Liberalized curfews. Sch & Soc 97:142+ Mr '69
On campus: getting away with it? Mlle 68:68 Mr '69
Penalties for campus disturbance. Sch & Soc 97:411-12 N '69
Protest and authority; symposium. il Newsweek 73:72-3 My 12 '69
Regulations for the maintenance of public order. Sch & Soc 97:458-61 N '69
Two roads to capitulation; acquiescence, or, clumsy use of police force. Chr Cent 86:637 My 7 '69
Universities in loco parentis; survey on campus conduct. Sch & Soc 97:146+ Mr '69

COLLEGE dormitories. See Dormitories

COLLEGE dropouts. See Dropouts

COLLEGE education
Academic revolution. W. Roberts; H. Zinn. il Sat R 52:80-2+ O 18 '69
Campus reform; numbers and quality. Life 66:36 My 30 '69
Education at the barricades, by C. Frankel. Review
    Bul Atom Sci 25:53 My '69. J. B. Platt
Ford grant for educational reform. Sch & Soc 97:90-1 F '69
Higher education and the disenchanted students; excerpts from Leaders, teachers and learners in academe; partners in the educational process. S. Lehrer. bibliog Sch & Soc 97:427-31 N '69
Higher education: dilemma, analysis, and prospect. C. H. Watts, 2d. Sch & Soc 97: 352-6 O '69
Involving students with life. J. Jerome. Cur 112:23-6 N '69
Is there a college in his future? with study-discussion program, by R. Strang. W. D. Boutwell. bibliog PTA Mag 63:10-12, 34 Je '69
Laying on of culture; faculty attempts to make working class students accept culture of the university world as their own. J. McDermott. il Nation 208:296-301 Mr 10 '69
New era for higher education; liberal education and governance; address. March 4, 1969. H. R. Bowen. Vital Speeches 35: 373-9 Ap 1 '69
Of many things, concerning views of S. Hook. D. R. Campion. America 120:inside cover Mr 22 '69
Private higher education in America today; adaptation of address, May 2, 1968. S. J. Wenberg. Sch & Soc 97:439-41 N '69
Radical new plan for college education. M. Mead. Redbook 133:55-6+ My '69
Social change in education and the change in educational concepts; excerpt from Approaches to education for character, ed. by C. H. Faust and J. Feingold. D. Bell. Sch & Soc 97:322-6 Sum '69
Student revolt; the hard core; statement before the House special subcommittee on education, March 20, 1969. B. Bettelheim. Vital Speeches 35:405-10 Ap 15 '69; Excerpts. il U S News 66:61-3 Ap 7 '69
Universities in crisis; the price of submission. W. V. Shannon. Cur 108:6-8 Je '69
What's going on in schools & colleges. See issues of Changing times
Whose university? The case for professionalism. R. Brustein. New Repub 160:16-18 Ap 26 '69; Discussion. 160:12-14+ My 17; 31+ My 24 '69
See also
Coeducation
Colleges and universities—Curriculum

Colleges and universities—Teaching
Humanities
Independent study
Junior colleges
Liberal education
Professional education
Technical education

Aims and objectives

Academic bankruptcy; alumni activists; address, January 24, 1969. R. W. Sarnoff. Vital Speeches 35:282-4 F 15 '69
Alienation and relevance. S. J. Tonsor. il Nat R 21:636-8+ Jl '69
And the second function of college is education; interview. P. Madison. Mlle 69:264+ Ag '69
Beyond campus chaos: a bold plan for peace. G. B. Leonard. il Look 33:73+ Je 10 '69
Christian perspective. Q. L. Quade. America 120:392-6 Ap 5 '69
Dignity and human fulfillment; address, June 1, 1969. P. A. Freund. Vital Speeches 35:556-8 Jl '69
Dilemma of good men. D. J. Wolf. il Cath World 209:103-6 Je '69
Education tube. J. A. Gengerelli. Sch & Soc 97:363-6 O '69
How did we get so confused? address, February 10, 1969. J. A. Howard. Vital Speeches 35:331-2 Mr 15 '69
Search for alternative models in education; address. D. Riesman. Am Scholar 38:377-88 Sum '69; Excerpts. Cur 112:26-9 N '69
Snare of preparation. P. Clecak. Am Scholar 38:657-67 Aut '69
Social change and the university. J. J. Corson. Sat R 53:76+ Ja 10 '70
Student revolt against liberalism. J. Eisen and D. Steinberg. bibliog f Ann Am Acad 382:83-94 Mr '69; Same abr. with title Revolt against liberalism. Cur 108:11-14 Je '69
Survival U: prospectus for a really relevant university. J. Fischer. Harper 239:12+ S; 36-7 D '69
There needs to be some kind of revolution in education; the black people are articulating that. . ; a student forum. Mlle 69: 266-7+ Ag '69
University and the student; address, December 22, 1968. W. W. Posvar. Vital Speeches 35:234-6 F 1 '69
What is a college for? J. Cass. Sat R 52:49 D 20 '69
What is a university? R. Sampson. Nation 208:560-5 My 5 '69; Same abr. with title Culture, power and knowledge. Cur 108:27-32 Je '69
Who is responsible for student violence? R. L. Means. America 120:352-5 Mr 29 '69

COLLEGE education, Cost of
Burn bursar, burn. A. Rooney. Life 66:20B Je 13 '69
California's academic fault. K. Mulherin. il Commonweal 90:281-6 My 23 '69
College cost picture: is it so grim? P. Lindberg. il Bet Hom & Gard 47:8+ Mr '69
College costs going up. il U S News 67:34-5 S 8 '69
High cost of college; how families meet it. il U S News 66:48-9 Ap 14 '69
How much you'll pay for college. il Bsns W p94 My 3 '69

COLLEGE education, Experimental
Survival U: prospectus for a really relevant university. J. Fischer. Harper 239:12+ S; 36-7 D '69

COLLEGE education and state
Campus unrest: riots bring danger of punitive backlash. P. M. Boffey. il Science 164: 161-5 Ap 11 '69

COLLEGE enrollment. See Colleges and universities—Attendance

COLLEGE entrance examination board
Lowdown on those college entrance tests; CEEB and ACT. il Changing T 23:37-40 S '69
See also
Colleges and universities—Entrance requirements
Scholastic aptitude test
How to score higher on college boards. M. Abramson. il Seventeen 28:132-3+ N '69

COLLEGE entrance requirements. See Colleges and universities—Entrance requirements

COLLEGE faculties. See College professors and instructors

COLLEGE fees. See Colleges and universities—Finance

COLLEGE football. See Football

COLLEGE football players. See Football players

COLLEGE fraternities
College fraternities: brotherhood and bally-hoo. J. L. Rodnitzky. bibliog f Sch & Soc 97:449-51 N '69
Letter from a far frat. H. Gold. Atlan 223: 85-7 My '69

COLLEGE gardens. See School gardens

COLLEGE girls. See College students. Women

COLLEGE glee clubs. See Choral groups and societies

COLLEGE graduates
Academic bankruptcy: alumni activists: address. January 24, 1969. R. W. Sarnoff. Vital Speeches 35:282-4 F 15 '69
All-America team of business students. il Time 93:97-8 Je 13 '69
Amid campus unrest, graduates rush for jobs. il U S News 66:49-51 Ap 7 '69
Catholic alumni: seven years after. A. M. Greeley. il America 120:96-100 Ja 25 '69; Reply. N. J. Rigall. 120:178 F 15 '69
Going the rounds with a Dow recruiter. S. Braun. il N Y Times Mag p27-9+ Ap 13 '69
Harvard MBAs of '49 assess their twenty years; 20th reunion. il Bsns W p62+ Je 14 '69
How youth is reforming the business world. W. S. Rukeyser. il Fortune 79:76-9+ Ja '69
News and views; black American community and the brain drain. J. Deedy. Commonweal 89:510 Ja 24 '69
Power in the academy. D. Rabinowitz. Commentary 47:42-9 Je '69; Discussion. 48:4+ Ag '69
Recruiters ride it out; corporate talent hunters on campus. il Bsns W p30 My 3 '69
Vintage college classes. il Life 67:73-8 N 28 '69
　　See also
American alumni council

Anecdotes, facetiae, satire, etc.
Alumnus. R. Harris. Look 33:87 Ap 29 '69

COLLEGE graduates, Negro
Black grad's problem: which job to take? il Ebony 24:132-4+ My '69

COLLEGE grounds. See Campus planning

COLLEGE housing. See College students—Housing

COLLEGE journalism. See College and school journalism

COLLEGE librarians. See Librarians

COLLEGE libraries
Academic librarian and the protocol of scholarship. D. Kaser. Library J 94:719-21 F 15 '69
Back to the cave; or, Some buildings I have known; address, March 1969. E. Ellsworth. il Library J 94:4353-7 D 1 '69
Changes in characteristics of librarians: academics. J. A. McCrossan. ALA Bul 63:910 Jl '69
Collective action and professional negotiation: factors and trends in academic libraries. R. P. Haro. ALA Bul 63:993-6 Jl '69
Ivory tower ghettoes. W. E. Hinchliff. il Library J 94:3971-4 N 1 '6
Library-college movement: dying of old age at thirty: a personal view. F. Blake. il Wilson Lib Bul 44:557-60 Ja '70
Library-college USA; address, April 2, 1969. L. Shores. ALA Bul 63:1547-53 D '69
Wiley college library, the first library for Negroes west of the Mississippi River. H. L. Totten. bibliog il Negro Hist Bul 32:6-10 Ja '69
Word of hortatory; adaptation of address. G. R. Lyle. Library J 94:3607-8 O 15 '69
World of libraries: past, present and future: symposium. bibliog il Wilson Lib Bul 43: 518-44 F '69
　　See also
Negro colleges and universities—Libraries
　also subhead Libraries or Library under names of colleges, e.g. Brooklyn college—Library

Administration
See College library administration

Architecture
See Library architecture

Automation
American automation updated. D. Fielding. bibliog il Library J 94:2881-5 S 1 '69
Automated circulation system at Midwestern university. C. D. Heineke and C. J. Boyer. il ALA Bul 63:1249-54 O '69
Automating Columbia's libraries. il Sch & Soc 97:276+ Sum '69

Censorship
Skirmish with the censors; Evergreen review episode in McMurry college library; address, June 1968. D. Gore. ALA Bul 63:193-203 F '69; Discussion. 63:553-6, 704, 889-90, 1512-13 My-Jl, D '69

Circulation, loans, etc.
Automated circulation system at Midwestern university. C. D. Heineke and C. J. Boyer. il ALA Bul 63:1249-54 O '69

Cooperation
Piedmont university center, N.C. H. Poole. il Library J 94:1841-3 My 1 '69; Discussion. 63:553-6, 704 My-Je '69

Fines
No-fine, student-faculty common loan policy; Rensselaer polytechnic institute library. J. A. McCrossan. ALA Bul 63:1531-2 D '69

Hours of opening
Let's discover electric lights. N. D. Stevens. Library J 94:4501 D 15 '69

Standards
California library association resolution on sanctions against the California state colleges. ALA Bul 63:1205-7 O '69
They had a dream: black colleges and library standards. H. L. Totten. il Wilson Lib Bu 44:75-9 S '69

Statistics
Academic library building in 1969. J. Orne. il Library J 94:4364-8 D 1 '69

COLLEGE libraries and research. See Libraries and research

COLLEGE library administration
Best defense: library now a target. J. Berry. Library J 94:1401 Ap 1 '69; Discussion. 94: 1923-4 My 15 '69
College libraries for students. R. P. Haro. Library J 94:2207-8 Je 1 '69
Grievance: first step in improved library government. E. Volkersz. bibliog ALA Bul 63:1566-9 D '69
How to start a library with nothing. P. Butler. Library J 95:44-5 Ja 1 '70

COLLEGE library architecture. See Library architecture

COLLEGE life. See Student life

COLLEGE newspapers. See College and school journalism

COLLEGE of cardinals. See Cardinals

COLLEGE of education at Fredonia. See New York (state). State university—College at Fredonia

COLLEGE officials
Few kind words for academic administrators. L. Wilson. Ed Digest 34:6-8 My '69

COLLEGE operas, revues, etc.
Music to my ears; Francis Poulenc's La voix humaine performed by Juilliard school of music. I. Kolodin. Sat R 52:41 My 3 '69
Musical events; Arthur Honegger's Antigone and Francis Poulenc's La Voix humaine, performed by Juilliard school of music. W. Sargeant. New Yorker 45:155-6 Ap 26 '69
Musical events; Donald Swann's Perelandra, performed by Bryn Mawr and Haverford music and drama departments and drama club. W. Sargeant. New Yorker 45:196+ D 6 '69
Musical events; Massenet's Thaïs by Manhattan school of music. W. Sargeant. New Yorker 45:137 My 17 '69
Report: Bloomington; Indiana university opera theater productions. W. Mootz. Opera N 34:22 S 20 '69
Report: Carbondale; premiere performance of Altgeld at Southern Illinois university. H. Blumenfeld. il Opera N 33:30 Ap 19 '69
Report: Hartford; performance of Boito's Mefistofele. L. Mazzola. Opera N 33:28 Ap 19 '69
Report: Los Angeles; UCLA's production of Harry Partch's Delusion of the fury. A. Goldberg. Opera N 33:32 Mr 8 '69
Report: Massenet's Manon presented by the University of Michigan school of music. J. Carr. Opera N 34:31 Ja 10 '70
Report: New York; American premiere of Emmanuel Chabrier's L'Etoile. W. D. Zimmer. Opera N 33:31 Mr 8 '69
Report: New York; Brooklyn college opera theater's performance of Cosi fan tutte. R. R. Schlein. Opera N 33:31 F 1 '69
Report: New York; production of Turco in Italia by Adelphia university opera workshop. W. D. Zimmer. Opera N 33:31 Ap 12 '69

COLLEGE operas, revues, etc—*Continued*
Report: production of Handel's Deidamia.
C. P. Speaks. Opera N 34:25 N 22 '69
Report: Tallahassee; productions at Florida
state university. W. Richards. il Opera N
33:25 My 17 '69
Something to sing about: fish, bait and
blondes; University of Iowa production of
opera called $4000. B. Asbille. il Sports
Illus 31:94+ S 15 '69
COLLEGE periodicals. See College and school
journalism
COLLEGE presidents
Campus battle need not be lost. N. Cousins.
Sat R 52:24 Je 21 '69
Cheek brothers, a new breed of college presi-
dent. il Ebony 24:35-8+ O '69
Columbia's missing president. Time 94:51 Ag
22 '69
Edwin D. Etherington, president of Wesleyan
university; with report by R. Woodley. il
Life 66:36-8 F 14 '69
Few kind words for academic administra-
tors. L. Wilson. Ed Digest 34:6-8 My '69
Hayakawa folk hero or enigma? P. J. Sam-
mon. America 121:10-12 Jl 5 '69
Ivory tower; ed. by M. Friedman. G. J.
Stigler. Newsweek 74:92 N 10 '69
Life and hard times of Parsons college. J. D.
Koerner. il Sat R 52:53-5+ Jl 19 '69
Men in the middle. il Time 93:48-9 Ap 18 '69
Needed immediately: 200 college presidents.
il U S News 67:46-7 Jl 28 '69
New junior college president. W. A. Harper.
Sch & Soc 97:120+ F '69
See also
Colleges and universities—Administration
Smith, C. C.

Anecdotes, facetiae, satire, etc.

Wanted: new heads for old ivy. R. Baker.
Life 66:28B My 23 '69

Inauguration

See Inaugurations
COLLEGE professors, Retired. See College pro-
fessors and instructors—Retirement
COLLEGE professors and instructors
Are teachers too arrogant? excerpts from
address, June 13, 1969. L. B. Mayhew. U S
News 66:10 Je 23 '69
Artist and the university. E. Larrabee. Harp-
er 238:12+ Je '69
British dons' ire raised by request to ac-
count for time. D. S. Greenberg. Science
166:1489 D 19 '69
Campus & its critics. G. Kateb. bibliog f
Commentary 47:40-8 Ap '69
Campus conflict & professorial egos. J. P.
Spiegel. il Trans-Action 6:41-50 O '69
Cost of unrest: educators quitting? il U S
News 66:13 Je 9 '69
Faculty exodus from universities. America
120:319 Mr 22 '69
Faculty is the heart of the trouble. M.
Ways. il Fortune 79:94-7+ Ja '69
Faculty-librarian conflict. M. P. Marchant.
bibliog il Library J 94:2886-9 S 1 '69
Faculty member as a forestry consultant.
J. A. Zivnuska. il Am For 75:24-5+ Jl '69
NEA's special project for higher education;
need for a representative professional or-
ganization. J. N. Terrey. Todays Ed 58:53
My '69
On the right; discrimination in favor of
Negroes. W. F. Buckley, jr. Nat R 21:40-1
Ja 14 '69
Postdoctoral research associate-instructor. A.
E. S. Green. bibliog il Phys Todays 22:23-6
Je '69
Power in the academy. D. Rabinowitz. Com-
mentary 47:42-9 Je '69; Discussion. 48:4+
Ag '69
Reforming college education; student targets:
professors next. F. Hechinger. Cur 107:34-5
My '69
Revolution (cont): at the University of Con-
necticut. E. Hill. il N Y Times Mag p28-9+
F 23 '69
Student power; on the other hand, student
complaint: undergraduate courses taught
by graduate assistants. J. R. Coyne, jr.
Nat R 21:432-3+ My 6 '69
University and student dissent. R. S. Morison.
Science 163:1013 Mr 7 '69
Why students revolt. S. Barr. Ed Digest 34:
4-5 My '69

Will teacher be the new drop-out? A. Beich-
man. bibliog f il N Y Times Mag p48-9+
D 7 '69
See also
Academic freedom
Colleges and universities—Administration
Colleges and universities—Teaching
Science teachers
Teachers and students

Education

Training the teachers of teachers; U.S. Office
of education's Triple T project for inservice
development of teacher trainers. P. A.
Olson. il Am Ed 5:13-14 F '69

Pensions

Retirement benefits in higher education;
adaptation of address, March 3, 1969. W. C.
Greenough. Sch & Soc 97:444-6 N '69

Political activities

Ivory tower; moral goal of a university,
ed. by M. Friedman. G. J. Stigler. News-
week 74:92 N 10 '69
Kraus case. J. Deedy. Commonweal 90:354
Je 13 '69
Laying on of culture; faculty attempts to
make working class students accept culture
of the university world as their own. J.
McDermott. il Nation 208:296-301 Mr 10 '69
Opposition to war put on record. M. Muel-
ler. Science 166:352 O 17 '69
Politics in academe. il Newsweek 75:42-3
Ja 12 '70
Professors and politics. Time 95:36 Ja 12 '70
Professors of the silent generation. L. A.
Downing and J. J. Salomone. bibliog il
Trans-Action 6:43-5 Je '69
See also
Teach-ins

Qualifications

New breed on the university campus. A.
Dickie. Ed Digest 34:52-3 F '69

Rating

Self-evaluating college teacher. J. L. Jarrett. il Todays Ed 58:40-1 Ja '69

Rating by students

Columbia L.S. students rate their instructors. Library J 94:2543-4 Jl '69; Discussion. 94:2541, 2985 Jl, S 15 '69

Retirement

Retirement benefits in higher education;
adaptation of address. March 3, 1969. W. C.
Greenough. Sch & Soc 97:444-6 N '69

Selection and appointment

Phasing out Mary Daly; incident at Boston college. M. Malec. Commonweal 90:
61-2 Ap 4 '69
See also
College professors and instructors—Qualifications

Tenure

Academic freedom and tenure, by L. Jough-
lin. Review
Bul Atom Sci 25:46-7 Ap '69. T. Dinell
COLLEGE recruiting. See Employment sys-
tems
COLLEGE sports. See College athletics
COLLEGE student activities. See Student ac-
tivities
COLLEGE student opinion. See Student opin-
ion
COLLEGE students
Academic citizenship in a time of campus
revolt. C. Bay. Trans-Action 6:4+ Ja '69
American youth: its outlook is changing the
world; symposium with editorial comment.
il Fortune 79:59-60, 66-116+ Ja '69
Antidote for cynicism; excerpt from ad-
dress, September 1969. K. Brewster, jr.
Time 94:47 S 26 '69
Campus mood: quiet so far; student photo-
graphers and writers illuminate their own
scene. il Life 67:40-6 D 12 '69
Campus stress. P. Woodring. Sat R 52:72 Mr
15 '69
Capp's cuts; creator of Li'l Abner, mocks
student idealism. il Time 93:67-8 Ap 11 '69
Changing campus and a changing society;
adaptation of address, November 12, 1968.
D. Riesman. Sch & Soc 97:215-22 Ap '69
College students: why they drop out. B.
Bard. Ed Digest 34:18-21 Mr '69
Counter curriculum. M. B. Bloy, jr. Common-
weal 91:8-12 O 3 '69
Ecology of discontent. L. J. Averill. Chr Cent
86:835-8 Je 18 '69

COLLEGE students—*Continued*
Freshman attitudes and values. Sch & Soc 97:199 Ap '69
In defense of young people. Sch & Soc 97: 264 Sum '69
Laying on of culture; faculty attempts to make working class students accept culture of the university world as their own. J. McDermott. il Nation 208:296-301 Mr 10 '69
Letter from Ann Arbor. A. Waugh. Nat R 21:1169+ N 18 '69
Letter from Europe. A. Burgess. Am Scholar 38:684-6 Aut '69
Mediation: a path to campus peace? S. Zagoria. Mo Labor R 92:9 Ja '69
New mood on campus; survey. il Newsweek 74:42-5 D 29 '69
On campus: Israeli students. K. Schwartz. Mlle 69:68 S '69
On misunderstanding student rebels. M. Duberman; discussion. Atlan 222:42-4+ D '68; 223:28+ Ja '69
On strike, shut it down; the crisis at San Francisco state college. J. McEvoy and A. Miller. il Trans-Action 6:18-23+ Mr '69
Post modern youth: address, November 18, 1968. W. B. Boyd. Vital Speeches 35:246-50 F 1 '69
Quiet majority; other side of campus revolt. il U S News 66:34-7 My 26 '69
Scratching the surface: campus unrest in 1968; adaptation of address, June 1968. E. D. Eddy. Sch & Soc 97:16-18 Ja '69
Student power, foreign-style. il U S News 66:56-7 Je 23 '69
Students and the 1970's: calm after the storm. J. P. Giusti. bibliog Sch & Soc 97:360-3 O '69
There's a new-time religion on campus; interest in the occult and witchcraft. A. M. Greeley. il N Y Times Mag p 14-15+ Je 1 '69
To an angry old man. L. Rosten. Look 33:14 Ap 29 '69
Twelve rebels of the student right. S. Burnham. il N Y Times Mag p32-3+ Mr 9 '69; Reply with rejoinder. L. Rossetto and S. Lehr. p22+ Mr 30 '69
University and the unstudent. J. F. Ohles. Ed Digest 34:44-6 Ja '69
What's happened to the American dream? dialogue between the generations; with group-discussion program. V. Block .il Parents Mag 44:28, 40-1+ Je '69
What's really wrong with colleges; with interview with student activist. K. M. Glazier. il U S News 66:36-8+ Je 16 '69
Why students are angry. M. Mead. Redbook 132:50+ Ap '69
Yale revisited. S. Alsop. Newsweek 73:120 My 19 '69
You can't turn off concern. il Am Ed 5:12-16 Ag '69
Zap! youthful invaders wreck town. Newsweek 73:42 My 19 '69
Zapping Zap; wrecking of North Dakota town. il Time 93:25 My 16 '69
See also
Coeducation
College athletics
College graduates
College students and war
Colleges and universities—Administration—Student participation
Cuban students
Foreign study
Graduate students
Negro students
Self government in education
Student Christian movements
Student demonstrations
Student ethics
Student life
Student militants
Student movement
Student unions
Students, Interchange of
Teachers and students
United States national student association

Adjustment

Afterthoughts of a prodigy; growing up smart at Chicago. E. Shorris. Esquire 72: 28+ D '69
And who are you? R. A. Schroth. America 121:167 S 13 '69; Reply. A. J. Lisska. 121:280 O 11 '69
Bright college years, then and now. A. Gingrich. Esquire 72:6 S '69
How to get along with a college freshman. J. N. Bell. il Todays Health 47:56-7+ My '69

Listen to the white graduate, you might learn something; University of Michigan. R. Rapoport il Esquire 72:99+ S '69
New stage of American man, almost endless adolescence. B. M. Berger. il N Y Times Mag p32-3+ N 2 '69; Discussion. p 142 N 23; 38+ N 30 '69
Students, drugs and protest. K. Keniston. Cur 104:5-19 F '69; Same abr. with title Drug problem among students; how bad, what's back of it? il U S News 66:90-2 Mr 24 '69
Survival for college freshmen. A. Henley. il Todays Health 47:20-3+ S '69

Aid
See Negro students—Aid; Student aid; Student loans

Communist activities
Obsolete communism: the left-wing alternative. by D. Cohn-Bendit and G. Cohn-Bendit. Review
Sat R il 52:23-5+ Mr 1 '69

Conduct of life
Acceptable campus behavior. Sch & Soc 97: 204 Ap '69
Campus tensions and evangelical response. R. J. Bartel. Chr Today 13:12-15 Je 6 '69
Different kind of campus: the experiment at Santa Cruz. J. Fischer. Harper 239:12+ Jl '69
Innocents. K. Crawford. Newsweek 73:42 My 19 '69
Intervisitation. P. Woodring. Sat R 52:68 Ap 19 '69
New mood on campus; survey. il Newsweek 74:42-5 D 29 '69
Oedipal revolt and the Laius reaction. S. Alsop. Newsweek 73:112 Je 23 '69
Protest, past and present; address, June 1969. J. Bronowski. Am Scholar 38:535-46 Aut '69
Revolt of the diminished man; excerpt from address. A. MacLeish. Sat R 52:16-19+ Je 7 '69
Student revolt; the hard core; statement before the House special subcommittee on education, March 20, 1969. B. Bettelheim. Vital Speeches 35:405-10 Ap 15 '69; Excerpts. il U S News 66:61-3 Ap 7 '69
Why students act that way; a Gallup study. il U S News 66:34-5 Je 2 '69
See also
College students, Women—Conduct of life

Discipline
See College discipline

Employment
Importance of parsley; or, summer-jobbing at a summer resort. J. Irving. Mlle 69: 209-10+ My '69
Urban corps goes national. B. B. Stretch. il Sat R 52:75 S 20 '69
Working-class collegians: the true believers. il Time 94:42 O 31 '69
See also
Interns (civil service)
Student business

Expenditures
See also
College education, Cost of

Federal aid
See Student aid

Grading
See Grading and marking (students)

Housing
College & careers. D. Klein. il Seventeen 28:88+ Ag '69
New style of campus living. W. McQuade. il Fortune 79:98-103 Ja '69
See also
Dormitories

Political activities
Are student rebels neo-Communists? M. Cranston. Cur 104:19-25 F '69
Beyond new leftism. S. Kelman. Commentary 47:67-71 F '69
Campus near-fascism; student radical movements. America 120:350-1 Mr 29 '69
Co-ops on campus: the militant consumers. B. W. Newell. Nation 209:635-6 D 8 '69
Crazies; extremist radicals believe in direct action. il Newsweek 73:88 Mr 24 '69
Critique of student activism. Sch & Soc 97: 138-40 Mr '69
Democracy and the student left, by G. F. Kennan. Review
Commonweal 89:569-71 Ja 31 '69. A. Wright

COLLEGES and universities—See also—*Cont.*
Liberal education
Negro colleges and universities
Summer schools
University presses
  also names of colleges and universities.
  e.g. Coumbia university; *also* types of colleges, e.g. Medical colleges

Accreditation

Accredit thyself, accreditor; Marjorie Webster junior college vs the Middle states association of colleges and secondary schools. R. Kirk. Nat R 21:1014 O 7 '69
  See also
Junior colleges—Accreditation

Administration

Academic citizenship in a time of campus revolt. C. Bay. Trans-Action 6:4+ Ja '69
Alienation and relevance. S. J. Tonsor. il Nat R 21:636-8+ Jl 1 '69
American university: how it runs, where it is going. by J. Barzun. Review.
  Cath World 208:235-6 F '69. J. T. Buckley
  Commonweal 89:569-71 Ja 31 '69. A. Wright
As school term ends, campus troubles stay alive. il U S News 66:13 Je 16 '69
As turmoil spreads, uneasy U.S. takes stock. il U S News 66:33-4 My 19 '69
Attitudes of college and university trustees. Sch & Soc 97:265 Sum '69
Beyond campus chaos: a bold plan for peace. G. B. Leonard. il Look 33:73+ Je 10 '69
Campus conflict & professorial egos. J. P. Spiegel. il Trans-Action 6:41-50 O '69
Campus crucible. N. Glazer; F. G. Hutchins. Atlan 224:43-56 Jl '69; Reply with rejoinder. J. S. Bruner. 224:47-8+ O '69
Campus reform: numbers and quality. Life 66:36 My 30 '69
Campus reform: the faculty role. Life 66:42 My 23 '69
Campus stress. P. Woodring. Sat R 52:72 Mr 15 '69
Campus unrest: riots bring danger of punitive backlash. P. M. Boffey. il Science 164:161-5 Ap 11 '69
Campus violence: plans to prevent it. il U S News 67:45-7 S 1 '69
Case study in student protest; excerpts from The first hundred years: a social history of Hampton institute. E. K. Graham. Am Scholar 38:668-82 Aut '69
College president speaks out; inaugural address, 1836. M. Hopkins. Nat R 21:372 Ap 22 '69
Colleges must outlaw terror; excerpts from address, May 1, 1969. J. N. Mitchell. U S News 66:75 My 12 '69
Columbia and the closed corporation. N. Von Hoffman. Commonweal 89:566-9 Ja 31 '69
Columbia recap: School of library service during and after the spring of 1968. B. R. Wilkinson. bibliog il Library J 94:2567-70 Jl '69; Reply. R. D. Kempner. 94:2985-6 S 15 '69
Controversy on the campus; address, February 18, 1969. G. S. Dumke. Vital Speeches 35:332-5 Mr 15 '69
Cooling it on campus; mediation of student disputes. il Bsns W p40-1 My 17 '69
Danger of legislative over-reaction; summary of statement. J. R. Coleman. Sch & Soc 97:241 O '69
Declaration on campus unrest; excerpt from statement, by the American council on education. Cur 108:8-11 Je '69
Democracy and the curriculum. C. Cohen. il Nation 208:334-8 Mr 17 '69; Discussion. 208:586+ My 12 '69
Dilemma of good men. D. J. Wolf. il Cath World 209:103-6 Je '69
Ecology of discontent. L. J. Averill. Chr Cent 86:835-8 Je 18 '69
Enter the judiciary. W. F. Buckley, jr. Nat R 21:559 Je 3 '69
Father Hesburgh's true position; concerning letter to the Nation's governors. America 120:291 Mr 15 '69
Guns of academe. J. B. Sheerin. Cath World 209:98-9 Je '69
Harvard ablaze. R. B. Griffin. America 120:586-8 My 17 '69
Hesburgh's law: the problems of campus, secular or Catholic. Commonweal 89:719-20 Mr 14 '69; Reply. W. J. Wilson. 90:151 Ap 18 '69
Hopeful bet on campus cool. Life 67:50B S 26 '69
How educators would deal with college rebels. il U S News 67:14 Jl 14 '69

How to deal with campus chaos; interview. W. P. Knowles. il U S News 66:31-3 Mr 3 '69
How to deal with student dissent. il Newsweek 73:66-71 Mr 10 '69
Indignation and a wrist slap. Sci N 95:425-6 My 3 '69
Is this your university? law, or disorder; address, April 27, 1969, A. Capp. Vital Speeches 35:634-6 Ag 1 '69
Joint commission on university life. Sch & Soc 97:204 Ap '69
Law and order on the Catholic campus. J. L. Walsh. Commonweal 90:562-3 S 19 '69
Liberating the campus from liberators. il Life 66:26B F 28 '69
Listen to the white graduate, you might learn something; University of Michigan. R. Rapoport. il Esquire 72:99+ S '69
Mediation: a path to campus peace? S. Zagoria. Mo Labor R 92:9 Ja '69
Needed immediately: 200 college presidents. il U S News 67:46-7 Jl 28 '69
New era for higher education; liberal education and governance; address, March 4, 1969. H. R. Bowen. Vital Speeches 35:373-9 Ap 1 '69
No vacation for the responsible. il Ebony 24:158-9 Je '69
Of many things; letter of Fr. T. Hesburgh to the university's faculty and student body. D. R. Campion. America 120:inside cover Mr 8 '69
On strike, shut it down; the crisis at San Francisco state college. J. McEvoy and A. Miller. il Trans-Action 6:18-23+ Mr '69
Opinion: calling cops on campus. J. S. Kunen. Mlle 69:26+ Ag '69
Prospects for peace, plans for defense. Time 94:50+ S 12 '69
Real crisis on the campus; interview. S. Hook. il U S News 66:40-4 My 19 '69; Excerpts. Read Digest 95:41-5 Ag '69
Rebels, amnesty and property. Chr Cent 86:307 Mr 5 '69; Discussion. 86:600 Ap 23 '69
Reforming college education; student targets: professors next. F. Hechinger. Cur 107:34-5 My '69
Reforms in governance. Time 94:47 S 26 '69
Repeat performance? Catholic universities. J. Hitchcock. Commonweal 89:556-9 Ja 31 '69
Revolt on the campus. R. MacLeish. Read Digest 94:71-6 Je '69
Riot bill halted. B. B. Stretch. Sat R 52:58 Jl 19 '69
Solution to college administration problems. A. B. Quall. Sch & Soc 97:358-60 O '69
Sour grapes statement. il Esquire 72:89-97 S '69
Students and the 1970's: calm after the storm. J. P. Giusti. bibliog Sch & Soc 97:360-3 O '69
Summons to campus moderates. America 120:390 Ap 5 '69
To stop campus violence; excerpts from remarks, April 29, 1969. R. M. Nixon. il U S News 66:74 My 12 '69
Trojan horse in the universities? S. Hook. Cur 108:24-7 Je '69
Twelve rebels of the student right. S. Burnham. il N Y Times Mag p32-3+ Mr 9 '69; Reply with rejoinder. L. Rossetto and S. Lehr. p22+ Mr 30 '69
Universities: a new balance of power; change at Harvard. il Time 93:42+ Ap 25 '69
Universities in crisis; the price of submission. W. V. Shannon. Cur 108:6-8 Je '69
Universities in crisis; what are the real issues? T. Wicker. Cur 108:4-6 Je '69
University and the student; address, December 22, 1968. W. W. Posvar. Vital Speeches 35:234-6 F 1 '69
University and the unstudent. J. F. Ohles. Ed Digest 34:44-6 Ja '69
University integrity; adaptation of address, May 17, 1968 K. S. Pitzer; reply. R. Schillace. Science 163:127-8 Ja 10 '69
What kind of world do you want? address, May 1, 1969. J. N. Mitchell. Vital Speeches 35:497-500 Je 1 '69; Same with title Colleges must outlaw terror; excerpts from address. U S News 66:75 My 12 '69
When, if ever, do you call in the cops? symposium. il N Y Times Mag p34-5+ My 4 '69; Discussion. p 12+ My 25 '69
Who runs the university? symposium. il Sat R 53:53-4+ Ja 10 '70
Whose university? M. Miles. New Repub 160:17-19 Ap 12 '69; Same. Cur 108:14-19 Je '69; Reply with rejoinder. D. Bell. New Repub 160:30-1 My 3 '69
Whose university? The case for professionalism. R. Brustein. New Repub 160:16-18 Ap 26 '69; Same. Cur 108:19-24 Je '69; Discussion. New Repub 160:12-14+ My 17; 31+ My 24 '69

COLLEGES and universities—Administration—
Continued
Why poison spreads amid the ivy. F. Morley.
Nations Bsns 57:23-4 S '69
　See also
College discipline
College presidents
College trustees
Self government in education
Student selection
Theological schools—Administration

Faculty participation
Faculty is the heart of the trouble. M. Ways.
il Fortune 79:94-7+ Ja '69

Student participation
California's academic fault. K. Mulhern. il
Commonweal 90:281-6 My 23 '69
College president speaks out; interview, ed.
by N. Seitz. G. L. Cross. Parents Mag 44:
62-3+ O '69
Education for the seventies; the crisis in
the university; excerpts from Students
without teachers. H. Taylor. Cur 111:40-7
O '69
Holy Cross innovates. America 120:660 Je 7
'69
No passing grade for Hayakawa. P. J. Sam-
mon. Commonweal 90:405-6 Je 27 '69
School's out. G. Marine and R. Erlich. il Ramp
Mag 7:19-25 D 14 '68
Tomorrow's university, back to the middle
ages? student power at Bologna and Paris.
J. Barzun. il Sat R 52:23-5+ N 15 '69

Admission standards
　See Colleges and universities—Entrance requirements

Appraisal
　See Evaluation (education)

Arts departments
　See Colleges and universities—Departments of the arts

Attendance
Class of '73: no loyalty oath yet; black ad-
missions. Newsweek 73:28-9 My 5 '69
Double trouble at CCNY; dual admissions. il
Newsweek 73:91-2 Je 9 '69
Explosive growth in college enrollments. il
U S News 67:38-9 O 20 '69
Soaring community college enrollments. Sch
& Soc 97:137-8 Mr '69
Statistics of attendance in American univer-
sities and colleges, 1968-69. G. G. Parker. il
Sch & Soc 97:43-61, 118 Ja-F '69
　See also
Student selection
Choice
　See College, Choice of

Commencements
　See Commencements

Computer installations
Campus computers: federal budget cuts hit
university centers. M. W. Oberle. Science
165:1337-9 S 26 '69

Cooperation
Oklahoma consortium strikes it rich. L. K.
Hayes and O. F. Henderson. Am Ed 5:26
Mr '69

Curriculum
Academic innovation. B. B. Stretch. Sat R 52:
70 Mr 15 '69
Anti-culture at public expense. R. Kirk. Nat
R 21:962 S 23 '69
Can the university survive the black chal-
lenge? J. Cass. il Sat R 52:68-71+ Je 21 '69
College provisions for minorities. Sch & Soc
97:84-5 F '69
Consumer report; course-evaluation booklets
written and produced by students. il News-
week 73:80-1 F 24 '69
Counter curriculum. M. B. Bloy, jr. Common-
weal 91:8-12 O 3 '69
Democracy and the curriculum. C. Cohen. il
Nation 208:334-8 Mr 17 '69; Discussion.
208:586+ My 12 '69
Education at Brown: making the system
work for you. R. Friedel. Seventeen 29:42
Ja '70
Environmental studies: OST report urges
better effort. L. J. Carter. Science 166:851
N 14 '69
Graduate student; what does he study? A.
A. Strassenburg and M. T. Llano. il Phys
Today 22:45-51 Mr '69
Innovations. Sch & Soc 97:4-5 Ja '69
Mini-semester at Redlands; offering new ex-
perimental courses. il Sch & Soc 97:144+
Mr '69

On campus the encyclicals are out. B. L.
Masse. America 121:5 Jl 5 '69
Patterns of reform. W. Roberts. il Sat R
52:80+ O 18 '69
School is not a place but a process; new
curricula, new colleges. M. Mauk. Mlle 69:
260+ Ag '69
Search for alternative models in education;
address. D. Riesman. Am Scholar 38:377-
88 Sum '69; Excerpts. Cur 112:26-9 N '69
Student evaluation of courses. Sch & Soc
97:272-3 Sum '69
Whose university? The case for profession-
alism. R. Brustein. New Repub 160:16-18 Ap
26 '69; Same. Cur 108:19-24 Je '69; Discus-
sion. New Repub 160:12-14+ My 17; 31+
My 24 '69
　See also
Area studies
Independent study
Junior colleges—Curriculum
Liberal education

Departments of dance
　See also
Hawaii. University, Honolulu—Department of
music and drama

Departments of the arts
Artist and the university. E. Larrabee. Harper 238:12+ Je '69

Desegregation
Bending standards. Time 93:56 Je 6 '69
Pressure on state colleges to integrate. il
U S News 66:32-3 Mr 31 '69
State universities: report terms desegrega-
tion largely token. B. Nelson. Science 164:
1155-6 Je 6 '69; Reply. L. G. Humphreys.
166:167 O 10 '69

Dining halls
Dining halls at human scale. il Arch Rec
145:120-1 F '69

Discipline
　See College discipline

Drama departments
　See Drama—Study and teaching

English departments
Decline and fall of English? il Newsweek 74:
77-8 O 13 '69

Enrollment
　See Colleges and universities—Attendance

Entrance requirements
Challenge of open admissions. T. S. Healy;
A. W. Astin. il Sat R 52:54-8+ D 20 '69
College admissions; the price of diversity. J.
C. Hoy. il Sat R 52:96-7+ F 15 '69
Coming of the common college. W. Roberts.
Sat R 52:67+ Je 21 '69
How to be interesting. il Time 93:43 Mr 28
'69
How to get into college by really trying.
S. Reice. il McCalls 97:52+ N '69
New undergraduate program; revision of the
Institutional testing program of the Gradu-
ate record examinations. Sch & Soc 97:266
Sum '69
Opening college doors to the disadvantaged.
E. Flattau. il Parents Mag 44:48-9+ D '69
So you want to go to college? il Ebony 24:
79-86 S '69
　See also
College entrance examination board
College entrance examination board—Scholas-
tic aptitude test
Student selection

Anecdotes, facetiae, satire, etc.
Excellence of Welby Stitch jr. R. Baker. Life
66:24 Mr 21 '69

Faculties
　See College professors and instructors

Federal aid
Budget cuts hurt many, but not as badly as
feared. Phys Today 22:67 Je '69
Campus computers: federal budget cuts hit
university centers. M. W. Oberle. Science
165:1337-9 S 26 '69
Congress, confusion, and indirect costs. L. K.
Pettit. bibliog il Science 163:1301-5 Mr 21
'69; Discussion. 164:629, 770 My 9-16 '69
Implementing the NSB proposals. Sci N 95:
306 Mr 29 '69
Institutional grants: Miller bill opens the de-
bate. L. J. Carter. Science 163:265-6 Ja 17 '69
Marshalling support for the grad school. il
Sci N 95:231-2 Mr 8 '69
Midwest colleges: united on national policy;
letter. H. A. Acres and S. Hayward. Sci-
ence 163:1145 Mr 14 '69

COLLEGES and universities—Federal aid—
Continued
Miller bill endorsed in hearings, but critics
muster. J Walsh. Science 163:1045 Mr 7 '69
New deal for graduate education. J. Lear. il
Sat R 52:78-9 My 17 '69
On-again, off-again funding of academic sci-
ence. B. C. Dees. Science 163:343 Ja 24 '69
Proliferation of bureaucracy. P. H. Abelson.
Science 163:883 F 28 '69
Recruiting educational Luddites. R. Kirk. Nat
R 21:76 Ja 28 '69
Siege of the house of reason; adaptation of
address, May 23, 1969. M. Tishler. bibliog il
Science 166:192-5 O 10 '69
Splitting the costs. Sci N 95:549-50 Je 7 '69
Student riot bill. W. F. Buckley, jr. Nat R 21:
662-3 Jl 1 '69
Support of scientific research and education
in our universities; adaptation of address,
December 6, 1968. F. A. Long. Science 163:
1037-40 Mr 7 '69
Vermont case in Supreme court. America 120:
459 Ap 19 '69

Finance

Amateur who beats the pros; Nuffield col-
lege at Oxford university il Forbes 103:
233-5 My 15 '69
Burn bursar, burn. A. Rooney. Life 66:20B
Je 13 '69
College on the cuff. il Time 94:93 S 26 '69
Fee equalization for public higher education.
J. P. Eddy and F. B. Zook. Sch & Soc 97:
443-4 N '69
Money squeeze. Time 94:37 Ag 29 '69
State tax appropriations growth and public
higher education. Sch & Soc 97:158-9+
Mr '69
Universities and endowment funds. Sch &
Soc 97:348-9 O '69
When colleges need money; Ford founda-
tion financial advice. U S News 66:92 My 5
'69
Whither higher education? A look at the
state college. G. M. Schurr. Chr Cent 86:
373-7 Mr 19 '69

See also
College education, Cost of
Colleges and universities—Gifts, legacies, etc.
Colleges and universities—Investments
Education and state
Fund raising

Gifts, legacies, etc.

Alumni; money and protest. Time 94:52 Jl
4 '69
Billion dollar brains: how wealth puts knowl-
edge in its pocket. D. Horowitz. il Ramp
Mag 7:36-44 My '69
Grants for undergraduate education improve-
ments. Sch & Soc 97:476 D '69
Holding the line; corporate aid to education.
L. L. L. Golden. Sat R 52:73 D 13 '69
Making endowments greener; University of
Rochester. Bsns W p66+ S 13 '69
Personal investing: for profit and for Yale.
W. Robertson. il Fortune 79:179 Mr '69
Richmond's bombshell; gift of $50 million by
E. C. Robins to Richmond university. News-
week 74:79 Jl 7 '69
Tax reform and education. J. Cass. Sat R
52:57 S 20 '69
Upgrading Negro colleges in the South. Sch
& Soc 97:350-1 O '69
Why college donors are uptight. il Bsns W
p 126+ N 8 '69

Graduate work

Changes in doctoral language requirements.
A. H. Scaff. Sch & Soc 97:453-4 N '69
Graduate student; symposium. il Phys Today
22:23-33+ Mr '69; Discussion. 22:9+ Jl '69
Italy: first Ph.D program stalled by new and
old politics; International studium of mo-
lecular biology. D. S. Greenberg. Science
163:1306-8 Mr 21 '69
Marshalling support for the grad school. il
Sci N 95:231-2 Mr 8 '69
New deal for graduate education. J. Lear. il
Sat R 52:78-9 My 17 '69
Postdoctoral education: report emphasizes re-
cognition problem. J. Walsh. il Science 166:
1129-30 N 28 '69
Toward a public policy for graduate education
in the sciences. F. W. Putnam. Science 163:
1147 Mr 14 '69

International cooperation

Toward a world university. H. Taylor. Sat R
52:24+ O 11 '69

Investments

Endowments: the pressure for income; report
of Advisory committee on endowment management. Duns R 94:13 D '69
Making endowments greener; University of
Rochester. Bsns W p66+ S 13 '69

Laws and legislation

Campus and the law. E. Van Den Haag. il
Nat R 21:1212-13 D 2 '69
Campus unrest: Congress ponders federal
sanctions on universities. J. Walsh. Science
165:46-9 Jl 4 '69
Campus unrest: riots bring danger of puni-
tive backlash. P. M. Boffey. il Science 164:
161-5 Ap 11 '69
Law-and-order vs. higher education. R. H.
Smith. Pub W 196:42 Jl 21 '69

Military training

See Military training

Physics departments

Graduate student; how does he see himself?
il Phys Today 22:24-33 Mr '69

Political control

Siege of the house of reason; adaptation of
address, May 23, 1969. M. Tishler. bibliog
Science 166:192-5 O 10 '69
Sinews of empire. D. Horowitz. il Ramp
Mag 8:32-42 O '69

Public relations

Amherst college statement. C. H. Plimpton.
New Repub 160:7 My 17 '69
Community college: counselor to the com-
munity? H. Heiner. Ed Digest 34:50-2 My
'69
Communiversity; address. January 18, 1969.
E. W. Weidner. Vital Speeches 35:277-9 F 15
'69
News media; campus unrest; address, Octo-
ber 4, 1969. J. R. Bittner. Vital Speeches
36:139-41 D 15 '69
Overlive: power, poverty, and the university,
by W. M. Birenbaum. Review
Sat R 52:83 My 17 '69. C. J. Calitri
Take a hand. New Repub 160:1+ My 17 '69
Un-fair Harvard? Faculty report surveys uni-
versity-city relations. R. J. Samuelson. Sci-
ence 163:658-61 F 14 '69
Widening gap between town and gown. P.
Woodring. Sat R 52:82 My 17 '69

Publications

See also
University presses

Religious life

Campus ministry: a new taste of the old
salt. J. Carroll. Cath World 210:59-61 N
'69
Campus ministry as normative. F. T. Trotter.
Chr Cent 86:766-7 Je 4 '69
English chaplaincy. E. E. Kelly. America 120:
101-2 Ja 25 '69
God and man on campus; Columbia university abolishes post of university chaplain.
il Newsweek 74:92 Jl 21 '69
On campus: the religious alternatives. Mlle
68:156 Ap '69

See also
Campus crusade for Christ (organization)
College students—Religion
University Christian movement

Research

Academic research in Germany; a new sup-
port program. B. R. Stein. bibliog Science
165:1096-100 S 12 '69
Can a weapons lab solve urban ills? il Bsns
W p 132+ N 1 '69
Can defense work keep a home on campus?
MIT panel calls for balance with nondefense
R&D. il Bsns W p68-71 Je 7 '69
Closed corporation: American universities in
crisis, by J. Ridgeway. Review
Ramp Mag 7:63-4 Ap '69. S. Weissman
Colleges in action. See issues of Science di-
gest
Confrontation at Stanford: exit classified re-
search. J. Walsh. Science 164:534-7 My 2 '69
Congress, confusion, and indirect costs. L.
K. Pettit. bibliog il Science 163:1301-5 Mr
21 '69; Discussion. 164:629, 770 My 9-16 '69
Controversy at MIT. Aviation W 91:61+ D 1:
55-6+ D 15 '69
Future of university research; excerpt from
address, December 3, 1968. L. A. DuBridge.
Bul Atom Sci 25:39 Ja '69
Go back! Go back! war research protest at
MIT. il Newsweek 74:79-80 N 17 '69
Growing cost of campus attacks on arms
research. il U S News 66:37-8+ Je 2 '69
Kickoff at Harvard: raid on the Center for
international affairs. H. Cox. Commonweal
91:64-5 O 17 '69
March 4 MIT; protest the government's use
of academic facilities for military or para-
military purposes. W. F. Buckley, jr. Nat
R 21:246-7 Mr 11 '69

COLLEGES and universities—Research—*Cont.*
M.I.T. and the Pentagon. Time 94:48+ N 7 '69
MIT under the gun. il Sci N 96:446 N 15 '69
Militarism and American democracy; the complex; address, April 8, 1969. J. W. Fulbright. bibliog f Vital Speeches 35:455-60 My 15 '69
New breed on the university campus. A. Dickie. Ed Digest 34:52-3 F '69
Pentagon promises to observe congressional curbs on research. M. J. Mansfield. Science 166:1386-8 D 12 '69
Physics lab goes relevant; MIT's Fluid mechanics laboratory. P. Gwynne. il Sci N 96:132-4 Ag 16 '69
Research stoppage focuses on national science goals. il Phys Today 22:81+ Ap '69
Siege of the house of reason; adaptation of address, May 23, 1969. M. Tishler. bibliog il Science 166:192-5 O 10 '69
Support of science on the university's own terms; adaptation of address, October 21, 1969. G. Piel. Science 166:1101 N 28 '69
Support of scientific research and education in our universities; adaptation of address, December 6, 1968. F. A. Long. Science 163: 1037-40 Mr 7 '69
Uneven effects of cuts in science funding. P. H. Abelson. Science 166:131 Ja 10 '69
University arsenal. R. Gelmis. il Look 33: 34-5 Ag 26 '69
Washington scene; the case for agency research. W. J. Price. Bul Atom Sci 25:34-6 Ap '69

Science departments
Materials science and applied science; interaction between multiple scientific disciplines. W. A. Tiller. il Science 165:469-75 Ag 1 '69

Security measures
Police on campus. M. Friedman. Newsweek 73:87 Ap 14 '69
To keep peace on campuses; a plan for action by federal courts. il U S News 66:6 Je 30 '69
When, if ever, do you call in the cops? symposium. il N Y Times Mag p34-5+ My 4 '69; Discussion. p 12+ My 25 '69

Statistics
See also
Colleges and universities—Attendance

Teaching
Case for radical change. H. Zinn. il Sat R 52:81-2+ O 18 '69
College teaching: an escape from teaching? M. K. Samples. Todays Ed 58:40 Ap '69
Education for the seventies; the crisis in the university; excerpts from Students without teachers. H. Taylor. Cur 111:40-7 O '69
Higher education and the disenchanted students; excerpts from Leaders, teachers, and learners in academe; partners in the educational process. S. Lehrer. bibliog Sch & Soc 97:427-31 N '69
In a time of campus crises, college publishers ponder future role. J. P. Young. Pub W 195:28-31 Ap 21 '69
Rebellion as education. K. Widmer. il Nation 208:537-41 Ap 28 '69
See also
College professors and instructors
Junior colleges—Teaching

Trustees
See College trustees

Alabama
See also
Birmingham-Southern college, Birmingham

Alaska
See also
Alaska. University

Arizona
See also
Arizona state university, Tempe

Arkansas
See also
Hendrix college, Conway
John Brown university, Siloam Springs

Belgium
Brussels: in aftermath of revolt, a medical school works at reform. D. S. Greenberg. Science 164:651-4 My 9 '69

Brazil
Brazil; subverting the universities; anti-subversive laws. F. Bandeira. New Repub 161: 17-19 N 8 '69

California
California backlash; public's attitude toward the state's campus disorders. Time 93:60 Mr 14 '69
California's academic fault. K. Mulherin. il Commonweal 90:281-6 My 23 '69
Chicano rebellion; demand for courses in Mexican-American studies. R. Bongartz. Nation 208:271-4 Mr 3 '69; Discussion. 208:386+ Mr 31 '69
Education of Ronald Reagan. R. Y. Keon. Nation 209:302-6 S 29 '69
Why the colleges blew up; California state colleges system. K. Widmer. il Nation 208: 237-41 F 24 '69
See also
California institute of technology, Pasadena
California. San Fernando Valley state college, Northbridge
California. State college, Dominguez Hills
California. State college, San Francisco
California. State college, San Jose
California. University
Colleges and universities, State—California
Merritt college, Oakland
Orange coast college, Costa Mesa
Redlands university, Redlands
San Francisco. City college
Southern California university, Los Angeles
Stanford university

Canada
Canadian look at nationalization of universities. J. A. McCarter. Bul Atom Sci 25:45-6 My '69
See also
Loyola college, Montreal
Trent university, Peterborough, Ontario

Colorado
See also
Colorado. University, Boulder

Connecticut
See also
Connecticut. University, Storrs

Cuba
Student power in action. A. Hochschild. il Trans-Action 6:16-21+ Ap '69
Unexpected star forward; University of Havana. R. Erlich. Ramp Mag 7:60-1 N 30 '68

England
University of East Anglia. il Arch Rec 146: 99-110 Jl '69
See also
Oxford. University

Europe
Tomorrow's university, back to the middle ages? student power at Bologna and Paris. J. Barzun. il Sat R 52:23-5+ N 15 '69

Florida
See also
Florida state university, Tallahassee
Florida. University
Miami. University, Coral Gables
South Florida. University, Tampa
Stetson university, Deland

France
Nanterre: a year later at campus where French student revolt began. D. S. Greenberg. Science 164:1261-4 Je 13 '69
Theology students rebel. X. W. Carroll. America 120:268-71 Mr 8 '69; Discussion. 120:437, 515 Ap 12, My 3 '69

Georgia
See also
Emory university, Atlanta
Spelman college, Atlanta

Germany
Decline of the German mandarins, by F. K. Ringer. Review
New Repub 160:27-9 F 22 '69. P. Gay

Great Britain
English chaplaincy. E. E. Kelly. America 120: 101-2 Ja 25 '69
Graduate student; how does he fare in Britain? C. C. Butler. bibliog il Phys Today 22: 39-42 Mr '69
Open university: Britain's new venture in higher education. D. S. Greenberg. Science 165:881-2 Ag 29 '69
Private university: academics seek to set up Britain's first. D. S. Greenberg. Science 163:458-60 Ja 31 '69

COLLEGES and universities—*Continued*

Illinois
See also
Illinois institute of technology, Chicago
Illinois. University
Loyola university, Chicago
Northwestern university, Evanston
Southern Illinois university

Indiana
See also
Butler university, Indianapolis
DePauw university, Greencastle
Indiana. University, Bloomington
Notre Dame, Ind. University
Purdue university, Lafayette, Ind.

Iowa
See also
Iowa. University. Iowa City
Parsons college, Fairfied

Ireland
New setting for rare books; exterior shell of
Trinity college's 18th-century library in
Dublin preserved around a modernized
inner core. N. McGrath. il Arch Forum 131:
70-5 D '69

Italy
Italy: first Ph.D program stalled by new and
old politics; International studium of molecular biology. D. S. Greenberg. Science
163:1306-8 Mr 21 '69

Japan
Battle of Tokyo U. il Time 93:32 Ja 31 '69
Fall of Todai. il Newsweek 73:52 F 3 '69
Oriental coming-of-age. S. Griffin. il Sci N
95:432-3 My 3 '69
Student protest in Japan. R. H. Drummond.
Chr Cent 86:1292-5, 1358-60 O 8, 22 '69
Teacher's guide to Japan. M. Mann. bibliog
il Sr Schol 94:Schol Teach 16-18 F 28 '69

Kansas
See also
Kansas. University

Kentucky
See also
Pikeville college

Louisiana
See also
Grambling college, Grambling
Southern university and agricultural and
mechanical college, Baton Rouge

Maryland
See also
Goucher college, Baltimore

Massachusetts
See also
Amherst college, Amherst
Brandeis university, Waltham
Harvard university
Massachusetts institute of technology, Cam-
bridge
Massachusetts. University. Amherst
Mount Holyoke college. South Hadley
Springfield college
Williams college, Williamstown
Woodstock college, Woodstock

Michigan
See also
Michigan state university, East Lansing
Michigan. University, Ann Arbor
Oakland university, Rochester
Wayne state university, Detroit

Minnesota
See also
Minnesota. University. Minneapolis

Mississippi
Mississippi muzzle. C. Wilkie. Nation 208:132-
3 F 3 '69
See also
Mississippi state university, State college
Mississippi. University
Tougaloo Southern Christian college

Missouri
See also
Missouri. University, Columbia
Westminster college, Fulton

Montana
See also
Montana. University, Missoula

New Hampshire
See also
Dartmouth college, Hanover
New Hampshire. University, Durham

New Jersey
See also
Princeton university
Seton Hall university, South Orange
Shelton college, Cape May

New Mexico
See also
New Mexico. University, Albuquerque

New York (state)
See also
Barnard college
Brooklyn college
Columbia university
Cornell university, Ithaca
Kirkland college, Clinton
Rensselaer polytechnic institute, Troy
Rochester, N.Y. University
Sarah Lawrence college, Bronxville
Vassar college, Poughkeepsie

North Carolina
Piedmont university center. H. Poole. il Li-
brary J 94:1841-3 My 1 '69
See also
Agricultural and technical college of North
Carolina. Greensboro
Black Mountain college
Duke university, Durham
Shaw university, Raleigh

Ohio
See also
Antioch college, Yellow Springs
Ohio. State university, Bowling Green

Oklahoma
Oklahoma consortium strikes it rich. L. K.
Hayes and O. F. Henderson. Am Ed 5:26
Mr '69
See also
Bacone junior college, Muskogee

Pennsylvania
See also
Bryn Mawr college, Bryn Mawr
Haverford college, Haverford
Pennsylvania. University, Philadelphia
Swarthmore college, Swarthmore
Temple university, Philadelphia

Rhode Island
See also
Brown university, Providence

South Carolina
See also
South Carolina. State college, Orangeburg

Southern states
See also
Negro colleges and universities

Sweden
Political extra-curricula at Uppsala and Cali-
fornia. G. L. Heath. il Sch & Soc 97:223-7
Ap '69

Tennessee
Graduate library wing for Joint university;
University center, composing George Pea-
body college, Scarritt college and Vander-
bilt university. il Library J 94:4401-2 D 1 '69
See also
Fisk university, Nashville
University of the South, Sewanee

Texas
See also
McMurry college, Abilene
Texas. Midwestern university, Wichita Falls
Texas southern university, Houston
Texas. University

United States
American academics: the right to a diploma;
address, June 1, 1969. D. J. Boorstin. Vital
Speeches 36:21-4 O 15 '69
Better coed than dead? Read Digest 94:41-2+
F '69
Campus & its critics. G. Kateb. bibliog f
Commentary 47:40-8 Ap '69
Campus communiqué. Time 94:34 D 26 '69
Campus communiqué; quiet so far. Time 94:
45 O 3 '69
Campus freedom, not destruction. Sch & Soc
97:204+ Ap '69
Campus mood; quiet so far; student photo-
graphers and writers illuminate their own
scene. il Life 67:40-6 D 12 '69
Changing campus and a changing society;
adaptation of address, November 12, 1968.
D. Riesman. Sch & Soc 97:215-22 Ap '69
Class of '69: the violent years. E. Diamond.
il Newsweek 73:68-73 Je 23 '69

COLLEGES and universities—United States
—*Continued*
Closed corporation, by J. Ridgeway. Review
  Bul Atom Sci 25:45-6 Ap '69. A. S. Miller
  Ramp Mag 7:63-4 Ap '69. S. Weissman
Colleges in action. See issues of Science digest
Commencement week, 1969. Fortune 79:97-8
  Je '69
Conciliation, and cops; survey of campuses
  involved in upheavals. il Newsweek 74:60+
  S 22 '69
Difficult times in higher education; adapted
  from Harvard university: The president's
  report, 1967-68. N. M. Pusey. Science 163:
  1403 Mr 28 '69
Dissenting academy, ed. by T. Roszak. Review
  Trans-Action 6:54-6 My '69. R. A. Nisbet
Education at the crossroads. H. Lindsell.
  Chr Today 13:3-5 Jl 4 '69
Graduate student; what does he study? A. A.
  Strassenburg and M. T. Llano. il Phys
  Today 22:45-51 Mr '69
Innovations. Sch & Soc 97:4-5 Ja '69
Ivory tower; moral goal of a university, ed.
  by M. Friedman. G. J. Stigler. Newsweek
  74:92 N 10 '69
New stage of American man, almost endless
  adolescence. B. M. Berger. il N Y Times
  Mag p32-3+ N 2 '69; Discussion. p 142
  N 23; 38+ N 30 '69
News media; campus unrest; address, October 4, 1969. J. R. Bittner. Vital Speeches 36:
  139-41 D 15 '69
Obsolete neutrality of higher education. N.
  Shimahara. bibliog f Sch & Soc 97:18-20 Ja
  '69
Our stake in the private liberal arts colleges.
  A. K. Smith. Todays Ed 58:51-2 Mr '69
Political university. il Time 93:54+ My 16 '69
Private higher education in America today;
  adaptation of address, May 2, 1968. S. J.
  Wenberg. Sch & Soc 97:439-41 N '69
Real revolution on campus. il U S News 68:
  28-31 Ja 12 '70
Schools make news. B. B. Stretch. il Sat R
  52:98 F 15 '69
Scratching the surface: campus unrest in 1968;
  adaptation of address, June 1968. E. D. Eddy.
  Sch & Soc 97:16-18 Ja '69
Square universities are rolling too. J. Main.
  il Fortune 79:104-7+ Ja '69
These colleges still have room. il Changing T
  23:17-20 My '69
Tomorrow's university, back to the middle
  ages? J. Barzun. il Sat R 52:23-5+ N 15 '69
Universities on collision course. D. Riesman. Trans-Action 6:3-4 S '69
University and social change; excerpts from
  Social welfare forum, 1969. N. E. Cohen.
  bibliog Sch & Soc 97:479-84 D '69
What's going on in schools & colleges. See
  issues of Changing times
What's really wrong with colleges; with
  interview with student activist. K. M.
  Glazier. il U S News 66:36-8+ Je 16 '69
Who owns New York? H. D. Babbidge, jr.
  Science 164:658-60 My 9 '69
Who runs the university? symposium. il Sat
  R 53:53-4+ Ja 10 '70
Will teacher be the new drop-out? A. Belchman. bibliog f il N Y Times Mag p48-9+
  D 7 '69
    See also
Coeducation
Colleges and universities, State
Free universities
Junior colleges
Negro colleges and universities
Small colleges
Summer schools
    also names of Colleges and universities, e.g. Harvard university

    Bibliography
Good old school days are gone. W. S. Lynch.
  Bul Atom Sci 25:38-41 O '69

    History
Lower depths of higher education. M. Bishop.
  il Am Heritage 21:26-31+ D '69

    Utah
    See also
Brigham Young university, Provo
Weber state college, Ogden

    Vermont
    See also
Bennington college, Bennington

    Virginia
    See also
Hampton institute, Hampton
Richmond, Va. University

    Washington, D.C.
    See also
American university
George Washington university
Howard university
Washington, D.C. Federal city college

    Wisconsin
    See also
Beloit college, Beloit
Wisconsin state university, Oshkosh
Wisconsin. University—Madison campus
Wisconsin. University—Milwaukee campus
COLLEGES and universities, Experimental
Experiment at Old Westbury. M. Novak.
  Commonweal 89:560-3 Ja 31 '69
New Eden; Johnston college at University
  of Redlands. il Time 94:45-7 O 3 '69
School is not a place but a process; new
  curricula, new colleges. M. Mauk. Mlle 69:
  260+ Ag '69
View from Nairobi. il Newsweek 74:91 D 8
  '69
    See also
California. University—Santa Cruz campus
Free universities
COLLEGES and universities, Municipal
    See also
Chicago city college
New York (city). City university of New
  York—City college
San Francisco. City college
COLLEGES and universities, State
Anti-culture at public expense. R. Kirk. Nat
  R 21:962 S 23 '69
State universities: report terms desegregation largely token. B. Nelson. Science 164:
  1155-6 Je 6 '69; Reply. L. G. Humphreys.
  166:167 O 10 '69
Whither higher education? A look at the
  state college. G. M. Schurr. Chr Cent 86:
  373-7 Mr 19 '69
    See also
Arizona state university, Tempe
Michigan state university. East Lansing
Ohio. State university, Bowling Green
Texas, University

    California
California higher education: the master plan
  faulted. J. Walsh. Science 164:811-13 My 16
  '69
California library association resolution on
  sanctions against the California state colleges. ALA Bul 63:1205-7 O '69
Equality fiction: bottom dogs subsidize top
  dogs. W. L. Hansen and B. A. Weisbrod.
  New Repub 161:23-4 S 6 '69
Quiet revolution: CLA sanctions against state
  colleges. R. D. Galloway. il ALA Bul 63:
  1257-61 O '69
Why the colleges blew up; California state
  colleges system. K. Widmer. il Nation 208:
  237-41 F 24 '69
COLLEGES for women
Watch out girls! pressure to go coeducational. D. M. Keezer. New Repub 161:30-1
  S 6 '69
    See also names of womens colleges, e.g.
  Bryn Mawr college, Bryn Mawr, Pa.
COLLEGIATE school, New York. See Private
  schools
COLLEY, George J.
New Europe. Vital Speeches 35:560-3 Jl 1
  '69
COLLIER, Peter
Apollo 11: the time machine. Ramp Mag
  8:56+ O '69
COLLIER, R. J. and Cole, H. A.
Diphtheria toxin subunit active in vitro.
  bibliog Science 164:1179-82 Je 6 '69
COLLIER, Richard
One man's finnan haddie is another's smoked
  eel. Holiday 45:22+ F '69
COLLINS, Bud
Tennis. Sports Illus 30:68+ Je 9; 31:44-5 S 1
  '69
COLLINS, Dabney Otis
Happening at Oglala. Am West 6:15-19 Mr '69
Wanted: tougher roses. Horticulture 47:30-1
  O '69
COLLINS, E. D.
Silent and sound film. Hobbies 74:113+ Ag
  '69
COLLINS, James
Karl Jaspers; a tribute. America 120:328-30
  Mr 22 '69
COLLINS, John Norman
Rainy day murders. il por Time 94:19 Ag 8
  '69

COLLINS, Judy
I've looked at life from both sides now; interview, ed. by B. Kevles. por Redbook 133:88-9+ O '69
I've looked at life from both sides now; interview, ed. by I. Neves. pors Life 66:40A-40B+ My 2 '69

COLLINS, Larry, and Lapierre, Dominique
Story behind the liberation of Paris a quarter of a century ago. N Y Times Mag p46-7+ S 7 '69

COLLINS, Michael
I rattled around in my mini-cathedral. por Life 67:27-9 Ag 22 '69
Man walks on another world. il Nat Geog 136:738-49 D '69
Space exploration; address, September 16, 1969. Vital Speeches 35:741-2 O 1 '69

about
Apollo 11's team: the three who will carry the flag. por U S News 67:33 Jl 21 '69
Astronaut joins the Rogers team. il por U S News 67:12 D 8 '69
Collins has cool to cope with space and the Easter bunny. D. Nevin. il pors Life 67:26-9 Jl 4 '69
Crew: men apart. il por Time 94:27-30 Jl 11 '69
Homage to the men from the moon. il pors Time 94:8-11 Ag 22 '69
Men for the moon. il por Newsweek 74:74 Jl 21 '69
We love you. il pors Newsweek 74:20B-23 Ag 25 '69
See also
Space flight to the moon—Manned flights—Armstrong-Aldrin-Collins flight, 1969

COLLINS, Richard L.
Accidental spin. Flying 85:49-52+ Je '69
Fine art of landing. Flying 85:68-9+ Ag '69
On top. See issues of Flying
Safety check. Flying 85:22-3 Ag; 96-7 O; 12-13+ N; 28-9 D '69
What about the Twin Comanche? Flying 84:46-50 Mr '69

COLLINS, Thomas
Inquiring about retiring; questions and answers. See issues of Harvest years

COLLINS, Thomas W.
Ruth Duckworth. Ceram Mo 17:18-21 S '69

COLLINS, William E. See Contacos, P. G. jt. auth.

COLLINS and Aikman corporation
Living happily alone, but still hoping; mergers with Springs mills and Chelsea industries called off. il Forbes 104:41 S 1 '69

COLLINS radio company
Little fish tries to gulp a big one. Bsns W p 123-4 Ap 12 '69

COLLISION avoidance systems. See Airplanes—Safety devices and measures

COLLISION cushion. See Automobiles—Safety devices and measures

COLLISIONS, Airplane. See Aviation—Accidents

COLLISIONS at sea
Anatomy of a collision; postmortem on the Evans disaster. il Newsweek 73:53 Je 23 '69
Another disaster for the navy but a tale of heroism. il U S News 66:12 Je 16 '69
Disaster by moonlight; H.M.A.S. Melbourne-U.S.S. Frank E. Evans collision. il Time 93:19-20 Je 13 '69
End of the Evans. il Newsweek 73:46+ Je 16 '69
Esquire's official court of inquiry into the present state of the U.S. navy. il Esquire 72:84-6 Jl '69

COLLOGRAPHS. See Prints

COLLOIDS
Collagen gels: design for a vitreous replacement. K. H. Stenzel and others. bibliog il Science 164:1282-3 Je 13 '69
Metallic colloids in molten salts. H. W. Kohn and T. E. Willmarth. bibliog il Science 163:924-5 F 28 '69
See also
Aerosols
Brownian movements
Electrophoresis
Micellar theory

COLLYER brothers
Does your room look like the Collyer brothers? R. Cowley. il Horizon 11:44-5 Wint '69

COLOBUS monkeys. See Monkeys

COLOMBEY-LES-DEUX-ÉGLISES, France
On French leave with de Gaulle. J. Barry. il Sat R 52:66+ Mr 8 '69

COLOMBIA
See also
Agriculture—Colombia
Cartagena
Education—Colombia
Indians of South America—Colombia
Leticia
Mines and mineral resources—Colombia
Periodicals—Colombia
Radio broadcasting—Colombia
Santa Marta

Economic conditions
Colombia creeps back from the brink. il Bsns W p 128 Ap 26 '69
See also
Colombia —Industries

Foreign relations
President Nixon and President Lleras of Colombia review common goals of the Americas; exchange of greetings, toasts and remarks, June 12, 13, 1969. R. M. Nixon; C. Lleras Restrepo. Dept State Bul 61:8-13 Jl 7 '69

Industries
Colombia. J. J. Parsons. bibliog il Focus 20:1-7 S '69

Native races
See Indians of South America—Colombia

Politics and government
Laying the groundwork. P. Kramer. Newsweek 73:38+ Mr 3 '69

COLONIAL architecture, Latin American. See Architecture, Latin American

COLONIAL life and customs
See also
Williamsburg, Va.

COLONIAL national invitation tournament. See Golf—Tournaments

COLONIALISM. See Colonies

COLONIES
Brief visit to the third world: Guyana and Vietnam. S. W. Mintz. Yale R 59:151-60 O '69
See also
United Nations—Special committee on the situation with regard to implementation of declaration on granting of independence to colonial countries and peoples
United Nations—Trusteeship council

COLONNELLO, Attilio
Trovatore sketchbook. il Opera N 33:14-15 F 15 '69

COLONSAY (island)
Profiles. J. McPhee. il New Yorker 45:69-70+ D 6; 61-2+ D 13 '69

COLOR
Colors 1970. il House & Gard 136:112-19 S '69
Discovering: color magic. B. Farmer. il Sch Arts 69:12-13 Ja '70
Well-tempered color-wheel. L. Campbell. il Art N 68:42-3+ Ap '69

Psychology
Color test; excerpts from The Lüscher color test. M. Lüscher. il Ladies Home J 86:70+ N '69

COLOR bar generators. See Television apparatus

COLOR blanking circuits. See Television circuits

COLOR codes
Color code charts. Electr World 82:29 O '69

COLOR films. See Photography—Films

COLOR filters. See Light filters

COLOR in gardens. See Gardens—Color

COLOR in house decoration
Brighten your rooms with sunshine yellow. il McCalls 96:82-5 F '69
Collect color with posters. il House & Gard 135:102-5 Mr '69
Color! il House B 111:107-27 My '69
Color and the look of today. il House & Gard 136:106-29 S '69
Color schemes that start from the floor. il Good H 168:124-31 My '69
Colors in action. il House & Gard 135:77-93 Mr '69
Decorating scrapbook. il House B 111:59-69 Mr '69
Decorating with fabric. il House & Gard 136:124-9 O '69
Do a daredevil room. il Seventeen 28:80-1 Ja '69
How to paint a room with light; with comments by J. L. Larsen and E. Reiback. il House & Gard 135:78-83 Ja '69
I love dazzle. il House & Gard 135:106-9 Mr '69

COLOR in house decoration—*Continued*
It's all a question of light and air and whiteness. il House & Gard 136:48-53 Jl '69
Moving in with paint, wallpaper, and fabric. il Am Home 72:64-7 Ja '69
One color scheme all the way! P. Rumely and N. Corats. il Bet Hom & Gard 47:56-61 Je '69
Punchy, pushy, pazzazzy! That's Pucci. V. D. Hahn. il Am Home 72:46-51 Je '69
Quiet colors that say a lot. P. Rumely. il Bet Hom & Gard 47:62-73 N '69
Surprise colors. V. D. Hahn. il Am Home 72:62-9 Mr '69
Sweet and sour oranges. il House & Gard 136:138:41 S '69
Trend to neutral colors: the quiet ones. il House & Gard 135:86-91 Ja '69
Tricolor a la mode. B. Plumb. il N Y Times Mag p70-1 Ja 19 '69
Urbane color-plotting in a manor. R. Fitzgerald. il House B 111:64-9 Ag '69
What to do about a nothing room. P. Rumely. il Bet Hom & Gard 47:68-77 F '69
Why naturals? il House & Gard 136:106-7 O '69
Young violet. il House B 111:52-3 Jl '69
COLOR in house painting. See House painting
COLOR measurement
See also
Colorimeters and colorimetry
COLOR names
Colors 1970. il House & Gard 136:112-19 S '69
COLOR of automobiles. See Automobiles—Color
COLOR of birds
Bird energetics: effects of artificial radiation. S. Lustick. bibliog il Science 163:387-90 Ja 24 '69
COLOR of flowers
Green flowers for St Patrick. il Sunset 142:218+ Mr '69
COLOR of food
See also
Coloring matter in food
COLOR of leaves
Nature's extravaganza of color. C. Winkelman. il Horticulture 46:38-9+ O '68
Tree choices for autumn color. il Sunset 143:240 O '69
Why leaves change color in the fall. R. Wolkomir. il Sci Digest 66:30-1 N '69
COLOR of man
"I lived six months as a black woman": Grace Halsell. il Ebony 25:124-6+ D '69
Science can change the color of your skin. W. Hartley and E. Hartley. il Sci Digest 66:45-9+ N '69
See also
Albinos and albinism
COLOR of plants
See also
Color of flowers
COLOR organs
New color-organ kit; Eico model 3440. il Electr World 81:80 My '69
Psychedelia 1. D. Lancaster. il Pop Electr 31:27-35+ S '69
Stereo color organ. B. Hollins. il Radio-Electr 40:33-7 O 69
COLOR perception. See Color sense
COLOR photography
Color clinic. D. B. Eisendrath. See issues of Popular photography
Ed Scully on color. E. Scully. See issues of Modern photography
Essence of color. R. Routh. il Travel & Camera 32:100-1+ F '69
Pictures that say summer. il Pop Phot 65:84-92 S '69
Polacolor paint box. il U S Camera 32:38-9 Ja '69
35; why I prefer it for color. N. Rothschild. il Pop Phot 65:85-93 Ag '69
Tom McCarthy. il Pop Phot 64:80-9 Ap '69
Use and abuse of color. J. Scully. il Mod Phot 33:50-5+ S '69
Wrong light color? E. Scully. il Mod Phot 33:118-19 O '69
COLOR photography printing. See Photography—Printing processes
COLOR print processor. See Photography—Processing—Apparatus and supplies
COLOR prints (photographs) See Photographs
COLOR sense
How you see color. W. Hanson. Pop Phot 64:110-11+ My '69
Opponent color cells in the cat lateral geniculate nucleus. A. L. Pearlman and N. W. Daw. bibliog il Science 167:84-6 Ja 2 '70
Studies of rods and cones in color vision. Sky & Tel 37:207 Ap '69
COLOR slides. See Transparencies

COLOR television. See Television, Color
COLOR television cameras. See Television cameras
COLOR television receivers. See Television receivers, Color
COLOR vision. See Color sense
COLORADO
See also
Architecture, Domestic—Colorado
Booksellers and bookselling—Colorado
Fishing—Colorado
Great Sand Dunes National Monument
Hunting—Colorado
Music festivals—Colorado
Prisons—Colorado
San Juan Mountains
Skis and skiing—Colorado
Wilderness areas—Colorado

Description and travel
Colorado: the Rockies' pot of gold. E. J. Linehan. il Nat Geog 136:157-201 Ag '69
Discovering Colorado's lofty Southwest. J. Higgins and S. K. Higgins. il Todays Health 47:42-7+ O '69

Industries
Colorado: the Rockies' pot of gold. E. J. Linehan. il Nat Geog 136:157-201 Ag '69

Photographs
Colorado the beautiful. Am For 75:10-11 S '69
COLORADO earthquakes. See Earthquakes—United States
COLORADO RIVER
Adventure on the Colorado River. B. Hughes. il Redbook 133:66+ My '69
As floods threaten in U.S, the Colorado runs low. il U S News 66:85-6 Mr 31 '69
Century of the wild Colorado. il Life 67:46-51 O 31 '69
Conquest of the Colorado; earth-movers, dam-builders, and the end of a free river. T. H. Watkins. bibliog il Am West 6:4-9+ Jl '69
Down the Colorado; excerpts. J. W. Powell. il Am Heritage 20:52-9+ O '69
On the Green and the Colorado a summerlong Powell centennial. il Sunset 142:64 My '69
Wildest boat trip in the world. R. P. Crossley. il Pop Mech 131:122-6 +Mr '69
See also
Glen Canyon
Grand Canyon

Photographs
Powell's River; Colorado portfolio; excerpts from Down the Colorado. E. Porter. Audubon 71:64-76 N '69
COLORADO SPRINGS

Cheyenne Mountain zoological park
See Zoological gardens

Gardens
Cooperation in Colorado Springs. L. Burgess. il Home Gard 56:6 My '69

History
Pikes Peak panorama. I. Hunt. il Am For 75:20-3 S '69

Music
Rock, etc. E. Willis. New Yorker 45:52-3 D 27 '69
COLORADO state prison. See Prisons—Colorado
COLORADO. University, Boulder

Libraries
Contribution of the library to improving instruction; reprint. R. E. Ellsworth. il Library J 94:1955-7 My 15 '69
COLORED light. See Light, Colored
COLORED people (South Africa)
Thin edge of the wedge; elections for the Colored people's representative council. il Newsweek 74:91 O 6 '69
COLORED races. See Race problems
COLORIMETERS and colorimetry
Colorimeter you can build. R. M. Benrey. il Pop Sci 195:163-6+ N '69
COLORING matter in food
Lab bench: identifying synthetic colors in food. il Chem 42:27-8 D '69
COLORS. See Color
COLOSSEUM, Rome
Cclosseum. J. Bryan, 3d. il Holiday 46:70-1+ D '69
COLQUITT, Betsy
Scene; poem. Chr Cent 86:1087 Ag 20 '69

COLSON, Frank A.
Barbara's birds. Ceram Mo 17:14-16 Ap '69

COLSON, Ralph B.
New pheasant policy. Cons 24:14-15 O '69
Why the long grouse season? Cons 24:9+ O '69

COLT, Jon
Build a power inverter. Pop Electr 30:65-7+ My '69

COLT, Thomas C. jr
How Dayton built its imaginable museum. Art N 67:44-9+ F '69

COLTED (comissão do libro técnico e didático)
See Textbooks—Brazil

COLTON, Esther V.
Art as a language. Sch Arts 69:14-15 S '69

COLTS (football club) See Football clubs

COLUM, Padraic
In Pilver park there walks a deer. New Yorker 45:35-8 My 31 '69

COLUMBIA, Md.
Bryant Woods: blueprint for flexibility. J. Freudenberger. il Library J 94:4225-7 N 15 '69
Growing pains of a new town. il Newsweek 74:51 Jl 14 '69
Profits in building well. il Fortune 80:40 Jl '69
Space-age transit system for a new town. Am City 84:160 Mr '69

COLUMBIA, Mo.
Beware of an informal communications network. D. K. Wanamaker. il Am City 84: 114+ Ap '69

COLUMBIA broadcasting system, incorporated
CBS tries a new team. Bsns W p46 F 22 '69
Doily for your mind. P. Collier. Ramp Mag 7:44+ Je '69
Duel at daybreak; CBS morning news with Joseph Benti. il Time 93:89 Ap 25 '69
I was there; CBS was there program. G. Ace. Sat R 52:6 S 20 '69
RCA puts TV in packs. il Bsns W p 106+ O 4 '69
Transmogrification of the Smothers brothers. W. Kloman. il Esquire 72:148-53+ O '69

COLUMBIA RIVER
Carbon dioxide partial pressure in the Columbia River. P. K. Park and others. bibliog il Science 166:867-8 N 14 '69
Dam Columbia! G. Laycock. il Audubon 71: 84-5 Ja '69
Death of a river. Nation 208:454 Ap 14 '69
Graywacke matrix minerals: hydrothermal reactions with Columbia River sediments. J. W. Hawkins, jr. and J. T. Whetten. bibliog il Science 166:868-70 N 14 '69

COLUMBIA university
Barnard girls at Columbia. il Vogue 153:146-7 My '69
Campus & its critics; interpreting the Cox commission report. G. Kateb. bibliog f Commentary 47:40-2 Ap '69
Campus, camera and me: filming of Come out, come out. L. Yellen. il Seventeen 28: 154-5+ My '69
Campus spring offensive. il Newsweek 73: 67-8 Ap 28 '69
Columbia and the closed corporation. N. Von Hoffman. Commonweal 89:566-9 Ja 31 '69
Columbia: to be a revolutionary or not to be? J. L. Avorn. il Look 33:13-14 My 13 '69
Columbia today. il Newsweek 73:82+ Mr 31 '69
Columbia's choice. il Newsweek 74:64 Ag 4 '69
Columbia's choice. il Time 94:62 Ag 1 '69
Columbia's missing president. Time 94:51 Ag 22 '69
God and man on campus. il Newsweek 74:92 Jl 21 '69
Hail, Columbia! How it sold out completely. il Ramp Mag 7:115-19 Ja 25 '69
Into the breach; twelve students charge university trustees with breach of contract. Nat R 21:61-2 Ja 28 '69
Merrily, merrily, merrily, merrily. J. Kunen. il Sports Illus 30:46-8+ Je 16 '69
New president of Columbia. Sch & Soc 97: 473-4 D '69
Notes from the journal of a gentle revolutionary; excerpt from The strawberry statement. J. S. Kunen. Atlan 223:50-4 F '69
On the steps of Low library: liberalism & the revolution of the young. D. Trilling; discussion. Commentary 47:4+ Mr; 19-20+ Ap '69
Opinion; calling cops on campus. J. S. Kunen. Mlle 69:26+ Ag '69
Polykarp Kusch; interview. P. Kusch. New Yorker 45:28-31 Mr 29 '69
Protest and the law. il Time 93:32 Ja 31 '69
Rebel on campus. G. Wilson. Parents Mag 44: 52-3+ Ap '69

Reluctant president. Newsweek 74:55 S 1 '69
Rising up in Morningside. J. E. O'Connell. Cath World 209:230-1 Ag '69
Twelve rebels of the student right. S. Burnham. il N Y Times Mag p32-3+ Mr 9 '69
What about majority rights. A. H. Sypher. Nations Bsns 57:31-2 Mr '69
See also
American assembly
Barnard college, New York
Teachers college, Columbia university

Graduate school of journalism
Dean of a school divided. Time 94:36 D 26 '69

Lamont-Doherty geological observatory
Investigations: rocks, dust, or data from the moon. New Yorker 45:54-5 D 6 '69

Libraries
Automating Columbia's libraries. il Sch & Soc 97:276+ Sum '69

School of library service
Columbia L.S. students rate their instructors. Library J 94:2543-4 Jl '69; Discussion. 94: 2541, 2985 Jl, S 15 '69
Columbia recap: during and after the spring of 1968. B. R. Wilkinson. bibliog il Library J 94:2567-70 Jl '69; Reply. R. D. Kempner. 94:2985-6 S 15 '69

COLUMBIAN rope company
How rope is made. B. D. Barker. 3d. il Yachting 125:72-3 My '69

COLUMBINES
Hummingbirds and flowers. D. E. Rose. Horticulture 47:46-7 O '69

COLUMBUS, Christopher

Drama
Beyond mutiny. M. N. Peterson. Plays 29: 61-6 O '69
Reluctant Columbus. H. Cable. Plays 29:1-13 O '69

COLUMBUS, Ind.

Architecture
Middletown U.S.A. and good architecture. W. H. Gordon. il Trans-Action 6:39-42 My '69

COLUMBUS, Ohio

Education
Demand for accountability. Sat R 52:64 D 20 '69

Galleries and museums
Ceramics from the Howald collection in Columbus; Ferdinand Howald collection at Gallery of fine arts. E. P. Birk. il Antiques 96:692+ N '69

Police department
How police confront disaster; simulation study. T. E. Drabek and J. E. Hass. il Trans-Action 6:33-8 My '69

COLUMNISTS. See Journalists

COLUMNS (newspapers) See Newspapers—Sections, columns, etc.

COLWELL, Milton Sweeney
Keeper of the key. Am Heritage 20:49-53 Je '69

COLWIN, Laurie
Man who jumped into the water; story. New Yorker 45:38-42 D 20 '69

COLYER, Marilyn
Multiple-use orchard, 7,800 feet up. Org Gard & Farm 16:39-41 Ag '69

COMBAT fatigue. See Neuroses

COMBINATION rooms. See Rooms

COMBINATIONS
Handful of combinatorial problems based on dominoes. M. Gardner. il Sci Am 221:122-7 D '69

COMBINED insurance company of America
American original. il Time 93:78 F 7 '69

COMBINES. See Harvesting machinery

COMBS, Ann Gowen
Ode to a neglected dustcloth. por Redbook 132:14+ F '69

COMBS, Leslie
Cousin Leslie goes to market. W. Tower. il por Sports Illus 31:44-5 Jl 21 '69

COMBUSTION
See also
Ignition

COMBUSTION, Spontaneous
See also
Silos—Fires and fire protection

COMBUSTION engineering, incorporated
Dark horse in the lead; CE's entry into nuclear power field. Forbes 104:27 O 1 '69

COME along with me; story. See Jackson, S.

COME summer; musical comedy. See Musical comedies, revues, etc.—Criticisms, plots, etc.

COMEAU, Andre. See Roelofs, W. L. jt. auth

COMECON. See Council for economic mutual assistance

COMEDIANS
See also
Allen, W.
Smothers brothers

COMEDY
Theory of comedy, by E. Olson. Review
New Repub 160:23-4+ Mr 15 '69. K. Burke
See also
Humor
Moving pictures—Comedy
Television broadcasting—Humor

COMETS
How fast do comets decay? G. S. Mumford.
Sky & Tel 37:221 Ap '69
Minor planets from comets. Sky & Tel 38:
302 N '69
News about comets. Sky & Tel 38:223-4 O
'69
On the brightness of comets. J. Bortle. il R
Pop Astron 63:10-13 F '69
Recent comet observations. J. E. Bortle and
C. Scovil. il Sky & Tel 38:426-7 D '69
Selection effects on comet discoveries. il
Sky & Tel 38:301 N '69
Some questionable comets. J. Ashbrook. bib-
liog il Sky & Tel 37:229-30 Ap '69
See also
Halley's comet

COMFORT, Alex
Excerpts from Theories of aging. Aging 180:6
O '69

COMFREY
Plant some comfrey. M. L. Champie. il Org
Gard & Farm 16:44-5 O '69

COMIC literature. See Humor

COMIC strips. See Comics (books, strips, etc)

COMICS (books, strips, etc)
But what goes after the third line? Little
Orphan Annie. R. Gehman. Sat R 52:4
Jl 12 '69
Krazy kat, by G. Herriman. Review
Life 67:12 D 12 '69. G. Weales
Not-so Peanuts world of Charles M. Schulz.
J. Tebbel; C. M. Schulz. il Sat R 52:72-4+
Ap 12 '69
Where are they now? creators of Buck
Rogers and Flash Gordon. il Newsweek 74:
8 Ag 4 '69
You're an adman's dream, Charlie Brown.
il Bsns W p44-6 D 20 '69
See also
Advertising mediums—Comics (books, strips,
etc)
Educational applications
Charlie Brown goes to school; study of
Peanuts. M. E. Miner. bibliog f Engl J 58:
1183-5 N '69

COMINGLING. See Communication

COMINS, Jeremy
Art motivation for ghetto children. il Sch
Arts 69:6-7 O '69

COMMAGER, Henry Steele
Americanization of history. Sat R 52:24-5+
N 1 '69
Crisis of the academic library; address,
November 1968. por Wilson Lib Bul 43:518-
25 F '69

COMMANDMENTS, Ten
Murder
Thou shalt not kill, but thou mayest. Chr
Cent 86:1365 O 22 '69

COMMANDOS. See Guerrillas

COMMEMORATIVE coins. See Coins

COMMEMORATIVE firearms. See Firearms

COMMEMORATIVE medals. See Medals

COMMEMORATIVE stamps. See Postage
stamps

COMMEMORATIVE volumes. See Festschriften

COMMENCEMENT addresses. See Baccalaureate addresses

COMMENCEMENTS
Anti-commencement day. il Newsweek 73:64
Je 16 '69
Class of '69. il Life 66:28-33 Je 20 '69
Class of '69: the violent years. E. Diamond.
il Newsweek 73:68-73 Je 23 '69
Commencement dilemma. W. F. Buckley,
jr. Nat R 21:663 Jl 1 '69
Commencement, 1969: pomp and protest. il
Time 93:42+ Je 20 '69

Goodbye, Harvard; June commencement. D.
R. Papke. Commonweal 91:13-15 O 3 '69;
Reply, D. P. Nicastro. 91:197+ N 14 '69
Graduation day. Newsweek 73:92 Je 9 '69

COMMERCE
Business around the globe. See occasional
issues of Fortune
C.I.T-type operation for the world; proposed
Private export finance corp. il Forbes 103:25
F 1 '69
Changing world trade patterns and America's
leadership role. R. F. Mikesell. Ann Am
Acad 384:35-44 Jl '69
Economic report of the President and annual
report of the Council of economic advisers;
excerpts. L. B. Johnson. il Dept State Bul
60:101-17 F 3 '69
Imperatives of world economic progress;
trade & investment; address, November 17,
1969. J. M. Roche. Vital Speeches 36:187-
90 Ja 1 '70
Trade, aid, and peace. L. B. Pearson. Sat R
52:23-6 F 22 '69
Worldwide recession? threat that Europe sees.
il U S News 67:42-3 S 15 '69
See also
Balance of payments
Balance of trade
Barter
Export trade
Free trade and protection
Import quotas
Ports
Reciprocity
Smuggling
Tariff
World trade week
also subhead Commerce under name of
countries, e.g. Russia—Commerce

COMMERCE committee. See United States—
Congress—House of representatives—Commerce. Committee on

COMMERCE department (United States) See
United States—Commerce, Department of

COMMERCIAL aeronautics. See Aeronautics,
Commercial

COMMERCIAL arbitration. See Arbitration,
Commercial

COMMERCIAL art. See Art, Commercial

COMMERCIAL associations
See also
Chamber of commerce of the United States
of America
International chamber of commerce

COMMERCIAL buildings
Designed for machines but mindful of people;
telephone buildings, one in Oakland, Calif.
the other in New York city. il Arch Rec 146:
123-30 Jl '69

COMMERCIAL credit company
Control data's Cinderella: CCC. il Forbes
104:19 D 15 '69

COMMERCIAL finance companies. See Finance
companies

COMMERCIAL law
See also
Attachment and garnishment
Trusts, Industrial—Law
Warranty

COMMERCIAL paper. See Negotiable instruments

COMMERCIAL photography. See Photography,
Commercial

COMMERCIAL products
Months ahead; news & ideas to help you plan
ahead, stay ahead. See issues of Changing
times
Thanks for the memory; revival of old prod-
ucts. il Newsweek 74:90 N 10 '69
Things are in the saddle. R. Lynes. il Hori-
zon 11:40-1 Wint '69
See also
Commodity exchanges
Marine resources
Products, New
Quality of products
Endorsements
See Advertising—Testimonials
Standards
What consumers need: show biz or hard
facts. A. Q. Mowbray. il Nation 209:245-8
S 15 '69
Testing
See also
Consumers union of United States

COMMERCIAL travelers. See Salesmen and
salesmanship

COMMERCIAL treaties and agreements
Making soft money into hard; switch dealing.
il Fortune 80:184 Ag 15 '69
They'd rather switch: switch trade and clearing dollars. Newsweek 73:71-2 Mr 3 '69

COMMERCIALS. See Television advertising

COMMINUTORS. See Refuse and refuse disposal—Apparatus

COMMISSION of fine arts. See United States—Commission of fine arts

COMMISSION of the European communities
U.S. European communities officials hold trade talks at Washington. Dept State Bul 60:514 Je 16 '69

COMMISSION on college physics
What shall we do for the Commission on college physics? R. Geballe and others. il Phys Today 22:120-1 N '69

COMMISSION on faith and order. See World council of churches

COMMISSION on obscenity and pornography. See United States—Commission on obscenity and pornography

COMMISSION on the assassination of President Kennedy. See United States—President's commission on the assassination of President Kennedy

COMMISSIONER of education. See United States—Education, Office of

COMMISSIONER of football. See Football clubs—Organization and administration

COMMISSIONS, independent regulatory. See Independent regulatory commissions

COMMISSIONS of the United Nations. See name of the commission as subhead under United Nations, e.g. United Nations—Commission on narcotic drugs

COMMISSIONS of the United States government. See name of the commission as subhead under United States, e.g. United States—Commission on intergovernmental relations

COMMITTEE for a sane nuclear policy. See National committee for a sane nuclear policy

COMMITTEE for economic development
Businessmen and Operation Bootstrap. R. L. Tobin. Sat R 52:30 O 25 '69
New directions for the American school; recommendations by the Research and policy committee. Sch & Soc 97:156-8 Mr '69
Who runs the university? symposium. il Sat R 53:52-4+ Ja 10 '70
Who speaks for business? G. R. Rosen. il Duns R 94:45-7+ N '69

COMMITTEE of concerned Asian scholars. See Association for Asian studies

COMMITTEE of twenty-four. See United Nations—Special committee on the situation with regard to implementation of declaration on granting of independence to colonial countries and peoples

COMMITTEE on assessing the progress of education
Happenings in education; national assessment of education. W. D. Boutwell. PTA Mag 63:34-5 My '69
National assessment, what, why, how. Ed Digest 34:14-17 Ap '69
National assessment, where is it now? first data on educational attainments of young Americans. E. L. Norris. il Am Ed 5:20-3 O '69
National science assessment. E. L. Norris. Ed Digest 35:46-8 N '69

COMMITTEE on invisibles and financing relating to trade. See United Nations conference on trade and development

COMMITTEE on new directions. See American library association—Committee on new directions

COMMITTEE on non-governmental organizations. See United Nations—Economic and social council

COMMITTEE on persistent pesticides. See National academy of sciences

COMMITTEE on science in the promotion of human welfare. See American association for the advancement of science—Committee on science in the promotion of human welfare

COMMITTEE on space research. See International council of scientific unions—Committee on space research

COMMITTEE on the challenges of modern society. See NATO

COMMITTEE on uniform security identification procedures
Unclogging paperwork jam. il Bsns W p 111 Je 28 '69

COMMITTEE to rescue Italian art
Venice preserved? J. McAndrew. il Art N 68: 54-8+ Sum '69

COMMITTEES
See also
Church committees

COMMITTEES, Congressional. See United States—Congress—Committees

COMMITTEES in management
Bill Verity's Monday afternoon club; Armco's executive committee. S. Blickstein. il Duns R 93:33-5 My '69

COMMODITY exchanges
Case of jitters in cocoa; brisk trading on New York cocoa exchange. il Bsns W p 122+ Ja 25 '69
Cattle futures jump higher. il Bsns W p 132 Mr 22 '69
Commodity futures: the markets for fast action. Bsns W p 109-10 N 1 '69
Don't phone your broker; go to Aqueduct! Forbes 104:54-5 Ag 1 '69
Using futures, facts you need to use them. F. Bailey, jr. il Suc Farm 67:36-7 D '69
Using futures, how the market works. F. Bailey, jr. il Suc Farm 67:30-1+ N '69

COMMODITY labels. See Labels

COMMON Bible. See Bible—Versions

COMMON colleges. See Colleges and universities

COMMON market in Central America. See Central American program of economic integration

COMMON market in western Europe. See European economic community

COMMONER, Barry
Frail reeds in a harsh world; with biographical sketch. Natur Hist 78:4, 44-5 F '69
Lake Erie, aging or ill? por Sci & Cit 10: 254-63+ D '68
Myth of omnipotence. Environ 11:8-13+ Mr '69
Technology and the natural environment. Arch Forum 130:68-73 Je '69
—and others
Electron spin resonance signals in injured nerve. bibliog Science 165:703-4 Ag 15 '69

about
Last refuge of scoundrels. W. Kornberg. Sci N 96:261 S 27 '69

COMMONS (college) See Colleges and universities—Dining halls

COMMONWEAL (periodical)
Commonweal's future? former editors reply; symposium. Commonweal 91:222+ N 14 '69
Idea for a magazine. Commonweal 91:197-8 N 14 '69

COMMONWEALTH Edison company
Early bird. il Forbes 104:38 S 15 '69

COMMONWEALTH of nations
Beneath the moon; problems of the British Commonwealth. G. Lichtheim. Commentary 47:69-75 Mr '69
See also
Prime ministers conferences

COMMONWEALTH united corporation
Mini-conglomerate finds the going rough. Bsns W p40-1 Ag 16 '69

COMMUNAL living. See Collective settlements

COMMUNAL settlements. See Collective settlements

COMMUNICABLE diseases
Asiatic diseases; are they a threat to Americans back home? E. M. Wylie. Good H 168:96-7+ Ap '69
See also
Quarantine
Streptococcal infections
Venereal diseases
Virus diseases
also names of communicable diseases, e.g. Rocky Mountain spotted fever

COMMUNICABLE diseases in animals
Checkup for cats' role in leukemia. Bsns W p65 D 27 '69
Hepatitis in marmosets; induction of disease with coded specimens from a human volunteer study. A. W. Holmes and others. bibliog il Science 165:816-17 Ag 22 '69
Viral infection across species barriers: reversible alteration of murine sarcoma virus for growth in cat cells. P. J. Fischinger and T. E. O'Connor. bibliog il Science 165: 714-16 Ag 15 '69

COMMUNICATION
Art of not listening; A. Kaplan's idea of "duologues." il Time 93:52-3 Ja 24 '69
Birth of a new science: non-verbal communication, or, comingling. America 120:236-7 Mr 1 '69
Can you give the public what it wants? by E. Dale. Review
Cath World 208:238-9 F '69. R. Steele
Communications. J. McLaughlin. America 122:16-18 Ja 10 '70
Communications; ed. by R. L. Tobin. See Communications issues of Saturday review
Confrontation and communication. R. Ruether. Chr Cent 86:1163-5 S 10 '69

COMMUNICATIONS satellites—*Continued*

Ground stations

Intelsat access system designed; time-division multiple-access system. B. M. Elson. il Aviation W 90:107+ Ap 14 '69

Satcom earth station business booming. il Aviation W 90:263+ Mr 10 '69

International aspects

Communications by satellite. S. Mickelson. For Affairs 48:67-79 O '69

Comsat, State dept. split on negotiations. K. Johnsen. Aviation W 90:24-5 Mr 31 '69

New bond of union; first satellite in the common service of the American nations. G. de Zéndegui. Américas 21.1 Mr '69

Television: the view from Europe; EBU general assembly. J. Tebbel. il Sat R 52:43-4 Ag 9 '69

U.S. accedes to establishment of regional satellite networks. K. Johnsen. Aviation W 91:23 D 22 '69

Military applications

Tactical satcom orbited by USAF. Aviation W 90:21 F 17 '69

Telcomsat, world's largest satellite. il Space World F-5-65:12-13 My '69

UHF, X-band studied in TacSatCom test. il Aviation W 90:84 Je 9 '69

COMMUNICATIONS satellites, Canadian

Satellite that talks Canadian. il Bsns W p50+ Ag 2 '69

COMMUNICATIONS satellites, Indian (East Indian)

Next decade: TV by satellite. S. K. Ghaswala. Sci N 96:136 Ag 16 '69

TV for India. J. McLaughlin. America 121:308+ O 11 '69

U.S., India agree on experiment in instructional television. Dept State Bul 61:334-5 O 20 '69

COMMUNION. See Catholic church—Eucharist: Lords Supper

COMMUNISM

Communism: a house divided, a faith fragmented; leaders of seventy-five Communist parties meet in Moscow. J. Schecter. il Time 93:24+ Je 13 '69

For greater unity of communism; address, June 7, 1969. L. I. Brezhnev. Vital Speeches 35:578-92 Jl 15 '69

History quiz for the young revolutionary; similarity to nazism. J. Jeffries. Nat R 21:488+ My 20 '69

Marxian revolutionary idea, by R. C. Tucker. Review
New Repub 161:29-31 Jl 26 '69. M. Harrington

Obsolete communism, by D. Cohn-Bendit and G. Cohn-Bendit. Review
Nat R 21:391-3 Ap 22 '69. W. S. Schlamm

Ratifying the right to dissent; communiqué presented at Communist summit meeting. il Time 93:26 Je 27 '69

Red summit in the palace of the czars. il Life 66:34-5 Je 20 '69

Revolution: the past and the future. il Life 67:100-12 O 10 '69

Soviet summit: high on trouble; first full-fledged international summit since downfall of Nikita Khrushchev. il Newsweek 73:38-40+ Je 16 '69

Unperfect society, by M. Djilas. Review
Commentary 48:102+ S '69. D. T. Bazelon
New Repub 160:22-4 My 17 '69. W. C. McWilliams

See also
Communist countries
Communist parties
Socialism
World peace council

Anti-Communist measures

See also
United States—Foreign relations—Anti-Communist measures

Study and teaching

Check of Czech theology: Comenius faculty in Prague. Chr Today 13:27 Ap 11 '69; Reply. Chr Cent 86:702-3 My 21 '69

Africa

Communist gains in Africa; where Moscow and Peking are scoring. U S News 66:11 Je 9 '69

Asia, Southeastern

Theory topples. Nation 209:270 S 22 '69

Vietnam and southeast Asia; symposium. bibliog f il Cur Hist 56:65-109+ F '69

When war ends, U.S. role in Asia. il U S News 66:34-6 Ap 14 '69

Which will be the next Vietnam? C. T. Rowan. il Read Digest 94:95-100 Mr '69

See also
Anti-Communist movements—Asia, Southeastern

Cambodia

Cambodia: growing problem for U.S. military men. il U S News 66:28 Ap 7 '69

Cambodia, growing trouble spot. il U S News 67:31 Ag 11 '69

China (People's Republic)

China's two decades of communism. il Time 94:30-1 O 3 '69

East Asian backgrounds. C. P. Fitzgerald. Nation 209:384-6 O 13 '69

Mao's troubled ark. A. S. Whiting. il Life 66:62D-62F+ F 21 '69

Peking way of life. il N Y Times Mag p7-9+ Je 1 '69

Where China stands now: an introduction. D. Wilson. Bul Atom Sci 25:4-10 F '69

See also
Communist party (China [People's Republic])

Cuba

Castro's Cuba: drums, guns, and the new man. J. Corry. Harper 238:37-45 Ap '69

Fidel Castro, by H. L. Matthews. Review
Sat R 52:23-5+ My 3 '69. P. Kidd

Some thoughts on the right way (for us) to love the Cuban revolution. S. Sontag. Ramp Mag 7:6+ Ap '69

Czechoslovakia

Rescaring the unscared; Soviet style. S. Alsop. Newsweek 73:112 Ap 28 '69

See also
Communist party (Czechoslovakia)

France

See also
Communist party (France)

Germany (Democratic Republic)

Behind the wall, the success story of Walter Ulbricht? J. H. Huizinga. il N Y Times Mag p36-7+ S 7 '69

See also
Berlin wall, 1961-

Great Britain

See also
Trade unions—Communist activities

Indonesia

See also
Communist party (Indonesia)

Italy

See also
Communist party (Italy)

Laos

Breaking the rules; Communists pressing their offensive. il Time 94:35 Ag 1 '69

Staking a claim; victory at Muong Soui. il Newsweek 74:42 Jl 14 '69

Unbalancing the seesaw; North Vietnam steps up war in Laos. il Newsweek 73:56-7 My 19 '69

Latin America

Early cold war period. R. E. Poppino. Cur Hist 56:340-5+ Je '69

Rumania

Rumanian game; with interview with P. Popescu. L. Gross. il Look 33:22-8 Ap 15 '69

See also
Communist party (Rumania)

Russia

Brezhnev sets the clock back. H. Kamm. il N Y Times Mag p 14-15+ Ag 10 '69; Discussion. p 12+ Ag 24; 40+ S 7 '69

Difference is the system; relative buying power of U. S. and Soviet workers. il Nations Bsns 57:63 O '69

Ideology in power, by B. D. Wolfe. Review
Nat R 21:1122-3 N 4 '69. G. Niemeyer

Living with the ghost of Stalin. il Newsweek 73:40-2 F 24 '69

See also
Communist party (Russia)

Tanzania

Eye to the West; situation in Zanzibar. S. Ungar. Newsweek 73:52+ My 19 '69

COMMUNISM—*Continued*

Thailand

Thailand's role in southeast Asia. K. Young. bibliog f Cur Hist 56:94-9+ F '69

Tibet

Tibet struggles to survive. H. S. Bradsher. For Affairs 47:750-62 Jl '69

United States

On communism, by J. E. Hoover. Review
America 120:286 Mr 8 '69. P. J. Henriot
See also
Communist party (United States)

Anti-Communist measures

FBI in our open society, by H. Overstreet and B. Overstreet; and Communism, by J. E. Hoover; reviews. M. S. Evans. Nat R 21:499-500 My 20 '69
Timely initiative; movement for the repeal of Title II of the Internal security act of 1950. Nation 208:716-17 Je 9 '69
See also
John Birch society
United States—Subversive activities control board

Vietnam (Democratic Republic)

Red ruler who refuses to be defeated; what he hopes to gain. il U S News 66:18-19 My 26 '69

Vietnam (Republic)

Hand down your head, Tom Dooley; Vietnamese Catholics, a pawn of American foreign policy. R. Scheer. il Ramp Mag 7: 15-19 Ja 25 '69

Anti-Communist measures

See also
Vietnamese war, 1957-

Yugoslavia

Fifty years of Yugoslavia. G. J. Prpic. America 120:499-502 Ap 26 '69
Why Russia fears Yugoslav communism. C. S. Foltz. il U S News 66:82-4 My 5 '69
Yugoslavia; Karl Marx in a Mercedes. E. Dunbar. il Look 33:23-9 F 18 '69
See also
Communist party (Yugoslavia)

Zanzibar

See Communism—Tanzania

COMMUNISM and art
Art and revolution, by J. Berger. Review
Commonweal 90:441-3 Jl 11 '69. M. Harrington

COMMUNISM and democracy
Changing profile of world communism. T. O. Yntema. Sat R 52:15-18 Je 14 '69
Convergence: the uncertain meeting of East and West; Time essay. il Time 95:18-19 Ja 12 '70
Does American foreign policy entail frequent wars? P. Findley. Ann Am Acad 384:45-52 Jl '69
Global containment: the Truman years. N. A. Graebner. Cur Hist 57:77-83+ Ag '69
Making foreign policy; the influence of men and events. J. K. Galbraith. Cur 113:54-61 D '69
Mediterranean crisis. F. S. Meyer. Nat R 21:75 Ja 28 '69
Soviet Union and the West. K. L. London. Cur Hist 57:193-200+ O '69
Tinkering with delicate relationships. il Time 95:24 Ja 19 '70

COMMUNISM and nationalism
Ground rules for national communism. Life 67:46B S 19 '69

COMMUNISM and religion
Christian-Communist dialogue, by R. Garaudy and Q. Lauer. Review
Cath World 209:86 My '69. P. Nobile
Christian-Marxist dialogue. A. T. van Leeuwen. Cath World 208:219-21 F '69
Communist ecumenism. America 121:3 Jl 5 '69
Cuba and religion: challenge and response. E. E. Gendler. Chr Cent 86:1013-16 Jl 30 '69
Expanding dialogue. H. Aptheker. Cath World 209:272-3 S '69
Marxism and Christianity, by A. MacIntyre. Review
New Repub 160:30-1 Ja 25 '69. B. Murchland
On Christian-Marxist dialogue. J. M. Lochman. il Chr Cent 87:11-16 Ja 7 '70
Openings for Marxist-Christian dialogue, ed. by T. W. Ogletree. Review
Chr Cent 86:685 My 14 '69. H. A. Durfee

World Communist leaders think positively about Christians. Chr Cent 86:895 Jl 2 '69

COMMUNISM and the Catholic church. See Catholic church and communism

COMMUNIST aggression. See Aggression (international law)

COMMUNIST countries
Djilas revisits Orwell; there'll be many different communisms in 1984. M. Djilas. il N Y Times Mag p28-9+ Mr 23 '69
Red bloc. D. L. Flaherty. America 122:12-14 Ja 10 '70
See also
China (People's Republic)
Europe, Eastern

Commerce

Moscow, Bonn forge new link; East-West trade deals. Bsns W p 130 My 10 '69
Needed: a realistic East West trade policy. E. M. Dirksen. Read Digest 94:129-33 Je '69
Western economic warfare 1947-1967, by G. Adler-Karlsson. Review
Bul Atom Sci 25:44-6 O '69. H. I. Schiller
When West trades with a red nation; doing business with Rumania. il U S News 66:46 Je 2 '69

Travel regulations

See Travel regulations

COMMUNIST countries and the West. See World politics, 1945-

COMMUNIST newspapers
See also
Daily world (newspaper)

COMMUNIST parties
Communism: a house divided, a faith fragmented; leaders of seventy-five Communist parties meet in Moscow. J. Schecter. il Time 93:24+ Je 13 '69
Communism and economic development. Trans-Action 6:7 Ap '69
Divided comrades at the summit; meeting of party leaders in Moscow. Time 93:36 Je 6 '69
Independent mood; world summit meeting. il Time 93:29 Je 20 '69
Little something for everyone; international conference. P. Wohl. il Nation 209:38-41 Jl 14 '69
Lost leader; Moscow summit. il Newsweek 73:44 Je 23 '69
Moscow loses its gamble. America 120:724-5 Je 28 '69
Pravda on the invasion of Czechoslovakia; excerpts, September 25, 1968. Cur Hist 56: 237-8+ Ap '69
Put on a happy face; Soviet-sponsored world conference issues communiqué. il Newsweek 73:55+ Je 30 '69
Ratifying the right to dissent; communiqué presented at Communist summit meeting. il Time 93:26 Je 27 '69
Red summit in the palace of the czars. il Life 66:34-5 Je 20 '69
Second best at Moscow; international Communist congress. Nat R 21:628+ Jl 1 '69
Soviet summit: high on trouble; first fullfledged international summit since downfall of Nikita Khrushchev. il Newsweek 73:38-40+ Je 16 '69
Statement of the world Communist conference; excerpts, June 17, 1969. Cur Hist 57: 234-6+ O '69

Purges

See also
Communist party (Russia)—Purges

COMMUNIST party (China [People's Republic])
China. H. Yu. Chr Cent 86:760, 912 My 28, Jl 2 '69
China's search for stability; opening of Chinese party congress in Peking. il Time 93: 30+ Ap 11 '69
China's second liberation in perspective. W. A. C. Adie. il Bul Atom Sci 25:12-16+ F '69
Chinese communist leadership. K. Y. Hsu. bibliog f Cur Hist 57:129-34+ S '69
Communist China 1969; foreign and domestic policy; address, April 1, 1969. P. Lin. Vital Speeches 35:485-97 Je 1 '69
Communist struggle; spiritual reawakening; address, January 1, 1969. K. S. Chiang. Vital Speeches 35:231-4 F 1 '69
Happy times; ninth congress; communiqué. Newsweek 73:60 Ap 28 '69
Man picked to succeed Mao. il U S News 66: 21 Ap 14 '69
Mao and the new mandate. E. Snow. New Repub 160:17-21 My 10 '69
Military cast; newly elected Central committee. Time 93:42-3 My 9 '69

COMMUNIST party (China [People's Republic])
—*Continued*
Moderating Mao; ninth congress convened. il Newsweek 73:58+ Ap 14 '69
New constitution of the Chinese communist party; excerpts. Cur Hist 57:176+ S '69
Red China: twenty years after. il Newsweek 74:48-9 O 13 '69
Republic of China today; mainland recovery; address, September 26, 1969. C. K. Yen. Vital Speeches 36:77-83 N 15 '69
United States-China relations; address, January 24, 1969. M. O. Hatfield. Vital Speeches 35:322-6 Mr 15 '69

COMMUNIST party (Czechoslovakia)
Dubcek talks; interview, ed. by D. Hunebelle. A. Dubcek. il Look 33:21-3 Jl 29 '69
Lesser of two evils; Central committee plenum. il Newsweek 73:52+ Je 9 '69
Our internationalist duty; address, October 28, 1969. L. I. Brezhnev. Vital Speeches 36: 101-5 D 1 '69
Revolution, reformation, reform. E. V. Kohax. Commonweal 91:378-82 D 26 '69
Soviet triumph. Dubcek's fall. U S News 66:9 Ap 28 '69

Purges
Confession; concerning A. London's first hand account. A. L. Moats. il Nat R 21: 846-8+ Ag 26 '69
Prague: no time for heroics. K. D. Huszar. il Newsweek 74:49-50 D 15 '69
Purging the purgers. Newsweek 74:27 D 29 '69

COMMUNIST party (France)
Obsolete communism, by D. Cohn-Bendit and G. Cohn-Bendit. Review
Nation 208:578-80 My 5 '69. L. Derfler
Reverse twist in France. Nat R 21:631-2 Jl 1 '69

COMMUNIST party (Germany)
Who shot Rosa? Newsweek 73:51 Ja 27 '69

COMMUNIST party (India)
As Bengal goes... E. Behr. il Newsweek 73: 55 Ap 21 '69

COMMUNIST party (Indonesia)
Indonesia: another Communist disaster. A. C. Brackman. bibliog f Cur Hist 56:156-60+ Mr '69
Reporter at large: rise and fall of PKI. R. Shaplen. New Yorker 45:42-6+ My 24; 39-44+ My 31 '69

COMMUNIST party (Italy)
Bottom's up. Time 93:34 F 28 '69
Case of the cautious Communists. T. J. Barbarie. il Nat R 21:389+ Ap 22 '69
Challenge to Moscow. il Newsweek 73:40 F 24 '69
Departing from the script. il Time 93:23 F 21 '69
Italy between governments. R. Meachum. New Repub 162:16-18 Ja 10 '70

COMMUNIST party (Rumania)
Shadow; tenth congress. Newsweek 74:36 Ag 25 '69

COMMUNIST party (Russia)
Battle inside the Kremlin. V. Zorza. Look 33:93-7+ Mr '69
Can Russia afford a U.S. deal? another challenge to the old men in the Kremlin. il U S News 66:51 Mr 31 '69
Djilas revisits Orwell; there'll be many different communisms in 1984. M. Djilas. il N Y Times Mag p28-9+ Mr 23 '69
For greater unity of communism; address, June 7, 1969. L. I. Brezhnev. Vital Speeches 35:578-92 Jl 15 '69
Middle way. Newsweek 75:22-3 Ja 5 '70
Moscow loses its gamble. America 120:724-5 Je 28 '69
New man in town: K. Katushev. il Time 93: 34+ Mr 28 '69
Our internationalist duty; address, October 28, 1969. L. I. Brezhnev. Vital Speches 36: 101-5 D 1 '69
Power in the Kremlin, by M. Tatu. Review
Nat R 21:494-5 My 20 '69. T. Szamuely
Pravda on the invasion of Czechoslovakia; excerpts, September 25, 1968. Cur Hist 56: 237-8+ Ap '69
Some guesses about the next Kremlin conspiracy. J. Fischer. Harper 238:12+ Mr '69
Thinking about the Soviet Union. W. F. Buckley, jr. Nat R 21:818 Ag 12 '69

Anecdotes, facetiae, satire, etc.
Chetsky-Davidov report. J. Jeffries. il Nat R 21:748 Jl 29 '69

Political bureau
Kremlinology: power and terror. D. Joravsky. Nation 209:84-6 Jl 28 '69

Purges
Great terror, by R. Conquest. Review
Esquire 71:36+ F '69. M. Muggeridge
Kremlinology: power and terror. D. Joravsky. Nation 209:84-6 Jl 28 '69

COMMUNIST party (United States)
Angelo Herndon story. H. N. Meyer. Chr Cent 86:221-2 F 12 '69
Bryn Mawr tells it not quite like it is: H. Aptheker to head program of black studies. Nat R 21:580-1 Je 17 '69
Communist-Catholic neurosis? Reflections on A long journey. C. A. Weber. Commonweal 90:389-93 Je 20 '69
Long journey, by G. B. Charney. Review
Commentary 48:98-100+ N '69. M. J. Goldbloom

Anecdotes, facetiae, satire, etc.
Happy Jack fish hatchery papers; letters. S. Allen and D. Trumbo. Esquire 73:73-7+ Ja '70

COMMUNIST party (Vietnam)
I quit. D. Duncan. Ramp Mag 7:41-6 Ja 25 '69
North Vietnam in transition; after Uncle Ho, what? Cur 112:55-8 N '69
Power struggle in Hanoi? V. Zorza. Cur 112: 58-63 N '69
Scuffling in Hanoi. il Newsweek 74:57 D 22 '69
What life's like in Vietcong territory. T. Buckley. il N Y Times Mag p48-9+ N 23 '69

COMMUNIST party (Vietnam [Democratic Republic])
After Ho Chi Minh. N. K. Huyen. America 121:265-7 O 4 '69
After Ho: shift in the war? il U S News 67:25-7 S 15 '69
Farewell to Ho. il Newsweek 74:30-1 S 22 '69
Hanoi without Ho; what U.S. can expect; interview. P. J. Honey. il U S News 67:38-40 S 22 '69
Legacy of Ho Chi Minh. il Time 94:22-6+ S 12 '69
President Ho chi Minh (1890-1969) who will succeed him? il Newsweek 74:30+ S 15 '69

COMMUNIST party (Vietnam [Republic])
Letter from South Vietnam. R. Shaplen. New Yorker 45:134+ Ap 12 '69

COMMUNIST party (Yugoslavia)
Prudential Mr Tito. M. M. Mestrovic. Commonweal 90:62-3 Ap 4 '69
Unperfect society, by M. Djilas. Review
Commonweal 90:324 My 30 '69. M. M. Mestrovic

COMMUNIST propaganda. See Propaganda, Communist

COMMUNIST strategy
Analysis: behind the Sino/Soviet dispute. D. Horowitz. il Ramp Mag 7:39-43 Je '69
How to defeat communism without war; letter to the editor. U S News 66:108+ F 17 '69
Sino-Soviet rivalry in the third world. E. K. Valkenier. bibliog f Cur Hist 57:201-6+ O '69
Some dilemmas of counterinsurgency. G. K. Tanham and D. J. Duncanson. For Affairs 48:113-22 O '69
Statement of the world Communist conference; excerpts, June 17, 1969. Cur Hist 57: 234-6+ O '69

COMMUNIST terror organization. See Guerrillas—Malaysia

COMMUNISTS
See also
Communist parties

COMMUNITIES (ecology) See Ecology

COMMUNITY
Organization is not the essence of community; excerpts from address, August 1969. I. M. Sussman. il Cath World 210:114-18 D '69

COMMUNITY action programs. See Anti-poverty program, 1964-

COMMUNITY and business. See Business—Social aspects

COMMUNITY and the college. See Colleges and universities—Public relations

COMMUNITY and the school. See School and the community

COMMUNITY antenna television systems. See CATV system

COMMUNITY bulletin boards. See Bulletin boards

COMMUNITY centers
Indoor agora; Dronten, Netherlands. il Arch
Forum 131:68-9 N '69
See also
Cultural centers
Recreation centers
Senior centers
    also subhead Community centers under
names of cities. e.g. Rochester, N.Y.—
Community centers

COMMUNITY chests
See also
United fund

COMMUNITY colleges. See Junior colleges

COMMUNITY control of schools. See School
management and organization

COMMUNITY counseling service. See Counseling

COMMUNITY development

United States
Co-ordinating the war on poverty. J. L.
Sundquist. Ann Am Acad 385:41-9 S '69
Is cooperative self-help enough? O. A. Ornati.
Cur 107:31-3 My '69
Making capitalism work in the ghettos. L. L.
Allen. il Harvard Bsns R 47:83-92 My '69
Planning workbook for the community. J.
M. Dixon. il Arch Forum 131:32-9 D '69
Urban design with soul; Urban design de-
velopment group, incorporated, Detroit.
J. Aumente. il Arch Forum 131:44-5 D '69
See also
New York (state)—Urban development cor-
poration

COMMUNITY development corporations
Community economic self-help; coopera-
tives against poverty. G. Alperovitz. Cur
107:27-31 My '69
Deghettoization; choice of the new militancy.
C. Funnyé. Arch Forum 130:74-7 Ap '69
Georgia's biggest bank wades into the
slums; Citizens & Southern national bank. il
Bsns W p90-1 My 24 '69
Limits of black capitalism. F. D. Sturdivant.
bibliog f il Harvard Bsns R 47:122-8 Ja '69
Urban renewal need not be a dirty word;
South Arsenal neighborhood development
corp; Hartford, Conn. E. P. Berkeley. il
Arch Forum 130:36-41 Ap '69

COMMUNITY flying clubs. See Air travel clubs

COMMUNITY health centers. See Health centers

COMMUNITY health service. See Medical service

COMMUNITY law offices. See Legal aid

COMMUNITY life
  See also
Neighborhoods

**COMMUNITY mental health center, Temple
university.** See Temple university, Philadelphia

COMMUNITY mental health centers. See Mental health centers

COMMUNITY mental health service. See Mental
health service

COMMUNITY news service
Ghetto wire service. Newsweek 74:86+ Jl 7
'69

COMMUNITY organization
Community action program: a strategy to
fight poverty. S. A. Levitan. bibliog f il
Ann Am Acad 385:63-75 S '69
Community power and community mobiliza-
tion; excerpts from The structure of com-
munity power: readings. M. Aiken. bibliog
f il Ann Am Acad 385:76-88 S '69
Maximum feasible participation: the origins,
implications, and present status; extracts
from paper. L. B. Rubin. bibliog f Ann
Am Acad 385:14-29 S '69
Planning workbook for the community. J.
M. Dixon. il Arch Forum 131:32-9 D '69
See also
Community power

COMMUNITY planning. See Regional planning

COMMUNITY power
Community power and community mobiliza-
tion; excerpts from The structure of com-
munity power: readings. M. Aiken. bibliog
f il Ann Am Acad 385:76-88 S '69
War on poverty: experiment in federalism.
R. H. Davidson. bibliog f Ann Am Acad
385:1-13 S '69
See also
Community organization

COMMUNITY schools
Community school, pattern for progress; ad-
dress, March 7, 1969. E. G. Olsen. Vital
Speeches 35:370-3 Ap 1 '69

COMMUNITY service
Community action (title varies) (cont) il Sun-
set 142:96-9 Mr; 104-5, 148 My; 90-1 Je '69
Community action program: a strategy to
fight poverty. S. A. Levitan. bibliog f il
Ann Am Acad 385:63-75 S '69
Community action: where has it been? Where
will it go? S. Kravitz and F. K. Kolodner.
Ann Am Acad 385:30-40 S '69
Evaluation of broad-aim programs: a cau-
tionary case and a moral; excerpts from
address. R. S. Weiss and M. Rein. Ann
Am Acad 385:133-42 S '69
Reaching out; Potentials project. A. Mo-
lina. Seventeen 29:84-5+ Ja '70
  See also
Community service society of New York
Volunteer service

COMMUNITY service organization. See Industrial areas foundation—Community service organization

COMMUNITY service society of New York
Serve; Project SERVE. C. Rice. il Har Yrs
9:34-7 F '69
SERVE's success invites imitation; serve and
enrich retirement by volunteer service. il
Aging 170:7-10 D '68

COMMUNITY shopping centers. See Shopping
centers

COMMUTER airlines. See Local service airlines

COMMUTER service. See Railroads—Passenger
service

COMMUTERS
Commuters and city income taxes. J. Fried-
gut. il Nations Bsns 57:66 O '69
How to move a nation: latest ideas in mass
transit. il U S News 66:82-4 My 19 '69
LIRR revolt. il Newsweek 73:78 F 17 '69
Ticket trouble; Long Island railroad commu-
ters arrested for refusal to show tickets. il
Time 93:54 Ja 24 '69
Uncle Sam's commuter-shopper car P. Weis-
sler. il Mech Illus 65:32-4+ Ag '69
See also
Suburban life

COMO, William
On the boards. See issues of Dance magazine

COMPACT cars. See Automobiles, Compact

COMPAGNIA tecnica industrie petroli. See
Petroleum industry and trade—Italy

COMPAGNIE Renaud-Barrault. See Theater—
France

COMPANION crops
Lettuce in the onion row! L. Riotte. il Org
Gard & Farm 16:40-1 S '69

COMPANY magazines. See House organs

COMPANY names. See Corporations—Names

COMPANY presidents (in business) See Executives

COMPANY treasurers. See Corporations—
Treasurers

COMPARATIVE anatomy. See Anatomy, Comparative

COMPARATIVE education. See Education, Comparative

COMPARATIVE physiology. See Physiology,
Comparative

COMPARATORS
Homebuilt machine for scanning plates; blink
comparator. H. Vehrenberg. il Sky & Tel 38:
186+ S '69

COMPASS
Basic course in navigating by compass. J. S.
Doherty. il Mech Illus 65:71-3+ Mr '69
Compass for small craft; mariner's com-
pass. F. M. Paulson. il Field & S 74:142-4+
My '69

COMPASS, Radio. See Radio compass

COMPATIBILITY (marriage) See Marriage

COMPENSATION (law)
$1 million end to an unjust exile. D. Wolf.
il Life 66:67 Je 27 '69
See also
Damages
Traffic accidents—Cases
Workmens compensation

COMPENSATION, Unemployment. See Insurance, Unemployment

COMPENSATION for victims of crime. See
Reparation

COMPENSATORY education
Dead end in American education. R. A. Free-
man. Nat R 21:22-4 Ja 14 '69; Same abr. Ed
Digest 34:9-12 My '69

COMPETITION, Unfair
Legal limits of competition; excerpts from
Managerial analysis in marketing. J. R.
Grabner, jr. bibliog Harvard Bsns R 47:
4-6+ N '69

COMPETITIONS
Popular science anti-car-theft device competition. il Pop Sci 195:68-71 Jl; 66-7 Ag; 82-5+ S; 92-5+ O; 80-3 N '69
Whooos and foghorns; hollering contest. il Time 94:55 Jl 11 '69
See also
Beauty contests
    also subhead Competitions under various subjects, e.g. Photography—Competitions

Anecdotes, facetiae, satire, etc.
Year I won the contest. L. Duncan. Good H 169:205 D '69

COMPETITIONS, International
See also
Free trade and protection

COMPETITIVE bidding. See Building—Contracts and specifications: Contracts. Government; Municipal contracts

COMPETITIVE sports. See Sports

COMPLAINTS
Bodies or ballots? need for ways and means to redress valid group grievances. Nation 208:101 Ja 27 '69
Grocery shoppers' forty-four pet peeves. il Changing T 23:13-14 O '69
If you want to complain effectively. Good H 168:162 Je '69
Keppler on the SLR; of Modern readers complaining about equipment or service. H. Keppler. Mod Phot 33:113-14 Jl '69
LIRR revolt. il Newsweek 73:78 F 17 '69

COMPLEMENT fixation
Virus-like antigen, antibody, and antigen-antibody complexes in hepatitis measured by complement fixation. N. R. Shulman and L. F. Barker. bibliog il Science 165:304-6 Jl 18 '69

COMPLEMENTATION, Allelic. See Allelomorphism

COMPLEMENTS (immunity)
Anaphylatoxin release from the third component of human complement by hydroxylamine. D. B. Budzko and H. Müller-Eberhard. bibliog il Science 165:506-7 Ag 1 '69
Complement-immunoglobulin relation: deficiency of C'1q associated with impaired immunoglobulin G synthesis. bibliog il Science 163:474-5 Ja 31 '69
Cytotoxic effects of leukocytes triggered by complement bound to target cells. P. Perlmann and others. bibliog il Science 163:937-9 F 28 '69
Human C'3: evidence for the liver as the primary site of synthesis. C. A. Alper and others. bibliog il Science 163:286-8 Ja 17 '69
Human serum inhibitor of C'1 esterase: identity with α₂-neuraminoglycoprotein. J. Pensky and H. G. Schwick. bibliog il Science 163:698-9 F 14 '69
Immune adherence by the fourth component of complement. N. R. Cooper. bibliog il Science 165:396-8 Jl 25 '69
Neutralization of sensitized virus by the fourth component of complement. C. A. Daniels and others. bibliog il Science 165:508-9 Ag 1 '69
Serum C'3 lytic system in patients with glomerulonephritis. R. E. Spitzer and others. bibliog il Science 164:436-7 Ap 25 '69

COMPONENTS construction. See Houses, Prefabricated

COMPOSERS
And then I (wish I) wrote; statements by some top creators of hit songs; ed. by D. Dachs. il Hi Fi 19:34-7 Je '69
Girls, letting go; rock song writers. H. Saal. il Newsweek 74:68-71 Jl 14 '69
In composers. B. Jacobson. il Hi Fi 19:54-7 Jl '69
See also
Children of composers
International rostrum of composers

Political activities
Scandalous politics of Hans Werner Henze. R. P. Morgan. Hi Fi 19:106-7 D '69

COMPOSERS, American
See also
American society of university composers
Amram, D.
Babbitt, M.
Billings, W.
Brown, E.
Cage, J.
Carmichael, H.
Castaldo, J.
Copland, A.
Harris, R. E.

Kirchner, L.
Loesser, F.
Powell, M.
Rorem, N.
Rudin, A.
Schmidt, H.
Sessions, R.
Weber, B. B.

COMPOSERS, Argentinian
See also
Ginastera, A.

COMPOSERS, Austrian
See also
Bruckner, A.
Haydn, F. J.
Mahler, G.
Mozart, J. C. W. A.
Schönberg, A.
Schubert, F. P.
Webern, A. von
Wolf, H.

COMPOSERS, British
See also
Walton, W. T.

COMPOSERS, Czech
Janáček, L.
Smetana, B.

COMPOSERS, English
See also
Bishop, H. R.
Byrd, W.
Delius, F.
Tallis, T.
Vaughan Williams, R.

COMPOSERS, French
See also
Berlioz, H.
Boulez, P.
Couperin, F.
Debussy, C.
Delibes, L.
Faure, G.
Lully, J. B.
Millet, J.
Ravel, M.

COMPOSERS, German
See also
Beethoven, L. van
Graun, K. H.
Händel, G. F.
Henze, H. W.
Hindemith, P.
Meyerbeer, G.
Orff, C.
Pfitzner, H.
Stockhausen, K.
Strauss, R.
Telemann, G. P.
Weber, K. M. von

COMPOSERS, Greek
See also
Xenakis, Y.

COMPOSERS, Hungarian
See also
Kodály, Z.
Szokolay, S.

COMPOSERS, Italian
See also
Bononcini, G.
Catalani, A.
Cavalli, P. F.
Donizetti, G.
Mascagni, P.
Montemezzi, I.
Rossini, G.

COMPOSERS, Japanese
See also
Takemitsu, T.

COMPOSERS, Polish
See also
Chopin, F. F.
Penderecki, K.

COMPOSERS, Russian
See also
Balakirev, M. A.
Borodin, A. P.
Khachaturian, A.
Rachmaninoff, S.
Skriabin, A. N.
Tcherepnin, A.

COMPOSERS children. See Children of composers

COMPOSITE materials
F-14 spurs advance in composites. M. L. Yaffee. il Aviation W 90.46-7+ Mr 17 '69
Lighter than aluminum, stronger than steel! W. Von Braun. il Pop Sci 194:98-100+ F '69
New composite offers uniform strength; boron-coated polyimide composite film. il Aviation W 90:51+ F 10 '69

COMPOSITE photography. See Photomontage

COMPUTER programming. See Programming (computers)

COMPUTER workers
Face to face with a computer expert. A. Koenig. Seventeen 28:30 D '69
IBM's unruly brood; lawsuit against Cogar corp. and former IBM staff to prevent use of confidential IBM information. il Newsweek 74:85-7 Jl 21 '69
Paroled into programming. Bsns W p 154 Je 28 '69
Prison is no bar to computer work; programming training course at state correctional institution, Walpole, Mass. Nations Bsns 57:15 D '69
Self-instruction cuts computer training. N. S. Himmel. il Aviation W 90:78+ F 10 '69
We created our own data-processing division; Huntington Beach, Calif. F. B. Arguello. il Am City 84:155-6 S '69

COMPUTERIZED typesetting. See Computers—Printing applications

COMPUTERS
Computers on the brain. M. Mayer. il Esquire 71:100-3+ Ja '69
Guerrilla war against computers. Time 94:66 S 12 '69
How computers are changing your life. il U S News 67:96-8 N 10 '69
How to keep down noise levels in computer facilities. L. L. Boyer. jr. bibliog il Arch Rec 145:165-6 My '69
IBM thinks small; System/3. Newsweek 74:56 Ag 11 '69
Quiet stir of thought; or, What the computer cannot do; adaptation of address, May 1969. J. H. Shera. bibliog il Library J 94:2875-80 S 1 '69
This computer age. D. Powills. il Hobbies 74:152-3 O '69

See also
Automatic speech recognition
Data preparation corporation
Data processing service centers
Electronic data processing
International business machines corporation
Memory devices (computers)
Perceptrons
Programming (computers)
Programming languages (computers)
Punched card systems

Aeronautic applications
Airborne data system nears test; AIDS systems. K. J. Stein. il Aviation W 90:81+ Ap 7 '69
Area navigation gains in airline favor. K. J. Stein. il Aviation W 90:251-3+ Mr 10 '69
Computer flight planning offered. Aviation W 91:73-4 N 24 '69
FAA moves step-by-step into automation; National airspace system. P. J. Klass. il Aviation W 90:243-4+ Mr 10 '69
FAA using new glide path monitor. P. J. Klass. il Aviation W 91:67+ D 15 '69
France increasing ATC automation. P. J. Klass. il Aviation W 90:71+ Je 30 '69
French pool efforts on digital computers. il Aviation W 90:315+ Je 2 '69
See also
Airlines—Reservation systems

Agricultural applications
If your wife balks at keeping the books. J. Carlson. il Farm J 93:52O Mr '69
What farmer-feeders can learn from their big-lot competition. D. Seim. il Farm J 93:B8-9+ Mr '69

Analog computers
Magic box tells you when one more is too many. R. M. Benrey. il Pop Sci 194:102-5 Ap '69

Architectural applications
Computer applications in architecture and engineering; ed. by G. N. Harper. Review Arch Rec il 145:77-8 Ja '69

Art applications
Computer use in arts, humanities and museums. Hobbies 74:125 Mr '69
Picture processing by computer. L. D. Harmon and K. C. Knowlton. bibliog il Science 164:19-29 Ap 4 '69
See also
Computers—Print-out equipment

Astrological applications
Horoscope by computer. il Pop Electr 30:69-71+ F '69

Astronomical applications
Computer simulation of evolving galaxies. il Sky & Tel 38:19 Jl '69
More computer studies of galactic evolution. il Sky & Tel 38:302 N '69
Solar observations processed by computer. il Sky & Tel 37:363 Je '69

Biological applications
Automated analysis of cellular change in histological sections; image analysis computer. L. E. Mawdesley-Thomas and P. Healey. bibliog il Science 163:1200 Mr 14 '69
Computer analysis of protein evolution. M. O Dayhoff. il Sci Am 221:86-95 Jl '69
Computer-assisted design of complex organic syntheses. E. J. Corey and W. T. Wipke. bibliog il Science 166:178-92 O 10 '69
Eye movement-retina delayed feedback. K. U. Smith and others. bibliog il Science 166:1542-4 D 19 '69
Spectre II: general-purpose microscope input for a computer. P. G. Stein and others. bibliog il Science 166:328-33 O 17 '69
See also
Computers—Medical applications

Business applications
Bad decisions on computer use; with chart. J. Diebold. Harvard Bsns R 47:14-16+ Ja '69
Computers can't solve everything. T. Alexander. il Fortune 80:126-9+ O '69
GE builds a robot cashier; TRADAR system. il Bsns W p70 My 10 '69
Get the computer system you want. R. N. Freed. bibliog f il Harvard Bsns R 47:99-108 N '69
New controllers: more than numbers. J. Poindexter. il Duns R 94:37-41 O '69
New management finally takes over; computer-minded executives. il Bsns W p58-60+ Ag 23 '69
Time sharing takes off. B. Allen. il Harvard Bsns R 47:128-36 Mr '69

Cataloging applications
See Libraries—Automation

Church applications
Religion converts to computers; Church records management, inc. il Bsns W p 164 O 11 '69

Circuits
Bubble computers; microscopic cylinders embedded in thin sheets of ferrite. Sci Am 221:46-7 O '69

City planning applications
Urban dynamics, by J. W. Forrester. Review Fortune 80:241-2 N '69. J. F. Kain; Reply. J. W. Forrester. 80:191-2 D '69

Control applications
See also
Machine tools—Control

Cooperative use
See Computers—Time sharing systems

Cost
IBM rewrites the price book. Bsns W p 102+ Je 28 '69

Counseling applications
Doctor IBM. Newsweek 75:44 Ja 5 '70

Criminal investigation applications
See also
United States—Federal bureau of investigation—National crime information center

Design
Computer whiz kid; R. Dodson. il Ebony 25:101-2+ D '69
How fast can computers add? S. Winograd; reply with rejoinder. B. Beizer. Sci Am 220:8+ Ja '69
Large-scale integration and the revolution in electronics. S. Triebwasser. bibliog il Science 163:429-34 Ja 31 '69

Educational applications
Are you ready for your own data processing center? C. E. Wilsey. Ed Digest 34:16-17 Ja '69
Classroom gadgetry; concerning report by Anthony G. Oettinger and Sema Marks. J. Featherstone. New Repub 160:10-11 My 31 '69
Computer and individualized instruction. W. W. Cooley and R. Glaser. bibliog il Science 166:574-82 O 31 '69

COMPUTERS—Educational   applications—
- *Continued*
Computer and the peripatetic teacher; job-locator service. O. A. Payne. Todays Ed 58:13 F '69
Computer-assisted instruction. P. Suppes and M. Morningstar. bibliog il Science 166:343-50 O 17 '69
Computer-assisted instruction; interview. P. Suppes. Ed Digest 34:6-8 F '69
Computer-managed instruction. H. J. Brudner; reply. R. E. Schutz. Science 163:1009-10 Mr 7 '69
Computers in physics instruction. G. Schwarz and others. bibliog il Phys Today 22:41-9 S '69
Learning and the computer. J. Morgan. il Sci Digest 66:60-3 D '69
Pictures, punchcards, and poetry; address; November 1968. Daigon. Engl J 58:1033-7 O '69
Socrates, the computer, and ivied walls. M. H. Goldberg. bibliog Sch & Soc 97:424-7 N '69
Teachers without tempers. B. Asbell. il Redbook 132:44+ Ja '69
Utilization of computing and data processing in education. J. W. Alspaugh. bibliog Clear House 43:455-7 Ap '69
See also
Colleges and universities—Computer installations
Teaching machines

Employment applications
Headhunting by computer; job placement. il Bsns W p 130+ S 27 '69
Job bank in a computer pays off and branches out. il Bsns W p70-1 Jl 5 '69
Needed: a national job-matching network. G. K. Davies. bibliog f Harvard Bsns R 47:63-72 S '69

Engineering applications
Computer-designed PC boards. J. A. Bauer. il Electr World 82:47-9 O '69

Errors
Great snafu. il Newsweek 74:79-80 S 15 '69
When the computer fouls up your charge account. il Changing T 23:7-10 S '69

Government applications
Call to revolt. S. Alsop. Newsweek 74:108 D 22 '69
Study of the impact of office automation in the IRS. H. J. Rothberg. il Mo Labor R 92:26-30 O '69
What happens if computers pick out your tax return il U S News 67:69-70 S 8 '69
When computer handles hiring; state employment job bank. U S News 66:84-5 Ap 14 '69

Hospital applications
Computerized intercom a factor in new tower design for Providence. il Arch Rec 145:156-8 Mr '69

Industrial applications
Analytic instruments in process control. F. W. Karasek. il Sci Am 220:112-20 Je '69
Building a corporate financial model. G. W. Gershefski. il Harvard Bsns R 47:61-72 Jl '69
See also
Machine tools—Control

Input-output equipment
Computer interfaced fast analyzers. N. G. Anderson. bibliog il Science 166:317-24 O 17 '69
Computers users' aid; COM. Bsns W p49 Jl 5 '69
Data taping gets a bit cheaper. il Bsns W p 134+ F 15 '69
Picture processing by computer. L. D. Harmon and K. C. Knowlton. bibliog il Science 164:19-29 Ap 4 '69
Spectre II: general-purpose microscope input for a computer. P. G. Stein and others. bibliog il Science 166:328-33 O 17 '69

Investment applications
Battling the big board to serve big traders; A. F. Kay of AutEx computer system. il Bsns W p 104+ Je 14 '69
Challenge to the brokers; Instinct system. W. Robertson. il Fortune 79:67-8+ Ap '69
Computer to bypass the broker; investors trade electronically. Bsns W p96+ Mr 8 '69
Digital speculator. il Forbes 103:75 Mr 15 '69
Picking stocks by computer. Bsns W p 142 My 10 '69

Private stock exchange? il Forbes 103:70+ Mr 15 '69
SEC closes in on computers. Bsns W p82 Ag 9 '69
Street's new paper cutter. il Bsns W p56-7+ N 1 '69

Leasing and renting
Looking for a hedge in the risky leasing game; leasing companies. il Bsns W p 148 Ap 26 '69
See also
Management assistance, incorporated
SSI computer corporation

Library applications
See Libraries—Automation

Medical applications
Automatic identification and measurement of cells by computer. S. A. Rosenberg and others. il Science 163:1065-6 Mr 7 '69
Computer and the psychiatrist; Rockland state hospital's research center. T. Fleming. il N Y Times Mag p44-5+ Ap 6 '69
Computer predictions help cut hospital deaths. Todays Health 47:19 Mr '69
Diagnosing disease by computer. il Sci Digest 65:38-9 My '69
Incubating babies by computer. il Sci Digest 66:92-3 O '69

Meteorological applications
Computer's role in weather forecasting. W. H. Klein. bibliog il Weatherwise 22:195-201+ O '69
Now it can be foretold; spring floods in the Mississippi basin. il Sci N 95:302-3 Mr 29 '69
Past tells the future. il Sci N 96:298+ O 4 '69

Military applications
SAC evaluates onboard data processing; PACCS-ADA system. B. M. Elson. il Aviation W 91:87+ Jl 21 '69

Miniaturization
Bubbles for the future; miniaturized, high-speed computer. Time 94:40+ S 5 '69

Municipal applications
Computer is the key; Monroe, La. M. J. Cook. il Am City 84:127-8 O '69
Computer programs a city's growth; Coffeyville. Kan. B. J. DeMoss. il Am City 84:100+ D '69
Computer tells what street to pave; Westland, Mich. R. A. Jackson. il Am City 84:94+ Ja '69
Computerized billing collects 98 per cent of the taxes; Milwaukee, Wis. J. J. Krueger. il Am City 84:115+ Ag '69
Computerized management; or, Jungle administration; using data processing in park administration, Vancouver, Wash. D. W. Bridges. il Parks Rec 4:37-8+ D '69
Don't let size keep your waterworks from using EDP; East Windsor, N. J. W. B. Harvey. il Am City 84:95-6+ D '69
Small computer for a little city; Centralia, Wash. L. Hackett. il Am City 84:114+ Je '69
Urban management needs computers; Saginaw, Mich. E. H. Potthoff, jr. il Am City 84:69-71 Mr '69
We created our own data-processing division; Huntington Beach, Calif. F. B. Arguello. il Am City 84:155-6 S '69

Musical applications
Analysis of musical-instrument tones. J.-C. Risset and M. V. Mathews. bibliog il Phys Today 22:23-30 F '69
See also
Phonograph records—Electronic music

Optical equipment
See also
Optical scanners

Paleontological applications
Fossil foraging behavior: computer simulation. D. M. Raup and A. Seilacher. il Science 166:994-5 N 21 '69

Photographic applications
Man who loves computers; interview, ed. by N. Goldberg. R. Kingslake. il Pop Phot 65:93+ S '69

Plotters
See Computers—Print-out equipment

COMPUTERS—*Continued*

Police applications

Communications system aids Ohio police in war on crime; LEADS. Electr World 81:53 Je '69

Computer foils fast-moving criminals. Am City 84:25 Ag '69

Kansas City's police computer. C. M. Kelly. il Am City 84:103-4 Ja '69

War against crime quickens; LEADS. Am City 84:16 Je '69

Prices

GE, Control data play their hands; price increases. Bsns W p90+ S 20 '69

Print-out equipment

Computer-designed PC boards. J. A. Bauer. il Electr World 82:47-9 O '69

Picture processing by computer. L. D. Harmon and K. C. Knowlton. bibliog il Science 164:19-29 Ap 4 '69

Space printout uses gray scale plotter. Aviation W 91:84 D 8 '69

Printing applications

Aesthetic considerations in computerized photocomposition. J. W. Seybold. Pub W 195:64-5 Ap 7 '69

Computer with the green eyeshade. R. L. Tobin. Sat R 52:69-70 My 10 '69

In-house tape composition; basic considerations. V. Strauss. il Pub W 195:78+ Mr 3 '69

Insiders' views on computerized composition. V. Strauss. Pub W 195:99-100 Je 9 '69

National printing equipment show; composition systems dominate. il Pub W 196:90-1 Jl 7 '69

New composition technology: promises and realities. V. Strauss. Pub W 195:62-5 My 5 '69; Reply with rejoinder. M. Horowitz. 196:94-5 Jl 7 '69

Of computers and blacksmiths. R. L. Tobin. il Sat R 52:73-4 N 8 '69

Planning for computer composition; address, February 13, 1969. S. Rice. il Pub W 195: 34-9 F 24 '69

Some effects of computer composition on the editorial process in book publishing; address, March 27, 1969. L. Shatzkin. Pub W 195:28-31 Ap 7 '69

Typesetting. G. O. Walter. il Sci Am 220: 60-9 My '69

University presses examine the new technology. Pub W 195:23-7 My 26 '69

Psychiatric applications

See Computers—Medical applications

Quality control

See Electronic data processing—Quality control

Religious applications

Ministry, computer style. Chr Today 14:37 N 21 '69

Retailing applications

Master machines of retailing. L. Geller. il Duns R 94:107-9+ O '69

Scientific applications

Automatic determination of crystal structure. Q. Johnson and others. bibliog Science 164:1163-4 Je 6 '69

Simulation programs

Computer on wheels promises perfect handling in future cars; GM Variable-response vehicle J. Dunne. il Pop Sci 195:76-9 Ag '69

EAI computer aided success of Apollo docking operations. il Space World F-8-68:30-1 Ag '69

Software of change; address, September 23, 1969. M. Tribus. Vital Speeches 36:14-17 O 15 '69

Social applications

Magic box tells you when one more is too many; monitoring alcohol intake. R. M. Benrey. il Pop Sci 194:102-5 Ap '69

On the scene: computer as cupid; ten results. il Seventeen 28:320-1+ Ag '69

Social science applications

Project Cambridge: another showdown for social sciences? J. Coburn. Science 166: 1250-3 D 5 '69

Space flight applications

Automatic checkout equipment, the Apollo Hippocrates. S. Sternberg. il Bul Atom Sci 25:84-7 S '69

Computer overload laid to radar mode. il Aviation W 91:87+ Ag 4 '69

EAI computer aided success of Apollo docking operations. il Space World F-8-68:30-1 Ag '69

Here's what's happening; unified flight analysis system. R. Thomas. il Space World F-9-69:43-6 S '69

In the news; Apollo DSKY. il Space World F-6-66:48-9 Je '69

In the news; team from Univac keeps Apollo computers operating. il Space World F-5-65:42 My '69

Landing aid proves reliability on Apollo 12. Aviation W 91:51 D 8 '69

Roadmap to the moon for Apollo 8 astronauts. Space World F-3-63:36-7 Mr '69

Sports applications

Baseball by computer. Newsweek 74:74 Jl 28 '69

Stock exchange applications

See Computers—Investment applications

Ticket selling applications

American plans self-service ticketer test. B. M. Elson. Aviation W 91:81-2+ N 10 '69

Instant ticketing. Time 94:63 Ag 29 '69

See also

Airlines—Reservation systems

Time sharing systems

Computers: shake-out in time sharing? B. Szuprowicz. il Duns R 93:87-8+ Ap '69

How time sharing brought home a market. il Bsns W p76 My 24 '69

Mini-computer cuts the costs of timesharing. il Bsns W p88 D 20 '69

Time sharing takes off. B. Allen. il Harvard Bsns R 47:128-36 Mr '69

Traffic control applications

Computer smooths Golden Gate toll collections. R. E. Shields. Am City 84:152 My '69

Smile! You just got a ticket; Orbis speed monitoring system. M. Lamm. il Pop Mech 132:73-6+ D '69

Traffic controller for any intersection; Santa Monica, Calif. il Am City 84:152 My '69

Transportation applications

Electric solution to the traffic problem; M.I.T.'s guideway system. il Esquire 71: 62-7 F '69

COMPUTERS leasing. See Computers—Leasing and renting

COMRESS, incorporated
Insider's bath. Newsweek 74:48-9 D 29 '69

COMSAT. See Communications satellite corporation

COMSAT laboratories. See Communications satellite corporation

COMSTOCK, Anthony
Comstock's complaint. S. Maloff. Commonweal 91:362-3 D 19 '69

COMSTOCK, Henry
Four-mile train with a mind in the middle. il Pop Mech 132:82-5+ D '69

COMSTOCK, Peter H.
World of Peter Comstock. il por Forbes 104: 51-2 D 1 '69

COMTE, Gilbert
Are there any conservative Africans? Nat R 21:491+ My 20 '69

Letter from Paris. Nat R 21:695+ Jl 15 '69

CON Edison. See Consolidated Edison company of New York

CON men. See Fraud

CONANT, Ralph W.
Future of public libraries: an urban expert's optimism. por Wilson Lib Bul 44:544-9 Ja '70

CONAWAY, Ray
Matter of style; story. Redbook 132:76-7 F '69

CONCANAVALINS
Immunosuppressive activity of concanavalin A. H. Markowitz and others. bibliog il Science 163:476 Ja 31 '69

CONCENTRATION. See Attention

CONCENTRATION camps

Germany

Theology and the death camps. L. T. Howe. Chr Cent 86:251-5 F 19 '69; Discussion. 86: 716-18, 1046 My 21, Ag 6 '69

Russia

More it changes..; revelations through transcripts smuggled abroad. J. Burnham. Nat R 21:845 Ag 26 '69

Open letter to the presidium of the supreme Soviet of the USSR. Y. Daniel and others. il Nat R 21:852-3 Ag 26 '69

CONCENTRATION camps—*Continued*
United States
Before the colors fade: the return of the exiles; interview, ed. by J. Stevenson. R. W. Kenny. il Am Heritage 20:22-5+ Je '69
Request for repeal; Title II of the security act. Time 94:19 D 12 '69
Timely initiative; movement for the repeal of Title II of the Internal security act of 1950. Nation 208:716-17 Je 9 '69
CONCERT halls
Musical events; Alice Tully Hall. W. Sargeant. New Yorker 45:96+ S 20 '69
See also
Opera houses
Acoustics
See Acoustics, Architectural
CONCERTOS
Current chronicle; E. Carter's piano concerto. K. Stone. bibliog f il Mus Q 55:559-72 O '69
Opening theme of Rachmaninoff's third piano concerto and its liturgical prototype. J. Yasser. bibliog f il Mus Q 55:313-28 Jl '69
See also
Phonograph records—Concertos
CONCERTS
Recorded portraits of the artist; live vs recorded performance. J. Starker. Hi Fi 19: 32+ N '69
See also
Dance concerts
CONCESSIONS (food, etc)
See also
Canteen corporation
CONCHOLOGY. See Shells (conchology)
CONCILIATION, Industrial. See Arbitration, Industrial
CON-COMP, Incorporated
Mini-computer cuts the costs of timesharing. il Bsns W p88 D 20 '69
CONCORD, Mass.
Historic houses, etc.
Concord and Cambridge confidential. W. Sullivan. il Sat R 52:41-2 S 27 '69
CONCORDATS
Church and state in Spain. J. E. Griffiss. jr. il Chr Cent 86:802-6 Je 11 '69
Revising the concordat; relations between the Vatican and Italy. Time 93:70+ F 21 '69
CONCORDE airliner. See Airplanes, Supersonic
CONCORDIA theological seminary, St Louis
Concord at Concordia? C. M. Bunce. Chr Today 13:37 Mr 14 '69
CONCRETE
Tough concrete; treatment with methyl methacrylate. Sci Am 220:50 Ap '69
See also
Cement
Chemistry
Concrete admixtures; updating specification background knowledge. J. J. Gilleran. il Arch Rec 146:143-4 D '69
Coloring
How to color concrete. R. Day. il Pop Mech 131:152-5+ Je '69
CONCRETE, Precast
Two new French towns, by Marcel Breuer and Robert F. Gatje. il Arch Rec 146:101-12 Ag '69
Two precast structures cushioned by neoprene. il Arch Rec 146:135-7 D '69
CONCRETE admixtures. See Concrete—Chemistry
CONCRETE construction
Make it out of concrete. V. Tripp. il Org Gard & Farm 16:72-4 S '69
Pointers for designing and specifying perlite roof decks. F. Coda. il Arch Rec 145:175-6 F '69
CONCRETE fence posts. See Fence posts
CONCRETE houseboats. See Houseboats—Materials
CONCRETE houses
Stack-sack houses, build 'em by the bag. il Pop Sci 195:172 N '69
CONCRETE pavements. See Pavements, Concrete
CONCRETE poetry. See Poetry
CONCRETE-routing machines. See Road machinery
CONCRETE work
Instant cement fills cracks for good. il Pop Mech 132:168 O '69

CONCRETIONS
Freshwater ferromanganese concretions; chemistry and internal structure. R. C. Harriss and A. G. Troup. bibliog il Science 166:604-6 O 31 '69
CONCUSSION. See Brain—Concussion
CONDEMNED books
See also
Prohibited books
CONDENSATION
See also
Atmospheric nucleation
CONDIE, Kent C. and others
Uranium distribution in separated clinopyroxenes from four eclogites. bibliog Science 165:57-9 Jl 4 '69
CONDIMENTS
See also
Pickles and relishes
CONDIT, Carl W.
Aesthetic stylist for the world. il Bsns W p58-61 Je 21 '69
CONDITION of servitude; story. See Thompson, J.
CONDITIONED response
Avoidance learning; long-lasting deficits after temporal lobe seizure. J. D. Belluzzi and S. P. Grossman. bibliog il Science 166:1435-7 D 12 '69
Evoked potentials; modifications by classical conditioning. H. Begleiter and A. Platz. bibliog il Science 166:769-71 N 7 '69
Operant conditioning of cortical unit activity. E. E. Fetz. bibliog il Science 163:955-8 F 28 '69
See also
Reinforcement (psychology)
CONDITIONING therapy. See Psychotherapy
CONDOMINIUM plan ownership. See Apartment houses—Condominium plan ownership
CONDON, Edward U.
Scientific study of UFOs; excerpts. Sat R 52: 53-5 F 1 '69
UFOs I have loved and lost; adaptation of address, April 1969. Bul Atom Sci 25:6-8 D '69
about
Condon report and UFO's. J. A. Hynek. Bul Atom Sci 25:39-42 Ap '69
Condon study rebuts UFOs; critics offer own version. Phys Today 22:67+ Mr '69
Edward Condon; a physicist never afraid of a fight. pors Phys Today 22:66-7 Mr '69
Reporter Edward Condon. G. M. Spruch. por Sat R 52:55-8+ F 1 '69
UFO study; Condon group finds no evidence of visits from outer space. P. M. Boffey. por Science 163:260-2 Ja 17 '69
UFOs and the evidence. F. J. Hooven. Sat R 52:16-17+ Mr 29 '69
CONDON, Rita
Fifty books for school libraries on the blacks. por Wilson Lib Bul 43:657-64, 946 Mr, Je '69
CONDON report. See Flying saucers
CONDOR (guided missile) See Guided missiles —Launching from airplanes
CONDORS
Fierce majesty of the condor. J. M. Fowler. il Life 66:74-6+ Je 13 '69
CONDUCT of life
Building of an outlook. B. W. Overstreet. PTA Mag 63:20-1 Je '69
Dad's last good-bye. G. Christy. Good H 168:89+ Ap '69
Dignity and human fulfillment; address, June 1, 1969. P. A. Freund. Vital Speeches 35: 556-8 Jl 1 '69
Good life on earth, views of fifteen outstanding women. il McCalls 97:29-38+ Ja '70
Have courage; adaptation of introd. to new edition of the essays and journals of Ralph Waldo Emerson. L. Mumford. Am Heritage 20:104-11 F '69
Intermediate battlefield. N. Cousins. Sat R 52:26 N 8 '69
Interval between. J. E. Hoover. Chr Today 14:3-5 D 19 '69
Public figures and their private lives; Time essay. il Time 94:28-9 Ag 22 '69
Vanity of humanism. R. Sampson. Nation 209:718-25 D 29 '69
World's richest man. P. P. Puckett. Har Yrs 9:34 Mr '69
See also
Advice
Charity
Christian life
College students—Conduct of life

CONDUCT of life—See also—*Continued*
Conscience
Courage
Courtesy
Culture
Duty
Ethics
Festivity
Forgiveness
Friendship
Happiness
Human relations
Humanity
Joy
Kindness
Leisure
Loneliness
Love
Loyalty
Obedience
Patriotism
Pleasure
Responsibility
Service
Temptation
Work

Anecdotes, facetiae, satire, etc.
How to make a great getaway. Harp Baz 102:
214-15 My '69
CONDUCTING (music)
Traditionalist; interview. ed. by J. Ardoin.
N. Rescigno. Opera N 33:16 F 15 '69
See also
Conductors (music)

Competitions
Von Karajan speaks his mind; interview. ed.
by P. Moor. H. von Karajan. Hi Fi 19:MA18-
19 N '69
CONDUCTIVITY, Electric. See Electric con-
ductivity
CONDUCTORS (music)
After Bernstein who? the new generation of
conductors; with photographs by A. Eisen-
staedt. Life 66:42-51 F 21 '69
Compelling gesture; how a conductor moves.
D. Vaughan. il Opera N 34:22-5 D 20 '69
Great conductors, by H. C. Schonberg. Re-
view
Am Rec G 35:504-7 F '69. R. Sabin
Rise and decline of the Boston symphony. A.
Chasins. il McCalls 96:34+ Mr '69
Young conductors. R. Gelatt. House & Gard
135:66+ My '69
See also
Ansermet, E.
Bernstein, L.
Boulez, P.
Groves, C.
Kertész, I.
Mehmedov, M. M.
Munch, C.
Ormandy, E.
Ozawa, S.
Shostakovich, M.
Skrowaczewski, S.
Solti, G.
Szell, G.

Caricatures and cartoons
Maestros by Leitner. B. Leitner. Opera N 33:
12-13 Mr 8 '69
CONDUITS. See Electric conduits

CONE, Alvina
Ponies in my parlor. Har Yrs 9:48-9 Jl '69
CONE, Edward Toner
Beethoven new-born. Am Scholar 38:389-400
Sum '69
CONE, Fairfax Mastick
Memo to tomorrow's Madison avenue; ex-
cerpts from With all its faults. por Sat R
52:71-4 O 11 '69
about
Fax Cone, the Honest Abe of ad world, tells
his story. por Bsns W p 155-6 N 15 '69
Straight pitchman. D. Holt. por Newsweek
74:106 N 17 '69
CONE, James H.
In search of a black Christianity. por Time
94:57-8 Jl 4 '69
CONE, Wayne
Preparing the park ranger for his job.
Parks & Rec 4:30-1+ D '69
CONES, Volcanic. See Volcanoes
CONEXPO '69. See Machinery—Exhibitions
CONFECTIONERY
Making a miracle. C. Claiborne. il N Y Times
Mag p72 F 9 '69

Sweet fruits of Christmas. G. Maddox. il
Todays Health 47:60-3 D '69
See also
Candy
Cookery, Ornamental
CONFÉDÉRATION Vietnamienne du travail.
See Trade unions—Vietnam (Republic)
CONFERENCE of governors. See Governors
conference, 1969
CONFERENCE on Christian approaches to de-
fense and disarmament. See Religious con-
ferences
CONFERENCE on diplomatic intercourse and
immunities. See United Nations conference
on diplomatic intercourse and immunities
CONFERENCE on law of treaties. See United
Nations conference on the law of treaties
CONFERENCE on the committee on disarma-
ment. See United Nations—Eighteen-na-
tion committee on disarmament
CONFERENCE on the problems of human envi-
ronment (proposed) See United Nations con-
ference on the problems of human environ-
ment (proposed)
CONFERENCE tables. See Tables
CONFERENCES
Coming events. See issues of Parks & recrea-
tion
Conventions; when & where. See issues of
American city
Report of a repentant symposiast. G. P.
Elliott. Nation 209:256+ S 15 '69
See also
Conventions
also names of conferences, e.g. White
House conference on food, nutrition and
health
CONFERENCES on science and world affairs.
See Pugwash conferences on science and
world affairs
CONFESSION
Sparring with God. L. N. Bell. Chr Today
13:24-5 Ap 25 '69
See also
Absolution
CONFESSION (law)
Annals of jurisprudence: Whitmore confes-
sions; Wylie-Hoffert case. F. C. Shapiro.
New Yorker 44:39-42+ F 8; 44-6+ F 15;
45:42-4+ F 22 '69
Mitchell v. Miranda. il Newsweek 74:23-4 Ag
11 '69
Victims; excerpts. B. Lefkowitz and K. G.
Gross. il Look 33:39-44+ Je 10; 39-44+ Je
24 '69
CONFESSION story. See Short story
CONFIDENCE men. See Fraud
CONFLICT, Social. See Social conflict
CONFLICT of interests (business)
Ex-officer job publicity sought. Aviation W
91:118 Ag 11 '69
Justice dept. action requested on ex-officers
hired by industry. Aviation W 90:20 Je 30
'69
CONFLICT of interests (public office)
Attorney at war. D. Welsh and D. Horowitz.
il Ramp Mag 7:132-4+ Ja 25 '69
Code for judges; stiffer code of financial
ethics for Supreme court judges. Time 93:
61 Je 20 '69
Confirmation marathon. Time 93:13 Ja 24 '69
Conflict of interest; the Packard case. Amer-
ica 120:88-9 Ja 25 '69
Conflict situation; cases of W. Hickel and
D. R. Packard. Commonweal 89:608-9 F 14
'69
Democrats lean on Budge. il Bsns W p80 Ag
9 '69
Dog bites man. Newsweek 73:90+ My 12 '69
Influence peddling in Washington; Time es-
say. Time 93:20-1 My 16 '69
Interior's Walter Hickel; frontier figure in a
Cabinet hot seat. U S News 66:14 F 3 '69
Justice Abe Fortas on the spot. il Newsweek
73:29-33 My 19 '69
Mr Hickel's dilemma. J. B. Craig. Am For
75:10 F '69
Mr Justice Fortas. A. M. Bickel. New Repub
160:9-10 My 17 '69
Murky men from the Speaker's office. W.
Lambert. il Life 67:52-4+ O 31 '69
New concern over ethics codes. U S News 66:
10 My 26 '69
New controversy on an old issue. U S News
66:15 My 12 '69
New guidelines on conflict of interest? il
U S News 66:27-30 Je 9 '69
On the fall of Fortas. Nat R 21:523-4 Je 3
'69
Packard dilemma. Nation 208:66-7 Ja 20 '69
Scandals in Congress; the record. il U S
News 67:25-7 N 10 '69

CONFLICT of interests (public office)—*Cont.*
Skolnick's guerrilla war; investigating judges.
il Time 94:43+ Ag 29 '69
Strom's little acres.   D. Walsh. il Life 67:
42-46A'S 19 '69
Testing of Willie Mae; director of Good
housekeeping institute appointed consultant
on consumer affairs. il Newsweek 73:25 F
24 '69
That wonderful feeling; nomination of indus-
trialist D. R. Packard. New Repub 160:9-10
Ja 25 '69
CONFORMITY
Big brother is dead too. K. Melvin. Nat R 21:
116-18 F 11 '69; Reply. F. S. Meyer. 21:180
F 25 '69
Rising above conformity. Chr Today 13:25 Ag
22 '69
See also
Dissenters
Eccentrics and eccentricities
CONFRATERNITY of Christian doctrine
Total religious education and the parish. W.
J. Tobin. America 121:33+ Jl 19 '69
CONGENITAL malformations. See Deformities
CONGER, Lesley
Off the cuff. See issues of Writer
CONGESTION of population. See Population,
Distribution of
CONGLOMERATE corporations
Action against Jim Ling. il Time 93:89 Ap 4
'69
And now a raid on the raiders? a hypo-
thetical case history. S. Sauerhaft. il Duns
R 93:56-8 My '69
Antitrust, Republican style; interview, ed.
by G. R. Rosen. R. McLaren. Duns R 94:
12-13+ O '69
Assault on the conglomerates. il Time 93:76+
F 21 '69
Attacking the giants; planned merger of In-
ernational telephone & telegraph with
Hartford fire insurance co. Time 94:72+ Jl
4 '69
Bid and lost; conglomerates losing investor
confidence. Time 95:52 Ja 5 '70
Business mergers, what's right, what's
wrong; interview. W. F. Rockwell, jr. il
U S News 66:70-3 My 19 '69
Comic conglomerates. il Forbes 104:50 N 1 '69
Conglomerate critic aims a blast; W. Mueller's
report. Bsns W 92B+ N 1 '69
Conglomerate; federal policy on mergers; ad-
dress. June 6, 1969. J. N. Mitchell. Vital
Speeches 35:592-4 Jl 15 '69
Conglomerate test is on. Bsns W p35-7 Mr 29
'69
Conglomerates at the crossroads. R. Lekach-
man. Duns R 93:11 Ap '69
Conglomerates in the music business. Sat R
52:62-3 F 22 '69
Conglomerates under fire; the drive for new
controls. il U S News 66:86-7 F 24 '69
Conglomerates' war to reshape industry. il
Time 93:75-80 Mr 7 '69
Conglomeration, Spanish style; Grupo Fierro.
Fortune 80:166 Ag 15 '69
Coping with the conglomerates. America 120:
682-3 Je 14 '69
Crackdown starts on conglomerates. il U S
News 66:92 Ap 7 '69
Diversification; the new road to world
competition; address, October 23, 1969. H.
S. Geneen. Vital Speeches 36:147-52 D 15
'69
Do mergers need a union label? question for
NLRB. Bsns W p86+ My 17 '69
Don't tar them all. M. Simons. Forbes 103:
98+ Ap 15 '69
Economy may be in danger. U S News 66:
10 Je 16 '69
Got a light, McLaren? M. Ways. Fortune 79:
61-2 My 1 '69
How to regulate the conglomerates. Bsns W
p 148 Je 14 '69
Merger movement rides high. G. Burck. il
Fortune 79:78-82+ F '69
Mergers under scrutiny; excerpts from Man-
agerial analysis in marketing. L. W. Stern.
bibliog il Harvard Bsns R 47:18-20+ Jl '69
Nixon's antitrust policy. W. F. Baxter. New
Repub 161:13-16 Ag 9 '69
SEC turns light on big divisions; conglom-
erates to reveal their lines of business. Bsns
W p74 Jl 19 '69
Signal; the careful conglomerate. J. B. Wein-
er. il Duns R 93:38-42+ Mr '69
Some candid answers from James J. Ling;
interview, ed. by J. McDonald. il Fortune
80:92-5+ Ag 1; 136-8+ S '69
Target: conglomerates. Newsweek 73:59-60
Ap 7 '69

Ten conglomerates and how they grew; with
editorial comment. A. M. Louis. il Fortune
79:135-6, 152-3+ My 15 '69
Washington wakes up to the conglomerates.
il Forbes 103:23-5 F 15 '69
What future for the conglomerate? D. T.
Carroll. Harvard Bsns R 47:4-6+ My '69
What's different about conglomerate man-
agement? N. A. Berg. bibliog f il Harvard
Bsns R 47:112-20 N '69
See also
Alco standard corporation
Commonwealth united corporation
Government investigations—Conglomerate cor-
porations
Grace, W. R. and company
Gulf and Western industries, incorporated
Japan—Industries
Ling-Temco-Vought, incorporated
Litton industries, incorporated
Norton Simon, incorporated
3M company
TRW incorporated

Anecdotes, facetiae, satire, etc.
Conglomeration of Newt Ogilvy. R. Baker.
Life 66:4 Ap 18 '69

Securities
Buy conglomerates? R. Brady. Duns R 94:
133-4 O '69
Conglomerates look up. C. Morgello. il News-
week 74:102 N 17 '69
CONGO (capital Kinshasa) See Congo (Dem-
ocratic Republic)
CONGO (Democratic Republic)
After years of violence the Congo is afloat
but who knows where it's headed? M. A
McConnell. il N Y Times Mag p26-7+
S 21 '69
Congo: country on the way back. A. J.
Meyers. il U S News 67:76-8 N 3 '69
CONGREGATION for the doctrine of the faith
Get going, and don't come back; Vatican in-
vestigations. Time 93:48+ F 14 '69
Questions about a questionnaire; controversy
over the Cuernavaca center, with text of
letter from I. Illich. L. M. Orsy. America
120:185-9 F 15 '69
CONGRESS (United States) See United States
—Congress
CONGRESS for change. See Library confer-
ences
CONGRESS for recreation and parks
Many new products featured at 1968 congress in Seattle. Parks & Rec 3:25-6 O '68
1968 highlights. il Parks & Rec 3:17-24 D '68
1969 Congress for recreation and parks, Chi-
cago, Illinois, September 14-18. il Parks
& Rec 4:55-66 S '69
1969 congress program shapes up. Parks &
Rec 4:61-3 My '69
1969 highlights. il Parks & Rec 4:27-38 N '69
When you're out at the inn; tips to ensure
hotel accommodations. R. C. Strobell. il
Parks & Rec 4:26-7+ Ag '69
CONGRESS of Angostura, 1818. See Latin Amer-
ica—History—Wars of independence, 1806-
1830
CONGRESS of racial equality
Roy Innis; nation builder. A. Poinsett. il
Ebony 24:170-4+ O '69
CONGRESS of writers, World. See PEN club
CONGRESS party. See Political parties—India
CONGRESSIONAL aides. See Public officers
CONGRESSIONAL campaigns. See Political
campaigns
CONGRESSIONAL committees. See United
States—Congress—Committees
CONGRESSIONAL committees on military af-
fairs. See United States—Congress—Com-
mittees
CONGRESSIONAL cup race. See Yacht racing
CONGRESSIONAL elections. See Elections—
United States
CONGRESSIONAL hearings. See United States
—Congress—Committees
CONGRESSIONAL immunity. See United
States—Congress—Privileges and immunities
CONGRESSIONAL investigations. See Govern-
ment investigations
CONGRESSIONAL page boys. See United
States—Congress—Pages
CONGRESSIONAL quarterly
Battle of Capitol hill. il Newsweek 73:100 Ap
14 '69
CONGRESSIONAL record
Missing from the Record; Richard Russell's
statement. New Repub 160:8-9 My 17 '69
CONGRESSIONAL reorganization. See United
States—Congress—Reorganization

CONGRESSMEN
Congressmen on campus; Republicans probe causes of unrest. P. R. Wieck. New Republic 160:9 Je 14 '69
Congressman's choice; investments. C. Morgello. il Newsweek 73:97 My 26 '69
Key men in the 91st Congress. il Sr Schol 94:8-9 F 28 '69
Lawbreaking lawmakers. Chr Today 13:22 Jl 4 '69
Other Democrats: Democratic congressmen who vote Republican. Nation 208:451 Ap 14 '69
Size up your man in Washington. il Changing T 23:45-7 S '69
Twenty-one; representatives who voted against the 1969 military appropriations measure. Nation 208:484 Ap 21 '69
Two Goldwaters in Congress now. il U S News 66:14 My 12 '69
Who speaks for the cities? il Newsweek 73: 48+ Ap 7 '69
Youth rebellion takes the floor; freshman congressmen. Bsns W p46-8 Je 28 '69
See also
Conflict of interests (public office)
Senators

Ethics
See Political ethics

Public relations
Lawmakers get the word. il Nations Bsns 57:28-32+ My '69
Profession: member of Congress; where the action is. F. Taddeo. il Sr Schol 94:10-13 F 28 '69
Reporter at large; new member: A. K. Lowenstein. F. Lewis. New Yorker 45:31-2+ Ja 10 '70
Taxed public temper; congressmen sample constituents mood. il Bsns W p41-2 Jl 12 '69

Religion
God on Capitol hill. J. Huffman. Chr Today 14:48-50 O 10 '69

Salaries, allowances, etc
Inflation by fiat. New Repub 160:10-11 F 1 '69
More money for the biplane set; proposed pay raises for the Vice-President and congressional leaders. il Time 94:17 S 5 '69
Raise for members of Congress, and that's not all. il U S News 66:38-9 F 17 '69
Slush storm; disclosure rule. New Repub 160: 7 My 31 '69
Tab for keeping Congress. il Bsns W p80+ N 15 '69

CONGRESSMEN, Letters to. See Lobbying

CONGRESSWOMEN
Women in Congress. F. L. Gehlen. bibliog il Trans-Action 6:36-40 O '69

CONIFERS
Conifers in the winter roof garden. P. Truex. il Horticulture 47:44-5 Ja '69
Not so well known conifers. il Sunset 143: 233-4 N '69
See also
Evergreens
Podocarpus. Fossil

CONIGLIARO, Tony
Conig's comeback. il por Time 93:84-5 Ap 11 '69
Now playing in right field. M. Mulvoy. il pors Sports Illus 30:26-8+ Ap 7 '69
Tony C can see to hit. D. Wolf. il pors Life 66:81 Ap 4 '69

CONIL-LACOSTE, Michel
Paris. See issues of Art news

CONJURING
See also
Magicians

CONKLE, E. P.
Day's end; drama. Plays 28:91-5 F '69

CONKLIN, Charlene
High adventure. Outdoor Life 143:84+ My '69

CONLAN, James
Priest in the cellar. Criticism
America 120:315-16 Mr 15 '69

CONLEY, Robert A. M.
Locusts: teeth of the wind. Nat Geog 136: 202-27 Ag '69

CONN, William M. See Crossley, E. I. jt. auth.

CONNAUGHTON, Charles A.
Preservation and conservation. por Am For 75:8 Mr '69

CONNECTICUT
See also
Airports—Connecticut
Architecture—Connecticut
Architecture, Domestic—Connecticut
Camping—Connecticut
Education—Connecticut
Law—Connecticut
Trials—Connecticut

Historic houses, etc.
A. Phelps' inn at North Colebrook. N. P. Blum. il Antiques 95:404-7 Mr '69
Connecticut home of Mary Allis. W. D. Garrett. il Antiques 96:754-62 N '69
Lawrence tavern in Canaan. J. A. Lyles. il Antiques 95:400-3 Mr '69

Politics and government
Doddering. New Repub 161:12 N 29 '69

CONNECTICUT commission on the arts
How to make the most of a shoestring; how Connecticut is becoming a state of dance. A. S. Keller. il Dance Mag 43:63-4+ Ap '69

CONNECTICUT opera association
Report: Hartford; production of Ciléa's Adriana Lecouvreur. W. D. Miranda. Opera N 34:24 D 6 '69
Report: Hartford; production of Walküre. W. D. Miranda. Opera N 33:32 Ap 5 '69

CONNECTICUT RIVER
How many sewers? How many dumps? B. Malarkey. il Seventeen 29:36 Ja '70

CONNECTICUT. University, Storrs
Revolution (cont): at the University of Connecticut. E. Hill. il N Y Times Mag p28-9+ F 23 '69; Discussion. p6+ Mr 16; 110+ Ap 13 '69

CONNECTING rods, Automobile. See Automobile engines

CONNECTIVE tissues
Acid polysaccharides from invertebrate connective tissue: phylogenetic aspects. R. L. Katzman and R. W. Jeanloz. bibliog il Science 166:758-9 N 7 '69

CONNECTORS
See also
Electric connectors

CONNELL, Charles A. Jr
Time for government bonds? Duns R 94:41-2+ Jl '69

CONNELL, Evan S. Jr
Mr Bridge; story. Esquire 71:173-6 My '69
Undersigned, Leon & Bébert; story. Esquire 72:232-3 D '69

CONNELLY, Marc
Expo '70-Osaka. Holiday 45:52-3+ Mr '69
Ninety-three days on a caviar bucket. Sat R 52:82+ S 13 '69
Taipei theater. Holiday 46:16+ N '69
Why women put to sea. McCalls 96:88+ S '69

CONNER, John W.
Book marks. Engl J 58:1255-8+, 1378-81+ N-D '69

CONNES, Keith
Winds aloft. See issues of Flying to December 1969

CONNIFF, James C. G.
Can you stay slim after dieting? Read Digest 94:69-72 F '69

CONNOLLY, Thomas Arthur, abp
Defender of the faith. il por Newsweek 74:75 Jl 28 '69

CONNOR, Albert Ollie
Army's desertion rate up, why; excerpts from testimony, House appropriations subcommittee, June 20, 1969. por U S News 67:61 Jl 7 '69

CONNOR, J. Robert
Fast way to modernize your bathroom. Mech Illus 65:95-7+ S '69

CONNOR, John Thomas
Allied chemical: a long rough road back. il por Forbes 103:205-8 My 15 '69

CONNORS, Joy
Building a career ladder. Am Ed 5:15-17 F '69
Interviewing techniques for trade journals. Writer 82:28-30 F '69

CONNORS, Peter G. and others
Structural studies on transfer RNA: the molecular conformation in solution. bibliog Science 166:1528-30 D 19 '69

CONOCO. See Continental oil company

CONOVER, Willis
Rare air. Sat R 52:64-5+ O 11 '69

CONQUES, France
Tale of the purloined saint. C. Cate. il Horizon 11:68-79 Wint '69

CONRAD, Barnaby
Peripatetic reviewer. E. Weeks. Atlan 224:98 Ag '69

CONRAD, Charles, 1930-
Apollo 12, by the crew. por Life 67:32-3 D 19 '69
Moonwalk; the sky was never as black as here. U S News 67:30 D 1 '69

CONRAD, Charles—*Continued*

about

Blithe spirits in space. por Time 94:30 N 21 '69

To the moon with a light touch. por Newsweek 74:90 N 17 '69

See also

Space flight to the moon—Manned flights— Conrad-Bean-Gordon flight, 1969

CONRAD, John P.
(ed) Future of corrections. bibliog f Ann Am Acad 381:1-158 Ja '69

CONRAD, Joseph
Teaching Conrad's Victory to superior high school seniors. S. I. Roody. Engl J 58:40-6 Ja '69

CONRAD, Linda
Knowledge; poem. Chr Cent 86:1514 N 26 '69

CONRAD, Max
If at first you don't succeed... J. Gilbert. il pors Flying 85:90-5 D '69

CONRAD, Thomas M.
Do-it-yourself A-bombs. Commonweal 90:455-7 Jl 25 '69

On the myths of liberalism and frustrations with change. Commonweal 89:531-2 Ja 24 '69

Vietnam: are there any lessons? Commonweal 90:78-80 Ap 4 '69

about

Bombs and bombast; Atomic energy commission released data on nuclear weapons. J. Deedy. Commonweal 90:450 Jl 25 '69

CONRATH, B. See Hanel, R. jt. auth.

CONROY, Hilary
(comp) Articles and other books received; East Asia. See issues of American historical review

CONSANGUINITY
Genetic drift in an Italian population. L. L. Cavalli-Sforza. il Sci Am 221:30-7 Ag '69

See also

Inbreeding
Kinship
Marriage of cousins

CONSCIENCE
Appeal to conscience. L. J. Van Til. Chr Today 13:6-8 My 23 '69

Conflict of consciences. T. C. Wright. America 120:332-4 Mr 22 '69

Paul VI and conscience. America 120:236 Mr 1 '69

See also

Liberty of conscience

CONSCIENTIOUS objectors
Choose your war; or, The case of the selective C.O. W. Goodman. il N Y Times Mag p34-5+ Mr 23 '69; Discussion, p 14+ Ap 13 '69; Discussion, p 142 Ap 27 '69

Christian neglect of political values: the case of selective objection. H. R. Davis. Chr Cent 86:1510-14 N 26 '69

Conflict of loyalties, the case for selective conscientious objection, ed. by J. Finn. Review

Sat R 52:50 My 24 '69. N. Dorsen

Conscientious objection; decision by the District court in Boston on the J. H. Sisson case. New Repub 160:9 My 3 '69

Counting them out; West German protest movement. il Time 93:40 Ja 24 '69

Court-martial of Dale Noyd. R. C. Kimball. Chr Cent 86:116-19 Ja 22 '69

Judaism, Israel and conscientious objection. S. Gottlieb. Chr Cent 86:1136-7 S 3 '69; Reply. J. Segal. 86:1286 O 8 '69

Latest challenge to the draft; who's a conscientious objector now. il U S News 66:52-3 Ap 14 '69

Mrs Eugene McCarthy tells why my son is a conscientious objector. A. Q. McCarthy. il Good H 169:98-9+ N '69

Moral objections; Massachusetts federal court ruling. Newsweek 73:44 Ap 14 '69

Moral objector wins a point; Massachusetts federal district court ruling. il Sr Schol 94:14 Ap 18 '69

No Jew nor Catholic need apply. M. Polner. Commonweal 90:386-7 Je 20 '69

Objection sustained; draft law interpretation. Time 93:46 Ap 11 '69

One war, yes; another, no. S. Rabinove. America 120:647-8 My 31 '69

Orthodoxy and favoritism: selective service dilemma. Chr Today 13:33 Ap 25 '69

Sisson's complaint, Wyzanski's ploy. I. Silver. Commonweal 90:385-9 Je 20 '69

Support means sanctuary and solidarity. G. F. Snyder. Chr Cent 86:120-1 Ja 22 '69

See also

Military service, Compulsory

Bibliography

CO and the draft. J. Coffman. il Library J 94:2059-65 My 15 '69

CONSCIOUSNESS
What would a scientific religion be like? H. G. MacPherson. il Sat R 52:46-7 Ag 2 '69

See also

Psychology

CONSCRIPTION. See Military service, Compulsory

CONSCRIPTION, Military. See Military service, Compulsory

CONSEIL européen pour la recherche nucléaire. See European organization for nuclear research

CONSERVATION associations
Conservationists: who conserves what; field guide to organization. il Changing T 23:24-7 Ag '69

See also

Environmental defense fund, incorporated
National wildlife federation
Sierra club

CONSERVATION education. See Conservation of resources—Study and teaching

CONSERVATION law. See Conservation of resources—Legal aspects

CONSERVATION of resources
Adirondacks; with paintings. Am Heritage 20:44-63+ Ag '69

All he wants to save is the world; efforts of V. J. Yannacone. G. Rogin. il Sports Illus 30:24-9 F 3 '69

America the beautiful doomed? interview. W. J. Hickel. il U S News 67:60-2+ N 10 '69

American land: an announcement. D. G. McCullough. Am Heritage 20:4-5 O '69

American land: symposium, ed. by D. G. McCullough. il Am Heritage 21:4-15+ D '69

Can man survive his environment? ed. by J. Mandelstam. il Sr Schol 95:2-3 O 27 '69

Can we keep our planet habitable? symposium. bibliog il UNESCO Courier 22:4-40 Ja '69

Citizen involvement, time for assessment! Parks & Rec 4:11 N '69

Conservation. M. Frome. See issues of Field & stream

Conservation and the Nixon years. M. Frome. Field & S 73:8+ Mr '69

Conservation at the crossroads; address. F. E. Moss. il Am For 75:20-3+ Ja '69

Conservation for conservation's sake? E. Rabinowitch. Bul Atom Sci 25:47-8+ My '69

Cultural imperative; stabilization of population and of natural areas. A. W. Smith. Nat Parks 43:2 O '69

Danger; America's environmental problems. A. Wolff. il Look 33:28-33 N 4 '69

Death row. G. Laycock. Audubon 71:106 Jl; 127 S '69

Destiny of conservation depends on truth. J. B. Craig. Am For 75:11 N '69

Disney imperative. W. Marx. Nation 209:76-8 Jl 28 '69

Earth is the Lord's... P. S. McElroy. il Am For 75:24+ My '69

Education of Wally Hickel; interview. ed. by R. Saltonstall. W. J. Hickel. Time 94:42+ Ag 1 '69

El Dorado beach project; Lake Ontario's shores. F. Eldridge. il Cons 24:6-8 O '69

For the Nixon cabinet, a path to follow. Audubon 71:4 Mr '69

Forming a nature corps for action; Susquehanna conservation council at Binghamton. N. Ayers. il Cons 24:2-5 O '69

How to avoid making our planet unlivable; address, August 15, 1969. K. Brandt. Vital Speeches 35:712-15 S 15 '69

Ike, the conservationist. C. Davis. il Am For 75:28-9+ Je '69

LaAdonoi haaretz umloah..; excerpt from address. J. Weinstein. il Am For 75:25+ My '69

Legacy from LBJ: controversy over national parks. il U S News 66:89 F 24 '69

Leverage against chaos. A. W. Smith. Nat Parks 43:2 Jl '69

Man in nature: model for a new radicalism. C. R. Harris. Nation 209:496-500 N 10 '69

Marshes, developers, and taxes, a new ethic for our estuaries. R. C. Clement. il Audubon 71:34-5 N '69

Mike Frome: President's call for volunteer effort in behalf of the national welfare. M. Frome. Am For 75:7+ S '69

National outlook. C. H. Callison. See issues of Audubon

National parks association; report of the president and general counsel, May 22, 1969. A. W. Smith. Nat Parks 43:15-18 My '69

CONSERVATION of resources—*Continued*
New conservation. R. L Means. Natur Hist 78:16+ Ag '69
New conservation; excerpts from address. F. Church. il Parks & Rec 4:36-40+ S '69
News and commentary. See issues of National parks magazine
Opportunity knocks but once. A. W. Smith. Nat Parks 43:2 Mr '69
Our environment; commitment or complacency; address, August 11, 1969. L. P. Weicker, jr. Vital Speeches 35:732-5 S 15 '69
Preservation and conservation. C. A. Connaughton. Am For 75:8 Mr '69
Record conservation congress. Parks & Rec 3:9 N '68
Turn-around year. M. A. Guitar. il Am Home 72:54+ N '69
Two modern challenges for every camp director. P. M. Ford. il Camp Mag 41:12-13 My '69
Washington report. L. S. Clapper. See issues of National Wildlife
What is the new conservation? interview. W. J. Hickel. il Nat Wildlife 7:8-9 Je '69
Where do we stand with Nixon? M. Frome. Field & S 73:38+ F '69
Why save the wilderness? M. Mead. Redbook 133:38+ Ag '69
See also
Conservation associations
Forest conservation
International union for the conservation of nature and natural resources
Landscape protection
Natural resources
Wilderness areas
Wildlife conservation

Bibliography

Nature and conservation. R. G. Lillard. bibliog il Wilson Lib Bul 44:158-77 O '69

Legal aspects

Conservation law I: seeking a breakthrough in the courts. L. J. Carter. Science 166:1487-91 D 19 '69
Conservation law II: scientists play a key role in court suits. L. J. Carter. Science 166:1601-6 D 26 '69
Hickel watching. D. R. Maxey. il Look 33:39+ N 4 '69
New say in court; suit against five major manufacturers of DDT. Time 94:54 O 24 '69
Wilderness: the last refuge. il Sr Schol 95:12-14 O 27 '69
See also
Wildlife conservation—Laws and legislation

Study and teaching

Camping can be unique; address, 1969. J. J. Kirk. Camp Mag 41:8-11 Je '69
Exploring the world around us; Middletown township, N.J. school children at Sandy Hook State Park. F. Sabin. il Am Ed 5:12-17 Je '69
Naturalist has a unique role. J. P. Hewitt. il Parks & Rec 4:39-40+ D '69
Truth or consequences. F. M. Washburn. Camp Mag 41:5 Je '69
When it rained cats in Borneo; excerpts from address. F. Mergen. il Am For 75:28-9+ Ja '69

Alaska

Alaskan prospect. A. W. Smith. Nat Parks 43:2 S '69
Hickel and the Arctic. M. Frome. il Field & S 74:12-14+ N '69
Progress may be unstoppable, but Alaska can be saved. Audubon 71:148-9 N '69
Whittling Alaska down to size. G. Laycock. il Audubon 71:66-8+ My '69

California

Beach for the ghetto; Cabrillo Beach. San Pedro. G. Laycock. il Audubon 71:107 Jl '69
Maximum feasible leakage; coastline in southern California. S. V. Roberts. Commonweal 89:667-8 F 28 '69
Mineral king, go or no go? R. Leadabrand. il Am For 75:32-5+ O '69
Protectionists vs. recreationists; the battle of Mineral King. A. Hano. il N Y Times Mag p24-5+ Ag 17 '69; Discussion. p79+ S 14 '69
Santa Barbarans cite an 11th commandment: thou shalt not abuse the earth. R. Macdonald and R. Easton. il N Y Times Mag p32-3+ O 12 '69

Florida

Assault on the Everglades. A Wolff. il Look 33:44-50+ S 9 '69

Folly in Florida; project to build jetport in the Everglades. A. W. Smith. Nat Parks 43:2+ Ja '69

Georgia

Battle for a Georgia island; conservation vs. development. il Bsns W p 128-9 S 6 '69

Illinois

Snakes and all; Goose Lake prairie. Newsweek 73:29 Mr 3 '69

Kentucky

Lonely war of a good angry man; H. M. Caudill. D. G. McCullough. il Am Heritage 21:97-113 D '69

Maine

Something up, down east. R. Pardo. il Am For 75:12-13+ My '69

Massachusetts

We can save our towns. C. Mangel. Look 33:50 N 4 '69

New England

Grass-roots conservation. il Time 94:51-2 O 17 '69

New York (state)

America the (formerly) beautiful; Storm King Mountain. J. N. Miller. il Read Digest 94:179-81+ F '69

Ohio

Big walnut. G. Laycock. Audubon 71:127 S '69
Rhododendron hollow; Clear creek program. G. Laycock. Audubon 71:106 Jl '69

Russia

USSR shares conservation headaches; articles and photographs provided by Novosti press agency of Moscow. il Parks & Rec 4:24-8+ Ja '69

Tanzania

Tanzanian marine parks? Nat Parks 43:33 Ap '69

Underdeveloped areas

Development in the poor nations: how to avoid fouling the nest. L. J. Carter. Science 163:1046-8 Mr 7 '69

CONSERVATION of wildlife. See Wildlife conservation
CONSERVATION of works of art. See Art—Conservation and restoration

CONSERVATISM
Are there any conservative Africans? G. Comte. Nat R 21:491+ My 20 '69
Elm street's new White House power. A. J. Reichley. il Fortune 80:70-3+ D '69
Enemies of the permanent things, by R. Kirk. Review
Nat R 21:862-3 Ag 26 '69. F. D. Wilhelmsen
Historical understanding of conservatism; situation in America. N. R. Phillips. il Nat R 21:278-81+ Mr 25 '69
Is conservatism dead? Nat R 21:317 Ap 8 '69
Libertarianism or libertinism? F. S. Meyer. Nat R 21:910 S 9 '69
See also
Right and left (political science)
Young Americans for freedom (organization)

Anecdotes, facetiae, satire, etc.

Our people's underworld movement exposed. T. J. Wheler. il Nat R 21:376-81 Ap 22 '69
CONSERVATIVE party (Great Britain)
Intellectuals and conservatism; situation in England. T. Szamuely. il Nat R 21:273-7 Mr 25 '69
Labor's chance: some unlikely Tories. K. Ovenden. Commonweal 91:348-9 D 19 '69
Richard III rides again; conservative party's annual meeting. Time 94:40 O 17 '69

CONSERVATORIES. See Greenhouses
CONSOLIDATED Edison company of New York
Con Ed runs out of clean energy. Bsns W p42-3 Ag 16 '69
Dilemmas of power. il Time 94:38 Ag 29 '69
Fish and power plants; Storm King Mountain pumped-storage project. A. C. Jensen. il Cons 24:2-5 D '69
Mile from Times square; adaptation of address, December 2, 1968. S. Novick. bibliog f il Environ 11:10-15+ Ja '69
Unholier than thou trio; Long Island rail road, Consolidated Edison and New York telephone. L. L. L. Golden. Sat R 52:30-1 O 11 '69
Utility crisis. il Newsweek 74:51-2 Ag 18 '69
We hire the hard-core unemployed. C. F. Luce. il Duns R 93:50-2 F '69
Woes of Con Edison. Nation 209:198 S 8 '69

CONSOLIDATED foods corporation
Coup at Consolidated. Newsweek 74:49+ D 29 '69
Why the head chef left Con foods. il Bsns W p21-2 D 20 '69
CONSOLIDATED freightways-Pacific Far East merger. See Business consolidations and mergers
CONSOLIDATIONS, Business. See Business consolidations and mergers
CONSORTIUM of publishers for employment. See Socially handicapped—Employment
CONSORTIUMS, College. See Colleges and universities—Cooperation
CONSPIRACY
See also
Trials (conspiracy)
CONSTABLE, John
Constable quotes; ed. by N. Kent. Am Artist 33:5 My '69
about
Caught moments; exhibit of illustrations at Washington's National gallery. il Time 93:70-1 My 9 '69
CONSTANT prince; drama. See Grotowski, J.
CONSTANTINE II, king of the Hellenes
Exiles: a clutch of feverish factions, and a coolly neutral monarch. il por Newsweek 75:36-7 Ja 19 '70
CONSTANTINE I, the Great, emperor of Rome
Constantine, by R. MacMullen. Review Sat R 52:28 D 27 '69. J. H. Plumb
CONSTANTS. See Units
CONSTELLATIONS
Action at Orion. W. K. Hartmann. il Natur Hist 78:90-3 F '69
See also
Zodiac
CONSTITUTION (United States) See United States—Constitution
CONSTITUTIONAL law
Constitutional liberty and the law of libel: a historian's view; address, December 1967. A. H. Kelly. bibliog f Am Hist R 74:429-52 D '68
See also
Civil rights
Due process of law
Privileges and immunities
CONSTRUCTION. See Building; Engineering
CONSTRUCTION contracts. See Building—Contracts and specifications
CONSTRUCTION for progress, incorporated
Cutting red tape and time in public housing; combining federal turnkey program with NYCHA's acquisition program. il Bsns W p48- Jl 26 '69
CONSTRUCTION industry. See Building industry
CONSTRUCTION industry foundation
Construction industry foundation sets up shop. Arch Rec 146:67 Jl '69
Trying to tackle industry troubles; CIF. Bsns W p33 My 31 '69
CONSTRUCTION industry manufacturers association
What municipal officials found at Conexpo '69. il Am City 84:125-6+ Ap '69
CONSTRUCTION machinery operators. See Building machinery operators
CONSTRUCTION workers. See Building machinery operators; Building workers
CONSULTANTS
See also
Business consultants
Forestry consultants
Recreation consultants
CONSULTATION on church union
Advance look at COCU. J. F. Nelson. Chr Today 13:40-1 Mr 28 '69
COCU and evangelical opportunity. C. N. Weisiger, 3d. Chr Today 13:22-3 Ap 11 '69
COCU: fervor and candor. H. E. Fey. Chr Cent 86:469-70 Ap 9 '69
COCU in the days ahead. Chr Today 13:29 Ap 11 '69
COCU maps multi-church parishes. D. E. Kucharsky. Chr Today 13:47-8 Ap 11 '69
Lumps for COCU. J. Adams. Chr Today 14:48-9 O 24 '69
Lutheran lament over creedless COCU. R. N. Ostling. Chr Today 13:44 F 28 '69
New C.O.C.U. parish. Chr Today 13:28 My 9 '69
Toward a superchurch. Time 93:75-6 Mr 28 '69
CONSUMER advertising. See Advertising
CONSUMER class actions. See Actions and defenses
CONSUMER complaints. See Complaints

CONSUMER credit
Buy now, pay later. Sr Schol 94:22 F 14 '69
Credit-cost table. Consumer Bul 52:22 O '69
Credit for the poor; drive to gain credit acceptance for welfare recipients. il Newsweek 74:67+ Jl 28 '69
Plenty of credit for the consumer. il Bsns W p39-40 Je 21 '69
See also
Credit cards

Laws and legislation
Battle breaks over buying on time; proposed Uniform consumer credit code. il Bsns W p80 Mr 29 '69
Consumer credit code for lenders. il Consumer Rep 34:121-6 Mr '69
Foggy first week for the lending law. il Bsns W p 13-14 Jl 5 '69
New key to credit shopping; Truth-in-lending act. il Consumer Rep 34:360-6 Jl '69
Revolving credit; Uniform consumer credit code. Nation 208:388 Mr 31 '69
Slum swindlers must go! J. N. Miller. Read Digest 95:169-70+ N '69
Truth in lending law; the way it will work. il U S News 66:100-2 Je 23 '69
Truth-in-lending: the new math. R. Krumme. Suc Farm 67:23 Je '69
What the new truth-in-lending law does for you. il Changing T 23:7-12 Je '69
What you must tell your customers; questions and answers. Nations Bsns 57:42-4 Je '69
Why not pay cash? Consumer Bul 52:13-14 Jl '69
Will your state pass this model credit law? Uniform consumer credit code. il Changing T 23:39-41 Mr '69
Z-day; Federal reserve board regulation blow at credit rackets. il Time 94:70 Jl 4 '69
CONSUMER credit legislation. See Consumer credit—Laws and legislation
CONSUMER frauds. See Fraud
CONSUMER goods. See Commercial products
CONSUMER price index. See Price indexes
CONSUMER protection
And now, a message from the customers. Fortune 80:103-4 N '69
Basically honest; White House consultant on consumer affairs director of the Good housekeeping institute. Nation 208:260-1 Mr 3 '69
Business can stand guard for the consumer. M. G. Jones. il Nations Bsns 57:52-4 N '69
Consumer revolution? Chr Cent 86:1269 O 8 '69
Consumer revolution; interview. V. H. Knauer. il U S News 67:43-6 Ag 25 '69
Consumer services for older Americans; assistance needed; address. May 24, 1969. J. J. Barry. Vital Speeches 35:649-52 Ag 15 '69
Consumers and the regulators. Life 67:34 O 3 '69
Consumer's impotent friend in Washington. Time 94:83 S 26 '69
Corporate deaf ear; address, December 5, 1968. E. B. Weiss. Vital Speeches 35:205-7 Ja 15 '69
Cost of living. B. Furness. McCalls 97:16+ Ja '70
Crusader widens range of his ire; Nader's targets: federal agencies and law firms. il Bsns W p 128-30 Ja 25 '69
Docket: notes on government actions taken to enforce consumer protection laws. See issues of Consumer reports
Giving the consumer class; consumer class actions. D. Sanford. New Repub 161:15-17 Jl 26 '69
Industry and the consumer. D. M. Kendall. Duns R 94:110-12 S '69
Let's take the politics out of consumerism. A. C. Fatt. il Nations Bsns 57:82-4+ Ja '69
Loaded odds; FTC investigation of promotional lures by food-chains and oil companies. il Time 93:86-7 Ap 18 '69
Nader's raiders. J. Newfield. il Life 67:56-56B+ O 3 '69
Nixon shops for consumer protection. Bsns W p32 N 1 '69
Protection message reaches more ears; with editorial comment. Bsns W p42+, 172 N 22 '69
Slum swindlers must go! J. N. Miller. Read Digest 95:169-70+ N '69
Toward a just marketplace. Time 94:92 N 7 '69
Where will Bess Myerson Grant strike next? J. Klemesrud. il N Y Times Mag p37+ O 12 '69
Will Virginia Knauer use her consumer power? Consumer Rep 34:326-7 Je '69

CONSUMER protection—*Continued*
Winners! Consumer challenge essays. G. L. Hart; G. W. Caldwell; L. W. Copits. il Har Yrs 9:16-17 Jl '69
See also
Consumers education and protective association
Packaging—Laws and regulations

Laws and legislation
Bill of rights? Newsweek 74:90 N 10 '69
Business responds to consumerism; with editorial comment. il Bsns W p94-6+, 132 S 6 '69
Headline hunting in the consumer's name. Consumer Bul 52:24-6 Je '69
Never underestimate the power of a consumer. il Newsweek 74:97-8+ O 20 '69
Product liability: tougher ground rules. D. L. Rados. Harvard Bsns R 47:144-52 Jl '69
Rush to help consumers. il U S News 67:47 Ag 25 '69
Slippery shoes; Mrs Hanberry vs. Good housekeeping. Time 94:66 N 21 '69
Swiss cheese; R. M. Nixon's buyer's bill of rights. R. Nader. New Repub 161:11-12 N 22 '69
U.S.'s toughest customer: R. Nader & raiders. il Time 94:89-92+ D 12 '69

CONSUMER reports (periodical)
Help prevent misuse of Consumer Reports. Consumer Rep 34:425 Ag '69
See also
Consumers union of the United States

CONSUMER surveys
How good are consumer pollsters? il Bsns W p 108-10 N 8 '69

CONSUMERS
Ann Arbor conference focuses on problems of older consumer. il Aging 178:5-10+ Ag '69
Chief political question of our time; reprint. W. Karp and H. R. Shapiro. ALA Bul 63: 165-7 F '69
Consumer services for older Americans; assistance needed; address, May 24, 1969. J. J. Barry. Vital Speeches 35:649-52 Ag 15 '69
Consumers rebudget. il Fortune 80:22+ S '69
Consumers: the buying goes on. il Bsns W p45-6 Je 14 '69
FTC: is it doing enough for consumers? il Changing T 23:17-19 Ap '69
Forgotten generation; over sixty-five market. il Forbes 103:22-4+ Ja 15 '69
Glow of affluence is fading fast. il Bsns W p33 D 13 '69
How consumer spending for automobiles creates jobs. R. E. Dempsey and D. F. Schmude. bibliog f il Mo Labor R 92:33-6 Mr '69
Less urge to splurge. Bsns W p43 Jl 12 '69
Prudent consumers. il Fortune 79:24+ Mr '69
Retail sales ring up riddle for economists; dramatic shifts in patterns of spending. il Bsns W p28-30 Mr 1 '69
Slowdown talk: a hot item. il Bsns W p 19 Ag 9 '69
Speaker for the house. C. Montgomery. See issues of Good housekeeping
Still buying but enjoying it less. il Bsns W p31-3 N 1 '69
What do we need as consumers? University of Michigan's Conference on aging discusses the aging consumer. C. Rice. il Har Yrs 9:46-8 S '69
Why Americans are buying less. il Time 94:90 O 3 '69
See also
Consumer protection
Stock exchange

CONSUMERS, Negro. See Negro market
CONSUMERS education and protective association
Defense against gouging. J. Carper. Nation 209:473-5 N 3 '69
Mrs Knauer's hometown. New Repub 160:9 My 17 '69

CONSUMERS preferences
Beyond market segmentation. N. L. Barnett. bibliog f il Harvard Bsns R 47:152-4+ Ja '69

CONSUMERS union of United States
Benchmark case; CU suit against Seagram's. Newsweek 74:89-90 D 15 '69
Partial victory in the hearing-aid case; CU vs VA on hearing aid data. Consumer Rep 34:492 S '69

CONSUMPTION (economics)
Harried leisure class, by B. Linder. Review Fortune 81:161-2 Ja '70. M. Ways
More fuel for inflation; the coming flow of cash. il U S News 67:29-30 O 6 '69
Price of the good life will get stiffer; forecast for the 1970s. il Bsns W p 196-7+ D 6 '69

What's happening to workers' purchasing power? il U S News 66:83-4 Ap 14 '69
Why people are buying less; reported from across U.S. il U S News 67:45-7 Ag 11 '69
See also
Advertising
Consumer surveys
Consumers
Supply and demand

CONTACOS, Peter G. and Collins, W. E.
Plasmodium malariae: transmission from monkey to man by mosquito bite. bibliog Science 165:918-19 Ag 29 '69

CONTACT lenses
Contact lenses anyone can wear; hydrophilic lenses. T. Bacon. il Pop Sci 194:84-6+ Ja '69

CONTAGION and contagious diseases. See Communicable diseases

CONTAINER corporation-Montgomery Ward merger. See Business consolidations and mergers

CONTAINER corporation of America
Containing the suitors. il Bsns W p94 Mr 22 '69
See also
Marcor, incorporated

CONTAINER gardening. See Gardening

CONTAINERIZATION (freight)
Moving to containers; Japan's role. S. Griffin. il Sci N 96:582 D 20 '69
Oceangoing drive-in; RO/RO container ships. J. Liston. il Pop Mech 132:100-3 N '69
Roll-on ships gather more cargo; roll-on/roll-off trailer ship. il Bsns W p74-6 My 10 '69
Transport: the container revolution. il Newsweek 74:62-62B S 1 '69
Why more Scotch is getting tanked. il Bsns W p74+ D 13 '69

CONTAINERS
Harvest of trash; reclaimed cans. il Time 94: 39 Ag 29 '69
See also
Beverage bottles
Vases

CONTAINERS for shipping
Refrigerated igloos studied by United on Hawaii flights. Aviation W 91:33 S 29 '69
See also
Containerization (freight)

CONTAINERSHIPS. See Freight vessels

CONTAMINATION of the earth. See Earth—Contamination

CONTEMPLATION. See Meditation

CONTEMPLATION, Religious. See Meditation

CONTEMPORARY music. See Music

CONTEMPORARY theology institute. See Religious institutes and workshops

CONTEMPT of court
Contempt in Chicago. Time 94:72+ N 14 '69
How militants try to destroy a court. il U S News 67:68-9 N 17 '69

CONTENTMENT
See also
Happiness

CONTERGAN. See Thalidomide

CONTEST; story. See Woiwode, L.

CONTESTS. See Competitions

CONTINENTAL airlines
Champagne on a beer budget. il Forbes 104: 61-2 S 15 '69
Unflown Hawaii route cost Continental $2 million. Aviation W 91:29 Jl 7 '69

CONTINENTAL can company
Separate ways. il Forbes 104:68 N 15 '69

CONTINENTAL copper and steel industries, incorporated
Pygmy among the giants. Forbes 103:44 F 1 '69

CONTINENTAL drift
Anorthosite belts, continental drift, and the anorthosite event. N. Herz. bibliog il Science 164:944-7 My 23 '69
Australarctica. Sci Am 221:50+ Ag '69
Brazil-Gabon geologic link supports continental drift. G. O. Allard and V. J. Hurst. bibliog il Science 163:528-32 F 7 '69
Clue to the past; lystrosaurus. il Sci N 96:549 D 13 '69
Continental drift. D. L. Turcotte and E. R. Oxburgh. bibliog il Phys Today 22:30-9 Ap '69; Reply with rejoinder. W. R. Cook. 22: 11+ Ag '69
Continental drift and evolution. B. Kurtén. il Sci Am 220:54-64 Mr '69
Drifting continents. il Chem 42:18-19 S '69
Geopoetry becomes geofact; evidence of breakup of two supercontinents called Gondwanaland and Laurasia. il Time 95: 46 Ja 5 '70

CONTINENTAL drift—*Continued*
Oceanic sediment volumes and continental drift. J. Gilluly. bibliog Science 166:992-4 N 21 '69
Origin of an obstacle; Bahama platform. il Sci N 96:473-4 N 22 '69
Origin of the oceanic ridges. E. Orowan. il Sci Am 221:102-8+ bibliog (p 166) N '69
Time for a theory. il Sci N 95:449-50 My 10 '69
Topological inconsistency of continental drift on the present-sized earth. R. Meservey. bibliog il Science 166:609-11 O 31 '69
See also
Continents

CONTINENTAL oil company
Conoco sharpens international image. Bsns W p64 Ag 30 '69

CONTINENTAL shelf
Continental shelves. K. O. Emery. il Sci Am 221:106-14+ bibliog (p285) S '69
Exploring the shelf; CNEXO laboratory at Ste-Anne-du-Portzic, Brittany. N. Hardy. il Sci N 95:366 Ap 12 '69
Late Cenozoic underthrusting of the continental margin of northernmost California. E. A. Silver. bibliog il Science 166:1265-6 D 5 '69
North Sea continental shelf: Court delivers judgment. UN Mo Chron 6:43-4 Mr '69
Offshore oil: channel blowout points up information gap. L. J. Carter. Science 164: 530-2 My 2 '69

CONTINENTS
Pre-drift continental nuclei. P. M. Hurley and J. R. Rand. bibliog il Science 164: 1229-42 Je 13 '69
See also
Continental drift

CONTINI, Edgardo
Perspective into the future. Sat R 52:35-8 F 22 '69

CONTINUITY testers. See Testing instruments

CONTINUOUS casting
Ribbon of steel cuts industry costs. il Bsns W p71-2 Ap 19 '69

CONTINUOUS sessions. See School year

CONTOSKI, Victor
(tr) See Harasymowicz. J.   Geometry

CONTOUR drawing. See Drawing

CONTRA COSTA COUNTY, Calif.
San Ramon Valley: unified school district. J. McHenry. il ALA Bul 63:260-1 F '69

CONTRABAND trade. See Smuggling

CONTRACEPTION. See Birth control

CONTRACEPTIVES
Balancing risks against benefits; birth control pills. Sci N 95:422 My 3 '69
Birth control: is male contraception the answer? Good H 168:201-3 Ap '69
Birth-control pills: safe, but—. U S News 67:10 S 15 '69
Caution on the pill; excerpt from Life, death and the doctor. L. Lasagna; reply with rejoinder. G. Langmyier. Sat R 52:60-1 Mr 1 '69
Doctor's view of birth-control pills. L. M. Hellman. Redbook 132:60+ Ap '69
Doubts about the pill. il Newsweek 73:118 My 19 '69
Further evidence on clots. Sci N 95:611 Je 28 '69
If not the pill, what? L. Lasagna. Vogue 154:102+ O 15 '69
New contraceptive society; findings of survey made in Sweden. J. R. Moskin. Look 33:50+ F 4 '69; Same abr. with title Sweden: the contraceptive society. Read Digest 94:225-6+ Ap '69
Only a yellow light; birth control pills. Sci N 96:198 S 13 '69
Oral contraceptives: government-supported programs are questioned. M. Mueller. Science 163:553-5 F 7 '69
Oral contraceptives: long-term use produces fine structural changes in liver mitochondria. V. Perez and others. bibliog il Science 165:805-7 Ag 22 '69
Pill and cancer; findings of Melamed-Dubrow study. il Newsweek 74:59 Ag 11 '69
Pill: cloudy verdict; FDA report. Newsweek 74:90 S 15 '69
Pill for men? il Newsweek 74:62 Jl 14 '69
Pill goes to Washington. Bsns W p31-2 Ja 10 '70
Prognosis for the development of new chemical birth-control agents; adaptation of address, October 22, 1969. C. Djerassi. bibliog il Science 166:468-73 O 24 '69; Discussion. 166:1575-6 D 26 '69
Pros and cons of the pill. il Time 93:58+ My 2 '69

Questions women ask most about the pill. R. W. Kistner. Good H 168:78-9+ F '69
Re-evaluating the pill; H. Lief's study findings. Newsweek 75:66 Ja 12 '70
Safe substitute for the pill. Sci Digest 66:60 Ag '69
Serum copper alteration after ingestion of an oral contraceptive. J. A. O'Leary and W. N. Spellacy; reply. E. Frieden and S. Osaki. Science 163:959 F 28 '69
7,000,000 American women take the pill. Very soon, now, it will be your turn; male pill. L. Aldridge. Esquire 71:92-3+ Ja '69
Something better than the pill? IUD and other devices. C. P. Gilmore. il N Y Times Mag p6-7+ Jl 20 '69; Discussion. p5+ Ag 10 '69
Substitute for the pill. B. J. Culliton. il Sci N 95:555-7 Je 7 '69
What's sure besides the pill? ed. by J. Fast. C. R. Garcia. Redbook 134:34+ Ja '70
Why birth control fails. L. Lader. il McCalls 97:74-5+ O '69

CONTRACT bridge. See Bridge (game)

CONTRACT labor
See also
Indentured servants

CONTRACTORS
When disaster strikes, they strike back; construction contractors' plan bulldozer. Nations Bsns 57:73 N '69
See also
Associated general contractors of America

CONTRACTS
Long arm law; an author's experience with a New York syndicate. W. Donaldson. Writers Digest 49:92-3 N '69
See also
Building—Contracts and specifications
Installment contracts
Labor contracts
Municipal contracts
Put and call transactions
Subcontracting
Teachers—Contracts
Trade agreements

CONTRACTS, Agricultural
Feeder pig contract that works for the little guy. R. Wilmore. il Farm J 93:42G S '69

CONTRACTS, Government
Anguish in the defense industry. R. M. Anderson. Harvard Bsns R 47:162-4+ N '69
Army cancels AH-56 production phase. Aviation W 90:24-6 My 26 '69
As Eisenhower was saying, we must guard against unwarranted influence by the military-industrial complex. R. F. Kaufman. il N Y Times Mag p 10-11+ Je 22 '69; Reply with rejoinder. J. R. L. Johnson, jr. p2+ Jl 6 '69
Blank check for the military; the need for control; address, March 10, 1969. W. Proxmire. Vital Speeches 35:400-5 Ap 15 '69
Building Lyndon Johnson. D. Welsh. il Ramp Mag 7:104-14 Ja 25 '69
Can defense work keep a home on campus? MIT panel calls for balance with nondefense R&D. il Bsns W p68-71 Je 7 '69
Competitors scramble to replace old fighter; air force contract sought by McDonnell Douglas, North American, and Fairchild Hiller. il Bsns W p 110+ My 17 '69
Contempt of Congress; Pentagon and the production contract for the top stage of Minuteman III ICBMs. Nation 209:36-7 Jl 14 '69
Crisis at Lockheed. il Newsweek 73:71-2 Je 2 '69
Defense contract: the money web. G. Astor. il Look 33:28-9 Ag 26 '69
Defense department lists leading 100 contractors for fiscal 1969; tables. Aviation W 91:104-5+ N 17 '69
Defense requirements for the 1970's; instant myths; address, April 3, 1969. J. J. Rhodes. Vital Speeches 35:460-2 My 15 '69
Dial-A-bomb: AT&T and the ABM. J. Goulden and M. Singer. il Ramp Mag 8:29-35+ N '69
Final appropriations for major weapon systems for fiscal 1970; tables. Aviation W 92:24-5 Ja 5 '70
For Lockheed, everything's coming up unknowns. H. B. Meyers. il Fortune 80:76-81+ Ag 1 '69
Forces affecting science policy; R&D address, August 30, 1968. D. E. Kash. Bul Atom Sci 25:10-17 Ap '69
GAO defense profit study asked. K. Johnsen. Aviation W 90:71-2 Je 9 '69
GAO urges prototype competition. K. Johnsen. il Aviation W 91:16-17 Jl 21 '69
Handling risk in defense contracting. R. M. Anderson. il Harvard Bsns R 47:90-8 Jl '69

CONTRACTS, Government—*Continued*

How to control the military. J. K. Galbraith. il Harper 238:31-46 Je '69

Incentive contract emphasis fades. K. Johnsen. Aviation W 91:65+ O 27 '69

Initial overrun review completed. C. Brownlow. il Aviation W 90:16-18 Je 30 '69

Joint 2707 work statements developing. il Aviation W 92:81-2 Ja 5 '70

Laird takes hard line with defense complex; with editorial comment. il Bsns W p82+, 182 My 10 '69

Let's internationalize defense marketing. R. E. McGarrah. Harvard Bsns R 47:146-55 My '69

Lockheed contract dropped. il Sci N 95:525 My 31 '69

Lockheed lands anti-sub plane. Bsns W p27-8 Ag 9 '69

Lockheed's casualties in the defense controversy. il Time 93:76-7 My 30 '69

Lockheed's ledger on the C-5A. Bsns W p35 Je 7 '69

MOL contractors attempt to assess action's impact. Aviation W 90:29-30 Je 16 '69

Military cutbacks will send tremors through industry; forecast for the 1970s. il Bsns W p91+ D 6 '69

Military-industrial complex. il Newsweek 73:74-6+ Je 9 '69

Military-industrial complex; an economic analysis; address, March 21, 1969. M. L. Weidenbaum. bibliog Vital Speeches 35:523-8 Je 15 '69

Military markets start to sag. il Bsns W p 140 O 25 '69

Mk. 2 hits severe cost problems. C. Brownlow. Aviation W 90:16-17 Mr 3 '69

More companies under the gun; Proxmire-Fitzgerald attack on Pentagon's procurement. Bsns W p42 Je 21 '69

Myth of war profiteering. G. E. Berkley. il New Repub 161:15-18 D 20 '69

NASA lists 100 top contractors. Aviation W 90:47+ Je 30 '69; 92:55 Ja 12 '70

News and views; L. M. Rivers and defense contracts. J. Deedy. Commonweal 90:58 Ap 4 '69

News and views; military-industrial romance. J. Deedy. Commonweal 90:92 Ap 11 '69

On uncovering the great nerve gas coverup; sheep killed near Dugway, the army's chemical and biological testing station, Skull Valley, Utah. S. Hersh. Ramp Mag 7:14-18 Je '69

100 top NASA contractors listed. il Aviation W 90:88-9 Mr 31 '69

Overlooked realities; excerpts from address. R. C. Gusman. Aviation W 90:11 Mr 3 '69

Plum for McDonnell Douglas; F-15 contract. Bsns W p22 D 27 '69

Power people; symposium. il Look 33:20-4+ Ag 26 '69

Raytheon: radar to refrigerators. il Forbes 103:28-32 Je 1 '69

Red and green in civil rights; Philadelphia plan. R. Kuttner. Commonweal 90:535 S 5 '69

Red ink alert; defense contractors running over cost estimates. Forbes 103:19 Ap 1 '69

S-3 program to test contracting concept. il Aviation W 91:34 Ag 11 '69

Son of the Phantom; F-15 contract. il Newsweek 75:50-1 Ja 5 '70

Talks started on C-5 contract revisions. D. C. Winston. Aviation W 91:29-30 Ag 4 '69

USAF contract for V/STOL propeller set. Aviation W 91:58 S 29 '69

USAF, Lockheed diverge over C-5A terms. Aviation W 90:20 Je 23 '69

Where the military contracts go; with charts. W. S. Rukeyser. il Fortune 80:74-5 Ag 1 '69

Who pulled in the big ones. il Bsns W p 130 N 8 '69

Why Nixon ordered construction cutback. U S News 67:15 S 15 '69

See also

Government spending policy

Insurance

No cover for catastrophes; aerospace contractors. il Bsns W p58+ O 18 '69

Labor problems

Political row erupts over fair employment. il Bsns W p20-1 Ap 5 '69

Roadmaster Volpe. New Repub 160:7 My 10 '69

TRB from Washington: Kennedy stands up; Senate hearing on contract compliance. New Repub 160:6 Ap 12 '69

Renegotiation

Gemini incentives emerge in renegotiation. K. Johnsen. il Aviation W 90:29-30 My 5 '69

Grumman fights excess Viet profits case. K. Johnsen. Aviation W 90:34 Ap 14 '69

SRAM cost overruns negotiated. C. Brownlow. Aviation W 90:16-17 Ja 27 '69

Sweet defense jobs sour at Lockheed; air force's C-5A, and army's AH-56A Cheyenne helicopter. il Bsns W p 122-3 My 17 '69

See also

United States—Renegotiation board

CONTRACTS, Teachers. See Teachers—Contracts

CONTRARY opinion theory (stock market) See Stockholders—Psychology

CONTRERAS, Gloria

Gloria Contreras dance company; 92nd street Y. J. Anderson. il Dance Mag 43:30-1 Ja '69

CONTRIBUTION; drama. See Shine, T.

CONTROL circuits. See Electronic control

CONTROL data corporation

Bail-out syndrome. C. Morgello. il Newsweek 74:87 N 10 '69

Control data tackles the giant. il Bsns W p 148+ Je 28 '69

Control data's Cinderella: CCC. il Forbes 104: 19 D 15 '69

GE, Control data play their hands; price increases. Bsns W p90+ S 20 '69

Plant for part-timers. Bsns W p 108 N 29 '69

CONTROL equipment. See Automatic control

CONTROL of credit. See Credit

CONTROL of insects. See Insects, Injurious and beneficial—Control

CONTROL panels (airplanes) See Airplanes—Instrument boards

CONTROL systems, Biological. See Biological control systems

CONTROLLED fusion. See Nuclear fusion

CONTROLLERSHIP

New controllers: more than numbers. J. Poindexter. il Duns R 94:37-41 O '69

CONTROVERSY: the Arthur Bader show; story. See Berger, T.

CONVALESCENT homes. See Nursing homes

CONVENTIONS

Conventions: when & where. See issues of American city

Freelance job idea: convention freelancing. E. Engle. il Writers Digest 49:42-3+ Ap '69

Great American get-together. il Forbes 103: 28-30+ F 15 '69

How I cover conventions; writing articles for businesspapers. N. I. Phillips. Writers Digest 49:44+ Ap '69

CONVENTIONS, Political. See National conventions (political)

CONVENTS and nunneries

Future for contemplatives? J. C. Haughev. America 121:261-4 O 4 '69; Discussion. 121: 343 O 25 '69

Irish nuns in the Mekong Delta. D. Warren. America 121:524-5 N 29 '69

New praying nun; House of prayer. J. M. Kann. Cath World 209:71-6 My '69

Renewal for the cloister; contemplative communities. il Time 94:64+ S 5 '69

CONVERSATION piece; drama. See Nicholson, J.

CONVERSATION radio programs. See Radio broadcasting—Conversation programs

CONVERSATION television programs. See Television broadcasting—Conversation programs

CONVERSE, Courtland

Floats. Flying 85:68-72 S '69

CONVERSION

Christianity's greatest challenge. C. G. Fry. Chr Today 14:9-12 N 7 '69

CONVERTERS. See Electric current converters

CONVERTERS, Radio. See Radio converters

CONVERTIBLE bonds. See Bonds, Convertible

CONVERTIBLE sofas. See Furniture, Convertible

CONVICTS. See Prisoners

CONVULSIONS

First aid; convulsions in children. C. J. Potthoff. Todays Health 47:80 Mr '69

CONWAY, Gordon R.

Consequence of insecticides; pests follow the chemicals in the cocoa of Malaysia. Natur Hist 78:46-51 F '69

CONWAY, Jack T.

New challenges to union leadership. Mo Labor R 92:56 Ap '69

CONWAY, T. F. and Johnson, L. F.

Nuclear magnetic resonance measurement of oil unsaturation in single viable corn kernels. bibliog Science 164:827-8 My 16 '69

CONWAY, William G.
Consumption of wildlife by man; reprint.
Parks & Rec 4:20-6+ F '69
CONYERS, John, 1929-
Politics and the black revolution. por Ebony
24:162-6 Ag '69
—See Armstrong, J. jt. auth.
COOK, Charles G.
Equestrian bridge. Parks & Rec 4:47+ Je '69
COOK, Charles W.
Web offset printing, a case history; excerpts
from address, November 1969. Pub W 196:
53-4+ D 1 '69
COOK, David W.
How we mapped the moon. por Nat Geog 135:
240-5 F '69
COOK, Don
Reports: Basel. Atlan 224:14-15+ Jl '69
Reports: France. Atlan 224:14+ N '69
COOK, Donald
High and the mighty. il por Newsweek 74:
42+ N 10 '69
6,900-mile skyjack. il por Time 94:29 N 7 '69
COOK, Donald C.
As I see it; interview. por Forbes 103:42+ F
1 '69
COOK, Fred J.
All-American frame-up. Nation 208:605-9 My
12 '69
Mobsters in pasture: Nostra Jersey. Nation
208:105-10 Ja 27 '69
about
Cook doctrine. Nation 209:5 Jl 7 '69
COOK, Greg
New Cincinnati kid. J. Pekkanen. il pors Life
67:141-2 O 10 '69
COOK, M. J.
Computer is the key. por Am City 84:127-8
O '69
COOK, Newell C.
Metalliding; with biographical sketch. Sci Am
221:12, 38-46 Ag '69
COOK, Robert E. and others
What have we done to Vietnam? New Repub
162:18-21 Ja 10 '70
COOK, Walter
NRPA expands service to members, here's
what it means to you. Parks & Rec 4:58-9
Mr '69
COOK, Whitfield
Only women can be wives; story. Redbook
132:70-1 Mr '69
COOK books. See Cookbooks
COOK COUNTY, III.
Keeper of the peace. il Newsweek 73:57 Mr 31
'69
COOK COUNTY Jail, Chicago. See Prisons—
Illinois
COOK STRAIT
Four-star paradise; Marlborough sounds. T.
R. Talamini. il Travel 131:60-1 F '69
COOKBOOKS
Authors & editors; Betty Crocker's cookbook.
B. A. Bannon. Pub W 196:25-6 S 15 '69
Delicious report on cookbooks. P. Simon. il
Redbook 132:96-7+ F '69
Gastronome's revenge; La cuisine des pro-
vinces de France; R. J. Courtine's foot-
notes. Newsweek 73:88 Ap 28 '69
Larder; excerpts from Great dinners from
Life; with editorial comment. E. Graves.
il Life 67:3, 54-61 O 24 '69
World's greatest cookery book: Beeton's
book of household management. E. Marlowe.
il Am Home 72:40+ D '69
See also
Booksellers and bookselling—Cookbooks

Bibliography
Cookbooks '69; a sampling. H. McCully. House
B 111:63-4+ N '69
Fall cookbooks preview. Pub W 196:36-44 S
15 '69
COOKE, Eileen D. See Krettek. G. jt. auth.
COOKE, Ian M. See Hartline. D. K. jt. auth.
COOKE, J. W.
Freedom in the thoughts of Fredrick Doug-
lass. 1845-1860. bibliog Negro Hist Bul 32:
6-10 F '69
COOKE, Jerry
Beauty to ornament the men of speed;
photographs. Sports Illus 30:22-7 Je 30 '69
COOKE, Terence James, cardinal
Out to lunch. Commonweal 91:62 O 17 '69
Two who agree on a way of life. il por U S
News 66:15 Je 9 '69
COOKERY
Accounting for tastes; packaged and frozen
foods. il Parents Mag 44:34-6 Mr '69
After the ball is over. N. S. Hazelton. Nat R
21:36 Ja 14 '69

Alice's cookbook. Time 94:67 O 24 '69
Big ideas for small equipment; with recipes.
il Redbook 134:76-7+ Ja '70
Bride makes... See issues of McCall's
Byline by Kriendler. P. Kriendler. Travel &
Camera 32:123 F '69
Camp chef. C. B. Colby. See issues of Outdoor
life
Celebrity cook book; with menus. il House &
Gard 13:90-1+ Jl '69
Celebrity cooks, their kitchens to enjoy;
symposium. il House & Gard 136:80-8 Jl '69
Company's coming. See issues of American
home
Complete weekend cookbook; with menus. il
Good H 168:108-23 My '69
Creative cooking for two; menus. il Good H
168:134-45 Ap '69
Date with a dish. See issues of Ebony
Dollars from doughnuts. il Seventeen 29:94-
5+ Ja '70
Easy-on-the-cook: recipes and timesaving ap-
pliances to help you cope, quickly in the
kitchen. il Good H 168:133-41 Mr '69
Eat. M Cantwell. See issues of Mademoiselle
Eat and run: what and how; food for your
party. il Seventeen 28:142+ Je '69
Fashion in the kitchen; recipes of ten fashion
luminaries. il Harp Baz 103:192-7+ D '69
Flaming issue. E. Greenberg and M. Green-
berg. Harp Baz 103:168-9 N '69
Food in Vogue. N. Lyon. Vogue 154:163 O 1;
69 O 15; 131 N 1; 71 N 15 '69; 155:85 Ja 1
'70
Food questions you ask; with answers. See
issues of American home
From our kitchen; with recipes. L. Driggs.
See issues of Harvest years
Hearty foods for hearty appetites. il Bet
Hom & Gard 47:34 D '69
Hearty winter fare with a welcome change
of pace. D. Brooks. il Home Gard 56:52
F '69
Hot pot cookery. il Sunset 143:102-5 O '69
How come they don't make them the way
they used to? make ahead main dishes. il
Redbook 133:106-7+ S '69
Ideas for an autumn calendar; with menus.
il McCalls 97:110-16+ O '69
Ladies write their own cookbooks. il Am
Home 72:86-8+ Mr '69
Learning to cook. See issues of American
home
Low-calorie cookery; with recipes. il McCalls
96:100-8+ F '69
Luscious low-cholesterol recipes. il Redbook
132:118-20+ Ap '69
Midsummer menus, right from the garden. D.
Brooks. il Home Gard 56:41 Jl '69
[Month] menus; with recipes. See issues of
Sunset
[Monthly column on cookery] G. Maddox.
See issues of Today's health
New foods that make cooking easier; with
recipes. il Redbook 132:88+ Ja '69
Nobody ever tells you these things, about
food and drink; questions and answers.
H. McCully. See issues of House beautiful
Oh food where is thy sting. N. S. Hazelton.
Nat R 21:911+ S 9 '69
On developing discriminating taste in food.
V. T. Habeeb. Am Home 72:50+ N '69
Orange flavor for meats, for fruits. il Sunset
142:137 F '69
Portfolio of new recipes, plans, equipment
and tips that save time, space, money &
you! symposium. il Good H 168:126-41 Mr
'69
Problem solvers. Parents Mag 44:96+ N '69
Questions you ask; with answers. Am Home
72:99-100 Mr '69
Redbook reader, cooking enthusiast. il Red-
book 133:105-10+ My '69
Redbook reader Mrs Diedrick S. Cassel: cook-
ing is her hobby; with recipes. il Redbook
134:100-3+ N '69
Redbook's timesaver cookbook. il Redbook
132:98-108 Mr '69
Redbook's wise woman's diet cookbook;
with menus. il Redbook 134:97-104 Ja '70
Simple joys of simple foods. il McCalls 97:
68-72+ Ja '70
Smart cook (cont) Bet Hom & Gard 47:132
Mr; 140-1 Ap; 135 My; 129 S '69
Stir up some fun, with refreshments everyone
helps make. il Good H 169:114+ Ag '69
Stop & go cooking. D. Eby. il Bet Hom &
Gard 47:92-9+ S '69
Summer-favorites cookbook. il Good H 168:
104-20 Je '69
Sunset's kitchen cabinet. See issues of Sunset
Sure-fire new ways to cook. il Parents Mag
44:68-71 Ap '69

COOKERY—*Continued*

Game

Art of cooking game birds. J. Jaffry. il Am Home 72:94-5 N '69

Band-tailed pigeon in wine. il Sunset 143:180 O '69

First you get yourself two rabbits. Sunset 143:196 O '69

Have a heart. C. B. Colby. il Outdoor Life 143:108 F '69

Prairie chicken. C. B. Colby. il Outdoor Life 144:33 O '69

Ptasty ptarmigan. C. B. Colby. il Outdoor Life 144:14 D '69

She's spooning up hasenpfeffer. il Sunset 142:213 Ap '69

Timberdoodle treats; woodcock terrapin. C. B. Colby. Outdoor Life 143:28 Mr '69

Venison benison. C. B. Colby. il Outdoor Life 144:16 N '69

Venison fit for a king. E. W. Piersol. il Outdoor Life 144:76+ N '69

Wild duck with apricot sauce. il Sunset 143:214 O '69

Leftovers

Leftovers, on purpose. Bet Hom & Gard 47:168 O '69

Yesterday's beef, supper today. il Sunset 142:185 Je '69

Liquors

How to mate food and spirits. E. Greenberg and M. Greenberg. House B 111:112-14 Mr '69

Maple syrup

Maple harvest: sweets from a tree; with recipes. E. Alston. il Look 33:60-1 Mr 4 '69

Meat

Beef at its best. C. Claiborne. il N Y Times Mag p 102 Ap 27 '69

Beefeater's cookbook. il McCalls 96:80-8+ Ja '69

Bottomless beef and vegetable pie. Sunset 142:218 Ap '69

Burger bonanza. il Ladies Home J 86:38-9+ F '69

Choice chops. C. Claiborne. il N Y Times Mag p36 Ag 31 '69

Complete sausage cookbook. il Good H 169:130-45 O '69

Consider the shank. C. Claiborne. il N Y Times Mag p86 Ap 20 '69

Cooking for two to eight. D. Eby. il Bet Hom & Gard 47:80-5+ F '69

Cooking with cool; meat loaf. il Seventeen 28:190 Mr '69

Devilishly delicious. J. McCloskey. il Bet Hom & Gard 47:109 Ap '69

Dozen ways to trap a man, or hold a husband; with menu and recipes. il McCalls 96:104-5+ My '69

Escalopes, a meal in minutes. P. S. Brown. il House & Gard 135:121-4+ Mr '69

Fast and fancy ways with burgers and franks. il Bet Hom & Gard 47:73-4 Jl '69

Fast ways with ham. il Bet Hom & Gard 47:111-12 My '69

Flight of fancy; veal birds. C. Claiborne. il N Y Times Mag p93 S 28 '69

Gastronomy recalled. M. F. K. Fisher. New Yorker 45:141-4 S 27 '69

Getting to know them; livers, kidneys, lungs, hearts and brains. C. Claiborne. il N Y Times Mag p68-9 Mr 2 '69

Great chili confrontation; condensation. H. A. Smith. il Read Digest 94:141-4 Je '69

Ground beef mix you can freeze. Farm J 93:46 Je '69

Ham that isn't-quite; with menu and recipes. E. Graves. il Life 66:76-8 Ap 4 '69

Hamburger. il Parents Mag 44:66-9+ Ja '69

It doesn't have to taste like liver! with recipes. B. Bryant. il Todays Health 48:60-3 Ja '70

It may be offal to some but to others it's sweetbreads, kidney pie and calf's liver. W. Clifford. il Holiday 46:68-9+ O '69

It's a ham and spinach roll. il Sunset 142:193 Mr '69

It's corned beef with peaches. il Sunset 143:222 O '69

It's leg of lamb; boned, rolled, tied. il Sunset 142:204 Mv '69

Meats for windy weather. G. Maddox. il Todays Health 47:60-5 Mr '69

Mexicans have some delicious ideas about lamb. il Sunset 142:172+ Ap '69

Mystery of foie gras. H. Gault and C. Millau. il Holiday 46:52-3+ D '69

New ways to cook chops. il Bet Hom & Gard 47:98 Mr '69

Pork is good eating. il Am Home 72:92+ Ja '69

Pork tenderloin, sweet and sour. Sunset 143:90 Ag '69

Pot roast, French style. V. T. Habeeb. il Am Home 72:94-5+ O '69

Quit murdering that hamburger! il Changing T 23:46 Ag '69

Recipes from Redbook readers private collection. il Redbook 133:102-10 Ja '69

Right honorable turnover; meat turnovers. C. Claiborne. il N Y Times Mag p 112 O 12 '69

Sausage, a food for all seasons. il Ebony 25:110+ Ja '70

Showoff steak; flaming pepper steak. il Sunset 143:190 O '69

Smoked tongue in a madeira sauce. il Sunset 142:184 Mr '69

Spring lamb in the pink, with menus and recipes. il McCalls 96:126-7 +Ap '69

Steak for the cook in a hurry. il Sunset 142:160 Je '69

Subject is veal; with recipes. H. McCully. il House B 111:124-6+ Ap '69

Summer ingenuity; chilled meat platters. il Sunset 143:86-7 Ag '69

Sweetbread gap. C. Claiborne. il N Y Times Mag p55 F 2 '69

Take a pound of ground beef. il Am Home 72:98+ My '69

These spareribs are sweet-sour. Sunset 142:129 F '69

Time to enjoy pork's palate-pleasing performance; with recipes. G. Maddox. il Todays Health 47:50-5 S '69

Try ham chaud froid. V. T. Habeeb. il Am Home 72:90-1 Ap '69

Twelve great recipes for pork. H. McCully. il House B 111:164-5+ O '69

Two hamburgers, both brash. il Sunset 142:210 Mv '69

Variations on three flavor classics. P. Pollock. il Bet Hom & Gard 47:102 Mr '69

Veal paupiettes duchesse. V. T. Habeeb. il Am Home 72:70-1 Je '69

Veal rolls with pâté inside. il Sunset 142:146 F '69

Veal scaloppine, white or red. Sunset 142:158+ Ap '69

Veal steaks with spinach on top. il Sunset 142:208 My '69

Versatile pot-au-feu. E. Lambert de Ortiz. il House & Gard 135:93-5+ F '69

Virtuosity with veal. C. Claiborne. il N Y Times Mag p90 O 19 '69

You call those hamburgers? with recipes. il McCalls 96:84-5 Ag '69

Your own pastrami with pepper, spices, smoke. il Sunset 142:138-9 F '69

See also
Barbecue cookery
Stew

Molasses

Make it with molasses. il Bet Hom & Gard 47:102 F '69

Mushrooms

How mushrooms dress an entrée; ham and mushroom crêpes. il Sunset 143:174 O '69

Mushroom menu-makers. il Bet Hom & Gard 47:136 S '69

Nuts

Cooking with chestnuts. E. Alston. il Look 33:97-8 N 18 '69

Nuts over chocolate. J. Hewitt. il N Y Times Mag p47 Jl 27 '69

What's cooking?
Homemade nut butter. B. T. Hunter. Org Gard & Farm 16:77-8 O '69

Poultry

Almond chicken with rice. Sunset 143:176 N '69

Bird for all seasons: chicken. il McCalls 96:128-35+ Ap '69

Boy, is it stuffed! turkey stuffing. C. Claiborne. il N Y Times Mag p 130 D 7 '69

Chicken big. C. Claiborne. il N Y Times Mag p81 Mv 18 '69

Chicken for every taste. C. Claiborne. il N Y Times Mag p 102 Mr 30 '69

Cooking for two to eight. D. Eby. il Bet Hom & Gard 47:80-5+ F '69

Eat: chicken and cêpes. M. Cantwell. Mlle 69:70+ Je '69

Epicures' choice; roast capon. C. Claiborne. il N Y Times Mag p47 D 21 '69

Fast and fancy ways with turkey. il Bet Hom & Gard 47:93-4 O '69

Festive laurel chicken for Easter dinner. il Sunset 142:192 Ap '69

First you pound your chicken. il Sunset 143:212 O '69

Food in Vogue; chicken and ginger sauce; chicken in chocolate sauce. N. Lyon. Vogue 154:69 O 15 '69

COOKERY, Foreign. See Cookery, International

COOKERY, French
Alexandre Dumas (père) invites you to the feast of Noël. R. A. DeGroot. il Esquire 73: 122-5+ Ja '70
Four classic French pastries. H. McCully and J. Pépin. il House B 111:108-10+ Mr '69
François-Xavier Lalanne: don't forget the stuffing. N. Lyon. Vogue 155:85 Ja 1 '70
French cooking à la Courtine. S. De Gramont. il N Y Times Mag p8-9+ Jl 6 '69
Grand bean-meat stew of southern France; cassoulet. il Sunset 143:134-5 D '69
Mystery of foie gras. H. Gault and C. Millau. il Holiday 46:52-3+ D '69
Napoleon's chicken marengo; with recipe. E. Alston. il Look 33:30-1 S 9 '69
Norman conqueror; chicken Vallee D'Auge. C. Claiborne. il N Y Times Mag p 100 N 2 '69
Pierre Androüet: insatiable with cheese and snails. N. Lyon. Vogue 154:131 N 1 '69
Pride of Provence; brandade de morus. C. Claiborne. il N Y Times Mag p 136 O 26 '69
Road to Périgord, a movable feast in more ways than one. M. Gough. il House B 111: 94+ N '69
Time off: to France on the France. P. O'Higgins. il McCalls 97:84+ Ja '70
What's cooking? shallots and leeks. il Org Gard & Farm 16:83-5 D '69
Yankee dinner for a royal collection; Boston Forsyth Wickes collection, French and English 18th-century antiques; with recipes. E. Alston. il Look 33:68-72 F 18 '69

COOKERY, Greek
From the Near East to our Far West, an all-appetizer midsummer party. il Sunset 143:70-3 Jl '69
Great Greek appetizers; with recipes. E. Alston. il Look 33:82-3 Mr 18 '69
Grecian favorite; moussaka. il Am Home 72: 100-1 S '69
Greek soup holds little meatballs. il Sunset 143:147 S '69

COOKERY, Hungarian
Toasted cabbage, just plain good. Sunset 143: 185 N '69

COOKERY, Indian (East Indian)
Spicy eats of India. M. Jaffrey. il Holiday 46: 40-1+ D '69
Taste of India. M. S. Atwood. il Ladies Home J 86:112-13+ N '69

COOKERY, International
Far-out foods from faraway lands. G. Maddox. il Todays Health 47:58-61 O '69
Merry eating and drinking. H. McCully. il House B 111:66-7+ D '69
Taste of the year. C. Claiborne. il N Y Times Mag p92-3 Ja 11 '70
World of curries. E. Lambert de Ortiz. il House & Gard 136:158-9+ S '69

COOKERY, Italian
Double-decker pizza. il Seventeen 28:104 Ja '69
Great Italian cooking; excerpts. L. Carnacina. il Ladies Home J 86:90-1+ F '69
Italian hand with tomato sauce. Sunset 142: 152-3 F '69
Our beautiful Christmas bread; pandoro. il Sunset 143:54-5 D '69
Pasta with peas and cheese. il Sunset 143:189 O '69
Pizza has a city cousin; calzone. il Sunset 142:178 Je '69
Presto, pesto; spaghetti sauce. C. Claiborne. il N Y Times Mag p58 Je 15 '69
Seafood Italian style; with recipes. E. Alston. il Look 33:40-1 F 4 '69
Tasting of savory Italian dishes. il House B 111:78-9 Jl '69
See also
Macaroni

COOKERY, Japanese
East meets West; shabu-shabu. C. Claiborne. il N Y Times Mag p42 Ja 4 '70
If you like sashimi and want to introduce it to guests. il Sunset 142:200-2 Ap '69
Make mine teppanyaki. P. Brooks. il Sat R 52:62+ S 13 '69
Soaring popularity of Japanese restaurants. B. Norman and K. Tatsumura. il Holiday 45:58-9+ Mr '69
What she's serving is Japanese me-zoo-ta-key. il Sunset 142:166-7 My '69

COOKERY, Jewish
Eat. M. Cantwell. Mlle 69:196+ Ag '69

COOKERY, Marine
Cooking up a storm. E. Slepian. il Motor B 124:52-3 S '69
Cool food for hot days. E. L. Slepian. il Motor B 124:64-5+ Ag '69
Dinner's on deck; sailing specials from a girl without a galley; with recipes. C. Goad. il Seventeen 28:340 Ag '69

Haut cuisine on the high seas. E. Slepian. il Motor B 123:70-3 My '69
How to eat well afloat. il Sunset 143:108-9+ Jl '69

COOKERY, Mexican
Chili to cry over; with menu and recipes by E. Graves. il Life 66:64-7 F 28 '69
Filled tortilla, but not a taco. il Sunset 143:135 Jl '69
Mexican pie with coconut. il Sunset 143:183 N '69
Mexicans have some delicious ideas about lamb. il Sunset 142:172+ Ap '69
September's the month to make chiles rellenos. il Sunset 143:164+ S '69

COOKERY, Middle Eastern
Eat; Lebanese and Turkish cooking. M. Cantwell. Mlle 69:88+ O '69
Khuroosh, it's a lamb and vegetable stew with rice. il Sunset 142:198 Ap '69

COOKERY, Muslim. See Cookery, Arabic

COOKERY, North African
Eat. M. Cantwell. Mlle 70:92 N '69

COOKERY, Norwegian
It's thin, flat, quick, foldable; lefse. il Sunset 143:153-4 D '69
Norwegian fish pudding. V. T. Habeeb. il Am Home 72:88-9 Ja '69

COOKERY, Oriental
Juicy Oriental pork balls. Sunset 142:181 Je '69
Stir-fry, meat with cabbage. Sunset 143:176 O '69
See also
Cookery, Chinese
Cookery, Japanese

COOKERY, Ornamental
Angel bright, silver white; Christmas tree cake. il Seventeen 27:124-5+ D '68
Art from the kitchen, baked candy ornaments. il Sunset 143:64-5 D '69
Candy house built of boxes. il Sunset 143:78 D '69
Candyland house. il McCalls 97:104+ D '69
Christmas in toyland. il Parents Mag 44:58-63+ D '69
How to make and use paper piping cones. il House B 111:98-9 D '69
Lights flicker inside this tasty castle. il Sunset 143:99 D '69
Merry mixer. il Seventeen 28:126-7+ D '69
Take a package of cake mix; Easter cakes. il Am Home 72:94+ Ap '69
These Easter eggs are cookies. il Sunset 142: 215-16 Ap '69
Treat for Easter Sunday; Jeweled egg in emerald nest. il Farm J 93:96-7 Ap '69
See also
Food as gifts

COOKERY, Outdoor
Cooking on six cylinders. H. W. Riggs. il Travel 132:65-7 O '69
Grate outdoors. C. Claiborne. il N Y Times Mag p85 My 25 '69
Great day for a snow picnic! il Seventeen 27:150-1+ N '68
See also
Barbecue cookery
Outdoor meals
Smoke ovens

Equipment and supplies
Some like it hot. il House & Gard 136:102 Ag '69
See also
Camp stoves

COOKERY, Portuguese
Specialties from the Portuguese kitchen. B. S. Brown. il Good H 168:131 F '69

COOKERY, Scandinavian
Effortless holiday smörgasbord. il Sunset 143: 120-1 D '69
Holiday dishes you make ahead. Sunset 143: 147+ D '69
Lace cookies and buttery spritz. Sunset 143: 150 D '69
See also
Cookery, Danish
Cookery, Swedish

COOKERY, Shaker. See Cookery, American

COOKERY, Southern. See Cookery, American

COOKERY, Spanish
Dining in Madrid; paella. M. Woodward. il Travel 132:26 N '69
It's paella with a crab on top. il Sunset 143: 112 D '69

COOKERY, Swedish
Sunday lunch with Swedish overtones. il House B 111:76-7 Jl '69

COOKERY, Swiss
It's earth apple soup. It's Swiss. il Sunset 142:201 My '69
She's biting into a big carnival cooky. il Sunset 143:220 O '69
COOKERY, Welsh
To eat in Wales. il McCalls 96:62-3+ Je '69
COOKERY, West Indian
Caribbean cooking. J. H. Winchester. il Travel 132:70-2 Jl '69
COOKERY books. See Cookbooks
COOKERY by children
Derek and Alexis make a tasty coffee spiral. il Sunset 143:148-9 N '69
One hostess is 8. The other is 9. And it's a real tea party. il Sunset 142:186-7 My '69
Our beginning cook. See issues of Good housekeeping
She's cooking with sunshine; two friends use the oven. il Sunset 142:76-7 Je '69
Young cooks make mistakes and discoveries. il Sunset 143:172-3 O '69
COOKERY by men
Chefs of the West. See issues of Sunset
Close-up: Father Robert F. Capon; calories are only a demon to be exorcised; interview, ed. by M. C. Wrenn. R. F. Capon il Life 66:39-40+ Mr 14 '69
Cook for all seasons: Episcopal priest, R. F. Capon. il Time 93:64 Ap 4 '69
COOKERY contests. See Cookery—Competitions
COOKERY in automobile engines. See Cookery, Outdoor
COOKERY on yachts. See Cookery, Marine
COOKERY programs. See Television broadcasting—Cookery programs
COOKIES
ABCs of drop cookies. F. Crawford. il Am Home 72:100 O '69
Bar cookies are good travelers. Sunset 142:188 My '69
Christmas sun cookie. il Good H 169:48 D '69
Lace cookies and buttery spritz. Sunset 143:150 D '69
Mass-producing cookies for a tea. Sunset 142:164-5 Je '69
One recipe, two kinds of cookies; shortbreads. il Sunset 142:206 Ap '69
Pinwheels from a date-nut roll. il Sunset 142:177 Je '69
She's biting into a big carnival cooky. il Sunset 143:220 O '69
These Easter eggs are cookies. il Sunset 142:215-16 Ap '69
These quick cookies travel well. Sunset 143:203 O '69
COOKING. See Cookery
COOKING, Pressure. See Pressure cooking
COOKING utensils. See Kitchen utensils
COOKS
Recipe for a high-paying job. L. David. il Mech Illus 65:47-9+ Mr '69
Who cooks for the White House chef? C. Meyer. McCalls 96:66+ Ag '69
Wonder Child; Julia in her French kitchen. M. R. Henry. il Vogue 153:128-31+ Je '69
See also
Kerr, G.
COOLEY, Denton Arthur
Act of desperation. il por Time 93:58 Ap 18 '69
Artificial heart. Time 93:46 Ap 11 '69
Case of the stolen heart. L. Edson. Esquire 72:170 D '69
Man with a plastic heart. il Newsweek 73:128-9 Ap 14 '69
Natural v. artificial hearts. il por Time 93:42 Ap 4 '69
Too much, too fast? il por Newsweek 73:76+ Ap 21 '69
COOLEY, James Franklin
Arkansas' rebel minister. il pors Ebony 25:82-6 N '69
COOLEY, Leslie J.
Margaret and Les Cooley retire from L.J, Bowker. por Library J 94:1084 Mr 15 '69
COOLEY, Margaret L.
—and others
(ed) Book review. See issues of Library journal to April 15, 1969

about

Margaret and Les Cooley retire from L.J, Bowker. por Library J 94:1084 Mr 15 '69
COOLEY, William W. and Glaser, Robert
Computer and individualized instruction. bibliog Science 166:574-82 O 31 '69
COOLING
See also
Air conditioning
Automobile engines—Cooling
Boats—Cooling
Marine engines—Cooling
Ventilation

COOLING equipment
Amateur scientists; old refrigerators are salvaged to build a laboratory cooler and a gas liquefier. C. L. Stong. il Sci Am 221:151-6 N '69
COON, Caroline
Britain's Release. pors Time 94:56 Jl 18 '69
Ex-model Caroline Coon runs an underground with office hours. H. Johnson. il pors Life 67:55-6+ Ag 22 '69
COON hounds. See Hounds
COONEY, Joan Ganz
Cooney & the kids. Look 33:100-2+ N 18 '69
COONEY, John, and Spitzer, Dana
Hell, no, we won't go! pors Trans-Action 6:53-62 S '69
CO-OP city, Bronx. See New York (city)—Housing
CO-OP colleges. See Education, Cooperative
COOPER, David
Teaching the disadvantaged. Clear House 43:444-6 Mr '69
COOPER, Edwin L.
Specific tissue graft rejection in earthworms. bibliog Science 166:1414-15 D 12 '69
COOPER, Frank A.
Eighty acres that grew to $1/2 million. Farm J 93:52A+ Ap '69
COOPER, Gloria (Vanderbilt) See Vanderbilt, G.
COOPER, Henry S. F. jr
Letter from the space center. New Yorker 45:76-80 Jl 12; 79-83 Jl 19; 85-92 Jl 26; 50-7 Ag 2; 82+ Ag 16; 63-70 Ag 23; 92+ O 11 '69; 46-56 Ja 3 '70
Reporter at large (cont) New Yorker 45:53-4+ Ap 12; 47-8+ Ap 19 '69
COOPER, Jack R. and others
Thiamine triphosphate deficiency in subacute necrotizing encephalomyelopathy. bibliog Science 164:74-5 Ap 4 '69
—See Itokawa, Y. jt. auth.
COOPER, James M. and Seidman, Earl
Helping new teachers focus on behavioral change. Clear House 43:301-6 Ja '69
COOPER, John A. D.
Growing crisis in health care; interview. por U S News 67:70-3 N 3 '69
COOPER, John Sherman
Need for NATO; address, December 9, 1968. Vital Speeches 35:194-6 Ja 15 '69
United Nations extends UNRWA to June 30, 1972; statement, December 6, 1968. Dept State Bul 60:39-42 Ja 13 '69
U.N. legal committee discusses the question of defining aggression; statements, November 19 and 25, 1968. Dept State Bul 59:664-72 D 23 '68
COOPER, L. John
Water and wastewater master plans. Am City 84:136+ O '69
COOPER, Nell R.
Immune adherence by the fourth component of complement. bibliog Science 165:396-8 Jl 25 '69
COOPER, Robert
Marker in a child's history of warfare; poem. Chr Cent 87:6 Ja 7 '70
COOPER, William B.
Ice fever. Parks & Rec 4:53+ S '69
COOPER, Wyatt, family
Merry Christmas at the Wyatt Coopers. il House & Gard 136:48-57 D '69
COOPER-Hewitt museum of decorative arts and design. See Cooper union for the advancement of science and art
COOPER laboratories, incorporated
Master plan at Cooper laboratories. S. Margetts. Duns R 93:72+ Ap '69
COOPER union for the advancement of science and art
Cooper union addition gives plaza as bonus. il Arch Rec 145:114-17 F '69
Incoming tenant; Cooper-Hewitt museum of decorative arts and design. New Yorker 45:32-3 O 4 '69
COOPERATION
See also
Fisheries, Cooperative
Industrial cooperation
International cooperation
Interracial cooperation
Library cooperation
Religious cooperation
COOPERATION, Inter-American. See Inter-American relations
COOPERATION in education. See Colleges and universities—Cooperation
COOPERATIVE associations
Black capitalism on the move. C. T. Rowan and D. Mazie. Read Digest 94:141-5 F '69

COOPERATIVE associations—*Continued*

India

Unknown saint of India: V. Ferrer, with photographs by C. Rentmeester. Life 66:36-44 F 28 '69

Latin America

Impressive gains for cooperatives. il Américas 21:45-6 F '69

COOPERATIVE education. See Education, Cooperative

COOPERATIVE housing. See Housing, Cooperative

COOPERATIVE living establishments. See Collective settlements

COOPERATIVE marketing. See Marketing, Cooperative

COOPERATIVE municipal purchasing. See Purchasing, Municipal

COOPERATIVE nursery schools. See Nursery schools

COOPERMAN, Stanley
Jenifer; poem. Nation 209:676 D 15 '69
Recognition; poem. Nation 208:672 My 26 '69

COOPERSMITH, Stanley, and Silverman, Jan
How to enhance pupil self-esteem. Todays Ed 58:28-9 Ap '69

COOPERSTOCK, Aryeh
How to plan business districts. Am City 84:121-2 Ap '69

COOPERSTOWN, N.Y.
Cooperstown, N.Y. J. Fairhurst. il Home Gard 56:90-1 Ap '69
See also
National baseball hall of fame and museum

COORS, Adolph, company
Ignoring the rules. Forbes 103:34 F 1 '69

COOT (motor vehicle) See Motor vehicles

COOVER, Robert
Magic poker; story. Esquire 72:87-91 Jl '69

COP-out; drama. See Guare, J.

COPAGE, Marc
Double life of Marc Copage. il pors Ebony 25:174-6+ D '69

COPE, Freeman W. See Ling, G. N. jt. auth.

COPE, Myron
(ed) Game that was; symposium. Sports Illus 31:86-8+ O 13; 84-8+ O 20 '69
Little love, and a few punches, make a team. Life 67:79-80+ S 19 '69

COPELAND, Suanne
On campus: student wives. Mlle 69:18 Jl '69

COPENHAGEN

Exhibitions

Sex '69. il Newsweek 74:52 N 3 '69

Music

Report: Copenhagen; production of Monteverdi's Return of Ulysses. J. H. Sutcliffe. Opera N 34:26-7 S 20 '69

COPITS, Louis W.
Winners! Consumer challenge essays. por Har Yrs 9:17 Jl '69

COPLAND, Aaron
Abe Lincoln in Britain. E. Greenfield. il por Hi Fi 19:28+ Mr '69
Brooklyn eagle. R. Evett. Atlan 224:135-6 O '69

COPLAND, Jeri
(ed) See Woodroof, R. H. Should your child go to summer school?

COPLANS, John
(ed) See Oldenburg, C. Artist speaks; Claes Oldenburg

COPLEY, William
New piece. Art in Am 57:36-7 Jl '69

COPPEDGE, Floyd L. See Bartel, R. A. jt. auth.

COPPELIA; ballet. See Ballets—Criticisms

COPPER
Copper, a metal known to ancient man. O. A. Battista. il Chem 42:6-7 S '69

Prices

Copper rises another notch. il Bsns W p37 My 17 '69
Nonferrous metals join the price parade. Bsns W p21-2 Ag 9 '69

COPPER compounds
See also
Azurin

COPPER enameling. See Enamel and enameling

COPPER in the body
Serum copper alteration after ingestion of an oral contraceptive. J. A. O'Leary and W. N. Spellacy; reply. E. Frieden and S. Osaki. Science 163:959 F 28 '69

COPPER industry and trade
See also
Halstead and Mitchell (firm)

Chile

Chile wants more copper cash. Bsns W p37 My 17 '69

United States

Copper's disappearing act. il Bsns W p34-5 N 1 '69

Zambia

Consolation; Zambian nationalization of RST. il Forbes 104:63 O 1 '69

COPPER luster. See Luster ware

COPPER mines and mining
See also
Anaconda copper mining company
Hecla mining company

Chile

Clamor over Chilean copper. il Time 93:75 Je 27 '69
Is anybody listening? il Newsweek 74:33 Jl 7 '69
Putting the squeeze on Anaconda; move to nationalize the copper industry. Bsns W p36 My 31 '69
See also
Continental copper and steel industries, incorporated

Zambia

Nationalization in Zambia foreign-owned copper mines. il Time 94:72 Ag 22 '69

COPROLITES
Another helping of beetles, please. il Sci Digest 66:32-3 N '69
Biological and cultural evidence from prehistoric human coprolites. R. F. Heizer and L. K. Napton. bibliog il Science 165:563-8 Ag 8 '69
See also
Paleopathology

COPULATORY behavior. See Sexual behavior

COPY editors. See Editors and editing

COPY preparation. See Printing—Copy preparation

COPYING processes
Challenge for top copier cats; plain-paper copiers. il Bsns W p 106 N 1 '69
Copyright legislation and you. D. M. Timpano. il Todays Ed 58:18-20 Ap '69
Inexpensive copying machines: Casual copier and Copymate. il Consumer Bul 52:19 D '69
Office machine helps to alert police about crimes; Detroit. il Am City 84:36+ Je '69
Taking on Xerox with a fast copier; AMCD, copier-duplicator. il Bsns W p78+ Ap 26 '69
What happened to the duplicating machine? D. L. Predovich. Ed Digest 34:52-3 Mr '69
See also
Microfilms
Mimeograph
Photography—Copying
Photomechanical processes
Transparencies—Copying
Xerox corporation

COPYRIGHT
ABPC-AEPI joint sessions: copyright: highlights of panel discussions. T. Brennan; L. Albert; B. Ringer. il Pub W 195-33-4 Je 9 '69
Franklin to open clearing house for rights. il Pub W 196:30 D 8 '69
International copyright group meets at Washington. Dept State Bul 61:358 O 27 '69
Israel's copyright chief urges new clearinghouse. Pub W 195:38 My 19 '69
New conference called on international copyright. Pub W 195:42 F 24 '69
1968 in review: copyright developments. Pub W 195:40-1 Mr 10 '69
Patent and copyright conventions transmitted to the Senate; message, March 12, 1969. R. M. Nixon. Dept State Bul 60:298 Ap 7 '69
Technology vs. copyright: form vs. content; report of meeting. Pub W 196:18-20 Ag 11 '69
See also
Royalties

Art

Artists' rights. P. Nathan. Pub W 196:56 O 20 '69

Broadcasting rights

Copyright reform and the CATV issue. R. H. Smith. Pub W 196:35 S 1 '69

Music

Music from the conglomerates. H. W. Heinsheimer. Sat R 52:61+ F 22 '69
Note from the Copyright office. Hi Fi 19:10 Mr '69

COPYRIGHT—*Continued*

Photographs

Pictures and questions; controversy over R. L. Haeberle's pictures of the Songmy massacre. Newsweek 74:57 D 1 '69

Television rights

See Copyright—Broadcasting rights

Titles

What's in a name? Protection of titles. H. F. Pilpel and K. P. Norwick. Pub W 196:21 Ag 11 '69

Unauthorized reprints

Copyright legislation and you. D. M. Timpano. il Todays Ed 58:18-20 Ap '69
European literary scene; behavior of certain American reprint publishers. R. J. Clements. Sat R 52:27 My 3 '69

Japan

Japan's inscrutable policies on royalties and copyrights. L. E. Kern. jr. il Pub W 195: 39-41 F 10 '69; Discussion. 195:44 Ap 7: 81 Ap 28: 11-12 My 26 '69

United States

Business pending with adjournment in the offing. G. Krettek and E. D. Cooke. Wilson Lib Bul 44:578-9 Ja '70
Congress passes interim copyright extension. S. Wagner. Pub W 196:18-19 D 15 '69
Copyright revision bill introduced in Senate. Pub W 195:46+ F 10 '69
Copyright: technology, ethics, and instruction. R. Gilkey. Clear House 44:255-6 D '69
Is this the year for the copyright bill? Pub W 195:75-6 Ja 27 '69
Music from the conglomerates. H. W. Heinsheimer. Sat R 52:61+ F 22 '69
Prospects wane for action on copyright. S. Wagner. Pub W 196:40 S 29 '69
Rights and permissions. P. Nathan. See issues of Publishers' weekly
Rights and permissions: definitions and basics; foreign rights; book club rights; permissions procedures; symposium. il Pub W 196:22-6 Ag 4 '69
Senate heads for possible copyright vote this fall. S. Wagner. Pub W 196:39 Ag 18 '69
Senate subcommittee votes copyright revision bill. S. Wagner. Pub W 196:39 D 29 '69
COPYRIGHT and television. See Copyright—Broadcasting rights
COPYRIGHT infringement
Speed is of the essence in infringement cases. H. F. Pilpel and K. P. Norwick. Pub W 195:24 My 5 '69
CORACLES. See Boats and boating
CORAL reefs and islands
Destruction of Pacific corals by the sea star acanthaster planci. R. H. Chesher. bibliog il Science 165:280-3 Jl 18 '69; Reply. J. L. Fischer. 165:645 Ag 15 '69
Park beneath the sea; John Pennekamp coral reef state park. M. Michaelson. il Todays Health 47:28-33 Mr '69
See also
Great Barrier Reef
CORALS
Reef coral from Aldabra: new mode of reproduction. B. R. Rosen and J. D. Taylor. bibliog il Science 166:119-21 O 3 '69
Tropical reef corals: tolerance of low temperatures on the North Carolina continental shelf. I. G. MacIntyre and O. H. Pilkey. bibliog il Science 166:374-5 O 17 '69
CORBET, Philip S.
Terrestrial microclimate: amelioration at high latitudes. bibliog Science 166:865-8 N 14 '69
CORBETT, J. Ralph
Corbett foundation, a chance to make good. S. Fleming. Hi Fi 19:MA6 Jl '69
Happiest angel. Q. Eaton. il por Opera N 34: 20-1 D 6 '69
CORBETT, Ralph. See Corbett, J. R.
CORBIT, John D.
Behavioral regulation of hypothalamic temperature. bibliog Science 166:256-8 O 10 '69
CORCHORUS
Corchorus pascuorum: transmission of chemically induced fruit formation with environmental change. A. S. Islam and R. Mughal. bibliog il Science 164:315-16 Ap 18 '69

CORCORAN gallery Dupont circle
Capital art. il Newsweek 74:117-117A N 24 '69
New look for old tradition; 31st biennial. il Time 93:60-1+ F 7 '69
CORDELL, Dick
Airflow facts; interview, ed. by J. Dianna. Hot Rod 22:48-50 N '69
CORDIALS. See Liqueurs
CORDIER, Andrew Wellington
New president of Columbia. por Sch & Soc 97:473-4 D '69
Reluctant president. por Newsweek 74:55 S 1 '69
CORDLESS shavers. See Razors
CÓRDOVA, France
Traveling with Mlle: *shalom*, we echo *shalom!* Mlle 69:346-7+ Ag '69
CORDS, Electric. See Electric cords
CORDTZ, Dan
Change begins in the doctor's office. Fortune 81:84-9+ Ja '70
COREY, E. J. and Wipke, W. T.
Computer-assisted design of complex organic syntheses. bibliog Science 166:178-92 O 10 '69
CORFU (island)
Corfu: from Caesar to Constantine. F. Shea. il Sat R 52:76+ Mr 8 '69
CORINTH, Kay, and Sargent, Mary
Do his manners need help? excerpts from Male manners. Seventeen 28:134-5 N '69
CORIOLANUS (literary character) See Shakespeare, W.—Characters
CORIOLANUS; drama. See Shakespeare, W.—Plays
CORITA, Sister. See Kent, C.
CORLEY, Bob
Dry-mount your favorite photos for display. Pop Mech 131:148-50 My '69
CORLISS, Allene
Girl to remember; story. Good H 168:70-1 F '69
CORLISS, Richard
Film chronicle. Nat R 21:82-3, 292-3, 606-7, 760-1, 970-1, 1177-9 Ja 28, Mr 25, Je 17, Jl 29, S 23, N 18 '69
Still Legion, still decent? Commonweal 90: 288-93 My 23 '69
CORMIER, Robert
Charlie Mitchell, you rat, be kind to my little girl; story. McCalls 96:106-7 Ap '69
CORMS. See Bulbs
CORN
Alcohol dehydrogenase in maize: genetic basis for isozymes. J. G. Scandalios. bibliog il Science 166:623-4 O 31 '69
Alcohol dehydrogenase in maize: genetic basis for multiple isozymes. D. Schwartz. bibliog il Science 164:585-6 My 2 '69
Androgenesis by a mutation in maize. J. L. Kermicle. bibliog il Science 166:1422-4 D 12 '69
Corn crop. D. Seim. Farm J 93:27 S '69
How to plan corn handling for cattle. Suc Farm 67:39 D '69
See also
Cornstalks

Cultivation

Extra bushels from 20-inch rows. il Farm J 93:24D Jl '69
How corn reacts to thicker planting. C. E. Sommers. il Suc Farm 67:30-1+ Je '69
How to get the corn stand you want. il Suc Farm 67:40-1+ Mr '69
173-bu. corn nets $106 an acre. il Farm J 93:36E My '69

Diseases and pests

Check now for corn insects. Suc Farm 67: 62 Jl '69
Weed control for corn and soybeans. Suc Farm 67:64+ F '69
See also
Corn rootworms
European corn borers

Harvesting

He broke the corn harvest bottleneck. P. B. Jones. il Suc Farm 67:26-7 Jl '69

History

Fossil maize from Panama. A. S. Bartlett and others. bibliog il Science 165:389-90 Jl 25 '69

Hybrids

Corn, what's coming in new hybrids? R. D. Wennblom. il Farm J 93:30-1+ Mr '69
High protein corn, just what's involved? C. E. Sommers. il Suc Farm 67:52 Ap '69

CORPORATE acquisitions—*Continued*
Mergers are on everybody's mind; seminar on Managing the moderate-sized company. il Bsns W p 150-2 Ap 26 '69
New light on takeover defense; Chemical bank's battle plan. il Bsns W p89-90+ N 22 '69
Peril-point acquisition prices. J. F. Crowther. il Harvard Bsns R 47:58-62 S '69
Pioneer on the sidelines; Wattles of Eltra corp. Forbes 103:22-3 My 1 '69
Piper proves elusive prize. il Bsns W p62+ Ag 16 '69
Play the who-makes-it game; quiz. Changing T 23:47 O '69
Signal: the careful conglomerate. J. B. Weiner. il Duns R 93:38-42+ Mr '69
Steinberg's complaint; attempt to acquire New York's Chemical bank. il Forbes 103: 179+ My 15 '69
That long, lively pursuit of A.B.C. C. J. Loomis. il Fortune 79:130-4+ Mr '69
Warning: it may be later than you think. il Forbes 103:65+ F 15 '69
What next? acquisition of Jones motor co. Forbes 103:218 My 15 '69
When a takeover runs out of gas; Liquidonics and UMC. Bsns W p32 O 4 '69
Why rain fell on Automatic sprinkler. W. S. Rukeyser. il Fortune 79:88-91+ My 1 '69
Will White unload its stake in Allis? FTC opposition to merger. Bsns W p31-2 Jl 26 '69
See also
Conglomerate corporations
Diversification in industry
CORPORATE budget. See Budget, Business
CORPORATE distributions
Spin-off; one minus one equals three? A. Hershman. il Duns R 93:31-3 Mr '69
CORPORATE giving. See Corporations—Charitable contributions
CORPORATE liability. See Liability (law)
CORPORATE planning. See Business management and organization
CORPORATION for public broadcasting
Building constituencies. R. L. Shayon. Sat R 52:44 My 3 '69
Public broadcasting. J. McLaughlin. America 120:510-11 Ap 26 '69
Senatorial goose bumps; subcommittee hearings on the Magnuson bill. R. L. Shayon. Sat R 52:36 My 24 '69
TV and the arts. J. Tebbel; P. H. Adler. Sat R 52:19-25+ Ap 26 '69
Whither public TV? Newsweek 73.104 Ap 21 '69
CORPORATION law
Cool, creative company lawyers. J. Poindexter. il Duns R 93:34-7 Mr '69
CORPORATION lawyers. See Lawyers
CORPORATION management. See Business management and organization
CORPORATION reports
Companies get gabbier, reports get flossier. Bsns W p84 Ap 19 '69
Corporate reports open wider. il Bsns W p56-8 Mr 29 '69

Anecdotes, facetiae, satire, etc.
Annual report of the National refractory & brake company. W. Zinsser. il Life 66: 59-60+ F 28 '69
CORPORATIONS
Age of discontinuity, by P. Drucker. Review Commentary 47:102-7 Je '69. F. F. Heilmann
Difficult years; next four years. L. L. L. Golden. Sat R 52:63 F 8 '69
Four dimensions of American business; with directories. il Forbes 103:56-60+ My 15 '69
Luxury of privacy. Forbes 103:186+ My 15 '69
Rise of the techno-corporate state in America. A. S. Miller. Bul Atom Sci 25:14-19 Ja '69
See also
Bonds
Business consolidations and mergers
Conglomerate corporations
Executives
Family corporations
Farm corporations
Holding companies
Investments
Monopolies
Negro corporations
Public utilities

Accounting
Accountants turn tougher. il Bsns W p 124-5+ O 18 '69
Bit of rouge for Allis-Chalmers. H. B. Meyers. Fortune 79:234+ My 15 '69

Conglomerates face an accounting. C. Morgello. Newsweek 73:66 Ap 7 '69
Cooking the books to fatten profits. il Time 93:96 Ap 11 '69
CSPC: reporting project progress to the top. A. R. Saltow. il Harvard Bsns R 47:88-97 Ja '69
How much is the help worth? Bsns W p37 D 27 '69
Materials management as a profit center. D. S. Ammer. bibliog f il Harvard Bsns R 47:72-82 Ja '69
Strategy for financial emergencies. G. Donaldson. il Harvard Bsns R 47:67-79 N '69

Advertising
Confessions of an ad manager. L. Geist. Duns R 93:54-6+ Ap '69

Cash position
See Corporations—Finance

Charitable contributions
We gave at the office. il Forbes 104:54+ D 1 '69
See also
Foundations, Charitable and educational

Directories
500 biggest corporations by market value. Forbes 103:78+ My 15 '69
500 biggest corporations by net profits. Forbes 103:119+ My 15 '69
500 biggest corporations by revenues. Forbes 103:63-4+ My 15 '69
Fortune directory; 200 largest industrials outside the U.S. C. Haight. il Fortune 80:106-11 Ag 15 '69
Fortune directory; with introd. by E. J. Tracy. Fortune 79:166-202 My 15 '69

Directors
Is executive insurance worth it? S. H. Lieberstein. Duns R 94:53-4+ Jl '69
Roster of the country's biggest corporations. Forbes 103:128-33+ My 15 '69
Rules of the game; how companies make the Forbes 500 directory. il Forbes 103:174 My 15 '69
Squeeze on the directors. C. J. Loomis. il Fortune 79:146-50+ My 15 '69
U.S. moneymen: no innocence abroad. J. Ross-Skinner. il Duns R 93:48-9+ My '69
What do you people want? transfer of big companies to black control. R. F. America, jr. il Harvard Bsns R 47:103-12 Mr '69

Finance
Beyond expectations. Time 93:85-6 F 14 '69
Big grow much bigger. Time 93:98 My 23 '69
Building a corporate financial model. G. W. Gershefski. il Harvard Bsns R 47:61-72 Jl '69
Business trends 1969: a trillion dollar economy. il Sr Schol 94:7 Ja 31 '69
Case against ROI control. J. Dearden. il Harvard Bsns R 47:124-35 My '69
Cash is for the banks; with table. Forbes 103:68 Je 15 '69
Cash-rich are different. W. Robertson. il Fortune 79:83-4+ My 15 '69
Casualty list; stock market casualties. il Forbes 104:24-5 S 1 '69
Cooking the books to fatten profits. il Time 93:96 Ap 11 '69
Cooling off shows in earnings. il Bsns W p38-9 O 18 '69
Do profit centers really work? G. J. Berkwitt. il Duns R 93:29-31+ My '69
Earnings sky is still sunny. il Bsns W p48+ F 22 '69
Final 1968 profits look rosy; corporate earnings above 1967 level. Bsns W p40 Ja 25 '69
Financial realities of mergers; excerpts from address, March 28, 1969. J. S. R. Shad. il Harvard Bsns R 47:133-46 My '69
Fourth-quarter profits: still at a record level. il U S News 66:52 F 17 '69
Hard-pressed treasurers. il Fortune 79:28 Mr '69
How business lives beyond its means; cash management. il Bsns W p72+ N 15 '69
How the profit squeeze is taking hold. il U S News 67:37 N 3 '69
How to analyze foreign investment climates. R. B. Stobaugh, jr. bibliog f il Harvard Bsns R 47:100-8 S '69
Is your company a take-over target? J. O. Vance. il Harvard Bsns R 47:93-8 My '69
Latest on profits: still rising, but for how long? il U S News 66:62 My 5 '69
Peril-point acquisition prices. J. F. Crowther. il Harvard Bsns R 47:58-62 S '69

CORPORATIONS—Finance—*Continued*
Pressure is on profits. Bsns W p58+ Ag 2 '69
Profits lose a little savor. il Bsns W p 102 My 10 '69
Profits may have a leaner look. Bsns W p29-30 Jl 19 '69
Profits take extra bounce. il Bsns W p28-9 F 8 '69
Profits up, as expected. il Bsns W p35 Ap 19 '69
Second-quarter profits: first sign of a squeeze. U S News 67:50 Ag 4 '69
Third-quarter earnings are leaner. il Bsns W p53 N 1 '69
Top 500: assets; with directory. il Forbes 103:90-2+ My 15 '69
Tough enough to join the EEC; British companies. il Bsns W p46-7 S 27 '69
Who owns the US? New Repub 160:6 Ap 5 '69
Worried swingers of high finance. J. Poindexter. il Duns R 93:43-7 My '69
See also
Budget, Business
Corporate distributions
Corporations—Accounting
Corporations—Valuation
Small business—Finance
Stock purchase options

Statistics
Top 500: net profits. il Forbes 103:102-4+ My 15 '69
Top 500: revenues; with directory. il Forbes 103:58-60+ My 15 '69

Foreign expansion
See Business—Foreign expansion

Foreign subsidiaries
Borderline industry; effect of industrialization program in Mexico. il Newsweek 73:82+ Je 23 '69
Challenge of multinational business. R. Lubar. Fortune 80:73-4 Ag 15 '69
Europeans defect from U.S. companies. Bsns W p62+ Je 7 '69
Go Mexican or else. . ; pressure to persuade subsidiaries of two U.S. mining companies to take in local partners. Bsns W p24 F 1 '69
In Latin America: growing threats to U.S. companies. J. Benham. il U S News 67:68-70 Jl 14 '69
Managers away from home; proconsuls. R. S. Diamond. il Fortune 80:56-8+ Ag 15 '69
Nassau basks in new business climate; lure: no taxes. il Bsns W p 118+ Mr 22 '69
Sophistication comes to the tax havens. R. Beardwood. il Fortune 79:94-7+ F '69
Subsidiary that rebelled; McKee and CTIP. il Time 94:68 Jl 25 '69
Trouble spots for U.S. firms. U S News 67:7 Jl 7 '69
U.S. moneymen: no innocence abroad. J. Ross-Skinner. il Duns R 93:48-9+ My '69
What strategy for the third world? R. Vernon. il Sat R 52:42-6 N 22 '69
What U.S. companies are doing abroad. See issues of U S news & World report

Laws and legislation
See Corporation law

Names
Corporate image. W. Zinsser. il Life 67:57-8+ N 7 '69
Doctors of the corporate ego. R. Beardwood. il Fortune 79:108-10+ My 1 '69
Image is money in the name game. il Bsns W p37-9 Ja 3 '70
What did you say the company's name was (is)? il Forbes 103:31-2 Ap 15 '69

Public relations
See Business—Public relations

Real estate operations
Big money plays in the snow; ski area investments. il Bsns W p 142+ O 25 '69
Making land holdings part of the business. Bsns W p92+ Ag 9 '69
Old formula, new Field. Time 93:92+ Ap 11 '69

Size
Bigness is a numbers game. S. Rose. il Fortune 80:112-15+ N '69
Bigness means efficiency. il Bsns W p 162+ F 22 '69

Social aspects
See Business—Social aspects

Taxation
Big companies foot big bills for U.S. Nations Bsns 57:55 Jl '69
Federal taxation; cost of capital; address, December 6, 1968. N. B. Ture. Vital Speeches 35:221-4 Ja 15 '69
Golden ox of antitrust; question of whether treble damage payments are deductible. M. Mintz. Nation 208:467-8 Ap 14 '69
Hitting the big taxpayers a bit harder; Canadian tax reform. Bsns W p 170 N 22 '69
Reform ticket for companies, too. il Bsns W p64+ Je 21 '69
Sophistication comes to the tax havens. R. Beardwood. il Fortune 79:94-7+ F '69
Surviving June 16; quarterly tax liabilities. Bsns W p39 Je 21 '69
Tax haven for the professions? New headache for revenue men. il U S News 67:70-1 Jl 7 '69
Welcome to the state of confusion; when a business crosses state lines. il Nations Bsns 57:72-4 Ag '69
Why doctors and lawyers call themselves Inc; fight for corporate tax status. il Bsns W p80+ Jl 12 '69

Treasurers
Worried swingers of high finance. J. Poindexter. il Duns R 93:43-7 My '69

Valuation
Loaded laggards: the list for 1969; with tables. Forbes 103:54-6 Je 15 '69
Most fleeting asset; stock-market value of Recognition equipment. il Forbes 103:84-5 Je 15 '69
Poets and prices. R. Brady. Duns R 93:119-20 My '69
Polaroid; market value of its stock. il Forbes 103:34-6+ Je 15 '69
Skeptic's stock market. R. Brady. il Duns R 93:105-7 Mr '69
Top 500: market value; with directory. il Forbes 103:74-6+ My 15 '69
Very special situations. R. Brady. Duns R 93:103-4 Ap '69

CORPORATIONS, Foreign
See also
Corporations, International

CORPORATIONS, International
Agfa-Gevaert, model merger? il Bsns W p62-7 Jl 5 '69
American business abroad; symposium. il Sat R 52:31-6+ N 22 '69
Global giants; study by S. E. Rolfe. Newsweek 73:88+ My 19 '69
Importing woe for the worker. il Bsns W p66-8 Jl 26 '69
Nationalism sets boundaries for multinational giants. il Bsns W p94-6+ Je 14 '69
New world symphony; excerpt from World business: promise and problems. C. C. Brown. Sat R 52:56 N 22 '69
Technology transfer by multinational companies. J. B. Quinn. bibliog f il Harvard Bsns R 47:147-61 N '69
See also
Philips of Eindhoven companies

CORPORATIONS, Nonprofit
See also
Rand corporation

CORPORATIONS, Private. See Corporations
CORPORATIONS and education. See Business and education
CORPORATIONS entertaining. See Business entertaining
CORPS of engineers. See United States—Army —Corps of engineers
CORPULENCE
Calories count. Sci Digest 66:72-3 N '69
Can you stay slim after dieting? J. C. G. Conniff. Read Digest 94:69-72 F '69
Fat child. il Good H 169:40+ Jl '69
Fat folks' hidden secrets. A. J. Snider. il Sci Digest 66:58-9 Jl '69
How to stop from going to pot; executives joining I can't afford to lose you club. il Time 93:80 My 30 '69
My mother made me fat; symposium, ed. by G. Krupp. Redbook 132:52-4+ Ja '69
New life for Helen Rogers. J. Wilkie. il Good H 169:20+ Ag '69
Obesity. A. Lake. Seventeen 28:128-9+ O '69
Obesity starts in childhood il Sci Digest 65:59-60 My '69
Overweight: what to do; interview. J. Mayer. il U S News 67:60-4 O 20 '69
See also
Weight (physiology)
Weight watchers, incorporated

CORRADINO, Joseph C.
Busways may woo the rider back to mass transit. Am City 84:98-9 F '69
CORRECTIONAL institutions. See Reformatories
CORRECTIVE teaching. See Remedial teaching
CORRELATION (education)
Teaming a first step for interdisciplinary teaching. J. A. Meyer. Clear House 43:406-10 Mr '69
See also
Art—Study and teaching—Projects
CORRELATION protected instrument landing system. See Airplanes—Landing
CORRESPONDENCE schools and courses
Learning by mail; courses for writers. il Writers Digest 49:43-7+ S '69
See also
Famous artists schools, incorporated
National home study council
CORRESPONDENTS association, United Nations. See United Nations correspondents association
CORRIGAN, Douglas
Where are they now? il pors Newsweek 74:16 D 1 '69
CORRIGAN, John J.
d-Amino acids in animals. bibliog Science 164:142-9 Ap 11 '69
CORROSION and anticorrosives
Corrosion and infestation. E. A. Zadig. il Motor R 123:56-9+ F '69
Electronics of corrosion. W. P. Ferren. il Electr World 82:42-5+ N '69
Salvaged DC-8 test-flown after overhaul. Aviation W 90:46 Ap 7 '69
Sea, a challenge for materials. D. Groves. il Sea Front 15:356-63 N '69
CORRUPTION in politics. See Politics, Corruption in
CORRY, John
Castro's Cuba: drums, guns, and the new man. Harper 238:37-45 Ap '69
God, country, and Billy Graham. Harper 238:33-9 F '69
Greece: the death of liberty. Harper 239:72-81 O '69
Los Angeles times. Harper 239:74-6+ D '69
Return of Ted Williams. Harper 238:73-8 Je '69
CORSARO, Frank
Frank Corsaro; interview, ed. by C. L. Osborne. Hi Fi 19:MA25 My '69

about

Corsaro, Capobianco, and Merrill. D. Hering. il por Dance Mag 43:28-30 Mr '69
CORSICA
Last colony. E. Behr. il Newsweek 74:31-2 Ag 11 '69
One morning in Corsica. H. Sutton. Sat R 52:49-50 S 20 '69

History

Thought and practice of enlightened government in French Corsica: adaptation of address, December 29, 1967. T. E. Hall. bibliog f Am Hist R 71:880-905 F '69
CORSINI, Gianfranco
Opinion: responsibilities of the American intellectual. por Mlle 69:24+ Je '69
CORSO, Gregory
Somewhere else with Allen and Gregory; excerpt from My son's father. D. Moraes. il pors Horizon 11:66-7 Wint '69
CORSON, John J.
Social change and the university. Sat R 53:76+ Ja 10 '70
CORT, John
Mopes; poems. Esquire 72:133 O '69
CORT, John C.
Catholic worker and the ugly-lovely face of poverty. Commonweal 90:114-16 Ap 11 '69
CORTADERIA argentia. See Pampas grass
CORTEGE burlesque: ballet. See Ballets—Criticisms
CORTÉS, Manuel
Man upstairs. por Time 93:29 My 2 '69
CORTEZ, SEA OF. See California, Gulf of
CORTICOSTEROIDS
Prostaglandin stimulation of rat corticosteroidogenesis. J. D. Flack and others. bibliog il Science 163:691-2 F 14 '69
CORTICOSTERONE
Corticosterone regulation of tryptophan hydroxylase in midbrain of the rat. E. C. Azmitia, jr. and B. S. McEwen. bibliog il Science 166:1274-6 D 5 '69
Potassium, corticosterone, and adrenocorticotropic hormone release in vitro. J. Kraicer and others. bibliog il Science 164:426 Ap 25 '69

CORTISOL. See Hydrocortisone
CORTISONE
See also
Hydrocortisone
CORVO, Frederick, baron, pseud. See Rolfe, F. W.
CORWIN, Ronald G.
Enhancing teaching as a career. Todays Ed 58:55 Mr '69
CORY, John M.
Ad hoc harmony. por Library J 94:264-6 Ja 15 '69
CORYELL, Schofield
OPLAN NR 1-10; excerpt from report. Ramp Mag 8:9 O '69
COS lettuce. See Lettuce
COSA nostra. See Mafia
COSBY, Bill
Bill Cosby on chicken football. por Look 33:94 N 4 '69

about

I am two people, man. T. B. Morgan. il pors Life 66:74-74B+ Ap 11 '69
Pleasures and problems of being Bill Cosby. L. Robinson. il pors Ebony 24:144-6+ Jl '69
COSGRAVE, Mary Silva
Outlook tower. Horn Bk 45:433-5, 552-3, 697-9 Ag-D '69
COSGROVE, John Edward
Toward assuring family security. America 121:580 D 13 '69
COSINDAS, Marie
Portrait of Hilary; photographs. Life 67:97-101 N 7 '69
COSMETIC creams. See Cosmetics
COSMETIC industry and trade
See also
Smith Kline and French laboratories
COSMETIC surgery. See Surgery, Facial; Surgery, Plastic
COSMETICS
Beauty checkout. See issues of Vogue
Burned: para-aminobenzoic acid as a sun screen agent. il Newsweek 74:62 Jl 14 '69
Drug prevents sunburn. il Sci Digest 66:61 O '69
Undertoners, they wake up make-up. il Redbook 132:82-3+ Mr '69
Your face on a fitness kick. il Harp Baz 102:178-9 My '69
See also
Deodorants
Make-up
Toilet preparations

Advertising

Drugstore love-in; campaign for promoting Love cosmetics. il Time 93:93 Mr 14 '69
COSMETICS for men
Dear beauty editors: questions and answers. McCalls 96:40 Je '69
Is the man in your life afraid? il Harp Baz 102:120-1 Jl '69
Men are spending money on beauty. C. Kriebel. il Harp Baz 102:168-9 O '69
Who was that man? il Mlle 69:140-1 Je '69
COSMIC abundances. See Chemical elements
COSMIC physics
See also
Astrophysics
Magnetic fields (cosmic physics)
COSMIC rays
Astrophysics of cosmic rays. V. L. Ginzburg. il Sci Am 220:50-63 bibliog (p 132) F '69
Five cosmic events; quarks. Sci N 96:198-9 S 13 '69

Measurement

Setting a trap for cosmic rays. il Bsns W p50 Ag 23 '69

Physiological effects

Great dinosaur disaster. D. Cohen. il Sci Digest 65:45-52 Mr '69
COSMOCHRONOTROPE
Cosmochronotrope. O. R. Hagans. il Hobbies 74:126-7+ D '69
COSMOGONY
Universe: did it begin? Will it end? H. C. Stubbs. il Todays Ed 58:26-8 S '69
See also
Universe
COSMOLOGY
Antimatter, quasi-stellar objects, and the evolution of galaxies. H. Alfvén and A. Elvius. bibliog il Science 164:911-17 My 23 '69
Hierarchical structures: report of symposium at the Douglas advanced research laboratories. Huntington Beach, Calif. T. Page. il Science 163:1228-30 Mr 14 '69; Reply. A. G. Wilson. 165:202 Jl 11 '69

COURTS martial and courts of inquiry—*Cont.*
  Court-martial of Lt. Susan Schnall. S. Streshinsky. Redbook 134:78-9+ N '69
  Curbing courts-martial; cases against servicemen charged with serious civil offenses. Time 93:66 Je 13 '69
  Dilemmas of duty. il Life 66:14F-23 F 7 '69
  Eighteen minute verdict. M. Polner. Commonweal 90:40-3; 91:3+ Mr 28, O 3 '69
  End of the affair; Pueblo case. il Newsweek 73:34-5 My 19 '69
  Fragments but no conclusion; investigating the destruction of the submarine Scorpion. il Sci N 95:163 F 15 '69
  Green Berets to trial. il Newsweek 74:41 S 29 '69
  I never surrendered; Pueblo's skipper. il Newsweek 73:27 Mr 24 '69
  In the matter of Lloyd Mark Bucher. B. Weinraub. il N Y Times Mag p25-7+ My 11 '69
  Investigations: catch-68; capture of U.S.S. Pueblo. il Time 93:19-20 F 7 '69
  Is Bucher to blame? New Repub 160:11-12 F 8 '69
  Korean roulette. Newsweek 73:25-6 F 24 '69
  Matthew Morgenthau's complaint. D. Sanford. New Repub 160:14-15 Mr 1 '69
  Message for deserters. il Newsweek 73:35-6 Mr 17 '69
  Military justice; learning from the Green Berets. E. F. Sherman. Nation 209:399-403 O 20 '69
  More on the strange story of the Pueblo. il U S News 66:33-4 F 10 '69
  Mutineers; penalties for men found guilty at Fort Ord, Calif. Time 93:17 Je 13 '69
  Mutiny in the Presidio; trial of army prisoners who staged sitdown protest in San Francisco. il Time 93:17-18 F 21 '69
  Other Harris; testimony of Pueblo's officer in charge of research center spaces. il Time 93:17 F 21 '69
  Pass the buck; testimony of Admiral Johnson on capture of the Pueblo. Newsweek 73:23-4 F 10 '69
  Presidio mutiny; sentences for those participating in sit-down demonstration at the San Francisco stockade. P. Barnes. New Repub 161:21-5 Jl 5 '69
  Proud men of the Pueblo. il Read Digest 94:54-61 Je '69
  Pueblo: an odyssey of anguish replayed. il Time 93:14-16 Ja 31 '69
  Pueblo and L.B.J. il Time 93:22 F 14 '69
  Pueblo case: an official decision, but still a lot of loose ends. il U S News 66:16 My 19 '69
  Pueblo: don't give up the ship, ever? il Newsweek 73:24-8+ F 3 '69
  Pueblo surrender: who made the mistakes? il U S News 66:58-9 F 24 '69
  Pueblo; whodunit? New Repub 160:7-8 F 15 '69
  Pueblo's chief spy. il Newsweek 73:32 F 17 '69
  Reporter at large; soldier government witness in court-martial proceedings against four American soldiers in rape-murder case. D. Lang. New Yorker 45:61-4+ O 18 '69
  Strange tale of the Pueblo. U S News 66:50-1 F 3 '69
  Tough test for military justice; Green Beret case. il Time 94:50-1 O 3 '69
  Twenty-seven Billie Budds; prisoners in stockade of the Presidio of San Francisco. Nation 208:261 Mr 3 '69
COURTS of inquiry. See Courts martial and courts of inquiry
COURTSHIP
  See also
  Bundling
  Dating
  Love
COURTSHIP of animals
  Courtship in the natural world. J. A. Weeks. il Cons 23:21-7 F '69
  Timber titan; battles of wapiti. W. Peterson. il Nat Wildlife 7:4-7 Je '69
COURTSHIP of birds
  Courtship in the natural world. J. A. Weeks. il Cons 23:21-7 F '69
COURTSHIP of insects
  Flashes and behavior of some American fireflies. J. E. Lloyd. bibliog il Cons 23:8-12 Je '69
COURTYARDS
  At home on a private plaza. il Life 66:68-70+ Je 20 '69
COUSCOUS. See Cookery, North African
COUSINS, Margaret
  How to foil the burglar. House B 111:72-3+ F '69

COUSINS, Norman
  How the U.S. spurned three chances for peace in Vietnam. Look 33:45-8 Jl 29 '69
  Vietnam: the spurned peace. Sat R 52:12-16+ Jl 26 '69; Same abr. with title How the U.S. spurned three chances for peace in Vietnam. Look 33:45-8 Jl 29 '69
COUSTEAU, Jacques Yves
  How we film under the sea. por Pop Sci 194:65-9+ F '69
COUSTEAU, Philippe
  Dangerous creatures of the deep. C. B. Jackson. il Nat Wildlife 7:50-5 Ag '69
COUSY, Bob
  Vintage Litwack spoiled the grand exit. W. F. Reed. jr. il por Sports Illus 30:50-1 Mr 31 '69
COUVE DE MURVILLE, Maurice Jacques
  Common touch might come in handy. E. Behr. il por Newsweek 73:44-5 Ja 27 '69
  Painful event. Newsweek 74:56+ N 10 '69
COVE; story. See Berriault, G.
COVENT Garden opera company. See Royal opera, Great Britain
COVER design. See Book covers
COVER plants
  Flowering groundcovers. J. W. Wilson. il Horticulture 47:26-9+ Jl '69
  Green carpets for your garden. B. C. Kilvert, jr. Am Home 72:86-7 My '69
  Groundcovers for the dry country. F. B. Widmoyer and D. T. Sullivan. il Horticulture 47:40-2 F '69
  What to put where grass won't grow; with list of ground covers. il Changing T 23:45-7 My '69
  See also
  Ice plants (botany)
COVERLETS
  Bedspread racks. il House & Gard 135:102-3 F '69
  Here and now; midsummer pickup for the bedroom doldrums. T. Bowman. il House B 111:80-1 Ag '69
  Stylish spread. T. Bowman. il House B 111:82-3 Mr '69
  See also
  Afghans (coverlets)
COVERS (philately)
  First day covers. H. Herst, jr. Hobbies 74:131+ S '69
COVEY, Barbara L.
  Turning in and turning on the nonverbals. Am Ed 5:9-11 Je '69
COVINGTON, Va.
  Parade, charade, crusade. il Am City 84:132+ Ag '69
  Programmed lighting a must. P. R. Kelley. il Am City 84:120 Ag '69
COWAN, Edward
  Oil on the waters. Nation 208:304-7 Mr 10 '69
COWAN, Zélide. See Teague, M. jt. auth.
COWARD, Noel
  Noel Coward at seventy; interview. pors Time 94:46 D 26 '69
        about
  Private lives. Criticism
    Commonweal 91:409 Ja 9 '70
    Nation 209:704 D 22 '69
    New Yorker 45:115 D 13 '69
    Newsweek il 94:117 D 15 '69
    Sat R 52:36 D 20 '69
    Time il 94:84 D 12 '69
COWBOYS
  See also
  Rodeos
COWBOYS (football club) See Football clubs
COWDEN, Jeanne
  Adventures with South Africa's black eagles. il pors Nat Geog 136:532-43 O '69
COWES week. See Regattas
COWLE, Irving
  Some goals for the seventies. Camp Mag 41:10-11 Ja '69
COWLEY, Robert
  Does your room look like the Collyer brothers? Horizon 11:44-5 Wint '69
COWNE, Leslie J.
  Approaches to the mental health manpower problem. bibliog Ment Hy 53:176-87 Ap '69
COWS
  See also
  Milking
        Care
  Keep your cows on their toes; hoof trimming. C. Peterson, jr. il Suc Farm 67:82 Mr '69
        Culling
  When to cull dairy cows. Suc Farm 67:A6 My '69

COWS—*Continued*

Diseases and pests
See also
Mastitis

Feeding
Cows, legumes, grasses, sure profit trio. J. R. Borcherding. il Suc Farm 67:46-7 D '69
Group feed in one corral. R. G. Fowler. il Farm J 93:D8-9 F '69
He gets more from silos and cows. J. R. Borcherding. il Suc Farm 67:34-5 Je '69
No silage for his cows. C. Paterson, jr. il Suc Farm 67:40 Je '69
They milk real tank-fillers. J. R. Borcherding. il Suc Farm 67:B6 Ap '69
See also
Antibiotic feed supplements

Milk production
See Milk—Production
COX, Allan
Geomagnetic reversals; adaptation of address, April 8, 1968. bibliog Science 163:237-45 Ja 17 '69
COX, Annis
For the defense; poem. Engl J 58:68 Ja '69
COX, Arthur M.
Is peace in Vietnam possible? Sat R 52:38-9 Mr 22 '69
Shadowboxing in Saigon. New Repub 160: 14-15 Ap 12 '69
COX, Bruce
Red nationalists and uncle tomahawks. Trans-Action 6:60-1 F '69
COX, Donald
Learning on the road. Sat R 52:71 My 17 '69
COX, Edward
Miners play rough. New Repub 161:13-14 Ag 2 '69
Noiseless, nontoxic steam engine. New Repub 160:12-14 Je 28 '69
COX, Elsie A.
Environment and plant diseases. Horticulture 48:32-3 Ja '70
COX, Harvey
Buckle down, John Harvard. Commonweal 90: 22-4 My 9 '69
In praise of festivity; excerpt from The feast of fools. Sat R 52:25-8 O 25 '69
Issues for the '70s. Commonweal 90:18-20 Mr 21 '69
Kickoff at Harvard. Commonweal 91:64-5 O 17 '69
Rubem Alves: hopeful radical. Chr Cent 86: 1417-19 N 5 '69
Symposium in Rome: is unbelief believable? Commonweal 90:159-60 Ap 25 '69
COX, James
When your child begins to date. Todays Health 47:48-9+ Jl '69
COX, James, d 1798
Fine clocks of a bygone age. O. R. Hagans. il Hobbies 74:48-9 Jl '69
COX, Joan Etchingham
Plain man's guide to aphrodisia. Holiday 46:22-3 O '69
COX, Peter W.
Trying to save Maine. il por Time 94:72+ O 31 '69
COX, Robert E.
(ed) Gleanings for ATM's. See issues of Sky and telescope
(ed) See Richter, J. L. Test for figuring Cassegrain secondary mirrors
COX, Rody P.
Hormonal induction of increased zinc uptake in mammalian cell cultures: requirement for RNA and protein synthesis. bibliog Science 165:196-9 Jl 11 '69
COXE, Donald G. M.
Trudeau, danger to the North. Nat R 21: 344-5 Ap 8 '69
COXE, Louis
Dark sister; poem. New Repub 161:25 Ag 23 '69
COY, Dale E.
$20 scope camera. Radio-Electr 40:52-4 Ap '69
COYA, Albert H.
Encapsulate your circuits. Pop Electr 31:82-3 Ag '69
COYLE, Joan Washburn
Cuisine Québecoise. Travel & Camera 32:68-9 Ap '69
COYLE, Joseph T. and Snyder, S. H.
Antiparkinsonian drugs: inhibition of dopamine uptake in the corpus striatum as a possible mechanism of action. bibliog Science 166:899-901 N 14 '69

COYNE, John R. Jr
Black power casualties. Nat R 21:701 Jl 15 '69
Business to the rescue. Nat R 21:744-5 Jl 29 '69
Cracks in the coalition. Nat R 21:166-7 F 25 '69
Grapes of wrath. Nat R 21:639 Jl 1 '69
Is John Lindsay ungovernable? Nat R 21:584-9+ Je 17 '69
New politics and old. Nat R 21:1106-7+ N 4 '69
Peace in our time. Nat R 21:285+ Mr 25 '69
Positively the last word on the People's park. Nat R 21:1003-5+ O 7 '69
Siege of San Francisco state. Nat R 21:67-8 Ja 28 '69
Student power. Nat R 21:432-3+ My 6 '69
COYNE, Patricia S.
Christmas in Alaska. Nat R 21:1320-1+ D 30 '69
Sixty-six cents a day: let them eat squid. Nat R 21:909 S 9 '69
COYNE, Thomas A.
Who will speak for the child? bibliog f Ann Am Acad 383:34-47 My '69
COYOTE hunting
Death all day in Kansas. R. Rhodes. il Esquire 72:146-9+ N '69
Horizontal ghost. E. Mason. il Outdoor Life 144:76+ Ag '69
COZUMEL ISLAND
Editor's report: cozy Cozumel. M. M. Davis. il Travel 131:74-5 My '69
CRABS
Crabs move ashore. M. Gruber and J. Shoup. il Sea Front 15:364-75 N '69
DDT residues absorbed from organic detritus by fiddler crabs. W. E. Odum and others. bibliog il Science 164:576-7 My 2 '69
Vibrio parahaemolyticus from the blue crab callinectes sapidus in Chesapeake Bay. G. E. Krantz and others. bibliog Science 164: 1286-7 Je 13 '69
See also
King crabs
CRABS eye vine
Abrus precatorius: pretty but poisonous. C. R. Gunn. Science 164:245-6 Ap 18 '69; Reply. R. S. Chakravarthy. 166:44 O 3 '69
CRABTREE, Alex
San Fernando hits the road. il Yachting 126: 58-9 Jl '69
CRABTREE, Bruce
Three in a row for Cal 40's. Yachting 126:44+ S '69
Trademark cruising. il Yachting 126:67+ O '69
CRAFT, Robert
Igor Stravinsky: on illness and death; excerpts from Retrospectives and conclusions. Harper 239:111-16+ N '69

about
Marriage of Craft and art. R. Evett. New Repub 162:25-7 Ja 10 '70
Stravinsky's alter ego. H. Saal. por Newsweek 75:80-1 Ja 19 '70
CRAFT shops. See Art trade
CRAFTS, Edward C.
Brinkmanship in our forests; excerpts from congressional testimony. por Am For 75:19+ Ag '69
Doctor Craft's resignation; February 25, 1969. Am For 75:4 Ap '69
High noon for the Bureau of outdoor recreation. pors Am For 75:12-15+ O '69

about
Crafts named special articles editor. por Am For 75:19+ Jl '69
Crafts receives top career award. por Am For 75:39 Ja '69
CRAFTS. See Arts and crafts; Handicraft
CRAFTSMANSHIP
On craftsmanship. N. Kent. Am Artist 33:5 F '69
See also
Arts and crafts
CRAGUN, Richard
Spotlight! ballet personality. pors Seventeen 28:82 O '69

about
Gypsy from Sacramento. W. Terry. il pors Sat R 52:37-8 Ag 2 '69
CRAIG, E. H.
Chickens fit my garden. Org Gard & Farm 16:90-1 Ag '69
CRAIG, Gordon A.
Johannes von Müller: the historian in search of a hero. bibliog f Am Hist R 74:1487-502 Je '69

CRAIG, James B.
Washington lookout. Am For 75:5+ Ja '69

CRAIG, Marjorie
Famous shape-up secrets from Miss Craig. il por Vogue 153:178-9 Mr 1 '69

CRAIN, J. Willard
What the doctor ordered. S. Margetts. por Duns R 94:87-8 N '69

CRAMPTON, Rollin McNeil
Rollin Crampton, modest master. A. Brunelle. il por Art N 68:52-5 My '69

CRANBERG, Gilbert
Voluntary press codes. Sat R 52:71-2 My 10 '69

CRANBERRIES
Cranberry harvest: photographs. D. A. Caccia. Natur Hist 78:54-7 N '69

CRANCER, Alfred, Jr, and others
Comparison of the effects of marihuana and alcohol on simulated driving performance. bibliog Science 164:851-4 My 16 '69

CRANDALL, Ken
Stalk to remember. Outdoor Life 144:48-51+ N '69

CRANE, H. Richard
Better teaching with better problems and exams. por Phys Today 22:134-5 Mr '69

CRANE, Hart
Bridge; poem; excerpts. il Travel & Camera 32:58 S '69

about

Divided being. J. Hart. Nat R 21:1119+ N 4 '69

Voyager, by J. Unterecker. Review
Commonweal 90:545-6 S 5 '69. S. Hazo
New Repub 161:24-6 Ag 9 '69. K. Burke
Newsweek il por 74:100+ Jl 21 '69. G. Wolff
Sat R por 52:27-9+ Jl 19 '69. L. Untermeyer
Time il por 94:80 Jl 18 '69

CRANE, Stephen
Stephen Crane's A mystery of heroism: some redefinitions. P. Witherington. Engl J 58: 201-4+ F '69

CRANE company
So I lost, so what? Forbes 104:44 Ag 15 '69

CRANES (birds)
Crane watching in New Mexico. il Sunset 143:48 O '69
How goes the battle of the whooping crane? reprint. M. J. Walker. il Sci Digest 65:15-18 F '69
It's time to halt the taking of wild whooping crane eggs. Audubon 71:122 S '69

CRANES, derricks, etc.
Cranes that pack much more muscle. il Bsns W p54 Ja 10 '70
Facts on a big-pay job. A. Markovich. il Mech Illus 65:71-3+ O '69

CRANHAM, Gerry
Where the horse abides; photographs. Sports Illus 30:36-42 My 19 '69

CRANKO, John
Cranko; interview. New Yorker 45:27-8 Je 21 '69
Dancing master; interview. ed. by J. Boutwell. por Opera N 34:17-20 O 11 '69

about

Bravo Cranko! H. Saal. il Newsweek 73:62 Je 23 '69
Cranko & co. O. Maynard. il por Dance Mag 43:50-9+ S '69
Gazelleschaft. Time 93:82 Je 20 '69
Mr Cranko and his castle. J. Anderson. il por Dance Mag 43:46-9 Je '69
Steps from Stuttgart. W. Terry. il por Sat R 52:40+ My 31 '69
Stuttgart's Cranko. G. Trotta. pors Harp Baz 102:246-7 O '69

CRANKS and crankshafts
Crankshaft fundamentals. J. Thawley. il Hot Rod 22:78-80 Jl '69
VW flywheel gefixen. D. LaFayette. il Hot Rod 22:100-1 Je '69

CRANKSHAW, Edward
Internal Russian pressures against war. Cur 112:52-4 N '69

CRANNELL, Hall, and others
Particle track enhancement in cellulose nitrate by application of an electric field. bibliog Science 166:606-7 O 31 '69

CRANSTON, Alan
World peace; address, January 29, 1969. Vital Speeches 35:358-60 Ap 1 '69

about

Lawmakers get the word. il pors Nations Bsns 57:31-2+ My '69
Letter from Washington. R. H. Rover. New Yorker 45:171-2 N 29 '69

CRANSTON, Maurice
Are student rebels neo-Communists? Cur 104: 19-25 F '69

CRAPANZANO, Vincent, and Kramer, Jane
World of saints and she-demons. N Y Times Mag p 14-15+ Je 22 '69

CRAPE myrtle
Crapemyrtle. R. B. Fisher. il Horticulture 46: 32-3+ S '68

CRAPPER, Thomas
Flushed with pride, by W. Reyburn. Review
Newsweek il por 74:63 D 1 '69. H. F. Waters

CRAPPIE fishing
Crappies for all, all year; Lake Tawakoni. J. N. Mannix. il Outdoor Life 143:60-1+ F '69
Hot bridge crappies; New York city's reservoirs. A. Glowka. il Field & S 74:66-7+ My '69

CRASE, Douglas
Democrats confront 1970. Nation 209:598-9 D 1 '69

CRASH diets. See Diets

CRATER LAKE
Side trips around Crater Lake. il Sunset 143: 36-7 Ag '69

CRATERS, Moon. See Moon—Surface

CRAVENS corporation
Handley Page gets a Missouri accent. il Bsns W p38 O 25 '69
Handley Page taken over by U.S. group. H. J. Coleman. Aviation W 91:25 O 27 '69

CRAWFORD, Betty Anne
Worms; story. Seventeen 28:83 Ja '69

CRAWFORD, Constance
Far from Blue Earth; story. Seventeen 28: 166-7 Ap '69

CRAWFORD, H. D.
Thoreau country. il Am For 75:20-3+ N '69

CRAWFORD, John S.
Blackie and the silver horde. Outdoor Life 143:76-9+ Ap '69
Getting along with grizzlies. por Outdoor Life 144:45-7+ N; 44-7+ D '69

CRAWFORD, Kathleen. See Crawford, R. jt. auth.

CRAWFORD, Kenneth
Reporter remembers the political Ike. Newsweek 73:25 Ap 7 '69
Washington. See issues of Newsweek

CRAWFORD, Michael
Michael of the movies; interview. ed. by E. Miller. pors Seventeen 28:104-5+ D '69

CRAWFORD, Ralph, and Crawford, Kathleen
Bali. Travel 132:42-5 O '69

CRAWLER vehicles
Sno-cat for springtime mud. il Sci Digest 65: 25 My '69

CRAY, Ed
Politics of blue power. Nation 208:493-6 Ap 21 '69

CRAYFISH
Photoperiod, endocrinology and the crustacean molt cycle. D. E. Aiken. bibliog il Science 164:149-55 Ap 11 '69
See also
Cookery—Shellfish

CRAYON drawing
Crayon illuminations. G. A. Petine. il Sch Arts 69:16-17 S '69

CREAL, Margaret
Lifeline; story. McCalls 96:54-5 Ag '69

CREAM
Cream, sweet and sour. il Ladies Home J 86:122 N '69

CREAM cheese. See Cheese; Cookery—Cheese

CREAMER, Lex. See Espy, H. C. jt. auth.

CREAMS (dessert) See Custards

CREASMAN, Ralph Dedrick
Performance is important, but so is a good night's sleep. por Forbes 104:82-3 O 15 '69

CREATINE kinase. See Kinases

CREATION
Witness of creation. L. N. Bell. Chr Today 13:29 Mr 28 '69
See also
Cosmogony
Earth

Anecdotes, facetiae, satire, etc.
Creatio ex nihilo. Chr Cent 86:1437 N 5 '69

CREATION (literary, artistic, etc)
  Art as intersecting fields of energy. J. Unter-
    ecker. Sat R 52:27-9+ Je 14 '69
  Centipede and the creative spirit; address,
    1967. M. L'Engle. Horn Bk 45:373-7 Ag '69
  Creative person and some dangerous streets;
    address. J. D. MacDonald. il Writers Dig-
    est 49:58-61+ Je '69
  Danger! Talent at work. R. Warfield. House
    & Gard 136:76-7+ Jl '69
  On creativity. R. J. Enquist; discussion. Chr
    Cent 86:389-90 Mr 19 '69
  On doing-one's-thing. W. Goodman. Am
    Scholar 38:240-7 Spr '69
  Opium and the romantic imagination, by
    A. Hayter. Review
      New Repub 160:30-1 F 15 '69. R. Freed-
      man
  Stories I guess I won't write. H. Gold. Atlan
    224:39-42 Ag '69; Same abr. Writer 82:27
    D '69
      See also
  Creative ability
  Creative writing

CREATIVE ability
  How creative are you? excerpts. M. Gattis
    and E. Raudsepp. il Writers Digest 49:61-
    5+ Mr '69

CREATIVE dramatics. See Dramatization in
  education

CREATIVE education
  Creative alternatives. N. J. Reyburn. bib-
    liog f Sch & Soc 97:23-4 Ja '69
  Creativity and creative teaching: a reappraisal
    M. S. Vaughan. bibliog f Sch & Soc 97:230-2
    Ap '69

CREATIVE photography
  Creative destruction. R. Hattersley. il Pop
    Phot 64:95-8 F '69
  Pictures you won't see in a viewfinder. il Pop
    Phot 64:72-9 F '69

CREATIVE teaching. See Creative education
CREATIVE thinking. See Thought and thinking
CREATIVE writing
  Composition as the expression of personality.
    P. F. Cummins. Engl J 58:92-5 Ja '69
  ERIC abstracts and ERIC indexes: short-
    cuts to creative writing documents. R. V.
    Denby. Engl J 58:139-44 Ja '69
  Maturing of novel ideas. M. Montgomery.
    Writer 82:22-4+ D '69
  Quoth the parrot, nevermore. L. Conger. Wri-
    ter 82:9-10 O '69
  Use your creative memory. J. Yolen. Writer
    82:16-17+ S '69
  Writing teacher appraises his students. H.
    Swados. Writer 82:17-18 Ag '69

      Study and teaching
  Concrete poetry; creative writing for all stu-
    dents. L. Mueller. bibliog il Engl J 58:1053-
    6 O '69
  Experiment in creativity. C. Lang. il Parents
    Mag 44:56-7+ S '69
  Five things I tell my class in article writing.
    J. Stocker. Writer 82:25-6 O '69
  Improving buzzard's luck: Tougaloo college.
    R. B. Hoffman. il Wilson Lib Bul 44:51-7
    S '69

CREDIT
  Arthur Burns on easier credit, business in
    '70; excerpts from the hearings held by the
    Senate committee on banking and cur-
    rency. A. F. Burns. U S News 68:56-9 Ja
    12 '70
  As tight money slows business; with inter-
    view with D. Rockefeller. il U S News 67:
    23-5 Jl 21 '69
  Bank profits boom, small business pines. il
    Newsweek 75:69-70 Ja 19 '70
  Borrowing costs up again; why? il U S News
    67:33-4 S 22 '69
  Brakes are getting red hot. il Bsns W p26-7
    N 29 '69
  Buying the good life on easy terms; Mexico.
    Bsns W p 126 Jl 12 '69
  Credit crunch: who is hurt. il U S News 66:
    60-1 Je 16 '69
  Credit squeeze; as people feel the effects. il
    U S News 66:29-31 Ap 21 '69
  Crunch comes closer; Federal reserve's credit
    squeeze. il Bsns W p42-3 Je 14 '69
  Crunch vs. crisis. J. W. Schulz. Forbes 104:
    69 Jl 1 '69
  Does the Fed really mean it this time?
    squeeze or a bear hug. il Bsns W p30-1 Ap
    12 '69
  Drastic new squeeze on money; meaning to
    borrowers. il U S News 66:72-3 Ap 14 '69
  Latest threat to the boom, money experts
    sound an alarm. il U S News 66:32-3 Je 23
    '69

No time for controls. Time 95:49 Ja 5 '70
Not enough money to go around; demand
  for credit in the 1970s. il Bsns W p 166-8+
  D 6 '69
One thing is clear: uncertainty. il Newsweek
  74:80+ D 15 '69
Out on the credit limb; credit capitalism.
  M. Tanzer. Nation 208:686-9 Je 2 '69
Ten most misunderstood points about bor-
  rowing money. P. Lindberg. Bet Hom &
  Gard 47:7-8 Ag '69
U.S. feels the pain of a demi-crunch. il
  Bsns W p33-4 Je 7 '69
What you should know about truth in lend-
  ing. G. Town. Har Yrs 9:22-3 N '69
Word on tight money; no relief. il U S News
  67:87-8 D 8 '69
    See also
Charge accounts (retail trade)
Consumer credit
Debt
Debtor and creditor
Discount
Export credit
Farm finance
Foreign exchange
Loans, Bank
Loans, Foreign
Monetary policy
Negotiable instruments

      Information services
    See Credit bureaus

      Rating
Your credit is an open book. O. Bay. Farm J
  93:52AA Mr '69

CREDIT bureaus
  Credit bureaus: what they know about you.
    il Good H 169:184 S '69

CREDIT cards
  Bankers scrap to charge it; vie for credit
    card business. Bsns W p 102 My 24 '69
  College on the cuff. il Time 94:93 S 26 '69
  Credit cards or cash? Consumer Bul 52:30-1
    Ap '69
  Here come the bank cards! il Forbes 103:
    39-40 F 15 '69
  Japan: a yen for on-the-cuff shopping. il
    Bsns W p78 D 20 '69
  Lure of instant cash. il Time 94:73 Jl 11 '69
  Santa Claus that makes you pay; bank credit
    cards. il Bsns W p76-9 D 20 '69
  Unity urged to combat credit card fraud.
    J. W. Carter. il Aviation W 90:39+ F 3 '69
  Wanna bet, MasterCharge? J. Middlebrook.
    New Repub 161:17-18 S 20 '69
  What else can you charge on your gas card?
    il Changing T 23:23-4 Jl '69
  Why the worry over credit cards. il U S News
    67:62-5 N 24 '69
    See also
  Diners' club, incorporated

CREDIT counseling. See Debtor and creditor
CREDIT mobilier of America
  Credit mobilier: construction company
    building government-backed railroads. J.
    L. Phillips. il Am Heritage 20:108-9 Ap '69

CREDIT unions
  Credit unions want a place in the sun. B. L.
    Masse. America 120:87 Ja 25 '69
  How & whys of credit unions. il Changing
    T 22:33-7 D '68

CREDITOR. See Debtor and creditor
CREECH, John L.
  Plant hunting in Formosa. il Horticulture
    47:34-5+ Ap '69

CREED, Virginia
  Now's the time for Christmas shopping in
    Europe. Travel 132:62-4+ O '69

CREEDENCE Clearwater Revival. See Rock 'n'
  roll music

CREELEY, Robert
  So big; poem. Poetry 115:113 N '69

      about
  Pieces by Robert Creeley. R. Whittemore.
    New Repub 161:25 O 11 '69

CREEPING Charlie. See Loosestrife
CRELIN, E. S.
  Interpubic ligament: elasticity in pregnant
    free-tailed bat. Science 164:81 Ap 4 '69

CREMATION; story. See Walker, T.
CREMER, Gérard de. See Mercator, G.
CRÊPES. See Griddle cakes
CRESCI, Giovanni Francesco
  Fine Italian hands. P. Standard. il Pub W
    195:92-3+ F 3 '69

CRESPI, David
  David Crespi's weed pots. D. Cyr. il Ceram
    Mo 17:20-2 Mr '69

CRESSEY, Donald Ray
Theft of the Nation; excerpt. Harper 238:
84-90 F '69
CRESTS. See Heraldry
CRETACEOUS period. See Paleontology—Cretaceous
CREUTZFELDT-Jakob disease. See Brain—Diseases
CREWE, Quentin
London (cont) Vogue 153:108+ Mr 1; 156+
Ap 1; 72+ Je; 154:68 Ag 1; 66 S 15; 60+ O
15; 60+ N 15 '69; 155:80 Ja 15 '70
On the road with the British gypsies. Vogue
155:182+ Ja 1 '70
CREWS, Mildred T.
Saint-maker from Taos. il Américas 21:33-7
Mr '69
CRIBS (beds)
Case against a Pride Trimble crib. il Consumer Rep 34:239 My '69
CRICHTON, J. Michael
Sci-fi and Vonnegut. New Repub 160:33-5
Ap 26 '69
about
New note: the novel as sci-non-fi. M. Maddocks. Life 66:15 My 30 '69
CRICHTON, Michael. See Crichton, J. M.
CRICHTON, Robert
Real secret of Santa Vittoria. Writer 82:13-
14+ Jl '69
CRICK, Francis Harry Compton
Quick climb up Mount Olympus. E. Chargaff;
discussion. Science 164:1537-9 Je 27 '69
CRICKET (game)
Not quiet cricket; decline of county cricket
in Britain. il Newsweek 74:53 Jl 28 '69
CRICKETS
Acoustic synchrony: two mechanisms in the
snowy tree cricket. T. J. Walker. bibliog
il Science 166:891-4 N 14 '69
Jiminy, crickets. H. G. Tapply. il Field & S
74:72 S '69
CRIHFIELD, Brevard, and Bell, G. A.
Budgeting for state and local government
services. Ann Am Acad 379:31-8 S '68
CRIME and criminals
Anatomy of violence; findings of Frank R.
Ervin and Lawrence Razavi. il Newsweek
75:60-1 Ja 12 '70
Chromosomes and crime. il Chem 42:22 Jl '69
XYY chromosome and criminal acts; letter.
K. McWhirter. Science 164:1117 Je 6 '69;
Discussion. 165:442, 967; 166:947-9 Ag 1,
S 5, N 21 '69
See also
Assassination
Brigands and robbers
Capital punishment
Crime and the press
Crime prevention
Criminal investigation
Embezzlement
Fraud
Fugitives from justice
Insane, Criminal and dangerous
Mafia
Murder
Parole
Police
Prisoners
Prisons
Punishment
Rape
Self defense
Shoplifting
Smuggling
Stealing
Thieves
Trial

Economic aspects
Surging vandalism, its expense to America.
il U S News 67:32-4 Ag 25 '69

Research
See Criminal research

Statistics
See Criminal statistics

Brazil
See also
Rio de Janeiro—Crime

California
Murder on route 79. K. Detzer. il Read Digest 94:126-30 F '69
See also
Justice, Administration of—California

Canada
See also
Montreal—Crime

France
Bodyguard; French scandal involving sex,
politics, murder and decadence. il Time
93:24 F 21 '69
Château gang; excerpt from The discriminating thief. D. Leitch. il Horizon 11:114-20
Spr '69

Great Britain
Paradise lost; lives of bandits who robbed
Glasgow-to-London royal mail train. il
Time 94:34 O 31 '69

India
See also
Thugs

Italy
Nonviolent cities. il Newsweek 75:33-4 Ja 5
'70
See also
Mafia

Missouri
See also
Mafia

New Jersey
Mob scene in Jersey. W. Schechner. Commonweal 89:514-15 Ja 24 '69
See also
Mafia

Ohio
See also
Mafia

Russia
See also
Moscow—Crime

Sicily
See also
Mafia

United States
Conspiracy of silence; public refuses to report many crimes. Time 93:60-1 F 14 '69
Cop! A closeup of violence and tragedy, by
L. H. Whittemore. Review
Newsweek il 74:91+ Jl 7 '69. A. Cooper
Crime, a nationwide FBI view. Am City
84:178+ O '69
Crime legislation; address, October 6, 1969. J
N. Mitchell. Vital Speeches 36:39-42 N 1 '69
Crime of punishment, by K. Menninger. Review
Commonweal 89:533-4 Ja 24 '69. W. Ryan
New Yorker 45:63-7 Ja 3 '70. R. Coles
Crime; the community and the corporation;
address, July 28, 1969. M. R. Wilkey. Vital
Speeches 35:718-20 S 15 '69
Crime, violence and the local church. L. E.
Schaller. Chr Cent 86:641-5 My 7 '69
Crime war: key senator launches a broad
attack; organized crime; excerpts from
Senate statement, March 11, 1969. J. L.
McClellan. U S News 66:14 Mr 24 '69
Fighting crime in America; interview. J. N.
Mitchell. il U S News 67:46-53 Ag 18 '69
Gangbusters; Richard Nixon's campaign
against organized crime. Newsweek 73:33
My 5 '69
Ganging up on the mob; federal war on organized crime. il Time 93:76 My 2 '69
Guns and crime, a '68 upswing. U S News
66:16 Mr 17 '69
Hooked! J. Leavitt. Nation 209:737-8 D 29
'69
If crime goes unchecked, what big cities will
be like; excerpts from statement, November 24, 1969. M. S. Eisenhower. U S News
67:41-2 D 8 '69
Judge Burger's philosophy on justice in U.S.
a key speech; excerpts, May 1967; reprint.
W. E. Burger. il U S News 66:82-5 Je 2
'69; Same abr. with title Rights and
wrongs of U.S. justice. Read Digest 95:
84-8 Ag '69
Law and order in public parks. F. L. Campbell and others. il Parks & Rec 3:28-31+
D '68
Learning to live with fear. il Newsweek 73:
62-3 Mr 24 '69; Same abr. with title Fear
in the streets. Read Digest 95:51-3 Jl '69
Man with ideas on fighting crime. U S News
66:13 F 3 '69
Mugger's tale. G. B. Porter. il Newsweek 73:
63+ My 19 '69
Organized crime in the United States; statement, March 11, 1969. J. L. McClellan. Vital
Speeches 35:388-400 Ap 15 '69; Excerpts
U S News 66:14 Mr 24 '69
Our criminal society, by E. M. Schur. Review
New Repub 161:24-6 N 15 '69. H. L.
Packer
Talk with Warren on crime, the Court, the
country; interview, ed. by A. Lewis. E.
Warren. N Y Times Mag p34-5+ O 19 '69

CRIPPLES
Uncle Tom and Tiny Tim: some reflections on the cripple as Negro. L. Kriegal. Am Scholar 38:412-30 Sum '69
CRISE, Sherman F.
House is not a hot rod. H. D. Whall. il Sports Illus 31:14-17 Jl 28 '69
CRISMOND, Linda F.
Computer system for periodicals. por Library J 94:3619-21 O 15 '69
CRISP, Freda
Scandalous and delightful. Dance Mag 43:29-31 Ag '69
CRIST, Judith (Klein)
Sex and violence in movies and TV: how harmful are they? Good H 169:59-61+ Ag '69
CRIST, Raymond E.
Our increasingly urban world. Américas 21:42 Ja '69
CRISWELL, Wallie Amos, 1909-
Battle of the book. Newsweek 73:96-7 My 5 '69
Southern Baptists and the Bible. Chr Today 13:34 Ap 25 '69
CRITCHFIELD, Richard
Feeding the hungry. New Repub 161:16-19 O 25 '69
CRITCHLOW, James
Ins and outs of de-Stalinization. Commonweal 90:191-2 My 2 '69
CRITES, Stephen
Metamorphosis; poem. Chr Cent 86:1637 D 24 '69
Radix; poem. Chr Cent 86:181 F 5 '69
Suspension; poem. Chr Cent 86:1483 N 19 '69
CRITICAL path analysis
Critical path of decision making. M. Hanan. il Harvard Bsns R 47:51-61 Ja '69
CRITICISM
See also
Art criticism
Critics
Literary criticism
Moving picture criticism
Television criticism
CRITICS
After forty years of writing about movies. I know something about cinema and, being a congenital critic. D. Macdonald. Esquire 72:80-3+ Jl '69
European literary scene; International association of literary critics meeting, Parma. R. J. Clements. Sat R 52:30 Jl 5 '69
How I became a custom critic for fun and profit. J. C. Thomas. il Writers Digest 49:66-7+ Je '69
Kill the first night, kill it dead. C. Barnes. Holiday 45:10+ F '69
Overachiever; C. Barnes, Times drama and dance critic. Time 93:98+ Ap 11 '69
Reviewers. Newsweek 74:76+ Ag 11 '69
Rise and fall of the man of letters, by J. Gross. Review
Nation 209:478-80 N 3 '69 D. Fanger
Theatre. W. Sheed. Esquire 72:42+ D '69
See also
Art critics
Gelles, G.
Literary criticism
Music critics
Rahv, P.
CROATS
See also
Yugoslavia
CROCHETING
Holiday-best vests. il Redbook 134:89 D '69
CROCKER, Arthur M.
Why Gooley number one? Liv Wildn 32:22-4 Wint '68
CROCKER, Dick
Dick Crocker composes from sketches; with biographical sketch. il por Am Artist 32:64-5+ N '68
CROCKETT, George William, 1909-
Church gun battle: police vs. blacks. il U S News 66:10 Ap 14 '69
Detroit's rebel judge Crockett. C. L. Sanders. il pors Ebony 24:114-16+ Ag '69
Fallout from a shootout. il por Time 93:43+ Ap 11 '69
CROCKETT, James Underwood
In your greenhouse. See issues of Horticulture
CROCODILES
Cautious crocodile; safari in Zambia. W. Page. il Field & S 74:72-3+ My '69
CROCUSES
See what you can do with a thousand crocus. il Home Gard 56:28-9 S '69
CROGHAN, Leo M.
Marriage law and real life. America 121:352-5 O 25 '69

CROLEY, Victor A.
Growing a 16-foot shade tree in a single season. Org Gard & Farm 16:108-12 Mr '69
Ozark memories persisted. Org Gard & Farm 16:38-40 Ja '69
CROMWELL, Richard
Forest: poem. Am For 75:63 Ja '69
CRONEMILLER, Lynn F.
Sheepshooters' tree. Am For 75:37+ Jl '69
CRONK, Gene E.
Water tank dons polyframe lid. Am City 84:76-7 Je '69
CRONKITE, Walter, 1916-
Unflappable Walter Cronkite. J. Reddy. por Read Digest 95:193-4+ D '69
CROOK, Mel
More power to you. See issues of Yachting
CROP drying. See Drying (crops)
CROP forecasts. See Agricultural forecasts
CROPS
News. See issues of Farm journal
What's new. See issues of Successful farming
See also
Companion crops
Forage plants
Harvesting
Milo
also names of Crops, e.g. Wheat
Drying
See Drying (crops)
Varieties
What the new varieties have to offer. L. D. Rawson. il Suc Farm 67:30-1 D '69
CROQUETTES
Golden croquette. K. S. Nelson. il House & Gard 135:99-101+ Ja '69
CROSBY, Bing
Fishing with Bing: tale of a marlin. D. Davis. il pors Travel & Camera 32:84-5+ Ag '69
CROSBY, Bing, tournament. See Golf—Tournaments
CROSBY, Charles W.
Providence: a community relations program. Wilson Lib Bul 43:892-3 My '69
CROSBY, James M.
Blocking an air raid. il Time 93:86 Mr 21 '69
Craps, roulette & Pan American airways. il por Forbes 103:27-9 Mr 15 '69
CROSBY, John
John Crosby, we can afford to take chances . . . S. Flemming. por Hi Fi 19:MA17+ Ag '69
CROSBY, Muriel
ASCD coup d'etat. D. L. Burleson. Sr Schol 94:Schol Teach 6 Ap 18 '69
CROSIER, W. Ron
Blow up! Sch Arts 69:20-1 N '69
CROSS, George L.
College president speaks out; interview, ed. by N. Seitz. por Parents Mag 44:62-3+ O '69
CROSS, J. D.
Scanning electron microscopy of evaporating ice. bibliog Science 164:174-5 Ap 11 '69
CROSS, Janet S. and Nagle, J. M.
Teachers talk too much! bibliog f Engl J 58:1362-5 D '69
CROSS, Jennifer
Groceries, gas and games. Nation 208:370-2 Mr 24 '69
Washington confronts the hungry. Nation 209:687-9 D 22 '69
Why the poor pay more. Nation 209:315-16 S 29 '69
CROSS, Mary Ann (Evans) See Eliot, G. pseud.
CROSS, Ronald
Chansons of Matthaeus Pipelare. bibliog f Mus Q 55:500-20 O '69
CROSS and crosses
Proof text of the pudding; wearing crosses as jewelry. Chr Cent 86:1653 D 24 '69
Seeing God through the cross. Chr Today 13:23 Jl 4 '69
CROSS breeding. See Hybridization
CROSS connections (plumbing) See Water distribution
CROSS country running. See Running
CROSS county skiing. See Skis and skiing
CROSS FLORIDA BARGE CANAL
Florida's new canal. E. White. il Yachting 126:58-60+ N '69
CROSS pollination. See Fertilization of plants
CROSS-stitch
See also
Samplers
CROSS ventilation. See Ventilation
CROSSBREEDING of cattle. See Cattle breeding

CROSSBREEDING of swine. See Swine breeding

CROSSING over (genetics)
Cytoplasmic DNA from petite colonies of saccharomyces cerevisiae: a hypothesis on the nature of the mutation. F. Carnevali and others. bibliog il Science 163:1331-3 Mr 21 '69
Multiplicity reactivation as a test for recombination function. R. J. Huskey. bibliog il Science 164:319-20 Ap 18 '69
Parasexual cycle in cultivated human somatic cells. G. M. Martin and C. A. Sprague. bibliog il Science 166:761-3 N 7 '69

CROSSLEY, Eugene I. and Conn, W. M.
Water and wastewater research in San Diego. Am City 84:91-3+ O '69

CROSSLEY, John P. Jr
Madness, comfort and love. Chr Cent 86:1542-6 D 3 '69

CROSSMAN, Carl L.
China trade paintings on glass. Antiques 95:376-82 Mr '69

CROSSMAN, Patricia
Life to live; story. Good H 168:112-13 Mr '69

CROSSOVER, Electronic. See Loud speaking apparatus

CROTCH ISLAND. See Cliff Island

CROWE, Beryl L.
Tragedy of the commons revisited. bibliog Science 166:1103-7 N 28 '69

CROWELL, Ann
Vicuña; the littlest camel. Américas 21:2-7 Mr '69

CROWELL, Suzanne
They stayed. Am Ed 5:22-5 Ag '69

CROWELL Collier and Macmillan, Incorporated
CCM announces new acquisitions. Pub W 195:75 Ja 27 '69
CCM plans anti-trust suit vs. Home study trade assn. Pub W 196:20 D 15 '69
Pursuit of opportunity. il Forbes 103:62-3 Mr 15 '69

CROWHURST, Donald
Mutiny of the mind. il por Time 94:45 Ag 8 '69
Sea lover. il por Newsweek 74:32 Ag 11 '69

CROWHURST, Norman H.
Build a three-way electronic crossover. Radio-Electr 40:42-4 O '69
Crossovers, electrical or electronic? Radio-Electr 40:32+ Mr '69

CROWLEY, Elmer S.
NCSEA evaluation: catalyst for change in state education associations. Todays Ed 58:36-7 D '69

CROWLEY, Regis F.
Teaching the slow learner. Todays Ed 58:48-9 Ja '69

CROWN college. See California. University—Santa Cruz campus

CROWN-of-thorns starfish. See Starfishes

CROWN Zellerbach corporation
Catching up with the times. Forbes 104:43 Jl 15 '69

CROWTHER, Carol
Crimes, penalties, and legislatures. bibliog f Ann Am Acad 381:147-58 Ja '69

CROWTHER, John F.
Peril-point acquisition prices. Harvard Bsns R 47:58-62 S '69

CROY, Paul
College detour. Todays Ed 58:33 F '69

CROYDEN, Margaret
Elder Burton. Sat R 52:51 My 10 '69

CRUCE, B. H.
Trouble with municipal purchasing agents. por Am City 84:101-2 N '69

CRUELTY
Options of modern man. Chr Today 14:30-1 N 7 '69
Peaceable kingdom. J. Kleinheksel. Chr Today 14:6-7 Ja 2 '70
See also
Sadism

CRUELTY to animals. See Animals—Treatment

CRUELTY to children
Battered child. G. F. Fruchtl and A. E. Brodeur. Cath World 209:156-9 Jl '69
Battering parent; Battered child syndrome. il Time 94:77+ N 7 '69
Shelter: Children's center deluged with child abuse cases. New Yorker 45:21-2 Jl 5 '69
What schools can do about child abuse. D. G. Gil. Am Ed 5:2-4 Ap '69

CRUICKSHANK, Alexander M.
Gordon research conferences: program for 1969. Science 163:1085-98+ Mr 7 '69
Gordon research conferences: winter program, 1970. Science 166:910+ N 14 '69

CRUIKSHANK, Dale P.
Moon: infrared studies of surface composition. bibliog Science 166:215-18 O 10 '69

CRUISE ships. See Steamships and steamboats

CRUISES. See Cruising

CRUISING
Airline ordering ship for air-sea cruises. J. W. Carter. Aviation W 90:29 Ap 7 '69
Alaska to Key West cruise; by outboard motorboat. il Travel 131:59-61 Je '69
Alaska's inside passage by ferry. Sunset 142:53 Ap '69
Around North America in Fram. H. Field. il Yachting 126:50-1+ Jl '69
Case for the mini-cruise. J. Roe. il Motor B 123:74-7 My '69
Charter sailing in Green Bay. B. Stephany and S. Stephany. il Yachting 125:56-7+ Ap '69
Cruises. M. Gough. il House B 111:108+ O '69
Cruising can be wonderful. Z. Taylor. il Motor B 123:129-31+ Ja '69
Cruising on the level. H. Estes. il Yachting 126:66-8+ Ag '69
Cruising on your new boat. il Motor B 123:114-15 Ja '69
Cruising the North Atlantic islands. D. M. H. Mellonie. Motor B 123:144+ My '69
Down east heritage cruise. W. R. Juettner. bibliog il Motor B 123:74-9+ Je '69
Down home on the high seas; cruise from the West coast. D. Butwin. Sat R 52:46+ Ap 26 '69
Encounter in the Caribbean. il Holiday 45:12+ Je '69
Eventide on the East coast. E. Newmark. il Yachting 126:68-70+ O '69
Evergreen isles; Pacific Northwest. B. Crabtree. il Yachting 125:50-2+ F '69
Florida's a new canal. E. White. il Yachting 126:58-60+ N '69
From coast to coast:
Leewards to Antigua. E. Newmark. il Yachting 125:94-6+ Ja; 62-4+ F '69
Great northwest cruise. C. West. il Motor B 123:142-6 Ja '69
Great triangle cruise; New York state to Canada. A. Brown. il Yachting 126:68-9+ D '69
Greek paragraphs. T. Capote. Travel & Camera 32:46+ My '69
Houseboat in Florida. J. Smith. Yachting 126:52-3+ N '69
How to get more cruising for less time and money. A. Gingrich. Esquire 71:6 Ap '69
Inland Florida cruising. K. Hunn. il Yachting 125:74-5+ D '69
Least Antilles. E. Bedell. il Motor B 124:60-1+ N '69
Little known western Caribbean. E. Newmark. il Yachting 126:54-5+ N '69
Maine windjamming; letter. K. Ward. il Motor B 123:78-9 Mr '69
Ninety-three days on a caviar bucket; Kungsholm's Pacific cruises. M. Connelly. il Sat R 52:82+ S 13 '69
Outboard on Vancouver Island. C. L. Cadieux. il Yachting 125:50-1 Je '69
Ride on the Renaissance; musical cruises. P. Witter. il Hi Fi 19:MA22-4+ D '69
Sail on, Yankee! A. Goetz and N. Goetz. il Motor B 123:133-40+ Ja '69
Sailor meets houseboat; Canada's Rideau waterway. P. Smyth. il Motor B 124:36-41+ D '69
Small boat to Block Island. C. R. Meyer. il Yachting 126:72-3+ Jl '69
Special section: armchair cruising; symposium. il Yachting 125:54-63+ Mr '69
This year from West coast ports, more than 200 cruises. il Sunset 142:48-50+ Mr '69
Touring England by narrow boat. il Sunset 142:42 Ap '69
Trademark cruising. B. Crabtree. il Yachting 126:67+ O '69
Way out; cruising in the Bahamas and Florida. W. Juettner. il Motor B 124:53-9+ N '69
Which cruise to Mexico? il Sunset 143:24+ O '69
Why women put to sea. M. Connelly. McCalls 96:88+ S '69
See also
River trips

Anecdotes, facetiae, satire, etc.
Take Jorgensen along; mythical character takes blame for boating mishaps. T. Bottomley. Motor B 123:162-3 Mr '69

History
We had them to ourselves; cruising the Virgins in the early '30s. D. Puleston. il Yachting 126:64-5+ N '69

CRUISING houseboats. See Houseboats

CRUM, Mildred Lackey
Instant jobs keep me hopping. Har Yrs 9:10 N '69

CRUMB, George
Contemporary contrasts. D. W. Moore. Am Rec G 36:69 S '69
George Crumb: Eleven echoes of autumn, 1965. D. J. Henahan. il Mus Q 55:280-5 Ap '69

CRUMBLISS, Alvin L. and Basolo, Fred
Monomeric cobalt-oxygen complexes. bibliog Science 164:1168-70 Je 6 '69

CRUMMERE, Maria Elise
Horoscope. Vogue 154:55 Ag 1; 28-9 Ag 15; 356 S 1; 70 S 15; 165 O 1; 67 O 15; 133 N 1; 69 N 15; 149 D'69; 155:87 Ja 1; 83 Ja 15 '70

CRUMP, Fred, Jr. See Hertzke, J. jt. auth.

CRUSTACEA
See also
Barnacles
Crabs
Crayfish
Eye (crustacea)
Isopods
Lobsters
Nervous system—Crustacea
Ostracods

CRUTCHER, Harold L. See Guttman, N. B. jt. auth.

CRUTTWELL, Patrick
Shakespeare is not our contemporary. Yale R 59:33-49 O '69

CRUXENT, José M. and Rouse, Irving
Early man in the West Indies; with biographical sketches. Sci Am 221:18, 42-52 bibliog(p 166) N '69

CRYING
When should a Christian weep? J. R. W. Stott. Chr Today 14:3-5 N 7 '69

CRYOBIOLOGY
See also
Cryonics
Insects. Freezing of

CRYOGENICS. See Low temperatures

CRYONICS
Never say die. il Newsweek 73:16 Mr 24 '69
No, thank you, I'd rather not live twice. L. R. Chevalier. il Ladies Home J 86:68+ Mr '69

CRYONICS society of New York
No, thank you, I'd rather not live twice. L. R. Chevalier. il Ladies Home J 86:68+ Mr '69

CRYPLEX industries, incorporated
Squirting the cost out of quality plastics; liquid injection molding. il Bsns W p 146-8 Ap 12 '69

CRYSTAL (glass) See Glassware

CRYSTAL ball; story. See González Ledo, L.

CRYSTAL diodes. See Diodes

CRYSTAL lattices. See Crystals—Lattices

CRYSTAL oscillators. See Oscillators, Crystal

CRYSTALLIZATION
Boron modifications produced in an induction-coupled argon plasma. D. B. Sullenger and others. bibliog il Science 163:935-7 F 28 '69
How growing of synthetic gems began. il Chem 42:24-5 F '69
Structural studies on transfer RNA; crystallization of formylmethionine and leucine transfer RNA's. J. D. Young and others. bibliog il Science 166:1527-8 D 19 '69
See also
Metal crystals

CRYSTALLOGRAPHY
Automatic determination of crystal structure. Q. Johnson and others. bbiliog Science 164:1163-4 Je 6 '69
Basic ferric phosphates: a crystallochemical principle. P. B. Moore. il Science 164:1063-4 My 30 '69
Garnet-like structures of high-pressure cadmium germanate and calcium germanate. C. T. Prewitt and A. W. Sleight. bibliog il Science 163:386-7 Ja 24 '69
Lab bench: effect of temperature on light absorption by crystalline cadmium sulfide. J. A. Isenberg. il Chem 42:26-8 Je '69; Correction. 42:32 Jl '69
Microphotometric determination of preferred orientation in underformed dolomites. E. Sass. bibliog il Science 165:802-3 Ag 22 '69
Structural studies on transfer RNA: preliminary crystallographic analysis. M. Labanauskas and others. bibliog il Science 166:1530-2 D 19 '69

Tuhualite crystal structure. S. Merlino. bibliog il Science 166:1399-401 D 12 '69
See also
Crystallization
International union of crystallography
Polymorphism

Neutron diffraction studies
Neutron analysis for proteins. B. J. Culliton. il Sci N 96:536-7 D 6 '69

X ray studies
Crystal structure of benzene II at 25 kilobars. G. J. Piermarini and others. bibliog il Science 165:1250-5 S 19 '69
New X ray crystallography. il Chem 42:25 F '69
X-ray diffraction studies of echinoderm plates. G. Donnay and D. L. Pawson. bibliog il Science 166:1147-50 N 28 '69

CRYSTALS
Crystal acts like a two-dimensional antiferromagnet; K_2NiF_4. G. B. Lubkin. Phys Today 22:69 Jl '69
Crystals. S. C. Abrahams. il Phys Today 22:30-7 Ag '69
In pursuit of the atom. il Chem 42:20-1 Mr '69
Oxytocin: crystal data of a seleno analog. C. C. Chie and others. bibliog il Science 163:925-6 F 28 '69
Single crystals of silver oxide. il Chem 42:24 O '69
Where the action is, in molecules; excitonics, new way to transfer energy. il Bsns W p 106+ Ap 12 '69

Lattices
Ion implantation studies in silicon. L. Eriksson and others. bibliog il Science 163:627-33 F 14 '69

CRYSTALS, Ice. See Ice

CRYSTALS, Metal. See Metal crystals

CRYSTALS, Piezoelectric
Power from crystals to drive strange new tools; sonic motors. A. P. Armagnac. il Pop Sci 195:70-3+ Ag '69

CRYSTALS, Snow. See Snow

CSIKSZENTMIHALYI, Mihaly
Rigors of play. Nation 208:210-12 F 17 '69

CTENOCYSTOIDEA. See Echinoderms, Fossil

CUADRA, Carlos A.
Libraries and technological forces affecting them; address, April 1968. ALA Bul 63:759-68 Je '69

CUBA
View from Cuba. J. Harvey. il Commonweal 91:351-61 D 19 '69
Visit to Cuba. K. Witker. Vogue 154:92+ O 1 '69
See also
Agriculture—Cuba
Art—Cuba
Aviation—Cuba
Colleges and universities—Cuba
Communism—Cuba
Medical service—Cuba
Morale, National—Cuba
Negroes in Cuba
Slavery—Cuba
Socialism—Cuba

Economic conditions
Revolution, for internal consumption only; excerpt from The transformation of political culture in Cuba. R. R. Fagen. il Trans-Action 6:10-15 Ap '69
Weather change in Cuba? R. W. Dietsch. il Nation 208:826-7 Je 30 '69
See also
Communism—Cuba

Economic policy
Moral economy of a revolutionary society. J. A. Kahl. bibliog il Trans-Action 6:30-7 Ap '69
Revolutionary offensive. C. Mesa-Lago. bibliog il Trans-Action 6:22-9+ Ap '69
Socialism in Cuba, by L. Huberman and P. Sweezy. Review
Nation 209:416-17 O 20 '69. E. Capouya

Foreign relations
For Castro: tighter Soviet ties as popularity ebbs. il U S News 67:9 Ag 4 '69
Making peace with Cuba. America 120:577-8 My 17 '69
United States-Cuba relations: beyond the quarantine. I. L. Horowitz. bibliog il Trans-Action 6:43-7 Ap '69

CUBA—Foreign relations—*Continued*
We should start talking with Castro. J. Plank. il N Y Times Mag p28-31+ Mr 30 '69; Same abr. with title Should we talk with Castro? Cur 107:10-17 My '69; Reply. P. D. Bethel. N Y Times Mag p 133 My 11 '69
Weather change in Cuba? R. W. Dietsch. il Nation 208:826-7 Je 30 '69

History

Invasion, 1961

Kennedy, Khrushchev. and Cuba. D. Pearson. il Sat R 52:12-15 Mr 29 '69

Politics and government

Castro's Cuba: drums, guns. and the new man. J. Corry. Harper 238:37-45 Ap '69
Cuba; American radical views the revolution after ten years of Castro. C. Oglesby. il Life 66:62D-62F+ F 14 '69
Cuba ten years after; symposium. bibliog il Trans-Action 6:8-47+ Ap '69
For Castro: tighter Soviet ties as popularity ebbs. il U S News 67:9 Ag 4 '69
See also
Communism—Cuba

Religious institutions and affairs

Cuba and religion: challenge and response. E. E. Gendler. Chr Cent 86:1013-16 Jl 30 '69

Social conditions

Cuba; American radical views the revolution after ten years of Castro. C. Oglesby. il Life 66:62D-62F+ F 14 '69
Revolution, for internal consumption only; excerpt from The transformation of political culture in Cuba. R. R. Fagen. il Trans-Action 6:10-15 Ap '69
See also
Communism—Cuba

CUBA and the United States
View from Cuba. J. Harvey. il Commonweal 91:351-61 D 19 '69

CUBAN crisis, 1962
Dean Acheson's version of Robert Kennedy's version of the Cuban missile affair. D. Acheson. Esquire 71:76-7+ F '69
Pavlovian liberals; reviews of Robert Kennedy's memoir of the Cuban missile crisis. S. Alsop. Newsweek 73:92 F 10 '69
Thirteen days, by R. F. Kennedy. Review America 120:225-6 F 22 '69. R. L. Walker
Thirteen days; a memoir of the Cuban missile crisis, by R. F. Kennedy. Review Schol Teach Sec Teach Sup p31 O 6 '69. T. Waye

CUBAN refugees. See Refugees. Cuban

CUBAN students
Student power in action. A. Hochschild. il Trans-Action 6:16-21+ Ap '69

CUBANS in the United States
Havana, Fla. il Newsweek 74:59 S 1 '69
See also
Refugees, Cuban

CUBS (baseball) See Baseball clubs

CUCCI, Frank
Ofay watcher. Criticism
New Republic 161:24+ O 11 '69
New Yorker 45:97-8 S 27 '69
Sat R 52:26 O 11 '69

CUCCIA, James W.
Build the SCR tester. Pop Electr 30:47-9 My '69
Build the UJT tester. Pop Electr 30:33-5+ Je '69

CUCKOOS
See also
Road runners (birds)

CUCUMBERS
King of cukes. A. C. Andrews. Home Gard 56:42-43A Ap '69
Never plant cucumbers next to . . . F. D. Schales. il Org Gard & Farm 16:46-7 My '69
These cucumbers behave themselves. il Sunset 142:227 Je '69

CUDDIHY, Michael
Bridging the darkness; poem. Commonweal 91:251 N 21 '69
Bud vase; poem. Commonweal 90:595 S 26 '69
Muse; poem. Commonweal 90:561 S 19 '69

CUERNAVACA, Mexico
Joyful place. il Time 94:48 Ag 29 '69

CUERNAVACA center. See Center of intercultural documentation

CUFF, Sergeant, pseud. See Winterich. J. T.

CULBERG ballet. See Ballet—Sweden

CULBERTSON, Nancy
Giant's earth; poem. Liv Wildn 32:29 Wint '68

CULHAM, W. B.
Equipment needed for a sanitary fill. Am City 84:100 Ja '69

CULHANE, Eugene K.
Nonviolence in Latin America. America 120: 331 Mr 22 '69
They'd rather decide for themselves. America 120:621-3 My 24 '69

CULHANE, J. L. and others
Soft X-ray observations from OSO-4. Sky & Tel 37:287+ My '69

CULHANE, John
Men behind Dastardly & Muttley. il N Y Times Mag p50-1+ N 23 '69

CULLIGAN, Glendy
Artist or craftsman? Sat R 52:46-7+ Ap 12 '69
USA. Sat R 52:31-3 O 11 '69

CULLING. See Cows—Culling

CULLMAN, Joseph Frederick, 1912-
Jilted American. il Forbes 104:36 Jl 1 '69

CULLY, John J.
Saturn 5 gave the Apollo 8 a leg up to the moon. W. Jury. il Space World F-3-63:31-3 Mr '69

CULP, Gordon
Better settling basin. bibliog Am City 84: 82-5 Ja '69

CULSHAW, John
Where do we go from hear? Hi Fi 19:56-60 N '69

CULTIVATION. See Tillage

CULTIVATION of soybeans. See Soybeans—Cultivation

CULTIVATORS
Garden tillers. B. C. Kilvert, jr. il Home Gard 56:72-3 Mr '69
Here's to Tilly the toiler; finding parts for old rotary tillers. D. L. Moyle. il Org Gard & Farm 16:41-2 Ap '69
They plan for easy cultivation. G. L. Earle. il Suc Farm 67:38 Je '69
Tiller makes it possible. G. L'Allemand. il Org Gard & Farm 16:35-7 My '69
Woman looks at her tiller. L. Shade. il Org Gard & Farm 16:38-40 Ap '69

CULTS
Ghost dance. J. Greenway. il Am West 6: 42-7 Jl '69
Ghost dance and cargo cult. P. Farb. il Horizon 11:58-65 Spr '69
Jai Baba! Hare Krishna, and all that. P. Rowley. il Mlle 70:136-7+ D '69

CULTS, Negro
See also
Black Muslim movement

CULTURAL centers
Culture thrives in Peoria; Lakeview center for the arts and sciences. R. E. Owens. il Parks & Rec 3:38-40 N '68
See also
Centers for the performing arts
John F. Kennedy Center for the performing arts. Washington, D. C.
Manila—Philippine cultural center

CULTURAL cooperation. See International cooperation

CULTURAL evolution. See Social change

CULTURAL exchanges. See Exchange of persons programs

CULTURAL migration. See Man—Migrations

CULTURAL revolution. See Social revolution

CULTURALLY deprived children. See Socially handicapped children

CULTURE
Working paper for man and nature. M. Mead. il Natur Hist 78:14-15+ Ap '69
See also
Civilization
Education
History
Language and culture
Popular culture

CULTURE, American. See United States—Civilization; United States—Intellectual life; United States—Popular culture

CULTURE, Primitive. See Indians of North America—Culture

CULTURE, South African. See South Africa—Intellectual life

CULTURE and Christianity. See Christianity and culture

CULTURE media
See also
Fungi—Culture media

CUMBERFORD, Robert
Is there a diesel in your future? Motor T 21:28-31 Mr '69
Novelty, vice or virtue? Motor T 21:70-2 F '69

CUMBERLAND ISLAND
Battle for a Georgia island; conservation vs. development. il Bsns W p 128-9 S 6 '69

CUMMING, Elizabeth C. See Cumming. W. P.
jt. auth.
CUMMING, William P. and Cumming, E. C.
Treasure of Alnwick castle. Am Heritage
20:22-33+ Ag '69
CUMMINGS, Edward Estlin
Twenty-three letters; ed. by F. W. Dupee
and G. Stade. Harper 238:71-80 Mr '69

about

Champion of freedom and the individual.
J. Hart. Nat R 21:864 Ag 26 '69
Quirky communications from an exuberant
unhero. L. Untermeyer. Sat R 52:25-6 Jl 5
'69
Small-eyed poet. J. Epstein. New Repub 160:
23-7 Je 7 '69
Typewriter art. R. A. Sokolov. il por News-
week 73:112-13 Je 9 '69
CUMMINGS, Mrs Frank
Charm is her business. N. Bowden. il pors
Farm J 93:84-5 Mr '69
CUMMINGS, Samuel
Arms dealer Sam; excerpts from The war
business. G. Thayer. Harper 238:92+ Ap
'69
CUMMINS, Paul F.
Composition as the expression of personality.
Engl J 58:92-5 Ja '69
CUMMINS engine company
No flowers please. il Forbes 103:30-1 Ja 15 '69
CUNARD, Nancy
Personal history. P. MacManus. por Sat R
52:24 Ag 30 '69
CUNARD steamship company
Riding out the storm; Cunard expected to
earn a profit. il Bsns W p44+ Ja 25 '69
CUNEO, Paul K.
Future of Catholic books. America 120:170-1
F 8 '69
CUNNEEN, Sally
She married a priest. Commonweal 90:440-1
Jl 11 '69
CUNNINGHAM, Ben
Well-tempered color-wheel. L. Campbell. il
por Art N 68:42-3+ Ap '69
CUNNINGHAM, Evelyn
Action: a beauty investment. B. Wysor. il
pop Harp Baz 102:158-61 Ag '69
CUNNINGHAM, John T.
Place to look, a time to listen. Audubon 71:
28-41 Mr '69
CUNNINGHAM, Katharine
Norman Walker: a romantic poet, a sculptor
in space. Dance Mag 43:42-5 D '69
CUNNINGHAM, Merce
Choreography of the object. N. J. Loftis.
il pors Craft Horiz 29:10-13+ Mr '69
Merce Cunningham and dance company. Billy
Rose theatre. M. Marks. Dance Mag 43:
86-7 Mr '69
Movement itself. D. McDonagh. New Repub
161:24+ D 6 '69
CUNNINGHAM, Merce, dance company. See
Merce Cunningham dance company
CUNNINGHAM, Phillip J.
Far-spent day. Cath World 209:84-5 My '69
CUNNINGHAM, William D.
Anto wicharti. por Library J 94:4496-9 D 15
'69
CUONY, Edward R.
Shadow study. Clear House 43:312-14 Ja '69
CUP flowers. See Cupflowers
CUPBOARDS
Build a spacemaker cupboard. il Mech Illus
65:84-5 F '69
CUPCAKES. See Cake
CUPFLOWERS
Good low perennial. R. D. Pearce. il Hor-
ticulture 46:39 D '68
CUPOLAS
Working cupola. il Mech Illus 65:120-2 O '69
CUPPS, Stephen
Evading gun control. New Repub 160:16-18
My 3 '69
Television and cigarettes; whither fairness?
Chr Cent 86:1085-7 Ag 20 '69
CUPS
Wager cups; 16th century German cups. Y.
Hackenbroch. il Antiques 95:692-5 My '69
CURB peddlers. See Street trades
CURIA romana. See Catholic church—Roman
curia
CURIOS. See Souvenirs
CURLERS, Hair. See Hair curlers
CURLEY McDimple; musical comedy. See Mu-
sical comedies, revues, etc.—Criticisms,
plots. etc.
CURLING
Curling: hottest sport on ice. M. Michaelson.
il Todays Health 47:56-9+ N '69
Curling in Scotland. il Travel & Camera
32:96-7+ F '69

CURRAN, Dolores
(ed) What's heroic about continence? Cath
World 209:21-3 Ap '69
CURRAN, Joseph Edwin
Viva Curran. Nation 209:428-9 O 27 '69
CURRENCY. See Money
CURRENCY black markets. See Black mar-
kets
CURRENCY convertibility
Play money; rates of exchange in eastern
Europe. Newsweek 73:77-8 F 3 '69
CURRENCY question
Après devaluation; impact of France's ac-
tion. il Newsweek 74:57 Ag 25 '69
Decision on a summer weekend; implica-
tions of France's devaluation. il Newsweek
74:31-2 Ag 18 '69
CURRENT events
Hilda Maehling fellowships; in world affairs.
Todays Ed 58:29 D'69
March of the news; front page of the week.
See issues of U.S. news & world report
Month in review. See issues of Current his-
tory
News & views. J. Deedy. See issues of Com-
monweal
Newsnames: 68. il Todays Ed 58:44-5 Ja '69
Parting shots; with photographs. Life 67:
95-8 N 14; 91-4 N 21; 81-4 N 28; 107-10+
D 5; 93-6 D 12; 66A-68 D 19 '69
People and events. See issues of Senior
scholastic
Press section; notes and comment on the
news. See issues of Reader's digest

Bibliography

Issues of the day; world in ferment. il Sr
Schol 94:Schol Teach 10-12+ My 2 '69
Views on current affairs; paperback books.
il Sr Schol 94:Schol Teach 12-14 Ja 31 '69

Study and teaching

Ambassadors report; Machias, Me, public
schools. A. W. Dodd. il Sr Schol 94:Schol
Teach 13 Mr 28 '69
CURRENT RIVER
Our first national river. L. Hall. il Audubon
71:48-51 Mr '69
CURRENTS, Ocean. See Ocean currents
CURREY, Stella Martin
To live the dream; story. Good H 169:90-1
N '69
CURRICULUM. See Catholic colleges and uni-
versities—Curriculum; Colleges and univer-
sities—Curriculum; Courses of study; High
schools—Curriculum
CURRICULUM development, Association for.
See Association for supervision and cur-
riculum development
CURRY
World of curries. E. Lambert de Ortiz. il
House & Gard 136:158-9+ S '69
CURSING. See Swearing
CURTAIN and drapery fixtures
Create your own window treatments. il House
& Gard 136:188-9 S '69
CURTAINS and draperies
Fresh look at café curtains. il Good H 169:
166 Jl '69
Great new looks for windows. il House &
Gard 136:40-7 Ag '69
Ten idea window treatments. P. Rumely and
C. Garner. il Bet Hom & Gard 47:52-7 Jl
'69
Through the bamboo curtain. il Sunset 142:
129-30 Je '69
Window dressing. il McCalls 96:114-23 Ap '69
CURTIS, Bob
Security: a challenge to shoplifters. Pub W
196:40-2 S 1 '69
CURTIS, Byrd C. and Johnston, D. R.
Hybrid wheat; with biographical sketches. Sci
Am 220:18, 21-9 bibliog(p 158) My '69
CURTIS, C. Michael
Deprived of liberty. Atlan 223:104-6 Ja '69
Peace and quiet. New Repub 160:23-5 Mr 8
'69
Travels with Mr Charlie. Atlan 224:31-8 Ag
'69
CURTIS, Carl Thomas
What the Bible says about government; ex-
cerpts from address. U S News 67:108 N
10 '69
CURTIS, J. E.
How parks will shape urban development.
por Am City 84:87-90 O '69
CURTIS, Margaret E.
One summer there were dragons; story. Good
H 169:68-9 Ag '69
CURTIS, Patrick
Stars. il por Time 93:92+ Ap 4 '69

CURTIS, Paul
 Focus on quail. Field & S 74:50-1+ S '69
 Lake of bragging fish. Field & S 74:44-5+ Jl '69
 Pre-season training pays off. Field & S 73: 184-5+ Mr '69
CURTIS, Richard, and Hogan, Elizabeth
 Myth of the peaceful atom; with biographical sketches. pors Natur Hist 78:4, 6-8+ Mr '69
CURTIS, Thomas B.
 Fiscal picture; address, December 11, 1968. Vital Speeches 35:240-3 F 1 '69
CURTIS publishing company
 Curtis affair. Newsweek 73:86+ F 17 '69
 I am Marty Ackerman..; excerpts from Decline and fall. O. Friedrich. il Harper 239: 92-100+ D '69
 Still fighting over Curtis. Bsns W p42 My 17 '69
  See also
 Saturday evening post
CURTO, Frank
 Phipps conservatory. Horticulture 46:38-9+ N '68
CURVATURE of the spine. See Spine—Abnormities and deformities
CUSACK, Isabel Langis
 Lot to learn; story. Redbook 133:76-7 Je '69
 Matter of kindness; story. Good H 168:104-5 My '69
CUSCUNA, Michael
 New music of political protest. Sat R 52:55-6 D 13 '69
CUSHION flight-240. See Air cushion vehicles
CUSHIONS
 Super pillow, it's grandma's hassock up to date. il Sunset 143:77 D '69
CUSTARDS
 Creams and custards. R. C. Bateman. il House & Gard 136:143-5+ O '69
CUSTODIAL account. See Trusts and trustees
CUSTODY of children. See Guardian and ward
CUSTOMER service
 Why customers complain: the breakdown in service. il U S News 67:50-2 D 1 '69
CUSTOMS. See Manners and customs
CUSTOMS informers. See Informers (law)
CUSTOMS service

United States
 Confessions of a canary; Customs informers. il Newsweek 74:48 Jl 28 '69
 Customs plan bypasses JFK jam J. W. Carter. Aviation W 91:28-9 Jl 7 '69
CUSTOMS service and tourists
 Customs and cameras. B. Kelly. il U S Camera 32:59+ Ja '69
 How to cross borders with your photo equipment. L. Barry. il Pop Phot 65:86-7+ O '69
CUT flowers. See Flowers—Cut flowers
CUT glass. See Glassware
CUTAK, Ladislaus
 Cacti. il Horticulture 46:36-7+ N '68
 Jardin botanique Les Cedres. il Horticulture 47:36-7+ F '69
 Unusual succulents. il Horticulture 47:28-9+ My '69
CUTHBERTSON, George, and Cassian, George
 Yachting interviews; ed. by B. Robinson. pors Yachting 125:124-5+ Ja '69
CUTLER, Carol
 Paris: Paul Klee. Art in Am 57:132-5 N '69
 Peru: the future of the Inca empire. Art in Am 57:80-2 My '69
 Paris gallery guide. Art in Am 57:88-93 Mr '69
CUTLER, Donald
 Religious cultures, high and low. Commonweal 91:156-60 O 31 '69
CUTLER, Rose
 Rose Cutler and Alexandra Gardner the great-great-nieces of the great Mrs Jack. il pors Vogue 153:174-5 My '69
CUTLER-Hammer, incorporated
  See also
 Airborne instruments laboratory
CUTTER, Curt
 What's with the new auto warranties? Pop Mech 131:98-101+ Mr '69
CUTTHROAT trout. See Trout
CUTTING costs. See Cost control
CUTTING machines
 Fitting automation to the garment trade; precise cutting machine, Gerbercutter. il Bsns W p 102+ My 3 '69
CUTTING tools
 All-purpose cutting tool. H. Wicks. il Pop Mech 132:222 S '69
 Here's a dovetailing device that's really different. J. Burroughs. il Pop Mech 132:170-2 Ag '69

Your guide to tin snips. R. J. De Cristoforo. il Pop Sci 195:174-6+ O '69
 Zippidi-do; cutting and sanding disk 7. il Consumer Bul 52:14+ S '69
CUTTINGS, Plant. See Plant propagation
CUYAHOGA RIVER
 Cities: the price of optimism; Cleveland's polluted Cuyahoga. il Time 94:41 Ag 1 '69
CYBERNETIC anthropomorphous machine. See Man amplifiers
CYBERNETICS
 Making machines into men and women. D. M. Rorvik. il Esquire 71:114-15 Ap '69
  See also
 Man amplifiers
 Perceptrons
CYBORGS. See Man amplifiers
CYCADS, Fossil
 Cycads: evidence from the upper Pennsylvanian. T. N. Taylor. bibliog il Science 164: 294-5 Ap 18 '69
 Cycads: fossil evidence of late paleozoic origin. S. H. Mamay. bibliog il Science 164: 295-6 Ap 18 '69
CYCASIN
 Cycasin: detection of associated mutagenic activity in vivo. M. G. Gabridge and others. bibliog il Science 163:689-91 F 14 '69
CYCLAMATES. See Sugar substitutes
CYCLES, Business. See Business cycles
CYCLING
 Bicycle built for you. R. Teeger. il Har Yrs 9:6-12 Mr '69
 Bicycling through Holland. K. Harris. il Mlle 69:195-8+ S '69
 Holiday on wheels. R. Hanneman. il Parks & Rec 4:26-8+ Je '69
 Personal business. Bsns W p 159-60 Ap 26 '69
 Try bicycle-camping. C. B. Colby. il Outdoor Life 143:18+ Mr '69
 What makes Audrey pedal? Tiga muk. D. Levin. il Sports Illus 31:68+ N 24 '69

Safety devices and measures
 Learning to ride a bike with safety and skill. il Good H 168:188-9 My '69
CYCLING trips
 Go, go, go by bike. P. Lowry. il Seventeen 28:176-7+ Ap '69
 HY travel editor cycles in Europe. N. D. Ford. il Har Yrs 9:13 Mr '69
CYCLONES
  See also
 Hurricanes
CYCLOPHOSPHAMIDE. See Endoxan
CYCLOTRONS.   See Accelerators (electrons, etc)
CYLINDER records. See Phonograph records
CYLINDERS (engines, etc)
 Strictly for stocks; cylinder bore finishing. J. Dianna. il Hot Rod 22:116 Jl '69
CYLINDERS, Automobile. See Automobile engines
CYMATICS. See Vibration
CYMBIDIUMS. See Orchids
CYNARA. See Artichokes
CYNICISM
 Antidote for cynicism; excerpt from address, September 1969. K. Brewster, jr. Time 94: 47 S 26 '69
CYPHOMANDRA betacea. See Tree tomatoes
CYPRIDINA. See Ostracods
CYPROTERONE. See Steroids
CYPRUS
 Amity for Cyprus? L. H. Dean. Chr Today 13:45-6 Ap 11 '69
  See also
 United Nations—Armed forces—Forces in Cyprus
CYR, Donald J.
 Coiling a pot in a pot. Ceram Mo 17:12-14 Ja '69
 David Crespi's weed pots. Ceram Mo 17:20-2 Mr '69
 (ed) See Rada, P. Pravoslav Rada
CYR, Helen
 Doing your own thing at Sobrante park school. ALA Bul 63:268-71 F '69
CYSTIC fibrosis
 Oyster ciliary inhibition by cystic fibrosis factor. B. Bowman and others. bibliog il Science 164:325-6 Ap 18 '69
 Unmasking the great impersonator, cystic fibrosis. P. A. Di Sant'Agnese. il Todays Health 47:38-41+ F '69

CYSTINE
Cystine: compartmentalization within lysosomes in cystinotic leukocytes. J. D. Schulman and others. bibliog il Science 166:1152-4 N 28 '69

CYSTINURIA
Amino acid uptake by kidney and jejunal tissue from dogs with cystine stones. P. G. Holtzapple and others. bibliog il Science 166:1525-7 D 19 '69

CYTOCHROMES
Cytochrome a3: destruction by light. B. Epel and W. L. Butler. bibliog il Science 166:621-2 O 31 '69
Cytochrome P-420: tubular aggregates from hepatic microsomes. D. W. Shoeman and others. bibliog il Science 165:1371-2 S 26 '69
Enzyme molecule in three dimensions. il Chem 42:22 D '69
Extraparticulate chain interaction between different electron transport particles. E. Bogin and others. bibliog il Science 165:1364-7 S 26 '69

CYTOKININS. See Kinins

CYTOPHAGA. See Myxobacteria

CYTOPLASM
See also
Microsomes
Mitochondria

CYTOSINE
Cytosine to thymine transitions from decay of cytosine-5-³H in bacteriophage S13. F. Funk and S. Person. bibliog il Science 166: 1629-31 D 26 '69

CYTOSINE arabinoside. See Cancer inhibiting substances

CZARNECKI, Edgar R.
Profit sharing and union organizing. Mo Labor R 92:61-2 D '69

CZECH authors. See Authors, Czech

CZECH journalists. See Journalists

CZECH refugees. See Refugees, Czech

CZECH students
See also
Student movement—Czechoslovakia

CZECHOSLOVAKIA
See also
Airlines—Czechoslovakia
Airplane industry and trade—Czechoslovakia
Astronomical observatories—Czechoslovakia
Censorship—Czechoslovakia
Communism—Czechoslovakia
Communist party (Czechoslovakia)
Morale, National—Czechoslovakia
Moving pictures—Czechoslovakia
Political crimes and offenses—Czechoslovakia
Russia—Armed forces—Forces in Czechoslovakia
Russia—Foreign relations—Czechoslovakia
Student movement—Czechoslovakia
Trials—Czechoslovakia

Commerce
Tense Prague holds the trade door open. il Bsns W p46+ Ag 16 '69

Diplomatic and consular service
Diplomatic exile. Time 94:14 D 26 '69

Economic conditions
Existentialist opposition. L. Chabrowe. Commonweal 89:585-7 F 7 '69
High price of repression. il Time 94:92+ O 10 '69
Is there a tomorrow? il Newsweek 73:88+ My 5 '69
Other rape of Czechoslovakia. L. Velie. Read Digest 95:187-8+ Jl '69

Foreign relations
Homilies for Husak; Moscow visit. il Newsweek 74:51 N 3 '69
See also
Czechoslovakia—Occupation, 1968

History
Masaryk case, by C. Sterling. Review Time 95:78 Ja 12 '70

Industries
See also
Czechoslovakia—Economic conditions

Occupation, 1968-
Anxiety in Bonn: German fears after Czechoslovakia. S. Muller. Bul Atom Sci 25:13-15 Mr '69
Czechoslovakia in transition. A. Z. Rubinstein. Cur Hist 56:206-11+ Ap '69
Czechoslovakia: one year later. il Newsweek 74:34-6 Ag 25 '69

Czechoslovakia's tense anniversary. Time 94: 32 Ag 22 '69
Czechs protest a dark anniversary. il Life 67:48-9 S 5 '69
Day of shame; observing first anniversary of Soviet invasion. il Time 94:27 Ag 15 '69
Death to remember. L. Gross. il Look 33:18-26 S 9 '69
Dubcek talks; interviews, ed. by D. Hunebelle. A. Dubcek. il Look 33:21-3 Jl 29 '69
Existentialist opposition. L. Chabrowe. Commonweal 89:585-7 F 7 '69
Face to face with a girl who saw freedom die in Czechoslovakia. S. Hruby. Seventeen 27:125 N '68
Future U.S.-Soviet relations; the lessons of Czechoslovakia. A. Shub. Cur 104:46-54 F '69
High price of victory; crisis after ice hockey victory. il Time 93:34 Ap 11 '69
In Soviet-occupied Czechoslovakia; a search for Ivan with a hidden camera. M. Durham. il Life 66:30-3 Ap 18 '69
Look homeward. R. Gormley. il Nat R 21:849-50+ Ag 26 '69
Nation violated. P. E. Zinner. Sat R 52: 21-3+ Mr 29 '69
NATO communiqué on Czechoslovakia; excerpts. November 16, 1968. Cur Hist 56:239-41+ Ap '69
New trouble in Prague; the lessons. il U S News 67:4 S 1 '69
Prague diary. S. T. Black. il McCalls 96: 74-5+ Ja '69
Russians lose a pair; and set off 100,000 Czechs. il Life 66:93-4 Ap 11 '69
Second thoughts in the Kremlin. America 120:209 F 22 '69
Soviet communiqué on Czechoslovakia; communiqué, October 5, 1968. Cur Hist 56:238-9+ Ap '69
Thinking about the Soviet Union. W. F. Buckley, jr. Nat R 21:818 Ag 12 '69
U.N. legal committee discusses the question of defining aggression; statements. November 19 and 25, 1968. J. S. Cooper. Dept State Bul 59:664-72 D 23 '68
Year under Russia's heel; first-hand report from Prague. A. Kucherov. il U S News 67: 78-80 Ag 25 '69
Year's end in Prague. F. Pauly. America 120:135-8 F 1 '69
Yugoslavia: the diplomacy of balance. S. S. Anderson. bibliog f il Cur Hist 56:212-17+ Ap '69

Protests, demonstrations, etc. against
Bells peal for a martyr in Prague. il Life 66:24-7 F 7 '69
Burning of Jan Palach. America 120:151 F 8 '69
Czech clampdown. Sr Schol 94:14-15 Ap 18 '69
Czechoslovakia: politics on ice; Soviet demands. il Newsweek 73:49 Ap 14 '69
Message in fire. il Time 93:22+ Ja 31 '69
Protest in Prague; protest singers and songs. il Newsweek 74:49 Jl 28 '69
Second Jan. il Newsweek 73:42 F 3 '69
Student sets self afire; with report by R. Hemming. il Sr Schol 94:12-13 F 7 '69
These are Czechs beating Czechs. il Newsweek 74:27-8 S 1 '69
Tighter vise on Czechoslovakia. il Time 94: 22-3 Ag 29 '69
Torch number one. Newsweek 73:51-2 Ja 27 '69
Youth in ferment: occupied Czechoslovakia; Jan Palach's protest in fire. R. Hemming. il Sr Schol 94:8-9 Mr 7 '69

Politics and government
Can new leader of Czechs turn back the clock? U S News 66:18 My 5 '69
Closer to normal. il Time 94:25 O 3 '69
Consolation prize; subscribing to the Brezhnev doctrine. Newsweek 74:56 N 10 '69
Czech clampdown. Sr Schol 94:14-15 Ap 18 '69
Czechoslovakia in transition. A. Z. Rubinstein. Cur Hist 56:206-11+ Ap '69
Czechoslovakia: politics on ice. il Newsweek 73:49 Ap 14 '69
Dubcek dumped. Sr Schol 94:18 My 2 '69
Dubcek falls and the Russians have their way. il Newsweek 73:48+ Ap 28 '69
End of the Dubček era. il Time 93:26+ Ap 25 '69
Not far from Novotný. Time 94:29-30 O 24 '69
Prague winter; crackdown on liberals. Newsweek 74:50 S 22 '69

CZECHOSLOVAKIA—Politics and government
—*Continued*
Tightening rule. il Time 94:24+ Jl 4 '69
Tying up some loose strings. il Time 94:52
D 5 '69

See also
Communism—Czechoslovakia
Communist party (Czechoslovakia)

Religious institutions and affairs
Ambiguous news on Czech church. America
121:250 O 4 '69
Czech church in limbo. E. V. Kohak. Commonweal 90:591-4 S 26 '69
Hromadka exit. J. J. Van Capelleveen. Chr
Today 14:35 D 19 '69
New calvaries ever. Chr Cent 86:1538-9 D 3
'69

See also
Christians in Czechoslovakia

Social conditions
Year's end in Prague. F. Pauly. America 120:
135-8 F 1 '69

Travel regulations
See Travel regulations
CZECHOSLOVAKIA-United States air agreement. See Aviation—International aspects
CZECHS
Nation of Schweiks. S. Bingham. Atlan 223:
119-21 F '69
CZURA, Pete
Saddle up to safe horsemanship. Todays
Health 47:48-53 Ap '69
Ten top camping sites. il por Todays Health
47:42-7 My '69
Vacation: country style. Pop Gard 20:30-3+
Spr '69

D

D day invasion. See World war, 1939-1945—
Campaigns and battles—Western
DAVI. See National education association—
Department of audio-visual instruction
DDC. See Classification, Decimal
DDC (defensive driving course) See Automobile driving—Study and teaching
DDT (insecticide)
Attack on DDT. Time 94:59 N 21 '69
Brushing off DDT; government's elimination program. il Newsweek 74:74 N 24 '69
DDT ban sprays a wilting business. Bsns
W p37 N 22 '69
DDT: criticism, curbs are on the upswing.
M. Mueller. Science 164:936-7 My 23 '69
DDT: where will the ban stop? il Bsns W
p 16-17 Ja 3 '70
DED and DDT: it is time to change. Audubon
71:5 My '69
Environment: focus on DDT, the uninvited
additive. J. Walsh. Science 166:975-7 N 21
'69
Gardening without DDT. J. B. Kring. il
Horticulture 47:22-3 N '69
How the government will phase out DDT.
il U S News 67:8 N 24 '69
It's time to blow the whistle on DDT. il
Sunset 143:58-9 Ag '69
Keep DDT out of gardens! Home Gard 56:
62-3 O '69
Legal remedy. Sci Am 220:57 Je '69
Nature's broken vase; Dutch elm disease
and DDT. R. Rood. il Audubon 71:6-12 My
'69
New say in court; suit against five major
manufacturers. Time 94:54 O 24 '69
Pesticides: pro and con. il U S News 67:102-
3 O 20 '69
Photochemical decomposition of DDT by a
free-radical mechanism. A. R. Mosier and
others. bibliog il Science 164:1083-5 My 30
'69
Photooxidation of DDT and DDE. J. R.
Plimmer and others. bibliog il Science 167:
67-9 Ja 2 '70
We've got them on the run. R. Rodale. Org
Gard & Farm 16:25-7 N '69
Yesterday cyclamates, today 2,4,5-T, tomorrow DDT? J. R. Kramer. Science 166:724
N 7 '69
Your garden is on the front line; poison-free
gardening. R. Rodale. il Org Gard & Farm
16:21-4 O '69

Injurious effects
Adenosine triphosphates sensitive to DDT in
synapses of rat brain. F. Matsumura and K.
C. Patil. bibliog il Science 166:121-2 O 3 '69
Alarming case against DDT; interview. ed. by
J. N. Miller. C. F. Wurster. Read Digest
95:99-104 O '69
Avian thyroid: effect of p,p'-DDT on size
and activity. D. J. Jefferies and M. C.
French. bibliog il Science 166:1278-80 D 5
'69
Beginning of the end for DDT. G. Laycock. il
Audubon 71:36-43 Jl '69
Beyond the bug; environment poisoning. il
Time 93:24-5 Ap 18 '69
Bringing down the giant; DDT banned in
U.S. Sci N 96:473 N 22 '69
Charge is biocide; DDT stands trial. C. F.
Wurster. il Audubon 71:128-35 S '69
DDT and the Constitution; petition to ban
use of DDT in Wisconsin. H. Henkin. il
Nation 208:308-10 Mr 10 '69
DDT on trial; Wisconsin pollution case. H.
Henkin. il Environ 11:14-17 + Mr '69
DDT: sublethal effects on brook trout nervous system. J. M. Anderson and M. R.
Peterson. bibliog il Science 164:440-1 Ap
25 '69
DDT: the critics attempt to ban its use in
Wisconsin. L. J. Carter. Science 163:548-51
F 7 '69; Reply. R. Van Den Bosch. 164:497
My 2 '69
Don't go near the water? Lake Michigan
coho salmon contaminated. il Newsweek
73:75 My 5 '69
Fight to ban DDT. G. W. Wormley. Farm
J 93:15+ Je '69
Living for the moment; problem of preserving nature's balances. J. Deedy. Commonweal 91:324 D 12 '69
New storm brewing over DDT; named in NCI
study as causing tumors. Bsns W p32 Mr
8 '69
Obituary for DDT (in Michigan) H. Higdon.
il N Y Times Mag p6-7+ Jl 6 '69
Pesticide into pest. il Time 94:56-7 Jl 11 '69
Pesticide pollution. C. Cottam. il Nat Parks
43:4-9 N '69
Slow death for DDT? H. Bloomfield. il Am
For 75:16-19+ N '69
Wisconsin DDT story in pictures and words.
R. Rodale. il Org Gard & Farm 16:19-23 Jl
'69

Residues
Academy of sciences lays another thin-shelled
egg; Committee on persistent pesticides. Audubon 71:103 Jl '69
Beginning of the end for DDT. G. Laycock. il
Audubon 71:36-43 Jl '69
DDT in humans. il Sci Digest 66:75 N '69
DDT residues absorbed from organic detritus by fiddler crabs. W. E. Odum and others. bibliog il Science 164:576-7 My 2 '69
DDT threatens you! E. Chaney. il Nat Wildlife 7:48-9 Ag '69
Degradation and disappearance of ortho, para
isomer of technical DDT in living and dead
avian tissues. M. C. French and D. J.
Jefferies. bibliog il Science 165:914-16 Ag
29 '69
Persistent pesticides. P. H. Abelson. Science
164:633 My 9 '69
Problems in ppm; DDT residues in Lake
Michigan coho salmon. H. Henkin. il Environ 11:24-33+ My '69
Regulating a monster. Sci N 95:423 My 3 '69
Spectrum: ban of DDT in Michigan. H.
Henkin. Environ 11:S1-3 Ap '69
DEW (distant early warning) See Radar defense networks
DGB (Deutscher gewerkschaftsbund) See Trade
unions—Germany (Federal Republic)
DMZ cabaret programs. See Cabarets
DNA
Actinomycin binding to DNA: inability of a
DNA containing guanine to bind actinomycin D. R. D. Wells. bibliog il Science
165:75-6 Jl 4 '69
Another messenger. Sci Am 221:53-4 D '69
Berberine: complex with DNA. A. K. Krey
and F. E. Hahn. bibliog il Science 166:
755-7 N 7 '69
Cell transformation by viruses. R. Dulbecco.
bibliog il Science 166:962-8 N 21 '69
Cellular factors in genetic transformation. A.
Tomasz. il Sci Am 220:38-44 bibliog(p 138)
Ja '69
Cytoplasmic DNA from petite colonies of
saccharomyces cerevisiae: a hypothesis on
the nature of the mutation. F. Carnevali
and others. bibliog il Science 163:1331-3
Mr 21 '69
DNA helix. M. F. Perutz and others. Science
164:1537-9 Je 27 '69

DNA—*Continued*
Deoxyribonucleic acid methylase activity in pea seedlings. F. Kalousek and N. R. Morris. bibliog il Science 164:721-2 My 9 '69
Double helix, by J. D. Watson. Review
Trans-Action 6:53-6 Mr '69. F. Davis
Enzyme from calf thymus degrading the RNA moiety of DNA-RNA hybrids; effect on DNA-dependent RNA polymerase. H. Stein and P. Hausen. bibliog il Science 166:393-5 O 17 '69
Fourier analysis and the structure of DNA. J. Donohue. bibliog il Science 165:1091-6 S 12 '69
Glimpse of the helix; DNA molecule photographed. il Time 93:51 Mr 14 '69
Histone synthesis in vitro by cytoplasmic microsomes from HeLa cells. D. Gallwitz and G. C. Mueller. bibliog il Science 163: 1351-3 Mr 21 '69
Human diploid cell transformation by DNA extracted from the tumor virus SV40. S. A. Aaronson and G. J. Todaro. bibliog il Science 166:390-1 O 17 '69
Mammalian DNA polymerase: separation of binding from incorporation of deoxyribonucleoside triphosphates. P. Ove and J. Laszlo. bibliog il Science 165:903-4 Ag 29 '69
Mapping of deletions and substitutions in heteroduplex DNA molecules of bacteriophage lambda by electron microscopy. B. C. Westmoreland and others. bibliog il Science 163:1343-8 Mr 21 '69
Microsome-associated DNA. H. E. Bond and others. bibliog il Science 165:705-6 Ag 15 '69
Mitochondrial DNA: advances, problems, and goals. M. M. K. Nass. bibliog il Science 165:25-35 Jl 4 '69
Plus and minus single-stranded DNA separately encapsidated in adeno-associated satellite virions. H. D. Mayor and others. bibliog il Science 166:1280-2 D 5 '69
Polyoma virus gene activity during lytic infection and in transformed animal cells. M. A. Martin and D. Axelrod. bibliog il Science 164:68-70 Ap 4 '69
Repairing the DNA. Sci N 96:348-9 O 18 '69
Short fragments from both complementary strands in the newly replicated DNA of bacteriophage SPP-1. M. Polsinelli and others. bibliog il Science 166:243-5 O 10 '69
Spinning the thread of life. J. Lear. il Sat R 52:63-6 Ap 5 '69
Temporal coordination of DNA replication with enzyme synthesis in diploid and heteroploid cells. R. R. Klevecz. bibliog il Science 166:1536-8 D 19 '69
DNA polymerase. See Polymerases
DOM. See Amphetamines
DOT. See United States—Transportation, Department of
DQ Herculis. See Stars, Variable
DSRV (deep submergence rescue vehicle) See Submarine boats
DAANE, J. Dewey
Impact of tight money, new clues; report U S News 67:107-8 S 22 '69
DA CRUZ, Daniel
Letter from Beirut. Nat R 21:332, 711+ Ap 8, Jl 15 '69
DACTYLOSCOPY. See Fingerprints
DADAISM
Art world; Arp retrospective exhibition at Guggenheim. H. Rosenberg. New Yorker 45:91-2+ Je 21 '69
DADD, Richard
Method onto madness; Fairy feller's masterstroke. il por Time 93:72-3 Ap 25 '69
DADDARIO, Emilio Quincy
Needs for a national policy. por Phys Today 22:33-8 O '69
Science and the federal government; address, February 12, 1969. Vital Speeches 35:341-6 Mr 15 '69
DADE COUNTY, Fla.
Helicopters cover all. R. L. Shelton. il Am City 84:44 Jl '69
DAGUERREOTYPES
Remarkable decade of daguerreotype. B. Newhall. Mod Phot 33:100-5 N '69
DAHDAH, Robert
Shirley or Curley? R. Schickel. il Life 66:81-2 Je 13 '69
DAHER GUERRA, Jorge
Moctezuma's musicians. C. C. Lieberman. il pors Américas 21:23-8 F '69
DAHLIAS
Green dahlia? P. A. Pavlik. il Org Gard & Farm 16:56-9 Mr '69
Variety is the spice of dahlias. il Home Gard 56:35-7 My '69
DAICHES, David
Observations. Commentary 48:80-3 O '69

about
Criticism as performance. R. Alter. Commentary 47:94+ My '69
DAIGON, Arthur
Literature and the schools. Engl J 58:30-9 Ja '69
Pictures, punchcards, and poetry; address, November 1968. Engl J 58:1033-7 O '69
DAIGRE, Bert
Lift for black businessmen. il Bsns W p68 N 1 '69
DAILEY, Elric Jack
Last of Boone's breed. D. J. Anderson. por Field & S 73:64-5+ Mr '69
DAILEY, John
Air piracy: they want a moment of power and glory. S. McBee. il Life 66:26-7 Ap 18 '69
DAILY express international boat show, London. See Boats—Exhibitions
DAILY mail transatlantic air race. See Airplane racing
DAILY news, New York
Many-faceted fact; reactions to poll and the mayoral race. Newsweek 74:98 N 10 '69
Poll-axed? il Newsweek 74:87 N 17 '69
DAILY news, Washington. See Washington daily news
DAILY world (newspaper)
Communism's family newspaper. D. Smith. Nation 208:631-4 My 19 '69
DAIMLER-Benz, ag. See Automobile industry and trade—Germany (Federal Republic)
DAINES, Robert H. See Otto, H. W. jt. auth.
DAIRY farm management
Big production from thirty-five cows. J. R. Borcherding. il Suc Farm 67:B2 O '69
Boost dairy income with dairy beef. J. R. Borcherding. il Suc Farm 67:34-5+ Ja '69
Dairying, what's ahead in the '70s. J. R. Borcherding. il Suc Farm 67:28-9+ My '69
Fancy production with low-cost ideas. J. R. Borcherding. il Suc Farm 67:B8 S '69
$5000 pay increase for Bill Oswalt. N. Reeder. il Farm J 93:D8+ Je '69
Ideas from a high-profit dairy. il Suc Farm 67:32-3 N '69
Ideas from a 60-60-60 partnership. il Suc Farm 67:B2 Je '69
Their ideas build profits; management program of Curtis and Earl Phillips. C. Peterson, jr. and J. R. Borcherding. il Suc Farm 67:46-7 F '69
DAIRY industry and trade
Dairy extra; symposium. See issues of Farm Journal
Hitchhiking dairymen: pay or get off. il Farm J 93:D8-9+ Ap '69
DAIRY products
See also
Ice cream ices, etc.
DAIRY research
Wanted: more results from the research dollar. Farm J 93:D14 F '69
DAIRYING
Dairy extra; symposium. See issues of Farm Journal
News. See issues of Farm Journal
What's new. J. R. Borcherding. See issues of Successful farming
See also
Cows—Feeding
Dairy farm management
Milking
Research
See Dairy research
DAISIES
See also
Shasta daisies
DAISY V/L rifle. See Rifles
DAKOTA (territory)
Dakota boyhood. J. E. Fraser. il Am Heritage 20:81-8 D '68
DAKOTA, SOUTH. See South Dakota
DAKOTA Indians
Happening at Oglala; Jesuit helps Sioux regain pride in their heritage. D. O. Collins. il Am West 6:15-19 Mr '69
D'ALBERT, Eugen. See Albert, E. d'
DALE, Edwin L. jr
After peace breaks out, what will we do with all that extra money? N Y Times Mag p32-3+ F 16 '69
Nixon's tax plan. New Repub 160:9-11 My 3 '69
Realities of tax reform. New Repub 160:12-13 F 15 '69
Revenues & reform in the tax bill. New Repub 162:12-14 Ja 3 '70
Something for the silent majority. New Repub 161:14-15 N 29 '69

DALE. H. Fred
Tree stumps. Horticulture 46:47-8 S '68
DALE, Margaret
Margaret Dale: TV ambassador. M. Harriton. il pors Dance Mag 43:24-7 N '69
DALEY, Austin C.
Junked-car air pollution. Am City 84:131+ O '69
DALEY, Eliot A.
Is TV brutalizing your child? Look 33:99-100 D 2 '69
DALEY, Mary Dowling
Mayor Stokes' West side story. Commonweal 91:270-1 N 28 '69
DALEY, Richard J.
Chairman Daley's maxims; excerpts from Quotations from Mayor Daley. Time 94: 15B-16 Jl 18 '69
about
Daley on the stand. por Newsweek 75:23-4 Ja 19 '70
Daley vs. the guerrilla theatre. R. Whitehead, jr. Nation 208:422-3 Ap 7 '69
Daley's revenge. Nation 208:420 Ap 7 '69
Democrats against Daley. il por Time 93:19-20 F 21 '69
Enter Adlai III. il por Newsweek 74:48+ D 8 '69
Green peril. R. A. Sokolov. Newsweek 74:79 Ag 11 '69
Mayor Daley: solvent but worried. D. Rose and D. S. Canter. Nation 209:169-73 S 1 '69
Of heart and spleen. Time 93:28 Mr 14 '69
Place where all America was radicalized. T. Wicker. il por N Y Times Mag p26-7+ Ag 24 '69; Reply with rejoinder. E. F. Berman. p58+ O 5 '69
Police riot? Chicago report; summary. Sr Schol 93:18 Ja 10 '69
Roof caves in on Mayor Daley's housing plan. il por Bsns W p56-7 Ag 30 '69
Squabble between two top Democrats. por U S News 66:19 Mr 17 '69
Witness for the defense. Time 95:17 Ja 19 '70
DALGLISH, William E.
Hocket in medieval polyphony. bibliog f Mus Q 55:344-63 Jl '69
DALI, Salvador
De Kooning's 300,000,000th birthday; tr. by J. Ashbery. Art N 68:56-7+ Ap '69
DALL sheep. See Mountain sheep
DALLAS
Style trends 1969. il Am City 84:126+ Ja '69

Airports
Mobile lounges cut walk to aircraft; Love field. Aviation W 91:47 S 29 '69
New Texas airport advancing. Aviation W 90:53 My 19 '69
Tomorrow's air terminal, today. H. Apter. il Travel & Camera 33:33-4 Mr '69

Churches
Edifice complex loses out; Highland Park church. J. C. Evans. Chr Cent 86:309-11 Mr 5 '69

Monuments, statues, etc.
Dealey plaza. L. Smith. il Holiday 46:78-9+ N '69

Parades
Jingoism confronted in Dallas. J. C. Evans. Chr Cent 86:830-1 Je 18 '69

Sanitary affairs
Hit-and-run squads clear sewer stoppages. A. E. Holcomb. il Am City 84:119+ Jl '69
DALLAS civic opera company
DCO: good news. J. Ardoin. il Hi Fi 19: MA27+ F '69
Report; production of Aida. J. Ardoin. Opera N 34:27 D 20 '69
DALLAS cowboys (football club) See Football clubs
DALLETT, Francis James
Thibaults, Philadelphia silversmiths. Antiques 95:547-9 Ap '69
DALLIN, Cyrus Edwin
Sculptor Cyrus E. Dallin, who knew the horse and knew the Indian. J. C. Ewers. il por Am West 6:22-3 N '69
DALLMER, Rolf
Anthracnose in sycamores. Horticulture 47: 22+ Je '69
DALLOS, P. and others
Cochlear distortion: effect of direct-current polarization. bibliog Science 164:449-51 Ap 25 '69
DAL POZZO, Nicoletta Avogadro
Porcelain of Naples. Antiques 95:270-4 F '69

DALRYMPLE, Byron W.
Fly fishing in a forest. Outdoor Life 144:64-7+ O '69
Homecoming buck hunt. Outdoor Life 144:52-5+ D '69
Mountain pike. Field & S 74:64-5+ My '69
Return of the bandtail. Outdoor Life 144:46-7+ S '69
DALURY, Jean McG.
Iberian itinerary. Travel 132:36-41 N '69
D'ALVAREZ, Marguerite
Historical records. A. Favia-Artsay. por Hobbies 74:35+ Mr '69
DALY, Mary
Mary Daly on the church. Commonweal 91: 215 N 14 '69
Return of the Protestant principle. Commonweal 90:338-41 Je 6 '69
about
Phasing out Mary Daly. M. Malec. Commonweal 90:61-2 Ap 4 '69
DALY, Maxine Lindley
Side trip into space. Travel 132:54-7 Jl '69
DAMADIAN, Raymond
Ion exchange in escherichia coli: potassium-binding proteins. bibliog Science 165:79-81 Jl 4 '69
DAMAGES
Honor on a ski lift; case of Ruth Friedman. Time 93:40 Ja 31 '69
Simon says; story of how a prosecutor took photographer L. Gunkel to court. Simon. il Mod Phot 33:46-7+ F '69
See also
Actions and defenses
Workmens compensation
D'AMBOISE, Jacques
Jacques D'Amboise; interview, ed. by O. Maynard. pors Dance Mag 43:34-9 O '69
DAMEREL, Paul
Miracles of plastic surgery. Parents Mag 44: 78-9+ N '69
DAMES at sea; musical comedy. See Musical comedies. revues. etc.—Criticisms. plots. etc.
DAMIANO, Victor V. See Laibson. P. R. jt. auth.
DAMPING (mechanics)
Control of vibration and noise. T. P. Yin. il Sci Am 220:98-106 Ja '69
DAMPNESS in buildings
Fixing up an older home. il Bet Hom & Gard 47:41 My '69
Moisture problems in house walls and troubles with blistering and peeling paint. C. M. Edwards. il Consumer Bul 52:12-14 My '69
DAMS
Cornplanter. can you swim? Kinzua Dam flooding Senecas' ancestral lands for Allegheny reservoir. A. M. Josephy. jr. il Am Heritage 20:4-9+ D '68
Crisis on the Columbia. by O. Bullard. Review Audubon il 71:84-5 Ja '69. G. Laycock
Kinzua Lake development. J. J. Lindsey. il Cons 23:2-5 Ap '69
Lo the poor salmon! (or, Is this dam necessary?) Middle-Snake River Dam. W. E. Towell. Am For 75:38 F '69
Marble Valley controversy. R. Lyle, jr. il Nat Parks 43:14-17 N '69
Must this be lost to the sight of man? proposed dams. Snake River. M. Frome. il Field & S 74:52-5+ Jl '69
Regional water supply; Rend Lake conservancy district. R. D. Jones and J. W. Rezek. il Am City 84:108+ Mr; 73-5 Ap '69
Why dam the Charlotte? H. S. Kernan. il Am For 75:28-31+ N '69
Why Gooley number one? A. M. Crocker. il Liv Wildn 32:22-4 Wint '68
See also
Flood prevention and control

Failures
Throwing cold water on marmes man. M. P. Works. Esquire 73:59-60+ Ja '70

Egypt
See also
Aswan High Dam

Mexico
See also
Amistad (dam)

Rhodesia
Kariba Dam; the ecological hazards of making a lake. T. Scudder. il Natur Hist 78:68-72 F '69

United States
See also
Amistad (dam)

DANCE, Stanley
Ellington at the White House. Sat R 52:48-9+
My 31 '69
New Orleans, jazz capital? Sat R 52:45-6 Jl
12 '69
Recordings reports; jazz LP's. See issues of
Saturday review
DANCE bands. See Bands (music)
DANCE companies
Ageless Pierrot; Gruppe motion Berlin at Ja-
cob's Pillow. W. Terry. il Sat R 52:36 Ag
30 '69
Alwin Nikolais dance company; Brooklyn
academy of music. J. Dowlin. Dance Mag
43:82+ Ja '69
Come dance for us; Northern Westchester
dance company. il Dance Mag 43:73-80 D
'69
Dancers from Dinkytown; Minnesota dance
theatre. D. Hering. il Dance Mag 43:66-72
D '69
Dancing in the rain; Repertory dance thea-
tre of the University of Utah, in New York
city. W. Terry. il(p63) Sat R 52:64 O 4 '69
Les Feux-follets. M. Siegel. il Dance Mag
43:64-7 S '69
Gruppe motion Berlin, Judson memorial
church. J. Anderson. Dance Mag 43:33+ Mr
'69
New America ballet co. St Bartholomew's
community club theatre. J. Anderson.
Dance Mag 43:74 Ag '69
Paul Sanasardo dance co. Hunter college
playhouse. J. Armstrong. Dance Mag 43:70
Ag '69
Repertory dance theatre; Delacorte theater.
D. Hering. il Dance Mag 43:38-9+ N '69
Theatre; Alwin Nikolais dance theatre. H.
Clurman. Nation 209:703 D 22 '69
Three films in the making. il Dance Mag
43:43-6 Ap '69
See also
Afro-American dance ensemble
Alvin Ailey American dance theater
Association of American dance companies
Gertrude Talcott dance company
Glen Tetley dance company
Huntington dance ensemble
Martha Graham and dance company
Merce Cunningham dance company
Murray Louis dance company
Paul Taylor dance company
Pearl Lang dance company
DANCE concerts
Ballet soiree, Fashion institute of technology.
M. Marks. Dance Mag 43:93 Je '69
Black chamber dance concert; Minor Latham
playhouse. M. Marks. Dance Mag 43:76 Jl
'69
ChoreoConcerts workshop; St Peter's church.
J. Dowlin. Dance Mag 43:76 Jl '69
Clann Gael; Hunter college assembly hall.
J. Anderson. Dance Mag 43:32 D '69
Claudia Melrose, Anna Nassif, Emery Her-
mans & Robert Solomon; the Cubiculo.
T. Borek. Dance Mag 43:77-8 Jl '69
Dance caravan, New York city center. M.
Marks. Dance Mag 43:94 Je '69
Dance uptown; Minor Latham playhouse. J.
Armstrong. Dance Mag 43:33+ D '69
Dance uptown; Minor Latham playhouse,
January 18 and 31, 1969. A. J. Fortney.
Dance Mag 43:32 Mr '69
Deborah Hay & a large group of people;
Damrosch park. J. Anderson. Dance Mag
43:73 D '69
Evening of firsts, Clark center for the per-
forming arts. J. Anderson. Dance Mag 43:
80 Ap '69
Group dance theatre; 92nd street Y. M.
Marks. Dance Mag 43:80 Ap '69
Helen McGehee; 92nd st. Y. J. Anderson
Dance Mag 43:87 My '69
Hunter college playhouse; Miguel Godreau
and dancers. D. Hering. Dance Mag 43:73
Ag '69
Jazz as dance; Al Minns and Leon James pro-
gram. J. Brin. Dance Mag 43:88+ Mr '69
June Lewis & Deborah Zall; NYU school of
education auditorium. T. Borek. Dance
Mag 43:74+ Ag '69
Kathryn Posin, Michael Ebbin & Ze'eva
Cohen the Cubiculo. J. Anderson. Dance
Mag 43:71 Ag '69
Lar Lubovitch; 92nd street Y. M. Marks.
Dance Mag 43:87 Jl '69
New choreography; Betsy Kagan, Susan
Matheke, Fran Snygg & Paul Plumadore;
the Cubiculo. J. Armstrong. Dance Mag
43:92 S '69
New dance group studio, 92nd st. Y. J. An-
derson. Dance Mag 43:82 Je '69
Reyes-Soler ballet español; Brooklyn college.
M. Marks. Dance Mag 43:73 D '69

Sabina Nordoff and Burt Supree; dances,
poems and films, Cubiculo theatre. J. Dow-
lin. Dance Mag 43:93 Je '69
School of performing arts dance concert;
Brooklyn academy of music. J. Anderson.
Dance Mag 43:81 Jl '69
Twelfth New choreographers concert. Clark
center for the performing arts. J. Dowlin.
Dance Mag 43:80 Ja '69
World of dance; L. Lubovitch at 92nd street
YM-YWHA. W. Terry. il Sat R 53:77 Ja 3
'70
DANCE conferences
Colloquy of colleagues: dance conventions
'69. N. M. Stoop. il Dance Mag 43:70-3 N
'69
Sixteen to sixty at Wichita; second annual
dance symposium. D. Hering. il Dance
Mag 43:80-1 O '69
World of dance; second American dance
symposium. W. Terry. il Sat R 52:53-4 S
20 '69
DANCE costume. See Costume. Theatrical
DANCE costume designers. See Costume de-
signers
DANCE critics. See Critics
DANCE festivals
Ageless Pierrot; Gruppe motion Berlin at
Jacob's Pillow. W. Terry. il Sat R 52:36
Ag 30 '69
Calendar of international summer dance
events. il Dance Mag 43:51-9 My '69 (to be
cont)
Dancing in the rain; Rebekah Harkness
foundation dance festival. W. Terry. il Sat
R 52:63 O 4 '69
Dancing on the (new) Thames; American
dance festival. W. Terry. Sat R 52:100 S
13 '69
From nadir to zenith; Center ballet of Buf-
falo in Jacob's pillow dance festival. W.
Terry. Sat R 52:39 S 6 '69
Harkness youth dancers; Delacorte theatre,
Central park. J. Anderson. il Dance Mag
43:36-7 N '69
Israel dances. R. N. Abramson. il Sr Schol
94:Schol Teach 12-13 Ap 25 '69
Jacob's Pillow sampler. il Dance Mag 43:30-3
S; 30+ O '69
Life in a chambered nautilus; Southeastern
regional ballet festival. D. Hering. il Dance
Mag 43:66-9 Ag '69
Next year, keep the baby; 22nd annual Ameri-
can dance festival, Connecticut college; the
school and the festival. D. Herine; S. Smo-
lair. Dance Mag 43:40-2+ O '69
Pickles and cones; fourth annual Pacific re-
gional ballet festival. D. Hering. il Dance
Mag 43:68-71 Jl '69
Rub-off factor; Southwestern regional ballet
festival. D. Hering. il Dance Mag 43:70-4
Je '69
Seven sweets and seven sours; Northeast
regional ballet festival. D. Hering. il Dance
Mag 43:73-6 S '69
Summer circuit; Jacob's Pillow; Beaupré
ballet; Caramoor festivals. W. Terry. il Sat
R 52:41-2 Jl 26 '69
World of dance; Jacob's Pillow festival. W.
Terry. il Sat R 52:54-5 Ag 23 '69
World of dance; second festival of Daven-
port college ballet society. W. Terry. il
Sat R 52:42-3 Mr 29 '69
DANCE films. See Moving pictures—Dance films
DANCE institutes and workshops
Dance theatre workshop; The cubiculo. M.
Marks. Dance Mag 43:83-5 F '69
Through dance's open door; Gloria Unti's
Performing arts workshop of San Fran-
cisco. R. Hartley. il Dance Mag 43:29-31 N
'69
Where do you store your confetti? New
York's dance theater workshop. D. Hering.
il Dance Mag 43:38-41 Ja '69
See also
Dancers workshop of San Francisco
DANCE literature
Dance books in my life; symposium. il Dance
Mag 43:38-42 Mr; 68-9 Ap '69
DANCE magazine
Dance magazine awards 1968. il Dance Mag
43:34-7+ Ap '69
Dunham, Bruhn, Fracci receive Dance mag-
azine awards. il Dance Mag 43:44-6 Jl '69
DANCE masters of America
Colloquy of colleagues: dance conventions
'69. N. M. Stoop. il Dance Mag 43:70-3 N
'69
Seventy years of Dance masters of America.
J. Anderson. il Dance Mag 43:68-71 F '69
DANCE music
See also
Ballet music
Bands (music)
Phonograph records—Dance music

DANCE notation
Choreology. R. Holden. il Opera N 33:8-12 Ap 19 '69
DANCE perspectives (periodical)
Dancer's bookshelf. J. Anderson. Dance Mag 43:69 Ja '69
DANCE production
Coppelia is light and breezy. il Dance Mag 43:42-5 Ja '69
Dances at a gathering; interview, ed. by E. Denby. J. Robbins. il Dance Mag 43:47-55 Jl '69
Lizzie Borden, by A. De Mille. Review Dance Mag 43:70 Ja '69. M. G. Swift
DANCE records. See Phonograph records— Dance music
DANCE schools
Dance teacher in the community. D. R. Sellars. See issues of Dance magazine
Dressing room dream. A. Fatt. Dance Mag 43:104 Ja '69
Next year, keep the baby; 22nd annual American dance festival, Connecticut college; the school and the festival. D. Hering; S. Smoliar. Dance Mag 43:40-2+ O '69
Outlook encouraging; Ballet center of Buffalo. B. Miller. il Dance Mag 43:68-9 Mr '69
Your own thing: join a dance class. il Seventeen 28:30 S '69
See also
California institute of the arts
DANCE teachers
Dance teacher in the community. D. R. Sellars. See issues of Dance magazine
See also
Dance masters of America
Holm, H.

Education
Wisconsin's new certification program. M. H. Nadel. Dance Mag 43:105-6 F '69
DANCE theater workshop, New York. See Dance institutes and workshops
DANCE therapy
Dance, a world of wonders to handicapped children; seminar conducted by Adventures in movement organization. R. Lert. il Dance Mag 43:60-3 S '69
Describing an elephant. M. B. Siegel. Dance Mag 43:92-3 Ja '69
DANCE workshops. See Dance institutes and workshops
DANCERS
Alumni in dance; dancers who are college graduates. J. F. Teitelman. il Dance Mag 43:39-44 F '69
Balanchine+girls=ballet. R. Kotlowitz. il Holiday 45:54-7+ Mr '69
Brief biography. S. Goodman. See issues of Dance magazine
Changes and interchanges. il Dance Mag 43:63 My '69
Dancers of dancing parents (cont) M. Marks. il Dance Mag 43:65-8 Ja; 70-2 S '69
For men only; experiment in a dance project at University of Wisconsin. E. Jacobs. il Dance Mag 43:78-81 My '69
Hide your daughters, here comes Russ Markert; creator of the Rockettes. R. Roman. il Dance Mag 43:46-9+ S '69
In the news; photographs. See issues of Dance magazine
New year's message from the publisher. R. Orthwine. Dance Mag 43:21 Ja '69
Presstime news. See issues of Dance magazine
See also
Children as dancers
also names of dancers, e.g. E. Bruhn
DANCERS workshop of San Francisco
Mythmaker. il Time 93:53 Ja 24 '69
DANCES at a gathering; ballet. See Ballets —Criticisms
DANCING
Are people dancing? il Vogue 153:240 My '69
Dance adventure with Mozart. W. Terry. il Sat R 52:42-3 Ja 25 '69
Dance, by L. Kirstein. Review Dance Mag 43:21+ N '69. J. Anderson
Ferment and controversy; new look in dance and the arts keeps changing its sights. J. Anderson. il Dance Mag 43:46-55 Ag '69
How to make the most of a shoestring; how Connecticut is becoming a state of dance. A. S. Keller. il Dance Mag 43:63-4+ Ap '69
Jazz dance, by M. Stearns and J. Stearns. Review Newsweek il 73:120+ Mr 17 '69. A. Goldman

Laying down some leather: jazz dance; interview. L. James and A. Minns. New Yorker 44:29-31 F 15 '69
Looking at the dance; excerpts. E. Denby. il Dance Mag 43:51-9 Ja '69
Presstime news. See issues of Dance magazine
Reviews. See issues of Dance magazine
Theatre. H. Clurman. Nation 208:710 Je 2 '69
They danced till they dropped; making of They shoot horses, don't they? D. Adler. il Life 67:58-61 Jl 25 '69
World of dance. W. Terry. See issues of Saturday review
See also
Ballets
Choreography
Dance therapy
Folk dancing
Hula (dance)
Moving pictures—Dance films
Rock 'n' roll dancing
Royal academy of dancing
Tap dancing
Television broadcasting—Dancing

Auditions
Anybody need 683 dancers? J. Barthel. il Life 67:61-2+ D 5 '69

Bibliography
Books in print; comp. by R. Fentress. il Dance Mag 43:51-8 Mr '69
Dancer's bookshelf (cont) J. Anderson. Dance Mag 43:25-7+ S; 21+ N; 22-3 D '69
Dancer's bookshelf. S. J. Cohen. Dance Mag 43-65+ Jl '69

Competitions
See also
Ballet—Competitions

History
Dancing Bach. W. Hilton; R. Tureck. il Dance Mag 43:47-51+ O '69

Photographs
Dance, a muse of fire; excerpts. T. Victor. Dance Mag 43:52-61 O '69
See also
Photography of dancing

Study and teaching
Alumni in dance; dancers who are college graduates. J. F. Teitelman. il Dance Mag 43:39-44 F '69
Capturing the spirit along with the steps; ethnic dance program at UCLA. V. H. Swisher. il Dance Mag 43:70-4 O '69
For men only: experiment in a dance project at University of Wisconsin. E. Jacobs. il Dance Mag 43:78-81 My '69
Open letter from Bruce King. B. King. il Dance Mag 43:89 Ag '69
Pied Pipers in leotards. R. Estrada. il Dance Mag 43:56-60 Jl '69
Project for the farthest-out college; problems of American college dance. J. Anderson. il Dance Mag 43:45-6+ F '69
See also
Dance schools
Dance teachers
DANCING, African
African dance company of Ghana, Felt forum, Madison Square Garden. J. Anderson. Dance Mag 43:81-2 Ja '69
Ghana; spontaneous and authentic; the African dance company of Ghana. R. A. Thom. il Dance Mag 43:24-5 My '69
Twelve wives of Chief Ogunde. il Ebony 24:106-8+ O '69
DANCING, Balinese
Tourist in Indonesia. A. Rechter. il Dance Mag 43:23-4 S '69
DANCING, English
Entertainment for Elizabeth; Caramoor festival. D. Hering. Dance Mag 43:78-9 Ag '69
DANCING, Indian (East Indian)
Dances of India; Vija Vetra & company, the Cubiculo. M. Marks. Dance Mag 43:92 Je '69
Indra-nila; the Cubiculo. J. Anderson. Dance Mag 43:78 Ag '69
Sukhendu Dutt & Loveleen Bhata; the Cubiculo. T. Borek. Dance Mag 43:29 S '69
See also
Chaki-Sircar, M.
DANCING, Indonesian
See also
Dancing, Balinese

DANCING, Israeli
Hebraica dancers; 92nd street Y. J. Dowlin. Dance Mag 43:30 Ap '69
Israel dances. R. N. Abramson. il Sr Schol 94:Schol Teach 12-13 Ap 5 '69
Israel: from pungent image to vivid life; Batsheva company. R. Gold. il Dance Mag 43:36-40 My '69
DANCING, Japanese
Japan folk dance group; 92nd street Y. J. Dowlin. Dance Mag 43:88 Mr '69
DANCING, Korean
National folk ballet of Korea, Hunter college assembly hall. M. Marks. Dance Mag 43:32 Ja '69
DANCING, Marathon. See Dancing
DANCING, Mexican
    See also
Ballet folklórico of Mexico
DANCING, Moroccan
Sacred and profane; hadra and belly-dance. J. Kramer. il N Y Times Mag p26 Je 22 '69
DANCING, Spanish
Rumba-flamenca; spectacular new stars; with photographs by R. de Larrain. Vogue 154:162-9 D '69
    See also
Mava. M.
DANCING, Swedish
Sweden: stirring up a commotion; American D. Feuer. M. Kats. il Dance Mag 43:46-8 My '69
DANCING, Venezuelan
Danzas Venezuela and Yolanda Moreno; Hunter college assembly hall. M. Marks. Dance Mag 43:26+ F '69
DANCING, West Indian
Merry, merry John Canoe in Jamaica. H. Diaz. il Dance Mag 43:16-17 D '69
DANCING, Yugoslav
Tamburitzans; Hunter college assembly hall. J. Dowlin. Dance Mag 43:32 Ap '69
DANCING Christmas tree lights. See Christmas tree lights
DANCING for the handicapped
    See also
Dance therapy
DANCING in religion, folklore, etc.
    See also
Folk dancing
DANCING in television. See Television broadcasting—Dancing
DANCING schools. See Dance schools
DANDELIONS
Dandelions: golden heralds of spring. A. Hechtlinger. il Read Digest 94:31-2+ Ap '69
DANFORTH, John Claggett
Sweepstakes of the '70s; five entries. il por Newsweek 73:27-8 F 24 '69
DANFORTH center. See Rochester, N.Y.—Community centers
DANGERFIELD, George
Churchill: impossible and impenetrable. Nation 208:637-8 My 19 '69
DANGERFIELD, Lance
Miami to Nassau, Aronow style. Motor B 124:15 D '69
DANGEROUS toys. See Toys, Hazardous
DANIEL, A. Mercer
Lovetts of Harpers Ferry, West Virginia. por Negro Hist Bul 32:14-19 F '69
DANIEL, James
Better way of paying respects to the dead. Read Digest 95:143-6 Ag '69
Call for action, new voice for the people. Read Digest 95:207-10+ O '69
Negative income tax, better than welfare? Read Digest 94:60-4 My '69
DANIEL, Margaret (Truman)
Qualified thanks. Ladies Home J 86:99 N '69
    about
Authors & editors. B. A. Bannon. por Pub W 196:25-6 S 8 '69
DANIEL, Oliver
Harvest from Martha's Vineyard. Sat R 52:103+ S 13 '69
If it pleases. Sat R 52:71+ N 29 '69
Loops and reels. Sat R 52:62-3+ Ap 12 '69
More from Poland. Sat R 52:54-5 Je 28 '69
DANIEL, Thase
Feathers in full bloom; photographs. Nat Wildlife 7:12-13 Ap '69
DANIEL, Yuli
Day in the life of Yuli Daniel. por Time 93:44 Je 6 '69
—and others
Open letter to the presidium of the supreme Soviet of the USSR. Nat R 21:852-3 Ag 26 '69

DANIEL Yankelovich, incorporated. See Yankelovich, Daniel, incorporated
DANIELIAN, Leon
Leon Danielian at the helm. R. Gold. il pors Dance Mag 43:60-3 Ag '69
DANIELS, Charles A. and others
Neutralization of sensitized virus by the fourth component of complement. bibliog Science 165:508-9 Ag 1 '69
DANIELS, David N. See Gilula, M. F. jt. auth.
DANIELS, George
Eighteen minute verdict. M. Polner. Commonweal 90:40-3 Mr 28 '69
DANIELS, M. E.
Build a fun barge. Mech Illus 65:70-3+ My '69
DANIELS, Robert D.
Adriana from five to four. Opera N 33:24-5 Ap 19 '69
Serious Donizetti. Opera N 33:24-5 F 1 '69
Three cheers for Tri-Cities. Opera N 33:14-16 Mr 1 '69
DANISH cookery. See Cookery, Danish
DANISH pastry. See Pastry
DANISH royal ballet. See Royal Danish ballet
DANNAY, Frederic, and Lee, M. B. See Queen, E. pseud.
D'ANNUNZIO, Gabriele. See Annunzio, G. d'
DANSGAARD, W. and Tauber, Henrik
Glacier oxygen-18 content and Pleistocene ocean temperatures. bibliog Science 166:499-502 O 24 '69
—and others
One thousand centuries of climatic record from Camp Century on the Greenland ice sheet. bibliog Science 166:377-81 O 17 '69
DANTO, Arthur C.
Columbia, the useless lesson. New Repub 160:25-6+ Ja 25 '69
D'ANTONIO, Emile
News & views; In the Year of the pig. J. Deedy. il Commonweal 90:250 My 16 '69
DANUBE RIVER
The Danube. N. Hordern. il Harp Baz 102:86+ Ag '69
DANVILLE, Ill.
Two cities built malls that bring new vitality to Main Street. G. M. Chamberlain. il Am City 84:78+ N '69
DANZAS Venezuela. See Dancing, Venezuelan
DANZIG, Sarah Palfrey
Why don't we try it again soon? E. Watson. il por Sports Illus 31:76+ O 20 '69
DAO, Thomas L.
Mammary cancer induction by 7,12-dimethylbenz(a)anthracene: relation to age. bibliog Science 165:810-11 Ag 22 '69
D'AOUST, Brian G.
Hyperbaric oxygen: toxicity to fish at pressures present in their swimbladders. bibliog Science 163:576-8 F 7 '69
DAPHNES
Success with dwarf daphne. M. S. Sperka. Home Gard 56:8 F '69
DAPPER, Gloria, and Murphy, Judith
Part-time teachers and how they work. Ed Digest 35:22-5 N '69
D'AQUINO, Iva Ikuko Toguri. See Tokyo Rose, pseud.
D'ARAZIEN, Steven
Advocate of people's wars. Nation 208:470-1 Ap 14 '69
DARBY, Kim
New name, a new life; ed. by E. Miller. il por Seventeen 28:116-17+ Je '69
D'ARCANGELO, Angelo, pseud.
On the fringe. H. Frankel. Sat R 52:30 Je 14 '69
DARCOURT, Pierre
Buildings in Hanoi crumble, Haiphong is ruined, ravaged; interview. por U S News 67:39-40 D 22 '69
DARDEN, Betty D.
Miniature daffodils. Horticulture 46:24-7+ S '68
DARDEN, Norman
My man André. Sat R 52:43-5 Jl 26 '69
DARIEN, Panama
Darien. M. Barraco Mármol. il Américas 21:23-31 Jl '69
DARK adaptation. See Eye—Accommodation and refraction
DARK glasses. See Sun glasses
DARKROOM equipment. See Photography—Processing—Apparatus and supplies
DARKROOM technique in photography. See Photography—Processing
DARKROOM timers. See Photography—Processing—Apparatus and supplies
DARLEY, John M. and Latané, Bibb
Why people don't help in a crisis. Read Digest 94:65-9 My '69

DAUMIER, Honoré
Daumier's great city. D. L. Shirey. il Newsweek 73:96 My 19 '69
DAVENPORT, C. Lothrop
Apples of yesteryear. Horticulture 46:16-17+ O '68
DAVENPORT, Guy
Last of the masters. Nat R 21:1017-18 O 7 '69
Lenin before he became the czar. Nat R 21: 78-80 Ja 28 '69
DAVENPORT, John, 1904-
Chemical industry pushes into hostile country. Fortune 79:108-15+ Ap '69
New new economics in Washington. Fortune 80:100-5+ Jl '69
W. R. Grace is still looking for that magic. Fortune 80:106-9+ O '69
DAVENPORT, Willie D.
Willie the predictable. Time 93:52 Mr 14 '69
Woes of Wee Willie Wisp. S. Myslenski. il pors Sports Illus 30:42-4+ Mr 17 '69
DAVID, F. S.
Your garden indoors. Home Gard 56:12 D '69
DAVID, Gerard
Cover; Nativity, with donors and patron saints. il Am Artist 32:6 D '68
DAVID, Hal
Popular records. D. Watt. New Yorker 44: 84-6 Ja 18 '69
DAVID, Jan
Park; poem. Seventeen 29:91 Ja '70
DAVID, Lester
Facts about moonlighting. Mech Illus 65:29-31+ Ag '69
High-paying blue collar jobs and how to get one. Mech Illus 65:31-3+ D '69
How could this happen to our daughter? Good H 169:86-7+ S '69
How to get out of debt. Mech Illus 65:49-51+ F '69
How to save money when you travel. Mech Illus 65:48-50+ Ap '69
Our hairy revolution, and what to do about it. pors Mech Illus 65:74-5+ O '69
Recipe for a high-paying job. Mech Illus 65:47-9+ Mr '69
What to do when you're arrested. Mech Illus 65:45-7+ N '69
What you should know about arthritis quacks. Good H 169:70-1+ Ag '69
DAVID, Saul
David and the network Goliaths. R. L. Shayon. Sat R 52:52 N 1 '69
DAVID, Sherrie May
We tied and dyed. Sch Arts 68:18-19 My '69
DAVID; story. See Thorp, E.
DAVIDOW, Mary C.
Journey from apple orchard to swallow thronged loft: Fern Hill. bibliog f Engl J 58:78-81 Ja '69
DAVIDS, Richard C.
How safe are no-calorie sweeteners? Read Digest 95:77-80 Jl '69
Light-work way to an indoor garden. Read Digest 94:120-3 Mr '69
Pigs, those true-blue Americans. Sci Digest 66:18-21 S '69
DAVIDS, Warner
No more muddy boots in the kitchen. Am City 84:111-12 Ag '69
DAVIDSON, Aarno
Saint or sorcerer? poem. Clear House 43:434 Mr '69
DAVIDSON, Abraham A.
William S. Mount: the mysterious stranger. Art N 68:34-7 Mr '69
DAVIDSON, Angus
(tr) See Moravia, A. Chase; Reconciliation
DAVIDSON, Basil
Rediscovery of Africa; reprint. UNESCO Courier 22:66-7 Ag '69
DAVIDSON, Bernice F.
Gentile da Fabriano's Madonna and Child with saints. Art N 68:24-7+ Mr '69
DAVIDSON, Bruce
Gallery; photographs. Life 67:4-7 Ag 15 '69
Portfolio of Welsh photographs. Horizon 11: 30-9 Wint '69

about

Antonioni: from super 8 to panavision. H. V. Fondiller. il Pop Phot 65:112-13 S '69
SRO for Uelsmann, Davidson at S. F. museum of art. M. Mann. Pop Phot 65:23-4+ S '69
DAVIDSON, Eric H. See Britten, R. J. jt. auth
DAVIDSON, Erika
(ed) See Cappuccilli, P. What's in a name
DAVIDSON, Henry A.
Double life of a psychiatric hospital; address, October 4, 1968. Ment Hy 53:17-20 Ja '69

DAVIDSON, Jeff
Family portrait on a bearskin rug. McCalls 96:69+ Mr '69; Same abr. with title I have a son! Read Digest 94:51-4 My '69
DAVIDSON, Joan
Psychiatric consultation in a school for problem girls. Ment Hy 53:280-8 Ap '69
DAVIDSON, Muriel
Ingrid Bergman: the new happiness in her life. Good H 168:82-3+ My '69
(ed) See Woodward, J. Joanne Woodward tells all about Paul Newman
DAVIDSON, R. Michael
Man's participatory evolution; living in a biological revolution. Cur 105:4-10 Mr '69
DAVIDSON, Raymond
Time for change. il New Yorker 45:48-9 S 20 '69
DAVIDSON, Robert
Aleutian runaway. Sci Digest 65:64-8 My '69
DAVIDSON, Roger H.
Politics of anti-poverty. Nation 208:233-7 F 24 '69
War on poverty: experiment in federalism. bibliog f Ann Am Acad 385:1-13 S '69
DAVIDSON, Ruth
Books about antiques. See issues of Antiques
European tapestry; an Antiques survey. Antiques 96:912-17 D '69
Museum accessions. See issues of Antiques
DAVIDSON, Sara
Jacqueline Susann: the writing machine. Harper 239:65-71 O '69
Militants for women's rights. Life 67:66D-70+ D 12 '69
Rock style: defying the American dream. Harper 239:53-62 Jl '69
DAVIDSON college, Davidson, N.C.
Nobody waits on this Lefty; Davidson Wildcats in NCAA playoffs. M. Cope. il Sports Illus 30:28-30+ Mr 10 '69
DAVIE, Donald
Brantome; poem. New Repub 160:24 Je 21 '69
Oak openings; poem. New Repub 160:25 Ap 26 '69
To certain English poets; poem. Harper 239:68 O '69
DAVIES, Alan T.
New approach to Judaism; excerpts from Anti-Semitism and the Christian mind. Cath World 210:74-7 N '69
DAVIES, Don
Education professions development. Am Ed 5:9-10 F '69
DAVIES, Gordon K.
Needed: a national job-matching network. bibliog f Harvard Bsns R 47:63-72 S '69
DAVIES, John Paton, 1908-
U.S. invented the imbalance of power. N Y Times Mag p50-1+ D 7 '69

about

John Paton Davies, jr: quiet end to a shabby era. L. Gross. Look 33:82 Mr 4 '69
Long trial of John Paton Davies. J. W. Finney. il pors N Y Times Mag p7-9+ Ag 31 '69; Reply. G. Fitch. p54+ O 5 '69
Out of the mists. il por Newsweek 73:29 Ja 27 '69
Refrocked diplomat. Time 93:15 Ja 24 '69
DAVIES, M. and others
Protein digestion in isolated lysosomes inhibited by intralysosomal trypan blue. bibliog Science 163:1454-6 Mr 28 '69
DAVIES, Peter J. See Galston, A. W. jt. auth.
DAVIES, Peter Maxwell
Music; interview, ed. by D. Hamilton. Nation 208:284-6 Mr 3 '69

about

Britten premiere and a mad King George E. Greenfield. il Hi Fi 19:MA26-7 Ag '69
Inescapable power. Peter Maxwell Davies. P. L. Miller. Am Rec G 35:1054 Jl '69
DAVIES, R. W. and Amann, R.
Science policy in the U.S.S.R; with biographical sketches. Sci Am 220:14, 19-29 Je '69
DAVIES, Ralph Kenneth
Old oil hand makes Natomas swing. il por Bsns W p 102-3 S 27 '69
DAVIES, Richard Llewelyn-. See Llewelyn-Davies, R.
DAVIS, A. E. and Bolin, T. D.
Milk intolerance in southeast Asia. Natur Hist 78:54-5 F '69
DAVIS, Al
Most hated winner in football. L. Shecter. por Look 33:50+ N 18 '69
DAVIS, Angela
Academic freedom again. Nat R 21:1103 N 4 '69
Case of Angela the red. por Time 94:64 O 17 '69

DAVIS, Angela—*Continued*
Changing times. Nation 209:460 N 3 '69
Communist and the governor. A. S. Kaufman. New Repub 162:21-4 Ja 3 '70
Hard on Communism. por Newsweek 74:101 O 6 '69
Russians are coming at UCLA. S. V. Roberts. Commonweal 91:174-5 N 7 '69

DAVIS, Arthur Vining
Pitch that made Alcoa grow. por Bsns W p40 Ja 18 '69

DAVIS, Barbara Derrick-. See Derrick-Davis, B.

DAVIS, Clinton Leon
Ike, the conservationist. Am For 75:28-9+ Je '69

DAVIS, Colin
Lively arts; interview, ed. by R. Hemming. por Sr Schol 94:20 Ap 11 '69
Trojans. Hi Fi 19:61-3 Mr '69

about
Davis's English-speaking Seasons. I. Kolodin. Sat R 52:49 Je 28 '69
Musician of the month. P. J. Smith. Hi Fi 19:MA4 F '69
Other side; Berlioz by Davis. T. Heinitz. Sat R 52:54 Jl 26 '69

DAVIS, Derek
College store's temporary solution to space problem. Pub W 195:47-8 My 26 '69

DAVIS, Dick
Fishing with Bing: tale of a marlin. Travel & Camera 32:84-5+ Ag '69

DAVIS, Douglas M.
Rauschenberg's recent graphics. Art in Am 57:90-5 Jl '69

DAVIS, Duff Hart-. See Hart-Davis, D.

DAVIS, Dwight
Cup in decline. il por Time 94:52 O 3 '69

DAVIS, Elise Miller
When someone is drowning, it's no time to teach him how to swim. Read Digest 95:104-6 N '69

DAVIS, Flora
How to read body language. Read Digest 95:127-30 D '69
Right way to fight a marriage. Read Digest 94:97-100 Je '69

DAVIS, Fred
Genetics of the discovery of DNA. Trans-Action 6:53-6 Mr '69

DAVIS, Gary, Jr
Build all-transistor TV camera for $100. Radio-Electr 40:23-6+ Jl '69

DAVIS, Gene
Double puzzle game. il Art in Am 57:72-3 N '69

DAVIS, George D. See Liles, S. L. jt. auth.

DAVIS, Glover
Giant; poem. Poetry 114:17-18 Ap '69

DAVIS, Gussie Nell
Don't turn off the TV at halftime. H. Weiskopf. il por Sports Illus 31:28 D 22 '69

DAVIS, Hamilton E.
Mr Nixon's urban ballet. Nation 209:45-8 Jl 14 '69

DAVIS, Harry R.
Christian neglect of political values: the case of selective objection. Chr Cent 86:1510-14 N 26 '69

DAVIS, Hugh C.
Recreation planning in the technological age; address, May 1968. bibliog f Parks & Rec 3:22-4+ N '68

DAVIS, James Kotsilibas
Mother Waddles; the gentle warrior. Life 66:87-9 Mr 21 '69

DAVIS, James W. Jr. See Dolbeare, K. M. jt. auth.

DAVIS, Jefferson
Southern gentlemen honored in glass. T. H Marsh. il por Hobbies 74:98N Ag '69

DAVIS, Jim
Just for fun take a minibike along. Pop Sci 195:98-101+ N '69
Kawasaki Mach III: the hottest thing on two wheels. Pop Sci 194:88-9+ My '69
Kit turns your motorcycle into a three-wheel sports car. Pop Sci 195:124-5 Ag '69
Riding Honda's fabulous four. Pop Sci 195:108-9+ S '69
SR 125: new mail-order beauty from Austria. Pop Sci 195:118-19+ Jl '69
Taking care of your ear. Pop Sci 195:170-1 D '69
Yamaha 125, small bike with big power. Pop Sci 194:102-3+ Ja '69

DAVIS, John A.
Love game; story. Redbook 133:84-5 S '69

DAVIS, John D.
Silver. Antiques 95:134-7 Ja '69

DAVIS, John H.
Bouviers; excerpts. pors Ladies Home J 86:123-30 F; 90-3+ Mr '69

DAVIS, Joseph E. Jr. and others
Surprising minicell. por Chem 42:26-8 Ap '69

DAVIS, Malcolm McTear
Vienease. Travel 132:58-9 Jl '69

DAVIS, Marilyn
Christmas crafts. Har Yrs 9:30-1 D '69

DAVIS, Mildred
Third half; story. Redbook 132:143-65 Ja '69

DAVIS, Miles Dewey
Miles Davis. M. Williams. por Sat R 52:75 O 25 '69

DAVIS, Millard C.
Suspension; poem. Liv Wildn 33:12 Spr '69

DAVIS, Murray
Bob Derecktor, chosen to build the next America's cup contender. il Motor B 123:110-11+ Je '69

DAVIS, Peter G.
For Verdi, scholarship and fresh air. Hi Fi 19:MA27-8 N '69
Fresh voice for Schubert. Hi Fi 19:94 Jl '69
Repeat performance. See issues of High fidelity incorporating Musical America
Total view of Traviata. Hi Fi 19:75-6 S '69

DAVIS, Rennard C.
How the prisoners were released. por Time 94:22 Ag 15 '69

DAVIS, Richard
Portrait of Tracy, a very personal view. Life 67:88-91+ O 17 '69

DAVIS, Stanley M.
U.S. versus Latin America: business & culture. bibliog f Harvard Bsns R 47:88-98 N '69

DAVIS, Wayne H.
Overpopulated America. New Repub 162:13-15 Ja 10 '70

DAVIS, William
London. Q. Crewe. Vogue 153:108+ Mr 1 '69

DAVIS, William Eugene
Stamp out commencement speakers! Ed Digest 35:32-4 N '69

DAVIS, Wynn
Best fishing in Canada. Outdoor Life 144:70-2+ Jl '69
How to carve a turkey. Mech Illus 65:60-1 N '69
Mini course in spinning. pors Mech Illus 65:53-5+ Mr '69
Outdoors. Mech Illus 65:70+ F '69
Outdoors with Wynn Davis. See issues of Mechanix illustrated
Summer special for campers. Mech Illus 65:52-5+ My '69

DAVIS cup. See Tennis

DAVISON, Peter
Making marks; poem. New Yorker 45:38 My 17 '69
Two of you; poem. Atlan 224:55 Jl '69
Under protection; Public garden; Grandmother; Visitant; poems. Poetry 114:304-7 Ag '69
Word in your ear on behalf of indifference; poem. Harper 238:44 Je '69

DAVY, John
Polluting the planet. Cur 103:59-62 Ja '69

DAW, Nigel W. See Pearlman, A. L. jt. auth.

DAWE, Albert R. and Spurrier, W. A.
Hibernation induced in ground squirrels by blood transfusion. Science 163:298-9 Ja 17 '69

DAWE, R. A. and Smith, E. B.
Viscosity of argon at high temperatures. bibliog Science 163:675-6 F 14 '69

DAWIDOWICZ, Lucy S.
Toward a history of the holocaust. Commentary 47:51-6 Ap '69

DAWSON, Charles
Famous Piltdown hoax. il Chem 42:21-2 O '69

DAWSON, Christopher Henry
Dawson at eighty. C. J. McNaspy. America 121:302 O 11 '69

DAWSON, Dice. See Dawson, Donald

DAWSON, Donald
Dice Dawson's luck. il Time 95:21-2 Ja 19 '70
Super scandal? il por Newsweek 75:63-4 Ja 19 '70

DAWSON, Fielding
Fragments from the Black Mountain book. Harp Baz 102:254-7+ O '69

DAWSON, George P.
How dangerous is TV violence? Parents Mag 44:60-1+ O '69

DAWSON, I. L.
What's in a fence? il Nat Parks 43:11 F '69

DAWSON, Ronald G. and McGaugh, J. L.
Electroconvulsive shock effects on a reactivated memory trace: further examination. bibliog Science 166:525-7 O 24 '69

DAY, A. Grove
Honolulu: still the paradise of the Pacific? Holiday 46:62-5+ O '69
DAY, Alice Taylor
Population increase. Parents Mag 44:56-7+ O '69
DAY, Beth
Homegrown Hoosier in Italy. McCalls 96:71+ Jl '69
Return of the midwife. Redbook 132:72-3+ Mr '69
DAY, Dorothy
Dorothy Day on hope. Commonweal 91:217-18 N 14 '69
about
Dorothy Day: a sign of contradiction. S. Vishnewski. por Cath World 209:203-6 Ag '69
DAY, Dorothy LaVerne
Library on the air. por Wilson Lib Bul 44: 320-5 N '69
DAY, Edward J.
Excerpt from Post office, inc. Cong Digest 48:91+ Mr '69
DAY, Margaret M.
Very young in art. Sch Arts 69:30-1 D '69
DAY, Mark
Clergy and the grape strike. America 121: 114-17 Ag 30 '69
DAY, Richard
All those new caulks. Pop Sci 195:148-52+ S '69
Brakes for your car; special report. Pop Sci 194:117-32 Mr '69
How to color concrete. Pop Mech 131:152-5+ Je '69
How to find your best buys in plywood. Pop Sci 195:156-67 S '69
How to get your car started in cold weather. Pop Sci 194:149-53 Ja '69
How to install gutters and downspouts. Pop Mech 132:164-9 S '69
Want a patio? Pop Sci 194:172-6+ Ja '69
Your next boat may be ferro-cement. Pop Sci 195:110-13+ S '69
DAY camps. See Camps
DAY care centers. See Day nurseries
DAY care for children. See Day nurseries
DAY lilies
Daylilies indoors. R. P. Merry. il Horticulture 46:26-7+ Ag '68
Daylilies span a slope. M. J. Rozell. il Org Gard & Farm 16:46-7 Ap '69
Day-lilies to plant now for next summer's bloom. Home Gard 56:14 Jl '69
New trends in daylilies. R. P. Merry. il Horticulture 47:28-9+ F '69
DAY nurseries
C is for care; day-care centers and programs. il Newsweek 74:64-5 Ag 4 '69
Child's play; funds for day-care centers. P Stern. New Repub 161:10-11 Jl 26 '69
Day care, not baby-sitting. B. B. Stretch. Sat R 52:75 S 20 '69
Five million children with part-time mothers and nowhere to go. V. H. Bernstein. Redbook 134:86+ N '69
DAY of the dying rabbit; story. See Updike, J.
DAY we lost Max; story. See Littke, L. J.
DAYAKS. See Borneo—Native races
DAYAN, Assaf
Young and stung with love and war. P. Devlin. por Vogue 154:130-1+ S 15 '69
DAYAN, Moshe
We must not return to the old map; interview, ed. by J. Boetsch. N Y Times Mag p32-3+ Je 8 '69
about
Invitation to a coup. il Newsweek 74:60+ O 27 '69
Moshe Dayan, by N. Lau-Lavie. Review Sat R 52:36 Ap 19 '69. G. Samuels
Yigal Allon has supporters, Moshe Dayan has disciples. J. Feron. il pors N Y Times Mag p30-1+ Ap 27 '69
DAYHOFF, Margaret Oakley
Computer analysis of protein evolution; with biographical sketch. Sci Am 221:16, 86-95 Jl '69
DAYLIGHT
See also
Skylights
DAYLILIES. See Day lilies
DAY'S end; drama. See Conkle, E. P.
DAYTON, Paul K. and others
Anchor ice formation in McMurdo Sound, Antarctica, and its biological effects. bibliog Science 163:273-4 Ja 17 '69

DAYTON, Ohio
Galleries and museums
See also
Dayton art institute
DAYTON art institute
How Dayton built its imaginable museum. T. C. Colt, jr. il Art N 67:44-9+ F '69
DAYTONA 500. See Automobile racing
DAYTONA motorcycle speedweek. See Motorcycle racing
DEACONS
Permanent diaconate program; workshop at Collegeville. D. Durken. America 121:140-1 S 6 '69
DEAD of the house; story. See Green, H.
DEAD reckoning (navigation)
Offshore passages on D.R. C. M. Blackford. il Motor B 123:54-5+ F '69
DEAD SEA scrolls
Dead Sea scrolls. by E. Wilson. Review
Esquire 72:44+ O '69. M. Muggeridge
Nat R 21:1070-1 O 21 '69. J. Neusner
Nation 209:321-2 S 29 '69. R. M. V. Kieft
Sat R 52:43 Ag 23 '69. F. G. Bratton
Reporter at large. E. Wilson. New Yorker 45:45-6+ Mr 22; 45-6+ Mr 29; 45-6+ Ap 5 '69
DEADLY sins
Seven new deadly sins. Life 67:46 N 7 '69
Singing sinners; seven deadly sins. M. E. Geib. il Opera N 34:6-7 D 13 '69
DEAF
Experts list listening tips for hard-of-hearing. Todays Health 47:14 D '69
See also
National theatre of the deaf
Education
Dumb children. J. Ridgeway. New Repub 161: 19-21 Ag 2 '69
Means of communication
Dumb children. J. Ridgeway. New Repub 161:19-21 Ag 2 '69
DEAF, Apparatus for
See also
Hearing aids
DEAF, Theater for the. See National theatre of the deaf
DEAF-mutes
Of many things; Fr. Roberts home for the deaf, Suhaile, Lebanon. V. S. Kearney. America 121:inside cover Jl 19 '69
DEAFNESS
How to handle a hearing loss. G. M. Knox. il Bet Hom & Gard 47:38+ Je '69
See also
Deaf
Hearing
Noise—Physiological effects
DEAK, Niklas
Gallery; photographs. Life 67:6-7 Ag 8 '69
DEALERS, Automobile. See Automobile dealers
DEALERS in antiques. See Antique dealers
DEAN, Beth
USSR's first International ballet competition. Dance Mag 43:27+ Ag '69
DEAN, James
Fan; interview. T. J. Brandes. New Yorker 45:21-3 Ag 2 '69
DEAN, Jim
Carolina Beach bunnies. Field & S 74:68-9+ S '69
Carolina shad comeback. Field & S 73:58-9+ Ap '69
Two quail for Curtis. Field & S 74:70-1+ N '69
DEAN, Macabee
Research that pays. Sci N 96:462 N 15 '69
DEAN, Pamela
After sorcery; poem. Seventeen 29:91 Ja '70
DEAN, Ralph Stanley, bp
Those unbalanced bishops. Chr Cent 86:1154 S 10 '69
DEANGELIS, Richard M.
Enter Camille. bibliog Weatherwise 22:172-9 O '69
DEANS, Mickey
Judy Garland: her last tragic months. por Look 33:84-7+ O 7 '69
DEAR world; musical comedy. See Musical comedies, revues, etc.—Criticisms, plots, etc.
DEARBORN, Mich.
New lights increase police efficiency. O. L. Hubbard. il Am City 84:34 Ag '69
See also
Henry Ford museum and Greenfield Village
DEARDEN, John
Case against ROI control. Harvard Bsns R 47:124-35 My '69

DECISION making—*Continued*
Decision theory: guide to choice-making; gambling experiment. il Time 93:80-1 Ap 18 '69
Du Pont's answer machine. il Bsns W p68-70 D 20 '69
Educational decision making. W. L. Pharis, jr and others. Todays Ed 58:52-4 O '69
How the man at the top avoids crises; excerpts from The game of business. J. McDonald. il Fortune 81:120-2+ Ja '70
Indomitable no man. D. K. Dunkel. il Nations Bsns 57:55 D '69
Lost on the moon; a decision-making problem. Todays Ed 58:55-6 F '69
New game of business. J. McDonald. il Fortune 79:142-5+ My 15 '69
Scenario society. Y. Blumenfeld. Nation 208:788-91 Je 23 '69
Top executive's advice: hang loose. F. L. Byrom. il Duns R 94:51-3+ S '69

DECISION making (political science)
Age of discontinuity, by P. F. Drucker. Review
  Nation 208:576-8 My 5 '69. A. S. Miller
Have civilians defaulted to the military? Cur 108:59-60 Je '69
International conflict for beginners; excerpts. R. Fisher. il Atlan 223:46-52 Je '69
Power, participation and the politics of disruption. R. B. Thigpen and L. A. Downing. Chr Cent 86:973-5 Jl 23 '69; Same abr. with title Future of American politics; participatory vs. disruptive politics. Cur 111:19-22 O '69
Public challenge of government action. E. B. Skolnikoff. Science 164:499 My 2 '69; Discussion. 165:544 Ag 8 '69; 166:167-8 O 10 '69
Use of labor statistics in national decision-making; excerpt from address, August 1969. G. P. Shultz. Mo Labor R 92:48-50 N '69

DECIUS, J. C. See Hancock, J. K. jt. auth.

DECK, John
Preface to anonymous Max; story. Atlan 224:91-5 S '69

DECKER, Albert
Like father, but not exactly like son; ed. by W. S. Ross. pors Todays Health 47:38-41+ D '69

DECKER, Alonzo Galloway, 1908-
A. G. Decker of Black & Decker; interview. pors Nations Bsns 57:64-9 D '69

DECKER, Isabelle M.
Novel ways with book reports. Sr Schol 94:Schol Teach 20 My 2 '69

DECKER, Larry E.
Recreation in correctional institutions. Parks & Rec 4:31-2+ Ap '69

DECKER, Wayne H.
Like father, but not exactly like son; ed. by W. S. Ross. pors Todays Health 47:38-41+ D '69

DECKS (outdoor rooms) See Outdoor rooms

DECLARATION of human rights. See Universal declaration of human rights

DECLARATION of independence. See United States—Declaration of independence

DE CLERCQ, E. and others
Interferon induction increased through chemical modification of a synthetic polyribonucleotide. bibliog Science 165:1137-9 S 12 '69

DECLINE & fall of Dingdong-Daddyland; story. See Algren, N.

DECOMPRESSION birth. See Childbirth

DECONTAMINATION (from gases, chemicals, etc)
  See also
Space vehicles—Sterilization

DE COPPET and Doremus (brokers)
Odd-lot firms set to merge. Bsns W p81 Ag 9 '69

DECORATION and ornament
American decorative arts. R. Davidson. il Antiques 95:58 Ja '69
Fraktur: the colorful art of the Pennsylvania Germans; an antiques survey. E. Shaffer. il Antiques 95:550-5 Ap '69
Napoleon's empire. E. P. Birk. il Antiques 96:464+ O '69
Summer shells; how to enjoy them all year long. il McCalls 96:64-5 Ag '69
  See also
Art objects
Arts and crafts
Christmas decorations
Cookery, Ornamental
Design, Decorative
Easter eggs
Enamel and enameling
House decoration
Monograms

Mosaics
Paneling
Pottery—Decoration
Stencil work
Table decoration
Wall hangings
Wallpaper

DECORATION and ornament, Architectural
Building watcher. J. B. Myers. il Craft Horiz 29:20-9 Jl '69
Entrance or exit? Design 70:19-22 mid-Wint '69
New installations at the Metropolitan; decorative arts of northern Europe in the renaissance. R. Davidson. il Antiques 95:218+ F '69

DECORATION of book edges. See Book ornamentation

DECORATIONS, Christmas. See Christmas decorations

DECORATIVE arts. See Decoration and ornament

DECORATIVE lighting. See Lighting, Architectural and decorative

DECORATIVE plants. See Plants, Ornamental

DECOYS (hunting)
International decoy Carvers' exhibit. N. Drahos. il Cons 24:10-11 D '69

DE CRISTOFORO, R. J.
Bulova's Roto-vise system. Pop Sci 194:132-4 Je '69
Candid look at Delta's Uniplane. Pop Sci 194:146-8 Ja '69
Color-coded arc welder makes the job easier. Pop Sci 194:173-4 F '69
How to build a desk-workbench for a youngster. Pop Sci 195:130-4 D '69
New belt sanders: smaller, lighter, tougher. Pop Sci 195:150-3 O '69
Personal-use report; this sander cuts the dust, too. Pop Sci 194:139 Je '69
Radial saws: are two arms better than one? Pop Sci 195:122-5 Jl '69
Shop power at your fingertips. Pop Sci 195:124-7+ N '69
You can mat your picture like a pro. Pop Sci 194:126-8 Je '69
Your guide to tin snips. Pop Sci 195:174-6+ O '69

DECTER, Midge
St Paul and the American condition. Harper 238:56-61 Je '69
Stevenson we lost. Harper 238:98+ F; 12 My '69

DE CUIR, Cathy
Earthbound; poem. Seventeen 29:90 Ja '70

DEDERICH, Charles E.
Close-up: Chuck Dederich. S. O'Quin. il pors Life 66:36-8 Ja 31 '69
Second coming of Synanon. J. Kobler. il por Sat Eve Post 242:32-4+ F 8 '69

DEDERICH, Chuck. See Dederich, C. E.

DEEDY, John
News & views. See issues of Commonweal
Sacco and Vanzetti. Commonweal 96:466-8 Jl 25 '69

DEEP diving simulators. See Simulators

DEEP injection wells. See Trade waste disposal

DEEP Quest (submersible) See Submarine research vehicles

DEEP sea currents. See Ocean currents

DEEP sea deposits. See Marine sediments

DEEP sea diving. See Diving, Submarine

DEEP sea drilling. See Underwater drilling

DEEP sea fishing. See Salt water fishing

DEEP sea photography. See Photography, Submarine

DEEP sea research vehicles. See Submarine research vehicles

DEEP sea sounding
Shallow scattering layer in the subarctic Pacific Ocean: detection by high-frequency echo sounder. W. E. Barraclough and others. bibliog il Science 166:611-13 O 31 '69

DEEP submergence rescue vehicle. See Submarine boats

DEEP tillage. See Tillage

DEEPSTAR See Submarine research vehicles

DEER
Catch them if you can; whitetail deer. I. Smith. il Field & S 74:58-9+ O '69
Durable deer. J. D. Scott. il Read Digest 95:217-22 D '69
How to age your deer. P. M. Kelsey. il Cons 24:48-9+ O '69
Incredible white deer herd. W. T. Hesselton. bibliog il Cons 24:18-19 O '69

DEFORD, Frank
Pro basketball. Sports Illus 31:66+ Ap 21; 44-5 Ag 18 '69
Tennis. Sports Illus 30:55-6 F 17 '69

DEFORD, Sara
In the cave of the giant despair; Sleeping beauty; poems. Poetry 114:170-1 Je '69
Japanese scroll painting; poem. Cath World 209:181 Jl '69
Quasimodo; poem. Cath World 210:10 O '69

DE FOREST, Lee
First electron tube. G. Shiers. il Sci Am 220:104-12 Mr '69; Reply with rejoinder. L. Espenschied. 221:8 Ag '69

DEFORESTATION
Dead land of the withered trees. F. F. Darling. il UNESCO Courier 22:28-33 Ja '69
Nitrification: importance to nutrient losses from a cutover forested ecosystem. G. E. Likens and others. bibliog il Science 163:1205-6 Mr 14 '69
Saving our vanishing forests; reprint. K. H. Oedekoven. il UNESCO Courier 22:6-9 Ag '69

DEFORMATION (mechanics)
Inflation of Kilauea volcano prior to its 1967-1968 eruption. R. S. Fiske and W. T. Kinoshita. bibliog il Science 165:341-9 Jl 25 '69
See also
Plasticity

DEFORMATION of rocks. See Rocks—Deformation

DEFORMITIES
Avenging father; battle for justice for Germany's 3,000 thalidomide children. A. Levy. il Good H 168:50+ Ap '69
Do mind-bending drugs cause serious birth defects? B. K. Houston. il Sci Digest 66:30-2+ O '69
Fallout from thalidomide. Time 94:47 Ag 15 '69
Miracles of plastic surgery. P. Damerel. Parents Mag 44:78-9+ N '69
New concern for the unborn. il Time 94:52 S 19 '69
New ways to prevent and treat birth defects. Good H 169:139-41 Jl '69
Now: a vaccine to conquer another crippler; prenatal rubella infection. S. L. Englebardt. Read Digest 94:123-7 Ap '69
Solving the mystery of birth defects; genetic counseling. H. A. Rusk and others. il Parents Mag 44:61-3+ N '69
See also
Cripples

DE FREES, Madeline
Barometer; poem. New Repub 160:24 F 8 '69
Domesticating two landscapes; poem. New Repub 161:30 S 27 '69
Lode; poem. Nation 209:182 S 1 '69

DEFREGGER, Matthias, bp
Bishop & the ghosts of Filetto. D. Berrigan. Commonweal 91:39-42 O 10 '69; Discussion. 91:171+ N 7 '69
Bishop Defregger case. America 121:52 Ag 2; 107 Ag 30 '69
Bishop who was a major. por Time 94:63-4 Jl 18 '69
Bishop's burden; with report by P. S. Cook. il pors Newsweek 74:56-7 Ag 18 '69
Case of Bishop Defregger. Chr Today 13:24 Ag 22 '69
Under the circumstances; suspected accomplice to Italian atrocity. por Newsweek 74:40 Jl 21 '69

DEFROSTERS, Windshield. See Automobiles—Windshield defrosters

DE GAULLE, Charles. See Gaulle, C. de

DEGENS, Egon T. See Hathaway, J. C. jt. auth.

DEGGINER, E. R.
It's a riot of fungi; photographs. Audubon 71:57-64 S '69

DE GIVRY, Jean
La participation; the new language of labour-management relations; summary. UNESCO Courier 22:13-19 Jl '69
People no longer machines in labour relations; excerpts. UNESCO Courier 22:20-3 Jl '69

DEGLER, Carl N.
Negro in America: where Myrdal went wrong. N Y Times Mag p64-5+ D 7 '69

DEGNAN, James P.
Nonsense of liberal Catholics. Chr Today 14:3-6 N 21 '69

DE GRAAFF, Jan
Lilies with an American heritage. Home Gard 56:26-8 Ag '69

DEGRADATION (chemistry)
Oil in the ecosystem. R. W. Holcomb. Science 166:204-6 O 10 '69

DE GRAMONT, Sanche
Bernini. Horizon 11:34-47 Spr '69
Don't try to hum along with Pierre Boulez. Esquire 71:102-5+ F '69

French cooking à la Courtine. N Y Times Mag p8-9+ Jl 6 '69
Life style of homo cinematicus. N Y Times Mag p 12-13+ Je 15 '69
Paris talks: and sometimes counsel take, and sometimes tea. N Y Times Mag p28-9+ Mr 16 '69

DE GRAZIA, Edward
Americans. Criticism
Sat R 52:16 S 13 '69

DEGREES, Academic
D. Phil. or D. Phys? R. H Ellis, jr. Phys Today 22:154 Ja '69; Reply. K. E. Rieckhoff 22:9+ Ap '69
Measure of accomplishment. M. S. Marshall. Sch & Soc 97:21-2 Ja '69
New doctoral program in extension education. Sch & Soc 97:210 Ap 69
New M.A.T. at NYU; Master of arts in teaching. Sch & Soc 97:210 Ap '69
On proceeding M.A. T. S. Matthews. Vogue 153:256 My 69
See also
Diplomas, Fraudulent

DEGREES, Honorary
How honorable are honorary degrees? S. Braudy. McCalls 96:86+ Je '69
Kudos (cont) Time 93:61 Je 6; 58+ Je 13; 44 Je 20 '69

DE GROOT, Roy Andries
Alexandre Dumas (père) invites you to the feast of Noël. Esquire 73:122-5+ Ja '70
How to get a great drink at a great bar. Esquire 71:108-11 Ja '69
How to get a great meal at a great restaurant. Esquire 71:112-17+ Ja '69
Is there great wine in California? Esquire 72:54+ O '69
Movable feast. Esquire 72:96+ D '69
Port and Madeira; history in a glass. House B 111:80+ D '69
Royal Riesling. House B 111:158+ My '69

DEGRUGILLIER, Maurice. See LaChance, L. E. jt. auth.

DE HARTOG, Jan
Children; story; excerpt. McCalls 96:151-4 Mr '69

DEHAVEN, John
Semiconductor breakdown tester. Pop Electr 31:47-52 D '69

DEHLENDORF, Robert O.
Real world in which we compete; excerpts from address. por Pub W 196:20-1 D 8 '69

DEHYDROGENASES
Alcohol dehydrogenase in maize: genetic basis for isozymes. J. G. Scandalios. bibliog il Science 166:623-4 O 31 '69
Alcohol dehydrogenase in maize: genetic basis for multiple isozymes. D. Schwartz. bibliog il Science 164:585-6 My 2 '69
Dihydroorotic acid dehydrogenase: introduction into erythrocyte by the malaria parasite. R. S. Krooth and others. bibliog il Science 164:1073-5 My 30 '69
Gene dosage at the lactate dehydrogenase b locus in triploid and diploid teiid lizards. W. B. Neaves and P. S. Gerald. bibliog il Science 164:557-9 My 2 '69
Homology of lactate dehydrogenase genes: E gene function in the teleost nervous system. G. S. Whitt. bibliog il Science 166:1156-8 N 28 '69
β-Hydroxybutyrate dehydrogenase: lack in ruminant liver mitochondria. N. C. Nielsen and S. Fleischer. bibliog il Science 166:1017-19 N 21 '69
Lactate dehydrogenase electrophoretic variant in a New Guinea highland population. N. M. Blake and others. bibliog il Science 163:701-2 F 14 '69
Lactate dehydrogenase isozymes in human cardiac transplantation. J. J. Nora and others. bibliog il Science 164:1079-80 My 30 '69
Lactate dehydrogenase isozymes: kinetic properties at high enzyme concentrations. T. Wuntch and others. bibliog il Science 167:63-5 Ja 2 '70
Linkage of lactate dehydrogenase B and C loci in pigeons. W. H. Zinkham and others. bibliog il Science 164:185-7 Ap 11 '69
Mammalian oocytes: X chromosome activity. C. J. Epstein. bibliog il Science 163:1078-9 Mr 7 '69
Molecular basis for heterosis. D. Schwartz and W. J. Laughner. bibliog il Science 166:626-7 O 31 '69
6-Phosphogluconate dehydrogenase: hemizygous manifestation in a patient with leukemia. P. J. Fialkow and others. bibliog il Science 163:194-5 Ja 10 '69
Testicular lactate dehydrogenase isozyme: cyclic appearance in bats. A. Blanco and others. bibliog il Science 164:835-6 My 16 '69

DEIHL, Henry C.
Bidding for building contracts. Parks & Rec 4:39-40+ F '69
DEITCH, David
Case for advocacy journalism. Nation 209: 530-2 N 17 '69
DEJECTION. See Depression, Mental
DEJONG, Meindert
New National book award for children's literature; address, March 12, 1969. Horn Bk 45: 286 Je '69

about

Book industry presents the 20th National book awards; with excerpts from acceptance address. il por Pub W 195:29-30 Mr 24 '69
Children's literature NBA goes to Dejong. por Library J 94:1695 Ap 15 '69
Milestone for children's books. Z. Sutherland. Sat R 52:38 Ap 19 '69
New National book award for children's literature. V. Haviland. Horn Bk 45:283-6 Je '69
DEKKER, Charles A. See Delk, A. S. jt. auth.
DE KOONING, Willem
De Kooning's women; interview. ed. by D. Sylvester. il por Ramp Mag 7:20-4 Ap '69

about

Art; exhibition at the Museum of modern art. L. Alloway. Nation 208:380-1 Mr 24 '69
De Kooning. C. Willard. il pors Look 33:54-9 My 27 '69
De Kooning and the old masters. B. Rose. Vogue 153:134 My '69
De Kooning in retrospect; traveling exhibition. A. Forge. il Art N 68:44-7+ Mr '69
De Kooning's masterwork: Women of 1950-55. il Time 93:61 Mr 7 '69
De Kooning's 300,000,000th birthday; tr. by J. Ashbery. S. Dali. il Art N 68:56-7+ Ap '69
De Kooning's year. il por Newsweek 73:88-93 Mr 10 '69
Fine arts. K. Kuh. Sat R 52:38-9 Mr 29 '69
New De Koonings; Woman-in-landscape theme on show at Knoedler gallery, N.Y. J. Perreault. il por Art N 68:48-9+ Mr '69
DELACORTE, George Thomas
Giving a geyser. il Time 93:54 Je 27 '69
DE LA GRANGE, Henry Louis
Festival at Royan. Sat R 52:56 Je 28 '69
Mahler: a new image. Sat R 52:47-9+ Mr 29 '69
DELAHOYD, Mary
Corot: classic romantic. Art N 68:36-41+ N '69
DELANEY, Arthur A.
Guidelines for the potential teacher-author. Clear House 44:210-13 D '69
DELANEY, Jack J.
What do they do besides check books in and out? por Wilson Lib Bul 43:773-5 Ap '69
DELANEY, Shelagh
Joan of Arc rises in Ireland. McCalls 96:30+ Ag '69
DELANO, Gerard Curtis
Gerard Curtis Delano, painter of the Navajo Indians. J. Jellico. il por Am Artist 33:54-9+ D '69
DELANO, Calif.
Clergy and the grape strike. M. Day. America 121:114-17 Ag 30 '69
Poisoning the wells. il Environ 11:16-23+ Ja '69
DELANY, Mary
Mrs Delany and her handiwork. S. M. Newton. il por Antiques 96:100-5 Jl '69
DE LARA, Lane E.
Effective in-school program for counselors. Clear House 44:115-17 O '69
Listening is a challenge; group counseling in the school. Ment Hy 53:600-5 O '69
DE LARRAIN, Raymundo
Infinity of Jimis; photographs. Life 67:72-5 O 3 '69
DELAWARE
See also
Brandywine Creek
Gardens—Delaware
DELAWARE, Fort. See Fort Delaware
DELAWARE national guard. See United States —National guard
DELAY devices
New acoustic devices developed for radar; microsound components based on ultrasonic surface wave propagation. B. M. Elson. il Aviation W 90:85-8+ My 5 '69
DELBRÜCK, Max
1969 Nobel prize for physiology or medicine. G. Stent. por Science 166:479-81 O 24 '69
Nobel threesome. por Time 94:84 O 24 '69

DELDERFIELD, Ronald Frederick
Birth of a saga. Writer 82:18-21 N '69
DE LERMA, Dominique-Rene
Black music; what is it? Where is it? Hi Fi 19:MA16-17 N '69
DELEVORYAS, T.
Glossopterid leaves from the middle Jurassic of Oaxaca, Mexico. bibliog Science 165:895-6 Ag 29 '69
DELFELD, Paula
Call me when your vegetables are ready. Org Gard & Farm 16:24-5 Ag '69
DELGADO, Eufemio
Truck that fled Cuba. W. Schulz. il Read Digest 95:98-103 Jl '69
DEL GUERCIO, Eligio, jr
Jo Jo, king of competition sport fishing. J. Hardie. il por Motor B 123:98+ Ap '69
DELIBES, Léo
First complete stereo Lakme: twenty melodies and other charms. G. Movshon. il Hi Fi 19:83-4 Mr '69
Joan Sutherland as Lakmé. P. L. Miller. Am Rec G 35:532-3 Mr '69
Likable Lakmé from London. R. Jacobson. Sat R 52:59 Mr 29 '69
Records:
Lakmé. Opera N 33:34 F 15 '69
DELINQUENTS. See Juvenile delinquency
DELIUS, Frederick
Charles Groves: a true successor to Beecham? P. L. Miller; J. Diether. por Am Rec G 36:8-9 S '69
DELIUS, Jean
Twenty-fifth ceramic national. Craft Horiz 29:30-5+ Ja '69
DELIVORIA-PAPADOPOULOS, Maria, and others
Oxygen-hemoglobulin dissociation curves; effect of inherited enzyme defects of the red cell. bibliog Science 165:601-2 Ag 8 '69
DELK, Ann S. and Dekker, C. A.
Rhapidosomes: absence of a highly 2'-O-methylated RNA component. bibliog Science 166:1646-7 D 26 '69
DELK, Ralph M.
Announcement; new business manager of the Christian century foundation. Chr Cent 86: 365 Mr 19 '69
DELLA FEMINA, Jerry
What a tough young kid with *fegataccio* can do on Madison avenue. C. Sopkin. il pors N Y Times Mag p32-4+ Ja 26 '69
DELLINGER, David
How the prisoners were released. Time 94:22 Ag 15 '69
Indicted diplomat. Nation 209:68 Jl 28 '69
Last idealist. S. Alsop. Newsweek 74:140 N 17 '69
DELMAN, David
In all the treasured ways; story. Good H 168: 78-9 Je '69
DELMAR wildlife research laboratory. See New York (state)—Conservation department
DELMAS, Jacques Pierre Michel Chaban-. See Chaban-Delmas, J. P. M.
DE LONE, Richard H.
Cool man in a hot seat. Sat R 52:67-9+ S 20 '69
DELORIA, Vine, jr
War between the redskins and the feds. N Y Times Mag p47+ D 7 '69

about

Authors & editors. D. N. Mount. por Pub W 196:7-9 D 1 '69
DELOUGAZ, Pinhas P. See Kantor, H. J. jt. auth.
DELPHINIUMS
Growing delphiniums from seed. W. S. Porter. il Org Gard & Farm 16:90-1 Ap '69
DELSEMME, A. H. and Wenger, A.
Superdense water ice. bibliog Science 167:44-5 Ja 2 '70
DELTA (booster) See Space vehicles—Propulsion systems
DELTA air lines
So rich it hurts. il Forbes 103:20 Ja 15 '69
Strike cuts American net; Delta counters tide. il Aviation W 90:37 My 5 '69
DELTA Queen (steamboat) See Steamships and steamboats
DELTAS
See also
Sacramento-San Joaquin Delta
DELUCA, H. F. See Olson, E. B. jt. auth.
DELUCIA, Clement A. See Siqueland, E. R. jt. auth.
DELUSIONS. See Errors, Popular
DEMAND and supply. See Supply and demand
DEMAND deposits. See Banks and banking—Checking accounts

DEMARCO, Marco
  Marco DeMarco's teaching. W. C. Libby. il
    por Am Artist 33:56-7+ Je '69
DEMAREE, Allan T.
  Business picks up the urban challenge. For-
    tune 79:102-4+ Ap '69
  Defense profits; the hidden issues. Fortune 80:
    82-3+ Ag 1 '69
  How judgment came for the plumbing con-
    spirators. Fortune 80:96-9+ D '69
  Our crazy, costly life with oil quotas. Fortune
    79:104-7+ Je '69
  What business wants from President Nixon.
    Fortune 79:84-7+ F '69
DEMAREST, Michael
  Wines of California. Travel & Camera 32:
    62-5+ Ag '69
DEMARIA, Fernando
  Life, lands, and thought of the gaucho. Amér-
    icas 21:38-40 Ja '69

            about

  Song to life. C. A. Salatino. il Américas 21:
    40-2 My '69
DE MARIA, Walter
  High priest of danger. por Time 93:54 My 2
    '69
DEMARIS, Ovid
  You and I are very different from Howard
    Hughes. Esquire 71:73-81+ Mr '69
DEMARS, Robert, and others
  Lesch-Nyhan mutation: prenatal detection
    with amniotic fluid cells. bibliog Science
    164:1303-5 Je 13 '69
DEMAW, Doug
  Sound-with-sound mixer. Pop Electr 30:59-
    61+ Mr '69
DEMBO, L. S.
  Individuality and numerosity. Nation 209:574-
    6 N 24 '69
DEMETRACOPOULOS, Elias P.
  Greece; a new Vietnam? address. April, 1969.
    Vital Speeches 35:568-74 Jl 1 '69
DEMIREL, Suleyman
  There is no major problem between our coun-
    tries; interview. por U S News 66:91-2 Je
    9 '69
DEMOCRACY
  Alexander Hamilton: uncommon patriot. il Sr
    Schol 94:17 Ja 17 '69
  American historians and the democratic idea;
    address. I. Kristol. Am Scholar 39:89-104
    Wint '69
  Crisis, challenge, change; excerpt from ad-
    dress. W. M. Young, jr. il Parks & Rec 4:
    42-3+ Ap '69
  Crisis of confidence, by A. M. Schlesinger, jr.
    Review
    Sat R 5:28-9 My 17 '69. J. H. Bunzel
  Defense of U.S. democracy. Sch & Soc 97:
    410-11 N '69
  Making democracy work. T. F. Lunsford. Cur
    106:44-53 Ap '69
  Misreading democracy. New Repub 161:9-10
    S 27 '69
  Omnipotence of the majority. R. L. Tobin.
    Sat R 52:18 S 27 '69
  Politics and society, by R. M. MacIver. Re-
    view
    Sat R 52:25-6+ My 17 '69. S. Brown
  War against the democratic process. S. Hook.
    Atlan 223:45-9 F '69; Discussion. 223:44-7
    Ap '69
      See also
  Communism and democracy
  Equality
  Liberty
  Representative government and representa-
    tion
DEMOCRACY and religion. See Religion and
  democracy
DEMOCRATIC convention. See National con-
  ventions, Democratic
DEMOCRATIC party
  Alabama branch. New Repub 161:10 S 6 '69
  And how are the Democrats doing? il News-
    week 75:15-16 Ja 12 '70
  Both parties split: the meaning. il U S News
    67:19-20 D 8 '69
  Club business on the Hill; insurgents in
    caucus. R. G. Sherrill. il Nation 208:102-4
    Ja 27 '69
  Democrat speaks to the question; watershed
    of politics. J. Unruh. Nation 208:199-202
    F 17 '69
  Democratic reform. New Repub 160:10-11 F
    8 '69
  Democrats after 1968. P. Kemble; discussion.
    Commentary 47:24+ My '69
  Democrats still divided. P. J. Lavin. America
    121:254 O 4 '69
  Did Chappaquiddick finish the Democrats?
    T. C. Sorensen. Look 33:84+ N 4 '69
  Hungry Democrats. New Repub 161:12-13 S
    27 '69

Ins go out; Democratic national committee.
    il Newsweek 73:27 Ja 27 '69
  Life of the party. C. B. Gans. Atlan 223:
    73-5 Ap '69
  Nowhere to go but up. il Time 93:13-14 Ja
    24 '69
  Party chairmen: ready for battle. il U S
    News 66:14-15 Ap 28 '69
  Party predicament. K. Crawford. Newsweek
    73:45 My 26 '69
  Reform or die; decline of G. McGovern. i¹
    Time 93:18 Je 27 '69
  Republican era ahead for U.S? Yes, if . . .
    il U S News 66:41-3 F 10 '69
  Retooling a party; symposium. Nation 209:
    594-602 D 1 '69
  Reveille for Democrats. B. Moyers. Atlan
    223:37-41 Mr '69
  Singing in the rain; Democratic national
    committee. New Repub 160:10 Ja 25 '69
  Squabble between two top Democrats. il U S
    News 66:19 Mr 17 '69
  Troubled times for the Democrats. il U S
    News 67:21-2 Ag 11 '69
  What happened to the Democratic coalition?
    G. Will. Nat R 21:325-7+ Ap 8 '69
  Which way the parties? Nation 208:194-5 F 17
    '69
  Whither the Democrats? H. Brandson. Sat R
    52:16+ O 4 '69
  Why Democrats are divided. il U S News
    67:43-4 O 6 '69
      See also
  National conventions, Democratic
DEMODEX folliculorum. See Follicle mites
DEMOGRAPHY
  Feedbacks in economic and demographic
    transition; adaptation of address, June
    1969. H. Frederiksen. bibliog il Science 166:
    837-47 N 14 '69
DEMONOLOGY
      See also
  Exorcism
DEMONQUE, Marcel
  Reformer stirs French business. il por Bsns
    W p 122+ Ap 26 '69
DEMONSTRATION schools
  Ocean Hill is alive, and, well. . . J. Feather-
    stone. New Repub 160:21-3 Ap 19 '69
  Wiping out the demonstration schools. J.
    Featherstone. New Repub 162:10-11 Ja
    10 '70
DEMONSTRATIONS against Vietnamese war.
  See Vietnamese war, 1957- —Protests, dem-
  onstrations, etc, against
DE MORINNI, Clara More
  Libraries: Americans in Paris. New Repub
    161:30-2 S 20 '69
DEMOSS, Billy J.
  Computer programs a city's growth. por Am
    City 84:100+ D '69
DEMOTT, Benjamin
  How existential can you get? N Y Times
    Mag p4+ Mr 23 '69
  The sixties: a cultural revolution. N Y Times
    Mag p28-31+ D 14 '69

            about

  Americans. R. Phillips. por Sat R 52:39-40
    S 20 '69
DEMPEWOLFF, Richard F.
  Bantu witch doctor: the influential psychol-
    ogist of modern South Africa. Sci Digest
    66:6-15 Ag '69
  HYDRA for bottom lowdown. Sci Digest 65:
    76-9 F '69
  You got to get used to Harry. pors Am For
    75:20-3+ My '69
DEMPSEY, David
  Bruno Bettelheim is Dr No. N Y Times Mag
    p22-3+ Ja 11 '70
  Doctor Guttmacher is the evangelist of birth
    control. N Y Times Mag p32-3+ F 9 '69
  Eighth Army Loveman award. Sat R 52:28
    Jl 12 '69
  Mrs Payson and her lovable Mets. Read Di-
    gest 94:201-2+ Je '69
  Only real live bookstore in New York. Holi-
    day 46:8+ N '69
  P.E.N. congress: letters and leisure on the
    Riviera. Sat R 52:42-4 O 18 '69
  Publishing scene. See issues of Saturday re-
    view
  Social comment and TV censorship. Sat R
    52:53-5 Jl 12 '69
DEMPSEY, Paul W.
  Royal palm. Horticulture 46:14-15 N '68
DEMUTH, Jerry
  Movie. Chr Cent 86:1169, 1487, 1673 S 10, N
    19, D 31 '69
DEMY, Jacques
  Current cinema. P. Kael. New Yorker 45:
    122+ F 22 '69

DEPARTMENT of housing and urban development. See United States—Housing and urban development, Department of

DEPARTMENT stores
See also
Federated department stores, incorporated
Retail trade
also subhead Stores under names of cities, e.g. Boston—Stores

Book departments
Stern's leaves the beat of 42nd street. il Pub W 195:63-4 F 10 '69

DEPAULA, Frankie
Frankie the banger gets bombed. M. Kane. il pors Sports Illus 30:46-7 F 3 '69

DEPAUW university, Greencastle, Ind.
Free university. R. H. Farber. il Sch & Soc 97:356-8 O '69

DE PIETRO, Albert
Sculptor; poem. Cath World 209:202 Ag '69

DEPORTATION
Exodus; expulsion from Ghana. il Time 95:22 Ja 12 '70

DEPOSITARY receipts, American. See Banks and banking—Securities handling

DEPRECIATION
Cooking the books to fatten profits. il Time 93:96 Ap 11 '69
Depreciation: which method, how fast? F. Bailey, jr. Suc Farm 67:64 Ja '69
Tax know-how: more money for architecture? P. B. Farrell, jr. Arch Rec 145:77+ F '69
See also
Amortization deductions
Investment tax credit

DEPRESSION, Business.   See Business depression

DEPRESSION, Mental
Three profiles of depression. Ladies Home J 86:62 F '69
Truth about those new mother blues; postpartum depression. S. G. Streshinsky. il Parents Mag 44:56-7+ Ap '69
Winston Churchill's black dog. A. Storr. Esquire 71:94-9+ Ja '69

DEPRIVATION, Sensory. See Sensory deprivation

DEPTH indicators
Sound sounding. L. Heiner. il Yachting 125:64-5+ Je: 126:66+ Jl '69

DEPTH of field. See Photography—Focusing

DEPTH sounders. See Depth indicators

DERBYSHIRE, Robert C.
MD's without education, how to spot them; excerpts from address, October 1968. Sci Digest 65:14-18 Mr '69

DERBYSHIRE, Robert L.   See Sata, L. S. jt. auth.

DERDERIAN, Constance E.
Indoor bonsai. Horticulture 47:28-9+ N '69

DERECKTOR, Robert E.
Bob Derecktor, chosen to build the next America's cup contender. M. Davis. il pors Motor B 123:110-11+ Je '69

DERECSKEY, Charles
To the tick of a different clock. Atlan 223:74-6+ F '69

DERFLER, Leslie
Criticism and self-criticism. Nation 208:578-80 My 5 '69

DERIAGIN, Boris Vladimirovich
Equivocal standard; excerpt. Sat R 52:54-5 S 6 '69
about
Polymerized water, is it or isn't it? J. Finney. Chem 42:20 Mr '69
Russia's exotic water grower. F. M. Fowkes. por Sat R 52:52-4 S 6 '69

DERIVATION of words. See English language—Etymology

DERMACENTOR albipictus. See Ticks

DERMATOGLYPHICS
Dermatoglyphics. L. S. Penrose. il Sci Am 221:72-4+ bibliog(p 152) D '69

DERMER, Irwin
Gallery; photographs. Life 67:8-9 O 31 '69
Last artisans; photographs Esquire 72:57-64 Jl '69

DERMESTID beetles. See Beetles

DERNBERGER, Robert F.
Economic realities and China's political economics. Bul Atom Sci 25:34-42 F '69

DEROGATIS, Al
Newest star in pro football; interview. ed. by J. Hess. por Holiday 46:90-1+ O '69

DERRICK-DAVIS, Barbara
Race to reclaim a dead man's eyes. Todays Health 48:42-3+ Ja '70

DERSHOWITZ, Alan M.
Protecting civil liberties; psychiatry's role in civil commitment cases. Cur 105:32-6 Mr '69

DE SADE illustrated; drama. See Bush, J.

DESAI, Morarji
India: gunning for Mrs Gandhi. il por Newsweek 74:47 Jl 28 '69

DESAI, Narayan
Birthday; interview. New Yorker 45:47-8 O 18 '69

DESALINATION of seawater. See Sea water—Desalting

DESALINIZATION. See Water purification—Desalting

DESALTING of sea water. See Sea water—Desalting

DE SANTILLANA, Giorgio, and Von Dechend, Hertha
Age of strong man Samson; excerpt from Hamlet's mill: an essay on myth and the frame of time. Sat R 53:103-5 Ja 10 '70

DE SCHAUENSEE, Max
Enigma of Boninsegna. Opera N 33:12-13 F 15 '69

DESCHIN, Jacob
Viewpoint. See issues of Popular photography

DESCRIPTION (rhetoric)
Look a little closer. R. Engelken. Writers Digest 49:52-3 Jl '69

DESCRIPTIVE writing. See Description (rhetoric)

DESEGREGATION. See Colleges and universities—Desegregation; Public schools—Desegregation

DESEGREGATION decision, 1954. See United States—Supreme court—Decisions

DESERT. See Deserts

DESERT candles
Most dramatic flower you can grow. P. Shedesky. il Home Gard 56:58-9 Jl '69

DESERT fauna
Landscaping with natives from the Plains and the Rockies. G. W. Kelly. il Horticulture 46:28-33 D '68
See also
Sand rats

DESERT flora. See Desert vegetation

DESERT flying. See Aviation—Desert flying

DESERT national wildlife range. See Wildlife sanctuaries—Nevada

DESERT research institute. See Nevada. University, Reno—Desert research institute

DESERT sheep hunting. See Mountain sheep hunting

DESERT tortoises. See Tortoises

DESERT vegetation
Wanted: a suitable herbivore to convert western scrubland to protein. P. S. Martin. il Natur Hist 78:34-9 F '69
See also
Succulent plants

DESERTION, Military. See United States—Armed forces—Desertions

DESERTION and non-support
Family desertion problem across state lines. W. J. Brockelbank. bibliog f il Ann Am Acad 383:23-33 My '69

DESERTS
Saving our vanishing forests; reprint. K. H. Oedekoven. il UNESCO Courier 22:6-9 Ag '69
Walk with me. K. Hillyard. il Har Yrs 9:26-9 S '69
See also
Atacama Desert
Death Valley
Kalahari Desert

DE-SHALIT, Amos. See Shalit, A. de

DESIGN
Design alla Milanese; with comments by P. J. Smith. il Life 66:48-54+ Mr 14 '69
See also
Designers
International design conference
Natural forms

Study and teaching
Abstract stage settings. F. J. Kraft. il Design 70:14 mid-Wint '69
Blow up! enlarging designs from nature. W. R. Crosier. il Sch Arts 69:20-1 N '69
Circle, triangle, rectangle. M. B. Bowman. il Design 70:35 Sum '69
Design experiments with natural materials. R. Moore. il Sch Arts 68:16-17 Mr '69

DESIGN. Book. See Book design

DESIGN, Decorative
Art deco. il Time 94:74 N 7 '69
Art style in furniture; excerpt from The aesthetic movement. E. Aslin. il Antiques 96:578-81 O '69

DESIGN, Decorative—*Continued*
Decorative arts. J. T. Butler. il Antiques 96:
375 S '69
Decorative arts at the Newark museum. T.
Kyle. il Antiques 95:838-41 Je '69
Decorative arts in the City art museum of
St Louis. C. E. Buckley. il Antiques 96:76-
81 Jl '69
Graphics. il House & Gard 136:112-13 O '69
Postage stamp as a mini-art form. R. J.
Saunders. il Sch Arts 69:30-1 N '69
Public places, private taste. H. Morrison. il
House B 111:142-3 O '69
Sophisticated eye. M. Gilliatt. il House B
111:122-3 O '69
See also
Arts and crafts
Book covers
Designers
Drawing
Lettering
Monograms
Pottery—Decoration
Textile design

Animal forms
Animals into toys. P. L. Martin. il Am Artist
33:68-73+ O '69
Barbara's birds. F. A. Colson. il Ceram Mo
17:14-16 Ap '69

Plant forms
Everything's coming up mushrooms. il House
& Gard 136:64-5 Ag '69

Study and teaching
See Design—Study and teaching
DESIGN, Environmental. See Environmental en-
gineering (buildings)
DESIGN, Garden. See Garden design
DESIGN, Industrial
Contemporary career: design detective. il
Design 70:28-30 mid-Wint '69
Mark of Max is everywhere. il Life 67:34-9
S 5 '69
Where East beats West; new Japanese art;
with photographs by D. Kirkland. Look 33:
36-9 O 21 '69
See also
Human engineering

Exhibitions
Smithsonian salute. B. Plumb. il N Y Times
Mag p66-7 F 23 '69
DESIGN in photography. See Composition (pho-
tography)
DESIGN-in-steel awards. See American iron
and steel institute
DESIGN of automobiles. See Automobiles—
Design
DESIGNERS
Design alla Milanese; with comments by
P. J. Smith. il Life 66:48-54+ Mr 14 '69
Great craftsmen of the new renaissance. il
Holiday 46:38-41 S '69
Role of the artist in contributing elements of
grandeur to our physical environment. il
Sch Arts 68:21-9 Mr '69
Those fabulous Italian designers. J. A.
Michener. il Read Digest 95:157-62+ S '69
Young designers. E. Sverbeyeff and H. Mor-
risson. il House B 111:43-9 Jl '69
See also
Costume designers
DE SILVA, Anil
Spread of Buddhist culture; reprint. UNESCO
Courier 22:22-5 Ag '69
DESIPRAMINE
Tricyclic antidepressants: evidence for an in-
traneuronal site of action. W. D. Reid and
others. bibliog il Science 164:437-9 Ap 25 '69
DESK furnishings
Desk set. N. Mandelbaum. il McCalls 96:104-5
Mr '69
DESK lamps. See Lamps
DESKS
Build this all-in-one kitchen planning center.
R. C. House. il Pop Mech 131:150-1 Je '69
Build this colonial cabinet-top desk. P. K.
Snook. il Pop Mech 131:132-3 F '69
Build this handsome bookcase desk. A. Alto-
mare. il Pop Mech 132:164-7 Ag '69
Build yourself the Delta desk. K. Isaacs.
il Pop Sci 195:1602 N '69
Desks to live with forever. R. Fitzgerald.
il House B 111:78-80 F '69
One more Salem secretary. D. A. Fales, jr.
il Antiques 95:399 Mr '69
DES MOINES

Galleries and museums
Des Moines: an enclosure for sculpture completes an open court; new sculpture wing
of art center. J. Bailey. il Arch Forum 130:
62-7 Je '69

Lighting
New and brighter lighting era. H. M. Batts.
il Am City 84:136+ F '69
DESMOND, Paul
Desmond on Desmond. B. Korall. por Sat R
52:102-3 S 13 '69
DESPAIR
Despair in the final hour. F. Buechner. Chr
Cent 86:340 Mr 12 '69
DES PLAINES, Ill.
Citizen band radio enlarges police. H. H.
Behrel. il Am City 84:28 Ap '69
DESPORTES, Ulysse
Great men of America in Roman guise; sculp-
tured by Giuseppe Ceracchi. Antiques 96:
72-5 Jl '69
DESSERTS
Baked igloos. il Sunset 143:128 Jl '69
Blended dessert treats. il Ebony 24:158+ My
'69
Dessert of the month. V. V. Voboril. See oc-
casional issues of Good housekeeping
Desserts with a touch of spring. G. Maddox.
il Todays Health 47:60-5 Ap '69
Desserts you keep on ice. il Bet Hom & Gard
47:98-9+ S '69
Dream desserts that come true every time.
il Good H 168:113-17+ Ap '69
Easy cereal confections. il Am Home 72:94+
Ja '69
Elegant chocolate mousse. V. T. Habeeb. il
Am Home 72:58-9 Jl '69
Fast strawberry desserts; fancy strawberry
desserts. il Bet Hom & Gard 47:91-2 Je '69
Fried Camembert on toast with jelly. il Sun-
set 142:197 Mr '69
Frothy wine and egg confection; chaudeau.
il Sunset 143:125 Jl '69
Great American desserts. H. McCully. il
House B 111:114-16+ Je '69
Halfway between torte and trifle; rum cream
trifle. il Sunset 143:178 O '69
Hot desserts. il Redbook 132:100-1+ F '69
It doesn't take much to make a great des-
sert. il Redbook 133:116-18+ Jl '69
It's your fruit dessert on the stem. il Sunset
142:146-7 Mr '69
Refreshing as the Alps on a hot summer
day. E. W. Manning. il Farm J 93:42-3
Ag '69
Show-off desserts. D. Eby. il Bet Hom &
Gard 47:92-7+ Mr '69
Special cherry desserts. M. White. il Bet
Hom & Gard 47:86 Mr 1 '69
See also
Cake
Cheesecake
Cookery—Fruit
Custards
Ice cream, ices, etc.
Meringue
Puddings
Shortcake
Tarts
DESTOUCHES, Louis Ferdinand
Fanatic of disaster. M. Maddocks. Atlan 223:
102-4 Ja '69
First to mine delirium. F. Morton. Nation
208:343 Mr 17 '69
Noodles and hatred. R. A. Sokolov. por News-
week 73:91-91A+ Ja 27 '69
DESTROYERS. See Warships
DESTRUCTION; story. See Ford, J. H.
DESTRUCTIVE art. See Art, Modern
**DETECTION of underground atomic bomb
tests.** See Atomic bombs—Testing, Detec-
tion of
DETECTIVE and mystery plays
Case for two detectives. J. Murray. Plays
28:13-22+ Ap '69
DETECTIVE and mystery stories
Close-up: Dick Francis, jockey with an eye
for intrigue. J. Newcombe. il Life 66:81-2
Je 6 '69
From puzzles to people: suspense novels. J.
Kahn. Writer 82:19-20 F '69
Who done it? A guide to detective, mystery,
and suspense fiction, by O. A. Hagen. Re-
view
Am Scholar 39:138+ Wint '69. J. Barzun
See also
Mystery writers of America, incorporated
Publishers and publishing—Detective and
mystery stories

Authorship
Close-up: Georges Simenon, excuse me, I
think I'm about to have a novel; with report by M. Mok. il Life 66:43-4+ My 9 '69
Murder is my business, sort of; ladies who
write of murder. L. Wright. McCalls 96:97-8
Ap '69

DETECTIVE and mystery stories—*Continued*

Bibliography

Criminal record. J. T. Winterich. See last issue of each month of Saturday review

First novelists: Gothic, guns, and games; statements by the writers, ed. by I. E. Stokvis. il Library J 94:583-4 F 1 '69

Mystery, detective and suspense. M. K. Grant. See first issue of each month of Library journal

Summer sleuthing. il Newsweek 74:80+ Jl 28 '69

Single works

Night before the wedding. M. Gordon and G. Gordon. il Good H 168:85-7 Mr '69

Technique

Conversation with Rex Stout; interview. ed. by A. Bester. R. Stout. Holiday 46:38-9+ N '69

Detective novel. C. Aird. Writer 82:11-14 Ag '69

Plots and people. H. Waugh. Writer 82:9-11+ D '69

Way to maintain success. D. Wheatley. Writer 82:22-4 O '69

Write me an adventure novel. B. Cassiday. Writer 82:11-14 Mr '69

Anecdotes, facetiae, satire, etc.

Books from the wood. H. F. Ellis. New Yorker 44:81-3 Ja 18 '69

DETECTORS

How to find leaks. C. V. King. il Chem 42:8-11 Mr '69

See also
Counters (electrons, ions, etc)
Gas detectors
Metal detectors
Storm detectors

DETECTORS, Infrared

Night infrared sensors win wider role; airborne FLIR systems. B. Miller. il Aviation W 91:63+ N 3 '69

DETENTION centers. See Concentration camps

DETENTION homes

Home for kids in trouble; Attention home, Boulder, Colo. D. Van Ark. il Parents Mag 44:76-7+ N '69

Youthful offenders: experiment in rehabilitation. Robert F. Kennedy youth center. R. Coles. New Repub 161:12-14 O 4 '69

DETERGENT pollution of rivers, lakes, etc. Dirty detergents? Time 94:29 D 26 '69

DETERGENTS

Bleachmakers slug back; challenge of enzyme detergents. il Bsns W p 146 S 13 '69

Cold-water detergent no longer claims germproofs: Cold power. il Consumer Bul 52:4+ S '69

Fact on fifty-four soaps, soaks & detergents. il Changing T 23:21-3 S '69

Phosphates on the spot; detergent phosphates cause of eutrophication? il Sci N 96:591-2 D 27 '69

What is detergent as opposed to soap? Sci Digest 66:81 S '69

See also
Procter and Gamble company

DETERIORATION of materials. See Materials —Deterioration

DETJE, Frederick W.
One small step for space science. Sci N 96: 434-5 N 8 '69

DE TOLEDANO, Ralph
Time marches on Haynsworth. Nat R 21: 1164-6+ N 18 '69

DETROIT
Perspective; concerning the ills of American cities. J. H. Plumb. Sat R 52:40-1 F 22 '69

Crime

Church gun battle: police vs. blacks. il U S News 66:10 Ap 14 '69

Detroit's rebel Judge Crockett. C. L. Sanders. il Ebony 24:114-16+ Ag '69

Education

Daddy and the family. Time 93:68+ F 7 '69

Schools & corporations: partners in Detroit. E. Logan. il Sr Schol 84:Schol Teach 14-15 Mr 21 '69

See also
Wayne state university

Elections

Lot of converts; mayoralty results. il Newsweek 74:49 N 17 '69

Galleries and museums

See also
Detroit institute of arts

Music

Report: Detroit; production of Menotti's Medium and Cherubini's Portuguese inn. J. Carr. Opera N 33:31 Ap 12 '69

Negroes

Detroit's Ditto. il Time 93:22 Je 13 '69

Explosive package ticks away in Detroit. il Bsns W p 102-3 Ag 2 '69

Job makes the man. il Nations Bsns 57:34-6+ Je '69

Schools & corporations: partners in Detroit. E. Logan. il Sr Schol 94:Schol Teach 14-15 Mr 21 '69

Trouble with uplift; New Detroit committee. il Newsweek 73:62 Je 2 '69

Verdicts of history; take the hatred away, and you have nothing left: O. and G. Sweet in white neighborhood. T. J. Fleming. il Am Heritage 20:74-80+ D '68

Newspapers

See also
Detroit news

Police

End of the love-in; cop dies during gun battle with black nationalists. il Newsweek 73:35-6 Ap 14 '69

Fallout from a shootout; conduct of Negro judge in police killing incident. il Time 93: 43+ Ap 11 '69

From Detroit, with love. il Time 93:17 Mr 28 '69

God help our city. W. Serrin. il Atlan 223: 115-21 Mr '69

Taking a chance on love. il Newsweek 73: 63 Mr 24 '69

Police department

Crime-solver in science lab; hematologist with Scientific bureau of the Detroit police dept. il Ebony 24:72-5+ Ap '69

Office machine helps to alert police about crimes. il Am City 84:36+ Je '69

Politics and government

Cavanagh of Detroit; interview, ed. by F. Powledge. J. Cavanagh. il Harper 239:83-6 N '69

Dim day in Detroit. Newsweek 74:36-7 Jl 7 '69

Explosive package ticks away in Detroit. il Bsns W p 102-3 Ag 2 '69

Testing the wind; mayoral primary. Newsweek 74:32-3 S 22 '69

Victory for reason; first black candidate. Time 94:24 S 19 '69

See also
Detroit—Elections

Religious institutions and affairs

Detroit: evolution of a revolution. J. C. Haughey. America 120:475-8 Ap 19 '69

Social conditions

Detroit: evolution of a revolution. J. C. Haughey. America 120:475-8 Ap 19 '69

Social work

Mother Waddles; the gentle warrior. J. K. Davis. il Life 66:87-9 Mr 21 '69

Transportation

50,000 miles without an oil change. R. McKay, 3d. il Am City 84:136+ Je '69

DETROIT diocese. See Catholic church—Dioceses

DETROIT institute of arts
One man's fancy; R. Tannahill's collection. il Time 94:68-9 N 28 '69

DETROIT LAKES, Minn.
From mud flats to beautiful shore. B. J. Revering. il Am City 84:93 Ja '69

Quick-starting standby equipment. il Am City 84:118 Je '69

DETROIT news
Crime and race in Detroit. Time 93:61 My 9 '69

Detroit newspaper comes on hip. il Bsns W p 122 O 11 '69

Shady lady. Newsweek 74:79-80 S 8 '69

DETROIT Red Wings (hockey team) See Hockey teams

DETTRE, John R.
Pride of workmanship. Clear House 43:323-7 F '69

DETZER, Karl
Murder on route 79. Read Digest 94:126-30 F '69

DEUEL, Leo
Their relics remain in the Americas; excerpt from Flights into yesterday. Sat R 63:105-8 Ja 10 '70

DEUTSCH, Armin J.
 Obituary
  Sky & Tel por 39:33 Ja '70. J. Ashbrook
DEUTSCH, Babette
 Cento; poem. New Repub 160:32 Mr 1 '69
 Literary scenes in the Soviet Union; excerpts from address. Am Scholar 38:300-2+ Spr '69
 Mermaid remembered; poem. Harp Baz 102:190 S '69
 1669? 1969; poem. Harp Baz 103:136 D '69
DEUTSCH, Herbert
 Hauppauge. ALA Bul 63:257-60 F '69
DEUTSCH, Martin, and others
 Racial factors in intelligence, a rebuttal. Trans-Action 6:6+ Je '69
DEUTSCH, Patricia, and Deutsch, Ron
 Heart attack you didn't know you had. Todays Health 47:42-3+ Jl '69; Same abr. with title Do you have silent heart disease? Read Digest 95:93-7 Jl '69
DEUTSCH, Ron. See Deutsch, P. jt. auth.
DEUTSCHE grammophon gesellschaft. See Phonograph record industry—Germany (Federal Republic)
DEUTSCHER gewerkschaftsbund. See Trade unions—Germany (Federal Republic)
DEUTSCHMAN, Paul
 More and better rice for Asia's hungry millions. Read Digest 94:25-6+ My '69
 Rebirth in the hollers. Travel & Camera 32:62-7 S '69
DEV, Mohan
 On the boards. W. Como. por Dance Mag 43:20 Jl '69
DEVALUATION of currency. See Currency question
DEVANEY, John
 Match your baseball IQ with Mayo Smith. Mech Illus 65:56-7+ My '69
DE VARONA, Donna
 Everybody into the water! il por Redbook 133:82-7 Je '69
DEVELOPING (photography) See Photography —Developing and developers
DEVELOPING nations. See Underdeveloped areas
DEVELOPMENT, Biological. See Morphogenesis
DEVELOPMENT, Economic. See Economic development
DEVELOPMENT concept papers. See United States—Defense, Department of—Development concept papers
DEVELOPMENT of children. See Children—Growth and development; Infants—Growth and development
DEVELOPMENT program of the United Nations. See United Nations—Development program
DEVIANT behavior. See Behavior (psychology)
DEVIL
 Anecdotes, facetiae, satire, etc.
 If dropouts turn on. L. Woodrum. Chr Today 14:18-19 O 24 '69
DEVIL in literature
 To conceive of the devil. S. Scoville. Engl J 58:673-5 My '69
DEVILFISH. See Whales
DEVILS of Loudun; opera. See Penderecki, K.
DEVINE, Joseph E.
 Truth about A separate peace. Engl J 58:519-20 Ap '69
DEVINE, Robert E.
 Build a psych-analyzer. Pop Electr 30:27-32+ F '69
DEVINE, Thomas G.
 What does research in reading reveal: about materials for teaching reading? bibliog Engl J 58:847-52 S '69
DE VITO, E. B.
 Via dolorosa; poem. Cath World 209:155 Jl '69
DEVLIN, Bernadette
 Girl afire; excerpts from The price of my soul. por McCalls 97:69+ N '69
 Interview. por Ramp Mag 8:20-1 Jl '69
 about
 Bernadette and the clashing values of old and new Ireland. P. Tracy. Commonweal 91:281-2 N 28 '69
 Bernadette becalmed. il por Time 95:29-30 Ja 5 '70
 Bernadette Devlin, M.P. P. Devlin. por Vogue 154:123+ Ag 1 '69
 Bernadette of the Irish. P. Tracy. Commonweal 90:583-4 S 26 '69
 Bernadette on Fifth avenue. T. M Gannon. America 121:137-9 S 6 '69
 Carpenter's daughter. R. A. Gross. por Newsweek 74:100B+ N 3 '69

Catholic rebels at the summit: the Bernadette-Berrigan encounter. J. Roddy. il por Look 33:81 O 7 '69
Gospel of Devlin. por Time 93:34 Ap 25 '69
Joan of Arc rises in Ireland. S. Delaney. por McCalls 96:30+ Ag '69
Maid of Bogside: she's here! il pors Newsweek 74:42-3 S 8 '69
Northern Ireland: edging toward anarchy. il por Time 93:22-3 My 2 '69
SR: books. M. Ward. il pors Sat R 52:32-3+ N 8 '69
Song of Bernadette. il por Newsweek 73:56 My 5 '69
Sure and it's Miss Devlin for a seat in Parliament; with report by T. Dozier. il pors Life 66:58A-58B My 2 '69
Travels of Bernadette. Time 94:29-30 S 5 '69
Ulster in turmoil. il por Sr Schol 94:12 My 9 '69
Ulster: the gospel as a club raised. J. D. Douglas. Chr Today 13:38 My 9 '69
DEVLIN, John C.
 Dispatches from the unpaved world. Natur Hist 78:70-2 My '69
DEVLIN, Josephine Bernadette. See Devlin, B.
DEVLIN, Polly
 Bernadette Devlin, M.P. Vogue 154:123+ Ag 1 '69
 Letter from cowboy and Canyon country. Vogue 153:50+ Mr 1 '69
 Maddox: House of Messel. Vogue 153:194-201 Mr 1 '69
 Mia Farrow, her thin skinned courage. Vogue 153:80+ My '69
 Space venture. Vogue 154:128-33 Ag 15 '69
 Young and stung with love and war. Vogue 154:130-1+ S 15 '69
DEVONIAN period
 See also
 Paleontology—Devonian
DEVOTIONAL medals. See Medals, Devotional
DEVRIES, Abraham
 Ignorant preachers. Chr Today 14:8-10 Ja 2 '70
DEVRIES, Arthur L. and Wohlschlag, D. E.
 Freezing resistance in some Antarctic fishes. bibliog Science 163:1073-5 Mr 7 '69
DE VRIES, Peter
 Man who read Waugh. Sat R 52:19-20 Mr 8 '69
DEVRIES, Ted
 Research and practice. Clear House 44:236-7 D '69
 —See Tovatt, A. jt. ed.
DEW line. See Radar defense networks
DEWAN, Wilfrid F.
 Starting with man as he is. Cath World 209:39-40 Ap '69
DEWART, Leslie
 Fact of death. Commonweal 91:206-8 N 14 '69
 Meaning of religious belief; excerpt from The foundations of belief. Commonweal 90:15-17 Mr 21 '69
 Views from earth on the odyssey into space. Look 33:78 F 4 '69
 about
 Dewart's new foundations. A. Gibson. Commonweal 90:101-4 Ap 11 '69
DEWEY, John
 John Dewey and Vatican council II. T. F. McGann. America 120:411-12+ Ap 5 '69
 Revolution within an evolution. R. R. Winkelmann. Chr Cent 86:1577-80 D 10 '69
DEWEY, Robert D.
 Religion at college these days. Chr Cent 86:1220-2 S 24 '69
DEWEY classification. See Classification, Decimal
DEWING, Rolland
 Is an NEA-AFT merger imminent? Ed Digest 35:35-7 N '69
DEWLEN, Al
 To our fallen son. Read Digest 94:49-53 Mr '69
DEWOLF, L. Harold
 International dimensions of the seminary. Chr Cent 86:545-7 Ap 23 '69
 Is transcendence expendable? Chr Cent 86:1017-19 Jl 30 '69
DE WYS, E. Christiaan. See Trueb, L. F. jt. auth.
DEXTROAMPHETAMINE. See Amphetamines
DEY, Joe
 Mr Commissioner speaks out; interview, ed. by P. Ryan. por Sports Illus 30:20-1 F 10 '69
DHAININ, Felix K.
 Planning a neighborhood park. Parks & Rec 4:69-70+ S '69

DIABETES
Diabetic sandrats. D. G. Robinson. jr. il Sci N 95:172-3 F 15 '69
First aid: insulin reaction.   C. J. Potthoff. Todays Health 47:74 O '69
Mitotic division in pancreatic beta cells. A. A. Like and W. L. Chick. bibliog il Science 163:941-3 F 28 '69
My husband's secret triumph; interview. ed. by H. Higdon.   A. Rowan. il Good H 169: 66-7+ Ag '69
New clues to the diabetes riddle.   J. D. Wassersug. il Sci Digest 66:76-9 O '69
Questions & answers about childhood diabetes. M. L. Moore. Parents Mag 44:80-1+ N '69

DIACONATE. See Deacons

DIAGHILEV, Sergei Pavlovich
Return to Monte Carlo. il Newsweek 73:93 Je 30 '69

DIAGNE, Pathé
Vernacular languages in changing Africa; reprint. UNESCO Courier 22:30-1 Ag '69

DIAGNOSIS
Revealing palm lines; diagnostic clues in an infant's hand. il Time 93:57 Je 27 '69
Symptoms: when to call the doctor? G. M. Knox. Bet Hom & Gard 47:22+ F '69
What is a doctor's toughest diagnosis? psychosomatic disease or nerves? W. E. O'Donnell. Good H 169:59+ Jl '69
See also
Cancer—Diagnosis
Children—Diseases—Diagnosis
Computers—Medical applications
Heart—Examination
Mental illness—Diagnosis

DIAGRAMS, Business. See Business management and organization—Charts, graphs, etc.

DIAL, Roger. See Rose, L. E. jt. auth.

DIAL-a-listener service. See Telephone

DIAL-a-poem. See Poetry readings

DIAL indicators for gas and oil engines.   See Indicators for gas and oil engines

DIALECT, Negro. See Negro-English dialects

DIALECTS
See also
English language—Dialects

DIALOGUE
Diction in Warren's All the king's men. R. G. Martin. Engl J 58:1169-74 N '69
How people stand. M. Lee. Writer 82:13-15+ S '69

DIALOGUES
See also
Imaginary conversations

DIALYSIS
See also
Kidneys, Artificial

DIAMOND, Bernard L.
Sirhan through the looking glass. Time 93: 28 Ap 4 '69
Sirhan's trance. por Newsweek 73:37 Ap 7 '69

DIAMOND, Edwin
True nightmare: the most terrifying psychic experience known to man. N Y Times Mag p56-7+ D 7 '69

DIAMOND, I. T. and Hall, W. C.
Evolution of neocortex. bibliog Science 164: 251-62 Ap 18 '69

DIAMOND, James J.
Humanizing the abortion debate. America 121:36-9 Jl 19 '69

DIAMOND, Leila, and Gelboin, H. V.
Alpha-naphthoflavone: an inhibitor of hydrocarbon cytotoxicity and microsomal hydroxylase. bibliog Science 166:1023-5 N 21 '69

DIAMOND, Seymour
Headaches. Todays Ed 58:63-4 O '69

DIAMOND mines and mining
See also
Diamonds

DIAMOND Shamrock corporation
Dream a little. Forbes 104:20-1 D 15 '69

DIAMONDS
Diamond dust in space. G. S. Mumford. Sky & Tel 37:151 Mr '69
Diamonds are a girl's most overpriced friend. J. McCarthy. il McCalls 96:108-9+ Mr '69
Liz's million-dollar rock.   il Life 67:65-66B N 14 '69
Something that's perfect: Cartier diamond sold to Richard Burton. il Newsweek 74: 106 N 10 '69
U.S. journal: Atlantic City auction galleries selling other merchandise as warmup. C. Trillin. New Yorker 45:104+ Je 14 '69

DIAMONDS, Artificial
Hanay's diamonds. il Chem 42:20-2 Je '69

DIAMONDS, Baseball. See Baseball fields

DIAMONDS, Industrial
Carbonado: natural polycrystalline diamond. L. F. Trueb and E. C. De Wys. bibliog il Science 165:799-802 Ag 22 '69
World's sharpest tool. A. S. Freese. il Pop Mech 132:100-3+ S '69

DIAMONSTEIN, Barbaralee
Emphasis. Harp Baz 103:200+ N '69

DIANETICS
See also
Scientology

DIANNA, John
Strictly for stocks. See issues of Hot rod

DIAPAUSE. See Insects—Development

DIAPERS, Infants
Great diaper battle: disposable diapers. il Time 93:69-70 Ja 24 '69
What every mother should know about diapers. il Good H 168:128 F '69

DIARIES
Décors of sound; musical thoughts on emotion and environment; excerpts from diary. N. Rorem. House B 111:102-3+ Ap '69
Diary: tranquilizer without side effects. E. Richey. Mlle 68:82+ Ap '69
Schaap shop; tape-recorded diaries. Time 94: 49-50 S 19 '69
You meet such interesting people; diary of a free-lancer. C. Schwalberg. U S Camera 32:64-5+ Ja '69
See also
Celiac disease

DIARRHEA
See also
Celiac disease

DIAS, Earl J.
Enter Mr Poe; drama. Plays 29:39-48 N '69
Some of my best friends are spies; drama. Plays 29:1-10 Ja '70

DIASIO, Bob
(ed) See Szasz, T. Mental illness is not a disease

DIATOMS
3,4-Dihydroxyproline: a new amino acid in diatom cell walls. T. Nakajima and B. E. Volcani. bibliog il Science 164:1400-1 Je 20 '69

DIAZ, Herma
Merry, merry John Canoe in Jamaica. Dance Mag 43:16-17 D '69

DIAZ DE LEÓN, Martha
Red flower; story. Américas 21:30-2 Mr '69

DIAZ ORDAZ, Gustavo
President Nixon and President Diaz Ordaz of Mexico dedicate the Amistad Dam; remarks, exchange of toasts, September 8, 1969. Dept State Bul 61:278-9 S 29 '69
about
United States and Mexico reaffirm bonds of friendship; exchange of toasts, December 13, 1968. Dept State Bul 60:22-3, 25-6 Ja 13 '69

DIBONA, D. R. and Civan, M. M.
Toad urinary bladder: intercellular spaces. bibliog Science 165:503-4 Ag 1 '69

DIBOS CHAPPUIS, Eduardo
Good news from the Andes. Fortune 80:120 Ag 15 '69

DI CAPUA, Michael
Uri Shulevitz: Caldecott winner. Library J 94:2068-9 My 15 '69

DICHLORODIPHENYLTRICHLOROETHANE. See DDT (insecticide)

DICHLOROPHENOXYACETIC acid. See Herbicides

DICK and Jane; drama. See Feiffer, J.

DICKENS, Charles
Tale of two cities; dramatization. See Thane, A.
about
Charles Dickens and today's reader. J. Gold. Engl J 58:205-11 F '69
Close reading of Hard times. J. F. Lincks. Engl J 58:212-18 F '69
Pip: a love affair. S. Simmons. Engl J 58:416-17 Mr '69

DICKENSON, Fred
Nature's little puzzler: the platypus. Read Digest 95:167+ Ag '69

DICKERSON, George
Auto-da-fé; poem. Mlle 68:146 Mr '69

DICKERSON, Reed
Few corrections concerning Bix Beiderbecke. Esquire 71:72+ Ap '69

DICKEY, Eldridge
Prayer for Oakland. il por Newsweek 74:66 Ag 4 '69

DICKEY, James
At Mercy manor; poem. Atlan 224:75-6 D '69
Blood; Diabetes; Venom. Cancer match; Pine: taste, touch and sight; poems. Poetry 114: 149-62 Je '69
Drums where I live; poem. New Yorker 45: 56 N 29 '69
Knock; poem. New Yorker 44:92 Ja 25 '69
Living there; poem. Harper 238:52-3 My '69

DIET—See also—*Continued*
Food
Food fads
Food habits
Iron in diet
Vitamins
Weight watchers, incorporated
   also headings beginning Nutrition
DIET, Deficient
In the wake of starvation, a wound food
  cannot heal. A. H. Moore. il Life 66:52 Ja
  24 '69
Miasma of malnutrition. Sci Digest 65:75
  My '69
Milk and blindness in Brazil. G. E. Bunce.
  Natur Hist 78:52-5 F '69
Nutrition and learning. H. F. Eichenwald
  and P. C. Fry. bibliog Science 163:644-8
  F 14 '69; Reply with rejoinder. H. Baker
  and O. Frank. 165:313 Jl 18 '69
   See also
Deficiency diseases
DIET food industry. See Food industry and
trade
DIET in disease
Bland diet; with recipes. L. Driggs. il Har
  Yrs 9:34-40 S '69
Bland diets need not be dull. E. M. Peltz. il
  Todays Health 47:50-4 Jl '69
Low-fat diet. Sci Am 221:98 S '69
Luscious low-cholesterol recipes. il Redbook
  132:118-20+ Ap '69
Should your family's diet be changed to
  prevent heart attacks? Good H 168:185-7
  My '69
Yemenites' exodus; effects of different diets
  and ways of life on the heart and arteries
  of immigrants in Israel. il Time 93:67 Mr
  14 '69
DIET pills. See Drugs—Physiological effects
DIETETIC foods. See Food industry and trade
DIETHER, Jack
Bernstein's personal vision of the Sibelius
  symphonies. Am Rec G 35:804-6 My '69
Second symphony of Sir Michael Tippett.
  Am Rec G 36:98-9 O '69
Vaughan Williams from Sir Adrian, outstand-
  ing. Am Rec G 36:214-16+ N '69
DIETRICH, John W.
Brains of automation. Radio-Electr 40:51-3
  F '69
Surprises from the moon; interview. por U S
  News 67:26-7 Ag 4 '69
DIETRICH, Marlene
Quintessential sultry female. R. Crinkley. por
  Nat R 21:134-5 F 11 '69
DIETRICK, Karl E.
Valedictory; poem. Nat R 21:537 Je 3 '69
DIETS. See Diet
DIETSCH, Robert W.
Half an eye on $20 billion. Nation 208:331
  Mr 17 '69
Hard-core blacks and the shiny auto. New
  Repub 160:10 Mr 1 '69
Merger boom; who owns what? New Repub
  160:14-16 F 22 '69
Weather change in Cuba? Nation 208:826-7
  Je 30 '69
DIETTERICH, Paul
Affective ministries in international affairs.
  Chr Cent 86:579-81 Ap 23 '69
DIETZ, Lew
Confessions of a Maine deer hunter. Field &
  S 73:66-7+ Ap '69
DIETZ, Robert S. and Dill, R. F.
Down into the sea in ships. il Sea Front
  15:2-9 Ja '69
—and Knebel, H. J.
First deep-sea sounding. pors Sea Front 15:
  212-18 Jl '69
DIEZ DE MEDINA, Fernando
White llama; story. Américas 21:31-5 Ag '69
DIFFERENCES, National. See National char-
acteristics
DIFFERENT ball game; story. See Friedman,
B. J.
DIFFERENTIAL generalization. See Generali-
zation (psychology)
DIFFERENTIATION (biology)
Cellular differentiation in the immune sys-
  tem; report of eighth Midwinter conference
  of immunologists. J. S. Garvey. Science 165:
  205-6+ Jl 11 '69
Phases in cell differentiation. N. K. Wessells
  and W. J. Rutter. il Sci Am 220:36-44 bib-
  liog(p 148) Mr '69
   See also
Morphogenesis
DIFFICULT children. See Problem children
DIFFRACTION
Isaac Asimov explains; refraction vs dif-
  fraction. I. Asimov. Sci Digest 66:74-5 Jl '69

Observed diffraction pattern and proposed
  models of liquid water. A. H. Narten and
  H. A. Levy. bibliog il Science 165:447-54
  Ag 1 '69
   See also
Neutrons—Diffraction
DIFFUSION
Direct pathway to the brain. M. R. Kare and
  others. bibliog il Science 163:952-3 F 28 '69
Intracranial drug implants: an autoradio-
  graphic analysis of diffusion. S. P. Gross-
  man and W. E. Stumpf. bibliog il Science
  166:1410-12 D 12 '69
Rate of intracellular diffusion as measured
  in barnacle muscle. W. H. Bunch and G.
  Kallsen. bibliog il Science 164:1178-9 Je 6 '69
DIGESTIVE system
   See also
Flatulence
DI GIOVANNI, Norman Thomas
  (tr) See Borges, J. L. Daybreak
  (tr) See Borges, J. L. Fragment
  (tr) See Borges, J. L. Heraclitus
  (tr) See Borges, J. L. Isidoro Acevedo
  (tr) See Borges, J. L. Six poems: Keeper of
    the books; June 1968; Cambridge; Invoca-
    tion to Joyce; In praise of darkness;
    Plain things
  (tr) See Borges, J. L. To a Saxon poet
  (tr) See Borges, J. L. Unending gift
  (tr) See Borges, J. L. and Guerrero, M.
    Imaginary beings
DIGITAL counters. See Counting machines and
devices
DIGITAL data transmission systems. See Data
transmission systems
DIGITAL timers. See Timing devices
DIGITOXIN
Digitoxin poisoning: prevention by spiron-
  olactone. H. Selye and others. bibliog il
  Science 164:842-3 My 16 '69
DIHYDROXYPROLINE. See Proline
DILCHER, David L.
Podocarpus from the eocene of North Ameri-
  ca. bibliog Science 164:299-301 Ap 18 '69
DILL, Robert F. See Dietz, R. S. jt. auth.
DILLINGER, William C.
Outward bound adventures. Nat Wildlife
  7:12-16 Je '69
DILLON, George
Sonnet; I am saved by love the way the
  fisherman. Poetry 113:412 Mr '69
DILLON, Jack
Weather, time and fitting-out. Motor B 123:
  73+ Ap '69
DILLON, Sister Johnell
Philistine asks for equal time. por Phys
  Today 22:38-9 My '69
DIMANCESCU, Dan
Americans afoot in Rumania. por Nat Geog
  135:810-45 Je '69
DIMBLEBY, David
Dimbleby the second. por Time 93:71-2 Mr 7
  '69
DIMETHYLBENZANTHRACENE
Mammary cancer induction by 7,12-dimethy-
  lbenz(a)anthracene: relation to age. T. L.
  Dao. bibliog il Science 165:810-11 Ag 22 '69
DINELL, Tom
Freedom and tenure. Bul Atom Sci 25:46-7
  Ap '69
DINERMAN, Beatrice
Women in architecture; excerpts from book.
  Arch Forum 131:50-1 D '69
DINERS' club, incorporated
Shuffling cards at Diners' club. Bsns W p20
  D 27 '69
DINGHIES. See Boats and boating
DINGHY racing. See Boat racing
DINGMAN, Paul R.
Day programs for children: a note on ter-
  minology. Ment Hy 53:646-7 O '69
DINH, Tran-van-. See Tran-van-Dinh
DINING. See Dinners and dining
DINING alcoves, etc.
   See also
Snack bars
DINING halls in colleges. See Colleges and
universities—Dining halls
DINING rooms
Balcony into outdoor dining room. il House
  & Gard 135:124-5 My '69
Chez Mlle: flash in the pad. P. Bartlett. il
  Mlle 70:66-7 D '69
Far-flung look at star-quality dining. il
  House B 111:99-109 N '69
Nonstop dining room. il Bet Hom & Gard
  47:70-1 O '69
Small wonders. il Redbook 132:90-2 Mr '69
Stimulating the appetite. B. Plumb. il N Y
  Times Mag p54-5 Ag 10 '69

DINING tables. See Tables

DINIS, Edmund S.
Autopsy hearing nears in the Teddy Kennedy accident. por U S News 67:11 S 29 '69
D.A. on the spot. il por Newsweek 74:23-4 Ag 25 '69
Inquest set in Kennedy case. por U S News 67:9 Ag 18 '69
On the record. Newsweek 74:39-40 N 3 '69
Rehearsal for an inquest. il por Time 94:16-17 O 31 '69

DINKINS, Stephanie
Gallery; photographs. Life 67:8-9 S 12 '69

DINNERS and dining
Black-tie dinners; with menus. H. McCully. il House B 111:148-9+ N '69
Company's coming to dinner; with menus (title varies) il Am Home 72:94 Mr; 96 Ap; 104 My '69
Dinner for two. J. Morales. Parents Mag 44:134 N '69
Dinners for two. il Ebony 24:160+ Je '69
Dress up your frozen dinners. J. Miller. Am Home 72:96 Mr '69
Eat: a June dinner. M. Cantwell. Mlle 69:70+ Je '69
GH's big cookbook of best holiday dinners. il Good H 169:106-26 N '69
Great dinners. E. Graves. See issues of Life
Hearty family dinners for fall; with menus. il Good H 169:106-21 S '69
How I give a party. A. Vanderbilt. Ladies Home J 86:103-4 O '69
Larder; excerpts from Great dinners from Life; with editorial comment. E. Graves. il Life 67:3, 54-61 O 24 '69
No time to cook; menu with recipes. See issues of McCall's
Quick one-skillet dinner. il Good H 169:134-5 D '69
Should children eat separately at holiday dinners? il Good H 169:180 D '69
Sit-down dinner; with recipes. il Ladies Home J 86:100-1+ O '69
Tempting dinners for two. il Redbook 132:116-17+ Ap '69
Yankee dinner for a royal collection; Boston Forsyth Wickes collection, French and English 18th-century antiques; with recipes. E. Alston. il Look 33:68-72 F 18 '69
See also
Christmas dinners
Gastronomy
Thanksgiving dinners

DINNERWARE. See Pottery; Tableware

DINNETAH; drama. See Winther, B.

DINOSAUR NATIONAL MONUMENT
Dinosaur monument to the age of reptiles. O. F. Oldendorph. il Nat Parks 43:4-10 S '69

DINOSAURS
Brownstone dinosaur. Sci Am 221:50 O '69
Great dinosaur disaster. D. Cohen. il Sci Digest 65:45-52 Mr '69
Missing ammosaurus; discovered in a stony quarry near Manchester, Conn. Time 94:53 N 7 '69

DINUCLEOSIDE phosphates. See Phosphates

DINUZZO, Sal
Printed-circuit technology. por Electr World 82:37-41 O '69

DIOCESAN newspapers. See Catholic press

DIOCESES
Dropping titular fictions. America 120:180 F 15 '69
See also
Catholic church—Dioceses

DIODES
Normal-state electron tunneling only qualitatively understood; report of meeting. J. A. Appelbaum and J. M. Rowell. Phys Today 22:89+ D '69
Solid-state diodes; symposium. il Electr World 82:35-53 Jl '69
Solid-state LSA microwave diodes. D. L. Heiserman. il Electr World 81:40+ F '69
Variable-voltage tuning. R. F. Scott. il Radio-Electr 40:58-60 Ap '69
Varicaps; voltage-variable capacitance diodes. A. A. Mangieri. il Pop Electr 30:69-71 My '69

DIOLS. See Glycols

DIONYSOS restaurant. See Athens, Greece—Hotels, restaurants, etc.

DIONYSUS in 69; drama. See Schechner, R.

DIORAMAS
Pioneer mining camp. S. A. Parvin. il Hobbies 74:118 Ap '69

DIORITES
Diorites from the mid-Atlantic ridge at 45°N. F. Aumento. bibliog il Science 165:1112-13 S 12 '69

DIPAOLO, Joseph A. and others
Sarcoma-producing cell lines derived from clones transformed in vitro by benzo[a]pyrene. bibliog Science 165:917-18 Ag 29 '69

DIPEGO, Gerald
It's never cold in daydreams; story. Redbook 133:80-1 S '69
Sunday; story. Redbook 133:78 Ag '69

DIPHENYL compounds
Global pollutant; polychlorinated biphenyls. Sci Am 220:44 F '69

DIPHOSPHONATES. See Phosphonates

DIPHTHERIA
Deadly diphtheria. Newsweek 74:67 D 22 '69
Mush against death; getting diphtheria antitoxin to Nome, 1925. L. M. Rhodes. il Todays Health 48:30-3+ Ja '70
Recurrence of a killer. Sci N 96:576 D 20 '69

DIPHTHERIA toxin. See Toxins and antitoxins

DIPLOMACY
See also
International relations
United States—Diplomatic and consular service
also subhead Foreign relations under names of countries, e.g. France—Foreign relations

DIPLOMAS
Measure of accomplishment. M. S. Marshall. Sch & Soc 97:21-2 Ja '69

DIPLOMAS, Fraudulent
Instant-minister racket. B. Bruns. il Life 67:67-8+ N 14 '69

DIPLOMATIC and consular service
See also subhead Diplomatic and consular service under names of countries, e.g. United States—Diplomatic and consular service

DIPLOMATIC conferences. See International conferences

DIPLOMATIC privileges and immunities
See also
United Nations conference on diplomatic intercourse and immunities

DIPLOMATIC recognition. See Recognition (international law)

DIPLOMATS
See also
United States—Diplomatic and consular service
United States—Foreign service

DIPOLE moments
Orientation of the dipole moments of hydroxyl groups in oxidized and unoxidized biotite. A. S. R. Juo and J. L. White. bibliog il Science 165:804-5 Ag 22 '69
Ultracold neutrons may refine electric-dipole-moment value. M. S. Rothenberg. il Phys Today 22:56+ N '69

DIPPEL, Johann Andreas
Dippel the debonair. M. J. Matz. il por Opera N 33:14-16 F 22 '69

DIPS. See Appetizers

DIRECT approach; story. See Harrison, W.

DIRECT election of presidents. See Presidents—United States—Election

DIRECTION, Theatrical. See Theatrical production and direction

DIRECTION books. See Instruction manuals

DIRECTION finding apparatus
See also
Radio beacons
Radio compass

DIRECTORIES
See also subhead under various subjects, e.g. Airplane industry and trade—Directories

DIRECTORS. See Corporations—Directors

DIRECTORS, Moving picture. See Moving picture directors

DIRECTORS and officers liability insurance. See Insurance, Liability

DIRIGIBLES. See Airships

DIRKSEN, Everett McKinley
Excerpts from debate, June 23, 1969. Cong Digest 48:203+ Ag '69
High government source; excerpts from news conference, ed. by F. Taddeo. Sr Schol 94:12-13 F 28 '69
If a man die, shall he live again? reprint. por U S News 67:110+ S 22 '69
Needed: a realistic East-West trade policy. Read Digest 94:129-33 Je '69
New plan to fight pornography. Read Digest 95:113-16 N '69
about
Appointees fall down on the Hill. il por Bsns W p46-7 My 10 '69
Dirksen and the White House; the senator's role has changed now. il por U S News 67:14 Jl 21 '69

DIRKSEN, Everett McKinley—about—*Cont.*
Dirksen charge: businessmen are harassed to give Negroes jobs. il por U S News 66:8 Ap 7 '69
Dirksen's new role. pors U S News 66:46-7 My 19 '69
Dirksen's rebellion. por Newsweek 73:36 My 12 '69
Everett Dirksen: American original. il pors Time 94:25-6 S 19 '69
Ev Dirksen, 1896-1969. por Newsweek 74:27 S 15 '69
Ev Dirksen: master politician. H. J. Sievers. America 121:181 S 20 '69
Everett Dirksen. RIP. W. F. Buckley. Nat R 21:950 S 23 '69
Ev's amendment. il por Time 94:18 Ag 8 '69
Extinct species. K. Crawford. Newsweek 74:38 S 22 '69
Last of a rare old breed. il pors Newsweek 74:34-5 S 22 '69
Nixon's secret protector. por Time 93:26-7 My 9 '69
Obituary
  U S News 67:25 S 22 '69
Other Ev Dirksen. C. Roberts. il por Newsweek 73:26-8 Je 16 '69
Pike, Ho, Dirksen, and Pearson. Chr Today 13:38 S 26 '69
Prayer amendment no. 3. Chr Today 13:46 F 28 '69
Pretty good place to be from, and go back to. R. B. Stolley. il por Life 67:4 S 19 '69
Semieulogy for a senator. Chr Cent 86:1214 S 24 '69
Summer theatrics. P. Lisagor. Nations Bsns 57:17-18 Jl '69

DIRT eating. See Pica (pathology)

DISABILITY
Measurement
Price-tagging our bodies. Sci Digest 65:64 Je '69

DISABILITY, Reading. See Reading disability

DISABLED. See Handicapped

DISADVANTAGED children. See Socially handicapped children

DI SANT'AGNESE, Paul A.
Unmasking the great impersonator, cystic fibrosis. Todays Health 47:38-41+ F '69

DISARMAMENT
Assembly adopts seven resolutions; with text of resolutions. UN Mo Chron 6:46-55 Ja '69
Chances for an end to the arms race. il U S News 66:32-3 F 3 '69
Disarmament; First committee receives six draft resolutions. UN Mo Chron 6:66-70 D '69
Fiendish vials; proposal that the U S take first steps in arms control. N. Cousins. Sat R 52:16-17 Ag 30 '69
Mild encouragement. Chr Cent 86:1339 O 22 '69
Next: a deal between U.S. and Russia? il U S News 66:25-6 Mr 10 '69
Right to kill; reprint. D. Lawrence. U S News 67:104 D 15 '69
Security through limitations. H. Brown. For Affairs 47:422-32 Ap '69
Thing to do after Vietnam is to tell the truth. J. J. Stone. Commonweal 90:10-11 Mr 21 '69; Same with title To tell the truth. Cur 109:54-5 Ag '69
U.S. positions at Eighteen-nation disarmament conference outlined by President Nixon; text of letter, March 15, 1969. R. M. Nixon. Dept State Bul 60:289-90 Ap 7 '69
See also
Arbitration, International
Armaments
Atomic weapons and disarmament
Peace
Strategic arms limitation talks
United Nations—Eighteen-nation committee on disarmament
War
United States
Danger in arms cuts: a senator's warning; excerpts from address, September 3, 1969. J. Stennis. il U S News 67:38-9 S 15 '69

DISARMAMENT agency. See United States—Arms control and disarmament agency

DISASTERS
How police confront disaster; Columbus, Ohio simulation study. T E. Drabek and J. E. Haas. il Trans-Action 6:33-8 My '69
When disaster strikes, they strike back; construction contractors' plan bulldozer. Nations Bsns 57:73 N '69
See also
Bridges—Accidents
Building failures

Earthquakes
Emergency communication systems
Explosions
Floods
Forest fires
Hurricanes
Insurance—Catastrophe coverage
Panic
Relief work
Shipwrecks

DISC brakes. See Brakes, Automobile

DISC jockeys
See also
Miller, H.

DISCHARGE of employees. See Employees—Dismissal

DISCHARGED prisoners. See Prisoners, Discharged

DISCIPLINE
Decline of authority. M. Smith. Ed Digest 35:5-7 O '69
Discipline firm and sane. H. Ginott. McCalls 97:42+ O '69
Discipline means to teach. W. E. Homan. il N Y Times Mag p93+ Mr 16 '69
Discipline shouldn't be demeaning; with study-discussion program, by R. Strang. D. Graves. bibliog il PTA Mag 64:9-11, 34 O '69
Effects of three kinds of discipline. B. Spock. Redbook 132:63+ F '69
Fathers as disciplinarians. B. Spock. il Redbook 132:26+ Ap '69
Parents and teachers are greasing the skids. A. Giglio. Todays Ed 58:30 D '69
Parents' guide to the age of revolt. D. Barr. il McCalls 97:73+ O '69
This permissiveness nonsense. B. Bettelheim. Ladies Home J 86:34+ S '69
When the young take liberties. A. H. Sypher. Nations Bsns 57:25-6 My '69
See also
Camp discipline
Children—Management and training
College discipline
School discipline

DISCIPLINE, Industrial. See Labor discipline

DISCIPLINE, Library. See Library administration

DISCIPLINE, Military
Another target of new left; the armed forces. il U S News 66:58-60 My 26 '69
Dilemma of military dissent; with interview with General Lewis W. Walt. il Life 66:28D-37 My 23 '69
Dissent and discipline in the thinking man's army. Life 66:38 My 9 '69
Most unforgettable character I've met. G. P. Morrill. il Read Digest 95:122-6 Ag '69
Off limits to rioters. il Nations Bsns 57:50-1 Ag '69

DISCONTENT
How could anything that feels so bad be so good? R. E. Farson. Sat R 52:20-1+ S 6 '69

DISCOTHEQUES, etc.
Drop-in night at the Electric circus; imaginary conversation with F. Liszt. D. Bar-Illan. Sat R 52:72-3 N 15 '69
See also
Rock 'n' roll groups

DISCOUNT
Deflation: an economic waiting game. il Newsweek 73:83 Ap 21 '69
Economy won't give in; Fed's new efforts to halt inflation. il Bsns W p29-30 Ap 12 '69
On accepting clergy discounts: psychological implications. W. R. Rogers. Chr Cent 86:1113-14 Ag 27 '69; Discussion. 86:1285-6 O 8 '69

DISCOUNT, Trade
Bookselling and the dollar squeeze. G. R. Smith. Pub W 195:41-5 My 5 '69
Discount and the minimum order: policies of publishing houses. G. R. Smith. Pub W 196:47-8 O 13 '69

DISCOUNT chain stores. See Chain stores

DISCOVERIES in science. See Research

DISCRIMINATION
See also
Anti-Semitism
United Nations—Sub-commission on prevention of discrimination and protection of minorities

DISCRIMINATION (psychology)
Attention shifts in a maintained discrimination. D. S. Blough. bibliog il Science 166:125-6 O 3 '69
Averaged evoked responses in vigilance and discrimination: a reassessment. W. Ritter and H. G. Vaughan, jr. bibliog il Science 164:326-8 Ap 18 '69
See also
Preferences (psychology)

DISCRIMINATION, Racial. See Race discrimination

DISCRIMINATION in education
Exclude whites? No, says top Negro educator. U S News 66:18 Je 2 '69
First in fight over segregation. U S News 66: 12 Ap 28 '69
Listen to the black graduate, you might learn something; Brown university. B. Beckham. il Esquire 72:98+ S '69

DISCRIMINATION in employment
Affirmative action; changing hiring policies of Equitable life. L. L. L. Golden. Sat R 52:127-8 Mr 8 '69
Barriers to hiring the blacks. J. R. Goeke and C. S. Weymar. il Harvard Bsns R 47: 144-6+ S '69
Black battleground; Pittsburgh. il Time 94:78 S 5 '69
Black Monday and white Friday. il Newsweek 74:105-7 O 6 '69
Black workers in white unions. W. B. Gould. Nation 209:203-6 S 8 '69
Building pickets to spread? U S News 67:79 S 8 '69
Can a black man fly? interviews. K. Connes. il Flying 85:53-7 Jl '69
Cracking the crafts; Pittsburgh demonstrations. il Newsweek 74:34-5 S 8 '69
Demonstrating again at Allen-Bradley. il Bsns W p44 Ag 16 '69
Dirksen charge: businessmen are harassed to give Negroes jobs. il U S News 66:8 Ap 7 '69
Job-quota plan survives attack; the Philadelphia plan. U S News 67:64 Ag 18 '69
Job seniority and discrimination; excerpt from Discrimination in the union and on the job. A. W. Blumrosen. Mo Labor R 92: 52-3 Mr '69
Packard's deal with the textile big three. B. Sellers. New Repub 160:9-11 Mr 22 '69
Political row erupts over fair employment. il Bsns W p20-1 Ap 5 '69
Red and green in civil rights; Philadelphia plan. R. Kuttner. Commonweal 90:535 S 5 '69
Soul power drive for jobs expands. il Bsns W p22+ Ag 30 '69
Space is not black. J. Robertson. Nation 208: 814-16 Je 30 '69
Stiffer rules against bias. U S News 66:86 Je 23 '69
TRB from Washington: Kennedy stands up; Senate hearing on contract compliance. New Repub 160:6 Ap 12 '69
Trade unions grapple with race prejudice. B. L. Masse. America 120:701 Je 21 '69
See also
Negroes—Employment
United States—Equal employment opportunity commission

DISCRIMINATION in housing
Attack against blockbusting; Chicago court action. U S News 66:8 Ap 7 '69
Black homeowning; Contract buyers league lawsuits for price exploitation. A. Boles. New Repub 161:7-9 D 13 '69
Caroline and Charnita; Justice department suits charge violations of Title VIII of the Civil rights act of 1968. D. Sanford. New Repub 161:12-13 N 8 '69
Chicago's quiet slum revolt. America 121:350 O 25 '69
Fair housing: Denver venture as model. J. Willy. Chr Cent 86:1143-5 S 3 '69
Fair housing laws, unfair housing practices. L. W. Eley. il Trans-Action 6:56-61 Je '69
Race, jobs, and cities: what business can do. J. R. Lowe; reply. E. L. Stoll. Sat R 52:32-3 F 22 '69
Spotlight on blockbusting; unscrupulous realtors and unthinking community; A Baltimore study. T. M. Gannon. America 120: 563-4 My 10 '69
Unbusted blocks. il Newsweek 74:55 D 1 '69
See also
Housing—Desegregation
Negroes—Housing

DISCRIMINATION learning. See Learning, Psychology of

DISCUS, pseud.
Music in the round. See issues of Harper's magazine

DISCUSSION
See also
Conferences

DISCUSSION method (education)
Little black box of teaching and learning: lectures vs. discussion sections. Trans-Action 6:10 O '69
Why don't pupils talk in class discussions. J. R. Applegate. il Clear House 44:78-81 O '69

DISEASE, Diet in. See Diet in disease
DISEASE prevention. See Medicine, Preventive
DISEASE resistance. See Immunity

DISEASES
Cat-scratch-fever mystery. E. Ubell. McCalls 97:93+ O '69
What's new in medicine. See issues of McCall's to July 1969
See also
Autoimmune diseases
Children—Diseases
Communicable diseases
Diagnosis
Mortality
also names of diseases, e.g. Influenza; also subhead Diseases under names of organs and parts of the body, e.g. Heart—Diseases

Causes and theories of causation
See also
Traumatism

Statistics
Dollars you give to fight disease. Changing T 23:6 O '69

DISEASES, Incurable

Psychological aspects
What to tell a child? emotional effect of a child's leukemia on parents, siblings and victim. Time 93:67 Mr 14 '69

DISEASES, Industrial
See also
Cancer
Lungs—Dust diseases

DISEASES, Mental. See Mental illness
DISEASES, Prehistoric. See Paleopathology
DISEASES, Psychosomatic. See Medicine, Psychosomatic

DISEASES of famous persons
Porphyria and King George III. I. Macalpine and R. Hunter. il Sci Am 221:38-46 Jl '69; Discussion. 221:8-9 D '69
Royal malady; medical records of George III. Time 94:60+ Ag 1 '69

DISH driers, Electric. See Dishwashing and drying machines

DISHES. See Pottery

DISHON, Colleen
Skeezer: the canine child therapist. Todays Health 48:16-18 Ja '70

DISHONESTY. See Honesty

DISHWASHING
Dishwashing in small space. il Sunset 143:105 Jl '69

DISHWASHING and drying machines
Consumer's guide to dishwashers. il Mech Illus 65:52 N '69
Problem-solving dishwashers. il Bet Hom & Gard 47:17+ Je '69
Protect your health with a dishwasher. S. Schuler. Am Home 72:88-90 My '69

DISINFECTION and disinfectants
Swimming pool chemicals. il Consumer Rep 34:367-71 Jl '69

DISMISSAL of students. See Expulsion from school and college
DISMISSAL of teachers. See Teachers—Dismissal

DISNEY, Dorothy Cameron
(ed) Can this marriage be saved? See occasional issues of Ladies home journal

DISNEY, Roy
Unforgettable Walt Disney. Read Digest 94: 212-18 F '69

DISNEY, Walt
Disney imperative. W. Marx. Nation 209:76-8 Jl 28 '69
Disney version, by R. Schickel. Review Am West 6:50+ Ja '69. J. E. Illick
Unforgettable Walt Disney. R. Disney. il por Read Digest 94:212-18 F '69

DISNEY, Walt, productions
Disney without Walt. il Newsweek 74:90 O 20 '69
Men who followed Mickey Mouse. T. Murray. il Duns R 94:34-8 D '69
Tripping on Disney; Fantasia revival and Disney fad. il Newsweek 75:88 Ja 19 '70
Unforgettable Walt Disney. R. Disney. il Read Digest 94:212-18 F '69

DISNEY world, Walt. See Amusement parks
DISNEYLAND East. See Amusement parks

DISNEYLAND park, Anaheim, Calif.
Disney version, by R. Schickel. Review Am West 6:50+ Ja '69. J. E. Illick
Disneyland on a lollypop and a camera. J. Farber and P. Farber. il Travel & Camera 32:58-61 Ag '69

DISOBEDIENCE. See Obedience
DISORDERLINESS. See Neatness
DISPATCH news service
Hip-pocket AP. il Newsweek 74:83-4 D 8
'69
Miscue on the massacre. Time 94:75 D 5 '69
DISPENSATIONS (canon law)
When a priest leaves the ministry. W. W.
Bassett. America 120:242-5 Mr 1 '69; Reply.
J. D. Gerken. 120:381-2 Ap 5 '69
DISPLAY of antiques, art objects, etc.
Art everywhere you look. J. Russell. il House
& Gard 136:84-91 N '69
Art in contrast. il House & Gard 136:92-3
N '69
Country casual for today. il Am Home 72:46-9
Jl '69
House of surprises in Palm Beach; home of
Mr and Mrs Bedford Davie. il Vogue 153:
190-3 Ja 15 '69
Live with your collection. il Am Home 72:52-5
Je '69
Merry Christmas at the Wyatt Coopers. il
House & Gard 136:48-57 D '69
Mission possible: decorate the impossible
home. V. D Hahn. il Am Home 72:72-7 My
'69
Porcelain as room decoration in eighteenth-
century England. R. J. Charleston. il An-
tiques 96:894-9 D '69
Traveler's trophies on display. il Sunset
142:138 Mr '69
DISPLAY of merchandise
See also
Show windows
DISPLAYS, Library. See Library exhibits
DISPLAYS, Window. See Show windows
DISPOSABLES marketing services corporation
New pitch for disposables. il Bsns W p 156
N 15 '69
DISPOSAL of radioactive waste. See Radioac-
tive waste disposal
DISPOSAL of refuse. See Refuse and refuse dis-
posal
DISPOSAL of surplus supplies. See Surplus
products
DISPOSAL of trade waste. See Trade waste
disposal
DISRAELI, Benjamin, 1st earl of Beaconsfield.
See Beaconsfield, B. D.
DISSENT, Freedom of. See Free speech
DISSENT, Right of. See Free speech
DISSENTERS
Agnew's ten commandments of protest; ex-
cerpts from remarks, December 3, 1969.
S. T. Agnew. U S News 67:14 D 15 '69
Civil rights and symbolic language. A. Neier.
Cur 104:29-34 F '69
Dear Mrs Mitchell . . . D. P. Riley. Common-
weal 91:329 D 12 '69
Different drummers: men and women who
changed the step of American history (cont)
il Sr Schol 93:15 Ja 10; 94:17 Ja 17; 11 F 7;
12-13 F 14; 16 Mr 7; 11 Mr 14; 19 Mr 21; 9
Ap 11; 13 Ap 18; 21 Ap 25; 16 My 2; 6 My 9;
95:2 O 6 '69
Dilemma of military dissent; with interview
with General Lewis W. Walt. il Life 66:
28D-37 My 23 '69
Discrimination among the activists. Chr Cent
86:1539-40 D 3 '69
Dissent and discipline in the thinking man's
army. Life 66:38 My 9 '69
Dissent and law enforcement; excerpts from
report Rights in conflict. D. Walker. Cur
103:33-40 Ja '69
In defense of chaos; address. B. Shahn.
Ramp Mag 7:12-13 D 14 '68
Intolerable allegories of dissent. J. P. Sisk.
Cath World 210:55-8 N '69
Nixon-eye view of dissent. il Newsweek 74:
35 O 27 '69
Passionate rebels. S. Harrington. il Vogue
153:146-51+ My '69
Protest in the sixties; symposium, ed. by J.
Boskin and R. A. Rosenstone. bibliog F
Ann Am Acad 382:1-144 Mr '69
Protest, past and present; address, June
1969. J. Bronowski. Am Scholar 38:535-46
Aut '69
Rebellion and repression, by T. Hayden. Re-
view
Nation 210:21-3 Ja 12 '70. P. Clecak
Responsible versus irresponsible dissent;
adaptation of address, March 27, 1969. J. W.
Gardner. Science 164:379 Ap 25 '69
Submarine conspiracy: Tallin document ad-
vocating radical changes in Soviet policy.
Time 94:26+ O 31 '69
Towards a new past, ed. by B. J. Bernstein.
Review
Am Hist R 74:529-33 D '68. A. S. Kradi-
tor; D. Donald

Unco-optables. il Esquire 72:103 S '69
Why dissent turns violent. K. Widmer. Na-
tion 208:425-9 Ap 7 '69
See also
Vietnamese war, 1957- —Protests, demonstra-
tions, etc, against

Anecdotes, facetiae, satire, etc.
Upsidedown man. J. Keefauver. il Nat R 21:
691+ Jl 15 '69
DISSENTERS, Religious
Believers' church: the history and character
of radical Protestantism, by D. F. Durn-
baugh. Review
Chr Cent 86:685-6 My 14 '69. R. S. Paul
C.U.A. board of inquiry report; academic
propriety of the dissenting theologians' ac-
tion. America 120:489 Ap 26 '69
Communist-Catholic neurosis? Reflections on
A long journey. C. A. Weber. Commonweal
90:389-93 Je 20 '69
Practically schismatic. Time 93:60+ Ap 11 '69
Resistance in the church. E. C. Bianchi.
Commonweal 90:257-60 My 16 '69; Reply with
rejoinder. P. Foote. 90:379+ Je 20 '69
Right, duty, and dissent. N. J. Rigali. Cath
World 208:214-18 F '69
Vindication at C.U; right of theological dis-
sent. Commonweal 90:155-6 Ap 25 '69
Wish you were there; Rome's attempt to de-
port dissenting bishops. Newsweek 73:88 Je
16 '69
DISSOCIATION
Dilute solutions of strong acids: the effect
of water on ph. P. H. Mogul and J. S.
Schmuckler. bibliog il Chem 42:14-17 O '69
DISTAVAL. See Thalidomide
DISTILLERS corporation-Seagrams limited
M-G-M cliff-hanger. il Newsweek 74:70-1+
Ag 4 '69
DISTILLING industries
Distillers get ready to serve light whiskey.
il Bsns W p58-9+ F 22 '69
See also
Brown-Forman distillers corporation
Publicker industries
DISTRIBUTION (probability theory)
Gaussian behavior of the electroencephalo-
gram: changes during performance of men-
tal task. R. Elul. bibliog il Science 164:328-
31 Ap 18 '69
Peculiar distribution of first digits. R. A.
Raimi. il Sci Am 221:109-13+ D '69
DISTRIBUTION, Physical. See Distribution of
goods
DISTRIBUTION of goods
New pitch for disposables. il Bsns W p 156
N 15 '69
Prevent blunders in supply and distribution;
with charts. R. Pirasteh. il Harvard Bsns
R 47:113-27 Mr '69
See also
Wholesale trade
DISTRIBUTION of population. See Population,
Distribution of
DISTRIBUTION of wealth. See Wealth, Dis-
tribution of
DISTRIBUTIVE education
Distributive education; the retail industry;
address, March 22, 1969. R. V. Guelich. Vital
Speeches 35:508-12 Je 1 '69
Relevance: a job, a future, a sense of dignity
(cont) E. B. Gold. Library J 94:818 F 15
'69
DISTRIBUTOR vacuum. See Automobile en-
gines—Ignition
DISTRICT attorneys
See also
Garrison, J.
DISTRICT 50, UMWA. See United mine workers
of America—District 50
DISTRICT OF COLUMBIA
See also
Geology—District of Columbia
Law—District of Columbia
DITCHING machinery. See Trenching machine-
ry
DITHIOTHREITOL. See Mercaptans
DITTMER, Bradford
Build this power hacksaw from a washing
machine. Pop Mech 132:188-91 N '69
DIURETICS and diuresis
See also
Spironolactone
DIVERSIFICATION in industry
Bold bet of British-American tobacco. J. Ross-
Skinner. il Duns R 94:32-3+ Jl '69
Corporate growth through internal spin-outs.
M. Hanan. Harvard Bsns R47:55-66 N '69
Determined Dutchmen of Philips lamp. J.
Ross-Skinner. il Duns R 94:52-5+ N '69
Diversify to beat the take-over; Armco steel's
strategy. il Bsns W p 168-9 O 11 '69

DOBY, Larry
  Black athlete in the golden age of sports. A.
  S. Young. il pors Ebony 24:66-8+ F '69
DOBYNS, Stephen
  Name-burning; Waking, the cheering begins;
  poems. Poetry 113:253-4 Ja '69
DOCKING in space. See Orbital rendezvous
  (space flight)
DOCKS
  See also
  Fishing docks and piers
DOCKS (plants)
  Rumex. R. D. Pearce. Horticulture 47:30 N
  '69
DOCKSTADER, Tod
  Reviews of records. Mus Q 55:136-9 Ja '69
DOCTOR, B. P. and others
  Nucleotide sequence of escherichia coli tyro-
  sine transfer ribonucleic acid. bibliog Sci-
  ence 163:693-5 F 14 '69
DOCTOR; story. See Dubus, A.
DOCTOR; story. See Ford, J. H.
DOCTORS. See Physicians
DOCTORS of philosophy. See Degrees, Aca-
  demic
DOCTORATES. See Degrees, Academic
DOCUMENTARY drama. See Drama
DOCUMENTARY films. See Moving pictures—
  Documentary films
DOCUMENTARY photography. See Photogra-
  phy, Documentary
DOCUMENTARY television programs. See Tele-
  vision broadcasting—Documentary programs
DOCUMENTATION
  See also
  American society for information science
DOCUMENTS
  See also
  Archives
  Government publications
DODD, Anne W.
  Ambassadors report. Sr Schol 94:Schol
  Teach 13 Mr 28 '69
DODD, Bella (Visono)
  Obituary
  Nat R 21:479 My 20 '69
DODD, Bill
  Piper; Apartment: Getting up and going to
  work; poems. Poetry 113:314-16 F '69
DODD, Thomas Joseph
  Excerpt from debate. June 25, 1969. Cong
  Digest 48:211+ Ag '69
         about
  Doddering. New Repub 161:12 N 29 '69
DODDS, Robert C.
  Jeshua, a basic encounter for young Israelis.
  America 121:630-2 D 27 '69
DODDS, W. J.
  Hepatic influence on splenic synthesis and
  release of coagulation activities. bibliog
  Science 166:882-3 N 14 '69
DODGE, Mary (Mapes)
  Americans not everybody knows. C. W. Fer-
  guson. por PTA Mag 63:10-12 Mr '69
DODGE, F. W. corporation
  F. W. Dodge construction outlook: 1970. il
  Arch Rec 146:69-70+ N '69
  F. W. Dodge 1969 regional construction out-
  look. R. M. Young. il Arch Rec 145:71 Ja '69
  F. W. Dodge weighs strength in 1980 con-
  struction market outlook. il Arch Rec 145:
  83-7 Mr '69
DODGE division. See Chrysler corporation—
  Dodge division
DODGE revolutionary union movement. See
  United automobile, aerospace and agricul-
  tural implement workers of America
DODGERS (baseball) See Baseball clubs
DODGSON, Charles Lutwidge. See Carroll, L.
  pseud.
DODSON, Calaway H. and others
  Biologically active compounds in orchid fra-
  grances. bibliog Science 164:1243-9 Je 13 '69
DODSON, Dan W.
  Public schools; address, July 8, 1969. bibliog f
  Vital Speeches 35:686-91 S 1 '69
DODSON, Robert
  Computer whiz kid. il por Ebony 25:101-2+
  D '69
DOENECKE, Arthur Lawrence
  Rate your date. Seventeen 28:152-3 My '69
DOERINGER, Peter B.
  Labor market report from the Boston ghet-
  to; excerpt from Ghetto labor markets
  and manpower programs. Mo Labor R 92:
  55-6 Mr '69
DOERNBACH, Marguerite E.
  Three-dimensional concepts. Sch Arts 68:24-5
  F '69

DOERY, J. C. G. and others
  Aspirin: its effect on platelet glycolysis and
  release of adenosine diphosphate. bibliog
  Science 165:65-7 Jl 4 '69
DOES a tiger wear a necktie? drama. See Peter-
  sen, D.
DOESBURG, Théo van
  Van Doesburg: Stijl and all; traveling ex-
  hibition. J. Leering. il por Art N 68:38-41+
  Mr '69
DOG breeding

        Anecdotes, facetiae, satire, etc.

  Beware of fierce breeders! guard dog breed-
  ers. J. Sanders. il Sports Illus 31:30-2 N
  10 '69
DOG hotels. See Kennels
DOG houses. See Kennels
DOG racing
  All the big money was on the red; grey-
  hounds at U.S. Challenge cup racing. D.
  Russell. il Sports Illus 31:62-3 N 3 '69
  Queen of the kennels; P. Wallis given Flag-
  ler track contract. il Newsweek 73:94-5 Je
  30 '69
DOG training. See Dogs—Training
DOG trials. See Field trials (dogs)
DOGFISH
  Glyceryl ether metabolism: regulation of
  buoyancy in dogfish squalus acanthias. D.
  C. Malins and A. Barone. bibliog il Science
  167:79-80 Ja 2 '70
DOGMATIC opinions. See Attitudes
DOGS
  Anyone who has a dog is just plain crazy. P.
  Simon. Redbook 133:90+ S '69
  Congratulations! It's a dog! excerpts from
  How to raise a dog in the city and in the
  suburbs. J. R. Kinney and A. Honeycutt.
  McCalls 96:66+ S '69
  Dogs. D. M. Duffey. See issues of Outdoor
  life
  Erythropoiesis in the dog: the periodic nature
  of the steady state. A. Morley and F. Stohl-
  man, jr. bibliog il Science 165:1025-7 S 5
  '69
  Genetic polymorphism of tetrazolium oxidase
  in dogs. E. W. Baur and R. T. Schorr. bibliog il Science 166:1524-5 D 19 '69
  Gun dogs. J. Griffen. See issues of Field &
  stream
  Indian dog. S. Burnford. Atlan 224:85-8 Ag '69
  Letters on a dog; ed. by D. Shane. Har Yrs
  9:48-9 S '69
  Living with a dog, and loving it. F. Ames.
  il Parents Mag 44:50-1+ F '69
  Mechanism and prevention of fixed high vascular resistance in autografted and allografted lungs. F. J. Veith and K. Richards.
  bibliog il Science 163:699-701 F 14 '69
  Most celebrated dog case ever tried in Johnson County, Missouri, or the world; Old
  Drum trial, 1869; C. Burden vs. L. Hornsby. G. Carson. il Natur Hist 78:6-8+ D '69
  Pulmonary gas transport time: larynx to
  alveolus. W. W. Wagner, jr. and others.
  bibliog il Science 163:1210-11 Mr 14 '69
  Skeezer: the canine child therapist. C. Dishon.
  il Todays Health 48:16-18 Ja '70
  Traube-Hering waves in the pulmonary cir-
  culation of the dog. J. P. Szidon and oth-
  ers. bibliog il Science 164:75-6 Ap 4 '69
  Ventricular arrhythmias related to antibiotic
  usage in dogs. T. J. Regan and others. bib-
  liog il Science 165:509-10 Ag 1 '69
  See also
  Dog racing
  Eskimo dogs
  Field trials (dogs)
  Hounds
  Shih tzus

        Breeding
  See Dog breeding

        Care
  Care for elderly dogs. P. O'Keefe. Am Home
  72:106-7 Ap '69
  How to keep a big dog. il Bet Hom & Gard
  47:48+ O '69
  In case of emergency. L. F. Whitney. Mc-
  Calls 97:44+ N '69
  Just how well do you take care of your dog
  or cat? il Bet Hom & Gard 47:86-7+ Mr '69
  Summertime dog care. D. M. Duffey. il Out-
  door Life 144:110+ Jl '69

        Diseases and pests
  See also
  Rabies

DOGS—*Continued*

Feeding

Feeding your dog. D. M. Duffey. il Outdoor Life 144:182-4+ O '69

Kennels

See Kennels

Purchasing

Orientation F.O.B; mail-order dog sales. S. Ferber. il Field & S 74:148-50+ Ag '69

Training

Championship grouse dog trainer, Dick Shear; interview, ed. by L. J. Bashline. R. C. Shear. il Field & S 74:122-4+ D '69

Deer proofing your hunting dog. J. Griffen. il Field & S 74:164-6 Je '69

Easy way to train your dog. il Mech Illus 65:60-3 F '69

How to make a lamb in police dog clothing. il Sci Digest 66:73-5 O '69

Never, never, never... J. Griffen. il Field & S 73:164-6+ F '69

Orientation F.O.B; mail-order dog sales. S. Ferber. il Field & S 74:148-50+ Ag '69

Pre-season training pays off. P. Curtis. il Field & S 73:184-5+ Mr '69

Send your dog to school? E. D. Craster. il Bet Hom & Gard 47:46+ N '69

Six keys to training your dog. J. N. Miller. il Read Digest 94:53+ Ap '69

Anecdotes, facetiae, satire, etc.

Slave to a shah; obedience schools for dogs. J. Bruce. il Sports Illus 30:86-92+ My 5 '69

DOGS as guides

Seeing eye dog for a dog. il Sci Digest 65:39 Mr '69

DOGS in rescue work

Incredible tracking dog. D. D. Ellis. il Outdoor Life 144:60-1+ S '69

DOHAN, F. C.

Is celiac disease a clue to the pathogenesis of schizophrenia? bibliog Ment Hy 53:525-9 O '69

DOHERTY, J. Peter

Kiel: how it was and can be. Yachting 126:52+ D '69

DOHERTY, John J.

German bishops cry heresy. Commonweal 89:634-5 F 21 '69

DOHERTY, John Stephen

Basic course in navigating by compass. Mech Illus 65:71-3+ Mr '69

Learn to sail. Mech Illus 65:27-9+ Ap '69

DOHERTY, R. S. See Gilinsky, A. S. jt. auth.

DOIG, Stewart

Schools that turn people off. Todays Ed 58:28-30 My '69; Same abr. Ed Digest 35:41-3 S '69

DOIRON, Peter M.

What's your choice? ALA Bul 63:1505 D '69

DOLAN, Anthony R.

On campus and off (cont) Nat R 21:127+, 492+, 648 F 11, My 20, Jl 1 '69

Push button, end war. Nat R 21:1116+ N 4 '69

DOLAN, Dan

Life of Ivan Illich. New Repub 160:18-19 Mr 1 '69

DOLBEARE, Kenneth M. and Davis, J. W. jr

Little groups of neighbors, American draft boards; excerpts from Little groups of neighbors: the selective service system. pors Trans-Action 6:34-7+ Mr '69

DOLESERPETON. See Amphibia, Fossil

DOLGER, Jonathan

Expense account diet; excerpt. Duns R 94:66-8+ N '69

about

Authors & editors. R. H. Smith. por Pub W 196:27-8 O 13 '69

DOLL clothes

Clothing for dolls of the 1890's. C. H. Fawcett. il Hobbies 74:44+ D '69

Easter bonnet for your antique doll. C. H. Fawcett. il Hobbies 74:39+ Ap '69

On dressing the bisque-headed, ball-jointed doll; interview, ed. by C. H. Fawcett. P. Mann. il Hobbies 74:42+ Ag '69

DOLL houses

Dutch cabinet dolls' house, 17th century. S. A. Parvin. il Hobbies 74:118 Ag '69

Dutch doll house. S. A. Parvin. il Hobbies 74:148+ S '69

Rooms stack up to make a dolls' habitat. il Sunset 143:98-9 N '69

See also

Rooms, Miniature

DOLLAR gap. See Balance of payments

DOLLARHIDE, Douglas F.

New test tube for black cities? il por U S News 66:10 Je 16 '69

DOLLIVER, Barbara

We're the lucky ones! Good H 169:90-1+ D '69

DOLLS

Diahann Carroll presents the Julia dolls. il Ebony 24:148-50+ O '69

Dollology. C. H. Fawcett. See issues of Hobbies

Doll's paintings made for Uncle Sam in the 1930's. C. H. Fawcett. il Hobbies 74:38+ My '69

Graveyard doll; child's grave, Warren, N.J. C. H. Fawcett. il Hobbies 74:38+ Mr '69

Magical world of trolls. G. Kent. il Read Digest 95:215-16+ N '69

Menace of the Barbie dolls. D. Bess il Ramp Mag 7:25-8 Ja 25 '69

New fashion doll. C. H. Fawcett. il Hobbies 74:46-7 O '69

On studying doll bodies. C. H Fawcett. il Hobbies 74:42-3+ Je '69

Some Indian arts and crafts, papa and mama dolls. C. Miles. il Hobbies 74:142-4 O '69

They make their own kachinas, using poster paints and mailing tubes. il Sunset 142:157 My '69

Repairing

Dump babies; parts found in a nineteenth century dump. E. Sallee. il Hobbies 74:46 N '69

DOLLS in literature

Dolls in books. M. L. Morris. bibliog il Hobbies 74:42+ Jl '69

DOLMETSCH, Joan M.

Maps and pictures. Antiques 95:138-44 Ja '69

DOLOMITE (mineral)

Microphotometric determination of preferred orientation in undeformed dolomites. E. Sass. bibliog il Science 165:802-3 Ag 22 '69

DOLPHINS (mammals)

Blind river dolphin: first side-swimming cetacean. E. S. Herald and others. bibliog il Science 166:1408-10 D 12 '69

Dolphin is born. il Sea Front 15:277 S '69

Respiration and deep diving in the bottlenose porpoise. S. H. Ridgway and others. bibliog il Science 166:1651-4 D 26 '69

Ugly dolphin: bouto, the Amazon dolphin. M. C. Caldwell and D. K. Caldwell. il Sea Front 15:308-14, 349-55 S-N '69

DOMES

Air house for big winter projects. E. F. Muehlmatt. il Pop Sci 194:134-5+ Ja '69

Largest cover supported by air pressure; water reservoir in Seal Beach, Calif. il Am City 84:53 Ag '69

Well-rounded way to live; geodesic domes, Nags Head, N.C. P. Knight. il Sports Illus 31:42-3 Ag 11 '69

See also

Cupolas

DOMESTIC animals

See also

Dogs
Domestication
Livestock
Pets

DOMESTIC appliances. See Electric apparatus and appliances, Domestic; Household appliances

DOMESTIC architecture. See Architecture, Domestic

DOMESTIC employees. See Household employees

DOMESTIC finance

Family money management. Suc Farm 66:57-9 D '68; 67:72-3 Ja; 77+ Ap '69

Family money management; ed. by P. Lindberg. See issues of Better homes and gardens

Five ages of man, familywise. il Changing T 23:29-30 F '69

Hidden meanings of money in marriage; excerpt from The first ten years of marriage: a guide to successful family living. N. M. Lobsenz and C. W. Blackburn. Read Digest 94:141-4 Mr '69

How much does a baby cost? K. D. Fury. il Redbook 133:46+ Jl '69

How to get out of debt. L. David. il Mech Illus 65:49-51+ F '69

Losers. D. Fletcher. il Redbook 133:12+ Jl '69

Make family finance a family affair. il Changing T 23:15-16 Jl '69

Making money work; questions and answers. E. Merillat. Har Yrs 9:41-2 Je '69

DOMESTIC finance—*Continued*
Money management. M. Feeley. See issues of American home
Spending your money. S. Porter. See issues of Ladies' home journal
To combat inflation, try making do! Consumer Bul 52:15-16 N '69
You can't wait for probate. I. Ladimer. Har Yrs 9:38-42 My '69
See also
Budget, Household
Budget, Personal
Cost of living
Saving and savings

DOMESTIC peace corps. See Volunteers in service to America

DOMESTIC relations
Future of family law. H. H. Foster, jr. bibliog f Ann Am Acad 383:129-44 My '69
Progress in family law; symposium, ed. by J. S. Bradway. bibliog f Ann Am Acad 383:1-158 My '69
See also
Family
Family life
Marriage
Marriage counseling
Quarrels

DOMESTIC relations courts
Family court, evolving concepts. J. T. Zukerman. bibliog f Ann Am Acad 383:119-28 My '69

DOMESTIC service. See Household employees

DOMESTICATION
Fauna of Catal Hüyük: evidence for early cattle domestication in Anatolia. D. Perkins, jr. bibliog il Science 164:177-9 Ap 11 '69

DOMICILE
Breakthrough on welfare; residency requirements. il Newsweek 73:33-4 My 5 '69
Welfare and the Court; residence requirements. E. Van Den Haag. Nat R 21:805 Ag 12 '69

DOMINGO, Placido
Two notable City alumni. P. L. Miller. il por Am Rec G 35:458-9 F '69

DOMINICAN art. See Art, Dominican

DOMINICAN REPUBLIC
See also
Art, Dominican
Catholic church in the Dominican Republic
Land tenure—Dominican Republic

Description and travel
Seashells from East and West. J. B. Martin. Life 66:14A My 2 '69

Economic conditions
Dominican farm workers; churchmen on economic matters. America 120:293 Mr 15 '69
Good house; address, January 27, 1969. J. Balaguer. Vital Speeches 35:327-9 Mr 15 '69
Yes, we have no bananas. R. Shereff. Commonweal 89:497-9 Ja 17 '69; Discussion. 90:35+ Mr 28 '69

Politics and government
Dominican Republic revisited. E. von Kuehnelt-Leddihn. Nat R 21:324 Ap 8 '69
Inflaming the inflammable. il Time 93:39 Mr 7 '69
Seashells from East and West. J. B. Martin. Life 66:14A My 2 '69
See also
Political parties—Dominican Republic

Religious institutions and affairs
See also
Catholic church in the Dominican Republic

DOMINICK, David D.
Water-pollution control: trouble at headquarters. L. J. Carter. por Science 165:572-3+ Ag 8 '69

DOMINIS, John
Antelope of East Africa; photographs. Life 67:74-85 D 5 '69
Dusty and the Duke; photographs. Life 67:36-45 Jl 11 '69
Gallery; photographs. Life 67:8-9 Ag 22 '69

DOMINO theory in international relations. See International relations

DOMINOES (game)
Handful of combinatorial problems based on dominoes. M. Gardner. il Sci Am 221:122-7 D '69

DOMNICK, Howard
What this generation needs is a rousing chorus of the woodshed blues. Todays Ed 58:38-9 Ap '69

DON Giovanni; opera. See Mozart, J. C. W. A.

DON Quixote (literary character) See Characters in literature

DONAHOE, J. Michael
What harm can a little ice do? Flying 84:76-7 F '69

DONAHUE, Mildred. See Donahue, R. jt. auth.

DONAHUE, Ralph, and Donahue, Mildred
Temperamental visitor to our gardens. il Horticulture 47:59 Ja '69

DONAHUE, Roger P. See Kennedy, J. F. jt. auth.

DONAHUE, Thomas R.
Future of bargaining in the federal government. Mo Labor R 92:67-9 Jl '69

DONAHUE, Wilma Thompson
Doctor Donahue honored at Michigan conference. Aging 178:10 Ag '69

DONALDSON, Gordon
Strategy for financial emergencies. Harvard Bsns R 47:67-79 N '69

DONALDSON, William
Long arm law. Writers Digest 49:92-3 N '69

DONALDSON, Lufkin and Jenrette, incorporated
Broker forces an issue. C. Morgello. il Newsweek 73:77 Je 2 '69
Buying a share of the broker. Time 93:78+ My 30 '69
Changing Wall Street's rules; bid by DLJ to go public; with editorial comment. il Bsns W p70-4, 108 My 31 '69
They're tearing up Wall Street. C. J. Loomis. il Fortune 80:88-91+ Ag 1 '69

DONATHAN, Judith
(ed) Books to come. Library J 95:86-90 Ja 1 '70
—and Fletcher, Janet
(eds) Books to come. Library J 94:2965-76, 3481-576, 4031-56 S 1, O 1, N 1 '69

DONCHESS, Barbara
New interest in astrology. Writers Digest 49:36-7+ Ag '69

DONELSON, Kenneth L.
Challenging the censor: some responsibilities of the English department: address, November, 1968. bibliog Engl J 58:869-76 S '69
Playing the game in English teaching. Clear House 43:479-82 Ap '69

DONER, H. E. and Mortland, M. M.
Benzene complexes with copper(II) montmorillonite. bibliog Science 166:1406-7 D 12 '69

DONIZETTI, Gaetano
Back on Seraphim, the Callas Lucia. P. L. Miller. Am Rec G 35:560 Mr '69
Glimpses of a great age. W. Weaver. il Hi Fi 19:MA28-9 Ag '69
Lucia di Lammermoor. Criticism
Nation 209:550 N 17 '69
New Yorker 45:169-71 O 18 '69
Opera N il por 33:17-20 F 1 '69
Sat R 52:54 O 25 '69
Time il 94:66 O 17 '69
Records:
Lucia di Lammermoor. Opera N 33:33 F 22 '69
Roberto Devereux. Opera N 34:34 Ja 17 '70
Serious Donizetti. R. D. Daniels. Opera N 33:24-5 F 1 '69

DONLEAVY, James Patrick
Joey and Sebastian grown up. S. O'Connell. Nation 208:85-6 Ja 20 '69
Old and the new. H. Kaye. New Repub 160:22-5 Mr 1 '69

DONNAY, Gabrielle, and Pawson, D. L.
X-ray diffraction studies of echinoderm plates. bibliog Science 166:1147-50 N 28 '69

DONNELLY, Desmond Louis
London. Q. Crewe. Vogue 153:72+ Je '69

DONNELLY, Ignatius
Ignatius Donnelly & the politics of discontent. R. G. Kennedy. bibliog il por Am West 6:10-14+ Mr '69

DONNELLY, James F.
Who knows? Who cares? America 120:250-2 Mr 1 '69

DONNER, Frank J.
Colleges play ball. Nation 209:111-15 Ag 11 '69
Injunction on campus. Nation 208:718-20 Je 9 '69
Labor movement: between two worlds. Nation 209:222-4+ S 8 '69
Thank you, Mr Director. Nation 209:448-50 O 27 '69
Trouble with muckraking. Nation 208:513-15 Ap 21 '69

DONOHUE, James C.
Are the Catholic schools dying? interview, ed. by J. Star. por Look 33:105-6+ O 21 '69

DONOHUE, Jerry
Fourier analysis and the structure of DNA. bibliog Science 165:1091-6 S 12 '69
Structure of polywater. bibliog Science 166:1000-2 N 21 '69

DONOIAN, Harry A.
New approach to setting the pay of federal blue-collar workers. bibliog Mo Labor R 92:30-4 Ap '69

DONORS, Eye. See Eye donors

DONORS, Heart. See Heart donors

DONORS, Kidney. See Kidney donors

DONOVAN, Francis
Sketches of Madrid. America 120:562 My 10 '69

DONOVAN, Harold J.
Apprenticeship, vestal style. Ed Digest 35:52-4 D '69

DONOVAN, Hedley
United States and world affairs; address, February 18, 1969. por Wilson Lib Bul 43: 734-9 Ap '69
Who is America? What are we all about? excerpt from address. Fortune 79:83-4+ Ap '69
about
Time; after Luce. R. Pollak. Harper 239:42-52 Jl '69

DONOVAN, James A. See Shoup, D. M. jt. auth.

DONOVAN, James B.
Conscription; with a choice. America 120:726-7 Je 28 '69

DONOVAN, John
Foreign exchange. Sat R 52:61-2 N 8 '69
—See Silberberg, S. C. jt. auth.

DONOVAN, John Dennis
Priests and priesthoods. Commonweal 91:141-4 O 31 '69

DONOVAN'S boots; story. See Walker, T.

DONS. See College professors and instructors

DOODLES (sketches) See Psychoanalysis

DOOHAN, Joseph E.
Physical education. Clear House 44:232-5 D '69

DOOLEY, Thomas Anthony
Splendid Americans; excerpts from The legacy of Tom Dooley. L. Elliott. il por Read Digest 95:215-24+ S '69

DOOR frames. See Doors

DOOR knobs. See Doorknobs

DOOR locks. See Locks and keys

DOOR opened; story. See Hoffman, C.

DOOR PENINSULA, Wis.
Wisconsin's Door Peninsula. W. S. Ellis. il Nat Geog 135:346-71 Mr '69

DOORKNOBS
Nice thing to hold on to. il House B 111:56 S '69

DOORMEN, Hotel. See Hotels, taverns, etc.— Employees

DOORS
Carved panels decorate a door. il Sunset 143: 84+ Jl '69
Entrance or exit? il Design 70:19-22 mid-Wint '69
Family tile-makers make a door. il Sunset 143:120 N '69
Save by making your own colonial door frame. J. Olivari. il Pop Mech 132:163 S '69
See also
Automobiles—Doors
Garage doors

DOORWAY planting. See Landscape gardening

DOORWAYS
Generous new entry deck and trellis. il Sunset 142:103 F '69
New entry walk, new entry doors. il Sunset 142:154 My '69

DOPA
Correcting brain chemistry. Time 94:77-8 N 28 '69
m-Hydroxyphenylacetic acid formation from L-dopa in man: suppression by neomycin. M. Sandler and others. bibliog il Science 166:1417-18 D 12 '69
Pill that lets shaking palsy patients eat jell-o. J. E. Randal. il Todays Health 48: 34-7+ Ja '70
Progress with L-dopa. il Newsweek 74:116 O 6 '69

DOPAMINE
Adrenal tyrosine hydroxylase: compensatory increase in activity after chemical sympathectomy. R. A. Mueller and others. bibliog il Science 163:468-9 Ja 31 '69
Antiparkinsonian drugs: inhibition of dopamine uptake in the corpus striatum as a possible mechanism of action. J. T. Coyle and S. H. Snyder. bibliog il Science 166: 899-901 N 14 '69

Lesions of central norepinephrine terminals with 6-OH-dopamine: biochemistry and fine structure. F. E. Bloom and others. bibliog il Science 166:1284-6 D 5 '69
Luteinizing hormone-releasing activity in hypophysial stalk blood and elevation by dopamine. I. A. Kamberi and others. bibliog il Science 166:388-90 O 17 '69

DOPE smuggling. See Smuggling

DOPING in sports
Breakfast of champions; hormone drugs and athletes. il Newsweek 74:37 D 29 '69
Drugs in sport. B. Gilbert. il Sports Illus 30: 64-72 Je 23; 30-2+ Je 30; 30-5 Jl 7 '69; Same abr. with title Drugs and the athlete. Read Digest 95:95-9 S '69
Whitewash in Kentucky; 1968 Kentucky Derby. W. F. Reed, jr. il Sports Illus 30: 12-14 F 17 '69

DORADO fishing
In search of el dorado. A. J. McClane. il Field & S 73:96-8+ F; 94-6+ Mr '69

DORAN, Dermot
Biafran tragedy. J. Deedy. por Commonweal 90:378 Je 20 '69

DORCHESTER, Mass.
Bulls & bears in Boston; North Dorchester McCormack middle school. A. J. Owens. il Sr Schol 94:Schol Teach 14 Ap 18 '69

DORCY, Michael M.
(ed) See Rahner, K. Conservation with Karl Rahner

DORÉ, Gustave
Gustave Doré, prolific illustrator. H. C. Pitz. il por Am Artist 33:48-53+ D '69

DOREMUS, R. H. and Turkalo, A. M.
Phase separation in pyrex glass. bibliog Science 164:418-19 Ap 25 '69

DORIOT, Georges F.
Very special affair. por Forbes 104:42 O 15 '69

DORMAN, Sonya
L'oeil verite; poem. Sat R 52:56 F 8 '69

DORMITORIES
Boys and girls together; coed dorms for graduate students. il Time 93:44 My 30 '69
Campus housing recommendations; Stanford university. Sch & Soc 97:201-3 Ap '69
Co-ed living. B. Rollin. il Look 33:22-4+ S 23 '69
College live-in. S. Van Der Ryn. il Trans-Action 6:63-9 S '69
Dorm city; University of Guelph, Canada. K. B. Smith. il Arch Forum 129:76-85 D '68
Dormitories for Kirkland college, Clinton, N.Y. il Arch Rec 145:140-1 Je '69
Liberalized curfews. Sch & Soc 97:142+ Mr '69
New trend to open dorms; student reports. il Seventeen 28:141 Ja '69
Residences; University of East Englia. il Arch Rec 146:108-10 Jl '69
Student living in a sunken garden; Brown university graduate center. il Arch Forum 131:24-31 D '69
See also
College students—Housing
Womens residences

DORN, Edward
I like to (B)eat people up. A. Hoyem. Poetry 113:426-7 Mr '69

DORNER, Alexander
Art. L. Alloway. Nation 208:774 Je 16 '69

DOROSKA, Robert
Garbage belongs to the land. pors Org Gard & Farm 16:43-5 Ap '69

DORSEY, Edna J.
Stream of consciousness drawing. Design 70:25-7 mid-Wint '69

DORSEY, William H. jr
Arab commandos. New Repub 161:19-21 N 22 '69

DORST, Jean
Biologist looks at the animal world (beasts and men) UNESCO Courier 22:16-21 Ja '69
Galapagos Islands: living laboratory of evolution; reprint. UNESCO Courier 22:18-19 Ag '69

DORVAL International airport. See Montreal —Airports

DOSAGE. See Drugs—Dosage

DOSIMETERS. See Radiometers

DOS PASSOS, John
John Dos Passos; inventor in isolation. A. Kazin. il Sat R 52:16-19+ Mr 15 '69

DOSTOEVSKII, Fedor Mikhailovich
Dostoevsky, the struggle to create. I. Howe. Harper 239:126-8+ O '69

DOTSON, Heyward
Bradley effect. il por Newsweek 75:64 Ja 19 '70

DOZIER, Thomas
Hold out a hand to your Protestant neighbor. Life 66:58B My 2 '69

DRAAYER, Donald R. and Teague, P. A.
Student lounge or study hall: how are grades affected? Clear House 44:141-4 N '69

DRABEK, Thomas E. and Haas, J. E.
How police confront disaster. Trans-Action 6:33-8 My '69

DRAFT, Military. See Military service, Compulsory

DRAFT lottery. See Military service, Compulsory

DRAFT resisters. See Military service, Compulsory—Draft resisters

DRAFTING boards, tables, etc. See Drawing boards, tables, etc.

DRAG racing. See Automobile racing

DRAGONS
Dragons: past and present. D. Cohen. il Sci Digest 66:36-43 D '69

DRAHOS, Mary
Reunion of sorts. Criticism
America 121:341-2 O 18 '69

DRAHOS, Nick
Cleanup folk festival. Cons 24:31 O '69
International decoy Carvers' exhibit. Cons 24:10-11 D '69
Wilderness biological station. Cons 23:18-20 F '69

DRAINAGE
Dry stream, especially useful when it's wet. il Sunset 143:258 O '69
Preplanned drainage pays big dividends. A. R. Pagan. il Am City 84:121 Je '69
See also
Sewerage
Trenching machinery

DRAINAGE, House
How to install gutters and downspouts. R. Day. il Pop Mech 132:164-9 S '69
Rainspout devices, to carry water from rain and melting snow away from the house. il Consumer Bul 52:39-40 Ap '69

DRAKE, Albert
Father to son; story. Redbook 133:77 Ag '69

DRAKE, Francis Vivian
New alarm: the submarine gap. Read Digest 95:54-8 Ag '69
—and Drake, Katharine
Arizona, nature's gaudiest paintpot. Read Digest 94:146-53 Mr '69

DRAKE, James A. jr
Dramatize your scenics; excerpts from Philadelphia, the intimate city, ed. by J. Dreyfuss. Mod Phot 33:62-5 S '69

DRAKE, Katharine. See Drake, F. V. jt. auth.

DRAMA
Psychical reality and the theater of fact; documentary drama. H. S. Rollman-Branch. bibliog Am Imago 26:56-70 Spr '69
Theatre of interpretations; the documentary play. E. Bentley. Nation 209:148-9+ Ag 25 '6
See also
Comedy
Dramatists
Historical drama
Monologues
Negro drama
Psychodrama
Publishers and publishing—Drama
Television broadcasting—Drama

Study and teaching
Helping actors to act human; History and techniques of stage movement course, University of Minnesota. R. Moulton. il Dance Mag 43:76-7 My '69
Medium is the absurd; address, November 1968. L. Mussoff. Engl J 58:566-70+ Ap '69
Teaching machine for drama; Birmingham-Southern college, Ala. il Arch Forum 130:78-83 Ap '69
Theater of the absurd: a child studies himself; address, November 1968. P. J. Sheehan. Engl J 58:561-5 Ap '69
See also
Yale university—Drama school

DRAMA, Documentary. See Drama

DRAMA, Influence of. See Literature, Influence of

DRAMA critics. See Critics

DRAMA critics circle. See New York drama critics circle

DRAMA festivals
Expansiveness vs. expensiveness; summer repertory schedule, 1969. H. Hewes. Sat R 52:29 Je 21 '69

Theater; American college theatre festival, Washington, D.C. Sat R 52:27 My 24 '69
See also
International festival of music and drama, Edinburgh
New York Shakespeare festival

Canada
Fair beginning; Victoria fair, British Columbia. H. Hewes. Sat R 52:26 S 20 '69

Ireland
Theatre in Dublin. C. Hughes. Nation 209:579-81 N 24 '69

DRAMA in education. See Dramatization in education

DRAMAS
Dick and Jane. J. Feiffer. il Ramp Mag 8:23-6 Ag '69
Operation sidewinder. S. Shepard. il Esquire 71:152-3+ My '69
See also
Detective and mystery plays
Franklin, B.—Drama
Oppenheimer, J. R.—Drama
Passion plays
also subhead Drama *under various subjects, e.g.* Easter—Drama

Criticisms, plots, etc.
Goings on about town. See issues of New Yorker
Life theater review. S. Kanfer. Life 66:10 Je 13 '69
Off Broadway. E. Oliver. See issues of New Yorker
Stage. G. Weales See issues of Commonweal
Theater (cont) Nat R 21:186-7, 500-1, 918, 1022-3, 1334-5 F 25, My 20, S 9, O 7, D 30 '69
Theatre. H. Clurman. See issues of Nation
Theatre. J. Fairfield. Vogue 154:60 Ag 1 '69
Theatre. B. Gill. See issues of New Yorker
Theatre. R. Gilman. New Repub 160:32-4 Ja 25; 29-30 F 22; 29-31 Ap 12 69
Theater. H. Hewes. See issues of Saturday review
Theater. S. Kauffmann. New Repub 161:24+ O 11; 22+ N 1; 22+ N 22 '69; 162:25+ Ja 3 '7
Theatre. T. Lewis. See issues of America
Time listings. See issues of Time
See also
London—Theatre

Single works
See name of author for full entry
Acropolis. J. Grotowski
Adaptation. E. May
Ah, wilderness! E. G. O'Neill
Americans. E. De Grazia
Apocalypsis cum figuris. J. Grotowski
Ardèle. J. Anouilh
Arf. D. Greenburg
Assassin. J. Boyd
Bacchae. Euripides
Back to Methuselah. G. B. Shaw
Barracks. H. Leonard
Billy Budd. A. Hall
Boy on the straight-back chair. R. Tavel
Butterflies are free. L. Gershe
Cage. R. Cluchey
Camino real. T. Williams
Ceremonies in dark old men. L. Elder, 3d
Che! L. Raphael
Cher Antoine. J. Anouilh
Cities in Bezique. A. Kennedy
Close the coalhouse door. A. Plater
Cock-a-doodle dandy. S. O'Casey
Constant prince. J. Grotowski
Contribution. T. Shine
Cop-out. J. Guare
Council of love. O. Panizza
De Sade illustrated. J. Bush
Dionysus in 69. R. Schechner
Does a tiger wear a necktie? D. Petersen
Early morning. E. Bond
Edward II. C. Marlowe
Electra. Sophocles
End of all things natural. G. Zoffer
Evening for Merlin Finch. C. Dizenzo
Fire! J. Roc
Five on the black hand side. C. L. Russell
Flea in her ear. G. Feydeau
Forty carats. R. Barillet and J. P. Grédy
Front page. B. Hecht and C. MacArthur
Geese. G. Weill
Ghost dancer. F. Gaines
Gingham dog. L. Wilson
Gloria and Esperanza. J. Bovasso.
Glory! Hallelujah! A. M. Barlow
Great airplane snatch. D. Greenburg

DRAMAS—Criticisms, plots, etc.—Single works
—*Continued*
Great career. C. Dizenzo
Great white hope. H. Sackler
Hadrian VII. P. Luke
Harry, noon and night. R. Ribman
Hedda Gabler. H. Ibsen
Hello and goodbye. A. Fugard
Home away from. G. A. Smith
Homecoming. H. Pinter
Honest-to-God schnozzola. I. Horovitz
House of Atreus. J. Lewin
In the bar of a Tokyo hotel. T. Williams
In the matter of J. Robert Oppenheimer. H. Kipphardt
In the wine time. E. Bullins
Increased difficulty of concentration. V. Havel
Indians. A. Kopit
Inner journey. J. Hanley
Invitation to a beheading. R. McGrath
Le jardin des delices. F. Arrabal
Jimmy Shine. M. Schisgal
King Herod explains. C. C. O'Brien
Landscape. H. Pinter
Last of the red hot lovers. N. Simon
Little boxes. J. Bowen
Little murders. J. Feiffer
Man in the glass booth. R. Shaw
Man with the flower in his mouth. L. Pirandello
Mercy street. A. Sexton
Metamorphoses. P. Sills
Millionairess. G. B. Shaw
Miser. J. B. P. Molière
Mr Tambo, Mr Bones. A. Panas
Moon dreamers. J. Bovasso
My daughter, your son. P. Ephron and H. Ephron
Narrow road to the Deep North. E. Bond
Next. T. McNally
No place to be somebody. C. Gordone
Les nonnes. E. Manet
Ofay watcher. F. Cucci
Oresteia. See House of Atreus, above
Our town. T. N. Wilder
Papp. K. Cameron
Passing through exotic places. R. Ribman
Patriot for me. J. Osborne
Peer Gynt. H. Ibsen
Penny wars. E. Baker
Philosophy in the bedroom. See De Sade illustrated, above
Play it again, Sam. W. Allen
Priest in the cellar. J. Conlan
Private lives. N. Coward
Prometheus bound. R. Lowell
Rabelais. J. L. Barrault
Reckoning. D. T. Ward
Resistible rise of Arturo Ui. B. Brecht
Reunion of sorts. M. Drahos
Rosencrantz and Guildenstern are dead. T. Stoppard
Ruling class. P. Barnes
Scent of flowers. J. Saunders
Serpent. J.-C. Van Itallie
Serpent. J. Chaikin
Seven days of mourning. S. Simckes
Silence. H. Pinter
Silhouettes. T. Harris
Slave ship. L. Jones
Someone's comin' hungry. M. Imbrie and N. Selden
Spiro who? W. Meyers
Spitting image. C. Spencer
Stop, you're killing me. J. L. Herlihy
String. A. Childress
Swift. E. McCabe
Tango. S. Mrozek
Three men on a horse. J. C. Holm and G. Abbott
Three sisters. A. P. Chekhov
Time of your life. W. Saroyan
Tiny Alice. E. Albee
To be young, gifted and black. R. Nemiroff
La turista. S. Shepard
Uncle Vanya. A. P. Chekhov
Waltz invention. V. Nabokov
Watering place. L. Kessler
Whistle in the dark. T. Murphy
Who's happy now? O. Hailey
Wozzeck. A. Berg
Wozzeck. G. Büchner
Year Boston won the pennant. J. F. Noonan

One-act plays
Texts
I want cocoanuts. D. Ross. il Mlle 70:164-5+ N '69
Poof! G. Schoenewolf. Esquire 72:209 D '69
DRAMATIC censorship
Nudity, obscenity and all that. C. Hughes. Chr Cent 86:1349-50 O 22 '69
DRAMATIC criticism
See also
Moving picture criticism
DRAMATIC critics. See Critics

DRAMATIC illusion
Max Waldman's art of anguish; photographs; with account by John Neary. Life 67:60-66B D 12 '69
DRAMATIC production. See Theatrical production and direction
DRAMATIC production in education. See Drama—Study and teaching
DRAMATICS in school. See College and school drama
DRAMATISTS
Where are the playwrights? C. Hughes. Nation 208:90-3 Ja 20 '69
Whose play is it? W. Kerr. il N Y Times Mag p66-7+ O 12 '69
DRAMATISTS, American
See also
Williams, T.
DRAMATISTS, Greek
See also
Euripides
DRAMATISTS, Irish
See also
Shaw, G. B.
DRAMATIZATION in education
Moon's place in the classroom. V. H. Ormsby. il Todays Ed 58:42-3 D '69
Revolution by Brother Alexis; living theater at Antonian high school, San Antonio. W. A. McWhirter. il Life 66:67-8+ Ja 31 '69
Role playing. H. Lamb. Todays Ed 58:67-8 Ja '69
DRAPEAU, Jean
Montreal's new test for Drapeau. il por Bsns W p60-2 O 11 '69
DRAPER, Arthur G.
Teach the process of writing. Engl J 58:245-8 F '69
DRAPER, Charles Stark
Go back! Go back! il por Newsweek 74:79-80 N 17 '69
Who made it possible; men behind the moon program. il por Time 94:29 Jl 18 '69
DRAPER, Theodore
Fantasy of black nationalism. bibliog f Commentary 48:27-54 S; 20+ D '69
Ghost of social-fascism. bibliog Commentary 47:29-42 F; 8+ My '69
DRAPERIES. See Curtains and draperies
DRAVIDIAN languages
Harappan may be Dravidian. Sci Am 221:62 N '69
DRAWER cabinets. See Cabinets (furniture)
DRAWER pulls
Nice thing to hold on to. il House B 111:56 S '69
DRAWING
Drawing in a candid way. S. Weissman. il Am Artist 33:28-31 Ag '69
Drawings of Malcolm Cameron. M. Cameron. il Am Artist 33:50-5+ Ja '69
Guillermo Acevedo: draughtsman. F. Whitaker. il Am Artist 33:26-31+ S '69
Outdoor sketching in miniature. R. Angeloch. il Am Artist 33:48-9 Je '69
Sketching in Israel. L. Krausz. il Am Artist 33:54-8+ Ap '69
Strange things with string. il Design 70:24 mid-Wint '69
Stream of consciousness drawing. E. J. Dorsey. il Design 70:25-7 mid-Wint '69
Vignette: a contemporary art format. E. A. Whitney. il Am Artist 33:40-4+ Je '69
See also
Architectural drawing
Black and white (art)
Crayon drawing
Drawings
Illustration of books and periodicals
Pastel drawing
Pen drawing
Perspective
Portrait drawing
Scratchboard drawing

Study and teaching
Boxed in creativity; producing figures with drawing mediums. E. M. Jacomo. il Sch Arts 68:32-4 Mr '69
Drawing for environmental awareness; sketching circular auditorium using contour drawing technique. A. P. Taylor. il Sch Arts 68:12-13 Mr '69
Learn your craft. N. Kent. Am Artist 33:5 Ag '69
Marco DeMarco's teaching. W. C. Libby. il Am Artist 33:56-7+ Je '69
Sharpening perception; pencil drawings of a paper matchbook. A. F. Geisert. il Sch Arts 69:10-11 N '69
DRAWING, Childrens. See Childrens art

DRAWING and photography. See Art and photography

DRAWING boards, tables, etc.
Drawing board that turns you into an artist; Klok perspective board. E. F. Lindsley. il Pop Sci 195:68 O '69

DRAWING instruments
Machine that adds a dimension to drawings. Pop Sci 195:169 D '69
T square. il Consumer Bul 52:40 Ap '69

DRAWINGS
American travels of a French botanist. P. Rouse, jr. il Antiques 96:763-7 N '69
Guillermo Acevedo: draughtsman. F. Whitaker. il Am Artist 33:26-31+ S '69
Inspired drawings of Lajos Szalay. N. Kent. il Am Artist 33:66-71+ D '69
[Portfolio of drawings of Ben Shahn] Ramp Mag 7:17-20 My '69
Rediscovery; an Indian sketchbook: Zo-tom's history of Indian prison life. il Art in Am 57:82-7 S '69
See also
Drawing

Exhibitions
Becoming is meaning; work of A. Gorky at Knoedler. L. Finkelstein. il Art N 68:44-7+ D '69
Man of infinite possibilities; a portion of the British royal collection of Leonardo da Vinci's work on view at Queen's gallery in Buckingham palace Time 93:66-9 Je 20 '69
Rembrandt, the unrealistic realist. K. Kuh. il Sat R 53:46-8 Ja 10 '70

DREAM, dreamed between midnight and 1 a. m, July 8, 1969; story. See Sissman, L. E.

DREAMING sleep. See Sleep

DREAMS
Dialogue with mothers: where do nightmares come from? B. Bettelheim. Ladies Home J 86:38 F '69
Sweet reprogramming. Sci Digest 66:36 N '69
True nightmare: the most terrifying psychic experience known to man. E. Diamond. il N Y Times Mag p56-7+ D 7 '69
See also
Sleep

DREAMS of a young girl; story. See McCartin, J. T.

DREDGE boats. See Fishing boats

DREESMANN, Cécile
Ten basic embroidery stitches to work into a modern sampler; excerpts from Embroidery. House & Gard 136:154-5 S '69

DREIFUS, Claudia
Which memo? The odor of fraud. Nation 208:176 F 10 '69

DREISER, Theodore
Two Dreisers, by E. Moers. Review New Repub 161:25-6+ Jl 19 '69. C. T. Samuels

DRENNEN, D. A.
[Book review] America 120:368 Mr 29 '69

DRESDEN
Air raids
Requiem to Billy Pilgrim's progress. W. Sheed. Life 66:9 Mr 21 '69

DRESNER, Simon
Polywater, the water that isn't. Pop Sci 195: 68-71+ D '69

DRESS. See Clothing and dress

DRESS accessories
See also
Belts

DRESS designers. See Costume designers

DRESS fabrics. See Textile fabrics

DRESSER, Louisa
Portraits owned by the American antiquarian society. Antiques 96:717-27 N '69

DRESSING of game. See Game. Dressing of

DRESSING of poultry. See Poultry, Dressing of

DRESSMAKER and the Queen; drama. See Feather, J.

DRESSMAKING
Big happening in home sewing. D. Wharton. Read Digest 95:25-8 Jl '69

DREW, Charles
Teaching black history via films. il por Sch & Soc 97:416-17 N '69

DREW, Elizabeth Brenner
Cigarette companies would rather fight than switch. N Y Times Mag p36-7+ My 4 '69
Reports: Washington (cont) Atlan 223:4+ Ja; 4+ Mr; 4+ Ap; 4+ My; 224:6+ Jl; 4+ N; 4+ D '69

DREWS, Rudolph J.
Day after the wedding night. il por Forbes 103:203-4 My 15 '69

DREYFUSS, Jane
Gallery snooping. Mod Phot 33:60+ F; 32+ Mr '69
(ed) See Drake, J. A. jr. Dramatize your scenics
—See Tausk, P. M. jt. auth.

DRICKAMER, H. G. and others
Oxidation state of iron at high pressure. bibliog Science 163:885-90 F 28 '69

DRIED flowers. See Flowers, Dried

DRIESELL, Charles
Nobody waits on this Lefty. M. Cope. il pors Sports Illus 30:28-30+ Mr 10 '69

DRIESSEN, Gerald
Fallacy of the untrained driver. Ed Digest 35:43-5 O '69

DRIFTING of continents. See Continental drift

DRIGGS, Louise
From our kitchen. See issues of Harvest years

DRILLING and boring (earth and rocks)
Deep earth sampling. P. H. Abelson; reply. R. Gerard. Science 163:232 Ja 17 '69
How you can dig a well for air conditioning. E. F. Luscinskas. il Pop Sci 195:130 Jl '69
See also
Underwater drilling

DRILLING and boring (woodwork)
Drilling big holes. R. J. De Cristoforo. il Mech Illus 65:74-6+ Jl '69

DRILLING and boring machinery
Guide to spade drills. il Mech Illus 65:92-3+ F '69
Here's a dovetailing device that's really different. J. Burroughs. il Pop Mech 132:170-2 Ag '69
How to mill on a drill press. K. B. Littlefield. il Pop Mech 131:180-4 Ja '69
How to sharpen twist drills like a pro. F. W. Schuleter. il Pop Mech 132:174-6 Jl '69
Lunar core tube changed for Apollo 12. Aviation W 91:18 O 6 '69
Make this simple fixture to set boring bars accurately. R. Kouhoupt il Pop Mech 131: 172-3+ Je '69
See also
Augers
Jigs

DRILLS, Fire. See Fire drills

DRINAN, Robert F.
American laws regulating the formation of the marriage contract. bibliog f Ann Am Acad 383:48-57 My '69
Children's rights. America 122:4-5 Ja 10 '70
Political freedom in Vietnam. America 120: 731-3 Je 28 '69
Problems and potential of shared time. America 120:503-5 Ap 26 '69
Semipublic school: Rhode Island study. America 121:467-8 N 15 '69
Ultimate form of corruption. New Repub 161: 15-16 Jl 19 '69

DRINK question. See Alcoholism; Liquor problem

DRINKING and traffic accidents
Drinking and driving: the record in Britain. il U S News 66:61 Je 9 '69
D.W.I.s anonymous; Phoenix, Ariz, offenders to attend Phoenix alcohol research and re-education project. il Time 95:32 Ja 5 '70
Seven roads to wrecks. Time 94:38 Jl 4 '69
Shocking facts about drinking and driving. W. Haddon. il Pop Sci 194:78-81+ My '69

DRINKING customs
Should children be taught to drink? questions and answers; ed. by T. Berland. il Todays Health 47:46-9+ F '69
Six authorities discuss pre-dinner drinking; symposium, ed. by J. Wilson. il House & Gard 136:142+ O '69

DRINKING horns. See Drinking vessels

DRINKING in literature
Drinking in print. M. J. Kempner. House B 111:136+ S '69

DRINKING vessels
Ceramic drinking horns. G. Hageman. il Ceram Mo 17:27-8 N '69
Glasses to use in many ways. J. A. Beard. il House & Gard 135:165 Ap '69
Some Scottish quaichs. R. L. McClenahan. il Antiques 96:402-5 S '69
See also
Mugs

Collectors and collecting
Worldwide stein collection. il Hobbies 74:114-15+ O; 108 D '69

DRINKS. See Beverages; Liquors

DRINNON, Richard
Rhetoric of evasion. Nation 209:370-4 O 13 '69

DRISCOLL, Joseph L.
Semper fi at SMU. por Newsweek 74:91-2
D 8 '69
DRISCOLL, Patrick A.
Summer remedial program for primary chil-
dren. Ed Digest 34:36-7 My '69
DRIVER training courses. See Automobile driv-
ing—Study and teaching
DRIVER training schools. See Automobile driv-
ing—Study and teaching
DRIVES (money raising) See Fund raising
DRIVEWAYS
I built this driveway for a mere $100. C.
Wilson. il Pop Mech 132:154-5+ S '69
DRIVING
Riding to nostalgia. il Sports Illus 31:30-5 Ag
4 '69
DRIVING, Automobile. See Automobile driving
DRIVING classes. See Automobile driving—
Study and teaching
DRIVING tests, Automobile. See Automobile
drivers—Testing
DROBISH, Diane G. See Paterson, P. Y. jt.
auth.
DROEMER Knaur (publisher) See Publishers
and publishing—Germany (Federal Repub-
lic)
DRONTEN, Netherlands

Architecture
Indoor agora. il Arch Forum 131:68-9 N '69
DROPKIN, Stan, and Castiglione, Lawrence
Teacher credentials: item preferences of re-
cruiters. Clear House 43:474-8 Ap '69
DROPOUTS
All's calm in the crow's nest: project for
potential dropouts. J. B. Hicks. il Am Ed
5:9-10 O '69
College students: why they drop out. B.
Bard. Ed Digest 34:18-21 Mr '69
Dropouts, college style. D. Klein. il Seven-
teen 27:67+ N '68
Employment of high school graduates and
dropouts. V. C. Perrella. bibliog il Mo La-
bor R 92:36-43 Je '69
Ghetto dropout; analysis and partial solu-
tion. S. Cohen. bibliog Clear House 44:
118-22 O '69
Keeping the dropouts in: adapting Job corps
teaching techniques. Sr Schol 94:Schol
Teach 7 F 14 '69
Rebellious school dropout. S. B. Brown and
T. T. Peterson. Sch & Soc 97:437-9 N '69
Rodman experience with dropouts. L. Besant.
il Todays Ed 58:52-5 F '69; Same abr. Ed
Digest 34:35-7 Ap '69
Street academies: one step off the sidewalk.
J. Black. il Sat R 52:88-9+ N 15 '69
They don't have to drop out. W. S. Kruger.
il Am Ed 5:6-8 O '69
Vocational live-in; Ohio's Mahoning Valley
vocational school. R. C. Bixler. il Am Ed 5:
7-9 Mr '69
What's a nice girl like you doing as a drop-
out? Six answers. il Mlle 69:265+ Ag '69
Where failures make the grade; Chicago's
CAM academy and New York's Harlem prep.
Ed Digest 34:21-4 Ja '69
DROPS
Subsurface phenomena and the splashing of
drops on shallow liquids. W. C. Macklin
and P. V. Hobbs. bibliog il Science 166:
107-8 O 3 '69
DROSOPHILA
Action spectra for phase shifts of a circadian
rhythm in drosophila. K. O. Frank and
W. F. Zimmerman. bibliog il Science 163:
688-9 F 14 '69
Lipids of drosophila: a newly detected lipid
in the male. F. M. Butterworth. bibliog il
Science 163:1356-7 Mr 21 '69
DROST, Willem
Rembrandt and his circle. B. A. Rifkin. il
Art N 68:33-4+ O '69
DROTTNINGHOLM court theater. See Theater
—Sweden
DROUGHTS
Disastrous drought; Chile. il Time 93:40 Ja
24 '69
DROWNPROOFING. See Swimming—Safety de-
vices and measures
DROZ, Bernard, and Barondes, S. H.
Nerve endings: rapid appearance of labeled
protein shown by electron microscope radio-
autography. bibliog Science 165:1131-3 S 12
'69
DRRDLA; story. See Morris, W.
DRUCKER, Peter F.
Management's new role; excerpts from ad-
dress, November 7, 1969. Harvard Bsns R
47:49-54 N '69
Sickness of government; excerpts from The
age of discontinuity. por Nations Bsns
57:52-61 Mr '69

about
New era of innovation. I. Kristol. por Fortune
79:189-90 F '69
Super-futurist. E. T. Chase.   New Repub
160:25-6+ Je 21 '69
DRUG abuse
Do Americans suffer from medicine-cabinet
addiction? Good H 169:195-7 N '69
Drug abuse education program. Sch & Soc
97:273 Sum '69
Drug scene. P. J. Riga. il Cath World 209:
176-81 Jl '69
Drugs and narcotics: illusions and realities. il
Sr Schol 94:5-10 Mr 21 '69
Growing drive against drugs. il U S News
67:38-40 D 15 '69
Growing menace of drugs. Nixon's plan to
fight it; message   to Congress, July 14,
1969. R. M. Nixon. il U S News 67:60-2 Jl
28 '69
Hooked! J. Leavitt. Nation 209:737-8 D 29
'69
Is the pot user driven, or in the driver's
seat? Time 94:64-5 Jl 25 '69
Marijuana, sleeping pills and other drugs:
peril for America; excerpts from testimony
before a subcommittee of the House ap-
propriations committee, June 25, 1969. S. F.
Yolles. il U S News 67:47-8 Jl 14 '69
Multiple action programs; New Hampshire
activities. PTA Mag 64:26 O '69
Narcotics and drug abuse: a presidential
prescription. J. Walsh. Science 165:377-8 Jl
25 '69
Penalties   and   programs;   national   drive
against narcotics and other drugs. Time 94:
65 Jl 25 '69
Perils of pill-popping with mood drugs. E. C.
Gottschalk. il Sci Digest 66:13-17 Jl '69
Pill popping. A. Talmey. il Vogue 154:104-5
N 15 '69
Search for definitions. Sci N 96:234 S 20 '69
Several million felons. New Repub 161:9 Ag 2
'69
Stoned age? H. N. Oliphant. Ed Digest 34:
32-5 My '69
Two doctors warn against the abuse of am-
phetamines; excerpts from testimonies be-
fore House select committee on crime, No-
vember 18, 1969. G. R. Edison; B. Sheppard.
U S News 67:24-5 D 29 '69
Worst sickness in American history. D. Law-
rence. U S News 67:84 Jl 28 '69
See also
Marijuana
Narcotics and youth
DRUG addicts. See Narcotic addicts
DRUG laws and legislation
Administration about-face. Sci N 96:371 O
25 '69
Battle for a nation's health; early twentieth
century fight for pure food and drug laws.
L. M. Rhodes. il Todays Health 47:36-9+
Ap '69
Cleaning out the medicine chest. il Time 94:
64 Jl 25 '69
Common sense solution. il Ebony 25:140-1 D
'69
Little less illegal; marijuana proposals. New
Repub 161:11 N 8 '69
See also
Narcotic laws
United States—Food and drug administration
DRUG research. See Pharmaceutical research
DRUG stores. See Drugstores
DRUG testing. See Drugs—Testing
DRUG trade
Doctor V. D. Mattia: a pill-giving maverick;
with interview, ed. by J. Gurovitz. il Life
66:39-40+ Mr 7 '69
Drug establishment; makers of prescription
drugs. J. L. Goddard. Esquire 71:117-21+
Mr '69
Drug testing: is time running out? W. M.
O'Brien. Bul Atom Sci 25:8-14 Ja '69; Dis-
cussion. 25:12-19 Je '69
Million-dollar bugs, by M. Pearson. Review
Sat R 52:36-7 N 1 '69. M. Potomacus
Pharmaceutical revolution: its impact on sci-
ence and society. L. Lasagna. bibliog Sci-
ence 166:1227-33 D 5 '69
Speed demons: treacherous pep pills. Time
94:18 O 31 '69
Times does it again; New York times reports
on testing of new drugs on prisoners. Na-
tion 209:100-1 Ag 11 '69

DRUG trade—*Continued*
Wooden box; synthetic-drug industry in Japan. il Newsweek 74:74 S 8 '69

See also
Government investigations—Drug trade
Johnson and Johnson (firm)
Pfizer, Charles, and company
Pharmaceutical manufacturers association
Schering corporation
Searle, G. D, and company
Smith Kline and French laboratories

Finance
He who hesitates: Searle story. Forbes 104: 64 S 15 '69
Healthy, wealthy, but worried. il Bsns W p39 Ag 16 '69

Laws and legislation
See Drug laws and legislation

DRUGS
Drug revolution; findings of the Nelson subcommittee and the Task force. P. A. Dickinson. Har Yrs 9:6-15+ S '69
Drugs from the sea. il Time 94:82 S 5 '69
Fifteen most important drugs. A. J. Snider. Sci Digest 66:72 S '69
Intracranial drug implants: an autoradiographic analysis of diffusion. S. P. Grossman and W. E. Stumpf. bibliog il Science 166: 1410-12 D 12 '69

See also
Barbiturates
Doping in sports
Hallucinogenic drugs
Pharmacology
Pharmacopeias
United States—Food and drug administration
also names of drugs, e.g. Primaquine

Dosage
One woman's ordeal: when too much medicine is a dangerous thing; case of Ellen Morgan Holl. B. Merson. Ladies Home J 85:50+ N '69
Toward personalized prescriptions. il Time 94:60 Ag 1 '69
Unpredictable dosages. Sci N 95:258 Mr 15 '69

Laws and legislation
See Drug laws and legislation

Metabolism
Antibiotics alter methotrexate metabolism and excretion. D. S. Zaharko and others. bibliog il Science 166:887-8 N 14 '69
Toward personalized prescriptions. il Time 94: 60 Ag 1 '69

Patents
Assault on the drug jam; patent policy. il Sci N 96:325 O 11 '69

Physiological effects
Auditory habituation and barbiturate-induced neural activity. W. R. Webster. bibliog il Science 164:970-1 My 23 '69
Caution on the pill; excerpt from Life, death and the doctor. L. Lasagna; reply with rejoinder. G. Langmyler. Sat R 52:60-1 Mr 1 '69
Diet pill hoax. Harp Baz 102:112+ Ja '69
Receptor pattern in drug design. il Chem 42: 25-6 Jl '69
Tricyclic antidepressants: evidence for an intraneuronal site of action. W, D. Reid and others. bibliog il Science 164:437-9 Ap 25 '69
Will there soon be a drug that might ultimately prolong your husband's life? L. Kavaler. Good H 169:112-13+ O '69
See also
Drugs—Metabolism

Prices
Doctor V. D. Mattia: a pill-giving maverick; with interview, ed. by J. Gurovitz. il Life 66:39-40+ Mr 7 '69
Drug makers offer to settle; antibiotic price suit. Bsns W p34 F 15 '69
Maybe you can pay less for prescriptions; generic drugs. il Changing T 23:19-20 Mr '69
$120 million settlement; five leading drugmakers to settle claims for allegedly rigging the price of tetracycline. Time 93:92 F 14 '69
Settling up; major drug firms offer $120 million. Newsweek 73:85-6 F 17 '69

Psychological effects
Afterflash! ed. by V. Whitman. J. Alison. Read Digest 95:81-5 D '69
Brain control: tomorrow's curse or blessing? J. Reinert. il Sci Digest 66:14-19 N '69

Hallucinogen-tranquilizer interaction: its nature. M. F. Halasz and others. bibliog il Science 164:569-71 My 2 '69
Marijuana, sleeping pills and other drugs: peril for America; excerpts from testimony before a subcommittee of the House appropriations committee, June 25, 1969. S. F. Yolles. il U S News 67:47-8 Jl 14 '69
Ways drugs are used to help children learn. il Good H 168:160 F '69

Testing
Drug reaction; Senate subcommittee hearings. Newsweek 74:71 Ag 25 '69
Drug safety: experimental programs. G. Zbinden. bibliog Science 164:643-7 My 9 '69
Drug test dilemma; Canadian agency. F. Poland. il Sci N 96:438 N 8 '69
Drug testing: is time running out? W. M. O'Brien. Bul Atom Sci 25:8-14 Ja '69; Discussion. 25:12-19 Je '69
How those new products are tested and developed: animal health products. J. C. Clark. Farm J 93:B24 My '69
Palliatives and revolution. Sci N 96:147 Ag 23 '69
Times does it again; New York times reports on testing of new drugs on prisoners. Nation 209:100-1 Ag 11 '69

DRUGS, Experimental
Forever young? KH3 and ribaminol. il Newsweek 74:88-90 S 15 '69
What's new in medical care. il U S News 67:8 D 15 '69

DRUGS and athletes. See Doping in sports

DRUGS and youth. See Narcotics and youth

DRUGSTORES
Personal touch; Eckerd drug chain. il Time 93:89 My 2 '69

DRUKKER, Leendert
No expo for Expo 69. Pop Phot 65:98-9+ Jl '69

DRUNKEN drivers. See Drinking and traffic accidents

DRUNKENNESS and traffic accidents. See Drinking and traffic accidents

DRURY, Allen
Best of the second-raters. Nat R 21:77-8 Ja 28 '69
Mr Nixon goes to Washington. Read Digest 94:57-63 F '69

DRURY, Michael
Drug trip: voyage to nowhere. Read Digest 95:61-3 Ag '69

DRURY, Newton B.
Redwoods, wonders of the world. Am For 75:24-7+ S '69

DRURY, Robert E.
Interaction of plant hormones. bibliog Science 164:564-5 My 2 '69

DRY, Stanley W.
Problem is: we have too many rights. New Repub 160:11 My 17 '69

DRY cell batteries. See Electric batteries

DRYERS. See Clothes dryers

DRYING
See also
Freeze drying

DRYING (crops)
Which drying system? R. Krumme. il Suc Farm 67:28-9 Jl '69

DRYING of fruit. See Fruit—Drying

DRYPOINT
Simplified etching. N. S. Saranovitz. il Sch Arts 69:14-15 D '69

DRYSDALE, Don
Departure of the big D. por Time 94:59 Ag 22 '69
Highlight. por Sports Illus 30:64 Je 30 '69

D'SOUZA, Jerome
India's Congress party at the crossroads. America 121:582-5 D 13 '69

DUBAL, David
Earl Wild's re-creation of The daemonic Liszt. Am Rec G 35:364-5 Ja '69

DUBAWNT sports club. See Sports clubs

DUBČEK, Alexander
Dubcek talks; interview, ed. by D. Hunebelle. por Look 33:21-3 Jl 29 '69

about
Diplomatic exile. Time 94:14 D 26 '69
Dubcek dumped. por Sr Schol 94:18 My 2 '69
Dubcek falls and the Russians have their way. il por Newsweek 73:48+ Ap 28 '69
Dubcek's fall. Newsweek 74:89-90 O 6 '69
End of the Dubček era. il por Time 93:26+ Ap 25 '69
Ground rules for national communism. Life 67:46B S 19 '69
Soviet triumph, Dubcek's fall. U S News 66:9 Ap 28 '69

DUBERMAN, Martin
Goal has been to protect property rather persons. N YTimes Mag p 140 My 4 '69
Immoral imperialism. New Repub 160:27-8+ Ap 19 '69

about
Voice for troubled intellectuals. W. M. Wiecek. por Sat R 53:23-5+ Ja 3 '70

DUBINSKY, David
ILGWU: fighting for lower wages. M. Myerson. Ramp Mag 8:51-5 O '69

DUBIVSKY, Barbara
Bermuda haute couture: trend-setting and popular. Travel & Camera 32:18+ S '69

DUBLIN
See also
Stock exchange—Dublin

Description
Bloomsday in Dublin; excerpts from Ulysses, with notes by A. Bester and photographs by M. Koner. il Holiday 45:40-5 Je '69
Spirits of Dublin. D. Butwin. il Sat R 52:63-5 N 29 '69

Music
Report: Dublin; world premiere of Gerald Victory's Music hath mischief. W. H. A. Williams. Opera N 33:32 F 1 '69

Social life and customs
Week of the Great Hooley; Dublin horse bash. B. Moore. il Holiday 46:26-9+ Ag '69

Theater
See also
Drama festivals—Ireland

DUBLIN horse show. See Horse shows

DU BOFF, Richard B.
Whatever happened to the new economics? Commonweal 91:94-8 O 24 '69

DUBOFSKY, Melvyn
Radical goad. Nation 209:218-21 S 8 '69

DU BOIS, William Edward Burghardt
Du Bois as historian. H. Aptheker. bibliog il pors Negro Hist Bul 32:6-16 Ap '69

DUBOS, Rene Jules
Biosphere. UNESCO Courier 22:6-15 Ja '69
Human landscape; Department of state science lecture. December 9, 1968; with introd. by D. Rusk. Dept State Bul 60:127-36 F 10 '69
Scientist talks about careers in science; interview, ed. by A. S. Freese. pors Todays Health 47:24-7+ S '69
Social design for science; adaptation of address, November 14, 1969. Science 166:823 N 14 '69

DU BOUCHET, André
To ripen; poem, tr. by A. Rudolf. Nation 209: 122 Ag 11 '69

DUBRIDGE, Lee Alvin
DuBridge discusses defense R & D; excerpt from address, March 20, 1969. Science 164: 168 Ap 11 '69
Future of university research; excerpt from address, December 3, 1968. Bul Atom Sci 25:39 Ja '69
Hornig's accomplishments. Science 163:759 F 21 '69
Science serves society; adaptation of address, April 29, 1969. Science 164:1137-40 Je 6 '69
Social control of science. Bul Atom Sci 25: 26-8+ My '69

about
DuBridge: Nixon's science aide takes a swing through Europe. D. S. Greenberg. Science 166:350-3 O 17 '69
How the President gets his science advice: a visit to OST. J. P. Wiley. Phys Today 22: 70-1+ Ag '69
Last refuge of scoundrels. W. Kornberg. Sci N 96:261 S 27 '69
Lee DuBridge passes Senate test. B. Nelson. Science 163:657 F 14 '69
Science adviser DuBridge makes his press debut, tells about Nixon's meeting with scientists. B. Nelson. Science 163:794-5 F 21 '69
View from DuBridge. il por Newsweek 73:61 F 24 '69

DU BROFF, Sidney
Germany no longer. Nation 208:269-71 Mr 3 '69

DUBROW, Hilliard
Pill and cancer. il por Newsweek 74:59 Ag 11 '69

DUBRULLE, Bernard
Leading the life of Killy. P. Ryan. por Sports Illus 30:32-3 Ap 28 '69

DUBUFFET, Jean
Dubuffet as a writer. J. Russell. il por Art in Am 57:86-9 My '69

DUBUS, Andre
Doctor; story. New Yorker 45:38-9 Ap 26 '69

DUCHAMP, Marcel
Duchamp's Young man and girl in spring; excerpt from The complete works of Marcel Duchamp. A. Schwarz. bibliog il Am Imago 25:296-308 Wint '68
Marcel Duchamp, 1887-1968. T. B. Hess. Art N 67:29 N '68
Marcel Duchamp 1887-1968; symposium, ed. by Cleve Gray. il pors Art in Am 57:20-43 Jl '69
Peep show. il por Time 94:58 Jl 11 '69

DUCHEIN, Charles F.
Mess in the merchant marine; address, January 17, 1969. Vital Speeches 35:303-6 Mr 1 '69

DUCK as food. See Cookery—Poultry

DUCK blinds
Nobody here but us chickens. H. G. Tapply. il Field & S 74:54 D '69

DUCK shooting
Carry a blind on your back. C. F. Rees. il Field & S 74:56-7+ S '69
Color the can red? hunting canvasbacks and redheads. R. C. Clement. il Audubon 71:42-5 Mr '69
Gunning the Atlantic coast; best duck and goose hunting. S. M. Miller. il Field & S 74:64-5+ N '69
Home on the bison range. E. A. Bauer. il Outdoor Life 144:62-5+ S '69
How to bag your duck limit. W. Davis. il Mech Illus 65:69+ O '69
Raw deal for ducks; early teal season. B. East. Outdoor Life 144:10+ S '69

DUCKBILLED platypus. See Platypuses

DUCKS
Punishment by response-contingent withdrawal of an imprinted stimulus. H. S. Hoffman and others. bibliog il Science 163:702-4 F 14 '69

DUCKS, Wild
Are duck laws outdated? J. O. Cartier. il Outdoor Life 143:45-7+ F '69
Bluebills on the St Lawrence. J. B. Robinson. il Outdoor Life 144:40-1+ D '69
Color the can red? hunting canvasbacks and redheads. R. C. Clement. il Audubon 71: 42-5 Mr '69
Fertilizer for ducks; pothole making. il Field & S 74:53 D '69
Lick creek shoot. H. L. Lawrence. il Outdoor Life 144:50-1+ D '69
Woodies; wood ducks. H. Borland. il Audubon 71:inside cover Ja '69
See also
Duck shooting

Diseases and pests
War on duck plague. J Mears and B. East. il Outdoor Life 144:41-3+ Ag '69

DUCKWEEDS
Ozone: depression of frond multiplication and floral production in duckweed. W. A. Feder and F. Sullivan. bibliog il Science 165:1373-4 S 26 '69

DUCKWORTH, Ruth (Windmüller)
Ruth Duckworth. T. W. Collins. il pors Ceram Mo 17:18-21 S '69

DUCTS
Bulge method used to form complex ducting for DC-10. il Aviation W 91:56+ N 3 '69
Integrating ducts with concrete floor structures. il Arch Rec 145:161-4 My '69

DUDLEY, Arthur J.
Contemporary industrial-arts programs. Ed Digest 34:41-3 Ja '69

DUDLEY, George A.
Rest of our lives. Craft Horiz 29:50-1+ S '69

DUDLEY, Tilford E.
Wrong question; arrest after making a crack about Cuba in an airplane. Time 94:56 Jl 18 '69

DUDMAN, Richard
AFL-CIO as paid propagandist: agent Meany. New Repub 160:13-16 My 3 '69
Search-and-destroy. New Repub 161:12 Jl 19 '69
Sweden's plans for future aid; excerpts from After Vietnam, Sweden makes plans. Cur 109:61-4 Ag '69

DUDMAN, W. F. and Heidelberger, M.
Immunochemistry of newly found substituents of polysaccharides of rhizobium species. bibliog Science 164:954-5 My 23 '69

DUNHAM, Katherine
Dance magazine award, 1968. por Dance Mag 43:37+ Ap '69
Report on Dance magazine award reception. il pors Dance Mag 43:44-6 Jl '69
DUNKEL, D. K.
Indomitable no man. Nations Bsns 57:55 D '69
DUNKELMAN, L. See Evans, D. C. jt. auth.
DUNKLE, Larry D. and others
Infection structures from rust urediospores: effect of RNA and protein synthesis inhibitors. bibliog Science 163:481-2 Ja 31 '69
DUNLOP, Donald D.
Northwest Passage to what? J. Lear. il Sat R 52:55-6+ N 1 '69
DUNLOP, Richard
Journey to sundown on the Santa Fe Trail. Todays Health 47:44-9+ S '69
DUNN, Harvey
Four disciples of Howard Pyle. H. C. Pitz. il por Am Artist 33:42-3 Ja '69
DUNN, Kenneth J. See Stafford, R. L. jt. auth.
DUNN, Richard B.
Sacramento peak's new solar telescope. Sky & Tel 38:368-75 D '69
DUNNE, John Gregory
Producer always had a mournful look; excerpts from The studio. Life 66:62+ F 14 '69
DUNSIRE, Charles
In the swim. Opera N 34:8-13 S 6 '69
DUNSTAN, Bernard
Some notes on composition. por Am Artist 33:70-5+ Mr '69
DUONG-van-Minh
Communists on the attack. il por Time 94:42 N 21 '69
General's gambit. por Newsweek 74:54 N 17 '69
DUPAGE COUNTY, Ill.
Gravel+refuse=recreation. H. C. Johnson. il Parks & Rec 4:46-8+ S '69
DUPEE, F. W.
(ed) See Cummings, E. E. Twenty-three letters
DU PLESSIX, Francine
For the love of Joan Riley; story. Mlle 68:200-1 Mr '69
Reporter at large. New Yorker 44:37-8+ Ja 25 '69; 45:32-40+ Ja 3 '70
DUPLICATING equipment. See Copying processes
DUPLICATING processes. See Copying processes
DUPLICATORS. See Copying processes
DU PONT, Eleuthere Irenée
Old garden of E. I. du Pont. H. Hover. il Horticulture 47:35+ S '69
DU PONT, Samuel Francis
Samuel Francis DuPont: a selection from his Civil war letters; ed. by J. D. Hayes. Review
America 121:74-5 Ag 2 '69. R. W. Daly.
DU PONT DE NEMOURS, E. I. and company
Du Pont. il Forbes 104:22-6+ D 15 '69
Dupont changes signals at the top. Bsns W p85+ Jl 12 '69
Du Pont's answer machine. il Bsns W p68-70 D 20 '69
Du Pont's troubled dynasty. il Time 95:50-1 Ja 5 '70
DUPONT-SOMMER, André
Reporter at large; Dead Sea scrolls scholar. E. Wilson. New Yorker 45:45-6+ Mr 22 '69
DU PRÉ, Jacqueline
Triangle: Daniel and Jacqueline Barenboim and the cello. M. Cleave. il pors N Y Times Mag p50-1+ Mr 16 '69
DUPUY, Jean
Visual energy of sound. Judson poets' theater. A. J. Fortney. Dance Mag 43:78 Ja '69
DUQUESNE club. See Pittsburgh—Clubs
DU QUOIN, Ill.
First in Du Quoin, with a second from Rome; Hambletonian day. W. F. Reed, jr. il Sports Illus 31:60+ S 8 '69
DURABLE press fabrics. See Textile fabrics, Wrinkle resistant
DURANT, Ariel
Philosopher and the school girl. J. Bishop. il Read Digest 95:132-4 O '69
DURANT, Will
Philosopher and the school girl. J. Bishop. il Read Digest 95:132-4 O '69
DURANTE, Jimmy
Pinocchio lives! C. Mangel. il pors Look 33:93-5+ Mr 4 '69
DURATION of life. See Longevity
DURBIN, Elizabeth
Wife in the wilderness. Todays Health 47:32-3+ Jl '69

DURDIN, Peggy
Bitter tea of Mao's Red guards. N Y Times Mag p28-30+ Ja 19 '69
DURELL, Ann
Goodies and baddies. por Wilson Lib Bul 44:456-7 D '69
Lloyd Alexander: Newbery winner. Library J 94:2066-8 My 15 '69
Who's Lloyd Alexander? Horn Bk 45:382-4 Ag '69
DURELL, Jack, and others
Acetylcholine action: biochemical aspects. bibliog Science 165:862-6 Ag 29 '69
DURFEE, David A.
Screenings: media mix. Library J 94:3905 O 15 '69
DURFEE, Harold A.
Discussion in progress. Chr Cent 86:685 My 14 '69
DURHAM, Joseph T.
Who needs it? Compensatory education. bibliog f Clear House 44:18-22 S '69; Same abr. Ed Digest 35:18-21 D '69
DURHAM, Malcolm
Strip blazer. B. Lang. il pors Hot Rod 22:64-6 N '69
DURHAM, Michael
Experiments in marriage. Life 67:38-48A Ag 15 '69
In Soviet-occupied Czechoslovakia; a search for Ivan with a hidden camera. Life 66:30-3 Ap 18 '69
Stolid square in Scandinavia; ed. by R. Graves. por Life 67:1 Ag 15 '69
DURHAM, N.C.
Education
Durham education improvement program. R. M. Brandt. Todays Ed 58:62-4 F '69
DURK, David B.
Support your local police. Atlan 223:103-4 Mr '69
DURKEN, Daniel
Permanent diaconate program. America 121:140-1 S 6 '69
DURKIN, Henry P.
Where it's also at. por Library J 94:1839-40 My 1 '69
DUROCHER, Leo
In Chicago the left field bleacher bums are chanting: abeebee! Ungowa! Cub powuh! H. Higdon. il pors N Y Times Mag p28-9+ Ag 24 '69
Leo's bums rap for the Cubs. R. H. Boyle. il por Sports Illus 30:14-19 Je 30 '69
Long and short of Leo and me. B. Farrell. Life 67:4 Jl 25 '69
DURRELL, Lawrence
Art is very curature, you purge yourself by putting down; interview, ed. by J. Burns. por Mlle 69:178-9+ S '69
Justine; behind the novels and the motion picture. Holiday 45:74-7 Ap '69
One place; poem. Vogue 155:183 Ja 15 '70
Sixties; poem. Harper 238:4 Mr '69
about
Art as intersecting fields of energy. J. Uterecker. Sat R 52:27-9+ Je 14 '69
Durrell's landscapes. G. Wickes. New Repub 160:23-4 Je 21 '69
Landscape of the heart. J. Goulianos. Nation 209:56-7 Jl 14 '69
DURSLAG, Melvin
Harness racing. Sports Illus 30:72+ Ap 21 '69
DURSO, Joseph
Marianne Moore, baseball fan. Sat R 52:51-2 Jl 12 '69
DURYEA, Diane
One way to charter. il Yachting 126:56-7+ N '69
DUSCHA, Julius
Chief Justice Burger asks: If it doesn't make good sense, how can it make good law? N Y Times Mag p30-1+ O 5 '69
Laird has not lowered his voice. N Y Times Mag p 10-11+ Je 29 '69
DÜSSELDORF, Germany
Music
Report: Düsseldorf; production of Krzysztof Penderecki's Passion according to St Luke. H. Koegler. il Opera N 33:24-5 Je 14 '69
DUST
Dust in the lower atmosphere of Venus. A. D. Anderson. bibliog il Science 163:275-6 Ja 17 '69
Rivers of dust. il Chem 42:24 D '69
DUST, Interstellar. See Matter, Interstellar
DUST, Radioactive. See Radioactive fallout
DUST diseases. See Lungs—Dust diseases
DUST jackets. See Book covers

DUSTY miller
All three go by the name of dusty miller. il Sunset 142:213 Mr '69
DUTCH art. See Art, Dutch
DUTCH bulbs. See Bulbs
DUTCH elm disease. See Elm—Diseases and pests
DUTCH GUIANA. See Surinam
DUTCH painting. See Painting, Dutch
DUTHIE, J. G. and others
Optical studies of pulsar NP 0532. bibliog Science 163:1320-2 Mr 21 '69
DUTIES, Childrens. See Occupations for children
DUTOURD, Jean
French institution: the mistress. McCalls 96: 91-2 Mr '69
DUTTER, Vera E.
Ancient art of fore-edge painting. il por Am Artist 33:56-7+ Ja '69
DUTTON, Gary R. and Barondes, S. H.
Microtubular protein: synthesis and metabolism in developing brain. bibliog Science 166:1637-8 D 26 '69
DUTY
Duty: question of what to do when your team is doing something you think wrong. P. A. Samuelson. Newsweek 74:108 D 8 '69
DUVALIER, François
Haiti: ripe for the marines? R. A. Joseph. Nation 208:392-7 Mr 31 '69
Papa Doc, by B. Diederich and A. Burt. Review
Newsweek il por 74:112+ S 22 '69. G. Wolff
Rum and rumors. E. Peer. il por Newsweek 73:51 Je 23 '69
DVORAK, Antonin
Colin Davis, beyond beauty, poise, and logic. M. N. Kanny. Am Rec G 35:740 My '69
Great Dvorák cello concerto, plus two rare treats. H. Goldsmith. por Hi Fi 19:88 Mr '69
DVORNIKOV, Evgenii
Russian house in outer space. Space World F-4-64:37 Ap '69
DWARF daphnes. See Daphnes
DWARF fruit trees. See Fruit trees, Dwarf
DWARF trees. See Trees, Dwarf
DWARFISM
Deprivation dwarfism. Time 93:39 F 7 '69
DWARFS
Little people of America. Trans-Action 6:6 Mr '69
See also
Graf, L.
DWELL meters
Simplicity+dwell meter. J. Saddler. il Pop Electr 31:33-5 Ag '69
DWELLINGS, Prehistoric
Paleolithic camp at Nice. H. de Lumley. il Sci Am 220:42-50 My '69
DWIGHT, Edward H.
Worthington Whittredge, artist of the Hudson River school. Antiques 96:582-6 O '69
DWIGHT David Eisenhower library, Abilene, Kan.
Dwight D. Eisenhower library. K. V. Hostick. Hobbies 74:108 Je '69
DWORKIN, Gertrude B.
Teaching the boys in the back rooms. Ment Hy 53:258-62 Ap '69
DWYER, Florence P.
Excerpt from remarks, August 11, 1969. Cong Digest 48:298+ D '69
DYAKS. See Borneo—Native races
DYES and dyeing
Tie-dye caper: custom-color fabrics for sew-your-own dresses! il Seventeen 28:224+ S '69
Tie it and dye it. P. Peterson. il N Y Times Mag p 104-5 S 7 '69
We tied and dyed. S. M. David. il Sch Arts 68:18-19 My '69
See also
Batik
Coloring matter in food
Hair—Dyeing and bleaching
Fluorescence
Organic lasers. P. Sorokin. il Sci Am 220: 30-40 F '69
DYLAN, Bob
Back to the roots. il por Time 93:70-1 Ap 11 '69
Bob Dylan revisited: Nashville skyline. E Sander. Sat R 52:76 Ap 26 '69
Dylan's Country pie. H. Saal. il por Newsweek 73:102+ Ap 14 '69

Folk hero speaks. il por Time 94:58 N 14 '69
Poet's return: it's what I do. il por Time 94:80-1 S 12 '69
Records: rock, etc. E. Willis. New Yorker 45:157+ Ap 26 '69
That angry kid has gone all over romantic. A. Goldman. Life 66:18 My 23 '69
DYMALE, Herbert R.
Theology of resistance. Chr Today 13:8-10 Ag 22 '69
DYMENT, Robert G.
Hottest line in the world. Pop Mech 132:148-9 N '69
DYOMIN, Mikhail
Mikhail Dyomin was a successful writer in Soviet Russia. Yet he defected. Why? D. Burg. il pors N Y Times Mag p34-5+ Ap 13 '69
DYSENTERY, Swine. See Swine—Diseases and pests
DYSLEXIA, Developmental. See Reading disability
DYSON, Freeman John
Case for missile defense. Bul Atom Sci 25:31-3 Ap '69
Comment on Sternglass thesis. Bul Atom Sci 25:27 Je '69
Human consequences of the exploration of space. por Bul Atom Sci 25:8-10+ S '69
DYSON-HUDSON, Neville. See Dyson-Hudson, R. jt. auth.
DYSON-HUDSON, Rada, and Dyson-Hudson, Neville
Subsistence herding in Uganda; with biographical sketches. Sci Am 220:12, 76-82+ bibliog(p 132) F '69
DYSTROPHY, Muscular
Five-minute surgery aids muscular dystrophy victims. Todays Health 47:15 D '69
Myotonic muscular dystrophy; abnormalities in fibroblast culture. M. R. Swift and M. J. Finegold. bibliog il Science 165:294-6 Jl 18 '69
DZIRKALS, Lilita I.
(tr) See Stepanov, L. One percent: the problem of economic aid

E

E. Haldeman-Julius publications. See Haldeman-Julius publications
E-cells. See Electrolytic cells
EADI (electronic attitude director indicator) See Aeronautic instruments—Display systems
EASEP (early Apollo scientific experiments package) See Moon—Exploration—Equipment
EBU. See European broadcasting union
EC-121. See Airplanes, Military—United States
EC-121 incident, 1969
Exercise in restraint. il Newsweek 73:27-9+ Ap 28 '69
Flying Pueblo. R. Hotz. Aviation W 90:11 Ap 28 '69
Korean assignment strains carrier force. C. Brownlow. Aviation W 90:18 Ap 28 '69
New lesson in the limits of power; navy EC-121 reconnaissance plane shot down by North Korean MIG. il Time 93:15-16 Ap 25 '69
North Korea making trouble again. il U S News 66:25-7 Ap 28 '69
President Nixon's news conference of April 18, 1969. R. M. Nixon. Dept State Bul 60: 377-81 My 5 '69
Pueblo syndrome. J. Burnham. Nat R 21:480 My 20 '69
Remember the EC-121; warships ordered to the Sea of Japan. Nat R 21:424+ My 6 '69
Spy plane spurs new debate. il Sr Schol 94: 17-18 My 2 '69
Unarmed U.S. reconnaissance plane in international airspace shot down by North Korea; Department of defense statement, with U.S. statement at Panmunjom, April 16 and 17, 1969. Dept State Bul 60:382-3 My 5 '69
Words and warships in the Sea of Japan; U.S. task force 71. Chr Cent 86:639 My 7 '69
ECAFE. See United Nations—Economic commission for Asia and the Far East
ECE. See United Nations—Economic commission for Europe
ECIB (extra corporeal irradiation of the blood) See Blood—Irradiation

ECLA. See United Nations—Economic commission for Latin America
ECS. See Education commission of the states
EDF. See Environmental defense fund, incorporated
EDP. See Electronic data processing
EDP technology, incorporated
Creative computer. Newsweek 74:100+ N 17 '69
EDPA institutes. See Teachers institutes
EDPA institutes for school librarians. See Library institutes and workshops
EDS. See Electronic data systems corporation
EDTA. See Ethylenediamine tetracetic acid
EEF (Eisenhower exchange fellowships) See Scholarships and fellowships
EEOC. See United States—Equal employment opportunity commission
EGD (electrogasdynamics) See Magnetohydrodynamics
EG&G, incorporated. See Edgerton, Germeshausen and Grier, incorporated
E. I. Du Pont de Nemours and company. See Du Pont De Nemours, E. I, and company
EJA. See Executive jet aviation, incorporated
ELDO. See European launcher development organization
ELF (extremely low frequency) radio waves. See Radio waves
EMG. See Electromyography
EMI. See Electric and musical industries, limited
ENI (Ente nazionale idrocarburi) See Petroleum industry and trade—Italy
E.P; story. See Stuart, J.
EPCOT (experimental prototype community of tomorrow). See Amusement parks
EPP (earnings protection plan) See Wage payment plans
ERA (electron ring accelerator) See Accelerators (electrons, etc)
ERCA. See Educational research council of America
ERE (Edison responsive environment) See Teaching machines
ERGS (experimental route guidance system) See Automobiles—Radio equipment
ERIC. See Eric
ERTS (earth resources technology satellite) See Artificial satellites—Use in research
ESC. See Engineers and scientists of California (trade union)
ESP. See Extrasensory perception
ESRO. See European space research organization
ESSA. See United States—Environmental science services administration
ESSA (environmental survey satellite) See Artificial satellites—Meteorological applications
ETS. See Educational testing service
ETV. See Television in education
EVR. See Electronic video recording
EVVA (extravehicular visor assembly) See Astronauts—Clothing
EADS, Harold
Thursday parade. New Yorker 45:26-7 Ag 16 '69
EADS, James Buchanan
Mr Eads spans the Mississippi. J. Gies. il por Am Heritage 20:16-21+ Ag '69
EAGLES
Adventures with South Africa's black eagles. J. Cowden. il Nat Geog 136:532-43 O '69
Golden eagle and the rearing of redtails. F. Hamerstrom. il Natur Hist 78:62-9 My '69
Golden eagle: killer or saint? B. Milek. il Field & S 74:10+ S '69
Short fracas at a carcass; activities of the bald eagle; photographs; with introduction. C. Scott and J. Swedberg. Audubon 71:16-19 Mr '69
EAKINS, Thomas
Portraiture with a scalpel. il Time 94:54-5 Ag 15 '69
EAMES, Charles
Anti-casting couch. il Time 95:37 Ja 5 '70
EAMES, Danny
Muscle parts; interview. por Motor T 21:68-70 Ag '69
EAMES-Wilder chaise. See Chairs
EAR
Cochlear distortion: effect of direct-current polarization. P. Dallos and others. bibliog il Science 164:449-51 Ap 25 '69
See also
Deafness
Hearing
Models
See Anatomical models

EAR wax. See Earwax
EARGLE, John
Dolby noise-reduction system, its impact on recording. Electr World 81:32-4 My '69
EARL lectures. See Pacific school of religion, Berkeley, Calif.
EARLE, Arthur
Is this tile pattern a new math discovery? Pop Sci 195:150-1+ Jl '69
EARLE, George L.
Do's and don'ts of snowmobile safety. Suc Farm 67:W2 D '69
EARLY, Margaret J.
What does research in reading reveal: about successful reading programs? bibliog Engl J 58:534-47 Ap '69
EARLY marriage. See Teen-age marriage
EARLY morning; drama. See Bond, E.
EARNINGS, Corporate. See Corporations—Finance
EARNINGS protection plan. See Wage payment plans
EARPHONES
FM stereo in this headset. C. H. Lawrence. il Radio-Electr 40:43-4 Ag '69
For tops in hi-fi listening; now it's back to earphones yet! H. Fantel. il Pop Mech 132:146-50+ O '69
Hi-fi stereo headphones. il Radio-Electr 40:38-41 O '69
New for you; Koss ESP-6, ESP-7 and ESP-9 stereo headphones. il Radio-Electr 40:32 Ag '69
EARTH
Brothers in the eternal cold. A. MacLeish. Read Digest 94:68-9 Mr '69
See also
Cosmogony
Geography
Geology
Geophysics

Contamination
Diseases from the moon? Why officials worry. U S News 67:53 Jl 7 '69
Heroes or the plague: Apollo 11 astronauts. il Sci N 95:611-13 Je 28 '69

Internal structure
Origin of the oceanic ridges. E. Orowan. il Sci Am 221:102-8+ bibliog(p 166) N '69
Seismic waves reflected from discontinuities within earth's upper mantle. E. R. Engdahl and E. A. Flinn. bibliog il Science 163:177-9 Ja 10 '69
Suboceanic mantle. F. Press. bibliog il Science 165:174-6 Jl 11 '69
Upper mantle of the earth. L. Knopoff. bibliog il Science 163:1277-87 Mr 21 '69

Mantle
See Earth—Internal structure

Motion around the sun
See Earth—Orbital motion

Orbital motion
Measuring earth's motion. il Time 94:66 Jl 4 '69

Photographs from space
Color infrared defines terrain features. Aviation W 90:50-3 My 26 '69
Sunglint patterns: unusual dark patches. C. J. Bowley and others. bibliog il Science 165:1360-2 S 26 '69
Views from Apollo contrast earth, moon. Aviation W 91:62B-62D Ag 18 '69
Zond 7 photographs earth from moon. Aviation W 91:19 S 1 '69

Radiation
Earth's broadcasting atmosphere. il Sci N 95:423-4 My 3 '69
Satellite observations of the earth's radiation budget. T. H. Vonder Haar and V. E. Suomi. bibliog il Science 163:667-9 F 14 '69

Rotation
Secular accelerations of the earth and moon. R. R. Newton. bibliog il Science 166:825-31 N 14 '69

Size
Topological inconsistency of continental drift on the present-sized earth. R. Meservey. bibliog il Science 166:609-11 O 31 '69

Surface
Imbalance of nature. C. J. Roy. il Todays Ed 58:26-8+ Ja '69
See also
Continents
Faults (geology)
Ocean bottom

EARTH, Effect of man on. See Man—Influence on nature

EARTH augers. See Augers

EARTH movements
Measuring earth strains by laser. V. Vali. il Sci Am 221:88-95 bibliog(p 152) D '69
Mounting danger to homes; floods, quakes and slides. il U S News 67:78-9 D 15 '69
See also
Earthquakes
Seismology

EARTH moving machinery. See Bulldozers (machines)

EARTH pollution. See Soil pollution

EARTH resources satellites. See Artificial satellites—Use in research

EARTH sciences
Earth sciences. See occasional issues of Science news
See also
Climate

EARTH sculpture. See Art, Modern

EARTH works. See Art, Modern

EARTHMOVING equipment division. See General motors corporation

EARTHQUAKE detectors. See Seismographs

EARTHQUAKE prediction
Earthquake prediction and control. L. C. Pakiser and others. bibliog il Science 166: 1467-74 D 19 '69
Earthquake prediction: United States-Japan cooperative science program; report of meeting. J. Oliver. Science 164:92-3 Ap 4 '69
Toward better quakecasting; work of R. Hofmann. Time 93:60 Ja 24 '69

EARTHQUAKE research. See Earthquakes—Research

EARTHQUAKES
Doomsday in the Golden state. il Time 93:59 Ap 11 '69
Earthquakes. C. F. Richter. il Natur Hist 78: 36-45 D '69
Seismic activity and faulting associated with a large underground nuclear explosion. R. M. Hamilton and others. bibliog il Science 166:601-4 O 31 '69
Warning! California will fall into the ocean in April! S. V. Roberts. il N Y Times Mag p 12+ Ap 6 '69

Prediction
See Earthquake prediction

Research
Aftershocks below, uncertainty above; Amchitka thermonuclear test. il Sci N 96:322-3 O 11 '69
Alaskan earthquake that shook five continents. il UNESCO Courier 22:22-5 Je '69
Can we stop earthquakes from happening? C. P. Gilmore. il Pop Sci 194:78-82+ Ap '69
Earthquake prediction and control. L. C. Pakiser and others. bibliog il Science 166: 1467-74 D 19 '69
H-bombs for earthquakes. Time 94:82+ O 17 '69
Keeping tabs on quakes. Sci N 95:113 F 1 '69
Messing with the mousetrap; San Andreas fault. il Sci N 95:138-9 F 8 '69
More than prayer. il Sci N 95:280-1 Mr 22 '69
Science tries to call the shocks; U.S. geological survey. il Bsns W p67-8 Ap 26 '69
Underground nuclear explosions and the control of earthquakes. C. Emiliani and others. bibliog il Science 165:1255-6 S 19 '69

Alaska
Alaskan earthquake that shook five continents. UNESCO Courier 22:22-5 Je '69

Aleutian Islands
Earthquakes and nuclear tests: playing the odds on Amchitka. L. J. Carter. il Science 165:773-6 Ag 22 '69; Reply with rejoinder. G. Davidson. 166:688+ N 7 '69

Iran
When the earth shook in Khorassan. R. Keating. il UNESCO Courier 22:30-5 F '69; Reply. J. B. W. Day and E. P. Wright 22:38 My '69

Jamaica
City that drowned; Port Royal, Jamaica. J. D. Ratcliff. il Read Digest 94:192-4+ My '69

United States
America's greatest earthquake; Mississippi River town of New Madrid, Mo. B. Clark. il Read Digest 94:110-14 Ap '69
Earthquakes in New York state. il Cons 23: 6-9 Ap '69

Quaking California. il Newsweek 73:50 F 10 '69
Science tries to call the shocks; U.S. geological survey. il Bsns W p67-8 Ap 26 '69
Seismicity of Colorado: consistency of recent earthquakes with those of historical record. R. B. Simon. bibliog il Science 165:897-9 Ag 29 '69
See also
Earthquakes—Alaska
San Francisco—Earthquake and fire. 1906

EARTHS, Rare
Rare-earth elements and high pressures. Z. Fisk and B. T. Matthias. il Science 165:279-80 Jl 18 '69

EARTHWORK
See also
Soil mechanics

EARTHWORMS
Build your own earthworm-casting factory. R. N. Coffman. il Org Gard & Farm 16:58+ My '69
Earthworm pits for ailing elms. I. O. Sternberg. il Org Gard & Farm 16:90-2 D '69
Earthworms turn horse fertilizer into rich humus. L. H. Helms. Org Gard & Farm 16:88 Ja '69
Earthworms used to reclaim sterile spoilbanks caused by coal stripmining. il Org Gard & Farm 16:65 Ag '69
Lowly earthworm. V. A. Tiedjens. Horticulture 46:50+ S '68
Specific tissue graft rejection in earthworms. E. L. Cooper. bibliog il Science 166:1414-15 D 12 '69
Walleye crawl. R. Slogar. il Outdoor Life 143: 74-5+ Ap '69
What ever happened to worms? P. McManus. il Field & S 73:66-7+ F '69

EARWAX
Cerumen types in Choctaw Indians. L. M. Martin and J. F. Jackson. Science 163: 677-8 F 14 '69

EASELS
Connoisseur's corner. See issues of House & garden incorporating Living for young homemakers

EASON, James M.
Ho! Ho! Ho! North Pole calling. por Parks & Rec 4:45-6+ O '69

EASON, Tracy
Selected bibliography of A-V media in library literature, 1958-69. por Wilson Lib Bul 44: 312-19 N '69

EAST, Ben
Gray balls of fire. Outdoor Life 144:60-3+ Ag '69
(ed) News: the Great Lakes states. por Outdoor Life 144:33-4 Jl '69
(ed) See Reynolds, M. Bear that wouldn't quit

EAST
See also
Asia
Middle East

EAST (United States) See Atlantic states

EAST AFRICAN FEDERATION (proposed)
East African experience. K. W. Grundy and R. Fulton. bibliog f Cur Hist 56:275-81 My '69

EAST and West
Ex oriente lux? F. Holck and E. Cate. Chr Cent 86:315-18 Mr 5 '69; Discussion. 86:624-5 Ap 30 '69
Sacred cows, Asian and American: the language of social behavior; address. July 17, 1969. R. T. Oliver. bibliog Vital Speeches 35:663-72 Ag 15 '69

EAST ANGLIA
See also
Norfolk Broads, England

EAST ANGLIA. University, Norwich. See Colleges and universities—England

EAST Bay municipal utility district. See Oakland, Calif.—East Bay municipal utility district

EAST BERLIN. See Berlin (East Berlin)

EAST BERLIN festival. See Music festivals—Germany (Democratic Republic)

EAST CHICAGO, Ind.
Plenty of daylight but no bad view. il Am City 84:44 Ja '69

Water supply
New plants need modernizing, too. V. J. Kirrin and J. Rakowski, jr. il Am City 84:110+ Jl '69

EAST EUROPEAN refugees. See Refugees, European

EAST GERMANY. See Germany (Democratic Republic)

EAST HAMPTON, N.Y.
Annals of agriculture. M. Hunt. New Yorker 45:57-8+ N 1 '69
Beach wife. N. Ephron. il Holiday 45:68-9+ My '69

EAST INDIA company
Trial of Warren Hastings. A. Nevins. il Horizon 11:110-15 Wint '69

EAST INDIANS in South Africa
Gandhi's South Africa settlement. J. Brewer. Chr Cent 86:950+ Jl 16 '69

EAST MEADOW CREEK wilderness area. See Wilderness areas—Colorado

EAST ORANGE, N.J.

City planning
Low-income residents rebuild a neighborhood. il Am City 84:105+ Jl '69

Housing
Low-income residents rebuild a neighborhood. il Am City 84:105+ Jl '69

EAST ST LOUIS, Ill.
City: the East St Louis blues. il Time 93:29 Ap 11 '69

EAST-West exchange agreements. See Exchange of persons programs

EAST-West relations. See International relations

EAST-West trade. See Communist countries—Commerce

EAST WINDSOR, N.J.
Don't let size keep your waterworks from using EDP. W. B. Harvey. il Am City 84:95-6+ D '69

EASTER
Easter, American style. Newsweek 73:95 Ap 14 '69
Four Easters. P. S. Rees. Chr Today 13:3-5 Mr 28 '69
Where the customs surrounding Easter originated. il Good H 168:207 Ap '69
    See also
Holy week

Drama
Wild rabbit chase. C. Boiko. Plays 28:35-43 Ap '69

EASTER business. See Retail trade

EASTER cookery. See Cookery, Ornamental

EASTER eggs
Delicious dishes from the Easter bunny. il Ebony 24:164+ Mr '69
Dip and dye Easter eggs. il Sunset 142:131 Ap '69
Elegant eggs for all seasons il House & Gard 135:116-17 Mr '69

EASTER ISLAND
Easter, island of mysteries. P. Mann. il Harp Baz 102:132+ My '69
Mysteries of Easter Island, by F. Mazièrre. Review
    Time 94:72+ Ag 8 '69
Mysterious hieroglyphs of Easter Island; reprint. A. Métraux. il UNESCO Courier 22:16-17 Ag '69

EASTER procession; story. See Solzhenitsyn, A.

EASTERLA, Patricia James
Land of the frozen fires. por Nat Parks 43:18-21 D '69

EASTERN airlines
Eastern asks V/STOL design proposals. K. J. Stein. Aviation W 91:34 Ag 18 '69
Eastern drafts STOL criteria from Northeast corridor tests. il Aviation W 90:30 F 3 '69
Eastern girds for N.Y.-Miami push. R. F. Coburn. Aviation W 90:37-8 My 12 '69
Eastern plans to contract some service to air taxis. J. W. Carter. Aviation W 90:28 Ap 21 '69
Heads you lose, tails you lose; Eastern famous for bad service. il Forbes 103:33-4 Ap 15 '69
Skyful of trouble. il Time 93:68 Ja 24 '69

EASTERN EUROPE. See Europe, Eastern

EASTERN gas and fuel associates
BURP and make money; urban housing rehabilitation venture. E. Goldston. bibliog il Harvard Bsns R 47:84-99 S '69
Man who taught a corporate elephant to dance. W. McQuade. il Fortune 79:122-4+ F '69

EASTERNERS
East is East and West is second, or is it? A. Hano. il N Y Times Mag p32-3+ Mr 16 '69

EASTLAKE, William
Whitey's on the moon now. Nation 209:238-9 S 15 '69

EASTMAN, John
Field guide to field guides. Natur Hist 78:28+ N '69
Swedenborg: scientific saint. Chr Cent 86:156+ Ja 29 '69

EASTMAN, Max
Max Eastman. C. Neider. Sat R 52:4+ My 17 '69
Obituary
    Nat R 21:320 Ap 8 '69

EASTMAN, Peter F.
Fourth doctor. Todays Health 47:28-9+ Ap '69

EASTMAN Kodak company
Helping others to help themselves; laboratory trainee program. C. E. Rowley. il Chem 42:8-10 F '69
Those inexpensive cameras are good. N. Goldberg. il Pop Phot 65:62+ S '69

EASTON, Robert. See Macdonald, R. jt. auth.

EASTWOOD, Clint
Don't call him little Clint; interview. ed. by E. Miller. pors Seventeen 28:116-17+ O '69

EATING
Gastronomy recalled (cont) M. F. K. Fisher. New Yorker 45:140-6+ Ap 26; 118+ Je 7; 154+ S 20; 114+ S 27 '69
How to get a great meal at a great restaurant. R. A. De Groot. il Esquire 71:112-17+ Ja '69
Unexpected adrenergic effect of chlorpromazine: eating elicited by injection into rat hypothalmus. S. F. Leibowitz and N. E. Miller. bibliog il Science 165:609-11 Ag 8 '69
    See also
Cookery
Diet
Gastronomy
Nutrition

EATING, Psychology of
Don't use food as punishment! D. B. Hunter. il Camp Mag 41:18 N '69
My mother made me fat; symposium. ed. by G. Krupp. Redbook 132-52-4+ Ja '69
Satiety factor; to make learning possible for children, feed them in school. B. Bettelheim. N Y Times Mag p140 Ap 13 '69

EATING habits. See Food habits

EATON, Cyrus Stephen, 1883-
Eaton nips away at Ohio bank. por Bsns W p 178 My 10 '69

EATON, Jerome A.
Home greenhouse. See issues of Home garden & flower grower

EATON, John, 1829-1906
John Eaton, educator (1829-1906) G. Smith. bibliog f Sch & Soc 97:108-12 F '69

EATON, Lloyd
No defeats, loads of trouble. P. Putnam. il por Sports Illus 31:26-7 N 3 '69

EATON, Quaintance
Juillard's dream. Opera N 34:8-13 S 20 '69
Meals at the Met. Opera N 33:12-15 Mr 29 '69

EAVES, John
U.N. condemns racial policies of Southern Rhodesia; statement. March 24, 1969. Dept State Bul 60:413-14 My 12 '69

EAVESDROPPING devices. See Electronics in criminal investigation, espionage, etc.

EBASCO industries
Behold the bridegroom. Forbes 103:41-2 Mr 15 '69

EBBELAAR, Han
Brief biography. S. Goodman. pors Dance Mag 43:58-9 N '69

EBBIN, Michael
On the boards. W. Como. por Dance Mag 43:20 Ag '69

EBEL, Robert L.
Prospects for evaluation of learning. Ed Digest 34:22-5 Mr '69

EBEN, Lois E.
Originality in the parade. Sch Arts 69:38-9 O '69

EBERHARD, Edward G.
Upside-down thing. Engl J 58:1192-3 N '69

EBERHARD, Hans J. Müller-. See Müller-Eberhard, H. J.

EBERHART, Richard
Track; poem. New Yorker 45:105 S 13 '69

EBERLE, Robert F.
Open space school. bibliog Clear House 44:23-8 S '69

EBERLE, William Denman
Radiator maker starts to swing. il por Bsns W p86-7 My 3 '69

EBERT, Roger
Just another horror movie, or is it? Read Digest 94:127-8 Je '69
Newman's complaint. Esquire 72:110-11+ S '69

EBLE, Kenneth
Scholarly life. Am Scholar 39:109-22 Wint '69

EBLE, Mary
Literary launchings. Library J 94:3789-91 O 15 '69

EBONY fashion fair. See Fashion shows

EBREY, Thomas G. and Clayton, R. K.
Phycomyces: stimulus storage in light-initiated reactions. bibliog Science 164:427-8 Ap 25 '69

EBSEN, Buddy
New breed of racing catamaran. por Pop Sci 194:86-9 F '69
Ocean racing catamaran. por Yachting 125: 84+ Ja '69

EBY, Cecil
For whom the bell tolled; excerpts from Between the bullet and the lie. Am Heritage 20:36-41+ Ag '69

ECCENTRICS and eccentricities
Fun people. B. Farber. Sat R 52:8+ S 20 '69
Sad state of eccentricity; Time essay. Time 93:31 Mr 14 '69

ECCLESIASTICAL architecture. See Church architecture

ECCLESIASTICAL courts
Civil lawyer in the church court. S. J. Kelleher. America 120:444-5 Ap 12 '69

ECCLESIASTICAL law
See also
Canon law

ECCLESIOLOGY. See Church

ECDYSONE
Ecdysone analog: conversion to alpha ecdysone and 20-hydroxyecdysone by an insect. J. N. Kaplanis and others. bibliog il Science 166:1540-1 D 19 '69
Hormonal termination of larval diapause in dermacentor albipictus. J. E. Wright. bibliog il Science 163:390-1 Ja 24 '69
Puparium formation in flies: contraction to puparism induced by ecdysone. P. Berreur and G. Fraenkel. bibliog il Science 164: 1182-3 Je 6 '69

ECDYSTERONE
Cellular response to ecdysterone in vitro. K. J. Judy. bibliog il Science 165:1374-5 S 26 '69
Cockroach leg regeneration: effects of ecdysterone in vitro. E. P. Marks and R. A. Leopold. bibliog il Science 167:61-2 Ja 2 '70

ECHEVERRIA ALVAREZ, Luis
Next president: not left, not right. il por Time 94:33 O 31 '69

ECHINODERMS
X-ray diffraction studies of echinoderm plates. G. Donnay and D. L. Pawson. bibliog il Science 166:1147-50 N 28 '69
See also
Sea cucumbers
Sea urchins
Starfishes

ECHINODERMS, Fossil
Ctenocystoidea: new class of primitive echinoderms. R. A. Robison and J. Sprinkle. bibliog il Science 166:1512-14 D 19 '69

ECHINOIDEA. See Sea urchins

ECHO sounding. See Deep sea sounding

ECHOLOCATION (physiology)
Blind river dolphin: first side-swimming cetacean. E. S. Herald and others. bibliog il Science 166:1408-10 D 12 '69
Wave-making by whirligig beetles (gyrinidae) V. A. Tucker. bibliog il Science 166:897-9 N 14 '69

ECKER, Jon
(ed) See Szasz, T. Mental illness is not a disease

ECKERD, John M.
Personal touch. por Time 93:89 My 2 '69

ECKERT, Roger. See Naitoh, Y. jt. auth.

ECKHARDT, Robert C. See Nelson, P. L. jt. auth.

ECKLER, A. Ross
Statisticians and shoemakers: applying their skills; excerpt from address, August 1969. Mo Labor R 92:43-7 N '69
about
Why the uproar over '70 census? U S News 66:10 Ap 14 '69

ECKMAN, Theda M.
Knitting patterns for living. Har Yrs 9:29-31 F '69

ECKRICH, Catherine
At Mary's well; poem. Cath World 210:73 N '69
O little lad! (for our David, dying); poem. Cath World 210:110 D '69
Tornado; poem. Commonweal 90:489 Ag 8 '69

ECKSTEIN, George
Black business, bleak business. Nation 209: 243-5 S 15 '69

ECKSTEIN, Max A. See Noah. H. J. jt. auth.

ECLIPSES
See also
Occultations

ECLIPSES, Solar
Available, total eclipse. A. Ewing. il Sci N 95: 484-5 My 17 '69
Eclipse survey for the Astronomical league. R. C. Maag. il Sky & Tel 39:28-30 Ja '70
Five Mayan eclipses in thirteen years. H. E. Harber. il Sky & Tel 37:72-4 F '69
In Siberia, an eclipse of the sun. Chem 42:5 F '69
Observations of the September solar eclipse. il Sky & Tel 38:351-2+ N '69
Observing Baily's beads at the March 7, 1970, eclipse. J. Bixby. il Sky & Tel 38:435 D '69
Secular accelerations of the earth and moon. R. R. Newton. bibliog il Science 166:825-31 N 14 '69
September's solar eclipse. il Sky & Tel 38: 161-2 S '69
Shadow-band experiment. R. D. Burgess and M. E. Hults. il Sky & Tel 38:95 Ag '69
Total solar eclipse of 7 March 1970. J. W. Stewart. bibliog il Weatherwise 22:100-6 Je '69
Travel and eclipse site guide for Mexico. il Sky & Tel 39:19-20 Ja '70
Weather prospects for next March's total eclipse. E. M. Brooks. il Sky & Tel 38:7-11 Jl '69

ECLIPSING stars. See Stars, Variable

ECOLOGICAL models
Biological oceanography: models; report of meeting. K. Banse and G. J. Paulik. Science 163:1362 Mr 21 '69

ECOLOGICAL research
Ecology: the new Jeremiahs. Time 94:38+ Ag 15 '69
New science tries to keep old balance. il Bsns W p64-5+ F 15 '69
Research void: Amazonia's confusion of life. C. Weathersbee. il Sci N 95:340-1 Ap 5 '69
See also
International biological program

ECOLOGY
Can man survive? J. A. Oliver. Parents Mag 44:40 Ag '69
Can man survive his environment? ed. by J. Mandelstam. il Sr Schol 95:2-3 O 27 '69
Can technology be humanized. in time? H. G. Rickover. il Nat Parks 43:4-7 Jl '69
Can we keep our planet habitable? symposium. bibliog il UNESCO Courier 22:4-40 Ja '69
Making economic aid effective: are we causing ecological harm? R. Cahn. Cur 104:41-5 F '69
Organic gardeners in the wilds. H. S. Buyukmihci. il Org Gard & Farm 16:56-8 F '69
Pesticide into pest. il Time 94:56-7 Jl 11 '69
Saving the world the ecologist's way. R. W. Stock. il N Y Times Mag p32-3+ O 5 '69
Some ecological benefits of woody plant control with herbicides. D. C. Barrons. bibliog il Science 165:465-8 Ag 1 '69; Discussion. 166:43, 310+, 1098 O 3, 17, N 28 '69
Strategy of ecosystem development; adaptation of address, August 1966. E. P. Odum. bibliog il Science 164:262-70 Ap 18 '69; Reply with rejoinder. R. P. McIntosh. 166: 403-4 O 17 '69
Unforeseen international ecologic boomerang; symposium. il Natur Hist 78:41-72 F '69
See also
Environment
Fishes—Ecology
Food chains (ecology)
Forest ecology
Fresh water ecology
Human ecology
Marine ecology
Paleoecology
Seashore ecology

Study and teaching
Ecology in the classroom: uniting the specialists. J. Potter. il Sci N 97:44-5 Ja 5 '70
Humanistic technology; excerpt from address, May 7, 1969. H. G. Rickover. il Am For 75:12+ Ag '69
See also
Nature study

California
Guarding the bay. P. Marshall. il Sci N 96: 102-3 Ag 2 '69

ECOLOGY—*Continued*

Canada

Task for ecologists around waterfalls in Labrador-Ungava. P. Kallio. bibliog il Science 166:1598-601 D 26 '69

Labrador

See Ecology—Canada

Latin America

Amazonia. C. Weathersbee. il Sci N 95:312-15, 338-41 Mr 29–Ap 5 '69

Underdeveloped areas

Development in the poor nations; how to avoid fouling the nest. L. J. Carter. Science 163:1046-8 Mr 7 '69

Side effects; report of a conference on ecological aspects of international development. H. Henkin. il Environ 11:28:35+ Ja '69

Vietnam

CW in Viet Nam? Defoliants and tear gas. il Sr Schol 94:7 F 7 '69

Deflowering process; fact sheet from clergy and laymen concerned on the herbicide war in Vietnam. J. Deedy. Commonweal 90:306 My 30 '69

Defoliation in Vietnam. F. H. Tschirley. bibliog Science 163:779-86 F 21 '69; Discussion. 164:373+ Ap 25 '69

Ravaging Vietnam. Nation 208:484-5 Ap 21 '69

What have we done to Vietnam? R. E. Cook and others. New Repub 162:18-21 Ja 10 '70

ECONOMETRIC models. See Economic models

ECONOMETRICS. See Economics, Mathematical

ECONOMIC and social council of the United Nations. See United Nations—Economic and social council

ECONOMIC assistance

Development: a balance sheet; address. November 20, 1968. W. S. Gaud. Dept State Bul 59:703-6 D 30 '68

See also

International bank for reconstruction and development

ECONOMIC assistance, American

Advice on foreign aid. America 120:86 Ja 25 '69

Allies for hire; Senate foreign relations subcommittee hearings on financial costs of Asian allies in Vietnam. New Repub 161:5-6 D 13 '69

Annual report on foreign assistance program transmitted to Congress; letter. January 15. 1969. L. B. Johnson. Dept State Bul 60:117 F 3 '69

Budget of the United States government fiscal year 1970; excerpts. L. B. Johnson. Dept State Bul 60:95-100 F 3 '69

Changes ahead in foreign aid? U S News 66:17 F 17 '69

Current effect of the American aid program; with questions and answers. W. S. Gaud. Ann Am Acad 384:73-84 Jl '69

Economic and military assistance proposals for fiscal year 1970; statement. House committee on foreign affairs on June 9, 1969. E. L. Richardson. Dept State Bul 60:569-74 Je 30 '69

Foreign aid: new ideas, less cash. U S News 66:8 Je 9 '69

Foreign aid program for fiscal year 1970: new directions in foreign aid; message to Congress, May 28, 1969. R. M. Nixon. Dept State Bul 60:515-19 Je 16 '69

Foreign-aid syndrome; NPA study. America 120:679-80 Je 14 '69

Foreign aid: the postwar record and targets for the 1970's; excerpts from A forward look at foreign aid. R. E. Asher. bibliog f il Mo Labor R 92:23-30 N '69

Foreign assistance program for fiscal year 1970; statement. July 14, 1969. W. P. Rogers. Dept State Bul 61:81-5 Ag 4 '69

Foreign policy aspects of the foreign aid program; statement. July 17, 1969. W. P. Rogers. Dept State Bul 61:116-19 Ag 11 '69

Guns for hire? cost of getting allies to commit troops to Vietnam. il Newsweek 74:26-7 D 15 '69

International liquidity and foreign aid. E. R. Fried. For Affairs 48:139-49 O '69

Making economic aid effective: are we causing ecological harm? R. Cahn. Cur 104:41-5 F '69

New look at the idea of foreign aid; National planning association statement. America 120:492 Ap 26 '69

New year's thoughts, 1969: prospects for progress and peace. E. Rabinowitch. Bul Atom Sci 25:2-4 Ja '69

Private enterprise and foreign aid. America 120:240-1 Mr 1 '69

Problems of impacted ghettos. N. Macrae. Cur 109:25-32 Ag '69

Who can afford our aid? Commonweal 89:665-6 F 28 '69

See also

United States—President's task force in international development

ECONOMIC assistance, British

Sniping at Springboks, a new British game. E. Huxley. Nat R 21:1265-6 D 16 '69

ECONOMIC assistance, Domestic

Fading peace dividend? D. P. Moynihan's statements. U S News 67:70-1 S 8 '69

Model city for Indian lands; Four Corners economic development region. il U S News 66:96-9 Je 23 '69

See also

Anti-poverty program, 1964-

Community development—United States

Community development corporations

Negative income tax

United States—Job corps

Volunteers in service to America

ECONOMIC assistance, French

Francozone Africa. K. Irvine. bibliog f Cur Hist 56:282-5+ My '69

ECONOMIC assistance, Swedish

Sweden's plans for future aid; excerpts from After Vietnam, Sweden makes plans. R. Dudman. Cur 109:61-4 Ag '69

ECONOMIC assistance, Taiwanese

Free China gives Africa a helping hand. O. K. Armstrong. il Read Digest 95:183-4+ N '69

ECONOMIC assistance in Africa

Free China gives Africa a helping hand. O. K. Armstrong. il Read Digest 95:183-4+ N '69

Sniping at Springboks, a new British game. E. Huxley. Nat R 21:1265-6 D 16 '69

ECONOMIC assistance in India

India: a giant country deep in trouble. J. N. Wallace. il U S News 66:77-80 F 17 '69

ECONOMIC assistance in Indonesia

Got ark: need Boston whaler; progress report on W. Sargent's project to save the Dyaks. Nat R 21:893 S 9 '69

Needed: an ark; Operation Dyak, project to aid head-hunters in Borneo. Nat R 21:581-2 Je 17 '69

ECONOMIC assistance in Latin America

Popolorum progressio; Vatican's initial contribution to the Popolorum progressio fund. G. de Zéndegui. Américas 21:1 Je '69

U.S. aid to Latin America; funding radical change. G. C. Lodge. For Affairs 47:735-49 Jl '69

What Nixon plan faces in Latin America. J. Benham. il U S News 67:42-4 N 24 '69

Who can afford our aid? Commonweal 89:665-6 F 28 '69

Why the Latins don't love us. il Life 67:28 Jl 18 '69

See also

Action for progress for the Americas

Alliance for progress

Inter-American development bank

ECONOMIC assistance in underdeveloped areas

At crisis point. il Time 94:41-2 O 10 '69

Businessmen and Operation Bootstrap; recommendations of the Committee for economic development. R. L. Tobin. Sat R 52:30 O 25 '69

Foreign aid: the battle rejoined; Pearson report. America 121:377 N 1 '69

How to stay the richest country in the world. J. H. Weaver. Commonweal 90:67-8 Ap 4 '69; Reply with rejoinder. P. G. Clark. 90:355+ Je 13 '69

It is only right; Pearson report. America 121:318-19 O 18 '69

One percent: the problem of economic aid; tr. by L. I. Dzirkals. L. Stepanov. bibliog f Ann Am Acad 386:41-53 N '69

Partnership stagnation: the Pearson report. Chr Cent 86:1338 O 22 '69

Technology and social change; adaptation of address. August 4, 1969. H. E. Hoelscher. bibliog Science 166:68-72 O 3 '69

Willing to help; World bank's Pearson report. Partners in development. H. Malmgren. New Repub 161:10-12 N 1 '69

World banking McNamara-style; aid to have-not lands. il Bsns W p96-8+ S 27 '69

ECONOMIC commission for Africa. See United Nations—Economic commission for Africa

ECONOMIC commission for Europe. See United Nations—Economic commission for Europe

ECONOMIC commission for Latin America. See United Nations—Economic commission for Latin America

ECONOMIC conditions
Business around the world. See issues of
U S news & World report
World economy; year of inflation. L. A.
Mayer. il Fortune 80:27-8+ Ag 15 '69
　See also
Business cycles
Business depression
Cost of living
Poverty
Standard of living
　also subhead Economic conditions under
names of countries, states, cities, e.g.
Brazil—Economic conditions
ECONOMIC consultants. See Business consultants
ECONOMIC cooperation. See International cooperation
ECONOMIC cycles. See Business cycles
ECONOMIC development
American challenge challenged; EEC, a threat
to U.S. business. J. B. Rhodes. il Harvard
Bsns R 47:45-57 S '69
Arrested development. Chr Cent 86:765 Je 4 '69
Birth control for economic development. S.
Enke. bibliog il Science 164:798-802 My 16
'69
Business trend now. il U S News 66:32-3 My
12 '69
Changing resource policies of the U.S.S.R.
T. Shabad. bibliog il Focus 19:7-8 F '69
Choice of technology in less developed countries; excerpt from address. N. Kaldor. Mo
Labor R 92:50-3 Ag '69
Development: a balance sheet; address, November 20, 1968. W. S. Gaud. Dept State
Bul 59:703-6 D 30 '68
Economy in the 1970's: what labor expects;
address, May 13, 1969. I. Stern. Vital
Speeches 35:531-4 Ag 1 '69
Ever-widening gap. P. M. S. Blackett. il Bul
Atom Sci 25:23-5 My '69
Feedbacks in economic and demographic
transition; adaptation of address, June 1969.
H. Fredericksen. bibliog il Science 166:837-
47 N 14 '69
Lessons of the 1960s. P. A. Samuelson. Newsweek 74:79 Jl 14 '69
Policy for orderly economic growth; address, March 5, 1969. P. W. McCracken. Vital Speeches 35:354-6 Ap 1 '69
Toward a new decade; excerpts from address,
July 14, 1969. Thant. America 121:57 Ag 2
'69
Trade, aid, and peace. L. B. Pearson. Sat R
52:23-6 F 22 '69
Where business stands now; after a half
century of growth. il U S News 66:70-1
My 26 '69
　See also
Industrial development programs
Underdeveloped areas
United States—Economic conditions
ECONOMIC education. See Economics—Study
and teaching
ECONOMIC forecasting. See Forecasts (economics)
ECONOMIC growth. See Economic development
ECONOMIC history
Economic history old and new. T. C. Cochran.
bibliog f Am Hist R 74:1561-72 Je '69
ECONOMIC models
Bad year for econometrics. il Bsns W p36-7+
D 20 '69
Computer and the economists: near unanimity; econometric model. Bsns W p26 My 31
'69
**Feedbacks in economic and demographic
transition; adaptation of address, June 1969.**
H. Fredriksen. bibliog il Science 166:837-47
N 14 '69
Inflation worries Wharton's computer. Bsns W
p34 Mr 8 '69
Wharton perceives a benign recession. il
Bsns W p35 N 22 '69
Wharton prints out its preview of 1970. Bsns
W p 14 Ag 30 '69
Why Nixon's advisers listen less to models.
Bsns W p 128+ N 15 '69
ECONOMIC opportunity, Office of. See United
States—Economic opportunity, Office of
ECONOMIC planning
　See also
National planning
ECONOMIC planning, International
　See also
European economic community
Inter-American economic and social council
United Nations—Economic and social council

ECONOMIC policy
Changing world trade patterns and America's
leadership role. R. F. Mikesell. Ann Am
Acad 384:35-44 Jl '69
　See also
Economic development
Industrialization
　also subhead Economic policy under
names of countries, e.g. United States—
Economic policy
ECONOMIC policy, Foreign. See International
economic relations
ECONOMIC policy, International. See International economic relations
ECONOMIC relations
　See also
Balance of payments
ECONOMIC research
Service economy grows, but does it? il Bsns
W p 126+ F 15 '69
　See also
Brookings institution
ECONOMIC security. See Social and economic
security
ECONOMIC statistics
When figures are stranger than fiction. il
Bsns W p42-4 O 4 '69
Where the money went; federal reserve system's flow-of-funds accounts. il Fortune 80:
159-60 Jl '69
　See also
Employment—Statistics
Market statistics
Unemployment—Statistics
ECONOMIC status
　See also
Students—Social and economic status
ECONOMIC surveys
　See also
Consumer surveys
ECONOMIC theory. See Economics
ECONOMIC zoology. See Zoology, Economic
ECONOMICS
Affluent society after ten years; introduction
to revised edition. J. K. Galbraith. Atlan
223:37-44 My '69
Classical look at the real cost of money;
price-interest rate relationship. il Bsns W
p 130-1 Je 28 '69
Economics in the news (cont) il Sr Schol
93:10-11 Ja 10; 94:19 Mr 7; 9-10 Mr 14; 17-18
Mr 21; 6-8+ Ap 11 '69
Great iconoclast has a shocking answer; M.
Friedman. Bsns W p82 Jl 19 '69
In defense of the new economics. J. Tobin.
Fortune 80:211-12 O '69; Reply. R. Harrod.
81:59 Ja '70
Lessons of the 1960s. P. A. Samuelson. Newsweek 74:79 Jl 14 '69
Time's Board of economists; symposium. il
Time 94:88-90 N 14 '69
Whatever happened to the new economics?
R. B. Du Boff. il Commonweal 91:94-8 O 24
'69; Reply. R. Eisner. 91:342-3 D 12 '69
Who's who among economists in the news.
il Sr Schol 94:12 Ja 31 '69
　See also
Business cycles
Commerce
Credit
Economic development
Economists
Employment
Free enterprise
Income
Supply and demand
Union for radical political economics
War—Economic aspects
Wealth, Distribution of

　　　History
　See also
Economic history

　　　Mathematical models
　See Economic models

　　　Philosophy
Outlook, three views: Keynesian, monetarist, and the cyclical. H. C. Wallich.
Newsweek 73:93 My 19 '69

　　　Study and teaching
Economics for elementary school pupils. R.
B. McKenzie. Ed Digest 35:44-7 S '69
Economics, good and bad. J. E. Maher. Clear
House 44:16-17 S '69
　See also
London school of economics and political
science

　　　Terminology
Getting on good terms with economics. Sr
Schol 94:25 Ja 31 '69
Poetic license for Potomac policymakers.
Bsns W p35 O 25 '69

ECONOMICS, Agricultural.   See Agriculture—Economic aspects

ECONOMICS, International.   See International economic relations

ECONOMICS, Mathematical
Bad year for econometrics. il Bsns W p36:7+ D 20 '69
Nobel laureates in economics, chemistry, and physics. L. R. Klein. il Science 166:715-17 N 7 '69
   See also
Economic models

ECONOMICS and politics
Nixon economy: four years of go-go or no-no for prosperity? il Sr Schol 94:10-11 Ja 31 '69

ECONOMIST (London)
Miracle in a mess; survey of the United States. il Newsweek 73:89 My 26 '69
Stiff upper lip over a massacre. P. Steinfels. Commonweal 91:350 D 19 '69

ECONOMISTS
Britain's economists; confused and confusing self-contradictory irresponsible, ignorant. S. Brittan. il Fortune 79:183-4 Ja '69; Correction. 79:67 Ap '69
Radicals try to rewrite the book; new left economists. il Bsns W p78-80+ S 27 '69
Stirrings from the new left. Time 95:66 Ja 12 '70
Who's who in economics. P. A. Samuelson. Newsweek 75:78 Ja 19 '70

ECONOMY in government.   See Government spending policy

ECOSYSTEMS. See Ecology

ECTOPLASM. See Psychical research

ECUADOR
   See also
Fishing—Ecuador
Galápagos Islands

ECUMENICAL movement
American churches in the ecumenical movement 1900-1968, by S. M. Cavert. Review Cath World 208:233 F '69 C. C. Wedel
Arizona Protestants, Catholics join hands. M. H. Walling. Chr Cent 86:724 My 21 '69
Black hatred at St Paul's. J. D. Douglas. Chr Today 13:35-6 F 14 '69
Cardinal Willebrands: a Dutchman in Rome. E. M. Jung. Cath World 210:27-31 O '69
Coming together, Texas-style; Texas conference of churches. Time 93:67 Mr 7 '69
Ecumenicalism: threat to Christian unity? J. A. Mackay. Chr Today 13:11-12 S 12 '69
Ecumenism between hope and despair. Chr Cent 86:1301 O 15 '69
Ecumenism: what is going wrong? Chr Today 13:22-3 Ag 1 '69
Ecumunity: a great new word. Chr Cent 86:1371 O 29 '69
Eyes upon Texas; state Conference of churches. Newsweek 73:113 Mr 17 '69
Flight from reality; excerpt from The ecumenical movement, whence? and whither? J. A. Mackay. Chr Today 13:14 Ja 31 '69
High ecumenical gestures and an even wider dialogue. America 120:123-4 F 1 '69
Middle East trends toward ecumenism. G. Fitch. Chr Cent 86:1461-2+ N 12 '69
NCC chief proposes general ecumenical council; with editorial comment. D. Kucharsky. Chr Today 14:22, 30-2 D 19 '69
NCC crisis: ecumenism at a Crossroads. D. Kucharsky. Chr Today 14:34 D 5 '69
Necessary ecumenism; with reply. R. McBrien. il Commonweal 91:145-9 O 31 '69
Never the Twain shall meet. D. Grumbach. Commonweal 89:616-18 F 14 '69
Return of the Protestant principle. M. Daly. Commonweal 90:338-41 Je 6 '69
Roman Catholic-Anglican dialogue; Permanent joint commission formed. America 121:407 N 8 '69
Texas goes all out for ecumenism. J. C. Evans. Chr Cent 86:366-7 Mr 19 '69
Too late for soundings. C. F. H. Henry. Chr Today 13:31-2 Mr 14 '69
Trends to intercommunion. C. J. Armbruster. America 121:455-6 N 15 '69; Discussion. 121: 575 D 15 '69
   See also
Church unity
Religious cooperation
World council of churches

EDDY, Alan
5½ years before the mast. il por Time 93: 40-1 F 7 '69

EDDY, Edward D.
Scratching the surface: campus unrest in 1968; adaptation of address, June 1968. Sch & Soc 97:16-18 Ja '69

EDDY, Gould
Man and his boat; Gould Eddy and Y Como. B. Crabtree. il Yachting 126:70-1+ D '69

EDDY, John Paul, and Zook, F. B.
Fee equalization for public higher education. Sch & Soc 97:443-4 N '69

EDELMAN, Edward
New financing tool. Am Ed 5:20 D '69

EDELMAN, Gerald Maurice
Deciphering a giant. Sci N 95:401-2 Ap 26 '69
Poetry: how and why. J. Jerome. Writers Digest 49:26+ Jl '69
—See Bennett. G. S. jt. auth.

EDELMAN, Peter
Mr and Mrs Peter Edelman. il por Vogue 153: 150-1 My '69

EDELSON, Edward. See Thomas, H. H; Weingold. A. B. jt. auths.

EDELSTEIN, J. M.
(comp) See Steinitz, K. T. Kate's writings; a selected bibliography

EDEMA
Hemoglobin as a tracer in hemodynamic pulmonary edema. G. G. Pietra and others. bibliog il Science 166:1643-6 D 26 '69

EDER, Richard
Spain is still afraid of itself. N Y Times Mag p23+ Mr 9 '69
(ed) See Paniker, S. What Spaniards say when they think aloud

EDGAR, Barry
Country and charming: Swiss inns. House & Gard 136:83-4+ O '69

EDGARTOWN, Mass.
Prelude to the season. H. B. Hough. il Travel & Camera 32:60-3+ Je '69

EDGERTON, Germeshausen and Grier, incorporated
Bombs for peace. il Forbes 104:71-2 S 15 '69

EDGERTON, William H.
Building costs. See issues of Architectural record

EDGETT, James Deyo
Moving a mobile America; interview. pors Nations Bsns 57:74-7+ F '69

EDGINGS, Garden. See Garden borders

EDIBLE greens. See Greens, Edible

EDINBURGH
Music
Report: operatic productions. G. Loney. Opera N 34:26 N 1 '69

EDINBURGH festival of music and drama. See International festival of music and drama. Edinburgh

EDINGER, Lois V. and Sand, Ole
Schools for the seventies and beyond. Todays Ed 58:74-5 S '69

EDISON, Charles
Obituary
Nat R 21:843 Ag 26 '69

EDISON, George R.
No other drug has this wide a group of hazards; excerpt from testimony before House select committee on crime, November 18, 1969. por U S News 67:24-5 D 29 '69

EDISON responsive environment. See Teaching machines

EDITH Henry shoes, incorporated
Miniskirts, maxi-heels. R. Levy. il Duns R 93:65-6 F '69

EDITING. See Editors and editing

EDITING amateur moving pictures. See Moving pictures, Amateur—Editing

EDITORS and editing
Editing a scientific encyclopedia. D. L. Sills. bibliog il Science 163:1169-75 Mr 14 '69
Making of anthologies. W. Cole. Writers Digest 49:48-52 Mr '69
Man across the desk. S. S. Vaughan. Writer 82:13-17 N '69
Not everyone likes dragons; a librarian-author's encounters with library periodical editors. C. E. Werkley. il Library J 94:4110-11 N 15 '69
Production editing at McGraw-Hill. V. Strauss. il Pub W 196:56-8+ O 6 '69
Real and the ideal editor; excerpts from address. C. Canfield. Pub W 195:24-7 Mr 31 '69
What do editors mean when they say... sorry, but, the motivation is missing. D. R. Koontz. il Writers Digest 49:42-7 Mr '69
Who'll do the work? from copy editor to freelancer. B. Lasky. Pub W 196:13-14 D 15 '69
   See also
International magazine conference

EDMAN, David
Committee folly. Chr Cent 86:1091-2 Ag 20 '69

EDMAN, K. A. P. See Cleworth, D. jt. auth.

EDMONDS. Anne C.
Library dedication conference. Mount Holyoke college. por Wilson Lib Bul 43:518 F '69

EDMONDS, Vaughan W. See Fertig. D. S. jt. auth.

EDMONDSON, Jan
On campus: summer on the hill. Mlle 69:104 O '69

EDMONTON, Alberta
Booming Edmonton, Alberta's surprise. il Sunset 143:49 Jl '69

Music
Report: Edmonton; production of Lucia di Lammermoor. J. W. Searchfield. Opera N 33:33 Mr 22 '69

EDMUNDS, Leland N. Jr, and Funch, R. R.
Circadian rhythm of cell division in euglena: effects of a random illumination regimen. bibliog Science 165:500-3 Ag 1 '69

EDSALL, Constance H.
Values and the poems of Marianne Moore. Engl J 58:516-18 Ap '69

EDSON, Lee
Jensenism, n. the theory that I.Q. is largely determined by the genes. N Y Times Mag p 10-11+ Ag 31; 14+ S 21; 72+ S 28 '69
Transplantation of the species. Esquire 72: 168-71+ D '69

EDUCATION
1970: education at the crossroads; symposium. il UNESCO Courier 23:4-32 Ja '70
Psychoanalysis and education. B. Bettelheim. Ed Digest 35:38-42 O '69

See also
Audio-visual instruction
Books and reading
College education
Communication in education
Culture
Educators
Elective system in education
Foreign study
Group work in education
Illiteracy
Intercultural education
Learning, Psychology of
Learning and scholarship
Liberal education
Libraries
Memory
Montessori method of education
Motivation (education)
Physical education and training
Psychology, Educational
Right to education
Self culture
Special classes and special schools
Study
Teaching
Telecommunication in education
also headings beginning Educational; School; also subhead Education under various subjects. e.g. Catholic church—Education; also Religious education; Scientific education; and similar headings

Aims and objectives
Accountability for results: a basic challenge for America's schools. L. M. Lessinger. Am Ed 5:2-4 Je '69
Appeal for agitators; reprint. H. Howe, 2d. Ed Digest 34:1-2 Ap '69
Can parents and teenagers negotiate? with study-discussion program, by C. Smallenburg and H. Smallenburg. D. B. Harris. bibliog il PTA Mag 63:2-5, 37 My '69
Contemporary concerns for the secondary school. J. Turano and E. T. Kelly. bibliog f Clear House 43:387-91 Mr '69
Contemporary education; a double view; address, December 1967. E. Mason. bibliog il Library J 94:4201-6 N 15 '69
Crisis in the high schools; the Life poll; with report by B. Hooper. L. Harris. il Life 66:22-35+ My 16 '69
Educated man in the year 2000; address, November 15, 1968. P. C. Ritterbush. Vital Speeches 35:295-300 Mr 1 '69
Education and the renaissance of state government; adaptation of address, January 9, 1968. J. E. Allen, jr. Sch & Soc 97:148-51 Mr '69
Education for the future. A. P. Ludka. il Sr Schol 93:Schol Teach 14-15 Ja 10 '69
Education professions development; investment in the future. D. Davies. il Am Ed 5:9-10 F '69
Education put to the question. P. Lengrand. il UNESCO Courier 23:27-31 Ja '70
English teachers in a world we never made; address. J. N. Hook. Engl J 58:185-92 F '69
Fiery vehemence of youth; with study-discussion program, by C. Smallenburg and H. Smallenburg. P. Marin. bibliog PTA Mag 63:15-17, 35 Je '69
Forecast for the 70's. H. G. Shane and J. G. Shane. Todays Ed 58:29-32 Ja '69

Gandhi's views on education; quotations. M. K. Gandhi. UNESCO Courier 22:30-2 O '69
Hook-up, plug in, connect; relevancy is all. C. F. Greiner. Engl J 58:23-9 Ja '69
Knowledge machine. E. C. Wilson. Ed Digest 34:1-5 F '69
Little bit of rebellion is good for the soul, and the school. A. A. Glatthorn. Seventeen 28: 324-5+ Ag '69
Middle class values, lower class rights. P. I. Freedman. bibliog Clear House 43:469-70 Ap '69
National assessment, what, why, how. Ed Digest 34:14-17 Ap '69
Our son is a campus radical. Anonymous. Read Digest 71:71-5 Ap '69
Pedagogian or anarchist? Educational change and the teacher. L. W. Kline. Clear House 43:527-9 My '69; Same abr. Ed Digest 35:16-18 N '69
Pride of workmanship. J. R. Dettre. Clear House 43:323-7 F '69
Prospectus on education; excerpts from address. R. Shuman. Clear House 44:67-71 O '69
Public school movement; phoenix or dodobird? R. Pratte. Ed Digest 35:1-4 D '69
Refresher course; new vistas for the methods prof. R. Whitworth. Clear House 43:436-8 Ap '69
Role of education in a changing world; address, April 9 and 11, 1969. L. C. Michelon. Vital Speeches 35:683-6 S 1 '69
Schools for the seventies and beyond. L. V. Edinger and O. Sand. Todays Ed 58:74-5 S '69
Special dimension to our responsibility. J. E. Allen, jr. Todays Ed 58:73 S '69
Student of tomorrow; towards a new global horizon. R. Habachi. il UNESCO Courier 23:16-20 Ja '70
Too much stress on college; annual report of the National advisory council on vocational education. il U S News 67:45-6 O 13 '69
Toward excellence? address, February 3, 1969. E. L. Harlacher. Vital Speeches 36: 691-5 S 1 '69
Vocational education in a new comprehensive system. M. Feldman. Todays Ed 58:47-8 N '69
What makes an effective high school, a principal gives his views. A. A. Glatthorn. Parents Mag 44:64-5+ S '69
World beyond the classroom. G. Bauer. Clear House 43:371-2 F '69

See also
College education—Aims and objectives
Educational sociology

Bibliography
Books for educators; U.S. and foreign. W. W. Brickman. Sch & Soc 97:301-2+, 501-2+ Sum, D '69
Book reviews. See issues of Clearing house
New books. J. Calam. See issues of Saturday review
New educational materials. See issues of Education digest
Outstanding education books of 1968; list prepared by Pi lambda theta. Todays Ed 58:59-60+ My '69
Second-class schools in a first-class power. I. Kraft. Nation 208:669-71 My 26 '69
Teacher's bookshelf (cont) Sr Schol 94:Schol Teach 30 My 2 '69

Economic aspects
See also
Colleges and universities—Finance

Exhibitions
Convention exhibit notes; NCSS, NCTE. W. Deering; D. L. Burleson. Sr Schol 93:Schol Teach 8 Ja 10 '69

Experimental methods
See Education, Experimental

Federal aid
See Federal aid to education

Finance
See School finance

History
1969 as a centennial year in the history of education. F. Parker. Sch & Soc 97:112-14 F '69
See also
Education—United States—History

EDUCATION—*Continued*

International aspects

Classroom tips from trips. R. C. Moscrip. il Todays Ed 58:20-4 S '69

International dimension of American education; remarks, June 26, 1969. E. L. Richardson. Dept State Bul 61:72-4 Jl 28 '69

Student to tomorrow; towards a new global horizon. R. Habachi. il UNESCO Courier 23:16-20 Ja '70

See also
Colleges and universities—International cooperation
International education

International cooperation

See also
Colleges and universities—International cooperation
Students, Interchange of

Laws

See School laws and legislation

Objectives

See Education—Aims and objectives

Organization by years

Are middle schools the answer? pro, con. S. P. Rollins; G. W. Ellis. il Sr Schol 94:Schol Teach 9-11 Mr 14 '69

Middle school. M. F. Compton. Ed Digest 34: 22-4 Ap '69

Middle school in practice. P. Brod. Clear House 43:530-2 My '69

Middle school in transition. A. H. Oestreich. Clear House 44:91-5 O '69

Middle schools in theory and in fact. il Ed Digest 35:26-8 S '69

Switching from junior high to middle school? J. Di Virgilio. Clear House 44:224-6 D '69

What about the middle school? M. T. Wilson; S. H. Popper. Todays Ed 58:52-4 N '69

What is a middle school? Conwell middle magnet school, Philadephia. M. T. Wilson. Clear House 44:9-11 S '69

Periodicals

Early educational journalists in America. C. L. Hall. Ed Digest 35:42-5 N '69

See also
American education (periodical)
School and society (periodical)

Philosophy

Educational essentialism thirty years after. G. Chambers. bibliog f Sch & Soc 97:14-16 Ja '69

Philosophy, educational philosophy, and the current crisis; excerpt from What is philosophy of education? C. J. Lucas. bibliog f Sch & Soc 97:180-6+ Mr '69

Students without teachers, by H. Taylor. Review
Sat R 52:60 Jl 19 '69. P. Woodring

Underachieving school, by J. Holt. Review
Sat R il 52:88-9 O 18 '69. G. B. Leonard

Research

See Educational research

Standards

More disruptions expected unless schools relate to students' needs. Sch & Soc 97:456-7 N '69

Pride of workmanship. J. R. Dettre. Clear House 43:323-7 F '69

See also
Committee on assessing the progress of education

Statistics

Magnitude of the American educational establishment, 1969-70. il Sat R 52:83 O 18 '69

Race between education & catastrophe. H. Brabyn. il UNESCO Courier 23:11-13 Ja '70

School outlook, autumn, 1969: changes, unrest. il U S News 67:36-8 S 8 '69

Statistic of the month. See Issues of American education

Statistical look at American education 1970. W. V. Grant. il Am Ed 5:24-5 O '69

What the public wants to know. W. D. Boutwell. PTA Mag 64:31 N '69

See also
School attendance

Terminology

Do you need a memo decoder? G. A. Silver. Ed Digest 35:31 D '69

Newer clichés in education. W. W. Brickman. Ed Digest 34:32-3 F '69

Africa

Educational progress in developing countries. Sch & Soc 97:119-20 F '69

Nairobi conference. R. Ochs. Ed Digest 34: 29-31 Mr '69

Nairobi conference on education in Africa. Sch & Soc 97:41-2 Ja '69

Strengthening teacher education. Sch & Soc 97:415 N '69

Appalachian Region

They stayed; Vista teachers in Appalachia. S. Crowell. il Am Ed 5:22-5 Ag '69

Arizona

Help for hang-ups: Alhambra and Tempe school districts. J. Stocker. il Am Ed 5:5-8 Je '69

Asia

Books and libraries in the Far East; address, June 24, 1968. D. Kaser. il Wilson Lib Bul 43:974-9 Je '69

Australia

See also
Private schools—Australia

Botswana

Teacher shortage in Botswana. R. Greenough. il Sch & Soc 97:386-8 O '69

California

Experiences with differentiated staffing; Fountain Valley school district. E. W. Beaubier. Todays Ed 58:56-7 Mr '69

Free choice; a voucher plan. R. Kirk. Nat R 21:598 Je 17 '69

Library study carrel; bilingual program with tutoring and self-pacing; Coalinga junior high school. R. E. Philips. il Library J 94: 840-2 F 15 '69

Reagan's revivalists; Board of education's morality report. Nation 208:685 Je 2 '69

San Ramon Valley: unified school district, Contra Costa County. J. McHenry. il ALA Bul 63:260-1 F '69

Schools and moral instruction. R. Kirk. Nat R 21:752 Jl 29 '69

Tuning in and turning on the nonverbals; summer English class at Marymount college. Palos Verdes estates, for Upward bound girls. B. L. Covey. il Am Ed 5:9-11 Je '69

Who's fit to teach; training and licensing bill. J. Featherstone. New Repub 161:19-21 D 13 '69

See also
Berkeley, Calif.—Education
Palo Alto, Calif.—Education

Canada

See also
Education—Ontario

Colombia

Don Quixote of the radio; Father Salcedo of Accion cultural popular; reprint. D. Behrman. il UNESCO Courier 22:73-4+ Ag '69

My teacher, the TV set. C. M. Fitch. il Américas 21:8-14 Mr '69

Colorado

See also
Denver—Education

Connecticut

Enfield's excited about living history; high school, Thompsonville. F. S. Gross. il Sr Schol 94:Schol Teach 13-14 My 9 '69

Lab-carts are rolling; Enfield program. F. S. Gross. il Schol Teach Sec Teach Sup p 14-15+ O 6 '69

School aid in Connecticut; parochial and other nonpublic schools. America 120:699 Je 21 '69

Set of attitudes; social studies laboratory at Enfield high school. K. Branan. Sat R 52:67 Ap 19 '69

Cuba

Moral economy of a revolutionary society. J. A. Kahl. bibliog il Trans-Action 6:30-7 Ap '69

New policies for Cuban education. G. H. Read. Sch & Soc 97:288 Sum '69

Recent developments in Cuban education. Sch & Soc 97:289-93 Sum '69

See also
Colleges and universities—Cuba

Denmark

See also
Private schools—Denmark

EDUCATION—*Continued*

District of Columbia
See Washington, D.C.—Education

England
See Education—Great Britain

Florida
Lottery; Pinellas County draw for kindergarten seats. il Newsweek 74:74 Ag 25 '69
See also
Broward County, Fla.—Education
Miami, Fla.—Education

Georgia
In Worth County. Nation 208:132 F 3 '69

Germany
History
Academic freedom and the Third Reich, can it happen here? L. L. Beall. Clear House 43:483-7 Ap '69

Germany (Federal Republic)
Foreign languages in Germany. Sch & Soc 97:389 O '69
Idea of Germany's Telekolleg, Bavarian television school. G. Mahlmann. il Sch & Soc 97:106 F '69

Great Britain
Britain's answer on mixed schools. il U S News 66:105 Ap 14 '69
Children want classrooms alive with chaos. B. Villet. il Life 66:50-2+ Ap 11 '69
New kind of school day. R. A. Sponberg. Ed Digest 34:46-8 Ap '69
Raging against reform. Time 94:42+ O 31 '69
Teaching English, the English way. B. Pollard. Engl J 58:586-90 Ap '69
See also
Adult education

Guatemala
Montessori in Guatemala. R. Bellak. il Sat R 52:47-9 Ag 16 '69

Haiti
Winds of change in Haitian education. G. P. Clark and D. Purcell. il Negro Hist Bul 32:7-10 O '69

Hong Kong
Education as enterprise in Hong Kong. G. S. C. Cheong. Sch & Soc 97:395-6+ O '69

Hungary
Three-dimensional history class in Hungary. P. Almasy. il UNESCO Courier 22:31 N '69

Iceland
Educational tradition and change in Iceland; excerpts from Education in Iceland. S. E. Fraser and B. S. Josephson. Sch & Soc 97:388-9 O '69

Illinois
House that Glenbrook built; student builders from two high schools. F. G. Weed. il Sr Schol 94:School Teach 12-13 Mr 21 '69
Reavis high school; Oak Lawn, Ill. R. Erbes. il Library J 94:4214-15 N 15 '69
See also
Chicago—Education

India
Blackboard satellite on a passage to India. il Bsns W p34-5 S 27 '69
Gandhi's views on education; quotations. M. K. Gandhi. UNESCO Courier 22:30-2 O '69
TV for India. J. McLaughlin. America 121:308+ O 11 '69

Indiana
Spohn: resource center, Hammond. J. Coleman and M. Liesse. il ALA Bul 63:266-7 F '69
See also
Indianapolis—Education

Iowa
Top EB library award goes to Iowa City schools. il Library J 94:1698+ Ap 15 '69

Iran
Iran's tent schools. il Todays Ed 58:62-3 Ja '69

Israel
Dilemmas in the process of educational administration in Israel. N. S. Glasman. bibliog f Sch & Soc 97:392-5 O '69

Italy
Transition and transformation: Italian education between fascism and democracy, 1943-45. G. L. Williams. bibliog Sch & Soc 97:390-2 O '69

Japan
See also
Colleges and universities—Japan

Kansas
Poetry made easy, in one week: high school English and journalism in McPherson. N. Tucker. il Sr Schol 94:Schol Teach 8+ F 14 '69

Kentucky
All's calm in the crow's nest; project for potential dropouts. J. B. Hicks. il Am Ed 5:9-10 O '69

Korea (Republic)
Helping meet the demand for knowledge. Sch & Soc 97:414-15 N '69

Latin America
Men of tomorrow. G. de Zéndegui. Américas 21:1 O '69
$7,600,000 for science and education development; multinational projects in Latin America. Américas 21:43 Ja '69

Long Island
See Education—New York (state)

Maine
Ambassadors report; Machias public schools. A. W. Dodd. il Sr Schol 94:Schol Teach 13 Mr 28 '69

Maryland
Bryant Woods: blueprint for flexibility, Columbia, Md. J. Freudenberger. il Library J 94:4225-7 N 15 '69
See also
Bethesda, Md.—Education

Massachusetts
Irony of early school reform, by B. Katz. Review
Sat R 52:71-2 Ap 19 '69. P. Lauter
See also
Boston—Education

Michigan
Michigan solons ponder reforms. Sat R 52:99 N 15 '69
Mount Clemens: high school resource center. E. Giambrone. il ALA Bul 63:262-5 F '69
Rambler Romney: the Edsel of politicians. J. Mahoney. Commonweal 89:546-7 Ja 31 '69
Schools and moral instruction. R. Kirk. Nat R 21:752 Jl 29 '69
See also
Detroit—Education

Middle East
Middle Eastern library workshop: report from Beirut. I. V. Hathorn. il Wilson Lib Bul 43:1002-7 Je '69

Mississippi
Chaos in public schools; the Mississippi story. il U S News 67:24-6 D 8 '69
Coming showdown in Mississippi. U S News 67:52 N 10 '69
Court, the schools, and the southern strategy. G. Orfield. Sat R 52:62+ D 20 '69
End of an era. il Time 95:14-16 Ja 19 '70
Integration plans delayed. America 121:148 S 13 '69
Mississippi: black and white together. il Newsweek 75:17-18 Ja 19 '70
Surrender in Mississippi. il Time 95:12 Ja 12 '70
TRB from Washington; ruling on desegregation. New Repub 161:8 N 8 '69
Time runs out in Mississippi. Time 94:24+ N 14 '69
Yes Virginia, there is a Constitution; Supreme court ruling for Mississippi districts. il Newsweek 74:35-7 N 10 '69
See also
Colleges and universities—Mississippi
Yazoo City, Miss.—Education

Missouri
See also
Kansas City, Mo.—Education
St Louis—Education

Nebraska
See also
Lincoln, Neb.—Education
Omaha, Neb.—Education

Nevada
See also
Las Vegas, Nev.—Education

EDUCATION—*Continued*

New Jersey

Is Title 1 worthwhile? remedial reading instruction; Sussex junior school. D. M. Callahan. Sr Schol 94:Schol Teach 17 My 2 '69
Where all the arts are lively. E. L. Raichle. il PTA Mag 63:27-8 Je '69

New York (state)

Hauppauge: senior high school. Long Island. H. Deutsch. il ALA Bul 63:257-60 F '69
Move to ban busing of pupils; New York state legislature bill. U S News 66:12 Ap 7 '69
Pin money conversion; Oak Drive elementary school. Plainview, N.Y. M. F. Boyd. il Library J 94:4228 N 15 '69
Students campaign to save school libraries; Mamaroneck, N.Y. Library J 94:4568 D 15 '69

See also
New York (city)—Education

Nigeria

School library workshop in Nigeria. E. D. Sinnette. il Wilson Lib Bul 43:997-1001 Je '69

North Carolina

[Harry Golden column; Christian academies] H. Golden. Nation 209:697 D 22 '69

Ohio

Secular schoolmen and Amish aims; excerpts from The old paths: a study of the Amish response to public schooling in Ohio. F. S. Buchanan. Sch & Soc 97:104-5 F '69
Vocational live-in; Mahoning Valley vocational school. R. C. Bixler. il Am Ed 5:7-9 Mr '69

See also
Cleveland—Education

Ontario

Dissociating religion and ethics; ending formal religious education in Ontario grade schools. A. Wice. Chr Today 13:35+ Ap 25 '69
Funding Catholic schools: a Canadian way. C. J. Matthews. America 121:231-2 S 27 '69

Oregon

Perils of pluralism: the background of the Pierce case. D. B. Tyack. bibliog f Am Hist R 74:74-98 O '68

See also
Portland, Ore.—Education

Pennsylvania

Bristol township schools: strategy for change; Intergroup education and sensitivity training programs. T. J. Cottle. il Sat R 52:70-1+ S 20 '69
PA. state education officials sued on ESEA-II administration. Library J 94:2034+ My 15 '69; Discussion. 94:3110+, 3769-70 S 15, O 15 '69

See also
Philadelphia—Education

Rhode Island

Semipublic school: Rhode Island study. R. F. Drinan. America 121:467-8 N 15 '69

Russia

Problem for the classless society: educational elite. Trans-Action 6:11 O '69

See also
Moscow—Education

South Africa

Current status of non-white education in South Africa. R. R. Ireland. bibliog f il Sch & Soc 97:381-6 O '69

Southern states

Politics of resegregation. G. Orfield. il Sat R 52:58-60+ S 20 '69
Reckoning postponed; orders to cut off federal aid to segregated Dixie school districts. Newsweek 73:21-2 F 10 '69
Report; southern desegregation. H. Leifermann. Atlan 223:12+ F '69
September song: a long, long time; resistance to integration. il Newsweek 74:23-4 S 15 '69
South's schools; still under fire. U S News 66:10 F 24 '69
Symbolic South; executive committee of the Leadership conference on civil rights meets with R. Finch. New Repub 160:12-13 Ap 5 '69

Tension on the guidelines. il Sat R 52:66 Ap 19 '69
Vanishing black principals and teachers in the South. Sch & Soc 97:470+ D '69

See also
Negroes—Education
Public schools—Desegregation

Sweden

See also
Colleges and universities—Sweden

Texas

TEA new brand of Texas education; Texas education agency. J. Egerton. il Am Ed 5:23-4 Je '69

Underdeveloped areas

Community schools in developing countries. Sch & Soc 97:169 Mr '69
Education: but for whom? And how? P. Rondiere. il UNESCO Courier 23:6-10 Ja '70

United States

Agnew: is a college degree necessary? excerpts from address, December 10, 1969. S. T. Agnew. U S News 67:14 D 22 '69
Appeal for agitators; reprint. H. Howe. 2d. Ed Digest 34:1-2 Ap '69
Crisis in city schools; interview. J. E. Allen, jr. il U S News 66:30-4 Je 30 '69
Critical issues in education. Sch & Soc 97:297-8 Sum '69
Dead end in American education. R. A. Freeman. Nat R 21:22-4 Ja 14 '69; Same abr. Ed Digest 34:9-12 My '69
Education for rural America. R. C. Stutz. PTA Mag 63:22-3 Mr '69
Education in America; ed. by P. Woodring and others. See issues of Saturday review
Education in 1968. W. W. Brickman. Sch & Soc 97:8-9 Ja '69
Educational problems in the United States; excerpts from address. E. Hendryson. PTA Mag 63:12-14 Ja '69
Great leap for education. P. B. Price. PTA Mag 64:20-1 N '69
Happenings in education. W. D. Boutwell. See issues of PTA magazine
How schools can get better teachers; interview. J. Koerner. U S News 67:48-51 S 15 '69
Impact of changing school enrollment. il U S News 66:54-5 Je 9 '69
Inequities between suburban and urban schools. A. Adkins. Ed Digest 34:50-1 F '69
International dimension of American education; remarks, June 26, 1969. E. L. Richardson. Dept State Bul 61:72-4 Jl 28 '69
Irrationalism and the new reformism. M. A. Raywid. Ed Digest 35:5-8 S '69
Knowledge machine. E. C. Wilson. Ed Digest 34:1-5 F '69
Middle school. M. F. Compton. Ed Digest 34:22-4 Ap '69
New Year's resolution to dispel myths in education. E. D. Doak. Clear House 43:288-90 Ja '69
News and trends. See issues of Today's education
Promising decade for education. Ed Digest 34:1-3 Ja '69
Reappraisal of the most controversial educational document of our time: Coleman report. C. Jencks. il N Y Times Mag p 12-13+ Ag 10 '69; Discussion. p74+ S 14; 12+ O 12 '69
School outlook, autumn, 1969; changes, unrest. il U S News 67:36-8 S 8 '69
Schools for the seventies and beyond. L. V. Edinger and O. Sand. Todays Ed 58:74-5 S '69
Schools make news. See issues of Saturday review
Schools vs. education; excerpt from Schooling and education. J. I. Goodlad. il Sat R 52:59-61+ Ap 19 '69
Second-class schools in a first-class power. I. Kraft. Nation 208:669-71 My 26 '69
Space race and the American educational system. il Sch & Soc 97:406-8 N '69
Underachieving school, by J. Holt. Review Sat R il 52:88-9 O 18 '69. G. B. Leonard
What's gone wrong in our big-city schools? il Changing T 23:43-7 Jl '69
When I look at American education . . . ; excerpts from statement, October 20, 1968. R. M. Nixon. Todays Ed 58:21-3 Ja '69
Who controls American education? by J. D. Koerner. Review
   Commonweal 90:122-4 Ap 11 '69. M. R. Berube

EDUCATION—United States—*Continued*
With education in Washington. See issues of
  Education digest
  See also
  Adult education
  Colleges and universities—United States
  Community schools
  Education—Southern states
  Education—Statistics
  Education and state
  Educational innovations
  Equalization, Educational
  High schools
  Indians of North America—Education
  Jews—Education
  Junior colleges
  Negroes—Education
  Private schools
  Public schools—United States
  Summer schools
  United States—Air force—Education
  Vocational education
    also subhead Education under names of
    cities, e.g. Philadelphia—Education

History
American textbook; an unscientific phe-
  nomenon, quality without control. W.
  Jovanovich. Am Scholar 38:227-39 Spr '69
Public schools: the myth of the melting pot;
  excerpt from Cobweb attitudes: essays in
  American education and culture. C. Greer.
  il Sat R 52:84-6+ N 15 '69

Vermont
Lamoille union high school: education for
  all; Hyde Park, Vt. C. L. Fortune, jr. il Sr
  Schol 94:Schol Teach 22:3 Mr 7 '69
EDUCATION, Adult. See Adult education
EDUCATION. Boards of. See School boards
EDUCATION, College. See College education
EDUCATION. Commissioner of. See United
  States—Education. Office of
EDUCATION, Comparative
How Russian schools compare with ours. M.
  Hope. il Parents Mag 44:56-7+ Ja '69
Toward a science of comparative education;
  excerpts. H. J. Noah and M. A. Eckstein.
  Sch & Soc 97:35-8 Ja '69
EDUCATION, Compensatory. See Compensa-
  tory education
EDUCATION, Compulsory. See Compulsory
  education
EDUCATION, Cooperative
Apprenticeship, vestal style. H. J. Donovan.
  Ed Digest 35:52-4 D '69
Piece of the action; work-study program
  L. P. Minear. il Am Ed 5:4-6 Mr '69
Schools & corporations: partners in Detroit.
  E. Logan. il Sr Schol 94:Schol Teach 14-15
  Mr 21 '69
Work-program college. D. Klein. il Seventeen
  28:112+ Ap '69
World of work; Lincoln learning center,
  Minneapolis, Minn. M. Tibbits. il Schol
  Teach Sec Teach Sup p 12+ S 22 '69
EDUCATION, Cost of. See School finance
EDUCATION. Distributive. See Distributive
  education
EDUCATION, Doctors of. See Degrees, Aca-
  demic
EDUCATION, Elementary
Where all is quiet in the schools. il U S News
  66:53-6 Ja 27 '69
  See also
  Education of children
  Montessori method of education
  School children
EDUCATION. Evaluation of. See Evaluation
  (education)
EDUCATION, Experimental
Building a career ladder; experimenting with
  methods and curriculum in Temple City
  schools. J. Connors. il Am Ed 5:15-17 F '69
Children want classrooms alive with chaos;
  British technique. B. Villet. il Life 66:50-
  2+ Ap 11 '69
Classroom tips from trips. R. C. Moscrip. il
  Todays Ed 58:20-4 S '69
Drew middle school: it shouts nontraditional,
  Miami, Fla. I. Solie. il Sr Schol 94:Schol
  Teach 20-1 My 9 '69
New kind of school day. R. A. Sponberg. Ed
  Digest 34:46-8 Ap '69
New sorts of institutions must be had; Si-
  mon's Rock: model for a new system. J.
  Steinberg. il Mile 69:262-3+ Ag '69
Reaching in; Bethesda school's experiment
  in free-form education. D. Leff. Seventeen
  29:84-5+ Ja '70

School where little kids teach the teachers;
  Far West laboratory for educational re-
  search and development, Berkeley, Calif.
  il Parents Mag 44:70-2 S '69
War in the classroom: mass media vs. educa-
  tion. L. Penfield. il Schol Teach Sec Teach
  Sup p 14-15+ S 22 '69
  See also
  College education, Experimental
  Progressive education
  Schools, Experimental
EDUCATION, Higher. See College education;
  Colleges and universities
EDUCATION, Individual. See Individual in-
  struction
EDUCATION. Liberal. See Liberal education
EDUCATION, Medieval
  See also
  Colleges and universities—Europe
EDUCATION, Moral. See Moral education
EDUCATION, Museum. See Museum education
EDUCATION, Office of. See United States—
  Education, Office of
EDUCATION. Professional. See Professional
  education
EDUCATION, Progressive. See Progressive
  education
EDUCATION, Rural
Big-school services for country kids. O.
  Bay and R. Black. il Farm J 93:22-3+ S '69
Education for rural America. R. C. Stutz.
  PTA Mag 63:22-3 Mr '69
EDUCATION, Secondary
Contemporary concerns for the secondary
  school. J. Turano and E. T. Kelly. bibliog
  f Clear House 43:387-91 Mr '69
High school graduate's reflections on sec-
  ondary education. E. Kaplan. Sch & Soc
  97:154-5 Mr '69
Secondary education: U.S.A. (cont) il Sr
  Schol 94:Schol Teach 30-1 Ja 17; 22-3 Mr 7;
  20-1 My 9 '69
Secondary school and occupational prepara-
  tion. R. N. Evans. Ed Digest 34:20-3 My '69
  See also
  High schools
  Private schools
EDUCATION, Technical. See Technical edu-
  cation
EDUCATION. Theological. See Theological edu-
  cation
EDUCATION, Urban
Crisis in city schools; interview. J. E. Allen,
  jr. il U S News 66:30-4 Je 30 '69
EDUCATION, Value of
Education put to the question. P. Lengrand.
  il UNESCO Courier 23:27-31 Ja '70
EDUCATION, Vocational. See Vocational edu-
  cation
EDUCATION and business. See Business and
  education
EDUCATION and democracy
  See also
  Citizenship, Education for
EDUCATION and economic problems. See
  School and social and economic problems
EDUCATION and industry. See Business and
  education
EDUCATION and manpower
Eye on tomorrow's jobs. G. Venn. il Am
  Ed 5:12-15 Mr '69
Search for uncommon people; address,
  November 18, 1968. W. Wiesman. Vital
  Speeches 35:215-18 Ja 15 '69
EDUCATION and politics. See Education and
  state
EDUCATION and social problems. See School
  and social and economic problems
EDUCATION and sociology. See Educational
  sociology
EDUCATION and state
Campus riots: limited U.S. crackdown; use
  of antiriot provisions of the 1968 Civil
  rights act. U S News 66:47 Mr 17 '69
Economics of inequality. D. K. Cohen. il
  Sat R 52:64-5+ Ap 19 '69
Education and the renaissance of state gov-
  ernment; adaptation of address, January
  9, 1968. J. E. Allen, jr. Sch & Soc 97:148-51
  Mr '69
Hidden bonus to education. W. B. Ball.
  Parents Mag 44:66-7+ Mr '69
Inequities between suburban and urban
  schools. A. Adkins. Ed Digest 34:50-1 F '69
Inequities of school finance. A. K. Camp-
  bell. Ed Digest 34:10-13 Ap '69
New guard takes over. J. Cass. Sat R 52:55
  Mr 15 '69
Nixon's crackdown on campus violence. il
  U S News 66:28-30 Mr 31 '69
Nonsectarian public parochial school. P.
  Jacobson. Chr Cent 86:769-74 Je 4 '69

EDUCATIONAL guidance—*Continued*
Role of education in a changing world; address, April 9 and 11, 1969. L. C. Michelon. Vital Speeches 35:683-6 S 1 '69
Teaching experience a must for counselors? C. W. Humes, jr. Clear House 44:245-8 D '69
See also
Personnel service in education
School children—Adjustment
Vocational guidance

EDUCATIONAL innovations
Change and the junior college; excerpt from Islands of innovation expanding. B. L. Johnson. bibliog f Sch & Soc 97:248-54 Ap '69
Characteristics for innovation. H. J. Eibler. bibliog f Clear House 43:523-6 My '69
Free enterprise teacher. P. H. Wagschal. Sch & Soc 97:228-30 Ap '69
How to stifle progress. J. M. Gray. Ed Digest 35:32-3 D '69
New directions for the American school; recommendations by the Research and policy committee. Sch & Soc 97:156-8 Mr '69
Pedagogian or anarchist? Educational change and the teacher. L. W. Kline. Clear House 43:527-9 My '69; Same abr. Ed Digest 35:16-18 N '69
Pressures for educational innovations. W. D. Boutwell. PTA Mag 63:13-14 Mr '69
Swinging with mini-projects; Bloomington, Minn. public school system. E. Cain and A. St Pierre. il Am Ed 5:5-8 D '69

EDUCATIONAL literature
See also
Publishers and publishing—Educational literature

EDUCATIONAL lobbyists. See Lobbyists

EDUCATIONAL materials. See Teaching—Aids and devices

EDUCATIONAL media personnel
Emerging role of the instructional materials specialist. W. H. King. Ed Digest 35:26-8 N '69

EDUCATIONAL organization. See School management and organization

EDUCATIONAL periodicals. See Education—Periodicals

EDUCATIONAL personnel training, Division of. See United States—Education. Office of—Educational personnel training. Division of

EDUCATIONAL philosophy. See Education—Philosophy

EDUCATIONAL planning
Power shift: policy formulation in transition. J. B. McAndrews. Clear House 44:161-3 N '69
See also
Educational innovations

EDUCATIONAL research
Education research: Academy cooperates in new venture. J. Welsh. Science 163:162+ Ja 10 '69
Federal control and basic research in education. J. M. Scandura. Sch & Soc 97:227-8 Ap '69
Ford grant for educational reform. Sch & Soc 97:90-1 F '69
How do we learn? excerpt from Schooling and education. J. I. Goodlad. il Sat R 52:74-5+ Je 21 '69
Language of research. S. Dobbs. Clear House 44:249-52 D '69
Research clues; questions and answers. See issues of Today's education
Research in name only. R. L. Armstrong. Clear House 43:298-300 Ja '69
U.S. Office of education: report on research projects. D. V. Gunderson. Engl J 58:611-13+ Ap '69
See also
American educational research association
Eric

EDUCATIONAL research council of America
Infiltrating the curriculum. T. Sheridan and D. L. Barlett. Nation 209:661-4 D 15 '69

EDUCATIONAL research council of Greater Cleveland. See Educational research council of America

EDUCATIONAL resource centers. See Instructional materials centers

EDUCATIONAL resources center, New Delhi, India. See New York (state)—Education. Department of—Center for international programs and services

EDUCATIONAL resources information center. See Eric

EDUCATIONAL secretaries. See School secretaries

EDUCATIONAL segregation. See Segregation in education

EDUCATIONAL service centers (proposed)
Educational service centers. W. R. Feezle. Ed Digest 35:52-4 O '69

EDUCATIONAL sociology
Public schools; a sociological perspective; address, July 8, 1969. D. W. Dodson. bibliog f Vital Speeches 35:686-91 S 1 '69
Social context and vocational education. R. A. Gibboney. bibliog f Sch & Soc 97:28-31 Ja '69
Some needed emphases in educational sociology. H. Putnam. bibliog f Sch & Soc 97:27-8 Ja '69
See also
College education—Aims and objectives
Education—Aims and objectives
School and social and economic problems
Socially handicapped children—Education

EDUCATIONAL standards. See Education—Standards

EDUCATIONAL statistics. See Education—Statistics

EDUCATIONAL study tours. See Travel study courses

EDUCATIONAL television. See Television in education

EDUCATIONAL television stations. See Television stations, Educational

EDUCATIONAL testing service
College boards: criticism of English test by Serge Lang. New Repub 160:8 My 24 '69
New undergraduate program; revision of the Institutional testing program of the Graduate record examinations. Sch & Soc 97:266 Sum '69
What affects learning? S. Holzman. Sr Schol 94:Schol Teach 4 Ap 25 '69
What's the IQ of the IQ tests. P. Pine. il Am Ed 5:2-4 N '69

EDUCATIONAL tests and measurements
Answer to Sally; multiple-choice tests. W. R. Link. Ed Digest 34:24-7 My '69
Guide for converting test scores. J. F. McNamara and E. D. Keyes. il Clear House 43:432-4 Mr '69
Reading programs; use of test data, a vital factor. W. S. Ames. il Clear House 43:515-18 My '69
Teacher-made test. B. Z. Bluestone and S. C. Ericksen. Ed Digest 35:22-5 O '69
Testing, testing .1. .2. .3. C. Buethe. Clear House 43:536-8 My '69
Tyranny of testing; excerpts from The underachieving school. J. Holt. il Parents Mag 44:60-1+ S '69
Utility of projective techniques and the function of the clinical psychologist; Rorschach test. J. L. Horn. Ment Hy 53:654-6 O '69
See also
Achievement tests
American college testing program
Aptitude tests
College entrance examination board—Scholastic aptitude test
Educational testing service
Intelligence tests

EDUCATIONAL toys. See Toys

EDUCATIONAL travel, Division of. See National education association—Division of educational travel

EDUCATIONAL workshops
Black studies Vatican; workshop on the black world at the Institute of the black world, Atlanta. il Newsweek 74:38 Ag 11 '69
High on teaching; summer workshop at the National college of education, Evanston, Ill. for selected high school students. M. Bonn. il Am Ed 5:5-7 N '69
Individualized in-service education; Kamehameha schools, Honolulu. L. L. Stillwell. il Todays Ed 58:44-5 D '69

EDUCATORS
Foreign languages and the educator. W. W. Brickman. Sch & Soc 97:136-7 Mr '69
Man's participatory evolution; psychoneurobiochemeducation. D. Krech. Cur 110:55-64 S '69
New breed in education. A. P. Salatino. Ed Digest 34:18-20 Ja '69
See also
College professors and instructors
Teachers

EDWARD VIII, king of Great Britain (abdicated 1936)
Reflections of a one-time Prince of Wales. pors McCalls 96:60-1+ Je '69

EDWARD II; drama. See Marlowe, C.

EDWARDS, Carl M.
Moisture problems in house walls and troubles with blistering and peeling paint. Consumer Bul 52:12-14 My '69
Step toward the plastic house; rigid vinyl house siding and accessories. Consumer Bul 52:14-16 Ap '69

EDWARDS, Clifford W.
From everyman to superman in Archibald Macleish. Cath World 210:165-9 Ja '70
Muhammad Ali on campus. Cath World 210: 69-73 N '69

EDWARDS, Clive A.
Soil pollutants and soil animals; with biographical sketch. Sci Am 220:12, 88-92+ Ap '69

EDWARDS, Harry. See Friedland, W. H; Scott, J. jt. auths.

EDWARDS, Mrs J. L.
Work; reprint. Hobbies 74:92 Ag '69

EDWARDS, John G.
Row-to-row carpeting in the garden. Org Gard & Farm 16:46-7 Ja '69

EDWARDS, L.
Build the PPFL. Pop Electr 31:68-70 Ag '69

EDWARDS, Leona
More than a mother. J. Robbins and J. Robbins. il Redbook 133:90-1+ My '69

EDWARDS, R. F.
Planning board sets the lot size. Am City 84: 90+ Mr '69

EDWARDS, Sherman
1776: creating the best of Broadway in a small-town public library. il por Wilson Lib Bul 43:1008-10 Je '69

EDWARDS, Virginia Lee
Story of Christmas. Américas 21:18-27 N '69

EDWARDS, Ward
Decision theory: guide to choice-making. il Time 93:80-1 Ap 18 '69

EELS
Eels take the prizes. G. Heinold. il Outdoor Life 144:54-5+ Ag '69

EFF, Johannes
Dandruff is a hard thing to get rid of: poem. Nat R 21:118 F 11 '69
Long live John Quixote de la Mancha! poem. Nat R 51:1112 N 4 '69
Moon landing at Harvard; poem. Nat R 21: 647 Jl 1 '69
Styx ball down by the river; poem. Nat R 21:437 My 6 '69

EFFICIENCY, Administrative
Using incentives to improve the effectiveness of government. C. L. Schultze. Mo Labor R 92:34-8 S '69

EFFICIENCY, Agricultural. See Farm management

EFFICIENCY, Industrial
Dry rot: the most elusive enemy. G. J. Berkwitt. il Duns R 94:57-9 O '69
Efficiency as a prod to social action; excerpt from address. K. B. Clark. Mo Labor R 92: 54-6 Ag '69
Ten most wanted men: the worker; address, March 14, 1969. K. M. Flake. Vital Speeches 35:441-4 My 1 '69
See also
Executive ability
Labor productivity
Schedules

EFFICIENCY experts. See Business consultants

EFFIGY MOUNDS NATIONAL MONUMENT
Effigy mounds. R. W. Meyer. il Nat Parks 43:4-7 Je '69

EFTIHIADES, Theodore D.
Community meetings in a prison setting. Ment Hy 53:289-94 Ap '69

EGAN, Dona
Great stork race. Good H 168:28+ F '69

EGAN, Edmund J.
[Book review] Commonweal 90:149-50 Ap 18 '69

EGAN, Ferol
Jornada del muerto; adaptation from The el dorado trail. bibliog Am West 6:12-19+ Jl '69
Twilight of the California. Am West 6:34-42 Mr '69

EGAN, James
How to speak real estatese. McCalls 96:98 Ap '69
Passionate skier. Sat R 52:42-4 D 27 '69
Spring in Sicily. Sat R 52:48+ Ap 12 '69
(ed) See Johnson. C. A. T. My life-after the White House

EGAÑA, Juan
Juan Egaña's Pan American dream. R. Silva Castro. il por Américas 21:28-32 Ap '69

EGEBERG, Roger Olaf
Curious case of Dr Knowles. il por Time 94: 12-13 Jl 4 '69
Egeberg for Knowles. por Sci N 96:27 Jl 12 '69

EGERTON, John
TEA new brand of Texas education. Am Ed 5:23-4 Je '69
about
State universities: report terms desegregation largely token. B. Nelson. Science 164: 1155-6 Je 6 '69

EGG decoration. See Easter eggs
EGG laying. See Oviposition
EGG production. See Poultry—Egg production

EGG shells
Dieldrin and DDT: effects on sparrow hawk eggshells and reproduction. R. D. Porter and S. N. Wiemeyer. bibliog il Science 165: 199-200 Jl 11 '69

EGG white
Conductivity and photoconductivity in egg white. G. M. Spruch and C. Peskin. bibliog il Science 163:1350-1 Mr 21 '69

EGGERS, Paul W.
Slicing the federal tax pie; interview. pors Nations Bsns 57:23-6 D '69

EGGLER, Bruce W.
Long way to go in Mississippi. New Repub 160:19-21 Je 28 '69
Plaquemines without the great white father. New Repub 160:11-12 My 24 '69
That old-time religion. New Repub 161:15-17 O 11 '69

EGGPLANT
See also
Cookery—Vegetables

EGGS
See also
Cookery—Eggs
Easter eggs
Embryology
Poultry—Egg production

EGGS, Fossil
Australia's embarrassing egg; football-sized bird's egg in Perth museum. H. Butler. il Sci Digest 65:70-3 Mr '69

EGGSHELLS. See Egg shells

EGLEVSKY, Marina
Dancers of dancing parents. M. Marks. il pors Dance Mag 43:65-8 Ja '69

EGOISM
See also
Self love

EGYPT
See also
Alexandria
Cairo
Petroleum industry and trade—Egypt
Qantara
Red Sea
Sinai (peninsula)
Suez Canal
United Arab Republic

Antiquities

Imhotep; seeking the tomb of Pharaoh Zoser's grand vizier. L. Casson. il Horizon 11:92-101 Sum '69
See also
Abu Simbel, Temples of

Description and travel

Tomorrow the apricots will bloom. D. Holden. il Holiday 46:34-5+ N '69

Economic conditions

Egyptians to Nasser: make war or make peace or get out! J. Law. il U S News 66: 56-7 Mr 24 '69
In Cairo: threats of war but business better than usual. il U S News 67:39-40 Jl 7 '69
Oil may soothe Egypt's wounds. il Bsns W p89+ Je 28 '69

Foreign relations

Israel

Shells across Suez. il Time 93:24+ Mr 21 '69
Talk with President Nasser; interview, ed. by A. de Borchgrave. G. A. Nasser. il Newsweek 73:33-4+ F 10 '69
Training for Armageddon. il Newsweek 73: 49 Mr 24 '69

Russia

Tension: Nasser and the Russians. A. de Borchgrave. Newsweek 74:89 O 6 '69

History

Saladin, the complete Mohammedan. P. W. Schmidtchen. il Hobbies 74:134-6 O '69

Ancient to 640 A.D.

Black emperor who saved Jerusalem: Pharaoh Taharqa. M. H. Levine. il Negro Hist Bul 32:19-20 My '69

Kings and rulers
See also
Pharaohs

EGYPT—*Continued*

Politics and government

Egyptians to Nasser: make war or make peace or get out! J. Law. il U S News 66: 56-7 Mr 24 '69

Nasser's risky role in the Middle East. il Time 93:29-30+ My 16 '69

Rumblings out of Cairo. il Newsweek 74:49 S 29 '69

Tension: Nasser and the Russians. A. de Borchgrave. Newsweek 74:89 O 6 '69

EGYPTIAN magic. See Magic

EGYPTIAN onions. See Onions

EGYPTIAN poetry

Translations into English

Two Songs of heart's ease: translated from the ancient Egyptian. J. L. Foster. Poetry 114:176-8 Je '69

EHLE, Robert C.
Make your own electronic music. Radio-Electr 40:52-4+ My '69

Plain and easy guide to practical electronic music. Hi Fi 19:50-3+ Ag '69

EHRENHAFT, George
Combatting apathy: literature and the general class. Engl J 58:840-6 S '69

EHRLICH, Paul R.
Countdown to disaster. Cur 103:62-4 Ja '69

Eco-catastrophe! Ramp Mag 8:24-8 S '69; Same abr. with title Our plundered planet; the end of the oceans. Cur 111:23-32 O '69

Overcrowding and us. Nat Parks 43:10-12 Ap '69

World population: is the battle lost? Read Digest 94:137-40 F '69

—and Raven, P. H.
Differentiation of populations. bibliog Science 165:1228-32 S 19 '69

EHRLICHMAN, John D.
Ehrlichman; the troubleshooter. R. B. Semple, jr. il N Y Times Mag p54+ Ag 3 '69

Mr Nixon's honest broker. por Newsweek 75:19-20 Ja 19 '70

Praetorians. il por Newsweek 74:36+ Jl 28 '69

Struggle for neatness. J. Osborne. New Repub 161:14-15 N 22 '69

Three in bloom. H. Brandon. Sat R 52:8 Ag 2 '69

Traffic cop. il por Newsweek 74:50 N 17 '69

White House who's who. J. Osborne. New Repub 161:13-15 O 18 '69

EIBLER, Herbert J.
Characteristics for innovation. bibliog f Clear House 43:523-6 My '69

EICHEL, Bertram, and Shahrik, H. A.
Tobacco smoke toxicity: loss of human oral leukocyte function and fluid-cell metabolism. bibliog Science 166:1424-8 D 12 '69

EICHENAUER, Harry
Nuisance-free sludge disposal. Am City 84: 116-17 F '69

EICHENWALD, Heinz F. and Fry, P. C.
Nutrition and learning. bibliog Science 163: 644-8; 165:313 F 14, Jl 18 '69

EICHHORN, Noel D. See Darling, F. F. jt. auth.

EICHMANN, Adolf
I was only following orders. Trans-Action 6: 7-8 My '69

EIDETIC imagery
Eidetic images. R. N. Haber. il Sci Am 220: 36-44 Ap '69

EIDT, Mary B. and Alwood, R. C.
Man, the creative artist: an experiment. Engl J 58:87-9 Ja '69

EIGHTEEN hundred and fifty-seven
1857. O. Jensen. il Am heritage 21:81-96 D '69

EIGHTEEN-nation committee on disarmament.
See United Nations—Eighteen-nation committee on disarmament

EIGHTEENTH century
See also
Enlightenment

EIGHTFOLD way (nuclear physics) See Particles (nuclear physics)

EIGHTS week races. See Rowing

EIGNER, E. A. See Loftfield, R. B. jt. auth.

EIGNER, Larry
Three poems; Strength of a wing; Dangerous; Air. Poetry 113:256-8 Ja '69

292; poem. Poetry 115:105 N '69

about

Comment. B. Berkson. Poetry 114:259 Jl '69

I like to (B)eat people up. A. Hoyem. Poetry 113:427-8 Mr '69

EILENBERGER, Robert F.
Decorating with coils. Ceram Mo 17:20-2 My '69

Hollow-built sculpture. Ceram Mo 17:25-8 Mr '69

Water whistle sculpture. Ceram Mo 17:16-19 F '69

EILERS, Hazel Kraft
At the sign of the crest. See issues of Hobbies

EIMERIA tenella. See Coccidia

EIMON, Pan Dodd
(ed) City tells its story. See issues of American city

EINBINDER, Harvey
International encyclopedia of the social sciences. por Library J 94:1592-4 Ap 15 '69

EINSTEIN theory. See Relativity (physics)

EINSTEIN'S theory of gravity. See Gravitation

EIRE. See Ireland

EISELEY, Loren
Activism and the rejection of history; excerpt from The unexpected universe. Science 165:129 Jl 11 '69

Innocent fox; excerpt from The unexpected universe; with biographical sketch. por Natur Hist 78:4, 10-12+ O '69

Man in a web; excerpts from The unexpected universe. Read Digest 95:116-18 D '69

about

Of skulls, spiders and small libraries. C. E. Werkley. bibliog il pors Wilson Lib Bul 44: 188-96 O '69

EISEMAN, Robert C.
Preventive maintenance. Yachting 126:70-1+ Ag '69

EISEN, Jonathan
Dukes up. New Repub 160:36+ Je 14 '69

Hippie weltanschauung. Cath World 209:44+ Ap '69

—and Steinberg, David
Student revolt against liberalism. bibliog f Ann Am Acad 382:83-94 Mr '69; Same abr. with title Revolt against liberalism. Cur 108:11-14 Je '69

EISENBERG, Arlene, and Eisenberg, Howard
Dangerous new cult of scientology. Parents Mag 44:48-9+ Je '69

EISENBERG, Howard. See Eisenberg, A. jt. auth.

EISENBERG, Lucy
What's new in medicine. McCalls 96:34+ Ja '69

EISENDRATH, David B. Jr
Color clinic. See issues of Popular photography

EISENFELD, Arnold J. See Stern, J. M. jt. auth.

EISENHART, Willy
Boston museum of fine arts. 1870-1970. Art N 68:34-47+ S '69

EISENHOWER, David
David Eisenhower on his own generation; interview. ed. by C. Karpel. il por Look 33: 14 F 18 '69

about

At home with Julie and David. N. Moran. il pors McCalls 96:66-7+ Je '69

EISENHOWER, Dwight David
Day I knew I belonged to the flag. Read Digest 94:93 Mr '69

Eisenhower's America: historic interview; reprint of March 28, 1952 issue. por U S News 66:65-7 Ap 14 '69

From Eisenhower's speeches and writings. Sr Schol 94:13 Ap 11 '69

We must avoid the perils of extremism. Read Digest 94:103-8 Ap '69

about

Dwight D. Eisenhower, 1890-1969. il pors Newsweek 73:18-21 Ap 7 '69

Dwight David Eisenhower; eulogy, March 30, 1969. R. M. Nixon. Vital Speeches 35:386-7 Ap 15 '69; Same abr. with title He came from the heart of America. Read Digest 94:87-90 Je '69

Dwight David Eisenhower: ranking an ex-President. J. Leo. Commonweal 90:95-6 Ap 11 '69

Eisenhower. Nation 208:418+ Ap 7 '69

Eisenhower: a lifetime of public service; with quotations. il pors Sr Schol 94:12, 14 Ap 11 '69

Eisenhower era in Asia. A. J. Cottrell. bibliog f Cur Hist 57:84-7+ Ag '69

Eisenhower era: transition years for science. J. Walsh. Science 164:50-3 Ap 4 '69

Eisenhower era; with excerpts from Public law 7, passed by Congress, March 9, 1957. J. A. Huston. bibliog f Cur Hist 57:24-30+. 49-50 Jl '69

EISENHOWER, Dwight David—about—*Cont.*
Eisenhower legacy. N. Cousins. Sat R 52:
30+ Ap 12 '69
Eisenhower: soldier of peace. il pors Time
93:19-25 Ap 4 '69
Eisenhower story. H. La Fay. il pors Nat
Geog 136:1-39 Jl '69
Eisenhower's forgotten tragedy. Chr Cent 86:
467 Ap 9 '69
Eisenhower's two careers; with photo report.
U S News 66:83-6 Ap 7 '69
Farewell to the faithful servant; reprint. D.
Lawrence. U S News 66:96 Ap 7 '69
Fateful friendship. S. E. Ambrose. il pors
Am Heritage 20:40-1+ Ap '69
First verdict; opinions of leading historians.
Time 93:24 Ap 4 '69
Five-star humanity marches on. H. J.
Sievers. America 120:441 Ap 12 '69
For Eisenhower: an operation, then pneu-
monia; record of illnesses and operations.
por U S News 66:3 Mr 10 '69
Greatness in a time of tempest. Chr Today
13:26 Ap 11 '69
Ike. Sports Illus 30:11-12+ Ap 7 '69
Ike, the conservationist. C. Davis. il pors
Am For 75:28-9+ Je '69
Ike the honest. New Repub 160:10 Ap 12 '69
Ike: the last years of a great American.
B. Hibbs. il por Read Digest 95:111-16 Jl
'69
Ike's biggest battle. Time 93:19 Mr 7 '69
Ike's faith. E. E. Plowman. Chr Today 13:
33 Ap 25 '69
Legacy of General Eisenhower. America 120:
442 Ap 12 '69
Notes and comment. New Yorker 45:27 Ap 5
'69
Obituary
Nat R 21:374-5 Ap 22 '69
U S News por 66:14 Ap 7 '69
On the way: new Eisenhower dollar. il U S
News 67:10 O 27 '69
Reporter remembers the political Ike. K.
Crawford. il por Newsweek 73:25 Ap 7 '69
Soldier to the last. il pors Newsweek 73:22-
4+ Ap 7 '69
This was Eisenhower, 1890-1969. il pors Life
66:53-8 Ap 4 '69
Top general's rebuttal to attacks on military;
excerpts from address, May 17, 1969. E. G.
Wheeler. por U S News 66:14 Je 9 '69
Tributes to President Dwight D. Eisenhower.
Thant. UN Mo Chron 6:62 Ap '69

Funeral rites and ceremonies
Dwight David Eisenhower; eulogy, March 30,
1969. R. M. Nixon. Vital Speeches 35:386-7
Ap 15 '69
Farewell to Eisenhower. il U S News 66:68-
9 Ap 14 '69
Flags in the rain. S. Alexander. Life 66:4
Ap 11 '69
Home to Abilene. D. Nevin. il pors Life
66:24-35 Ap 11 '69
Home to the heartland. il Time 93:26-7 Ap
11 '69
Ike returns to the heart of America. il News-
week 73:38-43 Ap 14 '69
World's last salute to a great American. W.
Graves and others. il por Nat Geog 136:40-
51 Jl '69

Religion
Religion of a president. M. Gustafson. Chr
Cent 86:610-13 Ap 30 '69; Reply. F. Fox. 86:
907 Jl 2 '69
EISENHOWER, Dwight David, 2d. See Eisen-
hower. D.
EISENHOWER, Dwight David, library. See
Dwight David Eisenhower library, Abilene,
Kan.
EISENHOWER, John Sheldon Doud
His father's voice. por Time 93:76-8 Ja 31 '69
EISENHOWER, Julie (Nixon)
At home with Julie and David. N. Moran.
il pors McCalls 96:66-7+ Je '69
Capital idea. Newsweek 74:30-1 Jl 21 '69
Let's travel with Mrs Nixon and Julie. F.
Koltun. il pors Mlle 69:110-11 S '69
President's daughters: they also serve. il pors
Newsweek 74:46-8 D 8 '69
Why Julie is the happiest Nixon. N. Robert-
son. il por Good H 168:76-7+ Je '69
EISENHOWER, Mamie Geneva (Doud)
Faith of Mamie Eisenhower. E. L. R. Elson.
McCalls 96:44+ Jl '69
EISENHOWER, Milton Stover
If crime goes unchecked, what big cities will
be like; excerpts from statement, Novem-
ber 24, 1969. por U S News 67:41-2 D 8 '69
EISENHOWER exchange fellowships. See
Scholarships and fellowships

EISENSTAEDT, Alfred
After Bernstein who? photographs. Life 66:
42-51 F 21 '69
Eye of Eisenstaedt; excerpts. Mod Phot
33:62-7 Ag '69
about
Eisenstaedt: a snapshot. A. Goldsmith. il
Travel & Camera 32:78-32+ Jl '69
Eye of Eisenstaedt. M. R. Weiss. il Sat R
53:13-15 Ag 2 '69
EISNER, Thomas, and others
Ultraviolet video-viewing; the television
camera as an insect eye. Science 166:1172-4
N 28 '69
—See Pliske, T. E; Silberglied. R. E. jt.
auths.
EISSLER, K. R.
Fortinbras and Hamlet. bibliog Am Imago
25:199-223 Fall '68
EJECTION devices (airplanes). See Airplanes
—Escape devices
EK, Niklas
Sweden: theatre child. M. Kats. il por Dance
Mag 43:49-50 My '69
EKMAN, Paul, and others
Pan-cultural elements in facial displays of
emotion. bibliog Science 164:86-8 Ap 4 '69
EKTACHROME films. See Photography—
Films
EL AL Israel airlines. See Airlines—Israel
ELANDS. See Antelopes
ELASTIC waves
Maser amplification of 9.5-gigahertz elastic
waves in sapphire doped with divalent nickel
impurity ions. P. D. Peterson and E. H.
Jacobsen. bibliog il Science 164:1065-7 My
30 '69
ELASTICITY
Elastic coefficients of animal bone. S. B.
Lang. bibliog il Science 165:287-8 Jl 18 '69
See also
Elastic waves
Plasticity
ELASTOMERS
Control of vibration and noise. T. P. Yin. il
Sci Am 220:98-106 Ja '69
EL-BAZ, Farouk. See Baz, F.
ELBRICK, Charles Burke, kidnapping case
Brazil: hardship post. Time 94:35 D 19 '69
Incident on Marquis street. por Newsweek
74:45 S 15 '69
Kidnaping, a power shift, headaches for
U.S. Brazil. por U S News 67:10 S 15 '69
Ransom for a U.S. ambassador. il por Time
94:18 S 12 '69
Terror's toll. por Newsweek 74:52-3 S 22
'69
ELDER, Lee
Lee Elder, hottest sophomore in pro golf.
L. Robinson. il pors Ebony 24:60-4 S '69
ELDER, Lonne, 3d
Ceremonies in dark old men. Criticism
Life 66:14 Ap 4 '69
Nation 208:253 F 24 '69
New Yorker 41:90+ F 15 '69
Sat R 52:29 F 22 '69
Time 93:62 F 14 '69
Vogue 153:32 Ap 15 '69
ELDER
Meet the elders. J. Plewes. il Org Gard &
Farm 16:66-7 Ag '69
ELDERBERRIES
Meet the elders. J. Plewes. il Org Gard &
Farm 16:66-7 Ag '69
ELDRED, Leonard J.
Rare woods from old trees. Org Gard & Farm
16:88-90 S '69
ELDRIDGE, Frank
El Dorado beach project. Cons 24:6-8 O '69
ELEANOR of Aquitaine, consort of Henry II,
king of England
This medieval winter. H. S. Hughes. Amer-
ica 120:156-8 F 8 '69; Discussion. 120:290 Mr
15 '69
ELECTION (theology)
Karl Barth on election. R. M. Brown. Chr
Cent 86:405-7 Mr 26 '69
ELECTION districts
See also
Apportionment (election law)
ELECTION expenses. See Campaign funds
ELECTION forecasts. See Political forecasts
ELECTION frauds. See Elections—Currupt
practices
ELECTION laws
See also
Literacy tests (election law)
Voters, Registration of

ELECTION laws—*Continued*

United States

Debt to Dixie: proposal to withdraw Voting rights act of 1965. il Newsweek 74:23-4 Jl 14 '69

Electoral college reform. C. Joyner and D. Anderson. America 120:401-2 Ap 5 '69

For voters: end to literacy tests everywhere in U.S? il U S News 67:32+ Jl 7 '69

National mood; the Administration and the Voting rights act of 1965. New Repub 161: 10-11 Jl 12 '69

New approach to voting rights. U S News 67:10 D 22 '69

New left and the electoral college. F. A. Picó. America 120:252-4 Mr 1 '69; Reply. L. W. Belter. 120:378-9 Ap 5 '69

One of those weeks; proposal to withdraw 1965 voting rights act. Newsweek 74:16-17 Jl 7 '69

Right to vote; section V of the Voting rights act of '65. New Repub 162:8-9 Ja 3 '70

This month's feature: Congress and voting rights controversy. Cong Digest 48:257-88 N '69

Voting rights. Time 94:16 Jl 11 '69

Voting rights in danger; Act of 1965. America 121:626 D 27 '69

Voting rights, or wrongs? proposed changes in 1965 voting rights act. il Newsweek 74: 19-20 D 22 '69

ELECTIONS

Four elections; their meaning. il U S News 67:12 N 10 '69

See also
Political campaigns
Referendum

Corrupt practices

Battle against vote fraud; Operation Integrity. L. B. Nichols. Read Digest 93:37-43 Jl '69; Same. U S News 67:72-4 Ag 25 '69

Punch-card voting may have a hole in it; back-room jugglers could change computerized ballot count. il Bsns W p38 Jl 19 '69

Australia

Rebuke to a high flyer. Time 94:42 N 7 '69

Brazil

New president: medium-hard. il Time 94:33-4 O 31 '69

Chile

Fading romance. Newsweek 73:59-60 Mr 17 '69

Frei's revolution in suspended animation. D. D. Ranstead. Commonweal 90:190-1 My 2 '69

Swing to the right. Time 93:44 Mr 14 '69

France

Gaullism without de Gaulle. R. Bosc. America 121:13-15 Jl 5 '69

Letter from Paris; runoff of its presidential elections. Genêt. New Yorker 45:98+ Je 14 '69

Nation in miniature; how Briare will vote April 27. il Time 93:32+ Ap 25 '69

Outlook for France: new kind of Gaullism. U S News 66:16 Je 16 '69

Painful event; by-election in les Yvelines. il Newsweek 74:56+ N 10 '69

Pom-pi-dou, Pom-pi-dou; first-round. Newsweek 73:44+ Je 16 '69

Round 1 to choose France's president. il Time 93:35 Je 6 '69

Without de Gaulle, France goes for his disciple. il Life 66:32-3 Je 13 '69

Germany (Federal Republic)

Brandt on the threshold. il Newsweek 74:46-7 O 13 '69

City on the spot. il Sr Schol 94:15 Mr 21 '69

Crisis that wasn't. Time 93:38+ Mr 14 '69

Germans for more of the same. il Newsweek 74:83-4 O 6 '69

Healthy democratic consensus in Germany. Life 67:38 O 10 '69

Hour we have waited for. il Newsweek 73: 57-8 Mr 17 '69

West Germany: outcasts at the helm; Social democrats to take power. il Time 94:24-6+ O 10 '69

West Germany: ready for the parlor. il Time 94:28+ S 26 '69

West Germany's decision for the 70s. il Time 94:24 O 3 '69

Willy Brandt looks ahead. J. A. Morris, jr. Nation 209:363-4 O 13 '69

Willy Brandt's wanderjahre are finished. D. Binder. il N Y Times Mag p34-5+ N 30 '69

Ghana

No redeemers need apply. il Newsweek 74:44 S 8 '69

Great Britain

Another setback for Socialists. U S News 66:10-11 Ap 7 '69

Don't be euphoric; five by-elections. il Newsweek 74:54+ N 10 '69

Harold Wilson's sound pound. A. Howard. New Repub 161:13-14 N 15 '69

How long can Wilson last? local elections. Newsweek 73:46-8 My 19 '69

Pensions and race: key British issues; general election which must be held by March 1971. U S News 66:10 F 10 '69

History

Political organization and canvassing; Yorkshire elections before the reform bill. R. W. Smith. bibliog f Am Hist R 74:1538-60 Je '69

India

India: another setback for Indira. il Time 93:26 F 21 '69

Out of touch; Congress party losses. il Newsweek 73:47+ F 24 '69

Swing to the left? Sr Schol 94:24 F 28 '69

Ireland

Playing it safe; Fianna fail victory. Newsweek 73:52 Je 30 '69

Staying right. il Time 93:37 Je 27 '69

Israel

Slight erosion. il Newsweek 74:48 N 10 '69

Voting under fire. Time 94:35 N 7 '69

Italy

Night the Communists won. il Time 93:34 Ap 18 '69

Japan

Socialism on the ropes. il Time 95:21 Ja 12 '70

Winning formula. il Newsweek 75:24-5 Ja 5 '70

Kenya

Wanachi speak. il Newsweek 74:50 D 22 '69

Northern Ireland

Back to square one. il Newsweek 73:46 Mr 10 '69

Bad day for the Irish. Time 93:38-9 Mr 7 '69

Critical election in Ulster. America 120:212 F 22 '69

From captain to major. Newsweek 73:50+ My 12 '69

Gospel of Devlin; lady M.P. from Mid-Ulster. Time 93:34 Ap 25 '69

Quiet man. Time 93:42 My 9 '69

Ulster vote disappointing. America 120:263 Mr 8 '69

Philippines

Making of a President. il Newsweek 74:63 N 24 '69

Philippine vote: meaning to U.S. il U S News 67:14 N 24 '69

Victory for Marcos. il Time 94:39 N 21 '69

Portugal

New style of tyranny. L. Jenkins. Nation 209:532-4 N 17 '69

Rhodesia

See also
Political campaigns—Rhodesia

South Africa

Thin edge of the wedge; elections for the Colored people's representative council. il Newsweek 74:91 O 6 '69

Trickery and bravery in South Africa. Chr Cent 86:1411 N 5 '69

Taiwan

Bolder politics in Taiwan. America 121:625 D 27 '69

Thailand

Democratic beginnings. Time 93:32 F 21 '69

Updating a tradition. Newsweek 73:44+ F 24 '69

United States

Cities and the election of 1928; partisan realignment? J. M. Clubb and H. W. Allen. bibliog f il Am Hist R 74:1205-20 Ap '69

Contrary U.S. voters; state and local results. Newsweek 74:47 N 17 '69

Financing better elections; excerpt from report of the Research and policy committee of the Committee of economic development. Cur 104:35-40 F '69

ELECTIONS—United States—Continued

Key races to watch in states and cities. il U S News 67:27-8 N 3 '69

Lindsay and others. New Repub 161:11-12 N 15 '69

Meanwhile, in America. Nat R 21:1156 N 18 '69

Nixon counts up a vote of cheer. il Bsns W p30-1 N 8 '69

Notes on the election. Nation 209:522-3 N 17 '69

Politics. D. MacDonald. Esquire 71:18+ Mr '69

President Nixon and the two-party system. M. Mead. Redbook 132:54+ Mr '69

Republican strategy for '70 election. il U S News 67:34-6 N 24 '69

Surprises in store in '70 election. il U S News 67:20-1 Jl 7 '69

Two key governors: getting set for '70. il U S News 67:9+ D 8 '69

What '69 elections show. il U S News 67:35-7 N 17 '69

See also
Municipal elections
Presidents—United States—Election
Public opinion polls
also subhead Elections under names of cities, e.g. Chicago—Elections

Vietnam (Republic)

Incomplete returns; local elections. il Newsweek 73:46 Ap 14 '69

Viet Cong no to an election bid. U S News 67:8 Jl 21 '69

ELECTIVE system in education

Course electives; improving selection through a system of parent-pupil-teacher conferences. R. P. Brimm. Clear House 43:417-20 Mr '69

Maxi learning from mini courses; Wilson high school, Portland, Ore. W. Reed. il Sr Schol 94:Schol Teach 10+ Mr 7 '69

ELECTORAL college

All power to the voters? Newsweek 74:36+ S 29 '69

Bad idea whose time has come; direct election of the President. I. Kristol and P. Weaver. ii N Y Times Mag p43+ N 23 '69; Reply. E. Celler. p4+ D 21 '69

Better way to elect presidents. Life 67:50B S 26 '69

Congress and electoral reform. E. D. Eshleman and R. S. Walker. Chr Cent 86:178-81 F 5 '69

Electing presidents. New Repub 160:9-10 F 22 '69

Electing the president; in defense of the electoral college. R. N. Goodwin. Cur 113:33-5 D '69

Electoral college reform. C. Joyner and D. Anderson. America 120:401-2 Ap 5 '69

Electoral college: reform ahead? U S News 66:55 Mr 3 '69

Erasing the blot, slowly. il Time 93:26 My 9 '69

Is electoral reform the answer? A. M. Bickel; reply with rejoinder. G. Tyler. Commentary 47:24+ Mr '69

Letter from Washington. R. H. Rovere. New Yorker 45:128-32 O 4 '69

Misreading democracy. New Repub 161:9-10 S 27 '69; Discussion. 161:32 O 11 '69

New left and the electoral college. F. A. Picó. America 120:252-4 Mr 1 '69; Reply. L. W. Belter. 120:378-9 Ap 5 '69

Notes and comment. New Yorker 44:25-6 F 8 '69

Political power in the '70s: gains to South and West. il U S News 66:52-3 Ap 7 '69

Presidential lottery, by J. A. Michener. Review
Sat R 52:33-6 Ap 12 '69. T. C. Sorensen

Presidential lottery; the reckless gamble in our electoral system; condensation. J. A. Michener. Read Digest 94:247-50+ My '69

Renovation scheme; Nixon's proposed electoral refinements. Newsweek 73:22 Mr 3 '69

'72 vote change? Sr Schol 94:16 Mr 14 '69

Step toward reform. Time 94:20 S 26 '69

Time for reforms? Nixon's faithless elector. Sr Schol 94:22-3 Ja 31 '69

Wait a minute! Popular election of future presidents. A. M. Bickel. New Repub 160:11-13 My 10 '69

ELECTRA; drama. See Sophocles

ELECTRETS

Not altogether forgotten electret. H. Cohen and P. Cohen. il Pop Electr 30:70-4+ Mr '69

ELECTRIC alarms

All-purpose alarm you can build from a kit. S. M. Gallager. il Pop Mech 131:181-3 F '69

Build the Riot restrainer; sound-trigger alarm. A. J. Lowe. il Pop Electr 30:47-50 Ap '69

To summon help, press the button; alarm system for campers in the Hamilton County park district, Ohio. J. A. Rollman. il Am City 84:16 Jl '69

See also
Burglar alarms

ELECTRIC analgesia. See Analgesia

ELECTRIC and musical industries, limited

Cassettes, profits, and EMI. J. Ross-Skinner. il Duns R 94:44-51 O '69

ELECTRIC apparatus and appliances

See also names of Electric apparatus and appliances, e.g. Electric current inverters; *also* headings beginning Electric

Maintenance and repair

Before you call the repairman. il Parents Mag 44:75-8 My '69

What to do before you call the serviceman. Redbook 132:46+ Mr '69

Repairing

See Electric apparatus and appliances—Maintenance and repair

ELECTRIC apparatus and appliances, Domestic

Big ideas for small equipment; with recipes. il Redbook 134:76-7+ Ja '70

Buyer's guide to table cookers. B. Karr. il Am Home 72:112-13 S '69

Compact appliances. S. Schuler. Am Home 72:108+ Ap '69

Electric blenders. il Consumer Bul 52:17-22+ N '69

Hazardous egg-cooker; Egg-a-matic. Consumer Rep 34:298-9 Je '69

Household help available. il Parents Mag 44:80-3 Ag '69

Keep your cool with portables; cook at the table. N. Craig. il House B 111:80-1 Jl '69

New switches to pull; with recipes. C. Brock. il Parents Mag 44:60-3+ My '69

Redbook guide to small kitchen appliances. il Redbook 133:55-62 S '69

See also names of domestic electric appliances, e.g. Washing machines

Maintenance and repair

Know-how you need to repair your small appliances. E. Powell. il Pop Sci 194:117-32 Ja '69

What home economists say about appliances; questions and answers. il Changing T 23:15-19 Ag '69

Storage

She has six appliance garages. il Sunset 143:76 Ag '69

ELECTRIC apparatus industry

See also
General electric company
Philco-Ford corporation

Finance

Litton's shattered image. il Forbes 104:26-8+ D 1 '69

ELECTRIC automobiles. See Automobiles, Electric

ELECTRIC batteries

Dry cell batteries for transistor radios. il Consumer Bul 52:28-30 Mr '69

Lab bench; surprising minicell. J. E. Davis. jr. and others. il Chem 42:26-8 Ap '69

See also
Fuel cells
Storage batteries

Care

Phototronics. E. Farber. Mod Phot 33:28+ N '69

Charging

It's coming on toward battery-charging time; report on nine chargers. il Consumer Bul 52:27-31 N '69

Testing

All-purpose battery tester. il Mech Illus 65:94-6 Ag '69

ELECTRIC bicycle. See Bicycles

ELECTRIC blenders. See Electric apparatus and appliances, Domestic

ELECTRIC bug killers. See Insect traps

ELECTRIC charges

Chick interferon: heterogeneity of electric charge. K. H. Fantes. bibliog il Science 163:1198-9 Mr 14 '69

Mechanism for multiplication of atmospheric ice crystals: apparent charge distribution on laboratory crystals. F. K. Odencrantz and others; reply. R. I. Smith-Johannsen. il Science 163:958 F 28 '69

See also
Electrets

ELECTRIC lighting
Five-way projection for the 70s. V. D. Hahn.
il Am Home 72:72-7+ O '69
How to paint a room with light; with comments by J. L. Larsen and E. Reiback. il House & Gard 135:78-83 Ja '69
Kitchen lighting is critical. il Sunset 142:128 My '69
Look at light! il Duns R 94:71-4 Jl '69
See also
Electric wire and wiring
Lighting, Architectural and decorative

Anecdotes, facetiae, satire, etc.
We bathed by candlelight. F. Sparks. McCalls 96:67+ Ag '69

Control
Build 200-watt dual flasher. J. S. Simonton. jr. il Pop Electr 30:50-2 F '69
Burglar deterrents. il Consumer Bul 52:29-31 F '69
Mannerly table lamp; time-delay trickery. J. Small. il Pop Electr 29:79+ N '68; Correction. 30:111 F '69
Tune-in with psychedelic light-show systems you can build. W. S. Bacon and S. Shatavsky. il Pop Sci 194:158-61 My '69
Vary your light level; solid state dimmers. W. F. Wilson. il Pop Phot 64.38 Mr '69
Your own private OWL; outside welcome light. J. A. Archer. il Pop Electr 30:51-3+ Je '69

ELECTRIC lines
Thunderbolt machine tests tomorrow's power lines; General electric's ultra high voltage laboratory at Pittsfield, Mass. W. S. Bacon. il Pop Sci 195:82-5+ O '69

Grounding
See Electric currents—Grounding

Poles
Power poles with grace; Chicago's Northwest tollway. il Am City 84:52 Mr '69

Underground
Cold power. Sci Am 221:48-9 Ag '69
Get the lines underground effortlessly; Palo Alto, Calif. il Am City 84:141+ Ag '69
Los Angeles goes underground. Am City 84:161-2 Mr '69
Setting the pace on underground wiring; Maryland public service commission. Nat Parks 43:24 D '69
Technology outlook; high voltage underground transmission lines. Bsns W p76 Je 28 '69

ELECTRIC measurements
See also
Potentiometers
Strain gages

ELECTRIC meters
Build a capacitance meter. S. Sula. il Pop Electr 31:66-9+ O '69; Correction. 32:9 Ja '70
Check low-value capacitors with the pF meter-mate. W. G. Miller. il Radio-Electr 40:57-9 F '69
See also
Ammeters
Ohmmeters
Voltohmmeters

ELECTRIC motor trucks. See Motor trucks, Electric

ELECTRIC motors
Power from crystals to drive strange new tools; sonic motors. A. P. Armagnac. il Pop Sci 195:70-3+ Ag '69

ELECTRIC motors, Induction
Coming: streamliners without wheels. J. A. Volpe. il Pop Sci 195:51-5+ D '69
Rail vehicle completed for test of linear induction propulsion. Aviation W 91:24 D 15 '69

ELECTRIC outlets. See Electric wire and wiring

ELECTRIC plants
Power generation and environmental change; AAAS symposium, December 28, 1969. D. A. Berkowitz. il Science 166:908 N 14 '69
Utilities face a generation gap. il Bsns W p30+ Ag 2 '69
See also
Atomic power plants
Electric utilities
Hydroelectric plants

ELECTRIC plugs. See Electric wire and wiring
ELECTRIC potential. See Potential, Electric

ELECTRIC power
Not enough electric power; what to do about it. il U S News 67:85-7 S 22 '69
Utility men get powerful message. il Bsns W p 104+ Mr 15 '69
See also
Electric utilities

Transmission
See Electric transmission

Canada
Hottest line in the world; Hydro-Quebec's power complex. R. Dyment. il Pop Mech 132:148-9 N '69

United States
See Electric power

ELECTRIC power distribution
Why utilities can't meet demand. il Bsns W p48-53+ N 29 '69

ELECTRIC power industry. See Electric utilities

ELECTRIC power lines. See Electric lines
ELECTRIC ranges. See Electric stoves
ELECTRIC rates. See Electric utilities—Rates
ELECTRIC recording instruments. See Recording instruments

ELECTRIC refrigerators. See Refrigerators. Electric

ELECTRIC research
First electron tube. G. Shiers. il Sci Am 220:104-12 Mr '69; Reply with rejoinder. L. Espenschied. 221:8 Ag '69

ELECTRIC resistance
Finding parallel resistances; Kirchhoff's law. R. L. Ives. il Pop Electr 30:61-2 Je '69
Resistivity; some definitions. J. Tusinski. il Electr World 82:86+ N '69
Temperature-dependence of resistance at an electrotonic synapse. B. W. Payton and others. bibliog il Science 165:594-7 Ag 8 '69
Using transistors as negative-resistance devices. W. A. Vincent. il Electr World 81:38-40+ Je '69
See also
Electric conductivity
Impedance (electricity)

ELECTRIC resistivity. See Electric resistance
ELECTRIC resistors
Matching resistors to close tolerances. E. D. Clark. il Radio-Electr 14:43 Ja '70
See also
Thermistors

ELECTRIC scissors. See Scissors and shears
ELECTRIC screw drivers. See Screw drivers
ELECTRIC shavers. See Razors
ELECTRIC shock
Accidents spur legislation; control of hospital instruments. Sci N 95:257-8 Mr 15 '69
Electric shock. J. Frye. Electr World 82:50-1 Ag '69
Electroconvulsive shock effects on a reactivated memory trace; further examination. R. G. Dawson and J. L. McGaugh. bibliog il Science 166:525-7 O 24 '69; Reply. D. J. Lewis. 166:772 N 7 '69
Safety in medical electronics. J. Frye. Electr World 82:58-9 Jl '69
Stimulus properties of reinforcing brain shock. R. M. Stutz and others. bibliog il Science 163:1081-2 Mr 7 '69
Too many shocks; hazard in hospitals. Time 93:58+ Ap 18 '69

ELECTRIC soldering gun. See Soldering apparatus

ELECTRIC stoves
Buying a range in '69. V. T. Habeeb. Am Home 72:84+ Ja '69
How to speed up a hot plate. L. A. Harlow. il Pop Sci 195:143 S '69
Problem-solving appliances. il Bet Hom & Gard 47:16+ Ap '69

ELECTRIC switches
Build the touch control; light switch turns on and off with a touch. L. G. Striggow. il Pop Electr 30:56-8 Ap '69
Getting to know the SCS. F. H. Tooker. il Pop Electr 31:75-8+ S '69
Rotary thumbwheel switches for digital applications. J. R. Squires. il Electr World 81:40-1+ My '69
See also
Electric wire and wiring

ELECTRIC tools
Electric tools under water? you gotta be kidding! J. Hand. il Pop Sci 195:98-9+ S '69

Safety devices and measures
Safety rules for power tools. il Pop Sci 195:142-3 Jl '69

ELECTRON microscope and microscopy—
Continued
Synaptic vesicles in electron micrographs of
freeze-etched nerve terminals. H. Moor
and others. bibliog il Science 164:1405-7
Je 20 '69
Y-modulation: an improved method of re-
vealing surface detail using the scanning
electron microscope. T. K. Kelly and oth-
ers. il Science 165:283-5 Jl 18 '69
ELECTRON optics
See also
Image intensifiers
ELECTRON paramagnetic resonance. See Mag-
netic resonance
ELECTRON ray indicator tubes. See Vacuum
tubes
ELECTRON ring accelerators. See Accelerators
(electrons, etc)
ELECTRON spectrometers. See Spectrometers
ELECTRON spin resonance. See Magnetic re-
sonance
ELECTRON tubes
First electron tube. G. Shiers. il Sci Am 220:
104-12 Mr '69; Reply with rejoinder. L. Es-
penschied. 221:8 Ag '69
ELECTRONIC alarms. See Electric alarms
ELECTRONIC apparatus and appliances
Alphanumeric fun box with a Nixie. K.
Greenberg. il Radio-Electr 40:56-8 Mr '69
Build a psych-analyzer; measuring galvanic
skin resistance. R. E. Devine. il Pop Electr
30:27-32+ F '69
EW lab tested. See issues of Electronics world
Equipment report. See issues of Radio-elec-
tronics
New avionic products. See occasional issues
of Aviation week & space technology
New in electronics. il Pop Mech 130:188-9 D
'68
New products. See issues of Radio-elec-
tronics
New products & literature. See issues of Elec-
tronics world
Product gallery. See issues of Popular elec-
tronics
See also
Blind, Apparatus for the
Computers

Cabinets
Metal boxes built to size. R. E. Brock. il
Electr World 81:84 Mr '69

Color codes
See Color codes

Design
Advanced ECM devices designed; new micro-
wave solid-state components. B. Miller. il
Aviation W 91:67+ S 8 '69

Maintenance and repair
In the shop, with Jack. J. Darr. See issues
of Radio-electronics
Medical electronics servicing. J. Frye. Electr
World 82:63-4 O '69
Service clinic; questions and answers. J.
Darr. See issues of Radio-electronics
Service 2000 A.D. J. Darr. Radio-Electr 40:47
Ap '69
Technical topics. R. F. Scott. il Radio-Electr
40:46-7 Je '69
Technotes. See issues of Radio-electronics

Power supply
Build VHV supply. P. H. Fuge. il Pop Electr
30:46 Ap '69
Build your own power supply. il Pop Electr
30:72 F '69
Circuits & power supplies. il Radio-Electr 40:
66-7 My '69
Electronic loadbank, tests power supplies
dynamically. L. H. Bengner. il Electr World
81:44-5+ Je '69
IC lab power supply. L. H. Anderson. il
Radio-Electr 40:49-93 Ag; 62-3+ S '69
RCA models WP-700A, WP-702A power sup-
plies. il Electr World 81:68-9 Mr '69
Series-pass regulators. G. V. Fay. il Electr
World 81:48+ Mr '69

Radiation effects
See Electronic apparatus and appliances,
Effect of radiation on

Reliability
Reliability and MTBF. Pop Electr 31:84+ Ag
'69

Storage
Home for ohms. A. J. Lowe. il Pop Electr
30:34-5 My '69

Testing
Electronic loadbank, tests power supplies
dynamically. L. H. Bengner. il Electr World
81:44-5+ Je '69
ELECTRONIC apparatus and appliances, Effect
of radiation on
Radiation-hardened avionics gain interest. P.
J. Klass. il Aviation W 91:88-90+ S 8 '69
ELECTRONIC apparatus industry and trade
They call it instant research; Maptek reports
on what's ahead in electronics. il Bsns W
p62+ Ja 25 '69
U.S. avionics firms in European struggle.
B. Miller. il Aviation W 90:310-14 Je 2 '69
See also
Canoga industries
Collins radio company
Computer industry
Electronics as a profession
Philips of Eindhoven companies
Teledyne, incorporated
Varian associates

Consolidations and mergers
Maxson, Riker join; company renamed. Aviation W 90:126 Ap 14 '69

Europe, Western
Europe's avionics firms fear space losses.
il Aviation W 90:286-7+ Je 2 '69
Europe's electronic scramble. il Bsns W p28-
30 Ja 3 '70
ITT European companies coagulating into
strong group. il Aviation W 90:318-19+
Je 2 '69
Modest gains seen for European avionics.
P. J. Klass. il Aviation W 90:300-4+ Je
2 '69

France
See also
Computer industry—France

Japan
Now the Japanese discover the IC. Bsns W
p39 D 13 '69
Scrutable Orient; service for Japanese im-
ports, with list of U.S. agents. R. Angus.
Hi Fi 19:63-5 O '69
Stereo scene; sayonara to the stigma, made
in Japan. C. Lincoln. il Pop Electr 31·65-8
Jl '69
TV in a cartridge sparks three-way tiff;
Sony's color videoplayer. il Bsns W p41
N 22 '69
See also
Computer industry—Japan

Russia
Soviets push microcircuit sales. P. J. Klass.
il Aviation W 90:65-6+ My 26 '69

Sweden
Sweden stresses electro-optics efforts. Aviation W 90:326 Je 2 '69

United States
Quiet growth of industrial electronics. I. Gel-
ler. il Duns R 93:75-6+ Mr '69
They gamble on new technology; risk man-
agement by New business resources. il
Bsns W p 128+ N 1 '69
U.S. avionics firms review MRCA roles. Avia-
tion W 91:29 S 15 '69
Where the action is in electronics. il Bsns W
p86-91+ O 4 '69
See also
Beckman instruments, incorporated
Bendix corporation
Energy conversion devices, incorporated
Fairchild camera and instrument corporation
General instrument corporation
Mite corporation
RCA corporation
ELECTRONIC circuits
Breadboard circuits from PC boards. J. M.
Firth. Electr World 82:65 O '69
High-voltage protection for transistors. F. H.
Tooker. il Radio-Electr 40:58 O '69
Noteworthy circuits. See issues of Radio-
electronics
Technical topics. R. F. Scott. il Radio-Electr
40:46-7 Je; 41-2 Ag; 63+ O '69
Twenty SCR circuits you can make. R. M.
Marston. il Radio-Electr 40:49-51 Je; 55-7+
Jl '69
See also
Electron tubes
Printed circuits
Radio circuits
Switching systems
Telephone circuits
Television circuits
Transistor circuits

ELECTRONIC circuits—*Continued*

Design

ABC's of circuit breadboarding. J. Ashe. il Radio-Electr 40:62-3+ N '69

Multi-layer substrate aids hybrid design. il Aviation W 91:85+ S 8 '69

Use the wired board technique. R. E. Brock. il Radio-Electr 40:23-6 Mr '69

Integrated circuits

All about IC's:

Making circuit components. B. Hibberd. il Radio-Electr 40:58-60 Jl '69

Making circuit components. B. Hibberd. il Radio-Electr 40:64-7 Ag '69

What makes them tick. B. Hibberd. il Radio-Electr 40:33-5+ Je '69

Experiment with 15-watt IC powerhouse. J. Ashe. il Radio-Electr 40:33-5 S '69

How IC logic circuits work. D. Lancaster. il Radio-Electr 40:32-6 My '69

IC logic families:

What they are, how they work. B. Hibberd. il Radio-Electr 40:59-61 S '69

Large-scale integration. D. L. Heiserman. il Electr World 82:37-40+ D '69

Large-scale integration and the revolution in electronics. S. Triebwasser. bibliog il Science 163:429-34 Ja 31 '69

Linear IC's for the experimenter. il Pop Electr 30:27-33+ Ap '69

Micro-mini IC's. R. F. Scott. il Radio-Electr 41:39 Ja '70

Now the Japanese discover the IC. Bsns W p39 D 13 '69

One-IC radio. L. Auer and H. Thanos. il Radio-Electr 40:49-51 N '69

Power IC's for hi-fi. D. V. Jones. il Radio-Electr 40:52-4 Jl '69

Supply sliced thin in silicon wafers; shortage threat to integrated circuit business. Bsns W p28 Ag 23 '69

Texas instruments: big opportunities in small packages. il Forbes 103:32-4+ Mr 1 '69

Use the PA-222 in audio circuits. J. Ashe. il Radio-Electr 40:54-6 F '69

Where the action is in electronics. il Bsns W p86-91+ O 4 '69

Manufacture

Simplified bipolar technique developed; base-diffusion isolation. il Aviation W 90:71 Mr 17 '69

Miniaturization

Soviets push microcircuit sales. P. J. Klass. il Aviation W 90:65-6+ My 26 '69

Use of hybrid microcircuity grows. B. M. Elson. il Aviation W 90:91+ My 19 '69

Protection

Encapsulate your circuits. A. H. Coya. il Pop Electr 31:82-3 Ag '69

RF circuit protection. I. Math. il Radio-Electr 40:45 Ag '69

ELECTRONIC clocks. See Clocks, Electronic

ELECTRONIC components. See Electronic apparatus and appliances

ELECTRONIC control

Multiple-function remote-control relay circuits. H. R. Mallory. il Electr World 82:36+ Ag '69

See also

Photoelectric cells—Control applications

ELECTRONIC countermeasures aircraft. See Airplanes, Military

ELECTRONIC counters. See Counting machines and devices

ELECTRONIC crossover. See Loud speaking apparatus

ELECTRONIC data processing

Accentuate the positive with EDP. P. M. Welsh. il Pub W 196:37-9 D 8 '69

Cost control for the professional service firm. H. E. McDonald and T. L. Stromberger. il Harvard Bsns R 47:109-21 Ja '69

Growing wildly without a blueprint; the data-processing and communications industries in the 1970s. il Bsns W p 192+ D 6 '69

Magnetic areas in thin plate store, process digital data. il Aviation W 91:107-9 Ag 18 '69

Man and the computer; excerpts. J. Diebold. il Nations Bsns 57:50-2+ Jl '69

Management machine, can it work? G. Berkwitt. il Duns R 94:25-9 D '69

See also

Computer-based service companies

Computers

Data processing service centers

Programming languages (computers)

Libraries

See Libraries—Automation

Quality control

Plugging the leaks in computer security. J. J. Wasserman. il Harvard Bsns R 47:119-29 S '69

ELECTRONIC data processing workers. See Computer workers

ELECTRONIC data systems corporation

Fastest rich Texan ever. A. M. Louis. Read Digest 94:131-4 F '69

Little fish tries to gulp a big one; EDS proposes to take over Collins radio co. Bsns W p 123-4 Ap 12 '69

Texas breeds new billionaire. Bsns W p73-4 Ag 30 '69

ELECTRONIC ear. See Anatomical models

ELECTRONIC fish calls. See Fish calling

ELECTRONIC flash meters. See Exposure meters

ELECTRONIC golf range. See Golf, Indoor

ELECTRONIC keyers. See Radio telegraph—Equipment

ELECTRONIC lawn mowers. See Lawn mowers

ELECTRONIC listening devices. See Electronics in criminal investigation, espionage, etc.

ELECTRONIC measurements

See also

Biotelemetry

ELECTRONIC medical apparatus. See Medical electronics

ELECTRONIC mixers. See Sound—Apparatus

ELECTRONIC music. See Music, Electronic

ELECTRONIC musical instruments. See Musical instruments, Electronic

ELECTRONIC organ. See Organ

ELECTRONIC ovens

Radiation hazards

Are there hidden radiation hazards in your home? H. Blatz. il Pop Sci 194:90-3 My '69

ELECTRONIC photoflash. See Photography—Electronic equipment

ELECTRONIC piano. See Piano

ELECTRONIC reading aids. See Blind, Apparatus for the

ELECTRONIC respirator. See Respiratory apparatus

ELECTRONIC service associations

Plea for a united service association; excerpts from address. R. W. Woodbury. Electr World 82:13 N '69

ELECTRONIC service shops

Scrutable Orient; service for Japanese imports, with list of U.S. agents. R. Angus. Hi Fi 19:63-5 O '69

ELECTRONIC shutters. See Camera shutters

ELECTRONIC technicians

Service 2000 A.D. J. Darr. Radio-Electr 40:47 Ap '69

ELECTRONIC test instruments. See Testing instruments

ELECTRONIC thermometers. See Thermometers and thermometry

ELECTRONIC timers. See Timing devices

ELECTRONIC toys. See Electric toys

ELECTRONIC traffic signal control. See Traffic signals—Control

ELECTRONIC vibrato. See Musical instruments, Electronic—Equipment

ELECTRONIC video recording

And now SelectaVision. Time 94:67 O 10 '69

Color TV on a cartridge. S. V. Jones. il Sci Digest 66:63 N '69

Color-TV tape player uses laser and holograms; SelectaVision system. M. S. Snitzer. il Electr World 82:31+ D '69

EVR: canned movies from your TV set. S. Shatavsky. il Pop Sci 194:72-4 Mr '69

EVR: no precedent. P. Nathan. Pub W 196:34 D 1 '69

Electronic video recording; potential in education. D. Molner. il Sr Schol 94:Schol Teach 10+ Ja 17 '69

EVR, what it means. D. Lachenbruch. il Radio-Electr 40:2+ F '69

Instant replay; SelectaVision. il Newsweek 74: 102 O 13 '69

Low-cost color TV tapes in your home; Selecta Vision. il Sci Digest 66:85-7 D '69

RCA puts TV in packs; SelectaVision home-video player. il Bsns W p 106+ O 4 '69

SelectaVision and EVR. D. Lachenbruch. Radio-Electr 40:2 D '69

You'll play color tapes on your TV screen; SelectaVision. H. Shuldiner. il Pop Sci 195: 112-13 D '69

ELECTRONIC warfare. See Electronics—Military applications

ELECTRONIC watches. See Watches, Electric

ELECTRONICS
Electronic materials and applications. H. C. Gatos. Science 164:137-41 Ap 11 '69
Recent developments in electronics. il Electr World 81:30-1 F '69
See also
Cathode ray tubes
Electron tubes
Medical electronics
Pulse techniques (electronics)
Semiconductors

Bibliography

Book reviews. See issues of Electronics world
Electronics library. See issues of Popular electronics
New books (cont) Radio-Electr 40:96 Mr; 66 Ap; 84 Ag; 103 S; 94 N '69; 41:93 Ja '70

Industrial applications

Quiet growth of industrial electronics. I. Geller. il Duns R 93:75-6+ Mr '69

Military applications

Electronic warfare. B. Miller. il Aviation W W 91:71+ Ag 25; 52-3+ S 1; 67+ S 8; 79-81+ S 15 '69

Patents

Fairchild scores a point on circuits; Fairchild-TI patent battle on integrated circuits. il Bsns W p 128 N 29 '69

Terminology

Some technical terms aren't. L. Stern. Electr World 81:21 Je '69

Tools

See Tools

ELECTRONICS as a profession
Careers in electronics. B. G. Wels. il Radio-Electr 40:69-70 D '69
Math, doorway to higher pay. D. L. Heiserman. il Pop Electr 30:67-9+ Mr '69

ELECTRONICS in art
Art as machine; Cybernetic serendipity exhibit at Corcoran gallery of art, Washington, D.C. D. L. Shirey. il Newsweek 74:81 Ag 11 '69
But is it art? R. Berenson. il Nat R 21:395-6 Ap 22 '69

ELECTRONICS in criminal investigation, espionage, etc.
Bugging: new action by court. U S News 66:13 Ap 7 '69
Bugging subversives; ruling that the government must hand over transcripts to defendants. New Repub 161:5-8 Jl 5 '69
Did John Mitchell hear the justices? Justice department's reaction to bugging ruling. R. Shogan. New Repub 160:11-13 Ap 26 '69
Don't let them bug you! B. G. Wels. il Radio-Electr 40:35-8 F '69
Electronic revolution; electronic surveillance by the Pueblo and the EC-121. New Repub 160:8-9 My 24 '69
Fundamental choice; Supreme court rules records of any illegal bugging must be shown to accused. Time 93:39-40 Mr 21 '69
Manual on the Mafia. Newsweek 73:37-8 Je 23 '69
Misunderstanding about bugs; ruling that the government must show defendant transcripts of eavesdropping. il Time 93:55 Ap 4 '69
Mob: meet me at the Armory and let's talk about it; excerpts from eavesdropped conversations of the Chicago mob. il Life 66:45-7 My 30 '69
More dirty business; bugging M. L. King. Nation 209:5 Jl 7 '69
Privacy vs. protection, the bugged society. J. W. Bishop, jr. il N Y Times Mag p30-1+ Je 8 '69; Discussion. p28 Je 29; 29 Jl 20 '69
Right to eavesdrop? Newsweek 73:37 Je 23 '69
Taping the Mafia. Time 93:22 Je 20 '69
See also
Wire tapping

ELECTRONICS in medicine. See Medical electronics

ELECTRONICS in navigation
See also
Radio compass

ELECTRONICS in photography
See also
Photography—Electronic equipment

ELECTRONICS in postal service
Will there be, an electronic mail service? W. H. Buchsbaum. il Electr World 82:30-2+ Ag '69

ELECTRONICS in printing
Printed word goes electronic. L. Lessing. Fortune 80:116-19+ S '69

ELECTRONICS in traffic control
LTV develops highway traffic speed monitor. il Aviation W 91:83 Jl 21 '69

ELECTRONICS industry and trade. See Electronic apparatus industry and trade

ELECTRONICS research center. See United States—National aeronautics and space administration—Electronics research center

ELECTRONS
Electron repulsion theory. W. F. Luder. bibliog il Chem 42:16-19 Je '69
Normal-state electron tunneling only qualitatively understood; report of meeting. J. A. Appelbaum and J. M. Rowell. Phys Today 22:89+ D '69
See also
Electromagnetic theory
Exciton theory
Fermi surfaces
Plasma (ionized gases)
Positrons

Beams

Electron beam recorder developed. B. M. Elson. il Aviation W 91:91+ S 22 '69
Intense MeV-Electron beams and prospects for accelerators. bibliog il Phys Today 22:59-60 Je '69
Polarized beams show promise for atomic collision experiments; report of meeting. B. Bederson. bibliog il Phys Today 22:87+ N '69

ELECTRONYSTAGMOGRAPH. See Medical electronics

ELECTRO-OPTICAL switching. See Switching systems

ELECTROOPTICS
Sweden stresses electro-optics efforts. Aviation W 90:326 Je 2 '69

ELECTRO-PAINTING. See Painting, Industrial and practical

ELECTROPHORESIS
Amateur scientist; antigens and antibodies are studied by their diffusion patterns in agar. R. La Fond. il Sci Am 221:248-50+ S '69
Heterogeneity of presumably homogeneous protein preparations. W. A. Susor and others. bibliog il Science 165:1260-2 S 19 '69
Prostaglandins E₁ and E₂ antagonize norepinephrine effects on cerebellar Purkinje cells; microelectrophoretic study. B. J. Hoffer and others. bibliog il Science 166:1418-20 D 12 '69

ELECTROPHORETIC coating. See Painting, Industrial and practical

ELECTROPHRENIC respirator. See Respiratory apparatus

ELECTROPHYSIOLOGY
Acetylcholine facilitation, atropine block of synaptic excitation of cortical neurons. R. Spehlmann. bibliog il Science 165:404-5 Jl 25 '69
Afferent discharges from osmoreceptors in the liver of the guinea pig. A. Niijima. il Science 166:1519-20 D 19 '69
Amino acid incorporation into rat brain proteins during spreading cortical depression. G. S. Bennett and G. M. Edelman. bibliog il Science 163:393-5 Ja 24 '69
Analysis of restricted neural networks. D. Kennedy and others. bibliog il Science 164:1488-96 Je 27 '69
Attention reduction and activation of cortical neurons. J. J. Tecce and N. M. Scheff. bibliog il Science 164:331-3 Ap 18 '69
Avoidance learning: long-lasting deficits after temporal lobe seizure. J. D. Belluzzi and S. P. Grossman. bibliog il Science 166:1435-7 D 12 '69
Calcium current and activation of contraction in ventricular myocardial fibers. H. Reuter Tasaki and others. bibliog il Science 163:399-401 Ja 24 '69
Condylactis toxin; interaction with nerve membrane ionic conductances. T. Narahashi and others. bibliog il Science 163:680-1 F 14 '69
Current-voltage relations during illumination; photoreceptor membrane of a barnacle. H. M. Brown and others. bibliog il Science 166:240-3 O 10 '69
Dendritic spikes and their inhibition in alligator Purkinje cells. R. Llinás and others; discussion. bibliog Science 163:96-7, 166:637-9 Ja 3, O 31 '69
Evoked potentials: modifications by classical conditioning. H. Begleiter and A. Platz. bibliog il Science 166:769-71 N 7 '69

ELIZABETH rose garden. See Hartford. Conn.
—Gardens
ELIZABETH 2 (ship) See Ocean liners
ELIZABETHAN portraits. See Portraits, British
ELK
Issue: tule elk. il Nat Parks 43:35 Ap '69
Rare elks lose a lottery. il Life 67:79-80 N 21 '69
Timber titan; battle of wapiti. W. Peterson. il Nat Wildlife 7:4-7 Je '69
ELK hunting
Astronaut elk hunt. H. Williams. il Field & S 74:44-5+ Ag '69
Elk hunter's elk. J. Rooney. il Outdoor Life 144:62-3+ N '69
Elk hunting aces. J. S. Parker. il Field & S 74:78-80+ S '69
King of Kishanina. A. Flick, jr. il Field & S 73:72-3+ Mr '69
Lazarus bull; Gros Ventre Range. W. Page. il Field & S 74:54-5+ O '69
Was elk hunting ever like this? with muzzle-loader. C. Elliott. il Outdoor Life 143:56-9+ F '69
ELKIN, Herbert
Build an automatic enlarger timer. Radio-Electr 40:50-2 D '69
ELKOFF, Marvin
Careers are alway greener on the other side of the fence. McCalls 96:87+ Je '69
ELLEGOOD, Donald R.
Fifty faces of Uncle Sam. Sat R 52:42-4 Je 21 '69
ELLENDER, Allen Joseph
Travels of Allen Ellender. S. S. Rosenfeld. New Repub 161:25-7+ S 27 '69
ELLER, Carl
Explosive grace, on defense or in a dashiki. D. Wittner. il por Life 67:31-3 N 28 '69
ELLER, Vernard
Who are these Blumhardt characters anyhow? Chr Cent 86:1274-8 O 8 '69
ELLING, Georg
Spies in surplices. por Time 95:29 Ja 19 '70
ELLINGER, Rory V.
Decline and fall of a student movement. Commonweal 89:548 Ja 31 '69
ELLINGTON, Duke
Duke at seventy. H. Saal. por Newsweek 73:117 My 12 '69
Duke Ellington. P. Garland. il pors Ebony 24:29-32+ Jl '69
Duke's party. New Yorker 45:31-3 My 10 '69
Ellington at the White House. S. Dance. il por Sat R 52:48-9+ My 31 '69
Homage to Ellington in the Nixon style. A. Gingrich. Esquire 71:10 Je '69
Jazz night at the White House honoring the Duke. il pors U S News 66:10-11 My 12 '69
Man who put the top hat on jazz. J. Reddy. por Read Digest 95:108-12 N '69
Medal for Duke and a kiss for the chief. il pors Life 66:97-8 My 9 '69
Notes and comment. New Yorker 45:23 Ag 9 '69
Soul night. il por Time 93:25 My 9 '69
Taking the A train. il pors Newsweek 73:34-5 My 12 '69
ELLIOT, Bob
Toughest of flying targets? Outdoor Life 144:56-7+ N '69
ELLIOT, Cass
Sink along with Mama Cass. W. Kloman. il por Esquire 71:102-4+ Je '69
What a way to lose 110 lbs! il pors Ladies Home J 86:76+ Mr '69
ELLIOT, Elisabeth
We were hoping. Chr Today 14:12 O 10 '69
ELLIOTT, Bob
Guitar babies. Newsweek 74:76+ Jl 28 '69
ELLIOTT, Charles
Minor poet with major fund of love. Life 67:13 Jl 4 '69
ELLIOTT, Charles
More fish to fry. Outdoor Life 144:66-7+ S '69
News: the Southeast (cont) por Outdoor Life 143:43-6 Mr '69
—and Lawrence, H. L.
News: the Southeast. pors Outdoor Life 144:41-4 N '69
ELLIOTT, Douglas
Front-yard garden Down-Under. il Horticulture 46:28-9+ O '68
ELLIOTT, George Paul
Nikki for a couple of months; story. Esquire 71:95-7 Je '69
Report of a repentant symposiast. Nation 209:256+ S 15 '69
Till (violent) death do us part. Writer 82:15-16 O '69
ELLIOTT, H. Chandler
One trillion times zero. Yale R 58:549-62 Je '69

ELLIOTT, Lawrence
Conscience is his co-pilot. Read Digest 95:207-8+ D '69
Splendid Americans; excerpts from The legacy of Tom Dooley. Read Digest 95:215-24+ S '69
ELLIOTT, Osborn
Guest in ghetto America. Newsweek 73:41-3 Je 9 '69
ELLIOTT, William I.
Two hermits; poem. Chr Cent 86:115 Ja 22 '69
ELLIS, Don D.
Incredible tracking dog. por Outdoor Life 144:60-1+ S '69
ELLIS, Gerald W.
Are middle schools the answer? con. Sr Schol 94:Schol Teach 9-11 Mr 14 '69
ELLIS, H. F.
Books from the wood. New Yorker 44:81-3 Ja 18 '69
Content of tables. New Yorker 45:102+ F 22 '69
Visual welfare state. New Yorker 45:103-4+ Ap 19 '69
Without whose unfailing encouragement. New Yorker 45:24-5 Ag 23 '69
ELLIS, James Reed
Leadership; the vital ingredient. il por Time 93:34 Ja 24 '69
Seattle's modern-day vigilantes. J. Fischer. Harper 238:14 My '69
ELLIS, Mel
Hounding deer with dogs. Field & S 74:56-7+ O '69
ELLIS, R. J.
Chloroplast ribosomes: stereospecificity of inhibition by chloramphenicol. bibliog Science 163:477-8 Ja 31 '69
ELLIS, Ray G.
Ray G. Ellis paints in a minor key; with biographical sketch. il por Am Artist 33:26-7+ Ag '69
ELLIS, Susanne D.
Graduate student. por Phys Today 22:53-7 Mr '69
ELLIS, William D.
This is our house. y'see. Read Digest 95:65-9 D '69
ELLIS, William S.
Atlanta, pacesetter city of the South. Nat Geog 135:246-81 F '69
Lonely Cape Hatteras, besieged by the sea. Nat Geog 136:392-421 S '69
Wisconsin's Door Peninsula. Nat Geog 135:346-71 Mr '69
ELLISON, Louise
Mathematics for the very young. Parents Mag 44:48-9+ Jl '69
ELLISON, Matt G.
Selling tomatoes from a hilltop farm. pors Org Gard & Farm 16:68-70+ Mr '69
ELLISON, Ralph
Ellison's ambitious scope in Invisible man. S. Lillard. bibliog f Engl J 58:833-9 S '69
ELLMAN, Larry
Trompe l'oeil restaurant. il Time 93:83 Je 13 '69
ELLMANN, Mary
In America, the great brain divide. Vogue 153:152+ My '69
New narcissism. Nation 208:409-10 Mr 31 '69
ELLSBERG, Helen
Meanie; story. Am West 6:14-15 Ja '69
ELLSBERG, William
Charles. thou art a rare blade. Am West 6:4-9 Mr; 40-3+ My '69
ELLSWORTH, Ralph E.
Contribution of the library to improving instruction: reprint. por Library J 94:1955-7 My 15 '69
ELLSWORTH, Robert Fred
Future of the Atantic alliance; address, May 10, 1969. Dept State Bul 60:511-14 Je 16 '69
ELLSWORTH, Rudolph C.
Eleventh Scandinavian library congress. por Wilson Lib Bul 43:778-83 Ap '69
ELM
American elm. J. Hudak. Horticulture 47:8-9 My '69
Elm avenue; General electric research and development center. Schenectady, N.Y. J. Laska. il Cons 23:37 Je '69
Diseases and pests
DED and DDT: it is time to change. Audubon 71:5 My '69
Earthworm pits for ailing elms. I. O. Sternberg. il Org Gard & Farm 16:90-2 D '69
Hope for elms. il Time 94:57-8 D 12 '69
Nature's broken vase: Dutch elm disease and DDT. R. Rood. il Audubon 71:6-12 My '69
ELMAN, Robert H.
B-school grad calls the tune. il pors Bsns W p 144+ My 17 '69

ELMER, Michael. See Bishop, J. jt. auth.
ELOCUTION
  See also
  Gesture
ELON, Amos
  Remnant. Commentary 47:75-6 F '69
EL PASO natural gas company
  Bennett's revenge. Newsweek 73:71-2 Je 30 '69
  New day? il Forbes 104:24-5 D 1 '69
  Twelve-year itch; merger with Pacific Northwest pipeline. Forbes 103:20-1 My 1 '69
ELSEWHERE people; story. See Gold, H.
ELSHTAIN, Jean B.
  Cowboys and Commager. Commonweal 91:249-51 N 21 '69
ELSON, Edward Lee Roy
  Faith of Mamie Eisenhower. McCalls 96:44+ Jl '69
      about
  U.S. Senate names Elson its 50th chaplain. W. Willoughby. Chr Today 13:39 Ja 31 '69
ELSON, John T.
  After the last run. Travel & Camera 32:58-63 D '69
  Flowery summerlike wines of Switzerland and the Tirol. Travel & Camera 32:16+ Jl '69
  Mexico, hot and harmonious. Travel & Camera 32:12 N '69
  Rhône: a river of big red wines. Travel & Camera 32:13-14 Je '69
  Rum in all its variety. Travel & Camera 32:13+ S '69
  Wines of Spain and Portugal. Travel & Camera 32:35-6+ My '69
ELTRA corporation
  Pioneer on the sidelines. Forbes 103:22-3 My 1 '69
ELUL, Rafael
  Gaussian behavior of the electroencephalogram: changes during performance of mental task. bibliog Science 164:328-31 Ap 18 '69
ELVES. See Fairies
ELVIUS, Aina. See Alfvén, H. jt. auth.
ELY, Laurence E.
  Principal: a Machiavellian guide. Clear House 43:519-22 My '69
EMANCIPATION of women. See Woman—Equal rights
EMBARGO
  Embargo dims French aerospace outlook. D. E. Fink. Aviation W 90:21-2 Ja 27 '69
  Timing on eased Israel embargo awaited. D. E. Fink. Aviation W 91:22-3 Jl 21 '69
EMBASSIES (buildings)
  U.S. embassy; our men in Paris. W. Manchester. il Holiday 45:34-9+ Mr '69
EMBASSIES (United States)
  See also
  United States—Diplomatic and consular service
EMBELLISHMENT (music)
  L'art de bien chanter (1666) of Jean Millet. A. Cohen. bibliog f il Mus Q 55:170-9 Ap '69
EMBEZZLEMENT
  Clerk's wild ride. il Newsweek 73:82+ Je 16 '69
  Rags to riches; investigations of poverty agency frauds in New York. Newsweek 73:30+ Ja 27 '69
  Rolling in pennies; shortage of funds in Idaho highway department. il Time 93:26 My 23 '69
EMBLEMS, State
  State symbols in related hobbies. D. F. Brown. il Hobbies 74.50-1 Mr '69
EMBODEN, William A. Jr
  Two portraits, a bouquet, and two Valentines. Wilson Lib Bul 44:535-7 Ja '70
EMBOLISM
  Can you prevent embolism? E. Di Cyan. il Har Yrs 9:35-7 Mr '69
  Umbrella of life; vena caval device to prevent pulmonary embolism. il Newsweek 74:85 O 20 '69
  See also
  Infarctions
EMBROIDERY
  Captivating designs to embroider for your home. il Good H 169:116-17 O '69
  Here's how to master five creative embroidery stitches. il Am Home 72:38 Je '69
  Mural is... story of a stitchery mural and a sixth grade class at the Anne Beers elementary school, Washington, D.C. S. Battist. il Sch Arts 68:24-5 My '69
  Print work; embroidered pictures. L. B. Carlisle. il Antiques 95:328+ Mr '69

Stylized birds in stitchery. V. Jackson and W. Radcliffe. il Sch Arts 68:20-1 My '69
  See also
  Needlework
  Samplers
        Study and teaching
  They do it with their eyes closed; free designs in stitchery. J. Riesen. il Sch Arts 68:22-3 My '69
EMBRY, J. C.
  Afro-American vs Negro; excerpts from Afro-American encyclopedia, ed. by J. T. Haley. Negro Hist Bul 32:18 Mr '69
EMBRYOLOGY
  See also
  Amniotic liquid
  Differentiation (biology)
  Fetus
  Morphogenesis
  Ovaries
        Coelenterates
  Unique envelope of a jellyfish ovum: the armed egg. D. Szollosi. bibliog il Science 163:586-7 F 7 '69
        Mammals
  Closing in on mammals; clonal reproduction. il Sci N 95:304 Mr 29 '69
EMERALDS
  Emeralds of Muzo. H. Forman. il Américas 21:8-14 Ja '69
EMERGENCIES. See Accidents
EMERGENCIES, Assistance in. See Assistance in emergencies
EMERGENCY communication systems
  Alert the citizen before the disaster strikes; Topeka, Kan. T. E. Wright. il Am City 84:101-2 Ag '69
  Instant help; Austin, Tex. il Am City 84:50 D '69
  Operation survival; systems that will survive almost any catastrophe. J. W. Foss and R. W. Mayo. il Electr World 82:41-3 Ag '69
  See also
  Radio communication—Emergency applications
  Telephone—Emergency applications
EMERGENCY services, Hospital. See Hospitals—Emergency services
EMERGENCY trucks. See Motor trucks, Municipal
EMERSON, Gloria
  Paris fashion openings. Holiday 46:64-6 Ag '69
EMERSON, Guy
  Obituary
      Audubon por 71:55 Mr '69. R. T. Peterson
EMERSON, Peter Henry
  Terrible tempered Dr Emerson; excerpts from Naturalistic photography, ed. by D. Vestal. P. H. Emerson. il Pop Phot 64:102-3+ My '69
EMERSON, Ralph L.
  Fastest prop in the world. Pop Mech 132:94-5 D '69
EMERSON, Ralph Waldo
  Flower power: a student's guide to pre-hippie transcendentalism. P. H. Wild. Engl J 58:62-8 Ja '69
  Have courage! L. Mumford. por Am Heritage 20:104-11 F '69
EMERSON, William Austin, 1923-
  Post script. O. Friedrich. Harper 239:99-100+ D '69
EMERY, K. O.
  Continental shelves; with biographical sketch. Sci Am 221:42, 106-14+ bibliog (p285) S '69
EMIGH, C. H.
  Indoor mountaineering. Parks & Rec 4:36-7 Jl '69
EMIGRATION. See Immigration and emigration
EMIGRATION and immigration law. See Immigration and emigration law
ÉMIGRÉS
  Exiles: a clutch of feverish factions, and a coolly neutral monarch; Greek émigrés. il Newsweek 75:36-7 Ja 19 '70
EMILIA, David A. and Heinrichs, D. F.
  Ocean floor spreading: Olduvai and Gilsa events in the Matuyama epoch. bibliog Science 166:1267-9 D 5 '69
EMILIANI, Cesare
  Interglacial high sea levels and the control of Greenland ice by the precession of the equinoxes. bibliog Science 166:1503-4 D 19 '69
—and others
  Underground nuclear explosions and the control of earthquakes. bibliog Science 165:1255-6 S 19 '69
EMINENT men. See Great men
—See Rona, E. jt. auth.

EMLEN, Stephen Thompson
Bird migration: influence of physiological state upon celestial orientation. bibliog Science 165:716-18 Ag 15 '69
Celestial guidance system of a migrating bird. Sky & Tel 38:4-6 Jl '69

about

Birds migrate by the stars. il Sci Digest 66: 43-4 O '69
EMMA Willard school. See Private schools
EMMAUS house. East Harlem. See New York (city)—Churches
EMMERICH, André
Art collectors beware. Travel & Camera 32: 56-9 N '69
EMMERSON, B. T. and Wyngaarden, J. B.
Purine metabolism in heterozygous carriers of hypoxanthine-guanine phosphoribosyl-transferase deficiency. bibliog Science 166: 1533-5 D 19 '69
EMMERTON, Bill
Man believed sane runs 105,000 miles. D. Levin. il por Sports Illus 31:36-8+ O 6 '69
EMMETT, J. A.
Boating. See issues of Outdoor life
EMMETT, Jim
Lost art of sculling. Mech Illus 65:80+ F '69
EMMONS, Richard W. and Lennette, E. H.
Isolation of western equine encephalomyelitis virus from an opossum. bibliog Science 163: 945-6 F 28 '69
EMMY awards. See Academy of television arts and sciences
EMORY, George
Those wild new bikes. Pop Mech 132:150-5+ Jl '69
EMORY university, Atlanta, Ga.

Libraries

Advanced studies library at Emory university; Robert W. Woodruff library. il Library J 94:4400 D 1 '69
EMOTIONAL maturity. See Maturity
EMOTIONALLY disturbed children. See Mentally ill children; Problem children
EMOTIONS
In my opinion; boys should cry too! C. Hrd-licka. Seventeen 28:202 O '69
See also
Anger
Anxiety
Envy
Facial expression
Fear
Love
Mind and body
Photography of emotions
Temper
Timidity
EMOTIONS and food. See Eating, Psychology of
EMPAIN group. See Belgium—Industries
EMPEROR'S nightingale: drama. See Winther. B.
EMPHYSEMA
Serum elastase inhibitor deficiency and α_1-antitrypsin deficiency in patients with obstructive emphysema. G. M. Turino and others. bibliog il Science 165:709-11 Ag 15 '69
EMPLOYEE absenteeism. See Absenteeism
EMPLOYEE benefits. See Non-wage payments
EMPLOYEE incentives. See Incentives in industry
EMPLOYEE morale
See also
Industrial relations
EMPLOYEE recreation. See Industrial recreation
EMPLOYEE rights. See Employees—Civil rights
EMPLOYEE rules. See Labor discipline
EMPLOYEE seniority. See Seniority, Employee
EMPLOYEE thefts. See Stealing
EMPLOYEE vacations. See Vacations. Employee
EMPLOYEES
See also
Job satisfaction
also subhead Employees under various subjects, e.g. Railroads—Employees; *also* classes of employees, e.g. Government employees

Civil rights

What are your rights as a jobholder? P. Lindberg. Bet Hom & Gard 47:10 N '69

Dismissal

Million-dollar back-pay bonanza: awards to mill workers. il Bsns W p29-31 Jl 26 '69
Why arbitrators reinstate discharged employees. M. Stone. il Mo Labor R 92:47-50 O '69
See also
Labor discipline
Layoff systems

Length of service

See Seniority, Employee

Promotion

Who will get that promotion? il Changing T 23:15-17 O '69

Qualifications

Rich man's qualifications for poor man's jobs. I. Berg. Trans-Action 6:45-50 Mr '69

Training

Back of delays in road building; highway-building contracts and employment programs. U S News 66:8 Ja 27 '69
Behavioral approach to industrial selling. J. W. Thompson and W. W. Evans. il Harvard Bsns R 47:137-51 Mr '69
Evolution of private manpower planning in Armour's plant closings. J. L. Stern. bibliog il Mo Labor R 92:21-8 D '69
Franklin U.S. a plan to enlist talent, provide training; adaptation of address, April 10, 1969. C. F. Bound. Pub W 195:32-4 Ap 21 '69
Helping others to help themselves; laboratory trainee program at Eastman Kodak co. C. E. Rowley. il Chem 42:8-10 F '69
Helping workers locate jobs following a plant shutdown. J. C. Ullman. bibliog Mo Labor R 92:35-40 Ap '69
Nixon's job-training plan: how it will work. il U S News 67:62-3 Ag 25 '69
Some investment-like aspects of employment and pay. R. A. Lester. Mo Labor R 92:62-5 N '69
Talent corps: career ladders for bottom dogs. J. Featherstone. New Repub 161:17-23 S 6 '69
Waves of the future: your career? address. May 13, 1969. J. D. Pecsok. Vital Speeches 35:553-6 Jl 1 '69
Window on the hard-core world; excerpts from address. T. V. Purcell and R. Webster. Harvard Bsns R 47:118-29 Jl '69
EMPLOYEES, Interchange of
Interchangeable union workers. U S News 67:98 N 17 '69
EMPLOYEES, Library. See Library staffs
EMPLOYEES, Relocation of
Helping workers locate jobs following a plant shutdown. J. C. Ullman. bibliog Mo Labor R 92:35-40 Ap '69
EMPLOYEES, Temporary
Big boom in temp help. T. J. Rakstis. Read Digest 94:189+ Mr '69
Instant jobs for instant people; with report by M. L. Crum. il Har Yrs 9:6-10 N '69
Instant jobs: how you can get them. il Har Yrs 9:11-13 N '69
EMPLOYEES, Training of. See Employees—Training
EMPLOYEES as stockholders
See also
Profit sharing
EMPLOYEES representation in management
See also
Industrial relations
EMPLOYERS liability
See also
Workmens compensation
EMPLOYMENT *
How good were manpower projections for the 1960's. S. Swerdloff. il Mo Labor R 92: 17-22 N '69
Report on employment related to exports; with tables. C. T. Bowman. bibliog Mo Labor R 92:16-20 Je '69
Where the jobs are. Mlle 69:152-7 S '69
Where the jobs are going to be. U S News 66:74 Je '69
See also
Age and employment
Exploitation
Mentally ill—Employment
Seasonal labor
Unemployment
also subhead Employment under various subjects, e.g. Youth—Employment

ENDOWMENTS
 See also
Colleges and universities—Gifts, legacies, etc.
ENDOXAN
Cyclophosphamide: effect on experimental allergic encephalomyelitis in Lewis rats. P. Y. Paterson and D. G. Drobish. bibliog il Science 165:191-2 Jl 11 '69
ENERGY conversion devices, Incorporated
Ovshinsky: promoter or persecuted genius? P. M. Boffey. il Science 165:673-7 Ag 15 '69
ENERGY resources. See Power resources
ENFIELD, Conn.
Enfield's excited about living history; high school, Thompsonville. F. S. Gross. il Sr Schol 94:Schol Teach 13-14 My 9 '69
ENFIELD rifle. See Rifles
ENFORCEMENT of law. See Law enforcement
ENGDAHL, Eric R. and Flinn, E. A.
Seismic waves reflected from discontinuities within earth's upper mantle. bibliog Science 163:177-9 Ja 10 '69
ENGEL, Celeste G. and Fisher, R. L.
Lherzolite, anorthosite, gabbro and basalt dredged from the Mid-Indian Ocean ridge. bibliog Science 166:1136-41 N 28 '69
ENGELBRECHT, Robert Martin
Win raves with a redwood camper. Pop Sci 194:162-4+ Mr '69
ENGELHARD, Charles
Walking conglomerate. P. Ryan. il pors Sports Illus 30:64-8+ Ap 28 '69
ENGELHARD industries-Minerals and chemicals Philipp corporation merger. See Business consolidations and mergers
ENGELMANN, Franz
Female specific protein: biosynthesis controlled by corpus allatum in leucophaea maderae. bibliog Science 165:407-9 Jl 25 '69
ENGELMANN, R. G.
Saunas out and in. Sat R 52:6+ S 13 '69
ENGELS, John
Chronicle of younger poets. J. Atlas. Poetry 113:431 Mr '69
ENGH, Jeri
Action on the Apple. Travel 131:55-9 My '69
ENGH, Rohn
Another day at the mailbox. il Pop Phot 65:71-3+ S '69
ENGINE models
Wonderful world of model engines. H. G. McEntee. il Pop Sci 194:142-6 Mr '69
 See also
Steam engine models
ENGINEERING
Engineering sciences. See occasional issues of Science news
 See also Environmental engineering; Systems engineering, and similar headings

Cost
High cost of destruction; excerpts from The diligent destroyers. G. Laycock. il Audubon 71:86-8+ N '69

Study and teaching
 See also
Engineering education
ENGINEERING, Biomedical. See Biomedical engineering
ENGINEERING, Medical. See Biomedical engineering
ENGINEERING as a profession
Bum steering about engineering. B. Whitehill. jr. il Nations Bsns 57:109 S '69
Consider the engineer, sympathetically. Am City 84:8 N '69
Engineering: renew its luster; letter. D. Rosenthal. Science 163:623 F 14 '69
ENGINEERING colleges
 See also
Dartmouth college, Hanover, N.H.—Thayer school of engineering
ENGINEERING education
Engineering the Thayer way. E. Gross. il Sci N 96:456-7 N 15 '69
 See also
American society for engineering education
ENGINEERING research
 See also
Automobile research
ENGINEERING societies
 See also
National academy of engineering
ENGINEERING standards. See Standards, Engineering
ENGINEERS
Engineers wear a union label. Bsns W p48 Jl 12 '69
 See also
Aviation engineers
Engineering as a profession
Petroleum engineers

Political activities
Today's engineer, building a bridge to the public; address. K. H. Hohenemser. Sci & Cit 10:250-3 D '68

Supply and demand
Hard times and a union. Sci N 96:200 S 13 '69
ENGINEERS, Indian (East Indian)
Using what's available; oversupply of engineers and scientists. S. K. Ghaswala. il Sci N 96:314 O 4 '69
ENGINEERS and scientists of California (trade union)
Hard times and a union; ESC affiliates with AFL-CIO. Sci N 96:200 S 13 '69
ENGINES
 See also
Automobile engines
Diesel engines
Gas and oil engines
Gas turbines
Heat engines
Locomotives
ENGLAND
More notes from England. N. S. Hazelton. Nat R 21:188 F 25 '69
 See also
Architecture, Domestic—England
Booksellers and bookselling—England
Canals—England
Castle Combe
Cathedrals—England
Churches—England
Colleges and universities—England
English
Flood prevention and control—England
Gipsies in England
Music—England
Newmarket
Norfolk Broads
Theater—Great Britain
Yorkshire

Antiquities
 See Great Britain—Antiquities

Church history
Anti-Catholicism in Victorian England, by E. R. Norman. Review
 Cath World 209:134-5 Je '69. W. J. Feeney

Description and travel
Country ramble. D. Butwin. il Sat R 52:42+ O 11; 58+ O 18 '69
England's north country. H. B. Little. Harp Baz 103:66+ Ja '70
Real England. G. L. Carter. il Travel & Camera 32:50-1+ Mr '69
Walk through Britain, by J. Hillaby. Review
 Travel & Camera 32:34-5+ '69. W. O. Douglas

Education
 See Education—Great Britain

Historic houses, etc.
Cry of the peacock. F. Megarity. il House B 111:72+ Ap '69
Duke of Wellington's search for a palace. E. Longford. il Horizon 11:106-13 Spr '69

Intellectual life
London. Q. Crewe. Vogue 153:72+ Je '69

National trust
 See National trust for places of historic interest or natural beauty

Religious institutions and affairs
Christianity in England. C. F. H. Henry. Chr Today 13:36-7 My 9 '69
Church at large. C. F. H. Henry. Chr Today 13:29-30 Jl 4 '69
World around us (cont) Chr Cent 86:270, 692+. 964 F 19. My 14. Jl 16 '69
 See also
Church of England
England—Church history
Oxford movement

Social history
Perspective. J. H. Plumb. Sat R 52:30 N 29 '69

Social life and customs
Beginnings of modern pleasures; eighteenth-century England. J. H. Plumb. il Horizon 11:20-5 Spr '69
Rise and fall of trad. Q. Crewe. Vogue 155:80 Ja 15 '70

ENGLAND, Church of. See Church of England

ENGLAND and the United States
See also
Americans in England
United States—Foreign opinion—British

ENGLANDER, Mike
Face to face with a New York cab driver. por Seventeen 29:106 Ja '70

ENGLANDER, Roger
Music on TV, what works, what doesn't. por Hi Fi 19:MA10-11+ O '69

ENGLE, Eloise
Freelance job idea: convention freelancing. Writers Digest 49:42-3+ Ap '69

ENGLE, John D. Jr
Serious look at light verse. Writers Digest 49:47-9+ Jl '69

ENGLE, Katherine
Right man: story. Good H 168:92-3 My '69

ENGLEBARDT, Stanley L.
Are you accident-prone? Read Digest 95:127-30 S '69
Now: a vaccine to conquer another crippler. Read Digest 94:123-7 Ap '69
Prevention: new look in dentistry. Read Digest 94:15-16+ F '69

ENGLEMAN, Finis E.
Big-city superintendent. Ed Digest 35:20-1 O '69

ENGLEWOOD CLIFFS, N.J.
Preplanned drainage pays big dividends. A. R. Pagan. il Am City 84:121 Je '69

ENGLISH, Fenwick
Ailing principalship. Ed Digest 34:13-16 F '69
Questions and answers on differentiated staffing. Todays Ed 58:53-4 Mr '69

ENGLISH, Margaret
Lead-poisoned kids. Look 33:114 O 21 '69

ENGLISH
More notes from England. N. S. Hazelton. Nat R 21:188 F 25 '69
Parting shots: mad dogs, horses and Englishmen; with photographs. Life 67:66A-68 D 19 '69
See also
Londoners

ENGLISH CHANNEL
See also
Channel Islands (English channel)

ENGLISH coins. See Coins

ENGLISH composition. See English language—Composition

ENGLISH cookery. See Cookery, English

ENGLISH departments, College. See Colleges and universities—English departments

ENGLISH drama
See also
London—Theater

ENGLISH fiction
See also
Gothic romances

ENGLISH furniture. See Furniture, English

ENGLISH glass. See Glassware

ENGLISH grammar. See English language—Grammar

ENGLISH humor. See Humor, English

ENGLISH language
Are you making yourself clear? N. Cousins. Sat R 52:30-2 F 22 '69
Euphemism: telling it like it isn't; Time essay. Time 94:26-7 S 19 '69
Murder, mayhem and the mother tongue; address, May 4, 1969. W. Carroll. Vital Speeches 35:542-4 Je 15 '69; Same abr. with title Murder and the mother tongue. Read Digest 95:57-9+ O '69
See also
Adjectives
Slang

Bibliography
More sources of free and inexpensive material (cont) J. R. Searles Engl J 58:928-37 S '69

Composition
Acrobats, plowmen, and the healthy sentence. J. L. Green. bibliog f Engl J 58:892-9 S '69
Beginning begets: making composition assignments. E. J. Farrell. Engl J 58:428-31 Mr '69
Building a background for high school composition. R. Rideout. Engl J 58:242-4 F '69
Compositions: assigned or developed? M. A. Kaplan. Engl J 58:1194-8 N '69
Making films with students. K. Scheufele. Engl J 58:426-7+ Mr '69
Method for teaching subskills in composition. D. Stoner and A. Anderson. Engl J 58:252-6 F '69
New concepts in composition. K. A. Andrews. Engl J 58:96-101 Ja '69

No wonder students can't write. J. Hovelsrud. Engl J 58:249-51 F '69
Research paper revisited; analyzing current movies. D. M. Paananen. il Sr Schol 94: Schol Teach 18-19 F 7 '69
Some structures for written English; adaptation of address, November 1968. A. MacLeish. bibliog f Engl J 58:877-8+ S '69
Teach the process of writing. A. G. Draper. Engl J 58:245-8 F '69
Teaching composition to the disadvantaged. D. Geyer. Engl J 58:900-7 S '69
This English is something else: Indianapolis oral-aural-visual program for teaching language arts. S. L. Sheeley. il Sr Schol 94: Schol Teach 14-16 Ja 17 '69
See also
Creative writing

Courses of study
Advice to the curriculum committee: begin with the three -cy's. B. Fillion. Engl J 58: 1230-2 N '69
Curriculum: new perspectives. R. Shafer. Engl J 58:752-6 My '69
English curriculum revitalized for junior high schools. D. Shillinglaw and D. E. Hayden. Clear House 44:33-4 S '69
Little change in English. D. L. Burleson. Sr Schol 95:Schol Teach 1-2 O 27 '69

Dialects
Harpin' boont in Boonville. T. Tyler. il Time 93:20-1 F 7 '69
Let's dump the uptight model in English. K. S. Goodman. Ed Digest 35:45-8 D '69
Old English survival in mountain speech. J. K. Fitzhugh. Engl J 58:1224-7 N '69
See also
Negro-English dialects

Dictionaries
AHD exists: a child of wrath. F. Jennings. Pub W 196:34-5 S 29 '69
American heritage dictionary of the English language, ed. by W. Morris. Review
Sat R il 52:25-6 S 27 '69. R. Girson
Defense of elegance: American heritage dictionary. il Time 94:50 Ag 22 '69
Is it an O.K. word, usewise? publication of the American heritage dictionary of the English language. W. Zinsser. Life 67:2 Ag 29 '69
Publishing scene; American heritage dictionary of the English language. D. Dempsey. Sat R 52:35 S 20 '69
So to speak: publication of the American heritage dictionary of the English language. M. Bishop. Horizon 11:44-7 Sum '69
What is a dictionary? (a meander) J. Ciardi. Sat R 52:38-9 My 24 '69

Etymology
Exaltation of larks: excerpts. J. Lipton. il Natur Hist 78:8-10+ Je '69
What is a dictionary? (a meander) J. Ciardi. Sat R 52:38-9 My 24 '69
Why you say it; excerpts. W. B. Garrison. il Todays Health 47:74-6 Mr '69

Grammar
About those sentence fragments. C. T. Shades. Engl J 58:1223+ N '69
Grammar should be groovier. T. A. Lund. Ed Digest 34:32-4 Mr '69
Grammar, usage, teachers of English, and Paul Roberts. R. J. Goba. bibliog f Engl J 58:886-91 S '69
Linguistics: where do we go from here? J. Algeo. Engl J 58:102-12 Ja '69
No wonder students can't write. J. Hovelsrud. Engl J 58:249-51 F '69
Passive mystique: we've been had. A. Wolk. bibliog f il Engl J 58:432-5 Mr '69
Some structures for written English; adaptation of address. November 1968. A. MacLeish. bibliog f Engl J 58:877-8+ S '69
See also
English language—Usage

Semantics
Un-isness of is; E-prime, name for the English language minus to be. il Time 93:69 My 23 '69

Study and teaching
Ability grouping in English. R. L. Kelly. Clear House 43:547-52 My '69
Advisory teacher program benefits beginning teachers; English teacher program for the Cleveland schools. R. J. Goodrich. Clear House 44:12-15 S '69
Bi-dialectalism: the linguistics of white supremacy. J. Sledd. Engl J 58:1307-15+ D '69

ENGLISHWOMEN. See English

ENGLUND, Richard
Pied Pipers in leotards. R. Estrada. il Dance
Mag 43:56-60 Jl '69

ENGRAVERS
See also
Hogarth, W.

ENGRAVING
Prints and visual communication, by W. M.
Ivins, jr. Review
Art in Am 57:29 S '69. J. Jacobs
See also
Mezzotint
Monotypes

ENGRAVINGS
See also
Prints
Wood engravings

ENGS, Robert F. and Williams, J. B.
Integration by evasion. Nation 209:537-40
N 17 '69

ENID, Okla.
Try an intersection extension. L. Smith. il
Am City 84:101 O '69

ENIGMA variations; ballet. See Ballets—Criticisms

ENKE, Stephen
Birth control for economic development.
bibliog Science 164:798-802 My 16 '69

ENLARGER timer. See Photography—Processing—Apparatus and supplies

ENLARGERS, Photographic. See Photography
—Enlargers and enlarging

ENLARGING exposure meters. See Exposure
meters

ENLIGHTENMENT
Science of freedom, by P. Gay. Review
Nation 209:733 D 29 '69; J. H. Plumb
Sat R 52:35-6 N 15 '69. J. W. Burrow

ENLOE, Cortez F. Jr
Malnutrition of affluence. por Todays Health
47:40-1 N '69

ENNES, Howard
Human ecology; address, November 1968. bibliog Vital Speeches 35:210-15 Ja 15 '69

ENOCH Pratt free library, Baltimore
Joseph Lewis Wheeler. C. W. Ferguson. PTA
Mag 63:5-7 Ap '69
Noon-hour talks for adults. J. A. McCros-
san. ALA Bul 63:1244-5 O '69

ENQUIRER. See National enquirer

ENRICHED flour. See Flour

ENRICHED food. See Food, Enriched

ENRIGHT, Elizabeth
Little citadel; story. Ladies Home J 86:84-5
Mr '69
about
Art of Elizabeth Enright. E. Cameron. il
Horn Bk 45:641-51 D '69 (to be cont)

ENROLLMENT, College. See Colleges and universities—Attendance

ENROLLMENT, School. See School attendance

ENSEMBLES (music) See Wind ensembles

ENSIGNS. See Flags

ENSTATITE. See Pyroxenes

ENSTROM, E. A.
Left-handed child. Todays Ed 58:43-4 Ap '69
Those questions on handwriting. Ed Digest
34:44-7 My '69

ENTER Mr Poe; drama. See Dias, E. J.

ENTEROBIUS vermicularis. See Pinworms

ENTERPRISE, Free. See Free enterprise

ENTERPRISE fire. See Aircraft carriers—Fires
and fire protection

ENTERPRISE fund. See Investment trusts

ENTERTAINERS
Lively arts; Grey for brightness; interview,
ed. by J. Mandelstam. J. Grey. il Sr Schol
94:18 Ja 17 '69
See also
Beatles
Geishas
Magicians

ENTERTAINING
Celebrity cooks, their kitchens to enjoy;
symposium. il House & Gard 136:80-8 Jl '69
Chez Mlle: the party system; with menus.
P. Bartlett. il Mlle 69:84-5+ O '69
From famous people; symposium. il House
& Gard 136:62-75 Jl '69
Host's corner. House B 111:112-14 Mr '69
How to give sporting parties. il House &
Gard 136:76-9 Ag '69
In focus: pre-party and the party. il Seven-
teen 28:150-3 N '69
Last minute! Last minute! L. Lerman. il
Mlle 70:108-9+ D '69

Merry Christmas parties. il Seventeen 27:
102-3 D '68
Mrs Goodman is a party planner. J. Kuh.
Ladies Home J 86:112 F '69
Notes for the hostess. M. M. Hemingway. See
issues of House & garden incorporating
Living for young homemakers
Nothing-to-it big party. il Sunset 142:80-5
Ap '69
One hostess is 8. The other is 9. And it's
a real tea party. il Sunset 142:186-7 My '69
Parties all around the house. il Seventeen
28:154-9+ F '69
Party scene; symposium. il Ladies Home
J 86:99-101+ O '69
Potomac party-givers; with account by A.
Chamberlin. il McCalls 96:62-5+ Jl '69
Shower power; with menu and recipes. il
McCalls 96:88-9+ Je '69
These are teas? il Bet Hom & Gard 47:127
Mr '69
They give other people's parties. N. Axelrad.
il Mlle 69:180-1+ O '69
This year, let the invitation read: bring the
children. C. L. Miller. il House B 111:130-
1+ N '69
Three imaginative hostesses delight in tradi-
tion breakers. il House & Gard 135:50-5 F
'69
Time to celebrate; with recipes. il Parents
Mag 44:54-7 Je '69
Toss a light-and-sound party. il Am Home
72:120-1 O '69
Under twenty-one; complete plans for ten
swinging summer parties. S. Reice. McCalls
96:48+ Jl '69
Wettest splashdown; celebrating the moon
flight. il Time 94:28 Ag 1 '69
Whole house works for a party. il House &
Gard 135:70-1 Ja '69
Wine tasting parties; with menus. il House
& Gard 136:128-32+ N '69
See also
Balls (parties)
Buffet meals
Business entertaining
Christmas meals
Dinners and dining
Games
Government entertaining
Luncheons
Menus
Suppers
Table setting

Anecdotes, facetiae, satire, etc.
Dream party nightmare. B. Pfizer. il Ladies
Home J 86:52+ O '69

ENTERTAINMENTS. See Amusements

ENTHOVEN, Alain C. and Smith, K. W.
What forces for NATO? And from whom?
For Affairs 48:80-96 O '69

ENTOMOLOGY
Study and teaching
Oceanic filter, game of chance. D. Cav-
agnaro. il Natur Hist 78:52-7 Mr '69

ENTRANCE drives. See Driveways

ENTRANCE halls. See Halls

ENTRANCE requirements, College. See Colleges and universities—Entrance requirements

ENTRANCES (doorways) See Doorways

ENTREMONT, Philippe
Art of Philippe Entremont. R. T. Jones. por
Am Rec G 35:538-40 Mr '69

ENTREPRENEURS
All-pro miniconglomerate. D. Snell. il Life
66:85-6 My 23 '69
As I see it; interview. D. C. McClelland. il
Forbes 103:53-7 Je 1 '69
Brother act stars at Loew's: L. and R. Tisch.
il Bsns W p 126-7+ Ap 12 '69
Citizenship with a shrug; address, December
3, 1968. J. H. Binns. Vital Speeches 35:
207-10 Ja 15 '69
Figure in the puzzle; nude jigsaw venture
of Tonair, ltd, England. il Newsweek 74:
51 D 29 '69
Gallery of business wonders. A. M. Louis. il
Fortune 79:80-3 Ja '69
Incurables. il Forbes 104:21-3+ Jl 1 '69
Oracle follows his own advice: consultant J.
Diebold. il Bsns W p60-2+ Ap 12 '69
Teaching business success; course held at
India's Small industries extension training
institute in Hyderabad. il Time 93:64 Ap
25 '69
See also
Fairchild, S. M.
Goldston, E.
Hurt, J. E. jr
Kerkorian, K.
Ovshinsky, S. R.

ENVELOPES (philately) See Covers (philately)

ENVELOPES, Franked. See Franking privilege

ENVIRONMENT
Can man survive? centennial exhibit at American museum of natural history. C. Peet. il Am For 75:4-7+ Ag '69
Ian L. McHarg. comments on man's environment. I. L. McHarg. il Parks & Rec 4:27-9 Jl '69
Nixon panel reports on environment. P. M. Boffey. Science 163:549 F 7 '69
Our national EQ: the first National wildlife federation index of environmental quality. T. L. Kimball. il Nat Wildlife 7:2-13 Ag '69
Perspective into the future. E. Contini. Sat R 52:35-8 F 22 '69
Pre-Copernican views of the city. G. Rand. il Arch Forum 131:76-81 S '69
Similarities in Mars, Venus and earth. V. R. Eshleman. il Space World F-6-66:34-5 Je '69
Tragedy of the commons revisited. B. L. Crowe. bibliog Science 166:1103-7 N 28 '69
UN and the environment; plans for global conference in 1972. Sci Am 221:48 Ag '69
Using what's in hand. Sci N 96:178 S 6 '69
World conference on the environment; projected U.N. conference in 1972. A. W. Smith. Nat Parks 43:2 Ag '69

See also
Adaptation (biology)
Ecology
Man—Influence of environment
Man—Influence on nature
Pennsylvania. University, Philadelphia—Institute for environmental studies
United States—Congress—Senate—Technology and the human environment, Select committee on (proposed)
United States—Council of environmental and population advisors (proposed)

Study and teaching
Environmental studies: OST report urges better effort. L. J. Carter. Science 166:851 N 14 '69

ENVIRONMENT and state. See Environmental policy

ENVIRONMENT quality council. See United States—Environment quality council

ENVIRONMENTAL art. See Art, Modern

ENVIRONMENTAL defense fund, incorporated
All he wants to save is the world. G. Rogin. il Sports Illus 30:24-9 F 3 '69
DDT and the Constitution; petition to ban use of DDT in Wisconsin. H. Henkin. il Nation 208:308-10 Mr 10 '69
DDT on trial; Wisconsin pollution case. H. Henkin. il Environ 11:14-17+ Mr '69
DDT: the critics attempt to ban its use in Wisconsin. L. J. Carter. Science 163:548-51 F 7 '69
Effluent of the affluent: direct legal action against offenders. C. Peet. il Am For 75:16-19+ My '69
Environmental defense fund: Yannacone out as ringmaster. L. J. Carter. Science 166:1603 D 26 '69
New say in court. Time 94:54 O 24 '69
Wisconsin DDT story in pictures and words. R. Rodale. il Org Gard & Farm 16:19-23 Jl '69

ENVIRONMENTAL engineering
Environment, and what to do about it; address, May 5, 1969. G. T. Seaborg. il Am For 75:38-9+ S; 22-3+ O '69
For full technological assessment. H. B. Glass. Science 165:755 Ag 22 '69
From geography to geotechnics, by B. MacKaye; ed. by P. T. Bryant. Review
Am For 75:11 Mr '69. M. Bush
Human settlements and environmental design; AAAS symposium, December 28-30, 1969. A. H. Esser and R. G. Studer. il Science 166:1186-8 N 28 '69
Quest for environmental quality; excerpts from address. W. E. Towell. il Am For 75:13+ Ag '69
Search for clean air; experimental atmosphere. F. Marley. il Sci N 95:292-3 Mr 22 '69
Upgrading our environment; address. October 14, 1968. H. S. Reuss. il Am For 75:28-9+ My '69
Visual squalor, social disorder or. A new vision of the city of man. B. Thompson. il Arch Rec 145:161-4 Ap '69

See also
Life support systems (space environment)

ENVIRONMENTAL engineering (buildings)
Architecture of the well-tempered environment. by R. Banham. Review
Nat R 21:809-10 Ag 12 '69. H. Kenner
Franzen unifies an architecture of fragments into good places for people; five new projects by U. Franzen. il Arch Rec 145:113-32 F '69
Planning notplace for nobody; excerpt from Personal space: the behavioral basis of design. R. Sommer. il Sat R 52:67-9 Ap 5 '69
Quality environment: upon what principles do we proceed? W. F. Wagner, jr. Arch Rec 145:9 Ap 69
Reaching up; environmental design. R. Zyne. il Seventeen 29:84-5+ Ja '70

Study and teaching
Educating the professionals of the built environment. R. Llewelyn-Davies. il Arch Rec 145:145-50 F '69

ENVIRONMENTAL policy
Environmental policy act: Congress passes a landmark measure—maybe. L. J. Carter. Science 167:35-6 Ja 2 '70
Environmental quality, time for decision! Parks & Rec 4:33 S '69
From the floor; questions and answers. il Am For 75:40-1 D '69
How much is enough? address. E. L. Peterson. il Am For 75:24-7 D '69
Human ecology; address, November 1968. H. Ennes. bibliog Vital Speeches 35:210-15 Ja 15 '69
Nixon's 1970 worries: economy and environment. il Time 95:9-10 Ja 12 '70
Soviet plan for nature; reprint. I. P. Gerasimov. il Natur Hist 78:24-35 D '69
Worries of a Nebraska farmer and a Missouri biologist. J. Olds. Org Gard & Farm 16:66-70 D '69

See also
Conservation of resources
Man—Influence on nature
Pollution—Control

ENVIRONMENTAL pollution. See Pollution

ENVIRONMENTAL science services administration. See United States—Environmental science services administration

ENVIRONMENTAL studies board. See National academy of sciences

ENVIRONMENTAL survey satellite. See Artificial satellites—Meteorological applications

ENVOY international town clubs, incorporated. See Businessmens clubs

ENVY
That green-eyed monster. and what to do about him. J. Brothers. Good H 169:144+ Ag '69

ENVY; or, Yiddish in America; story. See Ozick, C.

ENZYME laundry products
Great white hope; presoaks. il Time 93:93 Mr 21 '69

ENZYMES
Allantoinase: association with amphibian hepatic peroxisomes. L. P. Visentin and J. M. Allen. bibliog il Science 163:1463-4 Mr 28 '69
Enzyme from calf thymus degrading the RNA moiety of DNA-RNA hybrids: effect on DNA-dependent RNA polymerase. H. Stein and P. Hausen. bibliog il Science 166:393-5 O 17 '69
Enzyme regulation in mammalian tissues; report of meeting. G. Weber. Science 163:597-8 F 7 '69
Enzyme synthesis in synchronous cultures. J. M. Mitchison. bibliog il Science 165:657-63 Ag 15 '69
Enzymic differentiation in mammalian liver. O. Greengard. bibliog il Science 163:891-5 F 28 '69
Heterogeneity of presumably homogeneous protein preparations. W. A. Susor and others. bibliog il Science 165:1260-2 S 19 '69
Life-saving promise of enzymes. L. Lessing. il Fortune 79:118-21+ Mr '69
Ligand-induced maturation of threonine deaminase. G. W. Hatfield and R. O. Burns. bibliog il Science 167:75-6 Ja 2 '70
Metal ion activation of phosphate transfer by bidentate coordination. F. J. Farrell and others. bibliog il Science 164:320-1 Ap 18 '69
Molecular order of participation of inhibitors (or activators) in biological systems. R. B. Loftfield and E. A. Eigner. bibliog il Science 164:305-7 Ap 18 '69
Regulation of branched biosynthetic pathways in bacteria. P. Datta. bibliog il Science 165:556-62 Ag 8 '69

ENZYMES—*Continued*
Renal fructose-metabolizing enzymes: significance in hereditary fructose intolerance. J. F. Kranhold and others. bibliog il Science 165:402-3 Jl 25 '69
    See also
Adenosine triphosphatase
Asparaginase
Carboxylases
Coenzymes
Dehydrogenases
Esterases
Galactosidases
Glucanases
Hydroxylases
Isomerases
Kinases
Lysosomes
Lysozyme
Melatonin
Oxidases
Oxygenases
Papain
Phosphatases
Polymerases
Reductases
Ribonucleases
Sulfatases
Synthetases
Thrombin
Transferases
Trehalase
ENZYMES, Plant
Deoxyribonucleic acid methylase activity in pea seedlings. F. Kalousek and N. R. Morris. bibliog il Science 164:721-2 My 9 '69
Enzyme induction in higher plants. P. Filner and others. bibliog il Science 165:358-67 Jl 25 '69
ENZYMES in detergents. See Detergents
EOCENE period. See Paleobotany—Eocene
EOHIPPUS. See Horses, Fossil
EPEL, Bernard, and Butler, W. L.
Cytochrome as: destruction by light. bibliog Science 166:621-2 O 31 '69
EPEL, David, and others
β-1,3-Glucanase of sea urchin eggs: release from particles at fertilization. bibliog Science 163:294-6 Ja 17 '69
EPHRON, Henry. See Ephron, P. jt. auth.
EPHRON, Nora
Beach wife. Holiday 45:68-9+ My '69
Private world of Barbra Streisand. Good H 168:92-3+ Ap '69
Yossaria is alive and well in the Mexican desert. N Y Times Mag p30-1+ Mr 16 '69
EPHRON, Phoebe, and Ephron, Henry
My daughter, your son. Criticism
America 121:18 Jl 5 '69
EPHRUSSI, Boris, and Weiss, M. C.
Hybrid somatic cells: with biographical sketches. Sci Am 220:12, 26-35 bibliog(p 146) Ap '69
EPIC poetry
Lyrics, heroic and otherwise. R. D. Spector. Sat R 52:33-5 Mr 15 '69
EPIDEMICS
    See also
Dengue
Influenza
EPIDERMIS. See Skin
EPILOBIUMS
Dwarf epilobiums. R. D. Pearce. Horticulture 47:9 O '69
EPINEPHRINE. See Adrenalin
EPIPHYLLUMS
Flower to excite the indoor or outdoor gardener. F. W. Kline. il Home Gard 56:62 S '69
EPISCIAS
Exotic episcias. il Home Gard 56:35 F '69
EPISCOPAL church. See Protestant Episcopal church
EPISCOPAL Franciscans. See Franciscans
EPISTEMOLOGY. See Knowledge, Theory of
EPSTEIN, Charles J.
Mammalian oocytes: X chromosome activity. bibliog Science 163:1078-9 Mr 7 '69
EPSTEIN, Edward Jay
Final chapter in the assassination controversy? N Y Times Mag p30-1+ Ap 20; 133 My 18 '69
Truth in the courtroom. bibliog f Commentary 48:50-4 Ag '69
EPSTEIN, Emanuel. See LaHaye, P. A. jt auth.
EPSTEIN, Joseph
Coming of age in Chicago. Commentary 48: 61-7 D '69
No punches pulled. New Repub 161:27-9 Jl 26 '69

Small-eyed poet. New Repub 160:23-7 Je 7 '69
Stranger. New Repub 160:25-6+ Mr 1 '69
EPSTEIN, Leslie
Arithmetic of silence. Nation 209:119-21 Ag 11 '69
EPSTEIN, Mike
Highlight. por Sports Illus 30:87 Je 2 '69
EQUAL employment opportunity commission. See United States—Equal employment opportunity commission
EQUAL pay for equal work
Sweetening for the ladies; B. Castle's proposed law in Britain. Bsns W p 140 O 11 '69
EQUAL rights for women. See Woman—Equal rights
EQUALITY
Chief political question of our time; reprint. W. Karp and H. R. Shapiro. ALA Bul 63:165-7 F '69
Epistle to the Babylonians, by C. L. Fontenay. Review
    Nat R 21:654-5 Jl 1 '69. A. W. Green
Hidden costs of opportunity. E. Z. Friedenberg. Atlan 223:84-90 F '69
Reparations for blacks? the question of effective equality through preferential treatment. M. Green. Commonweal 90:359-62 Je 13 '69
    See also
Individualism
Race relations
EQUALITY in education. See Equalization, Educational
EQUALIZATION, Educational
American academics; the right to a diploma; address, June 1, 1969. D. J. Boorstin. Vital Speeches 36:21-4 O 15 '69
Ultimate in opportunity; comments by J. B. Parsons. J. Cass. Sat R 52:39 Ag 16 '69
EQUATIONS
Significance of a simple equation. $A_1=A_o e^{-kt_1}$. S. Y. Shen and others. il Chem 42:16-18 F '69
EQUATORIAL GUINEA
Fangs a lot. Time 93.31 Mr 21 '69
Fruits of freedom. J. Barnes. il Newsweek 73:49 Mr 31 '69
EQUATORIAL undercurrent. See Ocean currents
EQUESTRIAN games. See Horsemanship
EQUILIBRIUM
Coalescence of two immiscible liquid drops. S. Torza and S. G. Mason. bibliog il Science 163:813-14 F 21 '69
EQUILIBRIUM, Chemical. See Chemical equilibrium
EQUINE encephalomyelitis virus. See Encephalomyelitis virus
EQUINOXES, Precession of. See Precession
EQUIPMENT industries
    See also
Machine tool industry and trade
EQUITABLE life assurance society of the United States
Affirmative action; changing hiring policies. L. L. L. Golden. Sat R 52:127-8 Mr 8 '69
Equitable puts premium on social role. il Bsns W p68-9 N 29 '69
EQUITY funding corporation of America
Instant millionaire. il Forbes 103:66-7 Mr 1 '69
ERASMUS, Desiderius
Erasmus. J. C. Margolin. il pors UNESCO Courier 22:4-13 N '69
Erasmus (1469-1536) international educator. W. W. Brickman. Sch & Soc 97:409 N '69
Unheard mediator. por Time 93:69-70 Ap 25 '69
ERBES, Raymond
Reavis high school. Library J 94:4214-16 N 15 '69
ERDMAN, Woody
All-pro miniconglomerate. D. Snell. il por Life 66:85-6 My 23 '69
EREMURUS. See Desert candles
EREN, Nuri
Supply, demand, and the brain drain. Sat R 52:10-12+ Ag 2 '69
ERFERT, Erch L.
Bill Saunders shoots the works; story. Har Yrs 9:38-9 Jl '69
ERHARD, Ludwig
Alan Wood affair: a tale of intrigue. il por Bsns W p94-6+ Jl 12 '69; Reply. J. P. Bauer. p5 Ag 2 '69
ERIC
NCTE/ERIC clearinghouse on the teaching of English: a report to the profession. B. O'Donnell. Engl J 58:458-60+ Mr '69
NCTE/ERIC report on innovation in teaching English. R. G. Clark. Engl J 58:949-55 S '69
NCTE/ERIC report: oral/dramatics approach to teaching English. R. V. Denby. Engl J 58:614-21 Ap '69

ERICKSEN, Stanford C. See Bluestone, B. Z. jt. auth.

ERICKSON, Carlton W. H.
School and the media. Todays Ed 58:28-9 F '69

ERICKSON, Paul A. and Reynolds, J. T.
Ecology of a reservoir; with biographical sketches. pors Natur Hist 78:6, 48-53 N '69

ERICKSON, Ray Charles
From the brink of extinction. J. C. George. il Nat Wildlife 7:20-3 Ap '69; Same abr. Read Digest 94:214-15 Ap '69

ERIE, LAKE
Lake Erie, aging or ill? B. Commoner. il Sci & Cit 10:254-63+ D '68
Lake Erie will be a little bit cleaner. il Am City 84:14 N '69
Lake Erie's islands by air. B. Thomas. il Travel 131:50-4 My '69
Life on a dying lake. P. Schrag. il Sat R 52:19-21+ S 20 '69
Microparticulates: isolation from water and identification of associated chlorinated pesticides. R. M. Pfister and others. bibliog il Science 166:878-9 N 14 '69

ERIE Lackawanna railway
'Bye, Phoebe Snow, 'bye Buffalo. O. Jensen. il Am Heritage 20:10-15 D '68

ERIKSON, Erik Homburger
What role for non-violence today? excerpts from Gandhi's truth. Cur 112:42-7 N '69

ERIKSSON, L. and others
Ion implantation studies in silicon. bibliog Science 163:627-33 F 14 '69

ERITREA. See Ethiopia

ERLICH, Reese
Unexpected star forward. Ramp Mag 7:60-1 N 30 '68
—See Cannon, T; Horowitz, D; Marine, G. jt. auths.

ERMARTH, Fritz
Soviet Union in the third world: purpose in search of power. bibliog f Ann Am Acad 386:31-40 N '69

ERNST, Max
House to dream in; murals transferred to canvas shown at Paris' Galerie André-François Petit. il Time 94:54 Jl 4 '69

ERNST, Stanton G.
Puzzle of outdoor recreation. Cons 23:17-19+ Je '69

EROSION
Earth is the Lord's... P. S. McElroy. il Am For 75:24+ My '69
Saving our vanishing forests; reprint. K. H. Oedekoven. il UNESCO Courier 22:6-9 Ag '69
Stop winter erosion now! C. E. Sommers. il Suc Farm 67:W6 N '69
Story of Antonio Arango; soil erosion in Colombia; reprint. G. Nannetti. UNESCO Courier 22:6-7 Ag '69
    See also
Rivers—Bank protection

EROTIC art. See Sex in art

EROTIC literature
Pornography & propaganda. J. Thompson. Commentary 48:54-7 Ag '69
    See also
Immoral literature and pictures
Sex in literature

ERPF, Armand Grover
Knossos in the Catskills. il por Time 94:48 Ag 15 '69
Market drop. R. Brady. por Duns R 94:77-8+ Ag '69

ERRORS, Logical. See Fallacies (logic)

ERRORS, Popular
Football exercise foibles. Sci Digest 65:55-6 Ap '69
Has Smokey Bear outlived his usefulness? public perception of and attitude towards wild animals. F. G. Bowman; discussion. Am For 75:2-3+ Ja; 2 F '69
Intoxicating ideas for the tender mind. J. Miller. Vogue 153:70+ Ja 15 '69

ERSKINE, Alice Putnam
Joseph Lee. Painter. Antiques 95:806-11 Je '69

ERTEGUN, Mica
Space venture. P. Devlin. il pors Vogue 154:128-33 Ag 15 '69

ERVIN, Howard M.
As the spirit gives utterance. Chr Today 13:7-8+ Ap 11 '69

ERWIN, John
Hippies invade our town; poem. Seventeen 29:90 Ja '70

ERWIN mills, incorporated
The mill: a giant step for the southern Negro. R. Cleghorn. il N Y Times Mag p34-5+ N 9 '69

ERYTHROCYTES
Dihydroorotic acid dehydrogenase: introduction into erythrocyte by the malaria parasite. R. S. Krooth and others. bibliog il Science 164:1073-5 My 30 '69
Fluid drop-like transition of erythrocytes under shear. H. Schmid-Schönbein and R. Wells. bibliog il Science 165:288-91 Jl 18 '69
Glucose-6-phosphate dehydrogenase deficient red cells: resistance to infection by malarial parasites. L. Luzzatto and others. bibliog il Science 164:839-42 My 16 '69
Glycosphingolipids with Lewis blood group activity; uptake by human erythrocytes. D. M. Marcus and L. E. Cass. bibliog il Science 164:553-5 My 2 '69
Membrane alterations in hemolysis: internalization of plasmalemma induced by primaquine. F. L. Ginn and others. bibliog il Science 164:843-5 My 16 '69
    See also
Erythropoiesis

ERYTHROPOIESIS
Erythropoiesis in the dog: the periodic nature of the steady state. A. Morley and F. Stohlman, jr. bibliog il Science 165:1025-7 S 5 '69

ESCALAIS, Léonce Antoine
Tenor of the high C. R. Seeliger. por Opera N 33:16 Mr 29 '69

ESCALANTE CANYON, Utah. See Canyons

ESCALANTE wilderness area (proposed) See Wilderness areas—Utah

ESCALOPES. See Cookery—Meat

ESCANABA, Mich.
Save-our-air. B. Lando. New Repub 161:11-12 O 11 '69

ESCAPES
Eighty-eight got away. Nat R 21:60 Ja 28 '69
Irish 'who' in a British whodunit; escape of G. Blake from London's Wormwood Scrubs prison. M. Mok. il Life 66:59-62 Ja 24 '69
L.B.J. caper; rescue of G. Mylonas from Greek isle of Amorgos. Time 94:39-40 O 17 '69
Manhunt by water; attempted escape by boat. R. Marston. il Yachting 125:150 Mr '69
Mexican prisoner; case of D. A. Simmons. il Newsweek 73:39-40 Ap 21 '69
Papillon, by H. Charrière. Review
New Yorker 45:200+ N 15 '69. Genêt
Truck that fled Cuba. W. Schulz. il Read Digest 95:98-103 Jl '69

ESCAPES from death. See Survival after airplane accidents, shipwrecks, etc.

ESCHATOLOGY
Berdyaev: philosopher of hope. C. S. Calian. Chr Cent 86:924-6 Jl 9 '69
Eschatology; the New Testament teaching. V. P. McCorry. America 121:inside back cover N 22 '69
    See also
Second advent

ESCHENBACH, Christoph
Music to my ears; Hunter college recital. I. Kolodin. Sat R 52:51 Ap 5 '69

ESCHERICHIA coli
Altered ribosomal protein in streptomycin-dependent escherichia coli. E. A. Birge and C. G. Kurland. bibliog il Science 166:1282-4 D 5 '69
Crystalline L-asparaginase from escherichia coli B. P. P. K. Ho and others. bibliog il Science 165:510-12 Ag 1 '69
Cytosine to thymine transitions from decay of cytosine-5³H in bacteriophage S13. F. Funk and S. Person. bibliog il Science 166:1629-31 D 26 '69
Dye-sensitized photooxidation of the escherichia coli ribosome. R. T. Garvin and others. bibliog il Science 164:583-4 My 2 '69
Escherichia coli: strains that excrete an inhibitor of colicin B. S. K. Guterman and S. E. Luria. bibliog il Science 164:1414 Je 20 '69
N-Formylseryl-transfer RNA. W. S. Kim. bibliog il Science 163:947-9 F 28 '69
Immunological detection of single amino acid substitutions in alkaline phosphatase. G. T. Cocks and A. C. Wilson. bibliog il Science 164:188-9 Ap 11 '69
Induction of helical arrays of ribosomes by vinblastine sulfate in escherichia coli. E. W. Kingsbury and H. Voelz. bibliog il Science 166:768-9 N 7 '69
Ion exchange in escherichia coli: potassium-binding proteins. R. Damadian. bibliog il Science 165:79-81 Jl 4 '69
Nucleoside triphosphate termini from RNA synthesized in vivo by escherichia coli. S. E. Jorgensen and others. bibliog il Science 164:1067-70 My 30 '69

ESCHERICHIA coli—*Continued*
Nucleotide sequence of escherichia coli tyrosine transfer ribonucleic acid. B. P. Doctor and others. bibliog il Science 163:693-5 F 14 '69
Ribosomal protein conferring sensitivity to the antibiotic spectinomycin in escherichia coli. A. Bollen and others. bibliog il Science 165: 85-6 Jl 4 '69
Structural determinant of a ribosomal protein: K locus. E. A. Birge and others. bibliog il Science 164:1285-6 Je 13 '69

ESCOBEDO, Danny
Where are they now? il por Newsweek 74:8 Ag 11 '69

ESCOLA superior de guerra, Brazil. See Military schools

ESENIN, Sergei Aleksandrovich
European literary scene. R. J. Clements. Sat R 52:29 Jl 5 '69

ESHKOL, Levi
Eshkol: a reply to Nasser; interview. por Newsweek 73:49-50+ F 17 '69

about
Death of Israel's prime minister complicates Middle East crisis. J. Shaw. il por Life 66:54-6+ Mr 7 '69
Legacy of Joshua. il por Time 93:36 Mr 7 '69
Levi Eshkol: in memoriam. M. H. Vogel. Chr Cent 86:340-1 Mr 12 '69; Reply. B. J. Nichols. 86:656-7 My 7 '69
More than ever; parliamentary uproar over interview with Newsweek. il Newsweek 73:42-3 F 24 '69
Pioneer passes. il por Newsweek 73:41-2+ Mr 10 '69

ESHLEMAN, Clayton
Poem; I pressed the red. Nation 209:610 D 1 '69

ESHLEMAN, Edwin D. and Walker, R. S.
Congress and electoral reform. Chr Cent 86: 178-81 F 5 '69

ESHLEMAN, Von Russel
Atmospheres of Mars and Venus; with biographical sketch. Sci Am 220:14, 78-88 bibliog(p 148+) Mr '69
Similarities in Mars, Venus and earth. Space World F-6-66:34-5 Je '69

ESKIMO dogs
Mush against death; getting diphtheria antitoxin to Nome, 1925. L. M. Rhodes. il Todays Health 48:30-3+ Ja '70

ESKIMOS
Nomad in Alaska's outback. T. J. Abercrombie. il Nat Geog 135:540-67 Ap '69
Now that you own Alaska, friends, what are you going to do with it? A. Barry. il Esquire 71:119-25 Ap '69

Antiquities
Prehistoric cultural contacts in southwestern Alaska. D. E. Dumond. bibliog il Science 166:1108-15 N 28 '69

Games
Guessing games of the original Americans. C. Miles. il Hobbies 74:110-11 Ag '69
Sports & recreation of the original Americans. C. Miles. il Hobbies 74:142-4 S '69

Implements
Indian tools and miscellaneous. C. Miles. il Hobbies 74:142-3 D '69

Origin
Prehistoric cultural contacts in southwestern Alaska. D. E. Dumond. bibliog il Science 166:1108-15 N 28 '69

Sports
Indian & Eskimo games. C. Miles. il Hobbies 74:110-11+ Jl '69 (to be cont)

ESPALIERS. See Plants, Training of; Trees, Training of

ESPERANTO
Babies, bombs, and books; suggestion for control of bibliographic flood; all scholarship in one language. M. P. Wilson. Library J 94:1599 Ap 15 '69

ESPIONAGE
Fishing vessels, or fishy ones? flotilla of Soviet and Polish trawlers off the Atlantic coast. il Newsweek 73:26 F 24 '69
Russians bungle attempt to steal Mirage. Aviation W 91:23 O 13 '69
Sex trap; British board of trade pamphlet warning Britons doing business with the Communist bloc against personal indiscretion. il Newsweek 73:73+ Mr 24 '69

Spies in surplices; failure of Nazi espionage in Rome. Time 95:29 Ja 19 '70
See also
Radio in criminal investigation, espionage, etc.
Secret service
Spies
Trials (espionage)

ESPIONAGE, Industrial. See Spies, Industrial

ESPOSITO, Nancy. See Henninger, D. jt. auth.

ESPOSITO, Phil
We have the taste of victory; ed. by M. Kane. Sports Illus 31:44-6+ O 13 '69

ESPY, Hilda Cole, and Creamer, Lex
Active volcano is no place to picnic. Holiday 46:68-9+ D '69

ESPY, Robert Hamilton Edwin
NCC chief proposes general ecumenical council. D. Kucharsky. Chr Today 14:30-2 D 19 '69

ESQUIRE (periodical)
BCA-Esquire third annual business in the arts awards. Esquire 72:128-9 Jl '69
Esquire's eighth annual dubious achievement awards. il Esquire 71:53-61 Ja '69
Esquire's ninth annual dubious achievement awards. il Esquire 73:103-11 Ja '70
Everybody's happy but Esquire. R. P. Crossley. Pop Mech 132:48 N '69
See also
Business in the arts awards

ESSARY, Sandra
How to coddle and keep a babysitter. Parents Mag 44:40-1 D '69

ESSAYS
Competitions
History lessons on wheels; high school essayists winning AKA sorority travel scholarship. il Ebony 24:106-8+ S '69

ESSENCES, Flavoring. See Flavoring essences

ESSENCES and essential oils
See also
Aromatic plants
Nepetalactone

ESSENTIALISM (education) See Education—Philosophy

ESSEX, Martin
Getting through to the establishment. PTA Mag 64:2-5+ bibliog(p36) N '69

ESSEX COUNTY, Mass.
Historic houses, etc.
Living with antiques: Coggswell's Grant, the Essex County home of Mr and Mrs Bertram K. Little. A. Winchester. il Antiques 95:242-51 F '69

ESSIEN-UDOM, E. U.
E. U. Essien-Udom; interview. New Yorker 45:27-8 Mr 8 '69

ESSO education foundation
Grants for undergraduate education improvements. Sch & Soc 97:476 D '69

ESTATE planning
Executives, estates, and trouble. A. Hershman. il Duns R 93:52-4 My '69
Personal business. Bsns W p 137-8 Ja 25 '69
Personal business. Bsns W p77 Ja 3 '70
Personal business; changes in the seventies. Bsns W p 163 D 6 '69

ESTATE tax. See Inheritance tax

ESTENSSORO, Hugo
You can take Brazil out of Portugal, but—. Commonweal 91:5-6 O 3 '69

ESTERASE polymorphism. See Polymorphism (biology)

ESTERASES
Esterase heterogeneity: dynamics of a polymorphism. R. K. Koehn. bibliog il Science 163:943-4 F 28 '69
Human serum inhibitor of C'1 esterase: identity with α-neuraminoglycoprotein. J. Pensky and H. G. Schwick. bibliog il Science 163:698-9 F 14 '69

ESTERLA, David, and Esterla, Patricia
America's rarest mammal. pors Nat Wildlife 7:14-18 Ag '69

ESTERLA, Patricia. See Esterla, D. jt. auth.

ESTES, Hugh
Cruising on the level. Yachting 126:66-8+ Ag '69

ESTES, James E.
Guaranteed annual income. Nat R 21:953-5 S 23 '69

ESTES, Nolan
Educational excellence: an end to cultural isolation. ALA Bul 63:221-5 F '69

ESTES, Richard
Muted moments of hockey; paintings. Sports Illus 31:28-33 N 3 '69

ESTES, Richard—*Continued*
about
Super realism. il por Life 66:48-9 Je 27 '69
ESTES, Sue Horn
What the poor are up against in Texas.
New Repub 161:13-14 Jl 19 '69
ESTES, Vern
Man with a million rockets. N. Carlisle. il
por Mech Illus 65:64-5+ Ag '69
ESTHETICS. See Aesthetics
ESTRADA, Jackie
Science fiction market. Writers Digest 49:
48-52+ Ap '69
ESTRADA, Pepe
Geee meter, a dyno on your dash. Hot Rod
22:96-7 F '69
ESTRADA, Ric
France; the ballet world of Anna Galina.
Dance Mag 43:64-7 My '69
Freddy Wittop costumes and castanets.
Dance Mag 43:37-41 D '69
—and Estrada, Sigrid
New York public library dance collection gets
a computerized catalogue. il Dance Mag 43:
50+ Mr '69
ESTRADA, Sigrid. See Estrada, R. jt. auth.
ESTRADIOL
Estradiol: specific binding by pituitary nucle-
ar fraction in vitro. W. W. Leavitt and
others. bibliog il Science 165:496-8 Ag 1 '69
ESTROGENS
Are estrogens really the answer to femininity?
E. Ubell. McCalls 96:42+ Jl '69
See also
Estradiol
ESTUARIES
Diseased estuaries. New Repub 160:7 Mr 1 '69
Goleta slough. L. H. Wakefield. il Audubon
71:154 N '69
Marshes, developers, and taxes, a new ethic
for our estuaries. R. C. Clement. il Audu-
bon 71:34-5 N '69
ESZTERHAS, Joseph
(ed) Order was to destroy Mylai and every-
thing in it; symposium. Life 67:39-45 D 5
'69
ETCHEN, Frederick Rudolph, 1923-
His resume fit the job to a T. por Bsns W
p 116 O 25 '69
ETCHING
Unusual technique. J. Jellico. il Am Artist
33:32-7 N '69
See also
Drypoint
ETCHING of metals. See Metal etching
ETHANOLAMINE
Potential energy fields about nitrogen in
choline and ethanolamine: biological func-
tion at cellular surfaces. J. E. Zull and
A. J. Hopfinger. bibliog il Science 165:512-
13 Ag 1 '69
ETHEL Percy Andrus gerontology center. See
Southern California university, Los Angeles
—Ethel Percy Andrus gerontology center
ETHERINGTON, Edwin Deacon
Close up; with report by R. Woodley. il pors
Life 66:36-8 F 14 '69
ETHERS
Binding of alkali metal ions by cyclic poly-
ethers: significance in ion transport pro-
cesses. R. M. Izatt and others. bibliog il
Science 164:443-4 Ap 25 '69
Glyceryl ether metabolism: regulation of
buoyancy in dogfish squalus acanthias.
D. C. Malins and A. Barone. bibliog il Sci-
ence 167:79-80 Ja 2 '70
Juvenile hormone: activity of aromatic ter-
penoid ethers. W. S. Bowers. bibliog il
Science 164:323-5 Ap 18 '69
ETHICAL education. See Moral education
ETHICS
Morality gap, by P. H. Furfey. Review
Commonweal 90:149-50 Ap 18 '69. E. J.
Egan
Reason can save us. D. Lawrence. U S News
66:94 My 5 '69
See also
Christian ethics
Conduct of life
Conscience
Duty
Forgiveness
Humanity
Journalistic ethics
Labor ethics
Loyalty
Lying
Marriage
Medical ethics

Moral attitudes
Moral education
Obedience
Professional ethics
Responsibility
Sexual ethics
Social ethics
Teachers ethics
Television broadcasting—Moral aspects
Temptation
ETHICS and science. See Science and ethics
ETHIOPIA
Ethiopia's unknown war. J. Kramer. Nation
209:104-6 Ag 11 '69
Selassie land. S. Ungar. il Newsweek 74:39
Jl 14 '69
Vegetational change along altitudinal gradi-
ents. E. W. Beals. bibliog il Science 165:
981-5 S 5 '69
See also
Gondar

Foreign relations
See also
Italo-Ethiopian war, 1935-1936
ETHIOPIAN music. See Music, Ethiopian
ETHNIC minorities. See Minorities
ETHNOLOGY
See also
Anthropology
Culture
Navigation, Primitive
Racial differences
ETHNOMUSICOLOGY
Americans not everyone knows: Laura Boul-
ton. C. W. Ferguson. PTA Mag 63:16-18 Ja
'69
ETHNOPSYCHOLOGY
Is white racism the problem? M. Friedman;
discussion. Commentary 47:4+ Ap '69
See also
Negroes—Psychology
ETHOLOGY. See Animals—Habits and behav-
ior
ETHOXYQUIN
How a problem with fish meal was solved.
Chem 42:22 F '69
ETHRIDGE, James M.
National union catalog: another view. ALA
Bul 63:1104-5 S '69
ETHYLENE
Ethylene: a factor in defoliation induced
by auxins. M. Hallaway and D. J. Os-
borne. bibliog il Science 163:1067-8 Mr 7
'69
ETHYLENEDIAMINE tetraacetic acid
Please pass the calcium disodium ethyl-
enediaminetetracetic acid! EDTA in salad
dressings. il Consumer Bul 52:4+ Jl '69
ETIQUETTE
Manners are alive and well; excerpts from
Vogue's new Book of etiquette. Vogue 154:
80+ N 1 '69
Monthly column. A. Vanderbilt. See issues
of Ladies' home journal
Practical guide to good manners; excerpts
from Vogue's book of etiquette and good
manners. House & Gard 136:62-3 N '69
Rose for Emily. J. Kaplan. Harper 238:
106-9 Mr '69

Anecdotes, facetiae, satire, etc.
What etiquette books don't tell. N. S. Hazel-
ton. Nat R 21:1328 D 30 '69
ETIQUETTE for children and youth
Do his manners need help? excerpts from
Male manners. K. Corinth and M. Sargent.
il Seventeen 28:134-5 N '69
In defense of ceremony. F. Maynard. PTA
Mag 63:22-4 Ap '69
Short sortie; excerpt from Seventeen guide
to travel. M. S. Welch. Seventeen 28:462-
7+ Ag '69
ETTER, Dave
Crayola; poem. Nation 209:320 S 29 '69
ETTINGER, Albert C.
Who needs rudders? Yachting 126:70-1+
N '69
ETYMOLOGY. See English language—Etymol-
ogy: Language and languages—Etymology
ETZIONI, Amitai
Agency for technological development for do-
mestic programs. bibliog Science 164:43-50
Ap 4 '69
Can the military aid the home front? Cur
105:24-6 Mr '69
Fallacy of decentralization. Nation 209:145-7
Ag 25 '69
EUCALYPTUS
Secret of its shape is pruning. il Sunset 143:
157 Jl '69
EUCHARIST. See Catholic church—Eucharist;
Lords Supper

EUDERMA maculatum. See Bats
EUGENE O'Neill memorial theater foundation, Waterford, Conn.
Theatre: National playwrights' conference. J. Novick. Nation 209:357-8 O 6 '69
EUGENICS
New life for old: genetic decisions. M. Hamilton. Chr Cent 86:741-4 My 28 '69
Test tube generation. D. M. Rorvik. il Esquire 71:108-14 Ap '69
See also
Marriage of cousins
EUGLENA
Circadian rhythm of cell division in euglena: effects of a random illumination regimen. L. N. Edmunds, jr. and R. R. Funch. bibliog il Science 165:500-3 Ag 1 '69
EUGRAMMIA press. See Private presses
EULA, Joe. See Greene, M. jt. auth.
EUPHEMISM
Euphemism: telling it like it isn't; Time essay. Time 94:26-7 S 19 '69
EURATOM
Euratom: atomic agency foundering amidst squabbles of its partners. D. S. Greenberg. Science 163:552-3 F 7 '69
Nuclear safeguards, the peaceful atom, and the IAEA. L. Scheinman. bibliog f il Int Concil 572:5-64 Mr '69
EUREKA SPRINGS, Ark.
U.S. journal: site of Christ of the Ozarks, statue and a Passion play. C. Trillin. New Yorker 45:69-70+ Jl 26 '69
EURIPIDES
Bacchae; tr. by K. Cavander. Criticism
Life il 66:32-5 Ap 1 '69
Newsweek il 73:113 Mr 24 '69
Sat R 52:20 Mr 29 '69
Euripides' Hippolytus. A. V. Rankin. bibliog f Am Imago 25:333-46 Wint '68
EUROBONDS. See Bonds
EURODOLLAR. See Money—International aspects
EUROPE
See also
Americans in Europe
Art—Europe
Cities and towns—Europe
Festivals—Europe
Fishing—Europe
Music festivals—Europe
Radio broadcasting—Europe
Tourist trade—Europe

Economic conditions
Economics & Europe: shakeups East & West. il Sr Schol 94:20 Ja 31 '69
See also
United Nations—Economic commission for Europe

History
See also
European war, 1914-1918

Bibliography
Articles and other books received; comp. by R. E. Lindgren. See issues of American historical review

Historiography
Johannes von Müller: the historian in search of a hero. G. A. Craig. bibliog f Am Hist R 74:1487-502 Je '69

15th century
Fifteenth century: the prospect of Europe, by M. Aston. Review
Nat R 21:185-6 F 25 '69. P. P. Witonski

17th century
Crisis of the seventeenth century, by H. R. Trevor-Roper. Review
Commonweal 89:595-6 F 7 '69. J. Ratté

20th century
Europe, a restless continent remapped. il Nat Geog 135:778-9, sup(folded map) Je '69

Politics
Europe: superseding the past. il Time 94: 29-30 D 19 '69
Overseas scenes. H. Brandon. Sat R 52:16+ N 8 '69
See also
Balance of power
European federation
International security
Munich four power agreement, 1938

Union (proposed)
See European federation

EUROPE, EASTERN
East Europe; symposium. bibliog f il Cur Hist 56:193-229+ Ap '69
See also
Atomic power—Europe, Eastern
Christians in eastern Europe
Germany (Federal Republic)—Foreign relations—Europe, Eastern
Money—Europe, Eastern
Tourist trade—Europe, Eastern

Commerce
East reaches for markets. M. I. Goldman. For Affairs 47:721-34 Jl '69
See also
Czechoslovakia—Commerce

Defenses
See also
Warsaw pact. 1955

Foreign relations
Detente in the '70s; East-West relations. Z. Brzezinski. New Repub 162:17-18 Ja 3 '70
Fatigue at the top. il Time 95:17-18 Ja 12 '70
Germany looks East; reshaping Europe. il Newsweek 74:33-4 D 22 '69
Willy vs. Walter. Newsweek 75:24 Ja 5 '70

History
Bibliography
Articles and other books received; comp. by C. Morley. See issues of American historical review
Politics
Uneasy lies the bloc. Time 93:36 F 28 '69
See also
Czechoslovakia—Occupation, 1968

Treaties
See also
Warsaw pact. 1955

Union (proposed)
See European federation

EUROPE, WESTERN
See also
Aeronautics, Commercial—Europe, Western
Aeronautics, Military—Europe, Western
Aerospace industries—Europe, Western
Agricultural administration—Europe, Western
Air travel—Europe, Western
Airlines—Europe, Western
Airplane industry and trade—Europe, Western
Airplanes, Military—Europe, Western
Architecture—Europe, Western
Atomic power—Europe, Western
Atomic research—Europe, Western
Automobile industry and trade—Europe, Western
Automobile touring—Europe, Western
Biscay, Bay of
Business consolidations and mergers—Europe, Western
Electronic apparatus industry and trade—Europe, Western
Gardens—Europe, Western
Investments, Foreign (in Europe)
Journalism—Europe, Western
Labor laws and legislation—Europe, Western
Labor supply—Europe, Western
Meat industry and trade—Europe, Western
Newspapers—Europe, Western
Police—Europe, Western
Public opinion—Europe, Western
Publishers and publishing—Europe, Western
Research—Europe, Western
Rhine River
Science—Europe, Western
Shopping and shoppers—Europe, Western
Space research—Europe, Western
Strikes—Europe, Western
Taxation—Europe, Western
Television broadcasting—Europe, Western
Tourist trade—Europe, Western
Trade unions—Europe, Western
Trusts, Industrial—Europe, Western
Water pollution—Europe, Western
Yachts and yachting—Europe, Western
Youth—Europe, Western

Armed forces
See also
United States—Armed forces—Forces in Europe

Commerce
Trade: rift of reason; western Europe and the United States. G. E. Bradley. il Nations Bsns 57:96-9 S '69

EUROPEAN launcher development organization—*Continued*
Four ELDO members agree on launches. E. H. Kolcum. Aviation W 90:24-5 Ap 28 '69
Shaky but hopeful. T. Shoemaker. Sci N 96: 120 Ag 9 '69
EUROPEAN literature
European literary scene. R. J. Clements. See issues of Saturday review
EUROPEAN organization for nuclear research
Big machine; by R. Jungk. Review Bul Atom Sci 25:34-5 Mr '69. M. S. Livingston
See also
International conference on high energy physics
EUROPEAN painting. See Painting, European
EUROPEAN physical society
Growing European physical society includes 31,000 persons. R. H. Ellis. il Phys Today 22:63+ N '69
EUROPEAN poetry
New poetry from Europe. H. Taylor. Nation 209:260-1 S 15 '69
EUROPEAN pottery. See Pottery, European
EUROPEAN southern observatory. See Astronomical observatories—Chile
EUROPEAN space research organization
European satellite plans. R. N. Watts, jr. il Sky & Tel 38:231 O '69
ESRO defines five advanced science satellites. Aviation W 91.44 S 1 '69
EUROPEAN union. See European federation
EUROPEAN war, 1914-1918
Aerial operations
Flier's journal. G. C. Kenney. il Am Heritage 21:46-57 D '69
Personal narratives
Flier's journal. G. C. Kenney. il Am Heritage 21:46-57 D '69
Treaties
See also
Versailles, Treaty of, June 28, 1919
EUROPEAN war in art
Banner years; with paintings by C. Hassam. D. G. Lowe. Am Heritage 20:54-9 Je '69
EUROPEAN women. See Women—Europe
EUSTICE, Brockhurst
Cube house vs. the squares. J. Neary. il por Life 67:83-4+ N 14 '69
EUTHANASIA
Euthanasia at 80? proposal by British health official. Newsweek 73:77 My 12 '69
EUTROPHICATION. See Water pollution
EVACUATION, Civilian
Safer but sadder; Israel evacuates residents of occupied Qantara. M. Elkins. il Newsweek 73:40+ Ja 27 '69
EVALUATION (education)
Catholic alumni: seven years after. A. M. Greeley. il America 120:96-100 Ja 25 '69; Reply. N. J. Rigali. 120:178 F 15 '69
Demand for accountability. Sat R 52:64 D 20 '69
Education assessment begins. Sr Schol 94: Schol Teach 8 My 2 '69
Evaluation is a full-time job. D. Iwamoto and N. E. Hearn. Am Ed 5:18-19 Ap '69
If I could do what I wanted to, I'd start with grade school and revamp the whole system. M. A. Hyde and S. Kalter. Mlle 69:268-9 Ag '69
National assessment: are we ready? W. P. Moellenberg. Clear House 43:451-4 Ap '69
National assessment of education. Sch & Soc 97:208 Ap '69
National assessment of educational progress, a diffusion study. R. Kock. bibliog f Sch & Soc 97:95-7 F '69
Speaking out: school is bad for children. J. Holt. Sat Eve Post 242:12+ F 8 '69
What's the score on national assessment? G. B. Brain. il Todays Ed 58:18-21 O '69
EVALUATION (psychology) See Value (psychology)
EVAN, William M.
Why not portable pensions? Duns R 94:60-2 S '69
EVAN-Picone, incorporated
It's back to high style at Evan-Picone. S. Margetts. il Duns R 93:83-4+ Mr '69
EVANGELICAL church
See also
National association of evangelicals
National Negro evangelical association
North American Christian convention
EVANGELICAL church in Africa
Africa's evangelicals choose the middle way. O. W. Okite. Chr Today 13:42-3 Mr 14 '69

EVANGELICAL church in Germany
Dropouts or heathen? Newsweek 75:55 Ja 5 '70
EVANGELICAL covenant church of America
Evangelical covenant annual meeting. J. Lambert. Chr Cent 86:1048 Ag 6 '69
EVANGELICALISM
Evangelical unity and disunity. Chr Today 14:35 O 10 '69
Time to meet the evangelicals? R. E. Branson. Chr Cent 86:1640-3 D 24 '69
Who is dividing British evangelicals? British evangelical council. J. D. Douglas. Chr Today 14:35 D 19 '69
See also
Fundamentalism
EVANGELISTIC work
American evangelicals mount fresh offensive. Chr Today 13:35 My 23 '69
Anaheim crusade: at home with the Angels. R. Chandler. il Chr Today 14:40+ O 24 '69
Billy Graham plays the Garden. P. Tracy. Commonweal 90:457-9 Jl 25 '69
Billy Graham: spanning the decades; interview. B. Graham. Chr Today 14:34 N 7 '69
Billy in the Garden. B. Farrell. Life 67:2B Jl 4 '69
Billy's apostles; U.S. business establishment behind New York crusade. il Newsweek 73:65 Je 23 '69
Black power in Asia. E. Ramientos, jr. Chr Today 13:40-1 Mr 14 '69
Closest thing to a White House chaplain: B. Graham. E. B. Fiske. il N Y Times Mag p27+ Je 8 '69
Coral ridge story. R. E. Friedrich, jr. il Chr Today 13:32-3 Jl 18 '69
Developing a climate for evangelism. Chr Today 13:24-5 Mr 28 '69
Educating for evangelism. J. Bayley. Chr Today 13:30 Jl 18 '69
Evangelism and social concern. Chr Today 13:22 Jl 4 '69
Evangelism in a day of revolution. L. Ford. Chr Today 14:6-12 O 24 '69
Every Christian a minister. Chr Today 14: 36 O 10 '69
Gospel in the city. L. Ford. Chr Today 13:39 Jl 4 '69
Graham in New York: less of the same. T. Early. Chr Cent 86:1049 Ag 6 '69
Mellowing magic; B. Graham at Manhattan's new Madison Square Garden. il Time 93:48 Je 27 '69
New crusader evangelist B. J. Hargis on pilgrimage to the Holy Land. il Time 94:49 Ag 29 '69
Saved or damned? first congress on evangelism. Newsweek 74:121 S 22 '69
Six days in September; U.S. Congress on evangelism. D. E. Kuchsrsky. il Chr Today 14:42-3 O 10 '69
10,852nd inquirer; Graham's New York crusade. D. E. Kucharshy. il Chr Today 13: 32-3 Jl 18 '69
U.S. Congress on evangelism: a turning point? Chr Today 14:32-3 O 10 '69
U.S. congress on evangelism; much given, much required. D. E. Kucharsky. Chr Today 13:40-1 S 26 '69
U.S. evangelicals; moving again. il Time 94:58+ S 19 '69
What is evangelism? S. H. Moffett. Chr Today 13:3-5 Ag; 13-14 S 12 '69
See also
American scientific affiliation
Communication (theology)
Missions
Revivals
Salvation army
Youth for Christ international

Anecdotes, facetiae, satire, etc.
If dropouts turn on. L. Woodrum. Chr Today 14:18-19 O 24 '69
EVANOFF, Vlad
Best salt-water lures. Motor B 123:88+ My '69
Coho catches on. Motor B 124:63+ O '69
Drop a hook down east. Motor B 124:39+ Jl '69
Fish 'n ships. See issues of Motor boating
Fishing is hunting. Motor B 123:87+ Je '69
Fishing the southern circuit. Motor B 124: 23-4+ D '69
Fishing the summer surf. Motor B 124:76-7+ Ag '69
Fishing your way south. Motor B 124:83+ N '69
EVANS, Allan R.
Graduate student. por Phys Today 22:25-6 Mr '69
EVANS, Barry R.
What is a councilman? Am City 84:8 Mr '69

EVANS, D. C. and Dunkelman, L.
Airglow and star photographs in the day-time from a rocket. bibliog Science 164: 1391-3 Je 20 '69

EVANS, David M.
Pollution goes underground. Nation 209:632-5 D 8 '69

—and Bradford, Albert
Under the rug. bibliog Environ 11:3-13+ O '69

EVANS, Eason
You see, this is the way it is! M. W. Brown. il por Sch Arts 68:30-3 Ap '69

EVANS, Fred
Bad day in Cleveland. R. Bartimole. por Nation 209:41-5+ Jl 14 '69
Death penalty for a massacre. il por Newsweek 73:68 My 26 '69
Evans case. Nation 209:237 S 15 '69

EVANS, George Bird
How close, and how? Field & S 74:152-4+ S '69

EVANS, Glen
Freelance market report: the men's action adventure field. Writers Digest 49:48-52+ D '69
Men's magazines. Writers Digest 49:59-61+ F '69

EVANS, John W. See Williams, W. jt. auth.

EVANS, John Whitney
[Book review] America 120:227-8 F 22 '69

EVANS, Luther
World's best blue-water race. Motor B 123: 95-7+ Mr '69

EVANS, M. Stanton
Kennedy mystique. Nat R 21:81 Ja 28 '69

EVANS, Mary
Shakers: a gifted people. Am Home 72:88+ S '69
Singing bamboo, falling water. Am Home 72:110+ O '69

EVANS, Minnie
Beautiful dreamer. il Newsweek 74:85-6 Ag 4 '69

EVANS, Rick
Futuristic nostalgia; 2525. il por Time 94:59 Jl 18 '69

EVANS, Robert
Why should he have it? J. Mills. il pors Life 66:62-8+ Mr 7 '69

EVANS, Rupert N.
Secondary school and occupational preparation. Ed Digest 34:20-3 My '69

EVANS, Thomas Mellon
So I lost, so what? por Forbes 104:44 Ag 14 '69

EVANS, Toni
Protection; poem. Chr Cent 86:1614 D 17 '69

EVANS, William W. See Thompson, J. W. jt. auth.

EVANS collision. See Collisions at sea

EVANSTON, Ill.
Churches
Sanctuary in Evanston; Methodist churches accommodate Weathermen. Newsweek 74: 73+ O 27 '69

EVANSVILLE, Ind.
Multi-purpose lights for an all-purpose park. L. Torgerson. il Am City 84:130 Je '69

EVAPORATION
Evaporation retarded by monolayers. F. MacRitchie. bibliog il Science 163:929-31 F 28 '69; Reply. R. Kappesser and others. 166: 403 O 17 '69

EVENING and continuation schools
See also
Adult education

EVENING for Merlin Finch; drama. See Dizenzo, C.

EVERDING, August
Everding; interview. ed. by G. Loney. por Opera N 34:16 O 11 '69

EVERETT, Boyd N. jr
Death of Dhaulagiri. por Time 93:42 My 9 '69

EVERETT, Marjorie (Lindheimer)
Marje's late, late show. W. Tower. il por Sports Illus 31:32-4+ S 15 '69

EVERETT, Walter H.
Four disciples of Howard Pyle. H. C. Pitz. il Am Artist 33:38-9 Ja '69

EVERGLADES
America the raped; excerpt. G. Marine. il Ramp Mag 7:72-4 Ja 25 '69
Assault on the Everglades. A. Wolff. il Look 33:44-50+ S 9 '69
Coalition forms to fight Florida jetport. Nat Parks 43:28 My '69
Easy way to explore the Everglades; Loop road. G. X. Sand. il Sci Digest 65:37-41 F '69
Everglades jetport; appeal to prevent airport. M. Nadel. Liv Wildn 32:2 Aut '68

Flowing grass; excerpts from The Everglades: river of grass. M. S. Douglas. il Audubon 71:28-45 Ja '69
Folly in Florida; project to build jetport in the Everglades. A. W. Smith. Nat Parks 43:2+ Ja '69
Jetport and the Everglades: life or runaway? il Liv Wildn 33:13-20 Spr '69
Jetport or Everglades park? The Leopold report; summary. L. B. Leopold. il Audubon 71:151-3 N '69
Jets v. Everglades. il Time 94:42-3 Ag 22 '69
Jets vs. the call of the wild. il Bsns W p76-7 Ag 30 '69
Last chance to save the Everglades. J. D. MacDonald. il Life 67:58-61+ S 5 '69
Leopold report: Everglades jetport; with editorial comment. L. B. Leopold. Nat Parks 43:10, 11-13 N '69
Progress menaces the Everglades. il Nat Parks 43:8-15 Jl '69
Superjetport, or Everglades Park? P. Brooks. il Audubon 71:4-11 Jl '69

EVERGLADES experiment station. See Agricultural experiment stations

EVERGLADES NATIONAL PARK
Inland Florida cruising. M. Hunn. il Yachting 126:74-5+ D '69

EVERGREEN review (periodical)
Evergreen tempest: eye of a storm; Los Angeles public library. E. T. Moore. ALA Bul 63:1527-30 D '69
Los Angeles library commission bans Evergreen. Library J 94:3385 O 1 '69
Skirmish with the censors; espisode in McMurry college library; address, June 1968. D. Gore. ALA Bul 63:193-203 F '69; Discussion. 63:553-6, 704, 889-90, 1512-13 My-Jl, D '69

EVERGREENS
Evergreens for accent. C. E. Lewis. il Horticulture 47:40-1+ My '69
How to choose and plant evergreens. L. Grove. il Bet Hom & Gard 47:36-7 O '69
How to get the best shrubs and evergreens for your money. il Bet Hom & Gard 47:52+ Mr '69
See also
Christmas trees
also names of evergreens. e.g. China-fir

Diseases and pests
See also
Spraying and dusting

EVERLY, Don
Records: rocks, etc. country music. E. Willis. New Yorker 45:116-18 F 22 '69

EVERLY, Phil
Records: rocks, etc. country music. E. Willis. New Yorker 45:116-18 F 22 '69

EVERLY, Robert E.
Voter-planner's plea for sensible facilities. Parks & Rec 4:21-2+ Ag '69

EVERS, Charles
Notes and comment; address, May 1969. New Yorker 45:29 Je 14 '69

about
Black power, municipal style. J. E. Patterson. Commonweal 90:477-8 Ag 8 '69
Jubilee day. il por Newsweek 73:45-6 My 26 '69
Mayor of Fayette, Miss. J. Lelyveld. il pors N Y Times Mag p54-5+ O 26 '69
Mississippi muzzle. C. Wilkie. Nation 208: 132-3 F 3 '69
Mississippi smiles on Charles Evers. il por Life 66:40-1 My 23 '69
New black hope for a town in Mississippi. il por Bsns W p40 Jl 5 '69
New day. New Yorker 45:24-6 Ag 2 '69
Not doing you like you done us. il por Time 94:16 Jl 18 '69
Pledges of love and unity. il por Time 93:25 My 23 '69
Three-man klan. Newsweek 74:34+ S 22 '69
To live and die in Dixie. il por Newsweek 74:31-2 Jl 21 '69

EVERS, James Charles. See Evers, C.

EVERS, Mrs Medgar W.
Mississippi homecoming. por Ladies Home J 86:77+ O '69

EVERSON, William. See Antoninus, Brother

EVERSON museum. See Syracuse, N. Y.—Galleries and museums

EVETT, Robert
Music. Atlan 223:110-11 My; 224:107 Jl; 135-6 O; 172+ N: 160-2 D '69
Music. New Repub 161:28-30 N 1 '69
Rehabilitating Ravel. Atlan 223:146+ Mr '69

EVIDENCE
Truth and proof. A. Tarski. Sci Am 220:63-70 bibliog(p 144) Je '69

EVIDENCE (law)
Is a hypnotized witness reliable? il Time 93:70 Mr 28 '69
See also
Confession (law)
Wire tapping
EVIL. See Good and evil
EVISON, S. Herbert
Farming on the Blue Ridge parkway. Nat Parks 43:18-20 O '69
Finding a route for the Blue Ridge parkway. Nat Parks 43:11-13 S '69
EVOLUTION
Continental drift and evolution. B. Kurtén. il Sci Am 220:54-64 Mr '69
Earthlings in the space age; reprint. Lord Ritchie-Calder. il UNESCO Courier 22:4-6 Ag '69
Evolution of man and society, by C. D. Darlington. Review
Time il 94:74+ O 17 '69
Generation and maintenance of gradients in taxonomic diversity. F. G. Stehli and others. bibliog il Science 164:947-8 My 23 '69; Reply. L. Van Valen. 166:1656-8 D 26 '69
Man, one of evolution's mistakes? adaptation of address, September 1969. A. Koestler. il N Y Times Mag p28-9+ O 19 '69; Discussion. p 14 N 9; 52+ N 23 '69
Of ants and men; reprint. J. Gray. il UNESCO Courier 22:46-7 Ag '69
See also
Adaptation (biology)
Human genetics
Man—Influence of environment
Man—Origin and antiquity
Mutation (biology)
Phylogeny
Religion and science
Species
Stars—Evolution
Tennessee evolution controversy

Laws and legislation
End of the monkey war. L. S. De Camp. il Sci Am 220:15-21 bibliog (p 132) F '69
See also
Tennessee evolution controversy
EVOLUTION, Social. See Social change
EVOLUTION, Stellar. See Stars—Evolution
EVOY, John J.
Dialogue across the gap. America 120:356-9 Mr 29 '69
EVTUSHENKO, Evgenii Aleksandrovich
Pages from a Tashkent diary. R. Styron. Vogue 154:240+ S 1 '69
EWBANK, Weeb
Eub Weebank's mother hens. R. F. Jones. il por Sports Illus 31:26-9 N 10 '69
EWEN, Lois Stuart
This shining moment; story. Good H 168:90-1 Mr '69
EWEN, Paterson
New work from Montreal. B. Lord. il Art in Am 57:99-101 My '69
EWERS, Jean
Perth potters' club. Ceram Mo 17:28 Ap '69
EWERS, John C.
Red painting. Am West 6:54+ Ja '69
Sculptor Cyrus E. Dallin, who knew the horse and knew the Indian. Am West 6:22-3 N '69
EWING, J. I. See Jones, E. J. W. jt. auth.
EWING, Maurice. See Jacobs. M. B. jt. auth.
EWING, Yale
Expertise of Dr Wiesner. Nat R 21:746+ Jl 29 '69
EXAMINATIONS
Grades hinder education. America 120:237 Mr 1 '69
See also
College entrance examination board
Educational tests and measurements
Physical examinations
Psychological examinations
EXCAVATING machinery
See also
Trenching machinery
EXCAVATIONS (archeology)
Students underground. J. Marks. il Mlle 70: 150-1+ D '69
Throwing cold water on Marmes man. M. P. Works. Esquire 73:59-60+ Ja '70
See also
Archeology
Cities and towns, Ruined, extinct, etc.
Sybaris
Troy
also subhead Antiquities under names of continents, countries, states, cities, etc, e.g. Turkey—Antiquities

EXCEPTIONAL children. See Children, Exceptional
EXCESS profits, War. See War profits
EXCHANGE, Foreign. See Foreign exchange
EXCHANGE of persons programs
Detente among management men; Soviet-MIT exchange of Sloan fellows. il Bsns W p42 Je 7 '69
Our cultural exports: a view of the United States exchange program; with questions and answers. J. Canter. Ann Am Acad 384:85-95 Jl '69
University of Minnesota band returns from tour of Soviet Union; excerpts from remarks, May 23, 1969. R. M. Nixon; A. F. Dobrynin. Dept State Bul 60:540-2 Je 23 '69
See also
Educational exchanges
Students, Interchange of
Teachers, Interchange of
EXCHANGE students. See Students, Interchange of
EXCHANGES
See also
Chicago board of trade
Chicago mercantile exchange
Stock exchange
EXCHANGES, Commodity. See Commodity exchanges
EXCHANGES, Educational. See Educational exchanges
EXCITON theory
Fission of nonparticles; weak fluorescence in tetracene. Sci N 95:378 Ap 19 '69
Split concept; splitting of an exciton. Sci Am 220:56 My '69
Where the action is, in molecules; excitonics, new way to transfer energy. il Bsns W p 106+ Ap 12 '69
EXCLUSIVE agencies
See also
Franchise system
EX-CONVICTS. See Prisoners, Discharged
EXCURSION rates. See Travel—Economic aspects
EXCUSES
Arrrah!! My arquebus jammed. R. Starnes. Field & S 73:14+ F '69
EXECUTIONS and executioners
See also
Capital punishment
Hanging
EXECUTIVE ability
Theory of executive incompetence; the Peter principle. S. Blickstein. il Duns R 94:30-1 Jl '69
See also
Leadership
EXECUTIVE absenteeism. See Absenteeism
EXECUTIVE agreements
See also
United States—Foreign relations—Executive agreements
EXECUTIVE airlines, incorporated
Executive airlines reports Florida traffic expansion. J. W. Carter. Aviation W 90:44 Ap 14 '69
EXECUTIVE committees. See Committees in management
EXECUTIVE departments (United States) See United States—Executive departments
EXECUTIVE jet aviation, incorporated
End of a bizarre overseas venture; Executive jet severing links to Penn central. il Bsns W p 122-3+ Ag 16 '69
Executive jet aviation begins efforts to find new financing. J. P. Woolsey. Aviation W 91:49-50 N 10 '69
EXECUTIVE liability. See Liability (law)
EXECUTIVE office of the president. See United States—Executive office of the president
EXECUTIVE power
See also
Presidents—United States—Power and duties
EXECUTIVE psychoanalysis. See Psychoanalysis
EXECUTIVE responsibility. See Responsibility
EXECUTIVE secretaries. See Secretaries
EXECUTIVES
Absentee executive; AWOLism. il Newsweek 74:104-6 N 17 '69
Case of the fragmented manager. G. J. Berkwitt. il Duns R 93:49-51 Ap '69
Corporate search for soul; role of corporate urban affairs departments. J. Poindexter. il Duns R 94:36-9 Ag '69
Do executives live better abroad? il Duns R 93:46-8 F '69
Executive defenses: they cost plenty. D. E. Zand. Duns R 94:62-3+ O '69

EXERCISE—*Continued*

Anecdotes, facetiae, satire, etc.

Ford's physical unfitness program. C. Ford. Read Digest 94:80-2 My '69

EXERCISE Acid Test. See Military maneuvers

EXERCISE, Yoga. See Yoga

EXERCISING equipment
Build this jogger-walker for $30. J. Capotosto. il Pop Mech 131:156-9 Je '69
Build your own exerbike. J. Wiley. il Mech Illus 65:118 Ap '69
Getting fit by making others slim; fitness industry. il Bsns W p 140-1+ Mr 22 '69
Keep trim with this dual-action exerciser. J. A. McKee. il Pop Mech 131:181 My '69
New exercise gadgets to keep you fit. A. Markovich. il Mech Illus 65:43-5+ S '69
Tone up, fatso! il Esquire 72:154-5 O '69

EXERCISING machines. See Exercising equipment

EXHAUST gases. See Automobile engines—Exhaust

EXHAUST head pipes. See Automobile engines—Exhaust

EXHAUST systems
See also
Automobile engines—Exhaust

EXHIBITION buildings
Kahn in Venice; designs for the Esposizione internazionale d'arte. il Arch Forum 130:64-7 Mr '69
See also
Pavilions

EXHIBITIONS
Black Expo; trade fair in Chicago. il Ebony 25:106-8+ D '69
Exposition: Japan exposition at the Coliseum. New Yorker 45:45-7 N 8 '69
Hotel show: annual National hotel & motel exposition at the Coliseum. New Yorker 45:47-8 N 22 '69
Ivan the terrible salesman; trade fair at Kuala Lumpur. il Time 94:104+ O 17 '69
Personal business; Europe's top trade fairs. Bsns W p 133-4 Mr 15 '69
Please do touch the daisies; first International tactile sculpture symposium. il Time 94:54 Jl 25 '69
Single idea; Great singles affair at Hollywood palladium. il Newsweek 73:81 F 24 '69
Spirit of '76; cities vie to hold international exposition to mark 200th anniversary of the Declaration of independence. Newsweek 74:79-80 S 29 '69
World travel calendar, 1970; comp. by F. Shemanski. Sat R 53:53-6 Ja 3 '70
See also
Audio fairs
Dioramas
Garden exhibits
Library exhibits
Moving picture festivals
Museum techniques
also subhead Exhibitions under names of cities, e.g. Copenhagen—Exhibitions
also subhead Exhibitions under various subjects, e.g. Glassware—Exhibitions

EXHIBITIONS, Traveling
Andy Warhol's exhibition; traveling show of period art called Raid the icebox. D. Bourdon. il Art N 68:44-5+ O '69
Little Irvy; exhibition of refrigerated whale. F. Deford. il Sports Illus 31:50-7 Ag 11 '69

EXHIBITS
Can man survive? centennial exhibit at American museum of natural history. C. Peet. il Am For 75:4-7+ Ag '69
See also special types of exhibits, e.g.
Library exhibits

EXILES
How it looks from the colonies. D. W. Brogan. Esquire 72:48+ D '69
See also
Émigrés

EXISTENTIALISM
Bergman's Shame and Sartre's stare. R. E. Lauder. il Cath World 209:247-50 S '69
Existential autonomy and Christian freedom. R. C. Sproul. Chr Today 13:12-13 Jl 18 '69
Existential school counselor. G. J. Pine. Clear House 43:351-4 F '69
Existentialist prolegomena to a future metaphysics, by F. Sontag. Review
Commonweal 91:50-1 O 10 '69. E. V. Kohak

Anecdotes, facetiae, satire, etc.

How existential can you get? B. DeMott. il N Y Times Mag p4+ Mr 23 '69

EX NUNS, priests, etc.
Bishop and Mrs Shannon. il Newsweek 74:76 Ag 25 '69

Defector in the household; chaplain to the Pope to leave the priesthood and marry. il Time 93:62 Mr 21 '69
Halfway houses for clergy dropouts. Chr Today 13:34-5 Jl 18 '69
News and views; former priests rating by Gallagher presidents' report. J. Deedy. Commonweal 89:664 F 28 '69
Priests who live in sin; Gallagher survey of former priests. C. McCarthy. New Repub 160:16-18 Mr 1 '69
Time of the fugitive. C. A. Weber Commonweal 90:137-40 Ap 18 '69; Reply. M. L. Farrell. 90:221+ My 9 '69
Where ex-priests work. Time 93:75 F 7 '69

EXOBIOLOGY. See Life on other planets

EXORCISM
Beating the devil; Zurich trial of six people accused of beating to death a girl while trying to exorcise the devil from her body. il Time 93:30 F 7 '69
Devil trial; religious group administered fatal beating to girl in effort to exorcise the devil from her soul. Newsweek 73:40+ F 10 '69

EXORIBONUCLEASE. See Ribonuclease

EXOSKELETON. See Skeleton (invertebrates)

EXOSKELETON (man amplifier) See Man amplifiers

EXOTECH, Incorporated
Blasting rock with water; hydrotechnology research. il Bsns W p 130 Jl 19 '69

EXOTIC fishes. See Fishes

EXPANDING universe. See Universe

EXPANSION of industry. See Industrial expansion

EXPECTATION of life. See Longevity

EXPENDITURES, Family. See Domestic finance

EXPENDITURES, Personal. See Budget, Personal

EXPENDITURES, State. See State finance

EXPENSE accounts ((business)
Expense account diet; excerpt. J. Dolger. il Duns R 94:66-8+ N '69
Travel-expense rule; outdated? U S News 66:87-8 Je 16 '69

EXPERIENCE (religion)
On rediscovering Jesus. M. Muggeridge. il Esquire 71:122-6+ Je '69
See also
Conversion

EXPERIENCE (religion) and hallucinogenic drugs. See Hallucinogenic drugs and religious experience

EXPERIMENT in international living (organization)
Taste of summer Sweden; Experiment group of American college women. R. Hawkins. il Sr Schol 94:Schol Teach 21-2 F 28 '69

EXPERIMENTAL aircraft association
Rockford. P. Garrison. il Flying 85:52-5 N '69

EXPERIMENTAL airplanes. See Airplanes, Experimental

EXPERIMENTAL animals. See Laboratory animals

EXPERIMENTAL automobiles. See Automobiles, Experimental

EXPERIMENTAL colleges. See Colleges and universities, Experimental

EXPERIMENTAL education. See Education, Experimental

EXPERIMENTAL films. See Moving pictures, Experimental

EXPERIMENTAL music. See Music

EXPERIMENTAL route guidance system. See Automobiles—Radio equipment

EXPERIMENTAL schools. See Schools, Experimental

EXPERIMENTAL theater. See Theater, Experimental

EXPERIMENTATION on man. See Medical research—Experimentation on man

EXPERIMENTS. See Physics—Experiments

EXPLODING stars. See Stars, New

EXPLOITATION
Labor waste in New York; rural exploitation and migrant workers. W. H. Friedland. bibliog il Trans-Action 6:48-53 F '69

EXPLORATION, Underwater. See Underwater exploration

EXPLORATIONS
See also
America—Discovery and exploration
Arctic exploration
Latin America—Discovery and exploration

EXPLORERS, American
See also
Powell, J. W.

EXPLORERS, English
See also
Bailey, F. M.

EXPLORERS, Portuguese
Portugal story, by J. D. Passos. Review
Sat R 52:22-3 My 31 '69. J. H. Plumb

EXPLORERS, Scottish
See also
Livingstone, D.

EXPLORING expeditions. See United States—
Exploring expeditions

EXPLOSIONS
Tunnel: gas-filled void cause of explosion
along Delancey street. New Yorker 44:24-7
F 1 '69
See also
Shock waves

EXPLOSIVES
Aleutian runaway; scuttling of the Robert
Louis Stevenson. R. Davidson. il Sci Di-
gest 65:64-8 My '69
Getting there in time; forcible entry tool
called Jet-Axe. il Bsns W p 158 Mr 29 '69

Transportation
Explosions en route; transporting explosives
by road and rail. S. Morrison. il Nation
209:379-81 O 13 '69

EXPO 70. See Osaka, Japan—Worlds fair, 1970

EXPORT and import control. See Foreign trade
regulation

EXPORT controls
Department supports extension of Export control act; statement, May 28, 1969. J. A.
Greenwald. Dept State Bul 60:545-7 Je 23
'69

EXPORT credit
Textile bubble bursts in Madrid. il Bsns W
p82+ S 20 '69

EXPORT trade
Export sales trends; excerpts from address.
R. H. Warren. Aviation W 90:11 Ap 7 '69
Political factor increases in export market.
E. H. Kolcum. il Aviation W 90:93+ Je 2
'69
Report on employment related to exports;
with tables. C. T. Bowman. bibliog Mo La-
bor R 92:16-20 Je '69
U.S. transport export slowdown expected. W.
C. Wetmore. il Aviation W 90:135-8 Je 2 '69

EXPOS (baseball) See Baseball clubs

EXPOSÉ articles. See Periodical articles

EXPOSITIONS. See Exhibitions

EXPOSURE (photography) See Photography—
Exposure

EXPOSURE meters
Calumet M-100; flash meter. H. Zucker; W.
F. Wison. il Pop Phot 65:70+ Jl '69
Can eleven SLR meters all be right? il Mod
Phot 33:106-7 N '69
Design of a light meter & exposure calcula-
tor. J. L. Barnum. il Electr World 81:52-4+
My '69
Foto facts. P. Farber. il Travel & Camera
32:38 O '69
How sensitive is your meter? L. A. Mann-
heim. il Mod Phot 33:68-9+ Jl '69
How to read spots safely. C. W. Kennedy.
il Pop Phot 64:24+ F '69
Instructions are for experts. B. Schwalberg.
il Pop Phot 64:82-3+ F '69
Kramer's korner; Luna-pro enlarging meter.
A. Kramer. il Mod Phot 33:52+ Jl '69
Metering through the lens; interview, ed. by
B. Schwalberg. H. D. Ulffers. Pop Phot
65:104+ Ag '69
Meters get a closer check. W. F. Wilson. il
Pop Phot 64:72-3 Je '69
New look in meters. W. F. Wilson. il Pop
Phot 64:72-3+ Ap '69
1969 exposure meter guide. D. L. Miller. Mod
Phot 33:60-1 Ag '69
Phototronics; should a flash meter also
read existing light? E. Farber. il Mod Phot
33:50+ O '69
Wein flash meter WP-1000 with sonic-slave.
P. Farber. il Travel & Camera 32:76+ Mr '69
Zero in on lens speed. P. Farber. il Travel
& Camera 32:104 D '69

L'EXPRESS (periodical) See Periodicals—
France

EXPRESS companies
See also
American express company

EXPRESS highways
Ban the bridge? protests over Three Sisters
bridge plans, Washington, D.C. il Newsweek 74:68 N 3 '69
Biggest snarl on city highways; Baltimore
freeway program. il Bsns W p 144+ O 18
'69
Driving the new interstates. D. Wharton. il
Read Digest 95:174-6+ Ag '69

Freeway plans threaten nation's capital. Nat
Parks 43:21 Ja '69
Highway as a killer. il Life 66:24D-35 My 30
'69
How S.O.M. took on the Baltimore road gang.
J. Bailey. il Arch Forum 130:40-5 Mr '69
How to survive freeway on/off ramps. D. L.
Gregg. il Bet Hom & Gard 47:50-1+ Jl '69
Kill the hill! Pave that grass! P. O'Neil. il
Life 67:126-7+ O 10 '69
Trouble for freeways. il U S News 67:76-7
Ag 11 '69
Will it be the soaring seventies? argument
for automated guideways. H. Sutton and
D. Butwin. il Sat R 53:50-1 Ja 3 '70

Southern states
Farming on the Blue Ridge parkway. S. H.
Evison. il Nat Parks 43:18-20 O '69
Finding a route for the Blue Ridge park-
way. S. H. Evison. il Nat Parks 43:11-13
S '69
Highway in the sky; Blue Ridge parkway.
J. T. Starr. il Am For 75:8-11+ Ja '69
Take the Blue Ridge parkway to Shenandoah
Valley and the Great Smokies. C. Carter. il
Home Gard 56:62-4 Mr '69

EXPRESSION
See also
Rhetoric

EXPRESSIONISM (art)
De Kooning's 300,000.000th birthday; tr. by
J. Ashbery. S. Dali. il Art N 68:56-7+ Ap
'69
One cheer for expressionism; German ex-
pressionism. A. Goldin. il Art N 67:48-9+
N '68
See also
Abstract expressionism

EX-PRIESTS. See Ex-nuns, priests, etc.

EXPROPRIATION
Expropriation game. Nat R 21:891-2 S 9 '69
See also
Latin America—Expropriation policy
Peru—Expropriation policy

EXPULSION. See Deportation

EXPULSON from school and college
Dealing with campus chaos; Notre Dame: fif-
teen minutes and out; excerpts from letter,
February 17, 1969. T. M. Hesburgh. U S
News 66:34 Mr 3 '69; Same abr. with title
College president takes a stand on campus
chaos. Read Digest 94:104-7 My '69
Suspension: a valid disciplinary tool? C. E.
Harwood. bibliog f Clear House 44:29-32 S
'69
Teacher opinion poll; teachers' right to sus-
pend students. Todays Ed 58:35 F '69

EXTENSION cords. See Electric cords

EXTERIOR house decoration. See House decoration, Exterior

EXTERMINATION of mosquitoes. See Mosquito control

EXTINCT animals. See Animals, Extinct

EXTINCT birds. See Birds, Extinct

EXTINCTION of animals. See Animals, Extinct

EXTINCTION of man. See Man—Survival

EXTRA corporeal irradiation of the blood. See
Blood—Irradiation

EXTRACTS, Flavoring. See Flavoring essences

EXTRACURRICULAR activities. See Student
activities

EXTRASENSORY perception
Mind over matter, maybe. il Time 93:52 Ja 24
'69

EXTRATERRESTRIAL life. See Life on other
planets

EXTRAVEHICULAR visor assembly. See Astronauts—Clothing

EXTREME unction
Last rites, do they bring fear or reassurance?
A. J. Snider. il Sci Digest 65:60-1 Je '69

EXTREMELY low frequency radio waves. See
Radio waves

EXTREMISM. See Right and left (political science)

EXTRUSION process
Firm squeeze; hydrostatic process. Sci Am
221:49-50 O '69
Overlooked metal broadens its appeal; zinc.
il Bsns W p 124-5 My 17 '69

EYDE, Richard H. and Tseng, C. C.
Flower of tetraplasandra gymnocarpa hypo-
gyny with epigynous ancestry. bibliog Science 166:506-8 O 24 '69

EYE
See also
Retina
Sight
Vitreous humor

EYE—*Continued*

Accommodation and refraction

Dark adaptation: an interocular light-adaptation effect. T. G. Lansford and H. D. Baker. bibliog il Science 164:1307-9 Je 13 '69

Interocular effects in prism adaptation. J. E. Foley and K. Miyanshi. bibliog il Science 165:311-12 Jl 18 '69

Diseases and defects

What causes spots before your eyes? muscae volitantes, or flitting flies. il Good H 169: 145 Jl '69

X-ray and electron diffraction of ocular and bone marrow crystals in paraproteinemia. P. R. Laibson and V. V. Damiano. il Science 163:581-3 F 7 '69

See also
Blindness
Eyeglasses
Glaucoma
Myopia
Ophthalmology

Examination

Measuring eyes with sound waves. S. V. Jones. il Sci Digest 66:91 O '69

Anecdotes, facetiae, satire, etc.

Top of my head; open your eyes and say ah. G. Ace. Sat R 52:6 O 11 '69

Injuries

First aid. C. J. Potthoff. Todays Health 47: 80 F '69

Movements

Encephalic cycles during sleep and wakefulness in humans: a 24-hour pattern. E. Othmer and others. bibliog il Science 164:447-9 Ap 25 '69; Reply. R. J. Berger. 166:530-1 O 24 '69

Eye movement-retina delayed feedback. K. U. Smith and others. bibliog il Science 166: 1542-4 D 19 '69

Pigmentation

See Visual pigments

Surgery

New sight with sound; use of ultrasonics to remove cataracts. Sci Digest 65:53 Ap '69

Your eyes medical experiments you've never known before. A. Talmey. Vogue 153:104-5 Mr 15 '69

See also
Eye banks

Transplantation

Eye for an eye. Sci N 95:426 My 3 '69

Eye for an eye; operation carried out by Conrad D. Moore and Daniel Sigband. il Newsweek 73:73 My 5 '69

Eye to eye. Time 93:60 My 2 '69

Part of a whole eye. Sci 95:450 My 10 '69

EYE (animals)
See also
Sight (animals)

EYE (arthropods)

Optics of arthropod compound eye. S. R. Shaw. bibliog il Science 165:88-90 Jl 4 '69

EYE (crustacea)

Conductance changes associated with receptor potentials in limulus photoreceptors. T. G. Smith and others; reply with rejoinder. G. Duncan and S. L. Bonting. bibliog il Science 164:1188-9 Je 6 '69

Role for the sodium pump in photoreception in limulus. T. G. Smith and others; reply with rejoinder. G. Duncan and S. L. Bonting. bibliog il Science 164:1188-9 Je 6 '69

Visual receptors and retinal interaction; Nobel lecture December 12, 1967. H. K. Hartline. Science 164:270-8 Ap 18 '69

EYE (insects)

Vitamin A deficiency: effect on mosquito eye ultrastructure. J. D. Brammer and R. H. White. bibliog il Science 163:821-3 F 21 '69

See also
Sight (insects)

EYE (mollusks)

Circadian rhythm of optic nerve impulses recorded in darkness from isolated eye of aplysia. J. W. Jacklet. bibliog il Science 164:562-3 My 2 '69

Hyperpolarizing and depolarizing receptor potentials in the scallop eye. A. L. F. Gorman and J. S. McReynolds. bibliog il Science 165:309-10 Jl 18 '69

EYE bank networks. See Radio communication—Emergency applications

EYE banks

They listen so others might see; Eye bank network. H. Kantor. il Todays Health 47: 62-3 S '69

EYE donors

Race to reclaim a dead man's eyes. B. Derrick-Davis. il Todays Health 48:42-3+ Ja '70

EYE make-up. See Make-up

EYE movements. See Eye—Movements

EYE of the needle; story. See Bayer, A.

EYEBROW make-up. See Make-up

EYEGLASS cases

Foolish cases for sunglasses. il Sunset 143: 106 D '69

EYEGLASSES

Are eyeglasses inevitable? A. S. Markovits. Mech Illus 65:59 F '69

Fit your swimming mask with glasses. A. Browning. il Pop Mech 132:172+ Jl '69

Focus on spectacles. F. L. Remington. il Todays Health 47:50-3 Mr '69

How to see with glasses. N. Rothschild. il Pop Phot 65:83-5+ N '69

Viewing aids for the reclining TV-watcher. il Consumer Bul 52:4+ Mr '69

See also
Sun glasses

Anecdotes, facetiae, satire, etc.

Visual welfare state. H. F. Ellis. 45:103-4+ Ap 19 '69

EYELIDS

Eye job: blepharoplasty. il Vogue 154:104-5 Ag 15 '69

Non-bibulous baggy eyes; orbital herniation Sci Digest 65:53 Ap '69

EYESIGHT. See Sight

EYRIES. See Nests

EZERGAILIS, Andrew

Anglo-Saxonism and fascism. Yale R 58:481-506 Je '69

F

F-14s. See Airplanes, Military—United States

F-111. See Airplanes, Military—United States

FAA. See United States—Federal aviation administration

FAO. See Food and agriculture organization of the United Nations

FBI. See United States—Federal bureau of investigation

FCC. See United States—Federal communications commission

FDA. See United States—Food and drug administration

FET (field-effect transistors) See Transistors

FH/BUSA. See Freedom house/Books USA.

FHA loans. See United States—Federal housing administration

FHLBB. See United States—Federal home loan bank board

FIGHT (Freedom, independence, God, honor, today) See Civil rights organizations

FLIR (forward-looking infrared) sensors. See Detectors, Infrared

FM. See Radio frequency modulation

FM radio stations. See Radio stations, Frequency modulation

FM-stereo antennas. See Radio antennas

FMCS. See United States—Federal mediation and conciliation service

FPC. See United States—Federal power commission

FPC (fish protein concentrate) See Fish flour

FRB. See United States—Federal reserve board

FTC. See United States—Federal trade commission

FUDR (fluorodeoxyuridine) See Growth inhibiting substances (plants)

F. W. Dodge corporation. See Dodge, F. W. Corporation

F. W. Woolworth company. See Woolworth, F. W, company

FWPCA. See United States—Federal water pollution control administration

FABER, Nancy Gay

Sex for credit. Look 33:39-40+ Ap 1 '69

Tragedy touches their triumph. Look 33:78-9+ O 21 '69

FABIO, Rose Marie

Hi, mom, what's for lunch? Parents Mag 44:38+ Ja; 74+ F; 46 Mr; 78 Ap; 80 My; 58 Je; 60 Jl; 72 Ag '69

FABLES
See also
Bestiaries
FABRIANO, Gentile da. See Gentile da Fabriano
FABRIC softeners. See Softening agents
FABRIC wall coverings. See Wall coverings
FABRICA nacional automobiles. See Automobile industry and trade—Mexico
FABRICATED buildings. See Buildings, Prefabricated
FABRICATED houses. See Houses, Prefabricated
FABRICATION (meat cutting) See Meat cutting
FABRICS. See Textile fabrics
FABRITSKII, Veniamin, and Shmelyov, Igor
Utensils as works of art. UNESCO Courier 22:25-7 My '69
FABRY'S disease. See Angiokeratoma
FACADE; ballet. See Ballets—Criticisms
FACE
See also
Beauty, Personal
Physiognomy
FACIAL expression
Jolly is happy everywhere. Sci Digest 66:31-2 Jl '69
Pan-cultural elements in facial displays of emotion. P. Ekman and others. bibliog il Science 164:86-8 Ap 4 '69
FACIAL treatments. See Beauty, Personal
FACILITIES management companies. See Computer-based service companies
FACKNITZ, Konrad, and Kostikov, Lev
Mongolia. UNESCO Courier 22:14-17+ N '69
FACKRE, Gabriel
Blue collar white and the far right. Chr Cent 86:645-8 My 7 '69
FACSIMILE transmission
Fax: bright future for ageless wonder. D. M. Costigan. il Pop Electr 30:33-5+ F '69
His first million in sight? N. Bruckman's facsimile machine networks. Bsns W p94 My 24 '69
Mail by phone picks up new speed. il Bsns W p 120+ D 13 '69
FACSIMILES of rare books. See Book rarities—Facsimiles
FACTORIES
See also
Automobile factories
Branch factories
Textile mills
Design
Glass factory of large-scale precast units in Amberg, Germany. il Arch Rec 146:148-50 S '69
Porcelain factory in Selb with generous recreation facilities for workers. il Arch Rec 146:144-7 S '69
River cement company: the genesis of three buildings. il Arch Rec 145:164-6 F '69
History
City no one knew; the Amoskeag millyard, Manchester, N.H. R. Langenbach. il Arch Forum 130:84-91 Ja '69
Location
See Location in business and industry
Remodeling
There's new life for old factories. P. Busse. il Nations Bsns 57:68+ S '69
FACTORY management
See also
Production control
FACTORY produced houses. See Houses, Prefabricated
FACULTIES, College. See College professors and instructors
FACULTY clubhouses. See Clubhouses
FACULTY relationships. See Colleges and universities—Administration
FADOS
Queen of sorrows; A. Rodrigues. H. Saal. Newsweek 73:76-7 F 10 '69
FADS
Tripping on Disney. il Newsweek 75:88 Ja 19 '70
See also
College students fads
Food fads
FAEGENBURG, David H.
Radiologist talks about his work; with biographical sketch. ed. by W. S. Ross. pors Todays Health 48:44-7+ Ja '70
FAESSLER, Shirley
Basket of apples; story. Atlan 223:70-6 Ja '69

FAGEN, Richard R.
Revolution, for internal consumption only; excerpt from The transformation of political culture in Cuba. por Trans-Action 6:10-15 Ap '69
FAGER, Charles E.
Movies (title varies) Chr Cent 86:238, 1022, 1141, 1555-6, 1647; 87:24 F 12, Jl 30, S 3, D 3, 24 '69, Ja 7 '70
Movies, records. Chr Cent 86:386-8 Mr 19 '69
Records (title varies) (cont) Chr Cent 86: 522, 595-6, 622-3, 928-9, 1284-5, 1320, 1673-4 Ap 16-30, Jl 9, O 8-15, D 31 '69
FAGERSTROM, Stan
Bass man in steelhead country. Outdoor Life 143:94-6+ Ap '69
Cutthroat harvest. Outdoor Life 144:56-7+ Jl '69
Paradise for plunkers. Field & S 74:62-3+ Je '69
FAHERTY, William B.
Midwest meets Fr. Lombardi. America 121: 162-3 S 13 '69
FAHEY, John L. See Buell, D. N. jt. auth.
FAILURE (psychology)
Effect of school failure. W. E. Glasser. Ed Digest 35:13-17 D '69
FAILURE to assist in emergencies. See Assistance in emergencies
FAILURES in business. See Bankruptcy
FAIN, Samuel C. jr
Graduate student. por Phys Today 22:29-30 Mr '69
FAINTING
First aid. C. J. Potthoff. Todays Health 47:62 Jl '69
FAIR, Ronald L.
Thank God it snowed. Am Scholar 39:105-8 Wint '69
FAIR deal. See United States—Economic policy
FAIR trade. See Price maintenance by industry
FAIRBANK, Alfred John
Alfred Fairbank and his book of scripts. P. Standard. il Pub W 195:97-8 Je 9 '69
FAIRBANK, John King
Assignment for the '70's; address, December 29, 1968. bibliog f Am Hist R 74:861-79 F '69
China's foreign policy in historical perspective. For Affairs 47:449-63 Ap '69
FAIRCHILD, Sherman M.
Fairchild's ever-expanding universe. il pors Bsns W p 152-3+ F 22 '69
FAIRCHILD camera and instrument corporation
Between the idea and the reality. Forbes 104:25-7 O 15 '69
Fairchild scores a point on circuits; Fairchild-TI patent battle on integrated circuits. il Bsns W p 128 N 29 '69
FAIRCLOTH, Earl
Faircloth's law: a new way to nail elusive mobsters? D. Walsh. il por Life 67:62A-62B O 24 '69
FAIRFAX, Thomas, 3d baron Fairfax of Cameron. See Fairfax of Cameron, T. F.
FAIRFAX of Cameron, Thomas Fairfax, 3d baron
Oopon and ill husband; poem. Seventeen 28:92 My '69
FAIRFAX COUNTY, Va.
Negroes
Court's ruling on a suburban swimming pool. il U S News 67:19 D 29 '69
FAIRFIELD, John
Out of her time, Lady Ottoline. Vogue 154: 442-7+ S 1 '69
Theatre. Vogue 154:60 Ag 1 '69
FAIRFIELD COUNTY, Conn.
Fairfield County; New York's best address. S. Birmingham. il Holiday 45:58-63+ Ap '69
FAIRIES
Tracking down elves in folklore. M. Calhoun. Horn Bk 45:278-82 Je '69
FAIRNESS doctrine (television) See Television laws and regulations
FAIRS
Street fair in San Francisco. il Sunset 142:30 Je '69
See also
Audio fairs
Exhibitions
FAIRY plays
Princess and the greenies; dramatization of a fairy tale. E. B. Kane. Plays 29:74-8, 96 O '69
Villain and the toy shop. B. Winther. Plays 29:57-64 D '69

FAITH, Sister Mary. See Mary Faith, Sister
FAITH
  Abraham's faith and ours today. H. K. Stothard. Chr Today 14:8-10 D 19 '69
  Archimedes revisited. H. B. Kuhn. Chr Today 13:55-6 Ap 11 '69
  Beloved infidels; Rome conference to explore The culture of unbelief. Time 93:64+ Ap 4 '69
  Christian faith and secular faiths. L. Paul. Chr Cent 86:477-81 Ap 9 '69
  Christian values and a secular future. J. Hitchcock. America 121:155-9 S 13 '69
  Does the gospel make sense? Chr Today 13: 21-2 Ag 1 '69
  Fabric of modern faith. V. R. Ruggiero. Cath World 208:255-8 Mr '69
  Faith and conviction; excerpt from Faith under challenge. H. Fries. il Cath World 210:119-23 D '69
  Has God forsaken the world? Chr Today 14: 20-1 D 19 '69
  Justification by ignorance: a neo-Protestant motif? address, December 29, 1969. C. F. H. Henry. Chr Today 14:10-15 Ja 2 '70
  Layman and his faith. See issues of Christianity today
  Life's chief discoveries; reminiscences of an octogenarian. J. A. Mackay. Chr Today 14:3-5 Ja 2 '70
  Lord, I don't believe: help my belief! J. R. Nelson. Chr Cent 86:501-2 Ap 16 '69
  Meaning of religious belief; excerpt from The foundations of belief. L. DeWart. Commonweal 90:15-17 Mr 21 '69
  New year's prayer; reprint. D. Lawrence. U S News 68:76+ Ja 5 '70
  Paul's thorn and ours. N. V. Hope. Chr Today 14:14-15 D 5 '69
  Proof of the pudding. H. Richardson. Commonweal 91:205-6 N 14 '69
  Rational Christianity. E. Trueblood. Chr Today 13:3-5 F 14 '69
  Recovery of the positive; excerpt from address, February 26, 1969. L. Cassels. Chr Today 13:3-4 Ap 25 '69
  Talking with God. R. Coles. Commonweal 91: 330-4 D 12'69
  That question of faith. V. P. McCorry. America 120:456-inside back cover Ap 12 '69
  What difference does faith make? G. C. Berkouwer. Chr Today 14:52 D 5 '69
  What the Bible says to me. B. Graham. Read Digest 94:83-7 My '69
    See also
  Apostasy
  Trust in God
FAITH cure
  Brother A. A. Allen on the gospel trail: he feels, he heals, & he turns you on with God. W. Hedgepeth. il Look 33:23-31 O 7 '69
  Getting back double from God: faith healer A. A. Allen. il Time 93:64+ Mr 7 '69
  Soupçon of sorcery; faith healers under investigation in France. il Newsweek 75:41 Ja 5 '70
FAITH healing. See Faith cure
FAKERS. See Quacks and quackery
FALANA, Lola
  Dancers go dramatic. il pors Ebony 24:38-40+ S '69
FALCO, Louis
  Louis Falco & company of featured dancers; 92nd street Y. T. Borek. Dance Mag 43:78 Jl '69
FALCONER, Barbara
  Bright faith. Good H 168:88-91 My '69
  Movie report. See issues of Good housekeeping
FALCONER, Raymond E.
  How weather is made. Cons 24:22-31 D '69
  Windchill, a useful wintertime weather variable. bibliog Weatherwise 21:227-9+ D '68
FALCONRY
  Bustards at 12 o'clock high; peregrine patrol of runways. il Time 95:29 Ja 12 '70
FALCONS
  Examination of a worldwide disaster; population crash of peregrine falcons. G. H. Lowery, jr. Science 166:591 O 31 '69
    See also
  Kestrels
FALCONS (football club) See Football clubs
FALEK, Arthur. See Chen, A. T. L. jt. auth.
FALES, Dan
  Conquering Minnesota's wilderness by snowmobile. Pop Mech 132:150-3 D '69
  Jetting down Montana's mighty Missouri. Pop Mech 132:121-4 N '69
  '70 a fine-tuning year for outboards. Pop Mech 13:100-3 O '69
  '70, a sensational year coming up for snowmobiles. Pop Mech 132:142-5+ O '69

FALES, Edward D. Jr
  In case of crash, who is at fault? Read Digest 94:124-6 Mr '69
  Marooned at 12,000 feet. Pop Mech 131:86-90+ Je '69; Same abr. with title Impossible rescue. Read Digest 95:50-5 S '69
  New barriers that cushion the crunch in crashes. Pop Mech 132:91-3+ N '69
  What you should know about motor oils; questions and answers. Read Digest 95: 166-9 O '69
FALK, Edward
  Heart and both lungs. il por Time 95:40 Ja 5 '70
FALK, Richard A.
  Elements of settlement: Saigon notwithstanding. Nation 208:689-93 Je 2 '69
FALKENSTEEN, Erik
  Gallery; photographs. Life 67:8-9 D 12 '69
FALL. See Autumn
FALLACI, Oriana
  Close-up; interview, ed. by R. Stolley. pors Life 66:36-9 F 21 '69
  (ed) See Frishman, R. F. Two American POW's
  (ed) See Ingvalson, R. D. Two American POW's
  (ed) See Mailer, N. Interview with Norman Mailer
FALLACIES (logic)
    Anecdotes, facetiae, satire, etc.
  Puke ethics. il Esquire 72:100-1 S '69
FALLEDER, Arnold
  Man will come along, before long; poem. Chr Cent 86:413 Mr 26 '69
FALLER, James, and others
  Laser beam directed at the lunar retroreflector array: observations of the first returns. bibliog Science 166:99-102 O 3 '69
FALLER, Larry
  Relaxation methods in chemistry; with biographical sketch. Sci Am 220:18, 30-41 My '69
FALLON, Norman
  Tune in shortwave on that transistor portable. Pop Mech 132:154-5 N '69
FALLOUT, Radioactive. See Radioactive fallout
FALLOUT shelters. See Atomic bomb shelters
FALLS (accidents) See Accidents
FALLS. See Wigs
FALLS CHURCH, Va.
    Hospitals
  Fairfax expansion is designed around a driverless cart system. il Arch Rec 145:153-5 Mr '69
FALSE-color film. See Photography—Films
FALSE teeth. See Teeth, Artificial
FALTER, Mary Elizabeth
  Notes of a happy housekeeper. See issues of House & garden incorporating Living for young homemakers
FALTERMAYER, Edmund K.
  Better care at less cost without miracles. Fortune 81:80-3+ Ja '70
  Lifting farm policy out of its rut. Fortune 79:121+ My 15 '69
  We can afford a better America. Fortune 79: 88-91+ Mr '69
FAME
    See also
  Celebrities
FAMILIES of service men. See Service mens families
FAMILY
  Family in crisis; symposium. il Sci Digest 65: 56-69 Mr '69
  Five ages of man. familywise. il Changing T 23:29-30 F '69
  Working paper for man and nature. M. Mead. il Natur Hist 78:14-15+ Ap '69
    See also
  Birth control
  Birth order
  Mothers
  Sexual ethics
  Tribes and tribal system
  Widows
FAMILY, Size of
  How changes in household composition affect family income; excerpt from address, August 1969. M. L. Turner, jr. il Mo Labor R 92:59-61 N '69
FAMILY allowances
  Family allowances. America 120:489 Ap 26 '69
  Now it's instant welfare; impact across the U.S. il U S News 66:32-3 My 5 '69

FAMILY budget. See Budget, Household
FAMILY business. See Family corporations
FAMILY camping. See Camping
FAMILY camps. See Camps
FAMILY corporations
  Alabama couple builds $1 million-a-year factory. il Ebony 25:68-70+ Ja '70
  Empain: the durable dynasty. il Fortune 80: 191 Ag 15 '69
    See also
  Gates rubber company
  Retlaw enterprises, incorporated
FAMILY counseling. See Counseling
FAMILY courts. See Domestic relations courts
FAMILY desertion. See Desertion and non-support
FAMILY doctors. See Physicians
FAMILY enterprises. See Family corporations
FAMILY farm operating agreements. See Father-son farm operating agreements
FAMILY finance. See Domestic finance
FAMILY law. See Domestic relations
FAMILY life
  All-America all the way; E. M. Vandeweghe family of Los Angeles. R. F. Jones. il Sports Illus 30:82-6+ My 26 '69
  Art of family fighting. G. R. Bach and P. Wyden. il N Y Times Mag p61-2+ Ja 26 '69
  Day nature said no. J. K. Martine. il Good H 168:34+ Mr '69
  Joy of family life. B. Graham. il Good H 169:103+ O '69
  Life in the space age: attitudes of engineers and technicians at Cape Kennedy. il Time 94:38+ Jl 4 '69
  Sweet sound of silence. P. La Farge. il Redbook 133:75+ S '69
  Today's family: a balance of strengths and weaknesses; excerpt from The clergyman as counselor. J. C. Hirschberg. Sci Digest 65: 63-5 Mr '69
  Unwed couples: do they live happily ever after? D. Bloch and S. Blum. il Redbook 132:90-1+ Ap '69
  What makes a loving marriage? symposium. ed. by M. Mead. il Redbook 132:74-5+ F '69
  Why I like feeling trapped. L. Wohlberg. il Redbook 133:15+ S '69
    See also
  Children
  Love
  Marriage counseling
  Music in the home
  Parent-child relationship
  Stepparents

  Anecdotes, facetiae, satire, etc.
  Man next door. B. Hillis. See issues of Better homes & gardens

  Caricatures and cartoons
  It's all in the family. S. Berenstain and J. Berenstain. See issues of McCall's
FAMILY life. Education for
  High school courses for future parents. F. A. Holton. il Todays Health 47:38-41+ S '69
  How one city teaches sex education and family life. B. A. Hawkins. il PTA Mag 63:24-6 Je '69
    See also
  Parent education
FAMILY planning. See Birth control
FAMILY quarrels. See Quarrels
FAMILY records
  Bringing in the ancestors; family record vaults in Little Cottonwood Canyon. il Time 94:52 Ag 22 '69
FAMILY recreation. See Recreation
FAMILY rooms. See Living rooms; Rooms
FAMILY vacations. See Vacations
FAMOSE, Annie
  Annie doesn't ski here anymore. B. Ottum. pors Sports Illus 30:22-3 F 10 '69
FAMOUS artists schools, incorporated
  High-rolling schoolmaster. S. Margetts. Duns R 94:57-8+ D '69
FAMOUS men. See Great men
FAMOUS persons, Diseases of. See Diseases of famous persons
FAMOUS women. See Women, Famous
FANCHER, Betsy
  Warm Springs of FDR. Sat R 52:42+ Mr 8 '69
FANDEL, John
  B.C. parley a.d; poem. Cath World 209:209 Ag '69

Equanimity; poem. Cath World 210:123 D '69
Meteors; poem. Commonweal 89:673 F 28 '69
Narreme; poem. Commonweal 90:508 Ag 22 '69
Paradigm; poem. Cath World 209:167 Jl '69
FANE, Marlene
  Writing for the fan magazine field. Writers Digest 49:36-40 My '69
FANNIE Mae. See Federal national mortgage association
FANNIN, Paul Jones
  Cause and the cure; address, January 31. 1969. Vital Speeches 35:293-5 Mr 1 '69
FANON, Frantz
  Frantz Fanon and the radical left. E. W. Ranly. America 121:384+ N 1 '69
FANS, Baseball. See Baseball fans
FANTASIES; ballet. See Ballets—Criticisms
FANTASIES, Literary
  Brats and bayonets: the rhetorics of the children's campaign. A. H. Bell. bibliog f Engl J 58:1038-41 O '69
  Middle earth in the classroom: studying J. R. R. Tolkien. R. Roos. Engl J 58:1175-80 N '69
  The owl service: a study. E. Cameron. bibliog il Wilson Lib Bul 44:425-33 D '69
  Tolkien and the critics; ed. by N. Isaacs and R. Zimbardo. Review
    Nat R 21:605 Je 17 '69
FANTASTIC furniture. See Furniture, Fantastic
FANTASY
  In praise of festivity; excerpt from The feast of fools. H. Cox. Sat R 52:25-8 O 25 '69
    See also
  Childrens fantasies
  Play
FANTEL, Hans H.
  CATV: a perfect picture, and more channels, too. Pop Sci 194:68-70+ Ja '69
  For tops in hi-fi listening: now it's back to earphones yet! Pop Mech 132:146-50+ O '69
  Modern hi-fi speakers: big sound in a small box. Pop Mech 131:134-7+ Je '69
  Sound for the 70's. Opera N 34:14-15 N 1 '69
  Those tiny new recorders. Pop Mech 131: 132-7+ Mr '69
FANTES, K. H.
  Chick interferon: heterogeneity of electric charge. bibliog Science 163:1198-9 Mr 14 '69
FAR EAST
  Magic of serendipity. E. J. Hodges. Horn Bk 45:436-40 Ag '69
    See also
  Asia
  Asia, Southeastern
  Libraries—Far East
  United Nations—Economic commission for Asia and the Far East

  Description and travel
  Road to Osaka, an expogoer's guide to the Pacific; symposium. il Sat R 52:43-8+ S 13 '69

  Industries
    See also
  Textile industry—Far East

  Social life and customs
  Yes, the Orient hasn't changed. M. Berry. il Sat R 52:70+ S 13 '69
FAR EAST and the United States
    See also
  Pacific countries
FAR from Blue Earth; story. See Crawford, C.
FAR from my loving arms; story. See Shyer, M. F.
FAR right (politics) See Right and left (political science)
FARA, John W. and others
  Visceral and behavioral responses to intraduodenal fat. bibliog Science 166:110-11 O 3 '69
FARADAY effect
  Pioneer 6: measurement of transient Faraday rotation phenomena observed during solar occultation. G. S. Levy and others. bibliog il Science 166:596-8 O 31 '69
FARADAY rotation. See Faraday effect
FARB, Peter
  Ghost dance and cargo cult. Horizon 11:58-65 Spr '69
  Rise and fall of the wild West Indian; excerpts from Man's rise to civilization as shown by the Indians of North America from primeval times to the coming of the industrial state. Read Digest 94:212-14+ Je '69

FARBEN, I. G. See Interessengemeinschaft farbenindustrie ag

FARBER, Barry
Fun people. Sat R 52:8+ S 20 '69

FARBER, Charles
Screens of memory; poem. Commonweal 89: 732 Mr 14 '69

FARBER, Ed
Phototronics. por Mod Phot 33:42 Ag: 16+ S: 50+ O; 28+ N '69

FARBER, Jo, and Farber, P. R.
Disneyland on a lollypop and a camera. il Travel & Camera 32:58-61 Ag '69

FARBER, Leslie H.
My wife, the naked movie star. Harper 238: 49-55 Je '69

FARBER, Milton
Auto men gasp in the smog. il por Bsns W p76+ N 1 '69

FARBER, Norma
Summoning Hosannah! poem. Horn Bk 45: 700-1 D '69

FARBER, Paul R.
Foto facts. See issues of Travel & camera —See Farber, J. jt. auth.

FARBER, Robert H.
Free university. Sch & Soc 97:356-8 O '69

FARBER, Stephen
(ed) See Jacobs, A. Writer; interview

FAREED, Omar
Journey to California. N. Cousins. Sat R 52: 20-1 Mr 1 '69

FARES
See subhead Fares under various subjects. e.g. Airlines—Fares

FARGO, Frank
Hurry-up beautification. Am City 84:110-11 Ja '69

FARIÑA, Richard
Ringing out the old in happy Havana; story. Esquire 72:130-1 S '69

about

Rock-folk-protest scene. H. S. Resnik. il por Sat R 52:36+ Jl 5 '69

FARLEY, Reynolds, and Taeuber, K. E.
See the city: color it black. Trans-Action 6: 8+ Ja '69

FARLEY, William
Flicker ball: new program idea. Camp Mag 41:18 Ja '69

FARM animals. See Livestock

FARM bargaining. See Collective bargaining— Farmers

FARM buildings
See also
Barns and stables
Swine farrowing crates and pens
Swine houses

Air conditioning

Medicated air, a new way to hold down disease? A. Phelps. Farm J 93:70 F '69

FARM buildings, Remodeled
How to remodel pole buildings for hogs. R. J. Fee. il Suc Farm 67:47-9 N '69
New uses for old buildings. W. Waltner and E. Waltner. il Suc Farm 67:L6 O '69

FARM bureaus. See American farm bureau federation

FARM corporations
Are the corporate giants taking over farming? R. Krumme. il Suc Farm 67:30-2 S '69
Big feedlots merge to get bigger. C. E. Ball. Farm J 93:B10 Mr '69
Corporate farms, family style. R. Sanders. il Suc Farm 67:38-9 Ap '69
How corporate farmers think and act. R. Krumme. il Suc Farm 67:28-9 O '69
More information on corporate farms. D. Hanson. Suc Farm 67:22 Jl '69
Way you can afford to buy land; Agricultural investors, inc. V. Sanderson. Farm J 93:44B F '69

FARM costs. See Agriculture—Economic aspects

FARM equipment
Home-made and handy; photographs. See issues of Farm journal

Leasing and renting

What it costs to rent farm equipment. R. Krumme. il Suc Farm 67:34 D '69

FARM finance
Financial strategy for the '70s. R. Krumme. il Suc Farm 67:36-7 Mr '69
How do you want your farm credit system run? with editorial comment. C. W. Gifford. Farm J 93:28-9, 74 S '69
How much debt can your farm carry? R. Krumme. il Suc Farm 67:31 Ap '69

How to invest on the farm. R. Krumme. il Suc Farm 67:44 Ag '69
Tax loopholes; address, January 11, 1969. L. Metcalf. Vital Speeches 35:253-6 F 1 '69
Three new ideas in farm finance. Farm J 93: 59 Mr '69
Why it will be harder to borrow money. Farm J 93:45 My '69

FARM labor
Employment patterns and place of residence. H. J. Hilaski and H. M. Willacy. bibliog f il Mo Labor R 92:18-25 O '69
England's cruel earth; excerpt from Akenfield: portrait of an English village. R. Blythe. Harper 238:46-52+ Ap '69
How mechanization of harvesting is affecting jobs. L. J. Fulco. bibliog f il Mo Labor R 92:26-32 Mr '69
New source of help: people on retirement. Suc Farm 67:A2 N '69
Nixon plan for farm workers. U S News 66: 110 My 19 '69
Poisons, profits and politics; cases of death and severe illness due to pesticide poisoning in Calif. R. Harmer. Nation 209:134-7 Ag 25 '69
Wrath of grapes. il Time 93:24 My 16 '69
Wrath of grapes; unions want to organize all hired farm labor. G. Logsdon. Farm J 93:33+ F '69
See also
American federation of labor and Congress of industrial organizations—United farm workers organizing committee
Collective bargaining—Farm labor
Migrant labor
Strikes—United States—Farm labor

Wages and hours

How to compete with the factory for help. R. Sanders. il Suc Farm 67:26-7 My '69
Pay $4 an hour for unionized farm help? Farm J 93:641 Ap '69

FARM leases. See Leases

FARM life
Another day at the mailbox; secrets of a successful free lance. R. Engh. il Pop Phot 65:71-3+ S '69
How to keep your cool. J. Gillies. il Farm J 93:52-4 My '69 (to be cont)
Letters from farm women. See issues of Farm journal
Love, honor, and discuss! M. Longwell. Farm J 93:44A-44B Je '69
Plan a year-round health program. il Suc Farm 67:89 F '69
West is getting lonely again. R. A. Bartlett. il Read Digest 95:46-50 Ag '69
See also
Country life
Farm women

Anecdotes, facetiae, satire, etc.

In the go-go summertime. M. Longwell. il Farm J 93:36-7 Ag '69

FARM life in art. See Art—Themes

FARM machinery. See Agricultural machinery

FARM management
Do the $100 an hour jobs first. Suc Farm 67:14F F '69
Double-cropping; how it is working. C. E. Sommers. il Suc Farm 67:60 Ap '69
Eighty acres that grew to $1/2 million. F. A. Cooper. il Farm J 93:52A+ Ap '69
How they prepare for a bad year. W. T. Messerly. il Suc Farm 67:28-9 Je '69
How to fit hogs into a grain farm. R. C. Black. il Farm J 93:H24 F '69
Partnership feedlot; another way to get bigger. O. Bay. il Farm J 93:B16 Mr '69
Paying job all year round. J. Carlson. il Farm J 93:24-5 Ap '69
Successful farming 1969 livestock management guide; symposium. Suc Farm 67:40-1+ O '69
They double-crop soybeans. Suc Farm 67:B2 Jl '69
Troubled times for the family farm? R. Krumme. il Suc Farm 67:28-9 N '69
You can't afford to be average. R. Sanders. Suc Farm 67:23 My '69
See also
Dairy farm management
Farm corporations
Farm records
Father-son farm operating agreements

Anecdotes, facetiae, satire, etc.

Why aren't you farming? G. Logsdon. Farm J 93:64B-64C Ap '69

Study and teaching

Feedlot managers for the future. O. Bay. il Farm J 93:B10-11+ S '69

FARM mechanization
How mechanization of harvesting is affect-
ing jobs. L. J. Fulco. bibliog f il Mo Labor
R 92:26-32 Mr '69
More time for management. D. K. O'Brien.
il Farm J 93:B12-13+ S '69
FARM operating agreements. See Father-son
farm operating agreements
FARM ownership
Troubled times for the family farm? R.
Krumme. il Suc Farm 67:28-9 N '69
FARM partnership
Pitfalls of partnership. R. Sanders. il Suc
Farm 67:25 O '69
FARM policy. See Agricultural administration—
United States
FARM population. See Rural population
FARM produce
See also
Surplus products, Agricultural

Marketing
Can we save our export markets? L. Palmer.
il Farm J 93:20-1+ S '69
Is our market system outdated? R. Saunders.
il Suc Farm 67:25 Ag '69
Marketing management. R. Sanders. Suc
Farm 67:10 D '69
What's new. W. E. Swegle. See issues of
Successful farming
See also
Corn—Marketing
Roadside marketing
Vegetables—Marketing

Prices
See also
Agricultural administration—United States
FARM records
Keeping chemical records. Suc Farm 67:74
F '69
FARM subsidies. See Agricultural administra-
tion—United States
FARM tenancy
Who pays for new barns, landlord or tenant?
R. J. Fee. il Suc Farm 67:H4 S '69
See also
Leases
FARM tractors. See Tractors
FARM trucks. See Motor trucks in agriculture
FARM vacations. See Vacations
FARM women
American country woman. P. P. Leimbach. il
Farm J 93:34-5 Jl '69
How to keep your cool. J. Gillies. il Farm J
93:52-4 My '69 (to be cont)
Is mom an under-achiever? farm and ranch
women who are putting their ideas to
work. L. Lane. il Farm J 93:102-3+ F '69
Letters from farm women. See issues of Farm
journal
What the farm wife should know about in-
come tax. R. Krumme. il Suc Farm 67:90-1
F '69
FARMER, Betsy
Discovering: color magic. Sch Arts 69:12-13 Ja
'70
FARMER, James
Education is the answer; excerpts from ad-
dress, January 1969. Todays Ed 58:25-6 Ap
'69
about
CIA as an equal opportunity employer. D.
Schechter and others. il Ramp Mag 7:30-3
Je '69
James Farmer. por Parks & Rec 4:24-5 Ag '69
Why a top Negro agreed to join the Nixon
team. il por U S News 66:16 F 24 '69
Working from within. il por Time 93:15 F 21
'69
FARMERS
Get a lawyer before you need one. R. Krumme.
il Suc Farm 67:18-19 Je '69
They aren't worried, they just don't care. D.
Hanson. Suc Farm 67:18 N '69
See also
Collective bargaining—Farmers
Negro farmers
Rural population

Retirement
Will you be ready to retire at 65? H. Guither.
Suc Farm 67:B4 S '69
FARMER'S daughter (restaurant) See Orland
Park, Ill.—Hotels, restaurants, etc.
FARMERS markets. See Markets, Farmers
FARMERS' service society (India) See Co-
operative associations—India
FARMERS wives. See Farm women

FARMHOUSES
Designs and plans
They built half a new house, a Farmhouse
core. J. Gillies. il Farm J 93:90-1 Mr '69
FARMHOUSES, Remodeled. See Houses, Re-
modeled
FARMING, Tax loss. See Agriculture—Economic
aspects
FARMING on shares. See Share-cropping
FARMINGDALE, N.Y. public library
When Birches last in the dooryard swung;
excerpts from address, June 25, 1969; with
editorial comment. O. B. Dow. ALA Bul
63:1237-9 O '69
FARMINGTON, W. Va.
Church and Farmington no. 9. R. Bowyer.
Chr Cent 86:161-2 Ja 29 '69
Farmington no. 9: will the tragedy be com-
pounded? G. F. Massay. Chr Cent 86:871-4
Je 25 '69
FARMS
See also
Farm management
Horse farms
Swine farms
Taxation
See Real property—Taxation
FARMS, Incorporated. See Farm corporations
FARNAM, William F.
Considerable advantages of one-man refuse
collection. Am City 84:97-8 Ap '69
FARRANT, Alan W.
Do it with peanuts. Design 70:36 Sum '69
FARRANT, Marion
Should I retire now? letter. por Har Yrs 9:18
Mr '69
FARRAR, John N.
Chappaquiddick: the driver's story. por U S
News 67:33 N 3 '69
FARRELL, Barry
Case of Private Sood. Life 66:12A F 28 '69
Column. Life 66:4 Je 20; 67:2B Jl 4; 4 Jl 25;
16F Ag 8; 20B Ag 22; 4 S 5; 32 S 19; 4 O
24; 4 N 7; 32B N 21; 31 D 12 '69
Subversion but no manifestos. R. Graves. por
Life 66:3 Je 20 '69
FARRELL, Ed, and Ruth, Leo
(eds) The scene. Engl J 58:756-61, 1382-90
My, D '69
FARRELL, Edmund J.
Beginning begets: making composition as-
signments. Engl J 58:428-31 Mr '69
FARRELL, Francis J. and others
Metal ion activation of phosphate transfer
by bidentate coordination. bibliog Science
164:320-1 Ap 18 '69
FARRELL, Paul B. jr
Case for specialized registration. Arch Forum
130:50-1 Mr '69
FARRELL, Suzanne
Trouble in paradise. il por Newsweek 73:85-6
My 26 '69
FARRINGTON, Debby
Dreaming with a friend; poem. Horn Bk
45:447 Ag '69
FARRINGTON, William H.
Statewide outreach: desert booktrails to the
Indians. por Wilson Lib Bul 43:864-71 My
'69
FARRIS, S. H. See Whitney, H. S. jt. auth.
FARROW, Jesse M. and Pinney, B. M.
Comprehensive liability insurance. Camp Mag
41:24-5 My '69
FARROW, Mia
Mia Farrow. pors Vogue 153:156-7 My '69
Mia Farrow, her thin-skinned courage. P.
Devlin. Vogue 153:80+ My '69
Mia Farrow is a trip. D. Chapman. il pors
Look 33:46-50 Ag 26 '69
Moonchild and the fifth Beatle. il por Time
93:50+ F 7 '69
FARROW, Tisa
Checking out First avenue. pors Holiday 45:
38-41 My '69
FARROWING crates and pens. See Swine far-
rowing crates and pens
FARSON, Richard E.
As I see it; interview, ed. by E. Melton.
por Forbes 104:44-6 Ag 1 '69
How could anything that feels so bad be so
good? Sat R 52:20-1+ S 6 '69
Rage of women. Look 33:21-3 D 16 '69
FARWELL, Byron
Doctor Livingstone presumes. Horizon 11:104-
11 Sum '69
FARWELL, Edith Foster
Wattle fence. il Horticulture 46:14 D '68
FASCELL, Dante Bruno
United Nations budget for 1970; statement,
October 21, 1969. Dept State Bul 61:454-7
N 24 '69

FASCISM
Anglo-Saxonism and fascism. A. Ezergailis.
Yale R 58:481-506 Je '69
See also
National socialism

Europe
European fascism, ed. by S. J. Woolf. Review
Trans-Action 6:56-7 O '69. A. J. Gregor

Italy
Goals of Italian fascism; excerpts from The
fascist experience. E. R. Tannenbaum. bibliog f Am Hist R 74:1183-204 Ap '69

United States
Red, white and blue fascism? Commonweal
90:379-80 Je 20 '69
Systemic fascism. Nation 208:714-16 Je 9 '69

FASHION
Fashion: the way of all flesh; new nude look.
il Time 93:62-71 My 16 '69
Pucci sees motion, color and architecture
determining fashion. E. Pucci. Holiday 46:
73 S '69
See also
Clothing and dress
Costume design
Hairdressing

Anecdotes, facetiae, satire, etc.
I really will. E. Sheppard. Harp Baz 102:133
Ja '69

FASHION critics award. See Coty, incorporated

FASHION designers. See Costume designers

FASHION shows
Hold that mini line! il Time 94:60 Ag 8 '69
Important: reception at Indian consulate and
Peck & Peck fashion show. New Yorker
44:21-2 Ja 25 '69
Paris fashion openings. G. Emerson. il Holiday 46:64-6 Ag '69
Smart, safe, and sexy; clothes shown in
Paris. il Newsweek 73:47 F 10 '69
Soul look from the 30s; 12th annual Ebony
fashion fair. il Ebony 24:155-8+ S '69

FAST, Howard
In search of the Welsh. Esquire 72:142+ D
'69
about
False starts and distorted vision in April
morning. E. Collamore. Engl J 58:1186-8
N '69

FAST, Julius
(ed) See Garcia, C. R. What's sure besides
the pill?

FAST analyzers. See Chemical apparatus and
supplies

FASTEAU, I. Jack
State grants program; interview. Am Ed
5:18 F '69

FASTENINGS
Mod fittings; compact hydropneumatic fittings. B. Lang. il Hot Rod 22:76 Jl '69
See also
Heli-Coil corporation

FASTENINGS (machinery)
See also
Staples and stapling machines

FASTER reading. See Speed reading

FASTING
See also
Lent
Starvation

FASTS and feasts
See also
Ascension day
Passover

FAT
Visceral and behavioral responses to intraduodenal fat. J. W. Fara and others. bibliog Science 166:110-11 O 3 '69
See also
Corpulence

FAT bodies. See Adipose tissues

FATHER-child relationship. See Parent-child
relationship

FATHER-daughter relationship. See Parent-
child relationship

FATHER keeps house; drama. See Hark, M.
and McQueen, N.

FATHER-separated children. See Broken homes

FATHER-son farm operating agreements
Each partner adds a speciality. C. Peterson,
jr. il Suc Farm 67:14H F '69
See also
Farm corporations

FATHER-son relationship. See Parent-child
relationship

FATHER to son; story. See Drake, A.

FATHERHOOD of God. See God

FATHERS
Family portrait on a bearskin rug. J. Davidson. McCalls 96:69+ Mr '69; Same abr. with
title I have a son! Read Digest 94:51-4 My
'69
Father as non-parent; California's abortion
statute. D. W. Louisell and C. Carroll. il
Cath World 210:108-10 D '69
Fathers as disciplinarians. B. Spock. il Redbook 132:26+ Ap '69
Fathers know best. Chr Today 13:29 Je 6 '69
What is a father? excerpts. L. P. McGrath
and J. Scobey. Good H 168:100-1 Je '69; il
Read Digest 95:100-1 S '69
See also
Desertion and non-support
Stepparents

Anecdotes, facetiae, satire, etc
Fathers only journals; public diaries in
hospital obstetrical wards. B. Gillespie. il
Todays Health 47:16-17 D '69

FATHERS day gifts. See Gifts

FATIGUE
How to do more work with less fatigue. J. C.
Churchill. Read Digest 95:167-8 N '69
Ten real ways to combat fatigue. Todays
Health 47:78 F '69
What do you mean, tired? S. H. Bartley. il
Todays Ed 58:40-1 F '69

FATIGUE, Combat. See Neuroses

FATSIAS
Fatsia japonica. J. T. Neal. Horticulture 47:
53 Ja '69

FATT, Amelia
Dressing room dream. Dance Mag 43:104 Ja
'69
Flamboyant maestro. Dance Mag 43:62-5 O
'69
Landscape into danscape. Dance Mag 43:
49+ D '69

FATT, Arthur C.
Let's take the politics out of consumerism.
Nations Bsns 57:82-4+ Ja '69

FATTY acids. See Acids, Fatty

FATTY tissues. See Adipose tissues

FAULKNER, William
Requiem for Faulkner's home town. L. L.
King. il pors Holiday 45:60-1+ Mr '69

FAULTS (geology)
Crustal plates in the central Atlantic: evidence for at least two poles of rotation. P.
J. Fox and others. bibliog il Science 165:
487-9 Ag 1 '69
Messing with the mousetrap; San Andreas
fault. il Sci N 95:138-9 F 8 '69
Origin of the oceanic ridges. E. Orowan. il
Sci Am 221:102-8+ bibliog(p 166) N '69
Quaking California; area of San Andreas
fault. il Newsweek 73:50 F 10 '69
Warning! California will fall into the ocean
in April! S. V. Roberts. il N Y Times
Mag p 12+ Ap 6 '69

FAUPL, Rudolph
ILO at fifty: a trade union perspective. Mo
Labor R 92:44-6 My '69

FAURÉ, Gabriel
Gabriel Fauré, by E. Vuillermoz. Review
Am Rec G por 35:866-7 My '69. C. J.
Luten

FAUST, Carl R.
Seven keys to the flute. Opera N 34:22-3 Ja
17 '70

FAUST, Edna, and Faust, Howard
She sells sea shells by the seashore... por
Har Yrs 9:13-15 Ag '69

FAUST, George T. and others
Pecoraite, $Ni_6Si_4O_{10}(OH)_8$, nickel analog of
clinochrysotile, formed in the Wolf Creek
meteorite. bibliog Science 165:59-60 Jl 4 '69

FAUST, Howard. See Faust, E. jt. auth.

FAUST, Joan Lee
Forest fire shock troops. Am For 75:12-15
Ja '69

FAUST: opera. See Gounod, C. F.

FAUSTER, Carl U.
Collectible cut glass rarities. Hobbies 74:98L-
98N Jl '69
Cut glass and other lamps by Libbey. Hobbies
74:116-17+ D '69
Glass canes & other whimseys. Hobbies
74:116-18 S '69

FAUVET, Jacques
Successful sobriety. il por Newsweek 75:43 Ja
5 '70

FAUX, Eugene J. and Rowley, C. M.
Compartmentalized children's services in a
therapeutic community. bibliog Ment Hy
53:585-9 O '69

FEDERAL national mortgage association
All fired up; removal of R. H. Lapin. il
Newsweek 74:82-3 D 15 '69
Flap at Fannie Mae: Ross is in, but Lapin
keeps on fighting. Bsns W p94 D 13 '69
Ginnie Mae runs into delays; Fannie Mae
ponders construction loans. Bsns W p 128
Je 21 '69
Privacy becomes Fannie Mae. il Bsns W
p44+ Ag 30 '69

FEDERAL power commission. See United
States—Federal power commission

FEDERAL reserve banks
See also
United States—Federal reserve board

FEDERAL revenue sharing with states. See
Intergovernmental tax relations

FEDERAL sign and signal corporation
Signs of change. R. Levy. Duns R 94:78+
O '69

FEDERAL-state tax relations. See Intergovernmental tax relations

FEDERAL urban renewal program. See Urban
renewal

FEDERALISM. See Federal government

FEDERATED department stores, incorporated
Federated department stores: growing pains
at forty. E. Carruth. il Fortune 79:142-7+
Je '69
Huge retailer splits load at top. Bsns W p61
O 25 '69

FEDERATION of Europe. See European federation

FEDERATION of Jewish philanthropies of New
York
See also
Jewish association for services for the aging

FEDERATION of Malaysia. See Malaysia

FEDERATION of South Arabia. See Southern Yemen

FEE, Rodney J.
What's new. See issues of Successful farming

FEED supplements, Antibiotic. See Antibiotic
feed supplements

FEEDER pig contracts. See Contracts, Agricultural

FEEDERS (birds)
Would you like to make this architect-de-
signed bird feeder? il Home Gard 56:46 Je
'69

FEEDING and feeding stuffs
Look what they're doing to milo! popping
grain. C. E. Ball. il Farm J 93:B11+ My
'69
Which feed processing method fits your lot?
interview, ed. by O. Bay. J. Matsushima. il
Farm J 93:B18+ Mr '69
See also
Antibiotic feed supplements
Calves—Feeding
Cattle—Feeding
Corn
Cows—Feeding
Forage plants
Grain
Milo
Poultry—Feeding
Ralston Purina company
Silos
Thyroproteins
Urea

Grain
How much will feed grains cost? L. Simerl.
Farm J 93:B9+ S '69
Latest grain processing method: micronizing.
C. E. Ball. il Farm J 93:B14 Ag '69

Grass
He grass-feeds, and likes it. E. Stout. il
Suc Farm 67:56 O '69

Molasses
He gets more milk with molasses. W. Messerly. il Suc Farm 67:L4 O '69

Protein supplements
Comeback for real protein supplements. B.
Coffman. il Farm J 93:B7+ My '69
Take a new look at protein supplements. D.
Malena. il Suc Farm 67:32-3 Je '69

Soybeans
New idea in on-farm feed processing. R. J.
Fee. il Suc Farm 67:52 Ag '69
Process your soybeans for livestock. J.
Russell. Farm J 93:28 Ag '69

Testing
How those new products are tested and developed. J. G. Clark. Farm J 93:B24 My '69

FEELEY, Mary
Money management. See issues of American
home

FEELINGS. See Emotions

FEET. See Foot

FEET of animals. See Foot (animals)

FEEZLE, William R.
Educational service centers. Ed Digest 35:
52-4 O '69

FEIFFER, Jules
Dick and Jane; text. Ramp Mag 8:23-6 Ag '69
Jules Feiffer. See occasional issues of New
republic
about
Little murders. Criticism
Nation 208:94 Ja 20 '69
New Yorker 44:100 F 8 '69
Sat R 52:22 F 1 '69

FEIGE, Norman
What do you know about... Yachting 125:
80-1+ Ap '69

FEIGEN, G. M.
Bucky Fuller and the firewalk. il Sat R 52:
22-3 Jl 12 '69

FEIN, Leonard
Two voices; a dialogue on dissension. por
Time 93:58 Ja 31 '69

FEINBERG, Gerald
Defining the future. Nation 209:250-2 S 15
'69
Pulsar test of a variation of the speed of light
with frequency. bibliog Science 166:879-81 N
14 '69
about
Exceeding the speed limit. il por Time 93:
42+ F 14 '69

FEINBERG, Sheldon
Mopping up the mess at Perfect film. por
Bsns W p31 N 29 '69
Perfect wants a better image. por Bsns W
p 100+ Je 28 '69

FEININGER, Andreas
Feininger. por Mod Phot 33:58+ O '69
Forms of nature. il UNESCO Courier 22:18-19
Mr '69
Large camera. See issues of Modern photog-
raphy
Message of the tree; excerpts from Trees.
Audubon 71:25-7 Ja '69
Winter tree; photographs. Audubon 71:16-24
Ja '69

FEINSTEIN, Donald, and others
Hemophilia A; polymorphism detectable by
a factor VIII antibody. bibliog Science 163:
1071-2 Mr 7 '69

FEINSTEIN, Phyllis
Parent and child. N Y Times Mag p 122+
O 26; 132+ N 16 '69
—See Lang, W. R.; Lewis, G. C. jr. jt auths.

FEIS, Herbert
President's making of history. Atlan 224:64-5
S '69

FELCH, William C.
Internist talks about his work; ed. by W. S.
Ross. pors Todays Health 47:24-7+ F '69

FELD, Eliot
American ballet company? D. Hering. il
Dance Mag 43:34-6+ D '69
Brooklyn bow. W. Terry. Sat R 52:40 N 8 '69
Dance grows in Brooklyn. H. Saal. il por
Newsweek 74:91 N 3 '69
New company is born. W. Terry. il por Sat R
52:62-3 N 15 '69

FELD, Ross
Plum for Edward Dahlberg; Hindenburg; poems. Poetry 115:16-17 O '69

FELDMAN, Edward S.
Building aids research program. Cons 24:
17+ D '69

FELDMAN, Gerald D.
Social and economic policies of German big
business, 1918-1929. bibliog f Am Hist R 75:
47-55 O '69

FELDMAN, Marvin
Vocation education in a new comprehensive
system. Todays Ed 58:47-8 N '69

FELDMAN, Sandor S.
Patterns in obedience and disobedience. bibliog Am Imago 26:21-36 Spr '69

FELDMAN, Trude B.
(ed) See Nixon, P. R. Mrs Nixon tells how
she brought up Tricia and Julie

FELDSPAR
See also
Anorthosite

FELDSTEIN, Mark
Building watcher. J. B. Myers. il Craft Horiz
29:20-9 Jl '69

FELEPPA, Ernest J.
Biomedical applications of holography. bibliog por Phys Today 22:25-32 Jl '69

FELIX, David
Cause celebre at galactic remove. Nat R 21:446-7 My 6 '69

FELLAND, Norman
English independent study for high school. Engl J 58:591-3+ Ap '69

FELLIG, Arthur
Weegee; a lens on life, 1899-1968. H. V. Fondiller; N. Rothschild; D. Vestal. il pors Pop Phot 64:92-5+ Ap '69

FELLINI, Federico
Fellini at work. H. Alpert. il Sat R 52:14-17 Jl 12 '69
Old Rome *alla* Fellini. E. Hughes. il por Life 67:56-9+ Ag 15 '69

FELLOWSHIP. See Human relations

FELLOWSHIP of Christian athletes
Christian athletes flex muscles. R. Chandler. Chr Today 13:37-8 Ag 22 '69
Harnessing hero worship. Chr Today 13:25 Ag 22 '69

FELLOWSHIP of Christians in the arts, media, and entertainment. See Religion and the arts

FELLOWSHIPS. See Scholarships and fellowships

FELSENHELD, Robert, Jr
Filters for microwaves. por Electr World 81:45-7 Ap '69

FELSENSTEIN, Walter
Triumph of Felsenstein's La Traviata. G. R. Marek. por Hi Fi 19:MA28-9+ F '69

FELTON, James
Temple's tale of two tents. Hi Fi 19:MA24-5 O '69

FEMINA, Jerry Della. See Della Femina, J.

FEMINISM. See Woman; Woman—Equal rights; Woman—Social and moral questions

FEMINISTS. See Women's liberation movement

FENANDER, Elliot
Portfolio: circus. Atlan 223:53-60 Je '69

FENCE posts
On stepping-stones and fence posts. il Org Gard & Farm 16:110-11 F '69
Put your fence posts to work! R. Van Vorse. il Org Gard & Farm 16:74-6 Jl '69

FENCES
Fence yourself in. il Bet Hom & Gard 47:152-3 My '69
Fences; photographs. G. Christman. Am West 6:33-9 My '69
Five handsome fences and how they're put together. il Home Gard 56:54-5 Ag '69
For roadside privacy, they built this handsome fence. il Sunset 143:188 D '69
Fundamentals of fencing. il Am Home 72:53 My '69
Handsome and durable, that's the split-rail fence. J. Seginski. il Org Gard & Farm 16:106-9 F '69
Packaged fence panels offer both beauty and privacy. W. C. Leckey. il Pop Mech 132:156-8 S '69
Portable fences improve landfill housekeeping. il Am City 84:127 F '69
See-through screens. il Bet Hom & Gard 47:20 F '69
They fenced the pool but kept their view. il Sunset 143:90 Jl '69
Wattle fence. E. F. Farwell. il Horticulture 46:14 D '68
What's in a fence? I. L. Dawson. il Nat Parks 43:11 F '69
See also
Gates

FENCES, Electric
Beware the one-wire fence. T. Trueblood. il Field & S 73:36+ Mr '69

FENCING
En garde! Here comes Baby Ruthie. il Life 67:91-2 S 26 '69
Touché! Baltimore girl to win a national fencing championship. il Ebony 25:52-6 Ja '70

FENDELL, Robert
Whatever happened to Rolls-Royce? Motor T 21:42-5 Ap '69

FENNEL
Fennel, for flower and flavor. il Home Gard 56:36 Ap '69

FENNER, Mildred (Sandison)
Facts are . . . (cont) Todays Ed 58:87 Ja; 83 F '69

FENNER, Theodore
Making of an opera critic: Leigh Hunt. bibliog f Mus Q 55:439-63 O '69

FENSCH, Tom
Tapping the university community market. Writers Digest 49:54-7 Mr '69
Turning magazine articles into books. Writers Digest 49:53-5 D '69

FENSTER, Leo
Latin millstone. Nation 209:525-6 N 17 '69
Mexican auto swindle. Nation 208:693-7 Je 2 '69

FENTRESS, Roy
(comp) Books in print. Dance Mag 43:51-8 Mr '69

FENWICK, Patrick P.
Gibson ranch, a county facility. Parks & Rec 4:33-4 Ap '69

FENWICK, Sara
Variation on a common theme. Library J 94:1724-7 Ap 15 '69

FERAHIAN, R. H. and Hurst, W. D.
Construction equipment shakes. bibliog Am City 84:102-6 S '69

FERBER, Ellen
It's Y.O.U. Am Ed 5:17-21 Ag '69; Same abr. Ed Digest 35:32-4 O '69

FERBER, Stephen
Orientation F.O.B. Field & S 74:148-50+ Ag '69

FER-DE-LANCE. See Snakes

FEREBEE, Dorothy Boulding
Doctor Dorothy B. Ferebee, charms birds off trees. por Vogue 153:173 My '69

FERGUSON, C. Clyde, Jr
Department reviews U.S. efforts to aid victims of the Nigerian civil war; statement, July 15, 1969. Dept State Bul 61:97-100 Ag 4 '69
Nigerian relief effort improved by agreement on new surface route: statement, June 18, 1969. Dept State Bul 61:14 Jl 7 '69

FERGUSON, Charles Nathaniel Newton
Americans not everyone knows. C. W. Ferguson. PTA Mag 63:16-18 F '69

FERGUSON, Charles W.
Americans not everyone knows. See issues of PTA magazine

FERGUSON, James
Value engineering; address, September 29, 1969. Vital Speeches 36:29-31 O 15 '69

FERGUSON, Paul R.
Judicial farce. por Wilson Lib Bul 43:653-6 Mr '69

FERGUSON, Wanda
Carrots and peas, good neighbors. Org Gard & Farm 16:34-6 Ap '69
Space-saving onion patch. Org Gard & Farm 16:54-5 Mr '69
What's missing in commercial poultry feeds? Org Gard & Farm 16:46-8 D '69

FERLINGHETTI, Lawrence
Third world; poem. Nation 208:92 Ja 20 '69
Tyrannus Nix? poem. Ramp Mag 8:45-50 S '69

about
Fling with Ferlinghetti. R. O'Neill. Engl J 58:1025-7+ O '69

FERMAN, Louis A.
(ed) Evaluating the war on poverty. bibliog f Ann Am Acad 385:1-156 S '69
Some perspectives on evaluating social welfare programs. Ann Am Acad 385:143-56 S '69

FERMI, Laura
Cars and air pollution. Bul Atom Sci 25:35-7 O '69

FERMI surfaces
Electrons in metals; adaptation of address, October 1968. W. A. Harrison. bibliog il Phys Today 22:23-31 O '69

FERNBERGER, Ed
House party at Fernbergers. il Sports Illus 30:55-6 F 17 '69

FERNBERGER, Marilyn
House party at Fernbergers. il por Sports Illus 30:55-6 F 17 '69

FERNDALE, Mich.
First in fight over segregation. U S News 66:12 Ap 28 '69

FERNEA, Elizabeth W. See Fernea, R. A. jt. auth.

FERNEA, Robert A. and Fernea, E. W.
Iraq. bibliog Focus 20:1-12 O '69

FERNIG, Leo
1970, International education year. UNESCO Courier 23:4-6 Ja '70

FERNS
New antheridiogen from the fern onoclea sensibilis. U. Näf and others. bibliog il Science 163:1357-8 Mr 21 '69
Woodland ferns. P. L. Weinman. il Home Gard 56:56-7 Ap '69

FERNS, Fossil
Glossopterid leaves from the middle Jurassic of Oaxaca, Mexico. T. Delevoryas. bibliog il Science 165:895-6 Ag 29 '69

FERON, James
Israel has found a replacement for Golda Meir, it's Golda Meir. N Y Times Mag p52-3+ O 26 '69
Yigal Allon has supporters, Moshe Dayan has disciples. N Y Times Mag p30-1+ Ap 27 '69

FERRARA, Armand
He's got composting on his mind. Org Gard & Farm 16:42-5 N '69

FERRÉ, Frederick
[Book review] Commonweal 90:28-9 Mr 21 '69

FERRÉ, Luis Alberto
Puerto Rico: will it be the 51st state? interview. por U S News 66:104-5 Mr 17 '69

about
New era for Puerto Rico. A. T. Viglucci. il por Look 33:44 Mr 18 '69

FERREN, William P.
Electronics of corrosion. Electr World 82:42-5+ N '69

FERRER, Vincent
Unknown saint of India. il pors Life 66:36-44 F 28 '69

FERRIC phosphates. See Iron phosphates

FERRIS, J. P. and others
Photochemical reactions and the chemical evolution of purines and nicotinamide derivatives. bibliog Science 166:765-6 N 7 '69

FERRIS, John
Holy terror. Opera N 33:6-7 F 15 '69
No rallentare for Rocco. Sat R 52:2 Je 28 '69
Notes on Italian travel. Sat R 52:4+ Ag 23 '69
Urk, Limmen, Lisse, and other places. Sat R 52:4+ N 8 '69

FERRIS wheels
Big wheels of the fun business. K. Holiday. il Pop Mech 131:144-6+ Mr '69

FERRITES (magnetic materials)
Bubble computers; microscopic cylinders embedded in thin sheets of ferrite. Sci Am 221:46-7 O '69
Magnetic ferrites. il Chem 42:22-3 S '69

FERRO cement boats. See Boats— Materials

FERROMANGANESE
Freshwater ferromanganese concretions: chemistry and internal structure. R. C. Harriss and A. G. Troup. bibliog il Science 166:604-6 O 31 '69

FERTIG, Daniel S. and Edmonds, V. W.
Physiology of the house mouse; with biographical sketches. Sci Am 221:15, 103-8+ bibliog (p 148) O '69

FERTILITY (botany)
Hybrid wheat. B. C. Curtis and D. R. Johnston. il Sci Am 220:21-9 bibliog (p 158) My '69

FERTILITY, Human
Anabaptists explosion; adaptation of Pockets of high fertility in the United States. W. F. Pratt. il Natur Hist 78:8-10+ F '69

FERTILITY control. See Birth control

FERTILITY of soils. See Soil fertility

FERTILIZATION (biology)
β-1,3-Glucanase of sea urchin eggs: release from particles at fertilization. D. Epel and others. bibliog il Science 163:294-6 Ja 17 '69
Proteins synthesized before and after fertilization in sea urchin eggs. F. R. MacKintosh and E. Bell. bibliog il Science 164:961-3 My 23 '69
Sex control by bees: a voluntary act of egg fertilization during oviposition. H. S. Gerber and E. C. Klostermeyer. bibliog il Science 167:82-4 Ja 2 '70
See also
Spawning

FERTILIZATION (in vitro)
How to make babies: researchers fertilize ova outside the female body. Newsweek 73:61 F 24 '69
Human eggs in a test tube. il Sci N 95:209 Mr 1 '69
Test tube fertilization; the field of genetic research and moral theology. America 120:292 Mr 15 '69

FERTILIZATION, Artificial. See Artificial insemination; Artificial insemination, Human

FERTILIZATION of plants
Fig wasps: mechanism of pollen transfer. W. Ramirez B. bibliog il Science 163:580-1 F 7 '69
Never plant cucumbers next to..; mistaken notions about cross pollination. F. D. Schales. il Org Gard & Farm 16:46-7 My '69
Sex habits of the trigger flower. il Am For 75:4-7 Je '69
Unique pollination in orchids. D. Seibert. Horticulture 46:23 Ag '68

FERTILIZER industry and trade
Oil companies bail out of fertilizer surplus. il Bsns W p35 D 13 '69
Too much fertilizer. il Bsns W p32-3 My 31 '69

FERTILIZER spreaders
This month's cover story. P. Jones. il Suc Farm 67:58 Mr '69

FERTILIZERS and manures
Curing Amazonia's anemic jungle soils. C. Weathersbee. il Sci N 95:338-9 Ap 5 '69
Indians really knew something; for fine flowers, go dig yourself a fish! W. Corley. Org Gard & Farm 16:45 Ap '69
See also
Ammonia
Compost
Forage plants—Fertilizers and manures
Lawns
Lime
Liquid fertilizers and manures
Mulching
Nitrates
Soil fertility

Anecdotes, facetiae, satire, etc.
Letter from a little old lady in tennis shoes. il Org Gard & Farm 16:46-8 S '69

Handling
Making a manure tea dripalator. V. Talbot. il Org Gard & Farm 16:88-9 Ag '69
Manure management; symposium. with editorial comment. il Suc Farm 67:43-5+ My '69
Too much fertilizer. il Bsns W p32-3 My 31 '69

Injurious effects
Are fertilizers polluting our water supply? R. Coffman. Farm J 93:19+ My '69
Chemical fertilizers cause new concern. R. Rodale. Org Gard & Farm 16:29-31 Mr '69

Preservation and storage
Everything-goes composters. M. C. Goldman. il Org Gard & Farm 16:32-5 O '69
Our six compost bins, all different. L. R. Horsted. il Org Gard & Farm 16:69-71 Ap '69
Two compost bins, and a cart. L. M. Hardwick. il Org Gard & Farm 16:70+ O '69

Spray applications
It's still go for fall fertilization. il Suc Farm 67:32 Jl '69

Spreaders
See Fertilizer spreaders

FESSENDEN, Clara L.
Cabbages in your garden. por Org Gard & Farm 16:39-41 Mr '69
More onions, the better. Org Gard & Farm 16:66-7 My '69

FESTIVAL of contemporary music. See Music festivals—Michigan

FESTIVAL of two worlds. See Festivals—Italy

FESTIVALS
World travel calendar, 1970; comp. by F. Shemanski. Sat R 53:53-6 Ja 3 '70
See also
Carnival
Dance festivals
Drama festivals
International festival of music and drama, Edinburgh
Thanksgiving day

California
Flower festival, flower touring. il Sunset 142:52+ Je '69
Pilgrims triumphant; Festival pageant, Claremont. il Har Yrs 9:26-9 N '69

Europe
Europe's autumn wine festivals. E. Fried. il Travel 132:52-5+ S '69

Hawaii
It's not Samoa, it's April 19 in Honolulu. il Sunset 142:35 Ap '69

Indiana
Back home again in automaniana; 500 festival. il Sports Illus 30:30-5 My 26 '69

Italy
European literary scene: Festival of two worlds. R. J. Clements. Sat R 52:28 Je 7 '69
Report: Spoleto; productions at Festival of two worlds. F. Stevenson; T. Goth. Opera N 34:32 S 6 '69
Scandal over Rossini; Festival of two worlds. W. Weaver. il Hi Fi 19:MA30-1 O '69

FESTIVALS—*Continued*

Japan

Plan a festival tour. Travel & Camera 32:107-8 O '69

Kentucky

Court day. B. Thomas. il Travel 132:48-51 S '69

Massachusetts

Something nice in Boston; street festival. Newsweek 74:51-2 Jl 14 '69

Norway

See also
Music festivals—Norway

Spain

Sound of hooves; fiesta of San Fermin, Pamplona. J. McCormick. il Sports Illus 31:60-4+ Jl 7 '69

United States

Summer festivals, all around the country. Changing T 23:11 My '69
Twenty-five noted autumn festivals to visit. il Good H 169:179 S '69

FESTIVITY
In praise of festivity; excerpt from The feast of fools. H. Cox. Sat R 52:25-8 O 25 '69

FESTSCHRIFTEN
Fest me no schriften. P. Bohannan. Science 166:819 N 14 '69

FETCHIT, Stepin
Black power casualties. J. R. Coyne, jr. Nat R 21:701 Jl 15 '69

FETOLOGY. See Fetus

FETROS, John G.
How-to-do-it books; building the collection. Library J 94:1595-7 Ap 15 '69

FETUS
Artificial placenta: two days of total extrauterine support of the isolated premature lamb fetus. W. M. Zapol and others. bibliog il Science 166:617-18 O 31 '69
Defense of human fetus; unethical experimentation with prenatal life. il Sci Digest 66:61-2 O '69
Fetal growth and development; report of meeting. E. W. Page. Science 164:1193 Je 6 '69
Fetology; doctoring unborn babies. R. Winter. il Sci Digest 66:24-9 N '69
The unborn; surgery before birth. D. M. Rorvik. il Look 33:74-6+ N 4 '69
Watching the unborn. B. J. Culliton. il Sci N 96:12-13 Jl 5 '69
Watching the unborn inside the womb; new electronic monitoring device. il Life 67:63-5 Jl 25 '69
What doctors now know about your unborn baby. Y. Brandt. il Redbook 132:69-71+ F '69

FETUS, Death of
See also
Fetus, Effect of radiation on the

FETUS, Effect of radiation on the
Fetal and infant motality and the environment. A. R. Tamplin; E. J. Sternglass. il Bul Atom Sci 25:23-34 D '69

FETZ, Eberhard E.
Operant conditioning of cortical unit activity. bibliog Science 163:955-8 F 28 '69

FEUER, Donya
Sweden: stirring up a commotion. M. Kats. il por Dance Mag 43:46-8 My '69

FEUER, Lewis S.
From vulgar Marxism to crude psychological determinism. N. Birnbaum. Commonweal 90:238+ My 9 '69

Les FEUX-follets (organization) See Dance companies

FEVER
What you should know about fever. T. Irwin. Read Digest 94:137-40 Mr '69
See also
Dengue

FEY, Harold E.
Unbiased approach. Chr Cent 86:519 Ap 16 '69

FEYDEAU, Georges
Flea in her ear. Criticism
Nation 209:451 O 27 '69
New Repub 161:33 N 1 '69
New Yorker 45:86+ O 11 '69
Newsweek il 74:125 O 13 '69

FEYK, David E.
Incentive plan for good drivers. Travel 132:73-4 D '69

FIALKOW, Philip J. and others
6-Phosphogluconate dehydrogenase: hemizygous manifestation in a patient with leukemia. bibliog Science 163:194-5 Ja 10 '69

FIAT aviation. See Airplane industry and trade—Italy

FIBER optics
Light from a cable; macro shots. W. F. Wilson. il Pop Phot 65:70 O '69

FIBERGLASS boats. See Boats—Materials

FIBERGLASS coatings. See Protective coatings

FIBERS
Getting in on a new thing; carbon fibers in British industry. L. Miller. il Sci N 95:462 My 10 '69
Graphite fibers coming of age. E. Gross. il Sci N 95:601-2 Je 21 '69
Large plant urged in Britain for carbon fiber production. Aviation W 90:23-4 Mr 17 '69

FIBONACCI numbers
Fibonacci numbers. il Time 93:48+ Ap 4 '69
Multiple fascinations of the Fibonacci sequence. M. Gardner. il Sci Am 220:116-20 Mr '69

FIBREBOARD corporation
Reward of virtue. Forbes 103:36 F 15 '69

FICHTER, Joseph H.
Farewell general practitioner. Commonweal 91:144-5 O 31 '69

FICTION
Future of fiction; summary of discussion; March 11, 1969. il Pub W 195:32 Mr 24 '69
A look at the novel. G. Hicks. il Todays Ed 58:12-15 Ap '69
Novel reflections. M. C. Albrecht. Trans-Action 6:54-5 O '69
See also
Characters in literature
Gothic romances
Historical fiction
Jews in literature
Realism in literature
Science fiction
Sex in literature
Spies in literature
also American fiction; English fiction; etc.

Authorship

Borges on Borges; interview, ed. by R. Stern. J. L. Borges. Am Scholar 38:452-8 Sum '69
Company; novels of H. Robbins. New Yorker 45:45-8 N 29 '69
See also
Detective and mystery stories—Authorship

Bibliography

American fiction in the '60's; a list and some random thoughts. P. S. Prescott. Look 33:10 D 30 '69
Fiction (cont) W. B. Hill. America 120:536+; 121:530-2 My 3, N 29 '69
For fiction aficionados; paperback books. il Sr Schol 94:Schol Teach 26-7 Ja 31 '69
For fiction fans. il Sr Schol 94:Schol Teach 26-7 My 2 '69
1969, a rich year for the novel; comp. by G. Wolff. il Newsweek 74:97-8+ D 22 '69
Up for discussion: fiction for today's teens. D. G. Stavn. Library J 94:4305-6 N 15 '69

Competitions

1969 Scholastic writing awards: short stories. il Sr Schol 94:20-1+ My 9 '69
1969 WD short story contest. L. Reis. Writers Digest 49:37-8+ O '69

Technique

Birth of a saga. R. F. Delderfield. Writer 82:18-21 N '69
Elements of fiction. S. L. Rubinstein. Writer 82:21-4 Ja '69
Experience and fiction; excerpts from Come along with me. S. Jackson. Writer 82:9-14+ Ja '69
Exploration in writing. G. Gordon and M. Gordon. Writer 82:9-12 N '69
Fiction's all-seeing I. R. Somerlott. Writer 82:11-15 F '69
How not to write a short story; excerpts from Prize stories from Seventeen. B. Rosmond. Writer 82:22-4+ Ag '69
Isaac Babel talks about writing; excerpts from Years of hope. K. G. Paustovskii. Nation 208:406-7 Mr 31 '69
Keep it brief and blend it in. D. James. il Writers Digest 49:50-2+ Jl '69
Letter to a still unknown author: entertainment in political thrillers. M. Avallone. Writer 82:21-2+ F '69
Maturing of novel ideas. M. Montgomery. Writer 82:22-4+ D '69
Nature and aim of fiction; excerpt from Mystery and manners. F. O'Connor. Writer 82:11-14+ O '69

FILM critics. See Critics
FILM festival, Cannes. See Cannes international film festival
FILM festivals. See Moving picture festivals
FILM propaganda. See Moving pictures—Propaganda films
FILM scripts. See Moving picture scripts
FILM societies. See Moving picture societies
FILM strips
Anyone can make a filmstrip. R. Grillotti. il Sch Arts 69:12-13 D '69
Making film strips; applying images directly. P. James. il Sch Arts 68:36-7 F '69
New life for old authors; original sound filmstrips at junior high school, Rutland, Vt. D. P. Miller. il Sr Schol 94:Schol Teach 16-17 Ap 18 '69
Screenings: filmstrips (cont) D. Lembo. Library J 94:276+, 852-3, 1310-12, 1739, 2078-80+, 3154+, 3803-5, 4590 Ja 15, F 15, Mr 15, Ap 15, My 15, O 15, D 15 '69
FILMS
Evaporation retarded by monolayers. F. MacRitchie. bibliog il Science 163:929-31 F 28 '69; Reply. R. Kappesser and others. 166: 403 O 17 '69
See also
Photography—Films
Thin films

Deterioration
See Materials—Deterioration
FILMS, Metallic
Alloys that pose for a picture; Photoform process. il Bsns W p 116 Ag 16 '69
Laser coupled with thin-film. il Aviation W 91:91+ Ag 11 '69
Magnetic areas in thin plate store, process digital data. il Aviation W 91:107-9 Ag 18 '69
FILMS from books. See Film adaptations
FILMSTRIPS. See Film strips
FILNER, Philip, and others
Enzyme induction in higher plants. bibliog Science 165:358-67 Jl 25 '69
FILTER plants
New plants need modernizing, too; East Chicago, Ind. V. J. Kirrin and J. Rakowski, jr. il Am City 84:110+ Jl '69
FILTERS, Electric. See Electric filters
FILTERS, Light. See Light filters
FILTERS, Radio. See Radio filters
FILTERS and filtration
See also
Air filters
Oil filters
FINAL dwarf; story. See Roth, H.
FINAL fate of the alligators; story. See Hoagland, E.
FINANCE
See also
Church finance
Commerce
Credit
Farm finance
Inflation (finance)
Municipal finance
Negotiable instruments
Securities
Speculation
Stock exchange
Taxation
United Nations—Finance
    also subhead Finance under various subjects. e.g. Corporations—Finance

Study and teaching
Bulls & bears in Boston; North Dorchester McCormack middle school. A. J. Owens. il Sr Schol 94:Schol Teach 14 Ap 18 '69

Brazil
See also
Inflation (finance)
Stock exchange—Rio de Janeiro

Canada
See also
Banks and banking—Canada
Stock exchange—Toronto

France
Another French crisis; Rendezvous of March and wage demands. America 120:324 Mr 22 '69
See also
France—Economic conditions
Money—France

Great Britain
See also
Budget—Great Britain

Japan
See also
Japan—Economic conditions
Stock exchange—Tokyo

Mexico
Nice way to pioneer; J. B. Rhoads. il Forbes 103:58+ Ap 1 '69

United States
Financing democracy; symposium, ed. by A. G. Buehler. bibliog f il Ann Am Acad 379: 1-93 S '68
Ragged edges in finance. il Fortune 80:24+ O '69
See also
Budget—United States
Debts, Public—United States
Inflation (finance)
Stock exchange—New York (city)
Taxation—United States
United States—Appropriations and expenditures
United States—Federal reserve board
FINANCE, Housing. See Housing finance
FINANCE, International
American share in the stream of international payments; with questions and answers. R. V. Roosa. Ann Am Acad 384:21-34 Jl '69
America's money troubles hit the Europeans, too. U S News 66:61 Je 16 '69
Annals of finance; New deal. J. Brooks. New Yorker 45:107-26 S 13 '69
Economic report of the President and annual report of the Council of economic advisers; excerpts. L. B. Johnson. il Dept State Bul 60:101-17 F 3 '69
Reporter at large; four day celebration of Brown brothers Harriman & co. hundred-and-fiftieth anniversary. J. Brooks. New Yorker 45:97-8+ Ap 26 '69
U.S. alternate governor of IMF and international banks confirmed. Dept State Bul 61:261 S 22 '69
We're all in the same boat. F. Morley. Nations Bsns 57:17-18 Ja '69
When a world money system is out of date. il Bsns W p70-3+ F 22 '69
See also
Balance of payments
Bank for international settlements
Banks and banking, International
Inter-American development bank
International bank for reconstruction and development
International monetary fund
Investments, Foreign
Liquidity, International
Loans, Foreign
Money—International aspects
Special drawing rights
United Nations—Panel on foreign investment in developing countries
United Nations monetary and financial conference
FINANCE, Local. See Local finance
FINANCE, Personal
Putting one's own house in order; New York consulting firm helps executives. Bsns W p 124 Ja 25 '69
Spending your money. S. Porter. See issues of Ladies' home journal
See also
Budget, Personal
Estate planning

Study and teaching
What to teach your children about money. R. Krumme. il Suc Farm 67:59 Jl '69
FINANCE, School. See School finance
FINANCE, State. See State finance
FINANCE companies
C.I.T.-type operation for the world; proposed Private export finance corp. il Forbes 103:25 F 1 '69
See also
Benevest, incorporated
Commercial credit company
General acceptance corporation
FINANCIAL analysts. See Investments—Advisers
FINANCIAL directors. See Corporations—Directors
FINANCIAL news. See Newspapers—Financial news
FINANCIAL public relations. See Investor relations programs

FINNAIR. See Airlines—Finland
FINNEGAN, Bob
Picture post card. See issues of Hobbies
FINNEY, Ben R. and Houston, J. D.
Polynesian surfing; with biographical sketches. pors Natur Hist 78:4, 26-35+ Ag '69
FINNEY, John W.
Long trial of John Paton Davies. N Y Times Mag p7-9+ Ag 31 '69
Winds of change in the Senate. New Repub 160:21-3 Ap 5 '69
FINNISH baths. See Sauna
FINNISH pottery. See Pottery, Finnish
FINNISH students
Student capitalists; student-owned enterprises in Finland. Time 93:77 Je 27 '69
FIORENTINO, Imero
On the beam. il por Newsweek 73:70 Je 16 '69
FIORI, Pamela
High cost of flying. Holiday 46:63 Jl '69
FIR
See also
Douglas fir
FIRBANK, Arthur Annesley Ronald
Ronald Firbank, by M. J. Benkovitz. Review
Newsweek por 73:94+ Je 2 '69. R. A. Sokolov
Sat R 52:31-2 Je 7 '69. E. M. Potoker
FIRBANK, Ronald. See Firbank, A. A. R.
FIREI drama. See Roc, J.
FIRE alarms
What you should know about fire warning systems. J. P. Schenley. il Pop Mech 131: 176-80 F '69
FIRE apparatus
Getting there in time; forcible entry tool called Jet-Axe. il Bsns W p 158 Mr 29 '69
Volunteer firemen; heroes without pay. J. H. Winchester. il Pop Sci 194:94-7+ My '69
FIRE arms. See Firearms
FIRE balls. See Meteors
FIRE boats. See Fireboats
FIRE control (aerial gunnery)
Helmet-mounted display interest revives. B. Miller. il Aviation W 90:71+ F 24 '69
FIRE departments
Fireman under fire. il Newsweek 74:59-60 Jl 21 '69
See also
Firemen
FIRE drills
Home fire drills; they may save your life. Good H 168:158-9 F '69
FIRE-dwellers; novel. See Laurence, M.
FIRE extinguishers
Amazing new instantaneous fire extinguisher. A. Freese. il Pop Mech 132:93-5+ O '69
Cram course on fire extinguishers. A. J. Maher. Am Home 72:114 Ap '69
How to buy home fire extinguishers. R. C. Sickler. il Pop Sci 195:108-11 D '69
FIRE flies. See Fireflies
FIRE-following plants. See Plant succession
FIRE ISLAND
See also
Architecture, Domestic—Fire Island
FIRE making
How to build a better fire. il Bet Hom & Gard 47:166-7 N '69
FIRE pits. See Fireplaces, Outdoor
FIRE protection
If the house catches fire. il Changing T 23: 21-3 F '69
See also
Airplanes in fire protection
Fire alarms
Fire departments
Fire extinguishers
Fireboats
Firemen
Forest fire protection
Magnetic recorders and recording—Fire protection applications
also subhead Fires and fire protection under various subjects, e.g. School buildings —Fires and fire protection
FIRE screens. See Fireplace accessories
FIRE sprinklers
See also
Automatic sprinkler corporation of America
FIRE walking
Bucky Fuller and the firewalk. G. M. Feigen. il Sat R 52:22-3 Jl 12 '69
FIREARMS
Alarm and trap guns. C. G. Worman. il Hobbies 74:150-1 S '69

Firearms in civil disorders; excerpt from study by the Stanford research institute. Cur 103:40-3 Ja '69
Getting the range. J. O'Connor. See issues of Outdoor life
Shooting. J. O'Connor. See issues of Outdoor life
Shooting. W. Page. See issues of Field & stream
See also
Cartridges
Muskets
Revolvers
Rifles
Submachine guns

Collectors and collecting
Guns that remember. W. Page. il Field & S 74:56-9+ Ag '69

History
Guns on the California trails. C. G. Worman. Hobbies 74:150-1 N '69
John Hills, gunsmith of Vermont. M. B. Peladeau. il Antiques 96:234-6 Ag '69

Laws and regulations
Black power smoke; replicas not affected by Gun control act of 1968. W. Page. il Field & S 74:64-6+ D '69
Controlling violence; toward a less lethal environment; excerpts from Honest politician's guide to crime control. N. Morris and G. Hawkins. Cur 111:48-53 O '69
Evading gun control; public hearings on proposed rules. S. Cupps. New Repub 160:16-18 My 3 '69
Going armed; report of National commission on the causes and prevention of violence. Nation 209:621 D 8 '69
Gun control confusion; gun control act of 1968. Cong 23:36 Ap '69
Gun law enfeeblement. America 121:553 D 6 '69
Keeping up with the Gun control act of 1968. J. O'Connor. Outdoor Life 144:68-9+ S '69
New gun law does affect sportsmen; Gun control act of 1968. W. Page. il Field & S 73:126-8+ F '69
News and views; gun control act of 1968 amendments. J. Deedy. Commonweal 89:664 F 28 '69
90 million firearms, and rising rapidly; excerpts from statement by the National commission on the causes and prevention of violence, July 28, 1969. il U S News 67:40-1 Ag 11 '69
Playing American roulette. J. Rigert. Commonweal 90:72-5 Ap 4 '69

Manufacture
Musket production at Springfield, 1852. C. G. Worman. il Hobbies 74:122-3 My '69

Sights
Focus on rifle scopes. W. Davis. il Mech Illus 65:43+ D '69
How the army learned to see in the dark. M. Schultz. il Pop Mech 131:79-82+ Ja '69
Now they're making a no-guess telescopic sight. P. Wahl. il Pop Sci 194:144-5+ Ja '69
Using your scope. W. Page. il Field & S 74: 96-8+ O '69
FIREARMS industry and trade
See also
International armaments corporation
FIREBALLS. See Meteors
FIREBOATS
Twin hulled fireboat; Yokahama waterfront. il Am City 84:46 My '69
FIRECRACKER 400. See Automobile racing
FIREFLIES
Flashes and behavior of some American fireflies. J. E. Lloyd. bibliog il Cons 23:8-12 Je '69
FIREMAN, E. L.
Freshly fallen meteorites from Portugal and Mexico. Sky & Tel 37:272-5 My '69
FIREMEN
Fireman under fire. il Newsweek 74:59-60 Jl 21 '69; Same abr. Read Digest 95:144-6+ N '69
Volunteer firemen; heroes without pay. J. H. Winchester. il Pop Sci 194:94-7+ My '69
FIREMEN, Railroad. See Railroad—Employees
FIREPITS. See Fireplaces, Outdoor
FIREPLACE accessories
Hanging the tools. il Sunset 143:90 D '69
Spark catcher for wall fireplace. il Sunset 143:168 O '69

FIREPLACES
Ceramic fireplace is a one-day job. D. Huff. il Pop Sci 195:141 N '69
Fire coves. M. Spires. il Am Home 72:36 Ja '69
Fixing up an older home. il Bet Hom & Gard 47:28 My '69
Install a fireplace in a weekend? Here's how; prefabricated package. D. Huff. il Pop Sci 195:175-7 S '69
Ways to spark up a fireplace. il Bet Hom & Gard 47:150 My '69

FIREPLACES, Outdoor
Build this patio firepit. C. D. Hellyer. il Pop Mech 132:148-9 Jl '69
See also
Barbecue grills

FIREPROOF construction
Fire tests prove steel structure can be exposed; excerpts from address. A. F. Nassetta. il Arch Rec 146:199-202 S '69

FIRES
Arson suspected in fire at Yale art and architecture building. il Arch Rec 146:36 Jl '69
150 days of fire; dump fire, Milwaukee, Wis. il Am City 84:80+ Jl '69
Plutonium fire raises questions; investigation after fire at weapons plant, Rocky Flats, Colo. il Sci N 96:25 Jl 12 '69
Tragedy in a house that friends built; N. Fontenelle and son Kenneth die in fire. G. P. Hunt. il Life 66:3 My 2 '69
See also
Forest fires
Jerusalem—Fires
also subhead Fires and Fire protection under various subjects, e.g Airplanes—Fires and fire protection

FIRESTONE, Harvey Samuel, 1898-
Harvey S. Firestone jr; interview. pors Nations Bsns 57:54-9 Ag '69

FIRESTONE family
In the first family of tires, everybody works. il Bsns W p 176 Ap 26 '69

FIRESTONE tire and rubber company
Harvey S. Firestone jr; interview. H. S. Firestone, jr. il Nations Bsns 57:54-9 Ag '69
Paternalism pays off in Akron. il Bsns W p 174-6+ Ap 26 '69

FIREWALKING. See Fire walking

FIREWORKS
Less bang in the fireworks profits. il Bsns W p21 Jl 5 '69

FIRING
See also
Pottery—Firing
FIRING of employees. See Employees—Dismissal

FIRM names. See Business names

FIRST aid in illness and injury
Accidents and injuries. L. W. Sauer. il PTA Mag 63:13-14 Je '69
First aid. C. J. Potthoff. See issues of Today's health
First aid in the home. il Good H 169:212-13 O '69
Quick home guide to first aid. A. S. Markovits. il Mech Illus 65:44-5+ Jl '69
See also
Medicine cabinets

FIRST artists production company
New lunatics. il Newsweek 73:81 Je 23 '69

FIRST avenue. See New York (city)—Streets

FIRST-born children. See Children, First-born

FIRST committee of the General assembly. See United Nations—Political and security committee

FIRST day covers. See Covers (philately)

FIRST editions. See Book rarities

FIRST national bank of Chicago. See Chicago—Banks

FIRST national city corporation of New York. See Bank holding companies

FIRST night audiences. See Audiences

FIRST night performances. See Theater

FIRST Pennsylvania banking and trust company. See Philadelphia—Banks

FIRST Spanish Methodist church, East Harlem. See New York (city)—Churches

FIRST street school. See New York (city)—Education

FIRST year; story. See White, D.

FIRTH, J. M.
Breadboard circuits from PC boards. Electr World 82:65 O '69

FISCAL policy
Farther than ever from a fiscal policy; with editorial comment. il Bsns W p31-2, 124 D 13 '69

Fiscal policy at bay. H. C. Wallich. Newsweek 74:57 Ag 11 '69
Fiscal revolution in America, by H. Stein. Review
Commentary 48:80-2+ Jl '69. R. Lekachman
Mc Labor R 92:10-14 Ag '69. D. Dillard

FISCH, Harold
Faith in Israel. Commentary 47:64-7 F '69

FISCHER, George D.
NEA's new president. por Todays Ed 58:83 Mr '69

FISCHER, John
Easy chair. See issues of Harper's magazine

FISCHER, Margaret T.
Information retrieval research at Time inc; address, January 1969. por Library J 94: 1585-8 Ap 15 '69

FISCHER, R. A.
Stomatal opening: role of potassium uptake by guard cells. bibliog Science 160:784-5; 163:494 My 17 '68. Ja 31 '69

FISCHER, Robert E. and Walsh, F. J.
What the systems approach means to air conditioning. Arch Rec 145:197-204 Ap; 146: 151-8 Ag; 165:172 N '69

FISCHER, Roger A.
Ghetto and gown: the birth of black studies. Cur Hist 57:290-4+ N '69
Racial segregation in ante bellum. New Orleans. bibliog f Am Hist R 74:926-37 F '69

FISCHER, S. verlag. See Publishers and publishing—Germany (Federal Republic)

FISCHER, W. H. and others
Antarctic atmospheric chemistry: preliminary exploration. bibliog Science 164:66-7 Ap 4 '69

FISCHER-WILLIAMS, Barbara
Scots wha hae. Opera N 34:16-19 D 13 '69
(ed) See Barbirolli, J. Sir John

FISCHINGER, Peter J. and O'Connor, T. E.
Radiation leukemia virus: quantitative tissue culture assay. bibliog Science 165:306-9 Jl 18 '69
Viral infection across species barriers: reversible alteration of murine sarcoma virus for growth in cat cells. bibliog Science 165: 714-16 Ag 15 '69

FISH, Kenneth L.
Coping with student activism in secondary schools. Ed Digest 35:8-11 O '69

FISH, Lawrence W. Jr. and Peter, K. J.
New concepts in hi-fi receiver design. Electr World 81:32-4+ F '69

FISH, Robert L.
Plot, plot—who's got a plot? Writer 82:22-3+ Ap '69

FISH, Smoked
See also
Food—Smoking

FISH and game division. See New York (state)—Conservation department

FISH as food
One man's finnan haddie is another's smoked eel. R. Collier. il Holiday 45:22+ F '69
See also
Fish flour
Sea food

FISH calling
Electronic fish call. il Mech Illus 65:78-9+ Ap '69

FISH census
Salmon do their own counting; sonar used to count salmon. J. Rearden. il Outdoor Life 143:16-17+ Mr '69
Star on TV, too; fish counted and catalogued by TV. W. C. Whitt. il Outdoor Life 143:17 Mr '69

FISH chowder. See Chowder

FISH culture
Aquaculture. J. E. Bardach. bibliog il Science 161:1098-106 S 13 '68; Correction. 163:493 Ja 31 '69; reply. C. Adler. 162:956 N 29 '68
Catfish farms are booming, too. Bsns W p 186 S 20 '69
Catfish harvest: thriving catfish industry in the South. il Time 93:112 My 16 '69
Ponds stocked by airplane; listing of wilderness waters stocked with trout in 1968. il Cons 23:14-15+ Ap '69
Thermal aquaculture. C. E. Nash. il Sea Front 15:268-76 S '69
Trout by the bottleful. L. J. Bashline. il Field & S 73:70-1+ Mr '69
See also
Shellfish culture

FISH flour
Fish powder for the millions; fish protein concentrate. il Sea Front 15:112-15 Mr '69

FISH hatcheries. See Fish culture

FISH industry and trade
Catfish harvest; thriving catfish industry in the South. il Time 93:112 My 16 '69
Hooked on fish; seafood industry growth. il Forbes 104:44-5 S 1 '69
See also
Fisheries
Fisheries, Cooperative
FISH marking. See Fish tagging
FISH meal
How a problem with fish meal was solved. Chem 42:22 F '69
FISH pools, Garden. See Garden pools
FISH prints. See Prints
FISH products. See Marine resources
FISH protein concentrate. See Fish flour
FISH records. See Fishing records
FISH soups. See Chowder
FISH tagging
Coho marking. J. Laska. il Cons 23:37 Je '69
Fish tagging; marking trout in New York state. P. M. Kelsey. il Cons 24:32 D '69
FISHBACK, Glen
Bumblebee cannot fly; interview, ed. by P. Farber. il pors Travel & Camera 32:68-71+ Mr '69
FISHER, Adrian S.
U.S. submits draft treaty banning emplacement of nuclear weapons on the seabed; statement. May 22, 1969. Dept State Bul 60:520-4 Je 16 '69
U.S. views on nuclear weapon material cut-off agreement and verification of comprehensive nuclear test ban; statement. April 8, 1969. Dept State Bul 60:409-13 My 12 '69
—and Roshchin, A. A.
U.S., U.S.S.R. recommend admission of Japan and Mongolia to ENDC; statement. Dept State Bul 60:542-3 Je 23 '69
FISHER, Allan C. Jr
Investiture of Great Britain's Prince of Wales. Nat Geog 136:698-715 N '69
Kenya says *harambee!* Nat Geog 135:151-205 F '69
San Diego, California's Plymouth Rock. Nat Geog 136:114-47 Jl '69
FISHER, D. Jerome, and McConnell, Duncan
Aluminum-rich apatite. bibliog Science 164:551-3 My 2 '69
FISHER, David E. See Luyendyk, B. P. jt. auth.
FISHER, Donald W. and Reilly, E. M. Jr
Fossil bones, how to find them. Cons 24:48+ D '69
FISHER, Gail
Gail Fisher, the girl from Mannix. il pors Ebony 24:140-2+ O '69
FISHER, Graham, and Fisher, Heather
Coming of age of Britain's Prince Charles. Good H 169:68-9+ Jl '69
FISHER, Heather. See Fisher, G. jt. auth.
FISHER, John Hurt
Language as emblem. Sch & Soc 97:446-9 N '69
FISHER, Louis
Federal revenue sharing. New Repub 161:15-17 O 4 '69
FISHER, M. F. K.
Gastronomy recalled (cont) New Yorker 45:140-6+ Ap 26; 118+ Je 7; 154+ S 20; 114+ S 27 '69
Only in spots have we tamed the California coast. Holiday 46:40-5+ N '69
FISHER, Max M.
Volunteers get a volunteer. por Bsns W p 155 My 10 '69
FISHER, R. V. and Waters, A. C.
Bed forms in base-surge deposits; lunar implications. bibliog Science 165:1349-52 S 26 '69
FISHER, Robert B.
Crapemyrtle. Horticulture 46:32-3+ S '68
FISHER, Robert L. See Engel, C. G. jt. auth.
FISHER, Roger
International conflict for beginners; excerpts. Atlan 223:46-52 Je '69
FISHER, Russell S.
Let the dead help the living. Todays Health 47:88+ Ap '69
FISHER, Shelley May
In my opinion. por Seventeen 28:196 Je '69
NSA congress, 1969. America 121:218-22 S 27 '69
FISHERIES
Food resources of the ocean. S. J. Holt. il Sci Am 221:178-82+ bibliog(p286) S '69
See also
Fish culture

International aspects
Authority delegated to secretary on fisheries recommendations; executive order. R. Nixon. Dept State Bul 60:544 Je 23 '69
Fishing again with the Russians. A. C. Jensen and J. C. Poole. il Cons 23:10-13+ Ap '69
Red herring; Russian fishing vessels off North Carolina. il Time 93:25 Ap 18 '69
U.S. and Soviet Union sign new fisheries agreement. Dept State Bul 60:19-20 Ja 6 '69

Australia
Boosting the tuna catch; using maps of sea-surface temperatures. W. A. Scholes. il Sci N 96:338 O 11 '69

United States
Marine fisheries; landings of fish and shellfish in New York during 1967. Cons 23:36 F '69
New Atlantic tuna fishery. G. L. Beardsley, jr. il Sea Front 15:152-9 My '69
Senate asked to approve convention on conduct of North Atlantic fishing; message to the Senate, April 16, 1969. R. M. Nixon. Dept State Bul 60:425 My 19 '69
FISHERIES, Cooperative
Shrimp co-op makes blacks own bosses; Hilton Head fishing cooperative, inc. il Ebony 25:106-8+ N '69
FISHERMEN
Even pros have problems. J. Chiappetta. il Field & S 73:64-5+ F '69
How to live with a fisherman. C. Ford. il Read Digest 95:104-6 Ag '69
Ivan and the sportfishermen; Russian trawlers off Long Island. H. Uhland. il Motor B 124:19-20+ D '69
FISHERY laws and legislation
Fishing laws; United States and Canada (cont) Field & S 73:36+ Ap '69
Fishing seasons (cont) Outdoor Life 143:40+ Ap '69
FISHERY research
Fishing again with the Russians. A. C. Jensen and J. C. Poole. il Cons 23:10-13+ Ap '69
FISHES
Forebrain temperature activates behavioral thermoregulatory response in Arctic sculpins. H. T. Hammel and others. bibliog il Science 165:83-5 Jl 4 '69
Fresh water fishes for garden pools. P. W. Stetson. il Horticulture 47:35-6 Ag '69
Learning in fish with transplanted brain tissue. D. E. Bresler and M. E. Bitterman. bibliog il Science 163:590-2 F 7 '69
Microvolt electric signals from fishes and the environment. E. G. Barham and others. bibliog il Science 164:965-8 My 23 '69
More brain, better brain? Sci Am 220:54 My '69
Pacific's all-star cast. il Esquire 72:102-3 Ag '69
Tropical fish for your garden pool. Org Gard & Farm 16:83 Ag '69
See also
Cave fishes
Ichthyology
Nervous system—Fishes
also headings beginning Fish; *also* names of fishes, e.g. Grunion

Accidents and hazards
Fish and power plants. A. C. Jensen. il Cons 24:2-5 D '69
Impetus for action; fishkill in the Rhine. T. Shoemaker. Sci N 96:64 Jl 19 '69
Longest sewer; tons of dead fish in the Rhine. il Newsweek 74:30 Jl 7 '69
Rancid Rhine. il Time 94:26 Jl 4 '69

Anatomy
See also
Gills

Anecdotes, facetiae, satire, etc.
Sven, the remora. D. Kearns. il Yachting 125:61+ Mr '69

Ecology
Fish and power plants. A. C. Jensen. il Cons 24:2-5 D '69
Outwitting the patient assassin; the human use of lake pollution. H. B. Gotaas. Bul Atom Sci 25:8-10 My '69

Food and feeding
Fine kettle of kelt soup in Loch Shin; Atlantic salmon feed. C. Gammon. Sports Illus 31:57-8 N 3 '69
See also
Food chains (ecology)

FISHES—*Continued*

Geographical distribution

Exotics: new threat to U.S. waters. E. Buckow. il Field & S 74:16+ My '69
Interoceanic sea-level canal: effects on the fish faunas. R. W. Topp. bibliog Science 165:1324-7 S 26 '69

Habits and behavior

Bigmouths tell all; home aquarium. T. McNally. il Outdoor Life 144:64-7+ N '69
Secrets of the animal world. R. Petrow. il Pop Mech 132:84-7+ S '69

Migration

Atlantic salmon. A. Netboy. il Sea Front 15: 66-77 Mr '69
Round trip with the salmon. A. Netboy. il Natur Hist 78:44-51+ Je '69
Where the salmon go. L. A. Roser. il Field & S 73:62-3+ Ap '69

Physiology

Fishes that grow horns; breeding or nuptial tubercles. R. F. Denoncourt. il Cons 23:30-1 Ap '69
Luminescent systems in apogonid fishes from the Philippines. Y. Haneda and others. bibliog il Science 165:188-90 Jl 11 '69
Seawater teleosts: evidence for a sodium-potassium exchange in the branchial sodium-excreting pump. J. Maetz. bibliog il Science 166:613-15 O 31 '69

Reproduction

See also
Spawning

Research

See Ichthyological research

Stories

Exit laughing. E. Zern. See issues of Field & stream

Tagging

See Fish tagging

FISHES, Breathing of. See Respiration
FISHES, Effect of cold on. See Cold—Physiological effects
FISHES, Effect of sound on
Shark caller. il Time 93:75 Je 20 '69
FISHES, Fossil
They dig for fish. J. S. Flannery. il Pop Mech 131:152-3 Mr '69
FISHEYE lenses. See Lenses, Photographic
FISHING
Access: the key to public land recreation. B. Milek. il Field & S 73:20+ Ap '69
Bridge fishing primer. A. Reinfelder. il Field & S 74:80-3+ Je '69
Fish-fighting myths exploded. H. Wixom. il Field & S 73:74-5+ Ap '69
Fish 'n ships. V. Evanoff. See issues of Motor boating
Fishing. A. J. McClane. See issues of Field & stream
Fishing J. Brooks. See issues of Outdoor life
Float for first-class fishing. N. Strung. il Field & S 74:68-9+ Je '69
Gist of it; digest of the outdoor news; ed. by H. Moore. See issues of Outdoor life
Sportsman's notebook. H. G. Tapply. See issues of Field & stream
Try it, number two. T. Trueblood. il Field & S 73:24+ F '69
Where to go; ed. by V. T. Sparano. See issues of Outdoor life
See also
Casting (fishing)
Fisheries
Fishermen
Salt water fishing
Trawls and trawling

Accidents and injuries

Saga of survival. E. L. Rogers. il Field & S 74:78-9+ Je '69
See also
Fishing, Winter—Accidents and injuries

Anecdotes, facetiae, satire, etc.

Great cow plot; chase the fisherman. P. McManus. il Field & S 74:76-7+ My '69

Competitions

1968 winners: Field & stream fishing contest. Field & S 73:116+ Mr; 116+ Ap '69

Implements and appliances

Streamlined tackle boxes. C. Conley. il Field & S 73:153 Mr '69
See also
Fishing tackle

Law

See Fishery laws and legislation

Study and teaching

Georgia is helping America learn to fish. H. Bradshaw. il Field & S 73:10-13 F '69

Alaska

Alaska: unfinished pleasure. E. A. Bauer. il Outdoor Life 143:62-5+ My '69
Personal business; sportsmen's utopia. Bsns W p93-4 My 3 '69
Take the high road to Alaska. G. Laycock. il Field & S 74:50-3+ My '69

Arizona

Happiest fishing ground; Fort Apache Indian reservation. R. Cantwell. il Sports Illus 31: 37-41 Ag 4 '69

Arkansas

More fish to fry; fishing Dardanelle Lake. C. Elliott. il Outdoor Life 144:66-7+ S '69

Bahama Islands

Raps and strikes. G. Heinold. il Outdoor Life 144:86+ D '69
Spitmouth puffers in the living room; development of Walker's Cay by aerosol king, Bob Abplanalp. R. H. Boyle. il Sports Illus 31:28-30+ D 8 '69

Brazil

In search of el dorado. A. J. McClane. il Field & S 73:96-8+ F; 94-6+ Mr '69

California

Backpack jackpot. M. Hayden. il Outdoor Life 144:56-9+ O '69
Double take on bonito; Redondo Harbor. L. Green; J. R. Gregg. il Field & S 73:50-3 F '69
First report: California's new ice fishing season. R. Cobb. il Field & S 74:26-7+ D '69
Fishing for shad in the Feather. il Sunset 142:42-3 My '69
Fishing is great, when you get there; Beegum creek. il Sunset 143:34 Jl '69
Fishing should be great at Lassen. il Sunset 143:67-8 O '69
Good fishing on Lassen's shoulder. il Sunset 142:60+ Je '69
Jump-fishing for rainbows. J. Freeman. il Field & S 74:56-7+ My '69
Manhattan with mountains, and trout. J. Mears. il Field & S 73:162-4+ Mr '69
May fishing in the Devil's Garden. il Sunset 142:69 My '69
Rainbows and rattlers. J. R. Higley. il Outdoor Life 143:80-3+ My '69
To Sausalito for the herring. il Sunset 143: 24 D '69

Canada

Amazing Great Bear Lake! C. Conley. il Field & S 73:44-7+ F '69
Best fishing in Canada; with list of twenty favorite spots in eastern Canada. W. Davis. il Oudoor Life 144:70-2+ Jl '69
Big four of the North. J. Brooks. il Outdoor Life 144:34-5+ Ag '69
Fall: a time for pike. A. W. Prince. il Field & S 74:62-3+ O '69
Fisherman's paradise on workingman's budget. G. W. Bowers. il Outdoor Life 144:64-7+ Jl '69
High-flying fishing club. G. Gresham. il Field & S 74:60-3+ My '69
Jumping with bass. H. Bradshaw. il Outdoor Life 144:48-51+ Ag '69
Lunkers of Obre Lake. A. Spiers. il Field & S 74:166-8+ O '69
Madness for muskies. H. Bradshaw. il Field & S 73:66-7+ Mr '69
On the watery trail of the great grayling. W. Davis. il Mech Illus 65:34+ Jl '69
Strategy for smallmouths. T. McNally. il Outdoor Life 143:56-9+ My '69
Unsung giants of the Fraser; British Columbia. H. Williams. il Field & S 73:68-9+ F '69
We saw the ice go out. O. A. Frederickson. il Outdoor Life 143:52-5+ My '69

Colorado

Woman's touch. M. C. Gethman. il Field & S 74:58-9 Jl '69

Costa Rica

Slugger turns to tarpon. V. Dunaway. il Field & S 73:60-3+ F '69

FISHING—*Continued*

Ecuador

Record bigeye for a lady. H. C. King. il Field & S 74:40-1+ Jl '69

Europe

Je fische europeanski. J. A. Maxtone-Graham. Travel & Camera 32:25-6 D '69

Finland

Travel notes; Kuopio and vicinity. R. Joseph. Esquire 72:38 Jl '69

Florida

Fishing the thick stuff. C. F. Waterman. il Field & S 73:58-9+ F '69

High-flying tarpon. J. Brooks. il Outdoor Life 144:74-6+ Jl '69

How to fish Florida Bay. G. X. Sand. il Field & S 73:192-4+ Ap '69

Stripers down south. G. Laycock. il Field & S 73:54-5+ F '69

Georgia

Can anyone catch a new record bass? C. Nansen. il Field & S 73:42-3+ F '69

Lake of bragging fish. P. Curtis. il Field & S 74:44-5+ Jl '69

Great Lakes Region

News: the Great Lakes states; ed. by B. East. Outdoor Life 144:33-4 Jl '69

Powerboat revolution. F. T. Moss. il Yachting 125:52-3+ My '69

Idaho

One for the governor. C. Ormond. il Outdoor Life 143:70-1+ Mr '69

Indiana

Call of the bugle. J. Parry. il Field & S 74:70-1+ Je '69

Lunker-busting on the level. J. A. Brang. il Field & S 74:12-14+ Jl '69

Italy

Suddenly, you are fishing in Italy. P. Barrett. il Outdoor Life 143:72-5+ F '69

Kentucky

Ballard's bass boom. E. A. Bauer. il Outdoor Life 143:68-71+ Ap '69

Our old Kentucky houseboat. A. W. Prince. il Outdoor Life 143:68-71+ My '69

Louisiana

Toledo Bend: big new bass lake. L. A. Wilke. il Field & S 74:148-9+ Je '69

Maine

Drop a hook down east. V. Evanoff. il Motor B 124:39+ Jl '69

Maryland

Fly rods & hickory shad. C. B. Pfeiffer. il Field & S 74:74-5+ My '69

Training grounds for trout fishermen. L. Kreh. il Field & S 73:86-7+ Ap '69

Turtle clapping. C. Robinson. il Field & S 74:66-7 Je '69

Mexico

Marlin lover of Mazatlán. R. F. Jones. il Sports Illus 30:42-4+ Mr 31 '69

Michigan

Boom in steelhead; rainbow trout that live in Lake Michigan. J. O. Cartier. il Outdoor Life 143:60-3+ Mr '69

But is it fishing? il Newsweek 74:66 Jl 14 '69

Coho catches on. V. Evanoff. il Motor B 124:63+ O '69

Honor coho; Michigan conservation department. A. Stark. il Field & S 74:58-9+ My '69

Jigging Lake Michigan. H. F. Zeman. il Field & S 74:32-3+ D '69

Lake trout are back! J. O. Cartier. il Outdoor Life 143:88-9+ Ap '69

Middle western states

Bass like wildfire. J. Brang. il Outdoor Life 143:58-9+ Mr '69

Minnesota

Walleye crawl. R. Slogar. il Outdoor Life 143:74-5+ Ap '69

Montana

Fall: season of big trout. J. Brooks. il Outdoor Life 144:156-8+ O '69

Nevada

Stripers in the Big Red. C. C. Niehuis. il Field & S 73:68-9+ Ap '69

New Jersey

New way for surf stripers; kite fishing. J. Samson. il Field & S 74:22+ Je '69

Tuna party. T. Kelley. il Outdoor Life 144:48-9+ S '69

New Mexico

Mountain pike. B. Dalrymple. il Field & S 74:64-5+ My '69

100-mile campground. B. W. Dalrymple. il Field & S 74:42-3+ Jl '69

New York (state)

Boys and bullheads. A. Glowka. il Outdoor Life 144:72-5+ Ag '69

Charmed circle completed; Catskills trout streams. C. E. Heacox. il Outdoor Life 143:80-1+ Ap '69

Charmed circle of the Catskills. C. E. Heacox. il Outdoor Life 143:50-3+ Mr '69

Family fun fish. W. Davis. il Mech Illus 65:46+ Je '69

First trout, first lie. N. Lyons. il Field & S 73:48-9+ F '69

Hot bridge crappies; New York city's reservoirs. A. Glowka. il Field & S 74:66-7+ My '69

Playing the game. G. Heinold. il Outdoor Life 144:22+ Jl '69

Uncrowned king of caviar; excerpt from The Hudson River, a natural and unnatural history. R. H. Boyle. il Sports Illus 31:70-6+ N 3 '69

Wire for the the blues; Long Island Sound. A. Glowka. il Field & S 74:56-7+ Jl '69

New Zealand

Fishing in New Zealand. J. Brooks. il Outdoor Life 144:60-3+ D '69

Paradise/south of the South Pacific. A. J. McClane. il Field & S 74:152-6 O '69

North Carolina

Carolina shad comeback. J. Dean. il Field & S 73:58-9+ Ap '69

Northeastern states

News: the Northeast; ed. by T. Janes. Outdoor Life 144:37-40 Ag: 31-4 S: 25-8 D '69

Oregon

Fresh frozen ironheads. D. Holm. Outdoor Life 144:42-3+ D '69

Sport without limit. L. Miracle. il Outdoor Life 144:66-7+ Ag '69

Pacific countries

Intelligent angler's guide to the Pacific-Orient. R. Joseph. il Esquire 72:96-101 Ag '69

Pennsylvania

Keystone coho. L. J. Bashline. il Field & S 73:54-5+ Ap '69

Throw darts for winter trout. L. J. Bashline il Field & S 74:112-14+ D '69

Rhode Island

Little jumbos. G. Heinold. il Outdoor Life 144:164+ O '69

Scotland

Scotland for salmon. A. Oglesby. il Field & S 74:64-6+ O '69

Southern states

News: the Southeast. C. Elliott and H. L. Lawrence. Outdoor Life 144:41 N '69

Tennessee

What walleye secret? C. Vinson. il Outdoor Life 144:58-9+ Jl '69

Texas

Crappies for all, all year; Lake Tawakoni. J. N. Mannix. il Outdoor Life 143:60-1+ F '69

Fly fishing in a forest. B. W. Dalrymple. il Outdoor Life 144:64-7+ O '69

Toledo Bend: big new bass lake. L. A. Wilke. il Field & S 74:148-9+ Je '69

United States

Fall fishing. A. J. McClane. il Field & S 74:122-5 S '69

Let the whole family flounder! M. Michaelson. il Todays Health 47:14-15 Jl '69

Pleasant'st angling. J. G. Harmount. il Todays Health 47:56-9+ Mr '69

FISHING—*Continued*

Vermont

Reunion at Missisquoi Bay. T. Janes. il Outdoor Life 143:76-7+ My '69

Vietnam

Fishing under the V.C. guns. F. Turner. il Outdoor Life 144:37-9+ Jl '69

Virginia

Assateague: great fishing-camping combo. P. McLain. il Field & S 74:68-9+ My '69
Lunkers of the Roanoke. B. Cochran. il Outdoor Life 143:80-2+ Mr '69

Washington (state)

Bass man in steelhead country. S. Fagerstrom. il Outdoor Life 143:94-6+ Ap '69
Cutthroat harvest. S. Fagerstrom. il Outdoor Life 144:56-7+ Jl '69
Harvest trout. W. Blair. il Field & S 74:136-8+ Ag '69
Paradise for plunkers; Columbia River. S. Fagerstrom. il Field & S 74:62-3+ Je '69
September of the humpback. B. Behme. il Field & S 74:140-2 S '69
Trophy steelhead country. W. E. Kruse. il Field & S 73:148-51+ F '69

West Virginia

Swim a jig for summer bass. C. B. Pfeiffer. il Outdoor Life 144:44-5+ Jl '69

Western states

Carlyle Lake: midwestern hotspot. J. Lockhart. il Field & S 74:164-6+ My '69
News: the West (cont) L. Miracle; J. Martin. Outdoor Life 143:41-4 F '69

Wisconsin

New technique for big pike. A. Welsch. il Outdoor Life 143:54-5+ F '69
Quiet boom. D. Otto. il Outdoor Life 144:77-80+ N '69

Wyoming

Bargain pack trip. N. D. Weis. il Outdoor Life 143:49-51+ My '69
Fishing the split-personality river; Wind River canyon. B. Milek. il Field & S 74:54-5+ My '69
Lead leaders. T. Trueblood. il Field & S 73:28+ Ap '69

Yugoslavia

Fishing in Yugoslavia; strong-bodied trout, grayling, and huchen. J. Brooks. il Outdoor Life 144:42-5+ S '69

FISHING, Deep sea. See Salt water fishing
FISHING, Winter
Finding fish in winter. H. G. Tapply. il Field & S 73:72 F '69
First report: California's new ice fishing season. R. Cobb. il Field & S 74:26-7+ D '69
Jigging Lake Michigan. H. F. Zeman. il Field & S 74:32-3+ D '69
Snowmobiles put new go in ice fishing. il Pop Sci 194:139-41 Ja '69
Throw darts for winter trout. L. J. Bashline. il Field & S 74:112-14+ D '69

Accidents and injuries

Death waited in white; ed. by B. East. C. E. Brown. il Outdoor Life 144:58-9+ D '69

FISHING accidents. See Fishing—Accidents and injuries
FISHING boats
Dredge boats of the Chesapeake; our last fleet of working sail. E. H. Nabb. il Yachting 126:50-3+ S '69
Fish 'n ships. V. Evanoff. See issues of Motor boating
Fishing vessels, or fishy ones? flotilla of Soviet and Polish trawlers off the Atlantic coast. il Newsweek 73:26 F 24 '69
Ivan and the sportfishermen; Russian trawlers off Long Island. H. Uhland. il Motor B 124:19-20+ D '69
Powerboat revolution. F. T. Moss. il Yachting 125:52-3+ My '69
Sport fisherman; interview. ed. by F. Moss. R. M. Akin, jr. il Yachting 125:80 Ja '69
Yachting eyes a boat; St Thomian fisherman. il Yachting 125:42 Je '69

Design

Give up. il Yachting 126:56-7+ Ag '69
Welcome aboard Wild Duck. il Motor B 124:64-5 S '69

Equipment

Fish 'n ships. V. Evanoff. See issues of Motor boating

Testing

Trans-Caribbean delivery. F. Burke. il Yachting 126:61+ N '69
FISHING docks and piers
Happiness is a fishing pier and a place in the sun; San Diego's municipal fishing pier. J. Lucas and M. Miner. il Parks & Rec 4:31-2 My '69
FISHING flies. See Fishing lures, flies, etc.
FISHING guides. See Guides
FISHING industry. See Fish industry and trade
FISHING laws and legislation
U.S, Chile, Ecuador, Peru hold first session of fisheries talks; Department announcement with joint declaration. Dept State Bul 61:216-17 S 8 '69
FISHING lines. See Fishing tackle
FISHING lures, flies, etc.
Basic spinning lures. A. J. McClane. il Field & S 74:72-6 Jl '69
Best salt-water lures. V. Evanoff. il Motor B 123:88+ My '69
Bucktailing for cohos. D. Knowles. il Outdoor Life 144:54-7+ S '69
Fishing streamers and bucktails. J. Brooks. il Outdoor Life 143:32-3+ Mr '69
Fluff bugs for bass. L. Green. il Field & S 73:56-7+ F '69
Hidden hatch. V. C. Marinaro. il Outdoor Life 144:48-51+ Jl '69
How to fool April trout. F. McKinley. il Outdoor Life 143:61-3+ Ap '69
Jigging for bass, east Tennessee style. S. Sutton. il Field & S 74:58-9+ Je '69
Jigs and jigging. G. Heinold. il Outdoor Life 143:84+ Mr '69
Keel hook; revolution in fly fishing. A. J. McClane. il Field & S 73:94-5+ Ap '69
Mini course in spinning. W. Davis. il Mech Illus 65:53-5+ Mr '69
New gleam for streamers. C. F. Waterman. il Field & S 73:56-7+ Ap '69
Plastic worm from A to B. H. G. Tapply. il Field & S 74:60 Jl '69
Plugs and plugging. G. Heinold. il Outdoor Life 143:38+ My '69
Top-water dynamite. J. Brooks. il Outdoor Life 143:86-8+ My '69
Trout flies. E. Zern. il Nat Wildlife 7:43-7 Ap '69
Ways to keep a fly afloat. H. G. Tapply. il Field & S 73:76 Mr '69
When in doubt, try a bucktail. T. Trueblood. il Field & S 74:30+ My '69
Who says propellers are obsolete? L. Green. il Field & S 74:54-5+ Je '69
FISHING records
New world record fish. Field & S 73:70-1 F '69
FISHING rods. See Fishing tackle
FISHING stories
One that drove away. D. Simpson. Field & S 73:149 Ap '69
FISHING tackle
Fresh-water spinning tackle. il Consumer Rep 34:328-35 Je '69
It's more than luck. A. J. McClane. il Field & S 74:88-90+ My '69
Lead leaders. T. Trueblood. il Field & S 73:28+ Ap '69
Mini course in spinning. W. Davis. il Mech Illus 65:53-5+ Mr '69
You need bait casting, too. T. Trueblood. il Field & S 74:29-30+ Jl '69
Your first trout outfit. W. Davis. il Mech Illus 65:51+ Ap '69

Storage

Tripod rack keeps fish rods handy. J. Hand. il Pop Sci 194:129 Je '69
FISHING with bow and arrow
Bownanza. E. A. Bauer. il Outdoor Life 143:74-7+ Mr '69
FISHLOCK, David
Animal antibiotic attack. Sci N 97:26 Ja 3 '70
Britain's toe on the Continent. Sci N 96:566 D 13 '69
Insulin design traced. Sci N 96:307 O 4 '69
FISHMAN, Katharine Davis
Women's residences: halfway between home and on your own. Seventeen 28:106-7+ Je '69
FISHPONDS. See Fish culture
FISHWORMS. See Earthworms
FISK, Zachary, and Matthias, B. T.
Rare-earth elements and high pressures. bibliog Science 165:279-80 Jl 18 '69
FISK university, Nashville, Tenn.
At Fisk, the students are totally black and the administration is scared. J. J. Oliver. Newsweek 73:55 F 10 '69

FISK university, Nashville, Tenn.—*Continued*
Library
Library and media center for Fisk's future. il Library J 94:4404-5 D 1 '69

FISKE, Edward B.
Closest thing to a White House chaplain. N Y Times Mag p27+ Je 8 '69
Why priests marry. Read Digest 95:105-10 D '69

FISKE, Richard S. and Kinoshita, W. T.
Inflation of Kilauea volcano prior to its 1967-1968 eruption. bibliog Science 165:341-9 Jl 25 '69

FISSION (biology). See Reproduction, Asexual

FISSION, Atomic. See Nuclear fission

FISSION-track dating. See Radioactive dating

FISSIONABLE materials. See Radioactive substances

FITCH, Charles Marden
My teacher, the TV set. pors Américas 21: 8-14 Mr '69

FITCH, James Marston
Bank with a past in its future. Arch Forum 130:68-75 My '69

FITCH, Marguerite E.
Education of the educational secretary. Todays Ed 58:69 Ja '69

FITCH, Robert E.
Dictionary of contemporary delusions. Chr Cent 86:377-8 Mr 19 '69

FITCH, William
After four years, a launch. J. B. Reynolds. Chr Today 13:41 Mr 28 '69

FITHIAN, Janet H.
Baby takes over. Parents Mag 44:48-9+ Ag '69

FITNESS, Physical. See Health

FITZGERALD, Arthur Ernest
Ernest Fitzgerald, R.I.F. por Newsweek 74: 106+ N 17 '69
Pentagon gadfly on contract costs. por Bsns W p43 Je 21 '69
Pentagon loyalty. Nation 209:526 N 17 '69
Pentagon purgatory. por Time 94:16-17 Jl 11 '69

FITZGERALD, C. P.
East Asian backgrounds. Nation 209:384-6 O 13 '69
Revolutionary hiatus. Bul Atom Sci 25:53-60 F '69
River is not the issue. Nation 208:465-6 Ap 14 '69

FITZ-GERALD, Daniel Michael
Supermarket for builders. S. Margetts. il por Duns R 94:85-6+ S '69

FITZGERALD, Frances
Child's Christmas in Megalopolis. House & Gard 136:71+ D '69

FITZGERALD, Francis Scott Key
Fitzgerald and Hemingway: the difficult friend. J. Hart. Nat R 21:29-31 Ja 14 '69

FITZGERALD, Scott. See Fitzgerald, F. S. K.

FITZGIBBON, Constantine
Joys of industrialization. Nat R 21:429-31+ My 6 '69

FITZGIBBON, Larry
Where it all began. il Yachting 125:68-9+ Je '69

FITZHUGH, Jewell Kirby
Old English survival in mountain speech. Engl J 58:1224-7 N '69

FITZJARRALD, Sarah
Gardener's life after a heart attack. Org Gard & Farm 16:48-51 Ag '69

FITZPATRICK, Franklin E.
Missing ingredient in Catholic schools. America 120:406-7 Ap 5 '69

FITZPATRICK, Joseph P.
Poverty, politics and social studies. America 120:558-61 My 10 '69

FITZPATRICK, Robert L.
This is the army. New Repub 161:19-21 Jl 19 '69

FITZSIMMONS, Frank
Mr Clean and the outcast. por Time 93:104 Je 6 '69

FIVE-and-ten-cent stores
See also
Woolworth, F. W. company

FIVE on the black hand side; drama. See Russell, C. L.

FIXED base operators
See also
Southwest airmotive company

FIXES, Basketball. See Bribery

FIXTURES, Bathroom. See Bathroom fixtures

FIXX, James F.
Trade winds (cont) Sat R 52:12 Ja 25; 8-9 F 8; 18 F 22; 14-15 Mr 8; 18 Mr 22 '69

FLACK, J. D. and others
Prostaglandin stimulation of rat corticosteroidogenesis. bibliog Science 163:691-2 F 14 '69

FLACKS, Richard
Assault at Chicago. Newsweek 73:70-1 My 19 '69

FLAGELLATES
See also
Euglena

FLAG signals. See Signals and signaling

FLAGS
Banner years; with paintings by C. Hassam. D. G. Lowe. Am Heritage 20:54-9 Je '69
Furor over flag for militants. U S News 66:13 Je 9 '69

Haiti
Haiti and the national flag; reprint. il Negro Hist Bul 32:14-15 O '69

United States
Day I knew I belonged to the flag. D. D. Eisenhower. il Read Digest 94:93 Mr '69
Decalcomania over the American flag. il Life 67:32-3 Jl 18 '69
Ensign of reassurance. il Time 94:17 Jl 11 '69
Hail to the flag! T. J. Fleming. il Read Digest 94:185-6+ Ap '69
High-flying flags. il Newsweek 73:78 Je 30 '69
Of 195 flags going to moon, one stays. il Bsns W p 105 Jl 19 '69
One flag from many. T. Fleming. il Read Digest 95:143-7 S '69

FLAHERTY, Daniel L.
Red bloc. America 122:12-14 Ja 10 '70

FLAHERTY, Joe
Right to the jaw: that's black power. Esquire 71:112-14+ My '69

FLAHERTY, Peter F.
Bye-bye machine. R. W. Gibbons. Commonweal 90:381-4 Je 20 '69
Nobody's boy. il por Newsweek 74:49 N 17 '69

FLAINE, France
Flaine, a ski resort near Chamonix, France designed to function as a self-sustaining town. il Arch Rec 146:102-7 Ag '69

FLAKE, Keith M.
Ten most wanted men: the worker; address, March 14, 1969. Vital Speeches 35:441-4 My 1 '69

FLAKED grain. See Feeding and feeding stuffs—Grain

FLAMES
Mercury-filled doughnut and clouds on Venus. il Chem 42:25 Ap '69

FLAMHOLTZ, Elaine
Majorca; the haunted island. Travel & Camera 32:46-7+ Mr '69

FLAMING (cookery) See Cookery

FLAMINGOS
Africa's great flamingo roundup. il Sci Digest 66:70-3 D '69

FLANAGAN, William
Vocal music by American composers, William Flanagan: a style of his own. P. L. Miller. por Am Rec G 35:542-3 Mr '69

FLANIGAN, Peter M.
Head-hunter. por Newsweek 73:37 Ap 28 '69
Nixon's odd-jobs man. por Bsns W p62-3 S 27 '69

FLANNER, Hildegarde
Memo: poem. New Yorker 44:100 F 8 '69

FLANNER, Janet
Letter from Paris. See issues of New Yorker

FLANNERY, John S.
They dig for fish. Pop Mech 131:152-3 Mr '69

FLANSBURGH, Earl R.
Some thoughts on starting your own office. Arch Rec 145:149-60 Ap '69

FLAPS, Airplane
Wingtip flap system provides variable wing area, sweep. D. A. Brown. il Aviation W 90: 88-90 Ap 14 '69

FLARE (photography) See Photography—Exposure

FLARES, Solar. See Solar flares

FLASH meters. See Exposure meters

FLASHBULBS. See Electric lamps, Photoflash

FLASHCUBES. See Electric lamps, Photoflash

FLASHING lights. See Electric lamps, Flashing

FLASHLIGHT photography. See Photography, Flashlight

FLATS, etc. (horticulture)
$11 plant-starter. T. Anderson. il Org Gard & Farm 16:86-8 D '69
Good news for stiff backs and tender knees. V. Tripp. il Org Gard & Farm 16:86-7 Ag '69

FLATS, Optical. See Optical flats

FLATTAU, Edward
Opening college doors to the disadvantaged.
Parents Mag 44:48-9+ D '69

FLATULENCE
Gastrointestinal gas. Sci Am 221:95 S '69

FLATWARE. See Silverware

FLATWORMS
Complex synaptic configurations in planarian
brain. J. B. Best and J. Noel. bibliog il
Science 164:1070-1 My 30 '69
Fissioning in planarians: control by the
brain. J. B. Best and others. bibliog il
Science 164:565-6 My 2 '69
Gnathostomulida from America. R. J. Riedl.
bibliog il Science 164:445-52 Ja 31 '69; Dis-
cussion. 164:855-6 My 16 '69
Gnathostomulidology. Sci Am 220:52 Ap '69
Microtubules in spermatozoa of childia (tur-
bellaria, acoela) revealed by negative stain-
ing. D. P. Costello and others. bibliog il
Science 163:678-9 F 14 '69

FLAVOR
Give me that old-time flavor. J. Olds. il
Org Gard & Farm 16:26-9 Ag '69

FLAVORING essences
Key people; blind people test flavorings
and fragrances. K. B. Pomeroy. il Am For
75:30-1 Ag '69
See also
International flavors and fragrances, incor-
porated
Seasonings

FLEA in her ear; drama. See Feydeau, G.

FLEAS
Super flea meets mountain beaver. V. S.
Scheffer. il Natur Hist 78:54-5 My '69

FLECK, James C.
What to do about Joe Mulligan? America 121:
184-9 S 20 '69

FLEDDERMANN, Harry, and Ingram, F. L.
Morals, marriage and youth. America 120:194-6
F 15 '69

FLEECE. See Wool

FLEGENHEIMER, Arthur
Last words of Dutch Schultz; scenario. W
S. Burroughs. pors Atlan 223:72-6+ Je '69

FLEISCH, Herbert, and others
Diphosphonates inhibit hydroxyapatite dissolution in vitro and bone resorption in
tissue culture and in vivo. bibliog Science
165:1262-4 S 19 '69

FLEISCHER, Leonore
Who's that vetoing our past? Life 66:12
Je 6 '69
Yen for young authors. Life 67:76+ O 24 '69

FLEISCHER, R. L. and others
Nuclear tracks in solids; with biographical
sketches. Sci Am 220:14, 30-9 Je '69

FLEISCHER, Sidney. See Nielsen, N. C. jt.
auth.

FLEISCHMANN, Raoul Herbert
Obituary
New Yorker 45:27-8 My 17 '69

FLEISHER, Bruce
Bruce and his babies storm Augusta. C.
Kirkpatrick. il Sports Illus 30:28-9 Ap 21 '69

FLEMER, William, 3d
Weeping trees. Horticulture 46:24-5+ N '68

FLEMING, Alice
Frigidity, the myth that plagues too many
women. Redbook 132:68-9+ Mr '69
Learning to ski in Switzerland. House B 111:
79+ O '69

FLEMING, Sir Ambrose. See Fleming, J. A.

FLEMING, Denna Frank
Path to total destruction. N. L. Parks. Nation 208:153+ F 3 '69

FLEMING, Donald
On living in a biological revolution. Atlan
223:64-70 F '69; Same with title Mood of the
new revolutionaries. Cur 105:10-19 Mr '69

FLEMING, Edward Jude
Campus that kept its cool. B. Darrach. il
pors Life 67:80-80B+ N 7 '69

FLEMING, George
Where are they now? il pors Newsweek 75:
7 Ja 5 '70

FLEMING, J. Carl
Pupil tutors and tutees learn together. Todays
Ed 58:22-4 O '69; Same abr. Ed Digest 35:
33-40 D '69

FLEMING, Joe W. 2d
Appalachian economy; excerpts from address, September 25, 1968. Parks & Rec 4:
21-3+ Ja '69

FLEMING, Sir John Ambrose
First electron tube. G. Shiers. il por Sci Am
220:104-12 Mr '69; Reply with rejoinder. L.
Espenschied. 221:8 Ag '69

FLEMING, Rodney R.
Scrutinize your street-cleaning techniques.
Am City 84:115-16+ Mr '69
Tandem plowing eases snowrighters' problems. Am City 84:82-4+ Ag '69
(ed) See Johnson, E. Supply all the water
your customers desire

FLEMING, Shirley
Winner in the Philippines. Hi Fi 19:MA25+
D '69

FLEMING, Thomas James, 1927-
Can the Catholic revolution succeed? Red-
book 133:77+ My '69
Case history: I am the law. Am Heritage
20:32-48 Je '69
Computer and the psychiatrist. N Y Times
Mag p44-5+ Ag 6 '69
Hail to the flag! Read Digest 94:185-6+ Ap
'69
Hesburgh of Notre Dame: (1) he's destroying
this university; (2) he's bringing it into the
mainstream of American life. N Y Times
Mag p56-7+ My 11 '69
One flag from many. Read Digest 95:143-7
S '69
Rugged road to independence. Read Digest
95:82-8 Jl '69
Verdicts of history (cont) Am Heritage 20:
74-80+ D '68
When Jersey was the spa of presidents. Sat R
52:46-7+ Mr 8 '69

FLEMISH art. See Art, Flemish

FLESHREN, D. F.
Electrolytic-capacitor tester. Electr World 82:
82-3 O '69

FLETCHER, Diane
Losers. por Redbook 133:12+ Jl '69

FLETCHER, Homer L.
Goals for the asking; address. October
1968, ed. by J. F. Krug. ALA Bul 63:731-3
Je '69

FLETCHER, Janet. See Donathan, J. jt. ed.

FLEXIBLE shafting. See Shafting, Flexible

FLEXNER, Abraham
Abraham Flexner's medical bombshell. J. L.
Slattery and R. Gosswiller. il Todays
Health 47:44-5+ Mr '69

FLEXNER, J. B. and Flexner, L. B.
Puromycin: effect on memory of mice when
injected with various cations. bibliog Science 165:1143-4 S 12 '69

FLEXNER, James Thomas
Washington after the Revolution; excerpts.
Am Heritage 20:10-13+ F; 64-73 Ap; 72-9+
Je; 24-7 O; 21:32-3+ D '69

FLEXNER, L. B. See Flexner, J. B. jt.
auth.

FLICK, Art, jr
King of Kishanina. Field & S 73:72-3+ Mr
'69

FLICK, Friedrich
Durable Friedrich Flick. il pors Forbes 103:
39-41 F 1 '69

Der FLIEGENDE Holländer; opera. See
Wagner, R.

FLIES
Fantastic fly. D. Valentry. il Todays Health
47:56-7 Ag '69
Puparium formation in flies: contraction to
puparism induced by ecdysone. P. Berreur
and G. Fraenkel. bibliog il Science 164:
1182-3 Je 6 '69
See also
Drosophila
Fruit flies
Sandflies

FLIES, Artificial. See Fishing lures, flies, etc.

FLIGHT
See also
Birds—Flight

Physiological aspects
See Aviation—Physiological aspects

FLIGHT, Interplanetary. See Space flight

FLIGHT crews. See Airplane crews

FLIGHT fatigue. See Aviation—Physiological
aspects

FLIGHT instructors. See Air pilots—Training

FLIGHT simulators
Flight simulator to help train army pilots.
R. S. Kahn. Aviation W 90:90-1 Je 23 '69
I learned to fly without leaving the ground,
and so can you. R. M. Benrey. il Pop Sci
194:92-5+ Mr '69
New products; Link's light twin. il Flying
85:20-1 Jl '69
See also
Space flight simulators

FLIGHT tests. See Air pilots—Testing

FLINDT, Flemming
World of dance. W. Terry. il Sat R 52:32-3
Je 21 '69

FLINN, Edward A. See Engdahl, E. R. jt. auth.

FLINT, Florence E.
Right to fail. Todays Ed 58:39-40 Ap '69

FLINT, Mich.
Voluntary refuse-bag program gains strength. T. Kay. il Am City 84:78-9 Je '69

Rapid transit

Bus at every door. T. Kay. il Am City 84: 126+ Ag '69

Recreation

City cares. L. W. Tyler. il Parks & Rec 4:30-1+ Jl '69

FLINT, Mich, public library
Branch library programs: operation shoestring budget; Civic Park branch. H. Hoeffgen. il Wilson Lib Bul 43:545-51 F '69

FLINT implements and weapons. See Stone implements and weapons

FLINTKOTE company
Look-alikes. Forbes 103:41 Ja 15 '69

FLIPPER, Henry Ossian
Cover story. por(p 1) Negro Hist Bul 32:3 Mr '69

FLOAT fishing. See Fishing

FLOATING
Float to safety. W. S. Kals. il Todays Health 47:46-7 Je '69
  See also
Aquatic sports

FLOATING sculpture. See Sculpture

FLOATS. See Rafts

FLOATS, Seaplane. See Seaplanes—Floats

FLOOD, Curt
Flood tide. Newsweek 75:45 Ja 12 '70

FLOOD insurance. See Insurance, Flood

FLOOD lighting. See Light projection

FLOOD prevention and control
  See also
Rivers—Bank protection
Rivers—Regulation

Canada

U.S.—Canada flood control payment agreement transmitted to the Senate; message, October 14, 1969. R. M. Nixon. Dept State Bul 61:463 N 24 '69

England

Thwarting the surge; keeping North Sea from flooding London. L. Miller. il Sci N 95:483 My 17 '69

United States

Flood; sandbags along the great midwestern rivers; photographs by G. Brimacombe, with report by J. Pekkanen. Life 66:53-60 Ap 25 '69
How the Midwest braced for floods. il U S News 66:12-13 Ap 28 '69
New Corps. C. Weathersbee. il Sci N 95:122-3+ F 1 '69
North and West wait on the levees; dire flood threat. il Bsns W p 160+ Mr 22 '69
Now it can be foretold; spring floods in the Mississippi basin. il Sci N 94:302-3 Mr 29 '69
Water, water everywhere. il Newsweek 73: 81 Mr 31 '69
What to do until the flood comes; Crookston, Minn. and Grand Forks. N.Dak. il Time 93: 22-3 Ap 25 '69

FLOODLIGHTING. See Light projection

FLOODS

Italy

Florence floods. R. M. Klein. il Natur Hist 78:46-55 Ag '69

Tunisia

Big flood. il Time 94:32 D 19 '69
Flood. il Newsweek 74:34 D 22 '69

United States

As floods threaten in U.S. the Colorado runs low. il U S News 66:85-6 Mr 31 '69
Flood; sandbags along the great midwestern rivers; photographs by G. Brimacombe, with report by J. Pekkanen. Life 66:53-60 Ap 25 '69
Holiday weekend holocaust in Ohio. M. E. Miller and R. E. Hamilton. il Weatherwise 22:190-4 O '69
James River flood of August 1969 in Virginia. H. J. Thompson. il Weatherwise 22:180-3 O '69
Mouse that roared; Midwest floods. il Newsweek 73:44 Ap 28 '69
Mud bath; southern California declared a disaster area. il Newsweek 73:24 F 10 '69

Record floods on the way? U S News 66:13 Mr 24 '69
Satellites gave warning of Midwest floods. P. T. White. il Nat Geog 136:574-92 O '69
Southern California's trial by mud and water. N. T. Kenney. il Nat Geog 136:552-73 O '69
What to do until the flood comes; Crookston, Minn. and Grand Forks, N.Dak. il Time 93:22-3 Ap 25 '69

FLOOR coverings
Cushion vinyl floor coverings. il Consumer Bul 52:7-11 F '69
  See also
Rugs and carpets

FLOOR wax removers. See Wax removers

FLOOR waxes. See Waxes

FLOORING
Floors: new kinds, old kinds, many kinds. il Changing T 23:15-18 F '69

FLOORING, Plastic
Plastic flooring spreads through the house. J Hand il Pop Sci 194:154-8 Ap '69
Quiet comfort flooring; cushioned vinyl. il Good H 168:132+ F '69
Seamless: the floor you pour from a can. J. H. Ingersoll. il House B 111:142-3+ N '69

FLOORS
Fixing up an older home. il Bet Hom & Gard 47:22 My '69
Stain your floors any color. il House & Gard 135:110-11 Mr '69

FLOORS, Concrete
Integrating ducts with concrete floor structures. il Arch Rec 145:161-4 My '69

FLOORS, Wood
Today's floors, away from the wood tones. D. X. Manners. il Am Home 72:28+ N '69

FLORAL decoration. See Flowers, Arrangement of

FLORENCE

Description

Rebirth of Florence. A. Menen. il Holiday 46:28-33+ S '69
Seven walks. P. J. Martineau. il Holiday 46:34-5 S '69

History

Florence floods. R. M. Klein. il Natur Hist 78:46-55 Ag '69

Hotels, restaurants, etc.

Little wonder hotels. P. Dallas. Holiday 46: 35+ S '69

Music

Report: Florence; opera season closed with Gianni Schicchi, Poulenc's Voix humaine and Dallapiccola's Prigioniero. J. C. Adams. Opera N 33:32 Mr 15 '69

FLORENTINE painting. See Painting, Italian

FLORIBUNDAS. See Roses

FLORICULTURE
Gardener's month. See issues of House & garden incorporating Living for young homemakers
Here is winter bloom and spring bloom. il Sunset 143:106-7 O '69
In your greenhouse. J. U. Crockett. Horticulture 47:16+ Ag '69
Seeds you can sow outdoors now. Sunset 143:230 N '69
  See also
Bulbs
Greenhouses
Irises
Nurseries (horticulture)
Plant breeding

FLORIDA
Florida surprises. G. Bradshaw. il Vogue 153:184-5+ Ja 15 '69
  See also
Airports—Florida
Architecture, Domestic—Florida
Biscayne Bay
Camping—Florida
Conservation of resources—Florida
Everglades
Everglades National Park
Fishing—Florida
Gardens—Florida
Housing—Florida
Justice, Administration of—Florida
Oklawaha River
Roads—Florida
Wilderness areas—Florida

Description and travel

Down Florida's spine. B. Keating. il Travel & Camera 32:66-9+ N '69
Florida, twenty million vacationers. G. Bradshaw. Vogue 153:100+ Ja 15 '69
From tip to top in Florida. G. Bourke. See issues of Travel
Young-up Florida. il Vogue 153:150-61 Ja 15 '69

FLORIDA—*Continued*

Economic conditions
How the Florida boom is changing. il U S News 66:88-9 My 5 '69

Parks and reserves
Park beneath the sea: John Pennekamp coral reef state park. M. Michaelson. il Todays Health 47:28-33 Mr '69

FLORIDA Derby. See Horse racing

FLORIDA in art
Artists on a houseboat. M. L. Norwood. il Am Artist 33:20-7 Ap '69

FLORIDA Indians. See Seminole Indians

FLORIDA KEYS
At the Florida white house. il U S News 66:35 F 24 '69
Landlubber's guide to ocean driving. M. Michaelson. il Todays Health 48:56-9+ Ja '70
Nixon in Rebozoland. D. Butwin. il Sat R 52: 40-1+ Mr 8 '69
Winter white house; with photographs by G. Silk and L. Pelham. il Life 66:26-31 F 21 '69

FLORIDA state university, Tallahassee
Spectacular space in a university chapel. il Arch Forum 131:84-5 N '69

FLORIDA. University
Graduate student. J. Taube. il Phys Today 22: 26-8 Mr '69

FLORISSANT FOSSIL BEDS NATIONAL MONUMENT (proposed) See National monuments

FLORISTS
See also
Flowers—Marketing

FLORIT, Ermenegildo, cardinal
Letter from Isolotto. T. H. Stahel. America 121:418-21 N 8 '69

FLORY, Sheldon
Kindred of the wild; Portents; poems. Poetry 114:10 Ap '69

FLOTATION equipment. See Sailboats—Safety devices and measures

FLOUNDER fishing
Let the whole family flounder! M. Michaelson. il Todays Health 47:14-15 Jl '69

FLOUNDERS
Seawater teleosts: evidence for a sodium-potassium exchange in the branchial sodium-excreting pump. J. Maetz. bibliog il Science 166:613-15 O 31 '69

FLOUR
Health help for the ghetto. Bsns W p 124 S 20 '69

FLOW charts
Magnetic flow-charts speed urban-renewal work. il Am City 84:72 F '69

FLOW diagrams. See Flow charts

FLOW formations (geology) See Geology, Structural

FLOW meters
Portable aircraft hydraulic tester built. il Aviation W 90:85-6 My 12 '69

FLOW-of-funds data. See Economic statistics

FLOWER borders. See Garden borders

FLOWER boxes, planters, etc.
For living sculpture, plants in containers. il Home Gard 56:54-7 Je '69
For summer splendor: annuals in containers. H. Mason. il Bet Hom & Gard 47:74-7 Mr '69

FLOWER-bud development
Ring for flowers. J. W. Caddick. il Horticulture 47:18 My '69

FLOWER buds. See Buds

FLOWER exhibits
Almanac of flower shows, garden tours, and festivals. il House & Gard 135:74+ Mr '69
Camellia shows. il Horticulture 48:28-9 Ja '70
Flower show in Golden Gate park. Sunset 143:136 Ag '69
Garden events. See issues of Home garden & flower grower
Garden events [in month] (title varies) See issues of Sunset
What is a flower show like in Peru? L. McHamish. Horticulture 47:31 D '69
See also
Garden exhibits

FLOWER growing. See Floriculture

FLOWER markets
Flower market: wholesale flower store in New York city. New Yorker 45:33-5 Ap 26 '69

FLOWER photography. See Photography of flowers, plants, trees, etc.

FLOWER pots
Versatile gift, a bonsai pot. il Sunset 143: 180-1 D '69

FLOWER shows. See Flower exhibits

FLOWER stands
Plant stand. il Mech Illus 65:38+ Ap '69
Plant stands and holders. il House & Gard 135: 64-5 Mr '69

FLOWERING almonds
New flowering almonds. P. H. Wright. Horticulture 47:58 Ja '69

FLOWERING trees
Beautiful trees for today's smaller houses and lots. H. Mason and L. Grove. il Bet Hom & Gard 47:82-7 Ap '69
Spring flowers from small trees. il Home Gard 56:70 Mr '69
See also
Magnolias
Tetraplasandra

FLOWERPOTS. See Flower pots

FLOWERS, Nancy
Club Mediterranee: where the leisure is: photographs. Travel & Camera 32:58-9+ Mr '69
Royal fleece of the Andes; with biographical sketch. por Natur Hist 78:4, 36-43 My '69

FLOWERS
More 1969 introductions. il Horticulture 47: 22-3 F '69
See also
Annuals (plants)
Botany
Bulbs
Color of flowers
Gardens
Perennials
Plant breeding
Proteas
Wild flowers
also names of flowers. e.g. Azaleas

All America selections
See Plants—All America selections

Anatomy
Flower of tetraplasandra gymnocarpa hypogyny with epigynous ancestry. R. H. Eyde and C. C. Tseng. bibliog il Science 166:506-8 O 24 '69

Cut flowers
Grow flowers to wear. R. M. Peters. Horticulture 48:30+ Ja '70
Longer life for cut flowers. il Consumer Bul 52:4 Je '69
Tip sheet for indoor flower care. Vogue 153: 112 My '69
See also
Flowers—Marketing

Marketing
Flowers all over the house. il Vogue 153: 141 My '69
See Odors

Odors
FLOWERS, Arrangement of
Arranging the flowers that bloom in the spring. il McCalls 96:76-7 My '69
Fill your pitchers with spring. il Bet Hom & Gard 47:120 Ap '69
Flower arrangements yesterday and today. Mrs J. W. Knight, jr. il Horticulture 47:32-3 Mr '69
For your autumn bouquets fungus fantasies. il Farm J 93:45 Je '69
Party flowers; five experts tell how. E. McDonald. il House B 111:114-15+ N '69
Three R's of flower arrangement: repair, replace, remove. Mrs A. H. Smith. il Horticulture 46:38-9+ S '68
See also
Flowers, Dried
Vases

FLOWERS, Dried
Dried arrangements for place cards. R. T. Northen. il Horticulture 46:34-5+ D '68
Pick, dry and keep. il Am Home 72:82-3+ S '69
When you dry it, an orchid is forever. R. Schenley. Home Gard 56:74 Mr '69
You make these flowers using leaves, pods, cones. il Sunset 142:114 Ap '69

FLOWERS, Forcing of. See Forcing (plants)

FLOWERS in house decoration. See Plants in house decoration

FLOWMETERS. See Flow meters

FLOYD, Carlisle
Of mice and men. por Opera N 34:20-1 S 6 '69

FLOYD, Ray
Confidence man. il por Time 94:36 Ag 29 '69
Golf gets a look at the real world. D. Jenkins. il pors Sports Illus 31:24-6+ Ag 25 '69
FLU. See Influenza
FLUID dynamics
Applying a core discipline. J. Eberhart. il Sci N 95:618-19 Je 28 '69
See also
Hydrodynamics
FLUID level sensing devices. See Liquid level indicators
FLUID mechanics laboratory, MIT. See Massachusetts institute of technology, Cambridge
FLUID monitors. See Liquid level indicators
FLUIDS
Water on the moon and a new nondimensional number. J. A. O'Keefe. bibliog il Science 163:669-70 F 14 '69
See also
Hydraulic fluids
FLUORESCEIN
Cell sorting: automated separation of mammalian cells as a function of intracellular fluorescence. H. R. Hulett and others. bibliog il Science 166:747-9 N 7 '69
FLUORESCENCE
Fission of nonparticles; weak fluorescence in tetracene. Sci N 95:378 Ap 19 '69
Fluorescence changes during conduction in nerves stained with acridine orange. I. Tasaki and others. bibliog il Science 163:683-5 F 14 '69
Histochemical fluorescence as an index of spread of centrally applied neurochemicals; with reply by A. Routtenberg and W. Bondareff. R. B. Montgomery and G. Singer. bibliog il Science 165:1031-2 S 5 '69
Peroxidation of subcellular organelles: formation of lipofuscinlike fluorescent pigments. K. S. Chio and others. bibliog il Science 166:1535-6 D 19 '69
See also
Fluorometric analysis

Decay
Mode-locked lasers: measurements of very fast radiative decay in fluorescent systems. H. Merkelo and others. bibliog il Science 164:301-2 Ap 18 '69
FLUORESCENCE spectra. See Spectrum—Fluorescence spectra
FLUORESCENT lamps. See Electric lamps, Fluorescent
FLUORESCENT paint. See Paint, Luminous
FLUORIDATION. See Water supply—Fluoridation
FLUORIDE lenses. See Lenses, Photographic—Materials
FLUORIDES
Battle of the fluorides. il Newsweek 74:94 O 13 '69
New facts on fluoridation. J. Lear. il Sat R 52:51-6 Mr 1 '69; Discussion. 52:72-4 Ap 5, 57-9 My 3, 57 Je 7, 47-9 Jl 5 '69
Spot check for fluoride safety; electrode with rare earth fluoride crystal. S. V. Jones. Sci Digest 65:71 Je '69
See also
Sulfur fluorides
FLUORINE
Fluorine: a hostile element! J. D. Navratil. bibliog il Chem 42:11-15 F '69
FLUORINE compounds
See also
Fluorocarbons
FLUORINE in the body
Carbon-fluorine bond in compounds of biological interest. P. Goldman. bibliog il Science 164:1123-30 Je 6 '69
FLUOROCARBONS
Carbon-fluorine bond in compounds of biological interest. P. Goldman. bibliog il Science 164:1123-30 Je 6 '69
Inhaling aerosol propellant. Todays Health 47:78 Ap '69
FLUOROCITRATE
Acute axonal dystrophy caused by fluorocitrate: the role of mitochondrial swelling. H. Koenig. bibliog il Science 164:310-12 Ap 18 '69
FLUORODEOXYURIDINE. See Growth inhibiting substances (plants)
FLUOROMETRIC analysis
Cell microfluorometry: a method for rapid fluorescence measurement. M. A. Van Dilla and others. bibliog il Science 163:1213-14 Mr 14 '69
Cell sorting: automated separation of mammalian cells as a function of intracellular fluorescence. H. R. Hulett and others. bibliog il Science 166:747-9 N 7 '69

FLUOROURACIL
Cancer cream shows promise. Sci Digest 65:56 Ap '69
FLUSHING, Street. See Street cleaning
FLUTE music
See also
Phonograph records—Flute music
FLY, Sally
New taps on freedom. Nation 208:697-9 Je 2 '69
FLY. See Flies
FLY agaric. See Mushrooms
FLY ash. See Ashes
FLY casting
Billfish on the fly; interview, ed. by A. J. McClane. G. Valdene. il Field & S 74:126-8+ N '69
Fly fishing in a forest; Toledo Bend Lake, Tex. B. W. Dalrymple. il Outdoor Life 144:64-7+ O '69
Longest silence; fly-fishing for permit. T. McGuane. il Sports Illus 31:92-6+ D 1 '69
Look backward, angler. J. Brooks. il Outdoor Life 143:46-8+ Ap '69
FLY fishing. See Fly casting
FLY leaders. See Fishing tackle
FLY tying. See Fishing lures, flies, etc.
FLYING. See Aviation
FLYING ants. See Termites
FLYING boats. See Seaplanes
FLYING Dutchman; drama. See Olfson, L.
FLYING Dutchman; opera. See Wagner, R.
FLYING flies. See Eye—Diseases and defects
FLYING machines
Flying belt stretches its wings. il Pop Mech 131:122-3 Ja '69
What it's like to fly the new Jet belt. R. Courter. il Pop Sci 195:55-9+ N '69
See also
Autogiros
FLYING saucers
Closing the Blue Book; air force to call off UFO investigations due to Condon report. Time 94:28 D 26 '69
Condon report on UFO's, should you believe it? A. P. Armagnac. il Pop Sci 194:72-6 Ap '69
Condon study rebuts UFOs; critics offer own version. Phys Today 22:67+ Mr '69
Edward Condon: a physicist never afraid of a fight. il Phys Today 22:66-7 Mr '69
If you don't mind my saying so; inexplicable saucer reports. J. W. Krutch. Am Scholar 38:370+ Sum '69
Lost cause; Condon report. Nation 208:100 Ja 27 '69
New turn for flying saucers. U S News 67:7 D 29 '69
Scientific study of unidentified flying objects, by E. U. Condon. Review
Bul Atom Sci 25:39-42 Ap '69. J. A. Hynek
Scientific study of UFOs; University of Colorado report; excerpts. E. U. Condon. il Sat R 52:53-5 F 1 '69
Study grounds flying saucers. il Sr Schol 94:21-2 Ja 31 '69
UFO report rejects nonterrestrial origin. Aviation W 90:85 Ja 27 '69
UFO study: Condon group finds no evidence of visits from outer space. P. M. Boffey. Science 163:260-2 Ja 17 '69
UFOs and the evidence; Condon report. F. J. Hooven. Sat R 52:16-17+ Mr 29 '69
UFOs I have loved and lost; adaptation of address, April 1969. E. U. Condon. Bul Atom Sci 25:6-8 D '69
FLYING squirrels. See Squirrels
FLYING Tiger line Incorporated
Big push; air-freight business. il Forbes 103:28 My 1 '69
Flying Tiger inaugurates Pacific service. il Aviation W 91:39+ S 22 '69
Flying Tiger shows gains for four months. Aviation W 90:46 Je 9 '69
Japan may delay Flying Tiger flights. Aviation W 90:27 Ap 21 '69
FLYNN, Thomas E.
Teamster old guard wins with Flynn. por Bsns W p74 Mr 15 '69
FLYPAPER; story. See Musil, R.
FLYTYING. See Fishing lures, flies, etc.
FO, Dario
Italian incendiary. il por Time 93:72 Mr 21 '69
FOAM plastics in building. See Plastics in building
FOCCART, Jacques
Man of shadows. por Newsweek 74:32+ Ag 18 '69

FOCUSING. See Photography—Focusing

FOCUSING screens. See Photography—Focusing

FOG
Out of the fog; vanishing London peasouper. il Time 94:57 D 12 '69
Sea reek. C. Neumann. il Sea Front 15:10-11 Ja '69

FOG dispersal
Assault on fogs. E. Gross. il Sci N 96:165-7 Ag 30 '69
Chopping a hole in fog. il Time 93:42 F 14 '69
Clearing ground fog with helicopters. V. G. Plank. il Weatherwise 22:91-8+ Je '69

FOG-mist plant propagation. See Plant propagation

FOG navigation. See Navigation

FOG seeding. See Fog dispersal

FOGEL, Susan Lee
Unknown opera. Opera N 34:8-13 D 6 '69
Unusual sound. Opera N 34:14-16 S 20 '69
(ed) See Nagy, R. Heroic road

FOGEL, Yvonne
Over the meadows and between the trees. Parks & Rec 4:28-9+ D '69

FOGG museum. See Harvard university—Fogg museum

FOIL, Aluminum. See Aluminum foil

FOIL mulch See Mulching

FOLAND, Frances M.
Agrarian reform in Latin America. For Affairs 48:97-112 O '69

FOLDING beds. See Beds

FOLDING boats. See Boats and boating

FOLDING furniture. See Furniture

FOLDING paper. See Paper work

FOLDING roll film cameras. See Cameras

FOLEY, Charles
Delectations (cont) Nat R 21:859+, 963+ Ag 26, S 23 '69

FOLEY, Connie
Tarzan of the trail. pors Am For 75:34-5+ Ap '69

FOLEY, Cressie
I live alone here. Org Gard & Farm 16:84-5 Ag '69

FOLEY, Joan E. and Miyanshi, Kiyoko
Interocular effects in prism adaptation. bibliog Science 165:311-12 Jl 18 '69

FOLEY, Kathleen M. and others
White blood cell cultures in genetic studies on the human mucopolysaccharidoses. bibliog Science 164:424-6 Ap 25 '69

FOLIAGE. See Leaves

FOLIAGE plants. See Plants, Ornamental

FOLIES-Bergère, Paris. See Paris—Theater

FOLK, Hugh
Oversupply of the young. por Trans-Action 6:27-32 S '69

FOLK, R. L.
Spherical urine in birds: petrography. bibliog Science 166:1516-19 D 19 '69

FOLK art
Collectors: Edgar and Bernice Chrysler Garbisch. M. Black. il Art in Am 57:48-59 My '69
Cuzco's mystical dolls. G. de Zéndegui. il Américas 21:7-12 Je '69
Exhibition of folk art; Abby Aldrich Rockefeller folk art collection, in Williamsburg. P. A. G. Brown. il Antiques 95:252-7 F '69
Live with your collection. il Am Home 72: 52-5 Je '69
Provocative parallels; primitive and contemporary sculpture. il Art in Am 57:52-5 Jl '69
See also
Krans, O.
Williamsburg, Va.—Abby Aldrich Rockefeller folk art collection

FOLK dance festivals. See Dance festivals

FOLK dancing
Capturing the spirit along with the steps; ethnic dance program at UCLA. V. H. Swisher. il Dance Mag 43:70-4 O '69
Merry, merry John Canoe in Jamaica. H. Diaz. il Dance Mag 43:16-17 D '69
Tourist in Indonesia. A. Rechter. il Dance Mag 43:23-4 S '69

FOLK festivals. See Festivals

FOLK medicine. See Medicine, Popular

FOLK music
Americans not everyone knows: Laura Boulton. C. W. Ferguson. PTA Mag 63:16-18 Ja '69
Sight & sound of folk. R. Goldstein. il Travel & Camera 32:70-5 Je '69
See also
Phonograph records—Folk music

FOLK music, American
As Arlo Guthrie sees it...kids are groovy. Adults aren't. S. Braudy. il N Y Times Mag p56-7+ Ap 27 '69
First angry man of country singers; J. Cash. T. Dearmore. il N Y Times Mag p32-4+ S 21 '69
Johnny Cash, something rude showing. R. Goldstein. Vogue 154:46 Ag 15 '69
Profiles; R. Miller, songwriter and singer in the country music field. W. Whitworth. New Yorker 45:38-42+ Mr 1 '69
Restless ballad of Johnny Cash. C. S. Wren. il Look 33:68-72+ Ap 29 '69
Rock country, Dylan without metaphor. R. Goldstein. Vogue 153:130 F 1 '69

FOLK music, Mexican
See also
Mariachi festivals

FOLK singers. See Singers

FOLK songs, American
See also
Ballads, American

FOLK songs, Flemish
Chansons of Matthaeus Pipelare. R. Cross. bibliog f il Mus Q 55:500-20 O '69

FOLK songs, Portuguese
See also
Fados

FOLKLORE
See also
Mythology
Proverbs
Mexico
See also
Mariachi festivals

FOLKLORE of the moon. See Moon in religion, folklore, etc.

FOLLAIN, Jean
Cadences; Matter; The square; The tragic in time; The useful; The song of the dragoon; The secret; poems. tr. by W. S. Merwin. Atlan 224:78-9 Ag '69
Poems by Jean Follain. W. S. Merwin. Atlan 224:77 Ag '69

FOLLICLE mites
Uninvited guest; Demodex folliculorum. il Time 94:35 Ag 29 '69

FOLLIES (architecture)
Do-it-yourself Gothic; photographs. Horizon 11:118-19 Sum '69

FOLLMER, Patricia
Of gypsy race. Opera N 33:6-11 Mr 15 '69

FOLLOW Through from Head Start. See Project Head Start—Follow through programs

FOLLOW Through program. See Project Head Start—Follow through programs

FONDA, Jane
Conversation with Jane Fonda; interview, ed. by T. Burke. por Holiday 46:44-5+ S '69
about
Jane Fonda: shining in two new roles. H. Ehrlich. il pors Look 33:70-3+ My 13 '69
Whatever happened to Mr Fonda's baby Jane? M. W. Lear. il por Redbook 133:66-7+ Ag '69

FONDA, Peter
Not-so-easy riders: Dennis Hopper. Peter Fonda. por Vogue 154:129 Ag 1 '69

FONDILLER, Harvey V.
Film notes. See issues of Popular photography

FONDUES
Dish of many disguises; fondue bourguignonne. C. Claiborne. il N Y Times Mag p 129-30 N 16 '69
Easy-do fun-do fondue. il Seventeen 28:158-9+ N '69
It's fun to fondue. il Ebony 24:180+ O '69

FONER, Eric
Black cargo on road paved with promises. Sat R 52:78-9 Mr 22 '69

FONES, Guy Porter
Monsters of hurricane hole. Field & S 74:48-9+ Jl '69

FONSECA, Aloysius
Gandhi and nonviolence. America 121:257-60 O 4 '69

FONTAINE, Athanas Paul
Miracles take longer. Forbes 104:22-3 S 1 '69

FONTAINE, Jack. See Fontaine, A. P.

FONTAINE, Roger W.
Revolutionary, and banal. Nat R 21:31-2 Ja 14 '69

FONTENELLE, Norman
Tragedy in a house that friends built; N. Fontenelle and son Kenneth die in fire. G. P. Hunt. il Life 66:3 My 2 '69

FONTENETTE, Edward J.
Overdue. por Wilson Lib Bul 44:96 S '69
FONTEYN, Dame Margot
Tested and found not wanting; interview, ed.
by L. Joel. por Dance Mag 43:30-1 Jl '69

about

Fonteyn, a new-old heroine is added to her
repertoire. W. Terry. il pors Sat R 52:46
N 1 '69
Fonteyn; instant magic. W. Terry. il por Sat
R 52:45 My 17 '69
FONTINELL, Eugene
Eugene Fontinell on the future. Common-
weal 91:216 N 14 '69
FOOD
Poisonous ingredients in common foods. bib-
liog Consumer Bul 52:7-8 Ap '69
See also
Cookery
Diet
Dinners and dining
Indians of North America—Food
Meals
Mushrooms
Nutrition
Nutrition problems
Salads
Space flight—Food problems
Vitamins
Analysis
See also
Coloring matter in food
Flavor
Food additives
Irradiation
See Food, Effect of radiation on
Marketing
Brand name for organic foods. J. Olds. il
Org Gard & Farm 16:62-4 Jl '69
Group orders for more foods at lower costs.
B. T. Hunter. Org Gard & Farm 16:63-5
S '69
Teen age of organic food marketing. J.
Olds. Org Gard & Farm 16:66-7 Mr '69

New sources
See Food supply—New sources

Packaging
See also
Meat—Prepackaging

Prices
Costly market basket. Time 93:80 Je 20 '69
Food for thought. il Newsweek 75:33 Ja 5
'70
Food outlook for 1969. R. G. Murphy. il
Camp Mag 41:13+ Ap '69
Housewives' beef. il Time 93:94 Je 13 '69
How to save on camp food bills. R. Hodgson.
il Camp Mag 41:20+ Mr '69
Quiet shrinkage; hidden increases. il News-
week 74:75-6 Ag 4 '69
We're not the bad guys. Forbes 104:49 N 1
'69
What's happening to food prices. il U S
News 67:32-3 Jl 28 '69
Where food prices are headed; interview. C.
M. Hardin. il U S News 67:69-72 O 27 '69
Why the high price of food. il U S News
67:39-40 S 8 '69
Why the poor pay more. J. Cross. Nation
209:315-16 S 29 '69
See also
Meat—Prices
Psychology
See Eating, Psychology of

Ready-to-cook food
New foods that make cooking easier; with
recipes. il Redbook 132:88+ Ja '69

Smoking
Build this fish and meat smoker. A. L.
Ramos. il Pop Mech 132:186 S '69

Storage
All about food storage. il Good H 169:162+
O '69
Every home should be a food factory. R. Ro-
dale. il Org Gard & Farm 16:23-6 My '69
Food storage; the final wrap-up. N. Craig.
il House B 111:42+ S '69
How long can you keep it? il Redbook 133:
108-9+ Jl '69
Solving camp food storage problems. E. Rose.
Camp Mag 41:14 My '69
FOOD, Canned. See Canned food
FOOD, Cost of. See Food—Prices

FOOD, Effect of radiation on
Nuclear energy and edibility. E. Gross. il Sci
N 95:287-8 Mr 22 '69
FOOD, Enriched
Today's food: what's fortified and why; plus
recipes rich in iron. Good H 169:159-61 Ag
'69
FOOD, Frozen
Accounting for tastes. il Parents Mag 44:84-
6 Mr '69
Convenience foods? Paper service? P. An-
dron. il Camp Mag 41:18-19 Je '69
Dress up your frozen dinners. J. Miller. Am
Home 72:96 Mr '69
Frozen fruit pies. il Consumer Rep 34:568-72
O '69
See also
Freezing of food
Ice cream, ices, etc.
Vegetables, Frozen
FOOD, Irradiated. See Food, Effect of radiation
on
FOOD, Organic
Announcing the organic food shopper. J. Olds.
il Org Gard & Farm 16:38-40 F '69
Brand name for organic foods. J. Olds. il
Org Gard & Farm 16:62-4 Jl '69
Finding the right food in a big city. J. C.
Goldman. il Org Gard & Farm 16:50-4 Je
'69
Give me that old-time flavor. J. Olds. il Org
Gard & Farm 16:26-9 Ag '69
1969-1970 organic foods shopping guide. Org
Gard & Farm 16:27 My '69
Streamlines: health food; with recipes. il
Seventeen 28:349 Ag '69
Tonic for body and mind; raising and selling
organic beef and vegetables. R. J. Wynd-
ham. il Org Gard & Farm 16:92-3 N '69
Vacationing with organic foods. A. Cadwal-
ader. il Org Gard & Farm 16:38-40 Jl '69
Marketing
See Food—Marketing
FOOD, Sensitivity to. See Food allergy
FOOD, Synthetic. See Food substitutes
FOOD, Wild
Autobiographical note, that mail-bag again. E.
Gibbons. il Org Gard & Farm 16:74-8 F '69
Mailbag; wild-food adventure across Europe.
E. Gibbons. Org Gard & Farm 16:62-5 My
'69
Playing Indian. E. Gibbons. Org Gard &
Farm 16:88-91 N '69
Wild food adventures in the land of the
Pennsylvania Dutch. E. Gibbons. il Org
Gard & Farm 16:78-81 D '69
FOOD additives
Baby food additive may be next to go. Bsns
W p 114 O 25 '69
Chemicals and cancer. P. H. Abelson. Sci-
ence 166:693 N 7 '69
Delaney amendment. Sci N 97:8 Ja 3 '70
Doctor Jean Mayer: food watcher for a
nation. il Life 67:41-2+ N 28 '69
Food additives: blessing or bane? il Time
94:41-2 D 19 '69
This additive age. D. Sanford. New Repub
160:17-19 My 17 '69
See also
Coloring matter in food
Monosodium glutamate
Testing
Is your food safe? Dispute over testing;
with inteview with U. Saffiotti. il U S
News 67:44-7 D 15 '69
FOOD adulteration and inspection
See also
Food laws and legislation
Meat inspection
Poultry inspection
FOOD allergy
All about food allergies. il Good H 168:224+
Mr '69
Chinese restaurant syndrome. il Chem 42:4-5
S '69
Milk intolerance in southeast Asia. A. E.
Davis and T. D. Bolin. Natur Hist 78:54-5
F '69
Monosodium L-glutamate: its pharmacology
and role in the Chinese restaurant syndrome.
H. H. Schaumburg and others. bibliog il
Science 163:826-8 F 21 '69
What parents can do about food allergies;
excerpt from The children's doctor. L.
Smith. il Todays Health 47:55-6+ Jl '69
FOOD and agriculture organization of the
United Nations
Attacking hunger in a new way. R. L.
Tobin. Sat R 52:20 Je 28 '69
Feeding the hungry; indicative world plan.
R. Critchfield. New Repub 161:16-19 O 25
'69

FOOD substitutes—*Continued*
Imports and substitutes: are they really threats to your beef market? excerpts from address, ed. by J. A. Rohlf. K. Monfort. Farm J 93:B7 Mr '69
Marketing protein for the world's poor. J. L. Breeling. il Todays Health 47:42-5+ F '69
Now remember, with the oocystis polymorpha, red wine; with the viobin fish concentrate, white. il Esquire 71:74-5+ F '69
Three-star synthetic cuisine. A. N. Nesmeianov and V. Belikov. il UNESCO Courier 22:20-5 Mr '69
Work wonders with counterfeits. il Ladies Home J 86:108+ Mr '69
You can't believe everything you eat; soybean meat. H. T. Gordon. il Mech Illus 65:50-1 N '69

FOOD supplements. See Nutrition

FOOD supply
Anti-famine strategy: genetic engineering for food. S. S. Chase. il Bul Atom Sci 25:2-6 O '69
Ecology of hunger; the UN's development role in the 1970's. J. McLaughlin. America 121:414-17 N 8 '69
Food and people; FAO report. Sci Am 221: 50-1 D '69
New food revolution. G. Gregory. il UNESCO Courier 22:4-6+ Mr '69
Our overcrowded, underfed world. America 120:609 My 24 '69
Protein problem and national development; statement, November 20, 1968. A. E. Goldschmidt. Dept State Bul 59:673-7 D 23 '68
To fill the world's belly. il Sci N 96:422-3 N 8 '69
See also
Food and agriculture organization of the United Nations
Surplus products, Agricultural

New sources
Coming, lots of new foods. W. E. Swegle. Suc Farm 67:12 O '69
Marketing protein for the world's poor. J. L. Breeling. il Todays Health 47:42-5+ F '69
New challenges to world hunger; with photographs by F. Goro. Life 66:38-51 Ja 24 '69
See also
Fish flour

Political aspects
Politics of hunger. J. A. Hamilton. il Sat R 52:18-21+ Je 21 '69

India
Hope of conquering hunger. il Time 93:21-2 Ja 31 '69
India moves towards self-sufficiency in food. il UNESCO Courier 22:6-7 Mr '69

United States
Our food supply; AAAS symposium, December 28, 1969. T. C. Byerly. Science 166:408 O 17 '69
See also
Nutrition problems—United States

FOOD values
Let's talk about food; ed. by P. L. White. See issues of Todays's health
See also
Diet
Food
Nutrition

FOOD waste disposers. See Refuse grinders

FOOD wrapping materials. See Wrapping materials

FOOT, Michael
Young and angry talent. M. C. Shefftz. Nation 208:720-4 Je 9 '69

FOOT
Unfair to feet. A. J. Markle. Sat R 52:6 Ag 2 '69

Care and hygiene
Feet first. G. Hollander. il Todays Ed 58: 42-3 N '69

FOOT (animals)
Gecko grip. J. F. Gennaro, jr. il Natur Hist 78:36-43 Ag '69
Well fitted feet. N. Smith. il Nat Wildlife 7:39 Je '69

FOOT bridges. See Bridges, Foot

FOOTBALL
Air war in the South; Southeastern conference. il Newsweek 74:73 N 10 '69
All those eyes of Texas; Texas-Oklahoma football game. D. Jenkins. il Sports Illus 31:24-7 O 20 '69
Answer to a foolish question; Tennessee vs Ole Miss. P. Putnam. il Sports Illus 31: 50-1 N 24 '69

Arkansas gets set for its one-game season; undefeated Razorbacks vs second-ranked Texas. D. Jenkins. il Sports Illus 31:74+ N 17 '69
Bowls of new year cheer. il Time 95:48 Ja 12 '70
Bye-bye, no. 1; Michigan 24, Ohio State 12. K. Kessler and W. F. Reed. il Sports Illus 31:20-3 D 1 '69
Chuck Hixon presents his 1969 SMU aerial circus. D. Jenkins. il Sports Illus 31:101-4 S 22 '69
Cloudburst for Kentucky's Ray of sunshine; football coach. J. Underwood. il Sports Illus 31:56-8 S 29 '69
Football. See issues of New Yorker
Football unscrambled. F. Tarkenton. il Ladies Home J 86:49+ O '69
Getting by nicely without O.J; sophomore quarterback J. Jones. P. Putnam. il Sports Illus 31:32-4+ S 29 '69
Gone are sophomores who behave like sophs. P. Putnam. il Sports Illus 31:42-3 O 6 '69
Grambling college: where stars are made. W. Rogers. il Look 33:72-5 D 16 '69
Hey, that's Missouri and Oklahoma out there! R. Blount, jr. il Sports Illus 31:46-7 N 3 '69
It's football time again, girls. il Changing T 23:11-13 S '69
It's the biggest draw in Philadelphia; Army-Navy football game. P. Putnam. il Sports Illus 31:49-50 D 8 '69
Knute would have agreed, Ara; Notre Dame to the Rose bowl. D. Jenkins. il Sports Illus 31:26-8+ D 22 '69
Machine from OSU; Purdue and Ohio state. il Newsweek 74:97 N 24 '69
Make way for the Wild Bunch; USC defense. D. Jenkins. Sports Illus 31:70-1 D 1 '69
Missouri waltzes to victory; Tigers take the Oklahoma Sooners. R. Blount, jr. il Sports Illus 31:40-1 N 17 '69
1969 college football forecast. G. Astor. il Look 33:90+ S 23 '69
No one in Tennessee has heard of Ohio state; unbeaten Volunteers. S. Treadwell. Sports Illus 31:52+ N 10 '69
Ohio state: alone at the top; Buckeyes are no. 1. D. Jenkins. il Sports Illus 31:22-7 N 24 '69
62-0; Ohio state vs TCU. D. Jenkins. il Sports Illus 31:18-19 O 6 '69
Small school, but you can learn to hate it; little Doane the nation's biggest winner. S. Myslenski. il Sports Illus 31:50-1 O 13 '69
SEC catches on; Southeastern conference football players. P. Putnam. il Sports Illus 31:20-5 O 13 '69
Sporting scene; game between the Montana Grizzlies and the Montana state Bobcats. H. W. Wind. New Yorker 45:152+ D 13 '69
State stands tall with the aid of some zap; Penn state vs Syracuse. P. Putnam. il Sports Illus 31:50-1 O 27 '69
Texas hangs on to its no. 1; Notre Dame vs Texas Longhorns in Cotton bowl. D. Jenkins. il Sports Illus 32:26-9 Ja 12 '70
Two for the roses; USC and UCLA. il Newsweek 74:102 D 1 '69
USC Trojans shoot for Rose bowl with black quarterback. il Ebony 25:44-6+ D '69
Why mom supports the game; high school football. K. Carlson. il Sports Illus 31:48-51 S 8 '69
Worth the wait; Texas vs. Notre Dame in Cotton bowl. P. Axthelm. il Newsweek 75:44-5 Ja 12 '70
See also
Football players
Rugby football
Soccer

Accidents and injuries
Loose knees and football. A. J. Snider. Sci Digest 65:67-8 F '69

Anecdotes, facetiae, satire, etc.
Bill Cosby on chicken football. B. Cosby. il Look 33:94 N 4 '69
You've gotta be a football heroine. J. L. O'Neill. il Am Home 72:110+ N '69

Caricatures and cartoons
Hot off the gridiron. Read Digest 95:102-3 N '69

History
First 100 years; intercollegiate football. D. Jenkins. il Sports Illus 31:46-53 S 15 '69
That autumn madness. P. W. Schmidtchen. il Hobbies 74:134+ D '69

Photographs
Lot of kicks coming. N. Leifer. Sports Illus 31:62-71 S 22 '69

FOOTBALL—*Continued*

Rules

Wave goodby to defense. il Sports Illus 31: 56-7 S 15 '69

FOOTBALL, Commissioner of. See Football clubs—Organization and administration

FOOTBALL, Photography of. See Photography of sports

FOOTBALL clubs

Aftermath; game between Los Angeles Rams and Chicago Bears. E. Kaine. Esquire 71:8 Mr '69

Annual football roundup: holdouts shake the money tree. il Ebony 25:164-6+ N '69

Arararararargh! laugh of V. Lombardi, new coach of Washington Redskins. W. Johnson. il Sports Illus 30:28-30+ Mr 3 '69

Bachelors II. Time 94:49 Jl 25 '69

Big four head for the summit; Rams, Vikings, Cowboys and Browns. T. Maule. il Sports Illus 31:44-6+ N 17 '69

Death by inches; Green Bay Packers 1968 season. excerpt from Jerry Kramer's farewell to football; ed. by D. Schaap. J. Kramer. il Sports Illus 31:50-9 Ag 4 '69

Difference of opinion in the gentle state of Texas; Dallas Cowboys rivalry with Houston Oilers. E. Shrake. il Sports Illus 31: 18-21 S 8 '69

Eub Weebank's mother hens; Jet pass blockers. R. F. Jones. il Sports Illus 31:26-9 N 10 '69

Eye on the quarterback. R. Riger. il Travel & Camera 32:92-7 O '69

Fall of Joe Willie; New York Jets vs Kansas City Chiefs. il Newsweek 74:40 D 29 '69

First taste of O. J. is OK; Buffalo's first draft choice. E. Shrake. il Sports Illus 31:20-3 Ag 25 '69

Four Norsemen; Minnesota Vikings. il Time 94:62 O 17 '69

Hard days for Halas; Chicago Bears. il Newsweek 75:34 Ja 5 '70

I read Plimpton, I can't say it helped; Dallas Cowboys. C. Hill. il Sports Illus 31:38-9 O 20 '69

Impossible reality; New York Jets against Baltimore Colts. il Time 93:50 Ja 24 '69

Just call him super Daryle; Oakland Raiders quarterback. E. Shrake. il Sports Illus 32: 36-41 Ja 5 '70

KC had the hot hand; Kansas City Chiefs vs New York Jets. R. F. Jones. il Sports Illus 31:16-19 N 24 '69

Kapping the Browns; Joe Kapp's Vikings vs Cleveland Browns for NFL title. T. Maule. il Sports Illus 32:12-16 Ja 12 '70

Lamonica's moveable feast; he was the main dish; Kansas City Chiefs vs Oakland Raiders in American football league championship game. R. F. Jones. il Sports Illus 32:17-19 Ja 12 '70

Lance Alworth: Charger goes groovy. G. Astor. il Look 33:91-2+ D 2 '69

Mad dogs & football men; Kansas City Chiefs. W. J. McKean. il Look 33:114-16 O 7 '69

Merciless Minnesota; the Vikings. T. Maule. il Sports Illus 31:18-21 N 3 '69

Most hated winner in football; Oakland's A. Davis. L. Shecter. Look 33:50+ N 18 '69

New slant on an old game in Atlanta; professional Falcons R. Blount, jr. il Sports Illus 31:40-1 S 1 '69

Newest star in pro football; interview, ed. by J. Hess. A. DeRogatis. Holiday 46:90-1+ O '69

1969 forecast. G. Astor. Look 33:36 S 9 '69

No clink and no clank in Cincy; P. Brown, head coach, general manager and part owner of Bengals. P. F. Putnam. il Sports Illus 21:26-7 S 15 '69

Now the AFL owns the football; AFL vs NFL in Super bowl. E. Shrake. il Sports Illus 30: 28-32 Ja 27 '69

Prayer for Oakland; Raiders vs Cowboys. il Newsweek 74:66 Ag 4 '69

Pro football 1969: scouting reports of National football league, American football league. T. Maule. il Sports Illus 31:38-50+ S 22 '69

Purple gang rubs out L.A; Minnesota vs the Rams, Cleveland vs Dallas in NFL playoff games. T. Maule. il Sports Illus 32:10-17 Ja 5 '70

Putting Yale on the map; Dallas Cowboys. Newsweek 74:104 O 20 '69

Rams win one for memory's sake; L. A. beat Dallas Cowboys. T. Maule. il Sports Illus 31:30-3 D 1 '69

Ready if you are. O.J; hold-out from Buffalo Bills. F. Deford. il Sports Illus 30:16-19 Jl 14 '69

Replay of the 12th-man theme. P. Putnam. Sports Illus 31:50+ Jl 7 '69

Rookies give it a shot; college All-stars vs New York Jets. P. Putnam. il Sports Illus 31:12-15 Ag 11 '69

Rookies on a rampage. il Time 94:80+ O 10 '69

Rush and a penny; Rams vs Colts. T. Maule. il Sports Illus 31:16-21 S 29 '69

Say it's so, Joe; Jets whip Colts in Super bowl. T. Maule. il Sports Illus 30:10-15 Ja 20 '69

Season in the stands; watching the New York Giants. W. Phillips. Commentary 48: 65-9 Jl '69

Sports; predictions for 1969 season. il Newsweek 74:60+ S 15 '69

Super Jets; New York Jets vs Baltimore Colts. il Newsweek 73:56 Ja 27 '69

To the Bowl of their dreams; Green Bay Packers leaders in NFL's Central division. R. F. Jones. il Sports Illus 31:28-30+ O 6 '69

View from the bottom; Chicago Bears. R. F. Jones. Sports Illus 31:22-4 O 27 '69

Vikings' front four. L. J. Banks. il Ebony 25:83-6+ Ja '70

Violent Vikings. il Newsweek 74:89 D 8 '69

We're going to win, you better believe it; Lombardi's war cry to Redskins. J. Underwood. il Sports Illus 31:18-20+ Jl 28 '69

When the Saints go stumbling out; New Orleans Saints. T. Maule. il Sports Illus 31:24-5 O 27 '69

Whipping up the Redskins. Time 94:24 D 26 '69

Yard no. 4; temporary practice field for New York Jets at the New York city correctional institution for men, Rikers Island. New Yorker 45:44-7 O 11 '69

You can't top a good loser; standings in the point-spread league. NFL and AFL. M. Mulvoy. Sports Illus 31:36-8+ D 8 '69

Youth will have its . . . oops! Cincinnati Bengals vs San Diego Chargers. T. Maule. il Sports Illus 31:30-3 O 13 '69

Zorba the Viking; quarterback J. Kapp. L. Shecter. il Look 33:64-5+ D 30 '69

See also

American football league

National football league

Economic aspects

Pro football: does money run the game? K. Rote and J. Winter. il Look 33:93-4+ O 21 '69

Pro in football stands for profits. il Bsns W p56-8 Ja 10 '70

Ethical aspects

See Sports—Ethical aspects

History

Game that was; symposium. ed. by M. Cope. il Sports Illus 31:86-8+ O 13; 84-8+ O 20 '69

Organization and administration

Does Pete Rozelle run pro football? Ask Joe Namath. L. Shecter. il N Y Times Mag p30-1+ Ag 17 '69

Last of the Titans; H. Wismer's New York football team. A. Kroll. il Sports Illus 31: 106-8+ S 22 '69

Pro football's boom: from sport to glamour industry. il U S News 67:82-4 S 22 '69

FOOTBALL clubs, Professional. See Football clubs

FOOTBALL coaches. See Coaches (athletics)

FOOTBALL fans

High spirits, high kicks and college football. G. Astor. il Look 33:86-8 S 23 '69

FOOTBALL gambling. See Gambling

FOOTBALL players

Air war in the South; Southeastern conference. il Newsweek 74:73 N 10 '69

Alone for a passing moment; pro receiver. il Sports Illus 31:20-7 Ag 18 '69

Annual football roundup: holdouts shake the money tree. il Ebony 25:164-6+ N '69

Arkansas gets set for its one-game season; undefeated Razorbacks vs second-ranked Texas. D. Jenkins. il Sports Illus 31:74+ N 17 '69

Big four head for the summit; Rams, Vikings, Cowboys and Browns. T. Maule. il Sports Illus 31:44-6+ N 17 '69

Chuck Hixson presents his 1969 SMU aerial circus. D. Jenkins. il Sports Illus 31:101-4 S 22 '69

Eub Weebank's mother hens; Jet pass blockers. R. F. Jones. il Sports Illus 31:26-9 N 10 '69

FOOTBALL players—*Continued*

Fall of Joe Willie: New York Jets vs Kansas City Chiefs. il Newsweek 74:40 D 29 '69

First 100 years; intercollegiate football. D. Jenkins. il Sports Illus 31:46-53+ S 15 '69

Football exercise foibles. Sci Digest 65:55-6 Ap '69

Football heroes invade Hollywood. il Ebony 24:195-7+ O '69

Four Norsemen; Minnesota Vikings. il Time 94:62 O 17 '69

Game that was; symposium, ed. by M. Cope. il Sports Illus 31:86-8+ O 13; 84-8+ O 20 '69

Game within a game; rite of picking NFL and AFL all-star teams. R. F. Jones. il Sports Illus 31:16-21 D 22 '69

Gone are sophomores who behave like sophs. P. Putnam. il Sports Illus 31:42-3 O 6 '69

Gregg Cook; the new Cincinnati kid. J. Pekkanen. il Life 67:141-2 O 10 '69

Hey, that's Missouri and Oklahoma out there! R. Blount, jr. il Sports Illus 31:46-7 N 3 '69

Hot line: progress in pros of winning college linemen. H. L. Masin. il Sr Schol 95:28 O 27 '69

I read Plimpton, I can't say it helped; Dallas Cowboys. C. Hill. il Sports Illus 31:38-9 O 20 '69

KC had the hot hand; Kansas City Chiefs vs New York Jets. R. F. Jones. il Sports Illus 31:16-19 N 24 '69

Kapping the Browns; Joe Kapp's Vikings vs Cleveland Browns for NFL title. T. Maule. il Sports Illus 32:12-16 Ja 12 '70

Last of the Titans; H. Wismer's New York football team. A. Kroll. il Sports Illus 31 106-8+ S 22 '69

Lonesome cornerbacks. il Newsweek 74:108-9 N 3 '69

Make way for the Wild Bunch; USC defense. D. Jenkins. Sports Illus 31:70-1 D 1 '69

Merciless Minnesota; the Vikings. T. Maule. il Sports Illus 31:18-21 N 3 '69

1968 All-American H.S. football squad. H. L. Masin. il Sr Schol 94:28-9 F 28 '69

1969 Look All America. W. McKean. il Look 33:76+ D 16 '69

Now the AFL owns the football; AFL vs NFL in Super bowl. E. Shrake. il Sports Illus 30: 28-32 Ja 27 '69

Pro football 1969: scouting reports of National football league, American football league. T. Maule. il Sports Illus 31:38-50+ S 22 '69

Pro football's broken men; guards for quarterbacks. B. Surface. il N Y Times Mag p56-7+ O 26 '69

Pro football's double edge. G. Astor. il Look 33:32-5 S 9 '69

Pro football's purple gang; Minnesota's defensive front; with account by D. Wittner. il Life 67:30-3 N 28 '69

Replay of the 12th-man theme. P. Putnam. Sports Illus 31:50+ Jl 7 '69

Rise of Roman's empire; Gabriel and the Rams. il Time 94:84 N 7 '69

Rookies give it a shot; college All-stars vs New York Jets. P. Putnam. il Sports Illus 31:12-15 Ag 11 '69

Rookies on a rampage. il Time 94:80+ O 10 '69

SEC catches on; Southeastern conference football players. P. Putnam. il Sports Illus 31:20-5 O 13 '69

Sports; predictions for 1969 season. il Newsweek 74:60+ S 15 '69

Super All-American (cont) H. L. Masin. il Sr Schol 94:25 Ja 17 '69

Time's All-America: the pick of the pros (cont) pors Time 95:44-5 Ja 5 '70

Transformed by the transfer; quarterback D. Dummit, from Long Beach city college to UCLA. D. Jenkins. il Sports Illus 31:36-9 O 27 '69

Vikings front four. L. J. Banks. il Ebony 25:83-6+ Ja '70

Who gets the Oscar? Heisman trophy for college football. D. Jenkins. il Sports Illus 31:18-23 N 10 '69

Year of the rookies: bigger, faster, smarter; with photographs. R. H. Boyle. Sports Illus 31:30-7 O 20 '69

You have to be a little crazy to play on a suicide squad. B. Surface. il N Y Times Mag p80-1+ D 14 '69

Youth will have its. . . oops! Cincinnati Bengals vs San Diego Chargers. T. Maule. il Sports Illus 31:30-3 O 13 '69

Recruiting

Shortage of studs: combined draft of the National and American football leagues. il Time 93:40 F 7 '69

Salaries

Game that was; symposium, ed. by M. Cope. il Sports Illus 31:86-8+ O 13; 84-8+ O 20 '69

Ready if you are, O.J; hold-out from Buffalo Bills. F. Deford. il Sports Illus 31:16-19 Jl 14 '69

Real mean; mean salaries by team. il Sports Illus 30:19+ Ap 21 '69

What price heroes? F. Deford. Sports Illus 30:32-4+ Je 9 '69

FOOTBALL scouting

Pro football 1969: scouting reports of National football league, American football league. T. Maule. il Sports Illus 31:38-50+ S 22 '69

FOOTBALL stadiums. See Stadiums

FOOTBALL trophies. See Trophies, Sport

FOOTE, Timothy

Life book review. Life 67:12 O 3 '69

FOOTE, Cone and Belding, incorporated

Fax Cone, the Honest Abe of ad world, tells his story. Bsns W p 155-6 N 15 '69

FOOTMEN. See Household employees

FOOTPRINTS

See also

Dermatoglyphics

FOOTPRINTS, Fossil

Near Tuba City, dinosaurs. il Sunset 143:52 N '69

FOOTSTOOLS. See Stools

FOOTWEAR. See Shoes

FOR the love of Joan Riley; story. See Du Plessix, F.

FOR worse is better and sickness is in health; story. See Trillin, C.

FORAGE crops. See Forage plants

FORAGE plants

Make your forages pay. il Suc Farm 67:45 D '69

See also

Clover, Sweet

Millet

Milo

Diseases and pests

Foil these forage insects. G. L. Earle. Suc Farm 67:62B F '69

Fertilizers and manures

How to manage forages for best results. C. E. Sommers. il Suc Farm 67:50-2 D '69

FORAKER, David

Cheap insect trap that works. Org Gard & Farm 16:84+ S '69

Fruits you won't find in the supermarket. Org Gard & Farm 16:28-32 N '69

Let that seedling grow. Org Gard & Farm 16:44-5 Ag '69

FORAMINIFERA, Fossil

Alaskan upper miocene marine glacial deposits and the turborotalia pachyderma datum plane. O. L. Bandy and others. bibliog il Science 166:607-9 O 31 '69

Glacier oxygen-18 content and pleistocene ocean temperatures. W. Dansgaard and H. Tauber. bibliog il Science 166:499-502 O 24 '69

Recent planktonic foraminifera: dominance and diversity in North Atlantic surface sediments. W. F. Ruddiman. bibliog il Science 164:1164-7 Je 6 '69

FORBES, Calvin

Poem on my birthday. Poetry 115:42 O '69

Two sonnets: For the Greek girl in New York; For my mother. Am Scholar 38:402-3 Sum '69

FORBES, Robert B. and Hoskin, C. M.

Dredged trachyte and basalt from Kodiak seamount and the adjacent Aleutian Trench, Alaska. Science 166:502-4 O 24 '69

FORBIS, Bill

Uruguay says olé to cars of yesterday. Sports Illus 30:44-8 F 10 '69

FORCE (violence) See Violence

FORCED labor. See Labor, Compulsory

FORCING (plants)

Forcing lilies. N. Simoni. il Horticulture 46: 26-7+ D '68

Forcing woody twigs and keeping them in bloom. L. Pyenson. il Horticulture 47:26-7+ Ja '69

Seedlings in my cellar; Fluorescent light gardening. C. B. Lees. il Horticulture 47: 38-9 Mr '69

See also

Hotbeds

FORD, Barbara

Redesign your body: what changes would you make? Sci Digest 66:20-3 N '69

Safe City: apartment living inside a mountain. Sci Digest 66:16-19 Ag '69

FORD, Barbara—*Continued*
Strange world of night creatures. Sci Digest
66:38-42 O '69
Traffic safety's mystery man. Sci Digest
66:64-8 D '69
What psychological conditioning can do for
animals. Sci Digest 66:76-81 N '69

FORD, Charlotte
Charlotte: the latest model Ford. H. Ehrlich.
il pors Look 33:62-6+ Ag 12 '69

FORD, Corey
Ford's physical unfitness program. Read Di-
gest 94:80-2 My '69
How to live with a fisherman. Read Digest
95:104-6 Ag '69
Letter to a grandson; reprint. Field & S 74:
8+ O '69
Lower forty. See issues of Field & stream

FORD, Cristina. See Ford, M. C. V. A.

FORD, Edsel
Sun poem. Mlle 69:58 Jl '69

FORD, George Barry
Christian gentleman. K. L. Woodward. por
Newsweek 75:84-6 Ja 19 '69

FORD, Henry, 1917-
Hidden revolution; address, June 5, 1969. Vital
Speeches 35:566-8 Jl 1 '69

about

At Ford everyone knows who is the boss.
W. Serrin. il pors N Y Times Mag p25-7+
O 19 '69
Ford collides with Dearborn's mayor. il
Bsns W p66-8 Ja 10 '70

FORD, Henry, family
Fabulous Ford women. L. Smith. il pors Mc-
Calls 96:82-3+ My '69
Inside the Fords; concerning Ford: an uncon-
ventional biography of the men and their
times, by B. Herndon. il Newsweek 74:64-5
S 1 '69

FORD, Jesse Hill
Destruction; story. Esquire 72:96-8 Jl '69
Doctor; story. Atlan 223:86-8 Ja '69

FORD, Leighton
Evangelism in a day of revolution. Chr Today 14:6-12 O 24 '69

FORD, Lincoln E. and Podolsky, R. J.
Regenerative calcium release within muscle
cells. bibliog Science 167:58-9 Ja 2 '70

FORD, Maria Cristina Vettore Austin
Fabulous life of Mrs Henry Ford. por Ladies
Home J 86:94-5+ S '69

FORD, Norman D.
Europe and the Holy Land. bibliog por Har
Yrs 9:6-15 My '69

FORD, Phyllis M.
Two modern challenges for every camp di-
rector. por Camp Mag 41:12-13 My; 18-19
S '69

FORD, Walter B.
Build an electronic shutter control. Pop Electr
30:75-8 Ap '69

FORD foundation
ASEE-Ford foundation residencies program.
Sch & Soc 97:10 Ja '69
Durham education improvement program. R.
L. Spaulding. Todays Ed 58:62-4 F '69
Fellowships in practical politics; attracting
minority college graduates to careers in
government and politics. Sch & Soc 97:133+
Mr '69
Ford foundation funds Reading/book-owning
program. Library J 94:255-6 Ja 15 '69
Ford grant for educational reform. Sch & Soc
97:90-1 F '69
New class war. J. Hart. il Nat R 21:896-
901+ S 9 '69
Reading can be fun everywhere. K. W. Lum-
ley. il Sr Schol 94:Schol Teach 21 Ja 31 '69
Studying Latin American affairs; appropria-
tion for research on Cuba. Sch & Soc 97:
213 Ap '69
Washington, D.C.: reading is fun-damental.
J. Sandler. il Wilson Lib Bul 43:881-5 My
'69
When you choose your own; Reading is fun-
damental booklist for children, program. il
Library J 94:269+ Ja 15 '69
  See also
Council on library resources, incorporated
Fund for the Republic

FORD motor company
L'affaire Knudsen. il Newsweek 74:90 S 22
'69
At Ford, a corporate shake-up and Mr Knud-
sen goes out. il U S News 67:26 S 22 '69
At Ford everyone knows who is the boss.
W. Serrin. il N Y Times Mag p25-7+ O 19
'69
Behind the palace revolt at Ford. il Bsns W
p 138-41 S 20 '69

Bumps for hard core; cuts in Ford output
bring layoffs. Bsns W p41 Mr 22 '69
Europe's mini-Mustang. il Newsweek 73:67
F 10 '69
Ford builds a new shape in Europe: the Capri.
il Bsns W p52-4+ Ja 25 '69
Ford rejects layoff policy. U S News 66:66
Ap 28 '69
Ford's better idea scores in Europe. Bsns W
p66 D 20 '69
Ford's Maverick starts chasing the imports.
il Bsns W p48 Ap 26 '69
Hue and cry flusters Ford; Eagle shirtmaker
claims credit for Maverick's offbeat color
names. Bsns W p41 My 17 '69
Inside the Fords; concerning Ford: an uncon-
ventional biography of the men and their
times, by B. Herndon. il Newsweek 74:64-5
S 1 '69
Making of the Maverick. il Time 93:88+ Mr
21 '69
NAB's problem: fight inflation but give jobs.
B. L. Masse. America 120:520 My 3 '69
No cannibals, please. il Forbes 104:21 Jl 15 '69
Pray for Iacocca's baby. W. A. McWhirter. il
Life 66:68-72 Ap 11 '69
Some kind of animal! excerpt from The
strategy of change for business success;
ed. by S. Furst and M. Sherman. L. A.
Iacocca. il Nations Bsns 57:62-4+ F '69
Whatever happened to the Edsel. il U S News
66:16 My 26 '69
Why Knudsen was fired. il Time 94:88+ S
19 '69

FORD motor company, limited, Dagenham,
England
Britain's unions get out of hand; strike. il
Bsns W p70-2 Mr 22 '69
Report from London; wildcat strike at Brit-
ish Ford. P. Siekman. il Fortune 79:49-50
My 1 '69
Wildcat has nine lives; Ford plants in Britain
paralyzed. Time 93:90 Mr 21 '69

FORD museum. See Henry Ford museum and
Greenfield Village, Dearborn, Mich.

FORD of Europe, incorporated
Ford builds a new shape in Europe: the Capri.
il Bsns W p52-4+ Ja 25 '69

FORDHAM university
What's coming off at Fordham? R. J. O'Connell. il Cath World 209:59-63 My '69

FORD'S theatre. See Washington, D.C.—Theater

FORECASTS
Executives of the future. A. Uris. il Nations
Bsns 57:68-73 Ja '69
Forecast for the 70's. H. G. Shane and J. G.
Shane. Todays Ed 58:29-32 Ja '69
Forecasting the seventies. J. Tebbel. il Sat
R 52:80-1 N 8 '69
From the '60s to the '70s: dissent and dis-
covery. il Time 94:20-6 D 19 '69
Hope for the '70s; forecast by the Economist
of London. K. Crawford. Newsweek 75:24
Ja 19 '70
Newsgram. See issues of U.S. news & World
report
Prophets and loses. Time 95:33 Ja 5 '70
Unfinished business. D. R. Campion. Amer-
ica 122:26-7 Ja 10 '70
  See also
Nineteen hundred and seventies
Political forecasts
Prophecies
Two thousand (year)
Weather forecasts

FORECASTS (economics)
Appraisal of America's economic prospects;
interviews. M. Friedman; P. A. Samuelson;
H. Wallich. il Newsweek 75:52-3 Ja 12 '70
Bad year for econometrics. il Bsns W p36-7+
D 20 '69
Boom, bust, or what? How top economists
see '70; symposium. il U S News 68:56-63
Ja 5 '70
Bumpy decade with a social sense; 1970s. il
Bsns W p98-9+ D 6 '69
Can Mr Nixon stop the inflation? il News-
week 75:49-51+ Ja 12 '70
Cloud over forecasts: does the Fed mean it?
il Bsns W p33-4 Mr 8 '69
Divining the future. R. Lekachman. Duns
R 94:13 S '69
Economy. B. L. Masse. America 122:27-8 Ja
10 '70
End to hyperprosperity. il Fortune 80:21-2+
Jl '69
Forecasters raise the bets on slowdown. il
Bsns W p25-6 My 31 '69
Forecasts for 1970. H. C. Wallich. News-
week 75:54 Ja 5 '70
Games forecasters play. M. Seeger. il Duns R
93:42-3+ Ja '69

FOREIGN visitors in eastern Europe
Sex trap; British board of trade pamphlet warning Britons doing business with the Communist bloc against personal indiscretion. il Newsweek 73:73+ Mr 24 '69

FOREIGN visitors in Europe
Wet paint from Paris; American touring with recently purchased original. L. Lightbody. il Sr Schol 94:Schol Teach 94:10-11 Ap 25 '69

See also
Tourist trade—Europe

FOREIGN visitors in Hungary
To the tick of a different clock. C. Derecskey. il Atlan 223:74-6+ F '69

FOREIGN visitors in Liberia
Cultural safari; Chicago community sends teen girls on tour of Liberia. il Ebony 24:123-4+ My '69

FOREIGN visitors in Northern Ireland
Mission to Belfast. D. Butwin. il Sat R 52:66+ D 6 '69

FOREIGN visitors in Rumania
Americans afoot in Rumania. D. Dimancescu. il Nat Geog 135:810-45 Je '69

FOREIGN visitors in Russia
Religion behind the iron curtain. C. J. McNaspy. America 120:450-3 Ap 12 '69
Take her along; British government pamphlet for businessmen visiting Russia. Time 93:27 Mr 21 '69
To Russia with understanding; Atlanta teenagers study tour of Soviet Union. il Ebony 25:43-6+ N '69

FOREIGN visitors in Sweden
Taste of summer Sweden; Experiment group of American college women. R. Hawkins. il Sr Schol 94:Schol Teach 21:2 F 28 '69

FOREIGN visitors in the United States
Innocent abroad; English conservative writer. A. Waugh. il Nat R 21:1322-5+ D 30 '69

FOREIGN visitors in Vietnam (Democratic Republic)
Journey to North Vietnam; interview, with photographs. M. Riboud. Newsweek 74:32-4 O 20 '69
November in Hanoi. W. Meyers. Nation 209:622-4 D 8 '69

FOREIGN visitors in Vietnam (Republic)
University on the make; or, How MSU helped arm Madame Nhu; with introd. by S. K. Sheinbaum. W. Hinckle and others. il Ram Mag 7:52-60 Ja 25 '69
Vietnam: sojourn and sequel. J. Armstrong and J. Conyers, jr. il Chr Cent 86:1307-9 O 15 '69

FORELLA, Ronn
On the boards. W. Como. por Dance Mag 43:20 D '69

FOREMAN, Carl
Cognoscenti abroad: Carl Foreman's London. A. Goodfriend. Sat R 52:32-4 Ag 16 '69

FOREMAN, Percy
Against conspiracy. por Look 33:112 Ap 15 '69

about
There is no better than me. il por Time 93:39 Mr 21 '69

FOREMOST dairies-McKesson and Robbins, incorporated merger. See Business consolidations and mergers

FORENSIC chemistry. See Chemistry, Legal

FORENSIC psychiatry
Harsh verdict on courtroom psychiatry. Life 66:32B My 2 '69
Protecting civil liberties; psychiatry's role in civil commitment cases. A. M. Dershowitz. Cur 105:32-6 Mr '69
Why psychiatrists disagree in court. il Time 93:44+ Ap 4 '69

FOREST, Jim
Banned in prison; reading material. J. Deedy. por Commonweal 90:578 S 26 '69

FOREST, Linda
Moses and the Milwaukee fourteen. Commonweal 90:410-13 Je 27 '69

FOREST CITY, Ia.
Saving a small town. il Time 94:90 S 19 '69

FOREST conservation
Jail, fine, or plant trees. R. Leadabrand. Am For 75:31+ F '69
Kids, crime and conservation; youth forestry camps. M. J. Benoit. il Cons 23:18-20+ Ap '69
Mike Frome; Torrey pine. M. Frome. Am For 75:3+ N '69
Society of useful men: Ayres and his crowd; Society for the protection of New Hampshire forests; summary of address. S. Adams. il Am For 75:40-3+ Mr '69

FOREST crown canopy
Solar radiation profiles in openings in canopies of aspen and oak. P. C. Miller. bibliog il Science 164:308-9 Ap 18 '69

FOREST ecology
Dwellers of the forest floor. C. Necker. il Nat Wildlife 7:50-5 Ap '69
Fire of life; excerpts from The hidden forest. S. F. Olson. il Audubon 71:4-9 S '69
Forest as an ecosystem. F. G. Goff. il Am For 75:16-18+ D '69
Forest fires: suppression policy has its ecological drawbacks. M. Oberle. Science 165:568-71 Ag 8 '69; Discussion. 166:552, 945+ O 31, N 21 '69
Forest succession in Yellowstone National Park. D. T. Patten. il Nat Parks 43:21-2 S '69
Research to save the fragile Green hell; plight of the Amazonian jungle. il Sci N 95:134-5 F 8 '69

See also
Rain forests

FOREST fauna
Dwellers of the forest floor. C. Necker. il Nat Wildlife 7:50-5 Ap '69

FOREST fire patrol, Aerial
Forest fire shock troops; smokejumpers. J. L. Faust. il Am For 75:12-15 Ja '69

FOREST fire protection
Alaska burns; with editorial comment. J. B. Craig. il Am For 75:1-3+, 11 O '69
As I see the forest fire challenge. E. P. Cliff. il Am For 75:20-3+ Je '69
Disaster fires, why? W. E. Towell. il Am For 75:12-15+ Je '69
Fire awards. il Am For 75:8 Je '69
Forest fires: suppression policy has its ecological drawbacks. M. Oberle. Science 165:568-71 Ag 8 '69; Discussion. 166:522, 945+ O 31, N 21 '69
Laying it on the line. J. B. Craig. Am For 75:11 F '69
Legend of Smokey Bear. M. Hardy. il Nat Parks 43:18-20 Ja '69
Little fire that remained little; Sisar fire, Calif. L. Thorpe. il Am For 75:36-9+ N '69
More muscle for a noble edifice. J. B. Craig. il Am For 75:10-11 Je '69
Rural fires; let's control them. O. B. Capps. il Am For 75:18-19+ Je '69
Why CM-2 needs a boost; Clarke-McNary act of 1924. D. Nelson. il Am For 75:16-17+ Je '69

History
First wings over the forest. H. Clepper. il Am For 75:24-7+ Je; 20-3+ Jl '69

FOREST fires
After the fire. G. H. Harrison. il Nat Wildlife 7:36-9 F '69
Alaska burns; with editorial comment. J. B. Craig. il Am For 75:1-3+, 11 O '69
Cloud condensation nuclei from a simulated forest fire. P. V. Hobbs and L. F. Radke. bibliog il Science 163:279-80 Ja 17 '69
Disaster fires, why? W. E. Towell. il Am For 75:12-15+ Je '69
Fire of life; excerpts from The hidden forest. S. F. Olson. il Audubon 71:4-9 S '69
Fire war; Alaska. il Time 94:20 Jl 11 '69
Firefighter views the Sundance fire. G. S. Gorsuch. il Am For 75:4-5+ Mr '69
Little fire that remained little; Sisar fire, Calif. L. Thorpe. il Am For 75:36-9+ N '69

FOREST management
Alaska's green serge navy. D. McKinlay and H. E. McLean. il Am For 75:16-18 Mr '69
Bridger controversy; with reply. F. Iverson. W. E. Towell. Am For 75:45-7 N '69
Brinkmanship in our forests; excerpts from congressional testimony. E. C. Crafts. Am For 75:19+ Ag '69
Catherine May backs AFA. C. May. Am For 75:8 Ag '69
Cotta's preface; excerpt from Anweisung zum waldbau. H. Cotta. Am For 75:15 S '69
Fire Smokey? il Sr Schol 94:18 F 14 '69
Future of multiple use; address. J. S. Bethel. il Am For 75:32-4+ D '69
Has Smokey Bear outlived his usefulness? public perception of and attitude towards wild animals. E. G. Bowman; discussion. Am For 75:2-3+ Ja; 2 F '69
Mike Frome. M. Frome. Am For 75:3+ Mr '69
Reminiscing about the TVA. W. M. Baker. Am For 75:30-1+ My '69
Revisions urged for high yield timber fund. K. B. Pomeroy. Am For 75:11 Jl '69
Scandinavian forestry. K. B. Pomeroy. il Am For 75:24-7 Ag '69
Squire of poodle patch. F. L. Brunton. il Am For 75:37+ Ap '69

FOREST management—*Continued*
Their pines get the right food; organic tree farming. G. M. Hutton. il Org Gard & Farm 16:40-3 O '69
Upgrading our environment; address, October 14, 1968. H. S. Reuss. il Am For 75:28-9+ My '69
See also
Western forestry center

FOREST products
Our southern pines. C. E. Randall. il Am For 75:32-5+ Je; 30-1+ Jl '69
See also
Lumber industry and trade

FOREST products industry
See also
Mead corporation
Western forestry center

FOREST protection
Infrared locates diseased trees. R. Neubert. il Electr World 82:34-5 Ag '69

FOREST rangers
Buck ranger; national park rangers training program. G. D. Alexander. il Nat Parks 43:21-3 O '69
Preparing the park ranger for his job; Horace M. Albright training center. W. Cone. il Parks & Rec 4:30-1+ D '69
Those were the days. . . ; excerpts from Five golden summers. D. C. Stewart. il Parks & Rec 4:20-4 D '69

FOREST rangers. See United States—Forest service

FOREST rangers wives
Marked for greatness; National park service wife. E. B. Sandlin. Nat Parks 43:14-15 Mr '69
Those were the days. . . ; excerpts from Five golden summers. D. C. Stewart. il Parks & Rec 4:20-4 D '69

FOREST service (United States) See United States—Forest service

FORESTRY camps. See Camps

FORESTRY consultants
Faculty member as a forestry consultant. J. A. Zivnuska. il Am For 75:24-5+ Jl '69

FORESTRY research
McIntire-Stennis program. J. D. Sullivan and G. F. Burks. il Am For 75:16-19+ Ap '69

FORESTRY societies
Society of useful men: Ayres and his crowd; Society for the protection of New Hampshire forests; summary of address. S. Adams. il Am For 75:40-3+ Mr '69
Why state forestry associations? M. K. Goddard. il Am For 75:26-7+ Jl '69
See also
American forestry association

FORESTS, National. See National forests

FORESTS and forestry
See also
Deforestation
Forest conservation
Forest fires
Trees

Alaska
Alaska's green serge navy. D. McKinlay and H. E. McLean. il Am For 75:16-18 Mr '69

Germany (Federal Republic)
See also
Black forest

Israel
Making the desert bloom. I. Gindel. il Am For 75:32-5+ S '69

Lebanon
Cedars of the Lord; cedar of Lebanon. E. R. Yarham. il Am For 75:24-6+ Ja '69

Maine
Mike Frome. M. Frome. Am For 75:3+ Mr '69

Mexico
Forestry and the public domain; a Mexican point of view; address. E. Beltran. il Am For 75:36-7+ D '69 (to be cont)

New Hampshire
Society of useful men: Ayres and his crowd; Society for the protection of New Hampshire forests; summary of address. S. Adams. il Am For 75:40-3+ Mr '69

Scandinavia
Scandinavian forestry. K. B. Pomeroy. il Am For 75:24-7 Ag '69

Texas
Big Thicket: biological crossroads of North America; excerpt from The biological crossroads of North America. O. H. Bonney. il Liv Wildn 33:19-21 Sum '69

Tropics
See also
Rain forests

United States
Washington lookout. V. Trumbull. See issues of American forests
See also
Lumber industry and trade
National forests
United States—Forest service

Virginia
George Washington: our history-making forest. C. E. Randall. il Am For 75:20-3+ Mr '69

FOREVER kind of thing; story. See Cave, H.
FORGE, Andrew
De Kooning in retrospect. Art N 68:44-7+ Mr '69

FORGERY of works of art
Crackpots and forgeries in art and science. J. A. Wilson. il Sci Digest 66:40-4 N '69
Rembrandt, Vermeer, Hals, you name it, Bass says he's got it. il Life 67:44-5 O 24 '69

FORGING
Overlooked metal broadens its appeal; zinc. il Bsns W p 124-5 My 17 '69

FORGING machinery
Forging economies for small parts; new one-man forge. il Bsns W p 154+ Mr 29 '69

FORGIVENESS
Always difficult task; forgiveness. V. P. McCorry. America 121:inside back cover O 18 '69
Forgiveness for failed saints. F. Buechner. Chr Cent 86:244 F 19 '69
See also
Absolution

FORK lift trucks
When I was a boy. il Forbes 104:68 O 1 '69

FORM (aesthetics)
See also
Natural forms

FORM (art)
Library display: using simple geometric shapes. M. Garvey. il Wilson Lib Bul 44:390-1 D '69
New shapes to delight the eye. il UNESCO Courier 22:28-9 My '69

FORMAL dinners. See Dinners and dining

FORMALDEHYDE
Formaldehyde in outer space. Chem 42:24 Je '69
Formaldehyde in space. Sci Am 220:53-4 My '69
Life's building blocks in space; discovery of first polyatomic organic molecule. Sci N 95:351 Ap 12 '69

FORMAN, Harrison
Emeralds of Muzo. Américas. 21:8-14 Ja '69

FORMAN, Ian
Sex and family living. Am Ed 5:11-13 O '69

FORMAN, James
And now James Forman. Nat R 21:789-90 Ag 12 '69
Black bill collector. il Newsweek 73:74-5 My 19 '69
Black manifesto. il por Time 93:94 My 16 '69
Black manifesto declares war on churches. Chr Today 13:29 My 23 '69
Black manifesto: the great white hope. R. Goetz. Chr Cent 86:832-3 Je 18 '69; Discussion. 86:1046-7 Ag 6 '69
Black over white. Commonweal 90:308-9 My 30 '69
Black preacher looks at the Black manifesto. R. D. Abernathy. Chr Cent 86:1064-5 Ag 13 '69
Blacks bill the churches. il por Bsns W p54+ My 10 '69
Catalyst of conscience. Time 94:49 Ag 29 '69
Churches and James Forman. Chr Today 13:27 Je 6 '69
Forman box score. J. C. Haughey. America 120:689 Je 14 '69
How James Forman lost his cool but saved religion in 1969. A. Vorspan. Chr Cent 86:1042 Ag 6 '69
Incident at Riverside church. Nation 208:618-19 My 19 '69
Issue is economic justice. Chr Cent 86:861 Je 25 '69
James Forman's Black manifesto. America 120:605 My 24 '69
Manifesto and the magnificat. H. Schomer. Chr Cent 86:866-7 Je 25 '69
Manifesto maker. il por Chr Today 13:42 Je 6 '69
What to do if James Forman busts up your service; excerpts from letter, ed. by W. F. Buckley. Nat R 21:792 Ag 12 '69

FORMAN, W. R.
Japanese research submersibles. Sea Front 15:
78-85 Mr '69
FORMER priests. See Ex-nuns, priests, etc.
FORMICHI, Cesare
Historical records. A. Favia-Artsay. por
Hobbies 74:35 N '69
FORMOSA. See Taiwan
FORMS, Natural. See Natural forms
FORNEY, James S.
Twenty-five sticky strobe questions & an-
swers. Mod Phot 33:80-3 Mr '69
FORREST, James T.
White painting. Am West 6:53-4 Ja '69
FORREST, W. G.
Greece: a chance for democracy. Nation 209:
279-82 S 22 '69
FORREST CITY, Ark.
Arkansas' rebel minister. il Ebony 25:82-6
N '69
FORRESTER, Jay W.
Overlooked reasons for our social troubles.
Fortune 80:191-2 D '69
FORSTER, Edward Morgan
Nonagenarian's threefold philosophy. D. J.
Leary. Sat R 52:49+ F 15 '69
On the scene. C. Barnes. Holiday 45:18 Mr
'69
FORSTER, Herman
Those atomic power plants; excerpts from
letter. Liv Wildn 33:29-30 Spr '69
FORSYTH Wickes collection. See Boston muse-
um of fine arts
FORT, Joel
Drug use and the law. Cur 113:4-13 D '69
FORT APACHE Indian reservation. See Indi-
ans of North America—Reservations
FORT BRAGG, Calif.
Town in trouble; plague of drugs among
kids in California. J. Bonfante. il Life 66:
48-54+ Mr 21 '69
FORT DELAWARE
Fort Delaware, a bywater of history. B. Schill
and B. Schill. il Yachting 125:66-7 Je '69
FORT DETRICK, Frederick, Md. See Labora-
tories, Government
FORT DIX, N.J. See Military training camps
FORT GARRY, Canada. See Lower Fort Garry,
Canada
FORT KNOX gold depository. See United
States—Mint, Bureau of the
FORT LAUDERDALE, Fla.
Beach phones keep emergencies at low tide.
il Am City 84:20 Ja '69

Architecture
Florida minivillage. il Arch Forum 130:92-5
Ja '69

Description
Place of the month. il Holiday 45:98-101 Mr
'69

Religious institutions and affairs
Coral ridge story. R. E. Friedrich, jr. il Chr
Today 13:32-3 Jl 18 '69
FORT WAYNE, Ind.
Copartners! Foundations and city depart-
ments. H. Grabner. il Parks & Rec 4:19 D
'69

Parks and playgrounds
Growth of Fort Wayne's park system. G.
Tetherly. il Parks & Rec 3:32-5+ D '68
FORT WORTH, Tex.
City-school liaison brings mutual benefits.
Am City 84:54 Ja '69
Piercing tool speeds pipe work. G. O. Muller.
il Am City 84:72-3 D '69
Summer work programs; Richmond, Va. G.
M. Chamberlain. il Am City 84:92+ N '69

City planning
No more land-development tie-ups. H. D.
McMahan. il Am City 84:85+ Ag '69

Galleries and museums
Windows on medicine's past; Dr May Owen
Hall of medical science at the Museum of
science and industry. E. H. McCleary. il
Todays Health 47:70-2 O '69

Police
See also
Helicopters in police work
FORT WORTH opera association
Report: Fort Worth; production of Don Pas-
quale. O. Chism. Opera N 33:31 Mr 8 '69
Report: Fort Worth; production of Turandot.
O. Chism. Opera N 33:30-1 Ap 19 '69

FORTAS, Abe
Fortas on his resignation: there wasn't any
choice for a man of conscience. por U S
News 66:33 My 26 '69

about
American disease. Nation 208:650-1 My 26 '69
End of the Fortas affair. pors Life 66:38-9
My 23 '69
Fortas affair. il por Time 93:20-2 My 16 '69
Fortas and the future of the Court. America
120:642 My 31 '69
Fortas of the Supreme court: a question of
ethics and the stock manipulator. W. Lam-
bert. il pors Life 66:32-7 My 9 '69
Fortas resignation. New Repub 160:7 My 24
'69
Fortas verdict on Abe Fortas. il por News-
week 73:31-3 My 26 '69
Furor over Supreme court. il por U S News
66:31-2 My 26 '69
Judgment on a justice. il por Time 93:23-4
My 23 '69
Justice Abe Fortas on the spot. il pors News-
week 73:29-33 My 19 '69
Mr Justice Fortas. A. M. Bickel. New Repub
160:9-10 My 17 '69
New controversy over Justice Fortas and a
fee; what it's all about. il por U S News
66:21 My 19 '69
No peace for Fortas; involvement with Wolf-
son family foundation. por Time 93:28 My 9
'69
On the fall of Fortas. Nat R 21:523-4 Je 3
'69
TRB from Washington. New Repub 160:4
My 17 '69
Warren and Fortas: a sober, tough conclu-
sion. Chr Cent 86:734 My 28 '69
FORTIER, Norman
Bay and the Sound; photographs. Motor B
123:57-63 Je '69
FORTIFICATION
See also
Sacsahuaman (fort)
Walls (fortifications)
FORTIFIED food. See Food, Enriched
FORTINBRAS (literary character) See Shake-
speare. W.—Characters
FORTUNE, Carl L. jr
Lamoille union high school: education for
all. Sr Schol 94:School Teach 22-3 Mr 7 '69
FORTUNE society
New lobby, ex cons. G. Samuels. il N Y
Times Mag p36-8 O 19 '69; Reply. D. T.
Orsini. p32+ N 16 '69
FORTUNE telling
Your fortune in wax. S. Leek. Ladies Home
J 86:110+ O '69
See also
Astrology
FORTY carats; drama. See Barillet, P. and
Grédy, J. P.
FORUM of the twelve Caesars. See New York
(city)—Hotels, restaurants, etc.
FORUMS (discussion and debate)
See also
Center for the study of democratic institu-
tions, Santa Barbara, Calif.
FORWARDING of air freight. See Air freight
service
FOSBURGH, Hugh
All is not well at Baker. Am For 75:32-4 Mr
'69
Loons of Mink Pond; excerpt from A clearing
in the wilderness. Cons 23:2-5 Je '69
FOSBURY, Dick
Being backward gets results. R. Blount, jr.
il pors Sports Illus 30:24-7 F 10 '69
FOSDICK, Harry Emerson
Driving out the fundamentals. Chr Today
14:16 N 21 '69
Obituary
Chr Cent 86:1306 O 15 '69
Chr Today 14:31 O 24 '69
Time por 94:90 O 17 '69
FOSS, J. W. and Mayo, R. W.
Operation survival. Electr World 82:41-3 Ag
'69
FOSSE, Bob
Bob Fosse translates Sweet Charity from
stage to screen. V. H. Swisher. il pors Dance
Mag 43:22-5 F '69
FOSSEY, Dian
Making friends with mountain gorillas. pors
Nat Geog 137:48-67 Ja '70
FOSSIL algae; Fossil horses, etc. See Algae,
Fossil; Horses, Fossil, etc.
FOSSIL bones. See Paleontology
FOSSIL man. See Man, Prehistoric

FOSSIL plants. See Paleobotany
FOSTER, Bob
    Frankie the banger gets bombed. M. Kane.
    il por Sports Illus 30:46-7 F 3 '69
    Hungry Bobby Foster. il pors Ebony 24:124-
    6+ S '69
FOSTER, Claude R. Jr
    Reformation and revolution: the maturing
    East German view. Chr Cent 86:1380-2 O
    29 '69
FOSTER, David William
    Garcia Márquez and Solitude. Américas 21:
    36-41 N '69
FOSTER, Edward J.
    How we judge FM tuners. Hi Fi 19:64-7 N
    '69
FOSTER, Gertrude B.
    Grow your own seasonings. Horticulture 47:
    34-7+ My '69
FOSTER, H. Lincoln
    Blue gentian. Horticulture 46:13-15+ O '68
FOSTER, Henry H. Jr
    Future of family law. bibliog f Ann Am
    Acad 383:129-44 My '69
    —See Freed, D. J. jt. auth.
FOSTER, Herbert B. Jr
    Obituary
        Am City 84:36+ Ja '69
FOSTER, John D. and Tooley, J. W.
    We kept the sewer in service. Am City 84:97-
    9 N '69
FOSTER, John H. See Smith. J. D. jt. auth.
FOSTER, John L.
    (tr) Two Songs of heart's ease: translated
    from the ancient Egyptian. Poetry 114:176-8
    Je '69
FOSTER, John Stuart, 1922-
    Blunt warning; excerpts from address. Avia-
    tion W 91:11 S 8 '69
FOSTER, Laura Louise
    Container gardening. Horticulture 47:34-7 D
    '69
FOSTER, MacArthur
    Fighting marine they named MacArthur. M.
    Kane. il por Sports Illus 32:46-7 Ja 5 '70
FOSTER, Michael
    Fold and dip. Sch Arts 69:22-4 Ja '70
FOSTER, Richard
    Nine rooms in search of a view. il House
    & Gard 135:64-9 F '69
FOSTER, Richard T.
    Carrousel house. J. Peter. il por Look 33:
    32-4 My 27 '69
FOSTER, William C.
    Prospects for arms control. For Affairs 47:
    413-21 Ap '69
    U.S. proposes world wide seismic investiga-
    tion of underground nuclear explosions;
    statement, December 5, 1968. Dept State
    Bul 60:53-62 Ja 20 '69
    U.S. receives U.K. ratification of nonpro-
    liferation treaty; statement, November 27,
    1968. Dept State Bul 59:679 D 23 '69
FOSTER, William S.
    Urban misconceptions. bibliog por Am City
    84:73-5+ Je '69
    Water-resource communications gap. bibliog
    por Am City 84:83-6 O '69
FOSTER grandparent program
    Blessed be the foster grandparent. A. W.
    Birch. Read Digest 95:21-4+ N '69
    Foster grandparent among 100 honored in
    Chicago Hall of fame. Aging 176:10 Je '69
    Foster grandparents get high rating in five
    studies. Aging 170:14-15 D '68
    Foster grandparents get honors. il Aging 178:
    17 Ag '69
    No cure like love. H. Bottel. il Har Yrs 9:
    35-7 My '69
    Older people as a resource. il Aging 175:8-9
    My '69
    San Francisco foster grandparents tiny UN:
    born in fifteen nations outside U.S. il Aging
    170:12-13 D '68
FOSTER home care
    Paul Anderson can lift eight of you; Paul
    Anderson youth home inc. J. F. Ryan. il
    Esquire 72:69-71+ Jl '69
    School problems of emotionally disturbed
    foster children. A. N. Maluccio. bibliog
    Ment Hy 53:611-19 O '69
FOSTER Wheeler corporation
    Soul of caution; J. E. Kenney. Forbes 104:70
    D 1 '69
FOTHERGILLAS
    Fothergilla. K. S. Taylor. Horticulture 48:46
    Ja '70
FOUCAULT'S pendulum
    Simple recording Foucault tester. A. C. Haven,
    jr. il Sky & Tel 38:51-2 Jl '69

FOULKE, Adrienne
    (tr) See Jullian, P.   Fresh remembrance of
    Oscar Wilde
    (tr) See Moravia, A.   Reflections on the
    moon
FOUND art. See Found objects
FOUND objects
    Decorative ways to use summer collections. il
    Good H 169:142-3 Ag '69
    Painting found objects. M. Panchal. il Sch
    Arts 69:14-15 N '69
        See also
    Collage
FOUNDATION garments
        See also
    Brassieres

        Anecdotes, facetiae, satire, etc.
    What's going on in that lab, Dr Fu? W.
    Zinsser. Life 66:22 My 23 '69
FOUNDATION of thanatology
    Foundation of thanatology.   A. Kutscher.
    Ment Hy 53:338-9 Jl '69
FOUNDATIONS
        See also
    Piles and pile driving
FOUNDATIONS, Charitable and educational
    Billion dollar brains: how wealth puts know-
    ledge in its pocket. D. Horowitz. il Ramp
    Mag 7:36-44 My '69
    Foundations [charity begins at home] D. Ho-
    rowitz and D. Kolodney. il Ramp Mag 7:
    38-48 Ap '69 (to be cont)
    Foundations fight back. il Bsns W p35-6
    My 17 '69
    Handcuffing the foundations. D. Wolfle. Science
    165-9 Jl 4 '69
    Let's not fence in the foundations. I. Ross. il
    Fortune 79:148-50+ Je '69
    Story of what a foundation did; the opera-
    tions of the Mott foundation. C. S. Mott.
    U S News 67:101 O 20 '69
    Taxing experience; Americans building con-
    stitutionally. Time 94:57 Ag 8 '69
    Treasury misfires; prohibition of activities
    affecting a political campaign. New Repub
    160:8-9 My 31 '69
    Twenty long years: Kathryn Long courses.
    M. Rudolf. if Opera N 33:6-7 Je 14 '69
    U.S. journal: New Orleans: twentieth annual
    conference on the Council on foundations.
    C. Trillin. New Yorker 45:112+ My 3 '69
    Why I believe in philanthropy. J. D. Rocke-
    feller, 3d. Read Digest 95:185-6+ D '69
        See also names of foundations, e.g. Pearl
    S. Buck foundation

        Taxation
    Bill to kill foundations. I. Mothner. Look 33:
    83 D 16 '69
    Dismay over foundations. Sci N 96:326 O 11
    '69
    For eight RFK aides, foundation funds. U S
    News 66:12 F 24 '69
    Foundation or public charity. D. Wolfle. Sci-
    ence 165:1209 S 19 '69
    Foundations and tax reform. Chr Today
    14:25-6 N 21 '69
    Foundations and the tax bill: threat to the
    private sector? L. J. Carter. Science 166:
    1245-8 D 5 '69
    Foundations feel heat of tax reform; House
    committee to plug tax law loopholes. il
    Bsns W p72+ Mr 8 '69
    Foundations; the unity of charitable organiza-
    tions; address, November 21, 1969. A. Pifer.
    Vital Speeches 36:178-82 Ja 1 '70
    Foundations under fire in Congress. J. Walsh.
    Science 163:913 F 28 '69
    Last of the great Populists takes on the
    foundations, the banks, the Federal re-
    serve, the Treasury. R. Sherrill. il N Y
    Times Mag p24-5+ Mr 16 '69
    New class war. J. Hart. il Nat R 21:896-901+
    S 9 '69
    Patman's complaint; proposed legislation lay-
    ing tax on foundations' gross income. News-
    week 73:23-4 Mr 3 '69
    Rocking the foundations. D. Sanford. New
    Repub 161:17-20 N 29 '69
    Rooney reform. K. Crawford. Newsweek 73:29
    Mr 3 '69
    Society's scouts; the new role of foundations.
    il Life 66:36 Mr 7 '69
    Tax-free foundations; study starts in Con-
    gress. il U S News 66:81-2 F 10 '69
    Tax-free funds come under fire. il U S News
    66:84-5 Mr 3 '69
    Tax-free groups studied again. U S News
    66:100-1 Mr 10 '69
    Tax reform and the foundations. F. G. Jen-
    nings. Sat R 52:32 O 18 '69

FOUNDATIONS, Charitable and educational—
Taxation—*Continued*
Tax reform: House bill holds penalties for foundations. J. Walsh. Science 165:678-9 Ag 15 '69
This month's feature: Congress and tax status of foundations. Cong Digest 48:130-60 My '69
Tougher in principle than in fact. Sci N 96: 590-1 D 27 '69
What price tax reform. R. H. Smith. Pub W 196:43 O 27 '69

FOUNDLINGS
At the Foundling, the child is everything. T. M. Gannon. il America 121:331-3 O 18 '69; Reply. J Werner. 121:575 D 13 '69

FOUNDRY practice
See also
Continuous casting

Study and teaching
Exploration in pewter casting. J. D. Kain. il Sch Arts 69:16-17 Ja '70

FOUNTAIN, Lawrence H.
Excerpt from testimony before House committee on interstate and foreign commerce, April 15, 1969. Cong Digest 48:175+ Je '69

FOUNTAIN pens
Bich the ballpoint king. Fortune 80:122 Ag 15 '69
Tests of ball-point pens and refills. il Consumer Bul 52:32-6 Ap '69
See also
Waterman-Bic pen corporation

FOUNTAINS
First new fountain concept in 2,000 years. il Parks & Rec 4:48 My '69
Fountain scale model serves as an engineering design tool. R. Chaix. il Arch Rec 145: 165-7 Mr '69
Giving a geyser; G. T. Delacorte's gift to New York. il Time 93:54 Je 27 '69

FOUR-channel sound. See Sound—Stereophonic recording and reproducing

FOUR-day-week. See Hours of labor

FOUR-letter words. See Words

FOUR wheel drive automobiles. See Automobiles—Four wheel drive

FOUR-wheel-drive Grand prix. See Motor vehicle racing

FOURIER series. See Harmonic analysis

FOURNIER, Robert O.
Old Faithful: a physical model. bibliog Science 163:304-5 Ja 17 '69

FOURTH avenue. See New York (city)—Streets

FOURTH committee of the General assembly See United Nations —Trusteeship committee

FOURTH of July
It's still a hopping holiday; celebrations of Eveleth, Minn, Bexley, Ohio, Stonington, Me, and Kotzebue, Alaska. il Sports Illus 31:36-43 Jl 7 '69
One last boom; Independence day activities. C. Ford. il Field & S 74:8+ Jl '69

FOVEA centralis. See Retina

FOWKES, Frederick M.
Russia's exotic water grower. Sat R 52:52-4 S 6 '69

FOWKES, William J.
Double sessions; high cost of saving money. Clear House 44:76-7 O '69

FOWLER, Henry Hamill
Farewell to Fowler. R. Brady. Duns R 92:5 D '68

FOWLER, James M.
Fierce majesty of the condor. Life 66:74-6+ Je 13 '69

FOWLER, Leonard
Fowler dance group; 92nd st. Y. A. J. Fortney. Dance Mag 43:30+ Ap '69
Fowler dance group; 92nd street Y. D. Hering. Dance Mag 43:31 Ja '69

FOX, Claire Gilbride
Merits and morals. Horn Bk 45:80-4 F '69

FOX, Gary C.
Geography: sighted subject, sank same. Clear House 44:35-6 S '69

FOX, Gerald S.
Zubin Mehta conducts a magnificent recording of Ein heldenleben. Am Rec G 35:604-6 Ap '69

FOX, Lucía Ungaro de. See Ungaro de Fox, L.

FOX, Paul J. and others
Crustal plates in the central Atlantic: evidence for at least two poles of rotation. bibliog Science 165:487-9 Ag 1 '69

FOX, Philip
Moonshot: young Europe reacts. por Seventeen 28:110-11+ D '69
Young Englishman looks at New York. por Seventeen 28:126-7+ O '69

FOX, Richard W.
Black Panthers in Africa. Commonweal 91: 6-7 O 3 '69
Protracted *jihad* in Palestine. Chr Cent 86: 1450-3 N 12 '69

FOX, Terry J.
Fox's hunt. S. Blickstein. por Duns R 93:69+ Mr '69

FOX, Thomas O. and Pardee, A. B.
Animal cells: noncorrelation of length of G₁ phase with size after mitosis. bibliog Science 167:80-2 Ja 2 '70

FOX, Tom
Devil's island off Vietnam. Commonweal 90:432-5 Jl 11 '69
Operation uplift in Vietnam. Commonweal 90: 502-3 Ag 22 '69
Return to Tuy Hoa. Commonweal 91:177-80+ N 7 '69
Thieu-ing the loyal opposition. Commonweal 90:459-62 Jl 25 '69
Word from the front. Commonweal 90:485-6 Ag 8 '69

FOX, Uffa
Maple Leaf IV; excerpt from Seamanlike sense in powercraft. Yachting 126:56-8+ O '69

FOX, Virgil
Virgil Fox. C. F. Gilmore. il por Hi Fi 19: MA22-3 N '69

FOX, William L.
Afternoon kites; poem. Seventeen 28:211 Ag '69

FOX, William Price
Rockefeller center west: Hawaii's Mauna Kea. Holiday 45:54-5+ My '69

FOX hunting
Snarling tractors and no tallyho; winter fox hunt in Minnesota. R. F. Jones. il Sports Illus 30:28-30+ F 17 '69

FOX squirrel hunting. See Squirrel hunting

FOXES
Trailing the gray ghost; excerpt from The walking adventures of a naturalist. J. K. Terres. il Audubon 71:50-6 Ja '69
See also
Fox hunting

FOXFIRE (student magazine) See College and school journalism

FOXGLOVES
Foxglove on the rise. W. Masson. il Org Gard & Farm 16:68-9 Ag '69

FOXHOUNDS
Fabulous foxhound. D. M. Duffey. il Outdoor Life 144:136+ N '69

FOXTAIL lilies. See Desert candles

FOXTAIL pine. See Pine

FOY d'Agen, Saint
Tale of the purloined saint. C. Cate. il Horizon 11:68-79 Wint '69

FRACCI, Carla
Dance magazine award, 1968. por Dance Mag 43:35 Ap '69
Reports on Dance magazine award reception. il pors Dance Mag 43:44-6 Jl '69

FRACTURE of solids
Massive internal fracture of an amorphous polyester. I. V. Yannas. bibliog il Science 166:227-8 O 10 '69

FRACTURES (geology) See Faults (geology)

FRADY, Marshall
California: the rending of the veil. Harper 239:57-73 D '69
Cooling off with LBJ. Harper 238:65-72 Je '69
Gary, Indiana. Harper 239:35-45 Ag '69
Haynsworth of Greenville. Life 67:36-8+ O 31 '69
Hofheinz and the Astrodome. Holiday 45: 42-5+ My '69

FRAENKEL, G. See Berreur, P. jt. auth.

FRAGARIA. See Strawberries

FRAGRANCE. See Odors

FRAGRANT gardens. See Gardens, Fragrant

FRAKTUR design. See Decoration and ornament

FRAME, Janet
Birds of the air; story. Harp Baz 102:102-5 Je '69
Words; poem. Mlle 69:134 O '69
You are now entering the human heart; story. New Yorker 45:134+ Mr 29 '69

FRANC. See Money—France

FRANCE, Bill
Talladega: the principals and the principles. por Motor T 21:37+ N '69

FRANCE, Pierre Mendès-. See Mendès-France, P.

FRANCE
French face mediocrity. F. Ungeheuer. Time 94:34+ S 26 '69
    See also
Aeronautics, Commercial—France
Aerospace industries—France
Airlines—France
Airplane industry and trade—France
Architecture, Domestic—France
Automobile driving—France
Avignon
Ballet—France
Biscay, Bay of
Brittany
Budget—France
Business consolidations and mergers—France
Colleges and universities—France
Colombey-les-deux-Eglises
Computer industry—France
Conques
Corsica
Crime and criminals—France
Elections—France
Foreign students in France
French
Gardens—France
Helicopter industry and trade—France
Hotels, taverns, etc.—France
Investments, Foreign (in France)
Jews in France
Labor and laboring classes—France
Libraries—France
Liquor problem—France
Moving pictures—France
Munitions industries—France
Music festivals—France
National parks and reserves—France
Normandy
Oceanographic research—France
Police—France
Political campaigns—France
Port Grimaud
Provence
Public health—France
Public officers—France
Publishers and publishing—France
Railroads—France
Rance River
Research—France
Restaurants—France
Saint-Tropez
Shopping and shoppers—France
Strikes—France
Student demonstrations—France
Student movement—France
Textile industry—France
Tourist trade—France
Trials—France
Villefranche

Antiquities
Paleolithic camp at Nice. H. de Lumley. il Sci Am 220:42-50 My '69

Cabinet
Eternal *non*; new leftist into office. Time 94:40 N 7 '69
France: the next seven years; Gaullist ranks dissent over choices. Newsweek 73:51 Je 30 '69
France's new cabinet. il Time 94:25 Jl 4 '69
Something human; new cabinet. il Newsweek 74:28-30 Jl 7 '69

Colonies
    See also
Corsica
French Guiana
Martinique

Constitution
French referendum: the mask of de Gaulle; proposed reforms. C. Bourdet. Nation 208:526-9 Ap 28 '69

Defenses
France's new defense strategy and the Atlantic puzzle. M. J. Brenner. Bul Atom Sci 25:4-7 N '69
Maginot: the line that failed. il Newsweek 73:14 Mr 31 '69

Description and travel
Gone flying to St Tropez. J. Gilbert. il Flying 84:66-72+ Je '69
Road to Périgord, a movable feast in more ways than one. M. Gough. il House B 111:94+ N '69

Economic conditions
After devaluation and controls; another crisis for France? il U S News 67:58-9 Ag 25 '69
De Gaulle's troubles aren't over. il U S News 66:47 Mr 24 '69
Franc: not quite a crisis. il Newsweek 73:79-80 My 12 '69

France awaits the next storm. il Bsns W p88 Ag 16 '69
Money: après moi, la dévaluation. il Time 93:90 My 9 '69
Pompidou versus the flaming franc. il Bsns W p44+ Je 21 '69
    See also
Business conditions
Finance—France
Money—France

Economic policy
Facing realities; austerity measures. Newsweek 74:42+ S 15 '69
Is worse to come for the franc? il Bsns W p34+ S 6 '69
Painful re-entry. Time 94:32+ S 26 '69
Strategy for stability. Time 94:95 S 12 '69

Foreign relations
De Gaulle: Nixon's stumbling block? il U S News 66:21-3 Mr 3 '69
De Gaulle's successor; any better for U.S? il U S News 66:58-9 Je 30 '69
In the General's wake. H. Brandon. Sat R 52:4 My 24 '69
New France under Pompidou? U S News 67:16 Jl 21 '69
New hope for European unity. America 121:27 Jl 19 '69
Twilight of de Gaulle. J. Burnham. il Nat R 21:114-15 F 11 '69

Africa
Francozone Africa. K. Irvine. bibliog f Cur Hist 56:282-5+ My '69

Arab states
Armorers of Araby. Time 95:28 Ja 19 '70
Reinforcing a policy. Newsweek 75:28-9 Ja 12 '70
    See also
France—Foreign relations—Libya

Great Britain
Once more, de Gaulle v. Britain. Time 93:18 F 28 '69
Scandale diplomatique; de Gaulle's remarks on the future of Europe made to British ambassador. Newsweek 73:37 Mr 3 '69
Scrambling Europe? Sr Schol 94:16-17 Mr 14 '69

Israel
FOB Cherbourg: Israel gets its boats. il Newsweek 75:27-8 Ja 12 '70
Furor after a gunboat coup. il U S News 68:7 Ja 12 '70
Gunboat diplomacy, new style; embargoed ships leave Cherbourg. Newsweek 75:22 Ja 5 '70
Israel's fugitive flotilla. il Time 95:15-16 Ja 12 '70

Libya
Arms across the sea. il Newsweek 75:38 Ja 19 '70

United States
America and France. S. Hoffmann. New Repub 160:17-21 Ap 5; 20-3 Ap 12 '69
Arms across the sea; impact of Libyan Mirage deal. il Newsweek 75:38 Ja 19 '70
Future of Franco-U.S. relations. il Time 93:24 My 9 '69
Presidents Johnson and de Gaulle exchange New Year's greetings. L. B. Johnson; C. de Gaulle. Dept State Bul 60:77-8 Ja 27 '69
Reviving an old alliance. il Newsweek 74:24+ D 29 '69

History
    See also
World war, 1939-1945—France

Bibliography
Articles and other books received; comp. by B. F. Hyslop. See issues of American historical review

Revolution
Revolution: the past and the future. il Life 67:100-12 O 10 '69

February revolution, 1848
1848 again? J. Barry. il Horizon 11:66-83 Spr '69

Third Republic, 1870-1940
Collapse of the Third Republic, by W. L. Shirer. Review
    Atlan 224:143-4+ D '69. A. Sampson
    Sat R il 52:29-31+ N 8 '69. D. Schoenbrun

FRANCE—History—*Continued*

German occupation, 1940-1945

Battle of silence, by J. Bruller. Review
  New Yorker 45:203-6 N 8 '69. N. Bliven
Fall of France; excerpts from The collapse
  of the Third Republic. W. L. Shirer. il
  Look 33:33-8+ S 23 '69

Industries

National chemical giants emerge in Europe.
  il Bsns W p76+ Jl 19 '69
Pompidou may let Westinghouse in. Bsns W
  p49-50 S 20 '69
La ronde; Perrier water and candy company
  trying to expand into dairy industry. Time
  94:96 N 7 '69
Westinghouse, go home; efforts to acquire
  Jeumont-Schneider blocked by EEC.
  Bsns W p52+ My 10 '69
  See also
Glass industry
Tire industry and trade

Intellectual life

France: a struggle against the second-rate.
  F. Ungeheuer. Harper 239:122-8 D '69

Moral conditions

After de Gaulle, sex sells. il Newsweek 74:
  61 S 29 '69
French institution: the mistress. J. Dutourd.
  McCalls 96:91-2 Mr '69

Politics and government

Absent presence of General de Gaulle. P.
  Ben. New Repub 161:12-13 O 11 '69
Almost making it; one view on the meaning
  of France's revolution. S. Lynd. Common-
  weal 90:345-7 Je 6 '69; Reply. W. O'Con-
  nor. 90:474-5+ Ag 8 '69
Challenger, front and center; candidates for
  de Gaulle's successor. il Time 93:39-40 My 16
  '69
De Gaulle, a summing up. G. Lichtheim. Com-
  mentary 48:79-85 S '69
De Gaulle and his era. il Newsweek 73:48-50
  My 12 '69
De Gaulle's legacy to Pompidou. S. Hoffmann.
  New Repub 161:19-21 Jl 12 '69
De Gaulle's successor; any better for U.S? il
  U S News 66:58-9 Je 30 '69
De Gaulle's troubles aren't over. il U S News
  66:47 Mr 24 '69
End of an era: France after de Gaulle. il
  Newsweek 73:41-2+ My 12 '69
Enter President Pompidou. il Newsweek 73:
  42-3 Je 23 '69
Follow the leader. Nat R 21:528 Je 3 '69
For France: a new man, a new mood. I.
  Ross. Read Digest 95:132-6 N '69
France: a struggle against the second-rate.
  F. Ungeheuer. Harper 239:122-8 D '69
France after de Gaulle; with interview with
  R. Aron. il U S News 66:25-9 My 12 '69
France enters a new era. il Time 93:30+ My
  9 '69
France takes the exit in stride; de Gaulle's
  departure brings no deluge of problems. il
  Bsns W p82-5 My 3 '69
France: the birth of Pompidoulism. il Time
  93:41 Je 13 '69
France: the power passes to Pompidou. il
  Time 93:22+ Je 27 '69
France without de Gaulle. E. von Kuehnelt-
  Leddihn. Nat R 21:533 Je 3 '69
France without father. C. Bourdet. Nation
  208:589-90 My 12 '69
General's heir takes over. il Time 93:27 Je 20
  '69
Le grand Charles steps down; Pursuit of
  grandeur. Sr Schol 94:11-12 My 9 '69
Grand strategy of de Gaulle. S. K. Padover.
  il Sat R 52:25-7 Mr 8 '69
How will France change? S. Hoffmann. New
  Repub 161:21-4 Jl 26 '69
Ideology of May '68. P. Hebblethwaite. Cath
  World 209:112-14 Je '69
Letter from Paris; candidates for president.
  Genêt. New Yorker 45:128+ My 24 '69
Letter from Paris; de Gaulle's resignation.
  Genêt. New Yorker 45:129-33 My 10 '69
Letter from Paris; depressant atmosphere in
  March. Genêt. New Yorker 45:126-7 Mr 22
  '69
Letter from Paris; end of President de
  Gaulle's regime. Genêt. New Yorker 45:78+
  Je 28 '69
Letter from Paris; President G. Pompidou's
  first press conference. Genêt. New Yorker
  45:135-6 O 4 '69
Mandate of Monsieur Pompidou. Life 66:34
  Je 13 '69

Matter of style. Newsweek 74:40+ Jl 21 '69
Non-candidate. il Newsweek 73:46 My 19 '69
Now a pretender to the Gaullist throne;
  G. Pompidou. H. de Turenne. il N Y Times
  Mag p30-1+ F 23 '69
Once more, the ultimatum. Time 93:27 Ap 18
  '69
Perils of Pompidou. C. Bourdet. Nation
  208:812 Je 30 '69
Poher to power? E. Behr. il Newsweek 73:48+
  My 26 '69
Politics of risk; de Gaulle's ultimatum. Time
  93:32 Ap 25 '69
Reports: France. D. Cook. Atlan 224:14+ N
  '69
Toward regionalism. Time 93:31 F 14 '69
Twilight of de Gaulle. J. Burnham. il Nat
  R 21:114-15 F 11 '69
Why Pompidou? G. Comte. Nat R 21:695+ Jl
  15 '69
  See also
Communist party (France)
Elections—France
France—Cabinet
France—Constitution
Political campaigns—France
Presidents—France

Referendum

See Referendum

Religious Institutions and affairs

See also
Catholic church in France

Riots

New Poujadists. il Time 94:30+ O 24 '69
Obsolete communism, by D. Cohn-Bendit and
  G. Cohn-Bendit. Review
  Time il 93:76 Ja 31 '69
Red flag/black flag, by P. Seale and M. Mc-
  Conville. Review
  America 120:171-2 F 8 '69. R. L. Carol

FRANCE (ship) See Ocean liners

FRANCE-United States air agreement. See
  Aviation—International aspects

FRANCEKEVICH, Al
  In the darkroom. See issues of Popular photography

FRANCESCONI, Ralph P. and Mager. Milton
  Hypobaric hypoxia: effects on early development of tryptophan oxygenase in neonatal
  rats. bibliog Science 166:1412-13 D 12 '69

FRANCHISE system
  Business franchises: how they work. il Good
  H 169:218 O '69
  Business of your own, the growth of fran-
  chising; with interview with C. L. Vaughn.
  il U S News 67:56-9 D 8 '69
  Caveat emptor: keyword of the franchising
  boom. Pub W 196:49-51 Ag 18 '69; Reply.
  H. Kursh. 196:27-8 S 15 '69
  Franchising: new power for 500,000 small
  businessmen. il Time 93:88+ Ap 18 '69
  Great U.S. franchising boom. il Newsweek
  74:88-9 N 10 '69
  How to be your own boss: the $80-billion
  boom in franchising. C. Peet. il Pop Mech
  131:85-6+ F '69
  In the franchise business anything goes. il
  Fortune 80:34+ D '69
  Job franchiser; Snelling and Snelling place-
  ment agency. S. Margetts. il Duns R 94:59-
  61 Jl '69
  So you want to run a franchise? R. Levy. il
  Duns R 93:36-8 Ja '69
  See also
  Government investigations—Franchise sys-
  tem
  Restaurants—Franchise system

FRANCIS, Arlene
  Memorable minutes on What's my line? Mc-
  Calls 96:88-9 Mr '69

FRANCIS, Devon
  How to leave your family without leaving
  home. Pop Sci 194:140-3+ Ap '69
  Modern steam cars are really on the way.
  Pop Sci 194:45-9+ Je '69

FRANCIS, Dick
  Carrot for a chestnut; story. Sports Illus 32:
  48-59 Ja 5 '70
  Dick Francis; interview. New Yorker 45:29-
  30 Mr 15 '69
  about
  Close-up: jockey with an eye for intrigue.
  J. Newcombe. il pors Life 66:81-2 Je 6 '69

FRANCIS, Ed
  IC stereo amplifier in a phono arm. Radio-
  Electr 40:52-5 Mr '69
  Ten-watt PA amplifier. Pop Electr 31:55-60
  N '69

FRANCIS, Edward Guy
  (tr) Native language. Todays Ed 58:40-1 N
    '69
FRANCIS Joseph, Sister
  Children, art and literature. Sch Arts 69:28-9
    N '69
FRANCIS, Marion D. and others
  Diphosphonates inhibit formation of calcium
    phosphate crystals in vitro and pathologi-
    cal calcification in vivo. bibliog Science
    165:1264-6 S 19 '69
FRANCISCANS
  Episcopal Franciscans celebrate fifty years.
    T. Early. Chr Cent 86:1592-4 D 10 '69
FRANCK, Frederick
  Alfrink of Utrecht, legate from Utopia. Com-
    monweal 90:460-1 Jl 25 '69
  Nuances in the Netherlands. Commonweal 89:
    581-5 F 7 '69
  Post-marital priesthood. Commonweal 89:724-
    6 Mr 14 '69
  Roman windmill tilting. Commonweal 90:224-5
    My 9 '69
  St Peter's square, 1997. Commonweal 91:162+
    O 31 '69
FRANCKE, Master
  Germany's first master. il Time 94:56-56B
    N '69
FRANCO, Francisco
  Crackdown in Spain. Nat R 21:163-4 F 25 '69
  Franco deals with the succession question.
    Chr Cent 86:1059 Ag 13 '69
  Franco's last deal. L. Jenkins. Nation 209:
    689-92 D 22 '69
  Spain is still afraid of itself. R. Eder. il por
    N Y Times Mag p23+ Mr 9 '69
  Spanish regime cracks down; with report
    by R. Hemming. il por Sr Schol 94:16-17
    F 14 '69
FRANCO, Marjorie
  Rite of spring; story. Redbook 134:56-7 Ja
    '70
  Shy Emily; story. Redbook 132:74-5 Mr '69
FRANCOEUR, Robert
  Great American worker-priest movement.
    Commonweal 89:636-7; 90:85-6 F 21, Ap 4
    '69
FRANCOIS, Terry A.
  Black man looks at black racism. por Read
    Digest 95:209-14 S '69
FRANK, Anne
  House of silence. H. Frankel. Holiday 46:16+
    S '69
FRANK, Anne, museum. See Amsterdam,
    Netherlands—Historic houses, etc.
FRANK, Bernhard
  Department meeting; poem. Engl J 58:61 Ja
    '69
FRANK, J. A. See Sweeney, G. E. jt. auth.
FRANK, Jacob, and Seitz, M. W.
  Parking garage, mall and office complex.
    Am City 34:108-9+ Ag '69
FRANK, Jean Michel
  Relevance of Jean-Michel Frank. A. Auer-
    bach. il House B 111:144-7 O '69
FRANK, Kenneth D. and Zimmerman, W. F.
  Action spectra for phase shifts of a circadian
    rhythm in drosophila. bibliog Science 163:
    688-9 F 14 '69
FRANK Lloyd Wright school of architecture
  Frank Lloyd Wright was also a gifted land-
    scape architect; visit to Taliesin West near
    Phoenix. il Sunset 142:70-3 F '69
FRANK, M. and Pfaffmann, C.
  Taste nerve fibers: a random distribution of
    sensitivities to four tastes. bibliog Science
    164:1183-5 Je 6 '69
FRANKEL, Charles
  Out of touch in Washington; excerpt from
    High on foggy bottom: an outsider's in-
    side view of the government. Sat R 52:21-
    3+ N 1 '69; Same abr. with title Making
    democracy work. Cur 113:27-32 D '69
  Silenced majority. Sat R 52:22+ D 13 '69
FRANKEL, Haskel
  House of silence. Holiday 46:16+ S '69
  On the fringe (cont) Sat R 52:29 Mr 8; 30 Je
    14; 30 S 13; 45 N 29 '69
FRANKEL, Max, and Semple, R. B. Jr
  If it's Thursday, this must be Rashtrapati
    Bhavan. N Y Times Mag p26-7+ Ag 17 '69
FRANKEL, Raymond
  What's my line? por Forbes 104:72+ D 1 '69
FRANKENSTEIN, Alfred
  Continental harmony of William Billings. Hi
    Fi 19:79 S '69
  Fidelio to remember. Hi Fi 19:MA20 D '69
  Music of Vaughan Williams, round two. Hi
    Fi 19:105 S '69
FRANKENTHALER, Helen
  We talk to..; interview. ed. by A. Gins-
    berg. por Mlle 69:343-4 Ag '69

about
  Art world; exhibition at the Whitney muse-
    um. H. Rosenberg. New Yorker 45:116+
    Mr 29 '69
  Colorful gesture; exhibition at Whitney mu-
    seum. N. Y. H. Rosenstein. il Art N 68:29-
    31+ Mr '69
  Gestalts of color. D. L. Shirey. por News-
    week 73:101-2+ Mr 24 '69
  Heiress to a new tradition. il pors Time 93:
    64-9 Mr 28 '69
FRANKFORT on the Main

Music
  Report: Frankfurt; production of Die frau
    ohne schatten. D. Stevens. Opera N 34:28
    D 6 '69
FRANKFURT book fair. See Book fairs
FRANKFURTER, Jack
  Cover: From the artist's studio. il por Am
    Artist 32:6 N '68
FRANKFURTERS
  Looking after the hot dog; fat limit. Time
    93:17 Je 27 '69
  No stomach for the undercover chickenfur-
    ter; hot dog regulations. W. Zinsser. il
    Life 67:24B O 3 '69
    See also
  Cookery—Meat
FRANKING privilege
  It's a privilege; misuse by Senators Charles
    Percy and Robert Griffin. D. Sanford. New
    Repub 162:9-10 Ja 3 '70
  Penalty clause on franked envelopes. H.
    Herst, jr. Hobbies 74:131+ D '69
FRANKLIN, Ben A.
  Scandal of death and injury in the mines.
    N Y Times Mag p25-7+ Mr 30; p62+ My 4
    '69
FRANKLIN, Benjamin

Drama
  Ben Franklin plays cupid. M. A. Nicholson.
    Plays 28:63-7 My '69
FRANKLIN, Hal A. 2d
  Mississippi revisited; photographs. Ebony 24:
    46-9+ Jl '69
FRANKLIN, Pamela
  On my own at last! ed. by E. Miller. por
    Seventeen 28:96-7+ Ja '69
FRANKLIN, Viola
  We do not cry. Redbook 132:98-9+ Ap '69
FRANKLIN, William M.
  Future of the Foreign relations series; ad-
    dress. June 16, 1969. bibliog f Dept State
    Bul 61:247-51 S 15 '69
FRANKLIN (aircraft carrier) See Aircraft
    carriers
FRANKLIN book programs, incorporated
  Franklin to open clearing house for rights. il
    Pub W 196:30 D 8 '69
  Future of Franklin book programs. R. H.
    Smith. Pub W 195:47 Je 9 '69
  Harwood named chairman of Franklin book
    programs. Pub W 196:249 Ag 25 '69
FRANKLIN mint
  How to collect coin from coin collectors;
    commemorative medals and tokens for gas
    station games. il Bsns W p 150-1 My 24 '69
  Joe Segel's private mint. il Forbes 104: 28-9 O
    15 '69
FRANKLINIAS
  You can grow the rare franklinia. J. Krill. il
    House B 111:71+ S '69
FRANKLIN'S trees. See Franklinias
FRANNY; story. See Amft. M. J.
FRANTZ, John C.
  (ed) Outreach, or oblivion? bibliog por Wilson
    Lib Bul 43:848-903 My '69
FRANZ, Maurice
  Garden calendar. Org Gard & Farm 16:62-5
    Je; 64-7 O; 77-80 N '69
  Thanksgiving-day tomatoes. Org Gard &
    Farm 16:78-9 N '69
  What makes garden power tools tick? Org
    Gard & Farm 16:69-73 Ja '69
FRANZA, August
  Liveliest art in the classroom. Engl J 58:1233-
    7 N '69
FRANZEN, Ulrich
  Franzen unifies an architecture of fragments
    into good places for people. il Arch Rec
    145:113-32 F '69
FRANZMEIER, Stephen A.
  Driving under the influence of emotion. To-
    days Health 47:40-1+ O '69
FRAREY, Carlyle J. and Rosenstein, R. S.
  Placement & salary picture in 1968: onward
    and upward. Library J 94:2425-9 Je 15 '69
FRASER, Lady Antonia (Pakenham)
  Gilded travellers. Vogue 153:262 Ap 1 '69

FRASER, Charles Elbert
Battle for a Georgia island. il por Bsns W p 128-9 S 6 '69
FRASER, Dorothy
What's new in the social sciences curriculum. Ed Digest 35:29-31 N '69
FRASER, James
Children's literature as a scholarly resource: the need for a national plan. bibliog Library J 94:4490-1 D 15 '69
FRASER, James Earle
Dakota boyhood. Am Heritage 20:81-8 D '68
FRASER, Kennedy
Books. New Yorker 45:134+ Ap 5 '69
FRASER, R. D. B.
Keratins; with biographical sketch. Sci Am 221:12, 86-96 Ag '69
FRASER, Stewart E. and Josephson, B. S.
Educational tradition and change in Iceland; excerpts from Education in Iceland. Sch & Soc 97:338-9 O '69
FRATER, Alexander
Stick it on the wall in Stockholm. Holiday 45:85-6 F '69
FRATERNITIES. See College fraternities
Die FRAU ohne schatten; opera. See Strauss, R.
FRAUD
Airlines join to fight illegal charters. J. W. Carter. Aviation W 91:41-2+ Ag 4 '69
Credit mobilier; construction company building government-backed railroads. J. L. Phillips. il Am Heritage 20:108-9 Ap '69
Fine art of fran-chiseling; franchising frauds. R. Levy. Duns R 93:38 Ja '69
Getting your money's worth; unscrupulous salesmen and unethical business practices. il Sr Schol 94:24 My 2 '69
Gourmet pirate; con man J. P. Lafitte. il Time 94:18 D 19 '69
Ten traps the gypsters set for you. il Changing T 23:11-12 Mr '69
Unity urged to combat credit card fraud. J. W. Carter. il Aviation W 90:39+ F 3 '69
    See also
Diplomas, Fraudulent
Forgery of works of art
Impostors and imposture
Quacks and quackery
FRAUDULENT voting. See Elections—Corrupt practices
FRAUENKNECHT, Alfred
Israel using Atar tooling data to prolong Mirage usefulness. Aviation W 91:20 O 6 '69
FRAUMENI, Joseph F. jr, and others
Simian virus 40 in polio vaccine: follow-up of newborn recipients. bibliog Science 167: 59-60 Ja 2 '70
FRAYN, Michael
This earth, this realm, this plastic finnan haddie. Horizon 11:120 Sum '69
FRAZER, A. H.
High-temperature plastics; with biographical sketch. Sci Am 221:16, 96-100+ Jl '69
FRAZER, John
Kuwait: Aladdin's lamp of the Middle East. Nat Geog 135:636-67 My '69
FRAZIER, Alexander
Curriculum planners are doing their thing. PTA Mag 64:16-18 bibliog(p36) N '69
FRAZIER, Donald T. and others
Hemicholinium-3: noncholinergic effects on squid axons. bibliog Science 163:820-1 F 21 '69
FRAZIER, George, 4th
John Steinbeck! John Steinbeck! How still we see thee lie. Esquire 72:150-1+ N '69
Last artisans. Esquire 72:57-64 Jl '69
Opinion: on being a bachelor. por Mlle 69: 16+ S '69
Sense of style. Esquire 71:58+ Je: 72:191-5 S '69
'30s. Mlle 69:168+ My '69
FRAZIER, Joe
Flaunt it and you may lose it. M. Kram. il pors Sports Illus 31:26-9 Jl 7 '69
Frazier's quarry. il por Newsweek 74:84 Jl 7 '69
Joe Frazier: the six-state champ. G. Astor. il pors Look 33:88-9+ Je 24 '69
Winner, and still (partial) champ. il por Time 94:36 Jl 4 '69
FRAZIER, John E.
Gandhi: apostle of non-violence. Read Digest 95:102-7 S '69
FREBERG, Stan
Thyme (rhymes with time) il Newsweek 73:70 Mr 31 '69
FRED, James A.
Simple checker for semiconductors. Pop Mech 131:146-7 My '69
FREDERICK, Sue Ellen, and Newcomb, E. H.
Microbody-like organelles in leaf cells. bibliog Science 163:1353-5 Mr 21 '69

FREDERICKSON, Donald T.
Calling Dr Killjoy. il por Time 93:82+ My 9 '69
FREDERIKSEN, Harald
Feedbacks in economic and demographic transition; adaptation of address, June 1969. bibliog Science 166:837-47 N 14 '69
FREDRICKSON, Olive A.
Nightmare spring. Outdoor Life 144:40-3+ Jl '69
We saw the ice go out. Outdoor Life 143:52-5+ My '69
FREE, John R.
IC electronics for shutterbugs. Radio-Electr 40:39-42 F '69
FREE democratic party. See Political parties— Germany (Federal Republic)
FREE energy
Free-energy transfer in plants. J. S. Boyer. bibliog il Science 163:1219-20 Mr 14 '69
FREE enterprise
Consumer and the producer. P. J. McNulty. Yale R 58:537-48 Je '69
Difference is the system; relative buying power of U.S. and Soviet workers. il Nations Bsns 57:63 O '69
Sickness of government; excerpts from The age of discontinuity. P. F. Drucker. il Nations Bsns 57:52-61 Mr '69
Yugoslavs dabble in capitalism. il Bsns W p 108+ Ag 16 '69
FREE forms. See Natural forms
FREE-lance writers. See Authors
FREE-lance writing. See Authorship
FREE library of Philadelphia. See Philadelphia —Free library
FREE Methodist church of North America. See Methodist church in the United States
FREE ports and zones
Machiasport gets two new bidders; battle over building a refinery at Machiasport, Me. Bsns W p20 Jl 5 '69
FREE press. See Freedom of the press
FREE public library of the borough of Madison, N.J. See Madison, N.J.—Free public library
FREE radicals. See Radicals (chemistry)
FREE schools

Denmark

See Private schools—Denmark

FREE speech
Concerned citizen speaks about America's turmoil; address, May 22, 1969. J. L. Robertson. US News 66:96+ Je 9 '69
Dissent and reaction in Missouri; with letter by J. Bodger. R. McLeod. il Wilson Lib Bul 44:269-76 N '69
First amendment: alive and well; B. Spock, W. S. Coffin, jr, M. Goodman and M. Ferber freed from further prosecution. Chr Cent 86:971 Jl 23 '69
Is treason permissible as merely free speech? students wearing black armbands in the classroom. D. Lawrence. U S News 66:108 Mr 10 '69
Methodists, Brethren, F.O.R. rebuke the Vice-President; muzzling of the media by government. Chr Cent 86:1541 D 3 '69
Mississippi muzzle; stifling freedom of speech on campuses. C. Wilkie. Nation 208:132-3 F 3 '69
Soldiers on the war; supporters of Pentagon policy. New Repub 161:5-6 D 6 '69
Spiro Agnew explains himself. S. T. Agnew. Life 67:34-5 N 28 '69
Threat from Spiro. Commonweal 91:293-4 D 5 '69
    See also
Academic freedom
Blasphemy
Contempt of court
Libel and slander
FREE trade and protection
Foreign competition, biggest problem in the 1970s? comments of members of the president's panel. G. R. Rosen. Duns R 94:41-2+ D '69
New protectionism. H. Hazlitt Nat R 21:485-8+ My 20 '69; Reply. A. Barro. 21:730 Jl 29 '69
Nixon's stance; foreign trade policy. il Newsweek 74:72+ D 1 '69
    See also
Import quotas
Tariff
FREE universities
Free university. R. H. Farber. il Sch & Soc 97:356-8 O '69
Midpeninsula: the ivy league. K. Power. Nation 208:463-4 Ap 14 '69
Shadow schools. il Time 93:56+ Je 6 '69

FREE will and determinism
  See also
  Election (theology)
  Freedom (theology)
  Obedience
  Pelagianism
FREED, Doris Jonas, and Foster, H. H. Jr
  Divorce American style. bibliog f Ann Am
    Acad 383:71-88 My '69
FREED, Eleanor
  Windfall for Texas. Art in Am 57:78-85 N '69
FREED, Jeffrey P.
  Japan 1970: year of upheaval. Nation 209:
    374-9 O 13 '69
FREED, Richard
  Guide to Russcol's guide. Sat R 52:80 N 29 '69
FREED, Roy N.
  Get the computer system you want. bibliog
    f Harvard Bsns R 47:99-108 N '69
FREEDMAN, Philip I.
  Middle class values, lower class rights. bibliog
    Clear House 43:469-70 Ap '69
FREEDMAN, Richard
  Dabblers and addicts. New Repub 160:30-1
    F 15 '69
  Star-crossed Hector and his Harriet. Life 66:
    14 My 30 '69
  Synthesizing Johann S. Bach. Life 66:12 Ja
    24 '69
  Yonghy-bonghy-bo. New Repub 160:28-30 Ap
    5 '69
FREEDMEN
  More about Richard Stanup. George Washing-
    ton's chief of servants. il Negro Hist Bul 32:
    16-18 My '69
  Richard Stanup who had charge of George
    Washington's slaves. il Negro Hist Bul 32:
    12-13 F '69
  To my old master; excerpt from The freed-
    men's book. L. M. Child. Negro Hist Bul
    32:15 Ja '69
FREEDOM. See Liberty
FREEDOM (theology)
  Delusion and reality. C. D. Linton. Chr Today
    14:4-7 O 10 '69
FREEDOM, Intellectual. See Intellectual lib-
  erty
FREEDOM house (organization)
  Present state of freedom; survey on state of
    freedom throughout the world. America
    120:123 F 1 '69
FREEDOM house/Books USA
  Book hunger is insatiable. L. R. Sussman.
    ALA Bul 63:1577-81 D '69
FREEDOM, Integration, God, honor, today
  (organization) See Civil rights organizations
FREEDOM of conscience. See Liberty of con-
  science
FREEDOM of Information. See Information,
  Freedom of
FREEDOM of information act. See Informa-
  tion, Freedom of
FREEDOM of speech. See Free speech
FREEDOM of teaching. See Academic freedom
FREEDOM of the press
  Freedom in South Africa. il Time 94:46 Jl 18
    '69
  Let them write responsibly; freedom of the
    press in the high school. R. J. Sullivan. Ed
    Digest 34:50-1 Ja '69
  Right to moonlight; H. P. Leifermann sus-
    pended by UPI for uncensored article. Na-
    tion 209:37 Jl 14 '69
  Who owns journalism? movement to offer
    employees ownership, profits and a voice
    in management. il Time 95:60-1 Ja 19 '70
  World's press: just how free is it? excerpt
    from The best cause: free press-free people.
    J. Hohenberg. Sat R 52:70-2 D 13 '69
  See also
  Censorship
  Free speech
  Government and the press
  Libel and slander
  Newspapers
FREEDOM of the seas
  See also
  Territorial waters
FREEDOM of thought. See Intellectual liberty
FREEDOM riders. See Negroes—Segregation.
  Resistance to
FREEDOM to read. See Intellectual liberty
FREEDOM to travel. See Travel regulations
FREELANCE editing. See Editors and editing
FREEMAN, Anne Hobson
  What ever became of Agnes Mason? story.
    McCalls 96:76-7 Ja '69
FREEMAN, Bob A. See Lewis, A. C. jt. auth.
FREEMAN, Bud
  Hoagy; interview, ed. by I. Kolodin. Sat R
    52:43-5+ Je 28 '69

FREEMAN, Catherine (Dove)
  Catherine Freeman recollected; interview, ed.
    by B. Goldsmith. por Harp Baz 102:290-1
    S '69
FREEMAN, Frank
  Bravura in Brooklyn. C. Robinson. il Arch
    Forum 131:42-7 N '69
FREEMAN, Jean Todd
  Games children don't play; story. Ladies
    Home J 86:100-1 Mr '69
  Who am I? story. Redbook 132:88-9 Ap '69
FREEMAN, Jim
  Jump-fishing for rainbows. Field & S 74:56-7+
    My '69
  Topknot tactics. Field & S 74:60-1+ N '69
FREEMAN, Jo
  New feminists. Nation 208:241-4 F 24 '69
FREEMAN, John
  Ambassador extraordinary. il por Time 93:20
    Mr 7 '69
FREEMAN, John W. Jr
  Magnetospheric wind. bibliog Science 163:
    1061-2 Mr 7 '69
FREEMAN, Norman
  Gear and gadgets for the one design. Yacht-
    ing 125:64-5+ My '69
FREEMAN, Orville Lothrop
  Land to live in; toward an urban/rural bal-
    ance. Cur 111:33-9 O '69
FREEMAN, Roger A.
  Dead end in American education. Nat R 21:
    22-4 Ja 14 '69; Same abr. Ed Digest 34:9-12
    My '69
FREESE, Arthur S.
  Amazing Boston arm. pors Pop Mech 131:102-
    6+ Mr '69
  Amazing new instantaneous fire extinguish-
    er. Pop Mech 132:93-5+ O '69
  Crazy things they'll use to build your new
    house. Sci Digest 65:42-8+ F '69
  He was a medical dynamo. Todays Health 47:
    58-9+ My '69
  How they keep you safe; without getting
    you killed. Pop Mech 132:78-81+ Ag '69
  MHD: giant blowtorches promise cheaper elec-
    tric power. Pop Sci 194:88-91 Je '69
  Mayo: from frontier medicine to clinic fame.
    Todays Health 47:58-9+ D '69
  Mechanics of medicine: a 200-mph surgical
    drill, the steady beap of a heart monitor
    and an electronic voice box. Pop Mech 132:
    138-41+ O '69
  Medical engineers: doctor/designers for to-
    morrow's people. bibliog Sci Digest 66:46-
    8+ S '69
  Microsurgery: medicine's big new hope. Sci
    Digest 65:7-11 My '69
  Salmonella: food poison plus. Todays Health
    47:34-5+ Ap '69
  Time of your life. Pop Mech 130:108-13+ D
    '68
  Useful organ we can live without. Todays
    Health 47:65-7+ N '69
  World's sharpest tool. Pop Mech 132:100-3+
    S '69
  (ed) See Dubos, R. Scientist talks about
    careers in science
FREEWAYS. See Express highways
FREEZE-dried coffee. See Coffee, Freeze-dried
FREEZE drying
  I'm not stuffed. I'm freeze-dried! Smith-
    sonian's process. W. O'Neill. il Pop Mech
    132:78-81 D '69
  See also
  Coffee, Freeze-dried
FREEZERS
  New light on food freezers. Am Home 72:68
    Je '69
            Care
  Care and safekeeping of refrigerators and
    freezers. House & Gard 135:194-5 Ap '69
FREEZING
  Yes, Mpemba, hot water can freeze faster.
    Chem 42:3 D '69
FREEZING of food
  Du Pont goes to the freezer; Freon freezant
    system for fast-freezing foods. il Bsns W
    p 146+ F 22 '69
  Freeze it! Tips and techniques to help you
    make the best use of your freezer. il Good
    H 168:238-9 My '69
  Great freeze-ahead diet. il Ladies Home J
    86:104-5+ Mr '69
  Ground beef mix you can freeze. Farm J 93:46
    Je '69
  How to wrap food for your freezer. il Bet
    Hom & Gard 47:104 S '69
FREI, Eduardo
  Fading romance. il por Newsweek 73:59-60
    Mr 17 '69
  Latin-American showcase where reforms
    went sour. il por U S News 66:68-9 Mr 17
    '69

FREIGHT airplanes. See Airplanes, Freight
FREIGHT and freightage
   See also
  Air freight service
  Railroads—Freight service
  Shipping
FREIGHT handling
   See also
  Containerization (freight)
  Trucking
FREIGHT payment plan. See Banks and banking—Freight payment plan
FREIGHT trains. See Railroads—Freight trains
FREIGHT vessels
  Barges that cross the ocean; transportation of barge ships. il Time 94:94+ S 12 '69
  Oceangoing drive-in; RO/RO container ships. J. Liston. il Pop Mech 132:100-3 N '69
  One morning at the Pierre; U.S. Lines' conversion to containerization. il Forbes 104:30-1 N 1 '69
  Roll-on ships gather more cargo; roll-on/roll-off trailer ship. il Bsns W p74-6 My 10 '69
  U.S. shipping steers back into the money; use of container ships. Bsns W p52-3 D 13 '69
  Why barges break the mixing rule. il Bsns W p 104+ Ja 10 '70

      Chartering
  Convenient marriage on the high seas; Sealand to charter U.S. lines containerships. Bsns W p46 O 11 '69
FREIRE, Nelson
  Joyful discovery. il por Time 95:64 Ja 19 '70
  Music to my ears; performance at the Hollywood bowl. I. Kolodin. Sat R 52:45 S 6 '69
FREISER, Leonard H.
  Community, library, and revolution. Library J 95:39-41 Ja 1 '70
FREIT, Gina
  It takes courage to float through the air. por Seventeen 28:92+ Ja '69
FREMANTLE, Anne
  Balm in Gilead; story. New Yorker 45:41-5 S 13 '69
FRENCH, Charles
  Coin quiz. See issues of Hobbies
  Numismatics. See issues of Hobbies
FRENCH, M. C. and Jefferies, D. J.
  Degradation and disappearance of ortho, para isomer of technical DDT in living and dead avian tissues. bibliog Science 165:914-16 Ag 29 '69
  —See Jefferies, D. J. jt. auth.
FRENCH, Michael J. and others
  Laser beat frequency spectroscopy. bibliog Science 163:345-51 Ja 24 '69
FRENCH
  French, by S. de Gramont. Review
    Sat R 52:31-4+ S 20 '69. L. Galantiere
   See also
  Parisians
FRENCH art. See Art, French
FRENCH artificial satellites. See Artificial satellites, French
FRENCH bronzes. See Bronzes
FRENCH CANADIANS
  Quebec: uneasy province. C. De Mestral. Chr Cent 86:427-9 Mr 26 '69; Reply. K. Barker. 86:683 My 14 '69
  Stream of the past; lives of the voyageurs, excerpts from Open horizons. S. Olson. il Am West 6:28-33 Mr '69
   See also
  Acadians in Louisiana
FRENCH chansons. See Songs, French
FRENCH cookery. See Cookery, French
FRENCH CORSICA. See Corsica
FRENCH GUIANA
  France's pad in South America. il Time 93:42 Mr 14 '69
FRENCH house decoration. See House decoration, French
FRENCH in the United States

      History
  Louis Philippe in America. M. Bishop. il Am Heritage 20:42-5+ Ap '69
FRENCH language

    Study and teaching
  Grouping foreign language students. M. Hernick and D. Kennedy. Todays Ed 58:38-9 Ja '69
  Waning echo in Cajun country. D. Snell. Life 66:18B Mr 14 '69
FRENCH literary prizes. See Literary prizes

FRENCH literature
   See also
  Surrealism
FRENCH painting. See Painting, French
FRENCH pastry. See Pastry
FRENCH photographers. See Photographers, French
FRENCH poetry
   See also
  Poets, French

   Translations into English
  Cadences; Matter; The square; The tragic in time; The useful; The song of the dragoon; The secret; tr. by W. S. Merwin. J. Follain. Atlan 224:78-9 Ag '69
  Victor Hugo on the burning of a library, juin 1871; excerpt from L'annee terrible, tr. by M. Blind. V. Hugo. il Wilson Lib Bul 43:980-1 Je '69
   See also
  Provençal poetry—Translations into English
FRENCH poets. See Poets, French
FRENCH police. See Police—France
FRENCH Polynesia. See Polynesia
FRENCH quarter. See New Orleans
FRENCH revolution. See France—History—Revolution
FRENCH seamen. See Seamen
FRENCH songs. See Songs, French
FRENCH students
   See also
  Student demonstrations—France
FRENCH wines. See Wine
FRENKEL, J. K. and others
  Toxoplasma gondii: fecal forms separated from eggs of the nematode toxocara cati. bibliog Science 164:432-3 Ap 25 '69
FREON freezant system. See Freezing of food
FREQUENCY calibrators. See Calibrators
FREQUENCY counters. See Counting machines and devices
FREQUENCY distribution. See Distribution (probability theory)
FREQUENCY measurement
  Build the Popular electronics universal frequency counter. D. Lancaster. il Pop Electr 30:33-5+ Mr; 41-5 Ap '69
  Simple frequency counter. R. L. Carroll. il Electr World 82:82 Jl '69
FREQUENCY modulation. See Radio frequency modulation
FREQUENCY standards
  Audio equalization curves up-to-date. T. R. Haskett. il Electr World 82:44-6 D '69
FRERICHS, Allen H.
  Look at adolescent music. Clear House 43:435-8 Mr '69
FRESCOES
  Miracle from the desert; frescoes from Faras. il Time 94:68 S 5 '69
FRESH fruit. See Fruit
FRESH water biology
  Strontium-90 concentration factors of lake plankton, macrophytes, and substrates. Z. Kalnina and G. Polikarpov. bibliog il Science 164:1517-19 Je 27 '69
   See also
  Fresh water ecology
  Limnology
FRESH water ecology
  Ecology of a reservoir; Quabbin reservoir, Mass. P. A. Erickson and J. T. Reynolds. il Natur Hist 78:48-53 N '69
  Trailing Lewis and Clark. B. Jensen. il Natur Hist 78:8-10+ bibliog(75) Ag '69
FRESH water flora. See Aquatic plants
FRESH water mussels. See Mussels, Fresh water
FRESNO, Calif.
  Christmas fantasyland. T. Hoxie. il Am City 84:104 D '69
  City insures home mortgages. Am City 84:26 F '69
FREUD, Sigmund
  Freudian affair. Time 95:41 Ja 12 '70
FREUDENBERGER, John
  Bryant Woods: blueprint for flexibility. Library J 94:4225-7 N 15 '69
FREUDIANISM. See Psychoanalysis
FREUND, Paul A.
  Dignity and human fullfillment; address, June 1, 1969. Vital Speeches 35:556-8 Jl 1 '69
FREUND, Peter George Oliver
  Gravity and infinity. D. E. Thomsen. il por Sci N 95:512-13 My 24 '69

FREY, Sherman H.
Policy formulation: a plan involving teachers.
Clear House 43:259-63 Ja '69
FREY, Thomas J.
Private vehicle inspection. Am City 84:112-13
Ap '69
FRIBERG, H. Daniel
Why Christ died. Chr Today 13:8-11 Jl 4 '69
FRIBERG, Tennys E.
In this valley we believe. Org Gard & Farm
16:48-9 Ap '69
FRICKER, John
Foreign accent. See issues of Flying
FRIED, Anne
Today's counselors are different; address.
Camp Mag 41:8-9 F '69
FRIED, Edward R.
International liquidity and foreign aid. For
Affairs 48:139-49 O '69
FRIED, Eunice
Europe's autumn wine festivals. Travel 132:
52-5+ S '69
FRIED, Norman
How to make a better tripod than you can
buy. Pop Sci 194:159-63+ F '69
FRIEDBERG, Judith
Emperor's pastry shop. Travel & Camera 32:
60-1+ Jl '69
From Lisbon to Madrid to Spain's Costa Del
Sol. Club continental's travelers tried out
a new kind of tour. Travel & Camera 32:
86-8+ O '69
South of the border, silver is as good as
gold. Travel & Camera 32:10 N '69
FRIEDBERG, Maurice
Soviet Jewry today. Commentary 48:45-7 Ag
'69
FRIEDEL, Ludwig
Patterns: do people help? J. Scully. Mod
Phot 33:58-63 My '69
FRIEDEL, Robert
Education at Brown: making the system
work for you. Seventeen 29:42 Ja '70
FRIEDENBERG, Edgar Z.
Generation gap. bibliog f Ann Am Acad 382:
32-42 Mr '69
Hidden costs of opportunity. Atlan 223:84-90
F '69
FRIEDGUT, Jac
Commuters and city income taxes. por
Nations Bsns 57:66 O '69
FRIEDLAND, William H.
Labor waste in New York: rural exploita-
tion and migrant workers. bibliog por
Trans-Action 6:48-53 F '69
—and Edwards, Harry
Confrontation at Cornell. pors Trans-Action
6:29-36+ Je; 7:62-3 D '69
FRIEDMAN, B. H.
Ivory garage. Art N 68:52-5 Ap '69
Plastic resurrection. Art N 68:59-61+ N '69
FRIEDMAN, Bruce Jay
Different ball game; story. Esquire 72:229 D
'69
Don't dare put me in your play! Writer 82:
16-18 Je '69
Partners; story. Esquire 72:72-4 Ag '69
FRIEDMAN, Edward
Now's time to talk with China. Bul Atom
Sci 25:10-11+ Je '69
FRIEDMAN, Gilbert B.
Why automobile insurance rates keep going up;
excerpt from Are you being taken for a
ride? Atlan 224:58-63 S '69
FRIEDMAN, Joseph Joel
Community psychiatry: a bold new approach
Ment Hy 53:482-3 Jl '69
FRIEDMAN, Joyce
I now think of the American Indian as being
very artistic. por Wilson Lib Bul 44:64-8 S
'69
FRIEDMAN, Leon
Legal gouging. New Repub 160:40-1 F 1 '69
Sacco, Vanzetti and the Scottsboro boys.
New Repub 160:25-8 Mr 22 '69
FRIEDMAN, Lynne
Painting city walls. Sch Arts 69:28-9 Ja '70
FRIEDMAN, Milton
[Column on economic questions] por See
issues of Newsweek
End the surtax. por Newsweek 73:74 F 10 '69;
Same abr. with title Taxes, everybody's
headache; case against the surtax. Read
Digest 94:67-8 Je '69
Excerpt from The public be damned; re-
print. Cong Digest 48:95 Mr '69
about
Great iconoclast has a shocking answer. por
Bsns W p82 Jl 19 '69
Intellectual provocateur. il por Time 94:71 D
19 '69
FRIEDMAN, Murray
Is white racism the problem? Commentary 47:
61-5 Ja; 6 Ap '69

FRIEDMAN, Neil
(ed) Learning in black colleges. Wilson Lib
Bul 44:49-74 S '69
Under the leaking roof. por Wilson Lib Bul
44:69-74 S '69
FRIEDMAN, Paul
Like it really is. R. Hattersley. il Pop Phot
65:114-17+ D '69
FRIEDMAN, Ralph
High-level disaffection. Nation 209:398 O 20
'69
FRIEDMANN, Nadav, and Miller, S. L.
Phenylalanine and tyrosine synthesis under
primitive earth conditions. bibliog Science
166:766-7 N 7 '69
FRIEDRICH, Otto
I am Marty Ackerman..; excerpts from Dec-
line and fall. Harper 239:92-100+ D '69
FRIEND, Robert
Letter to P; poem. New Yorker 45:78 Ag 30
'69
FRIEND for a season; story. See Harrison, D.
FRIENDLINESS. See Kindness
FRIENDLY, Alfred
Fedayeen. Atlan 224:12+ S '69
FRIENDLY, Fred W.
Some sober second thoughts on Vice Presi-
dent Agnew. Sat R 52:61-2+ D 13 '69
FRIENDLY giant (television program)   See
Television broadcasting—Childrens pro-
grams
FRIENDS, Society of
Quaker movement west. H. B. Kuhn. Chr
Today 14:46-7 N 21 '69
See also
American Friends service committee
FRIENDSHIP
Personal friends. B. W. Overstreet. PTA
Mag 63:14-15 Ap '69
She's my best friend but . . . questions and an-
swers. A. Wood. Seventeen 28:180 S '69
See also
Love
Neighbors
Playmates
FRIERMAN, J. D. and others
X-ray fluorescence spectrography: use in field
archaeology. Science 164:588 My 2 '69
FRIES, Heinrich
Faith and conviction; excerpt from Faith
under challenge. Cath World 210:119-23 D
'69
FRIGATES, Atomic powered. See Warships,
Atomic powered
FRIGGENS, Paul
Gift of the glaciers. Read Digest 95:21-2+
O '69
Great Alaska oil rush. Read Digest 95:66-70
Jl '69
FRIGIDITY (psychology)
Frigidity, the myth that plagues too many
women. A. Fleming. il Redbook 132:68-9+
Mr '69
FRIMBO, Ernest M.
Mr Frimbo on the Metroliner; interview. New
Yorker 45:29-31 My 17 '69
FRINGE benefits. See Non-wage payments
FRINGS, Joseph, cardinal
Steely cardinal. por Newsweek 73:84 Mr 10
'69
FRISCH, Bruce H.
Aging, the disease with a cure. Sci Digest
65:32-6 F '69
Once we've reached the moon. il Sci Digest
65:42-51 Ap '69
They find moonscapes on the earth. Sci Di-
gest 66:18-23 O '69
FRISCH, Ragnar
Awards for the modelmakers. il por Time
94:96 N 7 '69
Models bring Nobel prize. Sci N 96:397 N 1
'69
Nobel laureates in economics, chemistry,
and physics. L. R. Klein. por Science 166:
715-17 N 7 '69
Two remarkable men. P. A. Samuelson.
Newsweek 74:108 N 17 '69
FRISHMAN, Robert Franchot
I was a prisoner in Hanoi; ed. by L. R.
Stockstill. Read Digest 95:111-15 D '69
Two American POW's; interview. ed. by O.
Fallaci. por Look 33:30-2 Jl 15 '69
FRISSELL, Toni
Lindsays of New York; photographs. Vogue
153:182-9 My '69
FRITCHEY, Clayton
Must the Democrats concede? Cur 110:30-1
S '69
FRITCHMAN, Stephen Hole
Controversial. Nation 210:5 Ja 12 '70
FRITO-Lay, incorporated
Ban the Bandito? il Newsweek 74:82+ D 22
'69

FRITZ, G. and others
X-ray pulsar in the Crab nebula. bibliog Science 164:709-12 My 9 '69

FRITZ, Jean
Mr Sterling, darling; story. Seventeen 27:112-13 D '68

FROEHLICH, Cathy
Fairy tale year; poem. Horn Bk 45:712 D '69

FROGS
Allantoinase; association with amphibian hepatic peroxisomes. L. P. Visentin and J. M. Allen. bibliog il Science 163:1463-4 Mr 28 '69
Bullfrog (rana catesbeiana) ventilation: how does the frog breathe? C. Gans and others. bibliog il Science 163:1223-5 Mr 14 '69
Celebrated bullfrogs of Dorchester County. E. H. Nabb. il Motor B 123:90-1+ F '69
Pars intermedia: unitary electrical activity regulated by light. K. Oshima and A. Gorbman. bibliog il Science 163:195-7 Ja 10 '69
Toxin from skin of frogs of the genus atelopus: differentiation from dendrobatid toxins. F. A. Fuhrman and others. bibliog il Science 165:1376-7 S 26 '69
Transplantation of pluripotential nuclei from triploid frog tumors. R. G. McKinnell and others bibliog il Science 165:394-6 Jl 25 '69
See also
Cookery—Frogs legs
Tadpoles

FROHMAN, Lawrence A. and others
Hypothalamic stimulation of growth hormone secretion. bibliog Science 162:580-2; 163:705 N 1 '68, F 14 '69

FROLIC, B. Michael
As the plane lands in Moscow the people cheer. N Y Times Mag p62-3+ O 26 '69

FROM the second city; musical comedy. See Musical comedies, revues, etc.—Criticisms, plots, etc.

FROME, Michael
Conservation. See issues of Field & stream
Conservation and the Nixon years. Field & S 73:8+ Mr '69
Must our campgrounds be outdoor slums? Read Digest 95:169-70+ S '69

FROMM, Erika
Manifest and the latent content of two paintings by Hieronymus Bosch. bibliog Am Imago 25:145-66 Sum '69

FRONT page; drama. See Hecht, B. and MacArthur, C.

FRONTIER and pioneer life

Alaska
Christmas in Alaska: in the first place, there was always snow. P. S. Coyne. il Nat R 21:1320-1+ D 30 '69

Canada
Nightmare spring; Canadian Northwest Territories. O. A. Fredrickson. il Outdoor Life 144:40-3+ Jl '69

United States
American land: as it was; with paintings by G. Harvey. W. Karp. Am Heritage 21:16-21 D '69
Appalachia: 1914. R. M. Ketchum. il Am Heritage 20:26-41+ F '69
Arizona vanquished; life on a military frontier. R. M. Utley. il Am West 6:16-21 N '69
Black man in the American West. D. T. Schoenberger. bibliog il Negro Hist Bul 32:7-11 Mr '69
Dakota boyhood. J. E. Fraser. il Am Heritage 20:81-8 D '68
Guns on the California trails. C. G. Worman. Hobbies 74:150-1 N '69
Louis Philippe in America. M. Bishop. il Am Heritage 20:42-5+ Ap '69
Pioneers and panthers. R. V. Anderson. bibliog il Cons 23:6-7 Je '69
See also
Trappers

FRONTIER broadcasting company. See Television stations

FROST, David
Newest host. por Newsweek 74:87 Ag 4 '69
What makes David Frost talk. P. Hellman. il pors N Y Times Mag p54-5+ D 7 '69

FROST, Everett C.
Adam's song. Chr Cent 86:711 My 21 '69

FROST, Lesley
Egg man's daughter. C. Baker. New Repub 161:30+ Ag 23 '69

FROST, Robert
Hidden terror of Robert Frost. C. B. Hands. Engl J 58:1162-8 N '69
I shan't be gone long. J. F. Light. Nation 210:26-8 Ja 12 '70

FROZEN desserts. See Ice cream, ices, etc.

FROZEN food. See Food, Frozen

FROZEN fruit juices. See Fruit juices, Frozen

FROZEN ground
Pipeline and permafrost; Alaska's north slope. Sci N 96:524 D 6 '69

FROZEN vegetables. See Vegetables, Frozen

FRUCHTL, Sister Gertrude F. and Brodeur, A. E.
Battered child. Cath World 209:156-9 Jl '69

FRUIT
Ecuador's edible jewels. M. B. Pomeroy. il Américas 21:33-7 Ap '69
Fresh fruits and compotes. E. Ross. il House & Gard 136:81-3+ Ag '69
Must great food be perfect. J. Olds. Org Gard & Farm 16:59 Ap '69
See also
Cookery—Fruit
also names of fruits, e.g. Peaches

Drying
Your own dried persimmons. il Sunset 143:172+ N '69

Pickling
6000 bottles of wine; excerpt from A farmhouse in Provence. M. R. Henry. Atlan 223:69-71 My '69

Preservation
How to preserve kumquats. il Sunset 142:126 F '69
See also
Canning and preserving

FRUIT, Canned
Dress-ups for canned fruits. il Bet Hom & Gard 47:139 Mr '69

FRUIT culture
Multiple-use orchard. 7,800 feet up. M. Colyer. il Org Gard & Farm 16:39-41 Ag '69
See also
Apple trees
Grafting
Spraying and dusting
also names of fruits. e.g. Pears

FRUIT cups. See Appetizers

FRUIT drinks. See Beverages

FRUIT flies
Irradiating the fruit fly. Bul Atom Sci 25:34+ D '69

FRUIT juices, Frozen
Orange flavor for meats, for fruits. il Sunset 142:137 F '69
Turning oranges into slabs; Tropicana quick-freeze technique. il Bsns W p94 Jl 26 '69

FRUIT salads. See Salads

FRUIT stands. See Roadside marketing

FRUIT trees
Taming wild fruits. E. Gibbons. Org Gard & Farm 16:67-9 Jl '69
To make citrus thrive all summer. Sunset 143:150 Jl '69
See also
Apple trees
Fruit culture
Grafting
Gustavia trees

FRUIT trees, Care of
Maypoles for fruit trees. V. Tripp. il Org Gard & Farm 16:76-7 D '69

FRUIT trees, Dwarf
Instant fruit and berries; dwarf varieties. P. E. Mahan. il Org Gard & Farm 16:86-7 N '69

Fertilization
See Fertilization of plants

FRUIT trees, Training of
See also
Fruit trees, Care of

FRUITCAKE. See Cake

FRUSH, James, Jr
Life care housing; interview. ed. by W. P. Dumont. por Har Yrs 9:6-13 D '69

FRUSTRATION
See also
Repression (psychology)

FRY, Amelia
Along the suffrage trail. Am West 6:16-25 Ja '69

FRY, C. George
Christianity's greatest challenge. Chr Today 14:9-12 N 7 '69
Day to remember. Chr Today 13:3-5 My 9 '69

FRY, Edward F.
Gerhard Richter, German illusionist. Art in Am 57:126-7 N '69
Inside the Trojan horse. Art N 68:36-9+ O '69

FRY, Gary F. and Moore, J. G.
 Enterobius vermicularis; 10,000-year-old human infection. bibliog Science 166:1620 D 26 '69
FRY, John R.
 No taste for truth. Senator McClellan? Chr Cent 86:1271 O 8 '69
FRY, Kenneth E.
 Central cities fight back. Nations Bsns 57: 60+ S '69
FRY, Peggy Crooke. See Eichenwald, H. F. jt. auth.
FRY, Ray MacNairn
 National topics for 1969 outlined by Ray Fry. Library J 94:927 Mr 1 '69
 Washington spring. K. Nyren. il Library J 94:1945-9 My 15 '69
 —and Carl, H. A.
 Washington reports. ALA Bul 63:576-7 My '69
FRYE, David
 On the griddle with Frye. il Time 95:47 Ja 5 '70
FRYE, John T.
 [Monthly article on electronics] See issues of Electronics world
FRYER, Jerome M.
 Gabriel's gamesman. S. Margetts. por Duns R 94:79-80+ O '69
FRYKOWSKI, Voyteck
 Tate set. il por Newsweek 74:24-5 Ag 25 '69
FUCHS, Estelle
 Free schools of Denmark. Sat R 52:44-6+ Ag 16 '69; Same abr. Ed Digest 35:5-8 D '69
FUCHS, Victor R.
 Service economy grows, but does it? il por Bsns W p 126+ F 15 '69
FUCHSIAS
 Easy way to root fuchsias. il Sunset 143:124-5 Ag '69
  See also
 Cape fuchsia
FUDALI, R. F.
 Coesite from the Richat dome, Mauritania: a misidentification. bibliog Science 166: 228-30 O 10 '69
FUEL
 Out of the bread, into the chips, and back again, and not even a dust of the hands! N. H. Miller. il Am West 6:44-8 Mr '69
FUEL cells
 Swedes see role for fuel cells growing in civil, military fields. il Aviation W 90:322 Je 2 '69
FUEL consumption of motor boats. See Marine engines—Fuel consumption
FUEL injection systems. See Automobile engines—Fuel feeding; Gas and oil engines, Outboard—Fuel feeding
FUEL pumps
 How it works: the mechanical fuel pump. C. Miller. il Motor B 124:140-1 N '69
FUEL systems of automobiles. See Automobile engines—Fuel feeding
FUEL systems of motor boats. See Marine engines—Fuel consumption
FUEL trucks. See Tank trucks
FUENTE, Luis
 Brief biography. S. Goodman. pors Dance Mag 43:68-9 S '69
FUENTES, Carlos
 Carlos Fuentes barred admission to U.S. Pub W 195:52 Mr 10 '69
 Fuentes case. R. H. Smith. Pub W 195:37 Mr 17 '69
FUERBRINGER, Otto
 Time: after Luce. R. Pollak. Harper 239:43-52 Jl '69
FUGARD, Athol
 Hello and goodbye. Criticism
  Nation 209:517-18 N 10 '69
  New Repub 161:24 O 11 '69
  New Yorker 45:97 S 27 '69
  Newsweek 74:106 S 29 '69
  Sat R 52:26 O 11 '69
FUGE, Paul H.
 Build VHV supply. Pop Electr 30:46 Ap '69
FUGITIVES from justice
 Denial of seat to militant spurs call for protests; R. F. Williams' passage. L. Doty. Aviation W 91:40 S 15 '69
 Hot cargo; R. F. Williams surrenders. Newsweek 74:37-8 S 22 '69
FUHRMAN, Frederick A. and others
 Toxin from skin of frogs of the genus atelopus: differentiation from dendrobatid toxins. bibliog Science 165:1376-7 S 26 '69
FUJI-Yawata merger. See Business consolidations and mergers—Japan
FUKUYAMA, Betty Adkins
 Come, Elijah, now; poem. Chr Cent 86:404 Mr 26 '69
FULBRIGHT, James William
 Excerpt from speech, May 19, 1969. Cong Digest 48:202+ Ag '69

 Foreign policy implications of the ABM debate. Bul Atom Sci 25:20-3 Je '69
 Militarism and the American democracy; address, April 8, 1969. bibliog f Vital Speeches 35:455-60 My 15 '69
 Most powerful country; address, January 1969. Vital Speeches 35:258-62 F 15 '69
 Vietnam: where do we go from here? por Sat Eve Post 242:24-5+ F 8 '69
 Wars in your future. Look 33:82+ D 2 '69
  about
 Doves and hawks; new clash. por U S News 66:8 Mr 17 '69
 Fulbright vs. Meany. K. Crawford. Newsweek 74:29 Ag 18 '69
 Mr Meany replies to Sen Fulbright. B. L. Masse. America 121:111 Ag 30 '69
 Neo-isolationism. K. Crawford. Newsweek 73:40 Ap 21 '69
 Nixon's knaves; reactions to address at the Air force academy. K. Crawford. Newsweek 73:38 Je 23 '69
 On tormenting Fulbright. W. F. Buckley, jr. Nat R 21:662 Jl 1 '69
 Vietnam: the lull hits home. il Newsweek 74:23-4 N 3 '69
FULL extent of the damage; story. See Lawrence, L.
FULL gospel businessmen's fellowship international
 Exercising charisma. R. E. Friedrich, jr. Chr Today 13:33 Ag 1 '69
FULLER, Buckminster. See Fuller, R. B.
FULLER, Curtis G.
 Recreation in flux; address, November 2, 1968. Am For 75:20+ Ag '69
FULLER, Eugene M.
 Big game. Parks & Rec 3:13-14+ N '68
FULLER, Louis J.
 Globe is circled with a girdle of filth; interview. por Forbes 104:55-7 D 15 '69
FULLER, Margaret. See Ossoli, S. M. F. d'
FULLER, Marietta Cain
 Corn shucks can make attractive baskets. Camp Mag 41:22 F '69
FULLER, Richard Buckminster
 Vertical is to live, horizontal is to die. Am Scholar 39:27-47 Wint '69
  about
 Bucky Fuller and the firewalk. G. M. Feigen. il Sat R 52:22-3 Jl 12 '69
 Dreams and invention. por UNESCO Courier 22:10-11 My '69
 Meet Bucky Fuller, ambassador from tomorrow. F. Warshofsky. por Read Digest 95:199-200+ N '69
FULLER, Roy
 Voice outside the cliques and politics of literature. Sat R 52:21-2+ Jl 26 '69
  about
 Comment. R. Skelton. Poetry 114:397-8 S '69
FULLER, Thomas
 On rereading Fuller. R. Kirk. Nat R 21:234 Mr 11 '69
FULLERTON, William
 Outstanding. W. F. Buckley, jr. Nat R 21:1130 N 4 '69
FULTON, David K.
 House of the singing driftwood. Radio-Electr 40:57 My '69
FULTON, Richard. See Grundy, K. W. jt. auth.
FULTON, Mo.
  See also
 Westminster college
FULTON fish market. See New York (city) —Markets
FUMIGATION
  See also
 Swine houses—Fumigation
FUNARO, George J.
 Team teaching: the danger and the promise. Clear House 43:396-400 Mr '69
FUNCH, Roy R. See Edmunds, L. N. jr. jt. auth.
FUNCTIONS, Harmonic. See Harmonic functions
FUNCTIONS, Potential. See Potential, Theory of
FUND for the Republic
 Freedom and the foundation, by T. C. Reeves. Review
  Sat R 53:33-5+ Ja 10 '70. H. Orlans
  See also
 Center for the study of democratic institutions, Santa Barbara, Calif.
FUND raising
 Ball game; charity dances, dinners, and shows collect millions. il Bsns W p44+ My 17 '69
 Biography of a charity ball. T. Meehan. il N Y Times Mag p 12-13+ Je 1 '69

FUND raising—*Continued*
Business of charity. Forbes 104:58 D 1 '69
Personal business. Bsns W p 149-50 S 20 '69
Student activists go for $110,000; Harrison-burg, Va. Chr Today 14:40 Ja 2 '70
Twelve helpful fund-raising ideas for your club. il Good H 169:198-9 N '69

Anecdotes, facetiae, satire, etc.
Fine art of fund-raising. Chr Cent 86:729 My 21 '69
Who remembers M.A.M.A? A. H. Reiss. Esquire 71:162-3 Mr '69

FUNDAMENTAL particles. See Particles (nuclear physics)

FUNDAMENTALISM
Riverside pastor responds to McIntire manifesto. Chr Cent 86:1241 O 1 '69
When conservatism is liberalism. G. H. Shriver. Chr Cent 86:7040-1 Ag 6 '69
See also
Evangelicalism

FUNDAMENTALIST controversy. See Tennessee evolution controversy

FUNERAL rites and ceremonies
Burial liturgy in Detroit. America 121:82 Ag 16 '69
Changing way of death. il Time 93:60 Ap 11 '69
Christian service for the dead. America 120:183-4 F 15 '69
See also
Eisenhower, D. D.—Funeral rites and ceremonies

FUNERAL services. See Funeral rites and ceremonies

FUNGI
Clue from under the eaves; soya-paste molds may cause stomach cancer. il Time 93:81 My 9 '69
Fungal endogenous rhythms expressed by spiral figures. J. A. Bourret and others. bibliog il Science 166:763-4 N 7 '69
Fungal morphogenesis; cell wall construction in mucor rouxii. S. Bartnicki-Garcia and E. Lippman. bibliog il Science 165:302-4 Jl 13 '69
Fungi associated with stalactite growth; cephalosporium lamellaecola. F. W. Went. il Science 166:385-6 O 17 '69
Gossypol detoxication by fungi. W. L. Baugher and T. C. Campbell. bibliog il Science 164:1526-7 Je 27 '69
It's a riot of fungi. A. H. Smith. il Audubon 71:56-65 S '69
See also
Basidiomycetes
Mushrooms
Mutation (fungi)
Phycomyces
Rusts (botany)
Truffles

Culture media
Sclerospora graminicola axenic culture. M. M. Tiwari and H. C. Arya. bibliog il Science 163:291-3 Ja 17 '69

FUNGI, Aquatic
Blastocladia and aqualinderella: fermentative water molds with high carbon dioxide optima. A. A. Held and others. bibliog il Science 165:706-9 Ag 15 '69

FUNGI, Effect of light on
Phycomyces; stimulus storage in light-initiated reactions. T. G. Ebrey and R. K. Clayton. bibliog il Science 164:427-8 Ap 25 '69

FUNGI, Fossil
Fossil mycelium with clamp connections from the middle Pennsylvanian. R. L. Dennis. bibliog il Science 163:670-1 F 14 '69; Reply. D. P. Rogers 164:726 My 9 '69

FUNGI, Pathogenic
Fungus diseases that fool the doctors. J. D. Wassersug. Sci Digest 66:81-4 Ag '69
Phenethyl alcohol and tryptophol: autoantibiotics produced by the fungus Candida albicans. B. T. Lingappa and others. bibliog il Science 163:192-4 Ja 10 '69
See also
Histoplasmosis

FUNGI, Sex in
Sexual hormones of achlya and other fungi. A. W. Barksdale. bibliog il Science 166:831-7 N 14 '69

FUNGICIDES
Birds give warning; mercury fungicides national pollution problem in Sweden. G. Löfroth and M. E. Duffy. bibliog il Environ 11:10-17 My '69

FUNK, Fred, and Person, Stanley
Cytosine to thymine transitions from decay of cytosine-5-³H in bacteriophage S13. bibliog Science 166:1629-31 D 26 '69

FUNK, Hal D.
Nonpromotion teaches children they are inferior. Ed Digest 35:38-9 N '69

FUNK, Peter
It pays to increase your word power. See issues of Reader's digest

FUNNIES. See Comics (books, strips, etc)

FUNNYÉ, Clarence
Deghettoization. Arch Forum 130:74-7 Ap '69

FUR
Glossary of furs. Good H 169:178 S '69
Skin game. il Time 94:52-4 O 31 '69

FUR bearing animals
See also
Minks

FUR coats, wraps, etc.
How to store and protect furs. il Good H 168:203 Ap '69
Natural enemy of wild cats: woman's fascination for feline furs. V. Kraft. il Sports Illus 31:42-4 Jl 14 '69

FUR industry
Jacques Kaplan: his own best ad. il Bsns W p38-9 D 27 '69

FUR trade
Stream of the past; lives of the voyageurs, excerpts from Open horizons. S. Olson. il Am West 6:28-33 Mr '69

FURADAN. See Insecticides

FURLONG, William Barry
Medicine. Sports Illus 30:52-3 Ja 27 '69
Reincarnation of Woody Hayes. Life 67:51-2+ N 21 '69
Trial of Chicago eight. Life 67:28D-31 O 10 '69

FURNACE filters. See Air filters

FURNACES
How safe is your furnace? il Bet Hom & Gard 47:149-50 O '69
Raytheon has a hot number; mini-furnace. il Bsns W p49 Jl 5 '69
See also
Electric furnaces
Solar furnaces

FURNESS, Betty
Cost of living. por McCalls 97:16+ Ja '70

FURNISHINGS, Household. See Household furnishings

FURNITURE
Box I: max use in mini space; modular living units. il Pop Sci 195:68 S '69
Contemporary with English accent. F. Heard. il House B 111:148-51 My '69
Don't bend, spindle, staple or mutilate, but do fold! B. Plumb. il N Y Times Mag p96-7 My 11 '69
Fabulous fold-ups. il House & Gard 136:170-1 N '69
Flip counters give them extra usable space. il Sunset 142:90 F '69
For small apartments. il House B 111:124-5 N '69
Furniture finds from $11 to $88. il House & Gard 35:114-15 My '69
Furniture that evokes a mood. H. Morrison. il House B 111:104-5 Ap '69
Graphic furniture, all shape, curve, color. il House & Gard 136:114-15 O '69
I call it all-in-one furniture. L. Walker. il Pop Sci 195:152-7 Jl '69
100 ideas under $100. il Bet Hom & Gard 47:18+ Ag '69
Same furniture, two looks; storage portables for the space age. il House & Gard 136:66-9 Ag '69
Swing to leather. L. Grundy. il House B 111:122-7 S '69
Today's furniture: a faithful reflection of the best traditional styles. il Good H 168:124-30 Je '69
When the action is at home. il House B 111:122-3 N '69
See also
Bedroom furniture
Cabinets (furniture)
Chairs
Desks
Kitchen furniture
Office furniture
Period rooms
Stools
Upholstery

Design
Art décoratif, alive and well. il House B 111:148-9 O '69
Art style in furniture; excerpt from The aesthetic movement. E. Aslin. il Antiques 96:578-81 O '69
China, Japan, and the Anglo-American chair. R. C. Smith. il Antiques 96:552-8 O '69

FURNITURE—Design—*Continued*
Design for living, Italian style. il Bsns W p92-4+ Mr 15 '69
Relevance of Jean-Michel Frank: yesterday, today, tomorrow. A. Auerbach. il House B 111:144-7 O '69

Exhibitions

Eighteen furniture firms will hold two-day open house to exhibit contemporary contract designs. il Arch Rec 146:209+ S '69

Finishing

Decorator's diary; Martin Dinberg's furniture-finishing studio in Manhattan. M. Gough. il House B 111:126+ Jl '69
Instant boiled oil finish. il Mech Illus 65:98-9 F '69
Quick tricks that give an exciting look to budget furniture. il Good H 169:108-13 Ag '69
Real oil finish for your furniture. il Mech Illus 65:130-1+ N '69

Materials

Stuff that stuffs furniture. il Changing T 23:29-30 N '69

FURNITURE, American
American furniture; Williamsburg, Va. M. M. Naeve. il Antiques 95:128-33 Ja '69
Fresh flowering of New England. il House B 111:88-91 Je '69
Masterpiece furniture made in America: from England's stately Woburn abbey. il House B 111:144-7 Mv '69
One more Salem secretary. D. A. Fales, jr. il Antiques 95:399 Mr '69
Shaker treasure house; home of Dr and Mrs C. Upton. il Am Home 72:76-9 S '69

FURNITURE, Arrangement of
Anti-collision kitchens. il House & Gard 135:132-5 Ap '69
Designer shapes space. M. Baughman. il House & Gard 135:120-5 Ap '69
Elegance in a one-room *pied-à-terre.* E. Kinard. il House B 111:78-9 Ag '69
How to keep a flow of space. il House & Gard 135:106-11 Ap '69
How to live more in the rooms you have! N. Cordts and M. Smith. il Bet Hom & Gard 47:58-9 O '69
Just moved in? You'd never know it. J. L. O'Neill. il Am Home 72:40+ Ja '69
Logic of the eye. W. Baldwin. House & Gard 135:72+ Ap '69
Same furniture, two looks; storage portables for the space age. il House & Gard 136:66-9 Ag '69

FURNITURE, Built in
Built-in buffets, three ways. il Bet Hom & Gard 47:130 Ap '69

FURNITURE, Childrens
Child's world: a place for play, for dreams, for growth. il House B 111:86-9 D '69
How to build a desk-workbench for a youngster. R. J. De Cristoforo. il Pop Sci 195:130-4 D '69
How to build the microdorm. K. Isaacs. il Pop Sci 194:138-41+ Mr '69
Roomful of pretty furniture. il House & Gard 136:106 D '69
When the baby becomes a boy the cabinet just comes apart. il Sunset 142:114 My '69

FURNITURE, Convertible
Convertible sofas. il Consumer Rep 34:61-5 F '69

FURNITURE, English
Art style in furniture; excerpt from The aesthetic movement. E. Aslin. il Antiques 96:578-81 O '69
Chippendale: some new discoveries. J. Stuart. il Antiques 95:46+ Ja '69
English furniture; Williamsburg, Va. B. A. Greenlaw. il Antiques 95:150-3 Ja '69
Gentlemen's Gothic. J. Gloag. il Antiques 95:682-8 My '69

FURNITURE, European
In the romantic idiom. il House B 111:125-7 My '69

FURNITURE, Fantastic
Mike Nevelson: the gender of wood. W. Castle. il Craft Horiz 29:16-21 Mr '69

FURNITURE, Gothic
Gentlemen's Gothic. J. Gloag. il Antiques 95:682-8 My '69

FURNITURE, Inflatable
Expandables and inflatables: a great look in furniture that's proud to be plastic. il Arch Rec 146:145+ D '69
Now: furniture you can blow up. L. E. Sabal. il Pop Mech 131:148-9 Je '69

FURNITURE, Italian
Design for living, Italian style. il Bsns W p92-4+ Mr 15 '69

FURNITURE, Miniature
Colonial rooms in miniature. S. A. Parvin. il Hobbies 74:148+ N '69
Victorian rooms in miniature; interview, ed. by S. A. Parvin. Mrs. C. B. Baxter. il Hobbies 74:148+ O '69

FURNITURE, Outdoor
Casual furniture for all seasons. C. Garner. il Bet Hom & Gard 47:30+ Je '69
Here and now: indoor/outdoor carpeting and furniture. L. Grundy and T. Bowman. il House B 111:106-8 Je '69
See also
Furniture, Summer

FURNITURE, Paper
Roomful of furniture for $100! il Mech Illus 65:88-9 N '69

FURNITURE, Plastic
Curves on the horizon. B. Plumb. il N Y Times Mag p20-1 D 28 '69
Expandables and inflatables: a great look in furniture that's proud to be plastic. il Arch Rec 146:145+ D '69
Plastics explosion in home furnishings. P. Rumely. il Bet Hom & Gard 47:59-73 Ap '69
Plastics make themselves at home. il Bsns W p50-2 F 8 '69
Through a glass brightly. il McCalls 96:90-3 My '69

FURNITURE, Spanish
Avoid mistakes when you buy Spanish. il Am Home 72:10+ My '69

FURNITURE, Summer
Good looks of summer furniture. H. Brown. il Am Home 72:50-3 Jl '69
Summer storehouse. B. Plumb. il N Y Times Mag p48-9 Je 1 '69

FURNITURE design. See Furniture—Design

FURNITURE designers
Design for living, Italian style. il Bsns W p92-4+ Mr 15 '69

FURNITURE finishing. See Furniture—Finishing; Wood finishing

FURNITURE industry and trade
Ninety miles of furniture: Piedmont plateau of North Carolina. il Am Home 72:20+ Jl '69

FURNIVALL'S hoopoe; story. See Warner, S. T.

FURS. See Fur

FURTH, Hans G.
Problem of Piaget. Commonweal 90:69-72 Ap 4 '69

FURY, Kathleen D.
How much does a baby cost? Redbook 133:46+ Jl '69

FUSELAGE of airplanes. See Airplanes—Fuselage

FUSIDIC acid
Fusidic acid: inhibition of factor T_2 in reticulocyte protein synthesis. M. Malkin and F. Lipmann. bibliog il Science 164:71-2 Ap 4 '69

FUSION, Nuclear. See Nuclear fusion

FUSION reactors. See Nuclear reactors

FUTURE
Defining the future. G. Feinberg. Nation 209:250-2 S 15 '69
Education for the future. A. P. Ludka. il Sr Schol 93:Schol Teach 14-15 Ja 10 '69
Environment and change: the next fifty years, ed. by W. R. Ewald, jr. Review
  Bul Atom Sci 25:54-5 My '69. A. Roberts
Generation in search of a future; address, March 4, 1969. G. Wald. Vital Speeches 35:410-13 Ap 15 '69; Same with title Our business is with life. Redbook 133:68+ Ag '69; Excerpts. New Yorker 45:29-31 Mr 22 '69
George Wald: the man, the speech. R. Todd. il N Y Times Mag p28-9+ Ag 17 '69
Nigerian debate on man. Sat R 52:24+ S 20 '69
Planning the future; futurology: a new science? A. Shonfield. Cur 105:41-53 Mr '69
Super-futurist. E. T. Chase. New Repub. 160:25-6+ Je 21 '69
Third international conference on science and society; Herceg Novi, Yugoslavia, June 1969. A. M. Weinberg. Bul Atom Sci 25:23-6 N '69
Toward a planetary society; excerpts from The future of the future. J. McHale. Cur 110:16-25 S '69
Wanted: professional futurists. S. Ramo. Sci N 36:321 O 11 '69
See also
Forecasts
Two thousand (year)

  Anecdotes, facetiae, satire, etc.

  See also
Nineteen hundred and seventy-six—Anecdotes, facetiae, satire, etc.

FUTURE life
Hereafter. L. Woodrum. Chr Today 14:14-15 D 19 '69
See also
Eschatology
Purgatory
Resurrection
FUTURES. See Commodity exchanges; Hedging
FUTURISM, Russian. See Russian poetry
FUZZ box. See Musical instruments, Electronic —Equipment

G

GAC. See General acceptance corporation
GAF corporation
History's heavy hand; getting rid of government ownership. Forbes 104:34 Jl 1 '69
GAO. See United States—General accounting office
GAR. See Grand army of the Republic
GARP (Global atmospheric research program) See Weather research
GATX. See General American transportation corporation
G. D. Searle and company. See Searle, G. D, and company
GE. See General electric company
GEMS (good emergency mother substitutes) See Baby sitters
G. Heileman brewing company. See Heileman, G, brewing company
GM. See General motors corporation
GMP. See Guanosine monophosphate
GNP. See Gross national product
GOP (grand old party) See Republican party
GT (Grand touring) cars. See Automobiles, Racing
GABETTI, Gianluigi
Take a modest step; address, April 1969. Vital Speeches 35:533-5 Je 15 '69
GABLE, Clark
What it was like to kiss Clark Gable. M. Astor. il Read Digest 94:49-53 Je '69
GABLE, Claudine
Texas gardener speaks. Horticulture 47:34+ Ag '69
GABLE, Dan
Pancake man flattens 'em. H. Weiskopf. Sports Illus 30:48 Mr 24 '69
GABLER, Arthur
Treasure by the wayside; poem. Hobbies 74: 116 My '69
GABLIK, Suzi
Light conversation. Art N 67:58-60 N '68
GABON
See also
Geology—Gabon
Hospitals—Gabon
Lambaréné
GABREE, John
And now a rock opera! Hi Fi 19:80 S '69
Beatles' ninety-minute bore, and the Rolling Stones' Beggars banquet. Hi Fi 19:84-5 Mr '69
Rock: art, revolution, or sell-out? Hi Fi 19:MA10-11 Ag '69
GABRIDGE, M. G. and others
Cycasin: detection of associated mutagenic activity in vivo. bibliog Science 163:689-91 F 14 '69
GABRIEL, Jack P.
Hong Kong. Travel 132:28-35 Ag '69
Tahiti up to date. Travel 131:50-7 Ap '69
GABRIEL, Roman
Rise of Roman's empire. il por Time 94:84 N 7 '69
GABRIEL Industries
Gabriel's gamesman. S. Margetts. Duns R 94:79-80+ O '69
GABRIELLE, Yolanda
Where are they now? por Newsweek 74:14 S 15 '69
GADDAFI, Muammar
Young men in a hurry. por Time 94:17-18 D 26 '69
GADDIS, Paul O.
Winning over indifferent youth. Harvard Bsns R 47:154-6+ Jl '69
GADGETS
Little but mighty kitchen tools. il House & Gard 136:182-3 S '69
GAELS
See also
Celts

GAETA, Vincente
But Lord forget me not; poem. Writers Digest 49:40 O '69
GAFUROV, Bobojan
Great civilization of the Kushans. UNESCO Courier 22:4-13 F '69
GAGE, Nicholas
Prisoner of Amorgos. N Y Times Mag p23-5+ S 21 '69
GAGE, Peter W. and Moore, J. W.
Synaptic current at the squid giant synapse. bibliog Science 166:510-12 O 24 '69
GAGES
Instruments: the eyes and ears of modern yachting. E. A. Zadig. il Motor B 123:52-65 Mr '69
Simmonds develops L-1011 fuel probe. Aviation W 90:74 Mr 3 '69
Solid-state your car gages. J. Saddler. il Radio-Electr 40:38-40 Ag '69
See also
Strain gages
GAGLIARDO, Ruth
Books for children (title varies) See issues of PTA magazine
GAGNON, Charles
New work from Montreal. B. Lord. il Art in Am 57:99-101 My '69
GAGNON, John Henry
—and Simon, William
Child molester: surprising advice for worried parents. Redbook 132:54+ F '69
Is a women's revolution really possible? No. McCalls 97:76-7+ O '69
—See Simon, W. jt. auth.

about
Anatomy is not destiny. Time 93:56+ Mr 28 '69
GAILAR, Joanne L.
Seven warning signals: a review of Soviet civil defense. Bul Atom Sci 25:18-22 D '69
GAILLARD, Agathe
SSSSTT! Famous postcards? Pop Phot 65:80-1 S '69
GAINES, Edith
(ed) Collectors' notes. See issues of Antiques
GAINES, Ervin J.
Urban library dilemma. por Library J 94:3966-70 N 1 '69
GAINES, Fred
Ghost dancer. Criticism
Sat R 52:20 N 15 '69
Tried and the untried. H. Hewes. Sat R 52: 40 My 10 '69
GAINESVILLE, Fla.
Practical data on composting. il Am City 84:84+ Mr '69
GAJDUSEK, Daniel Carleton. See Gibbs, C. J. jr, jt. auth.
GALACTIC clusters. See Stars—Clusters
GALACTIC systems
Antimatter, quasi-stellar objects, and the evolution of galaxies. H. Alfvén and A. Elvius. bibliog il Science 164:911-17 My 23 '69
Dead galaxies. Sci Am 220:50-1 Ap '69
Deep-sky wonders. W. S. Houston. See issues of Sky and telescope
On the origin of arms in spiral galaxies. H. Arp. il Sky & Tel 38:385-7 D '69
Quasistellar objects and Seyfert galaxies. S. A. Colgate. bibliog il Phys Today 22:27-35 Ja '69
Seyfert galaxies. R. J. Weymann. il Sci Am 220:28-37 Ja '69
Spiral structure of our galaxy. B. J. Bok. il Sky & Tel 38:392-5 D '69
See also
Magellanic clouds
Spectra
Galactic water vapor emission: further observations of variability. S. H. Knowles and others. bibliog il Science 166:221-4 O 10 '69
GALACTOSIDASES
Hurler's syndrome: deficiency of a specific beta galactosidase isoenzyme. M. W. Ho and J. S. O'Brien. bibliog il Science 165: 611-13 Ag 8 '69
Thermal lability of beta galactosidase from pink salmon liver. S. Gatt. bibliog il Science 164:1422-3 Je 20 '69
GALAGTIDES, Constantine
On the boards. W. Como. por Dance Mag 43:20 S '69
GALANTHUS nivalis. See Snowdrops
GALANTIÈRE, Lewis
What is the translator's proper share? Pub W 196:44-6 Jl 7; 33 S 22 '69

GALÁPAGOS ISLANDS
Enchanted islands; excerpts from Galápagos, the flow of wildness, ed. by K. Brower. il Américas 21:20-9 Mr '69
Exploring the Galapagos. N. Badger. il Yachting 126:64-6+ O '69
Oceanic filter, game of chance. D. Cavagnaro. il Natur Hist 78:52-7 Mr '69
See also
Zoology—Galápagos Islands
GALAXIES. See Galactic systems
GALAXY (Milky way) See Milky way
GALAXY tours. See Travel agencies
GALBRAITH, John Kenneth
Affluent society after ten years; introduction to revised edition. Atlan 223:37-44 My '69
Berkeley in the age of innocence. Atlan 223: 62-8 Je '69
Big defense firms are really public firms. N Y Times Mag p50-1+ N 16 '69
How to control the military. Harper 238:31-46 Je '69
John Steinbeck: footnote for a memoir. Atlan 224:65-7 N '69
Making foreign policy. Cur 113:54-61 D '69
1929 and 1969. Harper 239:55-62 N '69
Nosegay of Galbraithisms. Am Heritage 20: 112 O '69
Plain tales from the embassy; excerpts from diary. pors Am Heritage 20:6-13+ O '69

about
Diplomat. G. Wolff. il por Newsweek 74:120 O 20 '69
Passage to India. J. Lelyveld. Nation 209: 637-8 D 8 '69
Personal history. J. M. Burns. Sat R 52:27 D 20 '69
Professor Galbraith and Vietnam. W. F. Buckley, jr. Nat R 21:39 Ja 28 '69
Prophet with and without honor. R. H. Rovere. New Yorker 45:185-9 O 25 '69
Why Galbraith-hating is an impossible activity. W. F. Buckley, jr. il por Life 67:12 O 17 '69
GALE, W. A. and Sinclair, A. C. E.
Polar temperature of Venus. bibliog Science 165:1356-7 S 26 '69
—and others
Venus: an isothermal lower atmosphere? bibliog Science 164:1059-60 My 30 '69
GALEFFI, Carlo
Historical records. A. Favia-Artsay. por Hobbies 74:35 My '69
GALELLA, Ron
Jackie watcher. il por Newsweek 74:102+ O 13 '69
GALES. See Storms
GALILEI, Galileo
New case for Galileo. J. J. Langford. Cath World 208:259-60 Mr '69
GALINA, Anna
France; the ballet world of Anna Galina. R. Estrada. il pors Dance Mag 43:64-7 My '69
GALLAGER, Sheldon M.
All-purpose alarm you can build from a kit. Pop Mech 131:181-3 F '69
Drop-in film cartridge has come to stay. Pop Mech 131:148-50 F '69
Kit that almost puts itself together. Pop Mech 132:236+ N '69
GALLAGHER, Buell Gordon
Retreat of a reconciler. il Time 93:59 My 16 '69
Students and priorities. J. Deedy. por Commonweal 90:306 My 30 '69
Subway college strife. G. Wagner. Nat R 21:539-40 Je 3 '69; Reply with rejoinder. S. J. Robbins. 21:570+ Je 17 '69
GALLAGHER, Cornelius Edward
Technology and society; address. March 26, 1969. Vital Speeches 35:528-33 Je 15 '69
GALLAGHER, Mary Barelli
Crawfie strikes again. W. F. Buckley, jr. Nat R 21:767 Jl 29 '69
Enemy within; about My Life with Jacqueline Kennedy. il Time 94:17 Jl 18 '69
—and Leighton, F. S.
Postscript to My life with Jacqueline Kennedy. Ladies Home J 86:84+ N '69
GALLAGHER, Robert S.
South street seaport. Am Heritage 20:36-43+ O '69
GALLAGHER, Thomas
Blizzard in Indian country. Read Digest 95: 70-5 D '69
Intrepid midgets; condensation. Read Digest 95:249-52+ N '69
GALLANT, Mavis
Good deed; story. New Yorker 45:35-41 F 22 '69

New Year's eve; story. New Yorker 45:25-30 Ja 10 '70
Old friends; story. New Yorker 45:27-30 Ag 30 '69
Prodigal parent; story. New Yorker 45:42-4 Je 7 '69
Rejection; story. New Yorker 45:42-4 Ap 12 '69
Wedding ring; story. New Yorker 45:41-2 Ja 28 '69
GALLEGOS, Rómulo
Rómulo Gallegos, civilizer. G. R. Perez. il pors Américas 21:2-6 Je '69
GALLER, David
Orpheus; poem. Poetry 113:247 Ja '69
Two poems: Philoktetes; Sanctuaries. Yale R 58:581-3 Je '69
GALLER, Sidney R.
Biological warfare: is the Smithsonian really a cover? P. M. Boffey. il por Science 163: 791-6 F 21 '69
GALLERY of modern art, Washington, D.C.
See Corcoran gallery Dupont circle
GALLEY proofs. See Proofs (printing)
GALLI, Mario von
Conflict at Chur. America 121:68-70 Ag 2 '69
GALLICO, Paul
Liechtenstein. Travel & Camera 32:63-5 Jl '69
Poseidon adventure; story. Redbook 133:157-87 Ag '69
GALLIGAN, Edward. See Galligan, R. jt. auth.
GALLIGAN, Reni, and Galligan, Edward
Kenya without lions. Travel & Camera 32: 20 N '69
GALLISTEL, C. R. and others
Neuron function inferred from behavioral and electrophysiological estimates of refractory period. bibliog Science 166:1028-30 N 21 '69
GALLIVAN, James F.
Experiment in learning. Clear House 44:235 D '69
GALLO, Josephine
Certification for the educational secretary. Todays Ed 58:56 D '69
GALLO, Robert C. and others
Isopentenyladenosine stimulates and inhibits mitosis of human lymphocytes treated with phytohemagglutinin. bibliog Science 165: 400-2 Jl 25 '69
GALLOWAY, R. Dean
Quiet revolution. ALA Bul 63:1257-61 O '69
GALLUCCI, Raymond
Interview with Raymond Gallucci; ed. by J. Wandres. Ceram Mo 17:12-15 F '69
GALLUP, Gordon G. jr
Chimpanzees: self-recognition. Science 167: 86-7 Ja 2 '70
GALLWITZ, Dieter, and Mueller, G. C.
Histone synthesis in vitro by cytoplasmic microsomes from HeLa cells. bibliog Science 163:1351-3 Mr 21 '69
GALSTON, Arthur W. and Davies, P. J.
Hormonal regulation in higher plants. bibliog Science 163:1288-97 Mr 21 '69
GALSWORTHY, John
As the Victorian world turns. il Time 94:84 O 3 '69
Saga. New Yorker 45:15-17 Ja 10 '70
Seen any good Galsworthy lately? A. Burgess. il por N Y Times Mag p57+ N 16 '69
GALTON, Lawrence
For amputees, the Boston arm. Read Digest 94:151-4 F '69
GALVANIC corrosion. See Corrosion and anticorrosives
GALVIN, Hoyt R.
Mecklenburg County: reaching for the unreached. Wilson Lib Bul 43:899-900 My '69
—and Asbury, Barbara
Public library building in 1969. pors Library J 94:4369-87 D 1 '69

about
New ALA officer. F. B. Sessa. por ALA Bul 63:1166-8 S '69
GAMBACCINI, Louis J.
Excerpt from testimony before the Housing and urban affairs subcommittee. October 16, 1969. Cong Digest 48:313 D '69
GAMBATI-Norton competition for trumpeters.
See Music—Competitions
GAMBLE, Bertin Clyde
Great retail what-is-it. il Forbes 104:32-3 S 15 '69
GAMBLE-Skogmo, incorporated
See also
Gambles, incorporated
GAMBLES, incorporated
Great retail what-is-it. il Forbes 104:32-3 S 15 '69

GANDHI, Mohandas Karamchand—about—
—Continued
Gandhi's South African settlement. J. Brewer. Chr Cent 86:950+ Jl 16 '69
Gandhi's truth, by E. H. Erikson. Review
Nation 209:285-6 S 22 '69. R. Sampson
New Repub 161:24+ O 18 '69. J. Feather-stone
Newsweek il por 74:84+ Ag 18 '69. R. A. Gross
Vogue 154:138+ D '69. E. Hardwick
In the Mahatma's centenary year, India finds Gandhi inspiring and irrelevant. J. Lely-veld. il pors N Y Times Mag p27-9+ My 25 '69
Irreplaceable Gandhi; excerpt from The life and death of Mahatma Gandhi. R. Payne. il por Sat R 52:26-7+ O 4 '69
Sad centennial. il Time 94:37 O 3 '69
United Nations observes Gandhi centenary; summaries of statements. UN Mo Chron 6:96-9 N '69
What role for non-violence today? excerpts from Gandhi's truth. E. H. Erikson. Cur 112:42-7 N '69
Yogi and the commissar. A. Koestler. il pors N Y Times Mag p27-9+ O 5 '69; Discussion. p22+ N 2 '69

GANGEMI, Kenneth
New York poets. R. Whittemore. New Repub 161:23-4 D 13 '69

GANGES RIVER
Sacred Ganges; picture portfolio. R. Singh. Horizon 11:11-25 Sum '69

GANGLIOSIDOSIS. See Nervous system—Dis-eases

GANGS
Avenging Angels; Hell's Angels and hippies brawl ends in killing of Meredith Hunter. il Newsweek 75:16 Ja 5 '70
Chicago's Blackstone Rangers. J. A. McPher-son. il Atlan 223:74-84 My; 92-8+ Je '69
Guerrilla summer? a different pattern. il Time 93:16-17 Je 27 '69
House of Lords; East Harlem's First Span-ish Methodist church taken over by Young Lords. il Time 95:33 Ja 12 '70
New yellow peril; Chinatown gangs. T. Wolfe. Esquire 72:190-9+ D '69
Return of the rumble; Negro gang problem in Philadelphia. il Newsweek 74:51 S 8 '69
White gangs; excerpt. W. B. Miller. bibliog il Trans-Action 6:11-26 S '69
See also
Youth organizations united

GANN, Ernest Kellogg
My island in the sky. Flying 84:68-71 Ap '69

GANNETS
Rarest booby; Abbott's booby. B. Nelson. il Natur Hist 78:56-61 Ag '69

GANNON, Robert
Inhumane traffic in exotic pets. Read Digest 95:149-52 S '69
My wildest airplane ride. pors Pop Sci 194:82-5+ F '69
Rocks in my head. pors Pop Sci 194:94-7+ Ap '69
Wheeze machine tracks down allergies. pors Pop Sci 194:82-3+ My '69

GANNON, Ruth
Pleasant garden room. Horticulture 47:22-3 Ag '69

GANNON, Thomas M.
At the Foundling, the child is everything. America 121:331-3 O 18 '69
Balancing the books on the year of the peo-ple. America 121:632-4 D 27 '69
Bernadette on Fifth avenue. America 121:137-9 S 6 '69
Home scene. America 121:527+ N 29 '69
Report on the Vietnam Moratorium. America 121:380-3 N 1 '69
Spotlight on blockbusting. America 120:563-4 My 10 '69
Urbanology. America 122:8-10 Ja 10 '70
Welfare plan: two Washington views. America 121:118-19 Ag 30 '69
What the black community wants. America 121:558-62 D 6 '69

GANS, Carl, and others
Bullfrog (rana catesbeiana) ventilation: how does the frog breathe? bibliog Science 163:1223-5 Mr 14 '69

GANS, Curtis B.
Life of the party. Atlan 223:73-5 Ap '69

GANS, Herbert J.
How well does TV present the news? N Y Times Mag p30-1+ Ja 11 '70
We won't end the urban crisis until we end majority rule. N Y Times Mag p 12-15+ Ag 3 '69

GANSEVOORT limner. See Portraits, Ameri-can

GARAGE doors
Keep the swing in an overhead-type garage door. S. J. Howard. il Pop Mech 131:168-71 Ja '69
When garage doors sag or stick. il Sunset 143:148+ O '69

GARAGES
Another old garage gives a family room with a patio. il Bet Hom & Gard 47:78-81 My '69
From an old garage to a new style of living. il Bet Hom & Gard 47:78-9 N '69
Garage conversion starts this indoor-outdoor remodeling. il Bet Hom & Gard 47:62-3 My '69
Garage into entertainment center. il House & Gard 135:122-3 My '69
Great garage does more than store cars. il Bet Hom & Gard 47:142+ S '69
Make way for more cars. il Bet Hom & Gard 47:130+ S '69
Space-age discovery in a garage. il Am Home 72:74-6 Ap '69

GARAGES (service stations)   See Automobile service stations

GARAGES, Municipal
Ample garage space for $10 per foot; Garden City, N.Y. B. J. Gorman. il Am City 84:136+ S '69
Garages on city streets. il Arch Rec 145:165-72 Ap '69
Parking garage, mall and office complex; York, Pa. J. Frank and M. W. Seitz. il Am City 84:108-9+ Ag '69
Portable parking lots; Los Angeles trying new solution for traffic trauma. il Time 93:109 My 16 '69
Santa wouldn't provide 2,000 free parking spaces; Santa Monica, Calif. P. Scott. il Am City 84:145-6 My '69
We make off-street parking self supporting; Palo Alto, Calif. G. E. Morgan. il Am City 84:170+ O '69

GARBAGE. See Refuse and refuse disposal
GARBAGE as fertilizer. See Refuse as fertilizer
GARBAGE bags. See Refuse receptacles
GARBAGE collection and disposal. See Refuse and refuse disposal
GARBAGE dumps. See Municipal dumps
GARBAGE grinders. See Refuse grinders

GARBER, Robert S.
Two Philadelphia psychiatrists and a theory of American psychiatry. bibliog Ment Hy 53:131-40 Ja '69

GARBISCH collection. See Art—Private collec-tions

GARBO, Greta
Garbo and her court; excerpts from Garbo. N. Zierold. il pors McCalls 96:52-3+ Ag '69

GARCIA, Celso Ramon
What's sure besides the pill? ed. by J. Fast. Redbook 134:34+ Ja '70

GARCIA, S. Bartnicki-. See Bartnicki-Garcia, S.

GARCIA MARQUEZ, Gabriel
García Márquez and Solitude. D. W. Foster. il por Américas 21:36-41 N '69

GARDEN apartments. See Apartment houses—Garden apartments
GARDEN architecture. See Arbors
GARDEN barrows. See Wheelbarrows

GARDEN borders
Annuals for edgings. V. Howie. il Horticul-ture 47:30-3+ My '69
This border at Sunset is colorful all year. il Sunset 143:269 O '69
See also
Garden walls

GARDEN carts. See Carts

GARDEN catalogs.   See Catalogs, Seed and plant

GARDEN CITY, N.Y.
Ample garage space for $10 per foot. B. J. Gorman. il Am City 84:136+ S '69
Blowers replace front-end loaders for leaf collection. B. J. Gorman. il Am City 84:96-7 My '69

GARDEN clubs
See also
Horticultural societies

GARDEN contests. See Gardening—Competi-tions

GARDEN design
Art of bedding. D. A. Brown. il Horticulture 47:25-6+ O '69
Broadleaved evergreens for all-year effect. A. R. Ireys. il Horticulture 46:32-5 O '68
From bare ground to garden in a week; Home garden of ideas at Sterling Forest gardens. il Home Gard 56:50-1 S '69
Importance of water in garden design. C. C. Calkins. il Home Gard 56:40-8 My '69

GARDEN design—*Continued*
It took her just six months. il Sunset 143:
144+ Jl '69
Making the most of the gardening hour. E.
McDonald. il House B 111:44-6 Ag '69
Pygmy hedges. C. W. Cares. il Horticulture
47:32-3+ Je '69
Three previews of the Home garden of ideas;
display at Sterling forest gardens. il Home
Gard 56:58-9 Ag '69
Update your garden. J. Hudak. il Horticul-
ture 46:36-7+ S '68
See also
Gardening—Planting plans and tables
GARDEN exhibits
Coming events of interest to gardeners. See
issues of Horticulture
Garden events [in month] (title varies) See
issues of Sunset
Spring show time. il Horticulture 47:50-1
Mr '69
See also
Flower exhibits
GARDEN fences. See Fences
GARDEN files. See Files and filing (docu-
ments, etc)
GARDEN gates. See Gates
GARDEN GROVE, Calif.
Model administration for a medium-sized city.
Am City 84:34+ Ap '69
GARDEN houses, shelters, etc.
Build this double-deck gazebo. J. Hand. il
Pop Sci 195:178-83+ S '69
Enhance your yard with a garden work
center. il Pop Mech 132:160-2 S '69
Get away from it all, on your own property.
il Bet Hom & Gard 47:46-7 Jl '69
Next to the pool, a cool retreat. il Sunset
143:56-7 Ag '69
Proud-to-show garden sheds. il House B 111:
74-5 Jl '69
Sitting place in the garden. il Sunset 143:93
S '69
That room outdoors. il House & Gard 136:
72-5 Ag '69
Thornton Abell's garden work center: a shady
lathhouse with extensions out into the sun.
il Sunset 142:222 Je '69
See also
Arbors
Trellises
GARDEN literature
Authors & editors; views of H. V. Wilson.
B. A. Bannon. Pub W 196:25-7 Ag 18 '69
GARDEN ornaments
At home in the garden. See issues of Home
garden & flower grower
See also
Bird baths, etc.
Sundials
GARDEN paths. See Garden walks
GARDEN pools
Cool effect of falling water. il Sunset 143:
122-3 Ag '69
Fresh water fishes for garden pools. P. W.
Stetson. il Horticulture 47:35-6 Ag '69
How to drain a garden pool. il Sunset 142:
121-2+ My '69
Importance of water in garden design. C. C.
Calkins. il Home Gard 56:40-8 My '69
Lily pool from a washtub. M. A. Roche. il
Org Gard & Farm 16:55-7 My '69
Tropical fish for your garden pool. Org Gard
& Farm 16:83 Ag '69
GARDEN power equipment. See Garden tools,
equipment and supplies
GARDEN rooms. See Rooms
GARDEN scents. See Gardens, Fragrant
GARDEN shelters. See Garden houses, shelters,
etc.
GARDEN stakes and staking
See also
Fruit trees, Care of
GARDEN steps
On stepping-stones and fence posts. il Org
Gard & Farm 16:110-11 F '69
Steps that make you want to climb. il House
& Gard 136:280-1 N '69
GARDEN tillers. See Cultivators
GARDEN tools, equipment and supplies
Garden-power you can hold in your hand.
C. Kilvert, jr. il Home Gard 55:66-7 Ap '69
Garden toil is easier with the right tool.
il Good H 168:193 My '69
Getting set for winter; power equipment. il
House & Gard 136:262-3 O '69
Have you heard? See issues of Home garden
& flower grower
Lean-to for tools. il Mech Illus 65:96-7 Ap
'69
New for lawn & garden. A. Bernsohn. il
Mech Illus 65:109-10+ Ap '69

Preview of the 1970 equipment. il Home Gard
56:28-9 D '69
Tool rack for a garden cart. il Sunset 142:
107 Je '69
What makes garden power tools tick? M.
Franz. il Org Gard & Farm 16:69-73 Ja '69
See also
Cultivators
Hedge clippers
Leisure group, incorporated
Spraying apparatus
Tractors
Maintenance and repair
Horsepower for homeowners; prepare power
tools and plants for winter now. il Home
Gard 56:32 O '69
Late summer tune-up pays off. il Home Gard
56:44 S '69
Old garden tools get a fresh start. il Sunset
142:118+ Ap '69
Take care of your favorite tools. R. C.
Hands. Horticulture 46:52+ D '68
Storage
Build this in-a-fence tool storage. il Pop
Mech 131:164-5+ Ap '69
Carport closet for yard tools. D. Shiner. il
Pop Sci 194:130-1 Je '69
See also
Garden houses, shelters, etc.
GARDEN tours
Almanac of flower shows, garden tours,
and festivals. il House & Gard 135:74+ Mr
'69
Cabin cruising on the Thames leads to many
gardens. D. L. McFadden. il Home Gard
56:54-7 S '69
Take a summertime trip and see gardens
along the way. il Home Gard 56:46-9 Ag '69
Third-second annual Maryland house and
garden pilgrimage, May 2, 1969. Hobbies
74:116 My '69
GARDEN tractors. See Tractors
GARDEN umbrellas. See Umbrellas
GARDEN walks
Handsome garden paths and walkways. P.
Oldale. il Pop Mech 131:162-7 My '69
Here's a mulch to walk on; Chemical bank
home garden of ideas at Sterling forest
gardens. il Home Gard 56:24-5 N '69
In Japan a pathway is a work of garden art.
il Sunset 142:84-7 Je '69
In three gardens in Salt Lake City ... the
pleasure of walking on wood. il Sunset 142:
100 F '69
Irrigation bridge of building blocks. il Sunset
142:234 My '69
They made a mosaic path. il Sunset 142:266
My '69
GARDEN walls
Broken cement gardening. il Org Gard &
Farm 16:57 D '69
Joy of planting a wall. il House & Gard 136:
145-6 Jl '69
GARDENING
Container gardening. L. L. Foster. il Horti-
culture 47:34-7 D '69
Fall garden countdown. Bet Hom & Gard 47:
165 N '69
Friends of the garden. E. A. Mason. il
Horticulture 46:24-5+ Ag '68
Garden calendar. See issues of Organic gar-
dening and farming
Gardener's month. See issues of House &
garden incorporating Living for young
homemakers
Gardener's notebook. E. McDonald. See issues
of House beautiful
Handy ideas for spring. Home Gard 56:58
F '69
Memory jogger; your own garden file. V.
Calkins. Home Gard 56:66-7 F '69
[Month] in your garden. See issues of Sunset
Plant a garden: get exercise, and maybe
flowers and vegetables. Consumer Bul 52:
27-8 F '69
They grow flowers with vegetables. il Sunset
142:240 Ap '69
Twenty-one chores (and then some) you can
do with a garden tractor. il Home Gard 56:
50-1 Je '69
We garden in cans. G. Shearer. il Org Gard
& Farm 16:31-3 Ap '69
What to do in [month] See issues of Horti-
culture
Your garden in May. Am Home 72:108-9 My
'69

GARDENING—*Continued*
Your garden is on the front line; poison-free gardening. R. Rodale. il Org Gard & Farm 16:21-4 O '69
See also
Bulbs
Catalogs, Seed and plant
Childrens gardens
Flats, etc. (horticulture)
Floriculture
Fruit culture
Gardens
Greenhouses
Herbs
Horticulture
Hotbeds
Landscape gardening
Lawns
Mulching
Nurseries (horticulture)
Organic gardening
Plant propagation
Plants, Potted
School gardens
Seeding
Seedlings
Transplanting
Vegetable gardening
Watering of gardens, lawns, etc.

Bibliography

Book notes. House & Gard 136:282-3 N '69
Speaking of books. See issues of Home garden & flower grower

Competitions

Enter Home garden's $2500 contest now! Home Gard 56:16-17 D '69
Home garden mail-order nursery contest. Home Gard 56:58-61 My '69
How much can a gardener accomplish between spring and fall? garden contest winners. il Sunset 142:86-91 Ap '69
It took her just six months. il Sunset 143:144+ Jl '69
Join the sunflower set; 1969 OGF sunflower contest. M. C. Goldman. il Org Gard & Farm 16:82-3 Ap '69
Mail-order nursery contest. Home Gard 56:80-2+ Ap '69
Meet some people who started gardening at ages five to sixteen. il Sunset 142:100-2 Ap '69
Sunflower contest winners for 1969. il Org Gard & Farm 16:72-4 D '69
Three teen-age organic gardeners; Organic harvest awards contest. M. Franz. il Org Gard & Farm 16:52-6 D '69

Planting plans and tables

Garden guide for reluctant gardeners. See issues of Home garden & flower grower
In one narrow flower bed, seven months of continuous bloom. il Sunset 143:264 O '69
Inspiration for homeowners at Sterling Forest gardens. il Home Gard 56:46-7 Jl '69
Logistics of building a shade garden. il House & Gard 136:140-1 Ag '69
Planting plan for the secluded garden. il House & Gard 135:171 Ap '69
Planting plan for the sunny garden. il House & Gard 135:113 Je '69
See also
Garden design

Soil preparation

Fertilizing tips from the experimental farm. K. F. Polscer. il Org Gard & Farm 16:42-3 Mr '69
Getting your soil ready for planting. Sunset 142:248-9 My '69
Greenest thumb in Alaska; seaweed, sawdust. L. Nelson. il Org Gard & Farm 16:36-8 Mr '69

Study and teaching

British Columbia's student gardeners. A. Walton. il Horticulture 47:37-9 Ag '69
New idea center for gardeners in San Francisco's Golden Gate park. il Sunset 143:94-7 N '69

British Columbia

British Columbia's student gardeners. A. Walton. il Horticulture 47:37-9 Ag '69

Hawaii

Horticulture in Honolulu. D. P. Watson. il Horticulture 46:24-7+ O '68

Nevada

In this valley we believe. T. E. Friberg. il Org Gard & Farm 16:48-9 Ap '69

Texas

Texas gardener speaks. C. Gable. Horticulture 47:34+ Ag '69
GARDENING, Indoor. See Greenhouses

GARDENS
Fabric of gardens. B. Miles. il Horticulture 47:38-9+ Ja '69
Garden is a place to be. C. B. Lees. il Horticulture 46:26-9 N '68
H&G's answer gardens in spring bloom. il House & Gard 136:138-9 O '69
My railroad-tie terrace garden. V. J. Bogacz. il Org Gard & Farm 16:46-7 Ag '69
Pick a garden hideaway. E. Kondonellis. il Am Home 72:72-3 Ap '69
Some interesting garden features. il Horticulture 47:34-5 N '69
This little corner beside a terrace we call our mini-garden. J. Hersey. il Home Gard 56:54-5 Jl '69
See also
Bird gardens
Childrens gardens
City gardens
Garden design
Labyrinths
Roof gardens
School gardens

Color

Bright bloom of yellow. E. L. Sculthorp. il House B 111:68+ My '69
Bulb color. W. Meachem. il Horticulture 46:36-7+ O '68
Get the jump on summer color. il Bet Hom & Gard 47:136-7 Ap '69
Green garden: answer to the need for color all year. il House & Gard 135:84-5+ F '69
It's time to plant color, and there's new color to plant. il Sunset 142:90-3 Mr '69
Many-splendored colors of summer; and all from the magic of bulbs, corms and tubers. il Home Gard 56:46-54 Ap '69
Touch of gray. G. Taloumis. il Horticulture 47:28-31+ Mr '69

Austria

Austria, a land of music with a symphony of gardens. M. Perry. il Home Gard 56:54-6 My '69

California

See also
San Francisco—Gardens

Colorado

See also
Colorado Springs—Gardens

Delaware

Old garden of E. I. du Pont. H. Hover. il Horticulture 47:35+ S '69

Denmark

Surprising Denmark. D. McFadden. il Home Gard 56:78-9 Mr '69

England

Cabin cruising on the Thames leads to many gardens. D. L. McFadden. il Home Gard 56:54-7 S '69
See also
London—Gardens

Europe, Western

Rose gardens of Europe. D. L. McFadden. il Horticulture 47:18-19+ N '69

Florida

Florida's fabulous garden world. il Home Gard 56:80-2 Mr '69

France

Jardin botanique Les Cedres; estate of J. Marnier-Lapostolle at St Jean Cap Ferrat. L. Cutak. il Horticulture 47:36-7+ F '69

Georgia

Callaway gardens, year-round retreat. E. Stone. il Parks & Rec 4:20-2 Ap '69
Georgia's Callaway gardens. il Home Gard 56:76 Ap '69
Here are two of Georgia's great gardens; Callaway gardens and Stone Mountain park. il Home Gard 56:60-1 O '69

Hawaii

See also
Honolulu—Gardens

Japan

Going to Expo 70? See Japan's gardens while you're there! P. S. Parr. il Home Gard 56:28-30 O '69

GARDENS—*Continued*

Long Island, N.Y.

H&G's answer gardens; Old Westbury gardens. il House & Gard 135:82-5+ F; 142-5+ Ap; 98-9+ Je '69

Louisiana

See also
New Orleans—Gardens

Massachusetts

See also
Boston—Gardens
Ipswich, Mass.—Gardens

Mediterranean Region

Gardens to see around the Mediterranean. G. Taloumis. il Home Gard 56:62-4 Jl '69

New York (state)

From bare ground to garden in a week; Home garden of ideas at Sterling Forest gardens. il Home Gard 56:50-1 S '69
Here's a mulch to walk on; Chemical bank home garden of ideas at Sterling forest gardens. il Home Gard 56:24-5 N '69
Inspiration for homeowners at Sterling Forest gardens. il Home Gard 56:46-7 Jl '69
Three previews of the Home garden of ideas; display at Sterling forest gardens. il Home Gard 56:58-9 Ag '69
See also
Oyster Bay, N.Y.—Gardens

New Zealand

Front-yard garden Down-Under. D. Elliott. il Horticulture 46:28-9+ O '68

Norway

Gardens of Norway. M. Perry. il Home Gard 56:60-2 Ap '69

Pennsylvania

See also
Phipps conservatory, Pittsburgh

Spain

Gardens from Málaga to Morocco. F. Lemkowitz. il Home Gard 56:48-9 D '69

Sweden

Sweden, the land of Linnaeus and its bounty of beautiful gardens. M. Perry. il Home Gard 56:56-7 F '69

Tennessee

See also
Gatlinburg, Tenn.—Gardens

Virginia

Garden week in Virginia. C. T. Massie. il Horticulture 47:46-7+ Mr '69

GARDENS, Childrens. See Childrens gardens

GARDENS, Fragrant
In search of summer scents. A. M. Murphy. Home Gard 56:64 F '69

GARDENS, Indoor
Garden that came indoors. il Harp Baz 102:164-7 Ap '69
Light-work way to an indoor garden. R. C. Davids. il Read Digest 94:120-3 Mr '69
Why not an outdoor room inside! il Bet Hom & Gard 47:66-7 O '69

GARDENS, Japanese
Garden of serenity; North Salem, N.Y. E. McDonald. il House B 111:100-1 Ap '69
In Japan a pathway is a work of garden art. il Sunset 142:84-7 Je '69
Singing bamboo, falling water. M. Evans. il Am Home 72:110+ O '69
See also
Gardens—Japan

GARDENS, Miniature
Miniature garden, as a gift or for yourself. il Sunset 143:170 D '69
See also
Terrariums

GARDENS, Rock
Joy of planting a wall. il House & Gard 136:145-6 Jl '69
See also
Plants, Rock garden

GARDENS, School. See School gardens

GARDENS, Spanish
Gardens—Spain

GARDENS, Watering of. See Watering of gardens, lawns, etc.

GARDENS, Wild
In praise of natural gardening. V. V. Smiley. il Horticulture 47:36-7 Jl '69
My wild garden. D. E. Rose. Horticulture 47:56+ My '69

GARDENS of Mont-Saint-Michel; story. See Maxwell, W.

GARDINER, Harold Charles
Obituary
America 121:183 S 20 '69

GARDINIER, David E.
(comp) Articles and other books received; Africa. See issues of American historical review

GARDNER, Alexandra
Rose Cutler and Alexandra Gardner the great-great-nieces of the great Mrs Jack. il por Vogue 183:174 My '69

GARDNER, Beatrice T. See Gardner, R. A. jt. auth.

GARDNER, Dorothy
Mom to the rescue. Am Ed 5:25 D '69

GARDNER, Erle Stanley
Case of the hospitable houseboat. por Pop Sci 195:50-5+ Jl '69
Cast loose all cares. Motor B 123:267+ Ja '69
Down into Baja. il Travel & Camera 32:80-3 Ag '69

GARDNER, George
Atlantic City; photographs. Travel & Camera 32:94-8 Jl '69
Meanwhile, back at the inauguration; photographs. Trans-Action 6:32-3 Mr '69

GARDNER, George L.
Gold medal for Phoenix. Parks & Rec 4:24-8 My '69

GARDNER, Harrison
Internship in historical perspective. Ed Digest 34:42-5 Mr '69

GARDNER, Harvey
Fun games people play. Mech Illus 65:56-8+ S '69

GARDNER, Herman L. and Jacobs, Evelyn
Causes and treatment of vaginitis. Redbook 133:38+ Jl '69

GARDNER, John W.
Responsible versus irresponsible dissent; adaptation of address. March 27, 1969. Science 164:379 Ap 25 '69
Task to test our mettle; excerpts from address. Read Digest 94:205-8 F '69
Toward a self-renewing society; Time essay; excerpts from address. por Time 93:40-1 Ap 11 '69
What kind of society do we want? excerpts from The recovery of confidence. Read Digest 95:74-8 S '69
Will there ever be a housing boom? interview. por Forbes 104:72+ O 15 '69
You can remake this society. Look 33:85-6 Jl 15 '69
about
Mr Gardner speaks his mind. America 121:628-9 D 27 '69

GARDNER, Leonard
Short talk with a first novelist; ed. by M. Durham. pors Life 67:10 Ag 29 '69

GARDNER, Martin
Mathematical games. See issues of Scientific American

GARDNER, Mercedes, and Smith, J. S.
King Midas; dramatization of the Greek myth. Plays 28:59-67 Mr '69

GARDNER, Paul
George Orwell. Cath World 209:90-1 My '69

GARDNER, R. Allen, and Gardner, B. T.
Teaching sign language to a chimpanzee. bibliog Science 165:664-72 Ag 15 '69

GARDNER, Richard K.
Current French library scene. por Wilson Lib Bul 43:982-91 Je '69

GARDNER, Richard Newton
Hard choices for the embattled dollar. Sat R 52:46+ N 22 '69
Will success spoil Bretton Woods? Sat R 52:18 Jl 26 '69
about
In the news; development of a network of broadcast satellites. Space World F-6-66:47-8 Je '69

GARDNER, W. David
Heart is a lonely hunter. Ramp Mag 7:34-8 Je '69
Mister Rockefeller builds his dream house. Ramp Mag 8:36-9 S '69
New Hampshire's Union leader. Nation 208:397-401 Mr 31 '69

GARDNER, William D.
Proteas and their relatives. il Horticulture 47:26-9+ Ag '69

GARELIK, Sanford D.
Campus is not a sanctuary for crime and lawlessness. N Y Times Mag p 136-7 My 4 '69

GARFIELD, James Abram
When Jersey was the spa of presidents. T. Fleming. il Sat R 52:46-7+ Mr 8 '69

GARFINCKEL, Julius, and company. See
  Washington, D.C.—Stores
GARGALIANI, Greece
  Spiro, won't you please come home? B. An-
    gelo. il Time 94:21 N 14 '69
GARGAN, William
  Why me? condensation. Good H 168:92-5+
    Mr '69
        about
  Sweet use of adversity. J. E. O'Connell. Cath
    World 209:284 S '69
GARGOYLISM. See Lipochondrodystrophy
GARLAND, Judy
  End of the rainbow. il por Time 94:64-5 Jl
    4 '69
  Judy floats. W. Goldman. il por Esquire 71:
    78-80 Ja '69
  Judy Garland: her last tragic months. M.
    Deans. il pors Look 33:84-7+ O 7 '69
  Obituary
    New Yorker 45:19 Jl 5 '69
  Over the rainbow. il pors Newsweek 74:18-
    19 Jl 7 '69
  Who killed Cock Robin? A farewell to Judy.
    B. Schulberg. il pors Life 67:26-8 Jl 11 '69
GARLAND, Phyllis
  A. Philip Randolph: labor's grand old man.
    Ebony 24:31-4+ My '69
  Booker T. and the M.G.'s. Ebony 24:92-4+
    Ap '69
  Bossman of the blues. Ebony 25:54-6+ N '69
  Duke Ellington. Ebony 24:29-32+ Jl '69
  Nina Simone, high priestess of soul; excerpt
    from The sound of soul—the music and its
    meaning. Ebony 24:156-9 Ag '69
GARLIC
  Garlic galore. C. Claiborne. il N Y Times
    Mag p60+ Ag 24 '69
GARMENT factories
        Automation
  Where automating is not in fashion. il Bsns
    W D 150+ Ja 25 '69
GARMENT workers
    See also
  Clothing industry—Wages and hours
  International ladies' garment workers' union
GARNER, Alan
  The owl service; study. E. Cameron. bib-
    liog il Wilson Lib Bul 44:425-33 D '69
GARNER, James
  James Garner's new act. D. Wells. il pors
    Motor T 21:74-6 Je '69
GARNER, L. H.
  Low-cost   d.c.-voltage   calibrator.   Electr
    World 82:42 S '69
GARNER, Louis E. Jr
  Solid state. See issues of Popular electronics
GARNETS
  Olivine-garnet transformation in a meteorite.
    B. Mason and others; discussion. bibliog
    Science 163:828-30 F 21 '69
GARNISHMENT. See Attachment and garnish-
    ment
GARRELS, Robert M. and MacKenzie, F. T.
  Sedimentary rock types: relative proportions
    as a function of geological time. bibliog
    Science 163:570-1 F 7 '69
GARRETS. See Attics
GARRETT, Wendell D.
  Century of aspiration. Antiques 96:372 S '69
  (ed) Clues and footnotes. Antiques 96:808+
    D '69
  Living with antiques: Antiques 96:754-62 N
    '69
  —and others
  Arts in America: the nineteenth century; ex-
    cerpts. Antiques 96:372-5 S '69
GARRETT corporation
  Garrett expanding turbine family. D. A.
    Brown. il Aviation W 91:85+ N 3 '69
GARRICK, Emily D.
  How bigotry is born. PTA Mag 63:8-11 bib-
    liog (p35) F '69
GARRIGUE, Jean
  Song in Sligo; poem. New Yorker 44:79 F
    1 '69
GARRISON, Jim
  Beating the feds. New Repub 161:11 N 22 '69
  Covering big Jim. Newsweek 73:105 Mr 17
    '69
  Curtains for the D.A. Newsweek 73:27 Ja
    27 '69
  Final chapter in the assassination contro-
    versy? E. J. Epstein. il por N Y Times
    Mag p30-1+ Ap 20 '69
  Garrison under pressure. por Newsweek 74:
    42+ O 27 '69
  Garrison v. the people. il por Time 93:29 Mr
    14 '69
  Garrison's last gasp. il por Time 93:23 Mr
    7 '69

Mardi Gras season. il por Newsweek 73:34 F
  17 '69
Objection, your honors. Nat R 21:267 Mr 25
  '69
Persecution of Clay Shaw. W. Rogers. il por
  Look 33:53-6+ Ag 26 '69
Sideshow in New Orleans. Time 93:40 Ja 31 '69
Verdict in New Orleans. Nation 208:324 Mr
  17 '69; Reply with rejoinder. P. Boothby.
  208:450+ Ap 14 '69
What Garrison proved. New Repub 160:9
  Mr 15 '69
GARRISON, Lloyd
  Odumegwu Ojukwu is Biafra. N Y Times Mag
    p7-9+ Je 22 '69
GARRISON, Peter
  Back to basics. Flying 85:56-9 D '69
  Pro's nest. Flying 84:38 My '69
  Sniff; reasoning under pressure in emer-
    gencies. Flying 86:88-9 Ag '69
  U.S. vs. Europe. Flying 84:30-5+ Mr '69
GARRISON, Webb B.
  Medicine's happy accidents. Todays Health
    47:28-31+ F '69
  Pain: your body's early-warning system. To-
    days Health 47:28-9+ O '69
  Strange facts about the Bible; excerpts. To-
    days Health 47:64-5 S; 12-13 O '69
  Vitamin K, savior of bleeding babies. To-
    days Health 47:42-3+ S '69
  Why you say it; excerpts. Todays Health 47:
    74-6 Mr '69
GARRISON, William Lloyd
  Means and ends in American abolitionism,
    by A. S. Kraditor. Review
      Nation 208:214-15 F 17 '69. E. Magdol
      New Repub 160:31-2+ F 15 '69. F. Brodie
GARRISON, Winfred Ernest
  Desirable eavesdropping. M. E. Marty. Chr
    Cent 86:303 F 26 '69
  Obituary
    Chr Cent por 86:278 F 26 '69
GARROWAY, Dave
  Peace, old tiger. il por Time 94:71 Jl 18 '69
GARRY, Charles
  Panthers' honky lawyer. il por Time 95:30
    Ja 12 '70
GARTH, Midi
  Midi Garth, the Cubiculo. T. Borek. Dance
    Mag 43:94 Je '69
GARTH, Warner D.
  Marks, how much do they mean? PTA Mag
    63:2-4 bibliog (p35) Ap '69
GARTHWAITE, Marion
  Joel of the far hills; story. Horn Bk 45:
    652-8 D '69
GARTNER, John
  Wheels for sportsmen. Field & S 73:45-59
    Mr '69
GARVER, Juliet
  Turkey, anyone? drama. Plays 29:59-68 N '69
GARVEY, Joseph M.
  Touch and see. Parks & Rec 4:20-2 N '69
GARVEY, Mona
  Bulletin board display: using large circles
    as background design. por Wilson Lib
    Bul 43:776-7 Ap '69
  Library display: use of a basic cartoon
    figure. Wilson Lib Bul 44:152-3 O '69
  Library display: using simple geometric
    shapes. Wilson Lib Bul 44:390-1 D '69
GARVIN, David
  Suggestion: the minireview. Phys Today 22:
    13+ O '69
GARVIN, Robert T. and others
  Dye-sensitized photooxidation of the esche-
    richia coli ribosome. bibliog Science 164:
    583-4 My 2 '69
GARY, Romain
  To mon général: farewell, with love and
    anger. Life 66:26-9 My 9 '69; Same abr. with
    title Farewell, mon général. Read Digest
    95:74-7 Ag '69
GARY, Ind.
  Gary in black and white. il Newsweek 73:61
    Ap 21 '69
        Fire department
    See also
  Gary, Ind.—Strikes
        Politics and government
  Gary, Indiana. M. Frady. il Harper 239:35-45
    Ag '69
  Gary presses a claim. il Bsns W p40-1 Ag 23
    '69
  Hatcher of Gary faces a revolt. il Bsns W
    p40-1 Ap 19 '69
        Social conditions
  Gary, Indiana. M. Frady. il Harper 239:35-45
    Ag '69
        Strikes
  Playing with fire. il Newsweek 74:52 Ag 18 '69

GARZANTI, Aldo, casa editrice. See Publishers and publishing—Italy

GAS, Natural
Looming shortage of natural gas: the cause and effect. il U S News 68:80 Ja 12 '70
Soviet icebox yields treasure; oil and gas fields at Arctic Circle. il Bsns W p43-4 Je 21 '69
See also
Gas industry

Pipe lines
Red dividend; Italian-Soviet agreement. il Newsweek 74:76 D 22 '69
Russia plans biggest gas pipe; to tap giant Asian gas fields. il Bsns W p72 Ap 12 '69
Russia pushes gas sales westward. il Bsns W p94+ O 11 '69

Prices
See Gas rates

Transportation
See also
Gas, Natural—Pipe lines

GAS and oil engines
Rotary engines. W. Chinitz. il Sci Am 220: 90-9 bibliog(p 132) F '69
See also
Airplane engines

Design
Tri-dyne: slick new rotary engine could lick the Wankel. D. Scott. il Pop Sci 195:45-7+ Jl '69

Fuel
Two-cycle fuel mixes. il Mech Illus 65:104+ D '69

Ignition
Build a Dwell Extender. G. Meyerle. il Pop Electr 31:51-4+ O '69

GAS and oil engines, Inboard
Gasoline engines. il Motor B 124:34-40 O '69
Inboard engines. il Motor B 123:164-8 Ja '69

GAS and oil engines, Outboard
Here come the 1970 outboards. E. A. Zadig. il Motor B 124:94-6+ O '69
New racing outboards. D. Fales. il Pop Mech 131:24 Mr '69
1970 outboard preview. J. A. Emmett. Outdoor Life 144:38+ O '69
No limit to outboard motor size? il Motor B 123:266+ Ja '69
Outboard motors. il Motor B 123:188-91 Ja '69
Outboards 1970, sports power unlimited. F. M. Paulson. il Field & S 74:92-7 D '69
Outboards: 1970 style. M. Crook. il Yachting 126:59-61+ O '69
Preview of 1970 outboards. B. McKeown. il Mech Illus 65:50-2+ O '69
'70 a fine-tuning year for outboards. D. Fales. il Pop Mech 132:100-3 O '69
'70 outboards: more power, convenience, reliability. J. Roe. il Pop Sci 195:146-9 O '69
They're a bunch of corks! J. Martenhoff. il Yachting 126:66-7+ N '69

Fuel
Fuel for your outboard. W. Cloud. il Pop Sci 194:117-19+ F '69

Fuel feeding
How to check out your fuel system. H. B. Notrom. il Pop Mech 132:144-7 S '69

Ignition
How to check out your ignition system. H. B. Notrom. il Pop Mech 132:138-41+ Jl '69

Maintenance and repair
How the pros keep their outboards humming. B. Weis. il Mech Illus 65:79-80+ Mr '69
How to check out your ignition system. H. B. Notrom. il Pop Mech 132:138-41+ Jl '69
Outboard motor service guide. W. Heyman. il Motor B 123:81+ Ap '69
Outboard-motor service giude. H. B. Notrom. il Pop Mech 132:138-41+ Jl; 132-5+ Ag; 144-7 S; 140-3 N; 162-5 D '69

Starting
How to check out your starting system. H. B. Notrom. il Pop Mech 132:132-5+ Ag '69

GAS appliances
Ignition devices
See Gas burners—Ignition devices

GAS as fuel
See also
Gas stoves

GAS bubbles. See Bubbles

GAS burners
Ignition devices
Piezoelectric igniter generates instant flames D. Markeson. il Electr World 82:72 N '69

GAS centrifuges. See Centrifuges

GAS chromatography. See Chromatographic analysis

GAS clothes dryers. See Clothes dryers

GAS companies
See also
Coastal states gas producing company
El Paso natural gas company

GAS detectors
How to find leaks. C. V. King. il Chem 42: 8-11 Mr '69

GAS dynamics laboratory. See Princeton university—Gas dynamics laboratory

GAS exchange in plants. See Plants—Respiration

GAS explosions. See Explosions

GAS industry
Natural gas deal may deflate shortage. Bsns W p39 N 22 '69
Not enough gas in the pipelines. A. Liversidge. il Fortune 80:120-2+ N '69
Tempers flare over dwindling gas supply. il Bsns W p 109-10+ D 13 '69
Too good to last? looming crisis in natural gas supply. il Forbes 104:29-30 N 1 '69
See also
Northern natural gas company

Russia
Russia plans biggest gas pipe; to tap giant Asian gas fields. il Bsns W p72 Ap 12 '69
Russia pushes gas sales westward. il Bsns W p94+ 11 '69

GAS leaks, Detection of. See Gas detectors

GAS rates
Looming shortage of natural gas: the cause and effect. il U S News 68:80 Ja 12 '70

GAS stoves
Free-standing 30-inch gas ranges; gas or electricity for cooking? il Consumer Bul 52:27-32 My '69

GAS turbines
Industrial, marine gas turbine sales rise. Aviation W 90:58 Ap 7 '69

GAS turbines, Aircraft
Advanced V/STOL engine tested. Aviation W 91:21 O 6 '69
Aircraft engine revolution. R. Blodget. il Flying 84:66-72 F '69
French aim to improve engines for export. M. L. Yaffee. il Aviation W 90:270-1+ Je 2 '69
Garrett developing new turbofan. C. M Plattner. il Aviation W 90:92-3+ Ap 28 '69
MRCA engine choice keyed to U.K. drive. E. H. Kolcum. Aviation W 91:22-3 N 10 '69
New designation system set for military engines. Aviation W 90:82 F 10 '69
New GE engine aimed at F-5 replacement. il Aviation W 91:72 Ag 11 '69
Outlook cloudy for GE 12, ST9 progam despite added funding. il Aviation W 91:32 N 17 '69
Pratt & Whitney offering 51,000-lb.-thrust JT9D. C. M. Plattner. Aviation W 90:27 Ap 7 '69
Rolls-Royce's $2-billion hard sell. J. M. Mecklin. il Fortune 79:122-8+ Mr '69

Blades
Rolls-Royce expands blade cooling work. il Aviation W 90:82 Mr 31 '69

Design
Garrett expanding turbine family. D. A. Brown. il Aviation W 91:85+ N 3 '69
GE increasing thrust of GE4/J5 engine. M. L. Yaffee. il Aviation W 92:71+ Ja 5 '70
GE plans growth version of CF6. M. Yaffee. il Aviation W 91:52-3+ O 27 '69
GE12 to demonstrate advanced design, component technology. il Aviation W 91:26 O 27 '69
Germans pushing engine development. il Aviation W 90:262-3+ Je 2 '69
Inlet taps point to Tu-154 problem. M. L. Yaffee. il Aviation W 91:57+ Jl 21 '69
Quieter turbofans could hit cost snag. M. L. Yaffee. Aviation W 91:31+ O 27 '69

Failure
Helicopter hubbub. R. B. Weeghman. Flying 84:68-9 Mr '69

GAS turbines, Aircraft—*Continued*

Manufacture

JT9D engine production shown. il Aviation W **91:54-9** D 1 '69
Pratt & Whitney assembles JT9D. il Aviation W **91:33** O 20 '69
Rolls-Royce expands blade cooling work. il Aviation W **90:82** Mr 31 '69

Materials

Soviets using cast titanium in AI-25 engine. il Aviation W **91:63** O 6 '69

Specifications

Leading international gas turbines (cont) Aviation W **90:177-8** Mr 10 '69
U.S. gas turbine engines (cont) Aviation W **90:175-6** Mr 10 '69

Testing

Bristol begins testing M-45H at Patchway. il Aviation W **90:21** F 10 '69
GE tests advanced J85 turbojet engine. il Aviation W **91:58** Ag 18 '69
RB.211 engine given outdoor noise tests. il Aviation W **90:115** Ap 14 '69

GAS turbines, Automotive

On learning, Indy and Andy; interview, ed. by S. Kelly. A. Granatelli. il Hot Rod 22:48-50 Mr '69

GAS turbines, Marine

Jet-jet, boat of the future. B. McKeown. il Mech Illus **65:68-70+** Mr '69
Ships go the way of the jet. il Bsns W p 173 O 11 '69

GAS vacuoles. See Cells—Inclusions

GASES

Applications of electron spin resonance to gas-phase kinetics. A. A. Westenberg. bibliog il Science 164:381-8 Ap 25 '69
Lab bench; Charles' law; estimating absolute zero. M. Spritzer and J. Markham. il Chem 42:24-5 S '69
See also
Ethylene

Liquefaction

Amateur scientist; old refrigerators are salvaged to build a laboratory cooler and a gas liquefier. C. L. Stong. il Sci Am 221:151-6 N '69

GASES, Asphyxiating and poisonous

Academy changes army gas dump plan. P. M. Boffey. Science 165:45 Jl 4 '69
Casual gas dump. il Sci N 95:609-10 Je 28 '69
NAS suggests modifications; nerve gas disposal procedures. Sci N 96:26 Jl 12 '69
Nerve gas; too hot to handle. Sci N 95:499-500 My 24 '69
See also
Carbon monoxide
Chemical and biological weapons
Chemical warfare
Sarin
Tear gas

Accidents

U.S. owns up; stockpiles of lethal nerve gas overseas. Sci N 96:80 Jl 26 '69

Testing

Germs and gas as weapons; congressional hearings. S. M. Hersh. New Repub 160:13-16 Je 7 '69
On uncovering the great nerve gas coverup; sheep killed near Dugway, the army's chemical and biological testing station, Skull Valley, Utah. S. Hersh. Ramp Mag 7:14-18 Je '69

Transportation

Army is at sea over nerve gas; plan to dump unwanted chemical weapons in Atlantic stirs fear and controversy. il Bsns W p72+ Je 7 '69
Gas scare. Nation 209:684 D 22 '69
Germs and gas as weapons; congressional hearings. S. M. Hersh. New Repub 160:13-16 Je 7 '69
How not to do it; disposal of war materials. Nation 208:653 My 26 '69
Poison gas; 27,000-ton headache. il U S News 66:10 Je 2 '69
Stockpiles of death. il Newsweek 73:36+ My 19 '69
Transcontinental death trains; with editorial comment. L. H. Madaras. Chr Cent 86:800, 817-18 Je 11 '69

GASES, Rare
See also
Xenon

GASES in warfare
See also
Chemical warfare
Tear gas

GASHEL, Jean. See Gashel, L. jt. auth.

GASHEL, Len, and Gashel, Jean
Undiscovered New Jersey. Travel 131:52-5+ Je '69

GASKETS
Keep your cool; Chevy gasket trouble. B. Lang. il Hot Rod 22:106 Jl '69

GASKINS, Francis
Young man in a hurry. por Duns R 94:45 S '69

GASNER, Beverley
Girls' rules; story. Redbook 132:177-99 Mr '69

GASOLINE

Additives

New gas fuels pollution fight; new additive that eliminates pollutants from exhaust. Bsns W p 19 D 20 '69

Advertising

Ads are kooky, and they sell; Bonded oil's campaign. il Bsns W p50 F 15 '69
Changing the rules; FTC ruling on giveaway promotions at gasoline stations. il Newsweek 74:63 Ag 25 '69
Enticers, 1970. E. Kendall. Vogue 155:119+ Ja 15 '70

Marketing

Meanwhile, back at the gas pump, a battle for markets. J. Main. il Fortune 79:108-11+ Je '69

Rating

Octane numbers game. A. Q. Mowbray. Nation 209:659-61 D 15 '69

GASOLINE handling

Safety devices and measures

Carrying or storing gasoline? Use a safety can. il Consumer Bul 52:12-13 Je '69

GASOLINE industry. See Petroleum industry and trade

GASSER, Henry
Adolf Konrad; painter of the American scene. Am Artist 32:26-32+ N '68

GASTON, Miguel I.
Too many cooks. Flying 85:32 D '69

GASTON, Rosetta
Mrs Gaston, mother of Negro history in New York. por Negro Hist Bul 32:22 Ap '69

GASTROINTESTINAL gas. See Flatulence

GASTRONOMY
Close-up; Father Robert F. Capon; calories are only a demon to be exorcised; interview, ed. by M. C. Wrenn. R. F. Capon. il Life 66:39-40+ Mr 14 '69
Great gourmet boom. il Forbes 103:20-2+ Ap 1 '69
See also
Gluttony

GASTROPODS
See also
Sea hares

GATCH, Donald Eugene
Aftermath. B. Shaw. Esquire 72:12+ Jl '69

GATELY, Olive P.
Elephants have the right of way! Har Yrs 9:19-23 Ag '69
Lone ladies on the go. por Har Yrs 9:32-3 Mr '69

GATES, David M.
New science tries to keep old balance. il por Bsns W p64-5+ F 15 '69
Saving the world the ecologist's way. R. W. Stock. il por N Y Times Mag p32-3+ O 5 '69

GATES, Perry
East of Schoodic. Yachting 125:76-7+ Mr '69

GATES
Garden gates are in. il Home Gard 56:50-1 N '69
Portfolio of garden gates. F. Kaltenbach. il Horticulture 47:22-5 Mr '69
Three garden gates. California style. H. Sibley. il Pop Sci 195:168-9 S '69

GATES rubber company
Holdout wavers; may go public. il Forbes 103:30 My 1 '69

GATHERS, Marvin L.
Great air race. il pors Ebony 24:80-2+ Jl '69

GATLINBURG, Tenn.

Gardens

Christus gardens. il Travel 131:34-5+ Ap '69

GATORADE. See Beverages

GATOS, Harry C.
Electronic materials and applications. Science 164:137-41 Ap 11 '69

GATT, Shimon
Thermal lability of beta galactosidase from pink salmon liver. bibliog Science 164:1422-3 Je 20 '69

GATTI, Arlo
Underwater world of Arlo Gatti; photographs. Nat Wildlife 7:9-13 F '69

GATTIS, Murrah, and Raudsepp, Eugene
How creative are you? excerpts. Writers Digest 49:61-5+ Mr '69

GATTO, Dominick
(comp) Used camera buying guide. Mod Phot 33:91-106 Mr; 99-113 Ap '69

GATWICK airport. See Airports—Great Britain

GAUCHOS
Gaucho Martin Fierro, by J. Hernández. Review
Américas 21:38-40 Ja '69. F. Demaría

GAUD, William Steen, 1907-
Current effect of the American aid program; with questions and answers. Ann Am Acad 384:73-84 Jl '69
Development: a balance sheet; address. November 20, 1968. Dept State Bul 59:703-6 D 30 '68

GAUDNEK, Walter
Polymorphism; mystic crackpot. J. Gruen. Vogue 153:38 Ap 15 '69

GAUGUIN, Paul
Where do we come from? What are we? Where are we going? J. Jacobs. il por Horizon 11:52-65 Sum '69

GAULLE, Charles de
Presidents Johnson and de Gaulle exchange New Year's greetings. Dept State Bul 60:78 Ja 27 '69

about

Absent presence of General de Gaulle. P. Ben. New Rpub 161:12-13 O 11 '69
Après moi. . . il Newsweek 73:48 Mr 24 '69
Citizen de Gaulle. K. Crawford. Newsweek 73:38 My 12 '69
Common market after de Gaulle. H. van B. Cleveland. For Affairs 47:697-710 Jl '69
De Gaulle, a summing up. G. Lichtheim. Commentary 48:79-85 S '69
De Gaulle and his era. il pors Newsweek 73:48-50 My 12 '69
De Gaulle leaves a monetary hangover. il por Bsns W p23-5 My 3 '69
De Gaulle: Nixon's stumbling block? il por U S News 66:21-3 Mr 3 '69
De Gaulle's troubles aren't over. U S News 66:47 Mr 24 '69
Does de Gaulle matter? S. Alsop. Newsweek 73:108 Mr 31 '69
End of an era: France after de Gaulle. il por Newsweek 73:41-2+ My 12 '69
Exit the king. New Repub 160:5-6 My 10 '69
Farewell, mon général. R. Gary. por Read Digest 95:74-7 Ag '69
France: a struggle against the second-rate. F. Ungeheuer. Harper 239:122-8 D '69
France after de Gaulle; with interview with R. Aron. il pors U S News 66:25-9 My 12 '69
France enters a new era. il por Time 93:30+ My 9 '69
France rejects de Gaulle. por Time 93:20-1 My 2 '69
France with de Gaulle. E. von Kuehnelt-Leddihn. Nat R 21:538 Je 3 '69
France without father. C. Bourdet. Nation 208:589-90 My 12 '69
French referendum. C. Bourdet. Nation 208:526-9 Ap 28 '69
Gaullism without de Gaulle. R. Bosc. America 121:13-15 Jl 5 '69
Le grand Charles slept here. P. Ryan. il pors Sports Illus 31:46-8+ Jl 28 '69
Le grand Charles steps down; Pursuit of grandeur. por Sr Schol 94:11-12 My 9 '69
Grand strategy of de Gaulle. S. K. Pad-over. por Sat R 52:25-7 Mr 8 '69
Hermit of Heron Cove. Newsweek 73:53 My 26 '69
Letter from Paris (cont) Genêt. New Yorker 45:126-7 Mr 22; 129-33 My 10; 128+ My 24; 78+ Je 28 '69
Mandate of Monsieur Pompidou. Life 66:34 Je 13 '69
Not yet Josephine. . . . il Time 93:28 Ja 31 '69
On French leave with de Gaulle. J. Barry. il pors Sat R 52:66+ Mr 8 '69
Once more. the ultimatum. por Time 93:27 Ap 18 '69

Quiet end to grandeur; with farewell letters from R. Gary. il pors Life 66:24D-31 My 9 '69
Richard de Nixon, Gaullist? J. Burnham. Nat R 21:382 Ap 22 '69
Story behind the liberation of Paris a quarter of a century ago. L. Collins and D. Lapierre. il pors N Y Times Mag p46-7+ S 7 '69
Too close for comfort. Newsweek 73:54+ Ap 28 '69
Twilight of de Gaulle. J. Burnham. il Nat R 21:114-15 F 11 '69
Two ex-exiles hit it off; R. Nixon's visit. H. Sidey. il por Life 66:4 Mr 14 '69
Ugly question: anti-Israeli attitude. Newsweek 73:44 Ja 27 '69
Undramatic exit of Charles de Gaulle. Chr Cent 86:638 My 7 '69
World after de Gaulle. Bsns W p 112 My 3 '69
World after General de Gaulle. America 120:556 My 10 '69

Caricatures and cartoons
Farewell sampler. Time 93:31 My 9 '69

GAULT, Henri, and Millau, Christian
Mystery of foie gras. Holiday 46:52-3+ D '69
Which is the world's greatest restaurant? Holiday 45:32-3+ Je '69

GAULT, Robert
After the Olympics: buying off protest. J. Scott and H. Edwards. il por Ramp Mag 8:16-21 N '69

GAUSSIAN curve. See Distribution (probability theory)

GAVER, Mary Virginia
Is anyone listening? Significant research studies for practicing librarians. bibliog por Wilson Lib Bul 43:764-72 Ap '69
Librarian in the academic community, a new breed? address, November 1968. por Wilson Lib Bul 43:540-4 F '69

GAVIN, James M.
Can industry manufacture social solutions? Sat R 52:21-2 My 24 '69

GAVIN, Thomas F.
Simple rule of love. America 121:424-5 N 8 '69

GAVRAS, Costa-. See Costa-Gavras

GAY, Peter
Last of a dying species. New Repub 160:21-2 My 17 '69
Roots of kultur. New Repub 160:27-9 F 22 '69
Secrets of a genius. Sat R 52:32 F 1 '69

GAY Head, pseud.
Talking it over with Gay Head. questions and answers. See issues of Senior scholastic

GAYNOR, John, and Wicks, Harry
Finish your basement like a pro. Pop Mech 132:154-7 D '69

GAZEBOS. See Garden houses, shelters, etc.

GEARING
See also
Automobiles—Gearing
Motorcycles—Gearing

GEARY, Ida
Redwood forest as seen in plant prints. Audubon 71:52-7 Jl '69

GEBALLE, Ronald, and others
What shall we do for the Commission on college physics? por Phys Today 22:120-1 N '69

GEBHARD, David
Pop scene for profs. Arch Forum 130:78-85 Mr '69

GECKOS. See Lizards

GEDDY, James, family
James Geddy and sons. colonial craftsmen: evidence from the earth; Williamsburg, Va. I. Noël-Hume. il Antiques 95:106-11 Ja '69

GEDDY, James, house. See Williamsburg, Va.

GEDIMAN, Wallita
Big day. Sch Arts 69:40 N '69

GEEL, Belgium
Town for outpatients. il Time 93:74 Mr 14 '69

GEERLINGS, Gerald K.
Eight ways to get more off-street parking. Pop Mech 131:148-51 Mr '69

GEESE
See also
Cookery—Poultry

GEESE; drama. See Weill, G.

GEESE, Wild
Best bets for geese this fall. C. Nansen. il Field & S 74:42-3+ Ag '69
Devil's own geese. J. O. Cartier. il Outdoor Life 144:82-4+ O '69
From the brink of extinction. J. C. George. il Nat Wildlife 7:20-3 Ap '69; Same abr. Read Digest 94:214-15 Ap '69
Gone are the honkers. N. Buckingham. il Outdoor Life 143:78-9+ My '69

GEESE, Wild—*Continued*
Gunning the Atlantic coast; best duck and goose hunting. S. M. Miller. il Field & S 74: 64-5+ N '69
Hero in a sneak box; brant shooting. E. Bowen. il Sports Illus 31:46-50+ S 1 '69
Hotspot for honkers. J. R. Olt. il Outdoor Life 144:68-9+ N '69
Sneak preview from a happy hunting ground; James Bay, Quebec. V. Kraft. Sports Illus 31:68-9 O 27 '69
Unexpected goose shoot. P. McLain. il Field & S 74:38-9+ D '69

GEHLEN, Frieda L.
Women in Congress. bibliog por Trans-Action 6:36-40 O '69

GEHMAN, Betsy Holland
Inside acronyms. Esquire 72:64+ S '69

GEHMAN, Richard
Big little band in Toronto. Sat R 52:46-7 F 8 '69
But what goes after the third line? Sat R 52:4 Jl 12 '69

GEHRES, Leslie E.
Before the colors fade: captain of the Franklin; interview, ed. by D. Davidson. pors Am Heritage 20:60-3+ Ap '69

GEIB, M. Eugenia
Singing sinners. Opera N 34:6-7 D 13 '69

GEIGER, Helen M.
Zoo on the mountain. Parks & Rec 3:32-4 O '68

GEIGER-Müller counters. See Counters (electrons, ions, etc)

GEISELMAN, Bud
Cruising trimaran. Yachting 125:85+ Ja '69

GEISERT, Arthur F.
Sharpening perception. Sch Arts 69:10-11 N '69
Sheet lead for relief sculpture. Sch Arts 68: 18-20 Ap '69

GEISHAS
Where have all the geisha gone? C. Lucas. il Read Digest 94:39-40+ Mr '69

GEISLER, Norman L.
Let's drop unbiblical rules for church membership. Chr Today 13:17-18 Ja 31 '69

GEISMAR, Peter
Moratorium in Paris. Nation 209:627-8 D 8 '69
Wretched of Martinique. Nation 208:782-3 Je 23 '69

GEIST, Lee
Confessions of an ad manager. Duns R 93:54-6+ Ap '69

GEIST, Otto William
Aghvook, white Eskimo, by C. J. Keim. Review
Sat R 52:32 Jl 5 '69. K. Winslow

GELATIN
Gelatin jewels. il Am Home 72:62+ Jl '69

GELATT, Roland
Cannes after the events. Sat R 52:22-3+ Je 21 '69
Great recordings revisited. Sat R 52:61-2 S 27 '69
Looking and listening. House & Gard 135:16+ F; 66+ Mr; 66+ My; 40+ Je '69
SR goes to the movies. See issues of Saturday review
Will Maria Callas sing again? McCalls 96: 90-1 Mr '69
(ed) See Boulez, P. Conversation with Pierre Boulez

GELB, Richard Lee
Crime; address, April 28, 1969. Vital Speeches 35:639-40 Ag 1 '69

GELBOIN, H. V. See Diamond, L. jt. auth.

GELDZAHLER, Henry
Dictator or fantasy? por Time 94:81 O 24 '69
Modern masters amid the old. D. Bourdon. il Life 67:12 O 24 '69

GELINEAU, Victor A. See Kantor, D. jt. auth.

GELL-MANN, Murray
Mouse in the cathedral. por Newsweek 74:70 N 10 '69
Nobel laureates in economics, chemistry, and physics. M. L. Goldberger. il por Science 166:720-2 N 7 '69
Nobel prizes. por Sci N 96:421-2 N 8 '69
Order in the zoo. por Time 94:52 N 7 '69

GELLER, Bob
Dear Benjamin. Engl J 58:423-5 Mr '69

GELLES, George
Critic at large. Time 94:81 D 12 '69

GELS. See Colloids

GELTMAN, Max
Black power and national socialism. Nat R 21:132-3 F 11 '69
Marx, magic and John Calvin. Nat R 21: 343-4 Ap 8 '69
Open question. Nat R 21:438-9, 902 My 6, S 9 '69

GEM cutting. See Lapidary work

GEMS
Shopping tips: gems. il Changing T 22:29-31 D '68
See also
Diamonds
Emeralds
Precious stones
Tanzanite

GENCER, Leyla
To Britain with song. E. Rizzo. por Opera N 33:16-17 My 17 '69

GENDA, Minoru
Japan relies upon the U.S. too much for her defense; interview, ed. by K. M. Chrysler. U S News 67:93-4 O 27 '69

GENDEL, Milton
From Ricci to Tiepolo via Bencovich. Art N 68:58-60+ S '69
Rome (cont) Art N 68:8 Sum '69

GENDLER, Everett E.
Cuba and religion: challenge and response. Chr Cent 86:1013-16 Jl 30 '69

GENE flow. See Genes

GENE frequency. See Genes

GENEALOGY
Let's climb the family tree. M. Hinckley. il Har Yrs 9:38-41 Mr '69
See also
Family records

GENEEN, Harold Sydney
Diversification; address. Vital Speeches 36: 147-52 D 15 '69

GENERAL acceptance corporation
Loan company joins conglomerates. Bsns W p84+ S 6 '69

GENERAL American transportation corporation
At the crossroads; GATX leasing freight cars. il Forbes 104:50 O 1 '69

GENERAL assembly of the United Nations. See United Nations—General assembly

GENERAL aviation. See Aviation

GENERAL cable corporation
Copper's disappearing act. il Bsns W p34-5 N 1 '69

GENERAL development corporation
Chairman wouldn't sit down. Bsns W p52-3 D 20 '69

GENERAL dynamics corporation
After the brink, what? il Forbes 103:27-8 Mr 1 '69
General dynamics: in trouble again. il Bsns W p48-50+ O 4 '69
Storms signals fly at General dynamics. Bsns W p28 Ag 9 '69

GENERAL education. See Liberal education

GENERAL electric company
AT&T, Comsat oppose GE on domestic Satcom plan. K. Johnsen. Aviation W 90:21 Ap 21 '69
Boulware writes on Boulwarism. Bsns W p24+ Ag 30 '69
Boycott at G.E. Time 94:100 D 5 '69
Boycott of GE goods may prolong strike. Bsns W p32-3 N 29 '69
Can GE's unions exorcise Boulwarism? il Bsns W p73 O 18 '69
Costliest GE contract? il Bsns W p 132 Je 28 '69
Crisis bargaining looms in GE talks. Bsns W p62+ O 4 '69
Do you want a riot? GE strike. Nat R 21: 1205-6 D 2 '69
Domestic satcom proposal reopens FCC evaluation. K. Johnsen. Aviation W 90:24-5 Ap 7 '69
Federation steps up its attack on GE. il Bsns W p38-9 N 22 '69
GE and unions open wage battle. il Bsns W p96+ Ag 16 '69
GE bind tightens. Bsns W p48 S 6 '69
GE, Control data play their hands; price increases. Bsns W p90+ S 20 '69
GE expects facilities, employ expansion for production phase. Aviation W 92:88 Ja 5 '70
General electric; pattern for next year's labor gains? il U S News 67:97-8 O 27 '69
GE settles down to a long ordeal. il Bsns W p36 N 1 '69
GE shuffles its groups; recentralization of overseas activities. Bsns W p37 Ap 19 '69
GE steps on teletype's toes; TermiNet 300 is quieter and faster than teletypewriters. il Bsns W p52 Ap 5 '69
GE strike: it's starting to hurt. il Bsns W p 13-15 D 20 '69
GE strikers back their leaders; with editorial comment. il Bsns W p 102+, 154 N 8 '69
GE talks come to first crunch. Bsns W p43+ O 11 '69

GENERAL electric company—*Continued*
GE's great bulb caper. W. F. Mattes. il
Nation 208:823-5 Je 30 '69
G.E.'s heavy armful. il Time 93:60 Ja 31 '69
GE's hot idea for die-casting. il Bsns W
p88+ S 27 '69
Heat but no light at General electric. il Bsns
W p42 D 13 '69
Hint of a break in GE deadlock. il Bsns W
p44+ N 15 '69
Holiday hitch; boycott. Newsweek 74:100 D 8
'69
Hopes are flickering for GE settlement. Bsns
W p50 O 18 '69
Issue is Boulwarism. B. J. Widick. Nation
209:491 N 10 '69
Labor's opening fight for higher wages. il
Time 94:91 N 7 '69
Now the real war begins. il Newsweek 75:
74-6 Ja 19 '70
Prefab housing steals ideas from warheads.
il Bsns W p73 Ja 3 '70
Strike, and a spiral. il Newsweek 74:83 N 10
'69
Strike to boycott to what? GE case. Nat R
21:1256 D 16 '69
What happens in a big strike: both sides of
General electric story; interviews. il U S
News 67:37-9 D 29 '69
Who needs Wall Street? house mutual fund
open only to GE management. Forbes 103:
52-3 F 1 '69
Why not compulsory arbitration? America
121:520 N 29 '69
GENERAL electric strike. See Strikes—United
States—Electric workers
GENERAL foods corporation
We've turned a corner. il Forbes 103:46 Mr 15
'69
GENERAL host corporation
Greyhound makes a run for Armour. Bsns W
p 19 F 1 '69
High-stakes game. Newsweek 74:70+ Jl 7 '69
Over a barrel? Wins control of Armour.
Forbes 103:44 Mr 15 '69
Packing up at Armour. Bsns W p27 My 3
'69
Pistell packer? Newsweek 73:83-4 Ap 14 '69
Prince, the General and the Greyhound.
Time 93:94 My 9 '69
You can't lose 'em all. il Forbes 104:25-6 N
15 '69
GENERAL information tests. See Information
tests
GENERAL instrument corporation
General instrument bides its time. Bsns W
p 118-20 N 29 '69
GENERAL mills, incorporated
Where youth sets the style. il Bsns W p 118-
20 My 17 '69
GENERAL motors corporation
Big boondoggle at Lordstown; with editorial
comment. D. Sider. il Fortune 80:85-6, 106-
9+ S '69
Biggest recall. Newsweek 73:79-80 Mr 10 '69
Bill Mitchell brings style to GM with a capital
S. L. Levine. il Motor T 21:38-40 Mr '69
Fresh air at GM. J. C. Jones. il Newsweek
73:84-5 Ja 27 '69
G.M. takes the high ground in the new battle
of Detroit. T. O'Hanlon. il Fortune 79:70-
5+ My 1 '69
GM workers say Roche is wrong. U S News
66:88 My 12 '69
GM's new line-up; top-level appointments.
il Newsweek 73:85 F 17 '69
How GM helps itself by helping the GIs;
Project Transition. il Bsns w p92+ Ap
26 '69
Reasonable doubt; recall of 4.9 million cars
and trucks. Nation 208:325 Mr 17 '69
Record recall. il Time 93:23 Mr 7 '69
Rematch; GM's earthmoving equipment division. il Forbes 104:62+ O 15 '69
When nearly 5 million cars are recalled; General motors inspection of four-barrel car-
buretors. U S News 66:14 Mr 17 '69

Chevrolet division
Exit the Corvair. il Newsweek 73:99 My 26
'69
GM scraps the Corvair. Bsns W p41 My 17
'69

Oldsmobile division
John Beltz the new doctor Oldsmobile: in-
terview, ed. by R. Brock. J. Beltz. il Motor
T 21:62-4 Jl '69
GENERAL motors institute. See Automobile
industry and trade—Study and teaching
GENERAL motors research laboratories
See also
REACT (organization)
GENERAL practitioners. See Physicians

GENERAL telephone and electronics company
Try selling red ink; GT&E trying to get rid
of 42 per cent Argus stock. Forbes 103:
69 Ap 15 '69
GENERAL time corporation
General time's losing battle. H. B. Meyers.
Fortune 79:204 My 15 '69
GENERAL tire and rubber company
Hard part of the job; to know how to run
the businesses you acquire. il Forbes 103:
43-4 Ap 1 '69
GENERALIZATION (psychology)
Neural readout from memory during gen-
eralization. E. R. John and others. bibliog
il Science 164:1534-6 Je 27 '69
GENERALS
Fateful friendship. S. E. Ambrose. il Am
Heritage 20:40-1+ Ap '69
GENERATION gap. See Parent-child relation-
ship; Youth-adult relationship
GENERATIVE organs

Surgery
Maturing science of sex reassignment; transsexualism and sex surgery. H. Benjamin;
I. B. Pauly. Sat R 52:72-3 O 4 '69
GENERATORS, Electric. See Electric genera-
tors
GENES
Control of specific gene expression in higher
organisms. G. M. Tomkins and others.
bibliog il Science 166:1474-80 D 19 '69
Differentiation of populations; importance of
gene flow. P. R. Ehrlich and P. H. Raven.
bibliog Science 165:1228-32 S 19 '69
Elegant triumph; isolating the gene. il Time
94:80 D 5 '69
Genetic engineers; lac genes isolated. il News-
week 74:110+ D 8 '69
Homology of lactate dehydrogenase genes;
E. gene function in the teleost nervous
system. G. S. Whitt. bibliog il Science 166:
1156-8 N 28 '69
Molecular tour de force; isolation of single
gene. il Sci N 96:494 N 29 '69
Non-Darwinian evolution. J. L. King and
T. H. Jukes. bibliog il Science 164:788-98
My 16 '69
Portrait of a gene. il Chem 42:20-1 S '69
Spinning the thread of life. J. Lear. il Sat R
52:63-6 Ap 5 '69
Visualization of nucleolar genes. O. L. Mil-
ler, jr. and B. R. Beatty. bibliog il
Science 164:955-7 My 23 '69
See also
Allelomorphism
GENESCO, incorporated
Genesco heir tries on the shoe; F. M. Jarman.
il Bsns W p50-2 Jl 26 '69
GENÊT, pseud. See Flanner, J.
GENETIC counseling
Solving the mystery of birth defects. H. A.
Rusk and others. il Parents Mag 44:61-3+
N '69
Will the baby be normal? The genetic coun-
selor tries to find the answer. R. W. Stock.
il N Y Times Mag p25-7+ Mr 23 '69
GENETIC counseling clinics. See Health clinics
GENETIC drift. See Genes
GENETIC research
Designed genetic change. Sci Am 221:50-2
Jl '69
Elegant triumph; isolating the gene. il Time
94:80 D 5 '69
Frontier; genetic control. B. J. Culliton. il
Sci N 96:118-19 Ag 9 '69
Gene regulation for higher cells: a theory;
clue in organization of the genome. R. J.
Britten and E. H. Davidson. bibliog il Sci-
ence 165:349-57 Jl 25 '69; Reply. C. H. Wad-
dington 166:639 O 31 '69
Genetic code reconfirmed. Sci Am 221:58 N
'69
Genetic engineers; lac genes isolated. il News-
week 74:110+ D 8 '69
Hybrid somatic cells. B. Ephrussi and M. C
Weiss. il Sci Am 220:26-35 bibliog(p 146) Ap
'69
Mouse stage of the new biology. R. W. Stock.
il N Y Times Mag p8-9+ D 21 '69
New life for old; genetic decisions. M.
Hamilton. Chr Cent 86:741-4 My 28 '69
Test tube generation. D. M. Rorvik. il Es-
quire 71:108-14 Ap '69
Two mothers, two fathers; allophenic mice.
B. J. Culliton. il Sci N 95:361-3 Ap 12 '69
See also
Mutagenic substances

GENETICS
Genetic aspects of learning and memory in mice. D. Bovet and others. bibliog il Science 163:139-49 Ja 10 '69; Reply with rejoinder. K. R. Henry and others. 165:1148 S 12 '69

Genetic control of the antibody response: relationship between immune response and histocompatibility (H-2) type. H. O. McDevitt and A. Chinitz. bibliog il Science 163:1207-8 Mr 14 '69

Modern biology: a terrifying power. S. E. Luria. il Nation 209:406-9 O 20 '69

Not even good rats; highly inbred white rats for reliable research. B. J. Culliton. il Sci N 95:145-6 F 8 '69
    See also
Alleiomorphism
Chromosomes
Crossing over (genetics)
Heredity
Human genetics
Plant genetics

History
Soviet biology and the powers that were. T. Dobzhansky. Science 164:1507-9 Je 27 '69

Research
See Genetic research
GENETICS (botany) See Plant genetics
GENETICS (fungi)
Schizophyllum commune: gene controlling induced haploid fruiting. T. J. Leonard and J. R. Raper. bibliog il Science 165:190 Jl 11 '69
GENEVA, Switzerland

Music
Great opera houses. D. A. MacKinnon. il Opera N 33:26-9 Mr 22 '69
GENEVA auto show. See Automobiles—Exhibitions
GENGERELLI, Joseph Anthony
Education tube. Sch & Soc 97:363-6 O '69
GENNARO, Joseph F. Jr
Gecko grip; with biographical sketch. Natur Hist 78:4, 36-43 Ag '69
GENNARO, Peter
Dancing on TV. W. Terry. il Sat R 52:42-3 Mr 1 '69
GENOA

Art
Genoese mix; Baroque paintings at the Palazzo Bianco; tr. by S. Morini. M. Valsecchi. il Art N 68:28-30+ O '69

Description
La superba. C. Foley. il Nat R 21:963+ S 23 '69

GENOESE painting. See Painting, Italian
GENOME. See Chromosomes
GENOTYPE and phenotype
Genetics and phenogenetics of mitochondria. R. P. Wagner. bibliog Science 163:1026-31 Mr 7 '69; Reply. R. T. Hersh. 166:402 O 17 '69

Linkage of lactate dehydrogenase B and C loci in pigeons. W. H. Zinkham and others. bibliog il Science 164:185-7 Ap 11 '69

6-Phosphogluconate dehydrogenase: hemizygous manifestation in a patient with leukemia. P. J. Fialkow and others. bibliog il Science 163:194-5 Ja 10 '69
GENOVESE, Eugene D.
Black studies: trouble ahead. Atlan 223:37-41 Je '69; Same abr. with title Black studies: legitimacy versus propaganda. Cur 109:39-42 Ag '69
GENOVESE, Vito
Power struggle after a death in the family. S. Smith il pors Life 66:51+ F 28 '69
GENRE painting
German genre paintings from the Von Schleinitz collection. T. Atkinson. il Antiques 96:712-16 N '69

William S. Mount: the mysterious stranger. A. A. Davidson. il Art N 68:34-7+ Mr '69
GENTIANS
Blue gentian. H. L. Foster. Horticulture 46:13-15+ O '69
GENTILE da Fabriano
Gentile da Fabriano's Madonna and Child with saints. B. F. Davidson. il Art N 68:24-7+ Mr '69
GENTLE genius; drama. See Jackson, D.
GEODESIC domes. See Domes
GEOFFRION, Bernard
Rangers go boom. G. Astor. il pors Look 33:80-2 F 4 '69

GEOGRAPHERS
Fascinating new careers in geography. C. Peet. il Sci Digest 65:77-80 Je '69
GEOGRAPHICAL distribution of animals and plants
Generation and maintenance of gradients in taxonomic diversity. F. G. Stehli and others. bibliog il Science 164:947-8 My 23 '69; Reply. L. Van Valen. 166:1656-8 D 26 '69
    See also
Fishes—Geographical distribution
Forest ecology
Insects—Geographical distribution
Life zones
GEOGRAPHICAL myths
    See also
Podunk (imaginary town)
GEOGRAPHOS (asteroid) See Asteroids
GEOGRAPHY
    See also
Anthropogeography
Man—Influence of environment

Study and teaching
Geography: sighted subject, sank same. G. C. Fox. Clear House 44:35-6 S '69
Mystery island: a lesson in inquiry. J. Zevin. il Todays Ed 58:42-3 My '69
This geography is something to sing about. C. Watson. il Am Ed 5:14-18 O '69
GEOGRAPHY, Historical

Maps
Historical atlas of Latin America, by A. C. Wilgus. Review
    Américas il 21:39-40 Ap '69. M. B. Mármol
    See also
Maps, Early
GEOLOGICAL maps. See Geology—Maps
GEOLOGICAL research
Lunar and terrestrial exploration. P. H. Abelson. Science 166:1225 D 5 '69
    See also
International geophysical year
GEOLOGICAL society of America
Earth sciences. Sci N 96:478 N 22 '69
New social science. Sci N 96:447 N 15 '69
GEOLOGICAL survey (United States) See United States—Geological survey
GEOLOGICAL time
Sedimentary rock types: relative proportions as a function of geological time. R. M. Garrels and F. T. Mackenzie. bibliog il Science 163:570-1 F 7 '69
    See also
Radioactive dating
Radiocarbon dating
GEOLOGY
How good a geologist are you? J. Daugherty and M. Daugherty. il Sci Digest 65:86-8 Mr '69
    See also
Continents
Earth
Earthquakes
Faults (geology)
Geological research
Geological society of America
Geological time
Glacial geology
Loess
Metamorphism (geology)
Mountains
Ocean bottom
Petrology
Submarine geology
Volcanoes

Bibliography
Geologist's guide to the planet earth. W. H. Matthews, 3d. il Natur Hist 78:66-8+ D '69

Maps
Geology map for western travelers. il Sunset 143:38 O '69

Alaska
Alaskan upper miocene marine glacial deposits and the turborotalia pachyderma datum plane. O. L. Bandy and others. bibliog il Science 166:607-9 O 31 '69
Bentonite debris flows in northern Alaska. D. M. Anderson and others. bibliog il Science 164:173-4 Ap 11 '69

Antarctic Regions
Ellsworth Mountains: position in west Antarctica due to sea-floor spreading. J. M. Schopf. bibliog il Science 164:63-6 Ap 4 '69
Mawson tillite in Antarctica: preliminary report of a volcanic deposit of Jurassic age. H. W. Borns, jr. and E. A. Hall. bibliog il Science 166:870-2 N 14 '69

GEOLOGY—*Continued*

Appalachian Region

Zircon ages of felsic volcanic rocks in the upper Precambrian of the Blue Ridge, Appalachian Mountains. D. W. Rankin and others. bibliog il Science 166:741-4 N 7 '69

Arctic Regions

Paleozoic tectonic history of the Arctic basin north of Alaska. M. Churkin, jr. bibliog il Science 165:549-55 Ag 8 '69

Argentina

Glaciation in southern Argentina more than two million years ago. J. H. Mercer. bibliog il Science 164:823-5 My 16 '69

Brazil

Brazil-Gabon geologic link supports continental drift. G. O. Allard and V. J. Hurst. bibliog il Science 163:528-32 F 7 '69

California

California=New Zealand. Sci Digest 66:38 S '69

Late Cenozoic underthrusting of the continental margin off northernmost California. E. A. Silver. bibliog il Science 166:1265-6 D 5 '69

Caribbean Region

Origin of an obstacle; Bahama platform. il Sci N 96:473-4 N 22 '69

District of Columbia

Glacial age marsh, Lafayette park, Washington, D. C. A. S. Knox. bibliog il Science 165:795-7 Ag 22 '69

Gabon

Brazil-Gabon geologic link supports continental drift. G. O. Allard and V. J. Hurst. bibliog il Science 163:528-32 F 7 '69

Germany

Jadeite: shock-induced formation from oligoclase, Ries crater, Germany. O. B. James. bibliog il Science 165:1005-8 S 5 '69

Hawaii

Eolian origin of quartz in soils of Hawaiian Islands and in Pacific pelagic sediments. R. W. Rex and others. bibliog il Science 163:277-9 Ja 17 '69

Iceland

Iceland's thermal geology. J. Kane. il Natur Hist 78:48-51 Ja '69

Mauritania

Coesite from the Richat dome, Mauritania: a misidentification. R. F. Fudali. bibliog il Science 166:228-30 O 10 '69

Mexico

Solving the mystery of Mexico's great stone spheres. M. W. Stirling. il Nat Geog 136:294-300 Ag '69

New York (state)

How firm a foundation; New York city's bedrock. C. J. Schuberth. il Natur Hist 78:56-64 Ap '69

New Zealand

California=New Zealand. Sci Digest 66:38 S '69

Oceania

Macquarie Island and the cause of oceanic linear magnetic anomalies. R. Varne nd others. bibliog il Science 166:230-3 O 10 '69

Pacific Region

Circum-Pacific late Cenozoic structural rejuvenation: implications for sea floor spreading. R. H. Dott, jr. bibliog il Science 166:874-6 N 14 '69

GEOLOGY, Stratigraphic

How firm a foundation; New York city's bedrock. C. J. Schuberth. il Natur Hist 78:56-64 Ap '69

Cenozoic

Circum-Pacific late Cenozoic structural rejuvenation: implications for sea floor spreading. R. H. Dott, jr. bibliog il Science 166:874-6 N 14 '69

Late Cenozoic underthrusting of the continental margin off northernmost California. E. A. Silver. bibliog il Science 166:1265-6 D 5 '69

Jurassic

Mawson tillite in Antarctica: preliminary report of a volcanic deposit of Jurassic age. H. W. Borns, jr. and B. A. Hall. bibliog il Science 166:870-2 N 14 '69

Miocene

Alaskan upper miocene marine glacial deposits and the turborotalia pachyderma datum plane. O. L. Bandy and others. bibliog il Science 166:607-9 O 31 '69

Paleozoic

Paleozoic tectonic history of the Arctic basin north of Alaska. M. Churkin, jr. bibliog il Science 165:549-55 Ag 8 '69

Pleistocene

Glacial age marsh, Lafayette park, Washington, D.C. A. S. Knox. bibliog il Science 165:795-7 Ag 22 '69

Methane-derived marine carbonates of pleistocene age. J. C. Hathaway and E. T. Degens. bibliog il Science 65:690-2 Ag 15 '69

Pre-Cambrian

Zircon ages of felsic volcanic rocks in the upper Precambrain of the Blue Ridge, Appalachian Mountains. D. W. Rankin and others. bibliog il Science 166:741-4 N 7 '69

Tertiary

Solving the mystery of Mexico's great stone spheres. M. W. Stirling. il Nat Geog 136:294-300 Ag '69

GEOLOGY, Structural

Bed forms in base-surge deposits: lunar implications. R. V. Fisher and A. C. Waters. bibliog il Science 165:1349-52 S 26 '69

Bentonite debris flows in northern Alaska. D. M. Anderson and others. bibliog il Science 164:173-4 Ap 11 '69

Molasse facies: records of worldwide crustal stresses. F. B. Van Houten. bibliog il Science 166:1506-8 D 19 '69

New view of the world; unifying plate theory. K. Frazier. il Sci N 96:430-1+ N 8 '69

Paleozoic tectonic history of the Arctic basin north of Alaska. M. Churkin, jr. bibliog il Science 165:549-55 Ag 8 '69

Time for a theory; plate tectonics. il Sci N 95:449-50 My 10 '69

Transversely aligned seismicity and concealed structures. C. F. Richter. bibliog il Science 166:173-8 O 10 '69

See also

Faults (geology)

GEOMAGNETIC observatories

Geomagnetic observatories. L. G. Lawrence. bibliog il Electr World 81:41-4 F '69

GEOMAGNETISM. See Magnetism, Terrestrial

GEOMETRY

Non-Euclidean geometry before Euclid; famous problem of parallels. I. Toth. Sci Am 221:87-92+ N '69

Study and teaching

Dilemma in geometry. C. B. Allendoefer. Ed Digest 34:40-3 My '69

GEOMORPHOLOGY. See Geology, Structural

GEOPHAGIA. See Pica (pathology)

GEOPHYSICAL research

Tritium geophysics as an international research project. H. E. Suess. bibliog il Science 163:1405-10 Mr 28 '69

GEOPHYSICS

Secret of the spreading ocean floors. T. Alexander. il Fortune 79:112-17+ F '69

See also

American geophysical union

Earth—Internal structure

International geophysical year

Seismology

GEORGE III, king of Great Britain

Porphyria and King George III. I. Macalpine and R. Hunter. il Sci Am 221:38-46 Jl '69; Discussion. 221:8-9 D '69

Royal malady. por Time 94:60+ Ag 1 '69

GEORGE IV, king of Great Britain

Regency: a nine-year wonder. L. Kronenberger. il Atlan 224:87-90 N '69

GEORGE, Gerald. See Bromberg, W. jt. auth.

GEORGE, Jean Craighead

From the brink of extinction. Nat Wildlife 7:20-3 Ap '69; Same abr. Read Digest 94:214-15+ Ap '69

Grizzlies, the magnificent menace. Read Digest 95:117-21 Jl '69

Many voices of life. Nat Wildlife 7:34-7 Je '69; Same abr. with title Surprising signals in the wild. Read Digest 94:163-4+ Je '69

GEORGE, Jean Craighead—*Continued*
North goes the mocker. Audubon 71:48-9 Ja '69
Surprising signals in the wild; excerpts. Read Digest 94:163-4+ Je '69
GEORGE Allen and Unwin, limited. See Allen, George and Unwin, limited
GEORGE slept here, too: drama. See Martens, A. C.
GEORGE Washington bridge. See Hudson River bridges
GEORGE Washington national forest. See National forests
GEORGE Washington trail. See Trails
GEORGE Washington university, Washington, D.C.
University contractors cut ties with CRESS. HumRRO, army's two main centers of social, behavioral research. J. Coburn. Science 164:1039-41 My 30 '69
GEORGETOWN. See Washington, D.C.
GEORGIA
Threatened marshes of Glynn. il Life 67:88-93 N 14 '69
See also
Architecture, Domestic—Georgia
Conservation of resources—Georgia
Fishing—Georgia
Gardens—Georgia
Negroes—Georgia
Urban renewal—Georgia

Economic conditions
Defense contract: the money web. G. Astor. il Look 33:28-9 Ag 26 '69

Historic houses, etc.
See also
Atlanta—Historic houses, etc.

Politics and government
Julian Bond. D. Llorens. il Ebony 24:58-62+ My '69

Race problems
Surprising talk between a black leader and a top segregationist; ed. by B. Cohn and S. Ball, jr. J. Bond and R. V. Harris. il N Y Times Mag p34-5+ Ap 27 '69
GEORGIA-Pacific corporation
Watch that waistline! il Forbes 103:26 F 1 '69
GEOTHERMAL energy. See Steam, Natural
GERA, Bernice
Squeeze play. il por Time 94:61 Ag 15 '69
GERACI, Phil
How to get your boat to pose for better pictures. Pop Mech 132:112-5+ Jl '69
How you'll see our men on the moon. Pop Mech 132:92-3+ Jl '69
Zoom your way to bigger, better pictures. Pop Mech 132:160-3+ O '69
GERALD, John Bart
Blood letting; story. Atlan 223:88-90 My '69
GERALD, Park S. See Neaves, W. B. jt. auth.
GERANIUMS
How to winter geraniums. G. Taloumis. il Horticulture 46:33+ N '68
Multiply geraniums: use kitchen supplies. il Home Gard 56:58-9 O '69
New and tough, the carefree geraniums. il Sunset 142:268 Ap '69
Story of the miniature geraniums. M. E. Ross. il Horticulture 47:34-7+ Mr '69
GÉRARD, Maurice
Soupçon of sorcery. il por Newsweek 75:41 Ja 5 '70
GERASIMOV, Innokentii Petrovich
Soviet plan for nature; reprint; with biographical sketch. por Natur Hist 78:5, 24-35 D '69
GERASSI, Marysa N.
Uruguay's urban guerrillas. Nation 209:306-10 S 29 '69
GERBER, H. Joseph
Wunderkind's road to Seventh avenue. por Bsns W p 104 My 3 '69
GERBER, Henry S. and Klostermeyer, E. C.
Sex control by bees: a voluntary act of egg fertilization during oviposition. bibliog Science 167:82-4 Ja 2 '70
GERBER, Merrill Joan
Getting to where the story is. Writer 82:15-16 Ag '69
What do I want to do today? story. Redbook 134:100-1 D '69
GERBER, Rudolph J.
Catholic philosopher. Commonweal 90:105-6+ Ap 11 '69
GERBER scientific instrument company
Fitting automation to the garment trade; precise cutting machine. Gerbercutter. il Bsns W p 102+ My 3 '69

GERBERCUTTER. See Cutting machines
GERBERG, Mort
What really happened when a very nice team from Atlanta encountered a force known as the New York Mets; cartoons. Life 67:42-5 O 17 '69
GERBILS
Up to here in gerbils. P. Simon. il McCalls 97:39+ D '69
GERHARDT, John. See Toyli, M. jt. auth.
GERHARDT, Lillian N. and others
(ed) Book review. See issues of Library journal
GERHART, Marian R.
(comp) Bibliography for a top Broadway hit. por Wilson Lib Bul 43:1010-11 Je '69

about
1776: creating the best of Broadway in a small-town public library. il Wilson Lib Bul 43:1008-10 Je '69
GERIATRICS. See Aged—Care and hygiene; Old age
GERM cells
Human oocytes: maturation in chemically defined media. J. F. Kennedy and R. P. Donahue. bibliog il Science 164:1292-3 Je 13 '69
Mammalian oocytes: X chromosome activity. C. J. Epstein. bibliog il Science 163:1078-9 Mr 7 '69
See also
Gametogenesis
GERM free animals. See Germfree life
GERM-free isolators. See Hospitals—Isolation departments
GERM warfare. See Biological warfare
GERMAN, Ambrose A.
Black and crumbling. Org Gard & Farm 16:46 O '69
GERMAN artificial satellites. See Artificial satellites, German
GERMAN automobiles. See Automobiles, Foreign
GERMAN Evangelical church. See Evangelical church in Germany
GERMAN fingerling. See Potatoes
GERMAN invasion of Poland. See World war, 1939-1945—Poland
GERMAN literature
See also
German poetry
GERMAN measles. See Rubella
GERMAN occupied countries. See France—History—German occupation, 1940-1945
GERMAN painting. See Painting, German
GERMAN periodicals. See Periodicals—Germany
GERMAN poetry
Poet in the collective; works of W. Biermann. D. Kleinbard. Nation 208:438+ Ap 7 '69

Translations into English
Ballads by Wolf Biermann; Song of the worst thing; Hanns Eisler, or the anatomy of a sphere; Comrades, which of us wouldn't be against war; Devastating side effect of the Vietnam war; tr. by E. Bentley. W. Biermann. Nation 208: 440 Ap 7 '69
Birth of Christ; tr. by M. W. Hess. R. M. Rilke. Chr Today 14:12 D 5 '69
GERMAN reunification question. See Germany—Union (proposed)
GERMAN scientists. See Scientists, German
GERMAN songs. See Songs, German
GERMAN students
See also
Student demonstrations—Germany (Federal Republic)
GERMAN war criminals. See World war, 1939-1945—War criminals
GERMAN wine. See Wine
GERMANATES
Garnet-like structures of high-pressure cadmium germanate and calcium germanate. C. T. Prewitt and A. W. Sleight. bibliog il Science 163:386-7 Ja 24 '69
Modified spinel, beta-manganous orthogermanate; stability and crystal structure. N. Morimoto and others. bibliog il Science 165:586-8 Ag 8 '69
GERMANDER
It makes a great silvery hedge; bush germander. il Sunset 143:279 O '69
GERMANTOWN. See Philadelphia

GERMANY

Two Germanies: a nation with a state. H. A. Schmitt. Cur Hist 56:224-9+ Ap '69
See also
Archives—Germany
Berlin
Colleges and universities—Germany
Geology—Germany
Industry and state—Germany
Lakes—Germany
Opera—Germany
Paleontology—Germany

Economic history

Big business in German politics: four studies. bibliog f Am Hist R 75:37-78 O '69

Economic policy

Big business and German politics: a comment. E. Nolte. bibliog f Am Hist R 75:71-8 O '69

History

Kings depart. by R. M. Watt. Review
Time il 93:82+ Je 27 '69

Bibliography

Articles and other books received; comp. by A. H. Price. See issues of American historical review
Sources
See also
World war, 1939-1945—Documents, sources, etc.

1871-

Political leadership in the German Reichstag, 1871-1918. J. J. Sheehan. bibliog f Am Hist R 74:511-28 D '68

1918-1933

Weimar and the rise of Hitler, by A. J. Nicholls. Review
Bul Atom Sci 25:41-2 D '69. D. B. King
Weimar culture. by P. Gay. Review
Commonweal 89:621-2 F 14 '69. G. Lewy
Nat R 21:602-4 Je 17 '69. S. J. Tonsor
Weimar Germany's left-wing intellectuals, by I. Deak. Review
Commentary 48:94-6+ O '69. M. Jay

1933-1945

Devil's architect: Hitler's Armaments Minister A. Speer. J. P. O'Donnell. il N Y Times Mag p45-9+ O 26 '69; Discussion. p22+ N 30 '69
Secrets of the Nazi archives. D. Kahn. Atlan 223:50-6 My '69

Intellectual life

Weimar culture. by P. Gay. Review
Commonweal 89:621-2 F 14 '69. G. Lewy
Weimar Germany's left-wing intellectuals, by I. Deak. Review
Nation 208:442-3 Ap 7 '69. S. Warnecke

National socialist movement
See National socialism

Politics and government

Führer's master builder. il Time 94:40 S 12 '69
See also
Germany—Reichstag
National socialism

Reichstag

Political leadership in the German Reichstag, 1871-1918. J. J. Sheehan. bibliog f Am Hist R 74:511-28 D '68

Religious institutions and affairs
See also
Protestants in Germany

Social history

Decline of the German mandarins. by F. K. Ringer. Review
New Repub 160:27-9 F 22 '69. P. Gay

Union (proposed)

Letter from Germany: documentary-style film on reunification. L. R. Colitt. Nation 208:283-4 Mr 3 '69

GERMANY (Democratic Republic)
German Democratic Republic and the West. J. E. Smith. Yale R 58:372-87 Mr '69
Germany no longer. S. Du Broff. Nation 208:269-71 Mr 3 '69
See also
Berlin (East Berlin)
Leipzig
Music festivals—Germany (Democratic Republic)

Economic conditions

Making the best of a bad situation. il Time 94:42 O 17 '69
Why Communists get tough over Berlin. il U S News 66:25-6 Mr 3 '69

Foreign relations

Berlin jitters again. il Newsweek 73:39 F 24 '69
Once more, trouble in Berlin. il Time 93:22-3 F 21 '69
Tight leash on Ulbricht? U S News 66:20 Mr 17 '69

Intellectual life
See also
Leipzig—Intellectual life

Politics and government

After Ulbricht? il Newsweek 74:36-8 Ag 25 '69
Behind the wall, the success story of Walter Ulbricht? J. H. Huizinga. il N Y Times Mag p36-7+ S 7 '69
Walter Ulbricht: the unsinkable satrap. J. P. O'Donnell. Read Digest 94:115-19 Mr '69

Religious institutions and affairs

Are red rites wrong? J. van Capeneveen. Chr. Today 14:54 N 7 '69
East German churches warned to cut all ties with West. Chr Cent 86:342 Mr 12 '69
World around us (cont) Chr Cent 86:331-2, 851-2, 1466-8; 87:29-30 Mr 5, Je 18, N 12 '69, Ja 7 '70

GERMANY (Federal Republic)
West Germany; policies for the future; address, October 28, 1969. W. Brandt. Vital Speeches 36:105-14 D 1 '69
See also
Air travel—Germany (Federal Republic)
Airlines—Germany (Federal Republic)
Airplane industry and trade—Germany (Federal Republic)
Airplanes, Military—Germany (Federal Republic)
Architecture—Germany (Federal Republic)
Automobile industry and trade—Germany (Federal Republic)
Ballet—Germany (Federal Republic)
Berlin (West Berlin)
Bielefeld
Bonn
Düsseldorf, Germany—Music
Education—Germany (Federal Republic)
Elections—Germany (Federal Republic)
Foreign students in Germany
Hotels, taverns, etc.—Germany (Federal Republic)
Investments, Foreign (by Germany [Federal Republic])
Israel—Commerce—Germany (Federal Republic)
Jews in Germany
Kiel
Library schools and education—Germany (Federal Republic)
Lüneburger Heide
Military service, Compulsory—Germany (Federal Republic)
Money—Germany (Federal Republic)
Oceanographic research—Germany (Federal Republic)
Opera—Germany (Federal Republic)
Political campaigns—Germany (Federal Republic)
Political parties—Germany (Federal Republic)
Public opinion—Germany (Federal Republic)
Publishers and publishing—Germany (Federal Republic)
Research—Germany (Federal Republic)
Selb, Germany (Federal Republic)
Student demonstrations—Germany (Federal Republic)
Technology—Germany (Federal Republic)
Television broadcasting—Germany (Federal Republic)
Trade unions—Germany (Federal Republic)
Trials—Germany (Federal Republic)
Youth—Germany (Federal Republic)

Army

Orphan army. il Time 93:30-1 Je 20 '69
Who's right? morale crisis meeting. Newsweek 73:49-50+ Ap 21 '69

Commerce

Germany's export boom steams right ahead. il Bsns W p112-14+ N 1 '69
West Germany v. Japan. il Time 95:51-2 Ja 5 '70

Description and travel
See also
Black forest

Economic conditions

As I see it; interview. J. J. McCloy. Forbes 103:46-8+ Ja 15 '69
Germany catches its second wind. P. Siekman. il Fortune 79:88-91+ Ap '69
Tensions of too much success. il Time 93:102 Je 6 '69

GERMANY (Federal Republic)—*Continued*

Economic policy

Money crisis: on your mark, get set, hold it. il Newsweek 73:79-80 My 19 '69
West Germany's financial defiance. il Time 93:103-4 My 16 '69
Winners inherit a heated economy. il Bsns W p27 O 4 '69

Economic relations

Yugoslavs to train for jobs in West? U S News 67:87 Ag 11 '69

Foreign relations

After twenty-five years. New Repub 161:9-10 N 8 '69
Germany's changing role; interview, ed. by R. Haeger. W. Brandt. il U S News 67:28-32 D 29 '69

Europe, Eastern

Fatigue at the top. il Time 95:17-18 Ja 12 '70
Getting together in Europe. Time 94:34+ N 14 '69

Germany (Democratic Republic)

Fast drive to Bonn. Time 94:15 D 26 '69
Getting together in Europe. Time 94:34+ N 14 '69
Willy vs. Walter. Newsweek 75:24 Ja 5 '70

Russia

Anxiety in Bonn: German fears after Czechoslovakia. S. Muller. Bul Atom Sci 25:13-15 Mr '69
Germany looks East: reshaping Europe. il Newsweek 74:33-4 D 22 '69

United States

Economic, scientific, technological; political partnership between the United States and Europe; address, October 12, 1969. F. J. Strauss. Vital Speeches 36:144-7 D 15 '69
Nod to the home folks: K. Kiesinger's visit and talks agenda. il Newsweek 74:38+ Ag 18 '69
President Nixon meets with Chancellor Kiesinger of the Federal Republic of Germany; exchange of greetings, remarks, together with joint statement; August 7 and 8, 1969. R. M. Nixon; K. G. Kiesinger. Dept State Bul 61:211-14 S 8 '69
Why Kiesinger came to the U.S. il U S News 67:12 Ag 18 '69

Industries

Durable Friedrich Flick. il Forbes 103:39-41 F 1 '69

See also

Chemical industries—Germany (Federal Republic)
Interessengemeinschaft farbenindustrie ag
Krupp works, Essen

Politics and government

Brandt and the bogeyman. W. S. Schlamm. Nat R 21:1061-2 O 21 '69
Brandt era begins. Newsweek 74:59 N 10 '69
Chopper chancellor awaits air force one. J. P. O'Donnell. il N Y Times Mag p26-7+ F 16 '69
Foxes of Bonn. Nation 208:652 My 26 '69
Germany on a new path, which way will it lead? il U S News 67:20+ O 13 '69
New frontier. B. Van Voorst. il Newsweek 74:48 O 27 '69
New team. Newsweek 74:46+ N 3 '69
Open house on the Rhine. il Time 94:24+ O 31 '69
Thinking big for Germany. il Newsweek 73:50-2 Je 9 '69

See also

Elections—Germany (Federal Republic)
Political parties—Germany (Federal Republic)

Religious institutions and affairs

World around us. Chr Cent 86:490, 1074-5 Ap 9, Ag 13 '69

See also

Catholic church in Germany (Federal Republic)
Evangelical church in Germany
Protestants in Germany (Federal Republic)

GERMANY, EASTERN. See Germany (Democratic Republic)

GERMANY, WESTERN. See Germany (Federal Republic)

GERMFREE life
Survival of germfree rats without vitamin A. J. G. Bieri and others. il Science 163:574-5 F 7 '69

GERMINATION
   See also
Seeds

GERMOND, Jack W.
L.A.'s about to say so long, Sam. New Repub 160:10 My 24 '69

GERMS. See Microorganisms

GERNHARDT, Lillian N. and others
(ed) Best books of the spring. Library J 94:2072-4 My 15 '69

GERNREICH, Rudi
Fashions for the '70s. Life 68:115-18 Ja 9 '70

GERONTOLOGICAL society
Gerontological society to move to D.C; awards made, new officers installed. Aging 180:9 O '69

GERONTOLOGY
Excerpts from Theories of aging. A. Comfort. Aging 180:6 O '69
How to handle problems of aging. T. Irwin. il Todays Health 47:28-31+ Jl '69
Prospects for gerontology: psychology. J. E. Birren. Aging 180:7 O '69
Time for learning. il Har Yrs 9:46-8 Je '69
   See also
Institute of gerontology
Southern California university. Los Angeles—Ethel Percy Andrus gerontology center

Study and teaching

Minnesota gives ten degrees as masters in work for aging. il Aging 178:14-15 Ag '69

GERONTOLOGY workers
AoA funds program to train state aging agencies staff. Aging 178:12 Ag '69
Manpower needs in the field of aging. C. Tibbitts. Aging 173:3-5 Mr '69
Thirty-two new specialists in aging under AoA training plan listed. Aging 176:8 Je '69
Training. il Aging 175:10-11 My '69
U. of South Florida trains generalists in gerontology. il Aging 173:6-7 Mr '69

GERRY, Roger, and Butler, J. T.
Japanese export porcelain for the American market. Antiques 95:544-6 Ap '69

GERSH, Gabriel
Mafia: native sons. Sat R 52:57+ Mr 22 '69
Tragedy and dignity of man. Cath World 208:268-9 Mr '69

GERSHE, Leonard
Butterflies are free. Criticism
   America 121:545 N 29 '69
   Nation 209:518 N 10 '69
   New Yorker 45:127 N 1 '69
   Newsweek 74:93-4 N 3 '69
   Sat R 52:28 N 8 '69
   Time 94:55 O 31 '69

GERSHEFSKI, George W.
Building a corporate financial model. Harvard Bsns R 47:61-72 Jl '69

GERSHEN, Alvin E.
Stake in the system; address, May 28, 1969. Vital Speeches 35:763-5 O 1 '69

GERSHMAN, Carl
Isolation of the new left. Nation 208:665-8 My 26 '69

GERSONI, Diane
Up for discussion. Library J 94:4305-6 N 15 '69

GERST, Tom
Bali hi. Travel & Camera 32:52-3+ My '69

GERSTACKER, Carl Allan
Garbage burner; excerpt from interview, ed. by H. Downs. New Republic 161:7-8 Jl 26 '69

GERSTEIN, George L. and Perkel, D. H.
Simultaneously recorded trains of action potentials: analysis and functional interpretation. bibliog Science 164:828-30 My 16 '69

GERSTEIN, Kurt
Kurt Gerstein, by S. Friedländer. Review
   America 120:454 Ap 12 '69
   Chr Cent 86:875 Je 25 '69. D. Rogan
   Commentary 48:71-2+ Jl '69; G. Lewy
   Newsweek por 73:108+ Mr 24 '69. A. Cooper

GERSTENMAIER, Eugen
Preacher's fall. Newsweek 73:49 F 3 '69

GERSTER, Georg
Abu Simbel's ancient temples reborn. il Nat Geog 135:724-44 My '69

GERTRUDE F. Fruchtl, Sister. See Fruchtl, G. F.

GERTRUDE Stein's first reader; revue. See Musical comedies, revues, etc.—Criticisms, plots, etc.

GERTRUDE Talcott dance company
Gertrude Talcott dance company; Cubiculo theatre. J. Dowlin. Dance Mag 43:78+ Jl '69

GERTSEN, Aleksandr Ivanovich. See Herzen, A. I.

GERTWANGLER, Harry
ABCs of selling your house. Mech Illus 65:66-8+ Ap '69

GERTZ, Elmer
No work for the hangman. Nation 208:101-2
Ja 27 '69
GESELL, Gerhard Alden
Open city for abortion. il por Time 94:65
N 21 '69
GESNERIACEAE
See also
Smithiantha
GESSO block printing. See Block printing
GESTELAND, Norman
Driver education that's different. por Todays
Ed 58:60-1 S '69
GESTURE
Compelling gesture; how a conductor moves.
D. Vaughan. il Opera N 34:22-5 D 20 '69
Do gestures tell your secret thoughts? il
Good H 168:163 F '69
Flowering of the speaker's art; concerning
book, The speaker's ideal. J. L. Phillips. il
Am Heritage 20:101-3+ D '68
Man's silent signals; nonverbal vocabulary of
gestures and expressions. il Time 93:86
Je 13 '69
See also
Sign language
GETLEIN, Frank
Honorable discharge for God? Commonweal
90:194 My 2 '69
GETTY, Eugene Paul
Moroccan wake-up. il por Vogue 155:166-
71+ Ja 15 '70
GETTY, Jean Paul
Jean Paul Getty in his golden age. H. Law-
renson. il por Esquire 72:146-7+ O '69
GETTY, Talitha
Moroccan wake-up. il pors Vogue 155:166-
71+ Ja 15 '70
GEYER, Alan
Toward a convivial theology; excerpt from
address, December 1968. Chr Cent 86:541-4
Ap 23 '69
GEYER, Donna
Teaching composition to the disadvantaged.
Engl J 58:900-7 S '69
GEYSERS
Old Faithful: a physical model. R. O. Four-
nier. bibliog Science 163:304-5 Ja 17 '69
GHANA
See also
Elections—Ghana
Immigration and emigration—Ghana
Misconduct in office—Ghana
Presidents—Ghana

Foreign relations
Little Ghana takes on the Russians. D. C.
Steffen. il Life 66:20-5 F 21 '69

Politics and government
Friday's child; Premier Busia. Time 94:39 S 12
'69
Ghana: no more Nkrumahs. O. W. Okite. Chr
Today 13:48 F 28 '69
Nkrumah's gone; Ghana's agony remains.
Africanus. Commonweal 90:136 Ap 18 '69
Reformer removed; Ankrah replaced by
Afrifa. Time 93:39 Ap 11 '69
Return to civilian rule in Ghana. C. E.
Welch, jr. bibliog f Cur Hist 56:286-91 My
'69
See also
Elections—Ghana
GHASWALA, S. K.
Chaotic congress. Sci N 95:270 Mr 15 '69
Giant iron mine. Sci N 95:514 My 24 '69
Next decade: TV by satellite. Sci N 96:136
Ag 16 '69
Radiation safety. Sci N 95:126 F 1 '69
Toward breeder reactors. Sci N 95:603 Je 21
'69
GHENT, Henri
And so it is... por Sch Arts 68:21-6 Ap
'69
GHETTOS (slums) See Slums
GHIGLIONE, Angelo F.
Conquest of Darien. Américas 21:1 Jl '69
GHOST dancer; drama. See Gaines, F.
GHOST towns. See Abandoned towns
GHOST writing. See Authorship—Collaboration
GHOSTS
Contrary spirits: a possibly royal poltergeist,
and the bucksaw ghost. J. Fischer. Harper
239:12+ O'69
See also
Spiritualism
GIAMBRONE, Eunice
Mount Clemens. ALA Bul 63:262-5 F '69
GIANNINI, Dusolina
Pertile and Giannini. A. Favia-Artsay. por
Hobbies 74:35+ Ag '69

GIANT African snail. See Snails
GIANT pandas. See Pandas
GIANTS (baseball) See Baseball clubs
GIANTS (football club) See Football clubs
GIAP, Vo-nguyen-. See Vo-nguyen-Giap
GIBBERELLINS
Peanuts: gibberellin antagonists and gen-
etically controlled differences in growth
habit. A. H. Halevy and others. bibliog il
Science 164:1397-8 Je 20 '69
GIBBON, John, and Rutschmann, Ruth
Temporal order judgment and reaction time.
bibliog Science 165:413-15 Jl 25 '69
GIBBONEY, Richard A.
Social context and vocational education.
bibliog f Sch & Soc 97:28-31 Ja '69
GIBBONS, Euell
Camping the wild way. Nat Wildlife 7:34-8 Ap
'69
Organic nature-lover. See issues of Organic
gardening and farming
GIBBONS, Russell W.
Bye-bye machine. Commonweal 90:381-4 Je 20
'69
Catching up with Bismarck. Commonweal
91:238-40 N 21 '69
High noon in the hospital. Commonweal
91:406-7 Ja 9 '70
Splendid story. Nation 209:226-7 S 8 '69
SDS in the mills. Nation 209:215-17 S 8 '69
GIBBS, C. J. jr. and Gajdusek, D. C.
Infection as the etiology of spongiform en-
cephalopathy (Creutzfeldt-Jakob disease)
bibliog Science 165:1023-5 S 5 '69
GIBBS, June
Choosing the right vegetables. Horticulture
47:24-5 Je '69
GIBBS, Tony
Book shelf. See issues of Motor boating
GIBNEY, Frank
New face of world power. Look 33:28-9 O 21
'69
Nippon, the land of contrast. Travel &
Camera 32:56-65 O '69
GIBRALTAR
New controversy over the Rock. il U S News
66:14 Je 23 '69
Shutting the gate. Time 93:29-30 Je 20 '69
GIBSON, Alexander
Scots wha hae. B. Fischer-Williams. il por
Opera N 34:16-19 D 13 '69
GIBSON, Althea
Where are they now? il pors Newsweek 74:8
S 1 '69
GIBSON, Arthur
Dewart's new foundations. Commonweal 90:
101-4 Ap 11 '69
New heaven and new earth. Commonweal
91:117-122 O 31 '69
GIBSON, Bob
Why the brushback? pors Look 33:66-9 Jl 29
'69
GIBSON, Dick
Rare air; Aspen jazz parties. W. Conover.
il por Sat R 52:64-5+ O 11 '69
GIBSON, Everett K. See Moore, C. B. jt. auth.
GIBSON, John
Sea works, creative explorations. J. Gruen.
Vogue 154:64 S 15 '69
GIBSON, John S.
Needed: a revolution in citizenship edu-
cation; address, March 3, 1969. Vital
Speeches 35:473-8 My 15 '69
GIBSON, Richard
Our far-flung correspondents. W. Balliett.
New Yorker 45:175-6+ O 18 '69
GIBSON, Robert
Crushes. Todays Ed 58:15-16 D '69
GIBSON RANCH COUNTY park. See Ranches
GICCA, Francis A.
Communications satellites, success in space.
Electr World 82:23-7+ Jl; 44-8+ Ag '69
GIDEON, Clarence Earl
Where are they now? il por Newsweek 74:8
Ag 11 '69
GIES, Joseph
Mr Eads spans the Mississippi. Am Heritage
20:16-21+ Ag '69
GIESEKE, Haydee
Magic of mother love. C. Remsberg and B.
Remsberg. il por Good H 169:74-5+ Ag '69
GIFFORD, Bernard
Scientist with a cause; B. Gifford and FIGHT.
il por Ebony 25:73-6+ D '69
GIFT for the Christ child; story. See Marsden,
C. G.
GIFT of grass; story. See Adams, A.
GIFT of tongues
As the spirit gives utterance. H. M. Ervin.
Chr Today 13:7-8+ Ap 11 '69
Gift of tongues. Chr Today 13:27 Ap 11 '69
GIFT wrappings. See Wrapping of packages

GIFTED children. See Children, Gifted
GIFTS
Anniversary gift. A. Woodend. Har Yrs 9:40 Je '69
Gift show; semiannual show at the Coliseum. New Yorker 45:38-9 S 13 '69
Gifts for that special man. B. Ullmann. il Good H 168:152 Mr '69
Host of gifts for Father's day. B. Ullmann. il Good H 168:121-3 Je '69
Presents for the hostess. il House & Gard 136:104-5 N '69
Rewards of procrastination. il Esquire 73: 92-5 Ja '70
This just has to be the greatest new decade since creation. il Esquire 72:234-41 D '69
Two views of Father's day. il Esquire 71: 116-17 Je '69
See also
Christmas gifts
Colleges and universities—Gifts, legacies, etc.
Food as gifts
Giving
Museums—Gifts, legacies, etc.

Taxation
Estate tax changes coming. il U S News 66:72-4 Ap 7 '69
Why college donors are uptight. il Bsns W p 126+ N 8 '69
GIFTS for children
Silver gifts to use for a lifetime. il House & Gard 136:194-6+ S '69
See also
Christmas gifts for children
GIFTS for service men
See also
Christmas gifts for service men
GIGLIO, Alice
Parents and teachers are greasing the skids Todays Ed 58:30 D '69
GIL, David G.
What schools can do about child abuse. Am Ed 5:2-4 Ap '69
GILBERT, Bil
Confessions of a retarded Tiger. Sports Illus 30:72-6+ Je 2 '69
Drugs in sport. Sports Illus 30:64-72 Je 23; 30-2+ Je 30; 30-5 Jl 7 '69; Same abr. with title Drugs and the athlete. Read Digest 95:95-9 S '69
Exploring the world within. Sports Illus 31: 80-4+ N 10 '69
I hate horses. Read Digest 94:134-6 Mr '69
GILBERT, George
From concrete to cast iron to plastics. pors il Am City 84:88-9 N '69
GILBERT, James
Safety check. See issues of Flying
—See Berliner, D. jt. auth.
GILBERT, James Burkhart
Hassle of historians. Nation 208:77-9 Ja 20 '69
GILBERT, Joan
Next book I write. Writers Digest 49:53-5 O '69
GILBERT, Sandra M.
Her last sickness; poem. New Yorker 45:98 Je 21 '69
GILBERT, Sara Dulaney
Medieval detour. Travel 131:58-62 Ap '69
GILBERT and Sullivan operas
See also
Phonograph records—Operas
GILBREATH, Becky
Shard mosaics. Ceram Mo 17:23-4 Mr '69
GILCHRIST, Robert T.
Signs of change. R. Levy. por Duns R 94: 78+ O '69
GILDING
Uses of gold in the graphic and decorative arts; address. H. L. Hunter. Pub W 195: 76+ My 5 '69
GILGORE, Sheldon G.
Pharmaceutical testing: company view. Bul Atom Sci 25:12+ Je '69
GILHAM, P. T. See Weith, H. L. jt. auth.
GILINSKY, Alberta S. and Doherty, R. S.
Interocular transfer of orientational effects. bibliog Science 164:454-5 Ap 25 '69
GILKEY, Richard
Instructional media. Clear House 44:61-4 S '69
GILL, Brendan
Off Broadway. New Yorker 45:72+ Je 28 '69
Theatre. See issues of New Yorker
GILLELAN, G. Howard
Archery. See issues of Outdoor life
GILLERAN, John J.
Concrete admixtures: updating specification background knowledge. Arch Rec 146:143-4 D '69
GILLES, Genevieve
Genevieve's holiday in Barbados. il pors Harp Baz 102:182-91 My '69
Mind of one's own. pors Harp Baz 102:148-9 F '69

GILLESPIE, Alfred
Tonight at nine thirty-six; story. Redbook 132:78-9 Mr '69
GILLESPIE, Bete
Fathers only journals. Todays Health 47:16-17 D '69
GILLESPIE, Charles
Wet, happy life of Marvin Shackelford. Sports Illus 32:66-72 Ja 12 '70
GILLESPIE, Dizzy
Cool hand in Hollywood. il Time 94:53 Jl 25 '69
GILLESPIE, Gregory
Beyond nightmare. il por Time 93:74-5 Je 13 '69
GILLETTE, Arthur
Exercise of social responsibility. Sch & Soc 97:222-3 Ap '69
GILLETTE, Ed
Samaritan. Flying 85:80 N '69
GILLETTE company
Great razor blade war; Gillette vs Warner-Lambert. il Forbes 104:26-7 O 15 '69
Week on the razor's edge. il Bsns W p 164+ O 18 '69
GILLHAM, C. E.
Me and that groundhog. Audubon 71:24-6 My '69
To pack a moose. Field & S 74:58-9+ N '69
GILLIATT, Mary
Sophisticated eye. House B 111:122-3 O '69
GILLIATT, Penelope
Current cinema. See issues of New Yorker March 22 to September 20, 1969
Last to go; story. New Yorker 45:38-46 Ap 19 '69
Profiles; J. Renoir. New Yorker 45:34-6+ Ag 23 '69
GILLIS, Peter C.
Kneeling; poem. Poetry 114:372 S '69
GILLIS, Richard A.
Cardiac sympathetic nerve activity: changes induced by ouabain and propranolol. bibliog Science 166:508-10 O 24 '69
GILLON, Hadassah
Drug against a virus. Sci N 96:414 N 1 '69
Hearts and national origin. Sci N 95:342 Ap 5 '69
GILLS
Central neuron initiation of periodic gill movements. B. Peretz. bibliog il Science 166:1167-72 N 28 '69
GILLULY, James
Oceanic sediment volumes and continental drift. bibliog Science 166:992-4 N 21 '69
GILMAN, Carl
Reporter or informer? Nation 209:461+ N 3 '69
Wrong occupation. il por Time 94:69 N 14 '69
GILMAN, Richard
Susan Sontag and the question of the new. New Repub 160:23-6+ My 3 '69
Theatre (cont) New Repub 160:32-4 Ja 25; 29-30 F 22; 29-31 Ap 12 '69
Theater of ignorance. Atlan 224:35-42 Jl '69
GILMORE, Artis
Up, up and away go Artis and new J.U. J. Jares. il por Sports Illus 32:18-21 Ja 5 '70
GILMORE, Bob
Photo print washer rocks itself. Pop Sci 195: 148 N '69
GILMORE, C. P.
Can we stop earthquakes from happening? Pop Sci 194:78-82+ Ap '69
Decoding messages from outer space. Pop Sci 194:72-7+ Je '69
How you'll see Mars close up. Pop Sci 195: 76-9+ Jl '69
Instead of a heart, a man-made pump. Read Digest 95:241-2+ N '69
Something better than the pill? N Y Times Mag p6-7+ Jl 20; 60 Ag 10 '69
GILMORE, Clifford F.
Bach's B minor mass, does the concentus musicus' authenticity make musical sense? Yes. por Hi Fi 19:76+ Jl '69
GILMORE, Haydn
Expendable men; poem. Chr Cent 86:1669 D 31 '69
GILMORE, Kathryn
Colorado; poem. Am For 75:12 D '69
GILMORE, Kenneth O.
Great challenge: making our government work. Read Digest 94:86-91 F '69
GILMORE, Patrick Sarsfield
Big boom in Boston. R. Jarman. il por Am Heritage 20:46-51+ O '69
GILMORE, Warren
It's Y.O.U. E. Ferber. il por Am Ed 5:17-21 Ag '69
GILPIN, Laura
Enduring Laura Gilpin. D. Vestal. il Pop Phot 64:50 Je '69

GILRUTH, Robert R.
Putting comfort in orbit. por Space World F-2-62:42 F '69

GILSVIK, Robert
Early season grouse. Field & S 74:66-7+ Ag '69
North woods hot zone. Field & S 74:52-3+ O '69

GILULA, Marshall F. and Daniels, D. N.
Violence and man's struggle to adapt. bibliog Science 164:396-405 Ap 25 '69

GILVARRY, John J.
What are the mascons? Sat R 52:54-7 Je 7 '69

GIMENEZ, Joaquin Ruiz-. See Ruiz-Gimenez, J.

GIN
Pale but glorious fire. L. Dowst. il Holiday 46:32-3+ Ag '69

GINA between; story. See Hoag, M. D.

GINASTERA, Alberto
Artist life. D. J. Soria. por Hi Fi 19:MA4+ D '69

GINDEL, Israel
Making the desert bloom. il Am For 75:32-5+ S '69

GINGHAM dog; drama. See Wilson, L.

GINGIVITIS. See Gums (anatomy)—Diseases

GINGRICH, Arnold
Publisher's page. See issues of Esquire

GINKGO
You are old father ginkgo! Pray, how did you manage to do it? il Chem 42:5-6 N '69

GINKGO petrified forest state park. See Washington (state)—Parks and reserves

GINN, F. L. and others
Membrane alterations in hemolysis: internalization of plasmalemma induced by primaquine. bibliog Science 164:843-5 My 16 '69

GINNIE Mae. See United States—Housing and urban development, Department of

GINOTT, Haim G.
Between parent and child. McCalls 96:40+ Mr; 40+ Ap; 40 Jl; 40 Ag; 36+ S; 97:42+ O 35+ N; 14+ D '69
Between parent and teenager; excerpt. por McCalls 96:78-9+ My; 48+ Je '69
Discipline firm and sane. McCalls 97:42+ O '69
How to get along with your teen-ager: excerpts from Between parent and teenager. Read Digest 95:55-8 Jl '69
Parents talk about sex. Vogue 154:103+ O 15 '69

GINSBERG, Allen
By air Albany-Baltimore; poem. Look 33: 34 N 4 '69
We talk to . . .: interviews with Mlle's guest editors. por Mlle 69:343-5 Ag '69

about
Authors & editors. J. T. Robinson. por Pub W 195:18 Je 23 '69
Comment. B. Berkson. Poetry 114:251-6 Jl '69
Comment. D. Lehman. Poetry 114:403-5 S '69
Music of angels. P. Zweig. Nation 208:311-13 Mr 10 '69
Somewhere else with Allen and Gregory; excerpt from My son's father. D. Moraes. il pors Horizon 11:66-7 Winter '69

GINSBERG, Mitchell I.
New federalism; interview. New Yorker 45: 19-22 Ag 23 '69

GINSBURG, Benjamin
Dating English brass candlesticks. Antiques 96:907-11 D '69

GINSBURG, Isaac, and others
Group A streptococci; localization in rabbits and guinea pigs following tissue injury. bibliog Science 166:1161-3 N 28 '69

GINSBURG, Sonia
Notes of a scab librarian. bibliog Library J 94:1300-2 Mr 15 '69

GINSBURGS, George
Kremlin scene: politics in a cul-de-sac. Cur Hist 57:228-31+ O '69

GINZA cabaret. See Cabarets

GINZBURG, Aleksandr
Day in the life of Yuli Daniel. Time 93:44 Je 6 '69

GINZBURG, Ralph
Goldwater case: actual malice asserted. H. F. Pilpel and K. P. Norwick. Pub W 196:31-2 S 1 '69
On borrowed time. Newsweek 73:92 Je 23 '69

GINZBURG, Vitalii Lazarevich
Astrophysics of cosmic rays; with biographical sketch. Sci Am 220:12, 50-63 bibliog (p 132) F '69

GIORDAN, Alma R.
It's easy to grow an amaryllis. Org Gard & Farm 16:84-5 N '69

GIORDAN, Alma Roberts
No effort wasted. Writers Digest 49:88-9 Je '69

GIORDMAINE, J. A.
Nonlinear optics; with biographical sketch. bibliog por Phys Today 22:38-44 Ja '69

GIORNO, John
Dial-a-poem, new poetry rather than weather tips on the telephone. J. Gruen. Vogue 153: 116 Mr 1 '69

GIOVANNI, Nikki
To be a poet; with poem. S. Weller. por Mlle 70:90, 126-7+ D '69

GIPSIES
Of gypsy race. P. Follmer. il Opera N 33:6-11 Mr 15 '69

GIPSIES in England
On the road with the British gypsies. Q. Crewe. Vogue 155:182+ Ja 1 '70

GIPSY moths
Those hungry gypsies. il Am For 75:28-31 Mr '69

GIRASOLES. See Jerusalem artichokes

GIRDERS
How to make your own antique beams. B. Powell. il Pop Mech 132:182-5 N '69

GIRDLES. See Foundation garments

GIRDLES of chastity. See Chastity belts

GIRDLING of trees. See Trees, Ringing of

GIRI, Varahagiri Venkata
India: the lady v. the syndicate. il por Time 94:29 Ag 29 '69

GIRL athletes. See Women as athletes

GIRL scouts
Kitchen labor problems eased by use of convenience foods; San Francisco Bay Girl scout camps. il Camp Mag 41:24-5 Ja '69
Meet today's scouts. T. Irwin. il Parents Mag 44:64-5+ O '69

GIRL to remember; story. See Corliss, A.

GIRL who won an island; story. See Sharp, M.

GIRLS
Joe's girls. il Esquire 72:108-11 O '69
What boys look for in girls; panel discussion by seven boys. il Seventeen 28:152-3+ Mr '69
Young living: questions and answers. A. Wood. See issues of Seventeen
See also
Adolescence
College students, Women
Daughters
School children
Young women

GIRLS books. See Childrens literature

GIRLS in sport. See School athletics

GIRLS rooms. See Childrens rooms

GIRLS' rules; story. See Gasner, B.

GIRONA (warship) See Shipwrecks

GIRONELLA, Alberto
Gironella: tension, time, light. R. Squirru. il por Américas 21:7-13 My '69

GIRSON, Rochelle
What did the Nineteenth amendment amend? Sat R 52:29+ O 11 '69

GISELLE; ballet. See Ballets—Criticisms

GISH, Lillian
Prim star dollies in on her director. T. Prideaux. Life 66:8 My 2 '69
Stanley Kauffmann on films. S. Kauffmann. New Repub 160:22+ My 10 '69
True heart Gish. A. Croce. il Nat R 21:865-6 Ag 26 '69

GITCHOFF, Thomas. See Wilkins, L. T. jt. auth.

GITLIN, David, and Sasaki, Teruo
Immunoglobulins G, A, and M determined in single cells from human tonsil. bibliog Science 164:1532-4 Je 27 '69

GITLIN, Todd
New left: old traps. Ramp Mag 8:20+ S '69

GITTELL, Marilyn
Chronicle of conflict. Sat R 52:73-4 Mr 15 '69

GITTELSON, Natalie
Are you wearing last year's status symbol? McCalls 97:92+ O '69
Erotic life of the American wife. Harp Baz 102:76-91 Jl '69
Excitement over spelling. McCalls 96:89+ S '69
Great airlines food race. McCalls 96:95+ My '69
Needles and pins. See issues of Harper's bazaar
Please! Don't tell me he's well-adjusted! McCalls 96:96-7 Ap '69

GITTENS, David
Ikenga. il pors Ebony 24:114-16+ S '69

GITTINGS, John
Prospects of the cultural revolution in 1969. Bul Atom Sci 25:23-8 F '69

GIUSTI, Joseph P.
Students and the 1970's: calm after the storm. bibliog Sch & Soc 97:360-3 O '69
GIVEAWAY magazines. See Periodicals—United States
GIVEN names. See Names, Personal
GIVENCHY, Hubert de
Life-style Givenchy. il pors Vogue 154:144-9 N 15 '69
GIVING
Dollars you give to fight disease. il Changing T 23:6 O '69
How children learn the joys of giving. E. L. Schulte. il Parents Mag 44:50+ D '69
Model philanthropist; interview. S. R. Mott. New Yorker 45:28-31 S 6 '69
Money talks; activities of H. R. Perot. il Newsweek 74:57-8 D 8 '69
What Christmas means; remembering the less fortunate. il Good H 169:183 D '69
Why I believe in philanthropy. J. D. Rockefeller, 3d. Read Digest 95:185-6+ D '69
See also
Charities
Church finance
GLACIAL epochs
Another ice age? Sci Digest 65:39 My '69
GLACIAL geology
Glaciation in southern Argentina more than two million years ago. J. H. Mercer. bibliog il Science 164:823-5 My 16 '69
See also
Geology, Stratigraphic—Pleistocene
GLACIER BAY NATIONAL MONUMENT
Glacier Bay cruise in Alaska. il Bet Hom & Gard 47:116 F '69
GLACIER NATIONAL PARK
Grizzly bear in the national parks. E. G. Bowman. il Am For 75:16-19+ Jl '69 (to be cont)
Night of the grizzlies; condensation. J. Olsen. il Sports Illus 30:38-44+ My 12; 44-8+ My 19; 36-8+ My 26 '69
GLACIERS
Gift of the glaciers. P. Friggens. il Read Digest 95:21-2+ O '69
Glaciers in the American West. S. F. Arno. il Natur Hist 78:84-9 F '69
Glaciers on the move. G. A. Avsiuk and V. M. Kotliakov. il UNESCO Courier 22:16-21+ Je '69
GLADIATORS
Colosseum. J. Bryan, 3d. il Holiday 46:70-1+ D '69
GLADIOLUS
How to keep your glads glad. G. Campbell. il Org Gard & Farm 16:50-1 Mr '69
New look in gladiolus. G. A. Webster. il Horticulture 47:24-5 Ag '69
Try the miniature glads. B. Miles. il Horticulture 47:45 My '69
GLADSON, Myrtle M.
Little lead toys. Hobbies 74:48 D '69
GLADSON, Patricia L.
Just another off year? Todays Ed 58:55-6 O '69
GLADSTONE, Mo.
Independent water supply proves best. G. F. Hands. il Am City 84:106+ F '69
GLAESSNER, Martin F. and others
Precambrian columnar stromatolites in Australia: morphological and stratigraphic analysis. bibliog Science 164:1056-8 My 30 '69
GLANDS
See also
Mammary glands
Pituitary body
Secretion
Thymus gland
GLANVILLE, Brian
Memory of Mexico. Commentary 47:77-9 Mr '69
GLASCOCK, Martha McClain, and Scholer, E. A.
Two experts view camping for older adults. pors Camp Mag 41:15-16 Mr '69
GLASER, Milton
Design gourmet. H. Junker. il por Newsweek 73:78 F 10 '69
GLASER, Robert. See Cooley, W. W. jt. auth.
GLASMAN, Naftaly S.
Dilemmas in the process of educational administration in Israel. bibliog f Sch & Soc 97:392-5 O '69
GLASS, Billy P.
Silicate spherules from Tunguska impact area: electron microprobe analysis. bibliog Science 164:547-9 My 2 '69
GLASS, H. Bentley
For full technological assessment. Science 165:755 Ag 22 '69

GLASS
Moon glass: control sample for chemical analysis experiments. il Space World F-8-68: 38-9 Ag '69
Through a glass brightly. il McCalls 96:90-3 My '69
See also
Bottles
Glassware
Pyrex
Pyroceram
Tektites
Electric properties
All about ovonics. F. Shunaman. il Radio-Electr 40:41-3 My '69
GLASS, Cellular
Trypsin and papain covalently coupled to porous glass: preparation and characterization. H. H. Weetall. bibliog il Science 166:615-17 O 31 '69
GLASS, Porous. See Glass, Cellular
GLASS, Safety
Shattered glass that can't cut. il Sci Digest 65:19 Mr '69
Test set for frangible glass canopy. M. L. Yaffee. il Aviation W 91:57+ Ag 25 '69
GLASS, Stained. See Glass painting and staining
GLASS, Structural
See also
Glass construction
GLASS automobiles. See Automobiles—Materials
GLASS blowing and working
Glass workshop; Toledo museum of art. L. Bruner. il Am Artist 33:48-53+ F '69
GLASS buttons. See Buttons
GLASS casting. See Casting (sculpture)
GLASS ceramics. See Pyroceram
GLASS coloring. See Glass painting and staining
GLASS construction
Japan's Crystal palace; prefabricated Nagashima tropical garden. il Arch Forum 130: 76-83 My '69
See also
Walls, Glass
GLASS containers
See also
Anchor Hocking glass corporation
GLASS fibers
See also
Owens-Corning fiberglas corporation
GLASS Industry
L'affaire Saint-Gobain; Boussois-Souchon-Neuvesel offer to buy 30 per cent of stock. il Newsweek 73:77 F 3 '69
Great glass battle; Saint-Gobain beat takeover attempt by Boussois Souchon Neuvesel. Time 93:77-8 F 7 '69
See also
PPG industries, incorporated
GLASS-lined pipe. See Pipe lining
GLASS manufacture
See also
Anchor Hocking glass corporation
Glass blowing and working
PPG industries, incorporated
GLASS painting and staining
China trade paintings on glass. C. L. Crossman. il Antiques 95:376-82 Mr '69
Glass coloring; cased, stained, marbleized, and homogeneous. A. G. Peterson. Hobbies 74:98F N '69
Glass medallions of Carl Paulson. J. Canavan. il Am Artist 33:22-5 Ag '69
New stained glass in Germany. R. Sowers. il Craft Horiz 29:14-21+ My '69
Stained glass by a modern master. W. S. Ross. il Read Digest 95:146-52 D '69
Stained glass reflects today's spirit. C. Young. il Sch Arts 68:8 Ap '69
GLASS pictures. See Glass painting and staining
GLASS semiconductors. See Semiconductors
GLASS walls. See Walls, Glass
GLASSER, William E.
Effect of school failure. Ed Digest 35:13-17 D '69
GLASSES, Drinking. See Drinking vessels
GLASSES for the eyes. See Eyeglasses
GLASSMAN, James K.
Reports: SDS at Chicago. Atlan 224:30+ D '69
GLASSWARE
Cut glass and other lamps by Libbey. C. U. Fauster. il Hobbies 74:116-17+ D '69
Establishing factory attributions of glassware. T. H. Marsh. il Hobbies 74:98T-98U+ Je '69
Glass: America's historic designs today. il House B 111:96-7 Je '69

GLASSWARE—*Continued*
Glass canes & other whimseys. C. U. Fauster. il Hobbies 74:116-18 S '69
Glass patterns: Mignon, Monroe, Mikado, & Okay. A. G. Peterson. il Hobbies 74:98EE My '69
Guide to buying crystal. Good H 169:148 Jl '69
Luxury in English and Irish cut glass. P. Warren. il Antiques 96:882-8 D '69
Maize art glass. A. G. Peterson. il Hobbies 73:76+ F; 74:98R Ag '69
Southern gentlemen honored in glass. T. H. Marsh. il Hobbies 74:98N-98P Ag '69
See also
Drinking vessels
Tableware

Collectors and collecting
Collectible cut glass rarities. C. U. Fauster. il Hobbies 74:98L-98N Jl '69

Exhibitions
Glass national II; Toledo glass national II exhibition. il Ceram Mo 17:23-5 F '69
Marinot glass on exhibit at Corning museum. il Hobbies 74:118 S '69

Patents
Glassware patents by Charles Ballinger. A. G. Peterson. il Hobbies 74:98DD-98EE Je '69

Terminology
Antique glass glossary. Am Home 72:87 Je '69
GLASSWARE, Chemical. See Glassware, Laboratory
GLASSWARE, Laboratory
Christmas at the chemist's, glass gifts in interesting shapes. il Sunset 143:62-3 D '69
GLASSY state
Glass-transition temperature of water. A. A. Miller. bibliog il Science 163:1325-6 Mr 21 '69
GLATTHORN, Allan A.
Little bit of rebellion is good for the soul, and the school. Seventeen 28:324-5+ Ag '69
What makes an effective high school. Parents Mag 44:64-5+ S '69
GLAUCOMA
Progress on glaucoma. il Newsweek 74:115-16 D 8 '69
GLAZE, Andrew
Make room: poem. Sat R 52:38 D 27 '69
GLAZE, Eleanor
Shadows; story. Redbook 133:86-7 Jl '69
GLAZER, Nathan
Blacks, Jews & the intellectuals. Commentary 47:33-9 Ap; 48:10+ Jl '69
For white and black, community control is the issue. N Y Times Mag p36-7+ Ap 27 '69
Jewish role in student activism. Fortune 79:112-13+ Ja '69
Missing bootstrap. Sat R 52:19-21+ Ag 23 '69
School politics. Commentary 47:81-6 Mr '69
Student politics and the university. Atlan 224:43-53 Jl, 48+ O '69
GLAZER, Sidney
(comp) Articles and other books received; Near East. See issues of American historical review
GLAZES and glazing
Ash glazes for Cone 6. R. Behrens. il Ceram Mo 17:31 Ja '69
Cone 6 stoneware. R. Behrens. il Ceram Mo 17:32-3 Mr '69
Crackle glazes. R. Behrens. il Ceram Mo 17:23+ O '69
Oven and range-top clay bodies and glazes. R. Behrens. il Ceram Mo 17:27+ S '69
Raku glazes. R. Behrens. il Ceram Mo 17:29 N '69
GLAZIER, Kenneth M. Jr
What's wrong with colleges: an answer from a student activist; interview. por U S News 66:42-6 Je 16 '69
GLEASNER, Diana C.
Selling your first article. Writers Digest 49:51-3 My '69
GLEASON, Gene
Long Island. Travel 132:38-43 S '69
GLEDITSIA. See Honey locust
GLEE clubs. See Choral groups and societies
GLEICH, Gerald J. and others
Antigen combining activity associated with immunoglobulin D. bibliog Science 165:606 Ag 8 '69
GLEN CANYON
Another look at Glen Canyon. G. Alderson. il Am For 75:6-7+ Mr '69

Colorado's canyons today; excerpts from Down the Colorado. E. Porter. il Audubon 71:76-9 N '69
Lament for a lost Eden. E. Porter. il Am Heritage 20:60-1 O '69

Photographs
Powell's River; Colorado portfolio; excerpts from Down the Colorado. E. Porter. Audubon 71:64-76 N '69
GLEN Tetley dance company
Glen Tetley dance co; NY city center. M. Marks. Dance Mag 43:32-3 Jl '69
GLENDAY, Alice
Perfect day in spring; story. Good H 168:94-5 Ap '69
GLENDENING, Richard M.
Psychedelic multimedia happening. Sr Schol 94:Schol Teach 18-19 Ap 18 '69
GLENN, Morton Bernard
Safe, sure fourteen-day diet. Redbook 133:92-3+ O '69
What too many women don't know about dieting; interview. Redbook 133:82-3+ S '69
GLENNAN, Thomas Keith
Where are they now? il pors Newsweek 74:26 N 24 '69
GLENWOOD, Ill.
Developers boost our water supply. L. Komer. il Am City 84:85-6 Jl '69
GLIAL cells. See Nerve cells
GLICK, Ira D. See Mardikian, B. jt. auth.
GLICKSTEIN, Mitchell
Organization of the visual pathways. bibliog Science 164:917-26 My 23 '69
GLIDERS (aeronautics)
Low-cost sailplane you build from a kit. il Mech Illus 65:70-1 Ap '69
See also
Gliding and soaring

Models
Radio control
Now they're flying model gliders by radio. H. G. McEntee. il Pop Sci 195:154-7 O '69
GLIDING and soaring
Come soar with me. S. Parrasch. il Seventeen 28:108-9+ O '69
Personal business. Bsns W p 139-40 Je 21 '69
Soaring in Hawaii; $7.50 and up. il Sunset 142:39 Mr '69
GLINES, C. V.
(ed) See Tunner, W. H. Before the colors fade: Berlin airlift commander
GLINKA, Mikhail Ivanovich
Russlan and Ludmilla. Criticism
Newsweek il 73:102 Ap 14 '69
GLIXON, David M.
SR's semi-annual reference book roundup. Sat R 52:31-2+ My 17; 45-6+ D 6 '69
(ed) Your literary I.Q. See issues of Saturday review
GLOAG, John
Gentlemen's Gothic. Antiques 95:682-8 My '69
GLOBAL atmospheric research program. See Weather research
GLOBE stands. See Stands (furniture)
GLOBE tulips. See Mariposa lilies
GLOBOKAR, Vinko
New music for solo trombone, and for virtuoso trombonist. R. P. Morgan. il por Hi Fi 19:64-5 Ap '69
GLOBULINEMIA
Germ-free baby chamber. Sci Digest 65:61 My '69
GLOBULINS
See als
Blood—Proteins
Concanavalins
Myoglobin
GLOEOCAPSA. See Algae
GLOMAR Challenger (ship) See Ships, Research
GLOMERULONEPHRITIS. See Kidneys—Diseases
GLORIA and Esperanza; drama. See Bovasso, J.
GLORY! Hallelujah! drama. See Barlow, A. M.
GLOSSOLALIA. See Gift of tongues
GLOSSOPTERIS. See Ferns, Fossil
GLOVER, Fred
Freddie's in, gloom's out. G. Ronberg. il por Sports Illus 30:62+ Mr 10 '69
GLOW, Bernie
Profiles. W. Whitworth. por New Yorker 45:43-4+ D 20 '69
GLOW worms. See Fireflies

GLOWKA, Arthur
Boys and bullheads. Outdoor Life 144:72-5+
Ag '69
Hot bridge crappies. Field & S 74:66-7+ My
'69
Wire for the blues. Field & S 74:56-7+ Jl
'69
GLUCAGON
Glucagon-sensitive adenyl cylase in plasma
membrane of hepatic parenchymal cells.
S. L. Pohl and others. bibliog il Science
164:566-7 My 2 '69
GLUCANASES
β-1,3-Glucanase of sea urchin eggs: release
from particles at fertilization. D. Epel and
others. bibliog il Science 163:294-6 Ja 17 '69
GLÜCK, Louise
To be a poet; with poem. S. Weller. por Mlle
70:90, 126-7+ D '69
GLUCOSE
Do trehalose and trehalase function in renal
glucose transport? E. Van Handel. bibliog
il Science 163:1075-6 Mr 7 '69
GLUE
Glue-tempera relief. H. M. Stahl. il Sch
Arts 69:12-13 N '69
See also
Adhesives
GLUE guns. See Spraying apparatus
GLUECK, Grace
New York gallery notes. See issues of Art in
America
Paintings descending a ramp. N Y Times
Mag p36-8+ Ja 19 '69
Soft sculpture or hard, they're Oldenburgers.
N Y Times Mag p28-9+ S 21 '69
GLUECK, Nelson
Holy Land. Travel & Camera 32:70-5+ D '69
GLUSMAN, Paul
More Mao than thou. Ramp Mag 8:6+ S '69
GLUTAMATE. See Monosodium glutamate
GLUTAMIC acid
Monosodium L-glutamate: its pharmacology
and role in the Chinese restaurant syn-
drome. H. H. Schaumburg and others. bib-
liog il Science 163:826-8 F 21 '69
GLUTTONY
'Tis the season to be gluttonous. S. Paregien.
Chr Today 14:9-10 N 21 '69
GLYCERYL ethers. See Ethers
GLYCINE
Glycine in the spinal cord of cats with local
tetanus rigidity. T. Semba and M. Kano.
bibliog il Science 164:571-2 My 2 '69
GLYCOGEN
Rats enriched with odd-carbon fatty acids:
maintenance of liver glycogen during
starvation. T. B. VanItallie and A. K. Kha-
chadurian. bibliog il Science 165:311-13 Ag
22 '69
GLYCOLIPIDS
Glycosphingolipids with Lewis blood group
activity: uptake by human erythrocytes.
D. M. Marcus and L. E. Cass. bibliog il
Science 164:553-5 My 2 '69
GLYCOLS
Naturally occurring diol lipids: dialkoxypen-
tanes in porpoise (phocoena phocoena) jaw
oil. U. Varanasi and D. C. Malins. bibliog il
Science 166:1158-9 N 28 '69
Sex pheromone of the queen butterfly; chem-
istry. J. Meinwald and others. bibliog il
Science 164:1174-5 Je 6 '69
GLYCOPROTEINS
Glomerular sialoprotein. S. C. Mohos and L.
Skoza. bibliog il Science 164:1519-21 Je 27
'69
Golgi apparatus. M. Neutra and C. P. Leb-
lond. il Sci Am 220:100-7 bibliog (p 132) F
'69
Piscatorial antifreeze. Chem 42:23-4 N '69
GLYCOSPHINGOLIPIDS. See Glycolipids
GLYCYRRHIZIN. See Licorice
GLYNDEBOURNE festival. See Music festivals
—England
GLYPHS. See Hieroglyphics
GNATHOSTOMULIDA. See Flatworms
GNETACEAE
See also
Welwitschias
GNOMES. See Fairies
GNOMON. See Astronomical instruments
GNOUTCHEFF, Michael
(tr) See Marchenko, A. My testimony
GO-karts. See Karts (midget cars)
GOA
Goa, hypnotic mix. P. Tree. Vogue 153:56 F
15 '69
GOAD, Claudia
Dinner's on deck. por Seventeen 28:340 Ag
'69

GOAL values. See Value (psychology)
GOARD, Dotty
To daughter; poem. Chr Cent 86:1669 D 31 '69
GOAT carts. See Carts
GOBA, Ronald Joseph
Grammar, usage, teachers of English, and
Paul Roberts. bibliog f Engl J 58:886-91 S
'69
Poetry and the senses. Clear House 44:149-51
N '69
GOBLE, Emerson
Obituary
Arch Rec por 146:9 D '69. J. Davern
GOBLIN VALLEY. See Utah
GOD
God and other minds; by A. Plantinga. Re-
view
Commonweal 90:28-9 Mr 21 '69
God at summer school. B. S. Llamzon. Amer-
ica 120:216-19 F 22 '69
God, in the Christian sense. J. J. Vincent. Chr
Cent 86:1192-4+ S 17 '69
God the redeemer; sovereignty and suffer-
ing. D. L. Weddle. Chr Today 13:12-15 Ag
1 '69
Has God forsaken the world? Chr Today 14:
20-1 D 19 '69
Honorable discharge for God? F. Getlein.
Commonweal 90:194 My 2 '69
Jewish paganism; views of R. L. Rubenstein.
M. Fox. Commentary 47:92-4+ Je '69; Dis-
cussion. 48:10+ S '69
Men like gods; sermon delivered at St Aldate's
church, Oxford, on December 1, 1968. M.
Muggeridge. Chr Cent 86:176-8 F 5 '69
New ministry; bringing God back to life. il
Time 94:40-5 D 26 '69
Proof of the pudding. H. Richardson. Com-
monweal 91:205-6 N 14 '69
Reality and identity of God. C. F. H. Henry.
Chr Today 13:3-6 Mr 14; 12-16 Mr 28 '69
Reason and God. P. H. Monsma. Chr Today
14:7-8+ O 10 '69
Rumor of angels, by P. Berger. Review
Nat R 21:759 Jl 29 '69. S. J. Tonsor
Son and the Father. V. P. McCorry. America
120:570-inside back cover My 10 '69
Vanity of humanism. R. Sampson. Nation 209:
718-25 D 29 '69
See also
Atheism
Christianity
Creation
Death of God theology
Holy Spirit
Love (theology)
Theism
Theology
Trinity
Trust in God
Anger
See God—Wrath

Mercy
Sparring with God. L. N. Bell. Chr Today
13:24-5 Ap 25 '69
Wrath
Holy wrath. L. N. Bell. Chr Today 13:22-3 Mr
14 '69
Wrath of God. V. P. McCorry. America 121:
276-inside back cover O 4 '69
GOD in legal cases. See Law—Curiosa and
miscellany
GOD is dead (theology). See Death of God
theology
GODARD, Jean Luc
Struggle on two fronts; interview; reprint.
por Film Q 22:20-35 Wint '68

about
For and against Godard. W. S. Pechter. Commentary 47:59-63 Ap '69
Godard's Week-end, or the self critical cinema of cruelty. J. R. MacBean. il Film Q
22:35-43 Wint '68
Politics, painting, and the language of signs
in Godard's Made in USA. J. R. MacBean.
il Film Q 22:18-25 Spr '69
Splicing together Jean-Luc Godard; with interview. W. S. Ross. il pors Esquire 72:
72-5 Jl '69
GODDARD, James Lee
Drug establishment. Esquire 71:117-21+ Mr
'69
Should it be legalized? Soon we will know.
por Life 67:34 O 31 '69
GODDARD, Maurice K.
Why state forestry associations? Am For
75:26-7+ Jl '69

GODDARD, Robert Hutchings
Moon rocket, circa 1929. Space World F-7-67:
38-9 Jl '69
Pioneers. il por Time 94:24 Jl 18 '69
GODDEN, Rumer
Authors & editors. B. A. Bannon. por Pub W
196:17-20 N 10 '69
GODFREY, Arthur
Challenge of the seventies. Esquire 72:8+ N
'69
GODS and goddesses
Pop theology; those gods from outer space.
il Time 94:64 S 5 '69
GODSEY, John D.
Karl Barth: master theologian. Chr Cent 86:
402-5 Mr 26 '69
GOEDICKE, Patricia
Learning; poem. Nation 208:216 F 17 '69
GOEKE, Joseph R. and Weymar, C. S.
Barriers to hiring the blacks. Harvard Bsns R
47:144-6+ S '69
GOELLNER, Jack G.
New, critical look at scholarly paperbacks;
excerpt from address. June 23, 1969. por
Pub W 196:33-4 Jl 28 '69
GOETHE, Johann Wolfgang von
Classics revisited. K. Rexroth. Sat R 52:
21 Ap 19 '69
GOETTSCH, Roger A.
Teaching coil building. il Design 70:32-4 Sum
'69
GOETZ, Alex, and Goetz, Nancy
Sail on. Yankee! Motor B 123:138-40+ Ja '69
GOETZ, Dorianne
Death; poem. Nation 208:767 Je 16 '69
GOETZ, Nancy. See Goetz, A. jt. auth.
GOETZ, Ronald
Movie. Chr Cent 86:715-16 My 21 '69
GOFF, F. Glenn
Forest as an ecosystem. Am For 75:16-18+ D
'69
GOFFMAN, Erving
Birth of a new science. America 120:236-7
Mr 1 '69
GOGOL', Nikolai Vasil'evich
Life as it is and as it should be. E. J. Sim-
mons. Sat R 52:44-5 Ap 12 '69
GOJMERAC, W. L. and Slominski, J. W.
Recipe for winter bait. Field & S 74:50-1 D
'69
GOKAY, Margaret Whitehead
Your son has been wounded. Read Digest 95:
63-7 S '69
GOLA, Tom
On top with no place to go. C. Kirkpatrick.
il por Sports Illus 30:22-4+ F 17 '69
GOLD, Edward B.
Relevance: a job, a future, a sense of dignity
(cont) Library J 94:818 F 15 '69
GOLD, Herbert
Elsewhere people; story. Harp Baz 103:182-3 D
'69
How to find out if you are rich or poor with-
out actually having any money. Harp Baz
102:197+ Ag '69
Letter from a far frat. Atlan 223:85-7 My '69
My summer vacation in Biafra. por Harper
N 21 '69
Stories I guess I won't write. Atlan 224:39-42
Ag '69; Same abr. Writer 82:27 D '69
GOLD, Joseph
Charles Dickens and today's reader. Engl
J 58:205-11 F '69
GOLD, Michael, and Summerlin, Edgar
Month's jazz. Am Rec G 35:592-3 Mr '69
GOLD, Ronald
Israel: from pungent image to vivid life.
Dance Mag 43:36-40 My '69
Leon Danielian at the helm. Dance Mag 43:
60-3 Ag '69
Music hall medley. Dance Mag 43:28-9 Jl '69
GOLD, Thomas
Apollo 11 observations of a remarkable glaz-
ing phenomenon on the lunar surface. bib-
liog Science 165:1345-9 S 26 '69
GOLD, Victor
Defeat of an educator. Nat R 21:28-9 Ja 14
'69
Obscenity gap. Nat R 21:597 Je 17 '69
On disengagement. Nat R 21:790 Ag 12 '69
GOLD
See also
Gold buying
Gold mines and mining, Submarine
Prices
All that's gold does not glitter. il Forbes
104:58 D 15 '69
Bullion break. Time 94:90 N 21 '69
Crisis that almost happened. il Bsns W p31
Mr 15 '69
Dollar triumphant; U.S.-South Africa agree-
ment. Newsweek 75:68 Ja 12 '70
Dollar victorious. Newsweek 74:97-8 D 8 '69

Double standard. il Newsweek 73:76+ Je 23
'69
Fixing a floor. Time 94:49-50 D 26 '69
Now it's gold that may need support. U S
News 67:89-90 D 8 '69
Two gold markets with the price of one. il
Bsns W p41 D 13 '69
Why the luster went out of gold. il Bsns W
p44 N 15 '69
GOLD, Deep sea drilling of. See Gold mines
and mining, Submarine
GOLD as money
Crisis again? il Time 93:61-2 Ja 31 '69
Monetary seers hold a summit; Claremont
international monetary conference in Cali-
fornia. il Bsns W p32-3 Mr 15 '69
Reassurance on gold price. U S News 66:75
F 3 '69
Reassuring gold men; appointment of Walker
and Volcker to key monetary posts. il
Bsns W p 120 Ja 25 '69
GOLD bond stamp company. See Trading
stamps
GOLD buying
Gold blues. P. A. Samuelson. Newsweek 74:84
S 15 '69
Where the gold has gone; South Africa
selling abroad. il Time 94:69 Jl 25 '69
GOLD cup race of APBA. See Motor boat rac-
ing
GOLD depository, Fort Knox. See United
States—Mint, Bureau of the
GOLD leaf
Uses of gold in the graphic and decorative
arts; address. H. L. Hunter. Pub W 195:76+
My 5 '69
GOLD mines and mining

Alaska
Nome. W. Bronson. il Am West 6:20-31 Jl '69
See also
Klondike
South Africa
Where the gold has gone; South Africa
selling abroad. il Time 94:69 Jl 25 '69
GOLD mines and mining, Submarine
Gold in the sea. F. Libby. il Sea Frout
15:232-41 Jl '69
GOLD panning
Those were the days. H. D. Brown. il Hob-
bies 74:116 Ap '69
GOLD star. See Golden star
GOLDBEATING. See Gold leaf
GOLDBERG, Art
Documenting the ghetto. Ramp Mag 7:63-4
D 14 '68
—and Marine, Gene
O'Brien: I want to kill a nigger. Ramp Mag
8:10-18 Jl '69
GOLDBERG, Arthur Joseph
Arthur Goldberg writes about the Green
Berets. por Life 67:30D O 17 '69
GOLDBERG, Bennett C.
Build for your car, one-IC tachometer. Radio-
Electr 40:52-3 Je '69
—and Wilkins, R. G.
Add electronic ignition to your car. Radio-
Electr 40:32-4 Ap '69
GOLDBERG, Emanuel
Other Goldberg; a visit with Zeiss Ikon's
practical prodigy. N. Goldberg. por Pop Phot
65:88-9+ N '69
GOLDBERG, Leo
Ultraviolet astronomy; with biographical
sketch. Sci Am 220:14, 92-102 bibliog
(p 144) Je '69
GOLDBERG, Maxwell H.
Socrates, the computer, and ivied walls. bib-
liog f Sch & Soc 97:424-7 N '69
GOLDBERG, Norman
Lens faults and how to spot them. Pop
Phot 65:83-5+ Jl '69
Shop talk. See issues of Popular photog-
raphy
GOLDBERG, Reuben Lucius. See Goldberg,
Rube
GOLDBERG, Rube
He sculptures his satire; interview, ed. C.
Rice. il pors Har Yrs 9:18-21 O '69
GOLDBERG, Stephen B.
Coordinated bargaining: some unresolved
questions. Mo Labor R 92:56-8 Ap '69
GOLDBERG, Stephen R. and Schuster, C. R.
Nalorphine: increased sensitivity of monkeys
formerly dependent on morphine. bibliog
Science 166:1548-9 D 19 '69
—and others
Morphine: conditioned increases in self-
administration in rhesus monkeys. bibliog
Science 166:1306-7 D 5 '69
GOLDBERGER, M. L.
Nobel laureates in economics, chemistry, and
physics. Science 166:720-2 N 7 '69

GOLDBLOOM, Maurice J.
Contribution to Das kapital. Sat R 52:57 Ap 5 '69
Is there a backlash vote? Commentary 48: 17-26 Ag '69
Junta's year. Commonweal 89:613-15 F 14 '69
New York school crisis. Commentary 47:43-58 Ja; 28+ Ap '69

GOLDBLUM, Stan
Instant millionaire. pors Forbes 103:66-7 Mr 1 '69

GOLDEMBERG, Isaac
New York's new blood poets. por Américas 21:14-20 My '69

GOLDEN, Harry
[Harry Golden column] See issues of Nation

GOLDEN, L. L. L.
Public relations. See issues of Saturday review

GOLDEN, Lotti
Salty socking soul of Lotti Golden. T. Barry. pors Look 33:74-6+ S 9 '69

GOLDEN, Mark, and Bridger, Wagner
Refutation of Jensen's position on intelligence, race, social class, and heredity. bibliog Ment Hy 53:648-53 O '69

GOLDEN, William T.
Paul E. Klopsteg retires as treasurer; William T. Golden elected to the post. W. O. Roberts. Science 165:826 Ag 22 '69

GOLDEN asters
Chrysopsis. R. D. Pearce. Horticulture 47: 54 Ap '69

GOLDEN-cheeked warblers. See Warblers

GOLDEN Delicious. See Apples

GOLDEN eagles. See Eagles

GOLDEN Gate bridge. See San Francisco Bay bridges

GOLDEN Gate park. See San Francisco—Parks and playgrounds

GOLDEN Spike national historic site
Last rail, last spike. M. M. Moller. il Nat Parks 43:8-9 Je '69

GOLDEN star
Gold star. R. D. Pearce. Horticulture 47:15 Ja '69

GOLDEN worms; story. See Greenberg, B. L.

GOLDFARB, Robert W.
Positive action; address, October 3, 1968. Vital Speeches 35:315-18 Mr 1 '69
Why whitey is failing in the cities. Read Digest 95:139-44 O '69

GOLDFARB, Ronald L.
Conspiracy for correctional reform. New Repub 161:15 D 13 '69
Legal nonsense. New Repub 161:10-11 Ag 9 '69
Prison: the national poorhouse. New Repub 161:15-17 N 1 '69
Rapping with convicts. New Repub 161:21-3 Jl 19 '69

GOLDFARB, Sidney
Speech, for instance; poem. Mlle 68:190 Ap '69

GOLDIN, Amy
Harlem out of mind. Art N 68:52-3+ Mr '69
One cheer for expressionism. Art N 67:48-9+ N '68
Sweet mystery of life. Art N 68:46-51+ My '69

GOLDIN, Hyman H.
Television overlords. Atlan 224:87-9 Jl '69

GOLDING, William
African genesis and Lord of the flies: two studies of the beastie within. R. Lederer and P. H. Beattie. Engl J 58:1316-21+ D '69
Symbol hunting Golding's Lord of the flies. J. Martin. Engl J 58:408-13 Mr '69
Trust the tale: a second reading of Lord of the flies. L. Levitt. bibliog f Engl J 58:521-2 Ap '69

GOLDMAN, Albert
Apollo voodoo. Holiday 45:54-5+ F '69
Books (cont) Vogue 153:130 My '69; 155:82 Ja 1 '70
Close up: the old smut peddler. Life 67:49-53 Ag 29 '69
Life music review. Life 66:16 Mr 28; 18 My 23; 67:8 Jl 4; 12 Jl 25; 28 S 26; 20 O 17; 22 N 21; 16 D 12 '69
Pale voodoo hands across the sea. Life 66: 14 Mr 14 '69
Portnoy's complaint by Philip Roth looms as a wild blue shocker. Life 66:58B-58D+ F 7 '69
Posthumous stardom for a once and future lord. Life 67:13 D 19 '69
Purity, not parody, in a real rock revival. Life 66:8 My 9 '69

GOLDMAN, Bernard
Shreds of ancient Persia; with biographical sketch. por Nat Hist 78:4, 26-35 My '69

GOLDMAN, Eric F.
Liberals, the blacks and the war. N Y Times Mag p40-1+ N 30 '69
Nixon after six months. por N Y Times Mag p26-7 Jl 20 '69
about
Advising the President. W. Goodman. Commentary 47:76-9 Ap '69

GOLDMAN, Harvey
Conditions for coequality. bibliog f Clear House 43:488-91 Ap '69

GOLDMAN, Jerry
Creative slip casting. Ceram Mo 17:25-7 Ap '69

GOLDMAN, Lorraine
Reading and reporting: a tailor-made program for each student. Engl J 58:236-41 F '69

GOLDMAN, M. C.
California's unique farm on less than an acre. Org Gard & Farm 16:36-9 D '69
Everything-goes composters. Org Gard & Farm 16:32-5 O '69
Have your own bug-in! por Org Gard & Farm 16:59-64 Ag '69
King of the dates. Org Gard & Farm 16:36-41 N '69

GOLDMAN, Marshall I.
East reaches for markets. For Affairs 47: 721-34 Jl '69

GOLDMAN, Michael
Berryman: without impudence and vanity. Nation 208:245-6 F 24 '69

GOLDMAN, Peter
Carbon-fluorine bond in compounds of biological interest. bibliog Science 164:1123-30 Je 6 '69

GOLDMAN, William
Judy floats. Esquire 71:78-80 Ja '69
about
Season. P. Nathan. Pub W 195:47 Je 23 '69

GOLDOVSKY, Boris
Hour with Boris Goldovsky. H. E. Phillips. il por Opera N 34:24-5 Ja 17 '70

GOLDSCHMIDT, Arthur E.
Protein problem and national development; statement, November 20, 1968. Dept State Bul 59:673-7 D 23 '68
Reports of the World bank group and international monetary fund; statement, December 5, 1968. Dept State Bul 60:15-17 Ja 6 '69
U.N. General assembly rejects move to bar South Africa from membership in UNCTAD; statement, December 3, 1968. Dept State Bul 60:8-9 Ja 6 '69

GOLDSCHMIDT, S. J. See Miller, R. G. jt. auth.

GOLDSMITH, Ann, and Hellerson, Robert
Our commitment is to diversification of campers. Camp Mag 41:19+ Mr '69

GOLDSMITH, Arthur
Eisenstaedt: a snapshot. Travel & Camera 32:78-83+ Jl '69
How to read a contact sheet. Pop Phot 65: 78-9+ Ag '69

GOLDSMITH, Barbara
(ed) See Freeman, C. D. Catherine Freeman recollected
(ed) Spot check; comment on culture U.S.A. Harp Baz 102:122A-122X F '69

GOLDSMITH, Harris
Conductor Casals, passion and tension. Hi Fi 19:96 S '69
Great pianist's noncareer. Hi Fi 19:89 Jl '69
Instrumental recordings. Hi Fi 19:81-4 O '69
Sibelius' seven symphonies. Hi Fi 19:56-60 My '69
Stokowski continues to invade new territories: symphonie fantastique via London. Hi Fi 19:75 Jl '69
Tchaikovsky surprise package. Hi Fi 19:72-3 Ag '69
Toscanini treasures. Hi Fi 19:96-7 D '69

GOLDSMITH, Paul
Track-testing Dodge's new pony car. pors Pop Mech 132:96-9+ D '69

GOLDSMITHING
See also
Gilding

GOLDSTEIN, Abraham S.
Jail before trial. New Repub 160:15-18 Mr 8 '69

GOLDSTEIN, Harry
Lunar medicine; questions and answers. Sci Digest 65:19-20 F '69

GOLDSTEIN, L. Alan
Double exposure. Nation 208:640+ My 19 '69
Thrashing with doom. Nation 209:386-7 O 13 '69

GOLDSTEIN, Laurence
Constructions. Nation 208:472+ Ap 14 '69

GOLDSTEIN, R. M.
Superior conjunction of Pioneer 6. Science 166:598-601 O 31 '69

GOLDSTEIN, Richard
The band, the best? Vogue 155:160-1 Ja 15 '70
Guerrilla theatre. Vogue 153:164-5+ Mr 1 '69
Pop music (cont) Vogue 153:130 F 1; 44 Mr 15; 34 Ap 15; 68 Je; 154:46 Ag 15; 158 O 1; 126 N 1 '69
Sight & sound of folk. Travel & Camera 32:70-5 Je '69
Why the young killed movie superstars. por Vogue 154:128+ Ag 1 '69

GOLDSTEIN, S. J. Jr. and Meisel, D. D.
Frequency dependence of polarization of pulsar CP 0328. bibliog Science 163:810-12 F 21 '69

GOLDSTEIN, William
Divorce from intellect. Clear House 44:195-8 D '69
Team planning: heart transplant in teaching. Clear House 43:272-4 Ja '69

GOLDSTON, Eli
BURP and make money. bibliog Harvard Bsns R 47:84-99 S '69

about

Man who taught a corporate elephant to dance. W. McQuade. il pors Fortune 79: 122-4+ F '69

GOLDWASSER, Edwin L.
Science and man: breaking new ground at Batavia. por Bul Atom Sci 25:7-10 O '69

GOLDWASSER, Thomas
Coal mining. Atlan 224:28+ N '69
Poor and the powerful. Sat R 52:30-2 Mr 8 '69

GOLDWATER, Barry Morris, 1909-
Nuclear weapons; address, January 20, 1969. Vital Speeches 35:262-3 F 15 '69
Why a military-industrial complex? A senator's answer; excerpts from address, April 15, 1969. por U S News 66:88-90 Ap 28 '69

about

Goldwater case: actual malice asserted. H. F. Pilpel and K. P. Norwick. Pub W 196:31-2 S 1 '69
Goldwater plea for elderly. America 121: 149-50 S 13 '69
Open letter to Barry Goldwater. K. Hess. il Ramp Mag 8:28-31 O '69; Same abr. Cur 113:21-6 D '69
Two Goldwaters in Congress now. por U S News 66:14 My 12 '69

GOLDWATER, Barry Morris, 1939?-
Barry jr. scolds the older generation; interview. pors Nations Bsns 57:46-9 Ag '69

about

Goldwater and son. il por Time 93:29 My 9 '69
Son also rises. por Newsweek 73:43-4 Ap 14 '69
Two Goldwaters in Congress now. por U S News 66:14 My 12 '69

GOLEMAN, Barbara
Teacher of the year. C. Mangel. il pors Look 33:58-62 My 13 '69

GOLETA, Calif.
Goleta slough. L. H. Wakefield. il Audubon 71:154 N '69

GOLF
Call back the years; Negro golfer, Charlie Sifford. W. Johnson. il Sports Illus 30: 56-8+ Mr 31 '69
Crazy Fatso, the putting fool, may now be the world's best golfer. E. Asinof. il N Y Times Mag p32-3+ Ap 6 '69
Even the duffers have fun. G. Town. bibliog il Har Yrs 9:40-3 Ap '69
Has anybody here seen Billy? R. F. Jones. il Sports Illus 31:24-6+ Jl 14 '69
Is a sclaffing cleek worth still another bisque? il Esquire 71:146-7+ Ap '69
New generation of heroes. D. Jenkins. il Sports Illus 30:18-21 F 17 '69
Presenting the Ben-Hur Open; All-America intercollegiate invitation gold championships. C. Kirkpatrick. il Sports Illus 30:54-5+ Ap 28 '69
Super keen-o show by la grande Catherine; winner of U.S. amateur championship. R. Blount, jr. il Sports Illus 31:54-5 Ag 25 '69
Teeing off on the Continent. Bsns W p 114 Jl 12 '69
Thanks for the memories; photographs, with account by D. Jenkins. Sports Illus 31:28-35 S 1 '69

See also

Golf courses
Ladies' professional golfers' association
Professional golfers' association of America
Putting (golf)
Swing (golf)

History

Personalized history of Scottish golf; or, You'll not do that here, laddie. D. Jenkins. il Sports Illus 31:28-39 Ag 11 '69

Tournaments

Archer grabs the giveaway Masters; with account by D. Jenkins. il Sports Illus 30: 24-9 Ap 21 '69
Archer makes his bow; Masters tournament in Augusta, Ga. il Time 93:56 Ap 25 '69
Big victory for little Ben; Hogan's protégé, at Colonial national invitation tournament. D. Jenkins. il Sports Illus 30:67-8+ My 26 '69
Confidence man; 1969 Professional golfers' association title to R. Floyd. il Time 94:36 Ag 29 '69
Cool one turned the heat on; Women's Open. C. Kirkpatrick. Sports Illus 31:54 Jl 7 '69
Couple of hips, one hurrah; Palmer and Nicklaus in Las Vegas. A. Wright. il Sports Illus 31:70-1+ O 27 '69
Course that Jack built; Heritage golf classic, Hilton Head, S.C. il Time 94:52 D 12 '69
Fluffy makes it no contest; S. Melnyk winner of U.S. amateur championship at Oakmont. C. Kirkpatrick. il Sports Illus 31:26-7 S 8 '69
Golf gets a look at the real world; protesters at PGA championship. D. Jenkins. il Sports Illus 31:24-6+ Ag 25 '69
Golf pays debt to a real pro; C. Sifford wins Los Angeles Open. il Ebony 24:44-6+ Ap '69
Gundy's victory was no fluke; Burdine's invitational. P. Ryan. il Sports Illus 30:52-3 F 10 '69
Here's to you, Mr Robinson, the pros love you; Robinson Open golf classic. M. Mulvoy. Sports Illus 31:64-5 O 6 '69
I am a stupid; Calcutta pools on golf. C. Price. il Esquire 71:148-50+ Ap '69
Jack's course is Arnie's, too; Heritage classic in Hilton Head, S.C. D. Jenkins. il por Sports Illus 31:24-7 D 8 '69
King is asked to earn his way; A. Palmer at U.S. Open. C. Kirkpatrick. il Sports Illus 30:34-5 Je 16 '69
Lee Elder, hottest sophomore in pro golf; Professional golfers' association tournament. L. Robinson. il Ebony 24:60-4 S '69
Liege lord of golf; T. Jacklin wins the British Open. C. Kirkpatrick. il Sports Illus 31:12-15 Jl 21 '69
Mania for the Masters; Heroes and stupids. M. Mulvoy; D. Jenkins. il Sports Illus 30: 34-46+ Ap 7 '69
Mister X, the mainstay of the tour; M. Barber. M. Mulvoy. il Sports Illus 30:52 Mr 3 '69
Never the twain shall; Singapore Open golf championship. E. Shrake. il Sports Illus 30:66-77 Je 16 '69
New master. il Newsweek 73:110-11 Ap 28 '69
Nice course if you like snakes; U.S. Open on Cypress creek course. J. Nicklaus. Sports Illus 30:51-2+ Je 9 '69
Old Charlie jolts the new tour; Negro wins the first tournament, L.A. Open. D. Jenkins. il Sports Illus 30:16-17 Ja 20 '69
Old sarge cools it; O. Moody winner of U.S. Open at Houston. D. Jenkins. il Sports Illus 30:18-23 Je 23 '69
Pennies in a golden age; World cup matches. L. Griggs. Sports Illus 31:83-5 O 13 '69
Place of the month; Augusta; world's most famous golf classic. il Holiday 45:106-7 Ag '69
Polite no from Arnie and Jack; skipping the Greater Greensboro Open. W. Johnson. il Sports Illus 30:34-5 Ap 14 '69
Sarge takes charge; U.S. Open. il Newsweek 73:94 Je 30 '69
Shower power; Bing Crosby Pro-Am tournament. il Newsweek 73:60 F 10 '69
Sporting scene; Masters tournament in Augusta, Ga. H. W. Wind. New Yorker 45:129-32+ My 3 '69
Sporting scene; United States Open golf championship at Champions golf club, Houston. H. W. Wind. New Yorker 45:65-6+ Jl 5 '69
Sudden death on the 18th hole. P. Farber. il Travel & Camera 32:12-14 Mr '69
This is golf? Crosby tournament. D. Jenkins. il Sports Illus 30:12-15 F 3 '69
Tie may be like kissing your sister; biennial Ryder cup matches. G. S. Brown. il Sports Illus 31:67-8 S 29 '69
Trades becalm skinny Jack; the Hawaiian Open. M. Mulvoy. il Sports Illus 31:42-3 N 17 '69

GOLF—Tournaments—*Continued*
Unknown soldier; O. Moody. il Time 93:51
Je 27 '69
Westchester at $3,472.22 a hole. J. Skow. il
Holiday 45:34-7+ Je '69
What has gone wrong, Jack? M. Mulvoy.
Sports Illus 30:25-5 My 19 '69
Wide-open eyes are on Texas; tournament at
Champions in Houston. D. Jenkins. il
Sports Illus 30:42-5 Je 9 '69

GOLF, Indoor
Electronic golf range. S. Anderson. il Parks
& Rec 4:45+ S '69

GOLF, Miniature
Everybody do the putt-putt; miniature golf.
C. Kirkpatrick. il Sports Illus 31:28-31 S 15
'69

GOLF balls
Golf's underwater underworld; scavenging
for balls is a $1 million a week business.
P. Ryan. il Sports Illus 30:74-8+ My 19
'69; Same abr. with title Second life of a
golf ball. Read Digest 95:91-4 Ag '69
Solid success. Time 94:36 Ag 29 '69

GOLF carts. See Motor vehicles
GOLF clothes. See Clothing and dress—Sports
clothes

GOLF courses
Caribbean golfing. A Chapin. il Travel 132:
28-35 N '69
Just the place when it snows; Mid-Ocean
club in Bermuda. il Sports Illus 30:22-7
Ja 27 '69
Pointillist view of Houston's Champions;
reproductions of paintings by D. Moss;
with account by J. Nicklaus. Sports Illus
30:46-52+ Je 9 '69
Public golf courses, with a difference. S.
Sousa. il Parks & Rec 4:49-50+ My '69
Rockefeller center west: Hawaii's Mauna
Kea. W. P. Fox. il Holiday 45:54-5+ My
'69
Shortest wait; public golf courses. Esquire
71:151 Ap '69
Sporting scene; Masters tournament in Au-
gusta, Ga. H. W. Wind. New Yorker 45:129-
32+ My 3 '69
Sporting scene; United States Open golf
championship at Champions golf club, Hous-
ton. H. W. Wind. New Yorker 45:65-6+
Jl 5 '69
Wide-open eyes are on Texas; Champions
golf club in Houston. D. Jenkins. il Sports
Illus 30:42-5 Je 9 '69

GOLF gambling. See Gambling
GOLF shoes. See Shoes
GOLFERS
Archer grabs the giveaway Masters; with
account by D. Jenkins. il Sports Illus 30:24-
9 Ap 21 '69
Black athlete in the golden age of sports;
stereotypes, prejudices, other unfunny hilar-
ities. A. S. Young. il Ebony 24:114-16+
Je '69
Call back the years; Negro golfer, Charlie
Sifford. W. Johnson. il Sports Illus 30:56-8+
Mr 17 '69
Golf gets a look at the real world; protesters
at PGA championship. D. Jenkins. il Sports
Illus 31:24-6+ Ag 25 '69
Never the twain shall; Singapore Open golf
championship. E. Shrake. il Sports Illus
30:66-77 Je 16 '69
New generation of heroes. D. Jenkins. il
Sports Illus 30:18-21 F 17 '69
Pennies in a golden age; World cup matches.
L. Griggs. Sports Illus 31:83-5 O 13 '69
Super keen-o show by la grande Catherine;
winner of U.S. amateur championship. R.
Blount, jr. Sports Illus 31:54-5 Ag 25 '69
This is golf? Crosby tournament. D. Jenkins.
il Sports Illus 30:12-15 F 2 '69
Tie may be like kissing your sister; biennial
Ryder cup matches. G. S. Brown. il Sports
Illus 31:67-8 S 29 '69
See also
Ladies' professional golfers' association
Professional golfers' association of America
also names of golfers, e.g. G. Archer

Anecdotes, facetiae, satire, etc.
This is a grown-up, right? What do you
think he's doing? B. Rollin. il Look 33:79-
83 Jl 15 '69

GOLFINOPOULOS, Peter
Introducing Peter Golfinopoulos. H. Rosenstein. il por Art N 68:56-8+ My '69

GOLFMOBILES. See Motor vehicles
GOLGI apparatus
Cellulosic wall component produced by the
Golgi apparatus of pleurochrysis scherffelii.
R. M. Brown and others. bibliog il Science
166:894-6 N 14 '69

Golgi apparatus. M. Neutra and C. P. Leblond. il Sci Am 220:100-7 bibliog (p 132) F
'69

GOLIGHTLY, Henry O.
How to keep on target. Nations Bsns 57:75-
7 My '69

GOLL, Yvan
Critic of the month. L. Lieberman. Poetry
114:54-5 Ap '69

GOLLAN, David
How to stretch your air fare dollar. Travel &
Camera 32:38+ N '69

GOLOVIN, Nicholas E.
Technology, social change and the evalua-
tive function; address. bibliog Vital
Speeches 35:310-15 Mr 1 '69

GOLUB, Sheldon D.
Controversial park wins friends. Am City
84:70-1 Jl '69
Urban oasis; Flower avenue park. Parks &
Rec 4:31-2 F '69

GOMEL, Bob
Specter of the auto's gilded age; photographs. Life 66:58-63 Je 27 '69

GÓMEZ-SICRE, José
What Noah left behind. por Américas 21:
32-7 O '69

GOMUŁKA, Władysław
Polish way. K. Huszar. por Newsweek 73:
48+ My 5 '69

GONADOTROPINS
Changing sensitivity of the pubertal gonadal
hypothalamic feedback mechanism in man.
H. E. Kulin and others. bibliog il Science
166:1012-13 N 21 '69
Luteinizing hormone; action on the Graafian
follicle in vitro. P. L. Keyes. bibliog il
Science 164:846-7 My 16 '69
Luteinizing hormone-releasing activity in hypophysial stalk blood and elevation by
dopamine. I. A. Kamberi and others. bibliog il Science 166:388-90 O 17 '69

GONDAR, Ethiopia
Well traveled camera. H. Keppler. il Mod Phot
33:134+ F '69

GONDWANALAND. See Continental drift
GONZALES, Joseph M. See Alexis, Brother
GONZALES, Pancho. See Gonzales, R. A.
GONZALES, Richard Alonzo
Adios, Pancho. il por Newsweek 74:104-5 O
20 '69
El Pancho grande. K. Chapin. il por Sports
Illus 31:56-9 Jl 7 '69
This old pro is just too mean to quit. M.
Smith. il pors Life 67:77-80 S 12 '69

GONZALEZ, Arturo
Boating's dozen deadly sins. Mech Illus 65:
56-7+ Ag '69

GONZALEZ, Arturo F. Jr
Successful magazine article writing. Writer
82:15-16+ Jl '69
Vietcong's secret weapon; marijuana. Sci
Digest 65:14-18 Ap '69

GONZÁLEZ LEDO, Liliana
Crystal ball; story. Américas 21:37-8 Je '69

GOOCH, Bob
America's no. 2 game animal. Field & S 74:
68-9+ N '69

GOOD, Loren D.
Time at a different tempo; poem. Am For
75:29 Ag '69

GOOD, Paul
Race crisis at a marine camp. Life 67:46-51
S 26 '69
Requiem for Courtney Smith. Life 66:76B-
76D+ My 9 '69

GOOD, Thomas L. and Bates, D. A.
Politics and youth. bibliog f Clear House 43:
396-400 Mr '69

GOOD and evil
Look at the problem of evil. D. A. Hagner.
Chr Today 13:10-12 S 26 '69
New year's prayer; reprint. D. Lawrence.
U S News 68:76+ Ja 5 '70
See also
Sin

GOOD bye too soon; story. See Dowty, L.
GOOD deed; story. See Gallant, M.
GOOD emergency mother substitutes. See Baby
sitters

GOOD Friday
Today's faces on the cross. P. P. Leimbach.
Farm J 93:91 Ap '69

GOOD housekeeping Institute
Ballad of Willie Mae; with editorial comment.
Bsns W p45-6, 172 F 22 '69

GOOD neighbor policy. See United States—
Foreign relations—Latin America
GOOD samaritanism. See Assistance in emer-
gencies
GOOD soldier Schweik (literary character)
See Characters in literature

GOOD taste. See Aesthetics
GOODALE, Thomas L.
Manpower muddle. Parks & Rec 4:27-30+
F '69
GOODE, Richard
Tax burden in the United States and other
countries. bibliog f Ann Am Acad 379:83-
93 S '68
GOODELL, Charles Ellsworth
Biafra and the American conscience. por Sat
R 52:24-7+ Ap 12 '69
Excerpt from address, January 15, 1969. Cong
Digest 48:238+ O '69
Excerpt from debate, June 26, 1968. Cong
Digest 48:55+ F '69
Report on Biafra; interview. New Yorker
45:37-8 Ap 12 '69
Set a deadline for withdrawal! New Repub
161:13 N 22 '69

about

Goodell is no Bobby Kennedy, but he's try-
ing hard. R. L. Madden. il pors N Y Times
Mag p50-1+ O 26 '69
Goodell's conversion. il por Newsweek 74:
37 N 24 '69
Goodell's deadline. New Repub 161:8-9 N 1
'69
Lawmakers get the word. il pors Nations
Bsns 57:38-40+ My '69
President and senators clash. America 121:
287-8 O 11 '69
Word for Goodell. Commonweal 91:60 O 17
'69
GOODELL, Grace
Cloth of the Quechuas; with biographical
sketch. por Natur Hist 78:5, 48-55+ D '69
GOODFRIEND, Arthur
Cognoscenti abroad, Amalia Rodrigues's Lis-
bon. Sat R 52:42-3+ Mr 15 '69
Cognoscenti abroad: Carl Foreman's Lon-
don. Sat R 52:32-4 Ag 16 '69
Cognoscenti abroad, Gore Vidal's Rome.
Sat R 52:36-9 Ja 25 '69
Cognoscenti abroad, James Jones's Paris.
Sat R 52:36-8 F 1 '69
Cognoscenti abroad, Julián Marías's Madrid.
Sat R 52:39-41 Je 14 '69
Cognoscenti abroad Morris West's Rome. Sat
R 52:23-6 Jl 19 '69
Cognoscenti abroad; Yehudi Menuhin's Lon-
don. Sat R 52:42+ My 10 '69
GOODHEART, Barbara
Exit German measles? Todays Health 47:26-
8+ Je '69
GOODING, Ben
On the boards. W. Como. por Dance Mag
43:20 My '69
GOODING, Judson
Ondine-gastronomy, with a view. Travel &
Camera 32:86 Ag '69
GOODISON, Nicholas
Clockmaker and cabinetmaker. Antiques 95:
825-9 Je '69
GOODLAD, John I.
How do we learn? excerpt from Schooling
and education. Sat R 52:74-5+ Je 21 '69
Schools vs. education; excerpt from School-
ing and education. Sat R 52:59-61+ Ap 19
'69
GOODMAN, Anita
Mrs Goodman is a party planner. J. Kuh.
Ladies Home J 86:112 F '69
GOODMAN, Benny
B.G. at his best. B. Korall. il por Sat R 52:
48-9 Mr 15 '69
GOODMAN, Kenneth S.
Let's dump the uptight model in English. Ed
Digest 35:45-8 D '69
GOODMAN, Marjorie J.
Stock control is more than counting. Pub
W 196:155-7 Jl 14; 49-50 Jl 21 '69
GOODMAN, Mitchell
Waiting; poem. Poetry 113:248-9 Ja 25 '69
GOODMAN, Paul
New reformation. N Y Times Mag p32-3+ S
14 '69; Same abr. with title Living through
a new reformation. Cur 112:4-9 N '69
GOODMAN, Reba M. See Benjamin, W. B. jt.
auth.
GOODMAN, Robert L.
New! color TV circuits. Radio-Electr 41:40-
2+ Ja '70
New 1969 color-killers. Radio-Electr 40:43-
5+ F '69
GOODMAN, Saul
Brief biography. See issues of Dance magazine
GOODMAN, Walter
Advising the President. Commentary 47:76-9
Ap '69
Choose your war; or, The case of the selec-
tive C.O. N Y Times Mag p34-5+ Mr 23 '69
Controversy over sex education. Redbook 133:
78-9+ S '69

Hippiedom. Commentary 47:94-5 Mr '69
Liberal establishment faces the blacks, the
young, the new left. N Y Times Mag p8-
9+ D 29 '68; 12 Ja 19 '69
New mobe (i): who's who? What's what?
N Y Times Mag p25-7+ N 30 '69
On doing-one's-thing. Am Scholar 38:240-7
Spr '69
Why teachers are striking. Redbook 132:67+
Mr '69
GOODNICK, Benjamin
Plea unanswered; poem. Ment Hy 53:140 Ja
'69
GOODPASTER, Andrew Jackson
Nato today; address, October 1969. Vital
Speeches 36:141-3 D 15 '69

about

General who is expected to keep on rising.
por U S News 66:16 Mr 24 '69
Making haste slowly. il por Time 93:15 Mr
21 '69
Sigh of relief. por Newsweek 73:46-9 Mr 24
'69
GOODPASTURE, Wendell Williamson
W. W. Goodpasture retires from Kroch's
and Brentano's il por Pub W 196:51-2 Ag
18 '69
GOODRICH, B. F, company
Classic defense. il Newsweek 73:90 My 5 '69
Conglomerate fight widens. Bsns W p40 My
24 '69
Goodrich's four-ply defense. T. O'Hanlon. il
Fortune 80:110-13+ Jl '69
How companies fend off suitors. il Bsns W
p80+ Mr 15 '69
Last great battle? il Forbes 103:46+ Ap 15
'69
Merger bid bounces off Goodrich; Northwest
industries' proposed offer. il Bsns W p66 F
1 '69
Northwest calls it quits on Goodrich. Bsns
W p41 Ag 16 '69
Northwest-Goodrich battle nears finale. il
Bsns W p28-9 Ag 2 '69
Quiet purge at Goodrich. Time 94:48 D 26 '69
Raising the siege. Newsweek 74:57 Ag 25 '69
Takeovers: a classic counteroffensive. il Time
93:98+ My 23 '69
USAF. Proxmire A-7 brake views diverge.
K. Johnsen. Aviation W 91:75 Ag 18 '69
GOODRICH, David L.
Anybody want to buy Chicago? Sat Eve Post
242:36-9 F 8 '69
GOODRICH, Ronald J.
Advisory teacher program benefits beginning
teachers. Clear House 44:12-15 S '69
GOODRICH, Samuel Griswold
Higglety, Pigglety, pop! or, The man who
tried to murder Mother Goose. M. Maxwell.
bibliog f Horn Bk 45:392-4 Ag '69
GOODRUM, John
Alabama's mountain lakes. Travel 131:40-3+
Je '69
Biggest airplane ever built. Pop Sci 194:98-
100 My '69
GOODSPEED'S bookstore. See Booksellers and
bookselling—Massachusetts
GOODWIN, Donald W. and others
Alcohol and recall; state-dependent effects in
man. bibliog Science 163: 1358-60 Mr 21 '69
GOODWIN, Mary Stewart
Wondrous machine that salvages backward
kids. T. Irwin. il Todays Health 47:31-3+
Ag '69
—and Goodwin, T. C.
In a dark mirror. bibliog Ment Hy 53:550-63
O '69
GOODWIN, Richard Naradof
Electing the president. Cur 113:33-5 D '69
Letter from Peru. New Yorker 45:41-6+ My
17 '69
Marcuse and Goodwin tangle at Temple. J.
Groutt. Commonweal 90:279-80 My 23 '69
GOODWIN, T. Campbell. See Goodwin, M. S.
jt. auth.
GOODY, Richard M. See Hunten, D. M. jt.
auth.
GOODYEAR blimps. See Airships
GOODYEAR tire and rubber company
Goodyear gambles on polyglas, and wins.
il Bsns W p 118-21 O 11 '69
GOOKIN, Ralph Burton
New spice. il por Forbes 103:64 Ap 15 '69
GOOLEY DAM (proposed) See Dams
GOOSE as food. See Cookery—Poultry
GOOSE calling. See Bird calling
GOOSE LAKE prairie. See Prairies
GOOSE shooting. See Geese, Wild
GOOSEMAN, Mildred
Old Gabe of Her Majesty's English life guards.
Am West 6:14-15 N '69

GORBMAN, Aubrey. See Oshima, K. jt. auth.
GORBOVSKII, Aleksandr
Towards a new kind of involvement. UNESCO
Courier 22:28-9 Ap '69
GORDAN, John Dozier
Legend revisited: Elinor Wylie. Am Scholar
38:459-68 Sum '69
GORDON, Arthur
Gone home. Read Digest 94:115-18 Ap '69
Louisiana's quiet revolution in family plan-
ning. Todays Health 48:38-41+ Ja '70
Mini-maxims for my godson. Read Digest
95:135-8 Ag '69
Oregon: unspoiled splendor. Read Digest 94:
135-42 My '69
GORDON, Bernard K.
U.S. defense in the nuclear age. bibliog f
Cur Hist 57:100-4+ Ag '69
GORDON, Cyrus H.
Ancient letters to the dead and others. Natur
Hist 78:94-9 F '69
GORDON, Edward J.
On teaching the humanities. Engl J 58:681-
7 My '69
GORDON, Eric
End of the ordeal. Time 94:59-60+ O 24 '69
GORDON, Ethel Edison
House by the water; story. Redbook 133:179-
201 O '69
Special kind of love. Redbook 132:87+ Ap '69
GORDON, Gordon, and Gordon, Mildred
Exploration in writing. Writer 82:9-12 N '69
—See Gordon, M. jt. auth.
GORDON, Harold D.
Open stacks: a second look; reprint. por
Library J 94:1844-5 My 1 '69
GORDON, Howard Todd
You can't believe everything you eat. Mech
Illus 65:50-1 N '69
GORDON, James Stewart-. See Stewart-Gor-
don, J.
GORDON, Kenneth W.
Total-cost bidding saves in the long run. Am
City 84:104+ Ag '69
GORDON, Kermit
Agenda for a new administration. Cur 103:
16-18 Ja '69
GORDON, Malcolm W.
What film making is all about. America 121:
555-7 D 6 '69
GORDON, Michael A.
Worst of Two worlds. Ramp Mag 7:58+ Ap
'69
GORDON, Mildred, and Gordon, Gordon
Night before the wedding; novel. Good H
168:85-7 Mr; 98-9 Ap '69
—See Gordon, G. jt. auth.
GORDON, Richard F. 1929-
Apollo 12, by the crew. por Life 67:36-7 D
19 '69
Blithe spirits in space. por Time 94:30 N
21 '69
To the moon with a light touch. por News-
week 74:90 N 17 '69
See also
Space flight to the moon—Manned flights—
Conrad-Bean-Gordon flight, 1969
GORDON, Ruth
Curtain call; poem. Chr Cent 86:783 Je 4 '69
...20, 21, 73 and counting. Vogue 154:174-5+
N 1 '69
about
Faa-bu-lous long run of Gordon and Kanin.
S Lydon. il pors N Y Times Mag p64-5+
O 5 '69
GORDON, Sol
Mythology of disadvantage. Ed Digest 34:5-7
Mr '69
GORDON, Ted
(ed) Tricks of the trade. Clear House 44:188
N '69
GORDON, Whitney H.
Middletown U.S.A. and good architecture.
por Trans-Action 6:39-42+ My '69
GORDON research conferences
Gordon research conferences: program for
1969. A. M. Cruickshank. Science 163:1085-
98+ Mr 7 '69
Gordon research conferences; supplemental
information. Science 164:860 My 16 '69
Gordon research conferences: winter pro-
gram, 1970. A. M. Cruickshank. Science
166:910+ N 14 '69
GORDONE, Charles
Quiet talk with myself. por Esquire 73:78-81+
Ja '70
about
No place to be somebody. Criticism
America 121:145 S 6 '69
Nation 208:644 My 19 '69
New Yorker 45:112+ My 17 '69

New Yorker 45:64 Ja 10 '70
Newsweek il 73:101 Je 2 '69
Sat R 52:18 My '69
Time il 93:85-6 My 16 '69
GORDY, William D.
Plastics of architecture. Craft Horiz 29:14-
17+ Ja '69
GORE, Albert Arnold
Excerpt from debate, June 24, 1969. Cong
Digest 48:210+ Ag '69
GORE, Daniel
Join! Library J 94:2413-14 Je 15 '69
Skirmish with censors: address, June 1968.
ALA Bul 63:193-203 F '69
GORE, Louise
Miss Gore named U.S. member of executive
board of UNESCO. Dept State Bul 61:343 O
20 '69
GORE, Robert H.
Scavengers of the mud flats; with biograph-
ical sketch. por Sea Front 15:242-8, 254 Jl
'69
GORE RANGE-EAGLES NEST primitive area.
See Wilderness areas—Colorado
GOREN, Charles Henry
Bridge. See issues of Sports illustrated
How the nicest women cheat at Canasta.
McCalls 96:66+ Mr '69
Meet Mr Four no trump. McCalls 96:64+
Ap '69
Two lame ducks in the Bowl. Sports Illus 30:
63-4 My 5 '69
GOREN, E. N. and others
Killing medicine; letter. New Repub 161:40 N
29 '69
GORES, Harold B.
New schools at no cost. Parents Mag 44:
58-9+ O '69
GORGENYI, Imre
Triggered sweep for any scope. Electr World
82:76-8 N '69
GORILLAS
Making friends with mountain gorillas. D.
Fossey. il Nat Geog 137:48-67 Ja '70
Man who makes pets of gorillas. D. Both-
well and D. Coleman. il Sci Digest 65:26-31
F '69
GORKY, Arshile
Becoming is meaning; exhibition of draw-
ings at Knoedler. L. Finkelstein. il Art N
68:44-7+ D '69
**GORMAN, Anthony L. F. and McReynolds,
J. S.**
Hyperpolarizing and depolarizing receptor
potentials in the scallop eye. bibliog Sci-
ence 165:309-10 Jl 18 '69
—See Marmor, M. F. jt. auth.
GORMAN, Bernard J.
Ample garage space for $10 per foot. Am
City 84:136+ S '69
Blowers replace front-end loaders. Am City
84:96-7 My '69
GORMAN, Chester F.
Hoabinhian: a pebble-tool complex with early
plant associations in southeast Asia. bibliog
Science 163:671-3 F 14 '69
GORMAN, Paul A.
Penn central hands throttle to outsider. il
por Bsns W p32 S 27 '69
GORMLEY, Rita
Letter from Prague. Nat R 21:849-50+ Ag
26 '69
GORO, Fritz
New challenges to world hunger; photo-
graphs. Life 66:38-51 Ja 24 '69
GORSKII, Nikolai
Pollution of the ocean; reprint. UNESCO
Courier 22:33-5 Ag '69
GORSUCH, George S.
Firefighter views the Sundance fire. Am For
75:4-5+ Mr '69
GORSUCH family
Gorsuch coat-of-arms. H. K. Eilers. il Hob-
bies 74:146-7 O '69
GORTON, John Grey
Exchange of toasts; May 6, 1969. Nat R
21:472+ My 20 '69
Prime Minister Gorton of Australia visits
Washington, exchange of toasts; with re-
marks, May 6, 7, 1969. Dept State Bul 60:
436-9 My 6 '69
about
Clamor in Canberra. il por Newsweek 73:44+
Mr 31 '69
Rebuke to a high flyer. Time 94:42 N 7 '69
Report from Sydney. E. Shirley. il por Fortune
79:59+ Ap '69
GORTON, Richard A.
Parental resistance to modular scheduling.
Clear House 43:392-5 Mr '69
GOSLAR, Lotte
Lotte Goslar and co; Promenade theater. T.
Borek. Dance Mag 43:33 D '69

GOSNELL, John
He started something. por Forbes 103:92+
Je 15 '69
GOSPEL songs. See Negro songs
GOSPELS. See Bible—New Testament—Gospels
GOSSAGE, Howard Luck
[Advertisements for the Whiskey distillers of
Ireland] Ramp Mag 8:22-3 S '69
Tell me, doctor, will I be active right up to
the last? por Atlan 224:55-7 S '69

about

Advertorial: on Howard Gossage. D. Stermer.
por Ramp Mag 8:21 S '69
GOSSIP
Things they say about each other! J. Stein-
berg. Mlle 69:202+ O '69
See also
Rumor
GOSSIP columns. See Newspapers—Sections,
columns, etc.
GOSSWILLER, Richard
Girl becomes a doctor. Todays Health 47:29-33
Je '69
—See Slattery, J. L. jt. auth.
GOSSYPOL
Gossypol detoxication by fungi. W. L. Baug-
her and T. C. Campbell. bibliog il Science
164:1526-7 Je 27 '69
GOSTUŠKI, Dragutin
Third dimension of poetic expression; or,
Language and harmony. bibliog f Mus Q
55:372-83 Jl '69
GOTAAS, Harold Benedict
Outwitting the patient assassin: the human
use of lake pollution. Bul Atom Sci 25:8-
10 My '69
GOTHAM book mart. See Booksellers and
bookselling—New York (state)
GOTHIC furniture. See Furniture, Gothic
GOTHIC romances
Mood stood still on Strawberry Hill. P.
Quennell. il Horizon 11:112-17 Sum '69
GOTHIC sculpture. See Sculpture, Gothic
GOTTFRIED, Bert A.
Prospects for lower taxes. Sat R 52:33-5+
Mr 22 '69
GOTTFRIED, Martin
Grotowski: genius of the theatre. Vogue
155:154-5+ Ja 1 '70
New theatre is here, isn't it? Vogue 153:80-1+
Ap 15 '69
Theatre. Vogue 154:136 D '69
GOTTLIEB, A. Arthur
Macrophage ribonucleoprotein: nature of the
antigenic fragment. bibliog Science 165:
592-4 Ag 8 '69
GOTTLIEB, Ann
Farewells; poem. Am Scholar 38:404 Sum '69
GOTTLIEB, P. and others
Nonexistence of large mascons at Mare mar-
ginis and Mare orientale. bibliog Science
166:1145-7 N 28 '69
GOTTLIEB, Stuart
Judaism, Israel and conscientious objection.
Chr Cent 86:1136-7 S 3 '69
GOTTSCHALK, Earl C.
Perils of pill-popping with mood drugs. Sci
Digest 66:13-17 Jl '69
GOTTSCHALK, Louis Moreau
Yankee Doodle dandy; performance of sec-
ond symphony. il por Newsweek 74:130
O 20 '69
GOTTSEGEN, Robert
And gladly wolde he lerne, and gladly teche.
Science 164:373 Ap 25 '69
GOUCHER college, Baltimore
Untaught teachers and improbable poets. F.
Howe. il Sat R 52:60-2+ Mr 15 '69
GOUDE, Jean-Paul, and Lagarrigue, Jean
Crud art. Esquire 72:134-9 O '69
GOUDSMIT, Samuel A.
What happened to my paper? por Phys To-
day 22:23-5 My '69
GOUGH, Aidan R.
California shows how. Nation 210:17-20 Ja
12 '70
GOUGH, Marion
Decorator's diary. House B 111:126+ Jl '69
(ed) How to leave home and like it. See issues
of House beautiful
GOULANDRIS, Dolly
Psychiatrist and the bouzoukia. Vogue 155:
64+ Ja 1 '70
GOULD, Glenn
Oh, for heaven's sake, Cynthia, there must
be something else on. Hi Fi 19:MA13-14+
Ap '69

about

Glenn Gould in a brand-new role, good old
pianistic hair-standing. H. Goldsmith. il
por Hi Fi 19:82 Mr '69

GOULD, Heywood
Last tycoons. Commentary 48:74-7 Jl '69
Up from Liverpool. Commentary 47:79-83 Ap
'69
GOULD, Jack
Old fear of Gould and the new criticism of
Arlen. R. Burgheim. Harper 239:100 Ag '69
GOULD, Kenneth M.
Obituary
Sr Schol por 94:24 Mr 28 '69
Sr Schol por 94:Schol Teach 6 Ap 11 '69
GOULD, Peter R.
New geography. Harper 238:91-2+ Mr '69
GOULD, Robert E.
Understanding homosexuality. Seventeen 28:
90-1+ Jl '69
GOULD, Sir Ronald
City of God; adaptation of address, 1969.
PTA Mag 64:2-5 O '69
GOULD, Warren
New alumni council president. por Sch &
Soc 97:350 O '69
GOULD, William B.
Black workers in white unions. Nation 209:
203-6 S 8 '69
GOULD, William S. Baring-. See Baring-
Gould. W. S.
GOULDEN, Joseph C.
Indiscretions of Ma Bell. Nation 209:346-9
O 6 '69
—and Singer, Marshall
Dial-A-bomb: AT&T and the ABM. Ramp
Mag 8:29-35+ N '69
GOULIANOS, Joan
Landscape of the heart. Nation 209:56-7 Jl
14 '69
GOUNOD, Charles François
Faust. Criticism
Hi Fi 19:MA12-13 Mr '69
Hi Fi 19:MA11 D '69
Records:
Romeo and Juliet. Opera N 33:34 Mr 15
'69
GOURDINE, Meredith C.
High-powered idea goes to work. il por Bsns
W p156+ S 20 '69
GOURDS
Gourds, a summertime adventure. il Sunset
142:236+ My '69
Graceful gourds, fantasies of the garden.
A. W. Rooda. il Org Gard & Farm 16:36-7
Jl '69
GOURSE, Leslie
What a change of hair can do. N Y Times
Mag p66-7+ N 16 '69
GOUT
Relief from gout. Sci Digest 65:61-2 Je '69
GOUTWEED
Bishop's weed, a Utah marvel. il Sunset
142:232 My '69
GOVERNMENT. See Federal government; Pub-
lic administration; State, The
GOVERNMENT, Military. See Military admin-
istration
GOVERNMENT, Resistance to
As turmoil spreads, uneasy U.S. takes stock.
il U S News 66:33-4 My 19 '69
Civil disobedience and where it leads, two
sides; statement by the National commis-
sion on the causes and prevention of vio-
lence. il U S News 67:27-8 D 22 '69
Conscience and the community; excerpt from
Civil disobedience and the Christian. D. B.
Stevick. il Chr Cent 86:345-8 Mr 12 '69
Lull. Nation 209:266-7 S 22 '69
New left. S. Lynd. Ann Am Acad 382:64-72
Mr '69
Nonviolent direct action; ed. by A. P. Hare
and H. H. Blumberg. Review
Nation 208:314-15 Mr 10 '69. C. Horman
On establishment law and people's disorder.
R. Scheer. Ramp Mag 8:4+ Jl '69
Power, participation and the politics of dis-
ruption. R. B. Thigpen and L. A. Down-
ing. Chr Cent 86:973-5 Jl 23 '69; Same abr.
with title Future of American politics; par-
ticipatory vs. disruptive politics. Cur 111:
19-22 O '69
Public challenge of government action. E. B.
Skolnikoff. Science 164:499 My 2 '69; Dis-
cussion. 165:544 Ag 8 '69
Public challenge of government action. E.
B. Skolnikoff. Science 164:499 My 2 '69; Discussion. 166:167-8 O 10 '69
Response of police agencies. G. E. Misner.
bibliog f Ann Am Acad 382:109-19 Mr '69
Theology of resistance. H. R. Dymale. Chr
Today 13:8-10 Ag 22 '69
Toward a social ethic; bureaucrats becom-
ing vocal on behalf of the public. Nation
208:292 Mr 10 '69

GOVERNMENT, Resistance to—*Continued*
Urban guerrilla, by M. Oppenheimer.
Review
New Repub 160:26+ My 24 '69. N. Hentoff
See also
Coups d'état
Revolutions

Brazil

Brazil; subverting the universities; anti-subversive laws. F. Bandeira. New Repub 161: 17-19 N 8 '69

China (People's Republic)

Beating the system; peasant revolts. il Newsweek 73:42 Ap 7 '69
Who controls Shansi. Newsweek 74:53-4 S 22 '69

GOVERNMENT administrative efficiency. See Efficiency, Administrative
GOVERNMENT agencies. See United States—Executive departments
GOVERNMENT aid to business
See also
Government lending
GOVERNMENT and agriculture. See Agricultural administration
GOVERNMENT and art. See Art and state
GOVERNMENT and business. See Industry and state
GOVERNMENT and labor. See Labor laws and legislation
GOVERNMENT and science. See Science and state
GOVERNMENT and the press
Administration v. the critics. il Time 94:19-20 N 28 '69
Beat the press, round two. il Newsweek 74: 25-6 D 1 '69
Communications gap. il Newsweek 74:22+ Ag 18 '69
Failing newspapers; Newspaper preservation act. New Repub 160:8 Je 28 '69
Freedom to cheer; Vice President Agnew's Des Moines speech. Nation 209:586-7 D 1 '69
Government vs. press. K. Crawford. Newsweek 74:33 D 1 '69
Guarded White House; Nixon and the new reporters. il Time 93:32+ My 2 '69
I'll check it out; Nixon's press secretary. il Time 94:77 O 10 '69
LBJ confidential; off-the-record remarks. Newsweek 73:60 F 3 '69
L.B.J.'s musings about the media. Time 93:68 F 14 '69
Mob and the media; assault by Vice President Agnew. Nat R 21:1204 D 2 '69
Notes and comment; Agnew's attacks on television and newspapers. New Yorker 45: 51-3 D 6 '69
Press faces its critics. Life 67:46 D 5 '69
Snowballing effect; significance of the intellectual press. Nation 209:427-8 O 27 '69
Summer theatrics. P. Lisagor. Nations Bsns 57:17-18 Jl '69
Surprising asset of normality. H. Sidey. Life 66:4 Mr 21 '69
TRB from Washington. New Repub 161:6 N 29 '69
Washington scene: the news under new management? W. Hines. Bul Atom Sci 25:38+ Mr '69
Weekly Agnew special. Time 94:62+ N 28 '69
See also
Government information
Presidents—United States—Press conferences
GOVERNMENT appropriations and expenditures
See also subhead Appropriations and expenditures under names of countries, e.g. United States—Appropriations and expenditures
GOVERNMENT bonds. See Bonds, Government
GOVERNMENT buildings. See Public buildings
GOVERNMENT committees. See United States—Executive departments
GOVERNMENT consultants
See also
Scientists in government
GOVERNMENT contracts. See Contracts, Government
GOVERNMENT decentralization. See Decentralization in government
GOVERNMENT documents. See Government publications
GOVERNMENT employees
Labor troubles for government. U S News 67:67-8 Jl 21 '69
See also
Bureaucracy

Civil service
Collective bargaining—Government employees
Conflict of interests (public office)
Municipal employees
Nepotism
Patronage, Political
Postal employees
Public officers
State employees
Strikes—United States—Government employees

Anecdotes, facetiae, satire, etc.

Buster Big-Brain's revenge. R. Starnes. Field & S 74:22+ O '69

Pensions

See Civil service pensions

Political activities

Remember the Hatch act? C. O. Jones. Nation 209:411-13 O 20 '69

Salaries, allowances, etc.

Another hike in federal pay; millions are getting raises. il U S News 66:62-3 Je 30 '69
Federal pay bill that faces a veto. U S News 67:12 O 27 '69
Federal pay comparability procedures; BLS national survey of professional, administrative, technical, clerical pay. L. E. Lewis. bibliog f il Mo Labor R 92:10-13 F '69
How it pays now to work for the government. il U S News 66:93-4 Mr 10 '69
New approach to setting the pay of federal blue-collar workers. H. A. Donoian. bibliog Mo Labor R 92:30-4 Ap '69
Trying to keep up; federal government scientists. Sci N 95:211 Mr 1 '69

Canada

Canada's experience with the right of public employees to strike. J. D. Muir. bibliog Mo Labor R 92:54-9 Jl '69

Northern Ireland

Ulster's spoils system. Nation 209:269 S 22 '69

GOVERNMENT employees unions
Union war on postal reform. il Bsns W p97-8 S 20 '69
GOVERNMENT entertaining
Duke Ellington; he took the A train to the White House. P. Garland. il Ebony 24: 29-32+ Jl '69
Duke's party; White House celebration for D. Ellington. New Yorker 45:31-3 My 10 '69
Early bedtime at Blair House; P. Trudeau's two-day visit. H. Sidey. il Life 66:4 Ap 4 '69
Ellington at the White House. S. Dance. il Sat R 52:48-9+ My 31 '69
Jazz at the White House; Modern jazz quartet at state dinner. S. Dance. il Sat R 52: 73+ N 15 '69
Jazz night at the White House honoring the Duke. il U S News 66:10-11 My 12 '69
New way of life at the White House. il U S News 66:32-4 F 24 '69
Politics of reconciliation; Nixon's birthday party for LBJ. il Time 94:14+ S 5 '69
R.S.V.P; Pat and Dick; White House receptions for congressmen and their wives. il Time 93:15-16 Mr 21 '69
Social notes; the Nixons' style. il Newsweek 74:38 N 3 '69
Soul night; party in the White House. il Time 93:25 My 9 '69
Taking the A train; White House birthday party for D. Ellington. il Newsweek 73:34-5 My 12 '69
There was a storm outside and a bit of frost within; excerpts from TR and Will: a friendship that split the Republican party. W. Manners. il Am Heritage 21:24-5+ D '69
Welcome to the club; 61st birthday celebrations of LBJ. il Newsweek 74:27 S 8 '69
White House dining, Nixon style. il U S News 66:12 Ap 7 '69
White House party in Nixon style. il U S News 67:4 D 29 '69
See also
Washington, D.C.—Social life and customs
White House festival of the arts, 1965
GOVERNMENT housing projects. See Housing projects, Government
GOVERNMENT information
Briefings: a ritual of noncommunication; Time essay. Time 94:42-3 O 10 '69
Selling the ABM. Nation 208:259-60 Mr 3 '69

GOVERNMENT information—*Continued*
Ultimate form of corruption; discrepancy between State department assertions and the facts in South Vietnam. R. F. Drinan. New Repub 161:15-16 Jl 19 '69
See also
Government and the press
Information. Freedom of

GOVERNMENT investigations
Long trial of John Paton Davies. J. W. Finney. il N Y Times Mag p7-9+ Ag 31 '69; Reply. G. Fitch. p54+ O 5 '69
Mollenhoff mandate. Time 94:25 N 7 '69
TRB from Washington; Senate hearings under way. New Repub 161:4 Jl 26 '69
U.S.'s toughest customer: R. Nader & raiders. il Time 94:89-92+ D 12 '69
See also
United States—President's commission on the assassination of President Kennedy

Aerospace industries
Lockheed and the SEC. Nation 209:396-7 O 20 '69

American telephone and telegraph company
Private line; rate reduction decision. Nation 209:588 D 1 '69

Army investigation, 1954
See McCarthy-Army controversy, 1954

Automobile industry and trade
Price hearing stays in low. il Bsns W p46-7 S 20 '69

Chemical and biological weapons
Secret weapons; with excerpts from testimony. V. Brodine. bibliog il Environ 11:12-26 Je '69

Conglomerate corporations
Conglomerates under attack. il Newsweek 73:73-4 Mr 10 '69
Conglomerates under the gun. il Bsns W p27-9 Mr 8 '69
Congress hears how Leasco did it. Bsns W p37 O 25 '69
Congress hears the conglomerates. Bsns W p27-8 Ag 2 '69
It's open season on conglomerates, and established business couldn't be happier. J. Cameron. il Fortune 79:43-4 My 1 '69
Mergers face tough quiz. Bsns W p36 My 17 '69
Storm over conglomerates; latest plans for curbs; hearing by the House ways and means committee. il U S News 66:86-8 Mr 24 '69

Drug trade
Congressional hearing; ascertainment of facts or individual publicity; address, October 1, 1969. C. J. Stetler. Vital Speeches 36:53-6 N 1 '69
Drug revolution; findings of the Nelson subcommittee and the Task force. P. A. Dickinson. Har Yrs 9:6-15+ S '69
FDA and Panalba; a conflict of commercial, therapeutic goals? M. Mintz. Science 165:875-81 Ag 29 '69
Pill goes to Washington. Bsns W p31-2 Ja 10 '70

Franchise system
Franchising goes on the griddle. il Bsns W p 15-16 Ja 3 '70

Gambling
Dice Dawson's luck. Time 95:21-2 Ja 19 '70
Super scandal? il Newsweek 75:63-4 Ja 19 '70

Petroleum industry and trade
Battle over special privilege. il Time 93:98+ Je 13 '69
Dry hole; hearings on import quota system. il Newsweek 74:72B+ Ag 4 '69
Jousting with oil. D. Sanford. New Repub 161:17-19 Ag 23 '69
Octane numbers game. A. Q. Mowbray. Nation 209:659-61 D 15 '69

Riots
Brother McClellan. New Repub 160:4 My 24 '69
Riot review; McClellan report. il Newsweek 73:35-6 Je 9 '69

Songmy massacre
Larger issues. Nation 209:683 D 22 '69
Probing the massacre probe. il Time 94:16-17 D 12 '69

Song My; what is the truth? il Newsweek 74:52+ D 22 '69
Southern Gothic; L. M. Rivers' role. Nation 209:715-16 D 29 '69

Student demonstrations
Senate hearings on campus disorders. M. Mueller. Science 165:270 Jl 18 '69

Television industry
Looking & listening; violence on the home screen, commercial crossfire. P. Hudson. Sr Schol 94:24 Ap 11 '69

GOVERNMENT labor policy. See United States—Labor policy

GOVERNMENT lending
How to even the odds; loans to Negroes. H. Samuels. il Sat R 52:22-6 Ag 23 '69
New source of consumer loans; federal savings and loan associations for purchases of household equipment. U S News 66:89 Ap 7 '69
Other budget. H. C. Wallich. Newsweek 73:75 Je 30 '69

GOVERNMENT liability
Legal nonsense; immunity of state and local governments from responsibility to citizens for negligence of their employees. R. Goldfarb. New Repub 161:10-11 Ag 9 '69

GOVERNMENT lotteries. See Lotteries

GOVERNMENT national mortgage association. See United States—Housing and urban development, Department of

GOVERNMENT officials. See Public officers

GOVERNMENT ownership
Revolt of the little man; investors fear nationalization. Time 93:94+ My 9 '69
See also
Railroads and state

Bolivia
New arrangement; nationalization of U.S.-owned Gulf oil co. Newsweek 74:53-4 N 3 '69

Chile
Putting the squeeze on Anaconda; move to nationalize the copper industry. Bsns W p36 My 31 '69

Great Britain
Corporations of a different stamp. F. Morley. Nations Bsns 57:19-20 Ag '69
Nationalization mess; failure of state-owned industries. Time 94:74 Jl 11 '69

India
India hires pro managers. il Bsns W p92+ Ag 30 '69

Spain
INI puts out the welcome mat; Spain's Instituto nacional de industria. il Bsns W p96-7 F 15 '69

United States
Big defense firms are really public firms. J. K. Galbraith. il N Y Times Mag p50-1+ N 16 '69
History's heavy hand; getting rid of government ownership. Forbes 104:34 Jl 1 '69

Zambia
Consolation; Zambian nationalization of RST. il Forbes 104:63 O 1 '69
Nationalization in Zambia; foreign-owned copper mines. il Time 94:72 Ag 22 '69

GOVERNMENT procurement. See Purchasing, Government

GOVERNMENT publications
Future of the Foreign relations series; address, June 16, 1969. W. M. Franklin. bibliog f Dept State Bul 61:247-51 S 15 '69
Govt. vs. publisher; report of seminar sponsored by the Technical, scientific and medical book publishers group. Pub W 196:20-3 D 1 '69
Public domain? publishing of government documents. il Newsweek 74:88 Jl 7 '69

Bibliography
Congressional documents relating to foreign policy. See issues of Department of state bulletin
Publications of the Department of state. See issues of Department of state bulletin
Selected government publications. F. J. O'Hara. Wilson Lib Bul 43:679-83, 797+, 912-19, 1025-9; 44:111-14+, 214-16+, 338-45, 472-81, 570-6 Mr '69-Ja '70
Source material. D. Wasson. See issues of Foreign affairs

GOVERNMENT publicity
Selling the ABM. Nation 208:259-60 Mr 3 '69
See also
Government and the press
GOVERNMENT purchasing. See Purchasing,
Government
GOVERNMENT regulation of industry. See In-
dustry and state
GOVERNMENT research
Growing cost of campus attacks on arms
research. il U S News 66:37-8+ Je 2 '69
GOVERNMENT scientists. See Scientists in
government
GOVERNMENT service. See Civil service;
Public officers
GOVERNMENT spending, Waste in. See
United States—Appropriations and expen-
ditures
GOVERNMENT spending policy
Appraisal of federal fiscal policies: 1961-1967.
R. J. Saulnier. Ann Am Acad 379:63-71 S '68
Can taxes do more than raise revenue? H.
Babian. il Sat R 52:30-2+ Mr 22 '69
Cost of democracy. A. G. Buehler. il Ann
Am Acad 379:1-12 S '68
Government finances and citizen responsibil-
ity. A. Parker. bibliog f Ann Am Acad
379:123-31 S '68
How essential is essential? H. C. Wallich.
Vogue 153:46 Mr 15 '69
3.5-billion cut in federal spending. U S News
67:80 Ag 4 '69
What on earth? New Repub 161:7-8 Ag 2 '69
Wilbur Mills on taxes and spending: inter-
view. ed. by N. MacNeil. W. D. Mills.
Time 93:16 F 21 '69
See also
United States—Appropriations and expendi-
tures
United States—Economic policy
GOVERNMENT statistics, Economic. See Eco-
nomic statistics
GOVERNMENT surplus. See Surplus products
GOVERNORS
See also
Republican governors association
GOVERNORS conference, 1969
Governors' verdict on Nixon program: good,
but. il U S News 67:28-9 S 15 '69
New federalism. il Newsweek 74:24-5 S 15 '69
GOWANS, Alan
Painting and sculpture. Antiques 96:374 S '69
GOWLAND, Peter
Glamour by Gowland. See issues of Popular
photography
Our movies fought city hall, and won! Pop
Phot 65:124-5+ N '69
GOWON, Yakubu
Interview with General Gowon; ed. by C.
Eisendrath. por Time 94:32 Jl 4 '69
GOYA Y LUCIENTES, Francisco José de
Book reviews. J. Jacobs. Art in Am 57:123-4
My '69
GOYER, Jane
My two weeks in the book business. Har Yrs
9:14-15 D '69
GOYNE, Nancy A.
American windsor chairs: a style survey. An-
tiques 95:538-43 Ap '69
GRAAFIAN follicles. See Ovaries
GRABNER, Harry
Copartners! Foundations and city depart-
ments. Parks & Rec 4:19 D '69
GRABNER, John R. Jr
Legal limits of competition; excerpts from
Managerial analysis in marketing. bibliog
Harvard Bsns R 47:4-6+ N '69
GRACE Patricia, consort of Rainier III, prince
of Monaco
Princess Grace turns forty; interview, ed. by
W. B. Arthur. pors Look 33:96-100 D 16 '69
GRACE, W. R. and company
Beer and pretzels? Newsweek 73:71 Je 30 '69
Grace takes a bitter pill in Peru. il Bsns W
p62-3 D 20 '69
New plate upholds power of letterpress:
Letterflex plastic printing plate. il Bsns
W p68+ F 8 '69
W. R. Grace is still looking for that magic.
J. Davenport. il Fortune 80:106-9+ O '69
GRACE (theology)
Concept of grace in Jodo Shin Buddhism. H.
Hashimoto. Chr Cent 86:318-19 Mr 5 '69
GRACIOUSNESS. See Kindness
GRAD, Harold
Plasmas. bibliog por Phys Today 22:34-44 D
'69
GRADE labels. See Labels
GRADER, R. J. and others
Search for soft X-rays from the galaxy. Sky
& Tel 37:79-81 F '69

GRADING and marking (students)
Answer to Sally: multiple-choice tests. W. R.
Link. Ed Digest 34:24-7 My '69
Are grades necessary? D. Wolfle: discus-
sion. Science 162:745-6; 164:245, 1117-18 N
15 '68, Ap 18, Je 6 '69
Down with grades. S. B. Simon. Todays Ed
58:24 Ap '69
Grading game. B. P. McGuire. il Todays Ed
58:32-4 Mr '69
Marks, how much do they mean? with study-
discussion program, by E. Harris and D.
Harris. W. D. Garth. bibliog il PTA Mag
63:2-4, 34-5 Ap '69
Measure of accomplishment. M. S. Marshall.
Sch & Soc 97:21-2 Ja '69
More on grading; symposium. bibliog il Clear
House 43:331-43 F '69
Nonpromotion teaches children they are in-
ferior. H. D. Funk. Ed Digest 35:38-9 N '69
ROTC: under fire but doing fine. il U S News
66:38 My 19 '69
Student evaluation dilemma. P. M. Allen.
il Todays Ed 58:48-50 F '69
Student lounge or study hall: how are grades
affected? D. R. Draayer and P. A. Teague.
il Clear House 44:141-4 N '69
Team teaching and objective evaluation. M.
McLane and others. Clear House 44:174-8
N '69
See also
Ability grouping in education
GRADING of meat. See Meat—Grading and
standardization
GRADUATE degrees. See Degrees, Academic
GRADUATE schools. See Colleges and univer-
sities—Graduate work
GRADUATE students
Draft caused drop in graduate science en-
rollments. P. M. Boffey. il Science 165:162
Jl 11 '69
Grad-school blues; APSA report. Newsweek
74:70-1 S 15 '69
Graduate student; symposium. il Phys Today
22:23-33+ Mr '69; Discussion. 22:9+ Jl '69
More grad students liable to draft. M. Muel-
ler. Science 163:264 Ja 17 '69
New Brahmins: scientific life in America,
by S. Klaw. Review
Sci Am 220:139-40+ My '69. D. Zinberg
and P. Doty
Stalling tactics: effect on enrollments in
graduate school of draft calls. Nation 208:
197 F 17 '69

Sexual behavior
Unmarried marrieds on campus. A. Karlen.
il N Y Times Mag p28-9+ Ja 26 '69; Discussion. p 16+ F 16; 16+ F 23 '69

Statistics
Graduate student; where does he come from?
Where does he go? S. D. Ellis. il Phys
Today 22:53-7 Mr '69
GRADUATE work. See Colleges and univer-
sities—Graduate work
GRADUATED taxation. See Taxation, Progres-
sive
GRADUATES, College. See College graduates
GRADUATION. See Commencements
GRADUATION addresses. See Baccalaureate
addresses
GRADUATION certificates. See Diplomas
GRAEBNER, Clark
Profiles. J. McPhee. por New Yorker 45:45-
8+ Je 7; 44-8+ Je 14 '69
GRAEBNER, Norman A.
Global containment: the Truman years. Cur
Hist 57:77-83+ Ag '69
GRAEF, Hilda
Why I remain a Catholic. Cath World 209:
77-80 My '69
GRAF, Lya
Millionaire & the midget; excerpts from
Once in golconda: a true drama of Wall
Street, 1920-1938. J. Brooks. il por Am Heri-
tage 20:34-5 O '69
GRAF, Rudolf F.
Build low-cost touch alarm. Pop Electr 30:
92-3 F '69
—and Whalen, G. J.
Build a voltminder for your car. Pop Sci 195:
158-61+ O '69
Build your own fluid monitor. Sci Digest 66:
78-81 D '69
Electronic watchdog in a can. Pop Sci 195:
182+ N '69
—See Whalen, G. J. jt. auth.

GRAFFITI
Graffiti lives. B. O'Boyle. il Seventeen 28: 158-9+ S '69
Stick it on the wall in Stockholm. A. Frater. il Holiday 45:85-6 F '69
Walls remember. il Sci Digest 65:31-3 Je '69

Anecdotes, facetiae, satire, etc.
Editor's choice; graffiti in staff lounges of libraries. G. R. Shields; reply. R. P. Clark. ALA Bul 63:430 Ap '69

GRAFFMAN, Gary
Mr Graffman. H. Saal. por Newsweek 73:114-15 F 17 '69

GRAFTING
Fruits you won't find in the supermarket. D. Foraker. il Org Gard & Farm 16:28-32 N '69
It's time you learned grafting! E. A. Kulsar. il Org Gard & Farm 16:38-41 My '69

GRAFTON, Edward G.
Evolution of a new school design system. Arch Rec 146:154-68 O '69

GRAFTON, Samuel
What's happened to the family budget? Mc-Calls 96:42+ S '69

GRAFTON, North Dakota
Small town beefs up its snowfighting capacity. il Am City 84:109-10 S '69

GRAHAM, Bill
Capitalist of rock. il por Time 94:63-4 S 19 '69

GRAHAM, Billy
Answer to corruption. pors Nations Bsns 57:46-9 S '69
Billy Graham: spanning the decades; interview. Chr Today 14:34 N 7 '69
Graham in Melbourne: stones at Christians? S. E. Wirt. Chr Today 13:45 Ap 11 '69
Joy of family life. Good H 169:103+ O '69
Loneliness: how it can be cured. Read Digest 95:135-8 O '69
1969 Protestant inaugural prayers. Chr Today 13:27 F 14 '69
Sickness of Sodom. il por Time 94:65-6 Jl 11 '69
Something for youth to believe in. Read Digest 94:77-81 Je '69
Speaking to the issues; excerpts from sermons. Chr Today 13:31-2 Jl 4 '69
Three American illusions; excerpts from address, November 19, 1969. Chr Today 14:12-14 D 19 '69
What the Bible says to me. Read Digest 94: 83-7 My '69

about
Anaheim crusade: at home with the Angels. R. Chandler. il Chr Today 14:40+ O 24 '69
Billy Graham plays the Garden. P. Tracy. Commonweal 90:457-9 Jl 25 '69
Billy in the Garden. B. Farrell. Life 67:2B Jl 4 '69
Billy's apostles. il por Newsweek 73:65 Je 23 '69
Closest thing to a White House chaplain. E. B. Fiske. il pors N Y Times Mag p27+ Je 8 '69
15th annual Mr Travel award. il pors Travel 132:52-3 Jl '69
God, country, and Billy Graham. J. Corry. Harper 238:33-9 F '69
Graham in New York: less of the same. T. Early. Chr Cent 86:1049 Ag 6 '69
Graham in the garden: new challenges in New York. J. Huffman. Chr Today 13:35 Je 20 '69
Graham: just be yourself. J. D. Douglas. Chr Today 13:41 Mr 28 '69
Graham's Vienna visit. D. Foster. Chr Today 13:58-9 S 12 '69
Hiring for God. Nation 208:653 My 26 '69
Madison Garden revisited. Chr Today 13:46 Je 6 '69
Mellowing magic. il por Time 93:48 Je 27 '69
New Zealand; reprise of a crusade. R. M. O'Grady. Chr Cent 86:459-60 Ap 2 '69
Praying together, staying together. il Time 93:15-16 F 7 '69
Real miracle for 34th street. D. E. Kuchar-sky. Chr Today 13:31 Jl 4 '69
Still in business with the Lord. Nation 208: 814 Je 30 '69
White House preacher. Chr Today 13:32 F 14 '69

GRAHAM, Clive
From Charles to Elizabeth. Sports Illus 30:43 My 19 '69

GRAHAM, Desmond
(ed) See Watson, C. Very private person

GRAHAM, Edward K.
Case study in student protest; excerpts from The first hundred years: a social history of Hampton institute. Am Scholar 38:668-82 Aut '69

GRAHAM, Frank, 1925-
Ear pollution! Audubon 71:34-9 My '69
Hunting. Sports Illus 30:68+ My 19 '69
Saint John; New Brunswick's splendid river. Motor B 123:46-9+ F '69

GRAHAM, Grace
Influences of social classes in schools; excerpt from The public school in the new society. bibliog f Sch & Soc 97:169-80 Mr '69

GRAHAM, Grace L.
Teacher's adventures in programland. Engl J 58:261-6 F '69

GRAHAM, J. A. Maxtone-. See Maxtone-Graham, J. A.

GRAHAM, John P.
Visit New York, the Empire state. Pop Gard 20:18-21+ Spr '69

GRAHAM, Lola Beall
To redwood retreat; poem. Nat Parks 43:9 D '69

GRAHAM, Martha
At seventy-five, a new frontier. il pors Sat R 52:42-3 My 3 '69
Israel: from pungent image to vivid life. R. Gold. il por Dance Mag 43:36-40 My '69

GRAHAM, Martha, and dance company. See Martha Graham and dance company

GRAHAM, Robin Lee
World-roaming teen-ager sails on. il pors Nat Geog 135:449-93 Ap '69

GRAHAM, Ruth McCue (Bell)
Mrs Billy Graham: lunching with 11,000. Chr Today 14:45 O 24 '69

GRAHAM, Sheilah
Authors & editors. B. A. Bannon. por Pub W 195:32-4 Ap 28 '69

GRAHAM, W. Gordon
As it looks in Britain: finding the book buyer of the '70s. Pub W 195:39-40 F 3 '69

GRAIN
See also
Feeding and feeding stuffs—Grain

Cultivation
Green revolution: cornucopia, or Pandora's box. C. R. Wharton, jr. For Affairs 47:464-76 Ap '69

Diseases and pests
Beat small grain insects. G. L. Earle. Suc Farm 67:62H F '69
Fight weeds in small grain. Suc Farm 67:71 F '69

Handling
See Grain handling

Harvesting
Ten best ideas to harvest more grain. P. B. Jones and G. L. Earle. il Suc Farm 67:28-9 S '69

History
Loess and the origin of Chinese agriculture. P. T. Ho. bibliog f il Am Hist R 75:1-36 O '69

Storage
How much grain in your bins? P. Jones. il Suc Farm 67:33 S '69
Protect stored grain with aeration. P. B. Jones. il Suc Farm 67:34-5 N '69
Seven features of a good grain center. P. B. Jones. il Suc Farm 67:26-7 Je '69
Stored grain needs attention now! P. B. Jones. il Suc Farm 67:24 F '69
They built emergency grain storage. il Suc Farm 67:H10 S '69
See also
Corn—Storage
Grain elevators

Transportation
Revolution in grain movement by rail. your stake in it. R. Sanders. il Suc Farm 67:34-5+ S '69
Transportation competition helps move your grain. R. Sanders. il Suc Farm 67: 32-3+ O '69

GRAIN aeration
Protect stored grain with aeration. P. B. Jones. il Suc Farm 67:34-5 N '69

GRAIN elevators
How to sell corn to the elevator. B. Coffman Farm J 93:34A S '69
Vertical elevator makes this setup better. il Suc Farm 67:42 Jl '69

GRAIN handling
Here's portable continuous-flow drying. il Suc Farm 67:B8 O '69

GRAIN in photography. See Photography—Grain

GRAIN of wood. See Wood

GRAMBLING college. Grambling, La.
  Grambling college: where stars are made. W.
    Rogers. il Look 33:72-5 D 16 '69
GRAMMAR, English. See English language—
    Grammar
GRAMONT, Sanche de. See De Gramont, S.
GRANADOS, Enrique
  Report: New York; concert performance of
    Goyescas. H. E. Phillips. il Opera N 33:24
    My 17 '69
GRANATELLI, Andy
  On turbines, Indy, and Andy; interview, ed.
    by S. Kelly. pors Hot Rod 22:48-50 Mr '69

            about

La dolce Indy. K. Chapin. il por Sports Illus
    30:24-9 Je 9 '69
End of an Indy jinx. il Newsweek 73:97 Je 9
    '69
Italian 500; with editorial comment. J. Dian-
    na. il Hot Rod 22:8, 34-7 Ag '69
It's never been a question of whether I'd win
    at Indianapolis or not, but when. B. Mark-
    us. il por Motor T 21:57+ Ag '69
Mister 500; autobiography. They call me
    Mister 500. il Hot Rod 22:156 My '69
Wheeler who deals in STP. il por Bsns W
    p56-7 My 31 '69
GRAND army of the Republic
  Grand army of the Republic; G.A.R. buttons.
    D. F. Brown. il Hobbies 74:50-1 My '69
GRAND BAHAMA ISLAND
  Island that raises one crop: $$$. il News-
    week 73:90+ Ap 21 '69
GRAND CANYON
  Colorado's canyons today; excerpts from
    Down the Colorado. E. Porter. il Audubon
    71:77-9 N '69
  Down, down and away. L. Barry. il Pop
    Phot 64:14+ Mr '69
  Grand Canyon river run. J. V. Young. il
    Travel 131:40-5+ F '69
  Man who owned Grand Canyon. D. H. Strong.
    il Am West 6:33-40 S '69
  Pilgrim's pride; excerpts from The Grand
    Colorado: the story of a river and its can-
    yons. T. H. Watkins. il Am West 6:49-54
    S '69
  Retracing John Wesley Powell's historic voy-
    age down the Grand Canyon. J. Judge. il
    Nat Geog 135:668-713 My '69
  Shooting the Canyon. B. Belknap. il Travel
    & Camera 32:46-7 Je '69
  Squalor amid splendor: Havasupai Indians,
    Cataract Canyon, Ariz. il Time 94:21 Jl 11
    '69
GRAND CANYON NATIONAL PARK
  Canyon commemoration; observations of its
    50th birthday and Powell centennial. il
    Travel 131:39 F '69
  Preparing the park ranger for his job; Ho-
    race M. Albright training center. W. Cone.
    il Parks & Rec 4:30-1+ D '69
GRAND CENTRAL terminal, New York. See
    New York (city)—Stations
GRAND FALLS. See Churchill Falls
GRAND FORKS air force base. See Guided
    missile bases
GRAND prix of Le Mans. See Automobile rac-
    ing
GRAND RAPIDS, Mich.

            Social life and customs

Yesterdays in Grand Rapids. J. Thompson.
    Harper 238:43-51 My '69
GRAND TETON NATIONAL PARK
  Mountains by the minute; through Yellow-
    stone and Grand Teton. L. P. Stinnett. il
    Travel 132:48-51 Jl '69
GRAND TETONS. See Teton Range
GRANDE, Luke M.
  Dies irae; poem. Chr Cent 86:799 Je 11 '69
GRANDFATHER clocks. See Clocks
GRANDFATHERS. See Grandparents
GRANDMA and the pampered boarder; drama.
    See Watts, F. B.
GRANDMOTHERS. See Grandparents
GRANDPARENTS
  Grandma and the buck deer. J. M. Vance. il
    Field & S 74:74-5+ Je '69
  Grandparent syndrome. H. S. Arnstein. il
    N Y Times Mag p 101-3 F 23 '69
  Tonic for an old sailor. W. N. Moose. il Mo-
    tor B 123:53 F '69
  Treasure for grandma. G. O'Hara. il Redbook
    133:14+ Je '69
      See also
  Foster grandparent program
GRANET, Gilbert K.
  High-rolling schoolmaster. por S. Margetts.
    Duns R 94:57-8+ D '69

GRANFIELD, Patrick
  (ed) See Boyd, M. Interview with Malcolm
    Boyd
GRANGER, Kathleen (Buehr)
  My most unforgettable character. Read Di-
    gest 94:88-92 Ap '69
GRANGER, William
  (ed) See West, C. A. That was our orders
GRANITE
  Granites: relation of properties in situ to
    laboratory measurements. G. Simmons and
    A. Nur; reply with rejoinder. A. S. Orange.
    Science 165:202-3 Jl 11 '69
GRANT, Bess (Myerson)
  What makes Bess run? por Bsns W p 122+
    N 1 '69
  Where will Bess Myerson Grant strike next?
    J. Klemesrud. il pors N Y Times Mag p37+
    O 12 '69
GRANT, Bob
  Skydiving. Pop Sci 194:62-6+ Ja '69
GRANT, Bruce
  Toward a new balance in Asia: an Austra-
    lian view. For Affairs 47:711-20 Jl '69
GRANT, Inez
  Sweetest carrots ever. Org Gard & Farm 16:
    37 Ap '69
GRANT, Louis
  Norman Mailer: dialogue with a non-mayor.
    Ramp Mag 8:44-6 D '69
GRANT, Mary Kent
  Mystery, detective and suspense. See first
    issue of each month of Library journal
GRANT, Neville
  Legacy of the mad hatter. bibliog por En-
    viron 11:18-23+ My '69
GRANT, Robert England
  Name of the game. por Forbes 104:23 D 1 '69
GRANT, Ulysses Simpson, 1822-1885
  Grant takes command, by B. Catton. Review
    Nat R por 21:393-4 Ap 22 '69. M. E.
      Bradford
    Sat R por 52:29-30 Mr 1 '69. D. M. Potter
    Time il 93:103 Mr 14 '69
  Miracle on Missionary ridge; excerpt from
    Grant takes command; with introd. by the
    editors. B. Catton. il Am Heritage 20:60-73
    F '69
  When Jersey was the spa of presidents. T.
    Fleming. il por Sat R 52:46-7+ Mr 8 '69
GRANT, W. Vance
  Statistical look at American education 1970.
    Am Ed 5:24-5 O '69
GRANT, William R.
  Public schools feel the money pinch. Com-
    monweal 90:167+ Ap 25 '69
GRANT, Zalin B.
  Ford condom in India's future. New Repub
    161:14-16 S 6 '69
  It's that kind of war. New Repub 161:9-11
    D 20 '69
  Picking up the pieces in Pakistan. New
    Repub 161:11-12 O 18 '69
  Revolt in the Pentagon? New Repub 161:17-20
    O 4 '69
  What are we doing in Thailand? New Repub
    160:19-21 My 24 '69
GRANTS, N.Mex.
  Tell it like it is. H. D. Overby. Todays Ed
    58:55-6 N '69
GRANTS-in-aid
  Game of grantsmanship. Parks & Rec 3:17
    O '68
GRANTS to colleges and universities. See Col-
    leges and universities—Gifts, legacies, etc.
GRAPE boycott. See Boycott
GRAPE industry. See Viticulture
GRAPE pickers strike. See Strikes—United
    States—Farm labor
GRAPE vines. See Grapes
GRAPES
  Muscadines, scuppernongs and grapes. B. Ro-
    zell. il Org Gard & Farm 16:32-4 Je '69
  Royal Riesling; greatest of grapes for warm-
    weather wines. R. A. De Groot. House B
    111:158+ My '69
  Sheridan grapes for Christmas. A. P. Al-
    bright. il Org Gard & Farm 16:75 D '69
      See also
  Wine
              Picking
  See Fruit—Picking
GRAPHIC arts
  Living with art: art works in multiple. E.
    Munro. House & Gard 136:94+ S '69
  New applications for 3-D graphics; potential
    uses for lasers and holograms. il Pub W
    195:88+ F 3 '69

GRAPHIC arts—*Continued*
Question of identity. C. B. Grannis. Pub W 195:71 Je 9 '69
See also
Drawing
Etching
Prints
Push pin studios
Typophiles, The

Bibliography
Books about the graphic arts. il Pub W 195: 97-9 Mr 3; 82+ Ap 7; 196:76 Ag 4; 62 S 1; 68+ N 3 '69
Graphic arts books; an illustrated review. F. Johnson. il Am Artist 33:30-4 My '69
Graphic arts books; illustrated reviews. Am Artist 33:27-30 O '69

Terminology
Importance of correct terms. N. Kent. Am Artist 33:5 O '69
GRAPHIC arts research and engineering council. See Research and engineering council of the graphic arts industry, incorporated
GRAPHIC data processing. See Computer graphics
GRAPHIC methods
See also
Flow charts
GRAPHICS, Computer. See Computer graphics
GRAPHITE fibers. See Fibers
GRAPHOLOGY
Handwriting analysis. D. S. Anthonly. Mech Illus 65:58-60+ D '69
Handwriting tells the tale. H. Van Horne. McCalls 97:152-3+ N '69
How to read handwriting. W. J. Shanahan. Mech Illus 65:58-60+ D '69
GRASHEY, Hellmut
Who's right? por Newsweek 73:49-50+ Ap 21 '69
GRASS, Günter
On writers as court jesters; address, April 1966. Am Scholar 38:275-80 Spr '69

about
European literary scene. R. J. Clements. Sat R 52:40 D 6 '69
Grass at the roots. por Time 94:24+ S 5 '69
Politics of Günter Grass. M. Harrington. Atlan 223:129-31 Ap '69
Voice of Grass. R A. Sokolov. por Newsweek 73:120+ My 26 '69
GRASS
See also
Feeding and feeding stuffs—Grass
GRASS, Artificial. See Turf. Artificial
GRASS clippings. See Lawn thatch
GRASS seed. See Grasses—Seed
GRASS silage. See Silage
GRASSES
Flowing grass; excerpts from The Everglades: river of grass. M. S. Douglas. il Audubon 71:28-45 Ja '69
Grass; excerpt from Blue grass. J. J. Ingalls. il Am For 75:36-7 S '69
See also
Lawns
Pampas grass

Seed
For that lush, green lawn. Consumer Bul 52: 28-30 Ag '69
Label's the clue to lawn seed. R. W. Schery. il Horticulture 46:21+ S '69
GRASSHOPPERS

Control
Exit the voracious locust? il Chem 42:4 D '69
Locusts: teeth of the wind. R. A. M. Conley. il Nat Geog 136:202-27 Ag '69
Manic locust; FAO program. il Time 94:54+ S 5 '69

Migration
Locusts: teeth of the wind. R. A. M. Conley. il Nat Geog 136:202-27 Ag '69
GRATITUDE
See also
Thanksgiving
GRATUITIES. See Tipping
GRAUBARD, Mark
Under the spell of the zodiac; with biographical sketch. por Natur Hist 78:4, 10-12+ My '69

GRAUN, Karl Heinrich
Festival of baroque operas: Graun's Montezuma and Bononcini's Griselda. P. L. Miller. por Am Rec G 35:366-7 Ja '69
Karl Heinrich Graun: Montezuma (excerpts) P. H. Lang. Mus Q 55:278-80 Ap '69
GRAVEREAUX, Daniel
How we judge stereo cartridges. Hi Fi 19: 48-53 F '69
How we test turntables, arms, and changers. por Hi Fi 19:39-42 Ap '69
GRAVES, Charles M.
All-electric recreation center. Parks & Rec 4:36-7 My '69
GRAVES, Dorothy
Discipline shouldn't be demeaning. PTA Mag 64:9-11 bibliog(p34) O '69
Many-pressured pupil. PTA Mag 63:27-9 bibliog(p36) F '69
Right from the start. PTA Mag 63:22-4 bibliog(p36) My '69
GRAVES, Eleanor
Great dinners. See issues of Life
GRAVES, Elizabeth Minot
Selected list of children's books. Commonweal 91:252-4+ N 21 '69
GRAVES, Madeline
Hail and farewell! Testimony of a teacher's testimonial. Clear House 43:561-3 My '69
GRAVES, Michael P.
Plastic saint; poem. Chr Cent 86:1039 Ag 6 '69
San Francisco; poem. Chr Cent 86:1605 D 17 '69
GRAVES, Nancy
Camel as art. il por Time 93:70 Ap 4 '69
GRAVES, Ralph
Managing editor's imprint after 400 issues. Life 66:3 Je 13 '69

about
Change at Life. por Time 93:60 My 16 '69
Life memo goes public. Bsns W p42 My 17 '69
GRAVES, Robert
Carols for Christmas, 1969: Shepherds armed with staff and sling. N Y Times Mag p5 D 21 '69
Troublesome fame; poem. New Yorker 45:150 Ap 26 '69
Unicorn and the white doe; poem. Atlan 223:73 My '69

about
Malevolent muse. G. Wolff. il por Newsweek 74:79-80 Jl 28 '69
Voice outside the cliques and politics of literature. R. Fuller. Sat R 52:21-2+ Jl 26 '69
GRAVES, William
San Francisco Bay, the westward gate. Nat Geog 136:593-637 N '69
—and others
World's last salute to a great American. Nat Geog 136:40-51 Jl '69
GRAVESTONES. See Sepulchral monuments
GRAVIMETRIC titration. See Titration
GRAVITATION
Can anti-gravity really exist? I. Asimov. Sci Digest 65:86-7 My '69
Gravitating toward Einstein; findings of J. Weber. Time 93:75 Je 20 '69
Gravitational mechanism for sea-floor spreading. H. N. Pollack. bibliog il Science 163: 176-7 Ja 10 '69
Gravitational waves detected. il Sci N 95: 593-4 Je 21 '69
Gravity and infinity. D. E. Thomsen. il Sci N 95:512-13 My 24 '69
Science rediscovers gravity. T. Alexander. il Fortune 80:100-4+ D '69
Testing relativity, measuring corona. il Sci N 96:396 N 1 '69
Two problems in gravitation. H. J. Rood. il Sky & Tel 37:152-3, 225-7 Mr-Ap '69
See also
Weightlessness

GRAVITATIONAL mass. See Mass (physics)
GRAVITY
Experiment with gravity. T. Appleby. il Pop Electr 32:66 Ja '70
Gravitational field of the moon. W. M. Kaula. bibliog il Science 166:1581-8 D 26 '69
Gravity: first measurement on the lunar surface. R. L. Nance. bibliog il Science 166: 384-5 O 17 '69
Grip on the tides; the beauty of seascapes tossed and sculpted by the moon. il Life 67: 32-41 Jl 4 '69
Hidden perils of a lunar landing; Sjogren-Muller analysis; and interview with E. S. Schiesser, ed. by J. Lear. il Sat R 52:47-54 Je 7 '69; Discussion. 52:46 Jl 5 '69
Laser target on moon could determine force of gravity. R. G. O'Lone. il Aviation W 91:99+ Ag 4 '69
Up the down tube? Sci Am 220:48 Ja '69

GRAVITY free state. See Weightlessness

GRAVITY waves
Gravitating toward Einstein; findings of J. Weber. Time 93:75 Je 20 '69
Gravitational waves detected. Sky & Tel 38: 71+ Ag '69
Gravitational waves detected. il Sci N 95: 593-4 Je 21 '69
Universe makes waves. Newsweek 73:63 Je 30 '69
Weber reports 1660-Hz gravitational waves from outer space. G. B. Lubkin. il Phys Today 22:61-2 Ag '69

GRAY, Cleve
Experiments in three dimensions; Michael Ponce de Leon. Art in Am 57:72-3 My '69

GRAY, David E.
Case for compensatory recreation. Parks & Rec 4:23-4+ Ap '69

GRAY, Elisha, 1906-
Darkness before dawn. por Forbes 103:21 Ja 15 '69

GRAY, Francine du Plessix. See Du Plessix, F.

GRAY, Irwin
Employment effect of a new industry in a rural area. bibliog Mo Labor R 92:26-30 Je '69

GRAY, Jack
Economics of Maoism. Bul Atom Sci 25:42-51 F '69

GRAY, Sir James
Of ants and men: reprint. UNESCO Courier 22:46-7 Ag '69

GRAY, Jesse
Rent strikes: poor man's weapon. M. Lipsky. il Trans-Action 6:10-15 F '69

GRAY, John
Oregon's visionary land lover. D. Connelly. il por Sports Illus 30:40 Ap 28 '69

GRAY, John M.
How to stifle progress. Ed Digest 35:32-3 D '69

GRAY, Joseph H.
Notes of the fall show. Hobbies 73:49 F '69

GRAY, Paul Edward
My three weeks at the White House. New Yorker 45:32-3 My 17 '69

GRAY, Robert T.
Crucial business issues facing Congress. Nations Bsns 57:32-7 D '69

GRAY, T. Kenney, and Munson, P. L.
Thyrocalcitonin: evidence for physiological function. bibliog Science 166:512-13 O 24 '69

GRAY, Walter
Some aspects of word treatment in the music of William Byrd. bibliog f Mus Q 55:45-64 Ja '69

GRAY, Wood
(comp) Articles and other books received; United States. See issues of American historical review

GRAY foxes. See Foxes

GRAY lodge wildlife area. See Wildlife sanctuaries—California

GRAY seals. See Seals (animals)

GRAY whales. See Whales

GRAYLING fishing
Fishing in Yugoslavia; strong-bodied trout, grayling, and huchen. J. Brooks. il Outdoor Life 144:42-5+ S '69
On the watery trail of the great grayling. W. Davis. il Mech Illus 65:34+ Jl '69

GRAYSON, George W. jr
Era of the good neighbor. bibliog f Cur Hist 56:327-32+ Je '69

GRAYWACKES
Graywacke matrix minerals: hydrothermal reactions with Columbia River sediments. J. W. Hawkins, jr. and J. T. Whetten. bibliog il Science 166:868-70 N 14 '69

GRAZING
See also
Stock ranges

GRAZING lands. See Stock ranges

GREAT airplane snatch; drama. See Greenburg, D.

GREAT American insurance company
Dividend for the winner. il Time 93:75 F 7 '69

GREAT Atlantic and Pacific tea company
A & what? Newsweek 74:75 D 1 '69
Blacks wrap up slice of action at food chains; Operation Breadbasket's boycott of Chicago A&P stores. il Bsns W p 162-3+ Ap 26 '69

GREAT Baldini; story. See Wilson, E. and O'Connor, E.

GREAT BARRIER REEF
Battle for the reef. L. Bickel. il Sci N 96:218-20 S 13 '69

GREAT BRITAIN
Smuggling and the British tea trade before 1784. H. C. Mui and L. S. Mui. bibliog f il Am Hist R 74:44-73 O '68
See also
Aerospace industries—Great Britain
Airlines—Great Britain
Airports—Great Britain
Arts and crafts—Great Britain
Atomic power—Great Britain
Automobile industry and trade—Great Britain
Aviation—Great Britain
Ballet—Great Britain
Booksellers and bookselling—Great Britain
Budget—Great Britain
Business consolidations and mergers—Great Britain
Colleges and universities—Great Britain
Commonwealth of nations
Computer industry—Great Britain
Education—Great Britain
Government ownership—Great Britain
Industrial research—Great Britain
Investments, Foreign (by Great Britain)
Labor laws and legislation—Great Britain
Law—Great Britain
Libraries—Great Britain
Mass media—Great Britain
Motor boat racing—Great Britain
Moving pictures—Great Britain
Narcotic laws—Great Britain
National parks and reserves—Great Britain
Postal service—Great Britain
Prices—Great Britain
Prisons—Great Britain
Public opinion—Great Britain
Public welfare—Great Britain
Publishers and publishing—Great Britain
Railroads—Great Britain
Recreation—Great Britain
Secret service—Great Britain
Shopping and shoppers—Great Britain
Strikes—Great Britain
Student demonstrations—Great Britain
Taxation—Great Britain
Theater—Great Britain
Trade unions—Great Britain
Wages—Great Britain
Wales
Youth—Great Britain

Antiquities
Prehistoric find in Yorkshire. F. C. Livingstone. il Sci N 96:245-6 S 20 '69
See also
Avebury, England
Megalithic monuments
Stonehenge, England

Appropriations and expenditures
See also
Budget—Great Britain

Armed forces
British troubles with a volunteer army. il U S News 66:80 Ap 21 '69

Army
Scottish regiments
British tournament & tattoo; Madison Square Garden. J. Armstrong. Dance Mag 43:81+ N '69
Choreographed combat; British tournament and tattoo. W. Terry. il Sat R 52:64 O 18 '69

Atomic energy authority
Government labs: Britain's Harwell finds new role in industrial work. D. S. Greenberg. Science 163:1041-3 Mr 7 '69

Aviation, Ministry of
See also
Great Britain—Royal radar establishment

Colonies
From the ruins of empire. G. Lichtheim. bibliog f Commentary 48:75-81 D '69
See also
Anguilla (island)
Hong Kong

Commerce
Bit of cheer for Mr Wilson. il Bsns W p54+ S 20 '69
See also
European economic community

History
Smuggling and the British tea trade before 1784. H. C. Mui and L. H. Mui. bibliog f il Am Hist R 74:44-73 O '68

Constitutional history
See also
Magna carta

GREAT BRITAIN—*Continued*

Diplomatic and consular service

Goodbye to all that; Duncan report on British representation abroad. Time 94:34 Ag 1 '69

Economic conditions

Britain's resistance to painful cures. Time 93:104 Ap 25 '69

British credit stretches thin; seeks IMF aid. Bsns W p42+ My 24 '69

Will Britain turn right? P. Rowley. il Chr Cent 86:806-7 Je 11 '69

See also

Budget—Great Britain

Economic policy

Choice for socialism. R. Moore. Commonweal 90:363+ Je 13 '69

See also

Budget—Great Britain

Economic relations

Europe, Western

Economic policy; E.E.C. entry; address, October 1, 1969. M. Stewart. Vital Speeches 36:59-61 N 1 '69

Foreign opinion

American—Anecdotes, facetiae, satire, etc.

This earth, this realm, this plastic finnan haddie. M. Frayn. Horizon 11:120 Sum '69

Foreign relations

Powell enigma. E. Huxley. il Nat R 21:328-30 Ap 8 '69

Realism in British foreign policy. E. Heath. For Affairs 48:39-50 O '69

See also

Great Britain—Diplomatic and consular service

China (People's Republic)

Tit for tat; exchange of prisoners. il Newsweek 74:65 O 27 '69

France

Once more, de Gaulle v. Britain. Time 93:18 F 28 '69

Scandale diplomatique; de Gaulle's remarks on the future of Europe made to British ambassador. Newsweek 73:37 Mr 3 '69

Scrambling Europe? Sr Schol 94:16-17 Mr 14 '69

Nigeria

Empty gesture; H. Wilson's visit. il Newsweek 73:56-7 Ap 14 '69

Look around; H. Wilson visit. Newsweek 73:42+ Ap 7 '69

Loss of touch? Time 93:33 Mr 28 '69

Twin stalemates; H. Wilson's visit to Nigeria. il Time 93:36-7 Ap 4 '69

Spain

See also

Gibraltar

Foreign service

See also

Great Britain—Diplomatic and consular service

History

See also

Magna carta

Scotland—History

Wales—History

Bibliography

Articles and other books received; comp. by L. H. Carlson. See issues of American historical review

Lancaster and York, 1399-1485

Wars of the Roses. L. B. Smith. il Horizon 11:80-93 Wint '69

Wars of the Roses, 1455-1485

Wars of the Roses. L. B. Smith. il Horizon 11:80-93 Wint '69

15th century

See Great Britain—History—Lancaster and York, 1399-1485

Stuarts, 1603-1714

See also

Charles I, king of Great Britain

18th century

Beginnings of modern pleasures; eighteenth-century England. J. H. Plumb. il Horizon 11:20-5 Spr '69

1800-1837

See also

United States—History—War of 1812

Regency period, 1811-1820

Regency: a nine-year wonder. L. Kronenberger. il Atlan 224:87-90 N '69

Victorian period, 1837-1901

When Britains grandeur knew no bounds; excerpts from Pax Britannica: the climax of an empire. J. Morris. il Read Digest 94:82-6 Je '69

House of lords

See Great Britain—Parliament—House of lords

Industries

Tough enough to join the EEC. il Bsns W p46-7 S 27 '69

See also

Computer industry—Great Britain

Shipbuilding

Kings and rulers

See also

Elizabeth II, queen of Great Britain

Great Britain—Royal family

Mary, queen of Scots

Labor policy

Down with reforms. Time 93:75 Je 27 '69

Moral conditions

Our newfound shadiness. Q. Crewe. Vogue 154:66 S 15 '69

What is fair in this land of fair play? Q. Crewe. Vogue 154:60+ O 15 '69

National health service

Private alternative. il Time 94:23 D 26 '69

National trust

See National trust for places of historic interest or natural beauty

Navy

See also

United States—History—War of 1812—Naval operations

World war, 1939-1945—Naval operations

Nobility

See Great Britain—Peerage

Parishes

See Parishes

Parliament

House of lords

Cutting down the lords. A. Howard. New Repub 160:10-11 Mr 29 '69

Peerage

Hippies at the top. il Newsweek 73:46+ Ja 27 '69

Politics and government

Another setback for Socialists. U S News 66:10-11 Ap 7 '69

Chronic ambiguity in choosing sides. R. D. Masters. Sat R 52:38+ Ap 26 '69

Edentulous and the myopic; Wilson's Labor party in local elections. Time 93:40+ My 16 '69

Powell enigma. E. Huxley. il Nat R 21:328-30 Ap 8 '69

Rigor mortis. il Newsweek 73:53-4 My 26 '69

Wilson's about-face; anti-strike bill shelved. A. Howard. New Repub 160:7-8 Je 28 '69

See also

Conservative party (Great Britain)

Elections—Great Britain

Labor party (Great Britain)

Prime ministers

Younger Pitt, by J. Ehrman. Review

Newsweek 74:92F+ D 1 '69. R. A. Gross

Race problems

Britain's answer on mixed schools. il U S News 66:105 Ap 14 '69

Race problem in Britain; the Rose report. America 121:81 Ag 16 '69

Race relations in England. T. Land. Nation 208:116 Ja 27 '69

Race violence: is Britain next? findings of Institute of race relations. U S News 67:11 Jl 21 '69

Religious institutions and affairs

Roman Catholic-Anglican dialogue; Permanent joint commission formed. America 121:407 N 8 '69

World around us. Chr Cent 86:354 Mr 12 '69

See also

Church unity—Great Britain

England—Religious institutions and affairs

GREAT BRITAIN—*Continued*

Royal family

Britain's Royal family gets a new and popular image. il U S News 67:72-4 S 29 '69
Foreign accent; Sky-kings. J. Fricker. Flying 84:28+ F '69
Monarch for the moon age; the monarchy today. il Newsweek 74:30-1 Jl 14 '69
Perspective. J. H. Plumb. Sat R 52:32 Je 28 '69
Royalty: its money troubles. il U S News 67:16 N 24 '69
Tune in on life with Charlie. A. Howard. New Repub 161·13 Jl 5 '69
See also
Charles, prince of Wales

Royal radar establishment

U.K. infrared research gets civil emphasis. il Aviation W 91:111 Ag 18 '69

Science research council

Britain: new emphasis on industrial research. D. S. Greenberg. Science 166:485 O 24 '69

Social history

Akenfield: portrait of an English village, by R. Blythe. Review
Atlan 224:110-12 S '69. Y. Blumenfeld
England's cruel earth; excerpt from Akenfield: portrait of an English village. R. Blythe. Harper 238:46-52+ Ap '69

Social life and customs

Incorrigible games players: gambling spirit. Q. Crewe. Vogue 154:68 Ag 1 '69
See also
Great Britain—Peerage

Travel regulations

See Travel regulations

Treaties

See also
United States—Treaties—Great Britain
GREAT career; drama. See Dizenzo, C.
GREAT expectations. See Dickens, C.
GREAT LAKES
IJC holds meetings on pollution of Great Lakes connecting channels; Department announcement with text of report. Dept State Bul 60:234-5 Mr 17 '69
IJC issues interim report on Great Lakes water levels. Dept State Bul 60:186 Mr 3 '69
Outwitting the patient assassin: the human use of lake pollution. H. B. Gotaas. Bul Atom Sci 25:8-10 My '69
See also
Erie, Lake
Ontario, Lake
Superior, Lake
GREAT LAKES REGION
Land of the blue waters. A. Juntunen. il Travel 132:36-41+ Ag '69
See also
Birds—Great Lakes Region
Fishing—Great Lakes Region
Hunting—Great Lakes Region
GREAT men
Americans not everyone knows. C. W. Ferguson. See issues of PTA magazine
Stories of great Americans. il Schol Teach Sec Teach Sup p28+ S 22 '69
See also
Celebrities
Leadership
GREAT NECK, N. Y.
Busing at Great Neck. il Newsweek 73:70 F 17 '69
GREAT PLAINS
See also
Irrigation—Great Plains
Libraries—Great Plains
GREAT powers
Great power cannot treat every tremor as a major threat. S. Hoffmann. Commonweal 90:13-14 Mr 21 '69; Same with title Need for self restraint. Cur 109:59-61 Ag '69
Policy for the 70s; after the Vietnam war, how not to be the world's policeman. S. Hoffmann. Life 66:68-70 +Mr 21 '69
Shifting great power politics; the end of U S-Soviet hegemony. Cur 108:61-4 Je '69
Superpowers; U. S. and Russia. K. Crawford. Newsweek 74:32 Jl 21 '69
Two sentinels of the status quo. U.S. & U.S.S.R; address, July 11, 1969. F. Church. bibliog f Vital Speeches 35:614-17 Ag 1 '69
GREAT Samurai sword; drama. See Winther, B.

GREAT SAND DUNES NATIONAL MONUMENT
America's sandpile. H. Montgomery. il Travel 132:60-1 O '69
GREAT SMOKY MOUNTAINS
Autumn's acres. M. B. Mellinger. il Nat Parks 43:12-13 Ja '69
GREAT SMOKY MOUNTAINS NATIONAL PARK
Great Smoky Mountains delegation visits Secretary Hickel. Liv Wildn 33:36-7 Sum '69
Highway in the sky; Blue Ridge parkway. J. T. Starr. il Am For 75:8-11+ Ja '69
GREAT SWAMP, N.J.
Place to look, a time to listen. J. T. Cunningham. il Audubon 71:28-41 Mr '69
GREAT transatlantic air race. See Airplane racing
GREAT white hope; drama. See Sackler. H.
GREAT wolf and the good woodsman; story. See Hoover, H.
GREATER Greensboro Open golf tournament. See Golf—Tournaments
GREATER prairie chicken. See Prairie chickens
GREATER-Washington alliance to stop pollution, incorporated
GASP may bring some cleaner air. Nat Parks 43:24 N '69
GREAVES, Delia D.
Manhattan children through the pavements; poem. Library J 94:4578-9 D 15 '69
GREBANIER, Bernard
Life less one immortal lover. Sat R 52:34 Ap 26 '69
GREBES
Return of the grebe. Time 94:85 D 5 '69
GRECHKO, Andrei Antonovich
Enforcer. il por Newsweek 73:48+ My 19 '69
GRÉDY, Jean Pierre. See Barillet, P. jt. auth.
GREECE, Ancient
Ancient Greece. il Travel & Camera 32:43-4 My '69
See also
Hellenism

Antiquities

See also
Athens, Greece—Antiquities
Macedonia—Antiquities

History

See also
Alexander the Great
GREECE, Ancient, in literature
Alexander's ascent to greatness on a ladder of gore; the novels of M. Renault. Sat R 52:27-9+ N 29 '69
GREECE, Modern
Grandeur of Greece; symposium. il Travel & Camera 32:28-51+ My '69
See also
Aegean Islands
Athos, Moun
Civil rights—Greece, Modern
Gargaliani
Investments, Foreign (in Greece)
Morale, National—Greece, Modern
Newspapers—Greece, Modern
Police—Greece, Modern
Political prisoners—Greece, Modern
Prisoners—Greece, Modern
Shipping—Greece, Modern
Tourist trade—Greece, Modern

Armed forces

NATO's missing link. Nation 209:267 S 22 '69

Commercial treaties and agreements

United States and Greece sign new cotton textile agreement; Department announcement with text of agreement. Dept State Bul 60:430-1 My 19 '69

Constitution

Junta's year. M. J. Goldbloom. Commonweal 89:613-15 F 14 '69

Description and travel

Lands of Greece. F. Shea. il Travel & Camera. 32:45+ My '69
Travel. D. Messinesi. Vogue 154:344 S 1 '69

Foreign relations

Exit the colonels; from the Council of Europe. Newsweek 74:44+ D 22 '69

Politics and government

And now Onassis. Nation 208:525-6 Ap 28 '69
Climate of fear. A. de Borchgrave. Newsweek 74:28-9 S 1 '69
Comfort for the colonels. il Time 94:38+ N 28 '69
Greece: a chance for democracy. W. G. Forrest. Nation 209:279-82 S 22 '69

GREECE, Modern—Politics and government—
Continued
Greece; a new Vietnam? address, April, 1969.
E. P. Demetracopoulos. Vital Speeches 35:
568-74 Jl 1 '69
Greece and the Council. Nation 209:653 D
15 '69
Greece: government by torture; Asphalia, the
security police. C. S. Wren. il Look 33:19-21
My 27 '69
Greece: how free? Close-up of a military dic-
tatorship. C. S. Foltz. jr. il U S News 67:
60-1 Ag 18 '69
Greece: the death of liberty. J. Corry. Harper
239:72-81 O '69
Greece: the rack and the bomb. J. Becket.
Nation 209:6-7 Jl 7 '69
Greece: the torture goes on. C. S. Wren.
Look 33:63 O 7 '69
Greek colonels' regime. America 121:133 S 6
'69
Greek junta: no headway toward humaniza-
tion. Chr Cent 86:1010 Jl 30 '69
How the colonels run things. il Newsweek
75:32-3+ Ja 19 '70
Junta's year. M. J. Goldbloom. Commonweal
89:613-15 F 14 '69
Neighbors' verdict; Greece's departure from
Council of Europe. Time 94:30 D 19 '69
Notes and comment: torture. New Yorker
45:23 Jl 12 '69
Outlook in Greece, as Premier sees it. U S
News 67:8 D 29 '69
Portrait of the non-artists. Nat R 21:682-3
Jl 15 '69
Say it with bombs. Time 94:34 Ag 8 '69
What to do with the colonels? Nat R 21:1303-
4 D 30 '69

Social life and customs
Breaking an old habit; plate-smashing
banned. il Time 93:37 Ja 24 '69
Psychiatrist and the bouzoukia. D. Goulan-
dris, Vogue 155:64+ Ja 1 '70
Why Greece's colonels are that way. il Time
93:32-3 Ap 18 '69
GREEK art. See Art, Greek
GREEK cookery. See Cookery, Greek
GREEK drama
See also
Aeschylus
GREEK émigrés. See Émigrés
GREEK islands. See Aegean Islands
GREEK language
Ancient Greece, alive and well in south
of Italy? il Sci Digest 66:18-19 Jl '69
GREEK literature
See also
Classical literature
GREEK mythology. See Mythology, Greek
GREEK poetry
Translations into English
Beginning; Remaining; Painted; tr. by S.
Spender. C. P. Cavafy. Harp Baz 102:202-3
F '69
GREEKS
Mystique of the Greek male. S. Zotos. il
McCalls 96:79+ Ap '69
GREEKS in Italy
Ancient Greece, alive and well in south of
Italy? il Sci Digest 66:18-19 Jl '69
GREELEY, Andrew M.
Catholic alumni: seven years after. America
120:96-100 Ja 25 '69
Comment by Fr. Greeley. America 121:129 S
6 '69
There's a new-time religion on campus. N Y
Times Mag p 14-15+ Je 1 '69
GREEN, Alex E. S.
Postdoctoral research associate-instructor.
bibliog por Phys Today 22:23-6 Je '69
GREEN, Andrew Haswell
[Father of Greater New York] F. Low. Natur
Hist 78:26 Ap '69
GREEN, Arnold W.
Capital punishment: has it become cruel and
unusual? Nat R 21:384-5+ Ap 22 '69
GREEN, Bob
Building industry needs a new approach to
product design! Bet Hom & Gard 47:60
S '69
GREEN, Douglas
Tips on building a financial reserve. Mech
Illus 65:64-5+ O '69
What to do after an accident. Mech Illus 65:
61-3+ Ag '69
GREEN, Dwight E.
Six-year chase. por Outdoor Life 144:80-1+
O '69
GREEN, Edith
School busing: are we hurting the people
we want to help? excerpts from address,
July 31, 1969. por U S News 67:72-3 Ag 18
'69

GREEN, Frances
(comp) Adult paperbacks. Library J 94:2139-
63, 3166-91 My 15, S 15 '69
—See Putnam, J. jt. comp.
GREEN, George S. See Pearce, B. L. jt. auth.
GREEN, Gerald
Some modest proposals on the novel. Writer
82:19-23 Je '69
GREEN, Hannah
Dead of the house; story. New Yorker 45:
54-60+ O 11 '69
GREEN, Harris
Music (cont) Commonweal 89:652-3; 90:206-7,
488-9; 91-408-9 F 21, My 2, Ag 8 '69, Ja 9 '70
GREEN, Howard. See Matsuya, Y. jt. auth.
GREEN, James L.
Acrobats, plowmen, and the healthy sentence.
bibliog f Engl J 58:892-9 S '69
GREEN, Jon A. and others
Immune specific induction of interferon pro-
duction in cultures of human blood lympho-
cytes. bibliog Science 164:1415-17 Je 20 '69
GREEN, Joyce
It takes heart to inspire twenty-six ghetto
kids. por Seventeen 28:93+ Ja '69
GREEN, Larry
Double take on bonito. por Field & S 73:
50-1 F '69
Fluff bugs for bass. Field & S 73:56-7+
F '69
Who says propellers are obsolete? Field & S
74:54-5+ Je '69
GREEN, Louis C.
1968 Texas symposium: pulsars. Sky & Tel
37:214-18 Ap '69
Quasars six years later. Sky & Tel 37:290-4
My '69
GREEN, Mark
Reparations for blacks? Commonweal 90:359-
62 Je 13 '69
GREEN, Marshall
Look at Asian regionalism; address, October
20, 1969. Dept State Bul 61:445-8 N 24 '69
GREEN, Martin
Mailer and Amis: the new conservatism.
Nation 208:573-4 My 5 '69
GREEN, Michael D.
Politics of pesticides. Nation 209:569-71 N
24 '69
GREEN, Robert L. and Stachnik, T. J.
Money, motivation, and academic achieve-
ment. Ed Digest 34:8-10 Mr '69
GREEN, Ron
Printout; story. Esquire 73:126-7 Ja '70
GREEN, Roy E.
Easy ways to finish frames. Am Artist 33:
46-7 D '69
GREEN, Teddy
Stick that sickens. P. Axthelm. il por News-
week 74:95 O 6 '69
GREEN, Victor E. Jr
More and better corn. Américas 21:42-5 N
'69
GREEN BAY
Charter sailing in Green Bay. B. Stephany
and S. Stephany. il Yachting 125:56-7+ Ap
'69
GREEN BAY Packers (football club) See Foot-
ball clubs
GREEN Beret force. See United States—Army
—Special forces
GREEN men, go home; drama. See Martens,
A. C.
GREEN MOUNTAIN race track, Vt. See Race
tracks
GREEN sea turtles. See Turtles
GREENAMYER, Darryl
Fastest prop in the world. R. L. Emerson. il
pors Pop Mech 132:94-5 D '69
GREENAWALT, Kent
Freedom of speech for students; interview.
Seventeen 28:54+ My '69
GREENAWAY, Emerson
Public library lure. por Library J 94:263-
4 Ja 15 '69
GREENAWAY, Kate
Enduring charm of Kate Greenaway. D. F.
Brown. il Hobbies 74:128-9 S '69
GREENBANK, Anthony
Could you survive? questions and answers.
Outdoor Life 143:90-3 Ap '69
GREENBERG, Barbara L.
Admal; poem. Atlan 224:63 O '69
Game of animals; poem. New Repub 161:23
O 18 '69
Golden worms; story. Yale R 58:408-13 Mr
'69
GREENBERG, Clement
People are talking about... por Vogue 153:
166-7 Mr 1 '69
GREENBERG, Emanuel, and Greenberg, Made-
line
Flaming issue. Harp Baz 103:168-9 N '69
How to mate food and spirits. House B 111:
112-14 Mr '69

GREENBERG, Hayim
Forgotten voice. A. Hertzberg. Commentary 48:98+ S '69
GREENBERG, Irvin
Comments on community mental health programs. Ment Hy 53:306-8 Ap '69
GREENBERG, Irwin
Much depends on attitude; with biographical sketch. il por Am Artist 33:76-7+ Mr '69
GREENBERG, Joanne
Timekeeper; story. McCalls 96:70-1 Ja '69
GREENBERG, Joseph H.
Language universals: a research frontier. bibliog Science 166:473-8 O 24 '69
GREENBERG, Ken
Alphanumeric fun box with a Nixie. Radio-Electr 40:56-8 Mr '69
GREENBERG, Madeline. See Greenberg, E. jt. auth.
GREENBERG, Murray. See Greenberg, P. jt. auth.
GREENBERG, Pearl
Haute couture in paper dresses. Sch Arts 68:29-30 F '69
—and Greenberg, Murray
Painting with developer. Sch Arts 68:30-1 My '69
GREENBERG, Sanford
Creative computer. Newsweek 74:100+ N 17 '69
GREENBURG, Dan
Arf. Criticism
New Yorker 45:112 Je 7 '69
Great airplane snatch. Criticism
New Yorker 45:112 Je 7 '69
GREENE, Bob
Up on two wheels. See issues of Hot rod
GREENE, Daniel E.
Daniel E. Greene: pastellist. H. Rogoff. il por Am Artist 33:80-8 N '69
GREENE, Graham
Graham Greene: on the screen; interview, by G. D. Phillips. Cath World 209:218-21 Ag '69
Paraguay: where the living is easy, so. . . Holiday 45:68-71 Ap '69

about

Books. M. Muggeridge. Esquire 72:16+ Ag '69
Obsession with failure. J. Finn. New Repub 161:30-1 Jl 5 '69
Short Greene. R. A. Sokolov. por Newsweek 73:110+ My 19 '69
Tantalizing two-way mirrors of Graham Greene. N. L. Magid. Commonweal 90:567-8 S 19 '69
GREENE, Harold H.
Excerpt from testimony before Subcommittee on constitutional rights, January 21, 1969. Cong Digest 48:109+ Ap '69
GREENE, Jonathan
Where the blinding sun; Horror rations: a meditation; Where the comfort; poems. Poetry 114:388-90 S '69
GREENE, Lorenzo J.
Freedom documents from Cole County, Missouri. bibliog Negro Hist Bul 32:11-13 Ja '69
GREENE, Mark R.
How to rationalize your marketing risks. Harvard Bsns R 47:114-23 My '69
GREENE, Milton, and Eula, Joe
Tour of the zodiac; photographs. Life 67:60-8 S 26 '69
GREENE, Sheldon L.
Operation sisyphus; wetbacks, growers and poverty. Nation 209:403-6 O 20 '69
GREENE COUNTY, Ala.
Alabama: first steps. D. F. Ross. New Repub 161:14-15 S 27 '69
Black day in Eutaw: Negro election triumph. il Newsweek 74:24-5 Ag 11 '69
GREENEWALT, Crawford H.
How birds sing; with biographical sketch. Sci Am 221:18, 126-34+ N '69
GREENFELD, Josh
Man who gave us Hair. Life 66:50B-50D+ Je 27 '69
Marshmallow literature. Mlle 68:206-7+ Mr '69
GREENFIELD, Edward
Behind the scenes (cont of) Notes from our correspondents. See issues of High fidelity incorporating Musical America
Notes from our correspondents. See issues of High fidelity incorporating Musical America
GREENFIELD VILLAGE. See Henry Ford museum and Greenfield Village, Dearborn, Mich.
GREENGARD, Olga
Enzymic differentiation in mammalian liver. bibliog Science 163:891-5 F 28 '69

GREENHOUSE management. See Greenhouses
GREENHOUSES
Beating the season with greenhouses. J. Stuwe. il Org Gard & Farm 16:36-9 S '69
Blooming desert. C. O. Hodge. il Bul Atom Sci 25:32-3 N '69
$11 plant-starter. T. Anderson. il Org Gard & Farm 16:86-8 D '69
Face to face with a modern-day Johnny Appleseed. D. Tifford. il Seventeen 28:60 Je '69
Greenhouse all around you. il House & Gard 135:150-1 Ja '69
Greenhouse-kitchen space is prodigal. il House & Gard 135:58-61 Ja '69
Greenhouse profit sideline. C. H. Potter. il Horticulture 46:22-3+ S '69
Greenhouse rooms, and priced right. il Bet Hom & Gard 47:40-1 Jl '69
Home greenhouse. J. Eaton. See issues of Home garden & flower grower
In your greenhouse. J. U. Crockett. See issues of Horticulture
Japan's Crystal palace; prefabricated Nagashima tropical garden. il Arch Forum 130:76-83 My '69
Low-cost greenhouse you can build. il Mech Illus 65:90-3+ S '69
Once a greenhouse, now a plastic tent. il Sunset 142:234 Ap '69
Pleasures & profits from a small greenhouse. M. A. Guitar. il Home Gard 56:58-9 N '69
You can put a greenhouse in your future. R. M. Peters. il Home Gard 56:34-42 D '69
See also
Phipps conservatory, Pittsburgh

Heating and ventilation

Eden under a geodesic dome; St Louis' Climatron. B. O'Connell. il Sci Digest 65:68-72 Ap '69
GREENHOUSES, Miniature
Greenhouse that pays for itself in one season. B. Brinhart. il Org Gard & Farm 16:80-1 Ja '69
Pint-size greenhouse. il Parks & Rec 4:34 Je '69
GREENLAND

Climate

One thousand centuries of climatic record from Camp Century on the Greenland ice sheet. W. Dansgaard and others. bibliog il Science 166:377-81 O 17 '69
Secrets of the icecap. il Time 94:94 N 14 '69
GREENLAW, Barry A.
English furniture. Antiques 95:150-3 Ja '69
GREENLEE, Lyman C.
Build a blinky blinker. Pop Electr 31:51-4 S '69
Why play Edison roulette? Pop Electr 31:71-4 Ag '69
GREENOUGH, Richard
Teacher shortage in Botswana. Sch & Soc 97:386-8 O '69
GREENOUGH, William C.
Retirement benefits in higher education; adaptation of address, March 3, 1969. Sch & Soc 97:444-6 N '69
GREENS, Edible
Eating off the land; salad that's free for the picking. E. Alston. il Look 33:64-5 N 4 '69
Gardener's kitchen; green salads. D. V. Thompson. Horticulture 47:6+ My '69
Wild greens. Cons 23:35 Ap '69
See also
Chicory
Dandelions
Purslane
Sorrel
Water cress
GREENSPAN, Bud
Waiting for glory. P. Axthelm. il Newsweek 74:82 Jl 7 '69
GREENSPON, Muriel
Lot to give; interview, ed. by R. D. Daniels. por Opera N 33:21 Je 14 '69
GREENSTONE, J. David
Labor and politics. Nation 209:212-15 S 8 '69
GREENWALD, Frank L.
Build this Connecticut shelf clock. Pop Mech 131:150-3+ Ja '69
No attic? Shelves will do the job. Pop Sci 194:160-1 Mr '69
GREENWALD, Joseph A.
Department supports extension of Export control act; statement, May 28, 1969. Dept State Bul 60:545-7 Je 23 '69
GREENWAY, Hugh D.
Report; Laos. Atlan 223:20+ Mr '69
GREENWAY, John
Ghost dance. Am West 6:42-7 Jl '69
Will the Indians get Whitey? Nat R 21:223-8+ Mr 11 '69

GREENWICH, Conn.
Education
Special workshop for the gifted. R. D. Campbell. il Todays Ed 58:32-3 D '69
GREENWICH VILLAGE, New York.   See New York (city)—Greenwich Village
GREENWOOD, D. and O'Grady, F.
Antibiotic-induced surface changes in microorganisms demonstrated by scanning electron microscopy. bibliog Science 163:1076-8 Mr 7 '69
GREENWOOD, Ned H.
Outside view of wilderness preservation in British Columbia. bibliog il Liv Wildn 32: 30-42 Aut '68
Preserving the corn ladder: a Mt Baldy wilderness. Liv Wildn 33:22-8 Sum '69
GREER, Allen E. and Raizes, Gary
Green blood pigment in lizards. bibliog Science 166:392 O 17 '69
GREER, Colin
Man's relations to man; can we move beyond the pluralistic society? Cur 105:27-31 Mr '69
Public schools: the myth of the melting pot; excerpt from Cobweb attitudes: essays in American education and culture. Sat R 52: 84-6+ N 15 '69
GREETING cards
For any greeting, say it on film. D. B. Eisendrath. il Pop Phot 64:18+ My '69
Soul cards. il Newsweek 73:101 My 5 '69
UNICEF greeting cards. il UNESCO Courier 22:33 N '69
Yes, I write greeting cards, how did you know? L. Hardt. il Writers Digest 49:43-4 O '69
  See also
Christmas cards
Onyx enterprises, incorporated
Valentines
GREGG, Andy
Writers of Santa Fe. Writers Digest 49:54-9 Ap '69
GREGG, Duane L.
Cars in your family. See issues of Better homes and gardens
GREGG, James R.
Double take on bonito. Field & S 73:52-3 F '69
How to see better in the field. Field & S 74: 46-7+ Ag '69
GREGGS, Robert G. See Bartlett, G. A. jt. auth.
GREGOR, Arthur
Poem: Out of continued striving. Nation 208: 766 Je 16 '69
Release; poem. Nation 209:150 Ag 25 '69
Statue; poem. Poetry 115:18 O '69
Water; poem. New Repub 161:33 Jl 19 '69
Worldliness; poem. New Repub 160:21 Ap 26 '69
GREGORIAN university. See Rome (city)— Pontifical Gregorian university
GREGORY, Gene
New food revolution. UNESCO Courier 22:4-6+ Mr '69
GREGORY, John R.
Movie Q's and A's. See issues of Travel & camera
GREGORY, Masten
Masten Gregory lives! K. Purdy. il por Esquire 71:65-9+ Ja '69
GREIG, Howard
Where will everybody be going soon? The Pacific, that's where. Holiday 46:64-5 Jl '69
GREINER, Charles F.
Hook-up, plug in, connect: relevancy is all. Engl J 58:23-9 Ja '69
GREÑAS, Alfredo
Mosquito that stang. G. Arciniegas. il Américas 21:22-31 O '69
GRENNAN, Michael Dennis
Movie titles unlimited. Pop Phot 64:106-7 F '69
GRESHAM, Grits
High-flying fishing club. Field & S 74:60-3+ My '69
GREY, Anthony
End of the ordeal. por Time 94:59-60+ O 24 '69
End to the void. Time 94:41 O 10 '69
Tit for tat. il por Newsweek 74:65 O 27 '69
GREY, Joel
Lively arts; interview. ed. by J. Mandelstam. pors Sr Schol 94:18 Ja 17 '69
GREY advertising, incorporated
Insurers wince at drain on cash; policyholders borrowing on their insurance. il Bsns W p 104 My 24 '69
GREY gulls. See Gulls
GREYBER, Howard D.
Is Venus prolate? bibliog Science 163:1469-70 Mr 28 '69

GREYHOUND corporation
Greyhound makes a run for Armour. Bsns W p 19 F 1 '69
Greyhound winning race for Armour. Bsns W p 170 O 18 '69
High-stakes game. Newsweek 74:70+ Jl 7 '69
Why Greyhound's buses are now an embarrassment; diversification program. il Bsns W p 126+ Jl 19 '69
You can't lose 'em all. il Forbes 104:25-6 N 15 '69
GREYHOUND racing. See Dog racing
GRIBBINS, Joseph
(ed) Motor boating USA. Motor B 123:16+ My; 16+ Je; 124:16+ Jl; 16+ Ag '69
Rivers. Motor B 124:49-56+ Ag '69
GRIBBS, Roman S.
Lots of converts. il por Newsweek 74:49 N 17 '69
GRIDDLE cakes
Better breakfast ideas. il Bet Hom & Gard 47:124 My '69
Blintzes, blini & beluga. il McCalls 96:122-3+ Mr '69
How mushrooms dress an entrée: ham and mushroom crêpes. il Sunset 143:174 O '69
Learning to cook: pancakes and waffles. il Am Home 72:72 Ja '69
Little filled pancakes as appetizers. il Sunset 142:150 F '69
Pancakes for all occasions. il Ladies Home J 86:44 O '69
GRIEDER, Calvin
Catholic schools should carry their own burden. Ed Digest 35:26-7 O '69
GRIEF. See Bereavement
GRIEGO, Richard J. See Hersh, R. jt. auth.
GRIER, Roosevelt
This is our house. y'see. W. D. Ellis. por Read Digest 95:65-9 D '69
GRIEVANCE procedures
Individual rights under collective agreements. M. Sulg. bibliog Mo Labor R 92:40-2 Jl '69
Taking the grief out of grievances; voluntary arbitration wins favor with management and unions. il Bsns W p78+ Mr 8 '69
  See also
Librarians grievances
GRIEVANCES, Public. See Complaints
GRIFFEN, Jeff
Gun dogs. See issues of Field & stream
GRIFFIN, Charles H.
Excerpt from remarks, July 10, 1969. Cong Digest 48:286 N '69
GRIFFIN, James W.
Oscilloscope evolution. Electr World 82:25-7+ N '69
GRIFFIN, Laurence R.
Twelve things nobody ever knew about stone age and iron age men. Sci Digest 65:26-31 My '69
GRIFFIN, Merv
Battle of the talk shows. il por Newsweek 74:42-4+ S 1 '69
Talk, talk, talk. il por Time 94:52 Ag 29 '69
GRIFFIN, Olva R.
Our problem blackberry patch. Org Gard & Farm 16:53 Ja '69
GRIFFIN, Richard B.
Harvard ablaze. America 120:586-8 My 17 '69
GRIFFIN, Robert P.
Republicans in the Senate, new leaders, new directions. il por U S News 67:17 O 6 '69
GRIFFIN, Stuart
Malaysia. Travel 132:50-5+ N '69
Millenial mementos. Sci N 95:102 Ja 25 '69
Pushing radiation chemistry. Sci N 96:514 N 29 '69
Steel and nucleonics. Sci N 95:318 Mr 29 '69
GRIFFISS, James E. Jr
Church and state in Spain. Chr Cent 86:802-6 Je 11 '69
GRIFFITH, David Wark
Movies. Mr Griffith, and me, by L. Gish and A. Pinchot. Review
  Nat R il 21:865-6 Ag 26 '69. A. Crocé
GRIFFITH, Emile
Jose settles an old account. J. Kirshenbaum. il Sports Illus 31:40-1 O 27 '69
GRIFFITH, F. H.
Old mechanical banks. See issues of Hobbies
GRIFFITH, Milton
Pheasant tips. Field & S 74:62-3+ N '69
GRIFFITH, Patricia Browning
Nights at O'Rear's; story. Harper 238:81-4 Mr '69
GRIFFITH, W. L. See Boegly, W. J. jr. jt. auth.
GRIFFITH, William E.
American stake in the Russia-China confrontation. Read Digest 95:88-92 S '69

GRIFFITH, Winthrop
Mrs Humphrey sums it up this way; he is not what he was, and he is not yet what he will be. N Y Times Mag p32-3+ Mr 30 '69
People's park. 270' x 450' of confrontation. N Y Times Mag p5-7+ Je 29 '69
This is an atomic missile base. N Y Times Mag p29+ My 4 '69

GRIGGS, Lee
Golf. Sports Illus 31:83-5 O 13 '69

GRIGGSVILLE, Ill.
Purple martinstro. G. Schneider. il Am For 75:36-7+ F '69

GRIGORENKO, Petr Grigor'evich
Dissenter's fate. il por Newsweek 73:50 My 19 '69
Once too often; arrested for anti-Soviet agitation. Time 93-44+ My 16 '69
Start to demand! il por Newsweek 73:40+ Ap 7 '69

GRILLING. See Barbecue cookery

GRILLOTTI, Richard
Anyone can make a filmstrip. Sch Arts 69: 12-13 D '69

GRILLS, Barbecue. See Barbecue grills

GRIM, Paul F.
Psychotherapy by somatic alteration. bibliog Ment Hy 53:451-8 Jl '69

GRIM, Paul J. and Naugler, F. P.
Fossil deep-sea channel on the Aleutian abyssal plain. bibliog Science 163:383-6 Ja 24 '69

GRIMES, Sally
True death of Bessie Smith. Esquire 71:112-13+ Je '69

GRINDEA, Miron
Trade winds; concerning founder editor of Adam, the oldest British literary magazine. J. Beatty, jr. Sat R 52:14 F 1 '69

GRINDING
In the news; process for reducing weight of metal plate. Space World F-5-65:46 My '69

GRINDING machines
See also
Compost grinders and grinding

GRINDING wheels
How to mount grinding wheels with epoxy. J. Burroughs. il Pop Mech 132:184-6 Jl '69

GRINSPOON, Lester
Marihuana; with biographical sketch. Sci Am 221:15, 17-25 D '69

GRINSTEAD, Robert R.
No deposit, no return. Environ 11:17-23 N '69

GRIPPE. See Influenza

GRIST, Reri
Recordings. M. Mayer. Esquire 71:42 F '69

GRIZZLY bear hunting. See Bear hunting

GRIZZLY bears. See Bears

GRIZZLY bears, Photography of. See Photography of animals

GRJEBINE, Lois
Inside France. por Time 93:60 My 16 '69

GROCERY stores
Grocery shoppers' forty-four pet peeves. il Changing T 23:13-14 O '69
What ever happened to the neighborhood store? E. L. Horwitz. McCalls 96:70+ Jl '69
Women sound off about grocery stores; Consumer dialogs; discussion. il Changing T 22:41-3 D '68
See also
Seven-Eleven food stores

GROCERY trade
Grocery business. il Forbes 104:34-6+ N 1 '69
See also
Great Atlantic and Pacific tea company
Strikes—United States—Grocery trade

GROFF, Charles W.
Gentle look. il Pop Phot 65:112-15 Jl '69

GROL, Lini R.
Silhouettes and scissor cutting. Design 70: 27-31 Spr '69

GROLIER incorporated
Grolier inc. to acquire W. M. Jackson. Pub W 196:37 O 27 '69

GROMAN, G.
Valentines from Janice. Har Yrs 9:46-7 F '69

GROMMON, Alfred H.
Is the present structure of the NCTE adequate for today and tomorrow? Engl J 58:595-601 Ap '69
NCTE presidential address: one year later. bibliog f Engl J 58:345-59 Mr '69

GROMYKO, Andrei Andreevich
Soviet foreign policy: address. July 11, 1969. Vital Speeches 35:618-28 Ag 1 '69

about
Cheers for Andrei. il por Newsweek 73:44+ Je 23 '69
Gromyko to Nixon: a tough reply. U S News 67:12 S 29 '69
Rogers, Gromyko: deals in making? il por U S News 67:18 O 6 '69
Russian speaks softly. il por Time 94:35 Jl 18 '69
Sunshine through the clouds. Newsweek 74:35 Jl 21 '69

GRONBORG, Erik
New generation of ceramic artists. por Craft Horiz 29:26-9+ Ja '69

GRONOWICZ, Antoni
Melange. P. Nathan. Pub W 195:127 Je 2 '69

GROOMING. See Beauty, Personal

GROOMING of pets. See Pets—Care

GROOMS, Red
Anybody want to buy Chicago? D. L. Goodrich. il pors Sat Eve Post 242:36-9 F 8 '69

GROPIUS, Walter Adolf
Bauhaus. J. F. McCullogh. il Pub W 196:23-9 S 1 '69
Bauhaus is alive and well in soup plates and skyscrapers. J. R. Mellow. il por N Y Times Mag p34-5+ S 14 '69
Idea-giver. il por Time 94:49-50 Jl 18 '69
Last work of Walter Gropius. il pors Arch Rec 146:131-50 S '69
Testament of joy. D. L. Shirey por Newsweek 74:67 Jl 21 '69
Walter Gropius: 1883-1969. M. F. Schmertz. por Arch Rec 146:9-10 Ag '69
Walter Gropius, 1883-1969. il Arch Forum 131: 34-9 S '69

GROPPI, James Edward
Groppi's putsch. il por Newsweek 74:38 O 13 '69
Legislators and welfare protests. America 121: 407 N 8 '69

GROSS, Amy
Smoking; why you do it and how not to suffer when you stop. Mlle 69:166-7+ O '69
Young lovers of the world, unite! But don't get married yet. Mlle 69:151+ S '69

GROSS, C. G. and others
Visual receptive fields of neurons in inferotemporal cortex of the monkey. bibliog Science 166:1303-6 D 5 '69

GROSS, Francine
Face to face with a trinket tycoon. por Seventeen 28:80 S '69

GROSS, Franklin S.
Enfield's excited about living history. Sr Schol 94:Schol Teach 13-14 My 9 '69
Lab-carts are rolling. School Teach Sec Teach Sup p 14-15+ O 6 '69

GROSS, John
Balanced view. Commentary 47:84-5 Ap '69

GROSS, Kenneth G.
Angry and alone together. Nation 208:207-10 F 17 '69
Give peace a chance. Nation 209:591-4 D 1 '69
—See Lefkowitz, B. jt. auth.

GROSS, Ronald. See Murphy, K. jt. auth.

GROSS national product
Analysis of price changes in second quarter of 1969. W. J. Layng and T. Nakayama. il Mo Labor R 92:36-41 O '69
First signs of business lag. il U S News 66: 100 Mr 17 '69
Gross product by industry; table. Nations Bsns 57:30-1 N '69
Price changes in the first quarter of 1969 in perspective. J. Popkin. bibliog il Mo Labor R 92:26-30 Jl '69

Japan
Japan's economic dynamism and our common interests in East Asia; excerpts from address, March 18, 1969. R. W. Barnett. Dept State Bul 60:447-50 My 26 '69

GROSSE, Aristid V.
Amateur scientist; how to blow soap bubbles that last for months or even years. Sci Am 220:128-32+ My '69
Soap bubbles: two years old and sixty centimeters in diameter. bibliog Science 164:291-3 Ap 18 '69

about
Doctor Grosse and his wonderful bubble machine. F. Harvey. il Pop Sci 195:60-3 N '69

GROSSMAN, Bruce
Academic grind at age three. Ed Digest 34:26-8 Mr '69

GROSSMAN, Edward
Journal from Israel. Commentary 48:62-73 O '69

GROSSMAN, Nancy
Beyond nightmare. il por Time 93:74-5 Je 13 '69

GROSSMAN, Robert
King & his court. Ramp Mag 8:32-3 Ag '69

GROSSMAN, Sebastian P. and Stumpf, W. E.
Intracranial drug implants: an autoradiographic analysis of diffusion. bibliog Science 166:1410-12 D 12 '69
—See Belluzzi, J. D. jt. auth.

GROST, Michael
Child prodigies. il por Newsweek 73:18 Ap 28 '69

GROSVENOR, Donna K. and Grosvenor, G. M.
Bali by the back roads. Nat Geog 136:656-97 N '69

GROSVENOR, Gilbert M. See Grosvenor, D. K jt. auth.

GROSVENOR, Melville Bell
Melville Bell Grosvenor receives Distinguished service award. il pors Am For 75:8-9+ N '69

GROTELL, Maija
Maija Grotell. J. Schlanger. il por Craft Horiz 29:14-23 N '69

GROTESQUE in art
Beyond the nightmare; new grotesques. il Time 93:74-7 Je 13 '69

GROTOWSKI, Jerzy
Acropolis; adaptation of play by S. Wyspianski. Criticism
New Repub 162:25+ Ja 3 '70
New Yorker 45:164-5 N 15 '69
Newsweek 74:86 D 1 '69
Sat R 52:62-3 N 22 '69
Apocalypsis cum figuris. Criticism
New Repub 162:37 Ja 3 '70
New Yorker 45:85-6 N 29 '69
Sat R 52:72 D 6 '69
Time il 94:71 N 28 '69
Bone-deep truth. S. Kauffmann New Repub 162:25+ Ja 3 '70
Constant prince; adaptation of play by P. Calderón de la Barca. Criticism
New Repub 162:25 Ja 3 '70
New Yorker 45:139-41 O 25 '69
Newsweek il 74:137 O 27 '69
Sat R 52:12+ N 1 '69
Time il por 94:70 O 24 '69
Vogue 154:136 D '69
Grotowskerie. H. Hewes. Sat R 52:12+ N 1 '69
Grotowski: genius of the theatre. M. Gottfried. il por Vogue 155:154-5+ Ja 1 '70
Something to talk about. L. Lerman. il Mlle 68:210-11 Mr '69
Theatre. H. Clurman. Nation 209:642-3+ D 8 '69
Towards a poor theatre, revolutionary. J. Gruen. Vogue 153:132 F 1 '69

GROTOWSKI method. See Acting
GROUND cherries. See Husk tomatoes
GROUND covers. See Cover plants
GROUND effect machines. See Air cushion vehicles
GROUND hogs. See Woodchucks
GROUND squirrels
Hibernation induced in ground squirrels by blood transfusion. A. R. Dawe and W. A. Spurrier. il Science 163:298-9 Ja 17 '69
GROUND stations (communications satellites)
See Communications satellites—Ground stations
GROUND support systems (space flight)
New lunar display slide set. il Aviation W 90:57 Je 9 '69
GROUNDCOVERS. See Cover plants
GROUNDHOGS. See Woodchucks
GROUNDING (electricity) See Electric currents—Grounding
GROUP conflict. See Social conflict
GROUP counseling
See also
Group guidance in education
Group psychotherapy
GROUP guidance in education
Listening is a challenge; group counseling in the school. L. E. De Lara. Ment Hy 53:600-5 O '69
GROUP insurance. See Insurance, Group
GROUP living. See Collective settlements
GROUP marriage. See Marriage
GROUP medical practice. See Medicine—Group practice
GROUP method in teaching. See Group work in education

GROUP psychology. See Groups (sociology)
GROUP psychotherapy
Breaking the role barrier: a psychotherapeutic necessity. L. S. Sata and R. L. Derbyshire. bibliog Ment Hy 53:110-17 Ja '69
Community meetings in a prison setting. T. D. Eftihiades. Ment Hy 53:289-94 Ap '69
Group psychotherapy in the treatment of emotional disturbance. N. S. Brandes. bibliog Ment Hy 53:105-9 Ja '69
In the therapeutic community, patients are doctors. M. Scarf. il N Y Times Mag p32-3+ My 25 '69
Informal day-care program aids psychiatric patients; Temple university's Community mental health center. Todays Health 47:18 F '69
Marathon therapy is a psychological pressure cooker. K. Lamott. il N Y Times Mag p28-9+ Jl 13 '69
Sensory stimulation: an adjunct to group work with the disabled aged. I. M. Burnside. bibliog il Ment Hy 53:381-8 Jl '69
Volunteer-powered recreation for geriatric patients. R. H. Burrill. Ment Hy 53:389-92 Jl '69
We just want to help you: a note on anger in adolescent group therapy. J. G. May and W. Main. Ment Hy 53:638-40 O '69
See also
Psychodrama
GROUP relations training
Bristol township schools: strategy for change; Intergroup education and sensitivity training programs. T. J. Cottle. il Sat R 52:70-1+ S 20 '69
Group; joy on Thursday; encounter groups. il Newsweek 73:104+ My 12 '69
Group therapy games. il Sci Digest 66:44-5 D '69
How to have a bloodless riot; racial confrontation groups. G. B. Leonard. il Look 33:24-8 Je 10 '69
Sense about sensitivity training. M. Birnbaum. Sat R 52:82-3+ N 15 '69
Sensitivity training: fad, fraud, or new frontier? T. J. Rakstis. il Todays Health 48:20-5+ Ja '70
T-school for behaviorism Bsns W p62 Ja 10 '70
GROUP singing. See Choral singing
GROUP teaching. See Group work in education
GROUP work in education
Let's focus on the group. J. Kranser. il Sch Arts 68:8 Mr '69
Small-group training and the English classroom. D. M. Litsey. Engl J 58:920-7 S '69
Stop action; technique to help students become more effective group leaders and members. D. J. Mial and S. Jacobson. Todays Ed 58:68 Mr '69
GROUPIES
Groupies. il Time 93:48 F 28 '69
Rock style: defying the American dream; group named Rhinoceros. S. Davidson. il Harper 239:53-62 Jl '69
GROUPING by ability. See Ability grouping in education
GROUPS (sociology)
Prognosis for crackdown: the wheel of panic. T. J. Lowi. Nation 208:624-8 My 19 '68
Scapegoating. B. W. MacLennan. il Todays Ed 58:38-40 S '69
Should camp cabins be inter-aged and co-ed? experiments at Camp Thoreau, N.Y. K. Rodman. il Camp Mag 41:14-15 Ap '69
See also
Age groups
GROUPS, Age. See Age groups
GROUPS, Theory of
Hierarchical structures; report of symposium at the Douglas advanced research laboratories, Huntington Beach, Calif. T. Page. il Science 163:1228-30 Mr 14 '69
GROUSE
See also
Prairie chickens
GROUSE shooting
Big boom for old ruff. E. A. Bauer. il Outdoor Life 144:48-9+ D '69
Early season grouse. R. Gilsvik. il Field & S 74:66-7+ Ag '69
Hint of fall. T. Trueblood. il Field & S 74:30+ Ag '69
Sage grouse: forgotten pioneer. B. Milek. il Field & S 73:82-3+ Ap '69
Why the long grouse season? R. B. Colson. il Cons 24:9+ O '69
GROUTT, John W.
[Book review] Commonweal 89:506-7 Ja 17 '69
Marcuse and Goodwin tangle at Temple. Commonweal 90:279-80 My 23 '69

GROVE, Arthur S. Jr
Sweet and sinister. New Repub 160:10 Je 14
'69
GROVE, David C.
Olmec cave paintings: discovery from
Guerrero, Mexico. bibliog Science 164:421-3
Ap 25 '69
GROVE, David L.
Should exchange rates float? por Nations
Bsns 57:92 N '69
GROVE, Larry
Landscaping. Bet Hom & Gard 47:36-7 O '69
GROVE, Mary
Bad case of common sense. Good H 169:36+
Ag '69
GROVE, Pearce S. and Totten, H. L.
Bibliographic control of media: the librar-
ian's Excedrin headache. bibliog f pors
Wilson Lib Bul 44:299-311 N '69
GROVE press, incorporated
Close up: the old smut peddler; B. Rosset of
Grove press. A. Goldman. il Life 67:49-53
Ag 29 '69
GROVES, Charles
Charles Groves: a true successor to Bee-
cham? P. L. Miller; J. Diether. Am Rec G
36:8-9 S '69
GROVES, Don
Sea, a challenge for materials. Sea Front
15:356-63 N '69
GROVES, Harold M.
Canadian tax report and the American tax
system. bibliog f Ann Am Acad 379:94-101
S '68
GROVES, Wallace
Island that raises one crop: $$$. il por News-
week 73:90+ Ap 21 '69
GROWTH
Size of life. J. T. Bonner. il Natur Hist
78:40-5 Ja '69
See also
Children—Growth and development
Maturity
GROWTH (bacteria)
Bacterial growth rates above 90 degree C in
Yellowstone hot springs. T. L. Bott and
T. D. Brock. il Science 164:1411-12 Je 20 '69
GROWTH (plants)
Cebus monkeys: effect on branching of Gus-
tavia trees. J. R. Oppenheimer and G. E.
Lang. bibliog il Science 165:187-8 Jl 11 '69
Corchorus pascuorum: transmission of chem-
ically induced fruit formation with environ-
mental change. A. S. Islam and R. Mughal.
bibliog il Science 164:315-16 Ap 18 '69
Hormonal regulation in higher plants. A. W.
Galston and P. J. Davies. bibliog il Science
163:1288-97 Mr 21 '69
See also
Fungi. Effect of light on
Tillering (plants)

Anecdotes, facetiae, satire, etc.
Solving one problem nearly always leads
to another. Chem 42:5 Ap '69
GROWTH, Economic. See Economic develop-
ment
GROWTH hormone. See Pituitary hormones
GROWTH Inhibiting substances (bacteria)
See also
Methotrexate
GROWTH Inhibiting substances (plants)
Chloroplast replication and growth in to-
bacco; inhibition by 5-fluorodeoxyuridine.
R. Boasson and W. M. Laetsch. bibliog il
Science 166:749-51 N 7 '69
See also
Herbicides
Hormones, Plant
GROWTH of children. See Children—Growth
and development
GROWTH of cities and towns. See Cities and
towns—Growth
GROWTH promoting substances
See also
Androgens
GROWTH promoting substances (plants)
See also
Gibberellins
Hormones, Plant
Indolebutyric acid
Tryptophol
GROWTH stocks. See Stocks
GRUBER, Frank
Television and film writing. N. Vogel. Writ-
ers Digest 49:82-7 Ap '69
GRUBER, Michael
On owning the ocean. Sea Front 15:170-9 My
'69
—and Shoup, John
Crabs move ashore. Sea Front 15:364-75 N '69
GRUBER, Sheldon
Gold cup sweep at San Diego. Motor B 124:
17 D '69

GRUDZEN, Gerald
Reflections on priesthood and marriage. Cath
World 210:111-13 D '69
GRUEN, John
Movies. Vogue 155:76 Ja 15 '70
Underground (cont) Vogue 153:132 F 1; 114+
Mr 1; 28 Ap 15; 138 My; 154:66 Ag 1; 38 Ag
15; 340 S 1; 64 S 15; 160 O 1; 128 N 1; 64 N 15
'69
(ed) See Beckett, S. Samuel Beckett talks
about Beckett
GRUENBERG, Selma
Serape happy. Sch Arts 68:16-17 My '69
GRUENING, Ernest
Close-up of a leading man. Nation 208:407-8
Mr 31 '69
[Proposal for getting out of Vietnam] Nation
208:570-2 My 5 '69
Statehood for Micronesia. Nation 209:664-5
D 15 '69
Volunteers for Vietnam. Nation 208:165-6 F
10 '69
GRUENINGER, Walter F.
Phonograph records. See issues of Consumer
bulletin
GRUMBACH, Aileen
Watch on MacDougal; poem. Nation 208:742
Je 9 '69
GRUMBACH, Doris
Albany stows its first throne. Commonweal
90:333-4 Je 6 '69
Coming into maturity. Commonweal 90:429-
30 Jl 11 '69
Never the Twain shall meet. Commonweal 89:
616-18 F 14 '69
Sad, slow death of a cathedral. Commonweal
90:316-17 My 30 '69
Tigers of wrath at the MLA. Commonweal
89:564-6 Ja 31 '69
GRUMET, Gerald W.
Problems of the practicing psychiatrist. bib-
liog Ment Hy 53:410-14 Jl '69
GRUMMAN aircraft engineering corporation
F-14 spurs advance in composites. M. L. Yaf-
fee. il Aviation W 90:46-7+ Mr 17 '69
Grumman fights excess Viet profits case. K.
Johnsen. Aviation W 90:34 Ap 14 '69
New muscle for navy's air arm: the F-14A.
il Bsns W p58+ F 1 '69
Waste unit uses space techniques; integrated
heating, water recycling and sewage dis-
posal system for homes. W. H. Gregory.
il Aviation W 91:49-50 D 15 '69
GRUNBERGER, Dezider, and others
Codon recognition by enzymatically mis-
charged valine transfer ribonucleic acid.
bibliog Science 166:1635-7 D 26 '69
GRUNDY, Kenneth W. and Fulton, Richard
East African experience. bibliog f Cur Hist
56:275-81 My '69
GRUNEWALD, Eva R.
Che & Lizzie & Joe & Lola. Opera N 34:6-7
Ja 17 '70
GRUNFELD, Frederic V.
Call of India. Horizon 11:4-10 Sum '69
Chamber music of Paul Klee. Opera N 33:8-11
Mr 1 '69
Chopin without tears. Horizon 11:84-93 Spr
'69
Indian giving. Horizon 11:46-7 Wint '69
Music by Handel and Hogarth. Opera N 33:
12-15 F 8 '69
GRUNION
Grunion: the fish that spawns on land. C. P.
Idyll. il Nat Geog 135:714-23 My '69
Here come those crazy grunion. D. Valentry.
il Sci Digest 65:20-1 Je '69
GRUNWALD, Henry Anatole
Time: after Luce. R. Pollak. Harper 239:42-
52 Jl '69
GRUPPE motion Berlin. See Dance companies
GRUZINOV, Evgenii
Lunar cameraman. Space World F-8-68:34 Ag
'69
GRZIMEK, Bernhard
Plastic animals fool real ones in Africa. il Life
66:69-71 My 2 '69
GUACHAROS. See Oilbirds
GUADELOUPE (islands)
Guadeloupe. M. A. Mackay. il Travel 132:36-7
S '69
Liberté, egalité, fraternité; political assimi-
lation of French West Indies. Trans-Action
6:5 Jl '69
GUAM
Uncle Sam's proud nephew. S. G. Slappey.
il Nations Bsns 57:74-6+ N '69
GUANINE
Actinomycin binding to DNA: inability of a
DNA containing guanine to bind actinomy-
cin D. R. D. Wells. bibliog il Science 165:
75-6 Jl 4 '69

GUANOSINE monophosphate
Cyclic guanosine monophosphate: effects on short-circuit current and water permeability. J. Bourgoignie and others. bibliog il Science 165:1362-3 S 26 '69
GUARANTEED annual income
Guaranteed annual income. J. E. Estes. Nat R 21:953-5 S 23 '69
Guaranteed income for everybody? il U S News 67:20-2 Ag 18 '69
Guaranteed minimum income; study by National conference of Catholic charities. B. L. Masse. America 120:265 Mr 8 '69
Guaranteeing wages: a modest proposal. J. Kesselman. Commonweal 89:700-3 Mr 7 '69; Reply with rejoinder. H. Gallagher. 90:93+ Ap 11 '69
Public attitudes toward guaranteed annual income. P. Wogaman. Chr Cent 86:1037-9 Ag 6 '69
GUARANTEED income. See Guaranteed annual income
GUARANTEED wages. See Wages—Annual wage
GUARANTY. See Warranty
GUARDIAN and ward
Legal guardians for children. McCalls 96:50 Ap '69
Who will speak for the child? T. A. Coyne. bibliog f Ann Am Acad 383:34-47 My '69
GUARDS, Prison. See Prisons—Officials and employees
GUARE, John
Cop-out. Criticism
New Yorker 45:98 Ap 19 '69
GUARNERI string quartet. See String quartets
GUATEMALA
See also
Antigua
Education—Guatemala
Political parties—Guatemala

Description and travel
Guatemala ancient land of the jaguar. J. Dugdale. il Travel & Camera 32:24+ N '69

Politics and government
Flash point for terror. W. Sloat. Commonweal 91:37-8 O 10 '69
GUBER, Albert L.
Sedimentary phosphate method for estimating paleosalinities: a paleontological assumption. bibliog Science 166:744-6 N 7 '69
GUBERNATORIAL elections. See Elections—United States
GUCCI, Aldo
Gucci on the go. il por Time 94:72 Jl 25 '69
GUCCIONE, Robert
Chasing Playboy's golden bunny. il Bsns W p98 Ag 9 '69
Penthouse v. Playboy. il por Time 94:88 N 7 '69
GUDRIDGE, Beatrice M.
When your child dislikes his teacher. PTA Mag 63:14-16 bibliog(p37) My '69
GUELICH, Robert V.
Distributive education; address, March 22, 1969. Vital Speeches 35:508-12 Je 1 '69
GUELPH university, Ontario, Canada
Dorm city. K. B. Smith. il Arch Forum 129: 76-85 D '68
GUERIN, Ann
Dead-on dialogue as their cash runs out. Life 66:56+ My 9 '69
GUERNSEY, John
Rise and shine. Am Ed 5:20-1 N '69
GUÉRON, J.
Lack of scientific planning in Europe; adaptation of address, December 1968. Bul Atom Sci 25:10-14+ O '69
GUERRA, Jorge Daher. See Daher Guerra, J.
GUERRERO, Margarita. See Borges, J. L. jt. auth.
GUERRERO, Tony
One man's family of five old cars. J. Neary. il por Life 66:65 Je 27 '69
GUERRILLA warfare
Guerrilla warfare. C. Bartnett. il Horizon 11: 4-11 Wint '69
Out of the East, the people's war. A. Hope. il Life 67:58-66B O 17 '69
GUERRILLAS

Africa, Southern
Southern Africa: a smuggled account from a guerrilla fighter. il Ramp Mag 8:8+ O '69
War in southern Africa. R. W. Howe. il For Affairs 48:150-65 O '69

Angola
Angola; report from Hanoi II; with editorial comment. D. Barnett. il Ramp Mag 7:49-54 Ap '69

Arab states
Arab commandos: growing power in the Mideast. J. Law. il U S News 67:82-3 N 24 '69
Between devil and deep blue sea. America 121:410-11 N 8 '69
Children of the storm: the Arab commandos. il Newsweek 74:37-8+ D 22 '69
Fedayeen. A. Friendly. Atlan 224:12+ S '69
Israel gets set for prolonged war; a first-hand report. J. Fromm. il U S News 67:50-2 O 20 '69
Middle East: commitment and resistance. il Time 93:30 F 14 '69
Middle East: the fedayeen revisited. il Time 93:42+ Je 13 '69
Middle East Vietcong? J. Burnham. Nat R 21: 272 Mr 25 '69
Protracted jihad in Palestine. R. W. Fox. Chr Cent 86:1450-3 N 12 '69; Reply. G. B. Kliman. 87:18 Ja 7 '70
Revolt of the Arab refugees: we'll meet in Tel Aviv! C. S. Wren. il Look 33:27-36 My 13 '69
Unwelcome guests. il Newsweek 73:58 Je 30 '69
What Israel thinks of the guerrillas. il U S News 66:62 F 24 '69
See also
Guerrillas—Lebanon

Asia, Southeastern
Which will be the next Vietnam? C. T. Rowan. il Read Digest 94:95-100 Mr '69

Brazil
Guerrilla war in the streets; with interview with a leader of the National students union, ed. by P. Kramer. il Newsweek 74: 66-8 D 8 '69

Eritrea
See Guerrillas—Ethiopia

Ethiopia
Ethiopia's unknown war. J. Kramer. Nation 209:104-6 Ag 11 '69

Jordan
My country, my country. M. J. Kubic. il Newsweek 74:41-2 Ag 18 '69
With the Arab commandos; no peace for Israel; a campaign of terror. J. Law. il U S News 66:60-2 F 24 '69

Latin America
Latin American revolution. E. M. Smith. Chr Cent 86:674-7 My 14 '69
Urban guerrilla. il Time 94:38 S 19 '69

Lebanon
Arab commandos. W. H. Dorsey, jr. New Repub 161:19-21 N 22 '69
Calling the tune; Al Fatah; with report by M. J. Kubic. il Newsweek 74:47 N 10 '69
Feeding the wolf; problem of the Palestinian terrorist groups. il Newsweek 73:52 My 19 '69
Lebanon: along the Arafat trail. il Time 94: 30+ N 7 '69
Lebanon: army against guerrillas. il Time 94:23-4 O 31 '69
Lebanon: religious buffer; with editorial comment. Chr Today 14:26, 43-4 N 21 '69
Lebanon: target in a holy war. il Newsweek 74:45-6 N 3 '69
Mideast's latest hot spot: the squeeze on Lebanon. il U S News 67:30-1 Ag 25 '69
Shock waves. il Newsweek 75:38+ Ja 19 '70

Malaysia
On the borderline; Thai-Malay border activities of Communist terror organization. K. Buckley. il Newsweek 75:48 Ja 19 '70

Middle East
Operating from Athens to Acre. il Newsweek 74:66 D 8 '69
War nobody won. V. S. Kearney. America 120:664-7 Je 7 '69
See also
Guerrillas—Arab states
Guerrillas—Lebanon

Mozambique
Hydroelectric battle plan. T. Land. Nation 208:598 My 12 '69
Lost leader. il Newsweek 73:61-2 F 17 '69
Most wanted man; E. C. Mondlane. Sr Schol 94:23 F 28 '69
Murder by the book; Mozambique liberation front leader killed. il Time 93:35-6 F 14 '69
Premier and prodigal. Newsweek 73:59-60 Ap 28 '69

GUERRILLAS—*Continued*

Sudan

Anya'Nya revolt. D. Robison. il Newsweek 74:
60+ O 13 '69
Has the scorpion lost its sting? Anya Nya
independence movement. W. Smith. il Time
94:30 S 5 '69

Uruguay

Robin Hood guerrillas: the Tupamaros. National liberation movement. il Time 93:46
My 16 '69
Uruguay's urban guerrillas: the Tupamaros.
M. N. Gerassi. Nation 209:306-10 S 29 '69

Vietnam

See Vietnamese war, 1957- —Guerrillas

Vietnam (Republic)

See Vietnamese war, 1957- —Guerrillas

GUERRY, Dupont
Vitamin K, savior of bleeding babies. W. Garrison. il por Todays Health 47:42-3+ S '69
GUESS-for-fun alphabet; drama. See Johnson, G.
GUESSING games. See Games
GUEST, Barbara
Chronicle of younger poets. J. Atlas. Poetry 113:428-30 Mr '69
GUEST houses
A-frame for guests. V. H. Lamoy. il Mech Illus 65:67-9 Jl '69
GUESTS
Marked for greatness; National park service wife. E. B. Sandlin. Nat Parks 43:14-15 Mr '69
See also
Entertaining
GUESTS, Government. See Government entertaining
GUEVARA, Ernesto
CIA finds a publisher. por Ramp Mag 7:58-60 N 30 '68
In cold blood; how the CIA executed Che. M. Ray. il por Ramp Mag 7:142-9 Ja 25 '69
Revolutionary. S. Rodman. Sat R 52:38-9 O 25 '69
Revolutionary, and banal. R. W. Fontaine. Nat R 21:31-2 Ja 14 '69
GUGGENHEIM, Peggy
Lively arts; interview. ed. by E. Sparn. por Sr Schol 94:15 My 9 '69

about

Apotheosis of an art addict. por Harp Baz 102:118-19 Ja '69
Paintings descending a ramp. G. Glueck. il pors N Y Times Mag p36-8+ Ja 19 '69
Peggy Guggenheim's art comes to America. H. Ehrlich. il pors Look 33:34-7 F 4 '69
Peggy's back in town. D. L. Shirey. il pors Newsweek 73:70-3 Ja 27 '69
Taste of the Guggenheims. B. Rose. Vogue 153:152 Ap 1 '69
GUGGENHEIM, Peggy, collection. See Art—Private collections
GUGGENHEIM, Solomon R, museum, New York. See Solomon R. Guggenheim museum, New York
GUIANA, DUTCH. See Surinam
GUIANA, FRENCH. See French Guiana
GUIDANCE. See Educational guidance; Vocational guidance
GUIDE books. See Guidebooks
GUIDE Michelin. See Guidebooks
GUIDEBOOKS
Guide lines to Temple Fielding. N. Busch. il Travel 131:69-72 Mr '69
Guide to Temple Fielding. il Time 93:79-82+ Je 6 '69
Harvard's hip, pocket guide. M. Wright. il Travel & Camera 32:30+ Je '69
How to crack the Michelin. S. Wiedel. il Travel & Camera 32:30+ Je '69
Inside Paris; A Parisian's guide to Paris, by Henri Gault and Christian Millau. Newsweek 73:100+ Mr 17 '69

Anecdotes, facetiae, satire, etc.

Kentucky on $5 a day. D. Lowe. il Esquire 71:88+ Mr '69
GUIDED missile bases
ABM blues; opposition in North Dakota. Nation 208:586 My 12 '69
ABM comes to town; deploying Sentinel as an area defense system. P. Moldauer. il Bul Atom Sci 25:4-6+ Ja '69
Anti the anti-missile; communities fighting to block construction of sites. il Time 93:19 F 7 '69
Hard point vs. city defense. H. A. Bethe. Bul Atom Sci 25:25-6 Je '69

Is Safeguard worth the risk? G. W. Rathjens. Bul Atom Sci 25:23-4 Je '69
Life with the Minuteman; Grand Forks air force base. G. Alexander. il Newsweek 73: 76-9 Ap 7 '69
Missileland; Grand Forks air force base. R. Pollak. il Harper 239:82-6+ O '69
Nixon-tailored ABM looks like a fit. il Bsns W p37-8 Mr 22 '69
Revised ABM deployment plan envisions fourteen sites. C. Brownlow. Aviation W 90:27-8 Mr 24 '69
Sentinel in the backyard: the transitional reaction. M. Selk. Bul Atom Sci 25:7 Ja '69
Showdown on the ABM; proposed Sentinel anti-ballistic missile launch site at Libertyville, Ill; statement, January 13, 1969. S. R. Yates. Bul Atom Sci 25:29-32 Mr '69
This is an atomic missile base; what the ABM would safeguard. W. Griffith. il N Y Times Mag p29+ My 4 '69
Why one city is up in arms against a Sentinel base; Compton, Calif. il U S News 66:30-1 F 24 '69
GUIDED missile crews
Life with the Minuteman; Grand Forks air force base. G. Alexander. il Newsweek 73: 76-9 Ap 7 '69
GUIDED missile industries
Missile defense drags; rivalry between Mitsubishi and Toshiba. S. Griffin. Sci N 95: 586 Je 14 '69
Missile work hampered in France by shortage of funds. il Aviation W 90:278-81+ Je 2 '69
GUIDED missiles
Armed decoy study faces funding lag. Aviation W 90:24 Mr 17 '69
Arms control: the critical moment; U.S. to discuss possible limits on nuclear weapons with the Soviet Union. Time 93:13-15 Je 27 '69
British raise missile R&D expenditures. Aviation W 90:292+ Je 2 '69
Busload of megatons; MRVs and MIRVs. il Time 93:14 Je 27 '69
Clifford sees U.S. continuing nuclear superiority over Soviets. Aviation W 90:20 Ja 27 '69
Enter MIRV. N. H. Norman. il Newsweek 74: 52-3 Jl 14 '69
Europeans push air defense development. il Aviation W 90:216-18+ Je 2 '69
Heavyweight in balance of terror: the MIRV. il Bsns W p48-9 Je 28 '69
High stakes in U.S.-Russian arms talks. il U S News 67:88-9 N 17 '69
Kicking the weapons habit. Chr Cent 86:893 Jl 2 '69
Missile work hampered in France by shortage of funds. il Aviation W 90:278-81+ Je 2 '69
Missileland; Grand Forks air force base. R. Pollak. il Harper 239:82-6+ O '69
Nixon and the weapons talks; controversial questions of MIRV and the ABM. H. Brandon. Sat R 52:9-10+ Jl 5 '69
Oversell? Overkill? protracted controversy over the Safeguard ABM system and MIRV's. Newsweek 74:18 Jl 7 '69
SS-9 seen spurring Nixon ABM effort; Soviet Scarp ICBM. D. C. Winston. Aviation W 90:18-19 Mr 31 '69
See also
Jet propulsion

Control

Problems balk Condor production plans; television guidance system. Aviation W 90:18-19 F 17 '69
Quick turn system sought for navy Dogfight missile. Aviation W 90:19 Ap 21 '69

Cost

ABM cost. il New Repub 160:9-10 My 31 '69
Now a hard look at spending for arms, space, superplanes. il U S News 66:29-31 F 24 '69
SRAM cost overruns negotiated. C. Brownlow. Aviation W 90:16-17 Ja 27 '69

Crews

See Guided missile crews

Defenses

Action report: ABM; groups working to stop deployment. New Repub 160:10-11 Ap 26; 9 My 24 '69
Action report: ABM; Senate headcount. New Repub 161:18 Jl 12 '69
Activists take ABM fight to Congress, White House. J. P. Wiley. il Phys Today 22:69+ Je '69
After the ABM vote... il U S News 67:6+ Ag 18 '69
Air force eyes dual role for Minuteman. il Aviation W 90:44-5 Mr 31 '69

GUIDED missiles—Defenses—*Continued*

Missiles and anti-missiles; symposium. il Bul Atom Sci 25:20-8+ Je '69

Morton's first strike; Safeguard issue. Newsweek 73:37-8 Ap 28 '69

Myth of MIRV. L. Sartori. Sat R 52:10-15+ Ag 30 '69

National security; address, October 6, 1969. E. Brooke. Vital Speeches 36:44-7 N 1 '69

Nearing the moment of truth; questions regarding the Safeguard ABM. E. Teller. Nat R 21:630 Jl 1 '69

New peril for U.S; latest in the ABM debate. il U S News 66:10 Mr 31 '69

New schemes for missile defense; Project Defender. il Bsns W p36-8 Mr 15 '69

Nixon anticipates close passage of ABM. Aviation W 90:26-7 Mr 24 '69

Nixon-tailored ABM looks like a fit. il Bsns W p37-8 Mr 22 '69

Nixon's ABM decision: what it means; with text of statement, March 14, 1969. il U S News 66:38-9 Mr 24 '69

Nixon's ABM; very thin indeed. R. Rothstein. New Repub 160:15-18 Mr 29 '69; Same abr. with title Controlling nuclear arms; the ABM debate continues. Cur 107: 18-23 My '69

Nixon's first decision; go forward with antiballistic missile system. M. McGrory. America 120:349 Mr 29 '69

Notes and comment: Sentinel anti-ballistic-missile system with Spartan and Sprint missiles. New Yorker 44:27-8 F 15 '69

Nuclear accidents and the ABM. J. Larus. Sat R 52:10-13 My 31 '69

Nuclear logic. Commonweal 90:35-6 Mr 28 '69

Of many things: need for creative thinking on ABM debate. D. R. Campion. America 120:inside cover My 3 '69

Once more, into the gap; Russia's SS-9. il Newsweek 73:88 Ap 14 '69

One-year delay in ABM possible. D. C. Winston. Aviation W 90:16-17 F 17 '69

Oversell? Overkill? protracted controversy over the Safeguard ABM system. Newsweek 74:18 Jl 7 '69

Overtalk? Safeguard ABM debate. il Newsweek 73:37-8 My 26 '69

Paper war; ABM dispute. il Time 93:18-19 My 16 '69

Pillars. J. J. Stone; J. W. Warnock; J. Hill. Commonweal 90:536-9 S 5 '69

Plea for an extra button. Newsweek 74:39 Jl 28 '69

Politics. J. Leonard. Esquire 71:66+ Je '69

Politics of ABM. A Wildavsky. biblio Commentary 48:55-63 N '69

President Nixon discusses the Viet-Nam peace talks and the ABM safeguard system; remarks, March 25, 1969. R. M. Nixon. Dept State Bul 60:313-16 Ap 14 '69

President Nixon modifies ballistic missile defense system. R. M. Nixon. Dept State Bul 60:273-5 Mr 31 '69

President Nixon's news conference of March 14, 1969. R. M. Nixon. Dept State Bul 60: 275-80 Mr 31 '69

President Nixon's news conference of April 18, 1969. R. M. Nixon. Dept State Bul 60: 377-81 My 5 '69

Reflections on the ABM decision. R. Rothstein. New Repub 160:19-21 Mr 22 '69

Reluctant leader; E. M. Kennedy. Nat R 21: 476-7 My 20 '69

Report; Washington. E. Drew. il Atlan 223:4+ Mr '69

Russian leadership; the ABM; address, July 9, 1969. H. M. Jackson. Vital Speeches 35: 610-13 Ag 1 '69

SALT: can the strategic arms race be halted? R. E. Lapp. New Repub 161:14-17 N 15 '69

Safeguard: a question of priorities; ABM deployment. H. H. Humphrey. Sat R 52: 28-9 Ap 5 '69

Safeguard battle; controversy over anti-ballistic missile system. Time 93:18 My 2 '69

Safeguard debate opens. il Newsweek 73:24-5 Mr 31 '69

Safeguard: experts continue the debate. B. Richter. Science 165:576-8 Ag 8 '69

Safeguard faces stiff debate in Senate. il Aviation W 91:18 Jl 14 '69

Safeguard: pro and con; summary of report of the Senate armed services committee. il Newsweek 74:26-7 Jl 21 '69

Safeguard: public relations as a way of death. M. J. Rosenberg. Chr Cent 86:508-12 Ap 16 '69

Safeguard; the A.B.M. debate; address, April 28, 1969. S. R. Resor. Vital Speeches 35:574-6 Jl 1 '69

Scale tips against th ABM; Safeguard and the senators. Newsweek 74:25-6+ Jl 21 '69

Selling ABM the hard way. Nation 208:312-13 Je 30 '69

Selling the ABM. Nation 208:259-60 Mr 3 '69

Sentinel go-ahead? il Newsweek 73:34-5 Mr 17 '69

Sentinel rides again. Newsweek 73:22 Mr 3 '69

Showdown on the ABM; proposed Sentinel anti-ballistic missile launch site at Libertyville Ill; statement, January 13, 1969. S. R. Yates. Bul Atom Sci 25:29-32 Mr '69

Slippery chameleon. Chr Cent 86:704 My 21 '69

Soviets resume ABM work at Moscow. P. J. Klass. Aviation W 90:22-3 Je 23 '69

SS-9 seen spurring Nixon ABM effort; Soviet Scarp ICBM. D. C. Winston. Aviation W 90:18-19 Mr 31 '69

Steep Soviet missile rise feared; with editorial comment. C. Brownlow. Aviation W 91:10-11, 16-17 Jl 7 '69

Strike three and out. J. Burnham. Nat R 21:531+ Je 3 '69

T.R.B. from Washington; dearer than Vietnam; anti-missile screen. New Repub 160:6 Ja 25 '69

TRB from Washington; keep your shirt on. New Repub 160:4 Mr 29 '69

Tis death, and death, and death indeed. S. Alsop. Newsweek 73:136 My 26 '69

To ABM or not to ABM? Nat R 21:266 Mr 25 '69

To cap the volcano. M. Bundy. For Affairs 48:1-20 O '69

Toward compromise on ABM? bill before the Senate. il Time 94:15B Jl 18 '69

Trudeau's ABM doubts. il U S News 66:14 Ap 7 '69

USAF hard rock program halted. D. C. Winston. Aviation W 90:16-17 Ap 28 '69

U.S. journal: Lake County, Ill; reactions to future Sentinel anti-ballistic missile system site for Chicago. C. Trillin. New Yorker 44: 100-6 F 15 '69

Vicious acronyms. R. E. Lapp. il New Repub 160:15-19 Je 21 '69

Way out of the impasse on Safeguard; compromise. Bsns W p 138 Jl 19 '69

Where superpowers stand in arms race; Institute for strategic studies report. il U S News 67:56 S 22 '69

White House cop-out. Nation 208:386-7 Mr 31 '69

Why Congress is confused about ABM. il U S News 66:86 My 26 '69

Why we should go ahead with an ABM. H. Kahn. Fortune 79:120-1+ Je '69

Winds of change in the Senate; moderates question defense spending. J. Finney New Repub 160:21-3 Ap 5 '69

See also

Ballistic missile early warning system
Radar defense networks
United States—Defenses

Design

ASMS configuration evolving. il Aviation W 90:49 Mr 3 '69

French S-1 IRBM nears operation. D. E. Fink. il Aviation W 91:103-5+ Ag 4 '69

USAF advances MIRV technology. Aviation W 91:16-17 S 1 '69

Launching from airplanes

Maverick enters flight test; improved display planned. il Aviation W 92:22-3 Ja 5 '70

Problems balk Condor production plans; television guidance system. Aviation W 90:18-19 F 17 '69

SRAM production expected in mid-1970. D. A. Brown. il Aviation W 91:47+ D 1 '69

Launching from ships

ASMS configuration evolving. il Aviation W 90:49 Mr 3 '69

Bold new plan for national defense. J. G. Hubbell. il Read Digest 95:82-7 O '69

Extra protection for the U.S. fleet; ASMS development. Bsns W p32 N 29 '69

Launching pads

Air force plans further ICBM hardening. il Aviation W 90:78+ Ja 20 '69

Tougher shell for Minuteman; to bury the ICBMS in deeper and stronger silos. il Bsns W p36-7 Je 7 '69

USAF hard rock program halted. D. C. Winston. Aviation W 90:16-17 Ap 28 '69

Launching sites

See Guided missile bases

Propulsion

New Athena test vehicle designed; ballistic re-entry research rocket. W. C. Wetmore. il Aviation W 90:81+ My 12 '69

Protective measures

Air force plans further ICBM hardening. il Aviation W 90:78+ Ja 20 '69

GUIDED missiles—*Continued*

Specifications

Leading international missiles (cont) Aviation W 90:147-8 Mr 10 '69
USSR missiles (cont) Aviation W 90:146 Mr 10 '69
U.S. drones and target missiles (cont) Aviation W 90:160 Mr 10 '69
U.S. missiles (cont) Aviation W 90:139-40 Mr 10 '69

Terminology

Nuclear age glossary. il Newsweek 74:48-9 N 24 '69

Testing

Dry run for ICBMs; Minuteman tests. il Bsns W p50 S 27 '69
Shillelagh tested against armor. Aviation W 90:17 Je 23 '69

GUIDES
Behind the ranges; guiding in the Quetico-Superior; excerpt from Open horizons. S. F. Olson. il Audubon 71:6-15 Mr '69
Discoverer of the Hudson's source. M. MacKenzie. il Cons 23:28-31 F '69
What it takes to become a surefooted iceman. B. Spring and I. Spring. il Pop Mech 132:106-10 Ag '69
See also
Mountaineering

GUILES, Fred Lawrence
Marilyn Monroe: the untold story of her last years; excerpts from Norma Jean. Good H 169:62-5+ Jl '69

GUILLOT, Ellen Elizabeth
Undergraduate education for social work. Sch & Soc 97:25-7 Ja '69

GUINEA, Equatorial. See Equatorial Guinea

GUINEA pigs
Leukotactic factor produced by sensitized lymphocytes. P. A. Ward and others. bibliog il Science 163:1079-81 Mr 7 '69
Plague bacillus: survival within host phagocytes. W. A. Janssen and M. J. Surgalla. bibliog il Science 163:950-2 F 28 '69

GUINEY, Jack
Whale of a tale. Yachting 125:62+ Ap '69

GUINIER, André
Thirty years of small-angle X-ray scattering; adaptation of address, August 1968. por Phys Today 22:25-30 N '69

GUINNESS, Desmond
Personal view of Ireland. Art in Am 57:92-5 My '69

GUINNESS, Gloria
What shall I wear? Harp Baz 102:142-3 Ap '69
Young and crazy years. Harp Baz 103:124-5 D '69

GUITAR, Mary Anne
Care and feeding of the artist. Mlle 70:166-7+ N '69
Give your house a tranquilizer. Am Home 72:48+ O '69
Hackettstown is for the birds. Am Home 72:12+ S '69
How you can save the land we love. Am Home 72:75-6+ Mr '69
Mobile society: one out of five of us will move this year. Am Home 72:52-3 Ja '69
Ombudsman, new man on campus. Seventeen 28:22+ Je '69
Turn-around year. Am Home 72:54+ N '69

GUITAR

Instruction and study

Guitar babies; crash course for disadvantaged children. Newsweek 74:76+ Jl 28 '69
Let your child play the guitar. R. Gelatt. House & Gard 135:40+ Je '69

GUITAR amplifiers. See Musical instruments, Electronic—Equipment

GUITAR music
See also
Phonograph records—Guitar music

GUITRY, Sacha
French characters. H. Clurman. Nation 208:88-9 Ja 20 '69

GULF and Western industries, Incorporated
Escape clause. il Forbes 104:46 D 1 '69
Some glitter is gone at Gulf & Western. il Bsns W p34-5+ Jl '69

GULF ISLANDS NATIONAL SEASHORE (proposed) See National parks and reserves—United States

GULF OF CALIFORNIA. See California, Gulf of

GULF OF MEXICO. See Mexico, Gulf of

GULF OF TONKIN incident, 1964. See Tonkin Gulf incident, 1964

GULF oil corporation
Company town loses its boss. il Bsns W p30-1 Ja 3 '70
Long, perilous path; takeover of Reston. il Forbes 104:42 Ag 15 '69

GULF states

Description and travel

Sun 'n' fun spots on the Gulf coast. il Ebony 24:148-50+ Je '69

GULF STREAM
Drifters; journey of the Ben Franklin. il Newsweek 74:48 S 1 '69
From Florida to Cape Cod without moving. W. Cloud. il Pop Mech 131:128-31+ My '69
Getting the drift of the Gulf Stream. il Sci N 96:145-6 Ag 23 '69
Gulf Stream: river in the sea. J. Stark. il Travel 132:30-5+ D '69

GULIN, Angela
Musician of the month. D. J. Soria. por (pMA1) Hi Fi 19:MA4-5 Jl '69

GULLIVER'S travels. See Swift, J.

GULLS
Garuma, gull of the desert; Garuma gulls. G. M. Moffett, jr. il Sea Front 15:330-8 N '69
How an instinct is learned. J. P. Hailman. il Sci Am 221:98-106 bibliog(p 152) D '69
Inland sea gulls. G. S. Smith. il Sea Front 15:12-20 Ja '69
Laughing gull chicks: recognition of their parents' voices. C. G. Beer. bibliog il Science 166:1030-2 N 21 '69

GUM, Chewing. See Chewing gum

GUMERMAN, George J. See Schaber, G. G. jt. auth.

GUMS (anatomy)

Diseases

Periodontal disease: hidden threat to grown-ups' teeth. T. Berland. il Todays Health 47:28-30 Ag '69
Tooth decay and pyorrhea. il Consumer Rep 34:143-6 Mr '69

GUMS and resins
Amber: a botanical inquiry. J. H. Langenheim. bibliog il Science 163:1157-69 Mr 14 '69

GUN control legislation. See Firearms—Laws and regulations

GUN models
Mini-cannons from antique design. F. Worth. il Design 70:31-5 mid-Wint '69
Model this 24-pounder. W. E. Burton. il Pop Mech 131:134-9+ F '69

GUN sights. See Firearms—Sights

GUN stocks. See Gunstocks

GUNDERSEN, Robert C.
Use a planned progression of camping experiences to achieve your goals. Camp Mag 41:48-9 Mr '69

GUNDERSON, Doris V.
U.S. Office of education: report on research projects. Engl J 58:611-13+ Ap '69

GUNKEL, Louis J.
Simon says, Simon. il Mod Phot 33:46-7+ F '69

GUNN, Barbara A.
And they came out of their cotton-batting world; address, August 19, 1969. Vital Speeches 36:114-15 D 1 '69

GUNN, Charles R.
Abrus precatorius: pretty but poisonous. Science 164:245-6 Ap 18 '69

GUNN, M. Agnella
About reading and the teacher of English. bibliog Engl J 58:368-85 Mr '69

GUNN, Margaret M.
Get your Christmas tree out alive! Org Gard & Farm 16:49 D '69

GUNN, Nancy Reid
Artists on a houseboat. M. L. Norwood. il Am Artist 33:20-7 Ap '69

GUNN, Robert L. and Pearman, H. E.
Essence of mental hospitals. bibliog Ment Hy 53:422-7 Jl '69

GUNN effect. See Oscillators, Crystal

GUNNEMANN, Jon P. See Powers, C. W. jt. auth.

GUNNISON, Colo.
Mr Ed: the talking bus. J. R. Raine. il Sr Schol 94:Schol Teach 13 Ja 17 '69

GUNS (small arms) See Firearms; Revolvers

GUNSMITHS
See also
Hills, J.

GUNSTOCKS
Stock for the shotgun. J. O'Connor. il Outdoor Life 144:66+ D '69

GUNSTON, David
Only trees and tortoises live longer than people. Sci Digest 66:47-51 Ag '69

GUNTHARP, Walter A. and Oliver, C. T.
Concept of hemispheric defense. bibliog f Cur Hist 56:355-61+ Je '69

GUNTHER, John
Berlin: a tale of two cities. Read Digest 95: 106-11 O '69
Jerusalem: the sacred city. Read Digest 94: 141-4+ Ap '69

GUNTHER, Max
Choosing an article title. Writer 82:14-15 D '69
Types of modern articles; excerpt from Writing the modern magazine article. Writer 82: 12-14+ My '69

GUNTHER ISLAND
Off to Gunther Island on Humboldt Bay. il Sunset 143:3-4 Jl '69

GUPPIES
Guppies, the amazing millions fish. G. P. Nicholas. il Sci Digest 65:73 My '69

GUPTA, Sisir
Third world and the great powers. bibliog f Ann Am Acad 386-54-63 N '69

GUPTON, James A. jr
Easy to build high power electronic photoflash. Radio-Electr 40:23-6 F '69
How to make etched circuits. Radio-Electr 40:23-6 Je '69

GURLEY, Henry T.
How I built a home tune-up center. Pop Sci 195:40 Jl '69

GURNEY, Alan
Yachting interview; ed. by B. Robinson. por Yachting 126:74+ Jl '69

GURNEY, Dan
Drivin' with Dan; questions and answers. See issues of Popular mechanics
Road racing's big big league. Pop Mech 131: 77-9+ Je '69

GURRÍA LACROIX, Jorge
First news from new Spain. Américas 21: 15-19 Mr '69

GUSHCHENKOV, E. M.
Can the Pacific warm the Arctic? Bul Atom Sci 25:49 My '69

GUSMAN, Robert C.
Overlooked realities; excerpts from address. Aviation W 90:11 Mr 3 '69

GUSTAFSON, Eben H.
Build this plywood cutoff jig. Pop Mech 131: 194-5 Mr '69
Three-way bike stand. Pop Sci 195:139 D '69

GUSTAFSON, James M.
Ethical theory and moral practice. Chr Cent 86:1613-17 D 17 '69
Responsibility & utilitarianism. Commonweal 91:140-1 O 31 '69

GUSTAFSON, Kjell
1320 smorgasbord. Hot Rod 22:78 N '69

GUSTAFSON, Merlin
Religion of a president. Chr Cent 86:610-13 Ap 30 '69

GUSTAFSON, Ralph
Valley of the kings; At Geza; On the diadem of Princess Khnoumit: Cairo museum; poems. Harp Baz 103:116, 132 N '69

GUSTAVIA trees
Cebus monkeys: effect on branching of Gustavia trees. J. R. Oppenheimer and G. E. Lang. bibliog il Science 165:187-8 Jl 11 '69

GUTENBERG, Adam, pseud.
Fright before Christmas. Pub W 195:74-5 F 3 '69

GUTENBERG Bible. See Bible

GUTERMAN, Sonia K. and Luria, S. E.
Escherichia coli: strains that excrete an inhibitor of colicin B. bibliog Science 164: 1414 Je 20 '69

GUTHEIM, Frederick
Human environment. Nation 209:288-90 S 22 '69

GUTHRIE, Arlo
Hollywood scene; ed. by E. Miller. por Seventeen 28:42+ F '69

about

Alice's; family of folk song fame becomes a movie. J. Stickney. il pors Life 66:43-5+ Mr 28 '69
Alice's restaurant's children. il pors Newsweek 74:101-4+ S 29 '69
As Arlo Guthrie sees it... kids are groovy. Adults aren't. S. Braudy. il por N Y Times Mag p56-7+ Ap 27 '69
Joyful happening. il por Time 94:66 O 17 '69
Successful anarchist. W. Hedgepeth. il pors Look 33:60-2+ F 4 '69

GUTHRIE, Harold W.
Teachers in the moonlight. Mo Labor R 92: 28-31 F '69

GUTHRIE, Jackie (Hyde)
Joyful happening. il por Time 94:66 O 17 '69

GUTHRIE, Ramon
Lyrical discourse. G. Bree. Nation 209:24-5 Jl 7 '69

GUTHRIE, Woody
Woody Guthrie, songwriter; excerpt from The incompleat folksinger, ed. by J. Schwartz. P. Seeger Ramp Mag 7:28-33 N 30 '68

GUTMAN, Melvin
Emblems of fervor. il Time 93:70-1 Ap 4 '69

GUTMANN, Assia
(tr) See Amichai, Y. Out of three or four in a room
(tr) See Amichai, Y. Place where I've not been
(tr) See Amichai, Y. Two poems: My mother once told me; Song of resignation
(tr) See Amichai, Y. Two quatrains

GUTTENBERG, A. Z.
Planning semantics need improvement. Am City 84:134 O '69

GUTTERS, (roof)
How to install gutters and downspouts. R. Day. il Pop Mech 132:164-9 S '69

GUTTMACHER, Alan F.
How to succeed at family planning; excerpts from Birth control and love. Parents Mag 44:54-5+ Ja '69
Sex education in the schools. por Parents Mag 44:40 Ap '69

about

Doctor Guttmacher is the evangelist of birth control. D. Dempsey. il pors N Y Times Mag p32-3+ F 9 '69; Discussion. p 14+ Mr 16 '69
Parents' magazine awards for outstanding service to children. il por Parents Mag 44: 62 Ja '69

GUTTMAN, Nathaniel B. and Crutcher, H. L.
Wind and temperature effects on supersonic aircraft operations. bibliog Weatherwise 21: 220-6 D '68

GUTTMANN, Allen
Protest against the war in Vietnam. bibliog F Ann Am Acad 382:56-63 Mr '69

GUTZMAN, Stanley D.
Career-long sabbatical. bibliog Library J 94: 3411-15 O 1 '69

GUYANA
See also
Hunting—Guyana
Vietnamese in Guyana

GUYER, David L.
International student and faculty exchange. 1967-68. Sch & Soc 97:31+ Ja '69

GWINUP, Grant
The one sensible way to diet; interview, ed. by R. H. Berg. Look 33:84+ D 16 '69

GWYNNE, Peter
Physics lab goes relevant. Sci N 96:132-4 Ag 16 '69

GYMNASIUMS
Shaping up slim gym style: Miss Craig at Elizabeth Arden, Manya Kahn, Kounovsky's. J. A. Segal. il Look 33:94-8 Je 24 '69
Super-light, saddle-shaped roof is made of plastic foam over tensioned-steel web. il Arch Rec 145:170 F '69

GYMNASTICS
At the finish first is Finnish; M. Nissinen of University of Washington, winner of all-around title in NCAA gymnastics championships. D. Levin. il Sports Illus 30:92-5 Ap 14 '69
Shaping up slim gym style: Miss Craig at Elizabeth Arden, Manya Kahn, Kounovsky's. J. A. Segal. il Look 33:94-8 Je 24 '69
See also
Exercise

GYNECOLOGIC examinations. See Physical examinations

GYNECOLOGY
Like father, but not exactly like son; ed. by W. S. Ross. A. Decker; W. H. Decker. il Todays Health 47:38-41+ D '69

GYÖRGYI, Albert Szent-. See Szent-Györgyi, A.

GYOTAKU. See Prints

GYPSIES. See Gipsies

GYPSIES in England. See Gipsies in England

GYPSUM
See also
United States gypsum company

GYPSY moths. See Gipsy moths

GYROPLANES. See Autogiros

GYROSCOPES
Honeywell to test laser gyro unit. P. J. Klass. il Aviation W 91:71+ O 6 '69
Vibrating-beam rate sensor tested. P. J. Klass. il Aviation W 92:71-3+ Ja 12 '70

GYROSCOPIC instruments
Steadying images by bending light; gyro-stabilized lens system. il Time 93:57 F 7 '69
See also
Automatic pilot (airplanes)
Inertial guidance systems

H

H-bombs. See Hydrogen bombs

H and R Block, incorporated.   See Block, H.
and R, incorporated

HCC. See Harlem commonwealth council

HEW.   See United States—Health. education
and welfare, Department of

HI-FI systems.   See High fidelity sound systems

H. J. Heinz company. See Heinz, H. J, company

HOK.   See Hellmuth, Obata and Kassabaum
(firm)

H. R. Pufnstuf (television program) See Television broadcasting—Childrens programs

HUD. See United States—Housing and urban
development, Department of

H. W. Wilson company. See Wilson, H. W.
company

HYDRA (hydrographic positioning and recording system) See Hydrographic surveying

HAACK, Robert W.
Danger signs in the stock market; interview.
por U S News 67:62-5 Ag 4 '69

about

Wall Street: trouble in the private club. il
por Time 93:93-4 Je 13 '69

HAAS, Ernst
Italy: splash of color in a sparkling ski
setting; Pucci designs; photographs. Sports
Illus 31:60-72 N 17 '69

about

Ernst Haas, creative force in contemporary
color. I. Bondi. il Mod Phot 33:62-7+ Jl
'69

HAAS, J. Eugene. See Drabek, T. E. jt. auth.

HAAS, Robert
KS & KS. Wilson Lib Bul 44:528 Ja '70

HAAS, Walter A. 1916-
Style-setter in equal opportunity. por Esns
W p67 N 1 '69

HAAVIKKO, Paavo
Comment. B. Berkson. Poetry 114:263-5 Jl '69

HABACHI, René
Heritage of non-violence. UNESCO Courier
22-13-19 O '69
Student of tomorrow: towards a new global
horizon. UNESCO Courier 23:16-20 Ja '70

HABASH, George
Voice of extremism; interview, ed. by L.
Griggs. por Time 93:42 Je 13 '69

about

Headline hunters. il Newsweek 74:46 S 22 '69

HABEEB, Virginia T.
Norwegian fish pudding. Am Home 72:88-9
Ja '69

HABER, Alan H. and Rothstein, B. E.
Radiosensitivity and rate of cell division:
law of Bergonié and Tribondeau. bibliog
Science 163:1338-9 Mr 21 '69

HABER, Leo
Perils of record collecting. Hi Fi 19:58-61
F '69

HABER, Paul
Just like a Green Bay tree. P. Putnam. il
pors Sports Illus 31:28-9 D 1 '69
Win for booze and nicotine. P. Putnam. il
por Sports Illus 30:22-3 Mr 31 '69

HABER, Ralph Norman
Eidetic images; with biographical sketches.
Sci Am 220:12, 36-44 Ap '69

HABIB, Gabriel
Possibilities of Christian-Moslem dialogue;
excerpts from interview. Chr Cent 86:111
Ja 22 '69

HABIB, Philip Charles
[31st plenary session, August 13, 1969] Dept
State Bul 61:208-9 S 8 '69

HABITABLE worlds. See Life on other planets

HABITS of animals. See Animals—Habits and
behavior

HACKBRETT. See Dulcimer

HACKEN, Joe
Unjust exile of a superstar.   D. Wolf. il Life
66:52-52B+ My 16 '69

HACKENBROCH, Yvonne
English silver in Texas. Antiques 96:889-93
D '69
Wager cups. Antiques 95:692-5 My '69

HACKENSACK, N.J.
Voluntary joint public bidding. R. M. Belmonte. il Am City 84:162+ O '69

HACKER, Andrew
Is there a new Republican majority? bibliog
f Commentary 48:65-70 N '69

HACKETT, Alice Payne
Hardcover best sellers of 1968 in the U.S.
book trade. Pub W 195:30-2 Mr 10 '69

HACKETT, Lloyd
Small computer for a little city. Am City
84:114+ Je '69

HACKNEY, Sheldon
Southern violence. bibliog f Am Hist R 74:
906-25 F '69

HACKSAWS. See Saws

HADDOCK
See also
Cookery—Fish

HADDON, E. P.
Clues and clothing for snow survival. por
Pop Mech 132:104-7+ N '69
How to bring to life those forgotten snap-
shots: make a montage. por Pop Mech
132:144-6 N '69
New gear means new cheer for backpackers.
Pop Mech 131:132-5 Ap '69

HADDON, William, Jr
Shocking facts about drinking and driving. por
Pop Sci 194:78-81+ My '69

HADDY, Arthur, and Heinitz, Thomas
Music's debt to Ernest Ansermet. Sat R 52:
55+ Mr 29 '69

HADEN, Charlie
New music of political protest. M. Cuscuna.
Sat R 52:55-6 D 13 '69

HADLEY, G. L.
Farmer-feeders push for market protection.
D. Seim. por Farm J 93:B10+ My '69

HADLEY, Leila
Ameropeans; the new breed of expatriates.
Travel & Camera 32:32-3 Ap '69
Christmas shopping abroad in New York.
Travel & Camera 32:87-9 D '69
Why not stay in a castle? Travel & Camera
32:62+ Jl '69

HADRA (dance) See Dancing. Moroccan

HADRIAN VII; drama. See Luke, P.

HAEBERLE, Ronald L.
Massacre at Mylai; photographs. Life 67:36-
45 D 5 '69

about

Pictures and questions. por Newsweek 74:57
D 1 '69

HAEFLIGER, Ernst
Music to my ears; Haefliger's Schubert. I.
Kolodin. Sat R 52:74 D 6 '69

HAFFER, Jürgen
Speciation in Amazonian forest birds. bibliog Science 165:131-7 Jl 11 '69

HAFNER, Stefan S. and Virgo, David
Cooling history of orthopyroxenes. bibliog
Science 165:285-7 Jl 18 '69

HAFT, Stephen
This land is your land. Sr Schol 94:Schol
Teach 16-17 Ap 11 '69

HAGANS, Orville R.
On time. See issues of Hobbies

HAGEL, Raymond Charles
Pursuit of opportunity. il por Forbes 103:
62-3 Mr 15 '69

HAGEMAN, George
Ceramic drinking horns. Ceram Mo 17:27-8
N '69

HAGEN, Arnold
Fifty free (or almost free) research aids
and idea stimulators. Writers Digest 49:48-
50+ F '69

HAGEN, Dick
How to make alfalfa your big-money crop.
Farm J 93:52C-52D Ap '69

HAGGADAH. See Passover

HAGGAI, John
Indonesian phenomenon. Chr Today 14:40 N
21 '69

HAGGIN, Bernard H.
New records in review. See issues of Yale
review
Records (cont) Commonweal 89:593-4; 90:20-1,
170-1 F 7, Mr 21, Ap 25 '69

HAGLER, Ronald
Alienation, apathy, or antagonism? report.
Library J 94:497-8 F 1 '69

HAGNER, Donald A.
Look at the problem of evil. Chr Today 13:
10-12 S 26 '69

HAGON, Alf
Naked record. il por Hot Rod 22:132-3 F '69

HAGUE, Frank
Case history: I am the law. T. J. Fleming.
il pors Am Heritage 20:32-48 Je '69

HAGUE, The

International court of justice
See International court of justice, The
Hague

HAGUE philharmonic orchestra
Musical events; concert in Carnegie Hall.
W. Sargeant. New Yorker 44:106+ F 8 '69

HAHN, Emily
Big smoke. New Yorker 44:35-43 F 15 '69
Eddychan. New Yorker 44:33-9 Ja 18 '69
HAHN, Fred E. See Krey, A. K. jt. auth.
HAHN, Harlan
Violence: the view from the ghetto. Ment
Hy 53:509-12 O '69
HAHN, Nicolas F.
How to teach a delinquent. Atlan 223:66-
8+ Mr '69
HAHN, Vera D.
Decorating newsletter. See issues of Amer-
ican home
HAHNENKAMM. See Skis and skiing—Aus-
tria
HAID, Sara
Manhattan woman sixty-seven is chosen '69
Golden age painter in NY show. il por
Aging 180:15 O '69
HAIG, Frank R.
Ann Arbor, 1969. America 121:192-4 S 20 '69
HAIGHT-Ashbury district. See San Fran-
cisco
HAIGNEY, John E.
Beer ain't soap. por Forbes 103:198 My 15
'69
HAIKU. See Japanese poetry
HAILE Selassie I, emperor of Ethiopia
Emperor Haile Selassie of Ethiopia visits the
United States as guest of President Nixon;
exchange of greetings, toasts and remarks,
July 8 and 9, 1969. Dept State Bul 61:87-
91 Ag 4 '69
        about
Selassie land. S. Ungar. il por Newsweek
74:39 Jl 14 '69
HAILEY, Merna McMillan
Ride for the money! Read Digest 95:139-42
Ag '69
HAILEY, Oliver
Who's happy now? Criticism
Nation 209:675 D 15 '69
New Yorker 45:86+ N 29 '69
Sat R 62:72 D 6 '69
Time 94:72 N 28 '69
HAILMAN, Jack P.
How an instinct is learned; with biograph-
ical sketch. Sci Am 221:15, 98-106 bibliog
(p 152) D '69
HAIMOVICH, Joseph, and Sela, Michael
Protein-bacteriophage conjugates: applica-
tion in detection of antibodies and anti-
gens. bibliog Science 164:1279-80 Je 13 '69
HAINES, Edmund
Moscow state symphony. Hi Fi 19:MA26-7+
My '69
Week of new American music. por Hi Fi 19:
MA22+ Ag '69
HAINS, Frank
Burst of art at the crossroads. Hi Fi 19:MA28-
9+ My '69
HAIR, Donald
Experiences with differentiated staffing. To-
days Ed 58:57-8 Mr '69
HAIR
Law and hair down Mexico way. C. Manne.
Commonweal 91:36-7 O 10 '69; Reply with
rejoinder. J. A. Magner. 91:415 Ja 9 '70
Red hair as a way of life. il Vogue 153:44-7
Ap 15 '69
        See also
Baldness
Hairdressing
Hypertrichosis
Keratin
Wigs
        Anecdotes, facetiae, satire, etc.
On being a blonde. E. Sheppard. Harp Baz
102:204-5 S '69
        Care
Cosmic conditioning of hair. X. Pové. Harp
Baz 102:13 Jl; 68 Ag; 132 S '69; 103-144 Ja
'70
Get a head start. il Seventeen 28:244 Ag '69
Hair: how to get the hang of it. il Mlle 70:
118-21 D '69
Hot weather hair care. P. Van Wagenen. il
Parents Mag 44:32 Jl '69
Incredible mane: beauty out of infinite care.
il Vogue 154:174-5+ O 1 '69
Know your hair; Vogue's own beauty dic-
tionary. il Vogue 153:172-7+ Mr 1 '69
Redbook guide to hair styles, hair care,
hair color. il Redbook 133:111-18 My '69
        Dyeing and bleaching
Hair colour; who and how. il Vogue 153:230-
2+ Ap 1 '69
Highlights of hair coloring. P. Van Wagenen.
il Parents Mag 44:12 N '69
How to hype your hair color with a little
help from the sun. il Mlle 69:123-5+ Je '69

In every woman's life there could be a
winning streak. il Vogue 153:48-9 Ap 15 '69
Streaking the newest beauty status symbol. il
McCalls 96:84-7 My '69
        Anecdotes, facetiae, satire, etc.
Grandma Venie gets the works; letter. H.
Venie. Har Yrs 9:25 F '69
        Transplantation
Resodding the scalp. il Sci Digest 65:54 Ap '69
What a change of hair can do. L. Gourse.
il N Y Times Mag p79-80+ N 16 '69
HAIR; musical comedy. See Musical comedies,
revues, etc.—Criticisms, plots, etc.
HAIR, Removal of
Removing hair by electrolysis: is it wise to
do at home? Good H 169:6 O '69
Ways to remove unwanted hair. il Good H
168:201 Mr '69
HAIR curlers
Q.H.S. saga: the rollers still burn. Consumer
Rep 34:425-6 Ag '69
HAIR cutting. See Haircutting
HAIR dressing. See Hairdressing
HAIR rollers. See Hair curlers
HAIRCUTTING
How to give a haircut at home. il Good H
169:178 S '69
Long may it wave; long-hair-for-boys issue
in schools. W. D. Boutwell. PTA Mag 64:
14 D '69
HAIRDOS. See Hairdressing
HAIRDRESSING
Art of decorating ourselves; reprint. il
UNESCO Courier 22:52-3 Ag '69
Brunettes are back! il Seventeen 28:70-5 Ja
'69
Christmas coifs. il Seventeen 27:94-5+ D '68
Dear beauty editor; quick hair-doings. il
Seventeen 28:30 Ap '69
Different by a hair. il McCalls 97:92-5+ N '69
Fall fashions. P. Van Wagenen. il Parents
Mag 44:37 O '69
Hair? Help! questions and answers. C.
Bartel. Am Home 72:16+ N '69
Hairdos and makeup that complete the sea-
son's looks. il Good H 169:88-9, 171 D '69
Hairdos of the month. il Seventeen 28:164 Je
'69
Hairdos that work. il Mlle 68:163-5 Mr '69
Head to turn now. Harp Baz 102:203 O '69
His-her hair. J. A. Segal. il Look 33:52-5 F
18 '69
How to keep your hairdo in line: perma-
nents, body waves, straighteners. N. Heine-
man. il Parents Mag 44:36 Mr '69
New beauty book; twenty-five exciting hair-
dos, fall makeup forecast. il Good H 169:
120-9+ O '69
New directions. il Seventeen 28:286-9+ Ag '69
Our hairy revolution, and what to do about
it. L. David. il Mech Illus 65:74-5+ O '69
Portfolio of spring hairstyles. il McCalls 96:
76-85 Mr '69
Redbook guide to hair styles, hair care,
hair color. il Redbook 133:111-18 My '69
Round-the-clock beauty on a time budget.
il Good H 168:148-9 Mr '69
Seven super ways to look. S. Harney. il
Ladies Home J 86:108-11 S '69
Six beautiful new looks for summer. il
Good H 168:98-9 Je '69
Spring beauty book. il Good H 168:120-9+ Ap
'69
Sweet neglect. il Time 94:90 D 5 '69
Vibrant new beauty for five young women.
il Good H 168:116-17 F '69
Washerwoman hairdo. il Life 67:57-8 D 12
'69
Your hair: past, present, future. il Seven-
teen 28:130-1 Mr '69
        History
Dolls follow prevailing hair styles. C. H.
Fawcett. il Hobbies 74:43-4 S '69
HAIRPIECES. See Wigs
HAIRSTON, Sylvia
Horoscope for April. por Ebony 24:70 Ap '69
HAIRTRIGGER flower
Sex habits of the trigger flower. il Am For
75:4-7 Je '69
HAITI
Reports: Haiti. R. Steel. Atlan 224:20+ S '69
        See also
Education—Haiti
Flags—Haiti
Nutrition problems—Haiti
Tourist trade—Haiti
        Description and travel
Haiti: equatorial Africa in the Caribbean.
C. Stinnett. il Holiday 46:30-1+ N '69

HAITI—*Continued*

History

Haiti and the national flag; reprint. il Negro Hist Bul 32:14-15 O '69
Monuments to Haiti's only king. W. Jeffs. il Negro Hist Bul 32:11-13 O '69

Politics and government

Haiti: ripe for the marines? R. A. Joseph. Nation 208:392-7 Mr 31 '69
Rum and rumors. E. Peer. il Newsweek 73: 51 Je 23 '69

Religious institutions and affairs

See also
Voodooism

HAJDU, Étienne
Etienne Hajdu. H. Kramer. il Art in Am 57:98-101 Mr '69

HAJEK, Igor
(ed) See Sillitoe, A. Morning coffee with Sillitoe

HALABY, Najeeb E.
Superjet; interview. New Yorker 45:24-6 Ag 9 '69

about

Merger movement in the airline industry. il por Fortune 81:37-8+ Ja '70
Pan Am's new chief. il por Time 94:94 N 28 '69
Pilot-president. por Time 95:55 Ja 19 '70

HALAS, George Stanley
Hard days for Halas. il por Newsweek 75: 34 Ja 5 '70

HALASZ, Gyula. See Brassai

HALASZ, Michael F. and others
Hallucinogen-tranquilizer interaction: its nature. bibliog Science 164:569-71 My 2 '69

HALB, Bernard
Indonesian rhapsodies. Sat R 52:80+ S 13 '69

HALBERSTAM, David
Ask not what Ted Sorensen can do for you. . . . Harper 239:90-2 N '69
Farewell to the 60s. McCalls 97:85-92 Ja '70
Very expensive education of McGeorge Bundy. Harper 239:21-41 Jl '69

HALBERSTAM, Michael Joseph
M.D. should not try to cure society. N Y Times Mag p32-3+ N 9; 62+ D 7 '69
Modern medical myths; adaptation of address. Todays Health 47:72+ Jl '69
Norman Mailer as ennthnographer. Trans-Action 6:52-3 Mr '69
Stover at the barricades. Am Scholar 38: 470+ Sum '69

HALBFAS, Hubertus
German bishops cry heresy. J. J. Doherty. Commonweal 89:634-5 F 21 '69
News and views. J. Deedy. Commonweal 90: 130 Ap 18 '69

HALBOUTY, Michel Thomas
Where are they now? il Newsweek 74:24 S 22 '69

HALBREICH, Susan T.
(comp) Children's paperbacks. Library J 94: 3163-5 S 15 '69

HALDANE, John Burdon Sanderson
JBS, by R. W. Clark. Review
Time por 93:88 Mr 7 '69

HALDEMAN, Harry Robbins
Haldeman: the gatekeeper. R. B. Semple, jr. por(p9) N Y Times Mag p59+ Ag 3 '69
Praetorians. il por Newsweek 74:36+ Jl 28 '69
White House who's who. J. Osborne. New Repub 161:15-15 O 18 '69

HALDEMAN, L. W.
Once upon a time. Opera N 33:24-5 Mr 22 '69

HALDEMAN-Julius publications
Would you spend $2.98 for a college education? Little blue books. P. Butler. Sat R 52:23 Ap 12 '69

HALE, John
Full-time freelance writer. Writers Digest 49: 38-41 Mr '69

HALE, Lester, and La Rovera, William
Ansonia's public works complex. pors Am City 84:101-3 Jl; 94-6 Ag '69

HALE, Nancy
Other side. New Yorker 45:82+ Mr 1 '69

HALE, Robert
Colossus of roads; poem. Cath World 210:6 O '69
Punctuation personified. Todays Ed 58.27 Mr '69

HALEAKALA NATIONAL PARK
Gift at Haleakala. il Nat Parks 43:13 Mr '69
Laurance Rockefeller and the Nature conservancy make big land gifts to national park in Hawaii. il Parks & Rec 4:8 Mr '69

HALEVY, Abraham H. and others
Peanuts: gibberellin antagonists and genetically controlled differences in growth habit. bibliog Science 164:1397-8 Je 20 '69

HALEY, Bill
Birth of rock. il por Newsweek 73:12 Ap 7 '69

HALEY, James T.
(ed) See Embry, J. C. Afro-American vs Negro

HALEY, Sir William John
Overruled at Britannica. il por Newsweek 73: 77 My 5 '69

HALF dollars. See Money—United States

HALICTINE bees. See Bees

HALKIN, Hillel
Hebrew as she is spoke. Commentary 48:55-60 D '69

HALL, Adrian
Billy Budd; dramatization of novela by H. Melville. Criticism
Sat R 52:22 My 3 '69

HALL, Arthur
Philadelphia company finds its feet. D. Webster. il Dance Mag 43:62-4 Jl '69

HALL, B. A. See Borns, H. W. jr. jt. auth.

HALL, Charles Francis
Murder at Thank God Bay. Sci Am 220:52 Mr '69
Mystery in the Arctic. D. Jackson. il por Life 66:66B-67+ Ap 25 '69

HALL, Charles William
Predicts life span of 300 years. il Todays Health 47:18 O '69

HALL, Clarence W.
Their motto is: We build. Read Digest 95:19-20+ Jl '69

HALL, Clifton L.
Early educational journalists in America. Ed Digest 35:42-5 N '69

HALL, Donald
Dump; poem. New Yorker 45:46 Je 14 '69
Mount Kearsarge; poem. Nation 209:150 Ag 25 '69

HALL, Edward T. and Hall, Mildred
Language of personal space; excerpts from The hidden dimension. House & Gard 135: 103-5+ Ap '69

HALL, Floyd D.
Heads you lose, tails you lose. il por Forbes 103:33-4 Ap 15 '69

HALL, Glenn Henry
Sporting scene. H. W. Wind. New Yorker 45:140-51 Mr 15 '69

HALL, James Baker
Strange new world of Ralph Eugene Meatyard. Pop Phot 65:120-1+ Jl '69

HALL, James Byron
I like it better now; story. Atlan 224:80-4 Ag '69

HALL, John S. and Slettebak, Arne
Perkins 72-inch telescope in Arizona. Sky & Tel 37:222-4 Ap '69

HALL, Leonard
Our first national river. Audubon 71:48-51 Mr '69

HALL, Margaret C.
Simpleton Peter; dramatization of an English folk tale. Plays 28:81-3 Mr '69

HALL, Marv
Our crazy, mixed-up speed laws. Pop Mech 132:81-3+ S '69

HALL, Mary Harrington
(ed) See Urey, H. C. As I see it

HALL, Mildred. See Hall, E. T. jt. auth.

HALL, Peter
What's in a name; interview, ed. by V. Imm. por Opera N 34:19 N 1 '69

HALL, Richard
All around us and so easily overlooked. Life 66:50 F 7 '69
Stir of hope in Mound Bayou. Life 66:66-70+ Mr 28 '69

HALL, Richard W.
Patron today. Opera N 33:8-11 Ap 12 '69
Princesse Winnie. Opera N 34:28-31 D 27 '69

HALL, Robert E.
Child; his birth without permission; excerpt from Ethical issues in medicine. Sat R 51: 78-9 D 7 '68; 52:59-60 Mr 1 '69

HALL, Thadd E.
Thought and practice of enlightened government in French Corsica; adaptation of address, December 29, 1967. bibliog f Am Hist R 74:880-905 F '69

HALL, W. C. See Diamond, I. T. jt. auth.

HALL effect
Solid-state inductor. D. L. Heiserman. il Electr World 82:37+ S '69

HALL of fame, Baseball. See National baseball hall of fame and museum

HALL of the biology of man. See American museum of natural history, New York

HALLAWAY, Mary, and Osborne, D. J.
Ethylene: a factor in defoliation induced by auxins. bibliog Science 163:1067-8 Mr 7 '69

HALLECK, Charles W.
Excerpt from testimony before Subcommittee on constitutional rights, January 22, 1969. Cong Digest 48:116+ Ap '69

HALLECK, Seymour L.
Generation gap: a problem of values. Ed Digest 34:32-5 Ja '69

HALLER, Henry
Who cooks for the White House chef?   C. Meyer. McCalls 96:66+ Ag '69

Les HALLES market. See Paris—Markets

HALLEY, Edmond
Edmond Halley: genius in eclipse, by C. A. Ronan. Review
  Sky & Tel por 39:41-3 Ja '70. P. L. Brown

HALLEY'S comet
Christmas and the comet. M. Shatraw. il Am West 6:28-33+ N '69

HALLGREN, Christer
Gallery: photographs. Life 67:10-11 D 5 '69

HALLIBURTON company
Money isn't everything; acquisition of Brown & Root. il Forbes 104:42 S 1 '69
Servicing the seabed oil drillers. il Bsns W p 132-4 O 25 '69

HALLIDAY, E. M.
Leisure. Horizon 11:6-7 Spr '69

HALLIDAY, William R. and Anderson, C. H. Jr
Paradise ice caves. Nat Parks 43:13-14 O '69

HALLORAN, Daniel F.
Sino-Soviet tensions and American foreign policy. Cath World 209:151-5 Jl '69

HALLORAN, Richard
Japan's premier resort. Sat R 52:91-2+ Mr 8 '69

HALLOW, Ralph Z.
Blacks cry genocide. Nation 208:535-7 Ap 28 '69

HALLOWEEN
Drama
Sandy scarecrow's Halloween. H. L. Miller. Plays 29:53-60 O '69
Test for a witch. E. MacLellan and C. V. Schroll. Plays 29:79-84 O '69
Which is witch? A. C. Martens. Plays 29:15-24, 96 O '69
Poetry
Changelings. H. Langs. il Good H 169:198 O '69

HALLOWEEN masks. See Masks (for the face)

HALLOWELL, H. Thomas, Jr
Numbers game at SPS. por Duns R 94:26-8 Jl '69

HALLS
Enter with style! B. Duggan. il Mech Illus 65:84-6+ O '69
Welcoming hallway. il House B 111:154-7 O '69

HALLUCINATION and illusion producing plants
Hallucinogens of plant origin. R. E. Schultes. bibliog il Science 163:245-54 Ja 17 '69
See also
Peyote

HALLUCINOGENIC drugs
Do mind-bending drugs cause serious birth defects? B. K. Houston. il Sci Digest 66:30-2+ O '69
Drugs and narcotics: illusions and realities. il Sr Schol 94:5-10 Mr 21 '69
First aid; reactions to hallucinogens. Todays Health 47:80 D '69
Hallucinogen-tranquilizer interaction: its nature. M. F. Halasz and others. bibliog il Science 164:569-71 My 2 '69
News and views; question of military application of marijuana-type drugs. J. Deedy. Commonweal 90:2 Mr 21 '69
Students, drugs and protest. K. Keniston. Cur 104:5-19 F '69; Same abr. with title Drug problem among students; how bad, what's back of it? il U S News 66:90-2 Mr 24 '69
See also
Amphetamines
LSD
THC

HALLUCINOGENIC drugs and art
Painting under LSD. il Time 94:88 D 5 '69

HALLUCINOGENIC drugs and religious experience
Teachings of Don Juan, by C. Castaneda. Review
  Nation 208:184-6 F 10 '69. T. Roszak

HALLWORTH, Gerald L.
Are we handcuffing the police? America 120:128-9 F 1 '69
Myth of the jury trial. Commonweal 90:161-4, 351 Ap 25, Je 6 '69

HALOBATES. See Water striders

HALOS (meteorology)
Radio telescope and the heiligenschein. F. L. Whipple. il Sky & Tel 37:85 F '69

HALOTHANE
Side effects again. Sci N 95:449 My 10 '69

HALPER, Nathan
Yiddish poets in translation. Nation 208:154-6 F 3 '69

HALPERIN, Irving
Do you know what's happening? Engl J 58:1049-52 O '69

HALPERN, Seymour
In hock signo. il por Newsweek 74:23 Ag 11 '69

HALPERN, Seymour Lionel
What too many women don't know about dieting; interview. Redbook 133:82-3+ S '69

HALPERN, Werner I.
Community mental health aide. bibliog Ment Hy 53:78-83 Ja '69

HALPRIN, Ann
Environmental happening conducted by Ann Halprin; Universalist church. T. Borek. Dance Mag 43:80-1 N '69
Mythmaker. il Time 93:53 Ja 24 '69

HALSBAND, Robert
Giant four feet six. Sat R 52:44-5 F 22 '69

HALSELL, Grace
"I lived six months as a black woman." il pors Ebony 25:124-6+ D '69

HALSTEAD, Byron
Big test for a one-man show. por Bsns W p62+ S 13 '69

HALSTEAD and Mitchell (firm)
Big test for a one-man show. Bsns W p62+ S 13 '69

HAM
See also
Cookery—Meat

HAMAYA, Hiroshi
Hamaya's Japan. M. R. Weiss. il Sat R 52:46-7 Mr 15 '69

HAMBLETONIAN race. See Harness racing

HAMBLIN, Clifford W.
Recalcining lime sludge produces multiple benefits. por Am City 84:67-9+ N '69

HAMBLIN, Dora Jane
Burning question that splits our churches. Read Digest 94:112-16 F '69
Close watch on the men and their prizes. Life 67:54+ Jl 4 '69

HAMBLIN, Robert L. and others
Changing the game from get the teacher to learn. bibliog por Trans-Action 6:20-31 Ja; 65 Ap '69

HAMBRO, Edvard
Ambassador Hambro: interview. New Yorker 44:27-9 Ja 18 '69

HAMBURG
Music
Double bow for Devils of Loudun. J. H. Sutcliffe. il Hi Fi 19:MA22-3+ S '69
Menotti's globolinks. J. H. Sutcliffe il Hi Fi 19:MA27-8 Ap '69
Report: Hamburg; performance of Glinka's Ruslan and Ludmila. J. H. Sutcliffe. il Opera N 33:24 Je 14 '69
Report: Hamburg; Peter Ustinov's production of Die zauberflöte at the Staatsoper. J. H. Sutcliffe. il Opera N 33:34 F 1 '69
Report: Hamburg; premiere of Devils of Loudun. J. H. Sutcliffe. il Opera N 34:27-8 S 6 '69
Report: Hamburg; production of Lars Johan Werle's The journey. J. H. Sutcliffe. il Opera N 33:32-3 Ap 19 '69
Report: production of Handel's Giulio Cesare, with Joan Sutherland. J. H. Sutcliffe. il Opera N 34:32-3 Ja 10 '70
See also
Hamburg state opera company

HAMBURG state opera company
Report: Hamburg; Menotti's Globolinks. J. H. Sutcliffe. Opera N 33:33 F 8 '69
Report: production of Barber of Seville as Italian street theater. J. H. Sutcliffe. il Opera N 34:38-9 D 27 '69
Russian heaven. H. Saal. il Newsweek 73:102 Ap 14 '69

HAMBURGER hill. Battle of, 1969. See Vietnamese war, 1957- —Campaigns and battles

HAMBURGERS. See Cookery—Meat

HAMELOT; drama. See Alderman, E. R.

HAMERSTROM, Frances
Golden eagle and the rearing of redtails; with biographical sketch. por Natur Hist 78:62-9 My '69

HAMILL, Pete
Hangouts. Mlle 70:151+ N '69
Report from Olympic village. Ramp Mag 7:21-7 N 30 '68

HAMILTON, A. E. See Horita, A. jt. auth.

HAMILTON, A. Ian
Cell population kinetics: a modified interpretation of the graph of labeled mitoses. bibliog Science 164:952-4 My 23 '69

HAMILTON, Alexander
Alexander Hamilton: uncommon patriot. por Sr Schol 94:17 Ja 17 '69

HAMILTON, Andrew
High flying in the Pentagon. New Repub 160:16-18 My 31 '69
How the Pentagon hooks the Congress. New Repub 161:13-14 O 11 '69
Wiring Wisconsin. New Repub 160:8-9 Mr 22 '69

HAMILTON, Andrew Jackson
Business and the compulsive drinker. Read Digest 95:25-6+ N '69
It takes 350,000 people to put three on the moon. Sci Digest 65:22-6 Mr '69
Stop the TV-repair swindlers! Read Digest 94:100-3 F '69
Your teeth are here to stay. Sci Digest 65:22-6 Je '69

HAMILTON, Charles, autographs, incorporated
Hamilton galleries has another succesful season. H. K. Thompson, jr. il Hobbies 74:140 D '69

HAMILTON, Charles Vernon
Black rebels are not pranksters; they are raising vital issues. N Y Times Mag p 138+ My 4 '69
He doesn't want to be made into a little middle-class black Sambo. Newsweek 73:53-4 F 10 '69
How black is black? Ebony 24:44-8+ Ag '69

HAMILTON, David
Anyone for Furtwangler's 1942 Beethoven Ninth in stereo? Hi Fi 19:68 Ap '69
Bach's last keyboard works. Hi Fi 19:74-5 Ag '69
Big sound from Berlioz. Hi Fi 19:94-5 D '69
Britten's unchanged aesthetic. Hi Fi 19:90 N '69
Fascinating repertory opens up. Hi Fi 19:78-9 Je '69
John McCormack, musical raconteur. Hi Fi 19:110 My '69
Moses at Maggio, rebellion in ISCM. Hi Fi 19:MA24+ S '69
Music (cont) Nation 208:93-4. 218+, 284-6, 349-50, 413-14, 549-50; 209:93-4, 125, 157, 325-6, 388-9. 549-50, 707 Ja 20, F 17, Mr 3, 17, 31, Ap 28, Jl 28-Ag 25, S 29, O 13, N 17, D 22 '69
Now where did I put that Franck Sonata? Hi Fi 19:56-60 S '69
Records (cont) Nation 208:189-90, 475-6, 613-14, 677-8, 738-9; 209:190, 229-30, 453-4, 613-14, 673-4 F 10, Ap 14, My 12, 26, Je 9, S 1-8, O 27, D 1, 15 '69
Sound world of Salome, and a surprise from Caballé. Hi Fi 19:112 N '69
Verdi's Otello, a discographic survey. Hi Fi 19:79-81 N '69
Vocal recordings. Hi Fi 19:84 O '69

HAMILTON, John A.
Politics of hunger. Sat R 52:18-21+ Je 21 '69

HAMILTON, Lawrence S. and LaBastille, Ann
Taking stock of your rural property. por Cons 24:28-30 O '69

HAMILTON, Lee Herbert
Excerpt from remarks, August 5, 1969. Cong Digest 48:246+ O '69

HAMILTON, Michael
New life for old: genetic decisions. Chr Cent 86:741-4 My 28 '69

HAMILTON, Milo
Atlanta on edge. por Newsweek 74:129-30 S 29 '69

HAMILTON, R. M. and others
Seismic activity and faulting associated with a large underground nuclear explosion. bibliog Science 166:601-4 O 31 '69

HAMILTON, Richard
Rehabilitation through art. N. Kent. il por Am Artist 33:32+ S '69

HAMILTON, Robert E. See Miller, M. E. jt. auth.

HAMILTON, Walter C.
Crystallographers offer meetings within meetings. por Phys Today 22:23-7 Ag '69

HAMILTON, William F. 2d, and Nance, D. K.
Systems analysis of urban transportation; with biographical sketches. Sci Am 221:16. 19-27 Jl '69

HAMILTON, Mass.

Education

Maximum results from mini-courses: Hamilton-Wenham regional high school. R. R. Hayward. Todays Ed 58:55-7 S '69

HAMILTON college, Clinton, N.Y.
See also
Kirkland college. Clinton. N.Y.

HAMILTON RIVER
See also
Churchill Falls

HAMILTON-Wenham regional high school. See Hamilton, Mass.—Education

HAMLET (literary character) See Shakespeare. W.—Characters

HAMLET; drama See Shakespeare. W.—Plays

HAMLET; opera. See Searle. H.

HAMLIN, William O.
Perfect electronic keyer. Radio-Electr 40:69-72 N '69

HAMMARSKJÖLD, Dag
Dag Hammarskjöld and Teilhard de Chardin. M. Ward. por Cath World 210:159-64 Ja '70
Dag Hammarskjold, by B. Beskow. Review Sat R por 52:37 Je 14 '69. P. Frederick

HAMMARSKJÖLD memorial scholarship. See United Nations correspondents association

HAMMEL, H. T. and others
Forebrain temperature activates behavioral thermoregulatory response in Arctic sculpins. bibliog Science 165:83-5 Jl 4 '69

HAMMEL, Lisa
Home (cont) N Y Times Mag p 114-15 O 12 '69

HAMMER, Armand
How to win without playing the game. por Bsns W p86 O 25 '69

HAMMER, Donald P.
Casting for automation. bibliog Library J 94:4492-5 D 15 '69

HAMMER, Gerald
One man's meat; interview, ed. by B. van Voorst. Newsweek 74:49-50 S 22 '69

HAMMER, Richard
Case that could end capital punishment. N Y Times Mag p46-7+ O 12 '69
Role playing: a judge is a con. a con is a judge. N Y Times Mag p56-7+ S 14 '69

HAMMERS
Right hammer. il Bet Hom & Gard 47:42+ N '69

HAMMOND, George
Businessmen and their responsibilities to a changing society; address. April 23, 1969. Vital Speeches 35:595-8 Jl 15 '69

HAMMOND, Paul Y.
Presidents politics, and international intervention; excerpts from The cold-war years: American foreign policy since 1945. Ann Am Acad 386:10-18 N '69

HAMMOND, Robert
Summer hunt. Outdoor Life 144:64-5+ Ag '69

HAMMOND, Ind.
Half the fun; busing program of the First Baptist church. il Newsweek 75:55-6 Ja 5 '70
Spohn: resource center. J. Coleman and M. Liesse. il ALA Bul 63:266-7 F '69

HAMPERS, Clothes. See Clothes hampers

HAMPLE, Stuart, and Marshall, Eric
(comps) God is a good friend to have; excerpts. Good H 169:76-7 D '69

HAMPTON, Va.
Ho! Ho! Ho! North Pole calling. J. M. Eason. il Parks & Rec 4:45-6+ O '69

HAMPTON Institute, Hampton, Va.
Case study in student protest; excerpts from The first hundred years: a social history of Hampton institute. E. K. Graham. Am Scholar 38:668-82 Aut '69

HAMS (radio) See Radio operators, Amateur

HAMSTERS
Two visual systems. G. E. Schneider. bibliog il Science 163:895-902 F 28 '69
L-Tyrosine-3,5-³H assay for tyrosinase development in skin of newborn hamsters. S. H. Pomerantz. bibliog il Science 164:838-9 My 16 '69

HAMSUN, Knut
Books. J. Updike. New Yorker 45:90+ Je 28 '69
Stanley Kauffmann on Norway's forgotten giant. S. Kauffmann. New Repub 160:28+ F 1 '69

HAMWI, Adel. and Haskin, H. H.
Oxygen consumption and pumping rates in the hard clam Mercenaria mercenaria: a direct method. bibliog Science 163:823-4 F 21 '69

HANAN, Mack
Corporate growth through internal spin-outs. Harvard Bsns R 47:55-66 N '69
Corporate growth through venture management. Harvard Bsns R 47:43-61 Ja '69

HANAOKA, Masao, and others
Thymus-dependent lymphocytes: destruction by lymphocytic choriomeningitis virus. bibliog Science 163:1216-19 Mr 14 '69

HANAWAY, J. K.
Lysergic acid diethylamide: effects on the developing mouse lens. bibliog Science 164:574-5 My 2 '69

HANCOCK, J. K. and Decius, J. C.
Sound velocity in carbon suboxide. Science 164:587-8 My 2 '69
HANCOCK, Mass.

Historic houses, etc.
Model for the frontier; Shaker architecture. il Time 94:54-5 Jl 4 '69
HANCOCK center, Chicago. See Chicago—Buildings
HAND, A. J.
Why not buy a good paint brush? Pop Sci 195:86-8 D '69
HAND, Jackson
Build these power-tool stands for your shop. il Pop Mech 132:178-82 Jl '69
Build this double-deck gazebo. Pop Sci 195:178-8+ S '69
Electric tools under water? You gotta be kidding! Pop Sci 195:98-9+ S '69
New chemistry creates a better metal primer. Pop Sci 195:129+ D '69
New look in house siding. Pop Sci 194:154-8+ F '69
New mini chain saw does big jobs in tight spots. Pop Sci 195:206+ O '69
New robot lawn mower works while you rest. Pop Sci 194:136-8+ Ja '69
New roofing: sticks better, looks better. Pop Sci 195:128-31+ N '69
New twist in portable jigsaws. il Pop Sci 194:194-7+ F '69
Now you can solder galvanized pipe. Pop Sci 195:153 S '69
Picture frames you buy in a bag. Pop Sci 195:122-3 Ag '69
Plastic flooring spreads through the house. Pop Sci 194:154-8 Ap '69
Pressurized painting system without a compressor. Pop Sci 195:154-5 S '69
Redwood in plywood form. Pop Sci 194:142-3+ Ja '69
They paint your house between breakfast and lunch. Pop Sci 195:108-10 Jl '69
Tripod rack keeps fish rods handy. Pop Sci 194:129 Je '69
Walls that fool the eye. Pop Sci 194:176+ Mr '69
What about double insulaton for tools? Pop Sci 195:194+ O '69
HAND, Thomas G.
Challenge of Zen. America 120:159-61 F 8 '69
HAND
Fine show of hands. il Redbook 132:108-12 Ap '69
Knuckle-walking and the problem of human origins. R. H. Tuttle. bibliog il Science 166:953-61 N 21 '69
Revealing palm lines; diagnostic clues in an infant's hand. il Time 93:57 Je 27 '69
See also
Gesture
HAND bags. See Handbags
HAND care. See Hand
HAND luggage. See Luggage
HAND saws. See Saws
HAND tools. See Tools
HANDBAGS
It's burlap back to back; tote bag. il Sunset 142:123-4 Je '69
It takes two to travel, me and my gladbag. il Seventeen 28:284-5 Ag '69
Their new bag; handbags for men. il Time 94:58 S 26 '69
HANDBALL
Just like a Green Bay tree; P. Haber handball's singles champion. P. Putnam. il Sports Illus 31:28-9 D 1 '69
Win for booze and nicotine; P. Haber wins USHA handball championship. P. Putnam. il Sports Illus 30:22-3 Mr 31 '69
HANDEDNESS. See Left- and right-handedness
HÄNDEL, Georg Friedrich
Joshua not so fit; recorded by the Collegium Musicum of the University of Missouri. H. Weinstock. Sat R 52:51 Ag 30 '69

about

After a decade, Sir Malcolm Sargent's last word on Messiah. P. L. Miller. Am Rec G 36:172 N '69
From Germany: an English music drama. P. H. Lang. il Hi Fi 19:83-4 N '69
Great Handel recording. Discus. Harper 238:110 My '69
Greater Handel. H. Weinstock. Sat R 52:50 Mr 29 '69
Handel's Chandos anthems: ceremonial music that makes a glorious sound. P. H. Lang. il Hi Fi 19:65-6 Ap '69
Handel's Samson glorified. H. Weinstock. Sat R 52:51 D 27 '69

Misunderstood Messiah. il Time 94:39 D 26 '69
Records:
Messiah. Opera N 34:36 Ja 10 '70
Theodora. Opera N 34:34 S 6 '69
Reissue of Alexander's feast, plus first editions of two other oratorios by George Frideric Handel: Theodora & Joshua. J. W. Barker. il por Am Rec G 36:108-12 O '69
Report: Princeton; concert version of Amadigi. H. E. Phillips. Opera N 33:34 Ap 5 '69
Report: Waterloo Village, N.J; concert performance of Semele. S. L. Fogel. Opera N 34:22 S 20 '69
Reviews of records. Mus Q 55:132-6 Ja '69
Solomon as king of England and Handel's only Christian oratorio. P. H. Lang. il por Hi Fi 19:75-7 My '69
HANDGUNS. See Pistols
HANDICAPPED
Blindness; handicap, or characteristic? address, July 3, 1969. K. Jernigan. Vital Speeches 36:10-14 O 15 '69
Sensory stimulation: an adjunct to group work with the disabled aged. I. M. Burnside. bibliog il Ment Hy 53:381-8 Jl '69
See also
Camps for the handicapped
Children, Handicapped
Cripples
Disability—Measurement
Libraries—Work with handicapped
Mentally handicapped
Recreation for the handicapped

Travel
Helping the handicapped travel by air. M. McEachern. il Todays Health 47:66-8+ Mr '69
HANDICAPPED children. See Children, Handicapped
HANDICRAFT
Bring unique interest to your home with handcrafted accessories. il Good H 169:108-12 Jl '69
See also
Artisans
Arts and crafts
Jewelry making
Patchwork
Stencil work
HANDLER, Bruce
Reports: Surinam. Atlan 224:38+ N '69
HANDLER, Philip
Can Handler teach NAS evolution? il pors Bsns W p60-2 Ap 5 '69
On the edge of change. B. J. Culliton. il por Sci N 95:579-81 Je 14 '69
Will the science brain bank go conglomerate? J. Lear. il por Sat R 52:38-44 Jl 5 '69
HANDLES
Making bamboo handles. C. C. Miller. il Ceram Mo 17:28-9 O '69
HANDLEY, Catherine
Four point system for writing a selling query letter; interview. ed. by O. Henry, with suggestions by I. B. Harrell. Writers Digest 49:48-51 Ag '69
HANDLEY Page, limited
Dawson leaves Handley Page in top management shakeup. Aviation W 91:71 Jl 7 '69
Handley Page gets a Missouri accent. il Bsns W p38 O 25 '69
Handley Page taken over by U.S. group. H. J. Coleman. Aviation W 91:25 O 27 '69
Handley Page unions seeking British aid to protect jobs. Aviation W 91:96-7 Ag 25 '69
HANDLING of materials. See Materials handling
HANDMADE paper. See Paper making and trade
HANDPRINTS
See also
Dermatoglyphics
HANDS, Charles B.
Hidden terror of Robert Frost. Engl J 58:1162-8 N '69
HANDS, Glenn E.
Independent water supply proves best. Am City 84:106+ F '69
HANDS, Richard C.
Take care of your favorite tools. Horticulture 46:52+ D '68
HANDSAWS. See Saws
HANDWORK. See Handicraft
HANDWRITING. See Penmanship
HANDWRITING analysis. See Graphology
HANDWRITING on the wall; drama. See Nicholson, J.
HANDY, John L.
How to face being taken over. Harvard Bsns R 47:109-11 N '69

HANEDA, Yata, and others
Luminescent systems in apogonid fishes from the Philippines. bibliog Science 165:188-90 Jl 11 '69
HANEL, R. and Conrath, B.
Interferometer experiment on Nimbus 3; preliminary results. Science 165:1258-60 S 19 '69
HANES, Arthur J.
For conspiracy. por Look 33:104+ Ap 15 '69
HANEY, Sonja
On the boards. W. Como. por Dance Mag 43: 20 Je '69
HANFT, Adam
Tumulus; poem. America 120:477 Ap 19 '69
HANGING
Carnival in Baghdad; public hangings of Iraqi Jews in Baghdad. il Newsweek 73:31-2 F 10 '69
Death, diplomacy and diminishing peace; political executions in Baghdad. il Time 93: 22-3 F 7 '69
Death to hanging; government resolution outlawing hanging in Great Britain. Newsweek 74:28+ D 29 '69
Hangings in Iraq. Nat R 21:108 F 11 '69
In Britain, an end to hangings. U S News 67:6 D 29 '69
Interfaith scaffold in Iraq. Chr Today 13: 47 F 28 '69
Mass public executions in Iraq deplored by United States; text of letter to the president of the Security council, January 29, 1969. C. W. Yost. Dept State Bul 60:145-6 F 17 '69
Nixon's first foreign crisis: the boiling Mideast; public hangings in Baghdad. il U S News 66:35-6 F 10 '69
Sacking the hangman; Great Britain. il Time 94:15-16 D 26 '69
Terrible myth of internal affairs; public hanging of fourteen men convicted of spying for Israel. Chr Cent 86:205 F 12 '69
HANGING baskets. See Plants, Potted
HANGING of pictures. See Pictures, Hanging of
HANGINGS, Wall. See Wall hangings
HANKE, Susanne
Brief biography. S. Goodman. il pors Dance Mag 43:66-9 O '69
HANKS, Sarah E.
Pantaleon's pantalon: an 18th-century musical fashion. bibliog f Mus Q 55:215-27 Ap '69
HANLEY, James
Inner journey. Criticism Nation 208:477 Ap 14 '69
HANNA, William Denby
Men behind Dastardly & Muttley. J. Culhane. il por N Y Times Mag p50-1+ N 23 '69
HANNAH, John Alfred
Changes ahead in foreign aid? por U S News 66:17 F 17 '69
Exit Methuselah. il por Time 93:42 Mr 21 '69
HANNAY, James B.
Hannay's diamonds. Chem 42:20-2 Je '69
HANNAY, Roger
Current chronicle; performance of Live and in color at Philadelphia musical academy. D. Chittum. il Mus Q 55:401-7 Jl '69
HANNEMAN, Ralph
Holiday on wheels. Parks & Rec 4:26-8+ Je '69
HANNERZ, Ulf
Roots of black manhood. bibliog por Trans-Action 6:12-21 O '69
HANNIBAL, Mo.
How they see it in Hannibal, Mo. H. B. Meyers. il Fortune 80:74-5+ D '69
One thing and another. J. K. Hutchens. Sat R 52:23-4 My 31 '69
HANNON, Kent
Baseball's week. Sports Illus 31:122-3 S 15 '69
HANO, Arnold
East is East and West is second, or is it? N Y Times Mag p32-3+ Mr 16 '69
Protectionists vs. recreationists; the battle of Mineral King. N Y Times Mag p24-5+ Ag 17 '69
HANSBERGER, Robert Vail
Bob Hansberger shows how to grow without becoming a conglomerate; interview, ed. by J. McDonald. por Fortune 80:134-8+ O '69

about

Don't jump on us! por Forbes 103:41 Mr 15 '69
State of mind. por Newsweek 74:63 S 1 '69
HANSBERRY, Lorraine
My name is Lorraine Hansberry, I am a writer. il por Esquire 72:140-1 N '69

about

Losing the playwright. G. Weales. Commonweal 90:542-3 S 5 '69
Sweet Lorraine. J. Baldwin. Esquire 72:139-40 N '69
HANSEN, Bertie D. 3d
Graduate student. por Phys Today 22:30-1 Mr '69
HANSEN, Carl F.
When courts try to run the public schools. por U S News 66:94-6 Ap 21 '69
HANSEN, Chris A.
Water hygiene programs; the environmental control administration; address, March 20, 1969. Vital Speeches 35:444-6 My 1 '69
HANSEN, Clifford Peter
Excerpt from addresses, October 11, 1968, and January 22, 1969. Cong Digest 48:80+ Mr '69
HANSEN, Ernest, and Bell, J. G.
Bitterly opposed wastewater plant. Am City 84:76-8 Ap '69
HANSEN, Helen
Tillamook rock: beacon of silence. Sea Front 15:54-60 Ja '69
HANSEN, J. R.
Image-tube photography. R Pop Astron 63: 28-32 F '69
HANSEN, James
Children of the world; photographs. Look 33:50-5 D 30 '69
HANSEN, Niles M.
Urban alternatives for eliminating poverty; excerpt from address, May 2 and 3, 1969. Mo Labor R 92:46-7 Ag '69
HANSEN, W. Lee, and Weisbrod, B. A.
Equality fiction: bottom dogs subsidize top dogs. New Repub 161:23-4 S 6 '69
HANSEN'S disease. See Leprosy and lepers
HANSON, Carl H.
Teaching the handicapped child. Todays Ed 58:46-7 D '69
HANSON, Dick
Across the editor's desk. See issues of Successful farming
HANSON, Wallace
That 21-jewel, 24-karat, 35-mm camera in the sky. Pop Phot 65.80-1+ Ag '69
HANSON, William R.
Estimating the number of animals; a rapid method for unidentified individuals. bibliog Science 162:675-6; 165:825 N 8 '68, Ag 22 '69
HAPLOIDY. See Chromosomes
HAPPENINGS (art)
Art. L. Alloway. Nation 209:419-21 O 20 '69
Art teachers experience various sensations through happenings. R. J. Topping. il Sch Arts 69:32-3 N '69
HAPPENINGS (theater)
My very last happening. C. Oldenburg. il Esquire 71:154-7 My '69
HAPPIEST hat; drama. See Nolan, P. T.
HAPPINESS
What would really make you happy? S. Blum. il Redbook 132:49+ Ja '69
See also
Pleasure

Anecdotes, facetiae, satire, etc.
Happy days for you! August. '69. Esquire 72: 68-9 Ag '69
HAPPY birthdays; story. See Robinson, B.
HARAPPA culture
Harappan may be Dravidian. Sci Am 221:62 N '69
HARASYMOWICZ, Jerzy
Geometry; poem; tr. by V. Contoski. Nation 208:216 F 17 '69
HARASZTY, Eszter
Very personal Christmas. McCalls 97:58-75 D '69
HARBER, Hubert E.
Five Mayan eclipses in thirteen years. Sky & Tel 37:72-4 F '69
HARBORS
See also subhead Harbor under names of cities, e.g. New York (city)—Harbor

Australia
Blasting a nuclear haven; proposed harbor at Cape Keraudren. il Sci N 95:159-60 F 15 '69
Six questions for Australians; proposal to use nuclear explosives to dig a harbor. il Environ 11:16-19 Ap '69
Unsnug harbor; Australian Plowshare harbor still a possibility. V. Brodine. il Environ 11:34-6 My '69
HARD of hearing. See Deaf; Deafness
HARDENING of the arteries. See Arteriosclerosis

HARDIE, Dee
Christmas is a tree. House & Gard 136:69-70+
D '69
HARDIE, Jim
Jo Jo, king of competition sport fishing.
Motor B 123:98+ Ap '69
HARDIN, Clifford Morris
Where food prices are headed; interview.
por U S News 67:69-72 O 27 '69

about

Agriculture. por Sci N 95:111 F 1 '69
Hardin listens in O. Bay and G. Lorang. il
por Farm J 93:16-16A+ Je '69
Meal ticket for the hungry. Nation 208:452-3
Ap 14 '69
Meet the new secretary. D. Seim. il por
Farm J 93:36-7+ F '69
Mike Frome. M. Frome. Am For 75:3+ Ap '69
Washington report. W. Swegle. il por Suc
Farm 67:9 Ja; 7 F '69
HARDIN, Garrett
Economics of wilderness: adaptation of ad-
dress. March 15, 1969. Natur Hist 78:20+
Je '69
Finding lemonade in Santa Barbara's oil.
Sat R 52:18-21 My 10 '69
HARDIN, Martha Love Wood
New first lady of agriculture. E. W. Manning.
il por Farm J 93:107 F '69
HARDINESS in plants. See Plants—Hardiness
HARDING, George
Four disciples of Howard Pyle. H. C. Pitz.
il Am Artist 33:41 Ja '69
HARDING, John
Monster shark. il Sea Front 15:50-3 Ja '69
HARDING, Vincent
Achieving educational equality; stemming the
black brain drain. Cur 105:37-40 Mr '69
Educator's view; black students and the im-
possible revolution. por Ebony 24:141-6+
Ag; 97-8+ S '69

about

Black studies Vatican. il por Newsweek 74:38
Ag 11 '69
HARDING, Warren Gamaliel
Harding's Alaskan dream; excerpt from The
shadow of Blooming Grove. F. Russell.
il por Sat R 52:63-4 Mr 8 '69
How Harding saved the Versailles treaty.
R. K. Murray. il por Am Heritage 20:
66-7+ D '68
Shadow of Blooming Grove. by F. Russell.
Review
America 120:104-5 Ja 25 '69. F. K. Kelly
Nat R 21:77-8 Ja 28 '69. A. Drury
HARDT, Lorraine
Yes, I write greeting cards, how did you
know? Writers Digest 49:43-4 O '69
HARDWARE
See also
Curtain and drapery fixtures
Doorknobs
Drawer pulls
Household appliances
HARDWICK, Elizabeth
Books. Vogue 154:50 Jl; 138+ D '69
Going home is America: Lexington, Kentucky.
Harper 239:78-82 Jl '69
HARDWICK, Lillian M.
Sweet and acid for rhododendrons. Org Gard
& Farm 16:50-1 D '69
Two compost bins, and a cart. Org Gard &
Farm 16:70+ O '69
HARDY, Godfrey Harold
Books. J. Bernstein. New Yorker 44:80+ F
1 '69
HARDY, Hugh
Architecture of awareness for the perform-
ing arts. Arch Rec 145:117-22 Mr '69
HARDY, Jerome Spilman
Life seeks more spark. por Bsns W p 135
My 10 '69
HARDY, Mal
Legend of Smokey Bear. Nat Parks 43:18-20
Ja '69
HARDY, Noah
Exploring the shelf. Sci N 95:366 Ap 12 '69
One more for the 300 GeV. Sci N 96:486
N 22 '69
White corpuscle transfusion. Sci N 96:88 Jl 26
'69
HARDY, William D. Jr, and others
Feline leukemia virus: occurrence of viral
antigen in the tissues of cats with lym-
phosarcoma and other diseases. bibliog
Science 166:1019-21 N 21 '69
HARE, Burt
Mummies: man's drive for immortality. bib-
liog Sci Digest 66:16-22 D '69

HARE, Nathan
Case for separatism: black perspective. por
Newsweek 73:56 F 10 '69
Two black radicals report on their campus
struggles. por Ramp Mag 8:54-9 Jl '69
HARE hunting. See Rabbit hunting
HARES
Snowshoe rabbit: varying hare's change of
color due to reduced length of daylight.
Cons 23:27 F '69
HARGIS, Billy James
New crusader. il por Time 94:49 Ag 29 '69
HARGIS, Charles H. See Kingsley, R. F. jt.
auth.
HARITHAS, James
Painting at the degree zero. Art N 67:52-
3+ N '68
HARK, Mildred, and McQueen, Noel
Best year; drama. Plays 29:59-64 Ja '70
Father keeps house; drama, reprint from
1955 issue. Plays 28:25-35 My '69
Jingle bells; drama. Plays 29:48-56, 72 D '69
Lincoln reminders; drama. Plays 28:67-71 F
'69
HARKARVY, Benjamin
Another try at the inevitable direction. J. J.
O'Connor. por Dance Mag 43:65-7 N '69
HARKAVY, Oscar, and others
Family planning and public policy: who is
misleading whom? bibliog Science 165:367-73
Jl 25 '69
HARKER, David
Molecules of molecular biology. por(p32) Phys
Today 22:36 Ag '69
HARKNESS ballet
Another try at the inevitable direction.
J. J. O'Connor. il Dance Mag 43:65-7 N
'69
Dancing in the rain. W. Terry. il Sat R 52:63
O 4 '69
Hail, Harkness, hail! W. Terry. il Sat R 52:
42-3 F 8 '69
Harkness youth dancers; Delacorte theatre,
Central park. J. Anderson. il Dance Mag
43:36-7 N '69
Through the first gate; second New York
season. D. Hering. il Dance Mag 43:34-6+
Mr '69
HARKNESS foundation dance festival. See
Dance festivals
HARLACHER, Ervin L.
Toward excellence? address, February 3, 1969.
Vital Speeches 35:691-5 S 1 '69
HARLEM. See New York (city)—Harlem
HARLEM book company
Publishing scene. D. Dempsey. Sat R 52:33
D 13 '69
HARLEM commonwealth council
Harlem gets down to business. il Bsns W p70-
2 Ag 9 '69
HARLEM prep. See Private schools, Negro
HARLEM school of the arts. See New York
(city)—Education
HARLEY, Rufus
Rufus Harley's black bag. il pors Ebony 24:
101-2+ Jl '69
HARLOW, Bryce Nathaniel
Harlow: primus inter pares. R. B. Semple,
jr. il por N Y Times Mag p8-9 Ag 3 '69
New crisis in leadership. H. Hubbard. il
Newsweek 74:20-2 Jl 14 '69
Where is Pat? J. Osborne. New Repub 161:
15-17 N 29 '69
HARLOW, Lewis A.
How to speed up a hot plate. Pop Sci 195:
143 S '69
HARMAN, Sidney
Specialist at Jervis. S. Margetts. por Duns
R 93:73+ My '69
HARMATZ, Morton G. and Rasmussen, W. A.
Behavior modification approach to head
banging. Ment Hy 53:590-3 O '69
HARMER, Ruth
Poisons, profits and politics. Nation 209:134-7
Ag 25 '69
HARMON, Kenneth E.
Typhoon refurbished. Motor B 123:132-5+ Ja
'69
HARMON, Leon D. and Knowlton, K. C.
Picture processing by computer. bibliog Sci-
ence 164:19-29 Ap 4 '69
—and MacLean, D. J.
Stereo versus the concert hall. Electr World
81:34-6 Ap '69
HARMONIC analysis
Fourier analysis and the structure of DNA.
J. Donohue. bibliog il Science 165:1091-6
S 12 '69
HARMONIC functions
Brownian motion and potential theory. R.
Hersh and R. J. Griego. il Sci Am 220:66-
72+ Mr '69

HARMONY
Third dimension of poetic expression; or, Language and harmony. D. Gostuški. bibliog f il Mus Q 55:372-83 Jl '69
See also
Tonality

HARMOUNT, James Godfrey
Pleasant'st angling. Todays Health 47:56-9+ Mr '69

HARMS, Oliver Raymund
Missouri synod survives strain; 1969. R. Jensen. Chr Cent 86:1072-3 Ag 13 '69
One of the good guys. Chr Cent 86:1077 Ag 13 '69

HARMS, Philip E.
Portable pulse generator. Pop Electr 31:61+ N '69
Squaring with an IC. Pop Electr 31:43-6 Jl '69

HARNACK, Curtis
Film scene at Pula. Nation 209:676+ D 15 '69

HARNESS racing
Baby day at Du Quoin; Lindy's Pride wins Hambletonian. il Newsweek 74:61-2 S 8 '69
Dark horse was trottin' for Haughton; Gayblade at Goshen. W. F. Reed, jr. Sports Illus 31:46 Jl 14 '69
First in Du Quoin, with a second from Rome; Hambletonian day. W. F. Reed, jr. il Sports Illus 31:60+ S 8 '69
High one is hiding out. W. F. Reed, jr. Sports Illus 31:46+ Ag 11 '69
Horseman in the sky; B. Haughton. il Newsweek 73:98 Ap 14 '69
Pops wants to win his own golden anniversary present; 50th year as trainer and driver. E. Avery. W. F. Reed, jr. Sports Illus 30:64-5 Je 16 '69
Raging tempest over trotting; night racing in Hollywood park, Inglewood, Calif. M. Durslag. Sports Illus 30:72+ Ap 21 '69
Seven men on a Hambo horse. W. F. Reed, jr. il Sports Illus 31:40-1 Jl 28 '69
Take the longest way to win; International trot won by French challenger Une de Mai. W. F. Reed, jr. il Sports Illus 31:18-19 S 1 '69
Trials of a boy names Laverne; winner of Little Brown Jug, Delaware, Ohio. W. F. Reed, jr. il Sports Illus 31:70+ S 29 '69
Trot, trot, trot. P. Axthelm. il Travel & Camera 32:62-7 My '69

HARNETT, Ellen
Who moved that tree? House B 111:15+ Ap '69

HARNETT, William Michael
Music and good luck. A. Saarinen. il McCalls 96:90-1 F '69

HARO, Robert P.
Collective action and professional negotiation: factors and trends in academic libraries. por ALA Bul 63:993-6 Jl '69
College libraries for students. por Library J 94:2207-8 Je 1 '69
Overdue. por Wilson Lib Bul 43:561+ F '69
Professional status: the revolt of the nopros. por Wilson Lib Bul 44:555-6 Ja '70

HARPER, Carol L. See Brezonik, P. L. jt. auth.

HARPER, G. B.
New Orleans: '59; poem. Negro Hist Bul 32:27 N '69
Proud: Black lament; poems. Negro Hist Bul 32:7 My '69

HARPER, Harry
Landfall in Maine. Yachting 125:56-7+ Mr '69

HARPER, Robert
Cover materials; excerpts from address, November 1969. Pub W 196:53 D 1 '69

HARPER, Tommy
Highlight. por Sports Illus 30:95 My 19 '69

HARPER, William A.
New junior college president. Sch & Soc 97:120+ F '69

HARPER and Row, publishers, Incorporated
Harper, MARC sponsor urban affairs publishing program. Pub W 195:234 Ja 20 '69

HARPERS FERRY, W.Va.
Lovetts of Harpers Ferry, West Virginia. A. M. Daniel. il Negro Hist Bul 32:14-19 F '69

John Brown raid, 1859
To wash this land in blood. . . S. B. Oates. il Am West 6:24-7+ N '69

HARPSICHORD music
See also
Phonograph records—Harpsichord music

HARRAN, Don
Mannerism in the cinquecento madrigal? bibliog f Mus Q 55:521-44 O '69

HARRELL, Dorothy Tudor
Some button history. Hobbies 74:129 D '69

HARRELSON, Kenneth Smith
Highlight. por Sports Illus 30:100 My 5 '69
—and Hirshberg, Al
Hawk; excerpt. pors Sports Illus 31:54-64+ Jl 14; 22-8 Jl 21 '69

HARRIGAN, Anthony
Letter from Helsinki. Nat R 21:1311-14 D 30 '69

HARRIGAN, Lucille, and Harrigan, Robert
Monomoy, a day on the island. Liv Wildn 33:24-7 Spr '69

HARRIGAN, Robert. See Harrigan, L. jt. auth.

HARRIMAN, William Averell
Ambassador Harriman discusses the Paris talks on Viet-Nam; excerpts from press conference, December 4. 1968. Dept State Bul 59:650-2 D 23 '68
Final report submitted on observance of Human rights year 1968; letter of transmittal, January 30, 1969. Dept State Bul 60:450-1 My 26 '69
Harriman suggests a way out of Vietnam; interview, ed. by H. Smith. pors N Y Times Mag p24-5+ Ag 24 '69
Our security lies beyond weapons. Look 33:37 Ag 26 '69
U.S. gains in the Vietnam war, a top envoy's view; excerpts from address. February 5, 1969. por U S News 66:18 F 17 '69

about
First steps. Commonweal 90:355-6 Je 13 '69

HARRINGTON, John J.
One way to handle crime; interview. por U S News 67:62-5 D 22 '69

HARRINGTON, Lyn
World's end is home for Nan Chauncy. Horn Bk 45:441-5 Ag '69

HARRINGTON, Michael
No half-baked Bacchus from Saginaw. Commonweal 89:656-7 F 21 '69
Politics of Günter Grass. Atlan 223:129-31 Ap '69
Religion and revolution. Commonweal 91:203-4 N 14 '69
Role of compensatory justice. Cur 110:50-1 S '69
What's in a name? New Repub 160:30-2 F 8 '69
Who are the true redeemers? New Repub 160:25-7 Ap 12 '69

HARRINGTON, Michael J.
Bad sign for Nixon. il por Time 94:22 O 10 '69
Turnabout. il por Newsweek 74:36-7 O 13 '69
Vote that went against Nixon. U S News 67:16 O 13 '69

HARRINGTON, Richard
Unknown Niger. il Travel 132:46-9 N '69

HARRINGTON, Stephanie
Enticers, 1970: on TV, who do they think you are? Vogue 155:118+ Ja 15 '70
Passionate rebels. Vogue 153:146-51+ My '69

HARRIS, Albert J.
Research on aspects of comprehension. Ed Digest 34:48-51 Mr '69

HARRIS, Ann
End of November; poem. Ment Hy 53:432 Jl '69

HARRIS, Ann Sutherland
Florentine sunset. Art N 68:32-5+ My '69

HARRIS, Catherine Riegger
Man in nature: model for a new radicalism. Nation 209:496-500 N 10 '69

HARRIS, Chauncy D.
USSR resources for agriculture. bibliog Focus 20:1-7 D '69
U.S.S.R. resources for heavy industry. bibliog Focus 19:1-6 F '69

HARRIS, Cyril C.
Remarkable floribunda. House B 111:109+ Je '69

HARRIS, Dale B.
Can parents and teenagers negotiate? PTA Mag 63:2-5. bibliog(p37) My '69

HARRIS, Doris
Sources of manuscript material. Hobbies 74:139-41 S '69

HARRIS, Dorothy
Our Adirondack pony ranch garden. por Org Gard & Farm 16:61-3 Mr '69

HARRIS, Fred Roy
Mission unaccomplished. Look 33:72 Mr 18 '69
Need for a National social science foundation; remarks. January 22, 1969. Trans-Action 6:3+ My '69
Next election: what party chairmen see as big campaign issues. por Nations Bsns 57:36-7 N '69

about
Nowhere to go but up. il por Time 93:13-14 Ja 24 '69
Party chairmen: ready for battle. por U S News 66:14-15 Ap 28 '69

HARRIS, Fred Roy—about—*Continued*
　Remarkable Mr Harris. C. Mangel. il pors
　　Look 33:75-6+ Mr 18 '69
　Singing in the rain. New Repub 160:10 Ja 25
　　'69

HARRIS, Gerard G. and others
　Receptor potentials from hair cells of the
　　lateral line. bibliog Science 167:76-9 Ja 2
　　'70

HARRIS, Gypsy Joe. See Harris, J.

HARRIS, Janette Hoston
　Haiti, a black government. Negro Hist Bul
　　32:1 O '69
　Long road to where? por Negro Hist Bul 31:
　　16-17 D '68
　Toussaint L'Ouverture; poem. Negro Hist
　　Bul 32:18 O '69

HARRIS, Joe
　Blind man's buff. M. Kram. il por Sports
　　Illus 30:68-72+ Mr 10 '69

HARRIS, John Benton
　Make it happen! J. Scully. Mod Phot 33:
　　74-7 My '69

HARRIS, John M.
　Channel cats on a slack line. Field & S 74:
　　84+ Je '69

HARRIS, Kathryn
　Bicycling through Holland. Mlle 69:195-8+ S
　　'69

HARRIS, Louis
　Crisis in the high schools: the Life poll.
　　Life 66:22-33 My 16 '69
　Life poll. Life 68:102-6 Ja 9 '70

HARRIS, Mark
　Maybe what baseball needs is a Henry David
　　Thoreau. N Y Times Mag p66-7+ My 4 '69

HARRIS, Michael
　California weather breeder. Nation 208:110-13
　　Ja 27 '69

HARRIS, P. and others
　Mosquitoes feeding on insect larvae. Science
　　164:184-5 Ap 11 '69

HARRIS, Ramón I.
　Thomas Jefferson: female identification. bib-
　　liog Am Imago 25:371-83 Wint '68

HARRIS, Richard
　Just for laughs. Look 33:87 Ap 29 '69

HARRIS, Richard (English writer)
　One-man diplomacy? Bul Atom Sci 25:60-5
　　F '69
　—and Brugger, William
　Reader's guide to publications from and on
　　China. Bul Atom Sci 25:84-8 F '69

HARRIS, Richard E.
　Annals of politics. New Yorker 45:63-4+ N
　　8; 64-8+ N 15; 61-4+ N 22 '69

HARRIS, Robert A. and others
　Energized configurations of heart mitochon-
　　dria in situ. bibliog Science 165:700-3 Ag 15
　　'69

HARRIS, Roy Ellsworth
　Music. R. Evett. Atlan 224:160-2 D '69

HARRIS, Roy Vincent
　Surprising talk between a black leader and a
　　top segregationist; ed. by B. Cohn and S.
　　Ball, jr. pors N Y Times Mag p34-5+ Ap 27
　　'69
　　　　　　　about
　Bond on Harris. J. Bond. N Y Times Mag p
　　112 Ap 27 '69

HARRIS, Sheldon
　Meanwhile, back in the Valley. Commonweal
　　90:286-8 My 23 '69
　San Fernando's black revolt. Commonweal 89:
　　549-52 Ja 31 '69

HARRIS, Stephen R.
　Other Harris. il por Time 93:17 F 21 '69
　Pueblo's chief spy. il por Newsweek 73:32 F
　　17 '69

HARRIS, Ted
　Silhouettes. Criticism
　　New Yorker 45:90+ S 20 '69

HARRIS, Theodore Findley
　Crumbling foundation. il por Time 94:60 Jl 25
　　'69

HARRIS, Wilhelmina S.
　Brooks Adams I knew. Yale R 59:50-70 O
　　'69

HARRIS COUNTY, Tex.
　Thirty-four deaths; and 376 confirmed cases
　　of encephalitis; mosquito-control program.
　　R. E. Barnett. il Am City 84:127-8 F '69

HARRISBURG, Pa.
　　　　　　Negroes
　When women fight for freedom. S. Pitzer. il
　　Parents Mag 44:62-3+ Ap '69

HARRISON, Alton, jr. and Scriven, E. G.
　TV and youth. bibliog Clear House 44:82-90
　　O '69

HARRISON, Barbara
　What children learn from living in distant
　　lands. Redbook 132:95+ Ap '69

HARRISON, Charles H.
　Negro in America. Ed Digest 34:13-15 Ja '69

HARRISON, Deloris
　Friend for a season; story. Redbook 133:74-5
　　Ag '69

HARRISON, Gilbert A.
　McCarthy on his campaign. New Repub 161:
　　21-3 O 25 '69

HARRISON, Hal H.
　Wildlife along the Lewis and Clark trail.
　　Nat Wildlife 7:20-9 F '69

HARRISON, Howard
　One street one role; London's Portobello
　　road; photographs. Travel & Camera 32:
　　75-7 Ap '69

HARRISON, Lou
　Lou Harrison: Symphony on G. D. J. Hen-
　　ahhan. il Mus Q 55:285 Ap '69

HARRISON, Robert Emanuel
　Black power in Asia. E. Ramientos, jr. Chr
　　Today 13:40-1 Mr 14 '69

HARRISON, Robert S.
　Tunisia. bibliog Focus 19:1-7 Ja '69

HARRISON, Shirley
　Shoes of the fisherman: the shoes have a
　　new contour. Cath World 208:264-7 Mr '69

HARRISON, Walter A.
　Electrons in metals; adaptation of address,
　　October 1968. bibliog por Phys Today 22:
　　23-31 O '69

HARRISON, William
　Direct approach; story. Redbook 133:88-9 S
　　'69

HARRISS, C. Lowell
　Efficiency in state and local government
　　expenditures. Ann Am Acad 379:39-52 S
　　'68

HARRISS, Robert C. and Troup, A. G.
　Freshwater ferromanganese concretions:
　　chemistry and internal structure. bibliog
　　Science 166:604-6 O 31 '69

HARRITON, Maria
　Chicago has been lucky. Dance Mag 43:22+
　　Ag '69
　Film and dance. Dance Mag 43:42 Ap '69
　Giselle on film. with Fracci and Bruhn.
　　Dance Mag 43:24-7 D '69
　Margaret Dale: TV ambassador. Dance Mag
　　43:24-7 N '69

HARRITY, Richard
　Cardinal Leger. Look 33:37-8+ Jl 29 '69
　Windswept Irish edge of Europe. Look 33:
　　56-68 Mr 18 '69

HARRY S. Truman library, Independence, Mo.
　Harry Truman's Missouri. R. Pearman il
　　Travel 132:56-60+ Ag '69

HARRY, noon and night; drama. See Ribman,
　R.

HART, Alfred A.
　Muscle, the gold, and the iron: documenting
　　the construction of the Central Pacific:
　　stereographs. Am West 6:13-19 My '69

HART, Arch D.
　Nasturtium flower. Horticulture 47:32-3 D '69

HART, George L.
　Winners! Consumer challenge essays. por
　　Har Yrs 9:16 Jl '69

HART, Jack
　Concrete streets constructed in stages. Am
　　City 84:104+ My '69

HART, James MacDougal
　James M. Hart, his mark. E. Gaines. il
　　Antiques 95:852-3 Je; 96:737 N '69

HART, Jeffrey
　Dignity of the South. Nat R 21:340-1 Ap
　　8 '69
　Divided being. Nat R 21:1119+ N 4 '69
　Fitzgerald and Hemingway: the difficult friend.
　　Nat R 21:29-31 Ja 14 '69
　Hemingway: sunlight and night-face. Nat R
　　21:390-1 Ap 22 '69
　Nation-state foundation of civilization. Nat
　　R 21:184-5 F 25 '69
　New class war. Nat R 21:896-901+ S 9 '69
　Proletarianization of culture. Nat R 21:1329-
　　30 D 30 '69
　　　　　　about
　Heartless decision. S. J. Adamo. America
　　120:654-5 My 31 '69

HART, Jerry
　Race against winter; England to Gibraltar.
　　il Yachting 125:62-3+ Mr '69

HART, John
　Staking out a tough turf. il por Newsweek
　　74:94-5 Jl 14 '69

HART, Leslie A.
　Learning at random. Sat R 52:62-3 Ap 19 '69

HART, Philip
　Two Prokofiev symphonies, a logical second
　　and a lyrical fifth. Hi Fi 19:77-8 My '69

HART, Philip A.
　Total landscape of Sleeping Bear Dunes. Am
　　For 75:36-7+ Ja '69
　Your outrageous car-repair bills; inter-
　　view. ed. by H. Shuldiner. por Pop Sci 194:
　　62-5+ Je '69

HART, Robert Mayes
New talents test their mettle. por Bsns W
p36 Ja 3 '70
HART-DAVIS, Duff
Will the Welsh welch on the prince of Wales?
Holiday 45:16+ Je '69
HARTACK, Bill
Royal neck for Bill's fifth; photographs by
J. Cooke and N. Leifer; with account by
W. Tower. Sports Illus 30:14-19 My 12 '69
HARTFORD, John
John Hartford, poet. G. Lees. por Hi Fi 19:124
F '69
HARTFORD, Conn.

City planning

Urban renewal need not be a dirty word;
South Arsenal neighborhood development
corp. E. P. Berkeley. il Arch Forum 130:
36-41 Ap '69

Galleries and museums

See also
Wadsworth antheneum

Gardens

In Connecticut, oldest rose garden we have;
Elizabeth rose garden. il Home Gard 56:
66-7 My '69
**HARTFORD fire insurance company-Interna-
tional telephone and telegraph proposed
merger.** See Business consolidations and
mergers
HARTKE, Vance
Department of peace. Commonweal 89:631-2
F 21 '69
HARTKOPF, Roy
Printed circuits path of least resistance.
Pop Electr 30:63-4+ Je '69
HARTLAGE, Lawrence C. and others
Expediting admissions procedures. bibliog
Ment Hy 53:71-7 Ja '69
HARTLEY, Anthony
Antimilitarism can be too much of a good
thing. N Y Times Mag p30-1+ O 19 '69
HARTLEY, Ellen. See Hartley, W. jt. auth.
HARTLEY, Fred Lloyd
Maybe a few nuts. New Repub 160:8-9 F
22 '69
Tale of the birds. Newsweek 73:58+ Mr 3 '69
HARTLEY, Harry J.
Limitations of systems analysis. Ed Digest
35:28-31 O '69
HARTLEY, Russell
Through dance's open door. Dance Mag 43:
29-31 N '69
HARTLEY, William, and Hartley, Ellen
Gyotaku: ancient Japanese art of fishprint-
ing. Sci Digest 66:28-31 D '69
Light and your health. Pop Sci 194:78-80+
F '69
Science can change the color of your skin.
Sci Digest 66:45-9+ N '69
Transplant that saved my baby's life. Red-
book 132:76-7+ Mr '69
HARTLINE, Daniel K. and Cooke, I. M.
Postsynaptic membrane response predicted
from presynaptic input pattern in lobster
cardiac ganglion. bibliog Science 164:1082-
2 My 30 '69
HARTLINE, Haldan Keffer
Visual receptors and retinal interaction. Sci-
ence 164:270-8 Ap 18 '69
HARTLINE, Peter H. and Campbell, H. W.
Auditory and vibratory responses in the mid-
brains of snakes. bibliog Science 163:1221-3
Mr 14 '69
HARTMAN, Boyd K. and others
Chloramphenicol: effects on mouse myeloma
cells in tissue culture. bibliog Science 165:
297-8 Jl 18 '69
HARTMAN, Chester W. and Carr, Gregg
Housing the poor. bibliog pors Trans-Action
7:49-53 D '69
HARTMAN, Daniel S.
Florida's manatees, mermaids in peril. por
Nat Geog 136:342-53 S '69
HARTMAN, Elizabeth
Daydreamer talks; interview. ed by E. Miller.
pors Seventeen 27:130-1+ N '68
HARTMAN, Geoffrey
Sicilian sketch; poem. New Repub 161:33 N
29 '69
Wordsworth. Yale R 58:507-25 Je '69
HARTMAN, J. E.
Nature's kleptomaniac, the pack rat. Nat
Wildlife 7:22-3 Ag '69
HARTMAN, Morris N.
Annulment of marriage. Ann Am Acad 383:
89-100 My '69
HARTMAN, Sylvia
Newton school-lunch caper. McCalls 96:88+ S
'69
Should wives work? McCalls 96:57-8+ F '69

HARTMANN, Erich
Gallery; photographs. Life 67:12-13 S 19 '69
HARTMANN, William K.
Action at Orion; with biographical sketch.
por Natur Hist 78:4, 90-3 F '69
HARTUNG, Philip T.
Screen. See issues of Commonweal
HARTZOG, George B. jr
Let's save the Buffalo River. Parks & Rec
4:12-15+ Ag '69
National parks. Am West 6:4-5 S '69
Over the years with the National park ser-
vice. Nat Parks 43:13-14+ My '69
Parks are yours, take them home with you.
Travel & Camera 32:37 Je '69
HARVARD center for international affairs.
See Harvard university—Center for inter-
national affairs
**HARVARD center for Italian renaissance cul-
ture.** See Harvard university
HARVARD law school. See Harvard univer-
sity—Law school
**HARVARD school of education's pre-school
project.** See Harvard university—Graduate
school of education
HARVARD square. See Cambridge, Mass.
HARVARD university
Academic calm of centuries broken by a ram-
page; with photographs by Loengard. Life
66:24-35 Ap 25 '69
And now, Harvard. New Repub 160:6-7 Ap
26 '69
Black studies at Harvard; personal reflec-
tions concerning recent events. H. Rosov-
sky. Am Scholar 38:562-72 Aut '69
Buckle down, John Harvard. H. Cox. Com-
monweal 90:22-4 My 9 '69
Bust at Harvard. il Newsweek 73:102-3 Ap 21
'69
Calming the furor? program in Afro-Amer-
ican studies. il Sr Schol 94:14-15 F 7 '69
Campus spring offensive. il Newsweek 73:66-7
Ap 28 '69
Can hip Harvard hold that line? agreement
to merge with Radcliffe. il Time 93:57-8+
Mr 14 '69
Confrontation with a Harvard son. J. Krie-
ger. McCalls 96:97+ Ag '69
Diplomatic post. Newsweek 74:55 S 1 '69
Do you have to be black to teach black
courses? Newsweek 73:59 F 10 '69
Fair Harvard; proposals for Afro-American
studies. Newsweek 73:56 F 3 '69
Fairly old grad ('55) looks at Harvard (in
'69) J. A. Lukas. il N Y Times Mag p28-
9+ Je 8 '69; Discussion. p2+ Je 29 '69
Flare-up in campus revolt, a crucial test at
Harvard. il U S News 66:41-3 Ap 28 '69
Goodbye, Harvard; June commencement. D.
R. Papke. Commonweal 91:13-15 O 3 '69;
Reply. D. P. Nicastro. 91:197+ N 14 '69
Harvard ablaze. R. B. Griffin. America 120:
586-8 My 17 '69
Harvard and beyond: the university under
siege. il Time 93:47-8+ Ap 18 '69
Harvard and the police. W. F. Buckley, jr.
Nat R 21:454-5 My 6 '69
Harvard: faculty organizes in response to
crisis. M. W. Oberle. Science 165:49-51 Jl
4 '69
Harvard is also a summer school. S. Lerner.
il Holiday 46:16-19 Jl '69
Harvard on my mind. M. Holroyd. Harper
239:69-72 Ag '69
Harvard yard. New Yorker 45:33-5 Ap 19 '69
Harvard's answer to radicals; text of a
resolution adopted by faculty of arts and
sciences, June 9, 1969. U S News 66:91 Je
23 '69
Harvard's three cultures; Henry J. Friendly
committee proposals. Newsweek 74:77 S 29
'69
Hasty pudding à la Billy Wilson; dancer
directing famed Harvard troupe. il Ebony
24:134-6+ Mr '69
Hippies vs. Harvard à la Berkeley; in Forbes
plaza. U S News 67:11 S 8 '69
If Harvard can't hold the line. . ; interview.
S. M. Lipset. U S News 66:42-3 Ap 28 '69
Into the center ring. Nation 208:524-5 Ap 28
'69
Is I Tatti the keeper of the flame? Harvard
center for Italian renaissance culture. S.
Alexander. il Holiday 46:36-7+ S '69
Is this your university? law, or disorder;
address, April 27, 1969. A. Capp. Vital
Speeches 35:634-6 Ag 1 '69
Moralists against managers. F. G. Hutchins.
Atlan 224:53-6 Jl '69
New campus troubles; a final fling, or. . . il
U S News 66:8 Ap 21 '69
Opposition to war put on record. M. Mueller.
Science 166:352 O 17 '69

HARVARD university—*Continued*
President Pusey and the Harvard radicals
deserve one another. A. S. Kaufman. N Y
Times Mag p 140 My 4 '69
Un-fair Harvard? Faculty report surveys
university-city relations. R. J. Samuelson.
Science 163:658-61 F 14 '69
Universities: a new balance of power; change
at Harvard. il Time 93:42+ Ap 25 '69
Veeck vs. Harvard. Newsweek 74:40 D 29 '69

Anecdotes, facetiae, satire, etc.
Excellence of Welby Stitch jr. R. Baker.
Life 66:24 Mr 21 '69

Arnold arboretum
Arnold arboretum. S. Sutton. il Horticulture
47:20-1+ Je '69

Center for international affairs
Kickoff at Harvard; raid on the Center for
international affairs. H. Cox. Commonweal
91:64-5 O 17 '69

Fogg museum
Daumier's great city; Daumier sculpture ex-
hibition. D. L. Shirey. il Newsweek 73:96
My 19 '69

Graduate school of art and sciences
Harvard graduate school: the elite response
to enrollment pressures. M. Mueller. Science 165:480-2 Ag 1 '69

Graduate school of business administration
Harvard MBAs of '49 assess their twenty
years; 20th reunion. il Bsns W p62+ Je 14
'69

Graduate school of design
Harvard graduate school of design. il Arch
Forum 131:62-7 D '69

Graduate school of education
Gloom at the top; Advanced administrative
institute. P. Schrag. il Sat R 52:50-1+ Ag
16 '69
Why some three-year-olds get A's; and some
get C's; pre-school project. M. Pines. il
N Y Times Mag p4-5+ Jl 6 '69

Law school
Faculty offices and library. il Arch Rec 145:
136-7 Je '69

HARVEY, James
View from Cuba. Commonweal 91:351-61 D
19 '69

HARVEST festivals. See Festivals
HARVEST labor. See Farm labor
HARVESTING
Harvesting on time pays. C. E. Sommers. il
Suc Farm 67:25 Jl '69
Latest ideas on harvesting livestock feed. D.
Malena. il Suc Farm 67:45 Jl '69
See also
Grain—Harvesting
Threshing

HARVESTING machinery
Combine adjustment, corn, beans. Suc Farm
67:33 Jl '69
How to have a new combine every year. W.
Messerly. Suc Farm 67:49 S '69
Mechanical harvesting of food. J. H. Levin.
bibliog il Science 166:968-74 N 21 '69

HARVEY, Frank
Doctor Grosse and his wonderful bubble
machine. Pop Sci 195:60-3 N '69

HARVEY, George
American land as it was; paintings. Am
Heritage 21:17-21 D '69

HARVEY, Marian
Papier maché a la mode. Am Artist 33:38-41
F '69

HARVEY, Mose L.
Lunar landing and the U.S.-Soviet equation.
por Bul Atom Sci 25:28-32+ S '69

HARVEY, Ronald G.
Migratory habits of the scientific goose. Science 163:764-5 F 21 '69

HARVEY, William
Eighteen minute verdict. M. Polner. Commonweal 90:40-3 Mr 28 '69

HARVEY, William B.
Don't let size keep your waterworks from
using EDP. Am City '84:95-6+ D '69

HARVEY aluminum, incorporated
Harvey's battle in the fjords. B. Caplan. il
Duns R 94:91+ S '69

HARWIT, Martin. See Houck, J. R. jt. auth.

HARWOOD, Alan E.
Reduction firing for the classroom. Sch Arts
68:40-1 Ap '69

HARWOOD, Charles E.
Suspension: a valid disciplinary tool? bibliog f
Clear House 44:29-32 S '69

HARWOOD, Raymond C.
Harwood named chairman of Franklin book
programs. por Pub W 196:249 Ag 25 '69

HASHIMOTO, Hideo
Concept of grace in Jodo Shin Buddhism.
Chr Cent 86:318-19 Mr 5 '69

HASHIMOTO, Toru. See Katsuki, Y. jt. auth.

HASHISH. See Marijuana

HASIDISM
Jewish view of redemption: Buber's hallow-
ing the everyday. C. R. Shaffer. Commonweal 90:512-15 Ag 22 '69; Discussion 90:574-5
S 19 '69

HASKELL, Arnold L.
Leonide Massine: an appreciation. Dance Mag
43:40-53 N '69

HASKETT, Thomas R.
Audio equalization curves up-to-date. Electr
World 82:44-6 D '69
JFETS: how they work, how to use them.
Radio-Electr 40:23-6 My '69
MOSFET's. Radio-Electr 40:33-6 N '69 (to
be cont)
Tools for electronics. See issues of Radio-
electronics
Truth about FM. Electr World 82:37-40+ Ag
'69

HASKIN, Harold H. See Hamwi, A. jt. auth.

HASLEY, Louis
Seminary mass; poem. Cath World 210:164 Ja
'70

HASS, Robert
San Pedro road; Lines on last springs; Failure
of buffalo to levitate; pomes. Poetry 114:
12-14 Ap '69

HASSAM, Childe
Banner years; paintings. Am Heritage 20:54-9
Je '69

HASSEL, Odd
Nobel laureates in economics, chemistry, and
physics. E. L. Eliel. por Science 166:718-20
N 7 '69
Nobel prizes. por Sci N 96:421-2 N 8 '69

HASSELBLAD cameras. See Cameras

HASSENGER, Robert
Conflict in the Catholic colleges. bibliog f
Ann Am Acad 382:95-108 Mr '69
Reformation of the Catholic college. Sat R
52:47-9+ Jl 19 '69

HASSID, W. Z.
Biosynthesis of oligosaccharides and polysaccharides in plants. bibliog Science 165:
137-44 Jl 11 '69

HASSOCKS. See Cushions

HASTINGS, Warren
Trial of Warren Hastings. A. Nevins. il pors
Horizon 11:110-15 Wint '69

HASTY Pudding shows. See College and school
drama

HATCH, James V.
Left theatre in India. Nation 208:804-6 Je
23 '69

HATCH, John
Black studies: the real issue. Nation 208:755-8
Je 16 '69; Excerpts. Cur 109:33-8 Ag '69

HATCH, Robert
Films. See issues of Nation
Theater (cont) Nation 208:837 Je 30 '69

HATCH act. See Government employees—Political activities

HATCHER, Richard Gordon
Black role in urban politics. Cur Hist 57:287-
9+ N '69

about

City: black power in office. por Time 93:27
F 28 '69
Gary, Indiana. M. Frady. il Harper 239:38-45
Ag '69
Gary presses a claim. il por Bsns W p40-1 Ag
23 '69
Hatcher of Gary faces a revolt. il Bsns W
p40-1 Ap 19 '69

HATFIELD, G. Wesley, and Burns, R. O.
Ligand-induced maturation of threonine
deaminase. bibliog Science 167:75-6 Ja 2 '70

HATFIELD, Mark Odom
Noise; address, October 8, 1969. Vital Speeches
36:130-3 D 15 '69
Senator Hatfield argues that the draft is
wrong; a volunteer army is the answer.
N Y Times Mag p34-5+ Mr 30 '69
United States-China relations; address, January 24, 1969. Vital Speeches 35:322-6 Mr
15 '69

about

John Brown's student body. Chr Today 14:
43 N 21 '69

HATHAWAY, Henry
No pro like an old pro. A. Knight. Sat R
52:31 Je 21 '69

HATHAWAY, John C. and Degens, E. T.
Methane-derived marine carbonates of pleistocene age. bibliog Science 165:690-2 Ag 15 '69
HATHAWAY, Lodene Brown
Assignment; poem. Chr Cent 86:977 Jl 23 '69
HATHAWAY, Dame Sibyl Mary (Collings) Beaumont
Nothing like a dame. il por Time 94:34 Ag 8 '69
Sibyl of Stark. il por Newsweek 74:33 Ag 11 '69
HATHORN, Isabel V.
Middle Eastern library workshop: report from Beirut. por Wilson Lib Bul 43:1002-7 Je '69
HATS
Big brim, the big news; mens hats. il Vogue 153:143 My '69
Bowler butts; Lock & co, birthplace of the bowler. H. Van Ketel. il Travel & Camera 32:10 My '69
HATS. Doll. See Doll clothes
HATT, Harold E.
Mystery of death and the problem of transplants. Chr Cent 86:441-4 Ap 2 '69
HATTERAS NATIONAL SEASHORE, CAPE. See Cape Hatteras National Seashore Recreational Area
HATTERSLEY, Ralph
Hattersley class. See issues of Popular photography
Nature montages. Pop Phot 64:98-9+ My '69
HAUGHEY, John C.
Black Catholicism. America 120:325-7 Mr 22 '69
Black sisters become soul sisters. America 121:67 Ag 2 '69
Black theology. America 120:583 My 17 '69
Detroit: evolution of a revolution. America 120:475-8 Ap 19 '69
Forman box score. America 120:689 Je 14 '69
Future for contemplatives? America 121:261-4 O 4 '69
Papal infallibility revisited. America 119:592-4; 120:345 D 7 '68, Mr 29 '69
Priesthood. America 122:18-20 Ja 10 '70
U.S. Bishops' conference November, 1969. America 121:525-6 N 29 '69
—and Campion, D. R.
Bishops' conferences past and present. America 121:327-30 O 18 '69
HAUGHT, Alan
Laser-made plasmas. D. E. Thomsen. il Sci N 95:384-5 Ap 19 '69
HAUGHTON, Billy
Dark horse, was trottin' for Haughton. W. F. Reed, jr. Sports Illus 31:46 Jl 14 '69
Horseman in the sky. il por Newsweek 73:98 Ap 14 '69
HAUGHTON, Daniel Jeremiah
Courage to compete; excerpts from address. Aviation W 90:21 Ap 14 '69

about

For Lockheed, everything's coming up unkunks. H. B. Meyers. il Fortune 80:76-81+ Ag 1 '69
Two old friends who worked their way to first class. il por Fortune 80:80-1 Ag 1 '69
HAUGHTON, James
James Haughton wants 500,000 more jobs. M. K. Sanders. il por N Y Times Mag p30-1+ S 14 '69
HAUGHTON, Rosemary
Signs of the times. See issues of Catholic world
HAUPERT, John S.
United Arab Republic. bibliog Focus 19:1-8 Mr '69
HAUPPAUGE, N.Y.
Hauppauge: senior high school, Long Island. H. Deutsch. il ALA Bul 63:257-60 F '69
HAUPT, Christopher Lehmann-. See Lehmann-Haupt, C.
HAUSE, Richard G.
Teaching: eight parts of a good life. Clear House 44:185-7 N '69
HAUSEN, Peter. See Stein, H. jt. auth.
HAUSER, Ernest O.
Nero: history's most spectacular tyrant. Read Digest 95:37-8+ D '69
HAUSER, Rita E.
U.S. brings Hanoi's treatment of American prisoners of war to attention of U.N. committee; statements, November 11 and 12, 1969. Dept State Bul 61:471-6 D 1 '69
HAUSMAN, Leonard J.
Welfare tax rate; excerpt from Public and private manpower policies, ed. by A. Weber and others. por Trans-Action 6:48-53 Ap '69
HAUTZIG, Esther
To each his own. book. por Pub W 195:124-5 F 17 '69

HAVANA
Description
Visit to Cuba. K. Witker. Vogue 154:92+ O 1 '69
HAVANA university. See Colleges and universities—Cuba
HAVASU LAKE
See also
Lake Havasu City, Ariz.
HAVASUPAI Indians
Squalor amid splendor. il Time 94:21 Jl 11 '69
HAVEL, Vaclav
Increased difficulty of concentration. Criticism Nation 209:703-4 D 22 '69
New Yorker 45:116+ D 13 '69
HAVEMANN, Ernest
How to plan a successful vacation. Read Digest 94:99-102 Ap '69
HAVENS, Richie
Richie Havens: coffee house favorite becomes college crowd's folk rock star. D. E. Bogle. il pors Ebony 24:101-2+ My '69
HAVERFORD college, Haverford, Pa.
Musical events; Donald Swann's Perelandra. W. Sargeant. New Yorker 45:196+ D 6 '69
HAVERS, Ronald W. Lamont-. See Lamont-Havers, R. W.
HAVIGHURST, Robert J.
Metropolitanism and the schools. Ed Digest 34:3-6 Ap '69
HAVILAND, Robert P.
Space broadcasting; how, when, and why. Bul Atom Sci 25:39-42 Mr '69
HAVLICEK, John
Here comes Hondo! H. L. Masin. por Sr Schol 94:19 Mr 14 '69
HAWAII
Trapped in a mystique. W. L. Abbott. Nation 208:146-9 F 3 '69
See also
Airlines—Hawaii
Aviation—Hawaii
Chinese in Hawaii
Festivals—Hawaii
Geology—Hawaii
Haleakala National Park
Honolulu
Hotels, taverns, etc.—Hawaii
Kauai (island)
Kilauea (crater)
Land—Hawaii
Maui (island)
Mauna Kea
Sports—Hawaii
Tourist trade—Hawaii
Bibliography
Hawaii books. Sunset 143:30+ D '69
Capitol
Between mountain and sea. il Time 93:18-20 Mr 21 '69
Hawaii state capitol: beautiful and unique and fitting. il Arch Rec 145:118-23 My '69
Description and travel
Avoiding the madding crowd in Hawaii. Bsns W p 141-2 O 18 '69
Beautiful life in Hawaii, J. Weldon. il Vogue 155:126-7+ Ja 15 '70
Hawaii, go back to a new grass shack. B. Ottum. il Sports Illus 32:30-4+ Ja 12 '70
Hawaii: paradise in peril? G. Zimmermann and F. Trippett. il Look 33:23-32 Ap 29 '69
Hawaii '69: beauty and the bulldozer. S. C. S. Stone. il Sat R 52:51-2+ S 13 '69
Outer Hawaiian Islands. R. Carson. il Holiday 46:56-61+ O '69
Economic conditions
Fiftieth state: still soaring, but—. il U S News 67:70-3 N 10 '69
History
Endless summer, 1779. il Am Heritage 20:112 Ag '69
Industries
Hawaii: paradise in peril? G. Zimmermann and F. Trippett. il Look 33:23-32 Ap 29 '69
Social life and customs
See also
Hula (dance)
HAWAII. University, Honolulu
Department of dance
See Hawaii. University, Honolulu—Department of music and drama
Department of music and drama
Dance department with the aloha spirit. M. Brodsky. il Dance Mag 43:62-5 D '69
HAWAIIAN ISLANDS national wildlife refuge. See Wildlife sanctuaries—Society Islands

HAWAIIAN Open tournament. See Golf—Tournaments

HAWES, Elizabeth
Lady who marries the best people. McCalls 96:64-5+ Je '69

HAWES, Evelyn
I loved the way you described Aunt Mary. . . Writer 82:15-16+ Mr '69

HAWES, Richard D.
River-fed wells and new filter plant. Am City 84:119-21+ My '69

HAWK, David
Old and the young say no. M. McGrory. America 120:555 My 10 '69

HAWK, James
Control of R.F. interference. Electr World 82:41-3 D '69
Tape-recorder wow and flutter. Electr World 81:36-7+ Je '69

HAWK, Richard L.
Have turnips the year-round. Org Gard & Farm 16:52-3 Mr '69
Let us grow more lettuce. Org Gard & Farm 16:44-5 My '69
Radishes round the calendar. Org Gard & Farm 16:43-5 D '69

HAWKERS. See Peddlers and peddling

HAWKES, Alex Drum
World of vegetable cookery; excerpts. Ladies Home J 86:112-13+ S '69

HAWKES, John
Nightmare world of John Hawkes. W. Schott. Life 67:22 S 19 '69

HAWKINS, Barbara A.
How one city teaches sex education and family life. PTA Mag 63:24-6 Je '69

HAWKINS, Coleman
Farewell to the Hawk. il por Time 93:86+ My 30 '69
Obituary
New Yorker 45:27-8 My 31 '69

HAWKINS, Connie
Coming-out party for Lew and Connie. T. Maule. il por Sports Illus 31:26-7 O 6 '69
$1 million end to an unjust exile. D. Wolf. il pors Life 66:67 Je 27 '69
Two big men. il por Newsweek 74:108 N 3 '69
Unjust exile of a superstar. D. Wolf. il pors Life 66:52-52B+ My 16 '69

HAWKINS, E. T. and others
Were Molly Rodman's dice loaded? McCalls 97:93+ O '69

HAWKINS, Edwin
Back to God. il por Time 93:52 My 23 '69

HAWKINS, Erick
Erick Hawkins dance company Brooklyn academy of music. J. Anderson. Dance Mag 43:78 Ja '69
Erick Hawkins dance co; Theatre of the Riverside church. J. Anderson. Dance Mag 43:74+ D '69

HAWKINS, Gordon. See Morris, N. jt. auth.

HAWKINS, Harold L.
Next step? Teachers select principals. bibliog Clear House 44:169-73 N '69

HAWKINS, James W. Jr, and Whetten, J. T.
Graywacke matrix minerals: hydrothermal reactions with Columbia River sediments. bibliog Science 166:868-70 N 14 '69

HAWKINS, Roberta
Taste of summer Sweden. Sr Schol 94:School Teach 21-2 F 28 '69

HAWKRIDGE, Cornelius
For profiteers, what a lovely war. E. McCulloch. il por Life 67:46-8+ Ag 1 '69

HAWKS
See also
Falcons
Kestrels
Ospreys

HAWKS (basketball team) See Basketball teams

HAWN, Goldie
Girls from L-L. por Newsweek 73:62 Ja 27 '69
Goldie rush. T. Burke. por McCalls 97:81+ O '69
Goofy little Goldie. B. Rollin. il pors Look 33:75-6+ D 2 '69
People are talking about . . . por Vogue 153: 192-3 My '69

HAWTHORNE, Nathaniel
Feathertop; dramatization. See Thane, A.

about
Arthur Miller's The crucible and Nathaniel Hawthorne: some parallels. D. M. Bergeron. Engl J 58:47-55 Ja '69
Sins of the fathers; Hawthorne's psychological themes, by F. Crews. Review
Trans-Action 6:74-7 S '69. A. Rothenburg
To conceive of the devil. S. Scoville. Engl J 58-673-5 My '69

HAY, John
Little auk! Little auk! excerpt from In defense of nature. Audubon 71:13-15 Ja '69
Pace of the tides; excerpt from In defense of nature. Audubon 71:26-7 Mr '69
Sea of survival; excerpt from In defense of nature. Audubon 71:40-51 My '69
Shape of water; excerpts from defense of nature. Audubon 71:16-26 Jl '69

HAY rides. See Hayrack rides

HAYAISHI, Osamu, and Nozaki, Mitsuhiro
Nature and mechanisms of oxygenases. bibliog Science 164:389-96 Ap 25 '69

HAYAKAWA, Samuel Ichiyé
Gangsters cash in on student revolt; interview. por U S News 66:38-41 F 24 '69
Our son Mark. il por McCalls 97:78-9+ D '69
Permanence for Hayakawa. por Time 94:53 Jl 18 '69

about
Battle for a college. L. Litwak; J. H. Bunzel. il Look 33:61-2+ My 27 '69
Bonus for bushido. il por Time 93:25 My 23 '69
Containment and counterattack. Nat R 21: 215-16 Mr 11 '69
Cracks in the coalition. J. R. Coyne, jr. Nat R 21:166-7 F 25 '69
Doctor Hayakawa in thought and action. E. Shorris. il por Ramp Mag 8:38-42 N '69
Hayakawa, folk hero or enigma? P. J. Sammon. America 120:10-12 Jl 5 '69
Hayakawa on stage. New Repub 160:9 F 15 '69
No passing grade for Hayakawa. P. J. Sammon. Commonweal 90:405-6 Je 27 '69
San Francisco state. A. J. Langguth. il Harper 239:99-100+ S '69
Siege of San Francisco state. J. R. Coyne, jr. Nat R 21:67-8 Ja 28 '69
Styles of handling student demonstrations. M. Selk. il Bul Atom Sci 25:36-8 Je '69

HAYDÉE, Marcia
Heyday for Haydée. pors Newsweek 74:95 Jl 7 '69

HAYDEN, Don E. See Shillinglaw, D. jt. auth.

HAYDEN, H. W. and others
Superplastic metals; with biographical sketches. Sci Am 220:14, 28-35 bibliog(p 148) Mr '69

HAYDEN, Mike
Backpack jackpot. Outdoor Life 144:56-9+ O '69

HAYDEN, Page, and Lindberg, R. G.
Circadian rhythm in mammalian body temperature entrained by cyclic pressure changes. bibliog Science 164:1288-9 Je 13 '69

HAYDEN, Thomas Emmett
Metamorphosis in S.D.S. the new left is showing its age. T. R. Brooks. il por N Y Times Mag p 14-15+ Je 15 '69

HAYDEN planetarium. See Planetariums

HAYDN, Franz Joseph
Arturo Toscanini society's initial release. C. J. Luten. Am Rec G 35:615 Ap '69
Colin Davis: a man for The seasons. H. C. R. Landon. Hi Fi 19:73-4 Jl '69
Davis's English-speaking Seasons. I. Kolodin. Sat R 52:49 Je 28 '69
Four recordings of Haydn's The creation. S. Lincoln. il Am Rec G 35:610-14 Ap '69
Haydn & friends. J. Diether. Am Rec G 35: 647-8 Ap '69
Pair of early cello concertos, luminously performed. P. H. Lang. Hi Fi 19:92 S '69
Treasure for Haydn seekers. S. Lowe. Hi Fi 19:84 Ag '69
Two albums from Philips: Haydn and Berlioz by Colin Davis. J. W. Barker. il Am Rec G 35:936-8 Je '69
Unhesitatingly recommended: Leinsdorf's Haydn. M. N. Kanny. Am Rec G 35:406+ Ja '69

HAYDN, Hiram
Henry A. Murray. Am Scholar 39:123-36 Wint '69

HAYDN, Johann Michael
That other (M.) Haydn. M. N. Kanny; J. W. Barker. Am Rec G 35:562 Mr '69

HAYDN, Michael
Age of business; poem. Am Scholar 38:405 Sum '69

HAYES, C. R.
Light up and flame out. Flying 85:66 S '69

HAYES, Dea Ann
Now or forever; story. Seventeen 29:78-9 Ja '70

HAYES, Edward L.
Criteria for curricula. Chr Today 13:42-3 F 28 '69

HAYES, Jim
Jig-saw sculpture. Design 70:12-13 mid-Wint '69

HAYES, Larry K. and Henderson. O. F.
Oklahoma consortium strikes it rich. Am Ed 5:26 Mr '69

HAYES, Melvin L.
Teacher power; key to a better tomorrow. Sch & Soc 97:40-1 Ja '69

HAYES, Peter
Muse of Newark; story. Atlan 223:76-80 Ap '69

HAYES, Robert H.
Qualitative insights from quantitative methods. bibliog f Harvard Bsns R 47:108-17 Jl '69

HAYES, Samuel L. 3d, and Reiling, H. B.
Sophisticated financing tool; the warrant. bibliog f Harvard Bsns R 47:137-43+ Ja '69

HAYES, Wayne Woodrow
Reincarnation of Woody Hayes. W. B. Furlong. il pors Life 67:51-2+ N 21 '69

HAYES, Woody. See Hayes, W. W.

HAYLOCK, E. F.
Admiral's cup. Motor B 124:82+ N '69
1851 re-enacted. Motor B 123:110+ Ap '69
Look at Holland. Yachting 126:56-7+ D '69
Round Britain powerboat race. Motor B 124: 78-9+ N '69
'Round the world, nonstop and singlehanded. Motor B 124:75+ Ag '69

HAYMAN, D'Arcy
Arts and man. UNESCO Courier 22:4-10+ My '69

HAYMAN. Lee Richard
Trial; poem. Engl J 58:251 F '69

HAYMARKET square riot. See Chicago—Haymarket square riot

HAYNES, C. Vance, jr
Earliest Americans. bibliog Science 166:709-15 N 7 '69

HAYNES, Douglas M. and Meilach, D. Z.
Gynecologic examination. Redbook 133:30 My '69

HAYNSWORTH, Clement Furman, 1912-
Another gray man? Newsweek 74:40 Jl 28 '69
Anti-Haynsworth drive; how strong? por U S News 67:18 S 15 '69
As Haynsworth showdown nears. por U S News 67:13 N 3 '69
Countdown on Haynsworth. Newsweek 74:50 N 17 '69
Does it stand up? A. M. Bickel. New Repub 161:13-15 N 1 '69
Ganging up on Haynsworth. il por Bsns W p48 S 6 '69
Haynsworth. Nation 209:162-3 S 1 '69
Haynsworth at home. por Time 94:25 O 24 '69
Haynsworth flap. Nat R 21:1051+ O 21 '69
Haynsworth hassle. il por Time 94:16-17 O O 10 '69
Haynsworth: I'm going to stay on. il por U S News 67:12 D 15 '69
Haynsworth nomination. New Repub 161: 7-8 O 4 '69
Haynsworth of Greenville. M. Frady. il pors Life 67:36-8+ O 31 '69
Haynsworth record. il por Time 94:54 O 17 '69
Haynsworth showdown. por Time 94:27 N 14 '69
Haynsworth taint. New Repub 161:11 O 25 '69
Haynsworth tragedy. D. Lawrence. U S News 67:88 D 1 '69
Haynsworth under fire. Newsweek 74:76+ O 6 '69
Haynsworth: what the administration's defeat means; with account by C. M. Mathias. il por Time 94:14-16 N 28 '69
Haynsworth's odds; what history shows. il U S News 67:40 O 20 '69
Haynsworth's record as judge: what it could mean for Supreme court. por U S News 67:14 Ag 25 '69
Help for Haynsworth. Newsweek 74:36+ O 27 '69
In Fortas's seat, or shoes? il por Newsweek 74:35-6 O 20 '69
Judge come to judgment. il por Newsweek 74: 36-7 N 24 '69
Jury of his club mates. P. Owens. Nation 209: 462-4 N 3 '69
Making the case for Haynsworth. J. Osborne. New Repub 161:12-13 N 1 '69
Nixon fights back. Nat R 21:1102-3 N 4 '69
Nixon for the defense. Newsweek 74:26 N 3 '69
Nixon's Court. New Repub 161:8-9 Ag 23 '69
Nomination is rejected. il por Newsweek 74:21-4 D 1 '69
Nomination rejected: why, how and by whom. il por U S News 67:32-3 D 1 '69
On Haynsworth; the pro and con. il por U S News 67:12 S 29 '69
Outlook: big vote for Haynsworth. U S News 67:14 O 6 '69

Over the cliff. Time 94:23-4 O 17 '69
Pyrrhic victory? Commonweal 91:294 D 5 '69
Question of ethics. il por Time 94:21-2 S 26 '69
Senate and the Court. America 121:314 O 18 '69
Shadow of a doubt. il por Newsweek 74:35-6 S 29 '69
Sharpie judge. Commonweal 91:4 O 3 '69
Southern justice. il por Time 94:11-12 Ag 29 '69
Southern strategy and southern stigma. il por Life 67:38 N 28 '69
Symbolic logic. Newsweek 74:20 S 1 '69
Time marches on Haynsworth. R. de Toledano. il por Nat R 21:1164-6+ N 18 '69
Toward confirmation. Time 94:22 O 3 '69

HAYRACK rides
Hayride; teen-age group on ride offered by Clove Lake stables, Staten Island. New Yorker 45:28-30 Je 28 '69

HAYWARD, Robert R.
Maximum results from mini-courses. Todays Ed 58:55-7 S '69

HAYWOOD, Spencer
Titan from Olympus. T. Barry. il pors Look 33:86-9+ Mr 4 '69

HAZARDOUS substances
See also
Explosives
Transportation
See also
Gases, Asphyxiating and poisonous—Transportation

HAZELTON, Nika Standen
Delectations. See issues of National review

HAZLITT, Henry
New protectionism. Nat R 21:485-8+ My 20 '69
Welfarism out of control. Nat R 21:903+ S 9 '69

HAZO, Samuel
Countdown; poem. Sat R 52:40 My 3 '69

HAZOR
Hazor's hidden resource. il Time 93:78+ My 16 '69

HE that died of Wednesday; story. See Woods, W. C.

HEACOCK, Charlene
Papuan paradise. por Yachting 125:58-60+ Mr '69

HEACOX, Cecil E.
Charmed circle completed; Catskills trout streams. Outdoor Life 143:80-1+ Ap '69
Charmed circle of the Catskills. por Outdoor Life 143:50-3+ Mr '69

HEAD, Barry
Special vision; story. Redbook 133:80-1 Je '69

HEAD, Josef
Three designers talk about light. Am Home 72:42 O '69

HEAD, Mary
On campus: foreign students at Yale. Mlle 70:165 D '69

HEAD banging
Behavior modification approach to head banging. M. G. Harmatz and W. A. Rasmussen. Ment Hy 53:590-3 O '69

HEAD Start, Project. See Project Head Start

HEADACHE
Headaches. S. Diamond. il Todays Ed 58:63-4 O '69
How headaches happen. il Newsweek 74:80 O 13 '69
Splitting headaches. A. Talmey. Vogue 155: 158-9+ Ja 15 '70

HEADBOARDS. See Beds

HEADE, Martin Johnson
Introducing Martin Johnson Heade; show at the Whitney museum. T. E. Stebbins, jr. il Art N 68:52-3+ D '69

HEADERS. See Automobile engines—Exhaust

HEADGEAR
Art of decorating ourselves; reprint. il UNESCO Courier 22:52-3 Ag '69

HEADLIGHTS, Automobile. See Automobiles—Lighting

HEADLIGHTS, Movable. See Automobiles—Lighting

HEADPHONES. See Earphones

HEADS (engine) See Automobile engines

HEADS of state
Spring and the traveler; the first resorts; a roundup of vacationlands preferred by world leaders; symposium. il Sat R 52:39-42+ Mr 8 '69

HEADSETS. See Earphones

HEAGY, H. Lee
Magnets of fire; poem. Poetry 114:238-41 Jl '69

HEALEY, James S.
Lesson for librarians. por Wilson Lib Bul 43:554-7 F '69

HEALEY, Peter. See Mawdesley-Thomas, L.
E. jt. auth.
HEALING, Divine. See Faith cure
HEALING of wounds. See Wound healing
HEALTH
Exercise for physical fitness. J. A. Lovell,
jr. il Todays Ed 58:16-17 Ap '69
Family health. G. M. Knox. See issues of
Better homes and gardens
Health in the home. A. F. Benjamin. See
issues of American home
Medical marvels: space-age breakthroughs at
AMA convention. il Har Yrs 9:42-5 N '69
Plan a year-round health program; farm
wife's responsibility. il Suc Farm 67:89 F
'69
Questions you don't ask your doctor; with
answers. A. Lake. il Seventeen 27:108-9+
D '68
Today's health news. A. L. Blakeslee. See
issues of Today's health
Twenty-five ways to feel better, look better.
il Vogue 155:100-3 Ja 15 '70
See also
Aged—Care and hygiene
Longevity
Nutrition
Physical education and training
Public health
Sickness
Woman—Health and hygiene

Periodicals
See also
Todays health (periodical)
HEALTH, Mental. See Mental hygiene
HEALTH agencies, Voluntary
What happens to your health handouts? T.
Irwin. il Todays Health 47:20-3+ N '69
HEALTH aides. See School nurses
HEALTH benefit plans. See Insurance, Health
HEALTH centers
Health center with muscles; Hollywood-Wil-
shire district health center. E. McCoy. il
Arch Forum 130:60-3 Mr '69
Stir of hope in Mound Bayou; with editorial
comment, and photographs by H. Bing-
ham. R. Hall. Life 66:3, 66-70+ Mr 28 '69
See also
Mental health centers
HEALTH clinics
How are your genes? genetic counseling cen-
ters. Newsweek 73:90 F 10 '69
Mobile multi-purpose unit; Bergen County's
health bus. il Am City 84:80 F '69
Salud; clinic in Woodville, Calif. Nation 208:
133-4 F 3 '69
HEALTH clubs
Shake and bake; The sanctuary, Hollywood.
il Newsweek 73:104 My 19 '69
HEALTH education
Teaching adolescents about smoking, drinking,
drug abuse. G. M. Hochbaum. Ed Digest
34:28-31 Ja '69
See also
Health agencies, Voluntary
Health exhibits
Health workers—Training
Physical education and training
Television broadcasting—Health education
programs
HEALTH, education and welfare, Department
of. See United States—Health, education
and welfare, Department of
HEALTH examinations. See Physical examina-
tions
HEALTH exhibits
Hall of health puts life into learning. il To-
days Health 47:66-8 My '69
HEALTH fads. See Medical delusions
HEALTH food stores. See Food stores
HEALTH foods. See Food, Organic; Food fads
HEALTH insurance. See Insurance, Health
HEALTH resorts, watering places, etc.
Fountain of youth; Bosnia, Yugoslavia. News-
week 73:90+ My 19 '69
Spas: the healthy way to weekend. il Mlle
69:88-9 Jl '69
Spring and the traveler; the first resorts;
a roundup of vacationlands preferred by
world leaders; symposium. il Sat R 52:39-
42+ Mr 8 '69
Status-spa: La Costa, Calif. il Harp Baz 102:
216-17 Ap '69
HEALTH service. See Medical service
HEALTH superstitions. See Medical delusions
HEALTH workers
Training
Approaches to the mental health manpower
problem. L. J. Cowne. bibliog Ment Hy
53:176-87 Ap '69

HEALTH workers, Volunteer
Volunteers helping families of the mentally
ill. J. P. Cole and W. E. Cole. bibliog Ment
Hy 53:188-95 Ap '69
HEALY, Cletus
For a vote in the vineyards. America 121:482
N 22 '69
HEALY, George Peter Alexander
G.P.A. Healy; success story. F. Lewison. il
por Am Artist 32:54-9+ D '68
HEALY, Paul F.
Girl in Ted Kennedy's car. Ladies Home J
86:66+ O '69
HEALY, Timothy S.
Will everyman destroy the university? Sat
R 52:54-6+ D 20 '69
HEARD, Alexander
Columbia's choice. il por Newsweek 74:64 Ag
4 '69
Columbia's choice. il por Time 94:62 Ag 1 '69
HEARING
Auditory and vibratory responses in the mid-
brains of snakes. P. H. Hartline and H. W.
Campbell. bibliog il Science 163:1221-3 Mr
14 '69
Hearing is a way of touching. J. K. Lage-
mann. Read Digest 95:-107-10 Ag '69
Hearing, single-unit analysis, and vocaliza-
tions in songbirds. M. Konishi. bibliog il
Science 166-1178-81 N 28 '69
See also
Deafness
Ear
Echolocation (physiology)

Testing
How well does your baby hear? M. Kimmel. il
Parents Mag 44:40-1+ Jl '69
HEARING aids
Hearing aids: how to pick one. il Changing
T 23:40-2 My '69
Partial victory in the hearing-aid case; CU
vs VA on hearing aid data. Consumer Rep
34:492 S '69
What you should know about hearing aids.
L. M. Rhodes. il Todays Health 47:40-3+
Ag '69
HEARING loss. See Deafness
HEARN, Norman E. See Iwamoto, D. jt. auth.
HEARST, James
Cry shame; poem. America 121:393 N 1 '69
Home place; poem. Harp Baz 102:96 Ja '69
Wren logic; poem. America 120:531 My 3 '69
HEARST, William Randolph, 1863-1951
Hearst gardens. G. Taloumis. il Horticulture
46:40-3 D '68
HEARST-San Simeon state historical monu-
ment. See California—Parks and reserves
HEART
Abnormalities and deformities
See also
Heart—Surgery
Diseases
Heart and hard water. Sci Am 220:58 Je '69
Heart attack you didn't know you had.
P. Deutsch and R. Deutsch. il Todays
Health 47:42-3+ Jl '69; Same abr. with
title Do you have silent heart disease?
Read Digest 95:93-7 Jl '69
Heart disease linked to aggressive personal-
ity. Todays Health 47:83 Mr '69
Heart-saver squad; St Vincent's hospital and
Medical center, New York. R. H. Berg. il
Look 33:26-9 F 4 '69
Hearts and national origin. H. Gillon. il Sci
N 95:342 Ap 5 '69
Husbands: take care of her heart. R. Bugg.
il Todays Health 47:52-5+ N '69
Manly foods=heart attacks. il Sci Digest 66:
57 D '69
No more heart attacks. R. H. Berg. il Look
33:30-2 F 4 '69; Same abr. with title Heart
attacks can be prevented! Read Digest
94:76-81 Ap '69
Push-button pain reliever; anginal pain. Sci
Digest 65:62-3 Je '69
Saving vital time for victims of heart
attacks; mobile coronary care units. il
Bsns W p96-8+ F 22 '69
Should your family's diet be changed to prevent heart attacks? Good H 168:185-7 My
'69
Soft water and heart disease; worldwide
puzzle. Sci N 95:471 My 17 '69
What heart attacks are & what to do about
them. il Changing T 23:39-41 F '69
Will there soon be a drug that might ultimately prolong your husband's life? L.
Kavaler. Good H 169:112-13+ O '69
Yemenites' exodus; effects of different diets
and ways of life on the heart and arteries
of immigrants in Israel. il Time 93:67 Mr
14 '69

HEART—Diseases—*Continued*

Diagnosis
See also
Electrocardiography

Psychological aspects
Procrastinators. il Newsweek 74:110 D 8 '69

Examination
Heart doctors heed telltale voice; coronary-prone pattern in voice. il Bsns W p 130 My 24 '69

Muscle
Contracture and catecholamines in mammalian myocardium. M. Morad. bibliog il Science 166:505-6 O 24 '69
Rat heart papillary muscles: action potentials and mechanical response to paired stimuli. G. W. Mainwood and S. L. Lee. bibliog il Science 166:396-7 O 17 '69

Rhythm
See Heart beat

Surgery
Call for help from Vietnam; heart of 13-year-old Vietnamese boy restored by patch at Philadelphia Children's hospital. R. H. Berg. il Look 33:24-30+ D 16 '69
Inside the operating room with Dr Michael DeBakey; interview, ed. by L. Tornabene, M. E. De Bakey. il McCalls 96:42+ My '69
My battered heart; pacemaker. M. C. Janes. il Har Yrs 9:19-21 My '69
Nonworking heart tissue removed by surgery. Todays Health 47:76 Mr '69

Transplantation
Brotherhood of borrowed time; heart-transplant clubs. D. Snell. il Life 67:65-6+ O 24 '69
Christiaan Barnard: one life; excerpt. C. Barnard and C. B. Pepper. il McCalls 97:127-34 N '69
Consequences of science; heart transplants: a time to wait. H. B. Taussig. Cur 108:43-5 Je '69
First black man to survive heart transplant. V. J. Bradley. il Ebony 24:82-4+ My '69
Go-ahead for transplants. il Bsns W p70 Ja 10 '70
Heart is a lonely hunter. W. D. Gardner. il Ramp Mag 7:34-8 Je '69
Lactate dehydrogenase isozymes in human cardiac transplantation. J. J. Nora and others. bibliog il Science 164:1079-80 My 30 '69
Natural v. artificial hearts. il Time 93:42 Ap 4 '69
Reassessing transplants; P. Blaiberg's death, C. D. Boulogne's survival. il Newsweek 74:73 S 1 '69
Transplantation of the species. L. Edson. il Esquire 72:168-71+ D '69
Why Blaiberg died. Time 94:34 Ag 29 '69
See also
Heart donors

HEART beat
Ventricular arrhythmias related to antibiotic usage in dogs. T. J. Regan and others. bibliog il Science 165:509-10 Ag 1 '69
See also
Pacemaker, Artificial (heart)
HEART disease. See Heart—Diseases
HEART donors
Tragic shortage of transplant hearts. A. Q. Maisel. Read Digest 95:69-73 Ag '69
HEART massage. See Cardiac resuscitation
HEART muscle. See Heart—Muscle
HEART pump. See Hearts, Artificial
HEARTS, Artificial
Act of desperation; controversy over mechanical heart in H. Karp. il Time 93:58 Ap 18 '69
Artificial heart. Time 93:46 Ap 11 '69
Have a heart. il Newsweek 73:88 Je 23 '69
Heartbeat away from the assembly line; reliable man-made heart. il Bsns W p 130 Je 14 '69
Implanting a stopgap heart. il Sci N 95:375 Ap 19 '69
Instead of a heart, a man-made pump. C. P. Gilmore. il Read Digest 95:241-2+ N '69
Man-made parts for the body; bright future? il U S News 66:11 Ap 21 '69
Man with a plastic heart. il Newsweek 73:128-9 Ap 14 '69
Mechanics of medicine: new tools for mending hearts. K. N. Anderson. il Pop Mech 131:120-3 My '69
Natural v. artificial hearts. il Time 93:42 Ap 4 '69
Too much, too fast? questions raised about D. Cooley's handling of the Haskell Karp case. il Newsweek 73:76+ Ap 21 '69

HEARTZ, Daniel
Genesis of Mozart's Idomeneo. bibliog f Mus Q 55:1-19 Ja '69
HEAT, Waste. See Waste heat
HEAT accumulators. See Heat regenerators
HEAT engines
Dutch on the road to a pollution-free engine; Stirling engine. il Bsns W p52-3 Ja 10 '70
HEAT pollution. See Water pollution
HEAT pumps
Heat pump system combines features of unitary and central approaches. il Arch Rec 146:177-8 O '69
HEAT regenerators
Student body turns it on; heat reclaim system project; Johnstown campus of Pittsburgh university. B. F. Peters. il Am Ed 5:20-1 Ap '69
HEAT resistance of bacterial spores. See Temperature—Physiological effects
HEAT resistant materials
See also
Refractory materials
HEAT resisting materials
See also
Pyroceram
HEAT treatment of steel. See Steel—Heat treatment
HEATERS
How to warm up a chilly room. il Good H 169:274B+ N '69
Tent heaters. il Consumer Rep 34:537-40 S '69
See also
Automobile engines—Heaters
Electric heaters
HEATERS, Water. See Water heaters
HEATH, Aloise Buckley
Trapp family Christmas. Nat R 21:1317-19 D 30 '69

about
Inimitable Aloise. C. Marsh. Nat R 21:812-13 Ag 12 '69
HEATH, Dick
Here's to you, Mr Robinson, the pros love you. M. Mulvoy. por Sports Illus 31:64-5 O 6 '69
HEATH, Edward Richard George
Realism in British foreign policy. For Affairs 48:39-50 O '69

about
Labor's chance: some unlikely Tories. K. Ovenden. Commonweal 91:348-9 D 19 '69
Richard III rides again. Time 94:40 O 17 '69
HEATH, G. Louis
Lodestar international student experiment. Sch & Soc 97:372-4 O '69
Political extra-curricula at Uppsala and California. Sch & Soc 97:223-7 Ap '69
Racial pallor of Cairo. Nation 209:692-5 D 22 '69
HEATH, Ted. See Heath, E. R. G.
HEATHERS
Native American heathers. S. D. Allen. il Horticulture 47:24-5 F '69
HEATING
Ultimate indoor comfort. J. H. Ingersoll. il House B 111:88-9+ F '69
See also
Radiant heating
School buildings—Heating and ventilation

Control
Electronic control keeps home heater on the mark. L. B. Stein, jr. il Pop Sci 195:184-6+ S '69

Costs
Heating bills: a matter of cold statistics. Changing T 23:10 S '69
HEATING equipment
Fixing up an older home. il Bet Hom & Gard 47:38 My '69
Hints for warmer winter farm work. il Suc Farm 67:W4 N '69
How to install new heating ducts. il Mech Illus 65:112-15+ N '69
Update your heating system with fresh air. il Pop Mech 132:190-1 O '69
See also
Electric heaters
Heat pumps
HEAVEN
Promise of paradise. F. Buechner. Chr Cent 86:276 F 26 '69
See also
Future life

HEAVEN grand in amber orbit; musical comedy. See Musical comedies, revues, etc.—Criticisms, plots, etc.

HEAVENLY bamboo. See Nandina
HEAVY-ion accelerators. See Accelerators (electrons, etc)
HEBBLETHWAITE, Peter
Ideology of May '68. Cath World 209:112-14 Je '69
HEBENSTREIT, Pantaleon
Pantaleon's pantalon: an 18th-century musical fashion. S. E. Hanks. bibliog f il Mus Q 55:215-27 Ap '69
HEBERT, Paul J. See Sugg, A. L. jt. auth.
HEBRAISM
Hebraism & Hellenism now. M. Himmelfarb. Commentary 48:50-7 Jl '69; Discussion. 48: 20+ N '69
HEBREW illumination. See Illumination of books and manuscripts
HEBREW language
Hebrew as she is spoke. H. Halkin. Commentary 48:55-60 D '69
HEBREW legends. See Legends, Hebrew
HEBREW literature
See also
Hebrew poetry
HEBREW manuscripts. See Manuscripts, Hebrew
HEBREW poetry
Translations into English
Two poems: My mother once told me; Song of resignation; tr. by A. Gutmann. Y. Amichai. New Yorker 45:42 Mr 22 '69
Two quatrains; tr. by A. Gutmann. Y. Amichai. Mlle 68:146 Mr '69
HEBREW teachers colleges. See Teachers colleges
HEBRIDES
See also
Colonsay (island)
HECHINGER, Fred Michael
Reforming college education. Cur 107:34-5 My '69
HECHLER, Ken
Excerpt from remarks; July 18 and 29, 1968. Cong Digest 48:86 Mr '69
about
Hechler's bridge. K. Crawford. Newsweek 73: 39 Mr 17 '69
HECHT, Anthony
Black boy in the dark; poem. Harper 239:41 Jl '69
HECHT, Ben, and MacArthur, Charles
Front page. Criticism
America 120:673-4 Je 7 '69
America 121:434 N 8 '69
Commonweal 90:437-8 Jl 11 '69
Nation 208:676 My 26 '69
New Yorker 45:112 My 17 '69
Newsweek il 73:133 My 26 '69
Time il 93:75 My 23 '69
HECHT, George J. and McGarry, B. D.
State of the Nation's children. Parents Mag 44:47-9+ Ja '69
HECHT, S. M. and others
Cytokinin of wheat germ transfer RNA: 6-(4-hydroxy-3-methyl-2-butenylamino)-2-methylthio-9-β-D-ribofuranosylpurine. bibliog Science 166:1272-4 D 5 '69
HECHTLINGER, Adelaide
Dandelions: golden heralds of spring. Read Digest 94:31-2+ Ap '69
HECKER, Isaac Thomas
Thoreau and Hecker: freemen, friends, mystics. M. W. Hess. Cath World 209:265-7 S '69
HECKER, Philip C. and Novak, C. T.
Connectors for PC boards. pors Electr World 82:52-5 O '69
HECKSCHER, August
Refuge for people. Travel & Camera 32:49-56 S '69
HECLA mining company
Right package. il Forbes 104:24-5 D 1 '69
HECTOR, Juliann
L'envoi; poem. Mlle 69:244 Ag '69
HEDBERG, Haakan
Challenge rising in the East. por Bsns W p89 N 15 '69
HEDDA Gabler; drama. See Ibsen, H.
HEDGE clippers
Electric hedge and bush trimmers. il Consumer Bul 52:12-16 Ag '69
Hedge trimmer. il Home Gard 56:63 F '69
Two hot new yard tools; chain saw, hedge trimmer. E. F. Lindsley. il Pop Sci 195: 121 Jl '69
HEDGEHOGS
Evolution of neocortex: studies of visual cortex in hedgehogs and tree shrews. I. T. Diamond and W. C. Hall. bibliog il Science 164:251-62 Ap 18 '69

HEDGES, Morris
Thanksgiving; story. Commentary 48:33-49 Jl '69
HEDGES
Pygmy hedges. C. W. Cares. il Horticulture 47:32-3+ Je '69
HEDGING
Best time to hedge live hogs. J. Russell. Farm J 93:44D F '69
Hard times come to the hedge funds. C. J. Loomis. il Fortune 81:100-3+ Ja '70
HEDIN, Mary
Peculiar vision of Mrs Winkler; story. Redbook 133:82-3 My '69
HEDIN, Robert S.
Darkroom sink with a built-in print washer. Pop Mech 131:130-2 Ja '69
Weekend thinwall projects. Pop Mech 132: 164-7 O '69
HEDMAN, Richard
Kindergarten chats. il Arch Forum 130:52-3 Ap '69
HEERAMANECK, Nasli
Treasure from the Orient. il por Time 93:70 Mr 14 '69
HEEREN, Astrid
Ascent of Astrid. J. Hamilton. il pors Look 33:86-8 Ap 1 '69
HEESE, Sister Elizabeth
Do you believe in lesson plans? Clear House 43:492-3 Ap '69
HEEZEN, Bruce C.
Time clock in history. Sat R 52:87-90 D 6 '69
HEFFER, Eric Samuel
Young and angry talent. M. C. Shefftz. Nation 208:720-4 Je 9 '69
HEFFERNAN, Michael
Table; Rage seated; poems. Poetry 114:386-7 S '69
HEFFERS children's bookshop, Cambridge, England. See Booksellers and bookselling—Childrens literature
HEFFNER, Hubert B.
Nixon chooses OST deputy director. P. M. Boffey. por Science 164:1263 Je 13 '69
HEFLIN, Jean
How do you measure up as a member of the united teaching profession? Todays Ed 58: 64-5 Mr '69
HEFNER, Hugh Marston
Hugh Hefner faces middle age. il por Time 93:69-70 F 14 '69
HEGEMONY
Discord of the spheres. J. Burnham. Nat R 21:165 F 25 '69
HEGERMANN-LINDENCRONE, Lillie (Greenough) Moulton
Marvelous Mme Moulton. R. Rushmore. por Opera N 33:6-7 Ap 5 '69
HEIDELBERGER, M. See Dudman, W. F. jt. auth.
HEIDENRY, John
Stage. Commonweal 91:409 Ja 9 '70
Vladimir in dreamland. Commonweal 90:231-4 My 9 '69
HEIDT, Ann
Balloon pots. Ceram Mo 17:26-7 O '69
Optical illusions. Sch Arts 69:17 N '69
HEIFERS
Feeding
See Cattle—Feeding
HEIFETZ, Jascha
Fiddler on the shelf. R. Kahn. il pors Life 67:58B+ O 31 '69
HEIKAL, Mohammed Hassanein
Nasser's pal. il por Time 94:60-1 Jl 25 '69
HEIKKILÄ, Juhana E. Idänpään-. See Idänpään-Heikkilä, J. E.
HEILBRONER, Robert Louis
Priorities for the seventies; excerpt from address. Sat R 53:17-19+ Ja 3 '70
Socialism and the future. bibliog f Commentary 48:35-45 D '69
HEILEMAN, G. brewing company
Battle for survival. Forbes 104:95 S 15 '69
HEILIGENSCHEIN. See Halos (meteorology)
HEILNER, Van Campen
Hero in a sneak box. E. Bowen. il por Sports Illus 31:46-50+ S 1 '69
HEIMPEL, Bill
Marlin lover of Mazatlán. R. F. Jones. il por Sports Illus 30:42-4+ Mr 31 '69
HEIN, Piet
Shorter diving boards; excerpts from Grooks 11. Sat R 52:22-3 O 11 '69
HEINE, Heinrich
Flying Dutchman; dramatization. See Olfson, L.
HEINEKE, Charles D. and Boyer, C. J.
Automated circulation system at Midwestern university. pors ALA Bul 63:1249-54 O '69
HEINEMAN, Nancy
Stay young and beautiful. See issues of Parents' magazine & better family living

HEINEMANN, Arthur
Discoveries by hindsight. Writer 82:20-1+ O '69

HEINEMANN. Eric G. and others
Discriminative control of attention. Science 160:553-4; 164:198 My 2 '68, Ap 11 '69

HEINEMANN, Gustav
Winner Gustav Heinemann. il por Time 93: 40 Mr 14 '69

HEINER, Harold
Community college: counselor to the community? Ed Digest 34:50-2 My '69

HEINER, Lou
Sound sounding. Yachting 125:64-5+ Je; 126: 66+ Jl '69
Which radiotelephone is for you? Motor B 123:236-7+ Ja '69

HEINITZ, Thomas
Other side. See Recordings issues of Saturday review
Tape and the English market. Sat R 52:55 D 27 '69
—See Haddy, A. jt. auth.

HEINOLD, George
Salt water. See issues of Outdoor life

HEINRICHS, Donald F. See Emilia, D. A. jt. auth.

HEINS, Paul, and others
(comp) Booklist (title varies) See issues of Horn book magazine

HEINSHEIMER, Hans W.
Music from the conglomerates. Sat R 52:61+ F 22 '69

HEINSOHN, Tom
Two guys on a Boston hot seat. F. Deford. il por Sports Illus 31:22-5 N 3 '69

HEINZ, H. J, company
New spice; B. Gookin became president of H. J. Heinz. il Forbes 103:64 Ap 15 '69

HEINZE, W. O.
Equal rights for all children. por Parents Mag 44:12 Mr '69

HEISERMAN, David L.
Large-scale integration. Electr World 82:37-40+ D '69
Making water droplets generate electricity. Pop Sci 195:144-5 S '69
Math, doorway to higher pay. Pop Electr 30: 30:67-9+ Mr '69
Solid-state inductor. Electr World 82:37+ S '69
Solid-state LSA microwave diodes. Electr World 81:40+ F '69

HEISMAN memorial trophy. See Trophies, Sport

HEITMAN, Sidney
Shades of Gogol in the 1930s. Sat R 52:50 My 17 '69

HEITMANN, Vera
In praise of garden shredders. Horticulture 47:42+ D '69

HEIZER, Robert F. and Napton, L. K.
Biological and cultural evidence from prehistoric human coprolites. bibliog Science 165:563-8 Ag 8 '69

HELD, Abraham A. and others
Blastocladia and aqualinderella: fermentative water molds with high carbon dioxide optima. bibliog Science 165:706-9 Ag 15 '69

HELD, Edward E. See Beasley, T. M. jt. auth.

HELDE, Thomas T.
Kennedy-Johnson years. Cur Hist 57:31-5+ Jl '69

HELDENTENORS. See Opera singers

HELFER, Ralph
Lion's share. Newsweek 74:53 Ag 25 '69

HELI-Coil corporation
Booby prize. il Forbes 104:89 N 15 '69

HELICOPTER airlines
See also
New York airways incorporated
San Francisco and Oakland helicopter airlines
Washington airways

HELICOPTER association of America
Helicopter hubbub. R. B. Weeghman. Flying 84:68-9 Mr '69

HELICOPTER industry and trade

Canada
LOH production in Canada seen. Aviation W 91:20 S 8 '69

France
Alouette, Super Frelon work continues. il Aviation W 90:252-3 Je 2 '69
French expect 600 sales of SA 341. il Aviation W 90:246-7 Je 2 '69

United States
U.S. pressed to meet helicopter demand. il Aviation W 90:343-4 Je 2 '69

HELICOPTERS
See also
Autogiros

Accidents
National safety board report:
Factors in fatigue failure cited. Aviation W 91:116+ N 17 '69
Fatigue failure cited on S-61L. Aviation W 91:93+ N 10 '69
New disputes flare over Cheyenne. C. Brownlow. Aviation W 91:16-17 O 13 '69

Blades
See Helicopters—Rotors

Design
Army seeks fixes for AH-56 problems. Aviation W 90:18-19 Ap 21 '69
Lear jet sets output goals on helicopter. il Aviation W 91:80+ S 22 '69
New helicopter design shown by Lear jet. il Aviation W 91:34-5 S 15 '69

Electronic equipment
Iroquois night vision system set for use. il Aviation W 91:23-4 Ag 25 '69
Navy flight tests helicopter avionics. Aviation W 91:101 Ag 18 '69

Maintenance and repair
NTSB suggests modifications for Bell JetRanger helicopter; replacement of magnesium tail booms. Aviation W 90:25 Ap 7 '69

Manufacture
Alouette, Super Frelon work continues. il Aviation W 90:252-3 Je 2 '69

Military applications
AH-56 wreckage studied for cause of crash in sea. Aviation W 90:23 Mr 24 '69
AH-56A remains grounded as Lockheed answers army. C. M. Plattner. Aviation W 90: 33 My 5 '69
Army shoots down Cheyenne; cancellation of contract: il Bsns W p34-5 My 24 '69
Dual-mode specifications cited for Mi-12 payloads. Aviation W 90:23 Je 9 '69
Europe reviewing combat helicopter role. il Aviation W 90:250-1 Je 2 '69
Improved HueyCobra readied for marines. E. J. Bulban. il Aviation W 91:20-1 O 27 '69
Iroquois night vision system set for use. il Aviation W 91:23-4 Ag 25 '69
Kaman aims new helicopters at military. D. A. Brown. il Aviation W 90:24-5 F 24 '69
Lockheed contract dropped. il Sci N 95:525 My 31 '69
Lockheed's helicopter fights Pentagon battle; Cheyenne, army's first whirlybird gunship. il Bsns W p42 My 3 '69
Navy seeking off-shelf Lamps helicopter. D. A. Brown. il Aviation W 91:30-3 S 15 '69
New chopper in trouble; army's AH-56A Cheyenne armed helicopter. il Sci N 95:498-9 My 24 '69
Three drone helicopter programs aimed at surveillance, supply. Aviation W 91:24 D 1 '69
Why helicopter losses are up. il U S News 66:17 My 19 '69

Noise
Army quiet helicopter effort aimed at reduction in losses. Aviation W 91:33 S 15 '69

Rotors
Lockheed to test blade sweep, tightened controls on AH-56A. Aviation W 92:17 Ja 5 '70
New disputes flare over Cheyenne. C. Brownlow. Aviation W 91:16-17 O 13 '69
Vertol testing glass fiber rotor blades. W. C. Wetmore. il Aviation W 91:80-1+ Ag 11 '69

Specifications
Leading international rotary-wing aircraft (cont) Aviation W 90:150 Mr 10 '69
U.S. rotary-wing aircraft (cont) Aviation W 90:151 Mr 10 '69

Television apparatus
See Television apparatus on aircraft

Testing
Pilot report:
Bell 205A. R. B. Weeghman. il Flying 85: 60-4 O '69
Enstrom F-28A. R. B. Weeghman. il Flying 85:46-9 S '69

HELICOPTERS, Ambulance
See also
Helicopters in medical service

HELICOPTERS, Business
Copter users seek increases in utilization.
Aviation W 90:230-1 Mr 10 '69
HELICOPTERS, Military. See Helicopters—
Military applications
HELICOPTERS in business
Lear jet sets output goals on helicopter. il
Aviation W 91:80+ S 22 '69
HELICOPTERS in medical service
Help is a helicopter. M. J. Schultz. il Todays
Health 47:20-3+ Ap '69
Interest in air ambulance use increases. N.
S. Himmel. il Aviation W 90:71-2+ Mr 24
'69
Medical unit offers air ambulance plan. Avia-
tion W 91:113+ N 17 '69
HELICOPTERS in police work
Do police helicopters justify their cost?
Project Sky Knight, Los Angeles County,
Calif. H. K. Becker. il Am City 84:70-1 N
'69
Helicopter adds versatility to police work;
Fort Worth, Tex. H. D. McMahon. il Am
City 84:42 O '69
Helicopters cover all; tool to law enforce-
ment, Dade County, Fla. R. L. Shelton.
il Am City 84:41 Jl '69
Powerful searchlight focuses on nighttime
crime. il Am City 84:28 Mr '69
HELICOPTERS in rescue work
Covert night vision aids rescue mission. B.
Miller. Aviation W 91:73-4+ D 1 '69
Marooned at 12,000 feet. E. D. Fales, jr. il
Pop Mech 131:86-90+ Je '69; Same abr.
with title Impossible rescue. Read Digest
95:50-5 S '69
HELICOPTERS in traffic regulation
Helicopter adds versatility to police work;
Fort Worth, Tex. H. D. McMahon. il Am
City 84:42 O '69
HELICOPTERS in weather control
Chopping a hole in fog. il Time 93:42 F 14 '69
Clearing ground fog with helicopters. V. G.
Plank. il Weatherwise 22:91-8+ Je '69
HELIUM
Helium program runs into ill winds. Bsns W
p35 N 1 '69
HELIX nebula. See Nebulae
HELL
Anecdotes, facetae, satire, etc.
Toward a theology of garbage. M. O. Boyle.
il Commonweal 90:200-1 My 2 '69
HELLEBORE
Poke or Indian poke? Which one can we eat?
Org Gard & Farm 16:94 Ag '69
HELLENISM
Hebraism & Hellenism now. M. Himmelfarb.
Commentary 48:50-7 Jl '69; Discussion. 48:
20+ N '69
HELLER, Walter Wolfgang
Should the government share its tax take?
Sat R 52:26-9 Mr 22 '69
HELLERSON, Robert. See Goldsmith, A. jt.
auth.
HELLMAN, Geoffrey T.
Profiles; A. O. Sulzberger. New Yorker 44:
40-2+ Ja 18 '69
HELLMAN, Lillian
Unfinished woman; excerpt. pors Atlan 223:
90-122+ Ap '69
about
Experience as drama. D. Rabinowitz. Com-
mentary 48:95-6+ D '69
Lively lady. A. Grant. por Newsweek 73:
89-90 Je 30 '69
No punches pulled. J. Epstein. New Repub
161:27-9 Jl 26 '69
Peripatetic reviewer. E. Weeks. Atlan 224:106
Jl '69
Personal history. W. G. Rogers. por Sat R
52:30 Jl 5 '69
Rebel as writer. R. Kotlowitz. Harper 238:
87-8+ Je '69
Stern self-portrait of lady. V. S. Pritchett.
Life 66:12 Je 27 '69
HELLMAN, Louis M.
Doctor's view of birth-control pills. Redbook
132:60+ Ap '69
HELLMAN, Peter
What makes David Frost talk. N Y Times
Mag p54-5+ D 7 '69
HELLMUTH, Obata and Kassabaum (firm)
Three new office structures by HOK. il Arch
Rec 146:121-6 Ag '69
HELLO and goodbye; drama. See Fugard, A.
HELL'S Angels. See Gangs
HELLS CANYON
Hells Canyon-Snake National River? C. M.
Slansky. il Nat Parks 43:18-20 Ag '69
Landscape esthetics. L. B. Leopold. il Natur
Hist 78:36-45 O '69

HELLWIG, Monika
Christian revolution and the Christian edu-
cator. Chr Cent 86:1088-91 Ag 20 '69
Crash attack on prejudice. America 120:193-4
F 15 '69
HELLYER, Clement D.
Build this patio firepit. Pop Mech 132:148-9
Jl '69
HELLYER, David
(ed) See Bucher, R. Rose Bucher and the
ordeal of the Pueblo
HELMER, Paul
(tr) See Lewinski, W. E. von. Where do we
go from here? A European view
HELMETS
Are motorcycle safety helmets good enough?
E. H. Arctander. il Pop Sci 194:122-4+ F
'69
Better head and face protection for Baltimore
police. il Am City 84:16 Je '69
HELMS, J. Lynn
Scientific fallout from the space program.
Space World G-1-73:7-11 Ja '70
HELMS, Mercer
Movies sell a magic show. Pop Phot 65:106-7+
Ag '69
HELMS, Richard McGarrah
Spying on the spy. il Time 93:72 My 23 '69
HELMSLEY, Harry Brakmann
How Harry Helmsley speared Parkchester. il
por Arch Forum 130:110 Ja '69
HELP, help, the Globolinks; opera. See Menot-
ti, G. C.
HELPFULNESS. See Service
HELPRIN, Mark Henry
Because of the waters of the flood; story.
New Yorker 45:35 S 27 '69
HELSINKI festival. See Music festivals—Fin-
land
HELSINKI talks. See Strategic arms limitation
talks
HEME
Absence of heme-heme interactions in hemo-
globin; adaptation of address. February 28,
1969. R. G. Shulman and others. bibliog il
Science 165:251-7 Jl 18 '69
HEMENWAY, Robert
I am waiting; story. New Yorker 45:35-40 S
6 '69
HEMEROCALLIS. See Day lilies
HEMICHOLINIUM
Hemicholinium-3; noncholinergic effects on
squid axons. D. T. Frazier and others. bib-
liog il Science 163:820-1 F 21 '69
HEMINGS, Sally
Thomas Jefferson and James Thomson Cal-
lender: the myth of Black Sally. J. W.
Knudson. Negro Hist Bul 32:15-19 bibliog
(p22) N '69
HEMINGWAY, Ernest
Across the river and into the trees. G. Steiner.
New Yorker 45:147-50 S 13 '69
Authors & editors. R. H. Smith. Pub W 195:
15-17 Mr 31 '69
Ernest Hemingway, by C. Baker. Review
Harper 238:96-102 My '69. I. Howe
Look 33:6 Ap 29 '69. P. S. Prescott
Nat R 21:390-1 Ap 22 '69. J. Hart
Nation 208:671-4 My 26 '69. J. F. Light
New Repub 160:28-32 Ap 26 '69. C. T.
Samuels
Newsweek pors 73:112+ Ap 21 '69. A.
Goldman
Sat R por 52:31-3+ Ap 19 '69. G. Hicks
Time il pors 93:102-4 Ap 18 '69
Ernest Hemingway; living, loving, dying; ex-
cerpt from Ernest Hemingway; a life story.
C. Baker. il pors Atlan 223:45-67 Ja; 91-5+
F '69
Fitzgerald and Hemingway: the difficult friend.
J. Hart. Nat R 21:29-31 Ja 14 '69
From Cohn to Herzog. M. J. Hoffman. Yale
R 58:342-58 Mr '69
Hemingway in our time. A. Lebowitz. Yale
R 58:321-41 Mr '69
Hemingway's truth. R. A. Schroth. America
120:534 My 3 '69
Impotence of being Ernest. S. Maloff. Com-
monweal 90:235-6+ My 9 '69; Discussion.
90:451+ Jl 25 '69
Irony of situation in Ernest Hemingway's
Soldier's home. A. J. Petrarca. Engl J 58:
664-7 My '69
Late notes on camp plus Papa Hemingway.
C. Barnes. Holiday 45:8+ Je '69
None are to be found more clever than
Ernie. D. P. Reichard. Engl J 58:668-72
My '69
Sound of hooves; dedication of bust, Pam-
plona. J. McCormick. il pors Sports Illus
31:60-4+ Jl 7 '69
View of literature too often neglected. J.
M. Nagle. Engl J 58:399-407 Mr '69

HEMINGWAY, Mary Moon
Notes for the hostess. See issues of House & garden incorporating Living for young homemakers
HEMIPTERA
See also
Milkweed bugs
HEMLINE. See Clothing and dress
HEMLOCK
Carolina hemlock. L. J. Uttal. Horticulture 47:51 Ag '69
HEMLOCK, Poison. See Poison hemlock
HEMMING, Roy, and others
DIScussions. See issues of Senior scholastic
HEMOGLOBIN
Absence of heme-heme interaction in hemoglobin: adaptation of address, February 28, 1969. R. G. Shulman and others. bibliog il Science 165:251-7 Jl 18 '69
Hemoglobin as a tracer in hemodynamic pulmonary edema. G. G. Pietra and others. bibliog il Science 166:1643-6 D 26 '69
Hemoglobins A and A₂ in New World primates: comparative variation and its evolutionary implications. S. H. Boyer and others. bibliog il Science 166:1428-31 D 12 '69
Single chain alkali resistance in hemoglobin Rainer: β145 tyrosine→histidine. G. Stamatoyannopoulos and A. Yoshida. bibliog il Science 166:1005-6 N 21 '69
Tadpole antibodies against frog hemoglobin and their effect on development. G. M. Maniatis and others. bibliog il Science 165:67-9 Jl 4 '69
See also
Porphyria
HEMOPHILIA
Hemophilia A: polymorphism detectable by a factor VIII antibody. D. Feinstein and others. bibliog il Science 163:1071-2 Mr 7 '69
Hemophilia: role of organ homografts. T. L. Marchioro and others. bibliog il Science 163: 188-90 Ja 10 '69
HEMORRHAGE
Aerosol tissue adhesive. Chem 42:24 F '69
Antithrombin III: protection against death after injection of thromboplastin. L. T. Mann, jr. and others. bibliog il Science 166: 517-18 O 24 '69
First aid. C. J. Potthoff. Todays Health 47: 66 Je '69
See also
Infarctions
HEMP
Hallucinogens of plant origin. R. E. Schultes. bibliog il Science 163:247-8 Ja 17 '69
HEMPHILL, Noyes and company. See Hornblower and Weeks-Hemphill, Noyes and company
HEMPSTEAD, N.Y.
What a 20-inch snowstorm can teach. Am City 84:22 D '69
HENAHAN, Donal
Magic theater of Luciano Berio. Hi Fi 19:71-2 Ag '69
Philharmonicsville (pop. 106) N Y Times Mag p26-7+ S 28; 12+ O 19 '69
Reviews of records. Mus Q 55:424-6 Jl '69
HENAUX, René
Soupcon of sorcery. il Newsweek 75:41 Ja 5 '70
HENDERSON, Curtis
No, thank you, I'd rather not live twice. L. R. Chevalier. il Ladies Home J 86:68+ Mr '69
HENDERSON, David Newton
Excerpt from statement presented to House committee on interstate and foreign commerce, April 15, 1969. Cong Digest 48:177+ Je '69
HENDERSON, Earl E.
Seeing the world as it is. Todays Ed 58:72-3 Ja '69
HENDERSON, Everett S.
Seldom used vines. Horticulture 47:36-7+ S '69
HENDERSON, George Washington
George Washington Henderson. por Negro Hist Bul 32:20 F '69
HENDERSON, Hazel
Action: a beauty investment. B. Wysor. il por Harp Baz 102:158-61 Ag '69
HENDERSON, Ose F. See Hayes, L. K. jt. auth.
HENDERSON, Robert
Aftermath; story. New Yorker 45:33-7 Mr 8 '69
HENDLEY, H. Ray. See Burlage, J. D. jt. auth.
HENDLIN, D. and others
Phosphonomycin, a new antibiotic produced by strains of streptomyces. bibliog Science 166:122-3 O 3 '69

HENDRICK, James Pomeroy
Interpol; address, November 22, 1968. Vital Speeches 35:306-8 Mr 1 '69
HENDRICKSON, Anita
Electron microscopic radioautography: identification of origin of synaptic terminals in normal nervous tissue. bibliog Science 165:194-6 Jl 11 '69
HENDRICKSON, Robert
Dig your own shallow well. Org Gard & Farm 16:77-80 Je '69
Globe artichokes. Horticulture 47:52-3 Ap '69
Lifetime garden of vegetables and herbs. Am Home 72:110a My '69
Onions that grow on trees. Org Gard & Farm 16:84 Ap '69
HENDRIX, Jimi
Infinity of Jimis; interview, ed. by R. Richman. Life 67:72-5 O 3 '69

about

People are talking about . . . por Vogue 153: 188-9 F 1 '69
Tangible impact. C. E. Fager. Chr Cent 86: 595-6 Ap 23 '69
HENDRIX college, Conway, Ark.
Underground library. il Arch Rec 146:92-3 D '69
HENDRYSON, Elizabeth S.
Case for sex education. PTA Mag 63:20-1 My '69; Same abr. Ed Digest 35:34-5 S '69
Educational problems in the United States: excerpts from address. PTA Mag 63:12-14 Ja '69
Necklace. por PTA Mag 63:18-19 Je '69
President's message. See issues of PTA magazine
Value of the PTA. Todays Ed 58:31-3 My '69
HENISCH, H. K.
Amorphous-semiconductor switching; with biographical sketch. Sci Am 221:18, 30-41 bibliog(p 166) N '69
HENKEL, Donald D.
Researcher and practitioner, they must communicate. Parks & Rec 4:26+ Jl '69
HENKIN, Harmon
DDT and the Constitution. Nation 208:308-10 Mr 10 '69
DDT on trial. Environ 11:14-17+ Mr '69
Problems in ppm. Environ 11:24-33+ My '69
Side effects. Environ 11:28-35+ Ja '69
Three days of Mifflin street. Nation 208: 653-4 My 26 '69
HENLEY, Arthur
Delinquents are his patients. Todays Health 47:48-9+ N '69
Survival for college freshmen. Todays Health 47:20-3+ S '69
HENNE, Frances
Move to school autonomy. por Library J 94: 259-60 Ja 15 '69
HENNESSY, Bernard
Welcome, Spiro Agnew. New Repub 161:13-14 D 13 '69
HENNESSY, Thomas A.
Rebuff in Pittsburgh. New Repub 161:16-17 S 27 '69
HENNING, Paul
King of corn. il por Newsweek 74:94 Jl 14 '69
HENNINGER, Daniel
Alaska: share the oil. New Repub 160:15-17 Je 28 '69
Challenge to Mayor Stokes. New Repub 161: 12-14 Ag 23 '69
Murphy's late show. New Repub 161:11-12 N 8 '69
—and Esposito, Nancy
Indian schools. New Repub 160:18-21 F 15 '69
HENRI, Robert
Duality of the artist. Am Artist 32:5 N '68
HENRIOT, Peter J.
[Book review] America 120:286 Mr 8 '69
HENRY II, king of England
This medieval winter. H. S. Hughes. America 120:156-8 F 8 '69
HENRY, Carl F. H.
Justification by ignorance: a neo-Protestant motif? address, December 29, 1969. Chr Today 14:10-15 Ja 2 '70
Reality and identity of God. Chr Today 13: 3-6 Mr 14; 12-16 Mr 28 '69
HENRY, George J.
Overseas commentary. See issues of Forbes
HENRY, James Thurman
Xenia, Ohio. por Negro Hist Bul 32:21 Mr '69
HENRY, Mary Roblee
How to enjoy a vacation house an ocean away; excerpts from A farmhouse in Provence. House & Gard 135:72-3+ Je '69
Kirdis of Cameroon. Vogue 154:174-81+ D '69
6000 bottles of wine; excerpt from A farmhouse in Provence. Atlan 223:69-71 My '69
Wonder Child. Vogue 153:128-31+ Je '69

HENRY, Omer
(ed) See Handley. C. Four point system for writing a selling query letter
HENRY V; drama. See Shakespeare, W.—Plays
HENRY Ford museum and Greenfield Village, Dearborn, Mich.
Dearborn: American life as lived. E. P. Birk. il Antiques 96:38+ Jl '69
HENSHEL, Harry Bulova
Humming with Henshel. R. Levy. il Duns R 93:68-70 Mr '69
HENSLEY, Kirby James
Dispenser of divinity. pors Newsweek 73:96 My 5 '69
Mail-order ministers. il por Time 93:70 F 21 '69
HENTOFF, Margot
Books. Vogue 154:56 Jl '69
Performing arts. Harper 239:28+ N '69
Television. Vogue 154:144 D '69; 155:78 Ja 1 '70
Toward a new erotic environment? Cur 109: 15-18 Ag '69
HENTOFF, Nat
Opinion: dehumanized radicalism. por Mlle 69:16+ My '69
Profiles: J. V. Lindsay. New Yorker 45:44-8+ My 3; 42-6+ My 10 '69
Smothers brothers: who controls TV? Look 33:27-9 Je 24 '69
Temptations of a Boston atheist. Harper 238:81-6 Ap '69
What pop music means to kids. Parents Mag 44:46-7+ My '69
HENZE, Hans Werner
Scandalous politics of Hans Werner Henze. R. P. Morgan. por Hi Fi 19:106-7 D '69
HEPATICAE. See Liverworts
HEPATITIS
Hepatitis in marmosets: induction of disease with coded specimens from a human volunteer study. A. W. Holmes and others bibliog il Science 165:816-17 Ag 22 '69
Hepatitis, on the rise again. Consumer Rep 34:344-7 Je '69
HEPATITIS, Infectious
Dropping like flies; outbreak hits Holy Cross football team. Newsweek 74:85-6 O 20 '69
Virus-like antigen, antibody. and antigen-antibody complexes in hepatitis measured by complement fixation. N. R. Shulman and L. F. Barker. bibliog il Science 165:304-6 Jl 18 '69

Vaccines

Toward a hepatitis vaccine. Time 94:60-1 Jl 18 '69
HEPATITIS virus
Toward a hepititis vaccine. Time 94:60-1 Jl 18 '69
Virus identification promised. Sci N 95:574 Je 14 '69
HEPBURN, Anthony
Anthony Hepburn. T. Birks. Craft Horiz 29: 34-6 Jl '69
HEPBURN, Audrey
New life, a new love; Audrey Hepburn at forty. J. Barry. il pors McCalls 96:56-7+ Jl '69
People are talking about Audrey and Andrea. il pors Vogue 153:108-9 Mr 15 '69
HEPBURN, Katharine
Great Kate. K. Tynan. pors Vogue 153:86-9+ Ap 15 '69
Kate and Coco. H. Saal. il pors Newsweek 74:75-9 N 10 '69
Very expensive Coco. il por Time 94:86-7 N 7 '69
HEPPENSTALL, Rayner
(tr) See Roussel. R. Skate's scales
HERALD, Earl S. and others
Blind river dolphin: first side-swimming cetacean. bibliog Science 166:1408-10 D 12 '69
HERALDRY
At the sign of the crest. H. K. Eilers. See issues of Hobbies
Printers, printing and heraldry; adaptation of address. J. Moran. il Pub W 196:80-2+ Jl 7 '69
Use and abuse of family crests. il Good H 168:162 F '69
HERATH, Kent A.
Books for progress. Américas 21:21-2 Ja '69
HERBERG, Will
Case for heterosexuality. Nat R 21:1007-8+ O 7 '69
Obituary notice; erratum. Nat R 21:64 Ja 28 '69
HERBERT, Jay
Books to help you take a trip. House & Gard 135:78+ My '69
How to make the most of your public library. House & Gard 135:50+ Ap '69
On the books. House & Gard 136:53+ S '69
Our cities, their wretched present, their hopeful future. House & Gard 135:44+ Mr '69

HERBERT, Zbigniew
Critic of the month. L. Lieberman. Poetry 114: 52-3 Ap '69
HERBERT Hoover presidential library, West Branch, Ia.
Herbert Hoover library and museum. K. V. Hostick. il Hobbies 74:108-9 My '69
HERBICIDES
Herbicides: order on 2,4,5-T issued at unusually high level. B. Nelson. Science 166: 977-9 N 21 '69
He's fighting his jungle. il Sunset 143:200 S '69
How herbicides work, why some fail. Suc Farm 67:64 Ap '69
How now, Dow Jones: chemical-biological warfare. J. Deedy. Commonweal 90:306 My 30 '69; Reply. D. L. Coslett. 90:531+ S 5 '69
1969 corn-soybean herbicide selection guide. C. E. Sommers. Suc Farm 67:62+ F '69
Sewer root control, chemically; Sacramento County. N. R. Townley. il Am City 84:92-4 D '69
Some ecological benefits of woody plant control with herbicides. K. C. Barrons. bibliog il Science 165:465-8 Ag 1 '69; Discussion. 166:43, 310+, 1098, 1576 O 3, 17, N 28, D 26 '69
What have we done to Vietnam? R. E. Cook and others. New Repub 162:18-21 Ja 10 '70
See also
Weeds—Chemical control

Injurious effects

Defoliation in Vietnam. F. H. Tschirley. bibliog Science 163:779-86 F 21 '69; Discussion. 164:373+ Ap 25 '69
How to avoid herbicide injury this season. C. E. Sommers. il Suc Farm 67:60-1 F '69

Residues

Pesticide interaction creates hybrid residue. R. Bartha. bibliog il Science 166:1299-300 D 5 '69
HERBIVORA
Wanted: a suitable herbivore to convert western scrubland to protein. P. S. Martin. il Natur Hist 78:34-9 F '69
HERBS
Grow your own flavors. T. Merkert. il Har Yrs 9:26-8 Mr '69
Grow your own seasonings. G. B. Foster. il Horticulture 47:34-7+ My '69
Herbs for permanence. M. W. Bear. il Horticulture 47:26-7+ S '69
Herbs in salad. L. S. Alsberg. il Horticulture 46:33+ Ag '68
Miniature herb garden. il Mech Illus 65:83+ My '69
Season with herbs & spices; with recipes. il Good H 168:92-106 F '69
Some modern uses and ancient lore, and some sources. Har Yrs 9:29 Mr '69
Spice of life. il Ladies Home J 86:116-17+ S '69
Spices and things. il Redbook 133:114-15+ Jl '69
Taste of beauty. J. Larmoth. il Harp Baz 103:208-9+ N '69
There's always room for herbs. J. J. Meeker. il Org Gard & Farm 16:60-4 Ja '69
Treasury of flavor tricks. D. Eby. il Bet Hom & Gard 47:88-94+ Ap '69
See also
Comfrey
Garlic
Parsley
Rosemary
HERBST, Josephine
Obituary
Nation 208:229 F 24 '69
Pub W 195:53 F 10 '69
HERCEG NOVI conference. See International conference on science and society
HERCULES incorporated
Hercules unchained. il Forbes 103:51 My 1 '69
HERDING of cattle. See Cattle herding
HEREDITY
Genetics vs. headstart. Sci N 95:326-7 Ap 5 '69
Intelligence and race; theories of Arthur R. Jensen on IQ test scores. New Repub 160: 10-11 Ap 5 '69
Intelligence: is there a racial difference? Time 93:54+ Ap 11 '69
Jensenism, n. the theory that I.Q. is largely determined by the genes. L. Edson. il N Y Times Mag p 10-11+ Ag 31 '69; Discussion. p4+ S 21; 38+ S 28 '69
Jensen's complaint. M. R. Berube. Commonweal 91:42-4 O 10 '69
Let there be darkness; theories of A. R. Jensen. Nat R 21:996-7 O 7 '69

HEREDITY—*Continued*
Race and intelligence; findings of A. R. Jensen. J Cass. Sat R 52:67-8 My 17 '69
Refutation of Jensen's position on intelligence, race, social class, and heredity. M. Golden and W. Bridger. Ment Hy 53:648 53 O '69
See also
Albinos and albinism
Eugenics
Evolution
Genes
Genetics
HEREDITY counseling clinics. See Health clinics
HEREDITY of disease
Diabetes may be dad's. Sci Digest 65:55 Ap '69
Inheriting heart defects. Sci Digest 66:60 Ag '69
White blood cell cultures in genetic studies on the human mucopolysaccharidoses. K. M. Foley and others. bibliog il Science 164:424-6 Ap 25 '69
See also
Angiokeratoma
Mongolism
Porphyria
HEREROS. See Botswana—Native races
HERESY
Inqui 67: some reflections on the Lyndian heresy. H. A. Patin. bibliog f Sch & Soc 97:98-100 F '69
Is heresy dead? il Time 93:55 My 23 '69
Roman Catholic: visible and invisible; address, October 1969. F. Sontag. America 121:298-301 O 11 '69
See also
Apostasy
HERING, Doris
Next year, keep the baby. Dance Mag 43:40-1 O '69
HERITAGE golf classic. See Golf—Tournaments
HERKO, Berthold M.
Berthold M. Herko; former student of August Macke; with biographical sketch. il por Am Artist 33:66-7 O '69
HERLIHY, Ed
Ed Herlihy tests the Nation's boating knowhow. il Motor B 123:58 Ap '69
HERLIHY, James Leo
Stop, you're killing me. Criticism
Commonweal 90:204-5 My 2 '69
Nation 208:477-8 Ap 14 '69
New Yorker 45:99-100 Mr 29 '69
Newsweek il 73:105 Mr 31 '69
Time 93:55 Mr 28 '69
HERLIHY, John L.
Walk through the 13th century. Commonweal 91:279-81 N 28 '69
HERLONG, Albert Sydney, 1909-
Troubled SEC gets a Nixon Democrat. il por Bsns W p27-8 S 6 '69
HERMAN, M. Justin
Leaving a heart in San Francisco. il pors Bsns W p 110-12 My 10 '69
HERMAN, Stan
We talk to. ; interview. ed. by A. Ginsberg. por Mlle 69:345 Ag '69
HERMAN, Woody
Woody 'n' me. G. Lees. Hi Fi 19:118 S '69
HERMAN Miller, incorporated. See Miller, Herman, incorporated
HERMANS, Emery
Dance images of now and thensome; Martinique theatre. M. Marks. Dance Mag 43:76 Ap '69
HERMAPHRODITISM
Two unusual unionid hermaphrodites. H. Van Der Schalie. bibliog il Science 163:1333-4 Mr 21 '69
HERMENEUTICS, Biblical. See Bible—Hermeneutics
HERMES blind landing system. See Airplanes—Landing
HERNDON, Angelo
Angelo Herndon story. H. N. Meyer. Chr Cent 86:221-2 F 12 '69
HERNDON, E. Garland
If you want to stay healthy. ; interview. por Nations Bsns 57:56-8+ F '69
HERNDON, Terry E. and Law, Kenneth
Every teacher's responsibility. Todays Ed 58:59-60 Ja '69
HERNIA
Non-bibulous baggy eyes; orbital herniation. Sci Digest 65:53 Ap '69
Normal incidence of brain hernia in the mouse. R. Rugh. bibliog Science 163:407 Ja 24 '69
Sliding stomach; hiatal hernia. il Time 93:52 Mr 28 '69
HERNICK, Michael, and Kennedy, Dora
Grouping foreign language students. Todays Ed 58:38-9 Ja '69

HEROES
China; instant popularization of unknown heroes. H. Yu. Chr Cent 86:1532 N 26 '69
See also
Courage
Vietnamese war. 1957—Heroes
HEROES in literature. See Characters in literature
HEROIC poetry. See Epic poetry
HEROIN
Heroin and death. il Time 94:38 Jl 11 '69
Heroin diplomacy. il Time 95:28-9 Ja 19 '70
What are narcotic drugs? questions and answers. il Todays Ed 58:48-50 Mr '69
HEROISM. See Courage
HERPES simplex virus
Herpes simplex virus: dry mass. F. Lampert and others. bibliog il Science 166:1163-5 N 28 '69
Neutralization of sensitized virus by the fourth component of complement. C. A. Daniels and others. bibliog il Science 165:508-9 Ag 1 '69
HERPESVIRUS
Herpesvirus in Marek's disease tumors. G. Schidlovsky and others. bibliog il Science 164:959-61 My 23 '69
Is intercourse a factor? cancer of the uterus triggered by a common virus. Time 94:77 N 14 '69
Tumor induction in developing frog kidneys by a zonal centrifuge purified fraction of the frog herpes-type virus. M. Mizell and others. bibliog il Science 165:1134-7 S 12 '69
HERPESVIRUS infections
Interferon stimulated. Sci Am 220:46-8 Ja '69
HERR, Dan
Dan Herr on mistakes. Commonweal 91:220 N 14 '69
HERR, Kenneth C. and Pimentel, G. C.
Evidence for solid carbon dioxide in the upper atmosphere of Mars. Science 167:47-9 Ja 2 '70
Infrared absorptions near three microns recorded over the polar cap of Mars. bibliog Science 166:496-9 O 24 '69
HERR, Michael
Conclusion at Khesanh. Esquire 72:113-23+ O '69
Khesanh. Esquire 72:118-23+ S '69
HERRER, Aristides, and Telford, S. R. Jr
Leishmania braziliensis isolated from sloths in Panama. bibliog Science 164:1419-20 Je 20 '69
HERRESHOFF, Halsey C.
Thoughts on racing an S boat. Yachting 125:189+ F '69 (to be cont)
What did we learn? Yachting 125:56-8+ My '69
HERRIMAN, George
Anatomy of a love-hate klassic. G. Weales. il Life 67:12 D 12 '69
HERRING
See also
Cookery—Fish
HERRING fishing
To Sausalito for the herring. il Sunset 143:24 D '69
HERRNKIND, William
Queuing behavior of spiny lobsters. bibliog Science 164:1425-7 Je 20 '69
HERRON, Edward A.
Three to get ready. Space World F-2-62; 36-9 F '69
HERSCH, Sam
Make your own time of day. J. Scully. il Mod Phot 33:58-63 Mr '69
HERSCHEL, Sir John Frederick William
John Herschel's expedition to South Africa. J. Ashbrook. il por Sky & Tel 358+ Je '69
HERSCHMAN, Arthur, and others
New information program for AIP. por Phys Today 22:29-32 D '69
HERSEY, M. Leonard
Control points. See issues of Yachting
HERSH, Burton
Pay Arthur D. Little inc, and then start listening. Esquire 71:118-21+ Je '69
HERSH, Leroy S.
Adsorption of alkyl trimethylammonium chlorides at a porous glass-potassium chloride solution interface. bibliog Science 164:179-81 Ap 11 '69
HERSH, Reuben, and Griego, R. J.
Brownian motion and potential theory; with biographical sketches. Sci Am 220:14, 66-72+ Mr '69
HERSH, Seymour M.
Dare we develop biological weapons? N Y Times Mag p28-9+ S 28 '69
Germ warfare: for alma mater, God and country. Ramp Mag 8:20-8 D '69
Germs and gas as weapons. New Repub 160:13-16 Je 7 '69
On uncovering the great nerve gas coverup. Ramp Mag 7:12-18 Je '69
20,000 guns under the sea. Ramp Mag 8:40-4 S '69

HERSH, Seymour M.—*Continued*
about
Hip-pocket AP. por Newsweek 74:83-4 D 8
  '69
Miscue on the massacre. il por Time 94:75 D
  5 '69
HERSHEY, Alfred Day
  1969 Nobel prize for physiology or medicine.
    G. Stent. por Science 166:479-81 O 24 '69
  Nobel threesome. por Time 94:84 O 24 '69
HERSHEY, Lenore
  Compassion power. Ladies Home J 86:88+
    S '69
HERSHEY, Lewis Blaine
  Future of the draft; interview. pors U S
    News 66:76-9 Ap 21 '69
about
Stepping aside: the man who drafted 15
  million Americans. por U S News 67:20
  O 20 '69
Thorn plucker. por Newsweek 74:36+ O 20
  '69
Washington icons. Nation 209:165 S 1 '69
HERSKOVITS, Theodore T. and Jaillet, Helene
  Structural stability and solvent denaturation
    of myoglobin. bibliog Science 163:282-5 Ja
    17 '69
HERST, Herman, Jr
  Stamps. See issues of Hobbies
HERSTEN, P. J.
  Shifting sands of Bantangas. Sat R 52:69 S
    13 '69
HERTZ corporation
  Number oneski; deal with Russia. il News-
    week 73:82 My 5 '69
HERTZBERG, Arthur
  Forgotten voice. Commentary 48:98+ S '69
HERTZBERG, Robert
  Fantastic new films let you almost shoot
    in the dark! Pop Mech 131:138-40 Mr '69
HERTZKE, Jon, and Crump, Fred, Jr
  Styrofoam sandcasting. Sch Arts 69:16-17 O
    '69
HERTZOG, Albert
  Fight goes on. il por Time 94:36 O 24 '69
  New right. por Newsweek 74:73 D 8 '69
HERZ, Norman
  Anorthosite belts, continental drift, and the
    anorthosite event. bibliog Science 164:944-
    7 My 23 '69
HERZEN, Aleksandr Ivanovich
  Books. G. Steiner. New Yorker 44:114-16+ F
    8 '69
HERZOG, Frederick
  Political theology. Chr Cent 86:975-8 Jl 23 '69
HESBURGH, Theodore Martin
  Dealing with campus chaos: Notre Dame:
    fifteen minutes and out; excerpts from
    letter, February 17, 1969. U S News 66:
    34 Mr 3 '69; Same abr. with title College
    president takes a stand on campus chaos.
    Read Digest 94:104-7 My '69
  Now, a backlash on campus turmoil; ex-
    cerpts from letter, February 25, 1969. U S
    News 66:11 Mr 10 '69
about
Father Hesburgh's true position. America
  120:291 Mr 15 '69
Hesburgh fights. J. O'Connor. por Look 33:
  42+ N 18 '69
Hesburgh of Notre Dame: (1) he's destroying
  this university; (2) he's bringing it into the
  mainstream of American life. T. J. Fleming.
  il por N Y Times Mag p56-7+ My 11 '69
Hesburgh's law. Commonweal 98:719-20 Mr
  14 '69
In defense of young people. por Sch & Soc
  97:264 Sum '69
Of many things; letter to the university's
  faculty and student body. D. R. Campion.
  America 120:inside cover Mr 8 '69
HESCHEL, Abraham Joshua
  Pleas for love without cause. por Time 93:
    63 Mr 14 '69
HESS, Andrew C.
  Moriscos: an Ottoman fifth column in six-
    teenth-century Spain. bibliog f Am Hist R
    74:1-25 O '68
HESS, John
  (ed) See DeRogatis, A. Newest star in pro
    football
HESS, Karl
  Open letter to Barry Goldwater. Ramp Mag
    8:28-31 O '69; Same abr. Cur 113:21-6 D '69
  Who is Melvin Laird? Ramp Mag 8:27-31 Ag
    '69
about
You know he's right. por Newsweek 74:42
  S 29 '69

HESS, Leon
  Leon Hess never plays it safe. A. M. Louis.
    por Fortune 81:104-7+ Ja '70
  Southwest passage? por Forbes 104:50 O 15
    '69
HESS, Linda
  Peaceful soul of the poet. Sat R 52:36-7+
    My 10 '69
HESS, M. Whitcomb
  Thoreau and Hecker: freemen, friends, mys-
    tics. Cath World 209:265-7 S '69
  (tr) See Rilke, R. M. Birth of Christ
HESS, Thomas B.
  Outsider. Art N 69:34-7+ D '69
HESS, Wilmot N.
  Generation of an artificial aurora. Science
    164:1512-13 Je 27 '69
about
Disenchantment with Apollo. por Sci N 96:112-
  13 Ag 9 '69
—and others
  Exploration of the moon; with biographical
    sketches. Sci Am 221:14, 54-60+ bibliog
    (p 148) O '69
HESS-Amerada merger. See Petroleum indus-
    try and trade—Consolidations and mergers
HESS oil and chemical corporation. See Amer-
    ada Hess corporation
HESSE, Hermann
  Books. G. Steiner. New Yorker 44:87-90+ Ja
    18 '69
  Fanned by youth. A. Goldman. Vogue 155:
    82 Ja 1 '70
  How Hermann Hesse speaks to the college
    generation. H. S. Resnik. Sat R 52:35-7
    O 18 '69
HESSELTON, William T.
  Deer trapping and tagging. Cons 23:14-17
    F '69
  Incredible white deer herd. bibliog Cons 24:
    18-19 O '69
HESSEN, Robert
  What campus rebellions mean to you. Na-
    tions Bsns 57:30-2 Je '69
HESSING, Mona
  Tapestry by Mona Hessing. il Craft Horiz
    29:30-3 Jl '69
HESSLER, Robert R. See Sanders, H. L. jt.
    auth.
HETEROCHROMATIN. See Chromatin
HETEROSIS (biology)
  Molecular basis for neterosis. D. Schwartz
    and W. J. Laughner. bibliog il Science 166:
    626-7 O 31 '69
    See also
  Heterozygosis
HETEROZYGOSIS
  Genetic load and its varieties. A. M. Brues.
    bibliog Science 164:1130-6 Je 6 '69
  Obstructive lung disease and α_1-antitrypsin
    deficiency gene heterozygosity. F. Kuep-
    pers and others. bibliog il Science 165:899-
    901 Ag 29 '69
HETRICK, Emery
  Psychiatry gets off the couch and hits the
    streets. il pors Life 67:48-48C Ag 8 '69
HEUBLEIN, Incorporated
  Heublein pours a potent sales mix; Smirnoff
    vodka's success in wines and pre-mixed
    cocktails. il Bsns W p76-7+ Je 14 '69
  New talents test their mettle. Bsns W p33+
    Ja 3 '70
HEUMANN, Sylvan
  Amateur scientist. Sci Am 220:118-23 F '69
L'HEURE espagnole; opera. See Ravel, M.
HEUSINKVELD, Helen
  Is 202 housing for you? Har Yrs 9:46-9 Mr
    '69
HEUTTE, Frederic
  Fogging and misting plants. Horticulture 47:
    26+ My '69
  Southern magnolia. il Horticulture 47:20+ Ja
    '69
HEWES, Henry
  Theater. See issues of Saturday review
HEWITT, George
  False witness, by M. Rader. Review
    Nation 209:449-50 O 27 '69. F. J. Donner
HEWITT, Jean
  Food (cont) N Y Times Mag p70 F 23;
    95-6 Mr 16; 53 Je 29; 47 Jl 27; 58 Ag 10;
    120 S 7; 76 S 21; 90+ N 9; 124+ N 30 '69
HEWITT, John P.
  Naturalist has a unique role. Parks & Rec
    4:39-40+ D '69
HEYDENRYK, Henry
  Ten commandments for the proper framing
    of pictures; excerpts from The right frame.
    House B 111:110 O '69
HEYDT, Mary
  If you can't fight them, don't join them.
    por Redbook 134:24+ N '69
HEYEN, William
  Depth of field; King's men; poems. Poetry
    114:15-16 Ap '69

HEYERDAHL, Thor
Close is close enough. Sci N 96:78-9 Jl 26 '69
Linking the transoceanic cultures. Sci N 95:534-7 My 31 '69
Papyrus boat. Sat R 52:68 N 1 '69
What happened to the Ra? Sat R 52:90 D 6 '69

about
Kon-Tiki's famous skipper goes to sea in a ship of reeds, the Ra. il Life 66:89-90 Je 6 '69
Shock at sea. Time 94:40 Ag 15 '69
Stormy wreck of the paper ship Ra. il por Life 67:36-7 Ag 15 '69
Thor Heyerdahl's next voyage. J. Lear. il Sat R 52:49-56 My 3 '69; Discussion. 52:46-7 Jl 5; 42-3 Ag 2 '69
Voyage of the Ra. il por Newsweek 73:56+ My 26 '69

HEYES, Frank C.
Chicago to Bay Bea. Yachting 126:47+ S '69

HEYMAN, Wayne
Here's how to wake up your outboard motor. Motor B 123:81+ Ap '69

HEYMANN, Dieter. See Anders. E. jt. auth.

HEYNS, Roger William
Flower power. il Newsweek 73:92 Je 9 '69
We support you, Roger. You do it. il por Newsweek 73:68-9 Mr 10 '69

HEYSER, Wolfgang, and others
Translocation in perennial monocotyledons. bibliog Science 164:572-4 My 2 '69

HEYWOOD, Anne
New wave of sex epics makes actress Anne Heywood a star. il pors Life 66:76-7 Ja 31 '69

HEZEL, Francis
Peace corps volunteer or missionary, does it really make any difference? Cath World 208:205-7 F '69

HIBBARD, Lester T. and Wolfe, S. W.
How will you carry your baby? Redbook 133:56 O '69

HIBBERD, Bob
All about IC's. Radio-Electr 40:33-5+ Je; 58-60 Jl; 40:64-7 Ag '69
IC logic families. Radio-Electr 40:59-61 S '69

HIBBITT, Peyton
Three cheers for Tri-Cities. R. D. Daniels. il por Opera N 33:14-16 Mr 1 '69

HIBBS, Ben
Ike: the last years of a great American. Read Digest 95:111-16 Jl '69

HIBERNATION
Hibernation induced in ground squirrels by blood transfusion. A. R. Dawe and W. A. Spurrier. il Science 163:298-9 Ja 17 '69
Seven sleepers. P. M. Kelsey. Cons 23:35 F '69

HICCOUGHS. See Hiccups

HICCUPS
Annals of medicine. B. Roueché. New Yorker 45:105-17 Ap 5 '69
Hiccups. McCalls 96:50 Ap '69

HICKCOX, Charles Buchanan, 2d
Q. What makes Charlie swim? A. Jelly beans. W. F. Reed, jr. il pors Sports Illus 30:53-5 Mr 24 '69

HICKEL, Walter Joseph
America, the beautiful doomed? interview. por U S News 67:60-2+ N 10 '69
Education of Wally Hickel; interview, ed. by R. Saltonstall. por Time 94:42+ Ag 1 '69
Improving our living environment. Parks & Rec 4:18-20 Je '69
What is the new conservation? interview. por Nat Wildlife 7:8-9 Je '69

about
Apprentice Noah. il Time 93:18 Mr 21 '69
Confirmation marathon. Time 93:13 Ja 24 '69
Conflict situation. Commonweal 89:608-9 F 14 '69
Conservationist. New Repub 160:9 Ja 25 '69
Great Smokey Mountains delegation visits Secretary Hickel. Liv Wildn 33:36-7 Sum '69
Hickel and the Arctic. M. Frome. il Field & S 74:12-14+ N '69
Hickel backs strong pollution bill. Sci N 95:258 Mr 15 '69
Hickel controversy points up enviromental quality issue. L. J. Carter. Science 163:455 Ja 31 '69
Hickel passes test. Sr Schol 94:14 F 7 '69
Hickel watching. D. R. Maxey. il por Look 33:39+ N 4 '69
Interior. por Sci N 95:110 F 1 '69
Interior Secretary Hickel to visit Pacific Islands Trust Territory. Dept State Bul 60:424 My 19 '69
Interior's Walter Hickel: frontier figure in a Cabinet hot seat. por U S News 66:14 F 3 '69

Mr Hickel's dilemma. J. B. Craig. Am For 75:10 F '69
Secretary Hickel issues park policy guidelines. Nat Parks 43:20 Jl '69
Shaping the clean water act. por Sci N 95:208 Mr 1 '69
Silver lining. Parks & Rec 4:19 Ap '69
Wally Hickel's Christmas. il Time 95:41 Ja 5 '70
War between the redskins and the feds. V. Deloria, jr. il por N Y Times Mag p47+ D 7 '69

HICKEY, Tom
Psychologic rehabilitation for the normal elderly. bibliog Ment Hy 53:369-74 Jl '69

HICKEY, Vic
Man for all seasons. B. Thomas. il pors Motor T 21:26+ O '69

HICKMAN, Ernest E.
How I rescued an old vac. Pop Sci 194:144-5 My '69

HICKMAN, Geneva
Advice to new wives from a used one. Redbook 133:96-7+ O '69

HICKORY
Shagbark hickory. J. Hudak. il Horticulture 46:10+ O '68

HICKORY shad fishing. See Shad fishing

HICKS, Clifford B.
George Beadle talks about the new genetics. Todays Health 47:44-7+ Jl '69
—and Hicks, D. L.
Now: shoot underwater photos for under $20. Pop Mech 131:107-10+ Je '69

HICKS, Douglas L. See Hicks, C. B. jt. auth.

HICKS, Granville
Literary horizons. See issues of Saturday review
A look at the novel. Todays Ed 58:12-15 Ap '69

HICKS, J. B.
Ail's calm in the crow's nest. Am Ed 5:9-10 O '69

HICKS, Jim
Is that you in there, Ringo? Life 66:59-60+ Je 13 '69

HICKS, Sam
Aparejo; the perfect packsaddle. Am West 6:28-32 Ja '69

HICKS, Sonja J. and others
Preferential synthesis of ferritin and albumin by different populations of liver polysomes. bibliog Science 164:584-5 My 2 '69

HICTER, Marcel
Angry generation. UNESCO Courier 22:15-27 Ap '69

HIDDEN treasure. See Treasure trove

HIDES and skins
See also
Fur
Tanning

HIEROGLYPHICS
Mysterious hieroglyphs of Easter Island; reprint. A. Métraux. il UNESCO Courier 22:16-17 Ag '69
Mystery scripts: cuneiform script born from the point of a reed, the undeciphered disc from Phaistos; reprint. il UNESCO Courier 22:64-5 Ag '69

HI-FI speakers. See Loud speaking apparatus

HIGDON, Hal
In Chicago the left field bleacher bums are chanting: abeebee! Ungowa! Cub powuh! N Y Times Mag p28-9+ Ag 24 '69
Obituary for DDT (in Michigan) N Y Times Mag p6-7+ Jl 6 '69
Well, if not DDT, than what? N Y Times Mag p26-7+ Ja 11 '70
(ed) See Rowan, A. My husband's secret triumph

HIGGINS, Alice
Horse shows (cont) Sports Illus 30:60 Mr 24; 31:102 S 15; 64 D 8 '69

HIGGINS, Dick
Underground. J. Gruen. Vogue 154:160 O 1 '69

HIGGINS, George G.
George G. Higgins on a council. Commonweal 91:220 N 14 '69

HIGGINS, Jim, and Higgins, S. R.
Discovering Colorado's lofty Southwest. Todays Health 47:42-7+ O '69

HIGGINS, Robert P.
Tektite I; who can use it? letter. Science 163:1009 Mr 7 '69

HIGGINS, Shirley R. See Higgins, J. jt. auth.

HIGH altitude, influence of. See Altitude, Influence of

HIGH ASWAN DAM. See Aswan High Dam

HIGH blood pressure. See Hypertension

HIGH energy physics. See Nuclear physics

HIGH-energy scattering. See Scattering (physics)

HIGH fidelity incorporating Musical America (periodical)
High fidelity's electronic music contest. Hi Fi 19:57 Ag '69
HIGH fidelity shows. See Audio fairs
HIGH fidelity sound systems
Are your components compatible? R. Long. il Hi Fi 19:44-7 My '69
Equipment in the news. See issues of High fidelity incorporating Musical America
Equipment reports. See issues of High fidelity incorporating Musical America
Hi-fi compacts you can build from kits. J. A. Linkletter and S. M. Gallager. il Pop Mech 132:142-3 Ag '69
Hi-fi power-rating problems. W. A. Stocklin. Electr World 81:6 My '69
Hi-fi stereo kits. il Consumer Rep 34:127-37 Mr '69
House of the singing driftwood. D. K. Fulton. il Radio-Electr 40:57 My '69
New products for the new decade. R. Long. il Hi Fi 19:54-8+ O '69
Perfect hi-fi for today and for tomorrow. I. Berger. il Esquire 72:155 N '69
See also
KLH research and development corporation
Stereophonic sound systems

Terminology
Anecdotes, facetiae, satire, etc.
Poor man's glossary of audio terms. il Hi Fi 19:58 Jl '69
HIGH fidelity speakers. See Loud speaking apparatus
HIGH jumping. See Jumping
HIGH pressure. See Pressure
HIGH-pressure oxygenation. See Hyperbaric oxygenation
HIGH-rise apartment houses. See Apartment houses
HIGH school and college relations. See Educational cooperation
HIGH school athletics. See School athletics
HIGH school boys. See Boys
HIGH school diplomas. See Diplomas
HIGH school dropouts. See Dropouts
HIGH school football. See Football
HIGH school football players. See Football players
HIGH school fraternities
In my opinion: sororities are a waste of time. L. Savryn. Seventeen 28:256 S '69
HIGH school girls. See Girls
HIGH school graduates
Employment of high school graduates and dropouts. V. C. Perrella. bibliog il Mo Labor R 92:36-43 Je '69
HIGH school journalism. See College and school journalism
HIGH school libraries
Media center design; symposium. bibliog il Library J 94:4201-28 N 15 '69
See also
Knapp school libraries project
HIGH school publications. See College and school journalism
HIGH school sororities. See High school fraternities
HIGH school students
And now the high schools; disorders and fears. il Time 93:68 F 7 '69
Behind the unrest in high schools; racial conflict findings of the Urban research corporation. U S News 66:12 Je 2 '69
Coping with student activism in secondary schools. K. L. Fish. Ed Digest 35:8-11 O '69
Crisis in the high schools; the Life poll; with report by B. Hooper. L. Harris. il Life 66:22-35+ Mv 16 '69
How free should the high school press be? E. Einsiedler. il Todays Ed 58:52-4+ S '69
In my opinion: seniors should teach their own courses. S. Fisher. Seventeen 28:196 Je '69
Long and short of it; sideburns and mini skirts. il Newsweek 74:77 S 29 '69
On the scene: cities, summer and the lively arts; vacation activities for teen-agers. il Seventeen 28:94-5 Jl '69
Principals report on student protest. J. Hunt. il Am Ed 5:4-5 O '69; Same abr. Ed Digest 35:49-51 D '69
Recommendations on student activism in high schools. Sch & Soc 97:342-3 O '69
Revolt in the high schools; the way it's going to be. D. Divoky. il Sat R 52:83-4+ F 15 '69; Discussion. 52:56 Mr 15 '69
Revolutionaries who have to be home by 7:30. N. Pileggi. il N Y Times Mag p26-7+ Mr 16 '69; Discussion. p22+ Ap 6; 106+ Ap 13; 22+ Ap 20 '69

The scene. E. Farrell and L. Ruth. Engl J 58:1382-90 D '69
Student activism drama; roles for the principal. A. O. Boykin. bibliog Clear House 44:145-8 N '69
Talk with us, not at us. S. Holzman. il Schol Teach Sec Teach Sup p8-10 S 22 '69
Talking it over with Gay Head, questions and answers. Gay Head. See issues of Senior scholastic
Underachieving school, by J. Holt. Review Life 67:10 Jl 25 '69. J. Kozol
Young people of North Long Beach. J. Q. Wilson. Harper 239:83-90 D '69
See also
Student activities

Adjustment
Crushes; what should you do about them? with marginal comments. S. Berman; R. Gibson. Todays Ed 58:12-16 D '69
Society's children, by C. Nordstrom and others. Review
Science 163:169 Ja 10 '69. M. P. Dumont

Civil rights
See Students—Civil rights

Clothing
See Clothing and dress—Students

Dating
See Dating

Demonstrations
See Student demonstrations—United States

Employment
See Student employment

Reading
New literature for inner-city students. A. C. Brocki. Engl J 53:1151-61 N '69
Time enough to read; Horton Watkins high school, Ladue, St Louis, Mo. G. Stanford. il Sr Schol 94:Schol Teach 13+ Ap 18 '69
What does research in reading reveal; about reading and the high school student? R. Karlin. bibliog Engl J 58:386-95 Mr '69
See also
Supplementary reading

Travel
See Student travel
HIGH school students, Married. See Teen-age marriage
HIGH school students, Mentally superior
Residential high school for gifted disadvantaged students. W. J. Tisdall. Ed Digest 34:40-3 F '69
HIGH school students, Negro. See Negro students
HIGH school students, Socially handicapped. See Socially handicapped children
HIGH school students and drugs. See Narcotics and youth
HIGH school students and smoking. See Smoking and youth
HIGH school teachers. See Teachers
HIGH school teaching. See Teaching
HIGH school underground press. See College and school journalism
HIGH schools
Crisis in the high schools; the Life poll; with report by B. Hooper. L. Harris. il Life 66:22-35+ My 16 '69
Department head in the large senior high school. R. F. Thorum. Clear House 43:264-6 Ja '69; Same abr. Ed Digest 34:11-13 Mr '69
Residential high school for gifted disadvantaged students. W. J. Tisdall. Ed Digest 34:40-3 F '69
Trouble in the high schools. G. R. Anrig. Am Ed 5:2-4 O '69
Underachieving school, by J. Holt. Review Life 67:10 Jl 25 '69. J. Kozol
What makes an effective high school, a principal gives his views. A. A. Glatthorn. Parents Mag 44:64-5+ S '69
What's going on in schools & colleges. See issues of Changing times
Where all is quiet in the schools. il U S News 66:53-6 Ja 27 '69
See also
Education, Secondary

Administration
See School management and organization

Curriculum
Changes in high school curriculum. Sch & Soc 97:343-4 O '69
Course electives; improving selection through a system of parent-pupil-teacher conferences. R. P. Brimm. Clear House 43:417-20 Mr '69

HIGH schools—Curriculum—*Continued*
Curriculum for the 80's; address. 1968. D. W.
Allen. il Sr Schol 93:Schol Teach 13+ Ja 10
'69
Curriculum planners are doing their thing;
with study-discussion program, by C. Smal-
lenburg and H. Smallenburg. A. Frazier.
bibliog il PTA Mag 64:16-18, 36 N '69
ETS curriculum study. Sr Schol 95:Schol
Teach 1 O 27 '69
Reaching in; Bethesda school's experiment
in free-form education. D. Leff. Seventeen
29:84-5+ Ja '70
Subject articulation between high school and
college. J. Menacker. Clear House 44:220-3
D '69
Total curriculum a concern for all teachers.
L. J. Zahn and D. K. Zahn. Clear House
44:54-6 S '69
Toward reorganizing secondary school English.
R. B. Shuman. Sch & Soc 97:97-8 F '69
What does research in reading reveal; about
reading and the teacher of English? M. A.
Gunn. bibliog Engl J 58:368-85 Mr '69
See also
Elective system in education
Oriental studies
Schedules, School

Social rooms
See Student lounges
HIGH SIERRA camps. See Camps
HIGH speed trains. See Railroads—Passenger
service—High speed trains
HIGH speed transportation. See Transporta-
tion, High speed
HIGH-temperature batteries. See Storage bat-
teries
HIGH temperatures
Viscosity of argon at high temperatures.
R. A. Dawe and E. B. Smith. bibliog il
Science 163:675-6 F 14 '69
See also
Solar furnaces
HIGH voltage power lines. See Electric lines
HIGH voltage transmission. See Electric trans-
mission
HIGH wire walking. See Acrobats and acro-
batism
HIGHER education. See College education;
Colleges and universities; Junior colleges
HIGHET, Gilbert
Greeks and Romans at their ease. Horizon 11:
8-11 Spr '69
HIGHLAND PARK church. See Dallas—
Churches
HIGHTOWER, John B.
MOMA tries again. por Newsweek 75:95 Ja
19 '70
HIGHWAY, Pan American. See Pan American
highway
HIGHWAY accidents. See Traffic accidents
HIGHWAY engineering
Back of delays in road building: highway-
building contracts and employment pro-
grams. U S News 66:8 Ja 27 '69
Kill the hill! Pave that grass. P. O'Neil. il
Life 67:126-7+ O 10 '69
Let's put brakes on the highway lobby. G.
Denison and K. Y. Tomlinson. Read Digest
94:97-102 My '69
Roadmaster Volpe. New Repub 160:7 My 10
'69
Street construction & maintenance. See issues
of American city
See also
Traffic engineering
HIGHWAY law
See also
Rule of the road
HIGHWAY lighting. See Roads—Lighting
HIGHWAY lobby. See Lobbying
HIGHWAY location. See Roads—Location
HIGHWAY maintenance. See Roads—Mainten-
ance and repair
HIGHWAY maintenance equipment. See Mu-
nicipal equipment
HIGHWAY safety. See Roads—Safety devices
and measures
HIGHWAY signs. See Road signs
HIGHWAY transportation
See also
Transportation, Automotive
HIGINBOTHAM, William A.
Nuclear safeguards: the US program. bibliog
por Phys Today 22:40-4 N '69
HIGLEY, John R.
Hottest cottontails in the West. Field & S 74:
50-1+ Jl '69
Judie's cat. Outdoor Life 144:58-9+ S '69
Rainbows and rattlers. Outdoor Life 143:80-
3+ My '69

HIJACKING. See Robberies and assaults
HIJACKING of airplanes. See Airplane hijack-
ing
HIKING. See Walking
HILD, Walther J. See Walker, F. D. jt. auth.
HILDA Maehling fellowships. See Scholarships
and fellowships
HILDESHEIMER, Wolfgang
Apartment in the attic; Slightly bigger ac-
quisition; stories, tr. by E. Schlant. Harp
Baz 103:184-5, 240 N '69
HILDRETH, Reed C.
Who put the handprints on Prayer rock? Sci
Digest 65:54-6 Je '69
HILL, Adrian
Bad weather makes good painting. Design
70:8-9 mid-Wint '69
HILL, Calvin
I read Plimpton, I can't say it helped. por
Sports Illus 31:38-9 O 20 '69
Putting Yale on the map. Newsweek 74:104
O 20 '69
HILL, Charles Francis, 1923-
Parchment paper lion. R. Levy. il por Duns
R 93:52-4 Ja '69
HILL, Dean
Mixer. Hot Rod 22:40-2 Je '69
HILL, Evan
Revolution (cont): at University of Connec-
ticut. N Y Times Mag p28-9+ F 23 '69
HILL, Fran
Art from a sandbox. Design 70:20-3 Spr '69
HILL, Geoffrey
Comment. R. Skelton. Poetry 114:398-9 S '69
HILL, Gladwin
About 355 of those things have exploded in
Nevada. N Y Times Mag p6-7+ Jl 27 '69
Lake Superior, private dump. Nation 208:
795-6 Je 23 '69
HILL, Graham
Serenity on the edge of disaster: ed by
G. S. Brown. por Sports Illus 30:40-+ Mr
10 '69
HILL, John C.
Wall painting. Sch Arts 69:26-7 S '69
HILL, John Wiley
Survival lessons. L. L. L. Golden. Sat R 52:
49 Ag 9 '69
HILL, Joseph, pseud.
In the wake of John L. Lewis. Commonweal
90:430-1 Jl 11 '69
Labor shoots the breeze. Commonweal 91:
176 N 7 '69
Nixon-Meany; an odd couple. Commonweal
90:537+ S 5 '69
One big union for the blue Meanys. Common-
weal 90:37-8 Mr 28 '69
Stop the world. Commonweal 90:5-6 Mr 21
'69
Walter Reuther's gamble. Commonweal 90:261-
3 My 16 '69
HILL, Joseph A.
Presence of Christ: a contemporary view.
Chr Today 13:5-8 Je 20 '69
HILL, Phil
Inverted image of Phil Hill. J. G. Schmidt. il
pors Motor T 21:28-31 F '69
HILL, Rita
Monotype printing. Sch Arts 68:36-7 Mr '69
HILL, Robert L. See Turkington, R. W. jt.
auth.
HILL, Terrell L.
Earth cycle? poem. Bul Atom Sci 25:5 D '69
HILL, Tom W.
Electric fog to smother asthma. Sci Digest
65:74-7 Ap '69
HILL, William B.
Fiction (cont) America 120:536+: 121:530-2
My 3, N 29 '69
HILL-Burton act. See Hospitals—United States
HILL and Knowlton, incorporated
Survival lessons. L. L. L. Golden. Sate R 52:
49 Ag 9 '69
HILLARD, James M.
Profession gone mad. por Library J 95:42-3
Ja 1 '70
HILLEARY, D. T. See Wark, D. Q. jt. auth.
HILLEMAN, Maurice R.
Toward control of viral infections of man.
bibliog Science 164:506-14 My 2 '69
HILLEN, Karl Hermann Schulte-. See Schulte-
Hillen, K. H.
HILLENBRAND, Robert
First men on the moon. Sky & Tel 38:144-9
S '69
Send-off of Apollo 12. Sky & Tel 39:9-10 Ja
'70
HILLIES; story. See Updike, J.
HILLIS, Burton
Man next door. See issues of Better homes
& gardens
HILLIS, Dick
Locked-in generation. Chr Today 13:10-11 My
23 '69

HILLMAN, Elsie Mead (Hilliard)
Everybody here knows Elsie. por Forbes 104:
52 S 15 '69
HILLMAN, Henry Lea
Hillmans of Pittsburgh. il pors Forbes 104:
42-6+ S 15 '69
HILLMAN, James Frazer
Strip mine conservationist. por Forbes 104:44
S 15 '69
HILLMAN family
Hillmans of Pittsburgh; coal, iron and steel
business. il Forbes 104:42-6+ S 15 '69
HILLS, John
John Hills, gunsmith of Vermont. M. B. Pela-
deau. il Antiques 96:234-6 Ag '69
HILLS, Rust
How to do four dumb tricks with a package
of Camels. Esquire 72:144 S '69
HILLSIDE architecture
Bold angles; house built for J. Walker, Dal-
ton, Ga. F. Heard. il House B 111:102-5
S '69
Chalet: contemporary slant. il House B 111:
76-9 D '69
Family united in a house divided. il House &
Gard 135:136-41+ Ap '69
House of terraces on a rocky hill. il Arch Rec
145:141-6 Ja '69
House spectacular. il House & Gard 135:100-9
My '69
Houses on hillsides. il Am Home 72:54-5 Mr
'69
Meilleur house, Bellevue, Washington. il Arch
Rec 145:74-5 mid-My '69
Smart house for a steep lot. il Bet Hom &
Gard 47:154 N '69
Twin sky-lit pavilions, cantilevered out from
the hill to gain space. il Sunset 143:110 S
'69
HILLYARD, Kay
Just the two of us; poem. Har Yrs 9:26-30
O '69
Walk with me. Har Yrs 9:26-9 Ag; 26-9 S
'69
HILTON, Conrad N.
Widening father's footsteps. il por Time 94:
60 Ag 29 '69
HILTON, George W.
Decline of rail passenger traffic; address,
June 19, 1969. Vital Speeches 35:657-61 Ag
15 '69
HILTON, Wendy
Dancing Bach. por Dance Mag 43:47-9+ O '69
HILTON, William Barron
Widening father's footsteps. il por Time 94:
60 Ag 29 '69
HILTON HEAD fishing cooperative, incor-
porated. See Fisheries, Cooperative
HILTON hotel. See Washington, D.C.—Hotels,
restaurants, etc.
HILTON hotels corporation
Nighttime boss of capital inn; Washington
Hilton hotel. il Ebony 25:67-8+ N '69
Widening father's footsteps. il Time 94:60
Ag 29 '69
HILTS, Len
How to be an old salt in a new boat. Todays
Health 47:20-5 Je '69
HIMALAYAN art. See Art, Himalayan
HIMMELFARB, Gertrude
Will to believe. New Repub 160:26-30 My 10
'69
HIMMELFARB, Milton
Hebraism & Hellenism now. Commentary 48:
50-7 Jl; 22 N '69
Is American Jewry in crisis? Commentary 47:
33-42 Mr; 20+ Je '69
HIMMELFARB, P. and others
Spin filter culture: the propagation of mam-
malian cells in suspension. bibliog Science
164:555-7 My 2 '69
HIMMELREICH, Ferdinand
Ferdinand Himmelreich, the blind pianist. J.
Walsh. pors Hobbies 74:38-40+ N '69
HINCHLIFF, William E.
Ivory tower ghettoes. por Library J 94:3971-4
N 1 '69
Urban problems and higher education; Federal
city college; address, November 1968. por
Wilson Lib Bul 43:526-33 F '69
HINCHLIFFE, Stephen
Making money on leisure time. il pors Bsns
W p62-4+ Ja 18 '69
HINCKLE, Marianne
Last hurrah of Cardinal Patrick Aloysius
O'Boyle. Ramp Mag 7:28-31 D 14 '68
HINCKLE, Warren, 3d
Manning the Ramparts, or is it the Barricades?
il por Time 93:42 F 7 '69
Ramparts story; um, very interesting. J.
Ridgeway. il por N Y Times Mag p34-6+
Ap 20 '69; Reply with rejoinder. W. Hinckle.
p 132 My 11 '69
Two for one. New Repub 160:9-10 F 15 '69

HINCKLEY, George P.
How the package plans will work; interview.
por U S News 66:83-4 Je 30 '69
HINCKLEY, Mabel
Let's climb the family tree. por Har Yrs
9:38-41 Mr '69
HINCKLEY, Ohio. See Cleveland
HINDEMITH, Paul
Hindemith's so-called Brandenburgs: seven
pieces from the twenties. A. Frankenstein.
por Hi Fi 19:75 F '69
One of the season's best chamber-music re-
leases, Hindemith and Honegger quartets
on Crossroads. A. Cohn. Am Rec G 35:563
Mr '69
Paul Hindemith's kammermusiken. A. Cohn.
por Am Rec G 36:22-3 S '69
Revitalizing the viola; Walter Trampler plays
three works by a great fellow violist. A.
Cohn. il por Am Rec G 35:368-9 Ja '69
HINDLE, Will
Two films by Will Hindle. R. Corliss. il Film
Q 22:47-50 Spr '69
HINDS, Ilene
Welfare mother. Chr Cent 87:17-18 Ja 7 '70
HINDS, Jeannette
Security; poem. Chr Cent 86:642 My 7 '69
HINDSIGHT and foresight; story. See Hoyer,
L. G.
HINDU KUSH
High above the Land of light. R. Cantwell. il
Sports Illus 31:30-6 Jl 28 '69
HINDU medicine. See Medicine, Hindu
HINDUISM
See also
Mysticism—Hinduism
HINE, A!
Camparis, contessas and casanovas. Holiday
46:20-1 Jl '69
HINE, Daryl
Burnt out; poem. Harper 239:59 Ag '69
Elegiacs. Poetry 115:83-5 N '69
HINES, Jerome
I am the way. Criticism
Chr Cent por 86:649-50 My 7 '69
Pathetic pavement of good intentions. T. W.
Moore. por Chr Cent 86:649-50 My 7 '69
HINES, William
Washington scene. Bul Atom Sci 25:38+ Mr;
37-40 My '69
HINKLE, John E. and Ivey, A. E.
Rural attitudes toward mental health. Ment
Hy 53:295-7 Ap '69
HINKLEY, Horace R.
Mystery of the Hinkley deer. por Outdoor
Life 144:44-7+ Ag '69
HINRICHS, Marie A.
Doctor, I have a question; questions and
answers. See issues of Harvest years
HINTON, James Sidney
Black spokesman, or Republican pawn. R. D.
Snell. bibliog por Negro Hist Bul 32:6-10
N '69
HIPPIES
Are you listening, D. H. Lawrence? E. Wit-
ten. New Repub 161:15-17 O 18 '69
Avenging Angels; Hell's Angels and hippies
brawl ends in killing of Meredith Hunter.
il Newsweek 75:16 Ja 5 '70
Case of the hypnotic hippie. il Newsweek 74:
30-2+ D 15 '69
Charlie Manson: one man's family. S. V.
Roberts. il N Y Times Mag p 10-11+ Ja
4 '70
Communing in Meadville. R. Hourlet. Ramp
Mag 7:10+ N 30 '68
Condemnation and persecution of hippies. M.
E. Brown. bibliog il Trans-Action 6:33-46
S '69; Excerpts. Cur 112:9-13 N '69
Do not smoke Skippy peanut butter. T.
Burke. il Esquire 72:129-32+ O '69
Flower power: a student's guide to pre-hippie
transcendentalism. P. H. Wild. Engl J 58:
62-8 Ja '69
Flowering of the hippie movement. J. R.
Howard. bibliog f Ann Am Acad 382:43-55
Mr '69
Great hippie hunt. il Time 94:22-3 O 10 '69
Groovy revolution. H. S. Resnik. il Sat R
52:34+ D 13 '69
Haight-Ashbury today: a case of terminal
euphoria. J. Luce. il Esquire 72:65-8+ Jl '69
Hip establishment, tyrant kids. J. Marks.
Vogue 154:346+ S 1 '69
Hippie weltanschauung. J. Eisen. Cath World
209:44+ Ap '69
Hippies and violence. il Time 94:25 D 12 '69
Hippies as parents. W. Hedgepeth. il Look
33:69-74 Jl 15 '69
Hippies get Boston up tight. il Bsns W p 142-
3 My 17 '69
Hippies vs. skinheads; takeover of unused
buildings in London. il Newsweek 74:90 O
6 '69

HIPPIES—*Continued*
How to stay hip, happy and out of jail; with photographs. Life 67:81-4 N 28 '69
Kid-killers: a night with the drugged children of America. S. Labin il Nat R 21:434-5 My 6 '69
Life and death of a commune called Oz: a settlement near Meadville, Pa. R. Houriet. il N Y Times Mag p30-1+ F 16 '69; Discussion. p 12+ Mr 9 '69
Making of a hippie; with study-discussion program, by C. Smallenburg and H. Smallenburg. L. Wolf. bibliog il PTA Mag 63:6-9, 36-7 Ja '69; Same abr. Ed Digest 34:32-4 Ap '69
Monstrous Manson family; with statements by D. Smith and R. Smith. P. O'Neil and others. il Life 67:2A, 20-31 D 19 '69
Notes from the new underground; an anthology, ed. by J. Kornbluth. Review
Commentary 47:94-5 Mr '69. W. Goodman
Paradise rocked; community at Taos, N.Mex. il Time 93:55 Je 20 '69
Squat-in at no. 144 Piccadilly. il Life 67:52-3 O 3 '69
Trouble in paradise; off-beat rural community of Canyon, Calif. S. Stern. il Ramp Mag 8:22-8 N '69
War at home; intolerance towards the hippies. D. Wakefield. Atlan 224:119-24 O '69
Where have all the flowers gone? New York bombings, Sharon Tate murders. Nat R 21:1257 D 16 '69
Year of the commune. il Newsweek 74:89-90 Ag 18 '69

Political activities
"Free", by A. Hoffman. Review
Commonweal 89:596-7 F 7 '69. R. Howard
Inside the great pigasus plot; excerpts from Do it! J. Rubin. il Ramp Mag 8:10-12+ D '69
Making of a yippie; J. Rubin. J. A. Lukas. il Esquire 72:126-34+ N '69
Making of the yippie culture. G. Willis. Esquire 72:135-8+ N '69
My little Yippela, Jerry Rubin goes home. J. Kornbluth. il Look 33:20 O 7 '69

Religion
Preacher in the mud; rapping for Christ; West Palm Beach, Florida, Thanksgiving weekend rock festival. A. Taft. Chr Today 14:34 D 19 '69

HIPPLE, Theodore W.
Toward improved English department meetings. Engl J 58:440-2 Mr '69
HIPPLER, Arthur E.
Popular art styles in Mariachi festivals. bibliog Am Imago 26:167-81 Sum '69
HIPWELL, Philip
Phoebe Neville dances with Philip Hipwell; Judson memorial church. J. Armstrong. Dance Mag 43:84 N '69
HIRED men. See Farm labor
HIRING. See Employment systems
HIRN, Doris D.
Your riding program. Camp Mag 41:31 My '69
HIROSHIMA
Death in life; a statement. R. J. Lifton. Bul Atom Sci 25:39 Je '69
Return to Hiroshima; oh, what a lovely pandemonium. N. Cousins. il Sat R 53: 20-2 Ja 3 '70
HIROSHIMA maidens
Return to Hiroshima; oh, what a lovely pandemonium. N. Cousins. il Sat R 53:20-2 Ja 3 '70
HIRSCH, G. H. and Hook, J. B.
Maturation of renal organic acid transport: substrate stimulation by penicillin. bibliog Science 165:909-10 Ag 29 '69
HIRSCH, Julian D.
EW lab tests new stereo compacts. Electr World 82:27-30+ D '69
EW lab tests of new cassette tape recorders. Electr World 81:26-7+ Je '69
HIRSCHBERG, J. Cotter
Today's family; a balance of strengths and weaknesses; excerpt from The clergyman as counselor. por Sci Digest 65:63-5 Mr '69
HIRSCHFIELD, Robert Carl
Barrientos, the man who captured Che. Commonweal 89:609-10; 90:182 F 14, Ap 25 '69
Lima slum. Cath World 207:251-3; 208:196 S '68. F '69
HIRSCHHORN, Kurt, and others
Pompe's disease: detection of heterozygotes by lymphocyte stimulation. bibliog Science 166:1632-3 D 26 '69
HIRSCHL, Milton
Collographs without a press. Sch Arts 68:14-17 F '69

HIRSCHMAN, Albert, and Hirschman, Mildred
Soluble sulfatase in growing bone of rats. bibliog Science 164:834-5 My 16 '69
HIRSCHMAN, Mildred. See Hirschman, A. jt. auth.
HIRSHBERG, Al. See Harrelson, K. jt. auth.
HIRSHHORN, Joseph H.
Collector: Joseph H. Hirshhorn. J. Jacobs. por Art in Am 57:56-71 Jl '69
HIRSHHORN collection. See Art—Private collections
HISPANIOLA (island)
Early man in the West Indies. J. M. Cruxent and I. Rouse. il Sci Am 221:42-52 bibliog (p 166) N '69
HISS, Anthony
Concert records. New Yorker 45:119-23 O 4; 114+ D 20 '69
HISTAMINE
Histamine and spermidine content in brain during development. L. A. Pearce and S. M. Schanberg. bibliog il Science 166:1301-3 D 5 '69
HISTOCHEMISTRY
See also
Brain—Analysis and chemistry
HISTOCOMPATIBILITY. See Immunological tolerance
HISTONES
Chromatin and histones: binding of tritiated actinomycin D to heterochromatin in mealy bugs. L. Berlowiz and others. bibliog il Science 164:1527-9 Je 27 '69
Histone structure: asymmetric distribution of lysine residues in lysine-rich histone. M. Bustin and others. bibliog il Science 163: 391-3 Ja 24 '69
Histone synthesis in vitro by cytoplasmic microsomes from HeLa cells. D. Gallwitz and G. C. Mueller. bibliog il Science 163: 1351-3 Mr 21 '69
Similarity between calves and peas: histone IV. il Chem 42:23-4 Ja '69
HISTOPLASMOSIS
Exposing histo. disease in disguise. J. Carper. il Todays Health 47:30-1+ My '69
Fungus diseases that fool the doctors. J. D. Wassersug. Sci Digest 66:81-2 Ag '69
HISTORIANS
Hassle of historians. J. Gilbert. Nation 208: 77-9 Ja 20 '69
HISTORIANS, American
See also
Duberman, M.
HISTORIANS, German
See also
Müller, Johannes von
HISTORIC houses, etc.
Historic houses, landmarks, and museums. See issues of Antiques
See also subhead Historic houses, etc. under names of countries, states, cities, etc. e.g. Sacramento, Calif.—Historic houses, etc.

Conservation and restoration
See Architecture—Conservation and restoration
HISTORIC trails. See Trails
HISTORIC trees. See Trees, Historic
HISTORICAL drama
History as drama. J. Richardson. Commentary 47:22+ F '69
HISTORICAL fiction
Exclusive interview with Frances Parkinson Keyes; ed. by P. A. Brock. F. P. Keyes. il Writers Digest 49:56-9 O '69
Revising a historical novel. C. Holland. Writer 82:17-19+ O '69
Writing of historical novels. excerpt from address, August 1968. H. Burton. Horn Bk 45:271-7 Je '69
See also
Fiction—Technique
HISTORICAL films. See Moving pictures—Historical films
HISTORICAL libraries
See also
Presidential libraries
HISTORICAL museums
From Sabbathday Lake to Pleasant Hill. Am Home 72:94 S '69
HISTORICAL societies
See also
Historical society of Montana
HISTORICAL society of Montana
One thing and another. J. K. Hutchens. Sat R 52:42-3 O 4 '69
HISTORIOGRAPHY. See History—Historiography

HISTORY
Is there a lesson of Munich? E. Stillman.
  Horizon 11:32-3 Spr '69
Who needs history? R. L. Tobin. Sat R 52:
  22 S 6 '69; Same. Chr Today 14:14-15 N 21
  '69
    See also
Archeology
Civilization
Economic history
Historians
Historical drama
Historical fiction
Revolutions
Sociology
World history
    also subhead Antiquities; Foreign rela-
    tions; History; Politics and government un-
    der names of countries, states, etc. e.g.
    France—Antiquities; *also* subhead History
    under various subjects, e.g. Science—His-
    tory

Anecdotes, facetiae, satire, etc.
American history blown off course by eighth
  graders; excerpts from Then some other
  stuff happened. B. Lawrence. il Todays Ed
  58:51 S '69

Bibliography
History (cont) C. L. Hohl, jr. America 120:
  539-40; 121:538-40 My 3, N 29 '69

Historiography
Inductive unit on historiography. B. M.
  Ashcom and R. S. Beren. Ed Digest 34
  47-9 F '69
    See also
Europe—History—Historiography
Historians

Philosophy
Americanization of history. H. S. Commager.
  Sat R 52:24-5+ N 1 '69
Defense walls repeat themselves. P. W.
  Schmidtchen. il Hobbies 74:134-6 N '69

Sources
Uncompleted past, by M. Duberman. Review
  Sat R 53:23-5+ Ja 3 '70. W. M. Wiecek
    See also
Oral history
World war, 1939-1945—Documents, sources,
  etc.

Study and teaching
Historian and historical films. W. H. McNeill.
  Ed Digest 34:38-40 Ja '69
Inductive unit on historiography. B. M. Ash-
  com and R. S. Beren. Ed Digest 34:47-9 F '69
Teaching the art of history. B. Lippman.
  il Nat R 21:1214-18 D 2 '69
Three-dimensional history class in Hungary.
  P. Almasy. il UNESCO Courier 22:31 N '69
    See also
United States—History—Study and teaching

HISTORY, Ancient
    See also
Archeology

Bibliography
Articles and other books received; comp. by T.
  R. S. Broughton. See issues of American
  historical review

HISTORY, Biblical. See Bible—History of biblical events

HISTORY, Roman. See Rome—History

HISTORY, Universal. See World history

HISTORY and science. See Science and civilization

HISTORY in art
American travels of a French botanist. P.
  Rouse, jr. il Antiques 96:763-7 N '69

HITCH hiking. See Hitchhiking

HITCHCOCK, James
Christian and change. Chr Cent 87:7-11 Ja
  7 '70
Christian values and a secular future. Ameri-
  ca 121:155-9 S 13 '69
Comes the cultural revolution. N Y Times
  Mag p4-5+ Jl 27 '69
Repeat performance? Commonweal 89:556-9
  Ja 31 '69
Sex, church, and culture. Cath World 209:17-
  20 Ap '69

HITCHENS, Dolores
Collection of strangers; story. Redbook 133:
  159-81 S '69

HITCHES (automobile) See Automobiles—
  Equipment

HITCHHIKING
New rule of thumb. il Newsweek 73:63 Je 16
  '69

HITLER, Adolf
Big business and the rise of Hitler. H. A.
  Turner, jr. bibliog f Am Hist R 75:56-70 O
  '69
Devil's architect. J. P. O'Donnell. il pors
  N Y Times Mag p45-9+ O 26 '69; Discus-
  sion. p22+ N 30 '69

HNATT, Luciana
Parents' night at school. Parents Mag 44:58-
  9+ S '69

HO, Mae Wan, and O'Brien, J. S.
Hurler's syndrome: deficiency of a specific beta
  galactosidase isoenzyme. bibliog Science 165:
  611-13 Ag 8 '69

HO, Peter P. K. and others
Crystalline L-asparaginase from escherichia
  coli B. bibliog Science 165:510-12 Ag 1 '69

HO, Ping-ti
Loess and the origin of Chinese agriculture.
  bibliog f Am Hist R 75:1-36 O '69

HO, T. Y. and others
Radiocarbon dating of petroleum-impregnated
  bone from tar pits at Rancho La Brea,
  California. bibliog Science 164:1051-2 My 30
  '69

HOAG, M. De Koning
Gina between; story. Seventeen 27:134-5 N '68
Whole cookie; story. Seventeen 28:118-19 Je
  '69

HOAGLAND, Edward
Final fate of alligators; story. New Yorker 45:52-7 O 18 '69
Problem of the golden rule. Commentary
  48:38-42 Ag '69

HOAGLAND, Hudson
Beings from outer space, corporeal and
  spiritual. Science 163:625 F 14 '69
Technology, adaptation, and evolution; ex-
  cerpt from address. Bul Atom Sci 25:27-30
  Ja '69

HOARDING
String-saver strikes back. J. L. Langdon.
  il Good H 168:56+ Mr '69

HOAXES
Great moon hoax. J. Cottrell. il Sci Digest
  66:40-4 Jl '69
Greatest Halloween prank of them all; re-
  actions to 1938 broadcast of The war of
  the worlds. J. H. Burns. Read Digest 95:
  157-60 O '69
Life and times of Blind Orange Adams; mu-
  sical hoaxes. G. Lees. Hi Fi 19:126 O '69
    See also
Naked truth about the great novel hoax;
  Naked came the stranger. B. Bruns. il
  Life 67:69-70 Ag 22 '69
One every minute. H. Bowser. Sat R 52:16
  My 31 '69
Penelope's playmates; authors of Naked
  came the stranger. il Time 94:66+ Ag 15
  '69
Put-on. F. Maynard. il Seventeen 27:126-7+
  N '68
Stranger than fiction; concerning Naked
  came the stranger. il Newsweek 74:90-1
  Ag 18 '69
View of the moon from the Sun; 1835. J. L.
  Morrison. il Am Heritage 20:80-2 Ap '69
    See also
Literary forgeries and mystifications
Piltdown forgery

HOBBIES
Use and abuse of leisure. H. Van Horne.
  House B 111:48-9+ Ag '69
    See also
Art, Amateur
Tandy corporation

HOBBS, Cecil
(comp) Articles and other books received;
  South Asia. See issues of American historical review

HOBBS, Helen
Loneliest night of the year. por Redbook
  134:49-50 D '69

HOBBS, Peter V. and Radke, L. F.
Cloud condensation nuclei from a simulated
  forest fire. bibliog Science 163:279-80 Ja 17
  '69
—See Macklin, W. C. jt. auth.

HOBBS, Walter C.
Contemporary church: instrument or idol? Chr
  Today 13:7-8 Je 6 '69

HOBBY clubs. See Clubs

HOBOKEN, N.J.
City of the prophecies, a Hoboken perspective. E. Abbey Natur Hist 78:24+ Ap '69

HOBSON, Jesse E. and Robbins, M. E.
Catholic colleges: the cost spiral catches up.
  America 121:634-6 D 27 '69

HOCHBAUM, Godfrey M.
Teaching adolescents about smoking, drinking, drug abuse. Ed Digest 34:28-31 Ja '69

HO-chi-Minh
President Ho's letter to President Nixon,
  August 25, 1969. Dept State Bul 61:443-4 N
  24 '69

HO-chi-Minh—*Continued*

about

After Ho Chi Minh. N. K. Huyen. America 121:265-7 O 4 '69

After Ho; shift in the war? il por U S News 67:25-7 S 15 '69

After Uncle Ho, what? Cur 112:55-8 N '69

Ceasefire for Ho? Nat R 21:946 S 23 '69

Death of Ho; views from Saigon. T. Fox. Commonweal 90:581 S 26 '69

Farewell to Ho. il Newsweek 74:30-1 S 22 '69

Funeral in Hanoi, feud in Peking. il por Time 94:34+ S 19 '69

Ground rules for national communism. Life 67:46B S 19 '69

Hanoi without Ho; what U.S. can expect; interview. P. J. Honey. il U S News 67: 38-40 S 22 '69

Ho Chi Minh: a eulogy. F. Schurmann. por Ramp Mag 8:52+ N '69

Kindly Uncle Ho. K. Crawford. Newsweek 74:29 S 15 '69

Last of the Comintern. America 121:178 S 20 '69

Legacy of Ho Chi Minh. il pors Time 94:22-6+ S 12 '69

Legendary life of he who enlightens comes to an end at last. il pors Life 67:36-8 S 12 '69

Nguyen ai Quoc's second funeral. Chr Cent 86:1185 S 17 '69

Obituary
    Nation 209:237 S 15 '69

President Ho chi Minh (1890-1969) il pors Newsweek 74:30+ S 15 '69

Red ruler who refuses to be defeated; what he hopes to gain. il pors U S News 66:18-19 My 26 '69

Trying to read Ho. il Time 93:29-30 My 30 '69

HOCHMAN, Sandra
Looking around. por Look 33:22 Mr 4 '69
Postscript; poem. Atlan 224:42 Ag '69
This summer; poem. New Yorker 45:32 Jl 26 '69

HOCHMAN, Shirley D.
Introducing motion. Sch Arts 69:12-13 S '69

HOCHSCHILD, Adam
Teapot dome in the Rockies. Ramp Mag 7:75-8 Ja 25 '69

HOCHSCHILD, Arlie
Student power in action. por Trans-Action 6:16-21+ Ap '69

HOCHSTEIN, Rolaine
Affirming flame of Ardith Manners; story. Redbook 133:100-1 O '69

HOCHSTEIN, Rollie
Crusades and capers of Shirley MacLaine. Good H 168:52-4+ Je '69

Diahann Carroll's juggling act. Good H 168: 38+ My '69

Mike Douglas, TV's no. 1 ladies' man. Good H 169:30+ S '69

Pride of five women. Good H 168:84-7+ Je '69

—See Sugarman, D. A. jt. auth.

HOCKEY
Found a native who outplays the imports; Boston college's T. Sheehy. M. Mulvoy. il Sports Illus 30:38+ Ja 20 '69

Muted moments of hockey; paintings. R. Estes. Sports Illus 31:28-33 N 3 '69

Power play; Russian hockey team tour of Canada. Newsweek 73:58 F 3 '69

Russians lose a pair; and set off 100,000 Czechs. il Life 66:93-4 Ap 11 '69

Some pros go back to college; Denver wins the NCAA championship. G. Ronberg. il Sports Illus 30:56-7 Mr 24 '69
    See also
National hockey league

Accidents and injuries

Stick that sickens; T. Green incident. P. Axthelm. il Newsweek 74:95 O 6 '69

HOCKEY coaches. See Coaches (athletics)

HOCKEY fans. See Sports fans

HOCKEY players
Hockey '69; the rough get rougher. G. Ronberg. il Sports Illus 31:34-6+ O 13 '69

Icy love-in with the red-hot Blues; Stanley cup playoffs. G. Ronberg. il Sports Illus 30: 52-4+ Ap 7 '69

It's Bobby Orr & the animals; Bruins a threat to Montreal's reign. M. Mulvoy. il Sports Illus 30:18-23 F 3 '69

Some pros go back to college; Denver wins the NCAA championship. G. Ronberg. il Sports Illus 30:56-7 Mr 24 '69

Sporting scene; St Louis Blues success story. H. W. Wind. New Yorker 45:138+ Mr 15 '69

We have the taste of victory; from Chicago Black Hawks to Boston Bruins; ed. by M. Kane. P. Esposito. il Sports Illus 31:44-6+ O 13 '69
    See also
Hockey teams
Howe, G.
Orr, B.

HOCKEY rinks
Ice fever; Northbrook, Ill. W. B. Cooper. il Parks & Rec 4:53+ S '69

HOCKEY sticks
Day of the banana stick. il Time 93:50 F 21 '69

HOCKEY teams
Blood and ice; best defenseman in the most savage sport outside of bullfighting. B. Surface. il N Y Times Mag p26-26A+ F 2 '69

Bobby mines the mother lode; Boston Bruins' defenseman. M. Mulvoy. il Sports Illus 32:20-1 Ja 12 '70

Bobby says he wants to play the game; Chicago Black Hawks. G. Ronberg. il Sports Illus 31:60-1 N 3 '69

Boston roars back; Bruins even Stanley cup series with Canadiens. G. Ronberg. il Sports Illus 30:20-3 Ap 28 '69

Boston's Orr; fire on ice. il Newsweek 73: 64-7 Mr 24 '69

Down go the babbling Bruins; Boston Bruins vs Montreal Canadiens. G. Ronberg. il Sports Illus 31:24-5 N 10 '69

Freddie's in, gloom's out; coach of Oakland Seals. G. Ronberg. il Sports Illus 30: 62+ Mr 10 '69

Gordie Howe; hockey's marvelous Methuselah; Detroit Red Wings. D. MacDonald. il Read Digest 95:122-6 N '69

Grand Jean a mighty man is he; Montreal vs Boston Bruins in East's Stanley cup finals. G. Ronberg. il Sports Illus 30:24-7 My 5 '69

Hockey '69; the rough get rougher. G. Ronberg. il Sports Illus 31:34-6+ O 13 '69

Icy love-in with the red-hot Blues; Stanley cup playoffs. G. Ronberg. il Sports Illus 30: 52-4+ Ap 7 '69

It's Bobby Orr & the animals; Bruins a threat to Montreal's reign. M. Mulvoy. il Sports Illus 30:18-23 F 3 '69

Maple Leafs. J. Sayre. il Holiday 45:70-1+ F '69

Montreal and the golden Ruel; winning the East title. G. Ronberg. il Sports Illus 30: 74+ Ap 7 '69

Montreal ho-hums the Blues. G. Ronberg. il Sports Illus 30:61-2 My 12 '69

New Cadillac for Detroit. G. Ronberg. il Sports Illus 30:50+ F 24 '69

Open season on Bobby Hull; Chicago Black Hawks top goal scorer. G. Ronberg. il Sports Illus 30:18-19 Ja 20 '69

Philly takes a flyer on a rookie with heart; B. Clarke. G. Ronberg. il Sports Illus 31: 92+ N 17 '69

Rangers go boom. G. Astor. il Look 33:80-2 F 4 '69

Red-hot tune for the Kings; Los Angeles Kings defeat Oakland Seals. A. Wright. il Sports Illus 30:30-1 Ap 21 '69

Sporting scene; St Louis Blues success story. H. W. Wind. New Yorker 45:138+ Mr 15 '69

Stadiums aren't for sleeping; Toronto Maple Leafs vs Detroit Red Wings. P. Waldmeir and G. Ronberg. il Sports Illus 31:28-9 O 20 '69

Unsudden death; Canadiens and the Boston Bruins. Newsweek 73:98 My 5 '69

We have the taste of victory; from Chicago Black Hawks to Boston Bruins; ed. by M. Kane. P. Esposito. il Sports Illus 31: 44-6+ O 13 '69

Why the Bruins climb. il Time 93:74 Ap 4 '69

Won't somebody please get me out of here? W. Blair, coach of Minnesota's North Stars. G. Ronberg. Sports Illus 31:81-2+ D 1 '69

HOCKNEY, David
Hockney paints a portrait. D. Shapiro. il por Art N 68:28-31+ My '69

HODGE, Carle O.
Blooming desert. Bul Atom Sci 25:32-3 N '69

HODGE, Gerald P. See Ravin, J. G. jt. auth.

HODGE, Jane Aiken
English season. Travel & Camera 32:41-2+ Ag '69

HODGE, Jim
Surfers stoke streetsters. Hot Rod 22:62-3 My '69

HODGES, Allen. See Mahoney, S. C. jt. auth
HODGES, Elizabeth Jamison
In Transylvania; poem. Horn Bk 45:36 F '69
Magic of serendipity. Horn Bk 45:436-40
Ag '69
HODGES, Joseph E.
Letter. Sch Arts 68:40 F '69
HODGES, William H.
Bruised world still seeks Good Samaritans.
Chr Today 13:6-9 S 12 '69
HODGIN, Ellis
Virginia librarian fired by city manager; with
editorial comment. Library J 94:2853, 2855
S 1 '69; Reply. I. Webb and others. 94:3585
O 15 '69

about

Martinsville counterattack: Ellis Hodgin ac-
cused. Library J 94:4082 N 15 '69
HODGINS, Maibelle Dickey
Brown thrasher handsome songster and
gardener's friend. Home Gard 56:76+ F '69
Music in the garden. il Horticulture 47:38-9
Je '69
HODGKIN, Dorothy (Crowfoot)
Insulin design traced. D. Fishlock. il Sci N
96:307 O 4 '69
HODGKIN, Howard
London; influence of Matisse and The Moroc-
cans. J. Russell. Art N 68:43 My '69
HODGKIN'S disease
They're curing an incurable cancer. W. S.
Ross. il Read Digest 95:89-93 D '69
HODGKINSON, Peter
Kafka's castle. Arch Forum 131:35-41 N '69
HODGSON, Marshall G. S.
In the centre of the map: reprint. UNESCO
Courier 22:54-5 Ag '69
HODGSON, Richard G.
Search for Vulcan. R Pop Astron 63:10-12
Mr; 10-11 My '69
HODGSON, Ruth
How to save on camp food bills. Camp Mag
41:20+ Mr '69
HOE, R, and company
Sad story printed by R. Hoe. Bsns W p35-6
Jl 19 '69
HOEFFGEN, Helen
Branch library programs; operation shoe-
string budget. por Wilson Lib Bul 43:545-51
F '69
HOEH, David C.
Where are they now? il por Newsweek 74:8
S 8 '69
HOELSCHER, Harold Ewald
Technology and social change; adaptation of
address. August 4, 1969. bibliog Science
166:68-72 O 3 '69
HOFFA, James Riddle
Hoffa hears some bad news. por Bsns W p68
Jl 26 '69
HOFFER, Barry J. and others
Prostaglandins E₁ and E₂ antagonize
norepinephrine effects on cerebellar
Purkinje cells: microelectrophoretic study.
bibliog Science 166:1418-20 D 12 '69
HOFFER, Eric
Leisure and the masses; address. pors Parks
& Rec 4:31-4+ Mr '69

about

Man of sense. R. Mackenzie. Nat R 21:445 My
6 '69
On Eric Hoffer. P. Kemble. Commentary 48:
79-82 N '69
HOFFERT, Emily
Annals of jurisprudence. F. C. Shapiro. New
Yorker 44:39-42+ F 8; 44-6+ F 15; 45:42-
4+ F 22 '69
Victims; excerpts. B. Lefkowitz and K. G.
Gross. il por Look 33:37-42+ My 27; 39-
44+ Je 10; 39-44+ Je 24 '69
HOFFMAN, Abbie
Groovy revolution. H. S. Resnik. il pors Sat
R 52:34+ D 13 '69
HOFFMAN, Charles
Door opened; story. Ladies Home J 86:78-9
F '69
HOFFMAN, Daniel
Constraints and self-determinations. Poetry
114:335-44 Ag '69
Historian; Special train; Aphrodite; poems.
Poetry 115:101-4 N '69
Moonshot; poem. Nation 208:408 Mr 31 '69
HOFFMAN, Dustin
Dusty and the Duke; with editorial comment.
il pors Life 67:1; 36-45 Jl 11 '69
High-level acting. R. Gilman. New Repub
160:32-4 Ja 25 '69
Moonchild and the fifth Beatle. il por Time
93:50+ F 7 '69
HOFFMAN, Howard S. and others
Punishment by response-contingent withdraw-
al of an imprinted stimulus. bibliog Science
163:702-4 F 14 '69

HOFFMAN, Judith
On campus. Mlle 69:52 Ag '69
HOFFMAN, Julius J.
In re Bobby Seale. W. F. Buckley, jr. Nat R
21:1234-5 D 2 '69
Judge Hoffmann goes on trial. America 121:
486-7 N 22 '69
Julius the just. por Time 94:75 O 24 '69
Mockery of justice? il por Newsweek 74:41-2
O 27 '69
Theater of the conspiracy. P. A. Luce. Nat
R 21:1264 D 16 '69
Then there were seven. Newsweek 74:50+
N 17 '69
HOFFMAN, L. E.
Bush-anemone. Horticulture 47:50 S '69
HOFFMAN, Michael J.
From Cohn to Herzog. Yale R 58:342-58
Mr '69
HOFFMAN, Rosellen Brown
Improving buzzard's luck. por Wilson Lib Bul
44:51-7 S '69
HOFFMAN, William
Mother wants to meet you: story. McCalls
96:68-9 Jl '69
HOFFMANN, Dietrich. See Wynder, E. L. jt
auth.
HOFFMANN, Rita
Moving finger writes; story. McCalls 96:72-3
Mr '69
HOFFMANN, Stanley
America and France. New Repub 160:17-21
Ap 5; 20-3 Ap 12 '69
De Gaulle's legacy to Pompidou. New Repub
161:19-21 Jl 12 '69
French style of protest. New Repub 160:23-4
Ja 25 '69
Great power cannot treat every tremor as a
major threat. Commonweal 90:13-14 Mr 21
'69; Same with title Need for self restraint.
Cur 109:59-61 Ag '69
How will France change? New Repub 161:
21-4 Jl 26 '69
Policy for the 70s. Life 66:68-70+ Mr 21 '69
HOFHEINZ, Roy Mark
Greatest showman on earth, and he's the
first to admit it. T. Maule. il por Sports
Illus 30:36-8+ Ap 21 '69
Hofheinz and the Astrodome. M. Frady. il pors
Holiday 45:42-5+ My '69
HOFSTADTER, Robert
New detectors for high-energy physics. bib-
liog Science 164:1471-82 Je 27 '69
HOFSTEDT and Jean, and others; story. See
Brodkey, H.
HOFSTEIN, David
Sabbath is gone; poem; tr. by N. Halper.
Nation 208:154 F 3 '69
HOG cholera
Keep cholera eradication moving. R. Wil-
more. il Farm J 93:H12-14 Ap '69
HOG houses. See Swine houses
HOGAN, Elizabeth. See Curtis, R. jt. auth.
HOGAN, Frank
Categoric past, the personal present. House
B 111:124-7 Je '69
(ed) See Lillie, B. Night I sang Carmen
at the Met
HOGAN, Gary
Character boat, what is it? Motor B 123:173-5
My '69
HOGAN, Joseph S. See Stewart, R. W. jt.
auth.
HOGAN, Lester
Between the idea and the reality. pors
Forbes 104:25-7 O 15 '69
HOGARTH, William
Hogarth and the ladies. I. Smith. il Horticul-
ture 47:22-3 O '69
Music by Handel and Hogarth. F. V. Grunfeld.
il Opera N 33:12-15 F 8 '69
HOGIN, James L.
Active filters. por Electr World 81:58-60 Ap
'69
HOHENBERG, C. M.
Radioisotopes and the history of nucleosyn-
thesis in the galaxy. bibliog Science 166:
212-15 O 10 '69
HOHENBERG, John
Great press put-on. Sat R 52:120-1 Mr 8 '69
Image-makers' image. Sat R 52:53-4 F 8 '69
Watchman, what of the news? Stories the
papers miss. Sat R 52:56-7 Je 14 '69
What it's like to be a Czech newspaperman.
Sat R 52:78-80 N 8 '69
World's press: just how free is it? excerpt
from The best cause: free press-free people.
Sat R 52:70-2 D 13 '69
HOHENEMSER, Kurt H.
Today's engineer, building a bridge to the
public; address. por Sci & Cit 10:250-3 D '68
HOHL, Clarence Leonard, jr
History (cont) America 120:539-40; 121:538-40
My 3, N 29 '69

HÖHN, E. Otto
Phalarope; with biographical sketch. Sci Am 220:14, 104-9+ Je '69
HOISINGTON, David B.
What do you know about silencing aluminum spars. il Yachting 125:83+ Ap '69
HOISINGTON, William F.
Microwaves for the beginner. Pop Electr 31: 40-6+ N '69
HOISTING machinery
See also
Cranes, derricks, etc.
Forklift trucks
Mine hoisting
HOLBEIN, Hans, the younger
Jokes the old masters used to play. P. Brock. il Sci Digest 65:12-17 My '69
HOLBROOK, David
Second avenue to cow lane; poem. Harp Baz 102:262 Mr '69
HOLBROOK, Marion
Toe toasters of yesterday. Har Yrs 9:14-15 Jl '69
HOLCK, Frederick, and Cate, Eleanor
Ex oriente lux? Chr Cent 86:315-18 Mr 5 '69
HOLCOMB, A. E.
Hit-and-run squads clear sewer stoppages. Am City 84:119+ Jl '69
HOLDEN, David
Bad case of the troubles called Londonderry N Y Times Mag p 10-11+ Ag 3 '69
Beirut p.m. Holiday 45:60-1+ Je '69
Tomorrow the apricots will bloom. Holiday 46:34-5+ N '69
HOLDEN, Donald
New method of lost wax casting. Am Artist 32:74-9 N '68
HOLDEN, Joan
Wild West rock show: shooting up a rock bonanza. Ramp Mag 8:70-2+ D '69
—and Davis, R. G.
Living. Ramp Mag 8:62+ Ag '69
HOLDEN, Richard
Choreology. por Opera N 33:8-12 Ap 19 '69
HOLDER, Fred W.
Advances in automotive electronics. Radio-Electr 40:48-51 Ap '69
Electronic speed control for the '69 Ford. Electr World 81:35-8 My '69
Mariner spacecraft, explorers of Mars. Electr World 82:43-6 S '69
HOLDER, Richmond
How can I tell if I'm normal? questions and answers. Seventeen 28:172-3+ Ap '69
HOLDING companies
Conglomerates under fire: the drive for new controls. il U S News 66:86-7 F 24 '69
INI puts out the welcome mat; Spain's Instituto nacional de industria. il Bsns W p96-7 F 15 '69
Why insurers like holding companies. Bsns W p 118 Mr 15 '69
See also
Bank holding companies
CNA financial corporation
Greyhound corporation
International utilities corporation
Lykes corporation
Marcor, incorporated
Natomas company
Northwest industries, incorporated
HOLDING devices (machine work)
Mini-pump powers two new hydraulic work-holding tools. il Pop Mech 132:176-7 S '69
See also
Clamps
Jigs
Vises
HOLDSWORTH, John B.
Peccaries. Nat Wildlife 7:14-15 F '69
HOLFORD, D. J.
I want to be a spy. Mr CIA man. Pop Electr 31:51-2 Ag '69
HOLIDAY, Kate
Big wheels of the fun business. Pop Mech 131.144-6+ Mr '69
HOLIDAY (periodical) awards. See Landscape protection—Awards, prizes, etc.
HOLIDAY inns of America, incorporated
Seeing problems as opportunities; interview. W. E. Johnson. il Nations Bsns 57:62-6+ Mr '69
HOLIDAY parties. See Entertaining
HOLIDAY rider: story. See Boles, P. D
HOLIDAY travel. See Travel
HOLIDAYS
Holidays and children. H. G. Ginott. McCalls 97:14+ D '69
Whatever happened to the plan for more Monday holidays? il U S News 67:5 S 1 '69
See also
Labor day
Vacations
also names of holidays, e.g. Christmas

HOLIFIELD, Chet
Teaching bureaucrats how to buy. por Bsns W p84 My 10 '69
HOLINESS
Up tight about holiness. Chr Today 13:27 Mr 14 '69
HOLLABAUGH, Kathleen
Old metals. Hobbies 74:121+ S '69
HOLLAND, Alma Boice
Second thoughts. See issues of Writer's digest
HOLLAND, Barbara
Rescue: story. McCalls 96:58-9 Jl '69
HOLLAND, Cecelia
Revising a historical novel. Writer 82:17-19+ O '69
Russia through the time tunnel. Mlle 70: 110-11+ D '69
HOLLAND, Richard D.
Is this any way to run an opera house? America 120:690-1 Je 14 '69
HOLLAND festival. See Music festivals—Netherlands
HOLLANDER, Gilbert
Feet first. Todays Ed 58:42-3 N '69
HOLLANDER, John
From beyond the cigarette: notes of a redeemed smoker. Harper 238:87-91 Ap '69
Letter to Jorge Luis Borges: apropos of the golem; poem. Harper 238:79 Je '69
Sonnets to Roseblush; excerpts. Poetry 115: 1-5 O '69
HOLLANDER, Lorin
Into the Fillmore East. R. Kotlowitz. por Harper 238:106-9 My '69
Lively arts. R. Hemming. por Sr Schol 94: 18 Mr 14 '69
Rebel in velvet. por Time 93:82+ F 7 '69
HOLLANDER, Richard
Boys watching girls watching games. por Seventeen 28:102+ Ja '69
HÖLLDOBLER, Bert
Host finding by odor in the myrmecophilic beetle atemeles pubicollis bris (staphylinidae) bibliog Science 166:757-8 N 7 '69
HOLLERING contests. See Competitions
HOLLINGS, Ernest Frederick
Case to end hunger. Ment Hy 53:500-2 O '69
HOLLINS, Brian
Stereo color organ. Radio-Electr 40:33-7 O '69
HOLLIS, Marvin
Ansel Adams: a Pacific portfolio. il Travel & Camera 32:66-71 Ag '69
HOLLISTER, Charles A.
Why more school boards are landing in court, and losing. Ed Digest 35:16-19 O '69
HOLLISTER, William G.
Why adolescents drink and use drugs. PTA Mag 63:2-5 bibliog (p37) Mr '69
HOLLO, Anselm
Any news from Alpha Centauri; Poem: Painting with no background at all: Lights going on in the rooms strung out back through the years; poems. Poetry 113:259-61 Ja '69
Bang bang with a silencer; poem. Nation 209:414 O 20 '69
Different smile. Nation 209:666-7 D 15 '69
HOLLOWAY, Bruce Keener
SAC: dynamic deterrant; address. July 29, 1969. Vital Speeches 35:706-9 S 15 '69
HOLLY
Landscaping with hollies in the Deep South. J. V. Watkins. il Horticulture 47:18-19 D '69
HOLLY green, the ivy green; story. See Amft, M. J.
HOLLY mahonias. See Mahonias
HOLLYWOOD, Calif.

Industries
See also
Moving picture industry—United States

Police
Kid-killers: a night with the drugged children of America. S. Labin. il Nat R 21:434-5 My 6 '69
HOLM, Bernard J.
(comp) Articles and other books received: medieval. See issues of American historical review
HOLM, Don
Fresh frozen ironheads. Outdoor Life 144: 42-3+ D '69
Run for the blue water. Outdoor Life 144: 52-5+ N '69
HOLM, Hanya
Hanya Holm. by W. Sorell. Review Dance Mag il por 43:56+ Jl '69. S. J. Cohen
HOLM, John Cecil, and Abbott, George
Three men on a horse. Criticism
America 121:545 N 29 '69
New Yorker 45:138-9 O 25 '69

HOLM, L. G. and others
Aquatic weeds. bibliog Science 166:699-709 N
7 '69
HOLMAN, Ben
Halt integration; the view of a Negro official;
excerpts from remarks. por U S News 67:16
D 1 '69
HOLMAN, J. Alan
Predation and the origin of tetrapods. Science
164:588 My 2 '69
HOLMAN, John
Race maker: John Holman. S. Kelly. il
pors Hot Rod 22:74-6 Ag '69
Wizards of the wild wheels. C. Phinizy. il
por Sports Illus 31:30-2+ Jl 14 '69
HOLMES, Albert W. and others
Hepatitis in marmosets: induction of disease
with coded specimens from a human volun-
teer study. bibliog Science 165:816-17 Ag 22
'69
HOLMES, Anna-Marie
Anna Marie and David Holmes from Winnipeg
to the world. D. Jowitt. il pors Dance Mag
43:34-8 F '69
HOLMES, Clifford
California telescope makers' conference. por
Sky & Tel 37:353-5 Je '69
HOLMES, David
Anna Marie and David Holmes from Winnipeg
to the world. D. Jowitt. il pors Dance Mag
43:34-8 F '69
HOLMES, John Clellon
Mirror of Venice. Travel & Camera 32:68-74
S '69
HOLMES, Jonathan
Letter to Charles. Time 93:31 Je 27 '69; Same
abr. with title Contemporary speaks. Read
Digest 95:133 S '69
HOLMES, Mike
Tokyo. Motor T 21:62+ Mr '69
HOLOGRAMS. See Holography
HOLOGRAPHY
Acoustical holography. A. F. Metherell. il
Sci Am 221:36-44 O '69
Biomedical applications of holography. E. J.
Feleppa. bibliog il Phys Today 22:25-32 Jl
'69
Color-TV tape player uses laser and holo-
grams; SelectaVision system. M. S. Snitzer.
il Electr World 82:31+ D '69
Do it yourself laser holography. C. H.
Knowles. il Pop Electr 32:27-35+ Ja '70
Erasable hologram. Sci Am 221:98+ S '69
Incredible hologram. il Newsweek 74:41 D
29 '69
Low-cost color TV tapes in your home:
SelectaVision. il Sci Digest 66:85-7 D '69
Movies by hologram. D. E. Thomsen. il Sci
N 95:460-1 My 10 '69
New applications for 3-D graphics; potential
uses for lasers and holograms. il Pub W 195:
88+ F 3 '69
Signs you'll see appearing out of thin air;
Holosigns. E. H. Arctander. il Pop Sci 195:
80-2+ Ag '69
HOLOSIGNS. See Traffic signs
HOLOTHURIANS. See Sea cucumbers
HOLOTOXIN. See Toxins and antitoxins
HOLROYD, Michael
Harvard on my mind. Harper 239:69-72 Ag;
12+ N '69
HOLSENDOLPH, Ernest
Middle-class blacks are moving off the mid-
dle. Fortune 80:90-5+ D '69
HOLSTEIN Friesian cattle. See Cattle—Breeds
HOLT, John Caldwell
Speaking out. por Sat Eve Post 242:12+ F 8
'69
Tyranny of testing; excerpts from The under-
achieving school. Parents Mag 44:60-1+ S
'69
HOLT, Kelly
Kelly Holt: NYU school of education audi-
torium. T. Borek. Dance Mag 43:76 Ag '69
HOLT, Milford O.
Reading to learn. Clear House 43:267-71 Ja
'69
HOLT, S. J.
Food resources of the ocean; with biographi-
cal sketch. Sci Am 221:46, 178-82+ bib-
liog(p286) S '69
HOLTER, Patra
Kinetic art. Sch Arts 68:26-7 My '69
HOLTON, A. Linwood
South is developing a real two-party sys-
tem; interview. por U S News 67:40 N 17
'69
HOLTON, Felicia Antonelli
High school courses for future parents. To-
days Health 47:38-41+ S '69
HOLTZAPPLE, Philip G. and others
Amino acid uptake by kidney and jejunal
tissue from dogs with cystine stones. bib-
liog Science 166:1525-7 D 19 '69

HOLTZMAN, David, and others
1-Δ⁹-Tetrahydrocannabinol: neurochemical and
behavioral effects in the mouse. bibliog Sci-
ence 163:1464-7 Mr 28 '69
HOLWAY, Chester P.
Creeping Charlie. Horticulture 47:13 Jl '69
HOLY Cross college, Worcester, Mass.
Holy Cross innovates. America 120:660 Je 7
'69
HOLY Ghost. See Holy Spirit
HOLY LAND
Holy Land. N. Glueck. il Travel & Camera
32:70-5+ D '69
HOLY office, Congregation of the. See Con-
gregation for the doctrine of the faith
HOLY Spirit
God renews! Chr Cent 86:702 My 21 '69
Job for the Spirit. V. P. McCorry. America
120:550 My 3 '69
Power that never fails. Chr Today 13:24 Ag
22 '69
Two Pentecostal experiences; one Protestant
and the other Catholic. J. S. Phillipson.
America 120:360-3 Mr 29 '69
See also
Pentecost
Trinity
HOLY Trinity Russian Orthodox monastery.
See Monasteries
HOLY week
See also
Easter
Good Friday

**Anecdotes, facetiae,
satire, etc.**
Five editorials. C. D. Schutjer. Chr Cent 86:
449-50 Ap 2 '69
HOLZ, Peter
Kruger National Park; South Africa's prime
game sanctuary. Nat Parks 43:17-20 S '69
HOLZER, Jane
Girl of the year. pors Newsweek 73:22 My 19
'69
Jane Holzer, the lion-hearted in her New
York apartment. il pors Vogue 154:210-17
N 1 '69
HOLZMAN, Robert S.
How to stay out of trouble with IRS. Na-
tions Bsns 57:28-31 D '69
HOLZMAN, Seymour
Talk with us, not at us. Schol Teach Sec
Teach Sup p8-10 S 22 '69
Will the schools survive the attack on sex
education? Schol Teach Sec Teach Sup p
10-12 O 6 '69
HOMAGE volumes. See Festschriften
HOMAN, William E.
How to be a better parent; excerpts from
Child sense: a pediatrician's guide for to-
day's families. Read Digest 95:187-8+ O '69
Parent and child. N Y Times Mag p93+
Mr 16 '69
HOME
Tear down the walls. E. S. Muskie. il Am
Home 72:8 Ap '69
Where the past is prologue; life at Jacnor
farm. D. Straus. il House B 111:99+ Ap '69
See also
Family
Family life
HOME accidents. See Accidents
HOME and the school. See School and the home
HOME away from; drama. See Smith, G. A.
HOME bars. See Bars for the home
HOME builders, National association of. See
National association of home builders
HOME building. See House construction
HOME building industry. See Building industry
HOME building materials. See Building ma-
terials
HOME buying. See House buying
HOME capital funds, incorporated
Leg up for the short homebuyer; HCF. il Bsns
W p 106-7 My 3 '69
HOME care hospital service. See Hospitals—
Home care programs
HOME care programs, Hospital based. See
Hospitals—Home care programs
HOME decoration. See House decoration
HOME economics
Ask Rufus. R. Cartwright. See issues of
Mechanix illustrated
Keeping house with Emily Taylor. See issues
of Good housekeeping
Lifestyle. See issues of American home
Notes of a happy housekeeper. M. E. Falter.
See issues of House & garden incorporat-
ing Living for young homemakers
Occupation: homemaker. See issues of Mc-
Call's

HOME economics—*Continued*
Ode to a neglected dustcloth. A. G. Combs.
il Redbook 132:14+ F '69
Portfolio of new recipes, plans, equipment
and tips that save time, space, money &
you! symposium. il Good H 168:126-47+
Mr '69
See also
Budget, Household
Clothing and dress—Care
Kitchens
Moving
Storage in the home

History

Housekeeping and childkeeping in the olden
days. B. Spock. Redbook 133:44+ O '69

Study and teaching

Curriculum development challenges in home
economics. E. J. Simpson. Ed Digest 34:49-
51 Ap '69
Home economics moves ahead. P. G. Garrett.
Todays Ed 58:18 My '69
New switch. L. Strother. Todays Ed 58:50
S '69
See also
Nutrition education

HOME equipment. See Household appliances
HOME files. See Files and filing (documents,
etc)
HOME fire drills. See Fire drills
HOME furnishings. See Household furnishings
HOME garden contest. See Gardening—Com-
petitions
HOME grounds
All this happens around one house! H.
Mason and L. Grove. il Bet Hom & Gard
47:38-9 Jl '69
At home in the garden. See issues of Home
garden & flower grower
How to clear property and remain married.
P. L. Levin. il Home Gard 56:68-9 My '69
New gardens for old. E. Kondonellis. il Am
Home 72:78-9 My '69
Place in the shade. E. Kondonellis. il Am
Home 72:62-3 Je '69

Care

Four good tips to ease yard work. il Pop
Sci 194:163 Je '69
Make your grounds care-free! W. Brunig. il
Mech Illus 65:78-9 My '69

HOME improvements. See Houses—Mainte-
nance and repair
HOME industries. See Cottage industries
HOME labor
See also
Cottage industries
HOME libraries. See Libraries, Private
HOME life. See Family life
HOME made toys. See Toys
HOME morale. See Family life
HOME music. See Music in the home
HOME offices. See Offices
HOME ownership
Don't let your house get you down. M. C.
Huntoon, jr. Am Home 72:84-5 My '69
How to find the perfect fit in housing. Am
Home 72:82 Ja '69
Ideas to build on. il House B 111:34+ Ap '69
News for home owners. A. J. Maher. il Am
Home 72:44+ Ap; 56+ My; 24 Je '69
News for home owners. D. X. Manners. il Am
Home 72:58+ S '69
Your housing today: should you rent or buy?
T. Irwin. Am Home 72:48+ Ja '69
See also
House buying
House selling
Mortgages
HOME play. See Play
HOME safety devices and measures. See Safety
devices and measures
HOME selling. See House selling
HOME service industries. See Service industries
HOME storage. See Storage in the home
HOME study
Discipline of homework. B. Bettelheim. Ladies
Home J 86:34-5 O '69
Homework and study habits. R. E. Leibert.
bibliog f Clear House 43:413-16 Mr '69
How to help your child develop good study
habits. P. Parrish. il Parents Mag 44:62-3+
Mr '69
Tales of homework. H. G. Ginott. McCalls
96:36+ S '69
HOME study council, National. See National
home study council

HOME study courses. See Correspondence
schools and courses
HOME work. See Home study
HOME workshops. See Workshops
HOMECOMING; drama. See Pinter, H.
HOMEMAKING. See Home economics
HOMEOPATHY
Queen's homeopath. Newsweek 73:67 F 3 '69
HOMEOWNER policies. See Insurance—All risk
policies
HOMER
Homer's Achilles heel. il Time 94:65-6 Jl 4 '69
HOMER, Louise
Child in the golden age. S. Homer. il por
Opera N 33:6-7 Mr 8 '69
HOMER, Sidney
Child in the golden age   por Opera N 33:6-7
Mr 8 '69
HOMES, Broken. See Broken homes
HOMES, Institutional
Toward a technology of child care for chil-
dren in residence. H. Alt. bibliog Ment Hy
53:564-74 O '69
See also
Children—Institutional care
Nursing homes
Old age homes
HOMES for the aged. See Old age homes
HOMESICKNESS. See Nostalgia
HOMESTEAD law

United States

Homesteading at sea: claims to off-Florida
reefs. Time 93:55 Ja 24 '69
HOMEWORK. See Home study
HOMICIDE. See Murder
HOMILETICS. See Preaching
HOMING instinct. See Orientation
HOMO erectus. See Man, Prehistoric
HOMOLOGY (biology)
Homology as applied to proteins; letter. W.
P. Winter and others; discussion. bibliog
Science 163:127; 164:455-6 Ja 10, Ap 25 '69
HOMOSEXUALITY
Canada debates abortion and homosexual-
ity. J. C. Fleck. Chr Cent 86:354-8 Mr 12
'69
Case for heterosexuality. W. Herberg. Nat R
21:1007-8+ O 7 '69
Coming to terms. il Time 94:82 O 24 '69
Faces of the boys in the band; a changing
view of homosexuality? J. Star. il Look
33:62-8 D 2 '69
Homosexual: newly visible, newly understood.
il Time 94:56+ O 31 '69
Homosexuality: changes on the way. L. Mas-
sett. il Sci N 96:557-9 D 13 '69
Homosexuality in the Bible and the law. B.
L. Smith. bibliog Chr Today 13:7-10 Jl 18
'69
Homosexuals convene in Kansas City. J. S
Tinney. Chr Cent 86:1436 N 5 '69
Laws against homosexuals. Chr Today 14:
32 N 7 '69
New homosexuality. T. Burke. il Esquire 72:
178-9+ D '69
Operation to relieve perversion. T. Shoe-
maker. il Sci N 97:50 Ja 10 '70
Policing the third sex. il Newsweek 74:76+
O 27 '69
Same sex, ed. by R. W. Weltge. Review
Commonweal 91:338-9 D 12 '69. W. Gaylin
Uncomplaining homosexuals. D. Trilling.
Harper 239:90-5 Ag '69
Understanding homosexuality. R. E. Gould.
Seventeen 28:90-1+ Jl '69
See also
Lesbianism

Anecdotes, facetiae, satire, etc.

Confession. J. Braine. Nat R 21:1176 N 18
'69
HOMOSEXUALITY in literature
Death in Venice: the aesthetic object as
dream guide. R. Tarbox. bibliog Am Im-
ago 26:123-44 Sum '69
Thomas Mann's Death in Venice. H.
Slochower. bibliog f Am Imago 26:99-122
Sum '69
HON, Edward H.
Watching the unborn inside the womb. il por
Life 67:64-5 Jl 25 '69
HONAN, William H.
Art of oratory in the Senate of the United
States. Esquire 71:161-7+ My '69
He wows them in Washington. N Y Times
Mag p 113-14+ N 9 '69
Men behind Nixon's speeches. N Y Times
Mag p20-1+ Ja 19 '69

HONAN, William H.—*Continued*
Le mot juste for the moon. Esquire 72:53-6+
  Jl '69
Yesterday Edward Kennedy turned thirty-
  seven, is Teddy, as they say, ready? N Y
  Times Mag p25-7+ F 23 '69
HONDA motorcycles. See Motorcycles
HONDURAS
        Foreign relations
But the problem remains. Nation 209:101
  Ag 11 '69
Cease-fire in Central America; soccer war
  between Honduras and El Salvador. Chr
  Cent 86:1082 Ag 20 '69
Great fútbol war; El Salvador against Hon-
  duras. T. P. Anderson. Commonweal 90:
  479-80 Ag 8 '69
Honduran-Salvadoran conflict resolved by
  OAS; Department statement with resolu-
  tions and declaration. Dept State Bul 61:
  132-4 Ag 18 '69
Lock-in; OAS success in ending violence.
  Newsweek 74:34 Ag 11 '69
OAS halts war between El Salvador and
  Honduras. G. Meek. il Américas 21:42-5 S
  '69
Population explosion; Central American mini-
  war. il Time 94:29-30 Jl 25 '69
Resolutions for El Salvador and Honduras
  conflict. Américas 21:56 N '69
Soccer war. il Newsweek 74:54 Jl 28 '69
Soccer war; its causes and what's at stake;
  El Salvador and Honduras went to war
  on July 14. il U S News 67:6 Jl 28 '69
Walking on eggshells. il Newsweek 74:50-1 Ag
  4 '69

HONECKER, Erich
After Ulbricht? por Newsweek 74:36-8 Ag 25
  '69
HONEGGER, Arthur
One of the season's best chamber-music
  releases, Hindemith and Honegger quar-
  tets on Crossroads. A. Cohn. Am Rec G
  35:563 Mr '69
HONEST-to-God schnozzola; drama. See Horo-
  vitz, I.
HONESTY
Dealing with dishonesty. H. G. Ginott. Mc-
  Calls 96:40 Ag '69
HONESTY (plants)
Sheer elegance and easy to grow. il Home
  Gard 56:34 F '69
HONEY, Patrick J.
Hanoi without Ho; what U.S. can expect; in-
  terview. por U S News 67:38-40 S 22 '69
HONEY
Varied fare of the honeybee. R. A. Morse. il
  Natur Hist 78:58-65 Je '69
  See also
  Bees
HONEY bees. See Bees
HONEY locust
It's the placement and the pruning. il Sun-
  set 142:207 F '69
HONEY thieves; drama. See Burleson, C.
HONEYCOMB worms. See Annelids
HONEYCUTT, Ann. See Kinney, J. R. jt.
  auth.
HONEYMOON
Honeymoon havens. il Newsweek 73:90-1 Je
  23 '69
HONEYWELL, Incorporated
Honeywell rounds out its line; Information
  services div. Bsns W D 18 F 1 '69
HONG KONG
Home of the China-watchers. A. Campbell.
  New Repub 160:11-13 My 3 '69
  See also
  Clothing industry—Hong Kong
  Education—Hong Kong
  Libraries—Hong Kong
  New Territories
  Railroads—Hong Kong
  Yachts and yachting—Hong Kong
        Description
Hong Kong. J. P. Gabriel. il Travel 132:28-
  35 Ag '69
Hong Kong, easily worth a return trip. P.
  Gowland. Pop Phot 65:30+ D '79
      Economic conditions
Cheer in the Year of the rooster. il Time
  93:86 F 28 '69
Hong Kong; the complaisant haven. S. Salaff.
  Nation 209:409-11 O 20 '69
HONG KONG flu. See Influenza
HONIG, Edwin
Critic of the month. L. Lieberman. Poetry
  114:49-50 Ap '69
Yesterday; poem. Sat R 52:36 Mr 8 '69

        about
Double exposure. L. A. Goldstein. Nation 208:
  640+ My 19 '69
HONIGMANN, John J.
Psychological anthropology. bibliog f Ann
  Am Acad 383:145-58 My '69
HONING. See Sharpening
HONOLULU
        Airports
Honolulu enlarging airport for giant jets. R. G.
  O'Lone. il Aviation W 90:39-41 Je 30 '69
        Description
Honolulu: still the paradise of the Pacific?
  A. G. Day. il Holiday 46:62-5+ O '69
Look what's happened to Honolulu! J. Becker.
  il Nat Geog 136:500-31 O '69
        Education
Individualized in-service education. L. L.
  Stillwell. il Todays Ed 58:44-5 D '69
        Gardens
Horticulture in Honolulu. D. P. Watson. il
  Horticulture 46:24-7+ O '68
        Music
Report: Honolulu; production of Manon. W.
  Aguiar, jr. Opera N 33:31 Ap 5 '69
    Politics and government
Ripples from jet-generated traffic spread
  over Hawaii. W. H. Gregory. il Aviation
  W 91:96-7+ O 20 '69
HONOLULU international airport. See Honolulu
  —Airports
HONORARY degrees. See Degrees, Honorary
HONZIK, Marjorie P. and others
Sex differences in verbal and performance
  IQ's of children undergoing open-heart sur-
  gery. bibliog Science 164:445-7; 166:259-60
  Ap 25, O 10 '69
HOOD, Graham
New light on Bonnin and Morris. Antiques
  95:812-17 Je '69
HOOD, Horace
Holiday for hounds. Outdoor Life 144:56-7+
  D '69
HOOD ornaments, Automobile. See Automo-
  biles—Equipment
HOOK, J. N.
English teachers in a world we never made;
  address. Engl J 58:185-92 F '69
HOOK, Sidney
Real crisis on the campus; interview. por
  U S News 66:40-4 My 19 '69; Excerpts.
  Read Digest 95:41-5 Ag '69
Trojan horse in the universities? Cur 108:24-
  7 Je '69
War against the democratic process. Atlan
  223:45-9 F; 46-7 Ap '69
Who is responsible for campus violence?
  Sat R 52:22-5+ Ap 19 '69
        about
Of many things. D. R. Campion. America
  120:inside cover Mr 22 '69
HOOK, Thom
Fly your own plane, for no more than a
  new car. Pop Sci 194:58-61+ Je '69
HOOKED rugs. See Rugs and carpets
HOOPER, Bayard
Shapes of coalition and dissent. Life 68:102-6
  Ja 9 '70
Task is to learn what learning is for. Life 66:
  34-5+ My 16 '69
HOOPER, L. O.
Market comment. See issues of Forbes
HOOPES, Townsend
Fight for the President's mind, and the men
  who won it; excerpt from The limits of
  intervention. por Atlan 224:97-104+ O '69
HOOVEN, Frederick J.
UFOs and the evidence. Sat R 52:16-17+ Mr
  29 '69
HOOVER, Cynthia A.
Trumpet battle at Niblo's pleasure garden.
  bibliog f Mus Q 55:384-95 Jl '69
HOOVER, Helen
Great wolf and the good woodsman; story,
  excerpts. Parents Mag 44:44-7 D '69
HOOVER, Herbert, presidential library. See
  Herbert Hoover presidential library, West
  Branch, Ia.
HOOVER, Herbert Clark
Cold-war scholarship. P. S. Stern. il Nation
  209:176-80 S 1 '69
HOOVER, John Edgar
Interval between. Chr Today 14:3-5 D 19 '69
U.S. unrest, as FBI chief sees it; excerpts
  from report on 1969. por U S News 68:8 Ja
  12 '70

HOOVER, John Edgar—*Continued*

about

FBI in our open society, by H. Overstreet and B. Overstreet; and Communism, by J. E. Hoover; reviews. M. S. Evans. Nat R 21: 499-500 My 20 '69

F.B.I. in our open society, by H. Overstreet and B. Overstreet. Review
Commentary 48:78+ Jl '69. I. Silver

Happy birthday. il por Newsweek 75:20 Ja 12 '70

More dirty business. Nation 209:5 Jl 7 '69

Reactionary immortality: the private life in public testimony of John Edgar Hoover. Review
Trans-Action 6:64-70 Je '69. I. L. Horowitz

Thank you, Mr Director. F. J. Donner. Nation 209:448-9 O 27 '69

Washington icons. Nation 209:164-5 S 1 '69

What have they done since they shot Dillinger? T. Wicker. il pors N Y Times Mag p4-7+ D 28 '69

HOOVER institution on war, revolution and peace. See Stanford university. Stanford, Calif.—Hoover institution on war, revolution and peace

HOPE, A. D.
School of night; Apotelesm of W. B. Yeats; poems. Poetry 114:172-4 Je '69

HOPE, Adrian
Out of the East, the people's war. Life 67: 58-66B O 17 '69

HOPE, Arlene
When I was five. por Library J 94:3622-5 O 15 '69

HOPE, Bob
In support of Hope. D. R. Sharpless. il pors Parks & Rec 4:12-16+ D '69

HOPE, Marjorie
How Russian schools compare with ours. Parents Mag 44:56-7+ Ja '69

HOPE, Norman V.
Being Christian in an affluent society. Chr Today 13:7-8 F 14 '69
Does God lead us into temptation? Chr Today 13:13-14 Jl 4 '69
Paul's thorn and ours. Chr Today 14:14-15 D 5 '69

HOPE
We were hoping. E. Elliot. Chr Today 14: 12 O 10 '69
See also
Despair

HOPE (ship) See Hospital ships

HOPE is forever: story. See McKimmey, J.

HOPEWELL mounds. See Mounds and mound builders

HOPFINGER, A. J. See Zull, J. E. jt. auth.

HOPI Indians
Hopi Indians, inbreeding, and albinism. C. M. Woolf and F. C. Dukepoo. bibliog il Science 164:30-7 Ap 4 '69
See also
Pueblo Indians

HOPKINS, Joseph Martin
For lack of knowledge. Chr Today 13:10-11 Je 6 '69
Scientology: religion or racket? Chr Today 14:6-9 N 7; 10-13 N 21 '69

HOPKINS, Joseph S.
Unions in libraries. bibliog Library J 94:3403-7 O 1 '69

HOPKINS, Lee Bennett
Once upon a slaughterhouse: the Biblioteca publica de San Miguel de Allende. Horn Bk 45:37-9 F '69

HOPKINS, Mark
College president speaks out; inaugural address, 1836. Nat R 21:372 Ap 22 '69

HOPKINS, Terence K.
Third world modernization in transnational perspective. Ann Am Acad 386:126-36 N '69

HOPPE, Arthur Watterson
Reverse images. il por Time 93:54+ My 30 '69

HOPPER, Dennis
Not-so-easy riders: Dennis Hopper, Peter Fonda. por Vogue 154:129 Ag 1 '69

HOPPS, Walter
KS & KS. Wilson Lib Bul 44:528 Ja '70

about
Capital art. il por Newsweek 74:117-117A N 24 '69

HORACE M. Albright training center. See United States—National park service

HORAN, Ellen
With the racing classes. See issues of Yachting

HORDERN, Nicholas
The Danube. il Harp Baz 102:86+ Ag '69

HORDERN, William
Barth as political thinker. Chr Cent 86:411-13 Mr 26 '69

HORGAN, John
Life in Zambia: on the firing line. Commonweal 89:490-1 Ja 17 '69

HORITA, A. and Hamilton, A. E.
Lysergic acid diethylamide: dissociation of its behavioral and hyperthermic actions by DL-α-methyl-p-tyrosine. bibliog Science 164:78-9 Ap 4 '69

HORLER, Miklós
Historic quarter of Buda. Antiques 96:918-20 D '69

HORMAN, Charles
Pacifying California. Commonweal 90:356-7 Je 13 '69
Producers organize. Nation 208:634-6 My 19 '69
Violence and rhetoric. Nation 208:314-15 Mr 10 '69

HORMONE fattening of calves. See Calves—Hormone fattening

HORMONES
Hormonal induction of increased zinc uptake in mammalian cell culture: requirements for RNA and protein synthesis. R. P. Cox. bibliog il Science 165:196-9 Jl 11 '69
Hormones in development; report of meeting. M. Hamburgh. Science 164:1191-3 Je 6 '69
Hormones in social amoebae and mammals. J. T. Bonner. il Sci Am 220:78-84+ Je '69
Hypothalamic stimulation of growth hormone secretion. L. A. Frohman and others; reply with rejoinder. G. P. Smith and A. W. Root Science 163:705 F 14 '69
Molecular bomb for the war against insects; reprint. L. Lessing. il Am For 75:16-19+ Ja '69
See also
ACTH
Calcitonin
Corticosterone
Ecdysone
Glucagon
Hydrocortisone
Juvenile hormone
Neurosecretion
Oxytocin
Pheromones
Pituitary hormones
Prostaglandins
Stilbestrols
Vasopressin

HORMONES, Plant
Hormonal regulation in higher plants. A. W. Galston and P. J. Davies. bibliog il Science 163:1288-97 Mr 21 '69
Interaction of plant hormones. R. E. Drury. bibliog il Science 164:564-5 My 2 '69
Light and hormones: interchangeability in the induction of nitrate reductase. S. H. Lips and N. Roth-Bejerano. bibliog il Science 166:109-10 O 3 '69
New antheridiogen from the fern onoclea sensibilis. U. Näf and others. bibliog il Science 163:1357-8 Mr 21 '69
See also
Kinins

HORMONES, Sex
Breakfast of champions. il Newsweek 74:37 D 29 '69
Sexual hormones of achlya and other fungi. A. W. Barksdale. bibliog il Science 166:831-7 N 14 '69
See also
Estrogens
Gonadotropins
Progesterone
Testosterone

HORN, Andrew
Reflections of an old man's memory; poem. Ment Hy 53:77 Ja '69

HORN, B. Ray
Secret to achieving your camp goals. Camp Mag 41:13+ N '69

HORN, Eugene A. and others
School mental health services offered without invitation. bibliog Ment Hy 53:620-4 O '69

HORN, John L.
Utility of projective techniques and the function of the clinical psychologist. Ment Hy 53:654-6 O '69

HORN, William A.
Fishing for a pollution solution. Am Ed 5:14-16 Ap '69

HORN, CAPE
Our far-flung correspondents: the end beyond the end. R. Hough. il New Yorker 45: 151-4+ O 25 '69
Riding out a Cape Horn snorter. G. M. S. Tod. il Motor B 123:143+ Ap '69

HORN, CAPE—*Continued*
Rounding Cape Horn; excerpt from My lively lady. A. Rose. il Yachting 125:54-5+ Mr '69
Third time lucky; Tzu Hang braves Cape Horn. M. Smeeton. il Yachting 126:65-7+ D '69 (to be cont)
HORN band music. See Band music
HORN book magazine
Bertha Mahony Miller, 1882-1969; symposium. bibliog il Horn Bk 45:467-8+ O '69
Horn book reflections, ed. by E. W. Field. F. C. Sayers. Horn Bk 45:659 D '69
Innovation and tradition. P. H. Heins. Horn Bk 45:269 Je '69
HORN carving. See Carving (art industries)
HORN music, Russian. See Music, Russian
HORNBILLS
Inside a hornbill's walled-up nest. J. Root and A. Root. il Nat Geog 136:846-55 D '69
HORNBLOWER and Weeks-Hemphill, Noyes and company
Street's new paper cutter. il Bsns W p56-7+ N 1 '69
HORNBY, Lesley. See Twiggy (model)
HORNE, Bryant
If Jackson can do it. Horticulture 47:30-1 Ag '69
HORNE, Marilyn
Sense of timing; interview, ed. by R. D. Daniels. por Opera N 34:18-20 D 27 '69

about

Musical events; recital in Carnegie Hall. W. Sargeant. New Yorker 45:182 N 22 '69
HORNEY, Robert L.
Maintenance cost control. Parks & Rec 4:17-18+ D '69
Snomobility. Parks & Rec 4:29-32+ O '69
HORNIG, Donald Frederick
Hornig years: did LBJ neglect his science adviser? P. M. Boffey. por Science 163:453-4+ Ja 31 '69; Reply. L. A. Dubridge. 163:759 F 21 '69
United States science policy: its health and future direction; adaptation of address, December 29, 1968. Science 163:523-8 F 7 '69
HORNOCKER, Maurice G.
Stalking the mountain lion, to save him. Nat Geog 136:638-55 N '69
HORNS (animals)
Horns and antlers. W. Modell. il Sci Am 220:114-22 bibliog(p 146) Ap '69
HOROSCOPES. See Astrology
HOROVITZ, Carolyn
Fiction and the paradox of play. bibliog por Wilson Lib Bul 44:397-401 D '69
HOROVITZ, Israel
Feel it. Craft Horiz 29:14-15+ Mr '69
Three Austrians and the New Jersey turnpike. Craft Horiz 29:10-13+ Ja '69

about

Honest-to-God schnozzola. *Criticism*
New Yorker 45:108-9 My 3 '69
Newsweek il 73:118 My 5 '69
HOROWITZ, A, and son
Horowitz: fifty years of specialty binding. il Pub W 196:68+ O 6 '69
HOROWITZ, Al
Chess corner. See issues of Saturday review
HOROWITZ, David
Analysis: behind the Sino/Soviet dispute. Ramp Mag 7:39-43 Je '69
Billion dollar brains. Ramp Mag 7:36-44 My '69
Hand-me-down Marxism and the new left. Ramp Mag 8:16+ S '69
Rocky takes a trip. Ramp Mag 8:60-1 Ag '69
Sinews of empire. Ramp Mag 8:32-42 O '69
HOROWITZ, David, and Erlich, Reese
Big brother as a holding company. Ramp Mag 7:44-52 N 30 '68
Litton industries; proving poverty pays. Ramp Mag 7:40-9 D 14 '68
—and Kolodney, David
Foundations [charity begins at home] Ramp Mag 7:38-48 Ap '69 (to be cont)
HOROWITZ, Irving Louis
Young radicals & professorial critics. Commonweal 89:552-6 Ja 31 '69

about

New sociology. il por Time 95:38-9 Ja 5 '70
HOROWITZ, N. H. and others
Sterile soil from Antarctica: organic analysis. bibliog Science 164:1054-6 My 30 '69
HORR, David Agee
Our red-haired kin of the rain forest. por Life 66:88-9+ Mr 28 '69
HORRIDGE, G. A. and Tamm, S. L.
Critical point drying for scanning electron microscopic study of ciliary motion. bibliog Science 163:817-18 F 21 '69

HORROR films. See Moving pictures—Horror films
HORS d'œuvres. See Appetizers
HORSE breeding
Cousin Leslie goes to market; breeder of top-quality thoroughbreds. W. Tower. il Sports Illus 31:44-5 Jl 21 '69
Mare's nest; antitrust suit involving purchase of Kentucky's Maine chance farm. il Newsweek 73:82 Mr 10 '69
No reason for Bull to cry; Arthur (Bull) Hancock, of Claiborne farm. W. Tower. Sports Illus 30:99 Ap 14 '69
HORSE caravans. See Caravans
HORSE chestnut
Buckeye as a bonsai. il Sunset 143:195 D '69
HORSE farms
Stable full of dreams; untrained colts of Joe O'Brien's farm in Calif. P. Ryan. il Sports Illus 30:40+ F 17 '69
HORSE power. See Horsepower (mechanics)
HORSE race betting
Having a flutter, or andy capp lives; betting shops in London. Trans-Action 6:7-8 F '69
HORSE racing
After a battle, the Prince. W. Tower. Sports Illus 30:72 My 19 '69
Arts and Letters gets a degree; Derbybound colt at Hialeah. W. Tower. il Sports Illus 30:24-5 Mr 3 '69
Barnum's back. il Time 94:45 Jl 11 '69
Confirmation of a hero at Saratoga; Arts and Letters. W. Tower. il Sports Illus 31:16-19 Ag 25 '69
Conning the con men of Kentucky. J. McGinniss. il Sports Illus 30:36-8+ My 5 '69
Dick Francis: writer, former steeplechase jockey; interview. D. Francis. New Yorker 45:29-30 Mr 15 '69
Four hot chestnuts in a derby; Majestic Prince. W. Tower. il Sports Illus 30:28-30+ My 5 '69
From Charles to Elizabeth. C. Graham. Sports Illus 30:43 My 19 '69
Going after a tie at Laurel. W. Tower. il Sports Illus 31:64 N 3 '69
Good night, Sweet Prince; Belmont stakes. il Newsweek 73:67-8 Je 16 '69
Grandes dames of racing; proprietors of thoroughbred stables and breeding farms; with photographs by R. Meek. Sports Illus 31:46-54 S 29 '69
He took the biscuits for Seamus McGrath; Prix de l'Arc de Triomphe, Europe's richest race. W. Tower. il Sports Illus 31:72+ O 13 '69
In the pink; Top Knight wins Flamingo stakes. il Newsweek 73:77-8 Mr 17 '69
It may be a two-horse derby; Majestic Prince and Top Knight. W. Tower. il Sports Illus 30:22-5 Ap 7 '69
Last leg is the toughest; undefeated Majestic Prince at Belmont. W. Tower. Sports Illus 30:89 Je 9 '69
Man plus horse beats boy; Flamingo at Hialeah. W. Tower. il Sports Illus 30:52+ Mr 17 '69
Marje's late, late show; Arlington-Washington Futurity. W. Tower. il Sports Illus 31:32-4+ S 15 '69
Never? No, always on Sunday; Green Mountain thoroughbred and harness racing, Vermont. M. R. Werner. il Sports Illus 31:64-5 Ag 25 '69
No reason for Bull to cry; Arthur (Bull) Hancock, of Claiborne farm. W. Tower. Sports Illus 30:99 Ap 14 '69
Politics in the saddle at Utopia Downs; governors select racetrack officials. W. Tower. Sports Illus 30:52-3 Mr 31 '69
Prince ducks the big one; Majestic Prince passing up the Belmont. W. Tower. il Sports Illus 30:24-7 My 26 '69
Prince who would be king; Majestic Prince. W. Tower. il Sports Illus 30:14-15 F 17 '69
Race track. A. Minor. See issues of New Yorker
Recession ahead? No sign here. W. Tower. il Sports Illus 32:22-5 Ja 12 '70
Revenge was sweet; Arts and Letters defeat Majestic Prince at Belmont. W. Tower. il Sports Illus 30:24-7 Je 16 '69
Roses for the Prince; Kentucky Derby. il Newsweek 73:75 My 12 '69
Royal neck for Bill's fifth, photographs by J. Cooke and N. Leifer; with account by W. Tower. Sports Illus 30:14-19 My 12 '69
Saratoga; half hour of hope; event for two-year-olds. il Newsweek 74:66-68B Ag 25 '69
Sharp kid from the equine academy; three-year-olds competing in Florida Derby. M. R. Werner. il Sports Illus 30:24-5 Ap 7 '69
Sonny ... just like in money; Sonny Werblin. M. R. Werner. il Sports Illus 31:80 O 20 '69

HORSE racing—*Continued*
Spoiler; Arts and Letters wins Belmont stakes. il Time 93:57 Je 13 '69
Tantrum in victory; Laurel international. Newsweek 74:97 N 24 '69
Three could have stayed home; horse of the year; Arts and Letters. W. Tower. il Sports Illus 31:63 O 6 '69
Time has come to sort out the sprinters. W. Tower. il Sports Illus 30:48-9 F 3 '69
Top speed and a tender mouth; Majestic Prince a Derby favorite. W. Tower. Sports Illus 30:56 Mr 10 '69
Whitewash in Kentucky; 1968 Kentucky Derby. W. F. Reed. jr. il Sports Illus 30:12-14 F 17 '69
Winners are: Forum who? Karabas what? W. Tower. il Sports Illus 31:64-5 N 24 '69
Won't somebody help me buy this horse? Ring For Nurse. W. F. Reed. jr. il Sports Illus 31:86+ S 22 '69
See also
Harness racing
Race horses

Accidents and Injuries
Accident that kept Shoe out of the Derby; photographs. J. Deitz. Sports Illus 30:18-19 My 12 '69

HORSE shows
Emerald mare takes over My My's red roses; Kentucky state fair horse show. A. Higgins. Sports Illus 31:102 S 15 '69
Novelties and reform spark a rich finale; New York's National. A. Higgins. Sports Illus 31:64 D 8 '69
Onward the feminine invasion: lady jockeys. A. Higgins. il Sports Illus 30:60 Mr 24 '69
Week of the Great Hooley: Dublin horse bash. B. Moore. il Holiday 46:26-9+ Ag '69

HORSE stables. See Barns and stables
HORSE trainers
See also
Le Vine, D.

HORSE training
Agony of the walking horse. il Life 67:77-8 O 3 '69
Man who could talk to horses. T. McCarthy. il Am Heritage 20:58-9+ Ap '69
Pops wants to win his own golden anniversary present; 50th year as trainer and driver. E. Avery. W. F. Reed, jr. Sports Illus 30:64-5 Je 16 '69
Scientific view of Rarey: animal hypnosis. F. D. Klopfer. Am Heritage 20:89 Ap '69
See also
Horse racing

HORSEBACK riding. See Horsemanship
HORSEBACK trips
See Ireland slowly, by pony trek. il Sunset 142:36 Mr '69

HORSEMAN, pass by; revue. See Musical comedies. revues. etc.—Criticisms. plots. etc.

HORSEMANSHIP
Horse sense. J. S. Parker. il Field & S 74:72-3+ Je '69
Saddle up to safe horsemanship. P. Czura. il Todays Health 47:48-53 Ap '69
10th cavalry rides again; equestrian unit for cinema and television productions recreating Buffalo Soldiers. il Ebony 24:92-7 F '69
Your riding program; keeping it as safe as your waterfront. D. D. Hirn. Camp Mag 41:31 My '69
See also
Driving

HORSEMINT
Monardas. I. D. Jolly. Horticulture 46:51 Ag '68

HORSEPOWER (mechanics)
Crower power-times two. J. Thawley. il Hot Rod 22:94-6 Ag '69

HORSES
Agony of the walking horse. il Life 67:77-8 O 3 '69
Florida horse game. il Vogue 153:158-61 Ja 15 '69
I hate horses. B. Gilbert. il Read Digest 94:134-6 Mr '69
Wild horse: heritage, or pest? N. Wood. il Audubon 71:46-51 N '69
See also
Horse breeding
Horsemanship
Race horses

Stories
Meanie: story. H. Ellsberg. Am West 6:14-15 Ja '69

Training
See Horse training

HORSES, Fossil
Paleocene hyracothere from Polecat Bench formation. Wyoming. G. L. Jepsen and M. O. Woodburne. bibliog il Science 164:543-7 My 2 '69

HORSESHOE crabs. See King crabs
HORSESHOE pitching
Shoo-in for a young shoe pitcher; World horseshoe pitching championship. Erie. Pa. W. Paul. il Sports Illus 31:18-19 Ag 18 '69

HORST
Mrs Richard Milhous Nixon; photograph. Vogue 153:158-9 My '69

HORSTED, Leon R.
Our six compost bins, all different. Org Gard & Farm 16:69-71 Ap '69

HORTICULTURAL societies
Members' news. See issues of Horticulture

HORTICULTURE
Beauty and the beast; adaptation of address. D. G. Leach. Horticulture 46:22-3+ O '68
See also
Floriculture
Nurseries (horticulture)

Bibliography
Book reviews (cont of) Books and reviews. See issues of Horticulture

Hawaii
See Gardening—Hawaii

HORTICULTURE (periodical)
Garden club yearbook contest rules (cont) Horticulture 47:50 Ag '69
Garden club yearbook contest winners (cont) Horticulture 47:43-4 Je '69

HORTON, Jack
Amazing new lightweight turbine. Mech Illus 65:66-8+ F '69

HORTON, Louise
Five special research aids. Writers Digest 49:42-5+ F '69

HORTON, Willie
Highlight. por Sports Illus 31:122 S 15 '69

HORWICH, Frances R.
Fantasy and reality; children need both. PTA Mag 64:10-12 bibliog(p34) D '69

HORWITZ, Elinor Lander
What ever happened to the neighborhood store? McCalls 96:70+ Jl '69

HORWITZ, Julius
Portrait of New York's welfare population. in one month. 50,000 persons were added to the city's welfare rolls. N Y Times Mag p22-3+ Ja 26 '69

HOSFORD, Charles
Adventure in the Maine woods. il por Life 66:80-2+ Mr 21 '69

HOSIE, Stanley W.
Have you seen 'Shoes'? America 120:651-2 My 31 '69

HOSKIN, Charles M. See Forbes, R. B. jt. auth.

HOSPITAL automation. See Hospitals—Automation
HOSPITAL boards. See Hospitals—Trustees, boards, etc.

HOSPITAL care
Acute respiratory failure. P. M. Winter and E. Lowenstein. il Sci Am 221:23-9 N '69
Death in a cancer ward; psychological needs. Time 93:62+ Je 20 '69
See also
Children—Hospital care

HOSPITAL costs. See Medical service. Cost of
HOSPITAL libraries. See Libraries, Hospital
HOSPITAL nursing. See Nurses and nursing
HOSPITAL patients. See Sick, The
HOSPITAL service, Cost of. See Medical service, Cost of
HOSPITAL ships
Mission of Hope. M. Kraft. il Américas 21:29-35 S '69

HOSPITAL trustees. See Hospitals—Trustees, boards, etc.

HOSPITALITY
See also
Entertaining

HOSPITALIZATION insurance. See Insurance. Hospitalization

HOSPITALS
See also
Children—Hospitals
Computers—Hospital applications
Hospital care
Incurables
Medical centers
Missions, Medical

Administration
See Hospitals—Management and regulation

HOSPITALS—*Continued*

Architecture

Berlin university hospital: international design for optimum form and function. il Arch Rec 146:134-40 O '69

Automation

Building types study. il Arch Rec 145:149-64 Mr '69

Boards

See Hospitals—Trustees, boards, etc.

Emergency services

Heart-saver squad; St Vincent's hospital and Medical center, New York. R. H. Berg. il Look 33:26-9 F 4 '69
Portable heart hospital. Sci Digest 66:59 Jl '69
Saving vital time for victims of heart attacks; mobile coronary care units. il Bsns W p96-8+ F 22 '69

Equipment and supplies

See also
Medical instruments and apparatus

Finance

Blue cross pays the bills: problem of financing an anti-union campaign. J. Seldin. Nation 209:48-52 Jl 14 '69
Doctors' dilemma; Harlem hospital and budget cuts. il Newsweek 73:49 Ap 7 '69

Home care programs

High hospital costs: is home care the answer? il Good H 168:203 Mr '69
When the home makes the best hospital for a child. V. H. Bernstein. Redbook 133:91+ S '69

Isolation departments

Air curtain screens bacteria. Sci Digest 65:61 My '69
Germ-free baby chamber. Sci Digest 65:61 My '69

Management and regulation

Hospitals need management even more than money. J. M. Mecklin. il Fortune 81:96-9+ Ja '70
How to serve on a hospital board. J. M. Underwood. Harvard Bsns R 47:72-80 Jl '69

Maternity wards

Can we keep it? Woodland park hospital, Portland, Ore. il Good H 169:80-2+ O '69

Staff

See also
Strikes—United States—Hospital employees

Trustees, boards, etc.

How to serve on a hospital board. J. M. Underwood. Harvard Bsns R 47:73-80 Jl '69

Canada

See also
Toronto—Hospitals

Gabon

Lambaréné revisited; Albert Schweitzer hospital. N. Cousins. il Sat R 52:28-32 O 4 '69

United States

Hill-Burton on the block. Sci N 95:377 Ap 19 '69
Now you need a priority to get in a prestige hospital. il U S News 66:41-2 Mr 24 '69
Unless a remedy is applied at once . . . E. Switzer. il Redbook 133:65+ O '69

HOSPITALS, Childrens. See Children—Hospitals

HOSPITALS, Psychiatric
Adjustment of criminally insane patients to a civil mental hospital. L. White and others. bibliog il Ment Hy 53:34-40 Ja '69
Changing mental hospital, its perceived image and contact with the community. F. Baker and others. bibliog Ment Hy 53:237-44 Ap '69
Compartmentalized children's services in a therapeutic community; Utah state hospital, Provo. E. J. Faux and C. M. Rowley. bibliog Ment Hy 53:585-9 O '69
Computer and the psychiatrist; Rockland state hospital's research center. T. Fleming. il N Y Times Mag p44-5+ Ap 6 '69
Double life of a psychiatric hospital; address, October 4, 1968. H. A. Davidson. Ment Hy 53:17-20 Ja '69
Essence of mental hospitals. R. L. Gunn and H. E. Pearman bibliog Ment Hy 53:422-7 Jl '69

Lawyer in a mental hospital; the New York experiment. E. J. Meyer. Ment Hy 53:14-16 Ja '69
Lost and found: me! a teenager's nervous breakdown. L. Kapsand. il Seventeen 28:136-7+ N '69
Mental illness is not a disease; interview, ed. by J. Ecker and B. Diasio, T. Szasz. Sci Digest 66:7-14 D '69
Orientation video tape for psychiatric patients. P. E. Logue and others. Ment Hy 53:301-2 Ap '69
Patient-staff meetings: a study of some aspects of content, tone, and speakers. B. Mardikian and I. D. Glick. Ment Hy 53:303-5 Ap '69
Psychiatric patients as research interviewers in the mental hospital. A. Shiloh. Ment Hy 53:443-5 Jl '69
Sanctuary or prison, responses to life in a mental hospital. A. Shiloh; discussion. Trans-Action 6:4+ F '69
Some problems in helping patients in public mental hospitals. W. B. Simon. bibliog Ment Hy 53:428-32 Jl '69
Treating the mentally ill. A. Shiloh. Cur 106:36-43 Ap '69
See also
Mentally handicapped—Institutional care

Administration

Expediting admissions procedures. L. C. Hartlage and others. bibliog il Ment Hy 53:71-7 Ja '69

Employees

See Hospitals, Psychiatric—Staff

Staff

Mental health manpower dilemma. M. C. Bettis and R. E. Roberts. bibliog il Ment Hy 53:163-75 Ap '69

Volunteer workers

College companions for patients in mental institutions; program at Overbrook hospital, Cedar Grove, N.J. W. R. Nord. Todays Ed 58:28-9 D '69

HOSSLI, Walter
Steam turbines; with biographical sketch. Sci Am 220:12, 100-10 Ap '69

HOSTAGES
Tit for tat; exchange of prisoners. il Newsweek 74:65 O 27 '69

HOSTELS. See Youth hostels

HOSTESSES, Air. See Airlines—Hostesses

HOSTESSES gifts. See Gifts

HOSTICK, King V.
Autographs. See issues of Hobbies

HOT-dog regulations. See Meat industry and trade—Laws and legislation

HOT dogs (meat). See Frankfurters

HOT drinks. See Beverages

HOT plates, Electric. See Electric stoves

HOT rod (magazine)
Hot rod's 1968 top ten. B. Lang. il Hot Rod 22:58-9 Mr '69

HOT rod magazine championship drag races. See Automobile racing

HOT rod racing. See Automobile racing

HOT springs
Bacterial growth rates above 90°C in Yellowstone hot springs. T. L. Bott and T. D. Brock. il Science 164:1411-12 Je 20 '69

HOT water supply
See also
Water heaters

HOTBEDS
Electrically heated hotbed. H. Robinette. il Horticulture 47:26-7 Mr '69
Grow vegetables in a home hotbed. H. Robinette. il Org Gard & Farm 16:85-8 Ja '69
See also
Cold frames

HOTCHKISS school. See Private schools

HOTEL architecture. See Hotels, taverns, etc.

HOTEL corporation of America
Rocking the boat. il Newsweek 73:85+ My 19 '69

HOTELS, taverns, etc.
Holiday travel handbook. See issues of Holiday
Hotel headliners. See issues of Travel
U.S. hotels go abroad for jet-setting Joneses: hotel and motel chains start massive expansion overseas. il Bsns W p60-1 Ja 18 '69

HOTELS, taverns, etc.—*Continued*
Will it be the soaring seventies? tomorrow's hotels. H. Sutton and D. Butwin. il Sat R 53:41-2+ Ja 3 '70
See also
Airlines—Hotel operations
Hilton hotels corporation
Restaurants
also subhead Hotels, restaurants, etc. under names of cities, e.g. Boston—Hotels, restaurants, etc.

Designs and plans
Building types study: resort hotels. R. Jensen. il Arch Rec 146:119-23 D '69

Employees
Fixer. Roman style: concierge of the Excelsior hotel. A. Waugh. il Holiday 46:30-1+ Ag '69
Importance of parsley; or, summer-jobbing at a summer resort. J. Irving. Mlle 69:209-10+ My '69

Law
How can you be married, signore, when there are different names on your passports? R. Wolfe. il Holiday 46:92-3 O '69

Afghanistan
Adventures in Afghanland. D. Butwin. il Sat R 52:44+ O 25; 49-50+ N 1 '69

Austria
Why not stay in a castle? Travel & Camera 32:86-7 Jl '69

California
See Hotels, taverns, etc.—United States

France
Hotel welcome: Villefranche. A. Waugh. Nat R 21:753+ Jl 29 '69
Notes from a wayfaring ranger; Deauville; Bagnoles. D. Butwin. Sat R 52:23-4 Jl 5 '69

Germany (Federal Republic)
Why not stay in a castle? Travel & Camera 32:87-8 Jl '69
See also
Bonn—Hotels, restaurants, etc.

Hawaii
Hawaii now, beautiful and booming. D. Messinesi. Vogue 155:180-1 Ja 15 '70
Ripples from jet-generated traffic spread over Hawaii. W. H. Gregory. il Aviation W 91:96-7+ O 20 '69

Japan
Inn-thing in Japan: Kyoto *ryokan*. G. Cotler. il Holiday 46:48-51+ D '69

Lebanon
See also
Beirut—Hotels, restaurants, etc.

Portugal
Going places, finding things: Portugal's pousadas. D. Otis. il House & Gard 135:34+ Je '69

Puerto Rico
El Conquistador: siting and design to tell the guest how special he is. il Arch Rec 146:124-7 D '69
Puerto Rico guest houses. il Travel 131:30-1 Ap '69
See also
San Juan, Puerto Rico—Hotels, restaurants, etc.

Spain
Spain, a dither of cities. D. Messinesi. il Vogue 153:42+ Je '69

Switzerland
Country and charming: Swiss inns. B. Edgar. il House & Gard 136:83-4+ O '69

Tahiti
Tahara'a: the warm and magnificent view from Tahiti. il Arch Rec 146:130-1 D '69

United States
America's unique hotels. il Holiday 45:84-7+ Ap; 46:56-7+ S '69
Call me in the city: Singles week at a famous resort hotel. L. Tornabene. il McCalls 96:68-9+ Ja '69
Hotels and motels: all the comforts of home, and then some. Bet Hom & Gard 47:54+ N '69
Old inns on highway 49; from Nevada City to Coulterville. il Sunset 143:30-2 N '69
Reveille sounds for the hoteliers. R. Bearwood. il Fortune 80:110-15+ S '69

HOTELS for women. See Womens residences
HOTHAM, David
Return of Franz Josef Strauss. N Y Times Mag p36-7+ Mr 23 '69
HOTHOUSES. See Greenhouses
HOTTEN, Andy
Sixty mph in twenty-six seconds. E. Dahlquist. il por Motor T 21:78-80 Ag '69
HOTTI, G. and Tanner, R.
How European engineers design incinerators. Am City 84:107-8+ Je '69
HOTTLEMAN, Girard D.
Our curriculum is as solid as a mausoleum. Todays Ed 58:34-5 F '69
HOUBOLT, John
Apollo's unsung hero. il por Time 93:59-60 F 28 '69
How an idea no one wanted grew up to be the LEM; with report by D. Sheridan. il por Life 66:20-7 Mr 14 '69
Who made it possible; men behind the moon program. il por Time 94:29 Jl 18 '69
HOUCK, J. R. and Harwit, Martin
Far-infrared observations of the night sky. bibliog Science 164:1271-3 Je 13 '69
HOUDAILLE industries, incorporated
Tough mind of Gerry Saltarelli. S. Blickstein. Duns R 93:38-40+ F '69
HOUGH, Henry Beetle
Prelude to the season. Travel & Camera 32:60-3+ Je '69
HOUGH, Joseph C. Jr
Rules and the ethics of sex. Chr Cent 86:148-51 Ja 29 '69
HOUGH, Richard
Our far-flung correspondents. New Yorker 45:151-4+ O 25 '69
HOUGHTON, Mich.
Sewer had to be cleaned before snowfall. C. Knecht. il Am City 84:120+ O '69
HOUGHTON Mifflin company
Money: a big word in lexicography. il Bsns W p54+ F 8 '69
Part played by Boston publishers of 1860-1900 in the field of children's books. H. L. Jones. il Horn Bk 45:153-9 Ap '69
HOULTON, Loyce
Dancers from Dinkytown. D. Hering. il por Dance Mag 43:66-72 D '69
HOUNDS
Cooners: the best in the world. L. Mueller. il Field & S 74:184-5+ My '69
Hark, the hounds. C. G. Baldwin. il Outdoor Life 143:66-9+ Mr '69
Holiday for hounds. H. Hood. il Outdoor Life 144:56-7+ D '69
How a houndman picks his pups. L. Mueller. il Field & S 74:122-7 Jl '69
See also
Beagles (dogs)
Foxhounds
HOURIET, Robert
Life and death of a commune called Oz. N Y Times Mag p30-1+ F 16 '69
HOURS, Book of
Très riches heures of Jean, Duke of Berry. Review
Art in Am il 57:56-56A N '69. J. Jacobs
HOURS of labor
Comparing employment estimates from household and payroll surveys. G. P. Green. bibliog il Mo Labor R 92:9-20 D '69
Hours and earnings, private nonagricultural payrolls; tables. See issues of Monthly labor review
Play time eats into work time; four-day week. il Bsns W p 129 Je 28 '69
Quick lunch; changes in Italy. Newsweek 73:76 Ap 28 '69
Research summaries. See issues of Monthly labor review
See also
Overtime
Sunday labor
Vacations, Employee
also subhead Wages and hours under names of industries, e.g. Steel industry and trade—Wages and hours
HOUSE, Richard C.
Build this all-in-one kitchen planning center. Pop Mech 131:150-1 Je '69
HOUSE armed services committee. See United States—Congress—House of representatives—Armed services, Committee on
HOUSE boats. See Houseboats
HOUSE building. See House construction
HOUSE building industry. See Building industry
HOUSE building materials. See Building materials

HOUSE buying
Basic steps to take when buying a house. il Good H 168:166 F '69
How much house can you afford? A. M. Watkins. il Am Home 72:78 Ja '69
How to avoid the ten biggest home-buying traps, by A. M. Watkins. Review Consumer Bul il 52:27 Ag '69
How to buy a good old house. A. M. Watkins. il Pop Mech 132:139-42+ S '69
How to judge the house you want to buy. E. S. Oshin. House & Gard 135:70+ Mr '69
How to spot a bad house that looks good; excerpt from How to avoid the ten biggest homebuying traps. A. M. Watkins. il Pop Mech 131:144-6+ F '69
Is that older house worth buying? Bet Hom & Gard 47:14+ My '69
Is this a good time to buy a house? il Changing T 22:6-10 D '68
Put your money in the ground. T. Irwin. Am Home 72:38+ N '69
Quality or not? How to tell. J. H. Ingersoll. il House B 111:74-7+ F '69
Undaunted home buyers: expense doesn't stop them. il U S News 66:50-1 Ap 14 '69
What home buyers face now. il U S News 66:59 Mr 31 '69
What to expect in new housing. M. C. Huntoon. jr. Am Home 72:114+ Ja '69
See also
Mortgages

HOUSE by the water; story. See Gordon, E. E.

HOUSE cleaning
Thirty-four quick ways to a shining house. E. Kinard. House B 111:53+ Mr '69

HOUSE committees. See United States—Congress—House of representatives—Committees

HOUSE construction
Buy a lot and build a house? il Changing T 23:25-8 My '69
Can you have the house you want? il Parents Mag 44:92-5 Mr '69
Housing boom: how big? il U S News 66:86-8 Mr 17 '69
If you're trying to build a home of your own; higher costs, tighter credit. il U S News 66:45-6 Je 30 '69
MI's vacation home. il Mech Illus 65:77-92+ Je '69
Quality or not? How to tell. J. H. Ingersoll. il House B 111:74-7+ F '69
Signs of a boom in home building. U S News 66:10 Ja 27 '69
Tinkertoy houses; town houses. il Arch Forum 130:96-9 Ja '69
We built this house for $7500. R. R. Hunt. il Pop Mech 132:126-33+ N '69
Will you plan for the future in your next house? Bet Hom & Gard 47:152 S '69
See also
Concrete houses

Anecdotes, facetiae, satire, etc.
You got to get used to Harry; building a cabin, Pennsylvania's Pocono Mountains. R. Dempewolff. il Am For 75:20-3+ My '69

HOUSE decoration
All through the house (cont) N. Mandelbaum. il McCalls 96:32 Mr; 72 Ap '69
Architect's own; I. W. Colburn's house, Lake Forest, Ill. il House & Gard 135:94-101+ Mr '69
Art of the simple. B. Plumb. il N Y Times Mag p90-1 F 16 '69
Artful ambience; McIlhenny's house, Rittenhouse square, Philadelphia. B. Plumb. il N Y Times Mag p38-9 Jl 20 '69
Big pile-up. V. D. Hahn. il Am Home 72:68-73 N '69
Break out of the box; supergraphics. V. D. Hahn and A. C. Borg. il Am Home 72:55-63 Ap '69
Come in to Christmas. il House B 111:52-5 D '69
Comfort, rich color, and the things we love. il House Gard 136:42-7 Jl '69
Complete house and lot. il Am Home 72:56-61 Mr '69
Country casual for today. il Am Home 72:46-9 Jl '69
Décor and the psyche; effects of interior design on personality. G. Blaine. jr. House B 111:46+ Ap '69
Decorating clinic; questions and answers. See issues of American home
Decorating looks we like; symposium. il House & Gard 136:96-115 O '69
Decorating newsletter. V. D. Hahn. See issues of American home
Decorating notebook. il Ladies Home J 86:88-9 O '69

Decorating notebook. J. Macurdy. il Ladies Home J 86:82-3 F '69 (to be cont)
Decorating scrapbook. il House B 111:59-69 Mr '69
Decorator speaks his mind: change; lift or hang-up? W. Baldwin. House & Gard 136:12-13+ O '69
Decorator's diary. M. Gough. il House B 111:126+ Jl '69
Enchantment in a house of stone. F. Heard. il House B 111:112-17 Ap '69
Exercise in exorcising; East Hampton house. B. Plumb. il N Y Times Mag p50-1 Ja 4 '70
Exhilaration of up-and-coming ideas. il House & Gard 135:86-97 My '69
Fashion backgrounds. B. Plumb. il N Y Times Mag p88-9+ Ap 20 '69
Fresh ways to create space with fabrics. il House & Gard 135:146-9+ Ap '69
From famous people; symposium. il House & Gard 136:62-75 Jl '69
Go West, young family. il Am House 72:54-7 Ja '69
Good taste has no price tag. W. Baldwin. House & Gard 135:38+ My '69
Home for now. H. Brown. il Am Home 72:58-9 Ja '69
House full of decorating ideas. il Good H 169:154-61 O '69
House hunt with a happy ending. il Good H 168:108-15 F '69
House in the woods. B. Plumb. il N Y Times Mag p70-1 Ja 11 '70
House of history only five years old. M. Spires. il Am Home 72:78-81 N '69
House that sets us free. E. Saltzman and R. Saltzman. il House & Gard 136:78-87 D '69
House that's very Mary; Victorian brownstone in New York city. S. Nirenberg. il House B 111:74-7 Ag '69
How to keep a flow of space. il House & Gard 135:106-11 Ap '69
How to keep your city-cool. V. D. Hahn. il Am Home 72:42-5 Jl '69
Imagination gives an individual stamp; house of Mr and Mrs Saul Steinberg on Long Island. il House & Gard 135:44-9 F '69
In the romantic idiom. il House B 111:125-7 My '69
Inside way-out; home of William Howard Adams in Princeton. B. Plumb. il N Y Times Mag p90-1 Je 8 '69
Just moved in? You'd never know it. J. L. O'Neill. il Am Home 72:40+ Ja '69
Letting in the cheer; interior of E. Giobbi's country house. B. Plumb. il N Y Times Mag p 130-1 N 30 '69
Lively beat of young New Yorkers. il House B 111:38-9 Jl '69
Mission possible: decorate the impossible home. V. D. Hahn. il Am Home 72:72-7 My '69
Mood of sunny summers past; make-over of a Victorian farmstead in New England. R. Fitzgerald and M. Gough. il House B 111:76-81 Ap '69
New ways with windows. il Good H 168:98-109 Mr '69
1969 house of ideas. il House & Gard 135:46-71+ Ja '69
Renaissance on Long Island; mansion of E. J. Hughes. B. Plumb. il N Y Times Mag p98-9 D 14 '69
Romantic totality, past and present. F. Heard and J. DeLong. il House B 111:96-102 Mr '69
Six families make identical space unique. il House & Gard 135:126-31 Ap '69
Small wonders. il Redbook 132:90-2 Mr; 113-15+ Ap; 133:110-13+ Jl; 102-5+ S; 113-15+ O '69
Soft touch. B. Plumb. il N Y Times Mag p 102-3 Mr 16 '69
Space venture: the Ahmet Ertegün town house in New York. P. Devlin. il Vogue 154:128-33 Ag 15 '69
Start something. il McCalls 96:64-7 Ja '69
Steps to take when redecorating. il Good H 169:176-7 S '69
Sterility of perfection. W. Baldwin. House & Gard 135:38-9 Je '69
Summer by the water: four sites, four houses. il House B 111:54-67 Jl '69
Transferee's guide to home fix-up. A. J. Maher. Am Home 72:74-5 Ja '69
Twenty most frequently asked decorating questions. House B 111:70-2 Mr '69
Under one roof: personal space for three generations. il House & Gard 135:112-19 Ap '69
Unexpected touches give a home its personality. S. K. Stone. il Farm J 93:56-7 My '69
Visual arts at home. il House B 111:113-17 O '69
What to do about a nothing room. P. Rumely. il Bet Hom & Gard 47:68-77 F '69

HOUSE decoration—*Continued*
What's new for living. il House & Gard 135: 72-7 Ja '69
White on white. B. Plumb. il N Y Times Mag p96-7 Mr 23 '69
Why you need a decorator before you build. W. Baldwin. House & Gard 136:10-11 D '69
Young chic for the old sheik's lair. il House B 111:40-2 Jl '69
Young mood captured. F. Heard. il House B 111:136-41 O '69
Young-shot in decorating: California decorator, J. Steffy. P. Devlin. il Vogue 154:156-9+ Ag 1 '69
    See also
Apartments
Art in the home
Attics
Bathroom fixtures
Bathrooms
Bedrooms
Ceilings
Childrens rooms
Christmas decorations
Color in house decoration
Curtains and draperies
Dining rooms
Display of antiques, art objects, etc.
Furniture, Arrangement of
Halls
Household furnishings
Interior decorators
Kitchens
Lighting, Architectural and decorative
Living rooms
Mirrors
Period rooms
Pictures, Hanging of
Plants in house decoration
Pottery in house decoration
Screens (furniture)
Textile fabrics
Upholstery
Wall coverings
Window shades
Windows

HOUSE decoration, American
Sense of early America. N. Craig. il House B 111:122-3 Ap '69
    See also
Furniture, American

HOUSE decoration, Colonial and early American. See House decoration, American

HOUSE decoration, English
Aura of empire. Georgian manor house. il House B 111:90-1 Ap '69
    See also
House decoration, Victorian

HOUSE decoration, European
Splendor of decoration; nine beautiful period rooms. il House & Gard 136:58-67 D '69

HOUSE decoration, Exterior
Three dramatic face liftings. il Am Home 72:70-1 My '69
    See also
House painting

HOUSE decoration, French
On beauty bent. B. Plumb. il N Y Times Mag p 104-5 Mr 30 '69

HOUSE decoration, Italian
Fashions in living. il Vogue 153:161 Ap 1 '69
Magic under the skies of Milan. il House B 111:118-19 Ap '69

HOUSE decoration, Moroccan
Moroccan wake-up; the Paul Getty, jr. house in Marrakech. il Vogue 155:166-71+ Ja 15 '70

HOUSE decoration, Victorian
Very neo; neo-Edwardian apartment of Barbara and Fitz Fitzsimon. B. Plumb. il N Y Times Mag p68-9 Ag 17 '69

HOUSE fittings. See Building fittings

HOUSE heating. See Heating

HOUSE insulation. See Insulation (heat)

HOUSE lighting. See Electric lighting

HOUSE mice. See Mice

HOUSE of Atreus; drama. See Lewin, J.

HOUSE of lords. See Great Britain—Parliament—House of lords

HOUSE of prayer. See Convents and nunneries

HOUSE of representatives. See United States—Congress—House of representatives

HOUSE organs
Kaiser aluminum uncovers money in its PR efforts; Oscar winning documentary from material in house organ. il Bsns W p88-9 Jl 12 '69

HOUSE painting
Outdoor originality. il McCalls 97:106-9 O '69
They paint your house between breakfast and lunch; Hydraposit system. J. Hand. il Pop Sci 195:108-10 Jl '69
What to do before the painter comes. House & Gard 135:37+ Ap '69

HOUSE pets. See Pets

HOUSE placement. See Building sites

HOUSE plants
Care of houseplants when away. Good H 169: 148 Ag '69
Easy endeavors for fun and foliage indoors. il Home Gard 56:38-9 Jl '69
Flowers all over the house. il Vogue 153: 141 My '69
Gift plants will keep on giving, if you provide the easy care they need. H. V. Wilson. il Home Gard 56:68-9 F '69
Give your houseplants a summer vacation. C. Wallis. Horticulture 47:47 Jl '69
Group indoor plants for greater effect and easier maintenance. J. Hudak. il Horticulture 46:30-1+ N '68
Home garden's gallery of house plants. il Home Gard 56:8-9 N '69
House plants for every home. R. M. Peters. il Home Gard 56:32-40 N '69
Plant-in. B. Plumb. il N Y Times Mag p72-3 Ap 6 '69
Potted ornamentals for winter cheer. B. Wahlfeldt. il Org Gard & Farm 16:43-5 Ja '69
Regulating humidity in the home. D. A. Caccia. il Org Gard & Farm 16:112-16 F '69
Spray schedule for indoor plants. P. P. Pirone. il Horticulture 47:34-6 O '69
Tip sheet for indoor flower care. Vogue 153: 112 My '69
Your garden indoors. F. S. David. il Home Gard 56:12 D '69
    See also
Amaryllis
Artificial light gardening
Cactus
Coleus
Epiphyllums
Kalanchoes
Maranta
Poinsettias
Queen's tears
Shrimp plants

HOUSE prices. See Housing—Costs

HOUSE protection
    See also
Summer homes—Protection

HOUSE purchasing. See House buying

HOUSE rent. See Rent

HOUSE selling
ABCs of selling your house. H. Gertwangler. il Mech Illus 65:66-8+ Ap '69
Home for sale. H. B. Winsor. il PTA Mag 63: 26-8 Mr '69

HOUSE trailers. See Mobile homes

HOUSE ventilation. See Ventilation

HOUSE walls. See Walls

HOUSEBOAT racing
House is not a hot rod. H. D. Whall. il Sports Illus 31:14-17 Jl 28 '69

HOUSEBOAT seamanship. See Seamanship

HOUSEBOATS
Build this houseboat for under $1000. D. Fales. il Pop Mech 131:158-63 Ja '69
Case of the hospitable houseboat. E. S. Gardner. il Pop Sci 195:50-5+ Jl '69
Cast loose all cares. E. S. Gardner. il Motor B 123:267+ Ja '69
Cruising in a cottage. J. N. Miller. il Read Digest 94:37-8+ Je '69
Emergence of the houseboatman. D. Kirkpatrick. il Motor B 124:45 D '69
Evolution of the modern houseboat. D. Kirkpatrick. il Motor B 124:42-4 D '69
Good life afloat. Bsns W p68 Jl 19 '69
Hooked on houseboats. F. M. Paulson. il Field & S 74:88-91 Jl '69
House-boating. A. R. Roalman il Travel 132: 50-3 Ag '69
Houseboat. T. Johnson. il Yachting 125:301 Ja '69
Houseboat boom. J. Martenhoff. il Yachting 125:59-62+ My '69
Houseboat in Florida. J. Smith. Yachting 126:52-3+ N '69
Houseboat to Acapulco. P. Smyth. il Motor B 124:66-7 Ag '69
Houseboats. il Motor B 123:180-1 Ja '69
Mississippi houseboating. J. Ehresman. Outdoor Life 144:35-6 Jl '69
On the Columbia's Oregon shore, a floating two-family compound. il Sunset 143:62-5 Jl '69
Our old Kentucky houseboat. A. W. Prince. il Outdoor Life 143:68-71+ My '69
Personal business. Bsns W p 119-20 Jl 19 '69
Sailor meets houseboat; Canada's Rideau waterway. P. Smyth. il Motor B 124:36-41+ D '69

HOUSEBOATS—*Continued*
Sequel: Catamaran houseboat that grew. il Yachting 125:83 Je '69
Take your family houseboating. P. Plawin. il Bet Hom & Gard 47:145-6 My '69
When is a boat a home? When it's a house. F. Rohr. il Motor B 123:274-7+ Ja '69
Your new houseboat. il Motor B 123:106-7 Ja '69
See also
Houseboat racing

Design
Houseboats galore. il Motor B 124:64-6 D '69

Leasing and renting
Coyotes howl at midnight; Texas coast. P. Smyth. il Motor B 123:62-5+ My '69
Houseboat rental outfits across America. il Travel 132:73-4 Ag '69
Rent a floating vacation home. E. Kinard. il House B 111:68-70 S '69

Materials
How to build a concrete houseboat for $2,000. il Motor B 124:70-1+ N '69

Purchasing
Convert talks about houseboats; interview. O. L. McCurdy. il Motor B 124:48-9 D '69
Getting to know the modern houseboat; a shopper's guide. il Motor B 124:50-1+ D '69
HOUSECLEANING. See House cleaning
HOUSEHOLD accidents. See Accidents
HOUSEHOLD appliances
Are you polluting your own home? R. Winter. il Sci Digest 66:22-6 S '69
Exciting new products. C. Bilski. See issues of Popular mechanics
From a frosty refrigerator to a drier dryer; guide to appliance buying. il McCalls 96:78-9+ Ja '69
Household help available. il Parents Mag 44:80-3 Ag '69
How to save wear and tear on your home. W. C. Leckey. il Pop Mech 131:176-9+ My '69
If you're giving an appliance gift. Good H 169:223 D '69
It's worth mentioning. J. Polshek. See issues of House beautiful
What's new for living. See issues of House & garden incorporating Living for young homemakers
See also
Bathroom fixtures
Electric apparatus and appliances, Domestic
Kitchen utensils
Labor saving devices
also names of household appliances, e.g. Vacuum cleaners

Leasing and renting
Should you rent that major appliance? Am Home 72:98 Mr '69

Manufacture
From the frying pan into the... il Forbes 104:65-6 N 15 '69
HOUSEHOLD budget. See Budget. Household
HOUSEHOLD employees
American as indentured servant; working in a continental household as an au pair. L. Arking. Mlle 69:211+ My '69
Are you allowed to pay your maid's social security tax for her? McCalls 96:58 Ap '69
Arriving: the household professional. D. Mac-Donald. il House B 111:88-9 Mr '69
Care and feeding of the very rich. R. West. il McCalls 96:56-7+ Ag '69
Employer vs. domestic: the social security hassle. M. Feeley. Am Home 72:11+ Ja '69
In private service; a footman. H. J. Andrews. Vogue 153:151-3 F 15 '69
Village maids. Newsweek 73:79-80 F 3 '69

Anecdotes, facetiae, satire, etc.
My short and secret life as a cleaning woman. M. McSherry. il McCalls 97:78-9+ O '69
HOUSEHOLD expenses. See Domestic finance
HOUSEHOLD furnishings
At the sea and in the city. T. Capote. il House B 111:93-8 Ap '69
Bath boutique. il House & Gard 136:188-91 O '69
Bring unique interest to your home with handcrafted accessories. il Good H 169:108-12 Jl '69
Color game: how to score points. il House B 111:128-32 My '69
Connoisseur's corner. See issues of House & garden incorporating Living for young homemakers

Decorating newsletter. V. D. Hahn. See issues of American home
Decorating notebook. J. Macurdy. il Ladies Home J 86:82-3 F '69 (to be cont)
Decorating notebook. il Ladies Home J 86:88-9 O '69
Decorator crafts. M. Garrity. il Bet Hom & Gard 47:88-91 Mr '69
Decorator's diary. M. Gough. il House B 111:126+ Jl '69
Generation gap: two sets of interiors, Washington, D.C. B. Plumb. il N Y Times Mag p 134-5 N 16 '69
How to keep your city-cool .V. D. Hahn. il Am Home 72:42-5 Jl '69
I love the sunny colors and wide open spaces of my new apartment. il House & Gard 136:58-61 Ag '69
Ideas for entertaining. il House & Gard 136:168-9 O '69
Lifestyle. See issues of American home
Lilly look at home. il House & Gard 135:66-7 Je '69
New coordinates for decorating, in many moods. il House B 111:120-1 N '69
100 ideas under $100. il Bet Hom & Gard 47:18+ Ag '69
Plastics explosion in home furnishings. P. Rumely. il Bet Hom & Gard 47:59-73 Ap '69
Practical pleasures for night-and-day bedrooms. il House & Gard 135:80-1 F '69
Rooms that rise and shine. il McCalls 96:92-5 S '69
Setting up housekeeping? Here's what it costs. il Changing T 23:24-8 Mr '69
Sweet and sour oranges. il House & Gard 136:138-41 S '69
What's new for living. See issues of House & garden incorporating Living for young homemakers
Young optics. il House B 111:120-1 Ap '69
See also
Christmas gifts for the home
Color in house decoration

History
House furnishings of a Vermont family. F. W. Inman. il Antiques 96:228-33 Ag '69
Household accessories; Williamsburg, Va. B. T. Rumford. il Antiques 95:145-9 Ja '69
Textile furnishings; Williamsburg, Va. M. B. Lanier. il Antiques 95:121-7 Ja '69
HOUSEHOLD furnishings, Moving of. See Moving
HOUSEHOLD linens. See Linen, Household
HOUSEHOLD odors. See Odors
HOUSEHOLD pests

Control
What an exterminator can and cannot do. McCalls 96:52 Mr '69
HOUSEKEEPING. See Home economics
HOUSES
Ideas in houses (cont) il Life 66:70-2 F 21; 80-2+ Mr 21; 86-8+ Ap 11; 90-2+ My 9; 68-70+ Je 20; 67:56-61 Ag 1 '69
Whatever happened to the new building ideas of a few years back? il Bet Hom & Gard 47:62-3+ S '69
See also
Architecture, Domestic
Stone houses
Storage in the home

Maintenance and repair
Fixing up an older home. il Bet Hom & Gard 47:18+ My '69
Hammering headache of home repairs. il Time 94:67 Jl 25 '69
Home upkeep (title varies) Bet Hom & Gard 47:46 F; 42+ O '69
Homeowners' clinic; questions and answers. W. C. Lammey. See issues of Popular mechanics
How to save wear and tear on your home. W. C. Leckey. il Pop Mech 131:176-9+ My '69
Information almanac. McCalls 96.46 Mr '69
When the repairman won't come. A. M. Watkins. House B 111:84-6+ O '69
Wood and water don't mix. M. E. Dowd. Am Home 72:102-3 Mr '69

Prices
See Housing—Costs

Rating
Quality or not? How to tell. J. H. Ingersoll. il House B 111:74-7+ F '69

Ventilation
See Ventilation

HOUSING—*Continued*

Brazil

House is not a home. Trans-Action 6:8+
S '69

Florida

Gold coast booms again; Florida high-rise condominiums under construction. il Bsns W p 144+ Jl 12 '69

Trial run for instant housing; Modiflex homes. il Bsns W p 111-12 O 11 '69

Great Britain

Nowhere people; squatting in Britain. il Newsweek 74:37 Jl 7 '69

Latin America

Good house; address, January 27, 1969. J. Balaguer. Vital Speeches 35:327-9 Mr 15 '69

Slums of hope and despair. J. A. Casasco. il Américas 21:13-20 Je '69

Russia

Russia faces up to the realities of construction industry in reorganizing its approach to producing housing. J. Winkler. il Arch Rec 146:169-72 O '69

United States

As housing shortage grows. il U S News 67: 84-6 O 13 '69

Breakdown in our cities; interview. G. Romney. il U S News 67:48-51 Jl 28 '69

Church groups in housing. America 121:213 S 27 '69

Comsat for construction. Time 93:94 Je 13 '69

Fair housing laws, unfair housing practices. L. W. Eley. il Trans-Action 6:56-61 Je '69

Great U.S. housing shortage. il Newsweek 73: 68-70 Mr 31 '69

House shortage: what to do about it. il Good H 169:206 N '69

Housing shortage goes critical. L. A. Mayer. il Fortune 80:86-9+ D '69

Housing: the continuing crisis; symposium. il Arch Forum 131:44-93 Jl '69

Is a breakthrough near in housing? il Bsns W p80-2+ S 13 '69

Man builds a house. Nat R 21:317 Ap 8 '69

Recognizing market realities. Time 95:70 Ja 12 '70

Rush to apartments. il U S News 67:46-8 D 8 '69

Six men who share our concern about the problems of housing today. il Bet Hom & Gard 47:88-9 S '69

Toward a decent home for every American family. M. Farmer. il Arch Rec 146:131-4 O '69

Trees for people. G. Romney. Am For 75: 20-1 O '69

221 ways to save our cities. J. Bailey. Arch Forum 130:70-3 Ja '69

What to expect in new housing. M. C. Huntoon, jr. Am Home 72:114+ Ja '69

Why housing costs are going through the roof. il Time 94:82+ O 31 '69

Will there ever be a housing boom? interviews. J. W. Gardner and E. S. Callender. Forbes 104:72+ O 15 '69

See also
Building industry
Housing—Federal aid
Housing finance
Housing laws and legislation—United States
Housing projects, Government
Negroes—Housing
United States—Housing and urban development. Department of

HOUSING, Cooperative
Nine-G cooperative; brownstones in New York city. il Arch Forum 131:78-81 Jl '69

HOUSING, Discrimination in. See Discrimination in housing

HOUSING act of 1968. See Housing laws and legislation—United States

HOUSING and development administration. See New York (city)—Housing and development administration

HOUSING and urban development, Department of. See United States—Housing and urban development, Department of

HOUSING authorities
Housing the poor. C. W. Hartman and G. Carr. bibliog il Trans-Action 7:49-53 D '69

HOUSING construction. See Building industry

HOUSING finance
BURP and make money; urban housing rehabilitation venture. E. Goldston. bibliog il Harvard Bsns R 47:84-99 S '69

Lenders say: no relief near for house hunters. il U S News 67:86-8 O 27 '69

Managing a war on poverty; program in Roanoke, Va. il Nations Bsns 57:52-5 F '69

Money and housing; interview, ed. by G. R. Rosen. P. Martin. Duns R 94:12-15 Ag '69

Money is the root. Fortune 80:28+ O '69

Stake in the system: national urban bonds; address, May 28, 1969. A. E. Gershen. Vital Speeches 35:763-5 O 1 '69

What's the best way to get money for remodeling? il Bet Hom & Gard 47:9+ My '69

See also
Mortgages

HOUSING laws and legislation
See also
Building laws and regulations

United States

Changes in housing law; what they mean. il U S News 67:20 D 29 '69

Choice of housing bills. America 121:411 N 8 '69

Land law's fine print trips up developers; housing act of 1968 aimed at interstate land sales. il Bsns W p 184+ Ap 26 '69

HOUSING of students. See College students —Housing

HOUSING projects

Site planning

Enlightened builder creates a total environment. A. C. Borg. il Am House 72:50-3 Mr '69

Garden environments for apartment living; building types and study. Arch Rec 146:183-79 S '69

La Luz, N.Mex. il Arch Forum 131:66-71 Jl '69

Logical land use; housing in Vermont. E. P. Berkeley. il Arch Forum 131:40-3 D '69

Riverbend houses. P. Blake. il Arch Forum 131:46-55 Jl '69

Suburbs are changing. W. Langewiesche. il Read Digest 95:157-62+ N '69

Thamesmead. il Arch Forum 131:59-65 Jl '69

Urban housing: a comprehensive approach to quality: plans for New York city. il Arch Rec 145:97-118 Ja '69

HOUSING projects, Government
Crisis in public housing. il U S News 67: 66-7 N 24 '69

Is 202 housing for you? H. Heusinkveld. il Har Yrs 9:46-9 Mr '69

Mass-produced housing? G. Romney's plan. Commonweal 90:332 Je 6 '69

Operation Breakthrough. il Newsweek 74:78+ Jl 21 '69

Public housing in black and white; the Chicago housing authority. H. D. Shapiro. Commonweal 90:253-4 My 16 '69

HOUSING research
Research and development; the housing industry; address, July 7, 1969. H. B. Finger. Vital Speeches 35:652-4 Ag 15 '69

See also
Building research

HOUSING statistics. See Housing—Statistics

HOUSMAN, Alfred Edward
Swinburne; with introd. by J. Sparrow. Am Scholar 39:59-79 Wint '69

about

Housmaning into the seventies. R. Whittemore. New Repub 161:35-7 N 29 '69

HOUSTON, B. Kent
Do mind-bending drugs cause serious birth defects? Sci Digest 66:30-2+ O '69

HOUSTON, James D. See Finney, B. R. jt. auth.

HOUSTON, Walter Scott
Deep-sky wonders. See issues of Sky and telescope

Safe sun scope. R Pop Astron 63:27-8 F '69

HOUSTON, Tex.
Local association of the month. Todays Ed 58:65-6 F '69

New Houston blitzed Chicago; National association of home builders annual meeting. il Forbes 103:34-5 F 15 '69

Airports

Jetport for the supersonics. il Am City 84: 164 S '69

Soft landing in Houston. J. M. Dixon. il Arch Forum 131:60-9 S '69

Architecture

Bold tower for a utility company. il Arch Rec 145:151-4 F '69

Banks

Swinging with youth; First city national bank wooing young customers. il Time 94:69 Ag 22 '69

HOUSTON, Tex.—*Continued*

Description

Exciting cities, a Redbook vacation guide to sight-seeing with children; excerpts from America's exciting cities. A. Schwartz. il Redbook 132:39-40 Ap '69

Music

La Mancha's man; Massenet's Don Quixote. W. Starkie. il Opera N 33:14-16 Ap 19 '69
    See also
Houston grand opera association

Social life and customs

Single life: Houston. il Mlle 69:147+ S '69

Stores

Galleria Post Oak: Neiman-Marcus Houston store achieves quality identity in harmony with total-center architecture. il Arch Rec 146:143-50 Jl '69

Theater

Alley theater, Houston. W. Sheed. Life 66:10 Je 27 '69
Houston's Alley theater. J. M. Dixon. il Arch Forum 130:30-9 Mr '69

HOUSTON astrodome. See Stadiums

HOUSTON grand opera association
Report: Houston; production of Barber of Seville. A. Holmes. Opera N 33:32 F 22 '69
Report: Houston; production of Don Carlo. A. Holmes. Opera N 33:31 Ap 5 '69
Report: production of Turandot. A. Holmes. Opera N 34:27 D 13 '69

HOUSTON Oilers (football club) See Football clubs

HOUSTON space center. See United States—Manned spacecraft center

HOUSTON stadium. See Stadiums

HOUSTON tournament. See Golf—Tournaments

HOVDA, Robert
Prophets are made, not born. Commonweal 91:134-5 O 31 '69

HOVELSRUD, Joyce
No wonder students can't write. Engl J 58:249-51 F '69

HOVER, Herbert
Old garden of E. I. du Pont. Horticulture 47: 35+ S '69

HOVERCRAFT. See Air cushion vehicles

HOVEYDA, Amir Abbas
Prime Minister Hoveyda of Iran visits Washington; exchange of greetings and toasts, December 5, 1968. Dept State Bul 59:659-61 D 23 '68

HOVING, Thomas Pearsall Field
Our business is refreshment of the eye, the mind and the soul. por Holiday 45:56-9+ F '69

about

Harlem out of mind; exhibition at Metropolitan museum of art; with editorial comment. A. Goldin. il Art N 68:23, 52-3+ Mr '69
Hoving at the Met. B. Rose. Vogue 154:152 O 1 '69

HOVORKA, John
Magnetic flux-trapping experiment with a moving conductor. bibliog Science 166:877-8 N 14 '69

HOW, John B.
Art as an antidote for the boredom of retirement. por Am Artist 33:30-1+ N '69

HOW it turns out; story. See Rogin, G.

HOW-to-do-it books. See Instruction manuals

HOW will I know? story. See Briskin, J.

HOWARD, Anthony
Advice to the new boys. New Repub 160:29-30 F 1 '69
Cutting down the lords. New Repub 160:10-11 Mr 29 '69
Harold Wilson's sound pound. New Repub 161:13-14 N 15 '69
Odd and ugly noises from the Labor party. New Repub 160:13-14 Mr 8 '69
Time for heroes. Harper 238:91-2 F '69
Tune in on life with Charlie. New Repub 161:13 Jl 5 '69
Wilson's about-face. New Repub 160:7-8 Je 28 '69

HOWARD, Bob
You can edit sound movies. Pop Phot 64:100-1+ Je '69

HOWARD, Edward N.
Breaking the fine barrier. por ALA Bul 63: 1541-5 D '69
Terre Haute: no one has asked. Wilson Lib Bul 43:888-92 My '69

about

Train wreck in Terre Haute. G. R. Shields. il por ALA Bul 63:981-4 Jl '69

HOWARD, Frank
Fence-busters. il por Time 94:48 Jl 25 '69

HOWARD, Harry N.
Turkey: a contemporary survey. bibliog f Cur Hist 56:141-5+ Mr '69
United Arab Republic. Cur Hist 58:8-12+ Ja '70
U.S. in the Middle East today. bibliog f Cur Hist 57:36-41 Jl '69

HOWARD, Jane
Flowering of a late bloomer. Life 67:82-8 N 21 '69
For the long-distance runner who got caught: a twenty-year sentence. Life 67:30-1 O 31 '69
Growing up in America; Midwest. Mlle 68: 209+ Ap '69
Survival expert, Paul Petzoldt. Life 67:48-50+ D 19 '69
Up against the Peter principle. Life 67:59 Jl 18 '69

HOWARD, John A.
How did we get so confused? address, February 10, 1969. Vital Speeches 35:331-2 Mr 15 '69
Patriotism revisited; address, September 17, 1969. Vital Speeches 36:24-9 O 15 '69

HOWARD, John Robert
Flowering of the hippie movement. bibliog f Ann Am Acad 382:43-55 Mr '69

HOWARD, Loretta Hines
Tree; interview. New Yorker 45:31-2 D 20 '69

HOWARD, Lucille
All subjects are go with aerospace. Am Ed 5:5-8 Ap '69

HOWARD, Norman F.
Jordan: the commando state. bibliog f Cur Hist 58:16-20+ Ja '70

HOWARD, Richard
Critic of the month. Poetry 113:338-60 F '69
Demolition; Aubade: Donna Anna to Juan, still asleep; Freshwater: an idyll; poems. Poetry 114:289-97 Ag '69
May 26, 1969: the grievance; poem. Poetry 115:111 N '69
Revolution for the hell of it. Commonweal 89:596-7 F 7 '69
Second nature. Poetry 114:331-4 Ag '69

HOWARD, Robert C.
Speakers, present and future. por Hi Fi 19: 49-53 Je '69

HOWARD, Ruth
Requiem to Dr Martin Luther King, jr. Negro Hist Bul 32:17 Ap '69

HOWARD, Seymour
Small industrial buildings. Arch Rec 145:155 F '69

HOWARD, Steven J.
Keep the swing in an overhead-type garage door. Pop Mech 131:168-71 Ja '69
Those new tough-to-pick door locks. Pop Mech 132:134-8+ S '69
What you should know about home burglar alarms. Pop Mech 132:156-8 N '69

HOWARD, Theodore Roosevelt Mason
Doctor Howard's safari room. il pors Ebony 24:132-4+ O '69

HOWARD, Thomas
Human experience of death. Chr Today 14: 6-8 N 21 '69
Sodom and the city of God. Chr Today 13:8-10 Ja 31 '69

HOWARD university, Washington, D.C.
Cheek brothers, a new breed of college president. il Ebony 24:35-8+ O '69
Graduate student. M. J. Smith. il Phys Today 22:28 Mr '69
Howard U.'s oldest graduate. il Ebony 24:77-80 F '69

HOWARTH memorial park. See Santa Rosa, Calif.—Parks and playgrounds

HOWAT, John
John F. Kensett, 1816-1872. Antiques 96:397-401 S '69

HOWE, Fanny
Afterword; poem. Atlan 224:89 D '69
Growing up in America; New England. Mlle 68:206+ Ap '69

HOWE, Florence
Untaught teachers and improbable poets. Sat R 52:60-2+ Mr 15 '69

HOWE, Gordon
Gordie Howe: hockey's marvelous Methuselah. D. MacDonald. il Read Digest 95: 122-6 N '69
Stadiums aren't for sleeping. P. Waldmeir and G. Ronberg. il por Sports Illus 31:28-9 O 20 '69

HOWE, Harold 2d
Appeal for agitators; reprint. Ed Digest 34: 1-2 Ap '69
Excerpt from address, December 6, 1967. Cong Digest 48:45+ F '69

about

[Harry Golden column] H. Golden. Nation 208:181 F 10 '69

HOWE, Irving
Dostoevsky, the struggle to create. Harper 239:126-8+ O '69
New black writers. Harper 239:130-1+ D '69
Wounds of all generations. Harper 238:96-102 My '69

about

Parting of the ways. R. Williams. Commentary 47:73-5 F '69

HOWE, Leroy T.
Theology and the death camps. Chr Cent 86:251-5 F 19 '69

HOWE, Quincy
Mission to the White House. Sat R 52:37-9+ F 15 '69

HOWE, Russell Warren
Rising star, rising crescent. New Repub 161: 6-7 D 6 '69
War in southern Africa. For Affairs 48:150-65 O '69
Would-be leader of Arab militants. New Repub 160:11-12 F 15 '69

HOWELL, Betje
Herbert Ryman; California painter. Am Artist 33:66-71 Ap '69

HOWELL, Chauncey
Sight and sound. McCalls 96:10+ My '69

HOWELL, F. Clark
When man began. Newsweek 73:94 My 12 '69

HOWELL, Gordon S. and Weiser, C. J.
What makes plants hardy? Horticulture 46: 18-21+ D '68

HOWELL, Treva Turner
Feud in the hills. il por Time 94:21 S 12 '69

HOWES, Barbara
Harkness pavilion; poem. New Yorker 45: 48 N 1 '69
Lonely pipefish; poem. Atlan 224:90 N '69
Otis; poem. Sat R 52:6 F 22 '69

HOWIE, Virginia
Annuals for edgings. Horticulture 47:30-3+ My '69
Lilies for small gardens. Horticulture 47:18-19+ Je '69
Wild lilies. il Horticulture 46:30-1+ O '68

HOWLETT, William Porter
Coup at Consolidated. Newsweek 74:49+ D 29 '69
Why the head chef left Con foods. il por Bsns W p21-2 D 20 '69

HOWLEY, Frank Leo
Remembering liberated Paris. N Y Times Mag p22+ O 5 '69

HOY, John C.
College admissions; the price of diversity. Sat R 52:96-7+ F 15 '69

HOYEM, Andrew
I like to (B)eat people up. Poetry 113:426-8 Mr '69
Other people, other places; Chateau; poems. Poetry 113:389-90 Mr '69

HOYER, Linda Grace
Amish country: the promised land. Travel & Camera 32:66-71 Jl '69
Hindsight and foresight; story. New Yorker 44:30-7 F 1 '69

HOYLE, G. See Willows, A. O. D. jt. auth.

HOYMAN, H. S.
Should birth control be taught? Ed Digest 35:28-30 D '69
Should we teach about birth control in high school sex education? Ed Digest 34: 20-3 F '69

HOYT, Emerson M.
Second-guessing the pitch reference. Pop Electr 30:70-1 Je '69

HOYT, Mary Finch. See Muskie, J. jt. auth.

HRDLICKA, Connie
In my opinion. Seventeen 28:202 O '69

HROMADKA, Josef Luki
New calvaries ever. Chr Cent 86:1538-9 D 3 '69

HRONEK, Sharon
Battle of Omaha. Am West 6:10-11 Jl '69

HRUBY, Suzanne
Face to face with a girl who saw freedom die in Czechoslovakia. por Seventeen 27:125 N '68

HRUSKA, Roman Lee
Senate: the balancing act. J. Osborne. il New Repub 160:19-21 F 1 '69

HRYNIEWIECKI, Jerzy
Canaletto's paintings helped rebuild shattered Warsaw; reprint. UNESCO Courier 22:48-9 Ag '69

HSIEN, Ya. See Ya Hsien

HSU, Kai-yu
Chinese communist leadership. bibliog f Cur Hist 57:129-34+ S '69

HUA HIN, Thailand
Siam by-the-sea. P. Simms. il Sat R 52:86-8 Mr 8 '69

HUANG, Peter C. R.
Daring young men of acquisitions. J. Poindexter. il por Duns R 92:26-9+ D '68

HUANG, Yung-sheng
New star over Peking. Newsweek 74:44+ D 1 '69

HUBBARD, La Fayette Ronald
Dangerous new cult of scientology. A. Eisenberg and H. Eisenberg. Parents Mag 44: 48-9+ Je '69
Scientology: religion or racket? J. M. Hopkins. Chr Today 14:6-9 N 7 '69 (to be cont)
Total freedom and beyond. D. Bess. Nation 209:311-15 S 29 '69

HUBBARD, Orville
Ford collides with Dearborn's mayor. il por Bsns W p66-8 Ja 10 '70

HUBBARD squash. See Squashes

HUBBELL, John G.
Bold new plan for national defense. Read Digest 95:82-7 O '69
You'll never be afraid to try. Read Digest 94: 173-5+ Mr '69
(ed) See McCain, J. S. jr. In Vietnam, the enemy is beaten

HUBEL, Gordon
Rights and permissions; summary of address, June 23, 1969. por Pub W 196:22-3 Ag 4 '69

HUBERMAN, Michael
Experiment in university self-study. Sch & Soc 97:431-3 N '69

HUBS, Automobile. See Automobiles—Wheels

HUCKABY, Gerald
Bronc buster; poem. America 121:393 N 1 '69
Of one conception; poem. America 121:612 D 20 '69
Seal; poem. America 120:531 My 3 '69

HUDAK, Joseph
American elm. Horticulture 47:8-9 My '69
Group indoor plants. Horticulture 46:30-1+ N '68
Shagbark hickory. Horticulture 46:10+ O '68
Update your garden. Horticulture 46:36-7+ S '68

HUDSON, G. F.
[Book review] Commonweal 90:210-11 My 2 '69

HUDSON, Michael
Financing the world empire. Commonweal 91:243-5 N 21 '69

HUDSON, Neville Dyson-. See Dyson-Hudson, N.

HUDSON, Peggy
Look and listen. See issues of Scholastic teacher
Looking & listening. See issues of Senior scholastic

HUDSON, Rada Dyson-. See Dyson-Hudson, R.

HUDSON, William J. jr
His book steers merger hunters. il por Bsns W p98+ F 8 '69

HUDSON, Ohio
Plow on the front and a spreader on the rear. H. Kuchenbecker. il Am City 84:112+ F '69

HUDSON RIVER
Cleanup folk festival; visiting anti-Hudson-River-pollution sailing sloop Clearwater. N. Drahos. il Cons 24:31 O '69
Discoverer of the Hudson's source. M. MacKenzie. il Cons 23:28-31 F '69
Hope of the Hudson; project begun by the Hudson River sloop restoration to combat pollution. S. Atwater. il Cons 23:15-16 Je '69
Song of the open sewer; anti-pollution voyage aboard the sloop Clearwater. il Time 94:43 Ag 22 '69
To save the dying Hudson: Pete Seeger's voyage; with editorial comment by G. Goodman. P. Seeger. il Look 33:62-6 Ag 26 '69
Upper Hudson River bill signed. Liv Wildn 33:38 Sum '69
Upper Hudson: time for decision, reprint. P. Schaefer. il Liv Wildn 32:18-21 Wint '68
Why Gooley number one? A. M. Crocker. il Liv Wildn 32:22-4 Wint '68

HUDSON RIVER bridges
Bridge deck overlay gains stability with asbestos fibers; George Washington bridge. il Am City 84:87-9 F '69

HUDSON RIVER school. See Painting, American

HUDSON RIVER sloops. See Sloops

HUDSON'S corporate mergers. See Business consolidations and mergers—Directories

HUÉ, Vietnam
Anniversary thoughts. F. Sully. il Newsweek 73:40 F 17 '69
South Viet Nam: Hué revisited. il Time 93:34 F 14 '69
HUÉ massacre. See Vietnamese war, 1957- — Atrocities
HUELSENBECK, Richard
Reflections on leaving America for good. Am Scholar 39:80-5 Wint '69
HUEY, F. B. Jr
Being an idealist in a realist's world. Chr Today 13:6-7 Ja 31 '69
HUFF, Darrell
Ceramic fireplace is a one-day job. Pop Sci 195:141 N '69
Install a fireplace in a weekend? Here's how. por Pop Sci 195:175-7 S '69
Those way-out wall coverings. Pop Sci 194: 136-8+ My '69
HUFF, William H. and Brown, N. B.
Price indexes for 1969: Serial services. Library J 94:2572-3 Jl '69
HUFFMAN, James
Sex education in public schools. Chr Today 13:5-8 S 26 '69
HUGE, Harry. See Coles, R. jt. auth.
HUGGARD, Leslie
Build a different metal locator. Pop Electr 30:53-8 F '69
HUGGINS, Richard L.
Pithy petitionary prayer in Pennsylvania senate. Chr Cent 86:971 Jl 23 '69
HUGHES, Betty
Adventure on the Colorado River. Redbook 133:66+ My '69
HUGHES, Carrol C.
Administrative assistant. por Am City 84: 126+ S '69
HUGHES, Catharine R.
America's newest new theater. Cath World 209:123-5 Je '69
Art and responsibility. Cath World 209:210-12 Ag '69
Discovering Flann O'Brien. America 120:523-5 My 3 '69
John Osborne's generation gap. America 121: 295-7 O 11 '69
Pinter as Pinter does. Cath World 210: 124-6 D '69
Rabelais at the Old Vic. America 121:616-17 D 20 '69
Self-indulgent avant garde. Nat R 21:1022-3 O 7 '69
Theatre in Dublin. Nation 209:579-81 N 24 '69
Theatre of ritual? America 121:160-1 S 13 '69
Visiting Off off Broadway. America 121:30-2 Jl 19 '69
Where are the playwrights? Nation 208:90-3 Ja 20 '69
HUGHES, Charles Evans
How Harding saved the Versailles treaty. R. K. Murray. il por Am Heritage 20:66-7+ D '68
HUGHES, Edward
Hurricane warning! Read Digest 95:21-2+ S '69
HUGHES, Eileen Lanouette
Old Rome alla Fellini. Life 67:56-9+ Ag 15 '69
HUGHES, H. Stuart
Second year of the cold war. Commentary 48:27-32 Ag '69
HUGHES, Harold Everett
Harold E. Hughes: evangelist from the prairies. L. L. King. por Harper 238:50-7 Mr '69
Who's Hughes. W. Willoughby. Chr Today 13:40 Ja 31 '69
HUGHES, Herman S.
Soul. America 121:62-3 Ag 2 '69
This medieval winter. America 120:156-8 F 8 '69
HUGHES, Howard Robard
About 355 of those things have exploded in Nevada. G. Hill. il N Y Times Mag p6-7+ Jl 27 '69
Can AEC defuse Hughes? Bsns W 19-20 Ap 5 '69
Duel of aces in Las Vegas. il Bsns W p49-50 Jl 12 '69
Hi-yo, silver. il Newsweek 73:64 Mr 31 '69
You and I are very different from Howard Hughes. O. Demaris. il Esquire 71:73-81+ Mr '69
HUGHES, Jim
Amsterdam; photographs. Travel & Camera 32:52-3+ Mr '69
Which lenses do what. Travel & Camera 32: 94-7 S '69
HUGHES, John
Report. Atlan 223:4+ F '69
Reports: Okinawa. Atlan 224:30+ O '69
HUGHES, Langston
Black misery; excerpts. Good H 169:78-9 Jl '69
Misery of blackness; excerpts from Black misery. Read Digest 95:131 N '69

about
Hughes, Twain, Child, and Sanger: four who locked horns with the censors; adaptation of addresses. M. Meltzer. por Wilson Lib Bul 44:278-80 N '69
Langston Hughes and The brownies' book. D. C. Dickinson. bibliog il por Negro Hist Bul 31:8-10 D '68
HUGHES, Mary
Day in the life of a school nurse. Parents Mag 44:64-5+ Mr '69
HUGHES, Philip Edgcumbe
Reason, history, and Biblical authenticity. Chr Today 13:3-7 S 12 '69
HUGHES, Richard
Richard Hughes; interview. New Yorker 45:30-1 Je 28 '69
HUGHES, Thomas L.
On the causes of our discontents. For Affairs 47:653-67 Jl '69
HUGHES, Vernon W.
Atoms; with biographical sketch. por Phys Today 22:33-7 F '69
HUGHES tool company
Examiner backs Hughes-Air West pact. Aviation W 90:29 Ag 21 '69
Hughes seeks Air West revisions. Aviation W 91:26 N 3 '69
Losses, CAB terms imperil Hughes' Air West purchase. Aviation W 91:32 Ag 18 '69
HUGO, Victor Marie, comte
Les miserables; dramatization of excerpt. See Thane, A. Little Cosette and Father Christmas
Victor Hugo on the burning of a library, juin 1871; excerpt from L'annee terrible; poem, tr. by M. Blind. Wilson Lib Bul 43:980-1 Je '69
HUIE, William Bradford
Why James Earl Ray murdered Dr King. Look 33:102-4+ Ap 15 '69
HUITT, Ralph K.
Advising the President. Commentary 47:74-6 Ap '69
HUIZINGA, J. H.
Behind the wall, the success story of Walter Ulbricht? N Y Times Mag p36-7+ S 7 '69
European commentator looks at U.S. foreign policy today; America's lost innocence. N Y Times Mag p30-1+ Ja 26 '69
HUKBALAHAPS
Matter of revenge. il Time 93:32 F 21 '69
HULA (dance)
Hula; a paradoxical history. M. B. McGuire and E. W. Jacobs. il Dance Mag 43:58-61+ D '69
HULBECK, Charles Richard. See Huelsenbeck, R.
HULETT, H. R. and others
Cell sorting: automated separation of mammalian cells as a function of intracellular fluorescence. bibliog Science 166:747-9 N 7 '69
HULL, Bobby
Bobby says he wants to play the game. G. Ronberg. il por Sports Illus 31:60-1 N 3 '69
Open season on Bobby Hull. G. Ronberg. il pors Sports Illus 30:18-19 Ja 20 '69
HULL, Robert. See Taylor, K. I. jt. auth.
HULLS (naval architecture)
Built-in buoyancy saves lives. C. R. Meyer. il Pop Sci 194:114-16+ Ja '69
It's floatable, unflippable, even when flooded. J. Roe. il Pop Sci 194:106-8 Mr '69
New shapes underwater. B. D. Barker. 3d. il Yachting 125:68-9 Ap '69
Painting wooden hulls. P. Smyth. il Motor B 123:74-5+ Ap '69
What can go wrong with fiberglass hulls? W. Cloud. il Pop Sci 194:102-5+ Mr '69
What shape the hull? E. Monk. il Yachting 125:70-1 Je '69
HULME, Kathryn
Paradise isn't quite enough. por Holiday 45:64-5+ Ap '69
HULTS, Malcom E. See Burgess, R. D. jt. auth.
HUMAN behavior. See Behavior (psychology)
HUMAN beings. See Man
HUMAN body. See Body, Human
HUMAN ecology
Christian ecology. J. McLaughlin. America 121:103-5 Ag 16 '69
Ecology and the contemporary religious conscience. R. L. Means. Chr Cent 86:1546-9 D 3 '69
Human biological adaptability; excerpt from Evolution of man. G. W. Lasker. bibliog Science 166:1480-6 D 19 '69
Human landscape: Department of state science lecture, December 9, 1968; with introd. by D. Rusk. R. J. Dubos. Dept State Bul 60:127-36 F 10 '69

HUMAN ecology—*Continued*
Overpopulated America. W. H. Davis. New Repub 162:13-15 Ja 10 '70
Subsistence herding in Uganda. R. Dyson-Hudson and N. Dyson-Hudson. il Sci Am 220:76-82+ bibliog(p 132) F '69
Survival U: prospectus for a really relevant university. J. Fischer. Harper 239:12+ S; 36-7 D '69
Too many strangers. D. L. Allen. il Nat Parks 43:12-17 Ag '69
    See also
Environmental policy
Man—influence of environment
Man—Influence on nature
HUMAN engineering
Boats are for people. B. Robinson. il Yachting 126:71+ O '69
    See also
Human information processing
HUMAN environment, United Nations conference on the. See United Nations conference on the human environment (proposed)
HUMAN equality. See Equality
HUMAN fertility. See Fertility. Human
HUMAN figure in art
Richard Lindner; interview, ed. by D. Swanson. R. Lindner. il Vogue 154:124-7 Ag 15 '69
    See also
Action in art
Human figure in photography
Nude in art
Women in art
HUMAN figure in photography
Guide to figure photography; review. il Mod Phot 33:74-5 O '69
Natural nude; a portfolio. Pop Phot 65:88-97 O '69
New light on nudes. J. Scully. il Mod Phot 33:80-3 F '69
Stalking the sun set; with photographs by M. Newman. Travel & Camera 32:98-9 F '69
HUMAN genetics
Caucasian genes in American Negroes. T. E. Reed. bibliog il Science 165:762-8 Ag 22 '69; Reply with rejoinder. E. N. Anderson, jr. 166:1353 D 12 '69
Cloning: asexual human reproduction? D. M. Rorvik. il Sci Digest 66:6-13 N '69
Delayed radiation effects in atomic-bomb survivors; adaptation of address, March, 1969. R. W. Miller. bibliog Science 166:569-74 O 31 '69
Genetic drift in an Italian population. L. L. Cavalli-Sforza. il Sci Am 221:30-7 Ag '69
Genetic engineering: controlling man's building blocks; excerpts from 1970 Britannica yearbook of science and the future. J. Lederberg. il Todays Health 47:24-7+ N '69
Genetic load and its varieties. A. M. Brues. bibliog Science 164:1130-6 Je 6 '69
George Beadle talks about the new genetics. C. B. Hicks. il Todays Health 47:44-7+ Ji '69
Hopi Indians, inbreeding, and albinism. C. M. Woolf and F. C. Dukepoo. bibliog il Science 164:30-7 Ap 4 '69
Man's participatory evolution: living in a biological revolution. R. M. Davidson. Cur 105:4-10 Mr '69
Mapping the genes; man-mouse hybrid cells. il Sci N 96:323-4 O 11 '69
New life for old: genetic decisions. M. Hamilton. Chr Cent 86:741-4 My 28 '69
Parasexual cycle in cultivated human somatic cells. G. M. Martin and C. A. Sprague. bibliog il Science 166:761-3 N 7 '69
Repairing the DNA. Sci N 96:348-9 O 18 '69
Scanning genes for defects. A. J. Snider. il Sci Digest 66:71 N '69
Test tube generation. D. M. Rorvik. il Esquire 71:108-14 Ap '69
The unborn; genetic engineering. D. M. Rorvik. Look 33:82-3 N 4 '69
    See also
Genetic counseling
HUMAN geography. See Anthropogeography
HUMAN growth hormone. See Pituitary hormones
HUMAN information processing
Information and control processes in living systems; report of meeting. L. R. Troncale and D. M. Ramsey-Klee. Science 166:132+ O 3 '69
HUMAN interaction. See Social interaction
HUMAN nature. See Man
HUMAN race. See Anthropology; Man
HUMAN relations
Conference for human understanding. A. D. Mott. il Américas 21:38-9 Mr '69
Fund of sociability. R. S. Weiss. bibliog il Trans-Action 6:36-43 Jl '69

Gone home; day when the boundaries of understanding were enlarged. A. Gordon. il Read Digest 94.115-18 Ap '69
Healing touch of attention. D. E. Smith. Read Digest 94:175-6+ Ap '69
How to avoid making our planet unlivable; address, August 15, 1969. K. Brandt. Vital Speeches 35:712-15 S 15 '69
On permanent commitment. R. J. Westley. America 120:612-17 My 24 '69; Discussion. 121:1 Jl 5 '69
Problem of the golden rule. E. Hoagland. Commentary 48:38-42 Ag '69
Too many strangers. D. L. Allen. il Nat Parks 43:12-17 Ag '69
Touch and go. B. W. Overstreet. il PTA Mag 63:17-18 My '69
Toward an affirmative morality. J. F. Wharton. Sat R 52:11-13+ Jl 12 '69
When someone is drowning, it's no time to teach him how to swim. E. M. Davis. Read Digest 95:104-6 N '69
Who is our enemy? M. M. Shideler. Chr Cent 86:1609-13 D 17 '69
Words can hurt me; questions and answers. A. Wood. Seventeen 28:176+ My '69
You can meet them anywhere. B. W. Overstreet. il PTA Mag 63:22-4 Ja '69
    See also
Brotherhood of man
Friendship
Group relations training
Loneliness
Love
Marriage
Neighbors
Prejudice
Sex relations
Youth-adult relationship
HUMAN relations commission, Washington, D.C. See Washington, D.C.—Human relations commission
HUMAN rights. See Civil rights
HUMAN rights, Universal declaration of. See Universal declaration of human rights
HUMAN rights commission of the Council of Europe. See Council of Europe
HUMAN rights commission of the United Nations. See United Nations—Commission on human rights
HUMAN rights day and week
Human rights day, 10 December 1969; text of messages. A. Brooks; Thant. UN Mo Chron 6:i-iv D '69
Human rights week; proclamation. L. B. Johnson. Dept State Bul 59:690 D 30 '68
HUMAN rights year. See International year for human rights, 1968
HUMAN sacrifice. See Sacrifice, Human
HUMAN voice. See Voice
HUMANE treatment of animals. See Animals—Treatment
HUMANISM
Cult of iconoclasm: new menace to the West. L. S. Chang. Chr Today 13:5-6 Jl 4 '69
Erasmus: universal thinker of yesterday for today. J. C. Margolin. il UNESCO Courier 22:4-13 N '69
Image of man in Christian humanism. L. R. Ward. Cath World 209:12-16 Ap '69
Is transcendence expendable? L. H. DeWolf. Chr Cent 86:1017-19 Jl 30 '69
New humanisms for old. H. B. Kuhn. Chr Today 13:44 Ja 31 '69
Science as a humanistic discipline. J. Bronowski; reply with rejoinder. U. Neri. Bul Atom Sci 25:50 My '69
Toward a Christian humanism. R. Kysar. Chr Cent 86:706-8 My 21 '69; Reply. J. Voorhis. 86:1067 Ag 13 '69
Vanity of humanism. R. Sampson. Nation 209:718-25 D 29 '69
    See also
Hellenism
HUMANITIES
Humanities today. See issues of Clearing house
    See also
Liberal education
Science and the humanities

Study and teaching
Humanities at the crossroads; adaptation of address, March 4, 1968. V. K. Whitaker. Sch & Soc 97:278-80 Sum '69
Humanities: from Aeschylus to Antonioni; address, November 1968. A. H. Stern. Engl J 58:676-80 My '69
I now think of the American Indian as being very artistic; humanities course at Miles college, Birmingham. J. Friedman. il Wilson Lib Bul 44:64-8 S '69
NCTE/ERIC report on humanities instruction in secondary schools. R. V. Denby. Engl J 58:272-80 F '69

HUMANITIES—Study and teaching—Cont.
Negro literature for secondary English and humanities courses: an NCTE/ERIC report. R. V. Denby. bibliog Engl J 58: 767-72 My '69
On teaching the humanities. E. J. Gordon. Engl J 58:681-7 My '69
Scholarly life. K. Eble. Am Scholar 39:109-22 Wint '69

HUMANITY
Problem of the golden rule. E. Hoagland. Commentary 48:38-42 Ag '69

HUME, A. Britton
Coal mining. Atlan 224:22+ N '69

HUME, Ivor Noël-. See Noël-Hume, I.

HUMES, Charles W. Jr
Teaching experience a must for counselors? Clear House 44:245-8 D '69

HUMES, James C.
Dissent and involvement; address, October 18, 1969. Vital Speeches 36:183-4 Ja 1 '70

HUMIDITY
Regulating humidity in the home. D. A. Caccia. il Org Gard & Farm 16:112-16 F '69
See also
Plants, Effect of humidity on

HUMMINGBIRDS
Hummingbirds and flowers. D. E. Rose. Horticulture 47:46-7 O '69

HUMOR
How about humor? R. Armour. Writer 82: 24-6 Je '69
How to come out from under the putdown. K. Hurwitz. Seventeen 29:96 Ja '70
If you don't mind my saying so. J. Krutch. Am Scholar 38:188+ Spr '69
New humor. J. Marks. Esquire 72:213-20+ D '69
Popular records; L. Bruce's The Berkeley concert. D. Watt. New Yorker 45:92+ Je 14 '69
What ever happened to mother-in-law jokes? R. Orben. McCalls 96:93+ Mr '69
See also
Comedy
Music—Anecdotes, facetiae, satire, etc.
Television broadcasting—Humor

HUMOR, American
Reverse images: columnist, A. Hoppe. il Time 93:54+ My 30 '69

HUMOR, English
April fools' day delights. Q. Crewe. Vogue 153:156+ Ap 1 '69
London; British sense of humor. Q. Crewe. Vogue 153:108+ Mr 1 '69

HUMOR, Pictorial
See also
Comics (books, strips, etc)

HUMOR in art
Sculpture of Philip Kraczkowski; commentary on American humor series. P. Kraczkowski. il Am Artist 33:42-8 Ag '69

HUMORISTS
See also
Henning, P.

HUMPERDINCK, Engelbert
What's in a name? por Newsweek 73:117 My 5 '69

HUMPHREY, Hubert Horatio, 1911–
Four words to remember. McCalls 96:96-7 Mr '69
He's gonna get out; interview, ed. by S. Alsop. Newsweek 74:120 D 15 '69
Hubert Humphrey looks at the generation gap; address. por U S News 67:47-50 S 8 '69
No holy writ; address, June 26, 1969. Library J 94:3131-3 S 15 '69
Political power and the middle class in the '70s; interview. pors U S News 67:57-8 N 24 '69
President giveth and taketh away; interview, ed. by L. Janos. por Time 94:19 N 14 '69
Safeguard; a question of priorities. Sat R 52:28-9 Ap 5 '69
We came in peace for all mankind. special view of Christmas. Redbook 134:148 D '69

about
Big man on campus. il por Newsweek 73:30 Mr 10 '69
Democrats after 1968. P. Kemble; discussion. Commentary 47:35-41 Ja; 24+ My '69
Hubert rides again! Chr Cent 86:365 Mr 19 '69
Humphrey dumphrey. New Repub 161:8 O 25 '69
Job with a future. il por Time 93:20 Mr 7 '69
Mrs Humphrey sums it up this way; he is not what he was, and he is not yet what he will be. W. Griffith. il pors N Y Times Mag p32-3+ Mr 30 '69
Now the HHH of old: busy, vocal, acting like a candidate. il pors U S News 67:19-20 O 20 '69
Of heart and spleen. Time 93:28 Mr 14 '69
Squabble between two top Democrats. por U S News 66:19 Mr 17 '69

HUMPHREY, Ralph
To see, to feel. il Time 93:64-5 My 30 '69

HUMPHREY, Richard
FCC proposed rule making for 2-3 MHz marine band. Electr World 81:71 F '69
No place to go, but up. Pop Electr 30:75-9 Mr '69

HUMPHREY, William
Mrs Shumlin's cow Trixie; story. Esquire 72: 246-7 D '69

HUMPHRIES, Rolfe
Love at first sight; poem. New Repub 160:26 F 15 '69
Screaming meemies; poem. Nation 208:574 My 5 '69
With garb of proof; Song for Mortimer; poem. Poetry 113:407-8 Mr '69

HUNDLEY, Craig
Jazz is my bag! Seventeen 28:40 Ja '69

HUNEBELLE, Danielle
(ed) See Dubček, A. Dubček talks

HUNG, P. P. and others
Self-assembly of Qβ and MS2 phage particles; possible function of initiation complexes. bibliog Science 166:1638-40 D 26 '69

HUNGARIAN cookery. See Cookery, Hungarian

HUNGARIAN partridge shooting. See Partridge shooting

HUNGARY
See also
Catholic church—Relations (diplomatic)—Hungary
Education—Hungary
Foreign visitors in Hungary
Moving picture industry—Hungary

Economic conditions
Karl Marx doesn't work here anymore. L. Velie. Read Digest 94:93-4 Ap '69
Rewards of reform. A. Tillier. il Newsweek 74:75-6 D 1 '69

Politics and government
To the tick of a different clock. C. Derecskey. il Atlan 223:74-6+ F '69

HUNGATE, William L.
Excerpt from testimony before House committee on ways and means, February 24, 1969. Cong Digest 48:154+ My '69

HUNGER
Ecology of hunger; the UN's development role in the 1970's. J. McLaughlin. America 121:414-17 N 8 '69

HUNN, Max
Inland Florida cruising. Yachting 126:74-5+ D '69

HUNSBERGER, Donald
Wind ensemble grows up. Hi Fi 19:Ma14-15+ S '69

HUNT, Don
$5,000 a giraffe. il por Newsweek 73:84-5 F 17 '69

HUNT, Douglas W.
Induction of beginning teachers. Ed Digest 34: 34-7 F '69

HUNT, Evelyn Tooley
Protégé; poem. Chr Cent 86:711 My 21 '69

HUNT, George Pinney
Word from a departing M.E. Life 66:3 Je 6 '69

about
Change at Life. Time 93:60 My 16 '69
Life memo goes public. Bsns W p42 My 17 '69
Managing editor's imprint after 400 issues. R. Graves. por Life 66:3 Je 13 '69

HUNT, Haroldson Lafayette
H. L. Hunt and the Vatican. Chr Cent 86: 437 Ap 2 '69

HUNT, Inez
Pikes Peak panorama. por Am For 75:20-3 S '69

HUNT, J. McVicker
Black genes, white environment. por bibliog Trans-Action 6:12-22 Je '69

HUNT, James D.
Gandhi and the black revolution. Chr Cent 86:1242-4 O 1 '69

HUNT, James Henry Leigh. See Hunt, L.

HUNT, Jane
Principals report on student protest. Am Ed 5:4-5 O '69; Same abr. Ed Digest 35:49-51 D '69
We're glad you asked. America 121:453-5 N 15 '69

HUNT, Jane V.
Early detection of potential learning disorders. Ed Digest 35:12-15 O '69

HUNT, Jim
Yachting interview. por Yachting 126:72-3+ Ag '69

HUNT, Leigh
Making of an opera critic: Leigh Hunt. T. Fenner. bibliog f il por Mus Q 55:439-63 O '69

HUNT, Linda, and others
Nixon's guaranteed annual poverty. Ramp Mag 8:64-70 D '69
HUNT, Lyman C. jr
Decoding or meaning. Todays Ed 58:21-2+ Ap '69
HUNT, Morton M.
Affair; excerpts. Ladies Home J 86:141-8+ S; 159-66+ O '69
Annals of agriculture. New Yorker 45:57-8+ N 1 '69
Money and sex: two marital problems or one? Redbook 134:49+ Ja '70
Parenthood should wait! Read Digest 94:49-50+ F '69
HUNT, Naomi L.
Hosteler's way. Parks & Rec 4:44-6 Ag '69
HUNT, Richard
He seeks the soul in metal. il pors Ebony 24:80-2+ Ap '69
Richard Hunt. H. Ghent. il por Sch Arts 68: 26 Ap '69
HUNT, Robert Rex
We built this house for $7500. Pop Mech 132: 126:33+ N '69
HUNT, Rolfe Lanier
Teaching about religion in the public school. Todays Ed 58:24-6 D '69
HUNT, William
Entrance into the water; poem. Am Scholar 38:656 Aut '69
Moths at the window; Music in Michigan; poems. Nation 209:150 Ag 25 '69
HUNTEN, Donald M. and Goody, R. M.
Venus: the next phase of planetary exploration. bibliog Science 165:1317-23 S 26 '69
—See Belton, M. J. S. jt. auth.
HUNTER, Beatrice Trum
Getting organic lamb to the public. Org Gard & Farm 16:70-3 Ag '69
Group orders for more foods at lower costs. Org Gard & Farm 16:63-5 S '69
What cooking? Org Gard & Farm 16:77-8 O '69
HUNTER, Ben
Child market. il por Newsweek 73:70 Je 16 '69
HUNTER, Charlayne A.
New black businessmen. Sat R 52:27-9+ Ag 23 '69
HUNTER, Clementine
Primitive art of Clementine Hunter. S. Morris. il pors Ebony 24:144-8 My '69
HUNTER, D. Bruce
Don't use food as punishment! Camp Mag 41:18 N '69
HUNTER, Evan
Interview with Evan Hunter-Ed McBain. Writer 82:11-14 Ap '69
Wilt thou have this woman? story; excerpt from Sons. McCalls 96:58-9 Ag '69
HUNTER, Harold L.
Publishing color facsimiles of rare manuscripts and books. Pub W 196:92-3 Jl 7 '69
Uses of gold in the graphic and decorative arts: address. Pub W 195:76+ My 5 '69
HUNTER, Maxwell W. 2d
Are technological upheavals inevitable? Harvard Bsns R 47:73-83 S '69
HUNTER, Paul
Moonrise; poem. Poetry 114:364 S '69
HUNTER, Richard. See Macalpine, I. jt. auth.
HUNTER, Robert E.
Philco tries again. por Bsns W p72+ F 15 '69
HUNTER college, New York. See New York (city). City university of New York—Hunter college
HUNTERS
As others see us. P. Oberst. il Field & S 73:53+ Ap '69
HUNTING
Access: the key to public land recreation. B. Milek. il Field & S 73:20+ Ap '69
Big-game hunters of business. J. Poindexter. il Duns R 94:54-9 S '69
Gist of it; digest of the outdoor news; ed. by H. Moore. See issues of Outdoor life
How to see better in the field. J. R. Gregg. il Field & S 74:46-7+ Ag '69
Sportsman's notebook. H. G. Tapply. See issues of Field and stream
Way-out safaris. il Newsweek 73:95+ Ap 28 '69
What about hunting seasons? J. T. Shields and C. A. Buckmann. il Outdoor Life 144: 35-7+ S '69
Where to go; ed. by V. T. Sparano. See issues of Outdoor life
See also
Game
Hunting with bow and arrow
Poaching
Whaling
    also Deer hunting; Rabbit hunting, and similar headings

Accidents and injuries
Hunting accidents decline in 1968. B. E. Burgin. il Cons 23:32-3 Ap '69
Sunset to remember. G. C 'bright. il Outdoor Life 143:70-1+ F '69

Anecdotes, facetiae, satire, etc.
Rendezvous. P. McManus. il Field & S 74:48-9+ D '69

Equipment and supplies
See Hunting outfits

Safety devices and measures
Drown-proofing tips for hunters. il Todays Health 47:56-7 S '69

Statistics
Small game harvest up. H. F. Maguire. il Cons 24:6-7 D '69

Afghanistan
Breakfast at midnight. J. R. Mellon. il Outdoor Life 144:60-3+ Jl '69

Africa
Africa stares back. P. Barrett. il Field & S 74:42-7+ D '69
African safari: cabin class. R. Stavely. Travel 131:79-81 My '69
Picture it: a bargain safari. E. A. Bauer. il Outdoor Life 143:64-9+ F '69
Why hunt elephants? W. Page. il Field & S 74:52-3+ S '69

Africa, East
African safari. E. B. Thompson. il Ebony 24: 114-18+ F '69

Alaska
Float trip for moose. E. Park. il Outdoor Life 144:50-3+ S '69
Mountain rifle. J. O'Connor. il Outdoor Life 143:146+ Ap '69
Personal business; sportsmen's utopia. Bsns W p93-4 My 3 '69
Spring bear hunt. J. W. Valentine. il Outdoor Life 143:78-9+ Mr '69

Arizona
Pigs of the Cheery Cows; Chiricahua Mountains. W. A. Cartier. il Outdoor Life 143: 54-7+ Mr '69
Two guides and the no-peek sheep. G. Blair. il Field & S 74:54-5+ Ag '69

Atlantic states
Gunning the Atlantic coast; best duck and goose hunting. S. M. Miller. il Field & S 74:64-5+ N '69

California
Hottest cottontails in the West. J. R. Higley. il Field & S 74:50-1+ Jl '69
Judie's cat. J. R. Higley. il Outdoor Life 144:58-9+ S '69
Last grizzly in Shasta. E. Weigart. il Field & S 74:60-1+ Je '69
Notes on pheasant shooting. J. O'Connor. il Outdoor Life 143:92+ F '69
Topknot tactics. J. Freeman. il Field & S 74:60-1+ N '69

Canada
Alberta sharptail. C. F. Waterman. il Field & S 74:66-7+ S '69
Best bets for geese this fall. C. Nansen. il Field & S 74:42-3+ Ag '69
Blizzard moose; Ontario moose hunt. N. Karas. il Field & S 74:56-7+ N '69
Bluebills on the St Lawrence. J. B. Robinson. il Outdoor Life 144:40-1+ D '69
Hounding deer with dogs. M. Ellis. il Field & S 74:56-7+ O '69
King of Kishanina. A. Flick, jr. il Field & S 73:72-3+ Mr '69
Mark of the grizzly. R. V. Broadbent. il Outdoor Life 144:68-71+ Ag '69
Old naked face; British Columbia. R. S. Jackson. il Outdoor Life 144:52-5+ O '69
On the trail of the wary caribou. W. Davis. il Mech Illus 65:68-70+ N '69
Once is enough. J. Chiappetta. il Field & S 74:46-7+ S '69
Sneak preview from a happy hunting ground; James Bay, Quebec. V. Kraft. Sports Illus 31:68-9 O 27 '69
Stone rams in the Cassiar. J. O'Connor. il Outdoor Life 144:32-5+ D '69
We saw the ice go out. O. A. Frederickson. il Outdoor Life 143:52-5+ My '69

Colorado
Ambush tactics for mule deer. R. Tinsley. il Field & S 74:40-1+ Ag '69
Summer hunt. R. Hammond. il Outdoor Life 144:64-5+ Ag '69
We were in velvet. C. C. Niehuis. il Outdoor Life 144:52-5+ Jl '69

HUNTING—*Continued*

Great Lakes Region

News: the Great Lakes states; ed. by B. East. Outdoor Life 144:33-4 Jl '69

Guyana

Jungle challenge. S. E. Brock. il Outdoor Life 143:64-7+ Ap '69

Idaho

Elk hunting aces. J. S. Parker. il Field & S 74:78-80+ S '69
Fat cat. C. Ormond. il Outdoor Life 143:62-3+ F '69

Illinois

Hotspot for honkers. J. R. Olt. il Outdoor Life 144:68-9+ N '69

Indiana

Stop, listen, and look. C. Patterson. il Outdoor Life 144:68-9+ O '69

Iowa

Six-year chase. D. E. Green. il Outdoor Life 144:80-1+ O '69
To find a quail. H. Bradshaw. il Field & S 74:34-5+ D '69

Iran

Just back of Tehran. W. Page. il Field & S 74:72-3+ N '69

Kansas

Central Kansas mixed bag hunting. D. Pryce. il Field & S 74:36-7+ D '69
Shelterbelt squirrels. D. Pryce. il Outdoor Life 144:52-3+ Ag '69

Kentucky

Happy (deer) hunting grounds. C. Nansen. il Field & S 74:50-1+ O '69

Maine

Confessions of a Maine deer hunter. L. Dietz. il Field & S 73:66-7+ Ap '69
Mystery of the Hinkley deer. H. R. Hinkley. il Outdoor Life 144:44-7+ Ag '69

Maryland

Chucks above Antietam. D. Knight. il Outdoor Life 144:46-7+ Jl '69
Unexpected goose shoot. P. McLain. il Field & S 74:38-9+ D '69

Mexico

Bang-up time in Mexico. V. Kraft. Sports Illus 31:66+ O 6 '69

Michigan

Big track; Ottawa national forest. C. T. Johnson. il Outdoor Life 144:68-9+ Jl '69
Hunt those smart barnyard bucks. J. Chiappetta. il Field & S 74:108-10+ Jl '69

Minnesota

Early season grouse. R. Gilsvik. il Field & S 74:66-7+ Ag '69
New way to hunt deer. F. R. Martin. il Outdoor Life 144:29-31+ D '69
North woods hot zone. R. Gilsvik. il Field & S 74:52-3+ O '69
Snarling tractors and no tallyho: winter fox hunt in Minnesota. R. F. Jones. il Sports Illus 30:28-30+ F 17 '69
System for deer; stop and go. B. Cary. il Outdoor Life 144:70-1+ N '69

Missouri

Unforgettable hunt. J. O. Cartier. il Outdoor Life 143:72-5+ My '69

Montana

Elk hunter's elk. J. Rooney. il Outdoor Life 144:62-3+ N '69
Short order antelope. L. Miracle. il Outdoor Life 144:62-3+ O '69

Mozambique

Day of the leopard. P. L. Buckley. il Nat R 21:449-50 My 6 '69

Nebraska

Hill country antelope. T. Cacek. il Field & S 74:48-9+ S '69
Those shady sharpies. O. W. Larson. il Outdoor Life 144:60-1+ O '69

New England

Toughest of flying targets? B. Elliot. il Outdoor Life 144:56-7+ N '69

New Mexico

Cougar the hard way. E. S. Barker. il Field & S 74:70-1+ My '69
How to rattle whitetails and muleys! B. Brister. il Field & S 74:28-9+ D '69

New York (state)

Hell on hares. D. J. Anderson. il Field & S 74:30-1+ D '69

North Carolina

Bunny bop. C. Amory. il Holiday 46:20+ D '69
Carolina beach bunnies. J. Dean. il Field & S 74:68-9+ S '69
Holiday for hounds. H. Hood. il Outdoor Life 144:56-7+ D '69

North Dakota

Devil's own geese. J. O. Cartier. il Outdoor Life 144:82-4+ O '69

Northeastern states

News: the Northeast; ed. by T. Janes. Outdoor Life 144:37-40 Ag; 31-4 S; 25-8 D '69

Norway

Icy expedition; polar bear hunting, Spitzbergen islands. il Travel 131:19 Ap '69

Ohio

Big boom for old ruff. E. A. Bauer. il Outdoor Life 144:48-9+ D '69
It really isn't rabbit hunting without hounds. E. A. Bauer. il Outdoor Life 144:58-61+ N '69
Plight of the swampers. B. Thomas. il Field & S 74:76-7+ Je '69

Oklahoma

Gullible gobbler. C. Elliott. il Outdoor Life 143:64-5+ Mr '69

Oregon

Astronaut elk hunt. H. Williams. il Field & S 74:44-5+ Ag '69
Pheasant tips. M. Griffith. il Field & S 74:62-3+ N '69

Pennsylvania

Call of spring. K. C. Schuyler. il Outdoor Life 143:84-7+ Ap '69
No. 1 deer spot in the U.S? L. J. Bashline. il Field & S 74:54-5+ S '69

Portugal

Partridge in an olive tree. W. Page. il Field & S 73:70-1+ Ap '69

Russia

Spears instead of shotguns? il Parks & Rec 4:26-7 Ja '69

Scotland

Hunting in the Highlands. J. O'Connor. il Outdoor Life 144:96+ Ag '69

South Dakota

Plight of the people bird. V. Kraft. Sports Illus 31:87-8 N 17 '69

Southern states

News: the Southeast (cont) C. Elliott; H. L. Lawrence. Outdoor Life 143:43-6 Mr; 144: 41-4 N '69

Southwestern states

Return of the bandtail. B. W. Dalrymple. il Outdoor Life 144:46-7+ S '69

Tennessee

Challenge. C. Vinson. il Outdoor Life 143:60-1+ My '69
Lick creek shoot. H. L. Lawrence. il Outdoor Life 144:50-1+ D '69
Special rabbit hunt. G. X. Sand. il Outdoor Life 143:72-3+ Ap '69

Texas

Bowhunt for exotic sheep. G. H. Gillelan. il Outdoor Life 144:90-2 D '69
Homecoming buck hunt. B. W. Dalrymple. il Outdoor Life 144:52-5+ D '69
Meanwhile back at the Coffield ranch . . . V. Kraft. il Sports Illus 31:64-6 N 10 '69

United States

America's no. 2 game animal; with state chart of squirrels and recommended hunting areas. B. Gooch. il Field & S 74:68-9+ N '69
Hunt the trophy mule deer states. L. Stapleton. il Field & S 74:12+ O '69

HUNTING—*Continued*

Utah

Carry a blind on your back. C. F. Rees. il Field & S 74:56-7+ S '69
Smoothing the rough chukar road. F. A. Tinker. il Field & S 74:66-7+ N '69

Vermont

Green Mountain bear chase. D. Knight. il Outdoor Life 144:72-5+ O '69
The 100th rabbit. J. B. Robinson. il Outdoor Life 143:76-7+ F '69

Virginia

Bear by the ear. B. Cochran. il Outdoor Life 144:72-5+ N '69

Washington (state)

Stalk to remember. K. Crandall. il Outdoor Life 144:48-51+ N '69

Western states

Carlyle Lake: midwestern hotspot. J. Lockhart. il Field & S 74:164-6+ My '69
Great days on the desert; eastern Oregon and southern Idaho. T. Trueblood. il Field & S 74:39-40+ N '69
Hint of fall. T. Trueblood. il Field & S 74:30+ Ag '69
News: the West (cont) L. Miracle; J. Martin. Outdoor Life 143:41-4 F; 53-60 Ap '69

Wisconsin

Bear that wouldn't quit; ed. by B. East. M. Reynolds. il Outdoor Life 143:66-7+ My '69
New breed of mule deer. H. Wixom. il Outdoor Life 144:49-51+ O '69

Wyoming

High adventure. C. Conklin. il Outdoor Life 143:84+ My '69
Lazarus bull. W. Page. il Field & S 74:54-5+ O '69
Moose for the pot. B. Milek. il Field & S 74:56-7+ Je '69
Pre-hunt scouting: key to filling your license. G. Barrus. il Field & S 74:52-3+ Ag '69
Sage grouse: forgotten pioneer. B. Milek. il Field & S 73:82-3+ Ap '69
Tips for taking foothill muleys. B. Milek. il Field & S 74:44-5+ O '69
Was elk hunting ever like this? with muzzle-loader. C. Elliott. il Outdoor Life 143:56-9+ F '69

HUNTING creek. See Potomac River
HUNTING dogs
All-around dog? L. J. Bashline. il Field & S 74:178-80+ O '69
Dogs. D. M. Duffey. See issues of Outdoor life
Hounding deer with dogs; southern Ontario. M. Ellis. il Field & S 74:56-7+ O '69
See also
Beagles (dogs)
Bird dogs
Foxhounds
Hounds

Training

See Dogs—Training
HUNTING guides. See Guides
HUNTING lodges. See Lodges (architecture)
HUNTING outfits
Carry a blind on your back. C. F. Rees. il Field & S 74:56-7+ S '69
HUNTING rifles. See Rifles
HUNTING spaniels. See Spaniels
HUNTING trophies
Doctor Howard's safari room. il Ebony 24:132-4+ O '69
Put new life in your trophies. W. E. Anderson. il Outdoor Life 143:78-80+ F '69
Search for a trophy; mule deer shoot. R. V. Parke. il Outdoor Life 144:38-41+ S '69
HUNTING with bow and arrow
Archery. G. H. Gillelan. See issues of Outdoor life
How to hunt like an Indian. J. Palmer. il Field & S 74:62-3+ Ag '69
Jungle challenge. S. E. Brock. il Outdoor Life 143:64-7+ Ap '69
Keep archery safe. G. H. Gillelan. il Outdoor Life 144:90+ Jl '69
Of Bear, bow & buck. R. Kennedy. il Time 94:61 N 14 '69
Summer hunt. R. Hammond. il Outdoor Life 144:64-5+ Ag '69
Tune-up time. G. H. Gillelan. il Outdoor Life 143:114-17 Mr '69
HUNTINGTON, Collis Potter
For sale: an empire $1,500 down. D. Lavender. il pors Am West 6:6-12+ My '69

HUNTINGTON, Roger
How far can we go with the piston engine? Pop Mech 131:95-9+ Ja '69
What's new from Detroit in 1970? Consumer Bul 52:16-22 O '69
HUNTINGTON BEACH, Calif.
We created our own data-processing division. F. B. Arguello. il Am City 84:155-6 S '69
HUNTINGTON dance ensemble
Pied Pipers in leotards. R. Estrada. il Dance Mag 43:56-60 Jl '69
HUNTOON, Maxwell C. Jr
Don't let your house get you down. Am Home 72:84-5 My '69
What to expect in new housing. Am Home 72:114+ Ja '69
HUNTSVILLE, Ala.
See also
United States—National aeronautics and space administration
HUONG, Tran-van-. See Tran-van-Huong
HURDLE racing
Willie the predictable; W. D. Davenport. Time 93:52 Mr 14 '69
Woes of Wee Willie Wisp. S. Myslenski. il Sports Illus 30:42-4+ Mr 17 '69
HURLER'S syndrome. See Lipochondrodystrophy
HURLEY, Neil P.
Coming of the humanoids. Commonweal 91:297-300 D 5 '69
HURLEY, Patrick M. and Rand, J. R.
Pre-drift continental nuclei. bibliog Science 164:1229-42 Je 13 '69
HURLIMANN, Bettina
Picture book world author goes on U.S. tour. Library J 94:2036 My 15 '69
HUROK concerts, incorporated
Hurok 'n' roll? il por Newsweek 73:74+ Mr 10 '69
$. Hurok presents. . . por Forbes 103:29 Mr 15 '69
HURON, Ohio
Intergovernmental cooperation restores a downtown. D. E. Reis. il Am City 84:118+ S '69
HURRICANE control. See Hurricane protection
HURRICANE insurance. See Insurance. Hurricane
HURRICANE ISLAND outward bound school. See Outward bound schools
HURRICANE protection
Curbing hurricanes: the chances; interview. R. H. Simpson. il U S News 67:34-6 S 1 '69
Hurricane seeding: a quest for data. M. Mueller. Science 165:990 S 5 '69
Shrinking Debbie's eye. il Sci N 96:551 D 13 '69
Taming the hurricane; seeding Debbie. il Newsweek 74:47-8 S 1 '69
HURRICANES
Camille: a calamity at 205 miles an hour; with interview with R. H. Simpson. il U S News 67:33-6 S 1 '69
Camille at Columbia, Miss. il Weatherwise 22:184 O '69
Camille: did forecasters slip? il U S News 67:33 S 8 '69
La dame: Camille; survey by Mississippi library commission team of damage to public libraries. M. J. Morgan. ALA Bul 63:1583-5 D '69
Enter Camille. R. M. DeAngelis. bibliog il Weatherwise 22:172-9 O '69
From above: Camille. il Weatherwise 22:209 O '69
Gales at sea. J. Parkinson, jr. il Yachting 125:57-9+ F '69
How hurricanes are born; Camille and the BOMEX experiment. J. Lear. il Sat R 52:67-71 O 4 '69
Hurricane! il Motor B 124:50-1+ S '69
Hurricane loss; damage by Camille to Mississippi libraries. M. Love. ALA Bul 63:1502-4 D '69
Hurricane season of 1968. A. L. Sugg and P. J. Hebert. il Weatherwise 22:12-18 F '69
Hurricane warning! E. Hughes. il Read Digest 95:21-2+ S '69
In the wake of Camille. Chr Today 13:35 S 12 '69
In the wake of Camille; discriminatory use of federal funds for hurricane victims in Mississippi. D. Zwerdling. New Repub 162:8-10 Ja 10 '70
Killer Camille: the greatest storm. il Time 94:20-1 Ag 29 '69
Killer named Camille and her toll; with report by H. P. Leifermann. il Newsweek 74:16-19 S 1 '69
Report from the Gulf coast; hurricane Camille's toll. R. M. Williams. il Fortune 80:59+ O '69

HURRICANES—*Continued*
Tallying the damage in Camille's path: Mississippi after the storm. il Bsns W D33 Ag 23 '69
'38 hurricane; excerpts. J. McCarthy. il Am Heritage 20:10-15+ Ag '69
U.S. journal: Pass Christian, Miss; problems in recovering from hurricane Camille. C. Trillin. New Yorker 45:175-6+ N 29 '69
See also
Hurricane protection
HURST, Vernon J. See Allard, G. O. jt. auth.
HURST, William Donald. See Ferahian, R. H. jt. auth.
HURT, James E. Jr
He makes the ghetto make money. por Bsns W D 154-5 My 10 '69
HURT, N. Franklin
Integrating American history. Todays Ed 58: 18-20 Ja '69
HURTIG, M. G.
Solution to the special order problem. Pub W 196:271-2+ Ag 25 '69
HURTT, Jeffrey
American museum's youngest scientist. il pors Ebony 24:86-7+ O '69
HURWITZ, Ken
How to come out from under the putdown. por Seventeen 29:96 Ja '70
HUS, Jan
John Hus. by M. Spinka. Review
  Chr Cent 86:996-7 Jl 23 '69. T. G. Tappert
HUS, John. See Hus, Jan
HUSA, Karel
Musician of the month. S. Fleming. por(pMA1) Hi Fi 19:MA5 Ag '69
HUSAIN, Zakir
U.S. extends condolences on death of President Husain of India. Dept State Bul 60: 496 Je 2 '69
HUSÁK, Gustav
Can new leader of Czechs turn back the clock? por U S News 66:18 My 5 '69
Consolation prize. Newsweek 74:56 N 10 '69
Dubcek dumped. por Sr Schol 94:18 My 2 '69
End of the Dubcek era. il por Time 93:26+ Ap 25 '69
Homilies for Husak. il Newsweek 74:51 N 3 '69
Lesser of two evils. il por Newsweek 73:52+ Je 9 '69
Revolution, reformation, reform. E. V. Kohak. Commonweal 91:378-82 D 26 '69
Soviet triumph, Dubcek's fall. U S News 66:9 Ap 28 '69
Supreme Slovak. Newsweek 73:56+ F 17 '69
HUSBAND, Wilfrid Laurier
Mafia: the cartel. Sat R 52:55-6 Mr 22 '69
HUSBAND and wife. See Family life; Marriage; Wives
HUSBANDS
How men make women feel loved. J. Viorst. il Redbook 133:65+ Ag '69; Same abr. Read Digest 95:95-8 O '69
See also
Desertion and non-support
Marriage

Anecdotes, facetiae, satire, etc.

Husbands I'm glad aren't mine. E. Bombeck. il Good H 169:12+ N '69
Trouble with husbands; fishing widows. C. Ford. il Field & S 74:6+ S '69
HUSK tomatoes
What's a husk tomato? A. poha. il Sunset 142:226 My '69
HUSKEY, Robert J.
Multiplicity reactivation as a test for recombination function. bibliog Science 164: 319-20 Ap 18 '69
HUSKY oil, limited
Call of the wildcat. R. Levy. il Duns R 93: 56+ F '69
HUSSEIN, King of Jordan
King Hussein I of Jordan visits Washington; exchange of greetings: April 8, 1969. Dept State Bul 60:364 Ap 28 '69
Time is running out; ed. by L. Janos. Time 93:27 Ap 18 '69
about
Arabs, Jews and peace. New Repub 160:7-8 Ap 26 '69
Hussein in the middle. il por Newsweek 73: 42-4 Ap 21 '69
Hussein of Jordan, ed. by V. Vance and P. Lauer. Review
  Sat R il por 52:24-5 My 31 '69. B. B. Johansson
Troubled ruler with many lives: what he seeks in the U.S. il por U S News 66:22 Ap 14 '69

Uneasy heads. Newsweek 74:61+ O 20 '69
View from Allenby bridge. T. C. Sorensen. il Sat R 52:23-5+ O 4 '69
Visit from an Arab king. il por Time 93: 26-7 Ap 18 '69
HUSTON, Anjelica
Young and stung with love and war. P. Devlin. por Vogue 154:130-1+ S 15 '69
HUSTON, James T.
Eisenhower era. bibliog f Cur Hist 57:24-30+ Jl '69
HUSTON, John
Takes; interview. New Yorker 45:31-3 Je 14 '69
about
From book to film, via John Huston. H. Koningsberger. Film Q 22:2-4 Spr '69
HUTCHENS, John K.
Harry Scherman, 1887-1969. Sat R 52:23 N 29 '69
Man of the Times; Broadway's Sam Zolotow. Sat R 52:73-4 My 10 '69
One thing and another (cont) Sat R 52:42-3 F 22; 36-8 Ap 5; 23-4 My 31; 38+ Je 21; 42-3 O 4; 24-5 D 20 '69
HUTCHINS, Alice
Do-it-yourself sculpture in Paris. C. Cutler. il Art in Am 57:100 S '69
HUTCHINS, Francis G.
Moralists against managers. Atlan 224:53-6 Jl '69
HUTCHINS, Robert Maynard
Afterthoughts of a prodigy. E. Shorris. Esquire 72:28+ D '69
Off center? Newsweek 73:76-7 Je 30 '69
Technical education useless for rapid-change age of technology; excerpts. por Sch & Soc 97:71 F '69
HUTCHINSON, Art
On the boards. W. Como. por Dance Mag 43:20 O '69
HUTCHINSON, G. L. and Viets, F. G. jr
Nitrogen enrichment of surface water by absorption of ammonia volatilized from cattle feedlots. bibliog Science 166:514-15 O 24 '69
HUTCHINSON, Peter
Scuba sculpture. W. Johnson. il Art N 68:52-3+ N '69
Sea works, creative explorations. J. Gruen. Vogue 154:64 S 15 '69
HUTCHISON, Ira J. jr
Leisure time and the riots, are we contributing? Parks & Rec 4:23+ Jl '69
HUTH, Mary Jo
Catholic education: to be or not to be? bibliog f Sch & Soc 97:101-4 F '69
HUTS
See also
Dwellings, Prehistoric
HUTSALIUK, Liuboslav
Vibrant paintings of Hutsaliuk. J. H. Michel. il por Am Artist 33:32-8+ Ag '69
HUTSCHNECKER, Arnold A.
Mental health of our leaders. Look 33:51-4 Jl 15 '69
HUTTERITE Brethren
Anabaptist explosion; adaptation of Pockets of high fertility in the United States. W. F. Pratt. il Natur Hist 78:8-10+ F '69
Fertile folk. il Sci Digest 65:27-8 Mr '69
HUTTO, Henry Hubert
God of quasars; poem. Chr Today 13:9 My 9 '69
God (the poet) poem. Chr Today 14:4 O 24 '69
Near the Cambodian border; poem. Chr Cent 86:1659 D 31 '69
Teen part of the beach; poem. Chr Cent 86: 1011 Jl 30 '69
HUTTON, Ginger M.
Their pines get the right food. Org Gard & Farm 16:40-3 O '69
HUTTON, Winfield
Byways of Europe; Leipzig. Opera N 33: 6-7 Mr 29 '69
HUX, Samuel
Hero politics. Commentary 47:90+ My '69
HUXLEY, Elspeth
Letter from London. Nat R 21:328-30, 1265-5 Ap 8; D 16 '69
HUXLEY, H. E.
Mechanism of muscular contraction. bibliog Science 164:1356-66 Je 20 '69
HUXLEY family
Huxleys, by R. W. Clark. Review
  Commonweal 89:536-8 Ja 24 '69. M. Ward
HUYEN, N. Khac
After Ho Chi Minh. America 121:265-7 O 4 '69
HYACINTHS
Increasing hyacinth bulbs. B. Brinhart. il Horticulture 47:16-17+ My '69

HYACINTHS, Water. See Water hyacinths
HYBRID cells. See Cells
HYBRID corn. See Corn—Hybrids
HYBRID lilies. See Lilies
HYBRID vigor. See Heterosis (biology)
HYBRIDIZATION
Now seed growers do better than nature. il
Bsns W p 127 S 27 '69
Try your hand at hybridizing; iris. il Home
Gard 56:32 Je '69
See also
Allelomorphism
Heterosis (biology)
Plant breeding
also subhead Hybrids under various sub-
jects. e.g. Wheat—Hybrids
HYDE, J. A. Lloyd
Painted enamels of China. Antiques 96:567-
71 O '69
HYDE, Mary Anne, and Kalter, Suzy
If I could do what I wanted to, I'd start with
grade school and revamp the whole sys-
tem. Mlle 69:268-9 Ag '69
HYDE, Philip
Escalante Canyon; photographs. Natur Hist
78:58-63 N '69
Wilderness of slickrock. il Audubon 71:
44-9 S '69
HYDE PARK, Vt.
Lamoille union high school: education for
all. C. L. Fortune, jr. il Sr Schol 94:Schol
Teach 22-3 Mr 7 '69
HYDÉN, Holger, and Lange, P. W.
Protein synthesis in the hippocampal pyra-
midal cells of rats during a behavioral
test. bibliog Science 159:1370-3; 164:200-1 Mr
22 '68, Ap 11 '69
HYDRANTS
Hydra-hydrant works wonders. il Sunset 142:
242-3 My '69
HYDRATES
Clathrate hydrate of air in Antarctic ice. S.
L. Miller. bibliog il Science 165:489-90 Ag 1
'69
HYDRATION
Hydration of macromolecules. I. D. Kuntz,
jr. and others. bibliog il Science 163:1329-
31 Mr 21 '69
Portland cement: pseudomorphs of original
cement grains observed in hardened pastes.
R. B. Williamson. bibliog il Science 164:
549-51 My 2 '69
HYDRAULIC engineering
See also
Flood prevention and control
Underwater structure
HYDRAULIC flowmeters. See Flow meters
HYDRAULIC fluids
50,000 miles without an oil change; torque-
converter fluid in Detroit city buses. R.
McKay, 3d. il Am City 84:136+ Je '69
HYDRAULIC machinery
See also
Liquidonics industries, incorporated
HYDRAULIC mining
See also
Gold mines and mining, Submarine
HYDRAULIC presses
You can build a lightweight press for heavy-
weight jobs. il Pop Mech 132:200-3 O '69
HYDRAULICS
See also
Electrohydraulics
HYDRAZIDES
See also
Isoniazid
HYDROCARBONS
Hydrocarbons of blue-green algae: geochem-
ical significance. K. Winters and others.
bibliog il Science 163:467-8 Ja 31 '69
Solubility in water of normal C_9 and C_{10} al-
kane hydrocarbons. C. McAuliffe. bibliog il
Science 163:478-9 Ja 31 '69
Venus clouds: test for hydrocarbons. W. T.
Plummer. bibliog il Science 163:1191-2 Mr
14 '69
See also
Benzene

Physiological effects
Global pollutant; polychlorinated biphenyls.
Sci Am 220:44 F '69
HYDROCORTISONE
Cortisol induction of growth hormone syn-
thesis in a clonal line of rat pituitary tu-
mor cells in culture. P. O. Kohler and oth-
ers. bibliog il Science 166:633-4 O 31 '69
Mammary alveolar epithelial cells; effect of
hydrocortisone on ultrastructure. E. S.
Mills and Y. J. Topper. bibliog il Science
165:1127-8 S 12 '69

HYDRODYNAMICS
Convergence and strain waves caused by a
submerged turbulent disturbance in strati-
fied fluids. A. H. Schooley. bibliog il Sci-
ence 164:1393-4 Je 20 '69
See also
Fluid dynamics
Jets
Ships—Hydrodynamics
HYDROELECTRIC plants
Fish and power plants; Storm King Moun-
tain pumped-storage project. A. C. Jensen.
il Cons 24:2-5 D '69
Mountain power; largest in world to be built
at Northfield Mountain in western Mass.
Sci Am 221:52+ Jl '69
HYDROELECTRIC power
See also
Hydro-Quebec institute of research
Niagara Falls
Tide power
HYDROFOILS
Biggest, fastest flying boat yet! USS Plain-
view. R. Zimmerman. il Pop Mech 130:88-
91+ D '68
Can big hydrofoils give navy a lift? Bsns
W p42 D 20 '69
Fun on a foil. il Mech Illus 65:104-5 Mr '69
HYDROGEN
Hydrogen the simplest. E. Keller. il Chem
42:19-21 N '69
Local anesthetics: significance of hydrogen
bonding in mechanism of action. M. Sax
and J. Pletcher. bibliog il Science 166:1546-
8 D 19 '69
Superconducting hydrogen. Sci Am 220:44-5
F '69
Isotopes
See also
Tritium
HYDROGEN, Liquid
Liquid hydrogen emerging as most powerful
space fuel. Space World F-4-64:11 Ap '69
HYDROGEN bombs
Incredible, yes. True? (concerning) F. James'
reports of Chinese H-bomb installations. J.
Burnham. Nat R 21:687 Jl 15 '69
Men who play God, by N. Moss. Review
Sat R 52:19-21+ Ag 30 '69
See also
Nuclear fusion

Manufacture
Basement H-bombs; laser-triggered bombs.
S. Novick. il Sci & Cit 10:243-9 D '68
Testing
See Atomic bombs—Testing
HYDROGEN ion concentration
Dilute solutions of strong acids: the effect of
water on ph. P. H. Mogul and J. S.
Schmuckler. bibliog il Chem 42:14-17 O '69
Electronics of corrosion. W. P. Ferren. il
Electr World 82:42-5+ N '69
HYDROGRAPHIC surveying
HYDRA for bottom lowdown. R. Dempe-
wolff. il Sci Digest 65:76-9 F '69
HYDROIDEA. See Hydromedusa
HYDROLASES
Deoxycytidine and radiation response: exceed-
ingly high deoxycytidine aminohydrolase
activity in human liver. B. Zicha and L.
Bufič. bibliog il Science 163:191-2 Ja 10
'69
HYDROLOGIC research
World's growing water shortage; reprint. M.
Batisse. il UNESCO Courier 22:58-9 Ag '69
HYDROLYSIS
Metal ion activation of phosphate transfer
by bidentate coordination. F. J. Farrell
and others. bibliog il Science 164:320-1 Ap
18 '69
HYDROLYTIC enzymes. See Hydrolases
HYDROMECHANICS
See also
Hydrodynamics
HYDROMEDUSA
Inhibition of hydroid aging in campanularia
flexuosa. S. E. Toth. bibliog Science 166:
619-20 O 31 '69
HYDRON. See Plastics
HYDROPHOBIA. See Rabies
HYDROPLANE models. See Airplane models
HYDROPLANE racing. See Motor boat racing
HYDROPLANES
Maple Leaf IV; excerpt from Seamanlike
sense in powercraft. U. Fox. il Yachting
126:56-8+ O '69
HYDRO-QUEBEC institute of research
High powered research; Canada's new hydro-
power center. F. Poland. Sci N 95:174 F
15 '69

HYDROSKIMMER. See Air cushion vehicles
HYDROSTATIC extrusion process. See Extrusion process
HYDROSTATIC transmission. See Automobiles—Transmission
HYDROTHERMAL ore deposits. See Ore deposits
HYDROXYAPATITE
Diphosphonates inhibit formation of calcium phosphate crystals in vitro and pathological calcification in vivo. M. D. Francis and others. bibliog il Science 165:1264-6 S 19 '69
Diphosphonates inhibit hydroxyapatite dissolution in vitro and bone resorption in tissue culture and in vivo. H. Fleisch and others. bibliog il Science 165:1262-4 S 19 '69
HYDROXYCHOLECALCIFEROL. See Vitamins—Vitamin D
HYDROXYETHYLINDOLE. See Tryptophol
HYDROXYL
Hydroxyl and water masers in protostars. M. M. Litvak. bibliog il Science 165:855-61 Ag 29 '69
Interstellar masers. D. F. Dickinson and others. il Sky & Tel 39:4-7 Ja '70
Orientation of the dipole moments of hydroxyl groups in oxidized and unoxidized biotite. A. S. R. Juo and J. L. White. bibliog il Science 165:804-5 Ag 22 '69
HYDROXYLAMINE
Anaphylatoxin release from the third component of human complement by hydroxylamine. D. B. Budzko and H. Müller-Eberhard. bibliog il Science 165:506-7 Ag 1 '69
HYDROXYLASES
Adrenal tyrosine hydroxylase: compensatory increase in activity after chemical sympathectomy. R. A. Mueller and others. bibliog il Science 163:468-9 Ja 31 '69
Alpha-naphthoflavone: an inhibitor of hydrocarbon cytotoxicity and microsomal hydroxylase. L. Diamond and H. V. Gelboin. bibliog il Science 166:1023-5 N 21 '69
Corticosterone regulation of tryptophan hydroxylase in midbrain of the rat. E. C. Azmitia, jr .and B. S. McEwen. bibliog il Science 166:1274-6 D 5 '69
HYDROXYLATION
Enzymatic mechanism of steroid hydroxylation. C. J. Sih. bibliog il Science 163:1297-300 Mr 21 '69
HYDROXYTRYPTAMINE. See Serotonin
HYERS, M. Conrad
Ambivalent man and his ambiguous moon. Chr Cent 86:1158-26 S 10 '69
HYGIENE
    See also
Aged—Care and hygiene
Perspiration
Water pollution
Woman—Health and hygiene
HYGIENE, Public. See Public health
HYLAND, John Joseph, 1912-
Freeing the Pueblo: what happened. por U S News 66:12 F 17 '69
HYMAN, Dick
Hyman and the studio men. J. S. Wilson. il por Hi Fi 19:50-3 My '69
HYMAN, Joe
Rough sacking for Viyella chief. por Bsns W p23 D 20 '69
HYMAN, Sidney
Man on the moon, the Columbian dilemma. por Bul Atom Sci 25:18-22 S '69
HYMENOPTERA
Mimicry of hymenoptera by beetles with unconventional flight. R. E. Silberglied and T. Eisner. il Science 163:486-8 Ja 31 '69
    See also
Trichogramma
Yellow jackets
HYMENOSPORUM flavum. See Sweetshade
HYMNS

    Anecdotes, facetiae, satire, etc.
Silent majority sings. Chr Cent 86:1533 N 26 '69
HYNEK, Josef Allen
Condon report and UFO's. Bul Atom Sci 25:39-42 Ap '69
HYPERACTIVE children. See Problem children
HYPERBARIC oxygenation
Aping the ocean's deeps: high-pressure hyperbaric chamber. J. Eberhart. il Sci N 96:280-1 S 27 '69
High-pressure medicine. J. R. Berry. il Pop Mech 130 :99-103 D '68
Hyperbaric oxygen: toxicity to fish at pressures present in their swimbladders. B. G. D'Aoust. bibliog il Science 163:576-8 F 7 '69
O₂ for old age; relieving symptoms of senescence. Newsweek 74:80 O 13 '69

HYPERCALCEMIA
Thyrocalcitonin: evidence for physiological function. T. K. Gray and P. L. Munson. bibliog il Science 166:512-13 O 24 '69
HYPERPHAGIA
Hyperphagia and polydipsia in socially isolated rhesus monkeys. R. E. Miller and others. bibliog il Science 165:1027-8 S 5 '69
Hyperphagia in rats with cuts between the ventromedial and lateral hypothalamus. D. J. Albert and L. H. Storlien. bibliog il Science 165:599-600 Ag 8 '69
HYPERSENSITIVITY. See Allergy
HYPERSONIC aerodynamics. See Aerodynamics, Supersonic
HYPERTENSION
Giant step toward solving the mystery of high blood pressure. R. Winter. il Sci Digest 66:8-12 Jl '69
Vascular smooth muscle reactivity in normotensive and hypertensive rats. S. Spector and others. bibliog il Science 166:1300-1 D 5 '69
HYPERTRICHOSIS
Hairy people: hypertrichosis portrayed in art. J. G. Ravin and G. P. Hodge. il Sci Digest 66:14-17 S '69
HYPNOANALYSIS. See Hypnotism—Therapeutic use
HYPNOTISM
Hypnosis: what it can and can't do for you. R. F. Johnson. il Sci Digest 66:7-13 S '69
Is a hypnotized witness reliable? il Time 93:70 Mr 28 '69

    Therapeutic use
What hypnosis can do for you. R. Blackmon. Vogue 153:136-7+ Ja 15 '69
HYPOGAMMAGLOBULINEMIA. See Globulinemia
HYPOGLYCEMIA. See Blood sugar
HYPOPHYSIS. See Pituitary body
HYPOTENSION
Renin-aldosterone system in Parkinson's disease. A. Barbeau and others. bibliog il Science 165:291-2 Jl 18 '69
HYPOTHALAMUS
Hypothalamic motivational systems: fixed or plastic neural circuits? E. S. Valenstein and others. Science 163:1084 Mr 7 '69; Reply. R. A. Wise. 165:929-30 Ag 29 '69
Hypothalamic stimulation of growth hormone secretion. L. A. Frohman and others; reply with rejoinder. G. P. Smith and A. W. Root. Science 163:705 F 14 '69
Lateral hypothalamic stimulation: inhibition of aversive effects by feeding, drinking, and gnawing. J. Mendelson. bibliog il Science 166:1431-3 D 12 '69
Thermoregulation: effects of environmental temperature on turnover of hypothalamic norepinephrine. M. A. Simmonds and L. L. Iversen. bibliog il Science 163:473-4 Ja 31 '69; Reply with rejoinder. R. D. Myers. 165:1030-1 S 5 '69
Your chemical thermostat. C. H. Coleman. Sci Digest 65:81-4 My '69
HYPOXIA. See Anoxemia
HYPSOBLENNIUS gill. See Blennies
HYRACOTHERES. See Horses, Fossil
HYSLOP, Beatrice F.
(comp) Articles and other books received; France. See issues of American historical review
HYSTER company
When I was a boy. il Forbes 104:68 O 1 '69
HYSTERECTOMY. See Uterus—Surgery

I

IACC. See Inter-American cultural council
IACW. See Inter-American commission of women
IAEA. See International atomic energy agency
IA-ECOSOC. See Inter-American economic and social council
IAM. See International association of machinists and aerospace workers
IATA. See International air transport association
I am the way; opera. See Hines, J.
I am waiting; story. See Hemenway, R.
IBBY. See International board on books for young people
IBEC. See International basic economy corporation

IBM. See International business machines corporation

IBP. See International biological program

IBT. See International brotherhood of teamsters, chauffeurs, warehousemen and helpers of America

IC. See International controls corporation

ICAO. See International civil aviation organization

ICBM (intercontinental ballistic missiles) See Guided missiles

ICC. See United States—Interstate commerce commission

ICCC. See International council of Christian churches

ICFO. See International Catholic film office

ICFTU. See International confederation of free trade unions

ICI. See Imperial chemical industries, limited

ICMA. See International city management association

IDB. See Inter-American development bank

IDEA. See Institute for development of educational activities

I don't want to be like you; story. See McInerny, R.

IEEE. See Institute of electrical and electronics engineers

IFALPA. See International federation of air line pilots associations

IFCO. See Interreligious foundation for community organization

IFLA. See International federation of library associations

IFOR. See International fellowship of reconciliation

IFR flying. See Aviation—Instrument flying

I.G. farben. See Interessengemeinschaft farbenindustrie ag

IGY. See International geophysical year

IHM (Immaculate Heart of Mary, Missionary sisters of) See Sisterhoods

ILA. See International longshoremen's association

ILGWU. See International ladies' garment workers' union

ILO. See International labor organization

ILS (instrument landing system) See Airplanes—Landing

I like it better now; story. See Hall, J. B.

IMA. See International management association, incorporated

IMC. See Instructional materials centers

IMF. See International monetary fund

IMP (interplanetary monitoring platform) See Artificial satellites—Use in research

INI (Instituto nacional de industria) See Holding companies

IOS. See Investors overseas services, limited

IPI (individually prescribed instruction) See Individual instruction

IPI schools. See Individual instruction

IPSA. See Independent postal system of America

IQ. See Intelligence quotient

IRA. See Irish republican army

IRA-USM merger. See Business consolidations and mergers

IRBM (Intermediate range ballistic missiles) See Guided missiles

IRC. See International rostrum of composers

IRI (Istituto per la ricostruzione industriale) See Italy—Industries

IRRI. See International rice research institute

IRS. See United States—Internal revenue service

ISI. See International students, incorporated

IT and T. See International telephone and telegraph

ITT educational services incorporated. See International telephone and telegraph corporation

I Tatti center. See Harvard university

IUCN. See International union for the conservation of nature and natural resources

IUD. See American federation of labor and Congress of industrial organizations—Industrial union department

IUD (intra-uterine device) See Contraceptives

IUE. See International union of electrical, radio and machine workers

IUPAP. See International union of pure and applied physics

IWW. See Industrial workers of the world

I want cocoanuts; drama. See Ross, D.

I will not let thee go, except thou bless me; story. See Updike, J.

IACOCCA, Lee Anthony. See Iacocca, Lido Anthony

IACOCCA, Lido Anthony
Some kind of animal! excerpt from The strategy of change for business success; ed. by S. Furst and M. Sherman. por Nations Bsns 57:62-4+ F '69

about

Behind the palace revolt at Ford. por Bsns W p 139 S 20 '69

Ford's new Maverick. A. Rothenberg. il por Look 33:69+ Ap 15 '69

Pray for Iacocca's baby. W. A. McWhirter. il por Life 66:68-72 Ap 11 '69

IAGO (literary character) See Shakespeare, W. —Characters

IAKUBOVSKII, Ivan
Yakubovsky's travels. Newsweek 73:42+ Mr 3 '69

IBAÑEZ, Carlos
Carlos Ibanez company; 92nd street Y. J. Dowlin. Dance Mag 43:81 Jl '69

IBBOTSON, Eva
Why weep for Otto? story. Ladies Home J 86:104-5 S '69

IBISA. See Iviza (island)

IBIZA. See Iviza (island)

IBO tribe. See Nigeria—Native races

IBSEN, Henrik
Hedda Gabler. Criticism
Time il 94:58 D 19 '69
Peer Gynt. Criticism
Sat R 52:35-6 Ag 2 '69

ICARUS is coming; drama. See Murray, J.

ICE
Ice is nice; the automatic ice maker. il McCalls 96:126 Jl '69

Mechanism for multiplication of atmospheric ice crystals: apparent charge distribution on laboratory crystals. F. K. Odencrantz and others; reply. R. I. Smith-Johannsen. il Science 163:958 F 28 '69

Scanning electron microscopy of evaporating ice. J. D. Cross. bibliog il Science 164:174-5 Ap 11 '69; Reply. R. E. Ruskin. 166:906 N 14 '69

Superdense water ice. A. H. Delsemme and A. Wenger. bibliog il Science 167:44-5 Ja 2 '70

Water on the moon and a new nondimensional number. J. A. O'Keefe. bibliog il Science 163:669-70 F 14 '69

Polar Regions

Anchor ice formation in McMurdo Sound, Antarctica, and its biological effects. P. K. Dayton and others. bibliog il Science 163:273-4 Ja 17 '69

Clathrate hydrates of air in Antarctic ice. S. L. Miller. bibliog il Science 165:489-90 Ag 1 '69

Is the Arctic ice cap endangered? W. Sullivan. Cur 106:22-5 Ap '69

One thousand centuries of climatic record from Camp Century on the Greenland ice sheet. W. Dansgaard and others. bibliog il Science 166:377-81 O 17 '69

Secrets of the icecap. il Time 94:94 N 14 '69
See also
Glaciers

ICE age. See Glacial epochs

ICE boats and ice boating
Hot rods on ice. C. R. Meyer. il Motor B 124:10-12 D '69

ICE breaking vessels
Beat the freeze; Riverside, Conn. yacht club. R. Carrick. il Yachting 125:69+ F '69

Beefed-up tanker for Alaskan oil. il Pop Mech 132:30 Ag '69

$40 million gamble on the Northwest Passage; Manhattan's voyage. il Time 94:75 S 5 '69

Hard-charger to Alaska; tanker Manhattan. il Life 67:42-5 S 26 '69

It adds up to an icebreaker; supertanker Manhattan to open up route to Arctic oil. Bsns W p53 My 31 '69

Manhattan's epic voyage. J. Rychetnik. il Time 94:87 S 26 '69

New route to Alaska's oil? the S.S. Manhattan ice-breaking tanker. il U S News 67:10-11 Ag 25 '69

Northwest Passage; an ice-breaking tanker pioneers in opening the long-sought Arctic route. N. Wood. il Travel & Camera 32:14+ N '69

Northwest Passage to what? Manhattan's voyage. J. Lear. il Sat R 52:55-6+ N 1 '69

Northwest Passage; voyage of the Manhattan. Nation 09:301 S 29 '69

ICE breaking vessels—*Continued*
Oil, ice and ecology; voyage of the Manhattan through the Northwest Passage. il Sci N 96:265-6 S 27 '69
Search for Golconda; converting biggest tanker in the U.S. merchant fleet into an icebreaker to open route to Arctic oil. il Newsweek 73:77+ Mr 10 '69
Ship that beat the Arctic ice; the Manhattan experiment. il U S News 67:18 S 29 '69
Son of Northwest Passage; Manhattan's voyage. il Sci Digest 66:33-4 N '69
SS Manhattan's wake of questions. il Bsns W p33 S 27 '69

ICE capades. See Ice shows

ICE caves
Paradise ice caves; Mt Rainier glacial passageways. W. R. Halliday and C. H. Anderson, jr. il Nat Parks 43:13-14 O '69

ICE cream, ices, etc.
Banana split. il McCalls 96:128-30+ Mr '69
Hail to ice! C. Claiborne. il N Y Times Mag p70 Ag 17 '69
Ices are nice. il Sunset 143:84-5 S '69
Irresistible frozen treats; with recipes. il Redbook 133:96-8+ Ag '69
Jazzy ice cream. D. Eby and P. Pollock. il Bet Hom & Gard 47:62-8+ Ag '69
Let's end up with ice cream pie. il Sunset 143:196+ N '69
Summer desserts, cooling and easy. il Sunset 143:111 Ag '69
Two fresh fruit sundaes. il Sunset 142:187 Je '69

ICE cream pie. See Ice cream, ices, etc.

ICE cream sodas. See Beverages

ICE drinks. See Beverages

ICE fields. See Glaciers

ICE fishing. See Fishing, Winter

ICE hazards in aviation. See Airplanes—Ice protection

ICE hockey. See Hockey

ICE hockey rinks. See Hockey rinks

ICE on rivers, lakes, etc. See Lakes—Temperature

ICE plants (botany)
Ice plant. il Sunset 142:218-20+ My '69

ICE sculpture
Quebec's lively ice; Carnaval d'hiver de Quebec. R. Arnold. il U S Camera 32:56-8+ Ja '69

ICE shows
World of dance; the Ice capades. W. Terry. il Sat R 52:39-40 F 1 '69

ICE skating. See Skating

ICE skating rinks. See Skating rinks

ICEBOATS. See Ice boats and ice boating

ICEBREAKERS. See Ice breaking vessels

ICELAND
See also
Education—Iceland
Geology—Iceland
Reykjavik
Soils—Iceland
United States—Armed forces—Forces in Iceland

Description and travel
Iceland: fire and ice in a cold blue ocean. J. Morris. il Holiday 46:54-7+ D '69
Only in Iceland! K. Brown. il Travel 131: 44-9+ My '69
Sailing Iceland's rugged coasts. W. Britton. il Nat Geog 136:228-65 Ag '69
Stop and you'll want to stay in Iceland. S. Wiedel. il Travel & Camera 32:70-6 N '69
Two-day stopover in Iceland is an exciting trip to the Gullfoss and the Geysir country. E. Scully. il Mod Phot 33:120+ Je '69

Foreign relations
Reports. J. B. Ritch, 3d. Atlan 223:38+ Ap '69

History
Only in Iceland! K. Brown. il Travel 131: 44-9+ My '69

ICHTHYOLOGICAL research
Fishes that grow horns; breeding or nuptial tubercles. R. F. Denoncourt. il Cons 23:30-1 Ap '69

ICHTHYOLOGY
Oddballs of the deep sea; hunting for marketable seafood. C. Phinizy. il Sports Illus 31:24-7 Ag 4 '69

Research
See Ichthyological research

ICINGS
May takes the cake. il McCalls 96:102-3+ My '69

ICKERINGILL, Nan
Coolness of punches. House B 111:118-19 Je '69
Through Ireland by tinker wagon. Travel & Camera 32:35-6 Ap '69
Time-savers for the host. House B 111:47+ Ag '69

IDA Cason Callaway gardens. See Gardens—Georgia

IDAHO
See also
Fishing—Idaho
Hells Canyon
Hunting—Idaho
St Joe River
Wilderness areas—Idaho

Description and travel
Exploring Idaho. H. Bradshaw and V. Bradshaw. il Todays Health 47:34-7+ Je '69

IDÄNPÄÄN-HEIKKILÄ, Juhana E. and Schoolar, J. C.
LSD: autoradiographic study on the placental transfer and tissue distribution in mice. bibliog Science 164:1295-7 Je 13 '69
—and others
Relation of pharmacological and behavioral effects of a hallucinogenic amphetamine to distribution in cat brain. bibliog Science 164:1085-7 My 30 '69

IDE Adobe. See California—Historic houses, etc.

IDEA engineering. See Ideas in business

IDEA files. See Fiction—Technique

IDEAL couple; story. See Ingalls. S.

IDEAL toy corporation
Perils of going public. R. Levy. Duns R 94:46-7 S '69

IDEALISM
Being an idealist in a realist's world. F. B. Huey, jr. Chr Today 13:6-7 Ja 31 '69

IDEALISM in literature
See also
Romanticism

IDEAS in business
Management of ideas. M. Anshen. Harvard Bsns R 47:99-107 Jl '69

IDENTICAL twins. See Twins

IDENTIFICATION
Machine that takes security in hand; Identimat system. il Bsns W p 151 My 10 '69
When each person has only one number. U S News 66:15 My 5 '69
See also
Bertillon system
Voiceprints

IDENTIFICATION tags, bracelets, etc.
Bracelet that saves lives. T. Dowling. il Har Yrs 9:50 Ap '69

IDENTITY, Personal. See Personality

IDRIS I, king of Libya
How brave to be a king. por Newsweek 74: 40 S 15 '69

IDYLL, Clarence P.
Grunion: the fish that spawns on land. Nat Geog 135:714-23 My '69
New Florida resident, the walking catfish. Nat Geog 135:846-51 Je '69

IFNI
See also
United Nations—Ifni

IGEL, Howard J. and others
Mouse leukemia virus activation by chemical carcinogens. bibliog Science 166:1624-6 D 26 '69

IGLAUER, Edith
Profiles; P. Trudeau. New Yorker 45:36-42+ Jl 5 '69

IGNATOW, David
Communion; poem. Nation 208:183 F 10 '69

IGNEOUS rocks. See Rocks, Igneous

IGNITION
Ultraviolet radiation evaluated as igniter; studies by Air force office of scientific research. M. L. Yaffee. Aviation W 90:59-60 F 3 '69

IGNITION devices. See Automobile engines—Ignition; Gas and oil engines, Outboard—Ignition; Gas burners—Ignition devices; Marine engines—Ignition

IGOE, James
New in the Old Northwest. por Library J 94:4112-15 N 15 '69

IGUANAS
Lizard reflectivity change and its effect on light transmission through body wall. W. P. Porter and K. S. Norris. bibliog il Science 163:482-4 Ja 31 '69

IHDE, Aaron J.
Theodore William Richards and the atomic weight problem; adaptation of address, December 27, 1968. Science 164:647-51 My 9 '69

ILAN, Joseph. See Ilan, Judith, jt. auth.

ILAN, Judith, and Ilan, Joseph
Aminoacyl transfer ribonucleic acid synthetases from cell-free extract of plasmodium
berghei. bibliog Science 164:560-2 My 2 '69

ILEX. See Holly

ILIAD. See Homer

I'll be happy happy; story. See Bergstein, E.

ILLAN, David Bar-. See Bar-Illan, D.

ILLEGITIMACY
Forgotten victims of the war in Vietnam. D.
E. Ronk. il Parents Mag 44:43-5+ Ag '69
Japan's GI babies: a hard coming-of-age.
D. Moser. il Life 67:40-7 S 5 '69
Why bastard, wherefore base? H. D. Krause.
bibliog f Ann Am Acad 383:58-70 My '69
    See also
Mothers, Unmarried

ILLICH, Ivan D.
Monsignor Illich's letter to Cardinal Seper.
America 120:187-9 F 15 '69

            about
Camara and Illich. Commonweal 89:575-6 F
7 '69
Get going, and don't come back. por Time
93:48+ F 14 '69
Ivan Illich: the Christian as rebel. P. Schrag.
il pors Sat R 52:14-19 Jl 19 '69
Life of Ivan Illich. D. Dolan. New Repub
160:18-19 Mr 1 '69
Monsignor Illich leaves priesthood. Chr
Cent 86:503 Ap 16 '69
Of many things; Center for intercultural
documentation at Cuernavaca, out of bounds
to priests and religious. D. R. Campion.
America 120:120 F 1 '69

ILLICK, Joseph E.
Looking westward. See issues of American
west

ILLINOIS
    See also
Architecture, Domestic—Illinois
Conservation of resources—Illinois
Education—Illinois
Hunting—Illinois
Libraries—Illinois
Politics, Corruption in—Illinois
Prisons—Illinois
Trials—Illinois
Water supply—Illinois

        Politics and government
Democrats against Daley. il Time 93:19-20 F
21 '69
Democrats confront 1970: D. Rose and D. S.
Canter. Nation 209:595-7 D 1 '69
Enter Adlai III. il Newsweek 74:48+ D 8 '69
Filling the Dirksen gap. il Newsweek 74:33-4
S 22 '69
Ogilvie's offensive. Time 93:22 Ap 18 '69
    See also
Politics, Corruption in—Illinois

            Race problems
Black and poor in Cairo. R. Middeke. Com-
monweal 90:453-4 Jl 25 '69
Trouble in Cairo. Newsweek 73:41 My 5 '69

ILLINOIS central railroad company
Working for a different Johnson. il Time 93:
63-4 Ja 31 '69

ILLINOIS institute of technology, Chicago
New multi-use gymnasium for I.I.T. il Arch
Rec 146:111-13 Jl '69

ILLINOIS. University
Admission by lot. Newsweek 75:46 Ja 5 '70
Graduate student. S. C. Fain, jr. il Phys
Today 22:29-30 Mr '69
Now, a lottery to pick students. U S News
67:7 D 29 '69
Where student activists are VIP's; Volunteer
Illini projects. il Am Ed 5:27 Ag '69

        Chicago campus
Campus City continued; SOM's plan for the
Chicago circle campus Architecture and art
building. J. M. Dixon. il Arch forum 129:
28-43 D '68

    Krannert center for the per-
            forming arts
    See Urbana, Ill.—Krannert center for the
performing arts

ILLITERACY
Adult literacy programs and development;
conducted by Unesco. Sch & Soc 97:119 F
'69
Bookplates for literacy: a Unesco project. il
ALA Bul 63:835 Je '69

700 million forgotten minds; reprint. R.
Maheu. il UNESCO Courier 22:36-7 Ag '69
Some dimensions of illiteracy in the U.S:
one in fifty or fifty percent? M. Cohen.
bibliog il Wilson Lib Bul 44:45-8 S '69
24 million illiterates; U.S. Office of education's estimates. America 121:347 O 25 '69

ILLNESS. See Sickness

ILLUMINATED manuscripts. See Illumination
of books and manuscripts

ILLUMINATION. See Electric lighting

ILLUMINATION of books and manuscripts
Birds' heads and graven images. C. Roth.
Commentary 47:80-3 Je '69; Reply. R.
Wischnitzer. 48:12 Ag '69
    See also
Hours, Book of

ILLUSION, Dramatic. See Dramatic illusion

ILLUSIONS, Optical. See Optical illusions

ILLUSIONS and hallucinations
    See also
Flying saucers
Optical illusions

ILLUSTRATED books
    See also
Picture books
Publishers and publishing—Illustrated books

ILLUSTRATED songs. See Music, Popular
(songs, etc)

ILLUSTRATION of books and periodicals
Cartoonists Q's; spot drawing. J. Markow.
Writers Digest 49:16+ O '69
Children, art and literature. Sister Francis
Joseph. il Sch Arts 69:28-9 N '69
Confessions of a leprechaun. B. Turkle. il
Pub W 196:133-6 Jl 14 '69
Foreign exchange; Biennale of illustrations
Bratislava. J. Donovan. il Sat R 52:61-2 N
8 '69
George Bartell: California illustrator. F.
Whitaker. il Am Artist 33:64-9+ Mr '69
Illustrations of Peter Spier. J. H. Michel. il
Am Artist 33:49-55+ O '69
Illustrator talks; interview. ed. by W. Sleator.
B. Lent. il Pub W 195:126-8 F 17 '69
Working with a photographer; finding a good
photographer to illustrate your article. J.
Lawrence. il Writers Digest 49:60-3+ Jl
'69
    See also
Illumination of books and manuscripts
Picture books for children
Wood engravings

            History
World of fantasy; Alice in wonderland on
playing cards. D. Powills. il Hobbies 74:
152-3 D '69

ILLUSTRATORS
Art of the pen. H. C. Pitz. il Am Artist 32:
26-32 D '68
Millsap & Kinyon illustrator team. F.
Whitaker. il Am Artist 33:50-5+ Je '69
    See also
Bartell. G.
Celis, P.
Doré, G
Kossin. S.
Shulevitz, U.
Ungerer, T.
Wyeth. N. C.

IMAGE converters
    See also
Image intensifiers

IMAGE intensifiers
How the army learned to see in the dark. M.
Schultz. il Pop Mech 131:79-82+ Ja '69
Image-tube photography. J. R. Hansen. il
R Pop Astron 63:28-32 F '69

IMAGE of the dream; story. See Poston, P.

IMAGES and imagery (psychology)
    See also
After images

IMAGINARY animals. See Animal lore

IMAGINARY conversations
Drop-in night at the Electric circus;
imaginary conversation with F. Liszt. D.
Bar-Illan. Sat R 52:72-3 N 15 '69

IMAGINARY numbers. See Numbers, Complex

IMAGINATION
    See also
Creation (literary, artistic, etc)
Creative ability
Eidetic imagery
Fantasy

IMAI, Ryukichi
Non-proliferation treaty and Japan. Bul Atom
Sci 25:2-7 My '69

IMBRIE, McCrea, and Selden, Nell
Someone's comin' hungry. Criticism
Nation 208:478 Ap 14 '69
New Yorker 45:131-2 Ap 12 '69

IMHOTEP
 Imhotep. L. Casson. il Horizon 11:92-101 Sum
 '69
IMIDODIPHOSPHATES
 Imidodiphosphate and pyrophosphate: pos-
 sible biological significance of similar struc-
 tures. M. Larsenand others. bibliog il Sci-
 ence 166:1510-11 D 19 '69
IMITATION
 See also
 Influence (psychology)
IMITATION in art
 Copy cat; art of J. C. Clarke. D. L. Shirey.
 il Newsweek 73:105 Je 16 '69
IMLACH, George
 Knocking out punch. il por Newsweek 73:
 127-8 Ap 21 '69
IMM, Val
 (ed) See Hall, P. What's in a name
IMMACULATE Heart of Mary, Missionary
 sisters of. See Sisterhoods
IMMACULATE Heart sisters of Los Angeles.
 See Sisterhoods
IMMANENCE of God
 See also
 Transcendence of God
IMMATURITY, Emotional. See Maturity
IMMERMAN, Sol
 Pocket's art director tells goals for covers.
 il Pub W 195:70 Ap 7 '69
IMMERSION, Baptismal. See Baptism
IMMIGRANTS in Australia
 Reports: Australia. A. Koestler. Atlan 223:
 12+ Je '69
IMMIGRANTS in Denmark
 See also
 Jews in Denmark
IMMIGRANTS in Israel
 Promised land. il Newsweek 74:58+ O 27 '69
IMMIGRANTS in the United States
 See also
 Chinese in the United States
 Cubans in the United States
 Jews in the United States
 Russians in the United States

 Education
 See also
 Libraries—Work with foreign born
IMMIGRATION and emigration
 International migration of workers. P. Kuin.
 il UNESCO Courier 22:28-31 Jl '69

 Africa
 See also
 Back-to-Africa movements

 Australia
 See also
 Immigrants in Australia

 Cuba
 See also
 Cubans in the United States

 Ghana
 Exodus. il Time 95:22 Ja 12 '70

 Israel
 See also
 Immigrants in Israel

 Latin America
 Migration of scientists from Latin America;
 adaptation of address, 1968. H. M. Nussenzveig. Science 165:1328-32 S 26 '69; Reply.
 D. Schwartz. 166:820-1 N 14 '69

 Liberia
 Into the wilderness: group from Chicago's
 Alpha Beta Israel center. J. Barnes. il
 Newsweek 73:52 Ja 27 '69

 Poland
 Goodbye to Poland. G. Meretik. Commentary
 48:55-62 S '69
 Someone denounced us; with report by R.
 Z. Chesnoff. il Newsweek 75:32-3 Ja 12 '70

 Russia
 Next year in Jerusalem. L. Volkov. il Newsweek 74:52+ N 24 '69

 United States
 Operation sisyphus; wetbacks, growers and
 poverty. S. L. Greene. Nation 209:403-6 O
 20 '69
 Paper walls: America and the refugee crisis
 1938-1941. by D. S. Wyman. Review
 New Repub 160:25-6 F 15 '69. S. Adler
 See also
 Quarantine

 Vietnam (Republic)
 Vietnam exodus: a favored few. il Newsweek 73:41 Je 23 '69

IMMIGRATION and emigration law
 Where have all the busboys gone? il Time
 94:84+ N 21 '69
IMMORAL literature and pictures
 Clean sweep for a cleanup. Nations Bsns 57:
 20-1 D '69
 Close up: the old smut peddler; B. Rosset
 of Grove press. A. Goldman. il Life 67:49-
 53 Ag 29 '69
 Coming crackdown on smut peddlers; with
 excerpts from President Nixon's message
 to Congress, May 2, 1969. il U S News 67:
 52-3 Jl 21 '69
 Commission on obscenity files progress report. Library J 94:3591-2 O 15 '69
 Conversations on the new eroticism; symposium. il Time 94:64-5 Jl 11 '69
 Danes' bold experiment: legalized pornography. J. R. Moskin. Look 33:51+ Jl 29
 '69
 Does anything go? sex tabloids. il Newsweek
 74:80 Jl 14 '69
 For the only freak in Ohio; sex newspapers.
 B. Farrell. Life 67:32B N 21 '69
 Impact of offensive and obscene material on
 children and youth; excerpts from Sex edu-
 cation in the schools: a study of objectives,
 content, methods, materials, and evaluation.
 H. F. Kilander. Sch & Soc 97:326-30 Sum
 '69
 Isn't anything obscene any more? M. Man-
 nes. McCalls 96:64+ S '69
 Mental health pundits decry pornography
 threat. Library J 94:3392+ O 1 '69
 New plan to fight pornography. E. M. Dirk-
 sen. Read Digest 95:113-16 N '69
 Opinion: obscenity. G. Wolff. Mlle 69:148+
 Jl '69
 Poll about pornography. C. B. Grannis. Pub
 W 196:43 S 29 '69
 Pop sex among the squares. D. Smith. il
 Nation 209:142-5 Ag 25 '69
 Pop sex novel: new opiate of the masses.
 W. R. Miller. Chr Cent 86:152-3 Ja 29 '69
 Pornography & propaganda. J. Thompson.
 Commentary 48:54-7 Ag '69
 Prudes, lewds and polysyllables. J. H. Smylie.
 Commonweal 89:671-3 F 28 '69
 Reactionary view of obscenity and brutality;
 excerpts from Decent and indecent. B.
 Spock. Redbook 134:20+ Ja '70
 Richmond city attorney to be obscenity
 judge. Library J 94:2856 S 1 '69
 Riding the sexwelle; West Germany. il Time
 95:30 Ja 19 '70
 Sexploitation [sic]; new purveyors of por-
 nographic newspapers. S. Levinson. Ramp
 Mag 8:66-70 Ag '69
 Time for a halt; proposed anti-pornography
 measures. Newsweek 74:82 O 6 '69
 Tropic of conversation: Portnoy's complaint.
 S. Maloff. Commonweal 90:23-4 Mr 21 '69
 What is pornography, anyway? W. Sheed.
 Mlle 69:70-1+ Jl '69
 See also
 Censorship
 Obscenity (law)
 Sex in literature
 United States—Commission on obscenity and
 pornography
IMMORTALITY
 See also
 Death
 Eschatology
 Future life
IMMUNE response. See Immunological tolerance
IMMUNITIES and privileges. See Privileges
 and immunities
IMMUNITY
 Antigenicity: some molecular aspects. M.
 Sela. bibliog il Science 166:1365-74 D 12
 '69
 Cellular differentiation in the immune sys-
 tem; report of eighth Midwinter confer-
 ence of immunologists. J. S. Garvey. Sci-
 ence 165:205-6+ Jl 11 '69
 Cellular immunity; report of meeting. N. A.
 Mitchison. Science 165:931-2 Ag 29 '69
 Diffusible cytotoxic substances and cell-
 mediated resistance to syngeneic tumors;
 in vitro demonstration. K. Kikuchi and
 others. bibliog il Science 165:77-9 Jl 4 '69
 Dual immunology. Sci Am 220:42-3 F '69
 See also
 Antigens and antibodies
 Antiserum
 Complements (immunity)
 Globulinemia
 Immunosuppressive agents
 Inoculation
 Plants—Disease and pest resistance
 Vaccination

IMMUNOASSAY. See Biological assay

IMMUNOELECTROPHORESIS. See Electrophoresis

IMMUNOGLOBULIN. See Blood—Proteins

IMMUNOLOGICAL tolerance
Antigen-associated immunosuppressant: effect of serum on immune response. H. Y. Whang and E. Neter. bibliog il Science 163:290-1 Ja 17 '69
Genetic control of the antibody response: relationship between immune response and histocompatibility (H-2) type. H. O. McDevitt and A. Chinitz. bibliog il Science 163:1207-8 Mr 14 '69
Human leukocyte antigenic specificity HL-A3; frequency of occurrence. D. B. Amos and E. Yunis. bibliog il Science 165:300-2 Jl 18 '69
Immune response in vitro: independence of activated lymphoid cells. C. W. Pierce and B. Benacerraf. bibliog il Science 166:1002-4 N 21 '69
Immunity to cancer? Newsweek 73:76 My 12 '69
Immunological tolerance; report of meeting. R. S. Schwartz and S. Leskowitz. Science 163:1364+ Mr 21 '69
Rapid loss of tolerance induced in weanling NZB and B/W F_1 mice. P. J. Staples and N. Talal. bibliog il Science 163:1215-16 Mr 14 '69
Report on organ transplants. Chem 42:22-3 My '69
Specific tissue graft rejection in earthworms. E. L. Cooper. bibliog Science 166:1414-15 D 12 '69

IMMUNOLOGY
See also
Immunological tolerance

IMMUNOSUPPRESSIVE agents
Antiserum to lymphocytes and procarbazine compared as immunosuppressants in mice. P. B. Stewart and V. Cohen. bibliog il Science 164:1082-3 My 30 '69; Reply. J. H. Weisburger. 165:517 Ag 1 '69
See also
Concanavalins
Endoxan
Methotrexate

IMPALA. See Antelopes

IMPEDANCE (electricity)
Calculating input and output impedances. il Pop Electr 30:69+ Je '69
See also
Electric resistance

IMPERIAL chemical industries, limited
Two old foes may make up. Bsns W p30 Ja 10 '70

IMPERIALE, Tony
Violent man rises in Newark. C. Mangel. por Look 33:62-7 S 9 '69

IMPERIALISM
We honorable imperialists. J. Featherstone. New Repub 160:15-17 Ja 25 '69

IMPLEMENTS, utensils, etc.
See also
Handles
Household appliances
Indians of North America—Implements
Stone implements and weapons

IMPORT and export control. See Foreign trade regulation

IMPORT quotas
Bar to imports: Japanese and European steel producers agree to impose own restrictions. il Time 93:67 Ja 24 '69
Cheaper oil; subcommittee on antitrust and monopoly investigation into import controls. New Repub 161:9 Jl 19 '69
Coming crisis in oil; Battle over bigger imports. il U S News 68:77-80 Ja 12 '70
Dry hole; anti-trust hearings on oil. il Newsweek 74:72B+ Ag 4 '69
Erosion of union support for free trade. B L. Masse. America 120:463 Ap 19 '69
Fueling the debate on oil import quotas; with editorial comment. Bsns W p 19-20, 96 Ag 30 '69
How import quotas raise consumer prices. il Consumer Rep 34:270-4 My '69
If tariffs replace oil import quotas. il Bsns W p 17-18 D 20 '69
Importing woe for the worker; unions reappraising imports. il Bsns W p66-8 Jl 26 '69
Imports and substitutes: are they really threats to your beef market? excerpts from address. ed. by J. A. Rohlf. K. Monfort. Farm J 93:B7 Mr '69
Jousting with oil; Hart hearings. D. Sanford. New Repub 161:17-19 Ag 23 '69
Keep out. New Repub 160:9-10 Mr 15 '69
New protectionism. H. Hazlitt. Nat R 21:485-8+ My 20 '69

Our crazy, costly life with oil quotas. A. T. Demaree. il Fortune 79:104-7+ Je '69
Pressure for quotas may spark trade war; textiles next big battleground. il Bsns W p76-7 Mr 22 '69
Textiles pitch for import quotas; with editorial comment. il Bsns W p78+. 178 O 11 '69
Year oil gets its lumps. il Bsns W p98-9+ My 17 '69

IMPORT tax. See Tariff—United States

IMPORTANCE of being earnest; drama. See Wilde, O.

IMPORTATION of books. See Books—Importation

IMPORTS
Booming economy drains off the surplus. il Bsns W p26+ Ap 5 '69

IMPOSTORS and imposture
Leading the life of Killy; B. Dubrulle, Killy impostor. P. Ryan. il Sports Illus 30:32-3 Ap 28 '69
See also
Fraud
Quacks and quackery

IMPRESARIOS
Photographs
Opera bowl 1970. G. Fitzgerald. Opera N 34:22-3 Ja 10 '70

IMPRESSIONISM (art)
Yankee impressionists: impressive, impressionable. R. Pomeroy. il Art N 67:50-1+ N '68
See also
Painting, French

IMPRISONMENT. See Prisons

IMPROVED products. See Products, Improved

IMPROVISATION (music)
See also
Jazz music

IN all the treasured ways; story. See Delman, D.

IN due time; story. See Amft, M. J.

IN-flight periodicals. See Periodicals for airline passengers

IN-service librarian education. See Librarians—Education in service

IN-service teacher education. See Teachers—Education in service

IN service training of employees. See Employees—Training

IN the bar of a Tokyo hotel; drama. See Williams, T.

IN the land of morning calm, déjà vu; story. See Siegel, J.

IN the matter of J. Robert Oppenheimer; drama. See Kipphardt, H.

IN the reign of peace; story. See Nissenson, H.

IN the wine time; drama. See Bullins, E.

INAUGURATION day. See Inaugurations

INAUGURATIONS
Changing of the guard. il Ebony 24:29-32+ Mr '69
Civil religion; inaugural ceremony. il Newsweek 73:82 F 3 '69
Inauguration. New Yorker 44:27-8 F 1 '69
Inauguration amid religious trappings. W. Willoughby. Chr Today 13:30-1 F 14 '69
Inauguration ceremonies: dividends for dollars. R. Chandler. Chr Today 14:40-1 N 21 '69
Inaugurations 1789. 1969. il Sr Schol 94:2-3 Ja 17 '69
Let us, go forward together. il Newsweek 73:17-18 Ja 27 '69
Meanwhile, back at the inauguration; photographs. G. Gardner. Trans-Action 6:32-3 Mr '69
Never again? il Time 93:12-13 Ja 31 '69
Quiet, please. K. Crawford. Newsweek 73:35 F 3 '69
Rhetoric meets reality. il Life 66:18-31 Ja 31 '69
There was a storm outside and a bit of frost within; excerpts from TR and Will: a friendship that split the Republican party. W. Manners. il Am Heritage 21:24-5+ D '69
Washington after the Revolution; excerpts. J. T. Flexner. il Am Heritage 20:72-9+ Je '69
With lowered voice, enter Mr Nixon. il Newsweek 73:16-21 F 3 '69
See also
Nixon, R. M.—Inaugural address

INBREEDING
Hopi Indians, inbreeding, and albinism. C. M. Woolf and F. C. Dukepoo. bibliog il Science 164:30-7 Ap 4 '69
Polymorphism in an inbreeding population under models involving underdominance. S. K. Jain and K. B. L. Jain. bibliog il Science 166:1294-6 D 5 '69

INCOME Tax—United States—*Continued*
That's dedication? New Repub 160:10 Je 28 '69
Time for lower, fairer taxes is now! M. M. Caplin. Read Digest 95:39-44 S '69
Tough tax choice. Bsns W p38 Je 21 '69
Welfare tax rate; excerpt from Public and private manpower policies, ed. by A. Weber and others. L. J. Hausman. il Trans-Action 6:48-53 Ap '69
What the farm wife should know about income tax. R. Krumme. il Suc Farm 67:90-1 F '69
When you leave the honey jar open, you've got to expect ants. Nat R 21:220 Mr 11 '69
Where tax changes hit hardest. il U S News 67:23-5 Ag 18 '69
Your state income tax: how high. il U S News 66:73-5 Mr 31 '69
Your tax as voted by the House; chart. U S News 67:55 Jl 14 '69
See also
Tax evasion
Tax returns
INCORPORATED farms. See Farm corporations
INCORPORATION
Why doctors and lawyers call themselves Inc; fight for corporate tax status. il Bsns W p80+ Jl 12 '69
INCREASE of population. See Population, Increase of
INCREASED difficulty of concentration; drama. See Havel, V.
INCUBATOR babies. See Infants, Premature
INCUBATORS, Baby. See Infants, Premature
INCUNABULA
Incunabula and the New World. N. López Pellón. il Américas 21:11-17 N '69
See also
Printers marks
INCURABLE diseases. See Diseases, Incurable
INCURABLES
To die alone. L. J. Roose. Ment Hy 53:321-6 Jl '69
INDECENT assault
See also
Child molesters
INDENTURED servants
White servitude in America. L. Bennett, jr. il Ebony 25:31-4+ N '69
INDEPENDENCE, Declaration of. See United States—Declaration of independence
INDEPENDENCE day. See Fourth of July
INDEPENDENT postal system of America
Money in mail. il Newsweek 73:69+ Mr 3 '69
Private mail delivery? The postman rings twice. J. Tebbel. il Sat R 52:50-1 Je 14 '69
INDEPENDENT regulatory commissions
Conservative collar for the watchdogs; new appointments to the regulatory agencies. il Bsns W p47 S 20 '69
Consumers and the regulators. Life 67:34 O 3 '69
Decisions Nixon's watchdogs must make. Bsns W p27-8 Ja 10 '70
Hero among bureaucrats; elimination of some special agencies. Life 66:28 F 7 '69
Regulators, by L. M. Kohlmeier, jr. Review Sat R 53:37-8 Ja 10 '70. D. A. Swankin
Rules are changing; decisions which will affect businessmen. S. M. Aug. il Nations Bsns 57:76-8+ O '69
See also
United States—Federal commissions
INDEPENDENT study
English independent study for high school. N. Felland. Engl J 58:591-3+ Ap '69
Experiment in university self-study. M. Huberman. Sch & Soc 97:431-3 N '69
Independent study programs. R. V. Denby. bibliog Engl J 58:1396-1400+ D '69
Library-college USA; address, April 2, 1969. L. Shores. ALA Bul 63:1547-53 D '69
INDETERMINATE sentence
See also
Probation system
INDEX numbers
Forbes index. See issues of Forbes
INDEXES
Book, the bibliographer and the absence of mind. J. Barzun. Am Scholar 39:138+ Wint '69
See also
Audio-visual aids—Indexes
Science citation index
INDEXING
New indexing standard emphasizes principles. Library J 94:130 Ja 15 '69

INDIA
Wild elephant roundup in India. H. Miller. il Nat Geog 135:372-85 Mr '69
See also
Agriculture—India
Airlines—India
Atomic power—India
Birth control—India
Business education—India
Cooperative associations—India
Economic assistance in India
Elections—India
Food supply—India
Goa
Government ownership—India
Iron mines and mining—India
Khajuraho
Moving picture industry—India
Moving pictures—India
Natural resources—India
Political parties—India
Social science research—India
Space research—India
Udaipur
Unemployment—India
United States—Foreign relations—India

Antiquities
See also
Harappa culture

Civilization
Call of India. F. V. Grunfeld. il Horizon 11: 4-10 Sum '69
Importing India's educational riches; establishment of Educational resources center, New Delhi. W. Morehouse. il Am Ed 5:14-19 My '69

Cultural relations
Importing India's educational riches; establishment of Educational resources center, New Delhi. W. Morehouse. il Am Ed 5: 14-19 My '69

Description and travel
In India a visitor is caught up in history. il Sunset 143:41-2+ N '69
India for me. G. Trotta. il Harp Baz 102:40+ Jl '69
India; letters to Alwin Nikolais at the Henry st. playhouse. M. Louis. il Dance Mag 43: 44-5+ My; 83-4 Je '69

Economic conditions
Can India make it? R. R. R. Brooks. il Sat R 52:12-16 Ag 9 '69
India: a giant country deep in trouble. J. N. Wallace. il U S News 66:77-80 F 17 '69
Report from Mrs Gandhi's India. E. Behr. il Newsweek 74:55-7 D 15 '69
See also
Agriculture—India

Foreign relations
Nepal
Can a ministate find true happiness in a world dominated by protagonist powers? The Nepal case. L. E. Rose and R. Dial. bibliog f Ann Am Acad 386:89-101 N '69

Russia
India and the Soviet Union. D. Rothermund. bibliog f Ann Am Acad 386:78-88 N '69

United States
Second round of bilateral talks with India held at Washington; joint statement, October 17, 1969. Dept State Bul 61:403 N 10 '69

Hindu-Muslim relations
Fires of hatred. il Time 93:26+ F 21 '69
Hindu-Muslim conflict. Chr Today 14:51 O 24 '69
Sad centennial; religious riots in Ahmedabad. il Time 94:37 O 3 '69
Violence in nonviolent India. America 121: O 18 '69

History
In the Mahatma's centenary year, India finds Gandhi inspiring and irrelevant. J. Lelyveld. il N Y Times Mag p27-9+ My 25 '69
Yogi and the commissar. A. Koestler. il N Y Times Mag p27-9+ O 5 '69; Discussion. p22+ N 2 '69
See also
Kushan empire

British occupation, 1765-1947
Trial of Warren Hastings. A. Nevins. il Horizon 11:110-15 Wint '69

INDIA—*Continued*

Languages

India's continuing language problem. P. G. Altbach. Sch & Soc 97:107-8 F '69

Native races

Behind the Naga rebellion. P. C. Jain. Nat R 21:326 D 30 '69

Native states

Reporter at large. V. Mehta. il New Yorker 45:26-32+ Jl 19; 40-8+ Jl 26 '69

Politics and government

Another round for the lady. Time 94:31 S 5 '69
Divided they stand. A. Campbell. New Republic 160:15-19 Mr 22 '69
India: gunning for Mrs Gandhi. il Newsweek 74:47 Jl 28 '69
India: the lady v. the syndicate. il Time 94:29 Ag 29 '69
Infighter; Congress party bosses routed. Newsweek 74:34 S 1 '69
More troubles for India. il Time 94:28-9 Jl 25 '69
Radicalism on the cheap. Time 95:30+ Ja 19 '70
Report from Mrs Gandhi's India. E. Behr. il Newsweek 74:55-7 D 15 '69
Return of the enemies; victories in by-elections to India's House of commons. il Time 93:35 My 23 '69
Schismatic octopus; dominant Congress party. il Time 94:41 N 14 '69
See also
Communist party (India)
Elections—India
India—Hindu-Muslim relations
India—Native states
Political parties—India

Population
See also
Birth control—India

Religious institutions and affairs

Jai Baba! New Yorker 45:28-31 Je 21 '69
World around us. Chr Cent 86:688+. 1147-8 My 14, S 3 '69

Riots

Sad centennial; religious riots in Ahmedabad. il Time 94:37 O 3 '69
Violence in nonviolent India. America 121:315 O 18 '69

Social conditions

India that Nixon will not see. J. N. Wallace. il U S News 67:35-9 Ag 4 '69
INDIA ink. See Ink
INDIAN (East Indian) engineers. See Engineers, Indian (East Indian)
INDIAN (East Indian) rugs. See Rugs and carpets, Oriental
INDIAN affairs, Bureau of. See United States—Indian affairs, Bureau of
INDIAN art (East Indian) See Art, Indian (East Indian)
INDIAN arts and crafts. See Indians of North America—Industries
INDIAN-Chinese border dispute, 1957-. See Sino-Indian border dispute, 1957-
INDIAN cookery (East Indian) See Cookery, Indian (East Indian)
INDIAN dancing (East Indian) See Dancing, Indian (East Indian)
INDIAN mounds. See Mounds and mound builders
INDIAN OCEAN
See also
Christmas Island
INDIAN poke. See Hellebore
INDIAN reservations. See Indians of North America—Reservations
INDIAN rhinoceros. See Rhinoceros
INDIAN schools. See Indians of North America—Education
INDIAN science congress
Chaotic congress. S. K. Ghaswala. Sci N 95:270 Mr 15 '69
INDIAN symbols. See Symbolism
INDIAN weaving. See Weaving
INDIANA
See also
Education—Indiana
Festivals—Indiana
Fishing—Indiana
Hunting—Indiana
Music festivals—Indiana

Politics and government

Black spokesman, or Republican pawn; Indiana's first black legislator. R. D. Snell. bibliog Negro Hist Bul 32:6-10 N '69

INDIANA Pacers (basketball team) See Basketball teams
INDIANA. University, Bloomington
Close-up of student-soldiers; case study at one big university. il U S News 67:52-4 N 3 '69

Graduate library school

Library services and collections course. J. A. McCrossan. ALA Bul 63:1245-6 O '69

Institute for sex research

All they talk about is sex, sex, sex; Institute for sex research. T. Buckley. il N Y Times Mag p28-9+ Ap 20 '69

Libraries

Indiana's three-in-one. R. A. Miller. il Library J 94:4399 D 1 '69
INDIANAPOLIS

Description

Place of the month. il Holiday 45:80-1 My '69

Education

This English is something else; oral-aural-visual program for teaching language arts. S. L. Sheeley. il Sr Schol 94:Schol Teach 14-16 Ja 17 '69

Politics and government

Hoosier hotshot; creation of regional government. il Newsweek 75:32-3 Ja 5 '70
INDIANAPOLIS automobile races. See Automobile racing
INDIANAPOLIS 500. See Automobile racing
INDIANS

Art
See also
Indians of North America—Art
Petroglyphs

Education
See also
Indians of North America—Education

Poetry
Translations into English
Reality at white heat; with translations of American Indian poems. J. Rothenberg. Nation 209:444-6 O 27 '69

Weaving
See Weaving
INDIANS; drama. See Kopit, A.
INDIANS, Treatment of
Indians and others. Nation 209:682 D 22 '69
Sad lot of the Sioux. S. Alexander. Life 66:14E F 7 '69
INDIANS in art
Gerard Curtis Delano, painter of the Navajo Indians. J. Jellico. il Am Artist 33:54-9+ D '69
INDIANS of Bolivia. See Indians of South America—Bolivia
INDIANS of Canada. See Indians of North America—Canada
INDIANS of Central America
See also
Mayas

Antiquities

Rise of Mesoamerican civilization. F. L. Phelps. il Américas 21:46-8 N '69
See also
Mayas
Sculpture, Pre-Columbian

Medicine

Mini-hospital of the jungle; Choco Indians' mini-version of white man's hospital. il Todays Health 47:17-18 Ap '69

Music

Moctezuma's musicians. C. C. Lieberman. il Américas 21:23-8 F '69
INDIANS of Mexico
Olmec. M. W. Stirling. il Américas 21:2-10 N '69
See also
Mayas
Yaqui Indians

Antiquities

Settlement, farming technology, and environment in the Nochixtlan Valley. R. Spores. bibliog il Science 166:557-69 O 31 '69
See also
Mayas
Sculpture, Pre-Columbian

Art

Olmec cave paintings; discovery from Guerrero, Mexico. D. C. Grove. bibliog il Science 164:421-3 Ap 25 '69

INDIANS of North America
Almost ancestors, the first Californians, by
 T. Kroeber and R. F. Heizer. Review
  Américas 21:41-3 F '69. F. L. Phelps
Red power. W. E. Washburn. Am West 6:
 52-3 Ja '69
Will the Indians get Whitey? J. Greenway.
 il Nat R 21:223-8+ Mr 11 '69
   See also
Apache Indians
Cherokee Indians
Choctaw Indians
Dakota Indians
Eskimos
Havasupai Indians
Hopi Indians
Iroquois Indians
Nationalism—Indians of North America
Navaho Indians
Paleo-Indians
Pueblo Indians
Seminole Indians
Seneca Indians

Antiquities
Indian relics. C. Miles. See issues of Hobbies
   See also
Mounds and mound builders

Minnesota
Archeological evidence for utilization of wild
 rice. E. Johnson. bibliog il Science 163:276-7
 Ja 17 '69

New Mexico
Students underground. J. Marks. il Mlle 70:
 150-1+ D '69

South Dakota
Who put the handprints on Prayer rock?
 R. C. Hildreth. il Sci Digest 65:54-6 Je '69

Southwestern states
Ethnographic analogy and archeological inter-
 pretation. K. M. Anderson. bibliog il Sci-
 ence 163:133-8 Ja 10 '69
Southwestern archeological center. O. F.
 Oldendorph. il Nat Parks 43:4-7 F '69

Utah
Dusty secrets of Hogup cave. N. Wadsworth.
 il Sci Digest 65:34-8 Mr '69

Art
Red painting. J. C. Ewers. Am West 6:54+
 Ja '69
Rediscovery: an Indian sketchbook: Zo-tom's
 history of Indian prison life. il Art in Am
 57:82-7 S '69
Some Indian arts and crafts, papa and mama
 dolls. C. Miles. il Hobbies 74:142-4 O '69

Bibliography
Will the Indians get Whitey? J. Greenway.
 il Nat R 21:223-8+ Mr 11 '69

Civil rights
Apache doctor who sparked a new era for
 Indians; C. Montezuma (Wassaja) O.
 Arnold. il Todays Health 47:30-3+ O '69
Authors & editors; V. Deloria's crusade. D.
 N. Mount. Pub W 196:7-9 D 1 '69
Custer died for your sins, by V. Deloria, jr.
 Review
  Newsweek il 74:121-2 O 13 '69. R. A.
   Gross
  Sat R 52:39-41+ O 4 '69. N. O. Lurie
  Time il 94:102 O 10 '69
War between the redskins and the feds. V.
 Deloria, jr. il N Y Times Mag p47+ D 7 '69

Culture
Rise and fall of the wild West Indian; excerpts from Man's rise to civilization as
 shown by the Indians of North America
 from primeval times to the coming of the
 industrial state. P. Farb. il Read Digest
 94:212-14+ Je '69

Drama
Dinnetah. B. Winther. Plays 28:41-50 My '69

Economic conditions
Lagoon of excrement; Pine Ridge, an im-
 poverished reservation in South Dakota. R.
 G. Sherrill. Nation 209:500-3 N 10 '69
Model city for Indian lands; Four Corners
 economic development region. il U S News
 66:96-9 Je 23 '69
   See also
Indians of North America—Employment

Education
50,000,000 acre ghetto. R. Tunley. Seventeen
 28:122-3+ O '69
Indian schools. D. Henninger and N. Esposito. New Repub 160:18-21 F 15 '69; Discussion 160:31-3 Mr 22 '69

Pride of the reservation; Rough Rock demonstration school is working model for
 Indian community college. il Time 93:67 Ap
 11 '69
Tell it like it is. H. D. Overby. Todays Ed 58:
 55-6 N '69

Employment
American Indians come nearer mainstream.
 il Bsns W p 118-20 Je 7 '69
American Indians industrialize to combat
 poverty; excerpt from Manpower and in-
 dustrial development programs for Indian
 Americans. A. L. Sorkin. bibliog f il Mo
 Labor R 92:19-25 Mr '69

Food
Another helping of beetles, please. il Sci
 Digest 66:32-3 N '69
Archeological evidence for utilization of wild
 rice. E. Johnson. bibliog il Science 163:
 276-7 Ja 17 '69
Piki bread to see and taste. il Sunset 143:47
 Jl '69

Games
Guessing games of the original Americans.
 C. Miles. il Hobbies 74:110-11 Ag '69
Indian & Eskimo games. C. Miles. il Hobbies
 74:110-11+ Jl '69 (to be cont)
Sports & recreation of the original Americans.
 C. Miles. il Hobbies 74:142-4 S '69

Gifts
   See also
Potlatch

Government relations
American Indians: strangers in their own
 homeland? with biographical sketches. il
 Sr Schol 94:13-15+ Mr 7 '69
Apache doctor who sparked a new era for
 Indians; C. Montezuma (Wassaja) O.
 Arnold. il Todays Health 47:30-3+ O '69
Brothers of Passamaquodia: the royal screw-
 ing of the Passamaquodia. D. Welsh. Ramp
 Mag 7:98-103 Ja 25 '69
New flag over Alcatraz. il Time 95:20 Ja 5
 '70
Revolt on the reservation; OEO chief ban-
 ished from Navajo reservation. il Time 93:
 80 Mr 14 '69
Tribal rock; group of Indians claim Alcatraz.
 il Newsweek 74:52 D 8 '69
War between the redskins and the feds. V.
 Deloria, jr. il N Y Times Mag p47+ D 7
 '69
   See also
Indians of North America—Education
Indians of North America—Treaties

History
American Indians: strangers in their own
 homeland? with biographical sketches. il
 Sr Schol 94:13-15+ Mr 7 '69

Implements
Early American mills. C. Miles. il Hobbies
 74:110-11+ Mr; 110-12 Ap; 110-12 My '69
Ethnographic analogy and archeological inter-
 pretation. K. M. Anderson. bibliog il Science
 163:133-8 Ja 10 '69
Indian tools. C. Miles. il Hobbies 74:110-12
 Je '69
Indian tools and miscellaneous. C. Miles. il
 Hobbies 74:142-3 N; 142-3 D '69
Miscellaneous artifacts. C. Miles. il Hobbies
 73:110-11+ F '69

Industries
Adult western; Indian signs on the decorat-
 ing horizon. il McCalls 96:74-7 Je '69
Indian country is a frontier again. P.
 Mooney. il Nations Bsns 57:76-8 S '69

Legal status, laws, etc.
   See Indians of North America—Government relations

Libraries
Anto wicharti; dawn of a new day for In-
 dians in Region VI, the Great Plains. W.
 D. Cunningham. il Library J 94:4496-9 D
 15 '69
Statewide outreach: desert booktrails to the
 Indians; New Mexico state library. W. H.
 Farrington. il Wilson Lib Bul 43:864-71 My
 '69

Missions
Indian reservations about the church. J. Huff-
 man. Chr Today 13:54-5 S 12 '69
   See also
Jesuits—Missions

Pottery
Arikara Indian ceramics. L. A. Brown. il
 Ceram Mo 17:16-19 Mr '69
Native pottery of the Southwest. G. L.
 Downing. il Natur Hist 78:34-9 Je '69

INDIANS of North America—*Continued*

Religion and mythology

Ghost dance. J. Greenway. il Am West 6:42-7 Jl '69

Ghost dance and cargo cult. P. Farb. il Horizon 11:58-65 Spr '69

Happening at Oglala; Jesuit helps Sioux regain pride in their heritage. D. O. Collins. il Am West 6:15-19 Mr '69

See also

Native American church

Relocation

See Indians of North America—Government relations

Reservations

American Indians come nearer mainstream. il Bsns W p 118-20 Je 7 '69

American Indians industrialize to combat poverty; excerpt from Manpower and industrial development programs for Indian Americans. A. L. Sorkin. bibliog f il Mo Labor R 92:19-25 Mr '69

Brothers of Passamaquodia: the royal screwing of the Passamaquodia. D. Welsh. Ramp Mag 7:98-103 Ja 25 '69

50,000,000 acre ghetto. R. Tunley. Seventeen 28:122-3+ O '69

Happiest fishing ground; Fort Apache Indian reservation. R. Cantwell. il Sports Illus 31: 37-41 Ag 4 '69

Indian country is a frontier again. P. Mooney. il Nations Bsns 57:76-8 S '69

Social conditions

Florida's emerging Seminoles. L. Capron. il Nat Geog 136:716-34 N '69

Lagoon of excrement; Pine Ridge, an impoverished reservation in South Dakota. R. G. Sherrill. Nation 209:500-3 N 10 '69

Renaissance and repression: the Oklahoma Cherokee. A. L. Wahrhaftig and R. K. Thomas. il Trans-Action 6:42-8 F '69

See also

Indians of North America—Reservations

Social life and customs

See also

Potlatch

Treaties

Cornplanter, can you swim? Kinzua Dam flooding Senecas' ancestral lands for Allegheny reservoir. A. M. Josephy, jr. il Am Heritage 20:4-9+ D '68

Treatment

See Indians, Treatment of

Wars

Land of the frozen fires; scene of Modoc war, 1872-1873. P. J. Easterla. il Nat Parks 43: 18-21 D '69

See also

Seminole war. 2d, 1835-1842

Sullivan's Indian campaign, 1779

Canada

Public library services for Canadian Indians. J. A. McCrossan. ALA Bul 63:1243-4 O '69

See also

Kwakiutl Indians

INDIANS of North America in art. See Indians in art

INDIANS of Peru. See Indians of South America—Peru

INDIANS of South America

See also

Incas

Acculturation

As they sow; Amazon Indian suffers environmental depredations. C. Weathersbee. il Sci N 95:314-15 Mr 29 '69

Antiquities

Peru

Peru: the future of the Inca empire. C. Cutler. il Art in Am 57:80-2 My '69

Their relics remain in the Americas; excerpt from Flights into yesterday. L. Deuel. il Sat R 53:105-8 Ja 10 '70

Astronomy

See Astronomy, Indian

Calendar

Woven calendars of Peru; excerpt from Life, land, and water in ancient Peru. P. Kosok. il Sat R 53:109 Ja 10 '70

Costume and adornment

Tchikrin; bodily adornment expressing symbolic meaning. T. S. Turner. il Natur Hist 78:50-9+ O '69

Social conditions

Indian's birthright. T. D. Bernard, jr. il Américas 21:2-8 Jl '69

Bolivia

Bolivia; view from the Altiplano; ed. by G. de Zéndegui. il Américas 21:2-9 F '69

Cloth of the Quechuas. G. Goodell. il Natur Hist 78:48-55+ D '69

Brazil

Tchikrin: bodily adornment expressing symbolic meaning. T. S. Turner. il Natur Hist 78:50-9+ O '69

Colombia

As they sow; Amazon Indian suffers environmental depredations. C. Weathersbee. il Sci N 95:314-15 Mr 29 '69

Out of the jungle mists; lost Yuri tribe? il Sci N 96:175-6 S 6 '69

Peru

Reports: Peru. W. S. Just. Atlan 223:12+ My '69

See also

Incas

Surinam

Contact with the stone age. I. L. Schoen. il Natur Hist 78:10-18+ Ja '69

Into the stone age; Akuri tribe. il Newsweek 73:97 F 17 '69

INDIC languages

See also

Dravidian languages

INDICATORS for gas and oil engines

Dial indicating. J. Thawley. il Hot Rod 22:68-9 F '69

INDIGO buntings

Beacon for buntings; traveling orders from biological clock. il Time 94:94 N 14 '69

INDIVIDUAL and society

Epistle to the Babylonians, by C. L. Fontenay. Review

Sat R 52:58-9 Je 21 '69. M. R. Konvitz

Prognosis for crackdown: the wheel of panic. T. J. Lowi. Nation 208:624-8 My 19 '69

What the individual can do. il Time 93:33+ Ja 24 '69

INDIVIDUAL and state

Communication; lack of communication between the people and their government. D. Lawrence. U S News 67:96 N 24 '69

Ethics and social struggle. B. Dunham. Nation 209:726-9 D 29 '69

Hidden costs of opportunity. E. Z. Friedenberg. Atlan 223:84-90 F '69

Out of touch in Washington; excerpt from High on foggy bottom: an outsider's inside view of the government. C. Frankel. Sat R 52:21-3+ N 1 '69; Same abr. with title Making democracy work. Cur 113:27-32 D '69

What the individual can do. il Time 93:33+ Ja 24 '69

INDIVIDUAL differences

See also

Sex differences

INDIVIDUAL instruction

Classrooms come to the conference: National laboratory for the advancement of education. S. Holzman. Sr Schol 94:Schol Teach 6 Ja 17 '69

Computer and individualized instruction. W. W. Cooley and R. Glaser. bibliog il Science 166:574-82 O 31 '69

Individuals, front and center; teaching innovations presented at the National laboratory for the advancement of education. Washington, D.C. W. Leavitt. il Am Ed 5:4-6 F '69

One-to-one ratio; IPI schools. S. Holzman. il Sr Schol 94.Schol Teach 17 Mr 7 '69

See also

Special classes and special schools

INDIVIDUAL liberty. See Liberty

INDIVIDUALISM

Epistle to the Babylonians, by C. L. Fontenay. Review

Sat R 52:58-9 Je 21 '69. M. R. Konvitz

Irrepressible world revolt; excerpt from The irresponsible style in American politics. L. Benson; reply with rejoinder. M. Marien. New Repub 160:31-3 F 22 '69

See also

Conformity

INDIVIDUALITY
Sense of style. G. Frazier. Esquire 71:58+
Je '69
See also
Personality
INDIVIDUALIZED instruction. See Individual
instruction
INDIVIDUALLY prescribed instruction. See In-
dividual instruction
INDOCTRINATION
See also
Propaganda in the schools
INDOLE ethanol. See Tryptophol
INDOLEBUTYRIC acid
Corchorus pascuorum: transmission of chemi-
cally induced fruit formation with environ-
mental change. A. S. Islam and R. Mughal.
bibliog il Science 164:315-16 Ap 18 '69
INDONESIA
An act free of choice; annexation of West
Irian. il Time 94:36 Ag 22 '69
Indonesia's uncertain future. B. R. O. Ander-
son. bibliog f Cur Hist 57:355-60 D '69
See also
Bali
Economic assistance in Indonesia
Investments, Foreign (in Indonesia)
Petroleum—Indonesia
Petroleum industry and trade—Indonesia
Tourist trade—Indonesia

Economic conditions
Indonesia still struggling to strike it rich.
il U S News 67:52-4 D 29 '69
operating on a giant. il Time 93:38 Je 27 '69
Taking a Communist economy apart. S. G.
Slappey. il Nations Bsns 57:69-73 O '69

Industries
See also
Indonesia—Economic conditions

Politics and government
Army has it all. il Time 95:20-1 Ja 12 '70
Bottleneck. E. G. Martin. il Newsweek 73:
52-3 Je 23 '69
Indonesia: another Communist disaster. A.
C. Brackman. bibliog f Cur Hist 56:156-
60+ Mr '69
Indonesia: the greatest prize. A. Campbell.
New Repub 160:17-20 Ap 19 '69
Reporter at large (cont) R. Shaplen. New
Yorker 45:42-6+ My 24; 39-44+ My 31 '69

Religious institutions and affairs
Indonesian phenomenon; interdenominational
evangelistic crusade. P. Purukan. Chr Today
14:40 N 21 '69
INDOOR games. See Games
INDOOR gardening. See Greenhouses; House
plants
INDOOR plants. See House plants
INDOOR surfing. See Surf riding
INDOOR track. See Track athletics
INDUCTANCE
Solid-state inductor. D. L. Heiserman. il
Electr World 82:37+ S '69
INDUCTION (army) See United States—Army
—Recruiting and enlistment
INDUCTION motors. See Electric motors, In-
duction
INDUCTIVE reactance. See Inductance
INDULGENCES
See also
Absolution
INDUSTRIAL arbitration. See Arbitration, In-
dustrial
INDUSTRIAL areas foundation

Community service organization
Profiles; attempt of C. Chavez to interest
the C.S.O. in organizing farm labor. P.
Matthiessen. New Yorker 45:42-4+ Je 21;
43-4+ Je 28 '69
INDUSTRIAL arts
See also
Arts and crafts

Study and teaching
New switch. L. Strother. Todays Ed 58:50 S
'69
INDUSTRIAL arts education
Contemporary industrial-arts programs. A.
J. Dudley. Ed Digest 34:41-3 Ja '69
INDUSTRIAL buildings
Landlocked ship; maintenance depot. il
Arch Forum 130:64-7 My '69
Small industrial buildings; building types
study. S. Howard. Arch Rec 145:155 F '69
Upgrading industrial architecture with active
client support: Westinghouse plant, Pensa-
cola, Fla. il Arch Rec 146:126-30 N '69
See also
Commercial buildings

Designs and plans
Buildings for computers. il Arch Forum 131:
50-5 S '69
Walter Gropius, 1883-1969; Fagus shoe last
factory and administration building in Al-
feld-an-der-Leine. il Arch Forum 131:34-9
S '69
INDUSTRIAL conferences. See Business confer-
ences
INDUSTRIAL cooperation
Unexpected payoff of Project Apollo. T. Alex-
ander. il Fortune 80:114-17+ Jl '69
INDUSTRIAL decentralization. See Industry—
Decentralization
INDUSTRIAL design. See Design, Industrial
INDUSTRIAL designers. See Designers
INDUSTRIAL development programs
Industry tries to stir a Brazilian backwater.
il Bsns W p 146-8+ Mr 29 '69
INDUSTRIAL diamonds. See Diamonds, Indus-
trial
INDUSTRIAL districts
Industrial park: what it is, and isn't. H.
Bostwick, jr. il Nations Bsns 57:72-5 S '69
Parking place for industry. il Bsns W p 120+
S 20 '69
INDUSTRIAL diversification. See Diversifica-
tion in industry
INDUSTRIAL education
See also
Employees—Training
Technical education
Trade schools
Vocational education
INDUSTRIAL efficiency. See Efficiency, Indus-
trial
INDUSTRIAL electronics. See Electronics—In-
dustrial applications
INDUSTRIAL employment. See Employment
INDUSTRIAL equipment leasing. See Ma-
chinery—Leasing and renting
INDUSTRIAL espionage. See Spies, Industrial
INDUSTRIAL exhibitions. See Exhibitions
INDUSTRIAL expansion
Crisis of the $100-million companies. T. J.
Murray. Duns R 94:48-50+ D '69
INDUSTRIAL forecasting. See Business fore-
casting
INDUSTRIAL information service. See Infor-
mation services
INDUSTRIAL insurance. See Insurance, Indus-
trial
INDUSTRIAL laws and legislation
See also
Labor laws and legislation
INDUSTRIAL location. See Location in busi-
ness and industry
INDUSTRIAL management and organization
Collision at the interface. G. J. Berkwitt. il
Duns R 93:64-7 Mr '69
See also
American management association
Business management and organization
Controllership
Executives—Training
Industrial relations
Materials control
INDUSTRIAL migration. See Migrant labor
INDUSTRIAL noise. See Noise
INDUSTRIAL organization. See Industrial
management and organization
INDUSTRIAL painting. See Painting, Indus-
trial and practical
INDUSTRIAL parks. See Industrial districts
INDUSTRIAL pensions. See Pensions, Indus-
trial
INDUSTRIAL photography. See Photography
in industry
INDUSTRIAL production. See Production
INDUSTRIAL purchasing. See Purchasing, In-
dustrial
INDUSTRIAL recreation
Playing on the job; company-sponsored
sporting events. il Newsweek 73:100 Mr 17
'69
INDUSTRIAL relations
Descartes, guilt and shame. E. M. von Kueh-
nelt-Leddihn. Nat R 21:1066 O 21 '69
Developments in industrial relations. See
issues of Monthly labor review
New toughness at the bargaining tables. il
U S News 67:70-2 D 8 '69
Nixon's hands off policy; effect on unions,
companies. il U S News 67:57-8 D 1 '69
Outlook: a year of turmoil in labor. il U S
News 68:49-50 Ja 5 '70
La participation; the new language of la-
bour-management relations; summary. J.
de Givry. il UNESCO Courier 22:13-19 Jl
'69

INDUSTRIAL relations—*Continued*
People no longer machines in labour relations; excerpts. J. de Givry. il UNESCO Courier 22:20-3 Jl '69
Significant decisions in labor cases. See issues of Monthly labor review
Thou shalt nots for minority group rapport. il Nations Bsns 57:87 Je '69
Untouchable conglomerate; labor-union monopolies. D. Lawrence. U S News 66:108 Ap 14 '69
Why union leaders look for troubles in the '70s. il U S News 67:85-6 O 20 '69
Window on the hard-core world; excerpts from address. T. V. Purcell and R. Webster. Harvard Bsns R 47:118-29 Jl '69
See also
Business management and organization—Employee participation
Collective bargaining
Communication in management
Featherbedding (industrial relations)
Grievance procedures
Labor disputes
Layoff systems
Strikes
Trade agreements
United States—Labor policy
United States—National labor relations board

Great Britain
Industrial relations reform in Great Britain. N. Robertson and K. I. Sams. bibliog f Mo Labor R 92:35-40 Ja '69
INDUSTRIAL relations research association
IRRA conference papers; annual meeting: excerpts. Mo Labor R 92:47-57 Mr; 92:53-62 Ap '69
INDUSTRIAL research
Case of the straying scientist. J. S. Mendell. il Harvard Bsns R 47:4-6+ Jl '69
Inflation ups the R&D ante; McGraw-Hill survey. il Bsns W p78+ My 17 '69
See also
Little, Arthur D, incorporated
Products, New
Technology transfer

Great Britain
Britain: new emphasis on industrial research. D. S. Greenberg. Science 166:485 O 24 '69
Industrial innovation: how England sleeps. D. S. Greenberg. Science 164:54 Ap 4 '69
INDUSTRIAL revolution
Joys of industrialization. C. Fitzgibbon. il Nat R 21:429-31+ My 6 '69
INDUSTRIAL robots. See Automatons
INDUSTRIAL safety
Industrial safety: the toll of neglect. il Time 93:76-7 F 7 '69
Violence of omission. R. Nader. Nation 208:166-8 F 10 '69

Laws and regulations
Laws can't change attitudes. Nations Bsns 57:99-101 Ap '69
Nixon's call for job-safety rules. U S News 67:63 Ag 18 '69
Safety bill loses some of its bite; proposed occupational health & safety act of 1969. Bsns W p23-4 Ag 9 '69
INDUSTRIAL schools. See Trade schools
INDUSTRIAL secrets. See Trade secrets
INDUSTRIAL security measures. See Industry—Security measures
INDUSTRIAL spies. See Spies, Industrial
INDUSTRIAL statistics
See also
Input-output analysis
Unemployment—Statistics
INDUSTRIAL technicians. See Technicians in industry
INDUSTRIAL testing. See Testing
INDUSTRIAL trusts. See Trusts, Industrial
INDUSTRIAL union department. See American federation of labor and Congress of industrial organizations—Industrial union department
INDUSTRIAL waste disposal. See Trade waste disposal
INDUSTRIAL workers of the world
Radical goad. M. Dubofsky. Nation 209:218-21 S 8 '69
Rebels of the woods; the I.W.W. in the Pacific Northwest, by R. L. Tyler. Review
Am West 6:49 Jl '69. J. L. Shover
We shall not be moved, by M. Dubofsky. Review
Commonweal 91:412-14 Ja 9 '70. S. Lens

INDUSTRIALIZATION
Algeria hunts for new investors; attempt to lure U.S. capital il Bsns W p52+ Ap 12 '69
U.S.S.R. resources for heavy industry. C. D. Harris. bibliog il Focus 19:1-6 F '69
See also
Economic development
Underdeveloped areas
INDUSTRIES, Rural. See Rural industries
INDUSTRIES, Seasonal. See Seasonal industries
INDUSTRIES, Service. See Service industries
INDUSTRY
Changes of change: emerging industries; address, February 17, 1969. C. A. Anderson. Vital Speeches 35:360-3 Ap 1 '69
See also
Business enterprises, New
Cities and towns—Industries
Inventions

Decentralization
Employer manpower policies in the San Francisco Bay area; excerpt from Changing employer policies in a large urban labor market. M. Thal-Larsen. Mo Labor R 92:56-7 Mr '69

History
See also
Industrial revolution

Location
See Location in business and industry

Security measures
If strife hits the plants; NAM seminars. Bsns W p 137-8 Je 28 '69
When a secret is better than a patent. V. Block. il Pop Mech 132:110-12+ N '69
INDUSTRY, Nationalization of. See Government ownership
INDUSTRY and art. See Art and industry
INDUSTRY and education. See Business and education
INDUSTRY and state
Big brother as a holding company. D. Horowitz and R. Erlich. il Ramp Mag 7:44-52 N 30 '68
Biggest briefing yet; business leaders meet under White House auspices. Newsweek 74:74+ N 24 '69
Businessman's balance sheet on Nixon. il Bsns W p21-2 Ag 2 '69
But what is on the other side of the valley? businessmen and top government officials meeting, Washington. il Newsweek 74:71-2 D 1 '69
Challenge of multinational business. R. Lubar. Fortune 80:73-4 Ag 15 '69
Changes businessmen want. il U S News 66:58-61 Mr 3 '69
Corporate ideal in the liberal state, 1900-1918, by J. Weinstein. Review
Ramp Mag 8:38-40 D '69. M. Rothbard
Corporation in American politics, by E. M. Epstein. Review
Trans-Action 7:54-6 D '69. R. A. Bauer
Crucial business issues facing Congress. R. T. Gray. il Nations Bsns 57:32-7 D '69
Difficult years; next four years. L. L. L. Golden. Sat R 52:63 F 8 '69
Government, business, and the balance of payments; address, March 26, 1969. J. J. Powers, jr. Vital Speeches 35:430-4 My 1 '69
Is the administration crying wolf on controls? il Bsns W p 102+ Jl 12 '69
Laws can't change attitudes. Nations Bsns 57:99-101 Ap '69
Legal limits of competition; excerpts from Managerial analysis in marketing. J. R. Grabner, jr. bibliog Harvard Bsns R 47:4-6+ N '69
Let's take the politics out of consumerism. A. C. Fatt. il Nations Bsns 57:82-4+ Ja '69
Litton industries; proving poverty pays. D. Horowitz and R. Erlich. il Ramp Mag 7:40-9 D 14 '68
Memo from the editor. J. Wooldridge. il Nations Bsns 57:7-8 Jl '69
New realities of corporate power; interview, ed. by G. R. Rosen. A. A. Berle. il Duns R 92:43-5+ D '68
News-lines. See issues of U S news & World report
Nixon aides go to labor's summit. il Bsns W p38-9 Ap 19 '69
Nixon means to keep the lid on; Washington meeting of businessmen. il Bsns W p25-6 N 29 '69
Nixon's deconglomerater. Newsweek 73:69-70 Mr 24 '69
Nixon's prime goals. T. Trussell. Nations Bsns 57:7-8 Ap '69

INDUSTRY and state—*Continued*
President Nixon, a business judgment; with comments by business leaders. G. R. Rosen. Duns R 94:23-5 Ag '69
Rules are changing; decisions which will affect businessmen. S. M. Aug. il Nations Bsns 57:76-8+ O '69
Tough friend in the White House. il Time 93: 85-6 Mr 21 '69
Unexpected payoff of Project Apollo. T. Alexander. il Fortune 80:114-17+ Jl '69
Washington desk. G. R. Rosen. See issues of Dun's review
What business wants from President Nixon; with editorial comment. A. T. Demaree. il Fortune 79:71, 84-7+ F '69
What do you people want? transfer of big companies to black control. R. F. America, jr. il Harvard Bsns R 47:103-12 Mr '69
What is the military-industrial complex? Time 93:23 Ap 11 '69
Who will plan the future? D. Wolfle. Science 166:47 O 3 '69
Why is the building industry like the rebellious students? W. F. Wagner, jr. Arch Rec 146:9-10 O '69
See also
Contracts, Government
Free enterprise
Government ownership
Insurance companies—Regulation
Public utilities
Television laws and regulations
United States—Federal trade commission
United States—Interstate commerce commission
United States—Labor, Department of

Germany
Social and economic policies of German big business, 1918-1929. G. D. Feldman. bibliog f Am Hist R 75:47-55 O '69

Latin America
Threatening weather in South America. J. Cameron. il Fortune 80:98-101+ O '69
INDUSTRY and the arts. See The arts and industry
INDUSTRY wide collective bargaining. See Collective bargaining, Industry wide
INERTIA, Moments of. See Moments of inertia
INERTIA welders. See Welders
INERTIAL guidance systems
Boeing agrees to inertial navaid change. Aviation W 91:27 Jl 14 '69
Carousel 4 certificated for 707. Aviation W 90:29 Je 30 '69
Honeywell to test laser gyro unit. P. J. Klass. il Aviation W 91:71+ O 6 '69
Litton pushes navy inertial system; CAINS system. B. Miller. il Aviation W 90:91+ Je 16 '69
United planning use of carousel on Hawaii jets. Aviation W 91:43 S 15 '69
INERTIAL navigation systems
New navigator package for USAF studied. Aviation W 90:72+ Mr 17 '69
INFALLIBILITY, Papal. See Popes—Infallibility
INFANCY of animals. See Animals, Infancy of
INFANT baptism. See Baptism
INFANT feeding. See Infants—Nutrition
INFANT mortality
Death of all children; a footnote to the A.B.M. controversy. E. J. Sternglass. Esquire 72:1a-1d S '69; Excerpts. Cur 110:12-15 S '69
Ernest J. Sternglass: controversial prophet of doom. P. M. Boffey. Science 166:195-200 O 10 '69
Fetal infant mortality and the environment. A. R. Tamplin. E. J. Sternglass. il Bul Atom Sci 25:23-34 D '69
Infant mortality and nuclear tests. E. J. Sternglass. il Bul Atom Sci 25:18-20 Ap '69; Discussion. 25:27 Je; 26-32 O '69
Why babies die. il Time 93:81 My 9 '69
See also
Mortality
INFANT psychology. See Child study
INFANTILE autism. See Autism
INFANTS
Portrait in silverpoint of a grandchild. B. Plagemann. McCalls 96:66+ Ag '69
See also
Adoption
Fetus

Care and hygiene
First six weeks with baby. L. Merrick. il Parents Mag 44:66-7+ O '69
Pediatrician talks to mothers about that all-important first year. F. Kodl. il Parents Mag 44:68-70+ Mr '69

Second month of life: reaching out; excerpts from Infants and mothers: differences in development. T. B. Brazelton. il Redbook 134:75+ D '69
When infants come home; excerpts from Infants and mothers: differences in development. T. B. Brazelton. il Redbook 134: 82-3+ N '69
See also
Baby sitters
Child welfare
Infants, Premature
Thumb sucking

Clothing
See also
Diapers, Infants

Diseases
See Children—Diseases

Growth and development
Baby takes over. J. H. Fithian. il Parents Mag 44:48-9+ Ag '69
Conspiracy against childhood; excerpts. E. J. LeShan. Read Digest 94:111-14 Mr '69
Hatching out. J. A. Kleeman. il N Y Times Mag p67+ F 9 '69
Infants and mothers: differences in development; excerpts. T. B. Brazelton. il Redbook 133:85-7+ O '69
Pediatrician talks to mothers about that all-important first year. F. Kodl. il Parents Mag 44:68-70+ Mr '69
Third month: the baby is a person; excerpts from Infants and mothers: differences in development. T. B. Brazelton. il Redbook 134:52-3+ Ja '70
See also
Child study

Language
See Children—Language

Nutrition
Your child's health; bottle feeding. L. W. Sauer. il PTA Mag 63:19+ My '69
See also
Breast feeding
INFANTS, Cost of. See Domestic finance
INFANTS, Deformed. See Deformities
INFANTS, Disciplining of. See Discipline
INFANTS, Newborn
Fathers' hour; maternity ward at Manhattan's Flower and Fifth avenue hospitals. il Good H 169:22+ Jl '69
How to have a healthy baby. L. W. Sauer. il PTA Mag 63:29-30 Mr '69
Infants and mothers: differences in development; excerpts. T. B. Brazelton. il Redbook 133:85-7+ O '69
Urban poverty: effects on prenatal nutrition. R. L. Naeye and others. bibliog il Science 166:1026 N 21 '69
When infants come home; excerpts from Infants and mothers: differences in development. T. B. Brazelton. il Redbook 134:82-3+ N '69
INFANTS, Premature
Caring for a premature baby. J. L. Arehart. il Parents Mag 44:42-3+ Je '69
Incubating babies by computer. il Sci Digest 66:92-3 O '69
Mental retardation due to germinal matrix infarction. A. Towbin. bibliog il Science 164: 156-61 Ap 11 '69
Premature baby. L. Eisenberg. McCalls 96: 34+ Ja '69
Why babies die. il Time 93:81 My 9 '69
INFANTS food
Baby food additive may be next to go. Bsns W p 114 O 25 '69
INFANTS supplies
How much does a baby cost? K. D. Fury. il Redbook 133:46+ Jl '69
INFARCTIONS
Mental retardation due to germinal matrix infarction. A. Towbin. bibliog il Science 164:156-61 Ap 11 '69
INFAUSTO, Felix
Perspective on adoption. bibliog f Ann Am Acad 383:1-12 My '69
INFECTIOUS diseases. See Communicable diseases
INFECTIOUS hepatitis. See Hepatitis, Infectious
INFECTIOUS mononucleosis. See Mononucleosis, Infectious
INFERTILITY. See Sterility
INFLAMMABLE materials
Progress report on: flammable carpets. il Consumer Rep 34:72-3 F '69
INFLATABLE boats. See Boats and boating
INFLATABLE furniture. See Furniture, Inflatable

INFLATABLE structures (art) See Sculpture
INFLATED structures. See Domes
INFLATION (finance)
Another try at muffling the boom. Newsweek 73:65 Je 30 '69
Appraisal of federal fiscal policies: 1961-1967. R. J. Saulnier. Ann Am Acad 379:63-71 S '68
Backlash against the bankers; credit-tightening measures. Time 93:74 Je 27 '69
Big bite at inflation. Fortune 80:83 Jl '69
Big problem is still inflation. il Newsweek 73:90+ My 26 '69
Bleak day for inflation fighters. il Bsns W p61-2 D 6 '69
Business: no sign of a slowing. il Bsns W p44-5 Je 14 '69
Business roundup; signals of a turn. il Fortune 8:19 Ag 1 '69
Can Mr Nixon stop the inflation? il Newsweek 75:49-51+ Ja 12 '70
Can Nixon talk down inflation? il Bsns W p34-5 O 25 '69
Can the individual fight inflation? Chr Today 14:31-2 N 7 '69
Can they really stop inflation? interview; ed. by G. R. Rosen. Duns R 94:8-9 D '69
Can we control inflation? C. H. Madden. Nations Bsns 57:50-2 O '69
Chance of controlling inflation: as top money manager sees it; excerpts from testimony to Joint economic committee of Congress. W. M. Martin, jr. U S News 66:99-100 Mr 10 '69
Controlling inflation: a longer timetable. il Time 94:57 Ag 29 '69
Cost and price stability; address, January 15, 1969. R. J. Saulnier. Vital Speeches 35:243-6 F 1 '69
Critical fight against inflation. il Time 93:77-8+ Je 20 '69; Same abr. with title Inflation, will we stop it? Read Digest 95:85-8 S '69
Cure may prove worse than the disease. D. Lawrence. il U S News 67:88 D 22 '69
Deflate now, inflate later. il Fortune 80:21-2 S '69
Dime dollar; be honest; address, August 19, 1969. J. L. Jones. Vital Speeches 35:728-30 S 15 '69
Disinflation, not deflation. America 120:296 Mr 15 '69
Dividing the blame for higher prices. B. L. Masse. America 120:576 My 17 '69
Dollar squeeze; Life poll by L. Harris, with report on one family by J. McGinnis. il Life 67:18-29 Ag 15 '69
Don't bet on inflation. Fortune 79:62 My 1 '69
Economic perspective. M. Friedman. Newsweek 74:76 D 22 '69
Economic policy's crucial experiment; to end inflation without precipitating recession. Bsns W p 126 Mr 8 '69
Economic wringer: is it about to work? Newsweek 73:73 Je 16 '69
Economy won't give in; Fed's new efforts to halt inflation. il Bsns W p29-30 Ap 12 '69
Elephant in bed. H. C. Wallich. Newsweek 74:94 S 22 '69
End inflation with least pain. il Life 66:28 F 7 '69
Enough brake? Newsweek 73:60+ Ap 7 '69
Federal reserve head talks on inflation, interest, controls; excerpts from testimony before the Senate committee on banking and currency, September 10, 1969. W. M. Martin, jr. il U S News 67:103-4 S 22 '69
Gainers, losers in the battle with inflation. il U S News 66:71-2 Ja 27 '69
Good, and the bad. Newsweek 74:86 S 29 '69
GOP is thrown a price-job curve; Phillips curve. il Bsns W p60+ Mr 22 '69
Guessing game that saddles economists; forecasting what the Fed will do. Bsns W p35 Mr 8 '69
Hiding from inflation, nothing sure. H. C. Wallich. Vogue 153:70 Je '69
How gradual can gradualism get? Bsns W p23-4 Ag 23 '69
How safe is the dollar now? il U S News 67:19-21 S 1 '69
How Sweden slowed inflation: success story. il U S News 66:25 Ap 7 '69
How to handle your investments; interview. T. R. Price. il U S News 67:64-7 Jl 7 '69
Impotent jawbone? il Newsweek 74:76 N 3 '69
Inflation all over. Time 94:78+ S 5 '69
Inflation battle heats up; with editorial comment. il Bsns W p40-2, 170 Mr 29 '69
Inflation battle, Ottawa style. il Bsns W p39-40 Je 7 '69
Inflation curb, job cut, where the blow will fall. il U S News 66:74-5 F 17 '69

Inflation does not just happen; congressional education; address, October 3, 1969. R. W. Miller. bibliog Vital Speeches 36:152-4 D 15 '69
Inflation is government-made. Nat R 21:1101-2 N 4 '69
Inflation jawboning, Nixon-style. il Time 94:92-3 N 28 '69
Inflation jitters worry the bankers. il Time 93:101 Je 6 '69
Inflation or unemployment? F. Morley. Nations Bsns 57:25-6 Ap '69
Inflation prognosis. il Fortune 79:24+ F '69
Inflation '70: and the beat goes on. il Newsweek 74:103-4 O 6 '69
Inflation: what more can Nixon do? il Time 94:87 O 10 '69
Inflationary binge; address, October 18, 1969. R. H. Larry. Vital Speeches 36:115-18 D 1 '69
Inflationary slowdown. P. A. Samuelson. Newsweek 73:86 Je 23 '69
Inflationitis: a problem of psychology. Time 93:82 Mr 28 '69
Is economic crisis around the corner? E. P. Smith. Commonweal 91:62-4 O 17 '69
Is recession a cure now? U S News 66:23-5 Ap 7 '69
Is recession on the way? As top economists see it. il U S News 67:17-19 Ag 4 '69
Is the administration crying wolf on controls? il Bsns W p 102+ Jl 12 '69
Jawing over inflation; administration to retreat from hands-off policy on wages and prices. il Bsns W p29-30 Mr 15 '69
Labor keeps the wage pressure on; blamed for spiraling inflation. il Bsns W p 17-18 Ap 5 '69
Labor 1970: angry, aggressive, acquisitive. R. Armstrong. il Fortune 80:94-7+ O '69
Limits of economic policy. R. Lekachman. Duns R 94:11 Ag '69
Martin's views on controls; excerpts from message to the House banking committee, June 30, 1969. W. M. Martin, jr. U S News 67:57-8 Jl 14 '69
Medicine man; strategy in inflation fight. New Repub 161:10 N 1 '69
Memo from the editor. J. Wooldridge. il Nations Bsns 57:7-8 Jl '69
Mr Nixon's anti-inflation plea. America 121:377-8 N 1 '69
Money and inflation. M. Friedman. il Newsweek 73:105 My 26 '69
More fuel for inflation; the coming flow of cash. il U S News 67:29-30 O 6 '69
More it costs, the more you want. il Newsweek 73:63 Mr 31 '69
More, more, more. Time 94:90+ S 19 '69
Nixon jawbone. Nation 209:490 N 10 '69
Nixon moves to slow down wage rises; here's the plan. il U S News 67:98-9 S 22 '69
Nixon steps up his war on inflation; text of address, October 17, 1969. R. M. Nixon U S News 67:100-2 O 27 '69
Nixon's fight against economic problem no. 1. il Time 93:74-5 F 21 '69
Of war and inflation. il Time 93:18-19 Ap 11 '69
Ottawa steps up war on inflation. il Bsns W p21-2 D 27 '69
Outlook, three views; Keynesian, monetarist, and the cyclical anti-inflation theories. H. C. Wallich. Newsweek 73:93 My 19 '69
Painful process of slowing down. il Time 94:66+ Ag 1 '69
Patience may be the only strategy. C. Morgello. il Newsweek 73:83 Je 23 '69
Paying for the war. New Repub 161:3 Jl 5 '69
Persistent fever. il Time 93:88 My 2 '69
Pinch of inflation and unrest; R. M. Nixons anti-inflation proposals. il Newsweek 73:31-2 My 5 '69
Pocketbook pinch, personal side of inflation, '69. il U S News 66:64-6 My 19 '69
Policy for orderly economic growth; address, March 5, 1969. P. W. McCracken. Vital Speeches 35:354-6 Ap 1 '69; Excerpts. U S News 66:102 Mr 17 '69
President appeals to business and labor; text of letter, October 18, 1969. R. M. Nixon. U S News 67:102 O 27 '69
President's message. il Newsweek 74:93 O 27 '69
Progress on inflation. Time 93:19 Je 27 '69
Reaching the ceiling. il Fortune 79:15-16 Je '69
Ready to inflict pain. il Bsns W p25-6 S 6 '69
Republicans and inflation. P. W. McCracken. Duns R 93:19+ My '69
Rising risk of recession. il Time 94:66-70+ D 19 '69
Shift in the business mood. il Fortune 80:35-6 N '69

INFLATION (finance)—*Continued*
Showdown for the Fed; anti-inflation drive. il Bsns W p25-6 Mr 1 '69
Showdown on inflation control. Bsns W p 164 Je 7 '69
Signs of a turn. Time 94:70 Jl 4 '69
TRB from Washington: economic hurricane? New Repub 161:6 Ag 23 '69
Tax bill in the Senate; no painless way of stopping inflation. America 121:153-4 S 13 '69
Thinking the unthinkable. Duns R 94:88 Jl '69
Time's Board of economists: answering the hard questions; symposium. il Time 94:88-90 N 14 '69
To combat inflation, try making do! Consumer Bul 52:15-16 N '69
To guard the dollar. T. Trussell. Nations Bsns 57:7-8 Mr '69
Tough new fight on inflation. il Newsweek 73:77-8+ Ap 14 '69
Turmoil in the capital markets. il Time 94:96+ D 5 '69
Two cheers for direct controls. R. Lekachman. Duns R 93:11 My '69
Wages of inflation. Time 94:74 Jl 18 '69
Wages, prices, strikes; a new approach; interview. G. P. Shultz. il U S News 66:62-6 Je 2 '69
War on inflation: appeal to business. il U S News 67:8 D 1 '69
War on inflation; the outlook now. il U S News 66:25-7 Mr 31 '69
Warnings of money trouble. U S News 67:72 Jl 7 '69
We must get inflation under control; interview. D. M. Kennedy. U S News 66:56-60 My 5 '69
What inflation calls for. B. L. Masse. America 121:286 O 11 '69
What it takes to control inflation, the official word. il U S News 66:87-9 Ap 7 '69
What's happened to the family budget? S. Grafton. il McCalls 96:42+ S '69
What's really happening to the cost of living? il Nations Bsns 57:66-9 Jl '69
When inflation gets out of hand; the story of Brazil. il U S News 67:83-4 D 22 '69
Where high interest rates hurt: a look at the money squeeze. il U S News 66:34-5 F 17 '69
Where inflation hits hardest. il U S News 66:57 Mr 10 '69
Who started the spiral spinning? il Bsns W p 13-14 Ja 3 '70
Who's helped or hurt by inflation. il U S News 66:40-2 Mr 3 '69
Why interest rates keep going up. il U S News 67:64-6 Ag 11 '69
Why Nixon wants to wield the ax; repeal of the 7 per cent tax credit. il Bsns W p 108-10+ Ap 26 '69
Why recession will be avoided; interview. P. W. McCracken. U S News 68:52-5 Ja 12 '70
Why Wall Street is worried. il Time 94:73 Jl 18 '69
Will inflation be turned back? il U S News 66:19-20 Je 30 '69
Word from businessmen: boom cooling. U S News 66:69 My 19 '69
World economy; year of inflation. L. A. Mayer. il Fortune 80:27-8+ Ag 15 '69
See also
Currency question
Deflation (finance)

INFLUENCE (psychology)
Maternal influence in learning by observation in kittens. P. Chesler. bibliog il Science 166:901-3 N 14 '69

INFLUENCE of literature. See Literature, Influence of

INFLUENZA
Amantadine vs. Hong Kong flu. Sci N 95:613-14 Je 28 '69
Clean sweep for HK-68. il Time 93:74 Ja 31 '69
Flu may hide in animals. Sci Digest 65:62 Je '69
Flu that few will forget; Hong Kong flu and its impact on America. R. Bugg. il Todays Health 47:24-7+ Ap '69
Gripped by the grippe; Hong Kong flu sweeping across Europe. il Time 95:32 Ja 12 '70
Visitor from Hong Kong; epidemic in Europe. il Newsweek 75:62 Ja 12 '70

Anecdotes, facetiae, satire, etc.
Needling the doctor. G. Ace. Sat R 52:7 Mr 8 '69

Vaccines
On the way: vaccines to snuff out sniffles. R. Bugg. il Todays Health 47:36-7+ D '69
Turning virus into vaccine. il Todays Health 47:26-7 Ap '69

INFLUENZA viruses
How Hong Kong flu began. Newsweek 73:107 Mr 31 '69
Influenza virus: genetics and control; report of meeting. R. W. Simpson. Science 163:409-12 Ja 24 '69
Virus of the 1918 influenza pandemic era: new evidence about its antigenic character. P. Brown and others. bibliog il Science 166:117-19 O 3 '69

INFORMATION, Freedom of
Freedom of information act. P. Dickson. Writers Digest 49:44-7+ N '69
Not for publication; product information in the government's possession. E. Gross. il Sci N 95:508-10 My 24 '69
Open presidency: little enforcement of Freedom of information act. New Repub 160:7-8 Mr 1 '69
Operation Candor needed. R. Hotz. Aviation W 90:11 My 26 '69
Secrecy and dissemination in science and technology. bibliog Science 163:787-90 F 21 '69
See also
Freedom of the press
Government and the press
Intellectual liberty

INFORMATION, Government. See Government information

INFORMATION agency (United States) See United States—Information agency

INFORMATION display systems
Choosing a digital display. R. Bell. il Electr World 81:25-9 F '69
See also
Aeronautic instruments—Display systems

INFORMATION industry association
Information market. il Pub W 195:64-7 Ap 14 '69
Technology vs. copyright: form vs. content; report of meeting. Pub W 196:18-20 Ag 11 '69

INFORMATION libraries, Overseas. See American libraries abroad

INFORMATION processing, Human. See Human information processing

INFORMATION services
Five special research aids. L. Horton. il Writers Digest 49:42-5+ F '69
Information market. il Pub W 195:64-7 Ap 14 '69
Milking the most from auto sales; R. L. Polk & co. il Bsns W p84-6 Ap 26 '69
See also
Computer-based service companies

INFORMATION storage and retrieval systems
Communications. J. McLaughlin. America 122:16-18 Ja 10 '70
Data system speeds line troubleshooting. K. J. Stein. il Aviation W 90:63-5 Ap 21 '69
Information retrieval research at Time inc; address, January 1969. M. T. Fischer. il Library J 94:1585-8 Ap 15 '69
Speed and pre-selection aren't everything. R. E. Bye. Pub W 195:78 Ja 27 '69
See also
Electronic data processing
Eric
Libraries—Automation
Microforms
United States—National data center (proposed)

Science
Ask the men who know. G. Adelman. il por Library J 94:1413-15 Ap 1 '69
Chemical information test station. E. M. Arnett. il Chem 42:16-18 Mr '69
New information program for AIP. A. Herschman and others. il Phys Today 22:29-32 D '69
Plans for commercial bidding on standard reference data. S. Wagner. Pub W 195:105-6 Je 2 '69

INFORMATION systems, Management
Closing a gap at the top; Society for management information science. Bsns W p90 S 20 '69
Software of change; address, September 23, 1969. M. Tribus. Vital Speeches 36:14-17 O 15 '69

INFORMATION tests
Are you a wine whiz? oenological quiz. J. Wilson. House & Gard 136:156+ S '69
Changing times quiz (cont) Changing T 22:44 D '68; 23:47 Ag '69
Checkpoint. K. M. Binkley. See issues of Flying
Educators' quiz. M. Rosenberg. See issues of Education digest
[Electronics quiz] R. P. Balin. See issues of Popular electronics to September, 1969
Family quiz game. L. McCabe. See issues of Parents' magazine & better family living
Goren's Christmas quiz. C. Goren. il Sports Illus 31:80-2+ D 22 '69

INFORMATION tests—*Continued*
History quiz for the young revolutionary;
similarity of communism to nazism. J.
Jeffries. Nat R 21:488+ My 20 '69
How many ologies do you know? H. S.
Tucker. Sci Digest 66:39 Jl '69
Is a sclaffing cleek worth still another bisque?
il Esquire 71:146-7+ Ap '69
LCR circuits quiz. R. P. Balin. il Electr
World 82:99+ N '69
Lost on the moon: a decision-making prob-
lem. B. Luke. Todays Ed 58:55-6 F '69
Match your baseball IQ with Mayo Smith.
J. Devaney. il Mech Illus 65:56-7+ My
'69
Newsnames: 68. il Todays Ed 58:44-5 Ja '69
Play the who-makes-it game; quiz. Chang-
ing T 23:47 O '69
Quiz. J. Daugherty and M. Daugherty. See
issues of Science digest
Senior scholastic end-term review test (cont)
Sr Schol 93:31-2 Ja 10; 94:41-2 My 9 '69
Senior scholastic midterm review test. Sr
Schol 94:27-8 Mr 14 '69
Test your sports I.Q. H. L. Masin. il Sr Schol
94:18 Ap 11 '69
Test your ten-year memory span with the
wrap-up game. J. M. Flagler. il Look 33:
37+ D 30 '69
What do you know about the sea? quiz.
J. G. Vaeth. il Sci Digest 66:56-7+ N '69
Your literary I.Q; ed. by D. M. Glixon. See
issues of Saturday review
INFORMATION theory
See also
Human information processing
INFORMERS (law)
Confessions of a canary; Customs informers.
il Newsweek 74:48 Jl 28 '69
Crisis of silence. Time 94:25 O 17 '69
Gourmet pirate; con man J. P. Lafitte. il
Time 94:18 D 19 '69
How to stay out of trouble with IRS; tax in-
formers. R. S. Holzman. il Nations Bsns
57:28-31 D '69
Your role as eyes and ears for police. A.
Rosenthal. il Todays Health 47:58-61+ S '69
INFRARED apparatus and appliances
Binoculars contain infrared voice link. B.
Miller. il Aviation W 91:75-6+ N 10 '69
INFRARED detectors. See Detectors, Infrared
INFRARED films. See Photography—Films
INFRARED photography. See Photography,
Infrared
INFRARED photomicrography. See Photomi-
crography
INFRARED rays
Far-infrared observations of the night sky.
J. R. Houck and M. Harwit. bibliog il Sci-
ence 164:1271-3 Je 13 '69
Infrared astrophysics. F. J. Low. bibliog il
Science 164:501-5 My 2 '69
U.K. infrared research gets civil emphasis.
il Aviation W 91:111 Ag 18 '69
See also
Spectrum, Infrared

Industrial applications
See also
Infrared technology

Measurement uses
Infrared locates diseased trees. R. Neubert.
il Electr World 82:34-5 Ag '69
INFRARED technology
Putting infrared in the picture. il Bsns W
p80+ Ja 25 '69
INFRINGEMENT of copyright. See Copyright
infringement
INGALLS, John James
Grass; excerpt from Blue grass. Am For 75:
36-7 S '69
INGALLS, R. P. See Rogers, A. E. E. jt. auth.
INGALLS, Susan R.
Ideal couple; story. Seventeen 28:130-1 N '69
Perverse madonna in love; story. Seventeen
28:124-5 Je '69
INGERSOLL, John, jr
$5 for asparagus, $1 for hay. Org Gard &
Farm 16:97-9 Mr '69
Where can you find an organic Tahiti? por
Org Gard & Farm 16:51-3 O '69
INGERSOLL, John H.
Ideas to build on. See Issues of House
beautiful
Well-built, well-kept house. See issues of
House beautiful
INGLES, Frances
Row-to-row carpeting in the garden. J. G.
Edwards. il por Org Gard & Farm 16:46-7
Ja '69

INGLEWOOD, Calif.
Considerable advantages of one-man refuse
collection. W. F. Farnam. il Am City 84:
97-8 Ap '69
Dignified garage in a city's new civic center.
il Arch Rec 145:170-1 Ap '69
INGLEWOOD, Calif. public library
Prefab library. A. B. Stephenson and J. W.
Perkins. il Am City 84:126-7 Je '69
Record-breaking exhibit (library) by a group
of artists (black) A. Kerr. il Wilson Lib
Bul 43:756-9 Ap '69
INGLIS, Brian
Remarkable Ronald Laing. Vogue 154:132-
3+ S 15 '69
INGLIS, David R.
Nuclear models; adaptation of address, Oc-
tober 5, 1968. bibliog por Phys Today 22:
29-40 Je '69
INGRAM, Forrest L. See Fleddermann, H. jt.
auth.
INGRES, Jean Auguste Dominique
Ingres for Ingres sake. M. Levey. il Art N
68:46-7+ Ap '69
INGVALSON, Roger Dean
Two American POW's; interview, ed. by O.
Fallaci. por Look 33:32+ Jl 15 '69
INHERITANCE
See also
Estate planning
INHERITANCE tax
Estate tax changes coming. il U S News 66:
72-4 Ap 7 '69
INHIBITION
Lateral hypothalamic stimulation: inhibition
of aversive effects by feeding, drinking,
and gnawing. J. Mendelson. bibliog il Sci-
ence 166:1431-3 D 12 '69
See also
Repression (psychology)
INITIALISMS. See Acronyms
INJECTIONS
See also
Inoculation
INJECTIONS, Hypodermic
Automated injections. Sci Digest 65:71 F '69
INJUNCTIONS
Injunction on campus. F. J. Donner. Nation
208:718-20 Je 9 '69
New weapon on campus. il Time 93:72+
My 16 '69
INJURIES. See Accidents; First aid in illness
and injury; Traumatism; Wounds; *also* sub-
head Wounds and injuries under names of
organs and regions of the body, e.g. Brain—
Wounds and injuries
INK
Crayon illuminations; working with trans-
parent India inks. G. A. Petine. il Sch
Arts 69:16-17 S '69
Writing inks. il Consumer Bul 52:27-9 O '69
INLAND navigation
Alaska to Key West cruise; by outboard
motorboat. il Travel 131:59-61 Je '69
See also
River trips
INLAND waterway. See Intracoastal Waterway
INMAN, Pauline W.
House furnishings of a Vermont family. An-
tiques 96:228-33 Ag '69
INNER journey; drama. See Hanley, J.
INNER-tubing. See Aquatic sports
INNIS, Roy
Roy Innis: nation builder. A. Poinsett. il pors
Ebony 24:170-4+ O '69
Wilkins v. Innis. W. F. Buckley, jr. Nat R
21:140 F 11 '69
INNOVATION, Technological. See Technolog-
ical change
INNOVATIONS in education. See Educational
innovations
INNS. See Hotels, taverns, etc.
INOCULATION
Inoculations for travelers. il Sci Digest 66:75-
6 S '69
See also
Vaccination
INPUT-output analysis
Forecasters get some better props. il Bsns
W p 125-6+ N 22 '69
Rumania starts down model path. il Bsns W
p66 O 25 '69
They call it instant research; Maptek re-
ports on what's ahead in electronics. il
Bsns W p62+ Ja 25 '69
INQUIRER, Philadelphia. See Philadelphia in-
quirer
INQUIRY teaching. See Teaching
INSANE
See also
Mentally ill

Legal status, laws, etc.
See Mental health laws

INSANE, Criminal and dangerous
　Adjustment of criminally insane patients to a civil mental hospital. L. White and others. bibliog il Ment Hy 53:34-40 Ja '69
　Crime and mental illness: some problems in defining and labeling deviant behavior. S. A. Shah. bibliog Ment Hy 53:21-33 Ja '69

INSANITY
　Pleas of temporary insanity; letter. T. M. Cowan. Science 165:543-4 Ag 8 '69
　　See also
　Mental illness
　Psychiatry
　Psychology, Pathological
　Psychoses
　Schizophrenia

　　　　　Jurisprudence
　Insanity defense, by A. S. Goldstein. Review Commentary 47:100-1+ My '69. L. Radzinowicz
　　See also
　Forensic psychiatry
　Insane, Criminal and dangerous

INSANITY, Delusional. See Paranoia

INSANITY and crime. See Insane, Criminal and dangerous

INSCRIPTIONS
　　See also
　Graffiti
　Hieroglyphics

INSCRIPTIONS, Latin
　Origin of the serif, by E. M. Catich. Review Pub W il 195:83-4+ My 5 '69. P. Standard

INSCRIPTIONS, Roman. See Inscriptions, Latin

INSECT allergy. See Allergy

INSECT bites and stings
　R for insect and animal bites. G. M. Knox. Bet Hom & Gard 47:91-2 Jl '69
　Stinging insects, armed and dangerous. R. Wolkomir. il Todays Health 47:48-9+ Je '69

INSECT communication
　Dance versus smell; dance language of the bee. J. Chamblin. il Sci N 95:383 Ap 19 '69
　Honey bee recruitment to food sources: olfaction or language? A. M. Wenner and others. bibliog il Science 164:84-6 Ap 4 '69; Reply. R. Dawkins. 165:751 Ag 22 '69
　Secrets of the animal world. R. Petrow. il Pop Mech 132:84-7+ S '69

INSECT control. See Insects, Injurious and beneficial—Control

INSECT mating behavior. See Courtship of insects

INSECT populations
　Population explosion: a warning from the insects. J. Reinert. il Sci Digest 66:40-5 Ag '69

INSECT secretions. See Secretions

INSECT sex attractants
　Masking of the aggregation pheromone in dendroctonus pseudotsugae hopk. J. A. Rudinsky. bibliog il Science 166:884-5 N 14 '69
　Sex attractant of female dermestid beetle trogoderma inclusum le conte. J. O. Rodin and others. bibliog il Science 165:904-5 Ag 29 '69
　Sex pheromone of the queen butterfly: biology. T. E. Pliske and T. Eisner. bibliog il Science 164:1170-2 Je 6 '69
　Sex pheromone of the queen butterfly: chemistry. J. Meinwald and others. bibliog il Science 164:1174-5 Je 6 '69
　Sex pheromone of the queen butterfly: electroantennogram responses. D. Schneider and U. Seibt. bibliog il Science 164:1173-4 Je 6 '69
　Sex pheromone specificity: taxonomic and evolutionary aspects in lepidoptera. W. L. Roelofs and A. Comeau. bibliog il Science 165:398-400 Jl 25 '69
　Sex pheromones produced by male boll weevil: isolation, identification, and synthesis. J. H. Tumlinson and others. bibliog il Science 166:1010-12 N 21 '69
　Synthetic juvenile hormone: induction of sex pheromone production in ips confusus. J. H. Borden and others. bibliog il Science 166:1626-7 D 26 '69
　Western pine beetle: field response to its sex pheromone and a synergistic host terpene, myrcene. W. D. Bedard and others. bibliog il Science 164:1284-5 Je 13 '69
　　See also
　Propylure

INSECT societies
　Brood care in halictine bees. G. Knerer. bibliog il Science 164:429-30 Ap 25 '69
　　See also
　Insect populations

INSECT sounds
　Acoustic synchrony: two mechanisms in the snowy tree cricket. T. J. Walker. bibliog il Science 166:891-4 N 14 '69

INSECT-spraying machines. See Spraying apparatus

INSECT traps
　Cheap insect trap that works. D. Foraker. Org Gard & Farm 16:84-+ S '69
　Some safety bugs in electric bug-killers. il Consumer Rep 34:296 Je '69

INSECTICIDES
　Cotton-growers' dilemma; use of Azodrin upsets natural balance. Chem 42:6-7 Ap '69
　Garden insecticides. il Consumer Rep 34:407-10 Jl '69
　Keep DDT out of gardens! Home Gard 56:62-3 O '69
　Molecular bomb for the war against insects; reprint. L. Lessing. il Am For 75:16-19+ Ja '69
　New chemicals for mite control. Farm J 93:42D S '69
　New double-duty insecticide; Furadan. Farm J 93:39 My '69
　Pinpoint weapon for war on pests; VHZ the viral insecticides. il Bsns W p72+ Ap 26 '69
　Plant bites insect. R. M. Carleton. Horticulture 47:54-5 Ja '69
　　See also
　Aldrin
　DDT (insecticide)
　Pesticides

　　　　　Injurious effects
　Consumers get a break on pest control devices; warnings against lindane vaporizers and No-pest strip insecticide. Consumer Bul 52:20 S '69
　Dieldrin and DDT: effects on sparrow hawk eggshells and reproduction. R. D. Porter and S. N. Wiemeyer. bibliog il Science 165:199-200 Jl 11 '69
　Return of the grebe. Time 94:85 D 5 '69

　　　　　Residues
　　See also
　DDT (insecticide)—Residues

INSECTICIDES, Resistance to. See Insects, Injurious and beneficial—Resistance to control

INSECTS
　Night insects of West Bengal. S. Radinovsky. il Natur Hist 78:46-7 Ja '69
　　See also
　Fertilization of plants
　Hymenoptera
　Larvae
　Lepidoptera
　Nervous system—Insects
　　also names of insects, e.g. Butterflies

　　　　　Collection and preservation
　Oceanic filter, game of chance. D. Cavagnaro. il Natur Hist 78:52-7 Mr '69

　　　　　Control
　　See Insects, Injurious and beneficial—Control

　　　　　Development
　Cellular response to ecdysterone in vitro. K. J. Judy. bibliog il Science 165:1374-5 S 26 '69
　Puparium formation in flies: contraction in puparium induced by ecdysone. P. Berreur and G. Fraenkel. bibliog il Science 164:1182-3 Je 6 '69

　　　　　Egg laying
　　See Oviposition

　　　　　Flight
　Mimicry of hymenoptera by beetles with unconventional flight. R. E. Silberglied and T. Eisner. il Science 163:486-8 Ja 31 '69

　　　　　Food and feeding
　Mosquitoes feeding on insect larvae. P. Harris and others. il Science 164:184-5 Ap 11 '69
　Plant-herbivore coevolution; lupines and lycaenids. D. E. Breedlove and P. R. Ehrlich; discussion. Science 164:197; 165:415-16 Ap 11, Jl 25 '69
　　See also
　Food chains (ecology)

　　　　　Geographical distribution
　Indigens and immigrants; plants and animals in the New York city region. A. B. Klots. il Natur Hist 78:38-45 Ap '69

INSECTS—*Continued*

Habits and behavior
Alkali bees: response of adults to pathogenic fungi in brood cells. S. W. T. Batra and G. E. Bohart. bibliog il Science 165:607 Ag 8 '69
Pleasures of bumblebee petting and other garden adventures. M. M. Leister. il Home Gard 56:62 Ag '69
See also
Courtship of insects
Insect communication
Insect societies

Host plants
See Insects—Food and feeding

Metabolism
Insect metabolism of photoaldrin and photodieldrin. M. A. Q. Khan and others. bibliog il Science 164:318-19 Ap 18 '69

Migration
See also
Grasshoppers—Migration

Orientation
See Orientation

Protective equipment
See Defense mechanisms (biology)

Resistance to control
See Insects, Injurious and beneficial—Resistance to control

Sight
See Sight (insects)

INSECTS, Aquatic
See also
Water beetles

INSECTS, Effect of radiation on. See Insects, Injurious and beneficial—Control

INSECTS, Effect of temperature on
See also
Insects, Freezing of

INSECTS, Fossil
Permian insect wing from Antarctic Sentinel Mountains. P. Tasch and E. F. Riek. bibliog il Science 164:1529-30 Je 27 '69

INSECTS, Freezing of
Freezing tolerance in an adult insect. L. K. Miller. bibliog il Science 166:105-6 O 3 '69

INSECTS, Injurious and beneficial
Overhead sprinklers of Israel; how to provide a nice, wet place where insects you don't want thrive. E. Rivnay. bibliog il Natur Hist 78:56-61 F '69
There are monsters in your garden; with photographs. E. Ray. Am For 75:8-11 D '69
See also subhead Diseases and pests under names of crops, trees, plants, etc, e.g. Corn—Diseases and pests; *also* names of insects, e.g. Yellow jackets

Biological control
Are insects just accidents? J. I. Rodale. Org Gard & Farm 16:98-9+ Ag '69
Have your own bug-in! M. C. Goldman. il Org Gard & Farm 16:59-64 Ag '69
Insects guard your garden. J. Seginski. il Org Gard & Farm 16:95+ Ag '69
More ways than one to kill a bug: insect viruses. K. Frazier. il Sci N 96:334-6 O 11 '69
Pest control: report of meeting. D. L. Wood and others. Science 164:203-6+ Ap 11 '69
Pest plagues; viral pesticides. Sci Am 221:50 Ag '69
Well, if not DDT, then what? H. Higdon. il N Y Times Mag p26-7+ Ja 11 '70
See also
Trichoramma

Control
Corn rootworm. D. Seim. il Farm J 93:34+ F '69
Flower bugs and other fauna. Am Home 72:118 My '69
Garden insecticides. il Consumer Rep 34:407-10 Jl '69
Gardening without DDT. J. B. Kring. il Horticulture 47:22-3 N '69
Home garden notebook. insect control. B. C. Kilvert, jr. il Home Gard 56:37-8 Je '69
Irradiating the fruit fly. Bul Atom Sci 25:34+ D '69
Many paths to pest control. J. I. Rodale. Org Gard & Farm 16:99-101+ S '69
Molecular bomb for the war against insects; reprint. L. Lessing. il Am For 75:16-19+ Ja '69
We invited the bugs to dinner, but they never came! C. Skinner. il Org Gard & Farm 16:46-9 Mr '69

Weed and insect control guide. il Suc Farm 67:56-7+ F '69
With various plants and animals, invading insects can be chased away. V. M. Crill. il Home Gard 56:56-7 O '69
See also
Grasshoppers—Control
Household pests—Control
Insecticides
Insects. Injurious and beneficial—Biological control
Pesticides
Spraying and dusting

Resistance to control
Consequence of insecticides; pests follow the chemicals in the cocoa of Malaysia. G. R. Conway. il Natur Hist 78:46-51 F '69

INSECTS, Sound production by. See Insect sounds

INSECTS, Stinging
See also
Insect bites and stings

INSECTS as carriers of infection
See also
Cockroaches as carriers of infection
Mosquitoes as carriers of infection

INSECURITY, Feeling of. See Security and insecurity (psychology)

INSEMINATION, Artificial. See Artificial insemination; Artificial insemination, Human

INSERVICE teacher education. See Teachers—Education in service

INSOLVENCY. See Bankruptcy

INSOMNIA
Four kinds of insomniacs. Sci Digest 66:57 D '69
Insomnia, by G. G. Luce and J. Segal. Review
Sat R 52:23 Jl 26 '69. J. H. Plumb
See also
Sleep

Anecdotes, facetiae, satire, etc.
Ainmosni. R. Angell. New Yorker 45:32-4 My 31 '69

INSPECTION
Krypton flaw detection system designed. il Aviation W 90:85 Je 9 '69

INSPECTION of automobiles. See Automobiles—Inspection

INSPECTION of poultry. See Poultry inspection

INSPIRATION
See also
Creation (literary, artistic, etc)

INSTALMENT contracts
Buy now, pay later, no matter what. Consumer Rep 34:357-8 Jl '69
Installment contracts: what to check. il Good H 168:168 Je '69

INSTALMENT plan
Financing; boats. il Motor B 123:103 Ja '69
How to save money when you finance a car; excerpts from How to save money when you buy and drive your car. M. E. Dowd. il Pop Mech 130:94-8+ D '68
Why not pay cash? Consumer Bul 52:13-14 Jl '69
See also
Credit

INSTAMATIC cameras. See Cameras

INSTINCT
How an instinct is learned. J. P. Hailman. il Sci Am 221:98-106 bibliog (p 152) D '69
See also
Animal intelligence

INSTINET. See Institutional networks corporation

INSTITUTE for applied behavioral science. See National training laboratories

INSTITUTE for biomedical research. See American medical association—Institute for biomedical research

INSTITUTE for creative studies, Washington, D.C.
Don't call us geniuses. M. Melewicz. il Am Ed 5:22-5 N '69

INSTITUTE for development of educational activities
How to help your child do well in school. il U S News 67:49-50 O 6 '69

INSTITUTE for environmental studies. See Pennsylvania. University. Philadelphia—Institute for environmental studies

INSTITUTE for religious works. See Catholic church—Finance

INSTITUTE for sex research. See Indiana. University. Bloomington—Institute for sex research

INSTITUTE for strategic studies
Two Dutch treats and the arms race. A. Geyer. Chr Cent 86:1272-3 O 8 '69

INSTITUTE of electrical and electronics engineers
Engineers' turn; international convention. Nation 208:421 Ap 7 '69
Nuclear sciences. Sci N 96:427 N 8 '69
INSTITUTE of gerontology
Students in aging. E. Courter. il Har Yrs 9: 32-3 Je '69
INSTITUTE of high fidelity, incorporated
Fifteen years of the IHF. N. Spann. il Hi Fi 19:67-70 Mr '69
INSTITUTE of international education
Intermediate battlefield; annual meeting. N. Cousins. Sat R 52:26 N 8 '69
INSTITUTE of international studies. See United States—Education, Office of—Institute of international studies
INSTITUTES, Library. See Library institutes and workshops
INSTITUTES, Religious. See Religious institutes and workshops
INSTITUTES, Teachers. See Teachers institutes
INSTITUTIONAL homes. See Homes, Institutional
INSTRUCTIONAL materials centers
Impact of media centers on inner-city schools. J. A. McCrossan. ALA Bul 63:1532-4 D '69
Media center design; symposium. bibliog il Library J 94:4201-28 N 15 '69
INSTITUTIONAL networks corporation
Challenge to the brokers; Instinet system. W. Robertson. il Fortune 79:167-8+ Ap '69
Computer to bypass the broker; investors trade electronically. Bsns W p96+ Mr 8 '69
INSTITUTIONS, Nonprofit
Institutions, investments and integrity. C. W. Powers and J. P. Gunnemann. Chr Cent 86: 144-8 Ja 29 '69

Taxation
Milking the sacred cows. Newsweek 73:71 My 5 '69
INSTITUTIONS, Public. See State institutions
INSTITUTIONS, State. See State institutions
INSTITUTO nacional de industria. See Holding companies
INSTRUCTION. See Teaching
INSTRUCTION manuals

Bibliography
How-to-do-it books: building the collection. J. G. Fetros. Library J 94:1595-7 Ap 15 '69
INSTRUCTIONAL dynamics, incorporated
Taped newsletters sound off; cassette players. il Bsns W p58 Jl 26 '69
INSTRUCTIONAL materials centers
Big beyond promise; address, July 1968. R. L. Darling; reply. J. French. Library J 94: 817 F 15 '69
Criteria of excellence: the school library manpower project identifies outstanding school library centers. R. N. Case. ALA Bul 63:247-8 F '69
IMC network; Instructional materials center network for handicapped children and youth. L. Aserlind and J. J. McCarthy. Ed Digest 34:35-8 Mr '69
Marian, the media specialist. Sr School 94: Schol Teach 6 Ap 18 '69
Observations from abroad: the American scene. E. Roe. il Library J 94:835-9 F 15 '69
Pilot course on instructional materials centers; letter to the editor. A. M. Losse. Wilson Lib Bul 43:711-12 Ap '69
Promise of the new media standards; educational media center in each school. J. W. Brown. il Sr School 94:Schol Teach 34-5 Ja 17 '69
School libraries as school media centers: a portfolio; symposium, ed. by C. I. Whitenack. il ALA Bul 63:249-72 F '69
INSTRUCTORS, Aviation. See Air pilots
INSTRUCTORS, College. See College professors and instructors
INSTRUMENT boards (airplanes) See Airplanes—Instrument boards
INSTRUMENT flying. See Aviation—Instrument flying
INSTRUMENT landing. See Airplanes—Landing
INSTRUMENTAL music
See also
Chamber music
Phonograph records—Instrumental music
Trumpet music
INSTRUMENTS
See also
Aeronautic instruments
Nautical instruments
INSTRUMENTS, Drawing. See Drawing instruments

INSULATING materials
Amateur scientist; flow of blood, weather vanes, telescope mirrors and the conductivity of insulators. C. L. Stong. il Sci Am 221:137-8 O '69
INSULATION (electric)
What about double insulation for tools? J. Hand. il Pop Sci 195:194+ O '69
See also
Insulating materials
INSULATION (heat)
Insulated aluminum covers sheathe John Hancock building. il Arch Rec 145:168-70 Mr '69
Insulation deletion to cure glass fiber drift problem. Aviation W 90:77 Je 2 '69
Insulation for space vehicles. il Space World F-10-70:37 O '69
Which insulation should you use? B. Murphy. il Pop Mech 132:170-4 O '69
See also
Weather stripping
INSULIN
Insulin design traced. D. Fishlock. il Sci N 96:307 O 4 '69
Shape of insulin. Sci Am 221:47-8 O '69
Unraveling insulin; D. Hodgkin's structure findings. Newsweek 74:73-4 S 1 '69
INSULTS, Verbal. See Invective
INSURANCE
Who needs insurance? il Sr School 94:28 Ap 11 '69
See also
Estate planning
also subhead Insurance under various subjects, e.g. Contracts, Government—Insurance

Adjustment of claims
Hurricane claims whip up a storm; controversy over hurricane Camille claims. il Bsns W p36 N 29 '69
Stormy settlement; Gulf coast victims of last August's hurricane Camille. Time 94: 99 N 28 '69
When an insurance claim is made. il Good H 169:150 Jl '69

All risk policies
All-in-one insurance for householders. il Changing T 23:24-8 Ap '69
Homeowners get a break on insurance. Bsns W p 137 N 15 '69
Just how much does your personal insurance cover? Bet Hom & Gard 47:7 Je '69
New homeowners policies. Todays Ed 58:9 D '69

Catastrophe coverage
No cover for catastrophes; aerospace contractors. il Bsns W p58+ O 18 '69
See also
Insurance, Hurricane

Claims
See Insurance—Adjustment of claims

Policies
Fat cat executives, and insurance; umbrella policies. P. H. Durston. Duns R 94:75-6+ N '69
How to get more insurance for the same money. F. Bailey, jr. Suc Farm 67:A6 N '69

Reinsurance
Riot act irks underwriters; federal riot reinsurance program. Bsns W p 104 My 10 '69

Umbrella policies
See Insurance—Policies
INSURANCE, Automobile
Ahead; a new system of auto insurance? interview. W. O. Bailey. il U S News 66:54-6 Ap 28 '69
Changes coming in auto insurance. il U S News 66:40-1 Je 23 '69
Incentive plan for good drivers. D. E. Feyk. Travel 132:73-4 D '69
No risks preferred. J. Ridgeway. New Repub 160:18-21 F 22 '69
Progress report on: auto insurance. il Consumer Rep 34:70-2 F '69
Row over no fault auto insurance: Keeton-O'Connell system. il Changing T 23:7-11 My '69
Who's fit to drive? G. Town. il Har Yrs 9: 19-21 Mr '69
Why automobile insurance rates keep going up; excerpt from Are you being taken for a ride? G. B. Friedman. Atlan 224:58-63 S '69
Why car insurance costs so much. U S News 68:6 Ja 12 '70
INSURANCE, Aviation
Aviation insurance problem. R. Blodget. Flying 85:76-9 Ag '69

INSURANCE, Burglary
Personal business; fighting crime with help from insurance. Bsns W p89 Ag 23 '69

INSURANCE, Casualty
Insurance: the price you have to pay. il Newsweek 74:80+ N 24 '69
Who says casualty insurance is risky? il Forbes 103:56-7 Ap 1 '69
See also
Insurance, Automobile
Insurance, Hurricane
Insurance, Property

INSURANCE, Dental
Dental equipment picks up pace. il Bsns W p 140+ N 15 '69

INSURANCE, Flood
HUD wades in with flood aid; federally sponsored flood-insurance program. Bsns W p31 Mr 1 '69

INSURANCE, Group
Trends in negotiated health plans; broader coverage, higher quality care. D. M. Landay. bibliog Mo Labor R 92:3-10 My '69

INSURANCE, Health
See also
Insurance, Dental
Insurance, Hospitalization
Insurance, Mental health

Employees insurance
Insurance pitch with a union label. por Bsns W p88 Mr 29 '69

Great Britain
See also
Great Britain—National health service

United States
Better care at less cost without miracles. E. K. Faltermayer. il Fortune 81:80-3+ Ja '70
Catching up with Bismarck; Committee for national health insurance statement. R. W. Gibbons. Commonweal 91:238-40 N 21 '69
Cure-all? Committee for national health insurance proposal. Newsweek 74:68 O 27 '69
Health insurance, which plan for you? il Todays Health 47:54-7 D '69
Medical care: as costs soar, support grows for major reform. J. R. Kramer. Science 166:1126-9 N 28 '69
Right and left of medical insurance. J. Bockel. il Sci N 96:453 N 15 '69
TRB from Washington. New Repub 161:4 O 18 '69
Toward a national policy. Sci N 97:7 Ja 3 '70
Trends in negotiated health plans; broader coverage, higher quality care. D. M. Landay. bibliog Mo Labor R 92:3-10 My '69
Welfare plan of the future? proposed compulsory national health-insurance program. U S News 66:14 F 24 '69
See also
Medicaid program
Medicare program

INSURANCE, Hospitalization
Are you sure your hospital qualifies under your health insurance policy? Bet Hom & Gard 47:9 Je '69
Blue cross and the blues; adaptation of address, October 30, 1967. D. Rubin. Ment Hy 53:67-70 Ja '69
Blue cross pays the bills; problem of financing an anti-union campaign. J. Seldin. Nation 209:48-52 Jl 14 '69
How would you pay a $15,000 hospital bill? il Changing T 23:7-10 Ag '69

INSURANCE, Hurricane
Hurricane claims whip up a storm; controversy over hurricane Camille claims. il Bsns W p36 N 29 '69
Stormy settlement; Gulf coast victims of last August's hurricane Camille. Time 94:99-100 N 28 '69

INSURANCE, Industrial
Insurance pitch with a union label. Bsns W p88 Mr 29 '69
See also
Insurance, Group

INSURANCE, Liability
Is executive insurance worth it? S. H. Lieberstein. Duns R 94:53-4+ Jl '69
No cover for catastrophes; aerospace contractors. il Bsns W p58+ O 18 '69
See also
Insurance, Automobile
Insurance, Marine

INSURANCE, Life
Give your life insurance this checkup. il Changing T 23:17-19 Je '69
Low-cost life insurance. Todays Ed 58:76 F '69

Should you insure your wife and children? R. Krumme. il Suc Farm 67:46 Je '69
What you should know about life insurance. R. Krumme. il Suc Farm 67:69-76 Ap '69

Investments
See Insurance companies—Investments

Policies
How to choose your life insurance policy. il Suc Farm 67:72-3 Ap '69
If you quit paying on your life insurance. il Changing T 23:18 O '69

Policy loans
Insurers wince at drain on cash; policyholders borrowing on their insurance. il Bsns W p 104 My 24 '69

INSURANCE, Malpractice liability
Paying for error; proposed programs Sci N 96:552 D 13 '69

INSURANCE, Marine
Ahoy! Is that boat insured? Consumer Rep 34:314 Je '69
Insurance. il Motor B 123:107 Ja '69
Supertankers face troubles. Bsns W p47-8 Ja 10 '70
What do you know about yacht insurance? S. T. Chambers. Yachting 125:78-9+ Ap; 76-7+ My '69
See also
Lloyd's, London

INSURANCE, Medical. See Insurance, Health

INSURANCE, Mental health
Blue cross and the blues; adaptation of address. October 30, 1967. D. Rubin. Ment Hy 53:67-70 Ja '69

INSURANCE, Municipal
Cut costs through programmed insurance; Trenton, N.J. J. Matzer, jr. il Am City 84: 148+ Mr '69

INSURANCE, Property
Bad risk in schools. Time 94:49 D 26 '69
Profit before risk; insuring the ghettos. H. Shapiro. Commonweal 89:579-80 F 7 '69
Riot act irks underwriters; federal riot reinsurance program. Bsns W p 104 My 10 '69
See also
Insurance, Casualty

INSURANCE, Psychiatric. See Insurance, Mental health

INSURANCE, Social
More and more billions for workers' welfare. il U S News 66:72-3 Je 2 '69
See also
Social security taxes
Survivors benefits

United States
Adding $1-billion to spending power. il Bsns W p 12-13 Ja 3 '70
Answers to your questions about social security & medicare. F. Bailey, jr. il Suc Farm 67:72-3 Ja '69
Early retirement under social security. R. R. Jalbert. il Har Yrs 9:24-5 Mr '69
Employer vs. domestic: the social security hassle. M. Feeley. Am Home 72:11+ Ja '69
Find out what your social security will pay. il Changing T 23:47-8 Mr '69
For women: advice on social security. il Changing T 23:37-8 N '69
Free-lance writer and social security. J. Sword. Writer 82:27-9 Mr '69
How much can you earn and still collect social security? Bet Hom & Gard 47:7+ Je '69
One-upping Nixon on social security. il Bsns W p42-3 O 11 '69
Raise ahead for pensioners: only question is how big. il U S News 67:96-8 O 6 '69
Since you asked... R. R. Jalbert. Har Yrs 9:43-4 S '69
Social security: why pensions are smaller than people expect. il U S News 67:71 Ag 18 '69
Social security's galloping surplus. il Bsns W p41-2 O 18 '69
Writer and social security. L. Boggess. il Writers Digest 49:56-9+ D '69
See also
Old age pensions—United States
Old age, survivors' and disability insurance trust fund

INSURANCE, Strike
Construction industries to be insured against strikes? US News 66:66 Ap 7 '69
Contractors try strike insurance; employer weapon to counter labor's collective bargaining. Bsns W p56 Ap 5 '69

INSURANCE, Survivors. See Survivors benefits

INSURANCE, Unemployment
More help for the jobless: how the Nixon plan would work. U S News 67:65-6 Jl 21 '69

Canada
Jobless frauds, Canadian style. U S News 66:74 F 24 '69

United States
Feuding over jobless pay; proposed changes sent to Congress by President Nixon. Bsns W p47-8 Jl 12 '69
Railroads want to stop subsidizing their own strikers. Bsns W p34 D 20 '69
Status report on unemployment insurance laws; tables. J. A. Hickey. Mo Labor R 92:47-51 Ja '69

INSURANCE, Workmens compensation. See Workmens compensation

INSURANCE companies
Can fifty money managers all be wrong? conglomerates buying insurance companies. il Forbes 103:46-7 Mr 1 '69
Giants of black capitalism. il Ebony 24:164-6+ My '69
Heads you lose, tails. .? insurance companies moving into the computer business. il Forbes 104:25 O 1 '69
Insurance giants move into funds; control of Manhattan fund by CNA financial. il Bsns W p 114-16+ Mr 15 '69
Mutuals: publicly owned, but not stockholder owned. il Forbes 103:195 My 15 '69
Now the packaged estate: insurance plus stocks; with interview with G. P. Hinckley. il U S News 66:82-4 Je 30 '69
See also
American general insurance company
American income life insurance company
Equitable life assurance society of the United States
Kemper insurance group
Lloyd's, London
Pennsylvania life insurance company

Consolidations and mergers
He started something. Forbes 103:92+ Je 15 '69

Directories
Fifty largest life-insurance companies. Fortune 79:192-3 My 15 '69

Finance
Why automobile insurance rates keep going up; excerpt from Are you being taken for a ride? G. B. Friedman. Atlan 224:58-63 S '69
See also
Insurance companies—Investments

Investments
Are they compatible? mutual funds and life insurance. il Forbes 104:86+ Ag 15 '69
Great tax-free cash-in. il Forbes 104:52 N 1 '69
Insurance's belated awakening il Time 94:59 Ag '69
Why automobile insurance rates keep going up; excerpt from Are you being taken for a ride? G. B. Friedman. Atlan 224:58-63 S '69

Regulation
Insurance rates take new route. Bsns W p67 Ja 3 '70
Kemper officials see what makes Washington tick. il Bsns W p74 Je 28 '69

Securities
Lively stock group; life-insurance. C. Morgello. il Newsweek 74:88 N 3 '69

INSURANCE law
See also
Insurance companies—Regulation

INSURANCE of mutual funds. See Investment trusts—Insurance

INSURANCE policies. See Insurance—Policies

INSURRECTIONS. See Revolutions

INTEGRATED aircrew escape/rescue system capability. See Airplanes—Escape devices

INTEGRATED circuits. See Electronic circuits —Integrated circuits

INTEGRATED curriculum. See Correlation (education)

INTEGRATION of public schools. See Public schools—Desegregation

INTELLECT
See also
Brain
Intelligence
Thought and thinking

INTELLECTUAL liberty
ALA moves fast on freedom issue. Library J 94:2991 S 15 '69
Boll weevil six feet long; Mississippi librarian's action in battle against campus speaker ban. J. M. Carter. il Library J 94: 3615-18 O 15 '69
Booksellers' stake in intellectual freedom; excerpts from address. T. Sorensen. Pub W 195:61 Je 16 '69
Girl with the waterproof eyes; Statue of Liberty and liberal, but fired librarians. K. Nyren. Library J 94:1823 My 1 '69
I could no longer breathe. A. Kuznetsov. il Time 94:30-1 Ag 8 '69
Intellectual freedom. J. F. Krug. ALA Bul 63:1065-7 S '69
Martinsville counterattack: Ellis Hodgin accused. Library J 94:4082 N 15 '69
Missouri quicksand: an in-depth survey; free speech controversy. W. R. Eshelman. Wilson Lib Bul 44:266-8 N '69
President Nixon: intellectual freedom in danger; statement, March 23, 1969. R. M. Nixon. U S News 66:30 Mr 31 '69
Teaching the concept of intellectual freedom: the state of the art; address. January 14, 1967. D. Bendix. bibliog il ALA Bul 63:351-62 Mr '69
Virginia librarian fired by city manager; with editorial comment. Library J 94:2853, 2855 S 1 '69; Reply. I. Webb and others. 94:3585 O 15 '69
See also
Academic freedom
American library association—Intellectual freedom committee
National freedom fund for librarians

INTELLECTUAL life
See also
Books and reading
Enlightenment
also subhead Intellectual life under names of countries, states, cities, e.g. United States —Intellectual life

INTELLECTUAL property
See also
Royalties

INTELLECTUAL snobs. See Snobs and snobbishness

INTELLECTUALS
America and the world; a new fix? Princeton seminar. A. Schlesinger, jr. Vogue 153: 184-5+ F 1 '69
American power and the new mandarins, by N. Chomsky. Review
Commentary 47:35-44 My '69. L. Abel; Discussion. 48:12+ O '69
Dissident intellectuals; South Viet Nam. il Time 94:41-2 Jl 18 '69
From intellectuals, deliver us! R. Kirk. Nat R 21:128 F 11 '69
Heyday for intellectuals; growing force in America. il U S News 67:74-7 Jl 21 '69
Intellectuals and conservatism; situation in England. T. Szamuely. il Nat R 21:273-7 Mr 25 '69
Notes from the underground; Chronicle of current events. il Time 94:41-2 N 28 '69
Opinion: responsibilities of the American intellectual. G. Corsini. Mlle 69:24+ Je '69
Tortured role of the intellectual in America; Time essay. il Time 93:48-9 My 9 '69
Tragedy of Lyndon Johnson, by E. F. Goldman. Review
Sat R 52:37-9+ F 15 '69. Q. Howe
Very model of a modern intellectual. G. Stevens. Sat R 52:27 F 22 '69
Weimar Germany's left-wing intellectuals, by I. Deak. Review
Commentary 48:94-6+ O '69. M. Jay
Who is responsible for student violence? R. L. Means. America 120:352-5 Mr 29 '69
See also
Negro intellectuals
Scientists, American

INTELLIGENCE
Talk and intelligence; with study-discussion program, ed. by R. Strang. J. W. Kessler. bibliog il PTA Mag 64:15-17+, 34 S '69
See also
Memory

INTELLIGENCE, Air. See Military intelligence

INTELLIGENCE, Artificial. See Artificial intelligence

INTELLIGENCE, Military. See Military intelligence

INTELLIGENCE levels
Born dumb? theories of A. Jensen. il Newsweek 73:84 Mr 31 '69
Genetics vs. headstart. Sci N 95:326-7 Ap 5 '69
Nurture key to I.Q. P. McBroom. il Sci N 95:243-5 Mr 8 '69
Pygmalion in the classroom, by R. Rosenthal and L. Jacobson. Review
New Yorker 45:169-70+ Ap 19 '69. R. Coles

INTELLIGENCE levels—*Continued*

Negroes

Black power and the learning process. M. R. Berube. Commonweal 90:98-101 Ap 11 '69

Can Negroes learn the way whites do? findings of a top authority; with reactions to his conclusions. A. R. Jensen. il U S News 66:48-51 Mr 10 '69

Educational relevance and Jensen's conclusions. N. Anastasiow. Ed Digest 35:34-7 D '69

Furor over race and I.Q. Here's the latest chapter; response of seven educators to views of A. R. Jensen expressed in Harvard educational review. il U S News 66:54-6 Je 2 '69

Intelligence and race; theories of Arthur R. Jensen. New Repub 160:10-11 Ap 5 '69

Intelligence: is there a racial difference? il Time 93:54+ Ap 11 '69

IQ: God-given or man-made? theories of A. R. Jensen and J. Piaget. G. Voyat. il Sat R 52:73-5+ My 17 '69; Same abr. Ed Digest 35:1-4 O '69

Jensenism, n. the theory that I.Q. is largely determined by the genes. L. Edson. il N Y Times Mag p 10-11+ Ag 31 '69; Discussion. p4+ S 21; 38+ S 28 '69

Let there be darkness; theories of A. R. Jensen. Nat R 21:996-7 O 7 '69

On Negro inferiority. W. F. Buckley, jr. Nat R 21:350 Ap 8 '69

Racial factors in intelligence. a rebuttal; statement in response to Arthur R. Jensen's article in Harvard educational review. M. Deutsch and others. Trans-Action 6:6+ Je '69; Discussion 6:62-4 O '69

Refutation of Jensen's position on intelligence, race, social class, and heredity. M. Golden and W. Bridger. bibliog Ment Hy 53:648-53 O '69

Sense, and nonsense, about race. M. Mead. Redbook 133:35+ S '69

What color is IQ? intelligence and race; theories of A. R. Jensen. C. Jencks. New Repub 161:25-9 S 6 '69; Reply. J. D. Hyman. 161:30-1 O 25 '69

Women

You may be brighter than you think. D. Klein. il Seventeen 28:146-7+ Mr '69

INTELLIGENCE of animals. See Animal intelligence

INTELLIGENCE quotient

Black genes, white environment. J. M. Hunt. bibliog il Trans-Action 6:12-22 Je '69

Can Negroes learn the way whites do? findings of a top authority; with reactions to his conclusions. A. R. Jensen. il U S News 66:48-51 Mr 10 '69

Furor over race and I.Q. Here's the latest chapter; response of seven educators to views of A. R. Jensen expressed in Harvard educational review. il U S News 66:54-6 Je 2 '69

Intelligence and race; theories of Arthur R. Jensen on IQ test scores. New Repub 160:10-11 Ap 5 '69

Intelligence: is there a racial difference? il Time 93:54+ Ap 11 '69

IQ: God-given or man-made? theories of A. R. Jensen and J. Piaget. G. Voyat. il Sat R 52:73-5+ My 17 '69; Same abr. Ed Digest 35:1-4 O '69

Jensenism, n. the theory that I.Q. is largely determined by the genes. L. Edson. il N Y Times Mag p 10-11+ Ag 31 '69; Discussion. p4+ S 21; 38+ S 28 '69

Jensen's complaint. M. R. Berube. Commonweal 91:42-4 O 10 '69

Race and intelligence; findings of A. R. Jensen. J. Cass. Sat R 52:67-8 My 17 '69

Racial factors in intelligence. a rebuttal: statement in response to Arthur R. Jensen's article in Harvard educational review. M. Deutsch and others. Trans-Action 6: 6+ Je '69; Discussion. 6:62-4 O '69

Refutation of Jensen's position on intelligence, race, social class, and heredity. M. Golden and W. Bridger. bibliog Ment Hy 53:648-53 O '69

Sex differences in verbal and performance IQ's of children undergoing open-heart surgery. M. P. Honzik and others. bibliog il Science 164:445-7 Ap 25 '69; Reply with rejoinder. A. F. Paolino. 166:259-60 O 10 '69

What color is IQ? intelligence and race; theories of A. R. Jensen. C. Jencks. New Repub 161:25-9 S 6 '69; Reply. J. D. Hyman. 161:30-1 O 25 '69

What's the IQ of the IQ tests. P. Pine. il Am Ed 5:2-4 N '69

You may be brighter than you think. D. Klein. il Seventeen 28:146-7+ Mr '69

INTELLIGENCE service. See Secret service

INTELLIGENCE tests

Origin of IQ tests; excerpt from How much can we boost IQ and scholastic achievement? A. R. Jensen. Sat R 52:68 My 17 '69

See also
Aptitude tests
Intelligence quotient
Psychological examinations

INTELSAT. See International telecommunications satellite consortium

INTENSIFIERS, Image. See Image intensifiers

INTENSIVE care units. See Hospital care

INTER-AMERICAN children's institute

Men of tomorrow. G. de Zéndegui. Américas 21:1 O '69

INTER-AMERICAN commission of women

For women today. P. de Suro. il Américas 21:38-40 O '69

INTER-AMERICAN cooperation. See Inter-American relations

INTER-AMERICAN cultural council

Report from Port of Spain; sixth meeting. C. de Zéndegui. il Américas 21:2-5 Ag '69

$7,600,000 for science and education development; multinational projects in Latin America. Américas 21:43 Ja '69

INTER-AMERICAN development bank

Board of governors of the Inter-American development bank holds tenth annual meeting at Guatemala city; statement, April 22, 1969. D. M. Kennedy. Dept State Bul 60: 426-9 My 19 '69

INTER-AMERICAN economic and social council

Inter-American economic and social council meets at Port-of-Spain; statement, June 20, 1969, with President Nixon's message, and Declaration of Port-of-Spain. C. A. Meyer. Dept State Bul 61:21-6 Jl 14 '69

Latin American consensus of Viña del Mar; accepted at Port of Spain meeting. Américas 21:42-3 Ag '69

New bond of union; first satellite in common service of the American nations. G. de Zéndegui. Américas 21:1 Mr '69

INTER-AMERICAN education
See also
Center of intercultural documentation

INTER-AMERICAN highway. See Pan American highway

INTER-AMERICAN relations

Era of the good neighbor. G. W. Grayson, jr. bibliog f Cur Hist 56:327-32+ Je '69

Latin consensus. Newsweek 73:51-2 Je 23 '69

New approach to Pan American problems; remarks, April 14, 1969. R. M. Nixon. Dept State Bul 60:384-6 My 5 '69

New policy; closeness and cooperation with the countries of the hemisphere. G. de Zéndegui. Américas 21:1 My '69

President Nixon and President Lleras of Colombia review common goals of the Americas; exchange of greetings, toasts and remarks, June 12, 13, 1969. R. M. Nixon; C. Lleras Restrepo. Dept State Bul 61:8-13 Jl 7 '69

United States and Latin America; a special relationship; statement, January 9, 1969. L. B. Johnson. Dept State Bul 60:73-4 Ja 27 '69

See also
Action for progress for the Americas
Alliance for progress
Inter-American commission of women
Organization of American states

INTER-AMERICAN telecommunications commission. See Inter-American economic and social council

INTER-AMERICAN treaty of reciprocal assistance

Treaty of Rio de Janeiro. Cur Hist 56:363 Je '69

INTERARMCO. See International armaments corporation

INTERCHANGE of employees. See Employees, Interchange of

INTERCHANGE of persons. See Exchange of persons programs

INTERCHANGE of teachers. See Teachers, Interchange of

INTERCHURCH (newspaper)

New ecumenical newspaper in Indiana. Chr Cent 86:673 My 14 '69

INTERCITY transportation. See Transportation—United States

INTERCOLLEGIATE football. See Football

INTERCOMMUNICATING systems

Intercom network cuts city phone bill; Meriden, Conn. city hall. il Am City 84:56 Ja '69

Wire your house for intercoms, without wiring at all. W. G. Salm. il Pop Mech 132:130-3+ Jl '69

INTERCOMMUNION. See Lords Supper

INTERCONTINENTAL ballistic missiles. See Guided missiles

INTERCROPPING. See Companion crops

INTERCULTURAL education
Bristol township schools: strategy for change; Intergroup education and sensitivity training programs. T. J. Cottle. il Sat R 52:70-1+ S 20 '69

INTERDENOMINATIONAL cooperation. See Religious cooperation

INTERESSENGEMEINSCHAFT farbenindustrie ag
German chemicals' high-stakes game; Bayer, Hoechst, and BASF fragments of I. G. farben expanding fiercely. il Bsns W p82-4+ N 29 '69

INTEREST
Are interest rates about to turn down? il U S News 66:90-1 My 5 '69
As tight money slows business; with interview with D. Rockefeller. il U S News 67:23-5 Jl 21 '69
Backlash against the bankers; credit-tightening measures. Time 93:74 Je 27 '69
Banks try to dodge Fed's grasp; turn to loan participation certificates. il Bsns W p98 Ap 5 '69
Borrowing costs up again; why? il U S News 67:33-4 S 22 '69
Business loans won't slow down; soaring interest rates. il Bsns W p33-4 Mr 22 '69
Chance of controlling inflation: as top money manager sees it; excerpts from testimony to Joint economic committee of Congress. W. M. Martin, jr. U S News 66:99-100 Mr 10 '69
Classical look at the real cost of money; price-interest rate relationship. il Bsns W p 130-1 Je 28 '69
Fed pinch puts squeeze on Europe; foreign interest rates climb as U.S. banks tap Eurodollar market. il Bsns W p38 Mr 8 '69
Federal reserve head talks on inflation, interest, controls; excerpts from testimony before the Senate committee on banking and currency, September 10, 1969. W. M. Martin, jr. il U S News 67:103-4 S 22 '69
How high is eight per cent? H. C. Wallich. Newsweek 73:72 Ap 7 '69
Interest rates are up almost everywhere. U S News 66:33 Je 23 '69
Interest rates continue to rise. U S News 66:82 F 10 '69
Living with the squeeze; money available, at a price. il Bsns W p21-2 Ja 18 '69
Loosening a Fed rein; Regulation Q sets interest rate ceilings on bank deposits. il Bsns W p72-3 F 8 '69
Money marts feel pinch; interest rates moving up. il Bsns W p32 My 24 '69
Money turns cheaper. il Bsns W p44-5 My 10 '69
More it costs, the more you want. il Newsweek 73:63 Mr 31 '69
New way through the interest ceiling; First Pennsylvania's debt idea. Bsns W p31 Ja 10 '70
Say tight money, and rates soar. U S News 67:87 D 1 '69
Tight money beginning to ease? U S News 67:69-70 Ag 18 '69
U.S. feels the pain of a demi-crunch. il Bsns W p33-4 Je 7 '69
Where high interest rates hurt; a look at the money squeeze. il U S News 66:34-5 F 17 '69
Where the prime rate started its last climb; First national city bank. il Bsns W p38-40 Ja 25 '69
Why interest rates keep going up. il U S News 67:64-6 Ag 11 '69
Why the prime loses its power. il Bsns W p 119 D 13 '69
Will tight money drop interest rates? il Bsns W p 146+ Ap 19 '69
Word on tight money: no relief. il U S News 67:87-8 D 8 '69
See also
Bank deposits—Interest

INTERFACE management. See Industrial management

INTERFACES
Natural interfaces. Electr World 81:65 Ap '69

INTERFACES, Chemistry of. See Surface chemistry

INTERFAITH cooperation. See Religious cooperation

INTERFAITH service center, Portland. See Booksellers and bookselling—Oregon

INTERFERENCE, Radio. See Radio interference

INTERFEROMETRY
East-West baseline; Soviet and U.S. astronomers cooperate on small sources. D. E. Thomsen. il Sci N 96:437 N 8 '69
Interferometer experiment on Nimbus 3: preliminary results. R. Hanel and B. Conrath. il Science 165:1258-60 S 19 '69
Long-baseline interferometry. B. F. Burke. bibliog il Phys Today 22:54-63 Jl '69
Venus: mapping the surface reflectivity by radar interferometry. A. E. E. Rogers and R. P. Ingalls. bibliog il Science 165:797-9 Ag 22 '69

INTERFERON
Chick interferon: heterogeneity of electric charge. K. H. Fantes. bibliog il Science 163:1198-9 Mr 14 '69
Hard times for a panacea. Sci N 96:24-5 Jl 12 '69
Human trials with poly I:C. Sci N 96:574-5 D 20 '69
Immune specific induction of interferon production in cultures of human blood lymphocytes. J. A. Green and others. bibliog il Science 164:1415-17 Je 20 '69
Interfering with tumors. Sci Am 221:50 O '69
Interferon induction increased through chemical modification of a synthetic polyribonucleotide. E. De Clercq and others. bibliog il Science 165:1137-9 S 12 '69
Toward control of viral infections of man. M. R. Hilleman. bibliog il Science 164:511-12 My 2 '69

INTERGOVERNMENTAL fiscal relations
Efficiency in state and local government expenditures. C. L. Harriss. Ann Am Acad 379:39-52 S '68

INTERGOVERNMENTAL tax relations
Big bind in local taxes; look to Washington for help. il Bsns W p44+ Ag 9 '69
Can revenue sharing work? sharing federal tax revenues. Bsns W p 108 Ag 23 '69
Comeback of the states. il U S News 67:48-50 O 27 '69
Compelling idea of sharing the take; revenue sharing. Bsns W p24-5 Ag 9 '69
Enticing logic of revenue sharing. L. A. Mayer. Fortune 79:92-3 Mr '69
Federal revenue sharing. L. Fisher. New Repub 161:15-17 O 4 '69
Money matters; governors discussing welfare programs. Time 94:18-19 S 12 '69
New federalism; National governors conference. il Newsweek 74:24-5 S 15 '69
Nixon: we have to put the money where the problems are; excerpt from address, September 1, 1969. R. M. Nixon. U S News 67:82-4 S 15 '69
Revenue sharing: who would get what. il U S News 67:69-70 Ag 25 '69
Should the government share its tax take? W. W. Heller. il Sat R 52:26-9 Mr 22 '69
Slicing the federal tax pie; interview. P. W. Eggers. Nations Bsns 57:23-6 D '69
Spreading the buck; Richard Nixon's proposals for revenue sharing. K. Crawford. Newsweek 74:35 S 8 '69
This month's feature: federal revenue sharing with the states. Cong Digest 48:225-56 O '69
Toward a new fiscal federalism; local distribution of tax revenues: address, August 27, 1969. M. L. Weidenbaum. Vital Speeches 35:748-51 O 1 '69
Welfare, manpower training, revenue sharing; R. M. Nixon's proposed reforms. America 121:112-13 Ag 30 '69

INTERGROUP education. See Intercultural education

INTERIOR decoration
Design of interiors; a profile of emerging trends in practice. il Arch Rec 145:130-44 Je '69
Lifestyle. See issues of American home
See also
House decoration
Office decoration
Yacht decoration

INTERIOR decorators
Blue book of interior designers. House & Gard 135:56-8 Mr '69
It's up to you and your decorator. W. Baldwin. il House & Gard 136:12-13+ N '69
Vogue's choice; tips from famous decorators. Vogue 154:160 O 15 '69
See also
Braswell, J.

INTERIOR designers. See Interior decorators

INTERIOR monologue; story. See Oates, J. C.

INTERLIBRARY loans
Model interlibrary loan code. ALA Bul 63:513-16 Ap '69
WATS happening in North Carolina. B. A. Shuman. il Library J 94:945-7 Mr 1 '69

INTERMARRIAGE of races
Black and white couples: have attitudes changed? C. W. Childs. Redbook 133:90+ S '69
Pink is from mama. M. Booker. il Redbook 133:12+ O '69

INTERMARRIAGES, Religious. See Marriages, Mixed

INTERMEDIA performances. See Performing arts

INTERMEDINS
Pars intermedia: unitary electrical activity regulated by light. K. Oshima and A. Gorbman. bibliog il Science 163:195-7 Ja 10 '69

INTERMOUNTAIN conference on childrens literature. See Childrens literature

INTERMOUNTAIN observer. See Boise, Idaho —Newspapers

INTERNAL combustion engines. See Automobile engines; Gas and oil engines

INTERNAL revenue. See Taxation

INTERNAL revenue service. See United States —Internal revenue service

INTERNAL security
HEW blacklisting issue ignites again. B. Nelson. Science 166:357 O 17 '69
HEW security checks said to bar qualified applicants to PHS. B. Nelson. Science 165:269-71 Jl 18 '69
Prognosis for crackdown: the wheel of panic. T. J. Lowi. Nation 208:624-8 Mv 19 '69
Scientists increasingly protest HEW investigation of advisers. B. Nelson. il Science 164:1499-504 Je 27 '69
Search and destroy; proposed act of 1969. R. Dudman. New Repub 161:12 Jl 19 '69
Undeclared witch-hunt. T. Wicker. Harper 239:108-10 N '69
See also
Subversive activities

INTERNATIONAL agencies
See also
International cooperation

INTERNATIONAL agreements. See Treaties

INTERNATIONAL air race. See Airplane racing

INTERNATIONAL air transport agreements. See Aviation—International aspects

INTERNATIONAL air transport association
Governments threaten IATA role. L. Doty. Aviation W 91:27-8 O 27 '69
IATA establishes two-phase fare schedule. E. H. Kolcum. Aviation W 90:47 Ap 14 '69
IATA found to cast faint public image. Aviation W 91:33 N 10 '69
IATA slates North European fare raise. Aviation W 90:31-2 Mr 17 '69
National interests hobble action by IATA. L. Doty. il Aviation W 90:41+ Ja 27 '69
Revised IATA cargo rates to favor bulk containers. Aviation W 90:29 My 19 '69
Two-year Atlantic fare package set after lengthy IATA talks. Aviation W 90:32 F 10 '69

INTERNATIONAL animal exchange, incorporated
$5,000 a giraffe. il Newsweek 73:84-5 F 17 '69

INTERNATIONAL arbitration. See Arbitration, International

INTERNATIONAL armaments corporation
Arms dealer Sam; excerpts from The war business. G. Thayer. Harper 238:92+ Ap '69

INTERNATIONAL association for cultural freedom
America and the world; a new fix? Princeton seminar. A. Schlesinger, jr. Vogue 153:184-5+ F 1 '69
Liberal establishment faces the blacks, the young, the new left. W. Goodman; discussion. N Y Times Mag p4+ Ja 19 '69

INTERNATIONAL association of machinists and aerospace workers
Mr Smith goes to Washington for IAM. Bsns W p 102 Je 21 '69
National flights to fly. il Bsns W p78 F 8 '69
Push for new strike law; movement to reform Railway labor act. il Bsns W p45-6 S 6 '69

INTERNATIONAL astronomical union
Report from Rome: X-rays and gamma rays. G. S. Mumford. il Sky & Tel 38:96-8 Ag '69

INTERNATIONAL atomic energy agency
Assembly adopts resolution on IAEA. UN Mo Chron 6:107 Ja '69
General conference of the International atomic energy agency hold 13th session at Vienna; statement, September 24, 1969. G. T. Seaborg. Dept State Bul 61:329-33 O 20 '69
IAEA seeks better ways to detect nuclear-material diversion. J. P. Wiley. il Phys Today 22:69-70 Ag '69
Nuclear double-check; IAEA inspection of nuclear reprocessing plant facilities. il Bsns W p84 Je 28 '69

Nuclear safeguards; the IAEA program. B. W. Sharpe. il Phys Today 22:33-7 N '69
Nuclear safeguards, the peaceful atom, and the IAEA. L. Scheinman. bibliog f il Int Concil 572:5-64 Mr '69

INTERNATIONAL automobile show. See Automobiles—Exhibitions

INTERNATIONAL balance of payments. See Balance of payments

INTERNATIONAL ballet competition, Moscow. See Ballet—Competitions

INTERNATIONAL bank for reconstruction and development
IMF and IBRD boards of governors meet at Washington; statement, September 30, 1969. D. M. Kennedy. Dept State Bul 61:353-8 O 27 '69
It is only right; Pearson report. America 121:318-19 O 18 '69
Next five years. R. S. McNamara. Duns R 92:19+ D '68
Reports of the World bank group and international monetary fund; statement, December 5, 1968. A. E. Goldschmidt. Dept State Bul 60:15-17 Ja 6 '69
World banking McNamara-style; aid to have-not lands. il Bsns W p96-8+ S 27 '69

INTERNATIONAL banking. See Banks and banking, International

INTERNATIONAL basic economy corporation
Hard times hit a Rockefeller enterprise. il Bsns Wp60 Jl 26 '69

INTERNATIONAL biological program
Boost for IBP; letter. F. W. G. Baker. Science 164:245 Ap 18 '69
Keeping nature in balance. G. Alexander. il Newsweek 74:113-15 O 20 '69

INTERNATIONAL board on books for young people
Russians and Czechs at IBBY; skirting confrontation Library J 94:252+ Ja 15 '69

INTERNATIONAL book exhibition, Berlin. See Book exhibits

INTERNATIONAL book fair, Jerusalem. See Book fairs

INTERNATIONAL brotherhood of teamsters, chauffeurs, warehousemen and helpers of America
Teamster old guard wins with Flynn. Bsns W p74 Mr 15 '69
Teamsters open a labor school to process their local talent; IBT labor institute. il Bsns W p61 S 27 '69
Truckers' goals spark new worry over inflation. Bsns W p62 D 27 '69
See also
Alliance for labor action

INTERNATIONAL bureau of weights and measures
Measuring it better: a visit to Bureau international des poids et mesures. R. H. Ellis. il Phys Today 22:57+ D '69

INTERNATIONAL business machines corporation
Another great divide: major lawsuits against IBM. il Forbes 103:15-17 F 1 '69
Antitrust: U.S. vs. IBM. Newsweek 73:79 Ja 27 '69
Giants will stay that way. Bsns W p70 S 6 '69
IBM girds for battle; vs government's antitrust action. Bsns W p36-8 Ja 25 '69
IBM program for shaking off suits; IBM's court strategy. Bsns W p49 Je 14 '69
IBM questions; Justice department's antitrust suit. Time 93:63 Ja 31 '69
IBM rewrites the price book. Bsns W p 102+ Je 28 '69
IBM thinks small. Newsweek 74:56 Ag 11 '69
IBM's unruly brood: lawsuit against Cogar corp. and former IBM staff to prevent use of confidential IBM information. il Newsweek 74:85-7 Jl 21 '69
Now it's the Europeans versus I.B.M. P. Siekman. il Fortune 80:86-91+ Ag 15 '69
Performance comes first; philanthropic programs. L. L. L. Golden. Sat R 52:117 S 13 '69
Spy in the computer factory; a visit to the Watson research center in Ossining, N.Y. S. Hochman. Look 33:22 Mr 4 '69
Think. by W. Rodgers. Review
Sat R 52:44-5 O 4 '69. S. W. Clements
Washington's challenge to IBM. il Time 93:66 Ja 24 '69
When products fail IBM's tough test. il Bsns W p20-1 D 20 '69
Xerox: the McColough era; clashes with IBM. il Forbes 104:24-6+ Jl 1 '69

INTERNATIONAL Catholic film office
No Vatican Oscar for Teorema. L. J. Berry. Commonweal 90:292-3 My 23 '69

INTERNATIONAL chamber of commerce
Nationalism sets boundaries for multinational giants. il Bsns W p94-6+ Je 14 '69

INTERNATIONAL Christian broadcasters
Spiritual revolutionists. R. Chandler. Chr Today 13:32 Jl 4 '69

INTERNATIONAL city management association
City managers redirect to meet challenge of
70's. Am City 84:40+ Je '69

INTERNATIONAL civil aviation organization
ICAO notified of U.S. ratification of Tokyo
convention. Dept State Bul 61:275 S 22 '69
Sluggish traffic laid to global upheavals. Aviation W 90:47 Je 16 '69
U.S. offers updated approach on liability;
airline liability in international transportation. H. D. Watkins. Aviation W 91:45+ N
10 '69

INTERNATIONAL code signals. See Signals
and signaling

INTERNATIONAL coffee council
Fourth annual report on the International cof-
fee agreement transmitted to the Congress;
President's letter, with text of report. R.
M. Nixon. il Dept State Bul 61:262-7 S 22
'69
International coffee agreement: executive
order, January 17, 1969. L. B. Johnson. Dept
State Bul 60:126 F 10 '69

INTERNATIONAL committee of the Red cross.
See Red cross

INTERNATIONAL computers, limited. See
Computer industry—Great Britain

INTERNATIONAL confederation of free trade
unions
Mr Meany's full circle. Nation 208:291 Mr 10
'69
Stop the world; labor's establishment. J.
Hill. Commonweal 90:5-6 Mr 21 '69

INTERNATIONAL conference on high energy
physics
Theory falls behind experiments in high-
energy physics. M. J. Moravcsik. il Phys
Today 22:119+ Ja '69

INTERNATIONAL conference on public edu-
cation
Geneva conference on public education. Sch
& Soc 97:42+ Ja '69

INTERNATIONAL conference on science and
society
Third international conference on science and
society; Herceg Novi, Yugoslavia, June
1969. A. M. Weinberg. Bul Atom Sci 25:23-
6 N '69

INTERNATIONAL conference on the problems
of the human environment. See United
Nations conference on the problems of human environment (proposed)

INTERNATIONAL conferences
Calendar of international conferences. See Is-
sues of Department of state bulletin
Five principles, a new approach. M. Selk. Bul
Atom Sci 25:78 F '69
NLF asks the American left where are you?
ten-point proposal, and the Swedish inter-
national liaison committee conference,
Stockholm. F. Schurmann. Ramp Mag 8:14+
Ag '69
See also
International conference on science and so-
ciety
Midway conference, 1969

Anecdotes, facetiae, satire, etc.
Content of tables: conference tables, 1969-
2169. H. F. Ellis. New Yorker 45:102+ F
22 '69

INTERNATIONAL congress of gerontology.
See Aging, Conferences on

INTERNATIONAL controls corporation
Company on the make; R. L. Vesco's mini-
conglomerate. Forbes 103:29 Mr 1 '69

INTERNATIONAL convention on the elimina-
tion of all forms of racial discrimination
International day for the elimination of racial
discrimination; message March 21, 1969,
with summary of the convention. Thant.
UN Mo Chron 6:i-v Mr '69
Ratification procedures completed. UN Mo
Chron 6:81 Ap '69

INTERNATIONAL cookery. See Cookery, International

INTERNATIONAL cooperation
Let's internationalize defense marketing. R.
E. McGarrah. Harvard Bsns R 47:146-55
My '69
Quote, unquote. UNESCO Courier 22:12-13+
Ag '69
Soviets, West discuss think tank, proposed
international center for studies of the com-
mon problems of advanced societies. D. S.
Greenberg. Science 166:1382 D 12 '69
Trade, aid, and peace. L. B. Pearson. Sat R
52:23-6 F 22 '69

Unemployment of exile; is there a third
choice for the migrant worker? S. Parmar.
il UNESCO Courier 22:32-4 Jl '69
See also
Astronomy—International aspects
Inter-American economic and social council
International education
International university (proposed)
League of Nations
Patents—International aspects
Research—International aspects
Science—International aspects
United Nations

Anecdotes, facetiae, satire, etc.
Atlantic community; G. Swinger takes part
in discussions. D. S. Greenberg. Science
166:852-3 N 14 '69

INTERNATIONAL copyright. See Copyright

INTERNATIONAL corporations. See Corporations, International

INTERNATIONAL council of Christian churches
McIntire's complaint. il Newsweek 74:46 Ag
11 '69

INTERNATIONAL council of scientific unions

Committee on space research
International implications of weather modification. R. F. Taubenfeld and H. J. Taubenfeld. Bul Atom Sci 25:43-5 Ja '69

INTERNATIONAL court of arbitration, The
Hague
U.S. designates four new members of Permanent court of arbitration. Dept State Bul
61:54 Jl 21 '69

INTERNATIONAL court of justice, The Hague
Barcelona traction company case. UN Mo
Chron 6:54 My; 52-3 Je '69
Election of five members of International
court of justice. UN Mo Chron 6:80-1 N '69
Nominations to International court of justice
announced. Dept State Bul 61:218-19 S 8
'69
North Sea continental shelf: Court delivers
judgement. UN Mo Chron 6:43-4 Mr '69
Seeking a warmer venue; World court in The
Hague. Time 94:51 O 3 '69

INTERNATIONAL criminal police organization
Interpol; history & mission; address, November 22, 1968. J. P. Hendrick. Vital Speeches
35:306-8 Mr 1 '69

INTERNATIONAL design conference
Rest of our lives. G. A. Dudley. il Craft Horiz
29:50-1+ S '69

INTERNATIONAL economic policy. See International economic relations

INTERNATIONAL economic relations
Hard choices for the embattled dollar. R. N.
Gardner. il Sat R 52:46+ N 22 '69
Recent trends in international economics.
A. I. Bloomfield. bibliog f Ann Am Acad
386:148-67 N '69

INTERNATIONAL education
Human rights and international education.
C. Cosper. il Sch & Soc 97:457-8 N '69
International education in the 1970's. P. G.
Purcell. Sch & Soc 97:374-5 O '69
International education on a shoestring. W. W.
Brickman. Sch Soc 97:72-3 F '69
International studies for the professional
school. W. A. McCormack. bibliog f Sch &
Soc 97:114-16 F '69
Nairobi conference on education in Africa.
Sch & Soc 97:41-2 Ja '69
Planning and the development of education.
Sch & Soc 97:168 Mr '69
Special issue on international education. il
Am Ed 5:2-27 My '69
U.S. retrenchment in international education.
Sch & Soc 97:234-5 Ap '69
See also
American institute for foreign study
Area studies
International relations—Study and teaching
International university (proposed)
Students, Interchange of
Teachers, Interchange of
Travel study courses

Federal aid
Support for international education. il Am
Ed 5:27 My '69

INTERNATIONAL education year, 1970
International element in teacher education.
W. W. Brickman. Sch & Soc 97:474-5 D '69
1970, International education year. L. Fernig.
il UNESCO Courier 23:4-6 Ja '70
Preparation for International education year.
Sch & Soc 97:417+ N '69

INTERNATIONAL educational exchanges. See
Educational exchanges

INTERNATIONAL encyclopedia of the social sciences
Editing a scientific encyclopedia. D. L. Sills. bibliog il Science 163:1169-75 Mr 14 '69
International encyclopedia of the social sciences. H. Einbinder. il Library J 94:1592-4 Ap 15 '69
INTERNATIONAL expositions. See Exhibitions
INTERNATIONAL federation of air line pilots associations
IFALPA mounts anti-hijack drive. il Aviation W 91:22-4 S 8 '69
IFALPA pushing to thrust hijack issue before U.N; with editorial comment. H. J. Coleman. Aviation W 91:21, 39-40 S 15 '69
IFALPA threatens strike in push against hijackings. Aviation W 90:31 Mr 31 '69
Pilots call Kennedy facilities inadequate. Aviation W 90:32 Ap 7 '69
INTERNATIONAL federation of library associations
IFLA: Moscow; 1970 general council meeting. ALA Bul 63:1535 D '69
IFLA, 1969 at Copenhagen. R. C. Ellsworth. il Wilson Lib Bul 44:254+ N '69
INTERNATIONAL fellowship of reconciliation
I.F.O.R. accepts a wider role. C. Chatfield. Chr Cent 86:1288-90 O 8 '69
Nonviolence in Latin America. E. K. Culhane. America 120:331 Mr 22 '69
INTERNATIONAL festival of music and drama, Edinburgh
Scotland: the festival and Muggeridge. I. Logan. Chr Cent 86:1291-2 O 8 '69
INTERNATIONAL film festival, Cannes. See Cannes international film festival
INTERNATIONAL finance. See Finance, International
INTERNATIONAL flavors and fragrances, incorporated
Sex, hunger, and IFF. S. Margetts. il Duns R 94:93+ N '69
INTERNATIONAL geological congress
Prague: geologists' exodus. B. Nelson; reply. C. Hyman. Science 163:129 Ja 10 '69
INTERNATIONAL geophysical year
Prospects for international cooperation on the moon: the Antarctic analogy. P. M. Smith. il Bul Atom Sci 25:36-40 S '69
INTERNATIONAL high alpine ballooning week. See Balloon racing
INTERNATIONAL houses
See also
Lodestar international student center
INTERNATIONAL human rights year. See International year for human rights, 1968
INTERNATIONAL industrial conference
Business confers, SDS jeers. il Bsns W p56 S 20 '69
Rich confer; forthcoming convention. S. Weissman. Ramp Mag 8:58+ S '69
INTERNATIONAL joint commission (United States and Canada)
IJC asked to study pollution risks from Lake Erie oil spills; Department announcement, with text of U.S. letter, March 21, 1969. Dept State Bul 60:296 Ap 7 '69
IJC holds meetings on pollution of Great Lakes connecting channels; Department announcement with text of report. Dept State Bul 60:234-5 Mr 17 '69
IJC issues interim report on Great Lakes water levels. Dept State Bul 60:186 Mr 3 '69
U.S., Canada conclude agreements on Niagara Falls beautification; Department announcement; with exchange of notes, March 21, 1969. Dept State Bul 60:345-7 Ap 21 '69
U.S., Canada release IJC report on survey of Red River pollution. Dept State Bul 60:543 Je 23 '69
INTERNATIONAL labor day. See May day (labor holiday)
INTERNATIONAL labor organization
Building-blocks of social justice for 1,500 million workers; symposium. il UNESCO Courier 22:4-34 Jl '69
Church and the ILO. J. A. Lucal. America 120:644-6 My 31 '69
History
Fiftieth anniversary of ILO. UN Mo Chron 6:8-9 N '69
ILO and world peace; excerpts from address. D. A. Morse. UN Mo Chron 6:54-8 Je '69
ILO at fifty; how it began and how it functions. J. E. Lawyer. Mo Labor R 92:32-6 My '69
ILO at fifty; symposium. il Mo Labor R 92:30-53 My '69
ILO 50th anniversary; address, May 8, 1969. G. F. Pompei. il UNESCO Courier 22:4-7 Jl '69
ILO: fifty years of labor. J. A. Tijierino-Medrano. il Américas 21:16-22 Jl '69

International labor organization: fifty years of service; statement, October 29, 1969. G. P. Shultz. Dept State Bul 61:452-3 N 24 '69
Peace and justice; address, June 18, 1969. Thant. UN Mo Chron 6:96-101 Jl '69
Should U.S. business support the ILO? 50th anniversary of world body. il Bsns W p68+ Je 14 '69
INTERNATIONAL ladies' garment workers' union
ILGWU: fighting for lower wages. M. Myerson. Ramp Mag 8:51-5 O '69
INTERNATIONAL law
Programme of assistance in international law; advisory committee meets. UN Mo Chron 6:83 N '69
Programme of assistance in the field of international law; General assembly adopts resolution. UN Mo Chron 6:150 Ja '69
Role of world law in arms control. S. C. Yuter. Bul Atom Sci 25:23-5 O '69
Toward a new language; world law. N. Cousins. Sat R 52:24 My 24 '69
World law and the hijackers. K. M. Ruppenthal. Nation 208:144-6 F 3 '69
See also
Airspace (international law)
Aviation—Laws and regulations
League of Nations
Maritime law
Recognition (international law)
Sovereignty
Space law
United Nations—International law commission
United Nations—Legal committee
United Nations—Special committee on principles of international law concerning friendly relations and cooperation among states
War, Laws of
INTERNATIONAL law commission. See United Nations—International law commission
INTERNATIONAL license agreements
Does foreign licensing pay? A. Hershman. il Duns R 94:99-100+ O '69
INTERNATIONAL loans. See Loans, Foreign
INTERNATIONAL longshoremen's association
Peace comes to Boston; shippers and ILA end months-long tieup. Bsns W p58 Ap 5 '69
INTERNATIONAL magazine conference
Editors and publishers: a confrontation? J. Tebbel. Sat R 52:49-50 Jl 12 '69
INTERNATIONAL management association, incorporated
Briton charges the U.S. with managerial imperialism. il Bsns W p72 N 29 '69
INTERNATIONAL milling company
Old miller gets off the old grind. il Bsns W p54+ O 25 '69
Yeast maker; W. G. Phillips. J. Poindexter. Duns R 94:74-5 S '69
INTERNATIONAL monetary fund
British credit stretches thin; seeks IMF aid. Bsns W p42+ My 24 '69
Happy ending for gold drama. Ramp Mag 7:57-8 N 30 '68
IMF and IBRD boards of governors meet at Washington; statement, September 30, 1969. D. M. Kennedy. Dept State Bul 61:353-8 O 27 '69
IMF has a crisis agenda; with editorial comment. Bsns W p38+, 134 S 27 '69
Reports of the World bank group and international monetary fund; statement, December 5, 1968. A. E. Goldschmidt. Dept State Bul 60:15-17 Ja 6 '69
See also
Special drawing rights
INTERNATIONAL nickel company of Canada
Canadian strike squeezes the nickel; Canadian workers dig in their heels. il Bsns W p29-30 Ag 23 '69
Nickel's newest crisis; strike of nickel workers. il Bsns W p 106-8 Jl 19 '69
Steelworkers crusade in Canada. Bsns W p88 My 10 '69
INTERNATIONAL organization
Path to total destruction; books by D. F. Fleming. N. L. Parks. Nation 208:153+ F 3 '69
INTERNATIONAL organizations, Regional
See also
Southeast Asia treaty organization
INTERNATIONAL paper company
International paper sees the forest through the trees. E. Carruth. il Fortune 79:104-9+ Mr '69
INTERNATIONAL PEN club. See PEN club
INTERNATIONAL petroleum company
Challenging the U.S; dispute over seizure. Time 93:36 F 14 '69
Current U.S.-Peruvian problems; statement before the Subcommittee on western hemisphere affairs of the Senate committee on foreign relations; April 17, 1969. C. A. Meyer. Dept State Bul 60:406-8 My 12 '69

INTERNATIONAL petroleum company—*Cont.*
Heading for a showdown; seizure of property by Peruvian junta. Time 93:35 Ap 11 '69
Letter from Peru. R. N. Goodwin. New Yorker 45:41-6+ My 17 '69
New junta, but same old Peru. Ramp Mag 7:18+ N 30 '68
Peru turns tougher. il Bsns W p32-3 F 15 '69
Report from Lima. V. Clear. il Fortune 79: 55-6+ Mr '69
Second thoughts; Peruvian takeover. J. B. Utley. il Nat R 21:644-5+ Jl 1 '69
Washington over the oil barrel in Peru. D. Ross. New Repub 160:15-16 Ap 12 '69
INTERNATIONAL police
Frankenstein argument against peacekeeping. N. S. Barnes. Bul Atom Sci 25:16-18 My '69
INTERNATIONAL private investment advisory council. See Investments, Foreign
INTERNATIONAL Red cross. See Red cross
INTERNATIONAL relations
Blessed are the peacemakers. Esquire 72:250-2 D '69
Courage to compromise. Chr Cent 87:3 Ja 7 '70
Detente in the '70s; East-West relations. Z. Brzezinski. New Repub 162:17-18 Ja 3 '70
East-West relations: the process of gaining new evidence; address, June —, 1969. E. L. Richardson. Dept State Bul 60:557-61 Je 30 '69
European commentator looks at U.S. foreign policy today; America's lost innocence. J. H. Huizinga. il N Y Times Mag p30-1+ Ja 26 '69
Falling dominoes. il Newsweek 74:24 O 27 '69
Foreign policy of the Nixon administration: its aims and strategy; address, September 5, 1969. E. L. Richardson. Dept State Bul 61:257-60 S 22 '69
Gearing U.S. policy to the world's great trends. M. Ways. il Fortune 79:64-9+ My 1 '69
In quest of peace; excerpts from Britannica book of the year 1969. L. B. Johnson. il Read Digest 94:219-24+ F '69
Law, power and the pursuit of peace by E. V. Rostow Review
    Cath World 209:222-3 Ag '69. D. W. Louisell
Protagonists, power, and the third world: essays on the changing international system; symposium, ed. by W. Wilcox. bibliog f Ann Am Acad 386:1-147 N '69
Realism in international affairs; address, June 30, 1969. C. W. Yost. Vital Speeches 35:642-5 Ag 15 '69
Road to a third world war; reprint. D. Lawrence. U S News 66:96 Je 16 '69
Secretary Rogers' news conference of April 7, 1969. D. Rusk. Dept State Bul 60:357-63 Ap 28 '69
Slogans and realities. G. W. Ball. For Affairs 47:623-41 Jl '69
Toward a worldwide peace; address to U.N. September 18, 1969. R. M. Nixon. il U S News 67:98-101 S 29 '69; Same with title Establishment of peace. Vital Speeches 35: 738-41 O 1 '69; Same with title Strengthening the total fabric of peace. Dept State Bul 61:297-302 O 6 '69
Undiplomacy: or, The dark ages revisited; Time essay. il Time 93:40 F 28 '69
Way of Bapu; excerpt from Mahatma Gandhi: 100 years. H. Kabir. il UNESCO Courier 22:22-6 O '69
Where U.S. stands in world as top authorities see it. il U S News 66:50-1 Je 30 '69
    See also
Alliances
Balance of power
Disarmament
Europe and the United States
Great powers
Hegemony
International conferences
International cooperation
International economic relations
International labor organization
International law
International police
International security
Intervention (international law)
Italo-Ethiopia war, 1935-1936
League of Nations
Militarism
Nationalism
Pacific countries
Peace
Race problems
Sovereignty
Tariff
United Nations
War
World politics

Bibliography
Recent books on international relations; comp. by J. G. Stoessinger. See issues of Foreign affairs
Source material. D. Wasson. See issues of Foreign affairs
World scene (cont) V. S. Kearney. America 120:545-8; 121:540-3 My 3, N 29 '69
Study and teaching
Cincinnati airs world affairs. S. Aiken. il Am Ed 5:24-6 My '69
INTERNATIONAL rice research institute
From centuries of famine to years of plenty. Fortune 80:180 Ag 15 '69
More and better rice for Asia's hungry millions. P. Deutschman. Read Digest 94:25-6+ My '69
INTERNATIONAL rostrum of composers
Aid for the music of right now. R. McMullen. Hi Fi 19:MA27 S '69
INTERNATIONAL science fair. See Science fairs
INTERNATIONAL scientific radio union
URSI. Sci N 95:455 My 10 '69
INTERNATIONAL security
Kissinger: the uses and limits of power. il Time 93:17-22 F 14 '69
Must we stand alone? D. Lawrence. U S News 66:100 My 26 '69
Nuclear weapons; treaty on nonproliferation; address, January 20, 1969. B. Goldwater. Vital Speeches 35:262-3 F 15 '69
Question of security; Warsaw pact nations propose East-West conference. A. de Borchgrave. il Newsweek 74:65-6 N 17 '69
Space and senselessness; U.S. attitudes at the space science and technology conference, Denver, Colo. N. Cousins. Sat R 52:18 Jl 12 '69
Strategic arms limitation talks; address, November 13, 1969. W. P. Rogers. Dept State Bul 61:465-8 D 1 '69
Strengthening of international security; discussions in First committee. UN Mo Chron 6:28-33 N '69
    See also
Aggression (international law)
Disarmament
International police
International relations
League of Nations
Peace
United Nations—Security council
United Nations—Special committee on peacekeeping operations
INTERNATIONAL settlements, Bank for. See Bank for international settlements
INTERNATIONAL sky cab, Incorporated
Two carriers join Sky cab netwok plan. Aviation W 90:29 Je 30 '69
INTERNATIONAL social cooperation. See International cooperation
INTERNATIONAL society for general semantics
Doctor Hayakawa in thought and action. E. Shorris. il Ramp Mag 8:38-42 N '69
INTERNATIONAL students Incorporated
Reaching internationals. J. Novotney. Chr Today 13:45 S 26 '69
INTERNATIONAL studium of molecular biology. See Colleges and universities—Italy
INTERNATIONAL tapestry biennale. See Tapestry—Exhibitions
INTERNATIONAL telecommunications satellite consortium
Ambassador Marks holds press briefing on the Intelsat conference; February 20, 1969. L. H. Marks. Dept State Bul 60:224-30 Mr 17 '69
Can America stay no. 1 in global communications? U S News 66:12 Mr 24 '69
Comsat fights for a job; management of Intelsat. il Bsns W p60-1 My 3 '69
Comsat role major block to Intelsat pact. K. Johnsen. Aviation W 91:28-9 N 17 '69
Effort to cut Comsat's powers foreseen. K. Johnsen. Aviation W 90:22-3 F 24 '69
Intelsat conference opens at Washington; Department announcement, with welcoming remarks, February 24, 1969. E. L. Richardson; L. H. Marks. Dept State Bul 60:231-4 Mr 17 '69
Intelsat: flying high, but future course uncertain. R. J. Samuelson. Science 164:56-7 Ap 4 '69
Latins, Arabs hit Intelsat subcontracting. K. Johnsen. Aviation W 90:23 Ja 27 '69
New U.S. policy gives ground in the air. Bsns W p50 Je 14 '69
Revamping Intelsat. il Sci N 95:256 Mr 15 '69
Setting new rules for world communications; Intelsat conference in Washington. il Bsns W p32-3 Mr 1 '69
William W. Scranton to head U.S. delegation to Intelsat. Dept State Bul 60:367 Ap 28 '69

INTERNATIONAL telephone and telegraph corporation
Diversification; the new road to world competition; address, October 23, 1969. H. S. Geneen. Vital Speeches 36:147-52 D 15 '69
McLaren pours it on. Newsweek 73:89-90 My 12 '69
Money in the classroom; corporations sponsor vocational education. il Forbes 103:70+ Ap 15 '69
INTERNATIONAL telephone and telegraph-Hartford fire insurance company proposed merger. See Business consolidations and mergers
INTERNATIONAL textbook company
Intext buys Abelard-Schuman. Pub W 195:31 My 12 '69
INTERNATIONAL trade. See Commerce
INTERNATIONAL trade fairs. See Exhibitions
INTERNATIONAL trusteeships
See also
United Nations—Trusteeship council
INTERNATIONAL union for the conservation of nature and natural resources
IUCN; meetings to be in New Delhi, November 24-December 1, 1969. A. W. Smith. Nat Parks 43:2 N '69
National parks around the world. il Nat Parks 43:25-7 My '69
INTERNATIONAL union of crystallography
Crystallographers offer meetings within meetings. W. C. Hamilton. il Phys Today 22:23-7 Ag '69
INTERNATIONAL union of electrical, radio and machine workers
Engineers wear a union label. Bsns W p48 Jl 12 '69
GE and unions open wage battle. il Bsns W p96+ Ag 16 '69
Rival unions talk unity. Bsns W p80 F 8 '69
INTERNATIONAL union of pure and applied physics
International union of pure and applied physics. L. Kerwin. il Phys Today 22:53-5 My '69
INTERNATIONAL union of radio science. See International scientific radio union
INTERNATIONAL university (proposed)
Toward a world university. H. Taylor. Sat R 52:24+ O 11 '69
INTERNATIONAL university booksellers, incorporated
New imprint to specialize in African literature; Africana publishing corporation. Pub W 195:107 Je 2 '69
INTERNATIONAL utilities corporation
How to harvest a business farm. Bsns W p 141-2+ Ap 19 '69
INTERNATIONAL volunteer service. See Volunteer service. International
INTERNATIONAL year for human rights, 1968
Final report submitted on observance of Human rights year 1968; letters. R. M. Nixon; W. A. Harriman. Dept State Bul 60:450-1 My 26 '69
INTERNATIONALE buchausstellung, Berlin. See Book exhibits
INTERNATIONALISM
Beyond the Nation-state. L. B. Pearson. Sat R 52:24-7+ F 15 '69
See also
International cooperation
INTERNISTS. See Physicians
INTERNMENT camps. See Concentration camps
INTERNS (civil service)
On campus; summer on the hill. J. Edmondson. Mlle 69:104 O '69
INTERNSHIP (teaching) See Student teaching
INTEROCEANIC canal commission. See United States—Interoceanic canal commission
INTERPACE corporation
Fast stepping at Interpace. S. Margetts. il Duns R 93:79+ My '69
INTERPERSONAL relations. See Human relations
INTERPLANETARY communication
Messages from Mars. J. Lear. il Sat R 52:75-7 O 11 '69
INTERPLANETARY flight. See Space flight
INTERPLANETARY monitoring platform. See Artificial satellites—Use in research
INTERPOL. See International criminal police organization
INTERPRETERS and interpretation. See Translations and translating
INTERPUBIC ligament. See Ligaments
INTERRACIAL adoption. See Adoption
INTERRACIAL cooperation
Change in Birmingham. il Newsweek 74:79-80 D 8 '69
[Harry Golden column; on the labor front] H. Golden. Nation 109:217 S 8 '69
Why whitey is failing in the cities. R. W. Goldfarb. Read Digest 95:139-44 O '69

INTERRACIAL marriages. See Intermarriage of races
INTERRACIAL relations. See Race relations
INTERREGNUM, Presidential. See Presidents—United States—Transition periods
INTERRELIGIOUS foundation for community organization
Manifest(o) destiny: IFCO and the churches. R. Chandler. Chr Today 13:42 Je 6 '69
Without strings. H. E. Fey. Chr Cent 86:1239-40 O 1 '69
INTERSCHOLASTIC athletics. See School athletics
INTERSECTIONS of streets. See Streets—Intersections
INTERSTATE commerce commission. See United States—Interstate commerce commission
INTERSTATE highway system. See Express highways
INTERSTELLAR matter. See Matter, Interstellar
INTERVENTION (international law)
After Vietnam, what? symposium. il Commonweal 90:7-14 Mr 21 '69; Same. Cur 109:49-51 Ag '69
Intervention and revolution: America's confrontation with insurgent movements around the world, by R. J. Barnet. Review
Commentary 47:78-80 F '69. W. Pfaff
U.S. in Latin America to 1933: an overview. A. P. Whitaker. Cur Hist 56:321-6+ Je '69
INTERVIEWING
Better interviewing can mean better staff. P. Moon. Camp Mag 41:17 Ja '69
How to lose a job by an eyelash; interview. M. E. Campbell. Mlle 68:162-3 Mr '69
Interview for an art job. il Design 70:28-31+ Sum '69
Interviewing: ask the right questions. T. F. Koerner. Clear House 44:102-4 O '69
Interviewing techniques for trade journals. J. Connors. Writer 82:28-30 F '69
Ten rules for the incisive interview; suggestions for writers. J. T. Weiss. Writers Digest 49:41-3 My '69
See also
Employment systems
INTESTINAL and parasitic worms. See Worms Intestinal and parasitic
INTESTINES
See also
Flatulence
INTEXT. See International textbook company
INTOLERANCE. See Prejudice; Toleration
INTRACOASTAL WATERWAY
Eventide on the East coast. E. Newmark. il Yachting 126:68-70+ O '69
Way south. W. R. Juettner. il Motor B 124:52-5+ O '69
INTRAMERCURIAL planets. See Planets
INTRA-UTERINE device. See Contraceptives
INTROVERSION and extroversion
See also
Autism
INTRUDER alarms. See Burglar alarms
INUKAI, Tsuyoshi
Inukai Tsuyoshi: some dilemmas in party development in pre-World war II Japan; address, December 1966. T. Najita. bibliog f Am Hist R 74:492-510 D '68
INUVIK, Northwest Territories
Remotest realm. S. Libby. il Travel 131:55-7 F '69
INVASION, June 6, 1944. See World war, 1939-1945—Campaigns and battles—Western
INVECTIVE
How to insult everyone regardless of race, color, creed, or national origin. C. F. Berlitz. Horizon 11:120 Wint '69
INVENTIONS
Building a better mouse trap. il Time 93:46+ My 2 '69
Dreams and invention. il UNESCO Courier 22:10-11 My '69
New ideas from the inventors. See issues of Popular science monthly
So who's perfect? skeptics and progress. A. Abarbanel. Mech Illus 65:12+ S '69
See also
Patents
United States—Patent office

Exhibitions

Patexpo '69; world's biggest inventors show. S. M. Gallager. il Pop Mech 132:130-7 O '69
Rascal meets the spider; PATEXPO '69. B. Farrell. il Life 67:4 O 24 '69
When patents go on parade; Patexpo '69. il Bsns W p 148+ S 13 '69

INVENTORIES
Ahead of sales again. il Fortune 80:36+ N '69
Business roundup; hedging inventory bets. il
 Fortune 80:24 Ag 1 '69
Closer to avoiding recession; third annual
 survey by the McGraw-Hill economics dept.
 il Bsns W p88-9 My 24 '69
Less for the shelves. il Fortune 79:20+ My 1
 '69
Pileup of stocks. il Fortune 79:20+ F '69
Trimming stocks to fit sales. il Bsns W p29-30
 F 15 '69
 See also
Booksellers and bookselling—Stock
Materials control

INVENTORS
Face to face with an explosive Hawaiian
 inventor. A. Lum. Seventeen 28:34 Ja '69
 See also
De Forest, L.
Goldberg, E.
Inventions
Ovshinsky, S. R.

INVERTEBRATES
 See also
Nervous system—Invertebrates
Skeleton (invertebrates)

INVERTERS, Electric. See Electric current in-
 verters

INVESTIGATIONS, Government See Govern-
 ment investigations

INVESTMENT. See Investments

INVESTMENT advisory services. See Invest-
 ments—Advisers

INVESTMENT banking
Ice stocks in the winter? Forbes 103:62-3 Je
 1 '69
 See also
Hornblower and Weeks-Hemphill, Noyes and
 company

INVESTMENT clubs
Investment clubs pay double dividends. B.
 Watson. il Har Yrs 9:40-3 F '69

INVESTMENT companies. See Investment
 trusts

INVESTMENT counselors. See Investments—
 Advisers

INVESTMENT letter stocks. See Securities—
 Registration

INVESTMENT tax credit
Another blow, or boon? C. Morgello. il News-
 week 73:87 My 5 '69
Battle shaping up over investment credit. il
 U S News 66:93-4 My 12 '69
End of tax credit could curtail aircraft pur-
 chases. Aviation W 90:30 Ap 28 '69
House votes to terminate 7 per cent invest-
 ment tax credit. Aviation W 91:17 Jl 7 '69
If the 7 per cent credit goes. Bsns W p84
 Jl 19 '69
Investment tax credit. P. A. Samuelson.
 Newsweek 73:76 Mr 31 '69
Mid-autumn vote on tax credit bill seen.
 Aviation W 91:20 S 1 '69
New fight over investment credit. U S News
 66:73-4 Ap 14 '69
Retooling ahead for 7 per cent credit. il
 Bsns W p76+ Ap 5 '69
Senate unit backs easing tax credit end.
 Aviation W 91:23 S 29 '69
Tax debate resumes. il Bsns W p45-6 My 10
 '69
Tax trade-off; R. M. Nixon's proposals.
 Nation 208:554-5 My 5 '69
Tough tax choice. Bsns W p38 Je 21 '69
Why Nixon wants to wield the ax; repeal
 of the 7 per cent tax credit. il Bsns W
 p 108-10+ Ap 26 '69

Accounting
Quick depreciation grows among trunks.
 W. H. Gregory. il Aviation W 90:28-9 Ap 28
 '69

INVESTMENT trusts
Alibis, alibis; mutual funds. P. A. Samuelson.
 Newsweek 73:100 Ap 21 '69
Big funds offshore buy into the U.S; real
 estate from motels to factories. il Bsns W
 p 128-9+ Mr 22 '69
Double standard; closed-end funds and dual-
 purpose funds. il Forbes 103:65 Mr 1 '69
Fred Carr says: I've had enough. Bsns W
 p65 D 6 '69
Fund analysis finds its Freud; Arthur Lipper
 corp. il Bsns W p 128-30 S 13 '69
Fund retailers broaden their wares. Bsns W
 p88+ D 13 '69
Fund wizard builds an empire; F. Carr of
 Enterprise fund. il Bsns W p76-8 My 3 '69
Funds. See issues of Forbes
Funds are falling; mutual funds. Time 94:72
 Jl 11 '69
Funds get new rivals for pension billions;
 banks and insurance companies. il Bsns W
 p 140+ My 10 '69

Great fund explosion. il Fortune 79:131-3 My
 1 '69
Great margin maul; American mutual funds
 in Germany. W. Bremme. il Duns R 94:90+
 S '69
Hard times come to the hedge funds. C. J.
 Loomis. il Fortune 81:100-3+ Ja '70
Has Wall Street found this year's winner?
 mortgage trusts. Bsns W p 121-2 Ap 12 '69
How they fared. Time 93:67-8 Ja 24 '69
How to invest in mutual funds. R. Krumme.
 il Suc Farm 67:48-9 Ag '69
Insurance giants move into funds; control of
 Manhattan fund by CNA financial. il Bsns
 W p 114-16+ Mr 15 '69
Less demand for mutual funds. U S News
 67:71 Ag 18 '69
Less risky by the dozen? closed-end trusts.
 il Duns R 94:123-4 S '69
Letter stock is worth the worry; large hold-
 ings of unregistered shares by mutual
 funds. il Bsns W p 108+ Ja 18 '69
Midas of mutual funds. il Time 95:68-9 Ja 12
 '70
Mutual fund explosion. A. Hershman. Duns R
 94:21+ Jl '69
Mutual-fund mood. C. Morgello. il Newsweek
 73:81 Ap 28 '69
Mutual funds for retirement income. E. Meril-
 lat. il Har Yrs 9:14-17 Mr '69
Mutual funds: load or no-load. E. Merillat. il
 Har Yrs 9:46-9 Ap '69
Now the packaged estate; insurance plus
 stocks; with interview with G. P. Hinckley.
 il U S News 66:82-4 Je 30 '69
Performance, foreign style. il Fortune 81:147-
 8 Ja '70
Performance in reverse? il Forbes 103:58+
 Mr 15 '69
Quick guide to thirty no-load mutual funds.
 il Changing T 23:43-5 Je '69
Quiet revolution; Merrill Lynch selling mutual
 funds. Forbes 104:82 O 1 '69
Sleeper that soars; mortgage-investment
 trusts. C. Morgello. il Newsweek 73:80 Je 16
 '69
Smart, and sure of it; S. Stayman. Forbes
 104:59 D 15 '69
Vantage ten-ninety; mutual fund ratings.
 Bsns W p 124+ My 24 '69
Waiting for the market to move; mutual
 funds are eying stock drift with suspicion.
 il Bsns W p70-1 Ap 5 '69
Wall Street:
 Hedge funds decline. C. Morgello. il
  Newsweek 74:84 Jl 21 '69
 How to pick a fund. C. Morgello. il
  Newsweek 74:92-4 O 13 '69
 Money men's view; mutual fund buying
  and selling. C. Morgello. il Newsweek
  74:51 Ag 11 '69
What's ahead for mutual funds. il U S News
 67:80-1 S 29 '69
Who needs Wall Street? house mutual fund
 open only to GE management. Forbes 103:
 52-3 F 1 '69
Year the go-go funds went into reverse. il
 Bsns W p86-7 Ja 10 '70
You call it speculation: I call it investment;
 Enterprise fund. Forbes 104:56+ S 1 '69
 See also
Investors overseas services, limited
Oppenheimer fund, incorporated
Price, T. R.
Real estate investment trusts
Small business investment companies
Wellington management company

Finance
Mutual funds annual performance ratings. il
 Forbes 104:50-1+ Ag 15 '69
New funds, see how they run. Duns R 94:22-4
 Jl '69
Performance funds: under a cloud. il Forbes
 104:78+ Ag 15 '69

Insurance
Personal investing; insuring against catastrophe. Fortune 80:176-7 S '69
Sure thing; Harleysville plan. Newsweek 74:
 90 O 20 '69

INVESTMENTS
Advice for investors in 1970; interview. G.
 S. Johnston. il U S News 68:64-6 Ja 5 '70
Anyone can play, for fun and a bit of
 profit. il Newsweek 74:81 D 15 '69
Danger signs in the stock market; inter-
 view. R. W. Haack. il U S News 67:62-5
 Ag 4 '69
Executive investor. See issues of Dun's re-
 view
Family assets: where they are kept. il Good
 H 168:212 Ap '69
How Omaha beats Wall Street. Forbes 104:
 82+ N 1 '69

INVESTMENTS—*Continued*

How should a widow invest her money? il Changing T 22:17-19 D '68

How to cuddle up to money G. Trotta. Harp Baz 102:188-9 Ag '69

How to handle your investments; interview. T. R. Price. il U S News 67:64-7 Jl 7 '69

How to invest. R. Krumme. il Suc Farm 67: 43-50 Ag '69

Institutions, investments and integrity. C. W. Powers and J. P. Gunnemann. Chr Cent 86:144-8 Ja 29 '69

Investing in bonds, what you can get now. il U S News 66:73-5 Je 30 '69

Investors take a chance on chance; stocks of companies with stakes in Las Vegas and Bahamas. il Bsns W p 139-40 Ap 26 '69

Making it in the learning trade. Bsns W p74+ S 6 '69

Making money work; with questions and answers. E. Merillat. See issues of Harvest years

Money isn't funny; A. Linkletter's experience. il Forbes 104:60+ Jl 15 '69

Personal investing. See issues of Fortune

Security analysts size up today's markets. il U S News 66:66-9 My 26 '69

She's single, she's smart. Should she buy stocks? il Changing T 23:35-7 Ap '69

Stock market made simple; questions and answers. D. L. Markstein. Suc Farm 67: 50 N '69

Trends for investors to watch. il U S News 67:57-8 N 10 '69

Ways to invest your money now. il U S News 67:86-8 N 24 '69

Where the bears chase smart money. il Bsns W p 17 Ag 30 '69

Where to put the money. C. Morgello. il Newsweek 74:76 Jl 7 '69

With stocks in trouble, what about bonds? il U S News 66:102-4 Mr 10 '69

See also

Art investment companies
Bonds
Bonds, Government
Brokers
Capital investments
Equity funding corporation of America
Estate planning
Executives—Investment activities
Finance, Personal
Hedging
Insurance companies—Investments
Interest
Investment clubs
Investment trusts
Investor relations programs
Saving and savings
Securities
Speculation
Stockholders
Stocks

Advisers

Anyone with money can play. M. Mayer. Harp Baz 102:188-9 S '69

How to pick the acorns that will sprout; Institutional investment evaluation service. Bsns W p84 D 20 '69

InterCapitalists; Standard & Poor's Inter-Capital, inc. il Time 93:94-5 Mr 14 '69

Local scouts hunt for talented stocks; acting as the eyes and ears for institutional investors. il Bsns W p 128+ My 17 '69

Money men; interview. W. Van Devanter. Forbes 103:82-3 Ap 15 '69

New kid on the street. S. Mahoney. il Life 66:62-62B+ Je 6 '69

Putting one's own house in order; New York consulting firm helps executives. Bsns W p 124 Ja 25 '69

Sergeant wears two hats; R. A. Levy. il Forbes 103:80 Ap 15 '69

Stock chartist tries to pierce the foggy trend. il Bnsn W p66-7 Jl 5 '69

Wall Street's wizards of odds; securities analysts climbing from file room to councils of power. il Bsns W p 122-4+ Mr 15 '69

Watch the moneymen! views of M. Siebert. A. Hershman. Duns R 94:79-80 D '69

See also

Technological investors management corporation

INVESTMENTS, Foreign

Age of imperialism. by H. Magdoff. Review Nation 209:53-5 Jl 14 '69. J. O'Connor

Business around the globe. See occasional issues of Fortune

Comeback for overseas investments? il Duns R 93:81-2 Ja '69

Contributions of foreign investment to national development. E. M. Braderman. Dept State Bul 61:359-62 O 27 '69

Direct investment abroad; government policy. J. J. Powers, jr. Duns R 93:17+ Ap '69

Exchange controls. M. Friedman. Newsweek 73:76 Mr 24 '69

Government, business, and the balance of payments; address, March 26, 1969. J. J. Powers, jr. Vital Speeches 35:430-4 My 1 '69

How to analyze foreign investment climates. R. B. Stobaugh, jr. bibliog f il Harvard Bsns R 47:100-8 S '69

How U.S. industry is remaking the world. il U S News 67:58-60 O 27 '69

Imperatives of world economic progress; trade & investment; address, November 17, 1969. J. M. Roche. Vital Speeches 36:187-90 Ja 1 '70

Lifting the lid a bit, Nixon's revised overseas investment program. Bsns W p36-7 Ap 12 '69

More capital goes abroad; McGraw-Hill survey. il Bsns W p38 Ag 9 '69

Nationalism crimps the spending spree; issues of the 1970s. il Bsns W p206+ D 6 '69

New protectionism. H. Hazlitt. Nat R 21:485-8+ My 20 '69; Reply. A. Barro. 21:730 Jl 29 '69

Overseas commentary; Interest equalization tax. G. J. Henry. Forbes 103:60-1 F 1 '69

President Nixon reduces rates of interest equalization tax; White House announcement, with executive order by R. Nixon. il Dept State Bul 60:404-5 My 12 '69

Private enterprise and foreign aid; International private investment advisory council. America 120:240-1 Mr 1 '69

What U.S. companies are doing abroad. See issues of U S news & World report

See also

Business—Foreign expansion
Corporations—Foreign subsidiaries
Loans, Foreign

INVESTMENTS, Foreign (by Europe)

How U.S. industry is remaking the world. il U S News 67:58-60 O 27 '69

INVESTMENTS, Foreign (by Germany [Federal Republic])

Great margin maul; American mutual funds in Germany. W. Bremmme. il Duns R 94: 90+ S '69

INVESTMENTS, Foreign (by Great Britain)

American stocks, British style; interviews. M. deL. Belmont; A. J. S. C. Tennant. il Duns R 93:40-1+ Ja '69

Yanqui bankers feel competition's bite. il Bsns W p50-1 D 27 '69

INVESTMENTS, Foreign (by Italy)

Italy's hot export trade in lira. il Bsns W p74 D 27 '69

INVESTMENTS, Foreign (by Japan)

Asia's emerging industrial revolution. il Bsns W p60-1 D 13 '69

How U.S. industry is remaking the world. il U S News 67:58-60 O 27 '69

Japan comes on strong in Europe il Bsns W p88-9+ N 15 '69

INVESTMENTS, Foreign (in Algeria)

Algeria hunts for new investors; attempt to lure U.S. capital. il Bsns W p52+ Ap 12 '69

INVESTMENTS, Foreign (in Argentina)

Argentina steps up its tempo. il Bsns W p56-7+ My 17 '69

Dow wins a sí on Argentine plan. il Bsns W p64-5 D 6 '69

INVESTMENTS, Foreign (in Australia)

Report from Sydney. E. Shirley. il Fortune 79:89+ Ap '69

INVESTMENTS, Foreign (in Bolivia)

Can Gulf pick up the pieces in Bolivia? il Bsns W p44+ O 25 '69

Coup shakes up U.S. investors. il Bsns W p28 O 4 '69

INVESTMENTS, Foreign (in Brazil)

Industry tries to stir a Brazilian backwater. il Bsns W p 146-8+ Mr 29 '69

INVESTMENTS, Foreign (in Canada)

Investment chill from the North. Bsns W p50-1 Jl 12 '69

News and views; Nixon administration and U.S-owned businesses. J. Deedy. Commonweal 90:154 Ap 25 '69

INVESTMENTS, Foreign (in Europe)

European countdown for Westinghouse. Bsns W p64 D 6 '69

Japan comes on strong in Europe. il Bsns W p88-9+ N 15 '69

New Europe; opportunity for U. S. business? address, April 28, 1969. G. J. Colley. Vital Speeches 35:560-3 Jl 1 '69

INVESTMENTS, Foreign (in France)

They won't take *non* for an answer. Bsns W p39 D 13 '69

INVESTMENTS, Foreign (in Greece)

Twilight on Olympus; Litton international development corp. Forbes 104:38 D 1 '69

INVESTMENTS, Foreign (in Indonesia)

Taking a Communist economy apart. S. G. Slappey. il Nations Bsns 57:69-73 O '69

INVESTMENTS, Foreign (in Italy)
J. C. Penney, Italian-style. il Bsns W p48+ Ja 10 '70
Misadventure in Sicily. H. B. Meyers. Fortune 79:244+ My 15 '69

INVESTMENTS, Foreign (in Japan)
European money learns Japanese. il Bsns W p24-5 Ag 2 '69

INVESTMENTS, Foreign (in Latin America)
ADELA: capital idea for Latin America. S. Seegers. Read Digest 94:154-6+ Mr '69
Battening down for new storms. il Bsns W p 16-17 Jl 5 '69
Has Latin America a choice? J. L. Segundo. America 120:213-16 F 22 '69; Discussion. 120:211, 318 F 22, Mr 22 '69
In Latin America: growing threats to U.S. companies. J. Benham. il U S News 67: 68-70 Jl 14 '69
King ranch south of the border. C. J. V. Murphy. il Fortune 80:132-6+ Jl '69
Latin America: what are your priorities? address. May 6, 1969. C. A. Meyer. Dept State Bul 60:440-2 My 26 '69
Matter of vital interest; U.S. business and the Peruvian dispute. il Newsweek 73:53 Ap 14 '69
Multinational investment; excerpts from statement. G. Plaza. Américas 21:45 My '69
Nationalist wave hits Latin America; meaning to U.S. il U S News 66:36-7 Mr 10 '69
News and views; Nixon administration and U.S.-owned businesses; J. Deedy. Commonweal 90:143 Ap 25 '69
Threatening weather in South America. J. Cameron. il Fortune 80:98-101+ O '69
Where Yanqui companies are feeling the heat. il Bsns W p80-2+ N 22 '69
Yanqui bankers feel competition's bite. il Bsns W p50-1 D 27 '69

INVESTMENTS, Foreign (in Lebanon)
Beirut is beckoning. Bsns W p72 S 6 '69

INVESTMENTS, Foreign (in Libya)
Oilmen in Libya try to cap the jitters. il Bsns W p45-6 O 18 '69

INVESTMENTS, Foreign (in Mexico)
Jumping market below the border. il Bsns W p 120-1+ Jl 12 '69

INVESTMENTS, Foreign (in Northern Ireland)
Business is riding with the Irish storm; international companies in Northern Ireland. il Bsns W p32-3 Ag 23 '69

INVESTMENTS, Foreign (in Peru)
Peru: more troubles for U.S. il U S News 66:68 Mr 3 '69

INVESTMENTS, Foreign (in Russia)
Putting supermarkets on the steppes; Milan-based export-import company dealings with Moscow. il Bsns W p78+ S 20 '69

INVESTMENTS, Foreign (in Southeast Asia)
Asia's emerging industrial revolution. il Bsns W p60-1 D 13 '69

INVESTMENTS, Foreign (in Spain)
INI puts out the welcome mat; Spain's Instituto nacional de industria. il Bsns W p96-7 F 15 '69

INVESTMENTS, Foreign (in Thailand)
AID raises weeds in Thailand corn deal; government's Extended risk guarantee program. il Bsns W p78-9 Mr 22 '69
Next Vietnam; corporate investment. J. Deedy. Commonweal 90:578 S 26 '69

INVESTMENTS, Foreign (in the United States)
American stocks, British style; interviews. M. deL. Belmont; A. J. S. C. Tennant. il Duns R 93:40-1+ Ja '68
Big funds offshore buy into the U.S; real estate from motels to factories. il Bsns W p 128-9+ Mr 22 '69
Contributions of foreign investment to national development. E. M. Braderman. Dept State Bul 61:359-62 O 27 '69
Foreign aid for Wall Street. R. Ball. il Fortune 80:125+ Ag 15 '69
Foreign invasion. Forbes 103:55 F 1 '69
Foreigners up the ante. il Bsns W p56-8 Ag 16 '69
Salt in the wound. Fortune 80:104 N '69
U.S. antitrust muscle makes Europe wince. il Bsns W p84-6 N 8 '69
Wall Street: the stock market's foreign market. C. Morgello. il Newsweek 73:82 Ja 27 '69

INVESTMENTS, Foreign (in underdeveloped areas)
In the former colonies it's white man, come back. il U S News 66:102-4 My 19 '69
International financial challenges; address, October 16, 1969. D. Rockefeller. Vital Speeches 36:83-6 N 15 '69

Political economy of international oil and the underdeveloped countries, by M. Tanzer. Review
Nation 209:605-7 D 1 '69. R. Engler
U.S. agribusiness shows the way; American companies putting agricultural and marketing skills to work in poor lands. il Bsns W p52-6+ Ja 18 '69

INVESTOR relations programs
What's financial PR worth? il Duns R 94: 62-4 N '69
Why financial PR is booming. il Bsns W p 118+ N 15 '69

INVESTORS. See Stockholders

INVESTORS overseas services, limited
Bernie and his billions. il Newsweek 74:64-7 Jl 28 '69
Bernie Cornfeld: king of Europe's cash. il Bsns W p80-3 Ja 10 '70
Bernie, go back! IOS in Japan. il Forbes 104:21-2 D 1 '69
Cornfeld's cornucopia. il Time 94:94-5 O 3 '69
Croesus, American style. il Forbes 104:27-9 S 15 '69

INVITATION to a beheading; drama. See McGrath, R.

INVOLUTIONAL psychosis. See Psychoses

IODIDES
Lab bench; determining empirical formulas using radioisotopes. J. A. Sears and W. James. il Chem 42:29-30 O '69

ION bombardment
See also
Sputtering (physics)

ION chambers. See Ionization chambers

ION engines
Ion engine to be tested in orbit. Space World F-6-66:7 Je '69

ION exchange
Ion exchange in escherichia coli potassium-binding proteins. R. Damadian. bibliog il Science 165:79-81 Jl 4 '69

ION exchange electrodes. See Electrodes

IONESCO, Eugéne
European literary scene. R. J. Clements. Sat R 52:24 Ag 2 '69

IONIAN ISLANDS
Island that lived for a day; Levkas. M. Wilk. McCalls 96:94+ My '69
See also
Corfu (island)

IONIZATION chambers
Make your own ion chamber. H. Burgess. il Pop Electr 31:31-5 N '69

IONIZATION of gases
See also
Plasma (ionized gases)

IONOSPHERIC radio wave propagation
Ionospheric-propagation predictions. H. C. Wood. il Electr World 81:27-9+ Ap '69

IONS
Strange power of air ions. H. F. Burgess. Pop Electr 31:29-30+ N '69
See also
Electrolysis
Plasma (ionized gases)

Beams
Lamb-effect sources make better polarized ion beams. bibliog Phys Today 22:67+ Ja '69

Mobility
Motion of ions: principles and concepts; Nobel prize lecture, January 1969. L. Onsager. bibliog il Science 166:1359-64 D 12 '69

IOOSS, Walter, Jr
Roller derby; photographs. Sports Illus 30: 54-60 Mr 3 '69

IOWA
Big changes in America's small towns. il U S News 66:58-60 Ap 28 '69
See also
Architecture, Domestic—Iowa
Education—Iowa
Hunting—Iowa

Politics and government
Harold E. Hughes; evangelist from the prairies. L. L. King. Harper 238:50-7 Mr '69

IOWA beef packers, incorporated
Fighting over the cost of cutting meat. Bsns W p74+ N 22 '69
War at Iowa beef. il Newsweek 74:100 N 17 '69

IOWA. University, Iowa city
Changes in doctoral language requirements. A. H. Scaff. Sch & Soc 97:453-4 N '69

IPOMOEAS. See Morning glories

IPS confusus. See Beetles

IPSWICH, Mass.

Gardens

Whipple house, Ipswich; seventeenth century garden. I. Smith. il Horticulture 46:34-5+ Ag '68

IRAN

See also
Earthquakes—Iran
Education—Iran
Hunting—Iran
Libraries—Iran
Narcotic laws—Iran
Water supply—Iran

Antiquities

New light on the emergence of civilization in the Near East; revelations of the 5,000 year old city of Chogha Mish. H. J. Kantor and P. P. Delougaz. il UNESCO Courier 22:22-5+ N '69
See also
Persepolis

Description and travel

Iran, born Persia; excerpts from Persia. J. Morris. Vogue 154:212-13+ D '69

Economic conditions

Mideast victory for U.S, the boom in Iran; with interview with the Shah of Iran. il U S News 66:46-50 Ja 27 '69

Foreign relations

Mideast victory for U.S, the boom in Iran; with interview with the Shah of Iran. il U S News 66:46-50 Ja 27 '69
President Nixon and the Shah of Iran held talks at Washington; exchange of greetings, toasts and remarks, October 21 and 23, 1969. R. M. Nixon and Mohammed Reza Pahlevi. Dept State Bul 61:396-400 N 10 '69
Prime Minister Hoveyda of Iran visits Washington; exchange of greetings and toasts, with joint statement, December 5, 1968. L. B. Johnson; A. A. Hoveyda. Dept State Bul 59:659-62 D 23 '68

Social history

Persian diversions; sixteenth- and seventeenth-century customs. J. Morris. il Horizon 11:18-19 Spr '69

IRANIAN pottery. See Pottery, Iranian

IRANIANS
Iran: the Persian perspective. J. F. Harvey; reply. I. B. Occhino. Library J 94:1923 My 15 '69

IRAQ
See also
Jews in Iraq
Justice, Administration of—Iraq
Land tenure—Iraq
Natural resources—Iraq

Foreign relations

Nixon's first foreign crisis: the boiling Mideast. il U S News 66:35-6 F 10 '69

History

Iraq. R. A. Fernea and E. W. Fernea. bibliog il Focus 20:1-8 O '69

Industries

See also
Petroleum—Iraq

Religious institutions and affairs

See also
Christians in Iraq

IRELAND, Ralph R.
Current status of non-white education in South Africa. bibliog f Sch & Soc 97:381-6 O '69

IRELAND
See also
Aran Islands
Architecture, Domestic—Ireland
Art—Ireland
Aviation—Ireland
Camping—Ireland
Censorship—Ireland
Colleges and universities—Ireland
Country estates
Drama festivals—Ireland
Kilkenny
Music festivals—Ireland
Northern Ireland—Religious institutions and affairs
Shannon River
Taxation—Ireland
Tourist trade—Ireland
Wexford

Description and travel

Friendly Irish. J. Scofield. il Nat Geog 136: 354-91 S '69
Ireland & Scotland. M. MacLiammoir; E. Linklater. il Travel & Camera 32:120-1+ F '69
Personal view of Ireland. D. Guinness. il Art in Am 57:92-5 My '69
Shorthand notes on western Ireland. D. Messinesi. Vogue 154:64 O 15 '69

Anecdotes, facetiae, satire, etc.

Room and bored; why not rent an Irish castle for a week or two? S. J. Perelman. il Holiday 45:40-1+ Mr '69

Economic conditions

Perspective. J. H. Plumb. Sat R 52:37+ O 25 '69

Economic relations

New Europe; opportunity for U. S. business? address, April 28, 1969. G. J. Colley. Vital Speeches 35:560-3 Jl 1 '69

History

Ireland's clash of colors. R. W. Schleck. America 121:134-6 S 6 '69; Discussion. 121: 207-8 S 27 '69
1608 and all that. il Time 94:31 Ag 22 '69

Bibliography

Articles and other books received; comp. by L. H. Carlson. See issues of American historical review

Sinn Fein rebellion, 1916

Agony at Easter, by T. M. Coffee. Review Sat R 52:37+ O 25 '69. J. H. Plumb

Literary landmarks

See Literary landmarks

National library

Leabharlann: the national library of Ireland. W. Ready. il Wilson Lib Bul 43:954-8 Je '69

Politics and government

Evolutionaries. J. Barnes. Newsweek 73:48+ Je 23 '69
See also
Elections—Ireland
Ireland—History—Sinn Fein rebellion, 1916
Northern Ireland

Social life and customs

Conamara man, by S. Ridge. Review Sat R 52:35-6 Ap 19 '69. W. H. A. Williams

IRELAND, NORTHERN. See Northern Ireland

IREYS, Alice Recknagel
Broadleaved evergreens for all-year effect. il Horticulture 46:32-5 O '68

IRION, Mary Jean
Corner the sheep; poem. Chr Cent 86:439 Ap 2 '69
One winter world; poem. Chr Cent 86-341 Mr 12 '69

IRISES
Charming Dutch iris. B. Brinhart. il Home Gard 56:54-5 N '69
Delicate beauty, great stamina: Japanese iris. E. McDonald. il House B 111:68-9+ Jl '69
Flower of the iris comes in many lovely forms. il Home Gard 56:30-1 Je '69
Japanese iris for marvelous summer color. il Home Gard 56:67 Jl '69
Japanese iris likes it wet. il Sunset 143:239 N '69
Many pleasures of growing iris and exactly how to do it. il Home Gard 56:24-9 Je '69
Newer iris. K. I. Chambers. il Horticulture 47:30-1+ Je '69
Versatile iris. E. F. Steffek. il Horticulture 47:26-9+ Ap '69

IRISH
Irish sketches: Kilkenny. J. McCarten. New Yorker 45:95-6+ F 22 '69
Observations upon the Irish; Time essay. il Time 93:37-8 Je 20 '69

IRISH AMERICANS
Gra-a-nd parade; New York city's Saint Patrick's day parade. J. McCarthy. il Am Heritage 20:54-9+ F '69
Irish power on First avenue. P. Tracy. Commonweal 90:278-9 My 23 '69

IRISH art. See Art, Irish

IRISH Free State. See Ireland

IRISH glass. See Glassware

IRISH literature

Study and teaching

Case for the Irish. I. Sherwood. Engl J 58: 1181-2 N '69

IRISH republican army
Boys of the IRA. M. Kupfer. Newsweek 74:31 S 1 '69

IRISH silver. See Silverware

IRON
Oxidation state of iron at high pressure. H. G. Drickamer and others. bibliog il Science 163:885-90 F 28 '69
See also
Wrought iron

IRON age
Twelve things nobody ever knew about stone and iron age men. L. R. Griffin. il Sci Digest 65:26-31 My '69

IRON curtain. See Europe, Eastern

IRON in diet
Dishes to count on when you want to increase the amount of iron in your daily diet. Good H 169:160-1 Ag '69

IRON in the body
Growing concern about iron deficiency in women. il Good H 168:211 Ap '69

IRON industry and trade

Wages and hours
Unit labor costs of iron and steel industries in five countries: France, Japan, the United Kingdom, United States, and West Germany; with tables. P. C. Jackman. Mo Labor R 92:15-22 Ag '69

IRON mines and mining

Australia
Better than gold; iron ore from Mount Newman. il Time 94:76 Jl 4 '69

India
Giant iron mine; Bailadila project. S. K. Ghaswala. il Sci N 95:514 My 24 '69

Sweden
Swedish strike undermines a sales pitch; wildcat iron ore miners strike. Bsns W p63-4 D 27 '69

IRON ores
Trends and techniques; prereduced iron ores. F. C. F. Earney. Focus 19:12 Ap '69

Transportation
Iron ore gets piped aboard; slurry delivery. il Bsns W p118 Ag 16 '69

IRON phosphates
Basic ferric phosphates: a crystallochemical principle. P. B. Moore. il Science 164:1063-4 My 30 '69

IRON pipes. See Pipes, Iron

IRON rust. See Corrosion and anticorrosives

IRON stands. See Trivets

IRON workers
See also
Iron industry and trade—Wages and hours

IRONWORK
It's easy now to form your own wrought iron. R. Capotosto. il Pop Sci 194:196+ Mr '69
See also
Wrought iron

IROQUOIS Indians
End of the Iroquois. M. Bishop. il Am Heritage 20:28-33+ O '69
See also
Seneca Indians

IROQUOIS industries (firm)
Fox's hunt. S. Blickstein. Duns R 93:69+ Mr '69

IRRADIATED food. See Food, Effect of radiation on

IRRADIATED plastics. See Plastics, Irradiated

IRRIGATION
Use of arid lands. D. Wolfle. Science 164:1345 Je 20 '69
Warm-water irrigation: an answer to thermal pollution? L. J. Carter. Science 165:478-80 Ag 1 '69
See also
Irrigation, Overhead

Great Plains
Irrigation and climate. K. Frazier. il Sci N 96:599-600 D 27 '69

Israel
Overhead sprinklers of Israel: how to provide a nice, wet place where insects you don't want thrive. E. Rivnay. bibliog il Natur Hist 78:56-61 F '69

Tunisia
Majardah scheme. R. S. Harrison. il Focus 19:8-11 Ja '69

IRRIGATION, Overhead
Overhead sprinklers of Israel: how to provide a nice, wet place where insects you don't want thrive. E. Rivnay. bibliog il Natur Hist 78:56-61 F '69

IRRIGATION machinery
Ways to irrigate with less work. il Farm J 93:20-1+ Ag '69

IRRIGATION water
Blooming desert. C. O. Hodge. il Bul Atom Sci 25:32-3 N '69
Desalted seawater for agriculture: is it economic? M. Clawson and others. bibliog Science 164:1141-8 Je 6 '69; Discussion. 165:850-1 Ag 29 '69

Salt content
Desalting California; San Joaquin master drain controversy. F. M. Stead. il Environ 11:2-10 Je '69

IRVINE, Keith
Francozone Africa. bibliog f Cur Hist 56:282-5+ My '69

IRVING, Judy
Importance of parsley. Mlle 69:209-10+ My '69

IRWIN, John Nichol, 1913-
President appoints John N. Irwin as Special emissary to Peru. Dept State Bul 60:282 Mr 31 '69
Talking it over. por Time 93:31 Mr 21 '69

IRWIN, Theodore
Birth order, what it means to your children. Todays Health 47:26-7+ O '69
Helping children overcome learning disabilities. Todays Health 47:20-5+ My '69
How to handle problems of aging. Todays Health 47:28-31+ Jl '69
How to succeed as a step-parent. Parents Mag 44:37-9+ F '69
Hydron: new miracle plastic with a myriad of uses. Pop Sci 194:92-5 F '69
Meet today's scouts. Parents Mag 44:64-5+ O '69
Put your money in the ground. Am Home 72:38+ N '69
Scuba/com; now you can talk underwater. Pop Sci 195:120-1 Ag '69
What happens to your health handouts? Todays Health 47:20-3+ N '69
What you should know about fever. Read Digest 94:137-40 Mr '69
Wondrous machine that salvages backward kids. Todays Health 47:31-3+ Ag '69
Your housing today: should you rent or buy? Am Home 72:48+ Ja '69
(ed) See Finch, R. H. Inside look at HEW: what are the health goals?

ISAACS, Harold R.
Color in world affairs. Cur 105:57-64 Mr '69

ISAACS, John D.
Nature of oceanic life; with biographical sketch. Sci Am 221:44, 146-60+ bibliog (p285) S '69
—See Schwartzlose, R. A. jt. auth.

ISAACS, Kenneth
Build yourself the Delta desk. Pop Sci 195:160-2 N '69
Elegant dining: an I table and a sea of cube chairs. Pop Sci 195:162-6 O '69
How to build the microdorm. Pop Sci 194:138-41+ Mr '69
Security shelter for your snowmobile. Pop Sci 195:148-50+ D '69

ISANG Yun. See Yun, I.

ISBELL, Harold
Winter afternoon; poem. Nation 209:678 D 15 '69

ISCHIA (island)
Ischia. G. Blakeley. il Harp Baz 102:59+ Je '69

ISCHL, Austria. See Bad Ischl, Austria

ISD, incorporated
Interiors for business: an architectural response. Arch Rec 145:81 Je '69

ISENBERG, James A.
Lab bench. por Chem 42:26-8 Je '69

ISHIZAKA, Genkichi
Eyes have it. Time 93:39 Mr 7 '69

ISKANDER, pseud. See Herzen, A. I.

ISLAM, A. S. and Mughal, R.
Corchorus pascuorum: transmission of chemically induced fruit formation with environmental change. bibliog Science 164:315-16 Ap 18 '69

ISLAM
Determining Allah's will: conference in Kuala Lumpur to consider ways of accomodating to a changing world. Time 93:64+ My 9 '69
Rising star, rising crescent; militant Islam in Africa. R. W. Howe. New Repub 161:6-7 D 6 '69
World of Islam; symposium. bibliog f il Cur Hist 56:129-67+ Mr '69
See also
Moors (people)

ISLAM and Christianity. See Christianity and other religions
ISLAND airlines. See Local service airlines
ISLAND cruising club. See Yacht clubs
ISLAND of shadows; story. See Ogilvie, E.
ISLAND parks
By air, rail or water to an island park; Quinsippi Island; Quincy, Ill. K. W Kramer. il Am City 84:84-5 Ap '69
ISLANDS, Artificial. See Artificial islands
ISLANDS of the Adriatic Sea
Yugoslavia's Adriatic isles. H. P. Koenig. il Travel 131:56-8 Je '69
ISLANDS of the Pacific
Crossing the lonely latitudes. N. Morgan. il Sat R 52:46-7+ S 13 '69
Papuan paradise. C. Heacock. il Yachting 125:58-60+ Mr '69
See also
Bikini
Botany—Islands of the Pacific
Micronesia
Oceania
Polynesia
Truk Islands
Trust Territory of the Pacific Islands
ISLE OF WIGHT rock festival. See Music festivals—England
ISLE ROYALE NATIONAL PARK
Lake Superior's island wilderness. G. F. Stucker. il Nat Parks 43:4-9 Mr '69
Wilderness park for sportsmen. B. East. Outdoor Life 144:33-4 Jl '69
ISMAEL, Tareq Y.
Islam in Sub-Saharan Africa. bibliog f Cur Hist 56:146-50+ Mr '69
ISOBARIC spin
Isobaric analog resonances. W. R. Coker and C. F. Moore. bibliog il Phys Today 22: 53-61 Ap '69
ISOENZYMES. See Enzymes
ISOLATION, Sensory. See Sensory deprivation
ISOLATION, Social. See Social isolation
ISOLATIONISM (United States) See United States—Foreign relations
ISOMERASES
Are honeybees deficient in phosphomannose isomerase? S. A. Saunders and others. bibliog il Science 164:858-9 My 16 '69
ISOMERS
D-Amino acids in animals. J. J. Corrigan. bibliog il Science 164:142-9 Ap 11 '69
Determining the number of isomers from a structural formula. M. Orchin. il Chem 42: 8-12 My '69
ISON, Hobart
U.S. journal: Jeremiah, Ky. C. Trillin. New Yorker 45:178-83 Ap 12 '69
ISONIAZID
Cuprous complexes formed with isonicotinic hydrazide. A. F. Krivis and J. M. Rabb. bibliog Science 164:1064-5 My 30 '69
ISONICOTINIC acid hydrazide. See Isoniazid
ISOPENTENYLADENOSINE. See Kinins
ISOPODS
Learning sets in an invertebrate. J. E. Morrow and B. L. Smithson. bibliog il Science 164:850-1 My 16 '69
ISOTOPE separation
Isotope separation by thermal diffusion in liquid metal. A. Ott. bibliog il Science 164: 297 Ap 18 '69
ISOTOPES
See also
Radioactive tracers
Radioisotopes
ISRAEL, Adrian C.
Don't phone your broker; go to Aqueduct! pors Forbes 104:54-5 Ag 1 '69
ISRAEL
Another look at Israel. A. B. Southwick. Commonweal 89:516-22 Ja 24 '69; Discussion. 89:511-12, 665+, 719+ ; 90:55 Ja 24, F 28, Mr 14, 28 '69
First of the month. C. Amory. Sat R 52:4+ Ap 12 '69
Israel: an echo of eternity, by A. J. Heschel. Review
Time 93:63 Mr 14 '69
Journal from Israel. E. Grossman. Commentary 48:62-73 O '69
Perspective on Palestine. C. C. Ryrie. Chr Today 13:8-10 My 23 '69
Reports: Israel. E. Simon. Atlan 224:18+ D '69
See also
Airlines—Israel
Arabs in Israel
Atomic power—Israel
Ballet—Israel
Censorship—Israel
Children—Israel
Church and state in Israel
Collective settlements—Israel

Dancing—Israel
Education—Israel
Forests and forestry—Israel
Holy Land
Immigrants in Israel
Irrigation—Israel
Jerusalem
Masada (fortress) Israel
Public health—Israel
Publishers and publishing—Israel
Red Sea
Research—Israel
Television broadcasting—Israel
Tourist trade—Israel
Trials—Israel
United Nations—Israel
Women—Israel
Youth—Israel
Zionism

Air force
Soviet squadron. il Time 94:57 D 5 '69

Antiquities
See also
Masada (fortress) Israel

Armed forces
David's legacy. il Newsweek 73:48-9 F 17 '69

Cabinet
Cabinet of hawks Time 94:18 D 26 '69
Golda's brood. Newsweek 74:33-4 D 29 '69

Commerce
Germany (Federal Republic)
Should an Israeli buy a Volkswagen? il Time 93:92 Ap 11 '69

Defenses
Barlev line. il Newsweek 73:54+ My 26 '69
Israel and the nuclear non-proliferation treaty. G. H. Quester. il Bul Atom Sci 25:7-9+ Je '69
Israel's decision: security without peace; West Bank of the Jordan and Sinai. il Time 93: 24-5 F 7 '69

Description and travel
Israel, it's safe to eat the lotus. A. Chamberlin. Vogue 154:158 Jl '69
Israel onrush. A. Chamberlin. il Vogue 154: 106-11 Jl '69
Israel under siege. T. C. Sorensen. Holiday 46:90-1 D '69
Let's travel; the book of G.E.s. il Mlle 69: 230-2+ Ag '69
Teen travel talk. il Seventeen 28:32 F '69
Traveling with Mlle: *shalom*; we echo *shalom*! F. Córdova. il Mlle 69:346-7+ Ag '69

Diplomatic and consular service
Undiplomatic diversions; A. Ben-Natan first ambassador to West Germany. Newsweek 74:30+ Jl 7 '69

Economic conditions
Israel's war clouds have a silver lining. il Bsns W p42-4 F 1 '69

Foreign opinion
Another look at Israel. A. B. Southwick. Commonweal 89:516-22 Ja 24 '69; Discussion. 89:511-12, 665+, 719+; 90:55 Ja 24, F 28, Mr 14, 28 '69
Damn everybody sums up the angry mood of Israel. A. Rubinstein. il N Y Times Mag p24-7+ F 9 '69
On world reaction to developments in the Middle East. J. P. Rudin. Chr Cent 86:110 Ja 22 '69; Reply. J. N. Booth. 86:416 Mr 26 '69

Foreign population
See also
Immigrants in Israel

Foreign relations
Eshkol: a reply to Nasser; interview. L. Eshkol. il Newsweek 73:49-50+ F 17 '69
Israel: a passion for survival. M. E. Marty. Chr Cent 86:172-4 F 5 '69
Israel pays compensation claimed for men injured on U.S.S. Liberty. Dept State Bul 60: 473 Je 2 '69
Last thing we want is another war; interview, ed. by J. Fromm. G. Meir. il U S News 67:52-5 S 22 '69
Middle East: shifting into neutral. il Time 95:21-2 Ja 5 '70
Prime Minister Meir of Israel visits Washington; exchange of greetings, toasts and remarks, September 25 and 26, 1969. R. M. Nixon; G. Meir. Dept State Bul 61:318-22 O 13 '69

ISRAEL—Foreign relations—*Continued*

Egypt

Shells across Suez. il Time 93:24+ Mr 21 '69
Training for Armageddon. il Newsweek 73:49 Mr 24 '69

France

FOB Cherbourg: Israel gets its boats. il Newsweek 75:27-8 Ja 12 '70
Furor after a gunboat coup. il U S News 68: 7 Ja 12 '70
Gunboat diplomacy, new style: embargoed ships leave Cherbourg. Newsweek 75:22 Ja 5 '70
Israel's fugitive flotilla. il Time 95:15-16 Ja 12 '70

Jordan

Invitation to a coup. il Newsweek 74:60+ O 27 '69

Lebanon

Mideast's latest hot spot; the squeeze on Lebanon. il U S News 67:30-1 Ag 25 '69
U.N. Security council condemns Israel for attack on Beirut airport; statements with text of resolution, December 29 and 31, 1968. J. R. Wiggins. Dept State Bul 60:53-5 Ja 20 '69

Industries

Israel: the war-peace economy. G. R. Rosen, il Duns R 93:64-8+ Ap '69
Israel's war clouds have a silver lining. il Bsns W p42-4 F 1 '69

Intellectual life

Israel onrush; its surprises, pleasures, and people. A. Chamberlin. il Vogue 154:106-15 Jl '69

Military policy

Collective punishment; policy in occupied Arab lands. il Newsweek 74:40-2 D 1 '69
Israel: war without end? il Newsweek 74:53-4+ S 29 '69
Talk with General Barlev; interview, ed. by M. Elkins. H. Barlev. Newsweek 74:52 N 24 '69

Nationalism

Non-Jewish Jew and other essays, by I. Deutscher. Review
  Ramp Mag 8:66-8+ S '69. M. P. Lerner

Navy

FOB Cherbourg: Israel gets its boats. il Newsweek 75:27-8 Ja 12 '70
Furor after a gunboat coup. il U S News 68: 7 Ja 12 '70
Gunboat diplomacy, new style; embargoed ships leave Cherbourg. Newsweek 75:22 Ja 5 '70
Israel's fugitive flotilla. il Time 95:15-16 Ja 12 '70

Photographs

Photojournalism museum style; Israel: the reality. M. R. Weiss. Sat R 52:112-13 S 13 '69

Politics and government

Death of Israel's prime minister complicates Middle East crisis. J. Shaw. il Life 66:54-6+ Mr 7 '69
Golda. J. R. Moskin. il Look 33:94+ O 7 '69
In the running to lead Israel. il U S News 66:16 Mr 10 '69
Israel has found a replacement for Golda Meir, it's Golda Meir. J. Feron. il pors N Y Times Mag p52-3+ O 26 '69
Israel's image; new Minister of information. il Newsweek 75:59-60 Ja 19 '70
Middle East: the war and the woman. il Time 94:28-33 S 19 '69
New choices in the Middle East: changes in leadership. il Time 93:35-7 Mr 7 '69
Our Golda. Newsweek 73:63 Mr 17 '69
Yigal Allon has supporters. Moshe Dayan has disciples. J. Feron. il N Y Times Mag p30-1+ Ap 27 '69
  See also
  Elections—Israel
  Israel—Cabinet

Religious institutions and affairs

Jeshua, a basic encounter for young Israelis; with editorial comment. R. C. Dodds. America 121:626, 630-2 D 27 '69

Territorial expansion

Israel's decision: security without peace; West Bank of the Jordan and Sinai. il Time 93:24-5 F 7 '69

ISRAEL-Arab relations. See Jewish-Arab relations

ISRAEL in art
  Sketching in Israel. L. Krausz. il Am Artist 33:54-8+ Ap '69

ISRAELI-Arab war. 1967-
Border battles getting hotter in the Mideast. U S News 67:12 Jl 14 '69
Commando riposte. il Time 94:30 Jl 4 '69
Emboldened Arabs. Time 94:42+ N 28 '69
Forgotten lessons; commando raid on Green Island. il Newsweek 74:47-8 Ag 4 '69
Hussein of Jordan, ed. by V. Vance and P. Lauer. Review
  Sat R il 52:24-5 My 31 '69. B. B. Johansson
If Israel lost the war. by Chesnoff. Klein & Littell. Review
  Life 66:8 F 21 '69. U. Avnery
Israel: a garrison state. D. J. Simpson. il Cur Hist 58:1-7+ Ja '70
Israel gets set for prolonged war: a first-hand report. J. Fromm. il U S News 67:50-2 O 20 '69
Israel under siege. T. C. Sorensen. Holiday 46:90-1 D '69
King looks back in sorrow; concerning book by King Hussein. Newsweek 73:42-3 Ap 21 '69
Letter from Israel. B. Bernstein. New Yorker 45:133-40+ N 29 '69
Middle East: mounting violence. il Time 94: 29 Ag 1 '69
Mounting Mideast war fever. il U S News 67:6 Jl 21 '69
New flare-ups in the Mideast. il U S News 67:5 Jl 7 '69
Opening a second front? il Newsweek 74:27 Jl 7 '69
Operating from Athens to Acre. il Newsweek 74:65 D 8 '69
Our next Vietnam? J. Burnham. Nat R 21: 1002 O 7 '69
Paying the price for survival. P. Ben. New Repub 161:10-11 O 4 '69
Something must be done quickly. il Newsweek 73:43-4 My 5 '69
Toward open war in the Middle East. il Time 94:32+ Jl 18 '69
Undeclared war at Suez; with report by M. Mok and interview with G. Meir, ed. by R. Stolley. il Life 67:26-33 O 3 '69
U.S. policy in Middle East; address, December 9, 1969. W. P. Rogers. Vital Speeches 36:165-7 Ja 1 '70
View from the UN. G. Stevens. Atlan 224:4+ S '69
War in Mideast heats up anew. U S News 67:6 Ag 11 '69
War nobody won. V. S. Kearney. America 120:664-7 Je 7 '69

Aerial operations

Commanding the skies. il Time 94:35-6 Ag 22 '69
No middle ground; raids in the Salt area, Jordan. il Newsweek 73:39 Ap 7 '69
Opening a third front; Syria's riposte. il Time 94:33 Ag 8 '69
Preventive medicine. il Newsweek 74:42+ Jl 21 '69
Security council condemns Israeli air attacks; with text of resolution. UN Mo Chron 6:3-12 My '69
U.N. condemns Israeli air attacks on Lebanese villages; statements with text of resolution, August 14 and 26, 1969. C. W. Yost. Dept State Bul 61:272-4 S 22 '69

Campaigns and battles

Judicious bloodletting? il Newsweek 74:44-5 S 22 '69

Destruction and pillage

Collective punishment; policy in occupied Arab lands. il Newsweek 74:40-2 D 1 '69

Moral and religious aspects

More or less religious? Chr Cent 86:1129 S 3 '69; Discussion. 86:1354+ O 22 '69

Peace and mediation

Alternatives in the Middle East. N. Safran. Commentary 47:45-55 My '69; Discussion. 48:14+ S; 4+ O; 28+ D '69
Arab-Israeli confrontation; a challenge to international diplomacy; address, April 23, 1969. J. J. Sisco. Dept State Bul 60:443-6 My 26 '69
Arab-Israeli impasse. Z. B. Grant. New Repub 162:15-16 Ja 3 '70
Arabs, Jews and peace; King Hussein's offer. New Repub 160:7-8 Ap 26 '69
Cairo says no and so does Moscow. P. Ben. New Repub 161:11-12 Jl 26 '69
Cheers for Andrei; A. Gromyko in Cairo to sell Middle East peace package. il Newsweek 73:44+ Je 23 '69
Four-power exercise. Nat R 21:369 Ap 22 '69
Internationalize the Holy City. Nat R 21:738-9 Jl 29 '69; Reply. M. Geltman. 21:902 S 9 '69

ISRAELI-Arab war, 1967—Peace and mediation
—*Continued*
Israel: no war, no peace. S. Alsop. Newsweek 73:130 Ap 14 '69
Israel uptight. J. R. Moskin. il Look 33:30-6 Je 24 '69
Ivan the Arab; Soviet government suggestions for ending the conflict. New Repub 160:7-9 Ja 25 '69
King and the colonel. S. Alsop. Newsweek 73:96 Ap 7 '69
Letter from Washington. R. H. Rovere. New Yorker 45:161-3 Ap 19 '69
Long way to go; Big two talks. il Newsweek 73:51-2 My 19 '69
Middle East: direct talks v. imposed solution. Nat R 21:318 Ap 8 '69
Mideast: Moscow won't play; Russia-U.S. talks. il Newsweek 75:29 Ja 12 '70
Nixon and the Mideast. il Newsweek 75:21-2 Ja 5 '70
No middle ground; 1967 resolution and the Big four talks. il Newsweek 73:39 Ap 7 '69
Rhodes approach. il Newsweek 74:84+ O 6 '69
Small expectations; Big four meeting. il Newsweek 73:60 Ap 14 '69
Troubled ruler with many lives; what he seeks in the U.S. il U S News 66:22 Ap 14 '69
War or peace in Mideast? U S News 66:11 Ap 21 '69
ISRAELI dancing. See Dancing, Israeli
ISRAELI fiction
New Israeli fiction. R. Alter. Commentary 47:59-66 Je '69
ISRAELI literature
See also
Hebrew poetry
Israeli fiction
ISRAELI occupation of Jordan, 1967-. See Jordan—Israeli occupation, 1967-
ISRAELIS
Damn everybody sums up the angry mood of Israel. A. Rubinstein. il N Y Times Mag p24-7+ F 9 '69
Israel onrush; its surprises, pleasures, and people. A. Chamberlin. il Vogue 154:106-15 Jl '69
Israel uptight. J. R. Moskin. il Look 33:30-6 Je 24 '69
Jews and Arabs lie side by side, but not together, no man's land remains in Jerusalem. A. Rubinstein. il N Y Times Mag p30-1+ My 11 '69
ISSEI. See Japanese Americans
ISTANBUL
Music
House on the golden horn. C. E. Adelsen. il Opera N 34:22-3 O 11 '69
Riots
Bloody Sunday; anti-American demonstrators. il Newsweek 73:37 Mr 3 '69
ISTANBUL culture center. See Opera houses
ISTOMIN, Eugene
Recordings. M. Mayer. Esquire 72:76+ S '69
ITALIAN cookery. See Cookery, Italian
ITALIAN design. See Design
ITALIAN designers. See Designers
ITALIAN furniture designers. See Furniture designers
ITALIAN Grand prix. See Automobile racing
ITALIAN house decoration. See House decoration, Italian
ITALIAN philosophy. See Philosophy, Italian
ITALIAN poetry
Translations into English
Nothing new at Kindu; tr. by W. Alexander. R. Sanesi. New Repub 161:32 N 29 '69
ITALIAN pottery. See Pottery, Italian
ITALIAN students
See also
Student demonstrations—Italy
ITALIAN wines. See Wine
ITALIANS
Anecdotes, facetiae, satire, etc.
Duel of honor. J. Ciardi. Sat R 52:14-15 Mr 15 '69
ITALIANS in the United States
Seven men on a Hambo horse. W. F. Reed. jr. il Sports Illus 31:40-1 Jl 28 '69
ITALIC writing. See Writing, Italic
ITALO-AMERICANS. See Italians in the United States
ITALO-ETHIOPIAN war, 1935-1936
Civilizing missions, by A. J. Barker. Review Bul Atom Sci 25:51-2 My '69. L. Fermi

ITALY
See also
Airlines—Italy
Airplane industry and trade—Italy
Airplanes, Military—Italy
Architecture, Domestic—Italy
Automobile industry and trade—Italy
Bibliography, National—Italy
Booksellers and bookselling—Italy
Calabria
Catholic colleges and universities—Italy
Church unity—Italy
Divorce—Italy
Education—Italy
Elections—Italy
Festivals—Italy
Fishing—Italy
Floods—Italy
Florence
Investments, Foreign (by Italy)
Investments, Foreign (in Italy)
Ischia (island)
Lugano, Lake
Marriage—Italy
Morale, National—Italy
Moving pictures—Italy
Music—Italy
Music festivals—Italy
Opera—Italy
Parma (province)
Petroleum industry and trade—Italy
Postal service—Italy
Publishers and publishing—Italy
Rome (city)
Salerno
Science—Italy
Skis and skiing—Italy
Strikes—Italy
Student demonstrations—Italy
Theater—Italy
Trade unions—Italy
Tuscany
Val Gardena
Venice—Description
Youth—Italy

Antiquities
See also
Sybaris

Commerce
Putting supermarkets on the steppes; Milan-based export-import company dealings with Moscow. il Bsns W p78+ S 20 '69

Commercial treaties and agreements
Red dividend; Soviet gas deal. il Newsweek 74:76 D 22 '69

Description and travel
Italy: play places. L. Rasponi. il Vogue 153:212-15+ Ap 1 '69
Italy: sites to see, places to play. F. Lee. il Sports Illus 31:73 N 17 '69
Italy's five lands. B. Belford. il Travel 131:46-9 F '69
North of Italy. M. Edelson. il Travel & Camera 32:56-7+ Mr '69
Notes on Italian travel. J. Ferris. Sat R 52:4+ Ag 23 '69
Some random thoughts on downtown Italy. W. F. Wagner, jr. Arch Rec 145:9 Mr '69

Economic conditions
Il boom transforms Italy. G. Agnelli. Read Digest 94:195-8+ Ap '69
Crisis within a crisis. L. J. Berry. Commonweal 89:491-2 Ja 17 '69

Fascist movement
See Fascism—Italy

Foreign relations
Ethiopia
See also
Italo-Ethiopian war, 1935-1936
History
See also
Florence—History

Bibliography
Articles and other books received; comp. by E. P. Noether. See issues of American historical review

Industries
Il boom transforms Italy. G. Agnelli. Read Digest 94:195-8+ Ap '69
Hens nesting on rocks. Time 94:93+ S 19 '69
Motta goes American. M. A. Messina. il Duns R 93:95-6+ Mr '69
Revolt of the little man; investors fear nationalization. Time 93:94+ My 9 '69
See also
Chemical industries—Italy
Italy—Commerce
Petroleum industry and trade—Italy
Shoes—Trade and manufacture
Tire industry and trade

ITALY—*Continued*

Intellectual life

Italian heroines; the long shadow, cast by the poet D'Annunzio. A. Arbasino. il Vogue 153:202+ Ap 1 '69

Politics and government

Crisis within a crisis. L. J. Berry. Commonweal 89:491-2 Ja 17 '69

Italy between governments. R. Meachum. New Repub 162:16-18 Ja 10 '70

Last chance? il Newsweek 74:27-8 D 29 '69

No hope; minority government formed. Newsweek 74:41 Ag 18 '69

Rumor has it again. Time 94:32 Ag 15 '69

See also

Communist party (Italy)
Fascism—Italy
Socialist party (Italy)

Religious institutions and affairs

See also

Catholic church in Italy
Church unity—Italy

Social conditions

Storming the institutions; spreading social unrest. T. Terzani. Nation 208:751-2 Je 16 '69

ITEK corporation
Poor luck? Or poor management? il Forbes 103:15-16 Ap 1 '69

ITIL, Turan M. See Ulett, J. A. jt. auth.

ITKIN, Herbert
Crisis of silence. por Time 94:25 O 17 '69

ITOH, T. and Quastel, J. H.
Ribonucleic acid biosynthesis in adult and infant rat brain in vitro. bibliog Science 164: 79-80 Ap 4 '69

ITOKAWA, Y. and Cooper, J. R.
Thiamine release from nerve membranes by tetrodotoxin. bibliog Science 166:759-61 N 7 '69

IT'S never cold in daydreams; story. See Di-Pego, G.

IVENS, Dorothy, and Massee, W. E.
Getting stewed. Holiday 46:60-1+ N '69

IVERSEN, L. L. See Simmonds, M. A. jt. auth.

IVERSON, Floyd
Open letter to William E. Towell, re: the Bridger wilderness. Am For 75:46-7 N '69

IVES, Charles Edward
Alan Mandel plays all twenty-seven of the piano works of Ives. A. Cohn. Am Rec G 35:548-9 Mr '69
John Kirkpatrick: Concord revisited. D. W. Moore. Am Rec G 35-546-7 Mr '69
Shadow and substance in Ives. R. Evett. Atlan 223:110-11 My '69

IVES, Ronald L.
Finding parallel resistances. Pop Electr 30: 61-2 Je '69
Pathfinder of the Papagueria. Américas 21: 13-20 S; 14-21 O '69

IVEY, Allen E. See Hinkle, J. E. jt. auth.

IVEY, Jean Eichelberger
Current chronicle. Mus Q 55:87-91 Ja '69

IVIZA (island)
Ins and outs of islands. M. Berry. Sat R 52: 40+ Je 7 '69

IVORY
See also
Pratt, Read company

IVY
Easy-to-grow hardy ivies. R. Webber. Home Gard 56:77 Ap '69

IWAMOTO, David, and Hearn, N. E.
Evaluation is a full-time job. Am Ed 5:18-19 Ap '69

IZATT, Reed M. and others
Binding of alkali metal ions by cyclic polyethers: significance in ion transport processes. bibliog Science 164:443-4 Ap 25 '69

J

J.C. PENNEY company. See Penney, J. C. company

JFET (junction field-effect transistors) See Transistors

J. I. Case company. See Case, J. I. company

J MARKS. See Marks, J.

JOIDES (Joint oceanographic institutions deep earth sampling program) See Underwater drilling

JPL. See Jet propulsion laboratory

J. P. Stevens and company. See Stevens, J. P. and company

J. Walter Thompson company. See Thompson, J. Walter, company

JACK, Homer A.
When Russian and American peace groups talk peace. N Y Times Mag p28-9+ Mr 9 '69

JACK knives. See Knives

JACKETS. See Clothing and dress—Sports clothes

JACKLET, Jon W.
Circadian rhythm of optic nerve impulses recorded in darkness from isolated eye of aplysia. bibliog Science 164:562-3 My 2 '69

JACKLIN, Tony
Liege lord of golf. C. Kirkpatrick. il pors Sports Illus 31:12-15 Jl 21 '69

JACKS
ATA unit divided on equipment for retrieving disabled jets. Aviation W 91:32 S 29 '69

JACKSON, Billy Morrow
Jackson's prairie. G. R. Bradshaw. il por Am Artist 33:60-5 My '69

JACKSON, Brent. See Silva, B. J. jt. auth.

JACKSON, Charles B.
Dangerous creatures of the deep. Nat Wildlife 7:50-5 Ag '69

JACKSON, David
Comment. Poetry 114:411-12 S '69

JACKSON, Donald
Mystery in the Arctic. Life 66:66B-67+ Ap 25 '69
Threatened America. Life 67:33-43 Ag 1 '69
Whose wilderness? Life 68:109-10+ Ja 9 '70

JACKSON, Donald C.
Bouyancy control in the freshwater turtle, pseudemys scripta elegans. bibliog Science 166:1649-51 D 26 '69

JACKSON, Douglas
Gentle genius; drama. Plays 29:27-37 D '69

JACKSON, George F.
California's petroglyph canyons: a gallery of ancient Indian art. il Nat Parks 43:15-17 O '69

JACKSON, Henry Martin
Czechoslovakia and western security; statement. Bul Atom Sci 25:36-9 Ja '69
Excerpt from statement on National commitments resolution, June 25, 1969. Cong Digest 48:209+ Ag '69
Russia has not changed her ways; excerpts from address, March 17, 1969. Read Digest 94:91-5 Je '69
Russian leadership; address, July 9, 1969. Vital Speeches 35:610-13 Ag 1 '69

about

Fight over who cleans up. por Bsns W p46 Jl 12 '69
Policing the polluters. il por Time 94:42 Ag 1 '69

JACKSON, Howard E.
Don't bypass the Delta. Travel 131:36-41 Mr '69

JACKSON, Jean Jones
Flip side. il Time 93:44-5+ Ja 24 '69

JACKSON, Jeremy B. C.
Bivalves: spatial and size-frequency distributions of two intertidal species. bibliog Science 161:479-80; 162:1510; 163:830 Ag 2, D 27 '68, F 21 '69

JACKSON, Jesse L.
Black hope, white hope. J. Pekkanen. il pors Life 67:67-72+ N 21 '69
Blacks wrap up slice of action at food chains. il por Bsns W p 162-3+ Ap 26 '69
Jesse Jackson: heir to Dr King? R. Levine. por Harper 238:58-64+ Mr '69

JACKSON, John F. See Martin. L. M. jt. auth.

JACKSON, Joseph Harrison
Doctor Jackson delights the radical right. Chr Cent 86:1271 O 8 '69

JACKSON, Katherine Gauss
Books in brief. See issues of Harper's magazine to July 1969

JACKSON, L. Brewster
Draft boards in action. Nation 208:174-8 F 10 '69

JACKSON, Lawrence, and Miller, Robert
Deer take in 1968-69. Cons 23:13-14+ Je '69

JACKSON, Leonard
To become good readers. Am Ed 5:9-10 D '69

JACKSON, Louis
Westchester trustees warned against unions; summary of address, December 3, 1968. Library J 94:134-5 Ja 15 '69

JACKSON, Margaret A.
Viewpoint. Library J 94:2431 Je 15 '69

JACKSON, Norman
Blue nun; poem. New Yorker 45:172 O 18 '69

JACKSON, Reggie
Big A. il por Newsweek 74:84 Jl 7 '69
Fence-busters. il por Time 94:48 Jl 25 '69
Highlight. por Sports Illus 30:76 Je 23 '69
Home run king Reggie Jackson. il pors Ebony
24:92-4+ O '69
Maris and the Babe, move over! M. Mulvoy. il por Sports Illus 31:22-5 Jl 7 '69
JACKSON, Robert S.
Old naked face. por Outdoor Life 144:52-5+
O '69
JACKSON, Rupert A.
Computer tells what street to pave. Am City
84:94+ Ja '69
JACKSON, Samuel C.
New center for dispute settlement. Mo Labor
R 92:10 Ja '69
JACKSON, Shirley
Come along with me; story. McCalls 96:72-3
F '69
Experience and fiction; excerpts from Come
along with me. Writer 82:9-14+ Ja '69
JACKSON, Vera Ruth
Group pictures, group organization. Design
70:4-7 mid-Wint '69
—and Radcliffe, Woodward
Sponge painting. Sch Arts 68:9 F '69
Stylized birds in stitchery. Sch Arts 68:20-1
My '69
JACKSON, W. A. Douglas
Soviet collective farm. bibliog Focus 20:7-12
D '69
JACKSON, William Henry
Frontier photographers. D. Vestal. il Travel
& Camera 32:48-52+ Je '69
William Henry Jackson at ninety-nine. B.
Belknap. Travel & Camera 32:39 Je '69
JACKSON, William V.
Fifty million books for Brazil. bibliog por
Wilson Lib Bul 44:197-202 O '69
JACKSON, Mich.
Grass is greener. il Am City 84:114+ My '69

Music
Burst of art at the crossroads. F. Hains. il
Hi Fi 19:MA28-9+ My '69
JACKSON, Miss.
If Jackson can do it. B. Horne. il Horticulture 47:30-1 Ag '69
JACKSON, N.J.
Jackson, N.J. tells its story, 125 years old
and looking ahead. il Am City 84:112-13
D '69
JACKSONVILLE, Fla.

City planning
Business is solving a city's problems. H. G.
Tanzler, jr. il Nations Bsns 57:56-9 Jl '69

Metropolitan district
Metro has another fling. il Bsns W p 160-2
Mr 29 '69

Politics and government
Business is solving a city's problems. H. G.
Tanzler, jr. il Nations Bsns 57:56-9 Jl '69
JACKSONVILLE university, Jacksonville, Fla.
Up, up and away go Artis and new J.U.
J. Jares. il Sports Illus 32:18-21 Ja 5 '70
JACOB, Herbert
Winners and losers: garnishment & bankruptcy in Wisconsin; excerpts from Debtors in
court. Trans-Action 6:24-32 My '69
JACOBINIAS
Jacobinia carnea. J. T. Neal. Horticulture
47:14-15 F '69
JACOBS, Alexander
Writer; interview, ed. by S. Farber. Film Q
22:2-14 Wint '68
JACOBS, Elijah L.
Night's last look at the barn; poem. Farm J
93:52 S '69
JACOBS, Ellen W.
For men only. Dance Mag 43:78-81 My '69
—See McGuire, M. B. jt. auth.
JACOBS, Evelyn. See Gardner, H. L. jt. auth.
JACOBS, F. B.
Hospitality tray; poem. Horn Bk 45:693 D
'69
JACOBS, Harvey
Negotiators; story. Esquire 71:128-9 Ap '69
JACOBS, Hayes B.
New York market letter. See issues of
Writer's digest
JACOBS, Herb
Let's tell the people; address, March 24, 1969.
Vital Speeches 35:467-9 My 15 '69
JACOBS, Jane
Jane Jacobs: against urban renewal, for urban
life; interview, ed. by L. Kent. por N Y
Times Mag p34-5+ My 25 '69

about
City of man. il por Time 93:104 Je 13 '69
Inefficiency expert. L. S. Martz. il por Newsweek 73:63 Je 2 '69
Jane Jacobs, civic battler. S. Brownmiller.
il Vogue 153:180-1+ My '69
JACOBS, Jay
Collector: Joseph H. Hirshhorn. Art in Am
57:56-71 Jl '69
Where do we come from? What are we?
Where are we going. Horizon 11:52-65
Sum '69
JACOBS, John
Weather goes SDS? R. Whitehead. Commonweal 91:92 O 24 '69
JACOBS, Louis
Liberal beliefs. Commentary 48:89-91 N '69
JACOBS, Marian B. and Ewing, Maurice
Mineral source and transport in waters of
the Gulf of Mexico and Caribbean Sea. bibliog Science 163:805-9 F 21 '69
Suspended particulate matter: concentration
in the major oceans. bibliog Science 163:
380-3 Ja 24 '69
JACOB'S Pillow dance festival. See Dance
festivals
JACOBSEN, E. H. See Peterson, P. D. jt.
auth.
JACOBSEN, Josephine
Shade-seller; poem. Commonweal 90:22 Mr
21 '69
JACOBSON, Bernard
In composers. Hi Fi 19:54-7 Jl '69
Monteverdi's Orfeo, a true music-drama,
now complete and in stereo. Hi Fi 19:
66-7 Ap '69
JACOBSON, Marcus
Development of specific neuronal connections.
bibliog Science 163:543-7 F 7 '69
JACOBSON, Martin
Sex pheromone of the pink bollworm moth:
biological masking by its geometrical
isomer. bibliog Science 163:190-1 Ja 10 '69
JACOBSON, Philip
Nonsectarian public parochial school. Chr Cent
86:769-74 Je 4 '69
JACOBSON, Robert
Bach by the book. Sat R 52:53 Jl 26 '69
Fritz and Wally. Sat R 52:79-80 Ap 26 '69
From Bach to Bach. Sat R 52:79-80 O 25 '69
Likable Lakmé from London. Sat R 52:59
Mr 29 '69
McCracken as Canio. Sat R 52:105 S 13 '69
Mozart manifold. Sat R 52-72+ F 22 '69
Penderecki's Passion. Sat R 52:69+ Mr 22 '69
Pirates in stereo. Sat R 52:53 Je 28 '69
Renaissance revisited. Sat R 52:79 N 29 '69
Silla in sound. Sat R 52:58 D 27 '69
Under the shadow. Opera N 34:8-12 N 22 '69
Weekend with Rostropovich. Sat R 52:65 My
17 '69
JACOBSON, Stanley I. See Mial, D. J. jt. auth.
JACOBY, Harriette Weldon
Baby on the go. Parents Mag 44:54-5+ Ap '69
JACOBY, Susan
Who am I? Sr Schol 94:Schol Teach 16-17 F
7 '69
JACOMO, Edward M.
Boxed in creativity. Sch Arts 68:32-4 Mr '69
JACQUES, Jack
Four-channel audio mixer. Radio-Electr 40:
32-4 F '69
JACQUES, Michael
Big wheel. il por Newsweek 73:98 My 5 '69
JADEITE
Jadeite: shock-induced formation from oligoclase, Ries crater, Germany. O. B. James.
bibliog il Science 165:1005-8 S 5 '69
JAFFE, Dan
Voice of the poet: oracular, eerie, daring.
Sat R 52:28-9+ S 6 '69
JAFFE, Leonard D.
Lunar surface material: spacecraft measurements of density and strength. bibliog Science 164:1514-16 Je 27 '69
Strength-density relations in particulate silicates of complex shape and their possible
lunar significance. bibliog Science 165:1121-
3 S 12 '69
Surveyor lunar landings. bibliog Science 164:
774-88 My 16 '68
JAFFE, Louis L.
We need the Pastore bill. New Repub 161:
14-16 D 6 '69; 162:35-6 Ja 3 '70
JAFFREY, Madhur
Spicy eats of India. Holiday 46:40-1+ D '69
JAFFRY, Jacques
Art of cooking game birds. por Am Home
72:94-5 N '69
JAGGER, Mick
Mick Jagger, I love you. H. Lawrenson. pors
Esquire 71:132-5+ Je '69
JAGUAR hunting
Cat that kills with a single spring. S. E.
Brock. il Read Digest 94:152-4+ My '69

JAHR, El
Parliament of owls. R. D. Bonham. il Ceram Mo 17:23-5 Ja '69
JAILLET, Helene. See Herskovits, T. T. jt. auth.
JAILS. See Prisons
JAIN, K. B. L. See Jain, S. K. jt. auth.
JAIN, Prakash C.
Letter from India. Nat R 21:1326 D 30 '69
JAIN, S. K. and Jain, K. B. L.
Polymorphism in an inbreeding population under models involving underdominance. bibliog Science 166:1294-6 D 5 '69
JALBERT, Russell R.
Early retirement under social security. por Har Yrs 9:24-5 Mr '69
Medicare: three years of progress. por Har Yrs 9:24 Jl '69
Second hundred years. Har Yrs 9:40-1 N '69
Since you asked ... por Har Yrs 9:43-4 S '69
When daddy's in the kitchen. por Har Yrs 9:44-5 My '69
JAM. See Jelly, jam, etc.
JAMAICA
Black power and the archbishop. America 121:316 O 18 '69
Jamaica. A. J. Lowe. il Américas 21:2-13 O '69
See also
Aviation—Jamaica
Earthquakes—Jamaica
Montego Bay
JAMAICA-United States air agreement. See Aviation—International aspects
JAMBOREE, Boy scout. See Boy scouts
JAMBRO, Thomas A.
Collage. Sch Arts 68:10-11 Mr '69
Visual aids spark tripping calendar. Camp Mag 41:12 F '69
JAMES, Alan
Anti X-ray circuit. Radio-Electr 41:68-9 Ja '70
JAMES, Don
Keep it brief and blend it in. Writers Digest 49:50-2+ Jl '69
JAMES, Francis
Incredible, yes. True? J. Burnham. Nat R 21:687 Jl 15 '69
JAMES, Hatcher
Worst city in the world? Newsweek 74:38-9 D 29 '69
JAMES, Henry
Henry James: the treacherous years (1895-1901). by L. Edel. Review
Life 66:9 Je 6 '69. R. Freedman
Nation 209:55-6 Jl 14 '69. M. L. Krupnick
New Repub 160:33-4 Je 14 '69. D. Aaron
Newsweek por 73:100+ Je 23 '69. R. A. Gross
Sat R por 52:29 Je 7 '69. N. Kelvin
Time 93:104+ Je 13 '69
JAMES, Leon
Laying down some leather; interview. New Yorker 44:29-31 F 15 '69
JAMES, Odette B.
Jadeite: shock-induced formation from oligoclase, Ries crater, Germany. bibliog Science 165:1005-8 S 5 '69
Shock and thermal metamorphism of basalt by nuclear explosion, Nevada test site. bibliog Science 166:1615-20 D 26 '69
JAMES, Philip
Making film strips. Sch Arts 68:36-7 F '69
JAMES, Rosa
Primulas for your garden. Horticulture 47:49 Ja '69
JAMES Simon, pseud. See Kunen, J. S.
JAMES, William
Idea man. W. Arnold. Sat R 52:75-6 N 22 '69
—See Sears, J. A. jt. auth.
JAMES RIVER
James River flood of August 1969 in Virginia. H. J. Thompson. il Weatherwise 22:180-3 O '69
JAMESON, Richard T.
Manhandling the movies. Film Q 22:4-11 Spr '69
JAMIESON, John Kenneth
Jamieson and Brisco of Jersey Standard. por Fortune 80:39 O '69
JAMISON, Judith
Brief biography. S. Goodman. pors Dance Mag 43:64-5 Ag '69
JAMROG, Sandra
Sandra Jamrog; an evening of dance. J. Anderson. Dance Mag 43:87 Jl '69
JANáčEK, Leoš
House of the dead. S. Jenkins. Opera N 34:30 D 13 '69
Its true self. J. W. Freeman. il Opera N 34:14-15 O 11 '69
Rebirth of an eccentric. il por Time 94:82 D 5 '69
TV log. J. Chwat. il Opera N 34:17-19 D 6 '69

JANCSó, Miklós
Current cinema. P. Gilliatt. New Yorker 45:106+ Mr 29; 124+ My 17 '69
Films. R. Hatch. Nation 208:740-1 Je 9 '69
JANES, Kelly
Instinct of workmanship; poem. Chr Cent 86:472 Ap 9 '69
JANES, Mary C.
My battered heart. por Har Yrs 9:19-21 My '69
JANES, Ted
(ed) News: the Northeast (cont) por Outdoor Life 143:45-8 My; 144:37-40 Ag; 31-4 S; 41-8 O; 25-8 D '69
Reunion at Missisquoi Bay. Outdoor Life 143:76-7+ My '69
JANEWAY, Elizabeth
Subordinate sex. Sat R 52:27-9+ O 11 '69
Worlds of Jean Stafford. Atlan 223:136-8 Mr '69
JANIEC, Henry
Beethoven in a pup tent. Hi Fi 19:MA8-10 F '69
JANSEN, Udo H.
Grading practices in Nebraska. bibliog Clear House 43:335-7 F '69
JANSONISTS
See also
Bishop Hill, Ill.
JANSSEN, Werner A. and Surgalla, M. J.
Plague bacillus: survival within host phagocytes. bibliog Science 163:950-2 F 28 '69
JAPAN
Japan in transition; one hundred years of modernization. il Travel & Camera 32:87-90+ F '69
Japan on view; symposium. il Travel & Camera 32:48-85+ O '69
Japan '70; symposium. il Look 33:27-42+ O 21 '69
1970: the year of Japan. A. Geyer. Chr Cent 86:1660-1 D 31 '69
Non-proliferation treaty and Japan. R. Imai. il Bul Atom Sci 25:2-7 My '69
Sun up in Asia. A. Campbell. New Repub 161:16-18 Jl 5 '69
Three studies in Japanese tradition. M. Coleman. il Travel & Camera 32:18+ O '69
See also
Advertising—Japan
Airlines—Japan
Airlines, Military—Japan
Architecture—Japan
Atomic research—Japan
Automobile industry and trade—Japan
Baseball—Japan
Business consolidations and mergers—Japan
Chemical industries—Japan
Children—Japan
Colleges and universities—Japan
Computer industry—Japan
Electronic apparatus industry and trade—Japan
Festivals—Japan
Gardens—Japan
Gross national product—Japan
Hiroshima
Hotels, taverns, etc.—Japan
Investments, Foreign (by Japan)
Investments, Foreign (in Japan)
Japanese
Karuizawa
Labor supply—Japan
Marriage—Japan
Newspapers—Japan
Night clubs—Japan
Oceanographic resarch—Japan
Okinawa
Paper making and trade—Japan
Petroleum—Japan
Phonograph record industry—Japan
Photography—Japan
Piano industry and trade—Japan
Political parties—Japan
Public opinion—Japan
Publishers and publishing—Japan
Railroads—Japan
Restaurants—Japan
Science—Japan
Shopping and shoppers—Japan
Space research—Japan
Steel industry and trade—Japan
Student demonstrations—Japan
Tourist trade—Japan
United States—Armed forces—Forces in Japan
Water supply—Japan
Women—Japan
World war, 1939-1945—Japan
Yachts and yachting—Japan
Youth—Japan
Armed forces
Thinking the unthinkable. il Newsweek 74:68+ N 17 '69

JAPAN—*Continued*

Civilization

Japan's legacy and destiny of change. K. Aichi. For Affairs 48:21-38 O '69

What manner of men are these Japanese? C. Mydans and S. Mydans. il Fortune 80:100-2+ Ag 1 '69; Same abr. Read Digest 95:177-8+ O '69

Commerce

Hard bargaining with Japan. Time 93:82 My 30 '69

Japan's struggle to cope with plenty. il Time 94:69B-70 Ag 1 '69

Mission impossible; Far East cool to proposal for voluntary restrictions on textile exports to the U.S. il Newsweek 73:92 My 26 '69

Sharp side of the rising sun. il Bsns W p 124-6 S 6 '69

Showdown in trade with Japan. il Time 94:71-2 Jl 4 '69

View from the Pole; Alaska's best customer. il Forbes 104:36 N 15 '69

West Germany v. Japan. il Time 95:51-2 Ja 5 '70

See also
Japan—Industries
Joint United States-Japan committee on trade and economic affairs

Cultural relations

See also
Joint committee on United States-Japan cultural and education cooperation

Defenses

How Japan is reviving its military machine; with interview with M. Genda, ed. by K. M. Chrysler. il U S News 67:91-4 O 27 '69

Thinking the unthinkable. il Newsweek 74:68+ N 17 '69

Description and travel

Hamaya's Japan. M. R. Weiss. il Sat R 52:46-7 Mr 15 '69

Nippon, the land of contrast. F. Gibney. il Travel & Camera 32:56-65 O '69

Teacher's guide to Japan. M. Mann. bibliog il Sr Schol 94:Schol Teach 16-18 F 28 '69

Economic conditions

Japanese head for a bout with inflation. il Bsns W p67-8 D 6 '69

Japanese howdunit. M. Bronfenbrenner. il Trans-Action 6:32-6 Ja '69

Japan's struggle to cope with plenty. il Time 94:69B-70 Ag 1 '69

New face of world power. F. Gibney. Look 33:28-9 O 21 '69

Economic history

Japanese howdunit. M. Bronfenbrenner. il Trans-Action 6:32-6 Ja '69

Economic policy

Japan's economic dynamism and our common interests in East Asia; excerpts from address, March 18, 1969. R. W. Barnett. Dept State Bul 60:447-50 My 26 '69

Economic relations

Japan opens its doors, just a bit. il Fortune 80:33-4 Jl '69

See also
Joint United States-Japan committee on trade and economic affairs

United States

Steel industries of Japan and ECSC offer to limit exports to U.S; letter, with texts of steel industries' communications. D. Rusk. Dept State Bul 60:93-4 F 3 '69

Foreign population

Eddychan. E. Hahn. New Yorker 44:33-9 Ja 18 '69

Foreign relations

Japan beyond 1970. K. Wakaizumi. For Affairs 47:509-20 Ap '69

Asia, Southeastern

Invitation to greatness; U.S. pressures assume some responsibility for the security and welfare of the Pacific region. il Newsweek 47:30-1 Ag 11 '69

United States

Agreement on Okinawa. il Time 94:37 N 28 '69

American alliance in trouble? return of Okinawa. il U S News 66:8 Je 16 '69

Closing a chapter of the past; Okinawa agreement. il Newsweek 74:39-40 D 1 '69

Go; Okinawa agreement. New Repub 161:10 N 29 '69

Hour of apology; reprint. D. Lawrence. U S News 67:100 D 8 '69

Japan 1970: year of upheaval. J. P. Freed. il Nation 209:374-9 O 13 '69

Japan presses Pacific demands; U.S. airline expansion blocked. L. Doty. Aviation W 90:24-5 F 17 '69

New face of world power. F. Gibney. Look 33:28-9 O 21 '69

Okinawa mon amour. T. Oka. il N Y Times Mag p30-1+ Ap 6 '69

Pro-U.S. policy gets support. U S News 68:10 Ja 12 '70

Sato-Nixon pact; its meaning to U.S. and Japan. il U S News 67:18 D 1 '69

Sayonara, Okinawa. il Time 93:18 Je 13 '69

Short fuse in Japan. A. Axelbank. Nation 208:141-3 F 3 '69

Transpacific decision hardens JAL stand for gains in U.S. Aviation W 90:27 My 19 '69

U.S. Japan on a collision course? il U S News 67:84-5 N 24 '69

United States-Japanese relations today; address, October 22, 1969. U. A. Johnson. Dept State Bul 61:401-3 N 10 '69

Why we're returning Okinawa to Japan. A. Campbell. New Repub 160:11-13 Je 14 '69

Winning a round. il Newsweek 73:50 Je 16 '69

See also
Panay (gunboat) incident

History

Hour of the ox; burning of Sanjo palace in Heiji war as turning point in history. E. O. Reischauer. il Horizon 11:12-25 Wint '69

Japan in transition; one hundred years of modernization. il Travel & Camera 32:87-90+ F '69

1912-1945

Inukai Tsuyoshi; some dilemmas in party development in pre-World war II Japan; address, December 1966. T. Najita. bibliog f Am Hist R 74:492-510 D '68

Industries

Conglomerate way of life in Japan. il U S News 66:92-3 Je 2 '69

Japan's trade giant picks old U.S. hand; S. Wakasugi. Bsns W p 108+ My 24 '69

Linking the East; Pan-Asian bus and train routes. S. Griffin. Sci N 96:152 Ag 23 '69

Missile defense drags; rivalry between Mitsubishi and Toshiba. S. Griffin. Sci N 95:586 Je 14 '69

Pushing big-scale projects. S. Griffin. Sci N 96:14 Jl 5 '69

Still the brain drain. S. Griffin. il Sci N 96:362 O 18 '69

Travel notes. R. Joseph. Esquire 72:75-6+ D '69

See also
Airplane industry and trade—Japan
Automobile industry and trade—Japan
Computer industry—Japan
Electronic apparatus industry and trade—Japan
Japan—Economic conditions
Pearl industry and trade
Toy industry

Military policy

Testing ground in Tokyo; growing militarism and the Okinawa question. N. Cousins. il Sat R 52:28-9 D 6 '69

Photographs

100 years of Japanese photography. G. Konishi. il Travel & Camera 32:113-16+ O '69

Politics and government

Japan 1970: year of upheaval. J. P. Freed. il Nation 209:374-9 O 13 '69

Premier Sato would tap his way across a stone bridge to be sure it was safe. T. Oka. il N Y Times Mag p48-9+ N 16 '69; Reply. G. Berger. p 134 D 7 '69

See also
Political parties—Japan

Religious institutions and affairs

Money-changing temples; commercial ventures. il Newsweek 75:47 Ja 12 '70

See also
Buddha and Buddhism
Catholic church in Japan
Catholics in Japan
Soka Gakkai (sect)

Riots

Japan 1970: year of upheaval. J. P. Freed. il Nation 209:374-9 O 13 '69

JAPAN—*Continued*

Social conditions

Japan's U.S.-style boom, and U.S.-style problems. il U S News 67:62-3 Jl 7 '69

Social life and customs

Awaiting the explosion. B. Krisher. il Newsweek 75:25-6 Ja 5 '70
Inn-thing in Japan: Kyoto *ryokan*. G. Cotler. il Holiday 46:48-51+ D '69
Yes, the Orient hasn't changed. M. Berry. il Sat R 52:70+ S 13 '69
See also
Geishas
Marriage—Japan
Women—Japan

JAPAN-United States cooperative medical science committee. See Medical research—International cooperation

JAPAN air lines. See Airlines—Japan

JAPAN and the United States
Japan beyond 1970. K. Wakaizumi. For Affairs 47:509-20 Ap '69
1970: the year of Japan. A. Geyer. Chr Cent 86:1660-1 D 31 '69
See also
Hiroshima maidens

JAPAN center, San Francisco. See San Francisco—Japanese cultural and trade center

JAPAN Socialist party. See Political parties—Japan

JAPANESE
Eddychan. E. Hahn. New Yorker 44:33-9 Ja 18 '69
Japan '70; symposium. il Look 33:27-42+ O 21 '69
Japanese. D. Kurzman. Sat R 52:38+ N 15 '69
What manner of men are these Japanese? C. Mydans and S. Mydans. il Fortune 80: 100-2+ Ag 1 '69; Same abr. Read Digest 95:177-8+ O '69

JAPANESE AMERICANS
Americans from Asia: the East came to the West. il Sr Schol 94:12-17 Ap 25 '69
Before the colors fade: the return of the exiles; interview, ed. by J. Stevenson R. W. Kenny. il Am Heritage 20:22-5+ Je '69
Nisei, by B. Hosokawa. Review
Sat R 52:40-1 N 15 '69. J. Charyn

JAPANESE art. See Art, Japanese

JAPANESE artificial satellites. See Artificial satellites, Japanese

JAPANESE automobiles. See Automobiles, Foreign

JAPANESE baseball. See Baseball—Japan

JAPANESE baths. See Baths

JAPANESE beetles
Beetles and dieldrin; letter. C. F. Wurster, jr. Science 163:229 Ja 17 '69

JAPANESE cookery. See Cookery, Japanese

JAPANESE cultural and trade center. See San Francisco—Japanese cultural and trade center

JAPANESE dancing. See Dancing, Japanese

JAPANESE gardens. See Gardens, Japanese

JAPANESE in the United States
See also
Japanese Americans

JAPANESE irises. See Irises

JAPANESE music
See also
Phonograph records—Japanese music

JAPANESE poetry
Self-fulfilling prophecy and the haiku. H. L. Christ. Engl J 58:1189-91 N '69

JAPANESE pottery. See Pottery, Japanese

JAPANESE prints. See Prints

JAPANESE quail. See Quails

JAPANESE sculpture. See Sculpture, Japanese

JAPANESE students
Goodbye, Confucius. il Time 94:39 D 12 '69
See also
Student demonstrations—Japan
Student movement—Japan

JAQUES, Jack
50-watt booster amplifier. Radio-Electr 40:55-6 My '69
Make electronic bongos. Radio-Electr 40: 42-3 Jl '69
Solid-state fuzz box. Radio-Electr 40:40-1 D '69
Throbbing vibrato. Radio-Electr 40:45-6 Ap '69

JAQUITH, Lawrence C.
Cost index: working tool or trap? Arch Rec 145:75-6 F '69

JARAMILLO, Arthur
One man's battle. il por Time 93:15 Je 20 '69

Le JARDIN des delices; drama. See Arrabal, F.

JARES, Joe
Closing the missile gap in U.S. pubs. Sports Illus 31:66-72 S 8 '69
Track & field (title varies) (cont) Sports Illus 30:78+ My 5 '69

JARGON
See also
English language—Terms and phrases
Slang

JARMAN, Franklin Maxey
Genesco heir tries on the shoe. il pors Bsns W p50-2 Jl 26 '69

JARMAN, Rufus
Big boom in Boston. Am Heritage 20:46-51+ O '69

JARMUSZ, Robert T.
Some considerations in establishing a suicide prevention service. bibliog Ment Hy 53:351-6 Jl '69

JARRELL, Randall
Big pictures and little phrases. C. T. Samuels. New Repub 161:26-9 N 29 '69
Complete poems, by R. Jarrell. Review
Commonweal 90:146-7 Ap 18 '69. R. F. Deen
Melancholy monument. H. Carruth. Nation 209:19-20 Jl 7 '69

JARRETT, James L.
Self-evaluating college teacher. Todays Ed 58:40-1 Ja '69

JARRETT, Mary
Crime-solver in science lab. il pors Ebony 24:72-5+ Ap '69

JARRETT, Paul B.
IC stereo preamplifier. Pop Electr 30:52-4 Mr '69

JARRY, Madeleine
Design in Aubusson carpets. Antiques 95: 702-7 My '69

JARVIE, Ian
Media and manners: film and society in some current British films. Film Q 22:11-17 Spr '69

JARVIN, Stacey
Electronic aquarium heater. Pop Electr 32: 60-3 Ja '70

JASMINE
See also
Madagascar jasmine

JASPERS, Karl
One of Karl Jaspers' last commentaries: Gandhiji; excerpt from Mahatma Gandhi: 100 years. UNESCO Courier 22:26-7 O '69
about
Karl Jaspers; a tribute. J. Collins. por America 120:328-30 Mr 22 '69
Karl Jaspers: the inward path. N. J. Rigali. Commonweal 90:38-9 Mr 28 '69
Note on Karl Jaspers. D. von K. Jehle and H. Jehle. Bul Atom Sci 25:36 Mr '69
Obituary
Chr Cent 86:342 Mr 12 '69

JASTROW, Robert
Apollo's riches. por Newsweek 74:18 Ag 4 '69
Moon is a Rosetta stone. N Y Times Mag p25-7+ N 9 '69
Prize, or lunacy? statement on the eve of Apollo 11. il por Newsweek 74:60 Jl 7 '69
Travel plans; excerpts from address, 1969. New Yorker 45:17-18 Ja 10 '70
Venus and Mars; statements. New Yorker 45:29-31 My 10 '69

JAVELIN throwing
They're all out to launch. J. Kirshenbaum. il Sports Illus 31:38-41 Jl 21 '69

JAVELINA hunting. See Peccary hunting

JAVELINAS. See Peccaries

JAVITS, Jacob Koppel
Can President Nixon stop the arms race? Sat R 52:14-16+ Mr 1 '69
about
Where it's at: Los Angeles investigation by Senate committee on nutrition and human needs. il Time 93:23-4 My 16 '69

JAWS
Surgery
See Oral surgery

JAWS (animals)
Cynodont reptile with incipient mammalian jaw articulation. A. S. Romer. bibliog il Science 166:881-2 N 14 '69

JAXON, Valerie
Fashions for flattery. Har Yrs 9:42-4 O '69
Practically speaking. See issues of Harvest years

JAY, John
Jay papers II: the forging of the Nation; ed. by R. B. Morris. por Am Heritage 20:24-8+ D '68
Jay papers III: the trials of Chief Justice Jay; ed. by R. B. Morris. por Am Heritage 20:80-90 Je '69
JAY, Maurice
Slabs; poem. Poetry 115:33 O '69
JAYNES, Richard A.
Progress with chestnuts. Horticulture 46:16-17+ D '68
JAYS
Jaunty brigand: the Steller's jay. F. Weddle. il Nat Parks 43:9 Ja '69
JAY'S treaty. See United States—Treaties—Great Britain
JAZZ bands. See Bands (music)
JAZZ dance. See Dancing
JAZZ festivals. See Music festivals
JAZZ music
Early jazz, by G. Schuller. Review
Am Rec G 35:881-3 My '69. D. Heckman
Jazz (cont) W. Balliett. New Yorker 45:167-8+ Mr 18; 139-40+ My 17; 98+ My 31 '6
Jazz and the liberation of worship. Chr Cent 86:499 Ap 16 '69
Jazz is my bag! C. Hundley. Seventeen 28:40 Ja '69
Muscling in; rhythm and blues in Muscle Shoals. il Newsweek 74:90 S 15 '69
Music of militancy; a new breed assumes dominance. F. Kofsky. Commonweal 89:733-4 Mr 14 '69
Rare air; D. Gibson's Aspen jazz parties. W. Conover. il Sat R 52:64-5+ O 11 '69
See also
Blues (songs, etc)
Phonograph records—Jazz music
Rock 'n' roll music

History
Jazzman's last ramble; funeral of G. Lewis. J. Roddy. il Life 33:100-2 Mr 18 '69
Rebirth of the blues: soul. S. Booth. il Sat Eve Post 242:26-31+ F 8 '69
JAZZ musicians
Painting masters of jazz. D. Quinn. il Am Artist 33:39-41+ Ag '69
See also
Hawkins, C.
King, R. B.
JE t'aime (song) See Songs, French
JEALOUSY
See also
Envy
JEAN Marie Kann. Sister. See Kann. J. M.
JEANLOZ, Roger W. See Katzman, R. L. jt. auth.
JEANS. See Clothing and dress—Sports clothes
JEDEDIAH Smith redwoods state park. See California—Parks and reserves
JEDLICKA, Daniel A.
Gaining respect on Woodward avenue. Esquire 72:112-17+ S '69
JEEP automobiles
American motors will steer Jeep. il Bsns W p39-40 O 25 '69
Jeepster Commando thrives when the going gets rough. J. P. Norbye and J. Dunne. il Pop Sci 195:114-15 S '69
PM owners report:
Jeep Wagoneer. B. Hartford. il Pop Mech 132:106-9 S '69
JEFFERIES, D. J. and French, M. C.
Avian thyroid: effect of p,p'-DDT on size and activity. bibliog Science 166:1278-80 D 5 '69
—See French, M. C. jt. auth.
JEFFERSON, Thomas
Americanization of history. H. S. Commager. Sat R 52:24-5+ N 1 '69
Apostle of American democracy; Thomas Jefferson. P. W. Schmidtchen. il pors Hobbies 74:104-5+ Ag '69
Jefferson renounced: natural rights in the Old South. G. A. Cardwell. Yale R 58:388-407 Mr '69
President again; reprint from Recorder, Richmond, September 1, 1802. J. T. Callender. il Negro Hist Bul 32:20-1 N '69
Thomas Jefferson and James Thomson Callender: the myth of Black Sally. J. W. Knudson. por Negro Hist Bul 32:15-19 bibliog(p22) N '69
Thomas Jefferson: female identification. R. I. Harris. bibliog Am Imago 25:371-83 Wint '68
JEFFERSON COUNTY, Ky.
City-county merger in Kentucky; Louisville and Jefferson County combine park and recreation operations. C. Vettiner. il Parks & Rec 3:22-4+ O '68

JEFFERSON national forest, Va. See National forests
JEFFRIES, Jean
Chetsky-Davidov report. Nat R 21:748 Jl 29 '69
(ed) Dear Stalin, Dear Brezhnev, Dear... Nat R 21:590 Je 17 '69
History quiz for the young revolutionary. Nat R 21:488+ My 20 '69
Sticking the pigs. Nat R 21:236-8 Mr 11 '69
JEFFS, Wallace
Monuments to Haiti's only king. Negro Hist Bul 32:11-13 O '69
JEGART, Artemis
Artists on a houseboat. M. L. Norwood. il Am Artist 33:20-7 Ap '69
JEHOVAH'S Witnesses
Jehovah's Witnesses jailed in Spain. Chr Cent 86:1241 O 1 '69
Witnessing the end. il Time 94:62-3 Jl 18 '69
JELLEN, Mary Lou
On throwing out Ivanhoe. Clear House 43:316-18 Ja '69
JELLICO, John
Drawings of Nicolai Fechin. Am Artist 32:58-63+ N '68
Gerard Curtis Delano, painter of the Navajo Indians. Am Artist 33:64-9+ D '69
Realism of Ramon Kelly. Am Artist 33:58-63 Mr '69
Unusual technique. Am Artist 33:32-7 N '69
JELLINEK, George
How to build an opera record library. Opera N 34:18-19 N 22 '69
Songs by Verdi and Wagner. Opera N 33:24-5 Mr 29 '69
JELLINEK, Hedy D.
(comp) Guide to European music festivals, 1969. Sat R 52:68-9 Ap 26 '69
(comp) Music festivals USA, summer 1969. Sat R 52:42+ Je 14 '69
JELLY, jam, etc.
Gift from your kitchen: wine jelly. il Sunset 143:200+ N '69
If your jelly doesn't. Bet Hom & Gard 47:80 Ag '69
Low-sugar jams and jellies; with low-methoxyl pectin. E. Gibbons. Org Gard & Farm 16:96-9 Ja '69
Mailbag; low-sugar jams. E. Gibbons. Org Gard & Farm 16:62-5 My '69
There's nothing like homemade jam! il Changing T 23:41-2 Jl '69
See also
Canning and preserving
JELLY-rolls. See Cake
JELLYFISH
Unique envelope of a jellyfish ovum: the armed egg. D. Szollosi. bibliog il Science 163:586-7 F 7 '69
JENCKS, Christopher
Private schools for black children. Ed Digest 34:1-4 Mr '69
Reappraisal of the most controversial educational document of our time. N Y Times Mag p 12-13+ Ag 10; 76+ S 14; 12+ O 12 '69
What color is IQ? New Repub 161:25-9 S 6 '69
JENKINS, Bill
Strickler Trick. J. Dianna. il por Hot Rod 22:68-70 Mr '69
JENKINS, Dan
College football (cont) Sports Illus 31:101-4 S 22; 74+ N 17 '69
Golf (cont) Sports Illus 30:67-8+ My 26 '69
Skiing (cont) Sports Illus 30:58-9 Mr 17; 31:66 N 24 '69
JENKINS, David H.
Pesticides and man's environment; excerpts from address. Am For 75:30-1+ Ja '69
JENKINS, Leroy C.
It doesn't look like a police station. Am City 84:107-8 Jl '69
JENKINS, Loren
Franco's last deal. Nation 209:689-92 D 22 '69
New style of tyranny. Nation 209:532-4 N 17 '69
JENKINS, Lyll Becerra de
Saúl: story. Américas 21:34-6 F '69
JENKINS, Phyllis Adams
Moonhole, where time stands still. House B 111:38-43+ Ag '69
JENKINS, Speight, Jr
Basic books: a selection for the opera-lover. bibliog Opera N 34:14-15 D 6 '69
Loners. Opera N 33:24-5 Ap 5 '69
JENKINS, William A.
NCTE counciletter; addenda for the agenda. Engl J 58:1241-4 N '69
Will the real English teacher please stand? address, November 1968. Engl J 58:503-9 Ap '69
JENKINSON, Denis
Mercedes spins out an engine for the future. por Sports Illus 31:38-40+ S 15 '69

JENKINSON, Michael, and Bacon, Thorn
Voyage of the Green Witch. Motor B 124:84-5+ N '69
JENNER, Ann
Brief biography. S. Goodman. pors Dance Mag 43:66-7 Jl '69
JENNIE B. Zellerbach garden. See San Francisco—Gardens
JENNINGS, Anne
Visit of Mother Cloud; drama. Plays 28:76-80+ Mr '69
JENNINGS, Elizabeth
Port Meadow, Oxford; On writing an autobiography; Game of tennis; Workers; Summing-up; poems. Poetry 114:102-6 My '69
JENNINGS, Frank
AHD exists: a child of wrath. Pub W 196:34-5 S 29 '69
JENNINGS, James R.
Church and peace. America 120:304 Mr 15 '69
JENNINGS, Robert E. and Milstein, M. M.
School budget; achieving public support for education. Clear House 43:458-62 Ap '69
JENNISON, Peter S.
National book committee: work and progress. por Wilson Lib Bul 43:634-9 Mr '69
JENNY, Hans
Cymatics: the sculpture of vibrations. UNESCO Courier 22:4-12+ D '69
JENSEN, Albert C.
Fish and power plants. Cons 24:2-5 D '69
—and Poole, J. C.
Fishing again with the Russians. Cons 23:10-13+ Ap '69
JENSEN, Arthur Robert
Can Negroes learn the way whites do? por U S News 66:48-51 Mr 10 '69
Origin of IQ tests; excerpt from How much can we boost IQ and scholastic achievement? Sat R 52:68 My 17 '69

about

Born dumb? il por Newsweek 73:84 Mr 31 '69
Furor over race and I.Q. Here's the latest chapter. il por U S News 66:54-6 Je 2 '69
Genetics vs. headstart. Sci N 95:326-7 Ap 5 '69
IQ: God-given or man-made? G. Voyat. il por Sat R 52:73-5+ My 17 '69; Same abr. Ed Digest 35:1-4 O '69
Jensenism, n. the theory that I. Q. is largely determined by the genes. L. Edson. il por N Y Times Mag p 10-11+ Ag 31 '69; Discussion. p4+ S 21; 38+ S 28 '69
Jensen's complaint. M. R. Berube. Commonweal 91:42-4 O 10 '69
Let there be darkness. Nat R 21:996-7 O 7 '69
New rage at Berkeley. por Newsweek 73:69 Je 2 '69
Race and intelligence. J. Cass. Sat R 52:67-8 My 17 '69
What color is IQ? C. Jencks. New Repub 161:25-9 S 6 '69; Reply. J. D. Hyman. 161:30-1 O 25 '69
JENSEN, Belva
Trailing Lewis and Clark; with biographical sketch. por Natur Hist 78:4, 8-10+ bibliog (p75) Ag '69
JENSEN, Donald D. See Wasserman, E. A. jt. auth.
JENSEN, Eileen
Wisdom of the heart; story. Good H 169:80-1 S '69
JENSEN, H. James
English restoration attitudes toward music. bibliog f Mus Q 55:206-14 Ap '69
JENSEN, L. H. See Camerman, A. jt. auth.
JENSEN, Oliver
Anniversary. Am Heritage 21:3 D '69
'Bye, Phoebe Snow, 'bye Buffalo. Am Heritage 20:10-15 D '68
1857. Am Heritage 21:81-96 D '69
JENSEN, Robert
Building types study: resort hotels. Arch Rec 146:119-23 D '69
JEPSEN, Glenn L. and Woodburne, M. O.
Paleocene hyracothere from Polecat Bench formation, Wyoming. bibliog Science 164:543-7 My 2 '69
JEQUIRITY bean. See Crabs eye vine
JERNIGAN, Kenneth
Blindness; address. July 3, 1969. Vital Speeches 36:10-14 O 15 '69
JEROME, Bill
Shoot the sky. Travel & Camera 32:142 F '69
JEROME, Judson
Involving students with life. Cur 112:23-6 N '69
Poetry: how and why. See issues of Writer's digest
JERRARD, Margot
Long honeymoon; story. Redbook 133:94-5 O '69

JERSEY CITY, N.J.

Politics and government

Case history: I am the law; F. Hague. T. J. Fleming. il Am Heritage 20:32-48 Je '69

Stations

New transit center becomes focus of downtown renewal. il Am City 84:83+ Ap '69
JERUSALEM
Both sides of Arab-Israeli conflict agree; twilight war or holy war, but no peace. J. Fromm; J. Law. il U S News 67:24-5 S 8 '69
Crossroads of Jerusalem. H. Krosney. Nation 208:134-8 F 3 '69
Jews and Arabs live side by side, but not together, no man's land remains in Jerusalem. A. Rubinstein. il N Y Times Mag p30-1+ My 11 '69
Symbolic act; destruction by Arabs and Israelis. Time 93:26 Je 27 '69
United States reaffirms position on Jerusalem; statements. July 1 and 3, 1969; with text of resolution. C. W. Yost. Dept State Bul 61:76-8 Jl 28 '69

Description

Jerusalem: the sacred city. J. Gunther. il Read Digest 94:141-4+ Ap '69

Elections

Slight erosion. il Newsweek 74:48 N 10 '69

Fires

Arson in Jerusalem; al Aksa mosque. Chr Today 13:33 S 12 '69
Burning of al Aqsa. il Time 94:24 Ag 29 '69
Emotional Arab world aroused; reaction to al Aksa mosque fire. America 121:153 S 13 '69
Fire at mosque sparks new crisis. U S News 67:6 S 1 '69
Security council adopts resolution on al Aqsa mosque fire; with text of resolution. UN Mo Chron 6:3-33 O '69
U.S. abstains on security council resolution linking mosque fire to Middle East conflict; statement with text of resolution, September 15, 1969. C. W. Yost. Dept State Bul 61:307-9 O 6 '69

Mosques

Burning of al Aqsa. il Time 94:24 Ag 29 '69
Fire at a mosque sparks new crisis. U S News 67:6 S 1 '69
Security council adopts resolution on al Aqsa mosque fire; with text of resolution. UN Mo Chron 6:3-33 O '69
Trial of the new Moses; D. M. Rohan. A. Menen. il N Y Times Mag p54-5+ N 23 '69
U.S. abstains on security council resolution linking Mosque fire to Middle East conflict; statement with text of resolution, September 15, 1969. C. W. Yost. Dept State Bul 61:307-9 O 6 '69

Politics and government

Internationalize the Holy City. Nat R 21:738-9 Jl 29 '69; Reply. M. Geltman. 21:902 S 9 '69
Jerusalem II; Israeli occupation. Nat R 21:890 S 9 '69
Jerusalem III. Nat R 21:1302-3 D 30 '69
Letter from Israel. B. Bernstein. New Yorker 45:152-7 N 29 '69
Strange bedfellows. M. Elkins. il Newsweek 73:49-50 Je 16 '69

Yad va-shem

Toward a history of the holocaust. L. S. Dawidowicz. Commentary 47:51-6 Ap '69
JERUSALEM artichokes
Jerusalem artichoke, America's oldest vegetable. D. Reay. il Org Gard & Farm 16:102-3 Ja '69
See also
Cookery—Vegetables
JERUSALEM—Martyrs' and heroes' remembrance authority. See Jerusalem—Yad va-shem
JERVIS, Steven
Biafra has oil as well as starving children. New Repub 160:8-10 Mr 1; 30-1 Ap 5 '69
JERVIS corporation
Specialist at Jervis. S. Margetts. Duns R 93:73+ My '69
JESSE; story. See Williams, J.
JESSUP, John Knox
It's the third, not the fourth estate; farewell statement. por Life 66:3 Ap 4 '69
JESUIT universities. See Catholic colleges and universities

JESUITS
And now the Jesuits; M. Schoenenberger
leaving the order. Time 93:44 My 2 '69
Brothers not second-class citizens. C. J.
McNaspy. America 121:163 S 13 '69
New American Jesuits. J. L'Heureux. Atlan
224:59-64 N '69
Roman windmill tilting; problems of the
Amsterdam student parish. F. Franck. Com-
monweal 90:224-5 My 9 '69
What the black community wants; recom-
mended program of apostolic initiatives. T.
M. Gannon. America 121:558-62 D 6 '69
What to do about Joe Mulligan? J. C. Fleck.
America 121:184-9 S 20 '69; Discussion. 121:
360-2 O 25 '69
    See also
Kino, E. F.

Missions
Happening at Oglala; Jesuit helps Sioux re-
gain pride in their heritage. D. O. Collins.
il Am West 6:15-19 Mr '69
Unknown saint of India: V. Ferrer, with
photographs by C. Rentmeester. Life 66:
36-44 F 28 '69
JESUS CHRIST
Jesus of history and Christian faith. D. T.
Rowlingson; discussion. Chr Cent 86:121-2
Ja 22 '69
Married Christ? il Newsweek 73:90 Mr 24 '69
Presence of Christ: a contemporary view.
J. A. Hill. Chr Today 13:5-8 Je 20 '69
Sober question; Saviour of demonic connec
tions. V. P. McCorry. America 120:288-in
side back cover Mr 8 '69
That good shepherd image. V. P. McCorry
America 120:486 Ap 19 '69
    See also
Christianity
Cross and crosses
Salvation
Second advent

Apparitions and miracles (modern)
Image of Mr Christ; vision on door screen,
Port Neches, Tex. il Time 94:48 Jl 11 '69

Art
Gentile da Fabriano's Madonna and Child
with saints. B. F. Davidson. il Art N 68:
24-7+ Mr '69
Quest for a black Christ. A. Poinsett. il por
Ebony 24:170-2+ Mr '69
U.S. journal: Eureka Springs, Ark; site of
Christ of the Ozarks statue and a Passion
play. C. Trillin. New Yorker 45:69-70+ Jl 26
'69

Baptism
Beloved son and servant. V. P. McCorry.
America 122:28-inside back cover Ja 10
'70

Birth
See Jesus Christ—Nativity

Crucifixion
Why Christ died. H. D. Friberg. Chr Today
13:8-11 Jl 4 '69

Divinity
Responsibility: Christ's self-revelation. V. P.
McCorry. il America 120:176-7 F 8 '69

Drama
    See also
Passion plays

Forty days in the wilderness
See Jesus Christ—Temptations

Humanity
Unanswerable question V. P. McCorry. America 120:232-inside back cover F 22 '69

Incarnation
See Incarnation

Miracles
John and miracle. V. P. McCorry. America
121:311-12 O 11 '69

Nativity
Lord of the manger. E. P. Clowney. Chr
Today 14:3-5 D 5 '69
    See also
Incarnation

Passion
Thirst for fulfillment. F. Buechner. Chr Cent
86:364 Mr 19 '69

Poetry
Birth of Christ; tr. by M. W. Hess. R. M.
Rilke. Chr Today 14:12 D 5 '69
Penetrations to the Lord of the Resurrec-
tion. J. Chichetto. Chr Cent 86:443 Ap 2
'69
Servant's ballad. T. C. Arthur. Chr Cent 86:
446 Ap 2 '69

Resurrection and ascension
Is resurrection theology outdated? K. O'Shea.
Cath World 209:7-11 Ap '69
Journey's end. V. P. McCorry. America 120:
435-6 Ap 5 '69
Resurrection: joy and judgment. Chr Cent
86:435 Ap 2 '69
    See also
Ascension day

Teachings
Beware! substituting social gospel for the
Gospel of Jesus Christ. L. N. Bell. Chr To-
day 14:24-5 O 24 '69
Is the world view of Jesus outmoded? M. T.
Kelsey. Chr Cent 86:112-15 Ja 22 '69; Dis-
cusion. 86:454-5 Ap 2 '69
Teaching of Christ. V. P. McCorry. America
120:inside back cover Je 14 '69
That embezzler, again; Christ's teaching. V.
P. McCorry. America 121:48+ Jl 19 '69
What is the Gospel? L. N. Bell. Chr Today
13:28-9 F 14 '69

Temptations
Unanswerable question. V. P. McCorry.
America 120:232-3 F 22 '69

Transfiguration
On the holy mountain. V. P. McCorry. America 120:260-inside back cover Mr 1 '69

Trial
Two books, one question: was Jesus a zeal-
ot? J. L. McKenzie. Commonweal 90:26-7
Mr 21 '69
JESUS CHRIST in literature
Little prince, a story for our time. P.
Mooney. America 121:610-11+ D 20 '69
JET air travel. See Air travel
JET airplane engines
British see joint engine projects as key to
future sales. il Aviation W 90:256-8+
Je 2 '69
Inlets posed YF-12 design hurdle. C. M. Platt-
ner. il Aviation W 91:65+ Ag 11 '69
Navy pushing Ramjet propulsion studies. M.
L. Yaffee. Aviation W 90:51-2+ Ja 27 '69
RB.199 picked for MRCA; GE leads in A-
300B race. E. H. Kolcum. Aviation W 91:
19-20 S 8 '69

Exhaust
Rolls studies atomizer design in jet smoke
control effort. il Aviation W 90:51 F 24 '69

Fuel
Methane studied as fuel for SST. M. L.
Yaffee. Aviation W 91:47+ O 13 '69

Materials
Composite engine effort pushed. W. S.
Hieronymus, jr. il Aviation W 91:51+ N 3
'69
Two new alloys developed for jet engines.
Aviation W 91:64 S 8 '69

Starting devices
Turbine-powered starter unit developed for
air force jets. il Aviation W 90:63 Ja 20
'69

Testing
Improved jet engine tests seen; phase trim
balance systems. il Aviation W 90:64-5 Mr
3 '69
JET belt. See Flying machines
JET belts. See Flying machines
JET propelled airplanes. See Airplanes, Jet
propelled
JET propelled motor boats. See Motor boats,
Jet propelled
JET propulsion
Amazing new lightweight turbine. J. Horton.
il Mech Illus 65:66-8+ F '69
Navy pushing Ramjet propulsion studies. M.
L. Yaffee. Aviation W 90:51-2+ Ja 27 '69
United aircraft studying ramjet engines. M.
L. Yaffee. il Aviation W 90:75+ Je 16 '69
JET propulsion laboratory
Space age turns a new chapter; JPL's track-
ing network. il Bsns W p98-9+ Ap 12 '69
JET transports. See Airplanes, Jet propelled
JETS
Subsurface phenomena and the splashing of
drops on shallow liquids. W. C. Macklin and
P. V. Hobbs. bibliog il Science 166:107-8 O
3 '69
JETS (football club) See Football clubs
JETTER, Al
Laminated sailboat tiller. Mech Illus 65:117
O '69
JEWELL, Pliny, 3d
As the landscape architect sees it. Horticul-
ture 48:26-7 Ja '70

JEWISH theology
Liberal beliefs. L. Jacobs. Commentary 48:89-91 N '69
JEWISH way of life
Emphasis on a way of life. R. S. Rosen. il Sat R 52:42+ D 6 '69
See also
Hebraism
JEWISH wives. See Jewish women
JEWISH women
Jewish wife; excerpts. G. G. Schwartz and B. Wyden. il Ladies Home J 86:90-1+ O '69
Jewish wife vs Jewish mother-in-law; excerpts from The Jewish wife. G. G. Schwartz and B. Wyden. il Ladies Home J 86:106-7+ N '69
JEWS
Rethinking Judaism. A. A. Cohen. New Repub 160:28+ Mr 15 '69
Why are Jews successful? Chr Today 13:31 Ap 25 '69
See also
Anti-Semitism
Catholic church—Relations—Jews
Israel
Samaritans
Zionism

Civilization
See also
Hebraism

Education
Problems in Jewish teacher training. E. B. Levine. il America 120:398-401 Ap 5 '69

History
If I forget thee, O Jerusalem. S. Siegel. Sat R 52:34 F 1 '69
See also
Bible—Old Testament
Moses
World war, 1939-1945—Jews

Intellectual life
Blacks, Jews & the intellectuals. N. Glazer. Commentary 47:33-9 Ap '69; Discussion. 48: 4+ Jl '69

Liturgy and ritual
Curious case of Kol Nidre. H. Kieval; discussion. Commentary 47:10+ F '69
See also
Passover

Political and social conditions
Is American Jewry in crisis? M. Himmelfarb. il Commentary 47:33-42 Mr '69; Discussion. 47:6+ Je '69
Jewish role in student activism. N. Glazer. il Fortune 79:112-13+ Ja '69
See also
Zionism

Prayer books and devotions
Prayer in Judaism, by B. Martin. Review
Commentary 48:62+ Ag '69. E. Isaac

Religion
See also
Judaism
JEWS and Catholics. See Catholic church—Relations—Jews
JEWS and Christians. See Christianity and other religions
JEWS and Negroes
Black and the Jew: a falling out of allies. il Time 93:55-9 Ja 31 '69
Black anti-Semitism. J. Leo. Commonweal 89: 618-20 F 14 '69; Discussion. 89:695+; 90:3+ Mr 7, 21 '69
Black revolution & the Jewish question. E. Raab; discussion. Commentary 47:6+ Ap '69
Blacks, Jews & the intellectuals. N. Glazer. Commentary 47:33-9 Ap '69; Discussion. 48: 4+ Jl '69
Disappearing world of a New York Jew; Harry Kirschner of South Bronx. C. Mangel. il Look 33:66+ F 4 '69
Harlem on everybody's mind; with editorial comment. R. Berenson. il Nat R 21:106-7, 125 F 11 '69
How free the air? increasing anti-Semitism among New York's militant black community. il Newsweek 73:25-6 F 10 '69
Inflating the threat of black anti-semitism. J. Featherstone. New Repub 160:14-15 Mr 8 '69
Is American Jewry in crisis? M. Himmelfarb. il Commentary 47:33-42 Mr '69; Discussion. 47:6+ Je '69
Myth of black anti-Semitism. J. B. Sheerin. Cath World 209:50-1 My '69; Reply. A Gilbert. 209:196 Ag '69
JEWS and the World war. See World war, 1939-1945—Jews

JEWS in Arab states
Jews in the Arab world. il Time 93:23 F 7 '69
JEWS in Austria
Memoirs of an anti-Semite. G. Von Rezzori. New Yorker 45:42-52+ Ap 26 '69
JEWS in Denmark
Someone denounced us; with report by R. Z. Chesnoff. il Newsweek 75:32-3 Ja 12 '70
JEWS in France
Orleans witch-hunt; anti-Semitic group starts rumor and slander campaign. il Newsweek 73:52 Je 30 '69
JEWS in Germany
Post mortem: the Jews in Germany today, by L. Katcher. Review
Commentary 47:75-6 F '69. A. Elon
Weimar Germany's left-wing intellectuals, by I. Deak. Review
Commentary 48:94-6+ O '69. M. Jay
JEWS in Iraq
Let us out. Newsweek 73:32 F 10 '69
JEWS in literature
From Cohn to Herzog. M. J. Hoffman. Yale R 58:342-58 Mr '69
Odyssey of Saul Bellow. A. Bezanker. Yale R 58:359-71 Mr '69
Portnoy's compliance. P. Collier. il Ramp Mag 7:28-31 My '69
Waxing wroth. K. Amis. Harper 238:104+ Ap '69
Xerox withdraws Mother Goose; with editorial comment. Library J 94:2031, 2034 My 15 '69
JEWS in Morocco
Exodus from one's native land. B. W. Carlson. New Repub 160:14-15 Je 28 '69
Jews and Arabs in Morocco. Trans-Action 6: 5 Ap '69
JEWS in Poland
Goodbye to Poland. G. Meretik. Commentary 48:55-62 S '69
Old vice. Nation 209:461 N 3 '69
Second exodus. il Time 93:40+ Mr 14 '69
Someone denounced us. il Newsweek 75:32-3 Ja 12 '70
JEWS in Russia
Next year in Jerusalem. L. Volkov. il Newsweek 74:52+ N 24 '69
Soviet Jewry today. M. Friedberg. Commentary 48:45-7 Ag '69
Unredeemed, by R. I. Rubin. Review
Sat R 52:29-30 Ag 2 '69. E. Goldhagen
JEWS in textbooks. See Textbooks
JEWS in the United States
Disappearing world of a New York Jew; Harry Kirschner of South Bronx. C. Mangel. il Look 33:66+ F 4 '69
Downtown Jews, by R. Sanders. Review
Nation 210:24-6 Ja 12 '70. M. T. Gilmore
Emphasis on a way of life. R. S. Rosen. il Sat R 52:42+ D 6 '69
Generation gap in Judaism. Chr Cent 86:108 Ja 22 '69
Hillel vs. the elders. il Newsweek 74:118-20 D 8 '69
Is American Jewry in crisis? M. Himmelfarb. il Commentary 47:33-42 Mr '69; Discussion. 47:6+ Je '69
Jewish community & the Jewish condition. R. Alter. Commentary 47:55-9 F '69
Jews: ancient culture in a new land. il Sr Schol 94:12-15 My 2 '69
Portnoy's compliance. P. Collier. il Ramp Mag 7:28-31 My '69
See also
Central conference of American rabbis

JIGS
Build this plywood cutoff jig. E. H. Gustafson. il Pop Mech 131:194-5 Mr '69
How to sharpen tiny drills. F. H. Tracy. il Pop Sci 195:174 N '69
Router rides a track. P. Ashley. il Pop Sci 194:156+ Je '69
JIGSAWS
Jigsaw for a dime. W. G. Waggoner. il Pop Mech 132:160 D '69
New twist in portable jigsaws. J. Hand. il Pop Sci 194:194-7+ F '69
Variable speed jig saws. il Consumer Bul 52: 52:4+ O '69
JIMÉNEZ, Juan Ramón
Full consciousness; Oceans; Lumber wagons; Dawns of moguer; Road; Dawn outside the city walls; poems, tr. by R. Bly. Nation 209:18 Jl 7 '69
about
Private gardens, cloisters, silent women. R. Bly. Nation 209:17 Jl 7 '69
JIMMY; musical comedy. See Musical comedies, revues, etc.—Criticisms, plots, etc.
JIMMY Shine; drama. See Schisgal, M.
JINGLE bells; drama. See Hark, M. and McQueen, N.

JIU-Jitsu
See also
Judo
JOB banks. See Computers—Employment applications
JOB corps. See United States—Job corps
JOB discrimination. See Discrimination in employment
JOB instruction training. See Employees—Training
JOB interviews. See Interviewing
JOB mobility. See Occupational mobility
JOB performance standards. See Performance standards
JOB satisfaction
Job enrichment pays off; findings of studies carried out in British companies. W. J. Paul, jr. and others. il Harvard Bsns R 47:61-78 Mr '69
Make your job pay more than mere money. il Changing T 23:31-3 Ap '69
Making a job more than a job; AT&T's job enrichment program. il Bsns W p88-9 Ap 19 '69
Should you quit your job? R. Bugg. il Todays Health 47:26-9+ My '69
Some investment-like aspects of employment and pay. R. A. Lester. Mo Labor R 92:62-5 N '69
JOB tenure. See Seniority, Employee
JOB training. See Employees—Training
JOB transfers
Aerospace layoffs hardly hurt. il Bsns W p92 Jl 19 '69
Skill transfers: can defense workers adapt to civilian occupations? J. R. Cambern and D. A. Newton. il Mo Labor R 92:21-5 Je '69
JOBS. See Employment; Occupations
JOCK New York (periodical)
Sporting life. il Newsweek 74:78 O 20 '69
JOCKEYS
Four hot chestnuts in a derby; Majestic Prince. W. Tower. il Sports Illus 30:28-30+ My 5 '69
See also
Francis, D.
Horse racing
Shoemaker, W.
Women as jockeys
JODO Shin Buddhism. See Buddha and Buddhism
JOEL, Lydia
(ed) See Fonteyn, M. Tested and found not wanting
(ed) See Smok, P. Art must say something
JOEL, Yale
Black model breakthrough; photographs. Life 67:34-41 O 17 '69
JOEL of the far hills; story. See Garthwaite, M.
JOENS, Arnold C.
Assessment-district paving program. Am City 84:104-5 O '69
JOFFREY ballet. See City center Joffrey ballet
JOGGER-walkers. See Exercising equipment
JOGGING
Jog-in for dear life. T. Maule. il Sports Illus 31:26-9 Jl 28 '69
Warning to joggers from a leading physician; interview. H. J. Johnson. il U S News 67: 74-5 Ag 11 '69
JOHANNESBURG
Jo'burg builds on more than gold. il Bsns W p88-90+ F 15 '69
JOHANNSEN, Walter J.
Attitudes toward mental patients. bibliog Ment Hy 53:218-28 Ap '69
JOHANSEN, Gunnar
Diary of a miracle. il por Time 93:48 Ja 24 '69
JOHANSEN, John M.
Architecture through improvisation? S. Moholy-Nagy. il Arch Forum 131:40-7 S '69
JOHN XXIII, pope
Pope John and the sculptor; excerpts from An artist and the pope. C. B. Pepper. por Read Digest 94:200-4+ My '69
JOHN, Donald A.
Getting started in electronic organ servicing. Radio-Electr 40:76-8 Ag '69
JOHN, E. Roy, and others
Neural readout from memory during generalization. bibliog Science 164:1534-6 Je 27 '69
JOHN, Gospel of. See Bible—New Testament—John

JOHN Birch society
Sex ed flare-ups would ban courses, materials; with editorial comment. Library J 94:4185, 4187-8 N 15 '69
Sex in school: Watkins Glen, N.Y. and Anaheim, Calif. E. Dunbar. il Look 33:15-17 S 9 '69
When Birches last in the dooryard swung; Farmingdale public library; excerpts from address, June 25, 1969; with editorial comment. O. B. Dow. ALA Bul 63:1237-9 O '69
JOHN Brown raid, 1859. See Harpers Ferry, W.Va.—John Brown raid, 1859
JOHN Brown university, Siloam Springs, Ark.
John Brown's student body. Chr Today 14:43 N 21 '69
JOHN Cotton Dana publicity awards
John Cotton Dana publicity award winners. Wilson Lib Bul 44:370 D '69
JOHN F. Kennedy airport. See New York (city) —Airports
JOHN F. Kennedy center for the performing arts, Washington, D.C.
Kennedy center slowdown. il Newsweek 73: 109 Mr 10 '69
Whatever happened to the Kennedy cultural center? il U S News 67:17 S 22 '69
JOHN F. Kennedy library, Cambridge, Mass.
John F. Kennedy library. K. V. Hostick. Hobbies 74:108-9 Ag '69
JOHN F. Kennedy space center. See United States—John F. Kennedy space center
JOHN Hancock center, Chicago. See Chicago —Buildings
JOHN Muir historic site. See Martinez, Calif. —Historic houses, etc.
JOHN Pennekamp coral reef state park. See Florida—Parks and reserves
JOHN Ringling estate. See Sarasota, Fla.— Ringling center
JOHNELL Dillon, Sister. See Dillon, J.
JOHNIDES, Theodora. See Barisch, S. jt. auth.
JOHNNY get your gun; novel. See Ball, J.
JOHNNY question-mark; drama. See Boiko, C.
JOHNS, Jasper
Thoughts on Duchamp. Art in Am 57:31 Jl '69
JOHNS Hopkins medical book center. See College bookstores
JOHNS-MANVILLE
Company of the old school. il Forbes 103:18-19 F 1 '69
JOHNSON, Arnold R.
Instant freestanding shelves. Pop Mech 132: 164-5 Jl '69
JOHNSON, Arthur W.
Weather satellites: II; with biographical sketch. Sci Am 220:18, 52-68 Ja '69
JOHNSON, B. Lamar
Change and the junior college; excerpt from Islands of innovation expanding. bibliog f Sch & Soc 97:248-54 Ap '69
JOHNSON, Barbara Coe
Services an integrated hospital library can and cannot provide. ALA Bul 63:1554-9 D '69
JOHNSON, Bert W.
Evaluate the present and chart the future. por Am City 84:75-7 Ag '69
JOHNSON, Bruce
Paying the ultimate price. Chr Cent 86:1302 O 15 '69
JOHNSON, Carl T.
Big track. Outdoor Life 144:68-9+ Jl '69
JOHNSON, Carol
New world; poem. Commonweal 90:17 Mr 21 '69
JOHNSON, Carroll F.
Student unrest and racial confrontation at White Plains high school. Negro Hist Bul 32:20 O '69
JOHNSON, Claudia Alta (Taylor)
My life-after the White House; interview, ed. by J. Egan. por Good H 168:68-9+ F '69
about
Ruffles and flourishes; excerpts. E. Carpenter. McCalls 97:76-7+ D '69; 20+ Ja '70
JOHNSON, David B. and Stern, J. L.
Why and how workers shift from blue-collar to white-collar jobs. bibliog f Mo Labor R 92:7-13 O '69
JOHNSON, David Lee
Ruckus in Irasburg. H. Moffett. il por Life 66:62-4+ Ap 4 '69
JOHNSON, Donald R. and Powell, F. X.
Microwave spectrum and structure of sulfur difluoride. bibliog Science 164:950-1 My 23 '69
JOHNSON, Edwina
Black history: the early childhood vacuum. bibliog por Library J 94:2057-8 My 15 '69

JOHNSON, Elaine W.
Eyewitness. Sr Schol 94:Schol Teach 24-5 Ja 17 '69
JOHNSON, Eiden
Archeological evidence for utilization of wild rice. bibliog Science 163:276-7 Ja 17 '69
JOHNSON, Electa. See Johnson, I. jt. auth.
JOHNSON, Eric
Supply all the water your customers desire; interview, ed. by R. R. Fleming. pors Am City 84:101-3+ My '69
JOHNSON, Florence
Green thumb, junior style. Org Gard & Farm 16:61 Je '69
JOHNSON, Frances Kennon
Four-year hang-up. por Library J 94:1721-3 Ap 15 '69
JOHNSON, Franklyn A.
Leadership in the nuclear age; address, December 18, 1968. Vital Speeches 35:218-21 Ja 15 '69
JOHNSON, Fridolf
Typophiles and a keepsake. Am Artist 33: 66-9+ My '69
William Morris. bibliog Am Artist 32:43-9 D '68
JOHNSON, Gail
Guess-for-fun alphabet; drama. Plays 28:67-70+ Ap '69
JOHNSON, Gerald W.
Hopes and fears. New Repub 160:14 F 1 '69
Jacqueline's folks. New Repub 160:27-8 Ap 12 '69
Old Agnew we knew. New Repub 161:13-14 N 29 '69
Program for the mini-intellectual. Am Scholar 39:50-8 Wint '69
JOHNSON, Greg
Keeping up with Grape Juice. B. Gilbert. por Sports Illus 31:58-9 O 20 '69
JOHNSON, H. C.
Gravel+refuse=recreation. Parks & Rec 4:46-8+ S '69
JOHNSON, Harry J.
Warning to joggers from a leading physician; interview. por U S News 67:74-5 Ag 11 '69
JOHNSON, Herman F.
Tie bookshelf speaker. Pop Electr 31:69-71+ Jl '69
JOHNSON, Hiram
Diary of Hiram Johnson; excerpts, ed. by L. W. Levine. Am Heritage 20:64-76 Ag '69
JOHNSON, Horace
Ex-model Caroline Coon runs an underground with office hours. Life 67:55-6+ Ag 22 '69
JOHNSON, Howard Wesley
Man who cooled M.I.T. il por Time 94:68+ N 21 '69
JOHNSON, Hugh
Ardent apple. House & Gard 135:98+ Ja '69
Chianti. Holiday 46:62-3+ S '69
JOHNSON, Irving, and Johnson, Electa
Yankee cruises Turkey's history-haunted coast. Nat Geog 136:798-845 D '69
JOHNSON, Jack
Jack Johnson is alive and well on Broadway. J. E. Jones. il pors Ebony 24:54-6+ Je '69
JOHNSON, James A. and Radebaugh, B. F.
Excellent teachers: what makes them outstanding? Clear House 44:152-6 N '69
JOHNSON, James C.
How do you define urban success? interview; ed. by B. Foster. Am City 84:69-71 D '69
JOHNSON, James Weldon
Trumpets of the Lord. T. Lewis. America 120:599 My 17 '69
JOHNSON, Josephine Winslow
Earthly paradise. McCalls 97:40-1+ Ja '70
On March: time to take stock; excerpt from The inland islands. Nation 208:246-9 F 24 '69

about

Peripatetic reviewer. E. Weeks. Atlan 223: 104-5 My '69
JOHNSON, Kenneth L. See Zimering, S. jt. auth.
JOHNSON, L. C. and O'Shea J. P.
Anabolic steroid: effects on strength development. bibliog Science 164:957-9 My 23 '69
JOHNSON, L. F. See Conway, T. F. jt. auth.
JOHNSON, Lady Bird. See Johnson, C. A. T.
JOHNSON, LeRoy, jr
Obsidian hydration rate for the Klamath basin of California and Oregon. bibliog Science 165:1354-6 S 26 '69
JOHNSON, Les
Day my son grew a foot. Good H 168:34+ Je '69
JOHNSON, Louis
Louis Johnson dance theatre; Negro ensemble theatre. J. Anderson. Dance Mag 43:78-9 Ap '69

JOHNSON, Lucy (Taylor)
My most unforgettable character. R. J. Bunche. il Read Digest 95:45-9 S '69
JOHNSON, Lynda Bird. See Robb, L. B. J.
JOHNSON, Lyndon Baines
America at the crossroads; excerpts from Britannica book of the year 1969. por Read Digest 94:54-8 Mr '69
Amir of Kuwait visits Washington; exchange of greetings and toasts, with joint communique, December 11, 1968. Dept State Bul 59:691-5 D 30 '68
Annual report of the Peace corps transmittal to Congress; letter, January 7, 1969. Dept State Bul 60:118 F 3 '69
Annual report on foreign assistance program transmitted to Congress; letter, January 15, 1969. Dept State Bul 60:117 F 3 '69
Budget message of the President; excerpts. Dept State Bul 60:95-6 F 3 '69
Crew of U.S.S. Pueblo released at Panmunjom; U.S. position on facts unchanged; statement, December 22, 1968. Dept State Bul 60:1 Ja 6 '69
Death of Trygve Lie; statement, December 30, 1968. Dept State Bul 60:78 Ja 27 '69
Economic report of the President. Dept State Bul 60:101-3 F 3 '69
Flight of Apollo 8: international cooperation in space; remarks, January 9, 1969. Dept State Bul 60:76-7 Ja 27 '69
In quest of peace; excerpts from Britannica book of the year 1969. por Read Digest 94: 219-24+ F '69
Lighting of the Nation's Christmas tree; remarks, December 16, 1968. Dept State Bul 60:3 Ja 6 '69
LBJ speaks to Richard Nixon about what it is to be Mr President. por Look 33:23-5 F 4 '69
National conference on continuing action for human rights; remarks, December 4, 1968. Dept State Bul 59:685-6 D 30 '68
President Johnson joins appeal for holiday truce in Nigeria; statement, December 21, 1968. Dept State Bul 60:3 Ja 6 '69
President Johnson welcomes new talks on Viet-Nam; statement, January 16, 1969. Dept State Bul 60:91 F 3 '69
Presidents Johnson and de Gaulle exchange New Year's greetings. Dept State Bul 60:77 Ja 27 '69
Prime Minister Hoveyda of Iran visits Washington; exchange of greetings and toasts, December 5, 1968. Dept State Bul 59:659, 660 D 23 '68
State of the Union; address, January 14, 1969. Vital Speeches 35:228-31 F 1 '69; Excerpts. Dept State Bul 60:89-91 F 3 '69; Cur Hist 56:168+ Mr '69
United States and Latin America; a special relationship; statement, January 9, 1969. Dept State Bul 60:73-4 Ja 27 '69
United States and Mexico reaffirm bonds of friendship; exchange of toasts, December 13, 1968. Dept State Bul 60:21-2, 23-4 Ja 13 '69
U.S.-Japan medical science program report transmitted to Congress; letter, January 16, 1969. Dept State Bul 60:118 F 3 '69
Useful job for every American; excerpts from Britannica book of the year 1969. Read Digest 94:82-5 Ap '69
Why so much youth unrest today: LBJ's view; excerpts from interview. U S News 66:19 F 24 '69

about

As President Johnson bows out. America 120: 88 Ja 25 '69
Back at the ranch; summary of televised interview. por Newsweek 75:13-15 Ja 5 '70
Back home again in Johnson City. B. Porterfield. il por N Y Times Mag p22-3+ Mr 2 '69
Bitter aftertaste. por Newsweek 73:32 F 3 '69
Building Lyndon Johnson. D. Welsh. il Ramp Mag 7:104-14 Ja 25 '69
Cooling off with LBJ. M. Frady. Harper 238: 65-72 Je '69
Farewell to Mr Johnson. Chr Today 13:26 Ja 31 '69
Fight for the President's mind, and the men who won it; excerpt from The limits of intervention. T. Hoopes. il Atlan 224:97-104+ O '69
Great doer returns to Texas. Chr Cent 86: 140 Ja 29 '69
Hornig years: did LBJ neglect his science adviser? P. M. Boffey. Science 163:453-4+ Ja 31 '69
Inside story: LBJ's switch on Vietnam. il por Newsweek 73:32-3 Mr 10 '69
Kennedy-Johnson years. T. T. Helde. Cur Hist 57:31-5+ Jl '69

JOHNSON, Lyndon Baines—about—*Continued*
Last message, and adieu. il por Time 93:11-12 Ja 24 '69
Legacy from LBJ; controversy over national parks. il U S News 66:89 F 24 '69.
Legacy that LBJ is leaving to America. il por U S News 66:30-1 Ja 27 '69
LBJ and his critics. K. Crawford. Newsweek 73:35 Ja 27 '69
LBJ confidential. Newsweek 73:60 F 3 '69
L.B.J: hurting good. il por Time 93:18 Ja 31 '69
LBJ in retirement; still a busy man. il pors U S News 67:44-7 S 29 '69
L.B.J: telephone terror; Marriage of memos. il por Time 95:9 Ja 5 '70
LBJ's land grab. il por Newsweek 74:39 N 10 '69
L.B.J.'s musings about the media. Time 93:68 F 14 '69
Matter of memoirs; opposition to Vietnam policy. Commonweal 89:576 F 7 '69
Meanwhile, back at the L.B.J. ranch. D. Neff. il Time 94:15 S 5 '69
Meanwhile, back at the ranch. il por U S News 66:15 F 3 '69
My brother Lyndon; excerpts. ed. by E. H. Lopez. S. H. Johnson. il Look 33:49-52+ D 2; 43-6+ D 16 '69
Once they were political foes, but—. il por U S News 67:16 S 8 '69
One L.B.J. likes and the one he doesn't like. H. Sidey. pors Life 66:4 F 14 '69
Politics of reconciliation. il por Time 94:14+ S 5 '69
Requiem for LBJ. Commonweal 89:546 Ja 31 '69
Rose garden rubbish and other glorious compositions; presidential speech writer. P. Benchley. il Life 66:60B-60D+ My 23 '69
Ruffles and flourishes; excerpts. E. Carpenter. McCalls 97:76-7+ D '69; 20+ Ja '70
So long Lyndon. Nat R 21:59-60 Ja 28 '69
Summing up the LBJ years. il pors Sr Schol 93:3-9 Ja 10 '69
Tragedy of Lyndon Johnson. by E. F. Goldman. Review
Esquire 71:74+ Je '69. M. Muggeridge
Welcome to the club; 61st birthday celebrations. il por Newsweek 74:27 S 8 '69
When LBJ goes to his office now... il por U S News 66:12 F 10 '69
Wonders and woes of the LBJ economy. il pors Sr Schol 93:10-11 Ja 10 '69
Wrong man from the wrong place at the wrong time. E. F. Goldman; discussion. N Y Times Mag p 16+ Ja 26 '69

Anecdotes, facetiae, satire, etc.
My three weeks at the White House. P. E. Gray. New Yorker 45:32-3 My 17 '69

Messages
See also
Johnson, L. B.—State of the Union message, January 14, 1969

Public relations
Portrait of two presidents: Nixon and Johnson. B. Furlow. il por U S News 67:52-4 Jl 28 '69
Tragedy of Lyndon Johnson. by E. F. Goldman. Review
America 120:338 Mr 22 '69. F. K. Kelly
Commonweal 90:49-50 Mr 28 '69. R. G. Sherrill
Look 33:12 Mr 4 '69. P. S. Prescott
Nation 208:407- Mr 31 '69. E. Gruening
Sat R 52:37-9+ F 15 '69. Q. Howe
Time 93:104+ Mr 14 '69

State of the Union message, January 14, 1969
Auld lang syne. Nation 208:98 Ja 27 '69
Johnson tallies five-year score. il por Bsns W p 17 Ja 18 '69
Last message and adieu; State of the Union. il por Time 93:11-12 Ja 24 '69
Lyndon Johnson's last hurrah. il por Newsweek 73:22 Ja 27 '69

JOHNSON, Lyndon Baines, Library (proposed)
See Texas. University—Austin campus—Libraries

JOHNSON, Marjorie
We put it all on our living room wall. Pop Mech 130:150-3 D '68

JOHNSON, Maud B.
My mother, the celebrity. Todays Health 47: 56-7+ O '69

JOHNSON, Merel
Traveler's choice. Travel 132:18 S '69

JOHNSON, Miriam
Pride of five women. R. Hochstein. il por Good H 168:85-6 Je '69

JOHNSON, Neil
Low-cost a.c. ammeter. il Pop Electr 30: 50-2 My '69
Mini trouble light. Pop Electr 31:86 Ag '69
No more fuses. Pop Electr 30:59-60 Je '69

JOHNSON, Nicholas
Easy chair. Harper 238:14+ F '69
We need the Pastore bill; no, we don't. New Repub 161:16-19 D 6 '69

about
Nicholas Johnson vs. Broadcasting. R. L. Shayon. Sat R 52:82+ Ap 12 '69
Rippling the waves. Commonweal 90:60-1 Ap 4 '69
Tale of two speeches. P. Steinfels. Commonweal 91:272 N 28 '69
Trying to swat the FCC's gadfly. por Bsns W p21 Ag 30 '69

JOHNSON, Owen McMahon
Stover at the barricades. M. J. Halberstam. Am Scholar 38:470+ Sum '69

JOHNSON, Philip Cortelyou
New work of Philip Johnson. Arch Rec 146: 87-96 D '69

JOHNSON, Pyke, Jr
Book people: a West coast paperback wholesaler. Pub W 195:44-6 Je 23 '69

JOHNSON, Quintin, and others
Automatic determination of crystal structure. bibliog Science 164:1163-4 Je 6 '69

JOHNSON, Richard F.
Hypnosis: what it can and can't do for you. Sci Digest 66:7-13 S '69

JOHNSON, Robert
Slab pots from block forms. Ceram Mo 17: 20-1 F '69

JOHNSON, Rodney W.
Space, science, and scripture; interview. Chr Today 13:3-6 Jl 18 '69

JOHNSON, Roger N. and others
Intracranial self-stimulation and the rapid decline of frustrative nonreward. bibliog Science 164:971-2 My 23 '69

JOHNSON, Ronald
Good and the useful. M. Randall. Poetry 115:51-3 O '69

JOHNSON, Roswell D.
Why so many teenagers fall for marijuana. Parents Mag 44:58-61+ Mr '69

JOHNSON, Sam Houston
My brother Lyndon; excerpts. ed. by E. H. Lopez. Look 33:49-52+ D 2; 43-6+ D 16 '69

JOHNSON, Sandy
Sight, sound, and the research paper. Engl J 58:1061-3+ O '69

JOHNSON, U. Alexis
Department reviews history of international efforts governing activities on the seabed; statement. July 30, 1969. Dept State Bul 61: 191-4 S 1 '69
Pacific basin potential; address, May 16, 1969. Dept State Bul 60:488-92 Je 9 '69
United States-Japanese relations today; address, October 22, 1969. Dept State Bul 61: 401-3 N 10 '69

JOHNSON, Una E.
Intaglio prints of Bernard Childs. Art in Am 57:118-21 N '69

JOHNSON, Wallace Edward
Seeing problems as opportunities; interview. pors Nations Bsns 57:62-6+ Mr '69

JOHNSON, Wayne
Opera lives! Hi Fi 19:MA24-5 Ag '69

JOHNSON, William
Flying. Sports Illus 31:56-7 O 6 '69
Skiing. Sports Illus 32:60+ Ja 12 '70
Television and sport. Sports Illus 32:22-9 Ja 5; 44-52 Ja 12 '70 (to be cont)
TV made it all a new game. Sports Illus 31:86-90+ D 22 '69

JOHNSON, William (critic)
Face the music. Film Q 22:3-19 Sum '69
Scuba sculpture. Art N 68:52-3+ N '69

JOHNSON and Johnson (firm)
Calculated generosity. il Forbes 104:22-3 Ag 1 '69

JOHNSSON, Robert G.
Burning of the sea. Parks & Rec 4:31-3 Je '69

JOHNSTON, David R. See Curtis, B. C. jt. auth.

JOHNSTON, Denis F. and Wetzel, J. R.
Effect of the census undercount on labor force estimates. bibliog F Mo Labor R 92: 3-13 Mr '69

JOHNSTON, Edward E.
Trust Territory of the Pacific Islands; statements. June 6 and 13, 1969. Dept State Bul 61:223-7, 231-2 S 8 '69

JOHNSTON, Frances Benjamin
Gallery; photographs. Life 67:4-7 D 19 '69

JOHNSTON, George S.
Advice for investors in 1970; interview. por U S News 68:64-6 Ja 5 '70

JOHNSTON, Jill
  Jill Johnston, convoluted. J. Gruen. Vogue 154:38 Ag 15 '69
JOHNSTON, Madeline Steele
  Discipline or indulgence? Parents Mag 44:37-9+ Jl '69
JOHNSTON, Velda
  Phantom cottage; excerpts from novel. Redbook 134:169-91 D '69
JOHNSTONE, William C.
  Commitments in Asia: 1969. Cur Hist 57:93-9+ Ag '69
  Political-strategic significance of Vietnam. Cur Hist 56:65-70 F '69
JOINER, C. M.
  Bad days for wild ones. il por Time 94:76 Jl 11 '69
JOINT commission on mental health of children
  Action for the mental health of children: the Joint commission report and NAMH response. Ment Hy 53:497-9 O '69
JOINT committee on atomic energy. See United States—Congress—Joint committee on atomic energy
JOINT committee on society, development and peace
  SODEPAX and politics. Chr Cent 86:1034 Ag 6 '69
JOINT committee on United States-Japan cultural and education cooperation
  Committee on U.S.-Japan cultural cooperation meets at Honolulu. Dept State Bul 61:93 Ag 4 '69
JOINT computer conferences. See Computer industry—Exhibitions
JOINT oceanographic institutions deep earth sampling program. See Underwater drilling
JOINT tenancy
  Joint ownership: advantages and disadvantages. il Good H 169:150 Ag '69
JOINT United States-Canadian committee on trade and economic affairs
  U.S.-Canadian economic committee holds twelfth meeting; text of communique, June 26, 1969. Dept State Bul 61:38-40 Jl 14 '69
JOINT United States-Japan committee on trade and economic affairs
  U.S.-Japan joint economic committee meets at Tokyo; statement with text of communique, July 31, 1969. W. P. Rogers. Dept State Bul 61:121-4 Ag 18 '69
JOINT university libraries, Nashville, Tenn.
  Graduate library wing for Joint university; University center, composing George Peabody college, Scarritt college and Vanderbilt university. il Library J 94:4401-2 D 1 '69
JOINTS
      Diseases
    See also
  Arthritis
JOINTS (carpentry)
  Eight handy woodworking joints. R. Brightman. il Mech Illus 65:81-3 Ap '69
JOINTS (engineering)
  How to check ball joints. M. Schultz. il Pop Mech 132:132-5 D '69
JOKES. See Humor
JOKES, Practical. See Practical jokes
JOLLY, Iva D.
  Monardas. Horticulture 46:51 Ag '68
JONAS, Gerald
  Consumer report; poem. Sat R 52:7 Jl 26 '69
JONAS, Stephen
  Good and the useful. M. Randall. Poetry 115:47-9 O '69
JONATHAN, Will
  Three worlds of the camel. Sat R 52:70-1 Ap 5 '69
JONATHAN, Minn.
  New town: a proving ground for bold new ideas. il Bet Hom & Gard 47:70-3 S '69
JONES, Alan Pryce-. See Pryce-Jones, A.
JONES, Antony Charles Robert Armstrong-, 1st earl of Snowdon. See Snowdon, A. C. R. A.-J.
JONES, Booker T. Jr
  Booker T. and the M.G.'s P. Garland. il pors Ebony 24:92-4+ Ap '69
JONES, Charles O.
  Remember the Hatch act? Nation 209:411-13 O 20 '69
JONES, Chase B. See Bernstein, E. O. jt. auth.
JONES, Cleon
  Keeping up with Jones. il por Time 93:57 Je 13 '69
JONES. Cranston
  (ed) See Tange. K. Kenzo Tange
JONES, D. V.
  Power IC's for hi-fi. Radio-Electr 40:52-4 Jl '69
JONES, David Pryce-. See Pryce-Jones, D.
JONES, Dee Walker
  Opera's angels. Opera N 34:22-4 S 6 '69

JONES, E. J. W. and Ewing, J. I.
  Age of the Bay of Biscay: evidence from seismic profiles and bottom samples. bibliog Science 166:102-5 O 3 '69
JONES, Elizabeth Orton
  In remembrance: Bertha Mahony Miller. il Horn Bk 45:497-515 O '69
JONES, Gordon E.
  Planting fields arboretum. Horticulture 47:42-5+ Ap '69
JONES, Gwyneth
      Records
  Gwyneth Jones. Opera N 34:30 D 6 '69
JONES, H. McCoy
  Early influences in Turkish rugs. Antiques 95:847-51 Je '69
JONES, Helen
  What is a religious bookstore? Pub W 196:75-7 S 22 '69
JONES, Helen L.
  Part played by Boston publishers of 1860-1900 in the field of children's books. bibliog Horn Bk 45:20-8, 153-9, 329-36 F-Je '69
JONES, J. R.
  Few soft words for the Ku Klux klan. P. Young. il por Esquire 72:104-5+ Jl '69
JONES, James
  Cognoscenti abroad. James Jones's Paris. A. Goodfriend. il Sat R 52:36-8 F 1 '69
JONES, James Earl
  Jack Johnson is alive and well on Broadway. pors Ebony 24:54-6+ Je '69
  We talk to. .; interview, ed. by A. Ginsberg. por Mlle 69:344-5 Ag '69
  Whole issue of color becomes a fourth wall. pors Life 67:70-1 N 7 '69
JONES, James H.
  Surfacing of Pacific equatorial undercurrent: direct observation. bibliog Science 163:1449-50 Mr 28 '69
JONES, Jenkin Lloyd
  Dime dollar; address. August 19. 1969. Vital Speeches 35:728-30 S 15 '69
  Strangling picket line; address, October 30, 1969. Vital Speeches 36:136-9 D 15 '69
  Thinking the unthinkable; interview pors Nations Bsns 57:50-7 My '69
      about
  U.S. troubles: a business view. por U S News 66:18 My 5 '69
JONES, Jimmy
  Getting by nicely without O.J. P. Putnam. il por Sports Illus 31:32-4+ S 29 '69
  USC Trojans shoot for Rose bowl with black quarterback. il por Ebony 25:44-6+ D '69
JONES, John Kendrick-. See Kendrick-Jones, J.
JONES, John Paul
  John Paul Jones: father of the navy. por Sr Schol 95:2 O 6 '69
JONES, LeRoi
  Ameer (LeRoi Jones) Baraka. D. Llorens. il pors Ebony 24:75-8 +Ag '69
  Day LeRoi Jones spoke on Penn campus, what were the blacks doing in the balcony? G. Weales. il por N Y Times Mag p38-40+ My 4 '69
  Slave ship. Criticism
    New Yorker 45:168 D 6 '69
    Newsweek 74:86 D 1 '69
JONES, Margaret P.
  Opinions on collective bargaining. ALA Bul 63:803-9 Je '69
JONES, Margo
  Spirit power. H. Hewes. Sat R 52:41 F 8 '69
JONES, Marshall B. See Vierck, C. J. jr. jt. auth.
JONES, Mary Gardiner
  Business can stand guard for the consumer. pors Nations Bsns 57:52-4 N '69
JONES, Mary Lange
  New and gentle light; story. Good H 169:66-7+ Jl '69
JONES, Mike
  Rap 'n 'pinion. por Motor T 21:18 D '69
JONES, Phil B.
  What's new. See issues of Successful farming
JONES, Pirkle
  Black Panthers photographic essay. M. Mann. il Pop Phot 64:82-3+ My '69
JONES, Richard D. and Rezek, J. W.
  Regional water supply. Am City 84:108+ Mr; 73-5 Ap '69
JONES, Robert
  Advent; poem. Chr Cent 86:1637 D 24 '69
  Answer; poem. Chr Cent 86:502 Ap 16 '69
JONES, Robert A.
  Black vs. white in the station house. Nation 209:368-70 O 13 '69
  Fratricide in the Sierra club. Nation 208:567-70 My 5 '69
  Panthers' white conference. Nation 209:102-3 Ag 11 '69

JONES, Robert F.
　All-America all the way. Sports Illus 30:82-6+ My 26 '69
　Hail to king Jackie! Sports Illus 31:22-7 S 22 '69
　Motor sports. Sports Illus 31:78-81 O 13 '69
　Shocker at Daytona. Sports Illus 30:16-19 F 10 '69
　Snarling tractors and no tallyho. Sports Illus 30:28-30+ F 17 '69
JONES, Robert T.
　Janacek opera: another try for TV. Hi Fi 19:MA12-13 O '69
JONES, Robert W.
　Contemporary music project: it pays off. por Hi Fi 19:MA10-11+ N '69
JONES, Sally
　Macrame. Sch Arts 69:36-8 Ja '70
JONES, Stacy V.
　Inventions. See issues of Science digest
JONES, Tom
　Ladies' man. por Time 94:54-5 Jl 11 '69
　Tom Jones. B. Baer. il pors Look 33:96-100 N 4 '69
JONES, V. C.
　(ed) See Langdon, J. D. Before the colors fade: last of the Rough Riders
JONES and Laughlin steel corporation
　Ling finds a new twist; creates new concern to act as holding company. Bsns W p34+ F 8 '69
　Some candid answers from James J. Ling: interview, ed. by J. McDonald. il Fortune 80:92-5+ Ag 1; 136-8+ S '69
JONG, Erica Mann
　Slight cough; poem. Mlle 70:146 N '69
JONG, Petrus J. S. de
　President Nixon meets with prime minister and foreign minister of the Netherlands; exchange of greetings, and remarks, May 27, 28, 1969. Dept State Bul 60:561-3 Je 30 '69
JOPLIN, Janis
　Janis. H. Saal. pors Newsweek 73:84 F 24 '69
　Janis Joplin philosophy, every moment she is what she feels. M. Lydon. il pors N Y Times Mag p36-7+ F 23 '69
　Rebirth of the blues. il por Newsweek 73:82-5 My 26 '69
　Rock, etc. E. Willis. New Yorker 45:173 Mr 15 '69
JORDAN, Clarence
　Obituary
　　Chr Cent 86:1442 N 12 '69
JORDAN, Eileen Herbert
　Weekends; story. Redbook 132:63 Ja '69
JORDAN, Winthrop Donaldson
　Book industry presents the 20th National book awards; with excerpts from acceptance address. il por Pub W 195:27-9 Mr 24 '69
JORDAN
　　See also
　Guerrillas—Jordan
　Holy Land
　Israel—Foreign relations—Jordan
　Jerusalem
　Water supply—Jordan

　　　　Commerce
　Invisible occupation. M. Friedman. Newsweek 73:94 My 5 '69

　　　Foreign relations
　Jordan: the commando state. N. F. Howard. bibliog f Cur Hist 58:16-20+ Ja '70
　King Hussein I of Jordan visits Washington; exchange of greetings; with text of joint statement, April 8 and 10, 1969. King Hussein; R. M. Nixon. Dept State Bul 60:364-5 Ap 28 '69

　　　Israeli occupation, 1967-
　Invisible occupation. M. Friedman. Newsweek 73:94 My 5 '69
　Real Mideast problem; life in a refugee camp and Israeli occupation in Jordan. J. Law and A. Kucherov. il U S News 66:36-8 F 10 '69

　　　Politics and government
　Jordan: the commando state. N. F. Howard. bibliog f Cur Hist 58:16-20+ Ja '70
　Troubled ruler with many lives; what he seeks in the U.S. il U S News 66:22 Ap 14 '69
　Uneasy heads. Newsweek 74:61+ O 20 '69
JORDEN, Bill
　Virgin Islands. il Travel & Camera 32:102-5+ F '69
JORGENSEN, Sally E. and others
　Nucleoside triphosphate termini from RNA synthesized in vivo by escherichia coli. bibliog Science 164:1067-70 My 30 '69
JORGENSON, Lloyd P. See Meredith, M. M. jt. auth.

JOSEPH, Sister Francis. See Francis Joseph, Sister
JOSEPH, James
　Anchor you shoot from a gun. Mech Illus 65:123 N '69
　How soon a steam engine for your boat? Motor B 124:34-5+ Jl '69
JOSEPH, Lou
　Is a thumb for sucking? Todays Health 47:32-5 D '69
JOSEPH, Raymond Alcide
　Haiti: ripe for the marines? Nation 208:392-7 Mr 31 '69
JOSEPH, Richard
　(ed) Art of travel photography. Travel & Camera 32:78+ N '69
　Intelligent angler's guide to the Pacific-Orient. Esquire 72:96-101 Ag '69
　Japan's most closely watched train. Travel & Camera 32:66-7+ O '69
　Next Mediterranean Sea. Esquire 71:152-3+ Je '69
　Travel notes. See issues of Esquire
JOSEPH, Stephen M.
　Etc. Commonweal 91:101-2 O 24 '69
JOSEPH E. Seagram and sons. See Seagram, Joseph, E. and sons
JOSEPHS, Lois S.
　Disadvantaged: do not deprive them of the American literary heritage. bibliog f Clear House 44:105-9 O '69
JOSEPHSON, A.
　New York: poems because of Abra. Mlle 69:124 S '69
JOSEPHSON, Bragi S. See Fraser. S. E. jt. auth.
JOSEPHY, Alvin M. Jr
　Cornplanter, can you swim? Am Heritage 20:4-9+ D '68
JOSEY, E. J.
　Future of the black college library. por Library J 94:3019-22 S 15 '69
　Overdue. por Wilson Lib Bul 44:97-8+ S '69
JOSEY, William E. and Meilach, D. Z.
　How pregnancy affects your skin. Redbook 133:31+ Je '69
JOSTEN'S, incorporated
　Big wheel on campus. R. Levy. il Duns R 92:59-60 D '68
JOURNAL company
　Monopoly in Milwaukee? Newsweek 73:95-6 My 19 '69
JOURNALISM
　Best of times, the worst of times, plus the New York times. C. Barnes. Holiday 46:8+ Jl '69
　Freelance job idea: stringing for magazines. A. Napier. il Writers Digest 49:62-5+ F '69
　How to deal with four-letter words. il Time 93:63 Mr 7 '69
　What's wrong with news? It isn't new enough. M. Ways. il Fortune 80:110-13+ O '69
　When Jimmy told it like it was. W. Mc Whirter. Life 66:8 Ap 18 '69
　　See also
　Crime and the press
　Editors and editing
　Freedom of the press
　Interviewing
　Libel and slander
　News
　Newspaper court reporting
　Reporters and reporting
　Television broadcasting—News

　　Anecdotes, facetiae, satire, etc.
　View of the moon from the Sun: 1835. J. L. Morrison. il Am Heritage 20:80-2 Ap '69

　　　Study and teaching
　Journalism is my hang-up. B. J. Leonard. Engl J 58:1228-9+ N '69
　　See also
　Columbia university—Graduate school of journalism

　　　　Czechoslovakia
　What it's like to be a Czech newspaperman. J. Hohenberg. il Sat R 52:78-80 N 8 '69

　　　Europe, Western
　Who owns journalism? movement to offer employees ownership, profits and a voice in management. il Time 95:60-1 Ja 19 '70

　　　Greece, Modern
　　See also
　Newspapers—Greece, Modern

　　　　Japan
　　See also
　Airplanes in newspaper service

　　　　Russia
　Reed Whittemore on the news. R. Whittemore. New Repub 161:22-3 N 15 '69

JOURNALISM—*Continued*

United States

Image-makers' image. J. Hohenberg. il Sat R 52:53-4 F 8 '69

Reed Whittemore on the news. R. Whittemore. New Repub 161:22-3 N 15 '69

What's wrong with objectivity? H. Brucker. Sat R 52:77-9 O 11 '69

See also

Newspapers—United States

Periodicals—United States

JOURNALISM as a profession

Carve your niche with one of these newspaper jobs. Har Yrs 9:21 F '69

Journalism graduate and public relations. R. L. Tobin. Sat R 52:47-8 Jl 12 '69

JOURNALISTIC ethics

Checkbook journalism; L. Schiller and the S. Atkins story of the Tate murder. il Newsweek 74:45-6 D 29 '69

Voluntary press codes. G. Cranberg. Sat R 52:71-2 My 10 '69

See also

Crime and the press

JOURNALISTIC photography. See Photography, Journalistic

JOURNALISTS

Column right, column left. il Newsweek 73:58 Mr 3 '69

From Oscars to boredom, or is there any noticeable difference? C. Barnes. Holiday 45:8+ My '69

Image-makers' image. J. Hohenberg. il Sat R 52:53-4 F 8 '69

It's the third, not the fourth estate; farewell statement. J. K. Jessup. Life 66:3 Ap 4 '69

Leonard in the Lyons den. A. Bester. il pors Holiday 45:44-7+ Mr '69

What it's like to be a Czech newspaperman. J. Hohenberg. il Sat R 52:78-80 N 8 '69

JOURNALS. See Periodicals

JOURNALS, Personal. See Diaries

JOVANOVICH, Stefan

From fogged barracks; poem. Am Scholar 38:406 Sum '69

Poets have resigned; poem. Am Scholar 39:88 Wint '69

JOVANOVICH, William

American textbook; an unscientific phenomenon, quality without control. Am Scholar 38:227-39 Spr '69

JOWITT, Deborah

Anna Marie and David Holmes from Winnipeg to the world. Dance Mag 43:34-8 F '69

JOY

Sadness and joy. V. P. McCorry. America 120:514-inside back cover Ap 26 '69

See also

Festivity

JOYCE, James

Bloomsday in Dublin; excerpts from Ulysses, with notes by A. Bester and photographs by M. Koner. Holiday 45:40-5 Je '69

about

Pound/Joyce: the letters of Ezra Pound to James Joyce, ed. by F. Read. Review Cath World 209:91+ My '69. B. Wallenstein

Ulysses' tower. F. Russell. Horizon 11:48-51 Sum '69

JOYCE, Mary Rosera

Celibacy and sexual freedom. America 120:468-70 Ap 19 '69

JOYCE, Phyllis

Upon Julius' clothes; poem. Engl J 58:241 F '69

JOYNER, Conrad, and Anderson, Diane

Electoral college reform. America 120:401-2 Ap 5 '69

JUAN Carlos, prince of Spain

Back to the throne. W. F. Buckley, jr. Nat R 21:818-19 Ag 12 '69

Bonnie Prince Carlos? il por Newsweek 74:49-50 Jl 28 '69

Chosen prince. il por Time 94:33 Ag 1 '69

Clarifying the succession. il por Time 94:35+ Jl 25 '69

For Spain a royal restoration. il pors Life 67:33-4+ Ag 8 '69

Franco deals with the succession question. Chr Cent 86:1059 Ag 13 '69

Hard pill to swallow. il por Newsweek 74:48+ Ag 4 '69

King will reign in Spain again; Franco style. il por U S News 67:10 Ag 4 '69

JUDAH, Theodore Dehone

For sale: an empire $1,500 down. D. Lavender. il por Am West 6:6-12+ My '69

JUDAISM

Judaism, Israel and conscientious objection. S. Gottlieb. Chr Cent 86:1136-7 S 3 '69; Reply. J. Segal. 86:1286 O 8 '69

Myth of the Judeo-Christian tradition; excerpts. A. A. Cohen. Commentary 48:73-7 N '69

New approach to Judaism; excerpts from Anti-Semitism and the Christian mind. A. T. Davies. Cath World 210:74-7 N '69

Rethinking Judaism. A. A. Cohen. New Repub 160:28+ Mr 15 '69

See also

Bible—Old Testament

Church and state in Israel

Hebraism

Jewish theology

Passover

Philosophy, Jewish

Bibliography

Emphasis on a way of life. R. S. Rosen. il Sat R 52:42+ D 6 '69

Study and teaching

Double program of collegiate and rabbinical studies. il Sch & Soc 97:274-6 Sum '69

Jewish community & the Jewish condition; Segals centre. R. Alter. Commentary 47:55-9 F '69

JUDAISM and Christianity. See Christianity and other religions

JUDD, Donald

Don Judd: the complexities of minimal art. B. Rose. Vogue 153:105 Mr 1 '69

JUDEA

Death in the wilderness. il Time 94:47-8 S 12 '69

See also

Holy Land

JUDGE, Joseph

Retracing John Wesley Powell's historic voyage down the Grand Canyon. Nat Geog 135:668-713 My '69

JUDGES

Can Nixon's justices reverse the Warren court? F. Rodell. Look 33:38 D 2 '69

Chief Justice Burger asks: If it doesn't make good sense, how can it make good law? J. Duscha. il N Y Times Mag p30-1+ O 5 '69

Code for judges; stiffer code of financial ethics for Supreme court judges. Time 93:61 Je 20 '69

Code of ethics for U.S. judges. U S News 66:12 Je 23 '69

Furor over Supreme court. il U S News 66:31-2 My 26 '69

Good behavior of judges; who defines it? reprint of July 5, 1957 issue. D. Lawrence. U S News 66:116+ My 19 '69

Jinxed seat: who's next? il Newsweek 74:24 D 1 '69

Judges judged. Newsweek 73:30 Je 23 '69

Profiles of the nine justices. il Sr Schol 94:12-13 Mr 28 '69

Skolnick's guerrilla war; investigating judges. il Time 94:43+ Ag 29 '69

See also

United States—Supreme court

Appointment, qualifications, tenure, etc.

Chief justice. New Repub 160:7 My 31 '69

Haynsworth's record as judge; what it could mean for Supreme court. il U S News 67:14 Ag 25 '69

How Mr Nixon made his choice; selection of W. E. Burger as chief justice. il U S News 66:33 Je 2 '69

Invisible appointments; G. H. Carswell. New Repub 161:11 Jl 12 '69

Mr Nixon and the Court. D. Cobb. Chr Cent 86:1245-7 O 1 '69

Most important nomination that a president makes; selection of a new chief justice of the United States. il Life 66:40-1 My 30 '69

On Haynsworth; the pro and con. il U S News 67:12 S 29 '69

Senate and the Court. America 121:314 O 18 '69

Supreme court: no friends need apply. Life 66:33 Je 2 '69

Salaries, allowances, etc.

Outside income. New Repub 160:5-6 Je 7 '69

JUDGING of photographs. See Photography—Criticism

JUDGMENT

Man's judgment. Chr Today 14:27 N 21 '69

JUDGMENT day

Good news about judgment. Chr Today 13:29 My 9 '69

JUDGMENTS

See also

Arrest of judgment

JUDICIAL procedure. See Procedure (law)

JUDICIAL review
Congress versus the Supreme court. Sr Schol 94:20 F 28 '69

JUDICIARY. See Judges

JUDO
Judo: now it's a safe family sport. M. Michaelson. il Todays Health 47:32-7+ F '69

JUDSON, John
Goose Island; poem. Nation 209:122 Ag 11 '69

JUDY, Kenneth J.
Cellular response to ecdysterone in vitro. bibliog Science 165:1374-5 S 26 '69

JUETTNER, Walter R.
Down east heritage cruise. bibliog Motor B 123:74-9+ Je '69

JUILLIARD dance ensemble
Juilliard dance ensemble; Juilliard concert hall. M. Marks. Dance Mag 43:88-9 My '69
World of dance; last performance at Juilliard school of music on Claremont avenue. W. Terry. Sat R 52:60-1 Ap 12 '69

JUILLIARD school
Note:
For material after April 1969. See Lincoln Center for the performing arts—Juilliard school
Music to my ears: Francis Poulenc's La voix humaine. I. Kolodin. Sat R 52:41 My 3 '69
Musical events: Arthur Honegger's Antigone and Francis Poulenc's La Voix humaine. W. Sargeant. New Yorker 45:155-6 Ap 26 '69
Report: New York; all-Cocteau program at Juilliard opera theater. H. E. Phillips. Opera N 33:23 Je 14 '69
Report: New York; production of Il barbiere di Siviglia. S. Jenkins, jr. il Opera N 33:30 F 1 '69

JUKES, Thomas H. See King, J. L. jt. auth.

JULBER, Eric
Philosophy of Eric Julber of Santa Monica, California. por Esquire 71:122-3 Ja '69

JULIA dolls. See Dolls

JULIAN, Lesley T. and Julian, P. R.
Boulder's winds. bibliog Weatherwise 22:108-12+ Je '69

JULIAN, Paul R. See Julian, L. T. jt. auth.

JULLIAN, Philippe
Fresh remembrance of Oscar Wilde; tr. by A. Foulke. Vogue 154:176-9+ N 1 '69

JULY fourth. See Fourth of July

JUMPING
Being backward gets results; high jumper D. Fosbury. R. Blount, jr. il Sports Illus 30:24-7 F 10 '69
You can't keep a good high jumper down; V. Brumel. J. Schecter. il Sports Illus 31:72+ O 20 '69
See also
Trampolines

JUMPING spiders. See Spiders

JUNCTION diodes. See Diodes

JUNG, Carl Gustav
Faith and psyche: a role for Jung in theology. E. A. Merlin. Cath World 209:172-5 Jl '69

JUNG, Eva Maria
Cardinal Willebrands: a Dutchman in Rome. Cath World 210:27-31 O '69

JUNG, George J.
How to feed roses. Horticulture 47:48+ Mr '69

JUNG, Myrna Dunham
His roses; poem. Horticulture 46:42 S '68

JUNGK, Robert
Big machine. M. S. Livingston. Bul Atom Sci 25:34-5 Mr '69

JUNGKUNTZ, Richard
Lutheran quest for a more visible unity. Chr Today 13:5-6 Je 6 '69
Ouster in Missouri. Chr Today 14:38 N 21 '69

JUNGLE. See Rain forests

JUNIOR college presidents. See College presidents

JUNIOR colleges
Big grope; report of meeting on the two-year college market. Pub W 196:16-18 D 1 '69
Change and the junior college; excerpt from Islands of innovation expanding. B. L. Johnson. bibliog Sch & Soc 97:248-54 Ap '69
Community colleges; new frontier in education. il U S News 66:64-6 My 5 '69
Community colleges; the Williams bill. Ed Digest 34:58-9 Ap '69
Enrolling the disadvantaged. Sch & Soc 97:347-8 O '69
Junior college objectives: reactions and criticisms; excerpts from Dateline '79; heretical concepts for the community college. A. M. Cohen. bibliog Sch & Soc 97:330-3 Sum '69

Pride of the reservation; Navaho community college, Many Farms, Ariz. il Time 93:67 Ap 11 '69
Problems of the junior college. M. P. Sheridan. America 120:619 My 24 '69
Remedial program: teaching junior college students English, science, or math. R. M. Bossone. Clear House 43:364-7 F '69
Soaring community college enrollments. Sch & Soc 97:137-8 Mr '69
See also
National council of independent junior colleges

Accreditation
Landmark case is decided; Marjorie Webster junior college, Washington, D.C. J. D. Koerner. Sat R 52:74 S 20 '69

Curriculum
Junior college development in the United States; excerpts from Teaching in the community-junior college. W. Kelley and L. Wilbur. bibliog Sch & Soc 97:485-98+ D '69

Public relations
See Colleges and universities—Public relations

Teaching
Junior college development in the United States; excerpts from Teaching in the community-junior college. W. Kelley and L. Wilbur. bibliog Sch & Soc 97:485-98+ D '69

JUNIOR colleges, Catholic. See Catholic junior colleges

JUNIOR high schools

Curriculum
See also
English language—Courses of study

JUNIOR librarians. See Librarians

JUNK
String-saver strikes back. J. J. Langdon. il Good H 168:56+ Mr '69

JUNK cars. See Automobiles—Wrecking

JUNK sculpture. See Metal sculpture

JUNKER, Howard
As they used to say in the 1950's. . . Esquire 72:70-1+ Ag '69

JUNTUNEN, Arthur
Land of the blue waters. Travel 132:36-41+ Ag '69

JUO, A. S. R. and White, J. L.
Orientation of the dipole moments of hydroxyl groups in oxidized and unoxidized biotite. bibliog Science 165:804-5 Ag 22 '69

JUPITER (planet)
Jupiter and his satellites. D. D. Zahner. il R Pop Astron 63:7-9 My '69

Satellites
See Satellites

JURASSIC period. See Geology, Stratigraphic—Jurassic; Paleobotany—Jurassic

JURGENSEN, Sonny
Vincification of Sonny Jurgensen. G. Cartwright. il por Life 67:48-51 O 24 '69

JURICH, James P.
Worcester survey. America 120:649-51 My 31 '69
(ed) See Rahner, K. Conversation with Karl Rahner

JURIES, Art
Are juried exhibitions worth saving? G. R. Bradshaw. il Am Artist 33:56-7+ F '69

JURISDICTION
See also
Privileges and immunities

JURISDICTIONAL disputes. See Trade unions—Jurisdictional disputes

JURISPRUDENCE
See also
Sociological jurisprudence

JURKOWSKI, John
More things change; story. Redbook 133:73 Ag '69

JURY, William
Saturn 5 gave the Apollo 8 a leg up to the moon. Space World F-3-63:31-3 Mr '69

JURY
If you're called for jury duty. il Changing T 23:35-6 Jl '69
Myth of the jury trial; analysis of the Miranda v. Arizona decision. G. L. Hallworth. il Commonweal 90:161-4 Ap 25 '68; Reply with rejoinder. J. A. Ball. 90:331+ Je 6 '69
Ordeal of serving. il Time 93:35 F 7 '69
See also
Procedure (law)

JUST, Ward S.
Notes on losing a war. Atlan 223:39-44 Ja '69
Reports: Peru. Atlan 223:12+ My '69
Reports: Washington. Atlan 223:4+ Je '69

JUST what the doctor ordered; drama. See Miller, H. L.

JUSTICE, Donald
Confession; poem. New Yorker 45:193 N 29 '69
Lethargy; Portrait with brown hair; Assassination: poems. Poetry 113:329-31 F '69

JUSTICE, Administration of
See also
Bail
Criminal law
Criminal procedure
Due process of law
Judges
Legal aid
Public prosecutors
Punishment
Trials

California
Changing times; incidents at UCLA and San Jose. Nation 209:460 N 3 '69
Crimes, penalties, and legislatures. C. Crowther. bibliog f il Ann Am Acad 381:147-58 Ja '69
Jail, fine, or plant trees. R. Leadabrand. Am For 75:31+ F '69
New debate on death penalty. U S News 66: 13 My 5 '69
Nightmare for the innocent in a California jail. J. P. Ritter, jr. il **Life** 67:51-2+ **Ag** 15 '69
O'Brien; I want to kill a nigger. A. Goldberg and G. Marine. il Ramp Mag 8:10-18 Jl '69
Telltale trash; R. Edwards case. il Time 94: 54+ O 17 '69
Town on trial; Stockton and the case of the Watkins brothers. Nation 208:483 Ap 21 '69

Canada
Riding the Arctic circuit; administration of justice in Northwest Territories. il Time 93:68+ Je 6 '69

Florida
Faircloth's law; a new way to nail elusive mobsters? D. Walsh. il Life 67:62A-62B O 24 '69

Iraq
Carnival in Baghdad; public hangings of Iraqi Jews in Baghdad. il Newsweek 73: 31-2 F 10 '69
Death, diplomacy and diminishing peace; political executions in Baghdad. il Time 93: 22-3 F 7 '69
Hangings in Iraq. Nat R 21:108 F 11 '69
Interfaith scaffold in Iraq. Chr Today 13: 47 F 28 '69
Mass public executions in Iraq deplored by United States; text of letter to the president of the Security council, January 29, 1969. C. W. Yost. Dept State Bul 60:145-6 F 17 '69
Terrible myth of internal affairs; public hanging of fourteen men convicted of spying for Israel. Chr Cent 86:205 F 12 '69

Maryland
Damning blasphemy. il Time 93:72 My 16 '69

Mississippi
Something more than sympathy; Negro awarded damages from white law officer. Time 94:59 Ag 22 '69

North Carolina
Crime and punishment; twelve year sentences for Negro first-offenders upheld. Newsweek 73:35 Je 16 '69

Ohio
Death by agitation; James Nosis charged with manslaughter. Time 94:75 N 14 '69
Governor and the mobster; with report by D. Walsh. il Life 66:28-32A My 2 '69

South Africa
Immorality; an Afrikaner view. America 120: 579 My 17 '69
Terrorism act of South Africa; excerpts from statement by International commission of jurists. June 1968. Cur Hist 56:298-9+ My '69

United States
Administration of justice; halting the free press/fair trial debate; excerpts from address. C. Kirkpatrick. Cur Int 108:39-42 Je '69
Are courts more severe with black defendants? il Time 94:51 Jl 11 '69
Breakdown of courts in America. il U S News 66:58-60 Mr 10 '69
Court reform; Burger's role. U S News 67:14 Jl 14 '69

Crackdown; sentence of three and a half years in state prison for possession of marijuana. Nation 208:293-4 Mr 10 '69
Is crime chiefly a local problem? U S News 66:12 F 17 '69
Judge Burger's philosophy on justice in U.S, a key speech; excerpts. May 1967; reprint. W. E. Burger. il U S News 66:82-5 Je 2 '69; Same abr. with title Rights and wrongs of U.S. justice. Read Digest 95:84-8 Ag '69
Justice on trial. Chr Today 14:29-30 O 24 '69
No-nonsense man at the helm of justice. U S News 67:9-10 Jl 28 '69
Objection, your honors. Nat R 21:267 Mr 25 '69
On Eldridge Cleaver. K. Cleaver. Ramp Mag 7:4+ Je '69
Persecution of Clay Shaw. W. Rogers. il Look 33:53-6+ Ag 26 '69
Prison; the national poorhouse. R. Goldfarb. New Repub 161:15-17 N 1 '69
Slower justice; courts get blame; excerpts from address, May 1, 1969. W. R. Wilson. U S News 66:13 My 12 '69
What's past is prologue. R. A. McGee. bibliog f Ann Am Acad 381:1-10 Ja '69
See also
Courts—United States
Jury
Sacco-Vanzetti case
Scottsboro case
United States—Justice, Department of

Vermont
Ruckus in Irasburg; the case that had the gossips buzzing in Vermont. H. Moffett. il Life 66:62-4+ Ap 4 '69

Washington, D.C.
Crime war; the Nixon team's model plan. il U S News 67:8 Jl 21 '69

Wisconsin
Moses and the Milwaukee fourteen. L. Forest. Commonweal 90:410-13 Je 27 '69; Reply. J. Keelan. 90:572-4 S 19 '69

Zambia
Justice on trial; high court crisis. il Time 94: 32 Ag 15 '69

JUSTICE, Department of. See United States—Justice, Department of

JUSTICE and politics
Defense against Daley; the conspiracy on trial; case of the Chicago defendants. L. D. Nachman. Nation 208:752-4 Je 16 '69

JUSTICES. See Judges

JUSTIN was good; story. See Kolbeck, L.

JUTLAND
Enchanting Jutland. D. L. McFadden. il Travel 132:42-7 Ag '69

JUVENILE courts
Crisis in juvenile courts. il U S News 66:62-4 Mr 24 '69
First graders meet law and order. S. C. Pearson, jr. Chr Cent 86:681-3 My 14 '69; Discussion. 86:906-7, 997-8 Jl 2, 23 '69
Utopian world of juvenile courts. C. W. Tenney, jr. bibliog f Ann Am Acad 383:101-18 My '69
See also
Juvenile delinquency

JUVENILE delinquency
Delinquents are his patients. A. Henley. il Todays Health 47:48-9+ N '69
Educational programs for delinquents. Sch & Soc 97:477 D '69
Mother Nature vs. juvenile delinquency. D. Walker. il Field & S 73:60-3+ Mr '69
Some recent trends in juvenile delinquency. S. V. Didato. bibliog Ment Hy 53:545-9 O '69
Suddenly it happens to you; your son is arrested for vandalism. McCalls 96:74+ Ap '69
Throwaway children. by L. A. Richette. Review
Vogue 154:58 O 15 '69. J. Stafford
What we don't know about delinquency; with study-discussion program. by E. Harris and D. Harris. L. Vernon. bibliog il PTA Mag 63:5-8, 34-5 Je '69
See also
Detention homes
Gangs
Juvenile courts
Narcotics and youth
Police services for juveniles
Rehabilitation of juvenile delinquents

KALICHSTEIN, Joseph
Outstanding young artists win honors. por
Hi Fi 19:MA16 Ag '69
KALINS, Dorothy
Sauna: hot and healthy. Holiday 46:43+ D '69
KALKSTEIN, Marvin
Anti-ABM. bibliog por Trans-Action 6:23-8+
Je '69
KALLE, Kurt
Wheels of light. Sea Front 15:116-22 Mr '69
KALLEN, Lucille
Sex and the suburbs; or, Meet me at the
A&P. Mlle 69:132-3 Je '69
KALLIO, Paavo
Task for ecologists around waterfalls in
Labrador-Ungava. bibliog Science 166:1598-
601 D 26 '69
KALLIS, Stephen A. jr
Amateur scientist. Sci Am 220:123-6+ Ja '69
KALLMAN, Chester
Capital of away; Dead center; Matrix; Salome
dance; Like as not; poems. Poetry 115:178-84
D '69
KALLMANN and McKinnell, architects
After the Boston city hall. il Arch Forum
130:54-7 Ja '69
KALLSEN, Gene. See Bunch, W. H. jt. auth.
KALNINA, Z. and Polikarpov, G.
Strontium-90 concentration factors of lake
plankton, macrophytes, and substrates. bib-
liog Science 164:1517-19 Je 27 '69
KALODNER, Philip
Still fighting over Curtis. por Bsns W p42
My 17 '69
KALOUSEK, Frantisek, and Morris, N. R.
Deoxyribonucleic acid methylase activity in
pea seedlings. bibliog Science 164:721-2 My 9
'69
KALS, William S.
Bowditch. Motor B 123:136-7+ Ja '69
Float to safety. Todays Health 47:46-7 Je '69
Towing beats rowing. Pop Mech 131:174-7
Mr '69
KALTER, Suzy. See Hyde, M. A. jt. auth.
KALTMAN, Mary
Day the washing machine broke. H. Sidey. il
por Life 67:4 S 12 '69
KALVEN, Harry, jr
Image of justice: reflections on the Chicago
conspiracy trial. New Repub 161:20-3 N 8
'69
KAMAN aircraft corporation
Kaman designs ball bearing replacement;
ceramic fused sliding bearings. il Aviation
W 91:76-7+ Ag 18 '69
KAMBERI, Ibrahim A. and others
Luteinizing hormone-releasing activity in hy-
pophysial stalk blood and elevation by
dopamine. bibliog Science 166:388-90 O 17
'69
KAMIYA, Joe
Controlling the inner man. il por Time 94:
67 Jl 18 '69
KAMM, Henry
Brezhnev sets the clock back. N Y Times Mag
p 14-15+ Ag 10 '69
KAMMERER, Rafael
Two ways of looking at Debussy: Moravec
and Weissenberg. Am Rec G 36:20-1 S '69
KAMP, F. S. and Sondermeyer, J. C.
#200-watt stereo amp. Radio-Electr 40:71-3
O '69
KAMPALA, Uganda
Uganda awaits the Pope. il Newsweek 74:67
Ag 4 '69
KAMPION, Drew
Surfing: you don't have to be seventeen.
Motor B 123:89+ My '69
KANAB, Utah
Cowboys and Indians at Kanab. il Sunset 142:
68 Ap '69
KANDEL, Eric R. See Kupfermann, I; Pinsker,
H. jt. auths.
KANDINSKY, Wassily
In the beginning was Kandinsky. S. A. Kurtz.
il Art N 68:38-41+ My '69
Vasily Kandinsky: a space odyssey. R. C.
Washton. il Art N 68:46-9+ O '69
KANE, Eleanora Bowling
Children of Chocolate street; drama. Plays 29:
73-8 D '69
Paul Revere of Boston; drama. Plays 28:53-
60 Ap '69
Princess and the greenies; dramatization of a
fairy tale. Plays 29:74-8, 96 O '69
KANE, Julian
Iceland's thermal geology; with biographical
sketch. por Natur Hist 78:6, 48-51 Ja '69
KANE, Martin
Boxing. Sports Illus 30:46-7 F 3 '69; 32:46-7
Ja 5 '70
KANE, Sandi
Belle of the dumbbells. H. L. Masin. il por
Sr Schol 94:32 F 14 '69

KANEKO, Toshio, and others
Thyroid-stimulating hormone and prostag-
landin E₁ stimulation of cyclic 3',5'-adeno-
sine monophosphate in thyroid slices. bib-
liog Science 163:1062-3 Mr 7 '69
KANELBA, George S.
Adjustable shelf system for a show-off wall.
Pop Sci 194:158-9+ Mr '69
KANFER, Allen
Seven wonders of the world; poem. Poetry
115:12-13 O '69
KANFER, Stefan
Life theater review. Life 66:10 Je 13; 67 Ag 1
'69
KANIN, Garson
Faa-bu-lous long run of Gordon and Kanin.
S. Lydon. il pors N Y Times Mag p64-5+
O 5 '69
KANIN, Iurii
(ed) See Blagonravov, A. Flights to other
planets are becoming a realistic fact
KANN, Sister Jean Marie
New praying nun. Cath World 209:71-6 My '69
KANNON, Dorothy
Artists on a houseboat. M. L. Norwood. il
Am Artist 33:20-7 Ap '69
KANNY, Mark
Early Beethoven by Blumental. Am Rec G
36:16-17 S '69
Yale quartet's triumphant Beethoven: an
opus 127 from Cardinal. Am Rec G 36:100-1
O '69
KANO, Masaakira. See Semba, T. jt. auth.
KANOVITZ, Howard
Stardust on a spree. il Sports Illus 31:34-9
D 1 '69
about
Letter from the publisher. G. Valk. por Sports
Illus 31:4 D 1 '69
KANSAS
See also
Education—Kansas
Hunting—Kansas
Prisons—Kansas

Description and travel
Death all day in Kansas. R. Rhodes. il
Esquire 72:146-9+ N '69
KANSAS CITY, Mo.
No excess salt on the intersections. il Am
City 84:44 O '69
See also
Gladstone

Crime
Black crime, black victims. R. Pearman. il
Nation 208:500-3 Ap 21 '69

Education
Experiences with differentiated staffing; two
schools. D. Hair. Todays Ed 58:57-8 Mr '69

Police
Kansas City's police computer. C. M. Kelly.
il Am City 84:103-4 Ja '69

Water supply
New water plant on Rehab budget. W. G.
Riddle. il Am City 84:73-9 Ag '69
KANSAS CITY Chiefs (football club) See
Football clubs
KANSAS CITY Royals (baseball). See Baseball
clubs
KANSAS state penitentiary. See Prisons—
Kansas
KANSAS state teachers college, Emporia
See also
National outdoor leadership school
KANSAS. University
Rat pack; athletic team. il Newsweek 73:111
Ap 28 '69
KANTOR, David, and Gelineau, V. A.
Making chronic schizophrenics. Ment Hy 53:
54-66 Ja '69
KANTOR, Hal
They listen so others might see. Todays
Health 47:62-3 S '69
KANTOR, Helene J. and Delougaz, P. P.
New light on the emergence of civilization in
the Near East. UNESCO Courier 22:22-5+
N '69
KANTOR, Robert E. See Slomich, S. J. jt.
auth.
KANTROWITZ, Arthur
Test: meeting the challenge of new technol-
ogy; adaptation of address. Bul Atom Sci
25:20-2+ N '69
KAO, Fa-ten, and others
Complementation analysis on virus-fused
Chinese hamster cells with nutritional
markers. bibliog Science 164:312-14 Ap 18
'69
KAPER, J. M.
Nucleic acid-protein interactions in turnip
yellow mosaic virus. bibliog Science 166:
248-50 O 10 '69

KAPLAN, Abraham
Art of not listening. por Time 93:52-3 Ja 24 '69
KAPLAN, Edgar
Bidding like a Roman Blue with Benito. C. Goren. il Sports Illus 30:54 Mr 31 '69
KAPLAN, Elisabeth
High school graduate's reflections on secondary education. Sch & Soc 97:154-5 Mr '69
KAPLAN, Jack
Frauds who prey on shaky marriages. Todays Health 47:16-19+ Je '69
KAPLAN, Jacques
Jacques Kaplan: his own best ad. il por Bsns W p38-9 D 27 '69
Natural enemy of wild cats. V. Kraft. il Sports Illus 31:42-4 Jl 14 '69
KAPLAN, Johanna
Sour or suntanned, it makes no difference; story. Commentary 47:67-74 My '69
KAPLAN, Justin
Rose for Emily. Harper 238:106-9 Mr '69
KAPLAN, Milton A.
Compositions: assigned or developed? Engl J 58:1194-8 N '69
KAPLAN, Samuel
Bridging the gap from rhetoric to reality. Arch Forum 131:70-3 N '69
KAPLANIS, J. N. and others
Ecdysone analog: conversion to alpha ecdysone and 20-hydroxyecdysone by an insect. bibliog Science 166:1540-1 D 19 '69
KAPP, Joe
Violent Vikings. il Newsweek 74:89 D 8 '69
Zorba the Viking. L. Shecter. il pors Look 33:64-5+ D 30 '69
KAPSAND, Liz
Lost and found: me! Seventeen 28:136-7+ N '69
KAPUR, Harish
China's relations with India and Pakistan. bibliog f Cur Hist 57:156-63 S '69
KARACHI, Pakistan

Hotels, restaurants, etc.

International chef; a specialty of Chandni lounge. M. Woodward. il Travel 131:18 Mr '69
KARAJAN, Herbert von
Von Krajan speaks his mind; interview, ed. by P. Moor. Hi Fi 19:MA18-19 N '69

about

What happened to the new Karajan style? G. Movshon. il por Hi Fi 19:MA28-9+ Je '69
KARAS, Nicholas
Blizzard moose. Field & S 74:56-7+ N '69
KARASEK, F. W.
Analytic instruments in process control; with biographical sketch. Sci Am 220:14, 112-20 Je '69
KARE, Morley R. and others
Direct pathway to the brain. bibliog Science 163:952-3 F 28 '69
KARENGA, Maulana Ron
Black guns on campus. R. Rogers. il Nation 208:558-60 My 5 '69
KARIBA DAM. See Dams—Rhodesia
KARIBA LAKE
Kariba Dam: the ecological hazards of making a lake. T. Scudder. il Natur Hist 78:68-72 F '69
KARIM al Hussaini Shah. See Aga Khan IV
KARIMOJONG (native race) See Uganda—Native races
KARLE, Isabella L. and others
Crystal and molecular structure of a thymine-thymine adduct. bibliog Science 164:183-4 Ap 11 '69
2,3-cis-3,4-trans-3,4-dihydroxy-L-proline; mass spectrometry and X-ray analysis. bibliog Science 164:1401-2 Je 20 '69
KARLEN, Arno
Enrico's of San Francisco. Holiday 45:90+ Mr '69
Unmarried marrieds on campus. N Y Times Mag p28-9+ Ja 26 '69
KARLIN, Arthur. See Silman, I. jt. auth.
KARLIN, Robert
About reading and the high school student. bibliog Engl J 58:386-95 Mr '69
KARLINSKY, Simon
Heady past of futurism. Nation 208:182-3 F 10 '69
Pushkin in his real life. Nation 208:469-70 Ap 14 '69
KARLOFF, Boris
Gentle monster. pors Newsweek 73:100 F 17 '69
KARLOVSKY, C. C. Lamberg-. See Lamberg-Karlovsky, C. C.

KARNILOVA, Maria
I've always gone where fate led me. C. Barclay. il pors Dance Mag 43:34-7+ Ja '69
KARP, Haskell
Artificial heart. Time 93:46 Ap 11 '69
Implanting a stopgap heart. il Sci N 95:375 Ap 19 '69
Man with a plastic heart. il Newsweek 73:128-9 Ap 14 '69
KARP, Walter
American land: as it was. Am Heritage 21:16-21 D '69
Learned bureaucrats in China. Horizon 11:12-13 Spr '69
—and Shapiro, H. R.
Chief political question of our time: reprint. ALA Bul 63:165-7 F '69
KARPEL, Craig
Plastic reality. Esquire 72:221-8 D '69
(ed) See Eisenhower, D. David Eisenhower on his own generation
KARRAKER, William Henry
Brotherhood of borrowed time. D. Snell. il pors Life 67:65-6+ O 24 '69
KARSEN, Sonja P.
Jaime Torres Bodet. Américas 21:6-11 Ag '69
KARSH, Yousuf
Meeting with Dr DeBakey. Sat R 52:28-9 Ap 12 '69
KARTH, Joseph
Joe Karth's questions; excerpts from address, November 1969. Aviation W 91:21 N 17 '69
KARTS (midget cars)
How to turn a go-cart into a baby Chaparral. J. Capotosto. il Mech Illus 65:74-8 Ag '69
KARTUZ, Michael J.
Smithiantha. Horticulture 46:16-17+ N '68
KARUIZAWA, Japan
Japan's premier resort. R. Halloran. il Sat R 52:91-2+ Mr 8 '69
KARUME, Abeid Amani
Eye to the West. S. Ungar. por Newsweek 73:55 My 19 '69
KASER, David
Academic librarian and the protocol of scholarship. por Library J 94:719-21 F 15 '69
Books and libraries in the Far East; address, June 24, 1968. por Wilson Lib Bul 43:974-9 Je '69
KASH, Don E.
Forces affecting science policy: R&D; address, August 30, 1968. Bul Atom Sci 25:10-17 Ap '69
KASHA, Bernard
Fast way to make a boat unsinkable. Mech Illus 65:64-5+ Je '69
KASPER, Ed
Passion's wheels. il Sports Illus 31:52-7 O 20 '69
KASSALOW, Everett M.
Public employee bargaining in Europe; excerpt. Mo Labor R 92:47-9 Mr '69
KASTNER, Joe
Man and magazine grew in unison. G. P. Hunt. por Life 66:3 F 14 '69
KATCHALSKY, A. See Sussman, M. V. jt. auth.
KATCHEN, Julius
Julius Katchen (1926-1969) N. Rorem. Hi Fi 19:61 S '69
KATCOFF, Seymour
Alpha-recoil tracks in mica; registration efficiency. Science 166:382-4 O 17 '69
KATE herself; story. See Maier, W.
KATEB, George
Campus & its critics. bibliog f Commentary 47:40-8 Ap '69
KATHRYN Turney Long fund. See Foundations, Charitable and educational
KATIA
Katia's new clothes. il pors Newsweek 74:62-3 Ag 11 '69
KATIE Crawford; story. See West, A.
KATS, Madeleine
Sweden: stirring up a commotion. Dance Mag 43:46-8 My '69
Sweden: theatre child. Dance Mag 43:49-50 My '69
KATSUKI, Yasuji, and Hashimoto, Toru
Shark pit organs: enhancement of mechanosensitivity by potassium ions. bibliog Science 166:1287-9 D 5 '69
—and others
Shark pit organs: response to chemicals. bibliog Science 163:405-7 Ja 24 '69
KATUSHEV, Konstantin
New man in town. il por Time 93:34+ Mr 28 '69
Shadow. Newsweek 74:36 Ag 25 '69
KATZ, Bill
(ed) Magazines. See issues of Library journal

KATZ, George G.
Problem of the hit or myth approach to community mental health planning: reflections on George Albee's paper. bibliog Ment Hy 53:141-2 Ja '69

KATZ, Karl
Two in one. D. L. Shirey. il por Newsweek 73:84 F 3 '69

KATZ, Phyllis B.
(ed) Family clinic. See issues of Parents' magazine & better family living

KATZ, Raymond
Raymond Katz, master of mixed techniques. M. W. Dulac. il por Am Artist 33:58-61+ Ja '69

KATZ, William Loren
Let's set black history straight; interview. bibliog Read Digest 95:59-63 Jl '69

KATZENBACH, Nicholas deBelleville
Tragedy of Nigeria; address, December 3, 1968. Dept State Bul 59:653-8 D 23 '68

KATZENBERG, Barbara
In my opinion. por Seventeen 28:480 Ag '69

KATZMAN, Richard L. and Jeanloz, R. W.
Acid polysaccharides from invertebrate connective tissue: phylogenetic aspects. bibliog Science 166:758-9 N 7 '69

KAUAI (island)
Paradise isn't quite enough. K. Hulme. il Holiday 45:64-5+ Ap '69

KAUFFMANN, Stanley
Stanley Kauffmann on films. See issues of New republic
Theater. New Repub 161:24 O 11; 22+ N 1; 24+ N 8; 22+ N 22 '69; 162:25+ Ja 3 '70

KAUFMAN, Alvin B.
Constant-current ohmmeter. Pop Electr 30:53-5 Ap '69

KAUFMAN, Arnold Saul
Communist and the governor. New Repub 162:21-4 Ja 3 '70
President Pusey and the Harvard radicals deserve one another. N Y Times Mag p 140 My 4 '69
Role of compensatory justice. Cur 110:52-4 S '69

KAUFMAN, Daniel
Poems and photographs: Abstract; Lament for old men; O city of love; Seasons of the forest. Seventeen 28:154-5 S '69

KAUFMAN, Herbert
Creating a school crisis. Trans-Action 6:58-61 Ap '69

KAUFMAN, Irma
How to be a winner in cooking contests. Farm J 93:38 Jl '69

KAUFMAN, Lynne
Bedtime tale; story. Redbook 134:58-9 Ja '70
Before a girl marries; story. Redbook 133:72 Ag '69

KAUFMAN, P. B. and others
Silica in developing epidermal cells of avena internodes: electron microprobe analysis. bibliog Science 166:1015-17 N 21 '69

KAUFMAN, Richard F.
As Eisenhower was saying, we must guard against unwarranted influence by the military-industrial complex. N Y Times Mag p 10-11+ Je 22; 2+ Jl 6 '69
Billion-dollar grab bag. Nation 208:328-32 Mr 17 '69
Phoenix of obsolescence. Nation 208:656-60 My 26 '69

KAUFMAN and Broad building company
How a builder stays at the top. il Bsns W p 168-9 S 20 '69

KAUFMANN, Edgar, jr.
Frank Lloyd Wright: the eleventh decade Arch Forum 130:38-41 Je '69
2001 B.C. to 2001 Centre avenue. Arch Forum 131:54-7 O '69

KAUFMANN, Walter
Walter Kaufmann on Jacob Landau. Ramp Mag 8:20 O '69

KAULA, William M.
Gravitational field of the moon. bibliog Science 166:1581-8 D 26 '69

KAULENAS, M. S. and others
Ribosomal RNA synthesis during cleavage of ascaris lumbricoides eggs. bibliog Science 163:1201-3 Mr 14 '69

KAVALER, Lucy
Hidden conflicts in marriage. Parents Mag 44:35-7+ Je '69
Why some marriages fail. Parents Mag 44:46-7+ F '69
Will there soon be a drug that might ultimately prolong your husband's life? Good H 169:112-13+ O '69
(ed) See Squire, J. J. What women want to know about having a baby

KAVANAUGH, John Francis
Faith and philosophy. Cath World 208:282+ Mr '69

KAVANDAME, Lazaro
Premier and prodigal. por Newsweek 73:60 Ap 28 '69

KAWASAKI, Ichirō
Undiplomat; Japanese ambassador writes book about his fellow Japanese. Time 93:37 Ap 4 '69

KAY, Alan F.
Battling the big board to serve big traders. il por Bsns W p 104+ Je 14 '69

KAY, Jane Holtz
Artists as social reformers. Art in Am 57:44-7 Ja '69
Latin American art, New England setting. Américas 21:19-27 Ap '69

KAY, Thomas
Voluntary refuse-bag program gains strength. por Am City 84:78-9 Je '69

KAYAK racing
Ravaging mountain streams challenge white water canoeists. B. Thomas. il Pop Gard 20:12-17 Spr '69; Same abr. with title Whitewater canoe race. Travel 131:50-3+ Mr '69
Whitewater! National whitewater championships. J. B. Robinson. il Motor B 124:80-1+ Ag '69
Wild & wet canoe derby; White water derby, North Creek, N.Y. il Mech Illus 65:36+ My '69

KAYAKS
Skimmer-kayak, easy to build. il Sunset 143:64 Ag '69

KAYE, Howard
Delight and instruction. New Repub 160:19-20 F 8 '69
Old and the new. New Repub 160:22-5 Mr 1 '69

KAYE, Myrna
Art nouveau ceramics. Am Home 72:22+ N '69

KAZAKOVA, Rimma
Pattering rain set runlets flowing; tr. by T. Botting. Mlle 69:144 My '69

KAZAN, Elia
Current cinema. P. Kael. New Yorker 45:211-12+ N 22 '69

KAZANTZAKIS, Nikos
European literary scene; tomb desecration. R. J. Clements. Sat R 52:28 Je 7 '69
Nikos Kazantzakis, by H. N. Kazantzakis; tr. by A. Mims. Review
Nation 208:186-7 F 10 '69. J. Arthos

KAZIN, Alfred
Books (cont) Vogue 153:124+ F 1 '69
In the mind of Nabokov. Sat R 52:27-8+ My 10 '69
John Dos Passos: inventor in isolation. Sat R 52:16-19+ Mr 15 '69
Thoreau and American power. Atlan 223:60-4+ My '69
Walker in the city; excerpt. il Travel & Camera 32:59 S '69

KAZIN, Michael
Some notes on S.D.S. Am Scholar 38:644-55 Aut '69

KEACH, Stacy
I'm a good case study as a lesson in patience. pors Life 67:68-9 N 7 '69

about
Grand young man. J. Kroll. il pors Newsweek 74:135 N 24 '69

KEAN, Rick
Finding people who feel alienated and alone in their best impulses and most honest perceptions and telling them they're not crazy; letter. Wilson Lib Bul 44:36-44 S '69

KEANE, Mark E.
Recent city manager appointments. See issues of American city to July 1969

KEARNEY, Vincent S.
Asia. America 122:14-16 Ja 10 '70
Mission to the Middle East. America 120:495-8 Ap 26 '69
War nobody won. America 120:664-7 Je 7 '69
World scene (cont) America 120:545-8; 121:540-3 My 3, N 29 '69

KEARNS, Desmond
Before the mast in Bluenose II. il por Yachting 125:90-1+ Ja '69
Sea fight with time and a tempest. Motor B 123:95-7+ Ap '69
Sven, the remora. il Yachting 125:61+ Mr '69

KEAS. See Parrots

KEATING, Bern
America's gift to gastronomy. Holiday 45:46-7+ My '69
Down Florida's spine. Travel & Camera 32:66-9+ N '69

KEATING, Rex
When the earth shook in Khorassan. UNESCO Courier 22:30-5 F '69

KEATON, R. Roy
Strain, pain, is it bursitis? Har Yrs 9:45 S '69

KEATS, John
Frances G. Knight and the Passport office.
Holiday 46:48-9+ N '69
KECK, Herman
Instant-minister racket. B. Bruns. il pors
Life 67:67-8+ N 14 '69
KEEFAUVER, John
Sterilized puff and the great cancer scare.
Nat R 21:1168 N 18 '69
Upsidedown man. Nat R 21:691+ Jl 15 '69
KEEFE, John W.
English lusterware from the Duckworth col-
lection. Antiques 96:382-9 S '69
KEELER, Christine
Perils of Christine. por Time 94:77-8 O 10 '69
KEEN, Sam
Soft revolution explored. Chr Cent 86:
1667-9 D 31 '69
KEENAN, Martha
Princess with the broken heart; drama. Plays
28:63-6, 74 F '69
KEENE, Carolyn, pseud.
Secret of Nancy Drew, pushing forty and
going strong. A. Prager. il Sat R 52:18-19+
Ja 25 '69
KEENE, Paul
Profile of a pioneer in organic foods. M.
C. Goldman. il por Org Gard & Farm 16:
56-61 Jl '69
KEEPSAKES
Promoters hitch wagons to the moon. il Bsns
W p32 Ag 2 '69
Typophiles and a keepsake. F. Johnson. il
Am Artist 33:66-9+ My '69
See also
Souvenirs
KEESHAN, William
Magnin's moves East. il por Time 93:77 Je
27 '69
KEETON, William T.
Orientation by pigeons: is the sun necessary?
bibliog Science 165:922-8 Ag 29 '69
KEEZER, Dexter M.
Watch out girls! New Repub 161:30-1 S 6 '69
KEIFETZ, Norman
A U.S. youngster is infected with VD every
two minutes. N Y Times Mag p85+ Mr
9 '69
KEIFFER, Elisabeth
Bonnie Morgan's miracle baby. Good H 168:
62+ Mr '69
Trial of Elaine Murphy. Good H 168:12+ My
'69
KEITH, G. Stuart
Our local correspondents. E. Kinkead. New
Yorker 45:58+ Ag 2 '69
KEITH, Kay Whitcomb
Stuttgart: international handcraft. Craft
Horiz 29:20-3 S '69
**KEITH-SPIEGEL, Patricia. See Spiegel, D. E.
jt. auth.**
KELEMEN, Zóltan
Natural; interview. ed. by A. M. Lingg. por
Opera N 33:27 F 22 '69
KELF-COHEN, Reuben
Corporations of a different stamp. F. Morley.
Nations Bsns 57:19-20 Ag '69
KELLEHER, Stephen J.
Civil lawyer in the church court. America
120:444-5 Ap 12 '69
KELLER, Anthony S.
How to make the most of a shoestring. Dance
Mag 43:63-4+ Ap '69
KELLER, Eugenia
Chewing gum, a big industry. Chem 42:16-17
S '69
Early days of radioactivity in industry. Chem
42:16-17 My '69
Origin of life (cont) bibliog Chem 42:12-18
Ja; 8-13 Ap '69
KELLEY, Charles F.
Fresh water from the sea. Yachting 126:72-
3+ D '69
KELLEY, James B.
Law and order equals status quo? America
121:323-6 O 18 '69
KELLEY, James Bernard
Catholic colleges in the service of man. Cath
World 210:19-21 O '69
KELLEY, James W.
Case of the alcoholic absentee. Harvard Bsns
R 47:14-16+ My '69
KELLEY, Reeve Spencer
Men who fight in long wars; poem. Sat R
52:47 S 6 '69
School of fatal knocks; poem. Sat R 52:51
D 27 '69
KELLEY, Tom
Tuna party. Outdoor Life 144:48-9+ S '69
KELLEY, Win, and Wilbur, Leslie
Junior college development in the United
States; excerpts from Teaching in the
community-junior college. Sch & Soc 97:
485-9+ D '69
KELLOGG, Winthrop N.
Chimp human chit-chat. il Sci Digest 65:73-4
F '69

KELLOGG company
Kellogg diversifies beyond breakfast. Bsns W
p40 My 24 '69
KELLOGG peace plan. See War, Outlawry of
KELLSTADT, Charles H.
Chairman wouldn't sit down. por Bsns W
p52-3 D 20 '69
KELLY, Albert
Big ambulance for big birds. N. Sklarewitz.
il Pop Mech 132:124-7+ S '69
KELLY, Alfred H.
Constitutional liberty and the law of libel:
a historian's view: address. December 1967.
bibliog f Am Hist R 74:429-52 D '68
KELLY, Bob
Customs & cameras. U S Camera 32:59+ Ja
'69
I photograph a mountain. Travel & Camera
32:116-17+ F '69
KELLY, Clarence M.
Kansas City's police computer. por Am City
84:103-4 Ja '69
KELLY, Desmond
Desert sun circle. Travel 131:62-4 Mr '69
KELLY, Edward E.
English chaplaincy. America 120:101-2 Ja 25
'69
KELLY, Eugene T. See Turano, J. jt. auth.
KELLY, Frank K.
[Book review] America 120:104-5, 338 Ja 25,
Mr 22 '69
KELLY, George W.
Foxtail pine. Horticulture 47:17+ O '69
Landscaping with natives from the Plains
and the Rockies. il Horticulture 46:28-33
D '68
Pinyon pine. Horticulture 47:31 N '69
**KELLY, Grace. See Grace Patricia, consort of
Rainier III, prince of Monaco**
KELLY, Howard Atwood
He was a medical dynamo. A. S. Freese. il
por Todays Health 47:58-9+ My '69
KELLY, Inga
In-service: team approach. Library J 94:1733-
4 Ap 15 '69
KELLY, James
Floating guesthouse. Sat R 52:40 Ap 5 '69
KELLY, James J.
Master of air defense. il pors Ebony 24:124-
6+ O '69
KELLY, Jon R.
Speakers, present and future. por Hi Fi 19:
49-53 Je '69
KELLY, Paula
Paula adds zip to Sweet Charity. il pors
Ebony 24:86-8+ Je '69
KELLY, Perry, and Sarvis, Alva
Gesso cut for printmaking. il Sch Arts 69:8-11
D '69
KELLY, Ramon
Realism of Ramon Kelly. J. Jellico. il por
Am Artist 33:58-63 Mr '69
KELLY, Red
Red-hot tune for the Kings. A. Wright. il
por Sports Illus 30:30-1 Ap 21 '69
KELLY, Rob Roy
Collecting wood type. Pub W 196:64-6 N 3
'69
KELLY, Robert
Critic of the month. L. Lieberman. Poetry
114:51 Ap '69
KELLY, Robert L.
Ability grouping in English. Clear House
43:547-52 My '69
KELLY, Steve
Roundy-round corner. See issues of Hot rod
KELLY, T. K. and others
Y-modulation: an improved method of re-
vealing surface detail using the scanning
electron microscope. Science 165:283-5 Jl
18 '69

KELMAN, Steven
Beyond new leftism. Commentary 47:67-71
F '69
KELSEY, Morton T.
Is the world view of Jesus outmoded? Chr
Cent 86:112-15 Ja 22 '69
KELSEY, Paul M.
How to age your deer. Cons 24:48-9+ O '69
KEMBLE, Penn
Democrats after 1968. Commentary 47:35-41
Ja; 28+ My '69
On Eric Hoffer. Commentary 48:79-82 N '69
KEMENYFFY, Steven
Folding method for large slab constructions.
E. Chamness. il Ceram Mo 17:14-17 N '69
KEMP, Michael
Nightmare; poem. Negro Hist Bul 32:23 Mr
'69
KEMPER insurance group
Kemper officials see what makes Washington
tick. il Bsns W p74 Je 28 '69
KEMPLER, Walter
Pampered neglected child. Todays Health
47:46-9 Mr '69

KEMPNER, Mary Jean
Drinking in print. House B 111:136+ S '69
KEMPTON, Murray
Column right, column left. il por Newsweek 73:58 Mr 3 '69
KENDALL, Donald McIntosh
Business involvement; address, April 11, 1969. Vital Speeches 35:535-7 Je 15 '69

about

Hard-core jobless get a friend at the top. il por Bsns W p62+ Mr 8 '69
KENDALL, Elaine
Enticers, 1970. Vogue 155:119+ Ja 15 '70
Most, least, famous boring food in America. Vogue 154:258+ O 1 '69
Supermarket, demi-myth. Vogue 154:45+ N 15 '69
KENDRICK, John W.
Evaluating statistics on productivity. Mo Labor R 92:54-5 Ap '69
KENDRICK-JONES, John, and others
Paramyosin: molecular length and assembly. bibliog Science 163:1196-8 Mr 14 '69
KENEFICK, Donald P.
Has anyone seen my pertinent variable? bibliog Ment Hy 53:657-60 O '69
Past in the present. bibliog Ment Hy 53:472-6 Jl '69
KENISTON, Kenneth
Students, drugs and protest. Cur 104:5-19 F '69; Same abr. with title Drug problem among students; how bad, what's back of it? U S News 66:90-2 Mr 24 '69
You have to grow up in Scarsdale to know how bad things really are. N Y Times Mag p27-9+ Ap 27 '69
KENMORE, Carolyn
Model behavior. R. A. Gross. por Newsweek 74:127A+ D 8 '69
KENNEDY, Adrienne
Cities in Bezique. Criticism
New Yorker 44:77 Ja 25 '69
KENNEDY, Charles Edward
Chinese pipes for tobacco and opium. Antiques 95:408-9 Mr '69
KENNEDY, Cora Wright
Tools & techniques. See issues of Popular photography
KENNEDY, David Matthew
Board of governors of the Inter-American development bank holds tenth annual meeting at Guatemala city; statement, April 22, 1969. Dept State Bul 60:426-9 My 19 '69
IMF and IBRD boards of governors meet at Washington; statement, September 30, 1969. Dept State Bul 61:353-8 O 27 '69
We must get inflation under control; interview. por U S News 66:56-60 My 5 '69

about

Dog bites man. por Newsweek 73:90+ My 12 '69
High cost of David Kennedy. por Time 94:98 O 17 '69
New controversy on an old issue. por U S News 66:15 My 12 '69
Reassurance on gold price. por U S News 66:75 F 3 '69
Surtax fight gets rougher. il por Bsns W p42 Jl 12 '69
Tax reform: two rocky roads. il por Newsweek 74:73-4 S 15 '69
Tough new fight on inflation. il por Newsweek 73:77-8+ Ap 14 '69
Treasury's Kennedy. por Fortune 79:33 Ja '69
KENNEDY, Donald, and others
Analysis of restricted neural networks. bibliog Science 164:1488-96 Je 27 '69
KENNEDY, Dora. See Hernick, M. jt. auth.
KENNEDY, Edward Moore
Dealing with China; address, March 20, 1969. Cur 107:8-10 My '69
Shots that can save a million lives. por Ladies Home J 86:62+ S '69
Time for action on Biafra! Read Digest 94:75-7 My '69
Tragedy on Chappaquiddick; statements, July 18 and 25, 1969. U S News 67:21-2 Ag 4 '69

about

Achtung! Nat R 21:679 Jl 15 '69
As Kennedy plans for 1972. il por U S News 66:82-3 F 24 '69
Battle of the ABM. Newsweek 73:36 My 12 '69
Dirksen charge: businessmen are harassed to give Negroes jobs. il por U S News 66:8 Ap 7 '69
Disinvited. por Newsweek 74:38 S 29 '69
Emergence of EMK. Commonweal 90:331-2 Je 6 '69
How Americans rate Ted Kennedy. por U S News 66:19 Mr 17 '69
Is Teddy inevitable? S. Alsop. Newsweek 73:92 F 3 '69

Kennedy plan on Peking's role. U S News 66:15 Mr 31 '69
Last Kennedy. K. Crawford. Newsweek 75:24 Ja 12 '70
Letters from Hamburger hill; ed. by N. Sheehan. Harper 239:40-4+ N '69
Many thoughts, no conclusions. M. McGrory. America 121:86 Ag 16 '69
Nixon and Kennedy, as Gallup rates them now. il por U S News 67:13 Ag 18 '69
Nixon co-opts the middle. S. Alsop. Newsweek 73:104 Je 2 '69
Plea for mercy. Time 93:21 My 30 '69
Private loophole. il Newsweek 74:75-6 D 22 '69
Prodding destiny. K. Crawford. Newsweek 73:45 Ap 28 '69
Reluctant leader. Nat R 21:476-7 My 20 '69
Reports: Washington. W. S. Just. Atlan 223:4+ Je '69
Revival of Ted Kennedy. S. Wright. il pors Life 67:38-9 O 3 '69
Sanity and courage. Nation 208:684-5 Je 2 '69
Snow job? il por Newsweek 73:38 Ap 21 '69
Story of Teddy Kennedy. por U S News 67:20-1 Ag 4 '69
Ted Kennedy; focusing on '72? il por U S News 66:18 Ap 21 '69
Ted Kennedy talks about the past, and his future. W. Rogers. il pors Look 33:38-46 Mr 4 '69
Ted Kennedy's chances now: report from his home state. il pors U S News 67:30-4 N 3 '69
Teddy on China. por Newsweek 73:25-6 Mr 31 '69
Teddy on the attack. Newsweek 73:32+ Ap 7 '69
Teddy on the stump. il pors Newsweek 73:33 Je 2 '69
Teddy's realpolitik. W. F. Buckley, jr. Nat R 21:402 Ap 22 '69
Teddy's re-entry. W. F. Buckley, jr. Nat R 21:1079 O 21 '69
Ted's troubles in the tundra. il por Time 93:22-3 Ap 18 '69
Toll on Teddy. J. Deedy. Commonweal 90:498 Ag 22 '69
Troubled times for the Democrats. il por U S News 67:21-2 Ag 11 '69
Yesterday Edward Kennedy turned thirty-seven, is Teddy, as they say, ready? W. H. Honan. il pors N Y Times Mag p25-7+ F 23 '69

Accident, July 1969

After Chappaquiddick. W. F. Buckley, jr. Nat R 21:1026 O 7 '69
Anguish of Edward Kennedy. il por Time 94:19 Ag 29 '69
Back from Chappaquiddick. il por Time 94:20-1 O 10 '69
Columnist and Kennedy: J. Anderson's investigation. Newsweek 74:75 Ag 25 '69
D.A. on the spot. il Newsweek 74:23-4 Ag 25 '69
Disinvited. por Newsweek 74:38+ S 29 '69
Girl in Ted Kennedy's car. P. F. Healy. Ladies Home J 86:66+ O '69
Grief, fear, doubt, panic, and guilt. il pors Newsweek 74:22-6+ Ag 4 '69
Guilt by appearance. K. Crawford. Newsweek 74:34 Ag 4 '69
In dread of knowing more. B. Farrell. Life 67:16 F Ag 8 '69
Incident at the Dyke bridge. B. Brower. il pors Life 67:16B-27 Ag 1 '69
Journalists assume the role of assassins. S. J. Adamo. America 121:306 O 11 '69
Kennedy case: day by day since the fatal accident. il U S News 67:10-12 S 1 '69
Kennedy case: more questions. il por Time 94:14-16 Ag 8 '69
Kennedy ordeal. Nation 209:99-100 Ag 11 '69
Kennedy: reckoning deferred. Time 94:20-1 S 12 '69
Kennedy: the unanswered questions. Life 67:30 Ag 8 '69
Kennedy tragedy. Chr Today 13:23 Ag 22 '69
Kennedy's legal future: proposed inquest. il Time 94:34+ S 5 '69
Letter from Washington. R. H. Rovere. New Yorker 45:93-4 Ag 9 '69
Living with whispers. il por Time 94:13-14 Ag 22 '69
Massachusetts soap opera. Nat R 21:787 Ag 12 '69
Men who may decide Kennedy's fate. il U S News 67:18 S 15 '69
Moon and the Pond: press and TV coverage. il Newsweek 74:56-7 Ag 4 '69
Mysteries of Chappaquiddick. il Time 94:11B-15 Ag 1 '69
New light on Kennedy case? il por U S News 67:11 S 8 '69

KENNEDY, Edward Moore—Accident, July 1969—*Cont.*

New light on the tragedy; with interview with J. N. Farrar. U S News 67:32-3 N 3 '69

Occurrence at Dyke bridge; with editorial comment. F. Russell. il por Nat R 21:840, 854-7+ Ag 26 '69

On taking the Fifth. W. F. Buckley, jr. Nat R 21:870 Ag 26 '69

On the record. Newsweek 74:39-40 N 3 '69

Plea for secrecy. il por Newsweek 74:44 O 20 '69

Public reaction: charitable, skeptical; a Time-Harris poll. Time 94:17 Ag 8 '69

Questions about Kennedy; feedback between news and newsmen. L. Smith il Newsweek 74:56 Ag 4 '69

Rehearsal for an inquest. il Time 94:16-17 O 31 '69

Scandal that will not die? il por Newsweek 74:18-20 Ag 11 '69

Ted Kennedy. New Repub 161:12 S 20 '69

Teddy Kennedy story; the new chapter. il por U S News 67:30-1 S 15 '69

To bring Kennedy case up to date. il U S News 67:6 Ag 11 '69

Tragic turn for Teddy Kennedy. il por Newsweek 74:33-4+ Jl 28 '69

Walk in Chappaquiddick. H. Bruno. il Newsweek 74:20-2 Ag 11 '69

What voters think of Kennedy now. U S News 67:16 D 1 '69

Why the ferry is late. il Newsweek 74:23-4 S 1 '69

Wrong turn at the bridge. por Time 94:22 Jl 25 '69

Inquest

As inquest nears in the Kennedy car tragedy. il por U S News 67:14 D 22 '69

Autopsy hearing nears in the Teddy Kennedy accident. il por U S News 67:11 S 29 '69

Back to Chappaquiddick. il por Time 95:13-14 Ja 12 '70

Blueprint for the inquest. C. Roberts. il Newsweek 74:20-2+ S 8 '69

Calling the witnesses. Time 94:19 Ag 29 '69

Chappaquiddick mystery. il por Nat R 21:1158 N 18 '69

Inquest. il por Newsweek 75:21-2 Ja 19 '70

Inquest on Chappaquiddick. il por Time 95:18-19 Ja 19 '70

Inquest rules Kennedy wants. por U S News 67:15 O 20 '69

Inquest set in Kennedy case. U S News 67:9 Ag 18 '69

Kennedy inquiry: it's to be secret. U S News 67:16 N 10 '69

Kennedys: inquest of suspicions. il Time 94:20-1 Ag 15 '69

Kennedy's time of trial: pre-inquest hearing. il por Newsweek 74:19-20 S 8 '69

Listening to the lawyers; inquest postponed. il Newsweek 74:26 S 15 '69

No autopsy. Newsweek 74:28 D 22 '69

Order for an inquest. il por Newsweek 74:27-8 Ag 18 '69

Private inquest. il por Time 94:25-6 N 7 '69

Quiet inquest. il por Newsweek 74:40 N 10 '69

Rendezvous in Edgartown. por Newsweek 75:18 Ja 12 '70

Who's who at the Kennedy inquest. il Time 94:18-20 S 5 '69

KENNEDY, Ethel (Skakel)

Ethel Kennedy, a capacity for life. J. Bingham. por Redbook 133:86-7+ S '69

Kennedy of Hickory Hill. il pors Time 93:46-8+ Ap 25 '69

Lady of Hickory Hill. S. Sheehan. il pors N Y Times Mag p30-1+ N 30 '69

Lady of Hickory Hill. il por Newsweek 73:38+ Mr 24 '69

KENNEDY, Joan (Bennett)

Intimate portrait of Joan Kennedy. B. Kevles. il pors Good H 169:76-9+ S '69

KENNEDY, John Fitzgerald, 1917-1963

Artist sculptures JFK doodles. il por Ebony 24:46-8+ O '69

Growing involvement in Asia: 1960-1968. R. Butwell. bibliog f Cur Hist 57:88-92+ Ag '69

Kennedy-Johnson years. T. T. Helde. Cur Hist 57:31-5+ Jl '69

Tax cut in Camelot; excerpts from The fiscal revolution in America. H. Stein. il por Trans-Action 6:38-44 Mr '69

Assassination

Curtains for the D.A: physicians examine photographs and X-rays. Newsweek 73:27 Ja 27 '69

Dallas revisited. il Time 93:18-19 F 21 '69

Dealey plaza. L. Smith. il Holiday 46:78-9+ N '69

Final chapter in the assassination controversy? C. L. Shaw trial. E. J. Epstein. il N Y Times Mag p30-1+ Ap 20 '69; Reply with rejoinder. J. Thompson. p 133 My 18 '69

In the shadow of Dallas. D. Welsh and W. Turner. por Ramp Mag 7:61-71 Ja 25 '69

JFK assassination; Justice department publishes a report by doctors. New Repub 160:9-10 F 1 '69

JFK killing: new findings. U S News 66:4 Ja 27 '69

Jury clears Shaw. Sr Schol 94:16 Mr 21 '69

Kennedy conspiracy, by P. Flammonde. Review

Commonweal 89:712-14 Mr 7 '69. S. Meagher

Persecution of Clay Shaw. W. Rogers. il Look 33:53-6+ Ag 26 '69

Some disturbing parallels. W. Turner. il Ramp Mag 7:127-31 Ja 25 '69

What conspiracy? testimony of P. R. Russo. Newsweek 73:33 F 24 '69

What Garrison proved. New Repub 160:9 Mr 15 '69

Birthplace

Adding to the legend. il Time 93:30 Je 6 '69

Memorials

Dealey plaza. L. Smith. il Holiday 46:78-9 N '69

See also

John F. Kennedy library, Cambridge, Mass.

KENNEDY, John Fitzgerald, 1960-

Young John Kennedy got into Collegiate school; could your son? N. Moran. il por McCalls 96:70-1+ Mr '69

KENNEDY, John F, library. See John F. Kennedy library, Cambridge, Mass.

KENNEDY, Joseph F. and Donahue, R. P.

Human oocytes: maturation in chemically defined media. bibliog Science 164:1292-3 Je 13 '69

KENNEDY, Joseph Patrick, 1888-1969

Death of a dynast. il pors Newsweek 74:28-30 D 1 '69

Death of the founder. il por Time 94:21-2 N 28 '69

Where the Kennedy money is. R. J. Whalen. Time 94:23 N 28 '69

KENNEDY, Joseph Patrick, family

Death of a dynast. pors Newsweek 74:28-30 D 1 '69

In dread of knowing more. B. Farrell. Life 67:16F Ag 8 '69

Joe Kennedy dies at 81. por Life 67:36-7 N 28 '69

Kennedy dynasty: an appraisal. D. Brogan. Esquire 72:162-3+ N '69

KENNEDY, Joseph S.

Interscholastic sports: a balanced viewpoint. Clear House 43:471-3 Ap '69

KENNEDY, Lois J.

Age of Aronow. Motor B 124:81+ N '69

Congressional sweep for Henry Sprague. Motor B 123:166-7 Je '69

Tarring and feathering of Santa Barbara. Motor B 123:60-1 Ap '69

KENNEDY, Robert F, youth center, Morgantown, W.Va. See Detention homes

KENNEDY, Robert Francis, 1925-1968

Bobby books. E. B. Drew. Atlan 224:98-101 Jl '69

Mosaic of RFK. D. Young. Sat R 52:29-30 F 8 '69

RFK against himself. P. Goldman. il por Newsweek 73:32-3 F 17 '69

Robert F. Kennedy, the myth and the man, by V. Lasky. Review

Nat R 21:81 Ja 28 '69. M. S. Evans

Robert Kennedy: a memoir, by J. Newfield. Review

Life 66:8 Je 13 '69. V. S. Navasky

Newsweek il por 73:98+ Je 23 '69. A. Cooper

Sat R il por 52:19-21+ Ag 2 '69. G. Steinam

Time il por 93:84 Je 20 '69

Robert Kennedy as history. A. M. Bickel. New Repub 161:26-8 Jl 5 '69

Unfinished odyssey of Robert Kennedy, by D. Halberstam. Review

Esquire 71:82 Je '69. M. Muggeridge

Assassination

Assassins: who did it, and why? il Newsweek 73:28-9 Mr 24 '69

See also

Trials (murder)—Sirhan trial, 1969

Eulogies

Notes and comment. New Yorker 45:29 Mr 15 '69

KENNEDY, Robert Francis—*Continued*

Memorials

Mass for RFK; Arlington. il Newsweek 73: 35 Je 16 '69

Memorial in Arlington for RFK. U S News 66:12 F 17 '69

R.F.K. remembered. il por Time 93:30 Je 6 '69

Poetry

Lowering (Arlington cemetery, June 8, 1968) M. Swenson. New Yorker 45:46 Je 7 '69

KENNEDY, Robert Francis, 1954?- Bobby jr. in Africa. il pors Life 66:42-9 F 14 '69

KENNEDY, Robert Francis, family Kennedy of Hickory Hill. il pors Time 93: 46-8+ Ap 25 '69

KENNEDY, Roger G. Ignatius Donnelly & the politics of discontent. bibliog Am West 6:10-14+ Mr '69

KENNEDY, Rory Elizabeth Katherine Baptism of Rory Elizabeth Katherine Kennedy. il pors Life 66:56-56B Ja 24 '69

KENNEDY, Rose (Fitzgerald) Durable matriarch. por Time 94:15 Ag 8 '69

KENNEDY, Ted. See Kennedy, E. M.

KENNEDY, Wayne C. Living memorials, open space gifts. Parks & Rec 3:39-40 O '68

KENNEDY, William V. China: a positive policy. America 121:87-90 Ag 16 '69

Washington front. America 121:131 S 6 '69

KENNEDY, X. J. Ant trap; National shrine; Peace and plenty; poems. Poetry 113:325-8 F '69

Best seller; poem. Am Scholar 38:248-9 Spr '69

Devalued estate. Poetry 114:266-74 Jl '69

O'Riley's late-bloomed little son; poem. New Yorker 45:142 Ap 19 '69

Shorter view; poem. Commonweal 89:676 F 28 '69

KENNEDY, CAPE Apollo cuts trigger slump at Cape. Aviation W 91:63-4+ D 8 '69

Biggest Cape bash yet. il Bsns W p 18 Jl 5 '69

Eclipse on the ground. il Newsweek 73:75+ Je 2 '69

Heron and the astronaut; with editorial comment by G. Hunt, and photographs by S. Wayman and R. Morse. A. M. Lindbergh. Life 66:1, 14-26A F 28 '69

Life in the space age; attitudes of engineers and technicians at Cape Kennedy. il Time 94:38+ Jl 4 '69

Reversion to Cape Canaveral name urged. Aviation W 91:64 D 15 '69

Scene at the Cape; prometheus and a carnival; gathering for launch of Apollo 11. il Time 94:13 Jl 25 '69

Stay? No stay? Kennedy space center. J. Morgenstern. il Newsweek 74:24-26A Jl 28 '69

KENNEDY center for the performing arts. See John F. Kennedy center for the performing arts

KENNEDY family Ask not what Ted Sorensen can do for you... D. Halberstam. Harper 239:90-2 N '69

KENNEDY galleries, incorporated Art. L. Alloway. Nation 209:62 Jl 14 '69

KENNEDY half dollar. See Coins

KENNEDY international airport. See New York (city)—Airports

KENNEDY library. See John F. Kennedy library. Cambridge, Mass

KENNEDY space center. See United States— John F. Kennedy space center

KENNELS It's a dog's life? Aranwood hotel, Mahwah, N.J. il Newsweek 74:118D+ O 20 '69

Knock-down dog house. R. C. Sprint. il Pop Sci 195:140-1 Jl '69

KENNETH Readers' choice: abstraction by Robert Moore, jr. por Art in Am 57:51 N '69

KENNEY, George Churchill Flier's journal. pors Am Heritage 21:46-57 D '69

KENNEY, John Edward Soul of caution. por Forbes 104:70 D 1 '69

KENNEY, Nathaniel T. Southern California's trial by mud and water. Nat Geog 136:552-73 O '69

KENNISON, Hugh F. Fast stepping at Interpace. S. Margetts. il por Duns R 93:79+ My '69

KENNY, Robert W. Before the colors fade; the return of the exiles; interview, ed. by J. Stevenson. pors Am Heritage 20:22-5+ Je '69

KENSETT, John Frederick John F. Kensett, 1816-1872. J. Howat. il Antiques 96:397-401 S '69

KENT, Atwater What ever happened to Atwater Kent? F. Atlee. il Pop Electr 31:33-5+ Jl '69

KENT, Corita Naiveté of Corita. R. L. Sundbye. Chr Cent 86:186-7 F 5 '69

KENT, Francis B. Brazilian storm warning. Nation 208:178-9 F 10 '69

KENT, George Magical world of trolls. Read Digest 95:215-16+ N '69

KENT, Leticia (ed) See Jacobs, J. Jane Jacobs: against urban renewal, for urban life

(ed) See Mailer, N. Shoot-for-the-moon Mailer

KENT, Norman Inspired drawings of Lajos Szalay. pors Am Artist 33:66-71+ D '69

KENT, Robert L. Crystal filters. por Electr World 81:50-2 Ap '69

KENT, Thomas J. R. Angry voice from Red Lion. Pop Electr 31: 73-4 S '69

KENT COUNTY, Md.

Historic houses, etc.

Widehall in Chestertown, Kent County. E. Gaines. il Antiques 95:532-7 Ap '69

KENT memorial library. See Suffield, Conn.— Libraries

KENTUCKY
See also
Booksellers and bookselling—Kentucky
Conservation of resources—Kentucky
Education—Kentucky
Festivals—Kentucky
Fishing—Kentucky
Hunting—Kentucky
Mammoth Cave National Park
Red River

Anti-poverty program

Feud in the hills. il Time 94:21 S 12 '69

Description and travel

Anecdotes, facetiae, satire, etc.

Kentucky on $5 a day. D. Lowe. il Esquire 71:88+ Mr '69

Historic houses, etc.

Millwood: the Mercer County, Kentucky, residence of Mr and Mrs Robert McAlfee Brewer. il Antiques 96:82-7 Jl '69

Social conditions

Lonely war of a good angry man; H. M. Caudill. D. G. McCullough. il Am Heritage 21:97-113 D '69

U.S. journal: Kentucky; conditions in the strip-mining region of eastern Kentucky. C. Trillin. New Yorker 45:33-6 D 27 '69

KENTUCKY arts and crafts. See Arts and crafts—United States

KENTUCKY Colonels (basketball team) See Basketball teams

KENTUCKY Derby. See Horse racing

KENTUCKY mountaineers. See Mountaineers (southern states)

KENTUCKY state fair horse show. See Horse shows

KENTUCKY. University, Lexington Cloudburst for Kentucky's Ray of sunshine; football coach. J. Underwood. il Sports Illus 31:56-8+ S 29 '69

KENYA
See also
Asians in Kenya
East African Federation (proposed)
Elections—Kenya
Missions—Kenya
Nairobi
National parks and reserves—Kenya
Shopping and shoppers—Kenya
Trials—Kenya

Description and travel

Kenya says *harambee!* A. C. Fisher, jr. il Nat Geog 135:151-205 F '69

Native races

After Tom Mboya; tribal conflict. S. Meisler. Nation 209:106-8 Ag 11 '69

Model nation that may fall apart because of an assassin's bullet. il U S News 67:10 Jl 21 '69

Ominous oaths; outbreak of tribal tension set off by assassination of T. Mboya. Time 94:31 Ag 15 '69

Taking the oath. il Newsweek 74:42 Ag 25 '69

KENYA—*Continued*

Politics and government

After Tom Mboya; tribal conflict. S. Meisler. Nation 209:106-8 Ag 11 '69

Model nation that may fall apart because of an assassin's bullet. il U S News 67:10 Jl 21 '69

Tribal tinderbox. il Newsweek 74:46 Jl 21 '69

We will crush you; Kenyatta and the problem of tribalism. Time 94:42 N 7 '69

See also
Elections—Kenya
Political parties—Kenya

Race problems

Assassination of Tom Mboya. T. Woodward. Commonweal 90:501-3 Ag 22 '69

Riots

Pulling apart. il Newsweek 74:48+ N 10 '69

Under the ayieke tree; mourning T. Mboya. il Time 94:40-1 Jl 18 '69

KENYA people's union. See Political parties—Kenya

KENYAPITHECUS. See Man, Prehistoric

KENYATTA, Jomo
Tribal tinderbox. il por Newsweek 74:46 Jl 21 '69
We will crush you. por Time 94:42 N 7 '69

KEOGH, James
Keogh: the editor-in-chief. R. B. Semple, jr il por(p8) N Y Times Mag p64 Ag 3 '69

KEOHANE, Mary
Summerhill free school. New Repub 160:19-22 My 31 '69

KEON, Ross Y.
Education of Ronald Reagan. Nation 209: 302-6 S 29 '69

KEPLER, Johann
It is for us to grow... J. Lear. il Sat R 52:41-2 Ag 2 '69

KEPPEL, Francis
Governance of education; excerpts from address, August 1969. Ed Digest 35:9-12 D '69
Libraries and education; address, November 1968. bibliog por Wilson Lib Bul 43:534-9 F '69

KEPPLER, Herbert
Keppler on the SLR. See issues of Modern photography

KERATIN
Keratins. R. D. B. Fraser. il Sci Am 221:86-96 Ag '69

KERATOHYALIN. See Skin

KERBY, Phil
Democrats confront 1970. Nation 209:594-5 D 1 '69
Race, television and Yorty. Nation 208:403-5 Mr 31 '69

KERKORIAN, Kirk
Again the smiling cobra. Newsweek 74:84-5 N 3 '69
Coup that won MGM. Time 94:94 O 3 '69
Duel of aces in Las Vegas. il por Bsns W p49-50 Jl 12 '69
Eurodollars finance the new MGM drama. por Bsns W p41-2 Ag 16 '69
Glint in Kirk's eye. il por Forbes 104:27-9 Ag 15 '69
High ride on free time. por Time 94:70+ Jl 25 '69
Kirk Kerkorian doesn't want all the meat off the bone. I. Ross. il pors Fortune 80: 144-8+ N '69
M-G-M cliff-hanger. il por Newsweek 74:70-1+ Ag 4 '69
New lion roars on the MGM lot. por Bsns W p47 O 11 '69
New showdown looms at MGM. il por Bsns W p66+ Ag 2 '69
Return of smiling Jim. Time 94:80 O 31 '69
Western air lines opposing voice for Kerkorian on board. Aviation W 90:46 Ap 14 '69
Western must allow Kerkorian to inspect stockholder lists. Aviation W 90:28 Ap 21 '69

KERLAN, Robert Keith
Doc Kerlan: Rx for athletes. A. Wright. il pors Sports Illus 31:72-4+ N 24 '69

KERMICLE, J. L.
Androgenesis conditioned by a mutation in maize. bibliog Science 166:1422-4 D 12 '69

KERN, Edward
Can it happen here? Life 67:67+ O 17 '69

KERN, Lawrence E. jr
Japan's inscrutable policies on royalties and copyrights. Pub W 195:39-41 F 10 '69

KERN COUNTY, Calif. free library, Bakersfield
Do-it-yourself recruitment; letter to the editor. M. Dolby. ALA Bul 63:427 Ap '69

KERNAN, Alvin
Henriad: Shakespeare's major history plays. Yale R 59:3-32 O '69

KERNAN, Henry S.
Why dam the Charlotte? il Am For 75:28-31+ N '69

KERNAN, Michael
Will the real me please stand up? story. Ladies Home J 86:76-7 F '69

KERNER commission. See United States—National advisory commission on civil disorders

KERNS, Robert L.
Photograms: a teaching approach to creativity. Sch Arts 69:26-8 D '69

KEROES, Herbert I.
High-Q inductive electronic ignition system. Electr World 82:32-4+ Jl '69

KEROUAC, Jack
End of the road. Time 94:10 O 31 '69
Obituary
Nat R 21:1104 N 4 '69. J. Chamberlain

KERR, Adelaide
Record-breaking exhibit (library) by a group of artists (black) por Wilson Lib Bul 43: 756-9 Ap '69

KERR, Graham
Galloping gourmet. il por Newsweek 73:60 Mr 3 '69
Graham Kerr; Galloping gourmet of TV; with comments. ed. by M. C. Wrenn. P. O'Neil. il pors Life 67:51-2+ D 5 '69
Kitsch in the kitchen. il por Time 93:72+ F 28 '69

KERR, Jean
Christmas present: my 21-minute shape-up. Vogue 154:208-9 D '69
When your husband gives up smoking, leave town. McCalls 96:57+ Je '69

KERR, Russell
Animals in opera. Opera N 33:6-7 F 22 '69

KERR, Tamara
Camp counselor, me? Camp Mag 41:22 Ap '69

KERR, Walter
What can they do for an encore? N Y Times Mag p24-5+ F 2 '69
Whose play is it? N Y Times Mag p66-7+ O 12 '69

KERR, Walter B.
Newspapers and monopoly: S. 1312 and all that. Sat R 52:77-8 My 10 '69
Price-fixing, profit-pooling, and the newspaper business. Sat R 52:82-3 N 8 '69
When a PM paper goes AM. Sat R 52:58-9 F 8 '69

KERSTA, Lawrence George
Voice prints. R. E. Steinhauer. il Sat R 52:56-9 S 6 '69

KERTÉSZ, André
Gallery; photographs. Life 67:2-3 N 14 '69

KERTÉSZ, Istvan
Kertész at the Philharmonic. I. Kolodin. Sat R 52:24 D 27 '69
Musical events; concert performed by Philadelphia orchestra. W. Sargeant. New Yorker 45:152+ Ap 26 '69
Musician of the month. S. Fleming. por(pMA1) Hi Fi 19:MA5 D '69
Recordings. M. Mayer. il Esquire 72:22+ D '69

KERTESZ, Stephen D.
U.S. and Europe today. bibliog f Cur Hist 57:42-7+ Jl '69

KERWIN, Larkin
International union of pure and applied physics. por Phys Today 22:53-5 My '69

KESHISHIAN, Harold M.
Rugs of the Caucasus. Antiques 95:370-5 Mr '69

KESHISHIAN, John
Wilderness trail. Am For 75:44-5 S '69

KESSELMAN, Jonathan
Guaranteeing wages: a modest proposal. Commonweal 89:700-3; 90:93+ Mr 7, Ap 11 '69

KESSLER, Jane W.
Talk and intelligence. PTA Mag 64:15-17+ bibliog(p34) S '69

KESSLER, Jascha
Departure; poem. Sat R 52:18 Jl 26 '69

KESSLER, Kaye, and Reed, W. F.
Bye-bye, no. 1. Sports Illus 31:20-3 D 1 '69

KESSLER, Lyle
Watering place. Criticism
New Yorker 45:87 Mr 22 '69

KESTRELS
Dieldrin and DDT; effects on sparrow hawk eggshells and reproduction. R. D. Porter and S. N. Wiemeyer. bibliog il Science 165:199-200 Jl 11 '69
Faces from the past. Am Heritage 20:64-5 Je '69

KETCHLEDGE, Edwin H.
Recognizing woody plants in winter. Cons 24:20-7+ O '69

KETCHUM, Richard M.
Appalachia: 1914. Am Heritage 20:26-41+
F '69
KETONES
Sex pheromone of the queen butterfly: chemistry. J. Meinwald and others. bibliog il
Science 164:1174-5 Je 6 '69
KETTERING, Ohio
Water tank dons polyframe lid. G. E. Cronk.
il Am City 84:76-7 Je '69
KEULER, Francis H.
We beat business disruption. Am City 84:91-3
Ag '69
KEVLES, Barbara
Intimate portrait of Joan Kennedy. Good H
169:76-9+ S '69
Jobs in television production. Mlle 68:170-3+
Mr '69
(ed) See Collins. J. I've looked at life from
both sides now
KEY; story. See Singer, I. B.
KEYERS, Code. See Radio telegraph—Equipment
**KEYES, Erma D. See McNamara, J. F. jt.
auth.**
KEYES, Frances Parkinson
Exclusive interview with Frances Parkinson Keyes; ed. by P. A. Brock. Writers
Digest 49:56-9 O '69
KEYES, P. Landis
Luteinizing hormone: action on the Graafian
follicle in vitro. bibliog Science 164:846-7
My 16 '69
KEYES, Paul
Gagman's revenge. Newsweek 74:69 N 3 '69
KEYSERLING, Leon H.
Excerpt from Sharing revenue with the states;
reprint. Cong Digest 48:239+ O '69
Federal finances and the economy. Ann Am
Acad 379:53-62 S '68
**KHACHADURIAN, Avedis K. See VanItallie, T.
B. jt. auth.**
KHACHATURIAN, Aram
Stokowski continues to invade new territories. R. D. Darrell; H. Goldsmith. Hi Fi
19:75 Jl '69
Virtuoso festoon by Khachaturian. J. Diether.
Am Rec G 35:1134+ Ag '69
KHAJURAHO, India
Temple belles of India. A. Menen. il Holiday
45:48-9+ F '69
KHAMA, Sir Seretse
Botswana; address, September 1969. Vital
Speeches 36:121-4 D 1 '69
**KHAN, Agha Mohammed Yahya. See Yahya
Khan, A. M.**
KHAN, M. A. Q. and others
Insect metabolism of photoaldrin and photodieldrin. bibliog Science 164:318-19 Ap 18
'69
KHAN, Mohammad Ayub. See Ayub Khan. M.
KHATTAK, M. N. and Wang, S. Y.
Uracil photoproducts from uracil irradiated
in ice. bibliog Science 163:1341-2 Mr 21 '69
KHÊ, Trân-văn-. See Trân-văn-Khê
KHEEL, Theodore Woodrow
Can we stand strikes by teachers, police,
garbage men, etc? Read Digest 95:99-103 Ag
'69
Collective bargaining and community disputes. Mo Labor R 92:3-8 Ja '69
Resolving deadlocks without banning strikes.
Mo Labor R 92:62-3 Jl '69
KHIEM, Tran-thien-. See Tran-thien-Khiem
KHMER art. See Art, Khmer
KHMER sculpture. See Sculpture, Khmer
**KHORASSAN earthquake. See Earthquakes—
Iran**
KHRUNOV, Evgenii
Cosmonaut 14: Soyuz-5 Commander Boris
Volynov, cosmonaut 16: Yevgeny Khrunov.
il por Space World F-4-64:32 Ap '69
KHRUSHCHEV, Nikita Sergeevich
Battle inside the Kremlin. V. Zorza. Look
33:93-7+ Mr 18 '69
Power in the Kremlin. by M. Tatu. Review
Nat R 21:494-5 My 20 '69. T. Szamuely
Some guesses about the next Kremlin conspiracy. J. Fischer. Harper 238:12+ Mr '69
Who's who in Russia these days. U S News
66:18 F 17 '69
KHUROOSH. See Cookery, Middle Eastern
KIBBUTZIM. See Collective settlements—Israel
KIBIGER, Arthur H.
Hudsons that might have been. M. Lamm.
il Motor T 21:84-6 Mr '69
KIBLER, Robert F. and others
Encephalitogenic protein: structure. bibliog
Science 164:577-80 My 2 '69
KIDD, Paul
Price of achievement under Castro. Sat R 52:
23-5+ My 3 '69

KIDDE, Walter, nuclear laboratories, incorporated. See Walter Kidde nuclear laboratories, incorporated
KIDDER, Priscilla
Lady who marries the best people. E. Hawes.
il por McCalls 96:64-5+ Je '69
KIDNAPPING
My plea to Castro for return of my child. J.
Washington. il Ebony 24:66-8+ O '69
See also
Elbrick, C. B., kidnapping case
KIDNEY donors
Kidney donors decide fast. Sci Digest 65:76
Mr '69
Searching the reins. J. W. Montgomery. Chr
Today 13:41-2 Ag 1 '69
KIDNEY stones. See Calculi. Urinary
KIDNEYS
See also
Glomerulus
Urine

Diseases

Antigenic streptococcal components in acute
glomerulonephritis. G. Treser and others.
bibliog il Science 163:676-7 F 14 '69
Cystine: compartmentalization within lysosomes in cystinotic leukocytes. J. D. Schulman and others. bibliog il Science 166:1152-4
N 28 '69
Elution of glomerular bound antibodies in experimental streptococcal glomerulonephritis. L. H. Lindberg and K. L. Vosti. bibliog il Science 166:1032-3 N 21 '69
Intestinal calcium absorption: nature of defect in chronic renal disease. L. V. Avioli
and others. bibliog il Science 166:1154-6 N 28
'69
Serum C'3 lytic system in patients with
glomerulonephritis. R. E. Spitzer and others. bibliog il Science 164:436-7 Ap 25 '69

Transplantation

Bonnie Morgan's miracle baby. E. Keiffer.
il Good H 168:62+ Mr '69
New slant on transplants; Stanford investigators findings. Newsweek 74:79 D 15 '69
KIDNEYS, Artificial
It's time to die; patient asks doctor to take
him off artificial-kidney machine. il Newsweek 73:90-1 F 10 '69
New facts on fluoridation. J. Lear. il Sat R
52:51-6 Mr 1 '69; Discussion. 52:72-4 Ap 5,
57-9 My 3, 57 Je 7, 47-9 Jl 5 '69
KIDNEYS, Transplantation of. See Transplantation of organs, tissues, etc.
KIDNEYS as food
See also
Cookery—Meat
KIEL, Germany
Kai Kruger on Kiel: a look to the future;
preparation for 1972 Olympic games. K.
Kruger. il Yachting 126:53+ D '69
KIEL week. See Regattas
KIELY, Benedict
Ulster after the bludgeons. Nation 208:628-31
My 19 '69
KIENZ, Ethel
Choosing a mobile home park. Consumer
Bul 52:21-3 Mr '69
KIESEL, Stanley
Six candles for a cake: poem. Nation 209:190
S 1 '69
To a young man who has suddenly stopped
his car: poem. New Repub 161:24 O 4 '69
KIESINGER, Kurt Georg
President Nixon meets with Chancellor Kiesinger of the Federal Republic of Germany;
exchange of greetings, remarks. together
with joint statement; August 7 and 8, 1969.
Dept State Bul 61:211-14 S 8 '69

about

Chopper chancellor awaits air force one.
J. P. O'Donnell. il pors N Y Times Mag
p26-7+ F 16 '69
Foxes of Bonn. Nation 208:652 My 26 '69
Germany on a new path. which way will it
lead? il por U S News 67:20+ O 13 '69
Nod to the home folks. il por Newsweek 74:
38+ Ag 18 '69
Reassurance in Washington. il por Time 94:26
Ag 15 '69
West Germany's decision for the 70's. il por
Time 94:24 O 3 '69
Why Kiesinger came to the U.S. il por U S
News 67:12 Ag 18 '69
KIESLER, Charles A.
Applying pressure and changing attitudes.
Todays Ed 58:66-7 Mr '69
KIEVAL, Herman
Curious case of Kol Nidre. Commentary 46:
53-8 O '68; 47:14+ F '69

KIFNER, John
Spectator's guide to the troublemakers. Esquire 71:86-91 F '69
Vandals in the mother country. N Y Times Mag p 14-16+ Ja 4 '70

KIHN, Al
TV game. A. Alpert. New Repub 161:17-21 O 18 '69

KIKUCHI, Kokichi, and others
Diffusible cytotoxic substances and cell-mediated resistance to syngeneic tumors: in vitro demonstration. bibliog Science 165:77-9 Jl 4 '69

KILANDER, H. Frederick
Impact of offensive and obscene material on children and youth; excerpts from Sex education in the schools: a study of objectives, content, methods, materials, and evaluation. Sch & Soc 97:326-30 Sum '69

KILAUEA (crater)
Inflation of Kilauea volcano prior to its 1967-1968 eruption. R. S. Fiske and W. T. Kinoshita. bibliog il Science 165:341-9 Jl 25 '69
Kilauea volcano: the 1967-68 summit eruption. W. T. Kinoshita and others. bibliog il Science 166:459-68 O 24 '69

KILGORE, Thomas, Jr
Militant with love. Chr Today 13:43 Je 6 '69

KILGORE college, Kilgore, Tex.
Don't turn off the TV at halftime; Kilgore Rangerettes at the Cotton bowl. H. Weiskopf. Sports Illus 31:28 D 22 '69

KILIMANJARO
Blind students conquer Mt Kilimanjaro. il Ebony 24:44-6+ Je '69

KILKENNY, Ireland
Irish sketches. J. McCarten. New Yorker 45:95-6+ F 22 '69

KILLEBREW, Harmon
Ideal team in Harm's way. W. Leggett. il por Sports Illus 31:20-3 O 6 '69

KILLENS, John Oliver
Traveler's guide. bibliog Redbook 133:55-62 Jl '69

KILLER whales. See Whales

KILLIAN, Charles
Daniel A. Payne and the A.M.E. general conference of 1888: a display of contrasts. bibliog Negro Hist Bul 32:11-14 N '69

KILLIAN, James R.
ABM; excerpt from statement. Science 163:1310-11 Mr 21 '69

KILLIFISHES
Supermale fish from sex hormones. il Sci Digest 66:68-9 Jl '69

KILLY, Jean Claude
Jean-Claude Killy and the winter woman. il por Ladies Home J 86:37 N '69
My slopes. pors Travel & Camera 32:51-5 D '69

KILNS
Potter and his kiln; excerpt from Kilns: design, construction, and operation. D. Rhodes. il Craft Horiz 29:36-8 Mr '69

KILPATRICK, Bill
Detroit listening post. See issues of Popular mechanics

KILPATRICK, James Jackson
Report card for Richard Nixon. Nat R 21:532-7 Je 3 '69
Warren legacy. Nat R 21:794-800 Ag 12 '69

KILPATRICK, W. S.
Recollections of Karl Barth. Chr Cent 86:414-15 Mr 26 '69

KILSON, Martin
Negro militancy. Sat R 52:28-31 Ag 16 '69

KILVERT, B. Cory, Jr
Green carpets for your garden. Am Home 72:86-7 My '69
What you should know about starting a lawn; excerpt from Informal gardening. Home Gard 56:85-6 Ap '69

KIM, Il Sung
Asiatic Stalin who keeps on taunting U.S. por U S News 66:14 Ap 28 '69
Behind North Korea's belligerence. il por Time 93:24-5 Ap 25 '69
Cleaver in exile. S. Cloud. Time 94:27 O 24 '69
North Korea's new offensive. J. A. Kim. For Affairs 48:166-79 O '69
Why North Korea risks war with U.S. il U S News 66:37-8 My 5 '69

KIM, Joungwon A.
North Korea's new offensive. For Affairs 48:166-79 O '69

KIM, Sung-hou, and Rich, Alexander
Crystalline transfer RNA: the three-dimensional Patterson function at 12-angstrom resolution. bibliog Science 166:1621-4 D 26 '69

KIM, Untae
Metastasizing mammary carcinomas in rats: induction and study of their immunogenicity. bibliog Science 167:72-4 Ja 2 '70

KIM, W. S.
N-Formylseryl-transfer RNA. bibliog Science 163:947-9 F 28 '69

KIMBALL, Robert C.
Court-martial of Dale Noyd. Chr Cent 86:116-19 Ja 22 '69

KIMBALL, Thomas L.
Our national EQ. Nat Wildlife 7:2-13 Ag '69

KIMBERLEY, John
This is Radio Peking. Pop Electr 30:59-61+ Ap '69

KIMBERLY-Clark corporation
Closing the gap; K-C and Scott paper. il Forbes 104:26 S 1 '69

KIMBLE, Raymond L.
Social studies: a case for honest reflection. bibliog Clear House 43:428-31 Mr '69

KIMMEL, Mary
How well does your baby hear? Parents Mag 44:40-1+ Jl '69

KINARD, Epsie
Address book. See issues of House beautiful

KINASES
Adenosine 3', 5'-monophosphate-dependent protein kinase from brain. E. Miyamoto and others. bibliog il Science 165:63-5 Jl 4 '69
Creatine kinase and aldolase in serum: abnormality common to acute psychoses. H. Meltzer; reply with rejoinder. D. G. Warnock and G. L. Ellman. bibliog il Science 164:726-7 My 9 '69

KIND, Joshua
Chicago (cont) Art N 68.59 Ap '69

KIND, Roslyn
Lion's cub. H. Saal. por Newsweek 74:59 D 29 '69
Wonder Kind. por Time 93:61 Mr 28 '69

KINDERGARTEN
Classroom tips from trips. R. C. Moscrip. il Todays Ed 58:20-4 S '69
See also
Montessori method of education

KINDNESS
Rewards of a gracious heart. E. Byrd. Read Digest 94:106-8 Je '69
See also
Humanity

KINDSVATTER, Richard
Guidelines for better grading. Clear House 43:331-4 F '69

KINER, Steve
Players of the week. Sports Illus 31:59 O 27 '69

KINETIC art
Curving rhythms. il UNESCO Courier 22:30-1 My '69
Kinetic art. P. Holter. il Sch Arts 68:26-7 My '69

KINETIC light art
Kinetic light art. H. Wise. il Am Home 72:26+, 80-1 O '69

KING, A. D. Williams
Two drownings. Chr Cent 86:1033 Ag 6 '69

KING, Albert
Biggest, baddest bluesman: Albert King. A. Goldman. Life 66:16 Mr 28 '69

KING, Blues Boy. See King, B. B.

KING, Bruce
Open letter from Bruce King. por Dance Mag 43:89 Ag '69

KING, C. G.
Your health: food facts. Todays Ed 58:62-3 S '69

KING, Cecil V.
How to find leaks. por Chem 42:8-11 Mr '69

KING, Clyde
Pursuit of Willie and Clyde. M. Mulvoy. il por Sports Illus 31:22-5 S 15 '69

KING, Coretta (Scott)
He had a dream; excerpts from My Life with Martin Luther King, jr. pors Life 67:54-54B+ S 12; 82-6+ S 19 '69
Keeper of the dream. por Newsweek 73:38 Mr 24 '69
about
Doctor King's memorial. J. Osborne. New Repub 161:9-10 O 11 '69
Mrs Martin Luther King, jr; classic nobility. por Vogue 153:168-9 My '69
Queen is with us. il por Newsweek 73:37 My 12 '69

KING, Elbert Aubrey, 1935-
— and others
Meteorite fall at Pueblito de Allende, Chihuahua, Mexico; preliminary information. Science 163:928-9 F 28 '69
about
Trouble at NASA: space scientists resign. M. Mueller. il Science 165:776-7+ Ag 22 '69

KING, Helen C.
Record bigeye for a lady. pors Field & S 74:40-1+ Jl '69

KING, Jack Lester, and Jukes, T. H.
Non-Darwinian evolution. bibliog Science 164:
788-98 My 16 '69

KING, James W.
Router prepares concrete for overlay. Am
City 84:83+ Je '69

KING, John McCandish
Croesus, American style. il pors Forbes 104:
27-9 S 15 '69
King-size middleman of oil. por Bsns W
p92-3 Ag 16 '69

KING, Kendall W.
At a bargain price: help for the underfed. U S
News 66:84-5 F 3 '69

KING, Kenneth
Kenneth King; NYU Loeb student center.
T. Borek. Dance Mag 43:78+ D '69

KING, Larry L.
Harold E. Hughes: evangelist from the
prairies. Harper 238:50-7 Mr '69
Requiem for Faulkner's home town. por
Holiday 45:60-1+ Mr '69
Warren Burnett: Texas lawyer. Harper 239:
66-7+ Jl '69

KING, Martin Luther, 1929-1968
Dirty business. Nation 208:780 Je 23 '69
Doctor King, one year after: he lives, man!
G. Goodman. Look 33:29-31 Ap 15 '69
He had a dream; excerpts from My life with
Martin Luther King, jr. C. S. King. il pors
Life 67:54-54B+ S 12; 82-6+ S 19 '69
Martin Luther King: we shall overcome. il
pors UNESCO Courier 22:20-1 O '69
More dirty business. Nation 209:5 Jl 7 '69
My life with Martin Luther King, jr, by C.
S. King. Review
Sat R il 52:33 O 11 '69. A. Z. Silver
Time il por 94:100 O 3 '69
On bugging Martin Luther King. W. F Buck-
ley, jr. Nat R 21:714 Jl 15 '69
Some disturbing parallels. W. Turner. il
Ramp Mag 7:127-31 Ja 25 '69
Surfeit of surveillance. Chr Cent 86:917 Jl 9 '69
Updating sainthood. Chr Cent 86:606 Ap 30 '69

Assassination
Assassins: who did it, and why? Ray: ninety-
nine years and a victory. il Newsweek 73:
28-32 Mr 24 '69
Doctor King's murder: nagging questions re-
main. il U S News 66:13 Mr 24 '69
Martin Luther King and the right to know.
America 120:323 Mr 22 '69
Raising a whirlwind; Ray plea of guilty. il
Time 93:16-17 Mr 21 '69
Whole truth. il Ebony 24:56-7 My '69
Why James Earl Ray murdered Dr King.
W. B. Huie; A. J. Hanes; P. Foreman. il
Look 33:102-4+ Ap 15 '69
Year later: honors for Dr King; violence,
too. il por U S News 66:8 Ap 14 '69

Memorials
Anxious anniversary. il Time 93:19 Ap 11 '69
Doctor King: a year later; California Senate
refuses to honor Dr King's memory. Na-
tion 208:453 Ap 14 '69
Doctor King's memorial. J. Osborne. New
Repub 161:9-10 O 11 '69
Dream, still unfulfilled. il Newsweek 73:34-5
Ap 14 '69
Memorial for Dr King. W. F. Buckley, jr.
Nat R 21:1078 O 21 '69
Memorial to Dr King. America 121:315 O 18
'69
Pertinent memorials. Chr Cent 86:459 Ap 2
'69
That memorial. Nation 209:367 O 13 '69
Year of homage to Martin Luther King. il
pors Ebony 24:31-4+ Ap '69

Poetry
Requiem to Dr Martin Luther King, jr. R.
Howard. Negro Hist Bul 32:17 Ap '69

KING, Pamela
Secret; story. Seventeen 29:76-7 Ja '70

KING, Richard
Sopwith Pup. Flying 85:100-3 Jl '69

KING, Riley B.
Bossman of the blues. P. Garland. il pors
Ebony 25:54-6+ N '69
Rebirth of B. B. King. A. Goldman. por Life
67:16 D 12 '69

KING, Samuel
Samuel King of Newport. W. B. Stevens.
Antiques 96:728-33 N '69

KING, Terry Johnson
Miami's Troika talks about music? Hi Fi
19:MA20+ S '69
New trails through South America. Travel
131:62-5 Je '69

KING, William
Sack-race for the seventies. por Art in Am
57:74 N '69

KING, William H.
Emerging role of the instructional materials specialist. Ed Digest 35:26-8 N '69

KING Arthur: opera. See Purcell, H.

KING crabs
Visual receptors and retinal interaction;
Nobel lecture, December 12, 1967. H. K.
Hartline. Science 164:270-8 Ap 18 '69

KING family
Kings multiply and conquer. W. Murray. il
McCalls 97:72-3+ N '69

KING Herod explains; drama. See O'Brien.
C. C.

KING Lear; drama. See Shakespeare, W.—
Plays

KING Midas; drama. See Gardner, M. and
Smith, J. S.

KING ranch, incorporated
Fabulous house of Kleberg: a world of cattle
and grass. C. J. V. Murphy. il Fortune 79:
112-19+ Je '69
King ranch south of the border. C. J. V.
Murphy. il Fortune 80:132-6+ Jl '69
Treasures in oil and cattle. C. J. V. Murphy.
il Fortune 80:110-14+ Ag 1 '69

KING ranch, proprietary, limited
Fabulous house of Kleberg: a world of
cattle and grass. C. J. V. Murphy. il Fortune 79:112-19+ Je '69

KING resources company
Croesus, American style. il Forbes 104:27-9
S 15 '69
King-size middleman of oil. Bsns W p92-3
Ag 16 '69

KINGDON-WARD, Frank
F. Kingdon-Ward, plant hunter extraordinary.
D. S. Manks. il por Horticulture 46:20-1+
O '68

KINGETT, Robert P.
Avalon looks up. Motor B 123:242+ Ja '69

KINGMAN, Dong
Dong Kingman in South America: commen-
tary. N. Kent. il pors Am Artist 33:28-33+
Ap '69

KINGS and rulers
Whatever happened to the royalty of Europe.
il U S News 67:16 Jl 14 '69
See also
Heads of state

KINGS CANYON NATIONAL PARK
Interpreting the rattlesnake. S. F. Arno. il
Nat Parks 43:15-17 D '69

KINGSBURY, Elizabeth W. and Voelz, Herbert
Induction of helical arrays of ribosomes by
vinblastine sulfate in escherichia coli. bibliog Science 166:768-9 N 7 '69

KINGSLAKE, Rudolf
Man who loves computers; interview, ed. by
N. Goldberg. Pop Phot 65:93+ S '69

KINGSLEY, Ronald F. and Hargis, C. H.
Measuring counselors' needs aids success
prediction in camps for the handicapped.
Camp Mag 41:20 S '69; Correction. 41:30 N
'69

KINGSPORT press, incorporated
Arcata national corp. buying Kingsport press.
Pub W 195:74 Ja 27 '69

KINGSTON, N.Y., area library
Kingston, N.Y. firing blamed on censorship.
Library J 94:2991 S 15 '69

KININS
Cytokinin of wheat germ transfer RNA:
6-(4-hydroxy-3 - methyl - 2 - butenylamino)-
2-methylthio-9-β-D-ribofuranosylpurine. S.
M. Hecht and others. bibliog il Science 166:
1272-4 D 5 '69
Isopentenyladenosine stimulates and inhibits
mitosis of human lymphocytes treated
with phytohemagglutinin. R. C. Gallo and
others. bibliog il Science 165:400-2 Jl 25 '69

KINKEAD, Eugene
Our local correspondents. New Yorker 45:
58+ Ag 2 '69

KINNE, Russ
Probing the depths. Travel & Camera 32:96+
D '69

KINNELL, Galway
Hen flower; poem. Harper 239:90-1 D '69
Shoes; poem. Poetry 115:114-18 N '69

KINNEY, James R. and Honeycutt, Ann
Congratulations! It's a dog! excerpts from
How to raise a dog in the city and in the
suburbs. McCalls 96:66+ S '69

KINNICK, B. Jo
Emily Dickinson; poem. Engl J 58:229 F '69
Simplify, simplify; poem. Engl J 58:46 Ja '69

KINO, Eusebio Francisco
Pathfinder of the Papaguería. R. L. Ives. il
Américas 21:13-20 S '69 (to be cont)

KINOSHITA, Willie T. and others
Kilauea volcano: the 1967-68 summit erup-
tion. bibliog Science 166:459-68 O 24 '69
—See Fiske, R. S. jt. auth.

KINSHIP
  Elementary structures of kinship, by C. Levi-
    Strauss. Review
    New Repub 161:26-30 Jl 12 '69. R. Fox
KINSTLER, Everett Raymond
  Emphasizes expression over technique; with
    biographical sketch. il por Am Artist 33:
    54-5+ F '69
KINTNER, P. L. See Whittaker, A. G. jt.
  auth.
KINVILLE, Sam
  Why unionization? excerpts from address.
    Parks & Rec 4:28-30 Mr '69
KINYON, Robert C.
  Millsap & Kinyon illustrator team. F. Whitak-
    er. il Am Artist 33:50-5+ Je '69
KINZEL, Augustus F.
  Inner circle. il Time 93:74 Je 6 '69
KINZUA DAM. See Dams
KINZUA LAKE. See Lakes, Artificial
KIPNIS, Igor
  Igor Kipnis: another indispensable recording.
    J. W. Barker. Am Rec G 35:450 F '69
KIPPHARDT, Heinar
  In the matter of J. Robert Oppenheimer.
    Criticism
      America 120:430-1+ Ap 5 '69
      Commonweal 90:46-8 Mr 28 '69
      Life 66:16 Ap 25 '69
      Nation 208:379-80 Mr 24 '69
      New Yorker 45:131 Mr 15 '69
      Newsweek il 73:133 Mr 17 '69
      Sat R 52:72 Mr 22 '69
      Time 93:66 Mr 14 '69
KIRBY, Helen
  Children of Mexican-American migrants,
    aliens in their own homeland. Todays Ed
    58:44-5 N '69
KIRCHENTAG. See Religious conferences
KIRCHER, Donald P.
  New Singer makes a zigzag pattern. il por
    Bsns W p58-60+ N 22 '69
  New stitch for Singer. J. Poindexter. il por
    Duns R 93:28-32 Ja '69
KIRCHNER, Leon
  Musical events; Music for orchestra con-
    ducted by composer. W. Sargeant. New
    Yorker 45:147 O 25 '69
  New quartet player. I. Kolodin. por Sat R 52:
    45 Ag 30 '69
  Strings and electronics pack an emotional wal-
    lop. R. S. Brown. Hi Fi 19:104 O '69
  What's a composer, dad? P. D. Zimmerman.
    il por Newsweek 74:138 O 27 '69
KIRDIS. See Cameroon Republic—Native races
KIRK, David
  On the way to Emmaus. Commonweal 91:
    375-8 D 26 '69
                about
  Reporter at large. F. Du Plessix. New
    Yorker 44:40+ Ja 25 '69
KIRK, Edmund
  Where did the bedroom go? House B 111:
    38+ Je '69
KIRK, John J.
  New look for the standards program. por
    Camp Mag 41:6 Mr '69
                about
  Camping can be unique; address, 1969. por
    Camp Mag 41:3-11 Je '69
KIRK, Malcolm S.
  Journey into stone age New Guinea. il por
    Nat Geog 135:568-92 Ap '69
  New Guinea festival of faces. il Nat Geog
    136:148-56 Jl '69
KIRK, Russell
  From the academy. See issues of National re-
    view
  Nixon after six months. por(p27) N Y Times
    Mag p5 Jl 20 '69
KIRKLAND, Joseph Lane
  Heir apparent? Newsweek 73:92 My 26 '69
  Labor's Kirkland moves higher. America 120:
    639 My 31 '69
KIRKLAND college, Clinton, N.Y.
  Dormitories. il Arch Rec 145:140-1 Je '69
KIRKPATRICK, Clayton
  Administration of justice; halting the free
    press/fair trial debate; excerpts from ad-
    dress. Cur 108:39-42 Je '69
KIRKPATRICK, Curry
  College basketball (cont) Sports Illus 30:48-9
    Ja 27; 54-6 F 10; 48-9 Mr 3; 58+ Mr 10 '69
  Golf (cont) Sports Illus 30:54-5+ Ap 28; 64+
    My 12; 56-7 Je 16; 54 Jl 7 '69
  Tennis. Sports Illus 31:52-3 Ag 25 '69
KIRKPATRICK, Joel B.
  Microtubules in brain homogenates. bibliog
    Science 163:187-8 Ja 10 '69
KIRKPATRICK, John
  John Kirkpatrick: Concord revisited. D. W.
    Moore. por Am Rec G 35:546-7 Mr '69

KIRKPATRICK, Lyman B. Jr
  Spy with the old school tie. Trans-Action
    6:57-8 Ja '69
KIRKPATRICK, Ralph
  K. at the keyboard; performance of Scar-
    latti's sonatas in Alice Tully Hall. H. Saal.
    por Newsweek 74:133 N 24 '69
KIRKWOOD, Robert C.
  Robert C. Kirkwood of Woolworth; inter-
    view. por Nations Bsns 57:44-8 Jl '69
KIROV ballet
  American teacher in Leningrad: month at
    the Kirov's Vaganova choreographic tech-
    nicum. J. Anderson. il Dance Mag 43:24-7
    Ja '69
KIRRIN, Vincent J. and Rabowski, Joseph, Jr
  New plants need modernizing, too. Am
    City 84:110+ Jl '69
KIRSCHENBAUM, Gerry
  Sailing the waveless sea. Travel & Camera
    32:56-63 Ap '69
KIRSCHENBAUM, Lois
  Sweetest girl in New York. J. Weber. il por
    Opera N 33:26-7 Ap 19 '69
KIRSHENBAUM, Howard, and Simon, S. B.
  Teaching English with a focus on values.
    Engl J 58:1071-6+ O '69
KIRSHENBAUM, Jerry
  Boating. Sports Illus 31:44-5 Ag 11 '69
  Boxing's great white hoopla. Sports Illus 31:
    48-50+ Jl 21 '69
KIRSTEIN, George G.
  Trustee, resign! Nation 208:727-30 Je 9 '69
KIRVAN, John J.
  X equals what? Rating the new movie rat-
    ings. Cath World 210:15-18 O '69
KIRWAN, John D.
  School days; poem. Nat R 21:801 Ag 12 '69
KISHON, Ephraim
  First of the month. C. Amory. Sat R 52:4+
    My 3 '69
KISSINGER, Henry Alfred
  Kissinger primer on war and peace. News-
    week 74:23 D 22 '69
  New guidelines for foreign policy; excerpts
    from Agenda for the Nation. Cur 103:25-6
    Ja '69
                about
  At the President's elbow. P. Lisagor. Na-
    tions Bsns 57:17-18 Ag '69
  Autocrat in the action arena. D. Nevin. il pors
    Life 67:50-1+ S 5 '69
  Henry Kissinger: strategist in the White
    House basement. G. Astor. por Look 33:
    53-6 Ag 12 '69
  Kissinger plan for peace; Nixon's way out
    of Vietnam? U S News 66:26 Ap 7 '69
  Kissinger: the professor. R. B. Semple, jr.
    il por NY Times Mag p9+ Ag 3 '69
  Kissinger: the uses and limits of power. il
    pors Time 93:17-22 F 14 '69
  Kissinger to Rogers to Laird. il por News-
    week 73:35-6 Ap 21 '69
  Man with a pressure cooker job. il pors U S
    News 67:15-16 Jl 14 '69
  Managed propaganda, condoned disorder? J.
    Osborne. New Repub 160:10-11 My 10 '69
  Mr Nixon's professor. il pors Newsweek 74:
    21-5 D 22 '69
  Only power Kissinger has is the confidence of
    the President. P. Anderson. il por N Y
    Times Mag p 10-11+ Je 1 '69; Same abr.
    with title My only power is the confidence
    of the President. Read Digest 95:161-5 O '69
  Powerful Dr Kissinger. S. Alsop. Newsweek
    73:108 Je 16 '69
  Professor Bismarck goes to Washington. N.
    Beloff. por Atlan 224:77-82+ D '69
  Right of the individual vs. the right of the
    group. H. Sidey. il Life 66:4 My 9 '69
  TRB from Washington. New Repub 160:6 F
    22 '69
  Three in bloom. H. Brandon. Sat R 52:7-8
    Ag 2 '69
  Vietnam: the President's fading hope. J. Os-
    borne. New Repub 161:17-19 S 27 '69
  White House who's who. J. Osborne. New
    Repub 161:13-15 O 18 '69
  Who's making foreign policy for the United
    States? il por U S News 66:45-6 Ap 7 '69
KISTIAKOWSKY, George B.
  ABM; excerpt from statement. Science 163:
    1310 Mr 21 '69
                about
  Will the science brain bank go conglomer-
    ate? J. Lear. il por Sat R 52:41-4 Jl 5 '69
KISTNER, Robert W.
  Questions women ask most about the pill.
    Good H 168:78-9+ F '69
KIT air cushion vehicles. See Air cushion
  vehicles
KIT amplifiers. See Amplifiers
KIT boatbuilding. See Boatbuilding

KNIGHT, Mrs John W, Jr
Flower arrangements yesterday and today. il Horticulture 47:32-3 Mr '69
KNIGHT, Pamela
Design for sport (cont) Sports Illus 31:42-3 Ag 11; 60-1 O 6 '69
KNIGHTS and knighthood
See also
Chivalry
KNIGHTS of Columbus
Of many things. D. R. Campion. America 121: inside cover S 6 '69
KIPLING, Edward Fred
Well, if not DDT, then what? H. Higdon. il N Y Times Mag p26-7+ Ja 11 '70
KNISLEY, Phyllis E.
Dropout; poem. Engl J 58:1012 O '69
KNITTING
Knit an afghan in the gypsy spirit. il Good H 169:132+ S '69
Knitting patterns for living. T. M. Eckman. il Har Yrs 9:29-31 F '69
KNITTING machinery. See Textile machinery
KNIVES
All-purpose knives. il Consumer Bul 52:31-2 Je '69
Care of carving tools. Good H 169:204 N '69
Clam and oyster knife. il House & Gard 135:101 F '69
Garnishing knives. il House & Gard 135:130 Mr '69
Pocketknives. il Consumer Bul 52:22-6 S '69
KNOBS, Door. See Doorknobs
KNOBS, Drawer. See Drawer pulls
KNOCHE, H. and others
Allergenic component of a liverwort: a sesquiterpene lactone. bibliog Science 166: 239-40 O 10 '69
KNOCK-knees. See Leg
KNOETGEN, Jim
Traffic cop of the sky. C. Peet. il pors Pop Mech 130:104-7+ D '68
KNOPF, Terry Ann
Sniping a new pattern of violence? bibliog por Trans-Action 6:22-9 Jl; 5+ S '69
Violence and the press. Cur 107:36-47 My '69
KNOPOFF, L.
Upper mantle of the earth. bibliog Science 163:1277-87 Mr 21 '69
KNORR, Nathan H.
Witnessing the end. il por Time 94:62-3 Jl 18 '69
KNOTT, Bill
Pieces of a broken mirror. P. Zweig. Nation 209:20-2 Jl 7 '69
KNOTTING. See Macramé
KNOWLAND park zoo, Oakland, Calif. See Zoological gardens
KNOWLEDGE
See also
Education
Learning and scholarship
KNOWLEDGE, Sociology of
Knowledge is power. J. McDermott. Nation 208:458-62 Ap 14 '69
KNOWLEDGE, Theory of
Problem of Piaget. H. G. Furth. Commonweal 90:69-72 Ap 4 '69
KNOWLES, C. Harry
Do it yourself laser holography. Pop Electr 32:27-35+ Ja '70
Popular electronics exclusive experimenters' laser. Pop Electr 31:27-32 D '69
KNOWLES, Dick
Bucktailing for cohos. Outdoor Life 144:54-7+ S '69
KNOWLES, Edna
Capturing flower patterns with your camera. Horticulture 47:45 Jl '69
KNOWLES, John
Separate peace: meaning and myth. M. E. Mengeling. Engl J 58:1322-9 D '69
Truth about A separate peace. J. E. Devine. Engl J 58:519-20 Ap '69
KNOWLES, John H.
Man the A.M.A. cut down. pors Life 67:30-5 Jl 11 '69

about

AMA vs. Knowles. por Newsweek 73:68 Je 9 '69
Appointees fall down on the Hill. il por Bsns W p46-7 My 10 '69
Caught in a crunch: Secretary Finch. U S News 67:11 Jl 7 '69
Curious case of Dr Knowles. il por Time 94: 12-13 Jl 4 '69
Just what the doctor ordered? il por Newsweek 74:15-16 Jl 7 '69
NIH: another tight budget, fewer friends in high places. J. Walsh. il Science 164: 165-7 Ap 11 '69
Nixon-science gap. il por Sci N 95:451 My 10 '69
Party politics and public health. Bsns W p 164 My 17 '69

KNOWLES, S. H. and others
Galactic water vapor emission; further observations of variability. bibliog Science 166:221-4 O 10 '69
Spectra, variability, size, and polarization of H_2O microwave emission sources in the galaxy. bibliog Science 163:1055-7 Mr 7 '69
KNOWLES, Warren Perley
How to deal with campus chaos; interview. por U S News 66:31-3 Mr 3 '69
KNOWLTON, Kenneth C. See Harmon, L. D. jt. auth.
KNOWLTON, Perry
Rights and permissions; summary of address June 23, 1969. por Pub W 196:23-4 Ag 4 '69
KNOX, Arthur S.
Glacial age marsh, Lafayette park, Washington, D. C. bibliog Science 165:795-7 Ag 22 '69
KNOX, Clinton Everett
Black ambassador to Haiti. por Negro Hist Bul 32:28 N '69
KNOX, Gerald M.
Family health. See issues of Better homes and gardens
KNOX, John H.
Pope as Hamlet. Nat R 21:1058-60 O 21 '69
KNUDSEN, Semon Emil
L'affaire Knudsen. il por Newsweek 74:90 S 22 '69
At Ford, a corporate shake-up and Mr Knudsen goes out. il por U S News 67:26 S 22 '69
Behind the palace revolt at Ford. il por Bsns W p 138-41 S 20 '69
Public selects its transportation; address, January 15, 1969. Vital Speeches 35:279-82 F 15 '69
Why Knudsen was fired. il por Time 94:88+ S 19 '69
KNUDSON, Jerry W.
Thomas Jefferson and James Thomson Callender: the myth of Black Sally. Negro Hist Bul 32:15-19 bibliog(p22) '69
KOBAYASHI, Haruo. See Libet, B. jt. auth.
KOBLER, John
Second coming of Synanon. Sat Eve Post 242:32-4+ F 8 '69
KOBLICK, Freda
Freda Koblick. N. Znamierowski. il Craft Horiz 29:20-1 Ja '69
KOCH, Adrienne
Reform or revolution? Am Scholar 38:688+ Aut '69
KOCH, Edward I.
Excerpt from testimony before Housing and urban affairs subcommittee, July 23, 1969. Cong Digest 48:303+ D '69
KOCH, Kenneth
Change of hearts; an opera in one act. Harp Baz 102:180-1+ My '69
Sleeping with women; poem. Poetry 113:225-30 Ja '69

about

Comment. D. Lehman. Poetry 114:401-3 S '69
On verse. R. Whittemore. New Repub 161: 23 Ag 2 '69
KOCH, Roger
Grand tour. Space World F-12-72:16-17 D '69
KOCH, Stephen
Fiction and film: a search for new sources. Sat R 52:12-14+ D 27 '69
Warhol. New Repub 160:24-7 Ap 26 '69
KOCHMAN, Thomas
Rapping in the black ghetto. por Trans-Action 6:26-34 F '69
KOCIVAR, Ben
Six ways to make the going really great. Holiday 46:42-7 Jl '69
Sleek new private planes from across the seas. Pop Sci 195:88-91+ O '69
Your first flight on the fabulous 747. Pop Sci 195:76-9 D '69
KOCK, Reino
National assessment of educational progress, a diffusion study. bibliog f Sch & Soc 97:95-7 F '69
KODACHROME films. See Photography—Films
KODALY, Zoltán
Hary Janos, an entertainment with music. G. Movshon. Hi Fi 19:81-2 N '69
Recordings. M. Mayer. il Esquire 72:22+ D '69

Records:
Háry János. Opera N 34:36 Ja 10 '70
KODIAK hunting. See Bear hunting
KODL, Francis
Pediatrician talks to mothers about that all-important first year. Parents Mag 44:68-70+ Mr '69
KOEHLER, Charles R.
Bicycle trails of Cape Cod National Seashore. il Nat Parks 43:16-17 Ja '69

KOEHLER, Margaret H.
In the path of the Pilgrims. Travel 132:52-7 O '69

KOEHN, Richard K.
Esterase heterogeneity: dynamics of a polymorphism. bibliog Science 163:943-4 F 28 '69

KOENIG, Andrew
Face to face with a computer expert. por Seventeen 28:30 D '69

KOENIG, Duane
Magic of Malta. Travel 132:61-6 Ag '69

KOENIG, H. P.
Morocco's Atlantic coast. Travel 132:34-7+ O '69
Northern Ireland sampler. Travel 131:34-9 Je '69
Yugoslavia's Adriatic isles. Travel 131:56-8 Je '69

KOENIG, Harold
Acute axonal dystrophy caused by fluorocitrate: the role of mitochondrial swelling. bibliog Science 164:310-12 Ap 18 '69

KOENIG, Louis W.
Truman doctrine and NATO. bibliog f Cur Hist 57:18-23+ Jl '69

KOENIGSWALD, G. H. R. von
Peking man in the apothecary's shop: reprint. UNESCO Courier 22:76 Ag '69

KOEPPEN, Sheilah R.
Republican radical right. bibliog f Ann Am Acad 382:73-82 Mr '69

KOERNER, James D.
How schools can get better teachers; interview. por U S News 67:48-51 S 15 '69
Life and hard times of Parsons college. Sat R 52:53-5+ Jl 19 '69

KOERNER, Thomas F.
Interviewing: ask the right questions. Clear House 44:102-4 O '69

KOESTLER, Arthur
Man, one of evolution's mistakes? adaptation of address, September 1969. N Y Times Mag p28-9+ O 19 '69
Reports: Australia. Atlan 223:12+ Je '69
Reports: Fiji. Atlan 224:18+ O '69
Yogi and the commissar. N Y Times Mag p27-9+ O 5 '69

KOETHE, John
Boston is here, now. Art N 68:30-3+ S '69
Personal life; Satie's suits; Summer; Mission Bay; poems. Poetry 115:19-23 O '69

KOFFLER, D. and others
Antibodies to polynucleotides: distribution in human serums. bibliog Science 166:1648-9 D 26 '69

KOFSKY, Frank
Music of militancy. Commonweal 89:733-4 Mr 14 '69

KOH, Douglas
School libraries in Singapore. ALA Bul 63: 1596-9 D '69

KOHAK, Erazim V.
Czech church in limbo. Commonweal 90: 591-4 S 26 '69
Revolution, reformation, reform. Commonweal 91:378-82 D 26 '69

KOHLER, Carl
Live wire with a loot locator. Pop Electr 30: 45-9 Je '69

KOHLER, Peter F. and Müller-Eberhard, H. J.
Complement-immunoglobulin relation: deficiency of C'1q associated with impaired immunoglobulin G synthesis. bibliog Science 163:474-5 Ja 31 '69

KOHLER, Peter O. and others
Cortisol induction of growth hormone synthesis in a clonal line of rat pituitary tumor cells in culture. bibliog Science 166: 633-4 O 31 '69

KOHN, Hans
Agony of Peter's proud city. Sat R 52:28-9 F 1 '69

KOHN, Harold W. and Willmarth, T. E.
Metallic colloids in molten salts. bibliog Science 163:924-5 F 28 '69

KOKOSCHKA, Oskar
Love letters in pictures; decorated swanskin fans. il Time 93:70-3 Mr 14 '69

KOLÁŘ, Jiří
From pen to pastepot. il por Time 93:80 Mr 21 '69

KOLARS, John
Temptation of Anthony; poem. Commonweal 90:489 Ag 8 '69

KOLARS, John F.
Republic of Turkey. bibliog Focus 19:1-11 Ap '69

KOLBECK, Lisa
Justin was good; story. Seventeen 28:86-7 Ja '69

KOLER, Robert D. and others
Ontogeny of soluble and mitochondrial tyrosine aminotransferases. bibliog Science 163: 1348-50 Mr 21 '69

KOLKHOZ. See Collective farms—Russia

KOLLER, Ann Marie
American secondary student in the English university; address, November 1968. Engl J 58:719-25 My '69

KOLMAN, Ernest
Is space exploration worth while? Space World F-3-63:11-15 Mr '69

KOLODIN, Irving
Juilliard in transition. Sat R 52:65-7 Ap 26 '69
Music to my ears. See issues of Saturday review
Recordings in review. See issues of Saturday review
Recordings reports: miscellaneous LPs. See issues of Saturday review
Recordings reports: orchestral LPs. See issues of Saturday review
Santa Fe's operatic oasis. Sat R 52:39-40+ Ag 30 '69

KOLODNER, Ferne K. See Kravitz, S. jt. auth.

KOLODNEY, David. See Horowitz, D. jt. auth.

KOMBOLOI (worry-beads) See Beads

KOMEITO party. See Political parties—Japan

KOMER, Louis
Developers boost our water supply. Am City 84:85-6 Jl '69

KOMIVES, Margaret. See Whittaker, J. K. jt. auth.

KONER, Marvin
Bloomsday in Dublin; photographs. Holiday 45:40-5 Je '69

KONGO, Belgian. See Congo (Democratic Republic)

KONINGSBERGER, Hans
From book to film, via John Huston. Film Q 22:2-4 Spr '69

KONISHI, Gilbert
100 years of Japanese photography. Travel & Camera 32:113-16+ O '69

KONISHI, Masakazu
Hearing, single-unit analysis, and vocalizations in songbirds. bibliog Science 166:1178-81 N 28 '69

KONRAD, Adolf
Adolf Konrad writes about his painting, The anniversary. il Am Artist 32:30-1 N '68

about

Adolf Konrad: painter of the American scene. H. Gasser. il por Am Artist 32:26-32+ N '68

KONTARATOS, A. N.
(comp) Amazing 1865 moon shot of Jules Verne; excerpts from Verne's fantasy-Apollo reality. Look 33:74-8 My 27 '69

KONVITZ, Milton R.
Letter from Cornell, why one professor changed his vote. por N Y Times Mag p60-1 My 18 '69

KOOMEN, M. J. and others
Solar rocket observations on an eclipse day. Sky & Tel 37:356-7 Je '69

KOONTZ, Dean R.
What do editors mean when they say... sorry, but, the motivation is missing. Writers Digest 49:42-7 Mr '69

KOONTZ, Elizabeth Duncan
Needed: better teaching for slow learners. por Parents Mag 44:24 F '69
Profession and the media. por Todays Ed 58:17 F '69
Somebody needs you. por Ladies Home J 86: 74 O '69
Teen-agers speak out about sex; symposium; reply. Todays Ed 58:26 Mr '69

KOOPMAN John M.
Choosing binoculars. Motor B 123:62-5 F '69

KOOYMAN, Gerald L.
Weddell seal; with biographical sketch. Sci Am 221:12, 100-6 Ag '69

KOPECHNE, Joseph, family
Kopechnes: awaiting answers. il por Time 94:14 Ag 22 '69

KOPECHNE, Mary Jo
Autopsy hearing nears in the Teddy Kennedy accident. il U S News 67:11 S 29 '69
Blueprint for the inquest. C. Roberts. il Newsweek 74:20-2+ S 8 '69
Calling the witnesses. Time 94:19 Ag 29 '69
D.A. on the spot. il Newsweek 74:23-4 Ag 25 '69
Girl in Ted Kennedy's car. P. F Healy. Ladies Home J 86:66+ O '69
Girl next door. por Time 94:13A Ag 1 '69
Grief, fear, doubt, panic, and guilt. il por Newsweek 74:22-6+ Ag 4 '69
Inquest. il Newsweek 75:21-2 Ja 19 '70
Inquest set in Kennedy case. U S News 67:9 Ag 18 '69
Kennedy inquiry: it's to be secret. U S News 67:16 N 10 '69

KOPECHNE, Mary Jo—*Continued*
Kennedy ordeal. Nation 209:99-100 Ag 11 '69
Kennedy: reckoning deferred. Time 94:20-1 S 12 '69
Kennedy's legal future. il Time 94:34+ S 5 '69
Kennedy's time of trial; pre-inquest hearing. il por Newsweek 74:19-20 S 8 '69
Listening to the lawyers; inquest postponed. il Newsweek 74:26 S 15 '69
New light on Kennedy case? il U S News 67:11 S 8 '69
No autopsy. Newsweek 74:28 D 22 '69
On the record. Newsweek 74:39-40 N 3 '69
Order for an inquest. il Newsweek 74:27-8 Ag 18 '69
Plea for secrecy. il Newsweek 74:44 O 20 '69
Quiet inquest. il Newsweek 74:40 N 10 '69
Rehearsal for an inquest. il Time 94:16-17 O 31 '69
Rendezvous in Edgartown. Newsweek 75:18 Ja 12 '70
Ted Kennedy. New Repub 161:12 S 20 '69
Teddy Kennedy story; the new chapter. il U S News 67:30-1 S 15 '69
Tragedy on Chappaquiddick. E. M. Kennedy. il U S News 67:21-2 Ag 4 '69
Tragic turn for Teddy Kennedy. il por Newsweek 74:33-4+ Jl 28 '69
Two drownings. Chr Cent 86:1033 Ag 6 '69
Walk in Chappaquiddick. H. Bruno. il por Newsweek 74:20-2 Ag 11 '69
Who's who at the Kennedy inquest. il por Time 94:18-20 S 5 '69
Why the ferry is late. il Newsweek 74:23-4 S 1 '69
Wrong turn at the bridge. por Time 94:22 Jl 25 '69

KOPIT, Arthur
Indians. Criticism
America 121:432+ N 8 '69
Commonweal 91:185-6 N 7 '69
Dance Mag 43:30-1 D '69
Nation 209:485-6 N 3 '69
New Repub 161:24+ N 8 '69
New Yorker 45:149-50 O 18 '69
Newsweek il 74:137-8 O 27 '69
Sat R 52:24 Je 7 '69
Sat R il 52:55-6+ O 25 '69
Time il 93:96 Je 6 '69
Time il 94:68 O 24 '69
Vogue 154:58 N 15 '69

KOPKIND, Andrew
New culture of opposition. Cur 111:56-9 O '69

KORALL, Burt
B.G. at his best. Sat R 52:48-9 Mr 15 '69
Basie. Sat R 52:82-3 N 29 '69
Blood, sweat and tears. Holiday 46:39+ D '69
Can jazz-rock find happiness together? Sat R 52:42-3 Jl 12 '69
Desmond on Desmond. Sat R 52:102-3 S 13 '69
Realm of Mercer and Short. Sat R 52:66+ Ap 12 '69
Sinatra syndrome. Sat R 52:47+ F 8 '69

KORBONSKI, Andrzej
East Europe and the United States. bibliog f Cur Hist 56:200-5+ Ap '69
Warsaw pact. bibliog f por(back cover) Int Concil 573:5-73 My '69

KOREA
See also
United Nations—Korea

Union (proposed)
Signals from North Korea. B. Page. Nation 208:622-4 My 19 '69

KOREA (People's Republic)

Defenses
Electronic revolution; electronic surveillance by the Pueblo and the EC-121. New Repub 160:8-9 My 24 '69

Foreign relations
Asiatic Stalin who keeps on taunting U.S. U S News 66:14 Ap 28 '69
Behind North Korea's belligerence. il Time 93:24-5 Ap 25 '69
North Korea's new offensive. J. A. Kim. For Affairs 48:166-79 O '69
U.N. command in Korea submits report to the Security council; letter, with text of report. C. W. Yost. Dept State Bul 60: 497-9 Je 9 '69
Why North Korea risks war with U.S. il U S News 66:37-8 My 5 '69
See also
EC-121 incident, 1969
Pueblo incident, 1968

Politics and government
Asiatic Stalin who keeps on taunting U.S. U S News 66:14 Ap 28 '69
Behind North Korea's belligerence. il Time 93:24-5 Ap 25 '69

KOREA (Republic)
No war, no peace. il Time 93:31 My 2 '69
South Korea; success story in Asia. H. Sochurek. il Nat Geog 135:301-45 Mr '69
Success story in South Korea. E. Chapin. For Affairs 47:560-74 Ap '69
Why North Korea risks war with U.S. il U S News 66:37-8 My 5 '69
See also
Children—Korea (Republic)
Education—Korea (Republic)

Constitution
Constitutional change proposed. T. I. Moon. Chr Cent 86:1434-6 N 5 '69
Park stacks the cards; referendum on constitutional amendment. il Newsweek 74:58 O 27 '69

Foreign relations
President; C. H. Park's U.S. visit. il Newsweek 74:19 S 1 '69
President Nixon and President Park of the Republic of Korea hold talks at San Francisco; welcoming statement, exchange of remarks, toasts, together with joint statement, August 21 and 22, 1969. R. M. Nixon; C. H. Park. Dept State Bul 61:237-44 S 15 '69
South Korea and the US. A. Campbell. New Repub 160:9-11 Je 7 '69
We take the U.S. at its word; a Pacific power, here to stay. interview, ed. by K. M. Chrysler. C. H. Park. il U S News 67:23-5 Ag 25 '69

Industries
South Korea; success story in Asia. H. Sochurek. il Nat Geog 135:301-45 Mr '69

Politics and government
Full circle for Park. Time 94:29 O 24 '69
Lease on the Blue House. Time 94:33 Ag 8 '69
South Korea and the US. A. Campbell. New Repub 160:9-11 Je 7 '69
See also
Korea (Republic)—Constitution

Referendum
See Referendum

Religious institutions and affairs
World around us (cont) Chr Cent 86:164-5, 878 Ja 29, Je 25 '69
KOREA; story. See McGahern, J.
KOREA, NORTHERN. See Korea (People's Republic)
KOREAN dancing. See Dancing, Korean
KOREAN language

Alphabet
Completing 500 years of linguistic reform; dispensing with Chinese characters. il Sch & Soc 97:414 N '69

Writing
Completing 500 years of linguistic reform; dispensing with Chinese characters. il Sch & Soc 97:414 N '69
KOREAN war, 1950-1953

Peace and mediation
Whatever happened to peace talks with Korean reds? il U S News 67:14 N 10 '69
KOREANS
South Korea; success story in Asia. H. Sochurek. il Nat Geog 135:301-45 Mr '69
KORF, Willy
Willy Korf unsettles the steel goliaths. por Bsns W p68 Mr 29 '69
KORIYAMA, Naoshi
To P.M. on reading a commentary by P.M. on Hopkins' Spring; poem. Engl J 58:86 Ja '69
KORNBERG, Arthur
Active center of DNA polymerase. bibliog Science 163:1410-18 Mr 28 '69
What medicine can do for you; address, June 7, 1969. Vital Speeches 35:756-9 O 1 '69

about
Repairing the DNA. por Sci N 96:348-9 O 18 '69
KORNETSKY, Conan, and Eliasson, Mona
Reticular stimulation and chlorpromazine: an animal model for schizophrenic overarousal. bibliog Science 165:1273-4 S 19 '69
KORST, Donald R. See Clark, R. H. jt. auth.

KORTENAAR, Henry ten
Cardinals, thirty-five; aggiornamento. 0. Commonweal 90:277-9 My 23 '69
Divorce in the church through Italian eyes. Commonweal 89:696-8 Mr 7 '69
Synod of our discontent. Commonweal 91: 240-1 N 21 '69
Trial by headline. Commonweal 89:581-3 F 7 '69
Up against the Catholic wall. Commonweal 90:309-10 My 30 '69

KORTZ, Helen W.
Mini-tent keeps cabbage moths away. Org Gard & Farm 16:104-5 Ja '69

KORZYBSKI, Alfred
Un-isness of is. por Time 93:69 My 23 '69

KOSHETZ, Nina
Document of considerable value: Nina Koshetz. G. L. Mayer. por Am Rec G 35: 619 Ap '69
Historical records. A. Favia-Artsay. Hobbies 74:35+ My '69

KOSINSKI, Jerzy N.
From the other side of the moon. I. Howe. Harper 238:102-5 Mr '69

KOSMINSKY, Jane
Brief biography. S. Goodman. pors Dance Mag 43:68-9 My '69

KOSOK, Paul
Woven calendars of Peru; excerpt from Life, land, and water in ancient Peru. Sat R 53:109 Ja 10 '70

about
Their relics remain in the Americas; excerpt from Flights into yesterday. L. Deuel. il Sat R 53:105-8 Ja 10 '70

KOSSIN, Sandy
Interview with Sanford Kossin; ed. by H. Rogoff. il por Am Artist 33:54-9+ My '69

KOSTANTY, Raymond G.
IC color pattern generator. Radio-Electr 41: 44-5+ Ja '70

KOSTELANETZ, Richard
Fiddler (and drumbeater) of the new, new music. N Y Times Mag p30-1+ Mr 23 '69

KOSTROWISKY, Guillaume Apollinaire de. See Apollinaire, G. pseud.

KOSYGIN, Aleksei Nikolaevich
B and K: maintaining the status quo. il por Newsweek 74:45-6 O 27 '69
Battle inside the Kremlin. V. Zorza. Look 33:93-7+ Mr 18 '69
Surprise red summit after years of conflict. por U S News 67:11 S 22 '69
When good Communists get together. il por Newsweek 74:43 S 22 '69

KOTCHIAN, A. Carl
Two old friends who worked their way to first class. il por Fortune 80:80-1 Ag 1 '69

KOTLIAKOV, Vladimir Mikhailovich. See Avsiuk, G. A. jt. auth.

KOTLIER, Susan
Poem: I think sometimes. Mlle 69:300 Ag '69

KOTLOWITZ, Robert
Balanchine+girls=ballet. Holiday 45:54-7+ Mr '69
Performing arts. See issues of Harper's magazine
Rebel as writer. Harper 238:87-8+ Je '69
Taps at Utah Beach. Harper 239:104-12 O '69

KOTT, Jan
Shakespeare is not our contemporary. P. Cruttwell. Yale R 59:33-49 O '69

KOTZ, Nick
Hunger in America: let them eat words. Look 33:71 D 2 '69

KOUHOUPT, Rudy
Build this model walking-beam engine. Pop Mech 132:156-9+ Ag '69
Make this simple fixture to set boring bars accurately. Pop Mech 131:172-3+ Je '69
Open telescope travels with you. Pop Sci 195:138-42 Ag '69

KOUMANS, Alfred J. R.
Reaching the unmotivated patient. Ment Hy 53:298-300 Ap '69

KOUSSEVITZKY, Serge
Sixty-year-old controversy flares up again; Koussevitzky-Scriabin scandal. D. Cavallo; F. Bowers. il pors Hi Fi 19:54-61 Je '69

KOUTOUKAS, H. M.
Chamber theatre, touring living rooms. J. Gruen. Vogue 153:114+ Mr 1 '69

KOVACS, Malcolm
Who gives a damn? Nation 209:430-2 O 27 '69

KOVALY, Kenneth A.
What can you do with an avalanche of garbage? Sci Digest 66:70-3 Jl '69

KOWALCZYK, Robert
Teachers' advocate. Todays Ed 58:53-4 Ja '69

KOWALSKI, John J.
Music si, English no! poem. Clear House 44:205 D '69

KOZLICK, Joseph C.
Life in a Spanish boatyard. Motor B 123: 60-1+ F '69

KOZLOFF, Max
Art. Nation 208:347-8 Mr 17 '69

KOZLOWSKI, James
Creatures made from collapsed pots. Ceram Mo 17:16-19 O '69

KOZMETSKY, George
How a businessman ramrods a B-school. il por Bsns W p84-6 My 24 '69

KOZOL, Jonathan
Life book review. Life 67:10 Jl 25 '69

KRAAR, Louis
Southeast Asia builds for the post-Vietnam age. Fortune 80:76-80+ Ag 15 '69

KRACZKOWSKI, Philip
Sculpture of Philip Kraczkowski; with biographical sketch. il por Am Artist 33:42-8 Ag '69

KRAFT, Frank J.
Abstract stage settings. Design 70:14 mid-Wint '69

KRAFT, Ivor
Color in the classroom. Nation 208:71-3 Ja 20 '69
Second-class schools in a first-class power. Nation 208:669-71 My 26 '69

KRAFT, John A.
How to restring a tennis racket. Pop Mech 131:182-3+ Ap '69

KRAFT, Joseph
(ed) See Richardson, E. L. Under Secretary Richardson discusses Viet-Nam peace talks and U.S.-U.S.S.R. relations

KRAFT, Mike
Mission of Hope. Américas 21:29-35 S '69

KRAFT, Virginia
Hunting. Sports Illus 31:66+ O 6: 68-9 O 27: 64-6 N 10: 87-8 N 17 '69

KRAFT, William
True essence of percussion. A. Cohn. Am Rec G 35:1062-3 Jl '69

KRAHN, Fernando
Policeman's lot... il Atlan 223:100-2 Mr '69

KRAICER, Jacob, and others
Potassium, corticosterone, and adrenocorticotropic hormone release in vitro. bibliog Science 164:426 Ap 25 '69

KRAM, Mark
Blind man's buff. Sports Illus 30:68-72+ Mr 10 '69

KRAMER, Arthur
Kramer's korner. See issues of Modern photography

KRAMER, Hilton
Critic calls David Smith greatest of all American artists. N Y Times Mag p40-2+ F 16 '69
Emperor's new bikini. Art in Am 57:48-55 55 Ja '69
Etienne Hajdu. Art in Am 57:98-101 Mr '69
Rembrandt's vision, and ours. N Y Times Mag p32-5+ S 28 '69
Thirty years of the New York school. N Y Times Mag p28-31+ O 12 '69

KRAMER, Jack
Ethiopia's unknown war. Nation 209:104-6 Ag 11 '69

KRAMER, Jane. See Crapanzano, V. jt. auth.

KRAMER, Jerry
Death by inches; excerpt from Jerry Kramer's farewell to football; ed. by D. Schaap. Sports Illus 31:50-9 Ag 4 '69

KRAMER, Ken W.
By air, rail or water to an island park. por Am City 84:84-5 Ap '69

KRAMER, Lawrence
Miserere; poem. New Yorker 45:140 S 13 '69

KRAMER, Rita
Parent and child (cont) N Y Times Mag p97+ Mr 30: 77-8+ My 25: 93-4+ Je 8: 107+ S 7: 95+ N 2: 116+ D 7 '69

KRAMER, Victor A.
[Book reviews] Commonweal 90:211+ My 2 '69

KRAMER, William E.
How judgment came for the plumbing conspirators. A. T. Demaree. il Fortune 80:96-9+ D '69

KRANHOLD, Joseph F. and others
Renal fructose-metabolizing enzymes: significance in hereditary fructose intolerance. bibliog Science 165:402-3 Jl 25 '69

KRANNERT center for the performing arts. See Urbana, Ill.—Krannert center for the performing arts

KRANS, Olof
Prairie dream recaptured. D. G. Lowe. il pors Am Heritage 20:14-23+ O '69

KRANSER, Joel
Let's focus on the group. Sch Arts 68:8 Mr '69

KRANTZ, G. E. and others
Vibrio parahaemolyticus from the blue crab callinectes sapidus in Chesapeake Bay. bibliog Science 164:1286-7 Je 13 '69

KRAPF, Jim
Face to face with a contemporary Hercules. por Seventeen 28:68 Ag '69
KRATZ, Robert N.
Everyone has a sky. Clear House 43:349-50 F '69
KRAUS, Arthur James Israel
Kraus case. J. Deedy. por Commonweal 90: 354 Je 13 '69
KRAUS, Joseph Martin
Musical events; performance by Clarion concerts of funeral cantata for King Gustav III of Sweden. W. Sargeant. New Yorker 45:124-5 Mr 29 '69
KRAUSE, Harold A.
Selling a pitch to the pitchmen. il pors Bsns W p82-3 Je 21 '69
KRAUSE, Harry D.
Why bastard, wherefore base? bibliog f Ann Am Acad 383:58-70 My '69
KRAUSZ, Laszlo
Sketching in Israel. Am Artist 33:54-8+ Ap '69
KRAVITZ, Sanford, and Kolodner, F. K.
Community action: where has it been? Where will it go? Ann Am Acad 385:30-40 S '69
KREBS, Albert V. jr
American Catholic marriages and the church. Cath World 208:225-9 F '69
Justice for the rural poor. America 120:275-7 Mr 8 '69
KRECH, David
Man's participatory evolution. Cur 110:55-64 S '69
Psychoneurobiochemeducation; excerpts from address. PTA Mag 63:16-18 Ap; 6-8 My '69
KREH, Lefty
Training grounds for trout fishermen. Field & S 73:86-7+ Ap '69
KREIG, Raymond A.
Aerial photography: outdoor recreation. Parks & Rec 4:41-3 Ag '69
KREIGH, Helen D.
Censorship matters in Missouri; ed. by J. Krug. ALA Bul 63:570-2 My '69
KREIMER, Evered. See Mallas, J. H. jt. auth.
KREMS, Austria
Urban sites in Austria. J. Zykan. il Antiques 96:214-17 Ag '69
KREPS, Juanita M.
Time for leisure, time for work. Mo Labor R 92:60-1 Ap '69
KRESGE, S. S. company
Kresge's farewell. Newsweek 73:72+ F 3 '69
KRETTEK, Germaine, and Cooke, E. D.
ALA Washingon notes. See issues of Wilson library bulletin
Washington reports. See issues of ALA bulletin
KRETZ, Thomas
Backbiters; poem. Chr Cent 86:779 Je 4 '69
Old Tom's scruples; poem. Chr Cent 86:1449 N 12 '69
KREUTTNER, John
Herblock revisited. Nat R 21:1162-3 N 18 '69
KREY, Anne K. and Hahn, F. E.
Berberine: complex with DNA. bibliog Science 166:755-7 N 7 '69
KREYCHE, Gerald F.
Academic freedom and the Christian college. Chr Cent 86:1217-20 S 24 '69
KRICH, Percy
Education, servant of industry. Sch & Soc 97:280-1 Sum '69
KRIEBEL, Charles
His bazaar. Harp Baz 102:168-9 O; 103:144-5 N; 90-1 D '69; 72-3 Ja '70
KRIEBEL, Mahlon E. and others
Oculomotor neurons in fish: electrotonic coupling and multiple sites of impulse initiation. bibliog Science 166:520-4 O 24 '69
KRIEG, John G.
Purchasing guide for city employees. Am City 84:75+ Ja '69
Term purchasing cuts the purchasing cost. Am City 84:138 Jl '69
KRIEGEL, Leonard
Intellectual origins of Staughton Lynd. Commonweal 89:503-4 Ja 17 '69
Uncle Tom and Tiny Tim: some reflections on the cripple as Negro. Am Scholar 38:412-30 Sum '69
KRIEGER, Jane
Confrontation with a Harvard son. McCalls 96:67+ Ag '69
KRIEGER, Murray
Comment. M. L. Rosenthal. Poetry 114:130-2 My '69
KRIENDLER, Peter
Byline by Kriendler. por Travel & Camera 32:123 F; 20 Mr '69
KRILL, John
Try a self-weeding garden! Org Gard & Farm 16:28-9 Jl '69
You can grow the rare franklinia. House B 111:71+ S '69

KRING, James B.
Gardening without DDT. Horticulture 47: 22-3 N '69
Mulching with aluminum foil. Horticulture 47:27+ My '69
KRINOV, E. L.
New studies of the Sikhote-Alin meteorite shower. Sky & Tel 37:87-90 F '69
KRIPPENE, Urban M.
Marketing and capitalization; excerpts from address. Pub W 196:21-2 D 8 '69
KRISHNA MENON, Vengalil Krishnan
Return of the enemies. il por Time 93:35 My 23 '69
KRISHNA MURTI, C. R. and Brodie, A. F.
New light-sensitive cofactor required for oxidation of succinate by mycobacterium phlei. bibliog Science 164:302-4 Ap 18 '69
KRISLOV, Joseph. See Mead, J. F. jt. auth.
KRIST, Gary Steven
Manhunt by water. R. Marston. il Yachting 125:150 Mr '69
KRISTOL, Irving
American historians and the democratic idea; address. Am Scholar 39:89-104 Wint '69
Bilious sermon from a hero of the moral elite. Fortune 79:155-6 My 1 '69
Books & ideas. See issues of Fortune
Crisis behind the welfare crisis. Fortune 79: 227-8 Je '69
End of liberalism? Cur 103:6-15 Ja '69
Improbable guru of surrealistic politics. Fortune 80:191+ Jl '69
—and Weaver, Paul
Bad idea whose time has come; direct election of the President. N Y Times Mag p43+ N 23 '69
KRIVIS, Alan F. and Rabb, J. M.
Cuprous complexes formed with isonicotinic hydrazide. bibliog Science 164:1064-5 My 30 '69
KRIWANEK, Franz
Victor Spinski. Ceram Mo 17:24-5 O '69
KRIZ, Miroslav A.
Need for a reappraisal of American tax policies. Ann Am Acad 379:114-22 S '68
KROEKER, Russell
Electronic entrepreneur. il por Time 94:75A Jl 18 '69
KROLL, Alex
Last of the Titans. Sports Illus 31:106-8+ S 22 '69
KROLL, Ernest
Flood; poem. New Repub 162:38 Ja 3 '70
Homage to Frederick Law Olmsted; poem. Sat R 52:21 My 17 '69
KROLL, Judith
Poughkeepsie to New York; poem. New Repub 161:25 Ag 2 '69
Two poems: Textures; Dream of an antelope. Yale R 59:105-6 O '69
KRONAUER, Richard E. See O'Hare, M. jt. auth.
KRONENBERGER, Louis
Hadrian the seventh on stage and off. Atlan 223:62-5 Mr '69
Lady and the lion. Atlan 223:93+ Ja '69
Regency: a nine-year wonder. Atlan 224: 87-90 N '69
KRONMAN, Barry S. and others
Tumor-specific antigens detected by inhibition of macrophage migration. Science 165: 296-7 Jl 18 '69
KROOTH, Robert S. and others
Dihydroorotic acid dehydrogenase: introduction into erythrocyte by the malaria parasite. bibliog Science 164:1073-5 My 30 '69
KROPF, Richard Thomas
Thread of prosperity. S. Margetts. por Duns R 94:77-8+ S '69
KROSNEY, Herbert
Crossroads of Jerusalem. Nation 208:134-8 F 3 '69
TV comes to Israel. Nation 209:339-43 O 6 '69
KRUCKENHAUSER, Stefan
Infallible revelation by the pope of skiing. B. Ottum. il pors Sports Illus 30:24-6+ F 24 '69
KRUEGER, Arlin J.
Atmospheric absorption anomalies in the ultraviolet near an altitude of fifty kilometers. bibliog Science 166:998-1000 N 21 '69
KRUEGER, Edgar A.
Discord along the Rio Grande. J. C. Evans. il pors Chr Cent 86:397-400 Mr 26 '69
KRUEGER, Joseph J.
Computerized billing collects 98 per cent of the taxes. por Am City 84:115+ Ag '69
KRUEGER, Leo
U.S. bookselling: a European critique. Pub W 197:58 Ja 5 '70
KRUG, Judith F.
Intellectual freedom (cont) ALA Bul 63:320-1, 446-8, 570-2, 731-3, 1065-7 Mr-Je, S '69

KUNSTLER, William Moses—*Continued*
about
Few soft words for the rabble-rousers. C.
McCarry. il por Esquire 72:106-8+ Jl '69
Two for the show. il por Newsweek 74:41 N
10 '69
KUNTZ, I. D. jr, and others
Hydration of macromolecules. bibliog Science 163:1329-31 Mr 21 '69
KUPCINET, Irv
Wrigley bar. Holiday 45:18+ My '69
KUPFERBERG, Herbert
Bleeps in the night. Life 67:14 D 19 '69
Music; short reviews: records. See issues of
Atlantic
KUPFERMANN, I, and Kandel, E. R.
Neuronal controls of a behavioral response
mediated by the abdominal ganglion of
aplysia. bibliog Science 164:847-50 My 16 '69
KURGIN, Anatolii
Cosmonautics and space medicine. Space
World F-6-66:36-7 Je '69
KURLAND, C. G. See Birge, E. A. jt. auth.
KURTÉN, Björn
Continental drift and evolution; with biographical sketch. Sci Am 220:14, 54-64 Mr
'69
KURTZ, Emil S.
Trans-Pac: the race you sail by the
weather map. Weatherwise 22:185-9 O '69
KURTZ, Richard M.
Your body image: what it tells about you;
reprint. Sci Digest 66:52-5 Ag '69
KURTZ, Stephen A.
In the beginning was Kandinsky. Art N 68:
38-41+ My '69
KURZMAN, Dan
Japanese. Sat R 52:38+ N 15 '69
KUSCH, Polykarp
Polykarp Kusch; interview. New Yorker 45:
28-31 Mr 29 '69
KUSCH, R. W.
Sleep: Vienna: 11:46 p.m: poem. Yale R 59:
104-5 O '69
KUSHAN art. See Art, Kushan
KUSHAN empire
Great civilization of the Kushans. B. Gafurov.
il UNESCO Courier 22:4-13 F '69
KUSHMERICK, M. J. and Podolsky, R. J.
Ionic mobility in muscle cells. bibliog Science
166:1297-8 D 5 '69
KUTINA, Jan
Hydrothermal ore deposits in the western
United States: a new concept of structural
control of distribution. bibliog Science
165:1113-19 S 12 '69
KUTSCHER, Austin
Foundation of thanatology. Ment Hy 53:338-
9 Jl '69
KUTTNER, Robert L.
Recharging the peace movement. Commonweal
89:669-70 F 28 '69
Red and green in civil rights. Commonweal
90:535 S 5 '69
Shades of the past haunt an inaugural. Commonweal 89:576-8 F 7 '69
KUUSKOSKI, Helena
Magical world of trolls. G. Kent. il Read
Digest 95:215-16+ N '69
KUUSKOSKI, Martti
Magical world of trolls. G. Kent. il Read
Digest 95:215-16+ N '69
KUWAIT
Amir of Kuwait visits Washington: exchange
of greetings and toasts, with joint communique, December 11, 1968. L. B. Johnson;
Sabah al-Salim al-Sabah. Dept State Bul
59:691-5 D 30 '68
Kuwait: Aladdin's lamp of the Middle East.
J. E. Frazer. il Nat Geog 135:636-67 My
'69
See also
Petroleum industry and trade—Kuwait
KUZMA, Greg
In love with the bears; poem. New Yorker
45:48 Ap 12 '69
Looking for metaphor; poem. Commonweal 90:
393 Je 20 '69
My father and I steal an engine from a sawmill; poem. Poetry 114:368 S '69
KUZNETSOV, Anatolii Vasil'evich
I could no longer breathe. Time 94:30-1 Ag
8 '69
Why I left Russia. por Read Digest 95:73-8
N '69
about
Behind a desperate escape. Time 94:28 Ag
15 '69
Letter to Anatoly Kuznetsov. por Time 94:
49 D 5 '69
Salvation in Soho. il por Newsweek 74:30
Ag 11 '69
Soviet author's flight to the free word. il
por Time 94:29 Ag 8 '69

KWAKIUTL Indians
Indian giving. F. V. Grunfeld. il Horizon
11:46-7 Wint '69
KWASHIORKOR. See Deficiency diseases
KY. Nguyen-cao-. See Nguyen-cao-Ky
KYLE, Thomas
Decorative arts at the Newark museum. Antiques 95:838-41 Je '69
KYSAR, Robert
Toward a Christian humanism. Chr Cent
86:706-8 My 21 '69

L

L-dopa. See Dopa
LAPL. See Los Angeles public library
LARS (laboratory for agricultural remote sensing) See Purdue university, Lafayette, Ind.
—Laboratory for agricultural remote sensing
LC headings. See Subject headings
LDH (lactate dehydrogenase) See Dehydrogenases
LEAA. See United States—Justice, Department
of—Law enforcement assistance administration
LEADS (law enforcement automated data system) See Computers—Police applications
LEM (lunar excursion module) See Space vehicles—Landing systems—Moon
LIA (low income allowance) See Income tax—
United States
LM (lunar module) See Space vehicles—Landing systems—Moon
LPGA. See Ladies' professional golfers' association
LPIU. See Lithographers and photoengravers
international union
LSA (limited space charge accumulation) diodes. See Diodes
LSCA (Library services and construction act)
See Library laws and legislation
LSD
Afterflash! ed. by V. Whitman. J. Alison.
Read Digest 95:81-5 D '69
Biochemical clues to mental illness. G. Byinsky. il Fortune 80:124-7+ Jl '69
Drugs & the Caltech student; excerpts, with
editorial comment. il Chem 42:4, 13-14+ N
'69
LSD adapts to moon. America 120:643 My 31
'69
LSD and leukemia. Time 94:38 Jl 11 '69
LSD: autoradiographic study on the placental
transfer and tissue distribution in mice. J.
E. Idänpään-Heikkilä and J. C. Schoolar.
bibliog il Science 164:1295-7 Je 13 '69
Lysergic acid diethylamide: dissociation of its
behavioral and hyperthermic actions by
DL-α-methyl-p-tyrosine. A. Horita and A.
E. Hamilton. bibliog il Science 164:78-9 Ap
4 '69
Lysergic acid diethylamide: effects on the
developing mouse lens. J. K. Hanaway.
bibliog il Science 164:574-5 My 2 '69
Lysergic acid diethylamide: role in conversion of plasma tryptophan to brain serotonin (5-hydroxytryptamine) R. C. Lin
and others. bibliog il Science 166:237-9 O 10
'69
Painting under LSD. il Time 94:88 D 5 '69
What is LSD? questions and answers. il
Todays Ed 58:45-7 Mr '69
LSI (large scale integration) See Electronic
circuits—Integrated circuits
LTP. See American library association—Library technology program
LTV aerospace corporation. See Ling-Temco-
Vought. incorporated
LABANAUSKAS, Mindaugas, and others
Structural studies on transfer RNA: preliminary crystallographic analysis. bibliog Science 166:1530-2 D 19 '69
LABANOTATION. See Dance notation
LABARRE, Harriet
Days of our talented youth. McCalls 96:89+
S '69
Live alone and like it; 1969 style. McCalls
96:94+ My '69
Things we ate: or How did I live this long?
McCalls 96:86+ Je '69
LABASTILLE, Anne. See Hamilton, L. S. jt.
auth.
LABELING laws. See Labels—Laws and legislation

LABELS
If you can read this. .; bumper sticker mania. Chr Cent 86:1333 O 15 '69
Label's the clue to lawn seed. R. W. Schery. il Horticulture 46:21+ S '68
Practically speaking. V. Jaxon. Har Yrs 9:16 N '69
Sockeye, cling, & the Golden state; or, California labeled in the pantries of the world. R. Teiser. il Am West 6:20-5 Mr '69
Unit prices; grade-labeling. New Repub 161: 9 Jl 5 '69
See also
Wine labels

Laws and legislation
Caution: this hearing is hazardous; hearings on the cautionary warning on cigarette packages. il Newsweek 73:82-3+ Ap 28 '69
Neglected cure for phony price labels. Consumer Rep 34:493-4 S '69
Packaging and labeling; excerpts from address, October 9, 1968. F. J. Schlink. il Consumer Bul 52:27-8 Je; 15-17 Jl '69

LABIN, Suzanne
Kid-killers. Nat R 21:434-5 My 6 '69

LABÒ, Flaviano
Italian tenor: interview. ed. by F. Stevenson. por Opera N 33:16 F 8 '69

LABOR (obstetrics) See Childbirth

LABOR, Compulsory
My testimony; tr. by M. Gnoutcheff and R. Nacht. A. Marchenko. il Read Digest 95: 193-6+ Ag '69
Price of achievement under Castro; forced labor camps in Cuba. P. Kidd. Sat R 52: 23-4 My 3 '69

LABOR, Department of. See United States—Labor, Department of

LABOR absenteeism. See Absenteeism

LABOR agreements. See Trade agreements

LABOR and capital. See Industrial relations; Workmens compensation

LABOR and laboring classes
Foreign labor briefs. See issues of Monthly labor review
Politicizing the lower-middle. M. Novak. Commonweal 90:341-3 Je 6 '69
Ten most wanted men: the worker; address, March 14, 1969. K. M. Flake. Vital Speeches 35:441-4 My 1 '69
See also
Automobile factories—Employees
Church and labor
Coal miners
Farm labor
Hours of labor
Middle classes
Migrant labor
Skilled labor
Unemployment
Work
also headings beginning Industrial

Bibliography
Book reviews and notes. See issues of Monthly labor review

Education
Educational attainment of workers; with tables. E. Waldman. bibliog f il Mo Labor R 92:14-22 F '69

International aspects
See Trade unions—International aspects

Non-wage payments
See Non-wage payments

Political activities
See Trade unions—Political activities

Statistics
Current labor statistics. See issues of Monthly labor review
Effect of the census undercount on labor force estimates. D. F. Johnston and J. R. Wetzel. bibliog f il Mo Labor R 92:3-13 Mr '69
ILO at fifty; its role in improving labor statistics. H. Lacroix. bibliog Mo Labor R 92:47-50 My '69

Canada
See also
Trade unions—Canada

France
We're in no mood for barricades. il Bsns W p98 Je 14 '69
See also
Trade unions—France

Georgia
See also
Atlanta—Labor and laboring classes

Germany (Federal Republic)
See also
Trade unions—Germany (Federal Republic)

Great Britain
See also
Labor laws and legislation—Great Britain
London—Labor and laboring classes
Trade unions—Great Britain

Italy
See also
Trade unions—Italy

Japan
See also
Labor supply—Japan

New York (state)
Labor waste in New York: rural exploitation and migrant workers. W. H. Friedland. bibliog il Trans-Action 6:48-53 F '69; Reply. W. J. Haitigan. 6:64 My '69

Russia
Fire the workers? Newsweek 74:100+ O 27 '69
See also
Labor supply—Russia

Scandinavia
See also
Trade unions—Scandinavia

United States
A. Philip Randolph: labor's grand old man. P. Garland. il Ebony 24:31-4+ My '69
Blue collar white and the far right. G. Fackre. Chr Cent 86:645-8 My 7 '69
Labor in a year of expansion. B. V. Toth. Mo Labor R 92:11-19 Ja '69
Labor month in review. See issues of Monthly labor review
Labor trends 1969: spotlight on involvement. il Sr Schol 94:8 Ja 31 '69
Next decade for labor; face lifting and some new wrinkles. il Nations Bsns 57:44-6 N '69
Nixon and the new bourgeoisie; working class has become middle class. S. Alsop. Newsweek 73:96 Ja 27 '69
Perspectives on poverty; symposium. bibliog f il Mo Labor R 92:32-62 F '69
Research summaries. il Mo Labor R 92:66-8 F '69
Still forgotten: the working poor. D. Duggan. il Nation 208:724-6 Je 9 '69
Working poor; what libraries can do. K. Nyren. Library J 94:2989 S 15 '69
See also
American federation of labor and Congress of industrial organizations
Arbitration, Industrial—United States
Industrial workers of the world
Labor day
Labor laws and legislation—United States
Labor supply—United States
Negroes—Economic conditions
Negroes—Employment
Trade unions—United States
United States—Labor, Department of
Wages—United States

West Virginia
Strikers' lonely road; highway workers. il Bsns W p54+ S 27 '69

Yugoslavia
Yugoslavs to train for jobs in West? U S News 67:87 Ag 11 '69

LABOR and public welfare, Committee on. See United States—Congress—Senate—Labor and public welfare, Committee on

LABOR boards
See also
United States—National labor relations board

LABOR conferences
See also
International labor organization

LABOR contracts
Are employment contracts dead? M. F. Brdlik. il Duns R 93:32-3+ Ap '69
Nest egg is unscrambled; Polk's contract with MGM. Bsns W p63 Ja 10 '70
See also
Grievance procedures
Trade agreements

LABOR cost
High investment, bigger output; study on worker productivity. U S News 66:111 My 19 '69
Productivity and unit labor costs in 1968. S. W. Herman and L. J. Fulco. bibliog il Mo Labor R 92:11-15 Je '69

LABOR cost—*Continued*
Unit labor costs of iron and steel industries in five countries: France, Japan, the United Kingdom, United States, and West Germany; with tables. P. C. Jackman. Mo Labor R 92:15-22 Ag '69

LABOR courts
Australia's labor courts, model for U.S? U S News 66:84-5 F 10 '69

LABOR day
Labor day. H. Morgan. Sat R 52:18 Ag 30 '69
See also
May day (labor holiday)

LABOR discipline
Arbitrating the discharge and discipline of union officials. W. E. Baer. bibliog Mo Labor R 92:39-45 S '69
Why arbitrators reinstate discharged employees. M. Stone. il Mo Labor R 92:47-50 O '69

LABOR disputes
Now a rank-and-file revolt to worry unions and employers. il U S News 66:93-4 Mr 17 '69
See also
Arbitration, Industrial
Collective bargaining
Grievance procedures
Strikes
United States—Federal mediation and conciliation service
United States—National labor relations board

LABOR ethics
Politics. J. Leonard. il Esquire 71:10+ My '69

LABOR in politics. See Trade unions—Political activities

LABOR laws and legislation
Future of collective bargaining: close look by unions, employers. il U S News 66:91-3 My 26 '69
Nixon and the unions: can the honeymoon last? il U S News 66:82-4 Ap 21 '69
Toil and trouble. W. F. Buckley, jr. Nat R 21:88-9 Ja 28 '69
See also
Labor courts

Australia
Australia's labor courts, model for U.S? U S News 66:84-5 F 10 '69

Europe, Western
Union pact against U.S. auto invasion. U S News 67:79 D 22 '69

Great Britain
Britain facing taste of American labor law: white paper seeks to ease industrial strife. il Bsns W p72+ Ja 25 '69
British unions vs. U.S. firms; government's proposed laws to restrain wildcats. U S News 66:70-1 Mr 24 '69
Harold's hope; anti-strike law. il Newsweek 73:51+ Ap 28 '69
How long can Wilson last? reactions to Industrial reform bill. Newsweek 73:47-8 My 19 '69
Labor pains; anti-strike legislation shelved. Newsweek 73:52+ Je 30 '69
Mrs Castle's recipe. Time 93:63 Ja 31 '69
Wilson's about-face; anti-strike bill shelved. A. Howard. New Repub 160:7-8 Je 28 '69

Turkey
Factions of the Turkish labor movement differ over political role. B. H. Millen. bibliog Mo Labor R 92:31-5 Je '69

United States
Averting strikes; lawyers' plan. U S News 67:70-1 Jl 28 '69
Building industry: pattern for White House intervention? U S News 67:70-1 O 6 '69
Burger rulings on labor law. U S News 66:72 Je 9 '69
Can Nixon work with the unions? M. Seeger. Duns R 93:89-90+ Mr '69
Cause and the cure; the right to work; address. January 31, 1969. P. Fannin. Vital Speeches 35:293-5 Mr 1 '69
Changes coming in labor laws? U S News 66:95 Mr 17 '69
Curb on union democracy? the Pike bill on collective bargaining process. America 120:351 Mr 29 '69
Dock strike renews talk of tougher laws. il Bsns W p37 F 22 '69
Employee rights and union democracy; excerpt from Individual employee rights and union democracy. B. Aaron. Mo Labor R 95:50-2 Mr '69
How business hopes to change the Nation's labor laws; the Chamber of commerce proposals. U S News 66:68-9 Je 16 '69
How to live with Nixon, what union leaders say. il U S News 66:73-4 F 24 '69

Labor day, '69: some plain talk from George Meany; interview. G. Meany. U S News 67:77-8 S 8 '69
Nixon moves to slow down wage rises; here's the plan. il U S News 67:98-9 S 22 '69
Nixon's hands off policy; effect on unions, companies. il U S News 67:57-8 D 1 '69
Push for new strike law; movement to reform Railway labor act. il Bsns W p45-6 S 6 '69
Pushing to rewrite Labor relations act. Bsns W p50 O 11 '69
Readers' response: restraints unions need. Nations Bsns 57:80 Ja '69
Republicans and emergency strikes; anti-strike legislation. M. Seeger. il Duns R 93:81-2+ Ap '69
Review of state labor laws enacted in 1968. C. T. Sorenson. Mo Labor R 92:41-6 Ja '69
Significant decisions in labor cases. See issues of Monthly labor review
Unions and Nixon; harmony at the start. il U S News 66:62-3 Mr 3 '69
What Shultz inherits. il Bsns W p78 Ja 25 '69
What we need is a law. Nat R 21:15-16 Ja 14 '69
Will unions lose their political grip? il Nations Bsns 57:24-7 Ja '69
See also
Boycott
Insurance, Unemployment—United States
Workmen's compensation—United States

Taft-Hartley law
Dock strike renews talk of tougher laws; likelihood of major changes. il Bsns W p37 F 22 '69
Nixon plan for reform of Taft-Hartley. B. J. Masse. America 120:322 Mr 22 '69

LABOR leaders. See Trade unions—Officials

LABOR lobby. See Lobbying

LABOR-management relations. See Industrial relations

LABOR-management reporting and disclosure act of 1959. See Labor laws and legislation—United States

LABOR mobility
Job tenure: how it relates to race and age. E. J. O'Boyle. bibliog il Mo Labor R 92:16-23 S '69
See also
Occupational mobility

LABOR officials. See Trade unions—Officials

LABOR output. See Labor productivity

LABOR party (Great Britain)
Applications, not suppliants. Time 94:38+ O 10 '69
Choice for socialism. R. Moore. Commonweal 90:363+ Je 13 '69
Harold Wilson's sound pound. A. Howard. New Repub 161:13-14 N 15 '69
How long can Wilson last? Newsweek 73:46-8 My 19 '69
Labor v. labor. Time 94:35-6 S 19 '69
Labor's chance: some unlikely Tories. K. Ovenden. Commonweal 91:348-9 D 19 '69
Odd and ugly noises from the Labor party. A. Howard. New Repub 160:13-14 Mr 8 '69
Parlement of fooles; party conference. A. Waugh. Nat R 21:1063+ O 21 '69
Why one British Socialist turned conservative. J. Braine. il N Y Times Mag p24-5+ Mr 2 '69; Discussion. p 16 Mr 23 '69
Will Britain turn right? P. Rowley. il Chr Cent 86:806-7 Je 11 '69
Young and angry talent. M. C. Shefftz. Nation 208:720-4 Je 9 '69

LABOR productivity
As I see it; American workers more productive than Europeans; interview. E. F. Denison. il Forbes 104:48-50 Jl 1 '69
Evaluating statistics on productivity. J. W. Kendrick. Mo Labor R 92:54-5 Ap '69
High investment, bigger output; study on worker productivity. U S News 66:111 My 19 '69
New inefficiency; with editorial comment. il Bsns W p45, 188 S 20 '69
Productivity and unit labor costs in 1968. S. W. Herman and L. J. Fulco. bibliog il Mo Labor R 92:11-15 Je '69
Productivity rises as radio-TV output triples in eight years. J. E. Henneberger. il Mo Labor R 92:40-2 Mr '69
Productivity; tables. See issues of Monthly labor review
Pygmalion in management; excerpts from High expectations in management. J. S. Livingston. bibliog f il Harvard Bsns R 47:81-9 Jl '69
Report on productivity increases in the auto industry. C. Myslicki. il Mo Labor R 92:37-9 Mr '69

LABOR racketeering. See Racketeering

LABOR relations act, 1935. See Labor laws and legislation—United States

LABOR relations board, National. See United States—National labor relations board

LABOR saving devices
Take it easy. J. Polshek. See issues of House beautiful

LABOR statistics. See Labor and laboring classes—Statistics

LABOR statistics, Bureau of. See United States—Labor statistics, Bureau of

LABOR supply
Now. a monthly survey of jobs. U S News 66:65 F 3 '69
See also
Manpower
Unemployment

Europe, Western
Rising threat to west Europe: shortage of labor. il U S News 66:64-5 Ap 7 '69

Japan
Japanese head for a bout with inflation. il Bsns W p67-8 D 6 '69

Russia
Getting more output from fewer comrades. Bsns W p38-9 N 1 '69

United States
Employment effect of a new industry in a rural area. I. Gray. bibliog il Mo Labor R 92:26-30 Je '69
Employment patterns and place of residence. H. J. Hilaski and H. M. Willacy. bibliog f il Mo Labor R 92:18-25 O '69
How good were manpower projections for the 1960's. S. Swerdloff. il Mo Labor R 92:17-22 N '69
Human resource myopia. R. L. Brummet and others. Mo Labor R 92:29-30 Ja '69
Labor market report from the Boston ghetto; excerpt from Ghetto labor markets and manpower programs. P. B. Doeringer. Mo Labor R 92:55-6 Mr '69
Micro data in manpower study. M. S. Cohen. Mo Labor R 92:53-4 Ap '69
New directions in area labor force statistics; with charts and tables. H. V. Stambler. bibliog Mo Labor R 92:3-9 Ag '69
Persons not in the labor force: who they are and why they don't work; with charts and tables. P. O. Flaim. bibliog Mo Labor R 92:3-14 Jl '69
Reducing skill shortages in construction. E. Weinberg. bibliog f il Mo Labor R 92:3-9 F '69
See also
Education and manpower

LABOR turnover
Labor turnover rates; tables. See issues of Monthly labor review
Reducing skill shortages in construction. E. Weinberg. bibliog f il Mo Labor R 92:3-9 F '69
See also
Labor mobility
Occupational mobility

LABOR unions. See Trade unions

LABORATORIES
See also
Criminological laboratories
Medical laboratories
Photographic laboratories
Reading laboratories
Sandia laboratories
Testing laboratories
Underwater laboratories

Architecture
Flexible research laboratory complex for Inland steel. il Arch Rec 146:114-18 Jl '69
Lab for light: Center for advanced visual studies at MIT. il Arch Forum 130:62-3 My '69
Technique for designing the laboratory: user requirements and the development of alternatives. il Arch Rec 146:136-41 Ag '69
Tower expand research complex; Philip Morris research center. il Arch Rec 145:122-5 F '69

LABORATORIES, Government
Fort Detrick: redeployment? A. Hamilton. Science 166:1490 D 19 '69
Keeping track of a national asset. Sci N 95: 162-3 F 15 '69
See also
Atomic research laboratories
United States—Naval radiological defense laboratory

LABORATORY animals
Mouse stage of the new biology. R. W. Stock. il N Y Times Mag p8-9+ D 21 '69
Not even good rats; highly inbred white rats for reliable research. B. J. Culliton. il Sci N 95:145-6 F 8 '69
What do rats prove? il Time 93:64 F 21 '69
See also
Animal experimentation
Germfree life
also names of laboratory animals, e.g. Rats

LABORATORY for agricultural remote sensing. See Purdue university, Lafayette, Ind. —Laboratory for agricultural remote sensing

LABORATORY glassware. See Glassware, Laboratory

LABORATORY method
Set of attitudes; social studies laboratory at Enfield high school, Conn. K. Branan. Sat R 52:67 Ap 19 '69

LABORDE, Harold
Boat for world cruising. il Yachting 125:70-1+ My '69

LABRADOR
See also
Churchill Falls

LABRADOR dogs
All-around dog? L. J. Bashline. il Field & S 74:178-80+ O '69

LABRADOR retrievers. See Labrador dogs

LA BREA, Los Angeles
Death trap of the ages. J. R. MacDonald. il Nat Wildlife 7:24-9 Ag '69
Ice age dig in Hancock park and you are invited. il Sunset 143:58+ O '69
Radiocarbon dating of petroleum-impregnated bone from tar pits at Rancho La Brea, California. T. Y. Ho and others. bibliog il Science 164:1051-2 My 30 '69

LABYRINTHODONTS. See Amphibia, Fossil

LABYRINTHS
Knossos in the Catskills; largest maze in the world. il Time 94:48 Ag 15 '69

LACANILAO, Flor
Teleostean urophysis: stimulation of water movement across the bladder of the toad bufo marinus. bibliog Science 163:1326-7 Mr 21 '69

LACEWINGS
They feed on garden pests. il Sunset 143:142-3 Jl '69

LACH, Alma
On the trail of the white truffle. Travel & Camera 32:31-2+ Ag '69

LACHANCE, Leo E. and Degrugillier, Maurice
Chromosomal fragments transmitted through three generations in oncopeltus (hemiptera) bibliog Science 166:235-6 O 10 '69

LACHENBRUCH, David
Looking ahead. See issues of Radio-electronics

LACKEY, Lionel
Battle of Baby Doe. Opera N 33:9+ Mr 8 '69

LACOMBE, Olivier
Landmarks in an extraordinary life. UNESCO Courier 22:6-12+ O '69

LA COSTA, Calif. See Health resorts, watering places, etc.

LACOSTE, Catherine
Super keen-o show by la grande Catherine. R. Blount, jr. por Sports Illus 31:54-5 Ag 25 '69

LACOSTE, Michel Conil-. See Conil-Lacoste, M.

LACQUER and lacquering
Revival of an ancient art. il House & Gard 136:140-1+ O '69

LACROIX, Henri
ILO at fifty: its role in improving labor statistics. bibliog Mo Labor R 92:47-50 My '69

LACROIX, Jorge Gurría. See Gurría Lacroix, J.

LACROSSE
Assault and battery of lacrosse. R. Lardner. il Holiday 45:66-7+ Ap '69
Big sticks of the Midwest; Midwest lacrosse association. P. Carry. il Sports Illus 30:84-5 My 5 '69
Into combat with sticks, for more than a title; Army-Navy match. P. F. Putnam. il Sports Illus 30:30-1 Je 9 '69
Little brother of war. il Life 66:49-56 Ap 18 '69
Old boys are still best; photographs by R. De Carava; with account by G. Ronberg. Sports Illus 30:36-41 Mr 31 '69

LACTALBUMIN. See Albumins

LACTATE. See Lactic acid

LACTATE dehydrogenase. See Dehydrogenases

LACTATION
See also
Luteotropin
Suckling

LACTIC acid
Anxiety: the cheap neurosis for everyone. R. Signor. il Sci Digest 65:65-70 Je '69
Biochemistry of anxiety. F. N. Pitts, jr. il Sci Am 220:69-75 F '69
Drugs fight anxiety neurosis. Sci Digest 65: 58-9 My '69
LACTOGENIC hormone. See Luteotropin
LACTONES
Allergenic component of a liverwort: a sesquiterpene lactone. H. Knoche and others. bibliog il Science 166:239-40 O 10 '69
See also
Nepetalactone
LACTOSE synthetase. See Synthetases
LACY, Alex B. jr
White House staff bureaucracy. por Trans-Action 6:50-6 Ja '69
LACY, Edward A.
Electronic piano. Electr World 82:40-1+ N '69
Electronic type composition. E. A. Lacy. il Electr World 82:34-6 D '69
Omega, a V.L.F. radionavigation system. Electr World 82:47-9+ D '69
Static electricity, space age gremlin; reprint. Sci Digest 65:62-6 F '69
LA DANY, Louis
Religion in red China. America 120:282-3 Mr 8 '69
Revolution in China's power structure. America 121:8-9 Jl 5 '69; Excerpts. Cur 109:46-8 Ag '69
LADD, Everett Carll, jr
Professors and political petitions. bibliog Science 163:1425-30 Mr 28 '69
LADDERS
Bargain ladders, will they be safe? il Consumer Bul 52:31-2 O '69
Over the stile to the neighbors. il Sunset 142:146 My '69
LADENSON, Alex
Chicago: the public library reaches out. Wilson Lib Bul 43:875-81 My '69
LADER, Lawrence
Why birth control fails. McCalls 97:74-5+ O '69
LADIES' professional golfers' association
Put on your bracelets, Kathy is here. C. Kirkpatrick. Sports Illus 30:64+ My 12 '69
LADIMER, Irving
What did you say? Har Yrs 9:38-43+ Ag '69
You can't wait for probate. Har Yrs 9:38-42 My '69
LADOF, Nina Sydney
Freedom to read: a battlefield report, the censor knocks; address, June 1969. ALA Bul 63:903-5 Jl '69
LADUE, Mo.
Time enough to read; Horton Watkins high school. G. Stanford. il Sr Schol 94:Schol Teach 13+ Ap 18 '69
LADYBIRDS
Have your own bug-in! M. C. Goldman. il Org Gard & Farm 16:59-64 Ag '69
LADYBUGS. See Ladybirds
LAETSCH, W. M. See Boasson, R. jt. auth.
LA FARGE, Henry A.
Quiet Americans. Art N 68:34-5+ N '69
LA FARGE, Phyllis
Sweet sound of silence. Redbook 133:75+ S '69
LA FAY, Howard
Eisenhower story. Nat Geog 136:1-39 Jl '69
LAFAYETTE, Dick
VW flywheel gefixen. Hot Rod 22:100-1 Je '69
LAFAYETTE, Marie Joseph Paul Yves Roch Gilbert du Motier, marquis de
Lafayette in the French revolution, by L. Gottschalk and M. Maddox. Review Sat R 52:35 Jl 12 '69. L. Gershoy
LAFEBER, Walter
Before Pearl Harbor. Cur Hist 57:65-70+ Ag '69
LAFITTE, Jean Pierre
Gourmet pirate. il por Time 94:18 D 19 '69
LA FOND, Richard
Antigens and antibodies are studied by their diffusion patterns in agar. Sci Am 221:248-50+ S '69
LAFRANCHI, Robert. See Martinez, T. M. jt. auth.
LAGARRIGUE, Jean. See Goude, J.-P. jt. auth.
LAGEMANN, John Kord
Hearing is a way of touching. Read Digest 95:107-10 Ag '69
Self-fulfilling prophecy, a key to success. Read Digest 94:80-3 F '69
LAGERKVIST, Pär
Brats and bayonets: the rhetorics of the Children's campaign. A. H. Bell. bibliog f Engl J 58:1038-41 O '69

LAGERSTROEMIA indica. See Crape myrtle
LAGO, C. Mesa-. See Mesa, Lago, C.
LAGOONS, Manure. See Manure lagoons
LAGOS, Thomas
Summa cum velocitate. por Time 93:45 Je 27 '69
LAHAYE, P. A. and Epstein, Emanuel
Salt toleration by plants: enhancement with calcium. bibliog Science 166:395-6 O 17 '69
LAHR, Bert
Notes on a cowardly lion, by J. Lahr. Review
New Repub 161:20+ D 20 '69. S. Kauffmann
Newsweek por 74:123-123A+ N 24 '69. G. Wolff
Sat R por 52:31-3 N 15 '69. W. Kerr
Vogue 156:78 Ja 15 '70. A. West
LAHR, John
Reflections on the machine. Craft Horiz 29: 22-5+ Ja '69
LAI Ying
Escape. R. A. Gross. Newsweek 74:126+ N 24 '69
LAIBSON, Peter R. and Damiano, V. V.
X-ray and electron diffraction of ocular and bone marrow crystals in paraproteinemia. Science 163:581-3 F 7 '69
LAIDLAW, Angus
ATV with muscles. Mech Illus 65:48-9 N '69
LAING, Alexander
Fair Dartmouth. Nation 209:35-6 Jl 14 '69
LAING, Ronald David
Metaphysician of madness. il por Time 93: 64+ F 7 '69
Remarkable Ronald Laing. B. Inglis. por Vogue 154:132-3+ S 15 '69
LAINOFF, Harold M.
EMR campers gain from regular camp. Camp Mag 41:24-5 F '69
LAIRD, Charlton
Language: what to do about a drop-in; address, November 1968. Engl J 58:1199-205 N '69
LAIRD, Melvin R.
Dilemma for defense; excerpts. Aviation W 91:11 S 1 '69
Laird's official report on Vietnam: the basic problem remains; statement, March 19, 1969. U S News 66:35 Mr 31 '69
Power people; interview, ed. by F. Trippett. por Look 33:24+ Ag 26 '69
Role of defense; excerpts from address. Aviation W 90:17 My 5 '69
Secretary Laird urges Hanoi to release U.S. prisoners of war; statement, May 19, 1969. Dept State Bul 60:484 Je 9 '69
Trouble spots in the world; as Laird sees them; excerpts from testimony, July 15, 1969. por U S News 67:8 Jl 28 '69
What's the answer to ABM and the war? interview. pors U S News 66:30-6 Ap 7 '69
about
ABM counterattack. New Repub 160:9-10 Ap 12 '69
Defense. por Sci N 95:109-10 F 1 '69
How Laird is taking hold at the Pentagon. por U S News 66:12 Mr 3 '69
Kissinger to Rogers to Laird. il por Newsweek 73:35-6 Ap 21 '69
Laird has not lowered his voice. J. Duscha. il pors N Y Times Mag p 10-11+ Je 29 '69
Laird lowers sights on Pentagon spending. por Bsns W p36 Mr 22 '69
Laird plan. M. Parker. il Newsweek 73:44 Je 2 '69
Laird takes hard line with defense complex; with editorial comment. il Bsns W p82+. 182 My 10 '69
Managed propaganda, condoned disorder? J. Osborne. New Repub 160:10-11 My 10 '69
Mel the knife. il por Newsweek 74:38 N 10 '69
Mr Laird's stiffer posture. R. Hotz. Aviation W 90:11 Mr 24 '69
Negotiator and the confronter. por Time 93: 26-7 Ap 4 '69
Nixon says yes to arms talks; with report by L. Norman. il Newsweek 73:28-9 Je 23 '69
Nixon's dilemma in the war; defense secretary's visit. il U S News 66:30 Mr 17 '69
Political pro at the Pentagon. J. Cameron. por Fortune 79:116-10+ Ap '69
Politician at the Pentagon. il por Time 94:13-15+ Ag 29 '69
Pre-emptive strike. il por Newsweek 74:22B S 1 '69
Secretary Laird: on the other side of the table. por Time 93:13 Mr 28 '69
Strongman takes hold in top Pentagon job; with editorial comment. il por Bsns W p 110-12+, 156 Ap 19 '69
Waiting it out; pilgrimage to South Vietnam. il por Newsweek 73:42 Mr 24 '69

LAIRD, Melvin R.—about—*Continued*
  War: Nixon's big test. il por Newsweek 73:
    20-2 Mr 31 '69
  What Secretary Laird learned in Vietnam.
    il U S News 66:26-7 Mr 24 '69
  Who is Melvin Laird? K. Hess. por Ramp
    Mag 8:27-31 Ag '69
LAIRD, W. David, Jr
  Overdue. por Wilson Lib Bul 43:669+ Mr '69
LAISSEZ faire. See Free enterprise
LAITY
  Misplaced ministry of the laity; conflict in
    lay-clergy relations. Chr Cent 86:243 F 19
    '69; Discussion 86:523 Ap 16 '69

Catholic church

  Challenge of collegiality. W. L. Doty. Amer-
    ica 121:358-60 O 26 '69
  Coming into maturity; National association
    of laymen. D. Grumbach. Commonweal 90:
    429-30 Jl 11 '69
  Permanent diaconate program; workshop at
    Collegeville. D. Durken. America 121:140-1
    S 6 '69
  Tomorrow's Christian, by E. Marciniak. Re-
    view
      Commonweal 90:571 S 19 '69. J. A. Mc-
        Dermott
  Worcester survey; study of Vatican II's
    effect on the laity. J. P. Jurich. America
    120:649-51 My 31 '69
LA JOLLA, Calif.
  Riviera of the American West. C. Brossard. il
    Holiday 46:50-3+ Ag '69
LAKE, Alice
  Advice to women who are once-a-month
    witches. Redbook 132:94+ Ap '69; Same
    abr. Read Digest 95:117-20 Ag '69
  Does driver education save lives? McCalls
    97:153+ N '69
  How high can secretaries' salaries go?
    McCalls 96:95+ My '69
  Now that he's home again. McCalls 96:44-5+
    Ja '69
  Obesity. Seventeen 28:128-9+ O '69
  Questions you don't ask your doctor; with
    answers. Seventeen 27:108-9+ D '68
  VD: the greatest threat to teen-age health.
    Seventeen 28:146-7+ My '69
  What can be done about colds. Seventeen
    28:134-5+ F '69
  When the next bug bites, it may not be love.
    Seventeen 28:174-5+ Ap '69
LAKE COUNTY, Ill.
  U.S. journal: reactions to future Sentinel anti-
    ballistic missile system site for Chicago. C.
    Trillin. New Yorker 44:100-6 F 15 '69
LAKE ERIE. See Erie, Lake
LAKE ERIE islands. See Erie, Lake
LAKE GENEVA, Wis.

Hotels, restaurants, etc.

  Playboy: allusions to city tastes in a coun-
    try setting. il Arch Rec 146:128-9 D '69
LAKE GEORGE opera festival. See Music fes-
    tivals—New York (state)
LAKE HAVASU CITY, Ariz.
  How to build a river in the Arizona desert to
    flow under the London bridge. W. Robbins.
    il Esquire 71:78-83+ F '69
  Westward ho the station wagons; London
    bridge is going up in Arizona. D. Butwin.
    il Sat R 52:39-41 F 8 '69
LAKE HEMET. See Lakes—California
LAKE KINZUA. See Lakes, Artificial
LAKE LUGANO. See Lugano, Lake
LAKE MANYAS. See Manyas, Lake
LAKE MENDOCINO. Calif. See Lakes, Artificial
LAKE MICHIGAN. See Michigan, Lake
LAKE MOHONK. See Mohonk, Lake
LAKE OF THE OZARKS
  Elegance comes to the Ozarks; developers
    go after big spenders. il Bsns W p 104-5
    Ag 2 '69
LAKE ONTARIO. See Ontario, Lake
LAKE pollution. See Water pollution
LAKE POWELL. See Lakes, Artificial
LAKE shores. See Water fronts
LAKE SUPERIOR. See Superior, Lake
LAKE TAHOE. See Tahoe, Lake
LAKE trout fishing. See Trout fishing
LAKE WINNEBAGO, Mo.
  Concrete streets constructed in stages. J.
    Hart. il Am City 84:104+ My '69
LAKERS (basketball team) See Basketball
  teams

LAKES
  Nitrogen fixation in some anoxic lacustrine
    environments. P. L. Brezonik and C. L. Har-
    per. bibliog il Science 164:1277-9 Je 13 '69
  Strontium-90 concentration factors of lake
    plankton, macrophytes, and substrates. Z.
    Kalnina and G. Polikarpov. bibliog il Sci-
    ence 164:1517-19 Je 27 '69
    See also
  Water pollution

Temperature

  Temperatures and related factors in lakes.
    D. W. Webster. il Cons 24:12-16+ D '69
    (to be cont)

California

  Desert dwellers cool off here; Lake Hemet. il
    Sunset 143:21 Ag '69
    See also
  Tulare Lake

Finland

  Land of the endless lakes. D. Butwin. il Sat
    R 52:33-4 Ag 2 '69

Germany

  Königssee is a lake of surprises. il Sunset
    142:65 Ap '69
LAKES, Artificial
  Gravel+refuse=recreation; development of
    a lake in DuPage County, Ill. H. C. John-
    son. il Parks & Rec 4:46-8+ S '69
  Kinzua Lake development. J. J. Lindsey. il
    Cons 23:2-5 Ap '69
  Lake Mendocino: the fishing's improving. il
    Sunset 142:66 Ap '69
  Lake Powell; a spectacular test ground for
    Glastron's vagabond. D. Fales. il Pop Mech
    131:126-9+ F '69
  Lament for a lost Eden: Lake Powell. E.
    Porter. il Am Heritage 20:60-1 O '69
  New lakes: the beautiful and the dammed.
    H. R. Williams. il Parks & Rec 4:12-14+ N
    '69
  Regional water supply; Rend Lake conser-
    vancy district. R. D. Jones and J. W.
    Rezek. il Am City 84:108+ Mr; 73-5 Ap '69
    See also
  Kariba Lake
  Lake of the Ozarks
  Reservoirs
LAKESIDE buildings. See Building sites
LALANNE, François Xavier
  François-Xavier Lalanne; don't forget the
    stuffing. N. Lyon. Vogue 155:85 Ja 1 '70
L'ALLEMAND, Gordon
  Boysenberries, without the birds. por Org
    Gard & Farm 16:50 Ap '69
  Four-family garden co-op. Org Gard & Farm
    16:28-31 O '69
  Meyer lemons, garden treasure. Org Gard &
    Farm 16:108-9 Ja '69
  They garden in the darnedest places. Org
    Gard & Farm 16:43-5 Je '69
  Tiller makes it possible. Org Gard & Farm
    16:35-7 My '69
LALLY, Vincent E. and others
  Superpressure balloon flights in the tropical
    stratosphere. bibliog Science 166:738-9 N 7
    '69
LA LUPE
  Latin bombshell. P. D. Zimmerman. por
    Newsweek 74:128 O 13 '69
LA LUZ, N.Mex.
  La Luz, N.Mex. il Arch Forum 131:66-71 Jl '69
LA MAMA ETC (Experimental theater club)
  See New York (city)—Theater
LAMB, Howard
  Role playing. Todays Ed 58:67-8 Ja '69
LAMB, Willis E. Jr
  Operational interpretation of nonrelativistic
    quantum mechanics; adaptation of address,
    July 3, 1968. bibliog por Phys Today 22:23-
    8 Ap '69
LAMB (meat)
    See also
  Cookery—Meat

Marketing

    See Meat—Marketing
LAMBARÉNÉ
  Lambaréné revisited; Albert Schweitzer hos-
    pital. N. Cousins. il Sat R 52:28-32 O 4 '69
LAMBERG-KARLOVSKY, C. C.
  Selected aspects of archaeology, 1964-1968.
    bibliog f Ann Am Acad 379:132-50 S '68
LAMBERT, Darwin
  Escape to the Channel Islands. Nat Parks
    43:4-7 Ap '69
  Patterns in National parks association his-
    tory. Nat Parks 43:4-8 My '69
LAMBERT, John
  Politics and uranium. Sci N 95:438 My 3 '69

LAMBERT, William
Fortas of the Supreme court: a question of ethics and the stock manipulator. Life 66:32-7 My 9 '69
Murky men from the Speaker's office. Life 67:52-4+ O 31 '69
about
Coming to Life. il por Newsweek 73:95 My 19 '69

LAMBERT DE ORTIZ, Elisabeth
Versatile pot-au-feu. House & Gard 135:93-5+ F '69
World of curries. House & Gard 136:158-9+ S '69

LAMBOT, Jean Louis
What do you know about ferro cement? J. Smith. il Yachting 125:84-6+ Ap '69

LAMBRAKIS, Grigorios
J'accuse. R. Gelatt. Sat R 52:28 D 13 '69

LAMBRECHT, Dora. See Lambrecht, F. L. jt. auth.

LAMBRECHT, Frank L. and Lambrecht, Dora
Victorian fashions at the edge of the Kalahari; with biographical sketches. pors Natur Hist 78:4. 48-51 Mr '69

LAMBRIGHT, Donald
Black power casualties. J. R. Coyne, jr. Nat R 21:701 Jl 15 '69

LAMBS
Getting organic lamb to the public. B. T. Hunter. il Org Gard & Farm 16:70-3 Ag '69

LAME duck period. See Presidents—United States—Transition periods

LAMEL, Ellen
Face to face with a female mail carrier. por Seventeen 28:38 N '69

LA MESA, Calif.
Galleries and museums
Mini-museum of mom art. S. A. Parvin. il Hobbies 74:117-18 Jl '69

LAMM, John
Instant replay. il Motor T 21:78-9 D '69

LAMM, Michael
Bill Lear's steam car. Pop Mech 131:128-31+ Ar '69
Smile! You just got a ticket. Pop Mech 132:73-6+ D '69
Used cars. See issues of Motor trend

LAMMEY, W. Clyde
Homeowners' clinic; questions and answers. See issues of Popular mechanics
PM's handsome hall clock. Pop Mech 132 124-9 O; 176-80+ N '69

LAMONICA, Daryle
Just call him super Daryle. E. Shrake. il pors Sports Illus 32:36-41 Ja 5 '70
Lamonica's moveable feast: he was the main dish. R. F. Jones. il Sports Illus 32:17-19 Ja 12 '70

LAMONT-Doherty geological observatory. See Columbia university—Lamont-Doherty geological laboratory

LAMONT-HAVERS, Ronald W.
NIH grants cover page charges: letter. Science 163:622 F 14 '69

LAMOTT, Kenneth
Few hazards of the good life. Horizon 11:26-9 Spr '69
Marathon therapy is a psychological pressure cooker. N Y Times Mag p28-9 +Jl 13 '69

LAMOUREUX, C. E. See Waite. P. J. jt. auth.

LAMP cords. See Electric cords

LAMP flashers. See Electric lighting—Control

LAMP shades
Translucent lampshade. il Mech Illus 65:82 D '69

LAMPE, John M.
Look-in at the athletic program. PTA Mag 64:6-8 bibliog(p35) O '69

LAMPERT, Fritz, and others
Herpes simplex virus: dry mass. bibliog Science 166:1163-5 N 28 '69

LAMPS
How to make a mushroom light. il Sunset 143:84 D '69
How to make an extra camper lamp. R. K. Wallace. il Pop Sci 195:60 S '69
Make a lamp on your lathe. J. Capotosto. il Mech Illus 65:109+ O '69
Shopping tips; desk and study lamps. il Changing T 23:19-20 O '69
See also
Lighting fixtures
History
Cut glass and other lamps by Libbey. C. U. Fauster. il Hobbies 74:116-17+ D '69

LAMPS (light airborne multi-purpose system)
See Helicopters—Military applications

LAMPSHADES. See Lamp shades

LAMSON, Merle E.
Are we bandwagoneers? bibliog ALA Bul 63:1278-9 O '69

LANCASTER, Donald E.
Build the Popular electronics Universal frequency counter. Pop Electr 30:33-5+ Mr; 41-5 Ap '69
How IC logic circuits work. Radio-Electr 40:32-6 My '69
Paleomagnetism & archeomagnetism. Electr World 82:23-6+ S '69
Psychedelia 1. Pop Electr 31:27-35+ S '69
Thermoluminescence, theory & applications. Electr World 81:43-6 Mr '69

LANCASTER, Wilbert C. Jr
Yes! Bert is in, with go power. R. Blount, jr. il por Sports Illus 30:34-6+ Mr 3 '69

LANCASTER, Pa.
Tinkertoy houses: town houses. il Arch Forum 130:96-9 Ja '69

LAND, Edwin Herbert
Polaroid; market value of its stock. il por Forbes 103:34-6+ Je 15 '69

LAND, Irene Ellen (Stokvis) See Stokvis. I. E.

LAND, Thomas
Hydroelectric battle plan. Nation 208:598 My 12 '69
Race relations in England. Nation 208:116 Ja 27 '69

LAND
See also
Land utilization
Regional planning

Taxation
See Property tax; Real property—Taxation

Hawaii
Big and growing rush to buy land. il U S News 67:72-3 N 10 '69

Maryland
Planning against progress. J. T. Starr. il Am For 75:24-7+ Mr '69

New York (state)
Why dam the Charlotte? H. S. Kernan. il Am For 75:28-31+ N '69

United States
See also
Public lands—United States

LAND between the lakes national recreation area. See Recreation areas

LAND clearing. See Clearing of land

LAND companies. See Real estate business

LAND crabs. See Crabs

LAND drainage. See Drainage

LAND fills. See Filling (earthwork); Municipal dumps

LAND grant colleges
See also
Alaska. University
Washington, D.C. Federal city college

LAND management, Bureau of. See United States—Land management, Bureau of

LAND of the free; drama. See Block, B.

LAND planning. See Land utilization

LAND pollution. See Soil pollution

LAND reclamation. See Reclamation of land

LAND slides. See Landslides

LAND speculation
Land law's fine print trips up developers; housing act of 1968 aimed at interstate land sales. il Bsns W p 184+ Ap 26 '69

LAND tenure
See also
Homestead law

Alaska
Alaska: share the oil. D. Henninger. New Repub 160:15-17 Je 28 '69
Divvying up Alaska; natives claims bill. S. Brent. New Repub 161:11-13 D 13 '69
North Slope: oil rush. L. J. Carter. il Science 166:85-92 O 3 '69; Reply. F. F. Wright. 166:1220+ D 5 '69
Northwest Passage to what? J. Lear. il Sat R 52:55-6+ N 1 '69

Dominican Republic
Dominican bishop and president clash over land reform. Chr Cent 86:312 Mr 5 '69

Iraq
Land reform in modern Iraq. R. A. Fernea and E. W. Fernea. bibliog il Focus 20:9-12 O '69

Latin America
Agrarian reform in Latin America. F. M. Foland. For Affairs 48:97-112 O '69

LAND tenure—*Continued*

Rhodesia

Lame wife; legal fight between Chief Tangwena and European owners of neighboring Gaeresi ranch. Newsweek 73:46-7 Mr 10 '69

United States

La Raza: Mexican Americans in rebellion. J. L. Love. bibliog il Trans-Action 6:35-41 F '69

Vietnam (Republic)

Land for South Viet Nam's peasants. il Time 94:29 Jl 11 '69

Land reform in Vietnam. R. L. Prosterman. il Cur Hist 57:327-32+ D '69

LAND use. See Land utilization

LAND utilization

Competition will be fierce for future shares of land. R. Preston. il Nations Bsns 57:80-1+ S '69

Destiny of the public lands. J. B. Craig. il Am For 75:19 D '69

Disney imperative. W. Marx. Nation 209:76-8 Jl 28 '69

From the floor; questions and answers. il Am For 75:40-1 D '69

Future of multiple use; address. J. S. Bethel. il Am For 75:32-4+ D '69

Grazing lands must be restored; reprint. J. B. Craig. Am For 75:6-7 Ja '69

How much is enough? address. E. L. Peterson. il Am For 75:24-7 D '69

Living memorials, open space gifts. W. C. Kennedy. il Parks & Rec 3:39-40 O '68

Mike Frome. M. Frome. Am For 75:3+ Jl; 7+ D '69

Planning against progress. J. T. Starr. il Am For 75:24-7+ Mr '69

Rights or privileges? address. P. E. Terzick. il Am For 75:28-30+ D '69

Tightened landscape. W. H. Whyte. il Horizon 11:66-73 Sum '69

Tip from the conqueror: Soviet and American uses of land. J. T. Younger. Nation 208:275-6 Mr 3 '69; Same abr. with title Land to live in; do we need a new Domesday book? Cur 107:48-51 My '69

Uncle Sam's step-child acres. C. H. Stoddard. il Am For 75:16-19+ S '69

Why dam the Charlotte? H. S. Kernan. il Am For 75:28-31+ N '69

Wilderness and the American. A. Netboy. il Am For 75:12-15+ Ap '69

See also

City planning

History

Forestry and the public domain; a Mexican point of view; address. E. Beltran. il Am For 75:36-7+ D '69 (to be cont)

LAND values

Best land values: questions and answers. C. Norcross. House B 111:66-7+ F '69

Put your money in the ground. T. Irwin. Am Home 72:38+ N '69

LANDAIS, Hubert

Mini-monuments. bibliog Art N 67:30-3+ N '68

LANDAU, Jacob

Jacob Landau on art, etc; with paintings. Ramp Mag 8:20 O '69

about

Walter Kaufmann on Jacob Landau. W. Kaufmann. Ramp Mag 8:20 O '69

LANDAUER, Ali A. and others

Alcohol and amitriptyline effects on skills related to driving behavior. bibliog Science 163:1467-8 Mr 28 '69

LANDAZURI, Margarita

Young voices on advisory committees. Am Ed 5:26 Ag '69

LANDEGGER, Karl Francis

Paper mill king tries home market. il por Bsns W p 136-8 Mr 29 '69

LANDER, Toni

Toni Lander and Bruce Marks: on and off stage; interview, ed. by B. Coffey. pors Dance Mag 43:34-9+ Ag '69

LANDERS, Ann, pseud.

Men vs. women and vice versa; excerpts from Ann Landers says: truth is stranger... Read Digest 94:59-62 Mr '69

LANDFILLS. See Filling (earthwork); Municipal dumps

LANDING areas

Moon

See Moon—Surface

LANDING gear, Airplane. See Airplanes—Landing gear

LANDLORD and tenant

How we played monopoly in Washington, D.C. J. Viorst. il Redbook 133:94-5+ Jl '69

Now it's rent strikes. il U S News 67:31-3 O 20 '69

Rent strikes: poor man's weapon; Harlem rent strikes. M. Lipsky. il Trans-Action 6:10-15 F '69

Something new in student strikes; rent strike by University of Michigan students. D. Zwerdling. New Repub 160:13 My 31 '69

Tenants put the heat on the landlord. il Bsns W p72-3 N 8 '69

Tenants' revolt in Ann Arbor. N. C. Mills. Commonweal 91:294-5 D 5 '69

LANDMAN, Hedy Backlin-. See Backlin-Landman, H.

LANDMAN, Phyllis

Free-form coiling. Sch Arts 69:18-19 Ja '70

LANDMARKS, Literary. See Literary landmarks

LANDMARKS preservation commission. See New York (city)—Landmarks preservation commission

LANDO, Barry

It's a gas! New Repub 160:17-18 Je 28 '69

News you won't find in Brazil's newspapers. New Repub 161:11-12 Ag 2 '69

Save-our-air. New Repub 161:11-12 O 11 '69

LANDON, H. C. Robbins

Colin Davis: a man for The seasons. Hi Fi 19:73-4 Jl '69

LANDON, Kenneth P.

North Vietnam today and tomorrow. bibliog f Cur Hist 56:77-81+ F '69

LANDREAU, Anthony N. See Pickering, W. R. jt. auth.

LANDS, Public. See Public lands

LANDSCAPE; drama. See Pinter, H.

LANDSCAPE architecture

As the landscape architect sees it. P. Jewell, 3d. Horticulture 48:26-7 Ja '70

House spectacular. il House & Gard 135:100-9 My '69

See also

Landscape gardening

Study and teaching

Students involved in project at foot of Mendenhall glacier. F. Oehmichen and L. J. Reader. il Parks & Rec 4:50-2 S '69

LANDSCAPE design. See Landscape architecture

LANDSCAPE gardening

For a more livable landscape. il Home Gard 56:70-1 F '69

Garden happening took just three years. il Sunset 142:78-81 Je '69

Gardening for cliff dwellers. E. Kondonellis. il Am Home 72:38 Mr '69

House transformed by plants. L. Heitzman. il Home Gard 56:56-7 N '69

How retaining walls and raised beds do useful landscape jobs for you. il Sunset 143:238-9 O '69

In Mission Viejo they landscaped with old railroad ties. il Sunset 143:110-11 O '69

Landscaping. L. Grove. il Bet Hom & Gard 47:36-7 O '69

Logistics of building a secluded garden. House & Gard 135:170+ Ap '69

Secluded garden. il House & Gard 135:142-5+ Ap '69

Sunny garden: answer to the problem of all sun and no shade. il House & Gard 135:98-9+ Je '69

Two-faced garden: dignified in public, relaxed in private. il Sunset 142:256 My '69

Ways to beautify your farmstead. G. Logsdon. il Farm J 93:51 Ap '69

See also

Cemeteries

Evergreens

Garden design

Garden pools

Garden steps

Gardens

Gardens, Japanese

Golf courses

Home grounds

Landscape architecture

Lawns

Parks

LANDSCAPE improvement

Gravel+refuse=recreation: development of a lake in DuPage County, Ill. H. C. Johnson. il Parks & Rec 4:46-8+ S '69

To beautify America. See issues of Home garden & flower grower to August 1969

Urban oasis: Flower avenue park: Silver Spring, Md. S. D. Golub. il Parks & Rec 4:31-2 F '69

LANDSCAPE painting
Art; exhibition of T. Cole's art at the
Smithsonian. L. Alloway. Nation 209:158 Ag
25 '69
In pursuit of antiquity; exhibition of Wang
Hui's works. K. Kuh. il Sat R 52:60-2 O 4
'69
John F. Kensett, 1816-1872. J. Howat. il An-
tiques 96:397-401 S '69
Joseph Lee. Painter. A. P. Erskine. il An-
tiques 95:806-11 Je '69
Keep out of the mud! C. Waugh. il Am Artist
33:32-9 Je '69
Rediscovery: Van Dearing Perrine. J. I. H.
Baur. il Art in Am 57:76-9 Ja '69
Worthington Whittredge, artist of the Hud-
son River school. E. H. Dwight. il Antiques
96:582-6 O '69

Study and teaching
'Scapes, land, sea and city. A. Zaidenberg.
il Design 70:8-11 Spr '69

LANDSCAPE photography. See Photography—
Landscapes

LANDSCAPE protection
Arrogance toward the landscape: a problem
in water planning; excerpts from address,
September 4, 1969. R. L. Nace. il Bul Atom
Sci 25:11-14 D '69
Halting the highway men; urban highways
run into barriers. Bsns W p37 Jl 19 '69
How you can save the land we love. M. A.
Guitar. Am Home 72:75-6+ Mr '69
LaAdonoi haaretz umloah. . . ; excerpt from
address. J. Weinstein. il Am For 75:25+
My '69
Landscape esthetics. L. B. Leopold. il Natur
Hist 78:36-45 O '69
Must this be lost to the sight of man? pro-
posed dams, Snake River. M. Frome. il
Field & S 74:52-5+ Jl '69
Planning against progress. J. T. Starr. il
Am For 75:24-7+ Mr '69
Preservation and conservation. C. A. Con-
naughton. Am For 75:8 Mr '69
Threatened America. il Life 67:32-43 Ag 1;
58-61+ S 5; 126-7+ O 10; 88-93 N 14 '69
Turn-around year. M. A. Guitar. il Am Home
72:54+ N '69
War with the slobs. R. Starnes. Field & S
73:30+ Mr '69
We can save out towns. C. Mangel. Look
33:50 N 4 '69
White Cloud peaks; a time for decision. D. B.
Clement. il Am For 75:28-31+ S '69
See also
Conservation of resources
Landscape architecture
Regional planning
Roadside improvement

Awards, prizes, etc.
Holiday awards for a beautiful America. Holiday 45:28-9 My '69

Alaska
Alaska. M. Nadel. Liv Wildn 33:1 Spr '69
Cutting the inside Passage; letter. D. Butch-
er. Am For 75:63 Jl '69; Reply. J. B. Craig.
75:46-8 S '69
Letter from the Arctic. S. Wright. il Liv
Wildn 33:4-6 Spr '69

LANDSLIDES
Mounting danger to homes: floods, quakes
and slides. il U S News 67:78-9 D 15 '69
Mud bath; southern California declared a
disaster area. il Newsweek 73:24 F 10 '69
Southern California's trial by mud and water.
N. T. Kenney. il Nat Geog 136:552-73 O '69

LANDSVERK, George
Mexico. Bet Hom & Gard 47:17-22 D '69

LANDSVERK, Jean
Mexico. Bet Hom & Gard 47:17-22 D '69

LANDY, Edward
Dealing with disruptive pupils. PTA Mag
63:19-21 bibliog(p37) Mr '69

LANE, Belden C.
Yes, Virginia there is a God; poem. Chr
Cent 86:1608 D 17 '69

LANE, Margaret
(ed) See Menninger, C. W. What wives can
do to solve the communication problem

LANE, Mills B. 1912-
Georgia cracker's crackerjack bank. R. Loving, jr. il pors Fortune 80:134-7+ N '69
Georgia's biggest bank wades into the slums.
il por Bsns W p90-1 My 24 '69

about
Seed money in Georgia. il por Time 93:106
My 23 '69

LANE, Will
Should you buy a camera abroad? Travel
131:26 My '69
Vagabond camera. See issues of Travel

LANE COUNTY, Ore.
Encephalitis started the program of mosquito control. J. C. Stoner. il Am City
84:102+ Ap '69

LANG, Cynthia
Experiment in creativity. Parents Mag 44:
56-7+ S '69
Opinion: black friend. por Mlle 68:32+ Ap '69

LANG, Daniel
Reporter at large (cont) New Yorker 45:61-
4+ O 18 '69

LANG, Gerald E. See Oppenheimer, J. R. jt.
auth.

LANG, Kenneth R.
Interstellar scintillations of pulsar radiation.
bibliog Science 166:1401-3 D 12 '69

LANG, Mike
Mike Lang (groovy kid from Brooklyn) plus
John Roberts (unlimited capital) equals
Woodstock. R. Reeves. il por N Y Times
Mag p34-5+ S 7 '69; Reply. K. Roberts.
p54 O 5 '69

LANG, Nikolaus
Jig-saw sculpture. J. Hayes. il pors Design
70:12-13 mid-Wint '69

LANG, Paul Henry
Bach's B minor mass, does the concentus
musicus' authenticity make musical sense?
No. por Hi Fi 19:77-8 Jl '69
Critic answers his critics. Hi Fi 19:22 N '69
From Germany; an English music drama.
Hi Fi 19:83-4 N '69
Handel's Chandos anthems: ceremonial music
that makes a glorious sound. Hi Fi 19:65-6
Ap '69
Leinsdorf's Mozart, a feast for the ear.
Hi Fi 19:100 N '69
Pair of early cello concertos, luminously per-
formed. Hi Fi 19:92 S '69
Solomon as king of England and Handel's
only Christian oratorio. Hi Fi 19:75-7 My
'69

LANG, Pearl, dance company. See Pearl Lang
dance company

LANG, Sidney B.
Elastic coefficients of animal bone. bibliog
Science 165:287-8 Jl 18 '69

LANG, Warren R. and Feinstein, Phylis
What is a cervical erosion? Redbook 134:31
N '69

LANGDON, James J.
String-saver strikes back. Good H 168:56+
Mr '69

LANGDON, Jesse D.
Before the colors fade: last of the Rough
Riders; interview, ed. by V. C. Jones. por
Am Heritage 20:42-3+ Ag '69

LANGDON, Tom
10-second trip; interview. por Motor T 21:
39-40+ O '69

LANGE, Dale L. See Birkmaier, E. M. jt. auth.

LANGE, Norman J.
Johns Hopkins bookshop comes of age. Pub
W 196:73-4 N 17 '69

LANGE, Paul W. See Hydén. H. jt. auth.

LANGE, Victor
Thinking poetically. Atlan 223:138-41 Mr '69

LANGE, Walter. See Fifer, B. jt. auth.

LANGENBACH, Randolph
City no one knew. Arch Forum 130:84-91 Ja
'69

LANGENHEIM, Jean H.
Amber: a botanical inquiry. bibliog Science
163:1157-69 Mr 14 '69

LANGER, Don
Edit your travel films. Travel & Camera 32:
84-7 Je '69
Love that lens! Travel & Camera 32:110-11+
F '69
Shoot a story with one cartridge. Pop Phot
64-114-15+ Mr '69
Title your travel movies. Travel & Camera
32:121-5+ O '69
Zoom? Pop Phot 64:114-15+ My '69

LANGER, Elinor
Oakland seven. Atlan 224:76-82 O '69

LANGER, Henry C. Jr
What do you know about engine maintenance. Yachting 125:72-3+ Ap '69

LANGER, John B.
How's your memory of the good old days?
Har Yrs 9:18 My '69

LANGEWIESCHE, Wolfgang
Great American river cleanup. Read Digest
94:213+ My '69
Suburbs are changing. Read Digest 95:157-
62+ N '69

LANGFORD, Anna Riggs
Mrs Langford for the defense; reprint L.
Rockey. il pors Ebony 24:57-8+ Mr '69

LANGFORD, Arthur
Passion vine can be started now. Home Gard
56:68 S '69

LANGFORD, James J.
New case for Galileo. Cath World 208:259-60 Mr '69
LANGGUTH, A. J.
San Francisco state. Harper 239:99-100+ S '69
Vietnam: how do we get out? Sat Eve Post 242:19-21+ F 8 '69
LANGHAM, Maurice
Progress on glaucoma. il Newsweek 74:115-16 D 8 '69
LANGLAND, Joseph
Getting ready to really leave; poem. New Yorker 45:32 Ag 30 '69
LANGLEY, Lester D.
Military commitments in Latin America: 1960-1968. bibliog f Cur Hist 56:346-51+ Je '69
LANGS, Helen
Changelings; poem. Good H 169:198 O '69
LANGTON, Daniel J.
Today begins the week of her birthday; poem. Sat R 52:34 Jl 12 '69
LANGUAGE, Artificial
See also
Esperanto
LANGUAGE and culture
End of culture; with quotations. J. Thompson. Commentary 48:46-52 D '69
LANGUAGE and languages
Books; Chomskian revolution in linguistics. G. Steiner. New Yorker 45:217-18+ N 15 '69
Language universals: a research frontier. J. H. Greenberg. bibliog Science 166:473-8 O 24 '69
See also
Children—Language
Rhetoric
Semantics
Sign language
Slang
Style, Literary
Translations and translating

Etymology
If you don't mind my saying so. J. W. Krutch. Am Scholar 38:372+ Sum '69

Religious aspects
See Religion and language

Study and teaching
Solving problems presented by teaching linguistics. A. A. Lorentzen. Engl J 58:113-19 Ja '69
See also
English language—Study and teaching
Languages, Modern—Study and teaching
LANGUAGE and religion. See Religion and language
LANGUAGE and thought. See Thought and language
LANGUAGE arts
Gadfly and the dinosaur. T. Palmer. bibliog f Engl J 58:69-74 Ja '69
LANGUAGE laboratories
Static in the language lab. P. D. Smith; E. M. Birkmaier and D. L. Lange. Todays Ed 58:49-51 O '69
LANGUAGE of animals. See Animal communication
LANGUAGES. See Language and languages
LANGUAGES, Modern
Foreign languages and the educator. W. W. Brickman. Sch & Soc 97:136-7 Mr '69
See also
French language
Modern language association of America

Study and teaching
Asian and east European studies; University of Chicago. Sch & Soc 97:415 N '69
Changes in doctoral language requirements. A. H. Scaff. Sch & Soc 97:453-4 N '69
Foreign languages in Germany. Sch & Soc 97:389 O '69
Human dimension in foreign language instruction. L. B. Thomas. Clear House 43:425-7 Mr '69
Language programs are shortchanging our students! A. Caso. Ed Digest 34:48-9 My '69
Programed instruction in the language field. J. Ornstein. Ed Digest 34:9-12 F '69
Static in the language lab. P. D. Smith; E. M. Birkmaier and D. L. Lange. Todays Ed 58:49-51 O '69
See also
Spanish language—Study and teaching
LANIER, Mildred B.
Textile furnishings. Antiques 95:121-7 Ja '69
LANIER, Vincent
Teaching of art as social revolution. Ed Digest 34:42-5 Ap '69

LA NOUE, George R.
Church, state and the courts. Nation 209:656-9 D 15 '69
LANSDALE, Edward G.
Two steps to get us out of Vietnam. Look 33:64+ Mr 4 '69
LANSDOWNE, Fenwick. See Lansdowne, J. F.
LANSDOWNE, James Fenwick
Stunning birds of Fen Lansdowne. D. MacDonald. il Read Digest 95:147-52 Ag '69
LANSFORD, Henry
Weird things that happen when planes and birds collide. Sci Digest 65:32-6 My '69
LANSFORD, Theron G. and Baker, H. D.
Dark adaptation: an interocular light-adaptation effect. bibliog Science 164:1307-9 Je 13 '69
LANSKY, Meyer
Faircloth's law: a new way to nail elusive mobsters? D. Walsh. il por Life 67:62A-62B O 24 '69
LANTERN slides. See Transparencies
LANTERNS
See also
Electric lanterns
LANYON, Richard I.
Speech: relation of nonfluency to information value. bibliog Science 164:451-2 Ap 25 '69
LAOS
See also
China (People's Republic)—Foreign relations —Laos
Communism—Laos
United States—Air force—Forces in Laos
United States—Armed forces—Forces in Laos
United States—Foreign relations—Laos
Vientiane

Foreign relations
Beyond Vietnam borders; war moves a peace step il U S News 66:8 Ap 28 '69

History
Recurring problems in Laos. E. Urrows. bibliog f Cur Hist 57:361-3+ D '69

Politics and government
Anatomy of a crisis, by B. B. Fall. Review Nation 208:639-40 My 19 '69. R. J. Walton
Report; Laos. H. D. Greenway. Atlan 223:20+ Mr '69
Staking a claim. il Newsweek 74:42 Jl 14 '69
Tiger in the pagoda. il Time 94:26 S 26 '69
LA PAZ, Mexico
Bottom of Baja. il Sunset 142:76-85 Mr '69
LAPIDARY work
Getting started in gem cutting. E. Beason. il Mech Illus 65:114-16+ O '69
LAPIDE, Pinchas E.
It's still the land of the book. Chr Cent 86:1383-4 O 29 '69
LAPIERRE, Dominique. See Collins, L. jt. auth.
LAPIN, Al, jr
California flapjack flipper heads East to broaden his menu. por Bsns W p 130+ Je 21 '69
LAPIN, Raymond Harold
All fired up. il por Newsweek 74:82-3 D 15 '69
LAPIN, V.
(ed) See Mankin, V. Russia's gold medalist Valentin Mankin, talks of his training and racing experiences
LAPP, Ralph E.
Biography of the ABM. N Y Times Mag p29-30+ My 4 '69
Fear of a first strike. New Repub 160:21-4 Je 28; 161:34-5 Jl 19 '69
SALT: can the strategic arms race be halted? New Repub 161:14-17 N 15 '69
Send computers, not men, into deep space after the moon landing. N Y Times Mag p32-3+ F 2 '69
Vicious acronyms. New Repub 160:15-19 Je 21 '69
LAQUEUR, Walter
Reflections on youth movements. Commentary 47:33-41 Je '69; Same with title What the past reveals. Cur 109:3-14 Ag '69
LARAMEE, K. Helena
Have we lost our marbles? Sch Arts 69:36-7 N '69
LARDNER, George, jr
Faster! Faster! New Repub 161:9-11 O 18 '69
—and Loh, Jules
Wonderful world of George Wallace. Esquire 71:125-8+ My '69
LARDNER, Lon
Once in a while but not very often. R. L. Tobin. Sat R 52:4+ My 10 '69

LARDNER, Rex
Assault and battery of lacrosse. Holiday 45:
66-7+ Ap '69
1968 was the year of the knee. N Y Times
Mag p4+ Ja 26 '69
LARDNER, Susan
Current cinema. New Yorker 45:80-3 My 31
'69
LAREDO, Jaime
Musical events; recital at Alice Tully Hall.
W. Sargeant. New Yorker 45:162 N 1 '69
LARGE print books
See also
Publishers and publishing—Large print books
LARGE-scale integration. See Electronic cir-
cuits—Integrated circuits
LARGE space telescope. See Artificial satel-
lites—Astronomical applications
LARGEMOUTH bass. See Bass
LARGEMOUTH bass fishing. See Bass fishing
LARIONOV, Mikhail Fedorovich
Larionov and the Russian vanguard. L. H.
Schafran. il Art N 68:36-7+ My '69
LARKIN, Kathryn C.
Project Phantom; a class considers a change.
Yachting 126:66-7+ S '69
LARKIN, Richard
Sweet shivering rain; poem. Am Scholar 38:
407-8 Sum '69
LARMOTH, Jeanine
Taste of beauty. Harp Baz 103:208-9+ N '69
LARNER, Jeremy
Moratorium: a view from the inside. Life
67:52-6+ N 28 '69
Nobody knows, reflections on the McCarthy
campaign. Harper 238:62-72+ Ap; 71-88+
My; 239:6+ Ag '69
LAROCQUE, Geraldine E.
Book marks (cont) Engl J 58:288-97. 773-84
F, My '69
LA ROQUE, Lloyd
Why some programs don't work out well,
and what to do about it. por Camp Mag
41:8+ Ap '69
LAROUSSE (firm) See Publishers and pub-
lishing—France
LAROUSSE bookshop, New York. See Book-
sellers and bookselling—New York (state)
LA ROVERA, William. See Hale, L. jt. auth.
LARRABEE, Eric
Artist and the university. Harper 238:12+
Je '69
LARRAIN, Sergio
Sergio Larrain of Chile; excerpts from letter.
Pop Phot 65:94-7+ S '69
LARRICK, Nancy
Life ain't been no crystal stair; address,
1968. Library J 94:843-5 F 15 '69
Poetry is the natural language of children.
Parents Mag 44:46-7+ Ag '69
LARROCHA, Alicia de
Little lady from Spain. W. F. Rickenbacker.
Nat R 21:239 Mr 11 '69
Music to my ears; appearance in Carnegie
Hall. I. Kolodin. Sat R 52:24 D 27 '69
Musical events; recital in Carnegie Hall. W.
Sargeant. New Yorker 45:108+ D 20 '69
Musician of the month. H. Kupferberg.
por (pMA1) Hi Fi 19:MA6 O '69
LARRY, R. Heath
Inflationary binge; address, October 18, 1969.
Vital Speeches 36:115-18 D 1 '69
Something has to give; address, June 11,
1969. Vital Speeches 35:725-8 S 15 '69
LARSEN, Jack Lenor
Lausanne: International tapestry biennale.
Craft Horiz 29:14-19 S '69
New weaving. Craft Horiz 29:22-9+ Mr '69
Three designers talk about light. Am Home
72:42 O '69
LARSEN, Margaret Thal-. See Thal-Larsen. M.
LARSEN, Marlin, and others
Imidodiphosphate and pyrophosphate: pos-
sible biological significance of similar struc-
tures. bibliog Science 166:1510-11 D 19 '69
LARSON, Charles R.
Trial of Wole Soyinka. Nation 209:259-60 S 15
'69
LARSON, O. W.
Those shady sharpies. por Outdoor Life 144:
60-1+ O '69
LARSON, Roger L. and Spiess, F. N.
East Pacific rise crest: a near-bottom geo-
physical profile. bibliog Science 163:68-71;
165:618 Ja 3, Ag 8 '69
LARUS, Joel
Nuclear accidents and the ABM. Sat R 52:10-
13 My 31 '69
LARUSSO, Rudy
Brave words from a Hawk and a Warrior. A.
Wright. por Sports Illus 30:26-8+ Mr 24 '69

LARVAE
Mosquitoes feeding on insect larvae. P. Har-
ris and others. il Science 164:184-5 Ap 11 '69
Plant-herbivore coevolution: lupines and
lycaenids. D. E. Breedlove and P. R. Ehr-
lich; discussion. Science 164:197; 165:415-16
Ap 11, Jl 25 '69
See also
Insects—Development
LASAGNA, Louis
Caution on the pill; excerpt from Life, death
and the doctor. Sat R 51:64-9 N 2 '68;
52:61 Mr 1 '69
If not the pill, what? Vogue 154:102+ O 15
'69
Pharmaceutical revolution: its impact on
science and society. bibliog Science 166:
1227-33 D 5 '69
LA SCALA opera, Milan. See Milan, Italy—
La Scala
LASCAUX murals. See Cave drawings and
paintings
LASCH, Christopher
Reason appears to be helpless in the face of
violence. N Y Times Mag p 136 My 4 '69
LASER communication systems. See Light
communication systems
LASER gyro. See Gyroscopes
LASER holography. See Holography
LASER strain gages. See Strain gages
LASERS
Amateur scientist; how to construct an
argon gas laser with outputs at several
wavelengths. S. Heumann. il Sci Am 220:
118-23 F '69
Basement H-bombs; laser-triggered bombs.
S. Novick. il Sci & Cit 10:243-9 D '68
Continuous, but not portable. Sci N 96:448
N 15 '69
Continous-wave chemical laser requires no
external energy source. bibliog Phys To-
day 22:55 D '69
Hundred-joule lasers are producing high-
temperature plasmas. G. B. Lubkin. il Phys
Today 22:55-6 N '69
Laser hits device Apollo placed on moon.
Aviation W 91:31 Ag 11 '69
Laser-made plasmas. D. E. Thomsen. il Sci
N 95:384-5 Ap 19 '69
Laser scattering; report of meeting. B. Chu.
Science 163:967-8 F 28 '69
Lively laser. J. P. Robinson, jr. il Pop Electr
31:33-5+ D '69
Mode-locked lasers: measurements of very
fast radiative decay in fluorescent systems.
H. Merkelo and others. bibliog il Science
164:301-2 Ap 18 '69
New Apollo unit includes laser reflector:
Early Apollo scientific experiment package.
il Aviation W 90:52-3 F 24 '69
Organic lasers. P. Sorokin. il Sci Am 220:30-
40 F '69
Popular electronics exclusive experimenters'
laser. C. H. Knowles. il Pop Electr 31:27-32
D '69
Sandia operates picosecond laser at 50-joule
output. il Phys Today 22:60+ Je '69
Taking on bits by the trillion; laser record-
ing system. il Bsns W p78+ F 1 '69
They've taken the guesswork out of war
games. M. Schultz. il Pop Mech 132:84-7+
Ag '69
Under-$100 laser you can buy. il Pop Sci
194:92-3 Ap '69
See also
Nonlinear optics

Astronomical applications
Giant pancakes of laser light to measure
precise distance to moon. il Space World
F-10-70:30-2 O '69
Laser beam directed at the lunar retro-
reflector array: observations of the first
returns. J. Faller and others. bibliog il
Science 166:99-102 O 3 '69
Lunar target hit by second observatory.
Aviation W 91:19 Ag 25 '69

Manufacture
Bringing the laser down to earth; Spectra-
physics, inc. G. Bylinsky. il Fortune 80:126-
9+ S '69

Medical applications
Lasers for more than welding. Sci N 96:
296 O 4 '69

Military applications
French navy Jaguar to use self-test laser
rangefinder. il Aviation W 90:322-3 Je 2
'69
Laser weaponry seen advancing. Aviation W
92:16-17 Ja 12 '70

LASERS—*Continued*

Printing applications

Laser beam printing. S. V. Jones. il Sci Digest 65.72 F '69

New applications for 3-D graphics; potential uses for lasers and holograms. il Pub W 195:88+ F 3 '69

Safety devices and measures

Caution laser; safety rules. L. B. Lloyd. Pop Electr 31:41-2 D '69

Space flight applications

Experimental laser engines. L. G. Lawrence. bibliog il Electr World 81:30-2 Je '69

LASKER, Gabriel W.
Human biological adaptability; excerpt from Evolution of man. bibliog Science 166:1480-6 D '69

LASKY, Burton
Who'll do the work? Pub W 196:13-14 D 15 '69

LASSWELL, Thomas E.
Social stratification:1964-1968; excerpts from address March 24, 1969 and from Class and stratum. Ann Am Acad 384:104-34 Jl '69

LAST hours; story. See Taylor, G. A.

LAST Judgment. See Judgment day

LAST of the red hot lovers; drama. See Simon, N.

LAST rites. See Extreme unction

LAST to go; story. See Gilliatt. P.

LASTRA, Luis
Artists and astronauts. Américas 21:21-8 S '69

LAS VEGAS, Nev.
Absolutely free; Elvis Presley's opening performance. M. Hentoff. Harper 239:28+ N '69

Another Las Vegas. il Fortune 80:149-51 N '69

You and I are very different from Howard Hughes. O. Demaris. il Esquire 71:73-81+ Mr '69

Description

Las Vegas: the game is illusion. il Time 94:22 Jl 11 '69

Education

Roy W. Martin junior high school; where learning is interaction. C. O. Roundy. il Sr Schol 94:Schol Teach 30-1 Ja 17 '69

Hotels, restaurants, etc.

See also
Casinos

Negroes

Racial roulette. il Newsweek 74:48 O 20 '69

Riots

Racial roulette. il Newsweek 74:48 O 20 '69

LASZLO, John. See Ove, P. jt. auth.

LATANÉ, Bibb. See Darley, J. M. jt. auth.

LATERAL sclerosis. See Sclerosis

LATERAL thinking. See Thought and thinking

LATH houses. See Garden houses, shelters, etc.

LATHAM, G. and others
Apollo passive seismic experiment. bibliog Science 165:241-50 Jl 18 '69

LATHES
Add a rest to your lathe. W. E. Burton. il Pop Mech 131:200-3+ Mr '69

Boring indicator for lathe, shows where the tool point is. G. Douglas. il Pop Sci 194:130-2 My '69

Filing on a lathe. W. E. Burton. il Pop Mech 130:174-7 D '68

How to plane on a lathe. W. E. Burton. il Pop Mech 132:194-7+ O '69

Make a king-size toolpost for hefty turning bits. W. E. Burton. il Pop Mech 131:194-6 F '69

Make this back holder and use upside-down tool bits. W. E. Burton. il Pop Mech 132:180-4+ Ag '69

Make your own wood-turning lathe. il Mech Illus 65:86-8+ F '69

New wood planer attachment for your Unimat lathe. W. E. Burton. il Pop Mech 130:179-81 D '68

See also
Turning

LATIF, Patricia
My rooftop acre. pors Org Gard & Farm 16:33-5 N '69

LATIN AMERICA

See also
Aeronautics, Commercial—Latin America
Agricultural administration—Latin America
Air travel—Latin America
Automobile industry and trade—Latin America
Birth control—Latin America
Book industries and trade—Latin America
Catholic church in Latin America
Communism—Latin America
Cooperative associations—Latin America
Ecology—Latin America
Guerrillas—Latin America
Housing—Latin America
Immigration and emigration—Latin America
Industry and state—Latin America
Investments, Foreign (in Latin America)
Land tenure—Latin America
Monroe doctrine
Political parties—Latin America
Roads—Latin America
Rockefeller, N. A.—Visits to Latin America, 1969
Slums—Latin America
Social change—Latin America
Student demonstrations—Latin America
Taxation—Latin America
Technical assistance in Latin America
Tourist trade—Latin America
United States—Economic relations—Latin America
United States—Foreign relations—Latin America
Urban renewal—Latin America
Zoology—Latin America

Commerce

Not so dim/bright future of Latin America; excerpts from symposium on Contemporary economic problems and issues in Latin America. J. Villaverde. il Américas 21:16-22 F '69

Defenses

Hemispheric defense in World war II. P. B. Taylor. jr. Cur Hist 56:333-9 Je '69

Description and travel

Funny thing happened on the way to the jungle; sailing and flying the Amazon. S. Turner. il Sr Schol 94:Schol Teach 18-19 Ap 11 '69

Discovery and exploration

First news from new Spain; printed accounts of voyages of discovery. J. Gurría Lacroix. il Américas 21:15-19 Mr '69

Economic conditions

Development progress in Latin America. Américas 21:44 My '69

Economics & Latin America: more downs than ups? Sr Schol 94:19-20 Ja 31 '69

Has Latin America a choice? J. L. Segundo. America 120:213-16 F 22 '69; Discussion. 120:211, 318 F 22. Mr 22 '69

Not so dim/bright future of Latin America; excerpts from symposium on Contemporary economic problems and issues in Latin America. J. Villaverde. il Américas 21:16-22 F '69

Race against time; findings of report by Agency for international development. Commonweal 90:131-2 Ap 18 '69

Rockefeller report on Latin America. il Time 94:42 N 14 '69

Tinderbox in Latin America. S. M. Linowitz il Sat R 52:10-13 Ag 16 '69

Upturn in Latin American economy. Américas 21:43-4 Mr '69

See also
Inter-American economic and social council
United Nations—Economic commission for Latin America

Economic policy

Entering the second development decade; excerpts from address. G. Plaza. Américas 21:42 Ap '69

Latin America: what are your priorities? address, May 6, 1969. C. A. Meyer. Dept State Bul 60:440-2 My 26 '69

Seeds of transformation. G. Salgado. il Américas 21:12-18 Ap '69

Strengthening technical cooperation; OAS program. il Américas 21:43-4 Je '69

Threatening weather in South America. J. Cameron. il Fortune 80:98-101+ O '69

Economic relations

United States

For justice, if not for friendship; the Viña del Mar statement. America 120:703 Je 21 '69

LATIN   AMERICA—Economic   relations—
    United States—*Cont.*
U.S. versus Latin America: business & cul-
    ture. S. M. Davis. bibliog f il Harvard
    Bsns R 47:88-98 N '69
What Latin Americans want from U.S. il
    U S News 66:50 Je 23 '69

Expropriation policy

After Latin Americans seize foreign property
    then what? il U S News 67:55-6 N 3 '69
Where Yanqui companies are feeling the
    heat. il Bsns W p80-2+ N 22 '69

Foreign relations

Russians have come. il Time 93:39 F 28 '69

United States

Is anybody listening? il Newsweek 74:33 Jl
    7 '69
Latin America: challenge from the intel-
    lectuals. M. Maldonado-Denis. Nation 209:
    73-6 Jl 28 '69
Neighbors are restless; riots and demon-
    strations. il Bsns W p38-9 Je 7 '69
Their excellencies; position of U.S. ambassa-
    dors. Nation 209:268 S 22 '69
    See also
Inter-American relations
Rockefeller, N. A.—Visits to Latin America,
    1969

History

Early cold war period. R. E. Poppino. Cur
    Hist 56:340-5+ Je '69
Juan Egaña's Pan American dream. R. Silva
    Castro. il Américas 21:28-32 Ap '69
U.S. in Latin America to 1933: an overview.
    A. P. Whitaker. Cur Hist 56:321-6+ Je '69

Bibliography

Articles and other books received; comp. by
    D. E. Worcester. See issues of American
    historical review
First news from new Spain; printed accounts
    of voyages of discovery. J. Gurría Lacroix.
    il Américas 21:15-19 Mr '69

Wars of independence, 1806-1830

Angostura. A. U. Pietri. il Américas 21:2-6
    My '69

Industries

ADELA: capital idea for Latin America. S.
    Seegers. Read Digest 94:154-6+ Mr '69

Intellectual life

Latin America: challenge from the intel-
    lectuals. M. Maldonado-Denis. Nation
    209:73-6 Jl 28 '69
    See also
Center of intercultural documentation

Nationalism

Nationalist wave hits Latin America; mean-
    ing to U.S. il U S News 66:36-7 Mr 10 '69

Politics

Latin America: protest and progress. il Time
    94:29 Jl 4 '69
Latin American military elite. T. M. Mil-
    lington. bibliog f Cur Hist 56:352-4+ Je
    '69
Latin American radicalism. ed. by I. L.
    Horowitz and others. Review
    America 120:308+ Mr 15 '69. F. P. Le
    Veness
    Nation 208:277-8 Mr 3 '69. R. F. Smith
    Sat R 52:37-9 Je 7 '69. A. Lauterbach
Latin American revolution: Catholics and
    Protestants together on behalf of oppressed
    and dispossessed. E. M. Smith. Chr Cent
    86:674-7 My 14 '69
Neighbors are restless; riots and demon-
    strations. il Bsns W p38-9 Je 7 '69
New military. Newsweek 75:26-8 Ja 5 '70
New turmoil in Latin America: its meaning
    for U.S. il U S News 66:30-2 Je 16 '69

Population

2000: a no-space odyssey. L. Olivos. bibliog il
    Américas 21:15-21 Ag '69

Religious institutions and affairs

    See also
Catholic church in Latin America
Methodist church in Latin America
Protestants in Latin America

Social conditions

Anti-capitalism in Latin America. America
    120:266-7 Mr 8 '69
U.S. versus Latin America: business & cul-
    ture. S. M. Davis. bibliog f il Harvard
    Bsns R 47:88-98 N '69
    See also
Housing—Latin America

LATIN AMERICA and Europe. See Europe and
    Latin America
LATIN AMERICA and Spain. See Spain and
    Latin America
LATIN AMERICA and the United States
    See also
Action for progress for the Americas
Alliance for progress
Inter-American relations
Pan American day and week
LATIN AMERICAN airline service. See Airlines
    —International services—Latin America
LATIN AMERICAN architecture. See Architec-
    ture, Latin American
LATIN AMERICAN art. See Art, Latin Ameri-
    can
LATIN AMERICAN art objects. See Art ob-
    jects, Latin American
LATIN AMERICAN congress on evangelism.
    See Religious conferences
LATIN AMERICAN literature
    See also
Authors, Latin American
LATIN AMERICAN poetry
Five books of Latin American poetry. R.
    Squirru. il Américas 21:40-2 Jl '69
New York's new blood poets; with poems
    and translations. I. Goldemberg. il Américas
    21:14-20 My '69

Translations into English

Five books of Latin American poetry. R.
    Squirru. il Américas 21:40-2 Jl '69
LATIN AMERICAN scientists. See Scientists,
    Latin American
LATIN AMERICAN students
    See also
Student demonstrations—Latin America
LATIN AMERICANS
Nonviolence in Latin America. E. K. Culhane.
    America 120:331 Mr 22 '69
LATIN AMERICANS in the United States
Library needs for the Spanish-speaking;
    adaptation of address, 1968. A. D. Trejo.
    ALA Bul 63:1077-81 S '69; Reply. R. P. Haro.
    63:1518 D '69
Problems of Spanish-American minority aired
    for N.C.C. unit. G. F. Hall. Chr Cent 86:
    1498-500 N 19 '69
LATIN inscriptions. See Inscriptions, Latin
LATIN literature
    See also
Classical literature
LATITUDE
Terrestrial microclimate: amelioration at
    high latitudes. P. S. Corbet. bibliog il Sci-
    ence 166:865-6 N 14 '69
LATTIMORE, Owen
If you have tears. W. F. Buckley, jr. Nat R
    21:560 My 20 '69
LAU, Nguyen. See Nguyen Lau
LAUBER, Jean K.
Amateur scientist. Sci Am 221:122-6 Jl '69
LAUDER, Robert E.
Bergman's Shame and Sartre's stare. Cath
    World 209:247-50 S '69
LAUGH-in (television program) See Television
    broadcasting—Humor
LAUGHING gulls. See Gulls
LAUGHLIN, Michael S.
New-wave producer hits jackpot. por Bsns
    W p41 Ja 3 '70
LAUGHNER, William J. See Schwartz, D. jt.
    auth.
LAUNDRIES
Drip-dry cabinet in the laundry. il Sunset
    143:96+ Jl '69
Mini bath & laundry. B. Duggan. il Mech
    Illus 65:90-3 Ag '69
LAUNDRY
Spring house cleaning. il Redbook 132:77+
    Ap '69
LAUNDRY boxes, kits, etc.
Laundry box. R. L. Tobin. Sat R 52:6+ N
    22 '69
LAUNDRY equipment
    See also
Clothes dryers
Washing machines
Whirlpool corporation
LAUNDRY products, Enzyme. See Enzyme
    laundry products
LAURASIA. See Continental drift
LAUREL international. See Horse racing
LAURENCE, Margaret
Fire-dwellers; excerpts from novel. Ladies
    Home J 86:127-34 Mr '69
LAURENT, Pierre Henri
(comp) Articles and other books received;
    the Low Countries. See issues of American
    historical review
LAURENTS, Gene
Gallery; photographs. Life 67:8-9 O 3 '69

LAURITZEN, Frederick
Three California craftsmen. M. Angelino. il por Am Artist 33:45-7+ S '69

LAUSANNE
Description
Traveler's choice. A. Beresford. Travel 132:24 Jl '69

LAUTER, Paul
More things change. Sat R 52:71-2 Ap 19 '69

LAUTZENHEISER, Robert E.
Snowy winter of 1968-69 in New England. Weatherwise 22:68-71+ Ap '69

LAVA
Kilauea volcano: the 1967-68 summit eruption. W. T. Kinoshita and others. bibliog il Science 166:459-68 O 24 '69
See also
Basalt
Volcanoes

LAVA BEDS NATIONAL MONUMENT
Land of the frozen fires. P. J. Easterla. il Nat Parks 43:18-21 D '69

LAVARRE, Frank Provost
For the long-distance runner who got caught: a twenty-year sentence. J. Howard. il pors Life 67:30-1 O 31 '69

LAVENDER, David
For sale: an empire $1,500 down. Am West 6:6-12+ My '69

LAVENDER cotton
You can sculpt the sun-loving santolinas. il Sunset 143:196 S '69

LAVER, Rodney George
Another redheaded league. K. Chapin. il por Sports Illus 31:50-2 Jl 14 '69
Best in the world. il por Newsweek 74:70-1 S 22 '69
Concentration on the court. il por Time 94:57 S 19 '69
Why Rocket is better than the best. E. Asinof. il pors N Y Times Mag p58-9+ N 30 '69
You can play Laver but you can't beat him. R. Blount, jr. il por Sports Illus 31:99-100 S 15 '69

LAVI, Daliah
New fashion manna from Israel. il pors Vogue 154:116-21 Jl '69

LAVIN, Patrick J.
Washington front. America 121:254 O 4 '69

LAVIN, Richard
Simulation, standards, and the seventies. por Library J 94:4216-17 N 15 '69

LAVOISIER, Antonie Laurent
Visit with Antoine Lavoisier; tr. by R. E. Oesper. F. Szabadvary. por Chem 42:14-16 Ap '69

LAW, Kenneth. See Herndon, T. E. jt. auth.

LAW
See also
Confession (law)
Copyright
Criminal law
Informers (law)
International law
Judges
Juvenile courts
Lawyers
Libel and slander
Maritime law
Martial law
Military law
Police
Procedure (law)
Trials
    also law on special subjects, e.g. Boats and boating—Laws and regulations; Game laws; etc.
Curiosa and miscellany
God's little acre; case involving God in Sonoma County, Calif. Newsweek 73:79 Je 30 '69
Language
Glossary. Sr Schol 94:25 Mr 28 '69
Study and teaching
Formal education; address, May 15, 1969. E. H. Levi. Vital Speeches 35:563-6 Jl 1 '69
Students should be taught the law. H. B. McDaniel and B. A. Truce. il Todays Ed 58-23-4 Ap '69
Teenagers and the law. L. Blackwood. Schol Teach Sec Teach Sup p 18-19+ S 22 '69
See also
Law schools
Terminology
See Law—Language
Alabama
See also
Banking law

California
Abortion for whom? New Repub 161:12 O 25 '69
Guideline on abortion. Time 94:66 S 19 '69
See also
Justice, Administration of—California
Connecticut
Modernizing sex laws; new code in Connecticut. il Time 94:57 Ag 8 '69
District of Columbia
Open city for abortion. Time 94:65 N 21 '69
Great Britain
Death to hanging; government resolution outlawing hanging. Newsweek 74:28+ D 29 '69
In Britain, an end to hangings. U S News 67:6 D 29 '69
Sacking the hangman. il Time 94:15-16 D 26 '69
Lebanon
See also
Banking law
Massachusetts
Snob zoning. New Repub 161:7 D 20 '69
Minnesota
Great Minnesota compromise; censorship bill. J. Challman. Library J 94:3627 O 15 '69
Southern states
Profiles: C. Morgan, jr. F. Powledge. New Yorker 45:63-4+ O 25 '69
Texas
Warren Burnett: Texas lawyer. L. L. King. il Harper 239:66-7+ Jl '69
United States
Clarence Darrow: partisan of the unpopular. Sr Schol 94:13 Ap 18 '69
Evolution in the law. C. M. Whelan. America 122:11-12 Ja 10 '70
See also
American bar association
Courts—United States
Justice, Administration of—United States
Law enforcement
Legislation—United States
Transplantation of organs, tissues, etc.—Legal aspects
Uniform state laws
United States—Constitution
Wisconsin
See also
Justice, Administration of—Wisconsin

LAW, Medical. See Medical laws and legislation

LAW, Natural. See Natural law

LAW and mental illness. See Mental health laws

LAW and religion. See Religion and law

LAW and science. See Science and law

LAW and sex. See Sex and law

LAW and society. See Sociological jurisprudence

LAW enforcement
Annals of politics; attorney generals Clark and Mitchell on law and order issue. R. Harris. New Yorker 45:61-4+ N 22 '69
Annals of politics; R. Clark, attorney general. R. Harris. New Yorker 45:63-4+ N 8 '69
Are we handcuffing the police? G. L. Hallworth. America 120:128-9 F 1 '69
Campuses and courts. Nat R 21:477-8 My 20 '69
Crime prevention; citizen participation; address, February 3, 1969. J. N. Mitchell. Vital Speeches 35:290-3 Mr 1 '69
Crimes while on bail; the hunt for a remedy. il U S News 66:42 F 17 '69
Criminal-justice system in trouble; excerpts from address, October 1, 1969. C. H Rogovin. U S News 67:16 O 13 '69
End to big riots? Findings of a police survey. il U S News 66:42-4 Je 2 '69
Enforcement: illusion of security. G. E. Misner. il Nation 208:488-90 Ap 21 '69
Federal government and crime; excerpts from Agenda for the Nation. J. Q. Wilson. Cur 103:23-5 Ja '69
Fighting crime in America; interview. J. N. Mitchell. il U S News 67:46-53 Ag 18 '69
First graders meet law and order. S. C. Pearson, jr. Chr Cent 86:681-3 My 14 '69; Discussion. 86:906-7, 997-8 Jl 2, 23 '69
How to restore law and order. Nations Bsns 57:89-91 Mr '69
How to stay hip, happy and out of jail; with photographs. Life 67:81-4 N 28 '69

LAW enforcement—*Continued*
Is crime chiefly a local problem? U S News 66:12 F 17 '69
Law and order equals status quo? J. B. Kelley. il America 121:323-6 O 18 '69; Reply. J. P. Morgan, jr. 121:514 N 29 '69
Man with ideas on fighting crime. U S News 66:13 F 3 '69
New era for Supreme court. il U S News 66:30-2 Je 2 '69
New taps on freedom; Title III of the Omnibus crime control and safe streets act of 1968. S. Fly. il Nation 208:697-9 Je 2 '69
One way to handle crime; interview. J. J. Harrington. il U S News 67:62-5 D 22 '69
Police and the community. M. Mead. Redbook 133:38+ Je '69
Punishment before crime; President Nixon's proposal of a system of preventive detention. Life 66:32 F 14 '69
Response of police agencies. G. E. Misner. bibliog f Ann Am Acad 382:109-19 Mr '69
Revolution eats its parents. F. S. Meyer. Nat R 21:541 Je 3 '69
Unlawful seizure; student riots and seizure of college property, violations of the law. D. Lawrence. U S News 66:108 Mr 17 '69
  See also
Law—United States
Police

LAW enforcement assistance administration. See United States—Justice, Department of —Law enforcement assistance administration

LAW enforcement automated data system. See Computers—Police applications

LAW schools
Law schools and law firms. R. Nader. New Repub 161:20-3 O 11 '69; Discussion. 161:14-15 O 25: 31-3 N 8; 31 N 15 '69
Learning the white man's law; black enrollments in law schools. il Time 95:32-3 Ja 5 '70
  See also
Harvard university—School of law
Law—Study and teaching
Mississippi. University—School of law

LAW societies
  See also
American bar association

LAWFORD, Valentine
Choice of past. Vogue 154:244-9+ O 1 '69
Le style Pauline. Vogue 153:150-3 Je '69

LAWLESSNESS
Civil disobedience and where it leads, two sides; statement by the National commission on the causes and prevention of violence. il U S News 67:27-8 D 22 '69

LAWLOR, John D.
Safety education: an investment in our future. Parents Mag 44:28+ Ag '69

LAWN mowers
Amazing new Mowbot; it really mows your lawn by itself! L. E. Sabal. il Pop Mech 130:83 D '68
Gasoline-powered rotary mowers. il Consumer Rep 34:372-9 Jl '69
How to mow the lawn without really pushing. B. C. Kilvert, jr. il Home Gard 56:52-3 My '69
New robot lawn mower works while you rest. J. Hand. il Pop Sci 194:136-8+ Ja '69
News in power equipment. il House & Gard 135:172+ Ap '69
Random lawn mower; Mowbot. Sci Am 220:52 Ap '69
Riding mowers and garden tractors. E. McDonald. il House B 111:58+ Ap '69
Safety rules for mowers. il Suc Farm 67:60 Jl '69
Tethered mowers go around and around. R. P. Stevenson. il Pop Sci 195:144-6 Ag '69
Vortex mower promises a revolution in grass cutting. H. Birch. il Pop Sci 195:86-7+ O '69
What everyone should know about safety with power mowers. B. C. Kilvert, jr. il Home Gard 56:53 Jl '69

Anecdotes, facetiae, satire, etc.
Electronic coup de grass. W. Zinsser. il Life 67:10 Ag 22 '69

Maintenance and repair
How to keep your mower running at its best. il Home Gard 56:60-1 Jl '69
Winterize your mower. il Bet Hom & Gard 47:149 N '69

Safety devices and measures
Gasoline-powered rotary mowers. il Consumer Rep 34:378-9 Jl '69
Safer mower blade: it's worth considering. il Consumer Rep 34:424 Ag '69

LAWN mowing. See Lawns
LAWN seeds. See Grasses—Seed
LAWN sprinklers. See Sprinklers
LAWN thatch
Lawn thatch, what it's all about. R. W. Schery. il Horticulture 47:24-5+ S '69

LAWNS
At last! a lawn we're proud of! L. M. Belt. il Org Gard & Farm 16:80-1 Ag '69
For that lush, green lawn. Consumer Bul 52:28-30 Ag '69
How and when to fertilize your lawn. Home Gard 56:65 My '69
How to buy a lawn. E. McDonald. il House B 111:68-9+ F '69
How to grow a perfect lawn. J. N. Miller. il Read Digest 95:64-8 Ag '69
How, when and why you should de-thatch and aerate your lawn. il Pop Mech 132:174-8 Ag '69
Mystique of mowing. P. Keeney. il Home Gard 56:34 Mr '69
This young lawn can take it. il Sunset 143:163 Jl '69
What you should know about starting a lawn; excerpt from Informal gardening. B. C. Kilvert, jr. il Home Gard 56:85-6 Ap '69
Winter feeding of lawns. R. W. Schery. Horticulture 47:34+ Ja '69
Your old lawn can be made new again. il Home Gard 56:58-9 S '69
  See also
Sprinklers

LAWNS, Watering of. See Watering of gardens, lawns, etc.

LAWRENCE, Bill
American history blown off course by eighth graders; excerpts from Then some other stuff happened. Todays Ed 58:51 S '69

LAWRENCE, Carolyn
Art for black students; a change in objectives. Sch Arts 68:18-21 F '69

LAWRENCE, Chester H.
FM stereo in this headset. Radio-Electr 40:43-4 Ag '69

LAWRENCE, Ernest Orlando
Lawrence and Oppenheimer, by N. P. Davis. Review
  Bul Atom Sci 25:31-2 Ja '69. J. Wilson
  New Yorker 45:141-2+ My 10 '69. J. Bernstein

LAWRENCE, H. Lea
Lick creek shoot. Outdoor Life 144:50-1+ D '69
News: the Southeast (cont) por Outdoor Life 143:43-6 Mr '69
Wild boar of the Appalachians; with biographical sketch. por Natur Hist 78:4, 46-7 O '69
—See Elliott, C. jt. auth.

LAWRENCE, H. Sherwood. See Valentine, F. T. jt. auth.

LAWRENCE, James
Great sea battle; excerpts from Broke and The Shannon. P. Padfield. il por Am Heritage 20:29-65 D '68

LAWRENCE, Jim
On a hill far away. Chr Cent 86:1419-20 N 5 '69

LAWRENCE, Jodi
Working with a photographer. Writers Digest 49:60-3+ Jl '69

LAWRENCE, L. George
Electrohydraulic effect. Electr World 81:44-5+ My '69
Electronics and the living plant. bibliog Electr World 82:25-8 O '69
Experimental laser engines. bibliog Electr World 81:30-2 Je '69
Geomagnetic observatories. bibliog Electr World 81:41-4 F '69

LAWRENCE, Louisa
Full extent of the damage; story. McCalls 96:76-7 S '69

LAWRENCE, Paul R.
How to deal with resistance to change; reprint from May-June 1954 issue. Harvard Bsns R 47:4-6+ Ja '69

LAWRENCE, Robert
Ansermet's own valedictory. Sat R 52:50 D 27 '69
Ariadne reconsidered. Sat R 52:49 Ja 25 '69
Prokofiev's satiric Oranges. Sat R 52:47 Je 28 '69
Sibelius in perspective. Sat R 52:73 F 22 '69

LAWRENCE radiation laboratory, Berkeley, Calif. See California. University—Lawrence radiation laboratories

LAWRENSON, Helen
Jean Paul Getty in his golden age. Esquire 72:146-7+ O '69
Mick Jagger, I love you. Esquire 71:132-5+ Je '69
Sweet Julie. Esquire 71:62-4+ Ja '69

LEAK detectors. See Detectors

LEAKEY, Louis Seymour Bazett, and others
Age of bed V, Olduvai Gorge, Tanzania. bibliog Science 162:559; 163:1360 N 1 '68, Mr 21 '69

LEAKEY, Richard
On safari into the past; with photographs by J. Reader and report by R. Stolley. il pors Life 67:42-51 S 12 '69

LEALE, Antonio
North of Italy; photographs. Travel & Camera 32:56-7+ Mr '69

LEAR, Bill
What Bill Lear wants. Bill Lear invents. D. Shaw. il por Esquire 72:132-3+ S '69

LEAR, Edward
Edward Lear, by V. Noakes. Review
    Atlan 223:138 Ap '69. E. Weeks
    Nation 208:545-6 Ap 28 '69. T. Roszak
    New Repub 160:28-30 Ap 5 '69. R. Freedman
    Newsweek 73:87A+ Ap 7 '69. P. D. Zimmerman
    Time il por 93:98+ Ap 4 '69

LEAR, John
Messages from Mars. Sat R 52:75-7 O 11 '69
New deal for graduate education. Sat R 52: 78-9 My 17 '69
New facts on fluoridation. Sat R 52:51-6 Mr 1; 59 My 3 '69
Science & humanity. See issues of Saturday review
Thor Heyerdahl's next voyage. Sat R 52:49-56 My 3 '69

LEAR, Jonathan
Great admissions sweepstakes, how Yale selected her first coeds. N Y Times Mag p52-3+ Ap 13 '69

LEAR, Martha Weinman
Dick Benjamin and Paula Prentiss: to love, honor, and analyze. Redbook 134:54-5+ Ja '70
Whatever happened to Mr Fonda's baby Jane? Redbook 133:66-7+ Ag '69
(ed) See Matthau, W. Walter Matthau: juiciest actor in the West

LEAR, William Powell
Doctored Stanley, we presume? il Time 93: 74 Ap 11 '69
Lear trades steam for gas turbine. il por Bsns W p40-1 N 22 '69
Lear's steam dream: a reality? D. Wells. il por Motor T 21:26-9 Je '69
Let there be steam. B. Ottum. il pors Sports Illus 30:50-6 F 3 '69
Steam cars: jet tycoon, others, espouse the cause. A. Jamison. il Science 163:370-4 Ja 24 '69
Steam cars try to get back in the running. il pors Bsns W p 130-2 Mr 29 '69

LEARNING, Maze. See Maze tests

LEARNING, Psychology of
Accountability for results: a basic challenge for America's schools. L. M. Lessinger. Am Ed 5:2-4 Je '69
Architectonics of the mind. D. Melcher. il Library J 94:3785-8 O 15 '69
Early detection of potential learning disorders. J. V. Hunt. Ed Digest 35:12-15 O '69
Education for the future. A. P. Ludka. il Sr Schol 93:School Teach 14-15 Ja 10 '69
Gut learning; controlling visceral responses. Sci Am 220:49-50 Ap '69
IQ: God-given or man-made? theories of A. R. Jensen and J. Piaget. G. Voyat. il Sat R 52:73-5+ My 17 '69; Same abr. Ed Digest 35:1-4 O '69
Interaction briefs: team learning. Todays Ed 58:59 D '69
Intracranial self-stimulation and the rapid decline of frustrative nonreward. R. N. Johnson and others. bibliog il Science 164: 971-2 My 23 '69
Learning at random. L. A. Hart. il Sat R 52:62-3 Ap 19 '69
Man's participatory evolution; psychoneurobiochemeducation. D. Krech. Cur 110:55-64 S '69
Mathematics for the very young. L. Ellison. il Parents Mag 44:48-9+ Jl '69
Observations from abroad: the American scene. E. Roe. il Library J 94:835-9, 1291-3, 1715-18+ F 15, Mr 15, Ap 15 '69
Pygmalion in the classroom. by R. Rosenthal and L. Jacobson. Review
    New Yorker 45:169-70+ Ap 19 '69. R. Coles
Roy W. Martin junior high school: where learning is interaction; Las Vegas, Nev. C. O. Roundy. il Sr Schol 94:School Teach 30-1 Ja 17 '69
See how they learn! symposium. il Todays Ed 58:15-30 F '69

Tuning in and turning on the nonverbals; summer English class at Marymount college, Palos Verdes estates, Calif. for Upward bound girls. B. L. Covey. il Am Ed 5:9-11 Je '69
See also
Animal learning
Attention
Maze tests
Memory
Recall (psychology)
Transfer of training

LEARNING ability. See Ability

LEARNING and scholarship
Scholarly life. K. Eble. Am Scholar 39:109-22 Wint '69
See also
Education
Humanism
Humanities
Intellectuals
Research

Anecdotes, facetiae, satire, etc.

Florida fable. V. McGuire. Engl J 58:122-3 Ja '69

LEARNING disabilities. See Minimal brain dysfunction

LEARNING materials. See Teaching—Aids and devices

LEARNING theory. See Learning, Psychology of

LEARY, Daniel J.
Nonagenarian's threefold philosophy. Sat R 52:49+ F 15 '69
Personal history. Sat R 52:52-3 N 15 '69

LEARY, John P.
Revolution in religion; address, February 12, 1969. Vital Speeches 35:446-8 My 1 '69
Youth: the voice of prophecy. America 121: 190-2 S 20 '69

LEARY, Mary Ellen
Trouble with troubleshooting. Atlan 223:94-9 Mr '69

LEARY, Timothy
Founding fathers of LSD. il Newsweek 73: 26 Ap 21 '69
Key ruling on marijuana. il por U S News 66:11 Je 2 '69

LEASCO data processing equipment corporation
Congress hears how Leasco did it. Bsns W p37 O 25 '69
Fiery Robert Maxwell down and out at Pergamon. R. Maxwell. Pub W 196:43-4 O 20 '69
Leasco must still mop up at Pergamon. il Bsns W p42-3 O 18 '69
Leasco sues Maxwell, who denounces Ross meeting. Pub W 196:63 N 17 '69
Leasco's noisy battle for a British publisher; Leasco-Pergamon press proposed merger. il Bsns W p30-2 S 6 '69
Levitating with Leasco. il Newsweek 73:77-8 F 24 '69
New light on takeover defense; Chemical bank's battle plan. il Bsns W p89-90+ N 22 '69
Pergamon-Leasco squabble increasingly bitter. Pub W 196:39 S 29 '69
Steinberg's complaint; attempt to acquire New York's Chemical bank. il Forbes 103: 179+ My 15 '69
Tribulations of Saul. il Time 94:94 O 24 '69
Why Leasco failed to net Chemical. il Bsns W p 144-5+ Ap 26 '69

LEASES
New look at crop leases: cash rent. R. Sanders. il Suc Farm 67:26-7 D '69
See also
Automobiles—Leasing and renting
Farm equipment—Leasing and renting
Oil and gas leases
Railroads—Cars—Leasing and renting

LEAST squares
Estimating proportions in petrographic mixing equations by least-squares approximation. W. B. Bryan and others. bibliog il Science 163:926-7 F 28 '69

LEATHER
Swing to leather. L. Grundy. il House B 111: 122-7 S '69

LEATHER industry and trade
See also
Tandy corporation

LEATHER work
Button collecting. D. F. Brown. il Hobbies 73:50-1 F '69
New forms in leather. D. J. Willcox. il Sch Arts 68:10-13 Ap '69

LEATHERBEE, Mary
Island that's good to its guests and its gods. Life 66:56 Ja 31 '69

LEATHERNECK (periodical)
Semper fidelis: the ethic of the warrior. S. Cain. Chr Cent 86:677-81 My 14 '69

LEAUD, Jean Pierre
Alive and well in Paris. il por(cover) Sat R 52:18 F 8 '69

LEAVES
Guide to leaf watching. il Travel & Camera 32:26+ O '69
Light, leaves and life. B. Capon. il Horticulture 47:30-1+ Jl '69
Motor to the mountains to see fall's flaming foliage. M. Perry. il Home Gard 56:66-7 S '69
See also
Color of leaves
Defoliation
Forest crown canopy

LEAVES, Color of. See Color of leaves

LEAVITT, Jack
Hooked! Nation 209:737-8 D 29 '69

LEAVITT, W. W. and others
Estradiol: specific binding by pituitary nuclear fraction in vitro. bibliog Science 165:496-8 Ag 1 '69

LEAVITT, William
Individuals, front and center. Am Ed 5:4-6 F '69
Post-Apollo policy: a look into the 1970s. por Bul Atom Sci 25:41-44 S '69

LEBANESE students
See also
Student demonstrations—Lebanon

LEBANON
Eye for an eye in Mideast? Arab-Israeli flareup. il Sr Schol 94:13 Ja 17 '69
Shadow on Lebanon. J. B. Wolf. bibliog f Cur Hist 58:21-6+ Ja '70
See also
Airlines—Lebanon
Banks and banking—Lebanon
Forests and forestry—Lebanon
Guerrillas—Lebanon
Investments, Foreign (in Lebanon)
Israel—Foreign relations—Lebanon
Music festivals—Lebanon
Student demonstrations—Lebanon

Politics and government
Arab commandos. W. H. Dorsey, jr. New Repub 161:19-21 N 22 '69
Between devil and deep blue sea. America 121:410-11 N 8 '69
Lebanon government: walking the tightrope. L. H. Dean. Chr Today 13:45 Je 6 '69
Lebanon: religious buffer; with editorial comment. Chr Today 14:26, 43-4 N 21 '69
Lesson in Lebanon. il Time 93:24 My 2 '69
Shock waves. il Newsweek 75:38+ Ja 19 '70

Relief work
Of many things; Fr. Roberts home for the deaf. Suhaile, Lebanon. V. S. Kearney. America 121:inside cover Jl 19 '69

LEBANON, N. H. airport. See Airports—New Hampshire

LEBECK, Robert
Jack London's Klondike; photographs. Travel & Camera 32:45-57 Ag '69

LEBLOND, C. P. See Neutra, M. jt. auth.

LE BOEUF, Burney J. and Peterson, R. S.
Dialects in elephant seals. bibliog Science 166:1654-6 D 26 '69

LEBOWITZ, Alan
Hemingway in our time. Yale R 58:321-41 Mr '69

LECHLITNER, Ruth
December 31st; poem. Sat R 52:54 S 20 '69
Voice of the dolphin; poem. Sat R 52:23 Mr 8 '69

LECITHIN
Lecithin aerosols generated ultrasonically above 25°C. E. W. Merrill and others. bibliog Science 164:1167-8 Je 6 '69

LECKERTS, Steve
Automatic color tint control. il Radio-Electr 41:36-8 Ja '70

LE CLAIR, John
Clerk's wild ride. il por Newsweek 73:82+ Je 16 '69

LECTURE method in teaching
Little black box of teaching and learning; lectures vs. discussion sections. Trans-Action 6:10 O '69

LECTURES and lecturing
See also
Lecture method in teaching

LECYTHIDACEAE
See also
Gustavia trees

LEDDIHN, Erik Maria, ritter von Kuehnelt-. See Kuehnelt-Leddihn. E. M. von

LEDERBERG, Joshua
Genetic engineering controlling man's building blocks; excerpts from 1970 Britannica yearbook of science and the future. por Todays Health 47:24-7+ N '69
We need more research; excerpts from articles in the Washington post. Sat R 52:60 My 3 '69

LEDERER, Esther Pauline (Friedman) See Landers, A. pseud.

LEDERER, Richard, and Beattie, P. H.
African genesis and Lord of the flies: two studies of the beastie within. Engl J 58:1316-21+ D '69

LEDERIS, Karl
Teleostean urophysis: stimulation of contractions of bladder of the trout salmo gairdnerii. bibliog Science 163:1327-8 Mr 21 '69

LEDO, Liliana González. See González Ledo, L.

LEDOGAR, Robert J.
What about the new liturgy? America 120:408-11 Ap 5 '69

LE Duan
Scuffling in Hanoi. il Newsweek 74:57 D 22 '69

LEE, Al
How I came to rule Brooklyn; poem Yale R 58:414-17 Mr '69
Magical mystery submarine; Sturm und drang confessed in tranquility; poems. Poetry 113:391-2 Mr '69

LEE, Caroline
Do-it-yourself sculpture in Paris. C. Cutler. il Art in Am 57:100 S '69

LEE, Charles W.
Loitering permitted here. W. D. Boutwell. PTA Mag 64:13 D '69

LEE, Don L.
Black Don Lee; writer-in-residence at Cornell university. D. Llorens. il Ebony 24:72-8+ Mr '69

LEE, Howard Nathaniel
Breakthrough in Chapel Hill; Negro elected mayor. il por Time 93:26 My 16 '69
Mayor of Chapel Hill. Newsweek 73:41 My 19 '69

LEE, Joe A.
Inspiration; poem. Negro Hist Bul 32:27 N '69

LEE, Joseph
Joseph Lee. Painter. A. P. Erskine. il Antiques 95:806-11 Je '69

LEE, Kuan-yew
View from Singapore; interview, ed. by D. Greenway. por Time 94:28 Jl 25 '69
about
Why Singapore might make it. A. Campbell. New Repub 160:13-15 Ap 26 '69

LEE, Laurie
As I walked out one midsummer morning. New Yorker 45:32-40 Je 28; 25-33 Jl 5; 32-40+ Ag 2; 26-33 Ag 23 '69
Romance. Seventeen 27:104-5 D '68
about
Peripatetic reviewer. E. Weeks. Atlan 224:117 S '69

LEE, Luke T.
Vienna convention on consular relations. bibliog f por(back cover) Int Concil 571:41-76 Ja '69

LEE, Lydia
Dolorosa; poem. Am Scholar 38:273-4 Spr '69

LEE, Manfred B. and Dannay, Frederic. See Queen, E. pseud.

LEE, Marjorie
How people sound. Writer 82:13-15+ S '69

LEE, Peter James
Grace of comedy. New Repub 161:14-15 S 20 '69

LEE, Richard Borshay
Eating Christmas in the Kalahari; with biographical sketch. por Natur Hist 78:5, 14+ D '69

LEE, Richard Charles
Lee of New Haven; interview, ed. by F Powledge. por(p69) Harper 239:76-9 N '69

LEE, Robert E.
Self-regulation or censorship; address, July 31, 1969. Vital Speeches 35:730-2 S 15 '69

LEE, Robert Edward
American history blown off course by eighth graders. il Todays Ed 58:27 D '69
Southern gentlemen honored in glass. T. H. Marsh. il Hobbies 74:98N-98P Ag '69

LEE, S. L. See Mainwood, G. W. jt. auth.

LEE, Sherman Emery
Art museum in today's society. Art N 68:27+ Ap '69

LEE, Soo Keun
Reluctant spy. il por Newsweek 73:44 F 24 '69

LEE, Ta-ling. See London, M. jt. comp.
LEE, Ulysses G. Jr
  Obituary
    Negro Hist Bul por 32:21 My '69
LEE, Virginia
  Doubly blessed; story. Good H 169:78-9 D
    '69
LEE waves. See Winds
LEEK, Sybil
  Horoscopes. Ladies Home J 86:53-4 N '69
  Your fortune in wax; with biographical
    sketch. Ladies Home J 86:106, 110+ O '69
LEEKS
    See also
    Cookery—Vegetables
LEERING, J.
  Van Doesburg: Stijl and all. Art N 68:38-41+
    Mr '69
LEES, Al
  Widest choice ever in travel vehicles. Pop
    Sci 194:163+ My '69
  (ed) See Blum, E. Far-out flexible surfboard,
    the wave of the future?
LEES, David
  Is Venice doomed? photographs. Life 67:34-
    43 Jl 18 '69
LEES, Gene
  Lees side. See issues of High fidelity incor-
    porating Musical America
  Rock-and-rollers latch on to the blues.
    House & Gard 136:90+ O '69
LEESTMA, Robert
  OE's Institute of international studies. Am Ed
    5:5-8 My '69
LEEUWEN, Arend Th. van
  Christian-Marxist dialogue. Cath World 208:
    219-21 F '69
LEEWARD ISLANDS (French Oceania) See
    Society Islands
LE FAIVRE, Wesley G.
  Woods were not far; poem. Am For 75:63 Je
    '69
LEFF, Deborah
  Reaching in. por Seventeen 29:84-5+ Ja '70
LEFKOE, M. R.
  Do they have a right to strike? Nations Bsns
    57:78-80 Mr '69
LEFKOWITZ, Bernard, and Gross, K. G.
  Victims; excerpts. Look 33:37-42+ My 27;
    39-44+ Je 10; 39-44+ Je 24 '69
LEFT and right (political science) See Right
    and left (political science)
LEFT-and right-handedness
  Are left handers all right? N. Lo Bello. il
    Mech Illus 65:81-3+ O '69
  Guide sinister. Newsweek 74:114 O 13 '69
  Left-handed child. E. A. Enstrom. il Todays
    Ed 58:43-5 Ap '69
  When children are left-handed. il Good H
    168:159 Je '69
LEFT wing (politics) See Right and left (poli-
    tical science)
LEFTOVERS. See Cookery—Leftovers
LEG
  Time is R-x for bowlegs and knock-knees.
    il Todays Health 47:16 My '69
LEGAL aid
  Britain's Release: agency to protect youthful
    drug addicts and pot users in trouble with
    the law. il Time 94:56 Jl 18 '69
  Ex-model Caroline Coon runs an under-
    ground with office hours; British agency
    called Release. H. Johnson. il Life 67:55-6+
    Ag 22 '69
  Ghetto law; neighborhood legal services. il
    Newsweek 75:55-6 Ja 19 '70
  Justice for the rural poor; the California
    rural legal assistance. A. V. Krebs, jr.
    America 120:275-7 Mr 8 '69
  Legal aid for the poor; new directions. F. J.
    Parker. America 121:421-2 N 8 '69
  Murphy's late show; amending the Econom-
    ic opportunity act affecting Legal ser-
    vices program. D. Henninger. New Repub
    161:11-12 N 8 '69
  Politics of pesticides; petition of the CRLA.
    M. D. Green. Nation 209:569-71 N 24 '69
LEGAL aid societies
  Saturday's lawyers; Atlanta legal aid society.
    il Time 93:47 Mr 7 '69
LEGAL chemistry. See Chemistry, Legal
LEGAL confession. See Confession (law)
LEGAL education. See Law—Study and teach-
    ing; Law schools
LEGAL language. See Law—Language
LEGAL literature
    See also
    Publishers and publishing—Legal literature
LEGAL procedure. See Procedure (law)
LEGAL profession. See Lawyers
LEGATOR, M. S. and others
  Cytogenetic studies in rats of cyclohexyl-
    amine, a metabolite of cyclamate. bibliog
    Science 165:1139-40 S 12 '69

LEGENDS
  Age of strong man Samson; excerpt from
    Hamlet's mill: an essay on myth and the
    frame of time. G. De Santillana and H. Von
    Dechend. il Sat R 53:103-5 Ja 10 '70
    See also
    Mythology
    Saints
LEGENDS, Hebrew
  Biblical legends. D. Daiches. Commentary 48:
    80-3 O '69
LÉGER, Paul Émile, cardinal
  Cardinal and the lepers. il por Time 93:94+
    My 16 '69
  Cardinal Leger. R. Harrity. il pors Look 33:
    37-8+ Jl 29 '69
LEGGE, Roger
  English-language broadcasts to North Ameri-
    ca; tables. See issues of Popular electronics
LEGGETT, William
  Baseball. Sports Illus 30:38-9 F 3; 31:86+ D
    1 '69
LEGION, American. See American legion
LEGION of decency. See National Catholic
    office of motion pictures
LEGISLATION
    Terminology
    See Law—Language
    New York (state)
    See also
    School laws and legislation—New York
    (state)
    United States
  Behind the snafu in Washington. il U S
    News 67:23-4 D 22 '69
  Christmas tree bill. il Time 94:17-18 D 12 '69
  Contradictory 91st. S. Shaffer. Newsweek 75:
    12 Ja 5 '70
  Down to the wire. Newsweek 74:21 D 29 '69
  How a bill becomes a law. Todays Ed 58:28-9
    Mr '69
  How Congress really works. il Sr Schol 94:
    3-7 F 28 '69
  How to get a bill through Congress. C. H.
    Brown. Todays Ed 58:30-1 Mr '69
  Lawmaking in Washington. E. Bardach.
    Trans-Action 6:57-9 O '69
  Legislatures react; new laws aimed at curb-
    ing campus disruptions. Time 93:58 Je 13
    '69
  Robert A. Taft; Mr Republican. Sr Schol 94:
    16 My 2 '69
    See also
    United States—Congress
    United States—Supreme court
    also legislation on special subjects, e.g.
    Labor laws and legislation—United States
LEGISLATIVE bodies
    Germany
    See also
    Germany—Reichstag
    United States
    See also
    New York (state)—Legislature
    United States—Congress
LEGISLATIVE reorganization act of 1946. See
    United States—Congress—Reorganization
LEGISLATURES, State. See State legislatures
LEGITIMACY (law) See Illegitimacy
LEGLER, Philip
  Campus ROTC; poem. Nation 209:383 O 13 '69
  Manger scene; poem. Chr Cent 86:1637 D 24 '69
  Postcard of Taos Pueblo mailed in K.C;
    poem. Commonweal 91:76 O 17 '69
LEGS. See Leg
LEGS, Artificial. See Artificial limbs
LEGUM, Colin
  Breaking the Nigeria-Biafra deadlock. Amer-
    ica 120:624-7 My 24 '69 (to be cont)
  Building new nations. Cur 107:24-6 My '69
LEHMAN, David
  Comment. Poetry 114:401-9 S '69
  Poem: As the day cuts off the last of the
    visitors; Anatomy of your body; Excur-
    sion; poems. Poetry 114:247-50 Jl '69
LEHMAN, Lois
  Let there be art! Sch Arts 68:48 Ap '69
LEHMAN art collection. See Metropolitan mu-
    seum of art, New York
LEHMANN, Gary H.
  Low-cost precision scope & V.T.V.M. calibra-
    tor. Electr World 81:80-2 Mr '69
LEHMANN, John
  Looking after others. L. Graver. New Repub
    161:23-4+ Jl 12 '69
  Men and letters. L. Edel. Sat R 52:31+ Jl
    12 '69
LEHMANN-HAUPT, Christopher
  Going critical. por Newsweek 73:86-7 Mr 10
    '69

LEHNDORFF, Vera Gottlieb, gräfin von. See Veruschka

LEHNUS, Donald J.
Let's keep Dewey alive. por Wilson Lib Bul 43:552-3 F '69

LEHRBAUMMER, Andrew L.
Tips on purchasing. Am City 84:145-6 Mr '69

LEHRER, Stanley
Higher education and the disenchanted students; excerpts from Leaders, teachers, and learners in academe: partners in the educational process. bibliog Sch & Soc 97: 427-31 N '69

LEIB, Mani, pseud.
Christmas; To a gentile poet; poems; tr. by N. Halper. Nation 208:155 F 3 '69

LEIBERT, Robert E.
Homework and study habits. bibliog f Clear House 43:413-16 Mr '69

LEIBMANN, Victor
Conformal coatings for printed circuits. por Electr World 82:50-1 O '69

LEIBOWITZ, H. and others
Ponzo perspective illusion as a manifestation of space perception. Science 166:1174-6 N 28 '69

LEIBOWITZ, Sarah Fryer, and Miller, N. E.
Unexpected adrenergic effect of chlorpromazine: eating elicited by injection into rat hypothalamus. bibliog Science 165:609-11 Ag 8 '69

LEICA cameras. See Cameras

LEIDEN, Carl
Assassination in the Middle East. Trans-Action 6:20-3 My '69

LEIFER, Michael
Rebellion or subversion in Cambodia? bibliog f Cur Hist 56:88-93+ F '69

LEIFER, Neil
Lot of kicks coming; photographs. Sports Illus 31:62-71 S 22 '69

LEIFERMANN, Henry P.
Report. Atlan 223:12+ F '69
Year later in Memphis. Nation 208:401-3 Mr 31 '69

about
Right to moonlight. Nation 209:37 Jl 14 '69

LEIGH, Augusta (Byron)
Lady and the lion. L. Kronenberger. Atlan 223:93+ Ja '69

LEIGH, David J.
Church renewal in Canada. America 121:96-7 Ag 16 '69

LEIGHTON, Charles M. and Tod, G. R.
After the acquisition: continuing challenge. bibliog f Harvard Bsns R 47:90-102 Mr '69

LEIGHTON, Frances Spatz. See Gallagher, M. B. jt. auth.

LEIGHTON, Joseph. and others
Secretory activity and oncogenicity of a cell line (MDCK) derived from canine kidney. Science 163:472 Ja 31 '69

LEIGHTON, Robert B. and others
Mariner 6 and 7 television pictures: preliminary analysis. bibliog Science 166:49-67 O 3 '69
Mariner 6 television pictures: first report. Science 165:684-90 Ag 15 '69
Mariner 7 television pictures: first report. Science 165:788-95 Ag 22 '69

LEIMBACH, Patricia P.
American country woman. Farm J 93:34-5 Jl '69

LEINSDORF, Erich
Boston symphony: end of the Leinsdorf era. G. Movshon. il por Hi Fi 19:MA12-13 N '69

LEINSTER, Colin
Close-up: General Creighton Abrams; one day they will go it alone. Life 66:38-40+ Ap 25 '69
Education of a wanderer. G. P. Hunt. il pors Life 66:3 Ap 25 '69

LEIPZIG

Description
Byways of Europe; Leipzig. W. Hutton. il Opera N 33:6-7 Mr 29 '69

Intellectual life
Byways of Europe; Leipzig. W. Hutton. il Opera N 33:6-7 Mr 29 '69

LEIS
Hawaiian leis. D. P. Watson. il Horticulture 47:20-1+ D '69

LEISHMANIASIS
Growth pattern of leishmania in phlebotomine sandflies. M. Hertig and others. bibliog Science 165:1379-80 S 26 '69
Leishmania braziliensis isolated from sloths in Panama. A. Herrer and S. R. Telford, jr. bibliog il Science 164:1419-20 Je 20 '69

LEISURE
Educating for leisure: preparing for the year 2000. T. A. Mobley. Parks & Rec 3:41-2 N '68
83 billion dollars for leisure. il U S News 67: 58-61 S 15 '69
How to do what you like. R. Rodale. Org Gard & Farm 16:24-6 Ap '69
Leisure and the masses: address. E. Hoffer. Parks & Rec 4:31-4+ Mr '69
Leisure for lazy days. Chr Today 13:22 Jl 18 '69
Leisure; present and past; symposium. il Horizon 11:4-31 Spr '69
Leisure time and the riots, are we contributing? with editorial comment. I. J. Hutchison, jr. Parks & Rec 4:11, 23+ Jl '69
Our obsolescent leisure-time education; with study-discussion program, by C. Smallenburg and H. Smallenburg. W. D. Boutwell. bibliog il PTA Mag 64:12-14, 35-6 O '69; Same abr. Ed Digest 35:25-7 D '69
Too much is too little; excerpts from The harried leisure class. S. B. Linder. Time 94: 44 Ag 8 '69
Use and abuse of leisure. H. Van Horne. House B 111:48-9+ Ag '69
See also
Recreation
Time, Use of

LEISURE class
Too much is too little; excerpts from The harried leisure class. S. B. Linder. il Time 94:44 Ag 8 '69

LEISURE dynamics, incorporated
Leisure dynamics has very rich friends. il Bsns W p60-1 N 15 '69

LEISURE group, incorporated
Making money on leisure time. il Bsns W p62-4+ Ja 18 '69

LEITCH, Addison H.
Current religious thought. Chr Today 13:39 D 20 '68; 51 F 28 '69

LEITCH, David
Château gang; excerpt from The discriminating thief. Horizon 11:114-20 Spr '69

LEITNER, Bernhard
Maestros by Leitner. il Opera N 33:12-13 Mr 8 '69

LEJEUNE, Anthony
Letter from London (cont) Nat R 21:386, 747, 1009, 1273 Ap 22, Jl 29, O 7, D 16 '69
Student anarchy in France. Nat R 21:341-3 Ap 8 '69

LEKACHMAN, Robert
Economy. See issues of Dun's review
Flabbiness of national will. Cur 113:44-5 D '69
Nixon's program. Commentary 47:67-72 Je '69

LELAND, Dorothy E.
Books for boys and girls. See issues of Parents' magazine & better family living

LELYVELD, Joseph
In the Mahatma's centenary year, India finds Gandhi inspiring and irrelevant. N Y Times Mag p27-9+ My 25 '69
Mayor of Fayette, Miss. N Y Times Mag p54-5+ O 26 '69
Story of a soldier who refused to fire at Songmy. N Y Times Mag p32-3+ D 14 '69

LE MANS Grand prix. See Automobile racing

LEMAY, Curtis E.
Ideas by which we are ruled; excerpt from America is in danger. Harper 238:37 Je '69

about
LeMay disputes his boss's right to fire him. por Bsns W p 136 F 22 '69

LEMBO, Diana
Screenings: filmstrips (cont) Library J 94: 276+, 852-3, 1310-12, 1739, 2078-80+, 3154+, 3803-5, 4590 Ja 15, F 15, Mr 15, Ap 15, My 15, S 15, O 15, D 15 '69

LEMEN, W. T.
Build slot-car win detector. Pop Electr 30: 41-5 My '69

LEMKOWITZ, Florence
Tokyo's incredible shopping resorts. Travel & Camera 32:68-9+ O '69

LEMMINGS
Mysterious lemmings. il Chem 42:3 S '69

LEMNITZER, Lyman L.
Russia's growing power; interview, ed. by F. C. Painton. por U S News 66:44-6+ My 12 '69

LEMON trees
Meyer lemons, garden treasure. G. L'Allemand. il Org Gard & Farm 16:108-9 Ja '69

LEMONE, Evelyn
Records for teachers. See issues of Dance magazine

LEMONS
See also
Cookery—Fruit

LENCZOWSKI, George
Islam and the West in the Middle East. bibliog f Cur Hist 56:129-35+ Mr '69

LENDLE, H. G.
Maxi-plantings for the birds. Org Gard & Farm 16:53-4 N '69

L'ENGLE, Madeleine
Centipede and the creative spirit; address, 1967. Horn Bk 45:373-7 Ag '69

LENGRAND, Paul
Education put to the question. UNESCO Courier 23:27-31 Ja '70

LENGTH of life. See Longevity

LENGTH of service. See Seniority, Employee

LENGTH of skirts. See Clothing and dress

LENIN, Vladimir Il'ich
Encounters with Lenin, by N. Valentinov. Review
    Commonweal 90:210-11 My 2 '69
    Nat R 21:78-80 Ja 28 '69. G Davenport
Power was lying in the street; we picked it up. A. Parry. il pors N Y Times Mag p30-1+ S 28 '69; Discussion. p34+ D 14; 14+ Ja 11 '70
Variations on a theme by Marx. J. M. Cammett. Nation 208:733-5 Je 9 '69

LENINGRAD, Siege of, 1941-1944
900 days, by H. E. Salisbury. Review
    Atlan 223:134-6 Ap '69. E. Weeks
    Nation 208:341-3 Mr 17 '69. A. Werth
    Newsweek il 73:90-1 Ja 27 '69. P. D. Zimmerman
    Sat R 52:28-9 F 1 '69. H. Kohn
    Time il 93:96 F 14 '69
900 days; condensation. H. E. Salisbury. il Read Digest 94:201-7+ Mr; 243-56+ Ap '69

LENNEBERG, Eric H.
On explaining language. bibliog Science 164:635-43; 165:1065 My 9, S 12 '69

LENNETTE, Edwin H. See Emmons, R. W. jt. auth.

LENNON, John
John Lennon talks; interview. ed. by J. Cott. por Vogue 153:170-1+ Mr 1 '69

about

John and Yoko Ono Lennon: give peace a chance. E. Sander. il por Sat R 52:46-7 Je 28 '69
Peace anthem. Newsweek 74:02 D 1 '69
Top pop merger: Lennon/Ono inc. B. Rollin. il pors Look 33:36-42 Mr 18 '69

LENNON sisters
Tragedy touches their triumph. N. G. Faber. il pors Look 33:78-9+ O 21 '69

LENNOX, S. D.
Parade, charade, crusade. il Am City 84:132+ Ag '69

LENSES
Clarks and some of their refractors. J. Ashbrook. il Sky & Tel 37:74-5 F '69
Improved carrier landing light studied. il Aviation W 91:63 S 29 '69
Steadying images by bending light; gyro-stabilized lens system. il Time 93:57 F 7 '69

LENSES, Photographic
Auto-vivitar lenses. P. Farber. il Travel & Camera 32:50+ F '69
Camera; all about lenses. B. Pierce; P. Farber; J. Hughes. il Travel & Camera 32:90-7+ S '69
Dial your print's colors; Janpol enlarging lens. A. Francekevich. il Pop Phot 64:34+ F '69
Ed Scully on color; creative potential of flare. E. Scully. il Mod Phot 33:44+ O '69
Fisheyes: some are better than others. E. Scully and H. Keppler. il Mod Phot 33:68-71 Ap '69
Flare: bugaboo of fast lenses. E. Scully. il Mod Phot 33:78-9 F '69
Instructions are for experts. B. Schwalberg. il Pop Phot 64:82-3+ F '69
Keppler on the SLR; how to buy a lens. H. Keppler. Mod Phot 33:40+ Ag '69
Keppler on the SLR; superspeed lens. H. Keppler. Mod Phot 33:46+ S '69
Kramer's korner. A. Kramer. il Mod Phot 33:12+ Mr '69
Kramer's korner; Goerz lenses replaced by new Dagor S series. A. Kramer. Mod Phot 33:40+ My '69
Kramer's korner; lens covering power. A. Kramer. il Mod Phot 33:40+ F '69
Large camera. A. Feininger. il Mod Phot 33:58+ Je '69
Lens faults and how to spot them. N. Goldberg. il Pop Phot 65:83-5+ Jl '69
Long ones! H. Keppler. il Mod Phot 33:76-7 Ag '69
Love that lens! D. Langer. il Travel & Camera 32:110-11+ F '69
Metering through the lens; interview. ed. by B. Schwalberg. H. D. Ulffers. Pop Phot 65:104+ Ag '69

Meyers on technique; 50mm lens? E. Meyers. Mod Phot 33:30+ Ap '69
1969-70 interchangeable lens list; comp. by D. L. Miller. Mod Phot 33:68+ N '69
Stand back and look close. C. W. Kennedy. il Pop Phot 64:46+ My '69
Techniques tomorrow; making of a long lens. B. Sherman. Mod Phot 33:54+ Ap '69
Those wild, weird, wacky fish-eyes. N. Rothschild. il Pop Phot 65:116-19+ Jl '69
Two different Vivitar SLR lens systems. il Mod Phot 33:86+ Mr '69
What you should know about filter attachments. N. Rothschild. il Pop Phot 64:96-7+ My '69
Wide angle lens. R. Arnold. il Writers Digest 49:57-9+ S '69
Zero in on lens speed. P. Farber. il Travel & Camera 32:104 D '69
    See also
Zoom lenses

Care
Why lenses may lose their sharpness. N. Goldberg. il Pop Phot 64:62+ My '69

Materials
Techniques tomorrow; Canon and Zeiss fluoride lenses. B. Sherman. Mod Phot 33:146-8 Mr '69
Techniques tomorrow; Canon fluorite crystalline material vs. glass. B. Sherman. Mod Phot 33:104+ S '69
Techniques tomorrow; glass and fluorite in long lenses. B. Sherman. Mod Phot 33:38+ O '69

Testing
How to test your lenses. P. Farber. il Travel & Camera 32:92-3 S '69
Kramer's korner; super recticle, a quality tool. A. Kramer. il Mod Phot 33:138-9+ Je '69
Lens testing's better than ever. N. Goldberg. il Pop Phot 64:80-1+ F '69
Man who loves computers; interview. ed. by N. Goldberg. R. Kingslake. il Pop Phot 65:93+ S '69
Presenting the wild and woolly wanderings of a lens through Modern's testing labs. B. Sherman. Mod Phot 33:36+ Je '69
Techniques tomorrow; Ronchi test for telephoto lenses. B. Sherman. il Mod Phot 33:12+ My '69

Used lenses
View from Kramer. A. Kramer. Mod Phot 33:30+ O '69

LENSING, George, Jr
Peace corps volunteer or missionary, does it really make any difference? Cath World 209:121-2 Je '69

LENT, Ace
Uncrowned king of caviar; excerpt from The Hudson River, a natural and unnatural history. R. H. Boyle. il Sports Illus 31:70-6+ N 3 '69

LENT, Blair
Illustrator talks; interview. ed. by W. Sleator. Pub W 195:126-8 F 17 '69

LENT
[Meditations] F. Buechner. Chr Cent 86:244, 276, 309, 340, 364, 396, 436 F 19-Ap 2 '69
Suggestions for Lenten reading. America 120:197-202 F 15 '69
To fast or not to fast. V. P. McCorry. America 120:204-inside back cover F 15 '69

LENTFOEHR, Sister Thérèse
Out of a cloud; in memory of Thomas Merton; poem. America 121:585 D 13 '69

LENTZ, John J.
Biomedical engineering: new lifesaving science. Todays Health 47:20-3+ F '69

LENZ, Lee W.
Racho Santa Ana botanic garden. Horticulture 47:32-3 N '69

LEO, Anthony
Treble boost for your guitar. Pop Electr 31:59-60+ D '69

LEO, John
Black anti-Semitism. Commonweal 89:618-20 F 14 '69
Dwight David Eisenhower: ranking an ex-President. Commonweal 90:95-6 Ap 11 '69
Life and Times of Gay Talese. Commonweal 91:66-8 O 17 '69

LEON, Michael Ponce de. See Ponce de Leon, M.

LEÓN, Spain
Beginnings of the Cortes of León-Castile. J. F. O'Callaghan. bibliog f Am Hist R 74:1503-37 Je '69

LEONARD, Barbara J.
Journalism is my hang-up. Engl J 58:1228-9+ N '69

LEONARD, George B.
How to have a bloodless riot. Look 33:24-8 Je 10 '69

LEONARD, Hugh
Barracks. Criticism
    Nation 209:580-1 N 24 '69
LEONARD, James F.
    U.S. and U.S.S.R. agree on draft treaty
    banning emplacement of nuclear weapons
    on the seabed; statement, October 7, 1969.
    Dept State Bul 61:365-7 N 3 '69
    United States comments on revisions in
    draft treaty banning emplacement of
    nuclear weapons on the seabed; statement,
    October 30, 1969. Dept State Bul 61:480-3
    D 1 '69
    U.S. discusses verification procedures under
    the draft treaty banning emplacement of
    nuclear weapons on the seabed; statement,
    October 16, 1969. Dept State Bul 61:425-9
    N 17 '69
LEONARD, Jerris
    Apologist. il por Time 94:77 O 31 '69
    Commitment to the law? America 121:315 O
    18 '69
    Nixon, Mitchell and Leonard. Nation 208:162
    F 10 '68
    Provocative precedent. Newsweek 74:26-7 N
    3 '69
LEONARD, John
    Dangerous uneasiness with ideas. Life 66:18
    Mr 21 '69
    Frozen instants: TV at its best. Life 66:14
    Ja 31 '69
    Life book review. Life 66:12 Mr 28 '69
    Politics. See issues of Esquire
    Question of taste, or is it? Life 66:12 My 16
    '69
    Short rap with the moonmen: the Emmy
    awards. life 67:12- Jl 18 '69
LEONARD, Lillie
    Why must they die? Look 33:42-4 N 4 '69
LEONARD, Marianne
    Memphis; story. Harper 239:95-103 O '69
LEONARD, Marjorie R.
    Parent and child. N Y Times Mag p81+ Ap
    20 '69
LEONARD, Thomas J. and Raper, J. R.
    Schizophyllum commune: gene controlling in-
    duced haploid fruiting. bibliog Science 165
    190 Jl 11 '69
LEONARDO da Vinci
    Man of infinite possibilities; sampling of
    the Crown's fabulous collection of prints
    and drawings on view at Queen's gallery in
    Buckingham palace. Time 93:66-9 Je 20 '69
LEONCAVALLO, Ruggiero
    La Bohème with a mezzo Musetta. I. Kolo-
    din. Sat R 52:71 Ap 26 '69
    Case for the other La Bohème. C. L. Os-
    borne. por Hi Fi 19:78-9 My '69
    McCracken as Canio. R. Jacobson. Sat R 52:
    105 S 13 '69
    Pagliacci. Criticism
        Time il 95:64 Ja 19 '70
    Records:
        Pagliacci. Opera N 34:30 S 20 '69
LEONHARDT, Douglas J.
    Christian preaching. Cath World 208:234 F
    '69
LEONIAN, Phillip
    Silent image. il Travel & Camera 32:91-5
    D '69
    Trot, trot, trot; photographs. Travel &
    Camera 32:62-7 My '69
LEONIDS. See Meteors
LEONOV, Aleksei Arkhipovich
    My first steps in space; reprint. UNESCO
    Courier 22:28-9 Ag '69
LEONT'EV, Konstantin Nikolaevich
    Belated bow of tsarist classic. E. J. Simmons.
    Sat R 52:31-2+ My 3 '69
    Slightly to the right of the Czar. C. Brown.
    New Repub 160:25-7 Ap 19 '69
LEONTIEF, Wassily
    Revolutionary idea catches fire. por Bsns W
    p 126 N 22 '69
LEOPARD hunting
    Day of the leopard. P. L. Buckley. il Nat R
    21:449-50 My 6 '69
LEOPARDS
    Hun...what hot tin roof? leopard in a tree.
    J. Carrick. il Outdoor Life 143:72-3+ Mr
    '69
                    Photographs
    See Animals—Photographs
LEOPOLD, Aldo
    Aldo Leopold; a philosophy and a challenge.
    B. S. Tindall. il por Parks & Rec 3:28-30
    O '68
LEOPOLD, Luna B.
    Jetport or Everglades park? The Leopold
    report; summary. Audubon 71:151-3 N '69
    Landscape esthetics; with biographical
    sketch. por Natur Hist 78:4, 36-45 O '69
    Leopold report: Everglades jetport. Nat Parks
    43:11-13 N '69

LEOPOLD, R. A. See Marks, E. P. jt. auth.
LEPERS. See Leprosy and lepers
LEPIDOPTERA
    Sex pheromone specificity: taxonomic and
    evolutionary aspects in lepidoptera. W. L.
    Roelofs and A. Comeau. bibliog il Science
    165:398-400 Jl 25 '69
LEPPARD, Raymond
    Performing musicologist, a new breed. P. H.
    Lang. il por Hi Fi 19:82 Ag '69
LEPPLA, Bruce W. See Sattler, J. M. jt. auth.
LEPRECHAUNS. See Fairies
LEPROSY and lepers
    Cardinal and the lepers; Nyamsong in Came-
    roon. il Time 93:94+ My 16 '69
    Cardinal Leger; colony at Nyamsong and
    village of Nsimalen in Cameroon. R. Har-
    rity. il Look 33:37-8+ Jl 29 '69
LEPROSY research
    Long-lived rodent for research. Sci N 95:
    212 Mr 1 '69
LERMAN, J. C. and others
    Carbon-14 in Patagonian tree rings. bibliog
    Science 165:1123-5 S 12 '69
LERMAN, Leo
    Across the river and off, off, way off Broad-
    way. Mlle 68:218-21 Ap '69
    Catch up with. See issues of Mademoiselle
    Export-import. Mlle 69:114-17 Je '69
    Something to talk about (cont) Mlle 68:210-
    11 Mr '69
LERNER, Michael
    Respectable bigotry; reprint. Am Scholar 38:
    606-17 Aut '69
LERNER, Steve
    Harvard is also a summer school. Holiday
    46:16-19 Jl '69
LERT, Ruth
    Dance, a world of wonders to handicapped
    children. il Dance Mag 43:60-3 S '69
LESBIANISM
    Research with adolescents sheds new light on
    early lesbianism. Sci N 96:45 Jl 19 '69
LESCH-Nyhan syndrome
    Lesch-Nyhan mutation: prenatal detection
    with amniotic fluid cells. R. DeMars and
    others. bibliog il Science 164:1303-5 Je 13
    '69
    Purine metabolism in heterozygous carriers of
    hypoxanthine-guanine phosphoribosyltrans-
    ferase deficiency. B. T. Emmerson and J. B.
    Wyngaarden. bibliog il Science 166:1533-5
    D 19 '69
    Spotting finger-biters. Sci Digest 66:74-5 S
    '69
LESCHIN, Deborah
    Broadway, 1776 and me. por Seventeen 29:
    118+ Ja '70
LESHAN, Eda J.
    Conspiracy against childhood; excerpts. Read
    Digest 94:111-14 Mr '69
    Secret of having fun. Read Digest 95:116-20
    O '69
LE SHANA, David C.
    Quaker movement west. H. B. Kuhn. Chr
    Today 14:46-7 N 21 '69
LESIEUR, Fred G. and Puckett, E. S.
    Scanlon plan has proved itself. Harvard
    Bsns R 47:109-18 S '69
LESIONS, Brain. See Brain
LESKOV, Nikolai Semenovich
    Paronomasia and I'll tell you no lies. C.
    Brown. New Repub 160:30-2 Mr 1 '69
LESLIE, Cecilie
    What makes a writer write? Writer 82:17-20
    Jl '69
LESLIE, Charles
    Modern India's ancient medicine. por Trans-
    Action 6:46-55 Je '69
LESLIE, Lynne
    Lay renewal litany. Chr Cent 86:547 Ap 23
    '69
LESLIE, Robert L.
    Fanfare for Dr Leslie. C. B. Grannis. Pub W
    195:61 My 5 '69
LESLIE, and others; story. See Murray, C.
LESSER ANTILLES. See West Indies
LESSING, Doris May
    Authors & editors. B. A. Bannon. por Pub W
    195:51-4 Je 2 '69
    Four-gated city, ends with a catastrophe. E.
    Hardwick. Vogue 154:50 Jl '69
LESSING, Lawrence
    Life-saving promise of enzymes. Fortune 79:
    118-21+ Mr '69
    Molecular bomb for the war against insects;
    reprint. Am For 75:16-19+ Ja '69
    Power from the earth's own heat. Fortune
    79:138-41+ Je '69
    Printed word goes electronic. Fortune 80:116-
    19+ S '69
    Science takes a closer look at man. Fortune
    81:112-14+ Ja '70

LESSINGER, Leon M.
Accountability for results. Am Ed 5:2-4 Je '69

LESTER, David
Suicidal behavior in men and women. bibliog Ment Hy 53:340-5 Jl '69

LESTER, Elenore
Final decline and total collapse of the American avant-garde. Esquire 71:142-3+ My '69
Professor of the Dionysiac theater. N Y Times Mag p32-3+ Ap 27 '69
Yale school of drama: winter of their discontent? Holiday 46:50-1+ S '69

LESTER, Julius
Julius Lester: Newbery runner-up. E. Geller. il por Library J 94:2070-1 My 15 '69

LESTER, Richard
What's Richard Lester trying to do? B. Prelutsky. il pors Holiday 45:82-3+ Ap '69

LESTER, Richard A.
Some investment-like aspects of employment and pay. Mo Labor R 92:62-5 N '69

LESUEUR, Larry
Most unforgettable character I've met. Read Digest 94:92-6 My '69

LETICIA, Colombia
What Noah left behind. J. Gómez-Sicre. il Américas 21:32-7 O '69

LE TRIPLETT. See Triplett, L.

LET'S go guides. See Guidebooks

LETTER carriers. See Postal service—Letter carriers

LETTER paper. See Stationery

LETTER pictures
Words tell a picture. F. Worth. il Design 70:12-13 Spr '69

LETTER sorting. See Mail handling

LETTER stocks. See Securities—Registration

LETTERING
Lettering, art curriculum stepchild. J. S. Lorr. il Design 70:10-14 Sum '69
Origin of the serif, by E. M. Catich. Review
Pub W il 195:83-4+ My 5 '69. P. Standard
See also
Monograms

LETTERPRESS printing. See Printing

LETTERS
See also
Chain letters

LETTERS from servicemen
See also
Vietnamese war, 1957- —Personal narratives

LETTERS of complaint. See Complaints

LETTERS to congressmen. See Lobbying

LETTERS to editors. See Newspapers—Letters to the editor; Periodicals—Letters to the editor

LETTERS to the dead. See Magic

LETTON, Jennette
Allegra's child; story. Redbook 132:165-87 F '69

LETTUCE
Cos lettuce, tender all the way up. L. Porter. il Org Gard & Farm 16:92-3 Ap '69
Let us grow more lettuce. R. L. Hawk. il Org Gard & Farm 16:44-5 My '69
Lettuce in the onion row! L. Riotte. il Org Gard & Farm 16:40-1 S '69

LETTVIN, Jerome
(ed) See Sokolski, K. N. Annotated octopus

LEUCINE
Preferential synthesis of ferritin and albumin by different populations of liver polysomes. S. J. Hicks and others. bibliog il Science 164:584-5 My 2 '69

LEUCOPHAEA maderae. See Cockroaches

LEUKEMIA
Checkup for cats' role in leukemia. Bsns W p65 D 27 '69
Delayed radiation effects in atomic-bomb survivors; adaptation of address, March 1969. R. W. Miller. bibliog Science 166:569-74 O 31 '69
EB virus and leukemia. il Sci N 95:350-1 Ap 12 '69
LSD and leukemia. Time 94:38 Jl 11 '69
Leukemia-associated antigens in the mixed leukocyte culture test. M. L. Bach and others. bibliog il Science 166:1520-2 D 19 '69
Leukemia battle gains. Sci Digest 66:74 N '69
6-Phosphogluconate dehydrogenase: hemizygous manifestation in a patient with leukemia. P. J. Fialkow and others. bibliog il Science 163:194-5 Ja 10 '69
What to tell a child? emotional effect of a child's leukemia on parents, siblings and victim. Time 93:67 Mr 14 '69

Therapy
And not to yield; condensation. J. P. Blank. il Read Digest 94:221-4+ Je '69
Stronger arm in the arsenal; cytosine arabinoside. il Sci N 96:349 O 18 '69
Titillating but inconclusive. il Sci N 96:161-2 Ag 30 '69

LEUKEMIA viruses
Cat viruses clue to cancer. B. J. Culliton. il Sci N 97:23-4 Ja 3 '70
Feline leukemia virus: occurrence of viral antigen in the tissues of cats with lymphosarcoma and other diseases. W. D. Hardy, jr. and others. bibliog il Science 166:1019-21 N 21 '69
Hunt for cancer vaccine closes in. il Bsns W p68+ N 15 '69
Mouse leukemia virus activation by chemical carcinogens. H. J. Igel and others. bibliog il Science 166:1624-6 D 26 '69
Radiation leukemia virus: quantitative tissue culture assay. P. J. Fischinger and T. E. O'Connor. bibliog il Science 165:306-9 Jl 18 '69

LEUKOCYTES
Cationic protein-bearing granules of polymorphonuclear leukocytes: separation from enzyme-rich granules. H. I. Zeya and J. K. Spitznagel. bibliog il Science 163:1069-71 Mr 7 '69
Cystine: compartmentalization within lysosomes in cystinotic leukocytes. J. D. Schulman and others. bibliog il Science 166:1152-4 N 28 '69
Cytotoxic effects of leukocytes triggered by complement bound to target cells. P. Perlmann and others. bibliog il Science 163:937-9 F 28 '69
Hormones cause false mastitis. D. Braun. Farm J 93:D7 F '69
Leukemia-associated antigens in the mixed leukocyte culture test. M. L. Bach and others. bibliog il Science 166:1520-2 D 19 '69
Tobacco smoke toxicity: loss of human oral leukocyte function and fluid-cell metabolism. B. Eichel and H. A. Shahrik. bibliog il Science 166:1424-8 D 12 '69

LEURESTHES tenuis. See Grunion

LE VA, Barry
Barry Le Va and the non-descript distribution. L. Rosing. por Art N 68:52-3 S '69

LEVARIE, Siegmund
Epochs of opera. Opera N 34:32-7 D 27 '69; 24-9 Ja 10; 26-31 Ja 17 '70

LEVEAU, Carl Walter
Care and maintenance of aluminum boats. Motor B 123:77+ Ap '69

LEVEL indicators
See also
Liquid level indicators

LE VENESS, Frank Paul
[Book review] America 120:308+ Mr 15 '69

LEVER, Janet
Soccer: opium of the Brazilian people. Trans-Action 7:36-43 D '69

LE VERRIER, Urbain Jean Joseph
Search for Vulcan. R. G. Hodgson. por R Pop Astron 63:10-12 Mr '69

LEVERTOV, Denise
Invocation; Wings of a god; poems. Poetry 115:90-1 N '69
about
Poetry: how and why. J. Jerome. il Writers Digest 49:18-23 F '69

LÉVESQUE, René
Separatist maps a free Quebec. por Bsns W p85 Mr 1 '69

LEVEY, Michael
Ingres for Ingres sake. Art N 68:46-7+ Ap '69

LEVI, Clifford A. See Niblack, W. K. jt. auth.

LEVI, Edward H.
Formal education; address, May 15, 1969. Vital Speeches 35:563-6 Jl 1 '69

LEVI-MONTALCINI, Rita. See Chen, J. S. jt. auth.

LÉVI-STRAUSS, Claude
Rousseau, father of anthropology; summary of address, reprint. UNESCO Courier 22:61-3 Ag '69
about
Anatomy of mythology. C. Wilson. Atlan 224:95-6+ Jl '69
Levi-Strauss' unfinished symphony: the analysis of myth. B. Scholte. Natur Hist 78:24-6+ F '69

LEVI Strauss and company. See Strauss, Levi, and company

LEVIANT, Curt
Poignant polarity. Sat R 52:25-7 Jl 12 '69

LEVICK, W. R. and others
Rabbit lateral geniculate nucleus: sharpener of directional information. bibliog Science 165:712-14 Ag 15 '69

LEVIN, Charles J.
Freelance job idea: pharmacy newsletters. Writers Digest 49:48-50 My '69

LEVIN, Dan
Cycling. Sports Illus 31:68+ N 24 '69
Doo wa diddie squiggly wigglies: get lost! Sports Illus 31:22-3 D 8 '69
Gymnastics. Sports Illus 30:92-5 Ap 14 '69
Surfing. Sports Illus 30:58-9 Mr 24 '69

LEVIN, Henry M.
What's ahead for city schools. por Parents Mag 44:44 Ja '69

LEVIN, Ira
To conceive of the devil. S. Scoville. Engl J 58:673-5 My '69

LEVIN, Jordan H.
Mechanical harvesting of food. bibliog Science 166:968-74 N 21 '69

LEVIN, Kim
Samaras bound. Art N 67:35-7+ F '69

LEVIN, Martin
(ed) Phoenix nest. See issues of Saturday review

LEVIN, Meyer
Sinai adventure. Travel 131:36-9 Ap '69

LEVIN, Philip Jerome
Escape clause. por Forbes 104:46 D 1 '69

LEVIN, Phyllis Lee
(ed) Architecture without fingerprints. House B 111:96-7+ S '69

LEVIN, Robert J. See Lowen, A. jt. auth.

LEVIN, Ruth
Cardinal stays all winter; story. Redbook 134:102-3 D '69

LEVINE, Carol. See Silberstein, R. M. jt. auth.

LEVINE, David
Making fun of themselves. il pors Vogue 153:122-3 Je '69

LE VINE, Don
Won't somebody help me buy this horse? W. F. Reed, jr. il por Sports Illus 31:86+ S 22 '69

LEVINE, Etan B.
Problems in Jewish teacher training. America 120:398-401 Ap 5 '69

LEVINE, Jack
Ben Shahn, painter. Nation 208:390 Mr 31 '69

LEVINE, Lawrence W.
(ed) See Johnson, H. Diary of Hiram Johnson

LEVINE, Leo
Strange story of the man who shook Indy. Mech Illus 65:43-5+ My '69

LEVINE, Les
Artist speaks: Les Levine; interview, ed. by T. R. Newman. por Art in Am 57:86-93 N '69
Chess-checkers. Art in Am 57:75 N '69

about

Disposable art; plastic man. D Bourdon. il por Life 67:62-7 Ag 22 '69
In the worst of taste. D. L. Shirey. il Newsweek 74:125 N 10 '69

LEVINE, M. Herschel
Black emperor who saved Jerusalem. Negro Hist Bul 32:19-20 My '69

LEVINE, Philip
Comment. Poetry 115:187-9 D '69
What we did to what we were; Noon; poems. Poetry 114:88-90 My '69

LEVINE, R. P.
Mechanism of photosynthesis; with biographical sketch. Sci Am 221:15, 58-64+ D '69

LEVINE, Richard H.
Jesse Jackson: heir to Dr King? Harper 238:58-64+ Mr '69
They made a better school. Am Ed 5:8-10 N '69

LEVINSON, Boris M.
Pets and old age. bibliog Ment Hy 53:364-8 Jl '69
Psychoevaluation of the child in the home. Ment Hy 53:632-4 O '69

LEVINSON, Harry
On being a middle-aged manager. bibliog f Harvard Bsns R 47:51-60 Jl '69

LEVINSON, Sandy
Sexploitation [sic] Ramp Mag 8:66-70 Ag '69

LEVISTON, Merna
On frenetic writing. Writer 82:25-6 Jl '69

LEVITAN, Sar A.
Community action program: a strategy to fight poverty. bibliog f Ann Am Acad 385:63-75 S '69

LEVITIN, Sonia
Playgroup for preschoolers. Parents Mag 44:62-3+ S '69

LEVITON, Theodore S. and Bezazian, P. D.
Work-in strike. Duns R 93:18+ Ja '69

LEVITT, Leon
Trust the tale: a second reading of Lord of the flies. bibliog f Engl J 58:521-2+ Ap '69

LEVITT, Theodore
New markets, think before you leap; excerpts from The marketing mode—pathways to corporate growth. bibliog f Harvard Bsns R 47:53-67 My '69

LEVITT and sons, incorporated
Where are they now? il Newsweek 74:20 O 6 '69

LEVKAS. See Ionian Islands

LEVY, Alan
Avenging father; battle for justice for Germany's 3,000 thalidomide children. Good H 168:50+ Ap '69
Czech Jiri Menzel (Closely watched trains) directs a movie. N Y Times Mag p28-9+ F 9 '69
Is 'Petula Clark another Julie Andrews? Good H 168:88-9+ Mr '69
Sophia Loren: a woman was born to have children. Good H 169:86-9+ N '69
—See Levy, N. jt. auth.

LEVY, G. S. and others
Pioneer 6: measurement of transient Faraday rotation phenomena observed during solar occultation. bibliog Science 166:596-8 O 31 '69

LEVY, H. A. See Narten, A. H. jt. auth.

LEVY, Howard Brett
Captain Levy and the Green Berets. R. G. Sherrill. Nation 209:133 Ag 25 '69

LEVY, Jacques
Levy of Oh Calcutta! E. Dunbar. il pors Look 33:38-40 Ag 26 '69

LEVY, Leon
Leon Levy's view. R. Brady. por Duns R 94:127-8 N '69

LEVY, Natalie
$5 yacht club. il Yachting 125:97+ Ja '69
What do you know about varnishing. Yachting 125:82+ Ap '69
Wowee! It's a thrashin' bee! Har Yrs 9:26-9 Je '69
—and Levy, Alan
Scupper strainers. Motor B 123:112 My '69

LEVY, Robert A.
Sergeant wears two hats. il pors Forbes 103:80 Ap 15 '69

LEVY, Samuel, and Blair, W. L.
High-efficiency d.c.-d.c. converter. Electr World 81:35-7 F '69

LEVY, Walter James
Troubleshooter assays the politics of oil. por Bsns W p89 O 25 '69

LEWIN, John
House of Atreus; adaptation of Oresteia, by Aeschylus. Criticism
Commonweal 89:528 Ja 24 '69
Vogue 153:122 F 1 '69

LEWIN, Lee
Gentle art of nonteaching. Ed Digest 35:24-5 S '69

LEWIN, Seymour Z.
Paint-on preservation for ancient stone. B. O'Connell. il por Sci Digest 65:77-80 My '69

LEWINGTON, Peter
Fast new pregnancy test for sows. Farm J 93:H5 S '69

LEWINSKI, Wolf Eberhard von
Where do we go from here? A European view, tr. by P. Helmer. Mus Q 55:193-205 Ap '69

LEWIS, A. Carter, and Freeman, B. A.
Separation of type 2 toxins of vibrio cholerae. bibliog Science 165:808-9 Ag 22 '69

LEWIS, Anthony
(ed) See Warren, E. Talk with Warren on crime, the Court, the country

LEWIS, Bernard
Great powers, the Arabs and the Israelis. For Affairs 47:642-52 Jl '69

LEWIS, Bill
Underachievers measure up. Am Ed 5:27-8 F '69

LEWIS, Clarence E.
American arborvitae. Horticulture 48:43-4 Ja '70
Betula papyrifera. Horticulture 47:48-9 S '69
Black or sour gum. Horticulture 47:48+ Jl '69
Evergreens for accent. Horticulture 47:40-1+ My '69
Learn to look at trees. il Horticulture 46:28-31+ S '68
Pawpaw. Horticulture 47:10+ D '69
Sweet gum. Horticulture 46:14-15+ Ag '68

LEWIS, David
Navigation: by forgotten native lore. Yachting 126:54+ Ag '69

LEWIS, Edwin C.
Choice and conflict for the college woman. Ed Digest 35:52-4 N '69

LEWIS, Edwin R. and others
Studying neural organization in aplysia with the scanning electron microscope. bibliog Science 165:1140-3 S 12 '69
LEWIS, Elma
Elma Lewis, I am a breakthrough. por Vogue 153:172-3 My '69
LEWIS, Flora
Reporter at large. New Yorker 45:31-2+ Ja 10 '70
LEWIS, George
Genuine Dixieland: the old sound dies. S. V. Roberts. Commonweal 89:734-5 Mr 14 '69
Jazzman's last ramble. J. Roddy. il por Look 33:100-2 Mr 18 '69
LEWIS, George C. jr, and Feinstein, Phylis
What you should know about X-rays and pregnancy. Redbook 132:30+ F '69
LEWIS, Henry
Teenage travel abroad. Parents Mag 44:44-5+ My '69
LEWIS, John Llewellyn
Demon, sovereign and savior. pors Time 93:21-2 Je 20 '69
Exit John L. Lewis. il pors Newsweek 73: 31-2 Je 23 '69
In the wake of John L. Lewis. J. Hill. Commonweal 90:430-1 Jl 11 '69
John L: something of a man. S. D. Alinsky. por Nation 208:827-8 Je 30 '69
Obituary
Chr Cent 86:867 Je 25 '69
LEWIS, John Robert
Lewis of SNCC. il por Newsweek 73:12 F 10 '69
LEWIS, John W. and Werner, J. S.
New stage in Vietnam. Bul Atom Sci 25:21-6 Ja '69
LEWIS, Lorna
Love all my faces; story. Redbook 133:88-9 My '69
Merry Christmas, mother! Merry Christmas, Barracliff! story. Redbook 134:96-7 D '69
LEWIS, Matthew Gregory
Moon stood still on Strawberry Hill. P. Quennell. il Horizon 11:114-17 Sum '69
LEWIS, Meriwether
See also
Lewis and Clark expedition
LEWIS, Norman
Mafia: family men. Sat R 52:56-7+ Mr 22 '69
LEWIS, Oscar
Death of Dolores; excerpt from Six women. por Trans-Action 6:10-19 My '69
One can suffer anywhere; excerpt from Six women. Harper 238:54-60 My '69
Possessions of the poor; with biographical sketch. Sci Am 221:15, 114-24 O '69
LEWIS, Owen
Chex Chagall; poem. Seventeen 28:211 Ag '69
LEWIS, Reba
What's cooking? por Org Gard & Farm 16: 116+ Ja '69
LEWIS, Richard S.
Is a lunar landing in July lunacy? Sat R 52: 52+ My 10 '69
Our Terra-luna transit system: where will it take us? Bul Atomic Sci 25:22-3 Mr '69
Summer in space. Bul Atom Sci 25:29-30 Je '69
LEWIS, Robert, and Payson, M. F.
New dimension in library administration: negotiating a union contract. por ALA Bul 63:455-64 Ap '69
LEWIS, Roberta Bailey
Pride of five women. R. Hochstein. il por Good H 168:86 Je '69
LEWIS, Roger
Power people: interview. ed. by W. Rogers. por Look 33:21 Ag 26 '69
about
General dynamics: in trouble again. il por Bsns W p48-50+ O 4 '69
LEWIS, Theophilus
Theatre. See issues of America
LEWIS, Sir W. Arthur
Black man's route to the top. Read Digest 95:157-8+ Ag '69
Road to the top is through higher education, not black studies; reprint. N Y Times Mag p34-5+ My 11 '69
LEWIS, William H.
Libya: the end of monarchy. Cur Hist 58:34-8+ Ja '70
Politics and Islam in North Africa. Cur Hist 56:136-40+ Mr '69
LEWIS, Wyndham
Wyndham Lewis. M. McLuhan. Atlan 224:93-4+ D '69
LEWIS and Clark expedition
Trailing Lewis and Clark. B. Jensen. bibliog il Natur Hist 78:8-10+ Ag '69
Wildlife along the Lewis and Clark trail. H. H. Harrison. il Nat Wildlife 7:20-9 F '69

LEWIS and Clark trail. See Trails
LEWIS COUNTY, Mo.
No-paint water standpipe. il Am City 84:24 Je '69
LEWISON, Florence
G. P. A. Healy: success story. Am Artist 32:54-9+ D '68
LEWIT, Sarah. See Tietze, C. jt. auth.
LEWY, Guenter
Precarious glory amidst a rising sense of gloom. Commonweal 89:621-2 F 14 '69
LEXINGTON, Ky
Mare's nest; antitrust suit involving purchase of Kentucky's Maine chance farm. il Newsweek 73:82 Mr 10 '69
Description
Going home in America: Lexington, Kentucky. E. Hardwick. Harper 239:78-82 Jl '69
LEY, Herbert L. jr
FDA shake-up. Newsweek 74:37 D 29 '69
LEY, Willy
Historian of the space age. il por Sky & Tel 38:79 Ag '69
LEYH, Gene
Outdoor teaching. Todays Ed 58:27 My '69
L'HEUREUX, John
Carpenter, to his son; poem. Cath World 208:226 F '69
New American Jesuits. Atlan 224:59-64 N '69
Startled flower; poem. Cath World 209:16 Ap '69
LI, Frederick P.
Chemists and cancer. por Sci N 95:234 Mr 8 '69
LI, Hsien-nien
Next foreign minister? por Time 94:53+ D 5 '69
LIABILITY (law)
Legal traps of executives. S. H. Lieberstein. il Duns R 93:60-2+ My '69
Long reach of liability. Bsns W p95 S 6 '69
Problem of product liability; address, November 21, 1968. F. A. Fielder. Vital Speeches 35:202-5 Ja 15 '69
U.S. offers updated approach on liability; airline liability in international transportation. H. D. Watkins. Aviation W 91:45+ N 10 '69
What's your financial liability for your children? P. Lindberg. Bet Hom & Gard 47:8 Jl '69
See also
Government liability
Insurance, Liability
LIABILITY insurance. See Insurance, Liability
LIAO, Ho-shu
From C to Z. por Time 93:33 F 14 '69
LIBAL, Dobroslav, and Stach, Eduard
Prague. Antiques 95:842-6 Je '69
LIBBEY glass. See Glassware
LIBBY, Fred
Gold in the sea: with biographical sketch. por Sea Front 15:232-41, 255 Jl '69
LIBBY, Steve
Remotest realm. Travel 131:55-7 F '69
LIBBY, Willard Frank
Why is the moon gray? bibliog Science 166: 1437-8 D 12 '69
—See Berger, R. jt. auth.
LIBBY, William Charles
Marco DeMarco's teaching. Am Artist 33: 56-7+ Je '69
LIBBY, McNeill and Libby (firm)
Drastic measures. il Forbes 104:43-4 D 15 '69
LIBEL and slander
Constitutional liberty and the law of libel: a historian's view; address, December 1967. A. H. Kelly. bibliog f Am Hist R 74:429-52 D '68
Flip is not actual malice. H. F. Pilpel and K. P. Norwick. Pub W 196:33 O 6 '69
How far can you go in reporting legal cases? H. F. Pilpel and K. P. Norwick. Pub W 195:30 My 26 '69
Is public-interest discussion libel-proof? When can a publisher be sued for libel? H. F. Pilpel and K. P. Norwick. Pub W 195:37-8 F 3 '69
Single publication rule solves, raises problems. H. F. Pilpel and K. P. Norwick. Pub W 195:41 F 24 '69
See also
Trials (libel)
LIBERAL arts colleges. See Liberal education
LIBERAL education
Christian perspective. Q. L. Quade. America 120:392-6 Ap 5 '69
Educating tomorrow's leaders. H. W. Johnson. Duns R 94:25-6 N '69
End of the great tradition. P. Schrag. il Sat R 52:94-5+ F 15 '69

LIBERAL education—*Continued*
Liberalism, ancient and modern. by L.
  Strauss. Review
    Nat R 21:181-2 F 25 '69. H. Caton
New paths to new destinations. M. Meyerson.
  Sat R 53:54+ Ja 10 '70
Technical education useless for rapid-change
  age of technology; excerpts. R. M.
  Hutchins. Sch & Soc 97:71 F '69
    See also
Humanities

LIBERALISM
Decline of liberal politics. W. Pfaff. Com-
  mentary 48:45-51 O '69
Enemies of the permanent things, by R. Kirk.
  Review
    Nat R 21:862-3 Ag 26 '69. F. D. Wil-
    helmsen
Liberal establishment faces the blacks, the
  young, the new left. W. Goodman; discus-
  sion. N Y Times Mag p4+ Ja 19 '69
Liberalism, ancient and modern, by L.
  Strauss. Review
    Nat R 21:181-2 F 25 '69. H. Caton
Liberals, the blacks and the war. E. F.
  Goldman. il N Y Times Mag p40-1+ N 30
  '69
Our fractured politics; a liberal/new left con-
  frontation? H. S. Ashmore. Cur 113:14-21 D
  '69
Plight of the U.S. liberals; signs that an era
  is ending. il U S News 67:38-41 Jl 14 '69
    See also
Right and left (political science)

Anecdotes, facetiae, satire, etc.
Liberal's lexicon; excerpts from So you want
  to be a liberal? E. Angst. Nat R 21:1177
  N 18 '69

History
Best men: liberal reformers in the gilded
  age, by J. G. Sproat. Review
    Am Heritage 20:104-5 Ap '69. B. Catton

LIBERALISM (theology) See Modernism

LIBERIA
    See also
Foreign visitors in Liberia
Immigration and emigration—Liberia
Marriage—Liberia

LIBERMAN, Alexander
Grandeur of Greece; photographs. Travel &
  Camera 32:38-42 My '69
Italian hours; photographs. Vogue 153:188-93
  Ap 1 '69

LIBERTY, N.Y.
Nuisance-free sludge disposal. H. Eichenauer.
  il Am City 84:116-17 F '69

LIBERTY
Constitutional liberty and the law of libel:
  a historian's view; address, December 1967.
  A. H. Kelly. bibliog f Am Hist R 74:429-52
  D '68
Freedom bit; Christ has won for us. V. P.
  McCorry. America 120:316-17 Mr 15 '69
Freedom in the thoughts of Frederick Doug-
  lass, 1845-1860. J. W. Cooke. bibliog Negro
  Hist Bul 32:6-10 F '69
Liberty and punishment. N. S. Care. New
  Repub 161:26-8 N 1 '69
Options of modern man. Chr Today 14:30-1
  N 7 '69
Tragedy of the commons: adaptation of ad-
  dress, June 25, 1968. G. Hardin; discussion.
  Science 163:518-19 F 7 '69
    See also
Anarchism and anarchists
Civil rights
Democracy
Equality
Free speech
Intellectual liberty

LIBERTY (periodical)
Liberty years: 1924-1950. ed. by A. Churchill.
  Review
    Newsweek il 75:58-9 Ja 5 '70. G. Wolff

LIBERTY (ship) See Warships—United States

LIBERTY, Statue of. See Statue of liberty

LIBERTY of conscience
Discrimination Canadian style; William
  Petty's refusal to print Unitarian magazine.
  W. Fitch. Chr Today 13:71 S 26 '69

LIBERTY of the press. See Freedom of the
  press

LIBERTY ships. See Merchant marine—United
  States—History

LIBET, Benjamin, and Kobayashi, Haruo
Generation of adrenergic and cholinergic potentials in sympathetic ganglion cells. bibliog Science 164:1530-2 Je 27 '69

LIBIA. See Libya

LIBRARIANS
Academic librarian and the protocol of
  scholarship. D. Kaser. Library J 94:719-21
  F 15 '69
ALAiad; or, A tale of two conferences:
  Congress for change; with photographs.
  Wilson Lib Bul 44:80-95 S '69
Atlantic City conference: great show in two
  parts and a cast of thousands; Congress for
  change. il ALA Bul 63:931-53+ Jl '69
Career-long sabbatical. S. D. Gutzman. bib-
  liog il Library J 94:3411-15 O 1 '69
Casting for automation; new roles for: ad-
  ministrator, librarian, systems analyst pro-
  grammer. D. P. Hammer. bibliog il Library
  J 94:4492-5 D 15 '69
Changes in characteristics of librarians: aca-
  demics. J. A. McCrossan. ALA Bul 63:910
  Jl '69
Conference on personnel management; Association of British Columbia librarians. R.
  Hagler; D. Wilder; E. Smith. bibliog Li-
  brary J 94:497-506 F 1 '69
Ever see a squirrelputer, with legs? publish-
  er's investigation of treatment of his ma-
  terial by librarians; letter to the editor.
  ALA Bul 63:149-52 F '69; Reply. W. Mayo.
  63:426 Ap '69
Faculty-librarian conflict. M. P. Marchant.
  bibliog il Library J 94:2886-9 S 1 '69
Librarian in the academic community, a new
  breed? address, November 1968. M. V.
  Gaver. il Wilson Lib Bul 43:540-4 F '69
New constituency: Congress for change. J
  Berry. il Library J 94:2725-39 Ag '69; Dis-
  cussion. 94:3941-3 N 1 '69
New librarian to the rescue; address, April
  1969. J. Barzun. il Library J 94:3963-5 N 1
  '69
Overdue; a truly modest proposal: bringing
  their young members into more active
  roles. W. D. Laird, jr. Wilson Lib Bul 43:
  669+ Mr '69
Overdue; association participation for young
  professionals: bag or hang-up? J. K. Lutz.
  Wilson Lib Bul 43:1015-16 Je '69
Professional identity: revolt of the scientists.
  H. S. White. il Wilson Lib Bul 44:550-4 Ja
  '70
Telling of Congress for change. J Nelson.
  Library J 94:2759 Ag '69
Young librarians are concerned: Junior mem-
  bers round tables of Ohio and Michigan
  library associations. J. A. McCrossan. ALA
  Bul 63:910-12 Jl '69
    See also
Library assistants
Library staffs
National freedom fund for librarians
School librarians
Strikes—United States—Librarians

Anecdotes, facetiae, satire, etc.
A!L!A! A!L!A! Here we go! Rah! Rah! Rah!
  Conventions past. C. E. Werkley. il Library
  J 94:2421-4 Je 15 '69
Editor's choice; conversational tidbits for
  next library cocktail party. G. R. Shields.
  ALA Bul 63:1057 S '69

Caricatures and cartoons
We are all librarians. ALA Bul 63:1000-1 Jl
  '69

Education
    See Library schools and education;
  School librarians—Education

Education in service
Continuing education needs pegged by poll.
  Library J 94:4092+ N 15 '69
Continuing education plan reports success in
  N.Y. Library J 94:135 Ja 15 '69
O Mr Poole, where are you? library educa-
  tion vs. apprentices in libraries: letter to
  the editor. R. K. Strong. Wilson Lib Bul
  43:513-14 F '69
Signposts to disaster; or, Road to Utopia?
  personnel and staffing standards proposed
  in Maryland; address, November 8, 1968.
  R. Blasingame, jr. bibliog il Library J 94:
  715-18 F 15 '69
    See also
School librarians—Education in service

Placement
    See Librarians—Selection and appoint-
  ment

Recruiting
Consider the wife as librarian: availability of
  a position wherever her husband's work
  takes her; letter to the editor. P. Reamer.
  ALA Bul 63:309 Mr '69

LIBRARIANS—Recruiting—*Continued*
Do-it-yourself recruitment: Kern County library, Bakersfield, Calif; letter to the editor. M. Dolby. ALA Bul 63:427 Ap '69
Dropout reservoir. J. Berry. Library J 94: 479 F 1 '69

Salaries

Placement & salary picture in 1968: onward and upward. C. J. Frarey and R. S. Rosenstein. il Library J 94:2425-9 Je 15 '69
Widening sex gap. A. R. Schiller. bibliog il Library J 94:1098-100 Mr 15 '69

Selection and appointment

Consider the wife as librarian: availability of a position wherever her husband's work takes her; letter to the editor. P. Reamer. ALA Bul 63:309 Mr '69
Placement & salary picture in 1968: onward and upward. C. J. Frarey and R. S. Rosenstein. il Library J 94:2425-9 Je 15 '69

Supply and demand

Education and manpower for librarianship. L. E. Asheim; discussion. ALA Bul 62:1063, 1106-18, 1344-5; 63:23-6, 152-4, 310-11, 552-3, 705-7, O, D '68-Mr, My-Je '69
Elements in a manpower blueprint: library personnel for the 1970's; address, October 17, 1968. P. Wasserman. bibliog ALA Bul 63:581-99 My '69
Open hearings: manpower at ALA midwinter meeting. J. Berry and S. Havens. Library J 94:1108-9 Mr 15 '69
See also
Librarians—Recruiting

Tenure

Editor's choice; policy and procedure regarding tenure investigations by the board of directors of the Library administration division of the American library association. ALA Bul 63:1223-4 O '69

Trade unions
See Librarians unions

LIBRARIANS, Negro. See Negro librarians
LIBRARIANS as authors
Not everyone likes dragons; a librarian-author's encounters with library periodical editors. C. E. Werkley. il Library J 94: 4110-11 N 15 '69
LIBRARIANS grievances
Grievance: first step in improved library government. E. Volkersz. bibliog ALA Bul 63:1566-9 D '69
LIBRARIANS offices
Office landscape: a new concept for library planners. P. Barkey. il Library J 94:4358-9 D 1 '69
LIBRARIANS unions
ALA and collective bargaining. L. W. S. Auld; reply. D. Moulton. ALA Bul 63:431 Ap '69
Collective action and professional negotiation: factors and trends in academic libraries. R. P. Haro. ALA Bul 63:993-6 Jl '69
Does Freiser know best? letter to the editor. S. Mendlow; I. Morris; M. D. Leventer. Library J 94:475 F 1 '69
Laying it on the line; address, 1968. C. J. Reiter. Library J 94:1953-4 My 15 '69
Letter to organizers. E. Volkersz. Wilson Lib Bul 43:948 Je '69
Librarians' association at the University of California. E. Smith. ALA Bul 63:363-8 Mr '69
Los Angeles County P.L. votes in a union. Library J 95:19 Ja 1 '70
Negotiating a collective bargaining agreement, the union perspective; Brooklyn public library. M. Lubin and L. Brandwein. il ALA Bul 63:973-9 Jl '69
New dimension in library administration: negotiating a union contract; Brooklyn public library. R. Lewis and M. F. Payson. il ALA Bul 63:455-64 Ap '69
Opinions on collective bargaining; staff organizations round table survey. M. P. Jones. il ALA Bul 63:803-9 Je '69
Paid leave during strike urged by California L.A; Berkeley campus of the University of California. Library J 94:1404+ Ap 1 '69; Discussion. 94:2175 Je 1 '69
Teachers of library unite! letter to the editor. Library J 94:2537-8 Jl '69
Unionization is not inevitable. K. M. Cottam; discussion. Library J 93:4077; 94:11, 123 N 1 '68, Ja 1-15 '69
Unions in libraries. J. S. Hopkins. bibliog il Library J 94:3403-7 O 1 '69
Unions: what's in it for administrators? D. Mleynek. il Wilson Lib Bul 43:752-5 Ap '69
Westchester trustees warned against unions; summary of address, December 3, 1968. L. Jackson. Library J 94:134-5 Ja 15 '69

LIBRARIANSHIP
Aware. J. A. McCrossan. ALA Bul 63:741-4, 909-12, 1243-6+, 1531-2 Je-Jl, O, D '69
Bloomers of my aunt, or, Does the union suit? L. H. Freiser; reply. S. Mendlow; I. Morris; M. D. Leventer. Library J 94: 475 F 1 '69
Community, library, and revolution. L. H. Freiser. il Library J 95:39-41 Ja 1 '70
Goals for the asking; address, October 1968, ed. by J. F. Krug. ALA Bul 63:731-3 Je '69
Libraries and the need for understanding; address, June 27, 1969. W. S. Dix. ALA Bul 63:965-71 Jl '69
Libraries in a state: but is it art? symposium. il Wilson Lib Bul 44:538-60 Ja '70
Student guests; proposed research project evaluating library situations and new theories and techniques in library schools. C. Nill. Library J 94:729 F 15 '69
Turning the corner. K. Nyren. Library J 94: 127 Ja 15 '69

Anecdotes, facetiae, satire, etc.

Editor's choice; graffiti in staff lounges of libraries. G. R. Shields; reply. P. P. Clark. ALA Bul 63:430 Ap '69
Unique achievement, 1969. J. Berry, 3d, and others. Library J 94:4469 D 15 '69

International aspects

Lesson for librarians: visit by foreign librarians to Rhode Island during NLW. J. S. Healey. il Wilson Lib Bul 43:554-7 F '69
Russians and Czechs at IBBY; skirting confrontation. Library J 94:252+ Ja 15 '69
LIBRARIANSHIP as a profession
Career-long sabbatical. S. D. Gutzman. bibliog il Library J 94:3411-15 O 1 '69
Conference on personnel management; Association of British Columbia librarians R. Hagler; D. Wilder; E. Smith. bibliog Library J 94:497-506 F 1 '69; Reply. R. P. Haro. 94:1397 Ap 1 '69
Cooperation: strategy for evolution; ALA six-division joint meeting. K. Nyren. il Library J 94:2743-51 Ag '69
Education and manpower for librarianship. L. E. Asheim; discussion. ALA Bul 62:1063, 1106-18, 1344-5; 63:23-6, 152-4, 310-11, 552-3, 705-7, O, D '68-Mr, My-Je '69
Elements in a manpower blueprint: library personnel for the 1970's; address, October 17, 1968. P. Wasserman. bibliog ALA Bul 63:581-99 My '69
New breed; school librarians; letter to the editor. A. E. Leach. Library J 94:241-2 Ja 15 '69
Profession gone mad. J. M. Hillard. Library J 95:42-3 Ja 1 '70
Professional identity: revolt of the scientists. H. S. White. il Wilson Lib Bul 44: 550-4 Ja '70
Rose colored glasses: propaganda syndrome. J. Berry, 3d. Library J 94:3589 O 15 '69
Sexuality of the library profession: the male and female librarian. A. P. Sable. Wilson Lib Bul 43:748-51 Ap '69

Anecdotes, facetiae, satire, etc.

Professional status: the revolt of the nopros. R. P. Haro. il Wilson Lib Bul 44: 555-6 Ja '70
LIBRARIE Larousse. See Publishers and publishing—France
LIBRARIES
Libraries between decades. Wilson Lib Bul 44:511 Ja '70
Overdue; the public library, the death of an icy nonenvironment? D. Roberts. Wilson Lib Bul 44:203+ O '69
Quiet stir of thought; or, What the computer cannot do; adaptation of address. May 1969. J. H. Shera. bibliog il Library J 94:2875-80 S 1 '69
See also
Bookbinding
Books and reading
College libraries
Librarians
Municipal reference libraries
School libraries

Administration
See Library administration

Architecture
See Library architecture

Audio-visual materials
See Libraries and audio-visual materials

LIBRARIES—*Continued*

Automation

Casting for automation; new roles for: administrator, librarian, systems analyst, programmer. D. P. Hammer. bibliog il Library J 94:4492-5 D 15 '69

Computer system for periodicals; San Francisco public library. L. F. Crismond. il Library J 94:3619-21 O 15 '69

Libraries and technological forces affecting them; address, April 1968. C. A. Cuadra. ALA Bul 63:759-68 Je '69

New York public library dance collection gets a computerized catalogue. R. Estrada and S. Estrada. il Dance Mag 43:50+ Mr '69

Old and new design philosophies used in library automation. T. K. Burgess. ALA Bul 63:1265-7 O '69

See also
College libraries—Automation
Information storage and retrieval systems
United States—Library of Congress—Automation

Anecdotes, facetiae, satire, etc.

Machina versatilis; a modern fable. H. Wooster. il Library J 94:725-7 F 15 '69

Bibliography

Bibliography of library automation; comp. by C. Mason. ALA Bul 63:1117-34 S '69

Book mutilation

See Books—Mutilation, defacement, etc.

Book selection

See Book selection

Branches and stations

Branch power. F. Field. il Library J 94:3408-10 O 1 '69

Structure for service; why not autonomy? J. Berry. Library J 94:4079 N 15 '69

Censorship

Censorship matters in Missouri; report on conference, ed. by J. F. Krug. H. D. Kreigh. ALA Bul 63:570-2 My '69

Censorship pressure rising, Missouri librarians told; conference on censorship. Library J 94:2188-90 Je 1 '69

Confrontation in Memphis; with reply by H. Mitchell. C. L. Wallis. Library J 94:4101-3 N 15 '69

Editor's choice; Missouri university students' arrest and newspaper seizure, state library consultant's protest and dismissal. G. R. Shields. ALA Bul 63:561-2 My '69; Reply. H. Kreigh. 63:1049 S '69

Evergreen tempest: eye of a storm; Los Angeles public library. E. T. Moore. ALA Bul 63:1527-30 D '69

Freedom to read: a battlefield report, the censor knocks; St Charles County library; address, June 1969. N. S. Ladof. ALA Bul 63:903-5 Jl '69

Girl with the waterproof eyes; Statue of Liberty and liberal, but fired librarians. K. Nyren. Library J 94:1823 My 1 '69

Intellectual freedom; measures of defense. J. F. Krug. ALA Bul 63:446-8 Ap '69

Irresponsible purge; letter to the editor. B. Clark. ALA Bul 63:427-8 Ap '69

Kingston, N.Y. firing blamed on censorship. Library J 94:2991 S 15 '69

Los Angeles library commission bans Evergreen. Library J 94:3385 O 1 '69

Missouri quicksand: an in-depth survey; free speech controversy. W. R. Eshelman. Wilson Lib Bul 44:266-8 N '69

Richmond review; letter to the editor. L. Burley. Library J 94:1924 My 15 '69

When Birches last in the dooryard swung; Farmingdale public library; excerpts from address, June 25, 1969; with editorial comment. O. B. Dow. ALA Bul 63:1237-9 O '69

See also
American library association—Intellectual freedom committee
American library association—Office for intellectual freedom
College libraries—Censorship

Charging systems

See also
School libraries—Charging systems

Circulation, loans, etc.

Backlog to frontlog; scheme for circulating nonfiction books at the Orange public library. M. H. Scilken. il Library J 94:3014-15 S 15 '69; Reply. R. O. Laythe. 95:13 Ja 1 '70

Library or lending warehouse? letter to the editor. S. Billings. Wilson Lib Bul 43:512-13 F '69; Reply. R. G. Schipf. 44:28 S '69

San Antonio: books by phone. I. Sexton. il Wilson Lib Bul 43:885-7 My '69

See also
College libraries—Circulation, loans, etc.
Interlibrary loans
Libraries—Fines

Classification

See Classification

Cooperative service

See Library cooperation

Extension work

See Library extension

Federal aid

Administration slashes budget requests for education, libraries. C. B. Grannis. Pub W 195:43 Ap 21 '69

ALTA march on Washington. E. Sheahan. ALA Bul 63:907-8 Jl '69

Book industry groups prepare to fight cuts in federal education, library programs. il Pub W 195:36-7 My 19 '69

Bowl of rain: public library budget cuts. K. Nyren. Library J 94:2179 Je 1 '69

Business pending with adjournment in the offing. G. Krettek and E. D. Cooke. Wilson Lib Bul 44:577-8 Ja '70

Charge brunt of OE cuts borne by libraries; federal fund cuts seen catastrophic; with editorial comment. il Library J 94:1927, 1929-30+ My 15 '69; Reply. L. J. Brass. 94:2846 S 1 '69

Critical tests ahead for federal book and library programs. S. Wagner. Pub W 195:62-3 Ap 28 '69

Dumping the books. Nation 208:750 Je 16 '69

Early returns show lawmakers against budget cuts; Trustees storm Washington; protest budget cuts. Library J 94:2711-12 Ag '69

Educators speculate on Finch appointment. Library J 94:824 F 15 '69

Fate of federal book and library programs is still up in the air. S. Wagner. Pub W 196:29 D 8 '69

Federal library-related legislation; with chart. ALA Bul 63:1002-16 Jl '69

History written on House floor. G. Krettek and E. D. Cooke. il Wilson Lib Bul 44:119-21 S '69

House of representatives votes to restore federal library, education funds. S. Wagner. Pub W 196:23-4 Ag 11 '69

House reaffirms education priority. G. Krettek and E. D. Cooke. ALA Bul 63:1069-71 S '69

House votes to restore library funds. Library J 94:2291 S 15 '69

Library trustees march on Washington. S. Wagner. Pub W 196:39 Jl 21 '69

MIRVs and money; recurring theme at ALA Atlantic City. S. Havens. il Library J 94:2740-2 Ag '69

NACL bill introduced at opening of Congress; Library central to pursuit of knowledge. G. Krettek and E. D. Cooke. ALA Bul 63:174 F '69

New HEW secretary a library booster. Library J 94:129 Ja 15 '69

NYPL research libraries get first public funds. Library J 94:2544+ Jl '69

1970 budget. G. Krettek and E. D. Cooke. ALA Bul 63:322-3 Mr '69

1970 budget. G. Krettek and E. D. Cooke. Wilson Lib Bul 43:685-7 Mr '69

Nixon outlines positions on libraries and education; excerpts from preelection statement. Library J 94:247+ Ja 15 '69

No holy writ; address, June 26, 1969. H. H. Humphrey. il Library J 94:3131-3 S 15 '69

Pursuit of progress. G. Krettek and E. D. Cooke. Wilson Lib Bul 43:1031-2 Je '69

Status of 1970 appropriations; other legislation affecting libraries. G. Krettek and E. D. Cooke. ALA Bul 63:1537 D '69

Study of LSCA Title I heaps praise on states. Library J 94:1826 My 1 '69

U.S. book, library programs may depend on veto fight. S. Wagner. Pub W 197:49 Ja 5 '70

LIBRARIES—*Continued*

Finance

Editor's choice: message in the Newark affair: tax problems for all public libraries. G. R. Shields. ALA Bul 63:439 Ap '69; Reply. W. Brahm. 63:1050-3 S '69

One thing and another; concerning the budget crisis of New York public library. J. K. Hutchens. Sat R 52:42-3 F 22 '69

Systems building: a solution to the cost squeeze? A. R. Rogers. bibliog il Library J 94:4360-3 D 1 '69

Tax reform. G. Krettek and E. D. Cooke. ALA Bul 63:1240-1 O '69

Tax reform dangers hit by ALA-Washington. Library J 94:3950 N 1 '69

Urban library dilemma. E. J. Gaines. il Library J 94:3966-70 N 1 '69
  See also
Libraries—Federal aid
Libraries—Statistics

Fines

Breaking the fine barrier; Vigo County public library, Terre Haute, Ind. E. N. Howard. il ALA Bul 63:1541-5 D '69
  See also
College libraries—Fines

Information service

See Libraries—Telephone reference service

Intermediate departments

See also
Libraries—Work with young people

International aspects

Around the world with WLB; symposium. il Wilson Lib Bul 43:952-1007 Je '69

School libraries and international development; ed. by J. E. Lowrie. ALA Bul 63:603-9, 977-9, 1108-10, 1284-9, 1586-99 Mr, Jl, S-O. D '69

Layout

See Library architecture

Legislation

See Library laws and legislation

Management

See Library administration

Microfilm collections

ARL-USOE microfilm study pegs library use problems. Library J 94:3394 O 1 '69

Offices

See Librarians offices

Open and closed shelves

See Open and closed shelves

Organization

See Library administration

Paperback books

Black sheep in public libraries: paperbacks. D. L. Burleson. Sr Schol 94:Schol Teach 6 Ja 31 '69

Librarians for and against paperbacks: the buckram syndrome. Pub W 195:27-8 Mr 3 '69

Periodical collections

Computer system for periodicals; San Francisco public library. L. F. Crismond. il Library J 94:3619-21 O 15 '69

Where it's also at; suggested list from the responsible right. H. P. Durkin. il Library J 94:1839-40 My 1 '69; Reply. S. Berman 94 2706 Ag '69

Periodicals

See Library science—Periodicals

Phonograph and phonograph records

Pop/folk/jazz: guideposts to a basic record library; with discography. J. Lissner. il Library J 94:158-61 Ja 15 '69 Discussion. 94:1077 Mr 15 '69

Poetry

Manhattan children through the pavements. D. D. Greaves. Library J 94:4578-9 D 15 '69

Public relations

Twenty-two New York systems report P.R. confab. Library J 94:4478 D 15 '69
  See also
Adult education—Library participation

Radio programs

See Radio broadcasting—Library programs

Reference departments

How to make the most of your public library. J. Herbert. House & Gard 135:50+ Ap '69

Reference work

See also
Libraries—Telephone reference service
Reference books

Special collections

See also
New York public library—Special collections

Standards

Overdue, measuring library efficiency circulation-per-square-foot? J. R. Banister. Wilson Lib Bul 44:561+ Ja '70
  See also
School libraries—Standards

Statistics

Dilemma of statistics for public libraries. R. L. Boaz. ALA Bul 63:1572-5 D '69

Indexes of American public library statistics. ALA Bul 63:556 My '69

Opinion on collective bargaining: staff organizations round table survey. M. P. Jones. il ALA Bul 63:803-9 Je '69

Overdue; measuring library efficiency circulation-per-square-foot? J. R. Banister. Wilson Lib Bul 44:561+ Ja '70

Public library building in 1969. H. Galvin and B. Asbury. il Library J 94:4369-87 D 1 '69

Student assistants

See Library assistants

Technical processes

Libraries and technological forces affecting them: address. April 1968. C. A. Cuadra. ALA Bul 63:759-68 Je '69

Technology departments

Penntap: Carnegie library of Pittsburgh's mobile service to industry. D. R. Pfoutz. il Library J 94:1589-91 Ap 15 '69

Telephone reference service

WATS happening in North Carolina; Wide area telephone service. B. A. Shuman. il Library J 94:945-7 Mr 1 '69

Trustees, boards, committees, etc.

Trustee: reaching the advantaged. H. E. Wales. Wilson Lib Bul 43:859 My '69

Trustee think-in; meeting at Starved Rock lodge, Utica, Ill. D. D. Corrigan. Wilson Lib Bul 44:378 D '69

Trustees storm Washington; protest budget cuts. Library J 94:2711-12 Ag '69

Vandalism

See Vandalism

Work with foreign born

Library needs for the Spanish-speaking; adaptation of address, 1968. A. D. Trejo. ALA Bul 63:1077-81 S '69; Reply. R. P. Haro. 63:1518 D '69

Work with handicapped

Handicapped institute reported a success. Library J 94:3957 N 1 '69

Handicapped readers; summary of panel discussion by readers themselves. ed. by J. A. McCrossan. ALA Bul 63:1246 O '69

Work with young people

Library environment. R. Minudri and R. Coats. il Wilson Lib Bul 44:294-8 N '69

Round-up of children's and YA programs: summer innovative services. il Library J 94:2040+ My 15 '69

Santa Clara: the land of YAP; county systems' Federal young adult library services project. R. Coats. il Wilson Lib Bul 43:901-3 My '69

Teen underground library withstands attack; Federal young adult library services project in Santa Clara and Gilroy, Calif. Library J 94:1284+ Mr 15 '69

Terre Haute: no one has asked; Young people's advisory committee for Railroad car library. E. N. Howard. il Wilson Lib Bul 43:888-92 My '69
  See also
Libraries and students

Arizona

See also
Scottsdale, Ariz. public library

LIBRARIES—*Continued*

Australia

School libraries in Australia. L. H. Mc-Grath. ALA Bul 63:1108-10 S '69

California

Santa Clara: the land of YAP; county systems' Federal young adult library services. project. R. Coats. il Wilson Lib Bul 43:901-3 My '69

Teen underground library withstands attack; Federal young adult library services project in Santa Clara and Gilroy. Library J 94:1284+ Mr 15 '69

See also
Inglewood, Calif, public library
Los Angeles County public library
Los Angeles public library
Richmond, Calif, public library
San Francisco public library

Canada

Public library services for Canadian Indians. J. A. McCrossan. ALA Bul 63:1243-4 O '69

See also
Canadian library association

Denmark

What Americans can learn from the Danes. F. J. Mosher. il Wilson Lib Bul 43:959-73 Je '69

District of Columbia

See Washington, D.C.—Libraries

England

See also
Libraries—Great Britain

Far East

Books and libraries in the Far East; address, June 24, 1968. D. Kaser. il Wilson Lib Bul 43:974-9 Je '69

Florida

See also
Orlando, Fla, public library

France

Current French library scene. R. K. Gardner. il Wilson Lib Bul 43:982-91 Je '69

French library assn. hears call for change. Library J 94:3953-4 N 1 '69

Great Britain

Major changes seen ahead for British libraries. Library J 94:2855 S 1 '69

School libraries in the United Kingdom. H. R. Mainwood. ALA Bul 63:997-9 Jl '69

Great Plains

Anto wicharti; dawn of a new day for Indians in Region VI, the Great Plains. W. D. Cunningham. il Library J 94:4496-9 D 15 '69

Hong Kong

Nixon library serves children of Hong Kong. Library J 94:250+ Ja 15 '69

Illinois

Trustee think-in; meeting at Starved Rock lodge, Utica. D. D. Corrigan. Wilson Lib Bul 44:378 D '69

See also
Aurora, Ill, public library
Chicago public library

Indiana

See also
Vigo County, Ind, public library, Terre Haute

Iowa

See also
Sioux City, Ia, public library

Iran

Iran: the Persian perspective. J. F. Harvey; reply. I. B. Occhino. Library J 94:1923 My 15 '69

School libraries in Iran and the Near East. A. Lohrer. bibliog ALA Bul 63:1284-9 O '69

Ireland

See also
Ireland—National library

Kansas

See also
Dwight David Eisenhower library, Abilene

Kentucky

See also
Louisville free public library

Malaysia

Opening school library doors in Malaysia and Singapore. M. B. Wiese. ALA Bul 63:1586-95 D '69

Maryland

Signposts to disaster; or, Road to Utopia? personnel and staffing standards proposed; address, November 8, 1968. R. Blasingame, jr. bibliog il Library J 94:715-18 F 15 '69

Massachusetts

See also
Centerville, Mass, public library

Mexico

Once upon a slaughterhouse: the Biblioteca publica de San Miguel de Allende. L. B. Hopkins. Horn Bk 45:37-9 F '69

Michigan

See also
Flint, Mich, public library

Middle East

School libraries in Iran and the Near East. A. Lohrer. bibliog ALA Bul 63:1284-9 O '69

Middle western states

New in the Old Northwest: Region V, the Middle western states. J. Igoe. il Library J 94:4112-15 N 15 '69

See also
Libraries—Great Plains

Minnesota

Minnesota's first system closes its books; Dakota-Scott library system. Library J 94:481 F 1 '69

Mississippi

La dame: Camille; survey by library commission team of damage to public libraries. M. J. Morgan. ALA Bul 63:1583-5 D '69

Hurricane loss; damage by Camille. M. Love. ALA Bul 63:1502-4 D '69

Missouri

Reciprocal borrowing: suburban public libraries in St Louis County. J. A. McCrossan. ALA Bul 63:909-10 Jl '69

See also
Harry S. Truman library. Independence
Missouri state library. Jefferson City
St Charles County, Mo. library, St Charles

New England

When I was five; half a decade of LSCA in New England. A. Hope. il Library J 94:3622-5 O 15 '69

New Jersey

See also
Madison, N.J.—Free public library
Morristown and Morris Township, N.J. joint free public library
Newark, N.J, public library
Orange, N.J. public library

New Mexico

See also
New Mexico state library, Santa Fe

New York (state)

School library services discussed in New York state; with editorial comment. Library J 94:3115, 3118+ S 15 '69

Turn children's services over to school libraries? Library J 94:2386+ Je 15 '69

Twenty-two New York systems report P.R. confab. Library J 94:4478 D 15 '69

See also
Brooklyn public library
Farmingdale, N.Y, public library
Kingston. N.Y, area library
New York library association
New York public library
Schenectady County, N.Y, public library
Westchester library system

North Carolina

WATS happening in North Carolina; Wide area telephone service. B. A. Shuman. il Library J 94:945-7 Mr 1 '69

See also
Charlotte and Mecklenburg County, N.C, public library

Ohio

Book/jobs program. J. A. McCrossan. ALA Bul 63:741-2 Je '69

See also
Cleveland public library

Pennsylvania

See also
Philadelphia—Free library
Pittsburgh—Libraries

LIBRARIES—*Continued*

Rhode Island
Lesson for librarians: visit by foreign librarians during NLW. J. S. Healey. il Wilson Lib Bul 43:554-7 F '69
See also
Providence, R. I. public library

Scandinavia
Eleventh Scandinavian library congress. R. C. Ellsworth. il Wilson Lib Bul 43:778-83 Ap '69

Singapore
Opening school library doors in Malaysia and Singapore. M. B. Wiese. ALA Bul 63:1586-95 D '69
School libraries in Singapore. D. Koh. ALA Bul 63:1596-9 D '69

Sweden
Swedish library legislation: comprehensive libraries. Library J 94:701 F 15 '69

Tennessee
See also
Memphis, Tenn, public library

Texas
See also
San Antonio, Tex. public library

United States
Affluent ghetto; suburban libraries. K. R. Shaffer. bibliog il Library J 94:1093-7 Mr 15 '69
Aware. J. A. McCrossan. ALA Bul 63:741-4, 909-12, 1243-6+, 1531-2 Je-Jl, O, D '69
Dust gathers on the public library. P. Dunhill; reply. J. M. Smith. Wilson Lib Bul 43:715-16+ Ap '69
Future of public libraries: an urban expert's optimism. R. W. Conant. il Wilson Lib Bul 44:544-9 Ja '70
Libraries grow with the community. il Am Ed 5:17 Ap '69
Libraries in a state: but is it art? symposium. il Wilson Lib Bul 44:538-60 Ja '70
Nearsighted foresight. J. Berry, 3d. and others. Library J 95:17 Ja 1 '70
News report: 1969. K. Nyren. Library J 95:31-8 Ja 1 '70
See also
Council on library resources, incorporated
Indians of North America—Libraries
Libraries—Statistics
Libraries, Regional
Libraries and state
Library surveys
National library week
School libraries
Special libraries association

History
Carnegie libraries: their history and impact on American public library development. G. S. Bobinski; reply. H. V. Deale. ALA Bul 63:149 F '69

Virginia
See also
Norfolk, Va, public library

Washington (state)
Instant awareness: a governor's conference spreads the word. E. Mansfield. ALA Bul 63:773-7 Je '69

LIBRARIES, Business
Is that a fact? paperback fact books. S. Mechanic. il Library J 94:960-1 Mr 1 '69

LIBRARIES, Childrens
Nixon library serves children of Hong Kong. Library J 94:250+ Ja 15 '69

Projects
Round-up of children's and YA programs; summer innovative services. il Library J 94:2040+ My 15 '69

LIBRARIES, College. See College libraries
LIBRARIES, County
See also
Los Angeles County public library

LIBRARIES, Hospital
Services an integrated hospital library can and cannot provide. B. C. Johnson. ALA Bul 63:1554-9 D '69
Services in hospital and institution libraries. M. E. Monroe. ALA Bul 63:1280-3 O '69

LIBRARIES, Institution
Libraries in the therapeutic society; ed. by G. Casey. ALA Bul 63:1085-6, 1280-3, 1554-9 S-O, D '69

LIBRARIES, Municipal reference. See Municipal reference libraries

LIBRARIES, Negroes. See Libraries and Negroes
LIBRARIES, Private
Joy of Kate Steinitz; curator of Elmer Belt library of Vinciana. E. Belt. il Wilson Lib Bul 44:514-17 Ja '70
Kate's world: an awesome collage; curator of the Elmer Belt library of Vinciana. B. Lowry. il Wilson Lib Bul 44:520-2 Ja '70
Of skulls, spiders and small libraries. C. E. Werkley. bibliog il Wilson Lib Bul 44:188-96 O '69
On breaking up a library. A. Waugh. Nat R 21:554+ Je 3 '69
When a child a book & a teacher get together; Scholastic Lucky book club. il Sr Schol 94:Schol Teach 16 Ja 31 '69
See also
Book collecting

LIBRARIES, Regional
Penticton public library secedes from system. Library J 94:936 Mr 1 '69
Regional center of '70's seen in Pittsburgh study; summary. T. Minder. Library J 94:704+ F 15 '69
Regionalization has nine lives. M. R. Vale. il Library J 94:3016-18 S 15 '69

LIBRARIES, School. See School libraries
LIBRARIES, Special
See also
Libraries, Business
Municipal reference libraries
Special libraries association

LIBRARIES, Thefts from. See Library thefts
LIBRARIES, Traveling
See also
Bookmobiles
Library extension

LIBRARIES, University. See College libraries
LIBRARIES and adult education. See Adult education—Library participation
LIBRARIES and art
Record-breaking exhibit (library) by a group of artists (black) Inglewood, Calif, public library. A. Kerr. il Wilson Lib Bul 43:756-9 Ap '69

LIBRARIES and audio-visual materials
Organization and administration of multimedia resources. E. Clement. il Wilson Lib Bul 43:360-2 D '68; Correction. 43:500 F '69
Wait, come back! symposium. ed. by D. Roberts. bibliog il Wilson Lib Bul 44:287-325 N '69
See also
School libraries and audio-visual materials

LIBRARIES and communication. See Communication
LIBRARIES and moving pictures
See also
Libraries and audio-visual materials

LIBRARIES and Negroes
Bookmobile goes in Brooklyn. I. E. Moran. il Library J 94:4487-9 D 15 '69
Decentralization. J. Berry. Library J 94:699 F 15 '69
Outreach, or oblivion? symposium; ed. by J. C. Frantz. bibliog il Wilson Lib Bul 43:848-57+ My '69
Overdue; black aspirations, white racism, and libraries. E. J. Josey. Wilson Lib Bul 44:97-8+ S '69
Overdue; southern black studies drain. E. J. Fontenette. Wilson Lib Bul 44:96 S '69
Overdue; why didn't they burn the libraries? J. M. Cloud. Wilson Lib Bul 43:787+ Ap '69
Pied Piper in Chicago; Reading and study center. Z. Sutherland. Sat R 52:36 S 13 '69
Record-breaking exhibit (library) by a group of artists (black) Inglewood, Calif, public library. A. Kerr. il Wilson Lib Bul 43:756-9 Ap '69
Take five. add soul-boss reading; West Coast tour sponsored by three libraries and Children's book council. Library J 94:823-4 F 15 '69
Train wreck in Terre Haute; scrapped plans for youth library. G. R. Shields. il ALA Bul 63:981-4 Jl '69
See also
Negro colleges and universities—Libraries

LIBRARIES and publishers
Ever see a squirrelputer, with legs? publisher's investigation of treatment of his material by librarians; letter to the editor. ALA Bul 63:149-52 F '69; Reply. W. Mayo. 63:426 Ap '69

LIBRARIES and readers
Archaeology of serendip; art and science of higher browsing. F. Celoria. bibliog il Library J 94:1846-8 My 1 '69
Can this marriage be saved? D. Bass. il Library J 94:3023-7 S 15 '69; Reply. J. C. Pine. 94:4321-2 D 1 '69

LIBRARY architecture—*Continued*
New setting for rare books; exterior shell of Trinity college's 18th-century library in Dublin preserved around a modernized inner core. N. McGrath. il Arch Forum 131: 70-5 D '69
Underground library; Bailey library, Hendrix college, Ark. il Arch Rec 146:92-3 D '69
  See also
Buildings, Prefabricated

Bibliography

Towards systems building: supplementary bibliography. comp. by A. R. Rogers. Library J 94:4363 D 1 '69

LIBRARY assistants
Library employment of minority group personnel; LAD report. R. R. Frame and J. F. Anderson. il ALA Bul 63:985-7 Jl '69
Tech assistant survey reveals new trends. Library J 94:2714+ Ag '69
Vermont finds older library aides boon in 4-county, 2.500-mile area. Aging 173:9 Mr '69

Anecdotes, facetiae, satire, etc.

Professional status: the revolt of the nopros. R. P. Haro. il Wilson Lib Bul 44:555-6 Ja '70

Education

Criteria for programs to prepare library technical assistants; report. ALA Bul 63:787-94 Je '69
Education and manpower for librarianship. L. E. Asheim; discussion. ALA Bul 62: 1063, 1106-18, 1344-5; 63:23-6, 152-4, 310-11, 552-3, 705-7 O, D '68-Mr, My-Je '69
New technician standards released by LED. Library J 94:1830 My 1 '69
Paraprofessional course tested in Michigan. Library J 94:3956 N 1 '69
Signposts to disaster; or, Road to Utopia? personnel and staffing standards proposed in Maryland; address. November 8, 1968. R. Blasingame, jr. bibliog il Library J 94: 715-18 F 15 '69
Tuning in to summer; orientation for Youth opportunity campaign employees of federal libraries in Washington. E. Sheahan. bibliog il Library J 94:1294-7+ Mr 15 '69

LIBRARY associations
Model associations. R. Warncke. Library J 94:3029 S 15 '69
Overdue: association participation for young professionals: bag or hang-up? J. K. Lutz. Wilson Lib Bul 43:1015-16 Je '69
Unionization is not inevitable. K. M. Cottam; discussion. Library J 93:4077; 94:11, 123 N 1 '68, Ja 1-15 '69
Why organize? R. Warncke. Library J 94:1112 Mr 15 '69
  See also names of library associations, e.g. Special libraries association

LIBRARY bill of rights
Intellectual freedom; survey by Sacramento state college students on attitudes. J. F. Krug. ALA Bul 63:320-1 Mr '69

LIBRARY boards. See Libraries—Trustees, boards, committees, etc.

LIBRARY bookbinding. See Bookbinding

LIBRARY broadcasts. See Radio broadcasting—Library programs

LIBRARY budgets. See Libraries—Finance

LIBRARY buildings. See Library architecture

LIBRARY catalogs. See Catalogs, Library

LIBRARY censorship. See Libraries—Censorship

LIBRARY classification. See Classification

LIBRARY conferences
Alienation, apathy, or antagonism? Association of British Columbia librarians second conference; report. R. Hagler. Library J 94:497-8 F 1 '69
ALAiad; or, A tale of two conferences: Congress for change; with photographs. Wilson Lib Bul 44:80-95 S '69
Atlantic City conference: great show in two parts and a cast of thousands; Congress for change. il ALA Bul 63:931-53+ Jl '69
Calendar. See issues of Library journal
Censorship matters in Missouri; report on conference. ed. by J. F. Krug. H. D. Kreigh. ALA Bul 63:570-2 My '69
Censorship pressure rising. Missouri librarians told; conference on censorship. Library J 94:2188-90 Je 1 '69
Congress for change issues new manifesto. Library J 94:3596 O 15 '69
Eleventh Scandinavian library congress. R. C. Ellsworth. il Wilson Lib Bul 43:778-83 Ap '69

French library assn. hears call for change. Library J 94:3953-4 N 1 '69
Instant awareness: a governor's conference spreads the word; Washington state. E. Mansfield. ALA Bul 63:773-7 Je '69
Lobotomy and the future of the book: general adult books and reading in America, two-day conference. Wilson Lib Bul 43:931-2 Je '69
Meetings, courses, associations, etc. See issues of Wilson library bulletin
National call for library reform; Congress for change. ALA Bul 63:1207 O '69
New constituency: Congress for change. J. Berry. il Library J 94:2725-39 Ag '69; Discussion. 94:3941-3 N 1 '69
Overdue; association participation for young professionals: bag or hang-up? J. K. Lutz. Wilson Lib Bul 43:1015-16 Je '69
Overdue; members from the Congress for change at ALA convention. L. Lynch. il Wilson Lib Bul 44:326-7 N '69; Reply. T. L. Vince. 44:502-4 Ja '70
Participant's report on Pittsburgh reform meeting, October 3-5, 1969. P. Schuman. Wilson Lib Bul 44:244 N '69

LIBRARY cooperation
Cooperation: strategy for evolution; ALA six-division joint meeting. K. Nyren. il Library J 94:2743-51 Ag '69
Dilemma of statistics for public libraries. R. L. Vince. 44:502-4 Ja '70
Instant awareness: a governor's conference spreads the word; Washington state. E. Mansfield. ALA Bul 63:773-7 Je '69
New in the Old Northwest: Region V, the Middle western states. J. Igoe. il Library J 94:4112-15 N 15 '69
Reciprocal borrowing: suburban public libraries in St Louis County, Mo. J. A. McCrossan. ALA Bul 63:909-10 Jl '69
Regional center of '70's seen in Pittsburgh study; summary. T. Minder. Library J 94: 704+ F 15 '69
School-public library relations: where do we stand? symposium. il Library J 94:259-68 Ja 15 '69; Discussion. 94:245, 1267+ Ja 15, Mr 15 '69
Take five, add soul-boss reading; West Coast tour sponsored by three libraries and Children's book council. Library J 94:823-4 F 15 '69
  See also
Interlibrary loans
Medical library center of New York

LIBRARY education. See Library schools and education

LIBRARY education division. See American library association—Library education division

LIBRARY employees. See Library assistants; Library staffs

LIBRARY exhibits
Bodleian show: first extraterritorial show, at the Grolier club. New Yorker 45:20-2 Ja 3 '70
Bulletin board display: using large circles as background design. M. Garvey. il Wilson Lib Bul 43:776-7 Ap '69
Library display. il Wilson Lib Bul 44:30-1, 152-3, 262-3, 390-1, 506-7 S '69-Ja '70
Red ink on green paper: lists and exhibits before the public in December, compared with rest of the year. R. Warncke. il Library J 94:4117 N 15 '69
Sketching scriveners; exhibition of Berg collection of English and American literature at the public library. New Yorker 45:53-4 D 6 '69

LIBRARY extension
Libraries grow with the community. il Am Ed 5:17 Ap '69
  See also
Bookmobiles
Libraries, Regional

LIBRARY finance. See Libraries—Finance

LIBRARY furniture and equipment
Buyers' guide: ed. by T. W. McConkey. See (usually) first issue of each month of Library journal
Ltp news. ALA Bul 63:1611 D '69
LTP news (cont) M. E. Weissman. ALA Bul 63:274, 394, 520, 662, 1181, 1295 F-My, S-O '69
New products. A. A. Mendelsohn. See issues of ALA bulletin
Purchasing guide 1969; ed. by T. W. McConkey. Library J 94:1431-2+ Ap 1 '69

LIBRARY institutes and workshops
EDPA institutes announced. Library J 94: 1701+ Ap 15 '69
HEW approves training institutes; school, children's and young adult instruction. Library J 94:1272+ Mr 15 '69
Librarianship institutes announced for 1969-70. Library J 94:930+ Mr 1 '69

LIBRARY institutes and workshops—*Continued*
Meetings, courses, associations, etc. See issues of Wilson library bulletin
Middle Eastern library workshop: report from Beirut. I. V. Hathorn. il Wilson Lib Bul 43:1002-7 Je '69
School library workshop in Nigeria. E. D. Sinnette. il Wilson Lib Bul 43:997-1001 Je '69
Summer courses, institutes still available. Library J 94:1833-5 My 1 '69
Tomato as big as the Ritz; latest list of institutes for training in librarianship as issued by the Division of library programs. K. Nyren. Library J 94:925 Mr 1 '69
LIBRARY journal
Book review editor named by LJ. Library J 94:1565 Ap 15 '69
Former LJ editor to head Scarecrow. Library J 94:2381 Je 15 '69
Library press; address, September 1969. E. Moon. Library J 94:4104-9 N 15 '69
Margaret and Les Cooley retire from LJ, Bowker. il Library J 94:1084 Mr 15 '69
Who writes for LJ? A second look. E. Moon. il Library J 94:1101-3 Mr 15 '69
LIBRARY laws and legislation
ALA Washington notes. G. Krettek and E. D. Cooke. See issues of Wilson library bulletin
Washington reports. G. Krettek and E. D. Cooke. See issues of ALA bulletin
When I was five; half a decade of LSCA in New England. A. Hope. il Library J 94:3622-5 O 15 '69
See also
United States—National commission on libraries and information science (proposed)
LIBRARY literature
Who writes for LJ? A second look. E. Moon. il Library J 94:1101-3 Mr 15 '69
LIBRARY loans. See Interlibrary loans; Libraries—Circulation, loans, etc.
LIBRARY management. See Library administration
LIBRARY of Congress subject headings. See Subject headings
LIBRARY offices. See Librarians offices
LIBRARY patrons. See Libraries and readers
LIBRARY periodicals. See Library science—Periodicals
LIBRARY personnel. See Library assistants; Library staffs
LIBRARY publicity
See also
National library week
LIBRARY radio stations. See Radio broadcasting—Library programs
LIBRARY research. See Library science—Research
LIBRARY scholarships. See Library science—Scholarships and fellowships
LIBRARY schools, Association of American. See Association of American library schools
LIBRARY schools and education
Accredited library schools. ALA Bul 63:1451-3 N '69
Education for oblivion? M. A. Jackson. Library J 94:2431 Je 15 '69; Reply. B. L. Wimble. 94:3377 O 1 '69
Library science doctorate. J. A. McCrossan. ALA Bul 63:912 Jl '69
Meetings, courses, associations, etc. See issues of Wilson library bulletin
O Mr Poole, where are you? library education vs. apprentices in libraries; letter to the editor. R. K. Strong. Wilson Lib Bul 43:513-14 F '69
Open hearings: manpower at ALA midwinter meeting. J. Berry and S. Havens. Library J 94:1108-9 Mr 15 '69
Schools in transition. Library J 94:1735-7 Ap 15 '69
Student guests: proposed research project evaluating library situations and new theories and techniques in library schools. C. Nill. il Library J 94:729 F 15 '69
Teaching the concept of intellectual freedom: the state of the art; address, January 14, 1967. D. Bendix. bibliog il ALA Bul 63:351-62 Mr '69
See also
Association of American library schools
Library assistants—Education
Library institutes and workshops
also names of library schools, e.g. Columbia university—School of library service

Curriculum
A-V report card for librarianship. C. W. Stone. il Wilson Lib Bul 44:290-3 N '69

Denmark
What Americans can learn from the Danes. F. J. Mosher. il Wilson Lib Bul 43:962-73 Je '69

Germany (Federal Republic)
Library education in West Germany. F. L. Carroll. il Wilson Lib Bul 43:992-6 Je '69
LIBRARY science
See also
Cataloging
Librarianship

Bibliography
Professional reading. See issues of Library journal
Publications checklist. See issues of ALA bulletin

Periodicals
Library press; address, September 1969. E. Moon. il Library J 94:4104-9 N 15 '69
Not everyone likes dragons; a librarian-author's encounters with library periodical editors. C. E. Werkley. il Library J 94:4110-11 N 15 '69
See also
Library journal
Wilson library bulletin

Research
Is anyone listening? Significant research studies for practicing librarians; school libraries. M. V. Gaver. bibliog il Wilson Lib Bul 43:764-72 Ap '69
Observations from abroad; the American scene. E. Roe. Library J 94:1291-3 Mr 15 '69
Student guests: proposed research project evaluating library situations and new theories and techniques in library schools. C. Nill. il Library J 94:729 F 15 '69
Untested assumptions. R. Warncke. Library J 94:163 Ja 15 '69; Reply. L. Grundt. 94:921 Mr 1 '69

Scholarships and fellowships
Fellowship awards announced by DLP. Library J 94:1826+ My 1 '69
Fellowship awards: Office of education. Division of library programs. R. M. Fry and H. A. Carl. ALA Bul 63:576-7 My '69

Study and teaching
See Library schools and education

Terminology
War on words. R. Warncke. Library J 94:2575 Jl '69
LIBRARY services and construction act. See Library laws and legislation
LIBRARY services and educational facilities, Division of. See United States—Education. Office of—Library programs, Division of
LIBRARY services branch. See United States—Education, Office of—Library programs, Division of
LIBRARY staffs
Administrators fiddle while employees burn, or flee. E. W. Stone. ALA Bul 63:181-7 F '69
See also
Librarians unions
LIBRARY standards. See Libraries—Standards; School libraries—Standards
LIBRARY statistics. See Libraries—Statistics
LIBRARY surveys
Black decision-makers. K. Nyren. Library J 94:2203-6 Je 1 '69; Discussion. 94:2845 S 1 '69
Continuing education needs pegged by poll. Library J 94:4092+ N 15 '69
Opinions on collective bargaining: staff organizations round table survey. M. P Jones. il ALA Bul 63:803-9 Je '69
Placement & salary picture in 1968: onward and upward. C. J. Frarey and R. S. Rosenstein. il Library J 94:2425-9 Je 15 '69
See also
Libraries—Standards
LIBRARY technology program. See American library association—Library technology program
LIBRARY thefts
Protecting the library after hours. D. Sager. bibliog il Library J 94:3609-14 O 15 '69
LIBRARY trustees. See Libraries—Trustees. boards, committees, etc.
LIBRARY vandalism. See Vandalism
LIBRARY week. See National library week
LIBRARY work. See Librarians
LIBRARY workers. See Librarians; Library assistants
LIBRARY workshops. See Library institutes and workshops
LIBRETTISTS
See also
Libretto

LIBRETTO
Adriana from five to four; condensing the original story. R. D. Daniels. Opera N 33: 24-5 Ap 19 '69
Genesis of Mozart's Idomeneo. D. Heartz. bibliog f il Mus Q 55:1-19 Ja '69
Who's afraid of Azucena? O. Rachleff. il Opera N 33:8-11 Mr 29 '69

LIBY, Shirley
Case for curriculum in the arts. Sch Arts 69: 8-9 S '69

LIBYA
See also
Petroleum industry and trade—Libya
Water supply—Libya

Defenses
North African arms race. A. Smith. Atlan 223: 24+ F '69

Foreign relations
Another Arab country that worries U.S. il U S News 67:81-2 D 8 '69
If Libya lines up with Nasser. il U S News 67:36-7 S 15 '69

Politics and government
How brave to be a king; military coup. Newsweek 74:40 S 15 '69
If Libya lines up with Nasser. il U S News 67:36-7 S 15 '69
Libya: the end of monarchy. W. H. Lewis. il Cur Hist 58:34-8+ Ja '70
On the southern flank; military coup. J. Burnham. Nat R 21:952 S 23 '69
Textbook coup in a desert kingdom. il Time 94:34 S 12 '69
Widening ripples. Newsweek 74:46 S 22 '69
Young men in a hurry. Time 94:17-18 D 26 '69
Youth movement. A. de Borchgrave. il Newsweek 74:56+ O 20 '69

LICAVOLI, Thomas
Governor and the mobster; with report by D. Walsh. il Life 66:28-32A My 2 '69
Rhodes under fire. il por Time 93:18-19 My 2 '69

LICAVOLI, Yonnie. See Licavoli, T.

LICENSE agreements, International. See International license agreements

LICENSES
See also
Automobile drivers—Licenses

LICHTENSTEIN, Roy F.
Art and technology in California. F. Tuten. Vogue 153:36 Ap 15 '69
Art; borrowing techniques of other artists. L. Alloway. Nation 209:92-3 Jl 28 '69
Art world; retrospective exhibition at Guggenheim. H. Rosenberg. New Yorker 45: 167-70+ N 8 '69
Inside the Trojan horse; exhibition at the Guggenheim. E. F. Fry. il por Art N 68: 36-9+ O '69
Roy Lichtenstein, who paints with cool. D. Sylvester. il pors Vogue 154:142-5+ S 15 '69

LICHTHEIM, George
De Gaulle, a summing up. Commentary 48: 79-85 S '69
From the ruins of empire. bibliog f Commentary 48:75-81 D '69
Public affairs (cont) Commentary 47:69-75 Mr '69
World politics, 1969. Commentary 47:50-8 Je '69

LICORICE
Licorice; no longer seen as harmless flavoring. il Consumer Bul 52:4 Ap '69

LIDSTROM, Gwendolynn
Small town. Sat R 52:4-5 Jl 5 '69

LIE, Trygve
Death of Trygve Lie; statements, December 30, 1968. L. B. Johnson; D. Rusk; J. R. Wiggins. Dept State Bul 60:78-9 Ja 27 '69
Secretary-General sends message on death of Trygve Lie. UN Mo Chron 6:109 Ja '69

LIE detectors
Big lie in criminal investigation. il Chem 42:3-5 Jl '69
See also
Polygraph

LIEBERMAN, Carol C.
Moctezuma's musicians. Américas 21:23-8 F '69

LIEBERMAN, Irv
Could you be a hero? Mech Illus 65:98-9+ N '69

LIEBERMAN, Laurence
Critic of the month. Poetry 114:40-58 Ap '69
Underwater skin flight; peacock flounder; poem. Sat R 52:57 Ap 26 '69

about
Books that look out, books that look in. W. Stafford. Poetry 113:423 Mr '69

LIEBERMAN, Philip H. and others
Vocal tract limitations on the vowel repertoires of rhesus monkey and other non-human primates. bibliog Science 164:1185-7 Je 6 '69

LIEBERSTEIN, Stanley H.
How companies stay out of the courtroom. Duns R 94:64-6+ S '69
Is executive insurance worth it? Duns R 94:53-4+ Jl '69
Legal traps of executives. Duns R 93:60-2+ My '69

LIEBLING, Estelle
First lady of voice; interview, ed. by Q. Eaton. por Opera N 33:26-8 Mr 1 '69

LIECHTENSTEIN
Liechtenstein. P. Gallico. il Travel & Camera 32:63-5 Jl '69
See also
Tourist trade—Liechtenstein

LIEDER, Ruth
Sporting look (cont) Sports Illus 30:64-5 Mr 17; 72-3 Je 9; 52-3 Je 23; 31:60-1 D 8 '69

LIEDER. See Songs, German

LIEF, Harold
Re-evaluating the pill. Newsweek 75:66 Ja 12 '70

LIEMOHN, Harold B.
Optical observations of Apollo 8. Sky & Tel 37:156-60 Mr '69

LIERHEIMER, Alvin P.
Cast off the bowline? Todays Ed 58:62 Mr '69

LIES. See Lying

LIESEGANG rings
Amateur scientist; salts react in a gel to make the colorful Liesegang bands. R. Sassen. il Sci Am 220:131-5 Je '69

LIESSE, Melanie. See Coleman, J. jt. auth.

LIETZMANN, Sabina
Guilty optimists. Harper 238:92+ F '69

LIEVENS, Jan, the elder
Rembrandt and his circle. B. A. Rifkin. il Art N 68:31-4+ O '69

LIFCHEZ, Raymond
Brilliant museum reflects Mexico's cultural ambitions; Four museums in a park. Arch Rec 145:176-81 Je '69

LIFE
See also
Conduct of life

LIFE (biology)
Breakthroughs for better or worse; isolating the gene. America 121:580-1 D 13 '69
Major first for U.S. scientists. il U S News 66:6 Ja 27 '69
Moon could answer the riddle of life. I. Asimov. il N Y Times Mag p 12-15+ Jl 13 '69; Same with title Why we must explore the moon. Sci Digest 66:16-17 O '69
Size of life. J. T. Bonner. il Natur Hist 78: 40-5 Ja '69
Spinning the thread of life. J. Lear. il Sat R 52:63-6 Ap 5 '69
See also
Genetics
Reproduction

Origin
Life's building blocks in space; discovery of first polyatomic organic molecule. Sci N 95:351 Ap 12 '69
Origin of life (cont) E. Keller. bibliog il Chem 42:12-18 Ja; 8-13 Ap '69

LIFE (periodical)
Change at Life; new managing editor. Time 93:60 My 16 '69
Coming to life; News projects department. il Newsweek 73:95 My 19 '69
Hattersley class; looking at Life. R. Hattersley. il Pop Phot 64:103-6 Je '69
Have some more guacamole, said the President. R. Graves. Life 67:3 S 5 '69
It's the third, not the fourth estate; farewell statement. J. K. Jessup. Life 66:3 Ap 4 '69
Life memo goes public; changes. Bsns W p42 My 17 '69
Life seeks more spark. Bsns W p 135 My 10 '69
Pablo Picasso, this is your Life; fake interview quoted in special issue. T. B. Hess. Art N 67:27+ F '69
We open a new picture gallery. R. Graves. Life 67:1 Ag 1 '69
Word from a departing M.E. G. P. Hunt. il Life 66:3 Je 6 '69

Covers
See Periodical covers

LIFE, Duration of. See Longevity

LIFE, Length of. See Longevity

LIFE adjustment education. See Education—Aims and objectives

LIFE expectancy. See Longevity

LIFE guard; story. See Wain, J.

LIFE in other worlds. See Life on other planets

LIFE insurance. See Insurance, Life

LIFE insurance companies. See Insurance companies

LIFE insurance stocks. See Insurance companies—Securities

LIFE jackets. See Life preservers

LIFE on other planets
Animal life on Jupiter? Sci Digest 66:30-1 Jl '69
Contradictions in temperature data spark dispute about possibility of life on Mars. N. S. Himmel. il Aviation W 91:90-1+ Ag 18 '69
Lookout for life. H. P. Klein. il Space World F-2-62:42-3 F '69
New debate over life on Mars. U S News 67:9 Ag 18 '69
Origin of life. E. Keller. bibliog il Chem 42:8-13 Ap '69
Venus and Mars; statements. R. Jastrow. New Yorker 45:29-31 My 10 '69

LIFE preservers
Fall in? Don't worry. il Sunset 143:58-61 Jl '69
Primer for self-preservation. F. M. Paulson. il Field & S 74:146-8+ O '69

LIFE-saving equipment
Beachphones real lifesavers. il Parks & Rec 4:53+ My '69
Lifesaving devices for boats. il Consumer Rep 34:450-6 Ag '69
Safety and survival at sea; safety harnesses. G. B. Bleil. il Yachting 125:78-9+ My '69
Use your LSD; advice on life-saving devices. P. H. Spectre. il Yachting 125:122-3+ Ja '69

LIFE span. See Longevity

LIFE span (animals) See Age (animals)

LIFE support systems (space environment)
In the news; portable life support system. Space World F-6-66:50 Je '69
Project Apollo portable life support system. il Space World F-7-67:4-9 Jl '69
Water in space travel; water regeneration system. B. Adamovich and others. Space World F-6-66:8-9 Je '69
Year in starcraft on earth; Russian experiment. il Space World F-4-64:14-18 Ap '69

Testing
Soviets gain new data on closed ecology; yearlong life-support experiment. il Aviation W 90:74-6 Ja 20 '69

LIFE support systems (submarine environment)
In the news; emergency breathing system for DSRV. Space World F-8-68:46-7 Ag '69

LIFE to live; story. See Crossman, P.

LIFE zones
Vegetational change along altitudinal gradients. E. W. Beals. bibliog il Science 165:981-5 S 5 '69

LIFELINE; story. See Creal, M.

LIFETIME sports foundation
Gold medal for Phoenix. G. L. Gardner. il Parks & Rec 4:24-8 My '69

LIFSCHUTZ, Joseph E.
Does an analyst tell? por Newsweek 74:67 D 22 '69

LIFT (aerodynamics)
See also
Flaps, Airplane

LIFTING
See also
Weight lifting

LIFTING bodies. See Space vehicles—Landing systems

LIFTON, Betty Jean
Report on a thousand cranes. Horn Bk 45:148-52 Ap '69

LIFTON, Robert Jay
Birdbrains; excerpt from Birds. Atlan 224:46-7 Ag '69
Death in life: a statement. Bul Atom Sci 25:39 Je '69
Lifton's birds. il Nation 209:548 N 17 '69
Vietnam: betrayal and self-betrayal. Trans-Action 6:6-7 O '69
Why civilians are war victims; interview. por U S News 67:25-3 D 15 '69
Young and the old: notes on a new history; excerpts from History and survival. Atlan 224:47-54 S; 83-8 O '69

about
Book industry presents the 20th National book awards; with excerpts from acceptance address. por Pub W 195:29 Mr 24 '69

LIGAMENTS
Interpubic ligament: elasticity in pregnant free-tailed bat. E. S. Crelin. il Science 164:81 Ap 4 '69

LIGETI, György
Music; presentation of Atmosphères by New York philharmonic. D. Hamilton. Nation 209:549 N 17 '69

LIGHT, James F.
I shan't be gone long. Nation 210:26-8 Ja 12 '70

LIGHT
Look at light! il Duns R 94:71-4 Jl '69
New waves of the future. E. Bowen. il Am Home 72:69-71 O '69
See also
Diffraction
Fluorescence
Photochemistry
Photography—Light
Refraction
Sunlight

Physiological effects
Azotobacter cysts: reactivation by white light after inactivation by ultraviolet radiation. G. R. Vela and J. W. Peterson. bibliog il Science 166:1296-7 D 5 '69
Circadian clock action spectrum in a photoperiodic moth. V. G. Bruce and D. H. Minis. bibliog il Science 163:583-5 F 7 '69
Light and your health. W. Hartley and E. Hartley. il Pop Sci 194:78-80+ F '69
Snowshoe rabbit; varying hare's change of color due to reduced length of daylight. Cons 23:27 F '69
See also
Algae, Effect of light on
Photoperiodism

Velocity
Exceeding the speed limit; debate over existence of particle that travels faster than light. il Time 93:42+ F 14 '69
Isaac Asimov explains; traveling faster than light. I. Asimov. Sci Digest 66:74-5 Ag '69
Pulsar test of a variation of the speed of light with frequency. G. Feinberg. bibliog il Science 166:879-81 N 14 '69

LIGHT, Colored
Equipment report; Edmund scientific co.'s Motiondizer. B. Wells. il Radio-Electr 40:75 F '69
Tune-in with psychedelic light-show systems you can build. W. S. Bacon and S. Shatavsky. il Pop Sci 194:158-61 My '69

LIGHT, Photography of. See Photography of light

LIGHT airplanes. See Airplanes, Light

LIGHT amplifiers. See Lasers

LIGHT bulbs. See Electric lamps

LIGHT communication systems
Fire engine has a built-in traffic cop. il Pop Sci 195:93 N '69
Flight tests to evaluate laser data link. B. M. Elson. Aviation W 91:66-8 N 24 '69
Laser coupled with thin-film. il Aviation W 91:91+ Ag 11 '69
Laser effort swings to applications. B. M. Elson. il Aviation W 91:77+ Jl 7 '69
Real-time systems speed recon pictures; compass link and quick look systems. B. M. Elson. il Aviation W 91:95+ N 17 '69

LIGHT filters
Ed Scully on color; effect of price competition without adequate standards. E. Scully. Mod Phot 33:32+ Ag '69
Funny, you don't look like an 85C! D. B. Eisendrath. il Pop Phot 64:10+ Je '69
What you should know about filter attachments. N. Rothschild. il Pop Phot 64:96-7+ My '69

LIGHT flashers. See Electric lighting—Control

LIGHT in art
Light conversation; Soundings at the Museum of modern art. S. Gablik. il Art N 67:58-60 N '68

LIGHT intensification. See Image intensifiers

LIGHT meters. See Exposure meters; Photometers

LIGHT projection
Floodlights light an interchange; San Antonio, Tex. il Am City 84:154 My '69
Light you can touch; T. Torffield's creations called Interfusion. il Esquire 72:64-7 Ag '69

LIGHT shows. See Light, Colored

LIGHT verse. See Poetry

LIGHTBODY, Lucy
Wet paint from Paris. Sr Schol 94:Schol Teach 10-11 Ap 25 '69

LIGHTHOUSES
Now the Point Pinos lighthouse has a downstairs museum. il Sunset 142:43 Mr '69
Tillamook rock: beacon of silence. H. Hansen. il Sea Front 15:54-60 Ja '69
LIGHTING
Three designers talk about light. J. L. Larsen; L. Peabody; J. Head. Am Home 72: 42 O '69
See also
Electric lighting
Skylights
also subhead Lighting under various subjects, e.g. Photography—Lighting
LIGHTING, Architectural and decorative
Light box overhead. il Sunset 142:116 Mr '69
Light: the revealing dimension; interviews, ed. by J. H. Ingersoll. S. R. Shemitz; J. Maguire. il House B 111:106-10+ Ap '69
LIGHTING, Outdoor
Outdoor lighting. See issues of American city
To find the house entry. il Sunset 142:98 Je '69
Ways to light up the yard & garden. il Changing T 23:11-13 Jl '69
See also subhead Lighting under various subjects, e.g. Skating rinks—Lighting; also under names of cities, e.g. Los Angeles—Lighting
Control
See Electric lighting—Control
LIGHTING fixtures
Electrician in the house. M. Spires. il Am Home 72:34 O '69
Three designers talk about light. J. L. Larsen; L. Peabody; J. Head. Am Home 72: 42 O '69
See also
Street lighting fixtures
LIGHTING in house decoration. See Lighting, Architectural and decorative
LIGHTNING
Manmade lightning: Apollo 12 liftoff into electrically charged clouds. il Sci N 96: 574 D 20 '69
LIGHTNING, Artificial
Thunderbolt machine tests tomorrow's power lines; General electric's ultra high voltage laboratory at Pittsfield, Mass. W. S. Bacon. il Pop Sci 195:82-5+ O '69
LIGHTNING protection
How to lightning-proof your home. R. Capotosto. il Mech Illus 65:95-7+ F '69
What do you know about... T. G. Dickinson. il Yachting 125:74-5+ Ap '69
LIGHTPLANES. See Airplanes, Light
LIGNITE
Senckenberg lignite: a lignitized wood with apparently original cellulose and lignin. P. R. Morey and E. D. Morey. bibliog il Science 164:836-8 My 16 '69
LIGON, Ronald S.
Christus gardens. il Travel 131:34-5+ Ap '69
LIKE, Arthur A. and Chick, W. L.
Mitotic division in pancreatic beta cells. bibliog Science 163:941-3 F 28 '69
LIKENS, Gene E. and others
Nitrification: importance to nutrient losses from a cutover forested ecosystem. bibliog Science 163:1205-6 Mr 14 '69
LILACS
1968 lilac survey. F. J. Niedz. il Horticulture 47:42-4 My '69
LILES, Samuel L. and Davis, G. D.
Athetoid and choreiform hyperkinesias produced by caudate lesions in the cat. bibliog Science 164:195-7 Ap 11 '69
LILIENTHAL, David Eli
Long view. il por Newsweek 73:56-7 My 12 '69
Man of many careers. A. Cooper. il por Newsweek 73:102+ Mr 10 '69
South Vietnam after the war: how it could be rebuilt. il por U S News 66:34-5 Ap 21 '69
LILIES
And a wealth of lilies for $35. H. Mason. il Bet Hom & Gard 47:78-9 O '69
For this flower show, plant now. Sunset 143: 224 N '69
Lilies for small gardens. V. Howie. il Horticulture 47:18-19+ Je '69
Lilies: high style for your garden. E. McDonald. il House B 111:152-3+ My '69
Lilies with an American heritage. J. De Graaff. il Home Gard 56:26-8 Ag '69
Madonna lily. B. Brinhart. il Org Gard & Farm 16:42-3 Ag '69
Wild lilies. V. Howie. il Horticulture 46:30-1+ O '68
See also
Day lilies
Desert candles
Mariposa lilies
Water lilies

LILLARD, Richard G.
Nature and conservation. bibliog por Wilson Lib Bul 44:158-77 O '69
LILLARD, Stewart
Ellison's ambitious scope in Invisible man. bibliog f Engl J 58:833-9 S '69
LILLIE, Beatrice
Night I sang Carmen at the Met; ed. by F. Hogan. pors Opera N 33:12-15 Mr 15 '69
LILLY, Othelia
Our circuit preacher: poem. Chr Cent 86:679 My 14 '69
LILY pools. See Garden pools
LIMA, Peru
Flower exhibit
See Flower exhibits
Poor
Lima slum. R. C. Hirschfield; reply with rejoinder. W. C. Francis. Cath World 208: 196 F '69
LIMA beans
Bush lima beans, a luxury northern gardeners can afford. Org Gard & Farm 16:45-6 Jl '69
LIMA flower show. See Flower exhibits
LIMBACHER, James L.
On the record: Words. See issues of Library journal
Recordings. See second issue of each month of Library journal
LIMBOURG brothers
Très riches heures of Jean, duke of Berry. Review
Art in Am il 57:56-56A N '69. J. Jacobs
LIME
Recalcining lime sludge produces multiple benefits; St Paul. C. W. Hamblin. il Am City 84:67-9+ N '69
What you should know about lime. D. Barrows. Home Gard 56:54 Mr '69
LIMERICKS
Limericks are jovial things; excerpts from The lure of the limerick. W. S. Baring-Gould. Read Digest 94:84-5 F '69
LIMESTONE
See also
Dolomite (mineral)
LIMITATION of arms. See Disarmament
LIMITATION of population. See Population
LIMITED war. See War
LIMNOLOGY
Carbon dioxide partial pressure in the Columbia River. P. K. Park and others. bibliog il Science 166:867-8 N 14 '69
Temperatures and related factors in lakes. D. A. Webster. il Cons 24:12-16+ D '69 (to be cont)
LIMÓN, José
José Limón & dance co; Billy Rose theatre. J. Anderson. Dance Mag 43:92-3 Mr '69
Jose Limon and dance company. Brooklyn academy of music. M. Marks. Dance Mag 43:35 Je '69
LIMON, Mordechai
Israel's Mordechai Limon: a flair for derring-do. por Newsweek 75:28 Ja 12 '70
LIMULUS. See King crabs
LIN, Piao
Communist China 1969: address. April 1, 1969. Vital Speeches 35:485-97 Je 1 '69
about
Man picked to succeed Mao. il por U S News 66:21 Ap 14 '69
Mao's heir. Time 93:33 Ap 11 '69
LIN, Robert C. and others
Lysergic acid diethylamide: role in conversion of plasma tryptophan to brain serotonin (5-hydroxytryptamine) bibliog Science 166:237-9 O 10 '69
LINCKS, John F.
Close reading of Hard times. Engl J 58:212-18 F '69
LINCOLN, Abraham
Lincolniana in 1968. B. E. Wheeler. il por Hobbies 73:98M-98p F '69
Looking over Nixon's shoulder; dilemma during Civil war. D. M. Kudrec. Nat R 21:1155 N 18 '69
Two new Lincoln finds. S. Lorant. pors Look 33:117-18 O 21 '69
Drama
Day's end. E. P. Conkle. Plays 28:91-5 F '69
Lincoln heart. H. L. Miller. Plays 28:9-18 F '69
Lincoln reminders M. Hark and N. McQueen. Plays 28:67-71 F '69
LINCOLN, C. Eric
New black challenge. Redbook 133:78-9+ Je '69

LINCOLN, Charles
Stereo scene. See issues of Popular electronics, June 1969-
LINCOLN, Robert Todd
Forgotten Lincoln. L. Anderson. il por Read Digest 94:172-4+ F '69
LINCOLN, Neb.
Citizens' group collects discarded vehicles. L. Scherer. il Am City 84:145 S '69

Education
All subjects are go with aerospace. L. Howard. il Am Ed 5:5-8 Ap '69
LINCOLN Center for the performing arts, New York
Culture shock; financial troubles. il Newsweek 73:94-5 Ja 27 '69
Fantasies flickered; comments by teen-agers. il Seventeen 28:150 Je '69

Juilliard school
Complete; public début with televised concert followed by open house. New Yorker 45:48-50 N 8 '69
Fanfare for Tully Hall. H. W. Simon. il Hi Fi 19:MA8-9+ D '69
Jewel of a Juilliard. Time 94:46 O 31 '69
Juilliard at home. P. D. Zimmerman. il Newsweek 74:127-8 O 13 '69
Juilliard in transition. i. Kolodin. il Sat R 52:65-7 Ap 26 '69
Juilliard's dream. Q. Eaton. il Opera N 34:8-13 S 20 '69
Life and times of the Juilliard quartet. I. Kolodin. Sat R 52:66 N 15 '69
Music; opening of Alice Tully Hall. D. Hamilton. Nation 209:325-6 S 29 '69
New Juilliard; photographs. Hi Fi 19:MA16-17 S '69
See also
School of American ballet at Juilliard

Library and museum of the performing arts
Anniversary; Dance collection. W. Terry. il Sat R 52:64-5+ N 22 '69

Opera house
Meals at the Met; the Opera club and Café in the Metropolitan opera house. Q. Eaton. il Opera N 33:12-15 Mr 29 '69

Philharmonic Hall
Music; acoustic modifications. D. Hamilton. Nation 209:389 O 13 '69
Music to my ears; Philharmonic Hall revised. I. Kolodin. Sat R 52:53-4 O 11 '69
Musical events: improvement in hall's acoustics. W. Sargeant. New Yorker 45:118-19 O 4 '69

LINCOLN Center repertory theater company
First hippie; revival of Saroyan's The time of your life. Time 94:57 N 14 '69
LINCOLN heart; drama. See Miller, H. L.
LINCOLN reminders; drama. See Hark, M. and McQueen, N.
LIND, Jakov
Inside the monster. G. Wolff. por Newsweek 74:127A+ O 6 '69
LINDAUER, Dinah
Courtesy and planned cooperation. bibliog por Library J 94:266-8 Ja 15 '69
LINDBECK, John M. H.
Isolationist science policy. Bul Atom Sci 25:66-72 F '69
LINDBERG, Lois H. and Vosti, K. L.
Elution of glomerular bound antibodies in experimental streptococcal glomerulonephritis. bibliog Science 166:1032-3 N 21 '69
LINDBERG, Peter
(ed) Family money management. See issues of Better homes and gardens
LINDBERG, Robert G. See Hayden, P. jt. auth.
LINDBERGH, Anne (Morrow)
Heron and the astronaut. Life 66:14-26A F 28 '69
LINDBERGH, Charles Augustus
Letter from Lindbergh. pors Life 67:60A-61 Jl 4 '69
LINDBLAD, Jan
Bird of darkness; with biographical sketch. por Natur Hist 78:4, 80-3 F '69
LINDBLOOM, P. S.
Eighty-five acre-feet in a steel water tank. Am City 84:129+ Ap '69
LINDBURG, D. G.
Rhesus monkeys; mating season mobility of adult males. bibliog Science 166:1176-8 N 28 '69
LINDE, Ronald K. and Crewdson, R. C.
Shock waves in solids; with biographical sketches. Sci Am 220:18, 82-91 My '69

LINDEMAN, Bard
Twins who found each other; excerpt. Good H 169:106-9+ O '69
LINDEMAN, Jack
Glacial; poem. Commonweal 91:44 O 10 '69
Surgery, please; poem. Poetry 114:163 Je '69
LINDEN, Fred
My right side is better. il Am Artist 32:50-1+ D '68
LINDENBAUM, Arthur, and Smoler, M. H.
High-resolution autoradiography of intracellular plutonium. bibliog Science 165:192-4 Jl 11 '69
LINDER, Staffan Burenstam
Too much is too little; excerpts from The harried leisure class. por Time 94:44 Ag 8 '69
LINDGREN, Raymond E.
(comp) Articles and other books received; Northern Europe. See issues of American historical review
LINDHOLM, William Lawrence
Case for America; address, October 2, 1969. Vital Speeches 36:56-9 N 1 '69
LINDLEY, Daniel A. Jr
Heretical questions. Engl J 58:90-1 Ja '69
LINDNER, Richard
Richard Lindner; interview, ed. by D. Swanson. por Vogue 154:124-7 Ag 15 '69
LINDSAY, Cynthia
Wither the bra. McCalls 97:90-1+ N '69
LINDSAY, Franklin A.
Poor luck? Or poor management? il por Forbes 103:15-16 Ap 1 '69
LINDSAY, John P.
Lindsay's double shooting. C. G. Worman. il Hobbies 74:122-3 Jl '69
LINDSAY, John Vliet
Mayor; interview. New Yorker 45:27-8 Je 28 '69
Secretary Shultz; talks with Mayor Lindsay. New Yorker 45:28-30 My 24 '69
Visitor's New York. Travel & Camera 32:40 S '69

about
Announcement. New Yorker 45:27-8 Mr 29 '69
Another chance. il por Time 93:15 Mr 28 '69
Around city hall. A. Logan. New Yorker 45:164+ O 11; 184-90 N 15 '69
As New York goes? F. S. Meyer. Nat R 21:751 Jl 29 '69
Campaign ahead. Nat R 21:628 Jl 1 '69
Can you stand it? W. F. Buckley, jr. Nat R 21:766-7 Jl 29 '69
Civic responsibility; berating by Barry Gray. Time 93:23 Je 20 '69
Comedy of the theories. Nation 209:524 N 17 '69
Curtains for John Lindsay? F. S. Meyer. Nat R 21:383 Ap 22 '69
Dear Mayor Lindsay. T. J. Lowi. por Nation 209:624-7 D 8 '69
Downs and ups of John Lindsay. J. Newfield. por Life 67:30D N 14 '69
Elections 1969; the moderates have it. il por Time 94:23 N 14 '69
Fight for New York. il por Newsweek 74:27-8+ N 3 '69
Frivolous candidate. Nat R 21:948 S 23 '69
Golden boy and little people. P. Tracy. Commonweal 91:98-101 O 24 '69
Here comes the next mayor. R. Reeves. il pors N Y Times Mag p25-7+ N 2 '69
Hitler for mayor. Nat R 21:478 My 20 '69
Homestretch see John run. il Newsweek 74:28-9 N 3 '69
Is John Lindsay ungovernable? J. R. Coyne, jr. il pors Nat R 21:584-9+ Je 17 '69
Just one more time. il por Newsweek 73:31 Mr 31 '69
Lindsay campaigning. New Yorker 45:33-5 O 4 '69
Lindsay caper. D. Schaap. il por Holiday 45:46-7+ Je '69
Lindsay tries to stay in there, while... R. Reeves. il por N Y Times Mag p7-9+ Je 15 '69
Lindsay vs. the field. J. Wilson. il por Nation 208:332-4 Mr 17 '69
Lindsay's new friends. il por Newsweek 74 33-4 Ag 4 '69
Lindsay's non-future. Nat R 21:680+ Jl 15 '69
Mayor in motion. J. M. Flagler. il pors Look 33:82+ Je 24 '69
Mayor Lindsay and the Jewish community. W. F. Buckley, jr. Nat R 21:88 Ja 28 '69
Mayor Lindsay wins re-election and more problems. por U S News 67:37 N 17 '69
Muddled mandate. por Newsweek 74:47-8 N 17 '69
New Lindsay. il por Newsweek 73:35 Je 2 '69
New politics and old. J. R. Coyne, jr. Nat R 51:1106-7+ N 4 '69

LIPIDS—*Continued*
Myxovirus envelope proteins: a directing influence on the fatty acids of membrane lipids. J. M. Tiffany and H. A. Blough. bibliog il Science 163:573-4 F 7 '69
Naturally occurring diol lipids: dialkoxypentanes in porpoise (phocoena phocoena) jaw oil. U. Varanasi and D. C. Malins. bibliog il Science 166:1158-9 N 28 '69
See also
Glycolipids
Lipoproteins
LIPMANN, Fritz
Einar Lundsgaard. Science 164:246-7 Ap 18 '69
Polypeptide chain elongation in protein biosynthesis. bibliog Science 164:1024-31 My 30 '69
—See Malkin, M. jt. auth.
LIPOCHONDRODYSTROPHY
Hurler's syndrome: deficiency of a specific beta galactosidase isoenzyme. M. W. Ho and J. S. O'Brien. bibliog il Science 165: 611-13 Ag 8 '69
LIPOFUSCIN pigments. See Pigments (biology)
LIPOPROTEINS
Advances in lipoproteins. J. Chamblin. il Sci N 96:33-4 Jl 12 '69
Antithrombin III: protection against death after injection of thromboplastin. L. T. Mann, jr. and others. bibliog il Science 166: 517-18 O 24 '69
LIPOSARCOMA. See Sarcoma
LIPPAY, Alex
Balsa-cored fiberglass. il Yachting 125:116-17+ Ja '69
LIPPER, Arthur, 3d
Fund analysis finds its Freud. il por Bsns W p 128-30 S 13 '69
LIPPERT, Marion
Unknown princess; interview, ed. by S. Jenkins. jr. por Opera N 33:30 Mr 22 '69
LIPPINCOTT, Ellis R. and others
Polywater. bibliog Science 164:1482-7 Je 27 '69
LIPPINCOTT, Sarah Lee
Double star specialists meet. Sky & Tel 39: 31-3 Ja '70
LIPPINCOTT, J. B, company
New distribution center for Lippincott. il Pub W 196:29-30 O 6 '69
LIPPINCOTT and Margulies, incorporated
Doctor of the corporate ego. R. Beardwood. il Fortune 79:108-10+ My 1 '69
LIPPMAN, Bert
Teaching the art of history. Nat R 21:1214-18 D 2 '69
LIPPMAN, Eleanor. See Bartnicki-Garcia, S. jt. auth.
LIPPMANN, Walter
Problem of Vietnam. por Newsweek 74:27 D 1 '69
Talk with Walter Lippmann, at eighty, about this minor dark age; interview, ed. by H. Brandon. pors N Y Times Mag p25-7+ S 14 '69
about
Lippmann at eighty. New Repub 161:13-14 S 20 '69
Lippmann at eighty. S. W. Little. Sat R 52:81-2 O 11 '69
Trade winds; book collection, to the Centerville library, Mass. J. Beatty, jr. Sat R 52: 18+ O 25 '69
LIPS, S. Herman, and Roth-Bejerano, N.
Light and hormones: interchangeability in the induction of nitrate reductase. bibliog Science 166:109-10 O 3 '69
LIPSET, Seymour Martin
If Harvard can't hold the line. .; interview. por U S News 66:42-3 Ap 28 '69
Political thrust motivating campus turmoil. Sat R 52:23-5+ Mr 1 '69
Why cops hate liberals, and vice versa. Atlan 223:76-83 Mr '69
—and Raab, Earl
Wallace whitelash. Trans-Action 7:23-32+ D '69
LIPSKY, Michael
Rent strikes: poor man's weapon. por Trans-Action 6:10-15 F '69
—and Olson, D. J.
Riot commission politics. pors Trans-Action 6:8-21 Jl '69
LIPTON, James
Exaltation of larks; excerpts. Natur Hist 78: 8-10+ Je '69
LIQUEURS
Cordially yours. W. Clifford. House B 111: 166+ O '69
LIQUID assets. See Liquidity (economics)
LIQUID fertilizers and manures
New look at liquid fertilizer economics. C. E. Sommers. il Suc Farm 67:B2 D '69

LIQUID hydrogen. See Hydrogen, Liquid
LIQUID injection molding. See Plastics—Molding
LIQUID jets. See Jets
LIQUID level indicators
Build your own fluid monitor. R. F. Graf and G. J. Whalen. il Sci Digest 66:78-81 D '69
LIQUID propellant rockets. See Rocket engines
LIQUIDAMBAR styraciflua. See Sweet gum
LIQUIDITY (economics)
Out on the credit limb: credit capitalism. M. Tanzer. Nation 208:686-9 Je 2 '69
LIQUIDITY, International
International liquidity and foreign aid. E. R. Fried. For Affairs 48:139-49 O '69
See also
Special drawing rights
LIQUIDONICS industries, incorporated
When a takeover runs out of gas. Bsns W p32 O 4 '69
LIQUIDS
Subsurface phenomena and the splashing of drops on shallow liquids. W. C. Macklin and P. V. Hobbs. bibliog il Science 166: 107-8 O 3 '69
See also
Brownian movements
Emulsions
Hydrodynamics
Soap bubbles and films
LIQUOR industry
Slight dash of bitters in the eggnog. Bsns W p 15 D 27 '69

Advertising
Will TV take to drink? Bsns W p33-4 F 15 '69
LIQUOR laws and regulations

North Carolina
[Harry Golden column; liquor by the drink vote defeated] H. Golden. Nation 209: 110-11 Ag 11 '69

United States
Wet season. il Newsweek 73:33-4 F 3 '69
LIQUOR problem
See also
Temperance

France
A votre santé? French drinking problem. il Newsweek 73:104 Mr 17 '69

United States
Living down prohibition. Chr Today 14:33 N 7 '69
Should children be taught to drink? questions and answers; ed. by T. Berland. il Todays Health 47:46-9+ F '69
Why adolescents drink and use drugs; with study-discussion program, by C. Smallenburg and H. Smallenburg. W. G. Hollister. bibliog il PTA Mag 63:2-5, 27 Mr '69
LIQUORI, Marty
Pressure cooker. S. Myslenski. il por Sports Illus 31:18-21 Jl 7 '69
LIQUORS
After the last run: exotic drinks. J. T. Elson. il Travel & Camera 32:58-63 D '69
Alcohol: caloric content. P. S. Brown. il House & Gard 135:132+ My '69
Bottoms up. il Esquire 72:144-5 N '69
For Christmas wassailing, cheering drinks. H. McNulty. House & Gard 136:96+ D '69
Gay quenchers. S. Lord. Harp Baz 102:90-1 Je '69
Knack, with a bottle. J. Wilson. House & Gard 136:96 Jl '69
Mexico, hot and harmonious. J. T. Elson. Travel & Camera 32:12 N '69
What is your liquor I.Q? P. S. Brown. House & Gard 135:92+ F '69
See also
Champagne
Cocktails
Cookery—Liquors
Gin
Rum
Tequila
Vodka
Whiskey

Anecdotes, facetiae, satire, etc.
These drinks are on me! J. Trahey. il Harp Baz 103:190-200 D '69
LISAGOR, Peter
White House mood. See issues of Nation's business
LISBON, Portugal

Description
Cognoscenti abroad. Amalia Rodrigues' bon. A. Goodfriend. Sat R 52:42-3 '69

LISSNER, John
Pop/folk/jazz: guideposts to a basic record library. por Library J 94:158-61 Ja 15 '69

LISTENING. See Attention

LISTER, Merle
Merle Lister dance company, Hudson guild theatre. J. Dowlin. Dance Mag 43:93 Je '69

LISTON, Charles. See Liston, S.

LISTON, Sonny
Right to the jaw; that's black power. J. Flaherty. por Esquire 71:112-14+ Mr '69

LISZT, Franz
Drop-in night at the Electric circus; imaginary conversation. D. Bar-Illan. por Sat R 52:72-3 N 15 '69
Earl Wild's re-creation of The daemonic Liszt. D. Dubal. Am Rec G 35:364-5 Ja '69
Wild romantics. Discus. Harper 238:101 Je '69

LITANIES
Lay renewal litany. L. Leslie. Chr Cent 86:547 Ap 23 '69

LITEKY, Angelo
I never met any priest who suggested withdrawal. P. Nobile. Commonweal 90:196-7 My 2 '69; Reply with rejoinder. J. J. Fahey. 90: 307+ My 30 '69

LITERACY. See Illiteracy

LITERACY tests (election law)
For voters: end to literacy tests everywhere in U.S? il U S News 67:32+ Jl 7 '69

LITERARY ability. See Creation (literary, artistic, etc)

LITERARY agents
Care and feeding of the artist. M. A. Guitar. il Mlle 70:166-7+ N '69
Counteragent. Pub W 196:35-7 Ag 18 '69

LITERARY censorship. See Censorship

LITERARY characters. See Characters in literature

LITERARY clubs
Ralph Newman, Chicago, opens Book and bottle club. Pub W 195:64 My 19 '69
See also
PEN club

LITERARY collaboration. See Authorship—Collaboration

LITERARY criticism
Craters of the spirit, by N. A. Scott, jr. Review
Cath World 208:235 F '69. L. A. Rosini
How to criticise and revise a juvenile book. K. Mason. il Writers Digest 49:52-5+ Ag '69
In defense of the tall story. W. H. Auden. New Yorker 45:205-6+ N 29 '69
On Walter Benjamin. R. Alter. bibliog f Commentary 48:86-93 S '69
Poetry; how and why. J. Jerome. Writers Digest 49:22-9 Ag '69
Poets & critics & poet-critics. M. L. Rosenthal. Poetry 114:113-26 My '69
Reviewing for The New York times book review. F. Brown. Writer 82:21 N '69
See also
Book reviews
Critics

LITERARY critics. See Critics

LITERARY fantasies. See Fantasies, Literary

LITERARY festivals
Clothesline full of poetry; second annual Palm Beach poetry festival. D. Wilkening. il Sr Schol 94:Schol Teach 20-1 F 14 '69

LITERARY forgeries and mystifications
I am Penelope Ashe. B. Young. il McCalls 97:70+ N '69
Letters from an American mother: hoax by Holger A. Koppel in Baltimore evening sun. E. Lund. il Am Heritage 21:44-5 D '69
Who is Penelope Ashe? G. Sheehy. il McCalls 97:71+ N '69

LITERARY form. See Style, Literary

LITERARY hoaxes. See Hoaxes

LITERARY landmarks
One thing and another: Sam Clemen's Hannibal, Mo. J. K. Hutchens. Sat R 52:23-4 My 31 '69
Ulysses' tower; Sandycove tower near Dublin. F. Russell. il Horizon 11:48-51 Sum '69

LITERARY periodicals. See Literature—Periodicals

LITERARY prizes
European scene: French prizes. H. R. Lottman. il Pub W 196:28 D 29 '69
Literary prizes and awards, 1968. Pub W 195:47-51 Mr 10 '69

Prizes and awards. See issues of Publishers' weekly
Sarah O'Loughlin Foley award; with winning poem by A. Hanft. America 120:477 Ap 19 '69
See also
Anisfield-Wolf awards
Mystery writers of America, incorporated
National council on the arts selection (program)

LITERARY property. See Copyright

LITERARY research
Some modest proposals on the novel. G. Green. Writer 82:19-23 Je '69

LITERARY style. See Style, Literary

LITERARY topics. See Literature—Themes

LITERATURE
Your literary I.Q; ed. by D. M. Glixon. See issues of Saturday review
See also
Anthologies
Authorship
Bible—Literary character
Bible in literature
Biography
Books and reading
Censorship
Characters in literature
Childrens literature
Creation (literary, artistic, etc)
Fiction
Gothic romances
Humor
Immoral literature and pictures
Literary criticism
Poetry
Romanticism
Style, Literary
Symbolism in literature
Translations and translating
also national literature, e.g. Russian literature; also literature of special subjects, e.g. Religious literature

Appreciation and interpretation
Man, the creative artist; an experiment; at Vidalia high school, Concordia parish, La. M. B. Eidt and R. C. Alwood. Engl J 58: 87-9 Ja '69
Teaching Conrad's Victory to superior high school seniors. S. I. Roody. Engl J 58:40-6 Ja '69
See also
Poetry—Appreciation

Competitions
Contests & awards. See issues of Writer's digest
Winners: Writer's digest creative writing awards. Writers Digest 49:36-42+ O '69
See also
Fiction—Competitions

Periodicals
Books! If you'll excuse the expression; magazine: The outsider. G. R. Shields. ALA Bul 63:715 Je '69
See also
New American review
Us (periodical)

Prizes
See Literary prizes

Study and teaching
Challenging the censor: some responsibilities of the English department: address, November, 1968. K. L. Donelson. bibliog Engl J 58:869-76 S '69
Choral reading and the English teacher. M. E. Stassen. Engl J 58:436-9 Mr '69
Combatting apathy: literature and the general class. G. Ehrenhaft. Engl J 58:840-6 S '69
Do you know what's happening? teaching literary works with themes of racial conflict. I. Halperin. Engl J 58:1049-52 O '69
Heretical questions. D. A. Lindley, jr. Engl J 58:90-1 Ja '69
How to make literature come alive; NCTE panel on Literature programs for inner city schools. Sr Schol 93:Schol Teach 19+ Ja 10 '69
Literature and the schools. A. Daigon. Engl J 58:30-9 Ja '69
Pattern and process, a polemic; address. L. M. Rosenblatt. bibliog f Engl J 58:1005-12 O '69
Reading and reporting; a tailor-made program for each student. L. Goldman. Engl J 58:236-41 F '69

LITERATURE—Study and teaching—*Continued*
Small-group training and the English classroom. D. M. Litsey. Engl J 58:920-7 S '69
Time enough to read; Horton Watkins high school, Ladue, St Louis, Mo. G. Stanford. il Sr Schol 94:Schol Teach 13+ Ap 18 '69
See also
English language—Study and teaching
English literature—Study and teaching

Technique
Nicholas Monsarrat's working methods; interview, ed. by A. Monsarrat. N. Monsarrat. Writers Digest 49:59 Ag '69
Second thoughts about notebooks. A. B. Holland. Writers Digest 49:18 Mr '69
Use your creative memory. J. Yolen. Writer 82:16-17+ S '69
See also
Fiction—Technique

Themes
Adolescent initiation: a thematic study in the secondary school; address, November 1968. H. Agee. Engl J 58:1021-4 O '69
African genesis and Lord of the flies: two studies of the beastie within. R. Lederer and P. H. Beattie. Engl J 58:1316-21+ D '69
Appalachian heritage; address, November 2, 1968. R. Caudill. il Horn Bk 45:143-7 Ap '69
Arthur Miller's The crucible and Nathaniel Hawthorne: some parallels. D. M. Bergeron. Engl J 58:47-55 Ja '69
Building a background for high school composition. R. Rideout. Engl J 58:242-4 F '69
Celebration: the lyric poetry of Melville Cane. J. Robinson. Am Scholar 38:286-96 Spr '69
Changing confession market. H. P. Malmgreen. Writer 82:22-3 S '69
Experience and fiction: excerpts from Come along with me. S. Jackson. Writer 82:9-14+ Ja '69
Hemingway in our time. A. Lebowitz. Yale R 58:321-41 Mr '69
John Steinbeck, writer. W. C. McWilliams and N. R. McWilliams. Commonweal 90:229-30 My 9 '69
Mailer and his gods. R. A. Schroth. Commonweal 90:226-9 My 9 '69
Nonfiction, three to one. S. S. Baker. Writer 82:19-20+ Ja '69
People and place: regional writing. J. G. Rushing. Writer 82:9-12 S '69
Pushkin and parricide: The miserly knight. C. R. Proffer. biblioq f Am Imago 25:347-53 Wint '68
Second thoughts about topics. A. B. Holland. Writers Digest 49:18 Ap '69
Vladimir in dreamland. J. Heidenry. Commonweal 90:231-4 My 9 '69
Woman-hater; Mérimée's Carmen. M. Springer. Opera N 33:24-5 Mr 15 '69
See also
Death in literature
Greece, Ancient, in literature
Homosexuality in literature
Jesus Christ in literature
Jews in literature
Love in literature
Negroes in literature
Plots (drama, novel, etc)
Sex in literature
West in literature
LITERATURE, Childrens. See Childrens literature
LITERATURE, Immoral. See Immoral literature and pictures
LITERATURE. Influence of
Dance books in my life; symposium. il Dance Mag 43:38-42 Mr '69
Lively arts: interview, ed. by R. Hemming. Topol. Sr Schol 94:32 Ap 25 '69
See also
Childrens literature. Influence of
LITERATURE, Regional
See also
Publishers and publishing—Regional literature
LITERATURE and morals
Arthur Miller's The crucible and Nathaniel Hawthorne: some parallels. D. M. Bergeron. Engl J 58:47-55 Ja '69
LITERATURE and moving pictures. See Moving pictures and literature
LITERATURE and music. See Music and literature
LITERATURE and psychoanalysis. See Psychoanalysis and literature
LITERATURE and religion. See Religion and literature
LITERATURE and science
Poetry: how and why; science and poetry. J. Jerome. Writers Digest 49:26+ Jl '69
See also
Science fiction

LITERATURE as a profession. See Authorship
LITERATURE classification, Decimal. See Classification, Decimal
LITHIUM in the body
Lithium story. Chem 42:24-5 Ap '69
Lithium vs. mental illness. E. Diamond; discussion. N Y Times Mag p21-2+ Ja 26 '69
LITHOGRAPHERS and photoengravers international union
LPIU orders walkout at three Krueger plants. Pub W 196:39-41 Jl 21 '69
LITHOGRAPHS
California's pictorial letter sheets: excerpts. J. A. Baird, jr. il Antiques 96:412-17 S '69
Portfolio of lithographs by Stow Wengenroth. W. Caxton, jr. il Am Artist 33:62-7+ N '69
LITHOGRAPHY
Rauschenberg's recent graphics. D. M. Davis. il Art in Am 57:90-5 Jl '69
LITIGATION. See Actions and defenses
LITSEY, David M.
Small-group training and the English classroom. Engl J 58:920-7 S '69
LITTELL, Robert. See Klein, E. jt. auth.
LITTEN, Chester D.
Squire of poodle patch. F. L. Brunton. il pors Am For 75:37+ Ap '69
LITTER. See Refuse and refuse disposal
LITTKE, Lael J.
Day we lost Max; story. Ladies Home J 86:84-5 O '69
LITTLE, Arthur D, incorporated
Pay Arthur D. Little inc, and then start listening. B. Hersh. il Esquire 71:118-21+ Je '69
LITTLE, Bertram K. family
Living with antiques. A. Winchester. il Antiques 95:242-51 F '69
LITTLE, Clarence Cook
Excerpt from statement presented to House committee on interstate and foreign commerce, April 1969. Cong Digest 48:189+ Je '69
LITTLE, Elbert L. Jr
Native trees of Hawaii. Am For 75:16-17+ F '69
LITTLE, George
Hamlet's dilemma, or The generation gap; poem. Engl J 58:359 Mr '69
LITTLE, H. Bayliffe
England's north country. Harp Baz 103:66+ Ja '70
LITTLE, Ian M. D.
Amateur who beats the pros. pors Forbes 103:233-5 My 15 '69
LITTLE, Joan
Do-it-yourself coffeehouses. Parks & Rec 4:37-8+ Mr '69
LITTLE, Malcolm. See Malcolm X
LITTLE, Royal
Roy Little's latest Textron? Forbes 103:33-4 My 1 '69
LITTLE, Stuart W.
Books in communications. See issues of Saturday review
Children's television workshop. Sat R 52:60-2 F 8 '69
New York is going to make it: how to start a magazine. Sat R 52:52-3+ Je 14 '69
SR's 1969 Anisfield-Wolf awards. Sat R 52:23 My 24 '69
LITTLE blue books. See Haldeman-Julius publications
LITTLE boxes; drama. See Bowen, J.
LITTLE, Brown and company
Part played by Boston publishers of 1860-1900 in the field of children's books. H. L. Jones. biblioq il Horn Bk 45:329-36 Je '69
LITTLE citadel; story. See Enright, E.
LITTLE Cosette and Father Christmas; drama. See Thane, A.
LITTLE leagues
Baseball by computer. Newsweek 74:74 Jl 28 '69
Boy with a bat and a ball. Sports Illus 30:9 My 26 '69
Case against little league mothers. J. Robbins. il McCalls 96:55+ Jl '69
Look, mom! Just like the bigs; photographs by W. Iooss, jr. Sports Illus 30:32-7 My 12 '69
Tell it like it was; official rules. D. Williamson. Sat R 52:4+ Je 21 '69
LITTLE magazines. See Literature—Periodicals
LITTLE murders; drama. See Feiffer, J.
LITTLE orchestra society, New York
Music to my ears; performance of Prometheus. I. Kolodin. Sat R 52:45 N 1 '69
Musical events: performance of C. Orff's Prometheus. W. Sargeant. New Yorker 45:145-7 O 25 '69
Report: production of Prometheus. F. Merkling. Opera N 34:23 N 22 '69

LITTLE people of America, Incorporated
Little people of America. Trans-Action 6:6
Mr '69
LITTLE red hen; drama. See Bolko, C.
LITTLE ROCK, Ark.

Parks and playgrounds
Portable park brightens urban-renewal site.
il Am City 84:32 Ag '69
LITTLECOTT, Lorna C.
Hawaii first. Am For 75:12-15+ F '69
Social register of big trees. Am For 75:18-
25 F '69
LITTLEFIELD, Kenneth B.
How to mill on a drill press. Pop Mech 131:
180-4 Ja '69
LITTLEJOHN, David
More on the second sex. New Repub 160:
27-8 Mr 8 '69
LITTLER, Frank
Carnaby street. Sat R 52:6-7 O 25 '69
Polly wants a capsule. Sat R 52:4+ N 15 '69
LITTMAN, Larry
Changing face of Stockholm. Travel & Cam-
era 32:29-30+ Mr '69
LITTON industries, incorporated
Big brother as a holding company. D. Horo-
witz and R. Erlich. il Ramp Mag 7:44-52
N 30 '68
Conglomerates; second salvo; FTC an-
nouncing plans for antitrust suit. Time
93:91 Ap 18 '69
Litton industries; proving poverty pays. D.
Horowitz and R. Erlich. il Ramp Mag 7:
40-9 D 14 '68
Litton's shattered image. il Forbes 104:26-8+
D 1 '69
LITURGICAL movement
Liturgy the public hope; with reply. R. Neu-
haus. il Commonweal 91:129-35 O 31 '69
LITURGICAL week
Liturgical movements in tension. C. J. Mc-
Naspy. America 121:320-2 O 18 '69; Re-
ply. W. J. Leonard. 121:442+ N 15 '69
LITURGIES
Planning for common worship; proposed new
worship service for constituents of Con-
sultation on church union. America 120:207
F 22 '69
See also
Catholic church—Liturgy and ritual
LITURGY, Catholic. See Catholic church—
Liturgy and ritual
LITVAK, M. M.
Hydroxyl and water masers in protostars.
bibliog Science 165:855-61 Ag 29 '69
LITVINOV, Ivy
Call it love; story. New Yorker 45:54-60 N 29
'69
Wet spring; story. New Yorker 45:38-41 My
10 '69
LITVINOV, Pavel Mikhailovich
Orthodox priest and a Soviet writer. M.
Bourdeaux. Chr Cent 86:266-8 F 19 '69
LITWAK, Leo
Oath; story. Commentary 48:33-7 Ag '69
We needed a revolution. Look 33:62+ My 27
'69
LITZ, Katherine
Katherine Litz and company, Brooklyn
academy of music. J. Dowlin. Dance Mag
43:92 Je '69
Katherine Litz & dance co; Judson dance
theatre. J. Anderson. Dance Mag 43:85 F '69
LIVE bait. See Bait
LIVER
Enzymic differentiation in mammalian liver.
O. Greengard. bibliog il Science 163:891-5
F 28 '69
I am Joe's liver. J. D. Ratcliff. il Read
Digest 95:81-4 S '69
Diseases
See also
Hepatitis
Transplantation
Human C'3: evidence for the liver as the pri-
mary site of synthesis. C. A. Alper and oth-
ers. bibliog il Science 163:286-8 Ja 17 '69
LIVER as food
See also
Cookery—Meat
LIVER mitochondria. See Mitochondria
LIVERSIDGE, Anthony
Not enough gas in the pipelines. Fortune 80:
120-2+ N '69
LIVERWORTS
Allergenic component of a liverwort: a
sesquiterpene lactone. H. Knoche and oth-
ers. bibliog il Science 166:239-40 O 10 '69

LIVESTOCK
How your livestock business is changing. C.
W. Gifford. Farm J 93:R1 My '69
News. See issues of Farm journal
Successful farming 1969 livestock manage-
ment guide; symposium. Suc Farm 67:40-1+
O '69
See also
Stock ranges
Prices
Livestock boom rolls on. il Farm J 93:20-1
Je '69
Transportation
Special pens speed livestock shipment. Avia-
tion W 91:50 N 17 '69
Watering
Helpful winter ideas to keep stock water
thawed. G. L. Earle. il Suc Farm 67:S4
O '69
LIVESTOCK markets
See also
Denver union stock yard company
LIVING. See Conduct of life
LIVING, Cost of. See Cost of living
LIVING, Standard of. See Standard of living
LIVING expenses. See Cost of living
LIVING rooms
At last, a family room that lives up to its
name. il Bet Hom & Gard 47:62-3 O '69
High-style family room from a back porch.
il Bet Hom & Gard 47:50 Mr '69
Live-in room works twenty-four hours a
day. il House & Gard 135:62-4 Ja '69
Living room that really entertains! il Bet
Hom & Gard 47:60-1 O '69
Wood-paneled living room is open to green
vistas. il House & Gard 135:50-1+ Ja '69
LIVING rooms, Outdoor. See Outdoor rooms
LIVING theater group. See Theater, Experi-
mental
LIVINGSTON, Ann Ryan
Action: a beauty investment. B. Wysor. il
por Harp Baz 102:158-61 Ag '69
LIVINGSTON, Gordon S.
Letter from a Vietnam veteran. Sat R 52:22-3
S 20 '69
LIVINGSTON, J. Sterling
Pygmalion in management, excerpts from
High expectations in management. bibliog
f Harvard Bsns R 47:81-9 Jl '69
LIVINGSTON, Jane
West coast report. Art in Am 57:92-7 Ja '69
LIVINGSTON, Lida
Communecology; address, June 17, 1969. Vital
Speeches 35:765-8 O 1 '69
LIVINGSTON, M. Stanley
Big machine; review. Bul Atom Sci 25:34-5
Mr '69
LIVINGSTON, Myra Cohn
Tune beyond us: the bases of choice. bib-
liog por Wilson Lib Bul 44:448-55 D '69
LIVINGSTON, Patricia
I will love you; poem. Ladies Home J 86:70
O '69
LIVINGSTONE, David
Doctor Livingstone presumes. B. Farwell.
il por Horizon 11:104-11 Sum '69
LIVINGSTONE, F. C.
Getting science to pay off. Sci N 96:224 S 13
'69
Grapes of antiquity. Sci N 95:407-8 Ap 26 '69
LIZARDS
Dragons: past and present. D. Cohen. il Sci
Digest 66:36-43 D '69
Gecko grip. J. F. Gennaro, jr. il Natur Hist
78:36-43 Ag '69
Gene dosage at the lactate dehydrogenase b
locus in triploid and diploid teiid lizards.
W. B. Neaves and P. S. Gerald. bibliog il
Science 164:557-9 My 2 '69
Green blood pigment in lizards; skinks. A. F.
Greer and G. Raizes. bibliog Science 166:
392 O 17 '69
See also
Basilisks
Iguanas
LLAMZON, Benjamin S.
God at summer school. America 120:216-19
F 22 '69
LLANO, Margaret T. See Strassenburg, A.
A. jt. auth.
LLERAS RESTREPO, Carlos
President Nixon and President Lleras of
Colombia review common goals of the
Americas; exchange of greetings, toasts
and remarks, June 12, 13, 1969. Dept State
Bul 61:9, 11-13 Jl 7 '69
about
Colombia creeps back from the brink. il por
Bsns W p 128 Ap 26 '69
Laying the groundwork. P. Kramer. por
Newsweek 73:38+ Mr 3 '69

LLEWELYN-DAVIES, Richard
Educating the professionals of the built environment. il Arch Rec 145:145-50 F '69
LLINÁS, Rodolfo, and others
Preferred centripetal conduction of dendritic spikes in alligator Purkinje cells. bibliog Science 163:184-7 Ja 10 '69
LLORENS, David
Ameer (LeRoi Jones) Baraka. Ebony 24:75-8+ Ag '69
Black Don Lee. Ebony 24:72-8+ Mr '69
Julian Bond. Ebony 24:58-62+ My '69
Mississippi revisited. Ebony 24:46-9+ Jl '69
LLOYD, Earl
Earl Lloyd. por Motor T 21:24-5+ S '69
LLOYD, James E.
Flashes and behavior of some American fireflies. bibliog Cons 23:8-12 Je '69
LLOYD, John
Washington report. See issues of Scholastic teacher
LLOYD, Lewis B.
Caution laser. Pop Electr 31:41-2 D '69
LLOYD, Susan
How can we ask children to be better than we are? Redbook 133:56+ Je '69
LLOYD'S, London
Lloyd's rising risks. il Time 94:104+ O 17 '69
Risky future at Lloyd's of London. il Bsns W p 102-3+ O 18 '69
LOADING and unloading
L-500 cargo loading device evaluated. W. Hansen il Aviation W 90:32-3 Mr 24 '69
LOAN associations. See Credit unions; Savings and loan associations
LOAN sharks
Theft of the Nation; excerpt. D. R. Cressey. Harper 238:84-90 F '69
LOANS
See also
Credit
Government lending
Insurance, Life—Policy loans
Interest
Mortgage loans
Student loans
LOANS, Bank
Banks kick up the ante on loans; ask for fringe benefits. Bsns W p34 Je 7 '69
Banks try to dodge Fed's grasp; turn to loan participation certificates. il Bsns W p98 Ap 5 '69
Business loans won't slow down. il Bsns W p33-4 Mr 22 '69
Next place to tighten; possible new move to control bank credit. il Bsns W p45-6 Je 28 '69
Small-business loans: their cost. U S News 67:99 O 6 '69
Still lining up at the loan window. il Bsns W p47-8 S 13 '69
Swinging your weight at a loan window. Bsns W p 143-4 Mr 29 '69
Taking the squeeze in stride; bank lending to business. il Bsns W p 11-12 Jl 5 '69
LOANS, Foreign
Borrowing abroad: the smart money game. A. Hershman. il Duns R 94:30-2+ D '69
LOANS, Government. See Government lending
LOANS, interlibrary. See Interlibrary loans
LOANS, Personal
See also
Beneficial finance company of New York
Credit unions
LOANS, Student. See Student loans
LOBB, John Cunningham
Hatchet man for deadwood operations. por Bsns W p80 S 6 '69
LOBBYING
Congressional mailbag; mail from religious conservatives. Chr Today 14:48-9 O 10 '69
Environment; how to join the battle. M. Frome. Field & S 74:22+ D '69
Haynsworth tragedy. D. Lawrence. U S News 67:88 D 1 '69
How the mayors saved OEO. Bsns W p86 D 20 '69
Let's put brakes on the highway lobby. G. Denison and K. Y. Tomlinson. Read Digest 94:97-102 My '69
Personal business: taking your problems to Washington. Bsns W p 121 F 15 '69
Petitioners; letters to congressmen about Vietnam war. K. Crawford. Newsweek 74:39 N 24 '69
Speaking for the cities; urban lobby. America 121:552-3 D 6 '69
Union lobbying machine. W. Wingo. il Nations Bsns 57:52-4+ Ap; 58-62 My '69
What can I do? reprint. D. Lawrence. U S News 66:104 Je 23 '69

What Congress hears from the voters. U S News 66:30-1 Ap 28 '69
Write now; user charges. R. B. Parke. Flying 85:30 S '69
See also
Lobbyists
LOBBYISTS
Citizens' lobby; education budget. E. Geller. Library J 94:4563 D 15 '69
Influence peddling in Washington; Time essay. Time 93:20-1 My 16 '69
Loitering permitted here; lobby for education and library appropriations. W. D. Boutwell. PTA Mag 64:13 D '69
Vietnam lobby. R. Scheer and W. Hinckle. Ramp Mag 7:31-6 Ja 25 '69
LOBDELL, Jared C.
I am the martyr of the people. Nat R 21:80 Ja 28 '69
LO BELLO, Nino
Are left handers all right? Mech Illus 65:81-3+ O '69
LOBSENZ, Norman M.
Boy who knows too much. Redbook 133:74-5+ Je '69
Warm welcome in a New England town. Good H 168:81+ My '69
—and Blackburn, C. W.
Are you a trapped housewife? excerpts from How to stay married. Read Digest 95:68-71 S '69
Hidden meanings of money in marriage; excerpt from The first ten years of marriage; a guide to successful family living. Read Digest 94:141-4 Mr '69
LOBSTERS
America's gift to gastronomy. B. Keating. il Holiday 45:46-7+ My '69
Cyclic and geographic trends in seawater temperature and abundance of American lobster. R. L. Dow. bibliog il Science 164:1060-3 My 30 '69
Queuing behavior of spiny lobsters. W. Herrnkind. bibliog il Science 164:1425-7 Je 20 '69
See also
Cookery—Shellfish
LOCAL anesthetics. See Anesthetics
LOCAL church councils
See also
Protestant council of the city of New York
LOCAL employees. See Municipal employees
LOCAL finance
Budgeting for state and local government services. B. Crihfield and G. A. Bell. Ann Am Acad 379:31-8 S '68
See also
Municipal finance
LOCAL government
See also
Community power
Metropolitan government
Municipal government
LOCAL service airlines
Difficulties beset local service mergers. R. G. O'Lone. Aviation W 90:27-9 Mr 17 '69
Lake Erie's islands by air. B. Thomas. il Travel 131:50-4 My '69
Trend to profitability in 1969 seen possible for local airlines. Aviation W 90:43-4 F 24 '69
White-knuckle carriers. il Time 94:76 Jl 18 '69
See also
Aero commuter
Air taxi service
Air West, incorporated
Allegheny commuter service
Executive airlines, incorporated
International sky cab, incorporated
Pacific Southwest airlines
Universal airlines, incorporated
Washington airlines

Consolidations and mergers
Consolidation gains in commuter industry. R. S. Kahn. Aviation W 92:39+ Ja 12 '70
Merger could reshape California market; proposed Pacific Southwest airlines and Air California merger. N. S. Himmel. Aviation W 92:42+ Ja 12 '70

Federal aid
Industry, CAB to review subsidy program. Aviation W 91:38 D 8 '69

Finance
Poor traffic clouds locals' profit outlook. H. D. Watkins. il Aviation W 91:27 O 13 '69
Supplemental airline revenues and expenses, first six months of 1969; table. Aviation W 91:75 O 20 '69
LOCAL-state municipal relations. See Intergovernmental fiscal relations

LOCAL taxation
Big bind in local taxes. il Bsns W p44+ Ag 9 '69
High cost of living elsewhere. Nations Bsns 57:81-3 My '69
Should the government share its tax take? W. W. Heller. il Sat R 52:26-9 Mr 22 '69
Tax-exempt property: another crushing burden for the cities. H. B. Meyers. il Fortune 79:76-9+ My 1 '69
What the city needs. A. Stone. Nation 209:494-5 N 10 '69
See also
Assessment
Libraries—Finance

LOCALIZATION of brain functions. See Brain—Localization of functions

LOCASTRO, Richard, and Tutton, M. E.
Emphasis on current events. Clear House 44:231 D '69

LOCATION in business and industry
American Indians industrialize to combat poverty; excerpt from Manpower and industrial development programs for Indian Americans. A. L. Sorkin. bibliog f il Mo Labor R 92:19-25 Mr '69
Changing resource policies of the U.S.S.R. T. Shabad. bibliog il Focus 19:7-8 F '69
Employment effect of a new industry in a rural area. I. Gray. bibliog il Mo Labor R 92:26-30 Je '69
Industry's own space quest; symposium. il Nations Bsns 57:59-62+ S '69
Moving to New York's outer edges. il Bsns W p 158-60 N 15 '69
New plants dot the black slums. il Bsns W p 100+ Mr 22 '69
Urban alternatives for eliminating poverty; excerpt from address, May 2 and 3, 1969. N. M. Hansen. Mo Labor R 92:46-7 Ag '69
Where in the world should we put that plant? manufacturing operations in foreign countries. R. B. Stobaugh, jr. bibliog f il Harvard Bsns R 47:129-36 Ja '69
See also
Cities and towns—Industries
Roadside business

LOCATION of airports. See Airports—Location

LOCATIONS, Moving pictures. See Moving pictures—Setting and scenery

LOCH NESS monster
On the difficult art of monster stalking. il Chem 42:5 N '69

LOCHMAN, J. M.
On Christian-Marxist dialogue. Chr Cent 87:11-16 Ja 7 '70

LOCK, James and company. See London—Stores

LOCK-picking. See Locks and keys

LOCKABEY, Almon
Passage had her troubles. Yachting 126:45+ S '69
West coast upset for windward passage. Motor B 124:79+ Ag '69

LOCKERBIE, D. Bruce
Conscious rhetorician. Engl J 58:1057-60 O '69
We use great plainness of speech. Chr Today 14:12+ O 24 '69

LOCKHART, Jim
Carlyle Lake: midwestern hotspot. Field & S 74:164-6+ My '69

LOCKHEED aircraft corporation
AH-56A remains grounded as Lockheed answers army. C. M. Plattner. Aviation W 90:33 My 5 '69
Army cancels AH-56 production phase. Aviation W 90:24-6 My 26 '69
Army shoots down Cheyenne; cancellation of contract. il Bsns W p34-5 My 24 '69
Crisis at Lockheed. il Newsweek 73:71-2 Je 2 '69
For Lockheed, everything's coming up unknowns. H. B. Meyers. il Fortune 80:76-81+ Ag 1 '69
How C-5A cutback will hurt Lockheed. il Bsns W p41-2 N 22 '69
Lockheed and the SEC. Nation 209:396-7 O 20 '69
Lockheed chosen by Singapore to maintain military aircraft. Aviation W 91:25 D 8 '69
Lockheed lands anti-sub plane. Bsns W p27-8 Ag 9 '69
Lockheed mass cargo system. D. A. Brown. il Aviation W 91:24-6 D 22 '69; 92:30-2 Ja 12 '70 (to be cont)
Lockheed plans new transports. Aviation W 90:26-7 Ap 28 '69
Lockheed switches top-level officers. Aviation W 91:33 S 15 '69
Lockheed's casualties in the defense controversy. il Time 93:76-7 My 30 '69
Lockheed's helicopter fights Pentagon battle; Cheyenne, army's first whirlybird gunship. il Bsns W p42 My 3 '69

Lockheed's ledger on the C-5A. Bsns W p35 Je 7 '69
New disputes flare over Cheyenne. C. Brownlow. Aviation W 91:16-17 O 13 '69
Sweet defense jobs sour at Lockheed; air force's C-5A, and army's AH-56A Cheyenne helicopter. il Bsns W p 122-3 My 17 '69
USAF, Lockheed diverge over C-5A terms. Aviation W 90:20 Je 23 '69

LOCKHEED-California company. See Lockheed aircraft corporation

LOCKHEED missiles and space company
Lockheed sells first educational program. R. G. O'Lone. il Aviation W 90:121+ Ap 14 '69

LOCKRIDGE, Richard
Troubled journey; story. Good H 169:62-5 Ag '69

LOCKS and keys
Great new locks, bad news for burglars. R. M. Benrey. il Pop Sci 195:170-3+ S '69
Those new tough-to-pick door locks. S. J. Howard. il Pop Mech 132:134-8+ S '69

LOCKWOOD, Lee
Book marks: trips to Hanoi. Nation 208:374-7 Mr 24 '69

LOCOMOTION
See also
Animal locomotion

LOCOMOTIVES
Flier: owner of a steam locomotive called the Flying Scotsman; interview. A. Pegler. il New Yorker 45:43-4 N 29 '69

Control
Automating the railroads: radio-controlled slave locomotives. D. Selby. il Electr World 81:46-7+ F '69

Testing
Railroads' space-age helper; aerospace type of tester. il Bsns W p94 Jl 26 '69

LOCUSTS. See Grasshoppers

LOCUSTS, Seventeen year. See Cicadas

LODESTAR international student center
Lodestar international student experiment. G. L. Heath. Sch & Soc 97:372-4 O '69

LODGE, George C.
U.S. aid to Latin America: funding radical change. For Affairs 47:735-49 Jl '69

LODGE, Henry Cabot, 1902-
Ambassador Lodge discusses the Paris peace talks; remarks, May 15, 1969. Dept State Bul 60:465-7 Je 2 '69
[Plenary sessions] See issues of Department of state bulletin, February 10, 1969-

about
Fatigue in Paris. por Time 94:23 O 17 '69
Giving up at Paris. Nation 209:618 D 8 '69
Is the war lost? S. Alsop. Newsweek 73:120 My 5 '69
Letter from Washington. R. H. Rovere. New Yorker 45:169-71 N 29 '69
Lodge leaves Paris. por Time 94:20 N 28 '69
Lodge signal. por Newsweek 74:26 D 1 '69
Now that Lodge is resigning. U S News 67:17 D 1 '69
Parting words. Newsweek 74:62 D 8 '69
Patient man in frustrating job; why Lodge gets discouraged. por U S News 67:18 N 24 '69

LODGE, John
July 20, 1969; poem. America 121:166 S 13 '69

LODGES (architecture)
All-season ski lodges. il Pop Mech 132:176-80 O '69
Modern museum piece; hunting lodge, called St Hubert's. B. Plumb. il N Y Times Mag p94-5 S 14 '69

LOEB, Gerald Martin
Are there men for all seasons? il por Forbes 103:55 Ja 15 '69

LOENGARD, John
Hattersley class: looking at Life; photographs. Pop Phot 64:103-6 Je '69
Magic of a summer house; photographs. Life 66:48-57 My 2 '69
Rampage at fair Harvard; photographs. Life 66:24-35 Ap 25 '69
Threatened marshes of Glynn; photographs. Life 67:88-93 N 14 '69

about
Hattersley class: looking at Life. R. Hattersley. il Pop Phot 64:103-6 Je '69

LOENING, Grover
Make my supersonic jet a flying boat. Holiday 46:38-9+ Jl '69

LOESER, Katinka
Messy and windy; story. Redbook 132:90-1 F '69

LOESS
Loess and the origin of Chinese agriculture.
P. T. Ho. bibliog f il Am Hist R 75:1-36 O
'69
LOESSER, Arthur
In 660 easy lessons. Atlan 223:130-1 F '69
about
Great pianist's noncareer. H. Goldsmith.
Hi Fi 19:89 Jl '69
LOESSER, Frank
Melodies linger. il por Newsweek 74:82 Ag
11 '69
Obituary
Time il por 94:48 Ag 8 '69
LOEW'S theatres, incorporated
Brother act stars at Loew's. L. and R. Tisch.
il Bsns W p 126-7+ Ap 12 '69
LOFROTH, Göran, and Duffy, M. E.
Birds give warning. bibliog por Environ 11:
10-17 My '69
LOFTFIELD, R. B. and Eigner, E. A.
Molecular order of participation of inhibitors
(or activators) in biological systems. bib-
liog Science 164:305-7 Ap 18 '69
LOFTIN, Wayne
I'll add it up: poem. Cath World 210:21 O '69
My great grandfather; poem. Cath World
209:150 Jl '69
They call me boy; poem. Cath World 209:261
S '69
LOFTING, Christopher
When the heat's on. Flying 85:58-62 S '69
LOFTIS, Norman J.
Choreography of the object. Craft Horiz 29:
10-13+ Mr '69
LOFTS, Norah
Lost queen; novel Good H 168:76-7 F '69
LOG in the bog; drama. See Watts. F. B.
LOGAN, Andy
Around city hall. New Yorker 45:131-2+ S
13; 164+ O 11; 184-90 N 15 '69
LOGAN, Dee
Build a Happy hybrid. Pop Electr 30:48-51+
Mr '69
LOGAN, Edgar
Schools & corporations: partners in Detroit.
Sr Schol 94:School Teach 14-15 Mr 21 '69
LOGAN, John
Unpredictable as Grace. A. Poulin, jr. Na-
tion 209:734-5 D 29 '69
LOGAN CANYON, Utah. See Canyons
LOGARITHMS
Units for logarithmic scales. C. S. McCamy.
bibliog il Phys Today 22:42-4 Ap '69
LOGGIE, Helen A.
Tree drawings of Helen Loggie. il Am Artist
33:62-7 Je '69
LOGIC
See also
Evidence
Fallacies (logic)
LOGIC, Symbolic and mathematical
How IC logic circuits work. D. Lancaster.
il Radio-Electr 40:32-6 My '69
IC logic families:
What they are, how they work. B. Hib-
berd. il Radio-Electr 40:59-61 S '69
See also
Algebra, Boolean
**LOGIC of mathematics. See Mathematics—Phi-
losophy**
LOGSDON, Gene
Grow the earliest corn. Org Gard & Farm
16:54-6 Ja '69
Project for the chicken-hearted. Org Gard
& Farm 16:59-64 N '69
LOGUE, Edward J.
New York: are cities a bust? Look 33:70+
Ap 1 '69
about
Bridging the gap from rhetoric to reality.
S. Kaplan. Arch Forum 131:70-3 N '69
Master rebuilder. il por Newsweek 74:76 N
17 '69
LOGUE, P. E. and others
Orientation video tape for psychiatric pa-
tients. Ment Hy 53:301-2 Ap '69
LOH, Jules. See Lardner, G. jr. jt. auth.
LOHRER, Alice
School libraries in Iran and the Near East.
bibliog ALA Bul 63:1284-9 O '69
LOIRE, Gabriel
Stained glass by a modern master. W. S. Ross.
il Read Digest 95:146-52 D '69
LOJEK, John S. and Orlob, G. B.
Aphid transmission of tobacco mosaic virus.
bibliog Science 164:1407-8 Je 20 '69
LOLICH, Mickey
Highlight. il por Sports Illus 31:62 Ag 4 '69
LOMAX, Louis E.
Mississippi eyewitness. Ramp Mag 7:20-4 Ja
25 '69

LOMBARDI, Riccardo
Midwest meets Fr. Lombardi. W. B. Fa-
herty. America 121:162-3 S 13 '69
LOMBARDI, Vince
Ararararararargh! W. Johnson. il por Sports
Illus 30:28-30+ Mr 3 '69
Capital coach. por Newsweek 73:74 F 17 '69
Death by inches; Green Bay Packers 1968
season; excerpt from Jerry Kramer's fare-
well to football; ed. by D. Schaap. J.
Kramer. il Sports Illus 31:50-9 Ag 4 '69
Vincification of Sonny Jurgensen. G. Cart-
wright. il por Life 67:48-51 O 24 '69
We're going to win, you better believe it.
J. Underwood. il pors Sports Illus 31:18-
20+ Jl 28 '69
Whipping up the Redskins. Time 94:24 D 26
'69
LOMPOC, Calif.
Flower festival, flower touring. il Sunset 142:
52+ Je '69
LONDON, Arthur
Confession. A. L. Moats. il Nat R 21:846-8+
Ag 26 '69
LONDON, Ivan D.
Unusual library of radical literature at
Brooklyn college. por Sch & Soc 97:72-3
F '69
LONDON, Jack
Jack London's Klondike. I. Stone. il por
Travel & Camera 32:45-57 Ag '69
London revisited. L. Conger. Writer 82:6-8
N '69
LONDON, Kurt L.
Soviet Union and the West. Cur Hist 57:
193-200+ O '69
U.S.S.R. east Europe and the socialist com-
monwealth. bibliog f Cur Hist 56.193-9
Ap '69
LONDON, Miriam, and Lee, Ta-ling
(comps) Making of a Red guard. N Y Times
Mag p8-9+ Ja 4 '70
LONDON
Air pollution
London: victory over smog. il U S News
67:77 D 15 '69
Out of the fog; vanishing London pea-
souper. il Time 94:57 D 12 '69
Airports
Political backfires blocking new airport for
London. H. J. Coleman. il Aviation W 91:
130-1+ O 20 '69
Architecture
Bright new look of old England; J. Bannen-
berg's house on Carlyle Square. il House B
111:108-11 S '69
Landlocked ship; maintenance depot. il Arch
Forum 130:64-7 My '69
Art
London. J. Russell. See issues of Art news
Bridges
How to build a river in the Arizona desert
to flow under the London bridge. W. Rob-
bins. il Esquire 71:78-83+ F '69
Westward ho the station wagons; London
bridge is going up in Arizona. D. Butwin.
il Sat R 52:39-41 F 8 '69
Clubs
How to make millions without really work-
ing; the Clubman's club providing mem-
bership to clubs. il Time 93:94 Ap 11 '69
Covent Garden
See also
Royal opera, Great Britain
Description
Cognoscenti abroad: Carl Foreman's London.
A. Goodfriend. Sat R 52:32-4 Ag 16 '69
Cognoscenti abroad: Yehudi Menuhin's Lon-
don. A. Goodfriend. il Sat R 52:42+ My 10
'69
Notes from a wayfaring ranger: pirate cabs:
Hampstead. D. Butwin. Sat R 52:24 Jl 5 '69
Notes from London. N. S. Hazelton. Nat R
21:136 F 11 '69
Personal business; businessman's guide to
Europe: London. Bsns W p 135-6 My 24 '69
Galleries and museums
London galleries. A. Eliot. il Art in Am 57:
92-6 S '69
New gallery: opening of Gimpel gallery of
London branch in New York. New Yorker
45:28-9 My 31 '69
Today gallery for today's art; Hayward art
gallery. il Design 70:36 Spr '69
See also
Tate gallery

LONDON—*Continued*

Gardens
Rooftop English and Spanish gardens are a London surprise. il Sunset 142:229 My '69

Harbor
New trouble on London's docks. U S News 66:93-4 My 26 '69

Hotels, restaurants, etc.
When in Rome do as the roamers do; eight writers tell where they sleep, eat and shop; symposium; with editorial comment. Esquire 72:124-7+. 198-9 O '69

Ye olde Cheshire cheese. London. M. Woodward. il Travel 131:24 Je '69
See also
Night clubs

Housing
Nowhere people; squatting in Britain. il Newsweek 74:37 Jl 7 '69

Thamesmead. il Arch Forum 131:59-65 Jl '69

Labor and laboring classes
New trouble on London's docks. U S News 66:93-4 My 26 '69

Publishing game; excerpts from London labour and the London poor. H. Mayhew. il Nation 208:313 Mr 10 '69

Music
Behind the scenes (cont of) Notes from our correspondents. E. Greenfield. See issues of High fidelity incorporating Musical America

Britten premiere and a mad King George. E. Greenfield. il Hi Fi 19:MA26-7 Ag '69

Notes from our correspondents. E. Greenfield. See issues of High fidelity incorporating Musical America

Of orchestras and echoes. E. Greenfield. Hi Fi 19:MA27+ Je '69

Other side; Berlioz in the Strand. T. Heinitz. Sat R 52:47 Ag 30 '69

Report: London: Orfeo ed Euridice at Royal opera. F. G. Barker. Opera N 34:29 S 6 '69

Report: London; production of Humphrey Searle's Hamlet as an opera. F. G. Barker. Opera N 33:27 Je 14 '69

Rosie side of the street; Albert Hall concert of buskers. il Time 93:82 F 7 '69
See also
Royal opera, Great Britain
Sadler's Wells opera

Newspapers
See also
News of the world (newspaper)
Sun (newspaper)
Times, London

Photographs
One street one roll; Portobello road. Travel & Camera 32:75-7 Ap '69

Police
Gray ghost wins again; Scotland Yard's T. Butler tracked down the perpetrators of the biggest cash theft in history. J. Stewart-Gordon. Read Digest 95:229-34 Jl '69

Prisons
See Prisons—Great Britain

Religious institutions and affairs
Black hatred at St Paul's. J. D. Douglas. Chr Today 13:35-6 F 14 '69

Social life and customs
Is there nothing sacred here? Q. Crewe. Vogue 154:60+ N 15 '69

Perspective. J. H. Plumb. Sat R 52:30 N 29 '69
See also
Night clubs

Anecdotes, facetiae, satire, etc.
Encounter in London. R. Atcheson. Holiday 46:10-11 Ag '69

Stores
Beau Brummell shopped here; Burlington arcade. J. A. M. Graham. il Holiday 46:62-3+ N '69

Bowler buffs; Lock & co, birthplace of the bowler. H. Van Ketel. il Travel & Camera 32:10 My '69

Streets
Carnaby street. F. Littler. Sat R 52:6-7 O 25 '69

One street one role; Portobello road; photographs. il Travel & Camera 32:75-7 Ap '69

Theater
Editor's report; lively London; Show tours. M. M. Davis. Travel 131:14 F '69

English season. J. A. Hodge. il Travel & Camera 32:41-2+ Ag '69

London is still no. 1 (in theater, anyway) K. Tynan. il Holiday 46:74-7+ O '69

London show. Y. Blumenfeld. Atlan 224:99-101 Ag '69

Rabelais at the Old Vic; performance by the Compagnie Renaud-Barrault. C. R. Hughes. America 121:616-17 D 20 '69
See also
Sadler's Wells opera

LONDON, Ontario
Art
What London, Ontario, has that everywhere else needs. B. Lord. il Art in Am 57:103-5 S '69

LONDON boat show. See Boats—Exhibitions

LONDON bridge. See London—Bridges

LONDON bridge; drama. See Swortzell. L.

LONDON Economist. See Economist (London)

LONDON school of economics and political science
London school of economics; end of a year of upheaval. D. S. Greenberg. Science 164:1379-82 Je 20 '69

LONDON Times. See Times, London

LONDON zoo. See Zoological gardens

LONDONDERRY, Ireland
Bad case of the troubles called Londonderry. D. Holden. il N Y Times Mag p 10-11+ Ag 3 '69

LONDONERS
Notes from London. N. S. Hazelton. Nat R 21:136 F 11 '69

LONE Star cement corporation
Relative triumph. il Forbes 104:53 Jl 15 '69

LONE Star steel company
How a company keeps going in spite of violent strike. il U S News 66:85-6 My 12 '69

LONELINESS
Listeners; Davenport, Iowa, Dial-a-listener service. Time 94:56 Ag 1 '69

Loneliest night of the year. H. Hobbs. Redbook 134:49-50 D '69

Loneliness; how it can be cured. B. Graham. Read Digest 95:135-8 O '69
See also
Social isolation
Solitude

LONEY, Glenn
(ed) See Everding, A. Everding
(ed) See Osborn. D. Two California poster designers
(ed) See Woods. C. Two California poster designers

LONG, Franklin A.
Industrial impact of Apollo. por Bul Atom Sci 25:70-3 S '69

Support of scientific research and education in our universities; adaptation of address, December 6, 1968. Science 163:1037-40 Mr 7 '69

about
ABM and NSF. il por Sci N 95:421-2 My 3 '69

NSF director: Nixon admits he was wrong. P. M. Boffey and B. Nelson. Science 164:532-4 My 2 '69

NSF directorship: why did Nixon veto Franklin A. Long? P. M. Boffey and B. Nelson. Science 164:406-11 Ap 25 '69

Nixon and NSF: politics block appointment of Long as director. P. M. Boffey. por Science 164:283-4 Ap 18 '69

Political criteria for non-political jobs? E. Rabinowitch. Bul Atom Sci 25:2-3+ Je '69

LONG, Huey Pierce
Huey Long, by T. H. Williams. Review
Nation 209:480-2 N 3 '69. R. G. Sherrill
New Repub 161:24+ D 13 '69. B. W. Eggler
Newsweek por 74:100+ N 3 '69. G. Wolff
Sat R por 52:31-3+ N 1 '69. E. M. Yoder, jr

LONG, Priscilla
Turning points; the decision. McCalls 96:103+ Ja '69

LONG, Ralph Gerry
Introduction to music for the choreographer. Dance Mag 43:63-5 F '69

LONG. Robert
Are your components compatible? Hi Fi 19:44-7 My '69

Ping-ping-pong-pong. Hi Fi 19:62-3+ S '69

Turntables; renaissance of the manual. Hi Fi 19:34-8 Ap '69

Video topics. Hi Fi 19:36 My; 34 Jl '69

LONG, Russell Bilile
Plot thickens around the surtax. por Bsns W p32 Jl 19 '69
Relief and reform bill. por Time 94:21-2 N 7 '69
Tax surcharge hits a hurdle. il por Newsweek 74:77-8 Jl 21 '69

LONG BEACH, Calif.
Young people of North Long Beach. J. Q. Wilson. Harper 239:83-90 D '69

LONG BRANCH, N.J.
When Jersey was the Spa of presidents. T. Fleming. il Sat R 52:46-7+ Mr 8 '69

LONG-focus lenses. See Lenses. Photographic

LONG honeymoon; story. See Jerrard, M.

LONG ISLAND, N.Y.
Long Island. G. Gleason. il Travel 132:38-43 S '69
See also
Architecture, Domestic—Long Island
Gardens—Long Island

LONG ISLAND agricultural and technical institute, Farmingdale. See New York (state). State university—Agricultural and technical institute at Farmingdale, Long Island

LONG ISLAND railroad
LIRR revolt. il Newsweek 73:78 F 17 '69
Model of inefficiency. il Time 94:71 Ag 8 '69
Nation's finest comes up short; survey of commuter railroads around the country on Oct. 7. il Bsns W p44-5 O 11 '69
New cars for the Long Island. il Am City 84:144 F '69
Rocky Island line. Newsweek 74:50 Ag 25 '69
Rocky's Island line. Newsweek 74:72 O 20 '69
Summer of discontent for commuters. il Bsns W p74-6 Ag 2 '69
Ticket trouble; commuters arrested for refusal to show tickets. il Time 93:54 Ja 24 '69
Unholier than thou trio; Long Island railroad, Consolidated Edison and New York telephone. L. L. L. Golden. Sat R 52:80-1 O 11 '69
Urban transit picks up some speed. il Bsns W p66+ S 20 '69

LONG playing records. See Phonograph records

LONG-range shooting. See Shooting

LONG table; drama. See Boiko, C.

LONGANESI and company. See Publishers and publishing—Italy

LONGDEN, Johnny
Prince ducks the big one. W. Tower. il Sports Illus 30:24-7 My 26 '69
Prince who would be king. W. Tower. il Sports Illus 30:14-15 F 17 '69

LONGET, Claudine
Holiday with music. G. Christy. il pors Good H 169:40-2+ D '69

LONGEVITY
Aging, the disease with a cure. B. Frisch. il Sci Digest 65:32-6 F '69
Men die earlier than women. B. Urlanis. il UNESCO Courier 22:28-30 N '69
Only trees and tortoises live longer than people. D. Gunston. il Sci Digest 66:47-51 Ag '69
Predicts life span of 300 years. il Todays Health 47:18 O '69
Timing of our lives. H. L. Browning. il Trans-Action 6:22-7 O '69
Why men die sooner. Sci Digest 66:56 D '69
See also
Aging
Centenarians
Mortality
Old age

Anecdotes, facetiae, satire, etc.
Good things that undone poor Gum. R. Baker. Life 67:16B Ag 15 '69

LONGFELLOW, Henry Wadsworth
Concord and Cambridge confidential. W. Sullivan. il Sat R 52:40-1 S 27 '60
Longfellow, a veritable father image. P. W. Schmidtchen. il por Hobbies 74:135-6 S '69

LONGFIN tuna fishing. See Albacore fishing

LONGFORD, Elizabeth (Harman) Pakenham, countess of
Duke of Wellington's search for a palace. Horizon 11:106-13 Spr '69

LONGMEADOW, Mass.
Pass/fail at Longmeadow. J. Climo. il Clear House 43:341-3 F '69

LONGMONT, Colo.
Aluminum replaces wood for reservoir cover. il Am City 84:68 O '69
New lights for a new park. J. Pope. Am City 84:156 My '69

LONGO, Joan
She married a priest. S. Cunneen. Commonweal 90:440-1 Ji 11 '69

LONGSHOREMEN
West coast dockers move toward peace; PMA-ILWU wars over packing containers at West coast ports. Bsns W p 142 O 11 '69

LONGWORTH, Alice (Roosevelt)
Before the colors fade. J. Bingham. pors Am Heritage 20:42-3+ F '69

LONSDALE, Dame Kathleen
Developing nations and scientific responsibility. Bul Atom Sci 25:27-8 N '69

LOOK (periodical)
Greece; the torture goes on. C. S. Wren. Look 33:63 O 7 '69
Mayor v. the magazine. il Time 94:49 S 19 '69
1969 Look All America. W. McKean. il Look 33:76+ D 16 '69
Teacher of the year. C. Mangel. il Look 33: 58-62 My 13 '69
See also
All-America cities

LOOMER, Alice
Is your child proud of you? Parents Mag 44: 50-1+ Ja '69
Youngster who doesn't fit in. Parents Mag 44:35-7 D '69

LOOMIS, Carol J.
Hard times come to the hedge funds. Fortune 81:100-3+ Ja '70
Squeeze on the directors. Fortune 79:146-50+ My 15 '69
That long, lively pursuit of A.B.C. Fortune 79:130-4+ Mr '69
They're tearing up Wall Street. Fortune 80: 88-91+ Ag 1 '69

LOOMIS, Chauncey
Mystery in the Arctic. D. Jackson. il por Life 66:66B-67+ Ap 25 '69

LOONEY, Joe Don
Looney is playing a new tune. J. Murphy. il Sports Illus 31:20-2 Ag 4 '69

LOONS
Loons of Mink Pond; excerpt from A clearing in the wilderness. H. Fosburgh. il Cons 23:2-5 Je '69

LOOS, Anita
Unforgettable Tallulah. Read Digest 95:130-4 Jl '69

LOOS, James
Air traffic cop; on the hottest spot in aviation. R. Lindsey. il pors N Y Times Mag p28-9+ S 14 '69

LOOSESTRIFE
Creeping Charlie. C. P. Holway. Horticulture 47:13 Jl '69

LOPATA, Richard S.
Faster pace in wholesaling. Harvard Bsns R 47:130-43 Jl '69

LOPATIN, Lawrence H.
Motor trend interview. pors Motor T 21: 87-8+ S '69
about
Getting on the right track. il por Bsns W p70-1 Ag 30 '69

LOPEZ, Enrique Hank
Mexico. Am Heritage 20:4-39+ Ap '69
(ed) See Johnson, S. H. My brother Lyndon

LOPEZ, Frances
Regional program for migrant education. Ed Digest 34:10-12 Ja '69

LÓPEZ PELLÓN, Nivio
Incunabula and the New World. Américas 21:11-17 N '69
Mutis in New Granada. Américas 21:29-33 F '69

LOPEZ TIJERINA, Reies. See Tijerina, R. L.

LORAN
F-105 modified for blind bombing role. R. Miller. il Aviation W 90:64-5+ Ja 20 '69

LORANT, Stefan
Two new Lincoln finds. Look 33:117-18 O 21 '69

LORD, Barry
New work from Montreal. Art in Am 57:99-101 Mv '69
Three young Canadians. Art in Am 57:87-9 Ja '69
What London, Ontario, has that everywhere else needs. Art in Am 57:103-5 S '69

LORD, Daniel A.
Simple rule of love. T. F. Gavin. America 121:424-5 N 8 '69

LORD, Ed
IC digital clocks. Radio-Electr 40:43-6 S '69

LORD, John
Longest wait. Am Heritage 20:4-15+ Je '69

LORD, Lois
Middle ages in environmental sculpture. Sch Arts 68:32-5 F '69

LORD, Shirley
Gay quenchers. Harp Baz 102:90-1 Je '69
Nouveau vs d'habitude. Harp Baz 102:196 Ag '69
Tempus fugit; poem. Harp Baz 103:100H D '69
True love+shrewd love=99 per cent success. Harp Baz 102:146-7+ F '69
Where to go. Harp Baz 102:167 My '69
LORDS. See Gangs
LORD'S Supper
Judgment at the Lord's table. Chr Today 13:24 Jl 18 '69
One bread, by M. Thurian. Review
  Commonweal 91:189-90 N 7 '69. W. G. Storey
Trends to intercommunion. C. J. Armbruster. America 121:455-6 N 15 '69; Discussion. 121:575 D 15 '69
Utrecht eucharist; Catholic/Protestant intercommunion. Chr Cent 86:468-9 Ap 9 '69
LORDSTOWN, Ohio
Big boondoggle at Lordstown; with editorial comment. D. Sider. il Fortune 80:85-6, 196-9+ S '69
LOREN, Harold
What can we do about the camp drop out? Camp Mag 41:14+ N '69
LOREN, Sophia
Sophia Loren: a woman was born to have children. A. Levy il pors Good H 169:86-9+ N '69
Sophia Loren and Carlo Ponti talk about their new baby. S. Blum. por Redbook 133:80-1+ My '69
Sophia Loren's baby: the doctor who made it possible. J. Barry. il pors McCalls 96:124-5+ Ap '69
Sophia triumphant: her greatest role, wife and mother. il por Vogue 153:202-3 Ap 1 '69
Star is born at last. il pors Life 67:44-5 Ag 1 '69
LORENTZEN, Arthur A.
Solving problems presented by teaching linguistics. Engl J 58:113-19 Ja '69
LORENZ, James Douglas, jr
Justice for the rural poor. America 120:275-7 Mr 8 '69
LORENZ, Konrad Zacharias
Profiles. J. Alsop. New Yorker 45:39-42+ Mr 8 '69
LORENZO, Gene
Welcome to Cowtown. East. C. Phinizy. il pors Sports Illus 31:72-4+ D 8 '69
LORR, John S.
Lettering, art curriculum stepchild. Design 70:10-14 Sum '69
LOS ANGELES
Reports: Los Angeles. S. V. Roberts. Atlan 224:30+ S '69
Sidewalks of L.A; official contest to find a theme song. Newsweek 73:91 F 3 '69
  See also
La Brea

Air pollution
Smog at the bar. il Newsweek 74:67 N 10 '69

Airports
Day in the life of an airport. J. N. Miller. il Read Digest 94:146-50 F '69

Architecture
In Los Angeles, refined detail and bold pattern enliven an understated office block. il Arch Rec 146:126 Ag '69

Art
Los Angeles. L. D. Armstrong. See issues of Art news
Los Angeles: a view from the studios. P. Selz; W. Wilson. il Art in Am 57:144-7 N '69
Two generations in L.A. P. Selz; J. Livingston. il Art in Am 57:92-7 Ja '69

City planning
Sprawling Los Angeles gets a new skyline. il Bsns W p68-9+ D 13 '69
Workshop in Watts: the Urban workshop. E. P. Berkeley. il Arch Forum 130:58-63 Ja '69

Description
Exploring walk in old Los Angeles. il Sunset 142:40-2 Je '69

Elections
Bitter victory; Yorty reelected mayor. il Time 93:28-9 Je 6 '69
Bradley challenge. il Time 93:26 My 23 '69
Fallen angels. New Repub 160:7 Je 7 '69
Mayor Yorty's big upset. il Newsweek 73:31-2 Je 9 '69
Round one for Bradley; mayoralty primary results. Nation 208:485 Ap 21 '69

Sad Sam; Mayor Yorty came in second to T. Bradley in mayoral primary. Time 93:28 Ap 11 '69
Victory for a specter. P. Kerby. Nation 208:749-50 Je 16 '69

Finance
  See also
Los Angeles—Taxation

Galleries and museums
  See also
Los Angeles County museum of art

Hotels, restaurants, etc.
Eating well in southern California; organic food in gourmet style. J. Olds. il Org Gard & Farm 16:55-7 Je '69

Libraries
  See also
Los Angeles public library

Lighting
Los Angeles goes underground. Am City 84:161-2 Mr '69

Mayors
Negro mayor for Los Angeles? il U S News 66:12 Ap 14 '69

Music
San Francisco's opera returns to Los Angeles. I. Kolodin. Sat R 52:40 Mr 29 '69

Negroes
Thomas Bradley, rising political star in the West. il Ebony 24:126-8+ Je '69
Up from Watts. W. F. Buckley, jr. Nat R 21:610-11 Je 17 '69

Police
Chief Reddin: new style at the top. L. M. Mathews. il Atlan 223:84-6+ Mr '69
Operation Empathy; project in Covina. il Newsweek 74:104 D 15 '69

Politics and government
Black ballot power; mayoralty race. il Newsweek 73:36 Ap 14 '69
L.A.'s about to say so long. Sam. J. W. Germond. New Repub 160:10 My 24 '69
Race, television and Yorty; mayoralty candidates. P. Kerby. Nation 208:403-5 Mr 31 '69
That new black magic; mayoralty race. il Newsweek 73:40+ My 26 '69
Thomas Bradley, rising political star in the West. il pors Ebony 24:126-8+ Je '69
Voters are in; Los Angeles. S. V. Roberts. Commonweal 90:381 Je 20 '69
What Yorty's victory shows about the mood in Los Angeles. il U S News 66:36 Je 9 '69
  See also
Los Angeles—Elections

Public library
  See Los Angeles public library

Recreation
Ocean fishing for Los Angeles youth. J. Maghakian. il Parks & Rec 4:32 Jl '69

Street traffic
Interconnected signals speed traffic flow. il Am City 84:134 Je '69

Streets
The used car lot, where else but Sunset Strip? Rolls-Royces of the 1930s and other vintage gems for sale. B. Sanders. il Motor T 21:32-3 Jl '69

Taxation
Los Angeles' golden goose; taxation against profits of new Music Center. A. Strick. Nation 209:87-9 Jl 28 '69

Theater
Los Angeles' golden goose; taxation against profits of new Music Center. A. Strick. Nation 209:87-9 Jl 28 '69
LOS ANGELES COUNTY, Calif.

Police
Do police helicopters justify their cost? H. K. Becker. il Am City 84:70-1 N '69

Sheriffs department
Relating! Police with people. il Am City 84:142+ Ap '69
LOS ANGELES COUNTY art institute. See Otis art institute of Los Angeles County
LOS ANGELES COUNTY museum of art
Art and technology in California. F. Tuten. Vogue 153:36 Ap 15 '69
Treasure from the Orient; Heeramaneck Indian collection. il Time 93:70 Mr 14 '69

LOUISVILLE free public library
Library on the air; Wire network. D. L. Day.
il Wilson Lib Bul 44:320-5 N '69
LOUISVILLE orchestra
Changing of the guard, eight new recordings.
A. Cohn. il Am Rec G 35:462-7 F '69
LOUNASMAA, O. V.
New methods for approaching absolute zero;
with biographical sketch. Sci Am 221:15,
26-35 bibliog(p 152) D '69
LOUNGES (rooms)
See also
Student lounges
LOUVAIN, Belgium

Historic houses, etc.
Grand Béguinage at Louvain, Belgium. J.
Tordeur. il Antiques 96:592-4 O '69
LOUVIERE, Vernon
Panorama of the nation's business. Nations
Bsns 57:18-19 N; 15 D '69
LOUVRE, Paris
Through the Louvre with Barnett Newman;
interview, ed. by P. Schneider. B. New-
man. il Art N 68:34-9+ Sum '69
LOVASICH, Jeanne L. and others
Timing of the apparent effects of cloud seed-
ing. bibliog Science 165:892-3 Ag 29 '69
LÖVE, Askell
Avena magna: new oat species. bibliog Science
163:595 F 7 '69
LOVE, Iris Cornella
Action: a beauty investment. B. Wysor. il
pors Harp Baz 102:158-61 Ag '69
LOVE, Joseph L.
La Raza: Mexican Americans in rebellion.
bibliog por Trans-Action 6:35-41 F '69
LOVE, Mary
Hurricane loss. ALA Bul 63:1502-4 D '69
LOVE, Robert Alonzo
How to pick the acorns that will sprout. por
Bsns W p84 D 20 '69
LOVE
Can love outwait the army? questions and
answers. A. Wood. Seventeen 28:336+ Ag
'69
How men make women feel loved. J. Viorst.
il Redbook 133:65+ Ag '69; Same abr.
Read Digest 95:95-8 O '69
I love him, but do I like him? D. A. Sugar-
man and R. Hochstein. Seventeen 28:152-3+
F '69
Love. P. A. Samuelson. Newsweek 74:52 D 29
'69
Love and money. E. Sheppard. Harp Baz 102:
191 F '69
Love with skin on it. Chr Today 14:23 D 19 '69
Playing the love game; questions and an-
swers. A. Wood. Seventeen 28:148+ O '69
Real relationship. F. Maynard. il Seventeen
28:100-1+ D '69
Right from the start; tactile communication,
with study-discussion program, by R.
Strang. D. Graves. bibliog il PTA Mag 63:
22-4, 36 My '69
Special kind of love: affection. E. E. Gordon.
Redbook 132:87+ Ap '69
True love+shrewd love=99 per cent success.
S. Lord. Harp Baz 102:146-7 F '69
Youth, love and sex: the new chivalry. J. D.
Rockefeller, 3d. Look 33:32+ O 7 '69
See also
Courtly love
Marriage
LOVE (theology)
Madness, comfort and love. J. P. Crossley,
jr. Chr Cent 86:1542-6 D 3 '69
On Romans 8:28. Chr Today 13:36 S 12 '69
LOVE, Courtly. See Courtly love
LOVE, Maternal
Magic of mother love. C. Remsberg and B.
Remsberg. il Good H 169:74-5+ Ag '69
Who comes first, husband or child? J.
Brothers. Good H 169:30+ O '69
LOVE, Platonic
Eros, play and death in Plato. P. Plass. bib-
liog f Am Imago 26:37-55 Spr '69
LOVE all my faces; story. See Lewis. L.
LOVE field airport. See Dallas—Airports
LOVE game; story. See Davis, J. A.
LOVE in literature
In declaration of love. M. Rubin. Writer 82:
14-15 Je '69
LOVE in religion, folklore, etc.
Jai Baba! New Yorker 45:28-31 Je 21 '69
LOVE potions. See Aphrodisiacs
LOVE the whole girl; story. See Savage, J.
LOVELL, Ann, and Ransom, Ann
Grandma's gone to camp! Parks & Rec 3:15
N '68

LOVELL, Sir Bernard
Man moves into the universe. por Bul Atom
Sci 25:4-7 S '69; Same abr. with title Space
frontier; what new American initiatives?
Cur 111:4-9 O '69
LOVELL, James A. Jr
Exercise for physical fitness. por Todays Ed
58:16-17 Ap '69
Physical fitness. por Parents Mag 44:34 My
'69
See also
Space flight to the moon—Manned flights—
Borman-Lovell-Anders flight, 1968
LOVELORN columns. See Newspapers—Advice
columns
LOVEMAN, Amy, national award. See Amy
Loveman national award
LOVESTONE, Jay
Stop the world. J. Hill. Commonweal 90:
5-6 Mr 21 '69
LOVI, George
Vienna planetarium conference. Sky & Tel
38:236-9 O '69
LOVING, Rush, Jr
Georgia cracker's crackerjack bank. Fortune
80:134-7+ N '69
LOVOOS, Janice
Janice Lovoos describes her methods. il por
Am Artist 32:52-3+ D '68
Marine paintings of Arden von Dewitz. Am
Artist 33:54-60+ S '69
Serigraphs of Phil Paradise. Am Artist 33:
43-8+ O '69
Tempera paintings of Robert Clark. Am Art-
ist 33:60-5+ D '69
LOW, Frances
[Father of Greater New York] Natur Hist
78:26 Ap '69
LOW, Frank J.
Infrared astrophysics. bibliog Science 164:501-
5 My 2 '69
LOW blood pressure. See Hypotension
LOW-calorie soft drinks. See Beverages
LOW cost housing. See Housing
LOW fat diet. See Diet in disease
LOW temperature physics. See Low tempera-
tures
LOW temperatures
New methods for approaching absolute zero.
O. V. Lounasmaa. il Sci Am 221:26-35 bib-
liog(p 152) D '69
LOWE, A. J.
Build the Riot restrainer. Pop Electr 30:47-50
Ap '69
Home for ohms. Pop Electr 30:34-5 My '69
Stop-action photos. Electr World 81:47 Mr
'69
LOWE, Arbon Jack
Jamaica. Américas 21:2-13 O '69
São Paulo 1990. Américas 21:28-9 Ja '69
LOWE, David
Kentucky on $5 a day. Esquire 71:88+ Mr
'69
LOWE, David G.
Banner years. Am Heritage 20:54+ Je '69
Case of the vanishing records. Am Heritage
20:34-5+ Ag '69
Prairie dream recaptured. Am Heritage 20:
14-23+ O '69
Wooden delights. Am Heritage 20:18-23 D '68
LOWE, Gay
To a student of mine upon the creation
of his second poem. Engl J 58:256 F '69
LOWE, Steven
(comp) Buyer's guide to cassette tape equip-
ment. Hi Fi 19:48-51 Jl '69
Treasure for Haydn seekers. Hi Fi 19:84 Ag
'69
LOWELL, C. Stanley
Church wealth and tax exemptions. Ed Di-
gest 35:17-19 S '69
Tax funds for religious education? Chr To-
day 13:6+ Mr 28 '69
LOWELL, Robert
Liberalism & activism. Commentary 47:19 Ap
'69

about
Dinner at the Lowells'. D. Newlove. il Es-
quire 72:128-9+ S '69
Prometheus bound; adaptation of play by
Aeschylus. Criticism
Nation 209:156 Ag 25 '69
Sojourner of the self. J. Mazzaro. Nation
209:22+ Jl 7 '69
Voice of the poet: oracular, eerie, daring. D.
Jaffe. Sat R 52:28-9+ S 6 '69
White House and the intellectuals; excerpts
from The tragedy of Lyndon Johnson. E.
F. Goldman; discussion. Harper 238:4+
Mr '69
LOWEN, Alexander, and Levin, R. J.
Case against cheating in marriage. Redbook
133:70-1+ Je '69; Same abr. Read Digest
95:79-82 N '69

LOWENSTEIN, Allard K.
Reporter at large. F. Lewis. New Yorker 45: 31-2+ Ja 10 '70
LOWENSTEIN, Edward. See Winter, P. M. jt. auth.
LOWENTHAL, Julius, and Birnbaum, Henry
Vitamin K and coumarin anticoagulants: dependence of anticoagulant effect on inhibition of vitamin K transport. bibliog Science 164:181-3 Ap 11 '69
LOWER CALIFORNIA. See California, Lower
LOWER FORT GARRY, Canada
Lower Fort Garry. N. Shipley. il Nat Parks 43:10-11 Ja '69
LOWI, Theodore J.
Dear Mayor Lindsay; letter. Nation 209:624-7 D 8 '69
Prognosis for crackdown: the wheel of panic. Nation 208:624-8 My 19 '69
LOWIN, Leeam
New kid on the street. S. Mahoney. il pors Life 66:62-62B+ Je 6 '69
LOWRIE, Jean E.
(ed) School libraries and international development. ALA Bul 63:603-9, 997-9, 1108-10, 1284-9, 1586-95 My, Jl, S-O, D '69
LOWRY, Bates
Kate's world: an awesome collage. Wilson Lib Bul 44:520-2 Ja '70

about

Departure at the Modern. Time 93:93 My 16 '69
Editorial; resignation as director of Museum of modern art. T. B. Hess. Art N 68:25 Sum '69
Parting with a paragon. il por Newsweek 73:118-19 My 12 '69
LOWRY, Betty
Europe on a mini-budget. House & Gard 135:12+ Ja '69
LOWRY, Peter
Go, go, go by bike. Seventeen 28:176-7+ Ap '69
LOWRY, W. McNeil
Arts are in trouble. R. H. Smith. Pub W 195: 39 Mr 31 '69
LOWRY, William C.
Some innovations in the preparation of teachers. Ed Digest 34:28-31 F '69
LOY, Frank E.
Department discusses air transport agreement with South Africa; statement, April 2, 1969. Dept State Bul 60:394-5 My 5 '69
Department reviews problem of aircraft hijacking and proposals for international action; statement, February 5, 1969. Dept State Bul 60:212-15 Mr 10 '69
LOYALTY
Anatomy of loyalty. S. W. Niehaus. Clear House 43:283-7 Ja '69
Sibling chivalry: the other side of the coin. G. Orcate. il Parents Mag 44:54-5+ Mr '69
See also
Americanism
Patriotism
LOYALTY, Oath of
Joe doesn't pledge allegiance; excerpts. R. S. MacGorman. Ed Digest 34:24-5 F '69
LOYCE Houlton's Minnesota dance theatre.
See Dance companies
LOYD, F. Glen
Good emergency mothers are GEMS. Todays Health 47:12-13+ S '69
How you can help the hungry. Todays Health 48:50-1 Ja '70
Medicine's Mark Twain. Todays Health 47: 52-5 My '69
New break for the gym dropout. Todays Health 47:38-43+ Mr '69
One man's fight against hunger in the city. Todays Health 47:48-53+ D '69
(ed) See Schaefer, A. E. Finally, facts on malnutrition in the United States
LOYOLA college, Montreal
Professionals discuss contemporary theology. J. W. Montgomery. Chr Today 13:45-6 S 26 '69
LOYOLA University, Chicago
Column right, march! Loyola and ROTC program. J. Deedy. Commonweal 91:2 O 3 '69
Fine arts: the Martin D'Arcy gallery of art. C. J. McNaspy. America 120:632-4 My 24 '69
LUBBOCK, Tex.
New lighting for University avenue. il Am City 84:114+ Ja '69
LUBIN, Martin, and Brandwein, Larry
Negotiating a collective bargaining agreement, the union perspective. ALA Bul 63: 973-9 Jl '69
LUBIN, Maurice A.
Giant dies, leader of the Haitian thought. Negro Hist Bul 31:16-18 O '69

LUBOVITCH, Lar
Lar Lubovitch; 92nd street Y. M. Marks. Dance Mag 43:87 Jl '69
World of dance; at 92nd street YM-YWHA. W. Terry. il por Sat R 53:77 Ja 3 '70
LUBRICANTS. See Lubrication and lubricants
LUBRICATION and lubricants
What you should know about motor oils; questions and answers. E. D. Fales, jr. Read Digest 95:166-9 O '69
See also
Automobiles—Lubrication

Additives

Big profits in little cans; growing market for oil additives. il Time 94:70-1 Ag 8 '69
Oil additives. Mech Illus 65:48 S '69
See also
STP corporation
LUCAL, John A.
Church and the ILO. America 120:644-6 My 31 '69
LUCAS, C. Payne
Black pride; address, December 4, 1968. Vital Speeches 35:505-8 Je 1 '69
LUCAS, Christopher
Master builder for the world. Read Digest 94:155-60 F '69
Where have all the geisha gone? Read Digest 94:39-40+ Mr '69
LUCAS, Christopher John
Philosophy, educational philosophy, and the current crisis; excerpt from What is philosophy of education? bibliog f Sch & Soc 97:180-6+ Mr '69
LUCAS, Jerry
Power game in the city. A. Wright. il Sports Illus 31:36-9 N 17 '69
LUCAS, Joseph, and Miner, Mae
Happiness is a fishing pier and a place in the sun. Parks & Rec 4:31-2 My '69
LUCAS, Ruth
Air force's education expert. il pors Ebony 25:88-91 N '69
LUCAS COUNTY, Ohio
Elevating scraper digs trench on sanitary landfill. il Am City 84:123 F '69
LUCE, Charles Franklin
We hire the hard-core unemployed. Duns R 93:50-2 F '69

about

Con Ed runs out of clean energy. por Bsns W p42-3 Ag 16 '69
LUCE, Gay Gaer. See Segal, J. jt. auth.
LUCE, Henry Robinson
Time: after Luce. R. Pollak. Harper 239: 42-52 Jl '69; Discussion. 239:6 S '69
LUCE, Phillip Abbott
Great rock conspiracy. Nat R 21:959+ S 23 '69
Letter from Chicago. Nat R 21:1264 D 16 '69
LUCERNE, Switzerland
Lights of Lucerne. J. Wechsberg. il Travel & Camera 32:39-41+ Mr '69
LUCEY, Dan, and Lucey, Rose
Nation directed to peace? America 121:120-1 Ag 30 '69
LUCEY, Robert Emmet, abp
Church dissent: its rising toll. por U S News 66:18 Je 16 '69
LUCEY, Rose. See Lucey, D. jt. auth.
LUCEY, William L.
Home scene. America 120:535-6 My 3 '69
LUCIA di Lammermoor: opera. See Donizetti, G.
LUCIENTES, Francisco José de Goya y. See Goya y Lucientes, F. J. de
LUCIFERIN
Luminescent systems in apogonid fishes from the Philippines. Y. Haneda and others. bibliog il Science 165:188-90 Jl 11 '69
LUCKY stores, California. See Supermarkets
LUDER, W. Fay
Electron repulsion theory. bibliog Chem 42: 16-19 Je '69
LUDKA, Arthur P.
Education for the future. Sr Schol 93:Schol Teach 14-15 Ja 10 '69
LUDLUM, David M.
Hundred years of Boston snowstorms. Weatherwise 22:72-5 Ap '69
Snowfall at San Francisco. Weatherwise 21: 230-7 D '68
Snowfall season of 1967-68. Weatherwise 22: 26-31 F '69
LUDVIGSEN, Karl E.
Brazil's industry on show. il Motor T 21: 28-31 Ap '69
Daring Wankel Mercedes. Motor T 21:42-4+ O '69
Hark! Detroit mid-engine sports cars are coming. Motor T 21:62-7+ D '69

LUDVIGSEN, Karl E.—*Continued*
Racers on the road. Motor T 21:32-5 Mr '69
Studded growth. Motor T 21:76-7 D '69
Super stoppers. Motor T 21:36-9 Je '69
Swinging headlights. Motor T 21:38-9+ S '69
Twice the traction for your next car? Motor T 21:34-7 Jl '69
Un-invention of the steering wheel. Motor T 21:90-3 F '69

LUDY, Perry Joseph
America's Boy of the year. il pors Ebony 24:70-2+ Jl '69

LUFTHANSA. See Airlines—Germany (Federal Republic)

LUG wrench; story. See Roueché. B.

LUGANO, LAKE
Lake Lugano, the cruise to Gandria. il Sunset 143:76 N '69

LUGAR, Richard G.
Hoosier hotshot. il por Newsweek 75:32-3 Ja 5 '70

LUGER, Milton
Innovations in the treatment of juvenile offenders. Ann Am Acad 381:60-70 Ja '69

LUGGAGE
Bag & baggage. M. P. R. Thomas. il Travel & Camera 32:38 Ap '69
Luggage scene: a brand-new bag. J. Reedy. Bet Hom & Gard 47:48-9 Mr '69
Personal business; lightweight luggage. Bsns W p 129-30 O 4 '69
What's your bag? Mlle 69:352-3 Ag '69
See also
Packing of luggage

LUGGAGE carriers, Automobile. See Automobiles—Equipment

LUGGAGE handling, Airline. See Airlines—Luggage handling

LUGONES, Leopoldo
How the mountains talk; poem; tr. by S. Blackwell. Américas 21:18 Ja '69

about

Leopoldo Lugones; golden condor. M. Belloni. Américas 21:15-17+ Ja '69
Short biography of Leopoldo Lugones. Américas 21:20 Ja '69

LUITJENS, Helen
Stencil designs with spray paints. Sch Arts 68:76-8 F '69

LUKACS, John Adalbert
Night Stalin and Churchill divided Europe. N Y Times Mag p36-8+ O 5 '69

LUKAS, J. Anthony
Fairly old grad ('55) looks at Harvard (in '69) N Y Times Mag p28-9+ Je 8 '69
Making of a yippie. Esquire 72:126-34+ N '69

LUKE, Peter
Hadrian VII; dramatization of novel by F. W. Rolfe. Criticism
America 120:231-2 F 22 '69
Atlan 223:62-5 Mr '69
Commonweal 89:588-9 F 7 '69
Nat R 21:168-7 F 25 '69
Nation 208:124-5 Ja 27 '69
New Repub 160:32-4 Ja 25 '69
New Yorker 44:72 Ja 18 '69
Sat R il 52:40-1 Ja 25 '69
Vogue 153:54 F 15 '69

LUKENS, Donald
Time for action on Biafra! Read Digest 94:77-9 My '69

LULLY, Jean Baptiste
Most important single Lully recording ever? J. W. Barker. Am Rec G 35:566 Mr '69

LUMBER
See also
Wood

Drying

Green wood to seasoned boards, in minutes! press drying. F. A. Strenge. il Pop Sci 195:86-7 Ag '69

Grading and standardization

Old, reliable 2x4 may shrink again. il Bsns W p32+ Ag 2 '69

Prices

Cost of neglect. il Time 93:86-7 Mr 28 '69
No lid on wood prices. il Bsns W p44 Mr 29 '69

Standards

See Lumber—Grading and standardization

LUMBER drying. See Lumber—Drying

LUMBER industry and trade
Boom in wood that busted. il Bsns W p 138 O 25 '69
Raiding the forests; timber supply act. M. McCloskey. New Repub 161:10-11 D 13 '69

Why lumber stays scarce and prices stay high. il U S News 66:104-5 Ap 21 '69
See also
Boise Cascade corporation
Georgia-Pacific corporation
Weyerhaeuser company

LUMBER workers
See also
Strikes—United States—Lumber workers

LUMINAIRES. See Street lighting fixtures

LUMINESCENCE
Wheels of light; luminous apparitions in the Indian Ocean. K. Kalle. il Sea Front 15:116-22 Mr '69
See also
Bioluminescence
Luciferin
Thermoluminescence

LUMINESCENCE dosimetry. See Radiometers

LUMINOUS paint. See Paint, Luminous

LUMLEY, Henry de
Paleolithic camp at Nice; with biographical sketch. Sci Am 220:18, 42-50 My '69

LUMLEY, Kathryn W.
Reading can be fun everywhere. Sr Schol 94:Schol Teach 21 Ja 31 '69

LUNA, Charles
Yesterday's battles. por Forbes 104:39 O 15 '69

LUNAR bases
See also
Moon—Exploration

LUNAR communications satellites. See Communications satellites

LUNAR communication systems. See Space flight—Communication systems

LUNAR core sampler. See Drilling and boring machinery

LUNAR drilling apparatus. See Drilling and boring machinery

LUNAR exploration. See Moon—Exploration

LUNAR geology
Ancient moon samples exhilarate selenologists. il Sci N 96:160-1 Ag 30 '69
Apollo 11 experiments. J. Ashbrook. il Sky & Tel 38:149-51+ S '69
Apollo 11 photos assist lunar geology. il Aviation W 91:104-6 S 8 '69
Apollo returns: the work begins. il Sci N 96:95-6 Ag 2 '69
As old as any body in the solar system. il Sci N 96:145-6 N 15 '69
Bed forms in base-surge deposits: lunar implications. R. V. Fisher and A. C. Waters. bibliog il Science 165:1349-52 S 26 '69
Bits of another world; moon rocks. L. B. Taylor jr. il Space World F-9-69: 35-41 S '69
Bleak, varied moon yields wealth of information to its first explorers. W. J. Normyle. il Aviation W 91:30-3 Jl 28 '69
Controversy continues. il Sci N 96:176-7 S 6 '69
Doctor Urey talks about the moon findings; interview. H. C. Urey. il Space World F-12-72:35-43 D '69
Eagle's rich haul. il Newsweek 74:70-2 Jl 28 '69
Findings of the moon mission. il U S News 67:11 Ag 11 '69
First studies of lunar material. R. N. Watts, jr. il Sky & Tel 38:312-14 N '69
Geologists get new data of lunar surface. Aviation W 91:89+ Ag 4 '69
Inside the box. il Newsweek 74:20 Ag 4 '69
Investigations; rocks, dust, or data from the moon at Lamont geological observatory. New Yorker 45:54-5 D 6 '69
Letter from the space center; completion of initial survey of the rocks and dust from Apollo 11 mission. H. S. F. Cooper, jr. New Yorker 45:92+ O 11 '69
Letter from the space center; examination of astronauts and samples from Apollo 11 mission. H. S. F. Cooper, jr. New Yorker 45:82+ Ag 16 '69
Letter from the space center; first lunar walk of the Apollo 12 mission. H. S. F. Cooper, jr. New Yorker 45:46-56 Ja 3 '70
Letter from the space center; gathering and examination of moon samples from Apollo 11 mission. H. S. F. Cooper, jr. New Yorker 45:50-7 Ag 2 '69
Letter from the space center; testing of lunar rocks and dust from Apollo 11 mission. H. S. F. Cooper, jr. New Yorker 45:63-70 Ag 23 '69
Lunar debate swirls around soil samples. Aviation W 91:27 Ag 4 '69
Lunar igneous intrusions. F. Baz. bibliog il Science 167:49-50 Ja 2 '70
Lunar laboratory; with report by D. A. Hamblin. il Life 67:50-4+ Jl 4 '69

LYMPHOCYTES—*Continued*
Lymphocyte stimulation: transfer of cellular hypersensitivity to antigen in vitro. F. T. Valentine and H. S. Lawrence. bibliog il Science 165:1014-16 S 5 '69
Microspikes on the lymphocyte uropod. W. McFarland. bibliog il Science 163:818-20 F 21 '69
Polymethacrylic acid: effects on lymphocyte output of the thoracic duct in rats. S. Ormai and E. de Clercq. bibliog il Science 163:471-2 Ja 31 '69
Pompe's disease: detection of heterozygotes by lymphocyte stimulation. K. Hirschhorn and others. bibliog il Science 166:1632-3 D 26 '69
Thymus-dependent lymphocytes: destruction by lymphocytic choriomeningitis virus. M. Hanaoka and others. bibliog il Science 163:1216-19 Mr 14 '69
LYMPHOCYTIC choriomeningitis virus. See Viruses
LYMPHOID cells
Immune response in vitro: independence of activated lymphoid cells. C. W. Pierce and B. Benacerraf. bibliog il Science 166:1002-4 N 21 '69
LYNCH, J. Barry
Peace corps intrigue in the Philippines. G. H. Anderson. Chr Cent 87:4-6 Ja 7 '70
LYNCH, Kevin. See Carr, S. jt. auth.
LYNCH, Lawrence
Overdue. por Wilson Lib Bul 44:326-7 N '69
LYNCH, William S.
Good old school days are gone. Bul Atom Sci 25:38-41 O '69
LYND, Staughton
Almost making it. Commonweal 90:345-7 Je 6 '69
New left. bibliog f Ann Am Acad 382:64-72 Mr '69
about
Inqui 67: some reflections on the Lyndian heresy. H. A. Patin. bibliog f Sch & Soc 97:98-100 F '69
Intellectual origins of Staughton Lynd. L. Kriegel. Commonweal 89:503-4 Ja 17 '69
LYNDEN, Patricia
Why I'm a cop: interviews from a reporter's notebook. Atlan 223:104-8 Mr '69
LYNDON B. Johnson state park. See Texas—Parks and reserves
LYNDON Baines Johnson library (proposed) See Texas. University—Austin campus—Libraries
LYNES, Russell
After hours. See issues of Harper's magazine
Gentle tyranny of books. House B 111:142-3 My '69
State of taste. Art in Am 57:121 My; 23 S: 47 N '69
Things are in the saddle. Horizon 11:40-1 Wint '69
LYNGE, John E.
Borovets: Bulgaria's year-round resort. Travel 131:60-1 Mr '69
LYON, John W.
Mississippi ballot box. Sat R 52:20-1 My 17 '69
LYON, Ninette
Food in Vogue. Vogue 154:163 O 1: 69 O 15: 131 N 1: 71 N 15 '69: 155:85 Ja 1 '70
LYON, Peter
Europe and the third world. bibliog f Ann Am Acad 386:137-47 N '69
LYONS, Anne Nason
Tourism. Focus 19:8-11 My '69
LYONS, Joseph
Stimulus generalization as a function of discrimination learning with and without errors. Science 163:490-1 Ja 31 '69
LYONS, Leonard
Leonard in the Lyons den. A. Bester. il pors Holiday 45:44-7+ Mr '69
LYONS, Nick
First trout, first lie. Field & S 73:48-9+ F '69
LYONS, Paul J.
Torture in the USSR. Nat R 21:1259-60 D 16 '69
LYONS, France
Music
Report: productions at Lyons and Marseilles. D. Stevens. Opera N 34:29 D 20 '69
LYRA TAVARES, Aurelio de. See Tavares, A. de L.
LYRIC opera of Chicago
Lyric opera in the home stretch. B. Jacobson. il Hi Fi 19:MA26+ F '69
Report: Chicago; production of Mussorgsky's Khovanshchina. S. Jenkins. Opera N 34:23 N 1 '69

Report: Chicago productions. J. Stedman and G. McElroy. il Opera N 34:24 D 13 '69
Report: productions of Puritani and Don Giovanni. J. Stedman and G. McElroy. Opera N 34:40 D 27 '69
LYRIC poetry
Lyrics, heroic and otherwise. R. D. Spector. Sat R 52:33-5 Mr 15 '69
LYRIDS. See Meteors
LYSENKO, Trofim Denisovich
Rise and fall of T. D. Lysenko, by Z. A. Medvedev. Review
Nat R 21:1020-1 O 7 '69. T. H. Jukes
Soviet biology and the powers that were. T. Dobzhansky. Science 164:1507-9 Je 27 '69
LYSERGIC acid diethylamide. See LSD
LYSIMACHIA. See Loosestrife
LYSINE
Histone structure: asymmetric distribution of lysine residues in lysine-rich histone. M. Bustin and others. bibliog il Science 163:391-3 Ja 24 '69
LYSIS (bacteriology) See Bacteriolysis
LYSOSOMES
Cystine: compartmentalization within lysosomes in cystinotic leukocytes. J. D. Schulman and others. bibliog il Science 166:1152-4 N 28 '69
Protein digestion in isolated lysosomes inhibited by intralysosomal trypan blue. M. Davies and others. bibliog il Science 163:1454-6 Mr 28 '69
LYSOZYME
Life-saving promise of enzymes. L. Lessing. il Fortune 79:118-21+ Mr '69
Lysozyme retention by cockroach periplaneta americana L. D. R. A. Wharton. bibliog il Science 163:183-4 Ja 10 '69
Mechanism of lysozyme action. D. M. Chipman and N. Sharon. bibliog il Science 165:454-65 Ag 1 '69
LYSTROSAURUS. See Reptiles, Fossil

M

MARC. See Metropolitan applied research center, incorporated
MATV (master antenna television) See Television antennas
MBD. See Minimal brain dysfunction
MBT (main battle tank) See Tanks, Military
MCA, Incorporated
Strange romance? talking merger with Firestone. il Forbes 104:22-3 S 1 '69
MERBISC (most extraordinary recreation bargain in southern California). See Recreation—United States
MESBIC (minority enterprise small business investment companies) See Small business investment companies
MHD. See Magnetohydrodynamics
MIRV (multiple, individually targeted reentry vehicle) See Guided missiles
MIT. See Massachusetts institute of technology, Cambridge
MLA. See Modern language association of America
MLN (Movimiento de liberación nacional) See Guerrillas—Uruguay
MOL (manned orbiting laboratory) See Space stations
MPC. See Military payment certificates
MPCA. See Minnesota—Pollution control agency
MPLA (Popular movement for the liberation of Angola) See Guerrillas—Angola
MSG. See Monosodium glutamate
MSTS. See United States—Military sea transportation service
MSU. See Michigan state university, East Lansing
MTA. See Metropolitan transportation authority
MTX. See Methotrexate
MAAG, Russell C.
Arcadia observatory, a sliding-roof construction. R Pop Astron 63:24-6 F '69
MAAS, Peter
Return of the cigar. Holiday 45:42-3+ Mr '69
Steady drinkers at Toots Shor. Holiday 45; 73+ Je '69
MAASTRICHT, Netherlands
One way to look at Holland. M. Gough. il House B 111:24-6 Jl '69
MABLEY, Jack
Mabley's martyrs. Time 93:56+ Ap 4 '69

MABOGUNJE, Akin, L.
Agricultural development in Africa; adaptation of address, April 1968. Bul Atom Sci 25:21-3+ Ap '69

MABRY, Guy O.
Modular components; address, September 10, 1969. Vital Speeches 36:61-4 N 1 '69

MACALPINE, Ida, and Hunter, Richard
Porphyria and King George III; with biographical sketches. Sci Am 221:16, 38-46 Jl '69

MCANDREW, John
Venice preserved? Art N 68:54-8+ Sum '69

MCANDREWS, J. Briggs
Power shift: policy formulation in transition. Clear House 44:161-3 N '69

MCANDREWS, Suellen
My husband bought me for $40 and a chicken. Read Digest 94:163-6 F '69

MACAO
Macao. I. Stanger. il Harp Baz 102:152+ S '69
Macao clings to the bamboo curtain. J. B. Billard. il Nat Geog 135:520-39 Ap '69
Mao's Macao. F. Riley. il Sat R 52:69-70+ N 15 '69

MACARONI
Flourishes with food: pointers on pasta. il McCalls 97:80-1 Ja '70
Pasta: happy Italian gift; with recipes. il Am Home 72:86+ S '69
Seafood and cream in a spaghetti; with menu and recipes by E. Graves. il Life 66:64-6 My 2 '69

MACARONI sculpture. See Sculpture—Study and teaching—Materials

MACARTHUR, Charles. See Hecht, B. jt. auth.

MACARTHUR, John D.
John D. MacArthur's (very) private empire. il por Forbes 104:57-8+ N 15 '69

MACAULEY, Cathy
Do not smoke Skippy peanut butter. T. Burke. il por Esquire 72:129-32+ O '69

MCAULIFFE, Anthony Clement
Where are they now? il pors Newsweek 74:12 D 22 '69

MCAULIFFE, Clayton
Solubility in water of normal C_9 and C_{10} alkane hydrocarbons. bibliog Science 163:478-9 Ja 31 '69

MCBAIN. Ed, pseud. See Hunter, E.

MACBEAN, James Roy
Godard's Week-end, or the self critical cinema of cruelty. Film Q 22:35-43 Wint '68
Politics, painting, and the language of signs in Godard's Made in USA. Film Q 22:18-25 Spr '69

MCBEE, Susanna
Air piracy: they want a moment of power and glory. Life 66:26-7 Ap 18 '69

MACBETH; drama. See Shakespeare. W.—Plays

MCBRIDE, Patricia
Ballerina for all seasons. O. Maynard. il pors Dance Mag 43:42-5+ Je '69

MCBRIEN, Richard
Necessary ecumenism. Commonweal 91:145-8 O 31 '69

MACBRINN, Monica C. and others
Generalized gangliosidosis: impaired cleavage of galactose from a mucopolysaccharide and a glycoprotein. bibliog Science 163:946-7 F 28 '69

MCBURNEY, Helen
Not unlike love; the Delta. Motor B 124:57-61+ Ag '69

MCCABE, Bruce
On the vice beat. Atlan 223:122-6 Mr '69

MCCABE, Eugene
Swift. Criticism
Nation 209:580 N 24 '69

MCCABE, Gloria
Left at the altar. Good H 168:66+ My '69

MCCABE, Lucille
Family quiz game. See issues of Parents' magazine & better family living

MCCAFFREY, Nell
Records. Nat R 21:709-10 Jl 15 '69

MCCAHILL, Tom
Mail for McCahill. See issues of Mechanix illustrated
MI tests. See issues of Mechanix illustrated
Tom McCahill tests. See issues of Mechanix illustrated

MCCAIN, John Sidney, 1911-
In Vietnam, the enemy is beaten; interview, ed. by J. G. Hubbell. Read Digest 94:75-9 F '69

about
Talk with an admiral. W. F. Buckley, jr. Nat R 21:1338 D 30 '69

MCCALDIN, R. O. and others
Atmospheric aerosols. bibliog Science 166:381-2 O 17 '69

MCCALL'S (periodical)
Feminine eye. S. Alexander. McCalls 97:7 D '69
Feminine eye; S. Alexander, new editor. Time 93:78 Ap 25 '69

MCCAMY, Calvin S.
Units for logarithmic scales. bibliog por Phys Today 22:42-4 Ap '69

MACCANN, Donnarae
(ed) Valid criticism for children's books. bibliog por Wilson Lib Bul 44:394-457 D '69

MCCANN, Frank D. Jr
Modernist vs. traditionalist. Américas 21:41-2 Ja '69

MCCANN, Tedd
Summer in the parks. Parks & Rec 4:14-17 Jl '69

MCCARRAN act. See Communism—United States—Anti-Communist measures

MCCARRY, Charles
Few soft words for the rabble rousers. Esquire 72:106-8+ Jl '69

MCCARTEN, John
Irish sketches (cont) New Yorker 45:95-6+ F 22 '69

MCCARTER, J. A.
Canadian look at nationalization of universities. Bul Atom Sci 25:45-6 My '69

MCCARTHY, Abigail (Quigley)
Mrs Eugene McCarthy tells why my son is a conscientious objector. por Good H 169:98-9+ N '69

MCCARTHY, Barbara Powell
Who sets the standards in your house? Parents Mag 44:51-3+ O '69

MCCARTHY, Colman
Baseball strikes out. New Repub 160:8-9 Ap 19 '69
Hard-core rich. New Repub 160:14-15 Mr 15 '69
Job on the Job corps. New Repub 161:19-21 Jl 5 '69
Priests who live in sin. New Repub 160:16-18 Mr 1 '69
Sort of a free world. New Repub 160:16-18 F 8 '69
Sunday morning with the Rev Dr Peale. New Repub 160:14-15 Ja 25 '69
Youth: alienated, estranged, or just bratlike? Chr Cent 86:897-99 Jl 2 '69

MCCARTHY, Eugene Joseph
Are you running with me Jesus? poem. New Repub 161:21 D 20 '69
Ares; poem. McCalls 97:80 N '69
McCarthy talk; interviews, ed. by J. Roddy. pors Look 33:19-21 Ap 1 '69
One man's America. por McCalls 97:18 Ja '70
Role of the military; the power of the Pentagon. Cur 105:20-4 Mr '69
Young people revitalized America. Look 33:32 D 30 '69

about
Balancing the books on the year of the people: 1968 presidential campaign. T. M. Gannon. America 121:632-4 D 27 '69
Eleven months after Chicago; Gene McCarthy is waiting for a sign. S. Brownmiller. il pors N Y Times Mag p 10-11+ Jl 20 '69
Explaining McCarthy. il por Time 93:66 Ap 18 '69
McCarthy on his campaign. G. A. Harrison. New Repub 161:21-3 O 25 '69
McCarthy's future. il por Time 94:17 Ag 1 '69
New life. il por Newsweek 74:22B-23 S 1 '69
1968. W. Goodman. Commentary 48:83-6 D '69
Nobody knows, reflections on the McCarthy campaign. J. Larner. Harper 238:62-72+ Ap; 71-88+ My '69; Discussion. 239:6+ Ag '69
Politics '68. C. Kilpatrick. Sat R 52:36+ N 29 '69
Very private man. D. Brudnoy. pors Nat R 21:1280-1 D 16 '69

MCCARTHY, Glenn
Where are they now? il pors Newsweek 74:24 S 22 '69

MCCARTHY, James J. See Aserlind, L. jt. auth.

MCCARTHY, Joe
Diamonds are a girl's most overpriced friend McCalls 96:108-9+ Mr '69
Gra-a-nd parade. Am Heritage 20:54-9+ F '69
'38 hurricane; excerpts. Am Heritage 20:10-15+ Ag '69
What's a sports arena doing on top of a railroad station? Holiday 46:24-8 O '69

MCCARTHY, Joseph Raymond
Army vs. McCarthy. il por Newsweek 73:16-17 Mv 5 '69
McCarthy, by R. Cohn. Review
Trans-Action 6:58-60 Jl '69. N. W. Polsby
Memories of Joe McCarthy; excerpts from Present at the creation. D. Acheson. Harper 239:113+ O '69

MCCARTHY, Michael Benet
Mrs Eugene McCarthy tells why my son is a conscientious objector. A. Q. McCarthy. por Good H 169:98-9+ N '69

MCCARTHY, Richard Dean
Biological warfare as national policy; address, August 10, 1969. Vital Speeches 35: 681-3 S 1 '69
Poison for peace. Commonweal 90:335-7 Je 6 '69

about

Germs and gas as weapons. S. M. Hersh. New Repub 160:13-16 Je 7 '69
Stockpiles of death. il por Newsweek 73: 36+ My 19 '69
Tracking CBW. il Sci N 95:470-1 My 17 '69
Trade winds. C. Amory. Sat R 52:4-5 D 27 '69
Transcontinental death trains; with editorial comment. L. H. Madaras. Chr Cent 86:800, 817-18 Je 11 '69

MCCARTHY, Tom
Man who could talk to horses. Am Heritage 20:58-9+ Ap '69

MCCARTHY, Tom (photographer)
Gallery: photographs. Life 67:8-9 N 28 '69

about

Tom McCarthy. il Pop Phot 64:80-9 Ap '69
MCCARTHY-Army controversy, 1954
Army vs. McCarthy. il Newsweek 73:16-17 My 5 '69
Memories of Joe McCarthy; excerpts from Present at the creation. D. Acheson. Harper 239:113+ O '69

MCCARTIN, James T.
Dreams of a young girl; story. Good H 169: 60-1 Jl '69

MCCARTNEY, Linda Eastman
Mrs Paul McCartney. por Vogue 153:152-3 My '69

MCCARTNEY, Paul
I want to live in peace; interview, ed. by D. Bacon. pors Life 67:105-6 N 7 '69

about

Magical McCartney mystery. J. Neary. il pors Life 67:103-5 N 7 '69
Of rumor, myth and a Beatle. por Time 94: 41 O 31 '69

MCCARTNEY, Susan
Real England; photographs. Travel & Camera 32:50-1+ Mr '69

MCCAULL, Julian
Black tide. bibliog Environ 11:2-16 N '69

MCCLANE, A. J.
Fishing. See issues of Field & stream

MCCLEAN, Lydia
Lindsays of New York. Vogue 153:182-9 My '69

MCCLEARY, Elliott H.
Big friend to little people. Todays Health 47: 20-3+ Ag '69
Where combat medics train. Todays Health 47:38-45 Je '69
Windows on medicine's past. Todays Health 47:70-2 O '69

MCCLELLAN, John Little
Crime war: key senator launches a broad attack; excerpts from Senate statement, March 11, 1969. por U S News 66:14 Mr 24 '69
Organized crime in the United States; statement, March 11, 1969. Vital Speeches 35: 388-400 Ap 15 '69; Excerpts. por U S News 66:14 Mr 24 '69

about

Brother McClellan. New Repub 160:4 My 24 '69
No taste for truth. Senator McClellan? Chr Cent 86:1271 O 8 '69
Riot review. il Newsweek 73:35-6 Je 9 '69
Senate hearings on campus disorders. M. Mueller. Science 165:270 Jl 18 '69

MCCLELLAN committee. See United States—Congress—Senate—Government operations, Committee on—Permanent subcommittee on investigations

MCCLELLAND, David C.
As I see it; interview. por Forbes 103:53-7 Je 1 '69

about

Teaching business success. il Time 93:64 Ap 25 '69

MCCLELLAND, Elizabeth
How to care for paintings. House B 111:70 Ap '69

MCCLELLAND, John
REDSOD, explosive dozer moves a mountain in an hour. Pop Sci 195:68-9 Ag '69

MCCLENAHAN, Richard L.
Some Scottish quaichs. Antiques 96:402-5 S '69

MCCLENDON, Ernestine
Ex-actress with an eye for business. il pors Ebony 24:82-4+ Mr '69

MCCLENDON agency. See Theatrical agencies

MCCLINTON, William
No honky apostolate, say urban priests. Commonweal 90:254-5 My 16 '69

MCCLISH, Gerald F.
Bahamas bearings. See issues of Motor boating

MCCLISH, Jerry. See McClish, G. F.

MCCLOSKEY, Michael
Last battle of the redwoods. Am West 6:55-64 S '69
Raiding the forests. New Repub 161:10-11 D 13 '69

MCCLOSKEY, Robert James
U.S. urges Nigerian cooperation in relief efforts; statements, December 5 and 6, 1968. Dept State Bul 59:658 D 23 '68

MCCLOY, John J.
As I see it; interview. por Forbes 103:46-8+ Ja 15 '69

MCCLUGGAGE, Denise
Snow driving. Travel & Camera 32:56-7+ D '69

MCCLURE, Harold M. and others
Autosomal trisomy in a chimpanzee: resemblance to Down's syndrome. bibliog Science 165:1010-12 S 5 '69

MCCLURE, John
Classical bag. Hi Fi 19:58-61 Ag '69

MACCLUSKEY, James Thomas, 1931-. See MacCluskey, T.

MCCLUSKEY, Neil G.
Catholic schools. America 122:22-4 Ja 10 '70
Child support or wall of separation; excerpt from Catholic education faces its future. Chr Cent 86:775-9 Je 4 '69
Rome listens to the universities. America 121:58-60 Ag 2 '69

MACCLUSKEY, Thomas
Musical events; summary of article, ed. by W. Sargeant. New Yorker 45:211-13 N 15 '69

MCCOLOUGH, Charles Peter
Xerox: the McColough era. il pors Forbes 104: 24-6+ Jl 1 '69

MCCONATHY, Dale
(ed) See Finlay, I. H. Words are the poet's paint

MCCONKEY, Thomas W.
(ed) Buyers' guide. See (usually) first issue of each month of Library journal
(ed) Purchasing guide 1969. Library J 94: 1431-2 Ap 1 '69

MCCONNEL, Frances
Snow in the poem; poem. Nation 209:292 S 22 '69

MCCONNELL, Duncan. See Fisher, D. J. jt. auth.

MCCONNELL, Malcolm A.
After years of violence the Congo is afloat but who knows where it's headed? N Y Times Mag p26-7+ S 21 '69

MCCORD, Howard
Spirit dream; poem. Harp Baz 102:90 Ja '69

MCCORD, Thomas B. and Adams, J. B.
Spectral reflectivity of Mars. bibliog Science 163.1058-60 Mr 7 '69

MCCORKLE, Susanna
Cornelia; story. Mlle 69:304-5 Ag '69

MCCORMACK, John
John McCormack, musical raconteur. D. Hamilton. por Hi Fi 19:110 My '69

MCCORMACK, John William
Call Marty. Newsweek 74:36 O 27 '69
Club business on the Hill; effort to depose J. McCormack as Speaker. R. G. Sherrill. il Nation 208:102-4 Ja 27 '69
Is Congress being too generous? U S News 67: 70 Ag 25 '69
Look at government's top-ranking Democrat. il pors U S News 67:14+ S 8 '69
McCormack faces life. por Newsweek 74:36 N 3 '69
Murky men from the Speaker's office. W. Lambert. il por Life 67:52-4+ O 31 '69
Scandals in Congress: the record. il por U S News 67:25-7 N 10 '69
Speaker's family. Time 94:18+ O 31 '69
Voloshen connection. por Time 94:26-7 O 24 '69

MCCORMACK, T. M.
Love poem. Poetry 113:318 F '69

MCCORMACK, William A.
International studies for the professional school. bibliog f Sch & Soc 97:114-16 F '69

MCCORMICK, John
Sound of hooves. Sports Illus 31:60-4+ Jl 7 '69

MACDONALD, Robert B.
Eye in the sky for a hungry world. Sci Digest 66:63-6 Jl '69
MACDONALD, Ross, pseud.
Life with the blob. por Sports Illus 30:50-2+ Ap 21 '69
—and Easton, Robert
Santa Barbarans cite an 11th commandment: thou shalt not abuse the earth. N Y Times Mag p32-3+ O 12 '69
MCDONELL, Sister Ruth
Separation. confrontation. disenchantment. PTA Mag 64:4-5 D '69
MCDONNELL, Kilian
Liturgy and the perils of experience. America 121:93-5 Ag 16 '69
MCDONNELL and company
O'Brien's fast hurrah. il Bsns W p90 Ag 16 '69
Pulling in its horns. Newsweek 74:58+ Ag 25 '69
MCDONNELL Douglas corporation
Gemini incentives emerge in renegotiation. K. Johnsen. il Aviation W 90:29-30 My 5 '69
IAM wins and fights on. Bsns W p90 Ja 18 '69
McDonnell Douglas' billion-dollar gamble. il Forbes 104:28-34 Ag 1 '69
McDonnell Douglas modernizes machining capabilities. M. L. Yaffee. il Aviation W 91:98-102+ Jl 28 '69
McDonnell Douglas sales, earnings surge. S. P. Siciliano. Aviation W 90:22-3 F 10 '69
MOL fallout hurts McDonnell the most. Bsns W p47 Je 14 '69
Plum for McDonnell Douglas. Bsns W p22 D 27 '69
Son of the Phantom: F-15 contract. il Newsweek 75:50-1 Ja 5 '70
MCDONOUGH, Roger Henry
ALA: advancing the reach. por Wilson Lib Bul 43:858-9 My '69
State of the association message; excerpts, January 1969. por ALA Bul 63:334-8 Mr '69
MACDOUGALL, Allan Ross
Who was Isadora? excerpt from Isadora: a revolutionary in art and love. Dance Mag 43:58-9 Je '69
MCDOWELL, Bart
Deerfield keeps a truce with time. Nat Geog 135:780-809 Je '69
MCDOWELL, Edwin
Letter from Lima. Nat R 21:331 Ap 8 '69
MCDOWELL, Malcolm
Mark this man! ed. by E. Miller. por Seventeen 28:88-9+ Jl '69
MACE, Dean T.
Pietro Bembo and the literary origins of the Italian madrigal. bibliog f Mus Q 55:65-86 Ja '69
MACE, Chemical. See Chemical mace
MCEACHERN, Margaret
Helping the handicapped travel by air. Todays Health 47:66-8+ Mr '69
Wigs: medicine for morale. Todays Health 47:36-7+ N '69
MACEDONIA
Antiquities
Grapes of antiquity. F. C. Livingstone. il Sci N 95:407-8 Ap 26 '69

History
See also
Alexander the Great
MCELENEY, John J. abp
Black power in the Caribbean. America 121: 557-8 D 6 '69
about
Black power and the archbishop; cooperation in Jamaica. America 121:316 O 18 '69
MCELHANEY, Ronald N. and Tourtellotte, M. E.
Mycoplasma membrane lipids: variations in fatty acid composition. bibliog Science 164: 433-4 Ap 25 '69
MCELMURY, Audrey
What makes Audrey pedal? Tiga muk. D. Levin. il por Sports Illus 31:68+ N 24 '69
MCELROY, Neil H.
Opposites forge a working team. por Bsns W p54 Jl 19 '69
MCELROY, Paul Simpson
Earth is the Lord's... Am For 75:24+ My '69
MCELROY, William David
McElroy asks expanded NSF role. Science 166:1252 D 5 '69
about
McElroy proposed to head NSF; Branscomb, Bureau of standards. P. M. Boffey. por Science 164:1504-6 Je 27 '69
NSF: McElroy seeks to impart political headway to agency. P. M. Boffey. por Science 166:481-4+ O 24 '69

Spate of science appointments. por Sci N 96:5-6 Jl 5 '69
W. D. McElroy: an old incident embarrasses new NSF director. P. M. Boffey. Science 165:379-80 Jl 25 '69
MCENTEE, Howard G.
Now they're flying model gliders by radio. Pop Sci 195:154-7 O '69
Wonderful world of model engines. Pop Sci 194:142-6 Mr '69
MACEÓIN, Gary
Vatican council in perspective; interview, ed. by H. J. Cargas. America 121:289-94 O 11 '69
MCEVOY, James, and Miller, Abraham
On strike, shut it down; the crisis at San Francisco state college. pors Trans-Action 6:18-23+ Mr '69
MCEWEN, Bruce S. See Azmitia, E. C. jr, jt. auth.
MCFADDEN, Dorothy Loa
Enchanting Jutland. Travel 132:42-7 Ag '69
Rose gardens of Europe. Horticulture 47:18-19+ N '69
You can show these travel slides. Har Yrs 9:46-7 N '69
MACFALL, Russell P.
Wayside treasures. Nat Wildlife 7:43-7 Ag '69
MCFALL, Wilfred M.
Pietà: poem. Chr Cent 87:9 Ja 7 '70
MCFARLAN, Ethel
Olive jar; drama. Plays 29:76-84 N '69
MCFARLAND, Jim
Flow-er-power. il Hot Rod 22:76-8 My '69
Shop talk. See issues of Hot rod
MCFARLAND, William
Microspikes on the lymphocyte uropod. bibliog Science 163:818-20 F 21 '69
MCFARLAND, Calif.
Poisoning the wells. il Environ 11:16-23+ Ja '69
MCGAHAN, Martha
Ghirardelli square and the Cannery. Travel & Camera 32:28-9 Ag '69
MCGAHERN, John
Korea; story. Atlan 224:94-6 O '69
MCGANN, Jerome
Prescriptions; poem. Poetry 114:95 My '69
Religious poetry. Poetry 115:196-201 D '69
MCGANN, Thomas F.
John Dewey and Vatican council II. America 120:411-12+ Ap 5 '69
Soviet law on marriage. America 120:687-8 Je 14 '69
MCGARRAH, Robert E.
Let's internationalize defense marketing. Harvard Bsns R 47:146-55 My '69
MCGARRY, Barbara D. See Hecht, G. J. jt. auth.
MCGAUGH, James L. See Dawson, R. G. jt. auth.
MCGAVRAN, Donald
Advanced education for missionaries. Chr Today 13:3-5 S 26 '69
MCGEE, Gale W.
Excerpt from debate, June 20, 1969. Cong Digest 48:219+ Ag '69
MCGEE, Richard A.
What's past is prologue. bibliog f Ann Am Acad 381:1-10 Ja '69
MCGEHEE, Helen
Helen McGehee; 92nd st. Y. J. Anderson. Dance Mag 43:87 My '69
MCGHEE, George Crews
Toward a new partnership with Europe. Sat R 52:16-18 Mr 8 '69
MCGILL, Ralph
Death of a conscience. por Time 93:68 F 14 '69
Obituary
Nation 208:198+ F 17 '69
Passing the baton. R. L. Tobin. il por Sat R 52:117-18 Mr 8 '69
Simple Christian vision. J. B. Cumming, jr. por Newsweek 73:72 F 17 '69
MCGINNIS, George
Recruiter's delight. il por Newsweek 73:54 Ap 7 '69
MCGINNIS, Lila Sprague
This house, our home; story. Good H 169: 114-15 O '69
MCGINNISS, Joe
Conning the con men of Kentucky. Sports Illus 30:36-8+ My 5 '69
Drummers and dexedrine; excerpts from The selling of the President 1968. Newsweek 74: 29-30 Jl 21 '69
Family struggles to stay even. Life 67:26-9 Ag 15 '69
I was the guy writing a book. por Life 67:15 O 10 '69
Selling of the President 1968; excerpts. Harper 239:46-60 Ag '69
(ed) Vietnam: three who came home. Sat Eve Post 242:22-3+ F 8 '69

MCGINNISS, Joe—*Continued*

about

Understanding Nixon; concerning The selling of the President 1968. W. F. Buckley, jr. Nat R 21:1286-7 D 16 '69

MCGONAGLE, William Loren
Where are they now? il pors Newsweek 74: 22 S 29 '69

MACGORMAN, Ruth Stephens
Joe doesn't pledge allegiance; excerpts. Ed Digest 34:24-5 F '69

MCGOVERN, George Stanley
And now that the American dream is safely in the hands of the military-industrial establishment, we wake to a new decade. Esquire 72:188-9+ D '69
Are our military alliances meaningful? Ann Am Acad 384:14-20 Jl '69
Case against the ABM. Cath World 209:24-9 Ap '69
Ending the Vietnam war. Cur 111:13-18 O '69
Politics of the arms buildup. Cur 106:18-21 Ap '69

about

As Democrats get set for '72. il U S News 66:46-8 My 26 '69
Documenting the hungry. il por Sci N 95: 160-1 F 15 '69
Reform or die. il por Time 93:18 Je 27 '69

MCGOVERN, Robert
You now are Brigid; poem. Chr Cent 86: 1476 N 19 '69

MCGOWAN, Alan
Getting their feet wet. por Environ 11:24-7 N '69

MCGRADY, Mike
Penelope's playmates. il por Time 94:66+ Ag 15 '69

MCGRADY, Patrick M. jr
Art of manly face-lifting. Vogue 153·117+ Je '69

MCGRATH, Lawrence H.
School libraries in Australia. ALA Bul 63: 1108-10 S '69

MCGRATH, Lee Parr. See Scobey, J. jt. auth.

MCGRATH, Lee Parr, and Scobey, Joan
What is a father? excerpts. Good H 168: 100-1 Je '69; Read Digest 95:100-1 S '69
What is a mother? excerpts. Read Digest 94:108-10 My '69

MCGRATH, Russell
Invitation to a beheading; dramatization of novel by V. Nabokov. Criticism
Nation 208:477 Ap 14 '69
New Yorker 45:100+ Mr 29 '69
Time 93:55 Mr 28 '69

MACGRAW, Ali
Ali MacGraw; the making of a star. il pors Mcalls 96:78-81 S '69
Girl who has everything, just about. por Time 93:102 My 9 '69
New princess. il por Newsweek 73:108 My 5 '69
One film turns life upside down for the new star named Ali. pors Life 66:46-9 Je 20 '69
People are talking about. . . por Vogue 154: 82-3 Ag 15 '69

MCGRAW, John Joseph
Days of Mr McGraw, by J. Durso. Review
Newsweek por 74:83-83A+ Ag 25 '69. A. Cooper
Tyrant of Coogan's Bluff. il por Time 94:68 Ag 29 '69

MCGRAW-Hill, incorporated
McGraw-Hill, urban league launch school for dropouts. Library J 94:824-6 F 15 '69
Production editing at McGraw-Hill. V. Strauss. il Pub W 196:56-8+ O 6 '69

MCGREGOR, Alan
Zurich's stock market swingers. Duns R 94: 103-4 N '69

MACGREGOR, Linda F.
My year as a snob. il por Redbook 132:14+ Ap '69

MACGREGOR, Malcolm H.
Nucleon-nucleon scattering. bibliog por Phys Today 22:21-8 D '69

MCGRORY, Mary
Washington front. See issues of America

MCGUANE, Thomas
Longest silence. Sports Illus 31:92-6+ D 1 '69

MCGUIGAN, Frank E.
Social revolution and sex education. Clear House 43:421-4 Mr '69

MCGUIRE, Brian Patrick
Grading game. Todays Ed 58:32-4 Mr '69

MCGUIRE, Mabelle B. and Jacobs, E. W.
Hula; a paradoxical history. Dance Mag 43: 58-61+ D '69

MCGUIRE, Vincent
Florida fable. Engl J 58:122-3 Ja '69

MCGUIRE, William L.
Hormonal stimulation of lactose synthetase in mammary carcinoma. bibliog Science 165: 1013-14 S 5 '69

MCGURK, Richard
Fast train to D.C. Travel & Camera 32:27-8 Ap '69
Haiti; a fresh look. Travel & Camera 32:34 Je '69

MACHADO, Conceicao R. S. and others
Circadian rhythm of serotonin in the pineal body of immunosympathectomized immature rats. bibliog Science 164:442-3 Ap 25 '69

MCHALE, John
Toward a planetary society; excerpts from The future of the future. Cur 110:16-25 S '69

MCHAMISH, Lorna
What is a flower show like in Peru? Horticulture 47:31 D '69

MCHARG, Ian L.
Ian L. McHarg; with biographical sketch. por Parks & Rec 4:27-9 Jl '69
What would you do with, say, Staten Island? excerpts from Design with nature; with biographical sketch. por Natur Hist 78:6, 26-37 Ap '69

about

How to design with nature. il por Time 94: 70-1 O 10 '69
Ian McHarg vs. us anthropocentric clods; with excerpts from Design with nature. il pors Life 67:48B-48D Ag 15 '69

MCHENRY, Joanne
San Ramon Valley. ALA Bul 63:260-1 F '69

MCHENRY, Ill.
Conditioner improves sludge vacuum filtering. il Am City 84:77 S '69

MACHIAS, Me.
Ambassadors report; public schools. A. W. Dodd. il Sr Schol 94:Schol Teach 13 Mr 28 '69

MACHIASPORT, Me.
Machiasport gets two new bidders; battle over building a refinery. Bsns W p20 Jl 5 '69
Prospect of oil awakens a Maine town. il Bsns W p46-7+ Ja 3 '70

MACHINE billing. See Billing

MACHINE guns
See also
Submachine guns

MACHINE in politics. See Boss rule

MACHINE tool industry and trade
Toolmen on razor's edge. il Bsns W p66-7+ O 11 '69
See also
Warner and Swasey company

MACHINE tools
Big machines help hedge the big bets. il Bsns W p 152-3+ Je 21 '69
Handiest tool you can have in you shop; vertical belt sander-grinder. W. C. Leckey. il Pop Mech 132:166 Jl '69
See also
Jigs
Planing machines
Punches
Vises

Control

McDonnell Douglas modernizes machining capabilities; numerically controlled machine tools. M. L. Yaffee. il Aviation W 91:98-102+ Jl 28 '69

Leasing and renting

See also
Machinery—Leasing and renting

Numerical control

See Machine tools—Control

MACHINERY
Reflections on the machine. J. Lahr. il Craft Horiz 29:22-5+ Ja '69
See also machinery used in particular industries or for special purposes, e.g. Road machinery

Design

See also
Human engineering

Exhibitions

Big iron gets bigger, and cozier: Conexpo '69. il Bsns W p52-3 Mr 1 '69
What municipal officials found at Conexpo '69. il Am City 84:125-6+ Ap '69

Leasing and renting

Can leasing make ownership obsolete? renting plant and equipment. il Bsns W p50+ Mr 8 '69

Stands

Stand for radial-arm saws. il Mech Illus 65: 118-19 O '69

MACHINERY—*Continued*

Transportation

Oceangoing drive-in; RO/RO container ships. J. Liston. il Pop Mech 132:100-3 N '69

MACHINERY and civilization. See Technology and civilization

MACHINERY in art

Art world; Museum of modern art exhibition; The machine as seen at the end of the mechanical age. H. Rosenberg. New Yorker 44:86+ Ja 25 '69

MACHINERY in industry

See also

Unemployment, Technological

MACHINERY industry

See also

Case, J. I. company

Machine tool industry and trade

MACHINES. See Machinery

MACHINES, Copying. See Copying processes

MACHINISTS

See also

Building machinery operators

MACHINISTS union. See International association of machinists and aerospace workers

MACHIZ, Marc

One generation speaks to another. U S News 67:28 Jl 7 '69

MACHT, Lee B.

Community interaction with the Job corps. Ment Hy 53:521-4 O '69

MACHTA, Lester

Winds, pollution, and the wilderness. Liv Wildn 33:3-8 Sum '69

MCHUGH, Heather

Divorce; poem. New Yorker 45:110 Mr 1 '69

Ejection; poem. Mlle 69:244 Ag '69

MCILHENNY, Henry Plumer

Collector; Henry P. McIlhenny. A. Pryce-Jones. il Art in Am 57:94-103 N '69

MCINERNY, Ralph

I don't want to be like you; story. Redbook 133:72-3 Je '69

Past, present and always; story. Good H 168:90-1 F '69

There comes a day; story. Good H 169:74-5 Jl '69

MACINNES, Colin

Epistle to the mugs. por Time 93:114 My 16 '69

Sense of the great city. T. G. Rosenthal. New Repub 160:23-5 F 15 '69

MCINNIS, A. E.

In the ancient tradition. il Yachting 125:120-1+ Ja '69

MCINTIRE, Carl

ACCC; no longer doing its founder's will. D. Tinder. Chr Today 14:41 N 21 '69

Angry voice from Red Lion. T. J. R. Kent. il Pop Electr 31:73-4 S '69

Counter-present-ecumaniac. Chr Cent 86:1475 N 19 '69

Doctor McIntire's magic touch. il por Time 94:81 N 14 '69

McIntire's complaint. il por Newsweek 74:46 Ag 11 '69

Riverside pastor responds to McIntire manifesto. Chr Cent 86:1241 O 1 '69

MCINTIRE, Clifford Guy

Public interest: address. pors Am For 75:20-3 D '69

about

McIntire-Stennis program. J. D. Sullivan and G. F. Burks. il por Am For 75:16-19+ Ap '69

MCINTOSH, Harrison

Harrison McIntosh. R. Petterson. il por Ceram Mo 17:19-26 Je '69

MCINTOSH, Kim Hamilton. See Aird, C. pseud.

MCINTURFF, Raymond M. See Finger. F. G. jt. auth.

MCINTYRE, Edward F.

Magic machine. Hi Fi 19:44-9 Ag '69

Use your room to enhance your stereo. Hi Fi 19:50-5 S '69

MACINTYRE, Ian G. and Pilkey. O. H.

Tropical reef corals: tolerance of low temperatures on the North Carolina continental shelf. bibliog Science 166:374-5 O 17 '69

MCINTYRE, Thomas James

Compromise may become price for administration ABM victory. Aviation W 91:19-20 Jl 21 '69

MCIVER, Dorothy

I love science, teaching, and children. Todays Ed 58:50-2 Ja '69

MACK, C. D.

Closing your fun home. Mech Illus 65:87-9 O '69

MCKAIN, Walter C.

Will your marriage be successful? questions from Retirement marriage. Har Yrs 9:49 My '69

MCKAY, Arthur Raymond

Stetson loses its head; McCormick's McKay quits. A. Taft. Chr Today 13:46 Je 6 '69

MCKAY, Floyd

Kaffeeklatsch constituency. Nation 208:205-6 F 17 '69

MACKAY, John A.

Ecumenicalism: threat to Christian unity? Chr Today 13:11-12 S 12 '69

Flight from reality; excerpt from The ecumenical movement, whence? and whither? Chr Today 13:14 Ja 31 '69

Life's chief discoveries. Chr Today 14:3-5 Ja 2 '70

MACKAY, Margaret-Anne

Martinique and Guadeloupe. Travel 132:34-7 S '69

Shopping in France. Travel 132:42-7+ Jl '69

MCKAY, Vernon

Progress toward African unity. Cur Hist 56:257-62+ My '69

MACKAYE, Benton

Mike Frome. M. Frome. Am For 75:3+ My '69

MACKAYE, William R.

Semi-confronting the issues. Commonweal 91:269-70 N 28 '69

MCKAYLE, Donald

Donald McKayle dance co; NY city center. T. Borek. Dance Mag 43:34 Jl '69

MCKEAN, William J.

Encounter: how kids turn off drugs. Look 33:40-3+ Ap 15 '69

MACKECKNIE, Donna

On the boards. W. Como. il por Dance Mag 43:20 My '69

MCKEE, Arthur G, and company

Arthur G. McKee scares them away; professional employees unwilling to go along with acquisition. Bsns W p82 Mr 15 '69

Italians bite kid-gloved hand; McKee's takeover of CTIP. Bsns W p40 Ag 9 '69

Subsidiary that rebelled. il Time 94:68 Jl 25 '69

MCKEEVER, William W. Jr

Vocational education unsuited for the socially disadvantaged. bibliog f Clear House 44:43-4 S '69

MCKEITHEN, John Julian

Big shakedown in Baton Rouge. A. J. Reichley. il por Fortune 80:96-9+ Ag 1 '69

MCKELLEN, Ian

Double crown. por Time 94:71-2 S 19 '69

MCKELVEY, Vincent E.

August session of U.N. seabed committee held at New York; statements, August 15 and 20, 1969. Dept State Bul 61:287-93+ S 29 '69

MCKELWAY, St Clair

Presbyterian captives. New Yorker 45:45-52 Ap 12 '69

MCKENNA, Joseph C.

Elements of a Nigerian peace. For Affairs 47:668-80 Jl '69

MCKENNA, Paul

Muonium metal. D. E. Thomsen. il por Sci N 96:311 O 4 '69

MCKENNEY, Ruth

Small journey from New York. Travel & Camera 32:54-5+ Ap '69

MACKENZIE, Fred T. See Garrels, R. M. jt. auth.

MCKENZIE, John Lawrence

Two books, one question: was Jesus a zealot? Commonweal 90:26-7 Mr 21 '69

MACKENZIE, Mary

Discoverer of the Hudson's source. Cons 23:28-31 F '69

MACKENZIE, R. Alec

Management process in 3-D. bibliog f Harvard Bsns R 47:80-7 N '69

MCKENZIE, Richard B.

Economics for elementary school pupils. Ed Digest 35:44-7 S '69

MACKENZIE, Ross

Man of sense. Nat R 21:445 My 6 '69

MACKENZIE, Zoë

Sunday walk; poem. Liv Wildn 33:14 Sum '69

MCKENZIE RIVER

Their thing in the spring; white water boating. il Sports Illus 30:38-43 Mr 24 '69

MCKEOWN, Bill

Boats and boating. See issues of Mechanix illustrated

Sailing: the thrill of a lifetime. Pop Gard 20:6-11+ Spr '69

Secrets of camping. Travel & Camera 32:57+ Je '69

MCKEOWN, William Taylor. See McKeown. B.

MACKEREL fishing

Little jumbos. G. Heinold. il Outdoor Life 144:164+ O '69

MCKERN, Sharon S. and McKern, T. W.

Secrets that dead men's bones tell. Sci Digest 66:30-4 Ag '69

MCKERN, Thomas W. See McKern, S. S. jt.
auth.
MCKERNAN, John
Lenin; poem. Nat R 21:1211 D 2 '69
MCKESSON and Robbins-Foremost dairies, in-
corporated merger. See Business consolida-
tions and mergers
MACKEY, Richard A.
Personal concepts of the mentally ill among
caregiving groups. Ment Hy 53:245-52 Ap
'69
MCKIMMEY, James
Abiding heart; story. Good H 169:94-5 N
'69
Hope is forever; story. Good H 168:106-7
My '69
MACKINAC race. See Yacht racing
MCKINLAY, Douglas, and McLean, H. E.
Alaska's green serge navy. il Am For 75:16-18
Mr '69
MCKINLEY, Fred
How to fool April trout. Outdoor Life 143:
61-3+ Ap '69
Pocket cameras for sportsmen. Outdoor Life
144:36-9+ D '69
MCKINNELL, Robert G. and others
Transplantation of pluripotential nuclei from
triploid frog tumors. bibliog Science 165:
394-6 Jl 25 '69
MACKINNON, Douglas A.
Great opera houses: Geneva. Opera N 33:26-
9 Mr 22 '69
MCKINSEY and company
Europe's lush market for advice. American
preferred. R. C. Allbrook. il Fortune 80:
128-31+ Jl '69
MACKINTOSH, F. Roy, and Bell, Eugene
Proteins synthesized before and after fer-
tilization in sea urchin eggs. bibliog Sci-
ence 164:961-3 My 23 '69
MACKLIN, W. C. and Hobbs, P. V.
Subsurface phenomena and the splashing of
drops on shallow liquids. bibliog Science
166:107-8 O 3 '69
MCKNIGHT, Allan D.
IAEA seeks better ways to detect nuclear
material diversion. J. P. Wiley. il por Phys
Today 22:69-70 Ag '69
MCKUEN, Rod
Pop personality; ed. by E. Miller. pors Seven-
teen 28:408+ Ag '69
We came in peace for all mankind. special
view of Christmas. Redbook 134:151 D '69

about

Loner. por Time 93:98 My 16 '69
Money in art. L. Coxe. New Repub 162:32-3
Ja 3 '70
MCLACHLAN, Dan, 1905-
Depth-of-field law finally repealed?   T.
Shackleford. il por Mod Phot 33:133+ Je '69
MCLAIN, David
National conference on ballet in higher educa-
tion: a report on the meetings, May 15-17,
1969. Dance Mag 43:88 Jl '69

about

Dance, architecture, music. W. Terry. il Sat
R 52:38+ My 10 '69
MCLAIN, Denny
Highlight. Sports Illus 31:62 Ag 4; 58 S 1 '69
Will success spoil Dennis McLain? I. R. Mc-
Vay. il pors Look 33:89-91 Ap 15 '69
MCLAIN, Pete
Assateague: great fishing-camping combo.
Field & S 74:68-9+ My '69
Unexpected goose shoot. Field & S 74:38-9+
D '69
MACLAINE, Shirley
Crusades and capers of Shirley MacLaine.
R. Hochstein. il pors Good H 168:52-4+
Je '69
MCLANE, Mary, and others
Team teaching and objective evaluation.
Clear House 44:174-8 N '69
MCLAREN, Bruce
Cornering the market. il por Newsweek 74:
129 S 29 '69
MCLAREN, Richard Wellington
Antitrust, Republican style; interview, ed. by
G. R. Rosen. por Duns R 94:12-13+ O '69
Softening the harsh words; interview. por
Forbes 103:23-4 Je 1 '69

about

Conglomerate test is on. il por Bsns W p35-7
Mr 29 '69
Got a light, McLaren? M. Ways. Fortune
79:61-2 My 1 '69
McLaren talks tough about conglomerates.
Bsns W p38 Mr 15 '69
McLaren wades into merger tide. por Bsns W
p42+ Mr 22 '69
Man who says no to the giants. il Newsweek
74:73-4 Jl 14 '69

Nixon's antitrust chief vows firmness. Bsns
W p36 Ja 25 '69
Nixon's deconglomerater. por Newsweek 73:
69-70 Mr 24 '69
Scourge of the conglomerates. por Time
93:100 My 23 '69
MCLAUGHLIN, John
Communications (cont) America 120:174-5,
342-3. 510-11, 634+, 714+; 121:103-5, 173-4,
308+ F 8, Mr 22, Ap 26, My 24, Je 21, Ag
16, S 13, O 11 '69; 122:16-18 Ja 10 '70
Ecology of hunger. America 121:414-17 N 8
'69
Education in human sexuality: two Catholic
programs. America 121:494-7 N 22 '69
Public regulation and the news media. Ameri-
ca 121:586-9 D 13 '69
Report from Biafra. America 120:90-5, 138-
41, 162-7 Ja 25-F 8 '69
MCLAUGHLIN, John, 1898-
Painting at the degree zero. J. Harithas. il
Art N 67:52-3+ N '68
MCLAUGHLIN planetarium, Toronto. See
Planetariums
MACLEAN, D. J. See Harmon, L. D. jt. auth.
MCLEAN, Herbert E. See McKinlay, D. jt.
auth.
MACLEISH, Andrew
Some structures for written English; adapta-
tion of address, November 1968. bibliog f
Engl J 58:877-8+ S '69
MACLEISH, Archibald
Brothers in the eternal cold. Read Digest
94:68-9 Mr '69
Revolt of the diminished man; excerpt from
address. Sat R 52:16-19+ Je 7 '69

about

From everyman to superman in Archibald
Macleish. C. W. Edwards. Cath World
210:165-9 Ja '70
MACLEISH, Kenneth
Legacy from the age of faith: Chartres. Nat
Geog 136:856-82 D '69
MACLEISH, Roderick
Are we a nation of haters and wreckers?
Read Digest 95:92-6 N '69
Revolt on the campus. Read Digest 94:71-6
Je '69
MACLELLAN, Esther, and Schroll, C. V.
Best friends; drama. Plays 29:69-74 Ja '70
Test for a witch; drama. Plays 29:79-84 O
'69
MACLENNAN, Beryce W.
Scapegoating. Todays Ed 58:38-40 S '69
MCLENNAN, Kenneth, and Moskow, M. H.
Multilateral bargaining in the public sector.
Mo Labor R 92:58-60 Ap '69
MACLEOD, Donald S.
America's social balance sheet; address,
September 17, 1969. Vital Speeches 36:17-
21 O 15 '69
MCLEOD, Richard
Dissent and reaction in Missouri. por Wilson
Lib Bul 44:269-74+ N '69
MACLIAMMOIR, Michael
Ireland & Scotland. Travel & Camera 32:120-
1 F '69
MCLUHAN, Herbert Marshall
Wyndham Lewis. Atlan 224:93-4+ D '69

about

Fortune cookie. D. Duffy. Nation 209:638-9
D 8 '69
Gadfly and the dinosaur. T. Palmer. bibliog
f Engl J 58:69-74 Ja '69
MCLUHAN, Marshall. See McLuhan, H. M.
MCMAHAN, H. D.
No more land-development tie-ups. por Am
City 84:85+ Ag '69
MCMAHAN, John
Surrounded, by rhubarb! Org Gard & Farm
16:106-7 Mr '69
MCMAHON, Ed
Permanent second fiddles. il por Newsweek
74:45 S 1 '69
MCMAHON, Francis Murray Patrick
Man takes charge of his horse. W. Tower.
il pors Sports Illus 30:24-8+ Je 2 '69
MCMANMON, John J.
Where's the church headed? New Repub 160:
16-19 Je 7 '69
MCMANUS, Irene
Who killed the bird? Am For 75:24-7+ O '69
MCMANUS, Patrick
Great cow plot. Field & S 74:76-7+ My '69
Kid camping. Field & S 73:68-9+ Mr '69
Rendezvous. Field & S 74:48-9+ D '69
What ever happened to worms? Field & S
73:66-7+ F '69
MCMILLAN, Calvin
Photoperiod in three xanthium populations
from the tropic of Cancer in Mexico. bib-
liog Science 165:292-4 Jl 18 '69

MACMILLAN, Clifford M.
To cut costs think Machiavellian. Nations
Bsns 57:74-6 Ja '69
MCMILLAN, Edwin Mattison
Radlab adds another physics first. il por
Bsns W p64-6+ Ap 19 '69
MACMILLAN, Harold
Macmillan's middle years. T. J. Spinner, jr.
Nation 208:279-80 Mr 3 '69
MCMILLAN, Robert S.
Practice abroad: a rewarding study in com-
prehensive frustrations. Arch Rec 145:88-9
My '69
MCMULLAN, Mrs Andrew
We moved a farmhouse and saved on build-
ing costs. Camp Mag 41:26 Ja '69
MCMULLEN, John
McMullen's hornpipe. Forbes 104:31 N 1 '69
MCMULLEN, Maurice D.
Don't settle for second class plant struc-
tures. Am City 84:38-40 My '69
MCMULLEN, Roy
Aid for the music of right now. Hi Fi 19:
MA27 S '69
Berlioz-sur-Seine; pictorial essay. Hi Fi 19:
47-54 Mr '69
Lascaux puzzle. Horizon 11:94-105 Spr '69
Life and death of Bruges. Horizon 11:74-91
Sum '69
Stockhausen: I am a radio. Hi Fi 19:MA30+
Ag '69
MCMURRAY, Lynn
On the boards. W. Como. por Dance Mag
43:22 N '69
MCMURRIN, Sterling M.
Other voices, other views. Sat R 53:74 Ja 10
'70
MCMURRY college, Abilene, Tex.
Skirmish with the censors: Evergreen review
episode: address. June 1968. D. Gore. ALA
Bul 63:193-203 F '69: Discussion. 63:553-6,
704, 889-90, 1512-13 My-Jl, D '69
MCNAIL, Stanley
Old country churches; poem. Chr Cent 86:
543 Ap 23 '69
MCNAIR, Robert Evander
I do not think people are ready for a party
of extremism; excerpt from address. Septem-
ber 18, 1969. por U S News 67:44 O 6 '69
MCNALLY, Dave
Flying high. il por Time 94:45-6 Jl 11 '69
Highlight. por Sports Illus 30:80 Je 16 '69
MCNALLY, Terrence
Next. Criticism
Nation 208:282 Mr 3 '69
New Yorker 45:90+ F 22 '69
Sat R 52:45 Mr 1 '69
Time il 93:42 F 21 '69
Vogue 153:150 Ap 1 '69
MCNALLY, Tom
Bigmouths tell all. Outdoor Life 144:64-7+ N
'69
Strategy for smallmouths. Outdoor Life 143:
56-9+ My '69
MCNAMARA, James F. and Keyes, E. D.
Guide for converting test scores. Clear House
43:432-4 Mr '69
MCNAMARA, Patrick H.
Rumbles along the Rio. Commonweal 89:730-
2 Mr 14 '69
MCNAMARA, Robert Strange
Excessive population growth; address. May
1, 1969. Vital Speeches 35:500-5 Je 1 '69
Next five years. Duns R 92:19+ D '68
Population threat; excerpts from address,
May 1969. Todays Ed 58:20-3 D '69

about

McNamara at Notre Dame. America 120:579
My 17 '69
McNamara's selective memory. B. Brodie.
Trans-Action 7:59-60 D '69
Robert McNamara's new sense of mission. H.
Brandon. il pors N Y Times Mag p40-1+
N 9 '69
World banking McNamara-style. il por Bsns
W p96-8+ S 27 '69
MCNAMARA, William G.
Widening horizons. por Parks & Rec 4:20-3+
O '69
MCNAMEE, Thomas
Three poems: Civic conscience bugging my
joy: Points defining a line; Warning to my
fathers. Yale R 58:578-80 Je '69
MCNAMEE, Wally
Washington album: photographs. Newsweek
73:23-6 Ja 27 '69
MCNASPY, Clement J.
After 400 years an improved missal. America
120:592+ My 17 '69
Arts. America 122:20-1 Ja 10 '70
At last, the new English liturgy. America
121:554-5 D 6 '69
Fighting drugs in Puerto Rico. America 121:
61 Ag 2 '69

Fine arts. See occasional issues of America
Fracas about saints. America 120:608 My 24
'69
Henri Ayrout Egypt's loss and ours. Ameri-
ca 120:494 Ap 26 '69
Liturgical movements in tension. America
121:320-2 O 18 '69
Religion behind the iron curtain. America
120:450-3 Ap 12 '69
MCNEIL, Cathie
Where do we be going? poem. Seventeen
29:90 Ja '70
MCNEILL, William H.
Historian and historical films. Ed Digest
34:38-40 Ja '69
MCNERNEY, Walter James
Does America need a new health system? ad-
dress, February 3, 1969. Vital Speeches
35:363-70 Ap 1 '69
How to improve medical care; interview. il
U S News 66:42-6 Mr 24 '69
MCNISH, Alvin Greene
Preliminary report. Sci N 96:297-8 O 4 '69
MACNISH, Linda
We learn by loving; story. Good H 169:104-5
N '69
MCNULTY, Henry
For Christmas wassailing, cheering drinks.
House & Gard 136:96+ D '69
MCNULTY, Paul J.
Consumer and the producer. Yale R 58:537-48
Je '69
MCNUTT, N. Scott, and Weinstein, R. S.
Carcinoma of the cervix: deficiency of nexus
intercellular junctions. bibliog Science 165:
597-9 Ag 8 '69
MACOMBER, Marle
Yuccas, hardy and elegant. Org Gard & Farm
16:66-7 Ap '69
MCPHEE, John
Profiles: A. Ashe and C. Graebner. New
Yorker 45:45-8+ Je 7: 44-8+ Je 14 '69
Profiles: Colonsay: the island of the crofter
and the laird. New Yorker 45:69-70+ D 6;
61-2+ D 13 '69
MACPHERSON, H. G.
What would a scientific religion be like? Sat
R 52:44-7 Ag 2 '69
MCPHERSON, James Alan
Chicago's Blackstone Rangers. Atlan 223:74-
84 My: 92-8+ Je '69
Matter of vocabulary; story. Atlan 223:55-63
F '69
Of cabbages and kings; story. Atlan 223:57-
63 Ap '69
MCPHERSON, Jim
Opera in bright lights. Opera N 33:12-13 Ap
5 '69
MCPHERSON, Sandra
Autumnal; poem. Poetry 114:374-5 S '69
Worlds of different sizes; poem. Nation 209:
150 Ag 25 '69
MCPHERSON, Stephen M.
Scenic tribute to Stephen Mather; address,
April 17, 1969. por Nat Parks 43:14 Je '69
MCPHERSON, Kan.
Poetry made easy, in one week; high school
English and journalism. N. Tucker. il Sr
Schol 94:Schol Teach 8+ F 14 '69
MCQUADE, Walter
Assembly-line answer to the housing crisis.
Fortune 79:98-103+ My 1 '69: Same abr.
with title Answer to the housing crisis?
Read Digest 95:197-200+ S '69
Man who taught a corporate elephant to
dance. Fortune 79:122-4+ F '69
Monthly column. See issues of Architectural
forum
Urban expansion takes to the water. Fortune
80:131-5+ S '69
MACQUARIE ISLAND
Macquarie Island and the cause of oceanic
linear magnetic anomalies. R. Varne and
others. bibliog il Science 166:230-3 O 10 '69
MACQUARRIE, John
Self-transcending man. Commonweal 91:155 O
31 '69
MCQUEEN, Noel. See Hark, M. jt. auth.
MCQUEEN, Steve
Motor trend interview; ed. by B. Sanders.
pors Motor T 21:88+ N '69
MCQUILKIN, Frank
Amputation; poem. America 120:134 F 1 '69
Summons; poem. America 121:71 Ag 2 '69
MCQUINN, Pat
Short story market that's always ready for
more. Writers Digest 49:53-5 Je '69
MACRAE, Norman
Problems of impacted ghettos. Cur 109:25-32
Ag '69

about

Miracle in a mess. il por Newsweek 73:89 My
26 '69
MACRAMÉ
Macramé. S. Jones. il Sch Arts 69:36-8 Ja '70
This headboard is sailor's knots. il Sunset
143:126 O '69

MCREYNOLDS, John S. See Gorman, A. L. F. jt. auth.

MACRITCHIE, F.
Evaporation retarded by monolayers. bibliog Science 163:929-31 F 28 '69

MACROMOLECULES
Hydration of macromolecules. I. D. Kuntz, jr. and others. bibliog il Science 163:1329-31 Mr 21 '69

MACRONYSSID mites. See Mites

MACROPHAGES
Macrophage ribonucleoprotein: nature of the antigenic fragment. A. A. Gottlieb. bibliog il Science 165:592-4 Ag 8 '69
Tumor-specific antigens detected by inhibition of macrophage migration. B. S. Kronman and others. il Science 165:296-7 Jl 18 '69

MCSHEA, William P.
Cartoon for angels; poem. Chr Cent 86: 841 Je 18 '69

MCSHERRY, Mary
My short and secret life as a cleaning woman. McCalls 97:78-9+ O '69

MACURDY, Jack
Decorating notebook. Ladies Home J 86:82-3 F '69 (to be cont)

MCWHIRTER, William A.
Great telephone snarl. Life 67:86-86D+ D 5 '69
Pray for Iacocca's baby. Life 66:68-72 Ap 11 '69
Revolution by Brother Alexis. Life 66:67-8+ Ja 31 '69
Tom Benton at eighty, still at war with bores and boobs. Life 67:64-6+ O 3 '69
When (and if) better presidents are made. Harp Baz 102:148-9+ Ja '69
When Jimmy told it like it was. Life 66:8 Ap 18 '69

MCWILLIAMS, Carey
Belfast: in glorious remembrance. Nation 209: 137-42 Ag 25 '69

MCWILLIAMS, Nancy R. See McWilliams, W. C. jt. auth.

MCWILLIAMS, Wilson Carey
[Book review] Commonweal 89:598-9 F 7 '69
Heretic on the left. New Repub 160:22-4 My 17 '69
Military assistance, yes; unconditioned involvement, no. Commonweal 90:12-13 Mr 21 '69; Same with title On choosing to be involved. Cur 109:56-9 Ag '69
—and McWilliams, N. R.
John Steinbeck, writer. Commonweal 90:229-30 My 9 '69

MACY, John Williams, 1917-
Future of non-commercial TV; interview. por U S News 67:94-7 D 8 '69
Merit system today; address, October 21, 1968. Vital Speeches 35:196-200 Ja 15 '69

MADAGASCAR. See Malagasy

MADAGASCAR Jasmine
Stephanotis floribunda. W. Radcliffe. il Horticulture 47:54 O '69

MADAGASCAR periwinkles. See Periwinkles

MADDEN, Carl H.
Can we control inflation? Nations Bsns 57: 50-2 O '69
How much does money count? por Nations Bsns 57:71 Jl '69

MADDEN, John
Eye for an eye. il por Newsweek 73:73 My 5 '69

MADDEN, Richard L.
Goodell is no Bobby Kennedy, but he's trying hard. N Y Times Mag p50-1+ O 26 '69

MADDOCKS, Melvin
Close-up: Van Doren at seventy-five a complex poet. Life 66:64-7 Je 20 '69
Fanatic of disaster. Atlan 223:102-4 Ja '69
Mod Hamlet. Atlan 224:132-5 O '69
New note: the novel as sci-non-fi. Life 66: 15 My 30 '69

about
Books, bikes and Melvin Maddocks. R. Graves. il por Life 67:3 S 19 '69

MADDOX, Gaynor
[Monthly column on cookery] See issues of Today's health

MADDUX, Rachel
Walk in the spring rain; story. McCalls 96: 110-18 S '69

MADEIRA wine. See Wine

MADEMOISELLE (periodical)
Mlle's guest editors: 1969. C. Calvert. il Mlle 69:248-9 Ag '69

MADIGAN, Richard A.
Wave Hill; interview. New Yorker 45:47-8 N 8 '69

MADISON, James A.
Urban recreation problems. Parks & Rec 3: 14-16 D '68

MADISON, Peter
And the second function of college is education; interview. Mlle 69:264+ Ag '69

MADISON, N.J.

Free public library
Madison replaces romanesque with a fountain in the woods. il Library J 94:4393-4 D 1 '69

MADISON, Wis.

Education
Madison: Samuel Gompers and Robert M. La Follette junior high schools. K. I. Taylor. il ALA Bul 63:250-4 F '69

Riots
Three days on Mifflin street. H. Henkin. Nation 208:653-4 My 26 '69

MADISON Square Garden. See New York (city)—Madison Square Garden

MADOLE, Dena
Dena Madole: NYU school of education auditorium. J. Anderson. Dance Mag 43:72 Ag '69

MADONIA, Frank G.
Street paving spurs community improvements. Am City 84:71-2+ Ap '69

MADONNA lilies. See Lilies

MADRID

Description
Cognoscenti abroad. Julián Marías's Madrid. A. Goodfriend. Sat R 52:39-41 Je 14 '69
Sketches of Madrid. F. Donovan. America 120:562 My 10 '69

Galleries and museums
See also
Prado museum

Hotels, restaurants, etc.
Dining in Madrid. M. Woodward. il Travel 132:26 N '69

Markets
Looking and haggling in Madrid's famous flea market. il Sunset 142:53 My '69

MADRIGALS
Mannerism in the cinquecento madrigal? D. Harran. bibliog f il Mus Q 55:521-44 O '69
Pietro Bembo and the literary origins of the Italian madrigal. D. T. Mace. bibliog f il Mus Q 55:65-86 Ja '69

MADSEN, Egon
Brief biography. S. Goodman. il pors Dance Mag 43:66-9 O '69

MADSON, John
Last dance. Audubon 71:16-23 My '69

MAEHLING, Hilda fellowships. See Scholarships and fellowships

MAEROFF, Gene I.
Democrats confront 1970. Nation 209:599-600 D 1 '69

MAETZ, J.
Seawater teleosts: evidence for a sodium-potassium exchange in the branchial sodium-excreting pump. bibliog Science 166: 613-15 O 31 '69

MAFIA
Army tries to build a munitions factory in St Louis with the Mob on the payroll. D. Walsh. il Life 66:52-4+ F 14 '69
Broadway Joe: rebel with a nightclub for a cause; with report by S. Smith. il Life 66:22-7 Je 20 '69
City under indictment; Corruption by consent. il Time 94:10-11 D 26 '69
Conglomerate of crime; La Cosa nostra organization. il Time 94:17-22+ Ag 22 '69; Same abr. with title Cosa nostra: the poison in our society. Read Digest 95: 119-24 D '69
Corruption and crime, charges on a mass scale. il U S News 67:6 D 29 '69
Crackdown in New Jersey. Time 94:17 D 19 '69
Crisis of silence. Time 94:25 O 17 '69
Faircloth's law: a new way to nail elusive mobsters? D. Walsh. il Life 67:62A-62B O 24 '69
Game was up at Namath's. N. Pileggi. il Sports Illus 30:24-5 Je 23 '69
Ganging up on the mob; federal war on organized crime. il Time 93:76 My 2 '69
Governor and the mobster; with report by D. Walsh. il Life 66:28-32A My 2 '69
Gyp's last tape; conspiracy-extortion trial of A. DeCarlo. Newsweek 75:23 Ja 19 '70
Jersey bounce. il Newsweek 74:27 D 22 '69
Listening in on the Mafia; excerpts from transcript. il Time 95:20-1 Ja 19 '70

MAFIA—*Continued*
Man who plays alone, by D. Dolci, tr. by A. Cowan. Review
  Nation 208:831-2 Je 30 '69. E. Capouya
  Sat R 52:57+ Mr 22 '69. G. Gersh
Manual on the Mafia. Newsweek 73:37-8 Je 23 '69
Mayor in the dock. il Newsweek 74:21-2 D 29 '69
Mob; meet me at the Armory and let's talk about it; excerpts from eavesdropped conversations of the Chicago mob. il Life 66:45-7 My 30 '69
Mob's labors lost; investigation into reappearance in Las Vegas. Time 94:20-1 N 28 '69
Mobsters in pasture; Nostra Jersey. F. J. Cook. il Nation 208:105-10 Ja 27 '69
Mushroom Mafiosi; Montalto meeting. Time 94:41 N 7 '69
Organized crime robs all of us. il Changing T 23:25-9 Je '69
Politics. J. Leonard. Esquire 71:84+ Ap '69
Power struggle after a death in the family. S. Smith. il Life 66:51+ F 28 '69
Prosecutor as underdog; concerning The prosecutor, by J. Mills. il Time 94:36 S 5 '69
Rhodes under fire; commuted life sentence of Mafia mobster Yonnie Licavoli. il Time 93: 18-19 My 2 '69
Taping the Mafia. Time 93:22 Je 20 '69
That gang that couldn't shoot straight, by J. Breslin. Review
  Life 67:16 N 21 '69. R. Woodley
Theft of the Nation, by D. R. Cressey. Review
  Newsweek 73:120+ Ap 14 '69. A. Cooper
  Sat R 52:55-6 Mr 22 '69. W. L. Husband
Theft of the Nation; excerpt. D. R. Cressey. Harper 238:84-90 F '69
Valachi papers, by P. Maas. Review
  Life 66:8+ Ja 31 '69. R. Sackett
  Sat R 52.56-7+ Mr 22 '69. N. Lewis
Web that links San Francisco's Mayor Alioto and the Mafia. R. Carlson and L. Brisson. il Look 33:17-21 S 23 '69
MAGALANER, Marvin
  [Book review] Commonweal 90:81-2 Ap 4 '69
MAGAZINE advertising. See Advertising mediums—Periodicals
MAGAZINE art. See Illustration of books and periodicals
MAGAZINE articles. See Periodical articles
MAGAZINE cartoonists guild
  Cartoonist Q's. J. Markow. Writers Digest 49: 60-5 Ag '69
MAGAZINE covers. See Periodical covers
MAGAZINE editors. See Editors and editing
MAGAZINE publishers association
  Magazines, new, changing, growing. J. Tebbel. il Sat R 52:55-6 F 8 '69
  See also
  International magazine conference
MAGAZINE publishing. See Periodicals, Publishing of
MAGAZINE stands, racks, etc.
  Chairside companion. il Mech Illus 65:58+ O '69
MAGAZINE writers. See Authors
MAGAZINER, Ira Charles
  Peaceful revolutionary. por Time 94:52-3 Jl 4 '69
MAGAZINES. See Periodicals
MAGAZINES, Childrens. See Childrens periodicals
MAGDISON, Daniel T.
  Token from the teacher; photographs. Trans-Action 6:26-7 Ja '69
MAGDOL, Edward
  New look at abolitionists. Nation 208:214-15 F 17 '69
MAGEE, Donald Drew
  NRPA administrative services. Parks & Rec 4:66-9 Je '69
  NRPA's personal security program. Parks & Rec 4:73-4 S '69
MAGEE, James J.
  Poor in the early church. America 121:164-5 S 13 '69
MAGEE, R. Dale
  Fire fighters record the action. Radio-Electr 40:71 My '69
MAGELLAN, Ferdinand
  Magellan's voyage; excerpts, tr. by R. A. Skelton. A. Pigafetta. il Am Heritage 20: 62-75 O '69
  Travels with Magellan. Newsweek 74:108+ O 20 '69
  West to the Orient. A. Villiers. il Sat R 52:21-3+ D 20 '60
MAGELLANIC clouds
  Report on the Magellanic clouds. B. E. Westerlund. il Sky & Tel 38:23-7 Jl '69

Through rugged ways to the stars, by H. Shapley. Review
  Natur Hist 78:72+ N '69. P. Van De Kamp
MAGER, Milton. See Francesconi, R. P. jt. auth.
MAGGEROLI, Phyllis
  Thousand voices. ALA Bul 63:1270-3 O '69
MAGGIO musicale fiorentino. See Music festivals—Italy
MAGHAKIAN, John
  Ocean fishing for Los Angeles youth. Parks & Rec 4:32 Jl '69
MAGIC
  Ancient letters to the dead and others. C. H. Gordon. il Natur Hist 78:94-9 F '69
  See also
  Witchcraft
MAGIC flute; opera. See Mozart. J. C. W. A.
MAGIC mama; story. See Clifton, L.
MAGIC poker; story. See Coover, R.
MAGICIANS
  License to spell; Italian magicians seek professional status. Time 93:23-4 F 21 '69
MAGID, Nora L.
  Tantalizing two-way mirrors of Graham Greene. Commonweal 90:567-8 S 19 '69
MAGINOT line. See France—Defenses
MAGNA carta
  Modernizing Magna carta. il Time 93:68 Je 6 '69
MAGNESIUM
  Magnesium eyes lightweight crown. il Bsns W p52-3 My 31 '69
MAGNETIC catheters. See Catheters
MAGNETIC ferrites. See Ferrites (magnetic materials)
MAGNETIC fields
  Magnetic flux-trapping experiment with a moving conductor. J. Hovorka. bibliog il Science 166:877-8 N 14 '69
  Magnetic polarity of pillow basalts from Reykjanes ridge. J. De Boer and others. bibliog il Science 166:996-8 N 21 '69
MAGNETIC fields (cosmic physics)
  Detecting solar magnetic fields by filter photography. il Sky & Tel 37:363-4 Je '69
MAGNETIC-film holograms. See Holography
MAGNETIC materials
  See also
  Ferrites (magnetic materials)
MAGNETIC measurements
  See also
  Magnetometers
MAGNETIC memory (computers) See Memory devices (computers)
MAGNETIC recorders and recording
  Are cassettes here to stay? R. Angus and N. Eisenberg. Hi Fi 19:46-7+ Jl '69
  Best tape system for you: reel, cassette, or cartridge? S. Shatavsky. il Pop Sci 194:126-9 F '69
  Dolby system, how it works: cutting tape hiss. W. G. Salm. il Radio-Electr 40:52-3+ O '69
  Magic machine: how a tape recorder works. E. F. McIntyre. il Hi Fi 19:44-9 Ag '69
  Magnetic recording. V. E. Ragosine. il Sci Am 221:70+ bibliog(p 166) N '69
  More tape recorders I have known and loved. I. Berger. Sat R 52:49 Ag 30 '69
  Multichannel recording for creating the new sound. R. Wickersham. il Electr World 82: 38-9+S '69
  Plain and easy guide to practical electronic music. R. Ehle. il Hi Fi 19:50-3+ Ag '69
  Professional hints for amateur tape recordists. L. Zide. il Hi Fi 19:78-82 D '69
  Selecting a tape recorder. L. P. Kubiak. il Electr World 81:39+ My '69
  Tape-recorder wow and flutter. J. Hawk. il Electr World 81:36-7+ Je '69
  Tape recorders I have known and loved. I. Berger. Sat R 52:57-8 Je 28 '69
  Tape today: reel-to-reel, cartridge, or cassette? with comment by I. Kolodin. I. Berger il Sat R 52:48-55 S 27 '69
  See also
  Automobiles—Tape equipment
  Tape recordings
  Video tape recorders and recording

Educational applications
  Cassettes in the classroom. D. Molner. il Schol Teach Sec Teach Sup p 18 O 6 '69
  This English is something else; Indianapolis Oral-aural-visual program for teaching language arts. S. L. Sheeley. il Sr Schol 94: 14-16 Ja 17 '69

Equipment
  Buyer's guide to cassette tape equipment; comp. by S. Lowe. Hi Fi 19:48-51 Jl '69

MAGNETIC recorders and recording—Equipment—*Continued*
Make a time-taper. A. L. Sohl. il Radio-Electr 40:54 Je '69
Sound-with-sound mixer; with pre-record monitoring. D. DeMaw. il Pop Electr 30:59-61+ Mr '69

Fire protection applications
Fire fighters record the action. R. D. Magee. il Radio-Electr 40:71 My '69

Maintenance and repair
You take care of them, they'll entertain you; or, How to keep your music-picture-sound equipment in shape. il Redbook 133:51+ Ag '69

Stereophonic recorders
Face to face with a one-man band. D. Muro. Seventeen 28:133 F '69
Harman-Kardon CAD-4 stereo tape cassette deck. il Radio-Electr 41:22 Ja '70
Hi-fi product report; Allied TR-1080 stereo tape recorder. il Electr World 81:24-5+ Ap '69
Hi-fi product report; Ampex AG-600-2 tape deck. il Electr World 81:65-7 Mr '69
Hi-fi product report; Ampex 1461 tape recorder. il Electr World 82:85-6 S '69
Recorders for tape composition. il Hi Fi 19:54-5 Ag '69
Stereo tape decks. il Consumer Bul 52:15-18 D '69

Testing
AC voltmeter spots tape recorder wow. K. Larsson. il Radio-Electr 40:99 D '69
Hi-fi product report; TEAC A-6010 tape deck. il Electr World 81:60-1 F '69

Visual recordings
See Video tape recorders and recording

MAGNETIC recorders and recording, Portable
Cassette tape recorders, a new breed. L. P. Kubiak. il Electr World 81:23-7 Je '69
Cassettes:pop in/pop out flexibility. B. Evans. il Pop Phot 65:78+ N '69
Cueing without three hands; how to use a cassette recorder. H. Friedman. il Pop Phot 65:49+ O '69
It's an AM! It's an FM! its super tape. C. Conley. il Field & S 74:159 O '69
New in stereo cassettes '70. W. G. Salm. il Radio-Electr 40:37-9 D '69
Stereo scene; cassettes: not either/or, but and! C. Lincoln. il Pop Electr 30:65-8 Je '69
Taped newsletters sound off; cassette players. il Bsns W p58 Jl 26 '69
Those tiny new recorders: tape your fun where you find it. H. Fantel. il Pop Mech 131:132-7+ Mr '69

Educational applications
See Magnetic recorders and recording—Educational applications

Testing
EW lab tests of new cassette tape recorders. J. D. Hirsch. il Electr World 81:26-7+ Je '69

MAGNETIC resonance
Applications of electron spin resonance to gas-phase kinetics. A. A. Westenberg. bibliog il Science 164:381-8 Ap 25 '69
Electron spin resonance signals in injured nerve. B. Commoner and others. bibliog il Science 165:703-4 Ag 15 '69
Paramagnetic unit in spinach subchloroplast particles: estimation of size. E. C. Weaver and others. bibliog il Science 165:906-7 Ag 29 '69

MAGNETIC resonance, Nuclear. See Nuclear magnetic resonance

MAGNETIC tape
Are cassettes here to stay? R. Angus and N. Eisenberg. Hi Fi 19:46-7+ Jl '69
Cassettes are rolling. il Newsweek 73:90-1 Ap 28 '69
Professional hints for amateur tape recordists. L. Zide. il Hi Fi 19:78-82 D '69
Stereo cassette tape players with automatic changers. il Consumer Bul 52:29-32 S '69
Tape and how to buy it. il Am Home 72:128+ O '69
Tape today: reel-to-reel, cartridge, or cassette? with comment by I. Kolodin. I. Berger. il Sat R 52:48-55 S 27 '69

Stereophonic tape
Ping-ping-pong-pong: four-channel stereo. R. Long. il Hi Fi 19:62-3+ S '69

MAGNETISM
Crystal acts like a two-dimensional antiferromagnet; K₂NiF₄. G. B. Lubkin. Phys Today 22:69 Jl '69
Magnetic model of matter. J. Schwinger. bibliog il Science 165:757-61 Ag 22 '69

Magnetism in medical treatment. il Chem 42:21-3 Mr '69
See also
Magnetic fields

MAGNETISM, Terrestrial
Age of the Bay of Biscay: evidence from seismic profiles and bottom samples. E. J. W. Jones and J. I. Ewing. bibliog il Science 166:102-5 O 3 '69
East Pacific rise crest: a near-bottom geophysical profile. R. L. Larson and F. N. Spiess; reply with rejoinder. W. C. Kellogg. bibliog Science 165:617-18 Ag 8 '69
Electroculture in plant growth. M. Franz. il Org Gard & Farm 16:85-6+ F '69
Geomagnetic reversal in Brunhes normal polarity epoch. J. D. Smith and J. H. Foster. bibliog il Science 163:565-7 F 7 '69
Geomagnetic reversals; adaptation of address, April 8, 1968. A. Cox. bibliog il Science 163:237-45 Ja 17 '69
Macquarie Island and the cause of oceanic linear magnetic anomalies. R. Varne and others. bibliog il Science 166:230-3 O 10 '69
Ocean floor spreading: Olduvai and Gilsa events in the Matuyama epoch. D. A. Emilia and D. F. Heinrichs. bibliog il Science 166:1267-9 D 5 '69
Paleomagnetism & archeomagnetism. D. E. Lancaster. il Electr World 82:23-6+ S '69
See also
Auroras
Geomagnetic observatories
Magnetic fields

MAGNETOHYDRODYNAMIC generators. See Electric generators

MAGNETOHYDRODYNAMICS
High-powered idea goes to work: EGD paint sprayer. il Bsns W p 156+ S 20 '69
Support for a tarnished dream. Sci N 96:8 Jl 5 '69

MAGNETOMETERS
Lunar surface magnetometer. il Space World G-1-73:36-7 Ja '70

MAGNETOSPHERE. See Atmosphere, Upper

MAGNETS
See also
Electrets

MAGNIN, I. and company
Magnin's moves East. il Time 93:77 Je 27 '69

MAGNOLIAS
Now's the time to pick a magnolia; saucer magnolia. il Sunset 142:178 F '69
Southern magnolia. F. Heutte. il Horticulture 47:20+ Ja '69

MAGOWAN, Robin
Secrecies; On this day: poems. Poetry 114:98 My '69

MAGUIRE, H. F.
Small game harvest up. Cons 24:6-7 D '69

MAGUIRE, John
Light: the revealing dimension; interview, ed. by J. H. Ingersoll. House B 111:138-9 Ap '69

MAGUIRE, John W.
Political action and America's teachers. Sch & Soc 97:22-3 Ja '69

MAH JONG (game)
Mah-jong craze. il Newsweek 73:14 F 24 '69

MAHAN, Paul E.
Instant fruit and berries. Org Gard & Farm 16:86-7 N '69
Two-climate gardening. pors Org Gard & Farm 16:42-3 My '69
What's cooking? Org Gard & Farm 16:102-3 Ag '69

MAHAR, Mary Helen
Equalizing educational opportunity; address, June 1968. ALA Bul 63:226-30 F '69

MAHDESIAN, Zaven M.
Visit to Moscow's schools. Clear House 44:166-8 N '69

MAHER, Art
Use what the varmint shooters use. Pop Mech 132:116-19 D '69

MAHER, Arthur J.
Mainly for men. See issues of American home News for home owners. Am Home 72:44+ Ap: 56+ My: 24 Je '69

MAHER, John E.
Economics, good and bad. Clear House 44:16-17 S '69

MAHEU, René
700 million forgotten minds; reprint. UNESCO Courier 22:36-7 Ag '69

MAHLER, Alma Maria (Schindler) See Werfel, A. M. S. M.

MAHLER, Gustav
Closest approach yet to an ideal Mahler Third. J. Diether. il Am Rec G 35:1119-21 Ag '69
Gustav Mahler, by A. Mahler. Review
Am Rec G 35:896+ My '69. J. Diether

MAISONS, M. Jacques
  Training for Europe. Travel 131:60-3 My '69
MAIZE. See Corn
MAIZE art glass. See Glassware
MAJARDAH irrigation project. See Irrigation—
  Tunisia
MAJOR league baseball players association
  Game deserves the best; M. Miller as execu-
    tive director. R. Roberts. Sports Illus 30:
    46-7 F 24 '69
  Strike one; spring training boycott. Time 93:
    79 F 28 '69
MAJOR league baseball playoffs. See Baseball
  clubs
MAJORCA
  Majorca. R. Peck. il Travel 131:26-31 Mr '69
  Majorca; the haunted island. E. Flamholtz. il
    Travel & Camera 32:46-7+ Mr '69
MAJORITIES
  Elm street's new White House power. A. J.
    Reichley. il Fortune 80:70-3+ D '69
MAKBETH; drama. See Shakespeare, W. Plays
  —Macbeth
MAKE-up
  Beautiful eyes. il Good H 169:76-9 Ag '69
  Beauty life; campus beat. il Mlle 68:256-7 Ap
    '69
  Beauty problems you may have too, and new
    ways to solve them. il Seventeen 29:70-1 Ja
    '70
  Beauty things Mlle taught me. il Mlle 69:336
    9 Ag '69
  Brunettes are back! il Seventeen 28:70-5 Ja
    '69
  Expressive eye. il Seventeen 28:122-3+ N '69
  Extra dry bikini straight up. C. Twiss. il
    Holiday 45:50-3 F '69
  Eye lights. il Redbook 133:96-9 S '69
  Eyebrows make the difference. C. Bartel.
    il Am Home 72:36+ Ap '69
  Eyes of the desert. il Vogue 154:136-7 S 15
    '69
  Fall's change of face: let your skin shine
    through. il McCalls 97:100-3 O '69
  Four faces of beauty. il Seventeen 28:72-5 Jl
    '69
  Gel, the new consistency of beauty. il Vogue
    155:136-7+ Ja 1 '70
  Hairdos and makeup that complete the sea-
    son's looks. il Good H 169:88-9, 171 D '69
  How to make faces. il Harp Baz 102:190-1
    O '69
  Know your makeup colorscope. il McCalls
    96:92-5 F '69
  The look and how to get it. il McCalls 96:102-
    5 Ap '69
  Luminous face. C. Bartel. il Am Home 72:
    20+ D '69
  Models without makeup; Colleen Corby and
    Lucy Angle. il Seventeen 28:130-3 S '69
  New beauty book: twenty-five exciting hair-
    dos, fall makeup forecast. il Good H 169:
    120-9+ O '69
  New insights on the eye. il Vogue 153:234-
    9+ Ap 1 '69
  Six beautiful new looks for summer. il Good
    H 168:98-9 Je '69
  Snow glow; beau glow. il Seventeen 27:114-
    15 N '68
  Spring beauty book. il Good H 168:120-9+
    Ap '69
  Summer sun, summer shade. il McCalls 96:
    68-71 Je '69
  Vibrant new beauty for five young women.
    il Good H 168:116-17 F '69
  What's your eye-Q? Harp Baz 103:212 N '69
MAKE-up, Theatrical
  Godfrey Cambridge turns white; filming of
    The night the sun came out. E. Dunbar.
    il Look 33:57+ D 30 '69
MAKE-up bases. See Cosmetics
MALADIE verte. See Algae
MALAGA
  Apocrypha on the Costa del Sol. D. Butwin.
    il Sat R 52:44-5+ Mr 29 '69
MALAGASY
  Stirrings at the end of the world. J. Blashill.
    il Time 95:32-3 Ja 19 '70
MALAM Adi Bwaye
  Keeping one's head. por Newsweek 74:33 D
    29 '69
MALAMUD, Bernard
  Portrait of artist as escape-goat. R. Scholes.
    Sat R 52:32-4 My 10 '69
MALANGA, Gerard
  Good and the useful. M. Randall. Poetry
    115:56-7 O '69
MALAPROPISMS. See Blunders
MALARIA
  Glucose-6-phosphate dehydrogenase defi-
    cient red cells: resistance to infection by
    malarial parasites. L. Luzzatto and others.
    bibliog il Science 164:839-42 My 16 '69

Invasion of the plasmodia; outbreaks in the
  U.S. il Newsweek 73:50 Mr 3 '69
Plasmodium malariae: transmission from
  monkey to man by mosquito bite. P. G.
  Contacos and W. E. Collins. bibliog Science
  165:918-19 Ag 29 '69
Protective effect of antilymphocyte serum on
  mice infected with plasmodium berghei.
  J. N. Sheagren and A. P. Monaco. bibliog
  il Science 164:1423-5 Je 20 '69
  See also
Primaquine
MALARKEY, Burgess
  How many sewers? How many dumps? Seven-
    teen 29:36 Ja '70
MALAWI
            Industries
  Electronic entrepreneur; Nzeru radio co. il
    Time 94:75A Jl 18 '69
MALAY PENINSULA
  See also
Malaysia
MALAYSIA
  Crisis in Malaysia. G. P. Dartford. Cur Hist
    57:349-54+ D '69
  Malaysia. S. Griffin. il Travel 132:50-5+ N
    '69
  Malaysian political game. R. O. Tilman. Cur
    Hist 56:100-5+ F '69
  Rahman to Razak. Newsweek 73:55-6 Je 2 '69
  Saddest story. il Newsweek 73:58 My 26 '69
    See also
  Guerrillas—Malaysia
  Libraries—Malaysia
          Foreign relations
  Quiet cold war over Sabah. il Ramp Mag
    7:20+ N 30 '68
            Race problems
  Preparing for a pogrom. il Time 94:43 Jl 18
    '69
MALCOLM X
  Legacy of my husband, Malcolm X. B.
    Shabazz. il pors Ebony 24:172-4+ Je '69
  St Malcom X. por Newsweek 73:27-8 Mr 3
    '69
  Visit with the widow of Malcolm X; inter-
    view, ed. by F. Knebel. B. Shabazz. il Look
    33:74-7+ Mr 4 '69
MALCOLM X, Mrs. See Shabazz, B.
MALCOM, W. J.
  Low-pressure air tests for sewer lines; ques-
    tions and answers. por Am City 84:74-5 N
    '69
MALDONADO, M. Martinez-. See Martinez-
  Maldonado, M.
MALDONADO-DENIS, Manuel
  Latin America: challenge from the intellec-
    tuals. Nation 209:73-6 Jl 28 '69
  Puerto Ricans: protest or submission? Ann
    Am Acad 382:26-31 Mr '69
MALE birth control drug. See Contraceptives
MALE coiffure. See Hairdressing
MALE dancers. See Dancers
MALEC, Alexander B.
  Participant past imperfect. Writer 82:19-21
    Ag '69
MALEC, Michael
  Phasing out Mary Daly. Commonweal 90:61-
    2 Ap 4 '69
MALETSKOS, Constantine J. See Tang, C.
  W. jt. auth.
MALFORMATIONS. See Deformities
MALHEUR national wildlife refuge. See Wild-
  life sanctuaries
MALI (Republic)
  Foxes foretell the future in Mali's Dogon
    country. P. J. Meyer. il Nat Geog 135:430-
    48 Mr '69
    See also
Timbuktu
MALIBU, Calif.
  Welcome to Malibu! R. Reed. il Holiday 45:
    34-7+ My '69
MALIK, Adam
  Indonesia: the greatest prize. A. Campbell.
    New Repub 160:18-19 Ap 19 '69
MALIK, Hafeez
  Muslims of India and Pakistan. bibliog f Cur
    Hist 56:151-5+ Mr '69
MALIN, Irving
  [Book review] Commonweal 89:599-600 F 7
    '69
MALINA, Judith
  Theater of ignorance. R. Gilman. Atlan 224:
    35-42 Jl '69
MALINS, Donald C. and Barone, Anthony
  Glyceryl ether metabolism: regulation of
    buoyancy in dogfish squalus acanthias. bib-
    liog Science 167:79-80 Ja 2 '70
  —See Varanasi, U. jt. auth.

MALKIN, Martin, and Lipmann, Fritz
  Fusidic acid: inhibition of factor T₂ in
    reticulocyte protein synthesis. bibliog Science 164:71-2 Ap 4 '69
MALLAS, John H.
  Selected objects from the Mallas observer's
    catalogue. See issues of Review of popular
    astronomy
—and Kreimer, Evered
  Messier album. See issues of Sky and telescope
MALLORCA. See Majorca
La MALLORQUINA (restaurant) See San Juan,
    Puerto Rico—Hotels, restaurants, etc.
MALLORY, H. R.
  Build a photosensitive switch. Pop Electr
    31:55-6 D '69
  Multiple-function remote-control relay circuits. Electr World 82:36+ Ag '69
MALLS, Shopping. See Business districts
MALMGREEN, Henry P.
  Changing confession market. Writer 82:22-3
    S '69
MALMGREN, Harald
  Willing to help. New Repub 161:10-12 N 1 '69
MALNUTRITION. See Children—Nutrition;
    Diet, Deficient; Nutrition; Nutrition problems
MALOFF, Saul
  Writers & writing (cont) Commonweal 89:
    654-6; 90:23-4, 235-6+, 490-1; 91:362-3 F 21,
    Mr 21, My 9, Ag 8, D 19 '69
MALONE, Jerry
  Little Irvy. F. Deford. il pors Sports Illus 31:
    50-7 Ag 11 '69
MALONEY, Elbert S.
  New charts. See issues of Motor boating
MALONEY, George A.
  Rumania's opening to the churches. America
    121:490-3 N 22 '69
MALONEY, Mary A. and Patt, H. M.
  Origin of repopulating cells after localized
    bone marrow depletion. bibliog Science 165:
    71-3 Jl 4 '69
MALPRACTICE
  One woman's ordeal: when too much medicine is a dangerous thing; case of Ellen
    Morgan Holl. B. Merson. Ladies Home J
    86:50+ N '69
  Suing the doctor; epidemic of suits. Newsweek 75:93-4 Ja 19 '70
MALPRACTICE liability insurance. See Insurance, Malpractice liability
MALRAUX, André
  Hero politics. S. Hux. Commentary 47:90+
    My '69
  Tragedy and dignity of man. G. Gersh. por
    Cath World 208:268-9 Mr '69
MALTA
  Democracy's fortress: unsinkable Malta. E.
    Bradford. il Nat Geog 135:852-79 Je '69
  Letter from Europe. A. Burgess. Am Scholar
    38:297-9 Spr '69
  Magic of Malta. D. Koenig. il Travel 132:61-6
    Ag '69
  Up from antiquity. N. Braybrooke. il Sat R
    52:34+ Mr 1 '69
MALTHUSIANISM
    See also
  Population, Increase of
MALUCCIO, Anthony N.
  School problems of emotionally disturbed
    foster children. bibliog Ment Hy 53:611-19
    O '69
MAMA, La. See New York (city)—Theater
MAMARONECK, N.Y.
  Small police cars, big results. J. Geary. il Am
    City 84:68 F '69
  Students campaign to save school libraries.
    Library J 94:4568 D 15 '69
MAMAY, Sergius H.
  Cycads: fossil evidence of late paleozoic origin. bibliog Science 164:295-6 Ap 18 '69
MAMMALS
    See also
  Bats
  Cetacea
  Embryology—Mammals
  Herbivora
  Mountain beavers
  Primates
  Sand rats
  Shrews
  Whales
MAMMALS, Fossil
    See also
  Elephants, Fossil
MAMMARY cancer. See Cancer
MAMMARY glands
  Milk. S. Patton. il Sci Am 221:58-62+ bibliog (p 140) Jl '69
MAMMARY tumor virus. See Tumor viruses

MAMMOTH CAVE NATIONAL PARK
  Mammoth Cave. B. Surface. il Travel 132:62-
    5 S '69; Same abr. with title Mammoth
    Cave: nature's underground cathedral. Read
    Digest 95:189-92 S '69
MAMURO, T. and Matsunami, T.
  Plutonium-238 in fallout. bibliog Science 163:
    465-7 Ja 31 '69
MAN
  Ambivalent man and his ambiguous moon.
    M. C. Hyers. il Chr Cent 86:1158-62 S 10
    '69
  Brothers in the eternal cold. A. MacLeish.
    Read Digest 94:68-9 Mr '69
  By the Late John Brockman, by J. Brockman. Review
    Vogue 153:138 My '69. J. Gruen
  Dewart's new foundations. A. Gibson. Commonweal 90:101-4 Ap 11 '69
  Earth might be fair. Chr Cent 86:1009 Jl 30
    '69
  Evaded question: science and human nature.
    E. Becker. il Commonweal 89:638-42+ F 21
    '69; Reply with rejoinder. J. R. Pleasants.
    90:59+ Ap 4 '69
  In and out of Eden. C. F. H. Henry. Chr Today 13:38-9 Je 6 '69
  Man in a web; excerpts from The unexpected
    universe. L. Eiseley. Read Digest 95:116-
    18 D '69
  Man, one of evolution's mistakes? adaptation of address, September 1969. A. Koestler. il N Y Times Mag p28-9+ O 19 '69;
    Discussion. p 14 N 9; 52+ N 23 '69
  Men in groups, by L. Tiger. Review
    Life 66:9+ Je 20 '69. R. Ardrey
  Nature and dignity of man; AAAS symposium, December 28-30, 1969. P. N. Williams. Science 166:778 N 7 '69
  Nigerian debate on man. Sat R 52:24+ S 20
    '69
  Working paper for man and nature. M. Mead.
    il Natur Hist 78:14-15+ Ap '69
    See also
  Anthropology
  Civilization
  History
  Human relations
  Humanism
  Longevity
  Psychology
  Sociology
  Woman

Anecdotes, facetiae, satire, etc.
  Birdbrains; excerpt from Birds. R. J. Lifton.
    il Atlan 224:46-7 Ag '69

Food habits
    See Food habits

Influence of environment
  Biosphere: delicate balance between man and
    nature. R. Dubos. il UNESCO Courier 22:
    6-15 Ja '69
  Conservation at the crossroads; address. F.
    E. Moss. il Am For 75:20-3+ Ja '69
  Countdown to disaster. P. R. Ehrlich. Cur
    103:62-4 Ja '69
  Environment; what to do about it; address,
    May 5, 1969. G. T. Seaborg. Vital Speeches
    35:514-20 Je 15 '69
  Healthiest spot in America: central Nebraska.
    J. Y. Dickinson. il Holiday 45:52-3+ My '69;
    Same abr. Read Digest 95:241-2+ O '69
  Human environment. F. Gutheim. Nation 209:
    288-90 S 22 '69
  Making economic aid effective: are we
    causing ecological harm? R. Cahn. Cur 104:
    41-5 F '69
  Need for revolution. P. Bascio. il Cath
    World 209:207-9 Ag '69
  Technology, adaptation, and evolution; excerpt from address. H. Hoagland. il Bul
    Atom Sci 25:27-30 Ja '69
  Toward a new scientific era; address, November 15, 1968. G. T. Seaborg. Vital Speeches
    35:236-40 F 1 '69
  Violence: we can end it. J. Poppy. il Look
    33:21-3 Je 10 '69
  Visual squalor, social disorder or, A new
    vision of the city of man. B. Thompson.
    il Arch Rec 145:161-4 Ap '69
    See also
  Anthropogeography
  United Nations conference on the problems of
    human environment (proposed)

Influence on nature
  America the beautiful? with editorial comment. D. Perlman. il Look 33:25-7, 71 N 4
    '69
  America the (formerly) beautiful; Storm King
    Mountain. J. N. Miller. il Read Digest 94:
    179-81+ F '69

MAN—Influence on nature—*Continued*
America the raped, by G. Marine. Review
    Nat Parks 43:25 D '69. C. Weathersbee
    Natur Hist 78:72-3+ O '69. H. Gilliam
Can man survive? J. A. Oliver. Parents Mag
    44:40 Ag '69
Challenge of the seventies. A. Godfrey. Esquire 72:8+ N '69
Earthly paradise. J. W. Johnson. il McCalls
    97:40-1+ Ja '70
Eco-catastrophe! predictions. P. Ehrlich.
    Ramp Mag 8:24-8 S '69; Same abr. with
    title Our plundered planet; the end of the
    oceans. Cur 111:23-32 O '69
Ecology roadblock. Am City 84:8 S '69
Finding lemonade in Santa Barbara's oil. G.
    Hardin. il Sat R 52:18-21 My 10 '69
Gambling with nature; usages of pesticides
    and herbicides. Commonweal 89:512-13 Ja
    24 '69
Ian McHarg vs. us anthropocentric clods;
    with excerpts from Design with nature. il
    Life 67:48B-48D Ag 15 '69
In dubious, desperate battle. J. W. Krutch.
    il Audubon 71:52-4 Mr '69
King in the kingdom of things. W. Brueggemann. il Chr Cent 86:1165-6 S 10 '69
Man against nature. F. F. Darling. il UNESCO
    Courier 22:24-40 Ja '69
Man in nature: model for a new radicalism.
    C. R. Harris. Nation 209:496-500 N 10 '69
Modern science and ethical dimension. P. J.
    Riga. Cath World 209:213-17 Ag '69
Polluting the planet; time to stop the plunder.
    J. Davy. Cur 103:59-62 Ja '69
Strategy of ecosystem development; adaptation of address, August 1966. E. P. Odum.
    bibliog il Science 164:262-70 Ap 18 '69; Reply with rejoinder. R. P. McIntosh. 166:
    403-4 O 17 '69
Technology and the natural environment. B.
    Commoner. il Arch Forum 130-68-73 Je '69
Vandal ideology. S. Paradise. Nation 209:
    729-32 D 29 '69
When it rained cats in Borneo; excerpts from
    address. F. Mergen. il Am For 75:28-9+
    Ja '69
    See also
Environmental policy
United Nations conference on the human environment (proposed)

Migrations

Linking the transoceanic cultures. T. Heyerdahl il Sci N 95:534-7 My 31 '69
Prehistoric cultural contacts in southwestern
    Alaska. D. E. Dumond. bibliog il Science
    166:1108-15 N 28 '69

Origin and antiquity

Knuckle-walking and the problem of human
    origins. R. H. Tuttle. bibliog il Science
    166:953-61 N 21 '69
Man among men. Sci Am 221:101 S '69
Man is over 14,000,000 years old. il Sci Digest
    66:84-5 O '69
    See also
Archeology
Evolution
Man, Prehistoric
Neanderthal race
Stone age

Periodicity
    See Periodicity

Survival

Can man survive? J. A. Oliver. Parents Mag
    44:40 Ag '69
Conservation equals survival. W. Stegner. Am
    Heritage 21:12-15 D '69
Earthlings in the space age; reprint. Lord
    Ritchie-Calder. il UNESCO Courier 22:4-6
    Ag '69
Men in groups, by L. Tiger. Review
    Life 66:9+ Je 20 '69 R. Ardrey
What we must do. J. Platt. Science 166:1115-
    21 N 28 '69; Reply. W. D. McElroy. 167:9
    Ja 2 '70
MAN (theology)
    See also
Pelagianism
MAN, Effect of altitude on. See Altitude, Influence of
MAN, Prehistoric
Age of man: identification of Ramapithecus.
    il Time 94:50 Ag 29 '69
Anthropology: fossil find fills a gap;
    Australopithecus africanus. il Sci N 95:469-
    70 My 17 '69
Challenging Kenyapithecus: studies of the
    Ramapithecus. il Sci N 96:97 Ag 2 '69
Controversial taxonomy of fossil hominids.
    E. L. Simons and others. bibliog Science
    166:258-9 O 10 '69

Fossil evidence of human violence. T. D.
    Stewart. il Trans-Action 6:48-53 My '69;
    Reply with rejoinder. S. Parker. 6:60-1 O '69
Marmes man is 10,000. Sci Digest 66:36 S '69
Old Australopithecines. Sci Am 220:56-7 Je '69
Peking man in the apothecary's shop; reprint.
    G. H. R. von Koenigswald. UNESCO Courier
    22:76 Ag '69
Secrets of China's ancient men. D. Cohen. il
    Sci Digest 66:40-4 S '69
Throwing cold water on marmes man. M. P.
    Works. Esquire 73:59-60+ Ja '70
When man began: earliest trace of the Australopithecus man found in Ethiopia. Newsweek 73:94 My 12 '69
    See also
Cave drawings and paintings
Man—Origin and antiquity
Neanderthal race
Paleo-Indians
Petroglyphs
Piltdown forgery
Stone implements and weapons
MAN amplifiers
Debut of a metal giant; CAM, walking
    machine. il Time 93:51-2 Ap 11 '69
Fabulous walking truck. il Pop Sci 194:76-9
    Mr '69
Four-footed friend; cybernetic anthropomorphous machine. il Newsweek 73:80 Ap
    14 '69
Step up and meet a walking, kicking robot.
    il Sr Schol 94:15 Ap 18 '69
They're not robots, they're cyborgs. W. T.
    Spencer. il N Y Times Mag p40-1+ D 14 '69
You had better be kind to this four-legged
    friend. il Life 66:34-5+ My 2 '69
MAN and his world exhibition. See Montreal—
    Exhibitions
MAN and nature. See Man—Influence on nature
MAN better man; musical comedy. See Musical comedies, revues, etc.—Criticisms,
    plots, etc.
MAN in the glass booth; drama. See Shaw, R.
MAN-made fabrics. See Textile fabrics, Synthetic
MAN-made lakes. See Lakes, Artificial
MAN power. See Manpower
MAN that corrupted Hadleyburg; drama. See
    Nolan, P. T.
MAN who came to stay; story. See Stegner, P.
MAN who jumped into the water; story. See
    Colwin, L.
MAN who knew everything; story. See Rolfs,
    M. J.
MAN with the flower in his mouth; drama. See
    Pirandello, L.
MANAGEMENT
    See also
Business management and organization
MANAGEMENT, Business. See Business management and organization
MANAGEMENT, Industrial. See Industrial
    management and organization
MANAGEMENT assistance, incorporated
Dramatic rise and fall of MAI; computer-
    leasing industry. il Forbes 104:19-21 S 1
    '69
MANAGEMENT consultants. See Business consultants
MANAGEMENT information systems. See Information systems, Management
MANAGEMENT of children. See Children—
    Management and training
MANAGERIAL training. See Executives—
    Training
MANAGERS. See Executives
MANAGERS, Baseball. See Baseball managers
MANATEES
Florida's manatees, mermaids in peril. D. S.
    Hartman. il Nat Geog 136:342-53 S '69
MANCARI, Carla
Education of Carla ManCari. W. Peters. il
    por Good H 169:90-1+ S '69
MANCHESTER, Harland
Boom in mobile homes. Har Yrs 9:14-17 Ap
    '69; Same with title Homes that come off
    the assembly line. Read Digest 94:23-4+
    Ap '69
Cable TV, the hottest thing in television.
    Read Digest 94:19-20+ Je '69
Homes that come off the assembly line.
    Read Digest 94:23-4+ Ap '69
MANCHESTER, William
U.S embassy; our men in Paris. por Holiday 45:34-9+ Mr '69
MANCHESTER, N.H.

Historic houses, etc.

City no one knew; the Amoskeag millyard.
    R. Langenbach. il Arch Forum 130:84-91 Ja
    '69
Doomed industrial monument: Amoskeag
    mills. il Fortune 79:118-21 F '69

MANCHESTER, N.H.—*Continued*
Newspapers
See also
Manchester union leader

MANCHESTER union leader
New Hampshire's Union leader. W. D. Gardner. Nation 208:397-401 Mr 31 '69

MANDARINS in a farther field; story. See Casey, J.

MANDEL, Alan
Piano works of Ives. A. Cohn. por Am Rec G 35:548-9 Mr '69

MANDEL, Ernest
Lecture canceled. Time 94:38 D 5 '69

MANDEL, Sheila
Trade winds. J. Beatty, jr. Sat R 52:16 Ap 19 '69

MANDELBAUM, Arthur
Threats to the modern family. por Sci Digest 65:57-60 Mr '69

MANDELBAUM, Leonard
Apollo: how the United States decided to go to the moon. bibliog Science 163:649-54 F 14 '69

MANDELBAUM, Nathan
All through the house (cont) McCalls 96:32 Mr; 72 Ap; 40 My '69

MANDELL, Arnold J. See Morgan, M. jt. auth.

MANDELSTAM, Janet
Summer on the continental campus. Sat R 52:56+ F 15 '69

MANDER, John
In defense of the fifties. Commentary 48:63-7 S; 12+ D '69

MANDEVILLE, Paul F. and Maholick, L. T.
Changing points of emphasis in training the community's natural counselors. bibliog Ment Hy 53:208-13 Ap '69

MANDL, Matthew
Cure color TV gremlins. Radio-Electr 40:35-7 Ap '69

MANDRAKE book shop, Cambridge, Mass. See Booksellers and bookselling—Massachusetts

MANET, Eduardo
Les nonnes. Criticism
New Yorker 45:101-2 Je 14 '69

MANEUVERS, Military. See Military maneuvers

MANFREDI, Mario, and Castellucci, Vincent
C-Fiber responses in the ventrolateral column of the cat spinal cord. bibliog Science 165:1920-2 S 5 '69

MANGANESE
Large manganese deposit found in Lake Michigan. il Chem 42:23 F '69

MANGELSDORF, P. C. jr, and others
Potassium enrichments in interstitial waters of recent marine sediments. bibliog Science 165:171-4 Jl 11 '69

MANGER groups. See Christmas cribs

MANGIERI, Adolph A.
AA-C-D-battery charger. Pop Electr 31:33-5+ O '69
IC frequency spotter/standard. Pop Electr 31:27-32 Ag '69
Varicap front end AM tuner. Pop Electr 30:76-7+ My '69
Varicaps. Pop Electr 30:69-71 My '69

MANGIONE, Anthony Roy
Advice for beginning teachers. Clear House 44:41-2 S '69

MANGUM, Garth L.
Why, how, and whence of manpower programs. Ann Am Acad 385:50-62 S '69

MANGUS, Marlyn
Bend of the Niger River; with biographical sketch. por Natur Hist 78:6, 26-37 Ja '69

MANHATTAN. See New York (city)

MANHATTAN (tanker) See Ice breaking vessels

MANHATTAN project. See Atomic bombs—History

MANHATTAN school of music
Musical events; Massenet's Thaïs. W. Sargeant. New Yorker 45:137 My 17 '69
Report: New York; concert performance of E. Granados' Goyescas. H. E. Phillips. il Opera N 33:24 My 17 '69
Report: New York; production of Massenet's Thaïs. S. Jenkins. il Opera N 33:22 Je 14 '69
Report: New York; productions. W. D. Zimmer. Opera N 33:30-1 F 1 '69

MANHEIMER, Dean I. and others
Marijuana use among urban adults. Science 166:1544-5 D 19 '69

MANIATIS, George M. and others
Tadpole antibodies against frog hemoglobin and their effect on development. bibliog Science 165:67-9 Jl 4 '69

MANICURING
Dazzling show of hands. il Seventeen 28:102-3 O '69
Fine show of hands. il Redbook 132:108-12 Ap '69

MANIFOLDS
Big breather. B. Lang. il Hot Rod 22:48-9 Jl '69
Short stack to go! street tunnel ram manifolds. J. Dianna. il Hot Rod 22:54-6 My '69
Triple-duty dandy. J. Thawley. il Hot Rod 22:62-3 N '69

MANILA
Philippine cultural center
Manila's new cultural center. P. Brooks. il Art in Am 57:140-2 N '69
Winner in the Philippines; Cultural center. S. Fleming. Hi Fi 19:MA25+ D '69

MANIPULATION (securities)
More things change. il Forbes 104:76+ N 15 '69
Rise and fall of Parvin-Dohrmann. il Fortune 80:163-4+ D '69

MANIPULATORS
See also
Man amplifiers

MANKER, Don
Possessions; poem. Ladies Home J 86:32 F '69

MANKIEWICZ, Frank F.
Columnists; Washington's third pair. il por Time 94:68 Ag 15 '69

MANKIN, Valentin
Russia's gold medalist Valentin Mankin, talks of his training and racing experiences; interview, ed. by V. Lapin. por Yachting 126:63+ Jl '69

MANKS, Dorothy S.
F. Kingdon-Ward, plant hunter extraordinary. Horticulture 46:20-1+ O '68
George Washington, horticulturist. Horticulture 46:30-2 Ag '68

MANLEY, Norman Washington
Black power in the Caribbean. J. J. McEleney. America 121:557-8 D 6 '69

MANN, Dean L. and others
Molecular heterogeneity of human lymphoid (HL-A) alloantigens. bibliog Science 163:1460-2 Mr 28 '69

MANN, Lewis T. jr, and others
Antithrombin III: protection against death after injection of thromboplastin. bibliog Science 166:517-18 O 24 '69

MANN, Margery
View from the Bay. See issues of Popular photography
When the people draw a curtain. Pop Phot 65:91+ D '69
about
Can whitey do a beautiful black picture show? il Pop Phot 64:82+ My '69

MANN, Milton
Teacher's guide to Japan. bibliog Sr Schol 94:Schol Teach 16-18 F 28 '69

MANN, Murray Gell-. See Gell-Mann, M.

MANN, Peggy
Easter, island of mysteries. Harp Baz 102:132+ My '69

MANN, Polly
On dressing the bisque-headed, ball-jointed doll; interview, ed. by C. H. Fawcett. Hobbies 74:42+ Ag '69
about
Polly Mann has done it again! C. H. Fawcett. il Hobbies 73:38 F '69

MANN, Theodore
Trumpets of the Lord. T. Lewis. America 120:599 My 17 '69

MANN, Thomas
Death in Venice: the aesthetic object as dream guide. R. Tarbox. bibliog Am Imago 26:123-44 Sum '69
Thomas Mann's Death in Venice. H. Slochower. bibliog f Am Imago 26:99-122 Sum '69

MANN, Thomas Clifton
Excerpt from testimony before the subcommittee on Housing and urban affairs, October 15, 1969. Cong Digest 48:300+ D '69

MANN, William
How I got rid of monstrous Mildred; or, What I think about Die frau ohne schatten. Opera N 33:24-5 Mr 8 '69

MANNE, Cynthia, pseud.
Law and hair down Mexico way. Commonweal 91:36-7, 415 O 10 '69, Ja 9 '70

MANNED orbiting laboratory. See Space stations

MANNED orbiting space station. See Space stations

MANNED space flights. See Space flight—Manned flights

MANNED spacecraft center. See United States—Manned spacecraft center

MANNED undersea research stations. See Underwater laboratories

MANNERISM (art)
Mannerism in the cinquecento madrigal? D. Harran. bibliog f il Mus Q 55:521-44 O '69
MANNERS, David X.
News for home owners. Am Home 72:58+ S '69
Six ways to make bad water good. Pop Mech 131:184-7+ My '69
MANNERS, William
There was a storm outside and a bit of frost within; excerpts from TR and Will: a friendship that split the Republican party. Am Heritage 21:24-5+ D '69
MANNERS. See Etiquette
MANNERS and customs
In defense of ceremony. F. Maynard. PTA Mag 63:22-4 Ap '69
Leisure; present and past; symposium. il Horizon 11:4-31 Spr '69
    See also
Amusements
Culture
Dating
Festivity
Hairdressing
Marriage customs and rites
Society, Primitive
Tipping
MANNES, Marya
Isn't anything obscene any more? McCalls 96:64+ S '69
MANNHEIM, L. A.
How sensitive is your meter? Mod Phot 33: 68-9+ Jl '69
MANNING, Archie
Answer to a foolish question. P. Putnam. il Sports Illus 31:50-1 N 24 '69
MANNING, Elizabeth
Why colors run; poem. Nat R 21:648 Jl 1 '69
MANNING, Frank
Gettysburg address for art educators. Sch Arts 68:48 Je '69
MANNING, Gordon P.
Easy-to-build galley food locker. Motor B 124:126-7 S '69
MANNIX, James N.
Crappies for all, all year. pors Outdoor Life 143:60-1+ F '69
MANOMETERS
Amateur scientist; how to make photographs in polymer and build a sensitive pressure gauge. K. Adams. il Sci Am 221:132-3 D '69
MANON; opera. See Massenet, J.
MANPOWER
Forecasting manpower needs. J. W. Walker. bibliog f Harvard Bsns R 47:152-4+ Mr '69
    See also
Labor supply
Labor supply—United States
United States—Population
MANPOWER and education. See Education and manpower
MANSFIELD, Eileen
Instant awareness: a governor's conference spreads the word. por ALA Bul 63:773-7 Je '69
MANSFIELD, Michael Joseph
Critical look at Congress; interview. por U S News 67:25-7 D 1 '69
Excerpt from debate, June 19 and 23, 1969. Cong Digest 48:214+ Ag '69
Pentagon promises to observe congressional curbs on research. Science 166:1387-8 D 12 '69

about
Mansfield: a leader with a new look. por U S News 67:16 Ag 11 '69
New move to reduce U.S. forces in Europe. il por U S News 67:6 D 8 '69
Polite indictment. por Time 94:23 O 17 '69
Senate's responsibility. E. Gruening. Nation 208:748-9 Je 16 '69
Vietnam: the lull hits home. il Newsweek 74:23-4 N 3 '69
MANSON, Charles
Case of the hypnotic hippie. il por Newsweek 74:30-2+ D 15 '69
Charlie Manson: one man's family. S. V. Roberts. il pors N Y Times Mag p 10-11+ Ja 4 '70
Demon of death valley. il por Time 94:22+ D 12 '69
Family jams incorporated. por Newsweek 75:59 Ja 19 '70
Martian model. il por Time 95:44 Ja 19 '70
Monstrous Manson family; with statements by D. Smith and R. Smith. P. O'Neil and others. il pors Life 67:2A, 20-31 D 19 '69
MANTEL, Rudy
Man who made his dreams come true. J. Gilbert. il pors Flying 85:88-92 Jl '69

MANTELLI, Eugenia
Eugenia Mantelli. por Hobbies 74:36+ N '69
MANTEY, Julius R.
What of priestly absolution? Chr Today 13: 12+ Ja 31 '69
MANTHORNE, Jane
Outlook tower; books of interest to high-school students. See issues of Horn book magazine to June, 1969
MANTLE, Mickey
Mickey Mantles' decision; ed. by G. Astor. pors Look 33:28-32+ Mr 18 '69

about
Mantle of greatness. il por Time 93:52 Mr 14 '69
Mickey. Sports Illus 30:9 Mr 10 '69
MANUAL labor. See Work
MANUFACTURERS, National association of. See National association of manufacturers
MANUFACTURES
Labor turnover rates; tables. See issues of Monthly labor review
Manufacturing, missing link in corporate strategy. W. Skinner. il Harvard Bsns R 47: 136-45 My '69
    See also
Products, New

Statistics
Ratios of manufacturing; with table (cont) il Duns R 94:107-11 N '69

Wages and hours
Report on incentive pay in maufacturing industries. G. L. Stelluto. il Mo Labor R 92: 49-53 Jl '69
Report on wage developments in manufacturing, 1968; with tables. J. Kinyon. Mo Labor R 92:33-9 Ag '69
MANURE, Liquid

Handling
See Fertilizers and manures—Handling
MANURE handling. See Fertilizers and manures—Handling
MANURE lagoons
Labor-free manure disposal? R. Wilmore. il Farm J 93:26C-26D Ag '69
Ways to handle livestock waste; use a lagoon. il Suc Farm 67:48-9 My '69
MANURES. See Fertilizers and manures
MANUSCRIPT division. See United States—Library of Congress—Manuscript division
MANUSCRIPTS
Quarterly notes from the manuscript division of the Library of Congress. K. V. Hostick. Hobbies 74:140 O '69
Sources of manuscript material. D. Harris. Hobbies 74:139-41 S '69
    See also
Archives
Dead Sea scrolls

Prices
Hamilton galleries has another succesful season. H. K. Thompson, jr. il Hobbies 74:140 D '69
MANUSCRIPTS, Hebrew
Birds' heads and graven images. C. Roth. Commentary 47:80-3 Je '69; Reply. R. Wischnitzer. 48:1 Ag '69
MANUSCRIPTS, Illuminated. See Illumination of books and manuscripts
MANUSCRIPTS, Maya
Five Mayan eclipses in thirteen years. H. E. Harber. il Sky & Tel 37:72-4 F '69
MANUSCRIPTS, Preparation of. See Printing—Copy preparation
MANUSCRIPTS, Rejected. See Editors and editing
MANYAS, LAKE
Lake Manyas: a Turkish park for birds. C. E. Adelson. il Nat Parks 43:25-7 Ap '69
MANZANITAS. See Bearberries
MANZÙ, Giacomo
Monument for a humanist. il Time 94:54 Ag 15 '69
Pope John and the sculptor; excerpts from An artist and the pope. C. B. Pepper. Read Digest 94:200-4+ My '69
MAO, Tse-tung
Chinese communist leadership. K. Y. Hsu. bibliog f Cur Hist 57:129-34+ S '69
Economics of Maoism. J. Gray. il Bul Atom Sci 25:42-51 F '69
Locked in generation. D. Hillis. Chr Today 13:10-11 My 23 '69
Man picked to succeed Mao. il por U S News 66:21 Ap 14 '69
Mao and the new mandate. E. Snow. New Repub 160:17-21 My 10 '69
Mao papers: a new view of China's chairman. il por Time 94:32-3 D 12 '69

MAO, Tse-tung—*Continued*
Mao's health and China's leadership. il por Time 94:24 S 26 '69
Moderating Mao. il por Newsweek 73:58+ Ap 14 '69
One-man diplomacy? R. Harris. il Bul Atom Sci 25:60-5 F '69
Out of the East, the people's war. A. Hope. il por Life 67:58-66B O 17 '69
Peking puzzles. por Time 94:41 O 10 '69
Red China: twenty years after. il por Newsweek 74:48-9 O 13 '69
Thoughts of Mao. il Newsweek 74:54+ O 13 '69
MAOISM. See Communism—China (People's Republic)
MAP making. See Cartography
MAPLE
Count on maple trees for cooling summer shade. il Home Gard 56:52 O '69
MAPLE Leafs (hockey team) See Hockey teams
MAPLE syrup
See also
Cookery—Maple syrup
MAPPING, Aerial
Boosting the tuna catch: preparing isotherm maps with an airborne sensor. W. A. Scholes. il Sci N 96:338 O 11 '69
MAPS
Maps and pictures; Williamsburg, Va. J. M. Dolmetsch. il Antiques 95:138-44 Ja '69
See also
Atlases
Cartography
Geology—Maps
Ocean—Maps
Publishers and publishing—Maps
Weather maps
also subhead Maps under names of countries, states, etc. e.g. West Indies—Maps
MAPS, Early
Discovery of a world: early maps showing America. D. Pratt. il Antiques 96:900-6 D '69 (to be cont)
MAPS, Historical. See Geography, Historical—Maps
MAPS, Road. See Road maps, guides, etc.
MARABELLI, Vittorio M. and O'Donovan, L. J.
Children of Isolotto. America 120:706-9 Je 21 '69
MARANTA
Prayer plant. F. Kaltenbach. il(cover) Horticulture 46:8 N '68
MARANTZ, Robert, and others
Vinblastine-induced precipitation of microtubule protein. bibliog Science 165:498-9 Ag 1 '69
MARATHON dancing. See Dancing
MARATHON races. See Running
MARATHON water skiing. See Water skis and skiing
MARAVICH, Pete
I want to put on a show; ed. by C. Kirkpatrick. Sports Illus 31:39-42+ D 1 '69
about
Fastest gun in the west. H. L. Masin. il por Sr Schol 93:22 Ja 10 '69
Pete and Press Maravich. C. Coe. il pors Life 66:30-2+ F 7 '69
MARAVICH, Press
Pete and Press Maravich. C. Coe. il pors Life 66:30-2+ F 7 '69
MARAVIGNA, Maria. See Maravigna, P. jt. auth.
MARAVIGNA, Pietrina, and Maravigna, Maria
Mushrooms: wild and edible. il Horticulture 47:22-3+ S '69
MARBLE CANYON NATIONAL MONUMENT
Four additions to the National park system. Nat Parks 43:20 Mr '69
MARBLE PEAK trail. See Trails
MARBLE VALLEY dam (proposed) See Dams
MARBLEHEAD, Mass.
Christmas in the classroom. il Time 94:48 D 12 '69
MARBLES (game)
Secret of the Terribles; defending title of World marbles champions. il Time 93:84 Ap 11 '69
MARCELLA, Dennis
Face to face with an explosive Hawaiian inventor. A. Lum. por Seventeen 28:34 Ja '69
MARCH, B. E. and others
Reticulocytosis in response to dietary antioxidants. bibliog Science 164:1398-400 Je 20 '69
MARCH, Fred
Fund retailers broaden their wares. por Bsns W p88+ D 13 '69

MARCH, Joseph Moncure
Trade winds. J. Beatty, jr. Sat R 52:14 Je 7 '69
MARCH
On March: time to take stock: excerpt from The inland islands. J. W. Johnson. Nation 208:246-9 F 24 '69
MARCH on Washington, November 15, 1969.
See Vietnamese war, 1957- —Protests, demonstrations, etc. against—Marches on Washington, November 1969
MARCHANT, Maurice P.
Faculty-librarian conflict. bibliog por Library J 94:2886-9 S 1 '69
MARCHENKO, Anatolii
My testimony; tr. by M. Gnoutcheff and R. Nacht. Read Digest 95:193-6+ Ag '69
about
Behind the lines; story behind publishing of My testimony. Read Digest 95:15-16 Ag '69
MARCHES (music)
See also
Phonograph records—Marches (music)
MARCHESE, Dolores
Sand casting. Sch Arts 69:25 Ja '70
MARCHI, John Joseph
Around city hall. A. Logan. New Yorker 45:164+ O 11; 184-90 N 15 '69
Here comes the next mayor. R. Reeves. il pors N Y Times Mag p25-7+ N 2 '69
Marchi campaigning. New Yorker 45:37-8 S 20 '69
New politics and old. J. R. Coyne, jr. Nat R 21:1106-7+ N 4 '69
New York: the revolt of the average man. il por Time 94:15-20 O 3 '69
Who's for mayor. W. F. Buckley, jr. Nat R 21:299 Mr 25 '69
MARCHIORO, T. L. and others
Hemophilia: role of organ homografts. bibliog Science 163:188-90 Ja 10 '69
MARCIANO, Rocky
Rock showed 'em how, forty-nine out of forty-nine. il por Life 67:34 S 12 '69
Super fight. il Time 95:59 Ja 19 '70
MARCINKUS, Paul, bp
Counting Peter's pence; Institute for religious works. il Time 93:70 Ja 24 '69
MARCO Polo sheep hunting. See Argali hunting
MARCONA corporation
Iron ore gets piped aboard; slurry delivery. il Bsns W p 118 Ag 16 '69
MARCOR, incorporated
Marcor: how's it managing? one year after Montgomery Ward and Container corporation of America merger. R. Levy. il Duns R 94:26-9+ Ag '69
Ward's joins the now generation; merger with Container corp. il Bsns W p84-6+ Mr 22 '69
MARCOS, Ferdinand E.
Why the Philippines are drifting away from U.S; interview, ed. by K. M. Chrysler. por U S News 66:80-1 Mr 31 '69
about
Lawless and corrupt Philippines. A. Campbell. New Repub 160:15-17 My 17 '69
Making of a President. il por Newsweek 74:63 N 24 '69
Victory for Marcos. il por Time 94:39 N 21 '69
MARCOS, Imelda Romualdez
Winner in the Philippines. S. Fleming. por Hi Fi 19:MA+ D '69
MARCUS, Adrianne
Things you do not say; poem. Nation 208:278 Mr 3 '69
MARCUS, Donald M. and Cass, L. E.
Glycosphingolipids with Lewis blood group activity: uptake by human erythrocytes. bibliog Science 164:553-5 My 2 '69
MARCUS, Matthew
Boy who knows too much. N. M. Lobsenz. il por Redbook 133:74-5+ Je '69
MARCUS, Morton
Good and the useful. M. Randall. Poetry 115:57-60 O '69
MARCUS, Ruth
Small wonders. See issues of Good housekeeping
MARCUSE, Herbert
Student protest is nonviolent next to the society itself. N Y Times Mag p 137 My 4 '69
about
Herbert Marcuse or Milovan Djilas? I. Howe. Harper 239:84+ Jl '69
Improbable guru of surrealistic politics. I. Kristol. il por Fortune 80:191+ Jl '69
Marcuse. E. Stillman. il por Horizon 11:26-31 Sum '69

MARCUSE, Herbert—about—*Continued*
Marcuse and Goodwin tangle at Temple. J. Groutt. Commonweal 90:279-80 My 23 '69
Marcuse: ferment of hope. P. Clecak. Nation 208:765-8 Je 16 '69
Marcuse: the gospel of hate. J. Sparrow. Nat R 21:1068-9 O 21 '69
Marcuse's merits. D. Braybrooke. Trans-Action 6:51-4 O '69
Norman Vincent Peale of the left. M. Cohen. Atlan 223:108-10 Je '69

MARCZYNSKI, T. J. and others
Steady potential correlates of positive reinforcement: reward contingent positive variation. bibliog Science 163:301-4 Ja 17 '69

MARDER, Louis
Shakespeare through the ages. por Hobbies 74:98B-98E+ Ap; 98D-98E+ My '69

MARDIKIAN, Baitzar, and Glick, I. D.
Patient-staff meetings: a study of some aspects of content, tone, and speakers. Ment Hy 53:303-5 Ap '69

MAREK, George R.
Triumph of Felsenstein's La Traviata. Hi Fi 19:MA28-9+ F '69

MAREK's disease. See Poultry—Diseases and pests

MARGOLIES, John S.
Multimedia zoo. Arch Forum 130:86-91 Je '69
New town for New York city. Arch Forum 131:40-5 O '69
TV: the next medium. Art in Am 57:48-55 S '69

MARGOLIN, Jean Claude
Erasmus. UNESCO Courier 22:4-13 N '69

MARGOLIS, Art
Troubleshooter's casebook. Radio-Electr 40: 58-60 My '69

MARGOLIS, Ellen
What makes some children bad? Parents Mag 44:52-3+ My '69

MARGOLIS, Joseph Zalman
Margolis on responsibility in psychotherapy. A. M. Wheeler. bibliog Ment Hy 53:309-10 Ap '69

MARGOLSKEE, Jeanne
It takes brains to learn from forty-six black mice. por Seventeen 28:94+ Ja '69

MARGULIES, Stan
If it's Tuesday, this must be Belgium. Travel 131:72-5 Je '69

MARGULIS, Lynn, and others
Colchicine-inhibited cilia regeneration: explanation for lack of effect in tris buffer medium. bibliog Science 164:1177-8 Je 6 '69

MARIA Magdalena Barbara de Braganza, consort of Ferdinand VI, king of Spain
Queen's music master. R. Evett. Atlan 224: 172+ N '69

MARIA of New York. See Crummere, M. E.

MARIACHI festivals
Popular art styles in Mariachi festivals; San Francisco. A. E. Hippler. bibliog Am Imago 26:167-81 Sum '69

MARIAN Frances Brand, Sister. See Brand, M. F.

MARIANO Parra ballet español. See Ballet—Spain

MARIAS, Julian
Cognoscenti abroad. Julián Marías's Madrid. A. Goodfriend. Sat R 52:39-41 Je 14 '69

MARIE James Palmer, Sister. See Palmer, M. J

MARIGHELA, Carlos
Guerrilla war in the streets; with interview with a leader of the National students union, ed. by P. Kramer. il Newsweek 74: 66-8 D 8 '69

MARIGOLDS
Marigolds in the garden; preventing nematode damage to plants. P. M. Miller and J. F. Ahrens. il Horticulture 47:30-1 S '69
With various plants and animals, invading insects can be chased away. V. M. Crill. il Home Gard 56:56-7 O '69

MARIJUANA
Clinical and psychological effects of marihuana in man. A. T. Weil and others; discussion. bibliog Science 163:1144-5; 165:204 Mr 14, Jl 11 '69
Comparison of the effects of marihuana and alcohol on simulated driving performance. A. Crancer, jr. and others. bibliog il Science 164:851-4 My 16 '69; Discussion. 166: 640 O 31 '69
Crackdown; sentence of three and a half years in state prison for possession of marijuana. Nation 208:293-4 Mr 10 '69
Drug use and the law: a case for legalizing marijuana. J. Fort. Cur 113:4-13 D '69
How pot-smokers start. Sci Digest 66:57-8 Ag '69
In Vietnam: mama-san pushers vs. psyops. il Newsweek 73:108 Ap 21 '69

Is the pot user driven, or in the driver's seat? Time 94:64-5 Jl 25 '69
Little less illegal. New Repub 161:11 N 8 '69
Marihuana. L. Grinspoon. il Sci Am 221:17-25 D '69
Marijuana famine. B. Farrell. Life 67:20B Ag 22 '69
Marijuana legislation. America 121:378 N 1 '69
Marijuana paradox; with reports by J. Howard and J. Goddard. il Life 67:26B-35 O 31 '69
Marijuana use among urban adults. D. I. Manheimer and others. Science 166:1544-5 D 19 '69
Marijuana: what it is, and isn't. il U S News 67:48-50 O 13 '69
Mexico's war on marijuana. il U S News 67: 21-3 D 29 '69
Mild intoxicant. Sci Am 220:43-4 F '69
Nixon drug law: a crucial fault. Life 67:32 S 5 '69
Nixon's new plan to deal with the marijuana problem. U S News 67:14 O 27 '69
No marijuana for adolescents. K. Angel. il N Y Times Mag p 170+ N 30 '69
On smoking pot; report of the Indian hemp drugs commission. Trans-Action 7:8+ D '69
Operation showboat: Mexican border crackdown. Nation 209:365-6 O 13 '69
Penalties and programs; national drive against narcotics and other drugs. Time 94:65 Jl 25 '69
Personal business; if your teen-ager uses pot. Bsns W p 137-8 My 17 '69
Pinning down the weed. il Sci N 96:263-4 S 27 '69
Pondering pot: effects of pot-smoking. Chr Cent 86:1270 O 8 '69
Pop drugs: the high as a way of life. il Time 94:68-70+ S 26 '69
Pot spotters; U.S.-Mexican border. il Newsweek 74:81-2 O 6 '69
Pot: year of the famine; Mexican border crackdown. il Newsweek 74:36-7 S 22 '69
Scarcity, higher prices, crooks; effects of crackdown on drug trade. il U S News 67: 48-9 O 13 '69
Scientific report, the effects of marijuana on human beings; research by Boston university school of medicine. N. E. Zinberg and A. T. Weil. il N Y Times Mag p28-9+ My 11 '69; Discussion. p22+ Je 8 '69
Some questions and answers about marijuana. il Sr Schol 94:11-13 Mr 21 '69
Telltale trash; R. Edwards case. il Time 94: 54+ O 17 '69
Trial of Elaine Murphy. E. Keiffer. il Good H 168:12+ My '69
Vietcong's secret weapon: marijuana. A. F. Gonzalez, jr. il Sci Digest 65:14-18 Ap '69
Vogues in vice: views of Margaret Mead. K. Crawford. Newsweek 74:45 N 10 '69
Warning: steer clear of THC. R. H. Berg. Look 33:46 Ap 15 '69
What about marijuana? Nat R 21:268+ Mr 25 '69; Discussion. 21:451 My 6 '69
What is marihuana? questions and answers. il Todays Ed 58:39-41 Mr '69
Why so many teenagers fall for marijuana; with group-discussion program. R. D. Johnson. Parents Mag 44:22+, 58-61+ Mr '69
Will cigarettes take to pot? Bsns W p28 S 6 '69
Your adolescent's health: drug abuse among teenagers. L. W. Sauer. il PTA Mag 63: 25-6 F '69
See also
THC

MARIN, Peter
Fiery vehemence of youth. PTA Mag 63:15-17 bibliog(p35) Je '69

MARIN COUNTY, Calif.
Few hazards of the good life. K. Lamott. Horizon 11:26-9 Spr '69

Housing
High interest, medium density on a hillside site in semi-rural area. il Arch Rec 146: 184-5 S '69

MARINACCIO, Gene
Choreographer became: me! V. H. Swisher. il por Dance Mag 43:39-41 S '69

MARINARO, Ed
Players of the week. Sports Illus 31:59 O 27 '69

MARINARO, Vincent C.
Hidden hatch. Outdoor Life 144:48-51+ Jl '69

MARINAS
Crisis: land and water parking problems. Parks & Rec 4:15 O '69
Kai Kruger on Kiel: a look to the future; preparation of 1972 Olympic games. K. Kruger. il Yachting 126:53+ D '69

MARINAS—*Continued*
Marina expansion in the Med. K. Bramham.
il Yachting 126:58+ D '69
Marinas, marinas, and . . . A. Anable. jr.
il Motor B 123:238-41 Ja '69
MARINE, Gene
America the raped; excerpt. Ramp Mag 7:72-4
Ja 25 '69
—and Erlich, Reese
School's out. Ramp Mag 7:19-25 D 14 '68
—See Goldberg, A. jt. auth.
MARINE bacteria. See Bacteria, Marine
MARINE biology
Nature of oceanic life. J. D. Isaacs. il Sci
Am 221:146-60+ bibliog(p285) S '69
Oceanic drug chest. J. L. Arehart. il Sea
Front 15:98-107 Mr '69
See also
Benthos
Fresh water biology
Marine resources
Plankton
Spawning
MARINE cookery. See Cookery, Marine
MARINE corps. See United States—Marine
corps
MARINE corrosion. See Corrosion and anti-
corrosives
MARINE deposits. See Marine sediments
MARINE diesel engines. See Diesel engines,
Marine
MARINE ecology
Aquaculture. J. E. Bardach. bibliog il Science
161:1098-106 S 13 '68; Correction. 163:493
Ja 31 '69
Bivalves: spatial and size-frequency distri-
butions of two intertidal species. J. B. C.
Jackson; discussion. Science 162:1509-10;
163:830 D 27 '68. F 21 '69
Central American sea-level canal; possible
biological effects. L. Rubinoff; discussion.
Science 162:511-13, 1329; 163:760+ N 1, D 20
'68; F 21 '69
Ecology of the deep-sea benthos. H. L.
Sanders and R. R. Hessler. bibliog il Sci-
ence 163:1419-24 Mr 28 '69; Reply with re-
joinder. A. H. Clarke. 166:1033-4 N 21 '69
New canal: what about bioenvironmental re-
search? M. Mueller. Science 163:165-7 Ja
10 '69
Oil in the ecosystem. R. W. Holcomb. Sci-
ence 166:204-6 O 10 '69
Thermal pollution and aquatic life. J. R.
Clark. il Sci Am 220:18-27 bibliog(p 148)
Mr '69
MARINE engine belts. See Belting
MARINE engine parts
How to get replacement parts for your
ancient mariner. M. J. Schultz. il Motor
B 124:66-7 N '69
MARINE engineering
Technology and the ocean. W. Bascom. il
Sci Am 221:198-204+ S '69
See also
Nautical instruments
MARINE engines
How soon a steam engine for your boat? J.
Joseph. il Motor B 124:34-5+ Jl '69
Power picture. C. Miller. il Motor B 124:33-
45+ O '69
Stern drives. il Motor B 123:168-71 Ja '69
Yachting's boat show. il Yachting 125:133+
Ja '69
See also
Electric engines, Outboard
Gas and oil engines, Outboard
Gas turbines, Marine
Steam turbines, Marine

Cooling

Air cooled engine for your boat. J. Seville.
il Mech Illus 65:70-1+ Ag '69
Cooling. M. Schultz. il Motor B 124:128-9 S
'69

Fuel consumption

How many miles per gallon? C. Miller. il
Motor B 124:54-5 S '69

Fuel feeding

See also
Fuel pumps

Ignition

How it works: marine ignition. C. Miller.
il Motor B 123:103-4 Je '69

Maintenance and repair

Engine operation and tuning for peak ef-
ficiency. C. Miller. Motor B 123:97-8+ Je
'69
Now! Enjoy boating all winter. B. Weis. il
Mech Illus 65:96-7+ N '69
Readying your engine the relaxed way. C.
Miller. il Motor B 123:78-9 Ap '69
Use your engine ear. C. Miller. il Motor B
123:66-7+ Mr '69

What do you know about engine mainte-
nance. H. C. Langer. jr. il Yachting 125:
72-3+ Ap '69
MARINE fauna
Cruising in a marine zoo; Gulf of Cortez.
C. L. Cadieux. il Yachting 126:60-1+ S
'69
See also
Barnacles
Cetacea
Corals
Marine biology
Plankton
Sea horses
Starfishes
MARINE fauna, Conservation of. See Wildlife
conservation
MARINE festivals. See Regattas
MARINE flora
See also
Diatoms
Marine biology
MARINE fuel pumps. See Fuel pumps
MARINE gages. See Gages
MARINE gas turbines. See Gas turbines,
Marine
MARINE geology. See Submarine geology
MARINE instruments. See Nautical instru-
ments
MARINE insurance. See Insurance, Marine
MARINE language. See Naval art and science
—Terminology
MARINE law. See Maritime law
MARINE mineral resources
Gold in the sea. F. Libby. il Sea Front 15:
232-41 Jl '69
MARINE museums. See Naval museums
MARINE navigation. See Navigation
MARINE painting
Joseph Lee. Painter. A. P. Erskine. il An-
tiques 95:806-11 Je '69
Marine paintings of Arden von Dewitz. J.
Lovoos. il Am Artist 33:54-60+ S '69
Rehabilitation through art. N. Kent. il Am
Artist 33:32+ S '69
MARINE pharmacology. See Pharmacology
MARINE pollution. See Sea water—Pollution
MARINE radio telephone. See Radio telephone
on ships, boats. etc.
MARINE resources
Coastal waters and the Nation; address,
February 3, 1969. E. Wenk, jr. Vital
Speeches 35:349-52 Mr 15 '69
Drugs from the sea. il Time 94:82 S 5 '69
Food resources of the ocean. S. J. Holt. il
Sci Am 221:178-82+ bibliog(p286) S '69
Nurseries of the sea. W. Marx. il UNESCO
Courier 22:13-17+ Mr '69
Oceans: man's last great resource. C. Pell. il
Sat R 52:19-21+ Q 11 '69
Ocean's riches. W. M. Stephens. il Nat Wild-
life 7:4-11 Ap '69
Photosynthesis and fish production in the sea.
J. H. Ryther. bibliog il Science 166:72-6 O
3 '69
Physical resources of the ocean. E. Wenk,
jr. il Sci Am 221:166-76 bibliog(p286) S '69
20 billion dollars to tap riches of the sea? il
U S News 66:62-4 Mr 31 '69
See also
Fisheries
Marine mineral resources

Laws and legislation

Bare-bones program; marine policy. il Sci N
96:372 O 25 '69
MARINE rope. See Rope
MARINE science, engineering and resources,
Commission on. See United States—Marine
science, engineering and resources. Commission on
MARINE sciences council. See United States—
National council for marine sciences and
engineering development
MARINE sediments
Absolute dating of Caribbean cores P6304-8
and P6304-9. E. Rona and C. Emiliani; reply. W. S. Broecker and T. L. Ku. bibliog
il Science 166:404-6 O 17 '69; rejoinder. 166:
1551-2 D 19 '69
Carbonate sediments: oriented lithified
samples from the North Atlantic. G. A.
Bartlett and R. G. Greggs. bibliog il Science 166:740-1 N 7 '69
Florida submergence curve revised: its relation to coastal sedimentation rates. D. W.
Scholl and others. bibliog il Science 163:
562-4 F 7 '69
Geomagnetic reversal in Brunhes normal
polarity epoch. J. D. Smith and J. H. Foster. bibliog il Science 163:565-7 F 7 '69

MARINE sediments—*Continued*
Mineral source and transport in waters of the Gulf of Mexico and Caribbean Sea. M. B. Jacobs and M. Ewing. bibliog il Science 163: 805-9 F 21 '69
Oceanic sediment volumes and continental drift. J. Gilluly. bibliog Science 166:992-4 N 21 '69
Potassium enrichments in interstitial waters of recent marine sediments. P. C. Mangelsdorf, jr. and others. bibliog il Science 165: 171-4 Jl 11 '69
Suspended particulate matter: concentration in the major oceans. M. B. Jacobs and M. Ewing. bibliog il Science 163:380-3 Ja 24 '69
MARINE surveying. See Hydrographic surveying
MARINE surveyors. See Surveyors, Marine
MARINE worms
   See also
   Annelids
   Palolo worms
MARINE zoology. See Marine fauna
MARINER probes. See Space probes
MARINERS compass. See Compass
MARININ, [Urii]
   Maneuver in outer space. Space World F-3-63:48 Mr '69
MARINOT, Maurice
   Marinot glass on exhibit at Corning museum. il Hobbies 74:118 S '69
MARIOLOGY. See Mary, Virgin—Theology
MARIPOSA lilies
   Mariposa lilies. Horticulture 47:11+ My '69
MARIS, Roger
   Maris and the Babe, move over! M. Mulvoy. il Sports Illus 31:22-5 Jl 7 '69
MARITAL counseling. See Marriage counseling
MARITAL infidelity. See Sexual ethics
MARITIME air forces Mediterranean. See Nato —Armed forces
MARITIME day, National. See National maritime day
MARITIME industry. See Shipping
MARITIME law
   On owning the ocean. M. A. Gruber. il Sea Front 15:170-9 My '69
   Why barges break the mixing rule. il Bsns W p 104+ Ja 10 '70
   See also
   Boats and boating—Laws and regulations
   Insurance, Marine
MARITIME meteorology. See Meteorology, Maritime
MARITIME museums. See Naval museums
MARITIME workers
   See also
   Strikes—United States—Maritime workers
MARK, Richard E. and others
   Cellulose: refutation of a folded-chain structure. bibliog Science 164:72-3 Ap 4 '69
MARK Twain, pseud. See Clemens, S. L.
MARK (money) See Money—Germany (Federal Republic)
MARKERT, Russell
   Hide your daughters, here comes Russ Markert. R. Roman. il pors Dance Mag 43:46-9+ S '69
MARKESON, Don
   Piezoelectric igniter generates instant flames. Electr World 82:72 N '69
MARKET carts. See Carts
MARKET hunting. See Poaching
MARKET research
   New markets, think before you leap; excerpts from The marketing mode—pathways to corporate growth. T. Levitt. bibliog f il Harvard Bsns R 47:53-67 My '69
   Techniques in marketing research. J. F. Dash and C. Berenson. bibliog Harvard Bsns R 47:14-16+ S '69
   They call it instant research: Maptek reports on what's ahead in electronics. il Bsns W p62+ Ja 25 '69
   Women sound off about grocery stores; Consumer dialogs; discussion. il Changing T 22:41-3 D '68
   See also
   Nielsen, A. C, company
MARKET statistics
   Bigness is a numbers game. S. Rose. il Fortune 80:112-15+ N '69
MARKET surveys
   Beyond market segmentation. N. L. Barnett. bibliog f il Harvard Bsns R 47:152-4+ Ja '69
MARKETING
   Forgotten generation; over sixty-five market. il Forbes 103:22-4+ Ja 15 '69
   How to rationalize your marketing risks. M. R. Greene. il Harvard Bsns R 47:114-23 My '69

What's new. W. E. Swegle. See issues of Successful farming
   See also
   Auctions
   Distribution of goods
   Franchise system
   Negro market
   Retail trade
   Roadside marketing
   Sales promotion
   Wholesale trade
      also subhead Marketing under various subjects, e.g. Aluminum—Marketing
MARKETING, Cooperative
   House divided; success breeds conflicts in cooperative retail groups. Forbes 103:32-3 Je 15 '69
MARKETING research. See Market research
MARKETS, Black. See Black markets
MARKETS, Farmers
   We go to Farmers market. V. T. Habeeb. il Am Home 72:92-4+ My '69
MARKETS, Roadside. See Roadside marketing
MARKETS for authors. See Authors and publishers
MARKETTE, Frank
   Focus on sound. Pop Phot 64:18+ Mr '69
MARKHAM, James. See Spritzer, M. jt. auth.
MARKING (students) See Grading and marking (students)
MARKLE, A. J.
   Unfair to feet. Sat R 52:6 Ag 2 '69
MARKO, Harold
   SOS—no help needed. S. Margetts. por Duns R 93:53+ Ja '69
MARKOVIC, Stevan
   Bodyguard. il por Time 93:24 F 21 '69
MARKOVICH, Alexander
   ABCs of taking the misery out of moving. Mech Illus 65:56-8+ Je '69
   And now, non foods from test tubes. Mech Illus 65:67-9+ S '69
   Facts on a big-pay job. Mech Illus 65:71-3+ O '69
   It's in to own a truck. Am Home 72:30+ Ap '69
   Light trucks for work & play. Mech Illus 65:165-7+ F '69
   New exercise gadgets to keep you fit. Mech Illus 65:43-5+ S '69
   PM tests Ford's new $4800 motor home. Pop Mech 131:116-19+ Je '69
   Those small sporty sedans. Pop Mech 131: 106-9+ Ja '69
MARKOVITS, Andrew S.
   Are eyeglasses inevitable? Mech Illus 65:59 F '69
   Quick home guide to first aid. Mech Illus 65:44-5+ Jl '69
   Sensible weight-watching diet for men. Mech Illus 65:48-9 Ag '69
   What do those chest pains mean? Mech Illus 65:43-5+ Je '69
MARKOW, Jack
   Cartoonist Q's. See issues of Writer's digest
MARKOWITZ, Harold, and others
   Immunosuppressive activity of concanavalin A. bibliog Science 163:476 Ja 31 '69
MARKS, Bruce
   Toni Lander and Bruce Marks; on and off stage; interview. ed. by B. Coffey. pors Dance Mag 43:34-9+ Ag '69
MARKS, E. P. and Leopold, R. A.
   Cockroach leg regeneration: effects of ecdysterone in vitro. bibliog Science 167:61-2 Ja 2 '70
MARKS, J.
   New humor. Esquire 72:218-20+ D '69
   Pop music. Vogue 154:346+ S 1 '69
MARKS, Jane
   Students underground. Mlle 70:150-1+ D '69
MARKS, Leonard H.
   Ambasssador Marks holds press briefing on the Intelsat conference; February 20, 1969. Dept State Bul 60:224-30 Mr 17 '69
   Intelsat conference opens at Washington; with welcoming remarks, February 24, 1969. Dept State Bul 60:232-4 Mr 17 '69
MARKSMANSHIP. See Shooting
MARKUS, Bob
   It's never been a question of whether I'd win at Indianapolis or not, but when. Motor T 21:57+ Ag '69
MARLBORO festival of music. See Music festivals—Vermont
MARLBOROUGH sounds. See Cook Strait
MARLER, Peter
   Teaching songbirds how to sing. B. Ford. il pors Sci Digest 66:20-5 Jl '69
MARLEY, Doone
   Aegean Turkey. Harp Baz 102:144+ Mr '69
MARLEY, Faye
   Helping the doctors. Sci N 95:97-8 Ja 25 '69

MARLIN fishing
Fishing with Bing; tale of a marlin. D. Davis. il Travel & Camera 32:84-5+ Ag '69
Marlin lover of Mazatlán. R. F. Jones. il Sports Illus 30:42-4+ Mr 11 '69
Stalking the red-nosed captain. M. Shulman. il Field & S 73:60-1+ Ap '69

MARLOW, Peter O.
Paintings at the Wadsworth atheneum. Antiques 96:745-53 N '69

MARLOWE, Christopher
Edward II. Criticism
Time 94:71-2 S 19 '69

MARLOWE, Eleanor
World's greatest cookery book. Am Home 72:40+ D '69

MARMES man. See Man, Prehistoric

MARMOL, Mario Barraco. See Barraco Mármol, M.

MARMOR, M. F. and Gorman, A. L. F.
Membrane potential as the sum of ionic and metabolic components. bibliog Science 167:65-7 Ja 2 '70

MARMOSETS
Hepatitis in marmosets: induction of disease with coded specimens from a human volunteer study. A. W. Holmes and others. bibliog il Science 165:816-17 Ag 22 '69

MARNEY, Carlyle
Toward Judah. Chr Cent 86:1345-8 O 22 '69

MARPLES, Mary J.
Life on the human skin; with biographical sketch. Sci Am 220:18, 108-15 Ja '69

MARQUETTE school of medicine, Milwaukee, Wis.
Marquette school of medicine: state aid and self improvement. J. Walsh. Science 166:1491-4 D 19 '69

MARQUEZ, Gabriel Garcia. See García Márquez, G.

MARR, David
(tr) See Nguyen-van-Minh, pseud. Jail notes of a young Vietnamese

MARRAKESH
Marrakech. P. Bosworth. il Holiday 46:44-7+ D '69

MARRIAGE
Are we the last married generation? H. Van Horne. il McCalls 96:69+ My '69
Are you a trapped housewife? excerpts from How to stay married. N. M. Lobsenz and C. W. Blackburn. Read Digest 95:68-71 S '69
Battle of the sexes; theories of G. R. Bach and P. Wyden. Newsweek 73:58 F 24 '69
Can this marriage be saved? ed. by D. C. Disney. See occasional issues of Ladies home journal
Elementary structures of kinship, by C. Levi-Strauss. Review
New Repub 161:26-30 Jl 12 '69. R. Fox
Experiments in marriage; group families in Sweden and Denmark. M. Durham. il Life 67:38-48A Ag 15 '69
Fight together, stay together. il Time 93:64+ F 21 '69
Footloose, but not fancy-free; fugitive husbands. Time 94:57 Ag 22 '69
How to get alone with your husband. J. Bradford. Read Digest 94:71-4 My '69
How to plan a successful vacation; danger time for marriage. E. Havemann. Read Digest 94:99-102 Ap '69
I love him, but do I like him? D. A. Sugarman and R. Hochstein. Seventeen 28:152-3+ F '69
If your husband takes you for granted. J. Brothers. Good H 168:52+ My '69
In praise of May-December marriages; Time essay. il Time 93:34-5 F 21 '69
Losers. D. Fletcher. il Redbook 133:12+ Jl '69
Love, honor, and discuss! M. Longwell. Farm J 93:44A-44B Je '69
Love, honor, and obey. A. S. Bustanoby. Chr Today 13:3-4 Je 6 '69
Lovers in marriage, by L. Evely. Review
America 120:256-7 Mr 1 '69. M. Passantino
Man talk; all the things you are. D. Newman and R. Benton. il Mlle 70:44 D '69
Minister and his wife. R. M. Smucker. Chr Today 13:3-4 Je 20 '69
Morals, marriage and youth; discussion at the Dutch council. H. Fleddermann and F. L. Ingram. America 120:194-6 F 15 '69; Reply. H. McKemie. 120:317 Mr 22 '69
Newsletter of marriage (cont) G. Seaman and B. Seaman. Ladies Home J 86:56 Mr '69
Parenthood should wait! M. M. Hunt. Read Digest 94:49-50+ F '69
Problem of making connections. J. Didion. Life 67:34 D 5 '69

Reflections on God in marriage. G. Chamberlain and S. Chamberlain. il Cath World 210:11-14 O '69
Retirement; danger time for marriages? C. Rice. Har Yrs 9:46-8 My '69
Right way to fight a marriage. F. Davis. Read Digest 94:97-100 Je '69
Suspicion. il Good H 168:12+ Je '69
Timing of our lives. H. L. Browning. il Trans-Action 6:22-7 O '69
Under twenty-one; quiz about marriage. S. Reice and L. Singer. il McCalls 96:36+ Je '69
Wedding bells for the '70s; marriages booming again. il U S News 67:66-7 D 8 '69
What makes a loving marriage? symposium, ed. by M. Mead. il Redbook 132:74-5+ F '69
What wives can do to solve the communication problem; ed. by M. Lane. C. W. Menninger. Read Digest 95:211-12+ Jl '69
What would really make you happy? S. Blum. il Redbook 132:49+ Ja '69
Why some marriages fail. L. Kavaler. il Parents Mag 44:46-7+ F '69
Why we don't want children. L. Michels. Redbook 134:10+ Ja '70
Will your marriage be successful? questions from Retirement marriage. W. C. McKain. Har Yrs 9:49 My '69
You, too, can find connubial chaos. W. Stanton. il Read Digest 95:89-92 Jl '69
Young lovers of the world, unite! But don't get married yet. A. Gross. Mlle 69:151+ S '69
Young wife's world. H. Valentine. See issues of Good housekeeping
See also
Alimony
Celibacy
Illegitimacy
Intermarriage of races
Love
Sex relations
Sexual ethics
Teen-age marriage
War marriages
Weddings
Wives

Annulment

Annulment of marriage. M. N. Hartman. Ann Am Acad 383:89-100 My '69
What Catholic bishops voted. U S News 66:10 Ap 28 '69

Handbooks, manuals, etc.

Sex manual revolution. M. Seligson il Life 67:21 D 5 '69

Italy

Divorce in the church through Italian eyes. H. ten Kortenaar. Commonweal 89:696-8 Mr 7 '69

Japan

Eyes have it; professional matchmaker. Time 93:39 Mr 7 '69

Liberia

My husband bought me for $40 and a chicken. S. McAndrews. il Read Digest 94:163-6 F '69

United States

See Marriage

MARRIAGE (canon law)
Divorce in the church through Italian eyes. H. ten Kortenaar. Commonweal 89:696-8 Mr 7 '69
Marriage law and real life. L. M. Croghan. il America 121:352-5 O 25 '69
Promises in a mixed marriage. J. T. Catoir. America 120:446-9 Ap 12 '69

MARRIAGE brokers
Eyes have it; professional matchmaker of Japan. Time 93:39 Mr 7 '69

MARRIAGE counseling
Astrologers as useful marriage counselors. L. Sechrest and J. H. Bryan; reply. A. S. La Vey. Trans-Action 6:63-4 F '69
Can this marriage be saved? ed. by D. C. Disney. See occasional issues of Ladies home journal
Frauds who prey on shaky marriages. J. Kaplan. Todays Health 47:16-19+ Je '69
Hidden conflicts in marriage; case histories. L. Kavaler. il Parents Mag 44:35-7+ Je '69
Marriage game: interpersonal psychological bargaining game-test. S V Jones. il Sci Digest 65:79 Ap '69
Why some marriages fail. L. Kavaler. il Parents Mag 44:46-7+ F '69

MARRIAGE customs and rites
I take thee, baby; couples are breaking away from traditional marriage ceremonies. il Time 94:57 Jl 4 '69

MARRIAGE customs and rites—*Continued*
My husband bought me for $40 and a chicken. S. McAndrews. il Read Digest 94:163-6 F '69
New rites for old. F. Maynard. il Seventeen 28:154-5+ Mr '69
See also
Weddings

MARRIAGE law
See also
Marriage (canon law)

Russia

Soviet law on marriage. T. F. McGann. America 120:687-8 Je 14 '69

United States

American laws regulating the formation of the marriage contract. R. F. Drinan. bibliog f Ann Am Acad 383:48-57 My '69

MARRIAGE of cousins
Elementary structures of kinship, by C. Lévi-Strauss. Review
Sat R 52:52-3 My 17 '69. R. F. Murphy

MARRIAGE of kin. See Consanguinity

MARRIAGE of priests
Altar ego. Newsweek 73:78+ Ap 21 '69
Bishop and Mrs Shannon. il Newsweek 74:76 Ag 25 '69
Bishops in trouble. il Time 94:52+ Ag 22 '69
Post-marital priesthood; with editorial comment. F. Franck. Commonweal 89:720, 724-6 Mr 14 '69
Reflections on priesthood and marriage. G. Grudzen. il Cath World 210:111-13 D '69
Shannon's wedding bells. Chr Today 13:49 S 12 '69
She married a priest; the spouse of Father Longo. S. Cunneen. Commonweal 90:440-1 Jl 11 '69
Truth or compassion? R. Haughton. Cath World 208:245-6 Mr '69; Reply. W. C. Lilly. 209:148 Jl '69
When priests marry. R. A. McCormick. America 120:471-4 Ap 19 '69
Why priests marry. E. B. Fiske. Read Digest 95:105-10 D '69

MARRIAGE tribunal. See Ecclesiastical courts

MARRIAGES, Mixed
Boston archdiocese accents positive ecumenism on mixed marriages. Chr Cent 86:768 Je 4 '69
Marriage law and real life. L. M. Croghan. il America 121:352-5 O 25 '69
Promises in a mixed marriage. J. T. Catoir. America 120:446-9 Ap 12 '69

MARRIED college students. See College students, Married

MARRIED women
See also
Mothers

Employment

Five million children with part-time mothers and nowhere to go. V. H. Bernstein. il Redbook 134:86+ N '69
Happenings in education; parents are relevant. W. D. Boutwell. PTA Mag 64:31-2 O '69
Married women in the labor force: an analysis of participation rates. M. S. Cohen. bibliog f il Mo Labor R 92:31-5 O '69
Mothers who try to be all things. B. Spock. Redbook 132:60+ Mr '69
Real and pseudo problems of the working woman. P. Sartin. il UNESCO Courier 22:24-8 Jl '69
Should welfare mothers work? M. C. Bernstein. America 120:704-6 Je 21 '69
Should wives work? S. Hartman. il McCalls 96:57-8+ F '69
Women's work is never done. Trans-Action 6:8 Je '69
Working wives: revolution in American family life. il U S News 67:95-6 N 17 '69
See also
Part time employment

MARRIS, Hervé
Crack on more canvas, and more, and more. Motor B 124:81+ N '69

MARROW
Origin of repopulating cells after localized bone marrow depletion. M. A. Maloney and H. M. Patt. bibliog il Science 165:71-3 Jl 4 '69

Transplantation

Getting to the core of blood diseases: transplanting bone marrow. il Bsns W p92+ Ja 18 '69
Marrow grafting holds promise. B. J. Culliton. il Sci N 96:358-61 O 18 '69

MARS, David
Federal government and protest. bibliog f Ann Am Acad 382:120-30 Mr '69

MARS, Jean Price
Giant dies, leader of the Haitian thought. M. A. Lubin. por Negro Hist Bul 32:16-18 O '69

MARS (planet)
Apollo and the Mariners. il Sci Am 221:90+ S '69
Fearful omen in the sky. Time 94:24 Ag 8 '69
Focus on Mars. Sci N 95:233 Mr 8 '69
Mars close up; Mariners' findings. il Newsweek 74:59-60 Ag 18 '69
New debate over life on Mars. U S News 67:9 Ag 18 '69
Scientists seek advanced Mars sensors. Aviation W 91:25-6 S 22 '69
See also
Space flight to Mars
Space vehicles—Landing systems—Mars

Atmosphere

Atmospheres of Mars and Venus. V. R. Eshleman. il Sci Am 220:78-88 bibliog (p 148+) Mr '69
CO_2 in Mars' atmosphere. G. S. Mumford. Sky & Tel 37:221 Ap '69
Evidence for solid carbon dioxide in the upper atmosphere of Mars. K. C. Herr and G. C. Pimentel. il Science 167:47-9 Ja 2 '70
Mariner 6: ultraviolet spectrum of Mars upper atmosphere. C. A. Barth and others. bibliog il Science 165:1004-5 S 5 '69
Mariners 6 and 7: radio occultation measurements of the atmosphere of Mars. A. Kliore and others. bibliog il Science 166:1393-7 D 12 '69
Mars probe controversy. Sci N 96:129 Ag 16 '69
Mars revisited; detection of two gases by Mariner 7. il Time 94:45-6 Ag 15 '69
Mars: water vapor in its atmosphere. T. Owen and H. P. Mason. bibliog il Science 165:893-5 Ag 29 '69
Moisture on Mars. il Time 93:48 Ap 4 '69
Solar cycle variation of exospheric temperatures on Mars and Venus: a prediction for Mariner 6 and 7. R. W. Stewart and J. S. Hogan. bibliog il Science 165:386-8 Jl 25 '69
Water or mirage? Sr Schol 94:16 Ap 18 '69

Mass

Lunar and planetary mass concentrations B. T. O'Leary and others. bibliog il Science 165:651-7 Ag 15 '69

Observations

Blue shift in springtime; water on Mars. Sci N 95:328 Ap 5 '69
Planet Mars in 1969. C. F. Capen and V. W. Capen. il Sky & Tel 37:190-4 Mr '69
Some highlights of the current apparition of Mars. il Sky & Tel 38:72-4 Ag '69

Photographs from space

Details shown at edge of Martian icecap. Aviation W 91:87-9 Ag 18 '69
Mariner photos show Mars pole, equator. Aviation W 91:96 S 22 '69
Mariner 6 and 7 television pictures: preliminary analysis. R. B. Leighton and others. bibliog il Science 166:49-67 O 3 '69
Mariner 6 television pictures: first report. R. B. Leighton and others. Science 165:684-90 Ag 15 '69
Mariner 7 near-encounter photos show hills, craters above south polar icecap on Mars. Aviation W 91:26-7 Ag 11 '69
Mariner 7 television pictures: first report. R. B. Leighton and others. Science 165:788-95 Ag 22 '69
Mars observed; Mariners 6 and 7 findings. Newsweek 74:72-3 Ag 11 '69
Mars pictures from Mariners 6 and 7. il Sky & Tel 38:212-21 O '69

Spectra

Infrared absorptions near three microns recorded over the polar cap of Mars. K. C. Herr and G. C. Pimentel. bibliog il Science 166:496-9 O 24 '69

Surface

In space: focus on Mars. il U S News 67:58-9 Ag 11 '69
Mariner 6 and 7 television pictures; preliminary analysis. R. B. Leighton and others. bibliog il Science 166:49-67 O 3 '69
Mariners reveal details of Mars' surface. N. S. Himmel. il Aviation W 91:28-30 Ag 11 '69
Mars: a closer look at a nearby world. il Sci N 96:111-12 Ag 9 '69
Mars, a dynamic world. C. F. Capen. il R Pop Astron 63:4-7 F '69
Mars: correlation of optical and radar observations. J. C. Robinson. bibliog il Science 164:176-7 Ap 11 '69

MARS (planet)—Surface—*Continued*
Mars is like itself; Mariner television pictures. Sci Am 221:52-3 D '69
Mars: is the surface colored by carbon suboxide? W. T. Plummer and R. K. Carson. bibliog il Science 166:1141-2 N 28 '69
Mars observed; Mariners 6 and 7 findings. il Newsweek 74:72-3 Ag 11 '69
Mars pictures from Mariners 6 and 7. il Sky & Tel 38:212-21 O '69
Martian craters: comparison of statistical counts. A. B. Binder. bibliog il Science 164: 297-9 Ap 18 '69
Martian topography: large-scale variations. R. A. Wells. bibliog il Science 166:862-5 N 14 '69
Puzzling terrain. Sci N 96:234 S 20 '69
Radar observations of Martian relief. il Sky & Tel 38:222 O '69
Special place; Mariners 6 and 7 findings. il Newsweek 74:74+ S 22 '69
Spectral reflectivity of Mars. T. B. McCord and J. B. Adams. bibliog il Science 163: 1058-60 Mr 7 '69
Spectrographic detection of topographic features on Mars. M. J. S. Belton and D. M. Hunten. bibliog il Science 166:225-7 O 10 '69

Temperature
Contradictions in temperature data spark dispute about possibility of life on Mars. N. S. Himmel il Aviation W 91:90-1+ Ag 18 '69
Mariner 1969: preliminary results of the infrared radiometer experiment. G. Neugebauer and others. bibliog il Science 166:98-9 O 3 '69
Surface temperatures on Mars charted. G. S Mumford. il Sky & Tel 37:150 Mr '69

MARS probes. See Space probes

MARSAN, Barbara Ajmone-. See Ajmone-Marsan, B.

MARSCHNER, Hannelore
Hydrocalcite ($CaCO_3 \cdot H_2O$) and nesquehonite ($MgCO_3 \cdot 3H_2O$) in carbonate scales. bibliog Science 165:1119-21 S 12 '69

MARSDEN, Catherine G.
Gift for the Christ child; story. Américas 21: 28-9 N '69

MARSEILLES, France

Music
Report: productions at Lyons and Marseilles. D. Stevens. Opera N 34:29 D 20 '69

MARSH, Corinna
Costliest luxuries; poem. Nat R 21:1326 D 30 '69

MARSH, Felicia Meyer
Ceremony. New Yorker 45:38-9 Ap 12 '69

MARSH, Georgia
Communications-arts teams. Todays Ed 58: 39-41 D '69

MARSH, John
Briton charges the U.S. with managerial imperialism. il por Bsns W p72 N 29 '69

MARSH, Reginald
Ceremony: wife memorialized as a benefactor of NYPL. New Yorker 45:38-9 Ap 12 '69

MARSH, Robert G.
Cheers for a prairie acropolis. Hi Fi 19: MA20-1 Ag '69
Ozawa in transit. Sat R 52:45-6+ S 27 '69
Solti, at last. Hi Fi 19:MA26+ Ap '69

MARSH, Tracy H.
Establishing factory attributions of glassware. Hobbies 74:98T-98U+ Je '69
Southern gentlemen honored in glass. Hobbies 74:98N-98P Ag '69

MARSH and McLennan, incorporated
Who says casualty insurance is risky? il Forbes 103:56-7 Ap 1 '69

MARSH birds. See Water birds

MARSH plants. See Bog vegetation

MARSHAK, Robert E.
Atoms for peace awards; address, May 14, 1969. Science 164:1496-8 Je 27 '69

MARSHALL, Eleanor
First words are important. Writers Digest 49:63-5 Ap '69

MARSHALL, Eric. See Hample, S. jt. comp.

MARSHALL, Jack
Feeding machine; poem. Poetry 114:94 My '69

MARSHALL, John
John Marshall: he made the Court supreme. por Sr Schol 94:11 F 7 '69

MARSHALL, Max S.
Measure of accomplishment. Sch & Soc 97:21-2 Ja '69

MARSHALL, Mel
Delectable egg; excerpts. Ladies Home J 86: 106-7+ Mr '69

MARSHALL, Neil F. See Shepard, F. P. jt. auth.

MARSHALL, Pearl
Guarding the bay. Sci N 96:102-3 Ag 2 '69

MARSHALL, Thurgood
Supreme court, justice's warning to fellow Negroes; excerpts from address, May 4, 1969. por U S News 66:92-3 My 19 '69

MARSHALL, Calif.
Marshall's hotel once took a dip in Tomales Bay. il Sunset 143:36 N '69

MARSHALL COUNTY, Miss.
What the blacks found out; boycott. M. L. Berzon. Nation 208:793-5 Je 23 '69

MARSHALL ISLANDS
See also
Bikini

MARSHALL space flight center. See United States—Marshall space flight center

MARSHES
Waterfowl on the wane? M. Frome. Field & S 74:34+ Ag '69
Winter marsh. F. Russell. il Audubon 71:36-45 N '69
See also
Great Swamp, N.J.
Salt marshes

Reclamation
See also
New Jersey meadows

MARSHES, Salt. See Salt marshes

MARSTON, David W.
Bahrain. Travel 132:61-7 N '69

MARSTON, R. M.
Twenty SCR circuits you can make. Radio-Electr 40:49-51 Je; 55-7+ Jl '69

MARSTON, Red
Manhunt by water. Yachting 125:150 Mr '69

MARSZALEK, Donald S. See Small, E. B. jt. auth.

MARTARELLA, Frank David
Animated cinema. America 120:271-3 Mr 8 '69

MARTELL, E. A.
Plowing a nuclear furrow. bibliog Environ 11:2-10+ Ap '69

MARTENHOFF, Jim
Birth of a yacht. Yachting 126:52-4+ Jl '69
Find the best prop for your boat on paper, first. Pop Sci 194:104-6 Je '69
Houseboat boom. Yachting 125:59-62+ My '69
Key to performance. Yachting 125:70-1 Mr '69
Place for everything. il Yachting 125:72-3 F '69
Small boat piloting. il Yachting 125:98-9+ Ja '69
They're a bunch of corks! il Yachting 126:66-7+ N '69
Weather: outboarders' bug-a-boo? Yachting 125:66-7+ Ap '69

MARTENS, Anne Coulter
George slept here, too; drama. Plays 28:1-8, 34 F '69
Green men, go home; drama. Plays 28:45-52+ Ap '69
Santa Claus is twins; drama. Plays 29:39-47 D '69
Which is witch? drama. Plays 29:15-24, 96 O '69

MARTENS, Rachel
Keeping up to date. Farm J 93:52H-52I Mr '69

MARTENS
Elf of the Alpine. R. Belous. il Audubon 71: 52-7 N '69

MARTHA Graham and dance company
From A to B to Z; Graham company at Manhattan's City center. il por Time 93:73 Ap 18 '69
Journey from within; performance of Canticle for innocent comedians at the New York city center. W. Terry. il Sat R 52:54-5 Ap 26 '69
Musical events: Canticle for innocent comedians. The plain of prayer, and A time of snow. W. Sargeant. New Yorker 45:168 Ap 19 '69
Old gods and devils. D. Hering. il Dance Mag 43:32-3+ Je '69

MARTHA'S VINEYARD
See also
Chilmark, Mass.
Edgartown, Mass.

MARTI, Kurt
Solar-type xenon: a new isotopic composition of xenon in the Pesyanoe meteorite. bibliog Science 166:1263-5 D 5 '69

MARTIAL law
Spain is still afraid of itself. R. Eder. il N Y Times Mag p23+ Mr 9 '69

MARTIN, Billy
Little love, and a few punches, make a team. M. Cope. il pors Life 67:79-80+ S 19 '69
Torrid time for the Twins. R. Blount, jr. il pors Sports Illus 31:16-19 Jl 21 '69
Two managers and two teams. Sports Illus 30:82-3 Ap 14 '69

MARTIN, Buddy
Sox & Martin. B. Lang. il pors Hot Rod 22: 52-4 F '69

MARTIN, David
Is this man the country's best athlete? Life
66:48-54+ Je 6 '69
MARTIN, David, 1949-
Cemetery; Intercourse; poems. Poetry 114:20-
1 Ap '69
MARTIN, Dick
Era of Rowan and Martin? H. Van Horne.
por McCalls 97:80-1+ O '69
New partner for Dan Rowan, the werewolf.
D. Adler. il pors Life 66:54-60 My 23 '69
MARTIN, Frank R.
New way to hunt deer. Outdoor Life 144:29-
31+ D '69
MARTIN, G. M. and Sprague, C. A.
Parasexual cycle in cultivated human somatic
cells. bibliog Science 166:761-3 N 7 '69
MARTIN, Graham
International conference of the Red cross
calls for observance of the Geneva conven-
tion on prisoners of war; statement, Sept-
ember 10, 1969. Dept State Bul 61:323-5 O
13 '69
MARTIN, Jerome
Symbol hunting Golding's Lord of the flies.
Engl J 58:408-13 Mr '69
MARTIN, Jim
News: the West (cont) por Outdoor Life 143:
41-4 F; 53-60 Ap '69
MARTIN, John B.
Martin testifies on nutrition needs of aging.
Aging 180:12-13 O '69
Our man in Washington; interview, ed. by T.
Schuchat. pors Har Yrs 9:30-2 S '69
Welcome to delegates to the International
congress of gerontology. Aging 178:3 Ag
'69
about
Confirmed by Senate, Martin heads AoA:
he sees work vital to all generations. il
pors Aging 176:4-5 Je '69
MARTIN, John Bartlow
Another view. Life 66:16B Ja 31 '69
Icy taste of winter. Life 66:4 Mr 7 '69
In the house that Adlai loved. Life 66:24 Mr
28 '69
Seashells from East and West. Life 66:
14A My 2 '69
Strange quest that ended in Finland. Holiday
46:70-3+ O '69
MARTIN, John Henry
Kaleidoscope for learning. Sat R 52:76-7+ Je
21 '69
MARTIN, Kingsley
Kingsley Martin: a memoir. A. Werth. Na-
tion 208:294-5 Mr 10 '69
MARTIN, Lawrence M. and Jackson, J. F.
Cerumen types in Choctaw Indians. Science
163:677-8 F 14 '69
MARTIN, Lowell M.
Lowell Martin survey blasts Chicago P.L;
summary. por Library J 94:1825 My 1 '69
Our own modest genius. por Wilson Lib Bul
43:851-3 My '69
MARTIN, Malcolm A. and Axelrod, David
Polyoma virus gene activity during lytic in-
fection and in transformed animal cells.
bibliog Science 164:68-70 Ap 4 '69
MARTIN, Mary
Pages from my needlepoint book; excerpts.
McCalls 96:84-91 Ap '69
MARTIN, Paul S.
Wanted: a suitable herbivore to convert
western scrubland to protein; with bio-
graphical sketch. por Natur Hist 78:4, 34-9
F '69
MARTIN, Philip L.
Animals into toys. il Am Artist 33:68-73+
O '69
MARTIN, Preston
Money, and housing; interview, ed. by G.
R. Rosen. por Duns R 94:12-15 Ag '69
about
S&Ls look for sympathy at the top. por Bsns
W p72+ Mr 29 '69
MARTIN, R. Glenn
Diction in Warren's All the king's men. Engl
J 58:1169-74 N '69
MARTIN, Ralph P.
Brighter outlook in the New Testament
field. Chr Today 13:6-8 F 28 '69
MARTIN, Robert E.
Too much teaching; too little reading. Ed
Digest 35:38-40 S '69
MARTIN, Robert Wesley, 1908-
Message from the publisher. R. A. Hubley.
por Aviation W 92:5 Ja 12 '70
MARTIN, Sarah S. See Bosmann, H. B. jt.
auth.
MARTIN, Stephen P.
Sunset exposure calculator. Pop Phot 65:74-
5+ S '69

MARTIN, W. E.
Commensal sea cucumber. Science 164:855 My
16 '69
MARTIN, W. L. Jr
Georgia archsegregationist nominated as U.S.
marshal. Chr Cent 86:673 My 14 '69
MARTIN, Wilbur
Budding revolt in Congress? Nations Bsns
57:56-61 Je '69
MARTIN, William
Respecting the words of kids. Clear House
43:380-1 F '69
MARTIN, William McChesney, 1906-
Chance of controlling inflation: as top money
manager sees it; excerpts from testimony.
por U S News 66:99-100 Mr 10 '69
Economic problems; address, February 27,
1969. Vital Speeches 35:346-9 Mr 15 '69
Federal reserve head talks on inflation, in-
terest, controls; excerpts from testimony,
September 10, 1969. por U S News 67:103-4
S 22 '69
Martin's views on controls; excerpts from
message, June 30, 1969. U S News 67:57-8
Jl 14 '69
about
Disinflation not deflation. America 120:296
Mr 15 '69
Guessing game that saddles economists.
Bsns W p35 Mr 8 '69
Mr Nixon has a friend at the Fed. il por
Newsweek 74:88+ O 27 '69
Nixon's new maestro of money. por Time
94:89-90 O 24 '69
MARTIN houses. See Bird houses
MARTIN Luther King memorial center, At-
lanta
Institute of the black world
Black studies Vatican. il Newsweek 74:38
Ag 11 '69
MARTIN Marietta corporation
Europeans interested in Titan 3 proposal. C.
Brownlow. il Aviation W 90:18-19 Je 23 '69
MARTINDALE, Don
America's moral and ethical stature abroad.
Ann Am Acad 384:96-103 Jl '69
MARTINE, Jane Kinkead
Day nature said no. Good H 168:34+ Mr '69
MARTINELLI, Giovanni
Death of a lion. B. Hastings. il pors Opera N
33:14-16 Mr 22 '69
Giovanni Martinelli. A. Favia-Artsay. il
pors Hobbies 74:35+ Jl '69
Giovanni Martinelli's Otello. P. L. Miller. por
Am Rec G 35:384 Ja '69
MARTINEZ, Enrique
Coppelia is light and breezy. il pors Dance
Mag 43:42-5 Ja '69
MARTINEZ, Thomas M. and LaFranchi, Rob-
ert
Why people play poker. pors Trans-Action
6:30-5+ Jl '69
MARTINEZ, Calif.
Historic houses, etc.
John Muir's house, you are welcome. il
Sunset 143:50 O '69
MARTINEZ-MALDONADO, M. and others
Renal concentrating mechanism: possible
role for sodium-potassium activated ade-
nosine triphosphatase. bibliog Science 165:
807-8 Ag 22 '69
MARTINIQUE
Liberté, egalité, fraternité; political assimila-
tion of French West Indies. Trans-Action
6:5 Jl '69
Martinique. M. A. Mackay. il Travel 132:34-5
S '69
Wretched of Martinique. P. Geismar. Nation
208:782-3 Je 23 '69
MARTINO, Joseph P.
Science and society in equilibrium. bibliog
Science 165:769-72 Ag 22 '69
MARTINOLI, Giuseppe
Avena magna: new oat species. bibliog Sci-
ence 163:594 F 7 '69
MARTINSVILLE, Va.
How to design a city hall. T. B. Noland. il
Am City 84:93-4 Ap '69
MARTY, Martin E.
Gifted with impatience. PTA Mag 64:2-3 D
'69
How to tell a fad from a trend. Common-
weal 90:509-12 Ag 22 '69
MARTYRS' and heroes' remembrance authority.
See Jerusalem—Yad va-shem
MARUSI, Augustine Raymond
Easier said than done. il por Forbes 104:98
N 15 '69
MARX, György
Quasars and the birth of the universe; ex-
cerpts from addresses. UNESCO Courier 22:
32-4+ D '69

MARX, Karl
Catalyst. P. W. Schmidtchen. il por Hobbies
74:104-5+ Mr '69
Many faces of Karl Marx. J. W. Burrow. il
pors Horizon 11:52-7 Wint '69
Marx, Mao, and the dissenters. R. L. Tobin.
Sat R 53:26+ Ja 10 '70
Marxian revolutionary idea, by R. C. Tucker.
Review
  New Repub 161:29-31 Jl 26 '69. M. Har-
  rington
Marxism: the persistent vision; Time essay.
il Time 93:35-6 Je 13 '69
Marx's religion of revolution, by G. North.
Review
  Nat R 21:343-4 Ap 8 '69. M. Geltman
Social and political thought of Karl Marx,
by S. Avineri. Review
  Sat R 52:31-3+ Ap 5 '69. R. D. Masters
Two risings against the liberals. R. Kirk.
Nat R 21:1170 N 18 '69
MARX, Wesley
Disney imperative. Nation 209:76-8 Jl 28 '69
How not to kill the ocean. Audubon 71:27-
35 Jl '69
Nurseries of the sea. UNESCO Courier 22:13-
17+ Mr '69
Parks between the tides. il Parks & Rec 3:18-
20 O '68
Reports: deep-sea bed. Atlan 223:24+ Ap
'69
Scene of slaughter was exceedingly pictur-
esque. Am Heritage 20:66-71+ Je '69
MARXISM. See Communism; Socialism
MARY, Virgin

Art
Place, time, and painter; B. Montagna's Vir-
gin and Child in Worcester art museum.
K. Kuh. il Sat R 52:46-7 S 6 '69

Theology
Job for the Spirit; the cultus of the Mother
of Christ. V. P. McCorry. America 120:550
My 3 '69
MARY, queen of Scots
Mary queen of Scots, by A. Fraser. Review
  America 121:472+ N 15 '69. M. Adelman,
  jr
  Newsweek il 74:123-4+ O 20 '69. R. A.
  Gross
MARY Corita Kent, Sister. See Kent, C.
MARY Faith, Sister
Poem at night. America 121:497 N 22 '69
M. Paulinus Sullivan, Sister. See Sullivan, M. P.
MARY Stuart, queen of the Scots. See Mary,
queen of Scots
MARYANNA Childs, Sister. See Childs, M.
MARYKNOLL fathers. See Catholic church—
Missions
MARYLAND
  See also
Architecture, Domestic—Maryland
Assateague Island National Seashore
Chesapeake Bay
Education—Maryland
Fishing—Maryland
Hunting—Maryland
Justice, Administration of—Maryland
Land—Maryland
Libraries—Maryland
Prisons—Maryland

Historic houses, etc.
Living with antiques on Maryland's eastern
shore. E. Gaines; E. A. W. Miles. il An-
tiques 95:520-37 Ap '69
  See also
Anne Arundel County, Md.—Historic houses,
etc.
MARYLAND academy of sciences, Baltimore
Events of 1970 in the Graphic time table.
Sky & Tel 39:35-7 Ja '70
MARZIPAN. See Candy
MASADA (fortress) Israel
Reporter at large; Dead Sea scrolls. E. Wil-
son. New Yorker 45:45-6+ Ap 5 '69
MASARYK, Jan Garrigue
Convenient conclusion. Newsweek 74:49 D 22
'69
Masaryk case, by C. Sterling. Review
  Time por 95:78 Ja 12 '70
MASCAGNI, Pietro
Cavalleria rusticana. Criticism
  Time 95:64 Ja 19 '70
First-rate performance of a second-rate
opera. C. L. Osborne. por Hi Fi 19:77 Je '69
Fritz and Wally. R. Jacobson. Sat R 52:79-
80 Ap 26 '69
Melting charm: non-verismo Mascagni;
L'Amico Fritz. P. L. Miller. Am Rec G
35:1137 Ag '69
Records:
  L'Amico Fritz. Opera N 33:31 My 17 '69

MASCONS. See Moon—Mass
MASERS
Hydroxyl and water masers in protostars. M.
M. Litvak. bibliog il Science 165:855-61 Ag
29 '69
Interstellar masers. D. F. Dickinson and
others. il Sky & Tel 39:4-7 Ja '70
Maser amplification of 9.5-gigahertz elastic
waves in sapphire doped with divalent nic-
kel impurity ions. P. D. Peterson and E. H.
Jacobsen. bibliog il Science 164:1065-7 My
30 '69
MASEVICH, Alla
New quests ahead. Space World F-4-64:38-9
Ap '69
MASIN, Herman L.
Sports. See issues of Senior scholastic
MASKS (for the face)
Originality in the parade; Halloween cos-
tumes and masks. L. E. Eben. il Sch Arts
69:38-9 O '69
MASKS (sculpture)
Enameled masks. K. Berl. il Ceram Mo 17:22
F '69
MASLAND, C. H, and sons
Masland's magic carpet. S. Margetts. Duns R
93:77-8 Ap '69
MASLAND, Richard H.
Visual motion perception: experimental modi-
fication. bibliog Science 165:819-21 Ag 22 '69
MASLOW, Sophie
Group dance theatre; 92nd street Y. J. An-
derson. Dance Mag 43:77-8 Ap '69
MASON, Charles
New York's fish and game budget. Cons 23:
5-7 F '69
MASON, Ed
Horizontal ghost. Outdoor Life 144:76+ Ag
'69
MASON, Edwin A.
Friends of the garden. Horticulture 46:24-5+
Ag '68
MASON, Ellsworth
Back to the cave; or, Some buildings I have
known; address, March 1969. por Library
J 94:4353-7 D 1 '69
Contemporary education: a double view; ad-
dress, December 1967. bibliog por Library J
94:4201-6 N 15 '69
Unnatural places and practices. por Library J
94:3399-402 O 1 '69
MASON, Harold P. See Owen, T. jt. auth.
MASON, Herbert M. jr
Our next decade in space. Mech Illus 65:
43-5+ Ap '69
MASON, Jan
Heroes? Man, we haven't any heroes left!
R. Graves. por Life 67:1 D 12 '69
MASON, John
New color tubes! Radio-Electr 41:33-5 Ja '70
MASON, Joseph G.
How to delegate. Nations Bsns 57:60-1+ O
'69
MASON, Kathleen
How to criticise and revise a juvenile book.
Writers Digest 49:52-5+ Ag '69
MASON, S. G. See Torza, S. jt. auth.
MASONRY
Atrium house in Ireland. il Arch Forum 130:
46-9 Mr '69
MASS
Papal decree on church ritual. U S News 66:16
My 12 '69
MASS (music)
  See also
Phonograph records—Mass
MASS (physics)
Two problems in gravitation. H. J. Rood. il
Sky & Tel 37:152-3, 225-7 Mr-Ap '69
MASS communication. See Mass media
MASS culture. See Popular culture
MASS media
American media baronies, a modest Atlantic
atlas; with report by H. H. Goldin. Atlan
224:82-94 Jl '69
Changing news values in the megamind era;
address, February 19, 1969. E. H. Methvin.
Vital Speeches 35:462-7 My 15 '69
Communications. J. McLaughlin. America 122:
16-18 Ja 10 '70
Electronic vs. linear. J. McLaughlin. America
120:634+ My 24 '69
Five myths of consumership. D. Smythe. il
Nation 208:82-4 Ja 20 '69
Ghetto wire service; Community news ser-
vice sponsored by the Ford foundation
and the New York urban coalition. News-
week 74:86+ Jl 7 '69
Judging the fourth estate; a Time-Louis
Harris poll. il Time 94:38-9 S 5 '69
Mass communications and American empire,
by H. I. Schiller. Review
  Sat R 52:38 Ag 16 '69. R. L. Shayon
Media for mediacy. M. Ronan. Sr Schol 94:
Schol Teach 22 F 7 '69

MASS media—*Continued*
Mediacy: what it can do for you. W. D. Boutwell. Sr Schol 94:Schol Teach 2 F 7 '69
Media-ized English. R. Siegfried. il Sr Schol 94:Schol Teach 13 F 7 '69
Newspapers' death held exaggerated. il Forbes 104:30-2+ O 1 '69
Spiritual revolutionists: capturing the media; space age communications conference. R. Chandler. Chr Today 13:32 Jl 4 '69
What's wrong with news? It isn't new enough. M. Ways. il Fortune 80:110-13+ O '69
    See also
Moving pictures
Newspapers
Radio broadcasting
Television broadcasting

Social aspects
Our basic news medium; impact of TV and newspapers; Roper survey. Sat R 52:41-2 Ag 9 '69

Great Britain
Summer of discontent. J. Tebbel. il Sat R 52:110-11 S 13 '69

MASS media in religion
Mass media and catechetics. A. Nebreda. America 121:29 Jl 19 '69
Mass media and church reform. Chr Today 14:28-9 O 24 '69

MASS murder. See Murder
MASS spectrometry
Mass spectrometry. R. I. Reed and D. H. Robertson. bibliog il Chem 42:7-11 Je; 11-15 S '69
Mass spectrometry and carbon-13 labeling. S. Meyerson and E. K. Fields. bibliog il Science 166:325-8 O 17 '69
Photoionization and ion-molecule reactions; report of meeting. J. L. Franklin. Science 164:93-4 Ap 4 '69

MASS transit. See Rapid transit
MASSACHUSETTS
    See also
Architecture—Massachusetts
Architecture, Domestic—Massachusetts
Bakers Island
Booksellers and bookselling—Massachusetts
Camping—Massachusetts
Cape Cod
Conservation of resources—Massachusetts
Education—Massachusetts
Festivals—Massachusetts
Law—Massachusetts
Music festivals—Massachusetts
Tourist trade—Massachusetts

Description and travel
Let's travel: capes, bays, and college boys. B. Gillam. il Mlle 69:48-50+ Jl '69
Thoreau country. H. D. Crawford. il Am For 75:20-3+ N '69

Historic houses, etc.
Living with antiques: the Massachusetts home of Mr & Mrs Samuel Chamberlain. N. G. Chamberlain and S. Chamberlain. il Antiques 95:696-701 My '69
    See also
Essex County, Mass.—Historic houses, etc.
Hancock, Mass.—Historic houses, etc.

History
    See also
Plymouth, Mass.

Politics and government
Bad sign for Nixon; G.O.P. House seat lost to M. J. Harrington. il Time 94:22 O 10 '69
Case of Massachusetts; Republicans' problem. P. R. Wieck. New Repub 160:25-7 F 1 '69
Massachusetts test. New Repub 161:13 S 27 '69
Turnabout; sending M. J. Harrington to Congress. il Newsweek 74:36-7 O 13 '69
MASSACHUSETTS institute of technology, Cambridge
Cambridge: March 4, the movement, and M.I.T. R. Salloch. il Bul Atom Sci 25:32-5 My '69
Can a weapons lab solve urban ills? il Bsns W p 132+ N 1 '69
Can defense work keep a home on campus? MIT panel calls for balance with nondefense R&D. il Bsns W p68-71 Je 7 '69
Controversy at MIT. Aviation W 91:61+ D 1; 55-6+ D 15 '69
Day of reckoning: funding for military research. Nation 209:556 N 24 '69
Go back! Go back! war research protest. il Newsweek 74:79-80 N 17 '69
Ins and outs at M.I.T. R. Todd. il N Y Times Mag p32-3+ My 18 '69

Man who cooled M.I.T. il Time 94:68+ N 21 '69
March 4 at MIT; one-day research halt to dramatize over-militarization of research. New Repub 160:10-11 Mr 15 '69
M.I.T. and the Pentagon. Time 94:48+ N 7 '69
M.I.T.: panel on special labs asks more nondefense research. J. Walsh. Science 164:1264-5 Je 13 '69
M.I.T. reviews its military research policies. M. Mueller. Science 164:653 My 9 '69
MIT revises laboratory work emphasis. P. J. Klass. Aviation W 90:49-50+ Je 16 '69
MIT under the gun. il Sci N 96:446 N 15 '69
M.I.T.'s March 4: scientists discuss renouncing military research. B. Nelson. il Science 163:1175-8 Mr 14 '69
Misuse of science; research stoppage planned at M.I.T. and other universities. Nation 208:228 F 24 '69
More balanced program. Sci Am 221:50 Jl '69
No secrets. Sci Am 220:54 Je '69
Physics lab goes relevant; Fluid mechanics laboratory. P. Gwynne. il Sci N 96:132-4 Ag 16 '69
Policy of protest; university scientists and engineers concern about government overemphasis on scientific weapons research. Time 93:60 F 28 '69
Project Cambridge: another showdown for social sciences? J. Coburn. Science 166:1250-3 D 5 '69
Science policy meeting at M.I.T. B. Nelson. Science 163:797 F 21 '69
Scientists plan research strike at M.I.T. on 4 March. B. Nelson. Science 163:373 Ja 24 '69; Correction. B. Magasanik and others. 163:517 F 7 '69
When protest on war hit MIT. il U S News 67:12 N 17 '69

Alfred P. Sloan school of management
Detente among management men; Soviet-MIT exchange of Sloan fellows. il Bsns W p42 Je 7 '69

Center for advanced visual studies
Lab for light: Center for advanced visual studies at MIT. il Arch Forum 130:62-3 My '69

MASSACHUSETTS. University, Amherst
University store gets faculty rapport. B. Wilkes. Pub W 196:51 Ag 18 '69
MASSAQUOI, Hans J.
André Watts, a giant among giants at age twenty-two. Ebony 24:90-1+ My '69
Unconquerable Muhammad Ali. Ebony 24:168-70+ Ap '69
Warden who reformed the world's worst jail. Ebony 24:60-2+ Jl '69
MASSAR, Ivan
Design by design, and by nature; photographs. Fortune 80:82-5 D '69
MASSAY, Glenn F.
Farmington no. 9: Will the tragedy be compounded? Chr Cent 86:871-4 Je 25 '69
MASSE, Benjamin Louis
Arithmetic of poverty. America 121:356-7 O 25 '69
Economy. America 122:7-8 Ja 10 '70
Fringe benefits. America 120:168-9 F 8 '69
Social front. See issues of America
MASSEE, William E. See Ivens, D. jt. auth.
MASSELL, Sam, 1927-
In the mayor's seat. il por Newsweek 74:39 N 3 '69
MASSENET, Jules
Case for Massenet. G. Movshon. il Hi Fi 19:93-4 D '69
Manon. Criticism
    New Yorker 45:105 Mr 1 '69
Records:
    Werther. Opera N 34:42 D 27 '69
Thaïs. Criticism
    New Yorker 45:137 My 17 '69
MASSEY, Clarence
Sourdough bread for sportsmen. Field & S 74:40-1+ D '69
MASSIALAS, Byron G.
Teaching and learning through inquiry. Todays Ed 58:40-2 My '69
MASSIE, Charlotte Taylor
Garden week in Virginia. Horticulture 47:46-7+ Mr '69
MASSIE, Robert K.
Answer to our blood shortage. Read Digest 95:199-200+ O '69
MASSINE, Leonide
Leonide Massine: an appreciation. A. L. Haskell. il pors Dance Mag 43:40-53 N '69
MASSMAN, Virgil F.
From out of a desk drawer: the beginnings of ALA headquarters. bibliog por ALA Bul 63:475-81 Ap '69

MASSON, André
Food in Vogue; chicken and ginger sauce; chicken in chocolate sauce. N. Lyon. Vogue 154:69 O 15 '69

MASSON, Georgina
Dumbarton oaks; excerpts from Dumbarton oaks, a guide to the gardens. Horticulture 47:38-9 O '69

MASSON, Walter
Brussels sprouts stretch the vegetable season. Org Gard & Farm 16:60 Mr '69
Cabbage, Chinese style. Org Gard & Farm 16:80 Ap '69
Foxglove on the rise. Org Gard & Farm 16: 68-9 Ag '69
Potatoes between the rows. Org Gard & Farm 16:34 My '69

MASTECTOMY. See Breast—Surgery

MASTER antenna television system. See Television antennas

MASTER charge cards. See Credit cards

MASTER classes, Bayreuth. See Opera—Instruction and study

MASTER Francke. See Francke, Master

MASTERS, Roger D.
Chronic ambiguity in choosing sides. Sat R 52:38+ Ap 26 '69
What in Marx speaks to today's young iconoclasts? Sat R 52:31-3+ Ap 5 '69

MASTERS, William Howell
All they talk about is sex, sex, sex. T. Buckley. il por N Y Times Mag p28-9+ Ap 20 '69

MASTERS degrees. See Degrees, Academic

MASTERS golf tournament. See Golf—Tournaments

MASTHEADS. See Newspapers—Mastheads

MASTITIS
Can these new weapons whip mastitis? D. Braun. Farm J 93:48 Mr '69
Do-it-yourself mastitis test. C. E. Ball. il Farm J 93:D6-D7+ Je '69
Hormones cause false mastitis. D. Braun. Farm J 93:D7 F '69

MASTOMYS. See Rats

MASTS and rigging
Project Phantom: a class considers a change; deck aluminum spar. K. C. Larkin. il Yachting 126:66-7+ S '69
They sail to win; masts and spars; excerpt from Boats for sailing. I. Proctor. il Yachting 126:36-7 S '69
What do you know about silencing aluminum spars. D. B. Hoisington. il Yachting 125:83+ Ap '69

MASURSKY, Harold
Advance in science: enormous; interview. por U S News 66:33-4 J 9 '69

MATALON, Reuben, and others
Glycolipid and mucopolysaccharide abnormality in fibroblasts of Fabry's disease. bibliog Science 164:1522-3 Je 27 '69

MATCH-making by computers. See Computers—Social applications

MATERIALISM
Universe and two chairs; excerpt from Death in the city. F. A. Schaeffer. Chr Today 13:8-11 Ap 25 '69

MATERIALS
Electronic materials and applications. H. C. Gatos. Science 164:137-41 Ap 11 '69
Naturals. il House & Gard 136:108-11 O '69
See also
Building materials
Composite materials

Deterioration

Case of the vanishing records. D. G. Lowe. il Am Heritage 20:34-5+ Ag '69

Fatigue
See also
Fracture of solids

Testing
See Testing

MATERIALS control
Materials management as a profit center. D. S. Ammer. bibliog f il Harvard Bsns R 47: 72-82 Ja '69

MATERIALS handling
How Rohr learned to move the goods. il Bsns W p92-3 Jl 26 '69
Prevent blunders in supply and distribution; with charts. R. Pirasteh. il Harvard Bsns R 47:113-27 Mr '69
See also
Grain handling

MATERIALS management. See Materials control

MATERIALS research
Materials; report of National colloquy on the field of materials. D. Johnson. Science 166:780+ N 7 '69
Sea, a challenge for materials. D. Groves. il Sea Front 15:356-63 N '69

MATERNAL love. See Love, Maternal

MATERNITY wards. See Hospitals—Maternity wards

MATESA company. See Textile machinery industry—Spain

MATH, Irwin
Electronics in weighing systems. Electr World 82:46-7+ N '69

MATH, Parke F.
Snow disaster at Fallsvale, Calif. Weatherwise 22:107 Je '69

MATHEMATICAL analysis
See also
Harmonic functions
Numerical analysis

MATHEMATICAL economics. See Economics, Mathematical

MATHEMATICAL formulas. See Mathematics—Formulae

MATHEMATICAL instruments
See also
Abacus

MATHEMATICAL models
For more efficient refuse collection; try analyzing your system with a mathematical model. R. Stone and R. Stearns. il Am City 84:98-100 My '69
Some mathematical models in science. M. Kac. bibliog il Science 166:695-9 N 7 '69

MATHEMATICAL physics
See also
Potential, Theory of
Statistical mechanics

MATHEMATICAL recreations
Mathematical games. M. Gardner. See issues of Scientific American
Puzzles to devil the mind; excerpts from Riverside puzzles. I. Morris. il Vogue 153: 134-5 Mr 15; 252-3 My '69

MATHEMATICAL research
Mathematicians's apology, by G. H. Hardy. Review
New Yorker 44:80+ F 1 '69. J. Bernstein

MATHEMATICS
Math. doorway to higher pay. D. L. Heiserman. il Pop Electr 30:67-9+ Mr '69
See also
Approximate computation
Axioms
Combinations
Economics, Mathematical
Equations
Logarithms
Mathematical recreations
Mathematical research
Trigonometry

Formulae

Geee meter, a dyno on your dash. P. Estrada. il Hot Rod 22:96-7 F '69
Jetting with know-how; air density meter. J. Dianna. il Hot Rod 22:106-7 F '69
This computer age. D. Powills. il Hobbies 74:152-3 O '69

Philosophy

Mathematician's apology, by G. H. Hardy. Review
New Yorker 44:80+ F 1 '69. J. Bernstein

Study and teaching

How they're teaching math to your kids; new math. il Changing T 23:19-22 N '69
Mathematics for the very young. L. Ellison. il Parents Mag 44:48-9+ Jl '69
Motivation for mathematics. G. Knaggs. Clear House 43:553-4 My '69
Underachievers measure up. B. Lewis. il Am Ed 5:27-8 F '69
See also
Arithmetic—Study and teaching

MATHEMATICS, Logic of. See Mathematics—Philosophy

MATHEMATICS teachers

Education

Sorry state of mathematics teacher education. G. R. Rising. Ed Digest 35:48-50 S '69

MATHER, Stephen Tyng
Scenic tribute to Stephen Mather; addresses, April 17, 1969. H. M. Albright; S. M. McPherson. il Nat Parks 43:12-14 Je '69

MATHEWS, Linda McVeigh
Chief Reddin: new style at the top. Atlan 223:84-6+ Mr '69

MATHEWS, Max V. See Risset, J.-C. jt. auth.

MATHIAS, Charles McCurdy, Jr
One Republican's ordeal; decision to vote against Haynsworth. ed. by N. MacNeil. por Time 94:16 N 28 '69

MATHIS, Joyce
Music to my ears. I. Kolodin. Sat R 52:53
Ap 19 '69
MATILIJA poppies. See Poppies
MATING behavior. See Sex behavior
MATING instinct. See Courtship of animals
MATISSE, Henri
Matisse: a celebration of pleasure. J. R.
Mellow. il pors N Y Times Mag p 16-17+
D 28 '69
MATLOCK, Gene D.
Bread-and-butter Spanish. Todays Ed 58:46
Ap '69
MATRICES
Matrix isolation. il Chem 42:25-7 N '69
MATRIMONY. See Marriage
MATSON line. See Matson navigation company
MATSON navigation company
Sitting duck; California-to-Hawaii steamship
run. il Forbes 103:19 Ja 15 '69
MATSUDA, Don
Using controls to troubleshoot TV. Electr
World 81:32-4+ Mr '69
MATSUMURA, Fumio, and Patil, K. C.
Adenosine triphosphatase sensitive to DDT
in synapses of rat brain. bibliog Sci-
ence 166:121-2 O 3 '69
MATSUNAMI, T. See Mamuro, T. jt. auth.
MATSUSHIMA, John
Which feed processing method fits your lot?
interview, ed. by O. Bay. por Farm J 93:
B18+ Mr '69
MATSUYA, Yutaka, and Green, Howard
Somatic cell hybrid between the established
human line D98 (presumptive HeLa) and
3T3. bibliog Science 163:697-8 F 14 '69
MATTEL, Incorporated
Diahann Carroll presents the Julia dolls. il
Ebony 24:148-50+ O '69
Menace of the Barbie dolls. D. Bess. Ramp
Mag 7:25-8 Ja 25 '69
Toy makers' shares are a losing game. il
Bsns W p82 D 20 '69
MATTER
Magnetic model of matter. J. Schwinger.
bibliog il Science 165:757-61 Ag 22 '69
Matter and antimatter. W. P. Trower. bib-
liog il Chem 42:8-13 O '69
Space, time and elementary interactions in
relativity. M. Sachs. il Phys Today 22:51-60
F '69; Discussion. 22:13 S: 11+ N '69
Universe's missing antimatter. D. E. Thom-
sen. il Sci N 96:562-3 D 13 '69
See also
Materialism
Phases (chemistry)
Solids
MATTER, Interstellar
Ammonia in outer space. Chem 42:23-4 Mr
'69
Antimatter, quasi-stellar objects, and the
evolution of galaxies. H. Alvén and A.
Elvius. bibliog il Science 164:911-17 My 23
'69
Birth of an earth? Newsweek 73:81 Mr 31 '69
Detection of ammonia in interstellar space G.
S. Mumford. Sky & Tel 37:150-1 Mr '69
Diamond dust in space. G. S. Mumford. Sky
& Tel 37:151 Mr '69
Interstellar sulfur hydride: a search for the
111-megahertz lines. M. L. Meeks and oth-
ers. bibliog il Science 163:173-4 Ja 10 '69
Interstellar sulfur hydride next? G. S. Mum-
ford. Sky & Tel 37:151 Mr '69
Interstellar water and formaldehyde. Sky &
Tel 37:271+ My '69
Mystery of the dust. Newsweek 73:62 F 3 '69
Rain in space. Sci Am 220:50 An '69
Stardust. il Chem 42:23-4 Je '69
Water, silicates and diamond. Sci N 95:234-5
Mr 8 '69
Water vapor: observations of galactic
sources. M. L. Meeks and others. bibliog
il Science 165:180-4 Jl 11 '69
MATTER of kindness; story. See Cusack, I. L.
MATTER of style; story. See Conaway, R.
MATTER of vocabulary; story. See McPher-
son. J. A.
MATTES, W. F.
GE's great bulb caper. Nation 208:823-5 Je
30 '69
MATTHAU, Walter
Walter Matthau: juiciest actor in the West;
interview, ed. by M. W. Lear. por Redbook
132:68-9+ Ja '69
MATTHEW, Lester J.
Exploring sculpture. Sch Arts 69:37 O '69
MATTHEWS, Carl J.
Funding Catholic schools: a Canadian way.
America 121:231-2 S 27 '69
MATTHEWS, Jack
Last Jack; poem. New Repub 160:23 Mr 29 '69

MATTHEWS, John
Undersea world of Jonah and Thetis. Sci
Digest 66:66-70 N '69
MATTHEWS, Robert C.
Trends just ahead in book manufacturing: ex-
cerpts from address. November 1969. por
Pub W 196:46+ D 1 '69
MATTHEWS, T. S.
I'll say nothing; poem. Atlan 223:54 F '69
Invisible man; poem. Atlan 223:90 My '69
On proceeding M.A. Vogue 153:256 My '69
MATTHEWS, William
Faith of our fathers; poem. Nation 209:354
O 6 '69
MATTHEWS, William B. jr
Chesapeake log. See issues of Motor boating
MATTHEWS, William H. 3d
Geologist's guide to the planet earth. Natur
Hist 78:66-8+ D '69
MATTHIAS, Bernd T. See Fisk, Z. jt. auth.
MATTHIESSEN, Peter
Profiles; C. Chavez. New Yorker 45:42-4+ Je
21; 43-4+ Je 28 '69
MATTIA, Virginius Dante
Doctor V. D. Mattia: a pill-giving maverick;
with interview, ed. by J. Gurovitz. il pors
Life 66:39-40+ Mr 7 '69
MATTICK, Hans W. and Aikman, A. B.
Cloacal region of American correction. bib-
liog f Ann Am Acad 381:109-18 Ja '69
MATTRESSES
Crib mattresses. il Consumer Rep 34:380-3
Jl '69
Mattresses can be flame-resistant. Consumer
Rep 34:56 F '69
MATURITY
Christian answers to immaturity. O. S. Wal-
ters. Chr Today 13:3-6 My 23 '69
Maturity: when? Chr Today 13:5-8 Ag 1 '69
Testing for maturity. A. Bustanoby. Chr To-
day 14:22-3 N 21 '69
MATURITY, Sexual. See Puberty
MATUSOW, Harvey
Guerrilla war against computers. Time 94:66
S 12 '69
MATZ, Mary Jane
Dippel the debonair. Opera N 33:14-16 F 22
'69
Rubini of Bergamo. Opera N 33:12-13 F 1 '69
Tripping with children. Opera N 33:13-15 My
17 '69
(ed) See Pizzi, P. L. Enlightener
MATZER, John, jr
Cut costs through programmed insurance.
Am City 84:148+ Mr '69
MATZKIN, Myron A.
Matzkin on movies. See issues of Modern
photography
MAUERMANN, Mary Anne
Best things in life; story. Redbook 132:80-1
F '69
MAUI (island)
Hawaii's perfect island. N. Kuehnl. il Bet
Hom & Gard 47:118 F '69
See also
Haleakala National Park
MAUK, Marion
Black studies. New Repub 160:12-13 Mr 15 '69
School is not a place but a process. Mlle 69:
260 +Ag '69
MAUMENEE, Alfred Edward
Ophthalmologist talks about his work; ed.
by W. S. Ross. pors Todays Health 47:
40-1+ Ap '69
MAUNA KEA
Rockefeller center west: Hawaii's Mauna Kea.
W. P. Fox. il Holiday 45:54-5+ My '69
MAUNA KEA, Hawaii golf course. See Golf
courses
MAUNEY, Mike
Faces of hunger; photographs. Todays Health
47:20-3 O '69
MAUR, Karin von
Music of the spheres, and cubes. bibliog Art
N 68:62-6+ N '69
MAURA, Sister
Words out of darkness; poem. Nation 209:
122 Ag 11 '69
MAURICA, François
Letter from Paris. Genêt. New Yorker 45:
144-5 Ap 19 '69
MAURITANIA
See also
Geology—Mauritania
MAVERICK, Samuel Augustus
Maverick. O. Ulph. il Am West 6:44-8+ My
'69
MAVERICK (guided missile) See Guided mis-
siles—Launching from airplanes
MAVERICK (term)
Maverick: reflections on fact, fiction, fantasy,
and the ideology of the free man. O. Ulph.
il Am West 6:44-8+ My '69
MAVES, Harold J.
Insight through inservice. Todays Ed 58:42
Ap '69

MAWDESLEY-THOMAS, Lionel E. and Healey, Peter
Automated analysis of cellular change in histological sections. bibliog Science 163:1200 Mr 14 '69
MAX, Peter
Man in motion. il por Newsweek 73:112-13 Ap 14 '69
MAX Planck society for the advancement of science
Backbone of German science. T. Shoemaker. il Sci N95:386-8 Ap 19 '69
MAXICOATS. See Coats
MAXSON electronics corporation. See Riker-Maxson corporation
MAXTONE-GRAHAM, J. A.
Beau Brummell shopped here. Holiday 46:62-3+ N '69
Flying the English Channel: altitude 7 feet. Pop Mech 131:102-5+ Ja '69
Je fische europeanski. Travel & Camera 32:25-6 D '69
Queen Elizabeth 2. Pop Mech 131:100-3+ F '69
MAXWELL, Margaret
Higglety, pigglety, pop! or, The man who tried to murder Mother Goose. bibliog f Horn Bk 45:392-4 Ag '69
MAXWELL, Neville
China and the USSR on the brink. New Repub 161:17-19 Ag 9 '69
MAXWELL, Robert
Fiery Robert Maxwell down and out at Pergamon. Pub W 196:43-4 O 20 '69
Leasco sues Maxwell, who denounces Ross meeting. Pub W 196:63 N 17 '69
Pergamon affair. por Newsweek 74:74+ S 8 '69
Summer of discontent. J. Tebbel. il por Sat R 52:110 S 13 '69
Tribulations of Saul. por Time 94:94 O 24 '69
MAXWELL, William
Gardens of Mont-Saint-Michel; story. New Yorker 45:30-9 Ag 9 '69
MAXWELL, William Lee
Case that could end capital punishment. R. Hammer. il pors N Y Times Mag p46-7+ O 12 '69
MAY, Catherine Dean
Catherine May backs AFA. por Am For 75:8 Ag '69
MAY, Elaine
Adaptation. Criticism
Nation 208:281-2 Mr 3 '69
New Yorker 45:90+ F 22 '69
Sat R 52:45 Mr 1 '69
Time il 93:42 F 21 '69
Vogue 153:150 Ap 1 '69
MAY, Ernest Richard
Diplomatic post. Newsweek 74:55 S 1 '69
MAY, Henry F.
Living with crisis; a view from Berkeley. Am Scholar 38:588-605 Aut '69
MAY, Jack G. and Main, William
We just want to help you: a note on anger in adolescent group therapy. Ment Hy 53:638-40 O '69
MAY, Rollo
Opinion: on Bethel and after. Mlle 70:28+ N '69
MAY, Thomas
Risky business; a primer on stock market speculation. Atlan 224:68-72+ Jl; 72-6 Ag '69
MAY, Wong
Silence; Going; poems. Poetry 114:365-7 S '69
MAY-apples
May-apple. G. B. Greenwood. il Home Gard 58:32 Ap '69
MAY basket fantasia; drama. See Boiko, C.
MAY day

Drama
May basket fantasia. C. Boiko. Plays 28:36-40, 68 My '69
MAY day (labor holiday)
Hurray, hurray; May day and European Communists. il Newsweek 73:52 My 12 '69
Where are the tanks of yesteryear? il Time 93:41-2 My 9 '69
MAY festival of contemporary American music, Rochester. See Music festivals—New York (state)
MAY flies
See also
Caddis flies
MAY flies, Artificial. See Fishing lures, flies, etc.
MAY you live in interesting times; story. See Williams, G.
MAYA, Mario
Mario Maya and company; 92nd street Y. D. Hering. Dance Mag 43:80 F '69
MAYA architecture. See Architecture, Maya
MAYA astronomy. See Astronomy, Maya
MAYA manuscripts. See Manuscripts, Maya

MAYAKOVSKY, Vladimir Vladimirovich. See Maiakovskii, V. V.
MAYALL, Margaret W.
Director reports. See issues of Review of popular astronomy
MAYAS
Heritage of the Mayas; Metropolitan museum of art in New York presented Maya art from Guatemala. il Américas 21:23-7 Ja '69
Lost cities of the Maya. L. Payne. il Todays Health 47:56-9+ F '69
Mystifying Maya. K. Kuh. il Sat R 52:11-17 Je 28 '69
MAYDOLE, Chester Walter
Classics at Crystal palace; photographs. Motor T 21:58-9 Ap '69
MAYER, Albert
It's not just the cities. Arch Rec 145:151-62 Je; 146:171-82 S; 139-46 N; 105-10 D '69
MAYER, Christa C.
Masterpieces of western textiles. Antiques 95:264-9 F '69
MAYER, George Louis
Italian passion, German skill. Sat R 52:78 Ap 26 '69
Not from the singer, but for the singer. Sat R 52:65 F 22 '69
Orff-Schulwerk, a joyous note. Sat R 52:46-7 Jl 26 '69
MAYER, Jean
It's not eating that kills, but underexercising. por Forbes 104:64+ O 1 '69
Overweight: what to do; interview. por U S News 67:60-4 O 20 '69
Priorities for White House hunger conference. por Todays Health 47:38-9 N '69

about
Food as the first priority. il por Time 94:18-19 D 12 '69
Food watcher for a nation. il pors Life 67:41-2+ N 28 '69
MAYER, Lawrence A.
Enticing logic of revenue sharing. Fortune 79:92-3 Mr '69
Housing shortage goes critical. Fortune 80:86-9+ D '69
Why companies still bet on expansion. Fortune 80:106-9+ Jl '69
World economy; year of inflation. Fortune 80:27-8+ Ag 15 '69
Young America: by the numbers. Fortune 79:72-5 Ja '69
MAYER, Martin
All you know is facts; excerpts. Writer 82:20-2 Mr '69
Anyone with money can play. Harp Baz 102:188-9 S '69
Computers on the brain. Esquire 71:100-3+ Ja '69
Full and sometimes very surprising story of Ocean Hill, the teachers' union and the teacher strikes of 1968; excerpts from The teachers strike; New York, 1968. N Y Times Mag p 18-23+ F 2 '69
Questions and answers about taxes. Redbook 134:87+ N '69
Recordings. See issues of Esquire

about
Life of a free-lancer. Newsweek 73:72 F 17 '69
MAYER, Parm
Walk on shorter legs. Har Yrs 9:22-3 Je '69
MAYER, Ralph
Ralph Mayer's technical question & answer page. See issues of American artist
MAYFIELD, E. B. and others
New solar observatory in California. Sky & Tel 37:208-13 Ap '69
MAYFIELD, John S.
American bibliophiles; reprint. L. S. Thompson. Hobbies 73:108-9+ F '69
Internal revenue deductions. Hobbies 74:140-1 N '69
MAYFLOWER compact. See Pilgrim fathers
MAYHEW, Alice
Merton against himself. Commonweal 91:70-1+ O 17 '69
MAYHEW, David R. See Barber, J. D. jt. auth.
MAYHEW, Henry
Publishing game; excerpts from London labour and the London poor. Nation 208:313 Mr 10 '69
MAYHEW, Lewis Baltzell
Are teachers too arrogant? excerpts from address, June 13, 1969. por U S News 66:10 Je 23 '69
MAYHEW family
Mayhew coat-of-arms. H. K. Ellers. il Hobbies 74:114-15 Mr '69
MAYNARD, A. Lee
Nature as teacher. Sat R 52:76-7 My 17 '69

MAYNARD, Fredelle Bruser
In defense of ceremony. PTA Mag 63:22-4
Ap '69
New rites for old. Seventeen 28:154-5+ Mr
'69
Put-on. Seventeen 27:126-7+ N '68
Real relationship. Seventeen 28:100-1+ D '69
MAYNARD, Olga
Ballerina for all seasons. Dance Mag 43:42-5+
Je '69
Cranko & co. Dance Mag 43:50-9+ S '69
(ed) See Arova, S. Norway
(ed) See D'Amboise, J. Jacques D'Amboise
MAYNARD, Rona
In my opinion. por Seventeen 28:228 F '69
MAYNOR, Dorothy
Dorothy Maynor. C. W. Ferguson. il por
PTA Mag 64:10-12 N '69
Ever-fresh art of Dorothy Maynor. P. L.
Miller. por Am Rec G 35:1111 Ag '69
MAYO, R. W. See Foss, J. W. jt. auth.
MAYO, William Worrall
Mayo: from frontier medicine to clinic fame.
A. S. Freese. il Todays Health 47:58-9+
D '69
MAYOR, Heather D. and others
Plus and minus single-stranded DNA sepa-
rately encapsidated in adeno-associated
satellite virions. bibliog Science 166:1280-2
D 5 '69
MAYOR, Stephen J.
Memory in the Japanese quail: effects of
puromycin and acetoxycycloheximide. bib-
liog Science 166:1165-7 N 28 '69
MAYORAL elections. See Municipal elections
MAYORS
Aid to cities: a White House clash. il U S
News 66:12 My 5 '69
Cities: shattered election patterns. il Time
94:24-5 O 24 '69
Curt words for the Veep; White House con-
ference. Newsweek 73:42+ Je 30 '69
Mayors confront the administration. Bsns
W p36+ N 29 '69
Survey of mayors on ills and remedies. il
Nations Bsns 57:38-41 F '69
Tale of three cities; Pittsburgh, Los Angeles,
Minneapolis. S. V. Roberts; R. W. Gibbons;
B. Casserly. Commonweal 90:381-4 Je 20 '69
See also
Negro mayors
also subhead Mayors under names of
cities. e.g. Los Angeles—Mayors
MAYORS, Negro. See Negro municipal officers
MAYR, Johann Simon
Medea in Corinto. Criticism
Sat R 52:46 D 20 '69
MAYS, Willie
Leading man: wondrous Willie. R. Blount,
jr. il pors Sports Illus 30:32-4 Ap 21 '69
MAYSLE, Albert
That great territory in the sky. H. Alpert.
Sat R 52:75 Mr 22 '69
MAYSLE, David
That great territory in the sky. H. Alpert.
Sat R 52:75 Mr 22 '69
MAZE tests
Learning sets in an invertebrate. J. E. Mor-
row and B. L. Smithson. bibliog il Science
164:850-1 My 16 '69
MAZER, Wendy
What Head Start meant to our town. Par-
ents Mag 44:54-5+ O '69
MAZES
See also
Labyrinths
MAZIE, David M. See Rowan, C. T. jt. auth.
MAZOWIECKI, Arthur W.
Pin-point plowing. por Am City 84:89-90 Ja
'69
MAZRUI, Ali A.
Africa on the eve of tomorrow. Bul Atom
Sci 25:15-19 N '69
MAZUR, Ronald M.
Commonsense sex; excerpt. Redbook 133:83-
5+ Jl '69
MAZZI, Enzo
Children of Isolotto. V. M. Marabelli and L. J.
O'Donovan. America 120:706-9 Je 21 '69
Incident at Isolotto. E. Cochrane. Common-
weal 91:400-3 Ja 9 '70
Letter from Isolotto T. H. Stahel. America
121:418-21 N 8 '69
MBOYA, Thomas Joseph
Last words from a murdered African leader:
the American Negro cannot look to Africa
for an escape. pors N Y Times Mag p30+
Jl 13 '69
Mboya's rebuttal. por Ebony 24:90-1+ Ag '69
Assassination
After Tom Mboya. S. Meisler. por Nation
209:106-8 Ag 11 '69
Assassination of Tom Mboya. T. Woodward.
Commonweal 90:501-3 Ag 22 '69

Clashing symbols. Newsweek 74:36+ Jl 14
'69
Cry of grief for Mboya. il por Life 67:44-44A
Jl 18 '69
Death in the afternoon. il por Time 94:30
Jl 11 '69
Death of a democrat. America 121:22 Jl 19
'69
Kikuyu suspect; killer of T. Mboya. il Time
94:34-5 Ag 1 '69
Loss of Mboya. Nation 209:69 Jl 28 '69
Model nation that may fall apart because of
an assassin's bullet. il U S News 67:10 Jl
21 '69
Obituary
Chr Cent 86:942 Jl 16 '69
Taking the oath. il Newsweek 74:42 Ag 25
'69
Funeral rites and ceremonies
Tribal tinderbox. il por Newsweek 74:46 Jl
21 '69
Under the eyieke tree. il por Time 94:40-1 Jl
18 '69
MEACHEM, William L.
Bulb color. Horticulture 46:36-7+ O '68
Bulbs for intimate plantings. Horticulture
47:22-3+ Ap '69
—See Reynolds, M. jt. auth.
MEACHUM, Roy
Italy between governments. New Repub 162:
16-18 Ja 10 '70
Pope's firm hand. New Repub 161:15-16 N 22
'69
MEAD, Emerson Ernest
Will the real SCM please stand up? R. Levy.
il por Duns R 93:34-7+ Ap '69
MEAD, John F. and Krislov, Joseph
Drawing jurisdictional lines in mediation.
bibliog Mo Labor R 92:41-5 Ap '69
MEAD, Margaret
Generation gap; adaptation of address. Sci-
ence 164:135 Ap 11 '69
Margaret Mead answers. por Redbook 132:33+
Ja '69
[Monthly column] See issues of Redbook
Police and the community. por Redbook 133:
38+ Je '69
Postscript: the 1969 demonstrations; Hamp-
ton institute. Am Scholar 38:682-3 Aut '69
President Nixon and the two-party system.
por Redbook 132:54+ Mr '69
Prize, or lunacy? statement on the eve of
Apollo 11. il por Newsweek 74:61 Jl 7 '69
Public policy and behavioral science; ex-
cerpt from testimony before the U.S. Sen-
ate foreign relations committee, June 20,
1969. por Bul Atom Sci 25:8-10 D '69
Where American women are now; with bio-
graphical sketch. por Vogue 153:176-8+
My '69
Why students are angry. por Redbook 132:
50+ Ap '69
Working paper for man and nature; with
biographical sketch. por Natur Hist 78:6.
14-15+ Ap '69
Youth revolt: the future is now; excerpt
from Culture and commitment. Sat R 53:
23-5+ Ja 10 '70
about
Margaret Mead today: mother to the world.
il pors Time 93:74 Mr 21 '69
MEAD corporation
Save-our-air. B. Lando. New Repub 161:11-
12 O 11 '69
Unpapering of Mead. Forbes 104:32 Ag 15 '69
MEADE, Mrs Everard K. jr
Guild-hopping; a diary. por Opera N 34:6-7 S
20 '69
MEADLO, David Paul
Are we really shocked? relentless question-
ing by Mike Wallace. America 121:629 D 27
'69
MEADOR, Clifton K.
MIST in Alabama. il por Time 94:72 O 10 '69
MEADVILLE, Pa.
Communing in Meadville. R. Houriet. Ramp
Mag 7:10+ N 30 '68
Life and death of a commune called Oz. R.
Houriet. il N Y Times Mag p30-1+ F 16
'69; Discussion. p 12+ Mr 9 '69
MEAGHER, Sylvia
[Book review] Commonweal 89:712-14 Mr 7
'69
MEALS
Great American summer; family reunion,
supper at sea, lunch in a tree house,
church social, barbecue. il McCalls 96:
84-91+ Jl '69
How to give sporting parties. il House &
Gard 136:76-9 Ag '69
Ideas for an autumn calendar; with menus.
il McCalls 97:110-16+ O '69
Play it cool in the kitchen. il Parents Mag
44:67-70+ Ag '69

MEALS—*Continued*
Ready when you are. il Parents Mag 44:74-6 O '69
See also
Breakfasts
Buffet meals
Christmas meals
Cookery
Diet
Dinners and dining
Entertaining
Lunches
Outdoor meals
Snacks
Suppers
Table setting
Thanksgiving dinners

MEALY bugs
Chromatin and histones: binding of tritiated actinomycin D to heterochromatin in mealy bugs. L. Berlowitz and others. bibliog il Science 164:1527-9 Je 27 '69

MEANIE; story. See Ellsberg, H.

MEANING of words. See Semantics

MEANS, Richard L.
Ecology and the contemporary religious conscience. Chr Cent 86:1546-9 D 3 '69
New conservation; with biographical sketch. por Natur Hist 78:4, 16+ Ag '69
Who is responsible for student violence? America 120:352-5 Mr 29 '69

MEANY, George
Labor day, '69; some plain talk from George Meany; interview. por U S News 67:77-8 S 8 '69
Labor looks at government finances. Ann Am Acad 379:72-7 S '68
Walter Reuther's gamble. J. Hill. Commonweal 90:261-3 My 16 '69

about
AFL-CIO as paid propagandist: agent Meany. R. Dudman. New Repub 160:13-16 My 3 '69
Fulbright vs. Meany. K. Crawford. Newsweek 74:29 Ag 18 '69
Isolation of George Meany. B. J. Widick. Nation 209:398-9 O 20 '69
Meany & Reuther: labor's main bout. B. J. Widick. Nation 208:601-2 My 12 '69
Meany-Reuther showdown, with unity the likely loser. por Bsns W p34-5 Ag 30 '69
Meany, Romney; troubled start. U S News 66:64 F 3 '69
Mr Meany replies to Sen. Fulbright. B. L. Masse. America 121:111 Ag 30 '69
Mr Meany's full circle. Nation 208:291 Mr 10 '69
Nixon-Meany: an odd couple. J. Hill. Commonweal 90:537+ S 5 '69
One big union for the blue Meanys. J. Hill. Commonweal 90:37-8 Mr 28 '69

MEARNS, Pat
Waiting out the war, wife or widow? J. J. Fried. il pors Life 67:75-6+ N 7 '69

MEARS, Joe
Manhattan with mountains, and trout. Field & S 73:162-4+ Mr '69
—and East, Ben
War on duck plague. Outdoor Life 144:41-3+ Ag '69

MEASLES
Vaccines
British vaccine withheld; Wellcovax. Sci N 95:328 Ap 5 '69

MEASLES, German. See Rubella

MEASLES virus
Subacute sclerosing panencephalitis: propagation of measles virus from brain biopsy in tissue culture. T. T. Chen and others. bibliog il Science 163:1193-4 Mr 14 '69

MEASUREMENT
Exotic pursuit of precision. T. Alexander. il Fortune 79:80-7 My 1 '69
See also
Frequency measurement

MEASURING instruments
Exotic pursuit of precision. T. Alexander. il Fortune 79:80-7 My 1 '69

MEASURING instruments, Optical
See also
Optical flats

MEAT
See also
Cookery—Meat

Grading and standardization
Case against castration; with editorial comment. il Suc Farm 67:25, 26-7 S '69
Cube steak: often a doubtful buy; scraps run through tenderizer. il Consumer Rep 34:59 F '69

Marketing
Farmer-feeders push for market protection. D. Seim. Farm J 93:B10+ My '69
Getting organic lamb to the public. B. T. Hunter. il Org Gard & Farm 16:70-3 Ag '69
How Minnesota gets everyone involved in pork promotion. D. Seim. Farm J 93:H16 Ag '69

Prepackaging
Bottoms up at the meat counter. il Consumer Rep 34:448-9 Ag '69

Preservation
See also
Game—Preservation

Prices
Are meat bargains gone forever? il U S News 67:68 O 27 '69
Beef sales boom and so do prices. il U S News 66:68-9 Je 9 '69
Consumer revolt; meat boycotts. il Newsweek 74:74+ S 15 '69
Making hay on the hoof. il Bsns W p40-1 Je 21 '69
Meat buying guide: the kindest cuts of all. il Good H 169:210-11 O '69
Pricecast. See issues of Farm journal
Still beautiful, but... il Farm J 93:H15 S '69
What pushed up the prices? fed-beef prices. il Farm J 93:B23 Ag '69
What's happening to food prices. il U S News 67:32-3 Jl 28 '69

Smoking
See Food—Smoking

Terminology
Glossary of cold cuts. il Good H 168:165 Je '69

MEAT, Simulated. See Food substitutes

MEAT, Synthetic. See Food substitutes

MEAT boycotts. See Boycott

MEAT cutting
Fighting over the cost of cutting meat: fabrication issue. Bsns W p74+ N 22 '69

MEAT industry and trade
Beef sales boom and so do prices. il U S News 66:68-9 Je 9 '69
For the old meatpackers, things are tough all over. H. B. Meyers. il Fortune 79:88-93+ F '69
Just ahead: a turning point in the beef industry. D. Malena. il Suc Farm 67:32-3 Ap '69
Meatpackers beef it up. il Bsns W p82-4 Ag 30 '69
Your beef business. J. A. Rohlf. See issues of Farm journal
See also
American beef packers, incorporated
Armour and company
Iowa beef packers, incorporated
Meat—Prepackaging
Meat—Prices
Meat inspection
Strikes—United States—Meat industry and trade
Wilson and company

Advertising
How you're promoting your pork. R. Wilmore. il Farm J 93:H6-7+ Ag '69

Laws and legislation
No stomach for the undercover chickenfurter; hot dog regulations. W. Zinsser. il Life 67:24B O 3 '69

Argentina
Hoofing it out of the doldrums; marketing pre-cut, pre-cooked meat products. Bsns W p62 My 17 '69

Europe, Western
Hog business shoots for even better pork. J. Russell. il Farm J 93:H5 Je '69

MEAT inspection
How that tough new meat inspection law is working. R. C. Black. Farm J 93:B22 Mr '69

MEAT loaf, pies, etc. See Cookery—Meat

MEAT packaging. See Meat—Prepackaging

MEAT packing industry. See Meat industry and trade

MEAT prices. See Meat—Prices

MEAT stock. See Soups

MEAT substitutes. See Food substitutes

MEATYARD, Ralph Eugene
Strange new world of Ralph Eugene Meatyard. J. B. Hall. il Pop Phot 65:120-1+ Jl '69

MECHANIC, Sylvia
　Is that a fact? por Library J 94:960-1 Mr 1 '69
MECHANICAL banks. See Banks, Coin
MECHANICAL devices
　　See also
　Automatons
　Man amplifiers
MECHANICAL dishwashers. See Dishwashing
　and drying machines
MECHANICAL equipment of buildings
　Nine rooms in search of a view; R. Foster's
　revolving house in Connecticut. il House
　& Gard 135:64-9 F '69
MECHANICAL harvesting. See Harvesting ma-
　chinery
MECHANICAL hearts. See Hearts, Artificial
MECHANICAL horsepower. See Horsepower
　(mechanics)
MECHANICAL inventions. See Inventions
MECHANICAL models
　　See also
　Automatons
MECHANICS
　　See also
　Statistical mechanics
　Vibration
MECHANICS (persons)
　　See also
　Airplane mechanics
MECHANICS, Household
　Ask Rufus. R. Cartwright. See issues of
　Mechanix illustrated
MECKLIN, John M.
　Hospitals need management even more than
　money. Fortune 81:96-9+ Ja '70
　It's time to turn down all that noise. For-
　tune 80:130-3+ O '69
　Philippines: an ailing and resentful ally. For-
　tune 80:118-23+ Jl '69
　Rolls-Royce's $2-billion hard sell. Fortune 79:
　122-8+ Mr '69
MEDALIE, Sylvia
　Two housewives run a gallery. J. Kuh. por
　Ladies Home J 86:31 Mr '69
MEDALLIONS, Portrait. See Portrait medal-
　lions
MEDALS
　How to collect coin from coin collectors;
　commemorative medals and tokens for gas
　station games. il Bsns W p 150-1 My 24 '69
　　See also names of medals, e.g. National
　medal of science
MEDALS, Devotional
　Glass medallions of Carl Paulson. J. Canavan.
　il Am Artist 33:22-5 Ag '69
MEDEA in Corinto; opera. See Mayr, J. S.
MEDELLIN, Colombia
　Medellin and manufacturing. J. J. Parsons.
　il Focus 20:8-11 S '69
MEDIA buying services. See Advertising me-
　diums—Purchasing
MEDIA service personnel in education. See
　Educational media personnel
MEDIATION, Industrial. See Arbitration, In-
　dustrial
MEDIC-alert bracelets. See Identification tags.
　bracelets, etc.
MEDICAID program
　Auditing the doctors; question of overbilling
　medicare and medicaid patients. Time 94:
　38+ Jl 11 '69
　Breaking the bank. il Sci N 95:497-8 My 24
　'69
　Granting a reprieve; breathing spell for
　states. Sci N 96:97-8 Ag 2 '69
　High cost of health; Senate finance com-
　mittee hearings. il Newsweek 74:61 Jl 14 '69
　Medicaid's maladies. Time 93:76 My 23 '69
　Mess in medicaid. Time 95:32-3 Ja 12 '70
　Modest fees, large returns. Time 94:46 Ag 15
　'69
　New limits on doctor fees. il U S News 67:
　21-2 Jl 14 '69
　Profiteers are wrecking medicaid. A. Q.
　Maisel. Read Digest 95:151-6 O '69
　Toward a national policy. Sci N 97:7 Ja 3 '70
　Twin tots of national health insurance; what
　are they? Sr Schol 94:8 Ap 11 '69
　Useful changes in medicaid; recommendations
　of special study group. America 121:520 N
　29 '69
MEDICAL assistants. See Medical workers
MEDICAL care. See Medical service
MEDICAL centers
　Berlin university hospital: international de-
　sign for optimum form and function. il
　Arch Rec 146:134-40 O '69
　Medical schools: at the center, the problem
　is unreimbursed costs. J. Walsh. Science
　166:726-8 N 7 '69
　　See also
　Health clinics

MEDICAL colleges
　Brussels: in aftermath of revolt, a medical
　school works at reform. D. S. Greenberg.
　Science 164:651-4 My 9 '69
　France: attempt to slash numbers stirs
　medical school strike. D. S. Greenberg.
　Science 166:1381-3 D 12 '69
　　See also
　Marquette school of medicine, Milwaukee,
　Wis.
　Medical centers
　Medical education
　Meharry medical college, Nashville, Tenn.
MEDICAL columns. See Newspapers—Sections,
　columns, etc.
MEDICAL delusions
　Great bracelet fad; newest health fad.
　Newsweek 74:114-15 O 13 '69
MEDICAL education
　Behavioral sciences and the medical school;
　report of meeting. J. H. U. Brown. Science
　163:964-7 F 28 '69
　Expanding horizons in medical education;
　AAAS symposium December 28, 1969. R. M.
　Dowben. il Science 165:1382-3 S 26 '69
　Growing crisis in health care; interview. J.
　A. D. Cooper. il U S News 67:70-3 N 3 '69
　Medical students: healers become activists.
　M. G. Michaelson. il Sat R 52:41-3+ Ag 16
　'69
　Training Viet Nam's future doctors; Viet
　Nam medical school project. A. Rosenthal.
　il Todays Health 47:38-41+ Jl '69
　　See also
　Medical centers
　Medical colleges

　　　　　History
　Abraham Flexner's medical bombshell; report
　on early 20th century practices. J. L. Slat-
　tery and R. Gosswiller. il Todays Health 47:
　44-5+ Mr '69
MEDICAL electronics
　Costly machines to save lives. il Fortune 81:
　92-5 Ja '70
　Dizzy machine; electronystagmograph. D.
　Ware. il Pop Electr 30:51-2 Ap '69
　Mechanics of medicine; a 200-mph surgical
　drill, the steady beep of a heart monitor
　and an electronic voice box. A. Freese. il
　Pop Mech 132:138-41+ O '69
　Medical electronics servicing. J. Frye. Electr
　World 82:63-4 O '69
　Mini-eye on blood pressure; cardiovascular
　pressure transducer. Sci Digest 66:59 Ag
　'69
　Push-button pain reliever; anginal pain. Sci
　Digest 65:62-3 Je '69
　Safety in medical electronics. J. Frye. Electr
　World 82:58-9 Jl '69
　Someone to watch over you (for less than
　2¢ a day) Electronic stimulation of the
　brain. D. M. Rorvik. Esquire 72:164-7+ D
　'69
　Watching the unborn inside the womb; new
　electronic monitoring device. il Life 67:
　63-5 Jl 25 '69
MEDICAL engineering. See Biomedical engi-
　neering
MEDICAL ethics
　Doctors, ethics and stooges. Chr Cent 86:
　918 Jl 9 '69
　Does an analyst tell? Newsweek 74:67 D 22
　'69
　Heart is a lonely hunter. W. D. Gardner. il
　Ramp Mag 7:34-8 Je '69
　Lesson in ethics; University of Virginia
　medical students debate drug companies'
　free gifts. Nation 208:325 Mr 17 '69
　　See also
　Transplantation of organs, tissues, etc.—Mor-
　al and religious aspects
MEDICAL examinations. See Physical exami-
　nations
MEDICAL fakers. See Quacks and quackery
MEDICAL fees. See Medical service. Cost of
MEDICAL history. See Medicine—History
MEDICAL hypnosis. See Hypnotism—Therapeu-
　tic use
MEDICAL information service via telephone.
　See Telephone in medical service
MEDICAL instruments and apparatus
　Accidents spur legislation; control of hospital
　instruments. Sci N 95:257-8 Mr 15 '69
　Instrumentation and the delivery of health
　services. J. H. U. Brown and J. F. Dick-
　son, 3d. bibliog Science 166:334-8 O 17 '69
　Umbrella of life; vena caval device to pre-
　vent pulmonary embolism. il Newsweek
　74:85 O 20 '69
　　See also
　Medical electronics
　Respiratory apparatus

MEDICAL insurance. See Insurance, Health
MEDICAL jurisprudence
   See also
Insanity—Jurisprudence
Malpractice
MEDICAL laboratories
   New deadline for labs; cut-rate mail-order
   clinical laboratories. Sci N 95:451 My 10 '69
MEDICAL laws and legislation
   Human studies; need for protection of in-
   vestigator and subject. H. K. Beecher. bib-
   liog Science 164:1256-8 Je 13 '69
   Let the dead help the living; proposed Uni-
   form anatomical gift act. R. S. Fisher.
   Todays Health 47:88+ Ap '69
   Making transplants easier; legislation based
   on Uniform anatomical gift act. Time 93:
   61+ Ap 25 '69
   VD: consent for care. D. A. Dukelow. To-
   days Health 47:88 F '69
   See also
   Transplantation of organs, tissues, etc.—
   Legal aspects
MEDICAL libraries
   See also
   Medical library center of New York
MEDICAL library association
   Medical library association officers and
   awards; annual meeting. Wilson Lib Bul
   44:499 Ja '70
MEDICAL library center of New York
   Programming costs shared in medical library
   plan. Library J 94:1570 Ap 15 '69
MEDICAL literature
   See also
   Booksellers and bookselling—Medical litera-
   ture
   Medicine—Periodicals
   Psychiatric literature
MEDICAL missions. See Missions, Medical
MEDICAL news
   Medical briefs. See issues of Todays health
MEDICAL periodicals. See Medicine—Periodicals
MEDICAL philosophy. See Medicine—Philoso-
   phy
MEDICAL profession. See Medicine—Practice;
   Physicians
MEDICAL radiology. See Radiology, Medical
MEDICAL relief work

Alaska
   Mush against death; getting diphtheria antitoxin to Nome, 1925. L. M. Rhodes. il Todays Health 48:30-3+ Ja '70

Biafra
   ABC; Saturday review's Aid for Biafran
   children. N. Cousins. il Sat R 52:20-1+ F 1
   '69
   Moon over Owerri. N. Cousins. Sat R 52:
   16+ Ag 2 '69
   Report on ABC; Saturday review's Aid for
   Biafran children. N. Cousins. Sat R 52:20-1
   My 3 '69
MEDICAL research
   Air pollution medical research; report of
   meeting. J. R. Goldsmith and R. Hartman.
   Science 163:706-9 F 14 '69
   Drugs vs. vaccines; antiviral drugs. il Time
   93:57 Je 27 '69
   Instrumentation and the delivery of health
   services. J. H. U. Brown and J. F. Dick-
   son, 3d. bibliog Science 166:334-8 O 17 '69
   Science and social purpose; adaptation of ad-
   dress, December 27, 1968. J. A. Shannon.
   bibliog Science 163:769-73 F 21 '69
   Scientist talks about careers in science; inter-
   view, ed. by A. S. Freese. R. Dubos. il To-
   days Health 47:24-7+ S '69
   See also
   American medical association—Institute for
   biomedical research
   Animal experimentation
   Cancer research
   Dental research
   Drugs, Experimental
   Health agencies, Voluntary
   Laboratory animals
   Medical centers
   Ophthalmology
   Psychiatric research
   United States—National institutes of health

Experimentation on man
   Defense of the human fetus; unethical ex-
   perimentation with prenatal life. il Sci
   Digest 66:61-2 O '69
   Human guinea pigs, by M. H. Pappworth.
   Review
     Nation 208:117-20 Ja 27 '69. G. A. Silver
   Human studies; need for protection of investi-
   gator and subject. H. K. Beecher. bibliog
   Science 164:1256-8 Je 13 '69

Federal aid
   Cutting back on health. Nation 209:685-6
   D 22 '69
   Killing medicine; letter. E. N. Goren and
   others. New Repub 161:40 N 29 '69
   Something for everybody. il Sci N 95:90-1 Ja
   25 '69
   Surgery on research; cutback on NIH proj-
   ects. il Newsweek 74:68 S 22 '69
   Why a shift in medical aid. U S News 67:18
   S 22 '69
   Wrong place to cut; funds slashed for bio-
   logical and medical research. Nation 209:
   362-3 O 13 '69

International cooperation
   U.S.—Japan medical science committee meets
   at Washington; Department announcement,
   with text of joint communique. Dept State
   Bul 61:215-16 S 8 '69
   U.S.-Japan medical science program report
   transmitted to Congress; letter, January 16,
   1969. L. B. Johnson. Dept State Bul 60:118
   F 3 '69
MEDICAL schools. See Medical colleges
MEDICAL service
   Crisis warning in health care; HEW report.
   U S News 67:9 Jl 21 '69
   Does America need a new health system?
   address, February 3, 1969. W. J. McNerney.
   Vital Speeches 35:363-70 Ap 1 '69
   Growing crisis in health care; interview. J.
   A. D. Cooper. il U S News 67:70-3 N 3 '69
   Health care costs; patient doctor relationship;
   address, January 13, 1969. D. L. Wilbur.
   Vital Speeches 35:263-7 F 15 '69
   Hospital unit trains family doctors. Todays
   Health 47:87 F '69
   How to improve medical care; interview.
   W. J. McNerney. il U S News 66:42-6 Mr 24
   '69
   If you're black and sick. il Newsweek 74:
   83 Jl 7 '69
   It's time to operate; symposium. il Fortune
   81:78-99+ Ja '70
   Medical crisis and how to meet it. il U S
   News 67:34-6 Jl 28 '69
   M.D. should not try to cure society. M. J.
   Halberstam. il N Y Times Mag p32-3+ N
   9 '69; Reply with rejoinder. R. Karp. p62+
   D 7 '69
   Medical shortages abroad, too. il U S News
   67:73-5 N 3 '69
   Modern medical myths; adaptation of ad-
   dress. M. J. Halberstam. Todays Health
   47:72 +Jl '69
   Plight of the U.S. patient. il Time 93:53-8
   F 21 '69; Same abr. with title What's
   wrong with U.S. medicine? Read Digest
   94:145-6+ My '69
   TRB from Washington; health care crisis
   in the US. New Repub 161:4 O 18 '69
   See also
   Helicopters in medical service
   Hospitals
   Telephone in medical service

Cuba
   Cuba's revolutionary medicine. W. P. Butler.
   Ramp Mag 7:6+ My '69
MEDICAL service, Cost of
   Better care at less cost without miracles.
   E. K. Faltermayer. il Fortune 81:80-3+ Ja
   '70
   Health care costs; address, January 13, 1969.
   D. L. Wilbur. Vital Speeches 35:263-7 F 15
   '69
   Health dollar headache; plenty of grief for
   everybody? il Sr Schol 94:6-8+ Ap 11 '69
   How to improve medical care; interview.
   W. J. McNerney. il U S News 66:42-6 Mr 24
   '69
   Medical care; as costs soar, support grows
   for major reform. J. R. Kramer. Science
   166:1126-9 N 28 '69
   Medical schools; at the center, the problem
   is unreimbursed costs. J. Walsh. Science
   166:726-8 N 7 '69
   Modest fees, large returns. Time 94:46 Ag 15
   '69
   New limits on doctor fees. il U S News 67:
   21-2 Jl 14 '69
   Safe ways to cut your medical bills. il Chang-
   ing T 22:39-40 D '68
   Staggering practices; medicare and medicaid
   fees. Newsweek 74:55 Ag 18 '69
   Unless a remedy is applied at once... E.
   Switzer. il Redbook 133:65+ O '69
MEDICAL service, State
   See also
   Great Britain—National health service
   Medicaid program
   Medicare program

MEDICAL social work
   See also
Health agencies, Voluntary
MEDICAL societies
   See also names of medical societies, e.g.
National medical association
MEDICAL students
France: attempt to slash numbers stirs
   medical school strike. D. S. Greenberg.
   Science 166:1381-3 D 12 '69
Girl becomes a doctor. R. Gosswiller. il To-
   days Health 47:29-33 Je '69
Medical students healers become activists.
   M. G. Michaelson. il Sat R 52:41-3+ Ag 16
   '69
Shaking up the curriculum. il Fortune 81:86-
   9 Ja '70
Student activists; summer programs. il Time
   94:60 Jl 18 '69
MEDICAL superstitions. See Medicine, Magic,
   mystic, etc.
MEDICAL supplies
Medical-industrial complex. H. B. Meyers.
   il Fortune 81:90-1+ Ja '70
MEDICAL workers
Medical assistant; the health team ap-
   proach; address, January 23, 1969. E. F.
   Rosinski. Vital Speeches 35:438-41 My 1 '69
Physician's assistant; new help for the
   sick. il U S News 67:90 S 8 '69
MEDICARE program
Answers to your questions about social secur-
   ity & medicare. F. Bailey, jr. il Suc Farm
   67:73 Ja '69
Auditing the doctors; question of overbilling
   medicare and medicaid patients. Time 94:
   38+ Jl 11 '69
High cost of health; Senate finance commit-
   tee hearings. il Newsweek 74:61 Jl 14 '69
Is medicare worth the price? interview. R. M.
   Ball. il U S News 67:48-51 Jl 21 '69
Medicare hospital deductible increases Jan-
   uary 1, 1969. Aging 170:11 D '68
Medicare: three years of progress. R. R.
   Jalbert. Har Yrs 9:24 Jl '69
Mess in medicaid. Time 95:32-3 Ja 12 '70
Scandal brewing in medicare? findings from
   inquiry by Senate finance committee. U S
   News 66:10 My 26 '69
Senate diagnosis of medicare bills. Bsns W
   p52 Je 14 '69
Twin tots of national health insurance: what
   are they? Sr Schol 94:8 Ap 11 '69
MEDICI, Emilio Garrastazú
New president: medium-hard. il por Time
   94:33-4 O 31 '69
MEDICINE
Keep up with medicine. B. Yuncker. See
   issues of Good housekeeping
Medical marvels: space-age breakthroughs at
   AMA convention. il Har Yrs 9:42-5 N '69
Medical sciences. See issues of Science news
Medicine. A. J. Snider. See issues of Science
   digest
Medicine today. P. Wright and D. R. Zimmer-
   man. See issues of Ladies' home journal
News from the world of medicine. See issues
   of Reader's digest
What's new in medicine. See issues of Mc-
   Call's to July 1969
   See also
Bible—Medicine, hygiene, etc.
Biomedical engineering
Homeopathy
Indians of Central America—Medicine
Medical research
Missions, Medical
Moving pictures in medicine
Politics and medicine
Prescriptions
Quacks and quackery
Space medicine

Bibliography
Books to come; ed. by J. Donathan and J.
   Fletcher. Library J 94:4031-52 N 1 '69
Books to come; ed. by J. Putnam (cont)
   Library J 94:1025-55, 2647-66 Mr 1, Jl '69

Group practice
Change begins in the doctor's office. D. Cord-
   dtz. il Fortune 81:84-9+ Ja '70

History
Medicine's happy accidents. W. Garrison. il
   Todays Health 47:28-31+ F '69
Washington after the Revolution; excerpts.
   J. T. Flexner. il Am Heritage 21:32-3+ D
   '69
Windows on medicine's past; Dr May Owen
   Hall of medical science at the Museum of
   science and industry, Fort Worth, Tex.
   E. H. McCleary. il Todays Health 47:70-2
   O '69

Periodicals
Medical advice comes in a new package. il
   Bsns W p66-7+ S 27 '69

Philosophy
Fourth doctor. P. F. Eastman. il Todays
   Health 47:28-9+ Ap '69

Practice
Helping the doctors; physicians' assistants.
   F. Marley. il Sci N 95:97-8 Ja 25 '69
   See also
Chiropractic
Diagnosis
Malpractice
Medical service
Physicians
Quacks and quackery

Social aspects
M.D. should not try to cure society. M. J.
   Halberstam. il N Y Times Mag p32-3+ N
   '69; Reply with rejoinder. R. Karp. p62+
   D 7 '69

Study and teaching
Mission of Hope. M. Kraft. il Américas 21:
   29-35 S '69
   See also
Medical colleges
Medical education
Medical students

Terminology
Glossary of medical terms. McCalls 96:50 Ap
   '69

Cuba
Cuba's revolutionary medicine. W. P. Butler.
   Ramp Mag 7:6+ My '69

Egypt
   See also
Imhotep

India
   See also
Medicine, Hindu

United States
Inside American medicine (cont) il Todays
   Health 47:24-7+ F: 40-1+ Ap; 24-7+ S;
   38-41+ D '69; 48:44-7+ Ja '70
It's time to operate; symposium. il Fortune
   81:78-99+ Ja '70
Plight of the U.S. patient. il Time 93:53-8
   F 21 '69; Same abr. with title What's wrong
   with U.S. medicine? Read Digest 94:145-6+
   My '69

Vietnam (Republic)
Training Viet Nam's future doctors; Viet Nam
   medical school project. A. Rosenthal. il
   Todays Health 47:38-41+ Jl '69
MEDICINE, Biblical. See Bible—Medicine, hy-
   giene, etc.
MEDICINE, Hindu
Modern India's ancient medicine; Ayurvedic
   medicine. C. Leslie. il Trans-Action 6:46-55
   Je '69
MEDICINE, Magic, mystic, etc.
World of saints and she-demons; life in a
   small Arab town. V. Crapanzano and J.
   Kramer. il N Y Times Mag p 14-15+ Je 22
   '69
MEDICINE, Military
   See also
United States—Army—Medical corps
MEDICINE, Popular
Folk remedies: part wisdom, part hokum; ex-
   cerpts from Potions, remedies, and old
   wives' tales. W. W. Bauer. il Todays
   Health 48:6+ Ja '70
MEDICINE, Preventive
Disease prevention, tomorrow's best hope. J.
   Carper. il Todays Health 47:20-3+ Mr '69
Latest on health care and cures. il U S News
   67:5 Jl 28 '69
MEDICINE, Primitive
   See also
Medicine men
MEDICINE, Psychosomatic
Psychotherapy by somatic alteration. P. F.
   Grim. bibliog Ment Hy 53:451-8 Jl '69
What is a doctor's toughest diagnosis? W. E.
   O'Donnell. Good H 169:59+ Jl '69
   See also
Mind and body
MEDICINE, Space. See Space medicine
MEDICINE and politics. See Politics and
   medicine
MEDICINE and religion
   See also
Hallucinogenic drugs and religious experience
MEDICINE cabinets
Your medicine chest. il Parents Mag 44:46+
   N '69

MEDICINE men
Bantu witch doctor: the influential psychologist of modern South Africa. R. F. Dempewolff. il Sci Digest 66:6-15 Ag '69
MEDICINES. See Drugs
MEDICINES, Patent, proprietary, etc.
See also
Toilet preparations
MEDIEVAL architecture. See Architecture, Medieval
MEDIEVAL civilizaton. See Civilization, Medieval
MEDIEVAL music. See Music, Medieval
MEDINA, Ernest L.
My Lai killings; how army captain describes incident; excerpts from Pentagon news conference, December 4, 1969. por U S News 67:10 D 15 '69
about
Captain's nightmare. A. Deming. il por Newsweek 74:41 D 15 '69
Fallout from Song My. il Newsweek 74:40-1 D 15 '69
Probing the massacre probe. por Time 94:16-17 D 12 '69
MEDINA, Fernando Diez de. See Diez de Medina, F.
MEDINA, Ohio
Pumped water storage. F. W. Reusswig and C. F. Tavener. il Am City 84:72-4 Mr '69
MEDIOCRITY
Excellence: a vanishing virtue? Chr Today 13:36-7 S 26 '69
MEDITATION
Future for contemplatives? J. C. Haughey. America 121:261-4 O 4 '69; Discussion. 121:343 O 25 '69
Make an appointment with yourself. L. Finkelstein. Read Digest 95:108-10 S '69
New praying nun; House of prayer. J. M. Kann. Cath World 209:71-6 My '69
Renewal for the cloister; contemplative communities. il Time 94:64+ S 5 '69
MEDITERRANEAN fruit fly. See Fruit flies
MEDITERRANEAN REGION
Climate and history; excerpt from Discontinuity in Greek civilization. R. Carpenter. il Horizon 11:48-57 Spr '69
Mediterranean crisis. F. S. Meyer. Nat R 21:75 Ja 28 '69
Sail on, Yankee! A. Goetz and N. Goetz. il Motor B 123:138-40+ Ja '69
Sun coasts of the Mediterranean isles. G. Bush. il Bet Hom & Gard 47:165 Mr '69
See also
Gardens—Mediterranean Region
Malta
Middle East
Defenses
West faces rising Mediterranean threat. E. H. Kolcum. il Aviation W 90:20-1 F 3 '69
Description and travel
Sketches from the Med. W. Bagley. il Yachting 126:59-61+ D '69
MEDITERRANEAN SEA
Soviet sea power; latest threat to America; with interview with Vice Admiral D. C. Richardson. C. S. Foltz, jr. il U S News 67:56-61 Jl 21 '69
See also
Aegean Islands
MEDIUM; story. See Mountzoures, H. L.
MEDIUMS
See also
Spiritualism
MEDRANO, José A. Tijerino-. See Tijerino-Medrano, J. A.
MEE, Suzi
Sebastian; poem. Poetry 114:369-70 S '69
MEE, Thomas R.
Making clouds has a silver lining. il por Bsns W p82 D 27 '69
MEEHAN, Thomas
At Bennington the boys are the coeds. N Y Times Mag p 12-13+ D 21 '69
Biography of a charity ball. N Y Times Mag p 12-13+ Je 1 '69
Four fantasies. Mlle 70:124-5+ D '69
If you're still curious, here are advance reviews of three important upcoming movies (rating: Z) N Y Times Mag p 12-13 Je 29 '69
New mobe (II); the kids on bus no. 28 N Y Times Mag p28-9+ N 30 '69
Nothing personal; story. New Yorker 45:30-2 Mr 1 '69
Scram gets green light: Spiro Agnew to rise at Marshgrass. New Yorker 44:32-3 F 15 '69
MEEK, George
(comp) Hemisphere. See issues of Américas

MEEKER, John J.
Seeds from your own garden. Org Gard & Farm 16:30-4 Jl '69
There's always room for herbs. por Org Gard & Farm 16:60-4 Ja '69
MEEKS, M. L. and others
Interstellar sulfur hydride: a search for the 111-Megahertz lines. bibliog Science 163:173-4 Ja 10 '69
Water vapor: observations of galactic sources. bibliog Science 165:180-4 Jl 11 '69
MEETER, Glenn
Waiting for daddy; story. Redbook 134:76-7 N '69
MEETINGS
Run a meeting that gets things done. il Changing T 23:19-20 S '69
See also
Business meetings
Conferences
Conventions
Sales conventions
Stockholders meetings
MEFISTOFELE; opera. See Boito, A.
MEGALITHIC monuments
Megalithic plan underlying Canterbury cathedral. L. B. Borst. bibliog il Science 163:567-70 F 7 '69; Discussion. 164:769-70; 166:772-4 My 16, N 7 '69
See also
Stonehenge, England
MEGARITY, Ferris
Cry of the peacock. House B 111:72+ Ap '69
MEGIVERN, James
Anti-morality missile. Commonweal 90:357-8 Je 13 '69
MEHARRY medical college, Nashville, Tenn.
Ghetto medicine. il Newsweek 75:56-7 Ja 5 '70
MEHER, Baba
Jai Baba! New Yorker 45:28-31 Je 21 '69
MEHMEDOV, Mesru M.
Young conductor from Bulgaria. I. Kolodin. Sat R 52:51 F 15 '69
MEHTA, Ved
Reporter at large. New Yorker 45:26-32+ Jl 19; 40-8+ Jl 26 '69
MEHTA, Zubin
Music to my ears: performance of works of Beethoven, Mendelssohn, and Richard Strauss in New York city. I. Kolodin. Sat R 53:76 Ja 3 '70
MEIER, August
Street corner voices. Trans-Action 6:58-60 F '69
—and Rudwick, Elliott
Black boycotts before Montgomery. Ebony 24:154-6+ O '69
MEIER, Richard
People come to architects to improve the quality of their lives; interview. por House & Gard 136:12+ D '69
MEIER, Richard L.
Social impact of a nuplex. Bul Atom Sci 25:16-21 Mr '69
MEIERHENRY, Wesley C.
National media standards for learning and teaching. ALA Bul 63:238-41 F '69
Strategies and ploys. bibliog por Library J 94:1728-30 Ap 15 '69
MEIJER, R. J.
Dutch on the road to a pollution-free engine. il por Bsns W p52-3 Ja 10 '70
MEILACH, Dona Z. See Haynes, D. M; Josey, W. E. jt. auths.
MEINKE, Peter
Progress; poem. New Repub 161:36 N 29 '69
MEINWALD, J. and others
Sex pheromone of the queen butterfly: chemistry. bibliog Science 164:1174-5 Je 6 '69
MEIOSIS. See Cell division (biology)
MEIR, Golda
Last thing we want is another war; interview, ed. by J. Fromm. il por U S News 67:52-5 S 22 '69
Plain talk from Golda Meir; interview, ed. by H. Donovan and H. Grunwald. por Time 93:37 My 23 '69
Prime Minister Meir of Israel visits Washington: exchange of greetings, toasts and remarks, September 25 and 26, 1969. Dept State Bul 61:318-22 O 13 '69
We won our wars, we don't need victories; interview, ed. by R. Stolley. por Life 67:32-3 O 3 '69
about
Cabinet of hawks. Time 94:18 D 26 '69
Golda. J. R. Moskin. il pors Look 33:94+ O 7 '69
Golda goes shopping. il por Time 94:32 O 3 '69
Golda's odyssey. il por Time 94:23 O 10 '69
Israel has found a replacement for Golda Meir. it's Golda Meir. J. Feron. il pors N Y Times Mag p52-3+ O 26 '69

MEIR, Golda—about—*Continued*
  Israel's Meir; a plea for aid. il por U S News
    67:18 O 6 '69
  Israel's new premier. Time 93:34+ Mr 14 '69
  Middle East: shifting into neutral. il por
    Time 95:21-2 Ja 5 '70
  Middle East: the war and the woman. il por
    Time 94:28-33 S 19 '69
  New choices in the Middle East. il por Time
    93:35-7 Mr 7 '69
  Our Golda. Newsweek 73:63 Mr 17 '69
  Rhodes approach. il por Newsweek 74:84+ O
    6 '69
  She's tough and everyone knows she's tough;
    with report by R. Chesnoff. pors Newsweek
    74:55 S 29 '69
  Voting under fire. por Time 94:35 N 7 '69
MEISEL, Alan R.
  Focus on Albuquerque. Craft Horiz 29:46-9
    S '69
MEISEL, D. D. See Goldstein, S. J. jr, jt. auth.
MEISLER, Stanley
  After Tom Mboya. Nation 209:106-8 Ag 11
    '69
  Biafra: war of images. Nation 208:301-4 Mr
    10 '69
  Isolated successes. Nation 208:86-8 Ja 20 '69
  Kenya's Asian outcasts. Nation 209:173-6
    S 1 '69
  Report: Portuguese Africa. Atlan 223:14+
    Ja '69
  Reports: Nigeria and Biafra. Atlan 224:25-6+
    O '69
Die MEISTERSINGER von Nürnberg; opera. See
    Wagner, R.
MEJIA, Paul
  Trouble in paradise. il por Newsweek 73:85-6
    Mr 26 '69
MEKAKE. See Women—Japan
MEKONG development project. See United
    Nations—Economic commission for Asia
    and the Far East
MELADY, Margaret Badum. See Melady, T.
    P. jt. auth.
MELADY, Thomas Patrick
  Background to U.S.-Vatican relations. Cath
    World 209:107-11 Je '69
  From the radical left to the center. Cath
    World 209:168-71 Jl '69
—and Melady, M. B.
  Commonwealth of churches; excerpt from
    The house divided: poverty, race, religion
    and the family of man. Cath World 210:
    170-4 Ja '70
  Human rights and the Nixon administration.
    Cath World 209:55-8 My '69
MELAMED, Monte
  Dynamic camp design aids creative arts pro-
    gram. Camp Mag 41:8-9 S '69
MELAMED, Myron R.
  Pill and cancer. il por Newsweek 74:59 Ag
    11 '69
—and others
  Cytotoxic test automation: a live-dead cell
    differential counter. bibliog Science 163:
    285-6 Ja 17 '69
MELATONIN
  Hair color, molt, and testis size in male,
    short-tailed weasels treated with melatonin.
    C. C. Rust and R. K. Meyer. bibliog il Sci-
    ence 165:921-2 Ag 29 '69
MELBA, Dame Nellie
  Melba, by J. Hetherington. Review
    Am Rec G pors 35:884-5 My '69. A. F. R.
    Lawrence
MELBOURNE-Frank E. Evans collision. See
    Collisions at sea
MELCHER, Daniel
  Architectonics of the mind. por Library J
    94:3785-8 O 15 '69
MELCHER, Marguerite (Fellows)
  Obituary
    Pub W il por 195:42 Je 30 '69
MELCHETT, Julian Edward Alfred Mond, 3d
    baron
  Nationalization mess. por Time 94:74 Jl 11 '69
MELCHITES. See Catholic church—Byzantine
    rite
MELEWICZ, Melanie
  Don't call us geniuses. Am Ed 5:22-5 N '69
MELGES, Frederick T.
  Postpartum psychiatric reactions: time of
    onset and sex ratio of newborns. bibliog
    Science 166:1026-7 N 21 '69
MELKITES. See Catholic church—Byzantine
    rite
MELLARD, Joan McGuire
  Not-really-an-answer to poetry class III; poem.
    Engl J 58:211 F '69
MELLINGER, Marie B.
  Autumn's acres. il Nat Parks 43:12-13 Ja '69
MELLON, J. R.
  Breakfast at midnight. Outdoor Life 144:60-
    3+ Jl '69

MELLONIE, David M. H.
  Cruising the North Atlantic islands. Motor B
    123:144+ Mr '69
MELLOW, James R.
  Bauhaus is alive and well in soup plates and
    skyscrapers. N Y Times Mag p34-5+ S 14
    '69
  Matisse: a celebration of pleasure. N Y Times
    Mag p 16-17+ D 28 '69
  Rocky as a collector. N Y Times Mag p34-
    6+ My 18 '69
MELMAN, Seymour
  How to cut the military budget by $54 billion.
    Commonweal 91:273-6 N 28 '69
MELNYK, Steve
  Fluffy makes it no contest. C. Kirkpatrick.
    por Sports Illus 31:26-7 S 8 '69
MELONS
  Banana melon. B. Brinhart. il Home Gard
    56:92-4 Ap '69
    See also
  Cookery—Fruit
  Watermelons
MELTON, Ellen
  (ed) See Farson, R. E. As I see it
MELTON, Marjorie L. See Sheffield, H. G.
    jt. auth.
MELTZER, Herbert
  Creatine kinase and aldolase in serum: ab-
    normality common to acute psychoses.
    bibliog Science 159:1368-70; 164:726-7 Mr 22
    '68. My 9 '69
MELTZER, Milton
  Hughes, Twain Child, and Sanger: four who
    locked horns with the censors; adaptation
    of addresses. por Wilson Lib Bul 44:278-86
    N '69
MELVILLE, Herman
  Billy Budd; dramatization. See Hall, A.
                    about
  Do you know what's happening; Benito
    Cereno and present day problems. I. Hal-
    perin. Engl J 58:1049-52 O '69
  Sesquicentennial; Melville society meeting.
    New Yorker 45:34-5 S 20 '69
  Why isn't Melville for the masses? H. Cohen.
    il por Sat R 52:19-21 Ag 16 '69
MELVILLE shoe corporation
  Melville draws a bead on the $50-billion fash-
    ion market. R. Beardwood. il Fortune 80:
    110-14+ D '69
  Melville shoe; the octogenarian & the teen-
    ager. il Forbes 103:20-2+ F 1 '69
MELVIN, A. Gordon
  Natural history. See issues of Hobbies
MELVIN, Glen E.
  How to choose a plow. Suc Farm 67:B2 Ap
    '69
MELVIN, Kenneth
  Big brother is dead too. Nat R 21:116-18 F
    11 '69
MEMBERS of Parliament
  Canada's black member of Parliament. il
    Ebony 24:132-4+ Ap '69
    See also
  Devlin. B.
MEMBRANES (biology)
  Bacterial cell wall. N. Sharon. il Sci Am
    220:92-8 My '69
  Carcinoma of the cervix: deficiency of nexus
    intercellular junctions. N. S. McNutt and
    R. S. Weinstein. bibliog il Science 165:597-9
    Ag 8 '69
  Cellulosic wall component produced by the
    Golgi apparatus of pleurochrysis scherf-
    felii. R. M. Brown and others. bibliog il Sci-
    ence 166:894-6 N 14 '69
  Ciliary orientation: controlled by cell mem-
    brane or by intracellular fibrils? Y. Naitoh
    and R. Eckert. bibliog il Science 166:1633-
    5 D 26 '69
  Cyclic guanosin monophosphate: effects on
    short-circuit current and water permeabili-
    ty. J. Bourgoignie and others. bibliog il
    Science 165:1362-3 S 26 '69
  Diffusive and convective flow across mem-
    branes: irreversible thermodynamic ap-
    proach. E. H. Bresler and R. P. Wendt.
    bibliog il Science 163:944-5 F 28 '69; Reply
    with rejoinder. G. S. Manning. Science 166:
    1438 D 12 '69
  Energy flux and membrane synthesis in
    photosynthetic bacteria. G. A. Sojka and
    others. bibliog il Science 166:113-15 O 3 '69
  Glucagon-sensitive adenyl cylase in plasma
    membrane of hepatic parenchymal cells. S.
    L. Pohl and others. bibliog il Science 164:
    566-7 My 2 '69
  Ionic mechanisms controlling behavioral re-
    sponses of paramecium to mechanical
    stimulation. Y. Naitoh and R. Eckert. bib-
    liog il Science 164:963-5 My 23 '69

MEMBRANES (biology)—*Continued*
Macromolecular subunits in the walls of marine nitrifying bacteria. S. W. Watson and C. C. Remsen. bibliog il Science 163: 685-6 F 14 '69
Mammary alveolar epithelial cells: effect of hydrocortisone on ultrastructure. E. S. Mills and Y. J. Topper. bibliog il Science 165:1127-8 S 12 '69
Membrane alterations in hemolysis: internalization of plasmalemma induced by primaquine. F. L. Ginn and others. bibliog il Science 164:843-5 My 16 '69
Membrane potential as the sum of ionic and metabolic components. M. F. Marmor and A. L. F. Gorman. bibliog il Science 167:65-7 Ja 2 '70
Membranous structures associated with translation and transcription of poliovirus RNA. L. A. Caliguiri and I. Tamm. bibliog il Science 166:885-6 N 14 '69
Mycoplasma membrane lipids: variations in fatty acid composition. R. N. McElhaney and M. E. Tourtellotte. bibliog il Science 164:433-4 Ap 25 '69
Neutron diffraction of cell membranes (myelin) D. F. Parsons and C. K. Akers. bibliog il Science 165:1016-18 S 5 '69
Permeability and structure of junctional membranes at an electrotonic synapse. B. W. Payton and others. bibliog il Science 166:1641-3 D 26 '69
Postsynaptic membrane response predicted from presynaptic input pattern in lobster cardiac ganglion. D. K. Hartline and I. M. Cooke. bibliog il Science 164:1080-2 My 30 '69
Potential energy fields about nitrogen in choline and ethanolamine: biological function at cellular surfaces. J. E. Zull and A. J. Hopfinger. bibliog il Science 165:512-13 Ag 1 '69
Role of surface dipoles on axon membrane. L. Y. Wei. bibliog il Science 163:280-2 Ja 17 '69
Stability of asymmetric phospholipid membranes. D. Papahadjopoulos and S. Ohki. bibliog il Science 164:1075-7 My 30 '69
See also
Blood-brain barrier

MEMBRANES (technology)
Calibrated membranes with coated pore walls. W. J. Petzny and J. A. Quinn. bibliog il Science 166:751-3 N 7 '69
Divalent phosphate electrode. I. Nagelberg and others. il Science 166:1403-4 D 12 '69

MEMENTOS. See Keepsakes

MEMORANDUMS
Ways to organize reminders. il Good H 168: 187 My '69

MEMOREX corporation
Thanks for the Memorex. Newsweek 74:78 D 1 '69

MEMORIAL arts center, Atlanta. See Atlanta —Memorial arts center

MEMORIAL funds
Better way of paying respects to the dead. J. Daniel. Read Digest 95:143-6 Ag '69

MEMORIAL stadium, Memphis, Tenn. See Stadiums

MEMORIALS
Partying is such sweet sorrow; strange memorial of O. L. Nelms. il Time 93: 83-4 Je 13 '69
See also
Kennedy, J. F—Memorials
King, M. L.—Memorials

MEMORY
Alcohol and recall; state-dependent effects in man. D. W. Goodwin and others. bibliog il Science 163:1358-60 Mr 21 '69
Chemical transfer of learning? ed. by B. M. Murray. G. Ungar. il Todays Ed 58:44-7 F '69
Man's participatory evolution; psychoneurobiochemeducation. D. Krech. Cur 110:55-64 S '69
Memory and magnetism. Chem 42:26 O '69
Memory in the Japanese quail: effects of puromycin and acetoxycycloheximide. S. J. Mayor. bibliog il Science 166:1165-7 N 28 '69
Memory traces in the octopus. M. Wells. il Sea Front 15:295-307 S '69
Neurophysiology of remembering. K. H. Pribram. il Sci Am 220:73-80+ bibliog(p 138) Ja '69; Reply with rejoinder. R. W. Rodieck. 220:6-7 Je '69
Puromycin: effect on memory of mice when injected with various cations. J. B .Flexner and L. B. Flexner. bibliog il Science 165: 1143-4 S 12 '69
Remembering machines of tomorrow. W. S. Merwin. il New Yorker 45:52-3 N 29 '69

What science has discovered about memory. il Changing T 23:25-8 N '69
See also
Amnesia
Eidetic imagery
Recall (psychology)
Reminiscence

MEMORY devices (computers)
Amorphous-semiconductor switching. H. K. Henisch. il Sci Am 221:30-41 bibliog(p 166) N '69
Magnetic tug toward the future. il Bsns W p78-9 Ag 9 '69
Taking on bits by the trillion; laser recording system. il Bsns W p78+ F 1 '69

MEMORY tests
How's your memory of the good old days? J. B. Langer. Har Yrs 9:18 My '69

MEMOS. See Memorandums

MEMPHIS, Tenn.
Colorful, splinter-free seating. N. Baxter. il Am City 84:52 Je '69
Rebirth of the blues; soul. S. Booth. il Sat Eve Post 242:26-31+ F 8 '69

Education
Memphis blues; demonstrations and school boycotts for desegregation of school administration. Newsweek 74:38-9 N 24 '69

Negroes
Memphis a year later: a proud city stunned but unmoved. W. Willoughby. Chr Today 13:42+ Ap 11 '69
Memphis blues; demonstrations and school boycotts for desegregation of school administration. Newsweek 74:38-9 N 24 '69
Year later in Memphis. H. P. Leifermann. Nation 208:401-3 Mr 31 '69

Parks and playgrounds
Fifty miniparks in three weeks. il Am City 84:121+ S '69

Politics and government
Year later in Memphis. H. P. Leifermann. Nation 208:401-3 Mr 31 '69

Religious institutions and affairs
Memphis a year later: a proud city stunned but unmoved. W. Willoughby. Chr Today 13:42+ Ap 11 '69

MEMPHIS, Tenn, public library
Confrontation in Memphis; with reply by H. Mitchell. C. L. Wallis. Library J 94:4101-3 N 15 '69

MEMPHIS; story. See Leonard, M.

MEN
See also
Boys
Cookery by men
Sex differences
Young men

Health and hygiene
Art of manly face-lifting. P. M. McGrady, jr. Vogue 153:117+ Je '69
Getting fat by making others slim; fitness industry. il Bsns W p 140-1+ Mr 22 '69
Warning to joggers from a leading physician; interview. H. J. Johnson. il U S News 67:74-5 Ag 11 '69
See also
Businessmen—Health and hygiene

Psychology
Feminized male, by C. Sexton. Review
Sat R 52:52-3 Ag 16 '69. P. Woodring
Great expectations. D. Newman and R. Benton. il Mlle 69:56 S '69
Men in groups, by L. Tiger. Review
Nation 209:286 S 22 '69. J. Leavitt
Newsweek il 74:89+ Jl 7 '69. G. Wolff
Redbook 134:62+ N '69. M. Mead
Science 165:883-4 Ag 29 '69. M. H. Fried
What makes a man lovable. T. I. Rubin. Ladies Home J 86:68+ O '69

MEN teachers. See Teachers

MENACKER, Julius
Subject articulation between high school and college. Clear House 44:220-3 D '69

MENAGERIES
Lingering of savages; roadside menageries. R. Caras. il Audubon 71:12-15 Jl '69
See also
Zoological gardens

MENARD, H. W.
Deep-ocean floor; with biographical sketch. Sci Am 221:42+, 126-32+ bibliog(p285) S '69

MENCHER, Alan G.
Scientists among diplomats. Bul Atom Sci 25:46-8 Ja '69

MENCKEN, Henry Louis
Books. E. Wilson. New Yorker 45:107-10+
My 31 '69
Mencken, by C. Bode. Review
Nation 209:513-14 N 10 '69. R. E. Long
Newsweek 74:120 S 29 '69. G. Wolff
Sat R por 52:27-9 S 13 '69. C. R. Dolmetsch
Time 94:96 N 21 '69
MENDEL, Arthur P.
Robots and rebels. New Repub 160:16-19
Ja 11; 32+ F 8 '69
MENDELEEV, Dmitrii Ivanovich
Mendeleev, his own man. J. Zimmerman.
Chem 42:32 D '69
MENDELL, Jay S.
Case of the straying scientist. Harvard Bsns
R 47:4-6+ Jl '69
MENDELS, J.
Common fears of childhood. Parents Mag 44:
42-3+ D '69
MENDELSOHN, Alfreda A.
New products. See issues of ALA bulletin
MENDELSOHN, Nathan K.
MERBISC: unique recreation bargain. R. C.
Taylor. il por Parks & Rec 4:35-8 Ap '69
MENDELSOHN, Robert S.
Following up on Head Start. New Repub 160:
12-13 Ap 12 '69
MENDELSON, Joseph
Lateral hypothalamic stimulation: inhibition
of aversive effects by feeding, drinking, and
gnawing. bibliog Science 166:1431-3 D 12 '69
MENDELSSOHN, Felix
About Claudio Abbado. M. N. Kanny; C. J.
Luten. Am Rec G 35:621 Ap '69
Bernstein, extraordinarily vital Mendelssohn,
marvelous Schubert. M. N. Kanny. Am
Rec G 36:194 N '69
For a monument, big shoulders; Elijah. P. L.
Miller. Am Rec G 35:1140-1 Ag '69
Records:
Elijah. Opera N 34:30 N 22 '69
MENDELSSOHN, Kurt
States of aggregation. por Phys Today 22:
46-51 Ap '69
MENDENHALL glacier recreation area. See
Recreation areas—Alaska
MENDÈS-FRANCE, Pierre
Mission of politics; tr. by D. Noakes. por
Sat R 52:14-15 My 31 '69
MÉNDEZ ARCEO, Sergio, bp
Joyful place; Catholic community in Cuernavaca. il por Time 94:48 Ag 29 '69
MENDING
Patching kit that often works; Patch-N-
Match. il Consumer Rep 34:58 F '69
MENDIVIL, Hilario
Cuzco's mystical dolls. G. de Zéndegui. il
Américas 21:7-12 Je '69
MENEN, Aubrey
City where the young still listen. McCalls
96:34+ F '69
Magnificent spectacle for a future king.
McCalls 96:58-9+ Je '69
Rebirth of Florence. Holiday 46:28-33+ S '69
Temple belles of India. Holiday 45:48-9+ F '69
Trial of the new Moses. N Y Times Mag
p54-5+ N 23 '69
MENGELING, Marvin E.
Separate peace: moaning and myth. Engl J
58:1322-9 D '69
MENINGITIS
Vaccines
Trial vaccine for meningitis. Sci N 95:501-2
My 24 '69
MENKE, Denis
Highlight. por Sports Illus 31:60 Ag 11 '69
MENNIN, Peter
Variation-symphony of Peter Mennin: clarity
and zest. A. Cohn. por Am Rec G 35:541
Mr '69
MENNINGER, Catharine W.
What wives can do to solve the communication problem; ed. by M. Lane. Read Digest
95:211-12+ Jl '69
MENNINGER, Karl Augustus
Psychiatrist looks at violence. Cath World
209:262-4 S '69
MENNONITES
Amish country: the promised land. L. G.
Hoyer. il Travel & Camera 32:66-71 Jl '69
Anabaptist explosion; adaptation of Pockets
of high fertility in the United States. W. F.
Pratt. il Natur Hist 78:8-10+ F '69
Gentle look; Amish of Lancaster, Pa. il Pop
Phot 65:112-15 Jl '69
Kind neighbor springs Amish bishop from
jail. Chr Cent 86:1132 S 3 '69
Secular schoolmen and Amish aims; excerpts
from The old paths: a study of the Amish
response to public schooling in Ohio. F. S.
Buchanan. Sch & Soc 97:104-5 F '69
MENON, Vengalil Krishnan Krishna. See
Krishna Menon, V. K.

MENOPAUSE
My dark journey through insanity; involutional psychosis. K. W. Seegers. Read Digest 95:67-71 N '69
MENOTTI, Gian Carlo
Point of contact. Opera N 34:8-11 D 27 '69
about
Help, help, the Globolinks! Criticism
Hi Fi 19:MA25+ N '69
Hi Fi il 19:MA27-8 Ap '69
Life il 67:14 D 19 '69
New Yorker 45:44 Ja 3 '70
Newsweek il 75:61-2 Ja 5 '70
Opera N il 33:32 F 8 '69
Sat R 52:52 Ag 30 '69
Operatic pied piper. P. D. Zimmerman. il
Newsweek 75:61-2 Ja 5 '70
MEN'S jewelry. See Jewelry
MENS shirts. See Shirts
MENS sweaters. See Sweaters
MENS underwear. See Underwear
MENSTRUATION
Advice to women who are once-a-month
witches. A. Lake. Redbook 132:94+ Ap '69;
Same abr. Read Digest 95:117-20 Ag '69
How the menstrual cycle affects behavior
and mood. Good H 168:167 Je '69
MENSTRUATION, Cessation of. See Menopause
MENTAL ability. See Ability; Intelligence
MENTAL arithmetic. See Arithmetic, Mental
MENTAL deficiency
See also
Mentally handicapped
MENTAL depression. See Depression, Mental
MENTAL development of children. See Children—Growth and development
MENTAL health. See Mental hygiene
MENTAL health aides. See Psychiatric personnel
MENTAL health centers
Community mental health centers in rural
areas: variations on a theme. S. C. Mahoney and A. Hodges. bibliog Ment Hy 53:
484-7 Jl '69
Way of acquainting people in the community with mental health facilities. A. V.
Monto and W. D. Miley. Ment Hy 53:480-1
Jl '69
Where the poor help the poor to help themselves; New York city's south Bronx. J.
Coudert. Read Digest 94:25-6+ Mr '69
MENTAL health laws
Dilemma of involuntary commitment; suggestions for a measurable alternative. N.
E. Penn and others. bibliog Ment Hy 53:
4-9 Ja '69
Some considerations for future mental health
legislation. N. E. Penn and others. il Ment
Hy 53:10-13 Ja '69
When a sick man needs a lawyer; legal influence on determining patient's mental
state. Trans-Action 6:8 O '69
MENTAL health literature. See Psychological
literature
MENTAL health service
Comments on community mental health programs. I. Greenberg. Ment Hy 53:306-8 Ap
'69
Community's use of family counseling as a
mental health service. B. Courtney. il Ment
Hy 53:90-9 Ja '69
Massachusetts plans for its retarded. E.
Newman and A. D. Spiegel. Ment Hy 53:
100-4 Ja '69
Problem of the hit or myth approach to
community mental health planning: reflections on George Albee's paper. G. G.
Katz. bibliog Ment Hy 53:141-2 Ja '69
Rural attitudes toward mental health; a
brief report. J. E. Hinkle and A. E. Ivey.
Ment Hy 53:295-7 Ap '69
Survey of the need for children's mental
health facilities. J. M. Sattler and B. W.
Leppla. Ment Hy 53:643-5 O '69
MENTAL health workers. See Health workers
MENTAL hospital attendants. See Hospitals,
Psychiatric—Staff
MENTAL hospitals. See Hospitals, Psychiatric
MENTAL hygiene
Children's emotional health project; National
institute of mental health progress report.
PTA Mag 63:25-6 My '69
Doldrums. A. F. Benjamin. Am Home 72:12
Ja '69
Problems in program evaluation: a ministers' workshop. E. R. Oetting and others.
Ment Hy 53:214-17 Ap '69
Psychiatrist's casebook. G. Caplan. See issues
of McCalls

MENTAL hygiene—*Continued*
Psychiatrist's notebook; questions and answers. T. Rubin. See issues of McCall's to March 1969
Work as a therapeutic goal; union-management clinical contributions to a mental health program. J. J. Sommer. Ment Hy 53:263-8 Ap '69
See also
Adjustment, Social
Businessmen—Health and hygiene
Psychiatric clinics
Psychiatry
Psychotherapy
School children—Adjustment
School children—Health and hygiene
Teachers—Health and hygiene
United States—National institute of mental health
Youth—Health and hygiene

Bibliography
Book reviews. See issues of Mental hygiene

History
Past in the present; a column on history. D. P. Kenefick. bibliog Ment Hy 53:472-6 Jl '69

Research
See Psychiatric research

Study and teaching
Teaching the boys in the back rooms. G. B. Dworkin. Ment Hy 53:258-62 Ap '69

MENTAL illness
Mental illness is not a disease; interview, ed. by J. Ecker and B. Diasio. T. Szasz. Sci Digest 66:7-14 D '69
Perceptions of mental illness among people in a rural area. W. K. Bentz and others. bibliog il Ment Hy 53:459-65 Jl '69
Postpartum psychiatric reactions; time of onset and sex ratio of newborns? F. T. Melges. bibliog il Science 166:1026-7 N 21 '69
See also
Autism
Neuroses
Paranoia
Psychiatric clinics
Psychiatry
Psychoses
Schizophrenia

Diagnosis
Dimensions of diagnosis and treatment. J. H. Kahn. bibliog Ment Hy 53:229-36 Ap '69

Prevention and control
Children's emotional health project; National institute of mental health progress report. PTA Mag 63:25-6 My '69

Research
See Psychiatric research

Social aspects
Attitude changes in psychiatric attendants following experience and training. M. W. Pryer and others. bibliog Ment Hy 53:253-7 Ap '69
Attitudes toward mental patients; a review of empirical research. W. J. Johannsen. bibliog Ment Hy 53:218-28 Ap '69
Personal concepts of the mentally ill among caregiving groups. R. A. Mackey. il Ment Hy 53:245-52 Ap '69
Rural attitudes toward mental health; a brief report. J. E. Hinkle and A. E. Ivey. Ment Hy 53:295-7 Ap '69

Therapy
Lithium vs. mental illness. E. Diamond; discussion. N Y Times Mag p21-2+ Ja 26 '69
See also
Bibliotherapy
Group psychotherapy
Psychotherapy

MENTAL illness and art. See Art and mental illness
MENTAL illness and law. See Mental health laws
MENTAL institutions. See Mentally handicapped—Institutional care
MENTAL suffering. See Suffering
MENTALLY handicapped
Mental retardation caused by physical trauma; report of meeting. E. A. Bering, jr. Science 164:460+ Ap 25 '69

Institutional care
Massachusetts plans for its retarded. E. Newman and A. D. Spiegel. Ment Hy 53:100-4 Ja '69

Rehabilitation
Independent living for the mentally handicapped; a program for young adults. T. R. Ames. Ment Hy 53:641-2 O '69
MENTALLY handicapped children
Caring enough for a cause: Hallmark's Teacher, teacher, featuring a retarded boy. R. L. Shayon. Sat R 52:46 Mr 1 '69
Retarded children. Trans-Action 6:6+ S '69
See also
Brain damaged children
Camps for the handicapped
Mentally ill children
Mongolism
Recreation for the handicapped
Slow learning children

Education
Program for handicapped children; British Honduras. il Sch & Soc 97:211-13 Ap '69
Vigorous plan for an institution; Bronx state school. il Arch Rec 145:126-32 F '69
Wondrous machine that salvages backward kids; talking typewriter, or ERE. T. Irwin. il Todays Health 47:31-3+ Ag '69
MENTALLY ill
Attitudes toward mental patients; a review of empirical research. W. J. Johannsen. bibliog Ment Hy 53:218-28 Ap '69
Psychiatric patients as research interviewers in the mental hospital. A. Shiloh. Ment Hy 53:443-5 Jl '69
Sanctuary or prison, responses to life in a mental hospital. A. Shiloh; discussion Trans-Action 6:4+ F '69
Sufficient versus necessary reasons for professional involvement. D. D. Simmons. Ment Hy 53:143-5 Ja '69
Suicide clues in psychotic patients. R. G. Singer and I. J. Blumenthal. Ment Hy 53:346-50 Jl '69
Treating the mentally ill. A. Shiloh. Cur 106:36-43 Ap '69
Why we came back; a study of patients readmitted to a mental hospital. D. E. Spiegel and P. Keith-Spiegel. Ment Hy 53:433-7 Jl '69
See also
Mentally handicapped

Care and treatment
College companions for patients in mental institutions; program at Overbrook hospital, Cedar Grove, N.J. W. R. Nord. Todays Ed 58:28-9 D '69
Community psychiatry: a bold new approach. J. J. Friedman. Ment Hy 53:482-3 Jl '69
Crisis intervention in the mental hospital. J. F. Samorajczyk. bibliog Ment Hy 53:477-9 Jl '69
Dimensions of diagnosis and treatment. J. H. Kahn. bibliog Ment Hy 53:229-36 Ap '69
Some problems in helping patients in public mental hospitals. W. B. Simon. bibliog Ment Hy 53:428-32 Jl '69
Town for outpatients; mental patients cared for by normal families in Geel, Belgium. il Time 93:74 Mr 14 '69
See also
Hospitals, Psychiatric

Employment
Work as a therapeutic goal; union-management clinical contributions to a mental health program. J. J. Sommer. Ment Hy 53:263-8 Ap '69

Legal status, laws, etc.
See Mental health laws

Rehabilitation
American and British mental health workers look at rehabilitation. A. R. Askenasy. Ment Hy 53:466-71 Jl '69
Psychiatric patients returned to military duty, an exploratory study. R. M. Blume. bibliog Ment Hy 53:438-42 Jl '69
Psychiatry gets off the couch and hits the streets; Gouverneur hospital's mobile unit in New York city. il Life 67:48-48C Ag 8 '69
Why does that man stare at me? N. T. Samet. Library J 94:156-7 Ja 15 '69
Work as a therapeutic goal; union-management clinical contributions to a mental health program. J. J. Sommer. Ment Hy 53:263-8 Ap '69
See also
Group psychotherapy
Schizophrenics—Rehabilitation
MENTALLY ill children
Film that jolts; Warrendale. J. McLaughlin. America 120:274 Mr 8 '69
Psychoevaluation of the child in the home. B. M. Levinson. Ment Hy 53:632-4 O '69

MENTALLY ill children—*Continued*
Starting point defined; improving mental
health of black children. il Ebony 25:136-7
N '69
See also
Child psychiatry

Care and treatment
Day programs for children: a note on terminology. P. R. Dingman. Ment Hy 53:
646-7 O '69
Survey of the need for children's mental
health facilities. J. M. Sattler and B. W.
Leppla. il Ment Hy 53:643-5 O '69

Education
Community nursery school program for hos-
pitalized children. N. I. Rieger and others.
Ment Hy 53:196-9 Ap '69
Work as therapy for emotionally disturbed
girls; Livingston school for girls, New
York city. E. P. Rothman. Ment Hy 53:
269-79 Ap '69

MENTALLY retarded children. See Mentally
handicapped children
MENTALLY superior children. See Children,
Gifted
MENTALLY superior college students. See Col-
lege students, Mentally superior
MENTLER, Sandor
Variable-rate windshield wiper. Electr World
82:76 O '69
MENUHIN, Yehudi
Cognoscenti abroad; Yehudi Menuhin's Lon-
don. A. Goodfriend. il por Sat R 52:42+ My
10 '69
MENUS
Celebrity cook book. il House & Gard 136:
90-1+ Jl '69
Ideas for an autumn calendar; with menus. il
McCalls 97:110-16+ O '69
Menus and recipes for holiday parties. House
& Gard 97-100 D '69
[Month] menus: with recipes. See issues of
Sunset
Party partnerships: serving both slim basics
and hearty extras; with recipes. il Seven-
teen 28:192-5+ Ap '69
Young couples who cook. H. McCully. il
House B 111:76-9+ Jl '69
See also
Buffet meals
Camp cookery
Dinners and dining
Luncheons
Lunches
Meals
Suppers
Thanksgiving dinners
MENZEL, Jiri
Czech Jiri Menzel (Closely watched trains)
directs a movie. A. Levy. il pors N Y Times
Mag p28-9+ F 9 '69
MENZEL, Randolf. See Wehner, R. jt. auth.
MERAS, Phyllis L.
Glamour's lineage. Sat R 52:46 Ap 12 '69
MERCANTILE exchange, Chicago. See Chicago
mercantile exchange
MERCAPTANS
Diphtheria toxin subunit active in vitro.
R. J. Collier and H. A. Cole. bibliog il
Science 164:1179-82 Je 6 '69
MERCATOR, Gerardus
Mercator and the lettering of maps. P. Stan-
dard. il Pub W 196:58+ N 3 '69
MERCE Cunningham dance company
Merce Cunningham & dance co; Brooklyn
academy of music. J. Anderson. il Dance
Mag 43:34-5 Je '69
La MERCED. See Mexico (city)—Markets
MERCENARIA. See Clams
MERCER, Austin, Jr
Exciting new rotary engine is piston-power-
ed. D. Scott. il por Pop Sci 195:45-9 D '69
MERCER, Harry E.
Tasmania. Travel 131:44-51 Je '69
MERCER, J. H.
Glaciation in southern Argentina more than
two million years ago. bibliog Science 164:
823-5 My 16 '69
MERCER, Mabel
Marvelous Miss Mercer. C. H. Simonds. il
Nat R 21:866-7 Ag 26 '69
Musical events: recital at Town Hall. W.
Balliett. New Yorker 45:103 My 31 '69
Popular records. D. Watt. New Yorker 45:
108-10 Mr 1 '69
Realm of Mercer and Short. B. Korall. il por
Sat R 52:66+ Ap 12 '69
MERCHANDISE, Quality of. See Quality of
products
MERCHANDISING
Everyone's gone to the moon; extravagant
tie-ins with Apollo 11 mission. il News-
week 74:69-70 Ag 4 '69

Promoters hitch wagons to the moon. il Bsns
W p32 Ag 2 '69
See also
Cash business
MERCHANT, Bruce, and Brahmi, Zacharie
Duplicate plating of immune cell products:
analysis of globulin class secretion by sin-
gle cells. bibliog Science 167:69-72 Ja 2 '70
MERCHANT, Jane
Tenth time is a nine day's wonder; poem.
McCalls 97:129 O '69
MERCHANT marine

Federal aid
Keeping a promise; President's proposals.
il Newsweek 74:83 N 3 '69

Russia
Mess in the merchant marine; address, January 17, 1969. C. F. Duchein. Vital Speeches
35:303-6 Mr 1 '69

United States
Keeping a promise; President's proposals. il
Newsweek 74:83 N 3 '69
Mess in the merchant marine; address, Jan-
uary 17, 1969. C. F. Duchein. Vital Speech-
es 35:303-6 Mr 1 '69
New pacts for maritime unions; tentative
settlement on the East coast. U S News
66:70 Je 16 '69
Requirements for defense; the U.S. merchant
marine in perspective; address, March 24,
1969. W. F. Schlech, jr. Vital Speeches 35:
425-30 My 1 '69
U.S. shipping lag; what's likely to be done
about it. il U S News 67:10 O 27 '69
See also
National maritime day
United States lines

History
Gallantry of an ugly duckling fight of liber-
ty ship Stephen Hopkins against cruiser
Stier and blockade runner Tannenfels. R.
L. Vargas. il Am Heritage 21:22-3+ D '69
MERCURY
Mercury-filled doughnut and clouds on Ve-
nus. il Chem 42:25 Ap '69
MERCURY (planet)
Lunar and planetary mass concentrations. B
T. O'Leary and others. bibliog il Science
165:651-7 Ag 15 '69
Mercury, up high Down Under. D. K. Brooks.
il R Pop Astron 63:13-15 Mr '69
MERCURY pesticides. See Pesticides
MERCURY poisoning
Birds give warning; mercury fungicides na-
tional pollution problem in Sweden. G.
Löfroth and M. E. Duffy. bibliog il Environ
11:10-17 My '69
Legacy of the mad hatter. N. Grant. bibliog
il Environ 11:18-23+ My '69
MERCY
See also
God—Mercy
MERCY street; drama. See Sexton, A.
MEREDITH, Freda
What's cooking? Org Gard & Farm 16:84-5
Je '69
MEREDITH, M. Marjorie, and Jorgenson, L.
P.
Admission of women to the University of
Missouri in 1868. bibliog f Sch & Soc 97:
282-5 Sum '69
MEREDITH, William
Earth walk; poem. Sat R 52:20 D 20 '69
Effort at speech; poem. New Yorker 45:58
D 6 '69
Fledglings; poem. New Yorker 45:40 My 10
'69
Waking dream about a lost child; poem. New
Yorker 45:32 Jl 12 '69
MERETIK, Gabriel
Goodbye to Poland. Commentary 48:55-62 S
'69
MERGEN, Francois
When it rained cats in Borneo; excerpts
from address. por Am For 75:28-9+ Ja
'69
MERGERS. See Business consolidations and
mergers; Trusts, Industrial
MERIDEN, Conn.
Intercom network cuts city phone bill. il Am
City 84:56 Ja '69

Lighting
Lighting brings a silver lining to the Silver
City. il Am City 84:144 O '69
MERILLAT, Emile, pseud.
Depressed bonds for high yields. Har Yrs
9:24-5 My '69
Making money work; with questions and an-
swers. See issues of Harvest years

MERILLAT, Emile, pseud—*Continued*
Mutual funds for retirement income. Har Yrs 9:14-17 Mr '69
Mutual funds: load or no-load? Har Yrs 9:46-9 Ap '69
MÉRIMÉE, Prosper
Woman-hater. M. Springer. Opera N 33:24-5 Mr 15 '69
MERINGUE
Ladyfingers with chocolate curls; chocolate ladyfinger torte. il Sunset 142:221 Ap '69
Springtime desserts, with strawberries and lemon. il Sunset 142:160 My '69
MERINO Y CORONADO, J.
Chemicals, the secret weapon in your shop. Radio Electr 40:60-1 N '69
MERIT certificates. See Rewards, prizes, etc.
MERIT pay. See Teachers—Salaries, allowances, etc
MERIT system (civil service) See Civil service
MERKELO, H. and others
Mode-locked lasers: measurements of very fast radiative decay in fluorescent systems. bibliog Science 164:301-2 Ap 18 '69
MERKER, Iris
Businessmen's expectations. Duns R 93:113 Mr; 94:131 S '69
MERKERT, Tilde
Grow your own flavors. pors Har Yrs 9:26-8 Mr '69
MERLIN, Eugene A.
Faith and psyche a role for Jung in theology. Cath World 209:172-5 Jl '69
MERLINO, Stefano
Tuhualite crystal structure. bibliog Science 166:1399-401 D 12 '69
MERMAIDS
If you don't mind my saying so. J. W. Krutch. Am Scholar 38:370+ Sum '69
MERMANN, Alan C.
Feed my sheep. Chr Cent 86:900-2 Jl 2 '69
When did we see thee hungry? Chr Cent 86:473-7 Ap 9 '69
MERRIAM, Eve
Wasp hymn. New Repub 161:24 Jl 12 '69
MERRIAM, Lawrence C. jr
Yosemite Valley revisited. Nat Parks 43:14-15 Ja '69
MERRICK, David
Dolly's dilemma: her $20 million movie is stuck on the shelf while producers argue. il por Life 66:58-60 F 14 '69
MERRICK, Iris
American teacher in Leningrad. J. Anderson. il por Dance Mag 43:24-7 Ja '69
MERRICK, Lee
First six weeks with baby. Parents Mag 44:66-7+ O '69
MERRIL, Judith
Merril-y we wave along. T. Sturgeon. Nat R 21:1174-5 N 18 '69
MERRILL, Anne
Private life of Ifor Tombs; story. Harp Baz 102:192-3 My '69
MERRILL, Edward W. and others
Lecithin aerosols generated ultrasonically above 25°C. bibliog Science 164:1167-8 Je 6 '69
MERRILL, James
Pola diva; Matinees; poems. Poetry 114:71-6 My '69
Summer people; poem. Atlan 223:51-8 Mr '69
Willowware cup; poem. Harper 239:89 S '69
MERRILL, Nathaniel
Corsaro, Capobianco, and Merrill. D. Hering. il por Dance Mag 43:28-30 Mr '69
Operas tightrope walker. il pors Time 93:68 Mr 14 '69
MERRILL college. See California. University —Santa Cruz campus
MERRILL Lynch, Pierce, Fenner and Smith, incorporated
Merrill Lynch buys Canadian. Bsns W p 126 My 24 '69
Performance is important, but so is a good night's sleep. Forbes 104:82-3 O 15 '69
Quiet revolution; Merrill Lynch selling mutual funds. Forbes 104:82 O 1 '69
We the people thinks bigger. Bsns W p27 My 3 '69
MERRIMAC and Monitor, Battle of. See United States—History—Civil war—Naval operations
MERRITT, Vernon
Great oil slick; photographs. Life 66:58-62B F 21 '69
That New York look; photographs. Life 67:32-41 Ag 22 '69
about
Very personal view of New York. R. Graves. por Life 67:3 Ag 22 '69
MERRITT college, Oakland, Calif.
This course is for black students only. Newsweek 73:57-8 F 10 '69

MERRY, Ruth Pierce
Daylilies indoors. Horticulture 46:26-7+ Ag '68
Fascinating begonias. Horticulture 47:26-9 Je '69
New trends in daylilies. il Horticulture 47:28-9+ F '69
MERRY Christmas, mother! Merry Christmas, Barracliff; story. See Lewis, L.
MERSON, Ben
One woman's ordeal: when too much medicine is a dangerous thing. Ladies Home J 86:50+ N '69
MERTON, Robert K.
Behavior patterns of scientists; address, December 1968. Am Scholar 38:197-225 Spr '69
MERTON, Thomas
Anti-poem; Plessy vs. Ferguson: theme & variations. Commonweal 89:592-3 F 7 '69
about
Bridge between two cultures. R. Haughton. Cath World 209:53-4 My '69
Critic of the month. L. Lieberman. Poetry 114:47-8 Ap '69
Merton against himself. A. Mayhew. Commonweal 91:70-1+ O 17 '69
Thomas Merton: the last three days. J. Moffitt. Cath World 209:160-3 Jl '69
Thomas Merton's early novel. Pub W 195:67 Ap 28 '69
MERWIN, W. S.
Beginning of the plains; poem. Harper 239:81 D '69
Death-defying Tartonis; story. New Yorker 45:20-4 Ja 10 '70
Edouard; poem. New Yorker 45:166 N 8 '69
February; poem. New Yorker 44:32 Ja 18 '69
Five poems: Signals; Different stars; Port; Banishment in winter; Envoy from D'Aubigné. New Yorker 45:62-3 N 15 '69
The tree; poem. New Yorker 45:58 O 25 '69
Hulk; poem. New Yorker 45:135 N 1 '69
Old room; poem. New Yorker 45:44 Ap 19 '69
Poems by Jean Follain. Atlan 224:77 Ag '69
Remembering machines of tomorrow. New Yorker 45:52-3 N 29 '69
Third psalm: the September vision; poem. Harper 239:79 O '69
Words from a totem animal; poem. Atlan 223:68-9 Ja '69
(tr) See Borges, J. L. Ars poetica
(tr) See Follain, J. Cadences; Matter; The square; The tragic in time; The useful; The song of the dragoon; The secret
about
Comment. P. Levine. Poetry 115:187-9 D '69
MÉRY, Hubert Beuve-. See Beuve-Méry, H.
MERYMAN, Richard
Cinematic assault. Life 67:65 N 7 '69
(ed) See West, M. Mae West
MESA-LAGO, Carmelo
Revolutionary offensive. bibliog por Trans-Action 6:22-9+ O '69
MESCAL buttons. See Peyote
MESELSON, Matthew
Why not poison? Science 164:413-14 Ap 25 '69
MESERVEY, R.
Topological inconsistency of continental drift on the present-sized earth. bibliog Science 166:609-11 O 31 '69
MESIANO, Lindalee
(comp) Audiovisual guide (cont) Library J 94:1741-2+ Ap 15 '69
MESIC, Michael
Three stanzas. Poetry 115:38-40 O '69
MESIROW, Leon F.
If you need a director, try placing a want ad. il por Bsns W p72+ Ja 18 '69
MESONS
One little, two little, A_2's. D. E. Thomsen. il Sci N 96:410-11 N 1 '69
Seeking the why of the muon. D. E. Thomsen. il Sci N 95:290-1 Mr 22 '69
See also
Muonium
MESOZOIC period. See Paleobotany—Mesozoic
MESSEL, Oliver
Maddox: House of Messel; with photographs by Snowdon. P. Devlin. Vogue 153:194-201 Mr 1 '69
MESSER, Alfred A.
Dissolution of long-standing marriages. Ment Hy 53:127-30 Ja '69
MESSER, Donald E.
Optional approach to clerical exemption. Chr Cent 86:921-4 Jl 9 '69
MESSER, Thomas M.
Impossible art: why it is. Art in Am 57:30-1 My '69

MESSERSCHMITT-BÖLKOW-BLOHM.   See
    Airplane industry and trade—Germany
    (Federal Republic)
MESSIAEN, Olivier
    Messiaen's monument. Time 93:52 Je 20 '69
MESSIAH (oratorio)
    Misunderstood Messiah. il Time 94:39 D 26
    '69
MESSINESI, Despina
    Travel. See issues of Vogue
MESSY and windy; story. See Loeser, K.
MESTROVIC, Matthew M.
    For eastern Europe: PR or policy? Common-
    weal 91:92-3 O 24 '69
    Prudential Mr Tito. Commonweal 90:62-3 Ap
    4 '69
    Renewal in Yugoslavia. America 121:488-90
    N 22 '69
METABOLIC chambers. See Physiological ap-
    paratus
METABOLISM
    Energetics of bird flight. V. A. Tucker. il
    Sci Am 220:70-6+ My '69
        See also
    Bacteria—Metabolism
    Drugs—Metabolism
    Oxidation, Physiological
METABOLISM, Disorders of
    Can you stay slim after dieting? J. C. G.
    Conniff. Read Digest 94:69-72 F '69
    Oxygen-hemoglobulin dissociation curves: ef-
    fect of inherited enzyme defects of the red
    cell .M. Delivoria-Papadopoulos and others.
    bibliog il Science 165:601-2 Ag 8 '69
    Pompe's disease: detection of heterozygotes
    by lymphocyte stimulation. K. Hirschhorn
    and others. bibliog il Science 166:1632-3 D
    26 '69
    Renal fructose-metabolizing enzymes: sig-
    nificance in hereditary fructose intolerance.
    J. F. Kranhold and others. bibliog il Sci-
    ence 165:402-3 Jl 25 '69
        See also
    Albinos and albinism
    Cystinuria
    Diabetes
    Gout
    Lesch-Nyhan syndrome
    Lipochondrodystrophy
    Porphyria
METABOLISM apparatus. See Physiological ap-
    paratus
METAL casting. See Foundry practice
METAL cleaning
    Copper and brass cleaners and polishes. il
    Consumer Bul 52:23-4 O '69
        See also
    Ultrasonic cleaning
METAL coating
    Metalliding. N. C. Cook. il Sci Am 221:38-46
    Ag '69
    Vinyl powder coatings protect and color steel
    paneling for walls and roofs. il Arch Rec
    145:171-2 My '69
METAL construction
    Three structural techniques use metals in-
    ventively. il Arch Rec 145:167-70 F '69
METAL crystals
    Electrons in metals; adaptation of address.
    October 1968. W. A. Harrison. bibliog il
    Phys Today 22:23-31 O '69
    Lighter than aluminum, stronger than steel!
    W. Von Braun. il Pop Sci 194:98-100+ F '69
METAL detectors
    Build a different metal locator. L. Huggard.
    il Pop Electr 30:53-8 F '69; Correction.
    31:98 Jl '69
    Carpenter's mate. J. S. Simonton, jr. il Pop
    Electr 31:69-72 S '69
    Hijacking spurs detector tests. Aviation W
    90:30-1 Mr 31 '69
            Anecdotes, facetiae, satire, etc.
    Live wire with a loot locator. C. Kohler.
    il Pop Electr 30:45-9 Je '69
METAL etching
    Alloys that pose for a picture: Photoform
    process. il Bsns W p 116 Ag 16 '69
    How to make etched circuits. J. A. Gupton,
    jr. il Radio-Electr 40:23-6 Je '69
METAL foils
        See also
    Aluminum foil
METAL locators. See Metal detectors
METAL polishes. See Polishing materials
METAL powders
        See also
    Aluminum. Powdered
METAL scrap. See Scrap metal
METAL sculpture
    Art; J. Olitski's aluminum sculpture. L. Allo-
    way. Nation 208:676-7 My 26 '69

Artist sculptures JFK doodles. il Ebony 24:
    46-8+ O '69
Bottle cap model maker. R. Wolfe. il Design
    70:4-7 Spr '69
He seeks the soul in metal. il Ebony 24:80-
    2+ Ap '69
Junk sculpture project. J. Walstrom. il Sch
    Arts 69:4-5 O '69
Me and my constructed self. T. R. Pokorny,
    jr. il Sch Arts 68:22-3 F '69
Rosati: masses in elevation, exhibition at
    Brandeis university. W. C. Seitz. il Art
    N 68:38-41+ D '69
Sheet lead for relief sculpture. A. F. Geiserf.
    il Sch Arts 68:18-20 Ap '69
Whimsical creatures; aluminum foil. R. Batch-
    eller. il Sch Arts 69:28 O '69
        See also
    Bronzes
METAL turning. See Turning
METAL whiskers. See Metal crystals
METAL work
    Bulge method used to form complex ducting
    for DC-10. il Aviation W 91:56+ N 3 '69
    Down the tube. J. Thawley. il Hot Rod
    22:58-60 Ap '69
    How to put holes of any shape into metal.
    W. E. Burton. il Pop Sci 194:123+ Je '69
        See also
    Ironwork
    Wire sculpture
            Projects
    Model this 24-pounder. W. E. Burton. il
    Pop Mech 131:134-9+ F '69
    Weekend thinwall projects. R. S. Hedin. il
    Pop Mech 132:164-7 O '69
METAL working industries
            Investments
    Tomorrow's materials. il Duns R 93:109-10 Mr
    '69
METAL working machinery
    New metal-working tool. il Mech Illus 65:112
    O '69
        See also
    Forging machinery
METALITZ, Beatrice R.
    Kibbutzim for the disadvantaged. Todays Ed
    58:17-19 D '69
METALLIC films. See Films, Metallic
METALLIDING process. See Metal coating
METALLURGICAL furnaces
        See also
    Electric furnaces
METALLURGY
    U.S. emphasizing metallurgy at air show. C.
    Brownlow. il Aviation W 90:62-3 Je 2 '69
        See also
    Alloys
    Extrusion process
METALS
        See also
    Alloys
    Fermi surfaces
    Muonium
    Scrap metal
        also names of metals, e.g. Copper
            Coating
        See Metal coating
            Prices
    Metals prices go on a spree. il Bsns W p23
    Ja 18 '69
        See also
    Copper—Prices
METALS, Liquid
    Liquid metals. N. W. Ashcroft. il Sci Am 221:
    72-82 bibliog(p 140) Jl '69
METALS, Nonferrous
            Prices
    Nonferrous miners are coining it. Bsns W
    p68 D 6 '69
METAMORPHISM (geology)
    Shock and thermal metamorphism of basalt
    by nuclear explosion, Nevada test site. O.
    B. James. bibliog il Science 166:1615-20 D
    26 '69
METAMORPHOSES; drama. See Sills, P.
METAMORPHOSIS; opera. See White, M.
METAMORPHOSIS (Insects) See Insects—De-
    velopment
METAPHYSICS
        See also
    Consciousness
    Existentialism
    Matter
METASTASEIS & Pithoprakta; ballet. See
    Ballets—Criticisms

METCALF, Aiden
Artist goes to Cape Kennedy to draw an Apollo launch. Space World F-11-71:19-22 N '69

METCALF, Lee
Tax loophole; address, January 11, 1969. Vital Speeches 35:253-6 F 1 '69
Tax reform now! New Repub 161:9 Jl 26 '69

METEORITES
Elements 112 to 119: were they present in meteorites? E. Anders and D. Heymann. bibliog il Science 164:821-3 My 16 '69
Enormous meteorite. Sky & Tel 38:222 O '69
Freshly fallen meteorites from Portugal and Mexico. E. L. Fireman. il Sky & Tel 37:272-5 My '69
Meteorite fall at Pueblito de Allende, Chihuahua, Mexico: preliminary information. E. A. King, jr. and others. il Science 163:928-9 F 28 '69
Meteorites and the early solar system. Chem 42:20-2 My '69
Murchison meteorite. il Sky & Tel 38:388 D '69
New studies of the Sikhote-Alin meteorite shower. E. L. Krinov. il Sky & Tel 37:87-90 F '69
Nitrogen abundances in chondritic meteorites. C. B. Moore and E. K. Gibson. bibliog il Science 163:174-6 Ja 10 '69
Pecoraite $Ni_3Si_4O_{10}(OH)_2$ nickel analog of clinochrysotile, formed in the Wolf Creek meteorite. G. T. Faust and others. bibliog il Science 165:59-60 Jl 4 '69
Phosphide from meteorites: barringerite, a new iron-nickel mineral. P. R. Buseck. bibliog il Science 165:169-71 Jl 11 '69
Radionuclide composition of the Allende meteorite from nondestructive gamma-ray spectrometric analysis. L. A. Rancitelli and others. bibliog il Science 166:1269-72 D 5 '69
Silicate spherules from Tunguska impact area: electron microprobe analysis. B. P. Glass. bibliog il Science 164:547-9 My 2 '69
Solar-type xenon: a new isotopic composition of xenon in the pesyanoe meteorite. K. Marti. bibliog il Science 166:1263-5 D 5 '69
Sprucefield meteorite. G. S. Mumford. il Sky & Tel 37:360 Je '69
Surveyor alpha-scattering data: consistency with lunar origin of eucrites and howardites. M. B. Duke. bibliog il Science 165:515-17 Ag 1 '69
See also
Meteors
Tektites

METEOROLOGICAL airplanes. See Airplanes, Meteorological

METEOROLOGICAL Instruments
Start him off on a home weather station. il Sunset 143:34-6+ D '69
See also
Storm detectors

METEOROLOGICAL optics
See also
Halos (meteorology)

METEOROLOGICAL research
See also
Artificial satellites—Meteorological applications
Balloons, Meteorological
Rain making
Weather control
Weather research

METEOROLOGY
How good are you as a meteorologist? quiz. J. Daugherty and M. Daugherty. il Sci Digest 65:82-4 Je '69
Tropics: a frontier in meteorology. H. Chronic. il Sea Front 15:288-94 S '69
See also
American meteorological society
Atmospheric nucleation
Auroras
Climate
Clouds
Computers—Meteorological applications
Lakes—Temperature
Precipitation (meteorology)
Rain and rainfall
Snow
Storms
Television in meteorology
Tornadoes
United States—Weather bureau
Weather
Weather forecasts
Weather maps
Winds
Bibliography
Selective bibliography in meteorology. Weatherwise 22:134-51 Ag '69

METEOROLOGY, Aeronautic
Concorde route study nears completion. H. J. Coleman. il Aviation W 90:34+ Mr 17 '69

Meteorology and the supersonic transport. F. G. Finger and R. M. McInturff. bibliog il Science 167:16-25 Ja 2 '70
Wind and temperature effects on supersonic aircraft operations. N. B. Guttman and H. L. Crutcher. bibliog il Weatherwise 21:220-6 D '68
See also
Airports—Visibility

METEOROLOGY, Maritime
High is the key; Transpac race. E. B. Mitchell. il Yachting 125:58+ Je '69
Storms that rage beneath the sea. W. Perkinson. il Sci Digest 65:7-11 Mr '69
Trans-Pac: the race you sail by the weather map. E. S. Kurtz. il Weatherwise 22:185-9 O '69
Wind & weather. See issues of Motor boating
Word about weather. il Motor B 123:111 Ja '69

METEORS
Favorable skies aid Perseid watchers. S. S. Ross. il Sky & Tel 38:265-8 O '69
Fine structure of a meteor train. il Sky & Tel 38:300 N '69
June Lyrids confirmed. il Sky & Tel 38:271 O '69
Look out for meteors. Sci Digest 65:23 F '69
November Leonid meteors observed. Sky & Tel 39:62-3 Ja '70
1,344 fireballs, catalogue. Sky & Tel 38:18 Jl '69
Perseid meteor spectra photographed in 1969. J. A. Russell. il Sky & Tel 38:424-5 D '69
Unusual meteor fall in Mexico. R Pop Astron 63:13 My '69
Widely photographed fireball. il Sky & Tel 39:8 Ja '70
See also
Space flight—Meteor hazards

METER reading
Don't let size keep your waterworks from using EDP; East Windsor, N.J. W. B. Harvey. il Am City 84:95-6+ D '69
No more muddy boots in the kitchen; remote meter reading; St Cloud, Minn. W. Davids. il Am City 84:111-12 Ag '69
One answer to the meter-reader shortage; woman meter reader, Oakland, N.J. N. D. Fagerlund. il Am City 84:12 Jl '69

METERS
See also
Dwell meters
Exposure meters
Flow meters
Micrometers
Odometers
Parking meters
Voltmeters

METHACRYLIC acid
Polymethacrylic acid: effects on lymphocyte output of the thoracic duct in rats. S. Ormai and E. de Clercq. bibliog il Science 163:471-2 Ja 31 '69

METHADONE
Key decisions coming: methadone therapy for heroin addicts. il Sci N 95:364-5 Ap 12 '69

METHANDROSTENOLONE
Anabolic steroid: effects on strength development. L. C Johnson and J. P. O'Shea. bibliog il Science 164:957-9 My 23 '69

METHANE
Approach to mine safety. il Sci N 95:570-1 Je 14 '69

METHEDRINE. See Amphetamines

METHEMOGLOBINEMIA. See Children—Diseases

METHERELL, Alexander F.
Acoustical holography; with biographical sketch. Sci Am 221:14, 36-44 O '69

METHODIST church
See also
United Methodist church

METHODIST church in Argentina
Argentina Methodists become autonomous. J. M. Swomley, jr. Chr Cent 86:1468 N 12 '69

METHODIST church in Australia
Three lives of one church; Central Methodist mission. A. Walker. Chr Cent 86:1594-6 D 10 '69

METHODIST church in England
Anglicans vote no; failure to reunite Methodist church of Great Britain with Church of England. il Time 94:62 Jl 18 '69
Church of England votes. W. J. O'Rourke. America 121:64-6 Ag 2 '69
See also
Church unity—Great Britain

METHODIST church in Latin America
Methodists in Latin America form council. M. Arias. Chr Cent 86:531-2 Ap 16 '69

METHODIST church in the United States
Free Methodist vitality. J. Huffman. Chr To-
  day 13:37 Jl 18 '69
    See also
United Methodist church
METHODIST church of Great Britain. See
Methodist church in England
METHODIST Episcopal church, Africa. See
African Methodist Episcopal church
**METHODIST publishing house, Nashville,
Tenn.**
Black Methodists appeal for boycott of pub-
  lishing house. Chr Cent 86:342 Mr 12 '69
METHOTREXATE
Antibiotics alter methotrexate metabolism
  and excretion. D. S. Zaharko and others.
  bibliog il Science 166:887-8 N 14 '69
METHVIN, Eugene H.
Changing news values in the megamind era;
  address, February 19, 1969. Vital Speeches
  35:462-7 My 15 '69
Is Congress destroying itself? Read Digest
  94:65-70 Ap '69
METHYLAZOXYMETHANOL. See Cycasin
METHYLCHOLANTHRENE
Carcinogen-induced immune depression; ab-
  sence in mice resistant to chemical on-
  cogenesis. O. Stutman. bibliog il Science
  166:620-1 O 31 '69
MÉTRAUX, Alfred
Mysterious hieroglyphs of Easter Island; re-
  print. UNESCO Courier 22:16-17 Ag '69
METRIC system
Foot is a four-letter word; what will the
  metric system mean to your photography?
  W. Hanson. Pop Phot 65:76-7+ O '69
New push for the metric system; will you
  give up pounds, feet, and inches? A. P.
  Armagnac. il Pop Sci 194:54-7+ Je '69
Preliminary report; NBS study of change-
  over problems. Sci N 96:297-8 O 4 '69
Whatever happened to plan to convert to
  metric system? U S News 67:8 D 8 '69
METRO-Goldwyn-Mayer, Incorporated
Again the smiling cobra. Newsweek 74:84-5
  N 3 '69
Coup that won MGM. Time 94:94 O 3 '69
Dash of bitters for a Bronfman. Bsns W p60
  N 8 '69
Eurodollars finance the new MGM drama.
  Bsns W p41-2 Ag 16 '69
Glint in Kirk's eye. il Forbes 104:27-9 Ag 15
  '69
James Aubrey makes comeback in movies.
  Bsns W p40 O 25 '69
Lawyer of the big deals; G. Bautzer. Bsns
  W p56+ N 8 '69
M-G-M cliff-hanger. il Newsweek 74:70-1+
  Ag 4 '69
New lion roars on the MGM lot. Bsns W p47
  O 11 '69
New showdown looms at MGM. il Bsns W
  p66+ Ag 2 '69
Return of smiling Jim; company's new presi-
  dent. J. T. Aubrey. Time 94:80 O 31 '69
Teaching MGM's lion new tricks. Bsns W
  p44 Ja 3 '70
METROLINER (train) See Railroads—Passen-
ger service—High speed trains
METRONIDAZOLE
Resistance to metronidazole by trichomonas
  foetus in hamsters infected intravaginally.
  P. Actor and others. bibliog il Science 164:
  439-40 Ap 25 '69
**METROPOLITAN applied research center, in-
corporated**
Harper, MARC sponsor urban affairs pub-
  lishing program. Pub W 195:234 Ja 20 '69
New teaching materials for the inner city.
  Sch & Soc 97:272 Sum '69
METROPOLITAN areas
Intraoccupational wage dispersion in metro-
  politan areas, 1967-68; with tables. J. E.
  Buckley. Mo Labor R 92:24-9 S '69
What would you do with, say, Staten Island?
  excerpts from Design with nature. I. Mc-
  Harg. il Natur Hist 78:26-37 Ap '69
    See also
City planning
Metropolitan government
Regional planning
Urban renewal
    also subhead Metropolitan district under
    names of cities, e.g. Seattle—Metropolitan
    district
METROPOLITAN government
Minnesota experiment; how to make a big
  city fit to live in. J. Fischer. Harper 238:
  12+ Ap '69
METROPOLITAN museum of art, New York
Anniversary. New Yorker 45:43-4 O 11 '69
Art: Harlem on my mind. L. Alloway. Nation
  208:156-7 F 3; 317 Mr 10 '69
Black magic at the Met; Harlem on my mind.
  P. P. Ardery, jr. il Nat R 21:240-1 Mr 11 '69

Books withdrawn from Met's Harlem exhibit. Pub W 195:32 Mr 17 '69
Centennial event at the Metropolitan; open-
  ing of two period rooms. E. P. Birk. il Antiques 96:700+ N '69
Fun city festival; exhibition of modern
  American painting and sculpture. T. B.
  Hess. Art N 68:23 D '69
Harlem catalog raises racist, censorship issues. Library J 94:1282+ Mr 15 '69
Harlem experiment; Harlem on my mind ex-
  hibition. il Time 93:44+ Ja 24 '69
Harlem on everybody's mind; with editorial
  comment. R. Berenson. il Nat R 21:106-7,
  125 F 11 '69
Harlem on my mind. D. Vestal. il Pop Phot
  64:79-81+ My '69
Harlem out of mind; exhibition. with edi-
  torial comment. A. Goldin. il Art N 68:23,
  52-3+ Mr '69
Harlem; sold out by Massa Hoving? photo
  exhibit Harlem on my mind. J. Dreyfuss.
  il Mod Phot 33:64-5+ My '69
Hoving at the Met. B. Rose. Vogue 154:152
  O 1 '69
How hip should a museum get? questioning
  the Harlem on my mind show. J. Stuart.
  Life 66:14 F 21 '69
Kabuki and the various Mets. C. J. Mc-
  Naspy. America 121:276 O 4 '69
Memoirs of a museum. E. Sheppard. Harp
  Baz 103:206-7 N '69
Metropolitan museum in New York cele-
  brates its first hundred years. il Arch Rec
  146:37 N '69
Metropolitan: worst foot forward; New York
  painting and sculpture 1940-1970. R. Beren-
  son. il Nat R 21:1281-3 D 16 '69
Modern masters amid the old. D. Bourdon.
  il Life 67:12 O 24 '69
New installations at the Metropolitan; deco-
  rative arts of northern Europe in the renaissance. R. Davidson. il Antiques 95:218+
  F '69
Our business is refreshment of the eye, the
  mind and the soul. T. Hoving. il Holiday
  45:56-9+ F '69
Patio party; reception by Brown-Forman
  distillers corporation to celebrate both
  centennials. New Yorker 45:45 N 29 '69
Splendor of decoration; nine beautiful period
  rooms. il House & Gard 136:58-67 D '69
Stompin' at the Met; Harlem on my mind exhibit. D. L. Shirey. il Newsweek 73:70+ Ja
  27 '69
Super-show; New York painting and sculpture, 1940-1970 show. D. L. Shirey. il Newsweek 74:80-4 O 20 '69
Tempest at the Met; Harlem on my mind controversy. Newsweek 73:84 F 3 '69
Thirty years of the New York school; exhibition, New York painting and sculpture;
  1940-1970 to open centennial celebrations. H.
  Kramer. il N Y Times Mag p28-31+ O 12
  '69
Treasure trove; gift of the Lehman art col-
  lection. il Newsweek 74:96-100 O 6 '69
Tree; Neapolitan baroque decorations. L. H.
  Howard. New Yorker 45:31-2 D 20 '69
What's an art museum for? questioning ex-
  hibition of Harlem on my mind. K. Kuh.
  Sat R 52:58-9 F 22 '69; Reply. A. Schoener.
  52:21 Mr 15 '69
Wing full of glory. il Am Home 72:64-72 D
  '69
Winner; announcement of Museum of primi-
  tive art transfer at Metropolitan's show.
  New Yorker 45:27-8 Je 7 '69
METROPOLITAN opera association
Discord at the Met; personnel want pay
  hikes. il Newsweek 74:89 S 8 '69
Discord keeps Met curtain down. il Bsns W
  p34-5 N 8 '69
Guild at work; financial & membership de-
  partments. J. Boutwell. il Opera N 33:20-3
  My 17 '69
Halls; light, dark, new. H. Saal. il Newsweek
  74:119 S 22 '69
Is this any way to run an opera house? R.
  D. Holland. America 120:690-1 Je 14 '69
Musical events; possible candidates for new
  general manager. W. Sargeant. New Yorker
  45:174+ Ap 12; 164 Ap 19; 152 Ap 26 '69
Old problems at the new Met. I. Kolodin.
  il Sat R 52:65-6+ O 25 '69
Singing is believing; prospects of peace be-
  tween New York's Metropolitan opera and
  the musicians' unions. Time 94:67D 12 '69
Thundering silence at the Met. il Time 94:55
  S 26 '69

History

Dippel the debonair. M. J. Matz. il Opera N
  33:14-16 F 22 '69

METROPOLITAN opera company
Bye-bye Brünnhilde; B. Nilsson walks out on the Met. il Time 93:77 Mr 21 '69
Discord at the Met; personnel want pay hikes. il Newsweek 74:89 S 8 '69
Discord keeps Met curtain down. il Bsns W p34-5 N 8 '69
Halls; light, dark, new. H. Saal. il Newsweek 74:119 S 22 '69
House united. Newsweek 74:107 D 22 '69
How long can the Met survive? I. Kolodin. il Sat R 52:47-9 D 27 '69
Met as museum. H. Green. Commonweal 90: 206-7 My 2 '69
Metropolitan opera (cont) il Hi Fi 19:MA11-13+ F; MA11-13 Mr; MA11-13 My; MA10-11+ Je '69
Music; labor troubles. D. Hamilton. Nation 209:707 D 22 '69
Musical events; back in business. W. Sargeant. New Yorker 45:67-70 Ja 10 '70
Musical events; performing arts in crisis. W. Sargeant. New Yorker 45:187-9 N 29 '69
New Rosenkavalier at the Met. G. Movshon. il Hi Fi 19:MA12 Ap '69
Old problems at the new Met. I. Kolodin. il Sat R 52:65-6+ O 25 '69
Opera's tightrope walker; N. Merrill, resident stage director. il Time 93:68 Mr 14 '69
Singing is believing; prospects of peace between New York's Metropolitan opera and the musicians' unions. Time 94:67 D 12 '69
Thundering silence at the Met. il Time 94:55 S 26 '69

METROPOLITAN opera guild
At the Colony club. il Opera N 34:17 D 27 '69
Festive guests; annual luncheon at Waldorf-Astoria. il Opera N 33:13 F 22 '69
Guild at work:
Director's office. J. Boutwell. il Opera N 33:18-20 Je 14 '69
Education department. J. Boutwell. il Opera N 33:26-9 Mr 15 '69
Financial & membership departments. J. Boutwell. il Opera N 33:20-3 My 17 '69
Opera news. J. Boutwell. il Opera N 33: 26-9 Mr 8; 26-9 Mr 15; 26-9 Mr 29 '69
Ticket service. J. Boutwell. il Opera N 33:26-9 Mr 8 '69
Guild's gala. il Opera N 33:14-16 Ap 5 '69
In service; the Guild rounds out a decade of teaching teachers. M. E. Peltz. il Opera N 33:6-7 F 8 '69
Metropolitan opera guild financial statement. Opera N 34:28 S 20 '69
See also
Metropolitan opera studio

METROPOLITAN opera national council
Council lights. il Opera N 34:22-3 D 13 '69
See also
Central opera service

METROPOLITAN opera on the air. See Radio broadcasting—Operas

METROPOLITAN opera studio
Bravos in Brooklyn; performances by Guild's education department. Q. Eaton. il Opera N 33:6-7 Ap 12 '69
Musical events; concert performance of Mozart's Don Giovanni at Town Hall. W. Sargeant. New Yorker 45:98 My 31 '69

METROPOLITAN transportation authority
Summer of discontent for commuters. il Bsns W p74-6 Ag 2 '69
Urban transit picks up some speed. il Bsns W p66+ S 20 '69

METS (baseball) See Baseball clubs

METZ, Johannes B.
Church and the world; excerpts from Theology of the world. bibliog f Cath World 208: 247-50 Mr '69

METZGER, H. Peter
Plutonium fire raises questions. il Sci N 96: 25 Jl 12 '69

METZGER, Stanley D.
Hero among bureaucrats. Life 66:28 F 7 '69

MEXICAN AMERICAN literature
Mexican-American literature. P. D. Ortego. Nation 209:258-9 S 15 '69

MEXICAN AMERICAN students
Chicano rebellion; demand for courses in Mexican-American studies. R. Bongartz. Nation 208:271-4 Mr 3 '69; Discussion. 208: 386+ Mr 31 '69

MEXICAN AMERICANS
Changing time; incidents at UCLA and San Jose. Nation 209:460 N 3 '69
Grapes of wrath. J. R. Coyne, jr. Nat R 21: 639 Jl 1 '69
Little strike that grew to *la causa.* il Time 94:16-21 Jl 4 '69; Same abr. with title Battle of the grapes. Read Digest 95:88-92 O '69
Mexican-Americans and la Raza. D. Post. Chr Cent 86:325-6+ Mr 5 '69

Mexican-Americans; the Nation's best-kept secret? il Sr Schol 94:10-12+ Ap 18 '69
Profiles; Cesar Chavez. P. Matthiessen. New Yorker 45:42-4+ Je 21; 43-4+ Je 28 '69
Rise and shine; Eastern Oregon program for migrant children. J. Guernsey. il Am Ed 5: 20-1 N '69
Rumbles along the Rio; U.S. civil rights commission hearings in San Antonio. P. H. McNamara. Commonweal 89:730-2 Mr 14 '69
Thorns on the yellow rose of Texas. R. Coles and H. Huge. New Repub 160:13-17 Ap 19 '69
Viva Sanchez! MAMA; Mexican-American minority against; letter, ed. by W. F. Buckley. R. V. Sanchez. Nat R 21:791-2 Ag 12 '69

Education
I am Mexican-American. J. J. Bernal. Todays Ed 58:51-2 My '69

MEXICAN cookery. See Cookery, Mexican

MEXICAN literature
See also
Mexican American literature

MEXICAN 1000. See Motor vehicle racing

MEXICAN pottery. See Pottery, Mexican

MEXICAN silver. See Silverware

MEXICAN students
See also
Student demonstrations—Mexico

MEXICANOS. See Mexican Americans

MEXICANS
Mexico. E. H. Lopez. il Am Heritage 20:4-39+ Ap '69

MEXICANS in the United States
No dice for braceros; imported farm labor, California. W. Turner. Ramp Mag 7:37-40 Ja 25 '69
See also
Mexican Americans

MEXICO
See also
Acapulco
Agriculture—Mexico
Art—Mexico
Automobile industry and trade—Mexico
Automobile touring—Mexico
California, Lower
Civil rights—Mexico
Cuernavaca
Finance—Mexico
Fishing—Mexico
Forests and forestry—Mexico
Geology—Mexico
Hunting—Mexico
Investments, Foreign (in Mexico)
La Paz
Libraries—Mexico
Mining industry and finance—Mexico
Monterrey
Oaxaca (state)
Pinacate, Sierra del
Poor—Mexico
Public lands—Mexico
Railroads—Mexico
Restaurants—Mexico
San Miguel De Allende
Student demonstrations—Mexico
Television broadcasting—Mexico
Tijuana
Tonalá
Tourist trade—Mexico
Yelapa
Zinacantán

Antiquities
See Indians of Mexico—Antiquities

Civilization
Crash program in Spanish and Mexican-American culture. il Sch & Soc 97:87-8 F '69
Mexico. E. H. Lopez. il Am Heritage 20:4-39+ Ap '69

Description and travel
Bush sculpture in Encarnacion de Diaz. L. Barry. il Pop Phot 65:60+ S '69
Exploring the land of the Mayas in Mexico. il Bet Hom & Gard 47:146 My '69
Groups can sometimes grab you. N. Rothschild. il Pop Phot 65:32+ N '69
Mexico; with editorial comment by P. Plawin. J. Landsverk; G. Landsverk. il Bet Hom & Gard 47:17-22 D '69
Mexico's mystery. J. R. Wilhelm. il Travel & Camera 32:51-5 N '69
South of the border. K. B. Pomeroy. il Am For 75:38-9 D '69
Tomorrow's Mexican Riviera? E. Silverman. il Travel 132:72-3 S '69
Travel and eclipse site guide for Mexico. il Sky & Tel 39:19-20 Ja '70

MEXICO—*Continued*

Economic conditions

Borderline industry; effect of industrialization program. il Newsweek 73:82+ Je 23 '69
Jumping market below the border. il Bsns W p 120-1+ Jl 12 '69
Measurement of modernism. by J. A. Kahl. Review
    Américas 21:41-2 Ja '69. F. D. McCann, jr
Report from Olympic village. P. Hamill. il Ramp Mag 7:21-7 N 30 '68

Foreign relations

President Nixon and President Díaz Ordaz of Mexico dedicate the Amistad Dam; remarks, exchange of toasts, September 8, 1969. R. M. Nixon; G. Díaz Ordaz. Dept State Bul 61:277-80 S 29 '69
Statue of Benito Juárez dedicated at Washington; remarks, January 7, 1969. D. Rusk. Dept State Bul 60:74-5 Ja 27 '69
United States and Mexico reaffirm bonds of friendship; border ceremony; with exchange of toasts, December 13, 1968. L. B. Johnson; G. Díaz Ordaz. Dept State Bul 60:21-6 Ja 13 '69

History

Mexico. E. H. Lopez. il Am Heritage 20:4-39+ Ap '69

Drama

Bell of Dolores. C. Campbell. Plays 28:75-86 Ap '69

1910-1946

Zapata and the Mexican revolution. by J. Womack, jr. Review
    Newsweek il 73:82+ F 10 '69. R. A. Sokolov
    Time 93:88+ F 7 '69

Industries

Borderline industry; effect of industrialization program. il Newsweek 73:82+ Je 23 '69
Jumpingest place in Mexico. il Bsns W p70-1 O 25 '69
    See also
Mexico—Economic conditions

Photographs

Viva Mexico. Travel & Camera 32:42-50 N '69

Politics and government

Next president: not left, not right. il Time 94:33 O 31 '69
    See also
Presidents—Mexico

MEXICO (city)

Architecture

Architecture in Mexico. N. Silver. Nation 209:121+ Ag 11 '69

Buildings

See also
Mexico (city)—Architecture

Description

Booked for travel. D. Butwin. il Sat R 52:39-40 My 3 '69

Galleries and museums

Brilliant museum reflects Mexico's cultural ambitions; Four museums in a park. R. Lifchez. il Arch Rec 145:176-81 Je '69

Markets

Market shopping in Mexico city; la Merced. il Sunset 142:66 My '69

Music

Report: productions of Manon and Nabucco. L. Frick. Opera N 34:28 D 6 '69

Parks and playgrounds

In Mexico city, the charisma of Chapultepec park. F. Lemkowitz. il Home Gard 56:66-7 Je '69

Rapid transit

See also
Mexico (city)—Subways

Subways

Mexico's subway is for viewing. il Fortune 80:105-9 D '69
Quintana's box. il Time 94:71 Ag 22 '69

MEXICO, GULF OF

Mineral source and transport in waters of the Gulf of Mexico and Caribbean Sea. M. B. Jacobs and M. Ewing. bibliog il Science 163:805-9 F 21 '69
    See also
Gulf states

MEYER, Alfred

In and out of the field. Natur Hist 78:8+ Ja; 6 F; 10+ Ap; 6 Ag '69

MEYER, Carolyn

Who cooks for the White House chef? Mc-Calls 96:66+ Ag '69

MEYER, Charles A.

Central American common market; initiative for development; address, April 30, 1969. Dept State Bul 60:421-3 My 19 '69
Current U.S.-Peruvian problems; statement before the Subcommittee on western hemisphere affairs of the Senate committee on foreign relations; April 17, 1969. Dept State Bul 60:406-8 My 12 '69
Future U.S. relations with Latin America; statement. Dept State Bul 60:473-4 Je 2 '69
Inter-American economic and social council meets at Port-of-Spain; statement, June 20, 1969, with President Nixon's message, and Declaration of Port-of-Spain. Dept State Bul 61:21-6 Jl 7 '69
Latin America: what are your priorities? address, May 6, 1969. Dept State Bul 60:440-2 My 26 '69
U.S. military assistance policy toward Latin America; statement, July 8, 1969. Dept State Bul 61:100-2 Ag 4 '69

MEYER, Charles R.

Built-in buoyancy saves lives. il Pop Sci 194:114-16+ Ja '69
Car-toppers and carriers: easiest way to boating fun. Pop Sci 194:100-3 Je '69
Choosing and using boat fenders. Pop Sci 194:122-4 My '69
Hot rods on ice. Motor B 124:10-12 D '69
How to choose and use a canoe. Pop Sci 194:108-11 Ap '69
How to survive in rough water. Pop Sci 194:110-13+ F '69
Small boat to Block Island. il Yachting 126:72-3+ Jl '69

MEYER, Daniel

Build the FET preamp. Pop Electr 30:27-33 My '69
Build the homesteader. Pop Electr 31:71-3+ O '69
Tigers that roar. Pop Electr 31:51-3+ Jl '69

MEYER, Edward Joel

Lawyer in a mental hospital. Ment Hy 53:14-16 Ja '69

MEYER, Frank S.

Principles and heresies. See issues of National review

about

Old man in the back of the room. W. F. Buckley, jr. Nat R 21:287-8 Mr 25 '69

MEYER, Henry

Lonely medical runner. Nation 209:493 N 10 '69

MEYER, Howard N.

Angelo Herndon story. Chr Cent 86:221-2 F 12 '69

MEYER, James A.

Programed learning: education's turkey? Ed Digest 34:8-9 Ja '69
Salvaging team teaching. bibliog Clear House 44:203-5 D '69
Teaming a first step for interdisciplinary teaching. bibliog f Clear House 43:406-10 Mr '69

MEYER, Karl E.

Dig. Esquire 71:94-5+ F '69

MEYER, Leonard S.

Desirable eavesdropping. M. E. Marty. Chr Cent 86:303 F 26 '69
Obituary
    Chr Cent 86:207 F 12 '69

MEYER, Pamela Johnson

Foxes foretell the future in Mali's Dogon country. il por Nat Geog 135:430-48 Mr '69

MEYER, Paul A.

Flight of Sergeant Meyer. Time 93:23 My 30 '69
I've got trouble. il por Newsweek 73:50+ Je 2 '69

MEYER, Roland K. See Rust, C. C. jt. auth.

MEYER, Roy W.

Effigy mounds. Nat Parks 43:4-7 Je '69

MEYER, Russ

Mister X. il por Newsweek 75:83 Ja 19 '70

MEYER, Susan E.

Pottery of Toshiko Takaezu. il Am Artist 33:42-7 F '69

MEYER lemons. See Lemon trees

MEYERBEER, Giacomo

Music to my ears. I. Kolodin. Sat R 52:38 My 31 '69
Some real rarities: the IRCC carries on. P. L. Miller. Am Rec G 36:7 S '69

MEYERHOFF, Arthur E.

Fighting the propaganda; address. Vital Speeches 35:469-73 My 15 '69

MEYERHOLD, Vsevolod Emil'evich
Doctor Dapertutto. H. Clurman. Nation 209:
608-9 D 1 '69
MEYERLE, George
Build a Dwell Extender. Pop Electr 31:51-4+
O '69
MEYERS, Dale
Dale Meyers advocates thorough preparation;
with biographical sketch. il por Am Artist
33:48-9+ Ja '69
MEYERS, Ed J.
World's richest man. P. P. Puckett. por Har
Yrs 9:34 Mr '69
MEYERS, Edward
Meyers on technique. See issues of Modern
photography
Protechniques. Pop Phot 65:58+ S; 54+ O;
52+ N; 60+ D '69
MEYERS, Harold B.
For Lockheed, everything's coming up unk-
unks. Fortune 80:76-81+ Ag 1 '69
For the old meatpackers, things are tough
all over Fortune 79:88-93+ F '69
Great nuclear fizzle at old B.&W. Fortune
80:123-5+ N '69
How they see it in Hannibal, Mo. Fortune
80:74-5+ D '69
Medical-industrial complex. Fortune 81:90-1+
Ja '70
Tax-exempt property: another crushing bur-
den for the cities. Fortune 79:76-9+ My 1
'69
MEYERS, Jeffrey
Personality of Belinda's baron: Pope's The
rape of the lock. bibliog f Am Imago 26:
71-7 Spr '69
MEYERS, Robert, Jr
Puppy love is mainly flowers; story. Red-
book 132:102-3 Ap '69
MEYERS, William
Nixon's history lesson: the myth of reprisals.
Nation 209:654-6 D 15 '69
November in Hanoi. Nation 209:622-4 D 8 '69
MEYERS, William (playwright)
Spiro who? Criticism
New Yorker 45:77 My 31 '69
MEYERSON, Martin
New paths to new destinations. Sat R 53:54+
Ja 10 '70
MEYERSON, Seymour, and Fields, E. K.
Mass spectrometry and carbon-13 labelling.
bibliog Science 166:325-8 O 17 '69
MEZEY, Robert
Reaching the horizon; poem. Harp Baz 102:
102 Ja '69
MEZZOTINT
Attribution for His Excellency and Lady
Washington; unsigned mezzotints. W. J.
Shadwell. il Antiques 95:240-1 F '69
MIAL, Dorothy J. and Jacobson, S. I.
Stop action. Todays Ed 58:68 Mr '69
MIAMI, Fla.

Architecture
Building types study: Miami's innovative
schools. il Arch Rec 146:153-68 O '69

Description
Exciting cities, a Redbook vacation guide to
sight-seeing with children; excerpts from
America's exciting cities. A. Schwartz. il
Redbook 132:40-1 Ap '69

Education
Drew middle school: it shouts nontraditional.
I. Solie. il Sr Schol 94:Schol Teach 20-1
My 9 '69

Foreign population
Havana, Fla. il Newsweek 74:59 S 1 '69

Galleries and museums
Rembrandt, Vermeer, Hals, you name it, Bass
says he's got it. il Life 67:44-5 O 24 '69

Harbor
Miami captures a fleet; new seaport. il Bsns
W p24-5 Ja 18 '69

Music
Miami's Troika talks about music? T. J.
King. Hi Fi 19:MA20+ S '69
Report: Miami; production of Die frau ohne
schatten. D. Reno. il Opera N 33:32 Mr 8 '69

Parks and recreation
Under-expressway playground. il Am City
84:46 O '69

MIAMI-Nassau powerboat race. See Motor boat
racing
MIAMI-Nassau race. See Yacht racing
MIAMI, University, Coral Gables, Fla.
Climate of learning. P. Schrag. il Sat R 52:57-
9+ Mr 15 '69

MICA
Alpha-recoil tracks in mica: registration ef-
ficiency. S. Katcoff. il Science 166:382-4 O
17 '69
See also
Biotite
MICE
Antigenic changes in lymph-node cells after
administration of antiserum to thymus
cells. M. Schlesinger and I. Yron. bibliog
il Science 164:1412-13 Je 20 '69
Antiserum to lymphocytes and procarbazine
compared as immunosuppressants in mice.
P. B. Stewart and V. Cohen. bibliog il
Science 164:1082-3 My 30 '69
Brain lesions, obesity, and other disturbances
in mice treated with monosodium glutamate. J. W. Olney. bibliog il Science 164:
719-21 My 9 '69; Reply with rejoinder. F. R.
Blood and others. 165:1028-9 S 5 '69
Carcinogen-induced immune depression: absence in mice resistant to chemical on-
cogenesis. O. Stutman. bibliog il Science
166:620-1 O 31 '69
Circadian rhythm in mammalian body temperature entrained by cyclic pressure
changes. P. Hayden and R. G. Lindberg.
bibliog il Science 164:1288-9 Je 13 '69
Communal nursing in mice: influence of multiple mothers on the growth of the young.
A. Sayler and M. Salmon. bibliog il Science 164:1309-10 Je 13 '69
Genetic aspects of learning and memory in
mice. D. Bovet and others. bibliog il Science 163:139-49 Ja 10 '69; Reply with rejoinder. K. R. Henry and others. 165:1148
S 12 '69
Genetic control of the antibody response: relationship between immune response and
histocompatibility (H-2) type. H. O. Mc-
Devitt and A. Chinitz. bibliog il Science 163:
1207-8 Mr 14 '69
Graft versus host inhibition: fetal liver and
thymus cells to minimize secondary disease.
M. M. Bortin and E. C. Saltzstein. bibliog
il Science 164:316-18 Ap 18 '69
Immunology of mouse mammary tumor virus; report of meeting. D. H. Moore. il Science 163:1230-1 Mr 14 '69
LSD: autoradiographic study on the placental transfer and tissue distribution in mice.
J. E. Idänpään-Heikkilä and J. C. Schoolar.
bibliog il Science 164:1295-7 Je 13 '69
Lysergic acid diethylamide: effects on the
developing mouse lens. J. K. Hanaway.
bibliog il Science 164:574-5 My 2 '69
Mitotic division in pancreatic beta cells.
A. A. Like and W. L. Chick. bibliog il
Science 163:941-3 F 28 '69
Normal incidence of brain hernia in the
mouse. R. Rugh. bibliog Science 163:407
Ja 24 '69
Pheromone-induced changes in the acidophil
concentration of mouse pituitary glands.
T. L. Avery. bibliog il Science 164:423-4 Ap
25 '69
Physiology of the house mouse. D. S. Fertig
and V. W. Edmonds. il Sci Am 221:103-8+
bibliog(p 148) O '69
Protective effect of antilymphocyte serum on
mice infected with plasmodium berghei. J.
N. Sheagren and A. P. Monaco. bibliog il
Science 164:1423-5 Je 20 '69
Puromycin: effect on memory of mice when
injected with various cations. J. B. Flexner
and L. B. Flexner. bibliog il Science 165:
1143-4 S 12 '69
Rapid loss of tolerance induced in weanling
NZB and B/W F₁ mice. P. J. Staples and
N. Talal. bibliog il Science 163:1215-16 Mr 14
'69
Slow aging. Sci Am 220:50+ Mr '69
1-Δ⁹-Tetrahydrocannabinol: neurochemical and
behavioral effects in the mouse. D. Holtzman and others. bibliog il Science 163:
1464-7 Mr 28 '69
Thymus-dependent lymphocytes: destruction
by lymphocytic choriomeningitis virus. M.
Hanaoka and others. bibliog il Science 163:
1216-19 Mr 14 '69
Two mothers, two fathers. B. J. Culliton.
il Sci N 95:361-3 Ap 12 '69
MICE as laboratory animals. See Laboratory
animals
MICELLAR theory
Micelle formation between 5-hydroxytrypta-
mine and adenosine triphosphate in platelet
storage organelles. K. H. Berneis and oth-
ers. bibliog il Science 165:913-14 Ag 29 '69
MICHAEL, Charles R.
Retinal processing of visual images; with
biographical sketch. Sci Am 220:18, 104-14
My '69
MICHAEL, Franz
Twenty years of Sino-Soviet relations. Cur
Hist 57:150-5+ S '69

MICHAELI, D. and others
Localization of antigenic determinants in the polypeptide chains of collagen. bibliog Science 166:1522-4 D 19 '69
MICHAELIAN, Al G.
Motorandom. See issues of Motor trend
MICHAELIS, John Hersey
Where are they now? il pors Newsweek 74: 26 D 8 '69
MICHAELMAS daisies. See Asters
MICHAELS, Ron
New automatic tint control colors it right. Pop Sci 195:116-17 S '69
MICHAELSON, Michael G.
Medical students: healers become activists. Sat R 52:41-3+ Ag 16 '69
MICHAELSON, Mike
Are you heading for a fall? Todays Health 47:52-5+ O '69
Curling: hottest sport on ice. Todays Health 47:56-9+ N '69
Family doctor, space-age style. il Todays Health 47:34-7+ S '69
Judo: now it's a safe family sport. Todays Health 47:32-7+ F '69
Landlubber's guide to ocean driving. Todays Health 48:56-9+ Ja '70
Let the whole family flounder! Todays Health 47:14-15 Jl '69
Park beneath the sea. Todays Health 47:28-33 Mr '69
MICHAUD, Roland
Gallery: photographs. Life 67:4-7 Ag 29 '69
MICHEL, Curtis
Trouble at NASA: space scientists resign. M. Mueller. il por Science 165:776-7+ Ag 22 '69
MICHEL, Joan Hess
Elaine Rapp, stone carver. Am Artist 33: 22-5+ Ja '69
Illustrations of Peter Spier. Am Artist 33: 49-55+ O '69
Vibrant paintings of Hutsaliuk. Am Artist 33: 32-8+ Ag '69
Visit with Tomi Ungerer. por Am Artist 33: 40-5+ My '69
MICHELIN, Francois
Enigmatic Monsieur Michelin. V. Lewis. il por Duns R 94:97-100 N '69
MICHELIN and company, France. See Tire industry and trade
MICHELIN guides. See Guidebooks
MICHELON, L. C.
Role of education in a changing world; address, April 9 and 11, 1969. Vital Speeches 35:683-6 S 1 '69
MICHELS, Lynnell
Why we don't want children. por Redbook 134:10+ Ja '70
MICHELSON, Irving
Space age phenomenon: the evolution of lunar studies. por Bul Atom Sci 25:52-5 S '69
MICHENER, James Albert
Madrid's fabulous Prado. Read Digest 94: 145-51 Je '69
Presidential lottery; the reckless gamble in our electoral system; condensation. Read Digest 94:247-50+ My '69
Those fabulous Italian designers. Read Digest 95:157-62+ S '69
about
Windfall for Texas. A. Freed. il por Art in Am 57:78-85 N '69
MICHENER collection. See Art—Private collections
MICHIGAN
See also
Architecture, Domestic—Michigan
Education—Michigan
Fishing—Michigan
Hunting—Michigan
Petroleum—Michigan

Capitol
Michigan state capitol: symbolic separatism, practical unity. il Arch Rec 145:124-8 My '69

Politics and government
Democrats confront 1970. D. Crase. il Nation 209:598-9 D 1 '69

Religious institutions and affairs
See also
Protestant Episcopal church
MICHIGAN, LAKE
DDT threatens you! E. Chaney. il Nat Wildlife 7:48-9 Ag '69
Large manganese deposit found in Lake Michigan. il Chem 42:23 F '69

Problems in ppm: DDT residues in Lake Michigan coho salmon. H. Henkin. il Environ 11:24-33+ My '69
Spectrum; ban of DDT in Michigan. H. Henkin. Environ 11:S1-3 Ap '69
See also
Green Bay
MICHIGAN Bell telephone company
Dial V for vengeance; class action suit. Newsweek 75:51+ Ja 5 '70
MICHIGAN library association
Young librarians are concerned: Junior members round tables. J. A. McCrossan. ALA Bul 63:910-12 Jl '69
MICHIGAN state university, East Lansing
Exit Methuselah. il Time 93:42 Mr 21 '69
MSU's choice: C. R. Wharton. Newsweek 74: 110-11 O 27 '69
University on the make; or, How MSU helped arm Madame Nhu; with introd. by S. K. Sheinbaum. W. Hinckle and others. il Ramp Mag 7:52-60 Ja 25 '69
MICHIGAN. University, Ann Arbor
Ann Arbor, 1969; Institute on college and university administration. F. R. Haig. America 121:192-4 S 20 '69
Co-ops on campus: the militant consumers. B. W. Newell. Nation 209:635-6 D 8 '69
Current chronicle; University of Michigan: Festival contemporary music. E. Borroff. il Mus Q 55:396-401 Jl '69
Letter from Ann Arbor. A. Waugh. Nat R 21:1169+ N 18 '69
Liberalized curfews. Sch & Soc 97:142+ Mr '69
Listen to the white graduate, you might learn something. R. Rapoport. il Esquire 72:99+ S '69
Real story of the '68 election; University of Michigan survey research center analysis. il U S News 67:74-5 O 27 '69
Something new in student strikes; rent strike. D. Zwerdling. New Repub 160:13 My 31 '69
Sports clinics at Michigan U. C. E. Oxley. il Parks & Rec 4:35-6 Mr '69
Tenants' revolt in Ann Arbor. N. C. Mills. Commonweal 91:294-5 D 5 '69
Universitas in loco parentis; survey on campus conduct. Sch & Soc 97:146+ Mr '69
See also
Institute of gerontology

Business hall of fame (proposed)
Is hall of fame a B-school bust? Bsns W p 132 S 27 '69

Conference on aging
See Aging, Conferences on

Hospital
Juvenile journalists find humor in a hospital. J. H. Pollack. il Todays Health 47:12-13 Ap '69

Medical center
Six long, long months; treatment at the Burn unit. J. P. Blank. Read Digest 95:97-101 N '69

School of library science
Paraprofessional course tested in Michigan. Library J 94:3956 N 1 '69
MICKELSON, Sig
Communications by satellite. For Affairs 48: 67-79 O '69
MICROBES. See Microorganisms
MICROCIRCUITS. See Electronic circuits—Miniaturization
MICROCOCCUS
Lysozyme retention by cockroach periplaneta americana L. D. R. A. Wharton. bibliog il Science 163:183-4 Ja 10 '69
MICROELECTROPHORESIS. See Electrophoresi
MICROFICHE. See Microforms
MICROFILM records
See also
Municipal records on microfilm
MICROFILMS
Microfilm: it pays to think small. I. Geller. il Duns R 94:101-4+ S '69
See also
Libraries—Microfilm collections
Municipal records on microfilm
Periodicals on microfilm
MICROFORMS
New aids to research; development of microfiche reader. Sch & Soc 97:475-6 D '69
UMF and the future; ultramicrofiche. N. Cousins. Sat R 52:26 Ap 19 '69
MICROMATION technology corporation
How to get in on a new issue early. A. Hershman. Duns R 93:25 F '69

MICROMETERS
Mike reading. J. Thawley. il Hot Rod 22:68 Ap '69

MICRONESIA
Coming of age in Micronesia. P. W. Quigg. il For Affairs 47:493-508 Ap '69
Promises, promises. il Commonweal 90:274 My 23 '69
Remembering an adopted cousin. il Time 93: 28 My 23 '69
Statehood for Micronesia. E. Gruening. il Nation 209:664-5 D 15 '69
Storm over Micronesia. F. Riley. il Sat R 52:56+ S 13 '69
Uncivil war afflicts the Peace corps: confronting the Pentagon in Micronesia. P. Stern. New Repub 161:14-16 Ag 23 '69
See also
Truk Islands
Trust Territory of the Pacific Islands

MICROORGANISMS
Life on man, by T. Rosebury. Review
Life 67:8 Jl 11 '69. H. Kenner
See also
Skin—Microorganisms
Unicellular organisms

MICROORGANISMS, Effect of drugs on
Antibiotic-induced surface changes in microorganisms demonstrated by scanning electron microscopy. D. Greenwood and F. O'Grady. bibliog il Science 163:1076-8 Mr 7 '69

MICROORGANISMS, Pathogenic
Indication of infectious cause; mycoplasma link to rheumatoid arthritis. il Sci N 96:397 N 1 '69

MICROPALEONTOLOGY
Fossil mycelium with clamp connections from the middle Pennsylvanian. R. L. Dennis. bibliog il Science 163:670-1 F 14 '69; Reply. D. P. Rogers. 164:726 My 9 '69

MICROPHONES
Five minute microphone housing. A. Traufter. il Radio-Electr 40:74 D '69
Linear IC's for the experimenter; FM wireless mike. il Pop Electr 30:27-33+ Ap '69
Sound advice. M. A. Matzkin. Mod Phot 33: 138-9 Mr '69

MICROPHONES in criminal investigation, espionage, etc. See Electronics in criminal investigation, espionage, etc.

MICROPHOTOGRAPHY
See also
Microforms

MICROSCOPE and microscopy
See also
Electron microscope and microscopy
Photomicrography

Study and teaching
American museum's youngest scientist; J. Hurtt. il Ebony 24:86-7+ O '69

MICROSOMAL oxidation. See Oxidation, Physiological

MICROSOMES
Cytochrome P-420: tubular aggregates from hepatic microsomes. D. W. Shoeman and others. bibliog il Science 165:1371-2 S 26 '69
Histone synthesis in vitro by cytoplasmic microsomes from HeLa cells. D. Gallwitz and G. C. Mueller. bibliog il Science 163: 1351-3 Mr 21 '69
Microsome-associated DNA. H. E. Bond and others. bibliog il Science 165:705-6 Ag 15 '69

MICRO-states. See States, Small

MICROSURGERY
Microsurgery: medicine's big new hope. A. S. Freese. il Sci Digest 65:7-11 My '69

MICROTUBULES. See Cells

MICROWAVE apparatus. See Radio apparatus, Short wave

MICROWAVE communications, incorporated
FCC plugs in a new AT&T rival. Bsns W p46 Ag 16 '69
Round AT&T lost; FCC's approval of MCI to carry voices and data. il Bsns W p68+ S 6 '69

MICROWAVE ovens. See Electronic ovens

MICROWAVE relay systems. See Radio relay systems

MICROWAVE spectrum. See Spectrum, Microwave

MICROWAVES
Microwaves: a technology in search of a market. I. Geller. il Duns R 92:63-4+ D '68
See also
Masers

Physiological effects
Microwaves and health effects. E. Gross. il Sci N 96:382-3+ O 25 '69
Radiation biology; report of symposium on the biological effects of microwave radiation. Sci N 96:276 S 27 '69

MIDDEKE, Raphael
Black and poor in Cairo. Commonweal 90: 453-4 Jl 25 '69

MIDDLE age
Middle age: for adults only; excerpts from I didn't come here to argue. P. Bracken. Read Digest 95:86-8 D '69
On being a middle-aged manager. H. Levinson. bibliog f il Harvard Bsns R 47:51-60 Jl '69
Should you quit your job? R. Bugg. il Todays Health 47:26-9+ My '69

MIDDLE age pregnancy. See Pregnancy

MIDDLE ages
This medieval winter. H. S. Hughes. America 120:156-8 F 8 '69; Discussion. 120:290 Mr 15 '69
See also
Architecture, Medieval
Chivalry

History
See also
Europe—History—15th century

Bibliography
Articles and other books received; comp. by B. J. Holm. See issues of American historical review

MIDDLE class Americans. See Americans

MIDDLE classes
Middle-class blacks are moving off the middle. E. Holsendolph. il Fortune 80:90-5+ D '69
Nixon and the new bourgeoisie; working class has become middle class. S. Alsop. Newsweek 73:96 Ja 27 '69
Social stability and black capitalism; matter of missing Negro middle class. M. Rein. Trans-Action 6:4+ Je '69

MIDDLE EAST
World of Islam; symposium. bibliog f il Cur Hist 56:129-67+ Mr '69
See also
Arab states
Bahrein
Central treaty organization
Education—Middle East
Iran
Libraries—Middle East
Prisoners of war in the Middle East
Suez Canal
United Nations—Middle East
United Nations relief and works agency for Palestine refugees in the Near East
United States—Foreign relations—Middle East
Water supply—Middle East

Bibliography
Middle East. M. H. Van Dusen. Cur Hist 56: 169+ Mr '69
Middle East roundup. M. Geltman. Nat R 21:655-6 Jl 1 '69

Foreign opinion
On world reaction to developments in the Middle East. J. P. Rudin. Chr Cent 86:110 Ja 22 '69; Reply. J. N. Booth. 86:416 Mr 26 '69

Foreign relations
Islam and the West in the Middle East. G. Lenczowski. bibliog f Cur Hist 56:129-35+ Mr '69
Middle East; symposim. bibliog f il Cur Hist 58:1-38+ Ja '70

History
Bibliography
Articles and other books received; comp. by S. Glazer. See issues of American historical review

Politics
Alternatives in the Middle East. N. Safran. Commentary 47:45-55 My '69; Discussion. 48:14+ S; 4+ O; 28+ D '69
Assassination in the Middle East. C. Leiden. il Trans-Action 6:20-3 My '69
Both sides take a hard look; Israel's leaders views. M. Elkins. il Newsweek 74:39-40 S 15 '69
Bubbling, but not yet boiling. Time 93:37 Ja 24 '69
Carnival in Baghdad; public hangings of Iraqi Jews in Baghdad. il Newsweek 73: 31-2 F 10 '69
Crumbling deterrent. Time 93:36 My 9 '69
Enter the big four. il Time 93:35 Ap 11 '69
Frayed patience. Newsweek 74:35-6 Jl 14 '69
Great power responsibilities. Commonweal 89: 487-8 Ja 17 '69
Great powers, the Arabs and the Israelis. B. Lewis. For Affairs 47:642-52 Jl '69
Hardening line. il Time 93:36 My 23 '69
Holy wars. Nation 209:194-5 S 8 '69
If Libya lines up with Nasser. il U S News 67:36-7 S 15 '69

MIDDLE EAST—Politics—*Continued*
In the Middle East, a new gathering of war clouds. il U S News 68:4 Ja 5 '70
Jerusalem III. Nat R 21:1302-3 D 30 '69
Looking for a way out. il Newsweek 73:40 Ja 27 '69
Middle East; symposium. bibliog f il Cur Hist 58:1-38+ Ja '70
Middle East; the storm gathers. il Time 93: 23-4 My 2 '69
Mideast: is compromise possible? il Newsweek 73:43-4 F 17 '69
Mideast moves closer to the brink. il U S News 67:51 S 22 '69
Mideast: new war tension. il U S News 67:23 S 8 '69
New choices in the Middle East. il Time 93:35-7 Mr 7 '69
Nixon's first foreign crisis: the boiling Mideast. il U S News 66:35-6 F 10 '69
On the southern flank. J. Burnham. Nat R 21:952 S 23 '69
Pride, fear, suspicion. A. de Borchgrave. Newsweek 73:42-3 F 24 '69
Prospects of war in the Middle East. G. C. AlRoy. Commentary 47:53-9 Mr '69
Rights reserved. Newsweek 73:52+ My 12 '69
Talk with President Nasser; interview, ed. by A. de Borchgrave. G. A. Nasser. il Newsweek 73:33-4+ F 10 '69
Uneasy heads Newsweek 74:61+ O 20 '69
U.S. in the Middle East today. H. N. Howard. bibliog f Cur Hist 57:36-41+ Jl '69
View from Allenby bridge. T. C. Sorenson. il Sat R 52:23-5+ O 4 '69
See also
Israeli—Arab war, 1967-
Jewish-Arab relations

Religious institutions and affairs

Middle East trends toward ecumenism. G. Fitch. Chr Cent 86:1461-2+ N 12 '69

MIDDLE EAST airlines. See Airlines—Lebanon
MIDDLE EASTERN cookery. See Cookery, Middle Eastern
MIDDLE schools. See Education—Organization by years

MIDDLE WEST
See also
Fishing—Middle western states
Libraries—Middle western states

Social life and customs

At the heart of the land ocean. H. Sidey. il Life 66:4 Je 13 '69
Growing up in America. J. Howard. il Mlle 68:209+ Ap '69

MIDDLEBROOK, Jonathan
Television as the medium of contempt. Ramp Mag 7:56+ Ap '69
Wanna bet, MasterCharge? New Repub 161: 17-18 S 20 '69

MIDDLEBROOKS, Glenna Parker
Another research tool. Writers Digest 49:45 F '69

MIDDLETON, Drew
Do the Arabs have a case? Sat R 52:23-5+ F 1 '69
Europe in a time of change. Sat R 52:14-15 Ag 16 '69

MIDDLETON, Sallie
Sallie Middleton works for weeks on a single painting; with biographical sketch. il por Am Artist 33:60-1+ Je '69

MIDDLETOWN, N. J.
Exploring the world around us; school children at Sandy Hook State Park. F. Sabin. il Am Ed 5:12-17 Je '69

MIDDLETOWN, Ohio
Steel shelters defy vandals. J. Paschal. il Am City 84:96-7 F '69

MIDGET automobile racing
Astro Grand prix. J. Thawley. il Hot Rod 22:96-7 Je '69
Poor li'l midgets, Texas style; midget-car races in Houston's Astrodome. B. Ottum. il Sports Illus 30:24-5 Mr 17 '69

MIDGET submarine boats. See Submarine boats

MIDGETS. See Dwarfs

MIDLOTHIAN, Va.

Historic houses, etc.

History in towns. B. W. Weaver. il Antiques 96:588-91 O '69

MIDNIGHT sun 600 snowmobile race. See Snowmobile racing

MID-OCEAN club course, Bermuda. See Golf courses

MIDPENINSULA free university. See Free universities

MIDWAY conference, 1969
Back from Midway. J. Osborne. New Repub 160:13-15 Je 21 '69

Confrontation at Midway. Newsweek 73:42-4 Je 2 '69
First step at Midway. Life 66:36 Je 20 '69
In mid-passage at Midway. il Time 93:14 Je 13 '69
Meaning of Midway; statement, June 10, 1969. R. M. Nixon. U S News 66:29 Je 23 '69
Meaning of the Midway conference. America 120:702 Je 21 '69
Midway meeting: the perils of peace. il Time 93:21-2 Je 6 '69
Nixon midway. New Repub 160:7 Je 7 '69
President Nixon and President Thieu confer at Midway Island; at the conclusion of the meeting with text of joint statement, June 8, 1969. R. M. Nixon; Nguyen-van-Thieu. Dept State Bul 60:549-54 Je 30 '69
President's mission to Midway. il Newsweek 73:23-4 Je 16 '69
Two presidents. Nation 208:778-9 Je 23 '69
Vietnam: the long, long way home. il Newsweek 73:25-7 Je 23 '69
What Midway means. il Bsns W p46-7 Je 14 '69
What U.S. plans after Midway. U S News 66:25 Je 16 '69

MIDWIVES
Return of the midwife. B. Day. Redbook 132: 72-3+ Mr '69
Return of the midwife. il Newsweek 73:107 Mr 31 '69

MIEHLE-Goss-Dexter, incorporated
Rockwell takes bumps out of road to merger. Bsns W p67 F 1 '69

MIERLAK, Henry J.
Electronic throttle. Radio-Electr 40:42-4 N '69

MIES VAN DER ROHE, Ludwig
Mies. W. McQuade. il Arch Forum 131:90 O '69
Mies and the closing of the Bauhaus. R. Stern. Nation 209:290 S 22 '69
Mies; his eloquent legacy: purity of structure. J. DeLong. por House B 111:132-5 N '69
Mies the master. D. L. Shirey. il por Newsweek 74:74-5 S 1 '69
Mies van der Rohe. P. Blake. il por Arch Forum 131:35-9 O '69
Mies van der Rohe: disciplinarian for a confused age. il por Time 94:46-7 Ag 29 '69
Obituary
Arch Rec por 146:9 S '69. W. F. Wagner, jr
Westmount square. E. P. Berkeley. il Arch Forum 131:82-9 S '69

MIGDOLL, Herbert
Landscape into danscape; photographs. Dance Mag 43:46-55 D '69

MIGNONETTES
For enticing fragrance. M. M. Leister. Home Gard 56:32 Mr '69

MIGRAINE. See Headache

MIGRANT labor
In support of migrants; Pope Paul's *motu-proprio*. America 121:447 N 15 '69
International migration of workers. P. Kuin. il UNESCO Courier 22:28-31 Jl '69
Labor waste in New York: rural exploitation and migrant workers. W. H. Friedland. bibliog il Trans-Action 6:48-53 F '69; Reply. W. J. Haltigan. 6:64 My '69
No dice for braceros; imported farm labor, California. W. Turner. Ramp Mag 7:37-40 Ja 25 '69
Operation sisyphus; wetbacks, growers and poverty. S. L. Greene. Nation 209:403-6 O 20 '69
Peonage in Florida. R. Coles and H. Huge. New Repub 161:17-21 Jl 26 '69
Self-help for the single farm worker. G. M. Bergman. Chr Cent 86:1426+ N 5 '69
TRB from Washington; intolerable conditions of poverty areas being explored by Senate subcommittee. New Repub 160:6 Ap 5 '69
Unemployment or exile; is there a third choice for the migrant worker? S. Parmar. il UNESCO Courier 22:32-4 Jl '69
See also
American federation of labor and Congress of industrial organizations—United farm workers organizing committee
Children of migrant laborers
Church work with migrants

MIGRATION, Internal
Breeding a national standard. il Sci N 95: 448 My 10 '69
Census report that set off a furor. U S News 66:11 Ap 28 '69
Changing resource policies of the U.S.S.R. T. Shabad. bibliog il Focus 19:7-8 F '69
End of the exodus; attempt of rural communities to win back urban migrants. il Time 93:28 Ap 4 '69
See also
Cities and towns—Growth
Negroes—Migration

MIGRATION from cities. See Migration, Internal

MIGRATION of animals. See Animals—Migration

MIGRATION of fishes. See Fishes—Migration

MIGRATION of Negroes. See Negroes—Migration

MIGRATION of teachers. See Teachers—Migration

MIGRATIONS of man. See Man—Migrations

MIGRATORY workers. See Migrant labor

MIKE Douglas show. See Television broadcasting—Programs

MIKESELL, Arthur
Trim tabs: do they really make a difference? Pop Mech 131:124-7 Ja '69

MIKESELL, Raymond F.
Changing world trade patterns and America's leadership role. Ann Am Acad 384:35-44 Jl '69

MILAM, Lorenzo W.
Defender of the faith. il por Newsweek 74:75 Jl 28 '69

MILAN, Italy
La Scala
Report: Milan; productions of Don Carlo and Die Walküre. P. Hoffer. Opera N 33: 33-4 F 8 '69
Sills & Horne triumph at La Scala; production of Rossini's L'assedio di Corinto. W. Weaver. il Hi Fi 19:MA25 Jl '69

Music
Report: Milan; production of Donizetti's Maria di Rohan. P. Hoffer. Opera N 33:33 Ap 19 '69
Report: Milan; production of Orfeo ed Euridice at Scala theater. P. Hoffer. Opera N 33:30-1 My 29 '69
Report: Milan; production of Rossini's Assedio di Corinto. P. Hoffer. Opera N 33: 28 Je 14 '69
See also
Milan, Italy—La Scala

MILANESE designers. See Designers

MILASI, Tony
Twins who found each other; excerpt. B. Lindeman. il pors Good H 169:107-9+ O '69

MILEAGE indicators. See Odometers

MILEIKOWSKY, Curt
Saab's new model. il por Duns R 93:97-8+ My '69

MILEK, Bob
Access: the key to public land recreation. Field & S 73:20+ Ap '69
Fishing the split-personality river. Field & S 74:54-5+ My '69
Golden eagle: killer or saint? Field & S 74: 10+ S '69
Meat hunting from A to Z. Field & S 74:64-5+ Ag '69
Moose for the pot. por Field & S 74:56-7+ Je '69
Sage grouse: forgotten pioneer. Field & S 73: 82-3+ Ap '69
Tips for taking foothill muleys. Field & S 74:44-5+ O '69

MILES, Al
Campus that kept its cool. B. Darrach. il pors Life 67:80-80B+ N 7 '69

MILES, Bebe
Birdwatching, the accommodating sport. Pop Gard 20:34-7+ Spr '69
Bulbs for autumn. Horticulture 46:36-7+ Ag '68
Fabric of gardens. Horticulture 47:38-9+ Ja '69
Try the miniature glads. Horticulture 47:45 My '69

MILES, Charles
Indian relics. See issues of Hobbies

MILES, Dick
Table tennis. Sports Illus 30:70+ My 5 '69

MILES, Eleanor Addison Williams
Blakeford, in Queen Anne's County. Antiques 95:526-31 Ap '69

MILES, Josephine
Family; poem. New Yorker 45:36 Ag 16 '69

MILES, Michael
Whose university? New Repub 160:17-19 Ap 12; 30-1 My 3 '69; Same. Cur 108:14-19 Je '69

MILES college, Birmingham, Ala.
I now think of the American Indian as being very artistic: humanities course. J. Friedman. il Wilson Lib Bul 44:64-8 S '69
Under the leaking roof; psychology and sociology. N. Friedman. il Wilson Lib Bul 44:69-74 S '69

MILEY, William D. See A. V. jt. auth.

MILFORD, Conn.
Administrative assistant. C. C. Hughes. il Am City 84:126+ S '69
Town where every kid can go to camp. M. Strumpf. il Parents Mag 44:42-3+ Jl '69

MILHAVEN, John Giles
Exit for ethicists. Commonweal 91:135-40 O 31 '69
Importance of being Roman Catholic. America 120:728-31 Je 28 '69

MILHORAT, Thomas H.
Choroid plexus and cerebrospinal fluid production. bibliog Science 166:1514-16 D 19 '69

MILHOUS family
Ancestors. New Yorker 45:30-2 Mr 15 '69

MILI, Gjon
American masterpiece: Dances at a gathering; photographs. Life 67:42-51 O 3 '69

MILITANT students. See Student militants

MILITARISM
Antimilitarism can be too much of a good thing. A. Hartley. il N Y Times Mag p30-1+ O 19 '69
Militarism and American democracy; the complex; address, April 8, 1969. J. W. Fulbright. bibliog f Vital Speeches 35:455-60 My 15 '69
Military complex: the unpleasant symptom. J. C. Dougherty. Bul Atom Sci 25:38+ Ap '69
New American militarism. D. M. Shoup and J. A. Donovan. Atlan 223:51-6 Ap '69; Same Abr. with title Role of the military; the rise of our militaristic culture. Cur 108:46-55 Je '69
New militarism in Peru. J. L. Klaiber. America 120:364-7 Mr 29 '69
Semper fidelis: the ethic of the warrior. S. Cain. Chr Cent 86:677-81 My 14 '69
That antimilitary mood. Life 66:38 Mr 21 '69
See also
Armaments
Armies
Disarmament
War
also subhead Military policy under countries, e.g. United States—Military policy

MILITARY administration
Latin American military elite. T. M. Millington. bibliog f Cur Hist 56:352-4+ Je '69
New military. Newsweek 75:26-8 Ja 5 '70

MILITARY alliances. See Alliances

MILITARY art and science
See also
Armaments
Armies
Chemical warfare
Guerrilla warfare
War
War games

MILITARY assistance, American
Allies for hire; Senate foreign relations subcommittee hearings on financial costs of Asian allies in Vietnam. New Repub 161: 5-6 D 13 '69
Economic and military assistance proposals for fiscal year 1970; statement, House committee on foreign affairs on June 9, 1969. E. L. Richardson. Dept State Bul 60:569-74 Je 30 '69
Eisenhower era; with excerpts from Public law 7, passed by Congress, March 9, 1957. J. A. Huston. bibliog f Cur Hist 57:24-30+, 49-50 Jl '69
Further exports sales dip seen by Pentagon officials. D. C. Winston. Aviation W 91:18 O 13 '69
Guns for hire? cost of getting allies to commit troops to Vietnam. il Newsweek 74: 26-7 D 15 '69
Military assistance program; foreign military sales; address, March 26, 1969. R. H. Warren. Vital Speeches 35:601-3 Jl 15 '69
Military assistance, yes; unconditioned involvement, no. W. C. McWilliams. Commonweal 90:12-13 Mr 21 '69; Same with title On choosing to be involved. Cur 109: 56-9 Ag '69
Military commitments in Latin America: 1960-1968. L. D. Langley. bibliog f Cur Hist 56:346-51+ Je '69
OV-10A export sales drive pushed. C. Brownlow. il Aviation W 91:67+ N 17 '69
Secret war; Laos. il Newsweek 74:92 O 6 '69
This month's feature: Congress & U.S. military commitments. Cong Digest 48:193-224 Ag '69
Truman doctrine and NATO; with excerpts from President's message to Congress, March 12, 1947. L. W. Koenig. bibliog f Cur Hist 57:18-23+, 49 Jl '69

MILK—*Continued*

Production

He got peak milk production. il Suc Farm 67:
18 Ap '69
Ways to keep milk quality high. D. Murray.
Suc Farm 67:T3 O '69

MILK, Acidophilus
See also
Yogurt

MILK, Filled
Vegetable fat in filled and imitation milks.
Consumer Bul 52:19-20 F '69

MILK, Human
See also
Breast feeding

MILK industry and trade
See also
Borden incorporated

MILKING
3X milking... quick way to jump production 15 per cent. N. Reeder. il Farm J 93:
D10-11+ Ap '69

MILKWEED bugs
Chromosomal fragments transmitted through
three generations in oncopeltus (hemiptera) L. E. LaChance and M. Degrugillier. bibliog il Science 166:235-6 O 10 '69

MILKY way
Mystery of the dust. Newsweek 73:62 F 3 '69
Radioisotopes and the history of nucleosynthesis in the galaxy. C. M. Hohenberg. bibliog il Science 166:212-15 O 10 '69
Spiral structure of our galaxy. B. J. Bok.
il Sky & Tel 38:392-5; 39:21-5 D '69-Ja '70

MILLAR, Kenneth. See Macdonald, R. pseud.

MILLAR, T. P.
Child who won't try. Parents Mag 44:44-5+
F '69

MILLAU, Christian. See Gault, H. jt. auth.

MILLAY, Edna St Vincent
Poet and her book, by J. Gould. Review
America 121:75-6 Ag 2 '69. J. J. McAleer
Sat R por 52:30-1 Je 7 '69. L. Untermeyer

MILLENNIAL cults. See Cults

MILLENNIUM
See also
Second advent

MILLER, A. A.
Glass-transition temperature of water. bibliog Science 163:1325-6 Mr 21 '69

MILLER, Abraham. See McEvoy, J. jt. auth.

MILLER, Ak
Yak with Ak; interview. ed. by J. Dianna. il
pors Hot Rod 22:50-2 Ap '69

MILLER, Alfred Jacob
Hunter and the artist. J. Monaghan. bibliog
il por Am West 6:4-13 N '69

MILLER, Arjay Ray
From executive suite to halls of ivy. il por
Bsns W p 122-3 Jl 19 '69

MILLER, Arthur
In Russia; excerpts. pors Harper 239:37-78 S
'69
Lines from California; poem. Harper 238:97
My '69

about
Arthur Miller's The crucible and Nathaniel
Hawthorne; some parallels. D. M. Bergeron.
Engl J 58:47-55 Ja '69

MILLER, Arthur Selwyn
Perils of pragmatism. Nation 208:576-8 My
5 '69
Rise of the techno-corporate state in Ameri-
ca. Bul Atom Sci 25:14-19 Ja '69
Universities in crisis. Bul Atom Sci 25:45-6
Ap '69

MILLER, Barbara
Screen. Commonweal 91:337-8 D 12 '69

MILLER, Bernard S.
More than a little is much too much; address.
November, 1968. Engl J 58:659-63 My '69

MILLER, Bertha E. (Mahony)
Bertha Mahony Miller, 1882-1969; symposium.
bibliog il por(p496) Horn Bk 45:467-8+ O
'69
Obituary
Horn Bk 45:371 Ag '69. P. Heins

MILLER, Bruce
Outlook encouraging. Dance Mag 43:68-9 Mr
'69

MILLER, C. Chapel
Making bamboo handles. Ceram Mo 17:28-9 O
'69

MILLER, C. John
Public-school Bible study: sectarianism in
disguise? Chr Today 13:3-5 Ag 1 '69

MILLER, Catherine Lanham
This year, let the invitation read: bring the
children. House B 111:130-1+ N '69
Yoga. Harp Baz 102:188-9+ Ap '69

MILLER, Charles
Royalty. Sat R 52:42-4 S 20 '69
What the black man's ancestors were up to.
Sat R 52:51-2+ Mr 22 '69

MILLER, Charles Leslie
Can a weapons lab solve urban ills? il por
Bsns W p 132+ N 1 '69

MILLER, Claude
What too many women don't know about
dieting; interview. Redbook 133:82-3+ S
'69

MILLER, Conrad
Hot prop for your boat. Mech Illus 65:81-
3+ F '69
Minimum program for readying your boat's
machinery. Motor B 123:80+ Ap '69
Pay her a mid-winter visit. Motor B 123:50-
2 F '69
Putting her to bed. Motor B 124:130-3 O '69
Readying your engine the relaxed way. Motor
B 123:78-9 Ap '69
Use your engine ear. Motor B 123:66-7+ Mr
'69

MILLER, Dana
Gabions harness flood waters. Am City 84:
80-1 Ag '69

MILLER, David M.
On being had by the radicals. Nat R 21:688-
90 Jl 15 '69

MILLER, Doris
Dorie Miller: first U.S. hero of World war II.
il por Ebony 25:132-4+ D '69

MILLER, Doris P.
New life for old authors. Sr Schol 94:Schol
Teach 16-17 Ap 18 '69

MILLER, Edwin
Real modern artist of our time. Seventeen
27:98-9+ D '68
Spotlight! See issues of Seventeen
(ed) See Franklin, P. On my own at last!
(ed) See Hartman, E. Daydreamer talks

MILLER, Harry
Wild elephant roundup in India. il Nat Geog
135:372-85 Mr '69

MILLER, Helen Louise
Christmas promise; drama. Plays 29:1-12, 26
D '69
Just what the doctor ordered; drama. Plays
29:17-26, 38 N '69
Lincoln heart; drama. Plays 28:9-18 F '69
Mother's day treasure hunt; drama. Plays
28:69-74, 88 My '69
Mount Vernon cricket; drama. Plays 28:35-43
F '69
Pilgrim who didn't care; drama. Plays 29:
69-75 N '69
Sandy scarecrow's Halloween; drama. Plays
29:53-60 O '69
Too many angels; drama. Plays 29:65-72 D '69

MILLER, Henry
Other people's bookshelves. L. Conger. Writer 82:9-10 Ag '69
Where are they now? por Newsweek 74:10 Ag
18 '69

MILLER, Herbert John, 1924-
Excerpt from remarks, February 13, 1969.
Cong Digest 48:122+ Ap '69

MILLER, Herman, Incorporated
Action Office is a movable feast. Bsns W
p 156 S 13 '69

MILLER, Howard
Howard power. il por Time 93:52 Ja 31 '69

MILLER, Irvin M.
Computer graphics for decision making.
Harvard Bsns R 47:121-32 N '69

MILLER, J.
(tr) See Molière, J. B. P. Miser

MILLER, J. Furman
Because Christ arose: the new man. Chr
Today 13:8-9 S 26 '69

MILLER, James Nathan
America the (formerly) beautiful. Read Digest 94:179-81+ F '69
Cruising in a cottage. Read Digest 94:37-8+
Je '69
Day in the life of an airport. Read Digest
94:146-50 F '69
How to grow a perfect lawn. Read Digest
95:64-8 Ag '69
Six keys to training your dog. Read Digest
94:53+ Ap '69
Slum swindlers must go! Read Digest 95:
169-70+ N '69
(ed) See Wurster, C. F. Alarming case
against DDT

MILLER, Joan
Dress up your frozen dinners. Am Home 72:
96 Mr '69

MILLER, John N.
Night game; Prince charming; poems. Poetry 114:378-9 S '69

MILLER, John S. and Stern, E. M.
Changes during pregnancy. Redbook 134:16+
D '69

MILLER, Jonathan
 Intoxicating ideas for the tender mind. Vogue
 153:70+ Ja 15 '69
 Sand, seals and shipwrecks. por Holiday 45:
 62-3+ Mr '69
MILLER, Josef M. and others
 Evoked potentials and auditory reaction time
 in monkeys. bibliog Science 163:592-4 F 7
 '69
MILLER, Joseph Irwin
 Business has a war to win; excerpts from
 address, December 5, 1968. Harvard Bsns
 R 47:4-6+ Mr '69

about

 Telling it as it really is. B. L. Masse. Amer-
 ica 120:389 Ap 5 '69
MILLER, L. Keith
 Freezing tolerance in an adult insect. bibliog
 Science 166:105-6 O 3 '69
MILLER, Larry
 Concorde challenge. Sci N 95:294 Mr 22 '69
 Getting in on a new thing. Sci N 95:462 My
 10 '69
MILLER, Linda B.
 New states and the international society. bib-
 liog f Ann Am Acad 386:102-12 N '69
MILLER, Louis J.
 Collage and collage prints. Sch Arts 69:32-4
 D '69
 Scratchboard drawing. Design 70:4-7 Sum '69
MILLER, Marilyn
 Graded curriculum. Library J 94:1731-3 Ap
 15 '69
MILLER, Marjorie, and Ankrum, Janet
 Trump school. Library J 94:4211-12 N 15 '69
MILLER, Marraine
 Potatoes you can't buy. por Org Gard &
 Farm 16:28-31 Je '69
MILLER, Marvin
 Game deserves the best. R. Roberts. il por
 Sports Illus 30:46-7 F 24 '69
MILLER, Marvin E. and Hamilton, R. E.
 Holiday weekend holocaust in Ohio. Weather-
 wise 22:190-4 O '69
MILLER, Mike
 How to help your campers overcome their
 fears. Camp Mag 41:20+ Je '69
 Tyro trailerite. Travel 131:64-70 My '69
MILLER, Neal E.
 Learning of visceral and glandular responses.
 bibliog Science 163:434-45 Ja 31 '69
 —See Leibowitz, S. F. jt. auth.

about

 Gut learning. Sci Am 220:49-50 Ap '69
MILLER, Nyle H.
 Out of the bread, into the chips, and back
 again, and not even a dust of the hands!
 Am West 6:44-8 Mr '69
MILLER, O. L. Jr, and Beatty, B. R.
 Visualization of nucleolar genes. bibliog Sci-
 ence 164:955-7 My 23 '69
MILLER, P. M. and Ahrens, J. F.
 Marigolds in the garden. Horticulture 47:30-1
 S '69
MILLER, Paul R.
 Chicago demonstrators: a study in identity
 adaptation of address, November, 1968.
 Bul Atom Sci 25:3-6 Ap '69
MILLER, Philip C.
 Solar radiation profiles in openings in cano-
 pies of aspen and oak. bibliog Science 164:
 308-9 Ap 18 '69
MILLER, Philip L.
 On the record: Music. See issues of Library
 journal
 William H. Seltsam; June 30, 1897– December
 27, 1968. Opera N 33:20 F 8 '69
MILLER, R. Alden
 Fall in the vegetable garden. Horticulture
 46:18-20+ S '68
 Rebuild worn-out soils. Horticulture 47:34+
 F '69
MILLER, R. G. and Goldschmidt, S. J.
 New idea is the ovals. Am City 84:101-2+
 Je '69
MILLER, Raymond Wiley
 Inflation does not just happen; address.
 October 3, 1969. bibliog Vital Speeches 36:
 152-4 D 15 '69
MILLER, Richard H.
 Synodic month: variations in the geologic
 past. bibliog Science 164:67-8 Ap 4 '69
MILLER, Robert. See Jackson, L. jt. auth.
MILLER, Robert A.
 Indiana's three-in-one. Library J 94:4399 D
 1 '69
MILLER, Robert E. and others
 Hyperphagia and polydipsia in socially iso-
 lated rhesus monkeys. bibliog Science 165:
 1027-8 S 5 '69

MILLER, Robert W.
 Delayed radiation effects in atomic-bomb
 survivors; adaptation of address, March
 1969. bibliog Science 166:569-74 O 31 '69
MILLER, Roger
 Profiles. W. Whitworth. por New Yorker 45:
 38-42+ Mr 1 '69
MILLER, Stanley L.
 Clathrate hydrates of air in Antarctic ice.
 bibliog Science 165:489-90 Ag 1 '69
 —See Friedmann, N. jt. auth.
MILLER, Stephen M.
 Gunning the Atlantic coast. Field & S 74:
 64-5+ N '69
MILLER, Sy
 Go-go decor fighting the back-office blahs.
 il Bsns W p70+ F 1 '69
MILLER, Vassar
 Critic of the month. L. Lieberman. Poetry
 114:48-9 Ap '69
MILLER, Walter B.
 White gangs; excerpt. bibliog por Trans-Ac-
 tion 6:11-26 S '69
MILLER, William G.
 Check low-value capacitors with the pF
 meter-mate. Radio-Electr 40:57-9 F '69
 Decibels without logs. Electr World 82:71 S
 '69
MILLER, William M.
 Fishbait and the Capitol pages. Sr Schol 94:
 11 F 28 '69
MILLER, William Robert
 Pop sex novel: new opiate of the masses.
 Chr Cent 86:152-3 Ja 29 '69
MILLER brewing company
 Worth fighting over; PepsiCo suing W. R.
 Grace & co. il Forbes 104:20-1 D 15 '69
MILLET, Jean
 L'art de bien chanter (1666) of Jean Millet.
 A. Cohen. bibliog f il Mus Q 55:170-9 Ap
 '69
MILLET
 Millet, a versatile, nutritious cereal. J.
 Plewes. il Org Gard & Farm 16:72-3 Je '69
MILLETT, John D.
 Other voices, other views. Sat R 53:74 Ja 10
 '70
MILLING
 How to mill on a drill press. K. B. Little-
 field. il Pop Mech 131:180-4 Ja '69
MILLING industry (grain)
See also
 International milling company
MILLINGTON, Thomas M.
 Latin American military elite. bibliog f Cur
 Hist 56:352-4+ Je '69
MILLIONAIRES
 How to make a million; three American suc-
 cess stories. il U S News 67:58-61 D 15 '69
See also
 Getty, J. P.
MILLIONAIRESS; drama. See Shaw, G. B.
MILLS, Dennis A.
 Keeping young down east. Motor B 124:82+
 N '69
MILLS, Elinor S. and Topper, Y. J.
 Mammary alveolar epithelial cells: effect of
 hydrocortisone on ultrastructure. bibliog
 Science 165:1127-8 S 12 '69
MILLS, Ernest Andrew
 Creative craft program in the summer camp.
 Sch Arts 68:34-5 My '69
MILLS, James
 Why should he have it? Life 66:62-8+ Mr
 7 '69
MILLS, Joan
 Five sales in one year to Reader's digest;
 ed. by L. Aigner. Writers Digest 49:38-43+
 Jl '69
 When fall begins. Read Digest 95:79-81 O '69
MILLS, Nicolaus C.
 Tenants' revolt in Ann Arbor. Commonweal
 91:294-5 D 5 '69
MILLS, Paul Chadbourne
 West coast report. Art in Am 57:108-9 S '69
MILLS, Ralph J. Jr
 Critic of the month. Poetry 113:262-84 Ja
 '69
 For the word, for the silence. Poetry 115:
 127-30 N '69
MILLS, Wilbur Daigh
 Excerpt from address, February 12, 1967.
 Cong Digest 48:233+ O '69
 Plan for new taxes; interview. por U S News
 66:40-5 My 26 '69
 Wilbur Mills on taxes and spending; inter-
 view, ed. by N. MacNeil. Time 93:16 F 21
 '69

about

 How Mills ran the tax makers' marathon. il
 pors Bsns W p70-1 D 27 '69
 If Wilbur Mills gets his way on spending and
 taxes. U S News 66:78-80 My 19 '69
 Mills squints at conglomerates. por Bsns W
 p30 Mr 8 '69

MILLS, Wilbur Daigh—about—*Continued*
Tax reform faces the Senate hurdles. il Bsns W p22-3 Ag 9 '69
Views from Wilbur Mills. Newsweek 73:80+ My 19 '69
Wilbur Mills has put together the biggest tax-reform package ever. J. L. Steele. il por Fortune 80:55+ S '69

MILLSAP, Darrel
Millsap & Kinyon illustrator team. F. Whitaker. il Am Artist 33:50-5+ Je '69

MILNE, Lorus, and Milne, Margery
Zoologist's library. Natur Hist 78:58-61 Ja '69

MILNE, Margery. See Milne, L. jt. auth.

MILNES, Sherrill
Recordings. M. Mayer. Esquire 71:58 Mr '69
Sherrill Milnes: a voice for tomorrow's golden age. G. Movshon. Hi Fi 19:102 Jl '69

MILO
He gets three-ton milo without irrigation; interview. ed. by C. E. Sommers and C. Peterson, jr. J. Nagel. il Suc Farm 67:26-7 Ag '69

MILO electronics corporation
Product parade at Milo electronics. S. Margetts. Duns R 93:73+ Ap '69

MILSTEIN, Mike M. See Jennings, R. E. jt. auth.

MILTON, John, 1608-1674
Milton: a biography, by W. R. Parker. Review Nation 210:23-4 Ja 12 '70. J. N. Morris

MILTON, John P.
Arctic walk; with biographical sketch. por Natur Hist 78:4, 44-53 My '69

MILTON, Nerissa L.
Writing on the wall; poem. Negro Hist Bul 32:19 Ap '69

MILWAUKEE

Center for the performing arts
Milwaukee center for the performing arts: facilities for orchestra, recital, opera, musical, drama and repertory in one building. il Arch Rec 146:148-57 N '69

City planning
How do we participate? the Model cities programs. M. O. Mohr. America 120:565-6 My 10 '69; Reply. D. K. Holland. 120:677 Je 14 '69

Finance
Computerized billing collects 98 per cent of the taxes. J. J. Krueger. il Am City 84:115+ Ag '69
Tips on purchasing. A. L. Lehrbaummer. il Am City 84:145-6 Mr '69

Housing
Fort Homeless. Newsweek 74:67-8 N 3 '69

Lighting
All out for alley lights. M. E. Bruening. il Am City 84:106 D '69

Politics and government
How do we participate? the Model cities programs. M. O. Mohr. America 120:565-6 My 10 '69; Reply. D. K. Holland. 120:677 Je 14 '69

Recreation
Indoor mountaineering. C. H. Emigh. il Parks & Rec 4:36-7 Jl '69
Year-round public tennis club. M. Wade. Parks & Rec 4:33-4 Jl '69

Riots
Groppi's putsch; protesting cutback in welfare. il Newsweek 74:38 O 13 '69

Sanitary affairs
Large-plastic tote barrels. il Am City 84:64 F '69
150 days of fire. il Am City 84:80+ Jl '69

MILWAUKEE art center
German genre paintings from the Von Schleinitz collection. T. Atkinson. il Antiques 96:712-16 N '69

MILWAUKEE center for the performing arts. See Milwaukee—Center for the performing arts

MILWAUKEE journal company. See Journal company

MILWAUKEE nature exhibition. See Photography—Exhibitions

MIME
See also
Avital, S.

MIMEOGRAPH

Anecdotes, facetiae, satire, etc.
KaPOOMcha: the mimeograph revolution. J. S. Kunen. Esquire 72:102 S '69

MIMICRY (biology)
Ecological chemistry. L. P. Brower. il Sci Am 220:22-9 F '69
Mimicry of hymenoptera by beetles with unconventional flight. R. E. Silberglied and T. Eisner. il Science 163:486-8 Ja 31 '69

MIND-altering drugs. See Hallucinogenic drugs

MIND and body
Are you really sick? F. L. Remington. il Mech Illus 65:94-5+ N '69
Deprivation dwarfism. Time 93:39 F 7 '69
When the mind makes the body sick. J. Brothers. il Good H 169:52+ S '69
See also
Consciousness
Faith cure
Medicine, Psychosomatic
Nervous system
Psychical research
Psychology, Physiological

MINDER, Thomas
Regional center of '70's seen in Pittsburgh study; summary. Library J 94:704+ F 15 '69

MINE accidents and explosions
See also
Coal mines and mining—Accidents and explosions

MINE gases
See also
Methane

MINE hoisting
Mineheads; photographs of winding gear towers in Europe. B. Becher and H. Becher. il Arch Forum 129:68-73 D '68

MINE labor. See Coal miners

MINEAR, Leon P.
Piece of the action. Am Ed 5:4-6 Mr '69

MINEAR, Paul
Karl Barth. New Repub 160:12-13 F 1 '69

MINER, Mae. See Lucas, J. jt. auth.

MINER, Marilyn E.
Charlie Brown goes to school. bibliog f Engl J 58:1183-5 N '69

MINER, Virginia Scott
Christmas service; poem. Good H 169:217 D '69

MINERAL industries
See also
Refractories industry

MINERAL King recreation area (proposed)
See Recreation areas—California

MINERAL resources, Marine. See Marine mineral resources

MINERALOGY
See also
Apatite
Concretions
Crystallography
Petrology
Precious stones

MINERALS and chemicals Philipp-Engelhard industries merger. See Business consolidations and mergers

MINERALS in diet
See also
Iron in diet

MINERALS in soils. See Soils—Mineral content

MINERALS in the body
See also
Trace elements

MINERS
So you'd like to be a miner. H. D. Brown. il Hobbies 73:121 F '69
See also
Coal miners
United mine workers of America

MINES and mineral resources
Riches under the earth's crust; with portfolio. C. Burck. il Fortune 80:92-101 Ag 15 '69
Tanzania to Tiffany's. T. Thompson. il Life 66:70-6 My 9 '69
See also
Coal mines and mining
Manganese
Ore deposits

Alaska
Alaska's $50-billion boom. il Forbes 104-30 3+ N 15 '69

Australia
Nuclear perseverance. W. A. Scholes. il Sci N 96:408-9 N 1 '69
See also
Nickel mines and mining—Australia

Canada
See also
Mining industry and finance—Canada

Colombia
Emeralds of Muzo. H. Forman. il Américas 21:8-14 Ja '69

MINES and mineral resources—*Continued*

Rhodesia
Rhodesian chrome caper. il Bsns W p50-1 Je 28 '69

United States
Affluence in jeopardy, minerals and the political economy, by C. F. Park and M. C. Freeman. Review
Am For 75:43-4 O '69. B. F. Grossling
See also
Coal mines and mining—United States

Zambia
See also
Copper industry and trade—Zambia

MINGUS, Charles
Musical events; appearances at Village Vanguard. W. Balliett. New Yorker 45:76-7 Je 28 '69

MINH, Duong-van-. See Duong-van-Minh

MINH, Ho-chi-. See Ho-chi-Minh

MINH, Nguyen-van-, pseud. See Nguyen-van-Minh, pseud.

MINH, Thiem. See Thiem Minh

MINIATURE bottles. See Bottles, Miniature

MINIATURE computers. See Computers—Miniaturization

MINIATURE gardens. See Gardens, Miniature

MINIATURE geraniums. See Geraniums

MINIATURE greenhouses. See Greenhouses, Miniature

MINIATURE objects
Exhibitions
Notes of the fall show. J. H. Gray. Hobbies 73:49 F '69

MINIATURE rooms. See Rooms, Miniature

MINIATURE roses. See Roses

MINIATURE trees. See Trees, Dwarf

MINIATURES (models) See Models and model-making

MINIBIKES. See Motor scooters

MINIBUSES. See Motor buses—Small size

MINICHIELLO, Raffaele
Anatomy of a skyjacker. il por Time 94:67-8+ D 5 '69
High and the mighty. il por Newsweek 74:42+ N 10 '69
Return of the native. il Time 94:30+ N 14 '69
6,900-mile skyjack. il por Time 94:29 N 7 '69

MINI-FINS. See Yachts—Stability and stabilizers

MINIHAN, Neil
School decentralization and racial integration. Sch & Soc 97:164-5 Mr '69

MINIMAL brain dysfunction
Helping children overcome learning disabilities. T. Irwin. il Todays Health 47:20-5+ My '69
Triumph for Kenny. I. R. Dickman. Read Digest 95:117-21 S '69
What makes some children bad? E. Margolis. il Parents Mag 44:52-3+ My '69

MINIMUM wage
United States
Do the poor benefit from wage floors? B. L. Masse. America 121:485 N 22 '69
Minimum wage: $2 an hour? U S News 66:73 Ja 27 '69
New idea on minimum wage: less for young people. il U S News 66:68-9 Mr 31 '69
Pay act widened for millions. U S News 66:66 F 3 '69

MINI-MUSEUM of mom art. See La Mesa, Calif.—Galleries and museums

MINING camps
Typical mining camp. H. D. Brown. il Hobbies 74:116-17 Mr '69

MINING engineering
Riches under the earth's crust; with portfolio. C. Burck. il Fortune 80:92-101 Ag 15 '69
So you'd like to be a miner. H. D. Brown il Hobbies 73:121 F '69

MINING industry and finance
Shell game; trading in penny mining stocks on the Salt Lake stock exchange. il Newsweek 73:70+ Mr 24 '69

Belgium
Belgium's new tempting target; Union miniere. Bsns W p 170 F 22 '69

Canada
Economic nationalism, free-enterprise style. il Forbes 103:36+ My 1 '69

Mexico
Go Mexican or else. . ; pressure to persuade subsidiaries of two U.S. mining companies to take in local partners. Bsns W p24 F 1 '69

MINING law
Breaking new ground to make mines safe. il Bsns W p 139-40+ N 8 '69
Is this mine necessary? W. E. Towell. Am For 75:31 S '69

MINING machinery
See also
Coal mining machinery

MINING research
Approach to mine safety. il Sci N 95:570-1 Je 14 '69

MINIS, Dorothea H. See Bruce, V. G. jt. auth.

MINISKIRTS. See Clothing and dress

MINISTERS of gospel. See Clergy

MINISTERS wives. See Clergymens wives

MINKOWSKI. See Nebulae

MINKS
At last, the mable; sable-like mink. il Time 93:49 Ja 31 '69

MINNEAPOLIS
Minnesota model; Twin Cities metropolitan council. Time 94:64-5 S 19 '69

Architecture
Federal reserve in suspense; new head office. il Arch Forum 130:100-5 Ja '69

City planning
New street scene; pedestrian mall. il Arch Forum 130:74-81 Ja '69

Economic conditions
Coalition splinters in Minneapolis. Bsns W p44+ Ag 16 '69

Education
World of work; Lincoln learning center. M. Tibbits. il Schol Teach Sec Teach Sup p 12+ S 22 '69

Elections
God is my co-pilot; mayoral results. Newsweek 73:32 Je 23 '69

Galleries and museums
See also
Minneapolis institute of arts

Music
Horspfal, a breakthrough; opera by E. Stokes. J. K. Sherman. il Hi Fi 19:MA30-1 My '69
Report: Minneapolis; production of Horspfal. P. Gainsley. il Opera N 33:30-1 Ap 5 '69

Politics and government
Another vote for law and order. U S News 66:18 Je 23 '69
Contagion in Minneapolis. il Time 93:24 Je 20 '69
Cop as candidate. Newsweek 73:63 My 12 '69
Minnesota experiment; how to make a big city fit to live in. J. Fischer. Harper 238:12+ Ap '69
Naftalin of Minneapolis; interview, ed. by F. Powledge. A. Naftalin. il Harper 239:72-6 N '69
One issue: L&O. B. Casserly. Commonweal 90:384 Je 20 '69
Resurgence of reaction? New Repub 160:6 Je 28 '69
See also
Minneapolis—Elections

Street traffic
New street scene; pedestrian mall. il Arch Forum 130:74-81 Ja '69

Theater
Company it's kept; Minnesota theatre company productions of The homecoming, Uncle Vanya and The ghost dancer. H. Hewes. Sat R 52:20 N 15 '69
Tried and the untried; Eastside theatre and Minnesota theatre company productions. H Hewes. Sat R 52:40 My 10 '69

Walker art center
See Walker art center, Minneapolis

MINNEAPOLIS institute of arts
Restoring reputations; The past rediscovered exhibition. D. L. Shirey. il Newsweek 74:85 Ag 4 '69

MINNELLI, Liza
Judy's daughter wants to be Liza. T. Thompson. il pors Life 67:51-2+ O 17 '69

MINNESOTA
See also
Booksellers and bookselling—Minnesota
Fishing—Minnesota
Hunting—Minnesota
Law—Minnesota
Libraries—Minnesota
Wilderness areas—Minnesota

Antiquities
See Indians of North America—Antiquities
—Minnesota

Politics and government
Minnesota experiment: how to make a big
city fit to live in. J. Fischer. Harper 238:
12+ Ap '69

Pollution control agency
Cooling it in Minnesota; report of Minnesota
committee for environmental information
on benefits and risks of nuclear reactors.
il Environ 11:21-5 Mr '69
Radioactive pollution; Minnesota finds AEC
standards too lax. P. M. Boffey. Science
163:1043-4+ Mr 7 '69
Who gets last radioactive word? Minnesota
vs Atomic energy commission. Bsns W p28
My 31 '69
MINNESOTA dance theatre. See Dance com-
panies
MINNESOTA mining and manufacturing com-
pany. See 3M company
MINNESOTA North Stars (hockey team) See
Hockey teams
MINNESOTA theatre company. See Minneapolis
—Theater
MINNESOTA Twins (baseball) See Baseball
clubs
MINNESOTA. University, Minneapolis
Helping actors to act human; History and
techniques of stage movement course. R.
Moulton. il Dance Mag 43:76-7 My '69
Sex for credit. N. G. Faber. il Look 33:39-
40+ Ap 1 '69
University of Minnesota band returns from
tour of Soviet Union; excerpts from re-
marks, May 23, 1969. R. M. Nixon; A. F.
Dobrynin. Dept State Bul 60:540-2 Je 23
'69
MINNESOTA Vikings (football club) See Foot-
ball clubs
MINNIG, Max Andrew
Happy specialist. R. Levy. il por Duns R 94:
76-7 S '69
MINNOWS
Minnows of New York. E. C. Raney. Cons
23:22-9 Ap, 21-9 Je '69
MINNS, Al
Laying down some leather; interview. New
Yorker 44:29-31 F 15 '69
MINOAN civilization. See Civilization, Minoan
MINOR, Audax, pseud.
Race track. See issues of New Yorker
MINOR, Larry
Major Minor. J. Thawley. il pors Hot Rod
22:48-50 Je '69
MINOR, Wilson
Gothic tale. por Newsweek 74:72 D 15 '69
MINOR league baseball. See Baseball
MINORITIES
Anatomy of a Chicago slum; study of a mul-
tiethnic community including Italians,
Mexicans, Negroes and Puerto Ricans. G.
D. Suttles. il Trans-Action 6:16-19+ F '69
Building new nations; self-determination for
whom? C. Legum. Cur 107:24-6 My '69
College provisions for minorities. Sch & Soc
97:84-5 F '69
How it looks from the colonies. D. W.
Brogan. Esquire 72:48+ D '69
Library employment of minority group per-
sonnel; LAD report. R. R. Frame and J. F.
Anderson. il ALA Bul 63:985-7 Jl '69
Minority employment in state and local gov-
ernments. il Mo Labor R 92:67-70 N '69
Minority groups in America. il Sr Schol 94:
13-15+ Mr 7; 6-8 Mr 14; 10-12+ Ap 18; 12-17
Ap 25; 12-15 My 2 '69
See also
Intercultural education
United Nations—Sub-commission on preven-
tion of discrimination and protection of
minorities
MINOST, Maurice
Paris: the Quartier du Marais. il Antiques
96:406-8 S '69
MINT, Bureau of the. See United States—Mint,
Bureau of the
MINT 400 race. See Motor vehicle racing
MINTZ, Edward N.
Celebrity spotlight. See issues of Travel
MINTZ, Morton
Golden ox of antitrust. Nation 208:467-8
Ap 14 '69

MINTZ, Sidney W.
Brief visit to the third world: Guyana and
Vietnam. Yale R 59:151-60 O '69
MINTZ, Walter
Skeptic's stock market. R. Brady. il por
Duns R 93:105-7 Mr '69
MINUDRI, Regina
(ed) Adult books for young adults. Library
J 94:3231-6, 4307-12, 4622-30 S 15, N 15, D
15 '69
—See Trahan, M. jt. ed.
—and Coats, Reed
Library environment. pors Wilson Lib Bul 44:
294-8 N '69
MINUTEMAN (guided missile) See Guided
missiles
MINUTEMAN silos. See Guided missiles—
Launching pads
MINYEN, Steve
God goes to high school. R. Taylor. Chr
Today 14:48 D 5 '69
MIOCENE period. See Geology, Stratigraphic—
Miocene
MIRA (star) See Stars, Variable
MIRACLE, Leonard
News: the West (cont) por Outdoor Life
143:41-4 F; 53-60 Ap '69
Short order antelope. por Outdoor Life 144:
62-3+ O '69
Sport without limit. Outdoor Life 144:66-7+
Ag '69
MIRACLES
See also
Jesus Christ—Miracles
Supernatural
MIRANDA, Ernesto A.
Where are they now? il por Newsweek 74:8
Ag 11 '69
MIRRORS
Beauty and the bath. S. Lindsay. il House
B 111:16+ O '69
Light up and look. il Seventeen 28:206 My
'69
Mirror, mirror. B. Plumb. il N Y Times Mag
p 104-5+ Ap 27 '69
MIRRORS for telescopes
Amateur scientist; flow of blood, weather
vanes, telescope mirrors and the conduc-
tivity of insulators. C. L. Stong. il Sci Am
221:136-7 O '69
Giant mirror blanks poured for Chile and
Australia. il Sky & Tel 38:140-3 S '69
Note on curved spiders. C. H. Werenskiold.
il Sky & Tel 38:262-3 O '69
Test for figuring Cassegrain secondary
mirrors, ed. by R. E. Cox. J. L. Richter.
il Sky & Tel 39:49-53 Ja '70
Testing a Schmidt corrector at a finite dis-
tance. J. J. Labrecque. il Sky & Tel 37:
250-1 Ap '69
MIRRORS in photography. See Composition
(photography)
MIRSKY, Jonathan
Easy job. Nation 208:556 My 5 '69
MIRV system. See Guided missiles
MISCARRIAGE. See Abortion
MISCEGENATION. See Intermarriage of races
MISCH, Robert Jay
How to select and serve the wine. House B
111:150+ N '69
In search of tequila, the new-old spirit.
House B 111:128-9 Ap '69
MISCONDUCT in office
Good behavior of judges; who defines it? re-
print of July 5, 1957 issue. D. Lawrence.
U S News 66:116+ My 19 '69

Ghana
Chairman bows out; J. A. Ankrah's offense.
Newsweek 73:57-8 Ap 14 '69
MISER; drama. See Molière. J. B. P.
MISKELL, David R.
How big tractors cut costs. Farm J 93:C2
Mr '69
MISNER, Gordon E.
Enforcement: illusion of security. Nation 208:
488-90 Ap 21 '69
Response of police agencies. bibliog f Ann
Am Acad 382:109-19 Mr '69
MISREPRESENTATION. See Fraud
MISS America contests. See Beauty contests
MISS Awful; story. See Cavanaugh, A.
MISS Black America contests. See Beauty con-
tests
MISS Elizabeth Landon, M.D; story. See
Schweitzer, G.
MISS Rose; story. See Boles, P. D.
MISSALS
After 400 years an improved missal. C. J.
McNaspy. America 120:592+ My 17 '69

MISSILE bases. See Guided missile bases
MISSILE silos. See Guided missiles—Launch-
ing pads
MISSILES, Guided. See Guided missiles
MISSING persons
See also
Tracers company of America
MISSION BAY park, San Diego. See San Diego,
Calif.—Parks and playgrounds
MISSION Bell 250. See Automobile racing
MISSION control (space flight) See United
States—Manned spacecraft center
MISSION de France. See Catholic church—
Missions
MISSION of the church
Exposing a false antithesis. Chr Today 13:
23-4 Jl 18 '69
Mission aborted. L. N. Bell. Chr Today 13:
34+ Je 6 '69
MISSION San Diego de Alcalá. See California—
Missions
MISSION San Luis Obispo de Tolosa. See
California—Missions
MISSIONARIES
Peace corps volunteer or missionary, does
it really make any difference? F. Hezel.
Cath World 208:205-7 F '69; Reply. G.
Lensing, jr. 209:121-2 Je '69

Training
Advanced education for missionaries. D. Mc-
Gavran. Chr Today 13:3-5 S 26 '69
MISSIONS
Mission and missionaries: 1969; statistics. il
Chr Today 13:20-1 Ap 25 '69
See also
Catholic church—Missions
Jesuits—Missions

Africa
See also
Catholic church—Missions

Asia
Encouraging missionary movement in Asian
churches. W. H. Chua. Chr Today 13:9-12
Je 20 '69

California
See California—Missions

France
See also
Catholic church—Missions

India
See also
Catholic church—Missions

Indians of North America
See Indians of North America—Missions

Kenya
It was beautiful to be in Nairobi. O. W.
Okite. Chr Today 13:41 My 9 '69

New Mexico
See New Mexico—Missions

Niger
Unexpected kudos. L. K. Tarr. Chr Today 14:
49-50 O 24 '69

Pakistan
Pakistan mission schools: up for grabs? Chr
Today 13:33-4 Ag 22 '69

Peru
See also
Catholic church—Missions
MISSIONS, Medical
Bruised world still seeks Good Samaritans.
W. H. Hodges. Chr Today 13:6-9 S 12 '69
MISSISSIPPI
Report from the Gulf coast; hurricane Ca-
mille's toll. R. M. Williams. il Fortune 80:
59+ O '69
Tallying the damage in Camille's path. il
Bsns W p33 Ag 23 '69
See also
Colleges and universities—Mississippi
Education—Mississippi
Justice, Administration of—Mississippi
Libraries—Mississippi
Negroes—Mississippi
Police—Mississippi

Race problems
Mississippi ballot box. J. W. Lyon. Sat R 52:
20-1 My 17 '69
Mississippi eyewitness. L. E. Lomax. il Ramp
Mag 7:20-4 Ja 25 '69

Social conditions
We need help; Mississippi's northern counties. R. Coles and H. Huge. New Repub
160:18-21 Mr 8 '69

State library commission
La dame; Camille; survey by team of damage
to public libraries. M. J. Morgan. ALA Bul
63:1583-5 D '69
MISSISSIPPI library commission. See Missis-
sippi—State library commission
MISSISSIPPI state university, State college
Boll weevil six feet long; librarian's action
in battle against campus speaker ban. J. M.
Carter. il Library J 94:3615-18 O 15 '69
MISSISSIPPI, University

School of law
Lawyers of Ole Miss. K. Vinson. Nation 208:
791-3 Je 23 '69
New dean at Ole Miss. Time 94:53+ Jl 18 '69
MISSOULA, Mont.
Hunger next door. N. Munro. il Redbook
132:21+ Mr '69
MISSOURI
See also
Architecture, Domestic—Missouri
Camping—Missouri
Hunting—Missouri
Lake of the Ozarks
Water supply—Missouri

Description and travel
Harry Truman's Missouri. R. Pearman. il
Travel 132:56-60+ Ag '69

History
Freedom documents from Cole County, Missouri. L. J. Greene. bibliog Negro Hist Bul
32:11-13 Ja '69

State library commission
Joan Bodger incident; statement; October
1969, ed. by G. R. Shields. R. Parker. ALA
Bul 63:1561-3 D '69
Missouri library commission defended by
Ralph Parker. Library J 94:4082 N 15 '69
Missouri quicksand: an in-depth survey;
free speech controversy. W. R. Eshelman.
Wilson Lib Bul 44:266-8 N '69
Ray of light in Missouri. Wilson Lib Bul 44:
498 Ja '70
MISSOURI botanical garden
Eden under a geodesic dome; St Louis' Cli-
matron. B. O'Connell. il Sci Digest 65:68-72
Ap '69
New science tries to keep old balance. il
Bsns W p64-5+ F 15 '69
MISSOURI library association
Censorship matters in Missouri; report on
conference, ed. by J. F. Krug. H. D. Kreigh.
ALA Bul 63:570-2 My '69
Censorship pressure rising. Missouri librar-
ians told; conference on censorship. Li-
brary J 94:2188-90 Je 1 '69
MLa 1969 conference, October 1-4: some high-
lights. H. Kreigh. Wilson Bul 44:277 N
'69
Stirrings in Missouri a state association
meets. G. R. Shields. ALA Bul 63:1560-3 D
'69
MISSOURI library commission. See Missouri—
State library commission
MISSOURI state library, Jefferson City, Mo.
Editor's choice; university students' arrest
and newspaper seizure, state library con-
sultant's protest and dismissal. G. R.
Shields. ALA Bul 63:561-2 My '69; Reply.
H. Kreigh. 63:1049 S '69
Missouri quicksand: an in-depth survey; free
speech controversy. W. R. Eshelman. Wil-
son Lib Bul 44:266-8 N '69
MISSOURI. University, Columbia
Admission of women to the University of
Missouri in 1868. M. M. Meredith and L. P.
Jorgenson. bibliog f il Sch & Soc 97:282-5
Sum '69
Dissent and reaction in Missouri; free speech
conflict; with letter by J. Bodger. R. Mc-
Leod. il Wilson Lib Bul 44:269-76 N '69
Editor's choice; university students' arrest
and newspaper seizure, state library con-
sultant's protest and dismissal. G. R.
Shields. ALA Bul 63:561-2 My '69; Reply.
H. Kreigh. 63:1049 S '69
Joan Bodger incident; statement; October
1969, ed. by G. R. Shields. R. Parker. ALA
Bul 63:1561-3 D '69
Missouri library commission defended by
Ralph Parker. Library J 94:4082 N 15 '69
Missouri waltzes to victory; Tigers take the
Oklahoma Sooners. R. Blount, jr. il Sports
Illus 31:40-1 N 17 '69

MIST (Medical information service via telephone) See Telephone in medical service
MR Bridge; story. See Connell, E. S.
MR Collier; story. See Morgan, B.
MR Sammler's planet; novel. See Bellow, S.
MR Sterling, darling; story. See Fritz, J.
MR Tambo, Mr Bones; drama. See Panas, A.
MR Travel award
  15th annual Mr Travel award; Billy Graham.
    il Travel 132:52-3 Jl '69
MR Wall Street. See Weinberg, S. J.
MISTEROGERS' neighborhood (television program) See Television broadcasting—Childrens programs
MISTLETOE
  Mistletoe. H. Rohrbach. il Horticulture 47:26-7 D '69
  Mystery of the mistletoe. H. W. Dengler. il Am For 75:1-3+ D '69
MRS Shumlin's cow Trixie; story. See Humphrey, W.
MITCHELL, Carleton
  Racing sailor's seagoing bungalow. Sports Illus 30:30-5 F 3 '69
  $2 million berth to Newport. Sports Illus 31:28-30+ N 24 '69
MITCHELL, Clint
  Cool-it man. il por Newsweek 74:69 O 13 '69
MITCHELL, Don
  Alcohol tripping; story. Harper 239:84-91 S '69
MITCHELL, E. B.
  High is the key. Yachting 125:58+ Je '69
MITCHELL, Edward H.
  Edward H. Mitchell post cards. B. Finnegan. il Hobbies 73:124-5 F '69
MITCHELL, Fanny Todd
  Road to Tarragona. Harp Baz 102:160+ O '69
MITCHELL, Henry
  [Reply to C. L. Wallis] Library J 94:4102-3 N 15 '69
MITCHELL, John Newton
  Conglomerate; address, June 6, 1969. Vital Speeches 35:592-4 Jl 15 '69
  Crime legislation; address, October 6, 1969. Vital Speeches 36:39-42 N 1 '69
  Crime prevention; address, February 3, 1969. Vital Speeches 35:290-3 Mr 1 '69
  Excerpt from testimony, June 26, 1969. Cong Digest 48:266+ N '69
  Fighting crime in America; interview. por U S News 67:46-53 Ag 18 '69
  How administration would broaden voting-rights act; excerpts from statement to House judiciary subcommittee on June 26, 1969. por U S News 67:32 Jl 7 '69
  Reasonable man; wiretapping, pretrial detention & civil rights; address, August 13, 1969. Vital Speeches 35:678-81 S 1 '69
  What kind of world do you want? address, May 1, 1969. Vital Speeches 35:497-500 Je 1 '69; Same with title Colleges must outlaw terror; excerpts from address. por U S News 66:75 My 12 '69
  Where attorney general draws the line on SDS and violence; excerpts from statement to subcommittee of the House committee on education and labor, May 20, 1969. por U S News 66:45 Je 2 '69

about

  Annals of politics. R. Harris. New Yorker 45:82+ N 15; 61-4+ N 22 '69
  Attorney General Mitchell's philosophy is: the Justice department is an institution for law improvement, not social improvement. M. Viorst. il pors N Y Times Mag p 10-11+ Ag 10 '69; Reply. L. Herman. p72+ S 14 '69
  Caretakers of justice. New Repub 160:9 F 1 '69
  Elm street's new White House power. A. J. Reichley. il Fortune 80:70-3+ D '69
  Law-and-order man. il pors Newsweek 74:29-30+ S 8 '69
  Man with ideas on fighting crime. por U S News 66:13 F 3 '69
  Mergers must toe the hard line. por Bsns W p48-9 Je 14 '69
  Mitchell's law and order. Nation 209:686 D 22 '69
  Nixon's antitrust policy. W. F. Baxter. New Repub 161:13-16 Ag 9 '69
  Nixon's heavyweight. il por Time 94:24 Jl 25 '69
  No-nonsense man at the helm of justice. por U S News 67:9-10 Jl 28 '69
  Pass for Mitchell. J. Osborne. New Repub 160:13 Ja 25 '69
  Pitchfork Ben, meet Wheelbarrow John. M. Ways. Fortune 80:84 Jl '69
  Politics. J. Leonard. Esquire 71:84+ Ap '69
  Pragmatist. il por Newsweek 74:45 D 8 '69
  Sharp new line on antitrust. il por Bsns W p 120-2 Je 21 '69

TRB from Washington. New Repub 161:4 D 13 '69
Three in bloom. H. Brandon. Sat R 52:7-8 Ag 2 '69
MITCHELL, Joni
  Into the pain of the heart; contemporary folk composer. il por Time 93:78+ Ap 4 '69
  Thumbs down, thumbs up. C. E. Fager. Chr Cent 86:1320 O 15 '69
MITCHELL, Louis D.
  Scranton: a short view, a microcosm. Cath World 210:7-10 O '69
MITCHELL, Martha
  Warbler of Watergate. por Time 94:37 D 5 '69

about

  Dear Mrs Mitchell... D. P. Riley. Commonweal 91:329 D 12 '69
MITCHELL, Victor
  Almost anonymous partner. C. Goren. il Sports Illus 30:58-9 My 12 '69
MITCHELL, William
  Billy Mitchell: the maverick general. por Sr Schol 94:21 Ap 25 '69
MITCHELL, William LeRoy
  Bill Mitchell brings style to GM with a capital S. L. Levine. il pors Motor T 21:38-40 Mr '69
MITCHELL, William R.
  Poet heareth the congregation chaunting a hymn. Chr Cent 86:546 Ap 23 '69
MITCHELL-BATEMAN, Mildred
  Doctor Mildred Mitchell-Bateman. por Vogue 153:170 My '69
MITCHISON, J. M.
  Enzyme synthesis in synchronous cultures. bibliog Science 165:657-63 Ag 15 '69
MITE corporation
  Booby prize. il Forbes 104:89 N 15 '69
MITES
  Macronyssid mites in oral mucosa of long-nosed bats: occurrence and associated pathology. C. J. Phillips and others. bibliog il Science 165:1368-9 S 26 '69
  See also
  Follicle mites
MITFORD, Jessica
  Guilty as charged by the judge; excerpt from The trial of Dr Spock. Atlan 224:48-66 Ag '69

about

  No reactionary he; analyzing the trial of Drs Coffin and Spock. Nat R 21:1054 O 21 '69
MITICIDES. See Insecticides
MITOCHONDRIA
  Acute axonal dystrophy caused by fluorocitrate: the role of mitochondrial swelling. H. Koenig. bibliog il Science 164:310-12 Ap 18 '69
  Energized configurations of heart mitochondria in situ. R. A. Harris and others. bibliog il Science 165:700-3 Ag 15 '69
  Genetics and phenogenetics of mitochondria. R. P. Wagner. bibliog Science 163:1026-31 Mr 7 '69; Reply. R. T. Hersh. 166:402 O 17 '69
  β-Hydroxybutyrate dehydrogenase: lack in ruminant liver mitochondria. N. C. Nielsen and S. Fleischer. bibliog il Science 166:1017-19 N 21 '69
  Mitochondrial autonomy: incorporation of monosaccharides into glycoprotein by isolated mitochondria. H. B. Bosmann and S. S. Martin. bibliog il Science 164:190-2 Ap 11 '69
  Mitochondrial DNA: advances, problems, and goals. M. M. K. Nass. bibliog il Science 165:25-35 Jl 4 '69
  Oral contraceptives: long-term use produces fine structural changes in liver mitochondria. V. Perez and others. bibliog il Science 165:805-7 Ag 22 '69
  Plague toxin. S. Kadis and others. il Sci Am 220:92-8+ Mr '69
MITOSIS. See Cell division (biology)
MITSUBISHI companies. See Japan—Industries
MITSUI and company. See Japan—Industries
MITTELSTAEDT, Arthur H. Jr, and others
  Appraisal of recreation standards. Parks & Rec 4:20-2+ Jl '69
MIXED marriages. See Marriages, Mixed
MIXED media performances. See Performing arts
MIXERS
  Blending fluids without a stir. il Bsns W p 156 Je 21 '69
  Mixer: static device developed by Kenics corporation and Arthur D. Little company. New Yorker 45:28 My 31 '69

MIXERS, Electronic. See Sound—Apparatus

MIXTEC Indians
Settlement, farming technology, and environment in the Nochixtlan Valley. R. Spores. bibliog il Science 166:557-69 O 31 '69

MIYAMOTO, Eishichi, and others
Adenosine 3',5'-monophosphate-dependent protein kinase from brain. bibliog Science 165:63-5 Jl 4 '69

MIYANSKI, Kiyoko. See Foley, J. E. jt. auth.

MIZE, D. Doyle
Zapata who? il por Forbes 103:46-7 Ap 1 '69

MIZELL, Merle, and others
Tumor induction in developing frog kidneys by a zonal centrifuge purified fraction of the frog herpes-type virus. bibliog Science 165:1134-7 S 12 '69

MIZELL, Wilmer
Curve for Vinegar Bend. W. Willoughby. Chr Today 13:47 F 28 '69

MIZUTAKI. See Cookery, Japanese

MLEYNEK, Darryl
Unions: what's in it for administrators? por Wilson Lib Bul 43:752-5 Ap '69

MOATS, Alice-Leone
Confession. Nat R 21:846-8+ Ag 26 '69

MOB violence
Wild in the streets; demonstrations in Chicago. il Newsweek 74:42+ O 20 '69

MOBERLY, Mo.
Money squeeze forces municipals to adapt. il Bsns W p68+ Ap 12 '69

MOBIL oil company
How to rob Peter; U.S gasoline business neglected. Forbes 103:30-1 Je 15 '69

MOBILE, Ala.
Auditorium
See Auditoriums

MOBILE coronary care units. See Hospitals—Emergency services

MOBILE health buses. See Health clinics

MOBILE home parks
Choosing a mobile home park. E. Kienz. il Consumer Bul 52:21-3 Mr '69
Growing boom in mobile homes; new style of living, the modern mobile-home park. il US News 67:48-51 S 1 '69
What living in a mobile home is like. il Changing T 23:7-11 O '69

MOBILE homes
Boom in mobile homes. H. Manchester. il Har Yrs 9:14-17 Ap '69; Same with title Homes that come off the assembly line. Read Digest 94:23-4+ Ap '69
Choosing a mobile home park. E. Kienz. il Consumer Bul 52:21-3 Mr '69
Homes that come off the assembly line. H. Manchester. il Read Digest 94:23-4+ Ap '69
Lesson from the Finns. S. Wrede. Am Home 72:118-19 S '69
Mobile millionaire; A. Decio. il Time 94:75 Jl 4 '69
Modular components; address, September 10, 1969. G. O. Mabry. Vital Speeches 36:61-4 N 1 '69
Posh pad on wheels. il Mech Illus 65:36 Jl '69
Tips for your home and family. Todays Health 47:69-70 Je '69
Towards a movable, livable mobile home. il Arch Forum 130:58-61 Ap '69
Vacation house for $6,000. il Parents Mag 44:68-71 Jl '69
What living in a mobile home is like. il Changing T 23:7-11 O '69
Winterize your home on wheels. B. F. Samuels. il Pop Sci 195:170-3+ O '69

MOBILE libraries. See Bookmobiles

MOBILE schools. See Schools, Traveling

MOBILES
Christmas mobile is cards on yarn. il Sunset 143:82 D '69
Dancing in the wind; Shingu mobiles at Osaka shipyard. il Time 93:47 Ja 24 '69
Wind sculptures. A. Albright. il Sch Arts 69:12-15 O '69

MOBILITY, Occupational. See Occupational mobility

MOBLEY, Tony A.
Educating for leisure. Parks & Rec 3:41-2 N '68

MOBS
See also
Mob violence
Panic

MOBUTU, Joseph Désiré
After years of violence the Congo is afloat but who knows where it's headed? M. A. McConnell. il por N Y Times Mag p26-7+ S 21 '69

MOCKINGBIRDS
North goes the mocker. J. C. George. il Audubon 71:48-9 Ja '69
This is a bird worth listening to. A. R. Giordan. il Home Gard 56:48-9 Jl '69

MOCZAR, Mieczyslaw
Polish way. K. Huszar. por Newsweek 73:48+ My 5 '69

MODEL, Leo
Ice stocks in the winter? por Forbes 103:62-3 Je 1 '69

MODEL cities program See City planning; Urban renewal

MODEL engines. See Engine models

MODEL gliders. See Gliders (aeronautics)—Models

MODEL making. See Models and modelmaking

MODEL towns
See also
Albert Lea, Minn.

MODELING
Sculpture of Philip Kraczkowski. P. Kraczkowski. il Am Artist 33:42-8 Ag '69
Water whistle sculpture; ceramic children's toys. R. F. Eilenberger. il Ceram Mo 17:16-19 F '69
See also
Wax modeling

MODELING clay. See Clay

MODELL, Walter
Horns and antlers; with biographical sketch. Sci Am 220:12, 114-22 bibliog(p 146) Ap '69

MODELMAKING. See Models and modelmaking

MODELS
See also
Airplane models
Anatomical models
Architectural models
Dioramas
Ecological models
Engine models
Mathematical models
Rocket models
Space vehicle models

MODELS (persons)
Beauty safari; Mona Grant and Margie Lindsay on a tour of Manhattan. il Seventeen 28:144-5 Mr '69
Black look in beauty. il Time 93:72+ Ap 11 '69
Black models breakthrough. il Life 67:34-41 O 17 '69
Hello, ugly! a new British model agency. il Esquire 72:92-3 Jl '69
It takes integrity to model and be yourself. L. Angle. Seventeen 28:95+ Ja '69
Make a model's portfolio. E. Scully. il Mod Phot 33:72-3 My '69
Models without makeup; Colleen Corby and Lucy Angle. il Seventeen 28:130-3 S '69
No time for the shelf. il Har Yrs 9:30-1 N '69
Rent an ugly. il Newsweek 73:96 Ap 28 '69
She's fifteen and fabulous; M. F. Boles. il Seventeen 28:150-1 My '69
Taking it off. il Newsweek 74:112+ O 13 '69
Thumb your nose at the stereotype! S. Nathan. il Pop Phot 65:56+ Ag '69
See also
Children as models
Katia
Shrimpton, J. R.

Competitions
Model of the year. il Seventeen 27:152-3 D '68

MODELS and modelmaking
Carousel. S. A. Parvin. il Hobbies 74:118-19+ Je '69
Tonsorial parlor. S. A. Parvin. il Hobbies 74:118-19 My '69

MODELS of cities, towns, etc.
Neon city: proposed bridge to Sicily and related amenities; project of T. Waddell. il Arch Forum 130:68-73 Ap '69

MODERN air transport (airline)
Modern air expands Berlin tour flights. E. H. Kolcum. il Aviation W 91:45-6 Ag 4 '69

MODERN architecture. See Architecture, Modern

MODERN art. See Art, Modern

MODERN art museum, New York. See Museum of modern art, New York

MODERN civilization. See Civilization

MODERN fiction. See Fiction

MODERN language association of America
Barbarians of virtue. Nat R 21:16 Ja 14 '69
Language as emblem. J. H. Fisher. Sch & Soc 97:446-9 N '69
Tigers of wrath at the MLA. D. Grumbach. Commonweal 89:564-6 Ja 31 '69
Unrest in the academy. W. Roberts. Sat R 52:69 Mr 15 '69

MODERN languages. See Languages, Modern

MODERN poetry. See Poetry
MODERNISM
How to tell a fad from a trend. M. E. Marty. il Commonweal 90:509-12 Ag 22 '69
Nonsense of liberal Catholics. J. P. Degnan. Chr Today 14:3-6 N 21 '69
Roman Synod: speaking with candor to the Pope. B. Bastien. il Chr Today 14:36-7 N 21 '69
When conservatism is liberalism. G. H. Shriver. Chr Cent 86:1040-1 Ag 6 '69
MODERNISM (art)
  See also
Art, Modern
Bauhaus
MODERNISM in the theater. See Theater, Experimental
MODERNIZATION. See Social change
MODERNIZATION, Housing. See Houses, Remodeled
MODERNIZATION of houses. See Houses, Remodeled
MODIFIED airplanes. See Airplanes, Remodeled
MODIFLEX homes. See Houses, Prefabricated
MODISETTE, Jerry L. and Novotny, J. E.
Buoyancy and solar spin-down. bibliog Science 166:872-4 N 14 '69
MODOC war, 1872-1873. See Indians of North America—Wars
MOELLENBERG, Wayne P.
National assessment: are we ready? Clear House 43:451-4 Ap '69
MOELLER, H. G.
Continuum of corrections. Ann Am Acad 381:81-8 Ja '69
MOENS, Peter B. and Perkins, F. O.
Chromosome number of a small protist: accurate determination. bibliog Science 166:1289-91 D 5 '69
MOFFETT, George M. Jr
Garuma, gull of the desert; with biographical sketch. por Sea Front 15:330-8, 383 N '69
MOFFETT, Hugh
Ruckus in Irasburg. Life 66:62-4+ Ap 4 '69
Sex movies? Chadron, Neb. tries gentle persuasion. Life 66:52B-52D+ My 30 '69
MOFFETT, Samuel H.
What is evangelism? Chr Today 13:3-5 Ag 22; 13-14 S 12 '69
MOFFITT, John
Edge of desert; poem. America 120:134 F 1 '69
(comp) Undergraduate poems. America 120:404-5 Ap 5 '69
Thomas Merton: the last three days. Cath World 209:160-3 Jl '69
MOGUL, Philip H. and Schmuckler, J. S.
Dilute solutions of strong acids: the effect of water on ph. pors Chem 42:14-17 O '69
MOHAMMED Reza Pahlevi, shah of Iran
Back of the boom in Iran: the Shah's own story; interview. ed. by W. MacDougall. por U S News 66:49-50 Ja 27 '69
President Nixon and the Shah of Iran hold talks at Washington; exchange of greetings, toasts and remarks, October 21 and 23, 1969. Dept State Bul 61:396-400 N 10 '69
MOHAMMEDANISM. See Islam
MOHAMMEDANISM and Christianity. See Christianity and other religions
MOHAWK airlines, incorporated
Mohawk discards variety flight series. Aviation W 90:32 F 3 '69
MOHOLY-NAGY, László
Inheritor and activator. K. Kuh. il Sat R 52:38-40 Jl 26 '69
Moholy. D. L. Shirey. il por Newsweek 73:105 Je 16 '69
Original in a white coat; retrospective exhibition at Chicago's museum of contemporary art. il por Time 94:50-1 Jl 18 '69
MOHOLY-NAGY, Sibyl
Architecture through improvisation? Arch Forum 131:40-7 S '69
Boston's city hall. Arch Forum 130:44-53 Ja '69
Making of non-architects. Arch Rec 146:149-52 O '69
MOHONK, LAKE
Climbing is not for amateurs; activities at the cliffs of Lake Mohonk. H. W. Trimm. il Cons 24:16-17 O '69
MOHOS, Steven C. and Skoza, Lorant
Glomerular sialoprotein. bibliog Science 164:1519-21 Je 27 '69
MOHR, M. O.
How do we participate? America 120:565-6 My 10 '69
MOISTURE
  See also
Dampness in buildings
Humidity
Water vapor

MOISTURE control in buildings. See Dampness in buildings
MOK, Michael
In Maigret's Paris with the man who invented it. Life 66:44+ My 9 '69
  about
You can stop snapping at my heels now. G. P. Hunt. il por Life 66:3 My 9 '69
MOLASSE deposits. See Sedimentation and deposition
MOLASSES
  See also
Cookery—Molasses
Feeding and feeding stuffs—Molasses
MOLBACH, Irving
Body; poem. Cath World 208:254 Mr '69
MOLDAUER, Peter
ABM comes to town. Bul Atom Sci 25:4-6+ Ja '69
MOLDED products
Squirting the cost out of quality plastics; liquid injection molding. il Bsns W p 146-8 Ap 12 '69
MOLDING. See Modeling
MOLDING (metals) See Foundry practice
MOLDING, Plastics. See Plastics—Molding
MOLDS (botany)
  See also
Fungi
Phycomyces
MOLDS (for ceramic products)
Creative slip casting. J. Goldman. il Ceram Mo 17:25-7 Ap '69
MOLE rats
Mole rat spalax enrenbergi: mating behavior and its evolutionary significance. E. Nevo. bibliog il Science 163:484-6 Ja 31 '69
Mole rat spalax: evolutionary significance of chromosome variation. J. Wahrman and others. bibliog il Science 164:82-4 Ap 4 '69
MOLECULAR asymmetry. See Stereochemistry
MOLECULAR biology
Italy: first Ph. D. program stalled by new and old politics; international studium of molecular biology. D. S. Greenberg. Science 163:1306-8 Mr 21 '69
Molecules of molecular biology. D. Harker. Phys Today 22:36 Ag '69
MOLECULAR synthesis. See Biosynthesis
MOLECULES
Molecular order of participation of inhibitors (or activators) in biological systems. R. B. Loftfield and E. A. Eigner. bibliog il Science 164:305-7 Ap 18 '69
Where the action is, in molecules; excitonics, new way to transfer energy. il Bsns W p 106+ Ap 12 '69
  See also
Polymers
MOLER, Murray M.
Last rail, last spike. Nat Parks 43:8-9 Je '69
MOLES (animals)
Bury the burrower. L. Guccini. Home Gard 56:29 Ag '69
MOLESTERS, Child. See Child molesters
MOLIÈRE, Jean Baptiste Poquelin
Miser; tr. by H. Baker and J. Miller. Criticism
America 120:674 Je 7 '69
Nation 208:675-6 My 26 '69
New Yorker 45:110+ My 17 '69
Sat R 52:27 My 24 '69
Time 93:86 My 16 '69
MOLINA, Anibal
Reaching out. por Seventeen 29:84-5+ Ja '70
MOLINARI, Guido
New work from Montreal. B. Lord. il Art in Am 57:99-101 My '69
MOLINAS, Jack
Unjust exile of a superstar. D. Wolf. il por Life 66:52-52B+ My 16 '69
MOLINOFF, Perry, and Axelrod, Julius
Octopamine: normal occurrence in sympathetic nerves of rats. bibliog Science 164:428-9 Ap 25 '69
MOLLENHOFF, Clark
House dick. por Newsweek 74:25 S 15 '69
Mollenhoff mandate. por Time 94:25 N 7 '69
MOLLENKOTT, Virginia Ramey
Christianity and aesthetics: conflict or correlation? Chr Today 13:6-9 My 9 '69
MOLLOY, Paul
Movies move into prime time. PTA Mag 63:27-9 My '69
MOLLUSKS
Agile mollusc. A. D. Ansell. il Sea Front 15:180-4 My '69
Bivalves: spatial and size-frequency distributions of two intertidal species. J. B. C. Jackson; discussion. Science 162:1509-10; 163:830 D 27 '68, F 21 '69

MOLLUSKS—*Continued*
Paramyosin: molecular length and assembly.
J. Kendrick-Jones and others. bibliog il
Science 163:1196-8 Mr 14 '69
Synaptic activation of an electrogenic sodium
pump. H. Pinsker and E. R. Kandel. bibliog
il Science 163:931-5 F 28 '69
See also
Eye (mollusks)
Mussels
Mussels, Fresh water
Nervous system—Mollusks
Oysters
Sea hares
Sea slugs
Shells (conchology)
Snails

MOLLUSKS, Fossil
Paleontological evidence of variations in
length of synodic month since late Cambrian. G. Pannella and others; discussion.
Science 163:1227; bibliog 164:201-2 Mr 14, Ap
11 '69
Tertiary climatic change in the marginal
northeastern Pacific Ocean. W. O. Addicott.
bibliog il Science 165:583-6 Ag 8 '69

MOLNER, Don
Cassettes in the classroom. Schol Teach Sec
Teach Sup p 18 O 6 '69
New audiovisual products. Sr Schol 94:Schol
Teach 10+ Ja 17 '69

MOLOTCH, Harvey
Santa Barbara: oil in the velvet playground.
Ramp Mag 8:43-51 N '69

MOLTEN salts. See Salts, Molten

MOLTING
Photoperiod, endocrinology and the crus-
tacean molt cycle. D. E. Aiken. bibliog il
Science 164:149-55 Ap 11 '69
See also
Ecdysone

MOLTON, Warren Lane
Eve's song. Chr Cent 86:711 My 21 '69
Mystery play; poem. Chr Cent 86:1643 D 24
'69
Prayers in the leap to the Lord of the yawp.
Chr Cent 86:1374-9 O 29 '69
Seed fruit; poem. Chr Cent 86:1518 N 26 '69

MOLTZ, Howard, and others
Prolactin in the postpartum rat; synthesis
and release in the absence of suckling
stimulation. bibliog Science 163:1083-4 Mr
7 '69

MOLYBDENUM
White Cloud peaks; a time for decision. D.
B. Clement. il Am For 75:28-31+ S '69

MOLZ, Kathleen
People call their crying rain. bibliog por Wilson Lib Bul 43:860-3 My '69

MOMENTS; ballet. See Ballets—Criticisms

MOMENTS of inertia
Variable moment of inertia for even-even
nuclei. il Phys Today 22:61+ Mr '69

MONACO, Anthony P. See Sheagren, J. N. jt.
auth.

MONACO, R. J.
You're only as young as they think you are.
Sat R 52:15-17 D 27 '69

MONACO
Royal family
Princess Grace turns forty; interview, ed.
by W. B. Arthur. Princess Grace. il Look
33:96-100 D 16 '69

MONAGHAN, Jay
Hunter and the artist. bibliog Am West 6:4-13
N '69

MONARCHY
See also
Kings and rulers

MONARDA. See Horsemint

MONASTERIES
Americanizing American religious life. S.
Poole. America 120:297-300 Mr 15 '69; Dis-
cussion. 120:457 Ap 19 '69
Downfall of Dom Besret; Abbaye de Boquen.
il Time 94:81 N 14 '69
End of an adventure; monastery of Toum-
line. il Time 93:56+ My 23 '69
Monks of San Lazzaro. W. Sargeant. il
Travel & Camera 32:22+ D '69
Mother Russia in New York state; Holy
Trinity Russian Orthodox monastery. Jor-
danville, N.Y. N. S. Hazelton. Nat R
21:1015 O 7 '69
See also
Athos, Mount
Convents and nunneries

MONASTICISM
Against all reason, by G. Moorhouse. Review
Commonweal 90:597-8 S 26 '69. K. Mc-
Donnell
Episcopal Franciscans celebrate fifty years.
T. Early. Chr Cent 86:1592-4 D 10 '69
See also
Trappists

MONAUNI, Hanno L.
Mini-cannons from antique design. F. Worth.
il por Design 70:31-5 mid-Wint '69

MOND, Julian Edward Alfred, 3d baron Melchett. See Melchett, J. E. A. M.

MONDADORI, Arnoldo, editore. See Publishers and publishing—Italy

Le MONDE. See Paris—Newspapers

MONDLANE, Eduardo Chivambo
Lost leader. il por Newsweek 73:61-2 F 17
'69
Mondlane: guerrilla Christian. Chr Cent 86:275
F 26 '69
Most wanted man. Sr Schol 94:23 F 28 '69
Murder by the book. il por Time 93:35-6 F 14
'69

MONDY, Lewis W.
Preparing children for psychologic evaluations. Ment Hy 53:635-7 O '69

MONELL chemical senses center. See Pennsylvania. University, Philadelphia

MONETARY fund. See International monetary
fund

MONETARY policy
Advise and dissent on monetary policy. Bsns
W p32 D 13 '69
Distant hopes for easier money. il Bsns W
p 13 D 27 '69
Fiscal and monetary policy. C. C. Balderston.
bibliog f Ann Am Acad 379:78-82 S '68
Gradualism hurts too. il Fortune 79:16+ My
1 '69
How gradual can gradualism get? Bsns W
p23-4 Ag 23 '69
Impact of tight money, new clues; report. J.
D. Daane. U S News 67:107-8 S 22 '69
Monetary overkill. M. Friedman. Newsweek
74:75 Ag 18 '69
Money and inflation. M. Friedman. il News-
week 73:105 My 26 '69
What Burns said that sparked a market
rally. U S News 67:8 D 29 '69
See also
Currency question
Fiscal policy

MONEY
How not to lose money carelessly. il Good H
168:164 Je '69
See also
Coins
Credit
Currency question
Foreign exchange
Inflation (finance)
Interest
Investments
Liquidity (economics)

International aspects
Another world money crisis on the way?
U S News 66:8 Mr 17 '69
Avoiding an international money squeeze.
Bsns W p 156 Mr 15 '69
Borrowing abroad: the smart money game;
Eurodollars. A. Hershman. il Duns R 94:
30-2+ D '69
Comeback of the dollar: why it leads the
world. il U S News 67:62-3 O 13 '69
Crawling peg. H. C. Wallich. Newsweek 74:84
N 3 '69
Crisis that almost happened. il Bsns W p31
Mr 15 '69
Fed pinch puts squeeze on Europe; foreign
interest rates climb as U.S. banks tap
Eurodollar market. il Bsns W p38 Mr 8
'69
Floating marks and paper gold. America
121:319 O 18 '69
Genie that escaped from the bottle; Euro-
dollar market. Time 93:104 My 16 '69
Happy ending for gold drama. Ramp Mag
7:57-8 N 30 '68
Hot market regains its cool. il Bsns W p37 N
1 '69
Inflation and the world money crisis. Bsns
W p82 F 1 '69
International liquidity and foreign aid. E.
R. Fried. For Affairs 48:139-49 O '69
International monetary system, and your
family. P. Lindberg. Bet Hom & Gard 47:
4+ D '69
Market fever zigzags down; foreign exchange
markets taking a breather. il Bsns W p25-7
Ag 23 '69
Mild repercussions of a deft devaluation. il
Time 94:68+ Ag 22 '69
Monetary seers hold a summit; Claremont
international monetary conference in Cali-
fornia. il Bsns W p32-3 Mr 15 '69
Monetary seesaw. Nation 208:651-2 My 26 '69
Money men worry; is the pound next? il Bsns
W p84-5 Ag 16 '69

New way to reform. Time 94:74 Jl 18 '69

MONEY—International aspects—*Continued*
Remedy for monetary crisis. S. Rose. il Fortune 80:102-5+ Ag 15 '69
Ripples from the franc. il U S News 67:59 Ag 25 '69
Thrust of history in international monetary reform. R. Triffin. For Affairs 47:477-92 Ap '69
When a world money system is out of date. il Bsns W p70-3+ F 22 '69
When the dollar gets new rivals; forecast for the 1970s. il Bsns W p 170+ D 6 '69
World trade and investment; address, March 10, 1969. R. A. Peterson. Vital Speeches 35: 413-16 Ap 15 '69
  See also
International monetary fund
Special drawing rights

Psychological aspects
How to find out if you are rich or poor without actually having any money. H. Gold. Harp Baz 102:197+ Ag '69
Love and money. E. Sheppard. Harp Baz 102: 191 F '69

Quotations, maxims, etc.
Money sampler; comp. by J. Sakol. Harp Baz 102:146-7 Ag '69

Canada
Canada's bittersweet float. Fortune 80:188 Ag 15 '69

Europe, Eastern
Play money; rates of exchange. Newsweek 73:77-8 F 3 '69

Europe, Western
Western Europe: mark of worry. il Time 93: 85-6 F 28 '69

France
Après devaluation. il Newsweek 74:57 Ag 25 '69
Bitter battle of the franc. il Time 93:86 Mr 14 '69
Cheaper franc for a smaller France. il Time 94:25 Ag 15 '69
Decision on a summer weekend; franc devalued. il Newsweek 74:31-2 Ag 18 '69
De Gaulle leaves a monetary hangover; devaluation of the franc likely. il Bsns W p23-5 My 3 '69
Franc at the barricades; battle over wage demands. Bsns W p33 Mr 15 '69
Franc: not quite a crisis. il Newsweek 73:79-80 My 12 '69
France sobering up; devaluing the franc. Nat R 21:841 Ag 26 '69
How business took the news; devaluation of the franc. Bsns W p85+ Ag 16 '69
Letter from Paris; midsummer devaluation of the franc. Genêt. New Yorker 45:134-5 N 1 '69
Mild repercussions of a deft devaluation. il Time 94:68+ Ag 22 '69
Money men worry: is the pound next? il Bsns W p84-5 Ag 16 '69
Rendezvous of March. Newsweek 73:88+ Mr 17 '69

Germany (Federal Republic)
Behind rush for German marks. il U S News 66:12 My 19 '69
Election pegged to the mark: whether to raise the parity of undervalued currency. il Bsns W p26 Ag 23 '69
Germany's export boom steams right ahead. il Bsns W p 112-14+ N 1 '69
If the D-mark had crawled. il Fortune 80:105 Ag 15 '69
Mark floats free and easy. il Newsweek 74: 83+ O 13 '69
Mark seeks an anchorage; with editorial comment. il Bsns W p25-6, 148 O 4 '69
Mark's golden mean. Time 94:79 O 31 '69
Monetary seesaw. Nation 208:651-2 My 26 '69
Money crisis: on your mark, get set, hold it. il Newsweek 73:79-80 My 19 '69
Money system reels out of its sixth crisis. il Bsns W p33-4 My 17 '69
Return of Franz Josef Strauss. D. Hotham. il N Y Times Mag p36-7+ Mr 23 '69
Revaluation ahead? Newsweek 73:67 Ap 7 '69
Weathering the storm. Newsweek 73:99+ My 26 '69
West Germany's financial defiance. il Time 93:103-4 My 16 '69

Great Britain
Britain's new money game. il Bsns W p50-1 N 1 '69

United States
Annals of finance; New deal. J. Brooks. New Yorker 45:107-26 S 13 69
Comeback of the dollar: why it leads the world. il U S News 67:62-3 O 13 '69
How much does money count? C. H. Madden. Nations Bsns 57:71 Jl '69
World money & trade: one big world of happy traders? il Sr Schol 94:13-15 Ja 31 '69
MONEY management. See Budget, Household; Budget, Personal; Domestic finance
MONEY plant. See Honesty (plants)
MONEY raising campaigns. See Fund raising
MONEY rates. See Interest
MONEYWORT. See Loosestrife
MONFORT, Kenneth
Imports and substitutes: are they really threats to your beef market? excerpts from address, ed. by J. A. Rohlf. por Farm J 93: B7 Mr '69
MONFORT packing, incorporated
In the vanguard with new ideas. il Bsns W p83 Ag 30 '69
MONGIARDINO, Renzo
Fashions in living. il por Vogue 153:161 Ap 1 '69
MONGOLIA
Mongolia. K. Facknitz and L. Kostikov. il UNESCO Courier 22:14-17+ N '69

Economic conditions
Steppe to the 20th century. il UNESCO Courier 22:18-19 N '69
MONGOLIAN race
Mongolia. K. Facknitz and L. Kostikov. il UNESCO Courier 22:14-17+ N '69
MONGOLISM
Ape with an extra chromosome. il Sci N 96: 26-7 Jl 12 '69
Autosomal trisomy in a chimpanzee: resemblance to Down's syndrome. H. M. McClure and others. bibliog il Science 165:1010-12 S 5 '69
Our son Mark. S. I. Hayakawa. il McCalls 97: 78-9+ D '69
MONGOLOIDS. See Mongolism
MONITOR and Merrimac, Battle of. See United States—History—Civil war—Naval operations
MONJOUR, Yvette
Yvette and Paris. W. Como. il por Dance Mag 43:20 Ag '69
MONK, Edwin
What shape the hull? Yachting 125:70-1 Je '69
MONK, Meredith
Meredith Monk and company. D. Hering. il Dance Mag 43:27+ Ap '69
MONKEY trial. See Tennessee evolution controversy
MONKEYS
Brain damage by asphyxia at birth. W. F. Windle. il Sci Am 221:76-84 O '69
Cebus monkeys: effect on branching of Gustavia trees. J. R. Oppenheimer and G. E. Lang. bibliog il Science 165:187-8 Jl 11 '69
City vs country monkeys; study of rhesus monkeys. il Sci Digest 66:75-6 D '69
Creative monkeys of Koshima. B. O'Connell. il Sci Digest 65:80-2 Ap '69
Evoked potentials and auditory reaction time in monkeys. J. M. Miller and others. bibliog il Science 163:592-4 F 7 '69
Hyperphagia and polydipsia in socially isolated rhesus monkeys. R. E. Miller and others. bibliog il Science 165:1027-8 S 5 '69
Morphine: conditioned increases in self-administration in rhesus monkeys. S. R. Goldberg and others. bibliog il Science 166:1306-7 D 5 '69
Nalorphine: increased sensitivity of monkeys formerly dependent on morphine. S. R. Goldberg and C. R. Schuster. bibliog il Science 166:1548-9 D 19 '69
Neurophysiology of remembering. K. H. Pribram. il Sci Am 220:73-80+ bibliog(p 138) Ja '69
Ontogeny of soluble and mitochondrial tyrosine aminotransferases. R. D. Koler and others. bibliog il Science 163:1348-50 Mr 21 '69
Operant conditioning of cortical unit activity. E. E. Fetz. bibliog il Science 163:955-8 F 28 '69
Orality, preference behavior, and reinforcement value of nonfood object in monkeys with orbital frontal lesions. C. M. Butter and others. bibliog il Science 164:1306-7 Je 13 '69

MONKEYS—*Continued*
Plasmodium malariae: transmission from monkey to man by mosquito bite. P. G. Contacos and W. E. Collins. bibliog Science 615:918-19 Ag 29 '69
Poliovirus crystals within the endoplasmic reticulum of endothelial and mononuclear cells in the monkey spinal cord. K. Blinzinger and others. bibliog il Science 163:1336-7 Mr 21 '69
Rare red monkey of Zanzibar; colobus monkeys. il Life 67:100-2 S 19 '69
Retention of delayed-alternation: effect of selective lesions of sulcus principalis. N. Butters and D. Pandya. bibliog il Science 165:1271-3 S 19 '69
Rhesus monkeys: mating season mobility of adult males. D. G. Lindburg. bibliog il Science 166:1176-8 N 28 '69
To fill the gaps in space medicine. il Sci N 95:569-70 Je 14 '69
Uncus and amygdala lesions: effects on social behavior in the free-ranging rhesus monkey. D. Dicks and others. bibliog il Science 165:69-71 Jl 4 '69
Undersea world of Jonah and Thetis; Arizona state university's Exotic environments laboratory. Tempe, Ariz. J. Matthews. il Sci Digest 66:66-70 N '69
Urban monkeys. S. D. Singh. il Sci Am 221:108-15 Jl '69
    See also
Chimpanzees
Marmosets
Orangutans
Primates
MONKS. See Monasticism
MONOBATH film processing. See Photography —Developing and developers
MONOGRAM industries, incorporated
Monogram nails down goals in National screw merger. il Bsns W p 103 My 31 '69
MONOGRAMS

Anecdotes, facetiae, satire, etc.

My three weeks at the White House. P. E Gray. New Yorker 45:32-3 My 17 '69
MONOLAYER films. See Films
MONOLOGUES
Day's end; an Abraham Lincoln portrait. E. P. Conkle. Plays 28:91-5 F '69
MONOMOY ISLAND. See Chatham. Mass.
MONONUCLEOSIS, infectious
EB virus and leukemia. il Sci N 95:350-1 Ap 12 '69
Hunt for cancer vaccine closes in; EBV implication in wide spectrum of cancers. il Bsns W p68+ N 15 '69
MONOPOLIES
Indiscretions of Ma Bell; with editorial comment. J. C. Goulden. Nation 209:333, 346-9 O 6 '69
Let's turn it loose; secret antitrust report. Newsweek 73:80+ Je 2 '69
    See also
Trusts, Industrial
MONOPRINTS. See Monotypes
MONORAIL railroads. See Railroads, Single rail
MONOSACCHARIDES. See Saccharides
MONOSODIUM glutamate
Baby food additive may be next to go. Bsns W p 114 O 25 '69
Brain lesions in an infant rhesus monkey treated with monosodium glutamate. J. W. Olney and L. G. Sharpe. bibliog il Science 166:386-8 O 17 '69
Brain lesions, obesity, and other disturbances in mice treated with monosodium glutamate. J. W. Olney. bibliog il Science 164:719-21 My 9 '69; Reply with rejoinder. F. R. Blood and others. 165:1028-9 S 5 '69
Chinese restaurant syndrome. il Chem 42:4-5 S '69
Monosodium L-glutamate: its pharmacology and role in the Chinese restaurant syndrome. H. H. Schaumburg and others. bibliog il Science 163:826-8 F 21 '69
Salting the pure-food mine; FDA report. Sci N 96:295 O 4 '69; Reply. J. W. Olney. 96:468 N 22 '69
MONOTYPES
Monotype printing. R. Hill. il Sch Arts 68:36-7 Mr '69
MONRO, John U.
Escape from the dark cave. Nation 209:434-9 O 27 '69
MONROE, Bill
(ed) See Prezioso, S. J. NRPA executive is guest on Today show
MONROE, Earl
Earl the Pearl Monroe. il pors Ebony 24:45-6+ F '69

MONROE, James W.
Recreation in flux; address, November 2, 1968. Am For 75:21+ Ag '69
MONROE, John N.
Slumping structures caused by organically derived gases in sediments. bibliog Science 164:1394-5 Je 20 '69
MONROE, Margaret E.
Services in hospital and institution libraries. por ALA Bul 63:1280-3 O '69
MONROE, Marilyn
Marilyn Monroe: the untold story of her last years; excerpts from Norma Jean. F. L. Guiles. il pors Good H 169:62-5+ Jl '69
Norma Jean, by F. L. Guiles. Review
    Commentary 48:100+ S '69. M. Wood
    Newsweek por 74:87+ Jl 14 '69. A. Keneas
MONROE, La.
Computer is the key. M. J. Cook. il Am City 84:127-8 O '69
MONROE, N.C.
U.S. journal; site of 1961 civil-rights movement led by R. F. Williams. C. Trillin. New Yorker 45:144+ O 11 '69
MONROE doctrine
U.S. in Latin America to 1933: an overview. A. P. Whitaker. Cur Hist 56:321-6+ Je '69
MONSANTO company
From pollution to profit. il Time 94:36 Ag 8 '69
MONSARRAT, Nicholas
Nicholas Monsarrat's working methods; interview, ed. by A. Monsarrat. Writers Digest 49:59 Ag '69
Yes, I write for money; reprint. por Writers Digest 49:56-9 Ag '69
MONSER, George
Build the pyramidal TV/FM antenna. Pop Electr 31:27-32 Jl '69
MONSMA, Peter H.
Reason and God. Chr Today 14:7-8+ O 10 '69
MONSTERS
    See also
Dragons
Loch Ness monster
MONTAGE
How to bring to life those forgotten snapshots: make a montage. E. P. Haddon. il Pop Mech 132:144-6 N '69
    See also
Collage
MONTAGNA, Bartolomeo
Place, time, and painter. il Sat R 52:46-7 S 6 '69
MONTAGNARDS
Highland reconciliation. il Time 93:35 F 14 '69
MONTAGU, Ashley
Admonishing Montagu. Chr Cent 86:1570-1 D 10 '69
MONTALCINI, Rita Levi-. See Levi-Montalcini, R.
MONTANA
    See also
Fishing—Montana
Glacier National Park
Hunting—Montana
National bison range

Description and travel

Montana is the message. R. Atcheson. il Holiday 45:56-9+ My '69
One thing and another. J. K. Hutchens. Sat R 52:42-3 O 4 '69
MONTANA state university, Bozeman
Sporting scene; game against Montana Grizzlies. H. W. Wind. New Yorker 45:152+ D 13 '69
MONTANA. University, Missoula
Sporting scene; game against Montana state Bobcats. H. W. Wind. New Yorker 45:152+ D 13 '69
MONTCLAIR, N.J.
City planning
Planning board sets the lot size; New Jersey planning law. R. F. Edwards. il Am City 84:90+ Mr '69
MONTE CARLO
Report: Monte Carlo; production of Debussy's Le martyre de Saint Sébastien. R. Raphael. il Opera N 33:27 My 17 '69
MONTECATINI complex. See Italy—Industries
MONTECATINI-Edison. See Chemical industries—Italy
MONTEGO BAY, Jamaica
Traveler's choice. M. Vandenburgh. Travel 132:15 N '69
MONTEJO, Esteban
Slave in our time. O. T. Myers. Nation 208:121-2 Ja 27 '69

MONTEMEZZI, Italo
Records:
L'amore dei trere. il Opera N 34:31 D13 '69
MONTEREY, Calif.
Historic Montery holds open house. il
Sunset 142:11 Ap '69

Parks and playgrounds
Where Dennis isn't a menace. il Todays
Health 47:50-1 Je '69
MONTEREY international pop festival. See
Music festivals—California
MONTERREY, Mexico
Jumpingest place in Mexico. il Bsns W p70-1
O 25 '69
MONTESSORI method of education
Montessori in Guatemala. R. Bellak. il Sat R
52:47-9 Ag 16 '69
MONTEVERDI, Claudio
From the dawn of opera. H. Weinstock. il
Sat R 52:80+ D 6 '69
Monteverdi's Orfeo, a true music-drama, now
complete and in stereo. B. Jacobson. Hi Fi
19:66-7 Ap '69
Records:
Orfeo. Opera N 33:34 Ap 12 '69
MONTEVIDEO, Minn.
Two cities built malls that bring new vitality
to Main Street. G. M. Chamberlain. il Am
City 84:78+ N '69
MONTEZ, Irina
On the boards. W. Como. por Dance Mag 43:
20 Mr '69
MONTEZUMA, Carlos
Apache doctor who sparked a new era for
Indians. O. Arnold. il por Todays Health
47:30-3+ O '69
MONTEZUMA, Ga.
100 per cent paper-bag collection. il Am City
84:14 O '69
**MONTEZUMA CASTLE NATIONAL MONU-
MENT**
Montezuma, it's south of Flagstaff. il Sunset
143:26 Ag '69
MONTGOMERY, Charlotte
Speaker for the house. See issues of Good
housekeeping
MONTGOMERY, Elizabeth
Secret magic of Elizabeth Montgomery. J.
Wilkie. il pors Good H 169:54-6+ O '69
MONTGOMERY, Frankie R.
Homemaker's prayer; poem. Farm J 93:52 S
'69
MONTGOMERY, Herbert
America's sandpile. Travel 132:60-1 O '69
MONTGOMERY, John Warwick
Demos and Christos. Chr Today 13:10-11 Jl
18 '69
MONTGOMERY, Marion
Maturing of novel ideas. Writer 82:22-4+ D
'69
MONTGOMERY, Parker G.
Master plan at Cooper laboratories. S. Mar-
getts. por Duns R 93:72+ Ap '69
MONTGOMERY, R. B. and Singer, G.
Histochemical fluorescence as an index of
spread of centrally applied neurochemicals.
bibliog Science 165:1031-2 S 5 '69
MONTGOMERY, Reggie
Color comes to the circus. il pors Ebony 25:
155-8+ N '69
MONTGOMERY, Roger
Acorn project. il Arch Forum 131:90-3 Jl '69
MONTGOMERY, William L.
Investing in today's youth. Parks & Rec 4:
29-31+ Ja '69
MONTGOMERY, Ala.

Negroes
Rosa Parks: she wouldn't move back. il Sr
Schol 94:6 My 9 '69
MONTGOMERY COUNTY, Md.

Police
Kid gloves and drugs. New Repub 160:11-12
Ap 12 '69
MONTGOMERY VILLAGE, Md.
Enlightened builder creates a total environ-
ment. A. C. Borg. il Am Home 72:50-3 Mr
'69
MONTGOMERY Ward and company
Ward's joins the now generation; merger
with Container corp. il Bsns W p84-6+ Mr
22 '69
See also
Marcor, incorporated
MONTHERLANT, Henry de
Blue blood and his women. L. Bersani. New
Repub 160:22+ F 8 '69
MONTICELLO (historic house)
Jefferson items; new exhibits at Monticello.
R. Davidson. il Antiques 95:500+ Ap '69

MONTMORILLONITE
Benzene complexes with copper(II)montmorill-
onite. H. E. Doner and M. M. Mortland.
bibliog il Science 166:1406-7 D 12 '69
MONTO, Alexander V. and Miley, W. D.
Way of acquainting people in the community
with mental health facilities. Ment Hy 53:
480-1 Jl '69
MONTREAL
Contract snowfighting. J. V. Arpin. il Am
City 84:98-9 D '69

Airports
Little plows play a big role at Dorval airport. il Am City 84:22 N '69

Architecture
Neat showcase for the arts; Saidye Bronf-
man cultural centre. P. Blake. il Arch
Forum 130:86-91 My '69

City planning
Vincent Ponte: a new kind of urban de-
signer. P. Blake. il Art in Am 57:62-7 S '69
Westmount square. E. P. Berkeley. il Arch
Forum 131:82-9 S '69

Crime
One touch of anarchy. il Newsweek 74:71 O
20 '69

Description
Rainy days in Montreal. D. Butwin. il Sat
R 52:41-2+ Mr 22 '69

Exhibitions
Let's travel: Man and his world. il Mlle 68:
98+ F '69

Newspapers
Noblesse oblige; how the Gazette staff were
informed of takeover. L. L. L. Golden.
Sat R 52:58+ Je 14 '69

Police
One touch of anarchy. il Newsweek 74:71
O 20 '69

Politics and government
Montreal's new test for Drapeau. il Bsns W
p60-2 O 11 '69

Riots
What happens when the police strike. G.
Clark. il N Y Times Mag p45+ N 16 '69

Saidye Bronfman cultural centre
See Saidye Bronfman cultural centre,
Montreal
MONTREAL Canadiens (hockey team) See
Hockey teams
MONUMENTS
See also subhead Monuments, statues,
etc. under names of cities, e.g. Washing-
ton, D.C.—Monuments, statues, etc.
MONUMENTS, Megalithic. See Megalithic mon-
uments
MOOD-changing drugs. See Psychopharmacol-
ogy
MOODY, Dwight Lyman
Dwight L. Moody, by J. F. Findlay, jr. Re-
view
Chr Cent 86:1093-5 Ag 20 '69. T. L. Smith
MOODY, Howard
Prudes, lewds and polysyllables. J. H. Smylie.
Commonweal 89:671-3 F 28 '69
MOODY, Orville
Old sarge cools it. D. Jenkins. il por Sports
Illus 30:18-23 Je 23 '69
Sarge takes charge. il por Newsweek 73:94
Je 30 '69
Unknown soldier. il por Time 93:51 Je 27 '69
MOODY, Ralph
Wizards of the wild wheels. C. Phinizy. il
por Sports Illus 31:30-2+ Jl 14 '69
MOODY memorial church, Chicago. See Chi-
cago—Churches
MOOG, Robert A.
Guide to electronic music terminology. por
Sat R 52:47 Ja 25 '69

about
Into our lives with Moog. il por Time 93:50-1
Mr 7 '69
Moog at the museum. J. Hiemenz. il por Hi
Fi 19:MA20-1 N '69
MOON, Eric
Eric Moon interviewed. por Wilson Lib Bul
44:140+ O '69
Library press; address, September 1969. por
Library J 94:4104-9 N 15 '69
Newfoundland revisited. por Library J 94:
2562-6 Jl '69
Who writes for LJ? A second look. Library J
94:1101-3 Mr 15 '69

MOON—*Continued*

Photographs

Diverse activity marks EVA on Apollo 12. Aviation W 91:50A-50H D 8 '69
Emerging face of the moon. il Time 94:20+ Ag 8 '69
EVA yields parts of Surveyor, samples. Aviation W 91:16-21 D 8 '69
First maps of the moon. J. Classen. Sky & Tel 37:82-3 F '69
Fra Mauro site selected for Apollo 13. Aviation W 91:16-19 D 15 '69
Intrepid on a sun-drenched Sea of storms. Life 67:34-9 D 12 '69
Men on the moon; pictures shot by the astronauts on the lunar surface. Life 67: 18-27 Ag 8 '69
Moon crater which lunar module evaded. Aviation W 91:21-3 Ag 18 '69
Moon, Mars and man. Newsweek 74:64-72 Ag 11 '69
Special color photos of man working on moon. Aviation W 91:1-2D Ag 11 '69
Views from Apollo contrast earth, moon. Aviation W 91:62B-62D Ag 18 '69
World sees astronauts Armstrong, Aldrin take man's steps on lunar surface. Aviation W 91:22-9 Jl 28 '69

Photographs from space

Apollo astronauts photograph the moon. Sky & Tel 37:136-46 Mr '69
Apollo 8 adds new perspective on moon. Aviation W 90:55-8 F 3 '69
Apollo 8 lunar album. R Pop Astron 63:4-6 Mr '69
Apollo 8 photographs; letter. Aviation W 90: 106 Ja 27 '69
Apollo 11 crew's farewell view of moon. Aviation W 91:35-8 Ag 25 '69
Awesome views of the forbidding moonscape; photographs by Lunar Orbiters. Nat Geog 135:231-9 F '69
Barnstorming the moon. Life 66:30B-43 Je 6 '69
How we mapped the moon. D. W. Cook. il Nat Geog 135:240-5, sup(folded map) F '69
Lunar detail documented by Apollo 10. Aviation W 90:35-40 Je 16 '69
Orbiter refrain. W. Clothier. Space World F-9-69:24-5 S '69
Pictures from Apollo 10. Sky & Tel 38:90-4 Ag '69
Primary, alternative sites for man's first landing on moon shown in Apollo 10 photos. Aviation W 90:16-21 Je 9 '69
Sequence photos to aid Apollo 11. W. C. Wetmore. Aviation W 90:53-4 Je 9 '69
To my great disappointment, I still do not know the color of the moon. A. Rothstein. Travel & Camera 32:35+ N '69
Uncluttered path to the moon. Time 93:64-7 Je 6 '69

Radiation

Alpha-particle emissivity of the moon: an observed upper limit. R. S. Yeh and J. A. Van Allen. bibliog il Science 166:370-2 O 17 '69

Rotation

Secular accelerations of the earth and moon. R. R. Newton. bibliog il Science 166:825-31 N 14 '69

Surface

Ancient giant craters. Sky & Tel 38:167 S '69
Ancient quest. J. Eberhart and S. Brouwer. il Sci N 96:56-7 Jl 19 '69
Apollo and the Mariners. il Sci Am 221:88-90 S '69
Apollo 11 observations of a remarkable glazing phenomenon on the lunar surface. T. Gold. bibliog il Science 165:1345-9 S 26 '69
Apollo 10 furnishes vivid lunar details. il Aviation W 90:58+ Je 9 '69
Astronauts' photos show rocks on moon. il Aviation W 91:64 Ag 25 '69
Chemical composition of the lunar surface in mare tranquillitatis. A. L. Turkevich and others. bibliog il Science 165:277-9 Jl 18 '69; Reply. E. Olsen. 166:401-2 O 17 '69
Early temperature history of the moon. H. C. Urey. bibliog il Science 165:1275 S 19 '69
Emerging face of the moon. il Time 94:20+ Ag 8 '69
Glazing the moon. il Time 94:72+ O 3 '69
Lunar maria: structure and evolution. W. G. Van Dorn. bibliog il Science 165:693-5 Ag 15 '69
Lunar riverbeds. il Sky & Tel 37:91-3 F '69
Lunar rivers. R. E. Lingenfelter and others; discussion. il Science 164:589; 165:201-2 My 2, Jl 11 '69
Lunar surface material: spacecraft measurements of density and strength. L. D. Jaffe. bibliog il Science 164:1514-16 Je 27 '69

Mining the moon. E. Shoemaker. il Newsweek 74:19 Ag 4 '69
Moon: electrical properties of the uppermost layers. D. W. Strangway. bibliog il Science 165:1012-13 S 5 '69
Moon glass; control sample for chemical analysis experiments. il Space World F-8-68: 38-9 Ag '69
Moon: infrared studies of surface composition. D. P. Cruikshank. bibliog il Science 166:215-18 O 10 '69
Moon is a Rosetta stone. R. Jastrow. il N Y Times Mag p25-7+ N 9 '69
Moon rivers; or, How water behaves in a vacuum. il Chem 42:25 O '69
Moon rivers? theories of P. M. Muller. il Newsweek 73:94 My 12 '69
Moonwalk: the sky was never as black as here. C. Conrad; A. Bean. il U S News 67:30 D 1 '69
Mysterious glaze on moon. Space World G-1-73:35 Ja '70
Next step will be the first; lunar landing. il Bsns W p78+ My 31 '69
Origin and history of the moon. H. C. Urey. il Bul Atom Sci 25:46-51 S '69
Primordial moon. il Time 94:40 S 5 '69
Scientists say lunar transients exist but little is known of origin. Aviation W 90:58 Mr 3 '69
Solar superflare? Sky & Tel 38:300 N '69
Some mysteries solved, some questions raised. il Time 94:21-2 Ag 1 '69
Space program and problems of the origin of the moon; address, December 26-31, 1968. H. C. Urey. Bul Atom Sci 25:24-6+ Ap '69
Standing waves on the moon. Sky & Tel 38: 166 S '69
Surveyor alpha-scattering data: consistency with lunar origin of eucrites and howardites. M. B. Duke. bibliog il Science 165:515-17 Ag 1 '69
Surveyor lunar landings. L. D. Jaffe. bibliog il Science 164:774-88 My 16 '69
Tale of the rocks. il Newsweek 74:59 S 8 '69
Water on the moon and a new nondimensional number. J. A. O'Keefe. bibliog il Science 163:669-70 F 14 '69; Reply. H. C. Urey. 164: 1088 My 30 '69
What we hope Apollo 11 will tell about the moon. il Life 67:24-7 Jl 18 '69
Why is the moon gray? W. F. Libby. bibliog Science 166:1437-8 D 12 '69

Temperature

Early temperature history of the moon. H. C. Urey. bibliog il Science 165:1275 S 19 '69
Lunar thermal anomalies: infrared observations. D. A. Allen and E. P. Ney. bibliog il Science 164:419-21 Ap 25 '69; Reply. D. R. Waldbaum. 166:531-2 O 24 '69

MOON, Flight to the. See Space flight to the moon
MOON dreamers; drama. See Bovasso, J.
MOON in religion, folklore, etc.
So long to the good old moon. P. O'Neil. il Life 67:46-8+ Jl 4 '69
MOON landing, Celebration of. See Celebrations
MOON landing, July 20, 1969. See Space flight to the moon—Manned flights—Armstrong-Aldrin-Collins flight, 1969
MOON landing mementoes. See Keepsakes
MOON landing systems. See Space vehicles—Landing systems—Moon
MOON lore. See Moon—Influence on plants; Moon in religion, folklore, etc.
MOON madness. See Moon—Influence on man
MOON movements. See Seismology
MOON photography. See Space photography
MOON probes. See Lunar probes
MOON vehicles. See Lunar vehicles
MOON worship. See Moon in religion, folklore, etc.
MOONEY, Joseph P.
Teachers' unions in Catholic schools. America 120:301-3 Mr 15 '69
MOONEY, Michael M.
Death of the Post. Atlan 224:70-6 N '69
MOONEY, Philip
Little prince, a story for our time. America 121:610-11+ D 20 '69
MOONEY, Prentice
Indian country is a frontier again. Nations Bsns 57:76-8 S '69
MOONEY, Stephen
Flying; poem. Nation 209:670 D 15 '69
MOONEY aircraft, Incorporated
Public financing considered for Mooney. D. A. Brown. il Aviation W 90:22-3 Je 30 '69
MOONEYHAM, W. Stanley
World vision's new chief. Chr Today 13:37 Mr 14 '69

MOONLIGHTING. See Supplementary employment

MOONMOBILES. See Lunar vehicles

MOONQUAKES. See Seismology

MOOR, H. and others
Synaptic vesicles in electron micrographs of freeze-etched nerve terminals. bibliog Science 164:1405-7 Je 20 '69

MOOR, Paul
Amid majestic ruins. Hi Fi 19:MA29-30 D '69
Blacher premiere; Karajan competition. Hi Fi 19:MA21+ D '69
High camp, low spirits. Hi Fi 19:MA26-7 Jl '69
Sexual hysteria set to music. Life 67:12 Ag 15 '69
(ed) See Karajan, H. von. Von Karajan speaks his mind

MOORE, Alicia Hills
In the wake of starvation, a wound food cannot heal. Life 66:52 Ja 24 '69

MOORE, Arch Alfred, jr
State road workers' strike becomes a political issue. Bsns W p 100 Je 21 '69

MOORE, Barrington, 1913-
Future of American politics. Cur 106:54-64 Ap '69

MOORE, Brian
Week of the Great Hooley. Holiday 46:26-9+ Ag '69

MOORE, C. Fred. See Coker, W. R. jt. auth.

MOORE, Carleton B. and Gibson, E. K.
Nitrogen abundances in chondritic meteorites. bibliog Science 163:174-6 Ja 10 '69

MOORE, Charles
In a little Spanish town; photographs. Pop Phot 65:96-9 Ag '69

MOORE, Charles (poet)
One day God spoke to me . . ; poem. America 120:692 Je 14 '69

MOORE, Charles Willard
Architect speaks his mind; interview. por House & Gard 136:30+ O '69

MOORE, David W.
Third and best recording of Biber's Rosary sonatas. Am Rec G 35:374-7 Ja '69

MOORE, Douglas Stuart
Ballad of Baby Doe. Criticism
Opera N 33:8+ Mr 8 '69
Battle of Baby Doe. L. Lackey. Opera N 33:9+ Mr 8 '69
New York city opera performance of Douglas Moore's Carry Nation. P. L. Miller. il por Am Rec G 35:452-4 F '69
Obituary
Opera N por 34:21 O 11 '69. J. Rudel
Records:
Carry Nation. Opera N 33:35 F 1 '69

MOORE, Edward H.
How to navigate around buoys. Cons 23:48-inside back cover Ap '69

MOORE, Everett T.
Evergreen tempest: eye of a storm. ALA Bul 63:1527-30 D '69

MOORE, G. E. and others
Lymphocytoid lines from persons with sex chromosome anomalies. bibliog Science 163:1453-4 Mr 28 '69

MOORE, Gerald, 1899-
EMI's star-studded birthday present for Gerald Moore. E. Greenfield. il pors Hi Fi 19:16+ Jl '69

MOORE, Grace
Toujours la Moore. V. Sheean. por Opera N 34:14-16 D 20 '69

MOORE, Henry
(ed) Gist of it. See issues of Outdoor life

MOORE, Henry Spencer
On the scene. C. Barnes. Holiday 45:16 F '69

MOORE, James L.
Selling the exposé article. Writers Digest 49:56-9+ Jl '69

MOORE, Jean Andre
Diamonds in the sky. bibliog Har Yrs 9:6-11 Ap '69

MOORE, John G. and others
Thorny-headed worm infection in American prehistoric man. bibliog Science 163:1324-5 Mr 21 '69
—See Fry, G. F. jt. auth.

MOORE, John W. See Gage, P. W. jt. auth.

MOORE, Kenneth E. See Carr, L. A. jt. auth.

MOORE, Marianne
Carols for Christmas, 1969: Santa Claus. N Y Times Mag p5 D 21 '69
Like a wave at the curl; poem. New Yorker 45:50 N 29 '69

about
Comment. M. L. Rosenthal. Poetry 114:126-7 My '69
Marianne Moore, baseball fan. J. Durso. por Sat R 52:51-2 Jl 12 '69

National medal for literature. M. Burke; W. H. Auden; G. Plimpton. il por Wilson Lib Bul 43:622-33 Mr '69
Preserving the greensward. New Yorker 45:28-30 Mr 8 '69
Values and the poems of Marianne Moore. C. H. Edsall. Engl J 58:516-18 Ap '69

MOORE, Mary Lou
Questions & answers about childhood diabetes. Parents Mag 44:80-1+ N '69

MOORE, Mary Louise
To an astronaut; poem. Negro Hist Bul 32:25 My '69

MOORE, Michele. See Sporich, G. jt. comp.

MOORE, Paul, bp, 1919-
Bishop militant. por Newsweek 74:69 D 22 '69

MOORE, Paul B.
Basic ferric phosphates: a crystallochemical principle. Science 164:1063-4 My 30 '69

MOORE, Philip W.
Wire taps: disclosed or leaked? Nation 209:432-4 O 27 '69

MOORE, Ralph
Movie. Chr Cent 86:842-3 Je 18 '69

MOORE, Richard
Thoughts of a voyeur; poem. Am Scholar 39:86-7 Wint '69

MOORE, Robert, jr
Readers' choice: abstraction by Robert Moore, jr. Kenneth. il Art in Am 57:51 N '69

MOORE, Rosanna
Design experiments with natural materials. Sch Arts 68:16-17 Mr '69

MOORE, Roy
Choice for socialism. Commonweal 90:363+ Je 13 '69

MOORE, Sam
Bible publisher multiplies the word. Chr Today 13:44 Je 6 '69

MOORE, Trevor Wyatt
Movies. Chr Cent 86:290+ F 26 '69
Opera. Chr Cent 86:649-50 My 7 '69

MOORE, W. A.
100, and going strong. E. E. Plowman. por Chr Today 13:46 S 26 '69

MOORE, Walter J.
What does research in reading reveal: About reading in the content fields? bibliog Engl J 58:707-18 My '69

MOORE, William J.
Howard U.'s oldest graduate. il pors Ebony 24:77-80 F '69

MOORE, Winston Erskine
New warden in Chicago. il por Newsweek 74:50 Ag 25 '69
Warden who reformed the world's worst jail. H. J. Massaquoi. il pors Ebony 24:60-2+ Jl '69

MOORE corporation
W. Herman Browne of Moore business forms; interview. W. H. Browne. Nations Bsns 57:80-4 N '69

MOOREA
Beyond Bali H'ai. W. A. Rusher. il Nat R 21:347+ Ap 8 '69

MOOREHEAD, Alan
Annals of discovery. New Yorker 45:31-4+ Ag 30; 41-4+ S 6 '69

MOORER, Thomas H.
How good are U.S. defenses? interview. por U S News 67:74-7 D 1 '69
Russian navy; address January 25, 1969. Vital Speeches 35:300-3 Mr 1 '69
Soviet navy; address, August 19, 1969. Vital Speeches 35:742-6 O 1 '69

MOORING of airplanes. See Airplanes—Mooring

MOORMAN, Elliott Duane
Benefit of anger. por Sat R 52:72-3+ Je 21 '69

MOORS (people)
Moriscos: an Ottoman fifth column in sixteenth-century Spain. A. C. Hess. bibliog f Am Hist R 74:1-25 O '68

MOOS, Malcolm Charles
Place in history. Nation 208:525 Ap 28 '69
When Ike said farewell. il por Newsweek 73:28 Ap 14 '69

MOOSE, Wayne N.
Tonic for an old sailor. Motor B 123.53 F '69

MOOSE
Anecdotes, facetiae, satire, etc.
To pack a moose. C. E. Gillham. il Field & S 74:58-9+ N '69

MOOSE hunting
Blizzard moose: Ontario moose hunt. N. Karas. il Field & S 74:56-7+ N '69
Float trip for moose. E. Park. il Outdoor Life 144:50-3+ S '69
Moose for the pot. B. Milek. il Field & S 74:56-7+ Je '69
On the trail of the wary caribou. W. Davis. il Mech Illus 65:68-70+ N '69

MOOSE tagging. See Animal tagging

MORAD, Martin
Contracture and catecholamines in mammalian myocardium. bibliog Science 166:505-6 O 24 '69

MORAES, Dom
Somewhere else with Allen and Gregory; excerpt from My son's father. Horizon 11:66-7 Wint '69

about

Peaceful soul of the poet. L. Hess. por Sat R 52:36-7+ My 10 '69

MORAL attitudes
Ethical theory and moral practice .J. M. Gustafson. Chr Cent 86:1613-17 D 17 '69
When the young take liberties. A. H. Sypher. Nations Bsns 57:25-6 My '69

MORAL conditions
Vanishing right to live, by C. E. Review Nat R 21:545-6 Je 3 '69. W. Herberg
See also
Moving pictures—Moral aspects
Television broadcasting—Moral aspects
also Moral conditions under names of countries, etc, e.g. Sweden—Moral conditions

MORAL education
Ethics and the school superintendent. il Sch & Soc 97:166-8 Mr '69
Parent teachers. C. N. Pickell. Chr Today 14:10-12 D 19 '69
Something for youth to believe in. B. Graham. Read Digest 94:77-81 Je '69
See also
Honesty

MORAL obligation. See Duty

MORAL philosophy. See Ethics

MORAL theology. See Christian ethics; Theology

MORALE
See also
United States—Army—Morale

MORALE, National

Cuba

Moral economy of a revolutionary society. J. A. Kahl. bibliog il Trans-Action 6:30-7 Ap '69

Czechoslovakia

Is there a tomorrow? il Newsweek 73:88+ My 5 '69
Prague: no time for heroics. K. D. Huszar. il Newsweek 74:49-50 D 15 '69

Greece, Modern

How the colonels run things. il Newsweek 75:32-3+ Ja 19 '70

Italy

Storming the institutions; spreading social unrest. T. Terzani. Nation 208:751-2 Je 16 '69

Russia

Internal Russian pressures against war. E. Crankshaw. Cur 112:52-4 N '69

United States

American militarism: what is it doing to us? E. Sevareid. il Look 33:14-16 Ag 12 '69
Case for America; address, October 2, 1969. W. L. Lindholm. Vital Speeches 36:56-9 N 1 '69
Comes the cultural revolution. J. Hitchcock. il N Y Times Mag p4-5+ Jl 27 '69; Discussion. p22-3 Ag 17 '69
Dissent and involvement; address, October 18, 1969. J. C. Humes. Vital Speeches 36:183-4 Ja 1 '70
Mood of America. F. Knebel. il Look 33:23-32 N 18 '69
Nation in trouble. C. F. H. Henry. Chr Today 13:37-8 S 12 '69
On the causes of our discontents. T. L. Hughes. For Affairs 47:653-67 Jl '69
Patriotism revisited; address, September 17, 1969. J. A. Howard. Vital Speeches 36:24-9 O 15 '69
Public happiness. E. McCarthy. McCalls 97:18 Ja '70
Restoration of confidence. New Repub 161:5-6 D 20 '69
Revolt of the middle class; with interview with H. H. Humphrey. il U S News 67:52-8 N 24 '69
Safeguard: public relations as a way of death. M. J. Rosenberg. Chr Cent 86:508-12 Ap 16 '69
Taxed public temper; congressmen sample constituents mood. il Bsns W p41-2 Jl 12 '69
Who is our enemy? M. M. Shideler. Chr Cent 86:1609-13 D 17 '69

Vietnam (Democratic Republic)

North Vietnam: plight of enemy. il U S News 67:37-8 D 22 '69
Rumblings from Hanoi. il Newsweek 73:56 My 12 '69

Vietnam (Republic)

Return to Tuy Hoa. T. Fox. il Commonweal 91:177-80+ N 7 '69
Vietnam: a degree of disillusion. L. Burrows. il Life 67:66-75 S 19 '69

MORALITY. See Ethics

MORALS and war. See War and morals

MORAN, Irene E.
Bookmobile goes in Brooklyn. Library J 94:4487-9 D 15 '69

MORAN, James
Printers, printing and heraldry; adaptation of address. Pub W 196:80-2+ Jl 7 '69

MORAN, Nancy
At home with Julie and David. McCalls 96:66-7+ Je '69
Young John Kennedy got into Collegiate school; could your son? McCalls 96:70-1+ Mr '69

MORATH, Inge
In Russia; photographs. Harper 239:37-78 S '69

MORATH. Max
Off Broadway; An evening with Max Morath, one-man show. E. Oliver. New Yorker 45:96-7 Mr 8 '69

MORATORIUM day, October 15, 1969. See Vietnamese war, 1957- —Protests, demonstrations, etc. against—Moratorium day, October 15, 1969

MORATORIUMS, November 1969. See Vietnamese war, 1957- —Protests, demonstrations, etc. against—November Moratoriums

MORAVIA, Alberto
Chase; Reconciliation; stories; excerpts from Command, and I will obey you, tr. by A. Davidson. Redbook 133:76-7 S '69
Reflections on the moon; tr. by A. Foulke. McCalls 97:42-3+ Ja '70

MORDY, Wendell Allen
Trouble at Nevada research center. P. M. Boffey. Science 165:880 Ag 29 '69

MORE things change: story. See Jurkowski. J.

MOREHEAD planetarium. See Planetariums

MOREHOUSE, Ward
Importing India's educational riches. Am Ed 5:14-19 My '69

MORELL, Anatol G. and others
Physical and chemical studies on ceruloplasmin: crystallization of desialized human ceruloplasmin asialoceruloplasmin. bibliog Science 166:1293-4 D 5 '69

MORELL, Barry
Two notable city alumni. P. L. Miller. il por Am Rec G 35:458-9 F '69

MORELLI, Carlo
Historical records. A. Favia-Artsay. Hobbies 74:35 Mr '69

MORELS. See Mushrooms

MORENCI, Ariz.
Semper fidelis: the marines of Morenci. il Time 95:14-15 Ja 5 '70

MOREY, Donald F.
Portrait: poem. Chr Cent 86:1637 D 24 '69

MOREY, Elsie D. See Morey, P. R. jt. auth.

MOREY, Philip R. and Morey, E. D.
Senckenberg lignite: a lignitized wood with apparently original cellulose and lignin. bibliog Science 164:836-8 My 16 '69

MORGAN, Berry
Mr Collier; story. New Yorker 45:58-60 O 18 '69
Robert: story. New Yorker 45:22-5 Jl 19 '69

MORGAN, Charles, jr
Profiles. F. Powledge. por New Yorker 45:63-4+ O 25 '69

MORGAN, George E.
We make off-street parking self supporting. Am City 84:170+ O '69

MORGAN, Graham J.
Ready and willing. por Forbes 103:196 My 15 '69

MORGAN, Henry
Labor day. Sat R 52:18 Ag 30 '69

MORGAN, Hugh G.
Closed-box speaker systems. bibliog Electr World 82:36-9 N '69

MORGAN, Jane
Learning and the computer. Sci Digest 66:60-3 D '69

MORGAN, John
Two poems; Dolphins of Atlantis; Suppressed. Yale R 59:103-4 O '69

MORGAN, John Pierpont, 1837-1913
New Haven railroad, its rise and fall, by J. L. Weller. Review
Bsns W il p54+ D 20 '69

MORGAN, John Pierpont, 1867-1943
Millionaire & the midget; excerpts from Once in golconda; a true drama of Wall Street. 1920-1938. J. Brooks. il por Am Heritage 20:34-5 O '69
MORGAN, Lael
Down east off season. Travel 132:61-5+ D '69
MORGAN, Madel Jacobs
La dame: Camille. ALA Bul 63:1583-5 D '69
MORGAN, Merrily, and Mandell, A. J.
Indole(ethyl)amine N-methyltransferase in the brain. bibliog Science 165:492-3 Ag 1 '69
MORGAN, Neil
Britain that was. Sat R 52:44+ Ap 19 '69
Crossing the lonely latitudes. Sat R 52:46-7+ S 13 '69
MORGAN, Robert
Lacuna; poem. Nation 209:668 D 15 '69
MORGAN, Robert E.
More avant-rock in the classroom. bibliog Engl J 58:1238-40 N '69
MORGAN, Robert P.
Big, seminal works of Karlheinz Stockhausen. Hi Fi 19:104+ Mr '69
Fresh music from the university laboratory. Hi Fi 19:75-6 Je '69
Late Beethoven, subtly nuanced. Hi Fi 19:78 Ag '69
New music for solo trombone, and for virtuoso trombonist. Hi Fi 19:64-5 Ap '69
Scandalous politics of Hans Werner Henze. Hi Fi 19:106-7 D '69
MORGAN, Robin
Meet the women of the revolution, 1969. P. Babcox. il pors N Y Times Mag p34-5+ F 9, 6+ Mr 2 '69
MORGAN, Thomas B.
I am two people, man. Life 66:74-74B+ Ap 11 '69
MORGAN library. See Pierpont Morgan library
MORGAN Stanley and company
Real estate gets a new blue chip. il Bsns W p40 D 13 '69
MORGANTON, N.C.
More light for Morganton. C. L. Brooks. il Am City 84:142 O '69
MORGELLO, Clem
Wall Street. See issues of Newsweek
MORGENS, Howard J.
Is the soap leader getting soft? il por Bsns W p52-4+ Jl 19 '69
MORGENTHAU, Hans J.
Congress and foreign policy. New Repub 160:16-18 Je 14 '69
MORGENTHAU, Matthew
Matthew Morgenthau's complaint. D. Sanford. New Repub 160:14-15 Mr 1 '69
MORGENTHAU, Robert Morris
Holdout. por Time 94:11-12 D 26 '69
One-man Roy Cohn lobby. W. Lambert. il por Life 67:26-31 S 5 '69
Tough act to follow. il por Newsweek 74:22-3 D 29 '69
Wall Street's crime-buster won't budge. por Bsns W p86+ Ag 2 '69
MORIMOTO, Nobuo, and others
Modified spinel, beta-manganous orthogermanate: stability and crystal structure. bibliog Science 165:586-8 Ag 8 '69
MORINI, Simona
Body sculpturing. Vogue 154:190-3 O 1 '69
(tr) See Valsecchi, M. Genoese mix
MORISON, Robert S.
Science and social attitudes; adaptation of address. April 1969. bibliog Science 165:150-6 Jl 11 '69
University and student dissent. Science 163:1013 Mr 7 '69
MORLEY, Alec, and Stohlman, Frederick, jr
Erythropoiesis in the dog: the periodic nature of the steady state. bibliog Science 165:1025-7 S 5 '69
MORLEY, Charles
(comp) Articles and other books received; Eastern Europe. See issues of American historical review
MORLEY, Felix
State of the Nation. See issues of Nation's business
MORLEY, Malcolm
Super realism. il Life 66:44-9 Je 27 '69
MORMONS and Mormonism
Bring in the ancestors; family record vaults in Little Cottonwood Canyon. il Time 94:52 Ag 22 '69
Mormons: visibly staking a witness. il Chr Today 13:48-9 My 9 '69
New Mormon history. M. Rischin. Am West 6:49 Mr '69
MORMONS and Mormonism, Negro
Mormons and the mark of Cain: charges of racism. Time 95:46+ Ja 19 '70
Second-class Mormons; restriction on priesthood. Newsweek 75:84 Ja 19 '70

MORNING glories
Wooden roses. F. Kaltenbach. Horticulture 46:16-17 S '68
MORNING newspapers. See Newspapers
MORNINGSTAR, Mona. See Suppes, P. jt. auth.
MOROCCAN house decoration. See House decoration, Moroccan
MOROCCO
World of saints and she-demons: life in a small Arab town. V. Crapanzano and J. Kramer. il N Y Times Mag p 14-15+ Je 22 '69
See also
Jews in Morocco
Marrakesh
Moors (people)
Tourist trade—Morocco
Defenses
North African arms race. A. Smith. Atlan 223:22+ F '69
Description and travel
Iberia & the Magreb. H. Apter. il Travel & Camera 32:40, 48-50 Ag '69
Morocco's Atlantic coast. H. P. Koenig. il Travel 132:34-7+ O '69
Two girls, Club Méd. les vacances extra. E. Count. il Mlle 69:148-50 Je '69
Politics and government
End of an adventure; monastery of Toumliline. il Time 93:56+ My 23 '69
MORPHINE
Morphine: conditioned increases in self-administration in rhesus monkeys. S. R. Goldberg and others. bibliog il Science 166:1306-7 D 5 '69
MORPHOGENESIS
Cell death during early morphogenesis: parallels between insect limb and vertebrate limb development. J. M. Whitten. bibliog il Science 163:1456-7 Mr 28 '69
Fungal morphogenesis: cell wall construction in mucor rouxii. S. Bartnicki-Garcia and E. Lippman. bibliog il Science 165:302-4 Jl 18 '69
Polyvinylsulfate: interaction with complexes of morphogenetic factors and their natural inhibitors. H. Tiedemann and others. bibliog il Science 164:1175-7 Je 6 '69
MORPHOLOGY
See also
Growth
MORRELL, Lady Ottoline Violet Anne (Cavendish-Bentinck)
Out of her time. Lady Ottoline. J. Fairfield. il pors Vogue 154:442-7+ S 1 '69
MORRILL, George P.
Most unforgettable character I've met. Read Digest 95:122-6 Ag '69
Use it up! Wear it out! Make it do! Read Digest 94:123-6 Je '69
MORRIS, Alice S.
Rooms with the power to enchant. House B 111:92+ Ap '69
MORRIS, Daniel Luzon
Music of new spheres. por Chem 42:10-12 D '69
MORRIS, David
'60s are dead! Long live the '50s! Commonweal 91:372-3 D 26 '69
MORRIS, Desmond
Must we have zoos? Yes, but. . . Read Digest 94:195-200 Mr '69
MORRIS, Effie Lee
Blowing in the wind. Library J 94:1298-300 Mr 15 '69
MORRIS, Ivan
Puzzles to devil the mind; excerpts from Riverside puzzles. Vogue 153:134-5 Mr 15; 252-3 My; 154:136 O 1 '69
MORRIS, James, 1926-
Iceland: fire and ice in a cold blue ocean. Holiday 46:54-7+ D '69
Iran, born Persia; excerpts from Persia. Vogue 154:212-13+ D '69
Persian diversions. Horizon 11:18-19 Spr '69
Wales? Horizon 11:26-9+ Wint '69
When Britain's grandeur knew no bounds; excerpt from Pax Britannica: the climax of an empire. Read Digest 94:82-6 Je '69
MORRIS, Joe Alex
To scare a thief. Read Digest 95:183-4+ S '69
MORRIS, Joe Alex, jr
Mutations left and right. Nation 208:423-5 Ap 7 '69
Willy Brandt looks ahead. Nation 209:363-4 O 13 '69
MORRIS, Jonas V.
Assateague Island. bibliog Nat Parks 43:15-20 F '69
Parde Island. bibliog Nat Parks 43:15-18 Je '69

MORRIS, M. D.
Out of Peking. Opera N 33:8-13 Mr 22 '69
MORRIS, Mary Louise
Dolls in books. bibliog Hobbies 74:42+ Jl
'69
MORRIS, N. Ronald. See Kalousek, F. jt. auth.
MORRIS, Norman S.
What's good about children's TV. Atlan 224:
67-71 Ag '69
MORRIS, Norval, and Hawkins, Gordon
Controlling violence; toward a less lethal
environment; excerpts from Honest poli-
tician's guide to crime control. Cur 111:48-
53 O '69
—and Zimring, Frank
Deterrence and correction. Ann Am Acad 381:
137-46 Ja '69
MORRIS, Patricia
In my opinion. por Seventeen 27:222 N '69
MORRIS, Philip, incorporated
Jilted American; competition for Canadian
breweries. il Forbes 104:36 Jl 1 '69
MORRIS, Richard Brandon
(ed) See Jay, J. Jay papers II: the forging
of the Nation
(ed) See Jay, J. Jay papers III: the trials of
Chief Justice Jay
MORRIS, Robert
Hard questions and soft answers. W. S. Wil-
son. il pors Art N 68:26-9 N '69
Mover and shaker. D. L. Shirey. il por News-
week 75:94-5 Ja 19 '70
MORRIS, Robert V.
Upheaval in the religious arena. Sat R 52:
64+ My 10 '69
MORRIS, Steven
How blacks upset the Marine corps. Ebony
25:55-8+ D '69
Primitive art of Clementine Hunter. Ebony
24:144-8 My '69
MORRIS, Terry
Can a young wife from Baltimore find ful-
fillment feeding turkeys on a farm in Is-
rael? Redbook 132:78-9+ F '69
Life-giving power of love. Good H 169:50+
D '69
MORRIS, William
William Morris. F. Johnson. bibliog il pors
Am Artist 32:43-9 D '69
MORRIS, Wright
Drrdla; story. Esquire 72:87-9 Ag '69
Green grass, blue sky, white house. New
Yorker 45:56-62 O 25 '69
Since when do they charge admission; story.
Harper 238:65-70 My '69

about

Books. R. Coles. New Yorker 45:205-6+ O 18
'69
Neglected seer. D. Madden. New Repub 162:
28-30 Ja 10 '70
Transforming the past. G. Wolff. por News-
week 75:69C+ Ja 12 '70
MORRISON, David
Venus: absence of a phase effect at a 2-centi-
meter wavelength. bibliog Science 163:815-17
F 21 '69
MORRISON, Gordon
Popcorn. Horticulture 47:21+ O '69
Watermelons for northern gardens. Horticul-
ture 47:40-1+ Ap '69
MORRISON, Joseph L.
View of the moon from the Sun: 1835. Am
Heritage 20:80-2 Ap '69
MORRISON, Karl R.
To scratch or not, for art. il por Am Artist
33:28-9+ My '69
MORRISON, Michael
[Book review] America 120:106-7 Ja 25 '69
MORRISON, Philip
Beneath civility: rage and fear. Life 66:16 Ap
25 '69
—and Morrison, Phylis
Children's books about science: an annual
Christmas selection. Sci Am 221:136-9+ D
'69

about

Two of a kind. Sci N 96:264 S 27 '69
MORRISON, Phylis. See Morrison, Philip, jt.
auth.
MORRISON, Sandy
Explosions en route. Nation 209:379-81 O 13
'69
MORRISON, William J.
Yachting interviews: Rear Admiral William J.
Morrison. W. T. Stone. por Yachting 125:
67+ Mr '69
MORRISTOWN and Morris Township, N.J.
Joint free public library
1766: creating the best of Broadway in a
small-town public library. il Wilson Lib Bul
43:1008-10 Je '69

MORRO BAY, Calif.
School library pot book stirs investigation;
discussion. Library J 93:3901; 94:241 O 15
'68, Ja 15 '69
MORROW, Anne Powers
Three faces of beauty; ed. by S. Harney. il
por Ladies Home J 86:88-9+ Mr '69
MORROW, Joseph E. and Smithson, B. L.
Learning sets in an invertebrate. bibliog Sci-
ence 164:850-1 My 16 '69
MORROW, William
Riding the Arctic circuit. il por Time 93:68+
Je 6 '69
MORROW, William, and company
Case history of a best seller. il Pub W 196:
16-17 D 15 '69
MORSE, David A.
ILO and world peace; excerpts from address.
UN Mo Chron 6:54-8 Je '69
ILO at fifty: its hopes for social progress.
Mo Labor R 92:51-3 My '69
World employment programme. UNESCO
Courier 22:8-12 Jl '69
MORSE, David E.
Avant-rock in the classroom. Engl J 58:196-
200+ F '69
MORSE, Joshua Marion, 3d
Lawyers of Ole Miss. K. Vinson. Nation
208:791-3 Je 23 '69
New dean at Ole Miss. por Time 94:53+ Jl
18 '69
MORSE, Ralph
Apollo 10; Apollo 11; crews with their families;
photographs. Life 66:44-51 My 16 '69
MORSE, Roger A.
Tapping a bee tree. Cons 23:10-11 F '69
Varied fare of the honeybee. Natur Hist 78:
58-65 Je '69
MORSE, Wayne Lyman
Perspectives on Latin America; address, Sep-
tember 9, 1969. Vital Speeches 36:86-90 N 15
'69
MORSE, William C.
Disturbed youngsters in the classroom. Todays
Ed 58:30-7 Ap '69
MORSE code. See Cipher and telegraph codes
MORSELL, John A.
Negro, black or Afro-American? reprint.
Negro Hist Bul 32:11 F '69
MORTALITY
Death & the physician. E. J. Cassell. Com-
mentary 47:73-9 Je '69
See also
Death
Infant mortality
MORTGAGE banks
Where a middleman is loved for what hap-
pens tomorrow. il Bsns W p 100-1 Jl 12
'69
See also
Home capital funds, incorporated
MORTGAGE companies. See Mortgage banks
MORTGAGE investment trusts. See Investment
trusts
MORTGAGE loans. See Mortgages
MORTGAGES
City insures home mortgages; Fresno, Calif.
Am City 84:26 F '69
Coping with the mortgage squeeze. il Chang-
ing T 23:13-14 Ag '69
Don't hurry to sign that mortgage until—.
D. L. Markstein. Suc Farm 67:42 D '69
Has Wall Street found this year's winner?
mortgage trusts. Bsns W p 121-2 Ap 12 '69
How housing rides out the storm; Washing-
ton is helping. il Bsns W p94+ My 31 '69
Is a home still a good investment? P. Lind-
berg. Bet Hom & Gard 47:46-7+ S '69
Leg up for the short homebuyer; HCF. il
Bsns W p 106-7 My 3 '69
Lenders say: no relief near for house hunters.
il U S News 67:86-8 O 27 '69
Mortgage rates; plan to lift ceiling. U S News
67:71 Ag 25 '69
See also
Mortgage banks
United States—Federal housing administra-
tion
MORTLAND, M. M. See Doner, H. E. jt. auth.
MORTON, C. R.
Digital photo enlarger timer. Radio-Electr
40:68-70 F '69
MORTON, Donald L. and others
Human liposarcomas: tissue cultures contain-
ing foci of transformed cells with viral
particles. bibliog Science 165:813-16 Ag 22 '69
MORTON, Frederic
First to mine delirium. Nation 208:343 Mr
17 '69
Sugarbush: Vermont's chic ski resort. Holi-
day 46:64-7 D '69
MORTON, Marcia
Elderly primipara, that's me! McCalls 97:
92+ O '69

MORTON, Rogers Clark Ballard
Next election: what party chairmen see as big campaign issues. por Nations Bsns 57: 36-7 N '69

about

Morton's first strike. por Newsweek 73:37-8 Ap 28 '69
Party chairmen: ready for battle. por U S News 66:14-15 Ap 28 '69
MORTON, Tom M.
New look for the Pentacon six. Travel & Camera 32:106-7 F '69
MOSAICS
Cloisonne or mosaic? il Design 70:32 Spr '69
Forty tons of mosaic; Mathematical sciences building. Westwood campus of the University of California. il Am Artist 33:18-21+ Ag '69
Objective: a work of permanent value. R. Wenger. il Sch Arts 69:14-15 Ja '70
Shard mosaics. B. Gilbreath. il Ceram Mo 17:23-4 Mr '69
Sparkling surfaces. S. R. Bailey. il Sch Arts 69:11 Ja '70
MOSAICS (biology)
Graft versus host inhibition: fetal liver and thymus cells to minimize secondary disease. M. M. Bortin and E. C. Saltzstein. bibliog il Science 164:316-18 Ap 18 '69
Two mothers, two fathers; allophenic mice. B. J. Culliton. il Sci N 95:361-3 Ap 12 '69
Wanted: capable ape to do janitor's work. D. M. Rorvik. il Esquire 71:114 Ap '69
MOSBACHER, Emil, 1922-
Skipper. il por Newsweek 73:43 Ap 14 '69
MOSCOW

Crime

Incident at the Kremlin; shooting at cars escorting the Soviet astronauts. Nat R 21: 104-5 F 11 '69
Shoot-up in Moscow; attack on motorcade of cosmonauts. il Newsweek 73:41 F 3 '69
Speculative silence; reverberations from shots fired by would-be assassin at cosmonauts' parade. Time 93:32+ F 14 '69
Unknown soldier; rumors after attack on cosmonauts and government leaders. Newsweek 73:56 F 17 '69

Description

As the plane lands in Moscow the people cheer. B. M. Frolic. il N Y Times Mag p62-3+ O 26 '69

Education

Visit to Moscow's schools. Z. M. Mahdesian. Clear House 44:166-8 N '69

Parades

Hurray, hurray; May day. il Newsweek 73:52 My 12 '69
MOSCOW state symphony orchestra
Moscow state symphony; concerts at Carnegie Hall. E. Haines. il Hi Fi 19:MA26-7+ My '69
Music, political and other; concerts at Carnegie Hall. C. J. McNaspy. America 120: 259-60 Mr 1 '69
Music to my ears: three-week visit to the East. I. Kolodin. Sat R 52:68 Mr 22 '69
Musical events; concerts in Carnegie Hall. W. Sargeant. New Yorker 45:114 F 22 '69
MOSCRIP, Ruth Cronkite
Classroom tips from trips. Todays Ed 58:20-4 S '69
MOSELEY, Katherine W.
Songs of an August night. Nat Wildlife 7: 32-4 Ag '69
MOSELEY, Monica
Duo, a remarkable new dance film. Dance Mag 43:22-3 Je '69
—See Snyder, A. F. jt. comp.
MOSER, Terry
Note to morning; poem. Nation 209:120 Ag 11 '69
MOSES
New Moses; and Christ the Saviour. V. P. McCorry. America 121:601 D 13 '69
MOSES, Harold L. and others
Adrennal cholesterol: localization by electron-microscopic autoradiography. bibliog Science 163:1203-5 Mr 14 '69
MOSES, Robert, 1888-
Master builder's plan; Atlantic village plan. il por Newsweek 73:64 My 12 '69
MOSES and Aaron; opera. See Schönberg, A.
MOSFET (metal oxide semiconductor field-effect transistor) See Transistors
MOSHER, Fredric J.
What Americans can learn from the Danes. por Wilson Lib Bul 43:959-73 Je '69

MOSHER, Ralph S.
You had better be kind to this four-legged friend. il pors Life 66:34-5+ My 2 '69
MOSIER, A. R. and others
Photochemical decomposition of DDT by a free-radical mechanism. bibliog Science 164: 1083-5 My 30 '69
MOSKIN, J. Robert
New contraceptive society. Look 33:50+ F 4 '69; Same abr. with title Sweden: the contraceptive society. Read Digest 94:225-6+ Ap '69
MOSKOW, Michael. H. See McLennan, K. jt. auth.
MOSLEY, James C.
Prosecutor, by J. Mills. Review
Newsweek il 74:83D-84 Ag 25 '69. G. Wolff
Time il por 94:36 S 5 '69
MOSLEY, Nicholas
Books. G. Steiner. New Yorker 45:89-91 Jl 12 '69
MOSQUES
See also
Jerusalem—Mosques
MOSQUITO control
Encephalitis started the program of mosquito control; Lane County, Ore. J. C. Stoner. il Am City 84:102+ Ap '69
Thirty-four deaths; and 376 confirmed cases of encephalitis; Harris County, Tex. R. E. Barnett. il Am City 84:127-8 F '69
To control mosquitoes, try to get them before they fly. il Sunset 143:148 Jl '69
MOSQUITOES
Bug off, bug. Motor B 124:63+ Ag '69
Mosquitoes feeding on insect larvae. P. Harris and others. il Science 164:184-5 Ap 11 '69
Vitamin A deficiency: effect on mosquito eye ultrastructure. J. D. Brammer and R. H. White. bibliog il Science 163:821-3 F 21 '69

Extermination

See Mosquito control

MOSQUITOES as carriers of infection
Fever in Hanoi; crippling epidemic of dengue-like fever. il Time 94:72 O 10 '69
MOSS, Dale N. and others
Carbon dioxide compensation points in related plant species. bibliog Science 164:187-8 Ap 11 '69
MOSS, Don
Pointillist view of Houston's Champions; reproductions of paintings. Sports Illus 30:46-50 Je 9 '69
MOSS, Frank Edward
Conservation at the crossroads; address. pors Am For 75:20-3+ Ja '69
Excerpt from address, January 31, 1969. Cong Digest 48:174+ Je '69
MOSS, Frank T.
Boats that fly. il Yachting 125:112-14+ Ja '69
New power catamaran. Yachting 125:54-6+ F '69
Powerboat revolution. Yachting 125:52-3+ My '69
With the sport fishermen. See issues of Yachting
MOSS, Howard
Ménage à trois; poem. New Yorker 45:56 O 11 '69
Where the castle is; poem. New Yorker 45:54 N 22 '69

about

Second nature. R. Howard. Poetry 114:331-4 Ag '69
MOSS, John Emerson
CAB role draws congressional interest. H. D. Watkins. Aviation W 91:38 D 1 '69
Congressmen plan to oppose fare increases. Aviation W 91:32 Ag 18 '69
MOSS, Norman
Bonfire in Ulster. New Repub 161:11-12 S 6 '69
MOSS, Stanley
Joy out of terror. New Repub 160:30-2 Mr 29 '69
Two fishermen; poem. New Repub 160:24 F 8 '69
MÖSSBAUER effect
Oxidation state of iron at high pressure. H. G. Drickamer and others. bibliog il Science 163:885-90 F 28 '69
MOSSES
To remove moss from paving. Sunset 142:116 My '69
MOSTEL, Zero
Making of The angel Levine. R. Kotlowitz. Harper 239:98-100 Jl '69
MOTELS
Hotels and motels: all the comforts of home, and then some. Bet Hom & Gard 47:54+ N '69
See also
Holiday inns of America, incorporated

MOTETS
Newly identified clausula-motets in the Las Huelgas manuscript. G. A. Anderson. bibliog f il Mus Q 55:228-45 Ap '69

MOTHER-child relationship. See Parent-child relationship

MOTHER Goose
Mother Goose: is the old girl relevant? J. Bodger. bibliog il Wilson Lib Bul 44:402-8 D '69
What comes after Mother Goose? P. Parker. Ed Digest 35:46-9 O '69

MOTHER-in-law jokes. See Humor

MOTHER love. See Love, Maternal

MOTHER of good fortune; story. See Rascoe, J.

MOTHER wants to meet you; story. See Hoffman, W.

MOTHERHOOD. See Mothers

MOTHERS
Happenings in education; parents are relevant. W. D. Boutwell. PTA Mag 64:31-2 O '69
Mothers who try to be all things. B. Spock. Redbook 132:60+ Mr '69
Older mother. B. Spock. Redbook 133:24+ S '69
Turning points; accident in the afternoon; a child's face cut by paring knife. M. Yusko. McCalls 96:14+ F '69
What is a mother? excerpts. L. P. McGrath and J. Scobey. Read Digest 94:108-10 My '69
Young mother's story. See issues of Redbook
See also
Pregnancy
Stepparents

Anecdotes, facetiae, satire, etc.
Elderly primipara, that's me! M. Morton. McCalls 97:92+ O '69
Who remembers M.A.M.A? A. H. Reiss. Esquire 71:162-3 Mr '69

Employment
See Married women—Employment

MOTHERS, Unmarried
I am an unwed mother. Seventeen 27:128-9+ N '68
Measuring morals; study of unwed mothers. il Time 93:74 Je 6 '69

MOTHERS and daughters. See Parent-child relationship

MOTHERS day
Drama
Conversation piece. J. Nicholson. Plays 28:1-12 My '69
Mother's day treasure hunt. H. L. Miller. Plays 28:69-74, 88 My '69

MOTHER'S day treasure hunt; drama. See Miller, H. L.

MOTHER'S helpers. See Household employees

MOTHERS-in-law, Jewish. See Jewish women

MOTHERWELL, Robert
Motherwell: the window and the wall. H. H. Arnason. il Art N 68:48-52+ Sum '69
Openness and Robert Motherwell; exhibition of large paintings. B. Rose. Vogue 154:62 Ag 1 '69

MOTHS
Circadian clock action spectrum in a photoperiodic moth. V. G. Bruce and D. H. Minis. bibliog il Science 163:583-5 F 7 '69
Sex pheromone of the pink bollworm moth; biological masking by its geometrical isomer. M. Jacobson. bibliog il Science 163:190-1 Ja 10 '69
See also
Gipsy moths

MOTION
See also
Vibration

MOTION in art. See Action in art

MOTION picture association of America
Films. S. Kauffmann. New Repub 161:22+ Jl 12 '69

MOTION sculpture. See Mobiles

MOTION study
See also
Movement, Psychology of

MOTIVATION (education)
Good scholarship: do students really care? K. Parrish and G. R. Weldy. il Clear House 43:275-9 Ja '69
Money, motivation, and academic achievement. R. L. Green and T. J. Stachnik. Ed Digest 34:8-10 Mr '69
Motivation for mathematics. G. Knaggs. Clear House 43:553-4 My '69

Teaching and learning through inquiry. B. G. Massialas; J. Zevin; M. Sugrue and J. A. Sweeney. il Todays Ed 58:40-4 My '69

MOTIVATION (psychology)
Are technological upheavals inevitable? M. W. Hunter. 2d. il Harvard Bsns R 47:73-83 S '69
As I see it; interview. D. C. McClelland. il Forbes 103:53-7 Je 1 '69
Job enrichment pays off; findings of studies carried out in British companies. W. J. Paul, jr. and others. il Harvard Bsns R 47:61-78 Mr '69
See also
Reinforcement (psychology)

MOTIVATION in literature. See Fiction—Technique

MOTIVE (periodical)
Nixed motives. Newsweek 73:89 Je 16 '69
Obscenity under a Methodist imprint? Chr Today 13:21-2 Je 20 '69

MOTO brousse. See Motor vehicles, Amphibious

MOTONEURONS. See Nerve cells

MOTOR boat insurance. See Insurance, Marine

MOTOR boat racing
Big shoot-out on Lake Havasu; outboard powerboat race. H. D. Whall. il Sports Illus 31:66 D 8 '69
Farewell to put-puts; Outboard world championship race at Lake Havasu. il Time 94:52 D 12 '69
Gold cup sweep at San Diego. S. Gruber. il Motor B 124:17 D '69
Master of those mad racers; D. Aronow, world champion ocean powerboat racer. J. Kirshenbaum. il Sports Illus 31:50-2+ N 17 '69
Miami to Nassau, Aronow style. L. Dangerfield. il Motor B 124:15 D '69
Month in yachting. See issues of Yachting
More power to you. M. Crook. See issues of Yachting
Motorboat racing records. Motor B 123:278+ Ja '69
On the racing circuit. See issues of Motor boating
Rooster tails; Gold cup hydroplane race. il Newsweek 74:70+ O 13 '69
Rooster tales. E. Rickman. See issues of Hot rod
Rugged world of offshore racing. B. McKeown. il Mech Illus 65:55+ Je '69
They all laughed when Peter turned left; Hennessy New York Grand prix powerboat race. J. Kirshenbaum. il Sports Illus 31:44-5 Ag 11 '69
Watersports. F. Rohr, jr. See issues of Motor boating
See also
Regattas

Great Britain
Round Britain powerboat race. E. F. Haylock. il Motor B 124:78-9+ N '69

MOTOR boats
All-American racing team; yachting's twentieth annual of outstanding power racing craft. M. Crook. il Yachting 125:64-6+ Mr '69
Classy, glassy '69 boats. D. Fales. il Pop Mech 131:168-72 Mr '69
Cruise your way to camping pleasure. N. Phillips. il Pop Gard 20:2-5+ Spr '69
Fast ski boat looks for work; Aquarius. il Bsns W p 124 Jl 19 '69
Inboards. il Motor B 123:148-63 Ja '69
Motor boating USA. See issues of Motor boating
New boats. See issues of Yachting
Pick the best boat for your wants and your waters. J. Roe. il Pop Sci 194:102-9 F '69
Rooster tales. E. Rickman. See issues of Hot rod
Skip o'er the waves on a scooter; aquascooter. il Changing T 23:20 Ag '69
Slow boat. M. Crook. il Yachting 125:68-9 Mr '69
Stern-drive. M. Crook. il Yachting 125:82 Ja '69
What's new in boating. il Pop Sci 194:144-16 F '69
Your new medium cruiser. il Motor B 123:102-3 Ja '69
Your new runabout. il Motor B 123:98-9 Ja '69
Your new small cruiser. il Motor B 123:100-1 Ja '69
See also
Catamarans
Hydrofoils
Hydroplanes

Anecdotes, facetiae, satire, etc.
They're a bunch of corks! J. Martenhoff. il Yachting 126:66-7+ N '69

MOTOR boats—*Continued*

Design
Designs. J. Atkin. il Yachting 125:78-82 Mr '69

Equipment
Boats are for people. B. Robinson. il Yachting 126:71+ O '69

Cruise your way to camping pleasure. N. Phillips. il Pop Gard 20:2-5+ Spr '69

Yachting's boat show. il Yachting 125:133+ Ja '69

See also
Nautical instruments

Exhibitions
Yachting's boat show. il Yachting 125:133+ Ja '69

Gages
See Gages

Testing
How much torture can your boat take? W. Cloud. il Pop Mech 131:146-50+ Ap '69

Jetting down Montana's mighty Missouri. D. Fales. il Pop Mech 132:121-4 N '69

Lake Powell: a spectacular test ground for Glastron's vagabond. D. Fales. il Pop Mech 131:126-9+ F '69

PM tests:
Chris-Craft's wave-piercing Lancer in the Florida Keys. D. Fales. il Pop Mech 132:112-14+ Ag '69

Chrysler's Sport Fury takes to the water. D. Fales. il Pop Mech 130:132-5 D '68

FrontRunner: the boat that wants to be a VW bus. D. Fales. il Pop Mech 131:138-41 Je '69

Sweet pair for '70: Sport Crowns. J. Roe. il Pop Sci 195:120-3 D '69

See also
Marine engines—Fuel consumption

MOTOR boats, Jet propelled
Jet boat you can build! L. Read. il Mech Illus 65:76-8 Mr '69

Jet-jet, boat of the future. B. McKeown. il Mech Illus 65:68-70+ Mr '69

MOTOR boats, Outboard
Outboard boats. il Motor B 123:182-7 Ja '69

Outboard runabout. D. Barker. il Yachting 125:81 Ja '69

Quick-change runabout: it's a fisherman, it's a camper. J. Roe. il Pop Sci 195:102-4 Ag '69

See also
Gas and oil engines, Outboard

Equipment
Power-tilt kit. il Field & S 73:140 Ap '69

Maintenance and repair
Tune up your outboard for water skiing. B. Weis. il Mech Illus 65:84-5+ Jl '69

Testing
Outboard boats. il Consumer Rep 34:306-16 Je '69

MOTOR bus drivers
Celestial omnibus: Sterling Tanks, the nicest bus driver in New York. New Yorker 45:47-8 O 11 '69

MOTOR bus engines
LTV testing pollution-free engine in bus; Freon vapor-driven propulsion system. Aviation W 90:20 Mr 3 '69

MOTOR bus lines
Busways may woo the rider back to mass transit. J. C. Corradino. il Am City 84:98-9 F '69

See also
Greyhound corporation

Passenger service
Free bus service increases summer fun; Santa Fe Springs, Calif. W. J. McCann. il Am City 84:128 Jl '69

Public relations
Free bus service increases summer fun; Santa Fe Springs, Calif. W. J. McCann. il Am City 84:128 Jl '69

MOTOR bus travel
Spreading out in South America; Amerbuspass. L. Zalamea. il Travel 132:58-9 O '69

Touring without a car. G. Pitman. il Travel 131:63-6 Ap '69

MOTOR buses
Will you commute in GM's new turbine-powered bus? J. Dunne. il Pop Sci 195:92-3 S '69

Small size
Little buses win big support; Racine, Wis. J. Erdmann. il Am City 84:134+ Mr '69

Small buses have a million uses. J. P. Norbye and J. Dunne. il Pop Sci 195:132-7 S '69

MOTOR camping. See Camping

MOTOR cars (railroad) See Railroads—Cars

MOTOR homes. See Campers and coaches. Truck

MOTOR lodges. See Motels

MOTOR oils. See Lubrication and lubricants

MOTOR response
Temporal order judgment and reaction time. J. Gibbon and R. Rutschmann. bibliog il Science 165:413-15 Jl 25 '69

Visual reinforcement of nonnutritive sucking in human infants. E. R. Siqueland and C. A. DeLucia. bibliog il Science 165:1144-6 S 12 '69

MOTOR scooters
Just for fun take a minibike along. J. Davis. il Pop Sci 195:98-101+ N '69

Notes for nomads. See issues of Travel

MOTOR sleds
Spiked wheel drives power sled. E. F. Lindsley. il Pop Sci 194:164-5 F '69

MOTOR State 500. See Automobile racing

MOTOR tractors. See Tractors

MOTOR transportation. See Transportation, Automotive

MOTOR trend awards
Motor trend's 1969 car of the year: Road Runner. il Motor T 21:32-4 F '69

1970 car of the year nominees. il Motor T 21:58-9 D '69

MOTOR truck drivers
How you look to a truck driver. E. D. Fales, jr. il Pop Mech 131:93-7+ My '69

MOTOR truck engines
Beep-beep jeep! pickup truck. E. Rickman. il Hot Rod 22:106-7 N '69

See also
Cummins engine company

MOTOR truck robberies. See Robberies and assaults

MOTOR truck trailers

Transportation
Piggybackers all fall down but railroads look for a pickup. il Bsns W p158 N 22 '69

MOTOR trucks
And the kitchen sink; recreational trucks. Time 94:76 Jl 11 '69

Dodge Adventurer. V. L. Oertle. il Motor T 21:96-8 F '69

It's in to own a truck. A. Markovich. il Am Home 72:30+ Ap '69

Light trucks for work & play. A. Markovich. il Mech Illus 65:165-7+ F '69

Longhorn: Chevy's hot new pickup. V. L. Oertle. il Motor T 21:48-50 My '69

Norbye-Dunne report: classy new pickups show pizzazz plus performance. J. P. Norbye and J. Dunne. il Pop Sci 194:92-7 Je '69

Tough new Internationals with style. J. P. Norbye. il Pop Sci 194:104-5 Ja '69

Trucks pick up new customers; pickup trucks for fun. il Bsns W p19-20 D 20 '69

What's new. P. B. Jones. See issues of Successful farming

Your second car may be a truck! B. Hartford. il Pop Mech 131:84-7+ Ja '69

See also
Tank trucks

MOTOR trucks, Electric
Municipal utility plugs all-electric trucks; Seattle. J. M. Nelson. il Am City 84:89 F '69

MOTOR trucks, Military
Army's flipflop truck under fire; M151 quarter-ton truck. il Bsns W p36 Je 7 '69

MOTOR trucks, Municipal
Ready for an emergency; special truck of Sioux Falls water department. P. V. Sanders. il Am City 84:98-9 Ja '69

MOTOR trucks, Remodeled
Beep-beep jeep! pickup truck. E. Rickman. il Hot Rod 22:106-7 N '69

383 into F-100. R. A. Hall. il Hot Rod 22:106-7 Ap '69

MOTOR trucks in agriculture
His forage wagons are self-propelled. il Suc Farm 67:38 Jl '69

MOTOR vehicle industry. See Automobile industry and trade

MOTOR vehicle racing
Baja, the second time around. J. Thawley. il Hot Rod 22:64-6 F '69

Bathtubs on wheels; all-terrain vehicle. il Time 94:60 Ag 22 '69

MOTOR vehicle racing—*Continued*
Buttercup buggy bash; imperial Valley Dunne buggy association's eighth annual winter-nationals. A. Hall. il Hot Rod 22:62-4 Mr '69
Dry lakes fiesta. E. Rickman. il Hot Rod 22:38-9 Jl '69
Far-out bug-in; Mexican 1000. J. Thawley. il Hot Rod 22:88-9 Ja '69
500 miles of Baja; off-road racers and would-be racers. J. Thawley. il Hot Rod 22:60-2 Ag '69
Mint 400. J. Thawley. il Hot Rod 22:66-8 Je '69
Motor trend interview; ed. by B. Sanders. S. McQueen. Motor T 21:88+ N '69
Mud, sweat and gears; closed-course circuit racing. C. Pendergast. il Motor T 21:84-5 N '69
Off-roading on a circle track? J. Thawley. il Hot Rod 22:146-7 O '69
Watery chow mein; Four-wheel-drive Grand prix. J. Thawley. il Hot Rod 22:62-4 Jl '69
You crazy gringos, you theenk you drive the Baja? Mexican 1000. R. Brock. il Motor T 21:86-9 F '69

MOTOR vehicles
Build this one-man golf cart. E. Alline. il Pop Mech 131:176-9 Je '69
Chevy heads for the hills; four-wheel-drive, off-the-road vehicle. J. G. Schmidt. il Motor T 21:32-3 Ap '69
Chevy's Blazer: a different four-wheel drive. V. L. Oertle. il Pop Mech 131:56+ Ap '69
Citroën Mehari: France's answer to the dune buggy. J. P. Norbye. il Pop Sci 195:118-19 D '69
Drive ya buggy. J. Thawley. See issues of Hot rod
Family funster. il Hot Rod 22:118-19 D '69
Growing rage for fun cars; dune buggies. V. L. Oertle. il Pop Sci 194:65-7+ Mr '69
Hill-and-gully riders; Coot off-the-road vehicle. il Time 93:90+ F 28 '69
Mini-boot, new four-wheel-drive dune buggy. J. Wright. il Pop Sci 195:179-81 Ag '69
Mini-Boot: the first 4x4 dune buggy for under $2500. V. L. Oertle. il Pop Mech 131:52 Je '69
Muckmobiles. il Hot Rod 22:120 My '69
Off-road going, in style. B. Kilpatrick. il Pop Mech 132:102-5 Ag '69
Snoopy, the mini dune buggy. H. Shuldiner. il Pop Sci 195:50 D '69
Starcraft's hefty haf-pint; all-terrain vehicle. D. Fales. il Pop Mech 132:110-13 S '69
Surfers stoke streetcars. J. Hodge. il Hot Rod 22:62-3 My '69
Youth gets bitten by the buggy; dune buggy craze. il Bsns W p66-7+ My 3 '69
See also
Automobiles
Crawler vehicles
Jeep automobiles
Snowmobiles

Bodies
Dune buggy bodies in ten brilliant colors. H. Shuldiner. il Pop Sci 195:45-7+ Ag '69

Laws and regulations
Your snowmobile and the law. H. Shuldiner. Pop Sci 195:134-5 N '69
See also
Automobile laws and regulations

Testing
PM tests:
OMC's secret green machine; all-terrain vehicle. B. Kilpatrick. il Pop Mech 131:102-5 Je '69

MOTOR vehicles, Amphibious
ATV with muscles; Moto brousse. A. Laidlaw. il Mech Illus 65:48-9 N '69
New ATV: twenty horses for the trail. E. F. Lindsley. il Pop Sci 195:102-3 N '69
This eagle can swim! il Mech Illus 65:63 D '69
Those amazing A.T.V.'s; all-terrain vehicle. B. Behme. il Field & S 74:48-51+ Ag '69
What kind of ATV is best for you? all-terrain vehicles. E. F. Lindsley. il Pop Sci 195:71-7+ S '69

MOTOR vehicles, Military
See also
Tanks, Military

MOTOR vehicles, Municipal
See also
Tractors, Municipal

MOTOR vehicles, Police
Station wagon most versatile police vehicle; Sioux City, Ia. il Am City 84:30 N '69

MOTORCYCLE brakes. See Brakes, Motorcycle
MOTORCYCLE helmets. See Helmets
MOTORCYCLE racing
Bake. D. Wells. Motor T 21:94-5+ O '69
Economy run with a twist. B. Greene. il Hot Rod 22:146-7 My '69
Hi-octane gas. B. Greene. il Hot Rod 22:136-7 D '69
Naked record. il Hot Rod 22:132-3 F '69
Space shot. B. Greene. il Hot Rod 22:108-11 Ja '69
Straightshooters; SCTA speed trials. B. Greene. il Hot Rod 22:102-3 N '69
Who really won Daytona? B. Greene. il Hot Rod 22:116-18+ Je '69
MOTORCYCLE riding. See Motorcycling
MOTORCYCLES
Collapsible motorbike fits in car trunk. T. Robinson. il Pop Sci 194:26 F '69
Commando! B. Greene. il Hot Rod 22:102-3 Mr '69
Ground-level flyin' machine. B. Greene. il Hot Rod 22:150-1 O '69
Honda's big four. B. Greene. il Hot Rod 22:112-13 My '69
Italian sidewinder. B. Greene. il Hot Rod 22:104-5 F '69
Japanese doll. T. Murphy. il Hot Rod 22:88-9 S '69
Join the navy, launch a bike; Japanese sales to sailors. B. Greene. il Hot Rod 22:134-5 N '69
Kawasaki Mach III. B. Greene il Hot Rod 22:104-5 Ap '69
Kawasaki Mach III: the hottest thing on two wheels. J. Davis. il Pop Sci 194:88-9+ My '69
Kit turns your motorcycle into a three-wheel sports car. J. Davis. il Pop Sci 195:124-5 Ag '69
Little big bike; Benelli Mini-Scrambler. B. Greene. il Hot Rod 22:108-9 Jl '69
Riding Honda's fabulous four. J. Davis. il Pop Sci 195:108-9+ S '69
Savage; Suzuki TS-250 Savage. B. Greene. il Hot Rod 22:102-4 Ag '69
Take five; five-cylinder scooter. B. Greene. il Hot Rod 22:128-9 S '69
This trail bike is really put together! B. Hartford. il Pop Mech 131:40+ Je '69
Trail bike you build from a kit. H. Luckett. il Pop Sci 194:106-7 Ap '69
Up on two wheels. B. Greene. See issues of Hot rod
Yamaha 125, small bike with big power. J. Davis. il Pop Sci 194:102-3+ Ja '69
See also
Motorcycling

Equipment
Add winter comfort to your cycle; fairing to reduce drag. H. Humphrey. il Pop Mech 132:194 N '69
Take the family along, with a sidecar. J. Davis. il Pop Sci 195:124-5 D '69

Frames
Pipe dream that came true. B. Greene. il Hot Rod 22:102-4 D '69

Gearing
Ready for a changer? il Hot Rod 22:108 D '69

Maintenance and repair
ABCs of servicing a motorbike. J. B. Nicholson. il Mech Illus 65:64-6 +Jl '69

Testing
SR 125: new mail-order beauty from Austria. J. Davis. il Pop Sci 195:118-19+ Jl '69
MOTORCYCLES, Remodeled
Hop-up for a motorbike. il Mech Illus 65:98-100 S '69
MOTORCYCLES, Used
How to buy a used motorcycle. il Pop Sci 194:110-11 Je '69
MOTORCYCLING
Midnight run. B. Greene. il Hot Rod 22:144-5 Jl '69
News on wheels; you and the motorcycle. M. Spiegel. Sr Schol 94:22 Mr 14 '69

Study and teaching
Fun and games on the freeway. B. Greene. il Hot Rod 22:140-1 Mr '69

Stunt cycling
Evel Knievel's cup of anguish. D. Lyle. il Esquire 73:88-91+ Ja '70
MOTORS. See Electric motors
MOTORS, Outboard. See Gas and oil engines, Outboard

MOTOWN record corporation
Detroit retools its rock; the Motown comeback. A. Goldman. Life 67:12 Jl 25 '69

MOTT, Charles Stewart
Story of what a foundation did. por U S News 67:101 O 20 '69

MOTT, Lucretia (Coffin)
Lucretia Mott: women also have rights. por Sr Schol 94:19 Mr 21 '69

MOTT, Stewart R.
Model philanthropist; interview. New Yorker 45:28-31 S 6 '69

MOTT foundation. See Foundations, Charitable and educational

MOTTA group. See Italy—Industries

MOTTOES
    See also
Newspapers—Mastheads

MOULD, Daphne D. C. Pochin. See Pochin Mould, D. D. C.

MOULTON, Lillie (Greenough) See Hegermann-Lindencrone, L. G. M.

MOULTON, Robert
Helping actors to act human. Dance Mag 43:76-7 My '69

MOUND BAYOU, Miss.
Stir of hope in Mound Bayou; with editorial comment, and photographs by H. Bingham. R. Hall. Life 66:3, 66-70+ Mr 28 '69

MOUNDS and mound builders
And the mound-builders vanished from the earth; Adena, Hopewell and Temple Indian mounds. R. Silverberg. il Am Heritage 20:60-3+ Je '69
    See also
Effigy Mounds National Monument

MOUNT, William Sidney
William S. Mount: the mysterious stranger. A. A. Davidson. il por Art N 68:34-7+ Mr '69

MOUNT ARARAT. See Ararat, Mount

MOUNT ATHOS. See Athos, Mount

MT BALDY wilderness area (proposed) See Wilderness areas—Arizona

MOUNT CLEMENS, Mich.
Mount Clemens: high school resource center. E. Giambrone. il ALA Bul 63:262-5 F '69

MOUNT HOLLY, N.J.
Gabions harness flood waters. D. Miller. il Am City 84:80-1 Ag '69

MOUNT Holyoke college, South Hadley, Mass.
Eldest sister starts to swing. B. B. Stretch. il Sat R 52:98 F 15 '69
    Library
World of libraries: past, present and future; symposium. bibliog il Wilson Lib Bul 43:518-44 F '69

MOUNT RAINIER NATIONAL PARK
Paradise ice caves; Mt Rainier glacial passageways. W. R. Halliday and C. H. Anderson, jr. il Nat Parks 43:13-14 O '69

MOUNT VERNON cricket; drama. See Miller, H. L.

MOUNTAIN beavers
Super flea meets mountain beaver. V. B. Scheffer. il Natur Hist 78:54-5 My '69

MOUNTAIN climbing. See Mountaineering

MOUNTAIN guides. See Guides

MOUNTAIN lions. See Pumas

MOUNTAIN men. See Trappers

MOUNTAIN plants. See Alpine flora

MOUNTAIN sheep
Once is enough. J. Chiappetta. il Field & S 74:46-7+ S '69

MOUNTAIN sheep hunting
Bowhunt for exotic sheep. G. H. Gillelan. il Outdoor Life 144:90-2 D '69
Just back of Tehran. W. Page. il Field & S 74:72-3+ N '69
Old naked face; British Columbia. R. S. Jackson. il Outdoor Life 144:52-5+ O '69
Stone rams in the Cassiar. J. O'Connor. il Outdoor Life 144:32-5+ D '69
Two guides and the no-peek sheep. G. Blair. il Field & S 74:54-5+ Ag '69

MOUNTAIN whites (southern states) See Mountaineers (southern states)

MOUNTAINEERING
Blind students conquer Mt Kilimanjaro; East Africans with training at Outward bound mountain school at Loitokitok. il Ebony 24:44-6+ Je '69
Climbing is not for amateurs; activities at the cliffs of Lake Mohonk. H. W. Trimm. il Cons 24:16-17 O '69
High above the Land of light. R. Cantwell. il Sports Illus 31:30-6 Jl 28 '69
Rocks in my head. R. Gannon. il Pop Sci 194:94-7+ Ap '69

What it takes to become a surefooted iceman. B. Spring and I. Spring. il Pop Mech 132:106-10 Ag '69
    Accidents
Death on Dhaulagiri; expedition headed by B. N. Everett. il Time 93:42 My 9 '69
Marooned at 12,000 feet. E. D. Fales, jr. il Pop Mech 131:86-90+ Je '69; Same abr. with title Impossible rescue. Read Digest 95:50-5 S '69
    Study and teaching
Indoor mountaineering. C. H. Emigh. il Parks & Rec 4:36-7 Jl '69
Thanks, I'll take the chair lift. C. W. Casewit. il Holiday 45:62-3+ My '69

MOUNTAINEERS (southern states)
U.S. journal: Jeremiah, Ky; killing of TV producer H. O'Connor by property owner H. Ison. C. Trillin. New Yorker 45:178-83 Ap 12 '69

MOUNTAINS
High ice, high rock; with photographs by A. Post. Audubon 71:28-33 My '69
Molasse facies: records of worldwide crustal stresses. F. B. Van Houten. bibliog il Science 166:1506-8 D 19 '69
    See also
Hindu Kush
Volcanoes

MOUNTAINS, Photography of. See Photography—Landscapes

MOUNTBATTEN, Louis, 1st earl Mountbatten of Burma. See Mountbatten of Burma, L. M.

MOUNTBATTEN of Burma, Louis Mountbatten, 1st earl
London; TV film series. The life and times of Lord Mountbatten. Q. Crewe. Vogue 153:110 Mr 1 '69

MOUNTED animals. See Hunting trophies

MOUNTZOURES, H. L.
Executor; story. New Yorker 45:44-7 S 20 '69
The medium; story. Redbook 134:72-3 N '69
1930 Olympics; story. New Yorker 45:127-30 Ap 5 '69

MOURNING dove shooting
Bang-up time in Mexico. V. Kraft. Sports Illus 31:66+ O 6 '69
Doves aren't dickey birds. G. X. Sand. il Field & S 74:60-1+ S '69
Gray balls of fire. B. East. il Outdoor Life 144:60-3+ Ag '69

MOUSSAKA. See Cookery, Greek

MOUSSE, Chocolate. See Desserts

MOUSSORGSKY, Modest Petrovich. See Musorgskii, M. P.

MOUSTERIAN culture. See Neanderthal race

MOUTH
Tobacco smoke toxicity: loss of human oral leukocyte function and fluid-cell metabolism. B. Eichel and H. A. Shahrik. bibliog il Science 166:1424-8 D 12 '69

MOUTH hygiene
    See also
Dentistry

MOVEMENT, Disorders of. See Movement disorders

MOVEMENT, Notation of. See Dance notation

MOVEMENT, Psychology of
Helping actors to act human; History and techniques of stage movement course. University of Minnesota. R. Moulton. il Dance Mag 43:76-7 My '69
How to read body language. F. Davis. il Read Digest 95:127-30 D '69

MOVEMENT disorders
Athetoid and choreiform hyperkinesias produced by caudate lesions in the cat. S. L. Liles and G. D. Davis. bibliog il Science 164:195-7 Ap 11 '69

MOVIE censorship. See Moving picture censorship

MOVIE shorts. See Moving pictures—Short subject films

MOVIES in the streets program. See New York (city)—Recreation

MOVING
ABCs of taking the misery out of moving. A. Markovich. il Mech Illus 65:56-8+ Je '69
Highway robbery. S. Raab. il McCalls 96:62-3+ Ja '69
Make your transfer easier. Am Home 72:76 Ja '69
Mobile society; one out of five of us will move this year. M. A. Guitar. Am Home 72:52-3 Ja '69
Moving to a different state? il Changing T 23:21-2 Je '69
Steps to take if you are moving. Good H 169:144 Ag '69
Transferee's guide to home fix-up. A. J. Maher. Am Home 72:74-5 Ja '69

MOVING and storage companies
Highway robbery. S. Raab. il McCalls 96:62-3+ Ja '69

MOVING finger writes; story. See Hoffmann, R.

MOVING of trees. See Tree planting

MOVING picture actors and actresses
Faces of the boys in the band. J. Star. il Look 33:62-7 D 2 '69
New ones: fresh and independent. il Time 93:50a-50f F 7 '69
On the vine in Hollywood. il Newsweek 74:116+ O 20 '69
Spotlight! E. Miller. See issues of Seventeen
Why the young killed movie superstars. R. Goldstein. Vogue 154:128+ Ag 1 '69
Writing for the fan magazine field. M. Fane. il Writers Digest 49:36-40 My '69
See also
Academy awards (moving pictures)
Make-up, Theatrical
Negro actors and actresses
also names of moving picture actors and actresses, e.g. R. Welch

MOVING picture adaptations. See Film adaptations

MOVING picture advertising. See Moving picture industry—Advertising

MOVING picture audiences
Art that matters. L. Cohen; S. Steiner. il Sat R 52:8-11+, 18-20 D 27 '69
Film as environment. A. Schillaci; discussion. Sat R 52:21+ Ja 25 '69
Have you seen 'Shoes'? S. W. Hosie. America 120:651-2 My 31 '69

MOVING picture authorship
Fiction and film: a search for new sources. S. Koch. il Sat R 52:12-14+ D 27 '69
Graham Greene: on the screen; interview, ed. by G. D. Phillips. G. Greene. Cath World 209:218-21 Ag '69
Television and film writing (cont) N. Vogel. Writers Digest 49:24-9 F; 82-7 Ap; 66-71 Ag '69
Writer; interview, ed. by S. Farber. A. Jacobs. il Film Q 22:2-14 Wint '68
Writers' dilemma; Writers guild of America conference discusses the question of writer control. A. Knight. Sat R 52:51 Ap 26 '69
See also
Moving picture scripts

MOVING picture awards
See also
Academy awards (moving pictures)
International Catholic film office

MOVING picture cameras
At last! Automatic camera focusing. il Mod Phot 33:90-1+ F '69
Expo '69: not much but something. il Mod Phot 33:56-61 S '69
Movie cameras are better than ever! S. Miller. il Mech Illus 65:62-3+ Jl '69
Movie equipment close-up; Beaulieu R16B. il Mod Phot 33:44 Ag '69
Movie equipment close-up; Eumig 308 zoom reflex super 8. il Mod Phot 33:81-2 O '69
Movie equipment close-up; Yashica super-60. il Mod Phot 33:159-60 Ap '69
Sensor introduces pressureless picture-taking; super compact super 8; Agfa's Microflexsensor. B. Schwalberg. il Pop Phot 65:100-1+ Jl '69
Which movie camera features do you really need? M. A. Matzkin. il Mod Phot 33:82-5+ Jl '69

Sound equipment
Matzkin on movies; super 8 sound. M. A. Matzkin. Mod Phot 33:26+ My '69

Testing
Canon Scoopic-16. J. J. Karamon. il U S Camera 32:60-2 Ja '69

MOVING picture cartoons. See Moving pictures—Animated cartoons

MOVING picture censorship
Sexy movies? Chadron, Neb. tries gentle persuasion. H. Moffett. il Life 66:52B-52D+ My 30 '69
Still Legion, still decent? R. Corliss. Commonweal 90:288-93 My 23 '69; Reply. J. P. Carrico. 90:423 Je 27 '69

MOVING picture criticism
After forty years of writing about movies, I know something about cinema and, being a congenital critic. D. Macdonald. Esquire 72:80-3+ Jl '69
Let us now praise Dwight Macdonald. J. Simon. Commonweal 91:68-70 O 17 '69
Manhandling the movies. R. T. Jameson. Film Q 22:4-11 Spr '69

MOVING picture criticisms. See Moving picture plays—Criticisms, plots, etc.

MOVING picture critics. See Critics

MOVING picture directors
And now some sacred cows to the kill. R. Reed. Holiday 45:22+ My '69
Artist risking all, a film to remember. R. Schickel. il Life 66:9 My 23 '69
Can this be America? personal statements of 1968 election campaign. R. L. Shayon. Sat R 52:51 F 22 '69
Film maker as ascendant star. il Time 94:46-51 Jl 4 '69
Five directors, five films. H. V. Fondiller. il Pop Phot 65:116-17+ O '69
See also
Antonioni, M.
Bergman, I.
Cassavetes, J.
Downey, R.
Fellini, F.
Godard, J L.
Huston, J.
Lester, R.
Pasolini, P. P.
Penn, A.
Renoir, J.
Resnais, A.
Sjöman, V.
Truffaut, F.

MOVING picture editing. See Moving pictures—Editing

MOVING picture festivals
Cats: first International cat film festival, or. Intercat '69. New Yorker 45:19-20 Ja 3 '70
Film festival farrago; New York. J. M. Wall. Chr Cent 86:1455-6 N 12 '69
Film festival; Lincoln Center. H. Clurman. Nation 209:389-90 O 13 '69
Film scene at Pula; Yugoslav film festival. C. Harnack. Nation 209:676+ D 15 '69
Films; New York film festival. W. Sheed. Esquire 71:34+ Ja '69
Foreshadowing an Esquire college film festival. A. Gingrich. Esquire 72:6 Ag '69
Leading back to Renoir; Lincoln Center festival. P. Gilliatt. New Yorker 45:96+ S 6 '69
Lively arts; seventh annual New York film festival. R. Hemming and W. Johnson. Sr Schol 95:23 O 27 '69
Man within: the New York film festival. G. D. Phillips. il Cath World 210:175-8 Ja '70
Modest fame; New York film festival. il Time 94:100+ O 10 '69
New York film festival. R. Corliss. Nat R 21:1177-9 N 18 '69
New York's film festival no. seven. il Newsweek 74:118+ O 6 '69
Opening; New York film festival. New Yorker 45:31-2 S 27 '69
Politics at the festival; the New York film festival. L. J. Berry. Commonweal 91:103 O 24 '69
What is a festival film? A. Knight. Sat R 52:99 S 13 '69
See also
Cannes international film festival

MOVING picture films
Matzkin on movies; faster Ektachrome EF super 8. M. A. Matzkin. Mod Phot 33:50+ N '69
Matzkin on movies; film for super 8 cameras. M. A. Matzkin. Mod Phot 33:26 F '69

MOVING picture holography. See Holography

MOVING picture industry
See also
Moving picture production and direction

Advertising
Laundering the sheets; movie-ad censorship. il Time 93:54 My 30 '69

Finance
Last days of Babylon? il Forbes 104:65-6+ N 1 '69
Why don't they get a new script? il Forbes 103:30-1 Je 15 '69

Regulation
See Moving picture laws and regulations

Hungary
New wave in Hungary. il Newsweek 75:75 Ja 12 '70

India
At home in Calcutta. B. Taper. Harper 239:40-2+ D '69
Indian cinema today. C. Das Gupta. il Film Q 22:27-35 Sum '69

United States
Darryl's antic; bill to prohibit military aid to commercial movies. New Repub 160:11 Je 28 '69

MOVING picture industry—United States—
Continued
Hollywood: myth, fact and trouble. J. Morgenstern. il Newsweek 73:82+ Je 30 '69
Last tycoons. H. Gould. Commentary 48:74-7
Jl '69
Movies get new moguls; conglomerates wooing
Hollywood. il Bsns W p29-30 F 8 '69
Multi-gadget movie van rolls into Hollywood; cinemobile. il Bsns W p 152-4 Mr 15
'69
New kind of movie shakes Hollywood; low-budget films made on location. il Bsns W
p40-1+ Ja 3 '70
Spot check: some observations on films in
America. J. Claman. il Harp Baz 102:122S
F '69
Stanley Kauffmann on films. S. Kauffmann.
New Repub 160:22+ My 10 '69
Studio, by J. G. Dunne. Review
Newsweek 73:114+ My 12 '69. P. D. Zimmerman
See also
Metro-Goldwyn-Mayer, incorporated
Paramount pictures corporation
Warner brothers pictures, incorporated

MOVING picture laws and regulations
Courts grant and deny film privacy injunctions: cases of the moving pictures. Boston
strangler and Titicut follies. H. F. Pilpel
and K. P. Norwick. Pub W 196:37-8 D 29
'69

MOVING picture literature
Movie-book boom. R. A. Sokolov. il Newsweek 74:90+ D 1 '69

MOVING picture make-up. See Make-up,
Theatrical

MOVING picture montage. See Photomontage

MOVING picture music. See Moving pictures
—Music

MOVING picture periodicals. See Moving pictures—Periodicals

MOVING picture photography
Antonioni: from super 8 to panavision. H. V.
Fondiller. il Pop Phot 65:112-13 S '69
First 100 feet are the hardest. i. Berger. Pop
Phot 64:112+ Ap '69
Let's make a movie. D. Molner. il Schol
Teach Sec Teach Sup p30+ S 22 '69
Matzkin on movies. M. A. Matzkin. See issues of Modern photography
Movie Q's and A's. J. R. Gregory. See issues
of Travel & camera
One movie image can be five. M. A. Matzkin.
il Mod Phot 33:108+ N '69
Pan, tilt, sweep, zoom, but shoot! W. Lane.
il Travel 132:76 O '69

Apparatus and supplies
Era of silent films ended for amateur travel
photographer. W. Clark. Holiday 46:49 O
'69
Movie equipment close-up (cont) Mod Phot
33:159-60 Ap; 147-9 Je: 44 Ag: 81-2 O '69
Movie Q's and A's. J. R. Gregory. See issues
of Travel & camera
You don't need an electric outlet to make
movies at night. H. Samuels. il Pop Sci
195:89 D '69

Copying
Matzkin on movies; good dupes from super
8 originals? M. A. Matzkin. Mod Phot
33:12+ Ag '69

Exposure
Manual override of the electric eye may get
you into big trouble instead of bailing you
out. M. A. Matzkin. il Mod Phot 33:46+
Je '69

Films
See Moving picture films

Focusing
For movies: let the action call the shot.
M. A. Matzkin. il Mod Phot 33:89-9+ N
'69
Zoom? D. Langer. il Pop Phot 64:114-15+
My '69

MOVING picture photography, Submarine
Dangerous creatures of the deep. C. B. Jackson. il Nat Wildlife 7:50-5 Ag '69
How we film under the sea. J. Cousteau. il
Pop Sci 194:65-9+ F '69

MOVING picture photography, Trick
Make a way-out movie. N. Rothschild. il
Pop Phot 64:104-5+ F '69

MOVING picture photography in advertising
Movies sell a magic show. M. Helms. il Pop
Phot 65:106-7+ Ag '69

MOVING picture plays
See also
Film adaptations
Moving pictures
Television broadcasting—Moving pictures

Anecdotes, facetiae, satire,
etc.
What should parents see? S. Robinson. Seventeen 28:42+ Ja '69

Criticisms, plots, etc.
At the movies. R. Reed. See issues of Holiday
Baker's dozen; comp. by J. Morgenstern. il
Newsweek 75:74 Ja 12 '70
Catch up with. L. Lerman. See issues of
Mademoiselle
Current cinema. P. Gilliatt. See issues of New
Yorker March 22 to September 20, 1969
Current cinema. P. Kael. See issues of New
Yorker January 18 to March 15, 1969; September 27—
Emphasis: on films. Harp Baz 103:226 N '69
Family movie guide; ed. by J. Ripp. See
issues of Parents' magazine & better family
living
Film chronicle. R. Corliss. il Nat R 21:82-3,
292-3, 1177-9 Ja 28, Mr 25, N 18 '69
Films. J. Brackman. See issues of Esquire
Films. R. Hatch. See issues of Nation
Films. W. Sheed. See issues of Esquire
Films. M. Walsh. See issues of America
Films for the popcorn brigade. R. Reed. il
Holiday 45:20+ Je '69
Flash-back on films. F. Tuten. Vogue 154:
62 S 15 '69
Following the films. M. Ronan. See issues of
Senior scholastic
Goings on about town. See issues of New
Yorker
Laurels and lemons; National society of film
critics annual awards. S. Kauffmann. New
Repub 160:22+ Ja 25 '69
Life movie review. R. Schickel. See issues
of Life
Look at the movies (cont) G. Shalit. il Look
33:66 F 18; 51 Mr 4; 84 Mr 18; 76 Ap 1; 60
Ap 29; 57 My 13; 16 Je 10; 20 Je 24; 20 Jl 15;
16 Jl 29; 14 Ag 26; 43 S 9; 65 S 23; 70 O
21; 92 N 4 '69
Media and manners; film and society in some
current British films. I. Jarvie. il Film Q
22:11-17 Spr '69
Motion picture previews. E. Whitehorn. See
issues of PTA magazine
Movie report. B. Falconer. See issues of
Good housekeeping
Movies. See issues of Consumer reports
Movies. A. Schlesinger, jr. See issues of
Vogue
Movies. D. Wakefield. See issues of Atlantic
New movies. See issues of Redbook
Ratings of current motion pictures. See issues of Consumer bulletin
SR goes to the movies. H. Alpert; R. Gelatt;
A. Knight. See issues of Saturday review
Screen. P. T. Hartung. See issues of Commonweal
Short notices. Film Q 22:58-64 Spr '69
Sight and sound. See issues of McCall's
Spotlight! E. Miller. See issues of Seventeen
Stanley Kauffmann on films. S. Kauffmann.
See issues of New republic
Three to skip. M. Walsh. America 120:656
My 31 '69
Time listings. See issues of Time
Today's movies. R. L. Coe. il Todays Ed 58:
20-2 Mr '69

Single works
Adalen 31
Life 67:15 N 7 '69
New Repub 161:20+ O 25 '69
New Yorker 45:164-5 N 8 '69
Sat R 52:28 N 1 '69
Alexander
Newsweek il 73:100A Ap 28 '69
Alfred the Great
America 121:600 D 13 '69
New Yorker 45:175 D 13 '69
Alice's restaurant
Atlan 224:170-2 N '69
Chr Cent 86:1555-6 D 3 '69
Esquire 72:82+ N '69
Life 67:8 Ag 29 '69
Mlle 69:54 O '69
Nat R 21:971 S 23 '69
Nation 209:294 S 22 '69
New Repub 161:22+ S 27 '69
New Yorker 45:96 S 6 '69
Newsweek il 74:68-9 S 1 '69
Newsweek il 74:101-4+ S 29 '69
Sat R 52:35 Ag 30 '69
Time il 94:64 Ag 29 '69
All neat in black stocking
Time 94:98 O 3 '69
All the loving couples
New Yorker 45:162 N 29 '69
Among the paths to Eden
Time 94:92+ N 21 '69
Andrei Rublev
New Yorker 45:179-81 D 13 '69

MOVING picture plays—Criticisms, plots, etc.—
   Single works—*Continued*
Angel Levine
   Ebony il 24:76-8+ O '69
April fools
   Commonweal 90:417 Je 27 '69
   New Yorker 45:83 Je 14 '69
   Newsweek 73:111 Je 9 '69
   Sat R 52:26 Je 14 '69
   Time 93:108 Je 6 '69
Arrangement
   New Yorker 45:211-12+ N 22 '69
   Newsweek il 74:118 N 24 '69
   Sat R 52:68 N 22 '69
   Time 94:92 N 21 '69
   Vogue 155:74 Ja 1 '70
Assassination bureau
   America 120:428-9 Ap 5 '69
   Time 93:104 Ap 11 '69
Baby love
   Commonweal 90:114 Ap 11 '69
   Time 93:92 Ap 4 '69
Barbarella
   Atlan 223:141 Ap '69
   Chr Cent 86:238 F 12 '69
Battle of Algiers
   Film Q 22:26-31 Spr '69
Battle of Britain
   America 121:399-400 N 1 '69
   Holiday 46:30 D '69
   Sat R 52:32 O 25 '69
   Sr Schol 95:24 O 27 '69
   Time 94:102+ O 24 '69
Bed sitting room
   Nation 209:452 O 27 '69
   New Repub 161:22+ O 18 '69
   New Yorker 45:159 O 11 '69
   Newsweek il 74:97-97A+ N 3 '69
Before winter comes
   America 120:550 My 3 '69
   Newsweek 73:120+ Ap 21 '69
   Sr Schol 94:26 Mr 7 '69
Ben-Hur
   Commonweal 90:515 Ag 22 '69
Bezhin meadow
   New Repub 160:20+ Mr 1 '69
Les biches
   Atlan 223:140 Ap '69
Big bounce
   America 120:344 Mr 22 '69
   Commonweal 90:114 Ap 11 '69
   Sat R 52:46 Je 7 '69
Birds of Peru
   Film Q 22:52-5 Wint '68
Birthday party
   Commonweal 89:591 F 7 '69
   Esquire 71:34 F '69
   Holiday 45:30 Mr '69
   McCalls 96:131 F '69
   Sr Schol il 94:26 Mr 7 '69
Bob & Carol & Ted & Alice
   America 121:267-9 O 4 '69
   Commonweal 91:247-9 N 21 '69
   Esquire 73:38+ Ja '70
   Holiday 46:53 O '69
   Life 67:17 O 3 '69
   Mlle 69:54 O '69
   New Repub 161:32 O 25 '69
   New Yorker 45:144+ O 4 '69
   Sat R 52:51+ O 11 '69
   Time il 94:94 S 26 '69
   Vogue 154:118 N 1 '69
Boom!
   Film Q 22:52-5 Wint '68
Boston strangler
   Esquire 71:32+ Mr '69
Boudu saved from drowning
   New Yorker 45:96+ S 6 '69
Boys of Paul street
   Commonweal 90:516 Ag 22 '69
   Newsweek il 74:85-85A Jl 14 '69
   Time il 93:81 Je 27 '69
Brain
   America 121:544 N 29 '69
   Newsweek 74:89 D 1 '69
   Time il 94:114 D 5 '69
Brotherhood
   America 120:144-6 F 1 '69
   Commonweal 89:654 F 21 '69
   New Repub 160:22 Ja 25 '69
   New Yorker 44:95-8 Ja 25 '69
   Newsweek il 73:89 F 3 '69
   Time il 93:62 Ja 24 '69
Bullitt
   Sr Schol il 94:29 Ja 31 '69
Buona sera. Mrs Campbell
   Holiday 45:40 Ap '69
Butch Cassidy and the Sundance Kid
   America 121:306-8 O 11 '69
   Life il 67:16 O 24 '69
   Look il 33:70 O 21 '69
   New Repub 161:32 O 25 '69
   New Yorker 45:127-9 S 27 '69
   Newsweek il 74:116 O 13 '69
   Sat R 52:30 S 20 '69
   Sat R 52:39 S 27 '69
   Time il 94:94 S 26 '69

Cactus flower
   Holiday 46:23 N '69
   Newsweek 74:55 D 29 '69
   Sat R 52:38 D 20 '69
   Time il 94:78 D 19 '69
   Vogue 154:118 N 1 '69
Can Heironymus Merkin ever forget Mercy
   Humppe and find true happiness?
   Chr Cent 87:24 Ja 7 '70
   Commonweal 90:144-5 Ap 18 '69
   Newsweek il 73:82 Ap 7 '69
   Sat R 52:50 Ap 5 '69
   Time il 93:88 Mr 28 '69
Candy
   Atlan 223:140-1 Ap '69
   Chr Cent 86:238 F 12 '69
   Harper 238:111 Mr '69
Castle
   Chr Cent 86:815 Je 11 '69
   Time il 93:88 Mr 28 '69
Castle keep
   Life 67:12 Ag 1 '69
   New Yorker 45:67 Jl 26 '69
   Newsweek 74:74 Ag 11 '69
   Sat R 52:22 Ag 9 '69
Chairman
   New Repub 160:26 Je 28 '69
   New Yorker 45:74-5 Jl 5 '69
   Time il 94:79 Jl 11 '69
La chamade
   Sat R 52:37 Ag 16 '69
   Time il 94:65 Ag 22 '69
Changes
   Atlan 224:109 Jl '69
   Commonweal 90:75 Ap 4 '69
   Esquire 72:130 Jl '69
   Sat R 52:59 Ap 12 '69
   Sr Schol 94:20 Mr 21 '69
Charge of the Light brigade
   Atlan 223:115-16 Ja '69
   Chr Cent 86:715.16 My 21 '69
Charly
   Nat R 21:607 Je 17 '69
Chastity
   Time il 94:77 Jl 18 '69
Che!
   Chr Cent 86:1045 Ag 6 '69
   Nation 208:806 Je 23 '69
   New Repub 160:22 Je 21 '69
   New Yorker 45:83 Je 14 '69
   Newsweek il 73:101-2 Je 16 '69
   Time 93:103+ Je 13 '69
Chitty chitty bang bang
   Commonweal 89:529 Ja 24 '69
Christmas tree
   America 121:308 O 11 '69
   Time 94:98 O 3 '69
Circus
   Newsweek 75:63 Ja 5 '70
   Time il 95:54 Ja 5 '70
Comic
   New Yorker 45:190+ D 6 '69
   Time il 94:103+ D 12 '69
Coming apart
   Esquire 72:16+ O '69
   Life 67:16 O 17 '69
   Nation 209:613 D 1 '69
   New Repub 161:32 N 15 '69
   New Yorker 45:142 N 1 '69
   Newsweek il 74:98 N 3 '69
   Sat R 52:39 N 8 '69
   Time il 94:105-6 N 7 '69
Les créatures
   Time 93:99 Mr 14 '69
Daddy's gone-a-hunting
   Sat R 52:21 Jl 5 '69
Damned
   America 121:642 D 27 '69
   New Yorker 45:61-2 Ja 3 '70
   Pop Phot il 65:117+ O '69
   Sat R 52:21 D 27 '69
   Time il 95:53 Ja 5 '70
Death of a gunfighter
   Time il 93:114+ My 23 '69
Decline and fall of a bird watcher
   Chr Cent 86:323 Mr 5 '69
   Commonweal 90:48 Mr 28 '69
   Nation 208:187 F 10 '69
   New Repub 160:22+ F 15 '69
   Sat R 52:50 F 15 '69
de Sade
   New Yorker 45:160-1 O 11 '69
   Time il 94:106 O 24 '69
Detour
   Commonweal 90:594 S 26 '69
   New Yorker 45:76 Ag 16 '69
Devil by the tail
   Time il 94:78 Jl 18 '69
Devil's bride
   Sr Schol il 94:20 Mr 21 '69
Dr?? Coppelius!!
   Time 93:75 Ja 31 '69
Doctor Glas
   New Repub 160:24+ Ap 19 '69
Don't drink the water
   America 121:544 N 29 '69
Double-stop
   Sat R 52:40 F 1 '69

MOVING picture plays—Criticisms, plots, etc.—
  Single works—*Continued*
  Downhill racer
    America 121:508 N 22 '69
    Life 67:18 D 5 '69
    New Yorker 45:179-81 N 15 '69
    Newsweek il 74:118+ N 24 '69
    Time il 94:101 N 14 '69
  Dracula has risen from the grave
    Sr Schol 94:29 Ja 31 '69
  Dream of kings
    Holiday 46:30 D '69
    Sat R 53:74 Ja 3 '70
  Duet for cannibals
    Commonweal 91:306-7 D 5 '69
    Nation 209:515+ N 10 '69
    New Repub 161:32 N 15 '69
    New Yorker 45:141-2 N 1 '69
    Time 94:96 S 26 '69
    Vogue 154:64 O 15 '69
  Easy rider
    America 121:126 Ag 30 '69
    Atlan 224:120-4 O '69
    Chr Cent 86:1169 S 10 '69
    Chr Cent 86:1491 N 19 '69
    Commonweal 90:487 Ag 8 '69
    Esquire 72:12+ S '69
    Esquire 72:14 O '69
    Holiday 46:14 Ag '69
    Life 67:10 Jl 11 '69
    Look il 33:16 Jl 29 '69
    Nat R 21:971 S 23 '69
    Nation 209:125-6 Ag 11 '69
    New Repub 161:22+ Ag 2 '69
    New Yorker 45:70-2 Jl 19 '69
    New Yorker 45:127 S 27 '69
    Newsweek il 74:95+ Jl 21 '69
    Sat R 52:20 Jl 12 '69
    Time il 94:73+ Jl 25 '69
    Vogue 154:64 Ag 1 '69
  End of the road
    Life il 67:64-72 N 7 '69
    Sat R 52:39 D 27 '69
    Vogue 155:76 Ja 15 '70
  Extraordinary seaman
    Sr Schol 94:24 Mr 14 '69
  Faces
    America 120:203 F 15 '69
    Chr Cent 86:352 Mr 12 '69
    Esquire 71:38+ Ja '69
    Film Q il 22:31-5 Spr '69
    Look 33:51 Mr 4 '69
  Fantastic plastic machine
    Commonweal 90:516 Ag 22 '69
  Fearless Frank
    Time 95:77 Ja 12 '70
  Une femme douce
    Time 94:96 S 26 '69
  La femme infidèle
    America 121:600 D 13 '69
    Commonweal 91:337-8 D 12 '69
    Nation 209:612 D 1 '69
    New Yorker 45:158 N 29 '69
    Newsweek 74:89 D 1 '69
    Sat R 52:68 N 22 '69
  Finian's rainbow
    Dance Mag il 43:94-5 Mr '69
  Firemen's ball
    Chr Cent 86:258 F 19 '69
  First time
    Sat R 52:59 Ap 12 '69
  Fixer
    America 120:117 Ja 25 '69
    Esquire 71:38+ Ap '69
    New Repub 160:22+ Ja 25 '69
    Sr Schol il 94:24 Ap 25 '69
  Futz
    Esquire 72:86+ D '69
    New Repub 161:21+ N 15 '69
    New Yorker 45:158-62 N 29 '69
    Newsweek 74:118 N 24 '69
    Sat R 52:55 N 29 '69
    Time 94:95 N 21 '69
  Gaily, gaily
    Holiday 46:28+ D '69
    Life 67:10 D 19 '69
    New Yorker 45:70 D 20 '69
    Newsweek 75:62 Ja 5 '70
    Sat R 52:38 D 20 '69
    Time il 94:52 D 26 '69
  Les Gauloises bleues
    New Yorker 45:122+ My 24 '69
  Goodbye, Columbus
    America 120:484-5 Ap 19 '69
    Atlan 224:108 Jl '69
    Chr Cent 86:960 Jl 16 '69
    Commonweal 90:172 Ap 25 '69
    Esquire 72:130 Jl '69
    Life 66:12 Ap 25 '69
    Look 33:60 Ap 29 '69
    Nation 208:550 Ap 28 '69
    New Repub 160:24+ Ap 12 '69
    New Yorker 45:171-3 Ap 12 '69
    Newsweek il 73:115-115A Ap 14 '69
    Sat R 52:50 Ap 19 '69
    Time il 93:104 Ap 11 '69

Goodbye, Mr Chips
  America 121:476 N 15 '69
  Life il 67:9 N 14 '69
  New Yorker 45:161-4 N 8 '69
  Newsweek il 74:122+ N 17 '69
  Sat R 52:64 N 15 '69
  Time il 94:100 N 7 '69
Graduate
  Commonweal 90:202-4 My 2 '69
Grazie zia
  Nation 208:126 Ja 27 '69
  Time il 93:62 Ja 24 '69
Great bank robbery
  Commonweal 90:465 Jl 25 '69
  Pop Phot il 65:117+ O '69
  Time 94:79 Jl 11 '69
Greetings
  Esquire 71:42 Ap '69
  Time il 93:75 Ja 31 '69
Guru
  America 120:549 My 3 '69
  Harper 238:116-17 Ap '69
  Life 66:16 My 16 '69
  Nation 208:582 My 5 '69
  New Yorker 45:135-8 My 10 '69
  Sr Schol il 94:20 Ap 18 '69
  Time il 93:105 My 9 '69
Gypsy moths
  America 121:144 S 6 '69
  Life 67:24 S 26 '69
  New Yorker 45:73 Ag 30 '69
  Newsweek 74:82 S 8 '69
Hail, hero
  America 121:508 N 22 '69
  Life 67:20 N 28 '69
  Newsweek il 74:112+ N 10 '69
  Time 94:100 N 7 '69
Hamlet
  Time il 95:73+ Ja 12 '70
Hannibal Brooks
  Time 93:93 My 2 '69
Happy ending
  Life 67:10 D 19 '69
  Sat R 52:40 D 27 '69
Hard contract
  Chr Cent il 86:842-3 Je 18 '69
  New Yorker 45:114+ Je 7 '69
  Sat R 52:37 Mr 24 '69
  Time il 94:79 Jl 11 '69
Hell in the Pacific
  America 120:288 Mr 8 '69
  Commonweal 89:707-8 Mr 7 '69
  Film Q il 22:52-6 Sum '69
  Holiday 45:40 Ap '69
  New Yorker 45:74 Mr 1 '69
  Newsweek il 73:98 F 24 '69
  Sr Schol il 94:24 Mr 14 '69
  Time il 93:87 F 21 '69
Hellfighters
  Holiday 45:40 Ap '69
  Newsweek 73:98+ F 24 '69
Hello, Dolly!
  New Yorker 45:57-8+ Ja 3 '70
  Sat R il 53:30 Ja 10 '70
  Time il 94:52 D 26 '69
Hello down there
  Holiday 45:23 Je '69
I am curious (blue)
  Film Q 22:42-5 Sum '69
I am curious (yellow)
  Commonweal 90:293-4 My 23 '69
  Film Q il 22:37-42 Sum '69
  Life 66:12 Mr 21 '69
  Look 33:80+ Ap 29 '69
  Nat R 21:760 Jl 29 '69
  Nation 208:381-2 Mr 24 '69
  New Repub 160:22+ Mr 15 '69
  New Yorker 45:97-8 Ap 5 '69
  Newsweek il 73:114-15 Mr 24 '69
  Sat R 52:54 Mr 15 '69
  Time il 93:98 Mr 14 '69
  Vogue 153:34 Ap 15 '69
Ice Station Zebra
  Harper 238:111 Mr '69
  McCalls 96:131 F '69
  Sr Schol il 93:26 Ja 10 '69
If. . .
  America 120:313-14 Mr 15 '69
  Chr Cent 86:905 Jl 2 '69
  Commonweal 90:21-2 Mr 21 '69
  Film Q il 22:48-52 Sum '69
  Harper 238:115-16 Ap '69
  Life 66:8 F 28 '69
  Look il 33:84 Mr 18 '69
  Nat R 21:606 Je 17 '69
  Nation 208:348-9 Mr 17 '69
  New Repub 160:22 F 15 '69
  New Yorker 45:152+ Mr 15 '69
  Newsweek il 73:95 Mr 31 '69
  Sat R 52:50 F 15 '69
  Time il 93:97 Mr 21 '69
  Vogue 153:40 Mr 15 '69
If it's Tuesday, this must be Belgium
  America 120:550 My 3 '69
  Time 93:105 My 9 '69
  Travel il 131:72-5 Je '69

MOVING picture plays—Criticisms, plots, etc.—
  Single works—*Continued*
  Midnight cowboy
    America 120:737-8 Je 28 '69
    Chr Cent 86:1400-2 O 29 '69
    Commonweal 90:393-4 Je 20 '69
    Esquire 72:14+ O '69
    Look il 33:20 Je 24 '69
    Mlle il 69:74 S '69
    Nation 208:774 Je 16 '69
    New Repub 160:20+ Je 7 '69
    New Yorker 45:80 My 31 '69
    New Yorker 45:127 S 27 '69
    Newsweek il 73:90+ Je 2 '69
    Newsweek il 74:85 Jl 28 '69
    Sat R 52:44 My 31 '69
    Time il 93:89 My 30 '69
    Vogue 154:52 Jl '69
  Milky way
    New Yorker 45:119-20 Ap 5 '69
    Sat R 52:28 D 13 '69
    Time il 94:103+ N 28 '69
    Vogue 155:80 Ja 1 '70
  Model shop
    Commonweal 90:75 Ap 4 '69
    New Yorker 45:122+ F 22 '69
    Sat R 52:60 F 22 '69
    Time il 93:99 Mr 14 '69
  More
    Chr Cent 86:1253-4 O 1 '69
    New Yorker 45:77-8 Ag 16 '69
    Newsweek 74:80 Ag 25 '69
  Morning
    America 121:555-6 D 6 '69
  My side of the mountain
    America 121:48 Jl 19 '69
    Commonweal 90:320 My 30 '69
    Life 67:10 Jl 4 '69
    Sat R 52:40 Mr 1 '69
    Sr Schol 94:21 Ap 11 '69
    Time 93:E9 My 2 '69
  Myra Breckinridge
    Time il 94:85-8 N 28 '69
  Nice girl like me
    Sat R 52:20 Jl 12 '69
  Night of the following day
    America 120:344 Mr 22 '69
    Commonweal 89:737 Mr 14 '69
    New Yorker 45:116-17 Mr 8 '69
    Time il 93:98 Mr 14 '69
  Night of the living dead
    Read Digest 49:127-8 Je '69
  Night they raided Minsky's
    Chr Cent 86:155 Ja 29 '69
    Harper 238:110 Mr '69
    New Yorker 44:76+ Ja 18 '69
  Number one
    Chr Cent 86:1283-4 O 8 '69
    New Yorker 45:152-3 S 20 '69
    Sat R 52:35 Jl 26 '69
  Oh! What a lovely war
    America 121:368-70 O 25 '69
    Holiday 46:23 N '69
    Life 67:17 O 10 '69
    Look il 33:92 N 4 '69
    Mlle il 69:74 S '69
    Nation 209:452 O 27 '69
    New Repub 161:22 O 18 '69
    New Yorker 45:157-8 O 11 '69
    Newsweek 74:116-17 O 13 '69
    Sat R 52:34 O 4 '69
    Vogue 154:150 O 1 '69
  Oliver!
    Commonweal 89:528-9 Ja 24 '69
    Dance Mag il 43:25 Je '69
    Holiday 45:30-1 Mr '69
    Life 66:16 Ap 4 '69
    Sr Schol il 94:22 F 7 '69
  On Her Majesty's secret service
    Newsweek 74:56 D 29 '69
    Sat R 53:30 Ja 10 '70
  Once upon a time in the West
    Commonweal 90:439 Jl 11 '69
    New Repub 160:22+ Je 21 '69
    Newsweek 73:108+ Je 9 '69
  100 rifles
    America 120:456 Ap 12 '69
  One Neetah and Mickey
    America 121:556 D 6 '69
  Only when I larf
    McCalls 96:131 F '69
  Otley
    America 120:429 Ap 5 '69
  Paint your wagon
    America 121:474-5 N 15 '69
    Dance Mag 43:31+ D '69
    Mlle 69:190-1 O '69
    New Yorker 45:176-9 O 25 '69
    Newsweek il 74:124 O 27 '69
    Sat R 52:64 N 15 '69
    Time il 94:100+ O 24 '69
  People meet and sweet music fills the heart
    Sat R 52:41 My 10 '69
    Time 93:116 My 23 '69

  Pierrot Le Fou
    Holiday 45:22 My '69
    Nation 208:126 Ja 27 '69
    New Repub 160:22+ F 22 '69
    Newsweek il 73:86 Ja 27 '69
  Place for lovers
    America 121:144 S 6 '69
    Time il 94:95 S 19 '69
  Popi
    America 120:675-6 Je 7 '69
    Chr Cent 86:1423-4 N 5 '69
    Commonweal 90:416 Je 27 '69
    Holiday 45:22-3 Je '69
    Life 66:16 My 30 '69
    Look 33:16 Je 10 '69
    New Yorker 45:81-2 My 31 '69
    Newsweek il 73:108 Je 9 '69
    Sat R 52:44 My 31 '69
    Sr Schol 94:25 My 9 '69
    Time il 93:108 Je 6 '69
  Prime of Miss Jean Brodie
    America 120:312-13 Mr 15 '69
    Atlan 224:123-4 S '69
    Chr Cent 86:521-2 Ap 16 '69
    Commonweal 90:48-9 Mr 28 '69
    Holiday 45:40 Ap '69
    Look il 33:76 Ap 1 '69
    Nat R 21:606 Je 17 '69
    New Repub 160:20 Mr 1 '69
    New Yorker 45:160-1 Mr 15 '69
    Newsweek 73:82+ Ap 7 '69
    Redbook 133:38 My '69
    Sat R 52:36 Mr 8 '69
    Sr School 94:25 My 9 '69
    Time 93:83 Mr 7 '69
    Vogue 153:154 Ap 1 '69
  La prisonnière
    Commonweal 90:294 My 23 '69
    Life 66:15 My 9 '69
    Nation 208:444 Ap 7 '69
    New Yorker 45:173 Ap 12 '69
    Newsweek il 73:115A+ Ap 14 '69
    Time 93:104 Ap 11 '69
    Vogue 153:136 My '69
  Putney Swope
    Chr Cent 86:1352 O 22 '69
    Commonweal 90:544 S 5 '69
    Life 67:16 Ag 22 '69
    Nation 209:126 Ag 11 '69
    New Repub 161:24+ Ag 23 '69
    New Yorker 45:46+ Ag 2 '69
    Newsweek il 74:85 Jl 28 '69
    Sat R 52:51 Ag 23 '69
    Time il 94:76 Ag 1 '69
    Vogue 154:342 S 1 '69
  Rain people
    Chr Cent 86:1673 D 31 '69
    Holiday 46:52 O '69
    Newsweek il 74:82 S 8 '69
    Pop Phot il 65:116+ O '69
  Red and the white
    Life 66:12 My 2 '69
    Nation 208:478 Ap 14 '69
    New Repub 160:24 Ap 19 '69
    New Yorker 45:106+ Mr 29 '69
    Newsweek il 73:85 Ap 7 '69
  Reivers
    Life 67:10 D 19 '69
    New Yorker 45:47 D 27 '69
    Newsweek il 75:63 Ja 5 '70
    Sat R 53:74 Ja 3 '70
    Time il 95:53 Ja 5 '70
  La religieuse
    Film Q il 22:44-7 Spr '69
  Report on the party and the guests
    Esquire 71:34+ Ja '69
  Ring of bright water
    America 121:48 Jl 19 '69
    Commonweal 90:321 My 30 '69
    Holiday 45:20+ Je '69
    Life 67:10 Jl 4 '69
    Time 93:E10 My 2 '69
  Riot
    New Repub 160:22 Ja 25 '69
    Time il 93:75 Ja 31 '69
  Ritual
    Time 94:94+ S 26 '69
  Romeo and Juliet
    Chr Cent 86:420-1 Mr 26 '69
  Rosemary's baby
    Film Q 22:35-8 Spr '69
  Round up
    Nation 208:740-1 Je 9 '69
    New Repub 160:22 My 24 '69
    New Yorker 45:124+ My 17 '69
    Time il 93:109+ My 23 '69
  Royal hunt of the sun
    America 121:340 O 18 '69
    Life 67:17 O 24 '69
    New Yorker 45:196 O 18 '69
    Newsweek 74:117-18 O 13 '69
    Sat R 52:34 O 18 '69
    Sr Schol 95:24 O 6 '69
    Vogue 154:124 N 1 '69

MOVING picture plays—Criticisms, plots, etc.—
Single works—*Continued*
Rules of the game
New Yorker 45:150-2 S 20 '69
Run, Angel, run
Time 93:112+ My 23 '69
Run wild, run free
America 121:48 Jl 19 '69
Commonweal 90:320 My 30 '69
Holiday 45:22 Je '69
Life 67:10 Jl 4 '69
Time il 94:76 Ag 15 '69
Sam Whiskey
Commonweal 90:439 Jl 11 '69
Satyricon
Time il 94:96-7 S 12 '69
Sea gull
Chr Cent 86:686-7 My 14 '69
Commonweal 89:591 F 7 '69
Holiday 45:26+ Mr '69
Life 66:12 F 14 '69
Sat R 52:22 Ja 25 '69
Vogue 153:128 F 1 '69
Secret ceremony
McCalls 96:131 F '69
Secret of Santa Vittoria
America 121:600 D 13 '69
Life 67:17 O 24 '69
New Yorker 45:140-1 N 1 '69
Newsweek 74:121A N 24 '69
Sat R 52:32 O 25 '69
Time 94:105 N 7 '69
Sergeant
America 120:116 Ja 25 '69
Commonweal 89:502 Ja 17 '69
Esquire 71:36+ Mr '69
New Repub 160:22 Ja 25 '69
New Yorker 44:78-80 Ja 18 '69
Session with The Committee
Newsweek 74:78+ Ag 25 '69
Shalako
McCalls il (p48) 96:131 F '69
Shame
America 120:202 F 15 '69
Cath World il 209:247-50 S '69
Commonweal 89:563 Ja 31 '69
Esquire 71:32 Mr '69
Sat R 52:22 Ja 25 '69
Shoes of the fisherman
America 120:651-2 My 31 '69
Cath World il 208:264-7 Mr '69
Chr Cent 86:290+ F 26 '69
McCalls il 96:48+ F '69
Sr Schol il 94:21 Ja 17 '69
Sign of the virgin
Newsweek il 74:108 N 10 '69
Simon of the desert
Chr Cent 86:452 Ap 2 '69
Commonweal 89:676 F 28 '69
Holiday 45:22+ My '69
New Repub 160:22 Mr 8 '69
New Yorker 44:109-12+ F 15 '69
Slaves
America 121:245 S 27 '69
Commonweal 90:544 S 5 '69
Newsweek il 73:113+ My 26 '69
Smith!
Holiday 45:23 Je '69
Song and the silence
Time 93:93 F 14 '69
Spirits of the dead
Life 67:12 S 5 '69
New Repub 161:22 S 27 '69
New Yorker 45:143-4 S 13 '69
Newsweek il 74:102 S 15 '69
Time il 94:96 S 12 '69
Staircase
America 121:144 S 6 '69
Life 67:19 S 19 '69
New Repub 161:32 S 6 '69
New Yorker 45:74 Ag 30 '69
Newsweek il 74:68 S 1 '69
Time il 94:64 Ag 29 '69
Stalking moon
America 120:146 F 1 '69
Commonweal 89:653 F 21 '69
Newsweek il 73:89 F 3 '69
Sat R 52:40 F 1 '69
Time il 93:93 F 14 '69
Star!
Dance Mag 43:26+ Mr '69
Sterile cuckoo
America 121:505; N 22 '69
Holiday 46:22 N '69
Life 67:18+ N 28 '69
New Yorker 45:138-40 N 1 '69
Newsweek il 74:97 N 3 '69
Time il 94:91 O 31 '69
Vogue 154:142 D '69
Stiletto
Time 94:76 Ag 1 '69
Stolen kisses
America 120:485 Ap 19 '69
Atlan 224:108 Jl '69
Commonweal 90:75 Ap 4 '69
Film Q 22:56-9 Sum '69
Harper 238:115 Ap '69
Holiday 45:25 My '69

Life 66:18 Mr 7 '69
Nation 208:126 Ja 27 '69
New Repub 160:22 F 22 '69
New Yorker 45:114 Mr 8 '69
Newsweek il 73:99-100 Mr 10 '69
Sat R 52:18 F 8 '69
Time il 93:97 Mr 21 '69
Vogue 153:48 Mr 15 '69
Subject was roses
Chr Cent 86:186 F 5 '69
Succubus
Sat R 52:41 My 10 '69
Support your local sheriff
America 120:549 My 3 '69
Life 66:16 Ap 11 '69
Sr Schol il 94:21 Ap 11 '69
Sweet body of Deborah
Sat R 52:46 Je 7 '69
Sweet Charity
America 120:455 Ap 12 '69
Dance Mag il 43:25-6 Ap '69
Holiday il 45:38+ Ap '69
Look il 33:57 My 13 '69
Newsweek 73:100+ F 17 '69
Sat R 52:39+ Mr 29 '69
Sr Schol 94:28 My 2 '69
Time il 93:87 F 21 '69
Take the money and run
Look 33:43 S 9 '69
New Repub 161:32+ S 6 '69
New Yorker 45:74-5 Ag 30 '69
Newsweek il 74:78 Ag 25 '69
Time 94:87 S 5 '69
Tell them Willie Boy is here
Life 67:18 N 28 '69
Nation 210:28-9 Ja 12 '70
New Repub 161:20+ D 6 '69
New Yorker 45:47-9 D 27 '69
Newsweek il 74:121-2 D 8 '69
Sat R 52:40 D 27 '69
Time 94:76+ D 19 '69
Teorema
America 120:569-70 My 10 '69
Chr Cent 86:1647 D 24 '69
Commonweal 90:265-6 My 16 '69
Commonweal 90:292-3 My 23 '69
Commonweal 89:706-7 Mr 7 '69
Nation 208:582 My 5 '69
New Yorker 45:91-2+ Ap 26 '69
Newsweek 73:108+ My 5 '69
Sat R 52:41 My 10 '69
Time 93:105 My 9 '69
Vogue 153:136 My '69
Thank you all very much
America 121:144 S 6 '69
Commonweal 90:344 Je 6 '69
That cold day in the park
Commonweal 90:487 Ag 8 '69
New Yorker 45:84-5 Je 14 '69
Newsweek il 73:101 Je 16 '69
Sat R 52:26 Je 14 '69
They came to rob Las Vegas
Commonweal 89:653 F 21 '69
They shoot horses, don't they?
America 121:642 D 27 '69
Nation 209:742 D 29 '69
New Yorker 45:62+ D 20 '69
Newsweek il 74:100-1 D 22 '69
Sat R il 52:21+ D 27 '69
Time il 94:76 D 19 '69
Three
Time il 95:67 Ja 19 '70
Three in the attic
Commonweal 90:113 Ap 11 '69
Newsweek 73:86 Ja 27 '69
New Yorker 45:115-16 Mr 8 '69
Time il 93:93 F 14 '69
3 into 2 won't go
Commonweal 90:594 S 26 '69
New Repub 161:26+ Jl 26 '69
New Yorker 45:74 Jl 12 '69
Newsweek il 74:98 Jl 21 '69
Three sisters
Commonweal 89:620-1 F 14 '69
Nation 208:220 F 17 '69
Toni
New Yorker 45:98-9 S 6 '69
Topaz
Nation 210:29 Ja 12 '70
New Yorker 45:49-50 D 27 '69
Newsweek 74:55 D 29 '69
Sat R 52:41 D 27 '69
Time 95:67 Ja 19 '70
Trans-Europ-express
Film Q 22:40-4 Spr '69
Trilogy
America 121:600 D 13 '69
True grit
America 121:47 Jl 19 '69
Atlan 224:123-4 S '69
Commonweal 90:464-5 Jl 25 '69
Holiday 46:25 Jl '69
Life 66:18 Je 20 '69
Nat R 21:970 S 23 '69
New Repub 161:26+ Jl 26 '69
New Yorker 45:67-8 Jl 26 '69
Newsweek il 73:95-6 Je 23 '69
Sat R 52:31 Je 21 '69
Time il 94:51 Jl 4 '69

MOVING picture plays—Criticisms, plots, etc.—
    Single works—*Continued*
Twisted nerve
    America 120:344 Mr 22 '69
    Commonweal 89:736-7 Mr 14 '69
    Sr Schol 94:28-9 Mr 28 '69
Two gentlemen sharing
    Time il 94:98 O 3 '69
Undefeated
    Life 67:17 O 24 '69
Up tight
    Life 66:6 Ja 24 '69
    Sr Schol 94:27 F 14 '69
Very happy Alexander
    America 120:288 Mr 8 '69
Walk with love and death
    America 121:400 N 1 '69
    Chr Cent 87:22+ Ja 7 '70
    Film Q 22:2-4 Spr '69
    Life 67:20 N 28 '69
    New Yorker 45:159-60 O 11 '69
    Sat R 52:28 N 1 '69
    Time 94:105 O 24 '69
    Vogue 154:130-1+ S 15 '69
Wanderer
    Newsweek 73:100+ Ap 28 '69
    Vogue 153:128 My '69
Weekend
    Esquire 71:36+ Ja '69
    Film Q il 22:35-43 Wint '68
What ever happened to Aunt Alice?
    Newsweek il 74:83 Ag 18 '69
Where eagles dare
    America 120:428 Ap 5 '69
    Life 66:12 Mr 28 '69
    Time il 93:89 Mr 28 '69
Where it's at
    Sat R 52:44 My 17 '69
Where's Jack?
    Sat R 52:44 My 17 '69
Who's that knocking at my door?
    Time il 94:97 S 19 '69
Wild bunch
    America 121:20 Jl 5 '69
    America 121:47-8 Jl 19 '69
    Chr Cent 86:1095+ Ag 20 '69
    Commonweal 90:465 Jl 25 '69
    Life 67:8 Jl 25 '69
    Nation 209:61 Jl 14 '69
    New Repub 161:24+ Jl 19 '69
    New Yorker 45:74-5 Jl 5 '69
    Newsweek il 74:85 Jl 14 '69
    Sat R 52:21 Jl 5 '69
    Sat R 52:39 S 27 '69
    Time 93:85+ Je 20 '69
Wind is driving him towards the open sea
    America 121:556-7 D 6 '69
Winning
    America 120:675 Je 7 '69
    Commonweal 90:368 Je 13 '69
    Holiday 46:24-5 Jl '69
    Life 66:16 Je 6 '69
    New Repub 160:32+ Je 14 '69
    New Yorker 45:80-1 My 31 '69
    Newsweek il 73:90C Je 2 '69
    Sat R 52:37 My 24 '69
    Time il 93:113 My 16 '69
You are what you eat
    Esquire 71:32+ F '69
You only love once
    Commonweal 90:594-5 S 26 '69
    New Yorker 45:87 Je 28 '69
Z
    America 121:619 D 20 '69
    Life 67:10 D 19 '69
    Nation 209:710 D 22 '69
    New Repub 161:22+ D 13 '69
    New Yorker 45:168+ D 13 '69
    Newsweek 74:105+ D 15 '69
    Sat R 52:28 D 13 '69
    Time il 94:113 D 5 '69
    Vogue 154:56 N 15 '69

MOVING picture production and direction
According to Pasolini. L. J. Berry. Common-
    weal 89:706-7 Mr 7 '69
After Faces, a film to keep the man-child
    alive; with report by A. Guerin. il Life 66:
    83-6+ My 9 '69
Alice's; family of folk song fame becomes
    a movie. J. Stickney. il Life 66:43-5+ Mr
    28 '69
Alice's restaurant's children. il Newsweek 74:
    101-4+ S 29 '69
American cinema, by A. Sarris. Review
    Commentary 48:89-92+ O '69. P. War-
    show
An ancient woman; M. Callas in Medea. J.
    Buckley. il Opera N 34:8-13 D 13 '69
Antonioni discovers America. P. Bosworth.
    il Holiday 45:64-5+ Mr '69
Antonioni's America; filming of Zabriskie
    Point. J. Hamilton. il Look 33:36-40 N 18
    '69
Ascent of Astrid; filming of Castle keep. J.
    Hamilton. il Look 33:86-8 Ap 1 '69

Barbra Streisand: on a clear day you can
    see Dolly. J. Hamilton. il Look 33:58-64
    D 16 '69
Belafonte plays angel on and off the screen.
    il Ebony 24:76-8+ O '69
Bob Fosse translates Sweet Charity from
    stage to screen. V. H. Swisher. il Dance
    Mag 43:22-5 F '69
Campus, camera and me: filming of Come
    out, come out; based on demonstrations at
    Columbia university. L. Yellen. il Seven-
    teen 28:154-5+ My '69
Cinematic assault; End of the road, a chal-
    lenge to the Hollywood system; symposium.
    il Life 67:64-72 N 7 '69
Cold-turkey month; Greenfield, Ia. Time 94:
    76 S 19 '69
Dancers go dramatic. il Ebony 24:38-40+ S
    '69
Director Arthur Penn takes on General Cus-
    ter. B. Weinraub. il N Y Times Mag p 10-
    11+ D 21 '69
Face of the husbands; films directed by J.
    Cassavetes. New Yorker 45:32-3 Mr 15 '69
Fellini at work; filming Satyricon. H. Alpert.
    il Sat R 52:14-17 Jl 12 '69
Film and dance. M. Harriton. Dance Mag
    43:42 Ap '69
Filming a day that will live in infamy;
    Tora! Tora! Tora! il Bsns W p68-70 Je
    28 '69
Godfrey Cambridge turns white; filming of
    The night the sun came out. E. Dunbar.
    il Look 33:57+ D 30 '69
Hollywood scene; making Alice's restaurant;
    ed. by E. Miller. A. Guthrie. Seventeen 28:
    42+ F '69
If it's Tuesday, this must be Belgium. S.
    Margulies. il Travel 131:72-5 Je '69
Is that you in there, Ringo? J. Hicks. il Life
    66:59-60+ Je 13 '69
Latest model Mailer; writer, now, actor and
    director of Maidstone. J. Roddy. il Look
    33:22-8 My 27 '69
Life style of homo cinematicus. S. De Gra-
    mont. il N Y Times Mag p 12-13+ Je 15 '69
M Truffaut makes it look so easy. R.
    Schickel. Life 66:18 Mr 7 '69
Making of The angel Levine. R. Kotlowitz.
    Harper 239:98-100 Jl '69
Man within; the New York film festival. G. D.
    Phillips. il Cath World 210:175-8 Ja '70
Movies, Mr Griffith, and me, by L. Gish
    and A. Pinchot. Review
    Nat R il 21:865-6 Ag 26 '69. A. Croce
My wife, the naked movie star. L. H. Farber.
    il Harper 238:49-55 Je '69
New wave of sex epics makes actress Anne
    Heywood a star. il Life 66:76-7 Ja 31 '69
Old Rome *alla* Fellini. E. Hughes. il Life
    67:56-9+ Ag 15 '69
Parts of some time spent with Abraham
    Polonsky. W. Pechter. il Film Q 22:14-19
    Wint '68
Paula adds zip to Sweet Charity. il Ebony
    24:86-8+ Je '69
Ponti; interview. C. Ponti. New Yorker 45:31-
    2 Ap 5 '69
Producer always had a mournful look; ex-
    cerpts from The studio. J. G. Dunne. il
    Life 66:62+ F 14 '69
Profiles; J. Renoir. P. Gilliatt. New Yorker
    45:34-6+ Ag 23 '69
Rescuing the Survivors. il Time 94:54 Ag 1
    '69
Return of Busby Berkeley. W. Murray. il
    N Y Times Mag p26-7+ Mr 2 '69
Screen and the voice; transferring opera to the
    moving-picture screen. H. Pleasants. il
    Opera N 34:8-13 Ja 17 '70
Sea gull from the wings. L. Blanch. il Vogue
    153:216-17+ Ap 1 '69
Shoes of the fisherman: the shoes have a
    new contour. S. Harrison. il Cath World
    208:264-7 Mr '69
Shooting it like it is; new documentarians. P.
    D. Zimmerman. il Newsweek 73:134-5 Mr 17
    '69
Successful anarchist; filming of Alice's res-
    taurant. W. Hedgepeth. il Look 33:60-2+
    F 4 '69
Takes: shooting scenes for The Kremlin let-
    ter; interview. J. Huston. New Yorker 45:
    31-3 Je 14 '69
That great territory in the sky; *cinéma
    vérité* technique of Salesman. H. Alpert.
    Sat R 52:75 Mr 22 '69
There's a catch; Catch-22. R. A. Sokolov. il
    Newsweek 73:52-5 Mr 3 '69
They danced till they dropped; making of
    They shoot horses, don't they? D. Adler.
    il Life 67:58-61 Jl 25 '69
Trash, art, and the movies. P. Kael. il
    Harper 238:65-8+ F '69; Ap 10 Discussion.
    238:6 Ap '69

MOVING picture production and direction—
—*Continued*
What it was like to kiss Clark Gable. M
  Astor. il Read Digest 94:49-53 Je '69
Writer; interview, ed. by S. Farber. A. Ja-
  cobs. il Film Q 22:2-14 Wint '68
Yossarian is alive and well in the Mexican
  desert; production of Catch-22. N. Ephron.
  il N Y Times Mag p30-1+ Mr 16 '69
  See also
Moving picture directors
Moving picture sound recording
Paramount pictures corporation

Study and teaching
You're only as young as they think you are;
  young film-makers and university courses.
  R. J. Monaco. il Sat R 52:15-17 D 27 '69
MOVING picture projectors
Let's make a movie. D. Molner. il Schol
  Teach Sec Teach Sup p30+ S 22 '69
MOVING picture scripts

Bibliography
Film scripts. A. Kauffmann. New Repub 160:
  26+ Je 28 '69
MOVING picture societies
Trade winds. C. Amory. Sat R 52:8-9 Jl 12
  '69
MOVING picture sound recording
Sound-on-film: historical footnotes. J. Wes-
  son. U S Camera 32:18 Ja '69
MOVING picture studios
Multi-gadget movie van rolls into Hollywood;
  cinemobile. il Bsns W p 152-4 Mr 15 '69
Paramount's lot; proposed sale of studios.
  il Newsweek 74:84 N 10 '69
MOVING picture theaters
Quads, sixplexes and up; AMCI's movie-
  house complexes. il Newsweek 74:71 S 8
  '69
Why the young killed movie superstars. R.
  Goldstein. il Vogue 154:128+ Ag 1 '69
MOVING pictures
Art that matters: a look at today's film
  scene by the under-thirties; symposium.
  il Sat R 52:7-20+ D 27 '69
Flaherty film seminar. H. V. Fondiller. il Pop
  Phot 65:132-3+ D '69
Screenings: 16mm. Library J 94:3153-4, 3801-
  2 4587-8 S 15, O 15, D 15 '69
Trash, art, and the movies. P. Kael. il
  Harper 238:65-8+ F '69; Discussion. 238:6
  Ap '69
What is a festival film? A. Knight. Sat R
  52:99 S 13 '69
  See also
Academy awards (moving pictures)
Moving picture production and direction
Museum of modern art, New York—Depart-
  ment of film
Negroes in moving pictures
Realism in moving pictures
Television broadcasting—Moving pictures

Abstract films
Secret life of John Chamberlain. E. C. Baker.
  il Art N 68:48-51+ Ap '69

Advertising
See Moving picture industry—Advertising

Animated cartoons
Animated cinema. F. D. Martarella. America
  120:271-3 Mr 8 '69
  See also
Disney, Walt, productions

Criticisms, plots, etc.
Boy named Charlie Brown
  Time 95:53-4 Ja 5 '70
Great Catherine
  Atlan 223:116 Ja '69
Windy day
  Newsweek il 73:96 Mr 31 '69
Yellow submarine
  Atlan 223:116 Ja '69
  Chr Cent 86:386-8 Mr 19 '69

Animal films
New movies. Time 93:93-E10 My 2 '69

Audiences
See Moving picture audiences

Bibliography
Books. C /C. Macauley. See issues of Film
  quarterly
Books on film. R. Sklar. Nation 209:702-3 D
  22 '69
Books to watch films by. R. Corliss. il Nat R
  21:1332-4 D 30 '69

Censorship
See Moving picture censorship

Children, Effect on
See Moving pictures and children

Classification
Can the new movie classification code bring
  back the customers? Consumer Bul 52:16 My
  '69
Films. S. Kauffmann. New Repub 161:22+
  Jl 12 '69
G as in good entertainment. A. Knight. il
  Sat R 52:40 Mr 1 '69
G, M, R and X; opinions on sex, violence,
  nudity in films and the new rating code;
  symposium, ed. by E. Miller. il Seventeen
  28:82-3+ Jl '69
In my opinion; new movie ratings are for
  the birds. S. Robinson. Seventeen 28:22 Mr
  '69
Keys to the new movie codes. il Good H
  168:162 Je '69
Motion picture industry has devised an
  audience-suitability rating system. E.
  Whitehorn. PTA Mag 63:39 Ja '69
Movies and the moral flux; MPAA code. J.
  Huffman. Chr Today 13:32-3 Jl 4 '69
Of ratings, psychos, etc. M. Walsh. America
  120:343-5 Mr 22 '69
X equals what? Rating the new movie
  ratings. J. J. Kirvan. il Cath World 210:15-
  18 O '69
X marks the spot. il Newsweek 73:101 F 24
  '69

Anecdotes, facetiae, satire, etc.
Let's have a symbol to protect pop; the
  new movie ratings. W. Zinsser. Life 66:11
  F 7 '69

Collectors and collecting
Silent and sound film; a growing hobby. E.
  D. Collins. il Hobbies 74:113+ Ag '69

Comedy
New partner for Dan Rowan, the werewolf.
  D. Adler. il Life 66:54-60 My 23 '69

Dance films
Connecticut film-in; a sit-in for establishing
  a dance film. il Dance Mag 43:65 Ap '69
Directory of 16mm dance films; comp. by
  A. F. Snyder and M. Moseley. il Dance
  Mag 43:47-62 Ap '69
Duo, a remarkable new dance film. M. Mose-
  ley. il Dance Mag 43:22-3 Je '69
Fabulous find in the files; Isadora Duncan
  and other dancers in movies. W. Terry. il
  Sat R 52:113-15 Mr 8 '69
Film and dance. M. Harriton. Dance Mag
  43:42 Ap '69
Giselle on film, with Fracci and Bruhn. M.
  Harriton. il Dance Mag 43:24-7 D '69
Three films in the making. il Dance Mag 43:
  43-6 Ap '69
Who can make them? How can we use them?
  findings of report on the relationship of
  film to dance. A. F. Snyder. il Dance Mag
  43:38-41 Ap '69

Detective and mystery films
Come out of the shower, and come out clean.
  T. S. Reck. Commonweal 90:588-91 S 26 '69

Documentary films
Flaherty film seminar. H. V. Fondiller. il Pop
  Phot 65:132-3+ D '69
Grand tour; Sir Kenneth Clark's series on
  the history of western civilization. il News-
  week 74:71 D 15 '69
Kaiser aluminum uncovers money in its PR
  efforts; Oscar winning documentary from
  material in house organ. il Bsns W p88-9
  Jl 12 '69
Screenings: 8mm (cont) A. Cohen. Library
  J 94:1309, 1739, 2083, 4589 Mr 15, Ap 15,
  My 15, D 15 '69
Shooting it like it is: new documentarians.
  P. D. Zimmerman. il Newsweek 73:134-5 Mr
  17 '69
  See also
Newsreel (organization)

Criticisms, plots, etc.
American revolution
  New Repub 161:34 S 30 '69
L'amour de la vie
  New Yorker 45:138+ O 4 '69
Birth and death
  Film Q 22:38-40 Spr '69
Chiefs
  New Yorker 45:121-2+ Mr 22 '69
Debrief: Apollo 8
  Science 163:371 Ja 24 '69
Deserter USA
  Commonweal 91:300-2 D 5 '69
Fantastic plastic machine
  Sat R 52:22 Jl 19 '69

MOVING pictures—Documentary films—Criticisms, plots, etc.—*Continued*
Float like a butterfly, sting like a bee
  Newsweek 74:122+ D 8 '69
High school
  Atlan 223:108 My '69
  Chr Cent 86:1141 S 3 '69
  New Repub 160:28-30 Je 21 '69
  New Yorker 45:199-204 O 18 '69
  Newsweek il 73:102 My 19 '69
  Sat R 52:57 Ap 19 '69
In the year of the pig
  Commonweal 90:250 My 16 '69
  New Repub 161:32 D 13 '69
  New Yorker 45:177-9 N 15 '69
  Newsweek il 74:108+ N 10 '69
King, Murray
  Esquire 72:130+ Jl '69
Married couple
  Vogue 154:143 D '69
Monterey pop
  Chr Cent 86:1022 Jl 30 '69
  Life 66:10 F 7 '69
  New Yorker 45:120-1 Mr 22 '69
No Vietnamese ever called me nigger
  Ramp Mag 7:63-4 D 14 '68
Popcorn
  New Yorker 45:163 N 29 '69
  Sat R 52:55 N 29 '69
  Time 94:113+ D 5 '69
Revolt at Columbia
  Ramp Mag 7:68+ N 30 '68
Salesman
  America 120:655-6 My 31 '69
  Atlan 223:107-8 My '69
  Chr Cent 86:1070 Ag 13 '69
  Commonweal 90:207-8 My 2 '69
  Esquire 71:56 Je '69
  Life 66:12 Mr 14 '69
  Nation 208:318 Mr 10 '69
  New Repub 160:24+ Ap 5 '69
  New Yorker 45:149-52 Ap 19 '69
  Newsweek 73:116+ Ap 21 '69
  Sat R 52:75 Mr 22 '69
  Time 93:83 Mr 7 '69
  Vogue 154:58 Jl '69
Terry Whitmore, for example
  Newsweek 74:89 D 1 '69
This is what Biafra is
  Sat R 52:10+ D 13 '69
Titticut follies
  Film Q 22:28-31 Spr '69
Warrendale
  America 120:274 Mr 8 '69

Editing
Technique of film editing, by K. Reisz and G. Millar. Review
  Film Q 22:50-5 Spr '69. C. C. Macauley

Educational aspects
See Moving pictures in education

Educational films
See Moving pictures in education

Historical films
Historian and historical films. W. H. McNeill. Ed Digest 34:38-40 Ja '69

History
Fabulous find in the files; Isadora Duncan and other dancers in movies. W. Terry. il Sat R 52:113-15 Mr 8 '69
Running away from myself, by B. Deming. Review
  New Repub 161:22+ O 4 '69. S. Kauffmann

Horror films
Just another horror movie, or is it? R. Ebert. Read Digest 94:127-8 Je '69

Laws and regulations
See Moving picture laws and regulations

Medical films
See Moving pictures in medicine

Meteorological films
Education film program of the American meteorological society. M. Toyli and J. Gerhardt. Weatherwise 22:152-5+ Ag '69

Moral aspects
G, M, R and X; opinions on sex, violence, nudity in films and the new rating code; symposium, ed. by E. Miller. il Seventeen 28:82-3+ Jl '69
Goodness, truth, and popcorn. Chr Today 13:22 Ap 25 '69
Graduate reclassified. T. S. Reck. Commonweal 90:202-4 My 2 '69
Homosexual movie. P. T. Hartung. Commonweal 89:502-3 Ja 17 '69
Pasolini's Teorema. America 120:518 My 3 '69

Screen. P. T. Hartung. Commonweal 90:486-7 Ag 8 '69
Sex and violence in movies and TV: how harmful are they? with opinions by celebrities. J. Crist. il Good H 169:59-61+ Ag '69
Sexy movies? Chadron, Neb. tries gentle persuasion. H. Moffett. il Life 66:52B-52D+ My 30 '69
Teorema; award withdrawal by the International Catholic film office. M. Walsh. America 120:569-70 My 10 '69
What do we mean by film art? R. Steele. il Cath World 209:35-8 Ap '69
  See also
Moving picture censorship
Moving pictures—Classification
National Catholic office for motion pictures
Sex in moving pictures

Music
Face the music. W. Johnson. il Film Q 22:3-19 Sum '69
Jazz; Camera three film about Jeremy Steig. W. Balliett. New Yorker 45:98+ My 31 '69

Musical films
Lively arts; change from escapism to serious themes. M. Ronan. il Sr Schol 94:16+ F 7 '69
Return of Busby Berkeley. W. Murray. il N Y Times Mag p26-7+ Mr 2 '69
Screen and the voice; transferring opera to the moving-picture screen. H. Pleasants. il Opera N 34:8-13 Ja 17 '70
Will the real Vera Hruba Ralston please stand up? R. Reed. il Holiday 45:38+ Ap '69

Opera films
See Moving pictures—Musical films

Periodicals
Writing for the fan magazine field. M. Fane. il Writers Digest 49:36-40 My '69

Propaganda films
USIA'S quickie; The silent majority. Nation 209:620-1 D 8 '69

Religious films
Cross and the switchblade: boon for the cinema. Chr Today 14:52-3 O 10 '69
What is a Catholic film? F. Clinton. Nat R 21:1125-6 N 4 '69

Science films
Films of the week. See issues of Science news
  See also
Moving pictures—Meteorological films

Setting and scenery
Justine; behind the novels and the motion picture. L. Durrell. il Holiday 45:74-7 Ap '69
New partner for Dan Rowan, the werewolf. D. Adler. il Life 66:54-60 My 23 '69
Remember the Alamo, please. G. Cartwright. il Life 66:62-4 Ap 25 '69
10th cavalry rides again; equestrian unit for cinema and television productions recreating Buffalo Soldiers. il Ebony 24:92-7 F '69

Sex films
See Moving pictures—Moral aspects; Sex in moving pictures

Short subject films
Films that turn kids on. V. Falconer. il Sr Schol 94:Schol Teach 8+ F 7 '69
Victory: short films at New York Republican County committee's Lincoln day dinner and ball. New Yorker 45:27-9 Mr 1 '69

Silent films
Quixote with a bowler. il Time 95:54 Ja 5 '70

Sound recording
See Moving picture sound recording

Sports films
How to succeed at racing without really racing; skiing movie; Downhill racer. D. Jenkins. il Sports Illus 31:66 N 24 '69
Motor trend interview; ed. by B. Sanders. S. McQueen. Motor T 21:88+ N '69

Study and teaching
Heritage of film. R. E. Sheratsky. bibliog Clear House 44:58-60 S '69
Matzkin on movies; teaching film making to first-graders. M. Matzkin. il Mod Phot 33:34+ S '69

MOVING pictures—*Continued*

Suspense films
See Moving pictures—Detective and mystery films

Themes
Last of the great outlaws: Butch Cassidy and the Sundance Kid. il Life 66:69-71 My 16 '69
See also
Sports in moving pictures
Youth in moving pictures

Travel films
Edit your travel films; with step-by-step splicing instructions. D. Langer. il Travel & Camera 32:84-7 Je '69

War films
News & views; managing the image; Emile D'Antonio's In the Year of the pig. J. Deedy. il Commonweal 90:250 My 16 '69

Westerns
Fool's gold; Paint your wagon. il Time 94: 100+ O 24 '69
10th cavalry rides again; equestrian unit for cinema and television productions recreating Buffalo Soldiers. il Ebony 24:92-7 F '69
See also
Canada—National film board

Czechoslovakia
Czech Jiri Menzel (Closely watched trains) directs a movie. A. Levy. il N Y Times Mag p28-9+ F 9 '69

Europe
Europe and America: a question of self-image. S. Steiner. il Sat R 52:18-20 D 27 '69

France
Profiles; J. Renoir. P. Gilliatt. New Yorker 45:34-6+ Ag 23 '69

Great Britain
Media and manners; film and society in some current British films. I. Jarvie. il Film Q 22:11-17 Spr '69

Hungary
See also
Moving picture industry—Hungary

India
Indian cinema today. C. Das Gupta. il Film Q 22:27-35 Sum '69

Italy
Ponti; interview. C. Ponti. New Yorker 45: 31-2 Ap 5 '69

United States
American cinema, by A. Sarris. Review Commentary 48:89-92+ O '69. R. Warshow
That great territory in the sky; *cinéma vérité* technique of Salesman. H. Alpert. Sat R 52:75 Mr 22 '69
See also
American film institute
Disney, Walt, productions
Moving picture industry—United States

MOVING pictures, Amateur
Foothill film festival; running people, symbolic seagulls. M. Mann. il Pop Phot 65: 26+ O '69
See also
Moving picture photography

Editing
Can a $5.95 splicer do a $299 job? M. A. Matzkin. il Mod Phot 33:72-3 S '69
Edit your travel films; with step-by-step splicing instructions. D. Langer. il Travel & Camera 32:84-7 Je '69
Matzkin on movies; editing super 8. M. A. Matzkin. Mod Phot 33:56 Ap '69
Mental notes aren't worth thinking about. D. B. Eisendrath il Pop Phot 65:16+ Ag '69
See also
Moving pictures, Amateur—Sound editing

Sound editing
You can edit sound movies. B. Howard. il Pop Phot 64:100-1+ Je '69

Sound recording
Wein Sound trigger. P. Farber. il Travel & Camera 32:47-8 F '69

Themes
Shoot a story with one cartridge. D. Langer. il Pop Phot 64:114-15+ Mr '69

Titles
Movie titles unlimited. M. D. Grennan. il Pop Phot 64:106-7 F '69
Title your travel movies. D. Langer. il Travel & Camera 32:121-5+ O '69

MOVING pictures, Childrens. See Moving pictures for children

MOVING pictures, Experimental
Underground movie thing. B. Ford. il Sci Digest 65:42-53 Je '69
What film making is all about. M. W. Gordon. America 121:555-7 D 6 '69

Anecdotes, facetiae, satire, etc.
Ninety-nine years is not forever. F. P. Tullitus. New Yorker 46:20-1 Jl 19 '69

MOVING pictures, Musical. See Moving pictures—Musical films

MOVING pictures and children
Just another horror movie, or is it? R. Ebert. Read Digest 94:127-8 Je '69
Sexy movies? Chadron, Neb. tries gentle persuasion. H. Moffett. il Life 66:52B-52D+ My 30 '69
See also
Moving pictures for children

MOVING pictures and literature
New audience: from Andy Hardy to Arlo Guthrie. L. Cohen. il Sat R 52:8-11+ D 27 '69

MOVING pictures and television
Why the young killed movie superstars. R. Goldstein. Vogue 154:128+ Ag 1 '69

MOVING pictures and youth
Art that matters: a look at today's film scene by the under-thirties; symposium. il Sat R 52:7-20+ D 27 '69
New expectations. D. R. Stevens. Seventeen 29:28 Ja '70

MOVING pictures for children
Family movie guide; ed. by J. Ripp. See issues of Parents' magazine & better family living
Films for children. M. Walsh. America 121:48 Jl 19 '69
Films for the popcorn brigade. R. Reed. il Holiday 45:20+ Je '69
Films that turn kids on. V. Falconer. il Sr Schol 94:Schol Teach 8+ F 7 '69

MOVING pictures in education
Film study in the secondary school. bibliog Engl J 58:1259-67 N '69
Films on ceramics. il Ceram Mo 17:28-9+ F '69
Liveliest art in the classroom. A. Franza. il Engl J 58:1233-7 N '69
Making films with students. K. Scheufele. Engl J 58:426-7+ Mr '69
Research paper revisited; analyzing current movies. D. M. Paananen. il Sr Schol 94: Schol Teach 18-19 F 7 '69
The scene. E. Farrell and L. Ruth. Engl J 58:756-61 My '69
Take 1 scene 1; sites selected for AFI grants. Sr Schol 94:Schol Teach 7 F 7 '69
Teaching black history via films. il Sch & Soc 97:416-17 N '69
See also
Moving pictures—Study and teaching

MOVING pictures in medicine
Reviews: books and films. Ment Hy 53:661-9 O '69

MOVING pictures in public relations
Our movies fought city hall, and won! use of films in preserving natural beauty. P. Gowland. il Pop Phot 65:124-5+ N '69

MOVSESIAN, Edwin A.
Reading music & reading words. Todays Ed 58:42-3 Ja '69

MOVSHON, George
Boston symphony: end of the Leinsdorf era. Hi Fi 19:MA12-13 N '69
Britten & Handel at Caramoor. Hi Fi 19: MA10-11 S '69
Case for Massenet. Hi Fi 19:93-4 D '69
Electric Karajan on the Yellow submarine. Hi Fi 19:16 Jl '69
Enriching recorded analysis of Wagner's Ring. Hi Fi 19:106 S '69
Enrico Caruso. Hi Fi 19:77-8 S '69
Hary Janos, an entertainment with music. Hi Fi 19:81-2 N '69
New Rosenkavalier at the Met. Hi Fi 19: MA12+ Ap '69
Parallel careers of Georg Solti. Hi Fi 19:66-70 O '69
Records to test your Woofer's crunchability. por Hi Fi 19:66-70 O '69
Sherrill Milnes: a voice for tomorrow's golden age. Hi Fi 19:102 Jl '69

MOVSHON, George—*Continued*
  Von Karajan's Siegfried: an Olympian approach. Hi Fi 19:79-80 O '69
  Wagnerian filet. Hi Fi 19:116 N '69
  What happened to the new Karajan style?
    Hi Fi 19:MA28-9+ Je '69

MOWAT, Farley
  Snow: beautiful, romantic, nostalgic, terrifying. Holiday 45:46-7+ F '69

MOWBRAY, A. Q.
  Octane numbers game. Nation 209:659-61 D
    15 '69
  Truth in packaging: how much a pound?
    Nation 208:730-2 Je 9 '69
  What consumers need: show biz or hard
    facts. Nation 209:245-8 S 15 '69

MOWBRAY, G. H. See Bird, J. F. jt. auth.

MOWING of lawns. See Lawns

MOWREY, Corma A.
  Value of the PTA. Todays Ed 58:31-3 My '69

MOYAL, Maurice
  Worker-priest for Christ. por Chr Cent 86:
    808-9 Je 11 '69

MOYERS, Bill D.
  Reveille for Democrats. Atlan 223:37-41 Mr
    '69
  White House staff versus the Cabinet; interview, ed. by H. Sidey. Cur 106:26-35 Ap '69

MOYLE, Donald L.
  Here's to Tilly the toiler. por Org Gard &
    Farm 16:41-2 Ap '69

MOYNIHAN, Daniel Patrick
  Fading peace dividend? statements. por U S
    News 67:70-1 S 8 '69
  NATO committee on the challenges of modern society: response to a common environmental peril; address, October 21, 1969. Dept
    State Bul 61:416-20 N 17 '69
  Politics as the art of the impossible; address,
    June 1, 1969. Am Scholar 38:573-83 Aut '69
  Soulless city; excerpts from address. Am
    Heritage 20:4-9+ F '69

about

Blaming Ophelia for not playing Hamlet. D.
  Yankelovich. il por Fortune 79:197-8 Ap
  '69
Compleat American pragmatist. R. Schickel.
  por Horizon 11:60-5 Wint '69
Mr Moynihan to head U.S. effort in NATO
  environmental study. Dept State Bul 61:261
  S 22 '69
Mr Nixon's urban ballet. H. E. Davis. Nation
  209:46-7 Jl 14 '69
Moynihan at work in the White House. J.
  Osborne. New Repub 160:11-13 Mr 22 '69
Moynihan: eminent Victorian. R. B. Semple,
  jr. il por(p9) N Y Times Mag p50+ Ag 3
  '69
Pat Moynihan: too much! And too little!
  B. Asbell. il pors N Y Times Mag p44-5+
  N 2 '69
Poverty, politics and social studies. J. P.
  Fitzpatrick. America 120:558-61 My 10 '69
Superelf in the basement. il por Time 93:24-5
  F 28 '69
TRB from Washington. New Repub 160:4 Je
  7 '69
Volcano in the cornfield. H. Sidey. il por
  Life 67:4 Ag 22 '69
Where is Pat? J. Osborne. New Repub 161:
  15-17 N 29 '69
White House's idea man for urban problems.
  il pors Bsns W p72-4+ S 27 '69

MOZAMBIQUE
  Mozambique: Hitler to Hunt. Ramp Mag 7:
    53-4 N 30 '68
  Report: Portuguese Africa. S. Meisler. Atlan 223:14+ Ja '69
  See also
  Guerrillas—Mozambique
  Hunting—Mozambique

MOZARABIC chant. See Chants (Gregorian,
  plain, etc)

MOZARABIC rite. See Catholic church—Mozarabic rite

MOZART, Johann Chrysostom Wolfgang Amadeus
  Casals, heroic, noble Mozart. M. N. Kanny.
    Am Rec G 36:136 O '69
  Conductor Casals, passion and tension. H.
    Goldsmith. Hi Fi 19:96 S '69
  Don Giovanni. Criticism
    Hi Fi 19:MA11 Mr '69
  Erich Leinsdorf's legacy, a superb feeling for
    Mozart. M. N. Kanny. Am Rec G 36:196 N
    '69
  Full-blooded and very funny performance of
    Cosi fan tutte. A. Sperber. il Am Rec G
    35:378-80 Ja '69
  Genesis of Mozart's Idomeneo. D. Heartz.
    bibliog f il Mus Q 55:1-19 Ja '69
  Leinsdorf's Mozart, a feast for the ear. P.
    H. Lang. il Hi Fi 19:100 N '69

Magic flute (Die zauberflöte) Criticism
  Opera N 34:17-20 Ja 17 '70
Mozart manifold. R. Jacobson. Sat R 52:72+
  F 22 '69
Music to my ears: Szell-Casadesus reconstruction of the D-major concerto. I. Kolodin.
  Sat R 52:50 D 13 '69
New Marriage on Deutsche Grammophon. A.
  Sperber. il Am Rec G 35:380-2 Ja '69
On Yehudi's 50th birthday, a gift from the
  whole family: M. N. Kanny. Am Rec G
  36:55 S '69
Price's Mozart: very beautiful singing. P. L.
  Miller. Am Rec G 36:195 N '69
Records:
  Requiem. Opera N 33:35 F 8 '69
  Requiem: Mozart's sacred drama. P. H.
    Lang. Hi Fi 19:92 O '69
Seven keys to the flute. C. R. Faust. il Opera
  N 34:22-3 Ja 17 '70
Silla in sound. R. Jacobson. Sat R 52:58 D
  27 '69
Twenty-one Mozart concerto recordings. M.
  Kanny. Am Rec G 35:768-70+ My '69

MRAK, Frank, family
  Family struggles to stay even. J. McGinniss.
    il pors Life 67:26-9 Ag 15 '69

MROZEK, Slawomir
  Tango. Criticism
    America 120:314 Mr 15 '69
    Nation 208:157-8 F 3 '69
    New Yorker 44:51-2 F 1 '69
    Time 93:73 Ja 31 '69

MU mesons. See Mesons

MUAN, Arnulf. See Ryall, W. R. jt. auth.

MUCH ado about nothing; drama. See Shakespeare, W.—Plays

MUCKRAKING
  Chop; journalistic karate. Nation 209:301
    S 29 '69

MUCOR. See Fungi

MUD rooms. See Rooms

MUD slides. See Landslides

MUEHLMATT, Ernest F.
  Air house for big winter projects. Pop Sci
    194:134-5+ Ja '69

MUELLER, Andrew J.
  (comp) CB troubleshooter's casebook (cont)
    Radio-Electr 40:77 F; 88-7 Je; 85 Ag; 82 O
    '69
  Fix CB fast. Radio-Electr 41:70-2+ Ja '70

MUELLER, George E.
  Goals of future explorers; interview. por
    U S News 67:30-1 Ag 4 '69
  Investigation of the moon: the 1970-71 plan.
    Bul Atom Sci 25:67 S '69
  Space program; address, October 23, 1969.
    Vital Speeches 36:170-5 Ja 1 '70

  about
  Musical chairs at NASA. Sci N 96:424 N 8 '69

MUELLER, Gerald C. See Gallwitz, D. jt. auth.

MUELLER, Larry
  Cooners: the best in the world. Field & S
    74:184-5+ My '69
  How a houndman picks his pups. Field &
    S 74:122-7 Jl '69

MUELLER, Lavonne
  Concrete poetry: creative writing for all students. bibliog Engl J 58:1053-6 O '69

MUELLER, Lisel
  Peace march; poem. New Yorker 45:24 Jl 19
    '69
  Sleepless; poem. Poetry 115:108 N '69

MUELLER, Robert A. and others
  Adrenal tyrosine hydroxylase: compensatory
    increase in activity after chemical sympathectomy. bibliog Science 163:468-9 Ja 31
    '69

MUELLER, Robert F.
  Planetary probe: origin of atmosphere of
    Venus. bibliog Science 163:1322-4 Mr 21 '69

MUELLER, Samuel A. and Sween, J. A.
  Omnis America in partes tres divisa est. Chr
    Cent 86:1342-4 O 22 '69; Correction. 87:18-19
    Ja 7 '70

MUELLER, Willard Fritz
  Conglomerate critic aims a blast. por Bsns W
    p98+ N 1 '69

MUENCH, Aloisius Joseph, cardinal
  American nuncio, Cardinal Aloysius Muench,
    by C. J. Barry. Review
      Commonweal 91:339-40 D 12 '69. P. Gleason

MUENCH, David
  Waters of the West; photographs. Nat Wildlife 7:42-7 Je '69

MUFFINS
  Sourdough English muffins, quickly. il Sunset
    143:208 O '69

MUFFLERS. See Automobile engines—Mufflers

MUGGERIDGE, Malcolm
Books. See issues of Esquire
Men like gods. Chr Cent 86:176-8 F 5 '69
On rediscovering Jesus. Esquire 71:122-6+ Je '69

about

Conversion of Malcolm Muggeridge. J. Hart. Nat R 21:1228-9 D 2 '69
Death-wish psychosis of the new left. Chr Today 13:26-7 My 9 '69
Jesus remuggeridged. W. Sheed. Commonweal 91:74+ O 17 '69
Personal history. H. Cox. Sat R 52:23-4 Ag 30 '69
Pilgrim's progress. G. Wolff. Newsweek 74: 85-S 8 '69
Scotland: the festival and Muggeridge. I. Logan. Chr Cent 86:1291-2 O 8 '69

MUGGERS (criminals) See Crime and criminals—United States
MUGGING (crime) See Assault and battery
MUGHAL, R. See Islam, A. S. jt. auth.

MUGS
Now it's mug time, summertime or anytime. W. Clifford. il House B 111:70-1+ Jl '69

MUHAMMAD Ali. See Clay, C.

MUHLEN, Norbert
[Book review] America 120:454-5 Ap 12 '69

MUHLFELD, Edward D.
From the tower. See issues of Flying

MÜHLHAUSEN, Germany
Wiedrigkeit and *verdriesslichkeit* in Mühlhausen; church music of eighteenth century. H. Serwer. bibliog f Mus Q 55:20-30 Ja '69

MUI, Hoh-cheung, and Mui, L. H.
Smuggling and the British tea trade before 1784. bibliog f Am Hist R 74:44-73 O '68

MUI, Lorna H. See Mui, H. C. jt. auth.

MUIR, J. Douglas
Canada's experience with the right of public employees to strike. bibliog Mo Labor R 92:54-9 Jl '69

MUIR, John, historic site. See Martinez, Calif.-Historic houses, etc.

MUIR, R. D.
Album of Canadian parks. il Liv Wildn 32:22-9 Je '69

MULADORE, H.
Youth labor movement. Nation 209:196-7 S 8 '69

MULCHING
About gardening and Rex and Harold, and then there's me! R. Stout. il Org Gard & Farm 16:44-7 F '69
Growing tricks with plastic sheeting. K. L. Armstrong. il Org Gard & Farm 16:40-2 Je '69
Make mine more mulch. R. Stout. il Org Gard & Farm 16:50-3 My '69
Mulch and edge your flower beds for easy maintenance. il Bet Hom & Gard 47:62-5 Je '69
Mulching with aluminum foil. J. B. Kring. Horticulture 47:27+ My '69
Mulching with newspapers. W. E. Osgood. Org Gard & Farm 16:106-7 Ja '69
Our problem blackberry patch. O. R. Griffin. il Org Gard & Farm 16:53 Ja '69
Plastic mulch; not so attractive but most efficient. il Home Gard 56:50-1 Ag '69
Row-to-row carpeting in the garden. J. G. Edwards. il Org Gard & Farm 16:46-7 Ja '69
To mulch, or not to mulch. C. Williamson. il Org Gard & Farm 16:28-30 Ap '69
Which mulch is best for potatoes? hay mulch. K. Polscer. il Org Gard & Farm 16:69-72 F '69
You have to improve it; instant compost plus permanent mulch. C. Allonby. il Org Gard & Farm 16:58-9 D '69
See also
Organic gardening

MULE deer hunting. See Deer hunting

MULHERIN, Kathy
California's academic fault. Commonweal 90:281-6 My 23 '69

MULL, Gary W.
Yachting interview; ed. by B. Robinson. por Yachting 125:70-1+ F '69

MULLER, George O.
Piercing tool speeds pipe work. Am City 84: 72-3 D '69

MÜLLER, German
Sedimentary phosphate method for estimating paleosalinities; limited applicability. Science 163:812-13 F 21 '69

MÜLLER, Johannes von
Johannes von Müller: the historian in search of a hero. G. A. Craig. bibliog f Am Hist R 74:1487-502 Je '69

MULLER, Paul M.
Hidden perils of a lunar landing. J. Lear. il Sat R 52:48-54 Je 7 '69
Moon rivers. il Newsweek 73:94 My 12 '69
—and Sjogren, W. L.
Information from deep-space tracking. bibliog Phys Today 22:46-52 Jl '69

MULLER, Steven
Anxiety in Bonn: German fears after Czechoslovakia. Bul Atom Sci 25:13-15 Mr '69

MÜLLER-EBERHARD, Hans J. See Budzko, D. B.; Kohler, P. F. jt. auths.

MULLIGAN, John
Baddest of the bad. J. Thawley. il pors Hot Rod 22:64-6 My '69

MULLIGAN, Joseph E.
What to do about Joe Mulligan? J. C. Fleck. America 121:184-9 S 20 '69

MULTILATERAL bargaining. See Collective bargaining, Industry wide
MULTI-media performances. See Performing arts
MULTINATIONAL corporations. See Corporations, International
MULTIPLE access computer. See Computers—Time sharing systems
MULTIPLE choice tests. See Educational tests and measurements
MULTIPLE, independently targeted re-entry vehicle system. See Guided missiles
MULTIPLE jobholding. See Supplementary employment
MULTIPLE printing. See Photography—Printing processes
MULTIPLE sclerosis. See Sclerosis, Multiple
MULTIPLE use plans. See Land utilization
MULTIPLEX radio broadcasting. See Radio broadcasting—Multiplex system
MULTIPLEX system in telecommunication. See Telecommunication—Multiplex system
MULTIPURPOSE furniture. See Furniture
MULTIPURPOSE rooms. See Rooms

MULTIVIBRATORS
Beeping a Sonalert. F. H. Tooker. il Electr World 82:79 D '69
Dual-rate sawtooth generator. F. H. Tooker. il Electr World 81:74 My '69
Dual UJT multivibrator. F. H. Tooker. il Electr World 82:74 D '69
SCS monostable multivibrator. F. H. Tooker. il Electr World 81:45 F '69
UJT monocycle multivibrator. il Electr World 81:61 Ap '69

MULVOY, Mark
Baseball (cont) Sports Illus 30:75-6+ My 26; 76+ Je 9; 31:48-9 Jl 14 '69
Golf (cont) Sports Illus 30:52 Mr 3; 31:64-5 O 6 '69
Hockey (cont) Sports Illus 30:38+ Ja 20 '69

MUMAW, Barton
Ageless Pierrot. W. Terry. por Sat R 52:36 Ag 30 '69

MUMFORD, George S. 3d
News notes. See issues of Sky and telescope
Report from Rome: X-rays and gamma rays. Sky & Tel 38:96-8 Ag '69

MUMFORD, Lewis
Have courage! Am Heritage 20:104-11 F '69
Prize, or lunacy? statement on the eve of Apollo 11. il por Newsweek 74:61 Jl 7 '69; Excerpts. Cur 110:6 S '69

MUMMIES
Mummies: man's drive for immortality. R. Hare. bibliog il Sci Digest 66:16-22 D '69

MUMS. See Chrysanthemums

MUNCH, Charles
From the late Charles Munch: a last word on one of his favorite works. J. W. Barker. por Am Rec G 35:475 F '69
Memories of Charles Munch. J. Szigeti. Hi Fi 19:MA15 Mr '69

MUNCH, Edvard
Three faces of Eve; exhibition of prints at Los Angeles County museum. il por Time 93:60-2 F 21 '69

MUNDELL, William D.
Autumn passing; poem. Am For 75:4-5 O '69
Fact of fire: poem. Am For 75:45 Ap '69
November beeches; poem. Am For 75:61 N '69
Sudden silence in the wood; poem. Am For 75:8 Jl '69

MUNDY, Fern
Peace corps: new challenges, more opportunities. Har Yrs 9:8-10 Jl '69

MUNGO, Raymond
Opinion: "I've got nothin', ma..." por Mlle 68:20+ F '69

MUNICH

Music

Report: Munich; Günther Rennert's production of Wagner's Ring des Nibelungen. F. J. Warnke. il Opera N 33:32-3 Mr 22 '69

MUNICH—Music—*Continued*
Report: Munich; productions at Bavarian state opera. F. J. Warnke. Opera N 33:25-6 Je 14 '69
MUNICH festival. See Music festivals—Germany (Federal Republic)
MUNICH four power agreement, 1938
Is there a lesson of Munich? E. Stillman. Horizon 11:32-3 Spr '69
MUNICIPAL administration. See Municipal government
MUNICIPAL advertising
City tells its story; ed. by P. D. Elmon. See issues of American city
MUNICIPAL and federal relations. See Federal and municipal relations
MUNICIPAL and state relations. See State and municipal relations
MUNICIPAL bonds
Bonds build cities, create jobs; Oklahoma City. il Am City 84:154+ O '69
Less cash for the cities. il Time 94:92 O 3 '69
Municipal-bond loophole. Am City 84:10 Ag '69
Municipal bond problems pose obstacles to airport funding. N. S. Himmel. Aviation W 91:56+ N 17 '69
Municipal bonds get Senate boost. U S News 67:80 O 20 '69
Municipal finance. See issues of American city
Tax-free bonds: a market in chaos. il U S News 67:77-9 S 29 '69
See also
Bonds, Revenue
MUNICIPAL buildings
Plenty of daylight but no bad view; East Chicago, Ind, Department of water works building. il Am City 84:44 Ja '69
See also
City halls
Police stations
MUNICIPAL centers
Small-city civic center; Sturgis, Mich. W. N. Yoder. il Am City 84:121-2 F '69
MUNICIPAL contracts
Contract snowfighting; Montreal. J. V. Arpin. il Am City 84:98-9 D '69
Total-cost bidding saves in the long run; Bristol, Conn. K. W. Gordon. il Am City 84:104+ Ag '69
Voluntary joint public bidding; Hackensack, N.J. R. M. Belmonte. il Am City 84:162+ O '69
MUNICIPAL corporations
Legal notes and decisions; prepared by National institute of municipal law officers. See issues of American city
MUNICIPAL dumps
Elevating scraper digs trench on sanitary landfill; Lucas County, Ohio. il Am City 84:123 F '69
150 days of fire; dump fire, Milwaukee, Wis. il Am City 84:80+ Jl '69
Ski hill from garbage dump. J. T. Riley. il Parks & Rec 3:37+ N '68
See also
Refuse and refuse disposal
MUNICIPAL elections
Cities: shattered election patterns. il Time 94:24-5 O 24 '69
Elections 1969: the moderates have it. il Time 94:23-4 N 14 '69
Is there a backlash vote? analysis of election results in Minneapolis, Los Angeles and New York city. M. J. Goldbloom. Commentary 48:17-26 Ag '69
Urban mood. J. Q. Wilson and H. R. Wilde. Commentary 48:52-61 O '69
What the voters want; environment issue in elections. Time 94:55 N 14 '69
When cities picked their mayors. il U S News 67:38 N 17 '69
Will forgotten voter decide? white middle class and mayoral elections. Sr Schol 95:15 O 27 '69
See also subhead Elections under names of cities, e.g. Los Angeles—Elections
MUNICIPAL employees
Minority employment in state and local governments. il Mo Labor R 92:67-70 N '69
Urban corps goes national. B. B. Stretch. il Sat R 52:75 S 20 '69
. . .Who collects the garbage. Am City 84:8 Je '69
See also
Municipal officers
Park employees
Police
Salaries, allowances, etc.
One reason your taxes keep going higher and higher. il U S News 66:37-9 Mr 3 '69
Supply and demand
Wanted: help! il Newsweek 74:51-2 S 15 '69

MUNICIPAL engineering
See also
Refuse and refuse disposal
Sewerage
Streets
MUNICIPAL equipment
Big red, something new in street maintenance; Bartlesville, Okla. B. Armstrong. il Am City 84:90-1 N '69
Equipment needed for a sanitary fill. W. B. Culham. Am City 84:100 Ja '69
New products and processes. See issues of American city
Quick service ditch cleaning; Scoopmobile with ditch-cleaning attachment, Clackamas County, Ore. il Am City 84:32 N '69
See also
Motor trucks, Municipal
Salt spreaders
Sand spreaders
Snow plows
Street cleaning apparatus
MUNICIPAL finance
Budgeting for state and local government services. B. Crihfield and G. A. Bell. Ann Am Acad 379:31-8 S '68
Municipal finance. See issues of American city
221 ways to save our cities. J. Bailey. Arch Forum 130:70-3 Ja '69
Welfare burden. Nation 208:67-8 Ja 20 '69
What the city needs. A. Stone. Nation 209:494-9+ N '69
See also
Local taxation
Municipal bonds
Municipal contracts

Federal aid
See Federal and municipal relations
MUNICIPAL garages. See Garages, Municipal
MUNICIPAL government
Black role in urban politics. Cur Hist 57:287-9+ N '69
City tells its story; ed. by P. D. Elmon. See issues of American city
Flight from city hall; interviews, ed. by F. Powledge. il Harper 239:69+ N '69
Model administration for a medium-sized city; Garden Grove, Calif. Am City 84:34+ Ap '69
Neighborhood government, by M. Kotler. Review
Ramp Mag 8:33-4 D '69. K. Hess
New urban-management science. E. S. Savas. Am City 84:156-9 Mr '69
No more book-type urban administrators. L. A. Rowe and S. P. Schoenberg. il Am City 84:83-4 D '69
Urban mood. J. Q. Wilson and H. R. Wilde. Commentary 48:52-61 O '69
. . .Who collects the garbage. Am City 84:8 Je '69
See also
Boss rule
Cities and towns—United States
Councilmen
Metropolitan government
Municipal finance
Municipal officers
National league of cities
Police
State and municipal relatons
also subhead Politics and government under names of cities, e.g. New York (city)—Politics and government

Public relations
Parade, charade, crusade; Pensacola, Fla; Covington, Va; and Lennox, S.D. il Am City 84:132+ Ag '69
MUNICIPAL improvement
Beauty and the beast; adaptation of address. D. G. Leach. Horticulture 46:22-3+ O '68
Color and comfort at streetside. L. Burgess. il Home Gard 56:40 Je '69
Hurry-up beautification; Stockton, Calif. F. Fargo. il Am City 84:110-11 Ja '69
If Jackson can do it. B. Horne. il Horticulture 47:30-1 Ag '69
See also
All-American cities
Business districts
City planning
Parks
Pavements
Refuse and refuse disposal
Streets
Urban renewal
Water fronts
also subhead Municipal improvement under names of cities, e.g. Trenton, N.J.—Municipal improvement

MUNICIPAL Insurance. See Insurance, Municipal

MUNICIPAL officers
Administrative assistant; Milford, Conn. C. C. Hughes. il Am City 84:126+ S '69
No more book-type urban administrators. L. A. Rowe and S. P. Schoenberg. il Am City 84:83-4 D '69
  See also
City managers
Councilmen
Mayors

MUNICIPAL ordinances
Legal notes and decisions; prepared by National institute of municipal law officers. See issues of American city

MUNICIPAL public relations.   See Municipal government—Public relations

MUNICIPAL publications

  Bibliography
Book reviews and reports. See issues of American city

MUNICIPAL purchasing. See Purchasing, Municipal

MUNICIPAL purchasing agents. See Purchasing agents

MUNICIPAL records on microfilm
Microfilm aperture cards. il Am City 84:106-8 Ja '69
Microfilm system that grows with the city; Phoenix, Ariz. D. Willis. il Am City 84:133-4 My '69

MUNICIPAL recreation. See Recreation

MUNICIPAL reference libraries
Have you tried a municipal reference library? Boulder, Colo. V. P. Boucher. il Am City 84:118-19 F '69

MUNICIPAL reports
Pequannock Picassos. il Am City 84:141-3 Je '69

MUNICIPAL service. See Public service

MUNICIPAL taxation. See Local taxation

MUNICIPAL transportation. See Rapid transit

MUNICIPAL utilities. See Public utilities

MUNITIONS
  See also
Atomic weapons
Weapons

  Manufacture
Army tries to build a munitions factory in St Louis with the Mob on the payroll. D. Walsh. il Life 66:52-4+ F 14 '69

MUNITIONS industries
Key issue; military demands vs. civilian needs. Nation 208:354 Mr 24 '69
War business, by G. Thayer. Review
Commonweal 90:598-9 S 26 '69. T. M. Conrad
Sat R 52:30 S 6 '69. J. B. Wiesner
  See also
Krupp works, Essen

  Employees
Cushioned cutback; effect of defense layoffs. il Newsweek 74:81-2 D 22 '69
Skill transfers: can defense workers adapt to civilian occupations? J. R. Cambern and D. A. Newton. il Mo Labor R 92:21-5 Je '69
Workers brace for the layoffs; reduction in defense contracts. il Bsns W p 166+ N 22 '69

  Finance
Myth of war profiteering. G. E. Berkley. il New Repub 161:15-18 D 20 '69

  Securities
Arms and the market. C. Morgello. il Newsweek 73:81 Je 9 '69

  France
Will French arms boom backfire? cutoff of military shipments to Israel. il Bsns W p22+ F 1 '69

  Russia
Military-industrial complex-Russian style. R. Armstrong. il Fortune 80:84-7+ Ag 1 '69

  United States
As Eisenhower was saying, we must guard against unwarranted influence by the military-industrial complex. R. F. Kaufman. il N Y Times Mag p 10-11+ Je 22 '69; Reply with rejoinder. J. R. L. Johnson, jr. p2+ Jl 6 '69
At play with the military-industrial complex; Air force association and Army association meetings. P Dickson and R. Skole. Esquire 73:66B+ Ja '70

Big defense firms are really public firms. J. K. Galbraith. il N Y Times Mag p50-1+ N 16 '69
Defense contract: the money web. G. Astor. il Look 33:28-9 Ag 26 '69
Defense profits: the hidden issues. A. T. Demaree. Fortune 80:82-3+ Ag 1 '69
M-I complex. K. Crawford. Newsweek 73:32 Mr 31 '69
Militarism and American democracy; the complex; address, April 8, 1969. J. W. Fulbright. bibliog f Vital Speeches 35:455-60 My 15 '69
Military-industrial complex. il Newsweek 73:74-6+ Je 9 '69
Military-industrial complex; an economic analysis; address, March 21, 1969. M. L. Weidenbaum. bibliog Vital Speeches 35:523-8 Je 15 '69
Top general's rebuttal to attacks on military; excerpts from address, May 17, 1969. E. G. Wheeler. il U S News 66:14 Je 9 '69
War work payrolls start heading down; civilian jobs in defense business have declined. il Bsns W p 134-5 Je 14 '69
What is the military-industrial complex? Time 93:23 Ap 11 '69
Why a military-industrial complex? A senator's answer; excerpts from address, April 15, 1969. B. Goldwater; W. Proxmire. U S News 66:88-90 Ap 28 '69
Witch hunt against military? A warning; excerpts from statement to a subcommittee of the Joint economic committee of Congress, June 11, 1969. D. Acheson. U S News 66:16 Je 23 '69

MUNITIONS purchasing. See Purchasing, Military

MUNITIONS workers. See Munitions industries —Employees

MUNRO, Donald
News from New Zealand. A. Alpers. il Opera N 33:26-8 Ap 5 '69

MUNRO, Eleanor
Framing pictures today. House & Gard 135:54+ Ap '69
How to light pictures and sculpture. House & Gard 135:72+ My '69
Living with art; art works in multiple. House & Gard 136:94+ S '69
Lunch for two women; poem. Harp Baz 102:132 Je '69
Spring; poem. New Yorker 45:40 My 24 '69

MUNRO, Nancy
Hanger next door. por Redbook 132:21+ Mr '69

MUNSON, Don
Influential onion. House B 111:34-5 F '69
Vesca the delicious. House B 111:98-100 O '69

MUNSON, Genevieve
Old raccoon; story. Seventeen 28:438-42 Ag '69

MUNSON, Gorham
Workshops for writers. Sat R 52:39-43 Ap 26 '69

MUNSON, Paul L. See Gray, T. K. jt. auth.

MUNZ, Walter
Lambaréné revisited. N. Cousins. il por Sat R 52:28-32 O 4 '69

MUONIUM
Muonium metal. D. E. Thomsen. il Sci N 96:311 O 4 '69

MUONS. See Mesons

MURAL painting and decoration
Mural painting for science & technology; lobby of Brooklyn polytechnic institute. A. J. Tobias. il Am Artist 33:46-52 Mr '69
Mural; peace, plenty, friendship, throughout the world. J. R. Tompkins. il Sch Arts 68:13 F '69
Painting city walls. L. Friedman. il Sch Arts 69:28-9 Ja '70
Painting mural portraits. C. B. Wilson. il Am Artist 33:56-61 N '69
Raymond Katz, master of mixed techniques. M. W. Dulac. il Am Artist 33:58-61+ Ja '69
Unknown treasures of Himalayan art. M. Singh. il UNESCO Courier 22:14-25+ F '69
Wall painting. J. C. Hill. il Sch Arts 69:26-7 S '69
Where art and science meet; story of mural describing development of science at the Polytechnic institute of Brooklyn. E. Keller. il Chem 42:17-20 D '69
  See also
Mosaics

MURCHLAND, Bernard
Marxist-Christian dialogue. New Repub 160:30-1 Ja 25 '69

MURDER
Annals of jurisprudence: Whitmore confessions: Wylie-Hoffert case. F. C. Shapiro. New Yorker 44:39-42+ F 8; 44-6+ F 15; 45:42-4+ F 22 '69

MURDER—*Continued*

Avenging Angels; Hell's Angels and hippies brawl ends in killing of Meredith Hunter. il Newsweek 75:16 Ja 5 '70

Case of the hypnotic hippie. il Newsweek 74:30-2+ D 15 '69

Charlie Manson; one man's family. S. V. Roberts. il N Y Times Mag p 10-11+ Ja 4 '70

Deadly venom; murder of Yablonski family. Time 95:19-20 Ja 19 '70

Death for a family; the Rohs family. il Time 94:27 N 21 '69

Death of a rebel; J. A. Yablonski, wife, daughter. il Newsweek 75:22 Ja 19 '70

Demon of death valley; Tate murders. il Time 94:22+ D 12 '69

Graves in the dunes; murder of two Rhode Island girls. il Time 93:29 Mr 14 '69

Hollywood murders; Sharon Tate and others. il Newsweek 74:28 Ag 18 '69

In Hollywood, the dead keep right on dying. B. Farrell. Life 67:4 N 7 '69

In the shadow of Dallas; mysterious deaths of those possessing crucial knowledge about the killings of President Kennedy, Officer J. D. Tippit or Lee Harvey Oswald. D. Welsh and W. Turner. Ramp Mag 7:61-71 Ja 25 '69

Marine's last battle; the case of F. Kulak. il Newsweek 73:44-5 Ap 28 '69

Mississippi eyewitness. L. E. Lomax. il Ramp Mag 7:20-4 Ja 25 '69

Monstrous Manson family; with statements by D. Smith and R. Smith. P. O'Neil and others. il Life 67:2A, 20-31 D 19 '69

Murder on route 79. K. Detzer. il Read Digest 94:126-30 F '69

Night of horror; Tate and LaBianca killings. il Time 94:16-17 Ag 22 '69

Nothing but bodies; murder of S. Tate. il Time 94:24 Ag 15 '69

Panther hunt; arrests in the Alex Rackley killing. Newsweek 74:22A-22B S 1 '69

Rainy day murders. il Time 94:19 Ag 8 '69

Southern violence. S. Hackney. bibliog f il Am Hist R 74:906-25 F '69

Susan and the elders; Bailey family of Parkersburg, W.Va. burned alive. il Newsweek 73:37 Je 23 '69

Tate set; Hollywood murders. il Newsweek 74:24-5 Ag 25 '69

There's a maniac loose out there; Cape Cod murders. K. Vonnegut, jr. il Life 67:53-4+ Jl 25 '69

Tragic house on the hill; Roman Polanski comes home to the scene of the Sharon Tate murders. T. Thompson. il Life 67:42-6+ Ag 29 '69

Victims; excerpts. B. Lefkowitz and K. G. Gross. il Look 33:37-42+ My 27; 39-44+ Je 10; 39-44+ Je 24 '69

Weekend on Cape Cod. il Newsweek 73:38 Mr 17 '69

Where have all the flowers gone? New York bombings; Sharon Tate murders. Nat R 21:1257 D 16 '69

See also
Assassination
Capital punishment
Commandments, Ten—Murder
Trials (murder)

MURDER in literature. See Literature—Themes

MURDER trials. See Trials (murder)

MURDERERS. See Murder

MURDOCH, Iris
Iris Murdoch, informally; interview, ed. by W. K. Rose. por Harp Baz 102:208-9+ My '69

about

Delight and instruction. H. Kaye. New Repub 160:19-20 F 8 '69

MURDOCH, Rupert
Stooping to conquer. il por Time 95:49 Ja 12 '70

MURDOCK, Steve
Real world comes to Wyoming. Nation 209: 535-7 N 17 '69

MÜRER, E. H.
Thrombin-induced release of calcium from platelets. bibliog Science 166:623 O 31 '69

MURFITT, Rex
Rock garden plants from seed. Horticulture 46:22-5 D '68
Silver saxifrages. Horticulture 47:24-5+ Ap '69

MURO, Don
Face to face with a one-man band. por Seventeen 28:133 F '69

MURPHY, Sister Agnes
Audubon's hummingbird: note for a history of gratitude; poem. Commonweal 90:561 S 19 '69

MURPHY, Burt
Look what you can do with a belt sander. Pop Mech 132:168-71 D '69
New mini-strobes; flashguns you can slip in a pocket. Pop Mech 132:128-31+ D '69
Which insulation should you use? Pop Mech 132:170-4 O '69

MURPHY, Charles J. V.
Fabulous house of Kleberg: a world of cattle and grass. Fortune 79:112-19+ Je '69
King ranch south of the border. Fortune 80: 132-6+ Jl '69
Treasures in oil and cattle. Fortune 80:110-14+ Ag 1 '69

MURPHY, Diana
Remember the zoo; poem. Seventeen 28:239 Mr '69

MURPHY, Elaine
Trial of Elaine Murphy. E. Keiffer. il por Good H 168:12+ My '69

MURPHY, Francis X.
Confrontation: curia style. America 121:91-3 Ag 16 '69

MURPHY, George Lloyd
Murphy's late show. D. Henninger. New Repub 161:11-12 N 8 '69

MURPHY, James
Love fell; poem. Seventeen 28:211 Ag '69

MURPHY, James F.
Recreation education; for white or black America. bibliog f Parks & Rec 4:28-9+ Ag '69

MURPHY, Judith. See Dapper, G. jt. auth.

MURPHY, Karen, and Gross, Ronald
All you need is love. Love is all you need. So writes a rock poet. But is that poetry? N Y Times Mag p36-8+ Ap 13 '69

MURPHY, Robert C. and others
Acidic components of Green River shale identified by a gas chromatography-mass spectrometry-computer system. bibliog Science 165:695-7 Ag 15 '69

MURPHY, Robert Cushman
Bird watching, an abiding avocation. Natur Hist 78:80+ Ap '69

MURPHY, Robert F.
Society where only cross-cousins wed. Sat R 52:52-3 My 17 '69

MURPHY, Roger G.
Food outlook for 1969. Camp Mag 41:13+ Ap '69

MURPHY, Seamus
Seamus Murphy dance company; NYU School of education auditorium. J. Anderson. Dance Mag 43:32 My '69

MURPHY, Thomas
Whistle in the dark. Criticism
Nation 209:518 N 10 '69
New Yorker 45:150-1 O 18 '69
Newsweek 74:129 O 20 '69
Time il 94:71-2 O 17 '69

MURPHY, Tony
Japanese doll. Hot Rod 22:88-9 S '69

MURRAH, Alfred Paul
Excerpt from testimony before Subcommittee on constitutional rights, January 30, 1969. Cong Digest 48:105+ Ap '69

MURRAY, Albert
Stonewall Jackson's Waterloo; story. Harper 238:59-64 F '69

MURRAY, Albert R.
Negro judge vs. white militants. U S News 66:15 Je 9 '69

MURRAY, Bain
Adventures in Poland. Hi Fi 19:MA26-7 D '69
Boulez at Blossom. Hi Fi 19:MA26-7 O '69

MURRAY, Bettie Jane
Two separate people; story. Redbook 134:80-1 N '69

MURRAY, Betty M.
(ed) See Ungar, G. Chemical transfer of learning?

MURRAY, Catherine
Leslie, and others; story. Cath World 209:268-9 S '69

MURRAY, Charles B.
Excerpt from statement submitted to Subcommittee on constitutional rights, January 30, 1969. Cong Digest 48:126 Ap '69

MURRAY, David J.
Future of southern white Africa. bibliog f Cur Hist 56:269-74+ My '69

MURRAY, Donald M.
Explorers of inner space. Engl J 58:908-11 S '69

MURRAY, Henry Alexander
Portrait. H. Haydn. Am Scholar 39:123-36 Wint '69

MURRAY, John
Airport adventure; drama. Plays 28:19-33 F '69
Case for two detectives; drama. Plays 28:13-22+ Ap '69
Icarus is coming; drama. Plays 28:13-26 Mr '69

MURRAY, John—*Continued*
Triumph for Trimbly; drama. Plays 29:49-58 N '69
MURRAY, John Courtney
Father Murray, extreme center. America 120: 124 F 1 '69
Of many things. D. R. Campion. America 120:148 F 8 '69
MURRAY, Philip
Fu on the owl; poem. Poetry 114:314-18 Ag '69
MURRAY, Robert K.
How Harding saved the Versailles treaty. Am Heritage 20:66-7+ D '68
MURRAY, Ruth Adams
Pick up my what, and what? poem. Chr Cent 86:926 Jl 9 '69
MURRAY, Spence
Like bounding gazelles. Motor T 21:62-3 Ag '69
MURRAY, Thomas Joseph
Our man out West. Duns R 94:3 D '69
MURRAY, Thomas M.
Private mail delivery? The postman rings twice. J. Tebbel. il Sat R 52:50-1 Je 14 '69
MURRAY, William
Kings multiply and conquer. McCalls 97:72-3+ N '69
Return of Busby Berkeley. N Y Times Mag p26-7+ Mr 2 '69
(tr) See Pirandello, L. Man with the flower in his mouth
MURRAY, William Henry Harrison
Adirondacks. il por Am Heritage 20:44-63+ Ag '69
MURRAY Louis dance company
India: letters to Alwin Nikolais at the Henry st. playhouse. M. Louis. il Dance Mag 43: 44-5+ My; 83-4 Je '69
MURRO, Mark
They're all out to launch. J. Kirshenbaum. il por Sports Illus 31:38-41 Jl 21 '69
MURROW, Edward R.
Ed Murrow in peacetime. R. L. Tobin. Sat R 52:67 Ap 26 '69
Most unforgettable character I've met. L. LeSueur. por Read Digest 94:92-6 My '69
Prime time, by A. Kendrick. Review
Atlan 224:131 O '69. E. Weeks
Nation 209:514-5 N 10 '69. D. Smith
New Repub 161:35-7 S 6 '69. J. Chancellor
Newsweek por 74:114 O 6 '69. L. Smith
Sat R por 52:21-3+ S 27 '69. F. W. Friendly
MURTI, C. R. Krishna. See Krishna Murti, C. R.
MURTON, Tom
One year of prison reform. Nation 210:12-17 Ja 12 '70
MURVILLE, Maurice Jacques Couve de. See Couve de Murville, M. J.
MUS, David
Four last poems. Poetry 114:107-12 My '69
Journey of the Magi; poem. Poetry 115:175-7 D '69
MUS musculus. See Mice
MUSANTE, Giovanni
Defector in the household. il por Time 93:62 Mr 21 '69
MUSCADINE grapes. See Grapes
MUSCAE volitantes. See Eye—Diseases and defects
MUSCAT, Victor
End of the Muscat trail. por Bsns W p70+ Je 21 '69
MUSCATINE, Doris
If you're starved for real old-fashioned bread, there's a little man in Paris. Holiday 46:74-5 S '69
MUSCLE
Ionic mobility in muscle cells. M. J. Kushmerick and R. J. Podolsky. bibliog il Science 166:1297-8 D 5 '69
Laser diffraction studies on single skeletal muscle fibers. D. Cleworth and K. A. P. Edman. bibliog il Science 163:296-8 Ja 17 '69
Mechanism of muscular contraction. H. E. Huxley. bibliog il Science 164:1356-66 Je 20 '69
Turbidity, birefringence, and fluorescence changes in skeletal muscle coincident with the action potential. L. D. Carnay and W. H. Barry. bibliog il Science 165:608-9 Ag 8 '69
Vascular smooth muscle reactivity in normotensive and hypertensive rats. S. Spector and others. bibliog il Science 166:1300-1 D 5 '69
See also
Heart—Muscle
Myoglobin

Proteins
Paramyosin: molecular length and assembly. J. Kendrick-Jones and others. bibliog il Science 163:1196-8 Mr 14 '69
MUSCLE SHOALS, Ala.
Muscling in. il Newsweek 74:90 S 15 '69
MUSCLE strength
Anabolic steroid: effects on strength development. L. C. Johnson and J. P. O'Shea. bibliog il Science 164:957-9 My 23 '69
Calcium uptake by isolated sarcoplasmic reticulum treated with dithiothreitol. W. Van Der Kloot. bibliog il Science 164:1294 Je 13 '69
MUSCLES
See also
Ligaments
Muscle strength
Diseases
Adenosine triphosphatase and myopathy. G. A. Klassen and R. Blostein. bibliog il Science 163:492-3 Ja 31 '69
See also
Dystrophy, Muscular
MUSCULAR dystrophy. See Dystrophy, Muscular
MUSCULAR fatigue. See Fatigue
MUSCULAR power. See Muscle strength
MUSCULAR sense
See also
Movement. Psychology of
MUSE of Newark; story. See Hayes, P.
MUSEUM education
Boston's museum a-go-go. R. Schiller. il PTA Mag 64:22-5 O '69; Same abr. with title This is a museum? Read Digest 95:225-9 N '69
MUSEUM of contemporary art, Chicago
All package; Christo wrapping. il Time 93: 60 F 7 '69
MUSEUM of contemporary crafts, New York
Advanced; environment: Feel it. New Yorker 44:28-9 F 15 '69
Feel it; exhibition explores anti-visual experience. I. Horovitz. il Craft Horiz 29:14-15+ Mr '69
Quarter century of arts & crafts. D. Preiss. il Am Artist 33:28-34 F '69
Tools: extenders of the mind. H. Aach. il Craft Horiz 29:10-13+ My '69
MUSEUM of modern art, New York
Art in space; exhibition. D. L. Shirley. il Newsweek 75:63 Ja 12 '70
Departure at the Modern. Time 93:93 My 16 '69
Editorial; resignation of B. Lowry. T. B. Hess. Art N 68:25 Sum '69
How modern the Modern museum? R. Berenson. il Nat R 21:656-8 Jl 1 '69
MOMA tries again; new director. Newsweek 75:95 Ja 19 '70
Museum shop thrives. M. Tarshish. il Pub W 195:123-5 Je 2 '69
Parting with a paragon. il Newsweek 73:118-19 My 12 '69
Department of film
Film library and how it grew. I. Barry. Film Q 22:19-27 Sum '69
Film library
See Museum of modern art, New York—Department of film
MUSEUM of natural history. See American museum of natural history, New York
MUSEUM of primitive art, New York
Winner: announcement of transfer to Metropolitan at Metropolitan's show. New Yorker 45:27-8 Je 7 '69
MUSEUM of science, Boston
Boston's museum a-go-go. R. Schiller. il PTA Mag 64:22-5 O '69; Same abr. with title This is a museum? Read Digest 95: 225-9 N '69
MUSEUM of science and industry, Fort Worth, Tex. See Fort Worth, Tex.—Galleries and museums
MUSEUM of the media. See New York (city) —Galleries and museums
MUSEUM of the sea, Long Beach, Calif. See Museums
MUSEUM techniques
Art; Can man survive? exhibition. L. Alloway. Nation 208:773-4 Je 16 '69
MUSEUM villages. See Villages, Restored
MUSEUMS
Museum world. J. L. Stoutenburgh. See issues of Hobbies
Now the Point Pinos lighthouse has a downstairs museum. il Sunset 142:43 Mr '69

MUSEUMS—*Continued*
Sea museum fit for a queen; planned Museum of the sea aboard the Queen Mary. D. Valentry. il Sea Front 15:234-7 S '69
Sensitively modest museums enrich historic sites: Flint ridge; Fort hill; Fort ancient museums, Ohio. il Arch Rec 145:182-5 Je '69
Ten fascinating vacation spots of interest to children. il Good H 168:188-9 My '69
See also
Art—Galleries and museums
Automobile museums
Historical museums
Military museums
Museum techniques
Natural history museums
Naval museums
Railroad museums
Zoological specimens—Collection and preservation

Architecture
Building types study. il Arch Rec 145:175-90 Je '69
Concrete frames for works of art: Syracuse, N. Y. and Des Moines. J. Bailey. il Arch Forum 130:54-67 Je '69
Impressive museum: Richard Kaselowsky museum. Bielefeld, Germany. il Arch Rec 146:94-5 D '69
Today gallery for today's art; Hayward art gallery, London. il Design 70:36 Spr '69

Finance
Can museums survive tax reform? T. B. Hess. Art N 68:27 O '69
See also
Museums—Gifts, legacies, etc.

Gifts, legacies, etc.
Art and taxes. Newsweek 74:75 S 1 '69
Of gifts and taxes. Time 94:47 Ag 29 '69

Work with children
New look in museums. P. M. Williams. il Parents Mag 44:44-5+ Je '69
See also
Art—Galleries and museums—Work with children

MUSEUMS, Natural history. See Natural history museums
MUSEUMS, Private
Art museum designed for living; home of Mr and Mrs David Lloyd Kreeger of Washington, D.C. R. Fitzgerald. il House B 111:58-65 F '69

MUSHROOMS
About mushrooms. T. Trueblood. il Field & S 74:34+ Je '69
Creek-fed mushrooms. J. Neff. il Org Gard & Farm 16:54 Ag '69
Hallucinogens of plant origin. R. E. Schultes. bibliog il Science 163:245-7 Ja 17 '69
It's a riot of fungi. A. H. Smith. il Audubon 71:56-65 S '69
Mushrooms, an unexpected organic dividend. E. E. Armitage. il Org Gard & Farm 16:100-2+ F '69
Mushrooms: wild and edible. P. Maravigna and M. Maravigna. il Horticulture 47:22-3+ S '69
Temperamental visitor to our gardens. R. Donahue and M. Donahue. il Horticulture 47:59 Ja '69
See also
Cookery—Mushrooms
Truffles
MUSHROOMS in design. See Design, Decorative—Plant forms

MUSIC
Artist life. D. J. Soria. See issues of High fidelity incorporating Musical America
Drop-in night at the Electric circus; imaginary conversation with F. Liszt. D. Barillan. Sat R 52:72-3 N 15 '69
Here & there. See issues of High fidelity incorporating Musical America
Lively arts; interview. ed. by R. Hemming. C. Davis. Sr Schol 94:20 Ap 11 '69
Musical events; avant-garde music. W. Sargeant. New Yorker 45:109 Mr 22 '69
Musical events; performance of avant-garde by Minnesota orchestra. W. Sargeant. New Yorker 45:162 Mr 15 '69
New sounds of music. Changing T 23:6 F '69
See also
Bands (music)
Chamber music
Choral singing
Church music
Composition (music)
Computers—Musical applications
Copyright—Music
Folk music

Negro music
Passion music
Radio broadcasting—Music
Rock 'n' roll music
Symbolism in music
Television broadcasting—Music
Tone

Acoustics and physics
Analysis of musical-instrument tones. J.-C. Risset and M. V. Mathews. bibliog il Phys Today 22:23-30 F '69
Music made visible in a film of liquid; cymatics. H. Jenny. il UNESCO Courier 22:10-12+ D '69
Of knees and noise. Chr Cent 86:1443 N 12 '69
Stereo versus the concert hall. L. D. Harmon and D. J. MacLean. il Electr World 81:34-6 Ap '69
Varnishing luthier. Sci Am 220:45-6 F '69
See also
Musical pitch

Anecdotes, facetiae, satire, etc.
Beethoven new-born. E. T. Cone. Am Scholar 38:389-400 Sum '69

Appreciation
Answer is chamber music! C. Wadsworth. Hi Fi 19:MA9+ S '69
Building better music audiences. B. R. Purrington. Clear House 43:497-9 Ap '69
Décors of sound; musical thoughts on emotion and environment; excerpts from diary. N. Rorem. House B 111:102-3+ Ap '69
See also
Music—Philosophy and aesthetics
Opera—Appreciation

Bibliography
Book reviews; ed. by P. J. Smith. il Hi Fi 19:MA29-31 Ap; MA28-30 Jl; MA29-31 N '69
Musical bookshelf for the Christmas shopper. R. Jacobson. Sat R 52:52-3 D 13 '69
Musical events; words and music. W. Sargeant. New Yorker 45:51-2 D 27 '69
See also
Opera—Bibliography

Competitions
Trumpet battle at Niblo's pleasure garden. C. A. Hoover. bibliog f il Mus Q 55:384-95 Jl '69

Copyright
See Copyright—Music

Criticism
Theory, etc.
See Music—History and criticism

History and criticism
Conforming with the avant-garde. Discus. Harper 238:112+ Ap '69
History of Russian music, by G. R. Seaman. Review
    Mus Q 55:408-17 Jl '69. M. Velimirović
Hocket in medieval polyphony. W. E. Dalglish. bibliog f il Mus Q 55:344-63 Jl '69
Music. W. F. Rickenbacker. Nat R 21:239 Mr 11 '69
Selected essays on music, by V. Stasov. Review
    Mus Q 55:580-3 O '69. B. Schwarz
Unusual sound; Berlioz' Les Troyens. S. L. Fogel. il Opera N 34:14-16 S 20 '69
Where do we go from here? A European view. tr. by P. Helmer. W. E. von Lewinski. Mus Q 55:193-205 Ap '69
See also
Motets
Opera—History and criticism

Instruction and study
Guide to music lessons. Good H. 169:141 Ag '69
Orff-Schulwerk, a joyous note. G. L. Mayer Sat R 52:46-7 Jl 26 '69
Reading music & reading words. E. A. Movsesian. Todays Ed 58:42-3 Ja '69
See also
Guitar—Instruction and study

Moving pictures
See Moving pictures—Music

Patronage
See Music patronage

Periodicals
See also
American musical digest
Opera news (periodical)

Philosophy and aesthetics
Der musikbegriff im deutschen barock, by R. Dammann. Review
    Mus Q 55:246-55 Ap '69. P. H. Lang

MUSIC—*Continued*

Reading

See Music reading

Study and teaching

See Music—Instruction and study

Theory

See also
Tonality

Argentina

See also
Buenos Aires—Music

Austria

See also
Opera—Austria
Salzburg festival
Vienna—Music

Belgium

See also
Brussels—Music

Brazil

See also
Rio de Janeiro—Music

Canada

See also
Edmonton, Alberta—Music

China

See also
Opera, Chinese

Denmark

See also
Copenhagen—Music

England

Other side: Phoenix at Snape, Berlioz by Davis. T. Heinitz. Sat R 52:54 Jl 26 '69

Ethiopia

See also
Music, Ethiopian

France

See also
Paris—Music
Strasbourg—Music

Germany

See also
Opera—Germany

Germany (Democratic Republic)

See also
Berlin (East Berlin)—Music

Germany (Federal Republic)

See also
Berlin (West Berlin)—Music
Frankfort on the Main—Music
Hamburg—Music
Munich—Music
Stuttgart, Germany—Music

Hungary

See also
Budapest—Music

Ireland

See also
Dublin—Music

Italy

Music on and off the track. W. Weaver. Hi Fi 19:MA28+ D '69
See also
Milan, Italy—Music
Naples—Music
Palermo—Music
Rome (city)—Music
Venice—Music
Verona, Italy—Music

Mexico

See also
Mexico (city)—Music

New Zealand

See also
New Zealand opera company

Norway

See also
Oslo—Music

Poland

See also
Warsaw—Music

Scotland

See also
Edinburgh—Music
Opera—Scotland

Sweden

See also
Stockholm—Music

Switzerland

See also
Zurich, Switzerland—Music

Turkey

See also
Istanbul—Music

United States

Current chronicle (cont) bibliog f il Mus Q 55:87-144, 396-407, 559-72 Ja, Jl-O '69
Spot check: some observations on music in America. J. Claman. il Harp Baz 102:122G-122I F '69
See also
Jazz music
Orchestras
    also subhead Music under names of cities, towns, etc. e.g. Jackson, Miss.—Music

Wales

See also
Cardiff, Wales—Music

MUSIC, American
See also
Jazz music
Phonograph records—American music
Songs, American
MUSIC, Aztec. See Aztecs—Music
MUSIC, Band. See Band music
MUSIC, Baroque
Dancing Bach. W. Hilton; R. Tureck. il Dance Mag 43:47-51+ O '69
Der musikbegriff im deutschen barock, by R. Dammann. Review
Mus Q 55:246-55 Ap '69. P. H. Lang
See also
Phonograph records—Baroque music
MUSIC, Chamber. See Chamber music
MUSIC, Chinese
See also
Opera, Chinese
MUSIC, Church. See Church music
MUSIC, Concrete
See also
Music, Electronic
MUSIC, Electronic
High fidelity's electronic music contest. Hi Fi 19:57 Ag '69
Make your own electronic music. R. C. Ehle. il Radio-Electr 40:52-4+ My '69
Moog at the museum. J. Hiemenz. il Hi Fi 19:MA20-1 N '69
On the off-beat. C. Susa. il Hi Fi 19:MA9-10 My; MA8-9 Ag '69
Plain and easy guide to practical electronic music. R. Ehle. il Hi Fi 19:50-3+ Ag '69
See also
Phonograph records—Electronic music

Terminology

Guide to electronic music terminology. R. A. Moog. Sat R 52:47 Ja 25 '69
MUSIC, English
English restoration attitudes toward music. H. J. Jensen. bibliog f il Mus Q 55:206-14 Ap '69
MUSIC, Ethiopian
Ethiopian music, by M. Powne. Review
Am Rec G 35:877 My '69. R. Kennedy
MUSIC, German
See also
Phonograph records—German music
MUSIC, Inca. See Incas—Music
MUSIC, Medieval
Hocket in medieval polyphony. W. E. Dalglish. bibliog f il Mus Q 55:344-63 Jl '69
MUSIC, National
See also
Folk music
MUSIC, Negro. See Negro music
MUSIC, Oriental
Non-acceptance of the unfamiliar: Oriental music-Occidental music. Trân-van-Khê. il UNESCO Courier 22:26-31 Je '69
MUSIC, Polish
See also
Phonograph records—Polish music
MUSIC, Popular (songs, etc)
All you need is love. Love is all you need. So writes a rock poet. But is that poetry? K. Murphy and R. Gross. il N Y Times Mag p36-8+ Ap 13 '69; Discussion. p22+ My 11 '69
And then I (wish I) wrote: statements by some top creators of hit songs; ed. by D. Dachs. il Hi Fi 19:34-7 Je '69
Beatles illustrated lyrics. ed. by A. Aldridge. Review
New Repub. 161:25-6 N 8 '69. R. Whittemore
Categoric past, the personal present. F. Hogan. House B 111:124-7 Je '69

MUSIC, Popular (songs, etc)—*Continued*
Chambers brothers; integrated group. il
Ebony 24:162-4+ O '69
Classical bag. J. McClure il Hi Fi 19:58-61
Ag '69
Cycles. G. Lees. il Hi Fi 19:100 Ap '69
Decade of pop completed. E. Sander. Sat R
52:59-60 D 27 '69
Janis Joplin philosophy, every moment she
is what she feels. M. Lydon. il N Y Times
Mag p36-7+ F 23 '69
Kicking out the jams; MC5. H. Saal. il News-
week 73:117 My 19 '69
Look at adolescent music. A. H. Frerichs.
Clear House 43:435-8 Mr '69
Musical events: influence of pop music. W.
Sargeant. New Yorker 45:138-9 Je 7 '69
On the off-beat C. Susa. il Hi Fi 19:MA9-10
My; MA8-9 Ag '69
Pop music (cont) R. Goldstein. Vogue 153:130
F 1; 44 Mr 15; 34 Ap 15; 68 Je; 46 Ag 15;
158 O 1; 126 N 1 '69
Pop personality; ed. by E. Miller. R. McKuen.
il Seventeen 28:408+ Ag '69
Rise of the self-love song. T. Prideaux. il Life
67:12 N 28 '69
Rock for sale. M. Lydon. il Ramp Mag 7:
19-24 Je '69
Secular music. R. Christgau. Esquire 71:62+
Ap '69
Sweet singing man; ed. by E. Miller. G.
Campbell. il Seventeen 28:148-9+ Mr '69
Taylor girls: nitty gritty twins. G. Zimmer-
mann. il Look 33:68-70+ Mr 4 '69
That angry kid has gone all over romantic:
about the new Dylan album. A. Goldman.
Life 66:18 My 23 '69
Times they are a-changin': the music of
protest. R. A. Rosenstone. bibliog f Ann
Am Acad 382:131-44 Mr '69
Upsy-downsies; pop lyrics. N. Gittelson.
Harp Baz 102:22-3+ Mr '69
What pop music means to kids: with group-
discussion program. N. Hentoff. Parents Mag
44:46-7+ My '69
Woody Guthrie, songwriter; excerpt from The
incompleat folksinger, ed. by J. Schwartz.
P. Seeger. Ramp Mag 7:28-33 N 30 '68
See also
Phonograph records—Music, Popular (songs,
etc)
Rock 'n' roll music

History

Grace notes in American history: popular
sheet music from 1820 to 1900, by L. S.
Levy. Review
Am Rec G 35:434-5 Ja '69. J. Ringo
Old lantern slides; the song plugger's best
friends. J. W. Ripley. il Hobbies 74:98L-98P
D '69

Czechoslovakia

Protest in Prague: protest singers and songs.
il Newsweek 74:49 Jl 28 '69
MUSIC, Renaissance
See also
Phonograph records—Renaissance music
MUSIC, Russian
History of Russian music, by G. R. Seaman.
Review
Mus Q 55:408-17 Jl '69. M. Velimirović
Russian horn bands. R. Ricks. bibliog f il
Mus Q 55:364-71 Jl '69
MUSIC, Slavic

History and criticism

Slavonic and romantic music, by G. Abraham.
Review
Mus Q 55:573-5 O '69. B. Krader
MUSIC, Spanish
See also
Phonograph records—Spanish music
MUSIC and children. See Children and music
MUSIC and color
See also
Color organs
MUSIC and literature
More avant-rock in the classroom; recorded
poetry set to music. R. E. Morgan. bibliog
Engl J 58:1238-40 N '69
MUSIC and moving pictures. See Moving pic-
tures—Music
MUSIC and race
Music of militancy. F. Kofsky. Commonweal
89:733-4 Mr 14 '69
See also
Ethnomusicology
MUSIC and religion. See Religion and music
MUSIC and romanticism. See Romanticism in
music
MUSIC and society
Can't eat politics, can't eat art. N. Rorem.
Vogue 154:92+ D '69

MUSIC and state
German forecast: fair skies ahead. J. H. Sut-
cliffe. Opera N 34:6-7 D 6 '69
MUSIC as recreation
Retirement in allegro; musicians past sixty.
H. Alpert. il Har Yrs 9:17-20 N '69
State by state, seniors are swinging! il Har
Yrs 9:21 N '69
MUSIC audiences. See Audiences
MUSIC boxes
All wound up. F. Stevenson. il Opera N
34:12-16 D 27 '69
MUSIC cabinets. See Cabinets (furniture)
MUSIC camps
Beethoven in a pup tent. H. Janiec. il Hi Fi
19:MA8-10 F '69
MUSIC conductors. See Conductors (music)
MUSIC corporation of America. See MCA, in-
corporated
MUSIC critics
Dissent in Boston; unfavorable reviews of the
Boston symphony. Nation 209:653-4 D 15
'69
Making of an opera critic: Leigh Hunt. T.
Fenner. bibliog f il Mus Q 55:439-63 O '69
MUSIC educators national conference
Contemporary music project; it pays off. R.
W. Jones. il Hi Fi 19:MA10-11+ N '69
MUSIC festivals

Austria

See also
Salzburg festival

California

Escape, but something missing. M. Bernheimer. il Hi Fi 19:MA23 Ag '69
Popular art styles in Mariachi festivals; San
Francisco. A. E. Hippler. bibliog Am Imago
26:167-81 Sum '69
When cinema shouldn't be vérité; film on
the Monterey pop festival. R. Schickel.
Life 66:10 F 7 '69
Wild West rock show: shooting up a rock
bonanza. J. Holden. Ramp Mag 8:70-2+ D
'69

Canada

Summer music festivals, 69. Hi Fi 19:MA17-
19 Mr '69

Colorado

Our far-flung correspondents; R. Gibson's
seventh annual subscription jazz party in
Aspen. W. Balliett. New Yorker 45:175-6+
O 18 '69

England

Britten premiere and a mad King George. E.
Greenfield. il Hi Fi 19:MA26-7 Ag '69
Poet's return: it's what I do; Isle of Wight
rock festival. il Time 94:80-1 S 12 '69
Report: Glyndebourne; productions. F. G.
Barker. Opera N 34:31 S 6 '69

Europe

Europe's festivals; sound of music. W. Sargeant. il Travel & Camera 32:56-9+ Jl '69
Guide to European music festivals, 1969;
comp. by H. D. Jellinek. Sat R 52:68-9 Ap
26 '69

Europe, Western

Summer evenings (cont) Opera N 33:33-4
Mr 29 '69

Finland

Report: Helsinki; 1969 Helsinki festival. A.
Swanson. Opera N 34:30 S 6 '69

France

Festival at Royan. H. L. De La Grange. Sat R
52:56 Je 28 '69
High camp, low spirits; Royan festival. P.
Moor. il Hi Fi 19:MA26-7 Jl '69
Report: Aix-En-Provence; twenty-second Aix
festival. M. E. Davies. Opera N 34:26 S 20
'69
Report: Bordeaux; production of La Damna-
tion de Faust. M. E. Davies. Opera N 34:
29-30 S 6 '69

Germany (Democratic Republic)

Report: productions at East Berlin festival.
J. H. Sutcliffe. Opera N 34:28-9 D 13 '69

Germany (Federal Republic)

Report: Munich; four new productions at
Munich festival. D. Graham. il Opera N
34:24-5 S 20 '69

Indiana

Romantic revival: Butler's second annual
festival of romantic music. il Time 93:85
My 30 '69

Ireland

Report: Wexford festival opera productions.
W. H. A. Williams. Opera N 34:29 D 13 '69

MUSIC festivals—*Continued*

Italy

Moses at Maggio, rebellion in ISCM. D. Hamilton. Hi Fi 19:MA24+ S '69
Report: Florence; performances at Maggio musicale. T. Goth. Opera N 34:30 S 6 '69
Report: production at Neapolitan musical autumn. E. Tellini. Opera N 34:38 D 27 '69

Latin America

Summer evenings. Opera N 33:33 Mr 29 '69

Lebanon

Amid majestic ruins: Baalbek festival of music and drama. P. Moor. il Hi Fi 19: MA29-30 D '69

Louisiana

New Orleans, jazz capital? S. Dance. il Sat R 52:45-6 Jl 12 '69

Massachusetts

Big boom in Boston; National peace jubilee, 1869. R. Jarman. il Am Heritage 20:46-52+ O '69
See also
Berkshire symphonic festival

Michigan

Current chronicle; University of Michigan: Festival of contemporary music. E. Borroff. il Mus Q 55:396-401 Jl '69

Netherlands

Music: productions of Reconstruction and Cosi fan tutte at the Holland festival. D. Hamilton. Nation 209:157 Ag 25 '69
Reconstruction, an opera by committee. F. Stevenson. il Hi Fi 19:MA25 S '69
Report: Amsterdam; performance of Reconstruction. J. Mindszenthy. il Opera N 34: 31 S 6 '69

New York (state)

Age of Aquarius; Woodstock music and art fair. il Newsweek 74:88 Ag 25 '69
All nature is but art; Woodstock music and art fair. il Vogue 154:194-201 D '69
Big Woodstock rock trip; with photographs by J. Dominis and B. Eppridge. Life 67: 14B-23 Ag 29 '69
Birth of a culture; Woodstock music and art fair's aquarian exposition. P. Tracy. Commonweal 90:532-3 S 5 '69
Bouquets to the flower cops; Woodstock music and art fair. Chr Cent 86:1130 S 3 '69
Britten & Handel at Caramoor. G. Movshon. il Hi Fi 19:MA10-11 S '69
I was there; Woodstock music and art fair. A. Sideman. il Seventeen 29:86-7+ Ja '70
Knocking rock-land; rock festival. J. Deedy. Commonweal 91:196 N 14 '69
Lively arts; second International university choral festival, at Lincoln Center. R. Hemming. il Sr Schol 94:18 Ap 18 '69
Mass infantilism, anyone? Woodstock music and art fair. W. A. Rusher. Nat R 21:1012 O 7 '69
Message of history's biggest happening; Woodstock music and art fair; Time essay. il Time 94:32-3 Ag 29 '69
Mike Lang (groovy kid from Brooklyn) plus John Roberts (unlimited capital) equals Woodstock. R. Reeves. il N Y Times Mag p34-5 S 7 '69; Reply. K. Roberts. p54 O 5 '69
Muddy grooving at White Lake, Woodstock music and art fair. E. H. Brill. Chr Cent 86: 1206-8 S 17 '69
New culture of opposition; Woodstock music and art fair. A. Kopkind. Cur 111:56-9 O '69
Notes and comment; Woodstock festival. New Yorker 45:17-21 Ag 30 '69
Opinion: on Bethel and after. R. May. il Mlle 70:28+ N '69
Part of the whole thing: name it Woodstock, name it Bethel. L. Lerman. il Mlle 70:160-1 N '69
Report: Glens Falls; productions at Lake George opera festival. A. M. Lingg. Opera N 34:22 S 20 '69
Report: Katonah, N.Y.; Caramoor festival. F. Merkling. Opera N 34:26 S 6 '69
Rock, etc; Woodstock music and art fair. E. Willis. New Yorker 45:121-4 S 6 '69
Rocky road to fame, if not fortune; Woodstock music & art fair. il Bsns W p78-80 Ag 23 '69
Second reading: bad vibrations from Woodstock. B. Farrell. Life 67:4 S 5 '69

Ultimate pop experience; Woodstock music and art fair. E. Sander. Sat R 52:59+ S 27 '69
Underground industrial complex; after Woodstock. Chr Cent 86:1237 O 1 '69
Upon a time in Woodstock. P. P. Ardery, jr. Nat R 21:908+ S 9 '69; Same abr. with title Woodstock scene revisited. Cur 111: 54-5 O '69
Week of new American music; Rochester May festival. E. Haines. il Hi Fi 19:MA22+ Ag '69
Whole new minority group; Woodstock music & art fair. il Newsweek 74:20-22A S 1 '69
Woodstock, grand slam rush. R. Goldstein. Vogue 154:158 O 1 '69
Woodstock in retrospect. M. Mead. Redbook 134:30 Ja '70
Woodstock weekend. Chr Today 13:37-8 S 26 '69

Norway

Poetic epic; Mot solen at the Bergen international festival. W. Terry. il Sat R 52:27-8 Je 28 '69

Ohio

Boulez at Blossom. B. Murray. il Hi Fi 19: MA26-7 O '69

Pennsylvania

Temple's tale of two tents; Temple university's musical festival and institute. J. Felton. il Hi Fi 19:MA24-5 O '69

Puerto Rico

Festival Casals and Ponce's Parthenon. C. J. McNaspy. America 121:17-18 Jl 5 '69

Rhode Island

Musical events; Newport notes. W. Balliett. New Yorker 45:73-4+ Jl 19 '69
Report: Newport; performance of Pauline Viardot's Cendrillon. Q. Eaton. Opera N 34: 24 O 11 '69
When rock buffs go marchin' in; Newport jazz festival. T Wainwright. Life 67:10 Ag 8 '69

Texas

Pop festivals and Pentecost. J. C. Evans. Chr Cent 86:1303-5 O 15 '69
Report: San Antonio; San Antonio grand opera festival. O. Chism. Opera N 33:28-9 Ap 19 '69

United States

More wrong than right; rock festivals across the U.S. Time 94:53 Jl 25 '69
Music festivals USA, summer 1969, comp. by H. Jellinek. Sat R 52:42+ Je 14 '69
Music on the home front. il Opera N 33:16-17 Je 14 '69
Sons of Bethel: rock festivals in Louisiana, Washington and Texas. il Time 94:81 S 12 '69
Summer evenings (cont) Opera N 33:33 Mr 29 '69
Summer music festivals, 69. Hi Fi 19:MA17-19 Mr; MA11 Ap '69
U.S. calendar. See issues of Opera news published during opera season

Vermont

Musical events; Music from Marlboro series at Town Hall. W. Sargeant. New Yorker 44:108-9 F 8 '69

Wisconsin

Peninsula music festival. J. Rudolph. il Hi Fi 19:MA26+ N '69

MUSIC for children
Operatic pied piper; G. C. Menotti's children's opera Help! Help! The Globolinks. P. D. Zimmerman. il Newsweek 75:61-2 Jan 5 '70
See also
Phonograph records—Childrens records

MUSIC halls (variety theaters, etc)
Apollo voodoo: Harlem's legendary variety house. A. Goldman. il Holiday 45:54-5+ F '69
See also
Discotheques, etc.
New York (city)—Radio City music hall

MUSIC history. See Music—History and criticism

MUSIC in art
Music by Handel and Hogarth. F. V. Grunfeld. il Opera N 33:12-15 F 8 '69

MUSIC in the home
Stimulant or tranquilizer; symposium. House & Gard 136:26+ Jl '69
See also
Music rooms and equipment

MUSIC libraries
See also
Libraries—Phonograph and phonograph records

MUSIC on television. See Television broadcasting—Music
MUSIC patronage
Princesse Winnie. R. W. Hall. Opera N 34: 28-31 D 27 '69
  See also
Opera patronage
MUSIC publishing
Music from the conglomerates. H. W. Heinsheimer. Sat R 52:61+ F 22 '69
MUSIC reading
Reading music & reading words. E. A. Movsesian. Todays Ed 58:42-3 Ja '69
MUSIC rooms and equipment
Handy home movie center. il Bet Hom & Gard 47:54 Ap '69
House that runs by itself. il House & Gard 136:54-7 Jl '69
Sound is glorious. D. Brubeck. il House & Gard 136:100 Jl '69
MUSIC schools
  See also
California institute of the arts
Manhattan school of music
North Carolina school of the arts, Winston-Salem
MUSIC writing. See Composition (music)
MUSICAL accompaniment
Plusses outweigh the minuses; recorded music in the dance studio. D. R. Sellars. Dance Mag 43:60-2+ N '69
MUSICAL boxes. See Music boxes
MUSICAL comedies, College. See College and school drama
MUSICAL comedies, revues, etc.
Guide to Modcom; commercial exploitation of modernity without regard for dramatic art. il Time 94:78 O 3 '69
  See also
Musical comedy, revue, etc.
Phonograph records—Musical comedies, revues, etc.
Zarzuelas
            Criticisms, plots, etc.
Billy
  New Yorker 45:99 Mr 29 '69
Canterbury tales
  America 120:316 Mr 15 '69
  Dance Mag 43:26+ My '69
  Nat R 21:918 S 9 '69
  New Yorker 44:90 F 15 '69
  Newsweek il 73:113 F 17 '69
  Time il 93:62 F 14 '69
  Vogue 153:42 Mr 15 '69
Caution: a love story (about a certain Duke and Duchess)
  Sat R 52:53-4 Ap 19 '69
Celebration
  America 120:315 Mr 15 '69
  Dance Mag 43:71 Mr '69
  Life il 66:82-4+ Mr 14 '69
  New Yorker 44:49 F 1 '69
  Time il 93:72 Ja 31 '69
Coco
  New Yorker 45:38 D 27 '69
  Newsweek il 74:75-9 N 10 '69
  Newsweek il 74:58 D 29 '69
  Sat R 53:88 Ja 10 '70
  Time il 94:86-7 N 7 '69
  Time il 94:35 D 26 '69
Come summer
  New Yorker 45:99 Mr 29 '69
Curley McDimple
  Life il 66:81-2 Je 13 '69
Dames at sea
  Commonweal 89:735-6 Mr 14 '69
  Dance Mag il 43:70-1 Mr '69
  Life 66:8 Mr 7 '69
  Nation 208:189 F 10 '69
Dear world
  America 120:512 Ap 26 '69
  Chr Cent 86:483-4 Ap 9 '69
  Dance Mag il 43:20+ Ap '69
  New Yorker 44:90 F 15 '69
  Newsweek il 73:113 F 17 '69
Fiesta in Madrid
  Dance Mag 43:71 Ag '69
  Newsweek 73:95-6 Je 9 '69
  Sat R 52:46 Je 14 '69
From the second city
  New Yorker 45:141-2 O 25 '69
Gertrude Stein's first reader
  New Yorker 45:39 D 27 '69
Hair
  Hi Fi il 19:108 Jl '69
  New Yorker 45:102 Je 14 '69
  Newsweek il 74:94 Jl 7 '69
  Opera N 34:8-13 D 20 '69
  Time 94:76 D 12 '69
Heaven grand in amber orbit
  Newsweek il 74:94 N 3 '69
Horseman, pass by
  New Yorker 44:77-8 Ja 25 '69

Jimmy
  America 121:544-5 N 29 '69
  Commonweal 91:382-3 D 26 '69
  New Yorker 45:128 N 1 '69
  Newsweek il 74:94 N 3 '69
Man better man
  New Yorker 45:58 Jl 12 '69
New music hall of Israel
  America 121:342 O 18 '69
  New Yorker 45:88+ O 11 '69
Oh! Calcutta!
  America 121:146 S 6 '69
  Commentary 48:24+ N '69
  Commonweal 90:463-4 Jl 25 '69
  Esquire 72:44 D '69
  Holiday 46:39+ D '69
  New Yorker 45:72+ Je 28 '69
  Newsweek il 73:107 Je 16 '69
  Newsweek il 73:81 Je 30 '69
  Sat R 52:51 Ap 26 '69
  Sat R 52:20 Jl 26 '69
  Time il 93:59 Je 27 '69
  Vogue 154:60 Ag 1 '69
Oklahoma!
  America 121:76-7 Ag 2 '69
Peace
  Dance Mag 43:23+ Ap '69
  New Yorker 44:98-100 F 8 '69
Promenade
  Life 67:8 Ag 1 '69
  Nation 208:837 Je 30 '69
  New Yorker 45:63 Jl 5 '69
  Newsweek il 73:107 Je 16 '69
Promises, promises
  America 120:146 F 1 '69
  Dance Mag 43:93-4 Ja '69
  Nat R 21:918 S 9 '69
  Nation 208:125 Ja 27 '69
Red, white and Maddox
  America 120:232 F 22 '69
  Nation 208:221 F 17 '69
  New Repub 160:29-30 F 22 '69
  New Yorker 44:49 F 1 '69
  Sat R 52:33 F 15 '69
  Vogue 153:42 Mr 15 '69
Salvation
  Chr Cent 86:1646-7 D 24 '69
  Dance Mag 43:84 N '69
  New Yorker 45:114 O 4 '69
  Newsweek il 74:133 O 6 '69
  Sat R 52:26 O 11 '69
Sambo
  New Yorker 45:43 Ja 3 '70
1776
  America 120:512-14 Ap 26 '69
  Dance Mag 43:92-3 My '69
  Nat R 21:919 S 9 '69
  Nation 208:443-4 Ap 7 '69
  New Yorker 45:87 Mr 22 '69
  Newsweek il 73:105 Mr 31 '69
  Sat R il 52:20 Ap 5 '69
  Time il 93:55 Mr 28 '69
  Vogue il 153:118-19 Je '69
South Pacific
  America 121:77-8 Ag 2 '69
Stomp
  Newsweek il 74:85-6 D 1 '69
  Newsweek il 74:138-9 D 8 '69
La strada
  New Yorker 45:57 D 20 '69
You never can tell
  Sat R 52:22 Mr 15 '69
Zorba
  Dance Mag 43:93 Ja '69
MUSICAL comedy, revue, etc.
Goings on about town. See issues of New Yorker
Successful musical combines the sound of today with a nonexistent story. C. Barnes. Holiday 45:12+ Mr '69
MUSICAL comedy production. See Theatrical production and direction
MUSICAL composition. See Composition (music)
MUSICAL cruises. See Cruising
MUSICAL education
  See also
Children and music
Music—Instruction and study
Music and children
Opera—Instruction and study
MUSICAL films. See Moving pictures—Musical films
MUSICAL form
  See also
Rondo
MUSICAL hoaxes. See Hoaxes
MUSICAL instruments
Analysis of musical-instrument tones. J.-C. Risset and M. V. Mathews. bibliog il Phys Today 22:23-30 F '69

MUSICAL instruments—*Continued*
Symphony of one: C. Tree's collection. il Time
93:58-9 Je 27 '69
See also
Band instruments
also names of musical instruments.
e.g. Piano
MUSICAL instruments, Electronic
Electric Bach; Moog synthesizer. H. Saal.
il Newsweek 73:90 F 3 '69
Electronic music-makers you can build from
kits. S. M. Gallager. il Pop Mech 132:124-6
D '69
Into our lives with Moog; electronic syn-
thesizer. il Time 93:50-1 Mr 7 '69
Make electronic bongos. J. Jaques. il Radio-
Electr 40:42-3 Jl '69
Switched-on Bach story; W. Carlos perform-
ing on a Moog electronic synthesizer. I.
Berger. il Sat R 52:45-7+ Ja 25 '69
Synthesizing Johann S. Bach. R. Freedman.
Life 66:12 Ja 24 '69

Equipment
For your guitar, a compression sustainer.
C. Anderton. il Pop Electr 30:63-4+ My
'69
Solid-state fuzz box. J. Jaques. il Radio-
Electr 40:40-1 D '69
Throbbing vibrato. J. Jaques. il Radio-Electr
40:45-6 Ap '69
Treble boost for your guitar. L. Anthony.
il Pop Electr 31:59-60+ D '69
Waa-waa. J. S. Simonton, jr. il Pop Electr
32:45-51 Ja '70
MUSICAL instruments, Mechanical
See also
Music boxes
MUSICAL intervals and scales
See also
Tonality
MUSICAL pitch
Second-guessing the pitch reference. E. M.
Hoyt. il Pop Electr 30:70-1 My '69
MUSICAL plagiarism. See Plagiarism in music
MUSICAL plays. See Operas
MUSICAL style. See Composition (music)
MUSICAL tone. See Tone
MUSICIANS
Artist life. D. J. Soria. See issues of High
fidelity incorporating Musical America
Debuts & reappearances; New York concerts.
See issues of High fidelity incorporating
Musical America
Here & there. See issues of High fidelity
incorporating Musical America
Musical America selects young artists, 1969;
photographs. Hi Fi 19:MA8-12+ Jl '69
Musical whirl; photographs. See issues of
High fidelity incorporating Musical Amer-
ica
Philharmonicsville (pop. 106) D. Henahan. il
N Y Times Mag p26-7+ S 28 '69; Discus-
sion. p 12+ O 19; 14+ N 16 '69
See also
Composers
Conductors (music)
Jazz musicians
Negro musicians
Street musicians

Salaries, allowances, etc.
Bargaining in major symphony orchestras. L.
E. Lunden bibliog Mo Labor R 92:15-19
Jl '69
Musical events: performing arts in crisis. W.
Sargeant. New Yorker 45:187-8 N 29 '69
MUSICIANS, American
See also
American federation of musicians
Bernstein, L.
Ellington, D.
Hawkins, C.
Hollander, L.
Istomin, E.
Jazz musicians
Negro musicians
MUSICIANS, Bolivian
See also
Laredo, J.
MUSICIANS, English
See also
Walton, W. T.
MUSICIANS, French
See also
Berlioz, H.
MUSICIANS, Italian
See also
Scarlatti, D

MUSICIANS, Negro. See Negro musicians
MUSICIANS, Russian
See also
Pachmann, V. de
Rostropovich, M.
MUSICIANS, Spanish
See also
Casals, P.
MUSICIANS in art. See Music in art
MUSICOLOGY
See also
Ethnomusicology
MUSIL, Robert
Flypaper; story, tr. by M. Roloff. Harp Baz
102:68 Je '69
MUSK oxen
These Alaskans like to butt things. il Sun-
set 142:46+ My '69
MUSKEGON, Mich.
Less than a minute a barrel. M. L. Leyrer.
il Am City 84:44 O '69
MUSKELLUNGE fishing
But is it fishing? il Newsweek 74:66 Jl 14 '69
Madness for muskies. H. Bradshaw. il Field
& S 73:66-7+ Mr '69
MUSKETS
Lindsay's double shooting. C. G. Worman.
il Hobbies 74:122-3 Jl '69
Musket production at Springfield, 1852. C. G.
Worman. il Hobbies 74:122-3 My '69
See also
Rifles
MUSKIE, Edmund Sixtus
Blocking the ABM. New Repub 160:11-12
Je 7 '69
Draft; address, February 17, 1969. Vital
Speeches 35:356-8 Ap 1 '69
Tear down the walls. por Am Home 72:8 Ap
'69
What happens when peace breaks out? Sat
R 52:12-15 My 24 '69

about
Battling governmental torpor. por Sci N 95:
450 My 10 '69
Can a poor man get to be president? S.
Alsop. Newsweek 73:136 Mr 17 '69
Congress: Muskie seeks committee on tech-
nological backlash. P. M. Boffey. Science
163:1179 Mr 14 '69
Ed for Ted. S. Alsop. Newsweek 74:88 Ag 4
'69
Educating Ed Muskie; challenge of running
for president. il por Time 94:23-4 Ag 15 '69
Fight over who cleans up. por Bsns W p46 Jl
12 '69
Muskie: the loser as a big winner. L. Berg-
quist. il pors Look 33:30-2+ F 18 '69
Shaping the clean water act. por Sci N 95:
208 Mr 1 '69
What I learned in 1968 about women, politics,
and my husband. J. Muskie and M. F.
Hoyt. il pors McCalls 96:92-3+ Ap '69
MUSKIE, Jane
What I learned in 1968 about women, politics,
and my husband; ed. by M. F. Hoyt. pors
McCalls 96:92-3+ Ap '69
MUSLIMS
See also
Islam
MUSLIMS, Black. See Black Muslim move-
ment
MUSLIMS in Africa
Islam in Sub-Saharan Africa. T. Y. Ismael.
bibliog f il Cur Hist 56:146-50+ Mr '69
Politics and Islam in North Africa. W. H.
Lewis. Cur Hist 56:136-40+ Mr '69
MUSLIMS in India
Muslims of India and Pakistan. H. Malik.
bibliog f il Cur Hist 56:151-5+ Mr '69
MUSLIMS in Nigeria
Religion in Nigeria's conflict: Islam in the
saddle. H. W. Turner. Chr Cent 86:1177-9
S 10 '69; Reply. E. Doerr. 86:1354 O 22 '69
MUSLIMS in Pakistan
Muslims of India and Pakistan. H. Malik.
bibliog f il Cur Hist 56:141-5+ Mr '69
MUSLIMS in Russia
Islam in the Soviet Union. J. B. Wolf. bib-
liog f Cur Hist 56:161-5+ Mr '69
MUSLIMS in Spain
Moriscos: an Ottoman fifth column in six-
teenth-century Spain. A. C. Hess. bibliog f
Am Hist R 74:1-25 O '68
MUSORGSKII, Modest Petrovich
Again, Boris by Kipnis. P. L. Miller. Am
Rec G 35:776 My '69
Great performance: Mussorgsky's Pictures.
M. N. Kanny. Am Rec G 35:629 Ap '69
Modest Mussorgsky, by M. D. Calvocoressi.
Review
Am Rec G por 36:146-8 O '69

MUSSELS
Two unusual unionid hermaphrodites. H. Van
Der Schalie. bibliog il Science 163:1333-4 Mr
21 '69
See also
Cookery—Shellfish
MUSSELS, Fresh water
Mussels on the move. J. J. Welsh. il Natur
Hist 78:56-9 My '69
MUSSOFF, Lenore
Medium is the absurd: address, November
1968. Engl J 58:566-70+ Ap '69
MUSTACHES
How I grew a mustache and found happiness.
A. Buchwald. il Ladies Home J 86:74 Mr '69
MUTAGENIC substances
Chemical mutagenesis; report of meeting held
at National institute of general medical sci-
ences. A. E. Heming and J. H. U. Brown.
Science 163:1361-2 Mr 21 '69
See also
Cycasin
MUTATION (bacteria)
Cellular factors in genetic transformation.
A. Tomasz. il Sci Am 220:38-44 bibliog
(p 138) Ja '69
Cycasin: detection of associated mutagenic
activity in vivo. M. G. Gabridge and others.
bibliog il Science 163:689-91 F 14 '69
Kasugamycin resistance: 30S ribosomal muta-
tion with an unusual location on the escheri-
chia coli chromosome. P. F. Sparling. bib-
liog il Science 167:56-8 Ja 2 '70
MUTATION (biology)
Hemoglobins A and A₂ in New World pri-
mates: comparative variation and its
evolutionary implications. S. H. Boyer and
others. bibliog il Science 166:1428-31 D 12 '69
Immunological detection of single amino
acid substitutions in alkaline phosphatase.
G. T. Cocks and A. C. Wilson. bibliog il
Science 164:188-9 Ap 11 '69
Non-Darwinian evolution. J. L. King and
T. H. Jukes. bibliog il Science 164:788-98
My 16 '69
See also
Heterozygosis
MUTATION (botany)
See also
Mutation (fungi)
Polymorphism (botany)
MUTATION (fungi)
Cytoplasmic DNA from petite colonies of sac-
charomyces cerevisiae: a hypothesis of the
nature of the mutation. F. Carnevali and
others. bibliog il Science 163:1331-3 Mr 21
'69
MUTILATION of books. See Books—Mutila-
tion, defacement, etc.
MUTINY
Company A; how history looks upon mu-
tinies. Commonweal 90:556-7 S 19 '69
Mutiny in the Presidio: trial of army prisoners
who staged sitdown protest in San Fran-
cisco. il Time 93:17-18 F 21 '69
MUTIS, José Celestino
Mutis in New Granada. N. López Pellón. il
por Américas 21:29-33 F '69
MUTUAL funds. See Investment trusts
MUTUAL insurance companies. See Insurance
companies
MUTUAL savings banks. See Savings banks
MUTUAL trust funds. See Investment trusts
MY brother who is dearly loved; story. See
Stevenson, K. L.
MY daughter, your son; drama. See Ephron,
P. and Ephron, H.
MY LAI massacre. See Vietnamese war, 1957-
—Atrocities—Songmy massacre
MY secret, your secret; story. See Soman, F. J.
MYCETOZOA. See Slime molds
MYCOBACTERIUM
New light-sensitive cofactor required for
oxidation of succinate by mycobacterium
phlei. C. R. Krishna Murti and A. F.
Brodie. bibliog il Science 164:302-4 Ap 18
'69
MYCOLOGY
See also
Fungi
MYCOPLASMA. See Microorganisms, Patho-
genic
MYDANS, Carl, and Mydans, Shelley
What manner of men are these Japanese?
Fortune 80:100-2+ Ag 1 '69; Same abr. Read
Digest 95:177-8+ O '69
MYDANS, Shelley. See Mydans, C. jt. auth.
MYELOMA. See Tumors
MYERS, Chauncie Kilmer, bp
Post-Pike era? E. E. Plowman. Chr Today 13:
44-5 F 28 '69
MYERS, John Bernard
Building watcher. Craft Horiz 29:20-9 Jl '69

MYERS, Oliver T.
Slave in our time. Nation 208:121-2 Ja 27 '69
MYERS, R. S. and O'Brien, J.
Light-emitting diodes. Elect World 82:41-5
Jl '69
MYERS, Tom
Can man afford to foul his environment?
photographs. Nat Wildlife 7:18-19 Je '69
MYERS, Walter
In the matter of James Whitcomb Riley.
Esquire 72:82+ S '69
MYERSON, Michael
ILGWU: fighting for lower wages. Ramp Mag
8:51-5 O '69
MYGATT, Peter
Atom at ease. Travel 132:68-70 N '69
MYLAR
Chez Mlle: flash in the pad. P. Bartlett. il
Mlle 70:66-7 D '69
MYLONAS, George
L.B.J. caper. por Time 94:39-40 O 17 '69
One man's odyssey. por Newsweek 74:54 O
20 '69
Prisoner of Amorgos. N. Gage. il pors N Y
Times Mag p23-5+ S 21 '69; Discussion.
p 16+ O 12; 16+ O 26 '69
MYOCARDIUM. See Heart—Muscle
MYOGLOBIN
Neutron analysis for proteins. B. J. Culliton.
il Sci N 96:536-7 D 6 '69
Structural stability and solvent denatura-
tion of myoglobin. T. T. Herskovits and
H. Jaillet. bibliog il Science 163:282-5 Ja
17 '69
MYOPATHIES. See Muscles—Diseases
MYOPIA
Kids who wear glasses; superior academic
performance of near-sighted children.
Trans-Action 6:10 Ja '69
MYOTONIC muscular dystrophy. See Dystro-
phy, Muscular
MYRBERG, Arthur A. jr
Shark caller. il por Time 93:75 Je 20 '69
MYRCENE. See Terpenes
MYRDAL, Gunnar. See Myrdal, K. G.
MYRDAL, Karl Gunnar
Soft states of South Asia: the civil servant
problem; address, November 14, 1968. Bul
Atom Sci 25:7-10 Ap '69
about
National image. Commonweal 90:36 Mr 28
'69
Negro in America: where Myrdal went wrong.
C. N. Degler. il por N Y Times Mag p64-5+
D 7 '69
MYRICK, Frank B.
As printers specialize. Pub W 195:68 Ap 7 '69
MYRMECOPHILIC beetles. See Beetles
MYROMYCETES. See Slime molds
MYRTLE, Crape. See Crape myrtle
MYSLENSKI, Skip
Cross-country. Sports Illus 31:69-70 D 8 '69
I do what I think is right. Sports Illus 30:
56-8+ Je 9 '69
Pressure cooker. Sports Illus 31:18-21 Jl 7
'69
Track & field (title varies) Sports Illus 30:52
F 17; 70-1 Je 2; 31:38 Jl 28 '69
Woes of Wee Willie Wisp. Sports Illus 30:42-
4+ Mr 17 '69
MYSTERIES, Religious
Mysteries. L. N. Bell. Chr Today 13:19 Jl 18 '69
MYSTERY of the gumdrop dragon; drama.
See Burtle, G. L.
MYSTERY stories. See Detective and mystery
stories
MYSTERY writers of America, incorporated
Mystery writers honor the best of 1968. Pub
W 195:66 Ap 28 '69
MYSTIC seaport museum, Mystic, Conn.
Mystic seaport. A. Rosenthal. il Todays
Health 47:42-7 Ap '69
MYSTICISM
Polymorphism, mystic crackpot. J. Gruen.
Vogue 153:138 Ap 15 '69
Search for faith. il Life 68:16-26+ Ja 9 '70
Hinduism
God-possessed: Sai Baba. il Newsweek 74:
110+ N 17 '69
Jai Baba! Hare Krishna, and all that. P.
Rowley. il Mlle 70:136-7+ D '69
MYSTROMYS
Long-lived rodent for research. Sci N 95:212
Mr 1 '69
MYTHOLOGY
Anatomy of mythology. C. Wilson. Atlan
224:95-6+ Jl '69
Flight of the wild gander, by J. Campbell.
Review
Commentary 48:108-10 D '69. R. Ackerman

MYTHOLOGY—*Continued*
Global myths record their passage. W. D. Stahlman. il Sat R 53:100-3 Ja 10 '70
Mystery of the mistletoe. H. W. Dengler. il Am For 75:1-3+ D '69
See also
Gods and goddesses
Legends

MYTHOLOGY, Classical
See also
Mythology, Greek

Study and teaching

See also
Mythology, Greek—Study and teaching

MYTHOLOGY, Greek
Greece, gods, and art, by A. Liberman. Review
Travel & Camera 32:62-3+ Mr '69. M. Wright

Study and teaching

All Greek? study of the Theseus myth in The king must die. J. M. Butcher. Engl J 58:1335-7 D '69

MYTHOLOGY, Pre-Columbian
Mythic symbols in two precolumbian myths. C. A. Sarnoff. bibliog il Am Imago 26:3-20 Spr '69

MYTHS. See Mythology

MYXOBACTERIA
Cytophaga that kills or lyses algae. J. R. Stewart and R. M. Brown, jr. bibliog il Science 164:1523-4 Je 27 '69

MYXOMYCETES. See Slime molds

MYXOVIRUSES. See Viruses

N

NAACP. See National association for the advancement of colored people
NAB. See National alliance of businessmen; National association of broadcasters
NACS. See National association of college stores
NADH. See Nicotinamide nucleotides
NADPH. See Nicotinamide nucleotides
NAE. See National academy of engineering; National association of evangelicals
NAEB. See National association of educational broadcasters
NAHB. See National association of home builders
NAM. See National association of manufacturers
NASA. See United States—National aeronautics and space administration
NASCAR (National association for stock car auto racing) See Automobile racing
NASPA. See National association of student planners and architects
NASSP. See National association of secondary school principals
NATA. See National aviation trades association
NATO. See National association of theatre owners; Nato
NAWAPA. See North American water and power alliance
NBA. See National basketball association; National book awards
NBAA. See National business aircraft association
NBC. See National book committee
NBEDC. See National black economic development conference
NCAA. See National collegiate athletic association
NCARB. See National council of architectural registration boards
NCC. See National council of churches
NCEA. See National Catholic educational association
NCOMP. See National Catholic office for motion pictures
NCSC. See National council of senior citizens
NCSEA. See National council of state education association
NCTE. See National council of teachers of English
NDEA (National defense education act) See School laws and legislation—United States
NDEA institutes. See Teachers institutes
NDHIA. See National dairy herd improvement association, incorporated

NDP (National democratic party) See Political parties—Germany (Federal Republic)
NEA. See National education association
NEA tours. See National education association—Division of educational travel
NERVA (nuclear engine for rocket vehicle application) See Rockets, Atomic powered
NET. See National educational television network
NFL. See National football league
NGO. See United Nations—Non-governmental organizations
NHL. See National hockey league
NHRA springnationals. See Automobile racing
NHSC. See National home study council
NICB. See National industrial conference board
NICEM (National information center for educational media) See Southern California university, Los Angeles
NIH. See United States—National institutes of health
NLC. See National league of cities
NLF. See National liberation front (Vietnam)
NLRB. See United States—National labor relations board
NLW. See National library week
NMU. See National maritime union of America
NNEA. See National Negro evangelical association
NOAA. See United States—National oceanic and atmospheric agency (proposed)
NOLS. See National outdoor leadership school
NORAD. See North American air defense command
NORI. See National office for the rights of the indigent
NPA. See National planning association
NPPC. See National pork producers council
NRP. See Neurosciences research program, Boston
NRPA. See National recreation and park association
NSA. See United States national student association
NSC. See National semiconductor corporation; United States—National security council
NSF. See United States—National science foundation
NSMC. See National student marketing corporation
NSRDS (national standard reference data system) See Information storage and retrieval systems—Science
NSTA. See National science teachers association
NSU-Wankel engines. See Automobile engines
NTL. See National training laboratories
NTSB. See United States—National transportation safety board
NWRO. See National welfare rights organization
NYLA. See New York library association
NYPL. See New York public library
NYSE (New York stock exchange) See Stock exchange—New York (city)
NYU. See New York university
NABB, Edward H.
Celebrated bullfrogs of Dorchester County. Motor B 123:90-1+ F '69
Dredge boats of the Chesapeake; our last fleet of working sail. Yachting 126:50-3+ S '69
Tighten your belt. Yachting 125:108-9+ Ja '69
NABI, Stanley
Poets and prices. R. Brady. por Duns R 93:119-20 My '69
NABISCO. See National biscuit company
NABOKOV, Peter
Peyote road. N. Y. Times Mag p30-1+ Mr 9 '69
NABOKOV, Vladimir
I have never seen a more lucid, more lonely, better balanced mad mind than mine; interview, ed. by M. Duffy. por Time 93:82-3 My 23 '69
Invitation to a beheading; dramatization. See McGrath, R.
Vladimir Nabokov talks about Nabokov; interview. Vogue 154:190-1 D '69

about

In the mind of Nabokov. A. Kazin. Sat R 52:27-8+ My 10 '69
Oh, my Lolita, I have only words to play with. P. S. Prescott. Look 33:6 My 27 '69
Prospero's progress. il pors Time 93:81-2+ My 23 '69

NABOKOV, Vladimir—about—*Continued*
Van loves Ada, Ada loves Van. J. Updike
New Yorker 45:67-75 Ag 2 '69
Vladimir in dreamland. J. Heidenry. Commonweal 90:231-4 My 9 '69
Waltz invention. Criticism
Sat R 52:22 F 1 '69
Time il 93:59 Ja 24 '69

NACE, Raymond L.
Arrogance toward the landscape: a problem in water planning; excerpts from address, September 4, 1969. Bul Atom Sci 25:11-14 D '69

NACHMAN, Larry David
Defense against Daley: the conspiracy on trial. Nation 208:752-4 Je 16 '69
Obituary for SDS. Nation 209:558-61 N 24 '69

NACHT, Ray
(tr) See Marchenko, A. My testimony

NADEL, Myron H.
Wisconsin's new certification program. Dance Mag 43:105-6 F '69

NADER, Ralph
Danger in toyland. Ladies Home J 86:81+ N '69
Law schools and law firms. New Repub 161: 20-3 O 11 '69
Swiss cheese. New Repub 161:11-12 N 22 '69
Violence of omission. Nation 208:166-8 F 10 '69
Yes, it is safe to fly, but is it safe to crash? por Holiday 46:56-7+ Jl '69

about

Crusader widens range of his ire. il pors Bsns W p 128-30 Ja 25 '69
Edible violence. Time 94:22-3 Jl 25 '69
Gadflies: report on Federal trade commission. Nation 208:69 Ja 20 '69
Lonely hero: never kowtow. Time 94:91 D 12 '69
Nader: from auto safety to a permanent crusade. M. Mueller. por Science 166:979-83 N 21 '69
Nader's raiders. J. Newfield. il pors Life 67: 56-56B+ O 3 '69
Nader's raiders and the traders. S. Watzman. Nation 209:317 S 29 '69
On top. R. L. Collins. Flying 85:24+ N '69
Toward a just market place. Time 94:92 N 7 '69
U.S.'s toughest customer. il pors Time 94: 89-92+ D 12 '69

NADLER, Paul S.
One-bank holding companies: the public interest. Harvard Bsns R 47:107-13 My '69

NAEGLERIA. See Amebas

NAESER, C. W.
Etching fission tracks in zircons. bibliog Science 165:388 Jl 25 '69

NAEVE, Milo M.
American furniture. Antiques 95:128-33 Ja '69

NAEVE, R. L. and others
Urban poverty: effects on prenatal nutrition. bibliog Science 166:1026 N 21 '69

NÄF, Ulrich. and others
New antheridiogen from the fern onoclea sensibilis. bibliog Science 163:1357-8 Mr 21 '69

NAFTALIN, Arthur
Naftalin of Minneapolis; interview, ed. by F. Powledge. por(p69) Harper 239:72-6 N '69

NAGAS. See India—Native races

NAGEL, Jack
He gets three-ton milo without irrigation; interview, ed. by C. E. Sommers and C. Peterson, jr. pors Suc Farm 67:26-7 Ag '69

NAGEL, Myra
Three scope explorers. Har Yrs 9:35-7 Ap '69

NAGELBERG, Irving, and others
Divalent phosphate electrode. Science 166: 1403-4 D 12 '69

NAGENDA, John
Have you seen Thomas? poem. Harper 238: 79 Ap '69

NAGLE, John M.
View of literature too often neglected. Engl J 58:399-407 Mr '69
—See Cross, J. S. jt. auth.

NAGRIN, Daniel
Peloponnesian war. Cubiculo theatre. A. J. Fortney. Dance Mag 43:85 Ja '69

NAGY, László Moholy-. See Moholy-Nagy, L.

NAGY, Robert
Heroic road; interview, ed. by S. L. Fogel. por Opera N 33:27 Ap 12 '69

about

Music to my ears. I. Kolodin. Sat R 52:41 My 3 '69

NAGY, Sibyl Moholy-. See Moholy-Nagy, S.

NAHUEL HUAPI NATIONAL PARK. See National parks and reserves—Argentina

NAILS (anatomy)
See also
Manicuring

NAIROBI, Kenya
Encounter in Nairobi. R. Atcheson. Holiday 46:14-17 O '69

NAIROBI college. See Colleges and universities, Experimental

NAITOH, Yutaka, and Eckert, Roger
Ciliary orientation: controlled by cell membrane or by intracellular fibrils? bibliog Science 166:1633-5 D 26 '69
Ionic mechanisms controlling behavioral responses of paramecium to mechanical stimulation. bibliog Science 164:963-5 My 23 '69

NAJITA, Tetsuo
Inukai Tsuyoshi: some dilemmas in party development in pre-World war II Japan; address. December 1966. bibliog f Am Hist R 74:492-510 D '68

NAKAJIMA, Tadashi, and Volcani, B. E.
3,4-Dihydroxyproline: a new amino acid in diatom cell walls. bibliog Science 164:1400-1 Je 20 '69

NAKAMURA, Kimpei
Kimpei Nakamura. M. Zimmerman and M. Zimmerman. il Ceram Mo 17:14-17 S '69

NAKANISHI, Miklye, and others
Phenoxyethanol: protein preservative for taxonomists. bibliog Science 163:681-3 F 14 '69

NAKED came the stranger hoax. See Hoaxes

NAKEDNESS. See Nudity

NALORPHINE
Nalorphine: increased sensitivity of monkeys formerly dependent on morphine. S. R. Goldberg and C. R. Schuster. bibliog il Science 166:1548-9 D 19 '69

NAMATH, Joe Willie
Bachelors II. Time 94:49 Jl 25 '69
Blues for Broadway Joe. il pors Newsweek 73:109-10 Je 23 '69
Broadcast Joe. il por Time 94:94 O 17 '69
Broadway Joe. P. O'Neil. il pors Life 66:24-9 Ja 24 '69
Broadway Joe: rebel with a nightclub for a cause; with report by S. Smith. il pors Life 66:22-7 Je 20 '69
Broadway Joe's return. il por Newsweek 74: 72+ Jl 28 '69
Bugging Joe Namath. Nat R 21:632-3 Jl 1 '69
Demi-god; symposium. il pors Esquire 72: 103-13+ O '69
Everybody's out to jolt Joe. il pors Life 67: 36-7 O 3 '69
Fall of Joe Willie. il Newsweek 74:40 D 29 '69
Game was up at Namath's. N. Pileggi. il Sports Illus 30:24-5 Je 23 '69
Impossible reality. il por Time 93:50 Ja 24 '69
Joe's tearful good-by. il por Newsweek 73:66 Je 16 '69
Mod man out; with editorial comment. W. Johnson. il por Sports Illus 30:10, 20-3 Je 16 '69
My son the quarterback; excerpts from letters, ed. by B. Verigan. R. Szolnoki. por Look 33:37-8 S 9 '69
Namath of the Jets. il por Newsweek 74: 57-8+ S 15 '69
Say it's so, Joe. T. Maule. il pors Sports Illus 30:10-15 Ja 20 '69
Super Jets. il pors Newsweek 73:56 Ja 27 '69
Surfeit of surveillance. Chr Cent 86:917 Jl 9 '69
To be a good Joe, it takes a hard sell. G. Ronberg. il por Sports Illus 31:12-13 Jl 28 '69

NAMES
See also
Corporations—Names

NAMES, Business. See Business names

NAMES, Fictitious. See Pseudonyms

NAMES, Literary. See Characters in literature

NAMES, Personal
Names people play. F. Remington. il Todays Health 47:50-1+ N '69

Anecdotes, facetiae, satire, etc.

Bible has a name for it. R. M. Walls. Har Yrs 9:45 O '69
Name of the game is names. Chr Cent 86:633 Ap 30 '69

NAMES, Scientific. See Botany—Nomenclature

NAMES of colors. See Color names

NAMES of newspapers. See Newspapers—Names

NAMIBIA
See also
United Nations—Namibia
United Nations council for Namibia

NANCARROW, Conlon
Music for piano, but not for pianist. R. P.
Morgan. Hi Fi 19:90 My '69
NANCE, Dana K. See Hamilton, W. F. 2d, jt.
auth.
NANCE, James J.
Renewal gadfly. por Bsns W p75 D 27 '69
NANCE, Ray
Musical events: Duke Ellington society con-
cert. W. Balliett. New Yorker 45:101+ My
31 '69
NANCE, Richard L.
Gravity: first measurement on the lunar sur-
face. bibliog Science 166:384-5 O 17 '69
NANCY Drew (literary character) See Char-
acters in literature
**NANCY Sayles Day collection of modern Latin
American art.** See Rhode Island school of
design, Providence, R.I.
NANDINA
It's good looking and well behaved. il Sunset
143:166-7 D '69
NANES, Allan S.
Congress and military commitments: an
overview. bibliog f Cur Hist 57:105-11+ Ag
'69
NANNETTI, Guillermo
Story of Antonio Arango; reprint. UNESCO
Courier 22:6-7 Ag '69
NANSEN, Charles
Best bets for geese this fall. Field & S 74:42-
3+ Ag '69
Can anyone catch a new record bass? Field
& S 74:42-3+ F '69
Happy (deer) hunting grounds. Field & S
74:50-1+ O '69
NANTUCKET HARBOR
Ahab wouldn't know it: modernization of old
whaling port. R. Carrick. il Yachting 125:
54-5+ My '69
NANTUCKET school of needlery. See Sewing
—Study and teaching
NANTUCKET SOUND, Mass.
Bay and the Sound; excerpts. J. Parkinson,
jr. il Motor B 123:57-63 Je '69
NAPA, Calif.
How parks build men. R. G. Pelusi. il Am
City 84:80-2 Je '69
NAPALM
Dow bows out. il Newsweek 74:78 D 1 '69
Dow drops napalm. il Time 94:100 N 28 '69
Garbage burner; excerpt from interview, ed.
by H. Downs. C. Gerstacker. New Repub
161:7-8 Jl 26 '69
Napalm: the image maker. il Forbes 103:39-40
Mr 15 '69
NAPHTHACENE
Fission of nonparticles; weak fluorescence in
tetracene. Sci N 95:378 Ap 19 '69
Split concept; splitting of an exciton. Sci Am
220:56 My '69
NAPIER, Arch
Freelance job idea: stringing for magazines.
pors Writers Digest 49:62-5+ F '69
NAPIER, James J. and Winters, S. B.
African trajedian in golden Prague. bibliog
Negro Hist Bul 32:23-6 N '69
NAPIER, Jeff. See Stone, R. jt. auth.
NAPKINS
Folding napkins. il Am Home 72:32+ Mr '69
NAPLES

Architecture
Down a hillside in Naples; Swiss school. il
Arch Forum 130:70-5 Mr '69

Music
Report: Naples; production of Donizetti's
Maria Stuarda. E. Tellini. il Opera N 33:32
F 15 '69
Report: Naples; productions of Giordano's
Andrea Chénier and Verdi's Otello. E.
Tellini. il Opera N 33:32 Mr 22 '69
Report: Naples; productions of Werther and
Ildebrando Pizzetti's Straniero. E. Tellini.
Opera N 33:31-2 Ap 19 '69
NAPOLEON I, emperor of the French
Bad case of Napoleonomania; 200th anniver-
sary of Bonaparte's birth. il Time 94:34 Ag
15 '69
Letter from Paris; exhibition at the Grand
Palais. Genêt. New Yorker 45:165-8 O 18 '69
Napoleon's empire. E. P. Birk. il Antiques
96:464+ O '69
NAPOLES, Jose
Jose settles an old account. J. Kirshenbaum.
il por Sports Illus 31:40-1 O 27 '69
NAPPING (sleep) See Sleep
NAPTON, Lewis K. See Heizer, R. F. jt. auth.
NARAGHI, Ehsan
Three-dimensional youth. UNESCO Courier
22:30-4 Ap '69
NARAHARA, Ikko
Gallery: photographs. Life 67:2-3 N 7 '69

NARAHASHI, Toshio, and others
Condylactis toxin: interaction with nerve
membrane ionic conductances. bibliog Sci-
ence 163:680-1 F 14 '69
NARAYAN, Rasipuram Krishnaswami
Uncle. New Yorker 45:54-60 D 13 '69
NARCISSISM. See Self love
NARCISSUS
Daffodils are a family affair. B. B. Brown.
il Home Gard 56:60-1 S '69
Miniature daffodils. B. D. Darden. il Horti-
culture 46:24-7+ S '68
**NARCOTIC addiction control commission of
New York state.** See New York (state)—
Narcotic addiction control commission
NARCOTIC addicts
Fighting drugs in Puerto Rico. C. J. Mc-
Naspy. America 121:61 Ag 2 '69
Of drunkards and junkies. Trans-Action 6:5-6
Jl '69
Physician as addict. Sci N 95:326 Ap 5 '69

Rehabilitation
Drug addiction is not physiologic. E. E.
Ramirez. il Sci Digest 65:20-4 My '69
Encounter: how kids turn off drugs. W. J.
McKean. il Look 33:40-3+ Ap 15 '69
Fighting drugs in Puerto Rico. C. J. Mc-
Naspy. America 121:61 Ag 2 '69
Five who came back from drugs. R. Tunley.
Seventeen 29:92-3+ Ja '70
I hurt! I hurt! I hurt! Encounter, inc. N.
Brereton. il Seventeen 28:144-5+ F '69
Key decisions coming; methadone therapy
for heroin addicts. il Sci N 95:364-5 Ap
12 '69
New York tries to kick the habit. il Ebony
24:29-32+ S '69
Town in trouble; plague of drugs among kids
in California; Awareness house. J. Bon-
fante. il Life 66:48-54+ Mr 21 '69
We're clean, are you? Phoenix house's photog-
raphy program for drug addicts. L. Druk-
ker. il Pop Phot 65:108-9+ N '69
See also
Synanon foundation, incorporated
NARCOTIC habit
Big smoke; becoming an opium addict in
China in 1935. E. Hahn. New Yorker 44:
35-43 F 15 '69
Drug trip: voyage to nowhere. M. Drury.
Read Digest 95:61-3 Ag '69
Town fights back against the teen-age drug
epidemic. C. Remsberg and B. Remsberg.
Good H 681:80-1+ Je '69
Turning on: two views; A teen-ager's trip;
A straight adult. il Time 94:72-3 S 26 '69
See also
Heroin
Narcotics and youth
NARCOTIC laws
Drug usage: a two-way attack. il U S News
67:9 N 3 '69
Drug use and the law; a case for legalizing
marijuana. J. Fort. Cur 113:4-13 D '69
New move for reform. Time 94:26 O 24 '69
Nixon drug law: a crucial fault. Life 67:32
S 5 '69
Nixon's drug bill. G. C. Stokes. Nation 209:
271-2 S 22 '69; Same with title What new
federal drug legislation? Cur 112:14-16 N
'69
Pondering pot. Chr Cent 86:1270 O 8 '69

Great Britain
Britain's Release: agency to protect youthful drug addicts and pot users in trouble
with the law. il Time 94:56 Jl 18 '69

Iran
Breaking the habit; first victims of the
world's toughest narcotics law. Time 94:18
D 26 '69
NARCOTIC trade. See Narcotics, Control of
NARCOTIC traffic. See Narcotics, Control of
NARCOTICS
See also
Heroin
Morphine
Opium
United Nations—Commission on narcotic
drugs
NARCOTICS, Control of
Abusing drugs. Nat R 21:1053-4 O 21 '69
Blueprint for a drug crackdown. U S News
67:16 S 22 '69
Dope control; reprint. R. Berrellez. U S News
67:108 O 20 '69
FAA proposes restraints on drug traffic.
Aviation W 91:112 Ag 18 '69
Growing drive against drugs. il U S News
67:38-40 D 15 '69

NASSER, Gamal Abdel—about—*Continued*
Rumblings out of Cairo. il por Newsweek 74:49 S 29 '69
Tension: Nasser and the Russians. A. de Borchgrave. por Newsweek 74:89 O 6 '69

NASSETTA, Anthony F.
Fire tests prove steel structure can be exposed; excerpts from address. Arch Rec 146:199-202 S '69

NASSIKAS, John N.
Too good to last? il por Forbes 104:29-30 N 1 '69

NASTURTIUMS
Nasturtium flower. A. D. Hart. il Horticulture 47:32-3 D '69

NAT Turner's insurrection. See Southampton insurrection. 1831

NATHAN, Leonard
Sorry; poem. New Repub 162:25 Ja 10 '70

NATHAN, Paul
Rights and permissions. See issues of Publishers' weekly

NATHAN, Simon. See Simon

NATHER, R. Edward, and Warner, Brian
DQ Herculis: synchronous photometry. bibliog Science 166:876-7 N 14 '69

NATION-wide auto auction, limited
Dealing out used-car dealers. il Bsns W p76-7+ O 25 '69

NATIONAL academy for school executives. See American association of school administrators

NATIONAL academy of engineering
National academy of engineering selects new members. M. Mueller. Science 164:162 Ap 11 '69
Technology assessment: NAE report explores the methodology. L. J. Carter. Science 166: 848-50+ N 14 '69

NATIONAL academy of sciences
Academy changes army gas dump plan. P. M. Boffey. Science 165:45 Jl 4 '69
Academy elects fifty new members. M. Mueller. Science 164:657 My 9 '69
Academy of sciences lays another thin-shelled egg; Committee on persistent pesticides. Audubon 71:103 Jl '69
Behavioral and social sciences: NAS report stresses applications. J. Walsh. Science 166: 585-6 O 31 '69
Can Handler teach NAS evolution? il Bsns W p60-2 Ap 5 '69
Education research: Academy cooperates in new venture. J. Walsh. Science 163:162+ Ja 10 '69
Everglades jetport: Academy prepares a model; report of Environmental studies board. M. Mueller. il Science 166:202-3 O 10 '69
Lunar report urges larger science role. Aviation W 91:92-3 N 17 '69
NAS suggests modifications; nerve gas disposal procedures. Sci N 96:26 Jl 12 '69
On the edge of change. B. J. Culliton. il Sci N 95:579-81 Je 14 '69
Will the science brain bank go conglomerate? J. Lear. il Sat R 52:37-44 Jl 5 '69
See also
Lunar science institute (proposed)
National research council

Space science board
Beyond Apollo: where? Bul Atom Sci 25:68 S '69
Science board seeks planetary emphasis. Aviation W 91:32 Ag 11 '69

NATIONAL accelerator laboratory
Science and man: breaking new ground at Batavia. E. L. Goldwasser. il Bul Atom Sci 25:7-10 O '69

NATIONAL advisory commission on civil disorders. See United States—National advisory commission on civil disorders

NATIONAL advisory council on the education of disadvantaged children. See United States —National advisory council on the education of disadvantaged children

NATIONAL advisory council on vocational education. See United States— National advisory council on vocational education

NATIONAL aeronautics and space administration. See United States—National aeronautics and space administration

NATIONAL air and space museum. See Smithsonian institution—National air and space museum

NATIONAL air races. See Airplane racing

NATIONAL airlines, incorporated
National airlines picks DC-10 for airbus order. Aviation W 91:198 O 20 '69
National fights to fly. il Bsns W p78 F 8 '69
Strike at National may delay Maimi-London service opening. Aviation W 91:36 D 8 '69

NATIONAL alliance of businessmen
Brighter vistas for hard core: NAB-JOBS program. Bsns W p44 Je 7 '69
Business involvement; address, April 11, 1969. D. M. Kendall. Vital Speeches 35:535-7 Je 15 '69
Hard-core jobless get a friend at the top; D. Kendall, chairman of NAB. il Bsns W p62+ Mr 8 '69
Hard-core program will widen its base; NAB Jobs '70 program. Bsns W p41 N 15 '69
Hard-sell push for hard-core hiring; Jobs-70. Bsns W p36 S 27 '69
How to hire the hard-core. il Newsweek 74:65-6 S 8 '69
Industry learns to train the hardcore. R. K. Peterson and B. B. Rash. Ed Digest 35:35-7 O '69
NAB's problem: fight inflation but give jobs. B. L. Masse. America 120:520 My 3 '69
Useful job for every American; excerpts from Britannica book of the year 1969. L. B. Johnson. Read Digest 94:82-5 Ap '69

NATIONAL amateur athletic union. See Amateur athletic union of the United States

NATIONAL arboretum. See Washington, D.C. —National arboretum

NATIONAL archives. See United States—National archives

NATIONAL assessment of education progress. See Committee on assessing the progress of education

NATIONAL association for mental health, incorporated
Action for the mental health of children; the Joint commission report and NAMH response. Ment Hy 53:497-9 O '69

NATIONAL association for the advancement of colored people
Color them traditional. Time 94:20 Jl 11 '69
N.A.A.C.P. executive urges churches to reject demands for reparations. Chr Cent 86:1413 N 5 '69
Purge at NAACP; publish and perish. M. L. Wulf; reply with rejoinder. R. Wilkins. Commonweal 89:575+ F 7 '69
There is no rest for Roy Wilkins. M. Arnold. il N Y Times Mag p40-1+ S 28 '69

NATIONAL association of broadcasters
Censorship bugaboo. Newsweek 73:90-1 Mr 31 '69
Down to the ash. Newsweek 74:82+ Jl 21 '69
Minuet over censorship. il Time 93:76 Ap 4 '69
Much ado about previews. Newsweek 73:55 Ap 7 '69
Switching and fighting; offer to phase out cigarette commercials. R. L. Shayon. Sat R 52:36 Ag 2 '69
Taking sides; opposition by Negro group to appointment of F. S. Weaver. R. L. Shayon. Sat R 52:65 N 15 '69

NATIONAL association of business economists
Monetarists dent conventional wisdom; seminar on role of money in forecasting. il Bsns W p86-8 Je 14 '69

NATIONAL association of college stores
Communications breakdown: publishers and booksellers. Pub W 195:29-30 Mr 17 '69
Impact of the 70s weighed at NACS regionals. Pub W 196:23-4 N 24 -'69
NACS national convention develops theme: reflect, renovate, activate. il Pub W 195: 27-35 My 19 '69
1968 in review. Pub W 195:44 Mr 10 '69

NATIONAL association of educational broadcasters
Day of reckoning; employment and program policy reports. R. L. Shayon. Sat R 52:37 D 20 '69

NATIONAL association of engine and boat manufacturers, incorporated
Yacht designers, how do they learn? P. Smyth. il Motor B 123:82-3+ Mr '69

NATIONAL association of evangelicals
NAE hits hard at pornography. J. L. Adams. Chr Today 13:46-7 My 9 '69
Standing for something; statement. Chr Today 14:52 N 7 '69

NATIONAL association of home builders
How Houston blitzed Chicago; annual meeting in Houston. il Forbes 103:34-5 F 15 '69

NATIONAL association of laymen. See Laity —Catholic church

NATIONAL association of manufactures
If strife hits the plants; NAM seminars. Bsns W p 137-8 Je 28 '69
Who speaks for business? G. R. Rosen. il Duns R 94:45-7+ N '69

NATIONAL association of secondary-school principals
Instructional system for training principals. Ed Digest 34:18-21 Ap '69
Meeting, 1969. D. L. Burleson. Sr Schol 94: Schol Teach 4 Ap 11 '69

NATIONAL association of state units on aging
Robinson, Chaskes, Blue are elected to head NASUA. il Aging 170:6 D '68
NATIONAL association of student planners and architects
Student architects and planners hope to continue action programs. R. E. Jensen. Arch Rec 145:36 Mr '69
NATIONAL association of theatre owners
NATO v. the monster. Time 94:71 S 12 '69
NATIONAL Audubon society
From birdwatching to the total environment. Audubon 71:4 My '69
St Louis notebook. J. Tripp. il Audubon 71: 58-9 Jl '69
See also
Audubon medal
Audubon nature camps
NATIONAL automobile dealers association
Viewpoint; auto repair business. L. Levine. Motor T 21:8 Mr '69
NATIONAL aviation trades association
From the tower. E. D. Muhlfeld. Flying 84:4 F '69
NATIONAL ballet
Fonteyn, a new-old heroine is added to her repertoire. W. Terry. il Sat R 52:46 N 1 '69
NATIONAL Baptist convention, USA, incorporated. See Baptists in the United States
NATIONAL baseball hall of fame and museum
Black athlete in the golden age of sports; the saga of Campy; elected to the baseball Hall of fame in Cooperstown, N.Y. A. S. Young. il Ebony 24:100-2+ Ap '69
NATIONAL basketball association
Four for the bundle; Baltimore, Philadelphia, New York and Boston in race for NBA stakes. J. Jares. il Sports Illus 30: 14-19 F 24 '69
NBA goodby to the old balance of power. F. Deford. il Sports Illus 31:26-33 O 27 '69
$1 million end to an unjust exile. D. Wolf. il Life 66:67 Je 27 '69
Thought for the NBA; blackballing of players. Sports Illus 31:9 Jl 21 '69
Tossing bombs into the hoops; ABA vs NBA. G. Ronberg. il Sports Illus 31:30-2+ S 22 '69
Unjust exile of a superstar; case of C. Hawkins. D. Wolf. il Life 66:52-52B+ My 16 '69
NATIONAL biscuit company
How Nabisco keeps its cookie crown; army of salesmen. il Bsns W p64-6 My 10 '69
NATIONAL bison range
Home on the bison range; duck hunting, trout, and more big-game shooting. E. A. Bauer. il Outdoor Life 144:62-5+ S '69
NATIONAL black economic development conference
Black bill collector. il Newsweek 73:74-5 My 19 '69
Black manifesto. il Time 93:94 My 16 '69
Black over white. Commonweal 90:308-9 My 30 '69
Blacks bill the churches; demand for reparations. il Bsns W p54+ My 10 '69
Breaking whitey's vice. il Time 93:29 My 9 '69
Forman bedevils the Episcopalians. W. Wallace. Commonweal 90:582-3 S 26 '69
Forman box score. J. C. Haughey. America 120:689 Je 14 '69
Group therapy; Episcopal church to fund. il Newsweek 74:105-6 S 15 '69
Incident at Riverside church. Nation 208: 618-19 My 19 '69
Issue is economic justice. Chr Cent 86:861 Je 25 '69
On Dow and calico. B. Thompson. Chr Cent 86:1571-2 D 10 '69
Putting it to the churches. S. C. Rose. New Repub 160:19-21 Je 21 '69
NATIONAL boat show. See Boats—Exhibitions
NATIONAL book awards
Book industry presents the 20th National book awards; with excerpts from acceptance addresses. il Pub W 195:26-30 Mr 24 '69
Children's literature NBA goes to Dejong. Library J 94:1695 Ap 15 '69
Children's NBA. E. Geller. Library J 94:1693 Ap 15 '69
Death in life: a statement; 1969 science award. R. J. Lifton. Bul Atom Sci 25:39 Je '69
Milestone for children's books. Z. Sutherland. Sat R 52:38 Ap 19 '69
National book awards: the winners; with excerpts from addresses. il Library J 94:1476-7 Ap 1 '69
NBA to be given for children's literature. Library J 94:250 Ja 15 '69

NBC announces NBA nominees and book award week program. Pub W 195:46 F 10 '69; Same. Library J 94:977 Mr 1 '69
New National book award for children's literature; with acceptance address by M. DeJong. V. Haviland. Horn Bk 45:283-6 Je '69
Seven writers win National book awards. il Pub W 195:32 Mr 17 '69; Same. Newsweek 73:104 Mr 24 '69; Willson Lib Bul 43:721 Ap '69
Trade winds. J. Beatty, jr. Sat R 52:8+ Mr 29 '69
NATIONAL book committee
National book committee reports 1968 activities. Library J 94:482+ F 1 '69
National book committee: work and progress. P. S. Jennison. il Wilson Lib Bul 43:634-9 Mr '69
1968 in review. Pub W 195:44 Mr 10 '69
NATIONAL budget. See Budget—United States
NATIONAL bureau of standards. See United States—National bureau of standards
NATIONAL business aircraft association
NBAA suit seeks stay of access limits. Aviation W 90:83 Ja 27 '69
NATIONAL can corporation
Small can maker is showing its mettle. il Bsns W p 102-3 Ja 10 '70
NATIONAL car rental system, incorporated
National tries hard to overtake no. 2. il Bsns W p85 N 1 '69
NATIONAL cartoonists society
Cartoonist Q's. J. Markow. Writers Digest 49:60-5 Ag '69
NATIONAL Catholic conference for interracial justice
PE suffers growing pains. America 121:446-7 N 15 '69
NATIONAL Catholic educational association
Meeting, 1969. J. Lloyd. Sr Schol 94:Schol Teach 5 My 9 '69
NCEA study a helpful tool; How good are Catholic schools? Study. America 120:263 Mr 8 '69
Private educational service center. il Sch & Soc 97:90 F '69
NATIONAL Catholic office for motion pictures
NCOMP charges Hollywood lacks black sensitivity. Chr Cent 86:1157 S 10 '69
NCOMP developments. America 120:460 Ap 19 '69; Reply. G. D. Phillips. 120:601 My 24 '69
Still Legion, still decent? R. Corliss. Commonweal 90:288-93 My 23 '69; Reply. J. P. Carrico. 90:423 Je 27 '69
NATIONAL Catholic reporter
Heartless decision; dismissal of J. Hart. S. J. Adamo. America 120:654-5 My 31 '69
NATIONAL Catholic welfare conference
See also
Catholic relief services
NATIONAL chamber foundation. See Chamber of commerce of the United States of America
NATIONAL championship air races. See Airplane racing
NATIONAL championship drag races. See Automobile racing
NATIONAL characteristics
Pictures in our heads; reprint. O. Klineberg. UNESCO Courier 22:49-51 Ag '69
NATIONAL children's book week. See Book week
NATIONAL church councils. See Councils and synods
NATIONAL cleanest town achievement contest
Fountains play key role in clean-up contest. il Am City 84:92+ Je '69
NATIONAL collection of fine arts, Washington, D.C. See Smithsonian institution—National collection of fine arts
NATIONAL collegiate athletic association
Hogwash; rules applicable to all student-athletes. Sports Illus 30:7 Ja 20 '69
Out of right field. Newsweek 75:35 Ja 5 '70
UCLA all the way. Newsweek 73:86-7 Mr 31 '69
NATIONAL collegiate basketball championship. See Basketball tournaments
NATIONAL commission on libraries and information science (proposed) See United States—National commission on libraries and information science (proposed)
NATIONAL commission on teacher education and professional standards
Determining professional standards. Sch & Soc 97:347 O '69
NATIONAL commission on the causes and prevention of violence. See United States—National commission on the causes and prevention of violence
NATIONAL commission on urban problems. See United States—National commission on urban problems

NATIONAL commitments resolution. See
United States—Congress—Resolutions

NATIONAL committee for a sane nuclear policy
Postscript on Negotiation now! safe but not
SANE. T. Ritt. Commonweal 90:134-5 Ap
18 '69; Reply with rejoinder. M. Temple.
90:413-15 Je 27 '69

NATIONAL committee of Black churchmen
Black churchmen plan NCC takeover; with
editorial comment. E. E. Plowman. Chr
Today 14:26, 33 D 5 '69
Black theology. il Chr Cent 86:1310 O 15 '69;
Discussion. 86:1523-4 N 26 '69
Disputed choices; nominating committee's
slate challenged. Chr Today 14:32 D 19 '69
Passing the buck. Newsweek 74:107 O 20 '69
Quest for a black Christ. A. Poinsett. il
Ebony 24:170-2+ Mr '69
Ultimatum and hope; black churchmen's convocation. G. S. Shockley. il Chr Cent 86:
217-19 F 12 '69
Without strings. H. E. Fey. Chr Cent 86:
1239-40 O 1 '69

NATIONAL conference of Catholic bishops
American bishops in Astrodome city; semi-annual meeting. W. Wallace. Commonweal
90:188-90 My 2 '69
Bishops move. il Time 93:69 Ap 25 '69
Bishops move slowly toward collaboration. R.
Chandler. Chr Today 14:44-6 D 5 '69
Bishops respond to change: is it fast enough?
R. Chandler. Chr Today 13:41-2 My 9 '69
Church and peace; the November pastoral.
J. R. Jennings. America 120:304 Mr 15 '69;
Reply. W. V. Kennedy. 120:379-80 Ap 5 '69
Embattled U.S. bishops demands for church
and social reform. il Time 94:62 N 21 '69
Ending catch 2222. Newsweek 74:58 D 1 '69
News and views; U.S. bishops in conference in Washington. J. Deedy; discussion.
Commonweal 89:511+ Ja 24 '69
Priest-bishop relations. America 121:372-3 N
1 '69
Scolding the press. S. J. Adamo; discussion.
America 120:30, 121 Ja 11, F 1 '69
Semi-confronting the issues. W. R. Mac-
Kave. Commonweal 91:269-70 N 28 '69
U.S. Bishops' conference November, 1969. J.
C. Haughey. America 121:525-6 N 29 '69

**NATIONAL conference of state executives on
aging.** See Aging, Conferences on

NATIONAL conference on religious architecture
Religious architecture: its function, future. R.
Jensen. Chr Cent 86:1002-4 Jl 23 '69

NATIONAL conference on social welfare
Behavioral sciences. Sci N 95:578 Je 14 '69
Choosing a new way. Sci N 95:549 Je 7 '69
Social workers move. Sci N 95:572-3 Je 14 '69
University and social change; excerpts from
Social welfare forum, 1969. N. E. Cohen.
bibliog Sch & Soc 97:479-84 D '69

NATIONAL congress for recreational parks.
See Congress for recreation and parks

NATIONAL congress of mothers. See National
congress of parents and teachers

NATIONAL congress of parents and teachers
Coping with change, a continuing PTA tradition. il PTA Mag 63:20-1 F '69
Necklace; the insignia of office. E. Hendryson.
il PTA Mag 63:18-19 Je '69

NATIONAL conventions (political)
Miami and the siege of Chicago. by N. Mailer.
Review
Nat R 21:129-30 F 11 '69. P. L. Buckley
Self-portrait: U.S.A. by D. D. Duncan. Review
Sat R il 52:38-9 N 29 '69. M. R. Weiss

NATIONAL conventions, Democratic
As Democrats get set for '72. il U S News
66:46-8 My 26 '69
Chicago demonstrators: a study in identity;
adaptation of address, November, 1968. P.
R. Miller. Bul Atom Sci 25:3-6 Ap '69
Chicago riots: sixteen indictments. U S News
66:11 Mr 31 '69
Confrontation at the Conrad Hilton; excerpts from the Walker commission report.
Rights in conflict. il Trans-Action 6:37-49
Ja '69
Convention fallout; indictments against
demonstrators and Chicago policemen. il
Newsweek 73:26 Mr 31 '69
Eight plus eight; demonstrators indicted.
Time 93:16 Mr 28 '69
How to reform? il Newsweek 73:39 My 5 '69
Place where all America was radicalized:
Chicago. T. Wicker. il N Y Times Mag
p26-7+ Ag 24 '69; Reply with rejoinder.
E. F. Berman. p58+ O 5 '69
Will it be the old Democratic donkey? Mc-
Govern commission's hearings on reforming the delegate selection process. P. R.
Wieck. New Repub 160:8-9 My 10 '69

NATIONAL corporation for housing partnerships
Comsat for construction. il Time 93:94 Je
13 '69

NATIONAL council for the social studies
Meeting, 1968. il Sr Schol 93:Schol Teach
4-8+ Ja 10 '69

NATIONAL council of architectural registration boards
N.C.A.R.B. pushes toward new exam bases.
Arch Rec 146:67 Ag; 83-4 S '69

NATIONAL council of Catholic bishops. See
National conference of Catholic bishops

NATIONAL council of churches
American churches in the ecumenical movement 1900-1968, by S. M. Cavert. Review
Cath World 208:233 F '69. C. C. Wedel
Black churchmen plan NCC takeover; with
editorial comment. E. E. Plowman. Chr.
Today 14:26, 33 D 5 '69
Crunch at the Council. Time 94:70 D 12 '69
Detroit assembly. Chr Cent 86:1506 N 26 '69
Disputed choices; nominating committee's
slate challenged. Chr Today 14:32 D 19 '69
Ecumenism as communication. Chr Cent 86:
1441 N 12 '69
Folding umbrella? general assembly. News-
week 74:97 D 15 '69
Issues behind church discord. il U S News
67:12 D 15 '69
Joy box with no joy: the N.C.C. at Detroit.
A. Geyer. il Chr Cent 86:1601-5 D 17 '69
Manifesto and the magnificat; strike called
against Interchurch center in New York.
H. Schomer. Chr Cent 86:866-7 Je 25 '69
May day in Manhattan; major items on the
agenda of General board. A. Geyer. Chr
Cent 86:671-2 My 14 '69
National council delegation visits Pope Paul.
Chr Cent 86:471 Ap 9 '69
NCC chief proposes general ecumenical
council; with editorial comment. D. Kuchar-
sky. Chr Today 14:22, 30-2 D 19 '69
NCC crisis: ecumenism at a Crossroads. D.
Kucharsky. Chr Today 14:34 D 5 '69
N.C.C. in Memphis. Chr Cent 86:204 F 12 '69
National council of churches: melancholia in
Memphis. D. E. Kucharsky. Chr Today
13:38 F 14 '69
NCC pledges half million while budget
shrinks. A. H. Matthews. Chr Today 14:
44-6 O 10 '69
Problems of Spanish-American minority
aired for N.C.C. unit. G. F. Hall. Chr Cent
86:1498-500 N 19 '69
Rethinking relevance. Chr Today 14:35-6 O 10
'69
Under the ecumenical umbrella. R. Chandler.
Chr Today 14:39 Ja 2 '70
Without strings. H. E. Fey. Chr Cent 86:
1239-40 O 1 '69

Division of Christian education
Christian educating in Chicago. M. Stone.
Chr Cent 86:422+ Mr 26 '69

**NATIONAL council of independent junior
colleges**
Promoting independent junior colleges. Sch &
Soc 97:476 D '69

NATIONAL council of senior citizens, incorporated
NCSC has biggest convention; backs broader
aging programs. Aging 178:13 Ag '69
Senior citizens denounce chiropractic cult.
Todays Health 47:55 Ap '69

NATIONAL council of state education association
NCSEA evaluation: catalyst for change in
state education associations. E. S. Crowley.
Todays Ed 58:36-7 D '69

NATIONAL council of teachers of English
Is the present structure of the NCTE adequate for today and tomorrow? A. H.
Grommon. Engl J 58:595-601 Ap '69
Meeting, 1968. Sr Schol 93:Schol Teach 3+
Ja 10 '69
NCTE councilletter; addenda for the agenda.
W. A. Jenkins. Engl J 58:1241-4 N '69
NCTE presidential address; one year later.
A. H. Grommon. bibliog f Engl J 58:345-59
Mr '69
Preliminary program; fifty-ninth annual meeting. Engl J 58:1077-111 O '69

**NATIONAL council of the churches of Christ
in the United States of America.** See National council of churches

**NATIONAL council of the Metropolitan opera
association.** See Metropolitan opera national council

NATIONAL council on the arts. See United
States—National foundation on the arts
and the humanities

NATIONAL council on the arts selection (program)
Up with arts at the UPS. H. R. Webber.
Sat R 52:44-6 Je 21 '69
NATIONAL council to repeal the draft. See
Military service, Compulsory
NATIONAL crime information center. See
United States—Federal bureau of investigation—National crime information center
NATIONAL dairy herd improvement association, incorporated
Change DHIA rules to allow thyroprotein?
O. Bay. Farm J 93:D5 Je '69
NATIONAL data center (proposed) See United
States—National data center (proposed)
NATIONAL debt (United States) See Debts,
Public—United States
NATIONAL defense
In place of war, by American Friends service committee. Review
Chr Cent 86:1456-7 N 12 '69. C. E. Fager
See also
United States—Defenses
NATIONAL defense education act. See School
laws and legislation—United States
NATIONAL democratic party. See Political
parties—Germany (Federal Republic)
NATIONAL education association
AASA-NEA. W. D. Boutwell and others.
Sr Schol 94:Schol Teach 3-4 Mr 21 '69
Desegregation, sex education, and other
critical issues. M. L. Hayes. Sch & Soc
97:455-6 N '69
Erratic winds of change: AEPI-NEA's joint
dilemma; report of meeting. il Pub W 196:
30-2 D 29 '69
From Dallas to Philadelphia; annual report.
il Todays Ed 58:65-72 S '69
Is an NEA-AFT merger imminent? R. Dewing. Ed Digest 35:35-7 N '69
NEA candidates to be voted on in Philadelphia. il Todays Ed 58:58-9 My '69
NEA changes leadership in mid-term. il Sr
Schol 94:Schol Teach 6 F 7 '69
NEA conference: a thoughtful note. W. D.
Boutwell. Sr Schol 94:Schol Teach 5 F 28
'69
NEA, POAU and tax exemptions. America
120:662 Je 7 '69
NEA president-elect. il Sch & Soc 97:349-50
O '69
NEA program. Ed Digest 34:56 F '69
NEA-related national groups. Todays Ed 58:
72-3 N '69
NEA special services. See issues of Today's
education
NEA's new president. Todays Ed 58:83 Mr
'69
NEA's special project for higher education;
need for a representative professional organization. J. N. Terrey. Todays Ed 58:53
My '69
Proposed amendments to the NEA bylaws
and standing rules. Todays Ed 58:63-5 Ap
'69
Summary financial report to members. Todays Ed 58:79 S '69
Teacher power: key to a better tomorrow;
discussion at National education association's meeting July 2-6, 1968. M. L. Hayes.
il Sch & Soc 97:40-1 Ja '69
See also
National commission on teacher education
and professional standards
National training laboratories

Meeting, 1969
NEA resolutions, 1969. il Todays Ed 58:42-6+
O '69
Time for decision. il Todays Ed 58:38-9 My
'69

Association of classroom teachers
ACT viewpoints; conference topic: Differentiated teaching assignments for classroom
teachers. Todays Ed 58:60-1 Mr '69

Committee on professional ethics
NEA committee acts on ethics complaint. E.
Faulconer and others. Todays Ed 58:34-5+
N '69

Department of audio-visual instruction
DAVI reorganization to create divisional
structure. Library J 94:3120 S 15 '69
DAVI '69: convention for commitment. R.
Gilkey. Clear House 44:61-4 S '69
Outstanding innovation: joint AASL-DAVI
standards for school media programs. L. O.
Vinson. il ALA Bul 63:235-7 F '69
Strategies and ploys; reactions to AASL-
DAVI standards for school media programs. W. Meierhenry. bibliog il Library J
94:1728-30 Ap 15 '69

Department of classroom teachers
See National education association—Association of classroom teachers

Division of educational travel
Fun on a freighter; or would you rather fly?
NEA tours in capsule. il Todays Ed 58:70-
4 Ja '69

Legislative commission
Our political power for good J. Sawaia. il
Todays Ed 58:31 D '69

NATIONAL educational television network
Janacek opera: another try for TV; NET's
Opera project. R. T. Jones. il Hi Fi 19:
MA12-13 O '69
Message about messages; failure of Vietnam
peace talks: a view from the other side to
illuminate relationships. R. L. Shayon. Sat
R 52:26 Jl 19 '69
Musical events: NET opera production of
Leoš Janáček's From the house of the
dead. W. Sargeant. New Yorker 45:186 D
13 '69
Sesame street opens. B. B. Stretch. il Sat
R 52:91 N 15 '69
NATIONAL enquirer
From worse to bad. il Newsweek 74:79 S 8
'69
Jury's privacy award affirmed on appeal. H.
F. Pilpel and K. P. Norwick. Pub W 195:
40-1 F 24 '69
NATIONAL farm bureau federation. See American farm bureau federation
NATIONAL federation of priests' councils
Priest-bishop relations. America 121:372-3 N
1 '69
NATIONAL film board, Canada. See Canada—
National film board
NATIONAL football league
Curse of the endless playoff; affliction of
pro hockey, basketball, and baseball, now,
spreading to pro football. T. Maule. il
Sports Illus 30:18-21 Ap 7 '69
They'd rather switch; Cleveland, Baltimore
and Pittsburgh move to AFL. T. Maule. il
Sports Illus 30:20-3 My 26 '69
Three for the money. il Newsweek 73:108 My
26 '69
NATIONAL forest service. See United States
—Forest service
NATIONAL forests
Battle for East Meadow Creek. P. I. Kain.
il Am For 75:36-9+ O '69
Big track; Ottawa national forest. C. T.
Johnson. il Outdoor Life 144:68-9+ Jl '69
Bridger controversy; with reply. F. Iverson.
W. E. Towell. Am For 75:45-7 N '69
George Washington: our history-making
forest. C. E. Randall. il Am For 75:20-3+
Mr '69
Jefferson's forest. C. E. Randall. il Am For
75:20-2+ Ap '69
National forests of America, by M. Frome
and D. L. Freeman. Review
Am For il 75:35+ Ja '69. W. E. Towell
Preserving the corn ladder: a Mt Baldy
wilderness; Apache national forest, Ariz.
N. H. Greenwood. il Liv Wildn 33:22-9 Sum
'69
Timber! campaign for overcutting the national forests. A. W. Smith. Nat Parks 43:
2 Je '69
Why not take to the woods this summer. B.
Thomas. il Parents Mag 44:60-1+ Ap '69
See also
National parks and reserves—United States

Roads
Logan Canyon: standards for destruction;
highway through the Cache national forest. Utah. G. Alderson. il Nat Parks 43:
18-20 N '69

Waterways
Alaska's green serge navy. D. McKinlay and
H. E. McLean. il Am For 75:16-18 Mr '69
**NATIONAL foundation on the arts and the
humanities.** See United States—National
foundation on the arts and the humanities
NATIONAL freedom fund for librarians
Hodgin thanks; letter to the editor. E. Hodgin. Library J 94:4465-6 D 15 '69
National freedom fund for librarians set. Library J 94:3592+ O 15 '69
National freedom fund to be incorporated.
il Library J 94:4082-3 N 15 '69
NATIONAL gallery of art, Washington, D. C.
Change at the National gallery. Time 93:70
My 9 '69
Orderly transfer in Washington; John Walker
retires succeeded by J. Carter Brown. T.
B. Hess. Art N 68:25 Sum '69

NATIONAL gallery of art, Washington, D.C.
—*Continued*
Self-service at the National gallery. Am Artist
33:8 Je '69
NATIONAL general corporation
Dividend for the winner. il Time 93:75 F 7 '69
NATIONAL gold medal awards program. See
Recreation—Awards, prizes, etc.
NATIONAL golf club, Augusta. See Augusta,
Ga.—Clubs
NATIONAL guard (United States). See United
States—National guard
NATIONAL gypsum company
Look-alikes. Forbes 103:41 Ja 15 '69
NATIONAL health insurance. See Insurance,
Health
NATIONAL health service (Great Britain)
See Great Britain—National health service
NATIONAL hockey league
To NHL or not to NHL. Sports Illus 31:15
N 17 '69
NATIONAL holidays. See Holidays
NATIONAL hollerin' contest. See Competitions
NATIONAL home study council
CCM plans anti-trust suit vs. Home study
trade assn. Pub W 196:20 D 15 '69
NATIONAL horse show. See Horse shows
NATIONAL hurricane center. See United
States—Environmental science services
administration
NATIONAL industrial conference board
Boom, bust, or what? How top economists
see '70; symposium. il U S News 68:56-63
Ja 5 '70
Mergers are on everybody's mind; seminar
on Managing the moderate-sized company.
il Bsns W p 150-2 Ap 26 '69
NATIONAL information center for educational
media. See Southern California university,
Los Angeles
NATIONAL institute of law enforcement and
criminal justice. See United States—Justice,
Department of—Law enforcement assis-
tance administration
NATIONAL institute of mental health. See
United States—National institute of mental
health
NATIONAL institutes of health. See United
States—National institutes of health
NATIONAL journal
Battle of Capitol hill. il Newsweek 73:100 Ap
14 '69
NATIONAL labor relations board. See United
States—National labor relations board
NATIONAL league of cities
Mayors confront the administration. Bsns W
p36+ N 29 '69
Mayors pan Nixon for dollar drought. Bsns
W p70+ D 6 '69
Small-town revolt. Newsweek 74:100 D 15 '69
NATIONAL legion of decency. See National
Catholic office for motion pictures
NATIONAL liberation front (Vietnam)
American view of a meeting with Vietnam's
NLF. T. Cannon. Ramp Mag 7:56 N 30 '68
Back from Midway. J. Osborne. New Repub
160:13-15 Je 21 '69
Communists on the attack. Time 94:42 N 21
'69
Elements of settlement: Saigon notwithstand-
ing. R. A. Falk. Nation 208:689-93 Je 2 '69
Many-sided politics of South Vietnam. R.
Butwell. bibliog f Cur Hist 56:71-6+ F
'69
NLF asks the American left: where are you?
ten-point proposal, and the Swedish in-
ternational liaison committee conference,
Stockholm. F. Schurmann. Ramp Mag 8:14+
Ag '69
National liberation front. P. Arnett. il Cur
Hist 56:82-7+ F '69
Negotiations or surrender? a coalition govern-
ment; address, January 30, 1969. Nguyen-
huu-Chi. Vital Speeches 35:318-20 Mr 1 '69
New stage in Vietnam; Tet offensive. J. W.
Lewis and J. S. Werner. Bul Atom Sci
25:21-6 Ja '69
Politics in South Vietnam. J. M. Silverman.
bibliog f Cur Hist 57:321-6+ D '69
Prospects for disengagement; direction of
President Nixon's strategy. il Time 93:17-
19 Je 20 '69
Ready to talk with the Viet Cong. il Time
93:31 Ap 4 '69
Reports; D. Warner. Atlan 224:12+ Ag '69
Seizing the initiative. Newsweek 73:49 Je 30
'69
This way out. W. Pfaff. Commonweal 89:611-
12 F 14 '69
Vietnam: the bloodbath argument. D. G.
Porter and L. E. Ackland. il Chr Cent 86:
1414-17 N 5 '69

War, peace, and the Viet Cong, by D. Pike.
Review
Nation 209:414-15 O 20 '69. J. Mirsky
What life's like in Vietcong territory. T.
Buckley. il N Y Times Mag p48-9+ N 23 '69
See also
Revolutionary provisional government
NATIONAL library week
Goals for the asking: address, October 1968,
ed. by J. F. Krug. ALA Bul 63:731-3 Je '69
Lesson for librarians: visit by foreign librar-
ians to Rhode Island during NLW. J. S.
Healey. il Wilson Lib Bul 43:554-7 F '69
Little stardust. R. Warncke. Library J 94:
1959 My 15 '69
National book committee: work and progress.
P. S. Jennison. il Wilson Lib Bul 43:634-9
Mr '69
NLW happenings, trends & evaluations. il Li-
brary J 94:2181-2+ Je 1 '69
NATIONAL liturgical conference, incorporated
Liturgy and social justice. Chr Today 13:41
S 26 '69
NATIONAL liturgical week. See Liturgical
week
NATIONAL lotteries. See Lotteries
NATIONAL manufacturers association. See
National association of manufacturers
NATIONAL maritime day
National maritime day, 1969; a proclama-
tion. R. M. Nixon. Dept State Bul 60:297
Ap 7 '69
NATIONAL maritime union of America
Viva Curran; fifteenth convention. Nation
209:428-9 O 27 '69
NATIONAL medal for literature
National medal for literature; symposium. il
Wilson Lib Bul 43:622-39 Mr '69
NATIONAL medal of science
National medal of science winners for 1968.
J. Walsh. Science 163:163 Ja 10 '69
NATIONAL medical association
Trying to be black; annual convention. il
Newsweek 74:71 Ag 25 '69
NATIONAL military establishment. See United
States—Defense, Department of
NATIONAL monuments
Big Thicket: biological crossroads of North
America; excerpt from The biological cross-
roads of North America. O. H. Bonney. il
Liv Wildn 33:19-21 Sum '69
Famous fossil beds are endangered; floris-
sant fossil beds in central Colorado. P. M.
Boffey. Science 164:1152 Je 6 '69
National parks, monuments and historic sites.
il Travel & Camera 32:77-80 Je '69
Treasure in danger; florissant fossils. il Sci N
95:594-5 Je 21 '69
See also names of national monuments,
e.g. Montezuma Castle National Monu-
ment
NATIONAL morale. See Morale, National
NATIONAL municipal league
See also
All-America cities
NATIONAL music service, incorporated
Dirge king. Newsweek 74:63 Ag 11 '69
NATIONAL Negro evangelical association
Black umbrella for evangelicals. D. Orme.
Chr Today 13:47-8 My 9 '69
NATIONAL oceanic and atmospheric agency
(proposed) See United States—National
oceanic and atmospheric agency (propos-
ed)
NATIONAL office for the rights of the in-
digent
Commandos into the ghetto. Time 93:66 My
23 '69
NATIONAL office of black Catholics. See Cath-
olic church—Negroes
NATIONAL outdoor leadership school
Survival expert, Paul Petzoldt. J. Howard
il Life 67:48-50+ D 19 '69
NATIONAL park service (United States). See
United States—National park service
NATIONAL park service academy. See United
States—National park service
NATIONAL parks and reserves
National parks around the world. il Nat Parks
43:25-7 My '69
Park idea and ecological reality. F. F. Darl-
ing. il Nat Parks 43:21-4 My '69
Photographs
Ansel Adams & the national parks. A. Adams.
Am West 6:17-23, 41-8, 65-72 S '69
Beyond what the eye sees. F. Tilden. Travel
& Camera 32:38-45 Je '69
Roads
Park road hearings. Nat Parks 43:32 Ap '69
Roadbuilding in national parks. Liv Wildn
32:36-8 Wint '68

NATIONAL parks and reserves—*Continued*

Trails

Bicycle trails of Cape God National Seashore. C. R. Koehler. il Nat Parks 43:16-17 Ja '69

Africa

Bobby jr. in Africa. il Life 66:42-7 F 14 '69

Argentina

Andean delight; Nahuel Huapi National Park. L. Zalamea. il Travel 132:75 S '69

Arizona

See also
Chiricahua National Monument

California

California's national parks; Yosemite, Kings Canyon, Sequoia and Lassen. J. J. McCoy. il Travel 131:66-9 Je '69
Park maintenance aided by modern equipment. R. D. Browne. il Parks & Rec 4:40-1 Jl '69

Canada

Album of Canadian parks. R. D. Muir. il Liv Wildn 32:22-9 Je '69

France

Mike Frome. M. Frome. Am For 75:3+ Ag '69

Great Britain

Britain's national parks. A. Netboy. il Am For 75:28-30+ F '69

Hawaii

See also
Haleakala National Park

Kentucky

See also
Mammoth Cave National Park

Kenya

Kenya says harambee! A. C. Fisher, jr. il Nat Geog 135:151-205 F '69

Maryland

See also
Assateague Island National Seashore

Montana

Montana is the message. R. Atcheson. il Holiday 45:56-9+ My '69
See also
Glacier National Park

North Carolina

See also
Cape Hatteras National Seashore Recreational Area

South Africa

See also
Kruger National Park

Sweden

Sweden's national parks. J. H. Winchester. il Travel 132:70-2 Ag '69

Tanzania

Life with the king of beasts; Serengeti National Park. G. B. Schaller. il Nat Geog 135:494-519 Ap '69

United States

Change on park planning. Nat Parks 43:21 Je '69
Conservation tragedy? Sleeping Bear Dunes. D. W. Scott. il Parks & Rec 4:24-6+ O '69
Escape to the Channel Islands. D. Lambert. il Nat Parks 43:4-7 Ap '69
Grizzly bear in the national parks. E. G. Bowman. il Am For 75:16-18+ Jl; 16-18+ Ag '69
How to save our national parks; excerpt from Desert solitarie; a season in the wilderness. E. Abbey. il Field & S 73:74-5+ Mr '69
Improving our living environment. W. J. Hickel. il Parks & Rec 4:18-20 Je '69
Legacy from LBJ; controversy over national parks. il U S News 66:89 F 24 '69
Let's get going at Sleeping Bear. J. J. Stophlet. il Nat Parks 43:21 N '69
Man and nature in the national parks; reprint; with preface by R. E. Train. F. F. Darling and N. D. Eichhorn. Nat Parks 43:13-24 Ap '69
Mike Frome; parks and people. M. Frome. Am For 75:3+ Ja '69
National park system enlarged. B. H. Thompson. il Parks & Rec 4:26-7 Mr '69
National parks association; report of the president and general counsel, May 22, 1969. A. W. Smith. Nat Parks 43:15-18 My '69

National parks, monuments and historic sites. il Travel & Camera 32:77-80 Je '69
National parks; symposium, ed. by D. C. Swain; with introd. by G. B. Hartzog, jr. il Am West 6:2-72 S '69
Parks are yours. take them home with you. G. B. Hartzog, jr. Travel & Camera 32:37 Je '69
Proposed Gulf Islands National Seashore. M. J. Stevens. il Nat Parks 43:16-19 Mr '69
Quandary on the campgrounds. H. Bloomfield. il Am For 75:4-7+ Jl '69
Secretary Hickel issues park policy guidelines. Nat Parks 43:20 Jl '69
Sonoran Desert National Park. D. W. Toll. il Nat Parks 43:4-8 Ja '69
This land is your land; camping with an automobile travel trailer. S. Haft. il Sr Schol 94:Schol Teach 16-17 Ap 11 '69
Total landscape of Sleeping Bear Dunes. P. A. Hart. il Am For 75:36-7+ Ja '69
Udall's last laugh. New Repub 160:10 F 1 '69
Udall's last stand. Nation 208:164-5 F 10 '69
See also
National forests
United States—National park service
also names of national parks and reserves, e.g. Yosemite National Park

Utah

See also
Canyonlands National Park
Dinosaur National Monument

Washington (state)

See also
Mount Rainier National Park

Wyoming

See also
Yellowstone National Park

NATIONAL parks association
Report of president and general counsel, May 22, 1969. A. W. Smith. Nat Parks 43:15-18 My '69

History

Patterns in National parks association history. D. Lambert. il Nat Parks 43:4-8 My '69
NATIONAL peace jubilee in 1869. See Music festivals—Massachusetts
NATIONAL planning
1967: agenda for tomorrow, by S. Udall. Review
Am For 75:38-9 Ja '69. M. Bush
Planning the future; futurology: a new science? A. Shonfield. Cur 105:41-53 Mr '69
NATIONAL planning association
Foreign-aid syndrome. America 120:679-80 Je 14 '69
New look at the idea of foreign aid; National planning association statement. America 120:492 Ap 26 '69
NATIONAL pork producers council
How you're promoting your pork. R. Wilmore. il Farm J 93:H6-7+ Ag '69
We've got the product, let's sell it hard! J. Russell. il Farm J 93:H16 Je '69
NATIONAL portrait gallery. See Smithsonian institution—National portrait gallery
NATIONAL psychology. See National characteristics
NATIONAL recreation and park association
Branches appoint advisors to regional directors. Parks & Rec 4:64-7 My '69
Bridging the gap between our human and natural resources. W. W. Brown. Parks & Rec 4:13 Jl '69
Can of worms; opposition to summer day camp sports program administered by the National collegiate athletic association. Parks & Rec 4:23 My '69
National awards recipients demonstrate public service. il Parks & Rec 4:24-6 N '69
National internship program expanding. Parks & Rec 4:33 F '69
National personnel inventory created. S. G. Lutzin. Parks & Rec 4:35-8 Ja '69
NRPA branch societies. il Parks & Rec 3:42-6 D '68; 4:42-5+ N '69
NRPA expands service to members, here's what it means to you. W. Cook. Parks & Rec 4:58-9 Mr '69
NRPA news. See issues of Parks & recreation
NRPA urban plan. Parks & Rec 4:47-9 N '69
NRPA's personal security program. D. D. Magee. il Parks & Rec 4:73-4 S '69
New NRPA membership and dues plan. Parks & Rec 3:31+ O '68
See also
Lifetime sports foundation

Meetings, 1968

Second national forum; summary highlights. il Parks & Rec 3:29-36 N '68

NATIONAL recreation and park association
—*Continued*

Meetings, 1969
Summary highlights, January 12-14, 1969; with editorial comment. Parks & Rec 4: 25, 39-46 Mr '69
Summary highlights; March 19-21; April 23-26, 1969. il Parks & Rec 4:35-46 Je; 33-40 Ag '69
NATIONAL register of scientific and technical personnel
National register looks at manpower. S. Barisch and T. Johnides. il Phys Today 22:48-52 O '69
NATIONAL research council
More than prayer; suggested program to minimize earthquake damage. il Sci N 95:280-1 Mr 22 '69

Space science board
See National academy of science—Space science board
NATIONAL resource lands. See Public lands —United States
NATIONAL responsibility. See Responsibility
NATIONAL review
Barth, Buckley and Herberg. Chr Cent 86: 431 Mr 26 '69
NATIONAL safety council
Challenge to the churches; slaughter on highways. America 120:320 Mr 22 '69
NATIONAL school lunch program. See School lunches
NATIONAL science foundation. See United States—National science foundation
NATIONAL science teachers association
Science for the seventies; Silver anniversary convention. il Sr Schol 94:Schol Teach 8 Ap 18 '69
NATIONAL screw and manufacturing company
Monogram nails down goals in National screw merger. il Bsns W p 103 My 31 '69
NATIONAL security. See Internal security
NATIONAL security council. See United States —National security council
NATIONAL semiconductor corporation
Millionaire bets on his chips; inventor. R. Widlar. Bsns W p52+ Ag 23 '69
NATIONAL service, Non-military. See Service, Compulsory non-military
NATIONAL social science foundation (proposed) See United States—National social science foundation (proposed)
NATIONAL socialism
Big business and the rise of Hitler. H. A. Turner, jr. bibliog f Am Hist R 75:56-70 O '69
Ghost of social-fascism. T. Draper. bibliog Commentary 47:29-42 F '69; Discussion. 47: 4+ My '69
History quiz for the young revolutionary; similarity of communism to nazism. J. Jeffries. Nat R 21:488+ My 20 '69
Nazi persecution of the churches, 1933-45, by J. S. Conway. Review
America 121:99-100 Ag 16 '69. J. F. Broderick
NATIONAL songs

United States
See also
Star spangled banner (song)
NATIONAL spelling bee. See Spelling—Competitions
NATIONAL standard reference data system. See Information storage and retrieval systems—Science
NATIONAL student association. See United States national student association
NATIONAL student conference on revolution
Striking back. il Newsweek 74:79 Jl 7 '69
NATIONAL student marketing corporation
Cash customers on campus. S. Blickstein. il Duns R 94:65-6+ Ag '69
Getting across to the young. il Bsns W p89-90 O 18 '69
NATIONAL teacher corps. See United States —National teacher corps
NATIONAL theatre of the deaf
National theatre of the deaf. Dance Mag 43: 92-3 My '69
NATIONAL training laboratories
T-school for behaviorism; NTL Institute for applied and behavioral science. Bsns W p62 Ja 10 '70
NATIONAL transportation safety board. See United States—National transportation safety board
NATIONAL trust for places of historic interest or natural beauty
Cry of the peacock. F. Megarity. il House B 111:72+ Ap '69

NATIONAL urban league
New thrust toward economic security; address, July 28, 1969. W. M. Young, jr. Vital Speeches 35:759-63 O 1 '69
Urban league conducts a guided tour. P. Bailey. il Ebony 24:48-50+ S '69
NATIONAL welfare rights organization
Welfare union steps up its demands. il U S News 66:36 Je 23 '69
NATIONAL wildlife federation
Awards for conservation achievement. il Nat Wildlife 7:28-31 Je '69
Call to battle; 33rd annual meeting highlights. il Nat Wildlife 7:17-19 Ap '69
Our national EQ; the first National wildlife federation index of environmental quality. T. L. Kimball. il Nat Wildlife 7:2-13 Ag '69
Public conservation interest. Nat Parks 43: 34 Ap '69
NATIONAL youth endowment program (proposed) See Student loans
NATIONAL youth service (proposed) See Service, Compulsory non-military
NATIONALISM
Beyond the Nation-state. L. B. Pearson. Sat R 52:24-7+ F 15 '69
Nationalism crimps the spending spree; issues of the 1970s. il Bsns W p206+ D 6 '69
Their NLFs and ours. J. Burnham. Nat R 21: 323 Ap 8 '69
Vietnam and the end of the age of superpowers. A. Schlesinger, jr. Harper 238:41-9 Mr '69; Discussion. 238:6+ My '69
See also
Americanism

Indians of North America
New Indians, by S. Steiner. Review
Trans-Action 6:60-1 F '69. B. Cox

Jews
See also
Zionism

Negro race
Ameer (LeRoi Jones) Baraka. D. Llorens. il Ebony 24:75-8+ Ag '69
Black nationalism. J. H. Blake. bibliog f Ann Am Acad 382:15-25 Mr '69
CIA as an equal opportunity employer. D. Schechter and others. il Ramp Mag 7:25-33 Je '69
Fantasy of black nationalism. T. Draper. bibliog f Commentary 48:27-54 S '69; Discussion. 48:14+ D '69
How black is black? C. V. Hamilton. il Ebony 24:44-8+ Ag '69
New black myths. P. Schrag. Harper 238:37-42 My '69
Rustin on black nationalism. America 120:152 F 8 '69
Searching for a new image. il Negro Hist Bul 32:4-5 F '69
Unity of blackness. il Ebony 24:42-3 Ag '69
We want Georgia, South Carolina, Louisiana, Mississippi and Alabama—right now. R. Sherrill. il Esquire 71:70-5+ Ja '69
Whitey's reaction; proposal of separate black state. R. Sherrill. Esquire 71:76+ Ja '69
See also
Black Muslim movement
Black power
NATIONALISM (philosophy)
John Dewey and Vatican council II. T. F. McGann. America 120:411-12+ Ap 5 '69; Discussion. 120:551 My 10 '69
NATIONALISM and communism. See Communism and nationalism
NATIONALIZATION of industry. See Government ownership
NATIONS
See also
States, Small
NATION'S business (periodical)
Memo from the editor. J. Wooldridge. il Nations Bsns 57:7-8 D '69
NATIVE American church
Peyote road. P. Nabokov. il N Y Times Mag p30-1+ Mr 9 '69
NATIVE races
See also
United Nations—Trusteeship council
NATIVE states of India. See India—Native states
NATIVITY groups. See Christmas cribs
NATIVITY of Christ. See Jesus Christ—Nativity
NATIVITY of Christ in art. See Jesus Christ —Art
NATKIN, Robert
Halfway house. il por Time 94:50-1 Ag 1 '69
NATO
After twenty good years, an identity crisis for NATO. Life 66:36 Ap 25 '69

NATURAL resources—*Continued*

United States

Conservation and the Nixon years. M. Frome. Field & S 73:8+ Mr '69

From here to oblivion? federal attitudes toward natural resources. M. Frome. Field & S 74:36+ O '69

Impossible gifts. T. Trueblood. il Field & S 74:16+ D '69

Land lovers; with photographs by P. Harrington. D. Chapman. Look 33:54-61 N 4 '69

Millions for defense but. . damn little for our land. M. Frome. Field & S 74:49+ Je '69

New York state. J. H. Thompson. bibliog il Focus 19:1-8 Je '69

Washington lookout. V. Trumbull. See also issues of American forests

Where conservation is a bad word; Soil conservation service. B. B. Blackburn, 3d; G. Laycock. il Field & S 74:12-14+ D '69

See also
Water supply—United States

NATURAL rights. See Natural law

NATURAL science. See Science

NATURAL steam. See Steam, Natural

NATURAL theology

Ecology and the contemporary religious conscience. R. L. Means. Chr Cent 86:1546-9 D 3 '69

NATURALISM (philosophy)

In and out of Eden. C. F. H. Henry. Chr Today 13:38-9 Je 6 '69

NATURALISTS

Naturalist at large. See issues of Natural history

Naturalist has a unique role. J. P. Hewitt. il Parks & Rec 4:39-40+ D '69

NATURE

Dispatches from the unpaved world. J. C. Devlin. Natur Hist 78:70-2 My '69

Man and nature in the city. B. S. Tindall. il Parks & Rec 4:39-40+ Ja '69

Public parks and private lives. I. J. Winn. Natur Hist 78:20-6 O '69

See also
Earth
Man—Influence on nature
Nature study
Outdoor life

Bibliography

Books in review. See issues of Natural history

For young naturalists. B. Neill. See issues of Audubon

Naturalist's bookshelf. See issues of Audubon

Nature books for a child's summer reading. Good H 169:147 Jl '69

NATURE (aesthetics)

Constable quotes; ed. by N. Kent. J. Constable. Am Artist 33:5 My '69

NATURE and art. See Nature (aesthetics)

NATURE and man. See Man—Influence on nature

NATURE books. See Nature literature

NATURE centers

New wilderness in Long Beach: El Dorado nature center. il Sunset 143:38 Ag '69

NATURE drawing. See Drawing

NATURE in art

Blow up! enlarging designs from nature. W. R. Crosier. il Sch Arts 69:20-1 N '69

See also
Landscape painting
Trees in art

NATURE literature

Field guide to field guides. J. Eastman. Natur Hist 78:28+ N '69

See also
Booksellers and bookselling—Nature literature

NATURE of man. See Man

NATURE outings. See Nature study

NATURE photography

Album of Canadian parks. R. D. Muir. il Liv Wildn 32:22-9 Aut '68

Ansel Adams: a Pacific portfolio. M. Hollis. il Travel & Camera 32:66-71 Ag '69

Ansel Adams, brilliant recorder of nature's magnificence. N. Newhall. il Mod Phot 33:66-71+ S '69

Eliot Porter, master of nature's color. A. Adams. Mod Phot 33:92+ O '69

Famed photographer to conduct workshop. W. Lane. il Travel 131:77 Ap '69

If you've got the eye, the technique is easy. M. A. Matzkin. il Mod Phot 33:84-9+ F '69

Matzkin on movies; shooting nature subjects. M. A. Matzkin. il Mod Phot 33:36+ Jl '69

Nature and the camera; selected prizewinners. il Natur Hist 78:28-33 Je '69

Nature's hidden patterns. il Am For 75:4-7 F '69

Selective focus; photographs. D. Stock. Travel & Camera 32:53-6 Je '69

Wilderness trail. J. Keshishian. il Am For 75:44-5 S '69

See also
Photography of animals
Photography of birds
Photography of flowers, plants, trees, etc.

NATURE sanctuaries. See Wilderness areas

NATURE study

A bird is not for throwing rocks at. G. Goodman. il Look 33:46-8 N 4 '69

Children's village experiments; nature and science program at Children's village. H. Romack. il Parks & Rec 4:39-41+ Ap '69

Forming a nature corps for action; Susquehanna conservation council at Binghamton. N. Ayers. il Cons 24:2-5 O '69

Mindsight; the aim of interpretation. F. Tilden. il Nat Parks 43:9-12 My '69

More ways to build nature interest. T. Stinson. il Camp Mag 41:15+ N '69

Recognizing woody plants in winter. E. H. Ketchledge. il Cons 24:20-7+ O '69

Song of the North; excerpt from Open horizons. S. F. Olson. il Audubon 71:6-12 Ja '69

Three scope explorers. M. Nagel. il Har Yrs 9:35-7 Ap '69

To stimulate campers' interest in nature. T. Stinson. il Camp Mag 41:16-17 S '69

Who killed the bird? I. McManus. il Am For 75:24-7+ O '69

See also
Audubon nature camps
Bird study
Camping—Educational aspects
Childrens gardens
Natural history museums
Nature
Nature literature
Outdoor education

NATURE trails. See Trails

NATURE trails for the blind. See Trails

NAUGLER, Frederic P. See Grim, P. J. jt. auth.

NAUTICAL astronomy

Astronomical pirate; observations from pilot's journal of 1680's. J. Ashbrook. Sky & Tel 38:75 Ag '69

NAUTICAL charts

Navigational aids and charts, you can buy them by mail. il Sunset 142:46-7 Mr '69

New charts. E. S. Maloney. See issues of Motor boating

Updating the charts; Latin American harbor charts. Sci N 95:574 Je 14 '69

Where to buy charts. Motor B 123:78-9+ F '69

NAUTICAL instruments

Instruments; the eyes and ears of modern yachting. E. A. Zadig. il Motor B 123:52-65 Mr '69

NAUTICAL terms. See Naval art and science—Terminology

NAVAHO Indians

Blizzard in Indian country. T. Gallagher. il Read Digest 95:70-5 D '69

Navajo's canyon of history. il Sunset 143:52-7 Jl '69

Revolt on the reservation; OEO chief banished from Navajo reservation. il Time 93:80 Mr 14 '69

NAVAJO demonstration school. See Indians of North America—Education

NAVAJO Indians. See Navaho Indians

NAVAL architecture

See also
Hulls (naval architecture)
Yacht building

NAVAL art and science

Terminology

Great sea battle; glossary; excerpts from Broke and The Shannon. P. Padfield. il Am Heritage 20:51 D '68

NAVAL battles

See also
United States—History—Revolution—Naval operations
World war, 1939-1945—Naval operations

NAVAL chaplains. See Chaplains, Military

NAVAL intelligence. See Military intelligence

NAVAL maneuvers

As reds shadow U.S. fleet. .; report from the Mediterranean. il U S News 66:43 My 12 '69

NAVAL museums
Star is reborn; Star of India in San Diego, Calif. S. Rice. il Yachting 125:66-7+ My '69
  See also
Mystic seaport museum, Mystic, Conn.

NAVAL offenses
United States
  See United States—Navy—Crimes and misdemeanors

NAVAL officers
  See also
United States—Navy—Officers

NAVAL power. See Sea power

NAVAL radio communication. See Radio communication, Naval

NAVAL radiological defense laboratory. See United States—Naval radiological defense laboratory

NAVASKY, Victor S.
Word game. N Y Times Mag p 14+ F 9 '69

NAVIGATION
Basic course in navigating by compass. J. S. Doherty. il Merch Illus 65:71-3+ Mr '69
Bowditch; American practical navigator. W. S. Kals. il Motor B 123:136-7+ Ja '69
Effect of leeway. F. Adams. il Yachting 125:63+ My '69
How to navigate around buoys. E. H. Moore. il Cons 23:48-inside back cover Ap '69
Navigation: for the yachtsman. R. C. McCurdy. il Yachting 126:55+ Ag '69
Position finding at sea. E. S. Szymanski. il Motor B 123:68-71 Ap '69
What makes a good helmsman? H. M. Scott, jr. Motor B 123:116+ Mr '69
What really caused the Torrey Canyon disaster? excerpts from In the wake of Torrey Canyon. R. Petrow. il Pop Mech 131:114-19+ Ap '69
When fog closes in. R. Witherill. il Yachting 125:74-5+ Je '69
  See also
Dead reckoning (navigation)
Lighthouses
Nautical astronomy
Nautical charts
Pilots and pilotage
Radio in navigation
Sailing
Seamanship
United States power squadrons, incorporated
Yachts and yachting

Aids and devices
Graph for estimating position errors. E. S. Szymanski. il Motor B 123:432-3 Ja '69
Navigational aids and charts, you can buy them by mail. il Sunset 142:46-7 Mr '69
  See also
Buoys
Radio in navigation

Competitions
Control points. M. L. Hersey. See issues of Yachting

Study and teaching
Mail order navigation. B. Crabtree. il Yachting 126:70+ S '69

NAVIGATION (space flight)
  See also
Computers—Space flight applications

NAVIGATION, Aerial
Area navigation control cited as air safety need for 1970s. il Aviation W 91:29 D 1 '69
Area navigation gains in airline favor. K. J. Stein. il Aviation W 90:251-3+ Mr 10 '69
FAA asks area navigation views in July. Aviation W 90:32 Je 30 '69
Safety check; wrong way, Corrigan. J. Gilbert. Flying 84:20 My '69
  See also
Airplanes—Piloting
Inertial guidance systems
Loran

Aids and devices
Manufacturers push area navaids. B. Miller. il Aviation W 91:28-9 Jl 21 '69

NAVIGATION, Primitive
Navigation: by forgotten native lore; methods used by South Sea natives without instruments. D. Lewis. il Yachting 126:54+ Ag '69

NAVIGATION instruments. See Nautical instruments

NAVONE, John
Gregorian university. America 120:584-6 My 17 '69

NAVRATIL, James D.
Fluorine; a hostile element! bibliog por Chem 42:11-15 F '69

NAVY football. See Football

NAVY yards and naval stations
NRPA representative visits Japan; conducting workshops at naval bases. P. O. Sturdivant. il Parks & Rec 4:49+ S '69

NAWAPA. See North American water and power alliance

NAZARETH, Israel
Homage to the incarnation; new Basilica of the incarnation and Church of the annunciation. il Time 93:62-4 Ap 4 '69

NAZI war criminals. See World war, 1939-1945—War criminals

NAZISM. See National socialism

N'DIAYE, Francine
Art of African pulleys. UNESCO Courier 22:18-24 My '69

NEAL, Harry Edward
In defense of writers' conferences. Writer 82:25-6 My '69

NEAL, Jay T.
Fatsia japonica. Horticulture 47:53 Ja '69
Jacobinia carnea. Horticulture 47:14-15 F '69

NEAL, Larry
Any day now: black art and black liberation. Ebony 24:54-8+ Ag '69

NEAL, Patricia
Does everybody love Patricia Neal? O, yes! G. Zimmermann. il pors Look 33:82-4+ F 18 '69

NEAL, Victor T. and others
Thermal stratification in the Arctic Ocean. bibliog Science 166:373-4 O 17 '69

NEAMAN, Samuel
Into retailing via Palestine. por Bsns W p 140 Je 14 '69

NEANDERTHAL race
Fossil evidence of human violence. T. D. Stewart. il Trans-Action 6:48-53 My '69; Reply with rejoinder. S. Parker. 6:60-1 O '69
Mousterian cultures in European Russia. R. G. Klein. bibliog il Science 165:257-65 Jl 18 '69

NEAPOLITAN musical autumn. See Music festivals—Italy

NEAR EAST. See Middle East

NEAR end; story. See Regnier, N.

NEARSIGHTEDNESS. See Myopia

NEARY, John
Cube house vs. the squares. Life 67:83-4+ N 14 '69
Magical McCartney mystery. Life 67:103-5 N 7 '69

NEATNESS
Anecdotes, facetiae, satire, etc.
Has anybody seen my hammer? M. Tupper. il Good H 169:48+ Ag '69

NEATROUR, Charles R.
In-service programs for JHS teachers. Clear House 44:187 N '69

NEAVES, William B. and Gerald, P. S.
Gene dosage at the lactate dehydrogenase b locus in triploid and diploid teiid lizards. bibliog Science 164:557-9 My 2 '69

NEBEL, Long John
Long John Nebel. I. Taves. il pors Look 33:86+ Mr 18 '69

NEBRASKA
Healthiest spot in America. J. Y. Dickinson. il Holiday 45:52-3+ My '69; Same abr. Read Digest 95:241-2+ O '69
  See also
Hunting—Nebraska

Description and travel
God's country and my people, by W. Morris. Review
  New Yorker 45:205-6+ O 18 '69. R. Coles

History
Battle of Omaha; fight for state capital. S. Hronek. il Am West 6:10-11 Jl '69

NEBRASKANS
God's country and my people, by W. Morris. Review
  New Yorker 45:205-6+ O 18 '69. R. Coles

NEBREDA, Alfonso
Mass media and catechetics. America 121:29 Jl 19 '69

NEBULAE
Deep-sky wonders; NGC 7293 Helix nebula. W. S. Houston. il Sky & Tel 38:272-3 O '69
Planetary nebulae. L. H. Aller. il Sky & Tel 37:282-6, 348-52; 38:12-18, 82-5, 152-5, 227-9, 306-9, 377-9; 39:15-18 My '69-Ja '70 (to be cont)
Pulsars and supernovas. Sci Am 220:46 Ja '69
X-ray pulsar in the Crab nebula. G. Fritz and others. bibliog il Science 164:709-12 My 9 '69

NEBULAE—*Continued*
X rays from crab have period of radio signals. il Phys Today 22:68-9 Jl '69
NECK
Diseases
Causes and cures for a pain in the neck. il Good H 168:165 F '69
NECKER, Claire
Dwellers of the forest floor. Nat Wildlife 7:50-5 Ap '69
NECKLACES
Ceramic necklaces. S. Nickle. il Ceram Mo 17:16-17 Je '69
NEEDHAM, James
Accountant to sit on SEC. Bsns W p28 My 31 '69
NEEDLEPOINT
Add a lively note with needlepoint. il Good H 169:104-5 Ag '69
Pages from my needlepoint book; excerpts. M. Martin. il McCalls 96:84-91 Ap '69
Very personal craft: needlepoint. il House & Gard 136:78-9 Jl '69
NEEDLEWORK
And this is yarn! M. Garrity. il Bet Hom & Gard 47:90-1 Mr '69
English needlework. R. Davidson. il Antiques 96:150 Ag '69
Kits for needle buffs. il House & Gard 136:108 D '69
Mrs Delany and her handiwork. S. M. Newton. il Antiques 96:100-5 Jl '69
Your own thing. il Seventeen 27:154 N '68
See also
Crocheting
Embroidery
Knitting
Needlepoint
Patchwork
Samplers
NEFEDOV, [Uril, and others
Problems of space exploration. Space World F-8-68:36-7 Ag '69
NEFF, James
Creek-fed mushrooms. Org Gard & Farm 16:54 Ag '69
NEGATIVE color films. See Photography—Films
NEGATIVE film files. See Files and filing (documents, etc)
NEGATIVE income tax
Choosing a new way. Sci N 95:549 Je 7 '69
Negative income tax, better than welfare? J. Daniel. Read Digest 94:60-4 My '69
Negative income tax: more minuses than pluses; Hawaii. il Nations Bsns 57:34-7 Jl '69
Poverty; the negative income tax; address, October 22, 1969. J. H. Smith. Vital Speeches 36:157-60 D 15 '69
NEGATIVE resistance. See Electric resistance
NEGATIVES, Photographic. See Photography—Negatives
NEGLIGENCE
Temptation; airplane as attractive nuisance. V. G. Wickham. Flying 85:84 Jl '69
See also
Liability (law)
NEGOTIABLE Instruments
Banks' paper route is coming to stop. Bsns W p35-6 N 8 '69
Money men put their bets on paper; short-term negotiable notes. il Bsns W p73 Jl 19 '69
They'd rather switch; switch trade and clearing dollars. Newsweek 73:71-2 Mr 3 '69
See also
Checks
NEGOTIATION now (organization) See Vietnamese war, 1957- —Peace and mediation
NEGOTIATORS; story. See Jacobs, H.
NEGRO (term)
Afro-American or Negro. O. R. Williams. Negro Hist Bul 32:18 Mr '69
Black, Negro, or Afro-American? What's in a name? Sr Schol 94:11 F 14 '69
Color them traditional. Time 94-20 Jl 11 '69
Identity crisis. Newsweek 73:62 Je 30 '69
Negro, black, or Afro-American? reprint. J. A. Morsell. Negro Hist Bul 32:11 F '69
Why black? D. Brudnoy. il Nat R 21:123-4 F 11 '69
NEGRO actors and actresses
Football heroes invade Hollywood. il Ebony 24:195-7+ O '69
See also
Aldridge, I. F.
Brown, J.
Cosby, B.
Fisher G.
Negroes in moving pictures
Negroes in television
Poitier, S.
St Jacques, R.

NEGRO air pilots
Can a black man fly? interviews. K. Connes. il Flying 85:53-7 Jl '69
NEGRO airline stewardesses. See Airlines—Hostesses
NEGRO American visitors in Liberia. See Foreign visitors in Liberia
NEGRO Americans in Africa. See Americans in Africa
NEGRO anti-Semitism. See Anti-Semitism
NEGRO architects
Urban design with soul; Urban design development group, incorporated, Detroit. J. Aumente. il Arch Forum 131:44-5 D '69
NEGRO art. See Art, Negro (American)
NEGRO artists
And so it is... H. Ghent. il Sch Arts 68:21-6 Ap '69
See also
Hunter, C
Negroes in art
NEGRO associations. See Negroes—Societies, etc.
NEGRO astrologers. See Astrologers
NEGRO athletes
After the Olympics: buying off protest. J. Scott and H. Edwards. il Ramp Mag 8:16-21 N '69
Black athlete in the golden age of sports (cont) A. S. Young. il Ebony 24:66-8+ F; 122-4+ Mr; 100-2+ Ap; 110-12+ My; 114-16+ Je '69
No defeats, loads of trouble; Wyoming's black football players suspended. P. Putnam. il Sports Illus 31:26-7 N 3 '69
Report from section 22; suspended black sprinters. R. Cochran and J. Scott. il Ramp Mag 7:6+ N 30 '68
Revolt of the black athlete, by H. Edwards. Review
New Repub 161:26-8 O 4 '69. P. Whitten
Trouble in Happy Valley; protesting BYU policy. il Newsweek 74:102-3 D 1 '69
See also names of Negro athletes, e.g. J. Jones
NEGRO authors
New black writers. I. Howe. Harper 239:130-1+ D '69
See also
Cleaver, E.
Du Bois, W. E. B.
Ellison, R.
Fanon, F.
Hansberry, L.
Hughes, L.
Novelists, Negro
Steptoe, J.
NEGRO bands. See Bands (music)
NEGRO banks. See Banks and banking—United States
NEGRO baseball players. See Baseball players
NEGRO basketball players. See Basketball players
NEGRO beauty contests. See Beauty contests
NEGRO boxers. See Boxers
NEGRO businessmen
Barriers to hiring the blacks. J. R. Goeke and C. S. Weymar. il Harvard Bsns R 47:144-6+ S '69
Black business, bleak business. G. Eckstein. Nation 209:243-5 S 15 '69
Economics of liberation. A. Poinsett. il Ebony 24:150-4 Ag '69
New black businessmen. C. Hunter. il Sat R 52:27-9+ Ag 23 '69
Olin corp. sows ghetto seed money. Nations Bsns 57:15 D '69
Profit versus pride; the trouble with black capitalism. A. F. Brimmer. il Nations Bsns 57:78-9 My '69
Speaking of business; black entrepreneurs with unusual enterprises. il Ebony 24:38-40+ Jl '69
See also
Black capitalism
Daigre, B.
Negro executives
NEGRO celebrities
Speaking of people: outstanding Negro women. il Ebony 24:6-7 Ag '69
NEGRO children
Black misery; excerpts. L. Hughes. il Good H 169:78-9 Jl '69
Shock of black recognition: recollections of famous Negroes; symposium. il Esquire 71:138-41 My '69
Starting point defined; improving mental health of black children. il Ebony 25:136-7 N '69
See also
Socially handicapped children
NEGRO children as actors
See also
Copage, M.

NEGRO children as authors. See Children as authors

NEGRO children as photographers. See Children as photographers

NEGRO children in literature
Black perspective in books for children. J. Thompson and G. Woodard. bibliog il Wilson Lib Bul 44:416-24 D '69
Especially for children (cont) H. Aldrich. il Negro Hist Bul 31:14-15 D '68; 32:13-14 Ja '69
Some 1969 books for and about Negro children. Pub W 197:76 Ja 5 '70
Stevie; realism in a book about black children. il Life 67:54-9 Ag 29 '69

NEGRO childrens literature. See Childrens literature

NEGRO childrens reading. See Childrens reading

NEGRO churches
Holy war of the Rev Trudie Trimm; minister of Chicago's New Testament missionary Baptist church. il Ebony 24:72-4+ S '69
Storefront churches; social stabilizers. W. Willoughby. il Chr Today 13:44-5 My 9 '69

NEGRO city managers. See City managers

NEGRO civil rights organizations. See Civil rights organizations

NEGRO clergy
Black Catholics. il Newsweek 73:55 Ja 27 '69
Black folk in white churches. G. H. Caldwell. il Chr Cent 86:209-11 F 12 '69
Storefront churches; social stabilizers. W. Willoughby. il Chr Today 13:44-5 My 9 '69
See also
Burgess, J. M.
National committee of Black churchmen

NEGRO clowns. See Clowns

NEGRO college graduates. See College graduates, Negro

NEGRO college presidents. See College presidents

NEGRO college students. See Negro students

NEGRO colleges and universities
Escape from the dark cave. J. U. Monro. il Nation 209:434-9 O 27 '69
Help for negro colleges. Sch & Soc 97:412 N '69
Ignorant armies. J. Stevenson. Atlan 224:57-63 O '69
Learning in black colleges; symposium. ed. by N. Friedman. il Wilson Lib Bul 44:49-74 S '69
Negro college. D. Klein. il Seventeen 28:86+ F '69
They had a dream: black colleges and library standards. H. L. Totten. il Wilson Lib Bul 44:75-9 S '69
Upgrading Negro colleges in the South. Sch & Soc 97:350-1 O '69
See also
Agricultural and technical college of North Carolina, Greensboro, N.C.
Fisk university, Nashville, Tenn.
Grambling college, Grambling, La.
Hampton institute, Hampton, Va.
Howard university, Washington, D.C.
Meharry medical college, Nashville, Tenn.
Miles college, Birmingham, Ala.
Shaw university, Raleigh, N.C.
South Carolina, State college, Orangeburg
Texas southern university, Houston
Tuskegee institute
Washington, D.C. Federal city college
Wiley college, Marshall, Tex

Libraries
Future of the black college library. E. J. Josey. il Library J 94:3019-22 S 15 '69

NEGRO comedians
See also
Cosby, B.

NEGRO companies
Blacks wrap up slice of action at food chains; Operation Breadbasket's boycott of Chicago A&P stores. il Bsns W p 162-3+ Ap 26 '69
Business to the rescue. J. R. Coyne, jr. Nat R 21:744-5 Jl 29 '69
Economics of liberation. A. Poinsett. il Ebony 24:150-4 Ag '69
Giants of black capitalism. il Ebony 24:164-6+ My '69
He makes the ghetto make money; black entrepreneur J. Hurt. Bsns W p 154-5 My 10 '69
Making capitalism work in the ghettos. L. L. Allen. il Harvard Bsns R 47:83-92 My '69
Soul cards; greeting card companies. il Newsweek 73:101 My 5 '69
Speaking of business; black entrepreneurs with unusual enterprises. il Ebony 24:38-40+ Jl '69

What do you people want? transfer of big companies to black control. R. F. America, jr. il Harvard Bsns R 47:103-12 Mr '69
See also
Black capitalism
Harlem commonwealth council
Onyx enterprises, incorporated
Terry manufacturing company

Federal aid
Black capitalism has a hollow ring. il Bsns W p51+ Ag 30 '69

NEGRO conferences
See also
National black economic development conference

NEGRO congressmen
New faces in Congress; Cleveland, St Louis, Brooklyn boost black representation to nine. il Ebony 24:56-61+ F '69

NEGRO congresswomen
See also
Chisholm, S. A.

NEGRO costume designers. See Costume designers

NEGRO criminals. See Negroes—Crime

NEGRO culture. See Negroes—Culture

NEGRO dancers
See also
Pomare, E.

NEGRO dialect. See Negro-English dialects

NEGRO directors. See Corporations—Directors

NEGRO dolls. See Dolls

NEGRO drama
Bar stool in a black hell. il Time 93:85-6 My 16 '69
No miracles; Black quartet. H. Junker. il Newsweek 74:82 Ag 11 '69
See also
Theater, Negro

NEGRO education. See Negroes—Education

NEGRO educators
See also
Negro teachers
Page, I. E.

NEGRO employees
Training
See Employees—Training

NEGRO-English dialects
Bi-dialectalism: the linguistics of white supremacy. J. Sledd. Engl J 58:1307-15+ D '69
Black dialect and history: NCTE warns of overreacting. Library J 94:1708 Ap 15 '69
Exploring the racial gap. il Time 93:75-6 My 9 '69
Rapping in the black ghetto. T. Kochman. il Trans-Action 6:26-34 F '69; Reply. R. D. Abrahams. 6:53+ My '69

NEGRO entertainers
See also
Falana, L.
Nicholas, F.

NEGRO executives
Crashing the barriers. il Fortune 79:105-7 Ap '69
See also
Lloyd, E.

NEGRO family corporations. See Family corporations

NEGRO family life. See Negroes—Social conditions

NEGRO farmers
Nixon's guaranteed annual poverty. L. Hunt and others. Ramp Mag 8:64-70 D '69
White agriculture; discrimination policy of the Agriculture department. New Repub 161:11 N 29 '69

NEGRO fiction
Black novelists: our turn. R. A. Gross. il Newsweek 73:94+ Je 16 '69

NEGRO gangs. See Gangs

NEGRO golfers. See Golfers

NEGRO historians
See also
Du Bois, W. E. B.

NEGRO history. See Negroes—History

NEGRO history week
Help change the pecking order. J. E. Wright. il Library J 94:153-5 Ja 15 '69
Making Negro history week last. il Negro Hist Bul 32:4-5 Ap '69

NEGRO intellectuals
Achieving educational equality; stemming the black brain drain. V. Harding. Cur 105:37-40 Mr '69
Crisis of the Negro intellectual, by H. Cruse. Review
Ramp Mag 8:36+ D '69. N. Hare

NEGRO journalism. See Negro press

NEGRO judges
    See also
    Crockett, G. W.
NEGRO labor. See Negroes—Employment
NEGRO lawyers
    See also
    Sanders, S.
NEGRO leadership
    Black governments and black power. il Negro Hist Bul 32:4-6 O '69
    New faces, new voices, new style. il Newsweek 73:24-6+ Je 30 '69
    Who speaks for Negroes now? A shift in leadership. il U S News 66:38-9 Je 23 '69
NEGRO legislators
    See also
    Hinton, J. S.
NEGRO librarians
    Black decision-makers. K. Nyren. Library J 94:2203-6 Je 1 '69; Discussion. 94:2845 S 1 '69
    Ivory tower ghettoes. W. E. Hinchliff. il Library J 94:3971-4 N 1 '69
    See also
    Libraries and Negroes
NEGRO life and history, Association for the study of. See Association for the study of Negro life and history
NEGRO literature
    American Negro, by U. Lee and others. Review
        Sat R 52:35-6+ Ag 23 '69. A. Nevins
    Book reviews. See issues of Negro history bulletin
    Ebony book shelf. See issues of Ebony
    Exhibit report; an estimate of importance; books on Negro life and history. F. Cohn. il Negro Hist Bul 31:6-7 D '68
    Overdue; southern black studies drain. E. J. Fontenette. Wilson Lib Bul 44:96 S '69
    Publishing the black experience. M. Thelwell. Ramp Mag 8:60+ O '69
    Take five, add soul-boss reading; West Coast tour sponsored by three libraries and Children's book council. Library J 94:823-4 F 15 '69
    See also
    Negro authors
    Negro fiction
    Negro poetry
    Negroes in literature

Study and teaching
Negro literature for secondary English and humanities courses; an NCTE/ERIC report. R. V. Denby. bibliog Engl J 58:767-72 My '69
Negro literature in the secondary school: problems and perspectives; address, November 1968. R. Bone. Engl J 58:510-15 Ap '69
Our guilt. M. Ylvisaker. bibliog Engl J 58: 193-5 F '69
Unit on black literature. J. S. Tinney. Engl J 58:1028-31 O '69
What's black and white and read all over? excerpts from address, November, 1968. D. Sterling. bibliog Engl J 58:817-32 S '69
NEGRO marines. See United States—Marine corps—Negroes
NEGRO market
    Black man in the gray flannel suit: Negro advertising agencies. il Time 93:76 Je 27 '69
    Will an ethnic pitch sell the black market? American dream soap aimed for the ghetto. il Bsns W p88+ Ap 12 '69
NEGRO mayors
    Breakthrough in Chapel Hill. il Time 93:26 My 16 '69
    Bright future for politicians. il Ebony 24:88-9 Jl '69
    Mayor of Chapel Hill. Newsweek 73:41 My 19 '69
    Mississippi smiles on Charles Evers. il Life 66:40-1 My 23 '69
    Not doing you like you done us; first black mayor of a racially mixed Mississippi town since Reconstruction. il Time 94:16 Jl 18 '69
    Pledges of love and unity; first black mayor of a Mississippi town since Reconstruction. il Time 93:25 My 23 '69
    To live and die in Dixie; C. Evers inauguration. il Newsweek 74:31-2 Jl 21 '69
    Xenia, Ohio. Negro Hist Bul 32:21 Mr '69
    See also
    Evers, C.
    Stokes, C. B.
NEGRO middle class. See Middle classes
NEGRO migration. See Negroes—Migration
NEGRO militants
    A. Philip Randolph: labor's grand old man, eighty-year-old black militant. P. Garland. il Ebony 24:31-4+ My '69

Church gun battle: police vs. blacks; black nationalists arrested in Detroit. il U S News 66:10 Ap 14 '69
End of the love-in; cop dies during gun battle with black nationalists. il Newsweek 73:35-6 Ap 14 '69
Furor over flag for militants. U S News 66:13 Je 9 '69
Myths of the black revolt. B. Rustin. il Ebony 24:96-8+ Ag '69
Negro militancy. M. Kilson. Sat R 52:28-31 Ag 16 '69
New faces, new voices, new style. il Newsweek 73-24-6+ Je 30 '69
New faces of racism. W. F. Buckley. jr. Nat R 21:558-9 Je 3 '69
New left in action. il U S News 66:35-7 My 19 '69
Reparations. D. Lawrence. U S News 67:104 O 13 '69
Sniping a new pattern of violence? T. A. Knopf. bibliog il Trans-Action 6:22-9 Jl '69; Reply with rejoinder. J. R. Corsi and L. H. Masotti. 6:5+ S '69
Tough new breed: ghetto blacks under thirty. il Newsweek 73:21 Je 30 '69
    See also
    Black Panther party
    Negro student militants
NEGRO militants and churches
    And now James Forman. Nat R 21:789-90 Ag 12 '69
    Black bill collector. il Newsweek 73:74-5 My 19 '69
    Black demands in Boston. il Newsweek 73: 88 Je 16 '69
    Black manifesto. il Time 93:94 My 16 '69
    Black manifesto declares war on churches. Chr Today 13:29 My 23 '69
    Black manifesto: the great white hope. R. Goetz. Chr Cent 86:832-3 Je 18 '69; Discussion. 86:1046-7 Ag 6 '69
    Black over white; the National black economic development conference. Commonweal 90: 308-9 My 30 '69
    Black preacher looks at the Black manifesto. R. D. Abernathy. Chr Cent 86:1064-5 Ag 13 '69
    Black threats move United church of Christ. J. Huffman. Chr Today 13:36 Jl 18 '69
    Blacks bill the churches; demand for reparations. il Bsns W p54+ My 10 '69
    Cardinal was in Connecticut. J. Deedy. Commonweal 90:534 S 5 '69
    Catalyst of conscience. Time 94:49 Ag 29 '69
    Churches and James Forman. Chr Today 13: 27 Je 6 '69
    Did we endorse the Black manifesto? Chr Cent 86:894 Jl 2 '69
    Forman box score. J. C. Haughey. America 120:689 Je 14 '69
    How James Forman lost his cool but saved religion in 1969. A. Vorspan. Chr Cent 86: 1042 Ag 6 '69
    In search of a black Christianity. Time 94: 57-8 Jl 4 '69
    Incident at Riverside church. Nation 208:618-19 My 19 '69
    Itemizing the reparations bill. Chr Today 13: 43 Je 6 '69
    James Forman's Black manifesto. America 120:605 My 24 '69
    Manifesto and the magnificat; strike called against Interchurch center in New York. H. Schomer. Chr Cent 86:866-7 Je 25 '69
    Preparation for separation and reparation: the churches' response to racism; demands on the World council of churches. J. R. Nelson. Chr Cent 86:862-5 Je 25 '69
    Putting it to the churches. S. C. Rose. New Repub 160:19-21 Je 21 '69
    Racism and revolt. Chr Today 13:33-4 Je 20 '69
    Violence justified. Time 93:88+ Je 6 '69
    What to do if James Forman busts up your service; excerpts from letter, ed. by W. F. Buckley. Nat R 21:792 Ag 12 '69
    White church and black business. N. Thomas. Commonweal 90:503-4 Ag 22 '69
    Will the Black manifesto help blacks? Chr Cent 86:701 My 21 '69
NEGRO militants and industry
    Plague on both your houses! black militants vs industry and organized labor. il Bsns W p54+ My 24 '69
    Some reflections on organized labor and the new militants. P. Henle. bibliog Mo Labor R 92:20-5 Jl '69
NEGRO military officers
    Air force's education expert. il Ebony 25: 88-91 N '69
    Master of air defense; J. J. Kelly, head of unit at Saglek Bay, Labrador. il Ebony 24:124-6+ O '69

NEGRO ministers. See Negro clergy

NEGRO models. See Models (persons)

NEGRO Mormons. See Mormons and Mormonism, Negro

NEGRO municipal officers
City: black power in office. il Time 93:27 F 28 '69
See also
Negro mayors

NEGRO music
Black music, by L. Jones. Review
Commonweal 90:372 Je 13 '69. H. S. Bryant, jr
Black music: what is it? Where is it? D.-R. De Lerma. Hi Fi 19:MA16-17 N '69
Blues people: Negro music in white America, by L. Jones. Review
Am Rec G 35:870+ My '69. R. Ellsworth
Revolution in sound. A. B. Spellman. il Ebony 24:84-9 Ag '69
See also
Blues (songs, etc)
Jazz music
Negro songs

NEGRO musicians
Black and white notes; discrimination charge against New York philharmonic by two black musicians. il Newsweek 74:82 Ag 18 '69
My man Andrué; classical pianist. A. Watts. N. Darden. il Sat R 52:43-5 Jl 26 '69
Revolution in sound. A. B. Spellman. il Ebony 24:84-9 Ag '69
See also
Ellington, D.
King, R. B.

NEGRO newspapers. See Negro press

NEGRO novelists. See Novelists, Negro

NEGRO nuns
Black sisters become soul sisters. J. C. Haughey. America 121:67 Ag 2 '69

NEGRO organizations. See Negroes—Societies, etc.

NEGRO periodicals
See also
Black scholar (periodical)
Brownies' book (periodical)

NEGRO physicians
See also
Drew, C.
National medical association

NEGRO poetry
Black lamps: white mirrors. il Time 94:60-71 O 3 '69
Life ain't been no crystal stair; address, 1968. N. Larrick. il Library J 94:843-5 F 15 '69

NEGRO poets
See also
Giovanni, N.
Lee, D. L.

NEGRO police
Black cop. il Newsweek 74:54 Ag 4 '69
Black lawman in KKK territory; Tallulah, La. C. L. Sanders. il Ebony 25:57-60+ Ja '70
Black vs. white in the station house. R. A. Jones. Nation 209:368-70 O 13 '69

NEGRO politicians. See Negroes—Politics and suffrage; Politicians

NEGRO press
Amsterdam news. J. K. Sale. il N Y Times Mag p30-1+ F 9 '69; Discussion. P 141 Mr 23 '69

NEGRO priests
Black Catholicism; meeting of Black Catholic clergy caucus. J. C. Haughey. America 120:325-7 Mr 22 '69

NEGRO prisoners
Black and proud behind bars; Swahili and soul program at Colorado prison. D. Bogle. il Ebony 24:64-6+ Ag '69
If you're black stay out of Tennessee. Trans-Action 6:11 O '69

NEGRO private schools. See Private schools, Negro

NEGRO professors. See College professors and instructors

NEGRO public officers
As black officials met; Black elected officials' institute conference. il U S News 67:37 S 29 '69
Black governments and black power. il Negro Hist Bul 32:4-6 O '69
Black power, municipal style. J. E. Patterson. Commonweal 90:477-8 Ag 8 '69
Black suspicion of Nixon. New Repub 160:12-13 F 8 '69
Cities outlook; ideas presented at Institute of black elected officials. Bsns W p 100 O 4 '69
Let's give him a chance; Negroes in the Nixon administration. il Ebony 24:52-3 Ap '69

Nixon makes two black appointees; E. D. Koontz and J. Farmer. il Negro Hist Bul 32:20-1 Ap '69
Spelling it out in black and white; Institute for black elected officials. il Newsweek 74:32 S 22 '69

NEGRO public opinion. See Public opinion—United States

NEGRO race
See also
Nationalism—Negro race

NEGRO schools
See also
Negro colleges and universities

NEGRO scientists
See also
Gifford, B.
Gourdine, M. C.

NEGRO seaside resorts. See Seaside resorts

NEGRO singers
Former Supreme talks a little. il Ebony 24:83-6+ F '69
See also
Allen, B.
Berry, C.
Brown, J.
Butler, J.
Havens, R.
Maynor, D.
Ross, D.
Simone, N.
Smith, B.
Terrell, T.

NEGRO slang. See Slang

NEGRO slum clearance. See Urban renewal

NEGRO songs
Beat of love; gospel song Oh happy day. Newsweek 73:117 My 19 '69
Trumpets of the Lord; soulfest of Negro spirituals. T. Lewis. America 120:599 My 17 '69
See also
Blues (songs, etc)

NEGRO spirituals. See Negro songs

NEGRO student demonstrations
Angry and alone together. K. G. Gross. Nation 208:207-10 F 17 '69
As guns are added to campus revolts; Cornell university surrenders to Negroes' demands. il U S News 66:30-1 My 5 '69
Benefit of anger. E. D. Moorman. Sat R 52:72-3+ Je 21 '69
Black against black; Negro activists shot at UCLA. Newsweek 73:30 Ja 27 '69
Black is beautiful, and belligerent. il Time 93:43 Ja 24 '69
Black mood on campus; symposium. il Newsweek 73:53-9 F 10 '69
Black moods on the campus. Life 66:32 Ja 31 '69
Black power play; report from Brandeis. D. Brudnoy. Nat R 21:66 Ja 28 '69
Blacks at Brandeis. M. Rosenthal and others. Commonweal 89:727-30 Mr 14 '69; Reply. E. Witten. 90:131 +Ap 18 '69
Brandeis: how a liberal university reacts to a black take-over. B. Nelson. Science 163:1431-4 Mr 28 '69
Campus spring offensive. il Newsweek 73:67-8 Ap 28 '69
Campus unrest: now force meets force. il U S News 66:8+ F 24 '69
Day in the troubled life of U.S. schools. il U S News 66:8 Ja 27 '69
Doves v. hawks on campus; Brandeis. D. Brudnoy. Nat R 21:172-4 F 25 '69
Guns come to Cornell; with report by C. Childs. il Life 66:20-7 My 2 '69
It can't happen here, can it? il Newsweek 73:26-30 My 5 '69
Negro leader's tough talk about Negro students; excerpts from address, April 27, 1969. B. Rustin. U S News 66:8 My 12 '69
Requiem for Courtney Smith. P. Good. il Life 66:76B-76D+ My 9 '69
San Fernando's black revolt. S. Harris. Commonweal 89:549-52 Ja 31 '69
Siege of Greensboro. il Newsweek 73:38 Je 2 '69
South Carolina: the movement finally arrives. D. Nolan. Nation 208:655-6 My 26 '69
Three days on Mifflin street; Madison, Wis. H. Henkin. Nation 208:653-4 My 26 '69
War of the flea at San Francisco state. J. H. Bunzel. il N Y Times Mag p28-9+ N 9 '69; Reply with rejoinder. B. Friedman. p44+ D 7 '69

NEGRO student militants
As guns are added to campus revolts; Cornell university surrenders to Negroes' demands. il U S News 66:30-1 My 5 '69
Battle for a college: Why San Francisco state blew up. L. Litwak; J. H. Bunzel. il Look 33:61-2+ My 27 '69

NEGRO youth—*Continued*
Tough new breed: ghetto blacks under thirty.
  il Newsweek 73:21 Je 30 '69
    See also
Negro students

NEGROES
American foreign affairs; black America; address, March 10, 1969. F. H. Williams. Vital Speeches 35:478-80 My 15 '69
Annual progress report: 1969; a year of marking time. il Ebony 25:103-6+ Ja '70
Black America: a historical survey; symposium. bibliog f Cur Hist 57:257-307 N '69
Black man's route to the top. W. A. Lewis. Read Digest 95:157-8+ Ag '69
Black pride; black action; address, December 4, 1968. C. P. Lucas. Vital Speeches 35:505-8 Je 1 '69
Build baby, build: why the summer was quiet. il Time 94:15-17 S 12 '69
Caucasian genes in American Negroes. T. E. Reed. bibliog il Science 165:762-8 Ag 22 '69; Reply with rejoinder. E. N. Anderson, jr. 166:1353 D 12 '69
Current events and branch news. See issues of Negro history bulletin
Identity crisis. Newsweek 73:62 Je 30 '69
New black myths. P. Schrag. Harper 238:37-42 My '69
Report from black America; with reports by R. M. Scammon; J. Rodgers; J. B. Cumming, jr. il Newsweek 73:16-26+ Je 30 '69
Shock of black recognition: recollections of famous Negroes; symposium. il Esquire 71:138-41 My '69
Troubled American: a special report on the white majority; with reports by K. Fleming and R. M. Scammon. il Newsweek 74:28-52+ O 6 '69; Same abr. Read Digest 95:94-9 D '69
    See also
Back-to-Africa movements
Black capitalism
Black Muslim movement
Black power
Boley, Okla.
Congress of racial equality
Freedmen
Interracial cooperation
National association for the advancement of colored people
National urban league
Negro authors
Negro history week
Negro market
Race relations
Revivals
United States—Army—Negroes
  also subhead Negroes under names of cities, e.g. Chicago—Negroes

Bibliography

Black bibliography. D. C. Dickinson. il Wilson Lib Bul 44:184-7 O '69
Black books; fourteen books covering the range of problems on the subject of race. D. Lockard. Trans-Action 6:53-8 Jl '69
Blowing in the wind; childrens books. E. L. Morris. Library J 94:1298-300 Mr 15 '69
Fifty books for school libraries on the blacks. R. Condon. il Wilson Lib Bul 43:657-64 Mr '69; Discussion. 43:946 Je '69
Help change the pecking order; booklist for Negro history week, February 9-15. J. E. Wright. il Library J 94:153-5 Ja 15 '69
Issues of the day: world in ferment. il Sr Schol 94:Schol Teach 10-11 My 2 '69
Paperback power. N. C. Polos. il Sr School 94:Schol Teach 32-5 Ja 31 '69
Read, baby, read: a first step to action. L. M. Ottaway. Chr Today 14:6-8 D 19 '69

Civil rights

A. Philip Randolph: labor's grand old man. P. Garland. il Ebony 24:31-4+ My '69
American history (white man's version) needs an infusion of soul; excerpt from address. C. V. Woodward. il N Y Times Mag p32-3+ Ap 20 '69
Civil rights push; with biographical sketches. il Sr Schol 93:12-14 Ja 10; 94:8-10 F 7 '69
Court's ruling on a suburban swimming pool. il U S News 67:19 D 29 '69
Doctor King, one year after: he lives, man! G. Goodman. Look 33:29-31 Ap 15 '69
Everybody in the pool; discrimination in community-owned recreational center, Virginia's Fairfax County. Time 94:23 D 26 '69
Firm against evasion: three Supreme court decisions involving racial injustice. il Time 93:66 Je 13 '69
From civil rights to black liberation: the unsettled 1960's. R. L. Zangrando. Cur Hist 57:281-6+ N '69

Gains in Negro rights; a fifteen year record. il U S News 66:51-4 My 19 '69
In my opinion: it isn't enough just to wear an Afro. G. Andrews. Seventeen 28:248 My '69
Martin Luther King: we shall overcome. il UNESCO Courier 22:20-1 O '69
Myths of the black revolt. B. Rustin. il Ebony 24:96-8+ Ag '69
Nixon, the Negro and the budget. il Time 93:19-20 Ap 18 '69
Of time, space and revolution; black rebellion at the crossroads. L. Bennett, jr. il Ebony 24:31-4+ Ag '69
Rebellion or revolution, by H. Cruse. Review Nat R 21:132-3 F 11 '69. M. Geltman
Spelling it out in black and white; administration's policy attacked by the Commission on civil rights and Justice department lawyers. il Newsweek 74:31-2 S 22 '69
Supreme court justice's warning to fellow Negroes; excerpts from address, May 4, 1969. T. Marshall. U S News 66:92-3 My 19 '69
To be truly free. L. M. Steel. Sat R 52:23-5+ Ja 25 '69
To the last drop; education, public accommodation and voting; Supreme court decisions. Newsweek 73:29 Je 16 '69
Tour's end: traveling journalists' conclusions. W. F. Buckley, jr. Nat R 21:611 Je 17 '69
Uncle Tom and Tiny Tim: some reflections on the cripple as Negro. L. Kriegel. Am Scholar 38:412-30 Sum '69
U.S. journal: Monroe, N.C; site of 1961 civil-rights movement led by R. F. Williams. C. Trillin. New Yorker 45:144+ O 11 '69
What Negro leaders want now; nationwide survey of Negro leaders and spokesmen. il U S News 66:44-6+ F 24 '69
When women fight for freedom. S. Pitzer. il Parents Mag 44:62-3+ Ap '69
Who speaks for Negroes now? A shift in leadership. il U S News 66:38-9 Je 23 '69
Writing off the blacks. Commonweal 91:62 O 17 '69
    See also
Race relations

History

Black boycotts before Montgomery. A. Meier and E. Rudwick. il Ebony 24:154-6+ O '69
Civil rights and the American Negro, ed. by A. P. Blaustein and R. L. Zangrando. Review
  Sat R 52:32-3 Ja 25 '69. A. Vorspan
Negro in America: 1901 to 1956. E. A. Toppin. bibliog f Cur Hist 57:269-74+ N '69
1950's: racial equality and the law. N. C. Amaker. bibliog f Cur Hist 57:275-80+ N '69

Clothing and dress
See Clothing and dress—Negroes

Colonization
See also
Back-to-Africa movements

Crime

Are courts more severe with black defendants? il Time 94:51 Jl 11 '69
Double jeopardy: black and poor; address, January 12, 1969. F. H. Williams. Vital Speeches 35:273-7 F 15 '69

Culture

Any day now: black art and black liberation. L. Neal. il Ebony 24:54-8+ Ag '69
Assimilation or cultural pluralism? concerning discussion at Duke university divinity school. C. L. Rice. Chr Cent 86:945-7 Jl 16 '69
Children who get cheated. T. Cade. il Redbook 134:64-5+ Ja '70
E. U. Easien-Udom: appearance on Black heritage; interview. E. U. Essien-Udom. New Yorker 45:27-8 Mr 8 '69
Exploring the racial gap. il Time 93:75-6 My 9 '69
Heart of soul. A. Dove. Read Digest 94:237-8+ Ap '69
Integrating culture; a credo for believers. B. Tate. bibliog il Library J 94:2053-6 My 15 '69
Last words from a murdered African leader: the American Negro cannot look to Africa for an escape. T. Mboya. il N Y Times Mag p30+ Jl 13 '69
Rebirth of the blues: soul. S. Booth. il Sat Eve Post 242:26-31+ F 8 '69
Soul. H. S. Hughes. America 121:62-3 Ag 2 '69
Soul. il Newsweek 73:22 Je 30 '69
Teaching black history. il Negro Hist Bul 32:4-6 Mr '69

NEGROES—*Continued*

Economic conditions

Black capitalism at work; what's happening in Philadelphia; interview. L. Sullivan. il U S News 66:60-4+ F 17 '69

Black revolution and the economic future of Negroes in the United States; excerpts from address, June 8, 1969. A. F. Brimmer. il Am Scholar 38:629-43 Aut '69

Dealing with the urban crisis; excerpts from Agenda for the Nation. K. B. Clark. Cur 103:21-3 Ja '69

Economics of liberation. A. Poinsett. il Ebony 24:150-4 Ag '69

Pattern for blacks. America 120:85 Ja 25 '69

Role of compensatory justice; black reparations, two views. M. Harrington; A. S. Kaufman. Cur 110:50-4 S '69

Social stability and black capitalism. M. Rein. Trans-Action 6:4+ Je '69

What Negro leaders want now; nationwide survey of Negro leaders and spokesmen. il U S News 66:44-6+ F 24 '69

See also
Black capitalism
Negroes—Migration

Education

Art for black students; a change in objectives. C. Lawrence. il Sch Arts 68:18-21 F '69

Battle to control black schools. A. Poinsett. il Ebony 24:44-6+ My '69

Black leaders speak out on black education; symposium. il Todays Ed 58:25-32 O '69

Black studies: an intellectual crisis; address. J. W. Blassingame. Am Scholar 38:548-61 Aut '69

Children who get cheated. T. Cade. il Redbook 134:64-5+ Ja '70

Educational attainment of workers; with tables. E. Waldman. bibliog f il Mo Labor R 92:14-22 F '69

Integrating culture; a credo for believers. B. Tate. bibliog il Library J 94:2053-6 My 15 '69

Long road to racial equality. M. Ways. Fortune 80:106 N '69

Media for the black curriculum. C. Robinson. bibliog il ALA Bul 63:242-6 F '69

NCTE focus: relevancy and racism. Sr Schol 93:Schol Teach 3 Ja 10 '69

NEA conference: a thoughtful note. W. D. Boutwell. Sr Schol 94:Schol Teach 5 F 28 '69

Negro moderates vs. militants; views of R. Wilkins and others. U S News 66:9 Ja 27 '69

Price of community control. D. K. Cohen. Commentary 48:23-32 Jl '69; Discussion. 48:4+ S; 12+ N '69

Reappraisal of the most controversial educational document of our time: Coleman report C. Jencks. il N Y Times Mag p 12-13+ Ag 10 '69; Discussion. p74+ S 14; 12+ O 12 '69

Researchers speak; AERA annual meeting. W. D. Boutwell. Sr Schol 94:Schol Teach 12+ Mr 14 '69

Road to the top is through higher education, not black studies; reprint. W. A. Lewis. il N Y Times Mag p34-5+ My 11 '69

Seven Dobbs against the odds. E. Dunbar. il Look 33:27-33 D 2 '69

They made a better school; community school in Providence. R. H. Levine. il Am Ed 5:8-10 N '69

Ultimate in opportunity; comments by J. B. Parsons. J. Cass. Sat R 52:39 Ag 16 '69

Uneasy peace at Valley state. D. Nevin. il Life 66:59-68+ Mr 14 '69

What seventy SEEK kids taught their counselor. L. W. Scheffler. il N Y Times Mag p54-5+ N 16 '69; Reply with rejoinder. M. Schuker. p 14 Ja 11 '70

See also
Catholic schools—Desegregation
Colleges and universities—Desegregation
Education—Mississippi
Negro colleges and universities
Private schools—Desegregation
Private schools, Negro
Public schools—Desegregation
Socially handicapped children—Education

History

John Eaton, educator (1829-1906) G. Smith. bibliog f Sch & Soc 97:108-12 F '69

Employment

ABPC seminar: minority manpower in publishing. Pub W 195:34-6 F 3 '69

Barriers to hiring the blacks. J. R. Goeke and C. S. Weymar. il Harvard Bsns R 47:144-6+ S '69

Black rage on the auto lines. il Time 93:89 Ap 11 '69

Confrontation in Pittsburgh; drive to crack building trades unions. C. C. Robb. il Nation 209:272-4 S 22 '69

Fomented conflict; black community and organized labor. L. L. Brown. Nation 208: 179-81 F 10 '69

James Haughton wants 500,000 more jobs. M. K. Sanders. il N Y Times Mag p30-1+ S 14 '69

Job makes the man; Detroit's inner city hiring program. il Nations Bsns 57:34-6+ Je '69

Jobs in building for Negroes: agencies split on rules. il U S News 67:91-2 N 24 '69

Negro job situation: has it improved? C. C. Hodge. bibliog f il Mo Labor R 92:20-8 Ja '69

Negro rights: Mr Nixon vs. labor; Congress repeals rider to Philadelphia plan. il Newsweek 75:49-50 Ja 5 '70

Opportunities: Job opportunities center, New York 1969; interview. R. Clarke. New Yorker 45:15-16 Jl 19 '69

Phillips curve; unemployment. il Newsweek 73:78 Ap 14 '69

Showdown on Negro jobs in the building trades. il U S News 67:95-7 S 29 '69

U.S. looks into building-job fight. U S News 67:100-1 S 22 '69

White institutions & black rage. D. Boesel and others. il Trans-Action 6:24-31 Mr '69

See also
Bedford-Stuyvesant restoration corporation, Brooklyn
Discrimination in employment
Negroes—Occupations
Opportunities industrialization centers, incorporated
Unemployment—Relief measures
United States—Equal employment opportunity commission

History

American history (white man's version) needs an infusion of soul; excerpt from address. C. V. Woodward. il N Y Times Mag p32-3+ Ap 20 '69

Birth of black America. L. Bennett, jr. il Ebony 24:31-4+ Je; 25:31-4+ N '69

Black America: a historical survey; symposium. bibliog f Cur Hist 57:257-307 N '69

Black dialect and history; NCTE warns of overreacting. Library J 94:1708 Ap 15 '69

Black history: a reappraisal, ed. by M. Drimmer. Review
Cath World 209:89-90 My '69. W. Schechner

Black history, or black mythology? P. Chew. il Am Heritage 20:4-9+ Ag '69

Black history: the early childhood vacuum. E. Johnson. bibliog il Library J 94:2057-8 My 15 '69

Center for black history. W. Raspberry. Negro Hist Bul 32:21 Mr '69

Congressional record, September 16, 1968; excerpts. Negro Hist Bul 32:17-22 Ja '69

Fantasy of black nationalism. T. Draper. bibliog f Commentary 48:27-54 S '69; Discussion. 48:14+ D '69

History and the black American (cont) il Sr Schol 93:12-13 Ja 10; 94:8-9 F 7; 7-11+ F 14 '69

Let's set black history straight; interview. W. L. Katz. bibliog Read Digest 95:59-63 Jl '69

Making the common into the uncommon; campaigns for black history. Negro Hist Bul 32:4-5 Ja '69

Racial segregation in ante bellum New Orleans. R. A. Fischer. bibliog f Am Hist 74:926-37 F '69

Teaching black history via films. il Sch & Soc 97:416-17 N '69

Teaching Negro history: one white experience. D. Walden. il Sch & Soc 97:232-3 Ap '69

They came in chains: Americans from Africa, by S. Redding. Review
Sat R 52:78-9 Mr 22 '69. E. Foner

Traveler's guide to two cities: Boston and New Orleans. J. O. Killens. bibliog il Redbook 133:55-62 Jl '69

Uses of history; how racist are we? C. V. Woodward. Cur 107:52-64 My '69

See also
Association for the study of Negro life and history
Slavery—United States

Historiography

American Negro, by U. Lee and others. Review
Sat R 52:35-6+ Ag 23 '69. A. Nevins

NEGROES—History—*Continued*

Sources

Availability of Negro source material in Philadelphia. Negro Hist Bul 32:17 Mr '69

Study and teaching

Advances of Negro history in community, school, and college. il Negro Hist Bul 31: 12-13+ D '68

Black revolution and black history. Negro Hist Bul 32:4-6 My '69

Integrating American history. N. F. Hurt. il Todays Ed 58:18-20 Ja '69

Negro in America. C. H. Harrison. Ed Digest 34:13-15 Ja '69

Negro role in U.S. history. Sch & Soc 97: 76+ F '69

Teaching black history. il Negro Hist Bul 32:4-6 Mr '69

To answer a letter; conference on teaching of Afro-American history. L. Christmas. il Sr Schol 94:Schol Teach 28 Ja 17 '69

See also
Afro-American studies

Housing

Breach of contract; Contract buyers league revolt. Newsweek 75:56 Ja 19 '70

Deghettoization; choice of the new militancy. C. Funnyé. Arch Forum 130:74-7 Ap '69

See also
Discrimination in housing

Intelligence

See Intelligence levels—Negroes

Language

See also
Negro-English dialects

Libraries

See Libraries and Negroes

Migration

Alaska: bonanza for blacks? il Ebony 25:123-6+ N '69

From inner city to suburbia: Negroes join in exodus. il U S News 67:17-19 D 29 '69

In the aftermath of city rioting; report by the Urban coalition and urban America inc. U S News 66:12 Mr 10 '69

See the city: color it black. R. Farley and K. E. Taeuber. il Trans-Action 6:8+ Ja '69

Occupations

Speaking of people. See issues of Ebony

Split-level challenge. W. M. Young, jr. il Sat R 52:16-18 Ag 23 '69

See also
Negro businessmen
Negro farmers
Negro librarians

Politics and suffrage

Alabama: first steps. D. F. Ross. New Repub 161:14-15 S 27 '69

Angelo Herndon story. H. N. Meyer. Chr Cent 86:221-2+ F 12 '69

Black day in Eutaw; Negro election triumph in Greene County, Ala. il Newsweek 74:24-5 Ag 11 '69

Black power at southern polls. il U S News 68:6 Ja 5 '70

Black power in politics. U S News 67:12 Ag 11 '69

Black role in urban politics. R. G. Hatcher. Cur Hist 57:287-9+ N '69

Bright future for politicians. il Ebony 24: 88-9 Jl '69

Debt to Dixie; proposal to withdraw Voting rights act of 1965. il Newsweek 74:23-4 Jl 14 '69

For voters: end to literacy tests everywhere in U.S? il U S News 67:32+ Jl 7 '69

Future of black leadership; Time essay. il Time 93:29-30 Ap 4 '69

Keeping a promise; Nixon administration's bill on voting-law reform. il Time 94:15 Jl 4 '69

Long way to go in Mississippi. B. W. Eggler. New Repub 160·19-21 Je 28 '69

Mississippi revisited; five years after the summer project; with photographs by H. A. Franklin, 2d. D. Llorens. Ebony 24:46-9+ Jl '69

Negro power; a built-in problem for Mr Nixon. il U S News 66:55-7 F 3 '69

Negro vote gains in South; by inches, not miles. U S News 66:16 My 26 '69

Negro voting power; how strong? il U S News 67:36-8+ S 29 '69

New approach to voting rights. U S News 67:10 D 22 '69

New test tube for black cities? il U S News 66:10 Je 16 '69

One of those weeks; proposal to withdraw 1965 voting rights act. Newsweek 74:16-17 Jl 7 '69

Politics and the black revolution. J. Conyers, jr. il Ebony 24:162-6 Ag '69

Right to vote; section V of the Voting rights act of '65. New Repub 162:8-9 Ja 3 '70

TRB from Washington:
Black feud; Nixon administration's alienation from the Negroes. New Repub 162:2 Ja 3 '70

Toxins are in. J. Deedy. Commonweal 91:394 Ja 9 '70

Voting rights, or wrongs? proposed changes in 1965 voting rights act. il Newsweek 74: 19-20 D 22 '69

Why a top Negro agreed to join the Nixon team. il U S News 66:16 F 24 '69

See also
Black power
Voters, Registration of

Psychology

Black children choose white dolls. il Sci Digest 66:28-9 Jl '69

Black power and achievement motivation. S. L. Woodard. Clear House 44:72-5 O '69

New black challenge. C. E. Lincoln. il Redbook 133:78-9+ Je '69

Psychiatrist looks at black power. A. F. Poussaint. il Ebony 24:142-4+ Mr '69

Roots of black manhood. U. Hannerz. bibliog il Trans-Action 6:12-21 O '69

Searching for a new image. il Negro Hist Bul 32:4-5 F '69

Recreation

Recreation education; for white or black America. J. F. Murphy. bibliog f il Parks & Rec 4:28-9+ Ag '69

Religion

Atlanta document: an interpretation. P. N. Williams. Chr Cent 86:1311-12 O 15 '69

Black theology. J. C. Haughey. America 120: 583 My 17 '69

Black theology; a statement of the National committee of Black churchmen. il Chr Cent 86:1310 O 15 '69; Discussion. 86:1523-4 N 26 '69

Black theology and black church. R. Reuther. America 120:684-7 Je 14 '69

Black voices in the church; symposium. il Chr Cent 86:209-22 F 12 '69

In search of a black Christianity. Time 94: 57-8 Jl 4 '69

See also
African Methodist Episcopal church
Mormons and Mormonism. Negro
National committee of Black churchmen
Negro churches

Reparations

Black militants: what Episcopalians voted. U S News 67:16 S 15 '69

Brother, can you spare $2 million? Chr Today 14:48 O 24 '69

Group therapy; Episcopal church to fund BEDC. il Newsweek 74:105-6 S 15 '69

N.A.A.C.P. executive urges churches to reject demands for reparations. Chr Cent 86:1413 N 5 '69

NCC pledges half million while budget shrinks. A. H. Matthews. Chr Today 14: 44-6 O 10 '69

Passing the buck. Newsweek 74:107 O 20 '69

Putting it to the churches. S. C. Rose. New Repub 160:19-21 Je 21 '69

Reparations for blacks? the question of effective equality through preferential treatment. M. Green. Commonweal 90:359-62 Je 13 '69

Reparations in black and white. Chr Today 13: 37 S 26 '69

Role of compensatory justice; black reparations, two views. M. Harrington; A. S. Kaufman. Cur 110:50-4 S '69

See also
Negro militants and churches

Segregation

Challenge to the court, by I. A. Newby. Review
Nat R 21:915-17 S 9 '69. A. W. Green

Gains in Negro rights; a fifteen year record. il U S News 66:51-4 My 19 '69

Halt integration; the view of a Negro official; excerpts from remarks. B. Holman. U S News 67:16 D 1 '69

Integration, or gilded ghettos? Bsns W p54 Ag 30 '69

Letters to a black boy; excerpts. B. Teague. il Redbook 132:55-62 Ja '69

NEGROES—Segregation—*Continued*
Mr Wilkins on the extremists; reinstitution of Jim Crow at urging of black people. Nat R 21:62 Ja 28 '69
Negro in America: 1901 to 1956. E. A. Toppin. bibliog f Cur Hist 57:269-74+ N '69
Racial segregation in ante bellum New Orleans. R. A. Fischer. bibliog f Am Hist R 74:926-37 F '69
Road to the top is through higher education, not black studies; reprint. W. A. Lewis. il N Y Times Mag p34-5+ My 11 '69
Surprising talk between a black leader and a top segregationist; ed. by B. Cohn and S. Ball, jr. J Bond and R. V. Harris. il N Y Times Mag p34-5+ Ap 27 '69
    See also
Church and race problems
Public schools—Desegregation
Segregation in education

Segregation, Resistance to

Black boycotts before Montgomery. A. Meier and E. Rudwick. il Ebony 24:154-6+ O '69
Long road to where? Southern university students participating in sit-ins in Baton Rouge, La. J. H. Harris. il Negro Hist Bul 31:16-17 D '68
Of time, space and revolution; black rebellion at the crossroads. L. Bennett, jr. il Ebony 24:31-4+ Ag '69
Restiveness on the right. W. F. Buckley, jr. Nat R 21:298 Mr 25 '69
Revolt of the urban ghettos, 1964-1967. J. Boskin. bibliog f Ann Am Acad 382:1-14 Mr '69
Rosa Parks: she wouldn't move back. il Sr Schol 94:6 My 9 '69

Social conditions

Beyond racism, by W. M. Young, jr. Review Newsweek 73:92+ Je 2 '69. A. Cooper
Beyond the burning: the life and death of the ghetto, by S. Tucker. Review America 120:172 F 8 '69. A. Buni
Crisis, challenge, change; excerpt from address. W. M. Young, jr. il Parks & Rec 4:42-3+ Ap '69
Guest in ghetto America. O. Elliott. il Newsweek 73:41-3 Je 9 '69
If you're black and sick. il Newsweek 74:83 Jl 7 '69
Letters to a black boy; excerpts. B. Teague. il Redbook 132:55-62 Ja '69
Middle-class blacks are moving off the middle. E. Holsendolph. il Fortune 80:90-5+ D '69
Negro in America: where Myrdal went wrong. C. N. Degler. il N Y Times Mag p64-5+ D 7 '69
Problems of impacted ghettos. N. Macrae. Cur 109:25-32 Ag '69
Roots of black manhood. U. Hannerz. bibliog il Trans-Action 6:12-21 O '69
Social stability and black capitalism. M. Rein. Trans-Action 6:4+ Je '69
Street corner voices. A. Meier. Trans-Action 6:58-60 F '69
To be truly free. L. M. Steel. Sat R 52:23-5+ Ja 25 '69
Travels with Mr Charlie; journalists look at the black American ghetto. C. M. Curtis. Atlan 224:31-8 Ag '69
Two shades of black; The Negro family; views of Andrew Billingsley and Herbert Hendin. Newsweek 74:119-20+ N 17 '69
Urban league conducts a guided tour. P. Bailey. il Ebony 24:48-50+ S '69
Where are they now? conditions of three, surveyed in 1966. il Newsweek 73:12 Je 30 '69
Window on the hard-core world; excerpts from address. T. V. Purcell and R. Webster. Harvard Bsns R 47:118-29 Jl '69
Yesterdays in Grand Rapids. J. Thompson. Harper 238:43-51 My '69
    See also
Alabama—Social conditions
Negroes—Segregation
United States—National advisory commission on civil disorders

Social life and customs

Black Wasps. Trans-Action 6:8-9 My '69
Harlem on my mind; the black renaissance. A. Nelson. il Harp Baz 102:214-18 F '69

Social status

Psychiatrist looks at black power. A. F. Poussaint. il Ebony 24:142-4+ Mr '69

Societies, etc.

Black guns on campus; Black Panthers and US. R. Rogers. il Nation 208:558-60 My 5 '69
    See also
Association for the study of Negro life and history
Black cultural development society
National association for the advancement of colored people
Society of African and Afro-American students

Statistics

Demographic profile, and where it points. R. M. Scammon. il Newsweek 73:18 Je 30 '69
See the city: color it black. R. Farley and K. E. Taeuber. il Trans-Action 6:8+ Ja '69

Suffrage

See Negroes—Politics and suffrage

Trade union membership

See Trade unions—Negro membership

Alaska

Alaska: bonanza for blacks? il Ebony 25:123-6+ N '69

Georgia

Seed money in Georgia; high-risk improvement loans from Citizens & Southern national bank. il Time 93:106 My 23 '69

Mississippi

Faces of hunger; photographs by M. Mauney; with report by F. G. Loyd. il Todays Health 47:20-3 O '69
In the wake of Camille; discriminatory use of federal funds for hurricane victims. New Repub 162:8-10 Ja 10 '70
Long way to go in Mississippi. B. W. Eggler. New Repub 160:19-21 Je 28 '69
Mississippi homecoming. M. Evers. il Ladies Home J 86:77+ O '69
Mississippi revisited; five years after the summer project; with photographs by H. A. Franklin, 2d. D. Llorens. Ebony 24:46-9+ Jl '69

Northern states

    See also
Cleveland—Negroes
New York (city)—Harlem

Southern states

Black boycotts before Montgomery. A. Meier and E. Rudwick. il Ebony 24:154-6+ O '69
The mill: a giant step for the southern Negro. R. Cleghorn. il N Y Times Mag p34-5+ N 9 '69
Nixon's guaranteed annual poverty. L. Hunt and others. Ramp Mag 8:64-70 D '69
Overdue; southern black studies drain. E. J. Fontenette. Wilson Lib Bul 44:96 S '69
South: changes deep and subtle. J. B. Cumming, jr. il Newsweek 73:34-5 Je 30 '69
    See also
Charleston. S.C.—Negroes
Negroes—Politics and suffrage
Scottsboro case
Tennessee—Race problems

Western states

Black man in the American West. D. T. Schoenberger. bibliog il Negro Hist Bul 32:7-11 Mr '69
NEGROES, Catholic. See Catholic church—Negroes
NEGROES, Discrimination against. See Race discrimination
NEGROES and Jews. See Jews and Negroes
NEGROES and libraries. See Libraries and Negroes
NEGROES and television. See Television broadcasting and Negroes
NEGROES as farmers. See Negro farmers
NEGROES in Africa
Mboya's rebuttal. T. Mboya. il Ebony 24:90-1+ Ag '69
Progress: Africa's untold story. E. B. Thompson. il Ebony 24:74-6+ Je '69
    See also
South Africa—Race problems
NEGROES in art
Black lamps: white mirrors. il Time 94:60-71 O 3 '69
NEGROES in business. See Negro businessmen
NEGROES in Canada
Canada's black member of Parliament. il Ebony 24:132-4+ Ap '69
Racial problem in Canada? A. Ages. Chr Cent 86:627-30 Ap 30 '69; Reply. M. Despland. 86:755 My 28 '69

NEGROES in childrens literature
Black history: the early childhood vacuum. E. Johnson. bibliog il Library J 94:2057-8 My 15 '69
Guidelines for black books: an open letter to juvenile editors; adaptation of address, May 8, 1969. A. Baker. Pub W 196:131-3 Jl 14 '69
Julius Lester: Newbery runner-up. E. Geller. il Library J 94:2070-1 My 15 '69
That ecstasy which comes from knowing that one is a human being; books on Negro life reviewed during 1968 by The horn book magazine. P. Heins. Horn Bk 45:141 Ap '69
Xerox withdraws Mother Goose; with editorial comment. Library J 94:2031, 2034 My 15 '69

NEGROES in Cuba
Fidel's tokenism. L. Stearns. Nat R 21:596-7 Je 17 '69

NEGROES in literature
Book reviews. See issues of Negro history bulletin
Ebony book shelf. See issues of Ebony
Racial understanding through literature. N. L. Arnez. bibliog f Engl J 58:56-61 Ja '69
Thesis and theme in Uncle Tom's cabin. D. S. Brown. bibliog f Engl J 58:1330-4+ D '69
   See also
Negroes in childrens literature

NEGROES in moving pictures
Black, white and technicolor. P. T. Hartung. Commonweal 90:543-5 S 5 '69
NCOMP charges Hollywood lacks black sensitivity. Chr Cent 86:1157 S 10 '69
   See also
Negroes in South Africa

NEGROES in South Africa
South Africa—Race problems

NEGROES in television
Black man's image; NBC film teleplay, Deadlock. R. L. Shayon. Sat R 52:48 Mr 22 '69
Black TV; its problems and promises. il Ebony 24:88-90+ S '69
Gail Fisher, the girl from Mannix, CBS show. il Ebony 24:140-2+ O '69
Living, breathing picture gallery; C. Brown on Laugh-in. il Ebony 24:54-6+ Ap '69
TV discovers the black man. L. Robinson. il Ebony 24:27-30+ F '69

NEGROES in textbooks. See Textbooks
NEGROES in the Peace corps. See United States—Peace corps
NEGROES in the United States army. See United States—Army—Negroes
NEGROES in trade unions. See Trade unions—Negro membership

NEIDER, Charles
Max Eastman. Sat R 52:4+ My 17 '69

NEIER, Aryeh
Civil rights and symbolic language. Cur 104:29-34 My '69

NEIGHBORHOOD law office plan. See Legal aid
NEIGHBORHOOD youth corps. See United States—Youth corps

NEIGHBORHOODS
Neighborhood government, by M. Kotler. Review
   Ramp Mag 8:33-4 D '69. K. Hess
Proper land planning, will we learn how at last? il Bet Hom & Gard 47:56+ S '69

NEIGHBORS
And who is my neighbor? R. Haughton. Cath World 210:53-4 N '69
Known for years! excerpts from Brave enough for life. B. W. Overstreet. PTA Mag 63:22-4 F '69

NEILAN, Edwin P.
ILO at fifty: a mangement assessment. Mo Labor R 92:41-3 My '69

NEILL, Barbara
For young naturalists. See issues of Audubon

NEILL, Humphrey B.
Opposites attract a following. il por Bsns W p 128-9 O 11 '69

NEILL, R. F.
Hands across the ice. Commonweal 91:302-3 D 5 '69

NEIMAN-Marcus store. See Houston, Tex—Stores

NEISSER, Edith G. and Bauling, Fay
What every preschooler needs. Parents Mag 44:49-51+ Ap '69

NEIZVESTNY, Ernst
Art and revolution, by J. Berger. Review
   Atlan 223:99-101 My '69. Y. Blumenfeld
   Commonweal 90:441-3 Jl 11 '69. M. Harrington

NEJGEBAUER, Aleksandar
America the poetical, and otherwise. New Repub 160:19-22+ Ap 26 '69

NEKHAMKIN, Iosif
New look in Soviet schools. UNESCO Courier 23:24-6 Ja '70

NELMS, Ocie Lee
Partying is such sweet sorrow. il por Time 93:83-4 Je 13 '69

NELSON, A'Lelia
Harlem on my mind: the black renaissance. Harp Baz 102:214-18 F '69

NELSON, Bert
Industry and education. Ed Digest 34:46-7 Mr '69

NELSON, Bryan
Rarest booby; with biographical sketch. Natur Hist 78:4, 56-61 Ag '69

NELSON, DeWitt
Why CM-2 needs a boost. Am For 75:16-17+ Je '69

NELSON, Gaylord Anton
Trails across America. Nat Wildlife 7:21-7 Je '69

NELSON, J. Robert
Farewell in Basel. Commonweal 89:526-7 Ja 24 '69
World council and race: give the black man his own turf! Cath World 209:256-61 S '69

NELSON, J. W.
Micro aspects of Manhattan tornado in Kansas on 8 June 1966. Weatherwise 22:113-17 Je '69

NELSON, James
Viewpoint. Library J 94:2759 Ag '69

NELSON, Janet
Ski bum's guide to winter grooving. Mile 70:198+ N '69

NELSON, Kay Shaw
Golden croquette. House & Gard 135:99-101+ Ja '69

NELSON, Leland
Greenest thumb in Alaska. Org Gard & Farm 16:36-8 Mr '69

NELSON, Peter
California: late afternoon; poem. Poetry 114:97 My '69

NELSON, Phillip L.
Some thoughts on a hike through Canyonlands Park. il Nat Parks 43:28-31 Ap '69
—and Eckhardt, R. C.
Sequoia, looking toward the King. Nat Parks 43:10-14 D '69

NELSON, Stanley
Letter to my pastor; poem. Chr Cent 86:919 Jl 9 '69

NELSON, Thomas, and sons (publisher)
Bible publisher multiplies the word. Chr Today 13:44 Je 6 '69

NELSON, Walter Henry
Monks' brew. Holiday 45:58-9+ Je '69

NELSON Rockefeller collection. See Art—Private collections

NEMATOCYSTS
Physalia nematocysts: utilized by mollusks for defense. T. E. Thompson and I. Bennett. bibliog il Science 166:1532-3 D 19 '69

NEMATODES
Learn to live with nematodes. Suc Farm 67:74 F '69
Marigolds in the garden; preventing nematode damage to plants. P. M. Miller and J. F. Ahrens. il Horticulutre 47:30-1 S '69
Nematodes, what they are all about. L. Pyenson. Horticulture 47:46-8 F '69
Ribosomal RNA synthesis during cleavage of ascaris lumbricoides eggs. M. S. Kaulenas and others. bibliog il Science 163:1201-3 Mr 14 '69
   See also
Roundworms

NEMEROV, Howard
Late butterflies; poem. New Yorker 45:38 O 4 '69

NEMIROFF, Robert
To be young, gifted and black. Criticism
   Commonweal 90:542-3 S 5 '69
   Nation 208:548 Ap 28 '69

NEMRUT DAG excavations. See Turkey—Antiquities

NEO-EDWARDIAN house decoration. See House decoration, Victorian

NEO-FASCISM. See Fascism

NEOCORTEX. See Cerebral cortex

NEOLOGISMS. See Words, New

NEOMYCIN
m-Hydroxyphenylacetic acid formation from L-dopa in man: suppression by neomycin. M. Sandler and others. bibliog il Science 166:1417-18 D 12 '69

NEON lamps. See Electric lamps, Neon

NEOPLASMS. See Tumors

NEOPRENE. See Rubber, Artificial

NEPAL
Foreign relations
Can a ministate find true happiness in a world dominated by protagonist powers? The Nepal case. L. E. Rose and R. Dial. bibliog f Ann Am Acad 386:89-101 N '69

NEPETALACTONE
Feline attractant, cis,trans-nepetalactone: metabolism in the domestic cat. G. R. Waller and others. bibliog il Science 164:1281-2 Je 13 '69

NEPOTISM
Case of the nettlesome nepot. R. W. Cambreleng. il Harvard Bsns R 47:14-16+ Mr '69
Going (half) public. il Forbes 103:26-7 Je 1 '69
Planned nepotism. il Forbes 103:26-7 Je 1 '69
Rules on relatives; who can be hired for a U.S. job? U S News 66:45 Ap 21 '69

NEPTUNE (planet)
Pluto's mass and the motion of Neptune. Sky & Tel 37:71+ F '69

NERO, emperor of Rome
Nero: history's most spectacular tyrant. E. O. Hauser. il por Read Digest 95:37-8+ D '69

NERO, Peter
Peter Nero as composer. M. N. Kanny. il por Am Rec G 35:782 My '69

NERO Wolfe (literary character) See Characters in literature

NERPEL, Charles E.
Now: air-cushion vehicle you can buy. Pop Sci 194:59-61 Ja '69

NERUDA, Pablo, pseud.
Poet who is too big for the Nobel prize. R. Christ. Commonweal 91:383-4 D 26 '69
Report from Chile: the left prepares for an election. J. Yglesias. il por N Y Times Mag p24-5+ Ja 11 '70

NERVA engine. See Rockets, Atomic powered

NERVE cells
Cyclic adenosine monophosphate: possible mediator for norepinephrine effects on cerebella purkinje cells. G. R. Siggins and others. bibliog il Science 165:1018-20 S 5 '69
Dendritic spikes and their inhibition in alligator Purkinje cells. R. Llinás and others; discussion. bibliog Science 163:96-7, 166: 637-9 Ja 3, O 31 '69
Development of specific neuronal connections. M. Jacobson. bibliog il Science 163:543-7 F 7 '69
Excitatory and inhibitory motoneurons in the central nervous system of the leech. A. E. Stuart. bibliog il Science 165:817-19 Ag 22 '69
Fast transport system of materials in mammalian nerve fibers. S. Ochs and others. bibliog il Science 163:686-7 F 14 '69
Generation of adrenergic and cholinergic potentials in sympathetic ganglion cells. B. Libet and H. Kobayashi. bibliog il Science 164:1530-2 Je 27 '69
Neuroglia electrically coupled to neurons. F. D. Walker and W. J. Hild. bibliog il Science 165:602-3 Ag 8 '69
Neuron function inferred from behavioral and electrophysiological estimates of refractory period. C. R. Gallistel and others. bibliog il Science 166:1028-30 N 21 '69
Operant conditioning of cortical unit activity. E. E. Fetz. bibliog il Science 163:955-8 F 28 '69
Perineurium: evidence for contractile elements. M. H. Ross and E. J. Reith. bibliog il Science 165:604-6 Ag 8 '69
Postsynaptic inhibition: intracellular effects of various ions in spinal motoneurons. H. D. Lux and P. Schubert. bibliog il Science 166:625-6 O 31 '69
Preferred centripetal conduction of dendritic spikes in alligator Purkinje cells. R. Llinás and others. bibliog il Science 163:184-7 Ja 10 '69
Protein synthesis in the hippocampal pyramidal cells of rats during a behavioral test. H. Hydén and P. W. Lange; reply with rejoinder. R. E. Bowman and G. Harding. bibliog Science 164:199-201 Ap 11 '69
Rabbit lateral geniculate nucleus: sharpener of directional information. W. R. Levick and others. bibliog il Science 165:712-14 Ag 15 '69
Synaptic activation of an electrogenic sodium pump. H. Pinsker and E. R. Kandel. bibliog il Science 163:931-5 F 28 '69
Taste nerve fibers: a random distribution of sensitivities to four tastes. M. Frank and C. Pfaffmann. bibliog il Science 164:1183-5 Je 5 '69
Unit activity: motivation-dependent responses from m'dbrain neurons. M. I. Phillips and J. Olds. il Science 165:1269-71 S 19 '69
Visual receptive fields of neurons in inferotemporal cortex of the monkey. C. G. Gross and others. bibliog il Science 166:1303-6 D 5 '69

NERVE conduction. See Electrophysiology

NERVE gases. See Gases, Asphyxiating and poisonous

NERVES
Nerve endings: rapid appearance of labeled protein shown by electron microscope radioautography. B. Droz and S. H. Barondes. bibliog il Science 165:1131-3 S 12 '69
See also
Electrophysiology
Nerve cells
Synapses
Injuries
Electron spin resonance signals in injured nerve. B. Commoner and others. bibliog il Science 165:703-4 Ag 15 '69

NERVOUS breakdown. See Neuroses

NERVOUS system
Attention as a concept in neurophysiology; report of meeting. C. R. Evans and T. B. Mulholland. Science 163:495-6 Ja 31 '69
Cardiac sympathetic nerve activity: changes induced by ouabain and propranolol. R. A. Gillis. bibliog il Science 166:508-10 O 24 '69
Controlling the inner man. il Time 94:67 Jl 18 '69
Electronics and psychology. J. Frye. Electr World 81:60-1 My '69
Gut learning; controlling visceral responses. Sci Am 220:49-50 Ap '69
Learning of visceral and glandular responses. N. E. Miller. bibliog il Science 163:434-45 Ja 31 '69
Mind over matter; animals learn to control their involuntary nervous responses . il Newsweek 73:91 F 10 '69
Neurophysiology of remembering. K. H. Pribram. il Sci Am 220:73-80+ bibliog(p 138) Ja '69; Reply with rejoinder. R. W. Rodieck. 270:6-7 Je '69
Next: you may control your own heartbeat. A. J. Snider. Sci Digest 65:57 My '69
See also
Biological control systems
Cerebral cortex
Electrophysiology
Minimal brain dysfunction
Neurosecretion
Psychology, Physiological
Spinal cord
Synapses
Amphibia
Receptor potentials from hair cells of the lateral line. G. G. Harris and others. bibliog il Science 167:76-9 Ja 2 '70

Annelids
Excitatory and inhibitory motoneurons in the central nervous system of the leech. A. E. Stuart. bibliog il Science 165:817-19 Ag 22 '69

Crustacea
Current-voltage relations during illumination: photoreceptor membrane of a barnacle. H. M. Brown and others. bibliog il Science 166:240-3 O 10 '69
Postsynaptic membrane response predicted from presynaptic input pattern in lobster cardiac ganglion. D. K. Hartline and I. M. Cooke. bibliog il Science 164:1080-2 My 30 '69
Temperature-dependence of resistance at an electrotonic synapse. B .W. Payton and others. bibliog il Science 165:594-7 Ag 8 '69

Diseases
Acute axonal dystrophy caused by fluorocitrate: the role of mitochondrial swelling. H. Koenig. bibliog il Science 164:310-12 Ap 18 '69
Axonal transport of proteins in experimental neuropathies. D. E. Pleasure and others. bibliog il Science 166:524-5 O 24 '69
Generalized gangliosidosis: impaired cleavage of galactose from a mucopolysaccharide and a glycoprotein. M. C. MacBrinn and others. bibliog il Science 163:946-7 F 28 '69
How to detect a faulty gene; Tay-Sachs disease. il Time 94:55 S 12 '69
Tay-Sachs disease: generalized absence of a beta-D-N-acetylhexosaminidase component. S. Okada and J. S. O'Brien. bibliog il Science 165:698-700 Ag 15 '69
See also
Lesch-Nyhan syndrome

Fishes
Acetycholine receptor: covalent attachment of depolarizing groups at the active site. I. Silman and A. Karlin. bibliog il Science 164:1420-1 Je 20 '69
DDT: sublethal effects on brook trout nervous system. J. M. Anderson and M. R. Peterson. bibliog il Science 164:440-1 Ap 25 '69
Homology of lactate dehydrogenase genes: E. gene function in the teleost nervous system. G. S. Whitt. bibliog il Science 166: 1156-8 N 28 '69

NERVOUS system—Fishes—*Continued*
Oculomotor neurons in fish: electrotonic coupling and multiple sites of impulse initiation. M. E. Kriebel and others. bibliog il Science 166:520-4 O 24 '69
Shark pit organs: enhancement of mechanosensitivity by potassium ions. Y. Katsuki and T. Hashimoto. bibliog il Science 166: 1287-9 D 5 '69
Shark pit organs: response to chemicals. Y. Katsuki and others. bibliog il Science 163: 405-7 Ja 24 '69
Teleostean urophysis: stimulation of contractions of bladder of the trout salmo gairdnerii. K. Lederis. bibliog il Science 163:1327-8 Mr 21 '69
Teleostean urophysis: stimulation of water movement across the bladder of the toad bufo marinus. F. Lacanilao. bibliog il Science 163:1326-7 Mr 21 '69

Insects
Axonal outgrowth and cell migration in vitro from nervous system of cockroach embryos. J. S. Chen and R. Levi-Montalcini. bibliog il Science 166:631-2 O 31 '69
Insect olfaction: deciphering system for chemical messages. D. Schneider. bibliog il Science 163:1031-7 Mr 7 '69

Invertebrates
Analysis of restricted neural networks. D. Kennedy and others. bibliog il Science 164:1488-96 Je 27 '69

Mollusks
Central neuron initiation of periodic gill movements. B. Peretz. bibliog il Science 166:1167-72 N 28 '69
Neuronal controls of a behavioral response mediated by the abdominal ganglion of aplysia. I. Kupfermann and E. R. Kandel. bibliog il Science 164:847-50 My 16 '69
Neuronal network triggering a fixed action pattern. A. O. D. Willows and G. Hoyle. bibliog il Science 166:1549-51 D 19 '69
Studying neural organization in aplysia with the scanning electron microscope. E. R. Lewis and others. bibliog il Science 165: 1140-3 S 12 '69
Synaptic current at the squid giant synapse. P. W. Gage and J. W. Moore. bibliog il Science 166:510-12 O 24 '69

Reptiles
Auditory and vibratory responses in the midbrains of snakes. P. H. Hartline and H. W. Campbell. bibliog il Science 163: 1221-3 Mr 14 '69

Surgery
Adrenal tyrosine hydroxylase: compensatory increase in activity after chemical sympathectomy. R. A. Mueller and others. bibliog il Science 163:468-9 Ja 31 '69
NERVOUS tension. See Stress (physiology)
NESBIT, Evelyn
Faces from the past. R. M. Ketchum. por Am Heritage 20:64-5 Je '69
NESBITT, John A.
Recreation in the UNICEF program. bibliog Parks & Rec 4:35-7 O '69
NESMEÎANOV, Aleksandr Nikolaevich, and Belikov, Vasilii
Three-star synthetic cuisine. UNESCO Courier 22:20-5 Mr '69
NESSEN, Ron
Journey to the moon: what health hazards? por Todays Health 47:16-21 Jl '69
NESTS
Golden eagle and the rearing of redtails; building of eyries. F. Hamerstrom. il Natur Hist 78:62-9 My '69
Inside a hornbill's walled-up nest. J. Root and A. Root. il Nat Geog 136:846-55 D '69
Nest of barn owls. J. Steeley, jr. il Cons 23: 20 Je '69
See also
Bird houses
NETBOY, Anthony
Atlantic salmon. Sea Front 15:66-77 Mr '69
Britain's national parks. Am For 75:28-30+ F '69
Round trip with the salmon. Natur Hist 78:44-51+ Je '69
Wilderness and the American. Am For 75:12-15+ Ap '69
NETER, E. See Whang, H. Y. jt. auth.
NETHERLANDS
See also
Architecture—Netherlands
Maastricht
Music festivals—Netherlands
Youth—Netherlands

Description and travel
Bicycling through Holland. K. Harris. il Mlle 69:195-8+ S '69
Look at Holland. E. F. Haylock. il Yachting 126:56-7+ D '69

Foreign relations
President Nixon meets with prime minister and foreign minister of the Netherlands; exchange of greetings, and remarks, May 27, 28, 1969. R. M. Nixon; P. J. S. de Jong. Dept State Bul 60:561-3 Je 30 '69

History
Bibliography
Articles and other books received; comp. by P. H. Laurent. See issues of American historical review

Industries
National chemical giants emerge in Europe. il Bsns W p76+ Jl 19 '69
See also
Philips of Eindhoven companies
Shipbuilding

Race problems
Pride and prejudice; attitudes towards the Amboinese. il Newsweek 74:62 N 17 '69

Religious institutions and affairs
Utrecht eucharist: Catholic/Protestant intercommunion. Chr Cent 86:468-9 Ap 9 '69
See also
Amsterdam, Netherlands—Religious institutions and affairs
Catholic church in the Netherlands
NETHERLANDS WEST INDIES
Netherlands Antilles: Holland in the Caribbean. J. Cerruti. il Nat Geog 137:114-46 Ja '70
See also
Bonaire (island)
NETO, Henrique Pereira
Cold blood in Brazil. T. E. Quigley. Commonweal 90:452-3 Jl 25 '69
NETSCHERT, Bruce C.
Antipollution technology: the electric car; excerpt from address. Bul Atom Sci 25:37 Ap '69
NETWORKS electronic corporation
LeMay disputes his boss's right to fire him. Bsns W p 136 F 22 '69
NEUBAUER, John
White House photographers. Pop Phot 65:108-11+ D '69
NEUBECK, Gerhard
Sex for credit. N. G. Faber. il pors Look 33: 39-40+ Ap 1 '69
NEUBERT, Robert W.
Infrared locates diseased trees. Electr World 82:34-5 Ag '69
Trees with temperatures. Am For 75:6-7+ Ap '69
NEUESTERN, Oscar
Neuestern's ultimate non-act; interview, ed. by K. Kundry. Art N 68:54-6+ S '69
NEUGEBAUER, G. and others
Mariner 1969: preliminary results of the infrared radiometer experiment. bibliog Science 166:98-9 O 3 '69
NEUGEBOREN, Jay
Finkel; story. Esquire 72:128 O '69
The pass; story. Mlle 69:164-5 O '69
NEUHAUS, Richard John
Liturgy the public hope. Commonweal 91:129-34 O 31 '69
Ministry to G.I.s in Sweden. Chr Cent 86: 378-80+ Mr 19 '69
NEUMANN, Bill
Dyno tunes in a kit. Hot Rod 22:84-6 Ja '69
Incalculable torque? il Hot Rod 22:152-3 O '69
NEUMANN, Conrad
Sea reek. il Sea Front 15:10-11 Ja '69
NEURINGER, Allen J.
Animals respond for food in the presence of free food. bibliog Science 166:399-401 O 17 '69
NEUROGLIA. See Nerve cells
NEURONS. See Nerve cells
NEUROPATHY. See Nervous system—Diseases
NEUROPHYSIOLOGY. See Nervous system
NEUROSCIENCES research program, Boston
Ask the men who know. G. Adelman. il Library J 94:1413-15 Ap 1 '69
NEUROSECRETION
Teleostean urophysis: stimulation of contractions of bladder of the trout salmo gairdnerii. K. Lederis. bibliog il Science 163:1327-8 Mr 21 '69
Teleostean urophysis: stimulation of water movement across the bladder of the toad bufo marinus. F. Lacanilao. bibliog il Science 163:1326-7 Mr 21 '69

NEUROSES

Anxiety: the cheap neurosis for everyone. R. Signor. il Sci Digest 65:65-70 Je '69

Biochemistry of anxiety. F. N. Pitts, jr. il Sci Am 220:69-75 F '69

Dividend from Viet Nam; new understanding of and approach to battle stress. il Time 94:60+ O 10 '69

Drugs fight anxiety neurosis. Sci Digest 65: 58-9 My '69

Glad news from Vietnam; combat fatigue. Nation 208:621 My 19 '69

How to be fit but neurotic. il Time 95:41 Ja 12 '70

Lost and found: me! a teenager's nervous breakdown. L. Kapsand. il Seventeen 28: 136-7+ N '69

Suddenly it happens to you; breakdown! N. C. Smith. McCalls 96:56+ My '69

See also
Depression, Mental
Mentally ill
Phobias
Psychoses

NEUROTICS. See Neuroses

NEUTRA, Marian, and Leblond, C. P.
Golgi apparatus: with biographical sketches. Sci Am 220:12, 100-7 bibliog(p 132) F '69

NEUTRINOS

Isaac Asimov explains; neutrino is a neutrino. I. Asimov. Sci Digest 66:87-8 O '69

Neutrino astrophysics discussed at Moscow. B. Kuchowicz. Sky & Tel 37:86 F '69

Neutrinos from the sun. J. N. Bahcall il Sci Am 221:28-37 bibliog(p 140) Jl '69

NEUTRON activation analysis. See Radioactivation analysis

NEUTRON diffraction. See Neutrons—Diffraction

NEUTRON stars. See Stars—Evolution

NEUTRONS

K-mesic atoms indicate a nuclear neutron skin. Phys Today 22:57 O '69

Neutronium. Sci Am 221:54 D '69

Ultracold neutrons may refine electric-dipole-moment value. M. S. Rothenberg. bibliog il Phys Today 22:56+ N '69

See also
Nucleons

Diffraction

Neutron diffraction of cell membranes (myelin) D. F. Parsons and C. K. Akers. bibliog il Science 165:1016-18 S 5 '69

See also
Crystallography—Neutron diffraction studies

NEVADA

See also
Fishing—Nevada
Gardening—Nevada
Wildlife sanctuaries—Nevada

Historic houses, etc.

Nevada's thirsty legacy; Rhyolite, Nev. F. Taylor. il Travel & Camera 32:32 D '69

NEVADA. University, Reno

Desert research institute

Trouble at Nevada research center. P. M. Boffey. Science 165:880 Ag 29 '69; Reply. P. C. Bettler and others. 166:1222 D 5 '69

NEVELSON, Mike

Mike Nevelson: the gender of wood. W. Castle. il por Craft Horiz 29:16-21 Mr '69

NEVES, Irene

(ed) See Collins, J. I've looked at life from both sides now

NEVI, Charles N.

Growth through English: another appraisal. Engl J 58:912-19 S '69

NEVILLE, Phoebe

Phoebe Neville dances with Philip Hipwell; Judson memorial church. J. Armstrong. Dance Mag 43:84 N '69

NEVILLE, Robert

Father Gibson's pop culture. Commonweal 91:122-3 O 31 '69

NEVILLE, Tam Lin

Wooden porch, summer in Japan; poem. Mlle 69:244 Ag '69

NEVIN, David

Collins has cool to cope with space and the Easter bunny. Life 67:26-9 Jl 4 '69

Home to Abilene. Life 66:24-35 Ap 11 '69

Uneasy peace at Valley state. Life 66:59-68+ Mr 14 '69

NEVINS, Allan

Trial of Warren Hastings. Horizon 11:110-15 Wint '69

NEVO, Eviatar

Mole rat spalax ehrenbergi: mating behavior and its evolutionary significance. Science bibliog 163:484-6 Ja 31 '69

NEW, Azalea Thorpe

Young Americans 1969. Craft Horiz 29:8-15+ Jl '69

NEW American ballet company. See Dance companies

NEW American review

Little mags and novelty. H. Kaye. New Repub 161:26+ Ag 2 '69

National journal. G. Wolff. Newsweek 74: 86 Ag 18 '69

NEW and gentle light; story. See Jones, M. L.

NEW BRUNSWICK, Canada

See also
St John River

Description and travel

Discovering New Brunswick. W. C. Brittain. il Travel 131:40-3+ Ap '69

NEW business enterprises. See Business enterprises, New

NEW church. See New Jerusalem church

NEW cities and towns

City: starting from scratch. il Time 93:25-6 Mr 7 '69

It's not just the cities. A. Mayer. Arch Rec 146:139-46 N '69 (to be cont)

MERBISC: unique recreation bargain; most extraordinary recreation bargain in southern California. R. C. Taylor. il Parks & Rec 4:35-8 Ap '69

New-city blues. il Newsweek 74:46+ Jl 14 '69

New New York for Jersey swamp. il U S News 66:96-7 Mr 24 '69

New towns: lessons Europe is teaching us. il Bsns W p 130-1 N 22 '69

New type of new town breaks ground for planners; Nuns' Island in St Lawrence River. il Bsns W p 132-4+ Jl 19 '69

Planning for the second America. J. Fischer. bibliog f Harper 239:21-4+ N '69

Strong boost for new towns; planned communities. Bsns W p50 My 31 '69

Two new French towns, by Marcel Breuer and Robert F. Gatje. il Arch Rec 146:101-12 Ag '69

Why new towns boom or fail flat. il Bsns W p 149 N 14 '69

See also
Columbia, Md.
Flaine, France
Jonathan, Minn.
Lake Havasu City, Ariz.
Lake Winnebago, Mo.
La Luz, N.Mex.
Montgomery Village, Md.
Panther Valley, N.J.
Port Grimaud, France
Reston, Va.
Tapiola, Finland

NEW dance group. See Dance schools

NEW deal. See United States—Economic policy

NEW Detroit committee. See Detroit—Negroes

NEW ENGLAND

See also
Architecture, Domestic—New England
Conservation of resources—New England
Hunting—New England
Libraries—New England
Skis and skiing—New England

Climate

Snowy winter of 1968-69 in New England. R. E. Lautzenheiser. il Weatherwise 22:68-71+ Ap '69

Description and travel

Bay and the Sound; excerpts. J. Parkinson, jr. il Motor B 123:57-63 Je '69

Down east heritage cruise. W. R. Juettner. bibliog il Motor B 123:74-9+ Je '69

Motor to the mountains to see fall's flaming foliage. M. Perry. il Home Gard 56:66-7 S '69

Social life and customs

Growing up in America. F. Howe. il Mlle 68:206+ Ap '69

NEW ENGLAND book show. See Book exhibits

NEW ENGLAND conservatory of music, Boston

Report: Boston, production of Debussy's Pelléas et Mélisande. M. Harris. il Opera N 33:32 Ap 5 '69

NEW ENGLAND cookery. See Cookery, American

NEW ENGLAND furniture. See Furniture, American

NEW ENGLAND hurricane. See Hurricanes

NEW ENGLAND transcendentalism. See Transcendentalism (New England)

NEW GUINEA

See also
United Nations—New Guinea
West Irian

NEW GUINEA—*Continued*

Description and travel
Journey into stone age New Guinea. M. S. Kirk. il Nat Geog 135:568-92 Ap '69

Native races
Journey into stone age New Guinea. M. S. Kirk. il Nat Geog 135:568-92 Ap '69
New Guinea festival of faces. M. S. Kirk. il Nat Geog 136:148-56 Jl '69

NEW HAMPSHIRE
See also
Airports—New Hampshire
Camping—New Hampshire
Forests and forestry—New Hampshire

NEW HAMPSHIRE. University, Durham
Dining halls at human scale. il Arch Rec 145:120-1 F '69

NEW HAVEN, Conn.

Architecture
Eastern press inc; renovation and expansion in an urban setting. il Arch Rec 145:162-3 F '69

Hospitals
See also
Yale university—Yale-New Haven medical center

Housing
New Haven: where federal dollars pay off. E. Selby. Read Digest 94:189-90+ Je '69

Politics and government
Lee of New Haven; interview, ed. by F. Powledge. R. C. Lee. il Harper 239:76-9 N '69

NEW HAVEN railroad. See New York, New Haven and Hartford railroad company

NEW HEBRIDES
New Hebrides. T. B. Lesure. il Travel 131:34-8 F '69

NEW JERSEY
See also
Education—New Jersey
Fishing—New Jersey
Great Swamp
New Jersey meadows
Pine Barrens
Politics, Corruption in —New Jersey
Port of New York authority
Public welfare—New Jersey

Historic houses, etc.
See also
Camden, N.J.—Historic houses, etc.

Parks and playgrounds
Exploring the world around us; Middletown township, N.J. school children at Sandy Hook State Park. F. Sabin. il Am Ed 5: 12-17 Je '69

Politics and government
1969 elections showed a movement to Republicanism; interview. W. T. Cahill. U S News 67:39 N 17 '69
See also
Politics, Corruption in—New Jersey

NEW JERSEY (battleship) See Warships— United States

NEW JERSEY meadows
New New York for Jersey swamp. il U S News 66:96-7 Mr 24 '69

NEW Jerusalem church
Swedenborg: scientific saint. J. A. Eastman. Chr Cent 86:156+ Ja 29 '69

NEW left (politics) See Right and left (political science)

NEW MADRID earthquake, 1811. See Earthquakes—United States

NEW mathematics. See Mathematics

NEW MEXICO
See also
Camping—New Mexico
Fishing—New Mexico
Hunting—New Mexico
Skis and skiing—New Mexico

Antiquities
See Indians of North America—Antiquities—New Mexico

Description and travel
Turquoise trail. M. Sonnenberg. il Harp Baz 102:60+ Ja '69

Land tenure
See Land tenure—United States

Missions
Spain in New Mexico, more than three centuries ago. il Sunset 143:22 O '69

NEW MEXICO state library, Santa Fe
Statewide outreach: desert booktrails to the Indians. W. H. Farrington. il Willson Lib Bul 43:864-71 My '69

NEW MEXICO. University, Albuquerque
Graduate student. B. D. Hansen, 3d. il Phys Today 22:30-1 Mr '69

NEW mobilization committee to end the war in Vietnam
Behind the coming march on Washington. il U S News 67:23-4 N 3 '69
Conflict in the movement. il Time 94:16 O 31 '69
Men behind the Mobe. il Newsweek 74:32 N 24 '69
New mobe. Newsweek 74:36+ N 3 '69
New mobe (1): who's who? What's what? W. Goodman. il N Y Times Mag p25-7+ N 30 '69
Nixon's the one. New Repub 161:7-8 N 1 '69
Reporter at large; the Moratorium and the New mobe. F. Du Plessix. New Yorker 45: 32-40+ Ja 3 '70

NEW music hall of Israel; revue. See Musical comedies, revues, etc.—Criticisms, plots, etc.

NEW ORLEANS

Architecture
Twenty-seven pieces make an office building. il Arch Forum 130:62-5 Ap '69

City planning
Will success spoil the Vieux Carre? il Arch Forum 130:78-83 Je '69

Crime
To catch a cop; charges of burglary filed against policemen. Time 94:23 O 10 '69

Description
Traveler's guide. J. O. Killens. bibliog il Redbook 133:55-62 Jl '69

Elections
Upset victory in New Orleans. America 121: 626 D 27 '69

Gardens
Restful charms of New Orleans gardens. E. McDonald. il House B 111:102-7 Mr '69

Music
Jazzman's last ramble; funeral of G. Lewis. J. Roddy. il Look 33:100-2 Mr 18 '69
See also
New Orleans opera house association

Negroes
History
Racial segregation in ante bellum New Orleans, R. A. Fischer. bibliog f Am Hist R 74:926-37 F '69

Newspapers
Covering big Jim. Newsweek 73:105 Mr 17 '69

Police
To catch a cop; charges of burglary filed against policemen. Time 94:23 O 10 '69

Politics and government
Beating the feds; J. Garrison's primary victory. New Repub 161:11 N 22 '69
Garrison under pressure; race for district attorney. Newsweek 74:42+ O 27 '69

Poor
Michael bit the archbishop; Witness social apostolate program. C. J. McNaspy. America 121:122 Ag 30 '69

Sanitary affairs
Flushing and sweeping; Vieux Carre, or French quarter. J. Cassreino. il Am City 84:80-1 Ap '69

Social conditions
See also
New Orleans—Poor

NEW ORLEANS Jazzfest. See Music festivals —Louisiana

NEW ORLEANS opera house association
Report: New Orleans: productions of Manon Lescaut and Norma. J. Belsom. Opera N 33:23 Je 14 '69
Report: productions of Don Pasquale and Bohème. J. Belsom. Opera N 34:31 Ja 10 '70
Report: Verdi's Attila. J. Belsom. Opera N 34:23 N 22 '69

NEW ORLEANS Saints (football club) See Football clubs

NEW products. See Products, New

NEW right (politics) See Right and left (political science)

NEW sources of food supply. See Food supply
　—New sources
NEW states. See States, New
NEW TERRITORIES
Journey through a borrowed land. F. Riley.
　il Sat R 53:91-2+ Ja 10 '70
NEW Tokaido line. See Railroads—Japan
NEW towns. See New cities and towns
NEW WINDSOR, N.Y.
Revolutionary war reminder; New Windsor
　cantonment, Vails Gate, N.Y. il Travel
　132:37-41 Jl '69
NEW words. See Words, New
NEW World. See America
NEW YEAR
When holiday pleasures turn to pressures. A.
　Wood. Seventeen 28:128 D '69
NEW Year's eve; story. See Gallant, M.
NEW YEARS resolutions

Anecdotes, facetiae, satire,
etc.
Resolved: for 1970. E. Sheppard. Harp Baz
　103:114-15 Ja '70
NEW YORK (city)
City to end all cities: Manhattan. M. Zwerin.
　Mlle 68:143+ F '69
Great white hang-up: crippling snowstorm. il
　Newsweek 73:28+ F 24 '69
New York city begins computerized traffic
　control. T. Karagheuzoff. il Am City 84:
　105-6 N '69
New York city: R.I.P. G. Lees. il Hi Fi 19:
　136+ N '69
Tenth street revisited; anti-establishment gal-
　leries in lower Manhattan. B. Rose. Vogue
　154:146 D '69
Theater: New York is a smash. D. Sullivan.
　il N Y Times Mag p 12-13 Je 22 '69
Why are we in New York? N. Mailer. il N Y
　Times Mag p30-1+ My 18 '69
　See also
Bronx
Staten Island
Welfare Island

Air pollution
Air pollution, N.Y. city; proposed reclassifica-
　tions to establish state and federal air qual-
　ity standards. Cons 24:41 O '69
Wave Hill; anti-air pollution project for high
　school students at Riverdale's Center for
　environmental studies. R. A. Madigan. New
　Yorker 45:47-8 N 8 '69

Airports
Cargo diverted by dock strike clogs N.Y.
　airfreight terminals. J. W. Carter. Aviation
　W 90:30 F 10 '69
Cost of restrictions: excerpts from address.
　S G. Tipton. Aviation W 90:11 F 10 '69
New York airport developments keyed to
　political scene. D. A. Brown. il Aviation
　W 91:118-20+ O 20 '69; Reply. W. A. Kuhrt.
　91:102 N 10 '69
New York jetport battle heats up. Bsns W
　p72 O 25 '69
N.Y. jetport still becalmed amid debate. J. W.
　Carter. Aviation W 90:28-9 My 19 '69
No way out, no way back; passengers
　stranded at John F. Kennedy airport due
　to snowstorm. il Time 93:47-8 F 21 '69
On top; general aviation facilities. R. L.
　Collins. Flying 85:12-14+ Jl '69
Pilots call Kennedy facilities inadequate.
　Aviation W 90:32 Ap 7 '69
Siege of Kennedy: thirty hours at the airport
　during snowstorm. E. J. Kahn, jr. il Travel
　& Camera 32:56-9+ My '69
Snow overwhelms airports at N.Y: 6,000
　stranded. Aviation W 90:31-2 F 17 '69
Tangled mess in aviation; with editorial
　comment. Bsns W p52-4+, 100 Ag 9 '69

Anecdotes, facetiae, satire, etc.
Urbanology. T. M. Gannon. America 122:8-10
　Ja 10 '70

Anti-poverty program
Rags to riches; investigations of poverty
　agency frauds. Newsweek 73:30+ Ja 27 '69

Architecture
Architectural interiors for banks with diver-
　gent problems: Banco do Brasil and Amer-
　ican bank and trust company. il Arch Rec
　146:113-20 Ag '69
Brownstoners. il Newsweek 74:56-9 S 1 '69
Building watcher. J. B. Myers. il Craft Horiz
　29:20-9 Jl '69
Design in the context of a changing city
　plan. il Arch Rec 145:182-5 Ap '69

Designing an office building for a particular
　client and his needs. il Arch Rec 145:186-91
　Ap '69
House that's very Mary; Victorian brown-
　stone in New York city. S. Nirenberg. il
　House B 111:74-7 Ag '69
In New York: a 20th-century fortress: tele-
　phone building. il Arch Rec 146:126-30 Jl
　'69
Manhattan's office building binge; with port-
　folio. E. Carruth. Fortune 80:114-25+ O
　'69
Rediscovery: a Tiffany room; Seventh regi-
　ment and armory. E. Robinson. il Art in
　Am 57:72-7 Jl '69
Space program: Manhattan brownstone. B.
　Plumb. il N Y Times Mag p54-5 Je 15 '69
Tiny place: with style and grace; city brown-
　stone. il House B 111:70-1 F '69
　See also
New York (city)—Buildings

Art
Art world (cont) H. Rosenberg. New Yorker
　44:86+ Ja 25; 45:107-8+ F 22; 110+ Mr
　21; 136+ Ap 19; 118+ My 17; 91-2+ Je 21;
　102+ S 27; 167-70+ N 8 '69
Art world: exhibition: New York painting
　and sculpture: 1940-1970. H. Rosenberg.
　New Yorker 45:171-2+ D 6 '69
Metropolitan: worst foot forward; exhibi-
　tion: New York painting and sculpture
　1940-1970. R. Berenson. il Nat R 21:1281-3
　D '69
Thirty years of the New York school; exhibi-
　tion, New York painting and sculpture:
　1940-1970 to open Metropolitan museum's
　centennial celebrations. H. Kramer. il N Y
　Times Mag p28-31+ O 12 '69
Variety of high traditions; exhibitions from
　Europe, Asia and Peru. R. Berenson. il Nat
　R 21:33-4 Ja 14 '69
　See also
New York (city)—Galleries and museums

Banks
Bankers in a cross fire; attempted takeover
　of Chemical bank by Leasco data process-
　ing equipment corp. il Fortune 79:43-4 Ap
　'69
Bankers team up to go abroad; Allied bank
　international. il Bsns W p88-9+ N 8 '69
Chase's tenth; artists from around the world
　invited. il Time 93:72 Ap 25 '69
End of a friendship: Chase Manhattan loses
　Tensor account. Newsweek 75:70 Ja 19 '70
Freight shippers enter the checkless society;
　Chase Manhattan bank's Computer oriented
　freight remittance system. Bsns W p33 My
　31 '69
Long road home; Charter New York corp.
　Forbes 103:69 Ap 15 '69
New light on takeover defense: Chemical
　bank's battle plan. il Bsns W p89-90+ N 22
　'69
Power shift at the Chase? il Bsns W p30-1
　Ja 10 '70
Reporter at large; four day celebration of
　Brown brothers Harriman & co. hundred-
　and-fiftieth anniversary. J. Brooks. New
　Yorker 45:97-8+ Ap 26 '69
Where the prime rate started its last climb:
　First national city bank. il Bsns W p38-40
　Ja 25 '69
Why Leasco failed to net Chemical. il Bsns
　W p 144-5+ Ap 26 '69

Battery park city (proposed)
Battery park city: a proposal for new hous-
　ing, new jobs, and new land. R. Jensen. il
　Arch Rec 145:145-50 Je '69
City within a city. il Newsweek 73:62 Ap 28
　'69
Design in the context of a changing city
　plan. il Arch Rec 145:182-5 Ap '69

Bellevue hospital
Happy days at Bellevue. W. A. Nolen. il Es-
　quire 72:170-1+ N '69

Birds
　See Birds—New York (state)

Bookstores
　See Booksellers and bookselling—New
York (state)

Bridges
　See also
Hudson River bridges

Buildings
I am in love with line. R. Welling. il Am
　Artist 33:56-8+ O '69
People who live in glass houses: United Na-
　tions Plaza. il Time 93:75 Ap 25 '69

NEW YORK (city)—*Continued*

Buses
See New York (city)—Rapid transit

Chinatown
Little wonder restaurants of New York's Chinatown. W. Clifford. il Holiday 45:72-3+ Ap '69

Churches
Ecumenical street theater on upper Broadway: Broadway United church of Christ to share facilities of St Paul the Apostle Roman Catholic church. Chr Cent 86:368 Mr 19 '69

Harlem's banker-priest; M. M. Weston of St Philip's Episcopal church. il Ebony 24:92-4+ Mr '69

House of Lords; east Harlem's First Spanish Methodist church taken over by the Young Lords. il Time 95:33 Ja 12 '70

How to stump theologians; Broadway United church of Christ to share facilities of Roman Catholic church of St Paul the Apostle. J. Evenson. il Chr Today 13:42-3 Mr 28 '69

On the way to Emmaus. D. Kirk. Commonweal 91:375-8 D 26 '69

Reporter at large; Emmaus house, radical Catholic community in East Harlem. F. Du Plessix. New Yorker 44:37-8+ Ja 25 '69

Riverside pastor responds to McIntire manifesto. Chr Cent 86:1241 O 1 '69

Sing a song of God; A. Carmines, of the Judson memorial church. il Newsweek 73:50 Ap 7 '69

City planning
Magnetic flow-charts speed urban-renewal work. il Am City 84:72 F '69

Master rebuilder; plan for Welfare Island. Newsweek 74:76 N 17 '69

New town for New York city. J. S. Margolies. il Arch Forum 131:40-5 O '69

New York: are cities a bust? E. J. Logue. Look 33:70+ Ap 1 '69

New York plan: the battle begins. il Bsns W p 134+ N 22 '69

New York's master plan. il Newsweek 74:71 N 24 '69

Notes on the margin of a master plan. Arch Forum 131:80 D '69

Planners try again to save New York. Bsns W p42 N 15 '69

So what's new? city planning commission study. Newsweek 73:39 F 17 '69

Tip from M. T. Cicero. W. McQuade. Arch Forum 130:96 Je '69

Urban housing: a comprehensive approach to quality. il Arch Rec 145:97-118 Ja '69

See also
New York (city)—Battery park city (proposed)

History
[Father of Greater New York] F. Low. Natur Hist 78:26 Ap '69

Colleges and universitites
See New York (city)—Education

Community centers
Where the poor help the poor to help themselves; New York city's south Bronx. J. Coudert. Read Digest 94:25-6+ Mr '69

Community service society
See Community service society of New York

Consumer affairs, Department of
Where will Bess Myerson Grant strike next? J. Klemesrud. il N Y Times Mag p37+ O 12 '69

Crime
House on Fourth street; bomb terrorists and explosions. il Newsweek 74:37-8 N 24 '69

Scare city; planting of bombs. Nat R 21:1206 D 2 '69

Shortage of Samaritans; plight of patrolman Alfredo Rivera. Newsweek 74:71-2 O 20 '69

They bombed in New York. il Time 94:26-7 N 21 '69

Wave of skyscraper bombings. il U S News 67:12 N 24 '69

See also
Mafia

Description
Blame it on the mayor. A. Waugh. Nat R 21:1006 O 7 '69

New York city: the magic is there. L. Shaver. il Pop Gard 20:26-9+ Spr '69

New York: the terrestrial city. Travel & Camera 32:84-5 S '69

Other city; excerpts. W. Boyd and others. il Ebony 24:90-1+ Jl '69

Two cities of light. M. Gough. il House B 111:80+ S '69

Visitor's New York. J. V. Lindsay. Travel & Camera 32:40 S '69

Where do we go? Try this. R. Kramer. il N Y Times Mag p77-8+ My 25 '69

Young Englishman looks at New York. P. Fox. Seventeen 28:126-7+ O '69

Economic conditions
Can you stand it? concerning J. V. Lindsay's speech on needs of New York city vs. Vietnamese war. W. F. Buckley, jr. Nat R 21:766-7 Jl 29 '69

How one middle-class family gets along in New York; Flushing, Queens. R. Rogin. il N Y Times Mag p32-4+ Ag 17 '69; Discussion. p 12+ S 7 '69

New York: are cities a bust? E. J. Logue. Look 33:70+ Ap 1 '69

Who can afford Manhattan? Time 94:49 D 26 '69

Education
Anarchy in the New York city schools? U S News 66:11 F 3 '69

Battle to control black schools. A. Poinsett. il Ebony 24:44-6+ My '69

Choking off community schools; bill to establish a community school system for New York city. J. Featherstone. New Repub 161:16-18 Jl 19 '69

Community control of schools; off to a bad start. J. Featherstone. New Repub 160:19-22 Mr 29 '69; Reply with rejoinder. M. Mayer. 160:39-40 Ap 26 '69

Decentralization fiasco and our ghetto schools. J. R. Everett; discussion. Atlan 223:36+ F '69

Dorothy Maynor; director of Harlem school of the arts. C. W. Ferguson. il PTA Mag 64:10-12 N '69

Environment to grow in; First street school; excerpt from The lives of children. G. Dennison. il Sat R 52:74-6 O 18 '69

For local control in the schools. R. A. Dentler. Atlan 223:77-9 Ja '69

For white and black, community control is the issue. N. Glazer. il N Y Times Mag p36-7+ Ap 27 '69

Lives of children, by G. Dennison. Review America 121:469-70 N 15 '69. F. Griffith Nation 209:447-8 O 27 '69. N. O'Gorman Newsweek 74:96+ D 1 '69. P. A. Janssen Sat R il 52:92-3 N 15 '69. P. H. Wagschal

McGeorge Bundy confronts the teachers; decentralization of New York schools. R. Armstrong. il N Y Times Mag p25-7+ Ap 20 '69; Discussion. p 118 My 25 '69

NYC unveils school decentralization plan. Sr Schol 94:Schol Teach 4 Ja 17 '69

N.Y. libraries fumbled teachers' strike role. Library J 95:20+ Ja 1 '70

New York school crisis. M. J. Goldbloom; Discussion. Commentary 47:22+ Ap '69

Notes and comment: city's troubled campuses. New Yorker 45:27-32 My 3 '69

Notes of a scab librarian: learning opportunities during the teachers strike. S. Ginsburg. bibliog il Library J 94:1300-2 Mr 15 '69; Discussion. 94:2028, 3107-8, 4559 My 15, S 15, D 15 '69

Ocean Hill is alive and well . . . J. Featherstone. New Repub 160:21-3 Ap 19 '69

110 Livingston street, by D. Rogers. Review Commentary 47:81-6 Mr '69. N. Glazer Trans-Action 6:58-61 Ap '69. H. Kaufman

Street academies: one step off the sidewalk. J. Black. il Sat R 52:88-9+ N 15 '69

Teachers strike, New York, 1968, by M. Mayer. Review Sat R 52:73-4 Mr 15 '69. M. Gittell

Valiant effort at compromise; decentralization issue. W. F. Buckley, jr. Nat R 21:192 F 25 '69

War for city schools; tomorrow everywhere; community control. I. Mothner. il Look 33:42-4+ My 13 '69

Why blame New York city schools? M. Zeldner. il Sch & Soc 97:152-4 Mr '69

Wiping out the demonstration schools. J. Featherstone. New Repub 162:10-11 Ja 10 '70

NEW YORK (city)—Education—*Continued*
Work as therapy for emotionally disturbed
girls; Livingston school for girls. E. P.
Rothman. Ment Hy 53:269-79 Ap '69
　See also
Brooklyn—Education
Brooklyn college
Cooper union for the advancement of science
and art
New York (city). City university of New York
—City college
New York (city). City university of New
York—Hunter college
New York city educational construction fund
Private schools, Negro

Education, Board of

Community control: down but not out. J.
Featherstone. New Repub 161:11-13 Ag 9
'69; Reply. A. Shanker. 161:26-8+ N 15 '69
Full and sometimes very surprising story
of Ocean Hill, the teachers' union and the
teacher strikes of 1968; excerpts from The
teachers strike: New York, 1968. M. Mayer.
il N Y Times Mag p 18-23+ F 2 '69; Discussion. p2+ F 23; 22+ Mr 16 '69
School managers. J. Featherstone. New Repub 160:13-14 F 8 '69

Elections

Comedy of the theories. Nation 209:524 N 17
'69
Countdown to November. Nat R 21:1053 O
21 '69
Elections 1969; the moderates have it. il Time
94:23 N 14 '69
Lindsay and others. New Repub 161:11-12
N 15 '69
Muddled mandate; mayoralty results. Newsweek 74:47-8 N 17 '69
New York: the day the liberals lost; mayoral primary. il Newsweek 73:39-40 Je 30
'69

Electric power

Utility crisis. il Newsweek 74:51-2 Ag 18 '69
　See also
Consolidated Edison company of New York

Elevated railroads

Old Myrt: final Myrtle avenue train. New
Yorker 45:48-9 O 18 '69

Finance

Bad news from a bigtime spender. Life 66:
36 Ap 18 '69
　See also
New York city educational construction
fund

Foreign population

　See also
Puerto Ricans in the United States

Fountains

　See Fountains

Galleries and museums

Art; artists; discontent about presentations
in galleries. L. Alloway. Nation 208:444+
Ap 7 '69
How to attend an opening. il Time 93:75 F
14 '69
New gallery: opening of Gimpel gallery of
London branch. New Yorker 45:28-9 My 31
'69
New York gallery notes. G. Glueck. See is-
sues of Art in America
Reviews and previews. See issues of Art news
South street seaport; maritime museum. R.
S. Gallagher. il Am Heritage 20:36-43+ O
'69
Underground; Museum of the media. J.
Gruen. Vogue 154:340 S 1 '69
　See also
American museum of natural history
Jewish museum
Kennedy galleries, incorporated
Metropolitan museum of art
Museum of contemporary crafts
Museum of modern art
Museum of primitive art, New York
Solomon R. Guggenheim museum
Whitney museum of American art

Geology

　See Geology—New York (State)

Greenwich Village

Artist and his fallen angels; paintings. il
Fortune 79:88-91 Ja '69

Harbor

South street seaport; maritime museum. R.
S. Gallagher. il Am Heritage 20:36-43+ O
'69
　See also
Statue of liberty

Harlem

Black magic at the Met; Harlem on my mind.
P. P. Ardery. jr. il Nat R 21:240-1 Mr 11
'69
Harlem on my mind. D. Vestal. il Pop Phot
64:79-81+ My '69
Harlem on my mind; the black renaissance.
A. Nelson. il Harp Baz 102:214-18 F '69
Harlem out of mind; exhibition at Metropolitan musem of art; with editorial comment. A. Goldin. il Art N 68:23, 52-3+ Mr
'69
Harlem: sold out by Massa Hoving? photo
exhibit Harlem on my mind at the Metropolitan museum. J. Dreyfuss. il Mod Phot
33:64-5+ My '69
Notes and comment; volunteer painting of a
storefront community center. New Yorker
45:27 F 22 '69
On the way to Emmaus. D. Kirk. Commonweal 91:375-8 D 26 '69
Rent strikes: poor man's weapon; Harlem
rent strikes. M. Lipsky. il Trans-Action 6:
10-15 F '69
Ruby's; interview. C. Watson. New Yorker
45:27-8 Jl 12 '69
Thursday parade; weekly parades organized
by Shalom, inc. New Yorker 45:26-7 Ag 1
'69
Who speaks for Harlem? proposed site of state
office building. America 121:284 O 11 '69
　See also
Harlem commonwealth council

History

Banner years; with paintings by C. Hassam
D. G. Lowe. Am Heritage 20:54-9 Je '69
Homestead: sixty years on Broadway and
157th street; interview. L. H. Southwick.
New Yorker 45:26-8 Ag 9 '69

Hospitals

Doctors' dilemma; Harlem hospital and bud
get cuts. il Newsweek 73:49 Ap 7 '69
Fathers' hour; maternity ward at Manhat-
tan's Flower and Fifth avenue hospitals.
il Good H 169:22+ Jl '69
Heart-saver squad; St Vincent's hospital and
Medical center. R. H. Berg. il Look 33:26-9
F 4 '69
Practical agitation; Society of urban phy-
sicians revolt against budget cuts. Nation
208:452 Ap 14 '69
Saving vital time for victims of heart at-
tacks; mobile coronary care units of St
Vincent's hospital & medical center. il Bsns
W p96-8+ F 22 '69
　See also
New York (city)—Bellevue hospital

Hotels, restaurants, etc.

Algonquin's sedate sitting room. L. Al-
dridge. il Holiday 45:110-11 Ap '69
Central park's fountain café. D. Allan. il
Travel & Camera 32:82 S '69
Checking out First avenue. T. Farrow. il
Holiday 45:38-41 My '69
Dining in/out with Esquire. Esquire 72:81
O '69
Downey's, the poor actor's Sardi's. A. Bester.
il Holiday 46:90-2 N '69
Farewell: Dixie Kitchen; cafeteria on Fifth
avenue and Forty-eight street. New York-
er 45:22-3 Ja 3 '70
Fashionable New York lunch-in. P. O'Hig-
gins. il Holiday 45:68-9+ F '69
For a change; Forum of the twelve Caesars
and Spats. N. S. Hazelton. Nat R 21:1118+
N 4 '69
Goings on about town. See issues of New
Yorker
Great eating outing. il Seventeen 28:128-9+
Je '69
How I became sad at La Caravelle. N. S.
Hazelton. Nat R 21:807+ Ag 12 '69
Little wonder restaurants of New York's
Chinatown. W. Clifford. il Holiday 45:
72-3+ Ap '69
Manhattan's foreign flavor. Travel & Camera
32:83-4 S '69
Meals at the Met; the Opera club and Café
in the Metropolitan opera house. Q. Eaton.
il Opera N 33:12-15 Mr 29 '69
Ruby's interview. C. Watson. New Yorker
45:27-8 Jl 12 '69
Safeguarding a symbol; 21 restaurant ac-
quired by Ogden development corp. il Time
93:106 Ap 25 '69
Soaring popularity of Japanese restaurants.
B. Norman and K. Tatsumura. il Holiday
45:58-9+ Mr '69
Steady drinkers at Toots Shor. P. Maas. il
Holiday 45:73+ Je '69

NEW YORK (city)—Hotels, restaurants, etc.
—*Continued*
Trompe l'oeil restaurant: Ellman's restaurants.
il Time 93:83 Je 13 '69
See also
Night clubs

Housing

Big picture; concerning articles in the Daily news and New York times. Nation 208: 557-8 My 5 '69
How Harry Helmsley speared Parkchester. il Arch Forum 130:110 Ja '69
Lessons of Co-op city. Time 93:30 Ja 24 '69
Manhattan madness. Time 93:75-6 F 21 '69
Nine-G cooperative. il Arch Forum 131:78-81 Jl '69
Riverbend houses. P. Blake. il Arch Forum 131:46-55 Jl '69
Urban housing: a comprehenisve approach to quality. il Arch Rec 145:97-118 Ja '69
Where landlord is king. Newsweek 73:110 Mr 10 '69

Housing and development administration

Raising the design quality of urban housing took commitment, and talent, and experience. il Arch Rec 145:98-9 Ja '69

Housing authority

Cutting red tape and time in public housing; combining federal turnkey program with NYCHA's acquisition program. il Bsns W p48-9 Jl 26 '69

Industries

Here come the buyers; garment industry. il Newsweek 73:83-4 Ja 27 '69
Moving to New York's outer edges. il Bsns W p158-60 N 15 '69
Parking place for industry. il Bsns W p 120+ S 20 '69

Landmarks preservation commission

Breuer two; battle over the future of Manhattan's Grand Central terminal. il Arch Forum 130:35 My '69
Grand central controversy; letter on the problem of preserving the terminal. D. Haskell. Arch Forum 130:16+ My '69
New York city's Landmarks commission gives Grand Central station a reprieve. il Arch Rec 146:37 O '69

Libraries

New York city library funds restored in part. Pub W 195:105 Je 2 '69
N.Y. libraries fumbled teachers' strike role. Library J 95:20+ Ja 1 '70
Overdue; local round tables for fast action. J. R. Clune. Wilson Lib Bul 43:905+ My '69
Social responsibility; a progress report. Library J 94:1950-2 My 15 '69
Surge of shock and dismay; cuts in budget for public library services. Pub W 195:19-20 My 12 '69
See also
Brooklyn public library
New York public library
Pierpont Morgan library

Madison Square Garden

What's a sports arena doing on top of a railroad station? new site. J. McCarthy. il Holiday 46:24-8 O '69

Markets

Fish story; Fulton fish market's new home. il Newsweek 73:92 My 5 '69
Flower market. New Yorker 45:33-5 Ap 26 '69

Mayors

Politics and chaos: the New York story. il U S News 66:36-8 Mr 31 '69
See also
Lindsay, J. V.

Metropolitan museum of art
See Metropolitan museum of art. New York

Monuments, statues, etc.
See also
Statue of liberty

Music

Debuts & reappearances. See issues of High fidelity incorporating Musical America
Halls: light, dark, new; New York city opera's season; Alice Tully hall opens. H. Saal. il Newsweek 74:119-20 S 22 '69
Into the Fillmore East. R. Kotlowitz. Harper 238:106-9 My '69
Lively arts. R. Hemming. il Sr Schol 93:20-1 Ja 10 '69

Music; series devoted to contemporary music. D. Hamilton. Nation 208:349-50 Mr 17 '69
Music to my ears. I. Kolodin. See issues of Saturday review
Musical events. W. Sargeant. See issues of New Yorker
Report: New York; Boston symphony orchestra in Carnegie Hall. S. Jenkins. Opera N 33:32 F 22 '69
Report: New York; Clark center opera workshop production of The magic flute. S. L. Fogel. Opera N 33:30 Mr 15 '69
Season past. H. Green. Commonweal 90:488-9 Ag 8 '69
Trumpet battle at Niblo's pleasure garden. C. A. Hoover. bibliog f il Mus Q 55:384-95 Ji '69
Week of Böhm, Karajan, Szell, Frühbeck de Burgos. I. Kolodin. Sat R 52:112+ Mr 8 '69
See also
Lincoln Center for the performing arts
Little orchestra society. New York
Metropolitan opera company
New York city opera company
Philharmonic-symphony society of New York

Newspapers
See also
Daily news, New York
New York post
New York sun
New York times

Night clubs
See Night clubs

Parades

Gra-a-nd parade; Saint Patrick's day parade. J. McCarthy. il Am Heritage 20:54-9+ F '69
Thursday parade; weekly parades organized by Shalom, inc. New Yorker 45:26-7 Ag 16 '69

Parks and playgrounds

Any Sunday; afternoon at Bethesda fountain, Central park. E. Coleman and L. Howard. il Newsweek 73:90 Je 9 '69
Our local correspondents; Central park bird walk. E. Kinkead. New Yorker 45:58+ Ag 2 '69
Playgrounds shape children shape playgrounds. il Am City 84:98-9 Ag '69
Preserving the greensward; press conference called by Save Central park committee. New Yorker 45:28-30 Mr 8 '69
Push and pull in the park; exhibition of sculpture in Bryant park, N.Y. il Arch Forum 130:68-9 Ja '69
Refuge for people; Central park. A. Heckscher. il Travel & Camera 32:49-56 S '69
See also
New York zoological park

Photographs

Other city; excerpts. W. Boyd and others. Ebony 24:90-1+ Jl '69
Photographer's New York. Travel & Camera 32:41-8 S '69

Planning, design and research, Office of
See New York (city)—Housing and development administration

Police

Cop as social scientist; Inspector Fink of Ninth precinct. S. Braun. il N Y Times Mag p46-7+ Ag 24 '69
Police power, by P. G. Chevigny. Review Commonweal 90:397-8 Je 20 '69. T. R. Brooks
New Repub 160:23-5 Mr 8 '69. C. M. Curtis
Policeman (anon) speaks up; letter; with reply by H. Klein. Nat R 21:436-7+ My 6 '69
Support your local police. D. B. Durk. Atlan 223:103-4 Mr '69

Police department

Politics of blue power. E. Gray. il Nation 208:493-6 Ap 21 '69
Requiem for the Centre street mafia. R. Dougherty. il Atlan 223:109-14 Mr '69

Politics and government

Al Smith day in New York. W. F. Buckley. jr. Nat R 21:1130-1 N 4 '69
Announcement: R. F. Wagner to run for mayor. New Yorker 45:32-3 Ap 19 '69
Another chance; J. Lindsay to run for re-election. il Time 93:15 Mr 28 '69
Answering November's big question: what is a Mario Procaccino? T. Buckley. il N Y Times Mag p7-9+ Ag 10 '69
Around city hall. A. Logan. New Yorker 45: 131-2+ S 13; 164+ O 11; 184-90 N 15 '69

NEW YORK (city)—Politics and government
—*Continued*
As New York chooses a mayor-. il U S
News 67:39-40 N 3 '69
As New York goes? F. S. Meyer. Nat R
21:751 Jl 29 '69
Campaign ahead. Nat R 21:628 Jl 1 '69
Candidate: L. M. Simon for borough president of Brooklyn. New Yorker 45:28-31 Je
7 '69
Countdown to November. Nat R 21:740 Jl
29 '69
Dear Mayor Lindsay; letter. T. J. Lowi. Nation 209:624-7 D 8 '69
Enough is enough; running for councilman
from twenty-third district, south-eastern
Brooklyn; interview. T. Silverman. New
Yorker 45:52-4 N 15 '69
Fight for New York: mayoral race. il Newsweek 74:27-8+ N 3 '69
Going for Lindsay; mayoral candidates. New
Repub 160:8 My 3 '69
Golden boy and little people. P. Tracy. Commonweal 91:98-101 O 24 '69
Here comes the next mayor. R. Reeves. il
N Y Times Mag p25-7+ N 2 '69
Is John Lindsay ungovernable? J. R. Coyne,
jr. il Nat R 21:584-9+ Je 17 '69
Just one more time. il Newsweek 73:31 Mr 31
'69
Law and order top the ballot; growing trend
toward conservatism in urban centers. il
Bsns W p41-2 Je 21 '69
Lindsay and the future. Nation 209:269 S 22
'69
Lindsay campaigning. New Yorker 45:33-5 O 4
'69
Lindsay tries to stay in there, while Wagner
tries a quiet comeback. R. Reeves; T. Buckley. il N Y Times Mag p7-11+ Je 15 '69
Lindsay vs. the field. J. Wilson. il Nation
208:332-4 Mr 17 '69
Lindsay's new friends; Democratic endorsements. il Newsweek 74:33-4 Ag 4 '69
Lindsay's non-future. Nat R 21:680+ Jl 15
'69
Literary ticket for the 51st state; Mailer-
Breslin campaign. R. Woodley. il Life 66:
71-2 My 30 '69
Mailer for mayor. il Time 93:21-2 Je 13 '69
Mayor in motion. J. M. Flagler. il Look 33:
82+ Je 24 '69
Mayor; interview. J. V. Lindsay. New Yorker
45:27-8 Je 28 '69
Mayor Lindsay wins re-election and more
problems. U S News 67:37 N 17 '69
New Lindsay. il Newsweek 73:35 Je 2 '69
New politics and old: mayoral campaign. J.
R. Coyne, jr. Nat R 21:1106-7+ N 4 '69
New York: dream or nightmare? G. Astor.
il Look 33:61-4 Ap 1 '69
New York primary. Nation 208:810-11 Je 30
'69
New York: the revolt of the average man. il
Time 94:15-20 O 3 '69
New York, too; law and order wins for conservatives. il U S News 66:21-2 Je 30 '69
New York's political pollution. Commonweal
90:427-8 Jl 11 '69
Nightmare for urban management. A. J.
Reichley. il Fortune 79:94-9+ Mr '69
Odd couple; mayoral candidates N. Mailer
and J. Breslin. il Newsweek 73:37-8 My 12
'69
On the steps of city hall; Mailer for mayor.
J. Pilati. Commonweal 90:255-6 My 16 '69
Politics and chaos: the New York story. il
U S News 66:36-8 Mr 31 '69
Politics of peevishness; mayoral campaign. il
Newsweek 74:28 S 15 '69
Profiles: J. V. Lindsay. N. Hentoff. New
Yorker 45:44-8+ My 3; 42-6+ My 10 '69
Reactionary trend in urban politics? Chr Cent
86:895 Jl 2 '69
Why it's the whites who worry the mayors.
il Bsns W p41 N 1 '69
See also
New York (city)—Elections

Poor

Portrait of New York's welfare population. in
one month, 50,000 persons were added to
the city's welfare rolls. J. Horwitz. il N Y
Times Mag p22-3+ Ja 26 '69; Discussion.
p34+ F 16 '69
Protest: opposition to budget cuts. New
Yorker 45:35-7 Ap 26 '69
Welfare in New York: let them eat cake. W.
Schechner. Commonweal 90:133-6 Ap 18
'69
Where the poor help the poor to help themselves; New York city's south Bronx. J.
Coudert. Read Digest 94:25-6+ Mr '69

Prisons and reformatories

Yard no. 4; temporary practice field for
New York Jets at the New York city
correctional institution for men, Rikers
Island. New Yorker 45:44-7 O 11 '69

Protestant council

See Protestant council of the city of New
York

Radio City music hall

Hide your daughters, here comes Russ Markert; creator of the Rockettes. R. Roman.
il Dance Mag 43:46-9+ S '69
Music hall medley. R. Gold. il Dance Mag
43:28-9 Jl '69

Rapid transit

50,000 seniors using NYC subways, buses with
dime half fare. il Aging 178:19 Ag '69
Urban transit picks up some speed. il Bsns
W p66+ S 20 '69
You can't get there from here; no complete
maps of New York city's transit system.
il Trans-Action 6:5-6 Ap '69
See also
New York (city)—Elevated railroads
New York (city)—Subways

Recreation

Street movies. New Yorker 45:36-8 S 13 '69
See also
New York (city)—Parks and playgrounds

Religious institutions and affairs

Non-prophet organization; church in the inner city. W. J. Duncan; discussion. Commonweal 89:607+ F 14 '69
See also
New York (city)—Churches

Restaurants

See New York (city)—Hotels, restaurants,
etc.

Rockefeller Center

Rockefeller Center; Christmas tree. il Holiday
46:76-7 D '69

Schools

See New York (city)—Education

Shops

See New York (city)—Stores

Social conditions

City to end all cities: Manhattan. M. Zwerin.
Mlle 68:143+ F '69
How free the air? increasing anti-Semitism
among New York's militant black community. il Newsweek 73:25-6 F 10 '69
New York: dream or nightmare? G. Astor.
il Look 33:61-4 Ap 1 '69
Only in New York. Chr Today 13:28 Je 6
'69
See also
New York (city)—Harlem
New York (city)—Poor

Social life and customs

See also
Night clubs

Social work

New York's Guidelines for social action; archdiocese's assessment. T. M. Gannon. America 121:98-9 Ag 16 '69
See also
New York (city)—Welfare, Department of

Stations

Breuer two; battle over the future of Manhattan's Grand Central terminal. il Arch
Forum 130:35 My '69
Grand Central controversy; letter on the problem of preserving the terminal. D. Haskell.
Arch Forum 130:16+ My '69
New York city's Landmarks commission
gives Grand Cental station a reprieve. il
Arch Rec 146:37 O '69

Stock exchange

See Stock exchange—New York (city)

Stores

Boutique with an art beat: ON 1st. J. Peter
and J. A. Segal. il Look 33:54-6 Mr 4 '69
Christmas runner; basement of F. A. O.
Schwarz. New Yorker 45:22-4 D 27 '69
Christmas shopping abroad in New York. L.
Hadley. il Travel & Camera 32:87-9 D '69
F.A.O. Schwarz: the store that kids built.
il Pub W 195:147-8 F 17 '69
Important; reception at Indian consulate
and Peck & Peck fashion show. New Yorker 44:21-2 Ja 25 '69
Stern's leaves the beat of 42nd street. il
Pub W 195:63-4 F 10 '69

NEW YORK (city)—*Continued*

Streets

Checking out First avenue. T. Farrow. il Holiday 45:38-41 My '69

Fourth avenue book trade. M. B. Tarshish. il Pub W 196:52-5 O 20; 50-3 O 27; 40-3 N 3 '69

I vote yes; remarks about special zoning district. W. McQuade. il Arch Forum 130: 96 My '69

South street seaport; maritime museum. R. S. Gallagher. il Am Heritage 20:36-43+ O '69

Wall Streeters rally to lunch-hour happening; Wall and Nassau streets. il Bsns W p 106-7 Jl 12 '69

See also

New York (city)—City planning

Strikes

What we need is a law. Nat R 21:15-16 Ja 14 '69

When public servants revolt. A. H. Raskin. Cur 103:27-32 Ja '69

See also

Strikes—United States—Teachers

Subways

Tunnel: gas-filled void cause of explosion along Delancey street. New Yorker 44:24-7 F 1 '69

Theater

Bad B.O. on Broadway. il Newsweek 74:92 D 22 '69

Chamber theatre, touring living rooms. J. Gruen. Vogue 153:114+ Mr 1 '69

Goings on about town. See issues of New Yorker

Irreverent themes invading reverent theaters. T. Tolnay. Chr Cent 86:1519-20 N 26 '69

Life with La Mama; first four productions in its new house. J. Kroll. il Newsweek 73: 109 Ap 28 '69

La Mama complex. H. Hewes. Sat R 52:53-4 Ap 19 '69

New home, new troupe, new play: In the wine time on off Broadway theater; reprint. L. Patterson. Negro Hist Bul 32:18-19 Ap '69

New season is off; list of shows scheduled to open before the end of 1969. H. Hewes. Sat R 52:37 Ag 30 '69

Offbeat-but on Broadway. T. Prideaux. il Life 66:82-4+ Mr 14 '69

Shaping up the season. il Newsweek 74:98+ S 22 '69

Spotlight. E. Miller. See issues of Seventeen

Theatre. W. Sheed. il Esquire 72:40+ S '69

Theater in '69. H. Hewes. il Sat R 52:19-23 Je 14 '69

Theater of crisis. J. Kroll. il Newsweek 73: 118 My 5 '69

Theatre: September overture; Broadway openings before Christmas. T. Lewis. America 121:242-4 S 27 '69

There's slow business in show business. il Bsns W p43-4 O 18 '69

Visiting Off off Broadway. C. Hughes. America 121:30-2 Jl 19 '69

Year ahead; hope tempered by reason; on or off Broadway. il Time 94:66-7 S 26 '69

See also

Lincoln Center repertory theater company

Theatre development fund

Transportation

Celestial omnibus: Sterling Tanks, the nicest bus driver in New York. New Yorker 45: 47-8 O 11 '69

See also

New York (city)—Rapid transit

New York (city)—Subways

Tunnels

Tunnel: gas-filled void cause of explosion along Delancey street. New Yorker 44:24-7 F 1 '69

Welfare, Department of

Chutzpah, in the first degree; misuse of welfare. Time 93:74 Je 6 '69

New federalism; interview. M. I. Ginsberg. New Yorker 45:19-22 Ag 23 '69

Portrait of New York's welfare population, in one month, 50,000 persons were added to the city's welfare rolls. J. Horwitz. il N Y Times Mag p22-3+ Ja 26 '69; Discussion. p34+ F 16 '69

Protest: opposition to budget cuts. New Yorker 45:35-7 Ap 26 '69

Shelter: Children's center deluged with child abuse cases. New Yorker 45:21-2 Jl 5 '69

Welfare in New York: let them eat cake. W. Scherbner. Commonweal 90:133-6 Ap 18 '69

World trade center

Greatest skyscraper of them all. J. D. Ratcliff. il Read Digest 95:217-21+ Jl '69

Once and future capital of world finance. il Fortune 80:118-25 O '69

Zoological park

See New York zoological park

NEW YORK (city). City university of New York

Buck stops where? budget cuts. il Newsweek 73:74 Ap 14 '69

CUMBIN at CUNY; closed circuit, talk-back television instruction system. il Sch & Soc 97:341-2 O '69

Regulations for the maintenance of public order. Sch & Soc 97:459-61 N '69

Socking it to 'em, or getting certified? SEEK students. Newsweek 73:58 F 10 '69

Swahili at City university of New York. Sch & Soc 97:86-7 F '69

Trustees under thirty. il Time 94:37 Ag 29 '69

What seventy SEEK kids taught their counselor. L. W. Scheffler. il N Y Times Mag p54-5+ N 16 '69; Reply with rejoinder. M. Schuker. p 14 Ja 11 '70

Will everyman destroy the university? T. S. Healy. il Sat R 52:54-6+ D 20 '69

City college

Bending standards. Time 93:56 Je 6 '69

Can the university survive the black challenge? J. Cass. il Sat R 52:70-1 Je 21 '69

Crisis at CCNY. il Newsweek 73:69-70 My 19 '69

Double trouble at CCNY; dual admissions plan. il Newsweek 73:91-2 Je 9 '69

Graduate student. J. Slevin. il Phys Today 22:31-2 Mr '69

High above the subway's rumble. D. Shaber. Holiday 45:20+ Mr '69

Retreat of a reconciler. il Time 93:59 My 16 '69

Students and priorities; Gallagher's resignation. J. Deedy. Commonweal 90:306 My 30 '69

Subway college strife; report from CCNY. G. Wagner. Nat R 21:539-40 Je 3 '69; Reply with rejoinder. S. J. Robbins. 21:570+ Je 17 '69

Hunter college

Lady is not for drowning. il Time 95:51 Ja 19 '70

Libraries

Blacks hit library at Queens college; action to protest changes in the SEEK program. Library J 94:481-2 F 1 '69

Queens college

Angry and alone together. K. G. Gross. Nation 208:207-10 F 17 '69

Blacks hit library at Queens college; action to protest changes in the SEEK program. Library J 94:481-2 F 1 '69

NEW YORK (state)

See also

Adirondack Mountains

Architecture, Domestic—New York (state)

Art—New York (state)

Automobile touring—New York (state)

Birds—New York (state)

Booksellers and bookselling—New York (state)

Camping—New York (state)

Education—New York (state)

Fishing—New York (state)

Geology—New York (state)

Hudson River

Hunting—New York (state)

Labor and laboring classes—New York (state)

Land—New York (state)

Libraries—New York (state)

Long Island

Music festivals—New York (state)

Public welfare—New York (state)

Recreation areas—New York (state)

School laws and legislation—New York (state)

Skis and skiing—New York (state)

Appropriations and expenditures

Protest: opposition to budget cuts. New Yorker 45:35-7 Ap 26 '69

Atomic and space development authority

Why New York worries utilities; plan to lease atomic cores from state. Bsns W p 17 D 27 '69

NEW YORK (state)—*Continued*

Climate

How weather is made; with map. R. E. Falconer. il Cons 24:22-31 D '69

Conservation department

Building aids research program; new addition at Delmar wildlife research laboratory. E. S. Feldman. il Cons 24:17+ D '69

New York's fish and game budget. C. Mason. il Cons 23:5-7 F '69

Description and travel

More to see in New York. il Pop Gard 20:22-5 Spr '69

Motor to the mountains to see fall's flaming foliage. M. Perry. il Home Gard 56:66-7 S '69

Visit New York, the Empire state. J. P. Graham. il Pop Gard 20:18-21+ Spr '69

Economic conditions

See also
Labor and laboring classes—New York (state)

Education, Department of

Importing India's educational riches; establishment of Educational resources center, New Delhi. W. Morehouse. il Am Ed 5:14-19 My '69

Fish and game division

See New York (state)—Conservation department

Fisheries

See Fisheries—United States

History

Changing concepts of party in the United States: New York, 1815-1828. M. Wallace. bibliog f Am Hist R 74:453-91 D '68

Industries

Manufacturing. J. H. Thompson. bibliog il Focus 19:8-12 Je '69

Legislature

Hearing: demonstration by women when Joint legislative committee on the problems of public health convened on abortion issue. New Yorker 45:28-9 F 22 '69

Narcotic addiction control commission

New York tries to kick the habit. il Ebony 24:29-32+ S '69

Natural resources

See Natural resources—United States

Parks and reserves

Upper Hudson: time for decision, reprint. P. Schaefer. il Liv Wildn 32:18-21 Wint '68
See also
Palisades Interstate Park

Politics and government

Changing concepts of party in the United States: New York, 1815-1828. M. Wallace. bibliog f Am Hist R 74:453-91 D '68

Democrats confront 1970. J. Wilson. Nation 209:597-8 D 1 '69

Urban development corporation

Bridging the gap from rhetoric to reality. S. Kaplan. Arch Forum 131:70-3 N '69

Youth, Division for

Innovations in the treatment of juvenile offenders. M. Luger. Ann Am Acad 381:60-70 Ja '69

NEW YORK (state). State university
Wilderness biological station; two units combine summer study in the Adirondacks. N. Drahos. il Cons 23:18-20 F '69

Agricultural and technical institute at Farmingdale, Long Island

Planting fields arboretum. G. E. Jones. il Horticulture 47:42-5+ Ap '69

College at Buffalo

Communications center. il Arch Rec 145:153-60 My '69

College at Fredonia

Academic center at Fredonia. J. Bailey. il Arch Forum 130:36-47 My '69

College at Old Westbury

Experiment at Old Westbury. M. Novak. Commonweal 89:560-3 Ja 31 '69

College at Purchase

Project for the farthest-out college; problems of American college dance. J. Anderson. il Dance Mag 43:45-6+ F '69

Long Island center, Stony Brook

Student power; demands for change at Stony Brook's talk-in. B. Nelson; discussion. Science 163:879 F 28 '69

NEW YORK (periodical)
New York is going to make it; how to start a magazine. S. W. Little. il Sat R 52:52-3+ Je 14 '69

Year of New York. Time 93:98 Ap 11 '69

NEW YORK airways incorporated
Pan Am plans to finance New York airways service. Aviation W 91:24 S 8 '69

NEW YORK Amsterdam news. See Negro press

NEW YORK automobile show. See Automobiles—Exhibitions

NEW YORK central railroad-Pennsylvania merger. See Railroads—Consolidations and mergers

NEW YORK city ballet
Balanchine+girls=ballet. R. Kotlowitz. il Holiday 45:54-7+ Mr '69

Ballerina for all seasons. O. Maynard. il Dance Mag 43:42-5+ Je '69

Is this man the country's best athlete? D. Martin. il Life 66:48-54+ Je 6 '69

Jerome Robbins prepares Dancers at a gathering for New York city ballet. il Dance Mag 43:40-1 Je '69

Musical events:
Dances at a gathering. W. Sargeant. New Yorker 45:96 My 31 '69
New creations at State theatre. W. Sargeant. New Yorker 44:95-7 F 15 '69

New York city ballet: some highlights. D. Hering. Dance Mag 43:85-6+ Ap '69

Prokofiev's perennial Peter. W. Terry. il Sat R 52:51-2 Ap 19 '69

Return to Monte Carlo. il Newsweek 73:93 Je 30 '69

Summer circuit; J. Robbin's production of Dances at a gathering. W. Terry. il Sat R 52:41-2 Jl 26 '69

Trouble in paradise. il Newsweek 73:85-6 My 26 '69

Two premieres; New York state theater. M. Marks. Dance Mag 43:33+ Ag '69

NEW YORK city educational construction fund
Building schools at no cost; leasing of air rights above new public schools. il Bsns W p 168+ Ap 26 '69

New schools at no cost. H. B. Gores. il Parents Mag 44:58-9+ O '69

NEW YORK city housing authority. See New York (city)—Housing authority

NEW YORK city opera company
Discographic postscript. J. Lyons. Am Rec G 35:459 F '69

Double devil. H. Saal. il Newsweek 74:132 O 6 '69

Music; performance of A. Boito's Mefistofele. D. Hamilton. Nation 209:388-9 O 13 '69

Music; performance of G. Donizetti's Lucia di Lammermoor. D. Hamilton. Nation 209:550 N 17 '69

Music to my ears; performance of A. Boito's Mefistofele. Sat R 52:53-4 O 11 '69

Music to my ears; presentation of Catulli carmina. I. Kolodin. Sat R 52:103 N 15 '69

Musical events:
Donizetti's Lucia di Lammermoor. W. Sargeant. New Yorker 45:169-71 O 18 '69
Orff's Catulli carmina and Ravel's L'heure espagnole. W. Sargeant. New Yorker 45:192-4 N 8 '69
Performance of A. Boito's Mefistofele. W. Sargeant. New Yorker 45:116-18 O 4 '69
Performance of Borodin's Prince Igor. W. Sargeant. New Yorker 45:98 Mr 8 '69
Performance of G. Verdi's Rigoletto. W. Sargeant. New Yorker 45:95 S 20 '69
Performance of Massenet's Manon. W. Sargeant. New Yorker 45:105 Mr 1 '69
Verdi's Rigoletto. W. Sargeant. New Yorker 45:122+ Mr 29 '69

New York city opera. il Hi Fi 19:MA14-15+ My; MA12-13 Je; MA10-12 D '69

Report: New York; production of Boito's Mefistofele. F. Merkling. il Opera N 34:20-1 N 1 '69

Report: New York; production of Prince Igor. F. Merkling. il Opera N 33:30 Ap 12 '69

Report: New York; production of Rigoletto. S. Jenkins, jr. il Opera N 33:29 Ap 19 '69

Report: presentations of Ravel's Heure espagnole, and Songs of Catullus. F. Merkling. il Opera N 34:25 D 13 '69

NEW YORK city opera company—*Continued*
Report: production of Lucia di Lammermoor with Beverly Sills. S. Jenkins, jr. il Opera N 34:22 N 22 '69
Reviews: opera Mefistofele; Capriccio. D. Hering. il Dance Mag 43:32+ N '69
NEW YORK city transit authority. See Metropolitan transportation authority
NEW YORK city-Vermont youth project. See Vermont-New York city youth project
NEW YORK daily news. See Daily news, New York
NEW YORK drama critics circle
New York drama critics circle choices. 1969. Sat R 52:51-2 Ap 19 '69
NEW YORK film festival. See Moving picture festivals
NEW YORK foundling hospital. See Foundlings
NEW YORK Giants (football club) See Football clubs
NEW YORK Jets (football club) See Football clubs
NEW YORK Knickerbockers (basketball team) See Basketball teams
NEW YORK library association
New York library assn. bans Vietnam statement. Library J 94:4477-8 D 15 '69
Pleasures of Lake Placid: the NYLA conference. A. Plotnik. il Wilson Lib Bul 44:373-4+ D '69; Discussion. 44:386-7 D '69
NEW YORK Mets (baseball) See Baseball clubs
NEW YORK, New Haven and Hartford railroad company
Down and out in New York, New Haven & Hartford. H. B. Meyers. Fortune 79:301+ My 15 '69
New Haven railroad, its rise and fall, by J. L. Weller. Review
Bsns W il p54+ D 20 '69
NEW YORK philharmonic. See Philharmonic-symphony society of New York
NEW YORK port authority. See Port of New York authority
NEW YORK post
Goodbye, Dolly! A reminiscence of the New York post. J. Newfield. Harper 239:92-8 S '69
NEW YORK public library
Ad hoc harmony; school-public library relations. J. M. Cory. Library J 94:264-6 Ja 15 '69
Budget cuts in a time of need. C. B. Grannis. Pub W 195:30 My 5 '69
Ceremony: F. M. Marsh memorialized as a benefactor. New Yorker 45:38-9 Ap 12 '69
NYPL research libraries get first public funds. Library J 94:2544+ Jl '69
One thing and another; concerning the budget crisis. J. K. Hutchens. Sat R 52:42-3 F 22 '69
See also
Lincoln Center for the performing arts, New York—Library and museum of the performing arts

Dance collection
New York public library dance collection gets a computerized catalogue. R. Estrada and S. Estrada. il Dance Mag 43:50+ Mr '69
See Lincoln Center for the performing arts, New York—Library and museum of the performing arts

135th Street branch
Harlem on my mind; Schomburg collection of Negro literature and history. S. Maloff. Commonweal 89:654-6 F 21 '69; Reply. H. Walter. 90:31 Mr 21 '69
NYPL sees new life for Harlem collection; Schomburg collection of Negro literature and history. il Library J 94:4094+ N 15 '69

Special collections
Sketching scriveners; exhibition of Berg collection of English and American literature at the public library. New Yorker 45:53-4 D 6 '69

NEW YORK Shakespeare festival
Romping through Ibsen. H. Hewes. il Sat R 52:35-6 Ag 2 '69
Theater; production of Electra. H. Hewes. Sat R 52:32 Ag 23 '69
NEW YORK souvenirs. See Souvenirs
NEW YORK state division for youth. See New York (state)—Youth, Division for
NEW YORK state library association. See New York library association
NEW YORK stock exchange. See Stock exchange—New York (city)
NEW YORK studio school
Breakaway art school. il Newsweek 73:121 Je 9 '69
NEW YORK sun
Great moon hoax. J. Cottrell. il Sci Digest 66:40-4 Jl '69

View of the moon from the Sun: 1835. J. L. Morrison. il Am Heritage 20:80-2 Ap '69
NEW YORK telephone company
Customers talk back. Time 94:60+ Ag 29 '69
Great telephone snarl. W. A. McWhirter. il Life 67:86-86D+ D 5 '69
Hello? Hello? Hello? overloaded circuits. il Newsweek 74:75+ Jl 7 '69
New York phone hangup. Bsns W p52 Ag 2 '69
Pl 8-6200, where are you? il Time 94:68 Jl 25 '69
Unholier than thou trio; Long Island railroad. Consolidated Edison and New York telephone. L. L. L. Golden. Sat R 52:80-1 O 11 '69
Utility crisis. il Newsweek 74:51-2 Ag 18 '69
Why you hear a busy signal at AT&T. il Bsns W p40-1+ D 27 '69
NEW YORK theological seminary
New leader, new motif for New York seminary. J. Evenson. Chr Today 13:42 Mr 28 '69
NEW YORK times
Beat the press, round two. il Newsweek 74: 25-6 D 1 '69
Best of Times, the worst of Times. A. M. Auerbach. Sat R 52:8+ O 11 '69
Change of the guard at the Times. Time 94: 45+ Ag 8 '69
Finis; new editorial assignments. il Newsweek 74:60-1 Ag 11 '69
Going critical; new movie critic and daily book critic. il Newsweek 73:86-7 Mr 10 '69
Kingdom and the power, by G. Talese. Review
Commentary 48:95-6+ S '69. J. Epstein
Esquire 72:20+ S '69. M. Muggeridge
Life 66:8 Je 27 '69. M. Kempton
Look 33:16 Jl 15 '69. P. S. Prescott
Nat R 21:810-12 Ag 12 '69. C. H. Simonds
Nation 209:254-6 S 15 '69. F. Powledge
New Repub 160:29-33 Je 28 '69. A. J. Langguth
Life and Times of Gay Talese. J. Leo. Commonweal 91:66-8 O 17 '69
Man of the Times; Broadway's Sam Zolotow. J. K. Hutchens. Sat R 52:73-4 My 10 '69
New York times; excerpt from The kingdom and the power (cont) G. Talese. il Harper 238:40-8+ F '69; Reply. A. Seeger. 238: 6+ Ap '69
Newspaper monopoly; address, November 20, 1969. S. T. Agnew. Vital Speeches 36:133-6 D 15 '69; Excerpts. U S News 67:12 D 1 '69
On the only hand. .; editorial page. Newsweek 73:90 Je 16 '69
Profiles: A. O. Sulzberger, president and publisher. G. T. Hellman. New Yorker 44:40-2+ Ja 18 '69
Quiet revolution in the palace; excerpts from The kingdom and the power. G. Talese. il Esquire 71:95-107+ Ap '69
Smoke signals. il Newsweek 74:66 S 15 '69
Strange Times. S. J. Adamo. America 120: 483-4 Ap 19 '69
Times does it again; reports on testing of new drugs on prisoners. Nation 209:100-1 Ag 11 '69
Weekly Agnew special. Time 94:62+ N 28 '69

Anecdotes, facetiae, satire, etc.
Who says a good newspaper has to be dull? il Esquire 72:200-8 D '69
NEW YORK transit authority. See Metropolitan transportation authority
NEW YORK university
Opening. New Yorker 45:30-1 S 27 '69
They're learning to be students again; School of continuing education and extension services. il Am Ed 5:14-19 N '69

Medical center
Pioneering nursery school. E. P. Berkeley. il Arch Forum 130:68-9 Mr '69
NEW YORK Yankees (baseball) See Baseball clubs
NEW YORK zoological park
Multimedia zoo: Bronx zoo. J. S. Margolies. il Arch Forum 130:86-91 Je '69
Strange world of night creatures. B. Ford. il Sci Digest 66:38-42 O '69
NEW YORK zoological society
Zoo meeting. New Yorker 45:26-7 Mr 1 '69
NEW YORKER (periodical)
New Yorker lists at this season some books by its contributors published during the year (cont) New Yorker 45:194-5 N 29 '69
Raoul Fleischmann. New Yorker 45:27-8 My 17 '69
Read all about it; table of contents. Newsweek 73:60 Mr 31 '69
Talk of the town; table of contents added to magazine. Time 93:46 Mr 28 '69

NEW YORKERS
Beauty safari; Mona Grant and Margie Lindsay on a tour of Manhattan. il Seventeen 28:144-5 Mr '69
Celestial omnibus: Sterling Tanks, the nicest bus driver in New York. New Yorker 45: 47-8 O 11 '69
Long-winded lady; drunk middle-aged woman in Times square. New Yorker 45:18-19 Ja 10 '70
Long-winded lady; reactions to visitor from California. New Yorker 45:16-19 Jl 19 '69
Moon hours: watching Apollo 11. New Yorker 45:25-30 Jl 26 '69
New York: making it where it's at; Essie Borden from Ames, Ia. B. Baer. il Look 33:66-9 Ap 1 '69
That New York look; photographs. V. Merritt. Life 67:32-41 Ag 22 '69
Why are we in New York? N. Mailer. il N Y Times Mag p30-1+ My 18 '69

NEW ZEALAND
New Zealand's ninety-mile beach. il Sunset 142:52 F '69
See also
Catholic church in New Zealand
Cook Strait
Fishing—New Zealand
Geology—New Zealand
Yachts and yachting—New Zealand

Description and travel
Four-star paradise; Marlborough sounds. T. R. Talamini. il Travel 131:60-1 F '69
New zip in New Zealand. T. R. Talamini. il Travel 132:60-1 S '69

Social life and customs
Britain that was. N. Morgan. il Sat R 52: 44+ Ap 19 '69

NEW ZEALAND opera company
News from New Zealand. A. Alpers. il Opera N 33:26-8 Ap 5 '69

NEWARK, Del.
Programmed lighting brings bright results. E. R. Stiff. il Am City 84:130 Ap '69

NEWARK, N.J.
City: problems of a prototype. il Time 93:21 Mr 21 '69

Crime
Crackdown in New Jersey. Time 94:17 D 19 '69

Economic conditions
Sick, sick city looks for a cure. il Bsns W p 16-17 D 27 '69

Moral conditions
See also
Newark, N. J.—Crime

Negroes
Violent man rises in Newark; T. Imperiale. C. Mangel. il Look 33:62-7 S 9 '69

Politics and government
Reports: T. R. Brooks. Atlan 224:4+ Ag '69
Violent man rises in Newark; T. Imperiale. C. Mangel. il Look 33:62-7 S 9 '69

Recreation
New pool helps keep city cool. il Am City 84: 36 D '69

Social conditions
Reports: T. R. Brooks. Atlan 224:4+ Ag '69

NEWARK, N.J. public library
Editor's choice. G. R. Shields. ALA Bul 63: 439 Ap '69; Reply. W. Brahm. 63:1050-3 S '69
Newark city council votes to drop library; with editorial comment. il Library J 94:1081, 1083 Mr 15 '69
Newark council rescinds library budget slash. il Library J 94:1403-4 Ap 1 '69
Reflections on the death of a library. P. Roth. il Wilson Lib Bul 43:746-7 Ap '69
Victory from the jaws of defeat: a tribute to the Newark public library. A. Plotnik. il Wilson Lib Bul 43:740-5 Ap '69

NEWARK museum
Decorative arts at the Newark museum. T. Kyle. il Antiques 95:338-41 Je '69

NEWBERGER, Babette
Plastics for everyday living. E. H. Varian. il Art in Am 57:104-7 Jl '69

NEWBERY medal
Here are the winners! R. Gagliardo. PTA Mag 63:32-3 Ap '69
Julius Lester: Newbery runner-up. E. Geller. il Library J 94:2070-1 My 15 '69
Lloyd Alexander: Newbery winner. A. Durell. il Library J 94:2070-1 My 15 '69

Newbery and Caldecott award winners announced. il Pub W 195:52 F 10 '69
Newbery award acceptance; address, June 24, 1969. L. Alexander. il Horn Bk 45:378-81 Ag '69
Newbery-Caldecott secret, not a secret any more. il Pub W 195:129-30 F 17 '69
Newbery-Caldecott winners announced at ALA midwinter. Library J 94:1280+ Mr 15 '69

NEWBORN Infants. See Infants, Newborn

NEWBURGH, N.Y.

Economic conditions
Cushioned cutback; effect of defense layoffs. il Newsweek 74:81-2 D 22 '69

NEWCOMB, Eldon H. See Frederick, S. E. jt. auth.

NEWCOMB, Don
New pitch for Newk. Sports Illus 30:14 Ap 14 '69

NEWCOMBE, Jack
Ascent of Prince Charles. Life 66:36-41 Je 27 '69
Close-up: Dick Francis jockey with an eye for intrigue. Life 66:81-2 Je 6 '69

NEWELL, Barbara W.
Co-ops on campus. Nation 209:635-6 D 8 '69

NEWFIELD, Jack
Downs and ups of John Lindsay. Life 67:30D N 14 '69
Goodbye, Dolly! Harper 239:92-8 S '69
Nader's raiders. Life 67:56-56B+ O 3 '69
New politics: more mood than movement. Nation 209:70-3 Jl 28 '69

about
Remembering Robert Kennedy. il por Time 93:84 Je 20 '69

NEWFOUNDLANDERS
This rock within the sea, by F. Mowat and J. de Visser. Review
Sat R 52:33+ Ap 26 '69. J. H. Plumb

NEWHALL, Beaumont
Remarkable decade of daguerreotype. il Mod Phot 33:100-5 N '69

NEWHALL, Nancy
Ansel Adams, brilliant recorder of nature's magnificence. Mod Phot 33:66-71+ S '69
Paul Strand, catalyst and revealer. Mod Phot 33:70-5 Ag '69

NEWHALL, Scott
I couldn't get anyone to arrest me. por Time 93:66+ Ap 18 '69

NEWLOVE, Donald
Dinner at the Lowells'. Esquire 72:123-9+ S '69
Dream of Tennessee Williams. Esquire 72:172-8+ N '69

NEWMAN, Barnett
Chartres and Jericho. il Art N 68:28-9 Ap '69
Through the Louvre with Barnett Newman; interview, ed. by P. Schneider. Art N 68: 34-9+ Sum '69

about
Art world. H. Rosenberg. New Yorker 45: 136+ Ap 19 '69
Barnett Newman in a new light. E. C. Baker. il Art N 67:38-41+ F '69
Barnett Newman, revolutionary genius into American classic. por Vogue 153:114-15 Mr 15 '69
Barney; show at New York's Knoedler gallery. D. L. Shirey. il por Newsweek 73:93-4 Ap 14 '69
Denials, affirmations, and art. K. Kuh. il Sat R 52:41-2 My 31 '69

NEWMAN, David, and Benton, Robert
Man talk. See issues of Mademoiselle

NEWMAN, Edward, and Spiegel, A. D.
Massachusetts plans for its retarded. Ment Hy 53:100-4 Ja '69

NEWMAN, Frank
Water pollution study. por Chem 42:28-9 Ja '69

NEWMAN, Gloria
No one-and-only way to go: Gloria Newman reflects on roots and influences. V. H. Swisher. il pors Dance Mag 43:56-8 Ag '69

NEWMAN, John Henry, cardinal
Newman: pioneer for the layman, by W. T. Patterson. Review
America 120:310 Mr 15 '69. J. Pick

NEWMAN, Marvin E.
Norway; fjords, fun, midnight sun; photographs. Travel & Camera 32:60-1+ Mr '69
Stalking the sun set; photographs. Travel & Camera 32:98-9 F '69

NEWMAN, Oscar
Countdown for small towns. Esquire 72:180-7 D '69

NEWMAN, Paul
How we turned Paul Newman into a winning driver. B. Bondurant. il pors Pop Sci 194: 50-3 Je '69
Joanne Woodward tells all about Paul Newman; interview, ed. by M. Davidson. J. Woodward. il pors Good H 168:72-5+ F '69
New lunatics. il por Newsweek 73:81 Je 23 '69
Newman's complaint. R. Ebert. il por Esquire 72:110-11+ S '69
NEWMAN, Paul Baker
Eavesdropping; poem. Chr Cent 87:6 Ja 7 '70
Sketch for a portrait; poem. Chr Cent 86: 1669 D 31 '69
NEWMAN, Ralph Geoffrey
Ralph Newman, Chicago, opens Book and bottle club. Pub W 195:64 My 19 '69
NEWMAN, Thelma R.
(ed) See Levine, L. Artist speaks: Les Levine
NEWMARK, Esther
Eventide on the East coast. il Yachting 126: 68-70+ O '69
From coast to coast (cont) il Yachting 125: 94-6+ Ja; 62-4+ F '69
Little known western Caribbean. Yachting 126:54-5+ N '69
NEWMARKET, England
From Charles to Elizabeth. C. Graham. Sports Illus 30:43 My 19 '69

Photographs
Where the horse abides. G. Cranham. Sports Illus 30:36-42 My 19 '69
NEWPORT, R.I.

Historic houses, etc.
House on John street; rejuvenation of a 1770 relic in Old Newport. A. Pryce-Jones. House & Gard 136:80+ S '69
Weekend in Newport and Providence. A. Stagg. il House & Gard 136:72-3+ S '69
NEWPORT, R.I. jazz festival. See Music festivals—Rhode Island
NEWQUIST, Roy
(ed) See Calisher, H. Interview with Hortense Calisher
NEWS
Watchman, what of the news? Stories the papers miss. J. Hohenberg. il Sat R 52: 56-7 Je 14 '69
What's wrong with objectivity? H. Brucker. Sat R 52:77-9 O 11 '69
See also
Community news service
Current events
Government and the press
Journalism
Reporters and reporting
Television broadcasting—News

Curiosa and miscellany
Good news. il Esquire 72:161 O '69
NEWS agencies
Front page revisited; City news bureau of Chicago. il Time 94:44+ Ag 22 '69
See also
Dispatch news service
NEWS commentators. See Television broadcasting—News
NEWS letters
Freelance job idea: pharmacy newsletters. C. J. Levin. il Writers Digest 49:48-50 My '69
NEWS media. See Mass media
NEWS of the world (newspaper)
Stooping to conquer. il Time 95:49 Ja 12 '70
NEWS periodicals. See Periodicals for men
NEWS photographers
See also
Eisenstaedt, A.
Galella, R.
NEWS photography. See Photography, Journalistic
NEWSCASTERS. See Television broadcasting—News
NEWSOM, David D.
Department presents views on Southern Rhodesia; statement, October 17, 1969. Dept State Bul 61:422-4 N 17 '69
NEWSOM, JON
Quarterly book-list. Mus Q 55:140-8, 286-93 Ja-Ap '69
NEWSPAPER censorship. See Censorship
NEWSPAPER columnists. See Journalists
NEWSPAPER columns. See Newspapers—Sections, columns, etc.
NEWSPAPER correspondents. See Reporters and reporting
NEWSPAPER court reporting
Administration of justice; halting the free press/fair trial debate; excerpts from address. C. Kirkpatrick. Cur 108:39-42 Je '69

From-the-hip delivery: N. Von Hoffman's style of reporting Chicago's Great conspiracy trial. Newsweek 74:112+ O 27 '69
NEWSPAPER ethics. See Journalistic ethics
NEWSPAPER mastheads. See Newspapers—Mastheads
NEWSPAPER men. See Journalists
NEWSPAPER mergers. See Newspapers—Consolidations and mergers
NEWSPAPER publishers and publishing
Computer with the green eyeshade. R. L. Tobin. Sat R 52:69-70 My 10 '69
Failing newspapers; Newspaper preservation act. New Repub 160:8 Je 28 '69
Knight in Philadelphia; Inquirer and News sold to Knight newspapers. il Newsweek 74: 98 N 10 '69
Letting go of a legacy; Philadelphia inquirer sold to Knight newspapers. Time 94:88 N 7 '69
Newspapers' death held exaggerated. il Forbes 104:30-2+ O 1 '69

Laws and legislation
Price-fixing, profit-pooling, and the newspaper business. W. B. Kerr. il Sat R 52:82-3 N 8 '69
NEWSPAPERS
For the only freak in Ohio ; sex newspapers. B. Farrell. Life 67:32B N 21 '69
When a PM paper goes AM; case of the Santa Fe New Mexican. W. B. Kerr. Sat R 52:58-9 F 8 '69
See also
Airplanes in newspaper service
Freedom of the press
Journalism
Journalistic ethics
News
News agencies
Publicity
Reporters and reporting

Advertising policy
Case to watch; ACWA vs. four Chicago newspapers. Nation 209:332-3 O 6 '69
Laundering the sheets; movie-ad censorship. il Time 93:54 My 30 '69
See also
Advertising mediums—Newspapers

Advice columns
Ask Dr Hip. il Newsweek 73:118-19 My 19 '69
Doctor HIP; medical advice column in underground newspapers. Time 93:49 Mr 7 '69
Men vs. women and vice versa; excerpts from Ann Landers says: truth is stranger... A. Landers. Read Digest 94:59-62 Mr '69

Bibliography
Underground and new left press. D. Tatko and C. Brown. il Wilson Lib Bul 43:648-52 Mr '69

Book reviews
See Book reviews

Consolidations and mergers
Failing newspaper probe: the press dummies up. A. E. Rowse. il Nation 208:816-20 Je 30 '69
Newspapers and monopoly: S. 1312 and all that. Sat R 52:77-8 My 10 '69

Crime reporting
See Crime and the press

Financial news
Recession fears; wild gyrations of financial opinion in the press. P. A. Samuelson. Newsweek 74:65 Ag 25 '69

Letters to editors
Letters to the world's editors; comp. by N. G. Balint. See issues of Saturday review
Who writes the letters to the editor? I. Rosenthal. Sat R 52:114-16 S 13 '69

Magazine sections
End of This week; Sunday supplement. Newsweek 74:75 Ag 25 '69
Newspaper feature market. W. J. Brier. Writer 82:27-9 Je '69

Mastheads
Newspaper mastheads. B. M. Bollas. Hobbies 74:159 N '69

Names
Lots in a name. New Repub 161:13 S 27 '69

NEWSPAPERS—*Continued*

Personal advertisements

There's gold in the fine print; personals columns as basis for stories. L. F. Reed. Writers Digest 49:51-3 F '69

Political activities

See Newspapers and politics

Political news

See also

Government and the press

Reader interest

D.N. creates a job. V. Sneider. il Har Yrs 9: 19-21 F '69

Sections, columns, etc.

Close up: the ladies who cover Washington society; interviews, ed. by deR. McQuade. M. Cheshire; B. Beale. il Life 66:30-3 F 28 '69

Columnists; Washington's third pair. il Time 94:68 Ag 15 '69

Detroit newspaper comes on hip; The other section of Detroit news. il Bsns W p122 O 11 '69

D.N. creates a job. V. Sneider. il Har Yrs 9: 19-21 F '69

Master of the epithet; W. Pegler's column. Time 94:68 Jl 4 '69

Medicine's Mark Twain. F. G. Loyd. il To-days Health 47:52-5 My '69

Return of the gossip; J. Haber's gossip column. il Time 93:66 Je 27 '69

See also

Newspapers—Advice columns

Society news

All brides aren't beautiful; leading society reporters. il Newsweek 73:60-1 Ja 27 '69

Sports news

See Sports journalism

Sunday supplements

See Newspapers—Magazine sections

Tabloid papers

Tabloid today. il Newsweek 73:69 My 12 '69

See also

National enquirer

Brazil

News you won't find in Brazil's newspapers. B. Lando. il New Repub 161:11-12 Ag 2 '69

Czechoslovakia

See also

Journalism—Czechoslovakia

Europe, Western

Notes from the European underground. il Mlle 69:118-22+ Je '69

France

See also

Paris—Newspapers

Great Britain

See also

News of the world (newspaper)

Sun (newspaper)

Times, London

Greece, Modern

Comfort for the colonels. il Time 94:38+ N 28 '69

What's up in Greece? proposed press law. Nat R 21:947 S 23 '69

Japan

Japanese air force. il Time 93:82 My 2 '69

Maine

Trying to save Maine; mission of the Maine times. il Time 94:72+ O 31 '69

Russia

Notes from the underground; Chronicle of current events. il Time 94:41-2 N 28 '69

United States

Admen groove on underground; in tabloids, the record industry has found a new advertising channel. il Bsns W p84-6 Ap 12 '69

Case for advocacy journalism. D. Deitch. Nation 209:530-2 N 17 '69

Mirror of the news and the big brother. R. L. Tobin. Sat R 52:59-60 D 13 '69

Newspapers' death held exaggerated. il Forbes 104:30-2+ O 1 '69

Public regulation and the news media. J. McLaughlin. America 121:586-9 D 13 '69

Tribe is restless; rebellion at underground newspaper, the Berkeley Barb. il Time 94: 46 Jl 18 '69

Underground press: symposium. il Wilson Lib Bul 43:640-56 Mr '69

Weekly and suburban press. C. E. Carlson. Writers Digest 49:60-2 Ap '69

See also

Negro press

also names of newspapers, e.g. New York times; *also* subhead Newspapers under names of cities, e.g. New Orleans—Newspapers

NEWSPAPERS, Childrens. See Childrens newspapers

NEWSPAPERS, Immoral. See Immoral literature and pictures

NEWSPAPERS, Publishing of. See Newspaper publishers and publishing

NEWSPAPERS, Ship. See Ship publications

NEWSPAPERS, Student. See College and school journalism

NEWSPAPERS and morals

See also

Newspapers—Advertising policy

NEWSPAPERS and politics

Case for advocacy journalism. D. Deitch. Nation 209:530-2 N 17 '69

NEWSPRINT industry. See Paper making and trade

NEWSREEL (organization)

Newsreel: a report. L. Braudy. Film Q 22: 48-51 Wint '68

Newsreel; comments by film-makers. il Film Q 22:43-8 Wint '68

NEWSWEEK (periodical)

Newsweek (a fact) is the new hot book (an opinion) C. Welles. Esquire 72:152-4+ N '69

NEWTON, Derek A.

Get the most out of your sales force. Harvard Bsns R 47:130-43 S '69

NEWTON, Huey P.

Black Panthers. por Ebony 24:106-8+ Ag '69

Selections from the biography of Huey P. Newton; with introd. by E. Cleaver. B. Seale; discussion. Ramp Mag 7:66+ Ap '69

NEWTON, Sir Isaac

Portrait of Isaac Newton, by F. E. Manuel. Review

Sat R por 52:32 F 1 '69. P. Gay

NEWTON, John

Prerequisites for preaching. J. D. R. Franklin. Chr Today 13:15 Ja 31 '69

NEWTON, Richard F.

Trustees: a look at some bureaucratic models. bibliog Sch & Soc 97:433-4 N '69

NEWTON, Robert R.

Secular accelerations of the earth and moon. bibliog Science 166:825-31 N 14 '69

NEWTON, Stella Mary

Mrs Delany and her handiwork. Antiques 96: 100-5 Jl '69

NEWTON, Mass.

Education

Newton school-lunch caper. S. Hartman. Mc-Calls 96:88+ S '69

Teaching man to children. il Time 95:50 Ja 19 '70

NEXT; drama. See McNally, T.

NEXT stop, spring! drama. See Boiko, C.

NEY, E. P. See Allen, D. A. jt. auth.

NEYMAN, Jerzy, and others

Areal spread of the effect of cloud seeding at the Whitetop experiment. bibliog Science 163:1445-9 Mr 28 '69

N'GAMILAND. See Botswana

NGO-dinh-Diem

Hang down your head, Tom Dooley. R. Scheer. il Ramp Mag 7:15-19 Ja 25 '69

University on the make; or, How MSU helped arm Madame Nhu; with introd. by S. K. Sheinbaum. W. Hinckle and others. il Ramp Mag 7:52-60 Ja 25 '69

Vietnam lobby. R. Scheer and W. Hinckle. Ramp Mag 7:31-6 Ja 25 '69

NGUYEN-cao-Ky

When war will end for U.S; interview, ed. by W. S. Merick. por U S News 67:58-61 O 13 '69

NGUYEN-huu-Chi

Negotiations or surrender? address, January 30, 1969. Vital Speeches 35:318-20 Mr 1 '69

NGUYEN-huu-Tho

Talk with the NLF leader; interview, ed. by M. Riboud. por Newsweek 74:33F O 20 '69

NGUYEN Lau

Dissident intellectuals. il por Time 94:41-2 Jl 18 '69

NGUYEN-van-Minh, pseud.

Jail notes of a young Vietnamese; tr. by D. Marr. Nation 208:359-62 Mr 24 '69

NGUYEN-van-Thieu

Mr Thieu has his day; excerpts from interview. Newsweek 75:64 Ja 5 '70

President Nixon and President Thieu confer at Midway Island; exchange of remarks, June 8, 1969. Dept State Bul 60:550-3 Je 30 '69

Thieu: determined and defiant; interview, ed. by M. Clark. Time 94:13 O 3 '69

—See Nixon, R. M. jt. auth.

about

Back to square one? M. Parker. il por Newsweek 73:58+ My 5 '69

Chances now for peace. il por U S News 66: 25-7 Je 2 '69

Diemist restoration. D. G. Porter. Commonweal 90:435-7 Jl 11 '69

No one can be sure what Thieu is thinking. K. P. Buckley. il pors N Y Times Mag p28-9+ Mr 2 '69

On the tightrope. il por Newsweek 74:21 Jl 7 '69

President Nixon hails Saigon proposals for political settlement in South Viet-Nam; statement. July 11, 1969. R. M. Nixon. Dept State Bul 61:61-2 Jl 28 '69

Seizing the initiative. Newsweek 73:49 Je 30 '69

Sigh of relief in Saigon. il por Time 94:29-30 N 14 '69

Strategy and tactics of peace in Viet Nam. il por Time 93:18-20+ Mr 28 '69

Thieu faces the kindergarten. il por Time 95:20 Ja 12 '70

Thieu-ing the loyal opposition. T. Fox. Commonweal 90:459-62 Jl 26 '69

Things worth doing. Newsweek 75:30 Ja 5 '70

War problems deepen as Nixon heads for Midway. il U S News 66:25-6 Je 9 '69

Word was never; South Korea visit. Newsweek 73:45-6 Je 9 '69

See also

Midway conference, 1969

NIAGARA FALLS

New look for an old landmark. il U S News 66:12 Je 23 '69

Senate approval asked of agreement for diversions from Niagara River; message to the Senate, April 14, 1969. R. M. Nixon. Dept State Bul 60:408 My 12 '69

U.S, Canada conclude agreements on Niagara Falls beautification; Department announcement; with exchange of notes, March 21, 1969. Dept State Bul 60:345-7 Ap 21 '69

Why they turned off Niagara's American Falls. W. S. Bacon. il Pop Sci 195:84-5+ Ag '69

NIARCHOS, Charlotte (Ford) See Ford, C.

NIARCHOS, Stavros Spyros

Charlotte: the latest model Ford. H. Ehrlich. il Look 33:62-6+ Ag 12 '69

The other Greek; with photographs by P. Boulat. il pors Life 66:58-65 Mr 28 '69

Shipping titans lock in battle. il por Bsns W p51 Jl 12 '69

When giants clash. Time 93:86 Mr 21 '69

NIBLACK, Walter K. and Levi, C. A.

Microwave power diodes. pors Electr World 82:49-53 Jl '69

NICHOLAS, Saint

See also

Santa Claus

NICHOLAS, Fayard

Dancers go dramatic. il pors Ebony 24:38-40+ S '69

NICHOLAS, George P.

Guppies the amazing millions fish. Sci Digest 65:73 My '69

NICHOLAS, Herb

How the designer helped an author-publisher. S. Salter. Pub W 195:98-9 F 3 '69

NICHOLS, Louis B.

Battle against vote fraud. Read Digest 95: 37-43 Jl '69; Same. U S News 67:72-4 Ag 25 '69

NICHOLS, Mike

There's a catch: Catch-22. R. A. Sokolov. il por Newsweek 73:52-5 Mr 3 '69

Yossarian is alive and well in the Mexican desert. N. Ephron. il pors N Y Times Mag p30-1+ Mr 16 '69

NICHOLSON, J. B.

ABCs of servicing a motorbike. Mech Illus 65:64-6+ Jl '69

NICHOLSON, Jessie

Conversation piece; drama. Plays 28:1-12 My '69

Handwriting on the wall; drama. Plays 28: 51-62 F '69

NICHOLSON, Mary Ann

Ben Franklin plays cupid; drama. Plays 28: 63-7 My '69

NICKEL

See also

International nickel company of Canada

Isotopes

Nickel-63 in marine and terrestrial biota, soil, and sediment. T. M. Beasley and E. E. Held. bibliog il Science 164:1161-3 Je 6 '69

Prices

Still betting on the spiral; price increase. Time 94:100 D 5 '69

NICKEL industry and trade

Big nickel shortage. il Time 94:89 N 21 '69

Nickel starvation brings the jitters. il Bsns W p42+ O 25 '69

Securities

Poseidon craze. Newsweek 74:51-2 D 29 '69

NICKEL mines and mining

Australia

Poseidon craze. Newsweek 74:51-2 D 29 '69

NICKEL strikes (Canada) See Strikes—Canada

NICKLAUS, Jack

Golf. See issues of Sports illustrated

about

Couple of hips, one hurrah. A. Wright. il por Sports Illus 31:70-1+ O 27 '69

Jack's course is Arnie's, too. D. Jenkins. il por Sports Illus 31:24-7 D 8 '69

Polite no from Arnie and Jack. W. Johnson. il por Sports Illus 30:34-5 Ap 14 '69

Trades becalm skinny Jack. M. Mulvoy. il por Sports Illus 31:42-3 N 17 '69

What has gone wrong, Jack? M. Mulvoy. por Sports Illus 30:24-5 My 19 '69

NICKLE, Suzanne

Ceramic necklaces. Ceram Mo 17:16-17 Je '69

NICOLL, Bruce H.

New, critical look at scholarly paperbacks; excerpt from address, June 23, 1969. por Pub W 196-34-5 Jl 28 '69

NICOTINAMIDE adenine dinucleotide phosphate. See Nicotinamide nucleotides

NICOTINAMIDE nucleotides

Enzymatic mechanism of steroid hydroxylation. C. J. Sih. bibliog il Science 163:1297-300 Mr 21 '69

NICOTINE

Nicotine hydrogen tartrate: effect on essential fatty acid deficiency in mature pigs. W. R. Allt and others. bibliog il Science 163:391 Ja 24 '69

NIDDRIE, David L.

Letter from Angola. Nat R 21:1064-5+ O 21 '69

NIDETCH, Jean

High priestess of the weight watchers. L. Botto. il pors Look 33:82-4+ My 27 '69

NIDORF, Patrick X.

Stoneware medallions. Ceram Mo 17:26-7 F '69

NIEBUHR, Helmut Richard

American academy of theology. Chr Cent 86: 395 Mr 26 '69

NIEBUHR, Reinhold

Toward new intra-Christian endeavors. por Chr Cent 86:1662-7 D 31 '69

NIEBURG, H. L.

Living with violent change; excerpts from Political violence. Cur 112:36-42 N '69

NIEDZ, Franklin J.

1968 lilac survey. Horticulture 47:42-4 My '69

NIEHAUS, Stanley W.

Anatomy of loyalty. Clear House 43:283-7 Ja '69

NIEHUIS, Charles C.

Stripers in the Big Red. Field & S 73:68-9+ Ap '69

We were in velvet. Outdoor Life 144:52-5+ Jl '69

NIEKRO, Phil

Atlanta tranquillity base here. R. Blount, jr. il por Sports Illus 31:46-9 Ag 4 '69

NIELSEN, A. C, company

Putting a measure on the market. il Bsns W p 104+ Ja 25 '69

NIELSEN, Bodil Schmidt-. See Schmidt-Nielsen, B.

NIELSEN, Carl

Wild romantics. Discus. Harper 238:103 Je '69

NIELSEN, Knut Schmidt-. See Schmidt-Nielsen, K.

NIELSEN, Niels C. and Fleischer, Sidney

β-Hydroxybutyrate dehydrogenase: lack in ruminant liver mitochondria. bibliog Science 166:1017-19 N 21 '69

NIELSEN, Waldemar August

United States and the challenge of Africa's development; statement, February 6, 1969 Dept State Bul 60:292-4 Ap 7 '69

NIEREMBERGIA. See Cupflowers
NIETZSCHE, Friedrich Wilhelm
Nietzsche in his letters. W. J. Dannhauser.
Commentary 48:86-93 D '69
NIGER
Unknown Niger. R. Harrington. il Travel 132:
46-9 N '69
  See also
Missions—Niger
NIGER RIVER
Bend of the Niger River. M. Mangus. il
Natur Hist 78:26-37 Ja '69
NIGERIA
  See also
Education—Nigeria

Civil war, 1967-
At the Umuapu front. G. Nnadi. il Newsweek
74:44+ Jl 21 '69
Attack on a village. J. Wilde. Time 93:36
Ap 4 '69
Backs to the wall. il Newsweek 74:68+ D 8
'69
Biafra has oil as well as starving children. S.
Jervis. New Repub 160:8-10 My 1; Discussion. 160:28+ Mr 22; 30-1 Ap 5 '69
Biafran tragedy. J. Deedy. Commonweal 90:
378 Je 20 '69
Challenge of Biafra. Commonweal 90:451-2 Jl
25 '69
Difficult choice; conflict between tribalism
and nationalism. P. Webb. il Newsweek 74:
52-3 N 3 '69
End the Nigeria-Biafra tragedy. America 120:
267 Mr 8 '69
End to a journey and an end to flight; interview, ed. by M. Kupfer and D. Robison. C.
O. Ojukwu. Newsweek 73:55 Mr 24 '69
Grim anniversary. Time 94:30+ Jl 4 '69
Inch by inch. Newsweek 73:56 My 5 '69
Letter from Biafra. R. Adler. il New Yorker
45:47-8+ O 4 '69
Moon over Biafra; a plea for priorities. S.
V. Roberts. Commonweal 89:489-90 Ja 17
'69
Nigeria-Biafra; a matter of accommodation.
J. McLaughlin. America 120:162-7 F 8 '69
Nigeria-Biafra military see-saw. America 120:
553 My 10 '69
Nigerian impasse. J. D. Chick. bibliog f
Cur Hist 56:292-7+ My '69
No reason to negotiate. Newsweek 75:45-6 Ja
19 '70
Odumegwu Ojukwu is Biafra. L. Garrison.
il N Y Times Mag p7-9+ Je 22 '69
Perspective on Nigeria. G. Arthur. America
120:221-5 F 22 '69
President Johnson joins appeal for holiday
truce in Nigeria; statement, December 21,
1968. L. B. Johnson. Dept State Bul 60:3
Ja 6 '69
Report from Biafra. J. McLaughlin. America 120:90-5 Ja 25 '69
Reports: Nigeria and Biafra. S. Meisler. Atlan 224:25-6+ O '69
Resurrection of Biafra. il Newsweek 73:50+
Mr 24 '69
Time for action on Biafra! E. M. Kennedy;
D. Lukens. Read Digest 94:75-9 My '69
Tragedy of Nigeria; address, December 3,
1968. N. deB. Katzenbach. Dept State Bul
59:653-8 D 23 '68
What hope in Nigeria? N. Cousins. Sat R 52:
16-17 Ag 16 '69

Aerial operations
How to build an instant air force; use of
Swedish single-engine aircraft, MFI-9B. il
Time 93:38 Je 6 '69
Operation Biafra baby. il Newsweek 73:60
Je 9 '69
Tragedy in the villages: air attacks on an
unarmed civilian population. il Time 93:37-
8 Mr 7 '69

Campaigns and battles
Closing the ring. il Newsweek 73:59 Ap 28
'69

Equipment and supplies
Cash and cocoa; Russian-made aircraft. Nation 208:357 Mr 24 '69

Peace and mediation
Britain's Wilson: peace envoy to a deadlocked
African war. U S News 66:16 Mr 31 '69
Elements of a Nigerian peace. J. C. McKenna. For Affairs 47:668-80 Jl '69
Look around; H. Wilson visit. Newsweek
73:42+ Ap 7 '69
Nigeria-Biafra talks collapse. America 120:
519 My 3 '69
One small step. il Newsweek 74:52 S 22 '69
Twin stalemates; H. Wilson's visit to Nigeria. il Time 93:36-7 Ap 4 '69

Propaganda
Biafra: war of images. S. Meisler. Nation 208:
301-4 Mr 10 '69

Relief work
Biafra and the American conscience. C. E.
Goodell. il Sat R 52:24-7+ Ap 12 '69
Biafran tragedy; Father Doran and relief
teams J. Deedy. Commonweal 90:378 Je 20
'69
Come on down and get killed; Biafra airlift.
il Time 93:32 Mr 21 '69
Conscience is his co-pilot; story of Count C.
G. von Rosen. il Read Digest 95:207-8+ D
'69
Department reviews U.S. efforts to aid victims of the Nigerian civil war; statements,
July 15, 1969. E. L. Richardson and C. C.
Ferguson, jr. Dept State Bul 61:94-100 Ag
4 '69
Left and right, young and old; United States
response to Biafra's plight. il Newsweek 73:
56 Mr 24 '69
Nigerian relief effort improved by agreement on new surface route; statement,
June 18, 1969. C. C. Ferguson, jr. Dept
State Bul 61:14 Jl 7 '69
Red cross insulted; ICRC plane shot down
by Nigerian government. America 121:27-8
Jl 19 '69
Relief flights into Biafra. America 121:4 Jl 5
'69
Secretary reports on U.S. efforts to help Nifería civil war victims; statement, November 12, 1969. W. P. Rogers. Dept State
Bul 61:469-70 D 1 '69
Special U.S. coordinator appointed for Nigerian relief efforts; statement. R. M.
Nixon. Dept State Bul 60:222-3 Mr 17 '69
Ultimate weapon; tightening of regulations
against relief organizations. il Newsweek
74:36 Jl 14 '69
U.S. makes new contribution to ICRC for
Nigerian relief operations. Dept State Bul
60:510 Je 16 '69
U.S. planes available to assist relief efforts in
Nigeria; Department announcement, December 27, with statement December 31,
1968. Dept State Bul 60:30-1 Ja 13 '69
U.S. pledges additional $6 million to ICRC
for Nigerian relief. Dept State Bul 60:281
Mr 31 '69
U.S. regrets Nigerian attack on relief flights
into Biafra; Department statement, June
6, 1969. Dept State Bul 60:556 Je 30 '69
U.S. seeks resumption of relief to victims of
Nigerian civil war; statement, July 2, 1969.
W. P. Rogers. Dept State Bul 61:51-2 Jl 21
'69
U.S. urges Nigerian cooperation in relief efforts; statements, December 5 and 6, 1968.
R. J. McCloskey. Dept State Bul 59:658 D
23 '68

War correspondents
More than a name; grandson of Sir Winston writes articles on the Nigerian war. il
Time 93:56 Ap 4 '69

Economic conditions
New country on the rise despite civil war.
il U S News 66:32-4 Je 16 '69
  See also
Nigeria—Industries

Industries
Oh, what a lovely war! il Newsweek 74:81-
2+ S 15 '69

Kings and rulers
Keeping one's head; controversy swirling
around king of the Jukuns reign. Newsweek
74:33 D 29 '69

Native races
Breaking the Nigeria+Biafra deadlock. C.
Legum. America 120:624-7 My 24 '69 (to be
cont)
Nigeria-Biafra: a matter of accommodation.
J. McLaughlin. America 120:162-7 F 8 '69
Perspective on Nigeria. G. Arthur. America
120:221-5 F 22 '69
Report from Biafra. J. McLaughlin. America
120:90-5 Ja 25 '69
Resurrection of Biafra; grim determination of
the Ibo tribe. il Newsweek 73:50+ Mr 24 '69

Politics and government
Breaking the Nigeria-Biafra deadlock. C.
Legum. America 120:624-7 My 24 '69 (to
be cont)
Building new nations; self-determination for
whom? C. Legum. Cur 107:24-6 My '69
New country on the rise despite civil war.
il U S News 66:32-4 Je 16 '69

NIGERIA—Politics and government—*Cont.*
Nigerian impasse. J. D. Chick. bibliog f Cur Hist 56:292-7+ My '69
Perspective on Nigeria. G. Arthur. America 120:221-5 F 22 '69

Religious institutions and affairs

World around us. Chr Cent 86:1177-9 S 10 '69
NIGERIAN teachers in the United States. See Foreign teachers in the United States
NIGHT animals. See Animals—Habits and behavior
NIGHT before the wedding; novel. See Gordon, M. and Gordon, G.
NIGHT clubs
Go-goville, N.Y; beautiful people retreating to privacy of membership clubs. il Newsweek 73:62 Mr 3 '69
Hangouts, U.S.A. il Mlle 70:158-9, 243 N '69
Home of the twist; New York's Peppermint lounge. il Newsweek 73:26 My 26 '69
Pubbing and clubbing. Sat R 52:74-6 F 15 '69
Teetotal nightclub where personal experience is all; Cerebrum, a cabaret for the mind. il Life 66:28-9 Ap 4 '69
Where are they now? The topless craze. il Newsweek 73:10 Mr 3 '69
Young places; New York. S. Weidel. il Travel & Camera 32:30+ S '69

Japan

Red-hot mama-san; Japan's cabaret hostesses. il Newsweek 74:123-4 O 27 '69
Where have all the geisha gone? C. Lucas. il Read Digest 94:39-40+ Mr '69

Puerto Rico

Puerto Rico; San Juan night life. il Travel 131:32-3+ Ap '69
NIGHT crawlers. See Earthworms
NIGHT driver; story. See Calvino, I.
NIGHT flying. See Aviation—Night flying
NIGHT insects. See Insects
NIGHT photography. See Photography, Night
NIGHTCLUBS. See Night clubs
NIGHTMARES. See Dreams
NIGHTS at O'Rear's; story. See Griffith, P. B.
NIHILISM
See also
Russia—History—19th century
NIIJIMA, A.
Afferent discharges from osmoreceptors in the liver of the guinea pig. Science 166: 1519-20 D 19 '69
NIILUS, Leopoldo Juan
World council names Niilus as international affairs director. Chr Cent 86:368 Mr 19 '69
NIKKI for a couple of months; story. See Elliott, G. P.
NIKOLAIS, Alwin
Globolinks' friend; interview, ed. by F. Rizzo. por Opera N 34:17 D 20 '69
NIKOLAIS, Alwin, dance company. See Dance companies
NILE RIVER
See also
Aswan High Dam
NILL, Carol
Viewpoint. Library J 94:729 F 15 '69
NILSSON, Birgit
My gypsy record collection. por Hi Fi 19: 22+ Jl '69
about
Bye-bye Brünnhilde. il por Time 93:77 Mr 21 '69
NILSSON, Lennart
Worlds within us; photographs. Life 68:40-56 Ja 9 '70
NIMBUS (satellite) See Artificial satellites—Meteorological applications
NIMS, John Frederick
(tr) See Bernart de Ventadorn. Era-m cosselhatz
about
Cheers of John Nims. J. Ciardi. Sat R 52:52 S 20 '69
NIMWES, Chutomu
Trust Territory of the Pacific Islands; statement, June 6, 1969. Dept State Bul 61:230-1 S 8 '69

NINETEEN hundred and fifties
In defense of the fifties. J. Mander. Commentary 48:63-7 S '69; Reply with rejoinder. A. M. Lahr. 48:10+ D '69
Up from silence; protest groups at Cornell. S. Brownmiller. il Esquire 71:100-4+ Mr '69

NINETEEN hundred and nine
Let's bring back 1909! R. S. Aldrich. Sat R 52:10 S 13 '69
NINETEEN hundred and seventies
Challenge of the seventies; thoughts of distinguished Americans. Esquire 72:8+ D '69
Forecasting the seventies. J. Tebbel. il Sat R 52:80-1 N 8 '69
From the '60s to the '70s: dissent and discovery. il Time 94:20-6 D 19 '69
Hope for the '70s; forecast by the economist of London. K. Crawford. Newsweek 75:24 Ja 19 '70
Into the seventies. il Harp Baz 103:141 Ja '70
Look at the 1970s. il U S News 67:90-3 D 15 '69
Nearsighted foresight; libraries. J. Berry, 3d, and others. Library J 95:17 Ja 1 '70
1970s: looking ahead; symposium. America 122:3-27 Ja 10 '70
Seventies: super but seething; with editorial comment. il Bsns W p76-7+, 214 D 6 '69
The 70's: what's coming in business, politics, labor and international affairs; symposium. il Nations Bsns 57:27-38+ N '69
Soar into the 70's. Seventeen 29:48-9 Ja '70
Young churchmen eye the seventies; symposium. il Chr Today 14:24-30 Ja 2 '70
NINETEEN hundred and seventy
As the new year moves in—. U S News 68: 17 Ja 5 '70

Anecdotes, facetiae, satire, etc.

Here it comes. Nat R 21:1308 D 30 '69
Reading the tea leaves: what will happen in 1970. L. Bergman. il N Y Times Mag p8-10+ D 28 '69
NINETEEN hundred and seventy-six
1976: agenda for tomorrow, by S. Udall. Review
Am For 75:38-9 Ja '69. M. Bush

Anecdotes, facetiae, satire, etc.

Who says a good newspaper has to be dull? il Esquire 72:200-8 D '69
NINETEEN hundred and sixties
Between despair and distracted joy. Chr Cent 86:1657 D 31 '69
Decade of the sixties. il Harp Baz 103:124-5 Ja '70
Decoding the decade, paying the bills. P. Steinfels. Commonweal 91:399 Ja 9 '70
Editor's choice; last corner. G. R. Shields. ALA Bul 63:1521 D '69
End of a year, end of a decade. America 121: 628 D 27 '69
Farewell to the sixties. Chr Today 14:21 D 19 '69
Farewell to the 60s. D. Halberstam. il McCalls 97:85-92 Ja '70
From the '60s to the '70s; dissent and discovery. il Time 94:20-6 D 19 '69
It can't happen here. Harp Baz 103:140 Ja '70
Nineteen-sixties: a not so fond farewell; poem. J. Walsh. Science 166:1605 D 26 '69
Notes and comment. New Yorker 45:19 Ja 3 '70
Religion: at sixes and sevens in the sixties and seventies. Chr Today 14:36-8 Ja 2 '70
The sixties. Nation 210:2-3 Ja 12 '70
Sixties. K. Auchincloss. il Newsweek 74:12-19 D 29 '69
The sixties: a cultural revolution. B. DeMott. il N Y Times Mag p28-31+ D 14 '69
'60s are dead Long live the '50s! D. Morris. Commonweal 91:372-3 D 26 '69
'60s: decade of tumult and change. il Life 67:8-9+ D 26 '69
'60s: story of an awesome decade. il U S News 68:66-9 Ja 12 '70
Sixties; symposium, ed. by P. Coffin and A. Hurlburt. bibliog il Look 33:10, 12-32+ D 30 '69
The sixties: this slum of a decade. R. H. Rovere. il N Y Times Mag p25-7+ D 14 '69
Souvenir for history; quotations. Harp Baz 103:138-9 Ja '70
Trivial trends that point the way. il Life 68: 78-81+ Ja 9 '70
Young and crazy years. G. Guinness. Harp Baz 103:124-5 D '69
NINETEEN hundred and sixty-eight
Apologia. il Ramp Mag 7:2-4 Ja 25 '69
Esquire's eighth annual dubious achievement awards. il Esquire 71:53-61 Ja '69
News pictures of the year: 1968 in review M. R. Weiss. il Sat R 52:122-3 Mr 8 '69
NINETEEN hundred and sixty-nine
Annual progress report: 1969; a year of marking time. il Ebony 25:103-6+ Ja '70
Esquire's ninth annual dubiuos achievement awards. il Esquire 73:103-11 Ja '70

NINETEEN hundred and thirties
'30s: appearance and reality. G. Frazier. 4th; H. Calisher. Mlle 69:168-9+ My '69
'30s spotting: where to see the thirties. il Mlle 69:170-1 My '69

1930 Olympics; story. See Mountzoures, H. L.

NISEI. See Japanese Americans

NISHIZUKA, Yasuaki, and Sakakura, Teruyo
Thymus and reproduction: sex-linked dysgenesia of the gonad after neonatal thymectomy in mice. bibliog Science 166:753-5 N 7 '69

NISSEN, Hans Ude
Crystal orientation and plate structure in echinoid skeletal units. bibliog Science 166: 1150-2 N 28 '69

NISSENSON, Hugh
In the reign of peace; story. Harper 239:63-5 Jl '69

NISSINEN, Mauno
At the finish first is Finnish. D. Levin. il por Sports Illus 30:92-5 Ap 14 '69

NITECKI, Joseph Z.
Speed cataloging; prudence and pitfalls. por Library J 94:1417-21 Ap 1 '69

NITRATE reductase. See Reductases

NITRATES
Pollution by fertilizer. Sci Am 220:48 Mr '69
Sweetclover-weevil feeding deterrent B: isolation and identification. W. R. Akeson and others. bibliog il Science 163:293-4 Ja 17 '69
See also
Water supply—Nitrogen content

NITRIFICATION
Nitrification: importance to nutrient losses from a cutover forested ecosystem. G. E. Likens and others. bibliog il Science 163: 1205-6 Mr 14 '69

NITROCELLULOSE
Particle track enhancement in cellulose nitrate by application of an electric field. H. Crannell and others. bibliog il Science 166: 606-7 O 31 '69

NITROGEN
Nitrogen abundances in chondritic meteorites. C. B. Moore and E. K. Gibson. bibliog il Science 163:174-6 Ja 10 '69
See also
Nitrification
Water supply—Nitrogen content

Fixation
Nitrogen fixation by gloeocapsa. J. T. Wyatt and J. K. G. Silvey. bibliog il Science 165: 908-9 Ag 29 '69
Nitrogen fixation in some anoxic lacustrine environments. P. L. Brezonik and C. L. Harper. bibliog il Science 164:1277-9 Je 13 '69

NITROGEN fixation. See Nitrogen—Fixation

NITROGEN oxides
Auto men gasp in the smog. il Bsns W p76+ N 1 '69
In the news; favorite oxidizer, nitrogen tetroxide. Space World F-5-65:41 My '69

NITROGEN tetroxide. See Nitrogen oxides

NITSCHKE, Robert A.
Peach George IV. Horticulture 47:32-3+ O '69

NIXIE tubes. See Vacuum tubes

NIXON, Edward C.
Kid brother. Newsweek 73:37 Ap 21 '69
Rules on relatives; who can be hired for a U.S. job? por U S News 66:45 Ap 21 '69

NIXON, John, Jr
World is an Janus-women; poem. Mlle 69:144 My '69

NIXON, Patricia (Ryan)
Mrs Nixon tells how she brought up Tricia and Julie; interview; ed. by T. B. Feldman. pors McCalls 96:74-5+ Mr '69
Pat Nixon, her first year as First lady; interview. ed. by H. Thomas. por U S News 67:13 D 22 '69
Power of a woman. Ladies Home J 86:93 S '69

about
Boosting volunteerism; four-day journey to publicize ten volunteer self-help projects on the West coast. il por Time 93:19 Je 27 '69
Compassion power. L. Hershey. il pors Ladies Home J 86:88+ S '69
First lady in the war zone. il por U S News 67:14 Ag 11 '69
First Lady with a style all her own. il pors U S News 66:17 Je 2 '69
House and home. il por Newsweek 73:22-3 F 3 '69

Let's travel: with Mrs Nixon and Julie. F. Koltun. il pors Mlle 69:110-11 S '69
Mrs Richard Milhous Nixon the First Lady; with photograph by Horst. il Vogue 153: 158-9 My '69
Pat's wardrobe mistress. il pors Time 95:28 Ja 12 '70
Redoing Pat; U.S. designers create wardrobe for new First Lady. il Time 93:56 Ja 24 '69
Traveling with Pat Nixon a different type of tour; volunteer projects in Oregon and California. il pors U S News 66:9 Je 30 '69
Women's rights a la Pat Nixon. il U S News 66:18 My 19 '69

NIXON, Richard Milhous
Ambassador Lodge discusses the Paris peace talks; remarks. May 15, 1969. Dept State Bul 60:465 Je 2 '69
America's role in the world; address, June 4, 1969. Vital Speeches 35:548-50 Jl 1 '69; Same. Dept State Bul 60:525-8 Je 23 '69; Excerpts. U S News 66:64-6 Je 16 '69
Broadcasting agreements with Mexico transmitted to the Senate; message, March 25, 1969. Dept State Bul 60:330 Ap 14 '69
Campus revolutionaries; the rights of students; address, June 3, 1969. Vital Speeches 35:546-8 Jl 1 '69; Excerpts. U S News 66: 66-7 Je 16 '69
Challenges of the third 100 million; message to Congress, July 18, 1969. U S News 68:34 Ja 12 '70
Defending the defenders; summary of address at U.S. air force academy. por Time 93:15 Je 13 '69
Draft, taxes, crime, welfare; Nixon asks for action now; text of message to Congress, October 13, 1969. por U S News 67:91-4 O 20 '69
Dwight David Eisenhower; eulogy, March 30, 1969. Vital Speeches 35:386-7 Ap 15 '69; Same abr. with title He came from the heart of America. Read Digest 94:87-90 Je '69
Emperor Haile Selassie of Ethiopia visits the United States as guest of President Nixon; exchange of greetings, toasts and remarks, July 8 and 9, 1969. Dept State Bul 61:86-91 Ag 4 '69
Exchange of toasts; May 6, 1969. Nat R 21: 472+ My 20 '69
Final report submitted on observance of Human rights year 1968; letter, April 29, 1969. Dept State Bul 60:450 My 26 '69
Food for peace report for 1968 transmitted to the Congress; message, April 22, 1969. Dept State Bul 60:547 Je 23 '69
Food, nutrition and health; address, December 2, 1969. Vital Speeches 36:162-5 J 1 '70
Foreign aid program for fiscal year 1970: new directions in foreign aid; message to Congress, May 28, 1969. Dept State Bul 60: 515-19 Je 16 '69
Governor Rockefeller reports on mission to Latin America; text of letter from President Nixon to Governor Nelson A. Rockefeller; September 3, 1969. Dept State Bul 61: 303-4 O 6 '69
Growing menace of drugs, Nixon's plan to fight it; message, July 14, 1969. U S News 67:60-2 Jl 28 '69
Inaugural address of President Nixon; January 20, 1969. por U S News 66:78-9 F 3 '69; Same. Vital Speeches 35:226-8 F 1 '69; Dept State Bul 60:121-3 F 10 '69; Cong Digest 48: 65-6+ Mr '69; Excerpts. PTA Mag 63:15 F '69; Life 66:20-9 Ja 31 '69
Interoceanic canal study commission submits fifth annual report; text of letter, August 6, 1969. Dept State Bul 61:218 S 8 '69
King Hussein I of Jordan visits Washington; exchange of greetings, April 8, 1969. Dept State Bul 60:364 Ap 28 '69
Lack of progress? summary of address, April 1969. Sr Schol 94:20 My 2 '69
Launching a new diplomacy: Nixon's report to the Nation; text of news conference, March 4, 1969. pors U S News 66:70-6 Mr 17 '69; Same with title President Nixon's news conference of March 4. Dept State Bul 60:237-47 Mr 24 '69
Meaning of Midway; statement. June 10, 1969. U S News 66:29 Je 23 '69
Nation's needs as Nixon sees them; text of message to Congress, April 14, 1969. por U S News 66:76-8 Ap 28 '69
Nelson Rockefeller begins mission to Latin America; remarks to news correspondents, May 11, 1969. Dept State Bul 60:470 Je 2 '69
New approach to Pan American problems; remarks, April 14, 1969. Dept State Bul 60:384-6 My 5 '69

NIXON, Richard Milhous—*Continued*
New theme: Action for progress; address, October 31, 1969; with introduction. por U S News 67:104-7 N 10 '69; Same. Dept State Bul 61:409-14 N 17 '69; Same abr. with title Action for progress. Vital Speeches 36: 70-3 N 15 '69

Nixon backs space future; excerpts from address. Aviation W 91:11 D 1 '69

Nixon: it is my duty; text of statement on the ABM program, March 14, 1969. U S News 66:39-40 Mr 24 '69; Same with title President Nixon modifies ballistic missile defense system. Dept State Bul 60:273-5 Mr 31 '69

Nixon on war: a plan and a warning; address, November 3, 1969. por U S News 67:110-14 N 17 '69; Same with title Vietnam plan. Vital Speeches 36:66-70 N 15 '69; Same with title Pursuit of peace in Viet-Nam. Dept State Bul 61:437-43 N 24 '69; Same with title President Nixon's statement on Vietnam, 1969. Cur Hist 58:42-6+ Ja '70

Nixon steps up his war on inflation; text of address, October 17, 1969. por U S News 67:100-2 O 27 '69

Nixon: the time has come to end this war; statement, September 16, 1969. U S News 67:32 S 29 '69

Nixon warns North Korea: U.S. flights will be protected; text of news conference, April 18, 1969. por U S News 66:72-5 Ap 28 '69

Nixon: we have to put the money where the problems are; excerpt from address, September 1, 1969. por U S News 67:82-4 S 15 '69

Nixon's blueprint for war on organized crime; excerpts from message to Congress, April 23, 1969. por U S News 66:43-4 My 5 '69

Nixon's case for tax reform; excerpts from message, April 21, 1969. U S News 66:29 My 5 '69

Nixon's four-front war on poverty; address, August 8, 1969. U S News 67:78-80 Ag 18 '69; Same. Vital Speeches 35:674-8 S 1 '69

Nixon's opening news session: Mideast. Vietnam, inflation; excerpts from news conference, January 27, 1969. por U S News 66: 55-6 F 10 '69; Same. Dept State Bul 60:141-4 F 17 '69

North Atlantic council celebrates the 20th anniversary of the signing of the North Atlantic treaty; address, April 10, 1969. Dept State Bul 60:351-4 Ap 28 '69; Same with title: NATO: the need for unity. Vital Speeches 35:418-20 My 1 '69

Only people can turn back the tide; protecting children against exposure to erotic publications; excerpts from message to Congress, May 2, 1969. U S News 67:53 Jl 21 '69

Patent and copyright conventions transmitted to the Senate; message, March 12, 1969. Dept State Bul 60:298 Ap 7 '69

President appeals to business and labor; text of letter, October 18, 1969. U S News 67:102 O 27 '69

President discusses responsibility for decisions on Viet-Nam policy; letter. Dept State Bul 61:371 N 3 '69

President explains his risks for peace; remarks, December 15, 1969. por U S News 67:15-16 D 29 '69

President hails tenth anniversary of Economic commission for Africa; text of message, February 3, 1969. Dept State Bul 60: 211 Mr 10 '69

President names Nelson Rockefeller for special mission to Latin America; statement, February 17, 1969. Dept State Bul 60:198 Mr 10 '69

President Nixon and President Diaz Ordaz of Mexico dedicate the Amistad Dam; remarks, exchange of toasts, September 8, 1969. Dept State Bul 61:277, 279-80 S 29 '69

President Nixon and President Lleras of Colombia review common goals of the Americas; exchange of greetings, toasts and remarks, June 12, 13, 1969. Dept State Bul 61: 8-9, 12 Jl 7 '69

President Nixon and President Park of the Republic of Korea hold talks at San Francisco; welcoming statement, exchange of remarks, toasts, together with joint statement, August 21 and 22, 1969. Dept State Bul 61:237-40, 243-4 S 15 '69

President Nixon and President Thieu confer at Midway Island; exchange of remarks, June 8, 1969. Dept State Bul 60:549-50, 552-3 Je 30 '69

President Nixon and Prime Minister Trudeau of Canada hold talks at Washington; exchange of greetings, toasts, March 24 and 25, 1969. Dept State Bul 60:319-23 Ap 14 '69

President Nixon and the Shah of Iran hold talks at Washington; exchange of greetings, toasts and remarks, October 21 and 23, 1969. Dept State Bul 61:396-400 N 10 '69

President Nixon calls for comprehensive efforts in multilateral disarmament negotiations; text of message, July 3, 1969. Dept State Bul 61:65-6 Jl 28 '69

President Nixon congratulates Chancellor Brandt of Germany; text of letter, October 21, 1969. Dept State Bul 61:415 N 17 '69

President Nixon discusses the objectives of his European trip; excerpts from remarks, February 21, 1969. Dept State Bul 60:217-19 Mr 17 '69

President Nixon discusses the Viet-Nam peace talks and the ABM safeguard system. remarks, March 25, 1969. Dept State Bul 60:313-16 Ap 14 '69

President Nixon extends greetings to Organization of African unity; text of message, September 6, 1969. Dept State Bul 61:280 S 29 '69

President Nixon greets leaders of People to people program; remarks, October 14, 1969. Dept State Bul 61:372-3 N 3 '69

President Nixon hails Saigon proposals for political settlement in South Viet-Nam; statement, July 11, 1969. Dept State Bul 61:61-2 Jl 28 '69

President Nixon hails sixth anniversary of Organization of African unity; remarks, May 25, 1969. Dept State Bul 60:539-40 Je 23 '69

President Nixon: intellectual freedom in danger; statement, March 23, 1969. por U S News 66:30 Mr 31 '69

President Nixon meets with Chancellor Kiesinger of the Federal Republic of Germany; exchange of greetings, remarks, together with joint statement; August 7 and 8, 1969. Dept State Bul 61:211-14 S 8 '69

President Nixon meets with foreign exchange students; remarks, July 22, 1969. Dept State Bul 61:111-13 Ag 11 '69

President Nixon meets with prime minister and foreign minister of the Netherlands; exchange of greetings, and remarks, May 27, 28, 1969. Dept State Bul 60:561-3 Je 30 '69

President Nixon reduces troop ceiling in Viet-Nam; statement, September 16, 1969. Dept State Bul 61:302 O 6 '69

President Nixon: rights of majority abused; letter to Notre Dame's president. on campus turmoil. U S News 66:11 Mr 10 '69

President Nixon sends greetings to IA-ECOSOC; June 20, 1969. Dept State Bul 61:22 Jl 14 '69

President Nixon urges Senate action on nuclear nonproliferation treaty; message to the Senate. February 5, 1969. Dept State Bul 60:162 F 24 '69

President Nixon visits the Department of state; remarks, January 29, 1969. Dept State Bul 60:168-71 F 24 '69

President Nixon's letter to President Ho Chi Minh, July 15, 1969. Dept State Bul 61:443 N 24 '69

President Nixon's news conference:
March 14, 1969. Dept State Bul 60:275-80 Mr 31 '69
April 18, 1969. Dept State Bul 60:377-81 My 5 '69
September 26, 1969. Dept State Bul 61:313-16 O 13 '69
September 26, 1969. pors U S News 67: 76-81 O 6 '69
December 8, 1969. pors U S News 67:48-52 D 22 '69

President on his trip to Europe: only a first step to peace; excerpts from news conference, February 6, 1969. pors U S News 66:94-5 F 17 '69; Same. Dept State Bul 60: 157-61 F 24, '69

President reaffirms interest in International Peace corps; text of letter, September 24, 1969. Dept State Bul 61:325 O 13 '69

President sends Vienna convention on consular relations to the Senate; message, May 5, 1969. Dept State Bul 60:475 Je 2 '69

President's blueprint for peace in Vietnam; address, May 14, 1969. por U S News 66: 79-82 My 26 '69; Same with title War in Vietnam. Vital Speeches 35:482-4 Je 1 '69; Same with title Peace in Viet-Nam. Dept State Bul 60:457-61 Je 2 '69

President's remarks to the North Atlantic council, February 24, 1969. Dept State Bul 60:250-2 Mr 24 '69

Prime Minister Gorton of Australia visits Washington; exchange of toasts; with remarks, May 6, 7, 1969. Dept State Bul 60: 436-9 My 26 '69

NIXON, Richard Milhous—*Continued*

Prime Minister Meir of Israel visits Washington; exchange of greetings, toasts and remarks. September 25 and 26, 1969. Dept State Bul 61:318-22 O 13 '69

Problems of population growth; message to Congress, July 18, 1969. Dept State Bul 61: 105-11 Ag 11 '69

Promises that Nixon has made; excerpts from campaign proposals. pors U S News 66:50-2 Mr 3 '69

Redefining an Alliance; summary of address. Newsweek 74:50+ N 10 '69

[Remarks and statements during visit to Asia and Rumania, July 26-August 3, 1969] Dept State Bul 61:141-76 Ag 25 '69

[Remarks on departure, and during visit to western Europe, February 23-March 2, 1969] Dept State Bul 60:249-71 Mr 24 '69

Richard Nixon on the presidency; excerpts from address, 1968. Sr Schol 94:10-11 Ja 17 '69

Senate approval asked of agreement for diversions from Niagara River; message to the Senate, April 14, 1969. Dept State Bul 60:408 My 12 '69

Senate asked to approve convention on conduct of North Atlantic fishing; message to the Senate, April 16, 1969. Dept State Bul 60:425 My 19 '69

Special U.S. coordinator appointed for Nigerian relief efforts; statement. Dept State Bul 60:222-3 Mr 17 '69

Tenth anniversary of the St Lawrence Seaway; exchange of remarks, June 27, 1969. Dept State Bul 61:67-8, 70-1 Jl 28 '69

Text of the President's statement on the Cleveland public library centennial; February 17, 1969. Wilson Lib Bul 43:733 Ap '69

Threat to American freedom? excerpts from statement. Sr Schol 94:15 Ap 11 '69

Time for a change; excerpts from message to Congress, May 27, 1969. U S News 66:44 Je 9 '69

To stop campus violence; excerpts from remarks, April 29, 1969. por U S News 66:74 My 12 '69

Toward a worldwide peace; address to U.N. September 18, 1969. por U S News 67:98-101 S 29 '69; Same with title Establishment of peace. Vital Speeches 35:738-41 O 1 '69; Same with title Strengthening the total fabric of peace. Dept State Bul 61:297-302 O 6 '69

U.S. balance of payments; statement, April 4, 1969. Dept State Bul 60:403-4 My 12 '69

U.S.-Canada flood control payment agreement transmitted to the Senate; message, October 14, 1969. Dept State Bul 61:463 N 24 '69

U.S. extends condolences on death of President Barrientos of Bolivia; text of message, April 28, 1969. Dept State Bul 60:423 My 19 '69

U.S.-Netherlands estate tax convention transmitted to the Senate; message. October 13, 1969. Dept State Bul 61:386 N 3 '69

U.S. positions at Eighteen-nation disarmament conference outlined by President Nixon; text of letter, March 15, 1969. Dept State Bul 60:289-90 Ap 7 '69

University of Minnesota band returns from tour of Soviet Union; excerpts from remarks, May 23, 1969. Dept State Bul 60: 540 Je 23 '69

We are not Democrats, or Republicans; we are Americans; excerpts from address to House of representatives, November 13, 1969. por U S News 67:68 N 24 '69

When I look at American education . . ; excerpts from statement. October 20. 1968. por Todays Ed 58:21-3 Ja '69

When Nixon talked to the Senate; excerpts from address, November 13, 1969. U S News 67:69 N 24 '69

World weather program; plan for U.S. participation; letter of transmittal, March 13, 1969. Dept State Bul 60:368 Ap 28 '69

—and Nguyen-van-Thieu

President Nixon and President Thieu confer at Midway Island; joint statement, June 8, 1969. Dept State Bul 60:550-2 Je 30 '69

about

Accelerated presidency. H. J. Sievers. America 121:450 N 15 '69

Administration: tenuous balance. il Time 94: 14-16 Jl 11 '69

Air routes: Nixon reverses Johnson. U S News 66:12 F 3 '69

Alive and well in California. il por Newsweek 74:17-18 Ag 25 '69

And, now, two peace plans. Commonweal 90:307-8 My 30 '69

Annals of politics. R. Harris. New Yorker 45:64-8+ N 15; 61-4+ N 22 '69

Answering Mr Nixon; analysis of speech on Vietnam. Nation 209:524-5 N 17 '69

At the Florida white house. il por U S News 66:35 F 24 '69

Australia looks to Nixon. J. M. Van Der Kroef. il Nat R 21:119-21 F 11 '69

Battle for the mind of Nixon. Nation 208:98-9 Ja 27 '69

Bearable burden. Time 94:17 S 26 '69

Behind all the Nixon activity. U S News 67: 10 Jl 28 '69

Behind Nixon's Vietnam stand. H. Sidey. Life 67:4 N 21 '69

Benchmarks to judge Nixon by: measuring the first six months. Life 67:30 Jo 25 '69

Bite on inflation? Sr Schol 94:17 Ap 11 '69

Brooke says no. Sr Schol 94:23-4 F 28 '69

Businessman's balance sheet on Nixon. il por Bsns W p21-2 Ag 2 '69

Campus: backbone and backlash. il por Newsweek 73:31 My 12 '69

Can Nixon's justices reverse the Warren court? F. Rodell. Look 33:38 D 2 '69

Chances now for peace. il por U S News 66:25-7 Je 2 '69

Change ahead under Nixon; with photo report. U S News 66:23-8 F 3 '69

Change in degree, not kind. America 121:452 N 15 '69

Change of heart. il Newsweek 73:33-4 My 19 '69

Changing of the guard. il pors Ebony 24:29-32+ Mr '69

Changing role of U.S. in world. por U S News 67:29-30 S 29 '69

Commander in chief reports to the nation: analysis of November 3 address. Nat R 21: 1153-4 N 18 '69

Cool and calm by the Potomac. H. J. Sievers. America 120:182 F 15 '69

Course we're on; autumnal State of the Union report. Commonweal 91:35-6 O 10 '69

Crackdown. Nation 208:587-8 My 12 '69

Crisis syndrome? character analysis by James Barber. Newsweek 74:25-6 S 15 '69

Decision on ABM. il por Newsweek 73:24-5+ Mr 24 '69

De-escalating the rhetoric. P. Schrag. Sat R 52:20 Mr 15 '69

Demonsterization of Nixon. S. Alsop. Newsweek 73:104 F 24 '69

Did Mr Nixon make his job harder? Life 67: 44 N 14 '69

Do Republicans have the courage to become the majority party? O. R. Reid. Look 33: 76+ My 13 '69

Doubts about Vietnamization; messages of December 8 and 15, 1969. J. Osborne. New Repub 162:11-12 Ja 3 '70

Down-to-work week of Richard Nixon. U S News 67:8 O 6 '69

Duke's party; White House celebration for D. Ellington. New Yorker 45:31-3 My 10 '69

Each day like another town. Time 93:21 Mr 14 '69

Early bedtime at Blair house; P. Trudeau's two-day visit. H. Sidey. il por Life 66:4 Ap 4 '69

Economy: what will Nixon do? G. L. Perry. il New Repub 160:19-31 Je 14 '69

Elm street's new White House power. A. J. Reichley. il Fortune 80:70-3+ D '69

Encouraging words before Tet. il Newsweek 74:35 D 29 '69

Enter: the Nixon era. il pors Sr Schol 94: 6-7+ Ja 17 '69

Exercise in restraint; EC-121 incident. il por Newsweek 73:27-9+ Ap 28 '69

Eyeball to eyeball with the monster. H. Sidey. il por Life 66:4 My 23 '69

Fan dance. Nation 209:236-7 S 15 '69

First hundred days of Richard M. Nixon. T. C. Sorensen. il Sat R 52:17-19 My 17 '69

First two months: between brake and accelerator. il por Time 93:10-11 Mr 28 '69

First weeks: a sense of inner direction. il pors Time 93:13-14 F 7 '69

536 characters in search of a legislative program. A. Blaustein. Harper 238:28+ Mr '69

For the young and for the old. il por Newsweek 74:34 S 29 '69

For want of a program. Commonweal 89: 607-8 F 14 '69

Germ warfare and the arms race. N. Cousins. Sat R 52:26 D 13 '69

Headless phantom, boneless wonder. New Repub 161:7-8 Ag 9 '69

Homing in on domestic programs; with editorial comment. il por Bsns W p36-8, 130 Ag 16 '69

Hopes and fears. G. W. Johnson. New Repub 160:14 F 1 '69

NIXON, Richard Milhous—about—*Continued*

How Mr Nixon made his choice; selection of W. E. Burger as chief justice. il por U S News 66:33 Je 2 '69

How much trouble is Nixon in? S. Alsop. Newsweek 74:88 Jl 28 '69

How Nixon is trying to end the war. il por U S News 66:27-8 My 26 '69

How Nixon operates. P. Lisagor. Nations Bsns 57:17-18 My '69

How President rates now. por U S News 66:16 Ap 7 '69

How the world views Nixon. P. Lisagor. Nations Bsns 57:21-2 F '69

How Washington plans to stretch your tax dollar. il por Nations Bsns 57:72-5 Mr '69

How's he doing in the White House? J. Osborne. New Repub 160:14-16 F 8 '69

If Nixon were to speak to the Russian people. D. Lawrence. U S News 66:88 Mr 3 '69

I'll check it out. il por Time 94:77 O 10 '69

Imprimatur for the simple pleasures. H. Sidey. il por Life 66:4 My 16 '69

Inauguration. New Yorker 44:27-8 F 1 '69

It was good to be home. H. Sidey. il por Life 66:2 F 7 '69

It will depend on the Nixon personality. P. Lisagor. Nations Bsns 57:15-16 Ja '69

Jazz night at the White House honoring the Duke. il pors U S News 66:10-11 My 12 '69

Jessamyn West talks about her cousin President Nixon. J. West. il McCalls 96:69-70 F '69

Journey round a new landscape. por Life 67:30 Ag 8 '69

Let not your right hand. Nat R 21:838-9 Ag 26 '69

Let the fight begin. Nat R 21:1051 O 21 '69

Let us, go forward together. il por Newsweek 73:17-21 Ja 27 '69

Let's give him a chance. il Ebony 24:52-3 Ap '69

Letter from Washington (cont) R. H. Rovere. New Yorker 44:65-6+ F 1; 45:155-8+ Ap 19; 128+ My 17; 86+ Je 14; 69-73 Jl 12; 165-9 N 29 '69

Liberal toryism. K. Crawford. Newsweek 74:24 S 1 '69

Looking Latinward: paternalism or partnership? D. Peerman. Chr Cent 86:1606-8 D 17 '69

Looking over Nixon's shoulder; analogy with dilemma facing A. Lincoln during Civil war. D. M. Kudrec. Nat R 21:1155 N 18 '69

Low silhouette rising. il por Time 94:11-12 O 31 '69

LBJ speaks to Richard Nixon about what it is to be Mr President; with painting by N. Rockwell. L. B. Johnson. Look 33:23-5 F 4 '69

Making of the President 1968; excerpts. T. H. White. il pors Life 67:48-48B+ Jl 11; 44B-44D+ Jl 18 '69

Making the case for Haynsworth. J. Osborne. New Repub 161:12-13 N 1 '69

Man with the four-button phone. H. Sidey. il por Life 66:4 Ja 31 '69

Many things to many men. P. Lisagor. Nations Bsns 57:17-18 O '69

Many thoughts, no conclusions. M. McGrory. America 121:86 Ag 16 '69

Matter of priorities; views on the Alliance for progress. Commonweal 90:221-2 My 9 '69

Medal for Duke and a kiss for the chief; D. Ellington honored at White House. il pors Life 66:97-8 My 9 '69

Medicine man. New Repub 161:10 N 1 '69

Men Nixon is seeing. il por U S News 67:10 D 22 '69

Middle ground? il Sr Schol 94:23-4 Mr 28 '69

Mr Nixon and the draft. W. F. Buckley, jr. Nat R 21:140-1 F 11 '69

Mr Nixon changes tune; attack on campus rebels and anti-military critics. il pors Newsweek 73:24-5 Je 16 '69

Mr Nixon goes to Washington. A. Drury. Read Digest 94:57-63 F '69

Mr Nixon in trouble. il por Newsweek 74:30-2+ O 13 '69

Mr Nixon's tax reforms. W. F. Buckley, jr. Nat R 21:506-7 My 20 '69

Mr Nixon's waffles. New Repub 161:5-6 O 18 '69

More adrenalin; preparing for crucial Vietnam speech. il por Newsweek 74:37-8 N 10 '69

National mood. New Repub 161:10-11 Jl 12 '69

NSF director: Nixon admits he was wrong. P. M. Boffey and B. Nelson. Science 164:532-4 My 2 '69

New administration easing in. il pors Time 93:11-12 Ja 31 '69

New federalism. il por Newsweek 74:24-5 S 15 '69

New hope for Latin America? D. Ross. New Repub 161:17-19 N 22 '69

New leadership emerges. il por Time 93:15-16 F 14 '69

New policy. G. de Zeñdegui. Américas 21:1 My '69

New politics: more mood than movement. J. Newfield. Nation 209:70-3 Jl 28 '69

New president, new goals, new ways. il por U S News 66:23-5 Ja 27 '69

New President's inaugural. America 120:126 F 1 '69

Nixon after six months; six appraisals. il N Y Times Mag p4-5+ Jl 20 '69

Nixon and China: time to talk. J. C. Thomson, jr. Atlan 223:71-3 F '69

Nixon and Kennedy, as Gallup rates them now. il por U S News 67:13 Ag 18 '69

Nixon and the Moratorium. il por Newsweek 74:26-7 O 20 '69

Nixon and the new bourgeoisie. S. Alsop. Newsweek 73:96 Ja 27 '69

Nixon and the new Washington. il por Nations Bsns 57:32-4+ Ja '69

Nixon at the six-month mark. Nat R 21:734-5 Jl 29 '69

Nixon bounces back. J. Osborne. New Repub 161:10-11 Jl 5 '69

Nixon co-opts the middle. S. Alsop. Newsweek 73:104 Je 2 '69

Nixon diplomacy: a full schedule. il pors U S News 66:21 Ap 14 '69

Nixon economy: four years of go-go or no-no for prosperity? il por Sr Schol 94:10-11 Ja 31 '69

Nixon fights back. Nat R 21:1102-3 N 4 '69

Nixon gets ready to build. il pors Bsns W p45-7 Ap 26 '69

Nixon: how to win friends, etc. il pors Newsweek 73:19-21 F 10 '69

Nixon in Rebozoland. D. Butwin. il por Sat R 52:40-1+ Mr 8 '69

Nixon is choosing his new weapons. Bsns W p39 O 18 '69

Nixon jawbone. Nation 209:490 N 10 '69

Nixon library serves children of Hong Kong. Library J 94:250+ Ja 15 '69

Nixon looks abroad. il por Newsweek 73:27-8 F 17 '69

Nixon makes some hard decisions. R. Lekachman. Duns R 93:11 Mr '69

Nixon meets students. J. Osborne. New Repub 161:9-10 O 4 '69

Nixon method. pors Newsweek 73:24 F 24 '69

Nixon on Vietnam. Nat R 21:1302 D 20 '69

Nixon: past, present, and future. il Bsns W p 158+ O 11 '69

Nixon plan for reform of Taft-Hartley. B. J. Masse. America 120:322 Mr 22 '69

Nixon plan to fight hunger. U S News 66:12 My 19 '69

Nixon rejection increases confusion in Pacific case. L. Doty. il Aviation W 91:25-6 Jl 14 '69

Nixon rhythm; problem of campus unrest. Nation 208:418 Ap 7 '69

Nixon-science gap. il Sci N 95:451 My 10 '69

Nixon sets the stage. il por Bsns W p33-4 Ja 25 '69

Nixon shows the pattern. il por Bsns W p33-5 Ap 19 '69

Nixon starts down the run. H. Brandon. Sat R 52:15 F 8 '69

Nixon steps fast into world arena. por Bsns W p25-6 F 15 '69

Nixon takes sides; letter concerning campus disorders. Time 93:57 Mr 7 '69

Nixon: the practical president. il pors U S News 67:24-8 Ag 11 '69

Nixon the predictable. Commonweal 90:251-2 My 16 '69

Nixon to tighten airline control. Aviation W 90:24-5 Mr 3 '69

Nixon watch: thought for food. J. Osborne. New Repub 161:7-9 D 6 '69

Nixon's affluence. New Repub 161-7-8 Ag 23 '69

Nixon's blueprint. E. Gruening. Nation 208:781 Je 22 '69

Nixon's contract for peace. il por Time 93:20-2 My 23 '69

Nixon's dog. G. Wills. il Esquire 72:91-5+ Ag '69

Nixon's first quarter; assessment. por Time 93:19-20 Ap 25 '69

Nixon's first six months. il pors Time 94:12-14 Jl 18 '69

Nixon's first test. G. Orfield. Nation 208:79-82 Ja 20 '69

Nixon's first year, how White House sums it up. il pors U S News 67:59-60 D 29 '69

Nixon's history lesson: the myth of reprisals. W. Meyers. Nation 209:654-6 D 15 '69

NIXON, Richard Milhous—about—*Continued*
Nixon's inch. New Repub 160:5-6 My 24 '69
Nixon's knaves. K. Crawford. Newsweek 73: 38 Je 23 '69
Nixon's new deal. il por Newsweek 74:17-19 Ag 18 '69
Nixon's new-found humor. Time 93:15 F 7 '69
Nixon's non-plan; analysis of TV address. New Repub 161:10-11 N 15 '69
Nixon's own ordeal in Latin America; May, 1958. il U S News 66:32 Je 16 '69
Nixon's presidency is a very private affair. R. B. Semple, jr. il pors N Y Times Mag p28-9+ N 2 '69
Nixon's prime goals. T. Trussell. Nations Bsns 57:7-8 Ap '69
Nixon's priorities. il pors U S News 66:23-5 F 10 '69
Nixon's program. R. Lekachman. Commentary 47:67-72 Je '69
Nixon's rating in the latest polls. U S News 67:13 O 13 '69
Nixon's Soviet approach. H. Brandon. Sat R 52:6 S 6 '69
Nixon's the one. New Repub 161:7-8 N 1 '69
Nixon's unsilent supporters. Time 94:25 N 21 '69
Nixon's workable proposals. W. F. Buckley, jr. Nat R 21:454 My 6 '69
Nixon's worst week. il por Time 94:15-16 O 10 '69
No deal. K. Crawford. Newsweek 73:42 My 5 '69
No disguised defeat? S. Alsop. Newsweek 73: 124 Je 9 '69
Notes and comment (cont) New Yorker 44: 25-6 F 8 '69
Notes and comment: official signature. New Yorker 45:15 Jl 19 '69
Now it's Nixon's turn. il por Sci N 95:109 F 1 '69
Number thirty-seven is ready. T. Wicker. il por N Y Times Mag p21+ Ja 19 '69
On the horns of a dilemma. il por Newsweek 74:31-2 S 29 '69
On tormenting Fulbright. W. F. Buckley jr. Nat R 21:662 Jl 1 '69
Once they were political foes, but—. il por U S News 67:16 S 8 '69
100 days, and four lessons. il Newsweek 73: 33-4 My 12 '69
One-liners for an open mind. H. Sidey. il Life 66:4 My 30 '69
One of those weeks; sacrificing principle to political expediency? Newsweek 74:16-17 Jl 7 '69
Open letter to President Nixon. Tran-van-Dinh. Chr Cent 86:313-14 Mr 5 '69
Order or conflict? P. Lisagor. Nations Bsns 57:23-4 Mr '69
Pending the Vietnam settlement. W. F. Buckley, jr. Nat R 21:403 Ap 22 '69
Pilot Nixon: and his copilot. H. J. Sievers. America 121:86 Ag 16 '69
Political pornography. J. Deedy. Commonweal 91:266 N 28 '69
Politics. J. Leonard. Esquire 71:66+ Je '69
Popularity: Nixon's still the one. U S News 66:12 Je 16 '69
Presidency. See issues of Time
Presidency under scrutiny. T. Wicker. Harper 239:92-4 O '69
President. See issues of Newsweek
President-elect sets his own style. il por Bsns W p80-2 Ja 18 '69
President Nixon, a business judgment. G. R. Rosen. pors Duns R 94:23-5 Ag '69
President Nixon's first thirty days. il por U S News 66:27-8 F 24 '69
President Nixon's horoscope. il Time 93:54-5 Mr 21 '69
President reiterates: nothing more for education. R. H. Smith. Pub W 196:253 Ag 25 '69
President settles in. il por Bsns W p 13-14 F 1 '69
President stumbles; concerning address at Air force academy. New Repub 160:7-8 Je 14 '69
Presidential performance; first news conference. il Newsweek 73:89 F 10 '69
President's analyst; summary of address. J. Barber. Time 94:58 S 12 '69
President's program and its chances in Congress. il U S News 66:68-9 My 12 '69
President's speech. P. Steinfels. Commonweal 91:242 N 21 '69
Pressures on Nixon now. il por U S News 66:28-30 Ap 28 '69
Professor Humphrey grades his rival. Time 94: 18 Ag 15 '69
Pullout: whose timetable? news conference. por Newsweek 73:40+ Je 30 '69

Putting the heat on Mr Nixon. J. Osborne. New Repub 160:11-12 Ap 19 '69
Question of belief in Hanoi, and at home. H. Sidey. il por Life 67:4 O 10 '69
Report card for Richard Nixon. J. J. Kilpatrick. il Nat R 21:532-7 Je 3 '69
Reports: Washington. W. S. Just. Atlan 223: 4+ Je '69
Republican era ahead for U.S? Yes, if... il U S News 66:41-3 F 10 '69
Richard de Nixon, Gaullist? J. Burnham. Nat R 21:382 Ap 22 '69
Right away, problems waiting around the world. il por U S News 66:38-41 Ja 27 '69
Road to the White House. il pors Sr Schol 94: 8-9 Ja 17 '69
Rockefeller's report. il Newsweek 74:68 N 17 '69
Sato-Nixon pact; its meaning to U.S. and Japan. il por U S News 67:18 D 1 '69
Search for end to the war; the emerging Nixon blueprint. il por U S News 67:8 D 22 '69
Seeking the role of peacemaker. Bsns W p 164 Ja 25 '69
Selling of the President 1968, by J. McGinniss. Review
    Nat R 21:1173 N 18 '69. V. Gold
    Nation 209:738-9 D 29 '69. R. MacNeil
    New Yorker 45:57-8 D 27 '69. L. E. Sissman
    Sat R 52:38-40+ O 18 '69. H. J. Telson
Selling of the President 1968; excerpts. J. McGinniss. Harper 239:46-60 Ag '69
Six views of Nixon; symposium. Sr Schol 94:4-5 Ja 17 '69
Social notes. il por Newsweek 74:38 N 3 '69
Sporting life. il por Time 94:21-2 Jl 4 '69
Strike troubles that LBJ left for the new President. il U S News 66:63-4 F 3 '69
Sudden shift in the capital mood. H. Sidey. il por Life 67:2 Jl 18 '69
Supreme court: no friends need apply. Life 66:44 Je 6 '69
Surprising asset of normality. H. Sidey. por Life 66:4 Mr 21 '69
T.R.B. from Washington. New Repub 160:6 Ja 25 '69
TRB from Washington; analysis of address on Vietnam. New Repub 161:8 N 15 '69
TRB from Washington; attack on the new isolationists. New Repub 160:6 Je 14 '69
TRB from Washington; Nixon meets the press. New Repub 160:6 F 15 '69
TRB from Washington; see Mr Nixon. New Repub 161:4 O 4 '69
Taking the A train. il pors Newsweek 73:34-5 My 12 '69
Three Nixons. S. Alsop. Newsweek 74:132 O 20 '69
Through his offices in search of the man. H. Sidey. Life 67:4 O 17 '69
Time for reforms? Nixon's faithless elector. Sr Schol 94:22-3 Ja 31 '69
Tough decisions for a new decade. il Newsweek 75:11-12 Ja 5 '70
Trick or trip; contrary moves and self-contradictory utterances. New Repub 161:9-10 Jl 12 '69
Ultimate Nixon. K. Crawford. Newsweek 73: 29 F 10 '69
Underbearing President? M. McGrory. America 121:26 Jl 19 '69
Understanding Nixon; concerning the selling of the President 1968, by J. McGinniss. W. F. Buckley, jr. Nat R 21:1286-7 D 16 '69
U.S. debt limit: Nixon's new plan. U S News 66:100 Mr 10 '69
Vietnam: how to get out? il Newsweek 74: 15-16 S 8 '69
Vietnam pullout. K. Crawford. Newsweek 73: 48 Je 30 '69
Vietnam: the moratorium ends. il por Newsweek 74:75 O 6 '69
Vietnam: the Nixon plan. il por Newsweek 73:33-6 My 26 '69
Vietnam: the President's fading hope. J. Osborne. New Repub 161:17-19 S 27 '69
Waiting for the word. New Repub 160:7-8 F 1 '69
War: Nixon's big test. il por Newsweek 73:20-2 Mr 31 '69
War on crime. Sr Schol 94:18-19 F 14 '69
War problems deepen as Nixon heads for Midway. il U S News 66:25-6 Je 9 '69
Washington report: how will education fare? J. Lloyd. Sr Schol 94:Schol Teach 6 Mr 7 '69
Washington waits for its social cue. il Bsns W p80-1 Ag 2 '69
We think we are on the right track. il por Newsweek 73:28-30 Ap 7 '69
Wealth of Richard Nixon. il U S News 66:56 My 26 '69

NIXON, Richard Milhous—about—*Continued*
Welcome to Mississippi. il por Time 94:20-1
S 19 '69
Welfare story, plot and subplot. J. Osborne.
New Repub 161:15-17 N 8 '69
What business wants from President Nixon;
with editorial comment. A. T. Demaree. il
por Fortune 79:71, 84-7+ F '69
What can we expect from the Nixon years?
K. E. Clarke. por Chr Cent 86:182-3 F 5 '69
What is Nixon's policy? Nat R 21:158+ F 25
'69
Who is Nixon? Nation 209:34-5 Jl 14 '69
Who's making foreign policy for the United
States? il por U S News 66:45-6 Ap 7 '69
Who's running the store downtown? il por
Newsweek 73:33-4 Ap 21 '69
Will he veto a better America? New Repub
162:7-8 Ja 10 '70
Will Nixon risk peace? New Repub 161:5-6 Ag
2 '69
Winter white house; with photographs by G.
Silk and L. Pelham. il pors Life 66:26-31
F 21 '69
With lowered voice, enter Mr Nixon. il pors
Newsweek 73:16-21 F 3 '69
See also
Midway conference, 1969

Anecdotes, facetiae, satire, etc.
Report from the future. Commonweal 91:239
N 21 '69
Welcome to the Nixon style. il pors Esquire
71:87-91 Je '69
Who is the man in the White House? R.
Baker. Look 33:92+ D 16 '69

Health
President's health; interview. W. R. Tkach.
il pors U S News 67:39-40 N 24 '69

Homes
California, here I come! il Newsweek 74:33 Ag
4 '69
Keeping up the presidential payments; White
House West, San Clemente, Calif. il Time
94:19-20 S 12 '69
Nixon in White House West; with photo-
graphs by A. Schatz. H. Sidey. Life 67:
18B-25 S 5 '69
Nixons go house-hunting; summer retreat at
Cotton Point, San Clemente, Calif. il pors
Life 66:63-6+ My 9 '69
Nixon's tranquility base: San Clemente,
Calif. il por Time 94:10-11 Ag 29 '69
Now, White House with a western tilt: San
Clemente, Calif. il por U S News 67:8-9 Ag
25 '69
Tab for Nixon's place in the sun; summer
White House, San Clemente, Calif. il por
Bsns W p24-5 Ag 23 '69
What it takes to run the western White
House. il pors U S News 67:24-5 S 1 '69
White House on the Pacific. il pors News-
week 74:18-19 Ag 25 '69
White House West; Cotton Point, San Cle-
mente, Calif. il Time 93:15 My 2 '69
White House West, San Clemente, Calif. il
Time 94:17-18 Ag 15 '69

Inaugural address
Inaugural; address. Nation 208:130 F 3 '69
Lower your voice. Time 93:39 Ja 31 '69
New President's inaugural. America 120:126
F 1 '69
Nixon as peacemaker. Chr Cent 86:171 F 5
'69
Nixon's message: let us gather the light. il
por Time 93:9-10 Ja 24 '69
Shades of the past haunt an inaugural. R. L.
Kuttner. Commonweal 89:576-8 F 7 '69

Messages
Administration: beginning to begin. Time
93:18-19 Ap 25 '69
Alive and well in California; highlights of
three domestic messages. il por Newsweek 74:17-18 Ag 25 '69
Nixon's new direction. il por Newsweek 73:
32+ Ap 28 '69

Press conferences
How the President gets ready for a news
conference. il por U S News 67:47 D 22 '69
TRB from Washington. New Repub 161:4 D 20
'69

Public relations
Betting on the silent majority. il pors News-
week 74:35-6 N 17 '69
Choosing up sides; reactions to Vietnam
policy speech. K. Crawford. Newsweek 74:
52 N 17 '69
Communications gap. C. Roberts. il pors
Newsweek 74:28-9 D 15 '69

Communications gap. il por Newsweek 74:22+
Ag 18 '69
Conciliation, confrontation; response to ad-
dress on war and peace in Viet Nam. il
por Time 94:15-16 N 14 '69
Disarray in the Nixon team. il por U S News
67:35-7 O 13 '69
Embattled White House. H. Sidey. il por
Life 67:31 O 24 '69
How Nixon rates now at home and abroad.
il por U S News 67:23-8 Ag 11 '69
How to watch Nixon on the tube. H. Sidey.
por Life 67:2 Jl 11 '69
Know your President. J. Osborne. New
Repub 161:13-14 O 25 '69
Love it or leave it; patriotic demonstrations
supporting Vietnam policy. il Newsweek 74:
34-5 N 24 '69
Marching and talking. H. Brandon. Sat R
52:16 D 6 '69
Nixon-eye view of dissent. il Newsweek
74:35 O 27 '69
Nixon shifts gears, from soft sell to action
now. il pors U S News 67:17-18 N 10 '69
Nixon strategy. K. Crawford. Newsweek 74:
58 D 8 '69
Nixon, the Negro and the budget. il Time
93:19-20 Ap 18 '69
Nixon turns to the attack. il pors U S News
67:22-4 D 1 '69
Nothing yet to mar the White House slum-
ber. H. Sidey. il por Life 67:8 S 26 '69
Politics of polarization. Time 94:16-17 N 21
'69
Portrait of two presidents: Nixon and John-
son. B. Furlow. il pors U S News 67:52-4
Jl 28 '69
Presidency and President. Nation 209:426-7
O 27 '69
President and the kids. S. Alsop. Newsweek
74:136 N 24 '69
President on Vietnam. S. Alsop. Newsweek
74:33 O 13 '69
Programming a president; views presented
in The selling of the President 1969. il Time
94:66-7 O 10 '69
Richard Nixon and collegians. M. McGrory.
America 121:286 O 11 '69
Selling of the President 1968, by J. McGinniss.
Review
Life 67:14 O 10 '69. M. Kempton
New Repub 161:26-8 O 11 '69. J. Osborne
Newsweek il por 74:119 O 13 '69. G. Wolff
Silenced majority; President's obligation to
public opinion. C. Frankel. Sat R 52:22+
D 13 '69
TRB from Washington. New Repub 161:6 O
25; 8 N 22; 6 N 29 '69
TRB from Washington; honeymoon's over.
New Repub 161:6 O 11 '69
Why it's no cinch to break a president. H.
Sidey. il Life 67:4 O 31 '69

Relations with Congress
Behind the snafu in Washington. il por U S
News 67:23-4 D 22 '69
Communications gap. C. Roberts. il pors
Newsweek 74:28-9 D 15 '69
Draft, taxes, crime, welfare; Nixon asks for
action now; text of message to Congress,
October 13, 1969. R. M. Nixon. por U S
News 67:91-4 O 20 '69
Gathering protest. il por Time 94:12+ O 3 '69
Gloves are off; fight over foreign and military
issues, ABM, taxes, and the budget. il
Bsns W p26-7 My 3 '69
How Congress sizes up Nixon. il pors U S
News 66:69-71 Mr 10 '69
Minority problem. P. Lisagor. Nations Bsns
57:19-20 Je '69
Mr Nixon changes tune; reactions to address
attacking the new isolationists. il News-
week 73:24-5 Je 16 '69
Moving ahead, Nixon style. il por Time 94:
13+ Ag 15 '69
New crisis in leadership; with report by H.
Hubbard. il por Newsweek 74:20-2 Jl 14 '69
Nixon and the liberal Republicans. J. Osborne.
New Repub 161:13-15 Jl 26 '69
Nixon shifts gears, from soft sell to action
now. il pors U S News 67:17-18 N 10 '69
Nixon turns to the attack. il pors U S News
67:22-4 D 1 '69
Nixon vs. Congress; what's involved. il U S
News 67:6 D 15 '69
Nixon's problem with Congress. il U S
News 67:22-3 S 1 '69
Polite indictment. Time 94:23 O 17 '69
Politics of polarization. Time 94:16-17 N 21
'69
President on Vietnam. S. Alsop. Newsweek
74:33 O 13 '69
President tries a harder line. il por Bsns W
p39-40 N 1 '69
Price of neglect. il Time 93:19-20 Je 20 '69

NIXON, Richard Milhous—Relations with Congress—Continued
Reports: Washington. E. B. Drew. Atlan 224:4+ N '69
Senate's cynical design. F. Morley. Nations Bsns 57:21-2 My '69
Surtax: in the balance. il Newsweek 74:69 Jl 7 '69

Religion

Rabbi's prayer about Nixon. il por U S News 67:12 Jl 14 '69
Religious services with the Nixons. il por U S News 66:11 F 10 '69
Sunday at the White House: watchers and worshipers. K. Huffman. il Chr Today 13:38-9 Ag 22 '69
Two who agree on a way to life; religious service, the sixth in a White House series. il U S News 66:15 Je 9 '69

Sports

Fan no. 1. il por Newsweek 74:70 D 22 '69

Statues, portraits, etc.

[Richard M. Nixon; painting] N. Rockwell. Look 33:24-5 F 4 '69

Travel

Lure of faraway places. P. Lisagor. Nations Bsns 57:19-20 S '69

Visit to Asia and Rumania, 1969

As Nixon charts his trip abroad. il por U S News 67:42 Jl 14 '69
Asia after Viet Nam. il por Time 94:15-16 Ag 1 '69
Debate on doctrine. il Time 94:26-7 Ag 15 '69
From Manila to Bucharest. il por Time 94:13 Jl 4 '69
Global showboating. Newsweek 74:31-2 Jl 14 '69
Half-farewell to Asia. H. Sidey. il Life 67:4 Ag 8 '69
If it's Thursday, this must be Rashtrapati Bhavan. M. Frankel and R. B. Semple, jr. il por s N Y Times Mag p26-7+ Ag 17 '69
Letter from Bucharest. T. Szulc. New Yorker 45:105-6+ S 6 '69
Letter from Washington. R. H. Rovere. New Yorker 45:89-93 Ag 9 '69
Mr Nixon's journeys. Nation 209:98 Ag 11 '69
Nixon in Asia: looking past Vietnam. il Newsweek 74:38-40 Ag 4 '69
Nixon's diplomacy. K. Crawford. Newsweek 74:25 Ag 11 '69
Nixon's sobering message to Asia. il pors Time 94:11-13 Ag 8 '69
Nixon's trip; aims, chances for success. il por U S News 67:32 Ag 4 '69
On the road with RMN. il por Newsweek 74:60 Ag 11 '69
President Nixon in Rumania. E. von Kuehnelt-Leddihn. Nat R 21:801 Ag 12 '69
President Nixon's round-the-world trip; texts of remarks and statements, July 26-August 3, 1969. R. M. Nixon. Dept State Bul 61:141-76 Ag 25 '69
Preview of Nixon's tour. il Time 94:27-8 Jl 25 '69
Problems the President will find on his trip to Asia. il por U S News 67:27-8 Jl 21 '69
Rich Richard's red Rumanians. P. Ben. New Repub 161:8-10 Ag 9 '69
Rumania; getting ready for Nixon. Time 94:30 Jl 11 '69
They loved him in Bucharest. il por Life 67:32-3 Ag 15 '69
Up, up and away. Newsweek 74:48-9 Jl 28 '69
Urrah Neek-son! il pors Newsweek 74:14-18 Ag 11 '69
Why's the President going to Bucharest? P. Ben. New Repub 161:16-17 Jl 12 '69

Anecdotes, facetiae, satire, etc.

Another open letter to President Nixon. Tranvan-Dinh. Chr Cent 86:1137-8 S 3 '69

Visit to Europe, 1969

Dutiful tourist. H. Sidey. il pors Life 66:22-7 Mr 7 '69
Eight-day whirlwinder. Sr Schol 94:22-3 F 28 '69
Europe after Nixon's visit. il pors U S News 66:26-9 Mr 10 '69
Journey to a different Europe. il por Time 93:13-14 F 21 '69
Launching a new diplomacy: Nixon's report to the Nation; text of news conference, March 4, 1969. R. M. Nixon. il pors U S News 66:70-6 Mr 17 '69; Same with title President Nixon's news conference of March 4. Dept State Bul 60:237-47 Mr 24 '69

Letter from Washington: President in Brussels. R. H. Rovere. New Yorker 45:103-4 Mr 1 '69
Listening to what Europe has to say. il Life 66:34 Mr 14 '69
Mission of modesty. il pors Newsweek 72:20-5 Mr 10 '69
Mr Nixon goes calling. Nation 208:322-3 Mr 17 '69
Mr Nixon goes to Europe. il pors Newsweek 73:17-19 Mr 3 '69
Mr Nixon's middle course. H. Brandon. Sat R 52:17 Mr 1 '69
Nixon builds a road to the summit. il pors Bsns W p31-2 Mr 8 '69
Nixon goes calling on European allies. il Bsns W p40-1 F 22 '69
Nixon in Europe: renewing old acquaintances. il pors Time 93:17-19 Mr 7 '69
Nixon lands on Willy Brandt's special island; interview. ed. by R. Meryman. W. Brandt. il por Life 66:28-9 Mr 7 '69
Nixon's Europe in the new era. J. Osborne. New Repub 160:17-19 Mr 15 '69
Nixon's preview of his trip. por U S News 66:10 Mr 3 '69
Nixon's quiet diplomacy. Bsns W p 100 Mr 1 '69
Notes and comment. New Yorker 45:25-7 Mr 8 '69; Same with title Making foreign policy; how to cooperate with Europe. Cur 107:3-7 My '69
President Nixon discusses the objectives of his European trip; excerpts from remarks, February 21, 1969. R. M. Nixon. Dept State Bul 60:217-19 Mr 17 '69
President Nixon makes eight day visit to western Europe; texts of remarks, February 23-March 2, 1969. R. M. Nixon. Dept State Bul 60:249-71 Mr 24 '69
President on his trip to Europe: only a first step to peace; excerpts from news conference, February 6, 1969. R. M. Nixon. il pors U S News 66:94-5 F 17 '69; Same. Dept State Bul 60:157-61 F 24 '69
Security shield for Nixon. il U S News 66:23 Mr 3 '69
Sure-footed step. Life 66:32 F 21 '69
Tour of the blue chips. H. Sidey. il por Life 66:2 F 28 '69
Two ex-exiles hit it off; visit with C. de Gaulle. H. Sidey. il por Life 66:4 Mr 14 '69
Voyage of rediscovery and reconciliation. il pors Time 93:17-22 F 28 '69
Why Nixon will go to Europe soon. il por U S News 66:45-7 F 17 '69
With Nixon on the grand tour; report from Berlin. J. Osborne. New Repub 160:9-10 Mr 8 '69

NIXON, Richard Milhous. family
Christmas at the Nixons'. il Time 94:6-7 D 26 '69
Mrs Nixon tells how she brought up Tricia and Julie; interview. ed. by T. B. Feldman. P. R. Nixon. il McCalls 96:74-5+ Mr '69

NIXON, Tom
Pork rind and bluegill. Field & S 74:64-5+ Je '69

NIXON, Tricia
Having a ball. il Newsweek 73:41 My 19 '69
President's daughters: they also serve. il pors Newsweek 74:46-8 D 8 '69

NIXON family
Ancestors. New Yorker 45:30-2 Mr 15 '69

NJENGA NJOROGE, Nahashon Isaac
Taking the oath. il por Newsweek 74:42 Ag 25 '69
Weight of evidence. Newsweek 74:50 S 22 '69

NJOROGE, Nahashon Isaac Njenga. See Njenga Njoroge. N. I.

NKOSI, Lewis
Forbidden dialogue; reprint. UNESCO Courier 22:69 Ag '69

NKRUMAH, Kwame
Nkrumah's gone; Ghana's agony remains. Africanus. Commonweal 90:136 Ap 18 '69
No redeemers need apply. il Newsweek 74:44 S 8 '69

NO-load mutual funds. See Investment trusts

NO place to be somebody; drama. See Gordone, C.

NOAH, Harold J. and Eckstein, M. A.
Toward a science of comparative education; excerpts. Sch & Soc 97:35-8 Ja '69

NOAH'S ark
Wood on Mount Ararat intrigues explorers. il Chr Today 13:48 S 12 '69

NOAKES, David
(tr) See Boulez, P. Berlioz and the realm of the imaginary
(tr) See Mendès-France, P. Mission of politics

NOBEL foundation
  Nobel symposium: super bowl of the world
    conference circuit. D. S. Greenberg. Science
    166:92-3 O 3 '69; Reply. E. M. Gurowitz.
    166:1097 N 28 '69
NOBEL prizes
  Awards for the modelmakers; first Nobel
    prize in economics. il Time 94:96 N 7 '69
  Biology Nobelists; Delbruck, Hershey. Luria.
    Sci N 96:370-1 O 25 '69
  How Nobel prizewinners get that way; science
    laureates. M. Wilson. il Atlan 224:69-74 D '69
  Kyrie eleison without God; award to S.
    Beckett. Time 94:55 O 31 '69
  Mouse in the cathedral; physics; chemistry;
    economics winners. Newsweek 74:70 N 10
    '69
  1969 Nobel prize for physiology or medicine.
    G. Stent. Science 166:479-81 O 24 '69
  Nobel laureates in economics, chemistry,
    and physics. L. R. Klein; E. L. Eliel; M.
    L. Goldberger. il Science 166:715-22 N 7
    '69
  Nobel prize for dismal science; new prize in
    economics. il Bsns W p44-5 O 18 '69
  Nobel prize: supreme sanction, or silly cere-
    mony? T. Berland. il Todays Health 47:
    24-7+ D '69
  Nobel prizes. Sci Am 221:48-50 D '69
  Nobel prizes in chemistry, and physics. il Sci
    N 96:421-2 N 8 '69
  Nobel: reward for econometricians. il Bsns
    W p42 N 1 '69
  Nobel threesome; prize in physiology and
    medicine. il Time 94:84 O 24 '69
  Nobels for phage group; three Americans
    share prize in medicine. il Newsweek 74:
    68 O 27 '69
  Order in the zoo; Nobel prize in physics.
    Time 94:52 N 7 '69
  Samuel Beckett: literature prize. T. Bishop.
    Sat R 52:26-7+ N 15 '69
  Samuel Beckett wins Nobel literature prize.
    Pub W 196:29-30 N 3 '69
  73,000 gallons of chicken soup; S. Beckett,
    winner of literature prize. K. Nyren. Li-
    brary J 94:4327 D 1 '69
  Two remarkable men; economics award win-
    ners R. Frisch and J. Tinbergen. News-
    week 74:108 N 17 '69
  View from the wasteland; literature award.
    Newsweek 74:54 N 3 '69
NOBILE, Philip
  Doping the book-makers. Commonweal 89:
    674-5 F 28 '69
  I never met any priest who suggested with-
    drawal. Commonweal 90:196-7, 307+ My 2,
    30 '69
  Innocents in Scandinavia. Commonweal 91:
    300-2 D 5 '69
  Renewal and destalinization. Cath World
    209:86 My '69
  Stage. Commonweal 91:382-3 D 26 '69
  US against them. Commonweal 90:566-7 S 19
    '69
NOBILITY
  See also
  Great Britain—Peerage
NOCHIXTLAN VALLEY. See Oaxaca (state),
    Mexico
NOCTILUCENT clouds. See Clouds
NOCTURNAL animals.   See Animals—Habits
    and behavior
NOCTURNAL insects. See Insects
NODELMAN, Sheldon
  After the high Roman fashion. Art N 67:34-
    7+ N '68
  David Smith. Art N 67:28-31+ F '69
NOEL, Mrs Carrington
  Stretching and enclosing space. Sch Arts 69:
    34 S '69
NOEL, J. See Best, J. B. jt. auth.
NOËL-HUME, Ivor
  James Geddy and sons, colonial craftsmen;
    evidence from the earth. Antiques 95:106-11
    Ja '69
  Pearlware: forgotten milestone of English
    ceramic history. Antiques 95:390-7; 96:922-3
    Mr, D '69
NOELL, Robert E.
  Man who makes pets of gorillas. D. Both-
    well and D. Coleman. il pors Sci Digest
    65:26-31 F '69
NOETHER, Emiliana P.
  (comp) Articles and other books received;
    Italy. See issues of American historical
    review
NOGUCHI, Thomas T.
  Examining the examiner. por Time 94:47 Ag
    15 '69

NOISE
  Noise: more than a nuisance. il U S News
    67:40-2 N 10 '69
    See also
  Sound
  Tractors—Noise

    Physiological effects
  Companies warned: quieter, please! Bsns W
    p28-9 Jl 26 '69
  Ear pollution! F. Graham, jr. il Audubon
    71:34-9 My '69
  Exuberant beetles of Brazil; small Volkswa-
    gens. il Time 94:63+ S 12 '69
  It's time to turn down all that noise. J. M.
    Mecklin. il Fortune 80:130-3+ O '69
  Noise is a slow agent of death. A. Bailey. il
    N Y Times Mag p46-7+ N 23 '69
  Noise: more than a nuisance. il U S News
    67:40-2 N 10 '69
  Noise; the gathering crisis; address, October
    8, 1969. M. O. Hatfield. Vital Speeches 36:
    130-3 D 15 '69
  Physiological effects of audible sound;
    AAAS symposium, December 28-30, 1969.
    B. L. Welch. il Science 166:533-4 O 24 '69
  Sounds of progress. Sr Schol 95:6 O 27 '69

    Psychological effects
  Environmental noise pollution: a new threat
    to sanity. D. F. Anthrop. Bul Atom Sci
    25:11-16 My '69
NOISE, Radio. See Radio interference
NOISE control
  Aircraft noise study set for city centers,
    suburbs. Aviation W 90:27 Ja 27 '69
  Are we hooked on noise? W. Zinsser. il Life
    67:12 O 31 '69
  Control of vibration and noise. T. P. Yin. il
    Sci Am 220:98-106 Ja '69
  Crusader for quiet. Time 94:85 D 5 '69
  Environmental noise pollution: a new threat
    to sanity. D. F. Anthrop. Bul Atom Sci
    25:11-16 My '69
  Give your house a tranquilizer. M. A.
    Guitar. il Am Home 72:48+ O '69
  Growing problem of airplane noise, what is
    being done. il Good H 168:155-7 F '69
  How to keep down noise levels in computer
    facilities. L. L. Boyer, jr. bibliog il Arch
    Rec 145:165-6 My '69
  How to noiseproof a room. il Mech Illus 65:
    100-2 Mr '69
  It's time to turn down all that noise. J.
    M. Mecklin. il Fortune 80:130-3+ O '69
  Noise is a slow agent of death. A. Bailey. il
    N Y Times Mag p46-7+ N 23 '69
  Noise; the gathering crisis; address, October
    8, 1969. M. O. Hatfield. Vital Speeches 36:
    130-3 D 15 '69
  Sound control in multi-purpose buildings.
    il Parks & Rec 4:46-7 My '69
  Supersonic boom. il Life 67:51-2 N 7 '69
  What do you know about silencing alumi-
    num spars. D. B. Hoisington. il Yachting
    125:83+ Ap '69

    Laws and legislation
  Companies warned: quieter, please! Bsns W
    p28-9 Jl 26 '69
  Ssh! ordinances on the books in New York
    and other cities. Newsweek 74:52 S 8 '69
NOISE measurement. See Sound measurement
NOISE prevention. See Noise control
NOLAN, Brian
  Discovering Flann O'Brien. C. R. Hughes. il
    America 120:523-5 My 3 '69
NOLAN, David
  South Carolina: the movement finally ar-
    rives. Nation 208:654-6 My 26 '69
NOLAN, Paul T.
  Happiest hat; drama. Plays 28:1-12+ Ap '69
  Man that corrupted Hadleyburg; dramatiza-
    tion of a story by Mark Twain. Plays 28:
    75-90 F '69
  Take it from the beginning; drama. Plays
    28:13-24 My '69
  Temporary job; drama. Plays 29:25-36, 96 O
    '69
  This younger generation; drama. Plays 28:
    89-98 My '69
  What's zymurgy with you? drama. Plays 28:
    1-12 Mr '69
  Wishing well or ill; drama. Plays 29:13-26 D
    '69
NOLAND, Kenneth
  Bold emblems. il por Time 93:74 Ap 18 '69
NOLAND, T. B.
  How to design a city hall. Am City 84:93-4
    Ap '69
NOLDE, O. Frederick
  Tribute to a diplomat. B. Thompson. Chr
    Cent 86:736 My 28 '69

NOLEN, William A.
Happy days at Bellevue. Esquire 72:170-1+ N '69

NOLL, Bink
Angel; poem. New Yorker 45:34 D 20 '69

NOLTE, Ernst
Big business and German politics: a comment. bibliog f Am Hist R 75:71-8 O '69

NOMA, Seiroku
Master-works of stone age Japan; reprint. UNESCO Courier 22:68 Ag '69

NOMA lite corporation
Turning on Christmas. il Newsweek 74:8 D 29 '69

NOME, Alaska
Nome. W. Bronson. il Am West 6:20-31 Jl '69

NOMOGRAMS. See Charts, Calculating

NOMURA, Masayasu
Ribosomes; with biographical sketch. Sci Am 221:14, 28-35 O '69

NONCOMMERCIAL television. See Television broadcasting, Noncommercial

NONCONFORMISTS. See Dissenters

NONCONFORMITY. See Conformity

NONDESTRUCTIVE testing. See Testing

NON-EUCLIDEAN geometry. See Geometry

NONFERROUS metals. See Metals, Nonferrous

NON-GOVERNMENTAL organizations of the United Nations. See United Nations—Nongovernmental organizations

NONGRADED classes. See Ungraded classes

NONLINEAR optics
Nonlinear optics. J. A. Giordmaine. bibliog il Phys Today 22:38-44 Ja '69

NON-MILITARY compulsory service. See Service, Compulsory non-military

NON-MUSICAL phonograph records. See Phonograph records—Spoken records

Les NONNES; drama. See Manet, E.

NONNUTRITIVE sucking. See Motor response

NON-OBJECTIVE art. See Art, Abstract

NONPROFIT organizations. See Institutions, Nonprofit

NON-PROLIFERATION treaty. See Atomic weapons—International control

NONSENSE verse
See also
Mother Goose

NON-SKID tires. See Tires, Automobile

NON-SUPPORT. See Desertion and non-support

NONVIOLENCE
Gandhi and nonviolence. A. Fonseca. America 121:257-60 O 4 '69
Gandhi: the heritage of non-violence; symposium. UNESCO Courier 22:4-32 O '69
Gandhi's truth, by E. H. Erikson. Review
New Repub 161:24+ O 18 '69. J. Featherstone
Latin American revolution; Catholics and Protestants together on behalf of oppressed and dispossessed. E. M. Smith. Chr Cent 86:674-7 My 14 '69
Letter from Delano. C. Chávez. Chr Cent 86:539-40 Ap 23 '69; Discussion. 86:110-11, 1115-16 Je 11, Ag 27 '69
Nonviolence in Latin America. E. K. Culhane. America 120:331 Mr 22 '69
Nonviolent direct action, ed. by A. P. Hare and H. H. Blumberg. Review
America 120:338+ Mr 22 '69. P. J. Weber Chr Cent 86:1068 Ag 13 '69. W. Saffen
Top Negro's plea for nonviolence; excerpts from remarks, May 6, 1969. A. P. Randolph. U S News 66:22 My 19 '69
What role for non-violence today? excerpts from Gandhi's truth. E. H. Erikson. Cur 112:42-7 N '69

NON-WAGE payments
Analysis of 1968 changes in wages and benefits; with chart and tables. J. E. Talbot, jr. Mo Labor R 92:43-8 Jl '69
Estimating the cost of collective bargaining settlements. L. M. David and V. J. Sheifer. bibliog il Mo Labor R 92:16-26 My '69
Fringe benefits. B. L. Masse. il America 120:168-9 F 8 '69
Golden fringe; benefits for executives abroad. il Time 93:84 Mr 28 '69
More and more billions for workers' welfare. il U S News 66:72-3 Je 2 '69
NRPA's personal security program; including life insurance benefits. D. D. Magee. il Parks & Rec 4:73-4 S '69
Negotiated retirement plans, a decade of benefit improvements. H. E. Davis. il Mo Labor R 92:11-15 My '69
New system fills in the blanks on benefits: individualized benefit report. il Bsns W p94-5 Mr 1 '69

Problems in selecting employee benefits. E. S. Willis. Mo Labor R 92:61-2 Ap '69
Should wages embrace fringes? Bsns W p53 F 15 '69
Where do you stand on employee benefits? Pub W 195:84-5+ Ap 14 '69
See also
Profit sharing

NONWOVEN textile fabrics. See Textile fabrics, Nonwoven

NOONAN, John Ford
Year Boston won the pennant. Criticism
Nation 208:741-2 Je 9 '69
New Yorker 45:77-8 My 31 '69

NOONAN, Joseph
How not to review anybody's book. Cath World 208:222-4 F '69
Something new. Cath World 210:78-9 N '69
Whither advertising? il Cath World 209:126-8 Je '69

NORA, James J. and others
Lactate dehydrogenase isozymes in human cardiac transplantation. bibliog Science 164: 1079-80 My 30 '69

NORANDA mines, limited
Economic nationalism, free-enterprise style. il Forbes 103:36+ My 1 '69

NORBYE, Jan P.
Sensational new Mercedes has triple-rotor Wankel engine. Pop Sci 195:73-7 O '69

NORCROSS, Carl
Best land values; questions and answers. House B 111:66-7+ F '69

NORD, Wayne R.
College companions for patients in mental institutions. Todays Ed 58:28-9 D '69

NORDAIR, limited. See Airlines—Canada

NORDBERG, E. Wayne
Marketing and capitalization; excerpts from address. Pub W 196:22-4 D 8 '69

NORDFORS, Margaret
Winter ferry crossing; poem. Yale R 59:108 O '69

NOREPINEPHRINE
Cyclic adenosine monophosphate: possible mediator for norepinephrine effects on cerebellar purkinje cells. G. R. Siggins and others. bibliog il Science 165:1018-20 S 5 '69
Cyclic adenosine monophosphate: stimulation of melatonin and serotonin synthesis in cultured rat pineals. H. M. Shein and R. J. Wurtman. bibliog il Science 166:519-20 O 24 '69
Facilitation of brain self-stimulation by central administration of norepinephrine. C. D. Wise and L. Stein. bibliog il Science 163:299-301 Ja 17 '69
Lesions of central norepinephrine terminals with 6-OH-dopamine: biochemistry and fine structure. F. E. Bloom and others. bibliog il Science 166:1284-6 D 5 '69
Norepinephrine: release from brain by d-amphetamine in vivo. L. A. Carr and K. E. Moore. bibliog il Science 164:322-3 Ap 18 '69
Prostaglandins E_1 and E_2 antagonize norepinephrine effects on cerebellar Purkinje cells: microelectrophoretic study. B. J. Hoffer and others. bibliog il Science 166:1418-20 D 12 '69
Thermoregulation: effects of environmental temperature on turnover of hypothalamic norepinephrine. M. A. Simmonds and L. L. Iversen. bibliog il Science 163:473-4 Ja 31 '69; Reply with rejoinder. R. D. Myers. 165: 1030-1 S 5 '69

NORFOLK, Va.
Style trends 1969. il Am City 84:126 Ja '69

Architecture
Sculptured precast tower paces downtown redevelopment; Virginia national bank. il Arch Rec 146:141-4 O '69

NORFOLK, Va, public library
International children's book day, 1969, at Norfolk public library, Virginia. L. R. Stone. il Horn Bk 45:461-3 Ag '69

NORFOLK and Western railway
It's getting late for the Cannonball. il Bsns W p 134+ Jl 12 '69

NORFOLK and Western railway-Chesapeake and Ohio merger (proposed) See Railroads —Consolidations and mergers

NORFOLK BROADS, England
Chartering in Ireland and England; cruising on the River Shannon and the Norfolk Broads. G. Stout; F. Adams; E. J. Durnall. il Yachting 126:54-5+ D '69

NORMAL curve. See Distribution (probability theory)

NORMAL person. See Normality

NORMALITY
How can I tell if I'm normal? questions and answers. R. Holder. Seventeen 28:172-3+ Ap '69

NORMAN, Barbara, and Tatsumura, Kazuko
Soaring popularity of Japanese restaurants. Holiday 45:58-9+ Mr '69

NORMAN, Douglas
Faster than a speeding bullet! Pop Mech 130: 130-1 D '68

NORMAN-Wilcox, Gregor
From the herds and flocks. Antiques 96:218-21 Ag '69

NORMANDY
Farewell to a Norman spring. D. Butwin. il Sat R 52:26-8 Je 21 '69

NORMANDY, Mo.
Local association of the month. M. Wagner. Todays Ed 58:81 S '69

NORMANDY invasion. See World war, 1939-1945—Campaigns and battles—Western

NORODOM Sihanouk, king of Cambodia (abdicated 1955)
Cambodia's strategy of survival. D. Chandler. bibliog f Cur Hist 57:344-8+ D '69
Mending fences. por Newsweek 73:46-7 Ap 28 '69
Rebellion or subversion in Cambodia? M. Leifer. bibliog f Cur Hist 56:88-93+ F '69
Report. J. Hughes. Atlan 223:4+ F '69

NORRIDGE, Ill.
Education
Trump school: a move toward recentralization; Ridgewood high school. M. Miller and J. Ankrum. il Library J 94:4211-12 N 15 '69

NORRING, Frances
In the pop bag. Am Rec G 35:1014-15 Je '69

NORRIS, Eleanor L.
National assessment. Am Ed 5:20-3 O '69
National science assessment. Ed Digest 35: 46-8 N '69

NORRIS, Kenneth S. See Porter, W. P. jt. auth.

NORSTAD, Lauris
General and the genius. il por Forbes 104: 48+ O 15 '69

NORTH, Harper Q. and Pyke, D. L.
Probes of the technological future. Harvard Bsns R 47:68-82 My '69

NORTH, Sandie
(ed) See Bucher, R. Rose Bucher and the ordeal of the Pueblo

NORTH, Sterling
Wolfling: story; excerpt from novel. Audubon 71:66-74+ S '69

NORTH AFRICAN cookery. See Cookery, North African

NORTH AMERICA
See also
Botany—North America
Water supply—North America

NORTH AMERICAN air defense command
Silent partner; Canada and the ABM issue. J. W. Warnock. Commonweal 90:536-9 S 5 '69

NORTH AMERICAN Christian convention
Undenominational Christians. J. Huffman. Chr Today 13:36 Ag 1 '69

NORTH AMERICAN Indians. See Indians of North America

NORTH AMERICAN Philips company
Orphan grown up. il Forbes 104:22-3 Jl 15 '69
Technologist of tomorrow? S. Margetts. il Duns R 94:53-4+ Ag '69

NORTH AMERICAN Rockwell corporation
Aero Commander adopts new sales plan; franchise financing. D. A. Brown. il Aviation W 90:68-9+ F 3 '69
Autonetics finds the right circuit. Bsns W p38 Mr 22 '69
Autonetics forms new company. Aviation W 91:117+ S 15 '69
Big machines help hedge the big bets. il Bsns W p 152-3+ Je 21 '69
North American may combine some units as space sales dip. Aviation W 91:97 Ag 25 '69
North American shifts divisions. Aviation W 92:23 Ja 12 '70
Rockwell takes bumps out of road to merger; close to acquisition of Miehle-Goss-Dexter. Bsns W p67 F 1 '69
Rockwell trims the giant. il Bsns W p33 Ja 10 '70

NORTH AMERICAN van lines, incorporated
Moving a mobile America: interview. J. D. Edgett. il Nations Bsns 57:74-7+ F '69

NORTH AMERICAN water and power alliance
Canada's water rights; NAWAPA water scheme. L. V. Smith. Bul Atom Sci 25:38 Ap '69

NORTH ATLANTIC council. See NATO

NORTH ATLANTIC fisheries. See Fisheries—United States

NORTH ATLANTIC islands
Cruising the North Atlantic islands. D. M. H. Mellonie. Motor B 123:144+ Mr '69

NORTH ATLANTIC treaty organization. See Nato

NORTH CAROLINA
See also
Cape Hatteras National Seashore recreational area
Colleges and universities—North Carolina
Education—North Carolina
Fishing—North Carolina
Hunting—North Carolina
Justice, Administration of—North Carolina
Libraries—North Carolina
Liquor laws and regulations—North Carolina

Constitution
Tarheelers, remember Torcaso, and Iredell! Chr Cent 86:703 My 21 '69

Description and travel
Climate fit for weathermen. D. Butwin. il Sat R 52:32+ My 31 '69

NORTH CAROLINA arts and crafts. See Arts and crafts—United States

NORTH CAROLINA school of the arts, Winston-Salem
New crop for Winston-Salem. J. M. Alfonte. il Opera N 33:6-7 F 1 '69

NORTH COLEBROOK. See Colebrook, Conn.

NORTH DAKOTA
See also
Hunting—North Dakota

NORTH KOREA. See Korea (People's Republic)

NORTH LAS VEGAS, Nev.
Area lights light a city street. D. K. Cooper. il Am City 84:138 F '69

NORTH LONG BEACH. See Long Beach, Calif.

NORTH POLE
Frosty trek across the Pole. il Sr Schol 96: 18 Ap 25 '69
See also
Airlines—International services—Great Circle route

NORTH SALEM, N.Y.
Gardens
Garden of serenity. E. McDonald. il House B 111:100-1 Ap '69

NORTH SEA
North Sea continental shelf: Court delivers judgment. UN Mo Chron 6:43-4 Mr '69

NORTH Stars (hockey team) See Hockey teams

NORTHBROOK, Ill.
New recreation complex results from overthrowing old taboos. J. Doud. il Am City 84:100+ Mr '69

NORTHEAST airlines, incorporated
Los Angeles Northeast route open. il Aviation W 91:30 O 6 '69
N.Y.-Miami competition intensifies. R. F. Coburn. il Aviation W 90:24-5 F 10 '69
Northeast reduces frequencies. Aviation W 91:34 D 1 '69

NORTHEAST airlines-Northwest merger. See Airlines—Consolidations and mergers

NORTHEAST regional ballet festival. See Dance festivals

NORTHEASTERN states
See also
Fishing—Northeastern states

NORTHEN, Rebecca T.
Dried arrangements for place cards. il Horticulture 46:34-5+ D '68

NORTHERN IRELAND
Belfast: in glorious remembrance; issues behind the troubles. C. McWilliams. il Nation 209:137-42 Ag 25 '69
Girl afire; excerpts from The price of my soul. B. Devlin. il McCalls 97:69+ N '69
John Bull's other island. J. D. Douglas. Chr Today 13:9-11 S 12 '69
See also
Civil rights—Northern Ireland
Elections—Northern Ireland
Foreign visitors in Northern Ireland
Government employees—Northern Ireland
Investments, Foreign (in Northern Ireland)
Londonderry
Protestants in Northern Ireland
Ulster
United Nations—Northern Ireland

Description and travel
Northern Ireland sampler. H. P. Koenig. il Travel 131:34-9 Je '69

NORTHERN IRELAND—*Continued*

Police

B-specials. Newsweek 74:30 S 1 '69

Politics and government

Backlash in Belfast. il Newsweek 74:54+ O 27 '69

Bad case of the troubles called Londonderry. D. Holden. il N Y Times Mag p 10-11+ Ag 3 '69

Battle of Bogside. il Newsweek 73:55 My 5 '69

Behind all the turmoil in Northern Ireland—. il U S News 66:10 My 5 '69

Bernadette and the clashing values of old and new Ireland. P. Tracy. Commonweal 91:281-2 N 28 '69

Bernadette Devlin, M.P. P. Devlin. il Vogue 154:123+ Ag 1 '69

Bonfire in Ulster. N. Moss. New Repub 161: 11-12 S 6 '69

Britain taking Ulster control. America 121: 344 O 25 '69

Cameron report. Nation 209:300 S 29 '69

Cameron report on Ulster. America 121:216-17 S 27 '69

Case of Ireland. Commonweal 90:579-80 S 26 '69

Clearing a political slum. Chr Today 13:25-6 F 14 '69

Coming winter of discontent. A. Boyd. Nation 209:566-9 N 24 '69

Cooling off Ulster: can Britain block civil war? U S News 67:5 S 1 '69

Divided Ireland: persistent trauma. J. Rockwell. Chr Cent 86:1494+ N 19 '69

Holy wars. Nation 209:194-5 S 8 '69

Human rights in Ulster. Cath World 210:2 O '69

Ireland; stage and the action. H. F. Woodhouse. Chr Cent 86:130-1 Ja 22 '69

Ireland's clash of colors. R. W. Schleck. America 121:134-6 S 6 '69; Discussion. 121: 207-8 S 27 '69

Madness; British intervention. Nation 209: 163-4 S 1 '69

Northern Ireland: edging toward anarchy. il Time 93.22-3 My 2 '69

Not Conor Cruise O'Brien. A. Lejeune. Nat R 21:1009 O 7 '69

Peace line; the Cameron report. il Newsweek 74:54 S 22 '69

State of siege. Newsweek 74:42-3 S 8 '69

Sure and it's Miss Devlin for a seat in Parliament; with report by T. Dozier. il Life 66:58A-58B My 2 '69

Tensions abate in Ulster. America 121:250-1 O 4 '69

Terence on a tightrope. il Newsweek 73:38+ F 10 '69

Their Irish is up. il Sr Schol 94:22 Ja 31 '69

To the polls. Newsweek 73:61 F 17 '69

Trouble in the land of Orange. il Time 93:26-7 Ja 31 '69

Two flags over Ulster. il Time 94:25-6 Ag 29 '69

Ulster after the bludgeons. B. Kiely. Nation 208:628-31 My 19 '69

Ulster in turmoil. il Sr Schol 94:12 My 9 '69

Ulster, still on the brink. T. E. Utley. Nat R 21:907 S 9 '69

Ulster under the microscope. J. D. Douglas. Chr Today 14:46 O 10 '69

Ulster: uneasy peace; British intervention. il Newsweek 74:29-31 S 1 '69

See also

Elections—Northern Ireland

Religious institutions and affairs

Divided Ireland: persistent trauma. J. Rockwell. Chr Cent 86:1494+ N 19 '69

Ireland; stage and the action. H. F. Woodhouse. Chr Cent 86:130-1 Ja 22 '69

Tragic charade. C. Northcott. Chr Cent 86: 1238-9 O 1 '69

Ulster after the bludgeons. B. Kiely. Nation 208:628-31 My 19 '69

Ulster: engulfed in sectarian strife. il Time 94:30-1 Ag 22 '69

Ulster: the gospel as a club raised. J. D. Douglas. Chr Today 13:38 My 9 '69

Riots

Bad case of the troubles called Londonderry. D. Holden. il N Y Times Mag p 10-11+ Ag 3 '69

Battle of Bogside. il Newsweek 73:55 My 5 '69

Business is riding with the Irish storm; international companies in Northern Ireland. il Bsns W p32-3 Ag 23 '69

Cameron report on Ulster. America 121:216-17 S 27 '69

Catholic vs. Protestant; Londonderry and Belfast. M. Kupfer. il Newsweek 74:39-40+ Ag 25 '69

Cooling off Ulster: can Britain block civil war? U S News 67:5 S 1 '69

For Ireland: specter of civil war. il U S News 67:6 Ag 25 '69

Irish ire. Chr Cent 86:1106 Ag 27 '69

Mad month begins; Londonderry's riots. il Newsweek 74:50+ Jl 28 '69

Storm over Stormont. il Newsweek 74:60 O 13 '69

Two flags over Ulster. il Time 94:25-6 Ag 29 '69

Ulster: engulfed in sectarian strife. il Time 94:30-1 Ag 22 '69

Ulster in turmoil. il Sr Schol 94:12 My 9 '69

Ulster: uneasy peace; British intervention. il Newsweek 74:29-31 S 1 '69

Social conditions

At the brink in Northern Ireland. J. A. Coulter. Cath World 209:164-7 Jl '69

NORTHERN natural gas company

Lean years. Forbes 103:210 My 15 '69

NORTHERN WESTCHESTER dance company. See Dance companies

NORTHSHIELD, Robert

Leeward Islands; with biographical sketch. por Natur Hist 78:4, 60-7 O '69

NORTHUMBERLAND, Hugh Algernon Percy, 10th duke of

Treasure of Alnwick castle; with maps. W. P. Cumming and E. C. Cumming. il pors Am Heritage 20:22-33+ Ag '69

NORTHUMBERLAND, Hugh Percy, 2d duke of

Treasure of Alnwick castle; with maps. W. P. Cumming and E. C. Cumming. il por Am Heritage 20:22-33+ Ag '69

NORTHWEST

Opening a new frontier. il U S News 67:36-8 Ag 18 '69

See also

Frontier and pioneer life—United States

Description and travel

Pacific Northwest 164 years after Lewis and Clark. R. Bongartz. il Holiday 45:48-51+ My '69

NORTHWEST, CANADIAN

Opening a new frontier. il U S News 67:36-8 Ag 18 '69

See also

Frontier and pioneer life—Canada

NORTHWEST airlines, incorporated

Northwest to contest decision in Pacific Islands route case. Aviation W 91:34 Ag 25 '69

Quarter net of Northwest Orient slumps. il Aviation W 90:40 My 12 '69

Quick depreciation grows among trunks. W. H. Gregory. il Aviation W 90:28-9 Ap 28 '69

Why Northwest puts on the ritz. il Bsns W p30-2 Jl 5 '69

NORTHWEST airlines-Northeast merger. See Airlines—Consolidations and mergers

NORTHWEST fur trade. See Fur trade

NORTHWEST industries, incorporated

Classic defense. il Newsweek 73:90 My 5 '69

Conglomerate fight widens. Bsns W p40 My 24 '69

Goodrich's four-ply defense. T. O'Hanlon. il Fortune 80:110-13+ Jl '69

How companies fend off suitors. il Bsns W p80+ Mr 15 '69

Last great battle? il Forbes 103:46+ Ap 15 '69

Merger bid bounces off Goodrich; Northwest industries' proposed offer. il Bsns W p66 F 1 '69

Northwest calls it quits on Goodrich. Bsns W p41 Ag 16 '69

Northwest-Goodrich battle nears finale. il Bsns W p28-9 Ag 2 '69

Raising the siege. Newsweek 74:57 Ag 25 '69

Takeovers: a classic counteroffensive. il Time 93:98+ My 23 '69

NORTHWEST Orient airlines. See Northwest airlines, incorporated

NORTHWEST PASSAGE

$40 million gamble on the Northwest Passage; Manhattan's voyage. il Time 94:75 S 5 '69

Hard-charger to Alaska; tanker Manhattan. il Life 67:42-5 S 26 '69

Latest search for Northwest Passage: the plan, the odds. il U S News 66:96-7 My 12 '69

Manhattan's epic voyage. il Time 94:84 S 26 '69

Northwest Passage; an ice-breaking tanker pioneers in opening the long-sought Arctic route. N. Wood. il Travel & Camera 32: 14+ N '69

NORTHWEST PASSAGE—*Continued*
Northwest Passage to what? Manhattan's voyage. J. Lear. il Sat R 52:55-6+ N 1 '69
Oil, ice and ecology; voyage of the Manhattan. il Sci N 96:265-6 S 27 '69
Ship that beat the Arctic ice; the Manhattan experiment. il U S News 67:18 S 29 '69
Who owns Northwest Passage? Bsns W p58 Ap 26 '69

NORTHWEST TERRITORIES, Canada
Report: Canadian north. J. Lotz. Atlan 223: 24-9 Je '69
See also
Inuvik, Northwest Territories

NORTHWESTERN university, Evanston, Ill.
Graduate student. J. Oberteuffer. il Phys Today 22:33 Mr '69

Transportation center
College that teaches how to move the goods. il Bsns W p 142+ Je 21 '69

NORTON, Don
NASA's tenth. Space World F-5-65:14-19 My '69
Want a summer house? Pop Sci 194:158-63 Ja '69

NORTON, Paul F.
Architecture. Antiques 96:373 S '69

NORTON Simon, incorporated
Norton Simon shuffle. Newsweek 74:65-6 S 1 '69
Simon says. . . Bsns W p64 Ag 30 '69

NORVO, Red
Mr Clean of jazz. N. McCaffrey. Nat R 21: 709-10 Jl 15 '69

NORWALK, Conn.
Notes from the Norwalk, Conn, underground; when things go wrong all blacks are black, and all whites are whitey. J. Sharnik. il N Y Times Mag p30-1+ My 25 '69

NORWAY
See also
Aeronautics, Military—Norway
Aluminum industry and trade—Norway
Ballet—Norway
Bergen
Gardens—Norway
Hunting—Norway
Music festivals—Norway
Performing arts—Norway
Publishers and publishing—Norway

Air force
Norwegian defense posture gives key role to air force. W. C. Wetmore. il Aviation W 90:40-1+ Mr 17 '69

Description and travel
Norway; fjords, fun, midnight sun. il Travel & Camera 32:60-1+ Mr '69

Industries
See also
Aluminum industry and trade—Norway

Religious institutions and affairs
See also
Lutheran church in Norway

NORWEGIAN air force. See Norway—Air force

NORWEGIAN ballet. See Ballet—Norway

NORWEGIAN cookery. See Cookery, Norwegian

NORWICK, Kenneth P. See Pilpel, H. F. jt. auth.

NORWOOD, Mary Lou
Artists on a houseboat. Am Artist 33:20-7 Ap '69

NOSEMA
Nosema cuniculi: in vitro isolation. J. A. Shadduck. il Science 166:516-17 O 24 '69

NOSHPITZ, Joseph D.
Phobias. Todays Ed 58:20-3 My '69

NOSTALGIA
Handling S.S. in camp; Separation syndrome or homesickness at Boy scout camp Yawgood, R.I. E. Ohlsen. Camp Mag 41:16 My '69

NOT an ordinary wife; story. See Rule, J.

NOTABLE books council. See American library association—Adult services division

NOTABLES. See Celebrities; Great men

NOTE paper. See Stationery

NOTE reading. See Music reading

NOTEBOOKS
Second thoughts about notebooks. A. B. Holland. Writers Digest 49:18 Mr '69

NOTES from a bottle; story. See Stevenson, J.

NOTHING personal; story. See Meehan, T.

NOTHING personal; story. See Packer, V.

NOTHING to hide; story. See Dash, J.

NOTRE DAME, Ind. University
Dealing with campus chaos: Notre Dame: fifteen minutes and out; excerpts from letter, February 17, 1969. T. M. Hesburgh. U S News 66:34 Mr 3 '69; Same abr. with title College president takes a stand on campus chaos. Read Digest 94:104-7 My '69
Hesburgh fights. J. O'Connor. Look 33:42+ N 18 '69
Hesburgh of Notre Dame: (1) he's destroying this university; (2) he's bringing it into the mainstream of American life. T. J. Fleming. il N Y Times Mag p56-7+ My 11 '69

NOTRE DAME cathedral. See Paris—Notre Dame (cathedral)

NOTROM, Henry B.
Outboard-motor service guide. Pop Mech 132: 138-41+ Jl; 132-5+ Ag; 144-7 S; 140-3 N; 162-5 D '69

NOTTS, Brian
Bottled art. Design 70:20-2 Sum '69

NOUNS
Exaltation of larks; excerpts. J. Lipton. il Natur Hist 78:8-10+ Je '69

NOVA SCOTIA
See also
Sable Island

NOVAK, Charles T. See Hecker, P. C. jt. auth.

NOVAK, Michael
Experiment at Old Westbury. Commonweal 89:560-3 Ja 31 '69
Politicizing the lower-middle. Commonweal 90:341-3 Je 6 '69
Vietnam's tomorrow. Commonweal 91:45-7 O 10 '69
Where did all the spirit go? Commonweal 90:540-2 S 5 '69

NOVELISTS
First novelists; spring-summer-fall 1969; statements by the writers, ed. by I. E. Stokvis. il Library J 94:570-84, 2254-61, 3473-9 F 1, Je 1, O 1 '69
Yen for young authors. L. Fleischer. il Life 67:76+ O 24 '69
See also
Women as authors

NOVELISTS, American
See also
Bellow, S.
Cheever, J.
Ellison, R.
Faulkner, W.
Hemingway, E.
Knowles, J.
Levin, I.
Oates, J. C.
O'Hara, J.
Potter, N. A. J.
Robbins, H.
Roth, P.
Steinbeck, J.
Stowe, H. B.
Susann, J.
Vonnegut, K. jr
Webb, C.

NOVELISTS, English
See also
Cary, J.
Forster, E. M.
Golding, W.
Lessing, D. M.
MacInnes, C.
Murdoch, I.
Renault, M. pseud.
Snow of Leicester, C. P. S.
Tolkien, J. R. R.

NOVELISTS, French
See also
Beyle, M. H.
Dumas, A.
Montherlant, H. de

NOVELISTS, Irish
See also
Nolan, B.
O'Brien, E.

NOVELISTS, Jewish
Portnoy's compliance. P. Collier. il Ramp Mag 7:28-31 My '69

NOVELISTS, Mexican
See also
Fuentes, C.

NOVELISTS, Negro
Black novelists: our turn. R. A. Gross. il Newsweek 73:94+ Je 16 '69

NOVELISTS, Norwegian
See also
Hamsun, K.

NOVELISTS, Swedish
See also
Lagerkvist, P.

NOVELISTS, Venezuelan
See also
Gallegos, R.

NOVELISTS, Welsh
See also
Thomas, G.
NOVELS. See Fiction
NOVELS, Israeli. See Israeli fiction
NOVELS, Religious. See Religious literature
NOVICH, Max
Pretend he's your sister. B. Gilbert. il pors Sports Illus 30:58-62+ F 17 '69
NOVICK, David
Paperwork mess goes into a think tank. por Bsns W p 126+ F 22 '69
NOVICK, Julius
Theatre. Nation 209:357-8 O 6 '69
Theatre. Vogue 153:150 Ap 1; 32 Ap 15 '69
NOVICK, Sheldon
Basement H-bombs. Sci & Cit 10:243-9 D '68
Mile from Times square; adaptation of address, December 2, 1968. bibliog f Environ 11:10-15+ Ja '69
New pollution problem: mercury contamination of food, air, and water. Environ 11:2-9 My '69
NOVOCAINE
Real truth behind the youth pill. E. Ubell. il McCalls 96:14+ Ag '69
NOVOTNY, John E. See Modisette, J. L. jt. auth.
NOW or forever; story. See Hayes, E. A.
NOYD, Dale E.
Court-martial of Dale Noyd. R. C. Kimball. Chr Cent 86:116-19 Ja 22 '69
NOYES, John Humphrey
Great Oneida love-in. M. Bishop. il Am Heritage 20:14-17+ F '69
NOYES, Judy
Chinook celebrates a birthday and an expansion. Pub W 196:52-3 S 15 '69
NOYES, Winninette A.
French Pete: lowland valley in Oregon's Cascades. Liv Wildn 32:25-9 Wint '68
NOZAKI, Mitsuhiro. See Hayaishi, O. jt. auth.
NUBIA

Antiquities
Miracle from the desert; frescoes from Faras. il Time 94:68 S 5 '69
NUBIANS
Disease in ancient Nubia. G. J. Armelagos. bibliog il Science 163:255-9 Ja 17 '69
NUCLEAR age. See Atomic age
NUCLEAR boilers. See Pressure vessels
NUCLEAR carriers. See Aircraft carriers, Atomic powered
NUCLEAR counters. See Counters (electrons, ions, etc)
NUCLEAR energy. See Atomic power
NUCLEAR engineering
See also
Atomic power industry
NUCLEAR excavation. See Atomic blasting
NUCLEAR fission
New insight is offered into the fission process. bibliog il Phys Today 22:64-5+ F '69; Reply. L. Pauling. 22:9+ Je '69
NUCLEAR fuels
Who'll own atom fuel supply? il Bsns W p 136+ Je 14 '69
Why New York worries utilities; plan to lease atomic cores from state. Bsns W p 17 D 27 '69
NUCLEAR fusion
Artsimovich talks about controlled-fusion research; ed. by J. L. Tuck and G. B. Lubkin. L. Artsimovich. il Phys Today 22:54-7 Je '69
Closer and closer; success at Tokamak. Sci N 96:424 N 8 '69
Cold octopole and hot Tokomak show long confinement times. Phys Today 22:55-6 D '69
Confinement among the rings. D. E. Thomsen. il Sci N 96:413 N 1 '69
Fusion power: optimism and a Tokamak gap at Dubna. R. W. Holcomb. Science 166:363-4 O 17 '69
Plasma confinement grows. il Sci N 95:397 Ap 26 '69
Quarks for neutrino-less fusion. Sci N 96:48 Jl 19 '69
Russia's H-bomb tamers; control of thermonuclear fusion for power. Bsns W p 176+ S 20 '69
Triumph for Tokamak. Newsweek 74:70 N 10 '69
US fusion experimenters want to try Tokomaks now. Phys Today 22:67-8 Jl '69
NUCLEAR industries. See Atomic power industry
NUCLEAR magnetic resonance
Hydration of macromolecules. I. D. Kuntz, jr. and others. bibliog il Science 163:1329-31 Mr 21 '69

Nuclear magnetic resonance measurement of oil unsaturation in single viable corn kernels. T. F. Conway and L. F. Johnson. bibliog il Science 164:827-8 My 16 '69
Phosphous-proton spin-spin coupling and conformation of a dinucleoside phosphate. M. Tsuboi and others. bibliog il Science 166:1504-6 D 19 '69
Polywater: proton nuclear magnetic resonance spectrum. T. F. Page, jr. and others. il Science 167:51 Ja 2 '70
NUCLEAR medicine. See Radiology, Medical
NUCLEAR non-proliferation treaty. See Atomic weapons—International control
NUCLEAR physics
Atoms. V. W. Hughes. il Phys Today 22:33-7 F '69
Gaps in high-energy physics; STU vs IBY physics. Sci N 96:162 Ag 30 '69
Into the nucleus. D. E. Thomsen. il Sci N 96:380-1 O 25 '69
Probing the depths of the nucleus; meson factories. D. E. Thomsen. il Sci N 96:332-3 O 11 '69
See also
Atomic nuclei
California. University—Lawrence radiation laboratories
International conference on high energy physics
Isobaric spin
Nuclear fission
Nuclear spin
Particles (nuclear physics)
Positrons
Radioactivity
Scattering (physics)
Time reversal

History
Three decades of fast-neutron experiments; adaptation of address, 1968. H. H. Barschall. bibliog por Phys Today 22:54-9 Ag '69
NUCLEAR physics institute, Akademgorodok. See Akademgorodok, Siberia
NUCLEAR power plants. See Atomic power plants
NUCLEAR propulsion. See Rockets, Atomic powered
NUCLEAR reactions
See also
Nuclear fission
NUCLEAR reactors
Asking the engineer; nuclear fusion reactor. Sci N 96:266-7 S 27 '69
On the sodium bandwagon; sodium-cooled fast breeder reactor. Sci N 95:233 Mr 8 '69
Possibility of successful nuplex for India's Thar Desert. R. D. Sharma. Bul Atom Sci 25:31 N '69
Ready for market; breeders. il Sci N 95:571-2 Je 14 '69
Social impact of a nuplex; advantages of nuclear-powered, industrial complexes. R. L. Meier. il Bul Atom Sci 25:16-21 Mr '69
Three plans approved; prototype liquid metal fast breeder reactor. Sci N 96:551-2 D 13 '69
Toward breeder reactors; India's choices. S. K. Ghaswala. il Sci N 95:603 Je 21 '69

Manufacture
When the music stops; problems of U.S. nuclear reactor producers. il Forbes 103:30+ F 1 '69

Safety devices and measures
Mile from Times square; adaptation of address, December 2, 1968. S. Novick. bibliog f il Environ 11:10-15+ Ja '69
Myth of the peaceful atom. R. Curtis and E. Hogan. il Natur Hist 78:6-8+ Mr '69; Discussion. 78:6+ My '69
NUCLEAR rocket development station. See Proving grounds
NUCLEAR rockets. See Rockets, Atomic powered
NUCLEAR spin
Nuclear spin thermodynamics in the rotating frame. A. G. Redfield. bibliog il Science 164:1015-23 My 30 '69
NUCLEAR technology and civilization. See Technology and civilization
NUCLEAR weapons. See Atomic bombs
NUCLEASES
See also
Ribonucleases
NUCLEATION, Atmospheric. See Atmospheric nucleation
NUCLEIC acids
See also
DNA
Nucleoproteins
RNA

NUCLEOLUS. See Cell nuclei

NUCLEONS
Nucleon-nucleon scattering. M. H. MacGregor. bibliog il Phys Today 22:21-8 D '69

NUCLEOPROTEINS
Altered ribosomal protein in streptomycin-dependent escherichia coli. E. A. Birge and C. G. Kurland. bibliog il Science 166:1282-4 D 5 '69

Assembly of protein and nucleoprotein particles from extracted tobacco rattle virus protein and RNA. J. S. Semancik and R. A. Reynolds. bibliog il Science 164:559-60 My 2 '69

Chloroplast ribosomes: stereospecificity of inhibition by chloramphenicol. R. J. Ellis. bibliog il Science 163:477-8 Ja 31 '69

Dye-sensitized photooxidation of the escherichia coli ribosome. R. T. Garvin and others. bibliog il Science 164:583-4 My 2 '69

Induction of helical arrays of ribosomes by vinblastine sulfate in escherichia coli. E. W. Kingsbury and H. Voetz. bibliog il Science 166:768-9 N 7 '69

Macrophage ribonucleoprotein: nature of the antigenic fragment. A. A. Gottlieb. bibliog il Science 165:592-4 Ag 8 '69

Phosphorylation of dipteran chromosomes and rat liver nuclei. W. B. Benjamin and R. M. Goodman. bibliog il Science 166:629-31 O 31 '69

Preferential synthesis of ferritin and albumin by different populations of liver polysomes. S. J. Hicks and others. bibliog Science 164:584-5 My 2 '69

Ribosomes. M. Nomura. il Sci Am 221:28-35 O '69

Satellite-like particle of tobacco ringspot virus that resembles tobacco ringspot virus. I. R. Schneider. bibliog il Science 166:1627-9 D 26 '69

Structure of ribosomes of chromatoid bodies; three-dimensional fourier synthesis at low resolution. R. S. Morgan; reply. D. J. DeRosier and A. Klug. Science 163:1470 Mr 28 '69
See also
Interferon

NUCLEOSIDE triphosphates. See Phosphates

NUCLEOTIDES
Interferon induction increased through chemical modification of a synthetic polyribonucleotide. E. De Clercq and others. bibliog il Science 165:1137-9 S 12 '69

Irreversible inhibition of nuclear exoribonuclease by thymidine-3'-fluorophosphate and p-haloacetamidophenyl nucleotides. M. B. Sporn and others. bibliog il Science 164:1408-10 Je 20 '69

Nucleotide sequence of escherichia coli tyrosine transfer ribonucleic acid. B. P. Doctor and others. bibliog il Science 163:693-5 F 14 '69
See also
Adenosine monophosphate
Adenosine triphosphate
Guanosine monophosphate
Nicotinamide nucleotides

NUDE in art
Sex as a spectator sport. il Time 94:61-3+ Jl 11 '69
See also
Sex in art

NUDE in photography. See Human figure in photography

NUDIBRANCHS. See Sea slugs

NUDITY
Conversations on the new eroticism; symposium. il Time 94:64-5 Jl 11 '69
Naked craze. H. E. Wright. Chr Cent 86:617-19 Ap 30 '69
Naked stage. il Newsweek 73:80 Mr 3 '69
Sex as a spectator sport. il Time 94:61-3+ Jl 11 '69
Taking it off. il Newsweek 74:112+ O 13 '69
To be or not to be nude. P. Bailey. Cur 109:18-19 Ag '69
What can they do for an encore? Theater of nudity. W. Kerr. il N Y Times Mag p24-5+ F 2 '69

Anecdotes, facetiae, satire, etc.
Nude scene: [BLIP] is beautiful. W. Zinsser. Life 67:16B Ag 8 '69

NUDITY, Theater of. See Theater, Experimental

NUDITY in the Bible
Nudity in biblical perspective. S. E. Smallman. Chr Today 13:6-8 Ag 22 '69

NUFFIELD college, Oxford. See Oxford. University

NUISANCES
See also
Odors

NUMBATS. See Anteaters

NUMBER work. See Arithmetic—Study and teaching

NUMBERING systems
Their number is up; army serial number replaced by social security number. Time 94:17 Jl 11 '69

NUMBERS, Complex
Imaginary numbers. I. Asimov. il Sci Digest 65:83-4 Mr '69

NUMBERS, Imaginary. See Numbers, Complex

NUMBERS, Symbolism of. See Symbolism of numbers

NUMBERS, Theory of
See also
Fibonacci numbers

NUMERALS
See also
Numeration

NUMERATION
Ordinary vs. binary numbers. I. Asimov. Sci Digest 65:83-4 Ap '69

NUMERIC identification. See Identification

NUMERICAL analysis
Rambling random walk and its gambling equivalent. M. Gardner. il Sci Am 220:118-20 My '69
Random walks, by semidrunk bugs and others, on the square and on the cube. M. Gardner. il Sci Am 220:122-4+ Je '69

NUMERICAL control. See Automatic control

NUMEROLOGY. See Symbolism of numbers

NUMISMATICS
How to make a buck with dimes and quarters. T. Powers. il Life 66:61-2+ My 2 '69
Numismatics. C. French. See Issues of Hobbies
See also
Coins

NUNCIOS, Papal
Bishop Shannon, exile? J. B. Sheerin. Cath World 209:194-5 Ag '69

NUNLEY, Jay
1-2-3 sequential turn signal. Radio-Electr 40:38-40 Ap '69

NUNS
Battling for nuns' rights: Vatican and the new militancy of secular nuns. il Newsweek 74:80-1 S 8 '69
Double bind in religious life today. A. Walters. il Cath World 210:22-6 O '69
Nuns and breast cancer. il Sci Digest 66:58 Ag '69
See also
Convents and nunneries
Negro nuns
Sisterhoods

NUNS' ISLAND
New type of new town breaks ground for planners. il Bsns W p 132-4+ Jl 19 '69

NUR, Amos. See Simmons, G. jt. auth.

NURBURGRING race. See Automobile racing

NURSE and patient
Dual role of comforter and bereaved; reactions of medical personnel to the dying child and his parents. E. Wallace and B. D. Townes. bibliog Ment Hy 53:327-32 Jl '69

NURSE midwives. See Midwives

NURSERIES (horticulture)
Denmark's nursery exhibits. M. C. Parsons, jr. Horticulture 46:32+ N '68
White flower farm. il House & Gard 136:48-53+ Ag '69
See also
Sun circle ranches

NURSERIES, Day. See Day nurseries

NURSERY rhymes
What comes after Mother Goose? P. Parker. Ed Digest 35:46-9 O '69
See also
Mother Goose

NURSERY schools
Early school admissions; a Baltimore best seller. A. C. Harding. il Todays Ed 58:57-8+ N '69
Hawaii's tiny-tot UN; Waiokeola. il Todays Health 47:50-3 F '69
Pioneering nursery school; one-room nursery school at New York university medical center's Institute of rehabilitation medicine. E. P. Berkeley. il Arch Forum 130:68-9 Mr '69
Playgroup for preschoolers. S. Levitin. il Parents Mag 44:62-3+ S '69
School where little kids teach the teachers; Far West laboratory for educational research and development, Berkeley, Calif. il Parents Mag 44:70-2 S '69
See also
Day nurseries

NURSES and nursing
Death in a cancer ward; psychological needs. Time 93:62+ Je 20 '69
Jobscope: for the science-minded. N. Axelrad. Mlle 69:218 My '69
Trauma for nurses; emergency decisions. il Sci Digest 66:59-60 Jl '69
See also
Nurse and patient
School nurses

NURSING (suckling) See Suckling

NURSING homes
Gold in geriatrics. il Time 93:103 Je 6 '69
Nursing-home chains: latest growth industry. il U S News 67:72-3 Ag 11 '69
Nursing-home fever. W. Robertson. il Fortune 79:170-1 Ja '69
Nursing homes; how to pick a good one. il Changing T 23:15-18 S '69
Personal business. Bsns W p 137-8 Je 7 '69
Who cares for the aged? R. E. Burger. il Sat R 52:14-17 Ja 25 '69; Discussion. 52:35 F 15 '69

NUSSENZVEIG, H. Moysés
Migration of scientists from Latin America; adaptation of address, 1968. Science 165:1328-32 S 26 '69

NUT torte. See Cake

NUTRITION
Accidents and what you eat. J. I. Rodale. Org Gard & Farm 16:93-5 D '69
And we still aren't eating right! il Changing T 23:11-13 N '69
Field studies of nutrition and behavior; AAAS symposium, December 27, 1969. A. P. Vayda and C. Lowman-Vayda. il Science 166:1312-13 D 5 '69
Let's talk about food; ed. by P. L. White. See issues of Today's health
People need fertilizers too. R Rodale. Org Gard & Farm 16:21-3 Ag '69
See also
Aged—Nutrition
Children—Nutrition
Food
Food habits
Iron in diet
Starvation
Vitamins

NUTRITION education
At a bargain price: help for the underfed; with report by K. W. King. il U S News 66:84-5 F 3 '69

NUTRITION problems
Is the world menaced by mass hunger? B. L. Masse. America 121:348 O 25 '69
Malnutrition, learning and behavior. P. H. Abelson. Science 164:17 Ap 4 '69
Protein problem and national development; statement, November 20, 1968. A. E. Goldschmidt. Dept State Bul 59:673-7 D 23 '68
See also
Food and agriculture organization of the United Nations

Biafra
ABC; Saturday review's Aid for Biafran children. N. Cousins. il Sat R 52:20-1+ F 1 '69
Challenge of Biafra. Commonweal 90:451-2 Jl 25 '69
Moon over Biafra: a plea for priorities. S. V. Roberts. Commonweal 89:489-90 Ja 17 '69
Nation is dying! D. Reed. il Read Digest 94:75-80 Mr '69
Report from Biafra. J. McLaughlin. America 120:90-5, 138-41 Ja 25-F 1 '69
Report on ABC; Saturday review's Aid for Biafran children. N. Cousins. Sat R 52:20-1 My 3 '69
Worsening conditions. il Time 94:26-8 Ag 29 '69

Haiti
At a bargain price: help for the underfed; with report by K. W. King. il U S News 66:84-5 F 3 '69

United States
Aftermath; more on Dr Gatch of South Carolina. B. Shaw. Esquire 72:12+ Jl '69
America's starving children. R. Coles and H. Huge. il Parents Mag 44:68-71+ N '69
Are we snacking our way to malnutrition? J. L. Breeling. il Todays Health 48:48-50+ Ja '70
Can the government abolish hunger and malnutrition? White House conference on food, nutrition and health (proposed) Consumer Bul 52:15-16 S '69
Case to end hunger. E. F. Hollings. Ment Hy 53:500-2 O '69
Doctor Jean Mayer: food watcher for a nation. il Life 67:41-2+ N 28 '69
Face of hunger; preliminary results of National nutrition survey. il Newsweek 73:66-7 F 3 '69

Faces of hunger; photographs by M. Mauney; with report by F. G. Loyd. Todays Health 47:20-3 O '69
Feed my sheep. A. C. Mermann. Chr Cent 86:900-2 Jl 2 '69
Finally, facts on malnutrition in the United States; interview, ed. by F. G. Loyd. A. E. Schaefer. il Todays Health 47:32-3+ S '69
Food, nutrition and health; address, December 2, 1969. R. M. Nixon. Vital Speeches 36:162-5 Ja 1 '70
Hunger amid plenty; summary of report. A. E. Schaefer. Sr Schol 94:13 F 7 '69
Hunger and affluence: the strange contradictions. il Sr Schol 95:6-10 O 6 '69
Hunger fighters. New Repub 160:4 My 17 '69
Hunger in America: let them eat words. N. Kotz. Look 33:71 D 2 '69
Hunger next door; program in Missoula, Mont. N. Munro. il Redbook 132:21+ Mr '69
Hunger, U.S.A. Commonweal 89:695-6 Mr 7 '69
It's there, all right. il Newsweek 73:28 Mr 3 '69
Let's talk about food; excerpts from report. P. L. White. Todays Health 47:8+ D '69
Making U.S. hunger a has-been; symposium, ed. by F. G. Loyd. il Todays Health 47:38-41 N '69
Nixon plan to fight hunger. U S News 66:12 My 19 '69
One man's fight against hunger in the city. F. G. Loyd. il Todays Health 47:48-53+ D '69
One-sixth of a nation. Time 93:74 Ja 31 '69
Reports: Washington; what the Nixon administration is doing. E. B. Drew. Atlan 224:6+ Jl '69
Starvation and the very rich. A. J. Snider. Sci Digest 66:60 O '69
Truth about hunger in America. il U S News 66:32-5 Ap 28 '69
Underdeveloped country. il Time 93:25 F 28 '69
When did we see thee hungry? A. C. Mermann. Chr Cent 85:473-7 Ap 9 '69
Where food prices are headed; interview. C. M. Hardin. il U S News 67:69-72 O 27 '69
Who are the hungry? il Newsweek 73:38+ Ap 28 '69
Who knows? Who cares? J. F. Donnelly. America 120:250-2 Mr 1 '69
Who's hungry? And for what? Nat R 21:265-6 Mr 25 '69
See also
United States—Congress—Senate—Nutrition and human needs, Select committee on
White House conference on food, nutrition and health

NUTRITION research
Effects of nutrition on behavior; AAAS symposium, December 30, 1969. J. Rosenblith. Science 166:909 N 14 '69
Malnutrition research; letter. J. A. Halsted. Science 165:543 Ag 8 '69
Miasma of malnutrition. Sci Digest 65:75 My '69
New challenges to world hunger; with photographs by F. Goro. Life 66:38-51 Ja 24 '69
Nutrition and learning. H. F. Eichenwald and P. C. Fry. bibliog Science 163:644-8 F 14 '69; Reply with rejoinder. H. Baker and O. Frank. 165:313 Jl 18 '69

NUTS
1968 not so nutty. E. M. Reilly, jr. il Cons 23:16 Ap '69
See also
Cookery—Nuts

NUTTER, G. Warren
Key defense aide who is known for calling the turn on Russia. por U S News 66:20 Mr 17 '69
Nuttering. New Repub 160:8 Mr 29 '69
Strange world of Mr Nutter. P. Steinfels. Commonweal 90:158-9 Ap 25 '69

NWOKORIE, Iheanacho Sunday
Doctor Sunday comes to town. L. Rich. il pors Am Ed 5:20-3 My '69

NYE, William B.
Discoverer of the Hudson's source. M. MacKenzie. il por Cons 23:28-31 F '69

NYERERE, Julius Kambarage
Tanzania; address, October 2, 1969. Vital Speeches 36:48-53 N 1 '69

about
Africa hails a president, prepares for Pope. O. Okite. Chr Today 13:30-1 My 23 '69

NYGREN, Malcolm
Church and political action. Chr Today 13:9-10+ Mr 14 '69

NYLON
Sad yarn for King Cotton. il Sr Schol 94:19 Mr 7 '69

NYLON shutters. See Shutters

O

OAO (orbiting astronomical observatory) See Artificial satellites—Astronomical applications

OAS. See Organization of American states

OAU. See Organization of African unity

OCR (optical character recognition) See Optical scanners

OECD. See Organization for economic co-operation and development

OEO. See United States—Economic opportunity, Office of

OGO (orbiting geophysical observatory) See Artificial satellites—Astronomical applications

OH radicals. See Hydroxyl

OIC. See Opportunities industrialization centers, incorporated

OSO (orbiting solar observatory). See Artificial satellites—Astronomical applications

OSS (orbiting space station) See Space stations

OST. See United States—Science and technology, Office of

O Tannenbaum; story. See Wood, P. S.

OAK
Diseases and pests
See also
Gipsy moths

OAK LAWN, Ill.
Reavis high school. R. Erbes. il Library J 94:4214-15 N 15 '69

OAK PARK, Ill.
Churches
Unity temple, Oak Park, Ill. H. Wright. bibliog f il Arch Forum 130:28-37 Je '69

OAKES, Chris
New mobe (II): the kids on bus no. 28. T. Meehan. il pors N Y Times Mag p28-9+ N 30 '69

OAKES, John Bertram
On the only hand. . . . por Newsweek 73:90 Je 16 '69

OAKLAND, Calif.
Architecture
In Oakland: simple mass, elegant precision new telephone equipment building. il Arch Rec 146:124-5 Jl '69

East Bay municipal utility district
We kept the sewer in service. J. D. Foster and J. W. Tooley. il Am City 84:97-9 N '69

Education
Doing your own thing at Sobrante park school. H. Cyr. il ALA Bul 63:268-71 F '69

Galleries and museums
New museum for the West; with editorial comment. J. Beyer. il Am West 6:34-9, 48 N '69
Oakland's brand new park-museum. il Sunset 143:12-5, 186 S '69
Regional art at Oakland. P. Selz; P. Mills. il Art in Am 57:108-9 S '69

Housing
Acorn project. R. Montgomery. il Arch Forum 131:90-3 Jl '69

Parks and playgrounds
Cavy has his day. il Am City 84:44 N '69
Park grows out of a reservoir. il Am City 84:63+ N '69

Police
Persecution and assassination of the Black Panthers as performed by the Oakland police under the direction of Chief Charles R. Gain, Mayor John Reading. et al. G. Marine. Ramp Mag 7:120-6 Ja 25 '69

OAKLAND Athletics (baseball) See Baseball clubs

OAKLAND museum. See Oakland, Calif.—Galleries and museums

OAKLAND Raiders. See Football clubs

OAKLAND Seals (hockey team) See Hockey teams

OAKLAND university, Rochester, Mich.
No feet on the floor. R. Kirk. Nat R 21:339 Ap 8 '69

OAKLEY, Thornton
Four disciples of Howard Pyle. H. C. Pitz. il Am Artist 33:40-1 Ja '69

OARSMANSHIP. See Rowing

OATES, James Franklin, 1899–
Affirmative action. L. L. L. Golden. Sat R 52:127-8 Mr 8 '69
SR's businessman of the year. R. L. Tobin. por Sat R 53:85-7 Ja 10 '70

OATES, Joyce Carol
Interior monologue; story. Esquire 71:84-5 F '69
Internal landscape; poem. Atlan 223:63 Ap '69
Interview with Joyce Carol Oates; ed. by L. Kuehl. por Commonweal 91:307-10 D 5 '69
Ordinary miracles; poem. Sat R 52:8 D 20 '69
Private life; story. Yale R 59:79-96 O '69
about
Writing as a natural reaction. il por Time 94:108 O 10 '69

OATES, Stephen B.
To wash this land in blood. . . Am West 6:36-41 Jl; 24-7+ N '69

OATH; story. See Litwak, L.

OATHS
Swearing in scientists. Chr Today 13:38-9 Mr 28 '69

OATHS (profanity) See Swearing

OATMEAL
Another kind of Swiss breakfast. il Sunset 142:162 My '69

OATS
Avena magna; new oat species. G. Martinoli; A. Löve; E. E. Terrell. bibliog Science 163:594-5 F 7 '69
Quick profits in big oat yields. D. Seim. il Farm J 93:36D My '69
Silica in developing epidermal cells of avena internodes: electron microprobe analysis. P. B. Kaufman and others. bibliog il Science 166:1015-17 N 21 '69
You can make money with oats. G. L. Earle. il Suc Farm 67:36-7 Ja '69

OAXACA (state), Mexico
Settlement, farming technology, and environment in the Nochixtlan Valley. R. Spores. bibliog il Science 166:557-69 O 31 '69

OBEDIENCE
I was only following orders; question of following orders to perform inhuman actions. Trans-Action 6:7-8 My '69
Patterns in obedience and disobedience. S. S. Feldman. bibliog Am Imago 26:21-36 Spr '69

OBEDIENCE (canon law)
Double bind in religious life today. A. Walters. il Cath World 210:22-6 O '69
New American Jesuits. J. L'Heureux. Atlan 224:59-64 N '69

OBEDIENCE schools for dogs. See Dogs—Training

OBERLIN, Ohio
Architecture
Oberlin printing: diverse functions within a single form. il Arch Rec 145:160-1 F '69

OBERST, Paul
As others see us. Field & S 73:53+ Ap '69

OBERTEUFFER, John
Graduate student. por Phys Today 22:33 Mr '69

OBERTH, Hermann
Pioneers. il por Time 94:24 Jl 18 '69

OBESITY. See Corpulence

OBEY, David
Laird country goes Democratic. por U S News 66:12 Ap 14 '69
Upset in Wisconsin. Time 93:29 Ap 11 '69

OBJECTIVES in education. See Education—Aims and objectives

OBLIGATION, Presidential. See Presidents—United States—Powers and duties

OBOLER, Eli M.
Case for ALA regional annual conferences. por ALA Bul 63:1099-101 S '69
Hold! Library J 94:2412-13 Je 15 '69

OBOTE, Milton
Shots above the music. Time 94:16 D 26 '69

O'BOYLE, Bonnie
Graffiti lives. Seventeen 28:158-9+ S '69

O'BOYLE, Patrick Aloysius, cardinal
L'affaire O'Boyle. America 121:24 Jl 19 '69
Last hurrah of Cardinal Patrick Aloysius O'Boyle. M. Hinckle. por Ramp Mag 7:28-31 D 14 '68

O'BRIEN, Brice
Coal industry; address, January 21, 1969. Vital Speeches 35:379-84 Ap 1 '69

O'BRIEN, Charles
Universities: industry links raise conflict of interest issue. J. Walsh. Science 164:411-12 Ap 25 '69

O'BRIEN, Conor Cruise
King Herod explains. Criticism
   Nation 209:580 N 24 '69
O'BRIEN, David J.
Needed: a new history. America 120:528-
   30 My 3 '69
Power to the students. Commonweal 91:15-
   18+ O 3 '69
O'BRIEN, Edna
Literary horizons. G. Hicks. Sat R 52:25-6 F
   1 '69
O'BRIEN, Flann, pseud. See Nolan, B.
O'BRIEN, J. See Myers, R. S. jt. auth.
O'BRIEN, James C.
Summer programs in the British Isles; ad-
   dress, November 1968. Engl J 58:726-34 My
   '69
O'BRIEN, John A.
Humanae vitae: reactions and consequences.
   Chr Cent 86:288-9 F 26 '69
It is time for a change. Read Digest 95:108-9
   D '69
Reform of the Roman curia. Chr Cent 86:
   868-71 Je 25 '69
Vatican speaks out. Chr Cent 86:1580-2 D 10 '69
O'BRIEN, John S. See Ho, M. W; Okada, S.
   jt. auths.
O'BRIEN, Lawrence Francis
Excerpt from address, April 3, 1967. Cong Di-
   gest 48:88+ Mr '69

about

O'Brien's fast hurrah. il por Bsns W p90
   Ag 16 '69
Pulling in its horns. por Newsweek 74:58+ Ag
   25 '69
O'BRIEN, Michael
O'Brien: I want to kill a nigger. A. Gold-
   berg and G. Marine. il por Ramp Mag 8:
   10-18 Jl '69
O'BRIEN, William M.
Drug testing: is time running out? Bul Atom
   Sci 25:8-14 Ja; 13-16 Je '69
OBSCENE literature. See Immoral literature
   and pictures
OBSCENITY (law)
Coming crackdown on smut peddlers; with
   excerpts from President Nixon's message
   to Congress, May 2, 1969. il U S News 67:
   52-3 Jl 21 '69
Communists are right about some things.
   Chr Today 13:26-7 Je 6 '69
Content no longer sole factor in obscenity.
   H. F. Pilpel and K. P. Norwick. Pub W
   195:32-3 Mr 31 '69
English lesson. Time 93:70+ Mr 28 '69
Home movies, anybody? Supreme court deci-
   sions. Newsweek 73:36 Ap 21 '69
Home movies: Stanley's conviction reversed.
   Time 93:78 Ap 18 '69
**** is no longer a dirty word. E. G. Romm.
   Esquire 71:135+ Ap '69
Mr Nixon on the trail of smut. R. H. Smith.
   Pub W 195:34 My 12 '69
Obscenity and public morality, by H. M.
   Clor. Review
   Sat R 52:80-1 My 10 '69. S. W. Little
Prudes, lewds and polysyllables. J. H. Smy-
   lie. Commonweal 89:671-3 F 28 '69
Variable obscenity laws popular in one third
   the U.S. Library J 94:4192+ N 15 '69
Warren court and whither obscenity. H. F.
   Pilpel and K. P. Norwick. Pub W 196:46-8
   Jl 7 '69
   See also
Censorship
Trials (obscenity)
United States—Commission on obscenity and
   pornography

Anecdotes, facetiae, satire, etc.
Obscenity gap. V. Gold. Nat R 21:597 Je 17
   '69
OBSERVATORIES
   See also
Astronomical observatories
Geomagnetic observatories
OBSIDIAN hydration dating. See Archeology—
   Methodology
OBSTETRICS
   see also
Midwives

O'CALLAGHAN, Joseph F.
Beginnings of the Cortes of León-Castile.
   bibliog f Am Hist R 74:1503-37 Je '69

O'CASEY, Sean
Cock-a-doodle-dandy. Criticism
   America 120:232 F 22 '69
   Nation 208:187-9 F 10 '69
   New Yorker 44:44+ F 1 '69
   Time il 93:72 Ja 31 '69
   Vogue 153:112 Mr 1 '69
OCCIDENTAL petroleum corporation
How to win without playing the game. Bsns
   W p86 O 25 '69
Libya adds water to its riches. il Bsns W
   p 168+ F 22 '69
OCCULT sciences
There's a new-time religion on campus. A.
   M. Greeley. il N Y Times Mag p 14-15+ Je
   1 '69
   See also
Astrology
Psychical research
Spiritualism
OCCULTATIONS
August occultation of the Pleiades. il Sky
   & Tel 38:269-70 O '69
Favorable grazing occultations, May-Au-
   gust, 1969. D. W. Dunham. il R Pop Astron
   63:26 My '69
1970 occultation supplement: predictions for
   the United States and Canada. il Sky &
   Tel 38:317-21+ N '69
Observations of the March Pleiades occulta-
   tion. il Sky & Tel 37:324-5 My '69
Observing tips for the August Pleiades oc-
   cultation. R. Abileah. Sky & Tel 38:130 Ag
   '69
Occultation highlights (cont) D. W. Dunham.
   il Sky & Tel 37:264; 38:204; 39:66-7 Ap, S,
   '69, Ja '70
Pleiades occultations: observations and pre-
   dictions. il Sky & Tel 37:197-9 Mr '69
This December's occultations of Pleiades
   stars. H. R. Povenmire. il Sky & Tel 38:
   432-4 D '69
OCCULTISM. See Occult sciences
OCCUPANCY
   See also
Squatters
OCCUPATIONAL education. See Vocational ed-
   ucation
OCCUPATIONAL guidance. See Vocational
   guidance
OCCUPATIONAL literature. See Vocational lit-
   erature
OCCUPATIONAL mobility
Conceptual framework for studying labor mo-
   bility: excerpt from address. August 1969.
   H. S. Parnes and R. S. Spitz. il Mo Labor
   R 92:55-8 N '69
Why and how workers shift from blue-collar
   to white-collar jobs. D. B. Johnson and
   J. L. Stern. bibliog f il Mo Labor R
   92:7-13 O '69
OCCUPATIONS
Black grad's problem: which job to take? il
   Ebony 24:132-4+ My '69
Courage and confusion in choosing a career;
   Time essay. Time 93:42-3 My 30 '69
Daring young girls: symposium. il Seven-
   teen 28:92-5+ Ja '69
Eye on tomorrow's jobs. G. Venn. il Am Ed
   5:12-15 Mr '69
Jobs in the 70's, where they'll be. il Changing
   T 23.43-5 Mr '69
New careers: problems and pitfalls. G. H.
   Weber and D. Palmer. il Am Ed 5:26-8 Ap
   '69
Obsessions of a late-bloomer. R. H. Boyle.
   il Sports Illus 31:32-6 Ag 18 '69
Students' preview of health professions;
   Philadelphia high school students working
   under different programs at the university.
   il Sch & Soc 97:267-8+ Sum '69
   See also
Professions
OCCUPATIONS, Choice of. See Occupations
OCCUPATIONS, Hazardous
   See also
Asbestos workers
OCCUPATIONS for children
Compartmentalized children's services in a
   therapeutic community. E. J. Faux and
   C. M. Rowley. bibliog Ment Hy 53:585-9
   O '69
OCEAN
How not to kill the ocean. W. Marx. il Au-
   dubon 71:27-35 Jl '69
Ocean; symposium. il Sci Am 221:54-86+ bib-
   liog(p284-7) S '69
Oceans: man's last great resource. C. Pell.
   il Sat R 52:19-21+ O 11 '69
Ocean's riches. W. M. Stephens. il Nat Wild-
   life 7:4-11 Ap '69
Sunglint patterns: unusual dark patches. C.
   J. Bowley and others. bibliog il Science
   165:1360-2 S 26 '69

OCEAN—*Continued*
What do you know about the sea? quiz. J. G. Vaeth. il Sci Digest 66:56-7+ N '69
See also
Arctic Ocean
Atlantic Ocean
Coast changes
Meteorology, Maritime
Oceanographic research
Oceanography
Pacific Ocean
Sea level changes
Sea water
Tides

Economic aspects
See Marine resources

Maps
Boosting the tuna catch; using maps of sea-surface temperatures. W. A. Scholes. il Sci N 96:338 O 11 '69

OCEAN bottom
Challenger's sixth leg. il Sci N 96:197-8 S 13 '69
Circum-Pacific late Cenozoic structural rejuvenation; implications for sea floor spreading. R. H. Dott, jr. bibliog il Science 166:874-6 N 14 '69
Crustal plates in the central Atlantic: evidence for at least two poles of rotation. P. J. Fox and others. bibliog il Science 165:487-9 Ag 1 '69
Deep-ocean floor. H. W. Menard. il Sci Am 221:126-32+ bibliog(p285) S '69
East Pacific rise crest: a near-bottom geophysical profile R. L. Larson and F. N. Spiess; reply with rejoinder. W. C. Kellogg. bibliog Science 165:617-18 Ag 8 '69
Fission track age of magnetic anomaly 10. a new point on the sea-floor spreading curve. B. P. Luyendyk and D. E. Fisher. bibliog il Science 164:1516-17 Je 27 '69
Fissure basalts and ocean-floor spreading on the East Pacific rise. E. Bonatti; reply with rejoinder. R. P. Herzen. bibliog il Science 166:1181-3 N 28 '69
Fossil deep-sea channel on the Aleutian abyssal plain. P. J. Grim and F. P. Naugler. bibliog il Science 163:383-6 Ja 24 '69
Gravitational mechanism for sea-floor spreading. H. N. Pollack. bibliog il Science 163:176-7 Ja 10 '69
Hands beneath the sea; proposed seabed treaty. Time 94:32+ O 17 '69
Ocean floor spreading: Olduvai and Gilsa events in the Matuyama epoch. D. A. Emilia and D. F. Heinrichs. bibliog il Science 166:1267-9 D 5 '69
Origin of the oceans. E. Bullard. il Sci Am 221:66-75 bibliog(p284) S '69
Secret of the spreading ocean floors. T. Alexander. il Fortune 79:112-17+ F '69
Ship that digs holes in the sea; Glomar Challenger. W. Cloud. il Pop Mech 131:108-11+ Mr '69
See also
Benthos
Continental shelf
Faults (geology)
Marine mineral resources
Marine sediments
Oceanographic research
Sounding and soundings
Submarine geology

International aspects
Ambassador Smith presents U.S. views on seabed proposal at Eighteen-nation disarmament conference; statement, March 25, 1969. G. Smith. Dept State Bul 60:333-7 Ap 21 '69
Another nuclear treaty ahead? U.S. and Russia propose a treaty to ban placement of nuclear weapons on the ocean floors. il U S News 66:12 Mr 31 '69
Big powers net seabed treaty. Bsns W p 108 O 11 '69
Delaying action on oceans; U.N. vote. Sci N 96:524 D 6 '69
Department reviews history of international efforts governing activities on the seabed; statement. July 30, 1969. U. A. Johnson. Dept State Bul 61:191-4 S 1 '69
Exercise in half-measure; banning nuclear weapons from seabeds. Commonweal 90:59-60 Ap 4 '69
Games powers play; seabed agreement between U.S. and Russia. Commonweal 91:91 O 24 '69
Narrow issues and large; sea-floor treaty. Sci N 96:495 N 29 '69
New world of the oceans; excerpt. D. Behrman. il UNESCO Courier 22:4-15 Je '69

Oceans: man's last great resource. C. Pell. il Sat R 52:19-21+ O 11 '69
Reports, deep-sea bed. W. Marx. Atlan 223:24+ Ap '69
U.S. and U.S.S.R. agree on draft treaty banning emplacement of nuclear weapons on the seabed; statement, with draft treaty, October 7, 1969. J. F. Leonard. Dept State Bul 61:365-8 N 3 '69
United States comments on revisions in draft treaty banning emplacement of nuclear weapons on the seabed; statement, October 30, 1969, with revised draft treaty. J. F. Leonard. Dept State Bul 61:480-3 D 1 '69
U.S. discusses verfication procedures under the draft treaty banning emplacement of nuclear weapons on the seabed; statement, October 16, 1969. J. F. Leonard. Dept State Bul 61:426-9 N 17 '69
U.S. submits draft treaty banning emplacement of nuclear weapons on the seabed; statement, May 22, 1969; with text of U.S. draft treaty. A. S. Fisher. Dept State Bul 60:520-4 Je 16 '69
U.S. views on nuclear weapon material cut-off agreement and verification of comprehensive nuclear test ban; statement, April 8, 1969. A. S. Fisher. Dept State Bul 60:409-13 My 12 '69
See also
United Nations—Committee on the peaceful uses of the seabed and the ocean floor

International control
Reservation of the sea-bed and ocean floor for peaceful purposes; with text of resolution. UN Mo Chron 6:56-62 Ja '69

OCEAN currents
Atmosphere and the ocean. R. W. Stewart. il Sci Am 221:76-86 bibliog(p284) S '69
Currents in La Jolla and Scripps submarine canyons. F. P. Shepard and N. F. Marshall. bibliog il Science 165:177-8 Jl 11 '69
Equatorial current history; Challenger: leg 8. Sci N 96:590 D 27 '69
Surfacing of Pacific equatorial undercurrent: direct observation. J. H. Jones. bibliog il Science 163:1449-50 Mr 28 '69
Transient circulation event near the deep ocean floor. R. A. Schwartzlose and J. D. Isaacs. bibliog il Science 165:889-91 Ag 29 '69
See also
Gulf Stream

OCEAN Eagle (tanker) See Shipwrecks
OCEAN fishing. See Salt water fishing
OCEAN in art
See also
Marine painting

OCEAN life. See Marine biology
OCEAN liners
Editor's report: QE2. M. M. Davis. il Travel 132:54-5 Ag '69
Hotel at sea; Queen Elizabeth 2. il Time 93:71 My 16 '69
New Queen's role: to lure more young travelers. il U S News 66:18 My 19 '69
Queen Elizabeth 2. B. Belford. il Travel & Camera 32:35+ Jl '69
Queen Elizabeth 2. J. A. Maxtone-Graham. il Pop Mech 131:100-3+ F '69
Queenly tour; visitors aboard the Queen Elizabeth. il Travel 131:13 Je '69
Riding out the storm; Cunard expected to earn a profit. il Bsns W p44+ Ja 25 '69
Sea museum fit for a queen; planned Museum of the sea aboard the Queen Mary. D. Valentry. il Sea Front 15:284-7 S '69
Seeing a ship off, it's fun and it's free. il Sunset 142:30+ Mr '69
Time off; to France on the France. P. O'Higgins. il McCalls 97:84+ Ja '70
Vibration aboard the Queen; trials of the Queen Elizabeth 2. Sci N 95:137-8 F 8 '69
See also
Steamship lines
Steamships and steamboats

OCEAN mineral resources. See Marine mineral resources
OCEAN mining
See also
Gold mines and mining, Submarine

OCEAN pollution. See Sea water—Pollution
OCEAN temperature
Cyclic and geographic trends in seawater temperature and abundance of American lobster. R. L. Dow. bibliog il Science 164:1060-3 My 30 '69
Thermal stratification in the Arctic Ocean. V. T. Neal and others. bibliog il Science 166:373-4 O 17 '69

OCEAN travel
1968 U.S. air, sea passengers; tables. Aviation W 91-42 Ag 4 '69
Travel notes. R. Joseph. Esquire 72:24 Ag '69
See also
Cruising
Ocean liners
Voyages
Voyages around the world

OCEAN yacht racing. See Yacht racing

OCEANIA
Islands of the South Pacific. G. Skinner. il Yachting 126:50-3+ Ag '69
South Pacific adventure; recreation and park specialists act as citizen ambassadors. T. S. Brungardt. il Parks & Rec 4:48-53+ Je '69
See also
Easter Island
Fiji
Geology—Oceania
Islands of the Pacific
Micronesia
Moorea
New Hebrides
Pitcairn Island
South Pacific commission
Tahiti

Description and travel
Road to Osaka, an expogoer's guide to the Pacific; symposium. il Sat R 52:43-8+ S 13 '69

OCEANIC basalt. See Basalt

OCEANIC water striders. See Water striders

OCEANOGRAPHERS
See also
Oceanography as a profession

OCEANOGRAPHIC instruments
Strange devices that found the sunken sub Scorpion; ed. by H. Shuldiner. C. L. Buchanan il Pop Sci 194:66-71+ Ap '69
Technology and the ocean. W. Bascom. il Sci Am 221:198-204+ S '69
See also
Oceanographic research—Equipment

OCEANOGRAPHIC research
Exploring the world's oceans. il UNESCO Courier 22:60 Ag '69
New world of the oceans; excerpts. D. Behrman. il UNESCO Courier 22:4-15 Je '69
Secret of the spreading ocean floors. T. Alexander. il Fortune 79:112-17+ F '69
20 billion dollars to tap riches of the sea? il U S News 66:62-4 Mr 31 '69
Undersea world of Jonah and Thetis; Arizona state university's Exotic environments laboratory, Tempe, Ariz. J. Matthews. il Sci Digest 66:66-70 N '69
See also
Underwater drilling
Underwater exploration
United States—National oceanic and atmospheric agency (proposed)

Equipment
Aping the ocean's deeps; high-pressure hyperbaric chamber. J. Eberhart. il Sci N 96: 280-1 S 27 '69
Pie in the sky (oceans division) il Forbes 104:36+ Jl 15 '69
Sensors in the deep sea. D. R. Caldwell and others. bibliog il Phys Today 22:34-42 Jl '69
See also
Submarine research vehicles

International aspects
Ocean and man. W. S. Wooster. il Sci Am 221: 218-20+ S '69

Antarctic Regions
Antarctic sub-ice observation; stationary manned submersible. J. R. Twiss, jr. il Sea Front 15:108-11 Mr '69

France
Exploring the shelf; CNEXO laboratory at Ste-Anne-du-Portzic, Brittany. N. Hardy. il Sci N 95:366 Ap 12 '69

Germany (Federal Republic)
Hat in the ring; Germany moving into study of oceans. T. Shoemaker. il Sci N 95:414 Ap 26 '69

Japan
Briskly and broadly. S. Griffin. il Sci N 95: 490 My 17 '69

OCEANOGRAPHY
Oceanography: an international laboratory, recommendation of Commission on marine science, engineering, and resources. H. Stommel and E. D. Goldberg. Science 165: 751-2 Ag 22 '69

Oceanology: first International oceanology conference. Sci N 95:262 Mr 15 '69
Oceanology; report of meeting. R. Yalkovsky. Science 164:862+ My 16 '69
20,000 guns under the sea; plans to militarize the ocean floor. S. Hersh. il Ramp Mag 8: 40-4 S '69
What do you know about oceanography? quiz. J. Daugherty and M. Daugherty. il Sci Digest 66:88-9+ D '69
See also
Marine resources
Meteorology, Maritime
Ocean
Oceanographic research
United States—Marine science, engineering and resources, Commission on
United States—National oceanic and atmospheric agency (proposed)

Bibliography
Science of the sea in books. See issues of Sea frontiers

Vocational guidance
See Oceanography as a profession

OCEANOGRAPHY as a profession
Fascinating new careers in oceanography. C. Peet. bibliog il Sci Digest 66:61-5 Ag '69

OCEANOLOGY. See Oceanography

OCHS, René
Nairobi conference. Ed Digest 34:29-31 Mr '69

OCHS, S. and others
Fast transport system of materials in mammalian nerve fibers. bibliog Science 163:686-7 F 14 '69

O'CONNELL, Adelyn
Prophet complains in time of drought; poem. Commonweal 91:204 N 14 '69

O'CONNELL, Barbara
Eden under a geodesic dome. Sci Digest 65: 68-72 Ap '69
Hypoglycemia, the disease that makes women tired. Sci Digest 65:40-4 Mr '69
Paint-on preservation for ancient stone. Sci Digest 65:77-80 My '69
Satellite weather forecasting. bibliog Sci Digest 65:43-8+ My '69
Wacky world of food fads. Sci Digest 65: 80-4 F '69

O'CONNELL, Richard
Burgher king; Ibid; Epigram: martial; poems. Nat R 21:174 F 25 '69
No hippies' lament; poem. Nat R 21:1271 D 16 '69

O'CONNELL, Robert J.
What's coming off at Fordham? Cath World 209:59-63 My '69

O'CONNELL, Shaun
Joey and Sebastian grown up. Nation 208: 85-6 Ja 20 '69

O'CONNOR, Edwin
—See Wilson, E. jt. auth.

about
Memoir. E. Wilson. Atlan 224:64-7, 74-5 O '69

O'CONNOR, Flannery
Nature and aim of fiction; excerpt from Mystery and manners. Writer 82:11-14+ O '69

about
Literary horizons. G. Hicks. Sat R 52:30 My 10 '69
On Flannery O'Connor. S. Maloff. Commonweal 90:490-1 Ag 8 '69
We have had our fall. J. Kellogg. Chr Cent 86:927 Jl 9 '69

O'CONNOR, Frank
Directions for my funeral; poem. Atlan 223: 120 F '69
Farce kept breaking in; excerpt from My father's son. Harper 238:81-4+ Je '69
Saint; excerpt from autobiography. Commonweal 90:364-5 Je 13 '69

about
Apostolic succession. K. Sullivan. Nation 209:668-70 D 15 '69
Heart of Ireland. A. H. Norman. por Newsweek 74:127 D 8 '69
Literary horizons. G. Hicks. por Sat R 52: 38 Ap 12 '69
O'Connor seen by himself and others. S. Kauffmann. New Repub 161:21-4 N 29 '69
Personal history. M. Ward. por Sat R 52:32-3 N 22 '69

O'CONNOR, Hugh
U.S. journal: Jeremiah, Ky. C. Trillin. New Yorker 45:178-83 Ap 12 '69

O'CONNOR, Jack
  Getting the range. See issues of Outdoor life
  Keeping up with the Gun control act of 1968.
    Outdoor Life 144:68-9+ S '69
  Shooting. See issues of Outdoor life
  Stone rams in the Cassiar. Outdoor Life 144:
    32-5+ D '69
O'CONNOR, John
  Hesburgh fights. Look 33:42+ N 18 '69
  Religious life and the religious layman. Cath
    World 208:199-204 F '69
O'CONNOR, John J.
  Another try at the inevitable direction.
    Dance Mag 43:65-7 N '69
O'CONNOR, Patrick
  Tap happening. Dance Mag 43:40-2 Ag '69
O'CONNOR, Timothy E. See Fischinger, P. J.
  jt. auth.
OCTAGONAL houses. See Houses. Octagonal
OCTANE rating. See Gasoline—Rating
OCTOPAMINE
  Octopamine: normal occurrence in sympa-
    thetic nerves of rats. P. Molinoff and J.
    Axelrod. bibliog il Science 164:428-9 Ap 25
    '69
OCTOPUS
  Annotated octopus; with notes, ed. by J.
    Lettvin. K. N. Sokolski. il Natur Hist 78:
    10-12+ N '69
  Memory traces in the octopus. M. Wells. il
    Sea Front 15:295-307 S'69
ODAJNYK, Walter
  (tr) See Symonenko, V. Diary of a Soviet
    Ukrainian poet: Vasyl Symonenko
ODD-lot brokers. See Brokers
O'DEA, Thomas F.
  Can Catholicism make it? Chr Cent 86:283-7
    F 26 '69
ODEAN, Donna M.
  Gee, mother, you're wonderful! Farm J 93:
    51 My '69
ODEGAARD, Charles H.
  Million-dollar ideas, for park and recreation
    departments. Parks & Rec 3:21+ O '68
O'DELL, Betty Young
  Suicide in children. Parents Mag 44:58-9+ Ja
    '69
ODEN, Thomas C.
  Visibility of the church. bibliog Chr Cent 86:
    613-16 Ap 30 '69
ODOM, John
  Highlight. por Sports Illus 30:100-1 My 26
    '69
ODOMETERS
  Great odometer raid. il Consumer Rep 34:
    250-3 My '69
O'DONNELL, Bernard
  NCTE/ERIC clearinghouse on the teaching
    of English: a report to the profession.
    Engl J 58:458-60+ Mr '69
O'DONNELL, James P.
  Chopper chancellor awaits air force one.
    N Y Times Mag p26-7+ F 16 '69
  Devil's architect. N Y Times Mag p45-9+ O
    26 '69
  Ghost of Brecht. Atlan 223:110-13 Ja '69
  Walter Ulbricht: the unsinkable satrap.
    Read Digest 94:115-19 Mr '69
O'DONNELL, Walter E.
  What is a doctor's toughest diagnosis?
    Good H 169:59+ Jl '69
O'DONOVAN, Leo J. See Marabelli, V. M. jt.
  auth.
ODORS
  Biologically active compounds in orchid
    fragrances. C. H. Dodson and others. bibliog
    il Science 164:1243-9 Je 13 '69
  Fragrance, the secret agent. S. Lindsay and
    L. Bohlig. il House B 111:22+ Ap '69
  How to keep your cool; questions and an-
    swers. il Seventeen 28:136-7 F '69
  Key people; blind people test flavorings and
    fragrances. K. B. Pomeroy. il Am For 75:
    30-1 Ag '69
  Olfactory stimuli and the pseudo-extinction
    effect. E. A. Wasserman and D. D. Jensen.
    bibliog il Science 166:1307-9 D 5 '69
    See also
  Perfumery
  Pheromones
ODUM, Eugene P.
  Strategy of ecosystem development: adapta-
    tion of address, August 1966. bibliog Sci-
    ence 164:262-70; 166:404 Ap 18, O 17 '69
ODUM, William E. and others
  DDT residues absorbed from organic detritus
    by fiddler crabs. bibliog Science 164:576-7
    My 2 '69
ODYSSEY. See Homer
OEDEKOVEN, Karl Heinz
  Saving our vanishing forests; reprint.
    UNESCO Courier 22:6-9 Ag '69
OEHMICHEN, Friedrich, and Reader, L. J.
  Students involved in project at foot of Men-
    denhall glacier. Parks & Rec 4:50-2 S '69

OERKE. Andrew
  Sparrows in the leafless willows; poem New
    Yorker 45:52 O 11 '69
OERTLE, V. Lee
  Chevy's Blazer: a different four-wheel drive.
    Pop Mech 131:56+ Ap '69
  Forty ways to test a camper before you
    buy it. Pop Mech 132:77-9+ Jl '69
  Growing rage for fun cars. Pop Sci 194:65-7+
    Mr '69
  MI tests. Mech Illus 65:58-9+ Ag '69
  Mini-Boot: the first 4x4 dune buggy for un-
    der $2500. Pop Mech 131:52 Je '69
  Plan a head. Pop Mech 130:140-4 D '68
  Portable power for camping comfort. Pop
    Mech 132:120-3 Ag '69
  Right way to winterize your camper. Pop
    Mech 132:116-19+ N '69
  Rugged new camper. Pop Mech 131:124-7+
    My '69
  Rules of the road and campsite tips. Pop Sci
    194:176+ My '69
  Selecting tires for recreational vehicles. Field
    & S 73:78-81+ Ap '69
  Trailer hitches: tips to keep you out of
    trouble. Pop Mech 132:134-7 Jl '69
  Trends in travel. See issues of Motor trend
  What you should know about trailer brakes.
    Pop Sci 195:111-13 Jl '69
OESCHGER, Helen
  Omaha. ALA Bul 63:255-7 F '69
OESPER, Ralph E.
  (tr) See Szabadvary, F. Great moments in
    chemistry
OESTREICH, Arthur H.
  Middle school in transition. Clear House 44:
    91-5 O '69
OETTING, E. R. and others
  Problems in program evaluation: a ministers'
    workshop. Ment Hy 53:214-17 Ap '69
OF cabbages and kings; story. See McPherson,
  J. A.
O'FAOLAIN, Julia
  Lots of ghastlies; story. Mlle 68:245 Ap '69
O'FAOLAIN, Seán
  Florentine hill towns: suburbs, Tuscan style.
    Holiday 46:42-3+ S '69
  Kitchen; story. Atlan 223:42-5 Je '69
  Planets of the years; story. Ladies Home J
    86:102-3 S '69
OFAY watcher; drama. See Cucci, F.
OFF-Broadway theater. See New York (city)
  —Theater
OFF-campus experience. See Education, Co-
  operative
OFF off Broadway theater. See New York
  (city)—Theater
OFF-road racing. See Motor vehicle racing
OFFENBACH, Jacques
  La Périchole. Criticism
    New Yorker 45:131 N 1 '69
OFFENSES against the person
    See also
  Assassination
  Assault and battery
OFFICE appliances
  Keeping up to date in your farm office. R.
    Martens. il Farm J 93:52H-52I Mr '69
    See also
  Computers—Business applications
OFFICE buildings
  Companies gasp for breathing space; office
    buildings in urban centers. il Bsns W p 160+
    Je 7 '69
  Service center for laundry machines; San
    Francisco. il Arch Rec 146:127-30 Ag '69
    See also
  Office layout
    also subhead Architecture under names
    of cities, e.g. New York (city)—Architec-
    ture
      Designs and plans
  Australia square. R. Boyd. il Arch Forum
    130:26-35 Ap '69
  Bold tower for a utility company. il Arch
    Rec 145:151-4 F '69
  Building types study. il Arch Rec 145:181-96
    Ap '69
  Ordered openness for corporate offices. il
    Arch Rec 145:141-8 Ap '69
  Powerful silhouette for a high-speed en-
    vironment; Pet plaza. il Arch Rec 146:163-
    70 S '69
  Suburban office building by TAC, designed as
    focal point and landmark. il Arch Rec 145:
    129-34 Mr '69
  Three new office structures by HOK. il Arch
    Rec 146:121-6 Ag '69
OFFICE decoration
  Go-go decor fighting the back-office blahs.
    il Bsns W p70+ F 1 '69

OFFICE decoration—*Continued*
Office landscape: no walls, no halls. il Design 70:14-18 Spr '69
Offices and showrooms for Herlinger Bristol, ltd, New York city; Air France ticket offices Fifth avenue, New York city. il Arch Rec 145:133-5 Je '69
Putting a new face on the office. il Bsns W p 152-3+ S 13 '69
OFFICE equipment industry
See also
Miller, Herman, incorporated
OFFICE for Intellectual freedom. See American library association—Office for intellectual freedom
OFFICE furniture
Keeping up to date in your farm office. R. Martens. il Farm J 93:52H-52I Mr '69
Putting a new face on the office. il Bsns W p 152-3+ S 13 '69
OFFICE holders. See Public officers
OFFICE layout
Office landscape: no walls, no halls. il Design 70:14-18 Spr '69
Ordered openness for corporate offices. il Arch Rec 145:141-8 Ap '69
Walls come tumbling down. il Nations Bsns 57:60-1+ Ap '69
OFFICE of economic opportunity. See United States—Economic opportunity, Office of
OFFICE of education. See United States—Education, Office of
OFFICE of minority business enterprise. See United States—Office of minority business enterprise
OFFICE of press relations of the Department of state. See United States—State, Department of
OFFICE of science and technology. See United States—Science and technology, Office of
OFFICE planning. See Office layout
OFFICE seekers. See Patronage, Political
OFFICE workers
Prospects for white-collar unionism; excerpt from address, September 1968. H. M. Douty. bibliog f il Mo Labor R 92:31-4 Ja '69
See also
Secretaries

Salaries, allowances, etc.
Federal pay comparability procedures; BLS national survey of professional, administrative, technical, clerical pay. L. E. Lewis. bibliog f il Mo Labor R 92:10-13 F '69
Salary levels continue sharp rise in white-collar occupations. E. J. Caramela. il Mo Labor R 92:46-8 Ap '69
Twenty white-collar jobs and what they pay. il Changing T 23:36 Je '69
White collar pay jumps again. il Nations Bsns 57:38-9 Jl '69
OFFICES
Adults only retreat. il Bet Hom & Gard 47:68-9 O '69
Economy and flair highlight six architects' own offices. il Arch Rec 146:111-18 D '69
Office in the kitchen. il Sunset 143:133-4 N '69
Put an office in your kitchen. il Parents Mag 44:134 S '69
See also
Librarians offices
Presidents—United States—Offices
OFFICIAL documents. See Government publications
OFFICIAL entertaining. See Government entertaining
OFFICIAL secrets
See also
Defense information, Classified
Government and the press
OFFSET printing. See Printing, Offset
OFFSHORE mutual funds. See Investment trusts
OFFSHORE oil fields. See Petroleum in submerged lands
OFFSHORE oil well drilling. See Oil well drilling, Submarine
O'FLAHERTY, Terrence
Murder on Saturday morning? McCalls 96:72-3+ S '69
OGBURN, Charlton, Jr
Catastrophe by the numbers. Am Heritage 21:114-17 D '69
Virginia: the state that has—well almost—everything. Holiday 46:46-9+ S '69
OGDEN, Bud
Simply dandy sibling rivalry. J. Jares. il por Sports Illus 30:30-4+ F 10 '69
OGDEN, Ralph
Simply dandy sibling rivalry. J. Jares. il por Sports Illus 30:30-4+ F 10 '69

OGDEN, Ralph E.
Storm King art center. E. S. Robbins. il Art in Am 57:108-9 My '69
OGDEN, Utah
Golden light for a golden spike celebration. B. Wolthuis. il Am City 84:132 Je '69
OGDEN corporation
Ogden engineers a total system; to solve Morocco's problems. il Bsns W p58+ Mr 15 '69
OGDEN house. See Connecticut—Historic houses, etc.
OGILVIE, Elisabeth
Island of shadows; story. Good H 169:83-5 N '69
OGILVIE, Philip W.
Making the most of our zoos. Parks & Rec 4:32-4+ Ja '69
OGILVIE, Richard Buell
Ogilvie's offensive. por Time 93:22 Ap 18 '69
OGILVY, David
View from the chateau; interview, ed. by S. Goldschlager. por Newsweek 74:16 Ag '69 18 '69
OGLESBY, Arthur
Scotland for salmon. Field & S 74:64-6+ O '69
OGLESBY, Carl
Cuba; a radical's view. por Life 66:62D-62F+ F 14 '69
Vietnamism has failed; the revolution can only be mauled, not defeated. Commonweal 90: 11-12 Mr 21 '69; Same with title Prospect for revolution. Cur 109:55-6 Ag '69
O'GORMAN, Ned
Books for children. Nation 209:670-2 D 15 '69
O'GRADY, F. See Greenwood, D. jt. auth.
OGUNDE, Hubert
Twelve wives of Chief Ogunde. il pors Ebony 24:106-8+ O '69
OH! Calcutta! revue. See Musical comedies, revues, etc.—Criticisms, plots, etc.
O'HANLON, Michael J.
Book clerk's view of things. Pub W 195:54-5 Ap 21 '69
Building a nature and sports section. Pub W 196:39-40 Ag 4 '69
O'HANLON, Thomas
G.M. takes the high ground in the new battle of Detroit. Fortune 79:70-5+ My 1 '69
Goodrich's four-ply defense. Fortune 80:110-13+ Jl '69
Who wins marketing promotion games? Fortune 79:104-8+ F '69
O'HARA, Frank
Pleasant thought from Whitehead; poem. New Repub 161:29 N 29 '69
Walking to work; Walking; Places for Oscar Salvador; Sudden snow; poems. Poetry 113: 332-7 F '69
O'HARA, Frederic James
Selected government publications. Wilson Lib Bul 43:679-83, 797+, 912-19, 1025-9; 44:111-14+, 214-16+ 338-45, 472-81, 570-6 Mr '69-Ja '70
O'HARA, Gloria
Treasure for grandma. por Redbook 133:14+ Je '69
O'HARA, James Grant
Excerpt from remarks, April 3, 1967. Cong Digest 48:235+ O '69
about
As Democrats get set for '72. il U S News 66: 46-8 My 26 '69
O'HARA, John
Sunroom; story. Sat Eve Post 242:40-2 F 8 '69
about
Joey and Sebastian grown up. S. O'Connell. Nation 208:85-6 Ja 20 '69
John O'Hara is alive and well in the first half of the twentieth century. D. A. Schanche. por Esquire 72:84-6+ Ag '69
O'HARE, Michael, and Kronauer, R. E.
Fence designs to keep wind from being a nuisance. Arch Rec 146:151-6 Jl '69
O'HIGGINS, Patrick
Fashionable New York lunch-in. Holiday 45:68-9+ F '69
Time off. McCalls 97:48+ D '69; 84+ Ja '70
OHIO
See also
Architecture, Domestic—Ohio
Booksellers and bookselling—Ohio
Conservation of resources—Ohio
Cuyahoga River
Hunting—Ohio
Justice, Administration of—Ohio
Libraries—Ohio
Politics, Corruption in—Ohio

OHIO—*Continued*

Politics and government

Democrats confront 1970. G. I. Maeroff. Nation 209:599-600 D 1 '69
See also
Politics, Corruption in—Ohio

Public works, Department of

Sensitively modest museums enrich historic sites: Flint ridge; Fort hill; Fort ancient museums, Ohio. il Arch Rec 145:182-5 Je '69

OHIO historical society

Sensitively modest museums enrich historic sites: Flint ridge; Fort hill; Fort ancient museums, Ohio. il Arch Rec 145:182-5 Je '69

OHIO library association

Young librarians are concerned: Junior members round tables. J. A. McCrossan. ALA Bul 63:910-12 Jl '69

OHIO. State university, Bowling Green

Beachcombers: Center for the study of popular culture. Newsweek 74:63 D 15 '69

OHKI, Shinpei. See Papahadjopoulos, D. jt. auth.

OHL, John F.
Reviews of books. Mus Q 55:120-5 Ja '69

OHLES, John F.
Supervision: essential and beneficial. Clear House 44:134-6 N '69
University and the unstudent. Ed Digest 34:44-6 Ja '69

OHLSEN, Elaine
Handling S.S. in a camp. Camp Mag 41:16 My '69

OHMMETERS
Constant-current ohmmeter. A. B. Kaufman. il Pop Electr 30:53-5 Ap '69

OHM'S law
How's your E=IR? quiz. R. P. Balin. il Pop Electr 30:32+ Mr '69

O'HORGAN, Tom
Tom's mix. H. Hewes. Sat R 52:21 Jl 12 '69

OIL and gas leases
Did money go where the oil is? il Bsns W p51-2 S 20 '69
Great Alaska oil sweepstakes. il Bsns W p43-4 S 13 '69
Great oil hunt; North Slope auction; with report by G. C. Lubenow. il Newsweek 74:80-2+ S 22 '69
North Slope showdown. il Newsweek 74:63-4 Ag 25 '69
Richest auction in history. il Time 94:87-8 S 19 '69
Santa Barbarans cite an 11th commandment: thou shalt not abuse the earth. R. Macdonald and R. Easton. il N Y Times Mag p32-3+ O 12 '69

OIL birds. See Oilbirds

OIL changes, Automobile. See Automobiles—Lubrication

OIL companies. See Petroleum industry and trade

OIL filters
Filtering the V-dub. J. Thawley. il Hot Rod 22:103 F '69

OIL imports. See Import quotas

OIL industries
See also
Petroleum industry and trade
Standard oil company (New Jersey)

Advertising

Games oil people play. il Bsns W p 132+ Ap 19 '69

OIL leases. See Oil and gas leases

OIL pollution of coastal waters. See Oil pollution of rivers, harbors, etc.

OIL pollution of rivers, harbors, etc.
Another oil slick; Santa Barbara subject to new onslaught. Newsweek 73:37 F 24 '69
Big oil leak leaves a messy legal residue: Santa Barbara slick. il Bsns W p30-2 F 15 '69
Black but clear lessons from Santa Barbara. Audubon 71:5 Mr '69
Black tide. J. McCaull. bibliog il Environ 11:2-16 N '69
Black tide; oil spills on the high seas. il Time 94:29 D 26 '69
California oil strike nobody wanted; oil slick along the Santa Barbara coast. il Life 66:30-1 F 14 '69
Can man afford to foul his environment? T. Myers. il Nat Wildlife 7:18-19 Je '69
Case of the oily waters; leaking oil well off the southern California coast. il Sr Schol 94:21-2 F 28 '69
Dead channel; oil off southern California. il Time 93:21 F 21 '69

Death from the sea; Santa Barbara oil spill. D. Snell. il Life 66:22-7 Je 13 '69
Environment: tragedy in oil; leak at Union oil platform in Santa Barbara Channel. il Time 93:23-5 F 14 '69
Fighting the oil on California's troubled waters. il Bsns W p60-1 F 8 '69
Finding lemonade in Santa Barbara's oil. G. Hardin. il Sat R 52:18-21 My 10 '69
GOO story. Newsweek 73:60 Je 16 '69
Great American river cleanup. W. Langewiesche. Read Digest 94:213+ My '69
Great blob; oil slick off Santa Barbara. il Newsweek 73:31-2 F 17 '69
Great oil slick; Southern California coast; with photographs by V. Merritt. Life 66:53-62B F 21 '69
Helpless birds, helpless technology; giant oil spill off Santa Barbara coast. il Sci N 95:183-4 F 22 '69
How not to kill the ocean. W. Marx. il Audubon 71:27-33 Jl '69
IJC asked to study pollution risks from Lake Erie oil spills; Department announcement, with text of U.S. letter, March 21, 1969. Dept State Bul 60:296 Ap 7 '69
Life with the blob; damage done by oil slick off Santa Barbara. R. Macdonald. il Sports Illus 30:50-2+ Ap 21 '69
Maximum feasible leakage; coastline in southern California. S. V. Roberts. Commonweal 89:667-8 F 28 '69
Not so deadly; study of Santa Barbara oil spill. Time 93:21 Je 13 '69
Oil in the ecosystem. R. W. Holcomb. Science 166:204-6 O 10 '69
Oil on the loose. B. Crabtree. Yachting 125:184+ Ap '69
Oil on the waters. E. Cowan. Nation 208:304-7 Mr 10 '69
Oil pressure; conservationists vs. Interior department. S. V. Roberts. New Repub 160:13-14 Mr 15 '69
Price of disaster; oil companies to pay damages for Torrey Canyon accident. il Time 94:59 N 21 '69
Runaway oil well; will it mean new rules in offshore drilling? Santa Barbara incident. il U S News 66:14 F 17 '69
Santa Barbara: oil in the velvet playground. H. Molotch. il Ramp Mag 8:43-51 N '69
Santa Barbarans cite an 11th commandment: thou shalt not abuse the earth. R. Macdonald and R. Easton. il N Y Times Mag p32-3+ O 12 '69
Still more trouble from oily waters; New York oil pollution conference. Bsns W p 18 D 20 '69
Tarring and feathering of Santa Barbara. L. J. Kennedy. il Motor B 123:60-1 Ap '69
Whittling Alaska down to size. G. Laycock. il Audubon 71:66-8+ My '69
Wreck of the Ocean Eagle. M. J. Cerame-Vivas. il Sea Front 15:224-31 Jl '69

OIL refineries
See also
Petroleum refineries

OIL royalties. See Oil and gas leases

OIL shales
Teapot dome in the Rockies. A. Hochschild. Ramp Mag 7:75-8 Ja 25 '69
Triterpene alcohol isolation from oil shale. P. Albrecht and G. Ourisson. bibliog il Science 163:1192 Mr 14 '69

OIL tankers. See Tank ships

OIL well drilling
Bad days for wild ones. il Time 94:76 Jl 11 '69
Great Alaska oil rush. P. Friggens. il Read Digest 95:66-70 Jl '69
Hot oil rush in Arctic Alaska. J. Main. il Fortune 79:120-5+ Ap '69
North Slope showdown. il Newsweek 74:63-4 Ag 25 '69
Oil in the Arctic; with report by J. Bonfante. il Life 66:20-9 F 14 '69
See also
Santa Fe international corporation

OIL well drilling, Submarine
California oil strike nobody wanted; oil slick along the Santa Barbara coast. il Life 66:30-1 F 14 '69
Camille and Hickel hit offshore drillers. Bsns W p20 Ag 30 '69
Fighting the oil on California's troubled waters. il Bsns W p60-1 F 8 '69
Finding lemonade in Santa Barbara's oil. G. Hardin. il Sat R 52:18-21 My 10 '69
GOO fishes in; Get oil out group fight companies drilling in the Santa Barbara Channel. il Newsweek 74:100 D 8 '69
GOO story. Newsweek 73:60 Je 16 '69
Lawsuits gush from oil disaster. Bsns W p41 Ap 19 '69

OIL well drilling, Submarine—*Continued*
Life with the blob; damage done by oil slick off Santa Barbara. R. Macdonald. il Sports Illus 30:50-2+ Ap 21 '69
Money isn't everything; acquisition of Brown & Root. il Forbes 104:42 S 1 '69
Oil-gathering octopus under the sea. il Pop Sci 194:84-5 Mr '69
Oil pressure; conservationists vs. Interior department. S. V. Roberts. New Repub 160:13-14 Mr 15 '69
Old oil hand makes Natomas swing; R. K. Davies. il Bsns W p 102-3 S 27 '69
Runaway oil well; will it mean new rules in offshore drilling? Santa Barbara incident. il U S News 66:14 F 17 '69
See also
Petroleum in submerged lands

OILBIRDS
Bird of darkness. J. Lindblad. il Natur Hist 78:80-4 F '69

OILS, Lubricating. See Lubrication and lubricants

OILS and fats, Edible
See also
Corn oil

OILSTONE. See Sharpening

OJAI festival. See Music festivals—California

OJUKWU, Chukwuemeka Odumegwu
End to a journey and an end to flight; interview, ed. by M. Kupfer and D. Robison. por Newsweek 73:55 Mr 24 '69

about
Nigeria-Biafra: a matter of accommodation. J. McLaughlin. America 120:162-7 F 8 '69
Odumegwu Ojukwu is Biafra. L. Garrison. il por N Y Times Mag p7-9+ Je 22 '69
Reprieve for eighteen. Time 93:44+ Je 13 '69

OKA, Takashi
Okinawa mon amour. N Y Times Mag p30-1+ Ap 6 '69
Premier Sato would tap his way across a stone bridge to be sure it was safe. il por N Y Times Mag p48-9+ N 16 '69

OKADA, Shintaro, and O'Brien, J. S.
Tay-Sachs disease: generalized absence of a beta-D-N-acetylhexosaminidase component. bibliog Science 165:698-700 Ag 15 '69

OKAI, John
Rosimaya; poem. il Atlan 224:104-5 S '69

OKAMOTO, Yoichi
White House photographers. J. Neubauer. il por Pop Phot 65:108-11+ D '69

O'KEEFE, Georgia
Hattersley class: looking at Life. R. Hattersley. pors Pop Phot 64:103-6 Je '69

O'KEEFE, John A.
Manned landings and theories of lunar formation. por Bul Atom Sci 25:56-8+ S '69
Water on the moon and a new nondimensional number. bibliog Science 163:669-70 F 14 '69

O'KEEFE, Patricia
Family pet. See issues of American home

OKINAWA
Agreement on Okinawa. il Time 94:37 N 28 '69
American alliance in trouble? il U S News 66:8 Je 16 '69
Closing a chapter of the past. il Newsweek 74:39-40 D 1 '69
Countdown on Okinawa. D. Reed. il Read Digest 95:117-21 N '69
Defenseless? Sarin gas incident. il Newsweek 74:65 Ag 4 '69
For SALT and Sato. Chr Cent 86:1476 N 19 '69
Go. New Repub 161:10 N 29 '69
Occupational problems; Tokyo students battling police on Okinawa day. il Time 93:43+ My 9 '69
Okinawa. M. Watkins. il Travel 131:54-9+ Mr '69
Okinawa mon amour. T. Oka. il N Y Times Mag p30-1+ Ap 6 '69
Okinawa: the island without a country. J. B. Billard. il Nat Geog 136:422-48 S '69
Passing the power; black GI's and militancy. B. Krisher. il Newsweek 74:49-50 D 22 '69
Reports: Okinawa. J. Hughes. Atlan 224:30+ O '69
Sato-Nixon pact; its meaning to U.S. and Japan. il U S News 67:18 D 1 '69
Sayonara, Okinawa. il Time 93:18 Je 13 '69
Short fuse in Japan. A. Axelbank. Nation 208:141-3 F 3 '69
Testing ground in Tokyo. N. Cousins. il Sat R 52:28-9 D 6 '69
Threat to a vital U.S. Pacific base. U S News 67:12 S 22 '69
U.S. Japan on a collision course? il U S News 67:84-5 N 24 '69
Why we're returning Okinawa to Japan. A. Campbell. New Repub 160:11-13 Je 14 '69
Winning a round. il Newsweek 73:50 Je 16 '69

OKLADNIKOV, A. P.
Petroglyphs of Siberia; with biographical sketch. Sci Am 221:12, 74-82 bibliog(p 136) Ag '69

OKLAHOMA
See also
Colleges and universities—Oklahoma
Hunting—Oklahoma
Paleontology—Oklahoma

Industries
Oklahoma's salesman-governor. Bsns W p 152+ O 11 '69

Parks and reserves
State parks where you don't have to rough it. il Bet Hom & Gard 47:147 My '69

OKLAHOMA CITY
No more mud for Sooner sports fans. il Am City 84:76-7 D '69

Finance
Bonds build cities, create jobs. il Am City 84:154+ O '69

OKLAHOMA Indians. See Indians of North America

OKLAHOMA! musical comedy. See Musical comedies, revues, etc.—Criticisms, plots, etc.

OKLAWAHA RIVER
Florida's new canal. E. White. il Yachting 126:58-60+ N '69

OKRA
We go for gumbo. V. Tripp. il Org Gard & Farm 16:54-5 Ap '69

OKUN, Arthur M.
Okun tells it like it might have been. por Bsns W p92 Ja 10 '70

OLAH, Franz
King's fall. por Newsweek 73:44-5 Ap 7 '69

OLCOTT, William
Wines that will improve with age. House & Gard 135:120+ Mr '69

OLCZEWSKA, Maria
Obituary
Opera N por 34:33 S 6 '69

OLD age
O₂ for old age; relieving symptoms of senescence. Newsweek 74:80 O 13 '69
Point of age. A. West. Vogue 153:56+ Ap 1 '69
Sensory stimulation: an adjunct to group work with the disabled aged. L. M. Burnside. bibliog il Ment Hy 53:381-8 Jl '69
See also
Aging
Centenarians
Gerontology
Old age assistance

OLD age assistance
AoA reports to state executives on work under Older Americans act. Aging 170:5+ D '68
Action line for aging; excerpts from address, October 24, 1968. W. J. Cohen. Aging 170:17 D '68
Dear Senator Williams, we've waited too long; letter. il Har Yrs 9:40-5 Jl '69
Goldwater plea for elderly. America 121:149-50 S 13 '69
House votes three-year extension, sends Senate Older Americans act amendments of 1969. Aging 176:3+ Je '69
New plan to help old people. il U S News 66:38 Ap 28 '69
News of state agencies. See issues of Aging
Nixon signs new law extending, expanding Older Americans act. AoA programs. il Aging 180:3-4 O '69
OAA bill delay tragic, Cohen tells state executives on aging; urges action in 1969. il Aging 170:3-5 D '68
Older Americans act: three years from the beginning. W. D. Bechill. Aging 171:3-4 Ja '69
Our man in Washington; interview, ed. by T. Schuchat. J. B. Martin. il Har Yrs 9:30-2 S '69
Research and demonstration. il Aging 175:6-7 My '69
State agencies on aging. Aging 175:14-15 My '69
State programs under the Older Americans act. il Aging 175:4-5+ My '69
Three years of progress under the Older Americans act. il Aging 175:5-6+ Ja '69
Who cares for the aged? R. E. Burger. il Sat R 52:14 17 Ja 25 '69; Discussion. 52:35 F 15 '69

OLD age centers. See Senior centers

OLD age homes
Among the aged. D. Rabinowitz. Commentary 47:61-6 Mr '69
See also
Nursing homes

OLSEN, Jack
Night of the grizzlies; condensation. Sports Illus 30:38-44+ My 12; 44-8+ My 19; 36-8+ My 26 '69

OLSEN, Jens
Astronomical clock of Jens Olsen, Danish astro-mechanic. O. Hagans. il por Hobbies 74:48-9+ Ap; 48-9+ My '69

OLSON, Charles E.
Way it looks to a classroom teacher. Todays Ed 58:59 Mr '69

OLSON, David J. See Lipsky, M. jt. auth.

OLSON, Dorothy C.
Perfectly normal spelling dilemma. Engl J 58:1220-2 N '69

OLSON, E. B. and DeLuca, H. F.
25-Hydroxycholecalciferol: direct effect on calcium transport. bibliog Science 165:405-7 Jl 25 '69

OLSON, John
Commune comes to America; photographs. Life 67:16B-23 Jl 18 '69

about

For exceptional courage and enterprise. G. P. Hunt. il por Life 66:3 Ap 11 '69
Two young men in a forest commune. R. Graves. por Life 67:1 Jl 18 '69

OLSON, Olof. See Krans, O.

OLSON, Ozzie
Wizard of Ozzie. C. Pendergast. il pors Motor T 21:26-8 N '69

OLSON, Paul A.
Training the teachers of teachers. Am Ed 5:13-14 F '69

OLSON, Sigurd F.
Battle for a wilderness; excerpt from Open horizons. Liv Wildn 32:4-13 Wint '68
Behind the ranges; excerpt from Open horizons. Audubon 71:6-15 Mr '69
Fire of life; excerpt from The hidden forest. Audubon 71:4-9 S '69
Song of the North; excerpt from Open horizons. Audubon 71:6-12 Ja '69
Stream of the past; excerpts from Open horizons. Am West 6:28-33 Mr '69

about

Dispatches from the unpaved world. J. C. Devlin. Natur Hist 78:70-2 My '69

OLSON, Toby
Game; poem. Nation 209:612 D 1 '69

OLT, James R.
Hotspot for honkers. Outdoor Life 144:68-9+ N '69
Outfoxing fox squirrels. Field & S 74:58-9+ S '69

OLYMPIA press
Olympia press starts hardcover series. Pub W 195:33-4 Mr 3 '69

OLYMPIC athletes. See Athletes

OLYMPIC games, 1968
After the Olympics: buying off protest. J. Scott and H. Edwards. il Ramp Mag 8:16-21 N '69
Report from Olympic village. P. Hamill. il Ramp Mag 7:21-7 N 30 '68
Report from section 22; suspended black sprinters. R. Cochran and J. Scott. il Ramp Mag 7:6+ N 30 '68
Year of turmoil and decision; Olympic boycott; ed. by J. Olsen. L. Alcindor. il Sports Illus 31:35-8+ N 10 '69

OLYMPIC games, 1972
Catch '72; controversy over flags and hymns. Newsweek 73:60 F 10 '69

OLYMPIC NATIONAL PARK
Olympic wilderness. il Sunset 142:64-75 Je '69

OLYMPIC rain forest. See Olympic National Park

OLYMPUS, MOUNT
See also
Olympic National Park

OMAHA, Neb.
Battle of Omaha: fight for state capital. S. Hronek. il Am West 6:10-11 Jl '69

Education

Omaha: Harry A. Burke high school. H. Oeschger. il ALA Bul 63:255-7 F '69

Hospitals

Continuous conveyor systems adapted to Nebraska Methodist. il Arch Rec 145:162-4 Mr '69

Music

Report: Omaha; performances of Carmen. R. Gainsley. Opera N 33:31 Ap 19 '69

Water supply

River-fed wells and a new filter plant. R. D. Hawes. il Am City 84:119-21+ My '69

OMAHA BEACH, Battle of. See World war, 1939-1945—Campaigns and battles—Western

O'MALLEY, Janet
Three's a crowd; story. Good H 169:80-1 Ag '69

O'MALLEY, Patrick
Plea to the bishops. Commonweal 91:267-8 N 28 '69

O'MALLEY, William
Polystyrene prints. Sch Arts 69:20-3 D '69

O'MARA, Richard
Rockefeller reports: half right on Latin America. Nation 209:602-4 D 1 '69

OMBUDSMAN
Answers East and West; Tucson, Ariz. and Trenton, N.J. il Am City 84:130+ F '69
Campus ombudsman. H. R. Rowland. il Todays Ed 58:37-9 O '69
No more land-development tie-ups; ombudsman concept to speed construction; Fort Worth, Tex. H. D. McMahan. il Am City 84:85+ Ag '69
Ombudsman, new man on campus. M. A. Guitar. il Seventeen 28:22+ Je '69
Ombudsmen. il Newsweek 74:100+ D 15 '69

OMEGA equities corporation
Story of a hot stock. C. Morgello. il Newsweek 73:85 My 12 '69

OMEGA-minus particles. See Particles (nuclear physics)

OMEGA system. See Radio in navigation

OMELETS
Eggs in your sky. il Am Home 72:84-5+ S '69
From Mexico, an oven omelet. il Sunset 142:163 Je '69

ON angels; story. See Barthelme, D.

ON-the-job training. See Employees—Training

ONASSIS, Aristotle Socrates
Shipping titans lock in battle. il por Bsns W p51 Jl 12 '69
When giants clash. Time 93:86 Mr 21 '69

ONASSIS, Aristotle Socrates, family
Jacqueline Kennedy Onassis' stepchildren. L. Smith. il McCalls 96:80-1+ Ap '69

ONASSIS, Jacqueline Lee (Bouvier) Kennedy
Bouviers; excerpts. J. H. Davis. il pors Ladies Home J 86:123-30 F: 90-3+ Mr '69
Crawfie strikes again. W. F. Buckley, jr. Nat R 21:767 Jl 29 '69
Enemy within; about My Life with Jacqueline Kennedy. il Time 94:17 Jl 18 '69
Jackie watcher. il por Newsweek 74:102+ O 13 '69
Jackie's judo caper. il por Life 67:94-6 O 17 '69
Postscript to My life with Jacqueline Kennedy. M. B. Gallagher and F. S. Leighton. Ladies Home J 86:84+ N '69

ONCOPELTUS fasciatus. See Milkweed bugs

ONDRA, Jaroslav
New calvaries ever. Chr Cent 86:1538-9 D 3 '69

ONE-bank holding companies. See Bank holding companies

ONE-of-a-kind regatta. See Regattas

ONE of my generation; story. See Updike, J.

ONE-room apartments. See Apartments

ONE summer there were dragons; story. See Curtis, M. E.

ONEIDA community
Great Oneida love-in. M. Bishop. il Am Heritage 20:14-17+ F '69

O'NEIL, Paul
Comedian in the kitchen. Life 67:51-2+ D 5 '69
Kill the hill! Pave that grass! Life 67:126-7+ O 10 '69
So long to the good old moon. Life 67:46-8+ Jl 4 '69
Who woulda thunk it? Life 67:34B-41 S 26 '69
—and others
Monstrous Manson family. Life 67:2A, 20-31 D 19 '69

O'NEIL, William Martin
One-to-one missions. America 121:357 O 25 '69

O'NEILL, Eugene, memorial theater foundation, Waterford, Conn. See Eugene O'Neill memorial theater foundation. Waterford. Conn.

O'NEILL, Eugene Gladstone
Ah, wilderness! Criticism
Sat R 52:62 N 22 '69

O'NEILL, Patricia
Spectacular succulent. Horticulture 48:47+ Ja '70

O'NEILL, Russell
Fling with Ferlinghetti. Engl J 58:1025-7+ O '69

O'NEILL, Terence Marne
Bad day for the Irish. Time 93:38-9 Mr 7 '69
Battle of Bogside. il Newsweek 73:55 My 5 '69

O'NEILL, Terence Marne—*Continued*
Ex-prime minister O'Neill praises ecumenical efforts of clergy. Chr Cent 86:705 My 21 '69
From captain to major. Newsweek 73:50+ My 12 '69
Terence on a tightrope. il Newsweek 73:38+ F 10 '69

O'NEILL, William
I'm not stuffed, I'm freeze-dried! Pop Mech 132:78-81 D '69

ONIONS
Influential onion. D. Munson. House B 111:34-5 F '69
Lettuce in the onion row! L. Riotte. il Org Gard & Farm 16:40-1 S '69
More onions, the better. C. Fessenden. il Org Gard & Farm 16:66-7 My '69
Onions against clots. il Time 93:52 Mr 28 '69
Onions that grow on trees; Egyptian, or top onions. R. Hendrickson. Org Gard & Farm 16:84 Ap '69
Space-saving onion patch. W. Ferguson. il Org Gard & Farm 16:54-5 Mr '69
See also
Alliums

ONLY women can be wives; story. See Cook, W.

ONO, Yoko
Peace anthem. Newsweek 74:102 D 1 '69
Top pop merger: Lennon/Ono inc. B. Rollin. il pors Look 33:36-42 Mr 18 '69

ONOCLEA. See Ferns

ONSAGER, Lars
Motion of ions: principles and concepts. bibliog Science 166:1359-64 D 12 '69

ONTARIO
See also
Education—Ontario

Religious institutions and affairs
Ontario. J. R. Mutchmor. Chr Cent 86:1626+ D 17 '69
World around us (cont) Chr Cent 86:196-8, 690+ F 5, My 14 '69

ONTARIO, LAKE
El Dorado beach project. F. Eldridge. il Cons 24:6-8 O '69

ONYX enterprises, incorporated
Putting soul in Christmas. il Bsns W p58 D 20 '69

OOCYTES. See Germ cells

OOGENESIS. See Gametogenesis

OOSTERMAN, Gordon
Tax funds for religious education? Chr Today 13:7+ Mr 28 '69

OP amps. See Amplifiers

OPALINA. See Ciliata

OPAQUE projectors. See Projectors

OPARIN, Aleksandr Ivanovich
Origin of life (cont) E. Keller. il Chem 42:12-18 Ja '69 (to be cont)

OPEN and closed shelves
Open stacks: a second look; reprint. H. D. Gordon. il Library J 94:1844-5 My 1 '69; Discussion. 94:2848, 3378+ S 1, O 1 '69

OPEN sandwiches. See Sandwiches

OPEN shelves in libraries. See Open and closed shelves

OPEN space planning. See Land utilization

OPEN theatre. See Theater, Experimental

OPENING of doors; story. See Regnier, N.

OPERA
People's choice; qualities that explain the popular favorite operas. I. Strasfogel. il Opera N 33:8-11 F 15 '69
Philosophy of innovation. G. Ross. il Opera N 34:14-16 S 6 '69
Recording as a medium; how does opera on the turntable differ from a live performance? E. T. Canby. il Opera N 33:8-11 F 8 '69
See also
Animals in opera
Libretto
Moving pictures—Musical films
Operas
Television broadcasting—Operas

Appreciation
Growing up with opera. N. S. Ross. Opera N 34:6-7 D 27 '69
Point of contact; reaching the people. G. C. Menotti. il Opera N 34:8-11 D 27 '69
R for opera. R. Palmai-Tenser. Opera N 34:14-15 D 13 '69

Bibliography
Basic books: a selection for the opera-lover. S. Jenkins, jr. bibliog Opera N 34:14-15 D 6 '69

Musical events. W. Sargeant. New Yorker 45:144-6 S 27 '69

History and criticism
Battle of Baby Doe. H. Blumenfeld. Opera N 33:8+ Mr 8 '69
Bridge to a new world; Das Rheingold is a fresh beginning. E. Downes. il Opera N 33:25-6 F 22 '69
Doctor Borodin's formula; pageantry and patriotism in Prince Igor. F. Rizzo. il Opera N 33:12-13 Mr 1 '69
Epochs of opera:
  France. S. Levarie. il Opera N 34:24-9 Ja 10 '70
  Germany and Austria. S. Levarie. il Opera N 34:26-31 Ja 17 '70
  Italy. S. Levarie. il Opera N 34:32-7 D 27 '69
How I got rid of monstrous Mildred; or, What I think about Die frau ohne schatten. W. Mann. Opera N 33:24-5 Mr 8 '69
Its true self: Janácek's Jenufa. J. W. Freeman. il Opera N 34:14-15 O 11 '69
Loners; Peter Grimes and Wozzeck. S. Jenkins, jr. Opera N 33:24-5 Ap 5 '69
Once upon a time; for Puccini, Turandot had to be more than a fairy tale. L. W. Haldeman. Opera N 33:24-5 Mr 22 '69
Operas of Benjamin Britten, by P. Howard. Review
  Am Rec G 36:70-2 S '69. J. Diether
Other Fidelio; Smetana's Dalibor. P. J. Smith. il Opera N 34:6-7 N 1 '69
Point of contact; reaching the people. G. C. Menotti. il Opera N 34:8-11 D 27 '69
Salvaging the past; A festival of baroque operas. H. Weinstock. Sat R 52:75 F 22 '69
Singing sinners; seven deadly sins. M. E. Geib. il Opera N 34:6-7 D 13 '69

Instruction and study
Corbett foundation, a chance to make good. S. Fleming. Hi Fi 19:MA6 Jl '69
In service; the Guild rounds out a decade of teaching teachers. M. E. Peltz. il Opera N 33:6-7 F 8 '69
Master's apprentices; Friedelind Wagner's Bayreuth master class tackled Aida. J. Rockwell. il Opera N 34:6-7 Ja 10 '69
National artists; Seattle opera's National artists program. F. Merkling. Opera N 34:25 S 6 '69
Report: New York; Clark center opera workshop production of The magic flute. S. L. Fogel. il Opera N 33:30 Mr 15 '69
Twenty Long years; Kathryn Long courses. M. Rudolf. il Opera N 33:6-7 Je 14 '69
See also
College operas, revues, etc.
North Carolina school of the arts, Winston-Salem

Stage scenery
Bright future? color and super-realism to sell Wagner. S. Jenkins, jr. il Opera N 33:8-12 F 22 '69
Dual control; interview, ed. by G. Loney. J. P. Ponnelle. Opera N 34:25 D 27 '69
Enlightener; interview, ed. by M. J. Matz. P. L. Pizzi. il Opera N 34:20-1 N 22 '69
Opera primer: who paints the scenery? F. Bowers. il Opera N 33:26-9 F 8 '69

Stories
See Libretto

Study and teaching
See Opera—Instruction and study

Australia
Report: Australia; productions of Madama Butterfly and Falstaff. W. L. Hoffmann. Opera N 33:29 Ap 12 '69
See also
Queensland opera company

Austria
Centennial of a shrine; Vienna's staatsoper. il Time 93:73 Je 6 '69
Epochs of opera: Germany and Austria. S. Levarie. il Opera N 34:26-31 Ja 17 '70
Hundred years' war; Vienna state opera at its centenary. J. Rockwell. Opera N 33:18-19 My 17 '69
In Vienna it's a 100th birthday, in three-four time. il Life 66:48-9 F 28 '69
One hundred years of the opera on the Ring, 1869-1969. I. Barea. il Sat R 52:45-7 My 31 '69

Bulgaria
Report: performance at Sofia. M. L. Eiland. Opera N 34:27 D 6 '69

China
See also
Opera, Chinese

OPERA—*Continued*

France

Epochs of opera; France. S. Levarie. il Opera N 34:24-9 Ja 10 '70

Germany

Epochs of opera: Germany and Austria. S. Levarie. il Opera N 34:26-31 Ja 17 '70

Germany (Federal republic)

German forecast: fair skies ahead. J. H. Sutcliffe. Opera N 34:6-7 D 6 '69
See also
Hamburg state opera company

Great Britain

See also
Royal opera, Great Britain
Sadler's Wells opera

Italy

Epochs of opera: Italy. S. Levarie. il Opera N 34:32-7 D 27 '69
See also
Milan. Italy—La Scala

Japan

Report: Tokyo; productions by Niki-Kai opera company. E. C. Wilkes. il Opera N 33:30 Mr 29 '69

New Zealand

See also
New Zealand opera company

Scotland

Scots wha hae; lyric theater in the land of the heather. B. Fischer-Williams. il Opera N 34:16-19 D 13 '69

United States

R for opera. R. Palmai-Tenser. Opera N 34:14-15 D 13 '69
U.S. calendar. See issues of Opera news published during opera season
U.S. opera survey: the multiest of media. M. F. Rich. il Opera N 34:13-16 N 22 '69
See also
American opera society
Central opera service
Clarion music society, incorporated
Metropolitan opera company
Metropolitan opera guild
New York city opera company
Opera guilds
San Francisco opera company
Santa Fe opera company
Television broadcasting—Operas
Tri-Cities opera

OPERA, Chinese
Out of Peking; Chinese opera preserves the many-splendored traditions of forty centuries. M. D. Morris. il Opera N 33:8-13 Mr 22 '69
Taipei theater. M. Connelly. Holiday 46:16+ N '69

OPERA, Paris. See Opera houses

OPERA, Spanish
See also
Zarzuelas

OPERA and state. See Music and state

OPERA broadcasting. See Radio broadcasting —Operas

OPERA company of Boston
Report: Boston; productions of Bluebeard's castle (opera), The wooden prince (ballet) and The miraculous mandarin (pantomime) M. Harris. Opera N 33:30 Mr 8 '69

OPERA critics. See Music critics

OPERA films. See Moving pictures—Musical films

OPERA for children. See Music for children

OPERA guilds
Guild-hopping; a diary. Mrs E. K. Meade, jr. Opera N 34:6-7 S 20 '69
See also
Metropolitan opera guild

OPERA houses
Centennial of a shrine; Vienna's staatsoper. il Time 93:73 Je 6 '69
Great opera houses:
Geneva. D. A. MacKinnon. il Opera N 33: 26-9 Mr 22 '69
House on the golden horn; Istanbul culture center. C. E. Adelsen. il Opera N 34:22-3 O 11 '69
Hundred years' war; Vienna state opera at its centenary. J. Rockwell. Opera N 33:18-19 My 17 '69
In Sydney: tours for opera house watchers. il Sunset 143:56 S '69
One hundred years of the opera on the Ring, 1869-1969. I. Barea. il Sat R 52:45-7 My 31 '69

Santa Fe's operatic oasis. I. Kolodin. il Sat R 52:39-40+ Ag 30 '69
Unknown opera; Théâtre national de l'opera. S. L. Fogel. il Opera N 34:8-13 D 6 '69
War memorial; San Francisco opera house. G. Fitzgerald. il Opera N 34:8-13 O 11 '69

OPERA news (periodical)
Guild at work. J. Boutwell. il Opera N 33: 26-9 Mr 29 '69

OPERA patronage
Happiest angel; J. R. Corbett. il Opera N 34: 20-1 D 6 '69
Patron today; donors who keep opera in good financial health. R. W. Hall. Opera N 33:8-11 Ap 12 '69

OPERA singers
Club 99 releases; recordings by Russian singers of the past. A. Favia-Artsay. il Hobbies 74:35-7 D '69
Opera and the stars. F. Stevenson and D. Brown. il Opera N 34:14-16 Ja 17 '70
Opera primer: how does a singer do it? J. Raskin. il Opera N 33:28-31 F 22 '69
Searching for heroes; L. Melchior's Heldentenor foundation. il Time 93:53 F 28 '69
See also
Singing
also names of opera singers, e.g. L. Homer

Photographs

Met jet. Opera N 33:12-13 Je 14 '69
Repress that release! photographs from press agents. Opera N 33:14-16 F 1 '69

OPERA society of Washington
Report: production of Rossini's Comte Ory. F. C. Smith. il Opera N 34:23 D 6 '69
Report: Washington; production of Manon Lescaut. F. C. Smith. Opera N 33:31 Ap 5 '69

OPERA tickets
Guild at work: ticket service. J. Boutwell. il Opera N 33:26-9 Mr 8 '69

OPERA workshops. See Opera—Instruction and study

OPERAKÄLLAREN (restaurant) See Stockholm—Hotels, restaurants, etc.

OPERAS
To wag the dog; new endings for old favorites. J. Freeman. il Opera N 34:6-7 N 22 '69
See also
Phonograph records—Operas
Video tape recordings—Operas

Criticisms, plots, etc

See name of composer for full entry
Adriana Lecouvreur. F. Cilea
Aida. G. Verdi
Ariadne auf Naxos. R. Strauss
Ballad of Baby Doe. D. S. Moore
Barber of Seville. G. Rossini
Il barbiere di Siviglia. See Barber of Seville, above
Capriccio. R. Strauss
Carmen. G. Bizet
Catulli carmina. C. Orff
Cavalleria rusticana. P. Mascagni
Devils of Loudun. K. Penderecki
Don Giovanni. J. C. W. A. Mozart
Faust. C. F. Gounod
Der fliegende Holländer. See Flying Dutchman, below
Flying Dutchman. R. Wagner
Die frau ohne schatten. See Woman without a shadow, below
Hamlet. H. Searle
Help, help, the Globolinks! G. C. Menotti
I am the way. J. Hines
King Arthur. H. Purcell
L'heure espagnole. M. Ravel
Lucia di Lammermoor. G. Donizetti
Magic flute. J. C. W. A. Mozart
Manon. J. Massenet
Medea in Corinto. J. S. Mayr
Mefistofele. A. Boito
Die Meistersinger von Nürnberg. R. Wagner
Metamorphosis. M. White
Moses and Aaron. A. Schonberg
Pagliacci. R. Leoncavallo
La Périchole. J. Offenbach
Peter Grimes. B. Britten
Prince Igor. A. P. Borodin
Das Rheingold. R. Wagner
Rigoletto. G. Verdi
Der Rosenkavalier. R. Strauss
Russlan and Ludmilla. M. I. Glinka
La straniera. V. Bellini
Thaïs. J. Massenet
Tosca. G. Puccini
La Traviata. G. Verdi
Il Trovatore. G. Verdi
Les Troyens. H. Berlioz
Turandot. G. Puccini
Twelfth night. D. Amram
Die Walküre. R. Wagner
Woman without a shadow. R. Strauss
Wozzeck. A. Berg
Die zauberflöte. See Magic flute, above

OPERAS—*Continued*

Scores

Something old, something new; discrepancies in the Rosenkavalier score. J. Rockwell. il Opera N 33:24-5 F 8 '69

OPERAS, Titles of. See Titles of operas

OPERATIC acting. See Acting

OPERATIC characters. See Characters in opera

OPERATIC composition. See Composition (music)

OPERATIC production and direction

Arena; photographs of Verdi's Don Carlo production, Verona. Opera N 34:18-21 S 20 '69

Bright future? color and super-realism to sell Wagner. S. Jenkins, jr. il Opera N 33:8-12 F 22 '69

Bring 'em back alive; key to revivals. P. Tavernia. il Opera N 33:8-11 F 1 '69

Challenge; photographs of Turandot. Opera N 33:21-3 Mr 22 '69

Cinderella out West; photographs of San Francisco opera's La Cenerentola. Opera N 34:26-7 D 27 '69

Corsaro, Capobianco, and Merrill; a sampler of opera directing today. D. Hering. il Dance Mag 43:28-30 Mr '69

Deadly affair; photographs of Adriana Lecouvreur. Opera N 33:21-3 Ap 19 '69

Dubious Don, an ingenious barber; Salzburg. G. Movshon. il Hi Fi 19:MA28-9+ O '69

Figures of Magic; photographs of Metropolitan production. Opera N 34:21 Ja 17 '70

Highland tragedy; photographs of Lucia di Lammermoor. Opera N 33:21-3 F 1 '69

In search of a shadow; photographs of Die frau ohne schatten. Opera N 33:21-3 Mr 8 '69

Is this any way to run an opera house? R. D. Holland. America 120:690-1 Je 14 '69

It reeks of blood; photographs of Wozzeck. Opera N 33:21-3 Ap 12 '69

Madonna and prima donna; photographs of Tosca. Opera N 33:21-3 F 15 '69

Moment of truth; photographs of Carmen. Opera N 33:21-3 Mr 15 '69

Mother's oath; photographs of Il Trovatore. Opera N 33:21-3 Mr 29 '69

Music; post-1954 stagings of Moses and Aron, by A. Schoenberg. D. Hamilton. Nation 209: 125 Ag 11 '69

New hall for Montezuma; R. Sessions' Montezuma. J. H. Sutcliffe. il Opera N 33:6-7 My 17 '69

Opera primer; why the director? F. Rizzo. il Opera N 33:26-30 F 15 '69

Opera's tightrope walker; N. Merrill, resident stage director of the Metropolitan opera. il Time 93:68 Mr 14 '69

Out of Peking; Chinese opera preserves the many-splendored traditions of forty centuries. M. D. Morris. il Opera N 33:8-13 Mr 22 '69

Out of the tempest; photographs of Peter Grimes. Opera N 33:21-3 Ap 5 '69

Rosenkavalier gallery; photographs. Opera N 33:21-3 F 8 '69

Scandal over Rossini; Festival of two worlds. W. Weaver. il Hi Fi 19:MA30-1 O '69

Tale of treachery; photographs of Das Rheingold. Opera N 33:21-4 F 22 '69

Tosca's shining stars. il Opera N 34:21 Ja 10 '70

Triumph of Felsenstein's La Traviata; Komische oper. G. R. Marek. Hi Fi 19:MA28-9+ F '69

Trovatore sketchbook. il Opera N 33:14-15 F 15 '69

U.S. opera survey: the multiest of media. M. F. Rich. il Opera N 34:13-16 N 22 '69

Verismo revisited; brand-new production of Cavalleria rusticana and Pagliacci at the Met. il Time 95:64 Ja 19 '70

Wotan's children; photographs of Die Walküre. Opera N 33:21-3 Mr 1 '69

Wozzeck at the Met. G. Perle. il Sat R 52:61-2 My 17 '69

See also
College operas, revues, etc.

OPERATIC training. See Opera—Instruction and study

OPERATION bookshelf

From Scarsdale to Korea: Operation bookshelf. M. B. Tarshish. il Pub W 195:28-9 My 26 '69

OPERATION Breadbasket. See Southern Christian leadership conference

OPERATION Breakthrough. See United States —Housing and urban development, Department of

OPERATION SEEK. See New York (city) City university of New York

OPERATION sidewinder; drama. See Shepard, S.

OPERATIONAL amplifiers. See Amplifiers

OPHTHALMOLOGY

Ophthalmologist talks about his work; ed. by W. S. Ross. A. E. Maumenee. il Todays Health 47:40-1+ Ap '69

OPHULS, Max

Artist risking all, a film to remember. R. Schickel. por Life 66:9 My 23 '69

Current cinema. P. Gilliatt. New Yorker 45: 137-8+ My 3 '69

OPINION, Public. See Public opinion

OPINION, Student. See Student opinion

OPINION, Teacher. See Teacher opinion

OPINION research. See Public opinion polls

OPINIONS, Personal. See Attitudes

OPIUM

Opium and the romantic imagination, by A. Hayter. Review
New Repub 160:30-1 F 15 '69. R. Freedman

OPIUM habit. See Narcotic habit

OPIUM pipes

Chinese pipes for tobacco and opium. C. E. Kennedy. il Antiques 95:408-9 Mr '69

OPIUM trade

U.N. to develop plans to control illegal narcotic drug crops; statement, December 17, 1968. D. F. Squire. Dept State Bul 60:64-5 Ja 20 '69

OPOSSUMS

Isolation of western equine encephalomyelitis virus from an opossum. R. W. Emmons and E. H. Lennette. bibliog Science 163:945-6 F 28 '69

OPPEN, George

Individuality and numerosity. L. S. Dembo. Nation 209:574-6 N 24 '69

OPPENHEIM, Dennis

Scuba sculpture. W. Johnson. il Art N 68:52-3+ N '69

OPPENHEIMER, Joel

Innocent breasts; poem. Poetry 113:310-13 F '69

OPPENHEIMER, John R. and Lang, G. E.

Cebus monkeys; effect on branching of Gustavia trees. bibliog Science 165:187-8 Jl 11 '69

OPPENHEIMER, Julius Robert

Atomization of the human spirit. J. Lear. por Sat R 52:25-7 D 27 '69

Lawrence and Oppenheimer, by N. P. Davis. Review
Bul Atom Sci 25:31-2 Ja '69. J. Wilson
New Yorker 45:141-2+ My 10 '69. J. Bernstein

Oppenheimer case, by P. M. Stern. Review
Atlan 224:158+ N '69. I. Asimov
New Repub 161:25-7 N 22 '69. C. Brown
Newsweek por 74:115-16 N 10 '69. G. Wolff

Drama

Theater. H. Hewes. Sat R 52:72 Mr 22 '69

OPPENHEIMER, Martin

Strategies for the ghetto wars; excerpt from The urban guerrilla. Nation 208:366-70 Mr 24 '69

OPPENHEIMER, Monroe

Car pool; story. Redbook 133:100-1 My '69

OPPENHEIMER fund, incorporated

Leon Levy's view. R. Brady. Duns R 94: 127-8 N '69

OPPORTUNITIES industrialization centers, incorporated

Business lobbies for ghetto program. Bsns W p56+ Je 28 '69

OPTICAL character recognition. See Optical scanners

OPTICAL communication systems. See Light communication systems

OPTICAL flats

Making optical flats with simple equipment. T. Caldwell. il R Pop Astron 63:26-32 Mr '69

OPTICAL illusions

Objective measure of the dynamics of a visual movement illusion. J. Thornson and others. bibliog il Science 164:1087-8 My 30 '69

Optical illusions. A. Heidt. il Sch Arts 69:17 N '69

Optical illusions; weird tricks your eyes play on you. B. Ford. il Sci Digest 66:45-55 Jl '69

Ponzo perspective illusion as a manifestation of space perception. H. Leibowitz and others. il Science 166:1174-6 N 28 '69

OPTICAL instruments
See also
Lenses
Recognition equipment, incorporated
Schlieren apparatus

OPTICAL reading machines. See Optical scanners

OPTICAL scanners

Optical scanning finally starts to pay off. il Bsns W p55-6 D 27 '69

OPTICON (optical tactical converter) See
Blind, Apparatus for the
OPTICS
More applications for coherent optics and
holography; report of meeting. R. E. Haskell. il Phys Today 22:103-7 Jl '69
See also
Diffraction
Nonlinear optics
Refraction
OPTICS, Nonlinear. See Nonlinear optics
OPTICS, Physiological
Optics of arthropod compound eye. S. R.
Shaw. bibliog il Science 165:88-90 Jl 4 '69
Organization of the visual pathways. M.
Glickstein. bibliog il Science 164:917-26 My
23 '69
See also
Optical illusions
OPTIMIST'S daughter; story. See Welty, E. E.
OPTIMUM population. See Population
OPTIONS
See also
Put and call transactions
Stock purchase options
OPTIONS, Stock purchase. See Stock purchase
options
OPUS Dei
Opus Dei: in Spain, a political force. W. E.
Greening. Chr Cent 87:27-9 Ja 7 '70
O'QUIN, Sally
Close-up: Chuck Dederich. Life 66:36-8 Ja
31 '69
ORAL behavior in infants. See Motor response
ORAL contraceptives. See Contraceptives
ORAL English. See English language—Study
and teaching
ORAL history
Enfield's excited about living history; high
school, Thompsonville, Conn. F. S. Gross.
il Sr Schol 94:Schol Teach 13-14 My 9 '69
ORAL reading. See Books and reading—Reading aloud
ORAL surgery
New faces for old. il Newsweek 73:94 Mr 10
'69
ORANGE, N.J., public library
Backlog to frontlog; scheme for circulating
nonfiction books. M. H. Scilken. il Library
J 94:3014-15 S 15 '69
ORANGE coast college, Costa Mesa, Calif.
Eight times two equals four; rowing squad
of OCC. H. D. Whall. il Sports Illus 30:
62+ My 26 '69
ORANGE COUNTY, Calif.

Parks and reserves

Parks between the tides; marine park preserves. W. Marx. il Parks & Rec 3:13-20
O '68
ORANGE juice, Frozen. See Fruit juices,
Frozen
ORANGEBURG, S.C.

Riots

Orangeburg incident. il Time 93:28 Je 6 '69
ORANGES
Your oranges don't shine. R. J. Wyndham. Org
Gard & Farm 16:66-7 S '69
See also
Cookery—Fruit
ORANGUTANS
Our red-haired kin of the rain forest; with
photographs by C. Rentmeester, and behavior study by D. A. Horr. Life 66:82-
9+ Mr 28 '69
ORATORIOS
Messiaen's monument; world première of The
transfiguration of Our Lord Jesus Christ.
Time 93:52 Je 20 '69
See also
Messiah (oratorio)
Phonograph records—Oratorios
ORBEN, Robert
What ever happened to mother-in-law jokes?
McCalls 96:93+ Mr '69
ORBIS speed monitoring system. See Computers
—Traffic control applications
ORBITAL motion of the earth. See Earth—
Orbital motion
ORBITAL rendezvous (space flight)
Apollo 9 rendezvous, docking plot shown. il
Aviation W 90:69 F 24 '69
Apollo probe, drogue exceed expectations. il
Aviation W 90:70 Mr 17 '69
Automatic docking in cosmos and its application to aviation safety and space stations; address at the first United Nations
space conference in Vienna, August 14-28,
1968. B. V. Raushenbakh. Bul Atom Sci
25:40-2 Ja '69

Control problems could have barred Soyuz
mission dockings. D. C. Winston. il Aviation W 91:18-19 O 27 '69
Docking transmitted live in first color TV
from space. W. C. Wetmore. il Aviation W
90:18-20 My 26 '69
Linkup in space; Soyuz 4 & 5. Sky & Tel 37:
163-4 Mr '69
Maneuver in outer space. IU. Marinin. Space
World F-3-63:48 Mr '69
Nuclear bulls-eye enables Apollo 9 astronauts
to dock right on button. il Space World
F-6-66:31-3 Je '69
Russians take new space path. il Bsns W
p40-1 Ja 25 '69
Russians' turn; first crew exchange in orbit.
il Time 93:60 Ja 24 '69
Soviet advances in orbital maneuvers. A.
Tumanov. Space World G-1-73:38-9 Ja '70
Soyuz versatility confirmed by docking;
Soyuz 4-5 flights, 1969. Aviation W 90:29
Ja 20 '69
Space lab progress. il Sci N 95:114 F 1 '69
Station no. 1; Soyuz union in orbit. il Newsweek 73:93 Ja 27 '69
ORBITAL workshop. See Space stations
ORBITING astronomical observatory. See Artificial satellites—Astronomical applications
ORBITING geophysical observatory. See Artificial satellites—Astronomical applications
ORBITING solar observatory. See Artificial
satellites—Astronomical applications
ORBITS
Spin-orbit resonance of the inner planets.
P. M. Campbell. bibliog Science 165:930 Ag
29 '69
See also
Space vehicles—Orbits
ORCATE, Gene
Sibling chivalry: the other side of the coin.
Parents Mag 44:54-5+ Mr '69
ORCHARDS. See Fruit culture
ORCHESTRA musicians. See Musicians
ORCHESTRAL conductors. See Conductors
(music)
ORCHESTRAL music
See also
Phonograph records—Orchestral music
ORCHESTRAS
Bargaining in major symphony orchestras.
L. E. Lunden. bibliog Mo Labor R 92:15-
19 Jl '69
Debuts & reappearances; New York concerts.
See issues of High fidelity incorporating
Musical America
Dreaming the possible dream; New Philharmonia orchestra conducted by M. Bialoguski, M.D. il Time 93:53+ My 9 '69
Impressive young orchestra from Westphalia;
Siegerland-orchester. D. Newlin. Am Rec
G 35:1033 Jl '69
Orchestras en route. il Hi Fi 19:MA17-19+
O '69
Retirement in allegro; musicians past sixty.
H. Alpert. il Har Yrs 9:17-20 N '69
Revolution in white tie and tails. R. Evett.
New Repub 161:28-30 N 1 '69
See also names of orchestras, e.g. Louisville orchestra

Finance

American orchestras: the sound of trouble;
financial burdens. il Time 93:71-2 Je 13 '69
Deficits bring sour note in world of music.
il Bsns W p77-8 Jl 12 '69
ORCHIDS
Biologically active compounds in orchid
fragrances. C. H. Dodson and others. bibliog il Science 164:1243-9 Je 13 '69
Getting a start on cymbidiums. il Sunset 142:
262 Ap '69
Orchid fundamentals. M. A. Reinikka. il
Horticulture 46:20-2+ Ag '68
Orchids around the year. G. J. Sessler. Horticulture 47:20-1 N '69; 48:34-5 Ja '70
They're not the least bit touchy; cymbidium orchids. il Sunset 142:226 Mr '69
Unique pollination in orchids. D. Seibert.
Horticulture 46:23 Ag '68
ORCHIN, Milton
Determining the number of isomers from a
structural formula. por Chem 42:8-12 My
'69
ORDAZ, Gustavo Díaz. See Díaz Ordaz, G.
ORDER processing
See also
Booksellers and bookselling—Order processing
Publishers and publishing—Order processing
ORDERLINESS. See Neatness
ORE deposits
Hydrothermal ore deposits in the western
United States: a new concept of structural
control of distribution. J. Kutina. bibliog il
Science 165:1113-19 S 12 '69

OREGON
See also
Booksellers and bookselling—Oregon
Columbia River
Crater Lake
Education—Oregon
Fishing—Oregon
Hells Canyon
Hunting—Oregon
Roads—Oregon
Wilderness areas—Oregon

Description and travel
Across Oregon's lonely corner. il Sunset 142:39 Je '69
Oregon: unspoiled splendor. A. Gordon. il Read Digest 94:135-42 My '69

Politics and government
Kaffeeklatsch constituency: Packwood's Dorchester conference. F. McKay. Nation 208:205-6 F 17 '69

OREGON. University

Medical school, Portland
Garage structure echoes shape of hill it replaces. il Arch Rec 145:165-7 Ap '69

OREGON historical society
Historical museum adds public amenity to urban setting; headquarters building. il Arch Rec 145:186-7 Je '69

OREGON hollygrape. See Mahonias

OREGON TRAIL
John Day ford at McDonald. il Sunset 143:30 S '69

O'REILLY, Jane
How much is enough? The Christmas tip. McCalls 97:40+ D '69
Jobs making television commercials. Mlle 68:174-5+ Mr '69

OREM, R. Calvert
Curse of crash education. Nations Bsns 57:60-2+ Ag '69

ORENGO, Charles
Fayard: one of the places where it is happening. H. R. Lottman. il por Pub W 195:36-8 Je 30 '69

ORESTEIA; drama. See Lewin, J.

ORFF, Carl
Catulli carmina. Criticism
New Yorker 45:192-3 N 8 '69
Sat R 52:103 N 15 '69
Music to my ears; performance of Prometheus. I. Kolodin. Sat R 52:45 N 1 '69
Musical events; Carmina burana performed by New York philharmonic, conducted by S. Ozawa. W. Sargeant. New Yorker 45:117 O 11 '69
Orff-Schulwerk, a joyous note. G. L. Mayer. Sat R 52:46-7 Jl 26 '69
Paramountcy of clarity. Roger Wagner's chorale: Catulli carmina. P. L. Miller. Am Rec G 36:198 N '69
Records:
Carmina burana. Opera N 33:35 F 8 '69
Report: production of Prometheus. F. Merkling. Opera N 34:23 N 22 '69

ORFIELD, Gary
Court, the schools, and the southern strategy. Sat R 52:62+ D 20 '69
Nixon's first test. Nation 208:79-82 Ja 20 '69
Politics of resegregation. Sat R 52:58-60+ S 20 '69

ORFORD, Horace Walpole, 4th earl of. See Walpole, H.

ORGAN
Getting started in electronic organ servicing. D. A. John. il Radio-Electr 40:76-8 Ag '69
Orchestra at your fingertips; electronic organ. E. McDonald. il House B 111:72+ O '69

History
Reed organs revisited; a glance into the past; reprint. J. J. Duga. Hobbies 74:98N-98O+ Je '69

ORGAN music
See also
Phonograph records—Organ music

ORGANELLES. See Plant cells and tissues

ORGANIC deposits. See Sedimentation and deposition

ORGANIC food. See Food, Organic

ORGANIC gardening
About gardening and Rex and Harold, and then there's me! R. Stout. il Org Gard & Farm 16:44-7 F '69
California's unique farm on less than an acre. M. C. Goldman. il Org Gard & Farm 16:36-9 D '69
Call me when your vegetables are ready. P. Delfeld. il Org Gard & Farm 16:24-5 Ag '69

Gardener's life after a heart attack. S. Fitzjarrald. il Org Gard & Farm 16:48-51 Ag '69
Happiness: organic gardening's bumper crop. C. Allonby. il Org Gard & Farm 16:33-5 S '69
Making three organic farms pay. M. Franz. il Org Gard & Farm 16:58-62 S '69
Organic food growers can make it on 50 acres or less. M. Franz. il Org Gard & Farm 16:51-5 Jl '69
Organic gardeners grow 'em big! M. C. Goldman. il Org Gard & Farm 16:32-5 Mr '69
Our Adirondack pony ranch garden. D. Harris. il Org Gard & Farm 16:61-3 Mr '69
Profile of a pioneer in organic foods. M. C. Goldman. il Org Gard & Farm 16:56-61 Jl '69
Retirement gardening, organic, of course. V. A. Croley; A. Cadwalader; E. Bauchilon. il Org Gard & Farm 16:38-42 Ja '69
We invited the bugs to dinner, but they never came! C. Skinner. il Org Gard & Farm 16:46-9 Mr '69
Where can you find an organic Tahiti? life in a small rural town in Massachusetts. J. Ingersoll. il Org Gard & Farm 16:51-3 O '69
Young man tells why he lives on the land; letter, ed. by R. Rodale. W. Rominger. il Org Gard & Farm 16:27-32 D '69
See also
Compost
Food, Organic
Mulching
Vegetable gardening, Home

Competitions
See Gardening—Competitions

ORGANIC harvest awards contest. See Gardening—Competitions

ORGANIZATION for economic cooperation and development
Italy: OECD report finally emerges. D. S. Greenberg. Science 166:587 O 31 '69
OECD ministerial council meets at Paris; statements, February 13 and 14, 1969; with text of communique. E. L. Richardson. Dept State Bul 60:192-6 Mr 10 '69
U. S. delegation named to OECD ministerial meeting. Dept State Bul 60:171 F 24 '69
World forecast: partly cloudy. il Bsns W p54 D 27 '69

ORGANIZATION for European nuclear research. See European organization for nuclear research

ORGANIZATION of African unity
President Nixon extends greetings to Organization of African unity; text of message, September 6, 1969. R. M. Nixon. Dept State Bul 61:280 S 29 '69
President Nixon hails sixth anniversary of Organization of African unity; exchange of remarks, May 25, 1969. S. E. Peal; R. M. Nixon. Dept State Bul 60:537-40 Je 23 '69

ORGANIZATION of American states
Alliance for progress and the O.A.S. H. J. Sievers. America 120:723 Je 28 '69
Hemisphere; comp. by G. Meek. See issues of Américas
Honduran-Salvadoran conflict resolved by OAS; Department statement with resolutions and declaration. Dept State Bul 61:132-4 Ag 18 '69
Jamaica becomes twenty-fourth member state. il Américas 21:41 Ag '69
Low profile in Latin America. il Time 94:36+ N 7 '69
New OAS council officers. il Américas 21:43 Ja '69
OAS halts war between El Salvador and Honduras. G. Meek. il Américas 21:42-5 S '69
See also
Inter-American children's institute
Inter-American cultural council
Inter-American economic and social council

ORGANIZED crime. See Crime and criminals—United States; Mafia; Racketeering

ORGANIZERS, Labor. See Trade unions—Officials

ORGANOMETALLIC compounds
Organotins as preservatives. il Chem 42:21 D '69

ORGANOTIN compounds. See Organometallic compounds

ORGANS, Artificial. See Prosthesis

ORGEL, Shelley
Iago. bibliog Am Imago 25:258-73 Fall '68

ORIENT. See Asia; Far East

ORIENT and occident. See East and West

ORIENTAL art. See Art, Oriental

ORIENTAL cookery. See Cookery, Oriental

ORIENTAL music. Music, Oriental

ORIENTAL poetry
Far Eastern chronicle. R. E. Teele. Poetry 114:196-201 Je '69

ORIENTAL poppies. See Poppies

ORIENTAL pottery. See Pottery, Oriental

ORIENTAL rugs. See Rugs and carpets, Oriental

ORIENTAL studies
Asian studies project in California. Sch &
 Soc 97:210-11 Ap '69
Parsippany dips a *maobi* in Asian studies.
 F. Sabin. il Am Ed 5:11-13 My '69

ORIENTAL zodiac. See Zodiac

ORIENTALS
See also
Asians

ORIENTATION
Bird migration: influence of physiological
 state upon celestial orientation. S. T.
 Emlen. bibliog il Science 165:716-18 Ag 15
 '69
Celestial guidance system of a migrating
 bird. S. T. Emlen. il Sky & Tel 38:4-6 Jl '69
Homing in the ant cataglyphis bicolor. R.
 Wehner and R. Menzel. bibliog il Science
 164:192-4 Ap 11 '69
Interocular transfer of orientational effects.
 A. S. Gilinsky and R. S. Doherty. bibliog
 il Science 164:454-5 Ap 25 '69
Orientation by pigeons: is the sun neces-
 sary? W. T. Keeton. bibliog il Science 165:
 922-8 Ag 29 '69
 See also
Echolocation (physiology)

ORIENTATION of teachers. See Teachers—
Adjustment

ORIENTATION programs for foreign students.
See Foreign students in the United States
 —Orientation

ORIGIN of man. See Man—Origin and antiquity

ORIGIN of species. See Evolution; Species

ORIGINAL sin. See Sin

ORIGO, Iris
Pursuit of happiness in a villa. Horizon 11:
 14-17 Spr '69

ORIOLES (baseball) See Baseball clubs

ORION (constellation) See Constellations

ORLAND PARK, Ill.

Hotels restaurants, etc.
Farmer's daughter, Orland Park. Illinois. Esquire 72:82 O '69

ORLANDO, Fla., public library
Composition in concrete. C. E. Wendell. il
 Am City 84:101+ Ap '69

ORLANS, F. Barbara
Animal experimentation by high school students; letter. Science 163:128-9 Ja 10 '69

ORLEN, Steven
New world, requesting nothing but peace;
 poem. Poetry 114:373 S '69
Over Newark; poem. Nation 208:610 My 12 '69
Policeman and the drunk; poem. Nation 208:
 512 Ap 21 '69

ORLOB, Gert B. See Lojek, J. S. jt. auth.

ORLOWSKI, Thomas O.
Stoned in the cradle of the deep. Esquire
 72:248-9+ D '69

ORLY airport. See Paris—Airports

ORMAI, S. and Clercq, E. de
Polymethacrylic acid: effects on lymphocyte
 output of the thoracic duct in rats. bibliog
 Science 163:471-2 Ja 31 '69

ORMANDY, Eugene
Musician of the month. S. Fleming. por(pMA1)
 Hi Fi 19:MA7 N '69
O plus O equals Ormandy and Ozawa. I.
 Kolodin. Sat R 52:66 O 18 '69
Philadelphia orchestra; RCA recordings. M.
 Kanny. il Am Rec G 35:44-7 F '69
Recordings. M. Mayer. Esquire 71:88+ Ap '69

ORME, Frank
TV world of violence. Parents Mag 44:52-
 3+ Ja '69

ORMOND, Clyde
Fat cat. por Outdoor Life 143:62-3+ F '69
One for the governor. Outdoor Life 143:70-
 1+ Mr '69

ORMOND BEACH. Fla.
Picture perfect. il Am City 84:140+ Mr '69

ORMSBY, Virginia H.
Moon's place in the classroom. Todays Ed 58:
 42-3 D '69

ORNAMENTAL cookery. See Cookery, Ornamental

ORNAMENTAL plants. See Plants, Ornamental

ORNAMENTS, Christmas tree. See Christmas
decorations

ORNATI, Oscar A.
Is cooperative self-help enough? Cur 107:
 31-3 My '69

ORNE, Jerrold
Academic library building in 1969. por Library
 J 94:4364-8 D 1 '69

ORNITHORHYNCHUS anatinus. See Platypuses

ORNSTEIN, Jacob
Programed instruction in the language field.
 Ed Digest 34:9-12 F '69

OROGENY. See Mountains

O'ROURKE, John
Hip to health foods. Org Gard & Farm 16:
 60-2 O '69

O'ROURKE, William J.
Church of England votes. America 121:64-6
 Ag 2 '69

OROWAN, Egon
Origin of the oceanic ridges; with biographical sketch. Sci Am 221:18, 102-8+ bib-
 liog(p 166) N '69

OROZCO, Reyes Arias
Amplification of Miranda. Time 93:55 Ap 4 '69

ORPHANS and orphan asylums
See also
Homes, Institutional

ORR, Bobby
Blood and ice. B. Surface. il por N Y Times
 Mag p26-26A+ F 2 '69
Bobby mines the mother lode. M. Mulvoy. il
 pors Sports Illus 32:20-1 Ja 12 '70
Boston's Orr: fire on ice. il pors Newsweek
 73:64-7 Mr 24 '69
It's Bobby Orr & the animals. M. Mulvoy.
 il por Sports Illus 30:18-23 F 3 '69

ORSINI, Armando
Snow-mass, best European skiing in America. Holiday 45:64-7 F '69

ORSY, Ladislas M.
Catholic presence. America 120:396-7 Ap 5 '69
Questions about a questionnaire. America 120:
 185-7 F 15 '69

ORTEGO, Philip Darraugh
Mexican-American literature. Nation 209:
 258-9 S 15 '69

ORTHODONTICS
New faces for old. il Newsweek 73:94 Mr 10
 '69

ORTHODOX Eastern church, Russian
Orthodox priest and a Soviet writer. M. Bourdeaux. Chr Cent 86:266-8 F 19 '69

ORTHODOX Eastern church, Russian, in the
United States
Mother Russia in New York state; Holy Tri-
 nity Russian Orthodox monastery, Jordan-
 ville, N.Y. N. S. Hazelton. Nat R 21:1015
 O 7 '69

ORTHOPEDIA
See also
American academy of orthopedic surgeons

ORTHOPYROXENES. See Pyroxenes

ORTHWINE, Rudolf
New year's message from the publisher. por
 Dance Mag 43:21 Ja '69

ORTIZ, Elisabeth Lambert de. See Lambert de
Ortiz, E.

ORTMAN, George
(ed) Artists' games. Art in Am 57:69-77 N
 '69
Backgammon game. il Art in Am 57:70-1 N
 '69

ORTON, Joe
Crimes of passion. Criticism
 Nation 209:546-7 N 17 '69
 New Yorker 45:156 N 8 '69

ORTUÑO, René Barrientos. See Barrientos Ortuño, R.

ORWELL, George, pseud.
Books. G. Steiner. New Yorker 45:139-40+
 Mr 29 '69
Books. M. Muggeridge. Esquire 71:51-2+ Mr
 '69
Djilas revisits Orwell; there'll be many dif-
 ferent communisms in 1984. M. Djilas. il
 N Y Times Mag p28-9+ Mr 23 '69
George Orwell. P. Gardner. Cath World 209:
 90-1 My '69
In his own image. P. Clecak. Nation 208:
 150-3 F 3 '69

ORYXES. See Antelopes

OSAKA, Japan

Worlds fair, 1970
Countdown for Expo '70. il Life 67:60D-60F
 N 28 '69
Design for Osaka: U.S. pavilion. il Time 94:
 68 N 28 '69
Expo '70: giving Osaka a chance at a come-
 back. il Bsns W p 138-9+ O 4 '69
Expo '70-Osaka. M. Connelly. il Holiday 45:
 52-3+ Mr '69
Expo 70, the first Asian world's fair. Sun-
 set 143:72 O '69
Going to Expo 70? See Japan's gardens while
 you're there! P. S. Parr. il Home Gard
 56:28-30 O '69

OSAKA, Japan—Worlds fair, 1970—*Continued*
Japan's Expo 70. il Newsweek 74:114+ S 29
'69
Kenzo Tange: interview, ed by C. Jones. K.
Tange. il Travel & Camera 32:52-5 O '69
Let's travel: Expo in Japan. il Mlle 70:80-1 D
'69
Meet me at the fair. D. Butwin. il Sat R 52:
44-5+ S 13 '69
Osaka & Expo '70. H. Ehrlich. il Look 33:
61-6 O 21 '69
Travel notes. R. Joseph. Esquire 72:75-6+
D '69

Architecture
Biggest big top. il Arch Forum 131:68-9 D '69

Religious exhibits
Holy emptiness at Expo '70. Chr Today 14:
51 O 10 '69
Time capsule
See Civilization—Preservation of records
OSBORN, David
Two California poster designers; interview,
ed. by G. Loney. il por Am Artist 33:48-
53+ My '69
OSBORN, Fairfield
Fairfield Osborn; Audubon medalist, 1968. por
Audubon 71:57 Ja '68
Obituary
Nat Parks 43:25 N '69
OSBORN, Robert
(ed) See Calder, A. Calder's international
monuments
OSBORNE, Conrad L.
Affiliate artists, a success story. Hi Fi 19:
MA18-19 D '69
Case for the other La Bohème. Hi Fi 19:78-9
My '69
First-rate performance of a second-rate
opera. Hi Fi 19:77 Je '69
From a rich heritage; the art of baritone
Mattia Battistini. Hi Fi 19:63-4 Ap '69
Opera reviewer strikes again. Hi Fi 19:20+
Ap '69
Perhaps not fabulous, but some excellent
singing anyway. Hi Fi 19:104 Je '69
OSBORNE, Daphne J. See Hallaway, M. jt.
auth.
OSBORNE, John, 1907-
Back from Midway. New Repub 160:13-15
Je 21 '69
Discipline and order but an open image. New
Repub 160:11-13 F 22 '69
How's he doing in the White House? New
Repub 160:14-16 F 8 '69
Making the case for Haynsworth. New Repub
161:12-13 N 1 '69
Managed propaganda, condoned disorder?
New Repub 160:10-11 My 10 '69
Moynihan at work in the White House. New
Repub 160:11-13 Mr 22 '69
Nixon and the liberal Republicans. New
Repub 161:13-15 Jl 26 '69
Nixon bounces back. New Repub 161:10-11
Jl 5 '69
Nixon meets students. New Repub 161:9-10
O 4 '69
Nixon watch: thought for food. New Re-
pub 161:7-9 D 6 '69
Nixon's command staff. New Repub 160:13-
15 F 15 '69
Nixon's Europe in the new era. New Repub
160:17-19 Mr 15 '69
Pass for Mitchell. New Repub 160:13 Ja 25
'69
President and the poor. New Repub 160:16-18
My 24 '69
Putting the heat on Mr Nixon. New Repub
160:11-12 Ap 19 '69
Reading the mind of the 91st Congress. New
Repub 160:11-13 Mr 29 '69
Rise of Harry Dent. New Repub 160:13-16 Je
14 '69
Senate: the balancing act. New Repub 160:
19-21 F 1 '69
Spiro Agnew's mission. il New Repub 161:17-
20 N 15 '69
Spiro the veep. New Repub 160:10-12 Mr 1 '69
Vietnam: the President's fading hope. New
Repub 161:17-19 S 27 '69
Welfare story, plot and subplot. New Repub
161:15-17 N 8 '69
White House who's who. New Repub 161:
13-15 O 18 '69
With Nixon on the grand tour; report. New
Repub 160:9-10 Mr 8 '69

OSBORNE, John, 1929-
John Osborne's generation gap. C. Hughes.
America 121:295-7 O 11 '69
Patriot for me. Criticism
Commonweal 91:185-6 N 7 '69
Nat R 21:1334-5 D 30 '69
Nation 209:451-2 O 27 '69
New Repub 161:22 N 1 '69
New Yorker 45:85 O 11 '69
Newsweek il 74:129 O 20 '69
Sat R 52:20 O 18 '69
Time il 94:71 O 17 '69
Vogue 154:58 N 15 '69
OSCARS (prizes) See Academy awards (moving
pictures)
OSCEOLA (Seminole chief)
Osceola: he wouldn't go. il por Sr Schol 94:
16 Mr 7 '69
OSCILLATIONS
Apollo mini-pogo remedy set; recommenda-
tion for early shutdown of center engine.
Aviation W 90:19 Ap 28 '69
Standing waves on the moon. Sky & Tel
38:166 S '69
See also
Damping (mechanics)
OSCILLATORS
JFETS. R. Clifton. il Radio-Electr 40:55-7
Je '69
Quick test horizontal oscillators. J. Darr.
il Radio-Electr 40:69 O '69
SCS crystal-controlled oscillator. F. H.
Tooker. Electr World 82:74 O '69
See also
Multivibrators
Pulse generators
OSCILLATORS, Crystal
FET sine-wave crystal oscillators. F. H.
Tooker. il Electr World 81:33+ Je '69
Solid-state LSA microwave diodes. D. L.
Heiserman. il Electr World 81:40+ F '69
OSCILLOGRAPHS
B&K 1450 diagnostic oscilloscope. J. Darr. il
Radio-Eelctr 40:93 Jl '69
Data instruments model 555 oscilloscope. il
Electr World 81:76-7 Ap '69
Hickok model CRO-5000 oscilloscope. il Electr
World 81:67 My '69
How to use triggered scopes. L. Allen. il
Radio-Electr 40:33-7 Ag '69
Jackson model CRO-4 oscilloscope. il Electr
World 81:69 Mr '69
Oscilloscope evolution. J. W. Griffin. il Electr
World 82:25-7+ N '69
Triggered sweep for any scope. I. Gorgenyi.
il Electr World 82:76-8 N '69
See also
Tektronix, incorporated
OSCILLOSCOPE calibrators. See Calibrators
OSCILLOSCOPE cameras. See Cameras
OSCILLOSCOPES. See Oscillographs
OSER, Janice Auritt
Running the country; drama. Plays 29:85-8
N '69
OSGOOD, William E.
Mulching with newspapers. Org Gard & Farm
16:106-7 Ja '69
O'SHEA, J. P. See Johnson, L. C. jt. auth.
O'SHEA, Kevin
Is resurrection theology outdated? Cath World
209:7-11 Ap '69
OSHIMA, Kiyoshi, and Gorbman, Aubrey
Pars intermedia: unitary electrical activity
regulated by light. bibliog Science 163:195-7
Ja 10 '69
—and others
Memory-blocking agents: effects on olfactory
discrimination in homing salmon. bibliog
Science 165:86-8 Jl 4 '69
OSHIN, Edith Sonn
How to judge the house you want to buy.
House & Gard 135:70+ Mr '69
OSLO
Description
Fishless days in fjordland. D. Butwin. il
Sat R 52:37-8 Ag 9 '69
Music
Report: Oslo; Norwegian opera's new version
of Tchaikovsky's Pique dame. W. Shank.
Opera N 33:28 My 17 '69
Report: Oslo; production of Falstaff. W.
Shank. Opera N 34:28 N 1 '69
Report: Oslo; production of Gluck's Iphigénie
en Tauride. W. Shank. Opera N 33:32 Mr
15 '69
OSMOSIS
Afferent discharges from osmoreceptors in the
liver of the guinea pig. A. Niijima. il Sci-
ence 166:1519-20 D 19 '69
Teleostean urophysis: stimulation of water
movement across the bladder of the toad
bufo marinus. F. Lacanilao. bibliog il Science 163:1326-7 Mr 21 '69

OSMUN, William G.
Airline warm fog dispersal program. Weatherwise 22:48-53+ Ap '69

OSPREYS
Osprey; endangered world citizen. R. T. Peterson. il Nat Geog 136:52-67 Jl '69; Same abr. with title Mystery of the vanishing osprey. Read Digest 95:86-9 N '69
Osprey refuge planned. il Nat Parks 43:23 S '69

L'OSSERVATORE romano. See Catholic press

OSSOLI, Sarah Margaret (Fuller) marchesa d'
Roman years of Margaret Fuller, by J. J. Deiss. Review
Sat R 52:27+ D 20 '69. G. Culligan

OSSORIO, Alfonso
Old hat no more. il por Time 94:47-8 D 19 '69
Plastic resurrection. B. H. Friedman. il por Art N 68:59-61+ N '69

OSTBY, Frederick P. and others
Small-scale precipitation network over central Connecticut. pors Weatherwise 22:60-3+ bibliog(p87) Ap '69

OSTER, Gerald
Amateur scientist. Sci Am 221:128-32 D '69

OSTERMAN, Paul
In high schools too. New Repub 160:13-14 Ap 5 '69

OSTLERE, Hilary
Plane and the single girl. Flying 84:74-5 F '69

OSTRACODS
Cypridina bioluminescence: light-emitting oxyluciferin-luciferase complex. O. Shimomura and others. bibliog il Science 164:1299-300 Je 13 '69

OSTRANDER, Kenneth H.
Divisive tendencies within NEA affiliates. bibliog f Sch & Soc 97:116-18 F '69

O'SULLIVAN, T. J.
Going. Travel & Camera 32:28 F; 26 Mr '69

O'SULLIVAN, Timothy T.
Frontier photographers. D. Vestal. il Travel & Camera 32:48-52+ Je '69

OSUNA, Rafael
Obituary
Sports Illus 30:10+ Je 16 '69

OSWALD, Charles
Big wheel on campus. R. Levy. il Duns R 92:59-60 D '68

OSWALD, Genevieve
Anniversary. W. Terry. Sat R 52:64-5+ N 22 '69

OSWALD, James R.
Make your own movie montages. Travel & Camera 32:108-9+ F '69

OTEPKA, Otto F.
Otepka and no-nonsense security. H. J. Sievers. America 120:681 Je 14 '69
Otto rides again. por Newsweek 73:27 Mr 31 '69
Search-and-destroy. R. Dudman. New Repub 161:12 Jl 19 '69
Solution to Otepka case? por U S News 66: 16 Mr 31 '69

OTERO, Alejandro
One man's vision, many men's skills. il por Fortune 80:102-5 O '69

OTHELLO; drama. See Shakespeare, W.—Plays

OTHELLO (literary character) See Shakespeare, W.—Characters

OTHMER, Ekkehard, and others
Encephalic cycles during sleep and wakefulness in humans: a 24-hour pattern. bibliog Science 164:447-9 Ap 25 '69

OTIS, Denise
Going places, finding things: Portugal's pousadas. House & Gard 135:34+ Je '69

OTIS, Harrison Gray
Harrison Gray Otis, by S. E. Morison. Review
America 120:424-5 Ap 5 '69. M. Cuddihy

OTIS art institute of Los Angeles County
Otis art institute at fifty. il Harp Baz 102: 103, 129 Ap '69

OTIS elevator company
Problem area; profit problems. il Forbes 104: 38 D 15 '69

O'TOOLE, Peter
Don't let anyone else play Henry; interview, ed. by M. Ronan. por Sr Schol 94:30 F 28 '69

OTT, Aadu
Isotope separation by thermal diffusion in liquid metal. bibliog Science 164:297 Ap 18 '69

OTT, George
Emperor of the floes. Nat Wildlife 7:42-7 F '69

OTTAWA
Canadian center for the performing arts
See Ottawa—National arts center

National arts center
Cultural center Canadian style. J. M. Dixon. il Arch Forum 131:46-53 O '69

OTTAWA national forest. See National forests

OTTAWAY, Lois M.
Read, baby, read: a first step to action. Chr Today 14:6-8 D 19 '69

OTTERS
Playful otters. T. Browne. il Nat Parks 43: 22-3 N '69
See also
Sea otters

OTTINGER, Richard Lawrence
Bounty on water polluters. A. R. Roalman. Motor B 123:78-81 My '69

OTTMAR, Jerome
Roy Little's latest Textron? por Forbes 103: 33-4 My 1 '69

OTTO, Christine
Western Samoa. Travel 132:34-6+ Jl '69

OTTO, Dave
Quiet boom. Outdoor Life 144:77-80+ N '69

OTTO, Harry W. and Daines, R. H.
Plant injury by air pollutants: influence of humidity on stomatal apertures and plant response to ozone. bibliog Science 163:1209-10 Mr 14 '69

OTTO, Herbert A.
New light on the human potential. Sat R 52:14-17 D 20 '69

OTTOMAN empire. See Turkey

OUABAIN
Cardiac sympathetic nerve activity: changes induced by ouabain and propranolol. R. A. Gillis. bibliog il Science 166:508-10 O 24 '69

OUELLETTE, C. A. See Strout, R. G. jt. auth.

OUR friend Pasquale; story. See Cornelisen, A.

OUR town; drama. See Wilder, T. N.

OURISSON, G. See Albrecht, P. jt. auth.

OURO PRETO, Brazil
Ouro Preto, gold, art and revolution in Brazil. D. Vestal. il Travel & Camera 32: 72-9 Ag '69

OUTBOARD electric engines. See Electric engines, Outboard

OUTBOARD motor boat racing. See Motor boat racing

OUTBOARD motor boats. See Motor boats, Outboard

OUTBOARD motors. See Gas and oil engines, Outboard

OUTDOOR carpets. See Rugs and carpets, Outdoor

OUTDOOR Christmas decorations. See Christmas decorations, Outdoor

OUTDOOR circle (organization)
Must we put up with billboards? D. P. Watson. il Horticulture 47:16-17+ N '69

OUTDOOR cookery. See Cookery, Outdoor

OUTDOOR education
Outdoor teaching; Frederick County, Md. G. Leyh. Todays Ed 58:27 My '69
See also
Camping—Educational aspects
Outward bound schools

OUTDOOR fireplaces. See Fireplaces, Outdoor

OUTDOOR furniture. See Furniture, Outdoor

OUTDOOR kitchens. See Kitchens, Outdoor

OUTDOOR life
Outdoors with Wynn Davis. W. Davis. See issues of Mechanix illustrated
Planning a backwoods experience; a wilderness trip. R. Walker. il Field & S 73:64-5+ Ap '69
Song of the North; excerpt from Open horizons. S. F. Olson. il Audubon 71:6-12 Ja '69
Survival expert, Paul Petzoldt: founder of National outdoor leadership school. J. Howard. il Life 67:48-50+ D 19 '69
See also
Camping
Country life
Fishing—United States
Houseboats
Hunting
Mountaineering
Nature
Outdoor meals
Picnics
Vacations
Walking
Wilderness survival

Bibliography
Books & flicks. Field & S 74:26 O; 10+ N; 20 D '69

OUTDOOR lighting. See Lighting, Outdoor

OUTDOOR meals
Movable feast. E. Alston. il Look 33:82-4 S 23 '69
See also
Barbecue cookery
Cookery, Outdoor
Picnics
OUTDOOR recreation. See Recreation

OUTDOOR rooms
Balcony into outdoor dining room. il House & Gard 135:124-5 My '69
Deck on the sunny side screens out heat, glare. il Sunset 143:95 S '69
Delights of summer at home; living room moves outdoors. il House & Gard 135:54-61 Je '69
Extending your living space. il Home Gard 56:52-3 S '69
Family landscape of many rooms. il House & Gard 136:196-7 D '69
Four great-looking patios. il Bet Hom & Gard 47:44-5 Jl '69
Glass doors make this new deck a wind shelter. il Sunset 142:145 Ap '69
Great American summer. il McCalls 96:73-5 Jl '69
Great outdoor living area from a do-nothing backyard. il Bet Hom & Gard 47:60-1 My '69
Indoor-outdoor fieldstone in the Pennsylvania farmlands. il Life 66:86-8+ Ap 11 '69
Lookout, a bridge, a grand deck. il Sunset 142:125 Ap '69
Nine suntraps on one beach house; Fire Island Pines, Long Island, N.Y. il House & Gard 135:68-71 Je '69
Outdoor living in Salt Lake City. it's done with a pair of patios. il Sunset 143:82-3 S '69
Outdoor living with all kinds of screening. il Bet Hom & Gard 47:42-3 Jl '69
Patio, Italian style. il Mech Illus 65:80-2+ My '69
Pointers for designing and specifying perlite roof decks. F. Coda. il Arch Rec 145:175-6 F '69
Rooftop patio. A. I. Sukor. il Pop Mech 131:166 Je '69
Rooms can be indoors or out. il Home Gard 56:56-8 Mr '69
Simple deck. M. Spires. il Am Home 72:22 Je '69
Six ways to expand living outdoors. House & Gard 135:44+ Je '69
Small wonders, the patio. il Redbook 133:96-9+ Je '69
Their new glass wall frames a canyon view, stops a canyon wind. il Sunset 142:98 F '69
They let the stair landing grow. il Sunset 143:66 Ag '69
To build a patio. il Am Home 72:55 My '69
Two stories of outdoor living. il Bet Hom & Gard 47:56 Ap '69
Want a patio? cast the tiles indoors. R. Day. il Pop Sci 194:172-6+ Ja '69
See also
Landscape gardening
Screens (sun)
OUTDOOR rugs. See Rugs and carpets, Outdoor
OUTDOOR speaking. See Street speaking
OUTDOOR stairways. See Stairways
OUTDOOR survival. See Wilderness survivial
OUTER space. See Space, Outer
OUTING clubs. See Clubs
OUTLAWRY of war. See War, Outlawry of

OUTLAWS
Last of the great outlaws: Butch Cassidy and the Sundance Kid. il Life 66:69-71 My 16 '69

OUTLER, Albert C.
[Book reviews] Commonweal 90:124-5 Ap 11 '69
OUTLETS, Electric. See Electric wire and wiring
OUTPUT (production) See Production
OUTPUT of workers. See Labor productivity

OUTWARD bound schools
Blind students conquer Mt Kilimanjaro; East Africans. il Ebony 24:44-6+ Je '69
East of Schoodic; deep water expedition. P. Gates. il Yachting 125:76-7+ Mr '69
Nature as teacher. A. L. Maynard. il Sat R 52:76-7 My 17 '69
This year, a different summer for the kids. il Changing T 23:31-3 Mr '69
To meet a challenge; Hurricane Island. P. O. Willauer. il Yachting 125:74-5+ Mr '69
You'll never be afraid to try; Hurricane Island. J. G. Hubbell. il Read Digest 94: 173-5+ Mr '69

OVANDO CANDIA, Alfredo
Exporting Perunismo. il por Time 94:38 O 3 '69

OVARIES
Luteinizing hormone: action on the Graafian follicle in vitro. P. L. Keyes. bibliog il Science 164:846-7 My 16 '69
Thymus and reproduction: sex-linked dysgenesis of the gonad after neonatal thymectomy in mice. Y. Nishizuka and T. Sakakura. bibliog il Science 166:753-5 N 7

OVE, Peter, and Laszlo, John
Mammalian DNA polymerase: separation of binding from incorporation of deoxyribonucleoside triphosphates. bibliog Science 165: 903-4 Ag 29 '69

OVENDEN, Keith
Labor's chance: some unlikely Tories. Commonweal 91:348-9 D 19 '69

OVENS
See also
Electronic ovens
Smoke ovens
OVER-the-counter market. See Stocks—Marketing

OVERBY, H. D.
Tell it like it is. Todays Ed 58:55-6 N '69
OVERDRIVE transmission. See Automobiles—Transmission
OVERDUE books. See Libraries—Fines
OVEREATING. See Hyperphagia
OVERHEAD irrigation. See Irrigation, Overhead
OVERHEAD projectors. See Projectors

OVERLAND journeys to the Pacific
Jornada del muerto; adaptation from The el dorado trail. F. Egan. bibliog il Am West 6:12-19+ Jl '69
OVERMEDICATION. See Drugs—Dosage
OVERPOPULATION. See Population—Overpopulation
OVERSEAS employees. See Americans in foreign countries—Employment
OVERSEAS forces. See United States—Armed forces—Forces in foreign countries

OVERSEAS national airways
Airline ordering ship for air-sea cruises. J. W. Carter. Aviation W 90:29 Ap 7 '69
Rockets bolster DC-9 payload capability. il Aviation W 90:70-2+ My 19 '69
OVERSEAS spending. See Investments, Foreign

OVERSETH, Oliver E.
Experiments in time reversal; with biographical sketch. Sci Am 221:14, 88-94+ bibliog (p 148) O '69

OVERSTREET, Bonaro W.
Building of an outlook. PTA Mag 63:20-1 Je '69
Known for years! excerpts from Brave enough for life. PTA Mag 63:22-4 F '69
People who know how; excerpts from Brave enough for life. PTA Mag 63:24-5 Mr '69
Personal friends. PTA Mag 63:14-15 Ap '69
Touch and go. PTA Mag 63:17-18 My '69
You can meet them anywhere. PTA Mag 63: 22-4 Ja '69

OVERTIME
Patterns in overtime hours and premium pay. J. Fenlon. il Mo Labor R 92:42-6 O '69

OVERTURES
See also
Phonograph records—Overtures
OVERWEIGHT. See Corpulence

OVID
Metamorphoses; dramatization. See Sills, P.

OVIPOSITION
Sex control by bees: a voluntary act of egg fertilization during oviposition. H. S. Gerber and E. C. Klostermeyer. bibliog il Science 167:82-4 Ja 2 '70

OVSHINSKY, Stanford R.
All about ovonics. F Shunaman il Radio-Electr 40:41-3 My '69
Effect of Stanford R. Ovshinsky. il pors Life 67:81-2+ O 17 '69
Glassy semiconductors show switching and memory effects. G. B. Lubkin. bibliog il Phys Today 22:63 Ja '69
Ovonics. J. P. Robinson, jr. il por Pop Electr 30:55-8 Mr '69
Ovshinsky: promoter or persecuted genius? P. M. Boffey. il por Science 165:673-7 Ag 15 '69

OWATONNA, Minn.
Best for the spring clean-up. M. R. Lueth. il Am City 84:32 Je '69

OWEN, Tobias, and Mason, H. P.
Mars: water vapor in its atmosphere. bibliog Science 165:893-5 Ag 29 '69

OWENS, Adam J.
Bulls & bears in Boston. Sr Schol 94:Schol Teach 14 Ap 18 '69

OWENS, Lowell D.
Toxins in plant disease: structure and mode of action. bibliog Science 165:18-25 Jl 4 '69

OWENS, Patrick
Bullmoose in the souvenir shop. Commonweal
91:349 D 19 '69
Jury of his club mates. Nation 209:462-4 N 3
'69
OWENS, Rhodell E.
Culture thrives in Peoria. Parks & Rec 3:38-
40 N '68
OWENS, Rochelle
Comment. B. Berkson. Poetry 114:256-7 Jl
'69
OWENS, Steve
Booming sooner. il por Time 94:79 D 5 '69
OWENS-Corning fiberglas corporation
General and the genius. il Forbes 104:48+
O 15 '69
OWL and the pussycat bookshop. See Book-
sellers and bookselling—Childrens litera-
ture
OWLS
Coffee-can owl; excerpt from Owl. W. Serv-
ice. il Read Digest 95:127-31 O '69
Nest of barn owls. J. Steeley, jr. il Cons
23:20 Je '69
Owl. W. Service. il Sports Illus 30:52-6+ Je
30 '69
OXALIS. See Wood sorrell
OXBURGH, E. Ronald. See Turcotte, D. L. jt.
auth.
OXFORD, Miss.
Requiem for Faulkner's home town. L. L.
King. il Holiday 45:60-1+ Mr '69
OXFORD movement
Oxford conspirators, by M. R. O'Connell. Re-
view
Commonweal 91:22-4 O 3 '69. K. Rexroth
OXFORD, University
Amateur who beats the pros; Nuffield col-
lege at Oxford university. il Forbes 103:
233-5 My 15 '69
On proceeding M.A. T. S. Matthews. Vogue
153:256 My '69
Revolting students. J. Sparrow. il Nat R
21:175-7+ F 25 '69
Bodleian library
Bodleian show: first extraterritorial show, at
the Grolier club. New Yorker 45:20-2 Ja 3
'70
OXIDASES
Genetic polymorphism of tetrazolium oxidase
in dogs. E. W. Baur and R. T. Schorr. bib-
liog il Science 166:1524-5 D 19 '69
L-Tyrosine-3,5-^{3}H assay for tyrosinase development in skin of newborn hamsters.
S. H. Pomerantz. bibliog il Science 164:838-
9 My 16 '69
OXIDATION
Peroxidation of subcellular organelles: forma-
tion of lipofuscinlike fluorescent pigments.
K. S. Chio and others. bibliog il Science 166:
1535-6 D 19 '69
Photooxidation of DDT and DDE. J. R.
Plimmer and others. bibliog il Science 167:
67-9 Ja 2 '70
OXIDATION, Physiological
Alcohol metabolism: role of microsomal oxi-
dation in vivo. T. R. Tephly and others.
bibliog il Science 166:627-8 O 31 '69
Dye-sensitized photooxidation of the esche-
richia coli ribosome. R. T. Garvin and
others. bibliog il Science 164:583-4 My 2 '69
New light-sensitive cofactor required for oxi-
dation of succinate by mycobacterium phlei.
C. R. Krishna Murti and A. F. Brodie. bib-
liog il Science 164:302-4 Ap 18 '69
See also
Cytochromes
OXIDATIVE phosphorylation. See Phosphory-
lation
OXIDES
See also
Nitrogen oxides
Silver oxide
OXLEY, Charles E.
Sports clinics at Michigan U. Parks & Rec
4:35-6 Mr '69
OXNARD, Calif.
We spray our odors away. S. G. Pateman. il
Am City 84:70 F '69
OXYGEN
Another pollution culprit; singlet oxygen. E.
Gross. il Sci N 96:538-40 D 6 '69
Structure of an oxygen-carrying cobalt com-
plex; Bis(3-fluorosalicylaldehyde) ethylene-
diimine cobalt(II) B. C. Wang and W. P.
Schaefer. bibliog il Science 166:1404-6 D 12
'69
See also
Hyperbaric oxygenation
OXYGEN deficiency. See Anoxemia
OXYGEN in the body
See also
Anoxemia
Asphyxia

OXYGEN in water. See Water—Analysis
OXYGEN therapy
See also
Hyperbaric oxygenation
OXYGENASES
Hypobaric hypoxia: effects on early develop-
ment of tryptophan oxygenase in neonatal
rats. R. P. Francesconi and M. Mager. bib-
liog il Science 166:1412-13 D 12 '69
Nature and mechanisms of oxygenases. O.
Hayaishi and M. Nozaki. bibliog il Science
164:389-96 Ap 25 '69
OXYGENATION, Hyperbaric. See Hyperbaric
oxygenation
OXYTETRACYCLINE. See Tetracyclines
OXYTOCIN
Oxytocin: crystal data of a seleno analog.
C. C. Chiu and others. bibliog il Science
163:925-6 F 28 '69
Oxytocin: effects of degradation on radio-
immunologic and biologic activity. P. Ku-
maresan and others. bibliog il Science 166:
1160-1 N 28 '69
Plasma saluretic activity: its nature and re-
lation to oxytocin analogs. E. Sedláková
and others. bibliog il Science 164:580-2 My
2 '69
OYSTER BAY, N.Y.
Gardens
Gardener's self-portrait; photographs by
Horst of his own garden. House & Gard
136:90-5 D '69
OYSTER boats. See Fishing boats
OYSTER CREEK nuclear power plant. See
Atomic power plants
OYSTER dredges. See Fishing boats
OYSTERS
Oyster ciliary inhibition by cystic fibrosis
factor. B. Bowman and others. bibliog il
Science 164:325-6 Ap 18 '69
See also
Pearls
OZARK air lines
Regional makes it to the big town; direct
service between Midwest and Washington
and New York. il Bsns W p 102+ Ap 26 '69
OZARK NATIONAL SCENIC RIVERWAYS
Our first national river. L. Hall. il Audubon
71:48-51 Mr '69
OZARKS, LAKE OF THE. See Lake of the
Ozarks
OZAWA, Seiji
Musical events; Orff's Carmina Burana per-
formed by New York philharmonic. W.
Sargeant. New Yorker 45:117 O 11 '69
O plus O equals Ormandy and Ozawa. I.
Kolodin. Sat R 52:66 O 18 '69
Ozawa in transit. R. C. Marsh. il por Sat R
52:45-6+ S 27 '69
Ozawa on Berlioz. I. Kolodin. Sat R 52:41-2
Mr 1 '69
OZICK, Cynthia
Envy; or, Yiddish in America; story. Com-
mentary 48:33-53 N '69
OZONE
See also
Plants. Effect of ozone on

P

PABA (para-aminobenzoic acid) See Aminobenzoic acid
PAC. See Pacific airmotive corporation
PACCS-ADA (post attack command control
system-airborne data automation) See Com-
puters—Military applications
PADRES (Padres asociados para derechos re-
ligiosos eclesiásticos) See Priests—Asso-
ciations, institutions, etc.
PAR (precision approach radar) See Radar in
aviation
PATCO. See Professional air traffic controllers
organization
PATROLS (patrol's automatic telecommunica-
tions rapid on-line system) See Police com-
munication systems
PBC (Public broadcasting corporation) See
Corporation for public broadcasting
PBL. See Public broadcast laboratory
PEBCO. See American library association—
Program evaluation and budget committee
PEN club
P.E.N. congress: letters and leisure on the
Riviera. D. Dempsey. Sat R 52:42-4 O 18
'69

PACKING of luggage
Art of painless deplaning. L. Barry. il Pop
Phot 65:66+ Jl '69
If carrying cameras is your bag. . . R. Arnold.
il Travel & Camera 32:16+ S '69
Planning and packing advice from experi-
enced travelers; symposium. il House &
Gard 136:98-9 Jl '69
Treks and the single girl; packing light for
European travel. il Sat R 52:72 F 15 '69
PACKSADDLES. See Pack transportation
PACKWOOD, Robert W.
Kaffeeklatsch constituency. F. McKay. Na-
tion 208:205-6 F 17 '69
PADFIELD, Peter
Great sea battle; excerpts from Broke and
The Shannon. Am Heritage 20:29-65 D '68
PADGETT, Ron
New York poets. R. Whittemore. New Repub
161:23-4 D 13 '69
PADOVER, Saul K.
Grand strategy of de Gaulle. Sat R 52:25-7
Mr 8 '69
PAELLA. See Cookery, Spanish
PAGAN, Alfred R.
Preplanned drainage pays big dividends. Am
City 84:121 Je '69
PAGE, Benjamin
Signals from North Korea. Nation 208:622-4
My 19 '69
PAGE, Inman E.
Inman E. Page outstanding educator. E. E.
Breaux and T. D. Perry. il pors Negro Hist
Bul 32:8-12 My '69
PAGE, Joseph A.
Mace for the masses. Commonweal 90:141-3
Ap 18 '69
March on Washington. Commonweal 91:268-9
N 28 '69
PAGE, Patricia Kathleen
Another space; Knitter's prayer; Fly; on webs;
Backwards journey; poems. Poetry 114:299-
302 Ag '69
PAGE, Roy C. and Benditt, E. P.
Collagen has a discrete family of reactive
hydroxylysyl and lysyl side-chain amino
groups. bibliog Science 163:578-9 F 7 '69
PAGE, Thomas F. Jr, and others
Polywater: proton nuclear magnetic resonance
spectrum. Science 167:51 Ja 2 '70
PAGE, Thornton Leigh
View from the outside. por Bul Atom Sci 25:
61-6 S '69
PAGE, Warren
Lazarus bull. Field & S 74:54-5+ O '69
Shooting. See issues of Field & stream
PAGEANTS
Pageant of the children and the wee animals.
J. Robbins and J. Robbins. il Redbook 134:
98-9+ D '69
Timely pageant; Virginia Thanksgiving fes-
tival. il Travel 132:16 N '69
PAGES, Congressional. See United States—
Congress—Pages
PAGLIACCI; opera. See Leoncavallo, R.
PAHLEVI, Mohammed Reza, shah of Iran. See
Mohammed Reza Pahlevi
PAHLEVI, Shams, princess of Iran. See Shams
Pahlevi
PAID holidays. See Vacations, Employee
PAIGE, Janis
I love dazzle. il pors House & Gard 135:106-
9 Mr '69
PAIGE, LeRoy. See Paige, S.
PAIGE, Ronald F.
Problem of responsibility for recreation.
Parks & Rec 4:27-8+ O '69
PAIGE, Satchel
Black athlete in the golden age of sports;
an old man makes baseball history. A. S.
Young. il pors Ebony 24:122-4+ Mr '69
Citation awarded baseball great. il por Aging
170:21 D '68
PAIN
Nerve jammer kills pain. il Sci Digest 66:72
N '69
Pain; search for understanding and relief.
il Time 93:63-4 Je 13 '69
Pain: your body's early-warning system. W.
Garrison. il Todays Health 47:28-9+ O '69
What do those chest pains mean? A. S.
Markovits. il Mech Illus 65:43-5+ Je '69
See also
Suffering
PAINE, Thomas
Thomas Paine. por Sr Schol 93:15 Ja 10 '69
PAINE, Thomas O.
As spacemen look beyond the moon; inter-
view. por U S News 67:48-53 Jl 7 '69
Flight of Apollo 11; statement, September 8,
1969. Dept State Bul 61:309-11 O 6 '69
Next steps in space. Nat Geog 136:793-7 D '69

about
Best man. Newsweek 73:74 Mr 17 '69
NASA's Tom Paine, is this a job for a
prudent man? T. Buckley. il pors N Y
Times Mag p34-8+ Je 8 '69
Paine named NASA administrator. por Science
163:1182 Mr 14 '69
Space station, lunar program urged by Paine.
Aviation W 90:278 Mr 10 '69
PAINT
How to choose one of today's wonder paints.
M. J. Schultz. il Pop Mech 131:196-8+ Ap
'69
See also
Enamel and enameling
PAINT, Antifouling. See Paint, Protective
PAINT, Effect of moisture on
Moisture problems in house walls and trou-
bles with blistering and peeling paint. C.
M. Edwards. il Consumer Bul 52:12-14
My '69
PAINT, Luminous
How to use fluorescent colors. D. G. Kuenze.
il Am Artist 33:74-5 O '69
PAINT, Protective
Antifouling boat paints. il Consumer Rep
34:223-7 Ap '69
New chemistry creates a better metal pri-
mer. J. Hand. il Pop Sci 195:129+ D '69
PAINT and varnish removers
How you can wash away old paint! il Bet
Hom & Gard 47:153 S '69
PAINT brushes
How to wash paint brushes with no fuss, no
muss, and very little solvent. D. Tinling.
il Motor B 123:124+ My '69
Pick the proper paintbrush. il Changing T
23:15-16 Je '69
Why not buy a good paint brush? A. J.
Hand. il Pop Sci 195:86-8 D '69
PAINT industry and trade
See also
Sherwin-Williams company

Consolidations and mergers
Germans brush aside Sherwin-Williams.
Bsns W p 19-20 D 27 '69
PAINT removers. See Paint and varnish re-
movers
PAINT sprayers. See Spraying apparatus
PAINT spraying
They paint your house between breakfast
and lunch; Hydraposit system. J. Hand.
il Pop Sci 195:108-10 Jl '69
PAINTED POST, N.Y.
Painted light poles for Painted Post. A. J.
Fuller. il Am City 84:158 My '69
PAINTED tin. See Tole
PAINTER, Hal
Mark is home to stay! por Good H 168:110-
11+ Mr '69
PAINTER, Mark
Mark is home to stay! H. Painter. il pors
Good H 168:110-11+ Mr '69
PAINTING
See also
Color
Expressionism (art)
Genre painting
Impressionism (art)
Landscape painting
Marine painting
Monotypes
Mural painting and decoration
Portrait painting
Realism in art
Stencil work
Tempera painting

Awards
See Art—Awards

Competitions
See Art—Competitions

Psychology
See Art—Psychology

Study and teaching
Painting found objects. M. Panchal. il Sch
Arts 69:14-15 N '69
See also
Water color painting—Study and teaching

Technique
Keep out of the mud! C. Waugh. il Am
Artist 33:32-9 Je '69
My painting technique. E. Carpenter. il Am
Artist 32:66-71 N '68
Raymond Katz, master of mixed techniques.
M. W. Dulac. il Am Artist 33:58-61+ Ja
'69
See also
Perspective

PAINTING—*Continued*

Themes
See Art—Themes

PAINTING, Abstract. See Art, Abstract

PAINTING, American

Ah, sweet mystery of gerontion; early and late paintings by artists from El Greco to Jackson Pollock at the Baltimore museum. L. Campbell. il Art N 67:38-41+ N '68

Ah, wilderness; nineteenth-century American romantic art revival. D. L. Shirey. il Newsweek 73:89 Mr 3 '69

American paintings. R. Davidson. il Antiques 95:156+ Ja '69

American prospects, American skies; exhibition of T. Cole paintings at Albany institute of history and art. il Time 93:76-7 Je 6 '69

Art; annual exhibition of contemporary American art at the Whitney museum. L. Alloway. Nation 210:29-30 Ja 12 '70

Flip side; three practitioners of miniature painting. il Time 93:44-5+ Ja 24 '69

Four disciples of Howard Pyle; excerpts from The Brandywine tradition. H. C. Pitz. il Am Artist 33:38-43 Ja '69

Painting and sculpture. A. Gowans. il Antiques 96:374 S '69

Quiet Americans; the mid-nineteenth century. H. A. LaFarge. il Art N 68:34-5+ N '69

Response to crisis in American art. D. Ashton. il Art in Am 57:24-35 Ja '69

Return to an older America. R. Berenson. il Nat R 21:813-15 Ag 12 '69

Spot check; some observations on painting and sculpture in America. J. Claman. il Harp Baz 102:122C-122F F '69

Thirty years of the New York school; exhibition, New York painting and sculpture; 1940-1970 to open Metropolitan museum's centennial celebrations. H. Kramer. il N Y Times Mag p28-31+ O 12 '69

Yankee impressionists; impressive, impressionable. R. Pomeroy. il Art N 67:50-1+ N '68

See also
Audubon, J. J.
Avery, M.
Beal, J.
Benton, T. H.
Berkowitz, L.
Blair, S.
Bluhm, N.
Broemel, C.
Buehr, K. A.
Caddell, F.
Cameron, M.
Christensen, D.
Clark, R.
Clarke, J. C.
Cole, T.
Costigan, J. E.
Crampton, R. M.
Crocker, D.
Cunningham, B.
De Kooning, W.
Delano, G. C.
Diebenkorn. R.
Dixon, M.
Dunn, H.
Eakins, T.
Ellis, R. G.
Estes, R.
Everett, W. H.
Frankenthaler, H.
Frankfurter, J.
Golfinopoulos. P.
Greene, D. E.
Hamilton, R.
Harding, G.
Harnett, W. M.
Heade, M. J.
Healy, G. P. A.
Humphrey, R.
Hunter, C.
Hutsaliuk, L.
Jackson, B. M.
Kahn, W.
Katz, R.
Kelly, R.
Kensett, J. F.
King, S.
Kingman, D.
Konrad, A.
Krans, O.
Krushenick, C.
Lee, J.
Lichtenstein, R. F.
McLaughlin, J.
Marsh, R.
Miller, A. J.

Motherwell, R.
Mount, W. S.
Natkin, R.
Newman, B.
Noland, K.
Oakley, T.
Olitski, J.
Perrine, V. D.
Pike, J.
Pollock, J.
Portrait painting
Portraits, American
Prentice, L. W.
Pyle, H.
Raffael, J.
Rauschenberg, R.
Rose, H.
Schapiro, M.
Schreyvogel, C.
Singer, C.
Steinberg, S.
Stella, F.
Still, C.
Tanner, H. O.
Von Dewitz, A.
Warhol, A.
Whitney museum of American art, New York
Whittredge, W.
Wyeth, A.
Young, P.

PAINTING, Argentine
See also
Pettoruti, E.
Salatino, C. A.

PAINTING, Baroque
After the high Roman fashion; show of baroque paintings at Wildenstein gallery, New York. S. Nodelman. il Art N 67:34-7+ N '68

PAINTING, British
See also
Constable, J.
Dadd, R.
Morley, M.
Morris, W.
Smibert. J.
Wagener, K.

PAINTING, Canadian
See also
Bolduc, D.
Ewen, P.
Gagnon, C.
Lansdowne, J. F.
Molinari, G.
Ristvedt, M.

PAINTING, Childrens. See Childrens art

PAINTING, Chinese
China trade paintings on glass. C. L. Crossman. il Antiques 95:376-82 Mr '69
See also
Wang, H.

PAINTING, Dutch
Rembrandt and his circle. B. A. Rifkin. il Art N 68:26-7+ My; 31-5+ O; 30-3+ N '69
See also
Bosch, H.
Doesburg, T. van
Rembrandt Hermanszoon van Rijn
Vermeer, J.

PAINTING, English
See also
Hockney, D.
Hodgkin, H.

PAINTING, European
Ah, sweet mystery of gerontion; early and late paintings by artists from El Greco to Jackson Pollock at the Baltimore museum. L. Campbell. il Art N 67:38-41+ N '68

Art world; European painters today at the Jewish museum. H. Rosenberg. New Yorker 45:107-8+ F 22 '69

PAINTING, Flemish
See also
Brueghel, P. the elder
David, G.

PAINTING, Florentine. See Painting, Italian

PAINTING, French
Before the deluge; pastels and watercolors by 18th-century French masters. J. Ashberg. il Art N 68:54-5+ N '69

Letter from Paris; biennial exhibition of seven canvases at Rue du Faubourg-St-Honoré gallery. Genêt. New Yorker 45:42+ D 27 '69

19th-century franc revalued; exhibition at the Minneapolis institute of arts. R. Rosenblum. il Art N 68:26-31+ Sum '69

Rediscovered riches; exhibition at the Minneapolis institute of arts. il Time 94:42-3 Jl 25 '69

PAINTING, French—*Continued*
Restoring reputations; The past rediscovered exhibition in Minneapolis. D. L. Shirey. il Newsweek 74:85 Ag 4 '69
See also
Corot, J. B. C.
Dubuffet, J.
Duchamp, M.
Dufy, R.
Gauguin, P.
Ingres, J. A. D.
Matisse, H.
Renoir, A.
Soutine, C.
Ungerer, T.
Vieira da Silva, M. H.
PAINTING, German
German genre paintings from the Von Schleinitz collection. T. Atkinson. il Antiques 96:712-16 N '69
One cheer for expressionism; German expressionism. A. Goldin. il Art N 67:48-9+ N '68
See also
Ernst, M.
Francke, Master
Klapheck, K.
Richter, G.
Schlemmer, O.
Schwitters, K.
PAINTING, industrial and practical
No-show for metal siding; prepainted fasteners by electrophoretic deposition, or electro-painting. Bsns W p 156 Je 21 '69
Should you do the painting yourself? Sunset 143:115+ N '69
See also
Boats—Painting
House painting
Paint, Protective
Paint brushes
Paint spraying

Equipment and supplies
Pressurized painting system without a compressor. J. Hand. il Pop Sci 195:154-5 S '69
PAINTING, Italian
Florentine sunset; exhibition of Florentine 17th-century painting at the Metropolitan museum. A. S. Harris. il Art N 68:32-5+ My '69
From Ricci to Tiepolo via Bencovich. M. Gendel. il Art N 68:58-60+ S '69
Genoese mix; Baroque paintings at the Palazzo Bianco; tr. by S. Morini. M. Valsecchi. il Art N 68:28-30+ O '69
See also
Bellotto, B.
Gentile da Fabriano
Montagna, B.
Pistoletto, M.
PAINTING, Landscape. See Landscape painting
PAINTING, Mexican
See also
Gironella, A.
PAINTING, Modern. See Art, Modern
PAINTING, Non-objective. See Art, Abstract
PAINTING, Romantic. See Romanticism
PAINTING, Russian
See also
Kandinsky, W.
Larionov, M. F.
PAINTING, Spanish
See also
Goya y Lucientes, F. J. de
Picasso, P.
PAINTING, Swiss
See also
Klee, P.
PAINTING, Symbolic. See Symbolism in art
PAINTING, Venetian. See Painting, Italian
PAINTING and photography. See Art and photography
PAINTING on book edges. See Book ornamentation
PAINTING on textiles. See Textile painting
PAINTINGS
Jokes the old masters used to play. P. Brock. il Sci Digest 65:12-17 My '69
Madrid's fabulous Prado. J. A. Michener. il Read Digest 94:145-51 Je '69
Masters in the art news. See issues of Art news
See also
Forgery of works of art

Appreciation
See Art—Appreciation

Care
How to care for paintings. E. McClelland. House B 111:70 Ap '69

Collections
See Art—Private collections

Copying
See Pictures—Copying
PAINTINGS, Reproductions of. See Reproductions of works of art
PAINTINGS, Theft of. See Art thefts
PAIROA, René
Wind, waves and stars; ed. by L. Zalamea. Américas 21:2-11 Ap '69
PAISANAS. See Road runners (birds)
PAISLEY, Ian
Bit of the bogus. J. D. Douglas. Chr Today 13:50-1 My 9 '69
Not defending the indefensible. J. D. Douglas. Chr Today 14:55 O 24 '69
Ulster after the bludgeons. B. Kiely. Nation 208:629-31 My 19 '69
PAK, Chung Hi. See Park, C. H.
PAKENHAM, Elizabeth (Harman) countess of Longford. See Longford, E. H. P.
PAKISER, L. C. and others
Earthquake prediction and control. bibliog Science 166:1467-74 D 19 '69
PAKISTAN
See also
Missions—Pakistan
United States—Foreign relations—Pakistan

Politics and government
Abdication, Asian style. il Newsweek 73:35-6 Mr 3 '69
Army takes over Pakistan. Time 93:32 Ap 4 '69
Ayub calls it quits. il Sr Schol 94:23 Mr 28 '69
Ayub's strategic retreat. il Time 93:29-30 F 21 '69
Back to democracy, on the double. il Time 94:34 D 12 '69
Developing society; address, December 1, 1968. M. Ayub Khan. Vital Speeches 35:200-2 Ja 15 '69
Divided they stand. A. Campbell. New Repub 160:15-19 Mr 22 '69
East is East; under martial law. il Newsweek 73:50 Ap 14 '69
Law & order in Pakistan. A. Ahmad. il Nation 208:455-8 Ap 14 '69
Not by bread alone. il Newsweek 73:43 F 10 '69
Old song; return to parliamentary democracy. Newsweek 73:50 Mr 24 '69
Pakistan: new leader, same troubles. il U S News 66:54 Ap 7 '69
Pakistan: why Ayub quit. il Newsweek 73:38-9 Ap 7 '69
Pakistan's Ayub steps down. il Time 93:29-30 F 28 '69
Precarious task. il Time 93:36 Mr 28 '69
Prophet of violence; riots inspired by Bhashani. il Time 93:39 Ap 18 '69

Riots
Developing society; address, December 1, 1968. M. Ayub Khan. Vital Speeches 35:200-2 Ja 15 '69
Not by bread alone. il Newsweek 73:43 F 10 '68
PALACES
Other Woodstock; a visit to Blenheim palace. D. Butwin. il Sat R 52:42+ O 11 '69
Taliesin in Teheran; palace planned for Princess Shams Pahlavi. W. W. Peters. il Art in Am 57:44-51 Jl '69
See also
Castles
PALACH, Jan
Bells peal for a martyr in Prague. il Life 66:24-7 F 7 '69
Burning of Jan Palach. America 120:151 F 8 '69
Message in fire. il por Time 93:22+ Ja 31 '69
Second Jan. il por Newsweek 73:42 F 3 '69
Student sets self afire; with report by R. Hemming. il Sr Schol 94:12-13 F 7 '69
Torch number one. Newsweek 73:51-2 Ja 27 '69
Youth in ferment; occupied Czechoslovakia. R. Hemming. il por Sr Schol 94:8-9 Mr 7 '69
PALEOANTHROPOLOGY. See Man, Prehistoric
PALEOBIOLOGY
See also
Paleoecology
PALEOBOTANY
Ancestral American forests. H. F. Becker. il Am For 75:12-15+ Mr '69
Fossil maize from Panama. A. S. Bartlett and others. bibliog il Science 165:389-90 Jl 25 '69
Some living plant fossils. H. F. Becker. il Am For 75:12-15+ Jl '69

PALEOBOTANY—*Continued*

Eocene

Podocarpus from the eocene of North America. D. L. Dilcher. Science 164:299-301 Ap 18 '69

Jurassic

Glossopterid leaves from the middle Jurassic of Oaxaca, Mexico. T. Delevoryas. bibliog il Science 165:895-6 Ag 29 '69

Mesozoic

140 million-year-old plant; cycadeoidea ingens. P. Clark. il Horticulture 47:41 S '69

Permian

Cycads: fossil evidence of late paleozoic origin. S. H. Mamay. bibliog il Science 164:295-6 Ap 18 '69

Quaternary

Carbon-14 trends in subfossil pine stubs. J. C. Vogel and others. bibliog il Science 166:1143-5 N 28 '69

China

Loess and the origin of Chinese agriculture. P. T. Ho. bibliog f il Am Hist R 75:1-36 O '69

Pennsylvanian

Cycads: evidence from the upper Pennsylvanian. T. N. Taylor. bibliog il Science 164:294-5 Ap 18 '69

PALEOCLIMATOLOGY

Environmental temperatures of tertiary penguins. B. Stonehouse. bibliog il Science 163:673-5 F 14 '69

Glacier oxygen-18 content and pleistocene ocean temperatures. W. Dansgaard and H. Tauber. bibliog il Science 166:499-502 O 24 '69

Tertiary climatic change in the marginal northeastern Pacific Ocean. W. O. Addicott. bibliog il Science 165:583-6 Ag 8 '69

PALEOECOLOGY

Recent planktonic foraminifera: dominance and diversity in North Atlantic surface sediments. W. F. Ruddiman. bibliog il Science 164:1164-7 Je 6 '69

PALEO-INDIANS

Biological and cultural evidence from prehistoric human coprolites. R. F. Heizer and L. K. Napton. bibliog il Science 165:563-8 Ag 8 '69

Earliest Americans. C. V. Haynes, jr. bibliog il Science 166:709-15 N 7 '69

Early man in the West Indies. J. M. Cruxent and I. Rouse. il Sci Am 221:42-52 bibliog (p 166) N '69)

PALEOMAGNETISM. See Magnetism, Terrestrial

PALEONTOLOGY

Continental drift and evolution. B. Kurtén. il Sci Am 220:54-64 Mr '69

Fossil bones, how to find them. D. W. Fisher and E. M. Reilly, jr. il Cons 24:48+ D '69

See also
Computers—Paleontological applications
Elephants, Fossil
Foraminifera, Fossil
Man, Prehistoric
Paleobotany

Methodology

Paleontological evidence of variations in length of synodic month since late Cambrian. G. Pannella and others; discussion. Science 163:1227; bibliog 164:201-2 Mr 14, Ap 11 '69

Sedimentary phosphate method for estimating paleosalinities: a paleontological assumption. A. L. Guber. bibliog il Science 166:744-6 N 7 '69

Synodic month: variations in the geologic past. R. H. Miller. bibliog Science 164:67-8 Ap 4 '69

Cambrian

Ctenocystoidea: new class of primitive echinoderms. R. A. Robison and J. Sprinkle. bibliog il Science 166:1512-14 D 19 '69

Cretaceous

Generation and maintenance of gradients in taxonomic diversity. F. G. Stehli and others. bibliog il Science 164:947-9 My 23 '69; Reply. L. Van Valen. 166:1656-8 D 26 '69

Devonian

Algal stromatolites: deepwater forms in the Devonian of Western Australia. P. E. Playford and A. E. Cockbain. bibliog il Science 165:1008-10 S 5 '69

Oldest known terrestrial arachnids. L. Størmer. bibliog il Science 164:1276-7 Je 13 '69

Permian

Lissamphibian origins: possible protolissamphiban from the lower Permian of Oklahoma. J. R. Bolt. bibliog il Science 166:888-91 N 14 '69

Permian insect wing from Antarctic Sentinel Mountains. P. Tasch and E. F. Riek. bibliog il Science 164:1529-30 Je 27 '69

Pleistocene

Glacier oxygen-18 content and pleistocene ocean temperatures. W. Dansgaard and H. Tauber. bibliog il Science 166:499-502 O 24 '69

Great dinosaur disaster. D. Cohen. il Sci Digest 65:45-52 Mr '69

Wanted: a suitable herbivore to convert western scrubland to protein. P. S. Martin. il Nature Hist 78:34-9 F '69

Pre-Cambrian

Precambrian columnar stromatolites in Australia: morphological and stratigraphic analysis. M. F. Glaessner and others. bibliog il Science 164:1056-8 My 30 '69

Triassic

Cynodont reptile with incipient mammalian jaw articulation. A. S. Romer. bibliog il Science 166:881-2 N 14 '69

Antarctic Regions

Clue to the past; lystrosaurus. il Sci N 96:549 D 13 '69

Permian insect wing from Antarctic Sentinel Mountains. P. Tasch and E. F. Riek. bibliog il Science 164:1529-30 Je 27 '69

Australasia

Environmental temperatures of tertiary penguins. B. Stonehouse. bibliog il Science 163:673-5 F 14 '69

Australia

Algal stromatolites: deepwater forms in the Devonian of Western Australia. P. E. Playford and A. E. Cockbain. bibliog il Science 165:1008-10 S 5 '69

Precambrian columnar stromatolites in Australia: morphological and stratigraphic analysis. M. F. Glaessner and others. bibliog il Science 164:1056-8 My 30 '69

California

Death trap of the ages; Rancho la Brea. J. R. MacDonald. il Nat Wildlife 7:24-9 Ag '69

China

Secrets of China's ancient men. D. Cohen. il Sci Digest 66:40-4 S '69

Germany

Oldest known terrestrial arachnids. L. Størmer. bibliog il Science 164:1276-7 Je 13 '69

Oklahoma

Lissamphibian origins: possible protolissamphibian from the lower Permian of Oklahoma. J. R. Bolt. bibliog il Science 166:888-91 N 14 '69

Utah

Ctenocystoidea: new class of primitive echinoderms. R. A. Robison and J. Sprinkle. bibliog il Science 166:1512-14 D 19 '69

See also
Dinosaur National Monument

Wyoming

Paleocene hyracothere from Polecat Bench formation, Wyoming. G. L. Jepsen and M. O. Woodburne. bibliog il Science 164:543-7 My 2 '69

They dig for fish. J. S. Flannery. il Pop Mech 131:152-3 Mr '69

PALEOPATHOLOGY

Disease in ancient Nubia. G. J. Armelagos. bibliog il Science 163:255-9 Ja 17 '69

Enterobius vermicularis: 10,000-year-old human infection. G. F. Fry and J. G. Moore. bibliog il Science 166:1620 D 26 '69

Thorny-headed worm infection in North American prehistoric man. J. G. Moore and others. bibliog il Science 163:1324-5 Mr 21 '69

PALEOSALINITIES. See Sedimentation and deposition

PALEOTEMPERATURE. See Paleoclimatology

PALEOZOIC period. See Geology, Stratigraphic —Paleozoic

PALERMO

Music

Report: Palermo; world premiere of Franco Manninos Luisella. J. Boraros. Opera N 33: 31 Ap 19 '69

PALESTINE

See also

Israel

Jerusalem

Popular front for the liberation of Palestine

Jewish-Arab problem

See Jewish-Arab relations

PALESTINE refugees. See Refugees, Arab

PALEY, Grace

Passionate rebels. S. Harrington. Vogue 153: 151+ My '69

PALEY, William

Classification of trivets. Hobbies 74:98R-98S Jl; 114-15 S '69

PALISADES interstate park

Defending Palisades park. Nat Parks 43:32 Ap '69

PALM BEACH, Fla.

Hard-core rich. C. McCarthy. New Repub 160:14-15 Mr 15 '69

Palm Beach; the rarest resort of them all. N. Busch. il Holiday 45:38-45 F '69

Description

Poor little Palm Beach. S. Birmingham. il Esquire 73:112-20+ Ja '70

PALM of the hand. See Hand

PALM trees. See Palms

PALMA, Robert J. and Pearson, K. H.

Coulometric titrations with halogens. bibliog pors Chem 42:28-31 N '69

PALMAI-TENSER, Rose

R for opera. Opera N 34:14-15 D 13 '69

PALME, Olof

Hot soup from Olof. il por Time 94:38 O 10 '69

I am curious (P.M.) il por Newsweek 74:47 O 13 '69

Letter from Stockholm. P. Siekman. por Fortune 80:67+ N '69

U.S. critic at Sweden's helm. por U S News 67:22 O 13 '69

PALMER, Arnold

Couple of hips, one hurrah. A. Wright. il por Sports Illus 31:70-1+ O 27 '69

Course that Jack Built. il por Time 94:52 D 12 '69

Jack's course is Arnie's, too. D. Jenkins. il por Sports Illus 31:24-7 D 8 '69

King is asked to earn his way. C. Kirkpatrick. il por Sports Illus 30:34-5 Je 16 '69

Polite no from Arnie and Jack. W. Johnson. il por Sports Illus 30:34-5 Ap 14 '69

Thanks for the memories; photographs, with account by D. Jenkins. Sports Illus 31:28-35 S 1 '69

PALMER, B. D.

Interhemispheric transport of atmospheric fission debris from French nuclear tests. bibliog Science 164:951-2 My 23 '69

PALMER, Diane. See Weber, G. H. jt. auth.

PALMER, Edward L.

Can television really teach? Am Ed 5:2-6 Ag '69

PALMER, Florence K.

Six ways to successful confessions. Writer 82:15-18 My '69

PALMER, Jeff

How to hunt like an Indian. Field & S 74: 62-3+ Ag '69

PALMER, Jim

Highlight. por Sports Illus 31:81 Ag 25 '69

PALMER, Joseph, 1914-

Africa; continent of change; address, December 5, 1968. Dept State Bul 59:696-702 D 30 '68

PALMER, L. F. jr

Out to get the Panthers. Nation 209:78-82 Jl 28 '69

PALMER, Sister Marie James

Forgetting; poem. Horn Bk 45:152 Ap '69

PALMER, Ted

Gadfly and the dinosaur. bibliog f Engl J 58:69-74 Ja '69

PALMER, William Jackson

Pikes Peak panorama. I. Hunt. il Am For 75: 20-3 S '69

PALMER, Winthrop

Mid-winter; poem. Commonweal 89:525 Ja 24 '69

PALMS

Big game of the plant world. G. White. il Am For 75:24-7+ N '69

Palms in the landscape. W. Radcliffe. il Horticulture 47:22-5+ Ja '69

Royal palm. P. W. Dempsey. il Horticulture 46:14-15 N '68

See also

Date palms

PALO ALTO, Calif.

Get the lines undergound effortlessly. il Am City 84:141+ O '69

Palo Alto's underground utility project. il Am City 84:172+ S '69

We make off-street parking self supporting. G. E. Morgan. il Am City 84:170+ O '69

Churches

Symbol and shelter; All Saints Episcopal church. il Arch Forum 131:76-9 O '69

Education

Psychedelic multimedia happening; Gunn senior high. R. M. Glendening. il Sr Schol 94:Schol Teach 18-19 Ap 18 '69

PALOLO worms

Night of the palolo. B. Smetzer. il Natur Hist 78:64-71 N '69

PALOMARES, Spain

Palomares after the fall. J. Blashill. il Time 93:39 Ja 24 '69

PAMPAS grass

Pampas grass, plumed beauty. B. Wahlfeldt. il Org Gard & Farm 16:82-3 D '69

PAMPHLETS

Best in booklets. See issues of House & garden incorporating Living for young homemakers

Booklets worth writing for. See issues of Good housekeeping

Books and booklets. See issues of American home

Fifty free (or almost free) research aids and idea stimulators. A. Hagen. il Writers Digest 49:48-50+ F '69

Guides for successful retirement. il Har Yrs 9: 34 My '69

Tell me more. See issues of House beautiful

Things to write for. See issues of Changing times

Worth writing for. Motor B 124:76 D '69

Anecdotes, facetiae, satire, etc.

KaPOOMcha: the mimeograph revolution. J. S. Kunen. Esquire 72:102 S '69

PAMPLONA, Spain

Sound of hooves; fiesta of San Fermin. J. McCormick. il Sports Illus 31:60-4+ Jl 7 '69

PAN, M. L. and others

Vitellogenic blood protein synthesis by insect fat body. bibliog Science 165:393-4 Jl 25 '69

PAN, Stephen C. Y.

China and southeast Asia. bibliog f Cur Hist 57:164-7+ S '69

PAN-AFRICANISM

Progress toward African unity. V. McKay. Cur Hist 56:257-62+ My '69

PANALBA. See Antibiotics

PAN AM (airline) See Pan American world airways

PANAMA

See also

Darien, Panama

Native races

See Indians of Central America

Politics and government

Day at the races. Time 94:16 D 26 '69

Exit Panama's lesser evil. Ramp Mag 7:16+ N 30 '68

What price democracy? il Newsweek 74:34 D 29 '69

PANAMA CANAL ZONE

See also

Barro Colorado Island

PAN AMERICAN agricultural school

Training tomorrow's farmers. P. Valle. il Américas 21:9-12 S '69

PAN AMERICAN airways. See Pan American world airways

PAN AMERICAN day and week

April 14: Pan American day. G. de Zéndegui. Américas 21:1 Ap '69

Pan American day and Pan American week, 1969; proclamation. R. M. Nixon. Dept State Bul 60:386 My 5 '69

PAN AMERICAN highway

Bridging the Darién gap. Américas 21:45 My '69

Conquest of Darien. A. F. Ghiglione. Américas 21:1 Jl '69

Darien. M. Barraco Mármol. il Américas 21: 23-31 Jl '69

PAN AMERICAN union

Hemisphere art. See issues of Américas

PAN AMERICAN world airways
Airlines prepare for introduction of 747. J. P. Woolsey. il Aviation W 91:36-41+ O 20 '69
Bid to takeover Pan Am blocked. L. Doty. Aviation W 90:26 Mr 17 '69
Blocking an air raid il Time 93:86 Mr 21 '69
Craps, roulette & Pan American airways. il Forbes 103:27-9 Mr 15 '69
End of bizarre overseas venture; Executive jet severing links to Penn central. il Bsns W p 122-3+ Ag 16 '69
Nuclear rocket development station. il Space World F-12-72:4-15 D '69
Pan Am feels competitive impact. L. Doty. Aviation W 91:27-8 D 1 '69
Pan Am finds the going's not great. il Bsns W p84-6 O 11 '69
Pan Am plans to finance New York airways service. Aviation W 91:24 S 8 '69
Pan Am prepares to receive first 747. R. G. O'Lone. Aviation W 91:36 N 24 '69
Pan Am reduces frequencies on West Coast-Hawaii routes. Aviation W 91:30 O 27 '69
Pan Am testing mobile loading system for 747. il Aviation W 90:43+ Je 9 '69
Pan Am to cut San Juan trips. Aviation W 91:26 N 10 '69
Pan Am to train 150 crews for 747s. Aviation W 90:46 Je 23 '69
Pan Am's new chief. il Time 94:94 N 28 '69
Troubles at Pan Am. Newsweek 74:90+ N 10 '69
Why Washington rode with Pan Am; CAB approval required on takeovers of airlines by non-transportation companies. Bsns W p40 Mr 15 '69

PAN AMERICANISM. See Inter-American relations

PANARABISM
See also
Arab states

PANAS, Alexander
Mr Tambo, Mr Bones. Criticisms
Sat R 52:33 F 15 '69

PANAY (gunboat) incident
Crew fought back. il Newsweek 73:11 F 3 '69

PANCAKES. See Griddle cakes

PANCHAL, Mansaram
Painting found objects. Sch Arts 69:14-15 N '69

PANCREAS
See also
Glucagon

PANDAS
Mary Simons; report on troubles in pandasville; Regent's park zoo, London. M. Simons. Look 33:22 O 21 '69

PANDION haliaetus. See Ospreys

PANDYA, Deepak. See Butters, N. jt. auth.

PANEL construction
See also
Sandwich construction

PANEL heating. See Radiant heating

PANEL on foreign investment in developing countries. See United Nations—Panel on foreign investment in developing countries

PANELING
Art panels with new Flair. il Pop Sci 194:134-9+ Ap '69
Paneled look. J. H. Ingersoll. il House B 111:158-9+ O '69
Walls that fool the eye; molded-plastic panels. J. Hand. il Pop Sci 194:176+ Mr '69
What's new in wall paneling. il Pop Sci 194:159 Ap '69

PANELS, Prefabricated. See Buildings, Prefabricated

PANHANDLING. See Begging and beggars

PANIC
Greatest Halloween prank of them all; reactions to 1938 broadcast of The war of the worlds. J. H. Burns. Read Digest 95:157-60 O '69
Sky is falling, but don't duck. D. Cohen. il Sci Digest 65:14-19 Je '69

PANIC in a desk drawer; drama. See Woster, A. C.

PANICS
See also
Stock exchange—Crisis, October 1929

PANIKER, Salvador
What Spaniards say when they think aloud; excerpts from Conversations in Madrid, ed. by R. Eder. N Y Times Mag p25+ S 28 '69

PANIZZA, Oskar
Council of love. Criticism
New Yorker 45:127-8+ Mr 22 '69

PANKOWSKI, Marian
European literary scene. R. J. Clements. Sat R 52:23 Ag 2 '69

PANNELLA, Giorgio, and others
Paleontological evidence of variations in length of synodic month since late Cambrian. bibliog Science 162:792-6; 164:202 N 15 '68, Ap 11 '69

PANORAMIC photography. See Photography, Panoramic

PANSIES
Pansies, last in the fall, and first in the spring. K. L. Carlsen. il Org Gard & Farm 16:68-9 O '69
See also
Violets

PANTALEON. See Dulcimer

PANTALON. See Dulcimer

PANTHER VALLEY, N.J.
Hackettstown is for the birds. M. A. Guitar. il Am Home 72:12+ S '69

PANTHERS
Pioneers and panthers. R. V. Anderson. bibliog il Cons 23:6-7 Je '69

PANTOMINE
See also
Gesture

PANTS. See Trousers

PANYARACHUN, Anand
Thailand. New Repub 160:31 Ap 19 '69

PANZER, Judith
On the boards. W. Como. por Dance Mag 43:20 S '69

PAOLOZZI, Eduardo
Paolozzi mix. C. Finch. il Art N 67:32-4+ F '69
Print man. il Newsweek 73:88-9 Mr 3 '69

PAPACY
Papacy. G. Baum. Cath World 209:64-6 My '69
St Peter's square, 1997. F. Franck. il Commonweal 91:162+ O 31 '69
See also
Popes

History
Bad popes, by E. R. Chamberlin. Review
Commonweal 90:599-600 S 26 '69. J. L. McKenzie

PAPADOPOULOS, George
Outlook in Greece, as Premier sees it. por U S News 67:8 D 29 '69
Why Greece's colonels are that way. il por Time 93:32-3 Ap 18 '69

PAPADOPOULOS, Maria Delivoria-. See Delivoria-Papadopoulos, M.

PAPAHADJOPOULOS, Demetrios, and Ohki, Shinpei
Stability of asymmetric phospholipid membranes. bibliog Science 164:1075-7 My 30 '69

PAPAIN
Trypsin and papain covalently coupled to porous glass: preparation and characterization. H. H. Weetall. bibliog il Science 166:615-17 O 31 '69

PAPAL infallibility. See Popes—Infallibility

PAPAL nuncios. See Nuncios, Papal

PAPAWS
Pawpaw. C. E. Lewis. Horticulture 47:10+ D '69

PAPAYAS
Florida sunshine and papaya. B. Brinhart. il Org Gard & Farm 16:62-4 D '69
Pistillate papaya flower: a morphological anomaly. W. B. Storey. bibliog il Science 163:401-5 Ja 24 '69

PAPER
Paper and the book; excerpts from address, November 1969. W. Chisholm. Pub W 196:50+ D 1 '69
See also
Photographic paper

Deterioration
See Materials—Deterioration

Preservation
Case of the vanishing records. D. G. Lowe. il Am Heritage 20:34-5+ Ag '69
Cooperative rethinking needed concerning permanent paper. C. B. Grannis. Pub W 195:67 Mr 3 '69

PAPER bag players. See Theater, Childrens

PAPER birch. See Birch

PAPER books. See Paperback books

PAPER cups, plates, etc.
Convenience foods? Paper service? P. Andron. il Camp Mag 41:18-19 Je '69

PAPER cutting. See Paper work

PAPER dresses. See Clothing and dress

PAPER gold. See Special drawing rights

PAPER making and trade
Making paper by hand. il Pub W 197:60-1
Ja 5 '70
See also
Boise Cascade corporation
Crown Zellerbach corporation
International paper company
Kimberly-Clark corporation
Mead corporation
Paper mills
Paterson parchment paper company
Scott paper company
Union camp corporation
Wood pulp

Consolidations and mergers
When publishers feud over newsprint; West
Tacoma newsprint co. merger into Boise
Cascade corp. Bsns W p39 O 25 '69

Japan
Wood chips ship out; to Japanese pulp and
paper makers. il Bsns W p 164+ Mr 29 '69
PAPER mills
Paper mill king tries home market; K. Lan-
degger plans North American mills. il Bsns
W p 136-8 Mr 29 '69
PAPER money
Paper money made into art you can bank
on. il Life 67:51-2+ S 19 '69
PAPER mulching. See Mulching
PAPER piping cones. See Cookery, Orna-
mental
PAPER products
See also
Fibreboard corporation
PAPER sculpture
Ah! Sunflower. M. J. Acosta. il Design 70:36
mid-Wint '69
Boxed in creativity; producing figures with
drawing mediums. E. M. Jacomo. il Sch
Arts 68:32-4 Mr '69
PAPER tableware. See Paper cups, plates, etc.
PAPER work
Backgrounds with a new look; wallpaper
pictures. M. Shaw. il Sch Arts 96:38 N '69
Fold and dip. M. Foster. il Sch Arts 69:22-4
Ja '70
Introducing motion. S. D. Hochman. il Sch
Arts 69:12-13 S '69
This is cardboard! M. Garrity. il Bet Hom &
Gard 47:88-9 Mr '69
See also
Paper sculpture
Papier-mâché
Silhouettes
PAPERBACK book covers. See Book covers
PAPERBACK books
AEP starts book club for young readers;
American education publications paperback
elementary school program. Library J 94:
4194-5 N 15 '69
Market for paperback originals. Writer 82:27-
9 Ap '69
Paperback best sellers of the year 1968. il Pub
W 195:33-6 Mr 10 '69
Writing paperback originals. M. Williams.
Writer 82:24-6 Ap '69
See also
Booksellers and bookselling—Paperback books
Libraries—Paperback books
Pocket books, incorporated
Publishers and publishing—Paperback books

Bibliography
Books to come; childrens and adult. J. Baumholtz; J. Putnam; F. Green. Library J 94:
324-59 Ja 15 '69
Books to come; childrens and adult; comp.
by J. Baumholtz; F. Green. Library J 94:
3135-63 My 15 '69
Books to come; childrens and adult; comp.
by S. T. Halbreich; F. Green. Library J 94:
3163-91 S 15 '69
Current and choice in paperbacks (cont of)
Picking the best of paperbacks. America
121:498-502 N 22 '69
Paperback bookshelf. See issues of Changing times
Paperbacks. See issues of Publishers' weekly
Paperbacks aplenty; symposium. Sr Schol
94:Schol Teach 12-14+ Ja 31 '69
Pick of the paperbacks. R. W. Saal. See issues of Saturday review
Quality paperbacks for children. R. Gag-
liardo. il PTA Mag 63:30-1 My '69
PAPERWEIGHTS
Glossary of paperweight terms. E. C. Cloak.
il Antiques 95:559-63 Ap '69
Paperweights; you can't judge their value
by their looks. McCalls 96:52 Ap '69

PAPIER-MACHÉ
Can we get the dinosaurs out of the cellar?
C. B. Xzeglin. il Sch Arts 68:18-20 Mr '69
Close up: Gerald Scarfe. il Life 66:40-1+ Ap
4 '69
Middle ages in environmental sculpture. L.
Lord. il Sch Arts 68:32-5 F '69
Papier maché a la mode. M. Harvey. il Am
Artist 33:38-41 F '69
PAPILLARY muscles. See Heart—Muscle
PAPKE, Davis R.
Good-bye, Harvard. Commonweal 91:13-15 O
3 '69
PAPP, Gilbert
Four R's. Todays Ed 58:59 N '69
PAPP, Joseph
Joseph Papp's Happening and the teaching
of Hamlet. P. Traci. Engl J 58:75-7 Ja '69
PAPP; drama. See Cameron, K.
PAPPAS, Lou Seibert
Picnic loaves and pastries. House & Gard
135:101-3+ Je '69
PAPPAS, Thomas Anthony
Greek for go-between. il por Time 93:86+
F 14 '69
PAPYRUS reed boats. See Boats—Materials
PARA-aminobenzoic acid. See Aminobenzoic
acid
PARACHUTING
It takes courage to float through the air. G.
Freit. il Seventeen 28:92+ Ja '69
Skydiving. B. Grant. il Pop Sci 194:62-6+
Ja '69
See also
Forest fire patrol, Aerial
PARADES
See also subhead Parades under names
of cities, e.g. New York (city)—Parades
PARADIS, H. James
Variations in form and technique. Ceram Mo
17:22-4 Ap '69
PARADIS, Marjorie B.
Alpha kappa; drama. Plays 29:33-44 Ja '70
PARADISE, Phil
Serigraphs of Phil Paradise. J. Lovoos. il
por Am Artist 33:43-8+ O '69
PARADISE, Scott
Vandal ideology. Nation 209:729-32 D 29 '69
PARADISE. See Heaven
PARADOXICAL sleep. See Sleep
PARAGUAY

Anecdotes, facetiae, satire, etc.
Paraguay. D. Barthelme. New Yorker 45:
32-4 S 6 '69

Description and travel
Paraguay: where the living is easy. so...
G. Greene. il Holiday 45:68-71 Ap '69

Politics and government
Indigestion in Paraguay; Stroessner regime
criticized by Catholic weekly Comunidad.
America 120:347-8 Mr 29 '69
Paraguay: where the living is easy, so...
G. Greene. il Holiday 45:68-71 Ap '69

Religious institutions and affairs
See also
Catholic church in Paraguay
Church and state in Paraguay
PARAKEETS. See Parrots
PARALLELS (geometry) See Geometry
PARALYSIS
See also
Cerebral palsied children
Parkinson's disease
PARAMECIA
Cell division: a second circadian clock sys-
tem in paramecium multimicronucleatum.
A. Barnett. bibliog il Science 164:1417-19
Je 20 '69
Ionic mechanisms controlling behavioral re-
sponses of paramecium to mechanical
stimulation. Y. Naitoh and R. Eckert. bib-
liog il Science 164:963-5 My 23 '69
PARAMOUNT pictures corporation
Paramount's lot; proposed sale of studios.
il Newsweek 74:84 N 10 '69
Why should he have it? Paramount's whiz-
kid studio boss. J. Mills. il Life 66:62-8+
Mr 7 '69
PARAMYOSIN. See Muscle—Proteins
PARANOIA

Anecdotes, facetiae, satire, etc.
Big P. M. Thomas. Look 33:14+ Ap 15 '69
PARAPROTEINEMIA. See Proteinemia
PARAPSYCHOLOGY
Man who reads nature's secret signals. T.
Bacon. il Nat Wildlife 7:4-8 F '69
Mind over matter, maybe. il Time 93:52 Ja
24 '69

PARASITES
See also
Coccidia
Follicle mites
Mealy bugs
Nematodes
Plasmodium (parasite)
Toxoplasma
Trematodes
Worms, Intestinal and parasitic

Fishes
Mussels on the move; transportation of parasitic larvae by host fish. J. H. Welsh. il Natur Hist 78:56-9 My '69

Insects
See also
Trichogramma

PARASITIC diseases
See also
Leishmaniasis
Schistosomiasis
Toxoplasmosis
Trypanosomiasis

PARC des Chaumont. See Paris—Parks and playgrounds

PARCEL post
Fight continues against bulk mailing rules. S. Wagner. Pub W 195:41-2 F 3 '69
Lots of ways to send a Christmas package. il Changing T 23:33-5 N '69

PARDE ISLAND NATIONAL SEASHORE
Parde Island; recreation plan. J. V. Morris. bibliog il Nat Parks 43:15-18 Je '69

PARDEE, Arthur B. See Fox. T. O. jt. auth.

PARDO, Richard
Something up, down east. Am For 75:12-13+ My '69

PAREE, Paul
Paul Paree. il Pop Phot 64:84-93 Mr '69

PAREGIEN, Stanley
'Tis the season to be gluttonous. Chr Today 14:9-10 N 21 '69

PARENT and child (law)
Children's rights. R. F. Drinan. America 122:4-5 Ja 10 '70
Father as non-parent; California's abortion statute. D. W. Louisell and C. Carroll. il Cath World 210:108-10 D '69
Mark is home to stay! H. Painter. il Good H 168:110-11+ Mr '69

PARENT-child relationship
Aren't two parents enough? questions and answers. A. Wood. Seventeen 28:196+ Ap '69
Art of listening to children; with group-discussion program. Y. Postelle. il Parents Mag 44:58-9+, 76 Ap '69
Between parent and child. H. G. Ginott. McCalls 96:40+ Mr; 40+ Ap; 40 Jl; 40 Ag; 36+ S; 97:42+ O; 35+ N; 14+ D '69
Between parent and teenager; excerpt. H. Ginott. il McCalls 96:78-9+ My; 48+ Je '69
Can parents and teenagers negotiate? with study-discussion program. by C. Smallenburg and H. Smallenburg. D. B. Harris. bibliog il PTA Mag 63:2-5, 37 My '69
Diahann Carroll's juggling act. R. Hochstein. il Good H 168:38+ My '69
Father and the fathers. M. M. Shideler. Chr Cent 86:1061-4 Ag 13 '69
Fathers' hour; maternity ward at Manhattan's Flower and Fifth avenue hospitals. il Good H 169:22+ Jl '69
Gee, mother, you're wonderful! D. M. Odean. Farm J 93:51 My '69
Growing away from home. D. A. Sugarman and R. Hochstein. il Seventeen 27:132-3+ N '68
How jet-set parents wreck their children's lives; interview. ed. by D. C. Disney. P. Popenoe. il Ladies Home J 86:12+ S '69
How to get along with your teen-ager; excerpts from Between parent and teen-ager. H. G. Ginott. Read Digest 95:55-8 Jl '69
How to help your child do well in school. il U S News 67:49-50 O 6 '69
If I had another chance at fatherhood. C. W. Chilman. il Todays Health 47:56-9+ Ap '69
Is your child proud of you? with group-discussion program. A. Loomer. il Parents Mag 44:16-17, 50-1+ Ja '69
Must mother be around all day? with study-discussion program. by R. Strang. M. W. Piers and B. Bowman. bibliog il PTA Mag 63:26-8, 34 Ap '69
My mother loved me! My mother loved me! L. Stinnett. il McCalls 96:70-1+ My '69
Now, while there's time. E. Bartley. il Read Digest 95:101-4 D '69
Oedipal revolt and the Laius reaction. S. Alsop. Newsweek 73:112 Je 23 '69

One thing sure, parenthood today is no bore! R. C. Albrook. Fortune 79:92-3+ Ja '69
Pampered neglected child. W. Kempler. il Todays Health 47:46-9 Mr '69
Parent and child, the hazards of equality. T. J. Cottle. il Sat R 52:16-19+ F 1 '69
Parent teachers. C. N. Pickell. Chr Today 14: 10-12 D 19 '69
Parents and privacy. J. Brothers. Good H 168:50+ F '69
Parents and teachers are greasing the skids. A. Giglio. Todays Ed 58:30 D '69
Parents' guide to the age of revolt. D. Barr. il McCalls 97:73+ O '69
Parents talk about sex. H. Ginott. Vogue 154:103+ O 15 '69
Perfect parent; survey of children's opinions. S. Blum. il McCalls 96:51+ Ag '69
Raising children by instinct. B. Spock. Redbook 133:24+ Ag '69
Right to be different. il Good H 168:14+ F '69
Salute to parents from teachers everywhere: if the shoe fits. bibliog il Todays Ed 58: 41-8 S '69
Son's discovery; excerpts from Ox bells and fireflies. E. Buckler. il Read Digest 95:127-30 N '69
State of the boy, 1969; findings of study by Daniel Offer. R. Kramer. il N Y Times Mag p97+ Mr 30 '69; Discussion. p 14+ Ap 27 '69
Suddenly it happens to you; the doctor makes an unexpected diagnosis. A. Kulish. McCalls 96:58+ Mr '69
Suddenly it happens to you; they're talking about your daughter. McCalls 96:50+ Jl '69
Trouble with parents is: young people's talkin; ed. by S. Reice. il McCalls 96:70-1+ S '69
Turning the world around; adaptation of address. May 1969. G. A. Olds. il PTA Mag 63:2-4 Je '69
When fathers drop out. M. R. Leonard. il N Y Times Mag p81+ Ap 20 '69
Why it's hard to love your parents. S. Blum. il Redbook 133:84-5+ My '69
Why students act that way; a Gallup study. il U S News 66:34-5 Je 2 '69
Why the generation gap? H. Brown. Sat R 52:20-2 Jl 19 '69
Why they can't talk to us. M. J. Bienvenu. il N Y Times Mag p87+ S 14 '69
Why you should make your kids miserable. P. Bracken. Redbook 133:69+ Ag '69
Young and the old; notes on a new history; excerpts from History and survival. R. J. Lifton. Atlan 224:47-54 S; 82-8 O '69
Youngster who doesn't fit in. A. Loomer. il Parents Mag 44:35-7 D '69
Youth revolt; the future is now; excerpt from Culture and commitment. M. Mead. il Sat R 53:23-5+ Ja 10 '70
See also
Broken homes
Children—Management and training
Family life
Fathers
Love, Maternal
Youth-adult relationship

Anecdotes, facetiae, satire, etc.
We're rotten, Laura. Rotten to the core. R. Baker. Life 66:18D F 21 '69

PARENT education
What schools can do about child abuse. D. G. Gil. Am Ed 5:2-4 Ap '69

PARENT participation in school management. See School management and organization—Parent participation

PARENT-pupil-teacher conferences. See Educational guidance

PARENT-teacher associations. See Parents and teachers associations

PARENT-teacher cooperation. See School and the home

PARENTAL love. See Love

PARENTHOOD, Planned. See Birth control

PARENTHOOD, Training for. See Parent education

PARENTS
Parenthood should wait! M. M. Hunt. Read Digest 94:49-50+ F '69
See also
Family
Mothers
Parent education
Stepparents

PARENTS and teachers associations
Constructive in controversy. E. Hendryson. PTA Mag 63:2-3 F '69
Getting through to the establishment; with study-discussion program. by E. Harris and D. Harris. M. Essex. bibliog il PTA Mag 64:5+, 35-6 N '69
Inaugural; address, May 21, 1969. P. B. Price. PTA Mag 64:18-19 S '69

PARENTS and teachers associations—*Cont.*
Is your PTA sagging? H. W. Quinton and R. B. Shuman. Clear House 43:307-11 Ja '69
Letter and spirit in the PTA. E. Hendryson. PTA Mag 63:20-1 Ap '69
Membership proclamation; right for the time. P. B. Price. PTA Mag 64:20-1 O '69
Noninterference in an interfering age. E. Hendryson. PTA Mag 63:16-18 Mr '69
PTA; where the action is. See issues of PTA magazine
Value of the PTA. E. S. Hendryson; C. A. Mowrey; D. Rich. Todays Ed 58:31-3 My '69
See also
National congress of parents and teachers

Student participation
Students in the PTA; with study-discussion program, by C. Smallenburg and H. Smallenburg. bibliog il PTA Mag 63:4-7, 36 F '69

PARENTS' magazine
Parents' magazine awards for outstanding service to children. il Parents Mag 44:62 Ja '69
See also
Youth group achievement awards
PARENTS responsibility (law) See Liability (law)
PARENTS school visiting. See School and the home
PARIN, Vasilii
Outer space helps man. Space World F-10-70:38-9 O '69
PARIS, Brenda
Brenda and the bandits. B. Sheridan. il por Good H 168:12+ Mr '69
PARIS, Harold
Final negation: Harold Paris' Koddesh-Koddashim. P. Selz. il por Art in Am 57:62-7 Mr '69
PARIS, James D.
APBA action report. See issues of Motor boating
PARIS, Wayne
Yvette and Paris. W. Como. il por Dance Mag 43:20 Ag '69
PARIS

Airports
All Orly needs now is a 747. il Bsns W p 106-7 N 15 '69
Orly to get special 747 passenger areas. il Aviation W 90:40-1 F 10 '69
Paris airport system plans are drafted. Aviation W 91:147+ O 20 '69
Paris delays laid to lack of controllers, congestion. D. E. Fink. Aviation W 91:139+ O 20 '69

Architecture
Paris: the Quartier du Marais. M. Minost. il Antiques 96:406-8 S '69

Art
Paris. M. Conil-Lacoste. See issues of Art news

Clubs
Travellers of Paris. il Esquire 71:106-7 F '69

Description
Cognoscenti abroad. James Jones's Paris. A. Goodfriend. il Sat R 52:36-8 F 1 '69
Down the old Parisian paths. D. Butwin. il Sat R 52:24-6 Je 28 '69
Two cities of light. M. Gough. il House B 111:80+ S '69

Galleries and museums
Paris gallery guide. C. Cutler. il Art in Am 57:88-93 Mr '69

Hospitals
American medicine's outpost in France. J. H. Winchester. il Todays Health 47:44-7 Ag '69

Hotels, restaurants, etc.
Brasserie Lipp, rendezvous for le tout Paris. W. Root. il Holiday 46:66-7+ O '69
When in Rome, do as the roamers do: eight writers tell where they sleep, eat and shop; symposium; with editorial comment. Esquire 72:124-7+, 198-9 O '69

Libraries
See also
American library in Paris

Maps
Anecdotes, facetiae, satire, etc.
Mark Twain's map of Paris; reprint. M. Twain. il UNESCO Courier 22:55 Ag '69

Markets
Au revoir les Halles. R. Bernier. il Travel & Camera 32:54-5 My '69

Belly leaves but the heart remains; move of les Halles. R. B. Stolley. il Life 66: 89-90 Mr 14 '69
Letter from Paris; les Halles in Rungis. Genêt. New Yorker 45:118-19 Ap 5 '69

Music
Report: Paris; production at Opéra Comique. D. Stevens. il Opera N 34:28-9 S 6 '69
Report: Paris; production of Puccini's La fanciulla del West. D. Stevens. Opera N 33: 27 Je 14 '69
Report: Paris; productions at Opéra comique. D. Stevens. Opera N 33:33 Mr 1 '69
Report: production of Les Troyens. D. Stevens. il Opera N 34:33-4 Ja 10 '70
Unknown opera: Théâtre national de l'opera. S. L. Fogel. il Opera N 34:8-13 D 6 '69

Newspapers
As Le Monde turns. il Time 94:36 D 26 '69
Inside France; English-language edition of Le Monde. Time 93:60 My 16 '69
Letter from Paris; Le Monde's new Weekly selection of its news in English translation. Genêt. New Yorker 45:133-4 N 1 '69
Revolt of the editors; Figaro strike. Newsweek 73:84 Je 2 '69
Successful sobriety; Le Monde's new editor. il Newsweek 75:43 Ja 5 '70

Notre Dame (cathedral)
Notre-Dame of Paris. W. A. H. Birnie. il Read Digest 95:184-6+ Ag '69
Paris; peace talks, and the flying of the Viet Cong flag. il Life 66:54-8 F 7 '69

Parks and playgrounds
Paris park with a view; Parc des Chaumont. il Sunset 143:66 N '69

Theater
European literary scene; Jean Mercure's production of L'engrenage. R. J. Clements. Sat R 52:27 My 3 '69
Folies Bergère; second hundred years. W. Root. il Holiday 45:92-3+ Ap '69
PARIS, Battle of, 1944
Story behind the liberation of Paris a quarter of a century ago. L. Collins and D. Lapierre. il N Y Times Mag p46-7+ S 7 '69; Reply. F. L. Howley. p22+ O 5 '69
PARIS air and space show. See Aviation—Exhibitions
PARIS fashion shows. See Fashion shows
PARIS international air show. See Aviation—Exhibitions
PARIS Opéra. See Opera houses
PARIS peace talks. See Vietnamese war, 1957——Peace and mediation—Negotiation meetings, May 1968—
PARISHES
Too much money. R. Haughton. Cath World 209:101-2 Je '69
PARISIANS

Anecdotes, facetiae, satire, etc.
Full blown roses. M. W. Wright. il Har Yrs 9: 30-1 My '69
PARK, Chung Hee
President Nixon and President Park of the Republic of Korea hold talks at San Francisco; welcoming statement, exchange of remarks, toasts together with joint statement, August 21 and 22, 1969. Dept State Bul 61:239-43 S 15 '69
We take the U.S. at its word; a Pacific power, here to stay; interview, ed. by K. M. Chrysler. por U S News 67:23-5 Ag 25 '69

about
Full circle for Park. por Time 94:29 O 24 '69
Lease on the Blue House. por Time 94:33 Ag 8 '69
Park stacks the cards. il por Newsweek 74: 58 O 27 '69
President; U.S. visit. il por Newsweek 74:19 S 1 '69
South Korea and the US. A. Campbell. New Repub 160:9-11 Je 7 '69
PARK, Ed
Float trip for moose. Outdoor Life 144:50-3+ S '69
PARK, James M.
Songs of the pioneers. Américas 21:21-8 My '69
PARK, Jeanne S.
They're sharing something special. Am Ed 5:23-5 Mr '69
PARK, P. Kilho, and others
Carbon dioxide partial pressure in the Columbia River. bibliog Science 166:867-8 N 14 '69

PARK administration. See Parks—Management

PARK and recreation consultants. See Recreation consultants

PARK buildings
New building designs for park, recreation and camping areas. il Parks & Rec 4:38-9 My '69

PARK crimes. See Crime and criminals—United States

PARK employees
How parks build men; Napa, Calif. R. G. Pelusi. il Am City 84:80-2 Je '69
Survey of retired recreation and park professionals; statistics and advice. G. D. Butler. il Parks & Rec 4:21-5+ Je '69

Salaries, allowances, etc.
NRPA acts on salary structures; minimum entry salary. S. G. Lutzin. Parks & Rec 4: 47+ Mr '69

PARK management. See Parks—Management

PARK naturalists. See Naturalists

PARK police. See United States—National park service—Park police

PARK rangers. See Forest rangers

PARK rangers wives. See Forest rangers wives

PARK roads. See National parks and reserves — Roads

PARK seed company
Getting to know the growers; flower days at Park seed co. il Home Gard 56:50-1 Jl '69

PARK shelters. See Shelters

PARK vandalism. See Vandalism

PARKE, Robert V.
Search for a trophy. Outdoor Life 144:38-41+ S '69

PARKER, Alfred
Government finances and citizen responsibility. bibliog f Ann Am Acad 379:123-31 S '68

PARKER, Frank J.
Legal aid for the poor; new directions. America 121:421-2 N 8 '69

PARKER, Franklin
1969 as a centennial year in the history of education. Sch & Soc 97:112-14 F '69

PARKER, Garland G.
Statistics of attendance in American universities and colleges, 1968-69. Sch & Soc 97: 43-61, 118 Ja-F '69

PARKER, Henry S. Jr
Make-ready gap. Yachting 125:76-8+ Je; 126: 70-1+ Jl '69

PARKER, John Conway
They work at rescue. Motor B 123:101+ Ap '69

PARKER, John S.
Elk hunting aces. Field & S 74:78-80+ S '69
Horse sense. Field & S 74:72-3+ Je '69

PARKER, Marlon H.
Care-Ring; interview. New Yorker 45:30-1 Je 14 '69

PARKER, P. L. See Sever, J. jt. auth.

PARKER, Patricia
What comes after Mother Goose? Ed Digest 35:46-9 O '69

PARKER, Ralph
Joan Bodger incident; statement; October 1969, ed. by G. R. Shields. ALA Bul 63: 1561-3 D '69

PARKER, Sanford S. and others
Business roundup. See issues of Fortune

PARKER, Stephen
The return; poem. Nation 208:156 F 3 '69

PARKER, Thomas
Troop withdrawal, the initial step; story. Harper 239:61-8 Ag '69

PARKING, Automobile. See Automobile parking

PARKING garages. See Garages

PARKING lots. See Automobile parking

PARKING meters
Meter revenue builds parking garages; Decatur, Ill. J. W. Loftus. il Am City 84:142 F '69
Token-dispensing parking meters; Barnesboro, Pa. G. Atkins. il Am City 84:125-6 Je '69

PARKINSON, C. Northcote
Proof of Parkinson. Time 94:66 Jl 18 '69

PARKINSON, John, Jr
Bay and the Sound; excerpts. Motor B 123:57-63 Je '69
Gales at sea. Yachting 125:57-9+ F '69

PARKINSON'S disease
Amantadine for Parkinsonism. Sci N 95:550 Je 7 '69

Antiparkinsonian drugs: inhibition of dopamine uptake in the corpus striatum as a possible mechanism of action. J. T. Coyle and S. H. Snyder. bibliog il Science 166:899-901 N 14 '69
Correcting brain chemistry. Time 94:77-8 N 28 '69
m-Hydroxyphenylacetic acid formation from L-dopa in man: suppression by neomycin. M. Sandler. and others. bibliog il Science 166:1417-18 D 12 '69
Pill that lets shaking palsy patients eat jell-o: L-dopa. J. E. Randal. il Todays Health 48:34-7+ Ja '70
Progress with L-dopa. il Newsweek 74:116 O 6 '69
Renin-aldosterone system in Parkinson's disease. A. Barbeau and others. bibliog il Science 165:291-2 Jl 18 '69

PARKS, Bert
There she is, Miss America. P. Ryan. il por Sports Illus 31:70-2+ O 6 '69

PARKS, F. Newton
Survival of the European headquarters. Harvard Bsns R 47:79-84 Mr '69

PARKS, Gordon, 1912-
Boy's life. J. Morgenstern. il por Newsweek 74:74 Ag 11 '69

PARKS, Gordon, 1935?-
Gallery; photographs. Life 67:6-7 S 5 '69

PARKS, Henry G. Jr
Up and out. por Time 93:62 Ja 31 '69

PARKS, Martha Smith
Whatever happened to radio? Space World F-3-63:16-21 Mr '69

PARKS, Norman L.
Path to total destruction. Nation 208:153+ F 3 '69

PARKS, Rosa
Rosa Parks: she wouldn't move back. il por Sr Schol 94:6 My 9 '69

PARKS, Wally
Motor Trend interview. pors Motor T 21: 101-2+ O '69

PARKS
How parks will shape urban development. J. E. Curtis. il Am City 84:87-90 O '69
Microcosms in a world apart. P. H. Abelson. Science 165:853 Ag 29 '69
Parks and recreation. See issues of American city
Planning a neighborhood park. F. K. Dhainin. il Parks & Rec 4:69-70+ S '69
Tightened landscape. W. H. Whyte. il Horizon 11:66-73 Sum '69
See also
Island parks
Landscape architecture
National parks and reserves
Zoological gardens

Administration
See Parks—Management

Finance
Million-dollar ideas, for park and recreation departments. C. H. Odegaard. Parks & Rec 3:21+ O '68

Lighting
Multi-purpose lights for an all-purpose park; Evansville, Ind. L. Torgerson. il Am City 84:130 Je '69
New lights for a new park; Longmont, Colo. J. Pope. Am City 84:156 My '69

Maintenance
Contracting for maintenance. C. C. Clegg. Parks & Rec 4:29-30+ My '69
Maintenance cost control. R. L. Horney. Parks & Rec 4:17-18+ D '69
Park maintenance aided by modern equipment. R. D. Browne. il Parks & Rec 4: 40-1 Jl '69

Management
Computerized management; or, Jungle administration; using data processing in park administration, Vancouver, Wash. D. W. Bridges. il Parks & Rec 4:37-8+ D '69
Evaluation of park and recreation operations; who should do it? A. V. Sapora. bibliog il Parks & Rec 4:35-6+ D '69
Mike Frome; parks and people. M. Frome. Am For 75:3+ Ja '69
National forum; park and recreation standards. il Parks & Rec 4:39-46 Mr '69
Quandary on the campgrounds. H. Bloomfield. il Am For 75:4-7+ Jl '69
See also
Park employees

United States
Bird's eye view can help park officials. R. D. Buechner. il Parks & Rec 3:27-8+ N '68

PARKS—United States—*Continued*
Law and order in public parks. F. L. Campbell and others. il Parks & Rec 3:28-31+ D '68
Mini-park on private property; Cedarhurst, N.Y. il Am City 84:51 Ap '69
Park practice program is seeking new ideas. Parks & Rec 3:44 O '68
Puzzle of outdoor recreation. S. G. Ernst. il Cons 23:17-19+ Je '69
  See also
National parks and reserves—United States
National parks association
  also subhead Parks and playgrounds under names of cities, e.g. Stamford, Conn. —Parks and playgrounds

PARKWAY program. See Philadelphia—Education

PARKWAYS. See Express highways

PARLIAMENT, Members of. See Members of Parliament

PARLIAMENTARY elections. See Elections— Great Britain

PARMA (province)
Genetic drift in an Italian population. L. L. Cavalli-Sforza. il Sci Am 221:30-7 Ag '69

PARMA, Italy

Music
Report: Parma; production of Verdi's Stiffelio. J. C. Adams. Opera N 33:32 F 15 '69

PARMAR, Samuel
Unemployment or exile. UNESCO Courier 22:32-4 Jl '69

PARNES, Herbert S. and Spitz, R. S.
Conceptual framework for studying labor mobility; excerpt from address, August 1969. Mo Labor R 92:55-8 N '69

PAROCHETUS communis. See Shamrock pea

PAROCHIAL schools. See Church schools

PAROCHIAL schools, Catholic. See Catholic schools

PAROLE
Designing for change; problems of planned innovation in corrections. H. B. Bradley. bibliog f Ann Am Acad 381:89-98 Ja '69

PARRA, Mariano
Mariano Parra ballet espanol; Town Hall. M. Marks. Dance Mag 43:90+ My '69

PARRASCH, Suzy
Come soar with me. por Seventeen 28:108-9+ O '69

PARRICIDE in literature. See Literature— Themes

PARRISH, Karen, and Weldy, G. R.
Good scholarship; do students really care? Clear House 43:275-9 Ja '69

PARRISH, Patricia
How to help your child develop good study habits. Parents Mag 44:62-3+ Mr '69

PARROTS
Keas; those fine-feathered villains of New Zealand. il Sci Digest 65:69 My '69
Last parakeet; Carolina parakeet. G. Laycock. il Audubon 71:20-5 Mr '69
Polly wants a capsule; import regulations for psittacine birds. F. Littler. Sat R 52: 4+ N 15 '69

PARRY, Albert
Power was lying in the street; we picked it up. N Y Times Mag p30-1+ S 28; 61+ D 14 '69

PARRY, Jack
Call of the bugle. Field & S 74:70-1+ Je '69

PARS intermedia. See Pituitary body

PARSEGHIAN, Ara
Knute would have agreed. Ara. D. Jenkins. il por Sports Illus 31:26-8+ D 22 '69

PARSIPPANY, N.J.

Education
Parsippany dips a maobi in Asian studies. F. Sabin. il Am Ed 5:11-13 My '69

PARSLEY
With us, parsley is permanent! L. Riotte. il Org Gard & Farm 16:70-2 N '69

PARSONS, Cynthia
Teacher or student? Sch Arts 69:38-9 S '69

PARSONS, Donald F. and Akers, C. K.
Neutron diffraction of cell membranes (myelin) bibliog Science 165:1016-18 S 5 '69

PARSONS, James Benton
Ultimate in opportunity. J. Cass. Sat R 52:39 Ag 16 '69

PARSONS, James J.
Colombia. bibliog Focus 20:1-7 S '69

PARSONS, Marsells C. Jr
Denmark's nursery exhibits. Horticulture 46:32+ N '68

PARSONS. See Clergy

PARSONS college, Fairfield, Ia.
Life and hard times of Parsons college. J. D. Koerner. il Sat R 52:53-5+ Jl 19 '69

PART time employment
How to make money in your spare time. J. Kuh. il Ladies Home J 86:112 F; 31 Mr; 151 O; 151 N '69
Plant for part-timers; Control data's subassembly plant in St Paul ghetto. Bsns W p 108 N 29 '69
Wanted: one safari guide, part-time. J. Scobey and L. P. McGrath. il McCalls 96:16+ Ja '69

PART time teachers. See Teachers, Part time

PARTHENOGENESIS
  See also
Androgenesis

PARTICLE accelerators. See Accelerators (electrons, etc)

PARTICLES
  See also
Brownian movements
Dust
Micellar theory

PARTICLES (nuclear physics)
Elementary particles. G. Veneziano. bibliog il Phys Today 22:31-6 S '69
Exceeding the speed limit; debate over existence of particle that travels faster than light. il Time 93:42+ F 14 '69
Five cosmic events; quarks. Sci N 96:198-9 S '13 '69
Form factors of elementary particles. R. Wilson. bibliog il Phys Today 22:47-53 Ja '69
Fundamental particles at high energy; report of meeting. L. M. Brown. il Phys Today 22:115-17 Ap '69
Hark, hark, a quark? il Chem 42:24-5 N '69
Is this a quark I see before me? Australian experiment. G. B. Lubkin. il Phys Today 22:55+ O '69
Isaac Asimov explains; a sizable universe. I. Asimov. Sci Digest 66:88-9 N '69
Isaac Asimov explains; do antiparticles produce antienergy? I. A. Asimov. Sci Digest 66:80-1 S '69
Isaac Asimov explains; how fast is infinite speed? tachyons. I. Asimov. Sci Digest 66: 82-3 D '69
Isaac Asimov explains; traveling faster than light. I. Asimov. Sci Digest 66:74-5 Ag '69
Magnetic model of matter. J. Schwinger. bibliog il Science 165:757-61 Ag 22 '69
Mouse in the cathedral; Nobel prize in physics to M. Gell-Mann for discovery of new particles. Newsweek 74:70 N 10 '69
Nobel laureates in economics, chemistry, and physics. M. L. Goldberger. il Science 166: 720-2 N 7 '69
Order in the zoo; Nobel prize in physics to M. Gell-Mann for discovery of particles. Time 94:52 N 7 '69
Particle physicists exchange facts, models and speculations; report of meeting. D. B. Lichtenberg. il Phys Today 22:93+ N '69; Discussion. bibliog 22:47-52 D '69
Particles beyond the light barrier. O.-M. Bilaniuk and E. C. G. Sudarshan. bibliog il Phys Today 22:43-51 My '69
Particles through the looking glass; tachyons. D. E. Thomsen. il Sci N 95:196-7 F 22 '69
Physics behind the looking glass; tachyons. Chem 42:23 Ap '69
Quark hunt still fruitless. H. N. Schwartz. il Sci N 95:538 My 31 '69
Quarks Down Under? Physicists have reservations. R. W. Holcomb. Science 165:1340 S 26 '69
Quarks for neutrino-less fusion. Sci N 96:48 Jl 19 '69
Recent developments in particle physics; Nobel lecture, January 1969. L. W. Alvarez. bibliog il Science 165:1071-91 S 12 '69
Symmetries and quarks raise more questions than solutions; report of meeting. J. A. Campbell. Phys Today 22:93-5+ O '69
Toward a dynamic theory. Sci N 95:136 F 8 '69
Track of the quark. Time 94:57 S 12 '69
Two xis from Brookhaven; new particles predicted by eightfold way theory. Sci Am 220:48+ Mr '69
  See also
Mesons
Neutrinos
Neutrons
Nucleons
Polarization of particles
Positrons
Scattering (physics)

Acceleration
Serpukhov data suggest asymptopia may be further away than ever. G. B. Lubkin. bibliog Phys Today 22:57+ O '69

Detection
Nuclear tracks in solids. R. L. Fleischer and others. il Sci Am 220:30-9 Je '69

PARTICLES, Elementary. See Particles (nuclear physics)

PARTIES. See Children's parties; Entertaining

PARTIN, Edward Grady
Big shakedown in Baton Rouge. A. J. Reichley. il por Fortune 80:96-9+ Ag 1 '69

PARTITIONS
This kitchen's new divider island provides privacy, display space. il Sunset 142:95 F '69

PARTNERS; story. See Friedman, B. J.

PARTNERSHIP
See also
Farm partnership

PARTON, Margaret
Personal history. Sa. R 52:44 O 4 '69

PARTRIDGE, Don
Rosie side of the street. por Time 93:82 F 7 '69

PARTRIDGE, John W.
Multiplexing audio entertainment for the Boeing superjet. Electr World 82:40-1+ S '69

PARTRIDGE shooting
Coming of the hun; Hungarian partridge C. F. Waterman. il Field & S 74:49-52+ N '69
Partridge in an olive tree. W. Page. il Field & S 73:70-1+ Ap '69
Smoothing the rough chukar road. F. A. Tinker. il Field & S 74:66-7+ N '69
See also
Grouse shooting

PARTY cards. See Place cards

PARTY favors
Happy party potpourri. il Seventeen 28:162+ F '69

PARTY toys. See Toys

PARVIN, Albert
Now, Douglas' dealings. il por Time 93:23 Je 6 '69

PARVIN, Stuart A.
Miniaturia. See issues of Hobbies

PARVIN-Dohrmann company
Parvin who? il Newsweek 73:72+ Je 2 '69
Rise and fall of Parvin/Dohrmann. il Fortune 80:163-4+ D '69

PARVIN foundation
Call Marty; investigation of Parvin-Dohrmann stock. Newsweek 74:36 O 27 '69
Justice Douglas's letter. Newsweek 73:36-7 Je 9 '69
Now, Douglas' dealings. il Time 93:23 Je 6 '69
Parvin who? il Newsweek 73:72+ Je 2 '69
Voloshen connection; investigation of Parvin/Dohrmann stock. il Time 94:26-7 O 24 '69

PAS de deux; la source; ballet. See Ballets—Criticisms

PASADENA art museum
Art bowl; new PAM. il Newsweek 74:138 D 8 '69

PASCAL, Marie Zimmerman
Unusual technique. J. Jellico. il Am Artist 33:32-7 N '69

PASCHAL, John
Steel shelters defy vandals. Am City 84:96-7 F '69

PASCOE, Jean
How weight watchers lose weight. Read Digest 95:143-4+ Jl '69

PASOLINI, Pier Paolo
According to Pasolini. L. J. Berry. Commonweal 89:706-7 Mr 7 '69
An ancient woman. J. Buckley. il por Opera N 34:8-13 D 13 '69
Pasolini's Teorema. America 120:518 My 3 '69

The PASS; story. See Neugeboren, J.

PASS CHRISTIAN, Miss.
It felt like fifteen or twenty tornadoes had caught us. H. P. Leifermann. il Newsweek 74:18 S 1 '69
U.S. journal: problems in recovering from hurricane Camille. C. Trillin. New Yorker 45:175-6+ N 29 '69

PASSAGEWAYS. See Halls

PASSAMAQUODDY Indians
Brothers of Passamaquodia: the royal screwing of the Passamaquodia. D. Welsh. Ramp Mag 7:98-103 Ja 25 '69

PASSANTINO, Myrtle
[Book review] America 120:256-7 Mr 1 '69

PASSENGER fares. See Airlines—Fares

PASSENGER loading systems. See Airports—Equipment

PASSENGER traffic (railroads). See Railroads—Passenger traffic

PASSIFLORA. See Passionflowers

PASSING through from exotic places; drama. See Ribman, R.

PASSION music
Modern Polish passion; premiere of Passion and death of Our Lord Jesus Christ according to St Luke. J. Evenson. Chr Today 13:39 Mr 28 '69
See also
Phonograph records—Passion music

PASSION plays
U.S. journal: Eureka Springs, Ark; site of Christ of the Ozarks statue and a Passion play. C. Trillin. New Yorker 45:69-70+ Jl 26 '69

PASSIONFLOWERS
Passion vine can be started now. A. Langford. il Home Gard 56:68 S '69

PASSIVE seismic experiment package. See Moon—Exploration—Equipment

PASSOVER
Radical Haggadah for Passover. A. Waskow. il Ramp Mag 7:25-33 Ap '69

PASSPORTS
U.S. passports remain invalid for travel to certain areas. Dept State Bul 61:362-3 O 27 '69
See also
United States—State, Department of—Passport division

PAST, The
Activism and the rejection of history; excerpt from The unexpected universe. L. Eiseley. Science 165:129 Jl 11 '69
In search of the past. P. Schrag. Sat R 52:24 S 13 '69

PAST, present and always; story. See McInerny, R.

PASTA. See Cookery, Italian

PASTAN, Linda
Each autumn; poem. Nation 209:546 N 17 '69
New England covered bridge; poem. America 120:307 Mr 15 '69

PASTED pictures. See Collage

PASTEL drawing
Before the deluge; pastels and watercolors by 18th-century French masters. J. Ashberg. il Art N 68:54-5+ N '69
Daniel E. Greene; pastellist. H. Rogoff. il Am Artist 33:80-8 N '69

PASTEL painting. See Pastel drawing

PASTEURELLA pestis
Plague bacillus: survival within host phagocytes. W. A. Janssen and M. J. Surgalla. bibliog il Science 163:950-3 F 28 '69

PASTIMES. See Amusements

PASTORAL counseling
Minister's workshop. See issues of Christianity today
Problems in program evaluation: a ministers' workshop. E. R. Oetting and others. Ment Hy 53:214-17 Ap '69
Psychiatric consultation to the clergy; a report on a group experience. L. H. Rockland. bibliog Ment Hy 53:205-7 Ap '69
Psychoanalytic notes on the disavowal of priestly authority. G. A. Benson. Chr Cent 86:738-41 My 28 '69; Reply. D. S. Smolen. 86:1322-3 O 15 '69

PASTORAL letters
Fifth mark; recent Pastoral on tourism in Guideline program. Commonweal 90:580 S 26 '69

PASTORAL psychology
See also
Pastoral counseling

PASTORAL theology
Theology of pastoral action. by K. Rahner. Review
America 120:312 Mr 15 '69. J. Gallen
Unresponsive pew. J. Richie. Chr Cent 86:1278-81 O 8 '69; Discussion. 86:1458+, 1549 N 12, D 3 '69

PASTORE, John O.
Christmas list. J. Fischer. Harper 239:26 D '69
Panic in TV censorship. J. Barthel. il Life 67:51-4 Ag 1 '69
Pastore bill. Nation 209:132 Ag 25 '69
Senator Pastore's TV proposal. America 120:440 Ap 12 '69

PASTORS. See Clergy

PASTRAMI. See Cookery—Meat

PASTRY
At last an easy strudel. il Sunset 142:156+ Mr '69
Bear claws, using a mix. il Sunset 142:154 Mr '69
Cook's pride; pie, cakes and cookies. J. Hewitt. il N Y Times Mag p90+ N 9 '69
Dazzling Danish pastry, from frozen puff patties and fruit. il Sunset 143:190+ N '69
Emperor's pastry shop; Zauner of Bad Ischl. J. Friedberg. il Travel & Camera 32:60-1+ Jl '69

PASTRY—*Continued*
Four classic French pastries. H. McCully and J. Pépin. il House B 111:108-10+ Mr '69
Pastry finishes. il Bet Hom & Gard 47:126 O '69
Picnic loaves and pastries. L. Seibert. il House & Gard 135:101-3+ Je '69
Strudels! M. Happel. il Ladies Home J 86:114-15+ N '69
Tiffany's on a tray; French pastry. il Mc-Calls 96:136-40+ Ap '69
Why Viennese women eat pastry every afternoon. J. Wechsberg. McCalls 96:71+ Jl '69
See also
Pie
Tarts

PATCH, F. William
Unusual window box plants. Horticulture 47:46 Jl '69

PATCH, Margaret Merwin
Travelogue. Craft Horiz 29:32-9+ S '69 (to be cont)

PATCHWORK
More about patchwork. il House & Gard 136:150-1 N '69
Patchwork beauties. il Redbook 134:60-1+ Ja '70

PATENT cooperation treaty. See Patents—International aspects

PATENT laws and legislation
Compromise on patent reform. Bsns W p23 Ag 9 '69
More things change; McClellan bill. Sci N 96:146-7 Ag 23 '69
Prospects grow dimmer for patent law reform. Bsns W p98 N 22 '69
See also
Patents—Licensing

PATENT lawyers
Choosing a career, patent law. H. E. Weisberger. il Chem 42:12-13 Mr '69

PATENT office (United States) See United States—Patent office

PATENTS
When patents go on parade; Patexpo '69. il Bsns W p 148+ S 13 '69
Zenith wins wedge of patent pool pie. Bsns W p39 My 24 '69
See also
Drugs—Patents
Electronics—Patents
Glassware—Patents
Patent laws and legislation
United States—Patent office

Infringement
Photon claims victory in suit against Mergenthaler. Pub W 196:45-6 S 15 '69

International aspects
Final touches on a draft; United international bureau for the protection of intellectual property sponsors treaty. Sci N 95:596 Je 21 '69
Foe of patent reform displaces the reformer; W. Schuyler takes over from Edward Brenner. il Bsns W p 167-8 My 10 '69
Patent and copyright conventions transmitted to the Senate; message March 12, 1969. R. M. Nixon. Dept State Bul 60:298 Ap 7 '69

Licensing
Assault on the drug jam; patent policy. il Sci N 96:325 O 11 '69
Inventor's best friends; patent middlemen. il Bsns W p 182+ S 20 '69

PATERSON, Philip Y. and Drobish, D. G.
Cyclophosphamide: effect on experimental allergic encephalomyelitis in Lewis rats. bibliog Science 165:191-2 Jl 11 '69

PATERSON, Thomas G.
Isolationism revisited. Nation 209:166-9 S 1 '69

PATERSON parchment paper company
Parchment paper lion. R. Levy. il Duns R 93:52-4 Ja '69

PATEXPO '69. See Inventions—Exhibitions

PATHOGENIC microorganisms. See Microorganisms, Pathogenic

PATHOLOGICAL psychology. See Psychology, Pathological

PATHOLOGY
See also
Paleopathology

PATHS. See Garden walks; Trails; Walks (paths)

PATIENT and nurse. See Nurse and patient

PATIENTS; story. See Strong, J.

PATIENTS, Hospital. See Sick, The

PATIENTS and physicians. See Physicians and patients

PATIL, K. C. See Matsumura, F. jt. auth.

PATIL, Sadashiv Kamoji
Return of the enemies. il por Time 93:35 My 23 '69

PATIN, Henry A.
Inqui 67: some reflections on the Lyndian heresy. bibliog f Sch & Soc 97:98-100 F '69

PATIO furniture. See Furniture, Outdoor

PATIOS. See Outdoor rooms

PATMAN, Wright
Excerpt from testimony before House committee on ways and means, February 18, 1969. Cong Digest 48:148+ My '69

about
Dog bites man. Newsweek 73:90+ My 12 '69
Last of the great Populists takes on the foundations, the banks, the Federal reserve, the Treasury. R. Sherrill. il pors N Y Times Mag p24-5+ Mr 16 '69
New class war. J. Hart. il Nat R 21:896-901+ S 9 '69
Patman's complaint. Newsweek 73:23-4 Mr 3 '69

PATON, Alan
Song of sorrow and thanksgiving. E. Callan. por Sat R 52:31-2+ N 8 '69

PATRIARCHS (Bible)
See also
Abraham (patriarch)

PATRICHI, Mihai D.
LeMay disputes his boss's right to fire him. Bsns W p 136 F 22 '69

PATRICK, Saint
Who was St Patrick? il Good H 168:200 Mr '69

PATRICOF, Alan J.
Daring young men of acquisitions. J. Poindexter. il por Duns R 92:26-9+ D '68

PATRICOF, Pat
Finland. Travel 131:34-9+ My '69

PATRIOT for me; drama. See Osborne, J.

PATRIOTISM
Is patriotism dead? Chr Today 13:20 Jl 4 '69
Is patriotism dying? il Nations Bsns 57:40 Jl '69
Patriotism revisited; address, September 17, 1969. J. A. Howard. Vital Speeches 36:24-9 O 15 '69
See also
Americanism
Citizenship
Loyalty

PATROL boats, Coast guard. See United States—Coast guard—Boats

PATROL boats, Navy. See United States—Navy—Boats

PATROL cars. See Automobiles, Police

PATROL'S automatic telecommunications rapid on-line system. See Police communication systems

PATRON saints. See Saints

PATRONAGE, Political
End to politics in postal system? il U S News 66:16 F 17 '69
Job drought; GOP patronage flap. Newsweek 73:28+ Mr 10 '69
Politics of patronage; spoils system. il Sr Schol 94:7-10 My 9 '69
See also
Nepotism

PATRONAGE of opera. See Opera patronage

PATT, Harvey M. See Maloney, M. A. jt. auth.

PATTEN, Duncan T.
Forest succession in Yellowstone National Park. Nat Parks 43:21-2 S '69

PATTERN perception
Pattern perception; AAAS symposium, December 29-30, 1969. P. C. Vitz. il Science 166:654-5 O 31 '69

PATTERN pictures. See Photography, Artistic

PATTERN recognition computers. See Perceptrons

PATTERSON, Charles
Stop, listen, and look. pors Outdoor Life 144:68-9+ O '69

PATTERSON, Ernest Minor
Obituary
Ann Am Acad 386:168 N '69

PATTERSON, Franklin
Other voices, other views. Sat R 53:74 Ja 10 '70

PATTERSON, Herbert Parsons
Power shift at the Chase? por Bsns W p30-1 Ja 10 '70

PATTERSON, Jack E.
Black power, municipal style. Commonweal 90:477-8 Ag 8 '69

PATTERSON, Lindsay
New home, new troupe, new play; reprint. Negro Hist Bul 32:18-19 Ap '69

PATTISON, William D.
Collector's choice; the photographs of A. J. Russell. Am West 6:20-3 My '69

PATTON, George Smith, 1885-1945
Fateful friendship. S. E. Ambrose. il pors Am Heritage 20:40-1+ Ap '69

PATTON, Stuart
Milk; with biographical sketch. Sci Am 221: 16, 58-62+ bibliog(p 140) Jl '69

PATTON, Thomas F.
Thomas F. Patton of Republic steel; interview. por Nations Bsns 57:54-9 O '69

PAUL, Saint

Teaching

In praise of Paul. R. Haughton. Cath World 210:101-2 D '69

PAUL VI, pope
Crisis of hope? Commonweal 89:488-9 Ja 17 '69
How Pope reacted to bids for change. il por U S News 67:13 N 10 '69
Little and late. Commonweal 90:187-8 My 2 '69
Papal decree on church ritual. U S News 66:16 My 12 '69
Paul VI and conscience. America 120:236 Mr 1 '69
Paul VI and violence. P. J. Riga. por Cath World 208:251-4 Mr '69
Pope as Hamlet. J. H. Knox. il Nat R 21: 1058-60 O 21 '69
Pope: firm in face of challenge. il por U S News 67:18 O 20 '69
Pope takes on a leading critic. U S News 67:10 Jl 7 '69
Pope's concern: church rebellion. U S News 66:16 Ap 14 '69
Pope's firm hand. R. Meachum. New Repub 161:15-16 N 22 '69
Princely promotions. il Time 93:62 Ap 4 '69
Problems of the papacy. Commonweal 90:132-3 Ap 18 '69
Roman Synod: speaking with candor to the Pope. B. Bastien. Chr Today 14:36-7 N 21 '69
Scandal and schism. il por Newsweek 73:95 Ap 14 '69
Tribute from an atheist. America 120:292 Mr 15 '69

Visit to Geneva, 1969

Church unity: the Pope's view. il por U S News 66:18 Je 23 '69
Our name is Peter. il por Time 93:70 Je 20 '69
Pope goes to Geneva. America 120:516 My 3 '69
Pope in Geneva: milestone or millstone? D. Foster. Chr Today 13:36-7 Jl 4 '69
Sign in Geneva. il por Newsweek 73:65-6 Je 23 '69
Together in spirit. G. Murray. Chr Cent 86: 931-2 Jl 9 '69

Visit to Uganda, 1969

Drumming in the Pope. il por Newsweek 74: 45-6 Ag 11 '69
Joy and frustration in Uganda. Chr Cent 86: 1058 Ag 13 '69
Papal sojourn in Africa. America 121:80 Ag 16 '69
Pope to visit Uganda in July. America 120: 385+ Ap 5 '69
Pope visits Uganda. il por Chr Today 13:33 Ag 22 '69
Pope's peace trip to black Africa. il por U S News 67:14 Ag 11 '69
Sacred safari for the Pope. il pors Time 94: 64 Ag 8 '69
Uganda awaits the Pope. il Newsweek 74:67 Ag 4 '69
Why the Pope is going to Africa. U S News 67:7 Ag 4 '69

PAUL, Leslie
Christian faith and secular faiths. Chr Cent 86:477-81 Ap 9 '69

PAUL, Richard W.
Somebody else's backyard; welfare and dissent. por Time 95:12 Ja 5 '70

PAUL, Robert S.
Saluting the sects. Chr Cent 86:685-6 My 14 '69

PAUL, Sherman
Something for everybody. Nation 209:672-3 D 15 '69

PAUL, William
Shoo-in for a young shoe pitcher. Sports Illus 31:18-19 Ag 18 '69

PAUL, William J. jr, and others
Job enrichment pays off. Harvard Bsns R 47:61-78 Mr '69

PAUL Bernat collection. See Art—Private collections

PAUL Revere corporation-Avco corporation merger. See Insurance companies—Consolidations and mergers

PAUL Revere of Boston; drama. See Kane, E. B.

PAUL Taylor dance company
Paul Taylor dance company, Brooklyn academy of music. J. Anderson. Dance Mag 43: 79-80 Ja '69
Paul Taylor dance co; NY city center. J. Anderson. Dance Mag 43:32 Jl '69

PAULEY petroleum, incorporated
To expand, sell the company; Rochester-Pauley petroleum merger. il Bsns W p 168+ O 18 '69

PAULING, Linus
Nuclear weapons and world sanity; excerpts from address, reprint. UNESCO Courier 22: 43-4+ Ag '69

PAULOWNIA
Growing a 16-foot shade tree in a single season. V. A. Croley. il Org Gard & Farm 16:108-12 Mr '69

PAULSON, Carl
Glass medallions of Carl Paulson. J. Canavan. il pors Am Artist 33:22-5 Ag '69

PAULSON, F. M.
Boating. See issues of Field & stream

PAULY, Franz
Year's end in Prague. America 120:135-8 F 1 '69

PAULY, Ira B.
Men who would be women. Sat R 52:73-8 O 4 '69

PAUSTOVSKII, Konstantin Georgievich
Isaac Babel talks about writing; excerpts from Years of hope. Nation 208:406-7 Mr 31 '69
Shades of Gogol in the 1930s. S. Heitman. Sat R 52:50 My 17 '69

PAVALON, Wes
Now he gets to shoot. P. Putnam. il pors Sports Illus 30:56-63 F 24 '69

PAVEMENT markings. See Traffic markings

PAVEMENTS
Handsome garden paths and walkways. P. Oldale. il Pop Mech 131:162-7+ My '69
Paving: theme and variations. il Sunset 143: 92 Jl '69
Street paving spurs community improvements; Springfield, Ill. F. G. Madonia. il Am City 84:71-2+ Ap '69
See also
Airports—Surfaces
Streets

Heating

Snow-free flagstone walk. il Mech Illus 65: 116-17 F '69
Snowmelting vs. serpentine street. il Am City 84:40 Ja '69

Maintenance and repair

Simplified crack sealer wins cash award; San Jose, Calif. il Am City 84:28 Ja '69
To remove moss from paving. Sunset 142:116 My '69
See also
Pavements—Surface treatment
Streets—Maintenance and repair

Slipperiness

Skidding will be scrutinized. il Am City 84:25 Jl '69

Surface treatment

Merchants in particular notice the difference; asbestos-asphalt for paving; Ventura, Calif. P. S. Pyles. il Am City 84:54 D '69
Paving cures dust and drainage ills; Albion, Neb. J. Lough. il Am City 84:97-8 Jl '69
Rubber stretches roadway life; Santa Fe, N.M. il Am City 84:24 F '69

Testing

Pavements tested for giant transports. J. W. Carter. il Aviation W 90:84-5 Mr 31 '69
Skidding will be scrutinized. il Am City 84: 25 Jl '69

Traffic lines

See Traffic markings

PAVEMENTS, Concrete
Concrete streets constructed in stages; Lake Winnebago, Mo. J. Hart. il Am City 84: 104+ My '69
Redwood frames a concrete walk. il Sunset 143:89 Jl '69
Want a patio? cast the tiles indoors. R. Day. il Pop Sci 194:172-6+ Ja '69

PAVIA, Philip
Five states of mind. il Art N 68:23-5+ My '69

PAVILIONS
Biggest big top; U.S. pavilion for Osaka's Expo 70. il Arch Forum 131:68-9 D '69

PAVLIK, John C.
Tea power. Sci Digest 65:72-6 Je '69
PAVLIK, Paul A.
Green dahlia? Org Gard & Farm 16:56-9 Mr '69
PAWLEY, Ray
Children's zoos. Parks & Rec 3:18-21+ N '68
PAWLIKOWSKI, John T.
Across a deep canyon. Commonweal 90:313-15+ My 30 '69
PAWLOWSKI, Robert S.
Men like Magellan; poem. Commonweal 91:407 Ja 9 '70
PAWPAWS. See Papaws
PAY-as-you see television. See Television broadcasting—Subscription programs
PAY differentials. See Wage differentials
PAY telephones. See Telephone
PAY television. See Television broadcasting—Subscription programs
PAYMENTS, Balance of. See Balance of payments
PAYNE, Daniel Alexander, bp
Daniel A. Payne and the A.M.E. general conference of 1888: a display of contrasts. C. Killian. bibliog por Negro Hist Bul 32:11-14 N '69
PAYNE, J. Barton
Bonanza in Old Testament studies. Chr Today 13:9-12 F 28 '69
PAYNE, Lee
Lost cities of the Maya. il Todays Health 47:56-9+ F '69
Visiting with California's memories. il Todays Health 47:42-7+ D '69
PAYNE, Osborne A.
Computer and the peripatetic teacher. Todays Ed 58:13 F '69
PAYNE, Robert
Irreplaceable Gandhi; excerpt from The life and death of Mahatma Gandhi. Sat R 52: 26-7+ O 4 '69
about
Man of 100 books. A. Grant. por Newsweek 73:109B-109D My 19 '69
PAYSON, Joan (Whitney)
Mrs Payson and her lovable Mets. D. Dempsey. por Read Digest 94:201-2+ Je '69
PAYSON, Martin F. See Lewis, R. jt. auth.
PAYTON, B. W. and others
Permeability and structure of junctional membranes at an electrotonic synapse. bibliog Science 166:1641-3 D 26 '69
Temperature-dependence of resistance at an electrotonic synapse. bibliog Science 165: 594-7 Ag 8 '69
PEA pods. See Cookery—Vegetables
PEABODY, Lawrence
Three designers talk about light. Am Home 72:42 O '69
PEABODY awards. See Television awards
PEACE
Blessed are the peacemakers. Esquire 72:250-2 D '69
Department of peace; Senator Vance Hartke's proposal. Commonweal 89:631-2 F 21 '69
If Christmas were only Christmas; reprint. D. Lawrence. U S News 67:68 D 29 '69
ILO and world peace; excerpts from address. D. A. Morse. UN Mo Chron 6:54-8 Je '69
In quest of peace; excerpts from Britannica book of the year 1969. L. B. Johnson. il Read Digest 94:219-24+ F '69
Nation directed to peace? D. Lucey and R. Lucey. America 121:120-1 Ag 30 '69
Peace and justice; address, June 18, 1969. Thant. UN Mo Chron 6:96-101 Jl '69
Peace on earth? K. Crawford. Newsweek 74:23 D 29 '69
Prayer for peace. Chr Today 14:31 N 7 '69
Secretary Rogers, bigger role in quest for peace. il U S News 67:12 D 22 '69
Strange indifference; to maintain peace. D. Lawrence. U S News 67:80 S 1 '69
Toward a worldwide peace; address to U.N. September 18, 1969. R. M. Nixon. il U S News 67::98-101 S 29 '69; Same with title Establishment of peace. Vital Speeches 35: 738-41 O 1 '69
True peace on earth. C. W. Yost. Parents Mag 44:30+ D '69
United Nations and the cause of peace; address, March 18, 1969. C. W. Yost. Dept State Bul 60:325-9 Ap 14 '69

World peace: the United Nations; address, January 29, 1969. A. Cranston. Vital Speeches 35:358-60 Ap 1 '69
See also
Disarmament
International relations
International security
League of Nations
United Nations—Special committee on peace-keeping operations
Women and peace

Anecdotes, facetiae, satire, etc.
Peace in our time; on campus and off. J. R. Coyne, jr. Nat R 21:285+ Mr 25 '69

Songs and music
Peace anthem: Give peace a chance. Newsweek 74:102 D 1 '69
PEACE (theology)
Peace on earth? Chr Today 14:22 D 19 '69
Peaceable kingdom. J. Kleinheksel. Chr Today 14:6-7 Ja 2 '70
PEACE, Department of (proposed) See United States—Executive departments
PEACE; musical comedy. See Musical comedies, revues, etc.—Criticisms, plots, etc.
PEACE conferences
New calvaries ever. Chr Cent 86:1538-9 D 3 '69
PEACE corps. See United States—Peace corps
PEACE societies
See also
Catholic association for international peace
War resisters league
World peace council
PEACE treaty, 1919. See Versailles, Treaty of, June 28, 1919
PEACEFUL coexistence. See World politics, 1945-
PEACEFUL uses of atomic power. See Atomic power—Economic aspects
PEACHES
Peach George IV. R. A. Nitschke. il Horticulture 47:32-3+ O '69
See also
Cookery—Fruit
PEAL, Christopher A.
English pewter collection. Antiques 96:202-8 Ag '69
PEAL, S. Edward
President Nixon hails sixth anniversary of the organization of African unity; remarks, May 25, 1969. Dept State Bul 60:537-8 Je 23 '69
PEALE, Norman Vincent
Looking at retirement problems. por Har Yrs 9:30-1 Je '69
about
Best medicine? por Chr Today 13:35 Jl 4 '69
Sunday morning with the Rev Dr Peale. C. McCarthy. New Repub 160:14-15 Ja 25 '69
PEANUT butter
Peanut butter's identity crisis. Changing T 23:34-5 Je '69
Peanuts and peanut butter. Am Home 72:97 Mr '69
PEANUT mold. See Fungi
PEANUTS
Do it with peanuts: picture for the wall. A. W. Farrant. il Design 70:36 Sum '69
Peanuts and peanut butter. Am Home 72: 97 Mr '69
Peanuts gibberellin antagonists and genetically controlled differences in growth habit. A. H. Halevy and others. bibliog il Science 164:1397-8 Je 20 '69
This year why not plant some peanuts? il Sunset 142:252+ Ap '69
PEANUTS (comic strip) See Comics (books, strips, etc)
PEARCE, Bernard L. and Green, G. S.
Local association of the month. Todays Ed 58:47-8 O '69
PEARCE, Bob, and Pearce, Sue
Snow cones and frankfurters. pors Library J 94:2415-18 Je 15 '69
PEARCE, Donn
Life-styles: building time. Esquire 71:130-4+ Ap '69
PEARCE, Larry A. and Schanberg, S. M.
Histamine and spermidine content in brain during development. bibliog Science 166: 1301-3 D 5 '69
PEARCE, Rex D.
Cape fuchsia. Horticulture 47:41 Jl '69
Chrysopsis Horticulture 47:54 Ap '69
Dwarf epilobiums. Horticulture 47:9 O '69
Gold star. Horticulture 47:15 Ja '69
Good low perennial. Horticulture 46:39 D '68
Rumex. Horticulture 47:30 N '69
Shamrock pea. Horticulture 46:49+ D '68

PEARCE, Sue. See Pearce, B. jt. auth.
PEARL HARBOR, Attack on, 1941
Dorie Miller; first U.S. hero of World war II.
il Ebony 25:132-4+ D '69
PEARL industry and trade
Luster regained; Japan's cultured-pearl industry. il Time 94:63 Ag 29 '69
PEARL Lang dance company
Pearl Lang and dance co; N Y city center.
M. Marks. Dance Mag 43:34 Jl '69
PEARL S. Buck foundation
Crumbling foundation; exposé articles.
Time 94:60 Jl 25 '69
PEARLMAN, Alan L. and Daw, N. W.
Opponent color cells in the cat lateral geniculate nucleus. bibliog Science 167:84-6 Ja 2 '70
PEARLMAN, Edith
Liniments of love; story. Seventeen 28:160-1 S '69
Ring out the new; story. Seventeen 28:96-7 D '69
Which Eleanor am I? story. Seventeen 28:148-9 My '69
PEARLS
Pearls as big as marbles. il Sci Digest 66:29 Ag '69
PEARLWARE. See Pottery, English
PEARMAN, H. Edgar. See Gunn, R. L. jt. auth.
PEARMAN, Robert
Behind the sentry gates. Travel 132:63-9 Jl '69
Black crime, black victims. Nation 208:500-3 Ap 21 '69
Harry Truman's Missouri. Travel 132:56-60+ Ag '69
PEARS, Peter
Youthful air. F. Rizzo. por Opera N 34:14-16 Ja 10 '70
PEARS
Pears are easy for us! K. F. Polscer. il Org Gard & Farm 16:25-7 S '69
See also
Cookery—Fruit
PEARSE, Benjamin H.
Dyslexia. Am Ed 5:9-13 Ap '69
PEARSON, Allen D.
Tornado season of 1968. Weatherwise 22:21-5 F '69
PEARSON, Drew
Drew Pearson: an interview, ed. by R. G. Sherrill. Nation 209:7-16 Jl 7 '69
about
Flat-earth liberals. Nat R 21:737-8 Jl 29 '69
He kept them honest. por Newsweek 74:65 S 15 '69
Kennedy, Krushchev, and Cuba. por Sat R 52:12-15 Mr 29 '69
Obituary
Nation 209:237-8 S 15 '69
Tenacious muckraker. Time 94:82 S 12 '69
PEARSON, Gaynor
Schoolrooms on the go. Am Ed 5:27-8 Mr '69
PEARSON, Karl H. See Palma, R. J. jt. auth.
PEARSON, Lester Bowles
Beyond the Nation-state. por Sat R 52:24-7+ F 15 '69
Trade, aid, and peace. Sat R 52:23-6 F 22 '69
about
Partnership stagnation: the Pearson report. Chr Cent 86:1338 O 22 '69
PEARSON, Samuel C. Jr
First graders meet law and order. Chr Cent 86:681-3 My 14 '69
PEAS
Pick a mess of peas by Memorial day. R. Tirrell. il Org Gard & Farm 16:41-3 F '69
See also
Cookery—Vegetables
PEASANTRY
Vietnam (Republic)
War, peace, and the Viet Cong, by D. Pike.
Review
Nation 209:414-15 O 20 '69. J. Mirsky
What life's like in Vietcong territory. T. Buckley. il N Y Times Mag p48-9+ N 23 '69
PEAT bogs
Medieval riddle of bodies in the bog. D. Cohen. il Sci Digest 65:9-14 F '69
PEAVY, Katherine B.
Traveler's choice. Travel 132:5 D '69
PECCARIES
Peccaries; funny little denizens of the Southwest. J. B. Holdsworth. il Nat Wildlife 7:14-15 F '69

PECCARY hunting
Pigs of the Cheery Cows; Chiricahua Mountains. W. A. Cartier. il Outdoor Life 143:54-7+ Mr '69
PECCEI, Aurelio
Doing business in a spaceship. por Forbes 104:56 Jl 15 '69
PECHTER, William S.
For and against Godard. Commentary 47:59-63 Ap '69
Parts of some time spent with Abraham Polonsky. Film Q 22:14-19 Wint '68
PECK, C. E.
Building communities; address, April 28, 1969. Vital Speeches 35:537-41 Je 15 '69
PECK, Ralph
Majorca. Travel 131:26-31 Mr '69
PECK, Richard
Nancy; poem. Sat R 52:6 Je 21 '69
PECKINPAH, Sam
Man and myth. il por Time 93:85+ Je 20 '69
PECORA, William Thomas
Keeping tabs on quakes. Sci N 95:113 F 1 '69
PECORAITE. See Serpentine
PECSOK, James D.
Waves of the future; your career? address. May 13, 1969. Vital Speeches 35:553-6 Jl 1 '69
PECTINS
Low-sugar jams and jellies; with low-methoxyl pectin. E. Gibbons. Org Gard & Farm 16:96-9 Ja '69
PECULIAR vision of Mrs. Winkler; story. See Hedin, M.
PEDDLERS and peddling
Publishing game; excerpts from London labour and the London poor. H. Mayhew. il Nation 208:313 Mr 10 '69
See also
Street trades
PEDESTRIAN accidents. See Traffic accidents
PEDESTRIAN bridges. See Bridges, Foot
PEDIATRICS
In a dark mirror. M. S. Goodwin and T. C. Goodwin. bibliog Ment Hy 53:550-63 O '69
When I was a boy. B. Spock. il Redbook 133:26+ Jl '69
See also
Sick children
PEDICORD, Larry C. See Pena, M. G. jt. auth.
PEDIGREED animals. See Pets
PEEBLES, Timothy
Bomb for Timothy. Newsweek 73:39 Mr 17 '69
PEEKE, Carroll E. B.
Cobra Fumando. Américas 21:9-15 Jl '69
PEER Gynt; ballet. See Ballets—Criticisms
PEER Gynt; drama. See Ibsen, H.
PEERAGE
See also
Great Britain—Peerage
PEERLESS quartet. See Choral groups and societies
PEERS, William R.
Probing the massacre probe. por Time 94:16-17 D 12 '69
PEET, Creighton
Can man survive? Am For 75:4-7+ Ag '69
Effluent of the affluent. Am For 76:16-19+ My '69
Fascinating new careers in geography. Sci Digest 65:77-80 Je '69
Fascinating new careers in oceanography. bibliog Sci Digest 66:61-5 Ag '69
How to be your own boss: the $80-billion boom in franchising. Pop Mech 131:25-6+ F '69
Traffic cop of the sky. Pop Mech 130:104-7+ D '68
PEGGY Guggenheim collection. See Art—Private collections
PEGLER, Alan
Flier; interview. New Yorker 45:43-4 N 29 '69
PEGLER, Westbrook
Master of the epithet. il por Time 94:68 Jl 4 '69
Obituary
Newsweek por 74:86 Jl 7 '69
Vote of no confidence; with editorial comment. D. Phelps. Nat R 21:685, 696-9+ Jl 15 '69
PEI, Ieoh Ming
Concrete frames for works of art. J. Bailey. Arch Forum 130:54-67 Je '69
PEIERLS, Sir Rudolf Ernst
Scientist in public affairs: between the ivory tower and the arena. Bul Atom Sci 25:28-30 N '69
PEINADO, Ricardo
On the boards. W. Como. por Dance Mag 43:20 F '69
PEJOVICH, Svetozar
Rhodesia tomorrow; address. bibliog Vital Speeches 35:338-41 Mr 15 '69

PEKING, China
Peking way of life. il N Y Times Mag p7-9+ Je 1 '69
PEKING man. See Man, Prehistoric
PEKKANEN, John
Black hope, white hope. Life 67:67-72+ N 21 '69
We just put on our boots and remember where the holes are. Life 66:60 Ap 25 '69
PELADEAU, Marius B.
John Hills, gunsmith of Vermont. Antiques 96:234-6 Ag '69
PELAGIANISM
Book reviews. A. C. Outler. Commonweal 90:124-5 Ap 11 '69
PELICANS
Pelicans: those high-diving fishermen. il Sci Digest 66:69-71 S '69
Where have all the pelicans gone? disappearance of the brown pelican from Louisiana. G. Laycock. il Audubon 71:10-17 S '69
PELL, Claiborne
Oceans; man's last great resource. Sat R 52:19-21+ O 11 '69

about

Senate: new leaders for health and education. B. Nelson. Science 163:654-8 F 14 '69
PELL CITY, Ala.
Muslims' farm. il Newsweek 74:52+ D 8 '69
PELLEAS and Mélisande; ballet. See Ballets—Criticisms
PELLEGRINESCHI, Paolo
Paolo Pellegrineschi. il Pop Phot 65:108-11 Jl '69
PELLEW, John C.
Cover. il Am Artist 33:6+ Mr '69
PELLISSIER, Hrissa
Wassmer 4/21. E. M. Miller. il Flying 84:52-4 My '69
PELLÓN, Nivio López. See López Pellón, N.
PELTZ, Edith M.
Bland diets need not be dull. Todays Health 47:50-4 Jl '69
PELTZ, Mary Ellis
In service. Opera N 33:6-7 F 8 '69
PELUSI, Robert G.
How parks build men. Am City 84:80-2 Je '69
PEN and ink drawing. See Pen drawing
PEN club. See PEN club
PEN drawing
Art of the pen. H. C. Pitz. il Am Artist 32:26-32 D '68
I am in love with line! R. Welling. il Am Artist 33:56-8+ O '69
See also
Black and white (art)
PEN names. See Pseudonyms
PENA, Mario G. and Pedicord, L. C.
What counselors get from camping. Camp Mag 41:11-12 Ap '69
PENAL colonies
Papillon, by H. Charrière. Review
New Yorker 45:200+ N 15 '69. Genêt
PENAL reform. See Prisons
PENANCE
See also
Absolution
PENCIL drawing. See Drawing
PENDERECKI, Krzysztof
Devils' advocate; interview. ed. by J. H. Sutcliffe. pors Opera N 33:14-15 Je 14 '69

about

Devils of Loudun. Criticism
Hi Fi 19:MA25 N '69
Life il 67:12 Ag 15 '69
Nation 209:93-4 Jl 28 '69
Newsweek il 74:85 Ag 25 '69
Sat R 52:42+ Ag 30 '69
Time 94:60-1 Ag 22 '69
Time il 94:65 Jl 4 '69
Modern Polish passion. J. Evenson. Chr Today 13:39 Mr 28 '69
Penderecki's Passion. R. Jacobson. Sat R 52:69+ Mr 22 '69
Sound of Poland. H. Saal. por Newsweek 73:114+ Mr 17 '69
PENDULUM
See also
Foucault's pendulum
PENETRANTS (zoology) See Nematocysts
PENFIELD, Louis
War in the classroom: mass media vs. education. Schol Teach Sec Teach Sup p 14:15+ S 22 '69
PENGUINS, Fossil
Environmental temperatures of tertiary penguins. B. Stonehouse. bibliog il Science 163:673-5 F 14 '69

PENICILLIN
Maturation of renal organic acid transport: substrate stimulation by penicillin. G. H. Hirsch and J. B. Hook. bibliog il Science 165:909-10 Ag 29 '69
PENINSULA music festival. See Music festivals—Wisconsin
PENKNIVES. See Knives
PENLAND school of crafts. See Art schools
PENMANSHIP
Alfred Fairbank and his book of scripts. P. Standard. il Pub W 195:97-8 Je 9 '69
Fine Italian hands; facsimile writing manuals published by Nattali & Maurice of London. P. Standard. il Pub W 195:92-3+ F 3 '69
Those questions on handwriting. E. A. Enstrom. Ed Digest 34:44-7 My '69
See also
Calligraphy
Graphology
Writing, Italic
PENN, Arthur
Alice's; family of folk song fame becomes a movie. J. Stickney. il Life 66:43-5+ Mr 28 '69
Director Arthur Penn takes on General Custer. B. Weinraub. il pors N Y Times Mag p 10-11+ D 21 '69
PENN, Elizabeth E.
Branch-weaving. Sch Arts 68:40 My '69
PENN, Irving
Kirdis of Cameroon; photographs. Vogue 154:174-81+ D '69
PENN, Nolan E. and others
Dilemma of involuntary commitment: suggestions for a measurable alternative. bibliog Ment Hy 53:4-9 Ja '69
Some considerations for future mental health legislation. Ment Hy 53:10-13 Ja '69
PENN central company
End of a bizarre overseas venture; Executive jet severing links to Penn central. il Bsns W p 122-3+ Ag 16 '69
Executive jet aviation begins efforts to find new financing. J. P. Woolsey. Aviation W 91:49-50 N 10 '69
Muddled merger: trouble on the Penn central. il Newsweek 74:105-6+ D 8 '69
Out of the rathole; disaster on the Penn Central commuter train, May 26, 1969. J. Ciardi. il Sat R 52:19-23+ S 13 '69
Penn central hands trottle to outsider; new president P. A. Gorman. il Bsns W p32 S 27 '69
Penn central sees a light in the tunnel. Bsns W p44 N 22 '69
Penn central tries a wider track; a plan to diversify. il Bsns W p 132 My 10 '69
Penn central's bad trip. il Bsns W p 122-4+ Je 28 '69
PENNEL, John
Crossing the bar. il por Time 94:36 Jl 4 '69
PENNEY, J. C, company
Can the last be first? il Forbes 103:30-1 Mr 15 '69
J. C. Penney, Italian-style. il Bsns W p48+ Ja 10 '70
PENNSYLVANIA
See also
Architecture, Domestic—Pennsylvania
Booksellers and bookselling—Pennsylvania
Brandywine Creek
Camping—Pennsylvania
Education—Pennsylvania
Fishing—Pennsylvania
Hunting—Pennsylvania

Parks and reserves

Bowman's Hill wildflower preserve. O. Stark. il Horticulture 47:22-5 My '69

Politics and government

Democrats confront 1970. A. S. Boynan, jr. Nation 209:600-2 D 1 '69
PENNSYLVANIA academy of the fine arts
Big big show; the cost of competitive exhibitions. N. Kent. Am Artist 33:5 D '69
PENNSYLVANIA avenue. See Washington, D.C.—Streets
PENNSYLVANIA engineering corporation
Building steel mills from top to bottom. il Bsns W p 126-8 Ja 18 '69
PENNSYLVANIA life insurance company
If nobody loves you, your company will. il Time 94:107 D 5 '69
PENNSYLVANIA New York central transportation company. See Penn central company
PENNSYLVANIA railroad-New York central merger. See Railroads—Consolidations and mergers
PENNSYLVANIA. University, Philadelphia
Day LeRoi Jones spoke on Penn campus, what were the blacks doing in the balcony? G. Weales. il N Y Times Mag p38-40+ My 4 '69

PENNSYLVANIA. University, Philadelphia
—*Continued*
Graduate student. J. R. Powers. Phys Today 22:32-3 Mr '69
Orphan senses; research at the Monell chemical senses center. C. Weathersbee. il Sci N 95:241-2 Mr 8 '69
Protest at Pen: a model for campus dissent? D. Sanford. New Repub 160:19-21 Mr 15 '69

Institute for environmental studies
Brandywine basin: defeat of an almost perfect plan. P. Thompson. il Science 163:1180-2 Mr 14 '69

PENNSYLVANIA university bookstore. See College bookstores
PENNSYLVANIAN period. See Paleobotany—Pennsylvanian
PENNY wars; drama. See Baker, E.
PENOLOGY. See Punishment
PENROSE, L. S.
Dermatoglyphics; with biographical sketch. Sci Am 221:15, 72-4+ bibliog(p152) D '69
PENS
See also
Fountain pens
PENSACOLA, Fla.
Parade, charade, crusade. il Am City 84:132+ Ag '69
PENSION funds. See Pensions—Finance
PENSION funds and funding. See Pensions—Finance
PENSION trusts
Punishing the successful. il U S News 67:84 Ag 25 '69
PENSIONS
See also
Baseball players—Salaries, pensions, etc.
Civil service pensions
College professors and instructors—Pensions
Old age pensions—United States
Trade unions—Benefit funds

Finance
Do-it-yourself pension fund. A. Hershman. il Duns R 93:21-3+ Ja '69
Funds get new rivals for pension billions; banks and insurance companies. il Bsns W p 140+ My 10 '69
How pension funds invest their money. U S News 67:50-1 D 29 '69
Pursuing pension money; investment middlemen allowed to sponsor employee benefit plans. il Bsns W p 108+ O 25 '69
When a pension fund runs out; actuarial goof on rail union funds. Bsns W p 128 O 25 '69
See also
Pension trusts

Laws and regulations
Pursuing pension money; investment middlemen allowed to sponsor employee benefit plans. il Bsns W p 108+ O 25 '69
PENSIONS, Industrial
How good is your company's pension plan? Changing T 23:6-10 Mr '69
Negotiated retirement plans, a decade of benefit improvements. H. E. Davis. il Mo Labor R 92:11-15 My '69
Rail unions split over pension policy. Bsns W p 108 N 29 '69
When a pension fund runs out; actuarial goof on rail union funds. Bsns W p 128 O 25 '69
Why not portable pensions? W. M. Evan. il Duns R 94:60-2 S '69
PENSKE, Roger
Motor trend profile. B. Thomas. il pors Motor T 21:32+ D '69
PENSKY, Jack, and Schwick, H. G.
Human serum inhibitor of C'1 esterase: identity with α_2-neuraminoglycoprotein. bibliog Science 163:698-9 F 14 '69
PENTAGON building, Arlington, Va.
Protecting the Pentagon. J. Deedy. Commonweal 90:530 S 5 '69
PENTAX gallery. See Tokyo—Galleries and museums
PENTECOST
Knowledge of the Spirit. V. P. McCorry. America 120:inside back cover My 24 '69
PENTECOSTAL churches
Two Pentecostal experiences; one Protestant and the other Catholic. J. S. Phillipson. America 120:360-3 Mr 29 '69
See also
Church of God
PENTECOSTAL churches in Asia
East Asia Pentecostals. S. H. Moffett. Chr Today 13:37 Ag 22 '69
PENTECOSTAL movement. See Pentecostal churches

PENTHOUSE (periodical)
Chasing Playboy's golden bunny. il Bsns W p98 Ag 9 '69
Penthouse v. Playboy. il Time 94:88 N 7 '69
PENTONY, DeVere E.
Case for black studies. Atlan 223:81-2+ Ap '69
PENTOTHAL sodium
Anesthetic helps locate brain disease. Todays Health 47:84 Mr '69
PEONIES
Breathtakers, larger than a man's hand, tree peonies. il Sunset 142:209-10 Mr '69
Make mine peonies. R. Van Vorse. il Home Gard 46:64-5 Je '69
Those other peonies. S. Saunders. il Horticulture 47:18-21+ S '69
PEOPLE, Single. See Single people
PEOPLE-to-people program
President Nixon greets leaders of People to people program; remarks, October 14, 1969. R. M. Nixon. Dept State Bul 61:372-3 N 3 '69
South Pacific adventure: recreation and park specialists act as citizen ambassadors. T. S. Brungardt. il Parks & Rec 4:48-53+ Je '69
PEOPLE'S liberation army. See China (People's Republic)—Armed forces
PEOPLE'S Republic of Southern Yemen. See Southern Yemen
PEP pills. See Amphetamines
PEPCO. See Potomac electric power company of Washington, D.C.
PEPPER, Curtis Bill
Making of a saint. Look 33:34+ Mr 4 '69
Pope John and the sculptor; excerpts from An Artist and the pope. Read Digest 94:200-4+ My '69
—See Barnard, C. N. jt. auth.
PEPPERIDGE. See Tupelos
PEPPERS
What's cooking?
Warm up to chili. G. Akers. Org Gard & Farm 16:77-8 Jl '69
See also
Cookery—Vegetables
PEPSI-COLA company
Beer and pretzels? tangle with R. R. Grace & co. Newsweek 73:71 Je 30 '69
PEPTIDES
Peptide antibiotics. M. Bodanszky and D. Perlman. bibliog il Science 163:352-8 Ja 24 '69
Polypeptide chain elongation in protein biosynthesis. F. Lipmann. bibliog il Science 164:1024-31 My 30 '69
See also
Bradykinin
PEQUANNOCK, N.J.
Pequannock Picassos. il Am City 84:141-3 Je '69
PEQUEGNAT, Arthur
Arthur Pequegnat clock company. R. Phillip. il por Hobbies 74:48-9+ Je '69
PERCEPTION
How to see better in the field. J. R. Gregg. il Field & S 74:46-7+ Ag '69
Visual motion perception: experimental modification. R. H. Masland. bibliog il Science 165:819-21 Ag 22 '69
See also
Body image
Cognition
Consciousness
Human information processing
Orientation
Pattern perception
Perceptrons
Sensory deprivation
Sound perception
Space perception
PERCEPTION, Disorders of
Visual information processing: early experience; report of meeting. F. A. Young. Science 163:1471-2 Mr 28 '69
PERCEPTRONS
Perceptrons, by M. Minsky and S. Papert. Review
Science 165:780-2 Ag 22 '69. A. Newell
See also
Automatic speech recognition
PERCH fishing
Family fun fish. W. Davis. il Mech Illus 65:46+ Je '69
Reunion at Missisquoi Bay. T. Janes. il Outdoor Life 143:76-7+ My '69
Walleye crawl. R. Slogar. il Outdoor Life 143:74-5+ Ap '69
What walleye secret? C. Vinson. il Outdoor Life 144:58-9+ Jl '69
PERCHIK, Simon
Poem: The only peaches I see. Nation 209:419 O 20 '69
PERCOLATORS, Coffee. See Coffee pots, percolators, etc.

PERCUSSION instruments, Electronic. See Musical instruments, Electronic
PERCUSSION music
    See also
Phonograph records—Percussion music
PERCY, Hugh, 2d duke of Northumberland. See Northumberland, H. P
PERCY, Hugh Algernon, 10th duke of Northumberland. See Northumberland, H. A. P.
PEREGRINE falcons. See Falcons
PERELMAN, Sidney Joseph
Be a cat's-paw! Lose big money! New Yorker 45:31-3 Jl 26 '69
Calling all moths: candle dead ahead. New Yorker 45:33-5 My 3 '69
Hark! whence came those pear-shaped drones? New Yorker 45:46-8 N 1 '69
Moonstruck at sunset. New Yorker 45:28-31 Ag 16 '69
Out of this nettle, danger. New Yorker 45:49-51 N 29 '69
Room and bored. por Holiday 45:40-1+ Mr '69
She walks in beauty, single file, eyes front, and no hanky-panky. New Yorker 45:32-4 F 22 '69
Three loves had I, in assorted flavors. New Yorker 45:34-7 Mr 22 '69
To err is human, to forgive supine. New Yorker 45:36-8 O 4 '69
    about
That Perelman of great price is sixty-five. W. Zinsser. il pors N Y Times Mag p24-7+ Ja 26 '69
PERENNIALS
Carefree flowers for summer. S. Fenell. il Home Gard 56:22-3 Ag '69
Late-blooming perennials. H. B. Aul. il Horticulture 47:20-1+ Ag '69
Plan now for early bloom with perennials. R. M. Peters. il Horticulture 47:18-19+ Ag '69
Three VIP's in my garden. E. M. Shroeder. Home Gard 56:73 S '69
Why are these eight perennials so popular? il Sunset 143:100-1 N '69
    See also
Chrysanthemums
Foxgloves
PERERA, Padma
Three is company; story. New Yorker 45:34-44 Mr 29 '69
PERETZ, Bertram
Central neuron initiation of periodic gill movements. bibliog Science 166:1167-72 N 28 '69
PERETZ, Martin
Protest politics; Peretz vs. Goodman. N Y Times Mag p4+ Ja 19 '69
PÉREZ, Galo René
Rómulo Gallegos, civilizer. Américas 21:2-6 Je '69
PEREZ, Leander Henry
Plaquemines without the great white father. B. W. Eggler. New Repub 160:11-12 My 24 '69
PEREZ, Rudy
Rudy Perez dance theatre; the Cubiculo. J. Anderson. Dance Mag 43:30 Ap '69
Rudy Perez dance theater; the Cubiculo. T. Borek. il por Dance Mag 43:86-7 Jl '69
PEREZ, Victor, and others
Oral contraceptives: long-term use produces fine structural changes in liver mitochondria. bibliog Science 165:805-7 Ag 22 '69
PERFECT day in spring; story. See Glenday, A.
PERFECT film and chemical corporation
Mopping up the mess at Perfect film. Bsns W p31 N 29 '69
Perfect wants a better image. il Bsns W p 100+ Je 28 '69
PERFECTIONISTS. See Oneida community
PERFORMANCE standards
Rich man's qualifications for poor man's jobs. I. Berg. il Trans-Action 6:45-50 Mr '69
PERFORMING animals. See Animals—Training
PERFORMING arts
Architecture of awareness for the performing arts. H. Hardy. il Arch Rec 145:117-22 Mr '69
Celebrity spotlight. E. N. Mintz. See issues of Travel
Export-import. L. Lerman. il Mlle 69:114-17 Je '69
Ferment and controversy: new look in dance and the arts keeps changing its sights. J. Anderson. il Dance Mag 43:46-55 Ag '69
On the scene. C. Barnes. See issues of Holiday to August 1969
On the scene: cities, summer and the lively arts; vacation activities for teen-agers. il Seventeen 28:94-5 Jl '69

Spot check: some observations on the state of the arts in America today. J. Claman. il Harp Baz 102:122B-122X F '69
    See also
Sex in the performing arts

    Study and teaching
Summer day art center; Usdan center for the performing arts. il Arch Forum 131:56-61 N '69

    Norway
Poetic epic, multi-media performance of Mot Solen at Bergen festival. W. Terry. il Sat R 52:27-8 Je '69
PERFORMING arts and industry. See The arts and industry
PERFORMING arts camps. See Camps
PERFORMING arts centers. See Centers for the performing arts
PERFUME holders. See Pomanders
PERFUMERY
All through the house; follow your nose. N. Mandelbaum. McCalls 96:40 My '69
Beauty of fragrance. il Good H 169:96-7 N '69
Follow your scent home. Harp Baz 103:177 N '69
Fragrant house. il House & Gard 135:168-9 Ap '69
Perfume ploy. Harp Baz 103:174 N '69
Perfume power. il Vogue 153:201-2 My '69
Perfume: the best of the bare fashion put-ons. il Vogue 154:86+ N 15 '69
Stars-and-scents quiz. il Mlle 70:122.3+ D '69
Where would you like to be scent game. il Mlle 69:202-3 My '69
    See also
International flavors and fragrances, incorporated
PERGAMON press, limited
Fiery Robert Maxwell down and out at Pergamon. Pub W 196:43-4 O 20 '69
Leasco must still mop up at Pergamon. il Bsns W p42-3 O 18 '69
Leasco sues Maxwell, who denounces Ross meeting. Pub W 196:63 N 17 '69
Leasco's noisy battle for a British publisher; Leasco-Pergamon press proposed merger. il Bsns W p30-2 S 6 '69
Pergamon affair. Newsweek 74:74+ S 8 '69
Pergamon-Leasco squabble increasingly bitter. Pub W 196:39 S 29 '69
Tribulations of Saul. il Time 94:94 O 24 '69
La PERICHOLE; opera. See Offenbach, J.
PERIOD rooms
Splendor of decoration; nine beautiful period rooms. il House & Gard 136:58-67 D '69
PERIODIC charts. See Chemical elements
PERIODIC law
Music of new spheres; development of periodic law of the elements. D. L. Morris. il Chem 42:10-12 D '69
PERIODICAL articles
All you know is facts; excerpts. M. Mayer. Writer 82:20-2 Mr '69
First words are important. E. Marshall. Writers Digest 49:63-5 Ap '69
Five things I tell my class in article writing. J. Stocker. Writer 82:25-6 O '69
Four point system for writing a selling query letter; interview, ed. by O. Henry, with suggestions by I. B. Harrell. C. Handley. il Writers Digest 49:48-51 Ag '69
Freelance job idea: convention freelancing. E. Engle. il Writers Digest 49:42-3+ Ap '69
Full-time freelancing in secondary magazines. N. Phillips. il Writers Digest 49:48-52+ Je '69
How I cover conventions; writing articles for businesspapers. N. I. Phillips. Writers Digest 49:44+ Ap '69
Idea a day. F. A. Dickson. See issues of Writer's digest
Make it personal; articles that communicate. G. Taher. Writer 82:15-17 Ap '69
1969 WD article contest. L. Whitt. Writers Digest 49:39+ O '69
Review of the journals. P. P. Witonski. Nat R 21:447-8 My 6 '69
Sell what you write. L. P. Zobel. Writer 82:26-7 N '69
Selling the exposé article; legal aspects. J. L. Moore. il Writers Digest 49:56-9+ Jl '69
Selling your first article. D. C. Gleasner. Writers Digest 49:51-3 My '69
Successful magazine article writing. A. F. Gonzalez, jr. Writer 82:15-16+ Jl '69
Tapping the university community market. T. Fensch. il Writers Digest 49:54-7 Mr '69
Turning magazine articles into books. T. Fensch. Writers Digest 49:53-5 D '69

PERIODICAL articles—*Continued*
Types of modern articles; excerpt from writing the modern magazine article. M. Gunther. Writer 82:12-14+ My '69
Writing and selling to city magazines. A. Bannon. Writer 82:24-6 S '69
See also
Newspapers—Magazine sections
PERIODICAL articles, Titles of. See Titles of books, stories, etc.
PERIODICAL cicadas. See Cicadas
PERIODICAL covers
Ten years that led to Apollo 11; thirty-two Life covers. R. Graves. il Life 67:3 Jl 25 '69
PERIODICAL literature
New York market letter. H. B. Jacobs. See issues of Writer's digest
Second thoughts about markets. A. Holland. Writers Digest 49:20 N '69
279 editors looking for writers. K. M. Sommers. il Writers Digest 49:48-51+ S '69
Writer's market; late news! See issues of Writer's digest
See also
Periodical articles
Trade journals
PERIODICALS
Critical eye; magazine photography. A. Rothstein. il Travel & Camera 32:100 O '69
See also
Blind, Periodicals for the
Childrens periodicals
Freedom of the press
House organs
Libraries—Periodical collections
Serial publications
Trade journals
also subhead Periodicals under various subjects, e.g. Moving pictures—Periodicals

Bibliography
Magazines; ed. by B. Katz. See issues of Library journal
Underground and new left press. D. Tatko and C. Brown. il Wilson Lib Bul 43:648-52 Mr '69
Where it's also at; suggested list from the responsible right. H. P. Durkin. il Library J 94:1839-40 My 1 '69; Reply. S. Berman. 94:2706 Ag '69

Letters to the editor
Four point system for writing a selling query letter; interview, ed. by O. Henry, with suggestions by I. B. Harrell. C. Handley. il Writers Digest 49:48-51 Ag '69
Letters and opinions. America 120:700 Je 21 '69
Letters from an American mother; hoax by Holger A. Koppel in Baltimore evening sun. E. Lund. il Am Heritage 21:44-5 D '69
Mike Frome; readers comments. M. Frome. Am For 75:3+ F '69
Of many things. D. R. Campion. America 121:278 O 11 '69

Prices
Price indexes for 1969; U.S. periodicals. H. W. Tuttle. il Library J 94:2571 Jl '69

Storage
See also
Magazine stands, racks, etc.

Argentina
Killing the front page; Primera plana banned. Newsweek 74:91 Ag 18 '69

Colombia
Mosquito that stang; El Zancudo. G. Arciniegas. il Américas 21:22-31 O '69

France
Behind the lines; A. Marchenko's article in L'Express. Read Digest 95:15-16 Ag '69

Germany
Weimar Germany's left-wing intellectuals, by I. Deak. Review
Nation 208:442-3 Ap 7 '69. S. Warnecke

Germany (Federal Republic)
Revolt of the editors; Stern agreement. il Newsweek 73:84 Je 2 '69

Great Britain
See also
Economist (London)
Punch (periodical)

United States
Chop; journalistic karate. Nation 209:301 S 29 '69
City and regional magazines. Writer 82:26-30 S '69

Everywhere market; regional magazines. D. W. Toll. il Writers Digest 49:48-52+ O '69
Giveaway magazines try hard to make it pay; consumer-oriented publications. il Bsns W p65 Jl 19 '69
Magazines, new, changing, growing. J. Tebbel. il Sat R 52:55-6 F 8 '69
Underground press; symposium. il Wilson Lib Bul 43:640-56 Mr '69
Where to sell manuscripts. See issues of Writer
See also
Periodicals for men
also names of periodicals, e.g. Antioch review
PERIODICALS, Immoral. See Immoral literature and pictures
PERIODICALS, Publishing of
Magazines, new, changing, growing. J. Tebbel. il Sat R 52:55- 6F 8 '69
Mixing the media; new publications. il Newsweek 73:101-2+ Je 9 '69
See also
Curtis publishing company
PERIODICALS, Trade. See Trade journals
PERIODICALS for airline passengers
In-flight magazine explosion. H. J. Teison. il Sat R 52:47-8+ Ag 9 '69
PERIODICALS for men
Freelance market report; the men's action adventure field. G. Evans. il Writers Digest 49:48-52+ D '69
Men's magazines. G. Evans. il Writers Digest 49:59-61+ F '69
See also
Penthouse (periodical)
Playboy (periodical)
PERIODICALS for women
See also
McCall's (periodical)
PERIODICALS on microfilm
Microfilm sales of American city magazine jumps. il Am City 84:30 My '69
PERIODICITY
Action spectra for phase shifts of a circadian rhythm in drosophila. K. D. Frank and W. F. Zimmerman. bibliog il Science 163: 688-9 F 14 '69
Beacon for buntings; traveling orders from biological clock. il Time 94:94 N 14 '69
Cell division: a second circadian clock system in paramecium multimicronucleatum. A. Barnett. bibliog il Science 164:1417-19 Je 20 '69
Circadian clock action spectrum in a photoperiodic moth. V. G. Bruce and D. H. Minis. bibliog il Science 163:583-5 F 7 '69
Circadian periodicity of bone marrow mitotic activity and reticulocyte counts in rats and mice. R. H. Clark and D. R. Korst. bibliog il Science 166:236-7 O 10 '69
Circadian rhythm in mammalian body temperature entrained by cyclic pressure changes. P. Hayden and R. G. Lindberg. bibliog il Science 164:1288-9 Je 13 '69
Ciradian rhythm of cell division in euglena: effects of a random illumination regimen. L. N. Edmunds, jr. and R. R. Funch. bibliog il Science 165:500-3 Ag 1 '69
Circadian rhythm of optic nerve impulses recorded in darkness from isolated eye of aplysia. J. W. Jacklet. bibliog il Science 164:562-3 My 2 '69
Circadian rhythm of serotonin in the pineal body of immunosympathectomized immature rats. C. R. S. Machado and others. bibliog il Science 164:442-3 Ap 25 '69
Cymatics: the sculpture of vibrations. H. Jenny. il UNESCO Courier 22:4-12+ D '69
Early experiences accelerate maturation of the 24-hour adrenocortical rhythm. R. Ader. bibliog il Science 163:1225-6 Mr 14 '69
Encephalic cycles during sleep and wakefulness in humans: a 24-hour pattern. E. Othmer and others. bibliog il Science 164:477-9 Ap 25 '69; Reply. R. J. Berger. 166:530-1 O 24 '69
Erythropoiesis in the dog: the periodic nature of the steady state. A. Morley and F. Stohlman, jr. bibliog il Science 165:1025-7 S 5 '69
Extraoptic phase shifting of circadian locomotor rhythm in salamanders. K. Adler. bibliog il Science 164:1290-2 Je 13 '69
Fungal endogenous rhythms expressed by spiral figures. J. A. Bourret and others. bibliog il Science 166:763-4 N 7 '69
Jetlag: walk, do not rush, and easy on the martinis. il Holiday 46:60-1 Jl '69
Paleontological evidence of variations in length of synodic month since late Cambrian. G. Pannella and others; discussion. Science 163:1227; bibliog 164:201-2 Mr 14, Ap 11 '69

PERIODICITY—*Continued*
Six cave explorers who lived outside of time.
W. S. Ross. il Sci Digest 65:8-13 Ap '69
Sleep and biorhythmicity; report of meeting.
A. Hobson. Science 165:932-3 Ag 29 '69
Time-zone effects. Sci Am 221:57 Ag '69
Time-zone effects. P. V. Siegel and others.
bibliog il Science 164:1249-55 Je 13 '69
See also
Photoperiodism
PERIODONTAL disease. See Gums (anatomy)
—Diseases
PERITZ, René
On southeast Asia. Cur Hist 56:106-8+ F '69
PERIWINKLES
What it likes and needs is heat; Madagascar
periwinkle, or vinca rosea. il Sunset 142:
236 Ap '69
PERKEL, Donald H. See Gerstein, G. L. jt.
auth.
PERKIN, Richard Scott
Builder of telescopes. Sky & Tel 38:3+ Jl
'69
PERKINS, Bradford
Inflation curbs: some progress, but no giant
steps. Arch Rec 146:55-6 D '69
PERKINS, Dexter, jr
Fauna of Çatal Hüyük: evidence for early
cattle domestication in Anatolia. bibliog
Science 164:177-9 Ap 11 '69
PERKINS, Frank O. See Moens, P. B. jt. auth.
PERKINS, James Alfred
It can't happen here, can it? il por News-
week 73:27-30 My 5 '69
PERKINS, Lawrence A.
Ancestral bones; poem. Cath World 209:120
Je '69
PERKINS, Stuart
He's got the bug. L. Levine. il pors Motor T
21:31-3 My '69
PERKINSON, William J.
Storms that rage beneath the sea. Sci Digest
65:7-11 Mr '69
PERLBERG, Mark
House tree; poem. New Yorker 45:44 My 17
'69
PERLE, George
Wozzeck at the Met. Sat R 52:61-2 My 17 '69
PERLMAN, Anne S.
Baleen; poem. Mlle 69:94 Je '69
PERLMAN, D. See Bodanszky, M. jt. auth.
PERLMAN, David
America the beautiful? Look 33:25-7 N 4 '69
PERLMANN, Peter, and others
Cytotoxic effects of leukocytes triggered by
complement bound to target cells. bibliog
Science 163:937-9 F 28 '69
PERMAFROST. See Frozen ground
PERMANENT court of arbitration. See Inter-
national court of arbitration, The Hague
PERMANGANIC acid
Crystalline permanganic acid. Chem 42:21-2
S '69
PERMIAN period. See Paleobotany—Permian;
Paleontology—Permian
PERMIT fishing. See Pompano fishing
PEROT, H. Ross
Fastest rich Texan ever. A. M. Louis. Read
Digest 94:131-4 F '69
Lone Star Santa. por Bsns W p94 Ja 10 '70
Money talks. por Newsweek 74:57-8 D 8 '69
Odyssey of Ross Perot. il por Time 95:12-13 Ja
12 '70
Parcels from Perot. il Newsweek 75:30 Ja 5 '70
Texas breeds new billionaire. por Bsns W
p73-4 Ag 30 '69
PEROXIDATION. See Oxidation
PEROXISOMES
Allantoinase: association with amphibian
hepatic peroxisomes. L. P. Visentin and
J. M. Allen. bibliog il Science 163:1463-4
Mr 28 '69
Peroxisome. Sci Am 221:52 Jl '69
PERREAULT, John
New De Koonings. Art N 68:48-9+ Mr '69
Plaster caste. Art N 67:54-5+ N '68
PERRIER company. See France—Industries
PERRINE, Van Dearing
Rediscovery: Van Dearing Perrine. J. I. H.
Baur. il Art in Am 57:76-9 Ja '69
PERRON, Robert
Dying marsh; photographs. Audubon 71:21-32
N '69
PERRONE, Glenn
Businessmen's expectations. Duns R 94:87 D
'69
PERROW, Charles B.
Birth of tolerance in the Soviet Union.
Trans-Action 6:60-2 Ja '69
PERRY, Deborah L.
Because I am black. Sat R 52:73 Je 21 '69
PERRY, George L.
Economy: what will Nixon do? New Repub
160:19-31 Je 14 '69

PERRY, Gregg
Utah upbeat. Travel 132:77 O '69
PERRY, Jay
Toughest kid in block trading. il pors Bsns
W p 114-16 O 4 '69
PERRY, Louis D. jr
Teaching vocabulary to slow learners. Clear
House 44:164-5 N '69
PERRY, Robin
It's a super system. Pop Phot 65:118-19+ D
'69
PERRY, Thelma D.
Knowing; poem. Negro Hist Bul 32:23 Ja '69
—See Breaux, E. E. jt. auth.
PERRYMAN, John N.
You can't teach a hungry child. Ed Digest
34:28-30 Ap '69
PERSECUTION
Nazi persecution of the churches, 1933-45,
by J. S. Conway. Review
America 121:99-100 Ag 16 '69. J. F. Brod-
erick
PERSEIDS. See Meteors
PERSEPOLIS
Shreds of ancient Persia. B. Goldman. il
Natur Hist 78:26-35 My '69
PERSIA. See Iran
PERSIAN architecture. See Architecture, Per-
sian
PERSIAN GULF
See also
Bahrein
PERSIANS. See Iranians
PERSICK, Roberta S.
Wedging board pots. Ceram Mo 17:13-15
Je '69
PERSIMMONS
Your own dried persimmons. il Sunset 143:
172 N '69
PERSON, Philip
Cartilaginous dermal scales in cephalopods.
bibliog Science 164:1404-5 Je 20 '69
PERSON, Stanley. See Funk, F. jt. auth.
PERSONAL advertisements. See Newspapers—
Personal advertisements
PERSONAL beauty. See Beauty, Personal
PERSONAL credit. See Consumer credit
PERSONAL finance. See Finance, Personal
PERSONAL liberty. See Liberty
PERSONAL names. See Names, Personal
PERSONAL opinions. See Attitudes
PERSONAL portfolios. See Applications for
positions
PERSONAL property. See Property
PERSONAL property insurance, All risk. See
Insurance—All risk policies
PERSONAL responsibility. See Responsibility
PERSONAL rights. See Civil rights
PERSONALITY
On doing-one's-thing. W. Goodman. Am
Scholar 38:240-7 Spr '69
See also
Body image
Human relations
Individuality
Leadership
Personality change
Psychology
PERSONALITY, Disorders of
See also
Autism
Schizophrenia
PERSONALITY change
How people change. A. Wheelis. Commentary
47:56-66 My '69
PERSONALITY tests
Utility of projective, techniques and the
function of the clinical psychologist. J. L.
Horn. Ment Hy 53:654-6 O '69
Who do you think he is? il Seventeen 27:122-
3+ D '68
Who do you think you are? il Seventeen 27:
120-1+ D '68
PERSONNEL management
Case of the nettlesome nepot. R. W. Cam-
breleng. il Harvard Bsns R 47:14-16+ Mr
'69
Case of the straying scientist. J. S. Mendell.
il Harvard Bsns R 47:4-6+ Jl '69
Forecasting manpower needs. J. W. Walker.
bibliog Harvard Bsns R 47:152-4+ Mr '69
How to deal with resistance to change; reprint from May-June 1954 issue, with retro-
spective commentary. P. R. Lawrence.
Harvard Bsns R 47:4-6+ Ja '69
Job enrichment pays off; findings of studies
carried out in British companies. W. J.
Paul, jr. and others. il Harvard Bsns R
47:61-78 Mr '69

PERSONNELL management—*Continued*
Pygmalion in management; excerpts from High expectations in management. J. S. Livingston. bibliog f il Harvard Bsns R 47:81-9 Jl '69
See also
Absenteeism
Communication in management
Employees—Promotion
Grievance procedures
Incentives in industry
Job satisfaction
Job transfers
Layoff systems
Library administration
PERSONNEL service in education
Entering the world of work; with study-discussion program, by C. Smallenburg and H. Smallenburg. H. J. Reed. bibliog il PTA Mag 63:8-10, 35-6 Ap '69
What professional guidance does for students. Good H 168:204-5 Ap '69
See also
Group guidance in education
Student counselors
PERSONS, Single. See Single people
PERSPECTIVE
Jokes the old masters used to play. P. Brock. il Sci Digest 65:12-17 My '69
PERSPIRATION
How to keep your cool; questions and answers. il Seventeen 28:136-7 F '69
Sweat in schizophrenic patients; identification of the odorous substance. K. Smith and others. bibliog il Science 166:398-9 O 17 '69
PERSUASION (propaganda) See Advertising—Social aspects
PERTILE, Aureliano
Pertile and Giannini. A. Favia-Artsay. por Hobbies 74:35+ Ag '69
PERU
See also
Agricultural administration—Peru
Airlines—Peru
Amazon River
Arts and crafts—Peru
Costume—Peru
Investments, Foreign (in Peru)
Poor—Peru
Puno
Sacsahuaman (fort)
Tourist trade—Peru

Antiquities
See Indians of South America—Antiquities—Peru

Commercial treaties and agreements
Sugaring off; first trade agreement between Peru and the Soviet Union. il Newsweek 73:38 Mr 3 '69

Description and travel
Peru: on top of the world. L. Blackwood. il Sr Schol 94:Schol Teach 13-14 Ap 11 '69

Expropriation policy
Back from the brink. Newsweek 73:52 Ap 21 '69
Challenging the U.S; dispute over seizure of International petroleum co, oilfields and refinery. Time 93:36 F 14 '69
Down to the wire; question of sanctions by the United States. Newsweek 73:45 Ap 7 '69
Grace takes a bitter pill in Peru. il Bsns W p62-3 D 20 '69
Heading for a showdown; seizure of International petroleum co. property. Time 93:35 Ap 11 '69
In the grip of a revolution; stakes involved in Peru's expropriation of U.S. oil investments. il Newsweek 73:52-4+ Ap 14 '69
Is anybody listening? il Newsweek 74:33 Jl 7 '69
Letter from Peru; takeover of International petroleum co. R. N. Goodwin. New Yorker 45:41-6+ My 17 '69
New junta, but same old Peru. Ramp Mag 7:18+ N 30 '68
Peru: more troubles for U.S; seizure of an American-owned oil firm without compensation. il U S News 66:68 Mr 3 '69
Peru turns tougher; takeover of International petroleum co. il Bsns W p32-3 F 15 '69
Peruvian crisis; sanctions by U.S. Nat R 21:371-2 Ap 22 '69
Postponed problem; expropriation of the U.S.-owned International petroleum co. il Time 93:40 Ap 18 '69
Report from Lima. V. Clear. il Fortune 79:55-6+ Mr '69

Second thoughts; case of the International petroleum corp. J. B. Utley. il Nat R 21:644-5+ Jl 1 '69
Washington over the oil barrel in Peru. D. Ross. New Repub 160:15-16 Ap 12 '69
Will we or won't we? expropriation of U.S.-owned International petroleum. E. McDowell. Nat R 21:331 Ap 8 '69

Foreign relations
Climate turns colder. Bsns W p34+ My 31 '69
Fish and oil. Time 93:40 My 30 '69
Gunboat diplomacy; private American tuna fleet accosted by Peruvian gunboat off coast of Peru. Newsweek 73:50 F 24 '69
Peru and the great colossus. Chr Cent 86:339 Mr 12 '69; Reply. H. C. Taylor. 86:654+ My 7 '69
Peru: more troubles for U.S. il U S News 66:68 Mr 3 '69
Peru's actions on Rockefeller visit and U.S. military missions regretted; Department statement. Dept State Bul 60:509-10 Je 16 '69
Report from Lima. V. Clear. il Fortune 79:55-6+ Mr '69
Talking it over; J. N. Irwin as U.S. emissary. Time 93:31 Mr 21 '69
United States and Peru hold round of talks at Washington; Department statement. Dept State Bul 60:472-3 Je 2 '69
U.S. and Peru resume talks on outstanding problems; Department statement. Dept State Bul 60:460-1 My 12 '69
U.S. expresses concern to Peru over fishing-boat incident; Department statement, February 14, 1969. Dept State Bul 60:184 Mr 3 '69

History
Spanish Peru: 1532-1560, by J. Lockhart. Review
Américas il 21:40-1 Mr '69. R. E. Crist
When civilizations collide. il Sr Schol 95:4-5 O 6 '69

Politics and government
New militarism in Peru. J. L. Klaiber. America 120:364-7 Mr 29 '69
Report from Peru; the reformers in brass hats. J. Yglesias. il N Y Times Mag p58-9+ D 14 '69
Two ears and a tail. P. Kramer. il Newsweek 74:43-4 S 8 '69

Religious institutions and affairs
In the shadow of the mountain; photographs. C. Andujar. Natur Hist 78:28-33 F '69
See also
Catholic church in Peru

Social conditions
Social reform in Peru. America 121:345 O 25 '69
PERUTZ, Max Ferdinand, and others
DNA helix. Science 164:1537-9 Je 27 '69
PERUVIAN folk art. See Folk art
PERUVIAN Indians. See Indians of South America—Peru
PERVERSE madonna in love; story. See Ingalls. S. R.
PESKIN, Charles. See Spruch, G. M. jt. auth.
PESSAH, Henry
New coax connector tops performance records. Electr World 82:28-9+ Ag '69
PESSIMISM
See also
Cynicism
PESTICIDES
Bald eagles and people; hearings before subcommittee on intergovernmental relations. New Repub 161:11 Jl 19 '69
Gardening without DDT. Time 94:41 Ag 8 '69
More ways than one to kill a bug; insect viruses. K. Frazier. il Sci N 96:334-6 O 11 '69
Pesticide research; industry, USDA pursue different paths. J. R. Kramer. Science 166:1383-6 D 12 '69
See also
Herbicides
Spraying and dusting

Injurious effects
Bug killers; a peril to health? U S News 66:14 My 5 '69
Fast way to clean pesticides out of cows. N. Reeder. Farm J 93:25 Ag '69
HEW examines cancer institute report. M. Mueller. Science 164:1503 Je 27 '69
Pesticide pollution. Consumer Rep 34:411-13, 478-82 Jl-Ag '69

PESTICIDES—Injurious effects—*Continued*
Pesticides and man's environment; excerpts from address. D. H. Jenkins. il Am For 75:30-1+ Ja '69
Poisons, profits and politics; cases of death and severe illness due to pesticide poisoning in Calif. R. Harmer. Nation 209:134-7 Ag 25 '69
Politics of pesticides. M. D. Green. Nation 209:569-71 N 24 '69
Side effects; report of a conference on ecological aspects of international development. H. Henkin. il Environ 11:28-35+ Ja '69
Soil pollutants and soil animals. C. A. Edwards. il Sci Am 220:88-92+ Ap '69
Thoroughly confused; letter, with reply. H. Magargle. W. H. Youngman. Am For 75:17-18 N '69

Laws and legislation

Politics of pesticides. Consumer Rep 34:478-82 Ag '69

Residues

Microparticulates: isolation from water and identification of associated chlorinated pesticides. R. M. Pfister and others. bibliog il Science 166:878-9 N 14 '69
New pollution problem: mercury contamination of food, air, and water. S. Novick. il Environ 11:2-9 My '69

PESYANOE meteorite. See Meteorites

PET Industries

Securities

Betting on real cats and dogs. il Bsns W p72-3 Ag 30 '69

PETER, Saint
Peter in Rome. by D. W. O'Connor. Review America 120:258-9 Mr 1 '69. H. Musurillo

PETER, Klaus J. See Fish, L. W. jr. jt. auth.

PETER, Laurence J.
Addition to the lexicon of management; hierarchiology. Bsns W p 134 F 22 '69
Glossary of incompetence. por Time 93:58 Mr 28 '69
Peter. sticks by his principle. por Bsns W p 115-16 D 13 '69
Science of hierarchiology. Sci Digest 65:89-90 Mr '69
Up against the Peter principle. J. Howard. por Life 67:59 Jl 18 '69

PETER, Robert
Letter from Uruguay. Nat R 21:700 Jl 15 '69

PETER and the wolf; ballet. See Ballets—Criticisms

PETER Grimes (operatic character) See Characters in opera

PETER Grimes; opera. See Britten, B.

PETER H. Wyden, incorporated. See Wyden, Peter H. incorporated

PETERS, Art
Ordeal of Tammi Terrell. Ebony 25:94-6+ N '69

PETERS, B. F.
Student body turns it on. Am Ed 5:20-1 Ap '69

PETERS, Charles Hamilton
Noblesse oblige. L. L. L. Golden. Sat R 52:58+ Je 14 '69

PETERS, Edward H.
Bishops of Rome in our time. Cath World 208:232-3 F '69

PETERS, Jean S.
Mom's in the driver's seat. Parents Mag 44:50+ Je '69

PETERS, Ruth Marie
Grow flowers to wear. Horticulture 48:30+ Ja '70
House plants for every home. Home Gard 56:32-40 N '69
Plan now for early bloom with perennials. Horticulture 47:18-19+ Ag '69
You can put a greenhouse in your future. Home Gard 56:34-42 D '69

PETERS, Thomas H.
Bookshop planned around social involvement. Pub W 195:44-6 Mr 3 '69

PETERS, William
Education of Carla ManCari. Good H 169:90-1+ S '69

PETERS, William Wesley
Taliesin in Teheran. Art in Am 57:44-51 Jl '69

PETERSEN, Don
Does a tiger wear a necktie? Criticism
America 120:433 Ap 5 '69
Nation 208:346-7 Mr 17 '69
New Yorker 45:94 Mr 8 '69
Newsweek il 73:96 Mr 10 '69
Sat R 52:22 Mr 15 '69

PETERSEN, Marjorie
Stornoway progress report. il Motor B 124:52-5+ D '69

PETERSON, Arthur G.
Glass coloring. Hobbies 74:98F N '69
Glass patterns: Mignon, Monroe, Mikado, & Okay. Hobbies 74:98EE My '69
Glassware patents by Charles Ballinger. Hobbies 74:98DD-98EE Je '69
Maize art glass. Hobbies 73:76+ F; 74:98R Ap '69

PETERSON, Bob
Les girls in Des Moines; photographs. Sports Illus 30:34-9 F 17 '69

PETERSON, Chester, jr
One-man assembly line for calving. Farm J 93:24F-24H Jl '69

PETERSON, Donald O.
Where are they now? il por Newsweek 74:8 S 8 '69

PETERSON, Eric
Program has helped me know that I don't know. Mlle 69:261+ Ag '69

PETERSON, Ervin L.
How much is enough? address. por Am For 75:24-7 D '69

PETERSON, George A.
Reacher: Don Redlich. il Dance Mag 43:60-3 Je '69

PETERSON, Harold
Baseball's Johnny Appleseed. Sports Illus 30:56-64+ Ap 14 '69
Down with the heathen. Sports Illus 30:38-40+ F 24 '69

PETERSON, J. W. See Vela, G. R. jt. auth.

PETERSON, Jeanne G.
How to quell the midnight halyard orchestra. Motor B 124:107 Ag '69

PETERSON, Jessie
New Mexico's sunspot. Travel 132:48-9 Ag '69

PETERSON, Margaret R. See Anderson, J. M. jt. auth.

PETERSON, Mary Nygaard
Beyond mutiny; drama. Plays 29:61-6 O '69

PETERSON, Paul D. and Jacobsen, E. H.
Maser amplification of 9.5-gigahertz elastic waves in sapphire doped with divalent nickel impurity ions. bibliog Science 164:1065-7 My 30 '69

PETERSON, Richard S. See Le Boeuf, B. J. jt. auth.

PETERSON, Robert
Little red schoolhouse reopens. Har Yrs 9:18 Je '69
Not her cup of tea. Flying 84:56-9 Je '69
Ready to copy? Flying 85:50-2+ S '69
(ed) See Cavalli, C. I retired to the library

PETERSON, Roger Tory
Osprey; endangered world citizen. il Nat Geog 136:52-67 Jl '69; Same abr. with title Mystery of the vanishing osprey. Read Digest 95:86-9 N '69
—See Buchheister, C. W. jt. auth.

about

Roger Peterson's whooping cranes. il Audubon 71:80-2 N '69

PETERSON, Rudolph Arvid
Mr Peterson to head task force on international development. Dept State Bul 61:284 S 29 '69
New boss for the biggest. por Time 94:50 D 26 '69
World trade and investment; address, March 10, 1969. Vital Speeches 35:413-16 Ap 15 '69

PETERSON, Russell K. and Rash, B. B.
Industry learns to train the hardcore. Ed Digest 35:35-7 O '69

PETERSON, Ted T. See Brown, S. B. jt. auth.

PETERSON, Willis
Timber titan. Nat Wildlife 7:4-7 Je '69

PETINA, Irra
Irra; interview, ed. by H. E. Phillips. por Opera N 34:17 S 6 '69

PETINE, George A.
Crayon illuminations. Sch Arts 69:16-17 S '69

PETITT, Dorothy
(ed) Professional publications (cont) Engl J 58:132-8, 281-7, 450-7, 602-6+, 945-8, 1250-4, 1391-5 Ja-Ap, S, N-D '69

PETRARCA, Anthony J.
Irony of situation in Ernest Hemingway's Soldier's home. Engl J 58:664-7 My '69

PETRIE, Paul
Dream; poem. Atlan 223:76 Ja '69
In praise of old stoves; poem. Poetry 114:313 Ag '69
Lament for the march king; poem. Atlan 224:68-9 N '69
Old pro's lament; poem. New Yorker 45:38 Je 28 '69

PETROCIK, Joe
Puerto Rico; outside San Juan. Travel 131:26-9+ Ap '69

PETROGLYPHS
California's petroglyph canyons: a gallery of ancient Indian art. G. F. Jackson. il Nat Parks 43:15-17 O '69

PETROGLYPHS—*Continued*
Petroglyphs of Siberia. A. P. Okladnikov. il Sci Am 221:74-82 bibliog (p 136) Ag '69
To see the maze. il Sunset 143:38 N '69
Unlocking the secrets graven on Mojave rock; Coso drawings. il Sunset 143:108-9 O '69
Who put the handprints on Prayer rock? R. C. Hildreth. il Sci Digest 65:54-6 Je '69

PETROLEUM

International aspects

Changing geopolitics of the world's oil. il U S News 66:98-100 Ap 14 '69
Jersey, Texaco, Gulf, meet BP. il Forbes 103:32+ Ap 1 '69
Oil deal strengthens link to Arab states; Hispanoil in French-American oil consortium. Bsns W p50+ O 11 '69
Political economy of international oil and the underdeveloped countries, by M. Tanzer. Review
 Nation 209:605-7 D 1 '69. R. Engler
Why the oil giants are under the gun. il Bsns W p82-3+ O 25 '69

Pipe lines

Billion-dollar pipeline to tap Alaskan oil. il U S News 68:79 Ja 12 '70
Interior sets limits on Alaska oil pipeline. Nat Parks 43:22 D '69
Laying it on the line for Alaskan oil; gamble on Trans-Alaska pipeline system. il Bsns W p31-2 N 29 '69
North Slope: oil rush. L. J. Carter. il Science 166:85-92 O 3 '69; Reply. F. F. Wright. 166:1220+ D 5 '69
Operation Hannibal: jungle oil for world markets. R. S. Diamond. il Fortune 79:109-11 F '69
Pipeline and permafrost; Alaska's north slope. Sci N 96:524 D 6 '69

Production methods
See Petroleum engineering

Prospecting

Bad days for wild ones. il Time 94:76 Jl 11 '69
Challenge of the North Slope. il Time 94:65 S 19 '69
Changing geopolitics of the world's oil. il U S News 66:98-100 Ap 14 '69
Underwater route to Arctic oil; plan of Marine resource consultants, inc; of Santa Monica, Calif. il Bsns W p47 Jl 12 '69
World's newest hunt for oil bonanza; the oil rush in southeast Asia. il U S News 67:66-8 D 1 '69

Transportation

Alaska's oil challenge. il Bsns W p 120+ S 13 '69
Real meaning of Alaskan oil finds. il U S News 66:66-7 Mr 3 '69
Southwest passage? to get crude out of Alaska. Forbes 104:50 O 15 '69
 See also
Petroleum—Pipe lines
Tank ships

Well drilling
See Oil well drilling

Alaska

Alaska: bonanza for blacks? il Ebony 25:123-6+ N '69
Alaskan prospect. A. W. Smith. Nat Parks 43:2 S '69
Bubble, bubble, Alaskan oil and trouble. Liv Wildn 33:37-8 Sum '69
Canada's oilmen stake claim in U.S. market; Alaska threaten Canadian sales in U.S. il Bsns W p24-5 Ap 5 '69
Challenge of the North Slope. il Time 94:65 S 19 '69
Driller's luck; Alaskan North Slope. Newsweek 74:94+ O 13 '69
Great Alaska oil rush. P. Friggens. il Read Digest 95:66-70 Jl '69
Great Alaska oil sweepstakes. il Bsns W p43-4 S 13 '69
Great oil hunt; North Slope auction; with report by G. C. Lubenow. il Newsweek 74:80-2+ S 22 '69
Hickel and the Arctic. M. Frome. il Field & S 74:12-14+ N '69
Interior sets limits on Alaska oil pipeline. Nat Parks 43:22 D '69
North Slope: oil rush. L. J. Carter. il Science 166:85-92 O 3 '69; Reply. F. F. Wright. 166:1220+ D 5 '69
North Slope showdown. il Newsweek 74:63-4 Ag 25 '69

Northwest Passage; an ice-breaking tanker pioneers in opening the long-sought Arctic route. N. Wood. il Travel & Camera 32:14+ N '69
Northwest Passage to what? Manhattan's voyage. J. Lear. il Sat R 52:55-6+ N 1 '69
Northwest Passage; voyage of the Manhattan. Nation 209:301 S 29 '69
Oil in the Arctic; with report by J. Bonfante. il Life 66:20-9 F 14 '69
Richest auction in history. il Time 94:87-8 S 19 '69
Rising stars; Hamilton brothers successful in Alaska bidding. Forbes 104:26-7 O 1 '69
Ultimate confrontation. R. Cantwell. il Sports Illus 30:66-70+ Mr 24 '69

Arctic Regions

It adds up to an icebreaker; supertanker Manhattan to open up route to Arctic oil. Bsns W p53 My 31 '69
Real meaning of Alaskan oil finds. il U S News 66:66-7 Mr 3 '69
Search for Golconda; converting biggest tanker in the U.S. merchant fleet into an icebreaker to open route to Arctic oil. il Newsweek 73:77+ Mr 10 '69
Underwater route to Arctic oil. il Bsns W p47 Jl 12 '69

Asia, Southeastern

World's newest hunt for oil bonanza. il U S News 67:66-8 D 1 '69

Indonesia

Japan the target for Indonesian oil; offshore oil. il Bsns W p60-1+ My 31 '69
Oil general. il Newsweek 73:81 Je 16 '69
World's newest hunt for oil bonanza. il U S News 67:66-8 D 1 '69

Iraq

Iraq. R. A. Fernea and E. W. Fernea. bibliog il Focus 20:1-8 O '69

Japan

Undersea oil for Japan? Sci Am 221:48 O '69

Michigan

Oil explorers find hope in Michigan. il Bsns W p46 O 18 '69

Russia

Soviet icebox yields treasure; oil and gas fields at Arctic Circle. il Bsns W p43-4 Je 21 '69

PETROLEUM engineering
They're mining oil with buckets. D. Fales. il Pop Mech 131:108-10 F '69

PETROLEUM engineers
Universities: industry links raise conflict of interest issue; questioning relation of petroleum engineering professors to oil industry. J. Walsh. Science 164:411-12 Ap 25 '69

PETROLEUM equipment industry
 See also
Halliburton company

PETROLEUM in submerged lands
Abyssal oil? Sci Am 221:54 Jl '69
Japan the target for Indonesian oil. il Bsns W p60-1+ My 31 '69
Offshore oil: channel blowout points up information gap. L. J. Carter. Science 164:530-2 My 2 '69
 See also
Oil well drilling, Submarine

PETROLEUM industry and trade
Why the oil giants are under the gun. il Bsns W p82-3+ O 25 '69
 See also
Government investigations—Petroleum industry and trade

Consolidations and mergers

Affair of state; Justice department suit to halt BP-Sohio merger. Newsweek 74:98B+ O 20 '69
Ashland oil scrambles hard to become an energy giant. il Bsns W p64-5 Ag 2 '69
BP's new boy has welcome mat yanked; BP-Sohio merger. Bsns W p48 O 11 '69
Marriage, divorce style; Atlantic Richfield co. and Sinclair oil corp. Newsweek 73:95-6 Mr 17 '69
Not so dumb; American petrofina's purchase of Cosden petroleum. Forbes 104:54-5 Jl 15 '69
Oil merger O.K. but; Justice dept. sanctions Atlantic Richfield-Sinclair oil merger. Bsns W p94 Mr 8 '69
Trustbusting and common sense; Justice department to block proposed merger of British petroleum and Standard oil co. of Ohio. Duns R 94:140 N '69
What price Hess? proposed Hess-Amerada merger. il Forbes 103:51+ Mr 1 '69

PETROLEUM industry and trade—*Continued*

Finance

Can we meet the expanding need for energy?
il Nations Bsns 57:32-3 N '69
King-size middleman of oil. Bsns W p92-3 Ag
16 '69

International aspects

See Petroleum—International aspects

Laws

See Petroleum laws and legislation

Securities

Investors gush over oil; oil stocks' boom. il
Bsns W p 130+ Je 7 '69
Oil funds: gusher or duster? il Duns R 94:68-
70+ O '69
Wall Steet beat. R. Brady. il Duns R 94:81-2
Jl '69
Wall Street: oil in a troubled market. C.
Morgello. il Newsweek 73:83 F 17 '69
Who are the winners? C. Morgello. il News-
week 74:88-90 S 22 '69

Taxation

Dry hole; threat is depletion allowance. il
Newsweek 74:72B+ Ag 4 '69
Oil and politics. R. Dugger. Atlan 224:66-78+
S '69; Discussion. 224:42+ D '69
Way to tax oil. New Repub 160:11-12 Ap 5
'69
Year oil gets its lumps. il Bsns W p98-9+
My 17 '69

Alaska

Alaska strikes it rich. il Bsns W p48-53 F 1
'69
Alaska's $50-billion boom. il Forbes 104:30-
3+ N 15 '69
Alaska's oil challenge. il Bsns W p 120+ S
13 '69
Assault on the North slope. J. Gooding. il
Fortune 81:108-11 Ja '70
Betting a billion on Alaskan oil. Bsns W
p43 Ag 16 '69
Billion-dollar pipeline to tap Alaskan oil. il
U S News 68:79 Ja 12 '70
Did money go where the oil is? il Bsns W
p51-2 S 20 '69
Hot oil rush in Arctic Alaska. J. Main. il
Fortune 79:120-5+ Ap '69
Laying it on the line for Alaskan oil; gamble
on Trans-Alaska pipeline system. il Bsns W
p31-2 N 29 '69
Real meaning of Alaskan oil finds. il U S
News 66:66-7 Mr 3 '69

Bolivia

Can Gulf pick up the pieces in Bolivia? il
Bsns W p44+ O 25 '69

Canada

Canada's oilmen stake claim in U.S. market;
Alaska threaten Canadian sales in U.S. il
Bsns W p24-5 Ap 5 '69

Egypt

Oil may soothe Egypt's wounds. il Bsns W
p89+ Je 28 '69

Great Britain

Burmah oil: another BP? J. Ross-Skinner. il
Duns R 94:60-2 Ag '69
See also
British petroleum company

Indonesia

Old oil hand makes Natomas swing; R. K.
Davies. il Bsns W p 102-3 S 27 '69

Italy

Italians bite kid-gloved hand; McKee's take-
over of CTIP. Bsns W p40 Ag 9 '69
Soviet gas salesmen sign up Italy's ENI.
Bsns W p36 D 13 '69
Subsidiary that rebelled. il Time 94:68 Jl 25
'69

Kuwait

Kuwait: Aladdin's lamp of the Middle East.
J. E. Frazer. il Nat Geog 135:636-67 My '69

Libya

Oilmen in Libya try to cap the jitters. il
Bsns W p45-6 O 18 '69

Spain

Oil deal strengthens link to Arab states:
Hispanoil in French-American oil consortium. Bsns W p50+ O 11 '69

United States

Battle over special privilege. il Time 93:98+
Je 13 '69

Cheaper oil; subcommittee on antitrust and
monopoly investigation. New Repub 161:9
Jl 19 '69
Coming crisis in oil: battle over bigger im-
ports. il U S News 68:77-80 Ja 12 '70
Costly beachheads; California oil market. il
Forbes 103:22-3 My 1 '69
Fill 'er up, and check the oil. Sr Schol
94:22 F 28 '69
Machiasport gets two new bidders; battle
over building a refinery at Machiasport,
Me. Bsns W p20 Jl 5 '69
Oil companies bail out of fertilizer surplus. il
Bsns W p35 D 13 '69
Our crazy, costly life with oil quotas. A. T.
Demaree. il Fortune 79:104-7+ Je '69
See also names of oil companies, e.g.
Pauley petroleum, incorporated

Venezuela

Venezuela: the race against time. J. Poindexter. il Duns R 94:62-5+ Jl '69

PETROLEUM laws and legislation
Oil and politics. R. Dugger. Atlan 224:66-
78+ S '69; Discussion. 224:4+ D '69
Oilmen feel the pressure; federal crackdown
after Union oil blowout. Bsns W p43 Mr 29
'69
Udall's last laugh; regulations allowing oil
imports to Hawaii. New Repub 160:10 F 1
'69
Year oil gets its lumps. il Bsns W p98-9+
My 17 '69
PETROLEUM pipe lines. See Petroleum—
Pipe lines
PETROLEUM refineries
Prospect of oil awakens a Maine town. il
Bsns W p46-7+ Ja 3 '70
PETROLOGY
Simulating conditions in deep earth. Chem
42:24 N '69
PETROSIAN, Tigran Vartanovich
Close-up; world chess champion. R. Chel-
minski. il pors Life 66:41-2+ Ap 11 '69
PETROV, Boris
Future belongs to space laboratories. Space
World F-7-67:11-12 Jl '69
PETROW, Richard
Death of World Glory. Pop Mech 132:106-
11+ Jl '69
In Florida today: ranchers get rough on
rustlers. Pop Mech 132:116-20 Jl '69
Secrets of the animal world. Pop Mech 132:
84-7+ S '69
What really caused the Torrey Canyon di-
saster? excerpts from In the wake of Tor-
rey Canyon. Pop Mech 131:114-19+ Ap
'69
PETROWSKY, Robert L.
Experiment with ten emitter-coupled circuits.
Radio-Electr 40:37-40 Mr '69
PETRUCCI, Ottaviano dei
Reviews of records. H. L. Clarke. Mus Q 55:
584-6 O '69
PETS
Authors & editors; M. Truman's White House
pets. B. A. Bannon. Pub W 196:25-6 S 8
'69
Family pet P. O'Keefe. See issues of Amer-
ican home
If you want to raise pedigreed animals. Good
H 168:157 F '69
Inhumane traffic in exotic pets. R. Gannon.
il Read Digest 95:149-52 S '69
Pet news. J. Kuh. See occasional issues of
Ladies' home journal
Pets. il Bet Hom & Gard 47:48+ O '69
Pets and old age. B. M. Levinson. bibliog
Ment Hy 53:364-8 Jl '69
Prescription: one puppy; pets for the aged.
Sci Digest 66:35 N '69
So your children want a pet? il Consumer
Bul 52:20-2 Jl '69
Turning pets into people. il Time 93:60 F
14 '69
Urban snakes: an identity crisis; snakes as
pets in New York apartments. H. G. Dowl-
ing. il Natur Hist 78:66-71 Ap '69
See also
Travel with pets
also names of animal pets, e.g. Dogs

Care

Good grooming for pets. P. O'Keefe. Am
Home 72:105 Mr '69
Health hints for exotic pets. Sci Digest 65:
41-2 My '69
Hot-weather grooming for pets. il Good H
169:144 Jl '69
PETSCHEK, Willa
Agatha Christie: the world's most mysterious
woman. McCalls 96:80-1+ F '69
PETTERSON, Richard
Harrison McIntosh. Ceram Mo 17:19-26 Je
'69

PETTIBONE, Dennis Lynn
Julius Caesar's poverty program. Nat R 21: 954-5 S 23 '69
PETTIS, Arthur H.
Distributed plates improve CRT response. Electr World 82:28 N '69
PETTIS, Jerry Lyle
Excerpt from testimony before House committee on interstate and foreign commerce, April 15, 1969. Cong Digest 48:176+ Je '69
PETTIT, Lawrence K.
Congress, confusion, and indirect costs. bibliog Science 163:1301-5 Mr 21 '69
PETTORUTI, Emilio
Reflections of an artist. R. Squirru. il Américas 21:37-41 F '69
PETTY, Richard
Talladega: the principals and the principles. por Motor T 21:37+ N '69
PETZNY, W. J. and Quinn, J. A.
Calibrated membranes with coated pore walls. bibliog Science 166:751-3 N 7 '69
PETZOLDT, Paul
Survival expert. Paul Petzoldt. J. Howard. il pors Life 67:48-50+ D 19 '69
PEWTER
English pewter collection. C. A. Peal. il Antiques 96:202-8 Ag '69
PEWTER casting. See Foundry practice
PEWTER pitchers. See Pitchers
PEWTER tableware. See Tableware, Pewter
PEYOTE
Peyote road. P. Nabokov. il N Y Times Mag p30-1+ Mr 9 '69
PFAFF, Richard C.
Africans question celibacy. America 120:305-6 Mr 15 '69
PFAFF, William
Decline of liberal politics. Commentary 48: 45-51 O '69
Lack of knowledge and leadership. Cur 113: 41-2 D '69
Like imperial Germany, we are tone-deaf in diplomacy. Commonweal 90:7-8 Mr 21 '69; Same with title Toward neo-isolationism? Cur 109:49-51 Ag '69
Mote in the eye. New Repub 160:36+ F 1 '69
World reformism. Commentary 47:78-80 F '69
PFAFFMANN, C. See Frank, M. jt. auth.
PFAU, Peter J.
Only one man per shift. Am City 84:112+ S '69
PFEIFFER, C. Boyd
Fly rods & hickory shad. Field & S 74:74-5+ My '69
Swim a jig for summer bass. Outdoor Life 144:44-5+ Jl '69
PFEIFFER, George
Page 48. Am West 6:48 N '69
PFEIFFER, John
Electronomusic. A. Cohn. por Am Rec G 35:627-8 Ap '69
PFEIL, Mary Pat
They got the feeling that everybody's somebody. Am Ed 5:21-4 D '69
PFINGSTON, Roger
Lost; poem. Nation 209:509 N 10 '69
PFISTER, Herbert R.
Air conditioner in a fireplace? Pop Sci 195: 38 Jl '69
PFISTER, Robert, and others
Microparticulates: isolation from water and identification of associated chlorinated pesticides. bibliog Science 166:878-9 N 14 '69
PFITZNER, Hans
Hans Pfitzner's near-miss: Von deutscher seele. G. L. Mayer. por Am Rec G 35:415-16 Ja '69
Mantle of Palestrina. F. G. Arnstein. por Opera N 34:20-1 D 13 '69
Records:
Von deutscher seele. Opera N 33:34 Mr 8 '69
PFIZER, Beryl
Dream party nightmare. Ladies Home J 86: 52+ O '69
End of a beautiful friendship with my friendly bank. McCalls 96:92-3 Mr '69
Poor woman's almanac. Ladies Home J 86:16 S; 24 O; 22 N '69
Why I don't buy wholesale any more. McCalls 96:87+ Je '69
PFIZER, Charles, and company
Still rolling along. il Forbes 104:44 D 1 '69
PFOUTZ, Daniel R.
Penntap. por Library J 94:1589-91 Ap 15 '69
(comp) Sci-tech books '68. por Library J 94:948-55 Mr 1 '69
PHAGOCYTES and phagocytosis
Plague bacillus: survival within host phagocytes. W. A. Janssen and M. J. Surgalla. bibliog il Science 163:950-3 F 28 '69
See also
Macrophages

PHALAROPES
Phalarope. E. O. Höhn. il Sci Am 220:104-9+ Je '69
PHAM-the-Truc
Appeal to the people of the United States. Nation 209:2 Jl 7 '69
PHANTOM cottage; novel. See Johnston, V.
PHARAOHS
Black emperor who saved Jerusalem: Pharaoh Taharqa. M. H. Levine. il Negro Hist Bul 32:19-20 My '69
Blood of the pharaohs. Sci Am 221:55 D '69
PHARIS, William L. jr, and others
Educational decision making. Todays Ed 58:52-4 O '69
PHARMACEUTICAL apparatus
To build a better pill counter. il Time 94: 102+ D 5 '69
PHARMACEUTICAL industry. See Drug trade
PHARMACEUTICAL manufacturers association
Battle to keep drugs on the market. Bsns W p30 O 4 '69
FDA and Panalba: a conflict of commercial, therapeutic goals? M. Mintz. Science 165:875-81 Ag 29 '69
PHARMACEUTICAL research
Pharmaceutical revolution: its impact on science and society. L. Lasagna. bibliog Science 166:1227-33 D 5 '69
PHARMACOLOGY
Oceanic drug chest. J. L. Arehart. il Sea Front 15:98-107 Mr '69
See also
Drugs

Research
See Pharmaceutical research

PHARMACOPEIAS
Information almanac. McCalls 96:52 Mr '69
PHASES (chemistry)
Measurements in the high-pressure environment; report of meeting. E. C. Lloyd and others. il Science 164:860-2 My 16 '69
States of aggregation. K. Mendelssohn. il Phys Today 22:46-51 Ap '69
PHAULKON, Constant
Constant and the King of Siam. M. Bishop. il por Horizon 11:58-9 Wint '69
PHEASANT shooting
Hunter alone. R. V. McCormick. il Field & S 74:70-1+ S '69
Notes on pheasant shooting. J. O'Connor. il Outdoor Life 143:92+ F '69
Pheasant tips. M. Griffith. il Field & S 74: 62-3+ N '69
Plight of the people bird. V. Kraft. Sports Illus 31:87-8 N 17 '69
PHEASANTS
New pheasant policy; artificial game propagation. R. B. Colson. il Cons 24:14-15 O '69
Where have all the pheasants gone? G. Laycock. il Field & S 74:60-1+ Ag '69
PHELAN, William D. jr
Authoritarian prescription. Nation 209:467-73 N 3 '69
PHÉLIZON, Georges
Communications on the moon. UNESCO Courier 22:26-31 Mr '69
PHELPS, Dale King
Girl becomes a doctor. R. Gosswiller. il pors Todays Health 47:29-33 Je '69
PHELPS, Donald
Westbrook Pegler, RIP. Nat R 21:696-9+ Jl 15 '69
PHELPS, Robert
Just whose art is primitive? Life 67:8 Ag 8 '69
PHENETHYL alcohol. See Alcohols
PHENOL oxidases. See Oxidases
PHENOTYPE. See Genotype and phenotype
PHENOXETOL. See Phenoxyethanol
PHENOXYETHANOL
Phenoxyethanol: protein preservative for taxonomists. M. Nakanishi and others. bibliog il Science 163:681-3 F 14 '69
PHENYLALANINE
Compulsive sexual activity induced by p-chlorophenylalanine in normal and pinealectomized male rats. A. Tagliamonte and others. bibliog il Science 166:1433-5 D 12 '69
Phenylalanine and tyrosine synthesis under primitive earth conditions. N. Friedmann and S. L. Miller. bibliog il Science 166:766-7 N 7 '69
See also
Dopa

PHEROMONES
Ant alarm pheromone activity: correlation with molecular shape by scanning computer. J. E. Amoore and others. bibliog il Science 165:1266-9 S 19 '69

PHEROMONES—*Continued*
Host finding by odor in the myrmecophilic beetle atemeles pubicollis bris. (staphyinidae) B. Hölldobler. bibliog il Science 166:757-8 N 7 '69
Pheromone-induced changes in the acidophil concentration of mouse pituitary glands. T. L. Avery. bibliog il Science 164:423-4 Ap 25 '69
Pheromone response in pine bark beetles; influence of host volatiles. G. B. Pitman. bibliog Science 166:905-6 N 14 '69
Sexual pheromone in some fishes of the genus hypsoblennius gill. G. S. Losey, jr. bibliog il Science 163:181-3 Ja 10 '69
See also
Insect sex attractants

PHILADELPHIA
Philadelphia story; Society hill. K. Chapin. il Am Home 72:58-61+ D '69

Archives
See Archives—United States

Banks
New way through the interest ceiling; First Pennsylvania's debt idea. Bsns W p31 Ja 10 '70

Bicentennial international exposition planning group, Philadelphia
Bicentennial commemoration 1976. D. S. Brown and R. Venturi. il Arch Forum 131:66-9 O '69

Churches
Barnhouse and Boice; Tenth Presbyterian church. Chr Today 13:41 Ja 31 '69

Crime
Return of the rumble; Negro gang problem. il Newsweek 74:51 S 8 '69

Education
Can urban schools be reformed? W. Roberts. il Sat R 52:70-2+ My 17 '69
Experiment: Philadelphia's school without walls; Parkway program. il Life 66:40-2 My 16 '69
High school; film about Northeast high school. J. Featherstone. New Repub 160:28-30 Je 21 '69
Learning on the road; Parkway project. D. Cox. il Sat R 52:71 My 17 '69
Philadelphia Free school. Sat R 52:98-9 N 15 '69
Stop making excuses and start that class library! Germantown high school. D. Weissberger. Sr Schol 94:Schol Teach 28 Ja 31 '69
What is a middle school? Conwell middle magnet school. M. T. Wilson. Clear House 44:9-11 S '69

Finance
Another big city facing a crisis. U S News 66:10-11 Mr 3 '69

Free library
Philadelphia: the Reader development program. J. A. Axam. il Wilson Lib Bul 43:894-7 My '69

Galleries and museums
See also
Pennsylvania academy of the fine arts

History
If all the world were Philadelphia; a scaffolding for urban history, 1774-1930. S. B. Warner, jr. bibliog f il Am Hist R 74:26-43 O '68

Hospitals
Call for help from Vietnam; heart of 13-year-old Vietnamese boy restored by patch at Philadelphia Children's hospital. R. H. Berg. il Look 33:24-30+ D 16 '69

Industries
If all the world were Philadelphia; a scaffolding for urban history, 1774-1930. S. B Warner, jr. bibliog f il Am Hist R 74:26-43 O '68

Lighting
Lights for America's Champs-Elysees. D. M. Smallwood. il Am City 84:158+ S '69

Music
Current chronicle: Philadelphia musical academy's concerts. D. Chittum. il Mus Q 55:91-5, 401-7 Ja, Jl '69
Report: Philadelphia; performances of Tosca and Madama Butterfly. M. De Schauensee. Opera N 33:32 F 22 '69
See also
Philadelphia grand opera company
Philadelphia orchestra

Negroes
Black capitalism at work; what's happening in Philadelphia; interview. L. Sullivan. il U S News 66:60-4+ F 17 '69
Mrs Knauer's hometown; how consumers get justice. New Repub 160:9 My 17 '69

Newspapers
Knight in Philadelphia; Inquirer and News sold to Knight newspapers. il Newsweek 74:98 N 10 '69
See also
Philadelphia inquirer

Photographs
Dramatize your scenics; excerpts from Philadelphia, the intimate city, ed. by J. Dreyfuss. J. A. Drake, jr. il Mod Phot 33:62-5 S '69

Rapid transit
Where commuters are happy; automated transit system between Philadelphia and Lindenwold, N.J. il Bsns W p81 My 10 '69

Recreation
1876 art gallery revitalized; Memorial hall recreation center. H. Schick. il Parks & Rec 4:38-9 Jl '69

Schools
See Philadelphia—Education

Streets
Rittenhouse square from riches to rags. C. Brossard. il Holiday 45:78-9+ Ap '69

Theater
Philadelphia street players; Society hill playhouse street theatre. J. Adcock. Nation 209:611-12 D 1 '69

Water department
From concrete to cast iron to plastics. G. Gilbert. il Am City 84:88-9 N '69

PHILADELPHIA (periodical)
Crumbling foundation; exposé articles. il Time 94:60 Jl 25 '69

PHILADELPHIA Flyers (hockey team) See Hockey teams

PHILADELPHIA gas works
Natural gas deal may deflate shortage. Bsns W p39 N 22 '69

PHILADELPHIA grand opera company
Report: Philadelphia; world premiere of Pietro Aria's Jericho road. M. De Schauensee. il Opera N 33:24-5 My 17 '69
Report: production of Faust. M. De Schauensee. Opera N 34:40 D 27 '69

PHILADELPHIA inquirer
Letting go of a legacy; Philadelphia inquirer sold to Knight newspapers. Time 94:88 N 7 '69

PHILADELPHIA lyric opera company
Report: productions of Nabucco and Rigoletto. M. De Schauensee. Opera N 34:40 D 27 '69

PHILADELPHIA orchestra
Music to my ears; performance of works of Beethoven, Mendelssohn, and Richard Strauss in New York city. J. Kolodin. Sat R 53:76 Ja 3 '70
Musical events; concert in Philharmonic Hall conducted by I. Kertész. W. Sargeant. New Yorker 45:152+ Ap 26 '69
Musical events; concerts in Philharmonic Hall (cont) W. Sargeant. New Yorker 44:80+ Ja 25 '69
Musical events; opening concert in Philharmonic Hall. W. Sargeant. New Yorker 45:118 O 11 '69
O plus O equals Ormandy and Ozawa. I. Kolodin. Sat R 52:66 O 18 '69
Ormandy's orchestra; new RCA recordings. H Kupferberg. Atlan 223:142+ Ap '69
Philadelphia orchestra; RCA recordings. M. Kanny. il Am Rec G 35:44-7 F '69

PHILADELPHIA Phillies (baseball) See Baseball clubs

PHILADELPHIA public library. See Philadelphia—Free library

PHILADELPHIA symphony orchestra. See Philadelphia orchestra

PHILANTHROPIC foundations. See Foundations, Charitable and educational

PHILANTHROPY. See Charities; Giving

PHILATELIC scrapbooks. See Scrapbooks

PHILATELY. See Postage stamps

PHILBIN, Regis
Permanent second fiddles. il por Newsweek 74:45 S 1 '69

PHILBY, Harold Adrian Russell
Spy with the old school tie. L. B. Kirkpatrick, jr. Trans-Action 6:57-8 Ja '69

PHILBY, Kim. See Philby, H. A. R.

PHILCO-Ford corporation
Philco gears down its line. Bsns W p50 S 20 '69
Philco tries again. Bsns W p72+ F 15 '69

PHILHARMONIC Hall. See Lincoln Center for the performing arts, New York—Philharmonic Hall

PHILHARMONIC-symphony society of New York
After Bernstein who? the new generation of conductors; with photographs by A. Eisenstaedt. Life 66:42-51 F 21 '69
Black and white notes; discrimination charge. il Newsweek 74:82 Ag 18 '69
Gospel of Beethoven as Szell is his prophet; performance of Ninth symphony. I. Kolodin. Sat R 52:62-3 N 29 '69
Kertész at the Philharmonic. I. Kolodin. Sat R 52:24 D 27 '69
Lebe wohl: rehearsals of G. Mahler's Third symphony for L. Bernstein's farewell appearance. New Yorker 45:30-1 My 24 '69
Music; new music commissioned for 125th anniversary season. D. Hamilton. Nation 208:218+ F 17 '69
Music; performance of Ligeti's Atmosphères and Scriabin's Prometheus. D. Hamilton. Nation 209:549-50 N 17 '69
Musical events:
Beethoven's Ninth symphony in Philharmonic Hall. W. Sargeant. New Yorker 45:188-9 N 29 '69
Concerts in Philharmonic Hall (cont) W. Sargeant. New Yorker 45:132-3 Ap 5; 177 Ap 12; 147 O 25; 163-4 N 1 '69
Gustav Mahler's Third symphony conducted by L. Bernstein in farewell appearance. W. Sargeant. New Yorker 45: 137 My 24 '69
Performance of Berlioz Requiem in Philharmonic Hall. W. Sargeant. New Yorker 45:114-15 F 22 '69
Performance of Bruckner's Ninth symphony in Philharmonic Hall. W. Sargeant. New Yorker 44:52 F 1 '69
Performance of concert version of Wagner's Tristan and Isolde in Philharmonic Hall. W. Sargeant. New Yorker 45:98+ Mr 8 '69
Performance of Carmina Burana conducted by S. Ozawa. W. Sargeant. New Yorker 45:117 O 11 '69
Performance of M. Babbitt's Relata II in Philharmonic Hall. W. Sargeant. New Yorker 44:80 Ja 25 '69
Season's opening concert. W. Sargeant. New Yorker 45:118-19 O 4 '69
Partisan pied piper. il Time 93:52 Je 20 '69
Philharmonic chooses. Newsweek 73:61-2 Je 23 '69
Philharmonicsville (pop. 106) D. Henahan. il N Y Times Mag p26-7+ S 28 '69; Discussion. p 12+ O 19; 14+ N 16 '69
Report: New York; concert performance of Tristan und Isolde. S. Jenkins, jr. Opera N 33:33 Ap 5 '69

PHILIP, consort of Elizabeth II, queen of Great Britain
Prince's rebuke to a protester. U S News 66:15 Je 9 '69
Royalty: its money troubles. il por U S News 67:16 N 24 '69

PHILIP Morris, Incorporated. See Morris, Philip, incorporated

PHILIPPINE cultural center. See Manila—Philippine cultural center

PHILIPPINE mahogany. See Mahogany

PHILIPPINE SEA, Battles of the, 1944
Damn the submarines! Turn on the lights! R. P. Crossley. il Pop Mech 131:111-15+ Je '69

PHILIPPINES
See also
Ballet—Philippines
Botany—Philippines
Hukbalahaps
Seaside resorts—Philippines
Student demonstrations—Philippines

Economic conditions
Letter from Manila. R. Shaplen. il New Yorker 45:87-96+ D 20 '69
Philippines: an ailing and resentful ally. J. M. Mecklin. il Fortune 80:118-23+ Jl '69

Foreign relations
Old friend turning from U.S. il U S News 66:63-4 Ja 27 '69
Quiet cold war over Sabah. il Ramp Mag 7:20+ N 30 '68
Reports: Bangkok, Manila. R. Terrill. Atlan 224:22-7 Jl '69
Why the Philippines are drifting away from U.S; interview, ed. by K. M. Chrysler. F. E. Marcos. U S News 66:80-1 Mr 31 '69

History
Insurrection, 1899-1901
Troop withdrawal: 1899. D. B. Schirmer. New Repub 161:19-20 S 27 '69

Moral conditions
Lawless and corrupt Philippines. A. Campbell. New Repub 160:15-17 My 17 '69

Nationalism
Philippines: an ailing and resentful ally. J. M. Mecklin. il Fortune 80:118-23+ Jl '69

Politics and government
Letter from Manila. R. Shaplen. il New Yorker 45:87-96+ D 20 '69
See also
Elections—Philippines
Politics, Corruption in—Philippines

Religious institutions and affairs
World around us (cont) Chr Cent 86:630-1, 1652 Ap 30, D 24 '69
See also
Catholic church in the Philippines

PHILIPS, Mack
How to duplicate small parts by plastic casting. Pop Sci 195:142-5 N '69
Slick finishes from new buffing kits. Pop Sci 195:126-9 Ag '69

PHILIPS, Robert E.
Library study carrel. Library J 94:840-2 F 15 '69

PHILIPS of Eindhoven companies
Determined Dutchmen of Philips lamp. J. Ross-Skinner. il Duns R 94:52-5+ N '69

PHILIPSON, Morris
New, critical look at scholarly paperbacks; excerpt from address, June 23, 1969. por Pub W 196:31-3 Jl 28 '69

PHILLIP, Robert
Arthur Pequegnat clock company. Hobbies 74: 48-9+ Je '69
Henry Playtner; excerpt from letter. Hobbies 74:48-9+ Ag '69

PHILLIPS, Anthony G. and others
Object-carrying by rats: an approach to the behavior produced by brain stimulation. bibliog Science 166:903-5 N 14 '69

PHILLIPS, Bernice
Getting to know you day. il por Newsweek 74:69 S 15 '69

PHILLIPS, Carleton J. and others
Macronyssid mites in oral mucosa of long-nosed bats: occurrence and associated pathology. bibliog Science 165:1368-9 S 26 '69

PHILLIPS, Charles William
Gray power. America 120:132-3 F 1 '69

PHILLIPS, Christopher H.
August session of U.N seabed committee held at New York; statements; August 11, 15 and 29, 1969. Dept State Bul 61:285-7+ S 29 '69
Trust Territory of the Pacific Islands; statements, June 6 and 13, 1969. Dept State Bul 61:220-3, 231-2 S 8 '69
United States urges negotiation and dialogue in Southern Africa; statement, October 16, 1969. Dept State Bul 61:458-9 N 24 '69

PHILLIPS, Gene D.
Man within: the New York film festival. Cath World 210:175-8 Ja '70
(ed) See Greene, G. Graham Greene: on the screen

PHILLIPS, Gifford
Cultural commercialism. Art N 68:29+ S '69

PHILLIPS, Harvey E.
Ravel's world. Opera N 34:8-13 N 1 '69
(ed) See Elgar, A. Go-getter
(ed) See Petina, I. Irra

PHILLIPS, John David
Master chef of management. S. Margetts. por Duns R 92:50-2+ D '68

PHILLIPS, John L.
Flowering of the speaker's art; concerning book, The speaker's ideal. Am Heritage 20:101-3+ D '68

PHILLIPS, Kevin P.
Future of American politics; excerpts from The emerging Republican majority. Cur 110:26-30 S '69

about
Abandon the cities? por Time 94:16-17 Ag 1 '69

PHILLIPS, M. Ian, and Olds, James
Unit activity: motivation-dependent responses from midbrain neurons. Science 165:1269-71 S 19 '69

PHILLIPS, Nancy Iran
How I cover conventions. Writers Digest 49:44+ Ap '69

PHILLIPS, Norman
Cruise your way to camping pleasure. Pop
Gard 20:2-5+ Spr '69
Full-time freelancing in secondary maga-
zines. Writers Digest 49:48-52+ Je '69
Make your next camp-out by boat. Pop Mech
131:178-80 Mr '69

PHILLIPS, Norman R.
Historical understanding of conservatism.
Nat R 21:278-81+ Mr 25 '69

PHILLIPS, Sam C.
Apollo 8: a most fantastic voyage. por Nat
Geog 135:593-631 My '69

PHILLIPS, Thomas L.
Raytheon: radar to refrigerators. il por
Forbes 103:28-32 Je 1 '69

PHILLIPS, William
Season in the stands. Commentary 48:65-9
Jl '69

PHILLIPS, William G.
Old miller gets off the old grind. il por
Bsns W p54+ O 25 '69
Yeast maker. J. Poindexter. por Duns R 94:74-
5 S '69

PHILLIPS curve. See Statistical methods

PHILLIPSON, John S.
Two Pentecostal experiences. America 120:
360-3 Mr 29 '69

PHILOLOGY
See also
Language and languages

PHILOSOPHICAL association, American Catholic. See American Catholic philosophical association

PHILOSOPHY
Catholic philosopher. R. J. Gerber. Common-
weal 90:105-6+ Ap 11 '69
Tragedy and philosophy. by W. Kaufmann.
Review
Commonweal 89:708-10 Mr 7 '69. K. Rex-
roth
See also
Atheism
Change
Civilization
Consciousness
Existentialism
God
Humanism
Knowledge, Theory of
Liberty
Man
Materialism
Music—Philosophy and aesthetics
Nationalism (philosophy)
Political philosophy
Science
Theism
Truth
Universe
also subhead Philosophy under various
subjects, e.g. Medicine—Philosophy

Anecdotes, facetiae, satire, etc.
My philosophy. W. Allen. New Yorker 45:25-6
D 27 '69

PHILOSOPHY, American
American philosophy and the future, ed. by
M. Novak. Review
America 120:368 Mr 29 '69. D. A. Drennen
Commonweal 90:180-2 Ap 25 '69. W. Ar-
nold
Have courage! adaptation of introd. to new
edition of the essays and journals of
Ralph Waldo Emerson. L. Mumford. Am
Heritage 20:104-11 F '69
See also
Blondel, M.
Santayana, G.

PHILOSOPHY, Ancient
See also
Avicenna
Science, Ancient

PHILOSOPHY, German
See also
Buber, M.
Jaspers, K.
Nietzsche, F. W

PHILOSOPHY, Greek
See also
Plato

PHILOSOPHY, Italian
Vico, one of the boldest innovators in the
history of human thought. I. Berlin. il
N Y Times Mag p76-7+ N 23 '69

PHILOSOPHY, Jewish
Jewish paganism; views of R. L. Rubenstein.
M. Fox. Commentary 47:92-4+ Je '69; Dis-
cussion. 48:10+ S '69

PHILOSOPHY, Roman
See also
Boethius, A. M. S.

PHILOSOPHY and religion
Dewart's new foundations; a sequel to The
future of belief. A. Gibson. Commonweal
90:101-4 Ap 11 '69
New themes in Christian philosophy, ed. by
R. M. McInerny. Review
Cath World 208:282+ Mr '69. J. F. Kava-
naugh
See also
Existentialism

PHILOSOPHY in the bedroom; drama. See
Bush, J.

PHILOSOPHY of education. See Education—
Philosophy

PHINIZY, Coles
Surfing. Sports Illus 31:74-8 N 10 '69

PHIPPS conservatory, Pittsburgh
Phipps conservatory. F. Curto. il Horticulture
46:38-9+ N '68

PHOBIAS
Facing phobias fearlessly. McCalls 96:50 Mr
'69
Phobias. J. D. Noshpitz. il Todays Ed 58:20-3
My '69

PHOCION
Phocion: a man for this season. J. Valenti.
Sat R 52:56-7 Ap 26 '69

PHOENIX, Ariz.
Instant ocean: it just keeps rolling along;
surfing indoors. C. Phinizy. il Sports Illus
31:74-8 N 10 '69
Microfilm system that grows with the city.
D. Willis. il Am City 84:133-4 My '69

City planning
Phoenix: the blemishes in boomtown. il
Bsns W p 144-5+ N 15 '69

Education
Help for hang-ups, Alhambra elementary
school district. J. Stocker. il Am Ed 5:6-8
Je '69

Parks and playgrounds
Gold medal for Phoenix. G. L. Gardner. il
Parks & Rec 4:24-8 My '69

Recreation
Gold medal for Phoenix. G. L. Gardner. il
Parks & Rec 4:24-8 My '69

PHONIC methods. See Reading—Study and
teaching

PHONOGRAPH
Phonographs of yesteryear. il Hobbies 74:42
S '69
Sound ideas. L. Zide. See issues of American
record guide
Sound-in! What's now. il Seventeen 28:142-5
S '69
See also
Radio receivers—Phonograph combination

Record changers
Garrard SL95 automobile turntable. C. H.
Lawrence. il Radio-Electr 40:32 Jl '69
Hi-fi product report; dual 1212 automatic
turntable. il Electr World 82:80-1 N '69
Hi-fi product report; Garrard SL 95 auto-
matic turntable. il Electr World 82:60 Jl '69
Hi-fi product report; Miracord 620 and 630
automatic turntables. il Electr World 82:
83-4 Ag '69
How we test turntables, arms, and changers.
D. Gravereaux. il Hi Fi 19:39-42 Ap '69

Stereophonic equipment
New look of stereo components. il House &
Gard 135:28+ Ja '69

Stereophonic pickup
Hi-fi product report; Shure M92E and M93E
stereo phono cartridges. il Electr World
82:86 O '69
How we judge stereo cartridges. D. Grav-
ereaux. il Hi Fi 19:48-53 F '69
Latest in Stereo cartridges. R. Angus. il Hi
Fi 19:54-7 F '69

Tone arm
How we test turntables, arms, and changers.
D. Gravereaux. il Hi Fi 19:39-42 Ap '69
IC stereo amplifier in a phono arm. E.
Francis. il Radio-Electr 40:52-5 Mr '69

Turntables
Hi-fi product report: Thorens TD-125 turn-
table. Electr World 82:12+ D '69
How we test turntables, arms, and changers.
D. Gravereaux. il Hi Fi 19:39-42 Ap '69
Turntables: renaissance of the manual? R.
Long. il Hi Fi 19:34-8 Ap '69

PHONOGRAPH in education
The scene. E. Farrell and L. Ruth. Engl J
58:756-61 My '69

PHONOGRAPH industry and trade
See also
Phonograph record industry
PHONOGRAPH radio combination. See Radio receivers—Phonograph combination
PHONOGRAPH record industry
High cost of gold; Columbia vs. RCA. il Time 93:86 Ap 25 '69
Rock for sale. M. Lydon. il Ramp Mag 7: 19-24 Je '69
Sound of music (jingle, jingle) tapes vs records. il Forbes 104:47-8 O 1 '69
Up Parnassus with Thud, Eros, The Good Rats, etc. il Esquire 71:84-8 Ja '69
See also
Bizarre, incorporated
Motown record corporation

Advertising
Admen groove on underground; in tabloids, the record industry has found a new advertising channel. il Bsns W p84-6 Ap 12 '69

Exhibitions
Music's uncommon market; Marché international du disque et de l'edition musicale fair. D. J. Soria. Sat R 52:62-3 My 17 '69

Canada
Canada enters the international recording picture. R. Angus. Hi Fi 19:24-5 My '69

Germany (Federal Republic)
DGG and Boston; Boston symphony and Boston Pops to record exclusively for the Deutsche grammophon gesellschaft. J. Hiemenz. Hi Fi 19:31 O '69

Great Britain
Other side; abandonment of Resale price maintenance. T. Heinitz. Sat R 52:47 Ag 30 '69
See also
Electric and musical industries, limited

Japan
Money-making music rocks Japan. il Bsns W p56 Ag 2 '69

PHONOGRAPH records
Artist who sang in choruses of Edison amberol cylinders. J. Walsh. il Hobbies 74: 36-7+ Ag '69
Berlioz on records. B. Jacobson. il Hi Fi 19:56-60+ Mr '69
Best records of the year. L. Marcus. il Hi Fi 19:67-72 D '69
Bounty from the golden age; Great recordings of the century. Hi Fi 19:81 O '69
Britten's unchanged aesthetic; Holy sonnets of John Donne, Songs and proverbs of William Blake. D. Hamilton. Hi Fi 19:90 N '69
Busoni by Petri, Ogdon, Glazer, and now David Bean. R. Kammerer; L. Richmond. il Am Rec G 35:1030-2 Jl '69
Checklist for a musical Christmas. il Seventeen 28:38+ D '69
Concert records. A. Hiss. New Yorker 45:119-23 O 4; 114+ D 20 '69
Contemporary contrasts: Wolpe: Trio, Crumb: Eleven echoes of autumn. D. W. Moore. Am Rec G 36:69 S '69
Continental harmony of William Billings. A. Frankenstein. Hi Fi 19:79 S '69
DISCussions. R. Hemming and others. See issues of Senior scholastic
Fanfare for Christmas. il Seventeen 27:18+ D '68
Favorite pioneer recording artists. J. Walsh. See issues of Hobbies
George Crumb: Eleven echoes of autumn, 1965. D. J. Henahan. il Mus Q 55:280-5 Ap '69
Good-bye mono, hello stereo. Bet Hom & Gard 47:41 Mr '69
Historic 1968 Hugo Wolf concert. P. L. Miller. il Am Rec G 35:944-6 Je '69
Historical records. A. Favia-Artsay. See issues of Hobbies
In brief (cont) Hi Fi 19:120 F; 96 Ap '69
Lighter side. M. Ames and others. See issues of High fidelity incorporating Musical America
Mid-month recordings. il Sat R 52:46-7 F 8; 48-9 Mr 15; 62-3+ Ap 12; 42-3 Jl 12; 102-3 S 13; 64-5+ O 11 '69
Music in the round. Discus. See issues of Harper's magazine
Music; short reviews: records. H. Kupferberg. See issues of Atlantic
New records in review. B. H. Haggin. See issues of Yale review
Not from the singer, but for the singer; records to teach vocalists correct pronunciation of texts of well known songs and arias in Italian, French, and German. G. L. Mayer. Sat R 52:65 F 22 '69

On the record: Music. P. L. Miller. See issues of Library journal
One for cinema buffs: The female prisoner. P. L. Miller. Am Rec G 36:179 N '69
Other reviews. See issues of American record guide
Other side. T. Heinitz. See Recordings issues of Saturday review
Parallel careers of Georg Solti; with discography. G. Movshon. il Hi Fi 19:66-71 O '69
Performer as composer: a symphony, a piano concerto, three folksong settings, a cantata, art songs, an early opera, and two solo sonatas by the many-faceted S. Rachmaninoff. M. N. Kanny; R. Kennedy; P. L. Miller. Am Rec G 35:616-18 Ap '69
Peter Nero as composer; Fantasy and improvisations. M. N. Kanny. il Am Rec G 35:782 My '69
Phonograph records. W. F. Grueninger. See issues of Consumer bulletin
Preview of forthcoming recordings. Hi Fi 19: 22-3+ S '69
Profits of tragedy; Incident at Dyke bridge. We you you and Dad. Time 95:43 Ja 5 '70
Recent recitals by the stars of New York city opera. il Am Rec G 35:455-7 F '69
Record reviews. See issues of Consumer reports
Recorded portraits of the artist; live vs recorded performance. J. Starker. Hi Fi 19:32+ N '69
Recordings. M. Mayer. See issues of Esquire
Recordings in review. I. Kolodin. See issues of Saturday review
Recordings reports: miscellaneous LPs. I. Kolodin. See issues of Saturday review
Records:
 Arias and songs. Opera N 33:34 Ap 19 '69
 Covent Garden anniversary. il Opera N 33:35 Ap 5 '69
Records. D. Hamilton. Nation 208:189-90, 613-14, 738-9; 209:190, 229-30, 453-4, 613-14, 673-4 F 10, My 12. Je 9. S 1-8, O 27, D 1, 15 '69
Records. N. McCaffrey. Nat R 21:709-10 Jl 15 '69
Records (cont) B. H. Haggin. Commonweal 89:593-4; 90:20-1, 170-1 F 7, Mr 21, Ap 25 '69
Records (title varies) (cont) W. F. Rickenbacker. Nat R 21:658-9, 1073-4 Jl 1, O 21 '69
Reviews of records. See issues of Musical quarterly
Reviews of records: Petrucci, first printer of music. H. L. Clarke. Mus Q 55:584-6 O '69
Shaping things to come; influence of the long playing record. il Time 94:54-5 Ag 29 '69
Sight and sound. See issues of McCall's
Speaking of records. See issues of High fidelity incorporating Musical America
Spotlight! popular, classical. E. Miller. See issues of Seventeen
Time listings. See issues of Time
Toscanini treasures. H. Goldsmith. Hi Fi 19: 96-7 D '69
Well-tempura'd Bach; New sound from the Japanese Bach scene. A. Frankenstein. Hi Fi 19:88 O '69
Year on record. H. Saal. il Newsweek 74: 106-7 D 22 '69
Year's best recordings. Sat R 52:76-8 D 6 '69
See also
Libraries—Phonograph and phonograph records
Tape recordings

American music
Harvest from Martha's Vineyard. O. Daniel. Sat R 52:103+ S 13 '69
New spectrum series from Nonesuch; Americana, recent and otherwise. P. L. Miller. Am Rec G 35:940-1 Je '69

Arias
Art of la Divina. P. L. Miller. Am Rec G 36: 102-3 O '69
Artistry of Lawrence Tibbett. P. L. Miller. Am Rec G 35:385 Ja '69
Enrico Caruso. G. Movshon. Hi Fi 19:77-8 S '69
From a rich heritage: the art of baritone Mattia Battistini. C. L. Osborne. Hi Fi 19: 63-4 Ap '69
John McCormack, musical raconteur; arias, duets, and songs. D. Hamilton. Hi Fi 19: 110 My '69
Met of the 1940s; no duds? Fabulous forties at the Met. P. L. Miller. Am Rec G 35:1042 Jl '69
Perhaps not fabulous, but some excellent singing anyway; The fabulous forties at the Met. C. L. Osborne. Hi Fi 19:104 Je '69

PHONOGRAPH records—Arias—*Continued*
Price's Mozart: very beautiful singing. P. L.
  Miller. Am Rec G 36:195 N '69
Recitals. P. L. Miller and others. Am Rec G
  36:24-8, 222-3 S, N '69
Records:
  Alexander Kipnis. por Opera N 33:34 Mr
    22 '69
  Beverly Sills. Opera N 34:30 N 1 '69
  Ernestine Schumann-Heink. Opera N 33:
    30 Je 14 '69
  Giovanni Martinelli. Opera N 33:34 Mr 22
    '69
  Gwyneth Jones. Opera N 34:30 D 6 '69
  Hermann Prey. Opera N 33:30 Je 14 '69
  John McCormack; Lily Pons; Paul Robe-
    son; Richard Tauber, and Fritz
    Wunderlich; selections. Opera N 33:35
    Ap 5 '69
  Leontyne Price: Mozart arias. Opera N
    34:36 Ja 10 '70
  Norman Treigle. Opera N 33:35 F 1 '69
  Peter Schreier sings Mozart; Theo Adam
    sings Wagner. Opera N 33:31 My 17 '69
  Placido Domingo. Opera N 33:35 F 1; 34:
    28 O 11 '69
  Sherrill Milnes. Opera N 34:34 S 6 '69
  Victoria de los Angeles. Opera N 33:34 Mr
    15 '69
Records. D. Hamilton. Nation 208:475-6 Ap
  14 '69
Sherrill Milnes: a voice for tomorrow's gold-
  en age. G. Movshon. Hi Fi 19:102 Jl '69
Star status for Beverly Sills, a first recital
  disc; Bellini and Donizetti heroines. C. L.
  Osborne. il Hi Fi 19:76-7 F '69
Two notable city alumni; B. Morell and P.
  Domingo. il Am Rec G 35:458-9 F '69
Two programs by the great Schumann-
  Heink. P. L. Miller. Am Rec G 35:1105 Ag
  '69
Unforgettable. and unforgotten: performan-
  ces from the French and Italian operatic
  repertoire. P. L. Miller. il Am Rec G 35:
  1116-18 Ag '69

Ballet music
Ansermet's own valedictory; Stravinsky's
  L'oiseau de feu. R. Lawrence. il Sat R 52:50
  D 27 '69
Seven deadly sins. C. J. Luten. Am Rec G
  35:383 Ja '69

Band music
Sweet and swinging. F. Reynolds. See issues
  of American record guide
See also
Phonograph records—Marches (music)

Baroque music
Bread and lollipops. H. Weinstock. Sat R
  52:81 O 25 '69
Recordings; Concentus Musicus of Vienna
  releases. M. Mayer. Esquire 71:46 Ja '69

Blues (songs, etc)
Biggest, baddest bluesman: Albert King. A.
  Goldman. Life 66:16 Mr 28 '69
New music of political protest. M. Cuscuna.
  Sat R 52:55-6 D 13 '69
Rebirth of B. B. King. A. Goldman. Life
  67:16 D 12 '69

Cantatas
Epiphany cantata by Biber. J. W. Barker. Am
  Rec G 36:173-4 N '69
From Bach to Bach. R. Jacobson. Sat R 52:
  79-80 O 25 '69
Hans Pfitzner's near-miss: Von deutscher
  seele. G. L. Mayer. Am Rec G 35:415-16
  Ja '69
Paramountcy of clarity, Roger Wagner's cho-
  rale: Catulli carmina. P. L. Miller. Am
  Rec G 36:198 N '69
Records:
  Cantatas no. 56, 82. Opera N 34:36 Ja 10
    '70
  Carmina Burana. Opera N 33:35 F 8 '69
  Von deutscher seele. Opera N 33:34 Mr
    8 '69
Stradella's view of the Nativity. J. W. Bar-
  ker. Am Rec G 36:170 N '69

Care
You take care of them, they'll entertain
  you; or, How to keep your music-picture-
  sound equipment in shape. il Redbook 133:
  51+ Ag '69

Catalogs
Guide to Russcol's guide. R. Freed. Sat R 52:
  80 N 29 '69

Chamber music
Harvest from Martha's Vineyard; new Amer-
  ican music. O. Daniel. Sat R 52:103+ S 13
  '69
Paired for the first time: the two apothéoses.
  J. W. Barker. Am Rec G 36:11+ S '69
Paul Hindemith's *kammermusiken.* A. Cohn.
  Am Rec G 36:22-3 S '69
Records; recordings by the Contemporary
  chamber ensemble. D. Hamilton. Nation
  208:677-8 My 26 '69

Childrens records
On and off the avenue (cont) New Yorker
  45:225-30+ D 6 '69
Orff-Schulwerk, a joyous note. G. L. Mayer.
  Sat R 52:46-7 Jl 26 '69

Choral music
Big sound from Berlioz; Colin Davis' record-
  ing of Te Deum. D. Hamilton. il Hi Fi 19:
  94-5 D '69
L'enfance du Christ, Martinon's best buy
  Berlioz. J. W. Barker. Am Rec G 36:166
  N '69
Rheinberger: The star of Bethlehem. P. L.
  Miller. Am Rec G 36:170-1 N '69

Choral singing
Artist who sang in choruses of Edison amberol cylinders. J. Walsh. il Hobbies 74:36-
  7+ Ag '69

Christmas music
Seasonal recordings: music for Christmas. J.
  W. Barker. il Am Rec G 36:164-5 N '69

Church music
Handel's Chandos anthems: ceremonial mu-
  sic that makes a glorious sound. P. H.
  Lang. il Hi Fi 19:65-6 Ap '69
Reviews of records: music of the Russian
  Orthodox church. M. Velimirović. Mus Q
  55:586-94 O '69
Thomas Tallis: a pair of indispensable re-
  cordings. J. W. Barker. Am Rec G 36:95
  O '69
  See also
Phonograph records—Oratorios

Collectors and collecting
Collectors' releases. A. Favia-Artsay. il Hob-
  bies 74:35+ Ap; 35-6+ O '69
Collector's showcase; selected recordings of
  an individual collector. A. Favia-Artsay.
  il Hobbies 74:35+ Je '69
My gypsy record collection. B. Nilsson. Hi Fi
  19:22+ Jl '69
Perils of record collecting. L. Haber. il Hi
  Fi 19:58-61 F '69
Speaking of records. Hi Fi 19:28 My '69
Where do you start? symposium, ed. by R.
  Hemming. Sr Schol 95:16-17 O 6 '69

Concertos
Early Beethoven by Blumental. M. Kanny.
  Am Rec G 36:16-17 S '69
Great Dvořák cello concerto, plus two rare
  treats. H. Goldsmith. Hi Fi 19:88 Mr '69
Hindemith's so-called Brandenburgs: seven
  pieces from the twenties. A. Frankenstein.
  il Hi Fi 19:75 F '69
Indispensable album; Clavier concerti. M. N.
  Kanny. Am Rec G 36:36 S '69
Mostly serial, and mostly academic. D. New-
  lin. Am Rec G 35:1039-40 Jl '69
On Yehudi's 50th birthday, a gift from the
  whole family: Mozart's Two-piano con-
  certo in E flat, K. 365. M. N. Kanny. Am
  Rec G 36:55 S '69
Pair of early cello concertos, luminously
  performed. P. H. Lang. Hi Fi 19:92 S '69
Reviews of records; Ben Weber's concerto.
  D. Henahan. Mus Q 55:424-6 Jl '69
That other (M.) Haydn. M. N. Kanny; J.
  W. Barker. Am Rec G 35:562 Mr '69
Twenty-one Mozart concerto recordings. M.
  Kanny. Am Rec G 35:768-70+ My '69

Dance music
Companies that make & distribute dance re-
  cordings/dance record distributors. Dance
  Mag 43:63 N '69
Plusses outweigh the minuses; recorded mu-
  sic in the dance studio. D. R. Sellars. Dance
  Mag 43:60-2+ N '69
Records for teachers. E. LeMone. See issues
  of Dance magazine
Sweet and swinging. F. Reynolds. See issues
  of American record guide

Electronic music
Electronic music. D. Heckman. il Am Rec
  G 35:356-61 Ja '69

PHONOGRAPH records—Electronic music—
Continued
If it pleases. O. Daniel. il Sat R 52:71+ N
29 '69
Loops and reels. O. Daniel. il Sat R 52:62-3+
Ap 12 '69
Moog strikes Bach. J. Downs. Life 67:18 O 3
'69
Reviews of records; Morton Subotnick: The
wild bull and John Pfieffer: Electronomusic.
T. Dockstader. Mus Q 55:136-9 Ja '69
Strings and electronics pack an emotional
wallop. R. S. Brown. Hi Fi 19:104 O '69
Synthetic sonorities; Switched-on Bach. C.
E. Fager. Chr Cent 86:1673-4 D 31 '69
Tape music: the beginning, and now J. Pfeif-
fer's electronomusic. A. Cohn. il Am Rec
G 35:626-8 Ap '69

Flute music
New music by seven composers. A. Cohn. il
Am Rec G 35:1114-15 Ag '69

Folk music
Drunkenness, incest, murder, and rape, fa-la-
la la. O. B. Brummell. il Hi Fi 19:48-9
My '69
Folk music. H. Yurchenco and others. See
issues of American record guide
Records: rock, etc. country music: Everly
brothers. E. Willis. New Yorker 45:116-18
F 22 '69

German music
Lieder masters: songs by H. Wolf. Discus.
Harper 239:101-2 Jl '69

Guitar music
Four by Rodrigo. J. Diether. il Am Rec G
35:472-4 F '69
Guitar by Charlie Christian. M. Williams.
Sat R 52:65 My 17 '69
Guitars, guitars, seven virtuosi. R. T. Jones.
il Am Rec G 35:468-71 F '69
New adventures of the jazz guitar. M. Wil-
liams. Sat R 52:55 Jl 26 '69

Harpsichord music
Couperin, mostly, by Marlowe and others.
J. W. Barker. Am Rec G 36:10-11 S '69
Igor Kipnis: another indispensable recording;
Spanish music for harpsichord. J. W. Bar-
ker. Am Rec G 35:450 F '69

History
How to tell when Victor records were made
(cont) J. Walsh. il Hobbies 73:36+ F; 74:
36+ Mr: 36+ Ap '69

Instrumental music
Instrumental recordings. H. Goldsmith. il
Hi Fi 19:81-4 O '69
Veritably a dilly: the disc debut of com-
poser Terry Riley in C. A. Frankenstein.
Hi Fi 19:104 F '69

Japanese music
Music for conservative avant-gardists. P. L.
Miller. Am Rec G 35:811-12 My '69

Jazz music
Basie; with discography. B. Korall. il Sat R
52:82-3 N 29 '69
B.G. at his best. B. Korall. il Sat R 52:48-9
Mr 15 '69
Can jazz-rock find happiness together? B.
Korall. il Sat R 52:42-3 Jl 12 '69
Jazz. J. S. Wilson. See issues of High fidelity
incorporating Musical America
Mr Clean of jazz: R. Norvo. N. McCaffrey.
Nat R 21:709-10 Jl 15 '69
Mostly modernists (cont) M. Williams. Sat
R 52:56 Ja 25; 69+ F 22; 52 Mr 15; 55 Jl 26;
75 O 25 '69
Recordings reports: jazz LP's. S. Dance. See
issues of Saturday review
Year's best in jazz, mainly mainstream. S.
Dance. Sat R 52:56 D 13 '69

Marches (music)
Authentic Sousa performances from the
march king himself. R. D. Darrell. Hi Fi
19:113 S '69

Mass
Bach by the book; Mass in B minor. R.
Jacobson. Sat R 52:53 Jl 26 '69
Bach's B minor mass, does the concentus
musicus' authenticity make musical sense?
C. F. Gilmore; P. H. Lang. il Hi Fi 19:76-8
Jl '69
From Bach to Bach. R. Jacobson. Sat R 52:
79-80 O 25 '69

Records:
  Mass, etc. Opera N 34:31 D 13 '69
  Mass in B minor. Opera N 34:34 Ja 17 '70
  Mass in B minor. Opera N 33:35 F 1 '69
  Mass in C. Opera N 33:33 F 22 '69
  St Matthew passion. Opera N 34:28 O 11
  '69
  See also
Phonograph records—Requiems

Moving picture music
John Barry, movie music you can listen to;
Lion in winter and Deadfall. J. Diether.
il Am Rec G 35:550-1 Mr '69
Nino Rota's Romeo and Juliet music. J.
Diether. Am Rec G 35:429-30 Ja '69

Music, Popular (songs, etc)
Apple corps four. C. E. Fager. Chr Cent
86:386-8 Mr 19 '69
Back to the roots. il Time 93:70-1 Ap 11 '69
Detroit retools its rock; the Motown come-
back. A. Goldman. Life 67:12 Jl 25 '69
Follow that trend! Donovan's greatest hits.
C. E. Fager. Chr Cent 86:522 Ap 16 '69
Futuristic nostalgia; 2525. il Time 94:59 Jl
18 '69
Jefferson Airplane, steady, smooth. R. Gold-
stein. Vogue 153:44 Mr 15 '69
New music of political protest. M. Cuscuna.
Sat R 52:55-6 D 13 '69
Old timers: paint it blue. E. Sander. Sat R
52:74+ F 22 '69
Pale voodoo hands across the sea; Arthur
Brown and Dr John. A. Goldman. Life
66:14 Mr 14 '69
Pop: a fresh stash for summer. E. Sander.
Sat R 52:51+ Jl 26 '69
Popular records (cont) D. Watt. New Yorker
44:84-6 Ja 18: 108-10 Mr 1 '69
Records: rock, etc; B. Dylan. E. Willis. New
Yorker 45:157+ Ap 26 '69
Records: rock, etc. comparison of Beatles
with Stones. E. Willis. New Yorker 44:55-
6+ F 1 '69
Rock, etc. P. Townshend of group called the
Who. E. Willis. New Yorker 45:62-5 Jl 12
'69
Rolling Stones; Beggars' triumph. E. Sander.
il Sat R 52:48 Ja 25 '69
Slashing lampoonery; Mothers of invention.
C. E. Fager. Chr Cent 86:622-3 Ap 30 '69
Swinging singles. C. E. Fager. Chr Cent 86:
928-9 Jl 9 '69
Tangible impact. C. E. Fager. Chr Cent 86:
595-6 Ap 23 '69
Wisdom of their years; the Beatles. A. G.
Aronowitz. Life 66:12 Ja 31 '69

Musical comedies, revues, etc.
Everywhere, Hair. Time 93:73 Je 6 '69
Popular records: Promises, promises. D.
Watt. New Yorker 44:84-6 Ja 18 '69
Way they used to do musical comedy. Discus.
Harper 238:112 Mr '69

Negro music
Back to God. il Time 93:52 My 23 '69

Operas
Again, Boris by Kipnis. P. L. Miller. Am
Rec G 35:776 My '69
Ariadne auf Naxos. A. Sperber. il Am Rec
G 35:1108-10 Ag '69
Ariadne reconsidered. R. Lawrence. il Sat R
52:49 Ja 25 '69
Back on Seraphim. the Callas Lucia. P. L.
Miller. Am Rec G 35:560 Mr '69
Berlioz Troyens for the record; Royal opera's
production and recording. T. Heinitz. Sat R
52:70 N 29 '69
La Bohème with a mezzo Musetta; R. Leon-
cavallo's libretto. I. Kolodin. Sat R 52:71
Ap 26 '69
La Callas of yore, iridescence and marble. P.
L. Miller. Am Rec G 36:106 O '69
Case for Massenet; Werther, sung by De los
Angeles and Gedda. G. Movshon. il Hi Fi 19:
93-4 D '69
Case for the other La Bohème. C. L. Osborne.
Hi Fi 19:78-9 My '69
Club 99 releases; recordings by Russian sin-
gers of the past. A. Favia-Artsay. il Hobbies 74:35-7 D '69
DGG's Siegfried. C. J. Luten. il Am Rec G
36:4-6 S '69
Elektra; a stage work violated? Or a new
sonic miracle? C. L. Osborne; reply, J. Cul-
shaw. il Hi Fi 18:68-71 O '68; rejoinder. 19:
20+ Ap '69
Festival of baroque operas: Graun's Montezuma and Bononcini's Griselda. P. L. Miller. il Am Rec G 35:366-7 Ja '69
Fifty-one best-buy opera albums. il Changing T 23:41-4 N '69

PHONOGRAPH records—Operas—*Continued*

First complete stereo Lakme; twenty melodies and other charms. G. Movshon. il Hi Fi 19:83-4 Mr '69

First-rate performance of a second-rate opera; Gavazzeni conducts Mascagni's L'amico Fritz. C. L. Osborne. Hi Fi 19:77 Je '69

Fritz and Wally; new recordings of Mascagni's L'amico Fritz and Catalani's La Wally. R. Jacobson. Sat R 52:79-80 Ap 26 '69

From Angel: James McCracken's (and Sir John Barbirolli's) Otello. P. L. Miller. il Am Rec G 36:92-4 O '69

From the dawn of opera; Monteverdi's L' Orféo and Cavalli's L'Erismena. H. Weinstock. il Sat R 52:80+ D 6 '69

Full-blooded and very funny performance of Cosi fan tutte. A. Sperber. il Am Rec G. 35:378-80 Ja '69

Giovanni Bononcini: Girselda (excerpts) P. H. Lang. Mus Q 55:276-8 Ap '69

Giovanni Martinelli. A. Favia-Artsay. il Hobbies 74:35+ Jl '69

Giovanni Martinelli's Otello. P. L. Miller. Am Rec G 35:384 Ja '69

Hary Janos, an entertainment with music. G. Movshon. Hi Fi 19:81-2 N '69

Historical records. A. Favia-Artsay. Hobbies 74:35+ My; 35-6+ N '69

How to build an opera record library; with discography. G. Jellinek. Opera N 34:18-19 N 22 '69

Joan Sutherland as Lakmé. P. L. Miller. Am Rec G 35:532-3 Mr '69

Karl Heinrich Graun: Montezuma (excerpts) P. H. Lang. Mus Q 55:278-80 Ap '69

Likable Lakmé from London. R. Jacobson. Sat R 52:59 Mr 29 '69

Maazel's masterpiece: La Traviata. P. L. Miller. il Am Rec G 35:1192-4 Ag '69

McCracken as Canio; Leoncavallo's Pagliacci. R. Jacobson. Sat R 52:105 S 13 '69

Melting charm: non-verismo Mascagni; L' Amico Fritz. P. L. Miller. Am Rec G 35: 1137 Ag '69

Mindless masters; Mascagni's L'Amico Fritz, Leoncavallo's La Bohème, and Catalani's La Wally. H. Kupferberg. Atlan 224:101-3 Ag '69

Monteverdi's Orfeo, a true music-drama, now complete and in stereo. B. Jacobson. Hi Fi 19:66-7 Ap '69

Most important single Lully recording ever? J. W. Barker. Am Rec G 35:566 Mr '69

Mozart manifold. R Jacobson. Sat R 52:72+ F 22 '69

New marriage on Deutsche Grammophon. A. Sperber. il Am Rec G 35:380-2 Ja '69

New York city opera performance of Douglas Moore's Carry Nation. P. L. Miller. il Am Rec G 35:452-4 F '69

Opera on your own. Time 94:67 D 12 '69

L'Ormindo. J. W. Barker. il Am Rec G 35: 1024-7 Jl '69

L'Ormindo, a delicious 325-year-old operatic hit. S. T. Sommer. Hi Fi 19:88+ Je '69

Pirates in stereo. R. Jacobson. Sat R 52:53 Je 28 '69

Prokofiev's satiric Oranges. R. Lawrence. Sat R 52:47 Je 28 '69

Recording as a medium; how does opera on the turntable differ from a live performance? E. T. Canby. il Opera N 33:8-11 F 8 '69

Recordings. M. Mayer. Esquire 72:8+ Jl; 32+ N '69

Recordings; Verdi's Otello directed by J. Barbirolli. M. Mayer. Esquire 73:22+ Ja '70

Records:

L'Amico Fritz. Opera N 33:31 My 17 '69

L'amore dei tre re. il Opera N 34:31 D 13 '69

Blood wedding. Opera N 33:35 F 8 '69

La Bohème. Opera N 33:31 My 17 '69

Carry Nation. Opera N 33:35 F 1 '69

Eugene Onegin. Opera N 33:34 Mr 8 '69

Festival of baroque opera. Opera N 33:35 Mr 1 '69

Die frau ohne schatten. Opera N 33:34 Mr Mr 8 '69

French opera excerpts. Opera N 33:34 Ap 19 '69

Gambler and Love for three oranges. Opera N 34:30 D 20 '69

La Gioconda. Opera N 33:33 F 22 '69

Götterdämmerung. Opera N 33:35 Mr 1 '69

Háry János. Opera N 34:36 Ja 10 '70

Italian opera excerpts. Opera N 33:34 Ap 19 '69

Lakmé. Opera N 33:34 F 15 '69

Lucia di Lammermoor. Opera N 33:33 F 22 '69

Mefistofele (prologue) Opera N 34:42 D 27 '69

Orfeo. Opera N 33:34 Ap 12 '69

Ormindo. Opera N 33:30 Je 14 '69

Otello. il Opera N 34:30 N 1 '69

Pagliacci. Opera N 34:30 S 20 '69

Roberto Devereux. Opera N 34:34 Ja 17 '70

Romeo and Juliet. Opera N 33:34 Mr 15 '69

Salome. il Opera N 34:30 D 6 '69

Siegfried. Opera N 34:28 O 11 '69

Theodora. Opera N 34:34 S 6 '69

La Traviata. Opera N 34:30 N 22 '69

Von heute auf morgen; Erwartung, and Die glückliche hand. Opera N 33:34 Ap 12 '69

Die Walküre, act III. Opera N 33:34 Ap 19 '69

La Wally. Opera N 33:35 Mr 29 '69

Werther. Opera N 34:42 D 27 '69

Salvaging the past; A festival of baroque operas. H. Weinstock. Sat R 52:75 F 22 '69

Silla in sound; Mozart's Lucio Silla. R. Jacobson. Sat R 52:58 D 27 '69

Singing beautifully. Discus. Harper 239:102-3 Ag '69

Some real rarities: the IRCC carries on; Meyerbeer collection. P. L. Miller. Am Rec G 36:7 S '69

Sound world of Salome, and a surprise from Caballé. D. Hamilton. Hi Fi 19:112 N '69

Strauss's Ariadne; expertly conceived on all sides. C. L. Osborne. Hi Fi 19:110 F '69

Total view of Traviata. P. G. Davis. il Hi Fi 19:75-6 S '69

Two albums from Philips: Haydn and Berlioz by Colin Davis: Romeo and Juliet, and Seasons. J. W. Barker. il Am Rec G 35:936-8 Je '69

Van Karajan's Siegfried. I. Kolodin. Sat R 52:57 D 27 '69

Venice 1644 (?), Glyndebourne 1967. H. Weinstock. Sat R 52:57 My 31 '69

Verdi's Otello, a discographic survey; Barbirolli conducting. D. Hamilton. Hi Fi 19: 79-81 N '69

Von Karajan's Siegfried: an Olympian approach; Ring at three-quarter mark. G. Movshon. il Hi Fi 19:79-80 O '69

Wagnerian filet; excerpts from the Ring. G. Movshon. Hi Fi 19:116 N '69

La Wally, the first stereo edition. P. L. Miller. Am Rec G 35:734+ My '69

Oratorios

After a decade, Sir Malcolm Sargent's last word on Messiah. P. L. Miller. Am Rec G 36:172 N '69

Bargain-priced Christmas oratorio. P. L. Miller. Am Rec G 36:171 N '69

Colin Davis: a man for The seasons. H. C. R. Landon. Hi Fi 19:72-4 Jl '69

Davis's English-speaking Seasons. I. Kolodin. Sat R 52:49 Je 28 '69

For a monument, big shoulders; Elijah. P. L. Miller. Am Rec G 35:1140-1 Ag '69

Four recordings of Hadyn's The creation. S. Lincoln. il Am Rec G 35:610-14 Ap '69

From Germany: an English music drama; Karl Richter conducts Handel's Samson. P. H. Lang. il Hi Fi 19:83-4 N '69

Greater Handel; first recording of Theodora. H. Weinstock. Sat R 52:50 Mr 29 '69

Handel's Samson glorified. H. Weinstock. Sat R 52:51 D 27 '69

Joshua not so fit; recorded by the Collegium Musicum of the University of Missouri. H. Weinstock. Sat R 52:51 Ag 30 '69

One of the outstanding Bach releases of the year: Easter oratorio. Am Rec G 36:114 O '69

Records:

Christmas oratorio. Opera N 34:30 D 20 '69

Elijah. Opera N 34:30 N 22 '69

Messiah. Opera N 34:36 Ja 10 '70

Reissue of Alexander's feast, plus first editions of two other oratorios by George Frideric Handel: Theodora & Joshua. J. W. Barker. il Am Rec G 36:108-12 O '69

Reviews of records: Handel: Hercules. Mus Q 55:132-6 Ja '69

Scandalous politics of Hans Werner Henze; recording of The raft of Medusa. R. P. Morgan. Hi Fi 19:106-7 D '69

Solomon as king of England and Handel's only Christian oratorio. P. H. Lang. il Hi Fi 19:75-7 My '69

Two albums from Philips: Haydn and Berlioz by Colin Davis: Romeo and Juliet, and Seasons. J. W. Barker. il Am Rec G 35:936-8 Je '69

Orchestral music

Boulez in top form; performances of Bartók and Stravinsky. I. Kolodin. Sat R 52:51 Ja 25 '69

PHONOGRAPH records—Orchestral music—
  Continued
Great performance: Mussorgsky's Pictures.
  M. N. Kanny. Am Rec G 35:629 Ap '69
Newly-discovered Webern from Eugene
  Ormandy; Im sommerwind. A. Cohn. Am
  Rec G 35:1126 Ag '69
Philadelphia orchestra; RCA recordings. M.
  Kanny. il Am Rec G 35:44-7 F '69
Recordings. M. Mayer. Esquire 71:88+ Ap
  '69
Recordings reports: orchestral LPs. I. Kolo-
  din. See issues of Saturday review
  See also
Phonograph records—Symphonic poems

Organ music

At last the avant-garde remembers the or-
  gan. R. P. Morgan. Hi Fi 19:92 Ap '69
New popularity of organ music. R. Gelatt.
  House & Gard 135:66+ Mr '69

Overtures

Viennese overtures in a new sonic dressing. R. D. Darrell. Hi Fi 19:116 O '69

Passion music

Bach by the book; St Matthew passion. R.
  Jacobson. Sat R 52:53 Jl 26 '69
Penderecki's passion. B. Belt. Chr Cent 86:
  421 Mr 26 '69

Percussion music

True essence of percussion. A. Cohn. Am Rec
  G 35:1062-3 Jl '69

Periodicals

  See also
American record guide (periodical)

Piano music

Alan Mandel plays all twenty-seven of the
  piano works of Ives. A. Cohn. Am Rec G
  35:548-9 Mr '69
Art of Philippe Entremont. R. T. Jones.
  Am Rec G 35:538-40 Mr '69
Bach's last keyboard works; Charles Rosen,
  pianist. D. Hamilton. il por Hi Fi 19:74-5
  Ag '69
Bread and lollipops. H. Weinstock. Sat R 52:
  81 O 25 '69
Charles Rosen's Bach on the piano. il Am
  Rec G 35:939 Je '69
Claudio Arrau's Schumann. R. Kammerer
  and L. Richmond. il Am Rec G 36:62-3 S '69
Earl Wild's re-creation of The daemonic
  Liszt. D. Dubal. Am Rec G 35:364-5 Ja '69
Ferdinand Himmelreich, the blind pianist.
  J. Walsh. il Hobbies 74:38-40+ N '69
Great pianist's noncareer. H. Goldsmith. Hi
  Fi 19:89 Jl '69
John Kirkpatrick; Concord revisited. D. W.
  Moore. Am Rec G 35:546-7 Mr '69
Lively arts; interview, ed. by R. Hemming.
  A. Weissenberg. Sr Schol 94:21-2 Mr 7 '69
More on Ben Weber and Wuorinen. A. Cohn.
  il por Am Rec G 35:1040-1 Jl '69
Musica ex machina; studies for player piano
  only. W. F. Rickenbacker. il Nat R 21:658-
  9 Jl 1 '69
Pianists: standard and offbeat. Discus. Harper
  238:108+ F '69
Prize winners all: Cliburn's Chopin, his finest
  recording; Ogdon's rescue of Rachmaninoff;
  Sokolov's impetuous Schumann. H. Gold-
  smith. il Hi Fi 19:73-4 F '69
Schoenberg, Webern, Berg, and Amy. D. New-
  lin. Am Rec G 35:1037-8 Jl '69
Scriabin on record, blaze of a sunburst. F.
  Bowers. Vogue 153:106 Mr 1 '69
Two ways of looking at Debussy: Moravec
  and Weissenberg. R. Kammerer. il Am
  Rec G 36:20-1 S '69
  See also
Phonograph records—Concertos
Phonograph records—Sonatas

Poetry

  See Phonograph records—Spoken records

Polish music

More from Poland. O. Daniel. Sat R 52:54-5
  Je 28 '69

Prices

Fifty-one best-buy opera albums. il Chang-
  ing T 23:41-4 N '69
Good new budget-priced records. Changing
  T 23:23-4 Je '69

Recording

Archive reaches a milestone. K. Blaukopf.
  Hi Fi 19:16 S '69
Barenboim and Beethoven; recording of the
  Hammerklavier, Op. 106. E. Greenfield. Hi
  Fi 19:28 N '69

Bonynges star in a swinging Messiah; Decca/
  London recording. E. Greenfield. il Hi Fi
  19:18+ Je '69
Britten's Brandenburgs, straight out of a
  malt house. E. Greenfield. il Hi Fi 19:14
  Ap '69
Caballe's Verdi, more temperamental than
  tenors; London. E. Greenfield. Hi Fi 19:
  46+ D '69
Conductors at work. E. Greenfield. il Hi Fi
  19:14+ S '69
Critic answers his critics; Telefunken record-
  ing of Bach's B minor mass. P. H. Lang.
  Hi Fi 19:22 N '69
DGG and Boston; Boston symphony and
  Boston Pops to record exclusively for the
  Deutsche grammophon gesellschaft. J. Hie-
  menz. Hi Fi 19:31 O '69
DGG in Spain. E. Greenfield. Hi Fi 19:20 Ag
  '69
Dream quartet for Beethoven; Berlin. P.
  Moore. il Hi Fi 19:20+ D '69
EMI's month: from Haydn to Walton with
  stops in between. E. Greenfield. il Hi Fi
  19:30+ F '69
EMI's star-studded birthday present for
  Gerald Moore. E. Greenfield. il Hi Fi 19:16+
  Jl '69
Electric Karajan on the Yellow submarine;
  conducting Wagner's Siegfried. G. Mov-
  shon. il Hi Fi 19:16 Jl '69
High cost of gold; Columbia vs. RCA. il Time
  93:86 Ap 25 '69
Hyman and the studio men; free-lance
  recording musician. J. S. Wilson. il Hi Fi
  19:50-3 My '69
Music-business maverick. G. Lees. Hi Fi 19:
  116 My '69
Not from the singer, but for the singer; rec-
  ords to teach vocalists correct pronuncia-
  tion of texts of well known songs and arias
  in Italian, French, and German. G. L. Mayer.
  Sat R 52:65 F 22 '69
Projects operatic; London. E. Greenfield. il
  Hi Fi 19:26+ O '69
Richard Wagner and Richard Rodgers, as
  sung by Renata Tebaldi. E. Greenfield. Hi
  Fi 19:20 My '69
Spring laugh-in; London recording scene. E.
  Greenfield. il Hi Fi 19:16+ Ag '69
You're going to hear from her; B. J. Baker.
  G. Lees. Hi Fi 19:132 D '69

Reissues

Born losers; or, Ten records that never made
  it. W. Zakariasen. Hi Fi 19:24+ Ag '69
Five Toscanini reissues. C. J. Luten. il Am
  Rec G 35:544-5 Mr '69
Great recordings revisited. R. Gelatt. Sat R
  52:61-2 S 27 '69
Making doubles out of singles. J. Walsh. il
  Hobbies 74:36-7+ Jl '69
Records:
  Historical reissues. Opera N 34:31 D 20
    '69
  Stainer: The crucifixion; Fabulous for-
    ties at the Met; Dorothy Maynor; Ezio
    Pinza, and Fritz Wunderlich. Opera N
    34:30 S 20 '69
Repeat performance. P. G. Davis. See is-
  sues of High fidelity incorporating Musical
  America
Via Everest, glister from the golden age. P.
  L. Miller. Am Rec G 36:29-30 S '69

Religious records

Inescapable power, Peter Maxwell Davies; Revelation and fall. P. L. Miller. Am Rec G
  35:1054 Jl '69

Renaissance music

Renaissance revisited; discs by the Syn-
  tagma musicum of Amsterdam. R. Jacobson. il Sat R 52:79 N 29 '69

Requiems

Records:
  Requiem. Opera N 33:35 F 8 '69
Requiem; Mozart's sacred drama. P. H.
  Lang. Hi Fi 19:92 O '69
Solti's Verdi Requiem. P. L. Miller. Am Rec
  G 35:423-4 Ja '69

Rock 'n' roll groups

Beatles' Abbey road. A. Goldman. il Life 67:
  22 N 21 '69
Beatles: cheerful coherence. il Time 94:57
  O 3 '69
Cussin', cryin', gettin' it on; Jeff Beck
  group and Blind Faith albums. E. Sander.
  Sat R 52:43 Ag 30 '69
Mephisto in Hollywood; LPs under direction
  of F. Zappa. il Time 94:46+ O 31 '69

PHONOGRAPH records—*Continued*

Rock 'n' roll music (songs, etc)

And now a rock opera; the Who's Tommy. J. Gabree. il Hi Fi 19:30 S '69

Beatles' ninety-minute bore, and the Rolling Stones' Beggars banquet. J. Gabree. il Hi Fi 19:84-5 Mr '69

Brutal and beautiful; the Who's opera Tommy. C. E. Fager. Chr Cent 86:1284-5 O 8 '69

Can jazz-rock find happiness together? B. Korall. il Sat R 52:42-3 Jl 12 '69

Crosby, stills, and Nash: renaissance fare. E. Sander. Sat R 52:56 My 31 '69

Decade of pop completed. E. Sander. Sat R 52:59-60 D 27 '69

Nostalgia: oldies but goodies and a last ditch attempt; rock 'n' roll revival. E. Sander. Sat R 52:51 Mr 29 '69

Pop: a fresh stash for summer. E. Sander. Sat R 52:51+ Jl 26 '69

Rock, etc; Colorado Springs. E. Willis. New Yorker 45:52-3 D 27 '69

See also
Phonograph records—Rock 'n' roll groups

Rock 'n' roll songs

See Phonograph records—Music, Popular (songs, etc)

Russian church music

See Phonograph records—Church music

Sonatas

Glenn Gould in a brand-new role, good old pianistic hair-standing. H. Goldsmith. il Hi Fi 19:82 Mr '69

Prokofiev: three sonatas, three pianists. L. Richmond. Am Rec G 35:624-5+ Ap '69

Szeryng, Ricci, and Bach. B. Schwarz. Sat R 52:53+ My 31 '69

Third and best recording of Biber's Rosary sonatas. D. W. Moore. Am Rec G 35:374-7 Ja '69

Van Cliburn recital: the two Chopin sonatas. C. J. Luten. Am Rec G 35:373 Ja '69

Songs

Canadian collectors' releases. A. Favia-Artsay. il Hobbies 74:35-6 S '69

Charles Groves: a true successor to Beecham? P. L. Miller; J. Diether. il Am Rec G 36:8-9 S '69

Document of considerable value: Nina Koshetz. G. L. Mayer. Am Rec G 35:619 Ap '69

Ever-fresh art of Dorothy Maynor. P. L. Miller. Am Rec G 35:1111 Ag '69

Fascinating repertory opens up. D. Hamilton. Hi Fi 19:78-9 Je '69

Fresh voice for Schubert; Werner Krenn. P. G. Davis. Hi Fi 19:94 Jl '69

History of the Peerless quartet. J. Walsh. il Hobbies 74:38-40+ D '69

Italian passion, German skill; Elisabeth Schwarzkopf and Dietrich Fischer-Dieskau sing H. Wolf's Italian songbook. G. L. Mayer. Sat R 52:78 Ap 26 '69

New Straussian territory, explored by Fischer-Dieskau. P. G. Davis. Hi Fi 19:84 Ap '69

Pertile and Giannini. A. Favia-Artsay. il Hobbies 74:35+ Ag '69

Recitals. P. L. Miller and others. Am Rec G 36:24-8, 222-3 S, N '69

Records:
Christa Ludwig, Walter Berry. Opera N 34:30 S 20 '69
Felicia Weathers. Opera N 33:34 Ap 12 '69
Regina Resnik. Opera N 33:34 Mr 22 '69
Songs. Opera N 33:35 Mr 1 '69
Wolf: Italian song book; Penthesilea; nine songs. Opera N 34:30 D 6 '69

Records. D. Hamilton. Nation 208:476 Ap 14 '69

Schubert among friends. S. Fleming. Hi Fi 19:102 Je '69

Seventeen more songs by Americans. G. L. Mayer. Am Rec G 35:543+ Mr '69

Tenor who will bear watching; Werner Krenn singing Schubert lieder. P. L. Miller. Am Rec G 35:796+ My '69

Vocal music by American composers. William Flanagan: a style of his own. P. L. Miller. Am Rec G 35:542-3 Mr '69

Sounds

Sonic tonic. Newsweek 74:127 N 10 '69

Spanish music

Songs of Andalusia in the middle ages and renaissance. J. W. Barker. Am Rec G 35:362-3 Ja '69

Spoken records

Catch up with; Barrow poets from London. L. Lerman. il Mlle 68:84 F '69

Enriching recorded analysis of Wagner's Ring. G. Movshon. Hi Fi 19:106 S '69

Historical records: fabulous world of the theater. G. Pluck. il Hobbies 73:35+ F '69

On the griddle with Frye; political record album, I am the president. il Time 95:47 Ja 5 '70

On the record: Words. J. L. Limbacher. See issues of Library journal

Poetry parade. il Sr Schol 94:Schol Teach 18-19+ F 14 '69

Popular records; L. Bruce's The Berkeley concert. D. Watt. New Yorker 45:92+ Je 14 '69

Posthumous stardom for a once and future lord; the Lord Buckley phenomenon. A. Goldman. Life 67:13 D 19 '69

Recordings. J. L. Limbacher. See second issue of each month of Library journal

Words only. S. Potter. See issues of American record guide

Stereophonic records

Good-bye mono, hello stereo. Bet Hom & Gard 47:41 Mr '69

Other reviews. See issues of American record guide

Phonograph records. W. F. Grueninger. See issues of Consumer bulletin

Record reviews. See issues of Consumer reports

String quartet music

Four recordings: Schoenberg only. A. Cohn. Am Rec G 35:1034-7 Jl '69

From CRI, a memorial to Quincy Porter. A. Cohn. Am Rec G 35:1142 Ag '69

Haydn & friends. J. Diether. Am Rec G 35:647-8 Ap '69

Late Beethoven, subtly nuanced. R. P. Morgan. Hi Fi 19:78 Ag '69

Three new records by the Quartetto italiano. M. N. Kanny; C. J. Luten. il Am Rec G 35:622-3 Ap '69

Yale quartet's triumphant Beethoven: an opus 127 from Cardinal. M. Kanny. il Am Rec G 36:100-1 O '69

Symphonic poems

Also sprach Zarathustra; orchestra conducted by Zubin Mehta. G. S. Fox. il Am Rec G 35:606-7 Ap '69

Lorin Maazel's Don Quixote. G. S. Fox. il Am Rec G 35:386-8 Ja '69

Virtuoso festoon by Khachaturian. J. Diether. Am Rec G 35:1134+ Ag '69

Zubin Mehta conducts a magnificent recording of Ein heldenleben. G. S. Fox. Am Rec G 35:604-6 Ap '69

Symphonies

About Claudio Abbado. M. N. Kanny; C. J. Luten. Am Rec G 35:621 Ap '69

Ansermet's own valedictory; Albéric Magnard's no. 3 and Arthur Honegger's nos. 3 and 4. R. Lawrence. il Sat R 52:50 D 27 '69

Anyone for Furtwangler's 1942 Beethoven Ninth in stereo? D. Hamilton. il Hi Fi 19:68 Ap '69

Arturo Toscanini society's initial release: Haydn's London symphony. C. J. Luten. Am Rec G 35:615 Ap '69

Bernstein, extraordinarily vital Mendelssohn, marvelous Schubert. M. N. Kanny. Am Rec G 36:194 N '69

Bernstein's personal vision of the Sibelius symphonies. J. Diether. Am Rec G 35:804-6 My '69

Casals, heroic, noble Mozart. M. N. Kanny. Am Rec G 36:136 O '69

Closest approach yet to an ideal Mahler Third. J. Diether. il Am Rec G 35:1119-21 Ag '69

Colin Davis, beyond beauty, poise, and logic; conducting Dvořák's symphonic variations. M. N. Kanny. Am Rec G 35:740 Mr '69

Colin Davis' Romeo and Juliet, as near perfect as possible. B. Jacobson. Hi Fi 19:81 Mr '69

Conductor Casals, passion and tension. H. Goldsmith. Hi Fi 19:96 S '69

Erich Leinsdorf's legacy, a superb feeling for Mozart. M. N. Kanny. Am Rec G 36:196 N '69

From the late Charles Munch: a last word on one of his favorite works. Am Rec G 35:475 F '69

In progress, David Blum's Haydn series: symphonies nos. 90 and 91. P. Hart. Hi Fi 19:94 Mr '69

Leinsdorf's Mozart, a feast for the ear. P. H. Lang. il Hi Fi 19:100 N '69

PHONOGRAPH records—Symphonies—*Cont.*
Lou Harrison: Symphony on G. D. J. Henahan. il Mus Q 55:285 Ap '69
Magic theater of Luciano Berio. D. Henahan. Hi Fi 19:71-2 Ag '69
Music of Vaughan Williams, round two. A. Frankenstein. Hi Fi 19:105 S '69
Records:
Roméo and Juliette. Opera N 33:30 Je 14 '69
Vaughan Williams. Opera N 34:42 D 27 '69
Second symphony of Sir Michael Tippett. J. Diether. Am Rec G 36:98-9 O '69
Shostakovich's symphonies; appraisal of the music and the recordings. R. S. Brown. il Hi Fi 19:43-7+ Ap '69
Sibelius in perspective. R. Lawrence. Sat R 52:73 F 22 '69
Sibelius' seven symphonies; a critic's view of the recordings. H. Goldsmith. il Hi Fi 19:56-60 My '69
Smashing interpretation of Prokofiev's Second symphony. J. Diether. Am Rec G 35:785+ My '69
Stokowski continues to invade new territories. R. D. Darrell; H. Goldsmith. Hi Fi 19:75 Jl '69
Tchaikovsky surprise package; Igor Markevitch conducting. H. Goldsmith. il Hi Fi 19:72-3 Ag '69
Together at last, the Fantastique and its sequel. J. W. Barker. il Am Rec G 35:370-2 Ja '69
Treasure for Haydn seekers; Symphonies no. 88 and no. 102. S. Lowe. Hi Fi 19:84 Ag '69
Two by Balakirev. M. N. Kanny. Am Rec G 35:556 Mr '69
Two Prokofiev symphonies, a logical second and a lyrical fifth. P. Hart. il Hi Fi 19:77-8 My '69
Unhesitatingly recommended: Leinsdorf's Haydn. W. N. Kanny. Am Rec G 35:406+ Ja '69
Variation-symphony of Peter Mennin; clarity and zest. A. Cohn. Am Rec G 35:541 Mr '69
Vaughan Williams, first stereo editions of his great Fourth symphony. J. Diether. Am Rec G 35:534-5 Mr '69
Vaughan Williams from Sir Adrian, outstanding. J. Diether. il Am Rec G 36:214-16+ N '69

Tone poems
See Phonograph records—Symphonic poems

Trombone music
New music for solo trombone, and for virtuoso trombonist. R. P. Morgan. il Hi Fi 19:64-5 Ap '69

Viola music
Revitalizing the viola: Walter Trampler plays three works by a great fellow violist, Paul Hindemith. A. Cohn. il Am Rec G 35:368-9 Ja '69

Violin music
No violinist does unaccompanied Bach quite like Henryk Szeryng. M. Sherwin. Hi Fi 19:86 Mr '69

Vocal music
Vocal recordings. D. Hamilton. Hi Fi 19:84 O '69
See also
Phonograph records—Cantatas

Zarzuelas
Many pleasures of the Spanish zarzuela, arias by Victoria de los Angeles and duets (with her husband) by Montserrat Caballé. P. L. Miller. il Am Rec G 35:536-7 Mr '69
PHONOGRAPH records, Cataloging of. See Cataloging
PHOSPHATASES
Immunological detection of single amino acid substitutions in alkaline phosphatase. G. T. Cocks and A. C. Wilson. bibliog il Science 164:188-9 Ap 11 '69
Potassium ions asymmetrically activate erythrocyte membrane phosphatase. A. F. Rega and others. bibliog il Science 167:55-6 Ja 2 '70
See also
Adenosine triphosphatase
PHOSPHATES
Annals of medicine; cases of organic phosphate poisoning. B. Roueché. New Yorker 45:123-4+ O 11 '69
Nucleoside triphosphate termini from RNA synthesized in vivo by escherichia coli. S. E. Jorgensen and others. bibliog il Science 164:1067-70 My 30 '69
Phosphorus-proton spin-spin coupling and conformation of a dinucleoside phosphate. M. Tsuboi and others. bibliog il Science 166:1504-6 D 19 '69

Sedimentary phosphate method for estimating paleosalinities; limited applicability. G. Müller. il Science 163:812-13 F 21 '69
See also
Apatite
Imidodiphosphates
Iron phosphates
Phosphorylation
Pyrophosphates
PHOSPHATES in detergents. See Detergents
PHOSPHATES in the body
Metal ion activation of phosphate transfer by bidentate coordination. F. J. Farrell and others. bibliog il Science 164:320-1 Ap 18 '69
PHOSPHATIDES
Stability of asymmetric phospholipid membranes. D. Papahadjopoulos and S. Ohki. bibliog il Science 164:1075-7 My 30 '69
PHOSPHIDES
Phosphide from meteorites: barringerite, a new iron-nickel mineral. P. R. Buseck. bibliog il Science 165:169-71 Jl 11 '69
PHOSPHOGLUCONTE dehydrogenase. See Dehydrogenases
PHOSPHOLIPIDS. See Phosphatides
PHOSPHOMANNOSE isomerase. See Isomerases
PHOSPHONATES
Diphosphonates inhibit formation of calcium phosphate crystals in vitro and pathological calcification in vivo. M. D. Francis and others. bibliog il Science 165:1264-6 S 19 '69
Diphosphonates inhibit hydroxyapatite dissolution in vitro and bone resorption in tissue culture and in vivo. H. Fleisch and others. bibliog il Science 165:1262-4 S 19 '69
PHOSPHONIC acids
Carbon-phosphorus bond in nature. J. S. Kittredge and E. Roberts. bibliog il Science 164:37-42 Ap 4 '69
PHOSPHONOMYCIN. See Antibiotics
PHOSPHORESCENCE
See also
Bioluminescence
Luminescence
PHOSPHORUS compounds
Carbon-phosphorous bond in nature. J. S. Kittredge and E. Roberts. bibliog il Science 164:37-42 Ap 4 '69
New bond; carbon-phosphorus bond. Sci Am 220:58 Je '69
PHOSPHORYLATION
Oxidative and photosynthetic phosphorylation mechanisms. J. H. Wang. bibliog il Science 167:25-30 Ja 2 '70
Phosphorylation of dipteran chromosomes and rat liver nuclei. W. B. Benjamin and R. M. Goodman. bibliog il Science 166:629-31 O 31 '69
PHOTO copy stand. See Photography—Apparatus and supplies
PHOTO finishing. See Photographic finishing, Commercial
PHOTOCHEMICAL etching. See Metal etching
PHOTOCHEMICAL ignition. See Ignition
PHOTOCHEMISTRY
Amateur scientist; how to make photographs in polymer and build a sensitive pressure gauge. G. Oster. il Sci Am 221:128-32 D '69
Chemistry and light. G. Porter. il Chem 42:21 Ja '69
Photochemical decomposition of DDT by a free-radical mechanism. A. R. Mosier and others. bibliog il Science 164:1083-5 My 30 '69
Photochemical reactions and the chemical evolution of purines and nicotinamide derivatives. J. P. Ferris and others. bibliog il Science 166:765-6 N 7 '69
Uracil photoproducts from uracil irradiated in ice. M. N. Khattak and S. Y. Wang. bibliog il Science 163:1341-2 Mr 21 '69
PHOTOCHROMIC substances
Here come the strange-change products! J. R. Berry. il Mech Illus 65:56-8+ Ap '69
PHOTOCOMPOSITION. See Phototypesetting
PHOTOCOPYING. See Copying processes
PHOTOELECTRIC cells
Build slot-car Win detector. W. T. Lemen. il Pop Electr 30:41-5 My '69

Control applications
Build a photosensitive switch. H. R. Mallory. il Pop Electr 31:55-6 D '69
PHOTOELECTRICITY
See also
Image intensifiers
PHOTOFLASH lamps. See Electric lamps, Photoflash

PHOTOGRAMS. See Shadowgrams

PHOTOGRAPHERS
Classics of photography. See issues of Modern photography
Critical eye; decline of the amateur. A. Rothstein. Travel & Camera 32:36 Ag '69
Czech points on surrealism. P. M. Tausk and J. Dreyfuss. il Mod Phot 33:74-5+ S '69
Gallery snooping. J. Dreyfuss. il Mod Phot 33:60+ F '69
Incredible will of creativity. R. Graves. Life 66:3 Je 27 '69
Japanese photography today. W. L. Broecker. il Travel & Camera 32:72-86 O '69
Working with a photographer; finding a good photographer to illustrate your article. J. Lawrence. il Writers Digest 49:60-3+ Jl '69
See also
Women as photographers
also names of photographers, e.g. A. Adams

Public relations
How to promote yourself as a photographer. D. Vestal. il Pop Phot 64:63-5+ F '69

PHOTOGRAPHERS, French
It started with Daguerre; French primitive photography exhibit, Philadelphia. M. R. Weiss. il Sat R 52:23-5 D 13 '69

PHOTOGRAPHIC albums
Your travel album. B. Weber. il Travel & Camera 32:88-9 N '69

PHOTOGRAPHIC apparatus industry and trade
See also
Eastman Kodak company

Anecdotes, facetiae, satire, etc.
Birth of a salesman. D. Sutherland. il Travel & Camera 32:78-9+ Ap '69

PHOTOGRAPHIC chemicals
Reducers to the rescue. C. W. Kennedy. il Pop Phot 65:48+ Ag '69

PHOTOGRAPHIC chemistry
Foto facts. P. Farber. il Travel & Camera 32:22+ Ap '69
Take it away by bleaching; using potassium ferricyanide. A. Francekevich. il Pop Phot 64:26+ Je '69
Wolfman on printing; ferricyanide for overall, or local reduction. A. Wolfman. Mod Phot 33:54+ N '69
Wolfman on printing; intermixing stabilization papers and solutions from various suppliers. A. Wolfman. Mod Phot 33:38+ My '69
See also
Emulsions, Photographic
Photography—Processing

PHOTOGRAPHIC Christmas cards. See Christmas cards

PHOTOGRAPHIC collectors of North America, Society of. See Society of photographic collectors of North America

PHOTOGRAPHIC copying. See Photography—Copying

PHOTOGRAPHIC emulsions. See Emulsions, Photographic

PHOTOGRAPHIC enlargers. See Photography—Enlargers and enlarging

PHOTOGRAPHIC equipment. See Photography—Apparatus and supplies

PHOTOGRAPHIC exhibitions. See Photography—Exhibitions

PHOTOGRAPHIC files. See Files and filing (documents, etc)

PHOTOGRAPHIC films. See Photography—Films

PHOTOGRAPHIC finishing
See also
Photography—Retouching

PHOTOGRAPHIC finishing, Commercial
Ed Scully on color; GAF color print film. E. Scully. Mod Phot 33:46-8 N '69
Mail-order photofinishers. il Consumer Bul 52:7-11 Ag '69

PHOTOGRAPHIC greeting cards. See Greeting cards

PHOTOGRAPHIC illustration. See Illustration of books and periodicals

PHOTOGRAPHIC laboratories
Color print services; how good are they? H. C. Birnbaum. il U S Camera 32:54-5+ Ja '69
Ten tips from a top lab. H. Shaman. il Pop Phot 65:78-9 O '69

PHOTOGRAPHIC lenses. See Lenses, Photographic

PHOTOGRAPHIC meters
See also
Exposure meters

PHOTOGRAPHIC paper
Can custom printing make a difference? E. Scully. il Mod Phot 33:91+ Je '69
Stabilization: it's here to stay. P. Farber. il Travel & Camera 32:92-5+ F '69
Wolfman on printing. A. Wolfman. Mod Phot 33:38 Ap '69
Wolfman on printing; intermixing stabilization papers and solutions from various suppliers. A. Wolfman. Mod Phot 33:38+ My '69

Testing
Wolfman on printing; imported paper. A. Wolfman. Mod Phot 33:82+ S '69

PHOTOGRAPHIC processing. See Photography—Processing

PHOTOGRAPHIC reconnaissance systems
Real-time systems speed recon pictures; Compass link and Quick look systems. B. M. Elson. il Aviation W 91:95+ N 17 '69

PHOTOGRAPHIC reproduction. See Photography—Copying

PHOTOGRAPHIC slides. See Transparencies

PHOTOGRAPHIC supplies. See Photography—Apparatus and supplies

PHOTOGRAPHIC themes. See Photography—Themes

PHOTOGRAPHS
Accent on stillness. il Pop Phot 65:88-97 Jl '69
Fall into winter: a portfolio. Pop Phot 65: 97-105 N '69
Gallery:
American Gothic in North Carolina; photographs by S. Dinkins. Life 67:8-9 S 12 '69
André Kertész in Washington square. il Life 67:2-3 N 14 '69
Aussie Whiting makes rugby look as rough as it is. il Life 67:12-13 S 26 '69
Bruce Davidson in Spanish Harlem. il Life 67:4-7 Ag 15 '69
City scenes, by E. Falkensteen. Life 67: 8-9 D 12 '69
An eastern approach by R. Michaud. il Life 67:4-7 Ag 29 '69
Erich Hartmann photographs time in New York's Grand Central station. il Life 67:12-13 S 19 '69
Erwin Fieger in Japan. il Life 67:8-11 O 17 '69
Frances B. Johnston's seventy-year-old documentaries. il Life 67:4-7 D 19 '69
G. Laurents, photographer as a collagist. il Life 67:8-9 O 3 '69
Gordon Parks, jr. photographs his father's movie. il Life 67:6-7 S 5 '69
Ikko Narahara on timelessness. il Life 67: 2-3 N 7 '69
Irwin Dermer on motion. il Life 67:8-9 O 31 '69
Jerry Uelsmann in the darkroom. Life 67:8-11 N 21 '69
John Dominis photographs an assemblage of horses. il Life 67:8-9 Ag 22 '69
John Zielinski's black and white gaiety of the Amish. il Life 67:8-9 O 24 '69
Niklas Deak's apocalypse. il Life 67:6-7 Ag 8 '69
Nudes in action by Christer Hallgren. il Life 67:10-11 D 5 '69
Poetic imagery of T. Tanuma. il Life 67: 4-7 Ag 1 '69
Surrealistic vision of Bill Brandt. il Life 67:8-11 O 10 '69
Tom McCarthy's double exposures. il Life 67:8-9 N 28 '69
Goofs; by Modern editors. H. Keppler. il Mod Phot 33:86-7 Je '69
Ice & blue. Pop Phot 65:98-103 D '69
Readers' gallery. See issues of Travel & camera
See also
Copyright—Photographs
also subhead Photographs under various subjects, e.g. Vietnam (Democratic Republic)—Photographs

Collections
See also
Photographic albums

Editing
Photo-graphics; elimination of detail. E. C. Scully. il Mod Phot 33:76-7 S '69

Exhibitions
See Photography—Exhibitions

Framing
See Photographs—Trimming, mounting, etc.

PHOTOGRAPHS—*Continued*

Mounting

See Photographs—Trimming, mounting, etc.

Trimming, mounting, etc.

Dry-mount your favorite photos for display. B. Corley. il Pop Mech 131:148-50 My '69

Dry-mounting in a can. C. W. Kennedy. il Pop Phot 65:42+ O '69

Dry-mounting the hand-iron way. C. W. Kennedy. il Pop Phot 65:24+ N '69

Mounting and framing prints. D. Vestal. il Pop Phot 64:94-5+ Je '69

Wolfman on printing. A. Wolfman. il Mod Phot 33:30+ F; 46+ Mr; 48+ Je '69

You can mat your pictures like a pro. R. J. De Cristoforo. il Pop Sci 194:126-8 Je '69

PHOTOGRAPHS, Composite. See Photomontage

PHOTOGRAPHS, Hanging of. See Pictures, Hanging of

PHOTOGRAPHS, Judging of. See Photography—Criticism

PHOTOGRAPHS in books and periodicals. See Illustration of books and periodicals

PHOTOGRAPHS in education. See Pictures in education

PHOTOGRAPHY

Answers; questions and answers. R. Arnold. See issues of Travel & Camera

Are you as good as that box camera? N. Rothschild. il Pop Phot 65:73-5+ O '69

Assignment: seeing between the scenics. J. Scully. il Mod Phot 33:92-5+ F '69

Best ways to take seashore pictures. Good H 168:166 Je '69

Break the rules! J. Scully. il Mod Phot 33:64-73 Mr '69

Critical eye. A. Rothstein. Travel & Camera 32:86 My '69

Eisenstaedt: a snapshot. A. Goldsmith. il Travel & Camera 32:78-83+ Jl '69

Feininger. A. Feininger. Mod Phot 33:58+ O; 51-2+ N '69

Foto facts. P. Farber. See issues of Travel & camera

Hattersley class. R. Hattersley. See issues of Popular photography

If in doubt, try the horse's mouth; sources of information. N. Rothschild. il Pop Phot 65:38+ Jl '69

Photo answers; questions and answers. R. Arnold. Travel & Camera 32:88-9 Ap; 96-7 My; 96-7 Je '69

Picture sense. A. Rothstein. Travel & Camera 32:30 F; 24 Mr '69

Religion 1968. R. Hattersley; reply with rejoinder. B. M. Wallach. Pop Phot 64:94 F '69

Tools & techniques. C. W. Kennedy. See issues of Popular photography

Travel guide. See issues of Travel & camera

Vagabond camera. W. Lane. See issues of Travel

View from the bay; London activities. M. Mann. il Pop Phot 65:29-30+ N '69

View from the Bay; San Francisco activities. M. Mann. il Pop Phot 65:33+ Jl; 20+ Ag '69

We open a new picture gallery. R. Graves. Life 67:1 Ag 1 '69

See also
Astronomical photography
Color photography
Creative photography
Daguerreotypes
Microfilms
Moving picture photography
Nature photography
Photographs
Photomicrography
Society of photographic collectors of North America
Space photography
Stereophotography
Telephotography
Television—Photographic aspects
Transparencies
Vietnamese war, 1957- —Photography

Anecdotes, facetiae, satire, etc.

It's hard to shoot a bank in London. S. Nathan. il Pop Phot 64:70+ My '69

Apparatus and supplies

Behind the scenes. See issues of Modern photography

Camera guide (title varies) il Travel & Camera. 32:13-14+ F; 15-17 Mr; 19-20 Ap; 27-8 My; 27-8 Je '69

Camera news. See issues of Travel & Camera

Expo '69: not much but something. il Mod Phot 33:56-61 S '69

First look. See issues of Popular photography

Foot is a four-letter word; what will the metric system mean to your photography? W. Hanson. Pop Phot 65:76-7+ O '69

Get ready, get set, go! R. Arnold. Travel & Camera 32:13-14 Ag '69

If carrying cameras is your bag. R. Arnold. il Travel & Camera 32:16+ S '69

It really happened; Photo-expo 69 June 7-15 N.Y. coliseum. il Pop Phot 65:76-7+ S '69

It's back to the big negative. N. Goldberg il Pop Phot 65:64+ O '69

It's not that technical. N. Rothschild. il Pop Phot 64:36+ Ap '69

Kramer's korner; Lektra laboratories. A. Kramer. il Mod Phot 33:134+ Ap '69

Lab reports. See issues of Popular photography

Large camera; homemade light table. A. Feininger. il Mod Phot 33:82+ Ag '69

Meyers on technique. E. Meyers. il Mod Phot 33:56+ F '69

New products. See issues of Travel & camera

No expo for Expo 69. L. Drukker. il Pop Phot 65:98-9+ Jl '69

Once over lightly. See issues of Modern photography

Pack along with Rothschild. N. Rothschild. il Pop Phot 64:88-9+ Je '69

Photo copy stand. il Mech Illus 65:116-17 N '69

Photokina '68. T. Morton; M. Edelson; J. Hughes. il U S Camera 32:42-51 Ja '69

Reflectors that fill and fold. C. W. Kennedy. il Pop Phot 64:24+ Ap '69

Tools & techniques. C. W. Kennedy. See issues of Popular photography

T&C tests. See issues of Travel & camera

Watch out for bargain accessories. N. Goldberg. il Pop Phot 64:52+ Je '69

Why not get off the bandwagon? N. Rothschild. il Pop Phot 64:34+ My '69

See also
Camera tripods
Exposure meters
Lenses, Photographic
Light filters
Photography—Electronic equipment
Photography—Printing processes—Apparatus and supplies
View finders

Exhibitions

See Photography—Exhibitions

Maintenance and repair

Where for repairs? See issues of Modern photography

Storage

How storage can cause breakdowns. N. Goldberg. il Pop Phot 65:74+ Jl '69

Testing

Modern tests. See issues of Modern photography

Bibliography

Book reviews. See issues of Popular photography

Books in review. See issues of Modern photography

Books in review. See issues of Travel & camera

Christmas cards

See Christmas cards

Close-up

See Photography, Close-up

Cold weather conditions

Camera troubles in winter? Pro tells you what to do. J. Rychetnik. Mod Phot 33:142+ Ap '69

Common cures for the cold camera. L. Drukker. il Pop Phot 64:66-7+ F '69

Collectors and collecting

Photography considers its past. J. Deschin. il Pop Phot 64:28+ Ap '69

Picture sense. A. Rothstein. Travel & Camera 32:24 Mr '69

Competitions

Announcing the winners of our photo contest (cont) il Home Gard 56:25-7 O '69

In a time of cold neutrality an impartial judge is hard to find; thirteenth World press photo competition. A. Rothstein. il Travel & Camera 32:24-5 Je '69

Justice Douglas as a contest judge. J. Deschin. il Pop Phot 65:28+ S '69

Monthly contest. il Mod Phot 33:98-9 F '69

PHOTOGRAPHY—Competitions—*Continued*
Nature and the camera; selected prizewinners.
il Natur Hist 78:28-33 Je '69
News pictures of the year; 1968 in review;
winners in the 26th Annual pictures of the
year competition. M. R. Weiss. il Sat R
52:122-3 Mr 8 '69
1969 Scholastic photography awards. il Sr
Schol 94:17, 34-7+ My 9 '69
Photo contests. il Pop Phot 65:133 N '69
Photography contest/1969. Home Gard 56:62
Je '69
Winners in the teachers' photo competition.
il Todays Ed 58:46-7 My '69
World travel photo contest: the judging and
the judged. M. R. Weiss. il Sat R 53:58-66
Ja 3 '70

Composition
See Composition (photography)

Copying
If you print b&w, you can do color. E.
Meyers. il Pop Phot 65:60+ D '69
Large camera; 4x5-in. view camera for copy
work. A. Feininger. Mod Phot 33:30-1+
Mr '69
Matzkin on movies; stills from your movies.
M. A. Matzkin. il Mod Phot 33:32+ O '69
Photo copy stand. il Mech Illus 65:116-17
N '69
See also
Moving picture photography—Copying
Transparencies—Copying

Criticism
Feininger; a photograph and the viewer. A.
Feininger. Mod Phot 33:51-2+ N '69
Gallery snooping. J. Dreyfuss. il Mod Phot
33:60+ F '69
Open your eyes! R. Hattersley. il Pop Phot
65:102-5+ Jl '69
Seeing pictures. J. Scully. See issues of
Modern photography
Who can say what future will treasure? N.
Rothschild. il Pop Phot 65:24+ Ag '69

Darkroom technique
See Photography—Processing

Developing and developers
Ed Scully on color; color film. E. Scully.
Mod Phot 33:50+ Mr '69
Give and take of contrast cutting. C. W. Ken-
nedy. il Pop Phot 65:58+ Jl '69
Kramer's korner; development times for
personal film-developer combinations. A.
Kramer. il Mod Phot 33:30+ Ag '69
Kramer's korner; film-developer combination
for big negatives. A. Kramer. il Mod
Phot 33:80+ S '69
What! You haven't done your own color? E.
Scully. il Mod Phot 33:110+ Je '69
Whatever happened to monobaths? R. D.
Zakia. il Pop Phot 64:68-9+ F '69
You can overdo it, agitators. A. Francekevich.
il Pop Phot 65:72+ N '69
See also
Photographic chemistry
Photographic finishing, Commercial

Electronic equipment
AC supply for professional photoflash units.
J. Kyle. il Radio-Electr 40:101 S '69
Bare-bulb flash goes electronic. E. H. Ortner.
il Pop Sci 195:105 Ag '69
Build an electronic shutter control. W. B.
Ford. il Pop Electr 30:75-8 Ap '69
Do guide numbers guide? P. Farber. il US
Camera 32:40-1+ Ja '69
Easy to build high power electronic photo-
flash. J. A. Gupton, jr. il Radio-Electr 40:
23-6 F '69
IC electronics for shutterbugs. J. R. Free.
il Radio-Electr 40:39-42 F '69
Is full automation the future? N. Rothschild.
il Pop Phot 65:90-1+ N '69
Phototronics. E. Farber. Mod Phot 33:42 Ag;
16+ S; 28+ N '69
Voltage regulator for enlarger lamp. R. A.
Wolff. il Electr World 82:72 S '69
See also
Electric lamps, Photoflash

Enlargers and enlarging
Does your enlarger steal sharpness? H. Zuck-
er. il Pop Phot 64:98-9+ Mr '69
Foto facts. P. Farber. Travel & Camera 32:
82-3 Mr '69
It's a super system; super Chromega enlargers
and super Chromegatron analyzer. R.
Perry. il Pop Phot 65:118-19+ D '69
Six tips about enlargers. il Mod Phot 33:44
N '69

Equipment
See Photography—Apparatus and supplies

Exhibitions
Brandt's Britain. M. R. Weiss. il Sat R 52:52-
3 O 25 '69
Can whitey do a beautiful black picture
show? D. Vestal; M. Mann. il Pop Phot 64:
79-83+ My '69
Chicago's septuagenarian swinger; 75th anniversary exhibit at the Field museum of natural history, Chicago. K. Poli. il Pop
Phot 65:80 N '69
Click! Nature photography exhibit, Milwaukee. il Nat Wildlife 7:36-9 Ag '69
Critical eye. A. Rothstein. il Travel & Camera 32:86 Ap '69
Ed Scully on color; Photo expo '69. E.
Scully. Mod Phot 33:30+ S '69
Enduring Laura Gilpin; show at the Riverside museum, N.Y. D. Vestal. il Pop Phot
64:50 Je '69
Eyes on America; A. Clayton's show of social commentary at New York's Jewish museum. H. Junker. il Newsweek 73:80 Ap 7
'69
Eyes on America; Farm security administra-
tion's show, just before the war. H. Junker. il Newsweek 73:80 Ap 7 '69
Gallery snooping. See issues of Modern
photography
Harlem; sold out by Massa Hoving? photo
exhibit Harlem on my mind at Metropolitan museum. J. Dreyfuss. il Mod Phot
33:64-5+ My '69
In review. D. Vestal. il Travel & Camera
32:28+ D '69
Is over-design ruining photo shows? J.
Deschin. il Pop Phot 64:22+ My '69
It really happened; Photo expo 69 June 7-15
N.Y. coliseum. il Pop Phot 65:76-7+ S '69
It started with Daguerre; French primitive
photography exhibit, Philadelphia. M. R.
Weiss. il Sat R 52:23-5 D 13 '69
No expo for Expo 69. L. Drukker. il Pop Phot
65:98-9+ Jl '69
Photojournalism museum style; Israel: the
reality. M. R. Weiss. il Sat R 52:112-13 S 13
'69
Photokina; forecast of the future. A. Roth-
stein. U S Camera 32:16+ Ja '69
Photokina '68. T. Morton; M. Edelson; J.
Hughes. il U S Camera 32:42-51 Ja '69
Phototronics; Photo expo '69. E. Farber. Mod
Phot 33:16+ S '69
SRO for Uelsmann, Davidson at S.F. museum
of art. M. Mann. il Pop Phot 65:23-4+ S '69
Seeing pictures; good and bad ways to ex-
hibit pictures. J. Scully. il Mod Phot 33:
10+ S '69
Shows to see. See issues of Popular pho-
tography
Shows we've seen. See issues of Popular pho-
tography
What photo shows don't really show. N.
Rothschild. il Pop Phot 65:30+ O '69
Who is Callahan? D. Vestal. il Travel &
Camera 32:68-72+ My '69

Exposure
B/W exposure a snap; or, is it? J. Scully.
il Mod Phot 33:70-7 Jl '69
Do guide numbers guide? P. Farber. il U S
Camera 32:40-1+ Ja '69
Ed Scully on color; creative potential of
flare. E. Scully. il Mod Phot 33:44+ O '69
Flare: bugaboo of fast lenses. E. Scully. il
Mod Phot 33:78-9 F '69
Foto facts. P. Farber. il Travel & Camera
32:38 O '69
Give and take of contrast cutting. C. W. Ken-
nedy. il Pop Phot 65:58+ Jl '69
Metering through the lens; interview, ed. by
B. Schwalberg. H. D. Ulffers. Pop Phot 65:
104+ Ag '69
Short course on exposure. P. Farber. Travel
& Camera 32:32 N '69
Sunset exposure calculator. S. P. Martin. il
Pop Phot 65:74-5+ S '69
What to do if your meter breaks down? N.
Rothschild. Pop Phot 65:80-1+ O '69
What's your camera's TP? time parallax. N.
Goldberg. il Pop Phot 64:56+ F '69
When to outthink a thru-lens meter. E.
Scully. il Mod Phot 33:68-9 Ag '69
See also
Exposure meters
Moving picture photography—Exposure

Films
Agfapan 1000; not only fast, but designed for
pictures. B. Schwalberg. il Pop Phot 64:80-
3 Mr '69

PHOTOGRAPHY—Films—*Continued*

Coming soon: Agfa-Gevaert's pro films. B. Schwalberg. Pop Phot 64:64+ Mr '69

Ed Scully on color; accurate color. E. Scully. Mod Phot 33:32+ F '69

Ed Scully on color; GAF color print film. E. Scully. Mod Phot 33:46-8 N '69

Fantastic new films let you almost shoot in the dark! R. Hertzberg. il Pop Mech 131: 138-40 Mr '69

How red was my greenery. D. B. Eisendrath. il Pop Phot 65:18+ S '69

Infrared: difficult? Not really; Ektachrome infrared aero film. E. Scully. il Mod Phot 33:82-7 My '69

Mix 'n' match color materials; world of color negative photography. D. B. Eisendrath. il Pop Phot 65:20+ O '69

No more purple skies; Kodachrome-X. N. Rothschild. il Pop Phot 64:115 F '69

35 color film round-up. N. Rothschild. Pop Phot 65:94-5 Ag '69

Three negative color films compared. E. Scully. il Mod Phot 33:90+ Je '69

Which indoor color film suits you best? E. Scully. il Mod Phot 33:76-7 Mr '69

See also
Emulsions, Photographic
Moving picture films

Testing

Color tests: ours and theirs. D. B. Eisendrath. il Pop Phot 64:18+ F '69

Focusing

At last! Automatic camera focusing. il Mod Phot 33:90-1+ F '69

Depth-of-field law finally repealed? T. Shackleford. il Mod Phot 33:133+ Je '69

How to see with glasses. N. Rothschild. il Pop Phot 65:83-5+ N '69

Keppler on the SLR; can a 126 Instamatic SLR camera deliver sharp pictures with an f/1.9 lens? H. Keppler. il Mod Phot 33:40+ Ap '69

Portraits: from 20mm to 500mm. J. Scully; E. Scully. il Mod Phot 33:76-83 Ap '69

Screen scene; why all those crazy SLR screens got that way. N. Rothschild. il Pop Phot 64:100-1+ Mr '69

See also
Moving picture photography—Focusing

Galleries and museums

Add New York galleries: best yet; interview, ed. by J. Deschin. L. D. Witkin. il Pop Phot 65:38+ O '69

At last, photo museum for New York; plans to move Sipley collection from Philadelphia. J. Deschin. il Pop Phot 64:22+ Je '69

Grain

Foto facts. P. Farber. il Travel & Camera 32: 22+ Ap '69

Instant grain, to order. A. Francekevich. il Pop Phot 74:42+ Mr '69

Search for texture treasures. A. Francekevich. il Pop Phot 64:34+ Ap '69

History

Atget, the little man who influenced a generation of photographers. D. Vestal. il Pop Phot 64:86-91+ F '69

Goodbye, hello! E. Hannigan. U S Camera 32:33+ Ja '69

In London, the Victorians are still eminent. M. Mann. il Pop Phot 65:29-30+ N '69

100 years of Japanese photography. G. Konishi. il Travel & Camera 32:113-16+ O '69

Photography considers its past. J. Deschin. il Pop Phot 64:28+ Ap '69

Landscapes

Frontier photographers: O'Sullivan and Jackson. D. Vestal. il Travel & Camera 32: 48-52+ Je '69

I photograph a mountain: Cotopaxi in Ecuador. B. Kelly. il Travel & Camera 32:116-17+ F '69

Make your own time of day. J. Scully. il Mod Phot 33:58-63 Mr '69

Light

Portraits on the shady side. N. Rothschild. il Pop Phot 65:104-5+ S '69

Shadows can make the picture. C. W. Kennedy. il Pop Phot 64:38+ Je '69

Lighting

Light from a cable; macro shots. W. F. Wilson. il Pop Phot 65:70 O '69

Lightweight lighting for heavyweight shooting; Lowell link system. il Pop Phot 64:78-9 Ap '69

Reflectors that fill and fold. C. W. Kennedy. il Pop Phot 64:24+ Ap '69

Vary your light level; solid state dimmers. W. F. Wilson. il Pop Phot 64:38 Mr '69

Wrong light color? E. Scully. il Mod Phot 33:118-19 O '69

See also
Photography—Exposure
Photography, Flashlight

Marines

See also
Photography of ships

Negatives

Ed Scully on color; standard negative? E. Scully. Mod Phot 33:16+ Ap '69

You can't print that, or can you? C. W. Kennedy. il Pop Phot 64:74-5+ Ap '69

Care

Wolfman on printing; eliminating dust on negatives. A. Wolfman. Mod Phot 33:46+ Ag '69

News

See Photography, Journalistic

Portraits

Arbus, does she cater to the peeping Tom within us? M. Mann. Pop Phot 65:25-6+ D '69

Are four heads better? D. Becker. il Mod Phot 33:109 N '69

Brazil's beauties: girls from Ipanema, Copacabana and Gavea. C. Jones. Travel & Camera 32:60-3 N '69

Easy way to get good people pictures. N. Goldberg. il Pop Phot 65:80+ D '69

Glamour by Gowland. P. Gowland. See issues of Popular photography

Here's me. April Sheffield, with James Mason! A. Sheffield. Esquire 71:136-8+ Je '69

Large camera; large camera portraiture. A. Feininger. Mod Phot 33:48+ F '69

Make a model's portfolio. E. Scully. il Mod Photo 33:72-3 My '69

Non-events happen, even in Morocco; Miss Europe competition. Simon. il Pop Phot 65: 79+ D '69

Paolo Pellegrineschi. il Pop Phot 65:108-11 Jl '69

Portrait of Tracy, a very personal view. R. Davis. il Life 67:88-91+ O 17 '69

Portraits: from 20mm to 500mm. J. Scully; E. Scully. il Mod Phot 33:76-83 Ap '69

Portraits on the shady side. N. Rothschild. Pop Phot 65:104-5+ S '69

Seeing pictures. J. Scully. il Mod Phot 33:26+ Mr '69

Shadows can make the picture. C. W. Kennedy. il Pop Phot 64:38+ Je '69

Should you direct your portraits? E. Meyers. il Pop Phot 65:52+ N '69

Sight & sound of folk. R. Goldstein. Travel & Camera 32:70-5 Je '69

Strange new world of Ralph Eugene Meatyard. J. B. Hall. il Pop Phot 65:120-1+ Jl '69

Printing processes

Archival printing, push for permanence. J. Deschin. il Pop Phot 65:30+ Ag '69

Are four heads better? D. Becker. il Mod Phot 33:109 N '69

Can custom printing make a difference? E. Scully. il Mod Phot 33:91+ Je '69

Color the b&w, the easy way. A. Francekevich. il Pop Phot 65:46+ S '69

Ed Scully on color; color film. E. Scully. Mod Phot 33:50+ Mr '69

Foto facts; Heath/Mitchell color wheel system. P. Farber. il Travel & Camera 32: 24+ My '69

New photographic process uses color to make invisible visible. il Life 66:78-80 Mr 7 '69

Pro's guide to successful printing. E. Steinbicker. il Pop Phot 64:78-9+ Mr '69

Wolfman on printing. A. Wolfman. See issues of Modern photography

You can't print that, or can you? C. W. Kennedy. il Pop Phot 64:74-5+ Ap '69

See also
Photographic finishing, Commercial

Apparatus and supplies

Color printing in a breadboard darkroom. E. Scully. il Mod Phot 33:34+ O '69

It's a super system; super Chromega enlargers and super Chromegatron analyzer. R. Perry. il Pop Phot 65:118-19+ D '69

PHOTOGRAPHY—Continued

Processing

Are your prints fading away? D. Vestal. il Pop Phot 64:67-9+ Ap '69
Photo developing by mail: are costs less? Good H 168:206 Ap '69
Stabilization: it's here to stay. P. Farber. il Travel & Camera 32:92-5+ F '69
View from Kramer; achieving permanent color. A. Kramer. Mod Phot 33:38+ N '69
See also
Photographic finishing, Commercial

Apparatus and supplies

Build an automatic enlarger timer. H. Elkin. il Radio-Electr 40:50-2 D '69
Build the SCS darkroom timer. F. H. Tooker. il Pop Electr 31:52-4+ N '69
Color kit makes printing easy. A. Francekevich. il Pop Phot 65:40+ Ag '69
Darkroom sink with a built-in print washer. R. S. Hedin. il Pop Mech 131:130-2 Ja '69
Digital photo enlarger timer. C. R. Morton. il Radio-Electr 40:68-70 F '69
Does your enlarger steal sharpness? H. Zucker. il Pop Phot 64:98-9+ Mr '69
Footswitch for penniless photographers. B. Bruggemeyer. il Pop Phot 64:28 My '69
Foto facts; color canoe. P. Farber. il Travel & Camera 32:20+ F; 25 Jl '69
How to read a contact sheet. A. Goldsmith. il Pop Phot 65:78-9+ Ag '69
Now, color prints almost as easy as B&W; Unicolor kit. P. Wahl. il Pop Sci 195:184-5 Ag '69
Photo print washer rocks itself. B. Gilmore. il Pop Sci 195:148 N '69
Some tools make darkroom life easier. E. Meyers. il Pop Phot 65:58+ S '69
Those convenient cold-water washes. C. W. Kennedy. il Pop Phot 65:30+ S '69

History

How to print pictures on apples, and other best-forgotten photographic processes; excerpts from Photographic amusements. K. Poli. il Pop Phot 65:94-6 N '69

Retouching

Dark, lighter, bleached; Farmer's reducer. R. Hattersley. il Pop Phot 65:102-5+ O '69
Make your own time of day. J. Scully. il Mod Phot 33:58-63 Mr '69
Reducers to the rescue. C. W. Kennedy. il Pop Phot 65:48+ Ag '69
Take it away by bleaching; using potassium ferricyanide. A. Francekvich. il Pop Phot 64:26+ Je '69

Social aspects

Have camera will travel; P. Ragland photographing social and economic projects. il Ebony 24:112-14+ Mr '69
Photography is my very life. R. Hattersley. il Pop Phot 64:108+ Je '69

Study and teaching

Discovery through photography. R. Plumb. il Sch Arts 69:16-19 D '69
Try this short photo course; instructive show at New York's Hallmark gallery. J. Dreyfuss. il Mod Phot 33:92-7 Je '69
Who is Callahan? D. Vestal. il Travel & Camera 32:68-72+ My '69
See also
Shadowgrams

Themes

Angles and images. il Pop Phot 64:104-9 My '69
Critical eye; New York subjects. A. Rothstein. Travel & Camera 32:38 S '69
For any greeting, say it on film. D. B. Eisendrath. il Pop Phot 64:18+ My '69
Frederic Sommer. M. Mann. Pop Phot 65: 82-3+ O '69
Gentle look; Amish of Lancaster, Pa. il Pop Phot 65:112-15 Jl '69
He found a new life, a people, a book; work of J. A. Warner. J. Deschin. Pop Phot 65: 44+ N '69
Photo-symbolism. R. Hattersley. il Pop Phot 64:69-72 Mr '69
Pictures that say summer. il Pop Phot 65:84-92 S '69
Seeing pictures. J. Scully. il Mod Phot 33:16+ N '69
Shoot the sky; bring your camera to the airport. B. Jerome. il Travel & Camera 32:142 F '69
Students at work. R. Hattersley. il Pop Phot 65:110-13 N '69
Usual subjects, unusual images. J. Scully. il Mod Phot 33:72-5 Ap '69

Visit to a small town. R. Hattersley. il Pop Phot 64:117-20 My '69
Weegee; a lens on life, 1899-1968. H. V. Fondiller; N. Rothschild; D. Vestal. il Pop Phot 64:92-5+ Ap '69

Therapeutic use

We're clean, are you? Phoenix house's photography program for drug addicts. L. Drukker. il Pop Phot 65:108-9+ N '69

Japan

Japanese photography today. W. L. Broecker. il Travel & Camera 32:72-85 O '69

PHOTOGRAPHY, Aerial

Aerial photography: outdoor recreation. R. A. Kreig. il Parks & Rec 4:41-3 Ag '69
Bird's eye view can help park officials. R. D. Buechner. il Parks & Rec 3:27-8+ N '68
High ice, high rock; with photographs by A. Post. Audubon 71:28-33 My '69
How top pro cuts through the haze. D. B. Eisendrath. il Pop Phot 65:18+ N '69

PHOTOGRAPHY, Artistic

Ansel Adams: a Pacific portfolio. M. Hollis. il Travel & Camera 32:66-71 Ag '69
Copyright, Snowdon; with photographs by Lord Snowdon. J. Scully. Mod Phot 33:68-85 Je '69
Czech points on surrealism. P. M. Tausk and J. Dreyfuss. il Mod Phot 33:74-5+ S '69
Edward Weston dedicated to simplicity. C. Weston. il Mod Phot 33:66-71+ My '69
Ernst Haas, creative force in contemporary color. I. Bondi. il Mod Phot 33:62-7+ Jl '69
Essence of color. R. Routh. il Travel & Camera 32:100-1+ F '69
Frenzy of a cymatic ballet. il UNESCO Courier 22:13-15 D '69
Infinity of Jimis. J. Hendrix. il Life 67:72-5 O 3 '69
It's the picture that counts. N. Rothschild. il Pop Phot 64:38+ F '69
Max Waldman's art of anguish; photographs; with account by John Neary. Life 67:60-66B D 12 '69
Patterns: do people help? J. Scully. il Mod Phot 33:58-63 My '69
Photographs as sculpture and prints. P. C. Bunnell. il Art in Am 57:56-61 S '69
Pictures you won't see in a viewfinder. il Pop Phot 64:72-9 F '69
Tour of the zodiac; photographs. M. Greene and J. Eula. Life 67:60-8 S 26 '69
See also
Composition (photography)

PHOTOGRAPHY, Close-up

Close-ups without kicks: take a TLR. N. Rothschild. il Pop Phot 64:70-1+ F '69
Does your SLR really read close-ups? W. Hanson. il Pop Phot 65:92-3 D '69
If you've got the eye, the technique is easy. M. A. Matzkin. il Mod Phot 33:84-9+ F '69
Large camera; homemade light table for shadowless illumination. A. Feininger. il Mod Phot 33:82+ Ag '69
Nature's hidden patterns. il Am For 75:4-7 F '69
Open up when you're up close. E. Meyers. il Pop Phot 65:54+ O '69
Stand back and look close. C. W. Kennedy. Pop Phot 64:46+ My '69

PHOTOGRAPHY, Cold weather. See Photography—Cold weather conditions

PHOTOGRAPHY, Commercial

Cash-in on your photographs. A. Ahlers. Pop Phot 64:75-7+ Mr '69
SSSSTT! Famous postcards? il Pop Phot 65: 80-1 S '69
You meet such interesting people; diary of a free-lancer. C. Schwalberg. U S Camera 32:64-5+ Ja '69
See also
Moving picture photography in advertising
Photography as a profession
Photography in advertising

PHOTOGRAPHY, Composite. See Photomontage

PHOTOGRAPHY, Documentary

America in crisis, by M. Levitas. Review Mod Phot il 33:98-9+ O '69. J. Scully
Carl Purcell pictures for social change; foreign assignments photographing major foreign aid projects. C. Purcell. il Pop Phot 64:76-83+ Je '69
It started with Daguerre: French primitive photography exhibit, Philadelphia. M. R. Weiss. il Sat R 52:23-5 D 13 '69
Like it really is, how to tell it that way. R. Hattersley. il Pop Phot 65:114-17+ D '69
Paul Strand, catalyst and revealer. N. Newhall. il Mod Phot 33:70-5 Ag '69

PHOTOGRAPHY, Documentary—*Continued*
Sergio Larrain of Chile; excerpts from letter. S. Larrain. il Pop Phot 65:94-7+ S '69
White House photographers; how two men approach instant history. J. Neubauer. il Pop Phot 65:108-11+ D '69

PHOTOGRAPHY, Flashlight
Fill-in flash basics. E. Scully. il Mod Phot 33:78-9+ My '69
How square is the flashcube? N. Rothschild. il Pop Phot 65:85-7+ D '69
Professional studio lighting: convert a single flash unit into a versatile lighting tool. E. Meyers. il Mod Phot 33:144+ Je '69
Stop-action photos. A. J. Lowe. il Electr World 81:47 Mr '69

Electronic equpment
See Photography—Electronic equipment

PHOTOGRAPHY, Industrial. See Photography in industry

PHOTOGRAPHY, Infrared
Infrared: difficult? Not really. E. Scully. il Mod Phot 33:82-7 My '69
New look at infrared color. N. Rothschild. il Pop Phot 65:94-7 D '69

PHOTOGRAPHY, Journalistic
Critical eye; magazine photography. A. Rothstein. il Travel & Camera 32:100 O '69
Do you take honest pictures? N. Rothschild. il Pop Phot 64:26+ Mr '69
Emil Schulthess: chronicler of continents. il Mod Phot 33:62-7 Ap '69
Eye of Eisenstaedt. M. R. Weiss. il Sat R 52:13-15 Ag 2 '69
Farewell, sweet photojournalism. S. Nathan. il Pop Phot 64:60+ Je '69
Ingenuity of hijacked amateurs; picture-taking under the eyes of Cuban guards. G. P. Hunt. il Life 66:3 Ap 18 '69
Look before you shoot! R. Arnold. il Writers Digest 49:54-7 My '69
Make it happen! J. Scully. il Mod Phot 33:74-7 My '69
My 50,000-mile, three-year photographic education. J. Robaton. il Pop Phot 64:102-5+ Mr '69
News pictures of the year; 1968 in review. M. R. Weiss. il Sat R 52:122-3 Mr 8 '69
Photojournalism. R. Arnold. See every other issue of Writer's digest
Photojournalist-editor team. R. Arnold. il Writers Digest 49:64-7+ Jl '69
Self-portrait: U.S.A. by D. D. Duncan. Review
   Sat R il 52:38-9 N 29 '69. M. R. Weiss
What is an honest photograph? N. Rothschild. il Pop Phot 65:38+ S '69
Working with a photographer. J. Lawrence. il Writers Digest 49:60-3+ Jl '69

Awards
For exceptional courage and enterprise; Robert Capa award. G. P. Hunt. il Life 66:3 Ap 11 '69

PHOTOGRAPHY, Military
Picture sense. A. Rothstein. Travel & Camera 32:30 F '69

PHOTOGRAPHY, Nature. See Nature photography

PHOTOGRAPHY, Night
Shooting for the moon. D. B. Eisendrath. il Pop Phot 65:24+ Jl '69

PHOTOGRAPHY, Panoramic
Winterama Eastman Kodak and Ozzie. il Travel & Camera 32:114-15 F '69

PHOTOGRAPHY, Stereoscopic. See Stereophotography

PHOTOGRAPHY, Submarine
Art of shooting underwater. G. P. Hunt. il Life 66:3 Mr 7 '69
Now: shoot underwater photos for under $20. C. B. Hicks and D. L. Hicks. il Pop Mech 131:107-10+ Je '69
Silent image. P. Leonian. il Travel & Camera 32:91-5 D '69
Tips on underwater photography. W. Lane. il Travel 131:77 Mr '69
Underwater world of Ario Gatti; photographs. Nat Wildlife 7:9-13 F '69
With scuba and camera. il Motor B 123:89+ Je '69
   See also
Moving picture photography. Submarine

Apparatus and supplies
Probing the depths. R. Kinne. il Travel & Camera 32:96+ D '69

PHOTOGRAPHY, Three dimensional. See Stereophotography

PHOTOGRAPHY, Travel. See Travel photography

PHOTOGRAPHY, Trick
   See also
Moving picture photography. Trick

PHOTOGRAPHY and art. See Art and photography

PHOTOGRAPHY as a profession
Another day at the mailbox; secrets of a successful free lance. R. Engh. il Pop Phot 65:71-3+ S '69
Are you ready to turn pro? A. Goldsmith. Pop Phot 65:92-3+ N '69
Brassai comes to America; interview, ed. by J. Deschin. Brassai. Pop Phot 64:20+ Mr '69
Bumblebee cannot fly; interview, ed. by P. Farber. G. Fishback. il Travel & Camera 32:68-71+ Mr '69
Careers for photography fans. il Changing T 23:30-2 Jl '69
First step to successful professionalism: a portfolio that sells you and your work. J. Scully. Mod Phot 33:14+ O '69
It's not always fun for the pros. N. Rothschild. il Pop Phot 64:30+ Je '69
Paul Paree. il Pop Phot 64:84-93 Mr '69
They say you're talented, but. . . J. Deschin. il Pop Phot 65:32+ D '69
To see or not to see young hopefuls. J. Deschin. il Pop Phot 65:34+ Jl '69

PHOTOGRAPHY as therapy. See Photography —Therapeutic use

PHOTOGRAPHY by children. See Children as photographers

PHOTOGRAPHY in advertising
Art for ad's sake; Art directors club awards. M. R. Weiss. il Sat R 52:54-5 Je 14 '69
   See also
Moving picture photography in advertising

PHOTOGRAPHY in industry
Beauty in the awful; photographing industrial relics. il Time 94:68+ S 5 '69

PHOTOGRAPHY models. See Models (persons)

PHOTOGRAPHY of animals
Africa stares back. P. Barrett. il Field & S 74:42-7+ D '69
Blackie and the silver horde; black bear eating salmon. J. S. Crawford. il Outdoor Life 143:76-9+ Ap '69
Davy Jones' studio is in Miami. L. Barry. il Pop Phot 65:50+ D '69
Elephants have the right of way! African safari. O. Gately. il Har Yrs 9:19-23 Ag '69
Fall vacation. E. A. Bauer. il Outdoor Life 144:56-9+ Ag; 62-5+ S '69
Getting along with grizzlies. J. S. Crawford. il Outdoor Life 144:45-7+ N; 44-7+ D '69
How to photograph your pet. J. Kuh. il Ladies Home J 86:11 S '69
Safari. M. E. Scott. il Travel & Camera 32:79-83 My '69

PHOTOGRAPHY of birds
Shooting birds. C. Purcell. il Pop Phot 65:82-3 S '69

PHOTOGRAPHY of boats. See Photography of ships

PHOTOGRAPHY of buildings and structures
Building watcher. J. B. Myers. il Craft Horiz 29:20-9 Jl '69
Dramatize your scenics; excerpts from Philadelphia, the intimate city, ed. by J. Dreyfuss. J. A. Drake, jr. il Mod Phot 33:62-5 S '69
Prelude to the season; Edgartown. Martha's Vineyard. H. B. Hough. il Travel & Camera 32:60-3+ Je '69

PHOTOGRAPHY of children
How to get better pictures of children. il Bet Hom & Gard 47:14+ Jl '69
It's wings that make birds fly; the story of a boy. S. Weiner. Review
   Pop Phot 64:32+ F '69. J. Deschin
View from the Bay. M. Mann. il Pop Phot 65:33+ Jl '69

PHOTOGRAPHY of dancing
American masterpiece; ballet. Dances at a gathering; photographs by G. Mili. Life 67:42-51 O 3 '69
Landscape into danscape; photographs. H. Migdoll. Dance Mag 43:46-55 D '69

PHOTOGRAPHY of emotions
Accent on stillness. il Pop Phot 65:88-97 Jl '69
Find yourself in your pictures. il Pop Phot 65:100-3+ S '69
Must you be involved? R. Hattersley. il Pop Phot 64:101-4 Ap '69
Portrait of Tracy, a very personal view. R. Davis. il Life 67:88-91+ O 17 '69
Seeing pictures: probe beneath the surface. J. Scully. il Mod Phot 33:50+ Ap '69

PHOTOGRAPHY of flowers, plants, trees, etc.
Capturing flower patterns with your camera. E. Knowles. Horticulture 47:45 Jl '69
Fight formality in flower pictures! N. Rothschild. il Pop Phot 64:84-9+ My '69

PHOTOGRAPHY of flowers, plants, trees, etc.
—Continued
Five hundred miles to shoot a flower. D. E. Rose. Horticulture 47:56-7 Ja '69
Sex habits of the trigger flower. il Am For 75:4-7 Je '69
PHOTOGRAPHY of girls. See Photography—Portraits
PHOTOGRAPHY of light
Flashlight designs. Design 70:15 Sum '69
PHOTOGRAPHY of mountains. See Photography—Landscapes
PHOTOGRAPHY of moving objects
Stop-action photos. A. J. Lowe. il Electr World 81:47 Mr '69
PHOTOGRAPHY of nature. See Nature photography
PHOTOGRAPHY of ships
Delta Queen, last of the stern-wheelers. R. Arnold. il Travel & Camera 32:81-3 Je '69
How to get your boat to pose for better pictures. P. Geraci. il Pop Mech 132:112-15+ Jl '69
PHOTOGRAPHY of sports
Shooting the pros. R. Riger. Travel & Camera 32:108 O '69
Wonderful world of skiing. il Travel & Camera 32:41-50 D '69
See also
Football—Photographs
Sports—Photographs
PHOTOGRAPHY of the human figure. See Human figure in photography
PHOTOGRAPHY of weddings
Photographing the Alice's restaurant church wedding. B. Pabst. il Pop Phot 64:94-5+ My '69
PHOTOGRAPHY of works of art
How to photograph a statue. R. Arnold. il Travel & Camera 32:89 Jl '69
Vigeland in the viewfinder; D Finn's photography of sculptures. M. R. Weiss. il Sat R 52:52-3 Ag 23 '69
PHOTOJOURNALISM. See Photography, Journalistic
PHOTOKINA. See Photography—Exhibitions
PHOTOMECHANICAL processes
Five firms explain conversion systems. Pub W 195:87 Ap 7 '69
Prints and visual communication, by W. M. Ivins, jr. Review
Art in Am 57:29 S '69. J. Jacobs
PHOTOMETERS
Electronic-flash light meter you can build; ballistic photometer. R. M. Benrey. il Pop Sci 194:112-15 Mr '69
Further adventures with photometry. P. Farber. il US Camera 32:14+ Ja '69
See also
Exposure meters
PHOTOMETRY, Astronomical
DQ Herculis: synchronous photometry. R. E. Nather and B. Warner. bibliog il Science 166:876-8 N 14 '69
Ultraviolet photometry from a spacecraft. A. D. Code and others. il Sky & Tel 38:290-3 N '69
See also
Spectrophotometry
PHOTOMICROGRAPHY
Glimpse of the helix: DNA molecule photographed. il Time 93:51 Mr 14 '69
How to take pictures through a microscope. il Mech Illus 65:40-1 Je '69
Micro-mini photography; thermomicrograph. S. V. Jones. il Sci Digest 66:77 Jl '69
Worlds within us with photographs by L. Nilsson. Life 68:40-56 Ja 9 '70
PHOTOMONTAGE
From B&W to color posters. R. D. Routh. il Pop Phot 64:84-7 Je '69
Make your own movie montages. J. R. Oswald. il Travel & Camera 32:108-9+ F '69
Nature montages. R. Hattersley. il Pop Phot 64:98-9+ My '69
Photographs as sculpture and prints. P. C. Bunnell. il Art in Am 57:56-61 S '69
PHOTONS
See also
Exciton theory
PHOTOOXIDATION. See Oxidation
PHOTOPERIODISM
Photoperiod, endocrinology and the crustacean molt cycle. D. E. Aiken. bibliog il Science 164:149-55 Ap 11 '69
Photoperiod in three xanthium populations from the tropic of Cancer in Mexico. C. McMillan. bibliog il Science 165:292-4 Jl 18 '69
PHOTORECONNAISSANCE systems. See Photographic reconnaissance systems
PHOTOSYNTHESIS
Carbon dioxide compensation points in related plant species. D. N. Moss and others. bibliog il Science 164:187-8 Ap 11 '69

Ingenuities of nature; excerpt from Food resources; conventional and novel. N. W. Pirie. Sat R 52:49 Ag 2 '69
Light, leaves and life. B. Capon. il Horticulture 47:30-1+ Jl '69
Mechanism of photosynthesis. R. P. Levine. il Sci Am 221:58-64+ D '69
Photosynthesis and fish production in the sea. J. H. Ryther. bibliog il Science 166:72-6 O 3 '69
See also
Chloroplasts
PHOTOSYNTHETIC bacteria. See Bacteria, Photosynthetic
PHOTOTROPISM
See also
Fungi, Effect of light on
PHOTOTYPESETTING
Electronic type composition. E. A. Lacy. il Electr World 82:34-6 D '69
Front page afloat: all the news that's fit to ship. M. R. Weiss. il Sat R 52:84-5 N 8 '69
Typography for the future: applying the new technology, not refusing it; excerpts from address, October 10, 1969. H. Zapf. Pub W 196:54-6 N 3 '69
Word about this CRT madness. D. N. Mount. Pub W 196:55 Ag 4 '69
PHTHALOCYANINES
Phthalocyanines, contributors to the world of color. H. Gerson. il Chem 42:25-6 D '69
PHYCOMYCES
Blastocladia and aqualinderella: fermentative water molds with high carbon dioxide optima. A. A. Held and others. bibliog il Science 165:706-9 Ag 15 '69
Phycomyces: stimulus storage in light-initiated reactions. T. G. Ebrey and R. K. Clayton. bibliog il Science 164:427-8 Ap 25 '69
PHYLOGENY
L-Ascorbic acid synthesis in birds: phylogenetic trend. C. R. Chaudhuri and I. B. Chatterjee. bibliog il Science 164:435-6 Ap 25 '69
Computer analysis of protein evolution. M. O. Dayhoff. il Sci Am 221:86-95 Jl '69
PHYSALIS. See Husk tomatoes
PHYSICAL anthropology. See Somatology
PHYSICAL education and training
New break for the gym dropout; adapted-physical-education programs. F. G. Loyd. il Todays Health 47:38-43+ Mr '69
Physical fitness: a school-community responsibility. J. A. Lovell. Parents Mag 44:34 My '69
Playing fields of Ware. I. K. Bradley. il Todays Ed 58:24-6 My '69
See also
College athletics
Gymnastics
National outdoor leadership school
School athletics
PHYSICAL education for the aged
Good news for joggers. il Time 93:39 F 7 '69
PHYSICAL examinations
Gynecologic examination. D. M. Haynes and D. Z. Meilach. Redbook 133:30 My '69
Ounce of prevention...? il Newsweek 74:108+ N 24 '69
Why you should have an annual checkup. J. LemMon. il Suc Farm 67:E6 D '69
See also
Air pilots—Physical examinations
Heart—Examination
United States—Army—Physical examinations
PHYSICAL exercise. See Exercise
PHYSICAL fitness. See Health; Men—Health and hygiene
PHYSICAL geography
See also
Earth
Man—Influence on nature
Mountains
Volcanoes
PHYSICAL geology. See Geology, Structural
PHYSICAL review
What happened to my paper? S. A. Goudsmit. il Phys Today 22:23-5 My '69
PHYSICAL science. See Science
PHYSICAL therapists
Jobscope: for the science-minded. N. Axelrad. Mlle 69:218 My '69
PHYSICAL training. See Physical education and training
PHYSICALLY handicapped. See Handicapped
PHYSICIANS
Ahead: a comeback for the family doctor. il U S News 66:88-9 F 10 '69
Before you need a doctor... R. B. Scott. Todays Health 47:54-5+ Mr '69
Death & the physician. E. J. Cassell. Commentary 47:73-9 Je '69

PHYSICIANS—*Continued*
Doctors to watch doctors; **peer review system**. Sci N 96:524 D 6 '69
Family doctor, space-age style. M. Michaelson. il Todays Health 47:34-7+ S '69
Hospital unit trains family doctors. Todays Health 47:87 F '69
Inside American medicine (cont) il Todays Health 47:24-7+ F; 40-1+ Ap; 24-7+ S; 38-41+ D '69; 48:44-7+ Ja '70
Internist talks about his work; ed. by W. S. Ross. W. C. Felch. il Todays Health 47:24-7+ F '69
Medical assistant; the health team approach; address, January 23, 1969. E. F. Rosinski. Vital Speeches 35:438-41 My 1 '69
M.D. should not try to cure society. M. J. Halberstam. il N Y Times Mag p32-3+ N 9 '69; Reply with rejoinder. R. Karp. p62+ D 7 '69
Never marry a doctor. J. Robbins and J. Robbins. il McCalls 96:69+ S '69
Physician as addict. Sci N 95:326 Ap 5 '69
Sociatry: social psychiatry and the physician's calling. H. C. Shands. bibliog Ment Hy 53:393-402 Jl '69
What medicine can do for you; opportunities in biology; address, June 7, 1969. A. Kornberg. Vital Speeches 35:756-9 O 1 '69
Who is the doctor's doc? il Sci Digest 66:61 Jl '69

    See also
Alvarez, W. C.
American medical association
Kelly, H. A.
Malpractice
Medical education
Medical ethics
Medicine
National medical association
Psychiatrists
Surgeons
Women as physicians

Fees
See Medical service, Cost of

Political activities
See Politics and medicine

Supply and demand
Ahead: a comeback for the family doctor. il U S News 66:88-9 F 10 '69
Change begins in the doctor's office. D. Cordtz. il Fortune 81:84-9+ Ja '70
Medical shortages abroad, too. il U S News 67:73-5 N 3 '69
    See also
Brain drain

PHYSICIANS and patients
Dual role of comforter and bereaved; reactions of medical personnel to the dying child and his parents. E. Wallace and B. D. Townes. bibliog Ment Hy 53:327-32 Jl '69
Family medicine: a new concept of medical care. il Good H 168:195 My '69
How doctors choose a doctor. Time 94:46-7 Ag 15 '69
Internist talks about his work; ed. by W. S. Ross. W. C. Felch. il Todays Health 47:24-7+ F '69
My mother, the celebrity. M. R. Johnson. il Todays Health 47:56-7+ O '69
Patient must prescribe for the physician. C. H. H. Branch. bibliog Ment Hy 53:403-9 Jl '69
Reaching the unmotivated patient. A. J. R. Koumans. Ment Hy 53:298-300 Ap '69
What is a doctor's toughest diagnosis? psychosomatic disease or nerves? W. E. O'Donnell. Good H 169:59+ Jl '69
    See also
Psychiatrists and patients

PHYSICIANS assistants. See Medical workers

PHYSICIANS wives
Never marry a doctor. J. Robbins and J. Robbins. il McCalls 96:69+ S '69

PHYSICISTS
Isaac Asimov explains: what is theoretical physics? I. Asimov. Sci Digest 65:85-6 Je '69
Philistine asks for equal time. J. Dillon. il Phys Today 22:38-9 My '69
Privilege of being a physicist; adaptation of address. V. F. Weisskopf. il Phys Today 22:39-43 Ag '69
Who finds the job? R. H. Ellis, jr. Phys Today 22:112 Je '69; Discussion. 22:9 S; 9+ N '69
    See also
American physical society

Supply and demand
Employment crisis; letters to the editor. Phys Today 22:9+ Ag '69

PHYSICS
Big machine, by R. Jungk. Review
    New Yorker 45:154-8 O 4 '69. J. Bernstein
Frontiers of physics today. il Phys Today 22:38-44 Ja; 33-7 F; 46-51 Ap; 30-7 Ag; 31-6 S; 47-53 N; 34-44 D '69
How good are you as a physicist? quiz. J. Daugherty and M. Daugherty. il Sci Digest 66:78-80 Jl '69
Practical need for beauty. R. H. Ellis, jr. Phys Today 22:144 Ap '69
    See also
Astrophysics
European physical society
Geophysics
Gravitation
International conference on high energy physics
Magnetism
Matter
Music—Acoustics and physics
Nuclear physics
Quantum theory
Radioactivity
Relativity (physics)
Solids
Sound
Statistical mechanics
Symmetry (physics)
Units

Bibliography
Books. See issues of Physics today

Experiments
Experiments simulate space travel. K. M. Swezey. il Pop Sci 195:167-9 O '69

History
    See also
Nuclear physics—History

Research
Search and discovery. See issues of Physics today
Visit to the Semiconductor institute in Leningrad. G. B. Lubkin. Phys Today 22:69+ Ja '69
Where do we go from here? A. E. Ruark. bibliog il Phys Today 22:25-8 S '69

Study and teaching
Better teaching with better problems and exams. H. R. Crane. Phys Today 22:134-5 Mr '69
Computers in physics instruction. G. Schwarz and others. bibliog il Phys Today 22:41-9 S '69
    See also
Commission on college physics

PHYSICS students
Physics dropout: what turns him off? Phys Today 22:67 O '69

PHYSIOGNOMY
Man's silent signals; nonverbal vocabulary of gestures and expressions. il Time 93:86 Je 13 '69

PHYSIOLOGICAL age. See Age

PHYSIOLOGICAL apparatus
Amateur scientist; metabolic rate of small animals is measured in homemade apparatus. J. K. Lauber. il Sci Am 221:122-6 Jl '69
Oxygen consumption and pumping rates in the hard clam Mercenaria mercenaria; a direct method. A. Hamwi and H. H. Haskin. bibliog il Science 163:823-4 F 21 '69
Spin filter culture: the propagation of mammalian cells in suspension. P. Himmelfarb and others. bibliog il Science 164:555-7 My 2 '69
Thermal radiation in metabolic chambers. W. P. Porter. bibliog il Science 166:115-17 O 3 '69
White corpuscle transfusion; newly perfected continuous flow cell separator. N. Hardy. Sci N 96:88 Jl 26 '69
    See also
Respiratory apparatus

PHYSIOLOGICAL effects of alcohol; Physiological effects of noise; etc. See Alcohol—Physiological effects; Noise—Physiological effects; etc.

PHYSIOLOGICAL optics. See Optics, Physiological

PHYSIOLOGICAL research
    See also
Space flight—Physiological aspects

PHYSIOLOGY
   See also
  Anatomical models
  Body, Human
  Fatigue
  Growth
  Old age
  Respiration
  Secretion
  Stress (physiology)
  Weight (physiology)
    also names of organs of the body, e.g.
    Brain
PHYSIOLOGY, Comparative
  Size of life. J. T. Bonner. il Natur Hist 78:
   40-5 Ja '69
PHYTOHEMAGGLUTININS. See Agglutinins
PHYTOPATHOLOGY. See Plants—Diseases and
  pests
PIAF, Edith
  Je ne regrette rien. il por **Newsweek 74:46**
   O 27 '69
PIAGET, Jean
  Jean Piaget: mapping the growing mind. por
   Time 94:61-2 D 12 '69
  Problem of Piaget. H. G. Furth. Common-
   weal 90:69-72 Ap 4 '69
PIANISTS
   See also
  Brubeck, D.
  Ellington, D.
  Freire, N.
  Graffman, G.
  Hollander, L.
  Johansen, G.
  Katchen, J.
  Larrocha, A. de
  Somer, H.
  Watts, A.
PIANKOVA, Tatiana
  France; the ballet world of Anna Galina. R.
   Estrada. il pors Dance Mag 43:64-7 My '69
PIANO
  Electronic piano. E. A. Lacy. il Electr World
   82:40-1+ N '69
   See also
  In the news; scientific approach to piano
   design. il Space World F-7-67:46 Jl '69

       History

  Scottish encyclopedist and the piano forte.
   E. M. Ripin. bibliog f il Mus Q 55:487-99
   O '69
PIANO industry and trade

       Japan

  Anyone for chopsticks? il Newsweek 73:96+
   Mr 17 '69
PIANO music
  Romance of the piano, by E. Blom. Review
   Am Rec G 35:892+ My '69. W. Yost
   See also
  Concertos
  Phonograph records—Piano music
  Player piano music

    Interpretation (phrasing, dynamics, etc)

  In 660 easy lessons. A. Loesser. Atlan 223:
   130-1 F '69
PIANO playing
   See also
  Piano music—Interpretation (phrasing, dy-
   namics, etc)
PIANOFORTE. See Piano
PICA (pathology)
  Why some children eat dirt; problem of
   geophagia. Good H 169:146 Ag '69
PICASSO, Pablo
  Erotica at eighty-seven. il Time 93:66 Ja 31
   '69
  Pablo Picasso, this is your life; fake inter-
   view quoted in special issue. T. B. Hess.
   Art N 67:27+ F '69
PICCARD, Jacques
  Drifters. il Newsweek 74:48 S 1 '69
  From Florida to Cape Cod without moving.
   W. Cloud. il por Pop Mech 131:128-31+ My
   '69
PICHLER, Anton Alexander Benedetti-. See
  Benedetti-Pichler, A. A.
PICKELL, Charles N.
  Parent teachers. Chr Today 14:10-12 D 19 '69
PICKER, Jean
  Social aspects of development; statement,
   November 13, 1968. Dept State Bul 59:716-
   19 D 30 '68
PICKERING, W. R. and Landreau, A. N.
  Flat-woven rugs of the Middle East. Antiques
   96:390-6 S '69
PICKERING, William Hayward
  Space age turns a new chapter. il por Bsns
   W p98-9+ Ap 12 '69
PICKETING
  Protecting the Pentagon. J. Deedy. Common-
   weal 90:530 S 5 '69

PICKFORD, Rollin, Jr
  Rollin Pickford, Jr: philosophical approach
   to watercolor; with biographical sketch.
   il por Am Artist 33:68-9+ N '69
PICKLES and relishes
  Dill crock. E. Gibbons. Org Gard & Farm 16:
   86-9 Ap '69
  Glossary of relishes. Good H 169:144 Jl '69
  Ripe time to pickle and preserve. D. Brooks.
   il Home Gard 56:45 S '69
  Spicy collection of relishes they'll rave about.
   il Farm J 93:62-3 S '69
PICKPOCKETS. See Thieves
PICKUP campers. See Campers and coaches,
  Truck
PICKUP carts. See Carts
PICKUP trucks. See Motor trucks
PICNIC cookery. See Cookery, Outdoor
PICNICS
  For families on the go, new meal ideas and
   gear! D. Eby and H. A. Dawson. il Bet
   Hom & Gard 47:44-55 Je '69
  Glasgow picnic; just a spot o'wet. D. Shaber.
   il Holiday 46:37 Ag '69
  Kettle picnic at the beach. il Sunset 142:82-
   3 Je '69
  Picnic drinks. P. S. Brown. il House & Gard
   135:100+ Je '69
  Picnic loaves and pastries. L. S. Pappas. il
   House & Gard 135:101-3+ Je '69
  Picnic notebook; with recipes. il Seventeen
   28:100-7+ Jl '69
  Return of the adult picnic. il Esquire 72:76-9
   Jl '69
  Summer cool-off. J. Hewitt. il N Y Times
   Mag p58 Ag 10 '69
  Summer rushing in with picnics. il House
   & Gard 135:62-5 Je '69
  Tailgate picnics. V. T. Habeeb. il Am Home
   72:100-2+ N '69
  Treats to tote. G. Maddox. il Todays Health
   47:52-5 Je '69
   See also
  Outdoor meals
PICÓ, Fernando A.
  New left and the electoral college. America
   120:252-4 Mr 1 '69
PICONE, Joseph
  It's back to high style at Evan-Picone. S.
   Margetts. il Duns R 93:83-4+ Mr '69
PICTOGRAPHS. See Petroglyphs
PICTORIAL letter sheets. See Stationery
PICTURE books
  America in crisis, by M. Levitas. Review
   Mod Phot il 33:98-9+ O '69. J. Scully
  Authors & editors; D. D. Duncan's Self-
   portrait: U.S.A. M. R. Kraner. Pub W
   196:15-16 Ag 4 '69
  Emil Schulthess: chronicler of continents. il
   Mod Phot 33:62-7 Ap '69
  It's wings that make birds fly: the story of a
   boy, by S. Weiner. Review
   Pop Phot 64:32+ F '69. J. Deschin
  Paper filmstrip: photo books and paperbacks.
   H. F. Rogers. Library J 94:846-7 F 15 '69
  Seeing pictures. J. Scully. Mod Phot 33:50+
   F '69
  T&C books. See issues of Travel & camera
  Two by Strand. A. D. Coleman; M. Mann.
   il Pop Phot 65:90-1+ D '69

       Bibliography

  Groaning coffee table. C. H. Simonds. il
   Nat R 21:1278-81 D 16 '69
  Pictorial holiday sampler. M. R. Weiss. il
   Sat R 52:40-1 N 29 '69
PICTURE books for children
  Visual language of the picture book. O.
   Richard. bibliog il Wilson Lib Bul 44:434-
   47 D '69
   See also
  Caldecott medal

       Bibliography

  Look, Johnny, look. S. Nirenberg. House B
   111:34 D '69
PICTURE frames
  Custom picture frame. il Mech Illus 65:40 Mr
   '69
  Easy ways to finish frames. R. E. Green. il
   Am Artist 33:46-7 D '69
  Framing pictures today. E. Munro. House &
   Gard 135:54+ Ap '69
  Picture frames you buy in a bag. J. Hand.
   il Pop Sci 195:122-3 Ag '69
  Ten commandments for the proper framing of
   pictures; excerpts from The right frame.
   H. Heydenryk. House B 11:110 O '69
  Three thrifty ways to frame a picture. D. A.
   Ashe. il Bet Hom & Gard 47:78-9+ F '69
PICTURE writing
   See also
  Hieroglyphics

PICTURES
Do it with peanuts: picture for the wall.
A. W. Farrant. il Design 70:36 Sum '69
See also
Drawings
Landscape painting
Photographs

Copying
John Clem Clarke transmits a picture. W. S.
Wilson. il Art N 68:46-7+ Sum '69
See also
Imitation in art

Framing
See Picture frames
PICTURES, Framing of. See Picture frames
PICTURES, Glass. See Glass painting and
staining
PICTURES, Hanging of
Magnetize your home gallery. C. W. Kennedy.
il Pop Phot 64:36+ Mr '69
Some pointers on art walls. il Bet Hom &
Gard 47:42 Mr '69
PICTURES, Immoral. See Immoral literature
and pictures
PICTURES, Pasted. See Collage
PICTURES in education
Children's books for spring. Z. Sutherland. il
Sat R 52:53 My 10 '69
PIE
A la. mode, move over! il Bet Hom & Gard
47:66-7 Ag '69
Big pies. Farm J 93:106 F '69
Bride makes lemon meringue pie. il McCalls
96:48 Ag '69
Butterscotch treats. il Bet Hom & Gard 47:
97 Je '69
Festive one-crust pies. il Redbook 133:108-
10+ S '69
Here are cantaloupe pies. il Sunset 142:154
Je '69
It's strawberry pie. il Sunset 142:172 Je '69
Lyrical lime pie; with recipe by E. Graves.
il Life 67:60-1+ Jl 11 '69
Mexican pie with coconut. il Sunset 143:183
N '69
Pastry finishes. il Bet Hom & Gard 47:126
O '69
Pies on the rise; with recipes. il Seventeen
28:174-5+ Mr '69
Strawberry slices in a glaze. il Sunset 142:176
My '69
Very special pies and cakes. il Bet Hom &
Gard 47:85-96 My '69
See also
Pastry
PIE, Frozen. See Food, Frozen
PIEDMONT airlines
Court orders Piedmont's pilots back to work
pending hearing. Aviation W 91:28 Ag 25
'69
PIEL, Gerard
Support of science on the university's own
terms; adaptation of address, October 21,
1969. Science 166:1101 N 28 '69
PIENE, Nan R.
Buying art as an investment. House & Gard
136:68+ N '69
Collecting originals on a shoestring. House &
Gard 136:80-1+ O '69
New York exhibition notes. Art in Am 57:
102-7 Ja '69
PIERCE, Albert R.
From cornfield to cornucopia. Am City 84:
137+ My '69
PIERCE, Bill
Lens kit. Travel & Camera 32:90-1+ S '69
PIERCE, Carl W. and Benacerraf, Baruj
Immune response in vitro: independence of
activated lymphoid cells. bibliog Science
166:1002-4 N 21 '69
PIERCE, Edith Lovejoy
Eve; poem. Chr Cent 86:711 My 21 '69
Footprints on the moon; poem. Chr Cent 86:
1135 S 3 '69
Hidden hunger; poem. Chr Cent 86:902 Jl 2
'69
Written in Advent; poem. Chr Cent 86:1578
D 10 '69
PIERCE, Francis
Welfare on the cheap. New Repub 160:23-4
F 22 '69
PIERCE, Milton
How to build powered trim tabs for your
boat. Pop Sci 194:110-12 Ja '69
PIERCE, Paul
Frenzy on the freeways; excerpts from Take
an alternate route. Read Digest 94:205-6+
Ap '69
PIERIS
How to keep your pieris beautiful. il Home
Gard 56:24 Ag '69
PIERMARINI, G. J. and others
Crystal structure of benzene II at 25 kilobars.
bibliog Science 165:1250-5 S 19 '69

PIEROTTI, Roland
Under the wire; passing the big East-
ern banks internationally. il por Forbes 103:
61-2 Je 15 '69
PIEROVICH, Andrew L.
After the storm in St Louis. Commonweal 90:
500-1 Ag 22 '69
PIERPONT Morgan library
J.P.'s place. D. L. Shirey. il Newsweek 75:
64 Ja 12 '70
PIERS, Maria W. and Bowman, Barbara
Must mother be around all day? PTA Mag
63:26-8 bibliog(p34) Ap '69
PIERS
See also
Fishing docks and piers
PIERSOL, Edna Wagner
Venison fit for a king. Outdoor Life 144:76+
N '69
PIES. See Pie
PIES, Meat. See Cookery—Meat
PIETRA, G. G. and others
Hemoglobin as a tracer in hemodynamic
pulmonary edema. bibliog Science 166:1643-
6 D 26 '69
PIETRI, Arturo Uslar
Angostura. Américas 21:2-6 My '69
PIETROFESA, John J.
Self-concept: a vital factor in school and
career development. bibliog Clear House
44:37-40 S '69
PIETY
Toward authentic piety. Chr Today 13:20-1
Je 20 '69
PIEYRE DE MANDIARGUES, André
Food in Vogue. N. Lyon. Vogue 154:71 N 15
'69
PIEZOELECTRIC crystals. See Crystals, Piezo-
electric
PIEZOELECTRIC igniter. See Gas burners—
Ignition devices
PIFER, Alan
Foundations; address, November 21, 1969.
Vital Speeches 36:178-82 Ja 1 '70
PIGAFETTA, Antonio
Magellan's voyage; excerpts, tr. by R. A.
Skelton. Am Heritage 20:62-75 O '69
about
Travels with Magellan. Newsweek 74:108+ O
20 '69
West to the Orient. A. Villiers. il Sat R 52:21-
3+ D 20 '69
PIGEON shooting
Return of the bandtail. B. W. Dalrymple. il
Outdoor Life 144:46-7+ S '69
PIGEONS
Animals respond for food in the presence of
free food. A. J. Neuringer. bibliog il Sci-
ence 166:399-401 O 17 '69
Attention shifts in a maintained discrimina-
tion. D. S. Blough. bibliog il Science 166:
125-6 O 3 '69
Discriminative control of attention. E. G.
Heinemann and others; reply with rejoinder.
R. M. Gilbert. Science 164:198 Ap 11 '69
Linkage of lactate dehydrogenase B and C
loci in pigeons. W. H. Zinkham and others.
bibliog il Science 164:185-7 Ap 11 '69
Orientation by pigeons: is the sun neces-
sary? W. T. Keeton. bibliog il Science 165:
922-8 Ag 29 '69
Stimulus generalization as a function of dis-
crimination learning with and without er-
rors. J. Lyons. il Science 163:490-1 Ja 31
'69
PIGGOTT, Lester
Tantrum in victory. Newsweek 74:97 N 24
'69
PIGGYBACK transportation of trailers. See
Motor truck trailers—Transportation
PIGMENTATION (biology) See Color of man
PIGMENTS
See also
Phthalocyanines
PIGMENTS (biology)
Peroxidation of subcellular organelles: for-
mation of lipofuscinlike fluorescent pig-
ments. K. S. Chio and others. bibliog il
Science 166:1535-6 D 19 '69
See also
Heme
PIGMENTS (blood) See Blood—Pigments
PIGMENTS, Visual. See Visual pigments
PIGS. See Swine
PIGWEED. See Purslane
PIKE, Albert V.
Yuletide in England. Horticulture 47:28-30
D '69

PIKE, James Albert
Why I'm leaving the church. pors Look 33:
54-8 Ap 29 '69

about

Death in the desert. Chr Cent 86:1186 S 17
'69; Reply. L. Kinsolving. 86:1402 O 29 '69
Death in the wilderness. il por Time 94:47-8
S 12 '69
Grace of comedy. P. J. Lee. New Repub 161:
14-15 S 20 '69
James Pike: spiritual wanderer is laid to rest.
il por Chr Today 13:42-3 S 26 '69
Just plain Jim. il por Newsweek 73:78 Ap
21 '69
Man of faith, child of doubt. J. Cogley. il
pors Life 67:62A-64 S 19 '69
Newest thing down the Pike: conservatism?
Chr Today 13:35 Jl 18 '69
Pike and the church alumni. Chr Cent 86:605
Ap 30 '69
Pike, Ho, Dirksen, and Pearson. Chr Today
13:38 S 26 '69
Post-Pike era? E. E. Plowman. Chr Today
13:44-5 F 28 '69
The Rev Roderick Random. Nat R 21:949-50
S 23 '69
Tribute to James A. Pike. America 121:178
S 20 '69
Wrong turn in Judea. il por Newsweek 74:105
S 15 '69
PIKE, John
John Pike discusses teaching watercolor; with
biographical sketch. il por Am Artist 33:46-
7+ My '69
PIKE, Otis Grey
Curb on union democracy? America 120:351
Mr 29 '69
PIKE fishing
Fall: a time for pike. A. W. Prince. il Field
& S 74:62-3+ O '69
Fisherman's paradise on workingman's bud-
get. G. W. Bowers. il Outdoor Life 144:64-7+
Jl '69
Mountain pike. B. Dalrymple. il Field & S
74:64-5+ My '69
New technique for big pike. A. Welsch. il
Outdoor Life 143:54-5+ F '69
Wilderness park for sportsmen. B. East. Out-
door Life 144:33-4 Jl '69
PIKES PEAK race. See Automobile racing
PIKEVILLE college, Pikeville, Ky.
Campus revolt in reverse. J. F. Nelson. Chr
Today 13:37 Ja 31 '69
PILATI, Joe
On the steps of city hall. Commonweal 90:
255-6 My 16 '69
Underground GI press. Commonweal 90:559-61
S 19 '69
PILCHER, Frederick
Observing the asteroids. R Pop Astron 63:14-
16 F; 16-17 Mr; 22-3 My '69
PILEA cadieri. See Aluminum plants
PILEGGI, Nicholas
Behind the scenes with the big-city burglar.
Read Digest 94:101-5 Mr '69
Game was up at Namath's. Sports Illus 30:
24-5 Je 23 '69
Revolutionaries who have to be home by
7:30. N Y Times Mag p26-7+ Mr 16 '69
PILES and pile driving
Twenty-seven pieces make an office build-
ing. il Arch Forum 130:62-5 Ap '69
PILGRIM fathers
Heritage of Plymouth. T. A. Askew. Chr
Today 14:15 N 21 '69
In the path of the Pilgrims. M. H. Koehler.
il Travel 132:52-7 O '69
See also
Plimoth plantation, incorporated
PILGRIM village. See Plymouth, Mass.
PILGRIM who didn't care; drama. See Miller,
H. L.
PILGRIMS and pilgrimages
In the shadow of the mountain; photographs.
C. Andujar. Natur Hist 78:28-33 F '69
PILGRIMS triumphant festival pageant. See
Festivals—California
PILKEY, Orrin H. See MacIntyre, I. G. jt.
auth.
PILKINGTON, Betty
Big brothers in the UN. Commonweal 90:
564-5 S 19 '69
Non-proliferation: disarming but not disarm-
ing. Commonweal 89:721-2 Mr 14 '69
Pinch of SALT at the UN. Commonweal 91:
396-7 Ja 9 '70
PILL counter. See Pharmaceutical apparatus
PILLIN, William
Accident; poem. Nation 209:88 Jl 28 '69
PILLOW basalt. See Basalt
PILLOW cases
Pennsylvania German pillowcases. L. B. Car-
lisle. il Antiques 95:556-8 Ap '69

PILLOWS
See also
Cushions
PILOT ejection seats, capsules, etc. See Air-
planes—Escape devices
PILOT training. See Air pilots—Training
PILOTS and pilotage
Small boat piloting. J. Martenhoff. il Yacht-
ing 125:98-9+ Ja '69
PILPEL, Harriet F.
Right of abortion. Atlan 223:69-71 Je '69
—and Norwick, K. P.
But can you do that? See occasional issues
of Publishers' weekly
PILTDOWN forgery
Famous piltdown hoax .il Chem 42:21-2 O '69
PIMENTEL, George C. See Herr, K. C. jt.
auth.
PIMLOTT, Douglas H.
Wilderness in Canada. bibliog por Liv Wildn
32:4-21 Aut '68
PINACATE, Sierra del
Sonoran Desert National Park. D. W. Toll.
il Nat Parks 43:4-8 Ja '69
PINATEL, André
Worker-priest for Christ. M. Moyal. il por
Chr Cent 86:808-9 Je 11 '69
PINCH hitters. See Baseball players
PINCHOT, Gifford
Fight goes on. M. Bush. Am For 75:40+ O
'69
PINE, Gerald J.
Existential school counselor. Clear House 43:
351-4 F '69
PINE, Patricia
Our Mrs Brooks. Am Ed 5:9-10 My '69
Tune up for summer. Am Ed 5:16-20 Mr '69
What's the IQ of the IQ test? Am Ed 5:2-4
N '69
PINE
Collectors of centuries; bristlecone pines. G.
Burridge. il Américas 21:31-6 Je '69
Foxtail pine. G. W. Kelly. il Horticulture 47:
17+ O '69
Mike Frome; Torrey pine. M. Frome. Am For
75:3+ N '69
Our southern pines. C. E. Randall. il Am For
75:32-5+ Je; 30-1+ Jl '69
Pinyon pine. G. W. Kelly. Horticulture 47:31
N '69
Their pines get the right food; organic tree
farming. G. M. Hutton. il Org Gard &
Farm 16:40-3 O '69
PINE bark beetles. See Beetles
PINE BARRENS
Pine Barrens. by J. McPhee. Review
Liv Wildn 32:31-3 Wint '68. A. M. Carter
Undiscovered New Jersey. L. Gashel and J.
Gashel. il Travel 131:52-5+ Je '69
PINEAL body
Circadian rhythm of serotonin in the pineal
body of immunosympathectomized immature
rats. C. R. S. Machado and others. bibliog
il Science 164:442-3 Ap 25 '69
Cyclic adenosine monophosphate; stimu-
lation of melatonin and serotonin synthe-
sis in cultured rat pineals. H. M. Shein
and R. J. Wurtman. bibliog il Science 166:
519-20 O 24 '69
PINEAPPLES
Plucky pineapple. il Org Gard & Farm 16:
89 Ja '69
See also
Cookery—Fruit
PINES, Maya
Why some three-year-olds get A's; and some
get C's. N Y Times Mag p4-5+ Jl 6 '69
PING pong. See Table tennis
PING pong tables. See Tables
PINIELLA, Lou
Highlight. por Sports Illus 30:98 Ap 21 '69
PINK, Ed
Old Master. J. Thawley. il pors Hot Rod
22:50-2 S '69
PINK bollworm moth. See Moths
PINK pagoda; story. See Allen, E.
PINKHAM, Lawrence
Television and the ghetto audience. Cur 108:
33-8 Je '69
PINKING shears. See Scissors and shears
PINKVILLE massacre. See Vietnamese war,
1957- —Atrocities—Songmy massacre
PINNATED grouse. See Prairie chickens
PINNEY, Burt M. See Farrow, J. M. jt. auth.
PINSKER, Harold, and Kandel, E. R.
Synaptic activation of an electrogenic sodium
pump. bibliog Science 163:931-5 F 28 '69
PINSKY, Robert
Summoning the personal devil; Embassy
architecture; poems. Poetry 114:381-2 S '69

PINSON, Penelope
(comp) Books for parents. Parents Mag 44:42
Ap '69
PINTER, Harold
Homecoming. Criticism
Sat R 52:20 N 15 '69
Landscape. Criticism
Cath World 210:124-6 D '69
Time 94:67 Jl 18 '69
Pinter is as Pinter does. C. Hughes. Cath
World 210:124-6 D '69
Silence. Criticism
Cath World 210:124-6 D '69
Time 94:67 Jl 18 '69
PINTO, Vivian de Sola
Personal history. R. Halsband. Sat R 52:83-
4 N 22 '69
PINUS aristata. See Pine
PINWORMS
Enterobius vermicularis: 10,000-year-old hu-
man infection. G. F. Fry and J. G. Moore.
bibliog il Science 166:1620 D 26 '69
PINYON pine. See Pine
PIONEER (satellite) See Artificial satellites—
Astronomical applications
PIONEER life. See Frontier and pioneer life
PIONEER probes. See Space probes
PIONEERING. See Frontier and pioneer life
PIONEERS
See also
Frontier and pioneer life
PIPE laying
Piercing tool speeds pipe work; Fort Worth,
Tex. G. O. Muller. il Am City 84:72-3 D
'69
We kept the sewer in service; East Bay
municipal utility district, Oakland, Calif.
J. D. Foster and J. W. Tooley. il Am City
84:97-9 N '69
PIPE lines
Too much fertilizer. il Bsns W p32-3 My 31
'69
See also
Gas, Natural—Pipe lines
Petroleum—Pipe lines

Cleaning

Rubber giants of the underground. bibliog il
Sci Digest 66:45 S '69
PIPE lines, iron ore. See Iron ores—Transpor-
tation
PIPE lining
Glass linings avert stoppages. il Am City 84:20
Jl '69
Plastic sewer liner; Toronto. R. M. Bremner.
il Am City 84:98-101 S '69
PIPE smoking. See Smoking
PIPELARE, Matthaeus
Chansons of Matthaeus Pipelare. R. Cross.
bibliog f il Mus Q 55:500-20 O '69
PIPER, David
Dimensions 1969. Craft Horiz 29:28-31+ S
'69
PIPER aircraft corporation
Piper control battle headed for court. Avia-
tion W 90:23 F 10 '69
Piper proves elusive prize. il Bsns W p62+
Ag 16 '69
Struggle looming over control of Piper. Avia-
tion W 90:23 F 3 '69
PIPES
See also
Pipe lining

Maintenance and repair

Dent puller from pipe parts. W. E. Burton.
il Pop Mech 132:198-9 O '69
PIPES, iron
Now you can solder galvanized pipe. J. Hand.
il Pop Sci 195:153 S '69
PIPES, Opium. See Opium pipes
PIPES, Plastic
What you can make from plastic pipe. V. L.
Oertle. il Pop Sci 195:136-7 Ag '69
See also
Water pipes, Plastic
PIPES, Tobacco. See Tobacco pipes
PIPINELIS, Panayotis
Neighbors' verdict. por Time 94:30 D 19 '69
PIPPENGER, Ruthann
Roofthings, or View from a teachers' lounge;
poem. Engl J 58:1161 N '69
PIRANDELLO, Luigi
Man with the flower in his mouth; tr. by
W. Murray. Criticism
New Yorker 45:107-8 My 3 '69

PIRASTEH, Ross
Prevent blunders in supply and distribution. Harvard Bsns R 47:113-27 Mr '69

PIRATES
See also
Privateering
Ringrose, B.
PIRE, Dominique Georges Henri
Père Pire: in memoriam. America 120:184 F
15 '69
PIRELLI of Milan. See Tire industry and trade
PIRIE, N. W.
Ingenuities of nature; excerpt from Food re-
sources: conventional and novel. Sat R 52:49
Ag 2 '69
PIRONE, P. P.
How when and what of spraying roses.
Horticulture 47:38-9 My '69
Spray schedule for evergreens. Horticulture
47:42-5 Mr '69
Spray schedule for indoor plants. Horticul-
ture 47:34-6 O '69
Spray schedule for the flower garden. Horti-
culture 47:34-5 Je '69
Spray schedule for vegetables. Horticulture
47:33-5 Jl '69
Spraying small fruits. Horticulture 47:38-9+
Ap '69
PIRONE, Thomas P. See Wheeler, H. jt. auth.
PISANO, John J.
Carbon-14 labeled vasoactive peptides avail-
able. Science 165:203 Jl 11 '69
Radioactive peptide available. Science 163:
494 Ja 31 '69
PISTELL, Richard Chadwick
From board to bush. por Bsns W p94 Ja 10
'70
PISTOLETTO, Michelangelo
People are talking about . . . por Vogue 153:
218-19 Ap 1 '69
PISTOLS
Lindsay's double shooting. C. G. Worman. il
Hobbies 74:122-3 Jl '69
Pistol is for fun. T. Trueblood. il Field & S
74:34+ S '69
Plinking handgun. W. Page. il Field & S
74:86-8+ S '69
See also
Revolvers
PISTON engines. See Automobile engines
PISTONS
Magnesium pistons. J. Dianna. il Hot Rod
22:100 Jl '69
PITANGUY, Ivo
Body sculpturing. S. Morini. il Vogue 154:
190-3 O 1 '69
PITCAIRN ISLAND
Heritage of H.M.S. Bounty; reprint. H. L.
Shapiro. il UNESCO Courier 22:20-1 Ag '69
PITCH, Musical. See Musical pitch
PITCHERS
Aquamanilia: medieval vessels designed to
hold water for the washing of hands. New
Yorker 44:29-30 Ja 18 '69
Fill your pitchers with spring. il Bet Hom
& Gard 47:120 Ap '69
Pitchers for everything pourable. il House
& Gard 135:184-5 Ap '69
Tilting sets from steam-boat days. K. Hol-
labaugh. il Hobbies 74:121+ S '69
PITCHERS, Baseball. See Baseball players
PITCHERS mounds. See Baseball fields
PITCHESS, Peter J.
Adopt a deputy. Todays Ed 58:81-2 F '69
PITCHING (baseball)
Why the brushback? B. Gibson. il Look 33:
66-9 Jl 29 '69
PITMAN, Gary B.
Pheromone response in pine bark beetles:
influence of host volatiles. bibliog Science
166:905-6 N 14 '69
PITMAN, Georgene
Touring without a car. Travel 131:63-6 Ap '69
PITNEY-BOWES, Incorporated
Wrong reason, right results. il Forbes 103:
62-3 Ap 15 '69
PITT, William
Younger Pitt, by J. Ehrman. Review
Newsweek por 74:92F+ D 1 '69. R. A.
Gross
PITTS, Ferris N. Jr
Biochemistry of anxiety; with biographical
sketch. Sci Am 220:12, 69-75 F '69
PITTSBURGH

Air pollution

Pittsburgh cracks down on polluters. il Bsns
W p66-7 D 27 '69

City planning

One mayor's story of the mess in cities; excerpts from remarks. J. M. Barr. il U S
News 66:57-9 Ap 21 '69

Clubs

Clash of symbols at the clubhouse; Duquesne
club. il Bsns W p31-2 My 31 '69

PITTSBURGH—*Continued*

Description

Exciting cities, a Redbook vacation guide to sight-seeing with children; excerpts from America's exciting cities. A. Schwartz. il Redbook 132:41-2 Ap '69

Elections

Nobody's boy; mayoralty results. il Newsweek 74:49 N 17 '69

Finance

One mayor's story of the mess in cities; excerpts from remarks. J. M. Barr. il U S News 66:57-9 Ap 21 '69

Gardens
See also
Phipps conservatory

Industries

Mergers and the city. R. S. Ahlbrandt. Duns R 93:17 Ap '69

Labor and laboring classes
At the crossroads; with portfolio. il Newsweek 74:36-44 O 6 '69

Libraries

Regional center of '70's seen in Pittsburgh study; summary. T. Minder. Library J 94:704+ F 15 '69
See also
Carnegie library of Pittsburgh

Negroes

Black battleground. il Time 94:78 S 5 '69
Blacks cry genocide; opposition to the Planned parenthood association programs. R. Z. Hallow. Nation 208:535-7 Ap 28 '69
Confrontation in Pittsburgh; drive to crack building trades unions. C. C. Robb. il Nation 209:272-4 S 22 '69
Cracking the crafts. il Newsweek 74:34-5 S 8 '69
Pittsburgh blacks try negotiating. il Bsns W p32-3 S 6 '69
Rebuff in Pittsburgh; reactions to Black construction coalition. T. A. Hennessy. New Repub 161:16-17 S 27 '69
What unions are, and are not doing for blacks. il Time 94:88+ S 26 '69

Politics and government

Bye-bye machine. R. W. Gibbons. Commonweal 90:381-4 Je 20 '69
Everybody here knows Elsie; chairman of local Republican party. il Forbes 104:52 S 15 '69
See also
Pittsburgh—Elections

Rapid transit

Will Skybus get off the ground? il Bsns W p 146+ Mr 22 '69

Strikes
See also
Strikes—United States—Hospital employees

Transportation
See also
Pittsburgh—Rapid transit

PITTSBURGH steel company. See Wheeling-Pittsburgh corporation

PITTSBURGH symphony orchestra
Music to my ears; performance of Das lied von der erde. I. Kolodin. Sat R 52:63+ N 29 '69
Musical events; concert in Carnegie Hall. W. Sargeant. New Yorker 45:183-4 N 22 '69

PITTSBURGH. University

Johnstown campus

Student body turns it on; heat reclaim system project. B. F. Peters. il Am Ed 5:20-1 Ap '69

PITTSTON company
They call me lucky; Routh of Pittston. Forbes 104:34 S 15 '69

PITUITARY body
Estradiol: specific binding by pituitary nuclear fraction in vitro. W. W. Leavitt and others. bibliog il Science 165:496-8 Ag 1 '69
Luteinizing hormone-releasing activity in hypophysial stalk blood and elevation by dopamine. I. A. Kamberi and others. bibliog il Science 166:388-90 O 17 '69

Pars intermedia: unitary electrical activity regulated by light. K. Oshima and A. Gorbman. bibliog il Science 163:195-7 Ja 10 '69
See also
Gonadotropins
Pituitary hormones
Thyrotropin

PITUITARY hormones
Cortisol induction of growth hormone synthesis in a clonal line of rat pituitary tumor cells in culture. P. O. Kohler and others. bibliog il Science 166:633-4 O 31 '69
Human growth hormone release: relation to slow-wave sleep and sleep-waking cycles. J. F. Sassin and others. bibliog il Science 165:513-15 Ag 1 '69
Pituitary hormones: international colloquium. H. A. Bern and others. Science 163:200+ Ja 10 '69

PITZ, Henry C.
Art of the pen. Am Artist 32:26-32 D '68
Four disciples of Howard Pyle; excerpts from The Brandywine tradition. Am Artist 33:38-43 Ja '69
Gustave Doré, prolific illustrator. Am Artist 33:48-53+ D '69

PITZER, Daniel Lee
Animal called POW: my four years in a Vietcong prison; ed. by W. Rogers. il pors Look 33:46-51 F 18 '69

PITZER, Kenneth S.
Who says it's safe? Nation 208:556-7 My 5 '69

PITZER, Sara
When women fight for freedom. Parents Mag 44:62-3+ Ap '69

PIZARRO, Francisco, marqués
When civilizations collide. il Sr Schol 95:4-5 O 6 '69

PIZZA. See Cookery, Italian

PIZZI, Pier Luigi
Enlightener; interview, ed. by M. J. Matz. por Opera N 34:20-1 N 22 '69

PLACE cards
Dried arrangements for place cards. R. T. Northen. il Horticulture 46:34-5+ D '68

PLACEMENT bureaus. See Employment agencies

PLACENTA, Artificial
Artificial placenta: two days of total extrauterine support of the isolated premature lamb fetus. W. M. Zapol and others. bibliog il Science 166:617-18 O 31 '69

PLACENTIA, Calif.
Teenagers given voice in local affairs. R. R. Samp and T. G. Bond. il Parks & Rec 4:35+ My '69

PLAGEMANN, Bentz
Portrait in silverpoint of a grandchild. McCalls 96:66+ Ag '69

PLAGIARISM
W. D. McElroy: an old incident embarrasses new NSF director. P. M. Boffey. Science 165:379-80 Jl 25 '69

PLAGIARISM in music
Unholy Bishop; composer of Home, sweet home. R. Rushmore. Opera N 34:6-7 D 20 '69

PLAGUE bacilli. See Pasteurella pestis
PLAGUE toxin. See Toxins and antitoxins
PLAINS Indians. See Indians of North America
PLAINVIEW, N.Y.
Pin money conversion; Oak Drive elementary school. M. F. Boyd. il Library J 94:4228 N 15 '69

PLANARIANS. See Flatworms

PLANE trees
Anthracnose in sycamores. R. Dallmer. il Horticulture 47:22+ Je '69

PLANETARIUMS
Everyone has a sky; a planetarium helps the slow learner. R. N. Kratz. Clear House 43:349-50 F '69
Major planetarium for Toronto; McLaughlin planetarium. T. Dickinson. il R Pop Astron 63:8-9 F '69
Model VI; Hayden planetarium's new Zeiss projector. New Yorker 45:35-7 S 20 '69
Modernization at two eastern planetariums; Morehead planetarium and American museum-Hayden planetarium. R. S. Knapp; S. S. Ross. il Sky & Tel 38:382-4 D '69
Vienna planetarium conference. G. Lovi. il Sky & Tel 38:236-9 O '69

PLANETARY nebulae. See Nebulae
PLANETARY spectroscopy. See Astronomical spectroscopy

PLANETS
Astronomy. J. Stokley. See fourth issue of each month of Science news
Barnard's star and its planetary system. G. S. Mumford. Sky & Tel 37:360 Je '69

PLANETS—*Continued*
Mysterious companions of Barnard's star; system of planets in constellation Ophiuchus. il Time 93:93-4 Ap 25 '69
Other worlds, other planets; planet-like objects in the Barnard system. Sci N 95:398 Ap 26 '69
Search for Vulcan. R. G. Hodgson. R Pop Astron 63:10-12 Mr; 10-11 My '69
Similarities in Mars, Venus and earth. V. R. Eshleman. il Space World F-6-66:34-5 Je '69
Sun, moon, and planets this month. See issues of Sky and telescope
Two-planet solar system. Sci Am 220:58 Je '69
See also
Earth
Life on other planets
Orbits
Solar system
also names of planets, e.g. Pluto (planet)

Observations
Among the planets. See issues of Review of popular astronomy
Penetrating the secrets of the planets. G. Bylinsky. il Fortune 80:138-43 N '69
Some radio observations of the outer planets. Sky & Tel 38:301 N '69
See also
Mars (planet)—Observations

Rotation
Spin-orbit resonance of the inner planets. M. Campbell. bibliog Science 165:930 Ag 29 '69

PLANETS of the years; story. See O'Faolain, S.

PLANING hulls. See Hydrofoils

PLANING machines
Candid look at Delta's Uniplane. R. J. De Cristoforo. il Pop Sci 194:146-8 Ja '69
How to plane on a lathe. W. E. Burton. il Pop Mech 132:194-7+ O '69
New wood planer attachment for your Unimat lathe. W. E. Burton. il Pop Mech 130:179-81 D '68

PLANK, John
We should start talking with Castro. N Y Times Mag p28-31+ Mr 30 '69; Same abr. with title Should we talk with Castro? Cur 107:10-17 My '69

PLANK, Vernon G.
Clearing ground fog with helicopters. Weatherwise 22:91-8+ Je '69

PLANKTON
Shallow scattering layer in the subarctic Pacific Ocean: detection by high-frequency echo sounder. W. E. Barraclough and others. bibliog il Science 166:611-13 O 31 '69
Tiny creatures of the tides. il Life 67:43-5 Jl 4 '69
See also
Diatoms

PLANNED parenthood. See Birth control

PLANNERS, City. See City planners

PLANNING
See also
City planning
Educational planning
National planning
Rural planning

PLANNING, Business. See Business management and organization

PLANNING, Land. See Land utilization

PLANT ash
Ash glazes for Cone 6. R. Behrens. il Ceram Mo 17:31 Ja '69

PLANT boxes. See Flower boxes, planters, etc.

PLANT breeding
Don't complicate simple things. R. Rodale. Org Gard & Farm 16:21-3 Je '69
How new flowers are made. J. W. Wilson. il Horticulture 47:36-7+ Ja '69
Improving on nature to vanquish hunger. G. Bylinsky. il Fortune 79:126-31+ Ap '69
See also
Hybridization
Inbreeding
Plant genetics

PLANT catalogs. See Catalogs, Seed and plant

PLANT cells and tissues
Don't complicate simple things. R. Rodale. Org Gard & Farm 16:21-3 Je '69
Green plants that live without cellulose. R. D. Preston. il Chem 42:24-6 Ja '69
Microbody-like organelles in leaf cells. S. E. Frederick and E. H. Newcomb. bibliog il Science 163:1353-5 Mr 21 '69

Silica in developing epidermal cells of avena internodes: electron microprobe analysis. P. B. Kaufman and others. bibliog il Science 166:1015-17 N 21 '69
See also
Chloroplasts

Culture
Crop improvement through plant cell and tissue culture; report of meeting. L. G. Nickell and J. G. Torrey. Science 166:1068+ N 21 '69
Whole tree from a few cells. il Chem 42:20 My '69

PLANT cuttings. See Plant propagation

PLANT diseases. See Plants—Diseases and pests

PLANT enzymes. See Enzymes, Plant

PLANT genetics
Alcohol dehydrogenase in maize: genetic basis for isozymes. J. G. Scandalios. bibliog il Science 166:623-4 O 31 '69
Alcohol dehydrogenase in maize: genetic basis for multiple isozymes. D. Schwartz. bibliog il Science 164:585-6 My 2 '69
Androgenesis conditioned by a mutation in maize. J. L. Kermicle. bibliog il Science 166:1422-4 D 12 '69
Anti-famine strategy: genetic engineering for food. S. S. Chase. il Bul Atom Sci 25:2-6 O '69
Improving on nature to vanquish hunger. G. Bylinsky. il Fortune 79:126-31+ Ap '69

PLANT growth. See Growth (plants)

PLANT hormones. See Hormones, Plant

PLANT hunting. See Botanical exploration

PLANT inspection
Bringing plants in from Canada. il Sunset 142:232-3 Ap '69

PLANT introduction
Indigens and immigrants; plants and animals in the New York city region. A. B. Klots. il Natur Hist 78:38-45 Ap '69

PLANT lice
Aphid transmission of tobacco mosaic virus. J. S. Lojek and G. B. Orlob. bibliog il Science 164:1407-8 Je 20 '69

PLANT location. See Location in business and industry

PLANT names. See Botany—Nomenclature

PLANT pathology. See Plants—Diseases and pests

PLANT polysaccharides. See Polysaccharides

PLANT pots. See Flower pots

PLANT prints. See Prints

PLANT propagation
Air layering. il Home Gard 56:61 Ag '69
Boardwalk for the beans. N. H. Berlin. il Org Gard & Farm 16:35 Jl '69
Easy ways to propagate shrubs and perennials. O. Kruse. il Org Gard & Farm 16:41 Jl '69
Fogging and misting plants. F. Heutte. Horticulture 47:26+ My '69
Garden projects and pastimes for children. il Home Gard 56:33-40 Jl '69
Getting them off to a good start. il Home Gard 56:46-9 F '69
Growing plants from cuttings. il Sunset 143:141 Jl '69
Increasing hyacinth bulbs. B. Brinhart. il Horticulture 47:16-17+ My '69
Planting & growing. J. Viles. il Home Gard 56:44-5 Mr '69
Try cotton-ball planting for an early garden. K. J. Sewell. il Org Gard & Farm 16:102-3 Mr '69
See also
Seedlings

PLANT proteins
Cell wall protein in plants: autoradiographic evidence. D. Sadava and M. J. Chrispeels. bibliog il Science 165:299-300 Jl 18 '69
Improving on nature to vanquish hunger. G. Bylinsky. il Fortune 79:126-31+ Ap '69
Nucleic acid-protein interactions in turnip yellow mosaic virus. J. M. Kaper. bibliog il Science 166:248-50 O 10 '69

PLANT quarantine
See also
Plant inspection

PLANT research. See Botanical research

PLANT stands. See Flower stands

PLANT succession
Forest succession in Yellowstone National Park. D. T. Patten. il Nat Parks 43:21-2 S '69
What does the law of succession mean when referred to nature? Sci Digest 65:86-7 Je '69

PLANT viruses. See Viruses, Plant

PLANTAR warts. See Warts

PLANTE, Jacques
  Sporting scene. H. W. Wind. New Yorker 45:
    144-51 Mr 15 '69

PLANTERS (farm machines)
  Faster planters for narrow rows. il Farm
    J 93:26-9 Ap '69
  Pointers for planters. P. Jones and G. Earle.
    il Suc Farm 67:42-5 Mr '69
  Simple strawberry-planting aid. D. A. Abdalla.
    il Org Gard & Farm 16:74-5 Ap '69

PLANTERS (flower boxes) See Flower boxes,
    planters, etc.

PLANTING. See Plants. Space arrangement of;
    Seeding; Transplanting

PLANTING fields arboretum, Oyster Bay. See
    New York (state). State university—Agri-
    cultural and technical institute at Farm-
    ingdale, Long Island

PLANTING machinery. See Planters (farm ma-
    chines)

PLANTING plans and tables. See Gardening—
    Planting plans and tables

PLANTS
  Best plants. See issues of Home garden &
    flower grower
  Fabric of gardens. B. Miles. il Horticulture
    47:38-9+ Ja '69
  [Month] in your garden. See issues of Sunset
  New plants 1970. il Horticulture 48:18-21 Ja
    '70
  Plants for city gardens. P. Truex. il Horticul-
    ture 46:38-9+ Ag '68
  Plants that do well with very little sun. il
    Sunset 143:194-5 S '69
    See also
  Alpine flora
  Annuals (plants)
  Botany
  Bulbs
  Desert vegetation
  Herbs
  Perennials
  Seedlings
  Shrubs
  Succulent plants
  Transplanting
  Trees
    also names of plants, e.g. Pokeweed;
    also headings beginning Plant

  Absorption of water
  Free-energy transfer in plants. J. S. Boyer.
    bibliog il Science 163:1219-20 Mr 14 '69

  All America selections
  All-America rose selections, and what they can
    mean to you. il Home Gard 56:52 Jl '69
  All-America roses. il Pop Gard 20:42 Spr '69
  First prize, All-America rose for 1970. il Hor-
    ticulture 47:32 Jl '69
  It's time to plant color, and there's new
    color to plant. il Sunset 142:90-3 Mr '69
  New! For your 1969 garden. E. Kondonellis.
    il Am Home 72:14+ Ja '69

  Assimilation
    See also
  Photosynthesis

  Breeding
  See Plant breeding

  Collection and preservation
  Mutis in New Granada; iconographic collec-
    tion of regional flora. N. López Pellón. il
    Américas 21:29-33 F '69

  Disease and pest resistance
  Pathotoxin-induced disease resistance in
    plants. H. Wheeler and T. P. Pirone. bib-
    liog il Science 166:1415-17 D 12 '69
  Plants that protect themselves. R. Tirrell. il
    Org Gard & Farm 16:35-7 Je '69

  Diseases and pests
  Bring plants in clean. L. Pyenson. Horticul-
    ture 46:44+ O '68
  Environment and plant diseases. E. A. Cox.
    Horticulture 48:32-3 Ja '70
  Toxins in plant disease: structure and mode
    of action. L. D. Owens. bibliog il Science
    165:18-25 Jl 4 '69
  What causes plant disease? J. I. Rodale. Org
    Gard & Farm 16:82-3+ Jl '69
    See also
  Nematodes
  Snails
    also subhead Diseases and pests under
    names of plants, e.g. Corn—Diseases and
    pests

  Growth
    See Growth (plants)

  Hardiness
  What makes plants hardy? G. S. Howell and
    C. J. Weiser. il Horticulture 46:18-21+
    D '68

  Inspection
    See Plant inspection

  Metabolism
    See also
  Plants—Respiration

  Nutrition
    See also
  Photosynthesis
  Plants, Effect of calcium on

  Purchasing
  Choice plants are worth buying. K. Twomey.
    Horticulture 46:50+ D '68

  Reproduction
    See also
  Fertility (botany)

  Resistance to disease
    See Plants—Disease and pest resistance

  Respiration
  Carbon dioxide compensation points in re-
    lated plant species. D. N. Moss and others.
    bibliog il Science 164:187-8 Ap 11 '69

  Temperature
  Trees with temperatures. R. W. Neubert. il
    Am For 75:6-7+ Ap '69

  Translocation
  Translocation in perennial monocotyledons. W.
    Heyser and others. bibliog il Science 164:
    572-4 My 2 '69
    See also
  Plants. Motion of fluids in

  Water requirements
  Pretty green place with the big garden.
    M. Rhoda. il Org Gard & Farm 16:62-4 F '69

PLANTS, Climbing. See Climbing plants

PLANTS, Edible
  Stalking the wild etcetera. E. Gibbons. Org
    Gard & Farm 16:92-4 Ag '69
  Wild health food. E. Gibbons. il Org Gard &
    Farm 16:87-91 Mr '69
  Wild prejudice. E. Gibbons. Org Gard &
    Farm 16:76-9 S '69
    See also
  Food, Wild
  Greens, Edible
  Vegetables

PLANTS, Effect of air pollution on
  Custer's last stand; tree grower's livelihood
    threatened by air pollution. Time 94:51 D
    19 '69

PLANTS, Effect of calcium on
  Salt toleration by plants: enhancement with
    calcium. P. A. LaHaye and E. Epstein.
    bibliog il Science 166:395-6 O 17 '69

PLANTS, Effect of climate on
  Corchorus pascuorum: transmission of chemi-
    cally induced fruit formation with environ-
    mental change. A. S. Islam and R. Mughal.
    bibliog il Science 164:315-16 Ap 18 '69

PLANTS, Effect of humidity on
  Plant injury by air pollutants: influence of
    humidity on stomatal apertures and plant
    response to ozone. H. W. Otto and R. H.
    Daines. bibliog il Science 163:1209-10 Mr
    14 '69

PLANTS, Effect of light on
  Light and hormones: interchangeability in
    the induction of nitrate reductase. S. H.
    Lips and N. Roth-Bejerano. bibliog il Sci-
    ence 166:109-10 O 3 '69
    See also
  Algae, Effect of light on
  Artificial light gardening
  Fungi, Effect of light on

PLANTS, Effect of ozone on
  Ozone: depression of frond multiplication and
    floral production in duckweed. W. A. Feder
    and F. Sullivan. bibliog il Science 165:1373-
    4 S 26 '69
  Plant injury by air pollutants: influence of
    humidity on stomatal apertures and plant
    response to ozone. W. H. Otto and R. H.
    Daines. bibliog il Science 163:1209-10 Mr
    14 '69

PLANTS, Effect of radiation on
  Radiosensitivity and rate of cell division: law
    of Bergonié and Tribondeau. A. H. Haber
    and B. E. Rothstein. bibliog il Science 163:
    1338-9 Mr 21 '69

PLANTS, Effect of salt on
Salt toleration by plants: enhancement with calcium. P. A. LaHaye and E. Epstein. bibliog il Science 166:395-6 O 17 '69
PLANTS, Effect of temperature on
See also
Plants—Hardiness
PLANTS, Fossil. See Paleobotany
PLANTS, Geographical distribution of. See Geographical distribution of animals and plants
PLANTS, Indoor. See House plants
PLANTS, Industrial. See Industrial buildings
PLANTS, Motion of fluids in
Free-energy transfer in plants. J. S. Boyer. bibliog il Science 163:1219-20 Mr 14 '69
PLANTS, Ornamental
Instead of flowers, the colors and textures of leaves, wood, stone. il Sunset 142:272 Ap '69
Potted ornamentals for winter cheer. B. Wahlfeldt. il Org Gard & Farm 16:43-5 Ja '69
See also
Coleus
House plants
Maranta
PLANTS, Potted
Bring plants in clean. L. Pyenson. Horticulture 46:44+ O '68
Bulbs in pots for later indoor bloom il Sunset 143:260 O '69
Hang-ups look you right in the eye. il Sunset 142:94-7 My '69
More plants for hanging baskets. Sunset 142:194 Je '69
Portable garden in pots. Am Home 72:102-3 Ja '69
See also
Flower boxes, planters, etc.
Flower pots
House plants
PLANTS, Printing. See Printing offices
PLANTS, Protection of
See also
Garden houses, shelters, etc.
Mulching
PLANTS, Rock garden
Enjoy the unique appeal of rock garden plants without rocks. M. Helleiner. il Home Gard 56:52-3 Ag '69
Here are color ideas for your rock garden. il Sunset 142:242+ Ap '69
Rock garden plants from seed. R. Murfitt. il Horticulture 46:22-5 D '68
See also
Epilobiums
Gardens, Rock
PLANTS, Shade
Logistics of building a shade garden. il House & Gard 136:140-1 Ag '69
Shade garden. il House & Gard 136:70-1 Ag '69
What to put where grass won't grow; with list of ground covers. il Changing T 23:45-7 My '69
PLANTS, Space arrangement of
How corn reacts to thicker planting. C. E. Sommers. il Suc Farm 67:30-1+ Je '69
Is this the ultimate for narrow rows? C. Peterson, jr. il Suc Farm 67:32-3 My '69
They plan for easy cultivation. G. L. Earle. il Suc Farm 67:38 Je '69
PLANTS, Training of
Training; take advantage of the vertical. J. Viles. il Home Gard 56:48-9 Mr '69
See also
Trees, Training of
PLANTS, Water requirements of. See Plants—Water requirements
PLANTS, Watering of. See Watering of plants
PLANTS for shady places. See Plants, Shade
PLANTS in house decoration
Garden house with garden rooms. il House & Gard 136:34-9 Ag '69
Vacation house alive with exotic flowers. il House & Gard 136:112-17 N '69
PLAQUEMINES PARISH, La.
Plaquemines without the great white father. B. W. Eggler. New Repub 160:11-12 My 24 '69
PLASMA (ionized gases)
Closer and closer; success at Tokamak. Sci N 96:424 N 8 '69
Cold octopole and hot Tokomak show long confinement times. Phys Today 22:55-6 D '69
Confinement among the rings. D. E. Thomsen. il Sci N 96:413 N 1 '69
Fusion power: optimism and a Tokamak gap at Dubna. R. W. Holcomb. Science 166:363-4 O 17 '69
Hundred-joule lasers are producing high-temperature plasmas. G. B. Lubkin. il Phys Today 22:55-6 N '69

Laser-made plasmas, D. E. Thomsen. il Sci N 95:384-5 Ap 19 '69
Plasma confinement grows. il Sci N 95:397 Ap 26 '69
Plasmas. H. Grad. bibliog il Phys Today 22:34-44 D '69
Tokamak. Sci Am 221:51-2 D '69
PLASMODIUM (parasite)
Aminoacyl transfer ribonucleic acid synthetases from cell-free extract of plasmodium berghei. J. Ilan and J. Ilan. bibliog il Science 164:560-2 My 2 '69
PLASMODIUM infection. See Malaria
PLASMOGAMY
Complementation analysis on virus-fused Chinese hamster cells with nutritional markers. F. T. Kao and others. bibliog il Science 164:312-14 Ap 18 '69
PLASS, Paul
Eros, play and death in Plato. bibliog f Am Imago 26:37-55 Spr '69
PLASTER sculpture
Plaster caste. J. Perreault. il Art N 67:54-5+ N '68
PLASTIC artificial organs. See Prosthesis
PLASTIC bottles. See Bottles
PLASTIC flooring. See Flooring, Plastic
PLASTIC furniture. See Furniture, Plastic
PLASTIC hearts. See Hearts, Artificial
PLASTIC houses. See Houses, Plastic
PLASTIC metal coating. See Metal coating
PLASTIC modeling. See Modeling
PLASTIC mulch. See Mulching
PLASTIC panels. See Paneling
PLASTIC pipes. See Pipes, Plastic
PLASTIC printing plates. See Printing plates
PLASTIC sculpture
Plastics of sculpture: materials and techniques; reprint. N. Roukes. il Craft Horiz 29:18-19+ Ja '69
PLASTIC surgery. See Surgery, Plastic
PLASTIC swimming pools. See Swimming pools
PLASTIC water pipes. See Water pipes, Plastic
PLASTICITY
Superplastic metals. H. W. Hayden and others. il Sci Am 220:28-35 bibliog (p 148) Mr '69
PLASTICS
Hydron: new miracle plastic with a myriad of uses. T. Irwin. il Pop Sci 194:92-5 F '69
Plastic moves uptown. il Esquire 71:105-11 Je '69
Plastics explosion in home furnishings. P. Rumely. il Bet Hom & Gard 47:59-73 Ap '69
See also
Elastomers
Mylar
Polyethylene
Polymers
Styrofoam

Irradiation
See Plastics, Irradiated

Manufacture
Plastics that come on strong. Bsns W p76+ N 8 '69

Molding
How to duplicate small parts by plastic casting. M. Philips. il Pop Sci 195:142-5 N '69
Squirting the cost out of quality plastics; liquid injection molding. il Bsns W p 146-8 Ap 12 '69

Reinforcement
See Plastics, Reinforced

Testing
Predicting durability of plastics. il Chem 42:26 Ja '69
PLASTICS, Decorative
Vinyl word on kitchens! H. A. Dawson. il Bet Hom & Gard 47:76-7 Je '69
PLASTICS, Irradiated
Pushing radiation chemistry; Japanese isotope work. S. Griffin. il Sci N 96:514 N 29 '69
PLASTICS, Molding. See Plastics—Molding
PLASTICS, Reinforced
Where plastics get a lot of muscle; glass fiber reinforced thermoplastics. il Bsns W p71-2 Ja 3 '70
PLASTICS as an art form
Freda Koblick. N. Znamierowski. il Craft Horiz 29:20-1 Ja '69

PLASTICS as art material
Acrylics in the classroom. J. T. Brandstadter. il Sch Arts 68:28-9 Ap '69
Art; Plastic presence at the Jewish museum. L. Alloway. Nation 209:646 D 8 '69
Disposable art; the plastic man L. Levine. D. Bourdon. il Life 67:62-7 Ag 22 '69
Plastics for everyday living. E. H. Varian. il Art in Am 57:104-7 Jl '69
Shroud for Sydney's cliffs. il Life 67:46-7 N 14 '69
Three Austrians and the New Jersey turnpike; Laurids, Zamp and Pinter. I. Horovitz. il Craft Horiz 29:10-13+ Ja '69
Wrap-in Down Under; first natural landscape to be wrapped. il Time 94:56 N 14 '69

PLASTICS in art. See Plastics as art material

PLASTICS in building
Blow me a house in two days; polyurethane foam interior designed by F. R. R. Drury. il Vogue 154:138-43+ O 15 '69
Foam buildings. il Parks & Rec 4:44-5 My '69
Foamed plastic plans work as forms, insulation and ceiling. il Arch Rec 145:175-6 Mr '69

PLATE tectonics. See Geology, Structural

PLATELETS (blood) See Blood—Corpuscles and platelets

PLATER, Alan
Close the coalhouse door. Criticism Atlan 224:101 Ag '69

PLATES, Printing. See Printing plates

PLATNER, Warren
Two uncompromisingly modern buildings, designed and drawn, with old-fashioned care. Arch Rec 146:97-104 D '69

PLATO
Eros, play and death in Plato. P. Plass. bibliog f Am Imago 26:37-55 Spr '69

PLATONIC love. See Love, Platonic

PLATONOV, Andreĭ Petrovich
Third son; story, excerpt from The fierce and beautiful world. Harper 239:87-9 N '69

about
Fiction. M. Friedberg. Sat R 53:44 Ja 10 '70
People vs. the plan. R. A. Sokolov. por Newsweek 75:72 Ja 12 '70

PLATT, Anthony
Rise of the child-saving movement; a study in social policy and correctional reform; excerpt from The child-savers; the invention of delinquency. bibliog f Ann Am Acad 381:21-38 Ja '69

PLATT, David
Very, very Pleasence. Harp Baz 102:126-7 Ap '69

PLATT, John
University as a five-legged animal; adaptation of address, October 1968. Science 165:649 Ag 15 '69
What we must do. Science 166:1115-21 N 28 '69

PLATYHELMINTHES. See Flatworms

PLATYPUSES
Nature's little puzzler: the platypus. F. Dickenson. il Read Digest 95:167+ Ag '69

PLATZ, A. See Begleiter, H. jt. auth.

PLAVCAN, A. B.
$200 IC digital clock. Radio-Electr 40:23-6 Ap '69

PLAWIN, Paul
Family travel. See issues of Better homes & gardens

PLAY
Fiction and the paradox of play. C. Horovitz. bibliog il Wilson Lib Bul 44:397-401 D '69
Passive mastery of helplessness in games; psychoanalytic case study. M. D. Capell. bibliog Am Imago 25:309-32 Wint '68
Play for all seasons; with study-discussion program. R. Strang. bibliog PTA Mag 63:19-21, 35 Ja '69
Play groups for the preschool child. McCalls 96:52 Mr '69
Secret of having fun. E. J. LeShan. il Read Digest 95:116-20 O '69
What play reveals about your child. A. Schrut. il Parents Mag 44:54-5+ Ag '69
See also
Sports

PLAY apparatus. See Playgrounds—Equipment

PLAY groups. See Nursery schools

PLAY it again, Sam: drama. See Allen. W.

PLAY production. See Theatrical production and direction

PLAYBOY (periodical)
Penthouse v. Playboy. il Time 94:88 N 7 '69
Playboy puts a glint in the admen's eyes. il Bsns W p 142-4+ Je 28 '69

PLAYER piano music
Music for piano, but not for pianist. R. P. Morgan. Hi Fi 19:90 My '69
Musica ex machina; studies for player piano only. W. F. Rickenbacker. il Nat R 21:658-9 Jl 1 '69

PLAYFORD, Phillip E. and Cockbain, A. E.
Algal stromatolites: deepwater forms in the Devonian of Western Australia. bibliog Science 165:1008-10 S 5 '69

PLAYGROUND apparatus. See Playgrounds—Equipment

PLAYGROUNDS
Great places to play. il House & Gard 135:116-17 My '69
Parks and recreation. See issues of American city
See also
Parks

Equipment
Play cube. il Parks & Rec 4:42 My '69
Playgrounds shape children shape playgrounds; New York. il Am City 84:98-9 Ag '69
Their fathers built this obstacle course; Millbrae nursery school, Calif. il Sunset 143:76-7 S '69

Safety devices and measures
London bridge is falling down. Todays Health 47:77 Mr '69

PLAYGROUNDS, Home

Equipment
Dragon and a dinosaur's tail. il Sunset 143:142 N '69
Fun house for the backyard. il Mech Illus 65:77 Jl '69
Plato's platonic solids as giant toys. il Sunset 143:56-7 D '69
Tips on buying outdoor play equipment. il Good H 168:196 My '69
See also
Playhouses

PLAYHOUSES
Built in one busy weekend by three energetic adults for something under $75. il Sunset 142:94-5 Mr '69
It's a floating tree house. il Sunset 142:126 Je '69
Roomy a-frame play house, easily built, cost about $350. il Sunset 143:52-3 Ag '69

PLAYING cards. See Cards

PLAYMATES
Birthday present; Negro and white friends. Read Digest 94:109 Je '69

PLAYOFF in sports. See Sports

PLAYTHINGS. See Toys

PLAYTNER, Henry R.
Henry Playtner; excerpt from letter. R. Phillip. il por Hobbies 74:48-9+ Ag '69

PLAYWRIGHTS. See Dramatists

PLAZA, Galo
Entering the second development decade; excerpts from address. por Américas 21:42 Ap '69
Multinational investment; excerpts from statement. Américas 21:45 My '69
Plaza's European visit: highly productive. Américas 21:44 Jl '69
Trade, aid, and development; excerpts from address, October 6, 1969. Américas 21:54-5 N '69
Unions urged to increase skilled labor in Latin America. Américas 21:44 O '69
View North and South; excerpts from Today show interview. por Américas 21:44 Ag '69

PLEASANT POINT reservation. See Indians of North America—Reservations

PLEASANTS, Clarence
Spectacular oleander. Horticulture 47:38-40 Jl '69

PLEASANTS, Henry
Screen and the voice. Opera N 34:8-13 Ja 17 '70

PLEASENCE, Donald
Very, very Pleasence. D. Platt. il pors Harp Baz 102:126-7 Ap '69

PLEASURE, David E. and others
Axonal transport of proteins in experimental neuropathies. bibliog Science 166:524-5 O 24 '69

PLEASURE
Ordeal of fun. F. Trippett. il Look 33:24-34 Jl 29 '69; Same abr. with title Unending quest for fun. Read Digest 95:62-4 D '69
See also
Festivity
Happiness

PLEDGE of allegiance. See Loyalty. Oath of

PLÉE, Auguste
American travels of a French botanist. P. Rouse, jr. il Antiques 96:763-7 N '69

PLEISTOCENE period. See Geology, Stratigraphic—Pleistocene; Paleontology—Pleistocene

PLENDERLEITH, Harold J.
New science of art conservation; reprint. UNESCO Courier 22:56-7+ Ag '69

PLETCHER, J. See Sax, M. jt. auth.

PLEUROCHRYSIS scheffelii. See Algae

PLEWES, Jacqueline
Meet the elders. Org Gard & Farm 16:66-7 Ag '69
Millet, a versatile, nutritious cereal. Org Gard & Farm 16:72-3 Je '69

PLEWES, John
Making bird homes for the garden. Org Gard & Farm 16:82-4 Ja '69

PLIERS
Tools for electronics. T. R. Haskett. il Radio-Electr 40:39-42 S; 58-62 O '69

PLIMMER, Jack R. and others
Photooxidation of DDT and DDE. bibliog Science 167:67-9 Ja 2 '70

PLIMOTH plantation, incorporated
Reality of the Pilgrim fathers. J. Deetz. il Natur Hist 78:32-45 N '69

PLIMPTON, Calvin H.
Amherst college statement. New Repub 160:7 My 17 '69
Everything's rosy at Amherst; summary of statement. 1969. Nat R 21:529 Je 3 '69

PLIMPTON, Francis T. P.
Police must be called if other legal measures fail. N Y Times Mag p 135 My 4 '69

PLIMPTON, George
World series with Marianne Moore; reprint. Wilson Lib Bul 43:626-33 Mr '69

PLINY, the elder
Pliny's pheromonic abortifacients. H. McCully. Science 165:236-7 Jl 18 '69

PLISETSKAĬA, Maĭa Mikhaĭlovna
World of dance. W. Terry. il por Sat R 52:32 Je 21 '69

PLISHKA, Paul
Hooked on opera; interview, ed. by A. M. Lingg. por Opera N 33:13 Ap 19 '69

PLISKE, T. E. and Eisner, Thomas
Sex pheromone of the queen butterfly; biology. bibliog Science 164:1170-2 Je 6 '69

PLOMER, William
Axe in the orchard; poem. Harp Baz 102:130-1 Je '69

PLOSCOWE, Morris
Alimony. bibliog f Ann Am Acad 383:13-22 My '69

PLOTS (drama, novel, etc)
Brainstorming by yourself; plot cards. D. Whitcomb. il Writers Digest 49:54-8 F '69
Getting to where the story is. M. J. Gerber. Writer 82:15-16 Ag '69
Plot isn't a dirty word. Z. Popkin. Writer 82:11-12 Jl '69
Plot, plot—who's got a plot? R. L. Fish. Writer 82:22-3+ Ap '69
Plots and people. H. Waugh. Writer 82:9-11+ D '69
Recipe for a short story. Sister Christine. Writer 82:17-21 D '69
Sorry, your story's too pat. L. Ryker. Writers Digest 49:45-7 Je '69
Stories I guess I won't write. H. Gold. Atlan 224:39-42 Ag '69; Same abr. Writer 82:27 D '69
There's gold in the fine print, personals columns as basis for stories. L. F. Reed. Writers Digest 49:51-3 F '69
Who's afraid of Azucena? O. Rachleff. il Opera N 33:8-11 Mr 29 '69
See also
Dramas—Criticisms, plots, etc.
Moving picture plays—Criticisms, plots, etc.

PLOWING. See Tillage

PLOWS
How to choose a plow. G. E. Melvin. il Suc Farm 67:B2 Ap '69
See also
Snow plows

PLOWSHARE project. See Atomic blasting

PLUCK, George
Historical records. Hobbies 73:35+ F '69

PLUGS, Electric. See Electric wire and wiring

PLUM puddings. See Puddings

PLUM sauce. See Sauces

PLUM trees
Let that seedling grow. D. Foraker. il Org Gard & Farm 16:44-5 Ag '69

PLUMB, Barbara
Different life. Holiday 45:88-91 Ap '69
Home. See issues of New York times magazine

PLUMB, J. H.
Astrologers. Horizon 11:102-3 Sum '69
Beginnings of modern pleasures. Horizon 11:20-5 Spr '69
Perspective. See issues of Saturday review

PLUMB, Robert
Discovery through photography. Sch Arts 69:16-19 D '69

PLUMBING
Fixing up an older home. il Bet Hom & Gard 47:33 My '69
See also
Water distribution

PLUMBING fixture manufacturers association
Heading for costly bath; conviction of leading makers of plumbing supplies. Bsns W p52 My 10 '69
How judgment came for the plumbing conspirators. A. T. Demaree. il Fortune 80:96-9+ D '69
Tub of trouble; antitrust investigation of the bathroom fixtures industry. Time 93:110+ My 16 '69

PLUMBING fixtures. See Shower fixtures

PLUMER, Mary
Penny Plumer's bequest. Read Digest 95:215-16+ O '69

PLUMMER, William T.
Venus clouds: test for hydrocarbons. bibliog Science 163:1191-2 Mr 14 '69
—and Carson, R. K.
Mars: is the surface colored by carbon suboxide? bibliog Science 166:1141-2 N 28 '69

PLUMS
See also
Cookery—Fruit

PLURALISM (political science)
What kind of society do we want? excerpts from The recovery of confidence. J. W. Gardner. Read Digest 95:74-8 S '69

PLUTO (planet)
Pluto's mass and the motion of Neptune. Sky & Tel 37:71+ F '69
Will men ever explore the planet Pluto? J. Reinert. Sci Digest 65:87-8 My '69

PLUTONIUM
Plutonium, the lively element. J. M. Cleveland. il Chem 42:13-16 D '69 (to be cont)
Plutonium-238 in fallout. T. Mamuro and T. Matsunami. bibliog il Science 163:465-7 Ja 31 '69

PLYMOUTH, Mass.
Reality of the Pilgrim fathers. J. Deetz. il Natur Hist 78:32-45 N '69
See also
Pilgrim fathers

PLYWOOD
How to find your best buys in plywood. R. Day. il Pop Sci 195:156-67 S '69
Redwood in plywood form. J. Hand. il Pop Sci 194:142-3+ Ja '69

Prices
No lid on wood prices. il Bsns W p44 Mr 29 '69
Plywood: will peace mean higher prices? Bsns W p44 Je 7 '69
Wood takes a tumble. Bsns W p49 Ap 26 '69

PLYWOOD industry
Boom in wood that busted. il Bsns W p 138 O 25 '69

PLYWOOD siding. See Siding (building)

PNEUMOCOCCI
Cellular factors in genetic transformation. A. Tomasz. il Sci Am 220:38-44 bibliog (p 138) Ja '69

PNEUMOCONIOSIS. See Lungs—Dust diseases

POACHING
See you later, alligator. M. Kane. il Sports Illus 31:38-40+ S 29 '69

POAGE, William Robert
Should we limit government payments per farm? por Farm J 93:15+ Jl '69

about
Thorns on the yellow rose of Texas. R. Coles and H. Huge. New Repub 160:13-17 Ap 19 '69

POCHIN MOULD, Daphne D. C.
Irish air. Flying 84:50-1+ My '69

POCKET books, incorporated
Pocket's art director tells goals for covers. il Pub W 195:70 Ap 7 '69

POCONO MOUNTAINS, Pa.
Honeymoon havens. il Newsweek 73:90-1 Je 23 '69

PODELL, Bertram L.
Excerpt from remarks, August 13, 1969. Cong Digest 48:301+ D '69

PODHORETZ, Norman
Making it in America. J. P. Sisk. Atlan 224:63-8 D '69

PODOCARPUS, Fossil
Podocarpus from the eocene of North America. D. L. Dilcher. bibliog il Science 164:299-301 Ap 18 '69

PODOLSKY, Richard J. See Ford, L. E.; Kushmerick, M. J. jt. auths.

PODUNK (imaginary town)
How things are in Podunk. D. Snell. il **Life**
66:81-2 Ap 18 '69
POE, Edgar Allan
Tender touch. P. W. Schmidtchen. il **por**
Hobbies 73:104-5 F '69
POEM-prayers. See Prayers
POEMS set to music. See Music and literature
POETICAL criticism. See Literary criticism
POETICS
Poet in his poem; address, October 17, 1968.
H. Rago. Poetry 113:413-20 Mr '69
Poets on poetry. Writer 82:30 Mr '69
Poet's workshop. F. Trefethen. See issues
of Writer
Serious look at light verse. J. D. Engle, jr.
Writers Digest 49:47-9+ Jl '69
Students as poets. S. L. Sheeley. Engl J 58:
577-85 Ap '69
Teaching the writing of poetry. L. A. Arndt.
il Sr Schol 94:Schol Teach 16-17 F 14 '69
Third dimension of poetic expression; or, Lan-
guage and harmony. D. Gostuški. bibliog f
il Mus Q 55:372-83 Jl '69
POETRY
Concrete poetry: creative writing for all stu-
dents. L. Mueller. bibliog il Engl J 58:1053-
6 O '69
Poetry and physiology. C. Tomlinson. Po-
etry 114:193-5 Je '69
Poetry place. See issues of Mademoiselle
Serious look at light verse. J. D. Engle, jr.
Writers Digest 49:47-9+ Jl '69
Street works, theatre works enigmatic. J.
Gruen. Vogue 154:66 Ag 1 '69
Verse. R. Whittemore. New Repub 161:25 O
11 '69
Words are the poet's paint; interview, ed.
by D. McConathy. I. H. Finlay. Harp Baz
102:174+ Ap '69
See also
Childrens poems (by children)
Childrens poetry
Christmas poetry
Nursery rhymes
Poets
Political poetry
Religious poetry
Songs
Symbolism in literature
also subhead Poetry under various sub-
jects, e.g. Deer—Poetry; also American
poetry; Latin American poetry; etc.

Appreciation
Journey from apple orchard to swallow
thronged loft; Fern Hill. M. C. Davidow.
bibliog f Engl J 58:78-81 Ja '69

Authorship
Lyrics, heroic and otherwise. R. D. Spector.
Sat R 52:33-5 Mr 15 '69
Poetry: how and why. J. Jerome. See issues
of Writer's digest

Bibliography
Book marks. C. Stein. Nation 208:217 F 17 '69
Nation book marks. C. Stein. Nation 208:611
My 12 '69
Poetry: combatting society with surrealism.
Time 93:72-73A+ Ja 24 '69
Poetry parade. il Sr Schol 94:Schol Teach
18-19+ F 14 '69

Collections
See Anthologies

Competitions
1969 Scholastic writing awards. il Sr Schol
94:21-2 My 9 '69
1969 WD poetry contest. J. Chimsky. Writers
Digest 49:40-2+ O '69

Philosophy
Pop personality; ed. by E. Miller. R. McKuen.
il Seventeen 28:408+ Ag '69

Study and teaching
Benét's John Brown's body; for study. P. J.
Sheehan. Engl J 58:219-25 F '69
Life ain't been no crystal stair; address, 1968.
N. Larrick. il Library J 94:843-5 F 15 '69
Poetry and the senses. R. J. Goba. il Clear
House 44:149-51 N '69
Presenting poetry; symposium. il Sr Schol
94:Schol Teach 8+ F 14 '69
Students as poets. S. L. Sheeley. Engl J 58:
577-85 Ap '69
Untaught teachers and improbable poets. F.
Howe. il Sat R 52:60-2+ Mr 15 '69
Upside-down thing. E. G. Eberhard. Engl
J 58:1192-3 N '69

Values and the poems of Marianne Moore.
C. H. Edsall. Engl J 58:516-18 Ap '69
What comes after Mother Goose. P. Parker.
Ed Digest 35:46-9 O '69

Aids and devices
Avant-rock in the classroom. D. E. Morse.
Engl J 58:196-200+ F '69
Pictures, punchcards, and poetry; address,
November 1968. A. Daigon. Engl J 58:1033-
7 O '69
Presenting poetry; symposium. il Sr Schol
94:Schol Teach 8+ F 14 '69
Two Corys: a sample of inductive teaching.
L. J. Clifton. Engl J 58:414-15 Mr '69

Technique
See Poetics

Themes
See Literature—Themes

Translations and translating
Cheers of John Nims. J. Ciardi. Sat R 52:52
S 20 '69
POETRY (periodical)
Announcement of prize awards for 1969.
Poetry 115:133-5 N '69
For the word, for the silence. R. J. Mills,
jr. Poetry 115:127-30 N '69
Islands waited, wait still . . . H. Carruth.
Poetry 115:130-2 N '69
POETRY and music. See Music and literature
POETRY and science. See Literature and sci-
ence
POETRY contests. See Poetry—Competitions
POETRY editors. See Editors and editing
POETRY festivals. See Literary festivals
POETRY phonograph records. See Phonograph
records—Spoken records
POETRY readings
Dial-a-poem, new poetry rather than weath-
er tips on the telephone. J. Gruen. Vogue
153:116 Mr 1 '69
POETRY society of America, Catholic. See
Catholic poetry society of America
POETS
Poets & critics & poet-critics. M. L. Rosen-
thal. Poetry 114:113-26 My '69
See also
Women as poets
POETS, American
Alone with America, by R. Howard. Review
Nation 209:541-2 N 17 '69. C. Molesworth
America the poetical, and otherwise. A. Nej-
gebauer. New Repub 160:19-22+ Ap 26 '69
Marshmallow literature. J. Greenfeld. Mlle 68:
206-7+ Mr '69
More than jewelry and crystal. M. Williams.
Sat R 52:32-4 Je 14 '69
Poetry as merchandise. A. Caruba. Pub W
196:34 D 29 '69
Robert Lowell and the circle, by J. Mazzaro.
Review
New Repub 160:31-3 My 31 '69
Young poets. H. Junker. il Newsweek 73:83-4+
Mr 3 '69
See also
American poetry
Antoninus, Brother
Benét, S. V.
Berryman, J.
Bishop, E.
Blackburn, P.
Cane, M.
Crane, H.
Creeley, R.
Cummings, E. E.
Ferlinghetti, L.
Frost, R.
Ginsberg, A.
Giovanni, N.
Glück, L.
Jarrell, R.
Knott, B.
Lindsay, V
Logan, J.
Longfellow, H. W.
Lowell, R.
McKuen, R.
Macleish, A.
Merwin, W. S.
Millay, E. S.
Moore, M.
Oppen, G.
Padgett, R.
Poe, E. A.
Rago, H.
Ray, D.
Rexroth, K.
Robinson, E. A.
Roethke, T.

POETS, American—See also—*Continued*
　Schevill, J. E.
　Shapiro, K.
　Sissman, L. E.
　Snyder, G.
　Van Doren, M.
　Waldman, A.
　Weiss, T.
　Wright, J.
POETS, Argentine
　See also
　Borges, J. L.
　Demaria, F.
　Zapata, C.
POETS, British. See Poets, English
POETS, Canadian
　Four poets from Canada. M. Atwood. Poetry 114:202-7 Je '69
　See also
　Cohen, L.
POETS, Cuban
　New York's new blood poets; with poems and translations. I. Goldemberg. il Américas 21:14-20 My '69
POETS, English
　Devalued estate. X. J. Kennedy. Poetry 114: 266-74 Jl '69
　See also
　Auden, W. H.
　Blake, W.
　Brooke, R.
　Browning, R.
　Byron, G. G. N. B.
　English poetry
　Finlay, I. H.
　Fuller, R.
　Graves, R.
　Milton, J.
　Pope, A.
　Swinburne, A. C.
　Thompson, F.
　Wordsworth, W.
POETS, Finnish
　See also
　Haavikko, P.
POETS, French
　Unicorn French poets. D. Kleinbard. Nation 209:290-1+ S 22 '69
　See also
　Follain, J.
POETS, German
　See also
　Biermann, W.
　Goethe, J. W. von
POETS, Italian
　See also
　Annunzio, G. d'
POETS, Nigerian
　See also
　Soyinka, W.
POETS, Peruvian
　See also
　Vallejo, C.
POETS, Puerto Rican
　New York's new blood poets; with poems and translations. L. Goldemberg. il Américas 21:14-20 My '69
POETS, Russian
　See also
　Akhmadulina, B.
　Akhmatova, A. A.
　Russian poetry
POETS, Scottish
　See also
　Burns, R.
POETS, Spanish
　See also
　Jiménez, J. R.
POETS, Welsh
　See also
　Thomas, D.
POETS, playwrights, editors, essayists, novelists club. See PEN club
POFF, Richard H.
　Excerpt from Report on Voting rights act. Cong Digest 48:276+ N '69
POHA. See Husk tomatoes
POHER, Alain
　Caretaker who cares. por Time 93:33 My 9 '69
　France: and now the final vote. il por Newsweek 73:49-50 Je 9 '69
　General's heir takes over. il Time 93:27 Je 20 '69
　Non-candidate. il por Newsweek 73:46 My 19 '69
　Outlook for France: new kind of Gaullism. por U S News 66:16 Je 16 '69
　Poher pulls ahead in France. il por Time 93: 29-30 My 23 '69
　Poher to power? E. Behr. il por Newsweek 73:48+ My 26 '69
　Who'll sit in the Elysee? il por Newsweek 73:42 My 12 '69

POHL, Stephen L. and others
　Glucagon-sensitive adenyl cylase in plasma membrane of hepatic parenchymal cells. bibliog Science 164:566-7 My 2 '69
POILANE, Pierre
　If you're starved for real old-fashioned bread, there's a little man in Paris. D. Muscatine. il por Holiday 46:74-5 S '69
POINDEXTER, Joseph
　Our man in Venezuela. por Duns R 94:3 Jl '69
POINSETT, Alex
　Battle to control black schools. Ebony 24: 44-6+ My '69
　Crusade against the craft unions. Ebony 25: 33-6+ D '69
　Economics of liberation. Ebony 24:150-4 Ag '69
　Quest for a black Christ. Ebony 24:170-2+ Mr '69
　Roy Innis: nation-builder. Ebony 24:170-4+ O '69
POINSETTIAS
　How to keep a poinsettia. L. A. Deming. il Home Gard 56:14 Mr '69
　New poinsettia, the year-round house plant. il Home Gard 56:44-5 D '69
POINT Pinos lighthouse. See Lighthouses
POINTERS (dogs)
　Weimaraner comes of age. D. M. Duffey. il Outdoor Life 143:154+ My '69
POIRIER, Normand
　American atrocity. Esquire 72:59-63+ Ag '69
POIRIER, Richard
　Edward Villella. Vogue 153:192-5+ F 1 '69
POISON gas. See Gases, Asphyxiating and poisonous
POISON hemlock
　Plant that killed Socrates. il Sunset 143:126-7 Ag '69
POISONING. See Poisons
POISONOUS fungi. See Fungi
POISONOUS mushrooms. See Mushrooms
POISONOUS plants
　See also
　Cockleburs
　Poison hemlock
POISONOUS snakes. See Snakes
POISONS
　Abrus precatorius: pretty but poisonous. C. R. Gunn. Science 164:245-6 Ap 18 '69; Reply. R. S. Chakravarthy. 166:44 O 3 '69
　Annals of medicine; cases of organic phosphate poisoning. B. Roueché. New Yorker 45:123-4+ O 11 '69
　Poisonous ingredients in common foods. bibliog Consumer Bul 52:7-8 Ap '69
　See also
　Arsenic
　Botulism
　Lead poisoning
　Sarin
POISONS, Industrial
　See also
　Carbon tetrachloride
POITIER, Sidney
　New lunatics. il por Newsweek 73:81 Je 23 '69
　Walking with Sidney Poitier. L. Tornabene. il pors McCalls 96:52+ Jl '69
POITIERS, Diane de, duchesse de Valentinois
　Diane de Poitiers. B. Bergery. il pors Vogue 54:178-9+ O 1 '69
POKER
　Why people play poker. T. M. Martinez and R. LaFranchi. il Trans-Action 6:30-5+ Jl '69
POKER players
　Why people play poker. T. M. Martinez and R. LaFranchi. il Trans-Action 6:30-5+ Jl '69
POKEWEED
　Poke or Indian poke? which one can we eat? Org Gard & Farm 16:94 Ag '69
　Taming wild plants. E. Gibbons. Org Gard & Farm 16:68-71 Je '69
POKORNY, Theodore R. Jr
　Me and my constructed self. Sch Arts 68:22-3 F '69
POLACH, Jaroslav G.
　Nuclear power in Europe at the crossroads. Bul Atom Sci 25:15-18+ O '69
POLACHECK, Dem
　Physical anthropology. bibliog por Wilson Lib Bul 44:178-83 O '69
POLAND, Fred
　Drug test dilemma. Sci N 96:438 N 8 '69
　High powered research. Sci N 95:174 F 15 '69
　Pulling together. Sci N 96:188 S 6 '69

POLAND
Poland: myth versus reality. R. F. Staar. bibliog f il Cur Hist 56:218-23 Ap '69
   See also
Immigration and emigration—Poland
Jews in Poland
Theater—Poland
Warsaw
World war, 1939-1945—Poland

Foreign relations
Roses for the West Germans; 25th anniversary of Poland's Communist government. il Time 94:30 Ag 1 '69

German invasion
See World war, 1939-1945—Poland

Politics and government
Polish way. K. Huszar. il Newsweek 73:48+ My 5 '69
Roses for the West Germans; 25th anniversary of Poland's Communist government. il Time 94:30 Ag 1 '69

Religious institutions and affairs
   See also
Catholic church in Poland
POLANSKI, Roman
Tragic house on the hill. T. Thompson. il pors Life 67:42-6+ Ag 29 '69
POLANSKY, Sanford A.
Modest fees, large returns. Time 94:46 Ag 15 '69
Staggering practices. Newsweek 74:55 Ag 18 '69
POLAR Bear express. See Railroads—Canada
POLAR bear hunting. See Bear hunting
POLAR bears. See Bears
POLAR exploration
   See also
Antarctic exploration
Arctic exploration
POLAR ice. See Ice—Polar Regions
POLAR REGIONS
   See also
Antarctic Regions
Arctic regions
Glaciers
Ice—Polar Regions
POLAR research
Antarctic atmospheric chemistry; preliminary exploration. W. H. Fischer and others. bibliog il Science 164:66-7 Ap 4 '69
Antarctic research, a prelude to space research; adaptation of address, September 18, 1968. E. Stuhlinger. Space World F-5-65:5-11 My '69
Prelude to space research; Antarctic research program; excerpt from address, September 1968. E. Stuhlinger. Bul Atom Sci 25:24-7 Mr '69
POLARIZATION (electricity)
Cochlear distortion; effect of direct-current polarization. P. Dallos and others. bibliog il Science 164:449-51 Ap 25 '69
   See also
Dipole moments
POLARIZATION of particles
Polarized beams show promise for atomic collision experiments; report of meeting. B. Bederson. bibliog il Phys Today 22:87+ N '69
POLAROID corporation
Polaroid; market value of its stock. il Forbes 103:34-6+ Je 15 '69
Polaroid's big blitz; twelve-day promotion drive. il Bsns W p54 Mr 1 '69
Problems at Polaroid? Newsweek 73:90 F 17 '69
POLAROID Land cameras
Better low-priced camera from Polaroid; Colorpack II. il Consumer Rep 34:297-8 Je '69
Lab report; instrument readouts; model 180. N. Goldberg. il Pop Phot 64:109 Mr '69
Lab report; model 180. C. W. Kennedy. il Pop Phot 64:108+ Mr '69
New Polaroid Land cameras. il Consumer Bul 52:25-7 Ag '69
Polaroid's $30 color camera and five other new Polaroids. E. H. Ortner. il Pop Sci 94:88-90 Ap '69
POLAROID process. See Color photography
POLE vaulting. See Vaulting (sport)
POLES
   See also
Electric lines—Poles

POLICE
   See also
Negro police
Police questioning
Police unions
Policewomen

Bibliography
A basic reading list. Atlan 223:135 Mr '69
Scholarly cop watching. E. Bendiner. Nation 208:515-18 Ap 21 '69

Caricatures and cartoons
Policeman's lot. . . F. Krahn. Atlan 223:100-2 Mr '69

Electronic equipment
See Electronics in criminal investigation, espionage, etc.

Equipment and supplies
Nutcracker. Time 93:27 F 28 '69
Outcry; thoughts on being tear gassed. il Newsweek 73:37 Je 2 '69
   See also
Helmets

Political activities
Politics of blue power. E. Cray. il Nation 208:493-6 Ap 21 '69
Why cops hate liberals, and vice versa. S. M. Lipset. il Atlan 223:76-83 Mr '69

Public relations
Adopt a deputy. P. J. Pitchess. Todays Ed 58:81-2 F '69
Bouquets to the flower cops; Woodstock music and art fair. Chr Cent 86:1130 S 3 '69
Condemnation and persecution of hippies. M. E. Brown. bibliog il Trans-Action 6:33-46 S '69; Excerpts. Cur 112:9-13 N '69
Cop as social scientist; Inspector Fink of Ninth precinct. S. Braun. il N Y Times Mag p46-7+ Ag 24 '69
Cops; symposium. il Nation 208:486-509 Ap 21 '69
Law and order equals status quo? J. B. Kelley. il America 121:323-6 O 18 '69; Reply. J. R. Morgan, jr. 121:514 N 29 '69
People, the police and the park. J. A. Coleman. America 120:668-71 Je 7 '69
Police and Panthers; growing paranoia. il Time 94:14-16 D 19 '69
Police and the community. M. Mead. Redbook 133:38+ Je '69
Policing the third sex. il Newsweek 74:76+ O 27 '69
Relating! Police with people; Los Angeles County sheriff's department. il Am City 84: 142+ Ap '69
Trouble with troubleshooting; police community relations in San Francisco. M. E. Leary. il Atlan 223:94-9 Mr '69
Two cops on a tough beat; excerpts from COP! a closeup of violence and tragedy. L. H. Whittemore. il Life 66:52-4+ Je 20 '69
White institutions & black rage. D. Boesel and others. il Trans-Action 6:24-31 Mr '69

Salaries, allowances, etc.
Police salaries. il Atlan 223:81 Mr '69

Supply and demand
Policemen's lot: happier. il U S News 66: 42-3 Je 2 '69

Trade unions
See Police unions

Training
Disadvantaged youth may fill police vacancies. il Am City 84:66 F '69
Fun and games on the freeway. B. Greene. il Hot Rod 22:140-1 Mr '69
How police confront disaster; Columbus, Ohio simulation study. T. E. Drabek and J. E. Haas. il Trans-Action 6:33-8 My '69
Operation Empathy; project in Covina; Calif. il Newsweek 74:104 D 15 '69

Brazil
   See also
Rio de Janeiro—Police

California
Fastest gun in the West; highway patrol communications system. il Am City 84: 123 Je '69
Outcry; thoughts on being tear gassed. il Newsweek 73:37 Je 2 '69
People, the police and the park. J. A. Coleman. America 120:668-71 Je 7 '69
Terror in a teapot; Berkeley park confrontations. F. Berry and others. il Nation 208:784-8 Je 23 '69

Those little wars. Nation 208:715-16 Je 9 '69

POLICE—*Continued*

Canada

See also
Canada—Royal Canadian mounted police

Europe, Western

How the police work. G. Berkley. New Repub 161:15-18 Ag 2 '69

France

Letter from Paris; citizens on the streets in danger from the French police. Genêt. New Yorker 45:196 N 29 '69

Great Britain

See also
London—Police

Greece, Modern

Greece: government by torture; Asphalia, the security police. C. S. Wren. il Look 33:19-21 My 27 '69
Greece: the rack and the bomb. J. Becket. Nation 209:6-7 Jl 7 '69

Mississippi

Mississippi eyewitness. L. E. Lomax. il Ramp Mag 7:20-4 Ja 25 '69

Russia

See also
Secret service—Russia

South Carolina

Acquittal in Orangeburg; state troopers. Newsweek 73:37 Je 9 '69

United States

Authoritarian prescription. W. D. Phelan, jr. Nation 209:467-73 N 3 '69
Community control of the police. A. I. Waskow. Trans-Action 7:4-7 D '69
Cop! A closeup of violence and tragedy, by L. H. Whittemore. Review
  Newsweek il 74:91+ Jl 7 '69. A. Cooper
Cops; symposium. il Nation 208:486-509 Ap 21 '69
Five good cops. il Esquire 71:68-9 F '69
Guerrilla summer? a different pattern. il Time 93:16-17 Je 27 '69
How the police work. G. Berkley. New Repub 161:15-18 Ag 2 '69
Is the Court handcuffing the cops? J. Vorenberg; J. Q. Wilson. il N Y Times Mag p32-3+ My 11 '69
One way to handle crime; interview. J. J. Harrington. il por U S News 67:62-5 D 22 '69
Persecution and assassination of Black Panther party as directed by guess who. Nat R 21:1306-7 D 30 '69
Police and the rest of us; symposium. il Atlan 223:74-86+ Mr '69
Police: six sociological essays, ed. by D. Bordua. Review
  Trans-Action 6:72-4 S '69. M. Lipsky
Political surveillance: the invisible police. J. R. Lundy. il Nation 209:629-32 D 8 '69
Response of police agencies. G. E. Misner. bibliog f Ann Am Acad 382:109-19 Mr '69
  See also
Police power
Police—Public relations
  also subhead Police under names of cities, e.g. Chicago—Police

Vermont

Ruckus in Irasburg; the case that had the gossips buzzing in Vermont. H. Moffett. il Life 66:62-4+ Ap 4 '69

POLICE, Negro. See Negro police

POLICE, State
  See also
Police—California
Police—South Carolina

POLICE automobiles. See Automobiles, Police
POLICE buildings. See Police stations
POLICE chases
Murder on route 79: one of the most intensive manhunts in California's history. K. Detzer. il Read Digest 94:126-30 F '69
POLICE communication systems
Fastest gun in the West; California highway patrol communications system. il Am City 84:123 Je '69
Merchant's hot line on crime; Charlotte, N.C. il Am City 84:38 Ja '69
POLICE helicopters. See Helicopters in police work
POLICE helmets. See Helmets
POLICE informers. See Informers (law)
POLICE interrogation. See Police questioning
POLICE laboratories. See Criminological laboratories

POLICE motor vehicles. See Motor vehicles, Police
POLICE power
Abuses of police power; excerpt from Police power. P. Chevigny. Atlan 223:128 Mr '69
Are we handcuffing the police? G. L. Hailworth. America 120:128-9 F 1 '69
Mugged by the sheriffs, an anecdote. S H Wildstrom. il Nation 208:496-7 Ap 21 '69
Police power; police abuses in New York city, by P. Chevigny. Review
  Commonweal 90:397-8 Je 20 '69. T. R. Brooks
Those little wars. Nation 208:715-16 Je 9 '69
POLICE questioning
Amplification of Miranda; A. Orozco's case. Time 93:55 Ap 4 '69
Annals of jurisprudence; Whitemore confessions; Wylie-Hoffert. F. C. Shapiro. New Yorker 44:39-42+ F 8 '69
Two cops on a tough beat; excerpts from COP! a closeup of violence and tragedy. L. H. Whittemore. il Life 66:52-4+ Je 20 '69
POLICE services for juveniles
Kid gloves and drugs; Montgomery County, Md. New Repub 160:11-12 Ap 12 '69
POLICE spies. See Police—United States
POLICE state. See Totalitarianism
POLICE stations
It doesn't look like a police station; Racine, Wis. L. C. Jenkins. il Am City 84:107-8 Jl '69
POLICE statistics. See Criminal statistics
POLICE uniforms. See Uniforms, Police
POLICE unions
Card-carrying police? AFL-CIO offer to charter national union. Newsweek 73:66 Mr 3 '69
One big union for the blue Meanys. J. Hill. Commonweal 90:37-8 Mr 28 '69
Police unions and picket lines. U S News 67:96-7 N 17 '69
POLICEMEN. See Police
POLICEWOMEN
Cop teen-agers dig; policewoman P. Thompson. Rochester, N.Y. il Ebony 24:106-8+ Je '69
Heaven's angel; Marshal Winders constitutes the entire police force of University Heights, Ia. il Time 93:21 Ap 25 '69
POLICIES, Insurance. See Insurance—Policies
POLICY loans. See Insurance, Life—Policy loans
POLIGNAC, Winnaretta Eugénie (Singer)
princesse de
Princesse Winnie. R. W. Hall. por Opera N 34:28-31 D 27 '69
POLIKARPOV, G. See Kalnina, Z. jt. auth.
POLIOMYELITIS

Vaccines

Simian virus 40 in polio vaccine: follow-up of newborn recipients. J. F. Fraumeni, jr. and others. bibliog il Science 167:59-60 Ja 2 '70
POLIOMYELITIS virus
Poliovirus crystals within the endoplasmic reticulum of endothelial and mononuclear cells in the monkey spinal cord. K. Blinzinger and others. bibliog il Science 163:1336-7 Mr 21 '69; Discussion. 165:1381 S 26 '69
POLISH laboratory theatre. See Theater—Poland
POLISH theater. See Theater—Poland
POLISHES. See Polishing materials
POLISHING
  See also
Abrasives
POLISHING machines
What's new for polishing and buffing. J. Burroughs. il Pop Mech 132:188-91 S '69
POLISHING materials
Auto cleaner-polishes (cont) il Consumer Rep 34:75 F '69
Copper and brass cleaners and polishes. il Consumer Bul 52:23-4 O '69
Slick finishes from new buffing kits. M. Philips. il Pop Sci 195:126-9 Ag '69
POLITBURO. See Communist party (Russia)—Political bureau
POLITE, Frank
Small craft warnings: From the puritan cookbook: poems. Poetry 114:91-3 My '69
POLITENESS. See Etiquette
POLITICAL attitudes
Is there a backlash vote? analysis of election results in Minneapolis, Los Angeles and New York city. M. J. Goldbloom. Commentary 48:17-26 Ag '69
Orange County bug; white racism. S. Alsop. Newsweek 73:96 Je 30 '69

POLITICAL attitudes—*Continued*
Politics and youth; attitudes of young Americans. T. L. Good and D. A. Bates. bibliog f Clear House 43:396-400 Mr '69
We must avoid the perils of extremism. D. D. Eisenhower. Read Digest 94:103-8 Ap '69
See also
Public opinion

POLITICAL bosses. See Boss rule

POLITICAL bureau of the Communist party. See Communist party (Russia)—Political bureau

POLITICAL cabarets. See Cabarets

POLITICAL campaigns
From the streets to the polls; campaign for a peace Congress. J. D. Barber and D. R. Mayhew. New Repub 161:9-11 D 6 '69; Discussion. 162:33-5 Ja 3 '70
See also
Campaign funds
Television in politics
also subhead Politics and government under names of countries, states, cities, e.g. New York (city)—Politics and government

Chile
Report from Chile: the left prepares for an election. J. Yglesias. il N Y Times Mag p24-5+ Ja 11 '60

France
France: and now the final vote. il Newsweek 73:49-50 Je 9 '69
France: the making of a president. il Newsweek 73:47 Je 2 '69
Making of le president; final days of campaigning. il Time 93:37 My 30 '69

Germany (Federal Republic)
Germans for more of the same. il Newsweek 74:83-4 O 6 '69
On German election stump; a battle of personalities. il U S News 67:22 S 29 '69
Science a political issue. T. Shoemaker. il Sci N 96:252 S 20 '69
West Germany's decision for the 70's. il Time 94:24 O 3 '69
Wrestling under the rug. il Newsweek 74:42 S 15 '69

Rhodesia
Road to apartheid. il Newsweek 73:59 Je 30 '69

POLITICAL cartoons. See Caricatures and cartoons

POLITICAL clubs and associations
Ripon: left spur to the GOP. H. L. Reiter. Nation 208:202-5 F 17 '69
See also
Freedom house (organization)

POLITICAL conventions
See also
National conventions (political)
National conventions, Democratic

POLITICAL corruption. See Politics, Corruption in

POLITICAL crimes and offenses
See also
Anarchism and anarchists
Assassination
Terrorism

Czechoslovakia
Masaryk case, by C. Sterling. Review Time 95:78 Ja 12 '70

Greece, Modern
See also
Political prisoners—Greece, Modern

POLITICAL defectors. See Defectors, Political

POLITICAL ethics
Congressional dirty linen. Tattler. Commonweal 91:327-8 D 12 '69
Duty; question of what to do when your team is doing something you think wrong. P. A. Samuelson. Newsweek 74:108 D 8 '69
New concern over ethics codes. U S News 66:10 My 26 '69
New guidelines on conflict of interest? il U S News 66:27-30 Je 9 '69
Politician as loser. Commonweal 90:276 My 23 '69
See also
Politics, Corruption in
Subversive activities

POLITICAL exiles. See Exiles

POLITICAL forecasts
Crucial tests coming at the polls. il U S News 68:30-3 Ja 5 '70
Political power patterns are changing. il Nations Bsns 57:34-6+ N '69

Prospects of the cultural revolution in 1969. J. Gittings. il Bul Atom Sci 25:23-8 F '69
Realpolitik, 1970. K. Crawford. Newsweek 75:20 Ja 5 '70
See also
Public opinion polls

POLITICAL games. See Games

POLITICAL ghost writing. See Authorship—Collaboration

POLITICAL leadership. See Leadership

POLITICAL liberty. See Liberty

POLITICAL obligations. See Citizenship

POLITICAL parties
See also
Communist parties

Chile
Frei's revolution in suspended animation. D. D. Ranstead. Commonweal 90:190-1 My 2 '69
Report from Chile: the left prepares for an election. J. Yglesias. il N Y Times Mag p24-5+ Ja 11 '70

Czechoslovakia
See also
Communist party (Czechoslovakia)

Dominican Republic
Yes, we have no bananas. R. Shereff. Commonweal 89:497-9 Ja 17 '69; Discussion. 90:35+ Mr 28 '69

Germany
History
Ghost of social-fascism. T. Draper. bibliog Commentary 47:29-42 F '69; Discussion. 47:4+ My '69

Germany (Federal Republic)
Brandt on the threshold. il Newsweek 74:46-7 O 13 '69
Change in the heart of Europe; shift to S.P.D. government. Chr Cent 86:1337 O 22 '69
Demolishing a shibboleth; Free democratic party favors recognition of East Germany. Time 93:31 Ap 25 '69
Echoes from an unhappy past; National democratic party. Time 94:32 S 26 '69
Election pegged to the mark; whether to raise the parity of undervalued currency. il Bsns W p26 Ag 23 '69
Grass at the roots; crusade on behalf of the Social democratic party. Time 94:24+ S 5 '69
Healthy democratic consensus in Germany. Life 67:38 O 10 '69
Mutations left and right. J. A. Morris, jr. Nation 208:423-5 Ap 7 '69
One man's meat; NPD. Newsweek 74:49 S 22 '69
Thinking big for Germany. il Newsweek 73:51-2 Je 9 '69
West Germany: outcasts at the helm; Social democrats to take power. il Time 94:24-6+ O 10 '69
Wrestling under the rug; CDU-SDP battle. il Newsweek 74:42 S 15 '69

Great Britain
See also
Conservative party (Great Britain)
Labor party (Great Britain)

Guatemala
Flash point for terror. W. Sloat. Commonweal 91:37-8 O 10 '69

India
Coming apart; Congress party. il Newsweek 74:66+ N 17 '69
Going it alone; Congress party split. Newsweek 74:63+ N 24 '69
India's Congress party at the crossroads. J. D'Souza. America 121:582-5 D 13 '69
Two parties face to face. il Time 94:36 N 21 '69

Italy
See also
Socialist party (Italy)

Japan
Inukai Tsuyoshi: some dilemmas in party development in pre-World war II Japan; address, December 1966. T. Najita. bibliog f Am Hist R 74:492-510 D '68
Lotus power; emergence of the Komeito party. il Newsweek 75:46 Ja 19 '70
Socialism on the ropes. il Time 95:21 Ja 12 '70

Kenya
Pulling apart; government crackdown against the Kenya people's union. il Newsweek 74:48+ N 10 '69

POLITICAL parties—*Continued*

Latin America

Taps for Christian democrats? R. Peter. Nat R 21:700 Jl 15 '69

Russia

See also
Communist party (Russia)

South Africa

Fight goes on. il Time 94:36 O 24 '69
New right; Herstige nasionale party. Newsweek 74:73 D 8 '69

Sweden

Hot soup from Olof; new Social democratic leader. il Time 94:38 O 10 '69
I am curious (P.M.) Palme to head Social democratic party. il Newsweek 74:47 O 13 '69

United States

Cities and the election of 1928; partisan realignment? J. M. Clubb and H. W. Allen. bibliog f il Am Hist R 74:1205-20 Ap '69
End of American party politics. W. D. Burnham. bibliog il Trans-Action 7:12-22 D 69
End of liberalism? I. Kristol. Cur 103:6-15 Ja '69
George Wallace's goals for '72. il U S News 66:39 Je 9 '69
Now, NCASPAIPAPIPCPCPCP; right-wing groups form another conservative party. il Time 93:22 Mr 7 '69
President Nixon and the two-party system. M. Mead. Redbook 132:54+ Mr '69
South's changing politics. il U S News 66:32-4 Mr 24 '69
Wallace whitelash. S. M. Lipset and E. Raab. il Trans-Action 7:23-32+ D '69
See also
Communist party (United States)
Democratic party
National conventions (political)
Populist party
Republican party

History

Changing concepts of party in the United States: New York, 1815-1828. M. Wallace. bibliog f Am Hist R 74:453-91 D '68

Vietnam

Thieu-ing the loyal opposition; peace and parties of peace are unwelcome. T. Fox. Commonweal 90:459-62 Jl 25 '69
See also
Communist party (Vietnam [Republic])

Zambia

Life in Zambia: on the firing line. J. Horgan. Commonweal 89:490-1 Ja 17 '69

POLITICAL patronage. See Patronage, Political

POLITICAL philosophy
American historians and the democratic idea; address. I. Kristol. Am Scholar 39:89-104 Wint '69
Improbable guru of surrealistic politics. I. Kristol. il Fortune 80:191+ Jl '69
Politics as the art of the impossible; address, June 1, 1969. D. P. Moynihan. Am Scholar 38:573-83 Aut '69
Thought and practice of enlightened government in French Corisca; adaptation of address, December 29, 1967. T. E. Hall. bibliog f Am Hist R 74:880-905 F '69
See also
Communism and democracy
Democracy
Liberalism
Nationalism
Natural law
Political thought
Racism

POLITICAL poetry

Bibliography

Politics of poetry. A. Laing. Nation 209:26+ Jl 7 '69

POLITICAL power. See Power (political science)

POLITICAL prisoners
Brief visit to the third world: Guyana and Vietnam. S. W. Mintz. Yale R 59:151-60 O '69
Sort of a free world. C. McCarthy. New Repub 160:16-18 F 8 '69

China (People's Republic)

End of the ordeal. Time 94:59-60+ O 24 '69

Greece, Modern

Greece: the death of liberty. J. Corry. Harper 239:72-81 O '69
One man's odyssey; G. Mylonas leaves Greece. Newsweek 74:54 O 20 '69
Prisoner of Amorgos; G. Mylonas. N. Gage. il N Y Times Mag p23-5+ S 21 '69; Discussion. p 16+ O 12; 16+ O 26 '69
Torture; activities of the Greek junta; excerpts from report of the Human rights commission of the Council of Europe. il Newsweek 74:52 D 15 '69
Unmentionable issue: torture of prisoners. il Time 94:39-40 D 12 '69

Korea (People's Republic)

Crew of U.S.S. Pueblo released at Panmunjom; U.S. position on facts unchanged; statements, December 22, 1968, with North Korean document. L. B. Johnson; D. Rusk. Dept State Bul 60:1-3 Ja 6 '69
Moving finger rites; crew of the Pueblo. E. H. Brandt. il Esquire 72:253-6+ D '69

Russia

My testimony; tr. by M. Gnoutcheff and R. Nacht. A. Marchenko. il Read Digest 95:193-6+ Ag '69
Torture in the USSR. P. J. Lyons. il Nat R 21:1259-60 D 16 '69

Vietnam (Democratic Republic)

Two groups of prisoners: American captives in North Vietnam. Chr Cent 86:1010 Jl 30 '69

Vietnam (Republic)

Devil's island off Vietnam; the price of political dissent. T. Fox. Commonweal 90:432-5 Jl 11 '69
Jail notes of a young Vietnamese; tr. by D. Marr. Nguyen-van-Minh. Nation 208:359-62 Mr 24 '69
Political freedom in Vietnam. R. F. Drinan. America 120:731-3 Je 28 '69
Spotlight on Vietnam; findings of U.S. interreligous study team. Nation 209:2-3 Jl 7 '69
Ultimate form of corruption; discrepancy between State department assertions and the facts in South Vietnam. R. F. Drinan. New Repub 161:15-16 Jl 19 '69
Vietnam: sojourn and sequel. J. Armstrong and J. Conyers, jr. il Chr Cent 86:1307-9 O 15 '69

POLITICAL psychology
Elm street's new White House power. A. J. Reichley. il Fortune 80:70-3+ D '69
Emerging Republican majority, by K. P. Phillips. Review
Nat R 21:913 S 9 '69. M. S. Evans
See also
Political attitudes
Public opinion

POLITICAL publicity. See Propaganda; Television in politics

POLITICAL rhetoric. See Rhetoric

POLITICAL satire. See Politics—Anecdotes, facetiae, satire, etc.

POLITICAL science
See also
Anarchism and anarchists
Bureaucracy
Communism
Equality
Liberalism
Political philosophy
Politics
Power (social sciences)
Public administration
Socialism
State, The
Totalitarianism

POLITICAL theory. See Political philosophy

POLITICAL thought
End of liberalism? I. Kristol. Cur 103:6-15 Ja '69
Marcuse and Goodwin tangle at Temple; colloquium on Marxism, religion and the liberal tradition. J. Groutt. Commonweal 90:279-80 My 23 '69
Plight of the U.S. liberals; signs that an era is ending. il U S News 67:38-41 Jl 14 '69
Politicizing the lower-middle. M. Novak. Commonweal 90:341-3 Je 6 '69
Theology for radical politics, by M. Novak. Review
Commonweal 90:369-72 Je 13 '69. S. Max

POLITICIANS
Bright future for politicians. il Ebony 24:88-9 Jl '69
Sweepstakes of the '70s: five entries; young political figures. il Newsweek 73:27-8 F 24 '69
See also
Statesmen

POLITICO-military affairs, Bureau of. See United States—State, Department of

POLITICS
Mission of politics; tr. by D. Noakes. P. Mendes-France. Sat R 52:14-15 My 31 '69
   See also
Liberalism
Political parties
Politicians
Scientists—Political activities
Television in politics
   also subhead Politics and government under names of countries, states, etc., e.g. Spain—Politics and government

    Anecdotes, facetiae, satire, etc.
He wows them in Washington; political humorist M. Russell. il N Y Times Mag p 113-14+ N 9 '69
Mosquito that stang; El Zancudo. G. Arciniegas. il Américas 21:22-31 O '69

    Terminology
Nixon neologisms. Newsweek 73:33-4 Je 9 '69

POLITICS, Corruption in
Answer to corruption. B. Graham. Nations Bsns 57:46-9 S '69
Get Douglas, get the liberals. Nation 208:716 Je 9 '69
Soft states of South Asia; the civil servant problem; address, November 14, 1968. K. G. Myrdal. Bul Atom Sci 25:7-10 Ap '69
   See also
Boss rule
Conflict of interests (public office)
Misconduct in office
Patronage, Political

    California
Web that links San Francisco's Mayor Alioto and the Mafia. R. Carlson and L. Brisson. il Look 33:17-21 S 23 '69

    Illinois
Roof caves in on Mayor Daley's housing plan. il Bsns W p56-7 Ag 30 '69

    New Jersey
City under indictment; Corruption by consent. il Time 94:10-11 D 26 '69
Corruption and crime, charges on a mass scale. il U S News 67:6 D 29 '69
Gyp's last tape; conspiracy-extortion trial of A. DeCarlo. Newsweek 75:23 Ja 19 '70
Jersey bounce. il Newsweek 74:27 D 22 '69
Listening in on the Mafia; excerpts from transcript. il Time 95:20-1 Ja 19 '70
Mayor in the dock. il Newsweek 74:21-2 D 29 '69
Mob scene in Jersey. W. Schechner. Commonweal 89:514-15 Ja 24 '69
Mobsters in pasture; Nostra Jersey. F. J. Cook. il Nation 208:105-10 Ja 27 '69
Why New Jersey? Nation 209:716-17 D 29 '69

    Ohio
Governor and the mobster; with report by D. Walsh. il Life 66:28-32A My 2 '69

    Philippines
Lawless and corrupt Philippines. A. Campbell. New Repub 160:15-17 My 17 '69
POLITICS and art. See Art and politics
POLITICS and authors. See Authors and politics
POLITICS and economics. See Economics and politics
POLITICS and education
Governance of education; excerpts from address, August 1969. F. Keppel. Ed Digest 35:9-12 D '69
Politics of resegregation. G. Orfield. il Sat R 52:58-60+ S 20 '69
   See also
College professors and instructors—Political activities
College students—Political activities
Colleges and universities—Political control
Teachers—Political activities
POLITICS and food. See Food supply—Political aspects
POLITICS and justice. See Justice and politics
POLITICS and medicine
AMA: doctors and politics; annual meeting. il Newsweek 74:86-7 Jl 28 '69
POLITICS and newspapers. See Newspapers and politics
POLITICS and religion
Case for Christian biopolitics. K. Cauthen. Chr Cent 86:1481-3 N 19 '69
Case of the jail-bound Jesuit; D. Berrigan. J. Roddy. Look 33:63-5 Ap 15 '69

Political theology; relationship between theology and politics. F. Herzog. Chr Cent 86:975-8 Jl 23 '69
   See also
Church and state
POLITICS and science. See Science and state
POLITICS and war
Role of the military; the power of the Pentagon. E. J. McCarthy. Cur 105:20-4 Mr '69
POLK, Duvan
Promise of oranges; story. Good H 168:80-1 F '69
POLK, Judd
Rise of world corporations. Sat R 52:32-4+ N 22 '69
POLK, Louis Frederick, 1930-
Leisure dynamics has very rich friends. il por Bsns W p60-1 N 15 '69
Nest egg is unscrambled. Bsns W p63 Ja 10 '70
POLK, R. L, and company
Milking the most from auto sales. il Bsns W p84-6 Ap 26 '69
POLL of the people. See Referendum
POLLACK, Henry N.
Gravitational mechanism for sea-floor spreading. bibliog Science 163:176-7 Ja 10 '69
POLLACK, Jack Harrison
Juvenile journalists find humor in a hospital. Todays Health 47:12-13 Ap '69
POLLACK, Seymour
Other Sirhan. Newsweek 73:44-5 Ap 14 '69
POLLACK, Sidney S. and DeCarli, P. S.
Enstatite: disorder produced by a megabar shock event. bibliog Science 165:591-2 Ag 8 '69
POLLAK, Felix
Playing the bookmarket. pors Library J 94:2890-1 S 1 '69
POLLAK, Richard
Missileland. Harper 239:82-6+ O '69
Time: after Luce. Harper 239:42-52 Jl '69
POLLAK, Stephen J.
Excerpt from letter, June 26, 1969. Cong Digest 48:281+ N '69
POLLARD, Barbara
Teaching English, the English way. Engl J 58:586-90 Ap '69
POLLARD, Spencer Drummond
Hope's candidate. Sat R 52:40 Ap 12 '69
POLLARDING. See Pruning
POLLEN, Peregrine
As I see it; interview, ed. by W. Welch and S. Fogelson. por Forbes 103:50+ Ap 15 '69
POLLINATION. See Fertilization of plants
POLLMAN, Ernest W.
Casting with glass. Ceram Mo 17:26-7 Ja '69
POLLOCK, Jackson
Art; works in Peggy Guggenheim collection. L. Alloway. Nation 208:221-2 F 17 '69
POLLOCK, Shirley E.
Parent-student panels. Todays Ed 58:54 D '69
POLLUTION
• America the beautiful doomed? interview. W. J. Hickel. il U S News 67:60-2+ N 10 '69
• America the befouled. il Time 94:70 O 10 '69
Can man survive his environment? ed. by J. Mandelstam. il Sr Schol 95:2-3 O 27 '69
Can we keep our planet habitable? symposium. bibliog il UNESCO Courier 22:4-40 Ja '69
• Conservation equals survival. W. Stegner. Am Heritage 21:12-15 D '69
Danger; America's environmental problems. A. Wolff. il Look 33:28-33 N 4 '69
Environment, and what to do about it; address, May 5, 1969. G. T. Seaborg. il Am For 75:38-9+ S; 22-3+ O '69
Environmental contamination; address, February 1, 1969. M. V. Anthony. Vital Speeches 35:434-8 My 1 '69
Environmental pollution; address, November 6, 1969. J. E. Swearingen. Vital Speeches 36:118-21 D 1 '69
Good earth? J. G. Mitchell. il Newsweek 74:57-9 Jl 7 '69
If you don't mind my saying so. J. W. Krutch. Am Scholar 39:18+ Wint '69
Industrial pollution. America 120:574 My 17 '69
Obituary for DDT (in Michigan) H. Higdon. il N Y Times Mag p6-7+ Jl 6 '69
Our environment; commitment or complacency; address, August 11, 1969. L. P. Weicker, jr. Vital Speeches 35:732-5 S 15 '69
Our national EQ: the first National wildlife federation index of environmental quality. T. L. Kimball. il Nat Wildlife 7:2-13 Ag '69
Our poisoned planet; reprint. il UNESCO Courier 22:34-5 Ag '69
Polluting the planet; time to stop the plunder. J. Davy. Cur 103:59-62 Ja '69

POLLUTION—*Continued*
Pollution: worldwide problem. il U S News 66:42-3 Je 9 '69
Prosecuting pollution. Time 95:41 Ja 5 '70
Summer: long and hot, wet and dry, and freaky; questioning effect of man-made pollution. il U S News 67:4 Jl 28 '69
Technology and the natural environment. B. Commoner. il Arch Forum 130:68-73 Je '69
We must stop pollution now. G. M. Landau. il Parents Mag 44:74-5+ N '69
Worries of a Nebraska farmer and a Missouri biologist. J. Olds. Org Gard & Farm 16:66-70 D '69
Young eco-activists; concern with environmental damage. Time 94:43 Ag 22 '69
See also
Air pollution
Soil pollution
Space pollution
United States—Congress—Senate—Environmental pollution. Subcommittee on
Water pollution

Control
Clean up on clean up? pollution-control stocks. C. Morgello. il Newsweek 75:73 Ja 19 '70
Effluent of the affluent; direct legal action against offenders. C. Peet. il Am For 75: 16-19+ My '69
Energy for man and environmental protection. P. Sporn. Science 166:555 O 31 '69; Discussion. 166:1459-60+ D 19 '69
Environment: ACS report is practical anti-pollution guide P. M. Boffey. Science 165: 1104-7 S 12 '69
London: victory over smog. il U S News 67: 77 D 15 '69
New bag on campus. il Newsweek 74:72 D 22 '69
New conservation; excerpts from address. F. Church. il Parks & Rec 4:36-40+ S '69
Policing the polluters; National environmental policy act of 1969. il Time 94:42 Ag 1 '69
Pollution control: Sweden sets up an ambitious new program. D. S. Greenberg. Science 166:200-1 O 10 '69
Pollution: growing menace, what U.S. is doing about it. il U S News 66:40-3 Je 9 '69
Professor with the answers to pollution. Bsns W p65 Ja 3 '70
Saving the world the ecologist's way. R. W. Stock. il N Y Times Mag p32-3+ O 5 '69
Science yells for industry's help against pollution. il Bsns W p62-3 Ja 3 '70
Tackling the environment; Overview group formed by S. Udall. Time 93:18 F 7 '69
Under the rug; problems of toxic waste disposal in deep injection wells. D. M. Evans and A. Bradford. bibliog il Environ 11:3-13+ O '69
What you can do about pollution. A. R. Roalman. il Todays Health 47:24-7 Mr '69
See also
Aerospace industries—Pollution control activities

Economic aspects
Who will foot the cleanup bill? il Bsns W p63-4 Ja 3 '70

Laws and legislation
Fight over who cleans up; Muskie vs. Jackson. Bsns W p46 Jl 12 '69
Hickel backs strong pollution bill. Sci N 95: 258 Mr 15 '69
Let's pass some organic laws. J. Olds. Org Gard & Farm 16:46-7 N '69
What the polluters wanted. il Sci N 96:589 D 27 '69

Sweden
Pollution control: Sweden sets up an ambitious new program. D. S. Greenberg. Science 166:200-1 O 10 '69
POLLUTION of lakes. See Water pollution
POLLUTION of streams. See Water pollution
POLMAR, Norman
NC-4 preserved; letter. Aviation W 90:94 F 10 '69
POLNER, Murray
Eighteen minute verdict. Commonweal 90: 40-3; 91:3+ Mr 28, O 3 '69
Enemy of the people. Commonweal 90:560 S 19 '69
No Jew nor Catholic need apply. Commonweal 90:386-7 Je 20 '69
POLONSKY, Abraham
Parts of some time spent with Abraham Polonsky. W. Pechter. il por Film Q 22:14-19 Wint '68
POLOS, Nicholas G.
Paperback power. Sr Schol 94:Schol Teach 32-5 Ja 31 '69

POLSCER, Kenneth F.
Fertilizing tips from the experimental farm. Org Gard & Farm 16:42-3 Mr '69
Pears are easy for us! Org Gard & Farm 16: 25-7 S '69
Which mulch is best for potatoes? Org Gard & Farm 16:69-72 F '69
POLSHEK, Julie
It's worth mentioning. See issues of House beautiful
Take it easy. See issues of House beautiful
POLSINELLI, M. and others
Short fragments from both complementary strands in the newly replicated DNA of bacteriophage SPP-1. bibliog Science 166: 243-5 O 10 '69
POLTERGEISTS. See Ghosts
POLYANTHUS. See Primroses
POLYDIPSIA. See Thirst
POLYETHERS. See Ethers
POLYETHYLENE
Massive internal fracture of an amorphous polyester; polyethylene terephthalate. I. V. Yannas. bibliog il Science 166:227-8 O 10 '69
Polyethylene is up off the floor. il Bsns W p76+ N 8 '69
POLYGAMY
Twelve wives of Chief Ogunde. il Ebony 24:106-8+ O '69
POLYGRAPH
How a lie detector works. McCalls 96:52 Ap '69
Man who reads nature's secret signals. T. Bacon. il Nat Wildlife 7:4-8 F '69
POLYIMIDES. See Resinous products
POLYMERASES
Active center of DNA polymerase. A. Kornberg. bibliog il Science 163:1410-18 Mr 28 '69
Enzyme from calf thymus degrading the RNA moiety of DNA-RNA hybrids: effect on DNA-dependent RNA polymerase. H. Stein and P. Hausen. bibliog il Science 166:393-5 O 17 '69
Mammalian DNA polymerase: separation of binding from incorporation of deoxyribonucleoside triphosphates. P. Ove and J. Laszlo. bibliog il Science 165:903-4 Ag 29 '69
POLYMERIC water. See Water
POLYMERIZATION
Amateur scientist; how to make photographs in polymer and build a sensitive pressure gauge. G. Oster. il Sci Am 221:128-32 D '69
POLYMERS
Polymer from water. il Sci N 96:23-4 Jl 12 '69
Polywater. E. R. Lippincott and others. bibliog il Science 164:1482-7 Je 27 '69
Spectra suggest anomalous water is a stable polymer of H_2O. M. S. Rothenberg. bibliog il Phys Today 22:61-2 S '69
Water that won't freeze. J. Lear. il Sat R 52:49-52 S 6 '69
See also
Elastomers
Plastics
Polyethylene

Fracture
See Fracture of solids

Thermal properties
High-temperature plastics. A. H. Frazer. il Sci Am 221:96-100+ Jl '69
POLYMETHACRYLIC acid. See Methacrylic acid
POLYMORPHISM
Modified spinel, beta-manganous orthogermanate: stability and crystal structure. N. Morimoto and others. bibliog il Science 165: 586-8 Ag 8 '69
Sulfur melting and polymorphism under pressure: outlines of fields for twelve crystalline phases. G. C. Vezzoli and others. bibliog il Science 166:218-21 O 10 '69
POLYMORPHISM (biology)
Esterase heterogeneity: dynamics of a polymorphism. R. K. Koehn. bibliog il Science 163:943-4 F 28 '69
Genetic polymorprism of tetrazolium oxidase in dogs. E. W. Baur and R. T. Schorr. bibliog il Science 166:1524-5 D 19 '69
Glucose-6-phosphate dehydrogenase deficient red cells: resistance to infection by malarial parasites. L. Luzzatto and others. bibliog il Science 164:839-42 My 16 '69
Hemophilia A: polymorphism detectable by a factor VIII antibody. D. Feinstein and others. bibliog il Science 163:1071-2 Mr 7 '69

POLYMORPHISM (botany)
Polymorphism in an inbreeding population under models involving underdominance. S. K. Jain and K. B. L. Jain. bibliog il Science 166:1294-6 D 5 '69
POLYMORPHONUCLEAR leukocytes. See Leukocytes
POLYNESIA
Traveler's camera. L. Barry. il Pop Phot 65: 54+ N '69
See also
Easter Island

Antiquities
Polynesia raises her sites; restoration of ancient religious and ceremonial sites. il Travel 132:66-7 D '69
POLYOLS
Polyol pathway in aorta; regulation by hormones. R. S. Clements, jr. and others. bibliog il Science 166:1007-8 N 21 '69
POLYOMA virus. See Tumor viruses
POLYPEPTIDES. See Peptides
POLYRIBONUCLEOTIDES. See Nucleotides
POLYSACCHARIDES
Acid polysaccharides from invertebrate connective tissue: phylogenetic aspects. R. L. Katzman and R. W. Jeanloz. bibliog il Science 166:758-9 N 7 '69
Biosynthesis of oligosaccharides and polysaccharides in plants. W. Z. Hassid. bibliog il Science 165:137-44 Jl 11 '69
Immunochemistry of newly found substituents of polysaccharides of rhizobium species. W. F. Dudman and M. Heidelberger. bibliog il Science 164:954-5 My 23 '69
See also
Glycogen
POLYSOMES. See Nucleoproteins
POLYSTYRENE block printing. See Block printing
POLYTECHNIC institute, Brooklyn
Mural painting for science & technology. A. J. Tobias. il Am Artist 33:46-52 Mr '69
POLYVINYLSULFATE. See Vinyl compounds
POLYWATER. See Water
POMANDERS
All through the house; follow your nose. N. Mandelbaum. McCalls 96:40 My '69
How to make the traditional, scented pomander ball. il House B 111:28 D '69
POMARE, Eleo
Eleo Pomare. por Ebony 25:94-6+ D '69
POMERANTZ, Seymour H.
L-Tyrosine-3,5-³H assay for tyrosinase development in skin of newborn hamsters. bibliog Science 164:838-9 My 16 '69
POMEROY, Kenneth B.
Key people. Am For 75:30-1 Ag '69
Scandinavian forestry. por Am For 75:24-7 Ag '69
South of the border. Am For 75:38-9 D '69
POMEROY, Mary (Barnas)
Ecuador's edible jewels. il Américas 21:33-7 Ap '69
POMEROY, Ralph
Yankee impressionists: impressive, impressionable. Art N 67:50-1+ N '68
POMPANO fishing
Longest silence; fly-fishing for permit. T. McGuane. il Sports Illus 31:92-6+ D 1 '69
Permit: monarch of the flats. A. J. McClane. il Field & S 74:122-6 Ag '69
POMPEI, Gian Franco
ILO 50th anniversary; address, May 8, 1969. UNESCO Courier 22:4-7 Jl '69
POMPE'S disease. See Metabolism, Disorders of
POMPIDOU, Georges
De Gaulle's successor; any better for U.S.? il por U S News 66:58-9 Je 30 '69
End of an era: France after de Gaulle. il Newsweek 73:41-2+ My 12 '69
Enter President Pompidou. il por Newsweek 73:42-3 Je 23 '69
European literary scene. R. J. Clements. por Sat R 52:29 Jl 5 '69
For France: a new man, a new mood. I. Ross. por Read Digest 95:132-6 N '69
France: and now the final vote. il por Newsweek 73:49-50 Je 9 '69
France enters a new era. il por Time 93: 30+ My 9 '69
France takes the exit in stride. il por Bsns W p82-5 My 3 '69
France: the birth of Pompidoulism. il por Time 93:41 Je 13 '69
France: the making of a president. il Newsweek 73:47 Je 2 '69
France: the next seven years. il Newsweek 73:51 Je 30 '69
France: the power passes to Pompidou. il por Time 93:22+ Je 27 '69

French face mediocrity. F. Ungeheuer. Time 94:34+ S 26 '69
Gaullism without de Gaulle. R. Bosc. America 121:13-15 Jl 5 '69
General's heir takes over. il por Time 93:27 Je 20 '69
Letter from Paris; concerning first televised message. Genêt. New Yorker 45:45-6 D 27 '69
Letter from Paris; President's first press conference. Genêt. New Yorker 45:135-6 O 4 '69
Mandate of Monsieur Pompidou. Life 66:34 Je 13 '69
Matter of style. Newsweek 74:40+ Jl 21 '69
More practical and down to earth: the likely successor to de Gaulle. por U S News 66:16 My 12 '69
New France under Pompidou? por U S News 67:16 Jl 21 '69
Not yet, Josephine... il por Time 93:28 Ja 31 '69
Now a pretender to the Gaullist throne. H. de Turenne. il pors N Y Times Mag p30-1+ F 23 '69
Outlook for France: new kind of Gaullism. por U S News 66:16 Je 16 '69
Perils of Pompidou. C. Bourdet. Nation 208:812 Je 30 '69
Pom-pi-dou, Pom-pi-dou. Newsweek 73:44+ Je 16 '69
Pompidou versus the flaming franc. il por Bsns W p44+ Je 21 '69
Première at the Elysée. por Time 94:36+ Jl 18 '69
Something human; new cabinet. il por Newsweek 74:28-30 Jl 7 '69
Whispering campaign. il por Newsweek 73: 60+ Mr 17 '69
Who'll sit in the Elysee? il por Newsweek 73:43 My 12 '69
Why Pompidou? G. Comte. Nat R 21:695+ Jl 15 '69
Without de Gaulle, France goes for his disciple. il pors Life 66:32-3 Je 13 '69
PONCE DE LEON, Michael
Experiments in three dimensions. C. Gray. il Art in Am 57:72-3 My '69
PONCHIELLI, Amilcare
Records:
La Gioconda. Opera N 33:33 F 22 '69
POND, John
John Pond: sixth astronomer Royal. J. Ashbrook. bibliog il Sky & Tel 38:224-5 O '69
PONGE, Francis
Taking sides with things; tr. by F. Brown. Harp Baz 102:262-3 S '69
PONNELLE, Jean Pierre
Dual control; interview. ed. by G. Loney. por Opera N 34:25 D 27 '69
PONTE, Vincent de Pasciuto
Vincent Ponte: a new kind of urban designer. P. Blake. il Art in Am 57:62-7 S '69
PONTECORVO, Salvatore F.
Sandblaster that cleans all my spark plugs. Pop Sci 195:146-7+ S '69
PONTI, Carlo
Ponti; interview. New Yorker 45:31-2 Ap 5 '69
PONTIAC, III.
Pullman's plan to export garbage. Bsns W p38+ Ja 10 '70
PONTIAC, Mich.

Bridges
Aluminum pedestrian bridge a first. J. Koren. il Am City 84:49 F '69

Education
Sensitivity in Pontiac; human-relations institute. Time 94:44+ S 19 '69
PONTIFICAL commission for studies on Justice and peace
See also
Joint committee on society, development and peace
PONTIFICAL Gregorian university. See Rome (city)—Pontifical Gregorian university
POOFI drama. See Schoenewolf, G.
POOLE, Herbert
Piedmont university center. por Library J 94:1841-3 My 1 '69
POOLE, John C. See Jensen, A. C. jt. auth.
POOLE, Stafford
Americanizing American religious life. America 120:297-300 Mr 15 '69
POOLS. See Garden pools; Swimming pools
POOR
Poor in the early church. J. J. Magee. il America 121:164-5 S 13 '69
See also
Church and social problems
Housing
Legal aid
Poverty
Public welfare
Slums

POOR—*Continued*

Psychology

Poverty: the psychological effects. P. Douglas. Chr Today 14:13 N 21 '69

Social action, the therapy of poor folk. R. Bitensky. Ment Hy 53:503-8 O '69

Mexico

Mexico's other half: it's still poverty. il Bsns W p 130 Jl 12 '69

Possessions of the poor. O. Lewis. il Sci Am 221:114-24 O '69

Peru

Reports: Peru. W. S. Just. Atlan 223:12+ My '69

Puerto Rico

Death of Dolores; excerpt from Six women: three generations in a Puerto Rican family. O. Lewis. il Trans-Action 6:10-19 My '69

One can suffer anywhere; excerpt from Six women: a study of three generations in a Puerto Rican family. O. Lewis. Harper 238: 54-60 My '69

United States

American underclass; symposium. bibliog il Trans-Action 6:9-53 F '69; Reply with rejoinder. E. Van Den Haag. 6:62-4 Ap '69

Arithmetic of poverty. B. L. Masse. America 121:356-7 O 25 '69

Courts have failed the poor. J. S. Wright. il N Y Times Mag p26-7+ Mr 9 '69; Reply. M. B. Stecher. p86 Ap 6 '69

Employment developments in urban poverty neighborhoods. P. M. Ryscavage. bibliog il Mo Labor R 92:51-6 Je '69

Food, nutrition and health; address, December 2, 1969. R. M. Nixon. Vital Speeches 36:162-5 Ja 1 '70

George's Branch, Ky; Rado Combs, former miner and his family. W. Hedgepeth. il Look 33:25-33 Mr 4 '69

Inequality: a trend analysis. P. Roby. bibliog f Ann Am Acad 385:110-17 S '69

It's there, all right. il Newsweek 73:28 Mr 3 '69

Measuring unemployment and subemployment in the Mississippi Delta. R. A. White. il Mo Labor R 92:17-23 Ap '69

Men in poverty neighborhoods: a status report; with charts. H. M. Willacy. bibliog f Mo Labor R 92:23-7 F '69

Myth of American affluence. S. Thernstrom. Commentary 48:74-8 O '69

New thrust toward economic security; address, July 28, 1969. W. M. Young, jr. Vital Speeches 35:759-63 O 1 '69

OEO and the working poor; General accounting office report. America 120:391 Ap 5 '69

On behalf of the poor. Commonweal 91:395-6 Ja 9 '70

Perspectives on poverty; symposium. bibliog f il Mo Labor R 92:32-62 F '69

Poor and the powerful. T. Goldwasser. Sat R 52:30-2 Mr 8 '69

Poor are still with us. Trans-Action 7:8 D '69

Poor get fewer. Newsweek 74:62B S 1 '69

Poverty: America's enduring paradox, by S. Lens. Review
  America 120:257-8 Mr 1 '69. L. F. Buckley

Poverty; the negative income tax; address, October 22, 1969. J. H. Smith. Vital Speeches 36:157-60 D 15 '69

Remarkable Mr Harris. C. Mangel. il Look 33:75-6+ Mr 18 '69

State of the poverty war. America 120:610 My 24 '69

TRB from Washington; McGovern subcommittee hearings on heavy worm infestation of low-income families. New Repub 160:6 Mr 8 '69

Thorns on the yellow rose of Texas. R. Coles and H. Huge. New Repub 160:13-17 Ap 19 '69

Urban poverty: effects on prenatal nutrition. R. L. Naeye and others. bibliog il Science 166:1026 N 21 '69

We need help; Mississippi's northern counties. R. Coles and H. Huge. New Repub 160:18-21 Mr 8 '69

Welfare mother. I. Hinds. Chr Cent 87:17-18 Ja 7 '70

Who are the hungry? il Newsweek 73:38+ Ap 28 '69

Who's hungry? And for what? Nat R 21:265-6 Mr 25 '69

  See also
Anti-poverty program, 1964—
Economic assistance, Domestic
Labor and laboring classes—United States
Negroes—Social conditions
Nutrition problems—United States
Public welfare—United States

White House conference on food, nutrition and health
  also subhead Poor under names of cities, e.g. New York (city)—Poor

POOR darling; story. See Kjelgaard, B.

POOR laws

United States

  See also
Public welfare—United States

POOR relief. See Public welfare

POP art. See Art, Modern

POP lyrics. See Music, Popular (songs, etc)

POP music. See Music, Popular (songs, etc.)

POP sculpture. See Sculpture

POPCORN

Popcorn. G. Morrison. il Horticulture 47:21+ O '69

POPE, Alexander

Alexander Pope, by P. Quennell. Review
  New Yorker 45:128+ F 22 '69. W. H. Auden

Education of genius, 1688-1728, by P. Quennell. Review
  Atlan por 223:92-5 My '69. L. Kronenberger

Giant four feet six. R. Halsband. Sat R 52: 44-5 F 22 '69

Personality of Belinda's baron: Pope's The rape of the lock. J. Meyers. bibliog f Am Imago 26:71-7 Spr '69

Poetry, how and why. J. Jerome. Writers Digest 49:20+ S '69

POPENOE, Paul

How jet-set parents wreck their children's lives; interview, ed. by D. C. Disney. Ladies Home J 86:12+ S '69

POPES

Bad popes, by E. R. Chamberlain. Review
  Atlan 224:75-8 Jl '69 L. Kronenberger

Popes of the twentieth century, by C. Falconi. Review
  Cath World 208:232-3 F '69. E. H. Peters
  See also
Papacy

Election

No more cardinals? Commonweal 89:632-3 F 21 '69

History

  See Papacy—History

Infallibility

Not fathers, but brothers. G. Baum. Chr Cent 86:607-8 Ap 30 '69

Papal infallibility and all that. J. Bishop. Commonweal 90:481-4 Ag 8 '69

Papal infallibility revisited. J. C. Haughey; discussion. America 120:345 Mr 29 '69

Schismatic ferment. Chr Cent 86:500 Ap 16 '69

Primacy

Bishops' conferences past and present. J. C. Haughey and D. R. Campion. America 121: 327-30 O 18 '69

Council over Pope? towards a provisional ecclesiology, by F. Oakley. Review
  Chr Cent 86:1457-8 N 12 '69. J. H. Smylie

House divided. il Newsweek 74:73 O 27 '69

Letter from the Synod. D. R. Campion. America 121:351 O 25 '69

New roads for Rome. K. L. Woodward. il Newsweek 74:95-6 N 10 '69

Papacy enhanced. C. Northcott. Chr Cent 86: 1443-4 N 12 '69

Pope: firm in face of challenge. il U S News 67:18 O 20 '69

Pope under fire. Time 94:90 O 17 '69

Synod of our discontent. H. ten Kortenaar. Commonweal 91:240-1 N 21 '69

Voice for bishops? il Newsweek 74:107-8 O 20 '69

What happened at the Synod? J. B. Sheerin. Cath World 210:98-9 D '69

POPESCU, Petru

Liberty versus death: a young writer's struggle; interview, ed. by G. Goodman. por Look 33:38 Ap 15 '69

POPKIN, Zelda

Plot isn't a dirty word. Writer 82:11-12 Jl '69

POPLAR
  See also
Aspen

La POPOTTE (restaurant) See New York (city) —Hotels, restaurants, etc.

POPPER, David H.

U.N. seabed committee concludes spring session; statement, March 28, 1969. Dept State Bul 60:342-5 Ap 21 '69

POPPER, Samuel H.

What about the middle school? Todays Ed 58:52-4 N '69

POPPET; ballet. See Ballets—Criticisms

POPPIES

All matilija needs is room. il Sunset 142:188 F '69

Desert stopper, pricky poppy. il Sunset 143: 152 Jl '69

On the cover: the poppy story begins in August. il Home Gard 56:67 Ag '69

Oriental poppies. A. Viette. il Horticulture 47: 36-7 Je '69

Satin-petaled pink poppy. M. F. Kirby. il Home Gard 56:12 Mr '69

Trance of poppies. A. West. il Vogue 154:202-7+ D '69

POPPINO, Rollie E.

Early cold war period. Cur Hist 56:340-5+ Je '69

POPULAR culture

Books and culture: a reevaluation; address, June 22, 1968. J. M. Thompson. ALA Bul 63:603-9 My '69
    See also
United States—Popular culture

POPULAR errors. See Errors, Popular

POPULAR front for the liberation of Palestine

Exporting violence; bomb and skyjack plots by Arab terrorists. il Time 95:27-8 Ja 5 '70

Headline hunters. il Newsweek 74:45-6 S 22 '69

This is your captain; TWA plane hijacked. il Newsweek 74:37-8 S 8 '69

Voice of extremism; interview, ed. by L. Griggs. G. Habash. Time 93:42 Je 13 '69

POPULAR government. See Representative government and representation

POPULAR medicine. See Medicine, Popular

POPULAR movement for the liberation of Angola. See Guerrillas—Angola

POPULAR music. See Music, Popular (songs, etc)

POPULAR songs. See Music, Popular (songs, etc)

POPULATION

Cultural imperative; stabilization of population and of natural areas. A. W. Smith. Nat Parks 43:2 O '69

Is there an optimum level of population? AAAS symposium, December 29-30, 1969. S. F. Singer. il Science 166:270-1 O 10 '69

New-type course to prepare officers for field duties. UN Mo Chron 6:23-4 F '69

News and views; UN's population control program. J. Deedy. Commonweal 89:606 F 14 '69

World power and population. C. Clark. il Nat R 21:481-4 My 20 '69
    See also
Birth control
Demography
United Nations—Population commission
    also subhead Population under names of countries, states, cities, e.g. United States —Population

Overpopulation

Catastrophe by the numbers; American population. C. Ogburn, jr. Am Heritage 21:114-17 D '69

Catholics and the population explosion. Trans-Action 6:8+ Je '69

Crisis of our overcrowded world. M. Mead. Redbook 133:40+ O '69

Critical weakness; reprint. Am For 75:9 Ap '69

Excessive population growth; address, May 1, 1969. R. S. McNamara. Vital Speeches 35: 500-5 Je 1 '69

Explosive desire for children. Time 94:57 Ag 22 '69

McNamara at Notre Dame. America 120:579 My 17 '69

On a collision course. W. W. Porter, 2d. Am For 75:5+ Ap '69

Our overcrowded, underfed world. America 120:609 My 24 '69

Overcrowding and us. P. R. Ehrlich. il Nat Parks 43:10-12 Ap '69

Overpopulated America. W. H. Davis. New Repub 162:13-15 Ja 10 '70

Population bomb, by P. R. Ehrlich. Review Audubon 71:94+ Mr '69. P. B. Sears

Population firecracker. Nat R 21:999-1000 O 7 '69; Reply. J. G. Viner. Nat R 21:1199-200 D 2 '69

Population problem; in search of a solution. J. J. Spengler. bibliog Science 166:1234-8 D 5 '69

Population threat; excerpts from address, May 1969. R. S. McNamara. il Todays Ed 58:20-3 D '69

Problem of people pollution; with photographs by R. Crane. Life 68:8-15 Ja 9 '70

Race for (automobile) space; adaptation of address, April 17, 1969. E. Corning, 2d Bul Atom Sci 25:15-16 D '69

Standing room only on spaceship earth. M. K. Udall. Read Digest 95:131-5 D '69

Technology, adaptation, and evolution; excerpt from address. H. Hoagland. il Bul Atom Sci 25:27-30 Ja '69

Too many strangers. D. L. Allen. il Nat Parks 43:12-17 Ag '69

Unwanted people. New Repub 161:7 Ag 2 '69

Urgency of population control. Chr Today 13:20 Jl 18 '69

World population: is the battle lost? P. R. Ehrlich. Read Digest 94:137-40 F '69

World's no. 1 worry, too many people. il U S News 66:48 Mr 17 '69
    See also
Population, Increase of

POPULATION, Distribution of

Fastest-growing cities; latest census estimates. il U S News 66:55-7 Mr 31 '69

Land to live in; toward an urban/rural balance. O. L. Freeman. Cur 111:33-9 O '69

Where U.S. growth is fastest. il U S News 67:16 S 22 '69

POPULATION, Increase of

Affluence in jeopardy, by C. F. Park, jr. Review Focus 19:12 My '69. A. Lyons

Challenges of the third 100 million; President Nixon's message to Congress, July 18, 1969. il U S News 68:34 Ja 12 '70

Interdisciplinary communications: population; report of meeting. Lord Ritchie-Calder. Science 163:408-9 Ja 24 '69

Many more faces of the seventies. il Bsns W p82-3+ D 6 '69

1969 to 2019. New Yorker 45:29-31 F 22 '69

Population crisis: rising concern at home. L. J. Carter. Science 166:722-6 N 7 '69

Population increase: a grave threat to every American family. A. T. Day. Parents Mag 44:56-7+ O '69

Population: the biggest boom. il Sr Schol 95: 9+ O 27 '69

Problems of population growth; message to Congress, July 18, 1969. R. M. Nixon. Dept State Bul 61:105-11 Ag 11 '69

Tragedy of the commons; adaptation of address, June 25, 1968. G. Hardin; discussion. Science 163:518-19 F 7 '69

2000: a no-space odyssey; population estimates projected for Latin America. L. Olivos. bibliog il Américas 21:15-21 Ag '69
    See also
Population—Overpopulation

POPULATION commission. See United Nations —Population commission

POPULATION limitation. See Birth control

POPULATION pressure. See Population—Overpopulation

POPULIST party

Ignatius Donnelly & the politics of discontent; inquiry into the career of a Populist. R. G. Kennedy. bibliog il Am West 6:10-14+ Mr '69

POPULUS tremuloides. See Aspen

PORCELAIN. See Pottery

PORCELAIN, Chinese. See Pottery, Chinese

PORCELAIN figurines. See Figurines

PORCHES

Home screenings. il Am Home 72:60-1 Je '69

Solve the patio problem, add a screened porch. D. Shiner. il Pop Mech 131:170-4+ My '69

Want a screened porch? R. Sickler. il Pop Sci 194:168-71 Ja '69

PORK
    See also
Cookery—Meat
Swine

Prices
    See Meat—Prices

PORK rind (bait) See Bait

PORNOGRAPHY. See Immoral literature and pictures; Obscenity (law)

POROUS glass See Glass, Cellular

PORPHYRIA

Porphyria and King George III. I. Macalpine and R. Hunter. il Sci Am 221:38-46 Jl '69; Discussion. 221:8-9 D '69

Royal malady; medical records of George III. Time 94:60+ Ag 1 '69

PORPOISES. See Dolphins (mammals)

PORRAS TROCONIS, Gabriel

Heroic Cartagena. Américas 21:21-30 Je '69

PORST, Hannsheinz

Millionaire spy. por Newsweek 73:48 Je 2 '69

PORT, David M.
　Mental health consultation with a paramilitary
　　youth program. bibliog Ment Hy 53:513-20
　　O '69
PORT GRIMAUD, France
　Antiquity-sur-mer. il Time 94:70-1 Jl 18 '69
PORT of New York authority
　New York airport developments keyed to
　　political scene. D. A. Brown. il Aviation
　　W 91:118-20+ O 20 '69
　　　See also
　Jersey City, N.J.—Stations
PORT ROYAL earthquake, 1692. See Earth-
　quakes—Jamaica
PORT terminals. See Ports
PORT WASHINGTON, Wis.
　Obstinacy of Bill Schanen. J. Pekkanen. Life
　　67:59 S 26 '69
PORT wine. See Wine
PORTABLE electric tools. See Electric tools,
　Portable
PORTABLE fences. See Fences
PORTABLE garages. See Garages
PORTABLE pensions. See Pensions, Industrial
PORTABLE radio receivers. See Radio re-
　ceivers, Portable
PORTABLE swimming pools. See Swimming
　pools
PORTABLE television receivers. See Televi-
　sion receivers, Portable
PORTAGO, Carol, marquesa de
　Off the beaten track. il pors Vogue 153:118-21
　　Ap 15 '69
PORTER, D. Gareth
　Diemist restoration. Commonweal 90:435-7 Jl
　　11 '69
—and Ackland, L. E.
　Vietnam: the bloodbath argument. Chr Cent
　　86:1414-17 N 5 '69
PORTER, Eliot
　Colorado's canyons today; excerpts from
　　Down the Colorado. por Audubon 71:77-9
　　N '69
　Lament for a lost Eden. Am Heritage 20:60-
　　1 O '69
　Powell's River; Colorado portfolio; excerpts
　　from Down the Colorado. Audubon 71:64-76
　　N '69
　　　　　about
　Eliot Porter, master of nature's color. A.
　　Adams. Mod Phot 33:92+ O '69
PORTER, George
　Laws of disorder (cont) Chem 42:19 F '69
PORTER, Graham
　Moment can last forever. Read Digest 95:71-2
　　Jl '69
PORTER, J. W. and others
　Renovated wastewaters. Am City 84:140-2
　　My '69
PORTER, John H.
　Checkmate; story; excerpt from Winterkill.
　　Mlle 69:128-9 Je '69
PORTER, Katherine Anne
　Opinion: notes on writing. Mlle 69:14+ O '69
PORTER, Lorie
　Cos lettuce, tender all the way up. Org Gard
　　& Farm 16:92-3 Ap '69
PORTER, Quincy
　From CRI, a memorial to Quincy Porter. A.
　　Cohn. por Am Rec G 35:1142 Ag '69
PORTER, Richard D. and Wiemeyer, S. N.
　Dieldrin and DDT: effects on sparrow hawk
　　eggshells and reproduction. bibliog Science
　　165:199-200 Jl 11 '69
PORTER, Rod A.
　Mutual-aid radio expands firefighting ser-
　　vices. por Am City 84:128+ S '69
PORTER, Russell W.
　Financing outdoor recreation; excerpt from
　　address. Parks & Rec 4:23+ N '69
PORTER, Sylvia
　Spending your money. See issues of Ladies'
　　home journal
PORTER, W. Stan
　Growing delphiniums from seed. Org Gard &
　　Farm 16:90-1 Ap 69
PORTER, Warren P.
　Thermal radiation in metabolic chambers.
　　bibliog Science 166:115-17 O 3 '69
—and Norris, K. S.
　Lizard reflectivity change and its effect on
　　light transmission through body wall. bib-
　　liog Science 163:482-4 Ja 31 '69
PORTER, William W. 2d
　On a collision course. Am For 75:5+ Ap '69
PORTERFIELD, Bill
　Back home again in Johnson City. N Y
　　Times Mag p22-3+ Mr 2 '69
PORTFOLIOS, Personal. See Applications for
　positions

PORTLAND, Ore.
　　　　Description
　Exciting cities, a Redbook vacation guide
　　to sight-seeing with children; excerpts from
　　America's exciting cities. A. Schwartz. il
　　Redbook 132:42-3 Ap '69
　　　　Education
　Maxi learning from mini courses; Wilson
　　high school. W. Reed. il Sr Schol 94:Schol
　　Teach 10+ Mr 7 '69
　Pupil tutors and tutees learn together;
　　Student team action. J. C. Fleming. il
　　Todays Ed 58:22-4 O '69; Same abr. Ed
　　Digest 35:38-40 D '69
　　　　Hospitals
　Can we keep it? Woodland park hospital. il
　　Good H 169:80-2+ O '69
　　　　Music
　　　See also
　Portland opera association
PORTLAND cement. See Cement
PORTLAND opera association
　Report: Portland; performances of Mas-
　　senet's Manon. F. Kinkaid. Opera N 33:25
　　My 17 '69
　Report: Portland; production of Der fliegende
　　Holländer. F. Kinkaid. Opera N 33:31
　　Mr 8 '69
　Report: production of Aida. F. Kinkaid.
　　Opera N 34:24 D 6 '69
PORTLIGHT screens. See Boats—Equipment
PORTO CERVO. See Sardinia
PORTO ROTONDO
　This year it's Porto Rotondo. il Holiday 45:
　　48-53 Je '69
PORTRAIT drawing
　Portraiture enlargement. A. W. Sande. il De-
　　sign 70:24-6 Spr '69
　Sketching faces from the TV screen. M. Ryer-
　　son. il Am Artist 33:68-72 Je '69
PORTRAIT medallions
　Washington miniature R. Davidson. il Anti-
　　ques 96:318+ S '69
PORTRAIT painting
　Each demonstration is a challenge; interview,
　　ed. by H. Rugoff. H. Van Wyk. il Am
　　Artist 33:78-82+ Mr '69
　Hockney paints a portrait. D. Shapiro. il
　　Art N 68:28-31+ My '69
　My right side is better. F. Linden. il Am
　　Artist 32:50-1+ D '68
　Painting masters of jazz. D. Quinn. il Am
　　Artist 33:39-41+ Ag '69
　Painting mural portraits. C. B. Wilson. il
　　Am Artist 33:56-61 N '69
　　　See also
　Pastel drawing
PORTRAIT sculpture
　Great men of America in Roman guise;
　　sculptured by Giuseppe Ceracchi. U. Des-
　　portes. il Antiques 96:72-5 Jl '69
PORTRAITS
　Notebook of John Smibert; Antiques book
　　preview. il Antiques 95:366-9 Mr '69
　　　See also
　Photography—Portraits
　Silhouettes
　　　　Exhibitions
　Elizabethan portraiture; exhibition at the
　　Tate gallery in London. E. P. Birk. il
　　Antiques 96:848 D '69
PORTRAITS, American
　Attribution for His Excellency and Lady
　　Washington; unsigned mezzotints. W. J.
　　Shadwell. il Antiques 95:240-1 F '69
　Gansevoort limner. M. Black. il Antiques 96:
　　738-44 N '69
　Place, time, and painter; portrait of Mrs
　　Freake and baby Mary in Worcester art
　　museum. K. Kuh. il Sat R 52:46-7 S 6 '69
　Portraits owned by the American antiquarian
　　society. L. Dresser. il Antiques 96:717-27
　　N '69
　Samuel King of Newport. W. B. Stevens. An-
　　tiques 96:728-33 N '69
　Southern gentlemen honored in glass. T. H.
　　Marsh. il Hobbies 74:98N-98P Ag '69
　　　See also
　Smithsonian institution—National portrait
　　gallery
PORTRAITS, British
　Elizabethan portraiture; exhibition at the
　　Tate gallery in London. E. P. Birk. il
　　Antiques 96:848 D '69
PORTS
　Canada's superport for superships; Roberts
　　bank. il Bsns W p 120-2 S 27 '69

PORTS—*Continued*
Issues that threaten life of ports. U S News 66:70 Mr 31 '69
See also
Free ports and zones
Harbors
also subhead Harbor under names of cities, e.g. New York (city)—Harbor
PORTUGAL
See also
Algarve
Hunting—Portugal
Lisbon
Tourist trade—Portugal
United Nations—Portugal

Colonies
Fight to save the last big empire. il U S News 66:96-7 Ap 14 '69
Territories under Portuguese administration; Assembly adopts resolution; with text of resolution. UN Mo Chron 6:23-33 D '69
You can take Brazil out of Portugal, but—. H. Estenssoro. Commonweal 91:5-6 O 3 '69
See also
Angola
Macao

Description and travel
Beating the crowds to the Algarve. A. Chamberlin. Vogue 153:70+ F 1 '69
From Lisbon to Madrid to Spain's Costa Del Sol, Club continental's travelers tried out a new kind of tour. J. Friedberg. il Travel & Camera 32:86-8+ O '69
Iberia & the Magreb. H. Apter. il Travel & Camera 32:40, 46-7, 50-1 Ap '69
Iberian itinerary. J. M. Dalury. il Travel 132: 36-41 N '69
Let's travel; Portugal. Mlle 69:82-4+ Je '69

History
Bibliography
Articles and other books received; comp. by C. J. Bishko. See issues of American historical review

Politics and government
Cracks in the facade. Newsweek 74:53-4 O 27 '69
In a minor key. P. S. Cook. Newsweek 73: 48+ Je 2 '69
Shades of Salazar. il Time 94:30 O 31 '69
Smooth shift of gears. P. Witonski. Nat R 21:851 Ag 26 '69
You can take Brazil out of Portugal, but—. H. Estenssoro. Commonweal 91:5-6 O 3 '69
See also
Elections—Portugal

PORTUGUESE cookery. See Cookery, Portuguese
PORTUGUESE explorers. See Explorers, Portuguese
PORTUGUESE WEST AFRICA. See Angola
PORTUGUESE wines. See Wine
POSEIDON adventure; story. See Gallico, P.
POSEY, Sam
You can go as fast as your mind lets you. C. Coe. il pors Life 66:48-50+ My 23 '69
POSITION, Social. See Social status
POSITRONS
Positron beams. D. E. Yount. bibliog il Phys Today 22:41-9 F '69
Producing positrons. il Chem 42:24-5 Je '69
POSNER, Victor
Building steel mills from top to bottom. il por Bsns W p 126-8 Ja 18 '69
Errant genius of Victor Posner. por Forbes 103:60+ F 15 '69
POSSESSIONS. See Property
POSSONY, Stefan T.
Soviet economy close up. Nat R 21:394-5 Ap 22 '69
POST, Austin
High ice, high rock; photographs. Audubon 71:28-33 My '69
POST, Emily (Price)
Rose for Emily. J. Kaplan. Harper 238:106-9 Mr '69
POST, New York. See New York post
POST, Washington. See Washington post and Times herald
POST cards
Artist signed post cards. B. Finnegan. il Hobbies 74:125 Ap; 124-5+ My; 124-5 Je '69 (to be cont)
Edward H. Mitchell post cards. B. Finnegan. il Hobbies 73:124-5 F '69
Nostalgia?? You will find it in post cards of the past. il Hobbies 74:98Z-98AA Jl '69
POST exchanges. See United States—Armed forces—Post exchanges

POST-intelligencer, Seattle. See Seattle—Newspapers
POST office. See Postal service
POST office buildings
Will investors lose the post office game? il Duns R 94:73-4 N '69
POST office department (United States) See United States—Post office department
POSTAGE stamp designs. See Design, Decorative
POSTAGE stamps
Last great man: commemorative stamps featuring W. L. S. Churchill. D. F. Brown. il Hobbies 74:50-1 Je '69
Man on the moon; stamp with the greatest sale ever. il U S News 67:18 S 22 '69
More physics philately. D. M. Lasky. il Phys Today 22:19+ S '69
Stamp collection of Dirk Bach. D. Bach. il Ramp Mag 7:42-3 N 30 '68
Stamp explosion; stamps by and of blacks. il Ebony 25:142-4+ D '69
Stamps. H. Herst, jr. See issues of Hobbies
See also
Covers (philately)

Collectors and collecting
Collecting stamp errors, freaks, & minor varieties. H. Herst, jr. Hobbies 74:99+ Ap '69
Here comes a hobby that can drive you crazy; collecting sports stamps. P. Knight. il Sports Illus 31:60-1 O 6 '69
Your own thing; beginner's stamp collection. il Seventeen 28:56 N '69

Exhibitions
Postage stamp as a mini-art form. R. J. Saunders. il Sch Arts 69:30-1 N '69
POSTAL censorship
House subcommittee studies anti-obscenity measures. S. Wagner. Pub W 196:39-40 Ag 18 '69
Mr Nixon on the trail of smut. R. H. Smith. Pub W 195:34 My 12 '69

Anecdotes, facetiae, satire, etc.
Of prurient interest. Chr Cent 86:1233 S 24 '69
POSTAL employees
End to politics in postal system? il U S News 66:16 F 17 '69
See also
Postal service—Letter carriers

Salaries, allowances, etc.
Will the mail get even slower? Bsns W p65 D 13 '69
POSTAL laws and regulations. See Postal service—Laws and regulations
POSTAL rates
Another penny to mail a letter? U S News 66:10 My 5 '69

United States
Proposed postal increases; no hikes for books. S. Wagner. Pub W 195:31 My 12 '69
Some postal reminders; manuscript postage. Writers Digest 49:93-4 Ag '69
POSTAL scales. See Scales (weighing instruments)
POSTAL service
Notes and comment. New Yorker 44:21 Ja 25 '69
See also
Electronics in postal service
Mail boats

Laws and regulations
Jan. 1 is effective date for new bulk mailing regulation. S. Wagner. Pub W 196:29 N 3 '69
P.O. proposes relief on bulk mailing rules. R. H. Smith. Pub W 196:42 Ag 18 '69
Post office revises bulk mailing regulation. S. Wagner. Pub W 196:49 Jl 7 '69
Step toward postal freedom; proposed U.S. postal system authority. Bsns W p 19 D 27 '69
See also
Postal censorship

Letter carriers
Face to face with a female mail carrier. E. Lamel. il Seventeen 28:38 N '69

Great Britain
Britain's plan for untangling the mail. il U S News 66:44 Mr 31 '69
How to straighten out the U.S. post office? Duns R 94:63 D '69

POSTAL service—*Continued*

Italy

Mail does not get through. il Bsns W p51-2 Jl 12 '69

United States

Can the mails be managed? interview, ed. by G. R. Rosen. W. M. Blount. Duns R 94:14-17 S '69

Case for postal reform. W. M. Blount. il Nations Bsns 57:52-4 S '69

Crusading for postal reform. il Bsns W p74-5 Jl 5 '69

New postal system for U.S; here's the way it would work. il U S News 66:44-5 Je 9 '69

This month's feature: moves to reorganize the postal system. Cong Digest 48.67-96 Mr '69

What ails the U.S. mails? il Life 67:24F-29 N 28 '69

What's wrong with the mails; interview. W. M. Blount. il U S News 66:40-4 Mr 31 '69

See also
Air mail service
Franking privilege
Parcel post
Postal censorship
Postal employees
United States—Post office department

Anecdotes, facetiae, satire, etc.

Puny express. G. Ace. Sat R 52:6 Mr 29 '69

History

See also
Postmasters

POSTAL system of America, independent. See Independent postal system of America

POSTAL unions. See Government employees unions

POSTCARDS

SSSSTT; Famous postcards? il Pop Phot 65: 80-1 S '69

POSTDOCTORAL education. See Colleges and universities—Graduate work

POSTELLE, Yvonne

Art of listening to children. Parents Mag 44: 58-9+ Ap '69

Baby sitters money can't buy. Parents Mag 44:56-7+ Ag '69

POSTERS

Ads to hang in your home. il Bsns W p 104+ Jl 26 '69

Agit pop art of Cuba. D. Stermer. il Ramp Mag 7:32-7 D 14 '68

Collect color with posters. il House & Gard 135:102-5 Mr '69

From B&W to color posters. R. D. Routh. il Pop Phot 64:84-7 Je '69

Keeping posted on dance. il Dance Mag 43: 42-5 S '69

Man in motion. il Newsweek 73:112-13 Ap 14 '69

Two California poster designers; interview, ed. by G. Loney. D. Osborn; C. Woods. il Am Artist 33:48-53+ My '69

POSTGRADUATE work. See Colleges and universities—Graduate work

POSTMASTER General. See United States— Post office department

POSTMASTERS

Postman. H. Herst. jr. Hobbies 74:131+ N '69

POSTMEN. See Postal service—Letter carriers

POSTON, Patricia

Image of the dream; story. Good H 168:96-7 Je '69

POSTPARTUM depression. See Depression, Mental

POSTPARTUM mental illness. See Mental illness

POSTS, Fence. See Fence posts

POSVAR, Wesley W.

University and the student; address, December 22, 1968. Vital Speeches 35:234-6 F 1 '69

POT. See Marijuana

POT marigolds. See Calendulas

POT roasting. See Cookery—Meat

POTASH industry and trade

Potash: the need for a tariff. Bsns W p 149 N 22 '69

POTASSIUM

Stomatal opening: role of potassium uptake by guard cells. R. A. Fischer; reply with rejoinder. J. Levitt. bibliog Science 163:494 Ja 31 '69

POTASSIUM in the body

Potassium, corticosterone, and adrenocorticotropic hormone release in vitro. J. Kraicer and others. bibliog il Science 164:426 Ap 25 '69

Potassium ion: is the bulk of intracellular K+ adsorbed? G. N. Ling and F. W. Cope. bibliog il Science 163:1335-6 Mr 21 '69

Potassium ions asymmetrically activate erythrocyte membrane phosphatase. A. F. Rega and others. bibliog il Science 167: 55-6 Ja 2 '70

POTATO chips

Party gets rough for potato chippers. il Bsns W p36 N 8 '69

Pioneering in potato chips. il Chem 42:5 Mr '69

Potato-chip war. Time 94:106 O 17 '69

POTATOES

Potatoes between the rows. W. Masson. il Org Gard & Farm 16:34 My '69

Potatoes you can't buy; German fingerlings, Canadian purples. M. Miller. il Org Gard & Farm 16:28-31 Je '69

See also
Cookery—Vegetables

POTENTIAL, Electric

Field potentials generated by dendritic spikes and synaptic potentials. R. S. Zucker. bibliog il Science 165:409-13 Jl 25 '69

POTENTIAL, Theory of

Brownian motion and potential theory. R. Hersh and R. J. Griego. il Sci Am 220:66-72+ Mr '69

POTENTIOMETERS

Save with a single-turn pot. L. Caso. il Electr World 81:92 Ap '69

POTHERBS. See Greens, Edible

POTHIER, Richard J.

Tektite, two months beneath the sea. Sea Front 15:130-9 My '69

POTLATCH

Indian giving. F. V. Grunfeld. il Horizon 11:46-7 Wint '69

POTOMAC electric power company of Washington, D.C.

Whose need is greater? Pepco money problems. Forbes 104:58 O 15 '69

POTOMAC RIVER

Fishing for a pollution solution. W. A. Horn. il Am Ed 5:14-16 Ap '69

Mike Frome: efforts to save Hunting creek from land developers. M. Frome. Am For 75:3+ Je '69

Potomac considered as capital water source. Nat Parks 43:22-3 D '69

Ravaging mountain streams challenge white water canoeists. B. Thomas. il Pop Gard 20:12-17 Spr '69; Same abr. with title White-water canoe race. Travel 131:50-3+ Mr '69

POTS and pans. See Kitchen utensils

POTTED plants. See Plants, Potted

POTTER, Charles H.

Greenhouse profit sideline. Horticulture 46: 22-3+ S '68

POTTER, Daniel

Tell me about the wind; story. Redbook 132: 64-5 Ja '69

POTTER, David M.

Anomalous hero of Appomattox. Sat R 52: 29-30 Mr 1 '69

POTTER, Nancy A. J.

There won't be any scars at all; story. Mc-Calls 96:94-5 Mr '69

about

Literary horizons. G. Hicks. por Sat R 52: 25-6 F 1 '69

POTTER, Stephen

Words only. See issues of American record guide

POTTER, Stephen, 1900-1969

Gamesman. il por Newsweek 74:50 D 15 '69

Winning the game of life. por Time 94:78 D 12 '69

POTTER instrument company

IBM punch cards face a new rival; magnetic cards. Bsns W p 125 My 17 '69

POTTERS

Ceramactivities; people, places and things. See issues of Ceramics monthly

Perth potters' club. J. Ewers. il Ceram Mo 17:28 Ap '69

See also
Boggs, H. M.
Gallucci, R.
Jahr, E.
Kemenyffy, S.
McIntosh, H.
Schulps, J.

POTTERY

Findings on R S china; history, variety, marks. V. Duncan. il Hobbies 74:98M-98P Mr '69

Porcelain and pottery animals. L. F. Reals. il Hobbies 74:98N N '69

Serve it in the right dish. il House & Gard 135:150-1 My '69

POTTERY—*Continued*
Showoffs. S. Lindsay. il House B 111:58-9 D '69
See also
Animal pottery
Ceramic sculpture
Cloisonné
Drinking vessels
Glazes and glazing
Indians of North America—Pottery
Molds (for ceramic products)

Bibliography
New Books. See occasional issues of Ceramics monthly

Collectors and collecting
English lusterware from the Duckworth collection. J. W. Keefe. il Antiques 96:382-9 S '69

Decoration
Deck a gift with stencil jolly. il Seventeen 27: 148-9+ N '68
Decorating with coils. R. F. Eilenberger. il Ceram Mo 17:20-2 My '69
Free-form coiling: a technique for forming and decorating pottery simultaneously. P. Landman. il Sch Arts 69:18-19 Ja '70
News pots. E. D. Taylor. il Ceram Mo 17:15-18 Ja '69
Parliament of owls. R. D. Bonham. il Ceram Mo 17:23-5 Ja '69
Some oriental aspects of European ceramic decoration. H. Syz. bibliog il Antiques 95: 670-81; 96:91-9; 209-13 My, Jl-Ag '69

Exhibitions
Ceramics from the Howald collection in Columbus; Ferdinand Howald collection at Gallery of fine arts. E. P. Birk. il Antiques 96:692+ N '69
Cerritos annual; Fort Wayne invitational; Salt glaze show at Geneseo, N.Y.; San Francisco biennial. il Ceram Mo 17:30-1 Je '69
Craft dimensions Canada; exhibition of contemporary crafts at Toronto's Royal Ontario museum. il Ceram Mo 17:18-19 N '69
Creative crafts VI, Pacific dimensions. il Ceram Mo 17:31 S '69
DePauw ceramic show. il Ceram Mo 17:29 Mr '69
Itinerary. See issues of Ceramics monthly
Mid-South ceramics and crafts exhibition. il Ceram Mo 17:24-5 My '69
Twenty-fifth ceramic national. J. Delius. il Craft Horiz 29:30-5+ Ja '69
25th ceramic national exhibition. il Ceram Mo 17:19-22 Ja '69

Firing
Cone 6 stoneware. R. Behrens. il Ceram Mo 17:32-3 Mr '69
Potter and his kiln; excerpt from Kilns: design, construction, and operation. D. Rhodes. il Craft Horiz 29:36-8 Mr '69
Raku glazes. R. Behrens. il Ceram Mo 17:29 N '69
Reduction firing for the classroom. A. E. Harwood. il Sch Arts 68:40-1 Ap '69
Workshop: wet firing. G. Williams. il Craft Horiz 29:10-13 S '69

History
Ceramics: Williamsburg, Va. J. C. Austin. il Antiques 95:112-20 Ja '69

Study and teaching
Ceramics in junior high. G. M. Scheck. il Sch Arts 68:14-15 Ap '69
Films on ceramics. il Ceram Mo 17:28-9+ F '69
Junior high students can throw big pots. C. D. Rash. il Ceram Mo 17:22-3 S '69
Pottery goes pop. E. Stein. il Sch Arts 68: 35 Ap '69
Summer workshops. Ceram Mo 17:29+ Ap; 28-9+ My; 27+ Je '69
Teaching coil building. R. A. Goettsch. il Design 70:32-4 Sum '69

Teaching aids and devices
See also
Moving pictures in education

Technique
Anthony Hepburn. T. Birks. il Craft Horiz 29:34-6 Jl '69
Balloon pots. A. Heidt. il Ceram Mo 17:26-7 O '69
Barbara's birds. F. A. Colson. il Ceram Mo 17:14-16 Ap '69
Ceramic drinking horns. G. Hageman. il Ceram Mo 17:27-8 N '69

Changing the base on a wheel-thrown pot. N. H. Baldwin. il Ceram Mo 17:20-2 N '69
Coiling a pot in a pot. D. Cyr. il Ceram Mo 17:12-14 Ja '69
Creative slip casting. J. Goldman. il Ceram Mo 17:25-7 Ap '69
David Crespi's weed pots. D. Cyr. il Ceram Mo 17:20-2 Mr '69
Folding method for large slab constructions. E. Chamness. il Ceram Mo 17:14-17 N '69
Free-form coiling: a technique for forming and decorating pottery simultaneously. P. Landman. il Sch Arts 69:18-19 Ja '70
New generation of ceramic artists. E. Gronborg. il Craft Horiz 29:26-9+ Ja '69
News pots. E. D. Taylor. il Ceram Mo 17:15-18 Ja '69
Porcelains of Kit Snyder. J. Wandres. il Ceram Mo 17:12-15 O '69
Pottery in New Guinea; excerpts from Pottery in Australia. M. Tuckson. il Craft Horiz 28:27-31+ Jl '68; Correction. 29:47 Ja '69
Pravoslav Rada; interview, ed. by D. Cyr. P. Rada. il Ceram Mo 17:17-21 Ap '69
Sack casting. L. Wood. il Ceram Mo 17: 24-6 S '69
Slab pots from block forms. R. Johnson. il Ceram Mo 17:20-1 F '69
Teapots. B. Woodman. il Ceram Mo 17:12-15 Mr '69
Variations in form and technique. H. J. Paradis. il Ceram Mo 17:22-4 Ap '69
Wedging board pots. R. S. Persick. il Ceram Mo 17:13-15 Je '69
See also
Glazes and glazing
Modeling

POTTERY, American
Art nouveau ceramics. M. Kaye. il Am Home 72:22+ N '69
Interview with Raymond Gallucci; ed. by J. Wandres. R. Gallucci. il Ceram Mo 17:12-15 F '69
Maija Grotell. J. Schlanger. il Craft Horiz 29:14-23 N '69
New generation of ceramic artists. E. Gronborg. il Craft Horiz 29:26-9+ Ja '69
New light on Bonnin and Morris. G. Hood. il Antiques 95:812-17 Je '69

History
Excavation at the Worcester porcelain factory. G. Wills. il Antiques 96:242-5 Ag '69

POTTERY, Australian
Perth potters' club. J. Ewers. il Ceram Mo 17:28 Ap '69
Pottery in New Guinea; excerpts from Pottery in Australia. M. Tuckson. il Craft Horiz 28:27-31+ Jl '68; Correction. 29:47 Ja '69

POTTERY, Canadian
Craft dimensions Canada; exhibition of contemporary crafts at Toronto's Royal Ontario museum. il Ceram Mo 17:18-19 N '69

POTTERY, Chinese
Collector: Paul Bernat; rare collection of Chinese porcelain. A. Pryce-Jones. il Art in Am 57:68-75 S '69

POTTERY, English
Anthony Hepburn. T. Birks. il Craft Horiz 29:34-6 Jl '69
Pearlware: forgotten milestone of English ceramic history. I. Noël-Hume. il Antiques 95:390-7; 96:922-3 Mr, D '69
See also
Luster ware

POTTERY, European
Some oriental aspects of European ceramic decoration. H. Syz. bibliog il Antiques 670-81; 96:91-9; 209-13 My, Jl-Ag '69

POTTERY, Finnish
Red clay renaissance in Finland. D. J. Willcox. il Ceram Mo 17:13-17 My '69

POTTERY, Indian. See Indians of North America—Pottery

POTTERY, Iranian
Man & beast. il UNESCO Courier 22:26-7 N '69

POTTERY, Italian
Porcelain of Naples. N. A. Dal Pozzo. il Antiques 95:270-4 F '69

POTTERY, Japanese
Japanese export porcelain for the American market. R. Gerry and J. T. Butler. il Antiques 95:544-6 Ap '69
Kimpei Nakamura. M. Zimmerman and M. Zimmerman. il Ceram Mo 17:14-17 S '69
Pottery of Toshiko Takaezu. S. E. Meyer il Am Artist 33:42-7 F '69

POTTERY, Mexican
Pottery town, east of Guadalajara. il Sunset 143:79+ O '69

POTTERY, Oriental
Some oriental aspects of European ceramic decoration. H. Syz. bibliog il Antiques 95: 670-81; 96:91-9; 209-13 My, Jl-Ag '69

POTTERY clay. See Clay

POTTERY in house decoration
Porcelain as room decoration in eighteenth-century England. R. J. Charleston. il Antiques 96:894-9 D '69

POTTERY whistles. See Whistles

POTTHOFF, Carl J.
First aid. See issues of Today's health

POTTHOFF, E. H. jr
Urban management needs computers. Am City 84:69-71 Mr '69

POTTS, Larry
Cairo: love it or leave it. W. Willoughby. il Chr Today 14:46 O 24 '69

POUGHKEEPSIE, N.Y.
New use for an old incinerator. J. W. Nelson, jr. il Am City 84:22 D '69

POULIN, A. Jr
Dream; poem. Atlan 223:80 Ap '69
Unpredictable as Grace. Nation 209:734-5 D 29 '69

POULLAIN, Ludwig
Germany's banks flex muscles. il por Bsns W p96-8 My 24 '69

POULSON, Norris
Where are they now? il por Newsweek 73:24 Je 9 '69

POULSON, Thomas L. and White, W. B.
Cave environment. bibliog Science 165:971-81 S 5 '69

POULTRY
See also
Cookery—Poultry
Poultry houses

Anecdotes, facetiae, satire, etc.
Do chickens lay nest eggs? A. Purcell. il Har Yrs 9:30-2 Ag '69

Diseases and pests
Herpesvirus in Marek's disease tumors. G. Schidlovsky and others. bibliog il Science 164:959-61 My 23 '69

Egg production
Put organic eggs in your market basket! M. C. Goldman. il Org Gard & Farm 16:60-5 Ap '69

Feeding
What's missing in commercial poultry feeds? W. Ferguson. il Org Gard & Farm 16:46-8 D '69

POULTRY, Dressing of
Easy way to pluck ducks. J. B. Robinson. il Outdoor Life 144:70-1 O '69

POULTRY, Frozen
Now, a turkey that times itself; Norbest tender-timed turkeys. Consumer Rep 34:168-9 Ap '69
Self-basting turkey, good but expensive. Consumer Rep 34:57 F '69

POULTRY houses
Chickens fit my garden. E. H. Craig. il Org Gard & Farm 16:90-1 Ag '69
Project for the chicken-hearted. G. Logsdon. il Org Gard & Farm 16:59-64 N '69

POULTRY industry and trade
Put organic eggs in your market basket! M. C. Goldman. il Org Gard & Farm 16:60-5 Ap '69

POULTRY inspection
What the new poultry inspection law means. Good H 168:190 My '69

POUND, Charles E.
Sports center for bow, rod and gun enthusiasts. Parks & Rec 4:25-7 D '69

POUND, Ezra
Mirror of Venice. J. C. Holmes. il Travel & Camera 32:73-4 S '69
Pound/Joyce: the letters of Ezra Pound to James Joyce, ed. by F. Read. Review
Cath World 209:91+ My '69. B. Wallenstein

POURING vessels. See Pitchers

POUSSAINT, Alvin F.
Psychiatrist looks at black power. Ebony 24:142-4+ Mr '69

POVÉ, Xavora
Christmas. Harp Baz 103:100A D '69
Cosmic conditioning of hair. Harp Baz 102:13 Jl; 68 Ag; 132 S '69; 103:144 Ja '70
Eye on the sky. See issues of Harper's bazaar
Of planets and personalities. House B 111:82-11 Ap '69

POVERTY
Perspectives on poverty; symposium. bibliog f il Mo Labor R 92:32-62 F '69

Poverty as underdevelopment. P. L. Van Den Berghe. Trans-Action 6:3-4+ Jl '69
See also
Anti-poverty program, 1964-
Poor
Public welfare
Slums

United States
See Poor—United States

POVERTY (virtue)
All things in common. R. Haughton. Cath World 209:197 Ag '69

POVERTY, Voluntary
Dead faith and hunger; eating on welfare budgets. Chr Today 13:24 Jl 18 '69
Playing poor; Boston experiment organized by Paul Chapman. il Newsweek 73:66 Ap 14 '69
Sixty-six cents a day: let them eat squid. P. Coyne. Nat R 21:909 S 9 '69; Reply. W F. Buckley, jr. 21:1027 O 7 '69

POVEY, John F.
African arts for the school. Sch Arts 69:30-1 Ja '70

POWDER metallurgy
Aluminum gets a run in the powder derby. il Bsns W p 152 My 10 '69

POWDERED aluminum. See Aluminum, Powdered

POWELL, Adam Clayton, 1908-
Challenge to Congress; denying his congressional seat declared unconstitutional. por Time 93:17 Je 27 '69
Earl Warren vs. Warren Earl. New Repub 160:10 Je 28 '69
Maverick returns. por Sr Schol 94:15-16 Ja 17 '69
Powell decision. il por Newsweek 73:45-6 Je 30 '69
Unanswered questions in the Powell case. D. Lawrence. U S News 66:88 Je 30 '69
Warren court vs. Congress. il por U S News 66:23-4 Je 30 '69

POWELL, Art
Soul stamps. il por Time 94:74 Jl 11 '69

POWELL, Benjamin E.
Redoubled gothic for Duke. Library J 94:4397-8 D 1 '69

POWELL, Bernard W.
How to make your own antique beams. Pop Mech 132:182-5 N '69

POWELL, Boog
Highlight. por Sports Illus 31:60 Ag 18 '69

POWELL, Enoch
Powell enigma. E. Huxley. il pors Nat R 21:328-30 Ap 8 '69

POWELL, Evan
Keeping the cool in your room air conditioner. Pop Sci 195:153-9+ Ag '69
Know-how you need to repair your small appliances. Pop Sci 194:117-32 Ja '69
Secrets of keeping your automatic washer trouble-free. Pop Sci 194:131-46 F '69

POWELL, Francis X. See Johnson, D. R. jt. auth.

POWELL, John Wesley
Down the Colorado; excerpts. Am Heritage 20:52-9+ O '69

about
Century of the wild Colorado. il pors Life 67:46-51 O 31 '69
Conservation hall of fame. W. C. Darrah. por Nat Wildlife 7:48-9 Ap '69
Grand Canyon river run. J. V. Young. il Travel 131:40-5+ F '69
Powell's quest. M. C. Rabbitt. pors Am For 75:8-9+ S '69
Powell's River; Colorado portfolio; excerpts from Down the Colorado. E. Porter. Audubon 71:64-76 N '69
Retracing John Wesley Powell's historic voyage down the Grand Canyon. J. Judge. il por Nat Geog 135:668-713 My '69

POWELL, Mel
Music of Mel Powell. L. Thimmig. il Mus Q 55:31-44 Ja '69

POWELL, Robert S. jr
Participation is learning. Sat R 53:56+ Ja 10 '70

POWELL, Theodore
Age of Aquarius; address, October 11, 1969. Vital Speeches 36:90-2 N 15 '69

POWELL, LAKE. See Lakes, Artificial

POWELL centennial. See Centennials

POWER, Anne
Church in Cuba. Commonweal 89:704-5 Mr 7 '69

POWER, Keith
Midpeninsula: the ivy league. Nation 208:463-4 Ap 14 '69

POWER, Thomas Sarsfield
Ideas by which we are ruled; excerpt from Design for survival. Harper 238:37 Je '69

POWER (political science)
Altered shape of world power; address, June 9, 1969. E. L. Richardson. Dept State Bul 61:27-9 Jl 14 '69
POWER (social sciences)
American power and the New Mandarins, by N. Chomsky. Review
Nation 208:373-4 Mr 24 '69. R. Sklar
New Repub 160:27-8+ Ap 19 '69. M. Duberman
Anatomy of power. J. S. Brubacher. Ed Digest 35:1-4 N '69
Blessed are the powerful; address, 1968. J. L. Adams. Chr Cent 86:838-41 Je 18 '69
Old order is becoming old hat. il Bsns W p 120-2+ D 6 '69
Power, by A. A. Berle. Review
Time 94:92+ O 31 '69
POWER boat racing. See Motor boat racing
POWER boats. See Motor boats
POWER commission, Federal. See United States—Federal power commission
POWER distribution, Electric. See Electric power distribution
POWER drills. See Drilling and boring machinery
POWER garden tools. See Garden tools, equipment and supplies
POWER lawn mowers. See Lawn mowers
POWER line poles. See Electric lines—Poles
POWER lines. See Electric lines
POWER of attorney
What is a power of attorney? Good H 168:194 My '69
POWER plants
See also
Atomic power plants
Electric plants
Hydroelectric plants
POWER resources
Can we meet the expanding need for energy? il Nations Bsns 57:32-3 N '69
POWER saws. See Saws
POWER supply, Electric. See Electric power
POWER tools. See Electric tools
POWER tools, Portable. See Electric tools, Portable
POWER transmission
See also
Tractors—Transmission
POWERS, Charles W. and Gunnemann, J. P.
Institutions, investments and integrity. Chr Cent 86:144-8 Ja 29 '69
POWERS, Dennis
Books for young westerners. Am West 6:49-Ja '69
POWERS, Elizabeth
Three faces of beauty; ed. by S. Harney. il pors Ladies Home J 86:88-9+ Mr '69
POWERS, J. F.
Bill; story. New Yorker 45:34-40 My 17 '69
Priestly fellowship; story. New Yorker 45:36-46 S 27 '69
POWERS, John J. jr
Government, business, and the balance of payments; address, March 26, 1969. Vital Speeches 35:430-4 My 1 '69
POWERS, John R.
Graduate student. por Phys Today 22:32-3 Mr '69
POWERS, Lindy
Three faces of beauty; ed. by S. Harney. il pors Ladies Home J 86:88-9+ Mr '69
POWERS, Thomas
How to make a buck with dimes and quarters. Life 66:61-2+ My 2 '69
POWILLS, Dorothy
Playing cards. See issues of Hobbies
POWLEDGE, Fred
(ed) Flight from city hall; interviews. Harper 239:69+ N '69
Profiles. New Yorker 45:63-4+ O 25 '69
PRACTICAL jokes
Put-on. F. Maynard. il Seventeen 27:126-7+ N '68
PRADO museum, Madrid
Madrid's fabulous Prado. J. A. Michener. il Read Digest 94:145-51 Je '69
PRAEGER, Frederick Amos
Trade winds. J. Beatty, jr. Sat R 52:14 Ap 19 '69
PRAFKA, W. R.
What you can do to save more healthy pigs. por Farm J 93:H20 Ap '69
PRAGER, Arthur
Secret of Nancy Drew, pushing forty and going strong. Sat R 52:18-19+ Ja 25 '69
PRAGUE
Death to remember. L. Gross. il Look 33:18-26 S 9 '69
Historic houses, etc.
Prague; historic town reservations. D. Libal and E. Stach. il Antiques 95:842-6 Je '69

Theater
African trajedian in golden Prague; with some unpublished correspondence of Ira Aldridge. J. J. Napier and S. B. Winters. Negro Hist Bul 32:23-6 N '69
Czech stage: freedom's last barricade; report by H. Judson. il Time 94:56+ Jl 25 '69
PRAGUE ballet
Art must say something! interview, ed. by L. Joel. P. Smok. il Dance Mag 43:43-6 O '69
World of dance. W. Terry. Sat R 52:28 Je 28 '69
PRAGUE trials. See Communist party (Czechoslovakia)—Purges
PRAIRIE chicken shooting
Alberta sharptail. C. F. Waterman. il Field & S 74:66-7+ S '69
Those shady sharpies. O. W. Larson. il Outdoor Life 144:60-1+ O '69
PRAIRIE chickens
Last dance: threats to the pinnated grouse, or greater prairie chicken. J. Madison. il Audubon 71:16-23 My '69
See also
Cookery—Game
PRAIRIE CREEK redwoods state park. See California—Parks and reserves
PRAIRIE dogs
I'm a prairie dog. M. J. Walker. il Am For 75:35+ Mr '69
PRAIRIES
Snakes and all; Goose Lake prairie. Newsweek 73:29 Mr 3 '69
PRAOMYS. See Rats
PRATT, Charles
Sea of survival; photographs. J. Hay. Audubon 71:41-8 My '69
PRATT, Dallas
Discovery of a world: early maps showing America. Antiques 96:900-6 D '69 (to be cont)
PRATT, Eliot
Obituary
Nation 209:198 S 8 '69
PRATT, Read company
World of Peter Comstock; ivory business. il Forbes 104:51-2 D 1 '69
PRATT, William F.
Anabaptist explosion: adaptation of Pockets of high fertility in the United States; with biographical sketch. por Natur Hist 78:4, 8-10+ F '69
PRATTE, Richard
Public school movement: phoenix or dodobird? Ed Digest 35:1-4 D '69
PRAYER
Feedback from God. W. J. Samarin. Chr Today 14:10-11 O 10 '69
Let us pray. D. Lawrence. U S News 67:88 Ag 11 '69
New year's prayer; reprint. D. Lawrence. U S News 68:76+ Ja 5 '70
We need new ways to pray. A. Whitman. Read Digest 95:77-80 D '69
What's new in prayer. Chr Today 13:38 Mr 28 '69
PRAYER books
See also
Jews—Prayer books and devotions
PRAYER in the schools. See Public schools and religion
PRAYER plants. See Maranta
PRAYER rock, South Dakota. See Indians of North America—Antiquities—South Dakota
PRAYERS
New year's prayer; reprint. D. Lawrence. U S News 68:76+ Ja 5 '70
1969 Protestant inaugural prayers. B. Graham; C. E. Tucker. Chr Today 13:27 F 14 '69
Pithy petitionary prayer in Pennsylvania senate; prayer of R. L. Huggins. Chr Cent 86:971 Jl 23 '69
Prayer for Christmas day. R. L. Stevenson. il Good H 169:71 D '69
Prayers in the leap to the Lord of the yawp; the prayer-poem. W. L. Molton. il Chr Cent 86:1374-9 O 29 '69
PREACHERS. See Clergy
PREACHING
Announcing the word of God. by J. A. Jungmann. Review
Cath World 208:234 F '69. D. J. Leonhardt
Ministry of admonition. Chr Today 14:27 D 5 '69
Prerequisites for preaching. J. D. R. Franklin. Chr Today 13:15 Ja 31 '69
Shared preaching. J. McLaughlin. America 120:342-3 Mr 22 '69
We use great plainness of speech. D. B. Lockerbie. Chr Today 14:12+ O 24 '69
See also
Communication (theology)
Sermons

PREAMPLIFIERS, See Amplifiers

PREBINDING. See Bookbinding

PREBISCH, Raul
Resignation of Raul Prebisch; reply. K. de P. Hughes. Chr Cent 86:121 Ja 22 '69

PRE-CAMBRIAN period. See Geology, Stratigraphic—Pre-Cambrian; Paleontology—Pre-Cambrian

PRECAST concrete. See Concrete, Precast

PRECESSION
Interglacial high sea levels and the control of Greenland ice by the precession of the equinoxes. C. Emiliani. bibliog il Science 166:1503-4 D 19 '69

PRECIOUS stones
Gems and minerals. H. D. Brown. See issues of Hobbies
See also
Diamonds
Emeralds
Gems
Tanzanite

PRECIOUS stones, Artificial
How growing of synthetic gems began. il Chem 42:24-5 F '69
See also
Sapphires, Artificial

PRECIPITATION (chemistry)
Induction in vitro of microtubular crystals by vinca alkaloids. K. G. Bensch and others. bibliog il Science 165:495-6 Ag 1 '69
Vinblastine-induced precipitation of microtubule protein. R. Marantz and others. bibliog il Science 165:498-9 Ag 1 '69
See also
Liesegang rings

PRECIPITATION (meteorology)
See also
Rain and rainfall
Snow

Measurement
Small-scale precipitation network over central Connecticut. F. P. Ostby and others. il Weatherwise 22:60-3+ bibliog (p87) Ap '69

PRECISION approach radar. See Radar in aviation

PRECISION flying. See Aviation—Stunt flying

PRECISION instrument company
Taking on bits by the trillion; laser recording system. il Bsns W p78+ F 1 '69

PRECISION measurement. See Measurement

PRECISION valve corporation
Spitmouth puffers in the living room; development of Walker's Cay by aerosol king, Bob Abplanalp. R. H. Boyle. il Sports Illus 31:28-30+ D 8 '69

PRE-COLUMBIAN art. See Art, Pre-Columbian

PRE-COLUMBIAN mythology. See Mythology, Pre-Columbian

PRECONDITIONING of cattle. See Cattle, Beef—Preconditioning

PRECOOKED food, Frozen. See Food, Frozen

PREDATION (zoology)
Predation and the origin of tetrapods. J. A. Holman. Science 164:588 My 2 '69

PREDICTIONS. See Forecasts; Forecasts (economics)

PREDOVICH, Daniel L.
What happened to the duplicating machine? Ed Digest 34:52-3 Mr '69

PREFAB fireplaces. See Fireplaces

PREFABRICATED bathrooms. See Bathrooms

PREFABRICATED buildings. See Buildings, Prefabricated

PREFABRICATED cabins. See Cabins

PREFABRICATED houses. See Houses, Prefabricated

PREFABRICATION
Sculptured precast tower paces downtown redevelopment: Virginia national bank. il Arch Rec 146:141-4 O '69

PREFACE to anonymous Max; story. See Deck, J.

PREFACES
Anecdotes, facetiae, satire, etc.
Without whose unfailing encouragement. H. F. Ellis. New Yorker 45:24-5 Ag 23 '69

PREFERENCES (psychology)
Orality, preference behavior, and reinforcement value of nonfood object in monkeys with orbital frontal lesions. C. M. Butter and others. bibliog il Science 164:1306-7 Je 13 '69

PREFLIGHT inspection. See Airplanes—Inspection

PREGNANCY
Expectant mother:
Changes during pregnancy. J. S. Miller and E. M. Stern. Redbook 134:16+ D '69
Diet and weight during pregnancy. A. B. Weingold and E. Edelson. Redbook 132:40+ Mr '69
How a mother protects her infant from infectious diseases. V. Apgar. Redbook 133:46 Ag '69
How pregnancy affects your skin. W. E. Josey and D. Z. Meilach. Redbook 133:31+ Je '69
How will you carry your baby? L. T. Hibbard and S. W. Wolfe. Redbook 133:56 O '69
What you should know about X-rays and pregnancy. G. C. Lewis, jr. and P. Feinstein. Redbook 132:30+ F '69
How much weight to gain during pregnancy. il Good H 169:149 Ag '69
How to have a healthy baby. L. W. Sauer. il PTA Mag 63:29-30 Mr '69
New concern for the unborn. il Time 94:52 S 19 '69
Older mother. B. Spock. Redbook 133:24+ S '69
Pregnancy I couldn't face. il Good H 169:12+ S '69
See also
Abortion
Amniotic liquid
Fetus
Sex determination and control

PREGNANCY, Complications of
Bonnie Morgan's miracle baby. E. Keiffer. il Good H 168:62+ Mr '69

PREHISTORIC animals. See Animals, Extinct

PREHISTORIC man. See Man, Prehistoric

PREHISTORIC monuments. See Megalithic monuments

PREISS, David
Quarter century of arts & crafts. Am Artist 33:28-34 F '69

PREJUDICE
How bigotry is born; with study-discussion program, by R. Strang. E. D. Garrick. bibliog il PTA Mag 63:8-11, 35 F '69
Man's relations to man; can we move beyond the pluralistic society? C. Greer. Cur 105:27-31 My '69
People who know how; excerpts from Brave enough for life. B. W. Overstreet. il PTA Mag 63:24-5 Mr '69
War at home; intolerance towards the hippies. D. Wakefield. Atlan 224:119-24 O '69
See also
Race prejudice

PRELUTSKY, Burt
What's Richard Lester trying to do? Holiday 45:82-3+ Ap '69

PREMATURE infants. See Infants, Premature

PREMIUM pay. See Overtime

PREMIUMS
Premium race; offers for opening bank accounts. Newsweek 75:50 Ja 5 '70

PREMIXED cocktails. See Cocktails

PREMONITIONS. See Previsions

PRENATAL care. See Pregnancy

PRENATAL sex determination. See Sex determination and control

PRENTICE, Levi Wells
Decline of the Adirondack painters. W. K. Verner. por Cons 23:17+ Ap '69

PRENTISS, Karl
Don't say woman driver when you talk about Pat Carlsson. Holiday 46:64-5 S '69
Is the steam car ready for a comeback? Holiday 46:46-7 N '69
Luxury, Detroit style. Holiday 46:82-7+ O '69
Will the Mercedes C-111 be the world's most sought after sports car? Holiday 46:62-3+ D '69

PRENTISS, Paula
Dick Benjamin and Paula Prentiss: to love, honor, and analyze. M. W. Lear. il por Redbook 134:54-5+ Ja '70
Trade winds. C. Amory. Sat R 52:8 Jl 26 '69

PREPACKAGED meat. See Meat—Prepackaging

PREPARATION for college. See Colleges and universities—Entrance requirements

PREPARATION of manuscripts. See Printing—Copy preparation

PREPARATORY schools. See Private schools

PREPAREDNESS, Military
See also
Armaments
United States—Defenses

PREPAREDNESS, Military—*Continued*
China (People's Republic)
Preparing for the worst. il Newsweek 74: 32+ Jl 14 '69

PRESBYTERIAN church in Canada
Presbyterian church in Canada assembly. D. H. Rayner. Chr Cent 86:962-4 Jl 16 '69

PRESBYTERIAN church in the United States
Landmark case; Baker affair in Iowa City. Newsweek 73:73 Je 9 '69

PRESBYTERIAN church in the United States (general)
Unwarranted rebuke; grievance committee chastisement of G. A. Taylor. Chr Today 13:26 Mr 14 '69
See also
Associate reformed Presbyterian church
Reformed Presbyterian church
United Presbyterian church in the United States of America

PRESBYTERIAN church in the United States (South)
Ecumenical showdown for southern Presbyterians; proposed Reformed church in America merger. il Chr Today 13:36 Mr 14 '69
PCUS rally; determination without compromise. R. L. Love. Chr Today 14:40-1 Ja 2 '70
Presbyterians, U.S. reject backward view. T. M. McMillan, jr. Chr Cent 86:788-92 Je 4 '69
Relative discord. R. Chandler. Chr Today 13:49-50 Ap 11 '69
Serving notice; Declaration of commitment. Chr Today 14:45 O 24 '69
Southern Presbyterian cliffhanger; merger with Reformed church in America. Chr Today 13:45 F 28 '69
Southern Presbyterians: the gap widens. W. Henley. Chr Today 13:32 My 23 '69

PRESBYTERIAN church in the United States of America
Hands across the border; General Assembly. Newsweek 73:66 My 12 '69
Presbytery mergers win key vote. A. H. Matthews. Chr Today 13:43 My 9 '69
Whence division in the church? Chr Today 13:22 My 23 '69

PRESBYTERIAN general assembly. See Presbyterian church in the United States of America

PRESCHOOL children
How to help your child do well in school. il U S News 67:49-50 O 6 '69
Mathematics for the very young. L. Ellison. il Parents Mag 44:48-9+ Jl '69
Play for all seasons; with study-discussion program. R. Strang. bibliog PTA Mag 63: 19-21, 35 Ja '69
Play groups for the preschool child. McCalls 96:52 Mr '69
Pre-school: books for parents, teachers: summary of addresses. R. LaCrosse; L. E. Feldman. Pub W 195:28-9 Je 9 '69
What every preschooler needs. E. G. Neisser and F. Bauling. il Parents Mag 44:49-51+ Ap '69
See also
Child study
Kindergarten
Nursery schools
Socially handicapped children

Education
Academic grind at age three. B. Grossman. Ed Digest 34:26-8 Mr '69
Can television really teach? Sesame street, produced by the Children's television workshop. F. L. Palmer. il Am Ed 5:2-6 Ag '69
Early learning for what? B. Spodek. Ed Digest 34:13-15 My '69
Education of the infant and young child; AAAS symposium, December 28, 1969. V. H. Denenberg. il Science 166:131 O 3 '69
Happenings in education. W. D. Boutwell. PTA Mag 64:31-2 O '69
National commitment to early childhood education. J. E. Allen, jr. Parents Mag 44:34 O '69
Score on early reading; with study-discussion program. by R. Strang, B. Bowman and D. Anker. bibliog il PTA Mag 64:6-8, 35 N '69
Seedtime in the church: the nursery. M. Le Bar. Ch Today 14:19 D 19 '69
See also
Project Head Start

Nutrition
See Children—Nutrition

PRESCOTT, Orville
Authors & editors. B. A. Bannon. por Pub W 195:19-21 Mr 17 '69

PRESCOTT, Peter S.
Hemingway: the whole truth and nothing but. Look 33:6 Ap 29 '69
Two more American tragedies. Look 33:12 Mr 4 '69

PRESCOTT, Robert William
Big push. il por Forbes 103:28 My 1 '69

PRESCRIPTION drug industry. See Drug trade

PRESCRIPTIONS
Maybe you can pay less for prescriptions; generic drugs. il Changing T 23:19-20 Mr '69
Toward personalized prescriptions. il Time 94:60 Ag 1 '69

PRESENT, The
See also
Past, The

PRESERVATION of architecture. See Architecture—Conservation and restoration

PRESERVATION of landmarks, scenery, etc.
See Landscape protection

PRESERVATION of materials
Time in the palm of your hand. il House B 111:34-7+ Ag '69
See also
Paper—Preservation
Stone—Preservation

PRESERVATION of records. See Records —Preservation

PRESERVATION of zoological specimens. See Zoological specimens—Collection and preservation

PRESERVING. See Canning and preserving

PRESIDENTIAL advisers. See Public officers

PRESIDENTIAL airplanes. See Airplanes, Government

PRESIDENTIAL campaigns
See also
Campaign funds
National conventions (political)
National conventions, Democratic
Presidents—United States—Election
Television in politics

Anecdotes, facetiae, satire, etc.
When (and if) better presidents are made. W. A. McWhirter. Harp Baz 102:148-9+ Ja '69

1952
Nixon's dog. G. Wills. il Esquire 72:91-5+ Ag '69

1968
American melodrama, by L. Chester and others. Review
Cath World 209:270-1 S '69. J. Fisher
New Repub 160:24-6 My 31 '69. L. L. King
Newsweek il 73:110D My 5 '69. A. Cooper
Sat R 52:34 Je 28 '69. D. Young
Balancing the books on the year of the people; E. McCarthy's campaign. T. M. Gannon. America 121:632-4 D 27 '69
Drummers and dexedrine; excerpts from The selling of the President 1968. J. McGinniss. il Newsweek 74:29-30 Jl 21 '69
Making of the President 1968; excerpts. T. H. White. il Life 67:48-48B+ Jl 11; 44B-44D+ Jl 18 '69
Nobody knows. reflections on the McCarthy campaign. J. Larner. Harper 238:62-72+ Ap; 71-83+ My '69; Discussion. 239:6+ Ag '69
Real story of the '68 election: University of Michigan survey research center analysis. il U S News 67:74-5 O 27 '69
Selling of the President 1968, by J. McGinniss. Review
Life 67:14 O 10 '69. M. Kempton
What I learned in 1968 about women, politics, and my husband. J. Muskie. il McCalls 96:92-3+ Ap '69
Wonderful world of George Wallace; with editorial comment. G. Lardner, jr. and J. Loh. il Esquire 71:6, 125-8+ My '69

Anecdotes, facetiae, satire, etc.
Infiltrating Nixon. E. Rothschild. il Ramp Mag 7:38-9 D 14 '68

Bibliography
1968. W. Goodman. Commentary 48:83-6 D '69

1972
Operation Spiro: winning voters to Republican campaign. Nat R 21:1255-6 D 16 '69

PRESIDENTIAL candidates
If people were voting for president today. il U S News 66:14 My 12 '69
See also
Presidential campaigns

PRESIDENTIAL candidates—*Continued*

1968

Anecdotes, facetiae, satire, etc.

Doctor Matrix gives his explanation of why Mr Nixon was elected President. M. Gardner. il Sci Am 220:116-18+ Ja '69

1972

As Kennedy plans for 1972. il U S News 66:82-3 F 24 '69

Democratic hopes. K. Crawford. Newsweek 73:37 F 24 '69

George Wallace's goals for '72. il U S News 66:39 Je 9 '69

How Americans rate Ted Kennedy: Gallup poll findings. U S News 66:19 Mr 17 '69

Ted Kennedy: focusing on '72? il U S News 66:18 Ap 21 '69

Trouble times for the Democrats. il U S News 67:21-2 Ag 11 '69

PRESIDENTIAL communication. See Communication in government

PRESIDENTIAL conventions. See National conventions (political)

PRESIDENTIAL duties. See Presidents—United States—Powers and duties

PRESIDENTIAL elections. See Presidents—United States—Election

PRESIDENTIAL entertaining. See Government entertaining

PRESIDENTIAL inaugurations. See Inaugurations

PRESIDENTIAL libraries

Nixon impropriety. New Repub 160:8 My 31 '69

Presidential libraries. K. V. Hostick. il Hobbies 74:108-9 My; 108 Je; 108-9 Ag '69

President's making of history. H. Feis. Atlan 224:64-5 S '69

PRESIDENTIAL obligation. See Presidents—United States—Powers and duties

PRESIDENTIAL power. See Presidents—United States—Power and duties

PRESIDENTIAL transitions. See Presidents—United States—Transition periods

PRESIDENTIAL veto. See Presidents—United States—Powers and duties

PRESIDENTS

France

France: the making of a president. il Newsweek 73:47 Je 2 '69

How will France change? S. Hoffmann. New Repub 161:21-4 Jl 26 '69

More practical and down to earth: the likely successor to de Gaulle. U S News 66:16 My 12 '69

Ghana

Chairman bows out. Newsweek 73:57-8 Ap 14 '69

Mexico

Presidents of the twentieth century. D. Tunstell. il Am Heritage 20:38-9 Ap '69

United States

From Hayes to McKinley, by H. W. Morgan. Review

Sat R 52:31-2 Ag 9 '69. M. L. Coit

Man with the four-button phone. H. Sidey. il Life 66:4 Ja 31 '69

Spring and the traveler: the first resorts; a roundup of vacationlands preferred by world leaders; symposium. il Sat R 52:39-42+ Mr 8 '69

When LBJ goes to his office now.... il U S News 66:12 F 10 '69

See also
Inaugurations
United States—Executive office of the president
White House

Assassination

Our nation's martyrs. B. Finnegan. il Hobbies 74:158-9+ O '69

Social psychopathology of political assassination. S. J. Slomich and R. E. Kantor. Bul Atom Sci 25:9-12 Mr '69

Birthplaces

See also
Kennedy, J. F.—Birthplace

Children

Whatever happened to the children of five presidents? il U S News 68:14-15 Ja 5 '70

Communication

See Communication in government

Election

Bad idea whose time has come; direct election of the President. I. Kristol and P. Weaver. il N Y Times Mag p43+ N 23 '69; Reply. E. Celler. p4+ D 21 '69

Direct election of the President. America 121:318 O 18 '69

Electing presidents. New Repub 160:9-10 F 22 '69

Electing the president; in defense of the electoral college. R. N. Goodwin. Cur 113:33-5 D '69

Electoral reform. New Repub 160:8 Mr 15 '69

End of American party politics. W. D. Burnham. bibliog il Trans-Action 7:12-22 D '69

Hassle over the presidency. F. Morley. Nations Bsns 57:27-8 Mr '69

Modest reform. Time 93:26 F 28 '69

One person, one vote for president, a step nearer. il U S News 66:58 My 12 '69

Politics for every man; Hughes commission's recommendations. New Repub 160:11 Mr 8 '69

Popular vote is popular. il Nations Bsns 57:29-31 S '69

Presidential lottery; the reckless gamble in our electoral system; condensation. J. A. Michener. Read Digest 94:247-50+ My '69

Renovation scheme; Nixon's proposed electoral refinements. Newsweek 73:22 Mr 3 '69

Republican era ahead for U.S? Yes, if . . . il U S News 66:41-3 F 10 '69

Rush to report the race; book by London daily express team of reporters. Time 93:42+ F 7 '69

Wallace whitelash. S. M. Lipset and E. Raab. il Trans-Action 7:23-32+ D '69

What to watch out for; electoral reform. L. Wilmerding. il Nat R 21:69-72+ Ja 28 '69

See also
Electoral college

Presidential campaigns

Families

See also
Presidents—United States—Children

Families—Protection

How Lynda Bird was guarded by McCalls. E. Weston. McCalls 96:89-90 Mr '69

Health

Mental health of our leaders. A. A. Hutschnecker. Look 33:51-4 Jl 15 '69

See also
Nixon, R. M.—Health

Homes

See also
Nixon, R. M.—Homes

Inaugural addresses

See also
Nixon, R. M.—Inaugural address

Libraries

See Presidential libraries

Messages

See also
Johnson, L. B.—State of the Union message, January 14, 1969

Offices

Through his offices in search of the man. H. Sidey. il Life 67:4 O 17 '69

Portraits

One L.B.J. likes and the one he doesn't like. H. Sidey. Life 66:4 F 14 '69

Powers and duties

Accelerated presidency. H. J. Sievers. America 121:450 N 15 '69

Budding revolt in Congress? curb White House writing of legislation. W. Martin. il Nations Bsns 57:56-61 Je '69

Commitments resolution. il Time 94:14 Jl 4 '69

Congress and foreign policy; import of Resolution 85. H. J. Morgenthau. New Repub 160:16-18 Je 14 '69

Fulbright's revenge; plans to resurrect National commitments resolution. il Newsweek 73:38 Ap 14 '69

Is Nixon bound by Kennedy's Cuban pledge? C. D. Williams. Nat R 21:26+ Ja 14 '69

Limits and excesses of presidential power; excerpt from The crisis of confidence: ideas, power and violence in America. A. Schlesinger, jr. Sat R 52:17-19+ My 3 '69

LBJ speaks to Richard Nixon about what it is to be Mr President. L. B. Johnson. il Look 33:23-5 F 4 '69

Many things to many men. P. Lisagor. Nations Bsns 57:17-18 O '69

Move to limit president's power; national commitment resolution. U S News 67:6 Jl 7 '69

Presidency under scrutiny. T. Wicker. Harper 239:92-4 O '69

PRESIDENTS—United States—Powers and duties—*Continued*
President and the power to make war. M. J. Pusey. Atlan 224:65-7 Jl '69
Presidents, politics, and international intervention; excerpts from The cold-war years: American foreign policy since 1945. P. Y. Hammond. Ann Am Acad 386:10-18 N '69
Richard Nixon on the presidency; excerpts from address, 1968. R. M. Nixon. Sr Schol 94:10-11 Ja 17 '69
Silenced majority; President's obligation to public opinion. C. Frankel. Sat R 52:22+ D 13 '69
War, peace, and the presidency, by H. Paolucci. Review
Nat R 21:184-5 F 25 '69. J. Hart
What kind of president? D. Lawrence. U S News 66:84 Ja 27 '69

Press conferences
Great press put-on. J. Hohenberg. il Sat R 52:120-1 Mr 8 '69
One-sided game; Presidential press conferences. il Newsweek 74:90 D 22 '69
See also
Nixon, R. M.—Press conferences

Protection
Security shield for Nixon. il U S News 66:23 Mr 3 '69

Public relations
Cool and calm by the Potomac. H. J. Sievers. America 120:182 F 15 '69
Our President, Appalachian style. children's political attitudes. Trans-Action 6:6 F '69
Why so much youth unrest today; LBJ's view; excerpts from interview. L. B. Johnson. il U S News 66:19 F 24 '69
See also
Johnson, L. B.—Public relations
Nixon, R. M.—Public relations

Qualifications
Mental health of our leaders. A. A. Hutchnecker. Look 33:51-4 Jl 15 '69

Relations with Congress
Changing role of Congress (1789-1969) il Sr Schol 94:14-15+ F 28 '69
Congress and military commitments: an overview. A. S. Nanes. bibliog f Cur Hist 57: 105-11+ Ag '69
Diary of Hiram Johnson; excerpts. ed. by L. W. Levine. H. Johnson. Am Heritage 20: 64-76 Ag '69
Why the slow pace in Congress. il U S News 67:19-20 Jl 14 '69
See also
Nixon, R. M.—Relations with Congress

Relations with the press
See Government and the press

Religion
God and the White House. il Newsweek 74: 57 Jl 14 '69
Worship in the East room. il Time 94:48 Jl 11 '69
See also
Eisenhower. D. D.—Religion
Nixon, R. M.—Religion

Salaries, allowances, etc.
Inflation by fiat. New Repub 160:10-11 F 1 '69
Planes, boats, expenses; president's pay is many things. il U S News 66:32-4 Ja 27 '69

Speechwriters
See Public officers

Sports
Sporting life. il Time 94:21-2 Jl 4 '69
See also
Nixon, R. M.—Sports

Transition periods
Annals of politics; post of attorney general during the transition. R. Harris. New Yorker 45:64-8+ N 15 '69

Travel
Lure of faraway places. P. Lisagor. Nations Bsns 57:19-20 S '69

Wives
See also
Nixon, P. R.
PRESIDENTS, College. See College presidents
PRESIDENTS, Company. See Executives
PRESIDENT'S advisory commission on civil disorders. See United States—National advisory commission on civil disorders

PRESIDENT'S commission on postal organization. See United States—President's commission on postal organization
PRESIDENT'S commission on the assassination of President Kennedy. See United States —President's commission on the assassination of President Kennedy
PRESIDENT'S council of economic advisers. See United States—Council of economic advisers
PRESIDENT'S equal employment opportunity commission. See United States—Equal employment opportunity commission
PRESIDENT'S foreign intelligence advisory board. See United States—President's foreign intelligence advisory board
PRESIDENT'S park. See Washington, D.C.— Parks and playgrounds
PRESIDENTS press conferences. See Presidents—United States—Press conferences
PRESIDING officers. See Chairmen
PRESIDIO. See San Francisco
PRESLEY, Elvis
Absolutely free. M. Hentoff. Harper 239:28+ N '69
Presley: the product is sex. M. Ames. Hi Fi 19:104 Ap '69
Return of The Pelvis. il por Newsweek 74:83 Ag 11 '69
Rock, etc; engagement at the new International hotel, Las Vegas; first in nine years. E. Willis. New Yorker 45:76-8 Ag 30 '69
PRESNELL, Richard W.
How to harvest wild rice. Cons 23:48-9+ Je '69
PRESS, Frank
Suboceanic mantle. bibliog Science 165:174-6 Jl 11 '69
PRESS. See Journalism; News agencies
PRESS, Catholic. See Catholic press
PRESS agencies. See News agencies
PRESS and crime. See Crime and the press
PRESS and government. See Government and the press
PRESS conferences
See also
Presidents—United States—Press conferences
PRESS drying of wood. See Lumber—Drying
PRESS photography. See Photography, Journalistic
PRESS relations. See Publicity
PRESS releases
See also
Government and the press
PRESS secretaries. See Public officers
PRESSED flowers and leaves. See Flowers, Dried
PRESSES
See also
Hydraulic presses
PRESSURE
Measurements in the high-pressure environment; report of meeting. E. C. Lloyd and others. il Science 164:860-2 My 16 '69
See also
Manometers
PRESSURE cooking
Meals under pressure. il Farm J 93:58-9+ My '69
PRESSURE groups
Meet the women of the revolution, 1969. P. Babcox. il N Y Times Mag p34-5+ F 9 '69; Discussion p6+ Mr 2; 16+ Mr 23 '69
Nader's raiders. J. Newfield. il Life 67:56-56B+ O 3 '69
New feminists. J. Freeman. il Nation 208:241-4 F 24 '69
Spectator's guide to the troublemakers. J. Kifner. il Esquire 71:86-91 F '69
See also
Lobbying
PRESSURE of population. See Population—Overpopulation
PRESSURE vessels
Boilermaker loses its steam; production delays with nuclear boilers. il Bsns W p62+ O 25 '69
Great nuclear fizzle at old B.&W; pressure vessels for nuclear power plants. H. B. Meyers. il Fortune 80:123-5+ N '69
Pressure; B&W's production problems with nuclear reactor boilers. il Forbes 104:26-7 O 1 '69
PRESTON, Betty Brown
Summer spooks; story. Seventeen 28:92-3 Jl '69
PRESTON, Paula Sampson
Printed and painted cottons from the collection of Old Sturbridge village. Antiques 96: 546-51 O '69
PRESTON, Richard
Competition will be fierce for future shares of land. Nations Bsns 57:80-1+ S '69

PREUS, Jacob A. O.
 Missouri synod survives strain; 1969. R.
 Jensen. Chr Cent 86:1072-3 Ag 13 '69
 Missouri synod's new president. Chr Today
 13:35 Ag 1 '69
PREVENTION of crime. See Crime prevention
PREVENTION of cruelty to animals. See Ani-
 mals—Treatment
PREVENTIVE medicine. See Medicine, Preven-
 tive
PREVISIONS
 Dad's last good-bye. G. Christy. Good H
 168:89+ Ap '69
PREWITT, C. T. and Sleight, A. W.
 Garnet-like structures of high-pressure cad-
 mium germanate and calcium germanate.
 bibliog Science 163:386-7 Ja 24 '69
PREZIOSO, Sal J.
 Economic advantages of parklands to a com-
 munity; excerpts from address. Parks &
 Rec 3:27+ O '68
 NRPA executive is guest on Today show;
 interview, ed. by B. Monroe. il por Parks
 & Rec 4:17-18+ O '69
PRIBRAM, Karl H.
 Neurophysiology of remembering; with bio-
 graphical sketch. Sci Am 220:18, 73-80+
 bibliog(p 138) Ja; 6-7 Je '69
PRICE, Arnold H.
 (comp) Articles and other books received;
 Germany, Austria, and Switzerland. See is-
 sues of American historical review
PRICE, Charles
 Golf. Esquire 71:44+ Je '69
 I am a stupid. Esquire 71:148-50+ Ap '69
PRICE, Leontyne
 Speaking of records. por Hi Fi 19:28 My '69

 about

 Records:
 Mozart arias. Opera N 34:36 Ja 10 '70
PRICE, Nancy
 Hackberry; poem. Nation 209:512 N 10 '69
 Midstream; poem. Commonweal 90:595 S 26 '69
 Refugees; poem. America 121:613 D 20 '69
PRICE, Pearl B.
 President's message. por PTA Mag 64:18-19
 S '69
PRICE, Raye
 Ghosts of the golden spike. Travel 131:44-9
 Ap '69
PRICE, Sylvia
 Books for the counter-culture. bibliog por
 Library J 94:2193-202 Je 1 '69
PRICE, T. Rowe
 How to handle your investments; interview.
 por U S News 67:64-7 Jl 7 '69

 about

 Old curmudgeon's new era. pors Forbes 104:
 62-3 Jl 1 '69
PRICE, William J.
 Washington scene. Bul Atom Sci 25:34-6 Ap
 '69
 —and Bass, L. W.
 Scientific research and the innovative
 process. bibliog Science 164:802-6 My 16 '69
PRICE control. See Price regulation by government
PRICE-earnings ratios. See Stock—Price-earn-
 ings ratios
PRICE fixing, Resale. See Price maintenance
 by industry
PRICE indexes
 Analysis of price changes in second quarter
 of 1969. W. J. Layng and T. Nakayama. il
 Mo Labor R 92:36-41 O '69
 Consumer prices; tables. See issues of Month-
 ly labor review
 Pinch of inflation and unrest; consumer-
 price-index figures for March. il Newsweek
 73:31-2 My 5 '69
 Price changes in the first quarter of 1969
 in perspective. J. Popkin. bibliog il Mo
 Labor R 92:26-30 Jl '69
 Up and up. Newsweek 73:79 Je 2 '69
 Wholesale prices; tables. See issues of Month-
 ly labor review
PRICE maintenance by industry
 Do auto prices mean what they say? il
 Bsns W p60-1+ S 6 '69
 Fair trade is fair game; Germany. il Bsns
 W p50 Ja 10 '70
 Heading for costly bath; conviction of lead-
 ing makers of plumbing supplies. Bsns W
 p52 My 10 '69
 How judgment came for the plumbing con-
 spirators. A. T. Demaree. il Fortune 80:96-
 9+ D '69
 $120 million settlement; five leading drug-
 makers to settle claims for allegedly rig-
 ging the price of tetracycline. Time 93:92
 F 14 '69
 Settling up; major drug firms offer $120
 million. Newsweek 73:85-6 F 17 '69

Tub of trouble; antitrust investigation of the
 bathroom fixtures industry. Time 93:110+
 My 16 '69
PRICE regulation by government

 United States

 Curbs on wages and prices. America 120:
 702-3 Je 21 '69
 How government wields its pricing power. il
 Bsns W p46 Mr 29 '69
 Nixon's no on controls; wage and price con-
 trols. U S News 67:5 Jl 28 '69
 Politics of full employment. A. Altshuler. il
 Trans-Action 6:43-7 My '69
 Would guidelines work better? with editorial
 comment. Bsns W p 134-6, 172 O 18 '69
PRICE supports, Agricultural. See Agricultural
 administration—United States
PRICES
 See also
 Cost of living
 Inflation (finance)
 Profiteering
 Supply and demand
 also subhead Prices under various sub-
 jects, e.g. Books—Prices; also headings be-
 ginning Price

 Great Britain

 Other side; abandonment of Resale price
 maintenance in the record industry. T.
 Heinitz. Sat R 52:47 Ag 30 '69

 United States

 Business roundup; prospect for prices. For-
 tune 80:20+ Ag 1 '69
 Consumer prices; tables. See issues of Month-
 ly labor review
 First signs of a slowdown. il Time 93:89-90
 My 9 '69
 Green for greed; industry price-hikes. J.
 Deedy. Commonweal 91:2 O 3 '69
 How import quotas raise consumer prices.
 il Consumer Rep 34:270-4 My '69
 Inflation jawboning, Nixon-style. il Time 94:
 92-3 N 28 '69
 Latest on zooming prices. U S News 67:5
 D 29 '69
 Painful process of slowing down. il Time
 94:66+ Ag 1 '69
 Prices are up for almost everything. il U S
 News 67:28 O 6 '69
 Prices still rising; what a national survey
 shows. il U S News 67:29-31 D 8 '69
 Where the price spiral gets that extra twist.
 il Bsns W p 18-19 Ap 5 '69
 Wholesale prices; tables. See issues of Month-
 ly labor review
 Why Americans are buying less. il Time 94:
 90 O 3 '69
 See also
 Price indexes
 Price regulation by government—United States
 also subhead Prices under various sub-
 jects, e.g. Food—Prices
PRICHARD, Philip S.
 Photographers to a nation. Américas 21:36-41
 S '69
PRICKLY poppies. See Poppies
PRIDE, Benton
 Yale elects a wise janitor. il pors Life 67:
 99-100 D 5 '69
PRIDEAUX, Tom
 Cry from the past for an artistic conscience.
 Life 66:32-5 Ap 4 '69
 Offbeat-but on Broadway. Life 66:82-4+ Mr
 14 '69
 Rise of the self-love song. Life 67:12 N 28 '69
PRIEST, Roger
 Enemy of the people. M. Polner. Common-
 weal 90:560 S 19 '69; Reply. S. L. Wilcox.
 91:111 O 24 '69
PRIEST in the cellar; drama. See Conlan, J.
PRIEST workers. See Worker priests
PRIESTHOOD. See Priests
PRIESTLY fellowship; story. See Powers, J. F.
PRIESTS
 American pastor and social change. W. J.
 Byron. America 120:246-9 Mr 1 '69; Dis-
 cussion. 120:317-18 Mr 22 '69
 Conflict at Chur; meetings of European
 bishops and priests. with editorial comment.
 M. von Galli. America 121:52, 68-70 Ag 2
 '69
 Educating priests after the seminary. F. K.
 Scheets. America 120:526-8 My 3 '69
 Facing a new priesthood. R. A. Blake. Cath
 World 209:67-70 My '69
 Interview with Malcolm Boyd; ed. by P.
 Granfield. M. Boyd. Cath World 208:208-13
 F '69

PRIESTS—*Continued*
Man in the cutaway suit. L. R. Ward. il
Commonweal 90:165-7 Ap 25 '69
Of many things; future status of the clergy.
D. R. Campion. America 120:inside cover
Mr 1 '69
Priesthood. J. C. Haughey. America 122:18-20
Ja 10 '70
Priests and priesthoods; with reply. J. D.
Donovan. il Commonweal 91:141-5 O 31 '69
Priests for tomorrow, by R. J. Bunnik. Review
America 120:628 My 24 '69. R. J. Hauser
Commonweal 90:348-9 Je 6 '69. A. Atkins
Religious life and the religious layman. J.
O'Connor. Cath World 208:199-204 F '69
Reporter at large; Emmaus house, radical
Catholic community in East Harlem. F.
Du Plessix. New Yorker 44:37-8+ Ja 25 '69
When a priest leaves the ministry. W. W.
Bassett. America 120:242-5 Mr 1 '69; Reply.
J. D. Gerken. 120:381-2 Ap 5 '69
See also
Celibacy
Chaplains, Military
Ex-nuns, priests, etc.
Marriage of priests
Negro priests
Worker priests

Anecdotes, facetiae, satire, etc.
Where are you, Fr O'Brien? Where are you,
Fr Fitzgerald? J. Brennan. Nat R 21:231+
Mr 11 '69

Associations, institutions, etc.
News and views; National federation of
priests' councils. J. Deedy. Commonweal
90:34 Mr 28 '69
No honky apostolate, say urban priests. W.
McClinton. Commonweal 90:254-5 My 16 '69
Of many things; Padres, organization of
Spanish-speaking priests. C. J. McNaspy.
America 121:inside cover N 1 '69; Reply. E.
Rodriquez. 121:547 D 6 '69
Open letter from French priests. A. Woodrow.
Commonweal 89:610-11 F 14 '69
Priests for a free ministry; Society of priests
for a free ministry. America 120:348 Mr 29
'69
Priests versus bishops? America 120:180 F
15 '69; Reply. W. L. Doty. 120:234 Mr 1 '69
Togetherness is the word in Canada. D. J.
Roche. Commonweal 89:578 F 7 '69
See also
National federation of priests' councils

Political activities
Priests in public office. America 121:550 D
6 '69
PRIESTS conferences. See Clergy conferences
PRIETO, Carlos
Carlos Prieto writes about shells; excerpts
from address, ed. by A. G. Melvin. por Hobbies 74:145+ S; 145+ O; 144+ N; 146-7 D
'69
PRIETO, Mariana
What you should know about using the
flashback in fiction. Writers Digest 49:44-
7 My '69
PRIMACY of the Pope. See Popes—Primacy
PRIMAQUINE
Membrane alterations in hemolysis: internalization of plasmalemma induced by
primaquine. F. L. Ginn and others. bibliog
il Science 164:843-5 My 16 '69
PRIMARIES
See also subhead Politics and government under names of states, cities, e.g.
New York (city)—Politics and government
PRIMATES
Hemoglobins A and A₂ in New World primates: comparative variation and its evolutionary implications. S. H. Boyer and
others. bibliog il Science 166:1428-31 D 12 '69
Vocal tract limitations on the vowel repertoires of rhesus monkey and other nonhuman primates. P. H. Lieberman and
others. bibliog il Science 164:1185-7 Je 6
'69
You can't teach a monkey how to talk. il
Sci Digest 66:67-8 S '69
See also
Gorillas
Monkeys
PRIME ministers conferences
Love, and complaints, for teacher; Commonwealth Prime ministers conference. il
Time 93:38 Ja 24 '69
PRIME rate. See Interest
PRIMITIVE and early church. See Church history—Primitive and early church
PRIMITIVE areas. See Wilderness areas
PRIMITIVE art. See Art, Primitive
PRIMITIVE musical instruments. See Musical instruments, Primitive

PRIMITIVE navigation. See Navigation, Primitive
PRIMITIVE society. See Society, Primitive
PRIMROSES
First call for spring; the primroses. il House
& Gard 136:142-3 S '69
No other plant quite matches it; polyanthus
il Sunset 142:256 +Ap '69
Primula japonica. K. S. Taylor. il Horticulture 47:18-19 Jl '69
Primulas for your garden. R. James. Horticulture 47:49 Ja '69
Success with primroses. D. Rose. il Home
Gard 56:30 Ap '69
PRIMULAS. See Primroses
PRINCE, Alain Wood
Fall: a time for pike. pors Field & S 74:
62-3+ O '69
Our old Kentucky houseboat. Outdoor Life
143:68-71+ My '69
PRINCE, George M.
How to be a better meeting chairman. Harvard Bsns R 47:98-108 Ja '69
PRINCE, William Henry Wood
Prince, the General and the Greyhound. por
Time 93:94 My 9 '69
PRINCE Igor; ballet. See Ballets—Criticisms
PRINCE Igor; opera. See Borodin, A. P.
PRINCES and princesses
See also
Princes of Wales
PRINCES of Wales
Magnificent spectacle for a future king. A.
Menen. il McCalls 96:58-9+ Je '69
Of Wales and its princes. il Time 93:28 Je
27 '69
Reflections of a one-time Prince of Wales.
Edward VIII. il McCalls 96:60-1+ Je '69
See also
Charles, prince of Wales
PRINCESS and the greenies; drama. See Kane,
E. B.
PRINCESS with the broken heart; drama. See
Keenan, M.
PRINCETON, Ind.
Lighting transforms a square into a mall.
W. McConnell. il Am City 84:130 Mr '69
PRINCETON, N.J.
Nassau street. L. Stinnett. il Holiday 46:78-
80 S '69
PRINCETON chamber orchestra. See Chamber
orchestras
PRINCETON reservation. See Indians of North
America—Reservations
PRINCETON university
Gatsby lives; new student magazine Business
today. A. R. Dolan. Nat R 21:648 Jl 1 '69
Girls among the ivy. il Newsweek 73:71 My
12 '69
Integration by evasion. R. F. Engs and
J. B. Williams. Nation 209:537-40 N 17 '69
Lady into tiger. il Life 67:105-6 S 19 '69
Quest for academic relevance; enrollment for
sociology courses. Sat R 52:84 O 18 '69
214 to 1: coeds at Princeton. J. Steinberg.
il Mlle 68:232-3+ Ap '69

Art museum
Boudinot furnishings in the Art museum of
Princeton university. H. Backlin-Landman.
il Antiques 96:366-71 S '69

Gas dynamics laboratory
Hypersonic studies get new focus. M. L.
Yaffee. il Aviation W 91:34-5 D 22 '69

**Research center for urban and
environmental planning**
Planning workbook for the community. J. M.
Dixon. il Arch Forum 131:32-9 D '69
PRINCIPALS, School. See School superintendents and principals
PRINT washers. See Photography—Processing—
Apparatus and supplies
PRINT writing. See Penmanship
PRINTED circuits
How to make etched circuits. J. A. Gupton,
jr. il Radio-Electr 40:23-6 Je '69
Printed circuits, path of least resistance.
R. Hartkopf. il Pop Electr 30:63-4+ Je '69
Printed circuits; symposium. il Electr World
82:37-60 O '69

Coatings
See also Protective coatings
PRINTERS
See also
Typophiles, The
PRINTERS marks
Printers, printing and heraldry; adaptation
of address. J. Moran. il Pub W 196:80-2+
Jl 7 '69

PRINTING

Printing-image carriers for letterpress. V. Strauss. il Pub W 195:76+ F 3 '69
See also
Block printing
Computers—Printing applications
Electronics in printing
Lasers—Printing applications
Lithography
Photomechanical processes
Proofreading
Proofs (printing)
Textile printing
Typophiles, The

Copy preparation

Some effects of computer composition on the editorial process in book publishing; address, March 27, 1969. L. Shatzkin. Pub W 195:28-31 Ap 7 '69
Who'll do the work? B. Lasky. Pub W 196: 13-14 D 15 '69

Design

Otto Treumann graphic designer. I. Soifer. il Pub W 196:64+ Ag 4 '69
Typography for the future: applying the new technology, not refusing it; excerpts from address, October 10, 1969. H. Zapf. Pub W 196:54-6 N 3 '69
See also
Type and typefounding

History

Typesetting. G. O. Walter. il Sci Am 220: 60-9 My '69
See also
Incunabula
Printers marks

Legibility

Few thoughts on legibility. C. B. Grannis. Pub W 195:73 F 3 '69

Private presses

See Private presses

PRINTING (photography) See Photography— Printing processes

PRINTING, Linoleum. See Linoleum block printing

PRINTING, Offset
Web offset printing, a case history; excerpts from address, November 1969. C. W. Cook. Pub W 196:53-4+ D 1 '69

PRINTING conferences
New York printing week: new printing creativity from advanced technology. il Pub W 195:86-9 Mr 3 '69

PRINTING industries of America, Incorporated
PIA graphic arts awards. il Pub W 196:96 Jl 7 '69

PRINTING industry
As printers specialize. F. B. Myrick. Pub W 195:68 Ap 7 '69
Incunabula and the New World. N. López Pellón. il Américas 21:11-17 N '69
See also
Strikes—United States—Printers

PRINTING machinery
See also
Hoe, R. and company

PRINTING offices
Eastern press inc: renovation and expansion in an urban setting. il Arch Rec 145:162-3 F '69
Oberlin printing: diverse functions within a single form. il Arch Rec 145:160-1 F '69

PRINTING paper (photography) See Photographic paper

PRINTING plates
New developments in platemaking; summary of conference; January 15, 1969. il Pub W 195:90+ Mr 3 '69
New plate upholds power of letterpress: Letterflex plastic printing plate. il Bsns W p68+ F 8 '69
Printing-image carriers for letterpress. V. Strauss. il Pub W 195:76+ F 3 '69

PRINTING presses
Paperback printing speeds up; Cameron machine press turns paper into books in one operation. Bsns W p54 Ap 5 '69

PRINTOUT; story. See Green, R.

PRINTS
Gyotaku: ancient Japanese art of fishprinting. W. Hartley and E. Hartley. il Sci Digest 66:28-31 D '69
Intaglio prints of Bernard Childs. U. E. Johnson. il Art in Am 57:118-21 N '69
Maps and pictures; Williamsburg, Va. J. M. Dolmetsch. il Antiques 95:138-44 Ja '69

Paolozzi mix. C. Finch. il Art N 67:32-4+ F '69
See also
Block printing
Lithographs
Monotypes
Shadowgrams

Collectors and collecting

Two housewives run a gallery; Berman-Medalie art gallery, Newtonville, Mass. J. Kuh. il Ladies Home J 86:31 Mr '69

Exhibitions

Unknown masters in wood; Los Angeles' U.C.L.A. art gallery displaying Japanese ukiyo-e hanga. il Time 93:54-7 My 2 '69

Technique

Collographs without a press. M. Hirschl. il Sch Arts 68:14-17 F '69
Culinary print. R. Broner. il Craft Horiz 29: 52-3 My '69
Experiments in three dimensions: Michael Ponce de Leon. C. Gray. il Art in Am 57: 72-3 My '69
Pseudo woodcuts with acetate. P. E. Tobey. il Design 70:15 mid-Wint '69
Redwood forest as seen in plant prints. I. Geary. il Audubon 71:52-7 Jl '69
Texture prints with tile. M. T. Thomas. il Design 70:10-11 mid-Wint '69
See also
Linoleum block printing

PRINTS, Finger. See Fingerprints

PRINTS, Photographic. See Photographs

PRISCILLA of Boston. See Kidder, P.

PRISMS
Aberrations of a prism diagonal. F. J. Eastman, jr. il Sky & Tel 38:261-2 O '69

PRISON camps
Russia
My testimony; tr. by M. Gnoutcheff and R. Nacht. A. Marchenko. il Read Digest 95:193-6+ Ag '69
Torture in the USSR. P. J. Lyons. il Nat R 21:1259-60 D 16 '69

PRISON education. See Education of prisoners

PRISON escapes. See Escapes

PRISON guards. See Prisons—Officials and employees

PRISON management
Life-styles: building time. D. Pearce. il Esquire 71:130-4+ Ap '69
See also
Prisons—Officials and employees

PRISON psychology
Community meetings in a prison setting. T. D. Eftihiades. Ment Hy 53:289-94 Ap '69

PRISON recreation
Recreation in correctional institutions. L. E. Decker. il Parks & Rec 4:31-2+ Ap '69

PRISON wardens
New warden in Chicago. il Newsweek 74:50 Ag 25 '69
Warden who reformed the world's worst jail; Cook County jail. H. J. Massaquoi. il Ebony 24:60-2+ Jl '69

PRISONERS
Corrections and the violent offender. M. E. Wolfgang. bibliog f il Ann Am Acad 381: 119-24 Ja '69
See also
Escapes
Negro prisoners
Political prisoners
Prisons

Rehabilitation

Breaking the bars: work-release schemes. il Newsweek 73:108+ F 17 '69
Continuum of corrections; emergence of community-treatment centers, work-release, and furlough programs studies in New York and in New Jersey. H. G. Moeller. Ann Am Acad 381:81-8 Ja '69
Convict and the burgher: a case study of communication and crime; Salisbury jail and Patuxent institution, Jessup, Md; address. J. Whitehill. Am Scholar 38:441-51 Sum '69
Convicts bone up on stocks; Bache's investment course at San Quentin. Bsns W p22 Ja 18 '69
Designing for change: problems of planned innovation in corrections. H. B. Bradley. bibliog f Ann Am Acad 381:89-98 Ja '69
Jungle rats; convicts and judges swap roles at workshop on crime and correction in Annapolis, Md. il Time 93:78 Je 27 '69
Rapping with convicts; conference in Annapolis, Md. R. L. Goldfarb. New Repub 161: 21-3 Jl 19 '69

PRISONERS—Rehabilitation—*Continued*
Realism in community-based correctional services. M. Burdman. bibliog f Ann Am Acad 381:71-80 Ja '69
Role playing: a judge is a con, a con is a judge; Workshop on crime and correction, Annapolis, Md. R. Hammer. il N Y Times Mag p56-7+ S 14 '69; Reply. R. Korn and others. p54 O 5 '69
See also
Education of prisoners

Treatment

Address. E. Cleaver. Ramp Mag 7:6-10 D 14 '68
America's Devil's Island; inside the Army stockade at San Francisco's presidio. D. Duncan. Ramp Mag 7:8+ Ja 25 '69
Life-styles; building time. D. Pearce. il Esquire 71:130-4+ Ap '69
Night at Santa Rita; abuse by guards. R. Scheer. il Ramp Mag 6:50-1 Ag '69
Nightmare for the innocent in a California jail. J. P. Ritter, jr. il Life 67:51-2+ Ag 15 '69
Support your local police; abuse by guards at Santa Rita. New Repub 160:9 Je 21 '69
Warning from Berkeley; abuse by guards at Santa Rita rehabilitation center. Nation 208:747-8 Je 16 '69
See also
Prisons—Social work

Biafra

Reprieve for eighteen. Time 93:44+ Je 13 '69

Greece, Modern

Prisoner of Amorgos; G. Mylonas. N. Gage. il N Y Times Mag p23-5+ S 21 '69; Reply. G. D. Pappas. p 16+ O 12 '69

Russia

Three jailed churchmen feared dead in Ukraine. Chr Today 13:41 My 9 '69

PRISONERS, Discharged
Barbwire theater; ex-convicts produce The Cage. il Newsweek 75:66-7 Ja 12 '70

Rehabilitation

Lessons for Norman house; halfway house movement for resettlement of homeless offenders. M. Turner. Ann Am Acad 381:39-46 Ja '69
New lobby, ex cons; Fortune society. G. Samuels. il N Y Times Mag p36-8+ O 19 '69; Reply. D. T. Orsini. p32+ N 16 '69

PRISONERS, Education of. See Education of prisoners

PRISONERS as authors
Books; personal record of British prisoner Zeno. K. Fraser. New Yorker 45:134+ Ap 5 '69

PRISONERS of war
By the book; Code of the U.S. fighting man. il Newsweek 73:23 Mr 3 '69
International conference of the Red cross calls for observance of the Geneva convention on prisoners of war; statement, with text of resolution. G. Martin. Dept State Bul 61:323-5 O 13 '69
New compassion for the prisoner of war; Time essay. il Time 93:16-17 Ja 31 '69
See also
Vietnamese war, 1957- —Prisoners and prisons

PRISONERS of war, Returned
Blowing the whistle; treatment of R. Frishman. D. Hegdahl and W. Rumble in North Vietnamese prisons. il Time 94:31 S 12 '69
Indicted diplomat; D. Dellinger, American negotiator for release of three U.S. fliers. Nation 209:68 Jl 28 '69
Plight of the prisoners; three U.S. prisoners freed. il Time 94:21-3 Ag 15 '69
Prisoners; experiences of G. E. Smith and others. D. Duncan. Ramp Mag 8:51-6 S '69
Prisoners from Hanoi; were they tortured? with editorial comment. J. M. Van Dyke. Nation 209:332, 334-5 O 6 '69
Unanswered questions; three U.S. airmen released by North Vietnamese. il Newsweek 74:43 Ag 18 '69

PRISONERS of war in the Middle East
Rate of exchange. Time 94:42 D 12 '69

PRISONERS of war in Vietnam. See Vietnamese war, 1957- —Prisoners and prisons

PRISONS
See also
Crimes and criminals
Parole
Penal colonies
Prisoners
Probation system
Punishment

Officials and employees

Night at Santa Rita; abuse by guards. R. Scheer. il Ramp Mag 8:50-1 Ag '69
Support your local police; abuse by guards at Santa Rita. New Repub 160:9 Je 21 '69
Warning from Berkeley; abuse by guards at Santa Rita rehabilitation center. Nation 208:747-8 Je 16 '69
See also
Prison wardens

Social work

Some directions for citizen involvement in corrections. V. O'Leary. bibliog f Ann Am Acad 381:99-108 Ja '69

Arkansas

One year of prison reform. T. Murton. Nation 210:12-17 Ja 12 '70

California

Night at Santa Rita; abuse by guards. R. Scheer. il Ramp Mag 8:50-1 Ag '69
Support your local police; abuse by guards at Santa Rita. New Repub 160:9 Je 21 '69
Warning from Berkeley; abuse by guards at Santa Rita rehabilitation center. Nation 208:747-8 Je 16 '69

Colorado

Black and proud behind bars; Swahili and soul program at Colorado prison. D. Bogle. il Ebony 24:64-6+ Ag '69

Great Britain

Books; personal record of prisoner Zeno. K. Fraser. New Yorker 45:134+ Ap 5 '69
Irish 'who' in a British whodunit; escape of G. Blake from London's Wormwood Scrubs prison. M. Mok. il Life 66:59-62 Ja 24 '69

Illinois

New warden in Chicago; Cook County jail. il Newsweek 74:50 Ag 25 '69
Warden who reformed the world's worst jail; Cook County jail. H. J. Massaquoi. il Ebony 24:60-2+ Jl '69

Kansas

Kansas's Achilles' heel; power struggle at state penitentiary. il Newsweek 75:19-20 Ja 5 '70

Maryland

Convict and the burgher; a case study of communication and crime; Salisbury jail and Patuxent institution, Jessup; address. J. Whitehill. Am Scholar 38:441-51 Sum '69
Jungle rats; convicts and judges swap roles at workshop on crime and correction in Annapolis, Md. il Time 93:78 Je 27 '69
Role playing; a judge is a con, a con is a judge; Workshop on crime and correction, Annapolis. R. Hammer. il N Y Times Mag p56-7+ S 14 '69; Reply. R. Korn and others. p54 O 5 '69

New York (state)

See also
New York (city)—Prisons and reformatories

Russia

Day in the life of Yuli Daniel; labor camp at Potma in the Volga basin. Time 93:44 Je 6 '69
See also
Concentration camps—Russia

United States

Cloacal region of American corrections; prospects for local jail reform. H. W. Mattick and A. B. Aikman. bibliog f il Ann Am Acad 381:109-18 Ja '69
Conspiracy for correctional reform. R. Goldfarb. New Repub 161:15 D 13 '69
Correctional system: problems and prospects. C. Schrag. bibliog f Ann Am Acad 381:11-20 Ja '69
Crime hatcheries; Senate subcommittee hearings on juvenile delinquency and institutions for dealing with it. il Newsweek 73:36 Mr 17 '69
Prison system breaking down? Search for a better way; with interview by J. E. Ragen. il U S News 67:60-3 Ag 11 '69
Realism in community-based correctional services. M. Burdman. bibliog f Ann Am Acad 381:71-80 Ja '69

Vietnam (Republic)

Behind Vietnam's prison walls. D. Luce. Chr Cent 86:261-2+ F 19 '69
Devil's island off Vietnam; the price of political dissent. T. Fox. Commonweal 90:432-5 Jl 11 '69

PRISONS—Vietnam (Republic)—*Continued*
Jail notes of a young Vietnamese; tr. by D.
Marr. Nguyen-van-Minh. Nation 208:359-
62 Mr 24 '69
PRISONS, Military
  See also
United States—Army—Prisons
United States—Marine corps—Prisons
PRITCHARD, Allen E. jr
Excerpt from testimony before Housing and
urban affairs subcommittee, October 15,
1969. Cong Digest 48:309+ D '69
PRITCHARD, James B.
Archaeology; address, September 3, 1969.
Vital Speeches 35:754-6 O 1 '69
PRITCHETT, Victor Sawdon
Captain's daughter; story. New Yorker 45:
28-32 D 27 '69
Getting the Amazon right. Holiday 46:42-5
Ag '69
Stern self-portrait of a lady. Life 66:12 Je 27
'69
PRIVACY
Parents and privacy. J. Brothers. Good H
168:50+ F '69
Your privacy. J. Bingham. House & Gard 136:
116-17 O '69
  See also
Wire tapping
PRIVACY, Right of
Can you name an author in a blurb? H. F.
Pilpel and K. P. Norwick. Pub W 195:23-4
My 5 '69
Can you publish data improperly obtained?
H. F. Pilpel and K. P. Norwick. Pub W 195:
32-3 Mr 31 '69
Courts grant and deny film privacy injunc-
tions; case of the moving pictures, Boston
strangler and Titicut follies. H. F. Pilpel
and K. P. Norwick. Pub W 196:37-8 D
29 '69
Jury's privacy award affirmed on appeal;
National enquirer case. H. F. Pilpel and
K. P. Norwick. Pub W 195:40-1 F 24 '69
Libel and privacy cases explore free speech
limits. H. F. Pilpel and K. P. Norwick.
Pub W 196:27-8 N 3 '69
National data bank: its advocates try to
erase big brother image. L. J. Carter. Sci-
ence 163:160-2 Ja 10 '69
Privacy and the 1970 census. Nat R 21:220-1
Mr 11 '69
Privacy invaded? census, obscenity issues.
Sr Schol 94:18+ Ap 25 '69
Privacy vs. protection, the bugged society. J.
W. Bishop, jr. il N Y Times Mag p30-1+
Je 8 '69; Discussion. p28 Je 29; 29 Jl 20 '69
Squeezing even more out of tax returns; sell-
ing of Internal revenue service data and
Census data to private industry. il Bsns
W p69 D 6 '69
Supreme court rules obscenity in home legal.
Pub W 195:68 Ap 14 '69
Technology and society; the right to privacy;
address, March 26, 1969. C. E. Gallagher.
Vital Speeches 35:528-33 Je 15 '69
Vanishing right to live, by C. E. Rice Review
Nat R 21:545-6 Je 3 '69. W. Herberg
Verrry interesting. Nat R 21:268 Mr 25 '69
PRIVATE airplanes. See Airplanes—Private
ownership
PRIVATE cars. See Railroads—Private cars
PRIVATE clubs. See Clubs
PRIVATE colleges and universities. See Col-
leges and universities
PRIVATE corporations. See Corporations
PRIVATE employment agencies. See Employ-
ment agencies
PRIVATE enterprise. See Free enterprise
PRIVATE experimental schools. See Schools,
Experimental
PRIVATE export finance corporation (pro-
posed). See Finance companies
PRIVATE flying
Airways jam: threat to private flying. il U S
News 67:42-3 D 29 '69
Discover flying; with editorial comment. il
Flying 84:14-15, 40 Je '69
Irish air. D. D. C. Pochin Mould. il Flying
84:50-1+ My '69
My island in the sky; open cockpit of a
Bücker Jungmann. E. K. Gann. il Flying
84:68-71 Ap '69
Richard Bach (cont) R. Bach. il Flying 84:32-
3 Ap; 32-3 Je; 85:35+ Ag; 92-3 O; 14 N; 10-
12 D '69
  See also
Airplanes in business
PRIVATE libraries. See Libraries, Private
PRIVATE life; story. See Oates, J. C.
PRIVATE life of Ifor Tombs; story. See Mer-
rill, A.

PRIVATE lives; drama. See Coward, N.
PRIVATE museums. See Museums, Private
PRIVATE placement of securities. See Securi-
ties—Marketing
PRIVATE presses
Encino press: one man's tribute to the South-
west. J. G. Burke. il Pub W 195:96-7 My 5
'69
Paul Bennett, private press keepsake. il Pub
W 195:72-4 Ap 7 '69
Publishing color facsimiles of rare manu-
scripts and books; Eugrammia press. H. L.
Hunter. il Pub W 196:92-3 Jl 7 '69
Underground; avant-garde literature of Some-
thing else press. J. Gruen. Vogue 154:160
O 1 '69
PRIVATE property. See Property
PRIVATE schools
Allendale school: an expression of individu-
al spaces. il Arch Rec 145:171-4 Je '69
Barnes completes the first stage of Emma
Willard expansion. il Arch Rec 145:163-70
Je '69
Choate and Rosemary Hall schools' affiliation.
il Sch & Soc 97:88-9 F '69
Deerfield keeps a truce with time; Deerfield
academy. B. McDowell. il Nat Geog 135:
780-809 Je '69
[Harry Golden column; North Carolina's
Christian academies] H. Golden. Nation
209:697 D 22 '69
Last refuge; Sandy Run academy, Swansea,
S.C. il Time 94:50 N 14 '69
New sorts of institutions must be had; Simon's
Rock: model for a new system. J. Steinberg.
il Mlle 69:262-3+ Ag '69
Oldfields incident; Cockerham sisters defy
school rules. il Newsweek 73:65 Je 16 '69
Prep school world adjusts to the real world;
Choate and Rosemary Hall to coordinate
education. R. J. Margolis; discussion. N Y
Times Mag p4+ F 2 '69
Prep schools go coed. B. B. Stretch. il Sat
R 52:80 My 17 '69
Remnant (Is. 1:9) lives, and is headmaster
of Hotchkiss school; letter to Hotchkiss
parents. A. W. Olsen, jr. Nat R 21:998 O
7 '69
Semipublic school: Rhode Island study. R. F.
Drinan. America 121:467-8 N 15 '69
Surrender in Mississippi. il Time 95:12 Ja 12
'70
Why many private schools are zooming. il
U S News 67:50-2 N 10 '69
Will Catholic schools survive? America 120:
460 Ap 19 '69
Young John Kennedy got into Collegiate
school; could your son? N. Moran. il Mc-
Calls 96:70-1+ Mr '69
  See also
Education and state

        Desegregation
Why many private schools are zooming. il
U S News 67:50-2 N 10 '69

        Federal aid
Diversity in schooling. R. Kirk. Nat R 21:
542 Je 3 '69

        Australia
Bonnie Prince Charles in bush country; at-
tending Timbertop school; excerpt from
Prince Charles: the future king. Sat R 52:88
Mr 8 '69

        Denmark
Free schools of Denmark. E. Fuchs. il Sat
R 52:44-6+ Ag 16 '69; Same abr. Ed Digest
35:5-8 D '69

        England
Summerhill free school. M. Keohane. New
Repub 160:19-22 My 31 '69; Discussion. 160:
38-40 Je 14 '69
PRIVATE schools, Negro
From Harlem to Harvard; Harlem prepara-
tory school. il Nations Bsns 57:74-5 D '69
Private schools for black children. C. Jencks.
Ed Digest 34:1-4 Mr '69
PRIVATE secretaries. See Secretaries
PRIVATEERING
People on spits and other niceties. L. Kronen-
berger. il Atlan 224:106-9 S '69
PRIVETT, Katharine
Albert Camus; poem. Cath World 209:34 Ap
'69
Picasso's art is a dense, intermingled growth,
a jungle; poem. Cath World 209:76 My '69
PRIVILEGES and immunities
Legal nonsense; immunity of state and local
governments from responsibility to citizens
for negligence of their employees. R. Gold-
farb. New Repub 161:10-11 Ag 9 '69
  See also
United States—Congress—Privileges and im-
munities

PRIX de l'Arc de Triomphe. See Horse racing

PRIX de Rome. See American academy in Rome

PRIZE fighters. See Boxers

PRIZE fighting. See Boxing

PROBABILISTIC potential theory. See Potential, Theory of

PROBABILITIES
Rambling random walk and its gambling equivalent. M. Gardner. il Sci Am 220:118-20 My '69
See also
Distribution (probability theory)
Risk

PROBATION system
What's past is prologue. R. A. McGee. bibliog f Ann Am Acad 381:1-10 Ja '69
See also
Parole

PROBES, Space. See Space probes

PROBES, Testing. See Testing instruments

PROBLEM children
Changing the game from get the teacher to learn; making good students of the too aggressive, too young, and the autistic. R. L. Hamblin and others. bibliog il Trans-Action 6:20-31 Ja '69; Reply with rejoinder. L. Silverstein. 6:64-5 Ap '69
Dealing with disruptive pupils; with study-discussion program, by E. Harris and D. Harris. E. Landy. bibliog il PTA Mag 63:19-21, 36-7 Mr '69
Disturbed parents: a challenge to the school. J. P. Cangemi. Ed Digest 35:22-4 D '69
Disturbed youngsters in the classroom. W. C. Morse. il Todays Ed 58:30-7 Ap '69
Is there a tornado in the house? the hyperactive child. S. Olds. il Todays Health 47:33-5+ N '69
Psychiatric consultation in a school for problem girls; University mound school, San Francisco, Calif. J. Davidson. Ment Hy 53:280-8 Ap '69
School problems of emotionally disturbed foster children. A. N. Maluccio. bibliog Ment Hy 53:611-19 O '69
We must prevent emotional disturbance in children. S. F. Yolles. Parents Mag 44:56 N '69
See also
Child psychiatry
Juvenile delinquency
Special classes and special schools

Recreation
Children's village experiments; nature and science program. H. Romack. il Parks & Rec 4:39-41+ Ap '69

PROBLEM drinking. See Alcoholism

PROBLEM solving
Qualitative insights from quantitative methods. R. H. Hayes. bibliog f Harvard Bsns R 47:108-17 Jl '69

PROCACCINO, Mario Angelo
Answering November's big question: what is a Mario Procaccino? T. Buckley. il pors N Y Times Mag p7-9+ Ag 10 '69
Around city hall. A. Logan. New Yorker 45:131-2+ S 13: 164+ O 11: 184-90 N 15 '69
Here comes the next mayor. R. Reeves. il pors N Y Times Mag p25-7+ N 2 '69
Mario in motion. F. McCulloch. il por Time 94:17 O 3 '69
New politics and old. J. R. Coyne, jr. Nat R 51:1106-7+ N 4 '69
New York: the revolt of the average man. il por Time 94:15-20 O 3 '69
Procaccino campaigning. New Yorker 45:32-4 S 27 '69

PROCAINE. See Novocaine

PROCARBAZINE
Antiserum to lymphocytes and procarbazine compared as immunosuppressants in mice. P. B. Stewart and V. Cohen. bibliog il Science 164:1082-3 My 30 '69; Reply. J. H. Weisburger. 165:517 Ag 1 '69

PROCEDURE (law)
Guilty as charged by the judge; excerpt from The trial of Dr Spock. J. Mitford. il Atlan 224:48-66 Ag '69; Discussion. 224:50+ N '69
See also
Criminal procedure

PROCESS control equipment. See Automatic control

PROCESS refractometers. See Refractometers

PROCTER and Gamble company
Great diaper battle; disposable diapers. il Time 93:69-70 Ja 24 '69
Is the soap leader getting soft? il Bsns W p52-4+ Jl 19 '69

Procter & Gamble. il Forbes 103:36-40+ Ap 15 '69
Sudsy P&G lightens that dull D-J image. il Bsns W p30 N 8 '69

PROCTOR, Ian
Ian Proctor on buoyancy apparatus; excerpt from Boats for sailing. Yachting 125:59+ Ja '69
They sail to win; excerpts from Boats and sailing. Yachting 126:36-7 S '69

PROCUREMENT, Government. See Purchasing, Government

PROCUREMENT, Military. See United States —Armed forces—Procurement

PRODIGAL parent: story. See Gallant, M.

PRODIGIES. See Children, Gifted

PRODUCE exchanges. See Commodity exchanges

PRODUCE trade
See also
Surplus products, Agricultural

PRODUCT liability. See Liability (law)

PRODUCT segmentation. See Market surveys

PRODUCTION
Getting more output from fewer comrades. Bsns W p38-9 N 1 '69
See also
Gross national product
Input-output analysis
Labor productivity
Supply and demand

PRODUCTION, Agricultural
Green revolution revisited. J. A. Shellenberger. Cur 110:37-41 S '69
Hungry future, by R. Dumont and B. Rosier. Review
Nat R il 21:968-9 S 23 '69. E. B. Meyer
See also
Food supply
Surplus products, Agricultural

PRODUCTION, Theatrical. See Theatrical production and direction

PRODUCTION code, Motion picture. See Moving picture censorship

PRODUCTION control
Way to make diversity pay off; group technology. il Bsns W p 152+ O 18 '69
See also
Critical path analysis

PRODUCTION editing. See Editors and editing

PRODUCTIVITY, Labor. See Labor productivity

PRODUCTS, Commercial. See Commercial products

PRODUCTS, Improved
Building a better mouse trap. il Time 93:46+ My 2 '69

PRODUCTS, New
Good news for men. See issues of Better homes and gardens
Great rush for new products. il Time 94:92+ O 24 '69
Mainly for men. A. J. Maher. See issues of American home
New products. See issues of Popular electronics
New products. See issues of Radio-electronics
New products & literature. See issues of Electronics world
New products and processes. See issues of American city
New products of tomorrow; a 1975 sampler. C. G. Burck. Fortune 79:161+ My 15 '69
Occupation: homemaker. See issues of McCall's
Product gallery. See issues of Popular electronics
Some of the year's new products. il Fortune 79:154-61 My 15 '69
Technology's best for '69. Sci Digest 66:45-6 D '69
This just has to be the greatest new decade since creation. il Esquire 72:234-41 D '69
What's newest. See issues of Newsweek
When patents go on parade; Patexpo '69. il Bsns W p 148+ S 13 '69

PRODUCTS, Quality of. See Quality of products

PROFANITY. See Swearing

PROFESSION, Choice of. See Vocational guidance

PROFESSIONAL air traffic controllers organization
Both FAA, controller unit harden positions in dispute. Aviation W 91:30-1 Ag 4 '69
FAA to revise air controller programs. D. A. Brown. Aviation W 91:24-5 Ag 18 '69

PROFESSIONAL associations. See Trade and professional associations

PROFESSIONAL basketball players. See Basketball players

PROFESSIONAL corporations. See Corporations

PROFESSIONAL drivers association
Talladega's troubled baptism. L. Laye. il
Motor T 21:34-6 N '69
Talladega's troubled Sunday. S. Kelly. il Hot
Rod 22:44-6 D '69
PROFESSIONAL education
Combined engineering program. Sch & Soc
97:89 F '69
International studies for the professional
school. W. A. McCormack. bibliog f Sch
& Soc 97:114-16 F '69
See also
Library schools and education
Technical education
PROFESSIONAL ethics
Ethics and the school superintendent. il Sch
& Soc 97:166-8 Mr '69
See also
Architects, Professional ethics for
Medical ethics
Teachers ethics
PROFESSIONAL football clubs. See Football
clubs
PROFESSIONAL football players. See Football
players
PROFESSIONAL golf. See Golf
PROFESSIONAL golfers' association of America
Blacks on the greens. il Time 93:56 F 14 '69
Mr Commissioner speaks out; interview, ed.
by P. Ryan. J. Dey. il Sports Illus 30:20-1
F 10 '69
See also
Ladies' professional golfers' association
**PROFESSIONAL golfers' association tourna-
ment.** See Golf—Tournaments
PROFESSIONAL service
Cost control for the professional service firm.
H. E. McDonald and T. L. Stromberger.
il Harvard Bsns R 47:109-21 Ja '69
PROFESSIONAL women. See Business and pro-
fessional women
PROFESSIONAL workers
Why doctors and lawyers call themselves
Inc; fight for corporate tax status. il
Bsns W p80+ Jl 12 '69

Supply and demand

See also
Brain drain
PROFESSIONAL workers in state government.
See State employees
PROFESSIONALISM
Toward professionalism in business manage-
ment. K. R. Andrews. bibliog f il Harvard
Bsns R 47:49-60 Mr '69
PROFESSIONALISM (sports) See Amateurism
(sports)
PROFESSIONS
Careers are always greener on the other side
of the fence. M. Elkoff. McCalls 96:87+ Je
'69
See also
Occupations
Self employed
PROFESSOR X, pseud
Exclusive and unauthorized: the liberated
report of Professor X. Esquire 72:104-7+
S '69
PROFESSORS. See College professors and in-
structors
PROFFER, Carl R.
Pushkin and parricide: The miserly knight.
bibliog f Am Imago 25:347-53 Wint '68
PROFILES. See Silhouettes
PROFIT
First signs of a slowdown. il Time 93:89-90
My 9 '69
See also
Investments
Profiteering
Risk
PROFIT sharing
Another look at profit sharing. America 121:
288 O 11 '69
Booming benefits of profit sharing. I. Ross.
Read Digest 95:111-14 Ag '69
Profit sharing and union organizing. E. R.
Czarnecki. il Mo Labor R 92:61-2 D '69
PROFITEERING
Profiteers are wrecking medicaid. A. Q.
Maisel. Read Digest 95:151-6 O '69
See also
War profits
PROFUMO, John Dennis
Perils of Christine. Time 94:77-8 O 10 '69
PROGESTERONE
Endocrine control of adrenal progesterone
secretion in the ovariectomized rat. J. A.
Resko. bibliog il Science 164:70-1 Ap 4 '69
Lactose synthetase: progesterone inhibition
of the induction of d-lactalbumin. R. W.
Turkington and R. L. Hill. bibliog il Sci-
ence 163:1458-60 Mr 28 '69

PROGNER, Jean
New libraries. Sat R 52:28-30 Ap 19 '69
PROGRAM evaluation and budget committee.
See American library association—Program
evaluation and budget committee
PROGRAMMED instruction
Freelance job idea: writing programmed
instruction materials. B. Williams. il Writ-
ers Digest 49:36-42+ S '69
Library study carrel: bilingual program with
tutoring and self-pacing; Coalinga junior
high school, Calif. R. E. Philips. il Library
J 94:840-2 F 15 '69
Programed instruction in the language field.
J. Ornstein. Ed Digest 34:9-12 F '69
Programed learning; education's turkey? J.
A. Meyer. Ed Digest 34:8-9 Ja '69
Teacher's adventures in programland. G. L.
Graham. Engl J 58:261-6 F '69
See also
Computers—Educational applications
Teaching machines
PROGRAMMED teaching. See Programmed in-
struction
PROGRAMMERS, Computer. See Computer
workers
PROGRAMMING (computers)
Software of change; address, September 23,
1969. M. Tribus. Vital Speeches 36:14-17
O 15 '69
See also
Programming languages (computers)
PROGRAMMING languages (computers)
Developing computer language. E. Joseph.
Duns R 94:15 Jl '69
PROGRESS
See also
Change
Civilization
Inventions
Science and civilization
Social progress
PROGRESSIVE education
Progressive education should continue; ad-
dress, December 1968. P. D. Diederich. il
Todays Ed 58:12-19 Mr '69; Same abr. with
title Progressive education will continue.
Ed Digest 34:28-31 My '69
PROGRESSIVE taxation. See Taxation, Pro-
gressive
PROGRESSIVISM (United States politics)
Corporate ideal in the liberal state, 1900-1918.
by J. Weinstein. Review
Ramp Mag 8:38-40 D '69. M. Rothbard
PROHIBITED books

Bibliography

Unsuitable for use; proscribed books on USIA
list. il Newsweek 74:44 D 1 '69
PROHIBITION

United States

Wet season. il Newsweek 73:33-4 F 3 '69
PROJECT Apollo. See Space flight to the moon
moon
PROJECT Cambridge. See Computers—Social
science applications
PROJECT Defender. See Guided missiles—De-
fenses
PROJECT Equality. See National Catholic con-
ference for interracial justice
PROJECT Head Start
Black genes, white environment. J. M. Hunt.
bibliog il Trans-Action 6:12-22 Je '69
Devil has slippery shoes, by P. Greenberg.
Review
Newsweek 73:114+ Je 9 '69. A. Cooper
Sat R 52:93-4 N 15 '69. W. Roberts
Following up on Head Start. New Repub
160:12-13 Ap 12 '69
Head start for Patsy. P. Cleveland. il Am Ed
5:19 O '69
Head Start is under attack. Sr Schol 94:Schol
Teach 8 My 9 '69
Head Start to nowhere: Westinghouse learn-
ing corporation, Ohio university study. M.
R. Berube. Commonweal 90:311-13 My 30 '69
How head a Head Start? study of programs
by the Westinghouse learning corporation
and Ohio university. New Repub 160:8-9
Ap 26 '69
Hunger next door: program in Missoula,
Mont. N. Munro. il Redbook 132:21+ Mr '69
Job corps. Headstart reassigned. Sci N 95:
400 Ap 26 '69
Overhauling Head Start. B. B. Stretch. il
Sat R 52:80 My 17 '69
Politics of evaluation: the case of Head
Start. W. Williams and J. W. Evans. Ann
Am Acad 385:118-32 S '69
Poor Head Start and its children. C. Smith.
New Repub 160:11-13 Je 21 '69
Second thoughts about a study. Sci N 95:
424-5 My 3 '69
What Head Start meant to our town. W.
Mazer. il Parents Mag 44:54-5+ O '69

PROJECT Head Start—*Continued*
Follow through programs
Follow Through programs, 1969-70. il Am
Ed 5:26-7 N '69
PROJECT Rulison. See Atomic blasting
PROJECT Sanguine. See Radio communication,
Naval
PROJECT SERVE. See Community service
society of New York
PROJECT teaching
See also
Art—Study and teaching—Projects
PROJECT Tektite. See Underwater laboratories
PROJECT Transition. See Service men—Vocational education
PROJECTILES
Flying underground. il Sci Digest 66:67 Jl
'69
RAP: an old naval shell with a new kick;
rocket-assisted projectiles. M. Schultz. il
Pop Mech 130:84-7 D '68
PROJECTION apparatus. See Projectors
PROJECTION cabinets. See Cabinets (furniture)
PROJECTION screens
Projection screens. il Consumer Rep 34:95-7
F '69
Right screen? Travel & Camera 32:91 Ag '69
Screen that's six times brighter; Kodak Ektalite screen. il Pop Sci 194:90 Ap '69
PROJECTORS
Do-it-yourself overhead projector and a
cheap opaque projector. il Consumer Bul
52:31-2 Mr '69
Slide projectors. il Consumer Bul 52:21-6 F '69
Slide projectors; where do they go from here?
N. Rothschild. il Pop Phot 65:84-5+ O '69
See also
Moving picture projectors
Transparencies—Viewers
PROJECTS (teaching)
Art—Study and teaching—Projects
PROKOF'EV, Sergei Sergeevich
Prokofiev: three sonatas, three pianists. L.
Richmond. Am Rec G 35:624-5+ Ap '69
Prokofiev's satiric Oranges. R. Lawrence.
Sat R 52:47 Je 28 '69
Records:
Gambler and Love for three oranges.
Opera N 34:30 D 20 '69
Smashing interpretation of Prokofiev's Second
symphony. J. Diether. Am Rec G 35:785+
My '69
Two Prokofiev symphonies, a logical second
and a lyrical fifth. P. Hart. il Hi Fi 19:77-8
My '69
PROKOSCH, Eric
Conventional killers. New Repub 161:18-21
N 1 '69
PROLACTIN. See Luteotropin
PROLINE
3,-4-Dihydroxyproline: a new amino acid in
diatom cell walls. T. Nakajima and B. E.
Volcani. bibliog il Science 164:1400-1 Je 20
'69
2,3-cis-3,4-trans-3,4-dihydroxy-L-proline: mass
spectrometry and X-ray analysis. I. L.
Karle and others. bibliog il Science 164:
1401-2 Je 20 '69
PROMENADE; musical comedy. See Musical
comedies, revues etc.—Criticisms, plots, etc.
PROMETHEUS bound; drama. See Lowell, R.
PROMISCUITY. See Sexual ethics
PROMISE of oranges; story. See Polk, D.
PROMISES
On permanent commitment. R. J. Westley.
America 120:612-17 My 24 '69; Discussion.
121:1 Jl 5 '69
PROMISES, promises; musical comedy. See
Musical comedies, revues, etc.—Criticisms,
plots, etc.
PROMONTORY, Utah
When the country was united; centennial reenactment. il Time 93:25 My 16 '69
PROMOTERS and promoting
Boxing's great white hoopla; T. Brenner. J.
Kirshenbaum. il Sports Illus 31:48-50+ Jl
21 '69
Horse laughs: sports promotions of B. Veeck.
il Newsweek 74:65 Jl 14 '69
Now he gets to shoot; W. Pavalon's plan to
get Alcindor and big sport for Milwaukee.
P. Putnam. il Sports Illus 30:56-63 F 24 '69
Yes! Bert is in, with go power; promoting
AAU indoor track meet. R. Blount, jr.
il Sports Illus 30:34-6+ Mr 3 '69
PROMOTION, Sales. See Sales promotion
PROMOTION of employees. See Employees—
Promotion
PROMOTIONAL games. See Sales promotion
PROMOTIONS, School. See Grading and marking (students)

PRONENESS to accidents. See Accidents—
Psychological aspects
PRONGHORN hunting
High adventure. C. Conklin. il Outdoor Life
143:84+ My '69
Hill country antelope. T. Cacek. il Field &
S 74:48-9+ S '69
PRONGHORNS
Camels and elands: at home on the range? Sr
Schol 94:15 Ja 17 '69
PROOF. See Evidence
PROOF (law) See Evidence (law)
PROOFREADING
Considerations about galleys and proofreading. S. Salter. Pub W 196:66+ S 1 '69
Some effects of computer composition on the
editorial process in book publishing; address, March 27, 1969. L. Shatzkin. Pub W
195:28-31 Ap 7 '69
PROOFS (printing)
Considerations about galleys and proofreading. S. Salter. Pub W 196:66+ S 1 '69
PROPAGANDA
Fighting the propaganda; a war at home; address. A. E. Meyerhoff. Vital Speeches 35:
469-73 My 15 '69
How to defeat communism without war; letter
to the editor. U S News 66:108+ F 17 '69
Pentagon hucksterism. Nation 209:685 D 22
'69
Soldiers on the war; supporters of Pentagon
policy. New Repub 161:5-6 D 6 '69
See also
Moving pictures—Propaganda films
Nigeria—Civil war. 1967- —Propaganda
Vietnamese war. 1957- —Propaganda
PROPAGANDA, American. See Propaganda
PROPAGANDA, Anti-Jewish. See Anti-Semitism
PROPAGANDA, Communist
Deep feelings expressed in an umbrella; reprint. Nat R 21:283 Mr 25 '69
See also
Propaganda, Russian
PROPAGANDA, Russian
Are we in a Pavlovian box? U.S. policy
conditioned response to Soviet objectives?
A. C. Sutton. il Nat R 21:692-4 Jl 15 '69
Kremlin chill. Newsweek 74:38-9 Ag 25 '69
PROPAGANDA in the schools
Worst of Two worlds; program published by
Flick-Reedy education enterprises to educate the nation's youth in the dogma of
the radical right. M. A. Gordon. Ramp
Mag 7:58+ Ap '69
PROPAGATION of plants. See Plant propagation
PROPELLERS
Find the best prop for your boat on paper,
first. J. Martenhoff. il Pop Sci 194:104-6
Je '69
Hot prop for your boat. C. Miller. il Mech
Illus 65:81-3+ F '69
Key to performance. J. Martenhoff. il Yachting 125:70-1 Mr '69
See also
Airplane propellers
PROPER motion of the stars. See Stars—Motion
PROPERTY
Possessions of the poor. O. Lewis. il Sci
Am 221:114-24 O '69
See also
Air rights
Church property
Joint tenancy
PROPERTY, intellectual
See also
Copyright
PROPERTY rights. See Real property
PROPERTY tax
Change the property tax. G. C. Brewer. Duns
R 92:77 D '68
See also
Real property and taxation
PROPHECIES
Sky is falling, but don't duck. D. Cohen. il
Sci Digest 65:14-19 Je '69
See also
Astrology
Forecasts
PROPHETS
Revolution within an evolution. R. R. Winkelmann. Chr Cent 86:1577-80 D 10 '69
PROPORTION (art)
My right side is better. F. Linden. il Am
Artist 32:50-1+ D '68
PROPPING of fruit trees. See Fruit trees,
Care of
PROPRANOLOL
Cardiac sympathetic nerve activity; changes
induced by ouabain and propranolol. R. A.
Gillis. bibliog il Science 166:508-10 O 24 '69

PROPRIETY. See Decency

PROPYLURE
Sex pheromone of the pink bollworm moth: biological masking by its geometrical isomer. M. Jacobson. bibliog il Science 163: 190-1 Ja 10 '69

PROSCRIBED books. See Prohibited books

PROSECUTORS. See Public prosecutors

PROSPECTING
Tanzania to Tiffany's. T. Thompson. il Life 66:70-6 My 9 '69
See also
Petroleum—Prospecting

PROSPERITY
Crumbling foundations of prosperity. P. H. Abelson. Science 165:1069 S 12 '69; Reply. S. G. Fletcher. 166:819-20 N 14 '69

PROSTAGLANDINS
Prostaglandin stimulation of rat corticosteroidogenesis. J. D. Flack and others. bibliog il Science 163:691-2 F 14 '69
Prostaglandins E_1 and E_2 antagonize norepinephrine effects on cerebellar Purkinje cells: microelectrophoretic study. B. J. Hoffer and others. bibliog il Science 165: 1418-20 D 12 '69
Prostaglandins: enzymatic analysis. E. Anggård and others. bibliog il Science 163:479-80 Ja 31 '69

PROSTATE gland
See also
Prostaglandins

PROSTERMAN, Roy L.
Land reform in Vietnam. Cur Hist 57:327-32+ D '69

PROSTHESIS
Artificial features for disfigured faces. G. E. Toles. il Sci Digest 66:59-62 N '69
Man-made parts for the body; bright future? il U S News 66:11 Ap 21 '69
Quick-fitted artificial limbs. Sci Digest 65:63-4 Je '69
See also
Artificial limbs

PROSTITUTION
Everything's up to date in Lida Junction; brothels in Nevada. il Time 93:54 Je 27 '69
Open house in Terre Haute; State university president asks city to reduce prostitution. il Time 93:20-1 F 21 '69

PROTEAS
Proteas and their relatives. W. D. Gardner. il Horticulture 47:26-9+ Ag '69
Those crazy proteas. il Sunset 142:250-1 Ap '69

PROTECTION (tariff) See Free trade and protection

PROTECTION against burglary. See Burglary protection

PROTECTION circuits. See Electronic circuits

PROTECTION of stone. See Stone—Preservation

PROTECTIVE clothing. See Clothing, Protective

PROTECTIVE coatings
Conformal coatings for printed circuits. V. Leibmann. il Electr World 82:50-1 O '69
Heat shield comes in a tube. E. F. Lindsley. il Pop Sci 195:36 Ag '69
How to fiberglass anything. il Mech Illus 65:98-100+ D '69

PROTECTIVE mechanisms (biology) See Defense mechanisms (biology)

PROTECTIVE paint. See Paint, Protective

PROTEIN deficient diet. See Diet, Deficient

PROTEIN drinks. See Beverages

PROTEIN supplements. See Feeding and feeding stuffs—Protein supplements

PROTEINEMIA
X-ray and electron diffraction of ocular and bone marrow crystals in paraproteinemia. P. R. Laibson and V. V. Damiano. il Science 163:581-3 F 7 '69

PROTEINS
Computer analysis of protein evolution. M. O. Dayhoff. il Sci Am 221:86-95 Jl '69
Encephalitogenic protein: structure. R. F. Kibler and others. bibliog il Science 164: 577-80 My 2 '69
Fusidic acid: inhibition of factor T_2 in reticulocyte protein synthesis. M. Malkin and F. Lipmann. bibliog il Science 164:71-2 Ap 4 '69
Induction in vitro of microtubular crystals by vinca alkaloids. K. G. Bensch and others. bibliog il Science 165:495-6 Ag 1 '69
Nerve endings: rapid appearance of labeled protein shown by electron microscope radioautography. B. Droz and S. H. Barondes. bibliog il Science 165:1131-3 S 12 '69
Non-Darwinian evolution. J. L. King and T. H. Jukes. bibliog il Science 164:788-98 My 16 '69

Plague toxin. S. Kadis and others. il Sci Am 220:92-8+ Mr '69
Polypeptide chain elongation in protein biosynthesis. F. Lipmann. bibliog il Science 164:1024-31 My 30 '69
Protein subunits: a table, second edition. I. M. Klotz and D. W. Darnall. bibliog il Science 166:126-8 O 3 '69
Protein synthesis in the hippocampal pyramidal cells of rats during a behavioral test. H. Hydén and P. W. Lange; reply with rejoinder. R. E. Bowman and G. Harding. bibliog Science 164:199-201 Ap 11 '69
Proteins synthesized before and after fertilization in sea urchin eggs. F. R. MacKintosh and E. Bell. bibliog il Science 164:961-3 My 23 '69
Ribosomal protein conferring sensitivity to the antibiotic spectinomycin in escherichia coli. A. Bollen and others. bibliog il Science 165:85-6 Jl 4 '69
Structural determinant of a ribosomal protein: K locus. E. A. Birge and others. bibliog il Science 164:1285-6 Je 13 '69
Vinblastine-induced precipitation of microtubule protein. R. Marantz and others. bibliog il Science 165:498-9 Ag 1 '69
See also
Amino acids
Azurin
Collagen
Fish flour
Food substitutes
Glycoproteins
Histones
Insulin
Interferon
Keratin
Lipoproteins
Myoglobin
Nucleoproteins
Plant proteins
Skin—Proteins
Tryptophan

PROTEST songs. See Music, Popular (songs, etc)

PROTESTANT church-owned publisher's association
PCPA holds 19th annual meeting, elects officers. Pub W 195:35 Mr 24 '69

PROTESTANT churches
See also
Catholic church—Relations—Protestant churches
Ecumenical movement
Protestantism
Clergy
See Clergy
Missions
See Missions
Statistics
See Church statistics

Belgium
New church in Belgium; Protestant church of Belgium. Chr Cent 86:970 Jl 23 '69

England
See also
British council of churches

Germany (Federal Republic)
See also
Evangelical church in Germany

Spain
Landmark centennial; fourth evangelical congress in Barcelona. T. Goslin. Chr Cent 86: 1589-90 D 10 '69

United States
See also
National council of churches

PROTESTANT churches and race problems. See Church and race problems

PROTESTANT churches and social problems. See Church and social problems

PROTESTANT council of the city of New York
Family of man fuss. Chr Today 13:45 F 28 '69

PROTESTANT Episcopal church
Almoners' dilemma; schism over social action. il Newsweek 74:96-7 D 15 '69
Balking Episcopal parishes. Chr Cent 86:1306 O 15 '69
Black militants: what Episcopalians voted. U S News 67:16 S 15 '69
Commitment to battle; Episcopal church's special general convention. Time 94:48 S 12 '69
Episcopal woes: double trouble, cauldron bubble. Chr Today 14:50 N 7 '69
Episcopalians hold special convention. W. I. Maxwell. Chr Cent 86:1262-4 O 1 '69
Forman bedevils the Episcopalians. W. Wallace. Commonweal 90:582-3 S 26 '69

PROTESTANT Episcopal church—*Continued*
Giver$ revolt. Chr Today 14:50 O 10 '69'
Group therapy; special general convention.
il Newsweek 74:105-6 S 15 '69
Looking for bruises; agenda for the special
general convention. Newsweek 74:76-8 Ag
25 '69
Michigan Episcopalians grant votes to six-
teen-year-olds. Chr Cent 86:1445 N 12 '69
Passing the buck. Newsweek 74:107 O 20 '69
Reparations in black and white. Chr Today
13:37 S 26 '69
Squirming in South Bend. R. Chandler. Chr
Today 13:42-4 S 26 '69
Why I'm leaving the church. J. A. Pike. il
Look 33:54-8 Ap 29 '69
See also
American Episcopal church

Bishops
Bishop Burgess of Massachusetts. il Ebony
24:54-6+ O '69
Bishop militant; P. Moore. Newsweek 74:69
D 22 '69
PROTESTANT missions. See Missions
PROTESTANT monasticism. See Monasticism
PROTESTANT theologians. See Theologians
PROTESTANTISM
Believers' church: the history and character
of radical Protestantism, by D. F. Durn-
baugh. Review
Chr Cent 86:685-6 My 14 '69. R. S. Paul
Protest of a troubled Protestant, by H. O. J.
Brown. Review
Nat R 21:707-8 Jl 15 '69. M. S. Evans
Return of the Protestant principle. M. Daly.
Commonweal 90:338-41 Je 6 '69
Rome and reformation today. H. O. J. Brown.
Chr Today 14:3-5 O 24 '69
Thoughts for Protestants to be static by. W.
D. Wagoner. Chr Cent 86:249-51 F 19 '69;
Reply. H. F. Reissig. 86:524 Ap 16 '69
See also
Evangelicalism
Fundamentalism
PROTESTANTS and other Americans united
for separation of church and state. See
Americans united for separation of church
and state
PROTESTANTS in Germany
Struggle for the German church. H. O. J.
Brown. Nat R 21:334-7+ Ap 8 '69
PROTESTANTS in Germany (Federal Republic)
Changing role for the Kirchentag. F. Lupsen.
Chr Cent 86:1259-61 O 1 '69
PROTESTANTS in Latin America
Latin American Protestants: which way will
they go? W. D. Roberts. Chr Today 14:14-16
O 10 '69
PROTESTANTS in Northern Ireland
Not defending the indefensible. J. D. Doug-
las. Chr Today 14:55 O 24 '69
PROTESTANTS in the United States
See also
WASPS (white Anglo-Saxon Protestants)
PROTESTS against Vietnamese war. See Viet-
namese war, 1957- —Protests, demonstra-
tions, etc, against
PROTISTA. See Unicellular organisms
PROTONS
Crystallography with protons. C. S. Barrett.
il Phys Today 22:33 Ag '69
See also
Nucleons
PROTOPLASM
See also
Golgi apparatus
Micellar theory
PROTOSTARS. See Stars—Evolution
PROTOZOA
Scanning electron microscopy of fixed, frozen,
and dried protozoa. E. B. Small and D. S.
Marszalek. bibliog il Science 163:1064-5 Mr 7
'69
See also
Amebas
Ciliata
Coccidia
Euglena
Nosema
Paramecia
Plasmodium (parasite)
Slime molds, Cellular

Resistance and sensitivity
Resistance to metronidazole by trichomonas
foetus in hamsters infected intravaginally.
P. Actor and others. bibliog il Science 164:
439-40 Ap 25 '69
PROTOZOA, Pathogenic
See also
Toxoplasma

PROUST, Marcel
Letter from Paris. Genêt. New Yorker 45:202
N 29 '69
PROUTY, L. Fletcher
Green Berets and the CIA. New Repub 161:
9-10 Ag 23 '69
PROUTY, Winston Lewis
Plea for an extra button. por Newsweek 74:39
Jl 28 '69
PROVENÇAL poetry
Translations into English
Era-m cosselhatz, senhor; tr. by J. F. Nims.
Bernart de Ventadorn. Sat R 52:52 S 20 '69
PROVENCE
Provence still life. O. Carlisle. il Holiday 45:
26-31+ Je '69
PROVERBS
Wild flowers of thought. Time 93:74+ Mr 14 '69
PROVIDENCE, R.I.
Education
They made a better school. R. H. Levine. il
Am Ed 5:8-10 N '69
Galleries and museums
See also
Rhode Island school of design, Providence,
R.I.
Historic houses, etc.
Weekend in Newport and Providence. A.
Stagg. il House & Gard 136:72-3+ S '69
Hospitals
Computerized intercom a factor in new tower
design for Providence. il Arch Rec 145:156-8
Mr '69
Theater
Special Providence; Adrian Hall's staging of
Macbeth and Billy Budd. H. Hewes. il Sat
R 52:22 My 3 '69
PROVIDENCE, R.I. public library
Providence: a community relations program.
C. W. Crosby. il Wilson Lib Bul 43:892-3 My
'69
PROVIDENCIA (island) See Old Providence
Island
PROVING grounds
How the sheep died in Skull Valley; testing
of nerve gas. R. G. Fowler. il Farm J 93:
34B-34D S '69
Nuclear rocket development station. il Space
World F-12-72:4-15 D '69
On uncovering the great nerve gas coverup;
sheep killed near Dugway, the army's chem-
ical and biological testing station, Skull
Valley, Utah. S. Hersh. Ramp Mag 7:12-13
Je '69
Wind from Dugway; death of sheep near
Proving ground, testing poisonous agents.
V. Brodine and others. il Environ 11:2-9+
Ja '69
PROXIMITY warning indicators
Army plans proximity warning test. P. J.
Klass. il Aviation 91:109+ Ag 4 '69
PROXMIRE, William
Blank check for the military; address, March
10, 1969. Vital Speeches 35:400-5 Ap 15 '69
Why a military-industrial complex? A sena-
tor's answer; excerpts from address, April
15, 1969. U S News 66:88-90 Ap 28 '69
about
Proxmire drops the ax. il por Bsns W p29 My
31 '69
Proxmire queries defense panel. Aviation
W 91:24 N 3 '69
USAF, Proxmire A-7 brake views diverge.
K. Johnsen. Aviation W 91:75 Ag 18 '69
PRPIC, George J.
Fifty years of Yugoslavia. America 120:499-
502 Ap 26 '69
PRUNING
One good way to prune a tree rose. il Sun-
set 142:198 F '69
Pollarding, it's drastic, but sometimes it's
wise. il Sunset 143:218+ N '69
PRUNUS triloba. See Flowering almonds
PRYBYLA, Jan S.
China's economy: a balance sheet after twenty
years. bibliog f Cur Hist 57:135-41+ S '69
PRYCE, Dick
Central Kansas mixed bag hunting. Field &
S 74:36-7+ D '69
Shelterbelt squirrels. Outdoor Life 144:52-3+
Ag '69
PRYCE-JONES, Alan
Collector: Paul Bernat. Art in Am 57:68-75
S '69
House on John street. House & Gard 136:80+
S '69

PRYCE-JONES, David
Conversation with W. H. Auden. Holiday 45: 56-7+ Je '69
PRYER, Margaret W. and others
Attitude changes in psychiatric attendants following experience and training. bibliog Ment Hy 53:253-7 Ap '69
PRYOR, Samuel F.
Traffic in narcotics: address, December 8, 1968. Vital Speeches 35:308-10 Mr 1 '69
PSALMS. See Bible—Old Testament—Psalms
PSAMMOMYS obesus. See Sand rats
PSENCIK, Leroy F.
Interaction analysis improves classroom instruction. bibliog f Clear House 43:555-60 My '69
PSEUDOMONAS
Vaccines
Umbrella of life. il Newsweek 74:85 O 20 '69
PSEUDONYMS
Second thoughts about salesmanship. A. Holland. Writers Digest 49:20 Ag '69
PSEUDOSCIENTIFIC stories. See Science fiction
PSITTACINE birds. See Parrots
PSYCHEDELIC art. See Hallucinogenic drugs and art
PSYCHEDELIC drugs. See Hallucinogenic drugs
PSYCHEDELIC light-show systems. See Light, Colored
PSYCHIATRIC aides. See Hospitals, Psychiatric—Staff
PSYCHIATRIC clinics
Psychiatry's new approach: crisis intervention; Ann Arbor, Mich, Crisis walk-in clinic. il Time 93:74 My 9 '69
PSYCHIATRIC hospitals. See Hospitals, Psychiatric
PSYCHIATRIC literature
Approaches to the mental health manpower problem; a review of the literature. L. J. Cowne. bibliog Ment Hy 53:176-87 Ap '69
PSYCHIATRIC personnel
American and British mental health workers look at rehabilitation. A. R. Askenasy. Ment Hy 53:466-71 Jl '69
Community mental health aide. W. I. Halpern. bibliog Ment Hy 53:78-83 Ja '69
Mental health manpower dilemma. M. C. Bettis and R. E. Roberts. bibliog il Ment Hy 53:163-75 Ap '69
PSYCHIATRIC research
Biochemical clues to mental illness. G. Bylinsky. il Fortune 80:124-7+ Jl '69
Psychiatric patients as research interviewers in the mental hospital. A. Shiloh. Ment Hy 53:443-5 Jl '69
Relatives as informants in mental health research. C. A. Bentinck and others. bibliog Ment Hy 53:446-50 Jl '69
PSYCHIATRIC social work
See also
Pastoral counseling
PSYCHIATRIC social workers. See Social workers
PSYCHIATRISTS
Problems of the practicing psychiatrist. G. W. Grumet. bibliog Ment Hy 53:410-14 Jl '69
See also
Laing, R. D.
Medical ethics
Psychiatric personnel
Rush, B.
Strecker, E. A.
PSYCHIATRISTS and patients
Problems of the practicing psychiatrist. G. W. Grumet. bibliog Ment Hy 53:410-14 Jl '69
PSYCHIATRY
I have a friend who... T. I. Rubin. Ladies Home J 86:56 S; 16 N '69
Metaphysician of madness: existential analysis of R. Laing. il Time 93:64+ F 7 '69
Psychiatry gets off the couch and hits the streets: Gouverneur hospital's mobile unit in New York city. il Life 67:48-48C Ag 8 '69
Sociatry: social psychiatry and the physician's calling. H. C. Shands. bibliog Ment Hy 53:393-402 Jl '69
Two Philadelphia psychiatrists and a theory of American psychiatry. R. S. Garber. bibliog Ment Hy 53:131-40 Ja '69
See also
Child psychiatry
Group psychotherapy
Mental illness
Mentally ill
Neuroses
Psychoanalysis
Psychology, Pathological

Bibliography
Book reviews. See issues of Mental hygiene

History
Has anyone seen my pertinent variable? D. P. Kenefick. bibliog Ment Hy 53:657-60 O '69
Past in the present; a column on history. D. P. Kenefick. bibliog Ment Hy 53:472-6 Jl '69
PSYCHIATRY, Forensic. See Forensic psychiatry
PSYCHIATRY and religion
H. N. Wieman: his work perpetuated. C. L. Hepler. Chr Cent 86:1099 Ag 20 '69
Psychoanalytic notes on the disavowal of priestly authority. G. A. Benson. Chr Cent 86:738-41 My 28 '69; Reply. D. S. Smolen. 86:1322-3 O 15 '69
What is Christian psychiatry? B. H. Kuehn. Chr Today 13:34-5 My 23 '69
PSYCHICAL research
Beings from outer space, corporeal and spiritual. H. Hoagland. Science 163:625 F 14 '69
See also
Parapsychology
PSYCHOANALYSIS
Artist sculptures JFK doodles. il Ebony 24: 46-8+ O '69
Grid puts executives on the griddle; managerial grid. il Bsns W p 158-60 O 18 '69
Passive mastery of helplessness in games; psychoanalytic case study. M. D. Capell. bibliog Am Imago 25:309-32 Wint '68
Patterns in obedience and disobedience. S. S. Feldman. bibliog Am Imago 26:21-36 Spr '69
Psychoanalysis and education. B. Bettelheim. Ed Digest 35:38-42 O '69
Psychoanalysis: in search of its soul. il Time 93:68-9 Mr 7 '69
Psychoanalytic dialogue, with a commentary. J. P. Sartre. Ramp Mag 8:43-9 O '69
Psychoanalytic notes on the disavowal of priestly authority. G. A. Benson. Chr Cent 86:738-41 My 28 '69; Reply. D. S. Smolen. 86:1322-3 O 15 '69
See also
Defense mechanisms (psychology)
Dreams
PSYCHOANALYSIS and literature
Euripides' Hippolytus. A. V. Rankin. bibliog f Am Imago 25:333-46 Wint '68
Shakespeare: symposium. bibliog Am Imago 25:199-293 Fall '68
Sins of the fathers: Hawthorne's psychological themes, by F. Crews. Review
Trans-Action 6:74-7 S '69. A. Rothenburg
PSYCHOANALYSIS in literature
Prufrock's defenses and our response. L. Waldoff. bibliog f Am Imago 26:182-93 Sum '69
PSYCHOANALYSIS in poetry. See Psychoanalysis in literature
PSYCHOANALYSTS
See also
Bettelheim, B.
Medical ethics
PSYCHOBIOLOGY
Final solution for stupidity. R. K. Field. Esquire 71:64+ Mr '69
Genetic aspects of learning and memory in mice. D. Bovet and others. bibliog il Science 165:139-49 Ja 10 '69; Reply with rejoinder. K. R. Henry and others. 165:1148 S 12 '69
Tryptophan pyrrolase induction in patients with manic depression; with reply by A. J. Mandell. R. T. Rubin and B. R. Clark. bibliog il Science 165:1146-8 S 12 '69
PSYCHOCHEMICALS. See Chemical warfare
PSYCHODRAMA
Can TV crime shows prevent violence? W. Bromberg and G. George. Todays Health 47:88+ My '69
Rapping with convicts; conference in Annapolis, Md. R. L. Goldfarb. New Repub 161: 21-3 Jl 19 '69
Role playing: a judge is a con, a con is a judge; Workshop on crime and correction, Annapolis, Md. R. Hammer. il N Y Times Mag p56-7+ S 14 '69; Reply. R. Korn and others. p54 O 5 '69
Theater; The concept, by ex-narcotic addicts from Daytop Village. H. Hewes. Sat R 52:16 S 13 '69
PSYCHOLOGICAL anthropology

Bibliography
Psychological anthropology. J. J. Honigmann. bibliog f Ann Am Acad 383:145-58 My '69

PSYCHOLOGICAL counseling. See Counseling
PSYCHOLOGICAL examinations
Inner circle; theory of Psychiatrist A. F. Kinzel. il Time 93:74 Je 6 '69
Test case; S. Sirhan's responses. il Newsweek 73:94-5 Ap 7 '69
　See also
Personality tests
PSYCHOLOGICAL games. See Games
PSYCHOLOGICAL literature
Approaches to the mental health manpower problem; a review of the literature. L. J. Cowne. bibliog Ment Hy 53:176-87 Ap '69
PSYCHOLOGICAL research
　See also
Laboratory animals
PSYCHOLOGICAL societies
　See also
American psychological association
PSYCHOLOGICAL stress. See Stress (physiology)
PSYCHOLOGICAL tests. See Psychological examinations
PSYCHOLOGISTS
　See also
Counselors
Jung, C. G.
PSYCHOLOGY
New light on the human potential. H. A. Otto. Sat R 52:14-17 D 20 '69
　See also
Aggressiveness (psychology)
American psychological association
Animal intelligence
Anxiety
Attitudes
Behavior (psychology)
Child study
Cognition
Consciousness
Defense mechanisms (psychology)
Discrimination (psychology)
Eidetic imagery
Generalization (psychology)
Influence (psychology)
Knowledge, Theory of
Memory
Motivation (psychology)
Perception
Personality
Physiognomy
Psychiatry
Psychoanalysis
Psychobiology
Recall (psychology)
Repression (psychology)
Self love
Sex (psychology)
Social interaction
Social psychology
Vigilance (psychology)
　also subhead Psychology under various subjects, e.g. Woman—Psychology
Bibliography
　See also
Psychological literature
Experiments
What's in a glance? tests at England's Exeter university. Time 94:74 O 17 '69
Study and teaching
Under the leaking roof; psychology and sociology at Miles college. N. Friedman. il Wilson Lib Bul 44:69-74 S '69
PSYCHOLOGY, Educational
Teacher behavior and the destructive critics. L. N. Tanner. bibliog f Sch & Soc 97:366-7+ O '69
　See also
Intelligence levels
Learning, Psychology of
Mental hygiene—Study and teaching
PSYCHOLOGY, Experimental
　See also
Psychology—Experiments
PSYCHOLOGY, Forensic
　See also
Forensic psychiatry
PSYCHOLOGY, Industrial
　See also
Job satisfaction
PSYCHOLOGY, National. See National characteristics
PSYCHOLOGY, Pathological
Social psychopathology of political assassination. S. J. Slomich and R. E. Kantor. Bul Atom Sci 25:9-12 Mr '69
　See also
Autism
Head banging
Paranoia
Psychoanalysis

PSYCHOLOGY, Physiological
Information processing in the nervous system; report of meeting. K. N. Leibovic. Science 164:457-8+ Ap 25 '69
　See also
Body image
Brain—Localization of functions
Conditioned response
Inhibition
Mind and body
Pain
Reaction time
Reinforcement (psychology)
Sex (psychology)
PSYCHOLOGY, Religious
Faith and psyche: a role for Jung in theology. E. A. Merlin. Cath World 209:172-5 Jl '69
PSYCHOLOGY, Sex. See Sex (psychology)
PSYCHOLOGY of color. See Color—Psychology
PSYCHOLOGY of eating. See Eating, Psychology of
PSYCHOLOGY of gambling. See Gambling—Psychology
PSYCHOLOGY today (periodical)
Synergistic scheme of things. il Time 93:65+ F 14 '69
PSYCHOPATHOLOGY. See Psychology, Pathological
PSYCHOPHARMACOLOGY
Biochemical clues to mental illness. G. Bylinsky. il Fortune 80:124-7+ Jl '69
Highs, lows and both; doxepin hydrochloride combats anxiety and depression. J. Bockel. il Sci N 96:581 D 20 '69
Perils of pill-popping with mood drugs. E. C. Gottschalk. il Sci Digest 66:13-17 Jl '69
Use of mood pills is up; no decline foreseen. Todays Health 47:11 My '69
PSYCHOPHYSIOLOGY. See Psychology, Physiological
PSYCHOSES
Creatine kinase and aldolase in serum: abnormality common to acute psychoses. H. Meltzer; reply with rejoinder. D. G. Warnock and G. L. Ellman. bibliog il Science 164:726-7 My 9 '69
My dark journey through insanity; involutional psychosis. K. W. Seegers. Read Digest 95:67-71 N '69
　See also
Depression, Mental
Mentally ill
PSYCHOSOMATIC medicine. See Medicine, Psychosomatic
PSYCHOTHERAPY
Margolis on responsibility in psychotherapy. A. M. Wheeler. bibliog Ment Hy 53:309-10 Ap '69
New parents for schizophrenics. S. Shubin. il Sci Digest 66:68-73 Ag '69
Psychotherapy by somatic alteration. P. F. Grim. bibliog Ment Hy 53:451-8 Jl '69
Reinforcement therapy; short cut to sanity? il Time 94:52+ Jl 11 '69
Social action, the therapy of poor folk. R. Bitensky. Ment Hy 53:503-8 O '69
　See also
Group psychotherapy
Psychiatry and religion
Psychodrama
PSYCHOTROPIC drugs. See Psychopharmacology
PTARMIGANS
　See also
Cookery—Game
PUBERTY
Changing sensitivity of the pubertal gonadal hypothalamic feedback mechanism in man. H. E. Kulin and others. bibliog il Science 166:1012-13 N 21 '69
Under twenty-one; teen-age love. S. Reice. il McCalls 96:44+ F '69
PUBLIC address amplifiers. See Amplifiers
PUBLIC address systems. See Loud speaking apparatus
PUBLIC administration
Sickness of government; excerpts from The age of discontinuity. P. F. Drucker. il Nations Bsns 57:52-61 Mr '69
What the Bible says about government; excerpts from address. C. T. Curtis. U S News 67:108 N 10 '69
　See also
Bureaucracy
Government spending policy
Municipal government
　also subhead Politics and government under names of countries, states, etc. e.g. France—Politics and government
PUBLIC beaches. See Beaches
PUBLIC broadcast laboratory
Can this be America? personal statements of 1968 election campaign. R. L. Shayon. Sat R 52:51 F 22 '69

PUBLIC broadcasting corporation. See Corporation for public broadcasting
PUBLIC buildings
Sad state of federal architecture. W. Von Eckardt. il Sat R 52:20-1 Je 7 '69
See also
Capitols
City halls
Library architecture
Post office buildings
PUBLIC colleges and universities. See Colleges and universities
PUBLIC decency. See Decency
PUBLIC documents. See Government publications
PUBLIC domain. See Public lands
PUBLIC grievances. See Complaints
PUBLIC health
See also
Air pollution
Camp sanitation
Malaria
Meat inspection
Mosquito control
Quarantine
Refuse and refuse disposal
Water pollution

Laws and legislation
See also
Food laws and legislation

Africa
Immunizing the Dark Continent. il Todays Health 47:17-18 My '69

France
A votre santé? French drinking problem. il Newsweek 73:104 Mr 17 '69

Great Britain
See also
Great Britain—National health service

Israel
Hearts and national origin. H. Gillon. il Sci N 95:342 Ap 5 '69

United States
It's not eating that kills, but underexercising. J. Mayer. il Forbes 104:64+ O 1 '69
Medicaid's maladies. Time 93:76 My 23 '69
See also
Health agencies, Voluntary
Nutrition problems—United States
Television broadcasting—Health education programs
United States—Childrens bureau
PUBLIC health centers. See Health centers
PUBLIC health workers. See Health workers
PUBLIC high schools. See High schools
PUBLIC holidays. See Holidays
PUBLIC houses (United States) See Bars and barrooms
PUBLIC housing projects. See Housing projects, Government
PUBLIC information act. See Information, Freedom of
PUBLIC institutions. See State institutions
PUBLIC interest television programs. See Television broadcasting—Public service programs
PUBLIC land law review commission. See United States—Public land law review commission
PUBLIC lands
See also
Submerged lands

Mexico
Forestry and the public domain; a Mexican point of view. E. Beltran. il Am For 75:36-7+ D '69 (to be cont)

United States
Access: the key to public land recreation. B. Milek. il Field & S 73:20+ Ap '69
Disney imperative. W. Marx. Nation 209:76-8 Jl 28 '69
History of public land law development, by P. W. Gates and R. W. Swenson. Review
Am For 75:39-41 F '69. H. K. Pyles
Keynote on the public lands. W. N. Aspinall. il Am For 75:12-15+ N '69
LBJ's land grab; federal land deal in Austin, Tex. il Newsweek 74:39 N 10 '69
National resource lands. Liv Wildn 33:37 Spr '69
Public interest; address. C. G. McIntire. il Am For 75:20-3 D '69
Public lands conference called. il Am For 75:10-11 Ap '69

Test plot of the public lands. T. Trueblood. il Field & S 74:12+ Ag '69
Uncle Sam's step-child acres. C. H. Stoddard. il Am For 75:16-19+ S '69
See also
National forests
United States—Land management, Bureau of
United States—Public land law review commission
PUBLIC libraries. See Libraries
PUBLIC officers
American power and the new mandarins, by N. Chomsky. Review
Cath World 210:80-1 N '69. S. Melman
At the President's elbow. P. Lisagor. Nations Bsns 57:17-18 Ag '69
Californians: a new in group in Washington. il U S News 66:80-1 My 5 '69
Circulating elite. Nation 208:131 F 3 '69
Closed-door policy; Mrs Nixon's press secretary. il Newsweek 73:85 Je 2 '69
Discipline and order but an open image; expansion of executive branch of the federal government. J. Osborne. New Repub 160:11-13 F 22 '69
Eight of the political hammers of Washington. il Vogue 154:106-13 N 15 '69
End to indifference along the Potomac. H. Sidey. il Life 67:6 D 5 '69
Goodbys, some with regret; and hellos, mostly appreciative. il Life 66:30 Ja 24 '69
I'll check it out; Nixon's press secretary. il Time 94:77 O 10 '69
Key men around LBJ when he was president. il U S News 67:9 D 29 '69
Key men around Nixon; who's calling the signals. il U S News 66:70-3 My 12 '69
Key men at White House now. il U S News 67:64-6 N 17 '69
Man with a pressure cooker job; how Kissinger exercises power; assistant to the President for national security affairs. il U S News 67:15-16 Jl 14 '69
New administration easing in. il Time 93:11-12 Ja 31 '69
New faces on the Nixon team. U S News 66:18 Ap 21 '69
Nixon's odd-jobs man; White House staff's P. Flanigan. Bsns W p62-3 S 27 '69
No. 1 on White House staff, how he'll advise Nixon. U S News 66:15 F 3 '69
Order or conflict? P. Lisagor. Nations Bsns 57:23-4 Mr '69
Patriot in the basement; D. Blumenthal. H. Sidey. Life 66:4 Mr 28 '69
Praetorians: White House chief of staff H. R. Haldeman and presidential counsel J. Ehrlichman. il Newsweek 74:36+ Jl 28 '69
Public figures and their private lives; Time essay. il Time 94:28-9 Ag 22 '69
Reports: Washington; former officials of the Johnson administration. E. B. Drew. Atlan 224:10 Jl '69
Rose garden rubbish and other glorious compositions; presidential speech writer. P. Benchley. il Life 66:60B-60D+ My 23 '69
Spiro Agnew explains himself. S. T. Agnew. Life 67:34-5 N 28 '69
Struggle for neatness: White House staff changes. J. Osborne. New Repub 161:14-15 N 22 '69
Swingtime; Republicans in Washington. H. Brandon. Sat R 53:4+ Ja 3 '70
Time: 7:45 a.m. weekdays; place: Roosevelt room, West wing, White House. Nixon's inner circle meets. R. B. Semple, jr. il N Y Times Mag p6-9+ Ag 3 '69
Washington now: who's in, who's out of power. pors U S News 66:26-9 Ja 27 '69
When Ike said farewell; presidential speechwriters Malcolm Moos and Ralph Williams. Newsweek 73:28 Ap 14 '69
Where is Pat? reorganization of White House staff. J. Osborne. New Repub 161:15-17 N 29 '69
White House staff bureaucracy. A. B. Lacy, jr. il Trans-Action 6:50-6 Ja '69
White House staff versus the Cabinet; interview, ed. by H. Sidey. B. Moyers. Cur 106:26-35 Ap '69
White House who's who. J. Osborne. New Repub 161:13-15 O 18 '69
Who's left to do the dishes? J. B. Martin. Life 66:16B Ja 31 '69
Why a top Negro agreed to join the Nixon team; case of J. Farmer. il U S News 66:16 F 24 '69
See also
Cabinet officers
Conflict of interests (public office)
Misconduct in office
Negro public officers
Political ethics
United States—Executive office of the president

PUBLIC officers—*Continued*

Anecdotes, facetiae, satire, etc.

Gag rule: radio and television comedians as presidential speech writers. V. Gold. Nat R 21:680 Jl 15 '69

On disengagement: limit of former Johnson administration officials to their involvement in U.S. government affairs. V. Gold. Nat R 21:796 Ag 12 '69

Appointment, qualifications, tenure, etc.

Appointees fall down on the Hill; E. Dirksen blocks Administration appointees. il Bsns W p46-7 My 10 '69

Blues on the right; administration's ranks. Newsweek 73:32 Ap 7 '69

Getting a grip on the 'governaut.' H. Sidey. il Life 66:2 Ja 24 '69

Head-hunter. Newsweek 73:37 Ap 28 '69

Man of the A.M.A. cut down; personal account of the campaign that blocked his nomination. J. H. Knowles. il Life 67:30-5 Jl 11 '69

Otepka and no-nonsense security. H. J. Sievers. America 120:681 Je 14 '69

Political criteria for non-political jobs? E. Rabinowitch. Bul Atom Sci 25:2-3+ Je '69

Reports: Washington; the Nixon White House Staff. E. B. Drew. Atlan 223:4+ Ap '69

Rise of Harry Dent. J. Osborne. New Repub 160:13-16 Je 14 '69

Traffic cop; reorganization of White House staff. il Newsweek 74:50 N 17 '69

Dismissal

All fired up; removal of R. H. Lapin. il Newsweek 74:82-3 D 15 '69

Homes

Great house hunt. il Newsweek 73:59 Ja 27 '69

Salaries, allowances, etc.

Raises for U.S. officials: why so big. il U S News 66:35 Ja 27 '69

Tab for keeping Congress. il Bsns W p80+ N 15 '69

Training

Fellowships in practical politics; attracting minority college graduates to careers in government and politics. Sch & Soc 97:133+ Mr '69

France

Man of shadows; J. Foccart. Newsweek 74:32+ Ag 18 '69

PUBLIC opinion
See also
Public opinion polls
Student opinion
Teacher opinion
Vietnamese war, 1957- —Public opinion
  also subhead Foreign opinion under names of countries, e.g. United States—Foreign opinion

Australia
See also
United States—Foreign opinion—Australian

Europe, Western

Europe in a time of change. D. Middleton. Sat R 52:14-15 Ag 16 '69
  See also
United States—Foreign opinion—European

Germany (Federal Republic)

New frontier. B. Van Voorst. il Newsweek 74:48+ O 27 '69

Great Britain

Just how radical are the young? recent poll. U S News 66:8 Je 30 '69

On leaving the herd; changing from Socialist to Conservative. J. Braine. Nat R 21:749-50+ Jl 29 '69

Prince who'll bust the scene? views of young Britons on Charles and the monarchy. il Newsweek 74:30-1 Jl 14 '69
  See also
United States—Foreign opinion—British

Japan

Testing ground in Tokyo; growing militarism and the Okinawa question. N. Cousins. il Sat R 52:28-9 D 6 '69

Russia

Moscow report: . . . the more it remains the same. A. Carthew. il N Y Times Mag p28-9+ My 18 '69
  See also
China (People's Republic)—Foreign opinion—Russian

Spain

What Spaniards say when they think aloud; excerpts from Conversations in Madrid, ed. by R. Eder. S. Paniker. il N Y Times Mag p25+ S 28 '69; Reply. J. Eugui. p22 N 9 '69

Sweden
See also
United States—Foreign opinion—Swedish

United States

California backlash; public's attitude toward the state's campus disorders. Time 93:60 Mr 14 '69

Death to gooks; reactions to Pinkville massacre. J. Osborne. New Repub 161:17-18 D 13 '69

Divided opinion; poll on TV press bias. Newsweek 75:59 Ja 19 '70

How President rates now. U S News 66:16 Ap 7 '69

How they see it in Hannibal, Mo. H. B. Meyers. il Fortune 80:74-5+ D '69

Ideology of fed-upness: public apprehension over violence and disorder. Time 93:15-16 Je 27 '69

If people were voting for president today. il U S News 66:14 My 12 '69

Left and right, young and old; United States response to Biafra's plight. il Newsweek 73:56 Mr 24 '69

Mood of America. F. Knebel. il Look 33:23-32 N 18 '69

NR reader. New Repub 160:12 Ap 5 '69

Nixon's rating in the latest polls. U S News 67:13 O 13 '69

On the causes of our discontents. T. L. Hughes. For Affairs 47:653-67 Jl '69

Our basic news medium; impact of TV and newspapers; Roper survey. R. L. Tobin. Sat R 52:41-2 Ag 9 '69

Popularity: Nixon's still the one. U S News 66:12 Je 16 '69

Public schools' public; Gallup CFK poll. J. Cass. Sat R 52:73 O 18 '69

Report from black America; with reports by R. M. Scammon; J. Rodgers; J. B. Cumming, jr. il Newsweek 73:16-26+ Je 30 '69

Shapes of coalition and dissent; a new Life Harris poll. B. Hooper. il Life 68:102-6 Ja 9 '70

Silenced majority; President's obligation to public opinion. C. Frankel. Sat R 52:22+ D 13 '69

Taxed public temper; congressmen sample constituents mood. il Bsns W p41-2 Jl 12 '69

Toward a social ethic; bureaucrats becoming vocal on behalf of the public. Nation 208:292 Mr 10 '69

Troubled American; a special report on the white majority; with reports by K. Fleming and R. M. Scammon. il Newsweek 74:28-52+ O 6 '69; Same abr. Read Digest 95:94-9 D '69

What business thinks. A. M. Louis. il Fortune 80:93-5+ S '69

What business thinks; the Fortune 500-Yankelovich survey. R. S. Diamond. il Fortune 80:139-40+ O; 157-8 N; 115-16 D '69; 81:123-4 Ja '70

What's bothering people Congress learns at home. il U S News 67:26-8 S 8 '69

Why workers are casting protest votes. B. L. Masse. America 121:55 Ag 2 '69
  See also
Vietnamese war, 1957- —Public opinion

Vietnam (Democratic Republic)

November in Hanoi. W. Meyers. Nation 209:622-4 D 8 '69

Vietnam (Republic)

Preparing for the worst; how the South Vietnamese feel about U.S. withdrawal. M. Parker. il Newsweek 74:40 N 24 '69
  See also
United States—Foreign opinion—Vietnamese

PUBLIC opinion polls

Changing morality: the two Americas; a Time-Louis Harris poll. il Time 93:26-7 Je 6 '69

Life poll, a marriage of two techniques. G. P. Hunt. il Life 66:3 My 16 '69

Many-faceted fact; reactions to New York daily news poll and the mayoral race. Newsweek 74:98 N 10 '69

Poll-axed? New York mayoral election and the Daily news poll. il Newsweek 74:87 N 17 '69

Anecdotes, facetiae, satire, etc.

Pupwsss poll. Chr Cent 86:601 Ap 23 '69

PUBLIC ownership. See Government ownership

PUBLIC prosecutors
  Now a shortage of prosecutors; survey. il
    U S News 67:33-4 D 29 '69
PUBLIC relations
  Difficult years; past concepts and present
    trends. L. L. L. Golden. Sat R 52:79 My
    10 '69
  Public relations. L. L. L. Golden. See issues
    of Saturday review
    See also
  Church advertising
  Investor relations programs
  Moving pictures in public relations
  Radio broadcasting—Public service programs
  Television broadcasting—Public service pro-
    grams
    also subhead Public relations under vari-
    ous subjects, e.g. Motor bus lines—Public
    relations
              Bibliography
  Books in communications. S. W. Little. See
    issues of Saturday review
PUBLIC relations consultants
    See also
  Hill and Knowlton, incorporated
PUBLIC relations society of America
  Reforming PRSA. L. L. L. Golden. Sat R
    52:57-8 Jl 12 '69
PUBLIC school education, Assessment of. See
  Evaluation (education)
PUBLIC school libraries. See School libraries
PUBLIC school teachers. See Teachers
PUBLIC schools
    See also
  Education and state
  School children
  School management and organization
  Special classes and special schools
              Appraisal
    See Evaluation (education)
              Attendance
    See School attendance
              Desegregation
  Amber light on integration. il Time 94:13-14
    S 5 '69
  Apologist: J. Leonard arguing for delay of
    desegregation in Mississippi. il Time 94:
    77 O 31 '69
  As schools reopen: Nixon faces test on inte-
    gration. il U S News 67:44-5 S 15 '69
  At once, at last. Chr Cent 86:1442 N 12 '69
  Balancing act; S. T. Agnew statement. il
    Newsweek 74:35 S 29 '69
  Brown v. Board of education of Topeka;
    excerpts from 1954 decision. Cur Hist 57:
    297-8+ N '69
  Busing at Great Neck. il Newsweek 73:70 F
    17 '69
  Caught in a crunch: Secretary Finch. U S
    News 67:11 Jl 7 '69
  Change the law on segregation? il U S News
    67:8 D 8 '69
  Chaos in public schools; the Mississippi story.
    il U S News 67:24-6 D 8 '69
  Civil rights, the Nixon fiddle. B. Sellers.
    Nation 209:344-6 O 6 '69
  Clarification, please; HEW desegregation
    plan. New Repub 161:8 O 4 '69
  Court, the schools, and the southern strat-
    egy. G. Orfield. Sat R 52:62+ D 20 '69
  Dead letter. New Repub 161:6 Jl 26 '69
  Debt to Dixie; Administration inching back
    from September 1969 desegregation dead-
    line. il Newsweek 74:23-4 Jl 14 '69
  Desegregate now; but how to do it? il U S
    News 67:45-6 N 10 '69
  Desegregation guidelines; problem of south-
    ern school districts. il Time 94:14-16 Jl 11
    '69
  Desegregation or integration; what the row
    is all about. il U S News 67:46-8 O 6 '69
  Desegregation slow-down? New Repub 161:8-
    9 Jl 19 '69
  Dream is over; Denver's elementary schools
    are de facto segregated. Time 93:44 My 30
    '69
  End of an era; school desegregation in Mis-
    sissippi. il Time 95:14-16 Ja 19 '70
  Fifteen years of deliberate speed; excerpt
    from Argument. K. B. Clark. il Sat R 52:59-
    61+ D 20 '69
  Finch's guidelines. New Repub 160:7 My 3
    '69
  Freedom of choice; suspending federal aid to
    southern districts. il Newsweek 73:31 F 17
    '69
  Gains in Negro rights; a fifteen year record.
    il U S News 66:51-4 My 19 '69
  Has there been a change of pace? S. Holz-
    man. Sr Schol 95:Schol Teach 1-2 O 6 '69

Immediate compliance for school integration.
    Library J 94:4565 D 15 '69
  In Worth County. Nation 208:132 F 3 '69
  Integration now. Time 94:19-20 N 7 '69
  Key job for a backer of integration: U.S.
    commissioner of education, J. E. Allen. U S
    News 66:17 F 17 '69
  Mississippi; black and white together. il
    Newsweek 75:17-18 Ja 19 '70
  Mr Nixon and the South. B. B. Stretch. Sat
    R 52:74 S 20 '69
  Mitchell's law and order. Nation 209:686 D
    22 '69
  Mix schools by busing? Where voters said no.
    U S News 66:70 Ap 28 '69
  Mixed classes: now a crackdown in the
    North. U S News 66:6-7 Mr 3 '69
  Mixed schools: new guidelines? U S News
    66:8 F 10 '69
  New approach to integration? interview. R. H.
    Finch. il U S News 66:38-40+ Mr 10 '69
  New court test on school desegregation. R.
    H. Smith. Pub W 196:46 O 20 '69
  New ruling on mixed classes. il U S News 66:
    10 F 3 '69
  Nixon/Finch desegregation policy criticized.
    Library J 94:4190+ N 15 '69
  Nixon's first test. G. Orfield. Nation 208:79-82
    Ja 20 '69
  Now, more flexible rules for school desegrega-
    tion. il U S News 67:11 Jl 14 '69
  110 Livingston street; politics and bureau-
    cracy in the New York city schools, by D.
    Rogers. Review
    Commentary 47:81-6 Mr '69. N. Glazer
  One of those weeks; Administration's un-
    certain stand on southern school desegrega-
    tion guidelines. Newsweek 74:16-17 Jl 7 '69
  Outlook on mixed classes. U S News 67:7
    S 1 '69
  Provocative precedent; J. Leonard argues
    for delay in desegregation. Newsweek 74:
    26-7 N 3 '69
  Public schools; a sociological perspective;
    address, July 8, 1969. D. W. Dodson. bib-
    liog f Vital Speeches 35:686-91 S 1 '69
  Query from the South; why not desegregate
    in the North? excerpts from address, Octo-
    ber 16, 1969. J. C. Stennis. il U S News
    67:93-5 N 3 '69
  Racial, religious and educational liberty.
    America 121:451 N 15 '69
  Racial resegregation in education. W. W.
    Brickman. Sch & Soc 97:345 O 7 '69
  Reasonable man; wiretapping, pretrial deten-
    tion & civil rights; address, August 13,
    1969. J. N. Mitchell. Vital Speeches 35:678-
    81 S 1 '69
  Report; southern desegregation. H. Leifer-
    mann. Atlan 223:12+ F '69
  Road Nixon is taking on civil rights. il U S
    News 67:36-7 Jl 21 '69
  School bussing and parental anxiety; con-
    cerning Negro ghetto children. Sch & Soc
    97:5-6 Ja '69
  School decentralization and racial integration.
    N. Minihan. il Sch & Soc 97:164-5 Mr '69
  School desegregation policy, 1969; Excerpts.
    Cur Hist 57:303-5 N '69
  School problem that's nationwide. U S News
    68:4 Ja 12 '70
  School segregation in Abbeville. federal guide-
    lines vs. John C. Calhoun. R. Cleghorn. il
    N Y Times Mag p8-9+ Jl 20 '69
  September song; a long, long time; resistance
    to integration in the South. il Newsweek
    74:23-4 S 15 '69
  Setbacks for segregationists Time 94:34-5 D
    26 '69
  Speeding up desegregation. Chr Today 14:27
    N 21 '69
  Spelling it out in black and white; administra-
    tion's policy attacked by the Commission
    on civil rights and Justice department
    lawyers. il Newsweek 74:31-2 S 22 '69
  Sweet and sour; the administration's ges-
    tures. New Repub 160:11 Ap 12 '69
  Symbolic South; executive committee of the
    Leadership conference on civil rights meets
    with R. Finch. New Repub 160:12-13 Ap 5
    '69
  Teacher opinion poll; bussing. Todays Ed
    58:7 Mr '69
  Tension on the guidelines. il Sat R 52:66 Ap
    19 '69
  They are going to do it. W. F. Buckley, jr.
    Nat R 21:1234 D 2 '69
  They made a better school; community
    school in Providence. R. H. Levine. il Am
    Ed 5:8-10 N '69
  This month's feature: Congress & public
    school racial policy. Cong Digest 48:34-64
    F '69
  Time is running out; new school desegrega-
    tion policy. America 121:217 S 27 '69

PUBLIC schools—Desegregation—*Continued*
Time runs out in Mississippi. Time 94:24+
N 14 '69
TRB from Washington; ruling on desegre-
gation of Mississippi schools. New Repub
161:8 N 8 '69
U.S. journal: Denver. C. Trillin. New Yorker
45:85-9 My 31 '69
U.S. Supreme court ruling on school desegre-
gation, 1969. Cur Hist 58:40-1 Ja '70
Vanishing black principals and teachers in
the South. Sch & Soc 97:470+ D '69
What is the law of the land on racial im-
balance? D. Lawrence. U S News 66:96+
F 10 '69
What the Court said. New Repub 161:12 N
15 '69
What's gone wrong in our big-city schools?
il Changing T 23:43-7 Jl '69
When courts try to run the public schools.
C. F. Hansen il U S News 66:94-6 Ap 21 '69
Where Jim Crow is alive and well; Missis-
sippi. M. Zim. Time 94:21 S 19 '69
Why school busing is in trouble. il U S News
67:42-4 O 13 '69
With all deliberate speed; integration in the
South. Trans-Action 6:7 Jl '69
Yes Virginia, there is a Constitution; Su-
preme court ruling for Mississippi districts.
il Newsweek 74:35-7 N 10 '69
See also
School boycotts

Finance
See School finance

Health service
Day in the life of a school nurse. M. Hughes.
il Parents Mag 44:64-5+ Mr '69
School mental health services offered with-
out invitation. E. A. Horn and others. bib-
liog Ment Hy 53:620-4 O '69
See also
School nurses

Public relations
See School and the community

Statistics
See Education—Statistics

United States
Financing urban schools: a continuing crisis.
T. P. Wilbur. bibliog f Sch & Soc 97:286-8
Sum '69
Hunger problem and how one town is beat-
ing it; rural school, San Diego, Tex. il
U S News 66:53-4 F 10 '69
Private schools for black children. C. Jencks.
Ed Digest 34:1-4 Mr '69
Public school movement: phoenix or dodo-
bird? R. Pratte. Ed Digest 35:1-4 D '69
Public schools' public; Gallup CFK poll. J.
Cass. Sat R 52:73 O 18 '69
Public schools: the myth of the melting pot;
excerpt from Cobweb attitudes: essays in
American education and culture. C. Greer.
il Sat R 52:84-6+ N 15 '69
Urban school crisis gets top billing at AASA.
W. D. Boutwell and others. Sr Schol 94:
Schol Teach 3-4 Mr 21 '69
What's going on in schools & colleges. See
issues of Changing times
Where all is quiet in the schools. il U S News
66:53-6 Ja 27 '69
See also
Education—United States
Equalization, Educational
Propaganda in the schools
Rural schools—United States
School year

PUBLIC schools and religion
Bringing back devotions. Chr Today 13:21
Ap 25 '69
Christmas in the classroom; observances in
Marblehead, Mass. il Time 94:48 D 12 '69
God goes back to school. R. Kirk. Nat R
21:27 Ja 14 '69
God goes to high school. R. Taylor. Chr To-
day 14:48 D 5 '69
Let us pray. D. Lawrence. U S News 67:88
Ag 11 '69
Perils of pluralism: the background of the
Pierce case. D. B. Tyack. bibliog f Am Hist
R 74:74-98 O '68
Public-school Bible study: sectarianism in
disguise? C. J. Miller. Chr Today 13:3-5
Ag 1 '69
Public school religion course. America 121:
407 N 8 '69
Religious guidelines for public schools. Chr
Cent 86:401 Mr 26 '69
School prayer issue rears up again; Leyden,
Mass. Chr Cent 86:1215 S 24 '69

Teaching about religion in the public school.
R. L. Hunt. il Todays Ed 58:24-6 D '69
See also
Bible study
PUBLIC schools and the community. See
School and the community
PUBLIC service
Public services slipping, too. il U S News 67:
52 D 1 '69
See also
Civil service
Public officers
PUBLIC service advertising. See Advertising,
Public service
PUBLIC service radio programs. See Radio
broadcasting—Public service programs
PUBLIC service television programs. See Tele-
vision broadcasting—Public service pro-
grams
PUBLIC speaking
Pointers for neophyte speechmakers. il Chang-
ing T 23:47 Ap '69
See also
Gesture
Rhetoric
Street speaking
PUBLIC spirit. See Patriotism
PUBLIC television. See Television broadcast-
ing, Noncommercial; Television in educa-
tion
PUBLIC universities. See Colleges and uni-
versities
PUBLIC utilities
As I see it; interview. D. C. Cook. il Forbes
103:42+ F 1 '69
Fifty largest utilities. Fortune 79:198-9 My
15 '69
GE strike hits utilities lightly. il Bsns W
p36 Ja 10 '70
Palo Alto's underground utility project. il
Am City 84:172+ S '69
See also
Electric utilities
Pacific gas and electric company

Securities
Wall Street: Io, the utilities. C. Morgello.
Newsweek 73:93 Mr 17 '69
PUBLIC welfare
See also
Old age assistance

Law
Breakthrough on welfare; residency requirements. il Newsweek 73:33-4 My 5 '69
Mobile poor. Nation 208:555-6 My 5 '69
Welfare and the Court: residence requirements. E. Van Den Haag. Nat R 21:805 Ag
12 '69
Welfare backlash. il Newsweek 73:64+ Ap 14
'69

Great Britain
Britain shakes up welfare system. il U S
News 67:29 Ag 25 '69

New Jersey
Go power; income maintenance program.
Newsweek 73:57-8 Mr 31 '69

New York (state)
Toward a welfare breakdown. Fortune 79:72
F '69
Welfare backlash; benefits cut. il Newsweek
73:64+ Ap 14 '69

Texas
What the poor are up against in Texas. S. H.
Estes. New Repub 161:13-14 Jl 19 '69

United States
Action on welfare. Sci N 96:113 Ag 9 '69
As Nixon shifts to home front—. U S News
67:19-22 Ag 19 '69
Breeding a national standard. il Sci N 95:
448 My 10 '69
Choice and change in the American welfare
system. M. Rein. bibliog f il Ann Am Acad
385:89-109 S '69
Courts have failed the poor. J. S. Wright. il
N Y Times Mag p26-7+ Mr 9 '69; Reply.
M. B. Stecher. p86 Ap 6 '69
Debate begins on Nixon's reforms. Time 94:
15-16 Ag 22 '69
Doing something relevant; Center on social
welfare policy and law. il Time 93:27-8 My
9 '69
Governors' verdict on Nixon program: good,
but. il U S News 67:28-9 S 15 '69
High marks for a new boy; Finch-Moynihan-
Burns proposals. il Newsweek 73:29-30 Je 23
'69
Homing in on domestic programs; with
editorial comment. il Bsns W p36-8. 130
Ag 16 '69

PUBLIC welfare—United States—*Continued*
How the relief system works now. il U S News 67:76-8 S 22 '69
If you have questions on welfare plan—. il U S News 67:54-5 S 1 '69
Let not your right hand; Nixon program. Nat R 21:833-9 Ag 26 '69
Look at what ails welfare; San Diego report. Nations Bsns 57:42 O '69
Money matters; governors discussing welfare programs. Time 94:18-19 S 12 '69
New federalism; National governors conference. il Newsweek 74:24-5 S 15 '69
New look in welfare: the Nixon program. Chr Cent 86:1105 Ag 27 '69
New thrust toward economic security; address, July 28, 1969. W. M. Young, jr. Vital Speeches 35:759-63 O 1 '69
Nixon: we have to put the money where the problems are; excerpt from address, September 1, 1969. R. M. Nixon. U S News 67:82-4 S 15 '69
Nixon's affluence; reform proposals. New Repub 161:7-8 Ag 23 '69
Nixon's big decision on welfare; White House advisers battle over reform. il Bsns W p 110+ Je 21 '69
Nixon's four-front war on poverty; address, August 8, 1969. R. M. Nixon. U S News 67:78-80 Ag 18 '69; Same. Vital Speeches 35:674-8 S 1 '69
Nixon's guaranteed annual poverty. L. Hunt and others. Ramp Mag 8:64-70 D '69
Nixon's new deal; proposals. il Newsweek 74:17-19 Ag 18 '69
Nixon's welfare options. America 120:682 Je 14 '69
Now it's instant welfare: impact across the U.S. il U S News 66:32-2 My 5 '69
One cheer; R. M. Nixon's proposals. Nation 209:131-2 Ag 25 '69
Overhauling relief; the meaning. il U S News 67:26-8 Ag 25 '69
PTA in Washington. C. Ryan. PTA Mag 64:26-7 O '69
Pat Moynihan: too much! And too little! B. Asbell. il N Y Times Mag p44-5+ N 2 '69
Poverty profession. Nat R 21:739 Jl 29 '69
President's poverty plan. Chr Today 13:34-5 S 12 '69
Right job to do on welfare. Bsns W p 156 Je 28 '69
Rocky road to reforming welfare. Life 67:38 Ag 22 '69
Runaway boom in welfare. il U S News 66:52-4 F 3 '69
Second thoughts; objections to R. M. Nixon's reform proposals. Newsweek 74:18+ Ag 25 '69
Sixty-six cents a day; let them eat squid. P. Coyne. Nat R 21:909 S 9 '69; Reply. W. F. Buckley, jr. 21:1027 O 7 '69
Some perspectives on evaluating social welfare programs. L. A. Ferman. Ann Am Acad 385:143-56 S '69
Supreme court and welfare laws. America 120:521 My 3 '69
Test tube for relief reform; Work incentive program. il Nations Bsns 57:37-42 O '69
Tory men and Whig measures; President Nixon's program. F. S. Meyer. Nat R 21:1013 O 7 '69
Toward a guaranteed income; what's in the works. il U S News 66:34-5 Je 23 '69
Toward a working welfare system. il Time 94:14 Ag 15 '69
Toward assuring family security; J. E. Cosgrove's testimony. America 121:580 D 13 '69
TRB from Washington; where the money goes. New Repub 160:4 Mr 22 '69
Volcano in the cornfield; Nixon policy as shaped by D. P. Moynihan & co. H. Sidey. il Life 67:4 Ag 22 '69
Welfare and the suitable job; President Nixon's approach. Nat R 21:888 S 9 '69
Welfare burden. Nation 208:67-8 Ja 20 '69
Welfare, manpower training, revenue sharing; R. M. Nixon's proposed reforms. America 121:112-13 Ag 30 '69
Welfare mother. I. Hinds. Chr Cent 87:17-18 Ja 7 '70
Welfare plan: two Washington views. T. M. Gannon. America 121:118-19 Ag 30 '69
Welfare story, plot and subplot. J. Osborne. New Repub 161:15-17 N 8 '69
Welfare tax rate; excerpt from Public and private manpower policies, ed. by A. Weber and others. L. J. Hausman. il Trans-Action 6:48-53 Ap '69
Welfare union steps up its demands. il U S News 66:36 Je 23 '69
Welfarism out of control; Richard Nixon's program. H. Hazlitt. Nat R 21:903+ S 9 '69

White House's idea man for urban problems; D. P. Moynihan. il Bsns W p72-4+ S 27 '69
Whither welfarism? Nat R 21:61 Ja 28 '69
Why people go on welfare. Trans-Action 6:6 S '69
Why should the poor work? America 120:489 Ap 26 '69
You can go home again. il Ebony 24:104-5 O '69
   See also
Anti-poverty program, 1964-
Child welfare—United States
Economic assistance, Domestic

Wisconsin
Legislators and welfare protests. America 121:407 N 8 '69

PUBLIC welfare departments
   See also
New York (city)—Welfare, Department of

PUBLIC welfare workers. See Social workers

PUBLIC works
   See also subhead Public works under names of cities, e.g. Ansonia, Conn.—Public works

PUBLICATIONS, Ship. See Ship publications

PUBLICITY
Fourth estate: smoothing press relations. Bsns W p99-100 Ja 10 '70
   See also
Church advertising
Television in politics

PUBLICKER industries
Going (half) public. il Forbes 103:26-7 Je 1 '69

PUBLISHERS and authors. See Authors and publishers

PUBLISHERS and publishing
   See also
Best sellers
Book clubs
Books—Advertising
Books—Prices
Copyright
International magazine conference
Literary agents
Music publishing
Newspaper publishers and publishing
Newspaper publishing
Periodicals, Publishing of
Private presses
   also names of publishers, e.g. Doubleday and company

Art literature
Illustrative units enliven scholarly art text. il Pub W 196:73 O 6 '69
Oriental arts set gets top care in Japan. il Pub W 196:58 D 1 '69

Atlases
Producing Economic atlas at Toronto press. Pub W 196:71-2 N 3 '69

Biographies
Statesmen recollect, and collect; cost of publishing memoirs. Bsns W p30-1 F 8 '69

Catholic literature
Doping the book-makers. P. Nobile. il Commonweal 89:674-5 F 28 '69
Future of Catholic books. P. K. Cuneo. America 120:170-1 F 8 '69; Reply. G. MacEoin. 120:234 Mr 1 '69

Childrens literature
ABC D goldfish. V. Wehrum. Pub W 196:28 N 10 '69
Children's paperback explosion in Britain. J. Taylor. Pub W 196:25-6 N 3 '69
Part played by Boston publishers of 1860-1900 in the field of children's books. H. L Jones. bibliog il Horn Bk 45:20-8, 153-9, 329-36 F-Je '69

Consolidations and mergers
ABPC-AEPI joint sessions: mergers of book firms; highlights of panel discussions. il Pub W 195:31-2 Je 9 '69
Droemer Knaur: before the merger and after H. R. Lottman. il Pub W 196:39-41 O 20 '69
Wall Streets notes, 1968. Pub W 195:45-6 Mr 10 '69

Detective and mystery stories
Specialized needs at Doubleday: mystery-suspense and science fiction. L. P. Ashmead. Writer 82:23-4 My '69

Dictionaries
Money: a word in lexicography. il Bsns W p54+ F 8 '69

PUBLISHERS and publishing—Dictionaries—
Continued
Producing a $4 million book; American heritage dictionary. il Pub W 196:56-8 S 1 '69
Publishing scene. D. Dempsey. Sat R 52:35 S 20 '69

Drama

Play markets. Writers Digest 49:94-5 S '69
(to be cont)

Educational literature

PI publishers. Writers Digest 49:80-1 S '69

Employees

ABPC seminar: minority manpower in publishing. Pub W 195:34-6 F 3 '69
For the agenda of book trade associations. C. B. Grannis. Pub W 195:55 Mr 10 '69

Facsimiles

See Book rarities—Facsimiles

Finance

No longer for gentlemen. P. R. Reynolds. il Sat R 52:124-5 Mr 8 '69

Illustrated books

Fright before Christmas; picture books for the Christmas sales season. A. Gutenberg. Pub W 195:74-5 F 3 '69

International aspects

American book abroad; excerpts from address. W. B. Wiley. Pub W 196:19-20 D 8 '69
Publishing scene; Russian literature, copyright and royalties. D. Dempsey. Sat R 52:31 Je 14 '69
See also
Franklin book programs, incorporated
Publishers and publishing—Translations

Large print books

Watts ultratype editions: new 14pt. type series. il Pub W 195:42-3 F 3 '69

Legal literature

Law publishers relax certain sales policies. Pub W 195:70-1 Ap 14 '69

Maps

Mapmaking: the gentleman's business. J. Poindexter. il Duns R 94:56-61 N '69

Order processing

New distribution center for Lippincott. il Pub W 196:29-30 O 6 '69
Norwegian publisher has unusual order system; computerized order-control system. Pub W 195:28 My 5 '69

Paperback books

Children's paperback explosion in Britain. J. Taylor. Pub W 196:25-6 N 3 '69
Mixing the media; new publications. il Newsweek 73:101-2+ Je 9 '69
New, critical look at scholarly paperbacks; excerpts from addresses at annual meeting of AAUP. M. Philipson; J. G. Goellner; B. H. Nicoll. il Pub W 196:31-5 Jl 28 '69
Paperback printing speeds up; Cameron machine press turns paper into books in one operation. Bsns W p54 Ap 5 '69
Publishing scene; Doubleday's Projections; underground books. D. Dempsey. Sat R 52:31 My 10 '69

Poetry

Poetry as merchandise. A. Caruba. Pub W 196:34 D 29 '69

Reference books

Publishing scene; Larousse in New York. D. Dempsey. Sat R 52:35 S 20 '69

Regional literature

Fifty faces of Uncle Sam. D. R. Ellegood. Sat R 52:42-4 Je 21 '69

Religious literature

Religious publishing in the Soviet Union. M. Bourdeaux. Chr Cent 86:626-7 Ap 30 '69
See also
American book publishers council—Religious publishers group
Methodist publishing house, Nashville, Tenn.
Nelson, Thomas, and sons (publisher)
Protestant church-owned publisher's association

Reprints

Publishing scene. D. Dempsey. Sat R 53:36 Ja 10 '70
Reprint markets. Writers Digest 49:31-3+ Ag '69
See also
Books—Reprints

Science fiction

Science fiction market. J. Estrada. il Writers Digest 49:48-52+ Ap '69
Specialized needs at Doubleday: mystery-suspense and science fiction L. P. Ashmead. Writer 82:23-4 My '69

Scientific literature

Page charges and tight budgets; letter. H. Grundfest. Science 164:905 My 23 '69
What happened to my paper? S. A. Goudsmit. il Phys Today 22:23-5 My '69
When should a book not be a book? R. H. Smith. Pub W 196:66 N 17 '69

Securities

Book industry stock reports (cont of) Book industry stocks: a monthly report. See occasional issues of Publishers' weekly
Wall Street notes, 1968. il Pub W 195:45-6 Mr 10 '69

Statistics

ABPC 1968 sales survey: industry-wide total over $2 1/2-billion. Pub W 196:25-7 D 8 '69
American book title output January through March 1969; table. Pub W 195:27 My 5 '69
Marketing and capitalization; excerpts from addresses. U. M. Krippene; E. W. Nordberg. Pub W 196:22-4 D 8 '69
1967 census for books is issued. il Pub W 196:38-9 O 27 '69
1968 in review; statistics, news, trends. il Pub W 195:37-44 Mr 10 '69
1968: subject analysis of American book title output. il Pub W 195:28-9 Mr 10 '69

Textbooks

American textbook; an unscientific phenomenon, quality without control. W. Jovanovich. Am Scholar 38:227-39 Spr '69
Big grope: report of meeting on the two-year college market. Pub W 196:16-18 D 1 '69
Books for urban education: scratching the surface. R. H. Smith. Pub W 196:32 Ag 4 '69
In a time of campus crises, college publishers ponder future role. J. P. Young. Pub W 195:28-31 Ap 21 '69
Whatever happened to the textbook? Ed Digest 35:29-31 S '69
See also
American educational publishers institute

Translations

Publishing translations: contest or collaboration? R. H. Smith. Pub W 195:54 F 10 '69
Translations: impossible, expensive and ultimately essential; summary of panel discussions, January 13, 1969. F. A. Praeger; H. Wolff; P. Grushkin. Pub W 195:45 F 10 '69

Europe, Western

European scene. H. R. Lottman. Pub W 196: 22 Ag 11; 30 S 1; 38 S 29; 31 O 6; 33 O 13; 34:5 O 27; 61-2 N 17; 28 D 8; 15 D 15; 33 D 29 '69

France

Fayard: one of the places where it is happening. H. R. Lottman. il Pub W 195:36-8 Je 30 '69
Publishing scene; Larousse in New York. D. Dempsey. Sat R 52:35 S 20 '69

Germany (Federal Republic)

Droemer Knaur: before the merger and after. H. R. Lottman. il Pub W 196:39-41 O 20 '69
S. Fischer of Germany reactivates U.S. office. Pub W 195:33 Mr 3 '69

Great Britain

As it looks in Britain: finding the book buyer of the '70s. W. G. Graham. Pub W 195: 39-40 F 3 '69
European scene. H. R. Lottman. Pub W 196: 31 O 6; 33 O 13; 34-5 O 27 '69
See also
Allen, George and Unwin, limited

Israel

It's still the land of the book. P. E. Lapide. Chr Cent 86:1383-4 O 29 '69
Thirty years of growth; Book publishers' association of Israel. I. Soifer. il Pub W 196: 35-6 S 8 '69

Italy

Bompiani: the personal touch. H. R. Lottman. il Pub W 195:42-3 F 10 '69
House of Garzanti: publishing as an industry. H. R. Lottman. il Pub W 195:29-31 Mr 3 '69
Longanesi: publishing in a garden in Milan. H. R. Lottman. il Pub W 196:32-4 S 8 '69
Mondadori: Italy's biggest. H. R. Lottman. il Pub W 195:28-31 Mr 31 '69

PUERTO RICO—Politics and government—
Continued
Identity crisis. il Newsweek 75:23-4 Ja 12 '70
New era for Puerto Rico. A. T. Vigiucci. il Look 33:44 Mr 18 '69
Puerto Rico: will it be the 51st state? interview. L. A. Ferré. U S News 66:104-5 Mr 17 '69
Social conditions
One can suffer anywhere; excerpt from Six women: a study of three generations in a Puerto Rican family. O. Lewis. Harper 238:54-60 My '69
PUERTO RICO and the United States
Puerto Ricans: protest or submission? M. Maldonado-Denis. Ann Am Acad 382:26-31 Mr '69
PUFF pastry. See Pastry
PUFNSTUF (television program) See Television broadcasting—Childrens programs
PUGET SOUND
I come from where the bushes are singing. E. Crimmin. il Motor B 123:66-71+ Je '69
On Puget Sound, charter boats. Sunset 142: 41 My '69
See also
Bainbridge Island
PUGWASH conferences on science and world affairs
Science and society: the Pugwash papers. K. Lonsdale; R. E. Peierls. Bul Atom Sci 25: 27-30 N '69
Science and survival: the Pugwash conference at Sochi, U.S.S.R. A. Rich. Science 166:1445-6 D 12 '69
PULESTON, Dennis
We had them to ourselves. Yachting 126:64-5+ N '69
PULICH, Warren M.
Golden-cheeked warbler: threatened bird of the cedar brakes. por Nat Parks 43:10-12 Mr '69
PULLEYS
Art of African pulleys. F. N'Diaye. il UNESCO Courier 22:18-24 My '69
PULLMAN, incorporated
Pullman's plan to export garbage. Bsns W p38+ Ja 10 '70
PULLS, Drawer. See Drawer pulls
PULMONARY circulation. See Blood—Circulation
PULMONARY edema. See Edema
PULMONARY embolism. See Embolism
PULMONARY emphysema. See Emphysema
PULP mills. See Paper mills
PULSARS
Broad-band pulsar in the Crab. Sci N 95:552-3 My 31 '69
Catching a pulsar; first picture taken of a blinking pulsar. il Newsweek 73:61 F 24 '69
Coordinated X-ray and optical observations of a pulsar; NP 0532. Sky & Tel 38:167 S '69
Crab pulsar optically identified: other pulsars show slowdown. G. B. Lubkin. Phys Today 22:60-1 Mr '69
Decoding messages from outer space. C. P. Gilmore. il Pop Sci 194:72-7+ Je '69
Extraterrestrial civilization or a pulsating star? V. Vitkevich. Space World F-4-64:36 Ap '69
Finger on the pulsars. Newsweek 74:73 D 22 '69
First look at a pulsar. il Time 93:57 F 7 '69
Frequency dependence of polarization of pulsar CP 0328. S. J. Goldstein, jr. and D. D. Meisel. bibliog il Science 163:810-12 F 21 '69
Further observations of pulsars. Sky & Tel 37:339+ Je '69
Interstellar scintillations of pulsar radiation. K. R. Lang. bibliog il Science 166:1401-3 D 12 '69
1968 Texas symposium: pulsars. L. C. Green. il Sky & Tel 37:214-18 Ap '69
No gammas, no lighthouse. il Sci N 96:7 Jl 5 '69
Optical pulsars: light from dark neutron star. il Sci N 95:207-8 Mr 1 '69
Optical signals at last; pulsars. Sci N 95:111-12 F 1 '69
Optical studies of pulsar NP 0532. J. G. Duthie and others. bibliog il Science 163:1320-2 Mr 21 '69
Pulsar detected optically; NP 0532. Sky & Tel 37:135+ Mr '69
Pulsar may have a planet. Sci N 96:370 O 25 '69
Pulsar test of a variation of the speed of light with frequency. G. Feinberg. bibliog il Science 166:879-81 N 14 '69
Pulsars: a third class of star. D. E. Thomsen. Sci N 97:43 Ja 10 '70

Pulsars and supernovas (cont) Sci Am 220: 46 Ja '69
Pulsar's slowdown; NP 0532 in the Crab nebula. Sky & Tel 38:283 N '69
Pulsars speedup puzzles theorists. il Sci N 95:377-8 Ap 19 '69
Television observations of the Crab nebula pulsar. il Sky & Tel 37:231 Ap '69
Testing relativity, measuring corona. il Sci N 96:396 N 1 '69
Theorists offer explanation for pulsar speeding up. Phys Today 22:68 Jl '69
Two of a kind. Sci N 96:264 S 27 '69
Visible pulsar. il(p49) Sci Am 220:46 Mr '69
X-ray pulsar. Sci Am 221:52 Jl '69
X-ray pulsar in the Crab nebula. G. Fritz and others. bibliog il Science 164:709-12 My 9 '69
PULSE generators
Build a pos-neg pulse generator. F. H. Tooker. il Pop Electr 30:34-5 Ap '69
IC sine-wave clipper. F. H. Tooker. il Electr World 82:96-7 N '69
Portable pulse generator. P. Harms. il Pop Electr 31:61+ N '69
Repetitive ramp generator. A. Burns. il Electr World 82:87 O '69
Self-powered pulse generator. il Pop Electr 31:78 S '69
PULSE techniques (electronics)
Microvolt electric signals from fishes and the environment. E. G. Barham and others. bibliog il Science 164:965-8 My 23 '69
PUMA hunting
Cougar the hard way. E. S. Barker. il Field & S 74:70-1+ My '69
PUMAS
Stalking the mountain lion, to save him. M. G. Hornocker. il Nat Geog 136:638-55 N '69
Photographs
See Animals—Photographs
PUMPED-storage hydroelectric plants. See Hydroelectric plants
PUMPING machinery
See also
Pumping stations
PUMPING stations
In case of drought: pump; Springfield, Mass. G. E. Sweeney and J. A. Frank. il Am City 84:76-8 Ja '69
Pumped water storage; Medina, Ohio. F. W. Reusswig and C. F. Tavener. il Am City 84:72-4 Mr '69
PUMPING stations, Sewage. See Sewage pumping
PUMPKINS
Always room for a few pumpkin vines. W. Price. Org Gard & Farm 16:81 Ap '69
How to grow a pumpkin big enough to put your little brother in. il Sunset 142:244+ My '69
See also
Cookery—Vegetables
PUMPS
Empty caulking cartridge makes pump. R. Shoberg. il Pop Mech 131:174 Je '69
Mini-pump powers two new hydraulic workholding tools. il Pop Mech 132:176-7 S '69
See also
Air pumps
PUNCH (beverage)
Coolness of punches. N. Ilckeringill. House B 111:118-19 Je '69
For Christmas wassailing, cheering drinks. H. McNulty. House & Gard 136:96+ D '69
Punch is a problem solver. il Sunset 142:174 Je '69
PUNCH (periodical)
London; new editor of Punch. Q. Crewe. Vogue 153:108+ Mr 1 '69
PUNCHED card systems
Punch card pros; Philadelphians capitalize on nation's computer boom. il Ebony 24:113-14+ Ap '69
PUNCHES
Bell center punch. C. Martin. il Mech Illus 65:119 N '69
PUNCHINELLO puppet theatre. See Puppets and puppet plays
PUNDEFF, Marin
(tr) See Bolkhovitinov, N. N. Study of United States history in the Soviet Union
PUNISHMENT
Crime of punishment, by K. Menninger. Review
Atlan 223:104-6 Ja '69. C. M. Curtis
Cath World 208:276-7 Mr '69. W. Arnold
Crimes while on bail; the hunt for a remedy. il U S News 66:42 F 17 '69
Future of corrections; symposium. ed. by J. P. Conrad. bibliog f il Ann Am Acad 381: 1-158 Ja '69

PUNISHMENT—*Continued*
In defense of punishment. E. Van Den Haag; reply. R. Rabull. Fortune 79:52 Ja '69
Legal quackery in D.C; Nixon proposal of the Ball reform act. M. L. Wulf. Commonweal 89:668-9 F 28 '69; Reply. C. D. Hale. 90:151 Ap 18 '69
Liberty and punishment. N. S. Care. New Repub 161:26-8 N 1 '69
Punishment before crime: President Nixon's proposal of a system of preventive detention. Life 66:32 F 14 '69
See also
Crime and criminals
Probation system
School discipline
Torture

PUNKE, Harold H.
Brain drain a great historical asset. Sch & Soc 97:441-3 N '69

PUNO, Peru
Reports: Peru. W. S. Just. Atlan 223:12+ My '69

PUPAE. See Insects—Development

PUPIL assistants in libraries. See School libraries—Student assistants

PUPIL self evaluation. See Self evaluation

PUPIL transportation. See School children—Transportation

PUPPETS and puppet plays
Puppets charm away the violence on Saturday TV. il Life 67:71-2+ O 31 '69
Show; Punchinello puppet theatre in Central park. New Yorker 45:27 S 6 '69

PUPPY love is mainly flowers; story. See Meyers, R. jr

PURCELL, Ann
Do chickens lay nest eggs? Har Yrs 9:30-2 Ag '69

PURCELL, Arthur W.
Peace corps intrigue in the Philippines. G. H. Anderson. Chr Cent 87:4-6 Ja 7 '70

PURCELL, Carl
Carl Purcell pictures for social change. il Pop Phot 64:76-83+ Je '69
Shooting birds. Pop Phot 65:82-3 S '69

PURCELL, Donald. See Clark, G. P. jt. auth.

PURCELL, Henry
King Arthur. Criticism
Dance Mag il 43:46-9 Ja '69

PURCELL, Pearl G.
International education in the 1970's. Sch & Soc 97:374-5 O '69

PURCELL, Theodore V. and Webster, Rosalind
Window on the hard-core world; excerpts from address. Harvard Bsns R 47:118-29 Jl '69

PURCHASE college. See New York (state). State university—College at Purchase

PURCHASING
See also
Consumers
Consumption (economics)
Quality of products
Shopping and shoppers
also subhead Purhasing under various subjets, e.g. Airlines—Purchasing

PURCHASING, Cooperative
See also
Purchasing, Municipal

PURCHASING, Government
Blunt warning; excerpts from address. J. S. Foster, jr. Aviation W 91:11 S 8 '69
Early House action sought on procurement study unit. K. Johnsen. Aviation W 91:22 Jl 7 '69
House unit approves fifteen member procurement study commission. Aviation W 91:25 Ag 18 '69
Industry to support procurement study; proposed in-depth review of government procurement policies. D. C. Winston. Aviation W 90:23 Ap 21 '69
See also
Contracts, Government
United States—Federal aviation administration—Procurement

PURCHASING, Industrial
Get the computer system you want. R. N. Freed. bibliog f il Harvard Bsns R 47:99-108 N '69
See also
Materials control

PURCHASING, Military
Military assistance program; foreign military sales; address, March 26, 1969. R. H. Warren. Vital Speeches 35:601-3 Jl 15 '69
North African arms race. A. Smith. Atlan 223:20+ F '69
Prototype shopping comes off the shelf. il Bsns W p 162-3 S 20 '69

Row over U.S. weapons. il U S News 66:26-7 Je 30 '69
See also
United States—Air force—Procurement
United States—Armed forces—Procurement
United States—Defense. Department of—Procurement

PURCHASING, Municipal
Cooperative purchasing pays; Sparta, N.J. J. P. Brown. il Am City 84:88+ D '69
Purchasing guide for city employees; Cincinnati, Ohio. J. G. Krieg. il Am City 84:75+ Ja '69
Term purchasing cuts the purchasing cost; Cincinnati, Ohio. J. G. Krieg. Am City 84:138 Jl '69
Tips on purchasing; Milwaukee. A. L. Lehrbaummer. il Am City 84:145-6 Mr '69
Watch out for the friendly arrangement; guaranteed maintenance purchasing. H. R. Bone. il Am City 84:104 F '69
See also
Municipal contracts

PURCHASING agents
Trouble with municipal purchasing agents. B. H. Cruce. Am City 81:101-2 N '69

PURCHASING power bonds. See Bonds, Government

PURDUE university, Lafayette, Ind.
On being had by the radicals. D. M. Miller. Nat R 21:688-90 Jl 15 '69

Laboratory for agricultural remote sensing
Eye in the sky for a hungry world; LARS program. R. B. MacDonald. il Sci Digest 66:63-6 Jl '69

PURDY, Ken C.
Depreciation in reverse? Holiday 46:40-1+ Ag '69

PURDY, Ken W.
Masten Gregory lives! Esquire 71:65-9+ Ja '69

PURE food laws. See Food laws and legislation

PUREBRED pets. See Pets

PUREX corporation
Purex presses trust suits. Bsns W p44 My 24 '69
Safety in asparagus; Purex to market fresh vegetables. Forbes 104:71 O 15 '69

PURGATORY
That other world. V. P. McCorry. America 121:400-inside back cover N 1 '69

PURGES (political parties) See Communist party (Czechoslovakia)—Purges

PURGES, Russian. See Communist party (Russia)—Purges

PURIFICATION of water. See Water purification

PURINES
Photochemical reactions and the chemical evolution of purines and nicotinamide derivatives. J. P. Ferris and others. bibliog il Science 166:765-6 N 7 '69
Purine metabolism in heterozygous carriers of hypoxanthine-guanine phosphoribosyltransferase deficiency. B. T. Emmerson and J. B. Wyngaarden. bibliog il Science 166:1533-5 D 19 '69
Purines: active transport by isolated choroid plexus. R. D. Berlin. bibliog il Science 163:1194-5 Mr 14 '69
See also
Kinins

PURITANISM
Perils of puritanism. C. J. McNaspy. il America 120:175-6 F 8 '69

PURITANS
Admonishing Montagu. Chr Cent 86:1570-1 D 10 '69

PURKINJE cells. See Nerve cells

PURNELL, Karl H.
Army's kangaroo courts. Nation 208:432-4 Ap 7 '69

PUROMYCIN
Hepatic influence on splenic synthesis and release of coagulation activities. W. J. Dodds. bibliog il Science 166:882-3 N 14 '69
Memory in the Japanese quail: effects of puromycin and acetoxycycloheximide. S. J. Mayor. bibliog il Science 166:1165-7 N 28 '69
Puromycin: effect on memory of mice when injected with various cations. J. B. Flexner and L. B. Flexner. bibliog il Science 165:1143-4 S 12 '69

PURRINGTON, Bruce R.
Building better music audiences. Clear House 43:497-9 Ap '69

PURSEL, Sherlyn
Art students design computer. Sch Arts 68:6-7 Je '69

PURSLANE
Weed to woo. L. Servais. il Home Gard 56:
34 Ap '69
PUSEY, Merlo J.
President and the power to make war. Atlan
224:65-7 Jl '69
PUSEY, Nathan M.
Difficult times in higher education; adapted
from Harvard university: The president's
report, 1967-68. Science 163:1403 Mr 28 '69
PUSEYISM. See Oxford movement
PUSH button telephone. See Telephone, Push
button
PUSH pin studios
Design gourmet. H. Junker. il Newsweek 73:
77-8 F 10 '69
PUSHKIN, Aleksandr Sergeevich
Pushkin, by D. Magarshack. Review
Time por 93:85-6 F 21 '69
Pushkin and parricide: The miserly knight.
C. R. Proffer. bibliog f Am Imago 25:347-
53 Wint '68
Pushkin boom. C. Brown. Atlan 223:107-8
Ja '69
Pushkin in his real life. S. Karlinsky. Na-
tion 208:469-70 Ap 14 '69
PUT and call transactions
Puts and calls: maneuvering in the market.
Bsns W p85-6 Ag 9 '69
PUTNAM, Frank W.
Immunoglobulin structure: variability and
homology. bibliog Science 163:633-44 F 14
'69
Toward a public policy for graduate educa-
tion in the sciences. Science 163:1147 Mr 14
'69
PUTNAM, Howard
Some needed emphases in educational so-
ciology. bibliog f Sch & Soc 97:27-8 Ja '69
PUTNAM, Judith
(ed) Books to come (cont) Library J 94:587-
684, 1025-63, 2262-86+, 2647-70 F 1, Mr 1,
Je 1, Jl '69
—and Green, Frances
(comps) Adult paperbacks. Library J 94:
326-59 Ja 15 '69
PUTNAM, Patrick F.
College basketball. Sports Illus 30:40+ F 3 '69
Football. Sports Illus 31:50+ Jl 7 '69
Into combat with sticks, for more than a
title. Sports Illus 30:30-1 Je 9 '69
PUTTERMAN, Milton
Product parade at Milo electronics. S. Mar-
getts. por Duns R 93:73+ Ap '69
PUTTING (golf)
Do it the right way for once. J. Nicklaus. il
Sports Illus 30:63 Mr 17 '69
Putting it on the line. J. Boros. il Esquire
71:143-5 Ap '69
PUZZLES
Puzzles to devil the mind; excerpts from
Riverside puzzles. I. Morris. Vogue 154:136
O 1 '69
PYENSON, Louis
Bring plants in clean. Horticulture 46:44+
O '68
Forcing woody twigs and keeping them in
bloom. il Horticulture 47:26-7+ Ja '69
Nematodes, what they are all about. Horti-
culture 47:46-8 F '69
PYKE, Donald L. See North. H. Q. jt. auth.
PYLE, Howard
Four disciples of Howard Pyle: excerpts from
The Brandywine tradition. H. C. Pitz. il
Am Artist 33:38-43 Ja '69
PYLES, Hamilton K.
Our public lands, a history of fraud and
speculation. Am For 75:39-41 F '69
PYNCHON family
Pynchon coat-of-arms. H. K. Eilers. il Hob-
bies 73:112-13 F '69
PYORRHEA. See Gums (anatomy)—Diseases
PYREX
Phase separation in pyrex glass. R. H. Dore-
mus and A. M. Turkalo. bibliog il Science
164:418-19 Ap 25 '69
PYRIMIDINES
See also
Cytosine
Fluorouracil
Thymine
Uracil
PYROCERAM
Wonder glass delights cooks and astrono-
mers. il Pop Sci 195:138-9 S '69
PYROPHOSPHATES
Diphosphonates inhibit formation of calcium
phosphate crystals in vitro and pathologi-
cal calcification in vivo. M. D. Francis and
others. bibliog il Science 165:1264-6 S 19 '69
Diphosphonates inhibit hydroxyapatite dis-
solution in vitro and bone resorption in
tissue culture and in vivo. H. Fleisch and
others. bibliog il Science 165:1262-4 S 19 '69

Imidodiphosphate and pyrophosphate: possible biological significance of similar structures. M. Larsen and others. bibliog il Science 166:1510-11 D 19 '69
PYROXENES
Cooling history of orthopyroxenes. S. S.
Hafner and D. Virgo. bibliog il Science
165:285-7 Jl 18 '69
Enstatite: disorder produced by a megabar
shock event. S. S. Pollack and P. S. De-
Carli. bibliog il Science 165:591-2 Ag 8 '69
Uranium distribution in separate clinopyroxenes from four eclogites. K. C. Condie
and others. bibliog il Science 165:57-9 Jl 4
'69
See also
Jadeite

Q

QANTARA, Egypt
Safer but sadder; Israel evacuates residents
of occupied Qantara. M. Elkins. il News-
week 73:40+ Ja 27 '69
QUABBIN reservoir, Mass. See Reservoirs
QUACKS and quackery
Frauds who prey on shaky marriages. J. Kap-
lan. Todays Health 47:16-19+ Je '69
Great bracelet fad; newest health fad. News-
week 74:114-15 O 13 '69
Health books: reader beware. R. L. Smith
il Todays Health 47:30-3+ Ap '69
MD's without education, how to spot them;
excerpts from address, October 1968. R. C.
Derbyshire. il Sci Digest 65:14-18 Mr '69
Soupçon of sorcery; faith healers under in-
vestigation in France. il Newsweek 75:41 Ja
5 '70
What you should know about arthritis quacks.
L. David. Good H 169:70-1+ Ag '69
QUADE, Quentin L.
Christian perspective. America 120:392-6 Ap
5 '69
QUAICHS. See Drinking vessels
QUAIL shooting
Bobwhite holiday. C. Elliott. il Outdoor Life
143:52-3+ F '69
Focus on quail. P. Curtis. il Field & S 74:
50-1+ S '69
Meanwhile back at the Coffield ranch... V.
Kraft. il Sports Illus 31:64-6 N 10 '6
To find a quail. H. Bradshaw. il Field & S
74:34-5+ D '69
Topknot tactics. J. Freeman. il Field & S
74:60-1+ N '69
Two quail for Curtis. J. Dean. il Field & S
74:70-1+ N '69

Anecdotes, facetiae, satire, etc.
Great days on the desert; eastern Oregon
and southern Idaho. T. Trueblood. il Field
& S 74:39-40+ N '69
QUAILS
Bobwhite for western New York? S. B.
Robeson. il Cons 24:8-9 D '69
Memory in the Japanese quail: effects of
puromycin and acetoxycycloheximide. S. J.
Mayor. bibliog il Science 166:1165-7 N 28
'69
QUAKER oats company
Old guard lives! il Forbes 104:66 O 15 '69
QUAKER relief work. See American Friends
service committee
QUAKERS. See Friends, Society of
QUAKING aspen. See Aspen
QUALIFICATIONS of teachers. See Teachers
—Qualifications
QUALITY control
Warranties, and what should be done about
them; automobile warranties. il Consumer
Rep 34:177-81 Ap '69
See also
Electronic data processing—Quality control
QUALITY of products
Institute reports. See issues of Good house-
keeping
Keppler on the SLR: of Modern readers com-
plaining about equipment or service. H.
Keppler. Mod Phot 33:113-14 Jl '69
Not for publication; product information in
the government's possession. E. Gross. il
Sci N 95:508-10 My 24 '69
Product liability: tougher ground rules. D. L.
Rados. Harvard Bsns R 47:144-52 Jl '69
Speaker for the house. C. Montgomery. See
issues of Good housekeeping

QUALITY of products—*Continued*
What consumers need: show biz or hard facts. A. Q. Mowbray. il Nation 209:245-8 S 15 '69
   See also
Automobile industry and trade—Quality control
Products, Improved
Quality control
Testing

QUALL, Alvin B.
Solution to college administration problems. Sch & Soc 97:358-60 O '69

QUANTUM field theory
What is the point of so-called axiomatic field theory? adaptation of address, February, 1969. A. S. Wightman. bibliog il Phys Today 22:53-8 S '69

QUANTUM mechanics. See Quantum theory

QUANTUM theory
Lab bench; effect of temperature on light absorption by crystalline cadmium sulfide. J. A. Isenberg. il Chem 42:26-8 Je '69; Correction. 42:32 Jl '69
Liquid metals. N. W. Ashcroft. il Sci Am 221:72-82 bibliog(p 140) Jl '69
Operational interpretation of nonrelativistic quantum mechanics; adaptation of address, July 3, 1968. W. E. Lamb. jr bibliog il Phys Today 22:23-8 Ap '69; Reply. G. T. Trammell 22:9 O '69
States of aggregation. K. Mendelssohn. il Phys Today 22:46-51 Ap '69
   See also
Exciton theory
Isobaric spin
Quantum field theory
Relativity (physics)
Statistical mechanics
Time reversal

QUARANTINE
Contamination from the moon. P. H. Abelson. Science 164:1227 Je 13 '69
Decision on astronaut quarantine not expected before next month. Aviation W 91: 21 D 15 '69
Disease battlers at our borders; Foreign quarantine program. W. Cole. il Todays Health 47:48-51+ My '69
Diseases from the moon? Why officials worry. U S News 67:53 Jl 7 '69
Is the earth safe from lunar contamination? Apollo plans. il Time 93:78 Je 13 '69
Letter from the space center; examination of astronauts and samples from Apollo 11 mission. H. S. F. Cooper, jr. New Yorker 45:82+ Ag 16 '69
Quarantine method revised for recovery of Apollo 11. Aviation W 90:21 My 26 '69
Rigid quarantine awaits Apollo 11 return. Z. Strickland. il Aviation W 91:18-21 Jl 7 '69
   See also
United States—Manned spacecraft center—Lunar receiving laboratory

QUARKS. See Particles (nuclear physics)

QUARRELS
If you can't fight them, don't join them; children's quarrels. M. Heydt. il Redbook 134: 24+ N '69
Making the most of family fights. A. R. Roalman. il Todays Health 47:54-5+ F '69
Man talk; put 'em up. D. Newman and R. Benton. Mlle 69:141 Jl '69
Right way to fight a marriage. F. Davis. Read Digest 94:97-100 Je '69
Six fights you won't want to miss; excerpts from The intimate enemy. G. R. Bach and P. Wyden. Ladies Home J 86:64+ F '69

QUARRY, Jerry
Brawler at the threshold. M. Kram. il pors Sports Illus 30:28-30+ Je 16 '69
Flaunt it and you may lose it. M. Kram. il pors Sports Illus 31:26-9 Jl 7 '69
Frazier's quarry. il por Newsweek 74:84 Jl 7 '69
Winner, and still (partial) champ. il por Time 94:36 Jl 4 '69

QUARTERBACKS. See Football players

QUARTETS, Vocal. See Choral groups and societies

QUARTZ
Eolian origin of quartz in soils of Hawaiian Islands and in Pacific pelagic sediments. R. W. Rex and others. bibliog il Science 163:277-9 Ja 17 '69
   See also
Chalcedony

QUASARS
Antimatter, quasi-stellar objects, and the evolution of galaxies. H. Alfvén and A. Elvius. bibliog il Science 164:911-17 My 23 '69
Light variations of quasars. Sky & Tel 38:18 Jl '69

Quasars and the birth of the universe; excerpts from addresses. G. Marx. il UNESCO Courier 22:32-4+ D '69
Quasars: finding a handle for a complex problem. R. W. Holcomb. Science 166:1609-10 D 26 '69
Quasars six years later. L. C. Green. il Sky & Tel 37:290-4 My '69
Quasistellar objects and Seyfert galaxies. S. A. Colgate. bibliog il Phys Today 22:27-35 Ja '69
Seyfert galaxies. R. J. Weymann. il Sci Am 220:28-37 Ja '69
Two of a kind. Sci N 96:264 S 27 '69

QUASISTELLAR objects. See Quasars

QUASTEL, J. H. See Itoh, T. jt. auth.

QUATERNARY period. See Paleobotany—Quaternary

QUEBEC (city)
   Description
Walking tours of Canada's great cities. il Bet Hom & Gard 47:68 Je '69
   Hotels, restaurants, etc.
Cuisine Québecoise. J. W. Coyle. il Travel & Camera 32:68-9 Ap '69

QUEBEC (province)
   Economic conditions
Bombs rattle Quebec's economy. il Bsns W p84-5+ Mr 1 '69
   Politics and government
Bombs rattle Quebec's economy. il Bsns W p84-5+ Mr 1 '69
Quebec: uneasy province. C. De Mestral. Chr Cent 86:427-9 Mr 26 '69; Reply. K. Barker. 86:683 My 14 '69
   Religious institutions and affairs
World around us (cont) Chr Cent 86:529-30, 1098 Ap 16, Ag 20 '69

QUECHUA Indians. See Indians of South America—Bolivia

QUEEN, Ellery, pseud.
Authors & editors. B. A. Bannon. il por Pub W 195:19-21 Mr 10 '69

QUEEN, Hallie Elvera
To France; poem. Negro Hist Bul 32:18 O '69

QUEEN ANNES COUNTY, Md.
   Historic houses, etc.
Blakeford, in Queen Anne's County. E. A. W. Miles. il Antiques 95:526-31 Ap '69

QUEEN butterflies. See Butterflies

QUEEN Elizabeth (ship) See Ocean liners

QUEEN Mary (ship) See Ocean liners

QUEENS college. See New York (city) City university of New York—Queens college

QUEEN'S tears
Queen's tears, carefree houseplant. K. L. Carlsen. Org Gard & Farm 16:114-15 Ja '69

QUEENSLAND, Australia
   Music
   See also
Queensland opera company

QUEENSLAND opera company
Touring in the Outback. C. Brumby. Opera N 34:13 Ja 10 '70

QUENNELL, Peter
Moon stood still on Strawberry Hill. Horizon 11:112-17 Sum '69

QUERO CORTÉS, Manuel. See Cortés, M.

QUESTER, George H.
Israel and the nuclear non-proliferation treaty. Bul Atom Sci 25:7-9+ Je '69

QUESTIONING
   See also
Police questioning

QUESTIONNAIRES
Survey spurs action; Waterville, Ohio. il Am City 84:160+ My '69

QUETICO-SUPERIOR wilderness region. See Wilderness areas

QUEUING theory
Line-up. Time 94:54 Jl 11 '69

QUIGG, Philip W.
Coming of age in Micronesia. For Affairs 47:493-508 Ap '69

QUIGLEY, Thomas E.
Cold blood in Brazil. Commonweal 90:452-3 Jl 25 '69

QUILTS
   See also
Coverlets

QUINCY, Ill.
By air, rail or water to an island park; Quinsippi Island. K. W. Kramer. il Am City 84:84-5 Ap '69

QUINN, Anthony
Walking with Anthony Quinn; interview, ed. by L. Tornabene. pors McCalls 96:60+ Mr '69

about

Films. J. Brackman. Esquire 73:34+ Ja '70
Loving world of Anthony Quinn. M. Simons. il pors Look 33:48-51 Ap 1 '69
QUINN, Davis
Painting masters of jazz. Am Artist 33:39-41+ Ag '69
QUINN, J. A. See Petzny, W. J. jt. auth.
QUINN, James Brian
Technology transfer by multinational companies. bibliog f Harvard Bsns R 47:147-61 N '69
QUINN, John
Man from New York, by B. L. Reid. Review
Art in Am 57:23 Mr '69. J. Jacobs
Cath World 209:144 Je '69. W. J. Feeney
QUINN, John Robert
Maternal grandfather; poem. Chr Cent 86:922 Jl 9 '69
This brotherhood; poem. Chr Cent 86:253 F 19 '69
Winter; poem. Commonweal 91:403 Ja 9 '70
QUINTANA, Bernardo
Quintana's box. il por Time 94:71 Ag 22 '69
QUINTON, H. Wayne, and Shuman, R. B.
Is your PTA sagging? Clear House 43:307-11 Ja '69
QUITTING. See Athletes, Resignation of
QUIZZES. See Information tests
QUOTAS, Import. See Import quotas
QUOTATION
See also
Plagiarism
QUOTATIONS
Quotable quotes. See issues of Reader's digest
Quotations from the Vice President. S. T. Agnew. Newsweek 74:39 N 17 '69
See also
Children—Sayings
Money—Quotations, maxims, etc.
Proverbs

Anecdotes, facetiae, satire, etc.

Quiet, please, while I murmur a witticism. J. Bryan, 3d. Holiday 46:14-15 S '69

R

R. Hoe and company. See Hoe, R, and company
R. J. Reynolds foods, incorporated. See Reynolds, R. J. foods, incorporated
RCA corporation
Balancing act. il Forbes 104:28-9 N 15 '69
How color TV was born; excerpt from The strategy of change for business success, ed. by S. Furst and M. Sherman. D. Sarnoff. il Nations Bsns 57:70-3 F '69
Now, it's official. Bsns W p94 Ja 10 '70
RCA puts TV in packs. il Bsns W p 106+ O 4 '69
RCA telephone? to buy Alaska's long-distance telephone system. il Forbes 104:42 O 1 '69
RCA Victor division
How to tell when Victor records were made (cont) J. Walsh. il Hobbies 73:36+ F: 74: 36+ Mr: 36+ Ap '69
REA express. See Railway express agency, incorporated
REM (rapid eye movement) sleep. See Sleep
RFI. See Radio interference
RGA. See Republican governors association
RIF (Reading is FUN-damental) program. See Childrens reading
RLEA. See Railway labor executives' association
RNA
Another messenger. Sci Am 221:53-4 D '69
Built-in-virus-fighter. Sci Digest 65:78 Mr '69
Codon 'ecognition by enzymatically mischarged valine transfer ribonucleic acid. D. Grunberger and others. bibliog il Science 166:1635-7 D 26 '69
Control of specific gene expression in higher organisms. G. M. Tomkins and others. bibliog il Science 166:1474-80 D 19 '69
Crystalline RNA. Sci Am 220:50 Mr '69

Crystalline transfer RNA: the three-dimensional Patterson function at 12-angstrom resolution. S. H. Kim and A. Rich. bibliog il Science 166:1621-4 D 26 '69
Cytokinin of wheat germ transfer RNA: 6-(4 - hydroxy - 3 - methyl-2-butenylamino)-2-methylthio-9-β-D-ribofuranosylpurine. S. M. Hecht and others. bibliog il Science 166: 1272-4 D 5 '69
Genetic code reconfirmed. Sci Am 221:58 N '69
Genetic coding: oligonucleotide coding for first six amino acid residues of the coat protein of R17 bacteriophage. W. E. Robinson and others. bibliog il Science 166:1291-3 D 5 '69
Hormonal induction of increased zinc uptake in mammalian cell cultures: requirements for RNA and protein synthesis. R. P. Cox. bibliog il Science 165:196-9 Jl 11 '69
Hormonal regulation in higher plants. A. W. Galston and P. J. Davies. bibliog il Science 163:1288-97 Mr 21 '69
Infection structures from rust urediospores: effect of RNA and protein synthesis inhibitors. L. D. Dunkle and others. bibliog il Science 163:481-2 Ja 31 '69
Interferon stimulated. Sci Am 220:46-8 Ja '69
Membranous structures associated with translation and transcription of poliovirus RNA. L. A. Caliguiri and I. Tamm. bibliog il Science 166:885-6 N 14 '69
N-Formylseryl-transfer RNA. W. S. Kim. bibliog il Science 163:947-9 F 28 '69
Nucleic acid-protein interactions in turnip yellow mosaic virus. J. M. Kaper. bibliog il Science 166:248-50 O 10 '69
Nucleoside triphosphate termini from RNA synthesized in vivo by escherichia coli. S. E. Jorgensen and others. bibliog il Science 164:1067-70 My 30 '69
Nucleotide sequence of escherichia coli tyrosine transfer ribonucleic acid. B. P. Doctor and others. bibliog il Science 163:693-5 F 14 '69
Polynucleotide sequence analysis by sequential base elimination; 3'-terminus of phage Qβ RNA. H. L. Weith and P. T. Gilham. bibliog Science 166:1004-5 N 21 '69
Rhapidosomes: absence of a highly 2'-O-methylated RNA component. A. S. Delk and C. A. Dekker. bibliog il Science 166: 1646-7 D 26 '69
Ribonucleic acid metabolism of a single neuron: correlation with electrical activity. R. W. Berry. bibliog il Science 166:1021-3 N 21 '69
Ribosomal RNA synthesis during cleavage of ascaris lumbricoides eggs. M. S. Kaulenas and others. bibliog il Science 163:1201-3 Mr 14 '69
Self-assembly of Qβ and MS2 phage particles: possible function of initiation complexes. P. P. Hung and others. bibliog il Science 166:1638-40 D 26 '69
Spinning the thread of life. J. Lear. il Sat R 52:63-6 Ap 5 '69
Structural studies on transfer RNA: crystallization of formylmethionine and leucine transfer RNA's. J. D. Young and others. bibliog il Science 166:1527-8 D 19 '69
Structural studies on transfer RNA: preliminary crystallographic analysis. M. Labanauskas and others. bibliog il Science 166: 1530-2 D 19 '69
Structural studies on transfer RNA: the molecular conformation in solution. P. G. Connors and others. bibliog il Science 166: 1528-30 D 19 '69
RNA polymerase. See Polymerases
ROI (return on investment) See Corporations—Finance
RO/RO container ships. See Freight vessels
ROTC. See United States—Reserve officers training corps
RPI. See Rensselaer polytechnic institute, Troy, N.Y.
RT Hydrae. See Stars, Variable
RTCA. See Radio technical commission for aeronautics
RTSRL. See American library association—Round table on the social responsibilities of libraries
RA (boat)
Thor Heyerdahl's voyage. J. Lear. il Sat R 52:42-3 Ag 2 '69
Voyage of the Ra. il Newsweek 73:56+ My 26 '69
What happened to the Ra? T. Heyerdahl. il Sat R 52:90 D 6 '69
RA expedition, 1969
Close is close enough. T. Heyerdahl. il Sci N 96:78-9 Jl 26 '69

RA expedition, 1969—*Continued*
Kon-Tiki's famous skipper goes to sea in a ship of reeds, the Ra. il Life 66:89-90 Je 6 '69
Stormy wreck of the paper ship Ra. il Life 67:36-7 Ag 15 '69
Thor Heyerdahl's next voyage. J. Lear. il Sat R 52:49-56 My 3 '69; Discussion. 52:46-7 Jl 5; 68 N 1 '69
Thor Heyerdahl's voyage. J. Lear. il Sat R 52:42-3 Ag 2 '69
To prove a theory. il Sci N 95:524 My 31 '69
Voyage of the Ra. il Newsweek 73:56+ My 26 '69

RAAB, Earl
Black revolution & the Jewish question. Commentary 47:23-33 Ja; 10 Ap '69
—See Lipset, S. M. jt. auth.

RAAB, Lawrence
Hero on his way home; poem. Am Scholar 38:409-10 Sum '69
Sunday; Walking alone: poems. Poetry 113: 322-4 F '69
Voices answering back: the vampires; poem. Am Scholar 39:48-9 Wint '69

RAAB, Norman
Fashionably poor. por Forbes 104:72 S 15 '69

RAAB, Selwyn
Highway robbery. McCalls 96:62-3+ Ja '69
Pay a dollar, win a hundred thousand. McCalls 96:100-1 Ap '69

RABASCA, Iris M.
Predictable hazards of childhood. Todays Health 48:53-5+ Ja '70

RABB, Charles
Obsolescence on the Hill. Nation 208:390-2 Mr 31 '69

RABB, Ellis
Zombie Hamlet. il por Time 93:66 Mr 14 '69

RABB, John M. See Krivis, A. F. jt. auth.

RABBIS
See also
Central conference of American rabbis

RABBIT hunting
Bunny bop. C. Amory. il Holiday 46:20+ D '69
Carolina Beach bunnies. J. Dean. il Field & S 74:68-9+ S '69
Hell on hares. D. J. Anderson. il Field & S 74:30-1+ D '69
Hottest cottontails in the West. J. R. Higley. il Field & S 74:50-1+ Jl '69
Hunter alone. R. V. McCormick. il Field & S 74:70-1+ S '69
It really isn't rabbit hunting without hounds. E. A. Bauer. il Outdoor Life 144:58-61+ N '69
The 100th rabbit. J. B. Robinson. il Outdoor Life 143:76-7+ F '69
Plight of the swampers. B. Thomas. il Field & S 74:76-7+ Je '69
Special rabbit hunt. G. X. Sand. il Outdoor Life 143:72-3+ Ap '69

RABBITS
Lysergic acid diethylamide: dissociation of its behavioral and hyperthermic actions by DL-α-methyl-p-tyrosine. A. Horita and A. E. Hamilton. bibliog il Science 164:78-9 Ap 4 '69
Maturation of renal organic acid transport: substrate stimulation by penicillin. G. H. Hirsch and J. B. Hook. bibliog il Science 165:909-10 Ag 29 '69
Population explosion; question of cottontails. il Cons 23:29 Je '69
Rabbit lateral geniculate nucleus: sharpener of directional information. W. R. Levick and others. bibliog il Science 165:712-14 Ag 15 '69
See also
Cookery—Game
Hares

RABBITS in literature. See Animals in literature

RABBITT, Mary C.
Powell's quest. Am For 75:8-9+ S '69

RABELAIS; drama. See Barrault, J. L.

RABI, Isidor Isaac
Views from earth on the odyssey into space. Look 33:77-8 F 4 '69

RABIES
Terror of rabies; British measures after outbreak. il Newsweek 74:54 N 10 '69

RABINOVE, Samuel
One war, yes; another, no. America 120: 647-8 My 31 '69

RABINOWITCH, Eugene
Conservation for conservation's sake? Bul Atom Sci 25:47-8+ My '69
From Alamogordo to Apollo: will man heed the lesson? por Bul Atom Sci 25:14-16 S '69; Same abr. with title Space frontier; necessity to review priorities. Cur 111:9-11 O '69

New year's thoughts, 1969: prospects for progress and peace. Bul Atom Sci 25:2-4 Ja '69
Political criteria for non-political jobs? Bul Atom Sci 25:2-3+ Je '69
Reflections on Apollo 8. Bul Atom Sci 25: 2-3+ Mr '69
Responsibility of scientists in our age. Bul Atom Sci 25:2-3+ N '69
Science and violence; adaptation of address, October 14, 1969. Bul Atom Sci 25:2-4+ D '69
Scientists and youth in revolt. Bul Atom Sci 25:2+ Ap '69

RABINOWITZ, Dorothy
Among the aged. Commentary 47:61-6 Mr '69
Power in the academy. Commentary 47:42-9 Je; 48:8-9 Ag '69

RACCOONS
Mystery of Pignut Mountain. R. Starnes. Field & S 74:18+ Jl '69

RACE
See also
Anthropology

RACE and music. See Music and race

RACE car drivers. See Automobile drivers

RACE characteristics. See National characteristics

RACE cooperation. See Interracial cooperation

RACE differences. See Racial differences

RACE discrimination
Court ruling that opened a club. U S News 66:15 Je 16 '69
Crime and race in Detroit; accusing Detroit news of distorted reportings. Time 93:61 My 9 '69
In the wake of Camille; discriminatory use of federal funds for hurricane victims in Mississippi. D. Zwerdling. New Repub 162: 8-10 Ja 10 '70
1950's: racial equality and the law. N. C. Amaker. bibliog f Cur Hist 57:275-80+ N '69
No bells for Bill; Birmingham, Ala. G. Shockley. Chr Cent 86:1508 N 26 '69
See also
Discrimination in education
Discrimination in employment
Discrimination in housing
International convention on the elimination of all forms of racial discrimination
Negroes—Segregation
Race prejudice
United Nations—Sub-commission on prevention of discrimination and protection of minorities

RACE equality. See Equality

RACE horse training. See Horse training

RACE horses
After a battle, the Prince. W. Tower. Sports Illus 30:72 My 19 '69
Arts and Letters gets a degree; Derby-bound colt at Hialeah. W. Tower. il Sports Illus 30:24-5 Mr 3 '69
Beauty and the beast; race between Majestic Prince and Top Knight at Kentucky, Derby. il Time 93:73 My 2 '69
Confirmation of a hero at Saratoga; Arts and Letters. W. Tower. il Sports Illus 31:16-19 Ag 25 '69
Grandes dames of racing; proprietors of thoroughbred stables and breeding farms; with photographs by R. Meek. Sports Illus 31:46-54 S 29 '69
How to retire successfully after a twenty-eight month career; Dr Fager, a thoroughbred. B. Surface. il N Y Times Mag p30-2+ Mr 2 '69
In the pink; Top Knight wins Flamingo stakes. il Newsweek 73:77-8 Mr 17 '69
Laurels for Arts and Letters. Time 94:84 O 10 '69
Man takes charge of his horse; F. McMahon owner of Majestic Prince. W. Tower. il Sports Illus 30:24-8+ Je 2 '69
Race track. A. Minor. See issues of New Yorker
Saratoga: half hour of hope; event for two-year-olds. il Newsweek 74:66-68B Ag 25 '69
Sharp kid from the equine academy; three-year-olds competing in Florida Derby. M. R. Werner. il Sports Illus 30:24-5 Ap 7 '69
Stable full of dreams; untrained colts of Joe O'Brien's farm in Calif. P. Ryan. il Sports Illus 30:40+ F 17 '69
Time has come to sort out the sprinters. W. Tower. il Sports Illus 30:48-9 F 3 '69
Top speed and a tender mouth; Majestic Prince a Derby favorite. W. Tower. Sports Illus 30:56 Mr 10 '69
Trials of a boy named Laverne; winner of Little Brown Jug, Delaware, Ohio. W. F. Reed, jr. il Sports Illus 31:70+ S 29 '69
Walking conglomerate. P. Ryan. il Sports Illus 30:64-8+ Ap 28 '69

RACE horses—*Continued*
Won't somebody help me buy this horse?
Ring For Nurse. W. F. Reed, jr. il Sports
Illus 31:36+ S 22 '69

Photographs
Where the horse abides; Newmarket, England. G. Cranham. Sports Illus 30:36-42
My 19 '69
RACE improvement. See Eugenics
RACE prejudice
Black men before the Civil war. P. E. Wilson. bibliog f Cur Hist 57:257-62+ N '69
Double jeopardy; black and poor; address,
January 12, 1969. F. H. Williams. Vital
Speeches 35:273-7 F 15 '69
Ruckus in Irasburg; the case that had the
gossips buzzing in Vermont. H. Moffett. il
Life 66:62-4+ Ap 4 '69
Shock of black recognition; recollections of
famous Negroes; symposium. il Esquire 71:
138-41 My '69
    See also
Anti-Semitism
Negroes—Segregation
Race problems
Racism
RACE problems
American foreign affairs; black America; address, March 10, 1969. F. H. Williams. Vital
Speeches 35:478-80 My 15 '69
    See also
Business and race problems
Church and race problems
Intercultural education
Intermarriage of races
Minorities
Negroes in Africa
Race relations
    also subhead Race problems under names
of continents, countries, etc. e.g. United
States—Race problems
RACE relations
America's racial crisis: the advent of a new
consciousness? J. Rensenbrink. Cur 112:17-
22 N '69
As I see it; interview. W. M. Young, jr.
Forbes 104:79-80+ S 15 '69
Assimilation or cultural pluralism? concerning discussion at Duke university divinity
school. C. L. Rice. Chr Cetn 86:945-7 Jl 16 '69
Black and white balance sheet. il Time 93:
23 Ja 24 '69
Black history, or black mythology? P. Chew.
il Am Heritage 20:4-9+ Ag '69
Black man's route to the top. W. A. Lewis.
Read Digest 95:157-8+ Ag '69
Black pastiche; quotations. ed. by B. Geller.
Library J 94:821 F 15 '69
Black pride; black action: address. December 4, 1968. C. P. Lucas. Vital Speeches
35:505-8 Je 1 '69
Build baby, build: why the summer was
quiet. il Time 94:15-17 S 12 '69
Chauvinistic headings; accusing LC and Sears
of racist/colonial bias; letter to the editor.
S. Berman. Library J 94:695 F 15 '69
Color in world affairs. H. R. Isaacs. Cur 105:
57-64 Mr '69
Cops. H. Toch; W. P. Brown. il Nation 208:
491-3, 498-500 Ap 21 '69
Guns of August, 1969. W. J. McKean. il
Look 33:69-72 S 9 '69
How to have a bloodless riot; racial confrontation groups. G. B. Leonard. il Look
33:24-8 Je 10 '69
"I lived six months as a black woman":
Grace Halsell. il Ebony 25:124-6+ D '69
I see Atlanta burning. D. M. Knight. America
120:710-12 Je 21 '69; Discussion. 121:51, 127
Ag 2, S 6 '69
Integrating culture: a credo for believers. B.
Tate. bibliog il Library J 94:2053-6 My 15
'69
Kerner plus one; sequel to 1968 Kerner commission report. Newsweek 73:39 Mr 10 '69
Legacy of my husband, Malcolm X. B. Shabazz. il Ebony 24:172-4+ Je '69
Let's work together, by N. Wright, jr. Review
America 120:172 F 8 '69. A. Buni
Liberals, the blacks and the war. E. F. Goldman. il N Y Times Mag p40-1+ N 30 '69
Love thy neighbor. D. Lawrence. U S News
67:88 S 15 '69
Moral of a story; the good Samaritan. V. P.
Mc Corry. America 121:106+ Ag 16 '69
National image; views of G. Myrdal. Commonweal 90:36 Mr 28 '69
Negro in America; where Myrdal went wrong.
C. N. Degler. il N Y Times Mag p64-5+
D 7 '69
Notes and comment; address, May 1969. C.
Evers. New Yorker 45:29 Je 14 '69

Notes from the Norwalk, Conn. underground; when things go wrong all blacks
are black, and all whites are whitey. J.
Sharnik. il N Y Times Mag p30-1+ My 25
'69
Opinion: black friend. C. Lang. Mlle 68:32+
Ap '69
Quiet talk with myself. C. Gordone. Esquire
73:78-81+ Ja '70
Sensitivity in Pontiac; human-relations institute. Time 94:44+ S 19 '69
Should your child be color-blind? B. Bettelheim. Ladies Home J 86:30+ N '69
South: changes deep and subtle. J. B. Cumming, jr. il Newsweek 73:34-5 Je 30 '69
Spirit is a spirit. N. Gittelson. Harp Baz 102:
43+ S '69
Strategies for the ghetto wars; excerpt from
The urban guerrilla. M. Oppenheimer. Nation 208:366-70 Mr 24 '69
Thou shalt nots for mniority group rapport.
il Nations Bsns 57:87 Je '69
Tour's end: traveling journalists' conclusions.
W. F. Buckley, jr. Nat R 21:611 Je 17 '69
Toward an affirmative morality. J. F.
Wharton. Sat R 52:11-13+ Jl 12 '69
Uncle Tom and Tiny Tim; some reflections on
the cripple as Negro. L. Kriegel. Am Scholar
38:412-30 Sum '69
Visit with the widow of Malcolm X; interview, ed. by F. Knebel. B. Shabazz. il
Look 33:74-7+ Mr 4 '69
Whitey's reaction; proposal of separate black
state. R. Sherrill. Esquire 71:76+ Ja '69
    See also
Black power
Interracial cooperation
RACE track officials. See Sports officiating
RACE tracks
Never? No, always on Sunday; Green Mountain thoroughbred and harness racing.
Vermont. M. R. Werner. il Sports Illus
31:64-5 Ag 25 '69
Racetrack land rush. Newsweek 74:74+ Jl
14 '69
RACHLEFF, Owen
Anatomy of a masterpiece. Horizon 11:94-103
Wint '69
Who's afraid of Azucena? Opera N 33:8-11 Mr
29 '69
RACHMANINOFF, Sergei
Opening theme of Rachmaninoff's third piano
concerto and its liturgical prototype. J.
Yasser. bibliog f il Mus Q 55:313-28 Jl '69
Performer as composer: a symphony, a piano
concerto, three folksong settings, a cantata, art songs, an early opera, and two solo
sonatas by the many-faceted S. Rachmaninoff. M. N. Kanny; R. Kennedy; P. L. Miller. por Am Rec G 35:616-18 Ap '69
RACIAL differences
Negro and white children, by E. E. Baughman and W. G. Dahlstrom. Review
Science 163:461-2 Ja 31 '69. M. B. Smith
Sense, and nonsense, about race. M. Mead.
Redbook 133:35+ S '69
RACIAL equality. See Equality
RACINE, Wis.

Police department
It doesn't look like a police station. L. C.
Jenkins. il Am City 84:107-8 Jl '69

Transportation
Little buses win big support. J. Erdmann.
il Am City 84:134+ Mr '69
RACING. See Airplane racing; Automobile racing; Dog racing; Horse racing
RACING accidents. See Automobile racing—Accidents and injuries
RACING car drivers. See Automobile racing
drivers
RACING car engines. See Automobile engines
RACING car tires. See Tires, Automobile
RACING cars. See Automobiles, Racing
RACING clocks. See Timing devices
RACING fans

Photographs
See Sports fans—Photographs
RACING tires. See Tires, Automobile
RACING yachts. See Yachts and yachting
RACISM
Angry voices, harsh words. Nation 208:226-7
F 24 '69
Black man looks at black racism. T. A.
Francois. Read Digest 95:209-14 S '69
Blue collar white and the far right. G. Fackre. Chr Cent 86:645-8 My 7 '69
Coming holocaust. S. Alsop. Newsweek 73:
92 Mr 3 '69

RACISM—*Continued*

International racism; proposals of the World council of churches. America 120:662-3 Je 7 '69

Is white racism the problem? M. Friedman; discussion. Commentary 47:4+ Ap '69

Man's relations to man; can we move beyond the pluralistic society? C. Greer. Cur 105:27-31 Mr '69

Negro judge vs. white militants. U S News 66:15 Je 9 '69

Orange County bug; white racism. S. Alsop. Newsweek 73:96 Je 30 '69

Sociological racism. H. Schuman. il Trans-Action 7:44-8 D '69

To be truly free. L. M. Steel. Sat R 52:23-5+ Ja 25 '69

Uses of history; how racist are we? C. V. Woodward. bibliog Cur 107:52-64 My '69

White racism. J. F. Bresnahan. America 120: 278-80 Mr 8 '69

Who's a racist? Chr Cent 86:139 Ja 29 '69
See also
Race prejudice

RACK, Wine. See Wine racks

RACKETEERING

Army tries to build a munitions factory in St Louis with the Mob on the payroll. D. Walsh. il Life 66:52-4+ F 14 '69

Significant developments in tax administration; organized crime; address, October 6, 1969. R. W. Thrower. Vital Speeches 36:73-7 N 15 '69
See also
Mafia
Profiteering

RACKETS, Tennis. See Tennis rackets

RACKS, Bicycle. See Bicycle racks

RACKS, Magazine. See Magazine stands, racks, etc.

RACKS, Spice. See Spice racks

RADA, Pravoslav
Pravoslav Rada; interview, ed. by D. Cyr. por Ceram Mo 17:17-21 Ap '69

RADAR
See also
Great Britain—Royal radar establishment

Antenna and scanning mechanisms

ASMS ship radars proposed. il Aviation W 90:88 Ap 28 '69

Hughes to flight test phased array; electronically scanned airborne intercept radar antenna. B. Miller. il Aviation W 90:76-7+ Je 9 '69

Mapping applications

Side-looking radar used in civil mapping. il Aviation W 90:94-5+ Je 16 '69

Military applications

Determining the shape of an unknown satellite from its radar signature. il Space World G-1-73:16-17 Ja '70

Europeans push air defense development. il Aviation W 90:216-18+ Je 2 '69

Tactical approach radar designed. B. M. Elson. il Aviation W 91:67+ S 29 '69
See also
Airplanes, Military—Radar equipment

Miniaturization

New acoustic devices developed for radar; microsound components based on ultrasonic surface wave propagation. B. M. Elson. il Aviation W 90:85-8+ My 5 '69

RADAR aids to aviation
See also
Proximity warning indicators

RADAR astronomy. See Radar in astronomy

RADAR beacons. See Radar in aviation

RADAR defense networks

How a Cuban MIG sneaked into U.S. il U S News 67:17 O 20 '69

Master of air defense; J. J. Kelly, head of unit at Saglek Bay, Labrador. il Ebony 24: 124-6+ O '69

Whatever happened to the DEW line. il U S News 67:13 Ag 11 '69

RADAR in astronomy

Penetrating the secrets of the planets. G. Bylinsky. il Fortune 80:138-43 N '69

RADAR in aviation

Crashes focus attention on landing aids; precision approach radar. P. J. Klass. Aviation W 90:30-1 Ja 27 '69

Europeans close U.S. ground navaid lead. il Aviation W 90:143+ Je 2 '69

Moving target test planned. B. Miller. il Aviation W 91:89+ Ag 11 '69

Radar replacement studied for control of air traffic. Aviation W 90:28 Mr 31 '69

Super beacon concepts emerging; intermittent positive control concept. P. J. Klass. il Aviation W 91:75+ D 8 '69

Tactical approach radar designed. B. M. Elson. il Aviation W 91:67+ S 29 '69
See also
Airplanes—Radar equipment
Airplanes, Military—Radar equipment
Airports—Traffic control

RADAR in space flight

LM landing radar. il Space World F-10-70:26 O '69

RADAR interferometry. See Interferometry

RADCLIFFE, Ann (Ward)

Moon stood still on Strawberry Hill. P. Quennell. il Horizon 11:114-17 Sum '69

RADCLIFFE, Woodward

Attractive native. Horticulture 47:12 N '69

Palms in the landscape. Horticulture 47:22-5+ Ja '69

Stephanotis floribunda. il Horticulture 47:54 O '69

Trembling poplar. Horticulture 47:16-18+ F '69
—See Jackson, V. R. jt. auth.

RADCLIFFE college, Cambridge, Mass.

Can hip Harvard hold that line? il Time 93: 57-8+ Mr 14 '69

RADEBAUGH, Byron F. See Johnson, J. A. jt. auth.

RADEMACHER, James H.

Excerpt from address; reprint. Cong Digest 48:85+ Mr '69

RADER, Dotson

American Armageddon? R. A. Gross. il por Newsweek 73:108-108A My 12 '69

RADHUBER, Stanley

Song in a car. Poetry 114:96 My '69

RADIAL engines. See Automobile engines

RADIAL saws. See Saws

RADIANT heating

Radiant heat panel for your boat. Y. K. Adam. il Motor B 124:65 N '69

RADIATION
See also
Alpha rays
Electronic apparatus and appliances, Effect of radiation on
Ionization chambers
Radioactivity
Rayleigh radiation
Scattering (physics)
Solar radiation
Television receivers, Color—Radiation hazards

Industrial applications

Radiation: industry's versatile new specialty. I. Geller. il Duns R 93:83-4+ My '69

Laws and regulations

Dispute over the standards. Sci N 97:8 Ja 3 '70

Measurement

Atomic radiation: measuring techniques. J. H. Wujek, jr. il Electr World 82:28-30 Jl '69

Transition-radiation detector shows promise for high energy. Phys Today 22:59 N '69

Physiological effects

Deoxycytidine and radiation response: exceedingly high deoxycytidine aminohydrolase activity in human liver. B. Zicha and L. Bufič. bibliog il Science 163:191-2 Ja 10 '69

Myth of omnipotence; hidden costs of nuclear power. B. Commoner. il Environ 11:8-13+ Mr '69

Potentially lethal radiation damage: repair by mammalian cells in culture. J. A. Belli and Shelton. bibliog il Science 165:490-2 Ag 1 '69

Radiosensitivity in animals; report of meeting. V. P. Bond and T. Sugahara. Science 164:1428+ Je 20 '69

Xenon: effect on radiation sensitivity of HeLa cells. R. J. Schulz and others. bibliog il Science 163:571-2 F 7 '69
See also
Electronic ovens—Radiation hazards
Fetus, Effect of radiation on the
Microwaves—Physiological effects
Plants, Effect of radiation on
Space flight—Radiation hazards

Safety devices and measures

Dispute over the standards. Sci N 97:8 Ja 3 '70

Radiation safety; report of meeting in India. S. K. Ghaswala. il Sci N 95:126 F 1 '69

RADIATION chemistry. See Radiochemistry

RADIATION counters. See Counters (electrons, ions, etc)

RADIATION detectors. See Radiation—Measurement

RADIATION medicine. See Radiology. Medical

RADIATOR ornaments, Automobile. See Automobiles—Equipment

RADIATORS, Automobile. See Automobile engines—Radiators

RADICAL left (politics) See Right and left (political science)

RADICAL right (politics) See Right and left (political science)

RADICAL theology. See Theology

RADICAL tires. See Tires, Automobile

RADICALS (chemistry)
Matrix isolation. il Chem 25-7 N '69

RADICALS, Student. See Student militants

RADICALS and radicalism. See Right and left (political science)

RADINOVSKY, Syd
Night insects of West Bengal; with biographical sketch. il Natur Hist 78:6, 46-7 Ja '69

RADIO

History
Whatever happened to radio? M. S. Parks. il Space World F-3-63:16-21 Mr '69

RADIO advertising
Army may be hazardous to your health; San Francisco peace groups plan anti-recruitment ads. P. Barnes. New Repub 161:13-14 D 20 '69

Cigarettes
See Cigarettes—Advertising

RADIO altimeters. See Altimeters

RADIO amateurs. See Radio operators, Amateur

RADIO antennas
Build the pyramidal TV/FM antenna G. Monser. il Pop Electr 31:27-32 Jl '69
FM fringe antennas. Consumer Rep 34:66-7 F '69
How to improve your FM and TV reception. R. Gelatt. House & Gard 135:16+ F '69
Low-noise broadcast antenna. il Radio-Electr 40:94 Mr '69
Radio mirrors for communications; passive repeaters. R. D. Thrower. bibliog il Electr World 81:27-9+ My '69
Tune in shortwave on that transistor portable; home-built antenna selector. N. Fallon. il Pop Mech 132:154-5 N '69

Maintenance and repair
Repairing ferrite rods. P. E. Sutheim. il Radio-Electr 40:53 Ag '69

Tuning
Simplest antenna bridge. J. Ashe. il Pop Electr 30:66-7 Ap '69

RADIO apparatus
Jack in the box. A. T. Grahn. il Radio-Electr 40:94 D '69
New products. See issues of Popular electronics

Testing
Build the Eyeballer; signal monitoring. J. White. il Pop Electr 30:41-4 Je '69

RADIO apparatus, Short wave
Microwaves for the beginner. W. F. Hoisington. il Pop Electr 31:40-6+ N '69

RADIO apparatus industry and trade
Productivity rises as radio-TV output triples in eight years. J. E. Henneberger. il Mo Labor R 92:40-2 Mr '69
See also
Kent, A.

RADIO apparatus on aircraft
FAA studying new navaid system; Integrated navigation-communication-identification-separation equipment. P. J. Klass. il Aviation W 91:73+ Jl 28 '69
Hi fi in the sky? R. Angus. il Hi Fi 19:62-5 F '69
Swan song of the tube. A. Trammell. il Flying 84:79-80 Je '69

RADIO apparatus on ships, boats, etc.
See also
Radio telephone on ships, boats, etc.

RADIO apparatus on space vehicles
Whatever happened to radio? M. S. Parks. il Space World F-3-63:16-21 Mr '69

RADIO astronomy
Decoding messages from outer space. C. P. Gilmore. il Pop Sci 194:72-7+ Je '69
Frequencies in a squeeze. D. E. Thomsen. il Sci N 96:216-17 S 13 '69
Gamma-ray source. Sky & Tel 38:223 O '69
Interstellar sulfur hydride; a search for the 111-megahertz lines. M. L. Meeks and others. bibliog il Science 163:173-4 Ja 10 '69

Models of pulsating radio sources. J. W. Warwick. bibliog Science 163:959-61 F 28 '69
Observing solar flares by radio. C. H. Hossfield. il Sky & Tel 37:254-8 Ap '69
Point source of gammas. D. E. Thomsen. il Sci N 96:277 S 27 '69
Some radio observations of the outer planets. Sky & Tel 38:301 N '69
Space-Beacon mystery; P. Morrison's theory that quasars are giant pulsars. Newsweek 74:107 S 15 '69
They listen to the language of the universe. I. Wolfert. Read Digest 94:95-9 F '69
Two years and no action. il Sci N 96:200-1 S 13 '69
Venus: absence of a phase effect at a 2-centimeter wavelength. D. Morrison. bibliog il Science 163:815-17 F 21 '69
Watching an X-ray source. il Sci N 96:130 Ag 16 '69
See also
Pulsars
Quasars
Radio telescope

RADIO astronomy explorer (satellite) See Artificial satellites—Astronomical applications

RADIO beacons
Rescue beacon law faces court challenge. N. S. Himmel. Aviation W 91:84 D 15 '69

RADIO broadcasting

Conversation programs
Bigot victory; talk-show format canceled by KLIQ. Nation 209:557 N 24 '69
Civic responsibility; berating by Barry Gray. Time 93:23 Je 20 '69
Long John Nebel. I. Taves. il Look 33:86+ Mr 18 '69
Night call. il Newsweek 73:100+ My 12 '69
Trade winds; Night call. J. Beatty, jr. Sat R 52:10 Ap 26 '69

Frequency modulation
See Radio frequency modulation

International aspects
Broadcasting agreements with Mexico transmitted to the Senate; message, March 25. 1969. R. M. Nixon. Dept State Bul 60:330 Ap 14 '69
United States and Mexico sign broadcasting agreements. Dept State Bul 60:39-42 Ja 13 '69

Laws and regulations
See Radio laws and regulations

Library programs
Library on the air; Louisville free public library's Wire network. D. L. Day. il Wilson Lib Bul 44:320-5 N '69

Licenses
See Radio laws and regulations

Multiplex system
Multiplexed seat units designed for 747. B. Miller. il Aviation W 90:81-2+ F 17 '69
Multiplexing audio entertainment for the Boeing superjet. J. W. Partridge. il Electr World 82:40-1+ S '69

Music
Grooving with WABC. A. R. Dolan. il Nat R 21:127+ F 11 '69

Negro programs
Good book? Washington, D. C.'s station, WOOK to be investigated by FCC. Newsweek 74:82 Jl 7 '69

News
Sounding off; TV newscasters give views before radio mike. il Newsweek 73:54-5 Ap 7 '69

Operas
Word in time. Opera N 33:6 Ap 19 '69

Programs
Dupont-Columbia audit; survey of broadcast journalism, 1968-1969. J. McLaughlin. il America 121:573 D 6 '69
See also
Radio broadcasting—Public service programs

Public service programs
Message to broadcasters; industry's responsibility. S. Ross. Chr Cent 86:280-3 F 26 '69

Religious programs
Conservative broadcasts: a fair death? Chr Today 13:32 Jl 4 '69

RADIO broadcasting—Religious programs—
Continued
New York radio station bans church program; WABC, Bishop Armstrong and T. Cornell interview. Chr Cent 86:1132 S 3 '69

Social aspects

Airing the hang-ups; WBZ radio, Boston experiment in solving community problems. R. L. Shayon. Sat R 52:36 F 15 '69
Call for action, new voice for the people; WMCA's program. J. Daniel. Read Digest 95:207-10+ O '69
Greatest Halloween prank of them all; reactions to 1938 broadcast of The war of the worlds. J. H. Burns. Read Digest 95:157-60 O '69

Weather forecasts

Transcribed weather broadcast service. il Weatherwise 22:156 Ag '69

Youth programs

Grooving with WABC. A. R. Dolan. il Nat R 21:127+ F 11 '69

China (People's Republic)

This is Radio Peking. J. Kimberley. il Pop Electr 30:59-61+ Ap '69

Colombia

Don Quixote of the radio; Father Salcedo of Accion cultural popular; reprint. D. Behrman. il UNESCO Courier 22:73-4+ Ag '69

Europe

Long-wave broadcast band. H. Bennett. il Pop Electr 31:98-100+ Ag '69

United States

See also
United States—Federal communications commission

RADIO broadcasting, Short wave
English-language broadcasts to North America; tables (title varies) R. Legge. See issues of Popular electronics

RADIO circuits
New concepts in hi-fi receiver design. L. W. Fish, jr. and K. J. Peter. il Electr World 81:32-4+ F '69
Vacuum-tube superhets. C. Cohn. Radio-Electr 40:96 S '69

RADIO City book store. See Booksellers and bookselling—New York (state)

RADIO City music hall. See New York (city)—Radio City music hall

RADIO communication
See also
Ionospheric radio wave propagation
Space flight—Communication problems
Space flight—Communication systems

Emergency applications

Alert-monitor receiver warns of emergencies; Kalamazoo, Mich. il Am City 84:79 Ap '69
Cleaning up Camille. G. H. Reese. il Pop Electr 31:79-80+ D '69
Hams tackle a hurricane. D. Waters. il Pop Electr 31:72-3 D '69
Mutual-aid radio expands firefighting services; Winnetka, Ill. R. A. Porter. il Am City 84:128+ S '69
They listen so others might see; Eye bank network. H. Kantor. il Todays Health 47:62-3 S '69
See also
React (organization)

Interference

See Radio interference

RADIO communication, Naval
ELF: how we'll broadcast with mystery radio waves. K. V. Brown. il Pop Sci 195:104-7+ S '69
Project Sanguine short-circuited. N. Gruchow. Science 166:850 N 14 '69
Still Sanguine; navy's project. New Repub 161:13 N 29 '69
Wiring Wisconsin; Project Sanguine, underground transmitter complex for communicating with Polaris missile submarines. A. Hamilton. New Repub 160:8-9 Mr 22 '69
Wisconsin gets wired for sound; navy's Project Sanguine communications systems. il Bsns W p 116+ Ap 26 '69

RADIO communication, Short wave
See also
Citizens radio service
Radio apparatus, Short wave

RADIO communication, Underground
Project Sanguine short-circuited. N. Gruchow. Science 166:850 N 14 '69
Still Sanguine; navy's project. New Repub 161:13 N 29 '69

Wiring Wisconsin; Project Sanguine, underground transmitter complex for communicating with Polaris missile submarines. A. Hamilton. New Repub 160:8-9 Mr 22 '69
Wisconsin gets wired for sound; navy's Project Sanguine communications systems. il Bsns W p 116+ Ap 26 '69

RADIO compass
Davis HELP; radio/compass direction finder. W. Robberson and E. Robberson. il Yachting 126:198 O '69

RADIO control
Control your gasser, plane or boat with this full house kit; radio-control rig. L. E. Sabal. il Pop Mech 130:162-3 D '68
See also
Automobile models—Radio control
Locomotives—Control
Yacht models—Radio control

RADIO converters
First project; shortwave converter. J. White. il Pop Electr 31:75-9 Ag '69
Sine-wave to pulse converter. F. H. Tooker. il Pop Electr 31:50 Jl '69

RADIO corporation of America. See RCA corporation

RADIO filters
Filters; symposium. bibliog il Electr World 81:37-60 Ap '69

RADIO frequency
Experiment with gravity. T. Appleby. il Pop Electr 32:66 Ja '70

Allocation

See Radio frequency allocation

RADIO frequency allocation
Frequencies in a squeeze. D. E. Thomsen. il Sci N 96:216-17 S 13 '69
Very hazardous fraud; electronics expert questions new proposals on VHF for marine radio. J. White. Yachting 126:72+ N '69

RADIO frequency interference. See Radio interference

RADIO frequency modulation
Audio equalization curves up-to-date. T. R. Haskett. il Electr World 82:44-6 D '69
Has success spoiled FM? I. Alberts. Hi Fi 19:61-3 N '69
Truth about FM. T. R. Haskett. il Electr World 82:37-40+ Ag '69

RADIO generators. See Signal generators

RADIO in aviation
See also
Radio apparatus on aircraft
Radio beacons

RADIO in civil defense
This is a test. Nation 208:621 Mv 19 '69

RADIO in criminal investigation, espionage, etc.
I want to be a spy, Mr CIA man. D. J. Holford. il Pop Electr 31:51-2 Ag '69

RADIO in defense
See also
Radio communication, Naval

RADIO in navigation
Omega, a V.L.F. radionavigation sytem. E. A. Lacy. il Electr World 82:47-9+ D '69
Omega: the last word in electronic navigation. J. West. il Motor B 124:48-9+ S '69
Very hazardous fraud; electronics expert questions new proposals on VHF. J. West. Yachting 126:72+ N '69

RADIO interference
Control of R.F. interference. J. Hawk. il Electr World 82:41-3 D '69
R.F. interference filters. B. Rosen. il Electr World 81:48-9 Ap '69

RADIO laws and regulations
FCC proposed rule making for 2-3 MHz marine band. R. Humphrey. Electr World 81:71 F '69
Pastore bill; barring competitive license applications. Nation 209:132 Ag 25 '69
Taking sides; opposition by Negro group to Pastore bill on broadcasting licenses. R. L. Shayon. Sat R 52:65 N 15 '69
See also
United States—Federal communications commission

RADIO meteorology
See also
Ionospheric radio wave propagation

RADIO operators, Amateur
Amateur radio. H. S. Brier. il Pop Electr 30:87+ Mr '69
Hatfield hams and the CB McCoys. C. H. Allen. il Pop Electr 30:73-5+ F '69
No place to go, but up. R. Humphrey. il Pop Electr 30:75-9 Mr '69
Short-wave listening. H. Bennett. See issues of Popular electronics
They listen so others might see; Eye bank network. H. Kantor. il Todays Health 47:62-3 S '69
See also
React (organization)

RADIO phonograph combination. See Radio receivers—Phonograph combination

RADIO plays
Connecticut Yankee in King Arthur's court; dramatization of a novel by Mark Twain, reprint from May 1955 issue. L. Olfson. Plays 28:99-107 My '69
Importance of being earnest; drama; adapted by L. Olfson. O. Wilde. Plays 28:87-95 Ap '69
Johnny question-mark. C. Boiko. Plays 29:1-16, 38 N '69

RADIO receivers
Sound-in! What's now. il Seventeen 28:142-5 S '69

Design
New concepts in hi-fi receiver design. L. W. Fish, jr. and K. J. Peter. il Electr World 81:32-4+ F '69

Frequency modulation receivers
Another good FM radio, but—; Realistic FM Concertmaster. il Consumer Rep 34:562 O '69
How we judge FM tuners. E. J. Foster. Hi Fi 19:64-7 N '69

History
See also
Kent, A.

Manufacture
Testing insures performance. C. Lincoln. il Pop Electr 31:61+ D '69

Phonograph combination
Radio-phono consoles. il Consumer Rep 34:300-5 Je '69

Testing
FM/AM monophonic table radios. il Consumer Rep 34:564-7 O '69
Look at the HQ-200 & SX-122A. O. P. Ferrell. il Pop Electr 31:55-7 S '69
Low-noise receiver performance measurements. L. R. Bishop. il Electr World 81:38-9+ Mr '69

Tuning
Equipment report; Heathkit AJ-15 FM stereo tuner. J. R. Free. il Radio-Electr 40:71-2 F '69
How we judge FM tuners. E. J. Foster. Hi Fi 19:64-7 N '69
Last-word. IC stereo tuner. K. F. Buegel. il Radio-Electr 40:36-40 Je '69
Variable-voltage tuning. R. F. Scott. il Radio-Electr 40:58-60 Ap '69
Varicap front and AM tuner. A. A. Mangieri. il Pop Electr 30:76-7+ My '69

RADIO receivers, Portable
Hot, new multiband portables tune in almost anything. F. H. Belt; S. M. Gallager. il Pop Mech 132:46-7+ Jl '69
One-IC radio. L. Auer and H. Thanos. il Radio-Electr 40:49-51 N '69
Portable AM radios. il Consumer Rep 34:385-9 Jl '69

RADIO receivers, Short wave
Heathkit SB-310 shortwave receiver. J. R. Free. il Radio-Electr 40:74-6 Mr '69

RADIO receivers, Stereophonic
FM stereo in this headset. C. H. Lawrence. il Radio-Electr 40:43-4 Ag '69
Hi-Fi product report: Hallicrafters CR-3000 stereo/communications receiver. il Electr World 82:12-13+ Ag '69
Hi-fi product report: Scott LR-88 AM/FM-stereo receiver. il Electr World 81:17+ My '69
Kit that almost puts itself together. S. M. Gallager. il Pop Mech 132:236+ N '69
New for you: Allied model 395 solid-state stereo AM/FM receiver. C. H. Lawrence. il Radio-Electr 40:32 Je '69
1970 stereo receiver roundup; tables. Radio-Electr 40:50-1 O '69
Scott LR88 solid state AM-FM stereo receiver kit. S. H. Leckerts. il Radio-Electr 40:68+ Mr '69
Stereo receivers. il Consumer Bul 52:35-40 F '69

RADIO receivers, Superheterodyne
Look at the HQ-200 & SX-122A. O. P. Ferrell. il Pop Electr 31:55-7 S '69

RADIO reception
See also
Radio antennas

RADIO relay systems
Radio mirrors for communications; passive repeaters. R. D. Thrower. bibliog il Electr World 81:27-9+ My '69
See also
Communications satellites

RADIO stations
Bigot victory; talk-show format canceled by KLIQ. Nation 209:557 N 24 '69
Call for action, new voice for the people; WMCA's program. J. Daniel. Read Digest 95:207-10+ O '69
Good book? Washington, D.C's station, WOOK to be investigated by FCC. Newsweek 74:82 Jl 7 '69
Grooving with WABC. A. R. Dolan. il Nat R 21:127+ F 11 '69
See also
Pacifica foundation

RADIO stations, Amateur

Equipment
Amateur radio equipment, 1969-70. H. S. Brier. il Pop Electr 31:59-61+ Ag '69
Build the Eyeballer; signal monitoring. J. White. il Pop Electr 30:41-4 Je '69
See also
Radio transmitters

RADIO stations, Frequency modulation
Tuning in on underground radio. Bsns W p86 Ap 12 '69

RADIO stations, Library. See Radio broadcasting—Library programs

RADIO stations, Short wave
Angry voice from Red Lion; WINB. T. J. R. Kent. il Pop Electr 31:73-4 S '69
New operating schedules for international broadcasters; tables. Pop Electr 31:82 N '69
Short-wave listening, H. Bennett. See issues of Popular electronics

RADIO stations, Underground. See Radio stations, Frequency modulation

RADIO technical commission for aeronautics
Scanning-beam technique selected for landing aid. Aviation W 91:26 O 13 '69

RADIO telegraph
Equipment
Perfect electronic keyer. W. O. Hamlin. il Radio-Electr 40:69-72 N '69

RADIO telephone
Annual catalog of five-watt CB equipment. il Pop Electr 31:40-50+ Ag '69

RADIO telephone, Portable
What's new in 5-watt CB gear. L. Buckwalter. il Radio-Electr 40:48-51 My '69

RADIO telephone on ships, boats, etc.
Dial Operator 25; list of important phone numbers. il Motor R 124:28-9+ Ag '69
FCC proposed rule making for 2-3 MHz marine band. R. Humphrey. Electr World 81:71 F '69
Is CB for your boat? E. Robberson. il Yachting 125:60-1+ F '69
Which radiotelephone is for you? L. Heiner. il Motor B 123:236-7+ Ja '69

RADIO telescope
Astronomy: tight budget gains stranglehold on radio facilities. R. W. Holcomb. il Science 166:984-6 N 21 '69
Miracle in sound; tracking antenna at Goldstone, Calif. il Time 94:22 Ag 1 '69
New radio telescopes. D. E. Thomsen. il Sci N 95:434-5 My 3 '69
Radio telescope and the heiligenschein. F. L. Whipple. il Sky & Tel 37:85 F '69

RADIO transmission
Cloud antenna for world communication. S. V. Jones. il Sci Digest 66:83 S '69

RADIO transmitters
Build a Happy hybrid; low-cost, low-power 40-meter transmitter. D. Logan. il Pop Electr 30:48-51+ Mr '69

Safety devices and measures
Protection system for solid-state transmitters. C. Smith. il Electr World 81:38-9+ F '69

RADIO waves
ELF: how we'll broadcast with mystery radio waves. K. V. Brown. il Pop Sci 195:104-7+ S '69
See also
Ionospheric radio wave propagation
Microwaves
Pulse techniques (electronics)

RADIOACTIVATION analysis
Elimination of sodium-24 and potassium-42 interferences in activation analysis of biological samples. C. W. Tang and C. J. Maletskos. bibliog il Science 167:52-4 Ja 2 '70
Murder at Thank God Bay; early Arctic explorer's death solved by neutron activation analysis. Sci Am 220:52 Mr '69

RADIOACTIVE dating
Absolute dating of Caribbean cores P6304-8 and P6304-9. E. Rona and C. Emiliani; reply, W. S. Broecker and T. L. Ku. bibliog il Science 166:404-6 O 17 '69; rejoinder. 166:1551-2 D 19 '69

RADIOACTIVE dating—*Continued*
  Etching fission tracks in zircons. C. W. Naeser. bibliog il Science 165:388 Jl 25 '69
  Fission track age of magnetic anomaly 10: a new point on the sea-floor spreading curve. B. P. Luyendyk and D. E. Fisher. bibliog il Science 164:1516-17 Je 27 '69
  Nuclear tracks in solids. R. L. Fleischer and others. il Sci Am 220:30-9 Je '69
    See also
  Radiocarbon dating
RADIOACTIVE fallout
  Ernest J. Sternglass; controversial prophet of doom. P. M. Boffey. Science 166:195-200 O 10 '69
  Fetal infant mortality and the environment. A. R. Tamplin; E. J. Sternglass. il Bul Atom Sci 25:23-34 D '69
  Infant mortality and nuclear tests. E. J. Sternglass. il Bul Atom Sci 25:18-20 Ap '69; Discussion. 25:27 Je; 26-32 O '69; Cur 113:62-4 D '69
  Nuclear weapons and world sanity; excerpts from address, reprint. L. Pauling. il UNESCO Courier 22:43-4+ Ag '69
  Radionuclide concentrations in surface air: direct relationship to global fallout. M. T. Kleinman and H. L. Volchok. bibliog il Science 166:376-7 O 17 '69
  Testing the treaty; radiation from Nevada test site carried into Mexico and Canada. Environ 11:10-11 Ap '69
    See also
  Atomic bomb shelters

Measurement
  See Radioactivity—Measurement

Arkansas
  Interhemispheric transport of atmospheric fission debris from French nuclear tests. B. D. Palmer. bibliog il Science 164:951-2 My 23 '69

Atlantic Ocean
  Strontium-90: concentrations in surface waters of the Atlantic Ocean. V. T. Bowen and others. bibliog il Science 164:825-7 My 16 '69
RADIOACTIVE substances
  Disarming proposal; Soviets refuse agreement to halt production of fissionable materials. Newsweek 73:44+ Ap 21 '69
  Please don't steal the atomic bomb. A. M. Adelson. il Esquire 71:130-3+ My '69
    See also
  Radioisotopes
  Radium
  Radon
RADIOACTIVE substances in the body
  High-resolution autoradiography of intracellular plutonium. A. Lindenbaum and H. M. Smoler. bibliog il Science 165:192-4 Jl 11 '69
RADIOACTIVE tracers
  Carbon-14 labeled vasoactive peptides available. J. J. Pisano. Science 165:203 Jl 11 '69
  Cell population kinetics: a modified interpretation of the graph of labeled mitoses. A. I. Hamilton. bibliog il Science 164:952-4 My 23 '69
  Mass spectrometry and carbon-13 labeling. S. Meyerson and E. K. Fields. bibliog il Science 166:325-8 O 17 '69
  Nerve endings: rapid appearance of labeled protein shown by electron microscope radioautography. B. Droz and S. H. Barondes. bibliog il Science 165:1131-3 S 12 '69
  Occupancy principle for radioactive tracers in steady-state biological systems. J. S. Orr and F. C. Gillespie; discussion. bibliog Science 163:491-2; 166:260 Ja 31, O 10 '69
  Radioactive drugs: how they are used. il Good H 169:149 Jl '69
RADIOACTIVE waste disposal
  Cooling it in Minnesota; report of Minnesota committee for environmental information on benefits and risks of nuclear reactors. il Environ 11:21-5 Mr '69
  Radioactive pollution: Minnesota finds AEC standards too lax. P. M. Boffey. Science 163:1043-4+ Mr 7 '69
  Under the rug; problems of toxic waste disposal in deep injection wells. D. M. Evans and A. Bradford. bibliog il Environ 11:3-13+ O '69
  War over the peaceful atom; radioactive and thermal hazards. il Life 67:26B-33 S 12 '69
  Who gets last radioactive word? Minnesota vs Atomic energy commission. Bsns W p28 My 31 '69

RADIOACTIVITY
  Atomic radiation. J. H. Wujek, jr. il Electr World 81:46-7 My; 46-8 Je; 82:28-30 Jl '69
    See also
  Alpha rays
  Autoradiography
  Radiochemistry
  Radium
  Tritium

Industrial applications
  Early days of radioactivity in industry. F. E. Wall. il Chem 42:17-19 Ap '69 (to be cont)

Measurement
  Plutonium-238 in fallout. T. Mamuro and T. Matsunami. bibliog il Science 163:465-7 Ja 31 '69
    See also
  Counters (electrons, ions, etc)
  Radioactivation analysis
  Radiometers

Physiological effects
  About 355 of those things have exploded in Nevada. G. Hill. il N Y Times Mag p6-7+ Jl 27 '69
  Death of all children; footnote to the A.B.M. controversy. E. J. Sternglass. Esquire 72: 1a-1d S '69; Excerpts. Cur 110:12-15 S '69
  Delayed radiation effects in atomic-bomb survivors; adaptation of address, March 1969. R. W. Miller. bibliog Science 569-74 O 31 '69
  Effects of atomic radiation; assembly adopts resolution. UN Mo Chron 6:33-4 N '69
  Infant mortality and nuclear tests. E. J. Sternglass. il Bul Atom Sci 25:18-20 Ap '69; Discussion. 25:27 Je; 26-32 O '69; Cur 113: 62-4 D '69
    See also
  Radioactive fallout
  United Nations—Scientific committee on the effects of atomic radiation

Safety devices and measures
  Plutonium fire raises questions; investigation after fire at weapons plant, Rocky Flats, Colo. il Sci N 96:25 Jl 12 '69
    See also
  Atomic bomb shelters
  Nuclear reactors—Safety devices and measures
RADIOAUTOGRAPHY. See Autoradiography
RADIOBIOLOGY
    See also
  Plants, Effect of radiation on
RADIOCARBON dating
  Age of bed V, Olduvai Gorge, Tanzania. L. S. B. Leakey and others; discussion. Science 163:1360; 166:258-9 Mr 21, O 10 '69
  Carbon-14 in Patagonian tree rings. J. C. Lerman and others. bibliog il Science 165: 1123-5 S 12 '69
  Carbon-14 trends in subfossil pine stubs. J. C. Vogel and others. bibliog il Science 166:1143-5 N 28 '69
  Radiocarbon dating of petroleum-impregnated bone from tar pits at Rancho La Brea, California. T. Y. Ho and others. bibliog il Science 164:1051-2 My 30 '69
  Upgrading radiocarbon dating. il Sci N 96: 159-60 Ag 30 '69
RADIOCHEMISTRY
  Lab bench; determining empirical formulas using radioisotopes. J. A. Sears and W. James. il Chem 42:29-30 O '69
RADIOGRAPHY
    See also
  Autoradiography
RADIOISOTOPE thermoelectric generators. See Electric generators
RADIOISOTOPES
  Lab bench; determining empirical formulas using radioisotopes. J. A. Sears and W. James. il Chem 42:29-30 O '69
  Radionuclide composition of the Allende meteorite from nondestructive gamma-ray spectrometric analysis. L. A. Rancitelli and others. bibliog il Science 166:1269-72 D 5 '69
    See also
  Radioactive tracers
RADIOLOGISTS
  Radiologist talks about his work; ed. by W. S. Ross. D. H. Faegenburg. il Todays Health 48:44-7+ Ja '70
RADIOLOGY, Medical
  Alone in a body counter. J. R. Berry. il Pop Mech 131:80-3+ Je '69
  Rays of hope; extracorporeal blood irradiators. Newsweek 73:88 Je 23 '69
    See also
  Radiologists
RADIOMETERS
  In the news; SBRC radiometer to help unlock secrets of Mars. il Space World F-5-65:41 My '69

RADIOMETERS—*Continued*
Luminescence dosimetry; report of meeting. K. Becker and J. A. Auxier. Science 164: 974+ My 23 '69
RADIONUCLIDES. See Radioisotopes
RADIOS on airplanes. See Radio apparatus on aircraft
RADIOTHERAPY
   See also
X Rays—Therapeutic applications
RADISHES
Radishes round the calendar. R. L. Hawk. il Org Gard & Farm 16:43-5 D '69
   See also
Cookery—Vegetables
RADIUM

Physiological effects
Early days of radioactivity in industry. F. E. Wall. il Chem 42:17-19 Ap '69 (to be cont)
Early days of radioactivity in industry; aftermath. E. Keller. Chem 42:16-17 My '69
RADIUM poisoning. See Radium—Physiological effects
RADIUS, Alexandra
Brief biography. S. Goodman. pors Dance Mag 43:58-9 N '69
RADKE, L. F. See Hobbs, P. V. jt. auth.
RADON
Latest on chemistry of radon. Chem 42:22-3 D '69
RADOS, David L.
Product liability: tougher ground rules. Harvard Bsns R 47:144-52 Jl '69
RADOSH, Ronald
Labor and foreign policy. Nation 209:208-11 S 8 '69
Making the world safe for America. Nation 209:350-1 O 6 '69
RAFFAEL, Joseph
Unphotography. il por Time 93:80-1 Ap 11 '69
RAFTS
Two wavemakers for summer fun. A. Lees. il Pop Sci 195:160-4+ Ag '69
Wildest boat trip in the world. R. P. Crossley. il Pop Mech 131:122-6+ Mr '69
RAGEN, Joseph E.
What prisons can and can't do; interview. por U S News 67:62-3 Ag 11 '69
RAGLAND, Philida
Have camera will travel; photographer for United Presbyterian church. il pors Ebony 24:112-14+ Mr '69
RAGO, Henry
Four fragments: poem. Poetry 115:79-82 N '69
Poet in his poem; address, October 17, 1968. Poetry 113:413-20 Mr '69

about
For the word, for the silence. R. J. Mills. jr. Poetry 115:127-30 N '69
In memory of Henry Rago: poems. Poetry 115:83+ N '69
Islands waited, wait still. . . H. Carruth. Poetry 115:130-2 N '69
RAGOSINE, Victor E.
Magnetic recording; with biographical sketch. Sci Am 221:18, 71-80+ bibliog(p 166) N '69
RAHLFF, Holger
With the sun around the world. il por Yachting 125:46-8+ F '69
RAHNER, Karl
Conversation with Karl Rahner; ed. by M. M. Dorcy and J. P. Jurich. America 120: 733-5 Je 28 '69

about
News and views. J. Deedy. Commonweal 90: 130 Ap 18 '69
Of many things. D. R. Campion. America 120:inside cover Je 21 '69
RAHV, Philip
Big pictures and little phrases. C. T. Samuels. New Repub 161:26-9 N 29 '69
Criticism. N. A. Scott, jr. Sat R 53:27+ Ja 3 '70
Partisan and public man. M. L. Krupnick. Nation 209:607-8 D 1 '69
RAICHLE, Elaine L.
Where all the arts are lively. PTA Mag 63:27-8 Je '69
RAIDERS (football club) See Football clubs
RAIL fences. See Fences
RAILROAD accidents. See Railroads—Accidents
RAILROAD advertising. See Railroads—Advertising
RAILROAD cars. See Railroads—Cars
RAILROAD clubs
April look at old trolleys and trains; Bay area electric railroad association. il Sunset 142: 54-5 Ap '69

RAILROAD crossings. See Railroads—Crossings
RAILROAD law
Danger on the track; rail safety bill. il Bsns W p54-6 O 4 '69
Railroads want to stop subsidizing their own strikers. Bsns W p34 D 20 '69
   See also
United States—Interstate commerce commission
RAILROAD management. See Railroads—Management
RAILROAD models

Electric equipment
Electronic throttle. H. J. Mierlak. il Radio-Electr 40:42-4 N '69
RAILROAD motor cars. See Railroads—Cars
RAILROAD museums
Utah has a railroad village. il Sunset 143:56 O '69
   See also
Laws, Calif.
RAILROAD retirement benefits. See Pensions, Industrial
RAILROAD stocks. See Railroads—Securities
RAILROAD supplies industry
Bumpy track for car builders. il Bsns W p 116-17 N 8 '69
RAILROAD switches. See Railroads—Switches
RAILROAD towns
   See also
Rawlins, Wyo.
RAILROAD travel
Century of railroading: early demise or daring new designs? J. Goodman; discussion. Sat R 52:21 Ja 25 '69
How to do Europe by train. D. Ardrey. il Travel & Camera 32:13-14 Jl '69
Journey through a borrowed land; Kowloon-Lo Wu. F. Riley. il Sat R 53:91-2+ Ja 10 '70
   See also
Railroads—Passenger traffic
RAILROAD unemployment insurance act. See Railroad law
RAILROAD workers. See Railroads—Employees
RAILROADS

Accidents
Danger on the track; rail safety bill. il Bsns W p54-6 O 4 '69
Explosions en route; transporting explosives by road and rail. S. Morrison. il Nation 209:379-81 O 13 '69
Rolling fright; freight-train derailments involving hazardous chemicals. il Time 93:24 Mr 7 '69

Advertising
'Bye, Phoebe Snow, 'bye Buffalo. O. Jensen. il Am Heritage 20:10-15 D '68

Automatic train control
Four-mile train with a mind in the middle. H. Comstock. il Pop Mech 132:82-5+ D '69
   See also
Locomotives—Control

Cars
Bumpy track for car builders. il Bsns W p 116:17 N 8 '69
Rail vehicle completed for test of linear induction propulsion. Aviation W 91:24 D 15 '69
Will car builders miss San Francisco train? il Bsns W p62+ My 3 '69
   See also
Railroads—Private cars

Leasing and renting
At the crossroads; GATX leasing freight cars. il Forbes 104:50 O 1 '69

Consolidations and mergers
Big rival for Penn central; proposed N&W-C&O merger. il Bsns W p 134 Mr 29 '69
Darkest hour; Pennsylvania railroad-New York central merger. il Forbes 103:16-17 Ap 1 '69
Longest? Newsweek 73:64 Mr 31 '69

Crossings
Commuter's revenge; Windsor, Ont. incident. Newsweek 73:66+ My 5 '69
Smooth, sturdy rail crossings; Pittsburgh, Pa. il Am City 84:20 Ap '69

Employees
Adjusting to technology on the railroads; ed. by M. Levine. il Mo Labor R 92:36-42 N '69
Firemen renew fight to get back on trains. il Bsns W p52-3 F 15 '69

RAILROADS—Employees—*Continued*
Shopcraft contract gears are jammed by
composite mechanic. Bsns W p63 D 27 '69
   See also
Featherbedding (industrial relations)
Railroads—Wages and hours
Strikes—United States—Railroads

Finance

Decline of rail passenger traffic; the public
service obligation of railroads; address,
June 19, 1969 G. W. Hilton. Vital Speeches
35:657-61 Ag 15 '69
Railroads are running scared. G. Burck. il
Fortune 79:122-5+ Je '69
So it's crummy. So what? Boston & Maine.
Forbes 103:32-3 Je 15 '69
   See also
Railroads—Securities

Fires and fire protection

Out of the rathole; disaster on the Penn
Central commuter train, May 26, 1969. J.
Ciardi. il Sat R 52:19-23+ S 13 '69

Freight cars

See Railroads—Cars

Freight service

Penn Central's bad trip. il Bsns W p 122-4+
Je 20 '69
Revolution in grain movement by rail, your
stake in it. R. Sanders. il Suc Farm 67:34-
5+ S '69
   See also
Motor truck trailers—Transportation

Freight trains

Four-mile train with a mind in the middle.
H. Comstock. il Pop Mech 132:82-5+ D '69
Rolling fright; freight-train derailments in-
volving hazardous chemicals. il Time 93:24
Mr 7 '69

Government ownership

See Railroads and state

History

   See also
Railroads—United States—History

Management

One helluva way to run a railroad. E. Roper.
Sat R 52:18-19 Je 28 '69
Penn Central's bad trip. il Bsns W p 122-4+
Je 28 '69

Motor cars

See Railroads—Cars

Operation

See Railroads—Management

Passenger service

Canadian national cools on riders. Bsns W
p 134 Jl 12 '69
Decline of rail passenger traffic; the public
service obligation of railroads; address,
June 19, 1969. G. W. Hilton. Vital Speeches
35:657-61 Ag 15 '69
How to move a nation; latest ideas in mass
transit. il U S News 66:82-4 My 19 '69
It's getting late for the Cannonball. il Bsns
W p 134+ Jl 12 '69
Meanwhile, back on the passenger lines;
Penn Central program. Bsns W p 128 Je
28 '69
Nation's finest comes up short; survey of
commuter railroads around the country on
Oct. 7. il Bsns W p44-5 O 11 '69
Should railroad passenger service be abolish-
ed? pro and con discussion. il Sr Schol 94:
10-11 Ap 25 '69
Summer of discontent for commuters. il Bsns
W p74-6 Ag 2 '69
Training for Europe. M. J. Maisons. il Travel
131:60-3 My '69
Unloved passenger. il Time 95:48 Ja 5 '70
   See also
Commuters

High speed trains

Airlines watch Metroliner traffic. R. F. Co-
burn. Aviation W 90:26-7 Mr 31 '69
Communicating by rail; Metroliner shuttling
daily between New York and Washington.
R. L. Tobin. Sat R 52:51-2 F 8 '69
Do fast trains have a real future? Penn cen-
tral's Metroliner on New York-Washington
run. il Bsns W p92-4+ Ja 25 '69
Fast train to D.C; the Metroliner. R. Mc-
Gurk. il Travel & Camera 32:27-8 Ap '69
How new fast trains are doing; the Metro-
liner and Turboliner. il U S News 66:16-17
Ap 21 '69
Mr Frimbo on the Metroliner; interview. E.
M. Frimbo. New Yorker 45:29-31 My 17 '69

Those fast, new trains in U.S. and Canada,
they'd never make it in Japan! R. P. Cross-
ley. il Pop Mech 131:98-9+ My '69
Train don't stop here anymore; high speed
train service competitive with air travel.
Trans-Action 6:10 Je '69
Train of the future finally gets into service;
Metroliner from Washington to New York.
il U S News 66:42 Ja 27 '69
Turbo train lags as potential airline rival.
R. S. Kahn. il Aviation W 91:30-1+ O 13 '69
Will success spoil the Metroliner? il Bsns W
p74-5 O 18 '69

Passenger traffic

   See also
Commuters
Railroad travel

Private cars

All aboard! il Newsweek 73:92 Mr 31 '69

Public relations

Decline of rail passenger traffic; the public
service obligation of railroads; address,
June 19, 1969. G. W. Hilton. Vital Speeches
35:657-61 Ag 15 '69

Securities

Is it endsville for the railroads? il Forbes
104:30-4+ O 15 '69

Stations

   See also
Jersey City, N.J.—Stations

Strikes

See Strikes—United States—Railroads

Switches

Keeper of the key; P. Sweeney, switchman
on the Hudson River rail road during Civil
war. M. S. Colwell. il Am Heritage 20:49-53
Je '69

Ties

In Mission Viejo they landscaped with old
railroad ties. il Sunset 143:110-11 O '69
Where to look for railroad ties. Sunset 143:
262 O '69

Train speed

Those fast, new trains in U.S. and Canada,
they'd never make it in Japan! R. P.
Crossley. il Pop Mech 131:98-9+ My '69
Trains without wheels. E. Gross. il Sci N
95:358-60 Ap 12 '69
   See also
Railroads—Passenger service—High speed
trains

Trains

Century of railroading: early demise or dar-
ing new designs? J. Goodman; discussion.
Sat R 52:21 Ja 25 '69
Master train of France: the Mistral. J. R. Ro-
berson. il Holiday 46:60-1+ D '69
Speed and style on foreign rails. G. Burck.
il Fortune 79:126-33 Je '69
   See also
Railroads—Freight trains

Wages and hours

Shultz policy brings rail pact; model for
other disputes? il U S News 67:100-1 D
15 '69
   See also
Collective bargaining—Railroads

Canada

Canada's Polar bear express. G. Bush. il
Bet Hom & Gard 47:116 F '69
Canada's superport for superships; Roberts
bank. il Bsns W p 120-2 S 27 '69
Railroads spur urban renewal; Canadian Pa-
cific and Canadian national. il Bsns W
p 152-4+ Ap 12 '69
   See also
Canadian national railways

Europe

Training for Europe. M. J. Maisons. il Travel 131:60-3 My '69

France

Master train of France: the Mistral. J. R.
Roberson. il Holiday 46:60-1+ D '69

Great Britain

Flier; owner of a steam locomotive called
the Flying Scotsman; interview. A. Pegler.
il New Yorker 45:43-4 N 29 '69

Hong Kong

Journey through a borrowed land; Kowloon-
Lo Wu. F. Riley. il Sat R 53:91-2+ Ja 10
'70

RAILROADS—*Continued*

Japan

Japan's most closely watched train; New Tokaido line. R. Joseph. il Travel & Camera 32:66-7+ O '69

Mexico

Train to Pátzcuaro. il Sunset 143:48 N '69

United States

Adjusting to technology on the railroads; ed. by M. Levine. il Mo Labor R 92:36-42 N '69

Communicating by rail; Metroliner shuttling daily between New York and Washington. R. L. Tobin. Sat R 52:51-2 F 8 '69

Is it endsville for the railroads? il Forbes 104:30-4+ O 15 '69

Railroads are running scared. G. Burck. il Fortune 79:122-5+ Je '69

Railroads: can they survive the 20th century? il Sr Schol 94:6-9+ Ap 25 '69

Unloved passenger. il Time 95:48 Ja 5 '70

See also
Collective bargaining—Railroads
Railroads—Management
  also names of railroads, e.g. New York, New Haven and Hartford railroad company

History

'Bye, Phoebe Snow, 'bye Buffalo. O. Jensen. il Am Heritage 20:10-15 D '68

First 100 years; transcontinental railroad. il Newsweek 73:87-8 My 19 '69

Golden spike centennial. il Sr Schol 94:4-5 Ap 25 '69

Iron spine; the Union Pacific met the Central Pacific at Promontory. H. Sturgis. il Am Heritage 20:46-57+ Ap '69

Last rail, last spike. M. M. Moler. il Nat Parks 43:8-9 Je '69

Pacific railroad centennial; the transcontinental railroad; symposium. il Am West 6:4-32+ My '69

U.S. railroads' route through history. Sr Schol 94:8-9 Ap 25 '69

When the country was united; centennial re-enactment at Promontory, Utah. il Time 93:25 My 16 '69

RAILROADS, Nationalization of. See Railroads and state

RAILROADS, Single rail
Braniff monorail system at Dallas to begin soon. N. S. Himmel. Aviation W 90:85 Mr 31 '69

Space pod; Forest flite monorail Rainbow Springs, Fla. il Travel 132:13 Jl '69

RAILROADS and state

Argentina

How to wreck a railroad. il Bsns W p75-6 O 18 '69

Canada

See also
Canadian national railways

United States

Credit mobilier: construction company building government-backed railroads. J. L. Phillips. il Am Heritage 20:108-9 Ap '69

RAILROADS in war
Keeper of the key; P. Sweeney, switchman on the Hudson River rail road during Civil war. M. S. Colwell. il Am Heritage 20:49-53 Je '69

RAILWAY accidents. See Railroads—Accidents

RAILWAY express agency, Incorporated
Up from the pony. il Newsweek 73:76 Ap 28 '69

RAILWAY labor executives' association
Rail unions split over pension policy. Bsns W p 108 N 29 '69

RAIMI, Ralph A.
Peculiar distribution of first digits; with biographical sketch. Sci Am 221:15, 109-13+ D '69

RAIMONDI, Ruggero
Stars of the Italian stage visit Edinburgh and Glyndebourne. E. Rizzo. por Opera N 33:16-17 My 17 '69

RAIN and rainfall
Contaminated rain water. Bul Atom Sci 25: 43 Je '69

Electricity and rain. J. D. Sartor. bibliog il Phys Today 22:45-51 Ag '69

From above: heavy May rains in the Southeast. il Weatherwise 22:165 Ag '69

Irrigation and climate. K. Frazier. il Sci N 96:599-600 D 27 '69

Operation raincheck. D. T. Brissett. il Weatherwise 22:64-7 Ap '69

Rain; of all weathers, rain is a happening. A. Reid. il Holiday 45:48-9+ Mr '69

See also
Droughts
Floods
Rain forests
Storms

RAIN forests
Curing Amazonia's anemic jungle soils. C. Weathersbee. il Sci N 95.338-9 Ap 5 '69

Funny thing happened on the way to the jungle; sailing and flying the Amazon. S. Turner. il Sr Schol 94:Schol Teach 18-19 Ap 11 '69

Puerto Rico's rain forest. il Home Gard 56: 82-3 Mr '69

Rain forest, and other magical lures in Puerto Rico. il Travel & Camera 32:112-13 F '69

Research to save the fragile Green hell; plight of the Amazonian jungle. il Sci N 95:134-5 F 8 '69

Spoiling the jungle yields few riches; Amazonian rain forest. C. Weathersbee. il Sci N 95:312-13 Mr 29 '69

Thoughts on wilderness preservation and a Central American ethic. A. Carr. il Audubon 71:50-5 S '69

See also
Olympic National Park

RAIN leaders. See Drainage, House

RAIN making
Areal spread of the effect of cloud seeding at the Whitetop experiment. J. Neyman and others. bibliog il Science 163:1445-9 Mr 28 '69; Discussion. 164:1341; 165:618 Je 20, Ag 8 '69

Room with a built-in deluge; an electronic rainmaker, scientists cause a storm indoors. il Life 66:77-8 Je 6 '69

Science and politics of rainmaking. G. J. F. MacDonald; reply. J. Neyman. Bul Atom Sci 25:27+ Mr '69

Timing of the apparent effects of cloud seeding. J. L. Lovasich. bibliog il Science 165: 892-3 Ag 29 '69

Where rain making is a success; northern Iran. il U S News 67:73 S 15 '69

RAINBOW classic. See Basketball tournaments

RAINBOW SPRINGS, Fla.
Space pod; Forest flite. il Travel 132:13 Jl '69

RAINBOW trout. See Trout

RAINBOW trout fishing. See Trout fishing

RAINDROPS. See Rain and rainfall

RAINE, James R.
Mr Ed; the talking bus. Sr Schol 94:Schol Teach 13 Ja 17 '69

RAINE, Kathleen Jessie
Fruits of the two seasons. J. Bronowski. il Nation 209:700-1 D 22 '69

RAINER, Dachine
Mid season sonnet. New Repub 161:21 D 6 '69

RAINER, Yvonne
Yvonne Rainer with group. D. Hering. Dance Mag 43:29+ Ap '69

RAINES, Robert A.
Toward social change. Chr Cent 86:594-5 Ap 23 '69

RAINIER NATIONAL PARK. See Mount Rainier National Park

RAIZES, Gary. See Greer, A. E. jt. auth.

RAJA Rao
Gandhi. UNESCO Courier 22:4-6+ O '69

RAKHEL Kafri's interview; ballet. See Ballets —Criticisms

RAKOSI, Carl
Looking into my granddaughter's eyes; poem. Nation 209:646 D 8 '69

Two variations on a theme; poem. Nation 209:354 O 6 '69

RAKOWSKI, Joseph, Jr. See Kirrin, V. J. jt. auth.

RAKSTIS, Ted J.
Big boom in temp help. Read Digest 94:189+ Mr '69

Moonlighting: do you really profit? Todays Health 47:24-5+ O '69

Sensitivity training: fad, fraud, or new frontier? Todays Health 48:20-5+ Ja '70

Why you need a vacation. Todays Health 47:24-7+ Ag '69

RAKU glazes. See Glazes and glazing

RALEIGH, Sir Walter
Shepherd of the ocean, by J. H. Adamson and H. F. Folland. Review
  Cath World 209:235-6+ Ag '69. J. V. Reel

RALL, Ellene M.
My regards to Ustinov. Engl J 58:548-60 Ap '69

RALLIES, Automobile. See Automobile driving—Competitions

RALSTON Purina company
But where are the earnings? il Forbes 103:50 F 15 '69

RAMAPITHECUS. See Man, Prehistoric
RAMEY, John H.
 We need to try harder; inner-city children need active recruitment. Camp Mag 41:12+ F '69
RAMIREZ, Armando Socarras
 Survivor. il por Newsweek 73:69 Je 16 '69
RAMIREZ, Efren E.
 Drug addiction is not physiologic. Sci Digest 65:20-4 My '69
RAMIREZ B, William
 Fig wasps: mechanism of pollen transfer. bibliog Science 163:580-1 F 7 '69
RAMJET airplane engines. See Jet airplane engines
RAMJET propulsion. See Jet propulsion
RAMO, Simon
 Wanted: professional futurists. Sci N 96:321 O 11 '69
RAMOS, Mel
 It helps to have read comic books as a kid; paintings. Sports Illus 30:36-41 Mr 17 '69
RAMP generators. See Pulse generators
RAMPARTS (periodical)
 About this issue. il Ramp Mag 7:4 Ap '69
 Apologia. il Ramp Mag 7:2-4 Ja 25 '69
 Manning the Ramparts, or is it the Barricades? il Time 93:42 F 7 '69
 Ramparts gang. il Time 93:53+ Je 6 '69
 Ramparts story: um, very interesting. J. Ridgeway. il N Y Times Mag p34-6+ Ap 20 '69; Reply with rejoinder. W. Hinckle. p 132 My 11 '69
 Two for one; original Ramparts to compete with Barricades. New Repub 160:9-10 F 15 '69
 Uses of capitalism. Newsweek 73:100 Ap 14 '69
RAMPS
 Ramp control key to freeway efficiency. il Am City 84:138 Ap '69
RAMS (football club) See Football clubs
RAMSEGER, Georg
 New European bookstore; tr. by C. B. Anderson. Pub W 195:19-22 My 26 '69
RAMSEY, Judith
 Healthier bosom: all the latest medical & surgical news. Ladies Home J 86:82+ O '69
RAMSEY, Paul
 Five epigrams on philosophy. America 120:307 Mr 15 '69
             about
 Ramsey's just war. R. H. Springer. Commonweal 90:76-8 Ap 4 '69
RAMSEY, Paul, 1924-
 Mill; poem. Poetry 114:175 Je '69
RAMSEY, Peter
 Peace corps: sneakers and levis for me. Har Yrs 9:10+ Jl '69
RAMUS, Michael
 Golden days that sustain the dream; photographs. Sports Illus 30:34-9 Mr 10 '69
RANCE RIVER
 Tidal energy. R. H. Charlier. il Sea Front 15:339-48 N '69
RANCHES
 Gibson ranch, a county facility; Sacramento County, Calif. P. P. Fenwick. il Parks & Rec 4:33-4 Ap '69
RANCHO Santa Ana botanic garden. See Botanical gardens
RANCITELLI, L. A. and others
 Radionuclide composition of the Allende meteorite from nondestructive gamma-ray spectrometric analysis. bibliog Science 166:1269-72 D 5 '69
RAND, Ayn
 Court upholds use of author's name in blurb. Pub W 195:35 Mr 31 '69
             about
 Can you name an author in a blurb? H. F. Pilpel and K. P. Norwick. Pub W 195:23-4 My 5 '69
RAND, George
 Pre-Copernican views of the city. Arch Forum 131:76-81 S '69
RAND, John R. See Hurley, P. M. jt. auth.
RAND corporation
 Paperwork mess goes into a think tank. Bsns W p 126+ F 22 '69
 Rand sticks with New York. Bsns W p 112 My 10 '69
RAND McNally and company
 Rand McNally: more than a mapmaker. il Bsns W p66+ N 22 '69
RAND McNally international atlas. See Atlases

RANDAL, Judith E.
 Pill that lets shaking palsy patients eat jello. Todays Health 48:34-7+ Ja '70
RANDALL, Charles Edgar
 Distinguished Douglas-fir; excerpt from Enjoying our trees. Am For 75:28-30 O; 40-1+ N '69
 George Washington: our history-making forest. Am For 75:20-3+ Mr '69
 Jefferson's forest. Am For 75:20-2+ Ap '69
 Our southern pines. Am For 75:32-5+ Je; 30-1+ Jl '69
RANDALL, David Anton
 Booksellers and collectors: a dealer's apprenticeship; excerpts from Dukedom large enough. Pub W 196:35-8 Jl 21 '69
             about
 Bibliophile. V. A. Bradley. Sat R 52:33 S 6 '69
RANDALL, Margaret
 Good and the useful. Poetry 115:47-60 O '69
 Sad poem. Poetry 115:24 O '69
RANDELL, Cortes Wesley
 Cash customers on campus. S. Blickstein. il Duns R 94:65-6+ Ag '69
RANDOLPH, Asa Philip
 Top Negro's plea for nonviolence; excerpts from remarks, May 6, 1969. por U S News 66:22 My 19 '69
             about
 A. Philip Randolph: labor's grand old man. P. Garland. il pors Ebony 24:31-4+ My '69
 Marching on. Nation 208:485 Ap 21 '69
 To A. Philip Randolph. America 120:521-2 My 3 '69
RANDOLPH, Peyton, house. See Williamsburg, Va.
RANDOM walks (mathematics) See Numerical analysis
RANEY, Edward C.
 Minnows of New York. Cons 23:22-9 Ap; 21-9 Je '69
RANEY, Ona
 Mother's garden of yesteryear. Org Gard & Farm 16:48-52 Ja '69
 Our third-purpose walk. Org Gard & Farm 16:114-15 Mr '69
 Stalks off the cob. Org Gard & Farm 16:44 Jl '69
 What's that about strawberries? questions and answers. Org Gard & Farm 16:48-50 F '69
RANGE finder cameras. See Cameras
RANGE finders. See View finders
RANGERS (hockey team) See Hockey teams
RANGERS, Park. See Forest rangers
RANGES. See Stock ranges
RANGES, Kitchen. See Electric stoves; Gas stoves
RANKIN, Anne Vannan
 Euripides' Hippolytus. bibliog f Am Imago 25:333-46 Wint '68
RANKIN, D. W. and others
 Zircon ages of felsic volcanic rocks in the upper Precambrian of the Blue Ridge. Appalachian Mountains. bibliog Science 166:741-4 N 7 '69
RANKIN, Kenneth R. See Clampitt, M. O. jt. auth.
RANKING, Student. See Grading and marking (students)
RANLY, Ernest W.
 Frantz Fanon and the radical left. America 121:384+ N 1 '69
RANSFORD, Ann. See Lovell, A. jt. auth.
RANSFORD, H. Edward
 Who riots; summary of California study. Trans-Action 6:8 F '69
RANSOM
 Ransom for a U.S. ambassador; kidnapping of C. B. Elbrick by Brazilian terrorists. il Time 94:18 S 12 '69
RANSTEAD, Donald D.
 Frei's revolution in suspended animation. Commonweal 90:190-1 My 2 '69
RAO, Raja. See Raja Rao
RAPE
 Return of the phantom; arrest of M. Brookins. il Newsweek 74:24 Jl 14 '69
      See also
 Trials (rape)
RAPER, John R. See Leonard, T. J. jt. auth.
RAPHAEL, Lennox
 Che! Criticism
  Chr Cent 86:1349-50 O 22 '69
  Esquire 72:44+ D '69
  New Repub 160:29-31 Ap 12 '69
  Sat R 52:50 Ap 26 '69
  Time il 93:61 Ap 4 '69

RAPID CITY, S.D.

Water supply

Bitterly opposed wastewater plant. E. Hansen and J. G. Bell. il Am City 84:76-8 Ap '69

RAPID reading. See Speed reading

RAPID transit

Bright year for the rail rapid. il Am City 84:140 Ap '69

Electric solution to the traffic problem: M.I.T.'s guideway system. il Esquire 71:62-7 F '69

Fallacy of free transportation. L. M. Schneider. bibliog f Harvard Bsns R 47:83-7 Ja '69

Mass transit, and frustrated executives. M. F. Brdlik. il Duns R 93:30-3+ F '69

Mass transportation, what works and why. Am City 84:8 D '69

Public transportation users short-changed. Am City 84:150 My '69

Urban transportation tomorrow. J. A. Volpe. il Am City 84:59-62 N '69

See also

Motor buses

Systems analysis in rapid transit

   also subhead Rapid transit under names of cities, e.g. Cleveland—Rapid transit

Federal aid

How to pay for mass transit. Bsns W p72 O 25 '69

This month's feature: Congress and urban mass transportation. Cong Digest 48:289-314 D '69

Finance

Greasing the wheels; trust fund proposal. Newsweek 73:57-8 Je 16 '69

RAPID transit cars. See Railroads—Cars

RAPIDS shooting. See Boats and boating

RAPOPORT, Roger

Listen to the white graduate, you might learn something. Esquire 72:99+ S '69

RAPP, Elaine

Elaine Rapp, stone carver. J. H. Michel. il por Am Artist 33:22-5+ Ja '69

RARE animals

Vanishing wildlife (cont) il Life 66:66-9 F 7; 82-9+ Mr 28; 74-6+ Je 13; 67:54-7 Jl 18; 100-2 S 19 '69

RARE book dealers. See Booksellers and bookselling—Book rarities

RARE books. See Book rarities

RARE earths. See Earths, Rare

RAREY, John Solomon

Man who could talk to horses. T. McCarthy. il por Am Heritage 20:58-9+ Ap '69

Scientific view of Rarey. F. D. Klopfer. Am Heritage 20:89 Ap '69

RARICK, John R.

Soviet penetration of Latin America: address, June 12, 1969. Vital Speeches 35:699-704 S 1 '69

RASCOE, Judith

Mother of good fortune; story. Atlan 223:84-8 Je '69

RASER, John R.

ABM and the MAD strategy. Ramp Mag 8:36-7 N '69

Failure of fail-safe. por Trans-Action 6:11-19 Ja '69

RASH, Bryson B. See Peterson, R. K. jt. auth.

RASH, Charles D.

Junior high students can throw big pots. Ceram Mo 17:22-3 S '69

RASKIN, A. H.

Berkeley, five years later, is radicalized. Reaganized, mesmerized. N Y Times Mag p28-9+ Ja 11 '70

When public servants revolt. Cur 103:27-32 Ja '69

RASKIN, Judith

Opera primer: how does a singer do it? por Opera N 33:28-31 F 22 '69

RASKIN, Lee

Heist a minute. Nation 208:434-6 Ap 7 '69

RASKIN, Marcus G.

Epilogue and a judgment. Ramp Mag 7:97 Ja 25 '69

RASMUSSEN, Dana. See Chapellier, R. jt. auth.

RASMUSSEN, Warren A. See Harmatz, M. G. jt. auth.

RASOOL, S. I.

Venus, star of sweet confidences. Natur Hist 78:52-7+ Je '69

RASPBERRIES

Everbearers, raspberries that laugh at cold. G. Abraham. il Org Gard & Farm 16:44-5 Mr '69

Our ten money-making raspberry bushes. D. Bermes. il Org Gard & Farm 16:70-1 S '69

Raspberries, robins and rascals. K. A. Sullivan. il Org Gard & Farm 16:36-8 O '69

Reliable red raspberries. E. Van Wicklen. il Org Gard & Farm 16:36-8 Ag '69

RASPBERRY, William

Center for black history. Negro Hist Bul 32:21 Mr '69

RASPONI, Lanfranco

Italy: play places. Vogue 153:212-15+ Ap 1 '69

El RASTRO. See Madrid—Markets

RAT cages. See Cages

RAT control

Health help for the ghetto. Bsns W p 124 S 20 '69

News and views: federal rat control money. J. Deedy. Commonweal 89:544 Ja 31 '69

Pied pipers can retire; drug that renders male rats infertile. Sci Digest 66:48 D '69

Rats' alley. il Time 94:40 Ag 15 '69

RATCLIFF, John Drury

City that drowned. Read Digest 94:192-4+ My '69

Greatest skyscraper of them all. Read Digest 95:217-21+ Jl '69

I am Joe's liver. Read Digest 95:81-4 S '69

I am Joe's lung. Read Digest 94:71-4 Mr '69

(ed) See Anderson, H. L. Day the atomic age was born

RATCLIFFE, Bill

Alpine summer. Audubon 71:44-51 Jl '69

Winter marsh: photographs. Audubon 71:37-44 N '69

RATES. See Electric utilities—Rates; Telephone—Rates

RATHBUN, Ben

Labor arbitration: Britain and the U.S. Atlan 223:22+ Ja '69

RATHJENS, George W.

Dynamics of the arms race; with biographical sketch. Sci Am 220:12, 15-25 bibliog(p 146) Ap '69

Is Safeguard worth the risk? Bul Atom Sci 25:23-4 Je '69

RATHMANN, Jim

Keeping the pace. il Motor T 21:33+ Ag '69

RATING. See subhead Rating under various subjects, e.g. Houses—Rating

RATING of teachers. See College professors and instructors—Rating by students

RATING of television programs. See Television broadcasting—Program rating

RATING scales. See Educational tests and measurements

RATIONALISM

See also

Enlightenment

RATIOS, Financial. See Financial ratios

RATS

Amino acid incorporation into rat brain proteins during spreading cortical depression. G. S. Bennett and G. M. Edelman. bibliog il Science 163:393-5 Ja 24 '69

Animals respond for food in the presence of free food. A. J. Neuringer. bibliog il Science 166:399-401 O 17 '69

Central nervous system: recovery of function. D. G. Stein and others. bibliog il Science 166:528-30 O 24 '69

Circadian rhythm of serotonin in the pineal body of immunosympathectomized immature rats. C. R. S. Machado and others. bibliog il Science 164:442-3 Ap 25 '69

Compulsive sexual activity induced by p-chlorophenylalanine in normal and pineal-ectomized male rats. A. Tagliamonte and others. bibliog il Science 166:1433-5 D 12 '69

Cyclophosphamide: effect on experimental allergic encephalomyelitis in Lewis rats. P. Y. Paterson and D. G. Drobish. bibliog il Science 165:191-2 Jl 11 '69

Cytogenetic studies in rats of cyclohexylamine, a metabolite of cyclamate. M. S. Legator and others. bibliog il Science 165:1139-40 S 12 '69

Early experiences accelerate maturation of the 24-hour adrenocortical rhythm. R. Ader. bibliog il Science 163:1225-6 Mr 14 '69

Endocrine control of adrenal progesterone secretion in the ovariectomized rat. J. A. Resko. bibliog il Science 164:70-1 Ap 4 '69

Hyperphagia in rats with cuts between the ventromedial and lateral hypothalamus. D. J. Albert and L. H. Storlien. bibliog il Science 165:599-600 Ag 8 '69

Hypobaric hypoxia: effects on early development of tryptophan oxygenase in neonatal rats. R. P. Francesconi and M. Mager. bibliog il Science 166:1412-13 D 12 '69

Malignant argyrophilic gastric carcinoids of praomys (mastomys) natalensis. K. C. Snell and H. L. Stewart. bibliog il Science 163:470 Ja 31 '69

RATS—*Continued*
Metastasizing mammary carcinomas in rats: induction and study of their immunogenicity. U. Kim. bibliog il Science 167:72-4 Ja 2 '70

Object-carrying by rats: an approach to the behavior produced by brain stimulation. A. G. Phillips and others. bibliog il Science 166:903-5 N 14 '69

Octopamine: normal occurrence in sympathetic nerves of rats. P. Molinoff and J. Axelrod. bibliog il Science 164:428-9 Ap 25 '69

Olfactory stimuli and the pseudo-extinction effect. E. A. Wasserman and D. D. Jensen. bibliog il Science 166:1307-9 D 5 '69

Ontogeny of adrenergic arousal and cholinergic inhibitory mechanisms in the rat. B. A. Campbell and others. bibliog il Science 166:635-7 O 31 '69

Pituitary-adrenal influences on fear responding. J. M. Weiss and others. bibliog il Science 163:197-9 Ja 10 '69

Polymethacrylic acid: effects on lymphocyte output of the thoracic duct in rats. S. Ormai and E. de Clercq. bibliog il Science 163:471-2 Ja 31 '69

Positive contrast in the runway obtained with delay of reward. M. E. Shanab and others. bibliog il Science 164:724-5 My 9 '69

Prolactin in the postpartum rat: synthesis and release in the absence of suckling stimulation. H. Moltz and others. bibliog il Science 163:1083-4 Mr 7 '69

Prostaglandin stimulation of rat corticosteroidogenesis. J. D. Flack and others. bibliog il Science 163:691-2 F 14 '69

Protein digestion in isolated lysosomes inhibited by intralysosomal trypan blue. M. Davies and others. bibliog il Science 163:1454-6 Mr 28 '69

Rat brain: effects of environmental enrichment on wet and dry weights. E. L. Bennett and others. bibliog il Science 163:825-6 F 21 '69

Soluble sulfatase in growing bone of rats. A. Hirschman and M. Hirschman. bibliog il Science 164:834-5 My 16 '69

Stimulus properties of reinforcing brain shock. R. M. Stutz and others. bibliog il Science 163:1081-2 Mr 7 '69

Surgery in the rat during electrical analgesia induced by focal brain stimulation. D. V. Reynolds. bibliog il Science 164:444-5 Ap 25 '69

Unexpected adrenergic effect of chlorpromazine: eating elicited by injection into rat hypothalamus. S. F. Leibowitz and N. E. Miller. bibliog il Science 165:609-11 Ag 8 '69

Unit activity: motivation-dependent responses from midbrain neurons. M. I. Phillips and J. Olds. il Science 165:1269-71 S 19 '69

Vascular smooth muscle reactivity in normotensive and hypertensive rats. S. Spector and others. bibliog il Science 166:1300-1 D 5 '69

Visual stimuli and evoked responses in the rat. C. Fields. bibliog il Science 165:1377-9 S 26 '69
See also
Pack rats

Extermination
See Rat control

RATS as laboratory animals. See Laboratory animals

RATTE, John
Church and the systematization of demonology. Commonweal 89:595-6 F 7 '69

RATTI, John
Statues; poem. Harper 238:90 Mr '69

RATTLESNAKES
Interpreting the rattle snake: Cedar grove, Kings Canyon National Park, Calif. S. F. Arno. il Nat Parks 43:15-17 D '69

Venom neutralization by rattlesnake serum albumin. W. C. Clark and H. K. Voris. bibliog il Science 164:1402-4 Je 20 '69

Why does the rattlesnake rattle? il Sci Digest 66:66-7 O '69

RATTUS natalensis. See Rats

RAUCH, Hans George
Urban individualist. il Arch Forum 130:52-5 Mr '69

RAUCH, Thomas Morton
Is Love the answer? il Forbes 103:25 Je 1 '69

RAUDSEPP, Eugene. See Gattis, M. jt. auth.

RAUP, David M. and Seilacher, Adolf
Fossil foraging behavior: computer simulation. Science 166:994-5 N 21 '69

RAUSCH, Howard
Report. Atlan 223:28+ F '69

RAUSCHENBERG, Robert
Art. L. Alloway. Nation 208:677 My 26 '69
Light conversation. S. Gablik. il por Art N 67:58-60 N '68
Rauschenberg's recent graphics. D. M. Davis. il por Art in Am 57:90-5 Jl '69

RAUSHENBAKH, B. V.
Automatic docking in cosmos and its application to aviation safety and space stations; address, August 14-28, 1968. Bul Atom Sci 25:40-2 Ja '69

RAUTBORD, Clayton Lee
Turning a company around; interview. por Nations Bsns 57:62-3+ Je '69

RAVEL, Maurice
L'heure espagnole. Criticism
New Yorker 45:193-4 N 8 '69
Maurice Ravel, by H. H. Stuckenschmidt. Review
Am Rec G por 35:842-4 My '69. A. Orenstein
Atlan 223:146+ Mr '69. R. Evett
Ravel's world. H. E. Phillips. il pors Opera N 34:8-13 N 1 '69

RAVEN, Peter H. See Ehrlich, P. R. jt. auth.

RAVENHOLT, R. T.
AID's family planning strategy; letter. Science 163:124+ Ja 10 '69

RAVIN, James G. and Hodge, G. P.
Hairy people: hypertrichosis portrayed in art. Sci Digest 66:14-17 S '69

RAWLINS, Wyo.
Rawlins: profile of a railroad town. H. H. Smith. il Am West 6:24-8 My '69

RAWORTH, Tom
Provence; poem. Poetry 113:402-3 Mr '69

RAWSON, R. O. and others
Thermoregulatory responses to intra-abdominal heating of sheep. bibliog Science 165:919-20 Ag 29 '69

RAY, Carleton, and DeCamp, M. A.
Watching seals at Turtle Rock; with biographical sketches. pors Natur Hist 78:4, 26-35 Mr '69

RAY, David
Articulation; poem. Nation 208:123 Ja 27 '69
On resurrection; poem. Nation 208:248 F 24 '69
about
Priceless catch. E. Coleman. Nation 208:345-6 Mr 17 '69

RAY, Ernest
There are monsters in your garden. Am For 75:8-11 D '69

RAY, James Earl
Assassins: who did it, and why? Ray: ninety-nine years and a victory. il Newsweek 73:28-32 Mr 24 '69
Camouflaged killer? il por Newsweek 73:37-8 Mr 17 '69
Case not closed. Nation 208:356 Mr 24 '69
Doctor King's murder: nagging questions remain. il por U S News 66:13 Mr 24 '69
Gambit declined. il por Newsweek 73:38 Je 9 '69
Martin Luther King and the right to know. America 120:323 Mr 22 '69
Raising a whirlwind; Ray plea of guilty. il por Time 93:16-17 Mr 21 '69
Ray admits killing Dr King. por Sr Schol 94:21 Mr 28 '69
Ray changes his mind. Newsweek 73:26-7 Mr 31 '69
Request for a reprise. Time 93:16 Mr 28 '69
Strange case of James Earl Ray, by C. Blair, jr. Review
Ramp Mag 7:50-2 Je '69. W. W. Turner
Whatever happened to the assassins of Kennedy and King? por U S News 67:10 Ag 18 '69
Whole truth. il por Ebony 24:56-7 My '69
Why James Earl Ray murdered Dr King. W. B. Huie; A. J. Hanes; P. Foreman. il por Look 33:102-4+ Ap 15 '69

RAY, John
Cloudburst for Kentucky's Ray of sunshine. J. Underwood. il por Sports Illus 31:56-8+ S 29 '69

RAY, Michèle
In cold blood; how the CIA executed Che. Ramp Mag 7:142-9 Ja 25 '69

RAY, Satyajit
At home in Calcutta. B. Taper. Harper 239:40-2+ D '69

RAYLEIGH radiation
New acoustic devices developed for radar; microsound components based on ultrasonic surface wave propagation. B. M. Elson. il Aviation W 90:85-8+ My 5 '69

RAYMOND, Frank
Camping and self-concept. Camp Mag 41:18 My '69

RAYMOND, Robert
Has the market bottomed out? il por Newsweek 74:49-50+ Ag 11 '69

RAYTHEON company
Raytheon: radar to refrigerators. il Forbes 103:28-32 Je 1 '69

RAYWID, Mary Anne
Irrationalism and the new reformism. Ed Digest 35:5-8 S '69

RAZA movement. See Mexican Americans

RAZAK, Tun Abdul
Rahman to Razak. Newsweek 73:55-6 Je 2 '69

RAZOR blades
New razor edges into the market; chromium-edged blades in England. Bsns W p29 Ag 9 '69
See also
Gillette company
Wilkinson sword, limited

RAZORS
What we learned about electric shavers. E. H. Ortner. il Pop Sci 195:114-17 Jl '69

REACH, James
How to make it big as a writer. Writer 82:27 F '69

REACT (organization)
GM research labs new sponsor of REACT. il Electr World 81:66-7 Je '69
New program in Nebraska. G. H. Reese. il Pop Electr 31:79-80+ N '69
Two-way REACTions. G. H. Reese. See issues of Popular electronics. September 1969-

REACTANCE (electricity)
Reactance chart. Electr World 82:31 N '69
See also
Electric resistance
Impedance (electricity)

REACTION time
Temporal order judgment and reaction time. J. Gibbon and R. Rutschmann. bibliog il Science 165:413-15 Jl 25 '69

REACTOR pressure vessels. See Pressure vessels

REACTORS, Nuclear. See Nuclear reactors

READ, Albert C.
First to fly the Atlantic. B. A. Weisberger. il por Am Heritage 20:18-21+ Je '69

READ, Gerald H.
New policies for Cuban education. Sch & Soc 97:288 Sum '69

READ, Sir Herbert Edward
Necessity of art; excerpt from The arts and man. Sat R 52:24-7 D 6 '69

about
Will to believe. G. Himmelfarb. New Repub 160:26-30 My 10 '69

READ, Leo
Jet boat you can build! Mech Illus 65:76-8 Mr '69

READ, Merrill S.
Malnutrition and learning. Am Ed 5:11-14 D '69

READABILITY. See Printing—Legibility

READER, John
On safari into the past; photographs. Life 67:42-51 S 12 '69

READER, Lawrence J. See Oehmichen, F. jt. auth.

READER Interest. See Newspapers—Reader interest

READERS (books)
Native language; stories and illustrations from a Russian reader for first graders; tr. by E. G. Francis. Todays Ed 58:40-1 N '69

READERS and libraries. See Libraries and readers

READERS digest

Anecdotes, facetiae, satire, etc.
Life in these now United States. R. Angell. New Yorker 45:34-6 Mr 15 '69

READINESS for school
See also
Reading readiness

READING
Right and ability to read; views of J. E. Allen. C. B. Grannis. Pub W 196:40 O 13 '69
Right to read; challenge for local leadership; address, October 3, 1969. J. E. Allen, jr. Vital Speeches 36:42-4 N 1 '69
Target for the 70's: the right to read; excerpts from testimony, before the General subcommittee on education of the U.S. House of representatives committee on education and labor, and discussion, October 1969. J. E. Allen, jr. Am Ed 5:2-4 D '69
See also
Books and reading
Supplementary reading

Aids and devices
See also
Reading laboratories

Readiness
See Reading readiness

Remedial teaching
Is Title 1 worthwhile? remedial reading instruction; Sussex, N.J. junior school. D. M. Callahan. Sr Schol 94:Schol Teach 17 My 2 '69
Let's be practical about reading. C. B. Smith. il Am Ed 5:28-31 Ag '69
Reading program with lay aides and programmed material. C. D. Briscoe. Clear House 43:373-7 F '69
Slow readers can enjoy oral reading. E. Schwartz. Ed Digest 34:36-7 Ja '69
To become good readers. L. Jackson. il Am Ed 5:9-10 D '69
Toward a new understanding of youngsters with reading problems. P. D. Rome. il Parents Mag 44:72-3+ N '69
See also
Speed reading

Special groups of readers
Young militants
Books for the counter-culture. S. Price. bibliog il Library J 94:2193-202 Je 1 '69

Study and teaching
Beginning reading: where do we go from here? excerpts from Learning to read: the great debate. J. Chall. il Todays Ed 58:36-9 F '69; Reply. L. C. Hunt, jr. 58:21-2+ Ap '69
Challenge to teachers of reading. R. G. Strickland. Ed Digest 35:51-4 S '69
Developmental reading in the 60's. A. S. Artley. Ed Digest 34:38-41 Ap '69
Rash of ideas to meet the Nation's reading problem. il U S News 66:74-5 Je 23 '69
Reading problem; advantages of phonic method. M. Smith. Am Scholar 38:431-40 Sum '69
Reading programs; use of test data, a vital factor. W. S. Ames. il Clear House 43:515-18 My '69
Respecting the words of kids. W. Martin. Clear House 43:380-1 F '69
Teaching Johnny to read: breakthrough? Sullivan system. il U S News 66:98-9 F 17 '69
Teaching reading skills in the junior high school. S. M. Carriar. bibliog Engl J 58:1357-61 D '69
What does research in reading reveal about:
Attitudes toward reading? J. R. Squire. bibliog Engl J 58:523-33 Ap '69
Evaluation in reading? P. B. Diederich. bibliog Engl J 58:853-68 S '69
Materials for teaching reading? T. G. Devine. bibliog Engl J 58:847-52 S '69
Practices in teaching reading? C. M. McCullough. bibliog Engl J 58:688-706 My '69
Reading the content fields? W. J. Moore. bibliog Engl J 58:707-18 My '69
Successful reading programs? M. J. Early. bibliog Engl J 58:534-47 Ap '69
What does research in reading reveal; about reading and the high school student? R. Karlin. bibliog Engl J 58:386-95 Mr '69
What does research in reading reveal; about reading and the teacher of English? M. A. Gunn. bibliog Engl J 58:368-85 Mr '69
See also
Reading readiness

Anecdotes, facetiae, satire, etc.
Turning out non-readers; with study-discussion program, ed. by E. Harris and D. Harris. bibliog il PTA Mag 64:6-8, 34-5 S '69

READING, Supplementary. See Supplementary reading

READING air show. See Aviation—Exhibitions

READING aloud. See Books and reading—Reading aloud

READING books. See Readers (books)

READING by children. See Childrens reading

READING comprehension
Reading to learn. M. O. Holt. Clear House 43:267-71 Ja '69
Research on aspects of comprehension. A. J. Harris. Ed Digest 34:48-51 Mr '69
What does research in reading reveal: about evaluation in reading? P. B. Diederich. bibliog Engl J 58:853-68 S '69

READING disability
Dyslexia; what is it? What's being done about it? B. H. Pearse. il Am Ed 5:9-13 Ap '69
Learning disabilities. L. W. Sauer. PTA Mag 64:24 S '69

READING disability—*Continued*
Toward a new understanding of youngsters with reading problems. P. D. Rome. il Parents Mag 44:72-3+ N '69
Visual information processing: early experience; report of meeting. F. A. Young. Science 163:1471-2 Mr 28 '69
See also
Reading—Remedial teaching
READING is FUN-damental program. See Childrens reading
READING laboratories
To become good readers. L. Jackson. il Am Ed 5:9-10 D '69
READING lists
Book marks (cont) G. E. LaRocque. Engl J 58:288-97, 773-84 F, My '69
Book marks. J. W. Conner. Engl J 58:1255-8+, 1378-81+ N-D '69
PA. state education officials sued on ESEA-II administration. Library J 94:2034+ My 15 '69; Discussion. 94:3110+, 3769-70 S 15, O 15 '69
Red ink on green paper; lists and exhibits before the public in December, compared with rest of the year. R. Warncke. il Library J 94:4117 N 15 '69
See also
Books and reading—Best books
Childrens literature—Bibliography
READING of music. See Music reading
READING readiness
Score on early reading; with study discussion program, by R. Strang. B. Bowman and D. Anker. bibliog il PTA Mag 64:6-8, 35 N '69
READING research
Research on aspects of comprehension. A. J. Harris. Ed Digest 34:48-51 Mr '69
READING to children. See Books and reading—Reading aloud
READY, William
Book sale at Cabra. ALA Bul 63:989-91 Jl '69
Leabharlann: the national library of Ireland. por Wilson Lib Bul 43:954-8 Je '69
READY-to-cook food. See Food—Ready-to-cook food
REAGAN, Michael D.
Congress meets science: the appropriations process. bibliog Science 164:926-31 My 23 '69
REAGAN, Ronald
And now, a word from Governor Reagan; excerpts from address, June 13, 1969. N Y Times Mag p22 Je 29 '69
Should youths, or parents, be blamed for unrest? Governor Reagan's answer; excerpts from address, October 14, 1969. por U S News 67:18 O 27 '69
about
California: the rending of the veil. M. Frady. il Harper 239:57-73 D '69
Communist and the governor. A. S. Kaufman. New Repub 162:23-4 Ja 3 '70
Education of Ronald Reagan. R. Y. Keon. Nation 209:302-6 S 29 '69
Reagan on the rise. Newsweek 73:41-2 My 5 '69
Ronnie show. il por Time 93:29 F 14 '69
Two key governors: getting set for '70. il por U S News 67:9+ D 8 '69
REAL estate. See Real property
REAL estate advertising. See Real property—Advertising
REAL estate agents
Unbusted blocks. il Newsweek 74:55 D 1 '69
REAL estate business
Big funds offshore buy into the U.S; real estate from motels to factories. il Bsns W p 128-9+ Mr 22 '69
Big market in land stocks. W. Robertson. il Fortune 80:160+ Jl '69
Black homeowning; Contract buyers league lawsuits for price exploitation. A. Boles. New Repub 161:7-9 D 13 '69
Caroline and Charnita; Justice department suits charge violations of Title VIII of the Civil rights act of 1968. D. Sanford. New Repub 161:12-13 N 8 '69
Cry, Vermont. Time 94:50 S 26 '69
Land deals: new twists, what risks? C. Rice. il Har Yrs 9:18-23 Jl '69
Profits in building well. il Fortune 80:40 Jl '69
Suburbs are changing. W. Langewiesche. il Read Digest 95:157-62+ N '69
Tenneco makes a case for Case. il Bsns W p 166-8 S 13 '69
Thinking of buying some land? new federal laws. D. Sanford. New Repub 161:17-19 O 11 '69
See also
Corporations—Real estate operations
General development corporation

Finance
Real estate gets a new blue chip. il Bsns W p40 D 13 '69
REAL estate investment trusts
Real estate investment trusts. il Changing T 23:6-9 N '69
REAL property
Who owns the beaches? il Time 94:43 Ag 29 '69
See also
Air rights
Building sites
Joint tenancy
Local taxation
Advertising
Charnita bonanza. D. Sanford. New Repub 161:12-14 S 6 '69
Taxation
Property taxes are unfair to farmers. R. Krumme. il Suc Farm 67:27+ N '69
Waiting for the tax dust to settle. Bsns W p34 N 1 '69
Terminology
How to speak real estatese. J. Egan. McCalls 96:98 Ap '69
REAL property and taxation
Those unlevied taxes. Nation 208:619-20 My 19 '69
REAL Russian ikon; story. See Theroux, P.
REAL us; story. See Sterry, R.
REALISM
See also
Materialism
REALISM in art
Ivory garage; Scarpitta's academic realism through abstraction to racing cars. B. H. Friedman. il Art N 68:52-5 Ap '69
Super realism; it's hard to tell a painting from a photograph. il Life 66:44-9 Je 27 '69
Unphotography. il Time 93:80-1 Ap 11 '69
See also
Genre painting
REALISM in literature
Root and measure of realism; modern stories for children. V. L. Wolf. il Wilson Lib Bul 44:409-15 D '69
See also
Sex in literature
REALISM in moving pictures
Film of social reality. H. Alpert. il Sat R 52:43-4 S 6 '69
REALITY
Plastic reality. C. Karpel. il Esquire 72:221-8 D '69
Psychical reality and the theater of fact. H. S. Rollman-Branch. bibliog Am Imago 26:56-70 Spr '69
See also
Existentialism
REALLY? At your age? story. See Robinson, B.
REALS, Lucile Farnsworth
Antique dealers as educators. Hobbies 74:98EE Je '69
Porcelain and pottery animals. Hobbies 74:98N N '69
REANEY, James
Four emblem poems: Egypt; Farm; Within within; Free. Poetry 115:149-53 D '69
REAPPORTIONMENT. See Apportionment (election law)
REARDEN, Jim
Salmon do their own counting. por Outdoor Life 143:16-17+ Mr '69
REARDON, John Paul
Cloisonne or mosaic? il Design 70:32 Spr '69
REARDON, Paul Cashman
Men who may decide Kennedy's fate. por U S News 67:18 S 15 '69
REASONER, Harry
Man behind Harry. il Time 94:68 Jl 11 '69
Merry magazines. il Time 93:86 Ap 11 '69
REASONING
See also
Fallacies (logic)
Problem solving
REAUGH, Wanda
Traditional in one home; 100 Christmas trees. Hobbies 74:154-5 D '69
REAVLEY, William L.
Public rights vs. stockmen's rights. Nat Wildlife 7:40-1 Je '69
REAY, Devon
Jerusalem artichoke, America's oldest vegetable. Org Gard & Farm 16:102-3 Ja '69
What's cooking? Org Gard & Farm 16:24-7 Mr '69
REBEKAH Harkness foundation dance festival. See Dance festivals
REBELLIONS. See Revolutions
REBENNACK, Malcolm
Voodoo rock. M. Kasindorf. por Newsweek 73:93-4 Je 30 '69

REBUILT airplanes. See Airplanes, Remodeled
RECALL (psychology)
Retrograde amnesia in free recall. E. Tulving. bibliog il Science 164:88-90 Ap 4 '69
RECEPTIONS
Sky-high cost of hotel weddings. P. Battelle. il McCalls 96:54+ Je '69
RECEPTORS, Retinal. See Retina
RECESSION, Business. See Business depression
RECHTER, Anne
Tourist in Indonesia. Dance Mag 43:23-4 S '69
RECHY, John
GIs for peace. Nation 210:8-12 Ja 12 '70
RECIPE testing. See Cookery—Testing
RECIPES. See Cookery
RECIPROCATING engines (automobile) See Automobile engines
RECIPROCITY
Reciprocity: a dangerous game. Bsns W p 121 Je 21 '69
Small triumph for trade relations. Bsns W p21-2 Ag 30 '69
RECK, Tom S.
Come out of the shower, and come out clean. Commonweal 90:588-91 S 26 '69
Graduate reclassified. Commonweal 90:202-4 My 2 '69
RECKONING; drama. See Ward, D. T.
RECLAMATION, Bureau of. See United States —Reclamation, Bureau of
RECLAMATION of land
25,000 trees reclaim land; tree-planting program in Minnesota. C. Vindex. il Org Gard & Farm 16:57-9 Ja '69
See also
Deserts
Land utilization
United States—Reclamation, Bureau of
RECLASSIFICATION. See Classification
RECLUSES
See also
Collyer brothers
RECOGNITION (international law)
Open door policy for red China, pro and con. Nations Bsns 57:81-2 Ag '69
RECOGNITION (psychology)
Chimpanzees: self-recognition. G. G. Gallup, jr. il Science 167:86-7 Ja 2 '70
See also
Recall (psychology)
RECOGNITION equipment, Incorporated
Most fleeting asset; stock-market value. il Forbes 103:84-5 Je 15 '69
RECOLLECTION (psychology) See Recall (psychology)
RECOMBINATION of genes. See Crossing over (genetics)
RECONCILIATION
Churchmen debate farewell to arms. C. Bunce. Chr Today 14:47 O 24 '69
RECONCILIATION; story. See Moravia, A.
RECONNAISSANCE satellites. See Artificial satellites—Military applications
RECONSTRUCTION (Civil war)
Du Bois as historian. H. Aptheker. bibliog il Negro Hist Bul 32:6-16 Ap '69
Political strategies of the reconstruction. R. Walters. bibliog f Cur Hist 57:263-8+ N '69
RECONSTRUCTION (World war, 1939-1945)
See also
Albert Lea, Minn.
RECORD changers. See Phonograph—Record changers
RECORD photography. See Photography, Documentary
RECORD players. See Phonograph
RECORDING for the blind, Incorporated
Time for giving. il Good H 169:38+ N '69
RECORDING instruments
Electron beam recorder developed. B. M. Elson. il Aviation W 91:91+ S 22 '69
See also
Magnetic recorders and recording
RECORDING studios. See Sound—Recording and reproducing
RECORDS
See also
Fishing records
Sports records
Weather records
RECORDS, Phonograph. See Phonograph records
RECORDS, Preservation of
Bringing in the ancestors; family record vaults in Little Cottonwood Canyon. il Time 94:52 Ag 22 '69
Do you have a safe-deposit box? Do you use it right? il Changing T 23:35-9 My '69
See also
Archives
Civilization—Preservation of records

RECREATION
Jingle bells! Jingle bells! Jingle all the way! il Bet Hom & Gard 47:30-3 D '69
Recreation demand from wharf to waterfall. E. L. Shafer. bibliog f il Parks & Rec 4:18-20+ Ag '69
See also
Amusements
Childrens amusements
Festivity
Industrial recreation
Leisure
Outdoor life
Parks
Physical education and training
Play
Problem children—Recreation
Walking
Winter sports

Activities
Clown Alley; Lubbock, Tex; offers classes in clowning. L. Witcher. il Parks & Rec 4:37+ F '69
Do-it-yourself coffeehouses. J. Little. il Parks & Rec 4:37-8+ Mr '69
Recreation enrichment classes; program for grade schoolers in Pasadena. E. E. Bignell. il Parks & Rec 3:43 O '68
Urban recreation problems. J. A. Madison. il Parks & Rec 3:14-16 D '68
Weaving as a creative art; Baltimore recreation department program. V. M. West. il Parks & Rec 3:41-2+ O '68
See also
Boats and boating
Camping—Activities
Horsemanship
Music as recreation
Picnics
Recreation for the handicapped
Tennis

Administration
Across state lines; Lewiston, Idaho, and Clarkston, Wash. S. W. Bly. il Parks & Rec 4:41+ F '69
City-county merger in Kentucky; Louisville and Jefferson County combine park and recreation operations. C. Vettiner. il Parks & Rec 3:22-4+ O '68
Contact hour unit, new tool for outdoor recreation planning. L. L. Suhm. il Parks & Rec 4:33-4+ O '69
County government. J. E. Arles. Parks & Rec 4:30-2+ Ag '69
Evaluation of park and recreation operations, who should do it? A. V. Sapora. bibliog il Parks & Rec 4:35-6+ D '69
Four short months, summer '69 will be here. Parks & Rec 4:15 F '69
National forum; park and recreation standards. il Parks & Rec 4:39-46 Mr '69
Teenagers given voice in local affairs; Placentia, Calif. R. R. Samp and T. G. Bond. il Parks & Rec 4:35+ My '69

Aims and objectives
Case for compensatory recreation. D. E. Gray. Parks & Rec 4:23-4+ Ap '69
National forum; park and recreation standards. il Parks & Rec 4:39-46 Mr '69
Problem of responsibility for recreation. R. F. Paige. il Parks & Rec 4:27-8+ O '69

Awards, prizes, etc.
Gold medal for Phoenix. G. L. Gardner. il Parks & Rec 4:24-8 My '69
National awards recipients demonstrate public service. il Parks & Rec 4:24-6 N '69

Economic aspects
Fun part of the cost of living. M. Feeley. Am Home 72:10+ Mr '69
Making money in recreation. B. T. Wilkins and H. B. Brumsted. il Cons 24:18-21 D '69

Equipment and supplies
Cavalcade of mobile fun. L. Schreiner. il Parks & Rec 4:50-1 My '69
Many new products featured at 1968 congress in Seattle. Parks & Rec 3:25-6 O '68
Quick delivery. I. O. Spellman. il Parks & Rec 4:23+ Ag '69

Federal aid
Taking the fun out of fun. il Newsweek 74:56 Jl 28 '69

Finance
Economic advantages of parklands to a community; excerpts from address. S. J. Prezioso. Parks & Rec 3:27+ O '68
Financing outdoor recreation; excerpt from address. R. W. Porter. Parks & Rec 4:23+ N '69
Foundation support for park and recreation funding. Parks & Rec 4:40+ O '69

RECREATION—Finance—*Continued*
Million-dollar ideas, for park and recreation
departments. C. H. Odegaard. Parks & Rec
3:21+ O '68
National forum; new approaches to financ-
ing parks and recreation. il Parks & Rec 4:
33-40 Ag '69
New recreation complex results from over-
throwing old taboos; Northbrook, Ill. J.
Doud. il Am City 84:100+ Mr '69
  See also
Recreation—Federal aid

Study and teaching

Recreation education; for white or black
America. J. F. Murphy. bibliog f il Parks &
Rec 4:28-9+ Ag '69

Great Britain

Britain's elegant sports centers. D. Tollefsen.
il Parks & Rec 4:16-19+ F '69

Russia

Discovering the weekend in Russia. il Time
93:73 My 9 '69

United States

MERBISC: unique recreation bargain; most
extraordinary recreation bargain in south-
ern California. R. C. Taylor. il Parks & Rec
4:35-8 Ap '69
Puzzle of outdoor recreation. S. G. Ernst.
il Cons 23:17-19+ Je '69
Recreation planning in the technological
age; address. May 1968. H. C. Davis. bibliog
f Parks & Rec 3:22-4+ N '68
  See also
Automobile touring—United States
National recreation and park association
Recreation, Rural
Recreation centers
Sports—United States
United States—Army—Recreation
  also subhead Recreation under names of
cities, e.g. Louisville—Recreation

RECREATION, Rural
County's responsibilities for recreation. H. T.
Ball. Parks & Rec 3:35-6+ O '68

RECREATION areas
Appraisal of recreation standards. A. H.
Mittelstaedt and others. il Parks & Rec 4:
20-2+ Jl '69
Fishing and boating the Land between.
F. M. Paulson. il Field & S 74:36-9+ Jl '69
Hells Canyon-Snake National River? C. M.
Slansky. il Nat Parks 43:18-20 Ag '69
New lakes: the beautiful and the dammed.
H. R. Williams. il Parks & Rec 4:12-14+ N
'69
Vacation between the lakes: Land between
the lakes. R. Bugg. il Todays Health 47:
34-9 Ag '69
  See also
Parks

Lighting

Good lighting can relieve the recreation
crush. il Am City 84:96+ Mr '69
Lighting adds thrills to a toboggan chute. O.
D. Graham. il Am City 84:124 Ag '69

Alaska

Students involved in project at foot of Mendenhall glacier. F. Oehmichen and L. J.
Reader. il Parks & Rec 4:50-2 S '69

California

King besieged. J. Hope; discussion. Natur
Hist 78:68+ Ja '69
Mineral King, a golden opportunity. W. E.
Towell. il Am For 75:36+ Ap '69
Mineral king, go or no go? R. Leadabrand.
il Am For 75:32-5+ O '69
Mom vs. apple pie; Sierra club opposes
Disney's proposed Alpine village. il News-
week 73:25 F 10 '69
Protectionists vs. recreationists; the battle
of Mineral King. A. Hano. il N Y Times
Mag p24-5+ Ag 17 '69; Discussion. p79+
S 14 '69
Sequoia, looking toward the King; proposal
to add Mineral King to Sequoia National
Park. P. L. Nelson and R. C. Eckhardt. il
Nat Parks 43:10-14 D '69
Storm over Alps; lawsuit threatened against
Disney organization by Sierra club. il Sr
Schol 94:17 F 14 '69
To guard and preserve? Or open and enjoy?
proposed Mineral King village. il Time
93:17 F 7 '69

New York (state)

Kinzua Lake development. J. J. Lindsey. il
Cons 23:2-5 Ap '69

RECREATION buildings
New building designs for park, recreation and
camping areas. il Parks & Rec 4:38-9 My
'69

RECREATION centers
1876 art gallery revitalized: Memorial hall
recreation center. H. Schick. il Parks & Rec
4:38-9 Jl '69
Low-cost recreation centers: one design does
triple duty. C. Campbell. il Parks & Rec
3:16-17 N '68
New pool helps keep city cool; Newark, N.J.
il Am City 84:36 D '69
Sports center for bow, rod and gun enthusiasts; Westchester County, N.Y. C. E.
Pound. il Parks & Rec 4:25-7 D '69
  See also
Cultural centers
Recreation areas

Equipment

All-electric recreation center. C. M. Graves.
Parks & Rec 4:36-7 My '69

RECREATION clubs. See Clubs
RECREATION conferences
Coming events. See issues of Parks & recrea-
tion
  See also
Congress for recreation and parks
RECREATION consultants
Consultants, guidelines for selection. R. D.
Buechner. il Parks & Rec 4:54+ S '69
RECREATION education. See Recreation—
Study and teaching; Recreation workers—
Training
RECREATION for the aged
Grandma's gone to camp! day camp program
in Seattle. A. Lovell and A. Ransford. il
Parks & Rec 3:15 N '68
High-diving grandma. D. Bopf. Har Yrs 9:43
Je '69
Rochester senior citizens love life; Danforth
center. J. M. Caverly. il Parks & Rec 4:15+
N '69
Two experts view camping for older adults.
M. M. Glascock and E. A. Scholer. Camp
Mag 41:15-16 Mr '69
Volunteer-powered recreation for geriatric
patients. R. H. Burrill. Ment Hy 53:389-92
Jl '69
RECREATION for the blind
Touch and see; nature trail at the National
arboretum, Washington, D.C. J. M. Gar-
vey. il Parks & Rec 4:20-2 N '69
Unique recreationist: J. McCraw is blind but
far from handicapped. D. Samuels. il Parks
& Rec 4:35+ Jl '69
  See also
Sports for the blind
RECREATION for the handicapped
Expanding program services; activities for
handicapped children. R. E. Shipp. il Parks
& Rec 3:43-4+ N '68
Soap box derby, Southbury style. J. Zakrzew-
ski il Parks & Rec 3:37-8 O '68
  See also
Recreation for the blind
RECREATION for women
Recreational activities that are fun for
women. Good H 168:196-7 Mr '69
RECREATION for youth. See Youth—Recrea-
tion
RECREATION in church work
Recreation and the church. Parks & Rec
4:11 D '69
RECREATION research
Researcher and practitioner, they must com-
municate. D. D. Henkel. Parks & Rec 4:26+
Jl '69
RECREATION workers
As I see it. A. Sansom. il Parks & Rec 4:68+
S '69
National personnel inventory created. S. G.
Lutzin. Parks & Rec 4:35-8 Ja '69
NRPA's personal security program. D. D.
Magee. il Parks & Rec 4:73-4 S '69
People. See issues of Parks & recreation
Recreation interns. il Parks & Rec 3:48 N '68
Survey of retired recreation and park pro-
fessionals: statistics and advice. G. D. But-
ler. il Parks & Rec 4:21-5+ Je '69
Unique recreationist: J. McCraw is blind
but far from handicapped. D. Samuels. il
Parks & Rec 4:35+ Jl '69

Recruiting

Manpower muddle. T. L. Goodale. il Parks
& Rec 4:27-30+ F '69

Salaries, allowances, etc.

NRPA acts on salary structures; minimum
entry salary. S. G. Lutzin. Parks & Rec 4:
47+ Mr '69

Supply and demand

Associate professional recreation programs.
P. J. Verhoven. Parks & Rec 4:28-30+ Ap
'69

RECREATION workers—*Continued*

Training

Associate professional recreation programs. P. J. Verhoven. Parks & Rec 4:28-30+ Ap '69

Britain's elegant sports centers. D. Tollefsen. il Parks & Rec 4:16-19+ F '69

National internship program expanding. Parks & Rec 4:33 F '69

University training for park administrators. L. M. Reid. Parks & Rec 3:25-7+ D '68

RECREATIONAL vehicle industry. See Automobile industry and trade

RECRUITING agencies. See Employment agencies

RECRUITING and enlistment. See United States—Army—Recruiting and enlistment

RECRUITING for business and industry. See Employment systems

RECRUITING for librarianship. See Librarians—Recruiting

RECRUITING of teachers. See Teachers—Recruiting

RECRUITS, Examination of. See United States—Army—Physical examinations

RECTIFIERS. See Electric current rectifiers

RED blood cells. See Blood—Corpuscles and platelets

RED BLUFF, Calif.
Victorians in Red Bluff, on tour and on display. il Sunset 143:52+ S '69

RED clay. See Clay

RED cross
International conference of the Red cross calls for observance of the Geneva convention on prisoners of war; statement, with text of resolution. G. Martin. Dept State Bul 61:323-5 O 13 '69

Red cross insulted; ICRC plane shot down by Nigerian government. America 121:27-8 Jl 19 '69

Ultimate weapon; Nigeria's move against Biafran aid activities. il Newsweek 74:36 Jl 14 '69

U.S. pledges additional $6 million to ICRC for Nigerian relief. Dept State Bul 60:281 Mr 31 '69
See also
Nigerian—Civil war, 1967- —Relief work

RED flower; story. See Díaz de León. M.

RED guard. See Youth movement—China (People's Republic)

RED hair. See Hair

RED RIVER
Daniel Boone's river; Red River gorge saved from submersion. il Time 93:28 Ap 11 '69
Victory in the Red River gorge, and a time for real planning. Audubon 71:4-5 My '69

RED SEA
Red Sea floor origin: rare-earth evidence. J. G. Schilling. bibliog il Science 165:1357-60 S 26 '69

RED tape. See Bureaucracy

RED, white and Maddox; musical comedy. See Musical comedies, revues, etc.—Criticisms, plots, etc.

RED Wings (hockey team) See Hockey teams

REDBOOK magazine
We're looking for real writers. N. G. Stuart. Writer 82:25-7 D '69

REDDIG, William M. Jr
New multinational managers. Sat R 52:35-6+ N 22 '69

REDDIN, Thomas J.
Chief Reddin, new style at the top. L. M. Mathews. il por Atlan 223:84-6+ Mr '69
Cop out in L.A. Newsweek 73:58+ Ap 21 '69
From chief of police to chief pontificator. por Time 93:24 Ap 18 '69
$100,000 anchorman. Time 93:98 My 16 '69

REDDING, Saunders
Black youth movement. Am Scholar 38:584-7 Aut '69

REDDY, John
Arthur Clarke: prophet of the space age. Read Digest 94:134-6+ Ap '69
Man who put the top hat on jazz. Read Digest 95:108-12 N '69
Ted Williams: a legend returns to baseball. Read Digest 95:201-4+ Jl '69
Unflappable Walter Cronkite Read Digest 95: 193-4+ D '69

REDEMPTION. See Salvation

REDEVELOPMENT programs. See Economic assistance, Domestic

REDFIELD, Alfred G.
Nuclear spin thermodynamics in the rotating frame. bibliog il Science 164:1015-23 My 30 '69

REDFIELD, Peter
Last shall be first. por Forbes 104:47 Jl 1 '69

REDFIELD, William
Is your heart in your voice? Vogue 154:180-1+ N 1 '69

REDFORD, Robert
How to succeed at racing without really racing. D. Jenkins. il por Sports Illus 31; 66 N 24 '69
When things come together. il pors Time 94:75 D 12 '69

REDHEADS. See Ducks, Wild

REDL, Fritz
Aggression in the classroom; excerpts from address. Todays Ed 58:30-2 S '69; Same abr. Ed Digest 35:5-8 N '69

REDLANDS university, Redlands, Calif
Mini-semester at Redlands; offering new experimental courses. il Sch & Soc 97:144+ Mr '69
New Eden; Johnston college at University of Redlands. il Time 94:45-7 O 3 '69

REDLICH, Don
Don Redlich dance company. D. Hering. Dance Mag 43:92 Ap '69
Reacher: Don Redlich. G. A. Peterson. il pors Dance Mag 43:60-3 Je '69

REDMOND, James Francis
Why the government is threatening to sue Chicago. Time 94:15 Jl 18 '69

REDSKINS (football club) See Football clubs

REDSOD (repetitive explosive device for soil displacement) See Bulldozers (machines)

REDUCING. See Corpulence

REDUCING diet. See Diet

REDUCING exercises. See Exercise

REDUCTASES
Light and hormones: interchangeability in the induction of nitrate reductase. S. H. Lips and N. Roth-Bejerano. bibliog il Science 166:109-10 O '69
Polyol pathway in aorta: regulation by hormones. R. S. Clements, jr. and others. bibliog il Science 166:1007-8 N 21 '69

REDUCTION of armaments. See Disarmament

REDWOOD
Redwood forest as seen in plant prints. I. Geary. il Audubon 71:52-7 Jl '69
Redwoods, wonders of the world. N. B. Drury. il Am For 75:24-7+ S '69
See also
Sequoia, Giant

REDWOOD NATIONAL PARK
Last battle of the redwoods M. McCloskey. il Am West 6:55-64 S '69
Looking ahead in California's coast redwoods. D. Anderson. il Nat Parks 43:4-8 Ag '69
New Redwood National Park is not the victory it may yet become. il Sunset 142:90-1 My '69

REED, David
Bourguiba; wise voice of the Arab world. Read Digest 94:175-6+ Je '69
Countdown on Okinawa. Read Digest 95: 117-21 N '69
Nation is dying! Read Digest 94:75-80 Mr '69

REED, Harold J.
Entering the world of work. PTA Mag 63: 8-10 bibliog(p36) Ap '69

REED, J. D.
Five poems: Reports come in; WPA; Weather is brought to you; Lost silvertip; Pigs. New Yorker 45:38 Jl 12 '69

REED, John, 1887-1920
Troubadour of revolution. E. Bendiner. Nation 208:832-3 Je 30 '69

REED, Kit
Weddings; story. Ladies Home J 88:100-1 N '69

REED, Lena F.
There's gold in the fine print. Writers Digest 49:51-3 F '69

REED, Oliver
Real modern artist of our time. E. Miller. il pors Seventeen 27:98-9+ D '68

REED, R. I. and Robertson, D. H.
Mass spectrometry. bibliog pors Chem 42:7-11 Je; 11-15 S '69

REED, Rex
At the movies. See issues of Holiday
Last night at Joe's place. Esquire 72:106+ O '69
Welcome to Malibu! Holiday 45:34-7+ My '69

REED, T. Edward
Caucasian genes in American Negroes. bibliog Science 165:762-8; 166:1353 Ag 22, D 12 '69

REED, Watford
Maxi learning from mini courses. Sr Schol 94:Schol Teach 10+ Mr 7 '69

REED, William F. Jr
College basketball (cont) Sports Illus 30:62+ Mr 24; 50-1 Mr 31 '69

REED, William F. Jr—*Continued*
Football's week. Sports Illus 31:58+ S 29;
51+ O 13; 59-60+ O 20; 51-2+ O 27; 54+
N 10; 79-80+ N 17; 51-2+ N 24; 50+ D 8 '69
Harness racing. Sports Illus 30:64-5 Je 16;
31:46 Jl 14; 40-1 Jl 28; 46+ Ag 11; 60+ S
8; 70+ S 29 '69
Horse racing. Sports Illus 31:86+ S 22 '69
Pro basketball. Sports Illus 30:60-2 Ap 28 '69
Swimming. Sports Illus 30:53-5 Mr 24; 67-8+
Ap 7 '69
Warmup for the Canyon run. Sports Illus 30:
16-19 Ja 27 '69

REED boats. See Boats—Materials

REED organ. See Organ

REEF coral. See Corals

REEFS
See also
Coral reefs and islands

REES, Albert
Geographic wage patterns in the Chicago labor market; excerpt from Spatial wage differentials in a large city market. Mo Labor
R 92:53-5 Mr '69

REES, Clair F.
Carry a blind on your back. Field & S 74:
56-7+ S '69

REES, Paul S.
Four Easters. Chr Today 13:3-5 Mr 28 '69

REESE, G. H.
Two-way REACTions. See issues of Popular
electronics, September, 1969-

REEVE, F. D.
Seaside crucifix; Hands; poems. Poetry 115:
34-5 O '69
Verse chronicle. Poetry 115:61-6 O '69

REEVES, Richard
Here comes the next mayor. N Y Times Mag
p25-7+ N 2 '69
Lindsay tries to stay in there, while . . .
N Y Times Mag p7-9+ Je 15 '69
Mike Lang (groovy kid from Brooklyn) plus
John Roberts (unlimited capital) equals
Woodstock. N Y Times Mag p34-5+ S 7 '69

REEVES, Rosser
Annals of television. T. Whiteside. New
Yorker 45:47-50+ S 27 '69
Getting them to church. A. Cooper. il News-
week 74:113 O 6 '69

REFERENCE books
How to make the most of your public li-
brary. J. Herbert. House & Gard 135:50+
Ap '69
See also
Encyclopedias
Publishers and publishing—Reference books

Bibliography
Current reference books. F. N. Cheney. See
issues of Wilson library bulletin
For personal reference; writer's bookshelf.
P. A. Whitney. Writer 82:23-6 F '69
Is that a fact? paperback fact books for a
business library. S. Mechanic. il Library
J 94:960-1 Mr 1 '69
Library reference sources. J. Cannon. il
Writers Digest 49:46-7 F '69
Reference books of 1968; recommendations
of a committee of the Reference services
division of ALA. M. Smart. il Library J
94:1579-84 Ap 15 '69
Reference roundup. Sr Schol 94:Schol Teach
9-10+ Mr 28 '69
SR's semi-annual reference book roundup.
D. M. Glixon. il Sat R 52:31-2+ My 17; 45-
6+ D 6 '69

REFERENDUM
France rejects de Gaulle. Time 93:20-1 My
2 '69
French referendum: the mask of de Gaulle;
proposed reforms. C. Bourdet. Nation 208:
526-9 Ap 28 '69
Park stacks the cards; referendum on con-
stitutional amendment, South Korea. il
Newsweek 74:58 O 27 '69
Too close for comfort; French proposals.
Newsweek 73:54+ Ap 28 '69
Town that voted yes for justice. M. A.
Rodgers. Good H 168:67+ F '69

REFINERIES. See Petroleum refineries

REFINISHING furniture. See Furniture—Finishing

REFLECTION spectra. See Spectrum—Reflection spectra

REFLECTORS
See also
Prisms

REFLECTORS (photography) See Photography
—Apparatus and supplies

REFLEXES
See also
Reinforcement (psychology)

REFORM
See also
Prisons
Social problems

REFORM of criminals. See Probation system

REFORM of Sterling Silverheart; drama. See
Cable, H.

REFORMATION
Reformation and revolution: the maturing
East German view. C. R. Foster, jr. Chr
Cent 86:1380-2 O 29 '69
Rome and reformation today. H. O. J. Brown.
Chr Today 14:3-5 O 24 '69

REFORMATORIES
Realism in community-based correctional
services. M. Burdman. bibliog f Ann Am
Acad 381:71-80 Ja '69
Rise of the child-saving movement; a study
in social policy and correctional reform;
excerpt from The child-savers; the inven-
tion of delinquency. A. Platt. bibliog f Ann
Am Acad 381:21-38 Ja '69
See also
Childrens village, Dobbs Ferry, N.Y.

Recreation
See Prison recreation

REFORMED church in America
After bitter debates, the positive thinker. J.
Huffman. Chr Today 13:46-6 Jl 4 '69
Example of lay power; verdict on RCA-PCUS
merger. Chr Today 13:28 Ap 11 '69
Reformed church rejects merger. Chr Today
13:48-9 Ap 11 '69

REFORMED Presbyterian church
Soft answers at Lookout Mountain. Chr To-
day 13:31 Je 20 '69
See also
Associate reformed Presbyterian church

REFRACTING telescope. See Telescope

REFRACTION
Isaac Asimov explains; refraction vs diffraction. I. Asimov. Sci Digest 66:74-5 Jl
'69

REFRACTOMETERS
Analytic instruments in process control. F.
W. Karasek. il Sci Am 220:112-20 Je '69

REFRACTORIES. See Refractory materials

REFRACTORIES industry
Superheated world of refractories. il Duns R
94:113-14+ N '69

REFRACTORY materials
Superheated world of refractories. il Duns R
94:113-14+ N '69

REFRIGERATED cargo containers. See Containers for shipping

REFRIGERATION and refrigerating machinery
New methods for approaching absolute zero.
O. V. Lounasmaa. il Sci Am 221:26-35 bib-
liog(p 152) D '69

REFRIGERATORS, Electric
Buyers guide to refrigerators. S. Schuler. il
Am Home 72:38+ Jl '69
Mini-refrigerators. il McCalls 96:129 Je '69
No-frost side-by-side refrigerator-freezers. il
Consumer Rep 34:573-81 O '69
No-frost, top-freezer refrigerators. il Con-
sumer Rep 34:496-503 S '69
Problem-solving appliances. il Bet Hom &
Gard 47:16+ Ap '69

Care
Care and safekeeping of refrigerators and
freezers. House & Gard 135:194-5 Ap '69

REFUGEES, Arab
Lasting Middle East peace? The need for
double vision. I. F. Stone. Cur 105:54-6 Mr
'69
Mission to the Middle East; the work of
the Pontificial mission for Palestine and
UNRWA. V. S. Kearney. America 120:495-8
Ap 26 '69
Real Mideast problem; life in a refugee
camp and Israeli occupation in Jordan.
J. Law and A. Kucherov. il U S News 66:
36-8 F 10 '69
Revolt of the Arab refugees: we'll meet in
Tel Aviv! C. S. Wren. il Look 33:27-36 My
13 '69
U.S. reaffirms concern for Near East refugees;
exchange of telegrams between Secretary
Rusk and the executive committee, Near
East emergency donations. D. Rusk. Dept
State Bul 59:662 D 23 '68
U.S. supports continuation of aid to Near
East refugees; statement, November 18,
1968. J. R. Wiggins. Dept State Bul 59:677-9
D 23 '68
View from the UN. G. Stevens. Atlan 224:
10+ S '69
See also
United Nations relief and works agency for
Palestine refugees in the Near East

REFUGEES, Chinese
China. H. Yu. Chr Cent 86:430 Mr 26 '69
Long road from China; escapes from the
border of Kwantung to the New Territor-
ies. R. C. C. Wu. Nat R 21:806 Ag 12 '69
REFUGEES, Cuban
Cubans take off on SBA test run. il Bsns W
p41 Je 21 '69
Eighty-eight got away. Nat R 21:60 Ja 28 '69
How a Cuban MIG sneaked into U.S. il
U S News 67:17 O 20 '69
News and views; Small business administra-
tion backing Cuban refugee merchants.
J. Deedy. Commonweal 89:574 F 7 '69
Truck that fled Cuba. W. Schulz. il Read
Digest 95:98-103 Jl '69
Whatever happened to the Cuban airlifts. il
U S News 67:6 Jl 28 '69
REFUGEES, Czech
Danube blues. il Newsweek 74:44 S 15 '69
Step in the darkness; Czechoslovak tourists
applying for political asylum in Sweden.
Time 95:28 Ja 5 '70
Warm welcome in a New England town. N.
M. Lobsenz. Good H 168:81+ My '69
REFUGEES, European
People-smuggling. il Time 93:27 Ja 31 '69
REFUGEES, Jewish
Paper walls; America and the refugee crisis
1938-1941, by D. S. Wyman. Review
New Repub 160:25-6 F 15 '69. S. Adler
REFUGEES, Nigerian
Moon over Owerri. N. Cousins. Sat R 52:16+
Ag 2 '69
REFUGEES, Palestinian. See Refugees, Arab
REFUGEES, Political
See also
Émigrés
REFUGES, Bird. See Bird sanctuaries
REFUSE, Utilization of
Building with garbage. il Mech Illus 65:74-5
F '69
What can you do with an avalanche of gar-
bage? K. A. Kovaly. il Sci Digest 66:70-3 Jl
'69
See also
Filling (earthwork)
Refuse as fertilizer
REFUSE and refuse disposal
Bigger cities pay more for refuse collection.
Am City 84:34 Je '69
City and county should share solid-waste
responsibilities. Am City 84:45+ S '69
Considerable advantages of one-man refuse
collection; Inglewood, Calif. W. F. Farnam.
il Am City 84:97-8 Ap '69
Digging out from under; problems of solid
waste disposal. E. Gross. il Sci N 96:278-9
S 27 '69
Epic of garbage. F. Trippett. Look 33:66 N
4 '69
For more efficient refuse collection; try ana-
lyzing your system with a mathematical
model. R. Stone and R. Stearns. il Am City
84:98-100 My '69
Garbage can crisis. il Life 67:32-7 N 7 '69
Garbage explosion; recycling and other
methods; with editorial comment. C. A.
Schweighauser. il Nation 209:268, 282-4 S
22 '69
Garbage, or, Can we ever get away from it
all. R. Starr. il Horizon 11:48-51 Wint '69
Getting rid of trash and garbage. il McCalls
96:38 Mr '69
How to dispose of bulky wastes; with tables.
J. J. Baffa and N. Bartilucci. Am City 84:
64-6+ N '69
Land pollution; a heap of trouble. il Sr
Schol 95:10-11 O 27 '69
No deposit, no return; report of First Na-
tional packaging wastes conference. R. R.
Grinstead. il Environ 11:17-23 N '69
Pollution goes underground. D. M. Evans.
Nation 209:632-5 D 8 '69
Pullman's plan to export garbage. Bsns W
p38+ Ja 10 '70
Refuse collection & disposal. See issues of
American city
Summary of state laws governing watercraft
waste disposal. Motor B 123:270-1 Ja '69
Those litter bits can hurt less. Nations Bsns
57:16 D '69
War that's looming on trash. Bsns W p 148
N 8 '69
Why the U.S. is in danger of being engulfed
by its trash. il U S News 67:64-6 S 8 '69
See also
Cleaning of cities, towns, etc.
Municipal dumps
Radioactive waste disposal
Refuse collection trucks
Refuse grinders
Refuse incinerators
Refuse receptacles

Street cleaning
Trade waste disposal
Water pollution
Apparatus
Comminutors chew up bulky items. Am City
84:24 Ja '69
Statistics
Less refuse from multi-family dwellings;
Santa Clara County, Calif. Am City 84:16 N
'69
REFUSE as fertilizer
Announcing: compost that's not for sale. J.
Olds; discussion. Org Gard & Farm 16:76-
8 Ja '69
Garbage as you like it, by J. Goldstein. Re-
view
Am For 75:48-9 D '69. M. Bush
Linking the farms and cities; use of city
wastes on country soils. J. Olds. Org Gard
& Farm 16:79-80 My '69
Practical data on composting; Gainesville, Fla.
il Am City 84:84+ Mr '69
See also
Compost
REFUSE bags. See Refuse receptacles
REFUSE collection. See Refuse and refuse dis-
posal
REFUSE collection trucks
Barrel dumper speeds litter collection; Wash-
ington state. il Am City 84:58 My '69
REFUSE containers. See Refuse receptacles
REFUSE grinders
Down with garbage! or, How a disposer
puts an end to the garbage problem. il
Good H 169:172 Jl '69
If you were Woody Allen, what would you
do with all that garbage? il Redbook 133:
88-9+ Je '69
Inside story on disposers. il Bet Hom &
Gard 47:162 N '69
REFUSE incinerators
How European engineers design incinerators.
G. Hotti and R. Tanner. il Am City 84:107-
8+ Je '69
How to get rid of it all; incinerators. il Bet
Hom & Gard 47:142 N '69
REFUSE receptacles
Colorful litter boxes; Austin, Tex. C. Bark-
ley. il Am City 84:52 D '69
Containerized residential refuse collection;
Snyder, Tex. L. A. Patterson. il Am City
84:55 Ag '69
Large-plastic tote barrels; Milwaukee. il Am
City 84:64 F '69
100 per cent paper-bag collection; Montezuma,
Ga. il Am City 84:14 O '69
Plastic and paper refuse bags to undergo
major test. Am City 84:36+ Jl '69
Refuse sacks slash collection time; Smyrna,
Ga. V. Broyles. il Am City 84:79-80 Ja '69
Streetside enclosure for trash. il Sunset 142:
116 Je '69
Voluntary refuse-bag program gains
strength; Flint, Mich. T. Kay. il Am City
84:78-9 Je '69
REGA, Alcides F. and others
Potassium ions asymmetrically activate eryth-
rocyte membrane phosphatase. bibliog Sci-
ence 167:55-6 Ja 2 '70
REGAN, James D. and others
Serine requirement in leukemic and normal
blood cells. bibliog Science 163:1452-3 Mr
28 '69
REGAN, Timothy J. and others
Ventricular arrhythmias related to anti-
biotic usage in dogs. bibliog Science 165:
509-10 Ag 1 '69
REGATTAS
Ankles aweigh; Henley-on-Todd sandy riv-
erbed regatta. il Time 94:35 S 19 '69
Combat for keel boats. F. Rohr, jr. il Motor
B 124:36-8+ Jl '69
Cowes week west. P. Smyth. il Motor B
124:81 S '69
Going tradition; Block Island week. E. Ho-
ran. il Yachting 125:52-3 Je '69
Kiel; how it was and can be; 88th Kiel week.
J. P. Doherty. il Yachting 126:52+ D '69
Let yourself go; Caribbean one-design regat-
ta. E. Horan. il Yachting 125:54-5+ Ap '69
Little club, big regatta; Atlantic coast
lightning championship. M. Wiley. il Yacht-
ing 125:52-3+ Mr '69
Month in yachting. See issues of Yachting
On the circuit. il Yachting 126:46-9+ O '69
One design action; races in the Caribbean
midwinters. E. Horan. il Yachting 126:56-
7+ N '69
Penn's blades take a fourth; Intercollegiate
rowing association championship. H. Whall.
il Sports Illus 30:54+ Je 23 '69
Regatta results. See issues of Yachting

REGATTAS—*Continued*
Salty swingy sea festival; fourth annual watersports fête, Long Beach, Calif. L. J. Kennedy; H. Marris. il Motor B 124:80-1+ N '69
Sayville knows how; organizing regattas. E. Horan. il Yachting 125:110-11 Ja '69
Showdown at Chicago; One-of-a-kind regatta. il Yachting 126:68-9+ S '69
Soggy spree on Sammamish slough. E. Crimmin. il Motor B 123:84-5+ Je '69
Twenty years later; Thistle wins Yachting's seventh One-of-a-kind. B. Robinson. il Yachting 126:46-9+ N '69
See also
Rowing
Yacht racing

REGENCY period. See Great Britain—History —Regency period, 1811-1820

REGENERATION (biology)
Cockroach leg regeneration: effects of ecdysterone in vitro. E. P. Marks and R. A. Leopold. bibliog il Science 167:61-2 Ja 2 '70
Origin of repopulating cells after localized bone marrow depletion. M. A. Maloney and H. M. Patt. bibliog il Science 165:71-3 Jl 4 '69
See also
Wound healing

REGINA Siegfried, Sister. See Siegfried, R.

REGINA award
Acceptance of the Regina medal for Bertha Mahony Miller. R. H. Viguers. Horn Bk 45:516-24 O '69

REGIONAL airlines. See Local service airlines

REGIONAL cooperation. See International cooperation

REGIONAL libraries. See Libraries. Regional

REGIONAL periodicals. See Periodicals—United States

REGIONAL planning
Brandywine basin: defeat of an almost perfect plan. P. Thompson. il Science 163:1180-2 Mr 14 '69; Reply. G. E. Willeke. 164:769 My 16 '69
Cry, Vermont. Time 94:50 S 26 '69
Evaluate the present and chart the future; Arlington County, Va. B. W. Johnson. il Am City 84:75-7 Ag '69
How to design with nature. il Time 94:70-1 O 10 '69
It's not just the cities. A. Mayer. Arch Rec 145:151-62 Je; 146:171-82 S; 139-46 N; 105-10 D '69
Planning for the second America. J. Fischer. bibliog f Harper 239:21-4+ N '69
Tightened landscape. W. H. Whyte. il Horizon 11:66-73 Sum '69
Urban alternatives for eliminating poverty; excerpt from address, May 2 and 3, 1969. N. M. Hansen. Mo Labor R 92:46-7 Ag '69
See also
City planning
Landscape improvement
Metropolitan areas
Parks
Rural planning
Suburbs
also subhead Metropolitan district under names of cities, e.g. Seattle—Metropolitan district

United States
See Regional planning

REGIONAL technical schools. See Trade schools

REGISTER of scientific and technical personnel. See National register of scientific and technical personnel

REGISTRATION of architects. See Architects —Licenses and registration

REGISTRATION of voters. See Voters, Registration of

REGNIER, Nita
Near end; story. Redbook 132:96-7 Ap '69
Opening of doors; story. Redbook 134:159-81 N '69
Our rocking house. Redbook 134:50-1+ Ja '70
Someone special; story. Redbook 133:79 My '69

REGULATION Q. See Bank deposits—Interest

REGULATORS, Voltage. See Voltage regulators

REGULATORY commissions. See Independent regulatory commissions

REHABILITATION
Rehabilitation: new lives for the stricken and disabled. H. A. Rusk. Vogue 153:98-9+ F 15 '69

See also
American rehabilitation foundation
also subhead Rehabilitation under various subjects, e.g. Aged—Rehabilitation

REHABILITATION, Regional. See Regional planning

REHABILITATION centers
Mother Waddles; the gentle warrior; Detroit self-help centers. J. K. Davis. il Life 66:87-9 Mr 21 '69
See also
Narcotic addicts—Rehabilitation
Synanon foundation, incorporated

REHABILITATION of juvenile delinquents
Case for differential treatment of delinquents. M. Q. Warren. bibliog f Ann Am Acad 381:47-59 Ja '69
How to teach a delinquent: Warrendale youth development center. N. F. Hahn. Atlan 223:66-8+ Mr '69
Innovations in the treatment of juvenile offenders; New York state programs. M. Luger. Ann Am Acad 381:60-70 Ja '69
Kids, crime and conservation; youth forestry camps. M. J. Benoit. il Cons 23:18-20+ Ap '69
Youthful offenders; experiment in rehabilitation, Robert F. Kennedy youth center. R. Coles. New Repub 161:12-14 O 4 '69

REHEARSALS, Theatrical. See Theatrical production and direction

REHEIS, H. F.
Model A. Har Yrs 9:19-23 S '69

REICE, Sylvie
(ed) Trouble with parents is. McCalls 96:70-1+ S '69
Under twenty-one. See issues of McCall's

REICH, Herbert
Rights and permissions; summary of address. June 23, 1969. por Pub W 196:24-5 Ag 4 '69

REICHARD, Daniel P.
None are to be found more clever than Ernie. Engl J 58:668-72 My '69

REICHLEY, A. James
Big shakedown in Baton Rouge. Fortune 80:96-9+ Ag 1 '69
Elm street's new White House power. Fortune 80:70-3+ D '69
Nightmare for urban management. Fortune 79:94-9+ Mr '69
States hold the keys to the cities. Fortune 79:134-7+ Je '69

REICHSTAG. See Germany—Reichstag

REID, Alastair
Rain. Holiday 45:48-9+ Mr '69
Scotland, the most beautiful country in the world? Holiday 46:34-6+ Ag '69
(tr) See Borges, J. L. Embarking on the study of Anglo-Saxon grammar

REID, Caroline H.
50th anniversary for army service clubs. Parks & Rec 4:16-19+ N '69

REID, Dorothy
Greatest snow on earth. Travel 132:52-6 D '69

REID, Giorgina
Don't be a clutterbug. Pop Phot 64:74-5+ Je '69

REID, Joan Scott-Tallman
Cousin; poem. Sat R 52:123 S 13 '69

REID, Leslie M.
University training for park administrators. Parks & Rec 3:25-7+ D '68

REID, Ogden Rogers
Do Republicans have the courage to become the majority party? Look 33:76+ My 13 '69

REID, Stephen
Othello's jealousy. bibliog f Am Imago 25:274-93 Fall '68

REID, W. D. and others
Tricyclic antidepressants: evidence for an intraneuronal site of action. bibliog Science 164:437-9 Ap 25 '69

REID, W. Stanford
Dual crisis of the western world. Chr Today 13:10-11 My 9 '69

REIF, F.
Science education for nonscience students. Science 164:1032-7 My 30 '69

REIF, Rita
Home (cont) N Y Times Mag p54-6+ Je 22; 94-6 N 9 '69

REILING, Henry B. See Hayes, S. L. 3d, jt. auth.

REILLEY, Robert R.
Availability and usefulness of occupational materials. Clear House 43:439-41 Mr '69

REILLY, Edgar M. Jr
1968 not so nutty. Cons 23:16 Ap '69
—See Fisher, D. W. jt. auth.

REILLY, John H.
Drama (cont) Chr Cent 86:483-4 Ap 9 '69

REIN, Martin
    Choice and change in the American welfare
        system. bibliog Ann Am Acad 385:89-109
        S '69
    Social stability and black capitalism. Trans-
        Action 6:4+ Je '69
    —See Weiss, R. S. jt. auth.
REINER, Carl
    Homecoming; interview. New Yorker 45:47-9
        D 13 '69
                about
    Current cinema. P. Kael. New Yorker 45:190+
        D 6 '69
REINERT, Jeanne
    Brain control: tomorrow's curse or bless-
        ing? Sci Digest 66:14-19 N '69
    Population explosion: a warning from the in-
        sects. Sci Digest 66:40-5 Ag '69
REINFELDER, Al
    Bridge fishing primer. Field & S 74:80-3+ Je
        '69
REINFORCED plastics. See Plastics, Rein-
    forced
REINFORCEMENT (psychology)
    Animals respond for food in the presence of
        free food. A. J. Neuringer. bibliog il Sci-
        ence 166:399-401 O 17 '69
    Intracranial self-stimulation and the rapid
        decline of frustrative nonreward. R. N.
        Johnson and others. bibliog il Science 164:
        971-2 My 23 '69
    Positive contrast in the runway obtained
        with delay of reward. M. E. Shanab and
        others. bibliog il Science 164:724-5 My 9 '69
    Reinforcement therapy: short cut to sanity?
        il Time 94:52+ Jl 11 '69
    Steady potential correlates of positive rein-
        forcement: reward contingent positive varia-
        tion. T. J. Marczynski and others. bibliog
        il Science 163:301-4 Ja 17 '69
    Trance children. il Time 94:56+ Ag 1 '69
    Visual reinforcement of nonnutritive sucking
        in human infants. E. R. Siqueland and C. A.
        DeLucia. bibliog il Science 165:1144-6 S 12
        '69
        See also
    Incentives in education
REINIKKA, Merle A.
    Orchid fundamentals. Horticulture 46:20-2+
        Ag '68
REINSURANCE. See Insurance—Reinsurance
REIS, Donald E.
    Intergovernmental cooperation restores a
        downtown. Am City 84:118+ S '69
REIS, Lois
    1969 WD short story contest. Writers Digest
        49:37-8+ O '69
REISCHAUER, Edwin Oldfather
    Hour of the ox. Horizon 11:12-25 Wint '69
REISFELD, Ralph A. See Kahan, B. D. jt.
    auth.
REISIG, Hans
    Playing cards in popular use currently in
        Germany; tr. by F. G. Taylor. Hobbies
        73:114-15 F '69
REISS, Alvin H.
    Who remembers M.A.M.A? Esquire 71:162-3
        Mr '69
REISS, James
    Harry; poem. Sat R 52:39 My 10 '69
REISSUES of phonograph records. See Phono-
    graph records—Reissues
REITER, Charles J.
    Laying it on the line; address. 1968. Library
        J 94:1953-4 My 15 '69
REITER, Howard L.
    Ripon: left spur to the GOP. Nation 208:202-5
        F 17 '69
REITH, Edward J. See Ross, M. H. jt. auth.
REJECTED manuscripts. See Editors and edit-
    ing
REJECTION; story. See Gallant, M.
REJUVENATION
    Real truth behind the youth pill. E. Ubell. il
        McCalls 96:14+ Ag '69
RELATIVISITIC quantum field theory. See
    Quantum field theory
RELATIVITY (physics)
    Matter of overtime; Apollo-earth time equa-
        tion. il Time 93:42 Mr 7 '69
    Particles and geometry; concept of super-
        space. D. E. Thomsen. il Sci N 96:86-7 Jl
        26 '69
    Physical sciences; Midwest relativity confer-
        ence. Sci N 95:597 Je 21 '69
    Space, time and elementary interactions in
        relativity. M. Sachs. il Phys Today 22:51-
        60 F '69; Discussion. 22:13 S; 11+ N '69
    Speed limit 186,300 m.p.s. I. Asimov. il Holi-
        day 46:40-1+ Jl '69
        See also
    Gravitation
    Light—Velocity
    Quantum field theory

RELAY running. See Running
RELIABILITY (engineering)
        See also
    Electronic apparatus and appliances—Re-
        liability
    Space vehicles—Reliability
RELIABILITY of products. See Quality of
    products
RELICS and reliquaries
    Requiescant in pace. il Newsweek 73:95-6
        Ap 14 '69
    Tale of the purloined saint. C. Cate. il Hori-
        zon 11:68-79 Wint '69
RELIEF (sculpture)
    From illusion toward reality. B. Wasserman.
        il Sch Arts 69:26-7 N '69
    Sheet lead for relief sculpture. A. F. Geisert.
        il Sch Arts 68:18-20 Ap '69
RELIEF work
    Assistance in case of natural disasters; As-
        sembly extends experimental assistance ar-
        rangements. UN Mo Chron 6:121-2 Ja '69
    U.S. journal: Pass Christian, Miss; problems
        in recovering from hurricane Camille. C.
        Trillin. New Yorker 45:175-6+ N 29 '69
        See also
    American Friends service committee
    Disasters
    Red cross
        also subhead Relief work under names of
        wars, e.g. Vietnamese war, 1957- —Relief
        work
RELIGION
    Crisis of kairos? W. Birmingham. Common-
        weal 91:210-14 N 14 '69
    More or less religious? Chr Cent 86:1129 S
        3 '69; Discussion. 86:1354+ O 22 '69
    New ministry: bringing God back to life. il
        Time 94:40-5 D 26 '69
    Religion: at sixes and sevens in the sixties
        and seventies. Chr Today 14:36-8 Ja 2 '70
    Search for faith. il Life 68:16-26+ Ja 9 '70
    Soft revolution explored: secular religion. S.
        Keen. Chr Cent 86:1667-9 D 31 '69
        See also
    Atheism
    Christianity
    Church
    Ethics
    Faith
    God
    Humanism
    Mythology
    Natural theology
    Piety
    Public schools and religion
    Revelation
    Revivals
    Spirituality
    Supernatural
    Television broadcasting—Religious programs
    Theology
    Women and religion
    Worship
    Youth—Religion

                Bibliography
    Book briefs. See issues of Christianity today
    Books '68; symposium, with editorial com-
        ment. Chr Today 13:3-12+ F 28 '69
    Books to come; ed. by J. Donathan. Li-
        brary J 95:86-90 Ja 1 '70
    Books to come; ed. by J. Donathan and J.
        Fletcher. Library J 94:2965-75 S 1 '69
    Fall book forecast. Chr Today 13:21-4+ S
        12 '69
    Fall religious books. il Pub W 196:41-55 S
        22 '69
    Spring religious highspots; January through
        July. il Pub W 195:43-64 Ja 27 '69
        See also
    Religious literature

            Dictionaries and encyclopedias
    Sacramentum mundi: an encyclopedia of the-
        ology; ed. by K. Rahner and others. Review
        Cath World 209:39-40 Ap '69. W. F. Dewan

                Periodicals
    Publications; what's new. Chr Today 14:50
        O 24 '69
                Philosophy
    Hearers of the word, by K. Rahner. Review
        Commonweal 90:395-7 Je 20 '69. J. C. Cor-
        rigan
    John Dewey and Vatican council II. T. F.
        McGann. America 120:411-12+ Ap 5 '69;
        Discussion. 120:551 My 10 '69
        See also
    Philosophy and religion

RELIGION—*Continued*

Study and teaching

Teaching about religion in the public school. R. L. Hunt. il Todays Ed 58:24-6 D '69
See also
Chicago university—Federated theological faculty
Judaism—Study and teaching

RELIGION (games) See Games

RELIGION, Comparative. See Christianity and other religions

RELIGION, Personal. See Christian life

RELIGION, Primitive
See also
Moon in religion, folklore, etc.

RELIGION and art. See Art and religion

RELIGION and business. See Business and religion

RELIGION and communism. See Communism and religion

RELIGION and democracy
Demos and Christos. J. W. Montgomery. Chr Today 13:10-11 Jl 18 '69
Dual crisis of the western world. W. S. Reid. Chr Today 13:10-11 My 9 '69

RELIGION and education. See Public schools and religion

RELIGION and labor. See Church and labor

RELIGION and language
Language of the tribe. J. Blenkinsopp. il Commonweal 90:505-8 Ag 22 '69

RELIGION and law
What the Bible says about government; excerpts from address. C. T. Curtis. U S News 67:108 N 10 '69

RELIGION and literature
Christian approach to literature. L. Ryken. Chr Today 14:10-12 D 5 '69
Craters of the spirit, by N. A. Scott, jr. Review
    Cath World 208:235 F '69. L. A. Rosini

RELIGION and music
Pop festivals and Pentecost. J. C. Evans. Chr Cent 86:1303-5 O 15 '69

RELIGION and philosophy. See Philosophy and religion

RELIGION and politics. See Politics and religion

RELIGION and psychiatry. See Psychiatry and religion

RELIGION and psychology. See Psychology, Religious

RELIGION and science
Biology and the Christian faith. B. L. Smith. bibliog Chr Today 13:11-14 Ap 11; 11-14 Ap 25 '69
Case for Christian biopolitics. K. Cauthen. Chr Cent 86:1481-3 N 19 '69
Dangerous intersection. Chr Today 13:23 Ag 22 '69
Ecology and the contemporary religious conscience. R. L. Means. Chr Cent 86:1546-9 D 3 '69
New case for Galileo. J. J. Langford. Cath World 208:259-60 Mr '69
Science for clergymen; religion for scientists? J. Huffman. Chr Today 13:40-1 Ag 22 '69
Science, secularization and God, by K. Cauthen. Review
    Chr Cent 86:903-5 Jl 2 '69. J. C. Logan
Symposium in Rome: is unbelief believable? H. Cox. Commonweal 90:159-60 Ap 25 '69
What would a scientific religion be like? H. G. MacPherson. il Sat R 52:44-7 Ag 2 '69; Discussion. 52:60 S 6 '69
See also
American scientific affiliation
Space flight—Religious aspects
Tennessee evolution controversy

RELIGION and sex. See Sex and religion

RELIGION and social problems. See Church and social problems

RELIGION and socialism. See Socialism and religion

RELIGION and sociology
New ecclesiology; with reply. G. Baum. il Commonweal 91:123-9 O 31 '69
See also
Sociology, Christian

RELIGION and space flight. See Space flight —Religious aspects

RELIGION and state. See Church and state

RELIGION and technology
One giant leap for mankind: the moon venture. America 121:56 Ag 2 '69
See also
Computers—Religious applications

RELIGION and the arts
Art is long; meeting of Fellowship of Christians in the arts, media, and entertainment. A. H. Leitch. Chr Today 14:57-8 O 10 '69

Penetrating the media through Christian art; Fellowship of Christians in the arts, media, and entertainment. R. L. Cleath. Chr Today 14:38 D 19 '69

RELIGION and war. See War and religion

RELIGION in literature
See also
Bible in literature
Jesus Christ in literature

RELIGION in the public schools. See Public schools and religion

RELIGIONS
See also
Buddha and Buddhism
Cults

RELIGIOUS advertising
Spots for God. il Time 95:33+ Ja 12 '70

RELIGIOUS architecture. See Church architecture

RELIGIOUS art. See Christian art and symbolism

RELIGIOUS books. See Religious literature

RELIGIOUS cartoons. See Caricatures and cartoons

RELIGIOUS conferences
Africa's evangelicals choose the middle way; second Africa evangelical conference. O. W. Okite. Chr Today 13:42-3 Mr 14 '69
Agenda anxiety: corralling relevance; conference on The relevancy of organized religion. Chr Today 14:41 N 7 '69
Argentina argumentum; third Latin American Protestant congress. C. P. Wagner. Chr Today 13:36-7 Ag 22 '69
Bangkok conference loosens the western grip. W. T. Bray and G. E. Roffe. Chr Today 13:51-2 Ap 11 '69
Beloved infidels; Rome conference to explore The culture of unbelief. Time 93:64+ Ap 4 '69
Bogotá: Latin liaison; Latin American congress on evangelism. E. Rawlings. Chr Today 14:33 D 19 '69
Canadians plan national evangelism congress. Chr Today 14:49 N 7 '69
CICOP conference: uneasy gathering. G. F. Hall. Chr Cent 86:328+ Mr 5 '69
Christian educating in Chicago. M. Stone. Chr Cent 86:422+ Mr 26 '69
Denominational assemblies. Chr Cent 86:1327-8 O 15 '69
Gospel in east Europe; Pastors' conference in Novi Sad, Yugoslavia. C. F. H. Henry. Chr Today 14:39-40 O 10 '69
Historians debate God-and-country theme; Conference on faith and history. R. V. Pierard. Chr Today 14:51-2 N 7 '69
Kirchentag characterized by both polarization and solidarity. Chr Cent 86:1035 Ag 6 '69
Korean congress: Christ for 30 million. S. H. Moffett. Chr Today 13:36 Je 20 '69
Landmark centennial; Fourth evangelical congress in Barcelona. T. Goslin. Chr Cent 86:1589-90 D 10 '69
New unbelief; Culture of unbelief conference. Rome. Newsweek 73:50+ Ap 7 '69
Ottawa congress hits squall; Canadian congress on evangelism. L. K. Tarr. Chr Today 14:47 D 5 '69
Peace churches find identity in peace; Conference of historic peace churches, New Windsor, Md. M. Shelly. Chr Cent 86:132-4 Ja 22 '69
Priests' counter-Synod; meeting of Europe's reformist Roman Catholic priests. B. Bastien. Chr Today 14:46 N 7 '69
Profits of prophecy; unnecessary conferences on the future of religious institutions. Chr Cent 86:1338-9 O 22 '69
Six days in September; U.S. Congress on evangelism. D. E. Kucharsky. il Chr Today 14:42-3 O 10 '69
Thwarted again; third Latin American evangelical congress postponed. C. P. Wagner. Chr Today 13:38 Ja 31 '69
Two Dutch treats and the arms race; Conference on Christian approaches to defense and disarmament. A. Geyer. Chr Cent 86:1272-3 O 8 '69
U.S. Congress on evangelism: a turning point? Chr Today 14:32-3 O 10 '69
U.S. congress on evangelism; much given, much required. D. E. Kucharsky. Chr Today 13:40-1 S 26 '69
U.S. evangelicals: moving again; U.S. congress on evangelism. il Time 94:58+ S 19 '69
Vanderbilt congress: the Chicago school. W. A. Geier. Chr Cent 86:491-4 Ap 9 '69; Reply. H. W. Hansen. 86:756 My 28 '69
See also
Consultation on church union
World council of churches

RELIGIOUS contemplation. See Meditation

RELIGIOUS cooperation

Border consultation gets new perspective. R. R. Winkelmann. Chr Cent 86:460-2 Ap 2 '69

Commonwealth of churches; excerpt from The house divided: poverty, race, religion and the family of man. T. P. Melady and M. B. Melady. il Cath World 210:170-4 Ja '70

Ecumenical street theater on upper Broadway; Broadway United church of Christ to share facilities of St Paul the Apostle Roman Catholic church. Chr Cent 86:368 Mr 19 '69

How to stump theologians; Broadway United church of Christ to share facilities of Roman Catholic church of St Paul the Apostle. J. Evenson. il Chr Today 13:42-3 Mr 28 '69

RELIGIOUS drama
See also
Passion plays

RELIGIOUS education

Christian-education rut. D. L. McKenna. Chr Today 13:22-3 Mr 28 '69

Christian revolution and the Christian educator. M. Hellwig. Chr Cent 86:1088-91 Ag 20 '69; Reply. 86:1648-9 D 24 '69

Criteria for curricula. E. L. Hayes. Chr Today 13:42-3 F 28 '69

Dissociating religion and ethics; ending formal religious education in Ontario grade schools. A. Wice. Chr Today 13:35+ Ap 25 '69

Fresh theme for church publicists; educational programs. D. E. Kucharsky. Chr Today 13:20-1 Ag 22 '69

Living biblically: Institute for Christian studies, Toronto. Chr Today 14:37 D 19 '69

Teaching church. F. E. Gaebelein. Chr Today 13:22-3 Ja 31 '69

Total religious education and the parish. W. J. Tobin. America 121:33+ Jl 19 '69
See also
Bible study
Catholic schools
Missionaries—Training
Moral education
National council of churches—Division of Christian education
Sunday school lessons
Sunday schools
Theological education
Vacation schools, Religious

RELIGIOUS experience. See Experience (religion)

RELIGIOUS faith. See Faith

RELIGIOUS fiction. See Religious literature

RELIGIOUS films. See Moving pictures—Religious films

RELIGIOUS games. See Games

RELIGIOUS institutes and workshops

Permanent diaconate program; workshop at Collegeville. D. Durken. America 121:140-1 S 6 '69

Professionals discuss contemporary theology. J. W. Montgomery. Chr Today 13:45-6 S 26 '69

RELIGIOUS institutions and affairs

World around us. See Issues of Christian century
See also subhead Religious institutions and affairs under names of countries, states, etc. e.g. Northern Ireland—Religious institutions and affairs

RELIGIOUS intermarriages. See Marriages, Mixed

RELIGIOUS liberty
See also
Blasphemy
Church and state
Liberty of conscience

RELIGIOUS life. See Christian life

RELIGIOUS literature

Gloom-dispelling delights. M. E. Marty. Chr Cent 86:1385-6 O 29 '69

Power of the word; comp. by K. L. Woodward. il Newsweek 74:47 D 29 '69

Theological novel of modern Europe, by K. F. Reinhardt. Review
New Repub 160:23-5 Mr 22 '69. J. Finn
See also
Booksellers and bookselling—Religious literature
Protestant church-owned publisher's association
Publishers and publishing—Religious literature
Religion—Bibliography
Religious newspapers and periodicals
Religious poetry

Bibliography

Choice Evangelical books. Chr Today 13:15 F 28 '69

Volumes of volumes. R. L. Love. Chr Today 13:16-23 F 28 '69

RELIGIOUS medals. See Medals, Devotional

RELIGIOUS music. See Church music

RELIGIOUS mysteries. See Mysteries, Religious

RELIGIOUS newspapers and periodicals

Periodical changes and Motive's four-letter hangup. Chr Today 13:30-1 Je 20 '69

Religious press: what price prophecy? ACP/CPA convention. J. V. Lawing. Chr Today 13:30-1 Je 20 '69

279 editors looking for writers. K. M. Sommers. il Writers Digest 49:48-51+ S '69
See also
Associated church press (organization)
Christian century (periodical)
Christian ministry (periodical)
Christianity today (periodical)
Interchurch (newspaper)
Motive (periodical)

RELIGIOUS orders

Americanizing American religious life. S. Poole. America 120:297-300 Mr 15 '69; Discussion. 120:457 Ap 19 '69

Theology of the walk-out. N. J. Rigali. il Cath World 209:251-5 S '69; Reply. J. F. Kane. 210:100 D '69
See also
Franciscans
Jesuits
Sisterhoods
Trappists
Vocation in religion

RELIGIOUS persecution. See Persecution

RELIGIOUS poetry

Religious poetry. J. McGann. Poetry 115:196-201 D '69

RELIGIOUS poverty. See Poverty (virtue)

RELIGIOUS publishers group. See American book publishers council—Religious publishers group

RELIGIOUS radio programs. See Radio broadcasting—Religious programs

RELIGIOUS records. See Phonograph records—Religious records

RELIGIOUS revivals. See Revivals

RELIGIOUS rites and ceremonies. See Rites and ceremonies

RELIGIOUS schools. See Catholic schools; Church schools

RELIGIOUS statistics
See also
Church statistics

RELIGIOUS thought

Search for a usable future, by M. E. Marty. Review
America 120:228 F 22 '69. J. F. Cotter

Too late for soundings. C. F. H. Henry. Chr Today 13:31-2 Mr 14 '69
See also
Religion and democracy

RELIGIOUS vocations. See Vocation in religion

RELUCTANT Columbus; drama. See Cable, H.

RELYEA, Kenneth E.
How seeds are tested. Horticulture 47:40+ D '69

REMARRIAGE
Reconstituted families. il Newsweek 74:90-1 S 8 '69

REMBAR, Charles
Obscenity & the law. Commentary 47:18+ F '69

REMBRANDT Hermanszoon van Rijn
Cover; Portrait of a young man in a broad-brimmed hat. il Am Artist 33:6 Ja '69
Rembrandt and American art. C. J. McNaspy. America 121:370 O 25 '69
Rembrandt and his circle. B. A. Rifkin. il Art N 68:26-7+ My; 31-5+ O; 30-3+ N '69
Rembrandt and modern man. A. Werner. il pors Am Artist 33:32-7+ Ja '69
Rembrandt, the unrealistic realist. K. Kuh. il Sat R 53:46-8 Ja 10 '70
Rembrandts. New Yorker 45:25-6 Mr 1 '69
Rembrandt's vision, and ours. H. Kramer. il pors N Y Times Mag p32-5+ S 28 '69; Reply. S. Slive. p 16 O 19 '69
Rembrandt's year. il por Newsweek 73:88-92 Mr 10 '69

REMBRANDT controlling investment, limited. See Rothmans of Pall Mall Canada, limited

REMEDIAL reading. See Reading—Remedial teaching

REMEDIAL teaching
If it isn't boring, it isn't education. J. H. Bens. Engl J 58:418-22 Mr '69
Remedial program: teaching junior college students English, science, or math. R. M. Bossone. Clear House 43:364-7 F '69
See also
Reading—Remedial teaching
Tutors and tutoring

REMINDERS. See Memorandums

REMINGTON, Frank L.
Animal talk. Mech Illus 65:76+ F '69
Are you really sick? Mech Illus 65:94-5+ N '69
Focus on spectacles. Todays Health 47.50-3 Mr '69
Names people play. Todays Health 47:50-1+ N '69

REMINGTON rifles. See Rifles

REMINISCENCE
Booksellers and collectors: a dealer's apprenticeship; excerpts from Dukedom large enough. D. Randall. Pub W 196:35-8 Jl 21 '69
Childhood is a strange book; excerpts from address, 1969. V. Sorensen. il PTA Mag 64:13-15 N '69
Gastronomy recalled (cont) M. F. K. Fisher. New Yorker 45:140-6+ Ap 26; 118+ Je 7; 154+ S 20; 114+ S 27 '69
Going home in America: Lexington, Kentucky. E. Hardwick. Harper 239:78-82 Jl '69
Housekeeping and childkeeping in the olden days. B. Spock. Redbook 133:44+ O '69
Thrashin' time. M. E. Shatraw. Am West 6:32-5 Jl '69
Where the past is prologue; life at Jacnor farm. D. Straus. il House B 111:99+ Ap '69
Yesterdays in Grand Rapids. J. Thompson. Harper 238:43-51 My '69

REMODELED airplanes. See Airplanes, Remodeled

REMODELED houses. See Houses, Remodeled

REMODELING (architecture)
Go West, young family. il Am Home 72:54-7 Ja '69
    See also
Apartment houses, Remodeled
Apartments, Remodeled
Buildings, Remodeled
Factories—Remodeling
Farm buildings, Remodeled
Houses, Remodeled
School buildings, Remodeled

REMORAS
Sven, the remora. D. Kearns. il Yachting 125:61+ Mr '69

REMOTE control
Build WWRC; wired wireless remote control. J. S. Simonton, jr. il Pop Electr 30:27-32 Je '69
Sonic remote control relay. L. E. Wilson. il Radio-Electr 40:36-8 S '69
    See also
Photoelectric cells—Control applications
Radio control

REMOTE sensing systems
Resource satellite effort spurred; multispectral scanner. W. S. Hieronymus. il Aviation W 91:79+ N 17 '69
    See also
Infrared rays—Measurement uses
Purdue university, Lafayette, Ind.—Laboratory for agricultural remote sensing

REMSBERG, Bonnie. See Remsberg, C. jt. auth.

REMSBERG, Charles, and Remsberg, Bonnie
Magic of mother love. Good H 169:74-5+ Ag '69
They walk to feed the hungry. Good H 169:82-3+ S '69
Town fights back against the teen-age drug epidemic. Good H 168:80-1+ Je '69

REMSEN, C. C. See Watson, S. W. jt. auth.

RENAISSANCE
    See also
Civilization, Medieval

RENAULT, Mary, pseud.
Alexander's ascent to greatness on a ladder of gore. L. Casson. Sat R 52:27-9+ N 29 '69
All Greek? J. M. Butcher. Engl J 58:1335-7 D '69

RENCHARD, Stella Mae
Two hidden cemeteries in the Georgetown section of Washington, D. C. Negro Hist Bul 32:29-30 N '69

REND LAKE. See Lakes, Artificial

RENDEZVOUS (space) See Orbital rendezvous (space flight)

RENEGOTIATION board. See United States—Renegotiation board

RENEGOTIATION of government contracts. See Contracts, Government—Renegotiation

RENEWAL of the church. See Church renewal

RENO, Nev.
    Architecture
Sea & Ski corporation: the scale is for men not machinery. il Arch Rec 145:156-9 F '69

Music
Opera succeeds in a city of contrasts. R. R. Williams. Hi Fi 19:MA25-6 Je '69

RENO national championship air races. See Airplane racing

RENOIR, Auguste
I pet a picture. H. Junker. il Newsweek 73:90-2 Ap 14 '69
Vive Renoir. F. Daulte. il Art N 68:30-3+ Ap '69

RENOIR, Jean
Leading back to Renoir; Lincoln Center festival. P. Gilliatt. New Yorker 45:96+ S 6 '69
Profiles. P. Gilliatt. New Yorker 45:34-6+ Ag 23 '69

RENOIR, Pierre Auguste. See Renoir, A.

RENSENBRINK, John
America's racial crisis; the advent of a new consciousness? Cur 112:17-22 N '69

RENSSELAER polytechnic institute, Troy, N.Y.
No-fine, student-faculty common loan policy. J. A. McCrossan. ALA Bul 63:1531-2 D '69

RENT
Manhattan madness. Time 93:75-6 F 21 '69
One billion dollar subsidy for slums. J. M. Bailey, jr. and H. Schubart, jr. Arch Forum 131:56-7 Jl '69; Discussion. 131:56-9 S; 80-1 O; 10+ N '69
Your housing today: should you rent or buy? T. Irwin. Am Home 72:48+ Ja '69
    See also
Landlord and tenant
Leases

RENTAL services
From ax to zax. Newsweek 73:80+ Ap 14 '69
    See also subhead Leasing and renting under various subjects, e.g. Farm equipment—Leasing and renting

RENTMEESTER, Co
Hello Bali; photographs. Life 66:42-55 Ja 31 '69

RENZI, Ralph R.
Package deal offered by Williams college store. Pub W 195:85-6 Ja 27 '69

REORGANIZING, Congressional. See United States—Congress—Reorganization

REPAIR of tissues. See Wound healing

REPAIR shops
    See also
Automobile service stations

REPAIRING
    See also
Mending
    also subheads Repairing, and Maintenance and repair under various subjects. e.g. Roofs—Maintenance and repair

REPARATION
Help for the victim; proposed federal violent crimes compensation commission. il Newsweek 73:59 Je 23 '69
    See also
Negroes—Reparations

REPENTANCE
    See also
Confession

REPERTORY companies. See Theater—Great Britain

REPERTORY dance theatre of the University of Utah. See Dance companies

REPERTORY theater of Lincoln Center for the performing arts. See Lincoln Center repertory theater company

REPETITIVE explosive device for soil displacement. See Bulldozers (machines)

REPLACEMENT parts (marine engine) See Marine engine parts

REPORTERS and reporting
Assassins; group of journalists and T. Kennedy. S. J. Adamo. America 121:306 O 11 '69
Changing news values in the megamind era; address, February 19, 1969. E. H. Methvin. Vital Speeches 35:462-7 My 15 '69
Covering big Jim. Newsweek 73:105 Mr 17 '69
Front page revisited; City news bureau of Chicago. il Time 94:44+ Ag 22 '69
Gospel according to Blackman. S. G. Blackman. Sat R 52:45-6+ Ag 9 '69
On the road with RMN. il Newsweek 74:60 Ag 11 '69
Press faces its critics. Life 67:46 D 5 '69
Pueblo, inc. Newsweek 73:89 F 10 '69
Questions about Kennedy; feedback between news and newsmen over Senator Kennedy's accident. L. Smith. il Newsweek 74:56 Ag 4 '69
Reporter or informer? Nation 209:461+ N 3 '69
Self-criticism in Chicago; reporters as critics of newspapers. il Time 93:71 Mr 21 '69

REPORTERS and reporting—*Continued*
Tale of the birds; Union oil co. president misquoted by the New York times. Newsweek 73:58+ Mr 3 '69
Urban league conducts a guided tour. P. Bailey. il Ebony 24:48-50+ S '69
Violence and the press. T. A. Knopf. Cur 107:36-47 My '69
Wrong occupation; newsmen moonlighting for FBI. il Time 94:69 N 14 '69
     See also
Crime and the press
Government and the press
Journalism
Journalists
News
Newspaper court reporting
Sports journalism
Television broadcasting—News
United Nations correspondents association
Vatican and the press
Vietnamese war, 1957- —Press reports and censorship
     also names of reporters, e.g. C. L. Sulzberger

REPORTS
     See also
Corporation reports
Municipal reports

REPRESENTATIVE government and representation
Beginnings of the Cortes of León-Castile. J. F. O'Callaghan. bibliog f Am Hist R 74:1503-37 Je '69
     See also
Apportionment (election law)
Referendum

REPRESENTATIVES, Congressional. See Congressmen

REPRESSION (psychology)
Paradoxical fear-increasing effects of tranquilizers: evidence of repression of memory in the rat. L. Stein and B. D. Berger. bibliog il Science 166:253-6 O 10 '69

REPRINTS. See Books—Reprints

REPRODUCTION
Science, sex and morality; adaptation of The second Genesis; with Life poll on the procreation revolution by Louis Harris. A. Rosenfeld. il Life 66:37-40+ Je 13 '69
     See also
Artificial insemination, Human
Embryology
Gametogenesis
Ovaries
Spawning

REPRODUCTION, Asexual
Cloning: asexual human reproduction? D. M. Rorvik. il Sci Digest 66:6-13 N '69
Fissioning in planarians: control by the brain. J. B. Best and others. bibliog il Science 164:565-6 My 2 '69
Reef coral from Aldabra: new mode of reproduction. B. R. Rosen and J. D. Taylor. bibliog il Science 166:119-21 O 3 '69

REPRODUCTIONS of furniture. See Antiques. Reproductions of

REPRODUCTIONS of works of art
Let's make artists rich. F. Whitaker. Am Artist 33:3 Je '69

REPRODUCTIVE biology research foundation
All they talk about is sex, sex, sex; Institute for sex research. T. Buckley. il N Y Times Mag p28-9+ Ap 20 '69

REPTILES
     See also
Alligators
Lizards
Snakes

Food and feeding
     See Animals—Food and feeding

REPTILES, Effect of solar radiation on
Lizard reflectivity change and its effect on light transmission through body wall. W. P. Porter and K. S. Norris. bibliog il Science 163:482-4 Ja 31 '69

REPTILES, Fossil
Clue to the past; lystrosaurus. il Sci N 96:549 D 13 '69
Cynodont reptile with incipient mammalian jaw articulation. A. S. Romer. bibliog il Science 166:381-2 N 14 '69
Fossil find; lystrosaurus in Antarctica. Newsweek 74:77 D 15 '69
     See also
Amphibia, Fossil
Dinosaurs

REPUBLIC of Ireland. See Ireland

REPUBLIC of Korea. See Korea (Republic)

REPUBLIC of San Marino. See San Marino

REPUBLIC of the Niger. See Niger

REPUBLIC steel corporation
Thomas F. Patton of Republic steel; interview. T. F. Patton. Nations Bsns 57:54-9 O '69

REPUBLICAN governors association
Coming Republican drive to hold statehouse gains. il U S News 67:57-8 D 29 '69

REPUBLICAN party
Abandon the cities? Time 94:16-17 Ag 1 '69
Both parties split: the meaning. il U S News 67:19-20 D 8 '69
Crisis in Republican leadership. il U S News 67:35-6 S 22 '69
Dirksen and the White House; the senator's role has changed now. il U S News 67:14 Jl 21 '69
Do Republicans have the courage to become the majority party? O. R. Reid. Look 33:76+ My 13 '69
Down in Dixie; regional conference, New Orleans. J. Osborne. New Repub 161:7 D 20 '69
Emerging Republican majority, by K. P. Phillips. Review
     Nat R 21:913 S 9 '69. M. S. Evans
     Sat R 52:31+ S 13 '69. M. Levy
Future of American politics; excerpts from The emerging Republican majority; with comments by C. Fritchey. K. P. Phillips. Cur 110:26-31 S '69
Into the '70s, a GOP decade? R. M. Scammon. il Newsweek 74:68+ O 6 '69
Is there a new Republican majority? A. Hacker. bibliog f Commentary 48:65-70 N '69
Kaffeeklatsch constituency; Packwood's Dorchester conference. F. McKay. Nation 208:205-6 F 17 '69
Liberal Republicans: a shared concern; interview, ed. by L. Miller. T. J. Riley; J. S. Saloma, 3d. il Time 94:13 Jl 18 '69
Negro power: a built-in problem for Mr Nixon. il U S News 66:55-7 F 3 '69
Nixon and the new bourgeoisie. S. Alsop. Newsweek 73:96 Ja 27 '69
Nixon: past, present, and future. il Bsns W p 158+ O 11 '69
Party chairmen: ready for battle. il U S News 66:14-15 Ap 28 '69
Republican era ahead for U.S? Yes, if. . . il U S News 66:41-3 F 10 '69
Republican radical right. S. R. Koeppen. bibliog f Ann Am Acad 382:73-82 Mr '69
Republican strategy for '70 election. il U S News 67:34-6 N 24 '69
Republicans in the Senate, new leaders, new directions. il U S News 67:17 O 6 '69
Ripon: left spur to the GOP. H. L. Reiter. Nation 208:202-5 F 17 '69
Rise of Harry Dent. J. Osborne. New Repub 160:13-16 Je 14 '69
Robert A. Taft: Mr Republican. Sr Schol 94:16 My 2 '69
Victory: short films at New York County committee's Lincoln day dinner and ball. New Yorker 45:27-9 Mr 1 '69
Where's the GOP going? symposium. il New Repub 160:15-27 F 1 '69
Which way the parties? Nation 208:194-5 F 17 '69
Why Republicans won; interviews. W. T. Cahill; A. L. Holton. il U S News 67:39-40 N 17 '69
     See also
Republican governors association

REQUIEMS
Verdi's Liber scriptus rewritten. D. Rosen. bibliog f il Mus Q 55:151-69 Ap '69
     See also
Phonograph records—Requiems

RESCIGNO, Nicola
Traditionalist; interview, ed. by J. Ardoin. por Opera N 33:16 F 15 '69

RESCUE; story. See Holland, B.

RESCUE beacons. See Radio beacons

RESCUE work
     See also
Dogs in rescue work
Helicopters in rescue work
Telephone in rescue work
United States—Coast guard auxiliary

RESEARCH
Basic research and the common good. W. Weaver. Sat R 52:17-18+ Ag 9 '69
Ins and outs at M.I.T. R. Todd. il N Y Times Mag p32-3+ My 18 '69
Payoffs from research. Sci N 95:139 F 8 '69
Scientific research and the innovative process. W. J. Price and L. W. Bass. bibliog il Science 164:802-6 My 16 '69
Social control of science. L. A. DuBridge. il Bul Atom Sci 25:26-8+ My '69
Structure of discovery; adaptation of address, December 30, 1967. P. Caws. bibliog Science 166:1375-80 D 12 '69

RESEARCH—*Continued*
Traces. T. Benfey. Chem 42:4 Mr '69
TRACES: basic research links to technology appraised. P. Thompson. Science 163:374 Ja 24 '69
See also
Information services
Libraries and research
Little, Arthur D. incorporated
Neurosciences research program, Boston
also Geophysical research and similar headings; *also* subhead Research under various subjects, e. g. Colleges and universities—Research

Cost

British study development cost rise: cost of collaboration on joint European projects. il Aviation W 90:124-5 Je 2 '69
Inflation ups the R&D ante; McGraw-Hill survey. il Bsns W p78+ My 17 '69

Economic aspects

Science and budget cutting; address, September 10, 1969. A. Szent-Gyorgyi. Bul Atom Sci 25:16-17 D '69
Who pays the bills? R. H. Ellis, jr. Phys Today 22:124 My '69

Federal aid

Basic research: Congress on prowl. A. Hamilton. Science 166:849 N 14 '69
Changing research emphasis. D. Wolfle. Science 164:773 My 16 '69
Congress meets science: the appropriations process. M. D. Reagan. bibliog il Science 164:926-31 My 23 '69
Federal control and basic research in education. J. M. Scandura. Sch & Soc 97:227-8 Ap '69
Federal funding: what are the priorities? letter. S. F. Singer. Science 163:759-60 F 21 '69
Finding non-Defense money. Sci N 97:36 Ja 10 '70
Gasping from a one-two punch. il Sci N 96:236 S 20 '69
Institutional grants: Miller bill opens the debate. L. J. Carter. Science 163:265-6 Ja 17 '69
Johnson budget holds science to a cost-of-living raise. Phys Today 22:65 Mr '69
LBJ's last budget: R&D follows a status quo pattern. J. Walsh. il Science 163:368-70 Ja 24 '69
Needs for a national policy. E. Q. Daddario. il Phys Today 22:33-8 O '69
Nixon science budget cuts less severe than feared. M. Mueller. Science 164:409 Ap 25 '69
Science and the federal government; address, February 12, 1969. E. Q. Daddario. Vital Speeches 35:341-6 Mr 15 '69
Science lets out a yell for money; new federal budget calls for curtailing R&D spending plans. il Bsns W p86-7 Ja 25 '69
Slim pickings for research. il Sci N 95:87-91 Ja 25 '69
Technology, social change and the evaluative function; address. N. E. Golovin. bibliog Vital Speeches 35:310-15 Mr 1 '69
Uneven effects of cuts in science funding. P. H. Abelson. Science 163:131 Ja 10 '69
United States science policy: its health and future direction; adaptation of address. December 29, 1968. D. F. Hornig. Science 163:523-8 F 7 '69
View from DuBridge. il Newsweek 73:61 F 24 '69
Washington scene; the case for agency research. W. J. Price. Bul Atom Sci 25:34-6 Ap '69
See also
Astronomical research—Federal aid

International aspects

After the moon, the earth! address, December 28, 1969. W. O. Roberts. Science 167:11-16 Ja 2 '70
Technical cooperation: big boost from de Gaulle's resignation. D. S. Greenberg. Science 164:1042-3 My 30 '69

Study and teaching

Research paper revisited; analyzing current movies. D. M. Paananen. il Sr Schol 94: School Teach 18-19 F 7 '69
Sight, sound, and the research paper. S. Johnson. Engl J 58:1061-3+ O '69

Arab states

Acquisition of scientific and technological capabilities by Arab countries. A. B. Zahlan. Bul Atom Sci 25:7-10 N '69

Canada

Canadian look at nationalization of universities. J. A. McCarter. Bul Atom Sci 25:45-6 My '69

China (People's Republic)

Science travels the Mao road. C. H. G. Oldham. il Bul Atom Sci 25:80-3 F '69
See also
Atomic research—China (People's Republic)

Europe, Western

European science: financially, politically, it has trouble too. D. S. Greenberg. il Science 166:1122-6 N 28 '69
Technical cooperation: big boost from de Gaulle's resignation. D. S. Greenberg. Science 164:1042-3 My 30 '69
See also
NATO—Scientific affairs. Division of

France

France: profit rather than prestige is new policy for research. D. S. Greenberg. Science 165:1334-7 S 26 '69
French science: austerity drive ends rapid budget growth. D. S. Greenberg. Science 163:266-7 Ja 17 '69

Germany (Federal Republic)

Academic research in Germany: a new support program. B. R. Stein. bibliog Science 165:1096-100 S 12 '69
Doubling science research. T. Shoemaker. Sci N 95:246 Mr 8 '69
Germany: booming research effort turning to space and computers. D. S. Greenberg. Science 164:281-3 Ap 18 '69

Israel

Miracles at Rehovot. Time 94:52+ N 7 '69
Research that pays. M. Dean. Sci N 96:462 N 15 '69
See also

Rumania

Academy of the socialist republic of Romania

Russia

Science policy in the U.S.S.R. R. W. Davies and R. Amann. il Sci Am 220:19-29 Je '69
Soviet science: OECD reports a pattern of uneven development. B. Nelson. Science 163:917-18 F 28 '69
See also
Academy of sciences of the USSR
Atomic research—Russia

Underdeveloped areas

Developing nations and scientific responsibility. K. Lonsdale. Bul Atom Sci 25:27-8 N '69
Don't call us geniuses; projects of Institute for creative studies, Washington, D.C. M. Melewicz. il Am Ed 5:22-5 N '69

United States

Forces affecting science policy; R&D address, August 30, 1968. D. E. Kash. Bul Atom Sci 25:10-17 Ap '69
More progress at a higher price; key developments of the 1970s. il Bsns W p 154+ D 6 '69
United States science policy: its health and future direction: adaptation of address. uneven development. B. Nelson. Science 163:523-8 F 7 '69
See also
Colleges and universities—Research
Rand corporation
Stanford research institute

Yugoslavia

Yugoslavia: seeking to link science with development. A. Jamison. Science 165:1241-3 S 19 '69
RESEARCH airplanes. See Airplanes, Experimental
RESEARCH and engineering council of the graphic arts industry, incorporated
R&E council examines future technology, looks at current innovations. Pub W 195:101-2+ Je 9 '69
RESEARCH and industry. See Industrial research
RESEARCH center for urban and environmental planning. See Princeton university—Research center for urban and environmental planning
RESEARCH foundations. See Foundations, Charitable and educational
RESEARCH in colleges. See Colleges and universities—Research
RESEARCH laboratories
Flexible research laboratory complex for Inland steel. il Arch Rec 146:114-18 Jl '69

RESEARCH laboratories—*Continued*
Lab for light: Center for advanced visual studies at MIT. il Arch Forum 130:62-3 My '69
MIT revises laboratory work emphasis. P. J. Klass. Aviation W 90:49-50+ Je 16 '69
Research laboratories: designing the unpredictable; Building types study. il Arch Rec 146:135-50 Ag '69
Tower expands research complex; Philip Morris research center. il Arch Rec 145:122-5 F '69
See also
Abbott laboratories
Atomic research laboratories
Battelle Northwest laboratories, Richland, Wash.
Bell telephone laboratories
Sandia laboratories
United States—National aeronautics and space administration—Electronics research center
United States—Naval radiological defense laboratory
RESEARCH laboratories, Federal. See Laboratories, Government
RESEARCH ships. See Ships, Research
RESEARCH workers

Education

See also
Institute for creative studies, Washington, D.C.
RESEGREGATION of schools. See Segregation in education
RESERVATIONS, Indian. See Indians of North America—Reservations
RESERVE forces (United States) See United States—Armed forces—Reserves
RESERVE mining company
Lake Superior, private dump; Stoddard and FWPCA reports; hearings in Duluth. G. Hill. Nation 208:795-6 Je 23 '69
RESERVE officers training corps. See United States—Reserve officers training corps
RESERVOIRS
Aluminum replaces wood for reservoir cover; Longmont, Colo. il Am City 84:68 O '69
Beachcombing at a reservoir. il Sunset 143:30 O '69
Ecology of a reservoir; Quabbin reservoir, Mass. P. A. Erickson and J. T. Reynolds. il Natur Hist 78:48-53 N '69
New lakes: the beautiful and the dammed. H. R. Williams. il Parks & Rec 4:12-14+N '69
Park grows out of a reservoir; Oakland, Calif. il Am City 84:63+ N '69
Pumped water storage; Medina, Ohio. F. W. Reusswig and C. F. Tavener. il Am City 84:72-4 Mr '69
RESIDENCE (law) See Domicile
RESIDENCE halls. See Dormitories
RESIDENCES, Womens. See Womens residences
RESIGNATION of athletes. See Athletes, Resignation of
RESINOUS products
New composite offers uniform strength; boron-coated polyimide composite film. il Aviation W 90:51+ F 10 '69
See also
Vinyl compounds
RESINS. See Gums and resins
RESISTANCE, Electric. See Electric resistance
RESISTANCE in insect control. See Insects, Injurious and beneficial—Resistance to control
RESISTANCE to disease. See Immunity
RESISTANCE to government. See Government, Resistance to
RESISTANCE to Negro segregation. See Negroes—Segregation, Resistance to
RESISTIBLE rise of Arturo Ui: drama. See Brecht, B.
RESISTIVITY, Electric. See Electric resistance
RESISTORS, Electric. See Electric resistors
RESKO, John A.
Endocrine control of adrenal progesterone secretion on the ovariectomized rat. bibliog Science 164:70-1 Ap 4 '69
RESNAIS, Alain
Films of Alain Resnais. F. Tuten. Vogue 154:24+ Jl '69
RESNIK, Henry S.
Education. Vogue 154:68 S 15 '69
How Hermann Hesse speaks to the college generation. Sat R 52:35-7 O 18 '69
Revolution biz. Sat R 52:84-5 My 17 '69
RESNIK, Muriel
Movable feast. E. Alston. il pors Look 33:82-4 S 23 '69

RESOLUTIONS
See also
New Years resolutions
RESONANCE
See also
Nuclear magnetic resonance
RESOR, Stanley R.
Official U.S. report on My Lai investigation; statement before the Senate armed services committee, November 26, 1969. por U S News 67:78-9 D 8 '69
Safeguard; the A.B.M. debate; address, April 28, 1969. Vital Speeches 35:574-6 Jl 1 '69
RESORPTION (physiology) See Absorption (physiology)
RESORTS. See Seaside resorts; Winter resorts
RESORTS International
Bid to takeover Pan Am blocked. L. Doty. Aviation W 90:26 Mr 17 '69
Blocking an air raid. il Time 93:86 Mr 21 '69
Craps, roulette & Pan American airways. il Forbes 103:27-9 Mr 15 '69
Why Washington rode with Pan Am; CAB approval required on takeovers of airlines by non-transportation companies. Bsns W p40 Mr 15 '69
RESOURCES, Conservation of. See Conservation of resources
RESOURCES, Natural. See Natural resources
RESPIRATION
Blow of the pilot whale. C. R. Olsen and others. bibliog il Science 163:953-5 F 28 '69
Bullfrog (rana catesbeiana) ventilation: How does the frog breathe? C. Gans and others. bibliog il Science 163:1223-5 Mr 14 '69
Respiration and deep diving in the bottlenose porpoise. S. H. Ridgway and others. bibliog il Science 166:1651-4 D 26 '69
See also
Anoxemia
Asphyxia
Bacteria—Respiration
Plants—Respiration

Measurement

Oxygen consumption and pumping rates in the hard clam Mercenaria mercenaria: a direct method. A. Hamwi and H. H. Haskin. bibliog il Science 163:823-4 F 21 '69; Reply. J. Verduin. 166:1309-10 D 5 '69
RESPIRATORY apparatus
Acute respiratory failure. P. M. Winter and E. Lowenstein. il Sci Am 221:23-9 N '69
Breath of life; special respirator for babies developed by L. J. Arp. Newsweek 73:68 Je 9 '69
Pacemaker=easier breathing; electrophrenic respirator. Sci Digest 66:73-4 N '69
Wheeze machine tracks down allergies. R. Gannon. il Pop Sci 194:82-3+ My '69
See also
Life support systems (submarine environment)
RESPIRATORY intensive care units. See Hospital care
RESPIRATORY organs
Acute respiratory failure. P. M. Winter and E. Lowenstein. il Sci Am 221:23-9 N '69
See also
Cilia and ciliary motion
Gills
Lungs

Diseases

See also
Air pollution—Physiological effects
Asthma
Cold (disease)
Influenza
Sinus disease
RESPIRATORY pigments
See also
Cytochromes
RESPONSE, Motor. See Motor response
RESPONSIBILITY
Ailing world of work. C. F. H. Henry. Chr Today 14:22-3 Ja 2 '70
Exercise of social responsibility. A. Gillette. Sch & Soc 97:222-3 Ap '69
Great atrocity hunt; murder at Songmy and the American conscience. Nat R 21:1252+ D 16 '69
How to delegate. J. G. Mason. il Nations Bsns 57:60-1+ O '69
See also
Assistance in emergencies
RESPONSIBILITY (law) See Liability (law)
REST
See also
Fatigue
RESTAURANTS
Hangouts, U.S.A. il Mlle 70:158-9, 243 N '69
Holiday travel handbook. See issues of Holiday

RESTAURANTS—*Continued*
How to get a great meal at a great restaurant. R. A. De Groot. il Esquire 71:112-17+ Ja '69
International chef. M. Woodward. See issues of Travel
Which is the world's greatest restaurant? H. Gault and C. Millau. il Holiday 45: 32-3+ Je '69

Franchise system
Most, least, famous boring food in America. E. Kendall. Vogue 154:258+ O 1 '69

Canada
Holiday's choice of North American restaurants. S. Spitzer and H. Spitzer. il Holiday 46:81-90 Jl '69

France
L'Auberge de l'Ill: France's newest three-star restaurant. P. Salinger. il Travel & Camera 32:60-1+ My '69
French cooking à la Courtine. S. De Gramont. il N Y Times Mag p8-9+ Jl 6 '69

Japan
Make mine teppanyaki. P. Brooks. il Sat R 52:62+ S 13 '69
Restaurants are for discovering. F. Gibney. il Travel & Camera 32:70-1+ O '69

Mexico
Holiday's choice of North American restaurants. S. Spitzer and H. Spitzer. il Holiday 46:81-90 Jl '69

Puerto Rico
See also
San Juan, Puerto Rico—Hotels, restaurants, etc.

United States
Holiday's choice of North American restaurants. S. Spitzer and H. Spitzer. il Holiday 46:81-90 Jl '69
RESTON, Va.
Long, perilous path; Gulf takeover. il Forbes 104:42 Ag 15 '69
RESTORATION music. See Music, English
RESTORATION of buildings. See Architecture —Conservation and restoration
RESTORATION of works of art. See Sculpture—Conservation and restoration
RESTORE (corporation) See Bedford-Stuyvesant restoration corporation, Brooklyn
RESTORED villages. See Villages, Restored
RESTRAINT of trade
See also
Boycott
RESTREPO, Carlos Lleras. See Lleras Restrepo, C.
RESTRICTIONS on travel. See Travel regulations
RESUMES of employment. See Applications for positions
RESURRECTION
Living Christ. Chr Today 13:28 Ja 31 '69
See also
Jesus Christ—Resurrection and ascension
RESUSCITATION
See also
Cardiac resuscitation
RETAIL credit. See Credit; Consumer credit
RETAIL price maintenance. See Price maintenance by industry
RETAIL trade
Clothes are the silver lining. il Bsns W p48 S 20 '69
Easter was good, but not great. il Bsns W p32-4 Ap 12 '69
Fifty largest retailing companies. Fortune 79:194-5 My 15 '69
Retail sales ring up riddle for economists; dramatic shifts in patterns of spending. il Bsns W p28-30 Mr 1 '69
Slowdown creeps up on the small stores. il Bsns W p30-1 Jl 19 '69
Slowdown talk: a hot item. il Bsns W p 19 Ag 9 '69
Why people are buying less; reported from across U.S. il U S News 67:45-7 Ag 11 '69
See also
Cash business
Charge accounts (retail trade)
Christmas business
Computers—Retailing applications
Distributive education
Drugstores
Grocery stores
Grocery trade
Sears, Roebuck and company
Supermarkets

Finance
Great retail what-is-it; Gamble's retail stores. il Forbes 104:32-3 S 15 '69

Hours of business
See Store hours

Security measures
Security: a challenge to shoplifters. B. Curtis. Pub W 196:40-2 S 1 '69

Canada
See also
Simpsons-Sears limited
RETAINING walls
Gabions harness flood waters; Mount Holly, N.J. D. Miller. il Am City 84:80-1 Ag '69
RETARDED children. See Mentally handicapped children
RETI, Ladislao
Renaissance of a woman. Wilson Lib Bul 44: 524-5 Ja '70
RETICULOCYTOSIS. See Blood—Diseases
RETINA
Organization of the visual pathways. M. Glickstein. bibliog il Science 164:917-26 My 23 '69
Retinal processing of visual images. C. R. Michael. il Sci Am 220:104-14 My '69
Visual pigment density in single primate foveal cones. W. H. Dobelle and others. bibliog il Science 166:1508-10 D 19 '69
RETIRED military personnel
News and views; military-industrial romance. J. Deedy. Commonweal 90:92 Ap 11 '69

Employment
Executive recruits. il Newsweek 73:70+ Ap 7 '69
Generals for hire. B. Rice. Look 33:31 Ag 26 '69
Good life; industrial recruitment of officers. Nation 208:419 Ap 7 '69
Why a military-industrial complex? A senator's answer; excerpts from address. April 15, 1969. B. Goldwater; W. Proxmire. U S News 66:88-90 Ap 28 '69
RETIRED skippers race. See Yacht racing
RETIREMENT
Are emotional problems necessary? symposium. il Har Yrs 9:34-7 O '69
Early retirement under social security. R. R. Jalbert. il Har Yrs 9:24-5 Mr '69
I retired to the library; interview, ed. by R. Peterson. C. Cavalli. Har Yrs 9:41 S '69
Inquiring about retiring; questions and answers. T. Collins. See issues of Harvest years
Looking at retirement problems. N. V. Peale. Har Yrs 9:30-1 Je '69
News desk; retirement information. See issues of Harvest years
Old tenants vacate the room at the top. Bsns W p32-3 Ja 3 '70
Plight of retired people; second-class living standard; text of study made for the U.S. Senate's Special committee on aging. U S News 67:62-3 S 8 '69
Poor health not result, but cause, of retirement, Missouri study finds. Aging 173:11-12 Mr '69
Retirement: danger time for marriages? C. Rice. Har Yrs 9:46-8 My '69
Retirement gardening, organic, of course. V. A. Croley; A. Cadwalader; E. Bauchillon. il Org Gard & Farm 16:38-42 Ja '69
Should I retire now? letter. M. Farrant. Har Yrs 9:18 Mr '69
Survey of retired recreation and park professionals; statistics and advice. G. D. Butler. il Parks & Rec 4:21-5+ Je '69
Three scope explorers. M. Nagel. il Har Yrs 9:35-7 Ap '69
Tonic for aging brass; conference cruise for executives nearing retirement. il Bsns W p90 Mr 15 '69
See also
Basketball players—Retirement
Farmers—Retirement
Pensions, Industrial
Teachers, Retired
RETIREMENT housing. See Aged—Housing
RETIREMENT income
Can you retire on $4,100 a year? il Changing T 23:39-42 Ap '69
Check this; a tax-sheltered retirement program. R. Krumme. il Suc Farm 67:42 Je '69
Measuring retired couples' living costs in urban areas; with tables. M. H. Hawes. bibliog f Mo Labor R 92:3-16 N '69
Mutual funds for retirement income. E. Merillat. il Har Yrs 9:14-17 Mr '69

RETIREMENT income—*Continued*
Personal business. Bsns W p 147 My 10 '69
65+ incomes well under those of younger
groups. H. B. Brothman. il Aging 173:13-
14 Mr '69
Studies on retirement income continued by
Senate committee. Aging 180:10 O '69
When you retire: living costs in thirty-nine
places. il U S News 67:70 N 17 '69
RETIREMENT of college professors. See Col-
lege professors and instructors—Retirement
RETIREMENT residence, incorporated
Life care housing; interview, ed. by W. P.
Dumont. J. Frush, jr. il Har Yrs 9:6-13 D
'69
RETIREMENT systems. See Pensions, Indus-
trial
RETLAW enterprises, incorporated
What's in a name? Plenty! il Duns R 94:36
D '69
RETOUCHING. See Photography—Retouching
RETRAINING programs. See Employees—
Training
RETREATS, Spiritual
Midwest meets Fr. Lombardi; Movement for
a better world. W. B. Faherty. America
121:162-3 S 13 '69
RETRIEVER trials. See Field trials (dogs)
RETRIEVERS
See also
Labrador dogs
RETROACTIVE pay. See Wage payment plans
RETROGRADE amnesia. See Amnesia
RETTIE, Dwight F.
Park values and the city. Nat Parks 43:8-10
F '69
RETURN on investment. See Corporations—
Finance
REUNIFICATION question, German. See Ger-
many—Union (proposed)
REUNION of sorts; drama. See Drahos, M.
REUSABLE launch vehicles. See Space ve-
hicles—Propulsion systems
REUSS, Henry S.
Upgrading our environment; address, Octo-
ber 14, 1968. por Am For 75:28-9+ My '69
REUSSWIG. F. W. and Tavener, C. F.
Pumped water storage. Am City 84:72-4 Mr
'69
REUTER, Harald, and Beeler, G. W. Jr
Calcium current and activation of contraction
in ventricular myocardial fibers. bibliog
Science 163:399-401 Ja 24 '69
Sodium current in ventricular myocardial
fibers. bibliog Science 163:397-9 Ja 24 '69
REUTHER, Walter Philip
Meany & Reuther: labor's main bout. B. J.
Widick. por Nation 208:601-2 My 12 '69
Meany-Reuther showdown, with unity the
likely loser. Bsns W p34-5 Ag 30 '69
Mr Clean and the outcast. por Time 93:104
Je 6 '69
Reuther's grand alliance: meaning to busi-
ness and labor. il por U S News 66:70-1
Je 9 '69
Walter Reuther's gamble. J. Hill. Common-
weal 90:261-3 My 16 '69
REVE, Karel van het
Underground press. por Newsweek 75:31 Ja
12 '70
REVELATION
Justification by ignorance: a neo-Protestant
motif? address, December 29, 1969. C. F. H.
Henry. Chr Today 14:10-15 Ja 2 '70
Revelation, by H. Fries. Review
America 120:672-3 Je 7 '69. J. M.
Staudenmaier
REVELLE, Roger
Ocean; with biographical sketch. Sci Am
221:40, 54-65 S '69
REVENUE
See also
Taxation
REVENUE, Municipal. See Local taxation
REVENUE bonds. See Bonds, Revenue
REVENUE sharing. See Intergovernmental tax
relations
REVENUE stamps
Learn about revenue stamps & how they
differ from postage stamps. H. Herst, jr.
Hobbies 74:99+ Je '69
REVERE, Paul
Drama
Paul Revere of Boston. E. B. Kane. Plays
28:53-60 Ap '69
REVERING, Bernard J.
From mud flats to beautiful shore. Am City
84:93 Ja '69
REVERSAL of time. See Time reversal

REVIEWS of moving pictures. See Moving
picture plays—Criticisms, plots, etc.
REVISED standard version of the Holy Bible.
See Bible—Versions
REVISION, Literary. See Authorship
REVISION of manuscripts. See Authorship—
Copy preparation
REVIVALS
Brother A. A. Allen on the gospel trail: he
feels, he heals, & he turns you on with
God. W. Hedgepeth. il Look 33:23-31 O 7
'69
Revolution in religion; address, February
12, 1969. J. P. Leary. Vital Speeches 35:
445-8 My 1 '69
REVLON, incorporated
It's back to high style at Evan-Picone. S.
Margetts. il Duns R 93:83-4+ Mr '69
REVOLTS, Student. See Student demonstra-
tions
REVOLUTION, Industrial. See Industrial revo-
lution
REVOLUTION, Social. See Social revolution
REVOLUTIONARIES. See Revolutionists
REVOLUTIONARY action and movement. See
Terrorism
REVOLUTIONARY provisional government
Red move that may delay peace. U S News
66:8 Je 23 '69
REVOLUTIONISTS
Gangsters cash in on student revolt: inter-
view. S. I. Hayakawa. il U S News 66:38-41
F 24 '69
Intelligence report on today's new revolu-
tionaries. W. Schulz. Read Digest 95:121-6
O '69
Spotlight on SDS; case study of campus tur-
moil. il U S News 66:34-6 My 12 '69
REVOLUTIONISTS, Algerian
Where are they now? il Newsweek 74:12 Jl
14 '69
REVOLUTIONISTS, Latin American
Report from Brazil: what the left is saying.
J. Yglesias. il N Y Times Mag p52-3+ D 7
'69
REVOLUTIONISTS, Russian
My friend, the terrorist. M. K. Argus. Sat
R 52:26 My 24 '69
REVOLUTIONS
Almost making it; one view on the meaning
of France's revolution. S. Lynd. Common-
weal 90:345-7 Je 6 '69; Reply. W. O'Connor.
90:474-5+ Ag 8 '69
Cuba: American radical views the revolution
after ten years of Castro. C. Oglesby. il
Life 66:62D-62F+ F 14 '69
Danger of playing at revolution; Time essay.
il Time 93:40-1 Mr 28 '69
Need for revolution. P. Bascio. il Cath World
209:207-9 Ag '69
Revolution: the past and the future. il Life
67:100-12 O 10; 58-66B+ O 17 '69
Some dilemmas of counterinsurgency. G. K.
Tanham and D. J. Duncanson. For Affairs
48:113-22 O '69
Thomas Paine: to do good is my religion.
Sr Schol 93:15 Ja 10 '69
Vietnamism has failed; the revolution can
only be mauled; not defeated. C. Oglesby.
Commonweal 90:11-12 Mr 21 '69; Same with
title Prospect for revolution. Cur 109:55-6
Ag '69
War in southern Africa. R. W. Howe. il For
Affairs 48:150-65 O '69
See also
Coups d'état
France—History—February revolution. 1848

Historiography
Reformation and revolution: the maturing
East German view. C. R. Foster, jr. Chr
Cent 86:1380-2 O 29 '69
REVOLVERS
First Smith & Wesson revolver. C. G. Wor-
man. il Hobbies 74.122-3 Ap '69
Plinking handgun. W. Page. il Field & S 74:
86-8+ S '69
Smith and Wesson's no. 3 new model re-
volver. C. G. Worman. il Hobbies 74:150-1
D '69
REVOLVING buildings. See Buildings, Rotat-
ing
REVOLVING charge account. See Charge ac-
counts (retail trade)
REVSON, Charles Haskell
It's back to high style at Evan-Picone. S.
Margetts. il Duns R 93:83-4+ Mr '69
REVUE. See Musical comedy, revue, etc.
REWARDS, prizes, etc.
Merits and morals: nineteenth century re-
wards of merit cards. C. G. Fox. il Horn
Bk 45:80-4 F '69

REWARDS, prizes, etc.—*Continued*
Prize offers and awards. See issues of Writer
See also
American association of nurserymen
Atoms for peace awards
Boys clubs of America, incorporated
Competitions
Saturday review
Scholastic magazines, incorporated
also subhead Awards, prizes, etc. under various subjects, e.g. Agriculture—Awards, prizes, etc.

Anecdotes, facetiae, satire, etc.
Unique achievement, 1969. J. Berry, 3d, and others. Library J 94:4469 D 15 '69
REWARDS and punishments in education. See Incentives in education
REX, R. W. and others
Eolian origin of quartz in soils of Hawaiian Islands and in Pacific pelagic sediments. bibliog Science 163:277-9 Ja 17 '69
REXALL drug and chemical company
New prescription at Rexall; plan to sell Rexall drugstores. il Bsns W p 118-19 Ja 25 '69
REXROTH, Kenneth
Classics revisited. See issues of Saturday review
On making Christianity habitable. Commonweal 91:199-202 N 14 '69
Song at the winepresses. Commonweal 89:522 Ja 24 '69
Wisdom literature, with the earnestness of north Europe. Commonweal 89:708-10 Mr 7 '69
about
Hazards of art. R. Stock. Nation 208:378-9 Mr 24 '69
REY, Federico. See Wittop, F.
REYBURN, Noel J.
Creative alternatives. bibliog f Sch & Soc 97:23-4 Ja '69
REYES, Juan Vila. See Vila Reyes, J.
REYES BASUALTO, Neftali Ricardo. See Neruda, P. pseud.
REYKJAVIK, Iceland
Well traveled camera. E. Scully. il Mod Phot 33:110+ My '69
REYNOLDS, Barbara
You'd never believe he was a cop. Ebony 24:106-10+ Jl '69
REYNOLDS, D. A. See Semancik, J. S. jt. auth.
REYNOLDS, David V.
Surgery in the rat during electrical analgesia induced by focal brain stimulation. bibliog Science 164:444-5 Ap 25 '69
REYNOLDS, Debbie
Can we love Debbie too? S. Gordon. il pors Look 33:90+ N 18 '69
REYNOLDS, Fred
Sweet and swinging. See issues of American record guide
REYNOLDS, John T. See Erickson, P. A. jt. auth.
REYNOLDS, Marc
Uncommon tulips. Horticulture 47:18-20+ O '69
—and Meacham, W. L.
Long season enjoyment from minor bulbs. Horticulture 47:32-4+ S '69
REYNOLDS, Mike
Bear that wouldn't quit; ed. by B. East. Outdoor Life 143:66-7+ My '69
REYNOLDS, Orr E.
Bioscience programs in space. Space World F-9-69:4-15 S '69
REYNOLDS, Paul R.
No longer for gentlemen. Sat R 52:124-5 Mr 8 '69
REYNOLDS, R. J. foods, incorporated
Master chef of management. S. Margetts. Duns R 92:50-2+ D '68
REYNOLDS foods. See Reynolds, R. J. foods, incorporated
REYNOLDS metals company
Harvest of trash; reclaimed cans. il Time 94:39 Ag 29 '69
REZEK, Joseph W. See Jones, R. D. jt. auth.
RHAPIDOSOMES. See Cells—Inclusions
RHEAULT, Charles
Practical notes about binding; summary of address at AAUP meeting, June 24, 1969. por Pub W 196:57-8 Ag 4 '69
Textbooks: Dullsville and brighter spots. Pub W 195:68-70+ Mr 3 '69
RHEAULT, Robert Bradley
Case of the Green Berets. il Newsweek 74:42-3 Ag 18; 26+ Ag 25 '69
CIA talks. il Newsweek 74:18 S 8 '69

Colonel Robert Rheault, ex-Green Beret; with report by F. McCulloch and editorial comment by R. Graves. il pors Life 67:1, 34-9 N 14 '69
Green Berets and the CIA. L. F. Prouty. New Repub 161:9-10 Ag 23 '69
Mystery of the Green Berets. Time 94:28+ Ag 15 '69
Under restraint. il por Newsweek 74:35-6 S 1 '69
Will he ever get his star? por Newsweek 74:32-3 Ag 25 '69
RHEINBERGER, Josef Gabriel
Rheinberger: The star of Bethlehem. P. L. Miller. Am Rec G 36:170-1 N '69
Das RHEINGOLD; opera. See Wagner, R.
RHEINGOLD breweries, incorporated
Beer ain't soap. Forbes 103:198 My 15 '69
RHESUS monkeys. See Monkeys
RHETORIC
Conscious rhetorician. D. B. Lockerbie. Engl J 58:1057-60 O '69
De-escalating the rhetoric. P. Schrag. Sat R 52:20 Mr 15 '69
We use great plainness of speech. D. B. Lockerbie. Chr Today 14:12+ O 24 '69
See also
English language—Composition
RHEUMATOID arthritis. See Arthritis
RHINE RIVER
At mouth of Rhine: a new megalopolis. il U S News 66:58-9 Je 23 '69
Impetus for action; fishkill in the Rhine. T. Shoemaker. Sci N 96:64 Jl 19 '69
Longest sewer; tons of dead fish. il Newsweek 74:30 Jl 7 '69
Rancid Rhine. il Time 94:26 Jl 4 '69
Rhine. J. Carlysle. il Travel & Camera 32:65-7+ Mr '69
Where the Rhine drops seventy feet; Rheinfall near Schaffhausen, Switzerland. il Sunset 142:61 F '69
RHINOCEROS
Love may be the death of the Indian rhino. il Life 66:66-9 F 7 '69
RHIZOBITOXINE. See Toxins and antitoxins
RHIZOBIUM
Immunochemistry of newly found substituents of polysaccharides of rhizobium species. W. F. Dudman and M. Heidelberger. bibliog il Science 164:954-5 My 23 '69
RHOADES, Orille B.
Books reviewed. See issues of Hobbies
RHOADES, Verne
Obituary
Am For por 75:41 Ap '69
RHOADS, John B.
Nice way to pioneer. il pors Forbes 103:58+ Ap 1 '69
RHODA, Marguerite
Pretty green place with the big garden. Org Gard & Farm 16:62-4 F '69
RHODE, Bill
Wayward wheel. Flying 84:86-7 Ap '69
RHODE ISLAND
Junked-car air pollution. A. C. Daley. il Am City 84:131+ O '69
See also
Architecture, Domestic—Rhode Island
Block Island
Camping—Rhode Island
Education—Rhode Island
Fishing—Rhode Island
Libraries—Rhode Island
Music festivals—Rhode Island

Historic houses, etc.
See also
Newport, R.I.—Historic houses, etc.
RHODE ISLAND school of design, Providence, R.I.
Latin American art, New England setting. J. H. Kay. il Américas 21:19-27 Ap '69
RHODES, Daniel
Potter and his kiln; excerpt from Kilns: design, construction, and operation. Craft Horiz 29:36-8 Mr '69
RHODES, James Allen
Governor and the mobster; with report by D. Walsh. il pors Life 66:28-32A My 2 '69
RHODES, John B.
American challenge challenged. Harvard Bsns R 47:45-57 S '69
RHODES, John Jacob
Defense requirements for the 1970's; address, April 3, 1969. Vital Speeches 35:460-2 My 15 '69
RHODES, Lawrence
Another try at the inevitable direction. J. J. O'Connor. por Dance Mag 43:65-7 N '69
Performing true to prediction. W. Terry. il por Sat R 52:52 F 15 '69

RHODES, Lynwood Mark
Battle for a nation's health. Todays Health 47:36-9+ Ap '69
Compact circuit. Travel 132:28-33+ Jl '69
Mush against death. Todays Health 48:30-3+ Ja '70
Texas River road. Travel 132:38-41+ O '69
What you should know about hearing aids. Todays Health 47:40-3+ Ag '69

RHODES, Richard
Death all day in Kansas. Esquire 72:146-9+ N '69

RHODESIA
Forgotten Rhodesians. D. R. Smock. For Affairs 47:532-44 Ap '69
See also
Dams—Rhodesia
Kariba Lake
Land tenure—Rhodesia
Mines and mineral resources—Rhodesia
Political campaigns—Rhodesia
United Nations—Rhodesia

Constitution
Blueprint for injustice: Rhodesian hierarchy's objections to new constitution. America 121:6 Jl 5 '69
Closing the doors: draft of new constitution. Nat R 21:578 Je 17 '69
Department presents views on Southern Rhodesia; statement, October 17, 1969. D. D. Newsom. Dept State Bul 61:422-4 N 17 '69
Final break; end of link with Britain. il Time 93:37 Je 27 '69
Road to apartheid. il Newsweek 73:59 Je 30 '69
Smith's world-beater. Newsweek 73:44 Mr 3 '69
U.S. deplores minority rule in Southern Rhodesia; statements. June 13 and 24, 1969; with text of draft resolution. C. W. Yost. Dept State Bul 61:55-9 Jl 21 '69
Native races
See also
Rhodesia—Race problems

Politics and government
Big problems facing Ian Smith. U S News 67:11 Jl 7 '69
Challenge of Rhodesia. R. Zacklin. bibliog f il Int Concil 575:5-72 N '69
Rhodesia-Britain: a final break? the new Rhodesian constitution. U S News 66:13 Je 2 '69
Rhodesia tomorrow; an experiment in racial coexistence; address. S. Pejovich. bibliog Vital Speeches 35:338-41 Mr 15 '69
See also
Rhodesia—Constitution

Race problems
Rhodesia tomorrow; an experiment in racial coexistence; address. S. Pejovich. bibliog Vital Speeches 35:338-41 Mr 15 '69
Slum clearance. Salisbury-style. il Time 94:38+ S 26 '69
U.N. condemns racial policies of Southern Rhodesia; texts of U.S. statements; with text of resolution. J. Eaves; S. M. Finger. Dept State Bul 60:413-15 My 12 '69

RHODODENDRONS
For rhododendron-azalea keepers, or paper experts. il Sunset 143:176 D '69
Here's how to move an azalea or rhododendron. il Sunset 142:190-1 F '69
Problems people have with azaleas and rhododendrons; questions and answers. il Sunset 143:248+ O '69
Sweet and acid for rhododendrons. L. M. Hardwick. il Org Gard & Farm 16:50-1 D '69

RHUBARB
Surrounded, by rhubarb! J. McMahan. il Org Gard & Farm 16:106-7 Mr '69
Two vegetables for a permanent patch. M. G. Benzinger. il Org Gard & Farm 16:46-7 Je '69

RHYTHM
See also
Periodicity

RHYTHM and blues music. See Jazz music
RHYTHM and blues singers. See Singers
RHYTHMIC phenomena. See Periodicity
RIBICOFF, Abraham A.
Vietnamese. New Repub 161:30-1 O 18 '69

RIBMAN, Ronald
Harry, noon and night. Criticism
Sat R 52:44 D 27 '69
Passing through from exotic places. Criticism
Nation 209:739-41 D 29 '69
New Yorker 45:57 D 20 '69
Sat R 52:44 D 27 '69

RIBOFLAVIN. See Vitamins—Vitamin B₂
RIBONUCLEASES
First synthesis. Sci Am 220:46-8 Mr '69
First synthesis of an enzyme, ribonuclease. J. Zimmerman. il Chem 42:21-2 Ap '69
Irreversible inhibition of nuclear exoribonuclease by thymidine-3'-fluorophosphate and p-haloacetamidophenyl nucleotides. M. B. Sporn and others. bibliog il Science 164:1408-10 Je 20 '69
Major first for U.S. scientists. il U S News 66:6 Ja 27 '69
Making of an enzyme. il Newsweek 73:67 Ja 27 '69
Noncovalent binding of a spin-labeled inhibitor to ribonuclease. G. C. K. Roberts and others. bibliog il Science 165:504-6 Ag 1 '69
Opening the enzyme door; synthetic ribonuclease. il Sci N 95:112 F 1 '69
Synthesis of an enzyme. il Time 93:61 Ja 24 '69

RIBONUCLEIC acid. See RNA
RIBONUCLEOPROTEINS. See Nucleoproteins
RIBONUCLEOTIDES. See Nucleotides
RIBOSOMES. See Nucleoproteins
RIBOUD, Marc
In Ho country. il N Y Times Mag p40-1 Mr 9 '69
Journey to North Vietnam; interview, with photographs. Newsweek 74:32-4 O 20 '69
(ed) See Nguyen-huu-Tho. Talk with the NLF leader

RICCARDO, David, pseud.
Great 1970 market crash. Esquire 72:50+ D '69
RICCARDO, John J.
Shake-up at Chrysler. il por Newsweek 75:76 Ja 19 '70
RICE, Berkeley
Generals for hire. Look 33:31 Ag 26 '69
RICE, Carolyn
Retirement: danger time for marriages? Har Yrs 9:46-8 My '69
RICE, Charles L.
Assimilation or cultural pluralism? Chr Cent 86:945-7 Jl 16 '69
RICE, Ralph S.
Conscience and the income tax. Nation 209:695-9 D 22 '69
RICE, Skip
Star is re-born. Yachting 125:66-7+ My '69
RICE, Stanley
Planning for computer composition; address, February 13, 1969. Pub W 195:34-9 F 24 '69
RICE
See also
Cookery—Rice
International rice research institute
Wild rice

RICE, Wild. See Wild rice
RICE pudding. See Puddings
RICE trade
Tempest in the rice bowl: U.S. cracks down on Thai deal with Vietnam. il Newsweek 75:59-60 Ja 12 '70

RICH, Adrienne
Ghazals: homage to Ghalib; poem. Nation 208:188-9 F 10 '69
RICH, Alexander. See Kim, S. H. jt. auth.
RICH, Dorothy
Value of the PTA. Todays Ed 58:31-3 My '69
RICH, Leslie
Doctor Sunday comes to town. Am Ed 5:20-3 My '69
RICH, Maria F.
U.S. opera survey: the multiest of media. Opera N 34:13-16 N 22 '69
RICH, The
Care and feeding of the very rich. R. West. il McCalls 96:56-7+ Ag '69
Good, good life of the Alpine set. S. Birmingham. il McCalls 97:46-7+ Ja '70
Hard-core rich. C. McCarthy. New Repub 160:14-15 Mr 15 '69
How 381 super-rich Americans managed not to pay a cent in taxes last year. P. M. Stern. il N Y Times Mag p30-1+ Ap 13 '69; Reply. p22+ My 4 '69
Nouveau vs d'habitude. S. Lord. Harp Baz 102:196 Ag '69

Anecdotes, facetiae, satire, etc.
Too rich and too thin. N. Gittelson. Harp Baz 102:19+ Ag '69
RICHARD, Gabriel
America's only congressman-priest. C. Clemens. Hobbies 74:108-9 Ap '69
RICHARD, Olga
Visual language of the picture book. bibliog por Wilson Lib Bul 44:434-47 D '69
RICHARDS, Kenneth. See Veith, F. J. jt. auth.

RICHARDS, Stanley
Broadway pre-sell. Writers Digest 49:52-6+
S '69
RICHARDS, Theodore William
Theodore William Richards and the atomic
weight problem; adaptation of address.
December 27, 1968. A. J. Ihde. il por Science
164:647-51 My 9 '69
RICHARDSON, Brenda
West coast report. Art in Am 57:104-5 My
'69
RICHARDSON, David C.
We are stronger than reds; interview. por
U S News 67:59-61 Jl 21 '69
RICHARDSON, Elliot L.
Altered shape of world power; address,
June 9, 1969. Dept State Bul 61:27-9 Jl 14 '69
Department reviews U.S. efforts to aid vic-
tims of the Nigerian civil war; state-
ment, July 15, 1969. Dept State Bul 61:94-
7 Ag 4 '69
East-West relations; the process of gaining
new evidence; address, June 8, 1969. Dept
State Bul 60:557-61 Je 30 '69
Economic and military assistance proposals
for fiscal year 1970; statement. June 9, 1969.
Dept State Bul 60:569-74 Je 30 '69
Foreign policy of the Nixon administration:
its aims and strategy; address, September 5,
1969. Dept State Bul 61:257-60 S 22 '69
Intelsat conference opens at Washington;
with welcoming remarks, February 24, 1969.
Dept State Bul 60:231-2 Mr 17 '69
International dimension of American educa-
tion; remarks, June 26, 1969. Dept State Bul
61:72-4 Jl 28 '69
OECD ministerial council meets at Paris;
statements of February 13 and 14, 1969.
Dept State Bul 60:192-5 Mr 10 '69
Soviet-U.S. dialogue; address, November 20,
1969. Vital Speeches 36:167-9 Ja 1 '70
Under Secretary Richardson discusses Viet-
Nam peace talks and U.S.-U.S.S.R. rela-
tions; interview, April 30, 1969, ed. by J.
Kraft. Dept State Bul 60:417-18 My 19 '69
Under Secretary Richardson interviewed on
CBS television; news program July 2, 1969.
Dept State Bul 61:49-51 Jl 21 '69
RICHARDSON, Herbert
Proof of the pudding. Commonweal 91:205-6
N 14 '69
RICHARDSON, Jack
Groping toward freedom: the living theatre.
Commentary 47:79-81 My '69
History as drama. Commentary 47:22+ F '69
Joe Namath and the problem of heroic vir-
tue. Esquire 72:105+ O '69
RICHARDSON, Joseph Emanuel
Saba's youngest ruler. il pors Ebony 24:116-
18+ O '69
RICHARDSON, Larry
Larry Richardson & dance company; Theatre
80 St Marks. M. Marks. Dance Mag 43:
80 Ap: 32 My '69
RICHARDSON, Thomas Henry
Students beliefs and values; adaptation of
address, June 2, 1968. Sch & Soc 97:94-5
F '69
RICHARDSON, Tony
Theatre; production of Hamlet. B. Gill. New
Yorker 45:121-2 My 10 '69
RICHELIEU, Armand Jean du Plessis, cardinal,
duc de
Richelieu, by D. P. O'Connell. Review
America 120:567 My 10 '69. M. Cuddihy
RICHEY, Elinor
Diary; tranquilizer without side effects. Mlle
68:82+ Ap '69
RICHIE, Jeanne
Unresponsive pew. Chr Cent 86:1278-81 O 8 '69
RICHLER, Xavier
Château gang; excerpt from The discrimina-
ting thief. D. Leitch. il Horizon 11:114-20
Spr '69
RICHLER, Mordecai
Baseball à la Franglais. Holiday 46:54-6 Ag
'69
RICHMOND, Calif.
Mix schools by busing? Where voters said
no. U S News 66:70 Ap 28 '69
RICHMOND, Calif. public library
Richmond review; letter to the editor. L.
Burley. Library J 94:1924 My 15 '69
RICHMOND, Va.
Summer work programs. G. M. Chamberlain.
il Am City 84:92+ N '69

Historic houses, etc.
Living in the past; Westover house. B.
Plumb. il N Y Times Mag p86+ My 18
'69
RICHMOND, Va. University
Big bequest. Chr Today 14:42 Ja 2 '70
Richmond's bombshell; gift of $50 million by
E. C. Robins. Newsweek 74:79 Jl 7 '69

RICHTER, Charles F.
Earthquakes; with biographical sketch. por
Natur Hist 78:5, 36-45 D '69
Transversely aligned seismicity and concealed
structures. bibliog Science 166:173-8 O 10
'69
RICHTER, Gerhard
Gerhard Richter, German illusionist. E. F.
Fry. il por Art in Am 57:126-7 N '69
RICHTER, Hans
In memory of a friend. Art in Am 57:40-1 Jl
'69
RICHTER, John L.
Test for figuring Cassegrain secondary mir-
rors, ed. by R. E. Cox. Sky & Tel 39:49-
53 Ja '70
RICKENBACKER, William F.
Delectations. Nat R 21:84, 1171 Ja 28, N 18 '69
Little lady from Spain. Nat R 21:239 Mr 11
'69
Records (title varies) (cont) Nat R 21:658-9,
1073-4 Jl 1, O 21 '69
Toiling masses and a' that. Nat R 21:291 Mr
25 '69
RICKMAN, Eric
Rooster tales. See issues of Hot rod
RICKOVER, Hyman G.
Can technology be humanized, in time? Nat
Parks 43:4-7 Jl '69
Humanistic technology; excerpt from ad-
dress. May 7. 1969. por Am For 75:12+
Ag '69
about
Test subs run afoul of costly delays. il Bsns
W p47-8 Mr 8 '69
RICKS, R. Bruce
Next: rose-chip stock? por Forbes 104:100+
N 15 '69
RICKS, Robert
Russian horn bands. bibliog f Mus Q 55:364-
71 Jl '69
RIDDELL, Alan
Alas. Harp Baz 102:82 Ag '69
Patchwork quilt. Harp Baz 102:82 Ag '69
RIDDLE, William G.
New water plant on a rehab budget. Am
City 84:78-9 Ag '69
RIDEAU waterway. See Waterways—Canada
RIDENHOUR, Richard
My Lai massacre. il por Time 94:17-19 N 28
'69
RIDEOUT, Ray
Building a background for high school com-
position. Engl J 58:242-4 F '69
RIDGEFIELD PARK, N.J.
Fluorescent painting and tandem plowing. il
Am City 84:57 F '69
RIDGEWAY, James
Dumb children. New Repub 161:19-21 Ag 2 '69
No risks preferred. New Repub 160:18-21
F 22 '69
Ramparts story; um, very interesting. N Y
Times Mag p34-6+ Ap 20; 132 My 11 '69
RIDGWAY, Sam H. and others
Respiration and deep diving in the bottle-
nose porpoise. bibliog Science 166:1651-4
D 26 '69
RIDING. See Horseback trips; Horsemanship
RIDLAND, John
Elegy for Ike Eisenhower. Nation 209:384 O 13
'69
RIECKEN, Henry W.
Quick thimking. Science 164:633-5 My 9 '69
RIEDER, Kathryn Sanders
Writing songs for children. Writers Digest
49:56-7+ Je '69
RIEDL, R. J.
Gnathostomulida from America. bibliog Sci-
ence 163:445-52; 164:856 Ja 31, My 16 '69
RIEGER, Norbert I. and others
Community nursery school program for hos-
pitalized children. Ment Hy 53:196-9 Ap '69
RIEGLE, Donald W. Jr
Sweepstakes of the '70s: five entries. il por
Newsweek 73:27-8 F 24 '69
RIEK, Edgar F. See Tasch. P. jt. auth.
RIES, S. K. See Schweizer, C. J. jt auth.
RIESEBERG, Harry E.
You, too, can dive for sunken treasure. Pop
Sci 194:84-7 Je '69
RIESEN, Janet
They do it with their eyes closed. Sch Arts
68:22-3 My '69
RIESLING grapes. See Grapes
RIESMAN, David
Administrators can be scapegoats for un-
reachable targets. N Y Times Mag p 137-8
My 4 '69
Changing campus and a changing society;
adaptation of address, November 12, 1968.
Sch & Soc 97:215-22 Ap '69

RIESMAN, David—*Continued*
Search for alternative models in education;
address. Am Scholar 38:377-88 Sum '69; Excerpts. Cur 112:26-9 N '69
Universities on collision course. Trans-Action 6:3-4 S '69

RIFAMPICIN. See Antibiotics

RIFKIN, Benjamin A.
Rembrandt and his circle. Art N 68:26-7+ My;
31-5+ O; 30-3+ N '69

RIFLE cartridges. See Cartridges

RIFLE shooting. See Shooting

RIFLE sights. See Firearms—Sights

RIFLE stocks. See Gunstocks

RIFLES
Gun that caused a mutiny: the Pattern 1853
.577 Enfield rifle musket. C. G. Worman.
il Hobbies 73:122-3 F '69
How to buy a deer rifle. W Davis. il Mech
Illus 65:62+ S '69
Mountain rifle. J. O'Connor. il Outdoor Life
143:146+ Ap '69
Now, a .22 with caseless ammunition. P.
Wahl. il Mech Illus 65:78+ O '69
Rifle on a diet. W. Page. il Field & S 74:134-8
Je '69
Rolling blocks by Remington C. G. Worman.
il Hobbies 74:122-3 Je '69
Sentimental rifleman. W. Page. il Field &
S 73:162-4+ Ap '69
'73 Winchester. C. G. Worman. il Hobbies
74:122-3 Ag '69
Use what the varmint shooters use. A. Maher.
il Pop Mech 132:116-19 D '69

RIGA, Peter J.
Drug scene. Cath World 209:176-81 Jl '69
Modern science and ethical dimension. Cath
World 209:213-17 Ag '69
Moon theology; some reflections. Cath
World 210:151-4 Ja '70
Paul VI and violence. Cath World 208:251-4
Mr '69

RIGALI, Norbert J.
Karl Jaspers: the inward path. Commonweal
90:38-9 Mr 28 '69
Right, duty, and dissent. Cath World 208:
214-18 F '69
Theology of the walk-out. Cath World 209:
251-5 S '69

RIGER, Robert
Eye on the quarterback. Travel & Camera
32:92-7 O '69

RIGERT, Joe
Playing American roulette. Commonweal 90:
72-5 Ap 4 '69

RIGGING. See Masts and rigging

RIGGS, Donald. See Riggs, M. jt. auth.

RIGGS, Harriet Wheatly
Cooking on six cylinders. Travel 132:65-7
O '69

RIGGS, Margaret, and Riggs, Donald
Seed sprouting, unlimited. Org Gard & Farm
16:42-3 Jl '69

RIGGS, Norman D.
Organization for instruction. Clear House
44:45-9 S '69

RIGHT and left (political science)
Address. E. Cleaver. Ramp Mag 7:6-10 D 14
'68
Agony of the American left, by C. Lasch.
Review
Commentary 48:59-63 Jl '69. D. H. Wrong
Nation 208:797-9 Je 23 '69. J. McDermott
New Repub 160:25-7 Ap 12 '69. M. Har-
rington
American power and the new mandarins, by
N. Chomsky. Review
Fortune 79:155-6 My 1 '69. I. Kristol
Anglo-Saxonism and fascism. A. Ezergailis.
Yale R 58:481-506 Je '69
Another target of new left; the armed forces.
il U S News 66:58-60 My 26 '69
Beyond new leftism. S. Kelman. Commentary
47:67-71 F '69
Blue collar white and the far right. G.
Fackre. Chr Cent 86:645-8 My 7 '69
Campus near-fascism; student radical move-
ments. America 120:350-1 Mr 29 '69
Can it happen here? E. Kern. il Life 67:67+
O 17 '69
Crisis of confidence, by A. M. Schlesinger, jr.
Review
Sat R 52:28-9 My 17 '69. J. H. Bunzel
Death-wish psychosis of the new left. Chr
Today 13:26-7 My 9 '69
Decline of liberal politics. W. Pfaff. Com-
mentary 48:45-51 O '69
Essay on liberation, by H. Marcuse. Review
Nation 208:765-8 Je 16 '69. P. Clecak
Frantz Fanon and the radical left. E. W.
Ranly. America 121:384+ N 1 '69

"Free". by A. Hoffman. Review
Commonweal 89:596-7 F 7 '69. R. Howard
From the radical left to the center. T. P.
Melady. il Cath World 209:168-71 Jl '69
Gathering of the clans; three-day conference
in Oakland summoned and run by the Black
Panthers. il Newsweek 74:32 Ag 4 '69
Hand-me-down Marxism and the new left. D.
Horowitz. Ramp Mag 8:16+ S '69
Herbert Marcuse or Milovan Djilas? I. Howe.
Harper 239:84+ Jl '69
How can the left be relevant? W. A. Wil-
liams. Cur 109:20-4 Ag '69
In my opinion: the new left is a paste gem.
M. Cain. Seventeen 28:160 Jl '69
Intellectual origins of American radicalism.
by S. Lynd. Review
Commonweal 89:503-4 Ja 17 '69. L. Kriegel
Isolation of the new left. C. Gershman. Na-
tion 208:666-8 My 26 '69
Jewish role in student activism. N. Glazer.
il Fortune 79:112-13+ Ja '69
Latin American radicalism, ed. by I. L.
Horowitz and others. Review
America 120:308+ Mr 15 '69. F. P. Le
Veness
Nation 208:277-8 Mr 3 '69. R. F. Smith
Sat R 52:37-9 Je 7 '69. A. Lauterbach
Marcuse: prophet of the new left. E. Still-
man. il Horizon 11:26-31 Sum '69
Memo on the new left; campus scene. W. A.
Rusher. Nat R 21:803-4+ Ag 12 '69
New left. S. Lynd. bibliog f Ann Am Acad
382:64-72 Mr '69
New left and Negro extremism. D. Brudnoy.
il Nat R 21:640-3 Jl 1 '69
New left and the electoral college. F. A.
Picó. America 120:252-4 Mr 1 '69; Reply. L.
W. Belter. 120:378-9 Ap 5 '69
New left in action. il U S News 66:35-7 My
19 '69
New left: old traps. T. Gitlin. Ramp Mag 8:
20+ S '69
New left on the New deal. D. Brudnoy. Nat R
21:1072-3 O 21 '69
Obsolete communism, by D. Cohn-Bendit and
G. Cohn-Bendit. Review
Nat R 21:391-3 Ap 22 '69. W. S. Schlamm
On leaving the herd; changing from Socialist
to Conservative in England. J. Braine.
Nat R 21:749-50+ Jl 29 '69
Open letter to Barry Goldwater. K. Hess. il
Ramp Mag 8:28-31 O '69; Same abr. Cur 113:
21-6 D '69
Opinion: dehumanized radicalism. N. Hent-
off. Mlle 69:16+ My '69
Our fractured politics; a liberal/new left
confrontation? H. S. Ashmore. Cur 113:14-
21 D '69
Peripatetic sycophant. Nat R 21:319 Ap 8
'69
Politics; young leftists. J. Leonard. Esquire
71:50+ F '69
Radical and the mediator: their roles in
social change. R. Ruether. America 121:
521-3 N 29 '69
Radicals try to rewrite the book; new left
economists. il Bsns W p78-80+ S 27 '69
Rebellion and repression, by T. Hayden. Re-
view
Nation 210:21-3 Ja 12 '70. P. Clecak
Republican radical right. S. R. Koeppen. bib-
liog f Ann Am Acad 382:73-82 Mr '69
Resurgence of reaction? New Repub 160:5-6
Je 28 '69
Shall we let America die? both new left and
conservatism threats to liberalism. D. A.
Zoll. il Nat R 21:1261-3 D 16 '69; Reply. F.
S. Meyer. 21:1327 D 30 '69
Spectator's guide to the troublemakers. J.
Kifner. il Esquire 71:86-91 F '69
Styles of radical will, by S. Sontag. Review
Life 66:12 Mr 28 '69. J. Leonard
Temptations of a Boston atheist. N. Hent-
off. Harper 238:81-6 Ap '69
Their morals and ours: new leftists. J. Burn-
ham. Nat R 21:793 Ag 12 '69
Theology for radical politics, by M. Novak.
Review
Commonweal 90:369-72 Je 13 '69. S. Max.
Unhappy right; first weeks of the Nixon
administration. Nation 208:290 Mr 10 '69
Unwitting help for the new left. B. L. Masse.
America 120:210 F 22 '69
We must avoid the perils of extremism. D. D.
Eisenhower. Read Digest 94:103-8 Ap '69
Where are they now? J. Weinberg activist at
Berkeley in 1964. il Newsweek 73:18 Je 23
'69
Why cops hate liberals, and vice versa. S. M.
Lipset. il Atlan 223:76-83 Mr '69
Why one British Socialist turned conserva-
tive. J. Braine. il N Y Times Mag p24-5+
Mr 2 '69; Discussion. p 16 Mr 23 '69

RIGHT and left (political science)—*Continued*
Worst of Two worlds; program published by
Flick-Reedy education enterprises to edu-
cate the nation's youth in the dogma of
the radical right. M. A. Gordon. Ramp Mag
7:58+ Ap '69
Young and angry talent; England's new left;
Tribune versus Black dwarf debate. M.
C. Shefftz. Nation 208:720-4 Je '69
Young radicals & professorial critics. I. L.
Horowitz Commonweal 89:552-6 Ja 31 '69
See also
Conservatism
Liberalism

Anecdotes, facetiae, satire, etc.
Exclusive and unauthorized: the liberated
report of Professor X. Professor X. Es-
quire 72:104-7+ S '69
RIGHT hand; story. See Solzhenitsyn, A.
RIGHT man; story. See Engle, K.
RIGHT of asylum. See Asylum, Right of
RIGHT of dissent. See Free speech
RIGHT of government employees to strike. See
Strikes—United States—Government employ-
ees
RIGHT of privacy. See Privacy, Right of
RIGHT to education
Race between education & catastrophe. H.
Brabyn. il UNESCO Courier 23:11-13 Ja '70
Right and ability to read; views of J. E.
Allen. C. B. Grannis. Pub W 196:40 O 13 '69
Right to be educated. ed. by R. F. Drinan.
Review
America 120:227-8 F 22 '69. J. W. Evans
Right to read; challenge for local leadership;
address, October 3, 1969. J. E. Allen, jr. Vi-
tal Speeches 36:42-4 N 1 '69
Right to read: target for the 1970's. J. E.
Allen, jr. il PTA Mag 64:6-8 D '69
Target for the 70's: the right to read; ex-
cerpts from testimony, before the General
subcommittee on education of the U.S
House of representatives committee on ed-
ucation and labor, and discussion, October
1969. J. E. Allen, jr. Am Ed 5:2-4 D '69
Washington report; the right to read. J.
Lloyd. Sr Schol 95:School Teach 2+ O 27 '69
RIGHT to labor
Religion and right to work. Chr Today 13:37
Ja 31 '69
See also
Discrimination in employment
RIGHT to read. See Right to education
RIGHT to work laws

United States
See Labor laws and legislation—United
States
RIGHT wing (politics) See Right and left
(political science)
RIGHTER, Carroll
Astrology: fad and phenomenon. il por Time
93:53-4 Mr 21 '69
On the fringe. H. Frankel. Sat R 52:30 Je
14 '69
RIGHTS, Bill of (United States) See United
States—Constitution—Bill of rights
RIGHTS, Natural. See Natural law
RIGHTS of employees. See Employees—Civil
rights
RIGHTS of women. See Woman—Equal rights
RIGOLETTO; opera. See Verdi, G.
RIIS, Jacob August
Jacob Riis: crusader against slums. por Sr
Schol 94:9 Ap 11 '69
RIKER-Maxson corporation
Maxson, Riker join; company renamed. Avia-
tion W 90:126 Ap 14 '69
RIKLIS, Meshulam
Full circle. il por Time 93:86 Mr 28 '69
RILEY, David P.
Dear Mrs Mitchell . . . Commonweal 91:329
D 12 '69
RILEY, Frank
Journey through a borrowed land. Sat R
53:91-2+ Ja 10 '70
Mao's Macao. Sat R 52:69-70+ N 15 '69
Snows of Kosciusko. Sat R 52:38+ My 17 '69
Storm over Micronesia. Sat R 52:56+ S 13
'69
RILEY, J. T.
Ski hill from garbage dump. Parks & Rec
3:37+ N '68
RILEY, Jack
New voice for Apollo. por Time 93:74-5 My
30 '69
RILEY, James Whitcomb
In the matter of James Whitcomb Riley.
W. Myers. Esquire 72:82+ S '69
RILEY, John
Class in our time. Esquire 73:82-7+ Ja '70

RILEY, O. V.
Hey Ollie, have ya got the time? E. Rickman.
il pors Hot Rod 22:126-8 O '69
RILEY, Robert Q. See Carey, D. jt. auth.
RILEY, Terry
Veritably a dilly: the disc debut of com-
poser Terry Riley in C. A. Frankenstein.
Hi Fi 19:104 F '69
RILEY, Tom J.
Liberal Republicans: a shared concern: in-
terview. ed. by L. Miller. il por Time 94:
13 Jl 18 '69
RILKE, Rainer Maria
Birth of Christ; poem. tr. by M. W. Hess.
Chr Today 14:12 D 5 '69
RINEHART, John S.
Waterfall-generated earth vibrations. Sci-
ence 164:1513-14 Je 27 '69
RINEHART, Stanley M. Jr
Obituary
Pub W por 195:29 My 5 '69
RINFRET, Pierre A.
Slowdown: real or apparent? il por News-
week 74:74 D 22 '69
RING-a-day service. See Telephone
RING-necked pheasants. See Pheasants
RING of the Nibelung; operas. See Wagner, R.
RING out the new; story. See Pearlman, E.
RINGEL, Ilene T.
In my opinion we need a woman president.
por Seventeen 27:180 D '68
RINGING of trees. See Trees, Ringing of
RINGING out the old in happy Havana; story.
See Farina, R.
RINGLING museum of art. See Sarasota, Fla.—
Ringling center
RINGLING museum of the circus. See Sarasota,
Fla.—Ringling center
RINGO, James
Composer somewhat apart: Mily Alexeyevich
Balakirev. Am Rec G 35:578-82 Mr '69
RINGROSE, Basil
Astronomical pirate. J. Ashbrook. Sky & Tel
33:75 Ag '69
RINGS of trees. See Tree rings
RINK, Larry
Watercolor: beyond rendering. il por Am
Artist 33:72-4 D '69
RINKS, Hockey. See Hockey rinks
RINKS, Skating. See Skating rinks
RINTA, Eugene F.
Federal budget and expenditure control. Ann
Am Acad 379:22-30 S '68
RIO ARRIBA COUNTY, N.Mex.
La Raza: Mexican Americans in rebellion.
J. L. Love. bibliog il Trans-Action 6:35-41
F '69
RIO DE JANEIRO
See also
Stock exchange—Rio de Janeiro

Crime
Death squads of Rio; manned by off-duty
cops. il Time 93:61 Ap 25 '69

Music
Report: Rio de Janeiro; productions by Tea-
tro San Carlo of Naples. R. Kovacs. Opera
N 34:25 N 1 '69

Police
Death squads of Rio; manned by off-duty
cops. il Time 93:61 Ap 25 '69
RIO treaty. See Inter-American treaty of re-
ciprocal assistance
RIOT control
Antiriot sprays: are they safe, or hazardous?
U S News 66:10 Je 2 '69
Bigger riot role for the national guard. il U S
News 66:42-3 Je 30 '69

Anecdotes, facetiae, satire, etc.
Making contact in Baltimore. J. Sack. il Es-
quire 71:92-4+ Je '69
RIOT prevention. See Riot control
RIOTS
Leisure time and the riots, are we contri-
buting? with editorial comment. I. J.
Hutchison, jr. Parks & Rec 4:11, 23+ Jl '69
Why the riots all over the world. il U S
News 66:33-5 Je 16 '69
See also
Mob violence
Riot control
also subhead Riots under names of con-
tinents, countries, cities, etc. e.g. United
States—Riots

RIOTS—*Continued*

Safety devices and measures
Fighting fashions. Time 94:55 Jl 18 '69
RIOTTE, Louise
Bigger, better, and earlier; broccoli. **por Org
Gard & Farm** 16:40-2 D'69
Lettuce in the onion row! Org Gard & Farm
16:40-1 S '69
Tiniest farm in America. **por** Org Gard &
Farm 16:24-7 Je '69
With us, parsley is permanent! Org Gard &
Farm 16:70-2 N '69
RIPIN, Edwin M.
Scottish encyclopedist and the piano forte.
bibliog f Mus Q 55:487-99 O '69
RIPLEY, John W.
Old lantern slides. Hobbies 74:98L-98P D '69
RIPON society. See Political clubs and asso-
ciations
RIPP, Judith
(ed) Family movie guide. See issues of
Parents' magazine & better family living
RISCHIN, Moses
New Mormon history. Am West 6:49 Mr '69
RISING, Gerald R.
Sorry state of mathematics teacher educa-
tion. Ed Digest 35:48-50 S '69
RISK
Handling risk in defense contracting. R. M.
Anderson. il Harvard Bsns R 47:90-8 Jl '69
How to rationalize your marketing risks. M.
R. Greene. il Harvard Bsns R 47:114-23 My
'69
Social benefit versus technological risk; adap-
tation of address, November 1968. C. Starr.
bibliog il Science 165:1232-8 S 19 '69
See also
Hedging
RISSET, Jean-Claude, and Mathews, M. V.
Analysis of musical-instrument tones; with
biographical sketches. bibliog **pors Phys
Today** 22:23-30 F '69
RIST, Charlie
Charnita bonanza. D. Sanford. **New Repub**
161:12-14 S 6 '69
RISTVEDT, Milly
Three young Canadians. B. Lord. il Art in
Am 57:88 Ja '69
RITCH, John B. 3d
Reports: Iceland. Atlan 223:38+ Ap '69
RITCHIE, Doris M.
Sharing the wealth. Sch Arts 69:32-3 S '69
RITCHIE, Gary A.
Ginkgo: window to the past. il Nat Parks
43:12-14 F '69
RITCHIE-CALDER, Peter Ritchie Calder,
baron
Earthlings in the space age; reprint. UNESCO
Courier 22:4-6 Ag '69
RITE of spring; story. See Franco, M.
RITES and ceremonies
New rites for old. F. Maynard. il Seventeen
28:154-5+ Mr '69
See also
Baptism
Fire walking
Funeral rites and ceremonies
Marriage customs and rites
Passover
RITNER, John
Deflector puts heat on VW windshield. Pop
Sci 195:50 N '69
RITSCHL, Dietrich
Presence of Christ: a contemporary view. J.
A. Hill. Chr Today 13:5-8 Je 20 '69
RITT, Tom
Postscript on Negotiation now! Common-
weal 90:134-5, 415 Ap 18, Je 27 '69
RITTER, Ed
Green dahlia? P. A. Pavlik. il por Org Gard
& Farm 16:56-9 Mr '69
RITTER, Jesse P. Jr
Nightmare for the innocent in a California
jail. por Life 67:51-2+ Ag 15 '69
RITTER, Walter, and Vaughan, H. G. Jr
Averaged evoked responses in vigilance and
discrimination: a reassessment. bibliog Sci-
ence 164:326-8 Ap 18 '69
RITTER AISLÁN, Eduardo
Carmela's marriage; story. Américas 21:32-4
Jl '69
RITTERBUSH, Philip C.
Educated man in the year 2000; address,
November 15, 1968. Vital Speeches 35:
295-300 Mr 1 '69
RITTMASTER, Peter
They all laughed when Peter turned left. J.
Kirshenbaum. il por Sports Illus 31:44-5
Ag 11 '69
RITUAL. See Catholic church—Liturgy and
ritual; Liturgies; Marriage customs and
rites
RITZ-Carlton hotel, Boston. See Boston—
Hotels, restaurants, etc.

RIVER boats. See Steamships and steamboats
RIVER ecology. See Fresh water ecology
RIVER fronts. See Water fronts
RIVER trips
Adventure on the Colorado River. B. Hughes.
il Redbook 133:66+ My '69
Chartering in Ireland and England; cruising
on the River Shannon and the Norfolk
Broads. G. Stout; F. Adams; E. J. Durnall.
il Yachting 126:54-5+ D '69
Grand Canyon river run. J. V. Young. il
Travel 131:40-5+ F '69
Outboard recollection; cruise on Wisconsin
River. D. Olesen. il Yachting 126:69+ Ag
'69
Rivers. J. Gribbins. il Motor B 124:49-56+
Ag '69
Saint John; New Brunswick's splendid river.
F. Graham, jr. il Motor B 123:46-9+ F '69
Shooting the Canyon. B. Belknap. il Travel
& Camera 32:46-7 Je '69
Tennessee River heritage cruise. J. Gribbins.
il Motor B 123:62-7+ Ap '69
Up a steep Alaska river to British Columbia;
just for the fun of it. il Sunset 142:54-6+
My '69
Voyage of the Green Witch. M. Jenkinson
and T. Bacon. il Motor B 124:84-5+ N '69
Where the rapids run gently; rafting voyage
on Jamaica's Rio Grande. F. Rohr, jr. il
Motor B 124:72-3 S '69
See also
Canoe trips
RIVERFRONTS. See Water fronts
RIVERS, Joan
Rampaging Rivers. il por Newsweek 73:72
Ap 28 '69
RIVERS, Lucius Mendel
New warning that navy is getting obsolete;
excerpts from address, May 23, 1969. por
U S News 66:11 Je 9 '69
Power people; interview, ed. by R. Yoakum.
por Look 33:22-3 Ag 26 '69
about
Arms spending: powerful chairmen disagree
sharply, and then softly. por U S News
66:18 Je 2 '69
Death before dishonor. R. Goetz. Chr Cent
86:1083 Ag 20 '69
News and views. J. Deedy. Commonweal 90:
58 Ap 4 '69
Southern Gothic. Nation 209:715-16 D 29 '69
TRB from Washington. New Repub 160:4 Je
7 '69
RIVERS
Rivers. J. Gibbons. il Motor B 124:49-56+
Ag '69
Waters of the West. D. Muench. il Nat
Wildlife 7:42-7 Je '69
See also
Limnology
Water pollution
also names of rivers, e.g. Danube River

Bank protection
Gabions harness flood waters; Mount Holly,
N.J. D. Miller. il Am City 84:80-1 Ag '69

Regulation
Where conservation is a bad word; Soil con-
servation service. B. B. Blackburn, 3d; G.
Laycock. il Field & S 74:12-14+ D '69
See also
Colorado River
Dams
Flood prevention and control
RIVERSIDE, Calif.

Sanitary affairs
Programmed street cleaning. R. Carmack. il
Am City 84:78-9 Jl '69

Street traffic
Signal system that has them asking for more.
D. Darnell. il Am City 84:148+ O '69

Water supply
How we sold backflow prevention. E. C.
Ross. il Am City 84:148-50 S '69
RIVES, Lloyd
Micro-presence. por Time 94:63 D 5 '69
RIVIERA
See also
Saint-Tropez, France
RIVIERE, Donald
Staggering practices. Newsweek 74:55 Ag 18
'69
RIVNAY, E.
Overhead sprinklers of Israel; how to provide
a nice, wet place where insects you don't
want thrive. bibliog Natur Hist 78:57-61
F '69

RIZER, H. M.
Overland cruising. Motor B 123:64-5+ Je '69
RIZZO, Francis
Doctor Borodin's formula. Opera N 33:12-13 Mr 1 '69
Opera primer: why the director? Opera N 33:26-30 F 15 '69
RIZZO, Michael E.
Active activities program. Clear House 44: 182-4 N '69
RIZZOLI editore. See Publishers and publishing —Italy
ROAD accidents. See Traffic accidents
ROAD construction. See Highway engineering
ROAD machinery
Machine for all seasons. il Am City 84:51 Ag '69
Router prepares concrete for overlay. J. W. King. il Am City 84:83+ Je '69
ROAD maps, guides, etc.
Europe by car? you'll need maps. Sunset 143:41 D '69
ROAD runners (birds)
Marvel of speed and endurance. L. E. Hoffman. Home Gard 56:78 Ap '69
ROAD signs
Breakaway sign posts reduce traffic hazards. il Am City 84:112 Ja '69
ROAD traffic
See also
Electronics in traffic control
Rule of the road
Traffic engineering
Traffic signs

Automatic control
Silent Sam; robot flagman controlling traffic across the Triborough bridge; interview. D. Berne. il New Yorker 45:45-6 D 13 '69

Radio control
Frenzy on the freeways; excerpts from Take an alternate route. P. Pierce. il Read Digest 94:205-6 +Ap '69
ROAD transport. See Transportation, Automotive
ROADRUNNERS. See Road runners (birds)
ROADS
See also
Driveways
Highway engineering
National parks and reserves—Roads
Pavements
Snow and ice removal
Soil mechanics
Trails

Federal aid
Back of delays in road building; highway-building contracts and employment programs. U S News 66:8 Ja 27 '69

Lighting
Cantilevered light poles cut freeway accidents; entrance to Cleveland's Innerbelt south highway from Memorial shoreway. A. Nichols. il Am City 84:132 Ap '69
Lighting cuts accidents, reduces cost. il Am City 84:146 O '69

Location
Halting the highway men; urban highways run into barriers. Bsns W p37 Jl 19 '69
Running over the public; proposed regulations on selection of highway locations. New Repub 160:12 Ja 25 '69

Maintenance and repair
Highway as a killer. il Life 66:24D-35 My 30 '69
See also
Road machinery

Safety devices and measures
Crash barrier saves lives. il Sci Digest 66:48-9 O '69
Highway as a killer. il Life 66:24D-35 My 30 '69
New barriers that cushion the crunch in crashes. E. D. Fales, jr. il Pop Mech 132:91-3+ N '69
New controlled deceleration barrier tested. il Am City 84:168+ S '69
Sand and balloons. Time 93:66 My 2 '69
Sandpiles make 50-m.p.h. smashups kid stuff. E. H. Arctander. il Pop Sci 195:48-9 Jl '69

Snow and ice control
See also
Pavements—Heating

Superhighways
See Express highways

Traffic lines
See Traffic markings

Winter maintenance
See also
Pavements—Heating

British Columbia
See Roads—Canada

California
Only in spots have we tamed the California coast. M. F. K. Fisher. il Holiday 46:40-5+ N '69

Canada
Up B.C. 101, along the sunshine coast. il Sunset 143:24-5 Ag '69

Central America
See also
Pan American highway

Colombia
See also
Pan American highway

Florida
Easy way to explore the Everglades: Loop road. G. X. Sand. il Sci Digest 65:37-41 F '69

Latin America
History
Royal highway of the Incas; reprint. J. Carrera Andrade. il UNESCO Courier 22: 71-3 Ag '69

Oregon
Back roads in the Willamette Valley. il Sunset 142:70 My '69
John Day ford at McDonald. il Sunset 143: 30 S '69

South America
See Roads—Latin America
See also
Express highways—Southern states

Texas
Texas River road. L. M. Rhodes. il Travel 132:38-41+ O '69

United States
See also
Express highways

Western states
Truly, Winnemucca-to-the-sea highway. il Sunset 143:52+ O '69
ROADSIDE business
U.S. journal: lower Bucks County, Pa; buying and selling along Route 1. C. Trillin. New Yorker 45:169-75 N 15 '69
ROADSIDE improvement
How to remove billboards. il Time 94:72 O 31 '69
See also
Billboards
Cleaning of cities, towns, etc.
ROADSIDE marketing
His fruit stand motto: no poisons used. il Org Gard & Farm 16:78-9 Ag '69
New ideas for roadside retailing. G. Logsdon. il Farm J 93:18-19+ Ag '69
ROADSIDE menageries. See Menageries
ROADSIDE stands. See Roadside marketing
ROALMAN, A. R.
Bounty on water polluters. Motor B 123: 78-81 My '69
House-boating. Travel 132:50-3 Ag '69
Making the most of family fights. Todays Health 47:54-5+ F '69
What you can do about pollution. Todays Health 47:24-7 Mr '69
ROANOKE, Va.

Anti-poverty program
Managing a war on poverty. il Nations Bsns 57:52-5 F '69
ROARK, Gene E.
Call of the wildcat. R. Levy. il por Duns R 93:56+ F '69
ROASTING. See Cookery—Poultry
ROBACK, Herbert
Do we need a department of science and technology? bibliog Science 165:36-43 Jl 4 '69
ROBATON, John
My 50,000-mile, three-year photographic education. Pop Phot 64:102-5+ Mr '69
ROBB, Charles C.
Confrontation in Pittsburgh. Nation 209:272-4 S 22 '69

ROBB, Lynda Bird (Johnson)
Books they loved. McCalls 96:28+ Ja '69

about

How Lynda Bird was guarded by McCalls. E.
Weston. McCalls 96:89-90 Mr '69

ROBBERIES and assaults
Brenda and the bandits. B. Sheridan. il Good
H 168:12+ Mr '69
Brooklyn delicatessen caper: hijacking of
Wells Fargo armored truck. E. Shrake. il
Sports Illus 31:20-1 N 24 '69
Gray ghost wins again; Scotland Yard's
T. Butler tracked down the perpetrators
of the biggest cash theft in history.
J. Stewart-Gordon. Read Digest 95:229-34
Jl '69
Truck hijackers, latest crime problem. il U S
News 66:42-4 Mr 17 '69

ROBBERS. See Brigands and robbers

ROBBERSON, Elbert
Is CB for your boat? Yachting 125:60-1+
F '69
—See Robberson, W. jt. auth.

ROBBERSON, Winifred
Boating business. See issues of Yachting
Maintenance with new products. Yachting
125:70-1+ Ap '69
—and Robberson, Elbert
Davis HELP. Yachting 126:198 O '69

ROBBIN, Anthony
Smithson's non-site sights. Art N 67:50-3
F '69

ROBBINS, E. Clairborne
Big bequest. Chr Today 14:42 Ja 2 '70

ROBBINS, Eugenia S.
Storm King art center. Art in Am 57:108-9
My '69

ROBBINS, Harold, pseud.
Company; interview. New Yorker 45:45-8
N 29 '69

about

Bleak as Beckett. P. Nathan. Pub W 196:72
N 17 '69
Dream merchant. G. Wolff. il por Newsweek
74:126+ O 27 '69

ROBBINS, Jerome
Dances at a gathering; interview. ed. by E.
Denby. Dance Mag 43:47-55 Jl '69

about

J. Robbins, dance master. W. Terry. il por
Sat R 52:36 D 6 '69
Jerome Robbins prepares Dancers at a
gathering for New York city ballet. il pors
Dance Mag 43:40-1 Je '69
Robbins comes home. H. Saal. il por News-
week 73:103 Je 2 '69
World of dance; Dances at a gathering. W.
Terry. il Sat R 52:41-2 Jl 26 '69

ROBBINS, Jhan, and Robbins, June
More than a mother. Redbook 133:90-1+ My
'69
Never marry a doctor. McCalls 96:69+ S '69
Pageant of the children and the wee ani-
mals. Redbook 134:98-9+ D '69

ROBBINS, June
Case against little league mothers. McCalls
96:55+ Jl '69
—See Robbins, Jhan. jt. auth.

ROBBINS, Martin E. See Hobson, J. E. jt.
auth.

ROBBINS, Phillips W. See Losick, R. jt. auth.

ROBBINS, William
How to build a river in the Arizona desert
to flow under the London bridge. Esquire
71:78-83+ F '69

ROBERSON, John R.
Master train of France: the Mistral. Holiday
46:60-1+ D '69

ROBERT; story. See Morgan, B.

ROBERT Capa award. See Photography, Journalistic—Awards

ROBERT F. Kennedy youth center, Morgantown, W.Va. See Detention homes

ROBERT Joffrey ballet. See City center Joffrey
ballet

ROBERT S. Marx theater. See Cincinnati—Theater

ROBERT Tannahill's collection. See Detroit institute of arts

ROBERTS, Arthur O.
Our winter is a foggy drive; poem. Chr Today 14:13 D 19 '69

ROBERTS, Dewey Noble
D.N. creates a job. V. Sneider. il pors Har
Yrs 9:19-21 F '69

ROBERTS, Don
Libraries to the (electric) people. Wilson Lib
Bul 44:288-9 N '69

Overdue. Wilson Lib Bul 44:203+ O '69
(ed) Wait, come back! bibliog Wilson Lib
Bul 44:287-325 N '69

ROBERTS, Eugene. See Kittredge, J. S. jt.
auth.

ROBERTS, Glenn
Identity crisis on U.S. campuses. Commonweal 90:557-8 S 19 '69

ROBERTS, Gordon C. K. and others
Noncovalent binding of a spin-labeled inhibi-
tor to ribonuclease. bibliog Science 165:504-6
Ag 1 '69

ROBERTS, Janet
Family pottery. Ceram Mo 17:28-9 Je '69

ROBERTS, John
Mike Lang (groovy kid from Brooklyn) plus
John Roberts (unlimited capital) equals
Woodstock. R. Reeves. il por N Y Times
Mag p34-5+ S 7 '69; Reply. K. Roberts.
p54 O 5 '69

ROBERTS, John A.
I watched my baby being born. Parents Mag
44:60-1+ Ja '69

ROBERTS, Kenneth
Clock watching, 19th-century style; interview,
ed. by S. Nerenberg. il House B 111:50-1
Ag '69

ROBERTS, Millard George
Life and hard times of Parsons college. J. D.
Koerner. il por Sat R 52:53-5+ Jl 19 '69

ROBERTS, Nick
Ions on vacation. il Pop Electr 30:50 Je '69

ROBERTS, Oral
Oral Roberts: rousing return to TV. W. Willoughby. il por Chr Today 13:40 Mr 28 '69

ROBERTS, Paul
Grammar, usage, teachers of English, and
Paul Roberts. R. J. Goba. bibliog f Engl J
58:886-91 S '69

ROBERTS, Robert C.
Tree above price. Am For 75:36+ Jl '69

ROBERTS, Robert E. See Bettis, M. C. jt.
auth.

ROBERTS, Robin
Baseball. Sports Illus 30:46-7 F 24 '69

ROBERTS, Ronald
Of many things. V. S. Kearney. America 121:
inside cover Jl 19 '69

ROBERTS, Steven V.
Breaking ranks and breaking dissenters.
Commonweal 91:397-8 Ja 9 '70
Charlie Manson: one man's family. N Y
Times Mag p 10-11+ Ja 4 '70
Genuine Dixieland: the old sound dies. Com-
monweal 89:734-5 Mr 14 '69
Maximum feasible leakage. Commonweal 89:
667-8 F 28 '69
Moon over Biafra: a plea for priorities. Com-
monweal 89:489-90 Ja 17 '69
Oil pressure. New Repub 160:13-14 Mr 15 '69
Reports: Los Angeles. Atlan 224:30+ S '69
Russians are coming at UCLA. Commonweal
91:174-5 N 7 '69
Seventy-six and still Diamond Lil. N Y Times
Mag p64-5+ N 2 '69
Voters are in: Los Angeles. Commonweal 90:
381 Je 20 '69
Warning! California will fall into the ocean
in April! N Y Times Mag p 12+ Ap 6 '69
We had a baby. por Good H 168:102-3+ My
'69

ROBERTS, W. Dayton
Latin American Protestants: which way will
they go? Chr Today 14:14-16 O 10 '69

ROBERTS, Wallace I.
Battle for urban schools. Ed Digest 34:4-7
Ja '69
Can urban schools be reformed? Sat R 52:
70-2+ My 17 '69
Patterns of reform. Sat R 52:80+ O 18 '69
Thirty thousand innocents abroad. Sat R 52:
61-2+ F 15 '69
Voices in the classroom (cont) Sat R 52:69
Mr 15 '69
Young Protestants. Sat R 52:22-3 D 27 '69

ROBERTS, Walter Orr
After the moon, the earth! address, Decem-
ber 28, 1969. Science 167:11-16 Ja 2 '70
Next objective in space. Science 163:521 F
7 '69
—See Cadle. R. D. jt. auth.

ROBERTSON, C. A.
Oscilloscope kits. Electr World 82:26 N '69

ROBERTSON, D. H. See Reed, R. I. jt. auth.

ROBERTSON, Frank
Unhurried splendor of the Japanese bath.
Holiday 46:88-9+ O '69

ROBERTSON, Ian
Apartheid's empire. Nation 208:596-7+ My 12
'69

ROBERTSON, Jack
Remember the Pueblo. Nation 208:326-8 Mr
17 '69
Space is not black. Nation 208:14-16 Je 30
'69

ROBERTSON, Jaime. See Robertson, R.

ROBERTSON, James L.
Concerned citizen speaks about America's turmoil; address, May 22, 1969. U S News 66:96+ Je 9 '69
One generation speaks to another. U S News 67:29-31 Jl 7 '69

ROBERTSON, Josephine
We chose a college town. Har Yrs 9:19-21 Je '69

ROBERTSON, N. and Sams, K. I.
Industrial relations reform in Great Britain. bibliog f Mo Labor R 92:35-40 Ja '69

ROBERTSON, Nan
Why Julie is the happiest Nixon. Good H 168: 76-7+ Je '69

ROBERTSON, Robbie
Down to old Dixie and back. il por Time 95:42-6 Ja 12 '70

ROBESON, Stacy B.
Bobwhite for western New York? Cons 24: 8-9 D '69

ROBIN, Ralph
Sense of smiling; poem. New Repub 161:23 Ag 2 '69

ROBINETTE, Harry
Electrically heated hotbed. Horticulture 47: 26-7 My '69
Grow vegetables in a home hotbed. Org Gard & Farm 16:85-8 Ja '69

ROBINS, A. H. company
Treating people as individuals; interview. E. C. Robins. Nations Bsns 57:48-52 Ja '69

ROBINS, Corinne
(ed) See Bladen, R. Artist speaks; Ronald Bladen
(ed) See Krushenick, N. Artist speaks: Nicholas Krushenick

ROBINS, E. Claiborne
Treating people as individuals; interview. por Nations Bsns 57:48-52 Ja '69

about

Richmond's bombshell. Newsweek 74:79 Jl 7 '69

ROBINSON, A. Jean, and others
Hageman factor (factor XII) deficiency in marine mammals. bibliog Science 166:1420-2 D 12 '69

ROBINSON, Alfred S.
Fantasy Washington coin of Alfred S. Robinson. C. F. French. il Hobbies 73:102 F '69

ROBINSON, Barbara
Almost any Friday; story. McCalls 96:72-3 Je '69
Happy birthdays; story. McCalls 97:104-5 O '69
Louisa May and the facts of life; story. Redbook 132:92-3 Ap '69
Really? At your age? story. McCalls 96:96-7 F '69

ROBINSON, Betty
Checkpoint for travelers. See issues of House beautiful

ROBINSON, Bill
Editor's page. See issues of Yachting

ROBINSON, Carrie C.
Media for the black curriculum. bibliog ALA Bul 63:242-6 F '69

ROBINSON, Cervin
Bravura in Brooklyn. il Arch Forum 131:42-7 N '69

ROBINSON, Conway
Turtle clapping. Field & S 74:66-7+ Je '69

ROBINSON, Dillard
Newark cathedral elects Negro dean. Chr Cent 86:609 Ap 30 '69

ROBINSON, Eddie
Grambling college: where stars are made. W. Rogers. il por Look 33:72-5 D 16 '69

ROBINSON, Edwin Arlington
Two Corys: a sample of inductive teaching. L. J. Clifton. Engl J 58:414-15 Mr '69

ROBINSON, Elton
Rediscovery: a Tiffany room. Art in Am 57: 72-7 Jl '69

ROBINSON, Forrest
Nativity: a meditation. Chr Cent 86:1637 D 24 '69

ROBINSON, Frank
Have the hitters really gone? debate. Look 33:84+ My 13 '69

about

High flight for an Oriole. W. Leggett. il por Sports Illus 30:38-9 F 3 '69
West in a birdbath. W. Leggett. il Sports Illus 30:18-23 Je 2 '69

ROBINSON, J. C.
Mars: correlation of optical and radar observations. bibliog Science 164:176-7 Ap 11 '69

ROBINSON, Jeffrey
Celebration: the lyric poetry of Melville Cane. Am Scholar 38:286-96 Spr '69

ROBINSON, Jerome B.
Bluebills on the St Lawrence. Outdoor Life 144:40-1+ D '69
Easy way to pluck ducks. Outdoor Life 144: 70-1 O '69
The 100th rabbit. Outdoor Life 143:76-7+ F '69
Whitewater! Motor B 124:80-1+ Ag '69

ROBINSON, John Arthur Thomas, bp
Not radical enough? excerpts from Christian freedom in a permissive society. por Chr Cent 86:1446-9 N 12 '69
Protest of a troubled Protestant, by H. O. J. Brown. Review
Nat R 21:707-8 Jl 15 '69. M. S. Evans

ROBINSON, John P. jr
Lively laser. Pop Electr 31:33-5+ D '69
Ovonics. Pop Electr 30:55-8 Mr '69

ROBINSON, Louie
Lee Elder, hottest sophomore in pro golf. Ebony 24:60-4 S '69
Pleasures and problems of being Bill Cosby. Ebony 24:144-6+ Jl '69
TV discovers the black man. Ebony 24:27-30+ F '69

ROBINSON, Sally
In my opinion. por Seventeen 28:22 Mr '69
What should parents see? Seventeen 28:42+ Ja '69

ROBINSON, Thomas E.
One a penny, two a penny. Todays Ed 58:61 Ja '69

ROBINSON, Thomas W.
Peking's revolutionary strategy in the developing world: the failures of success. bibliog f Ann Am Acad 386:64-77 N '69

ROBINSON, William E. and others
Genetic coding: oligonucleotide coding for first six amino acid residues of the coat protein of R17 bacteriophage. bibliog Science 166:1291-3 D 5 '69

ROBINSON, Willie
Brotherhood. il por Newsweek 74:51 S 15 '69

ROBINSON Open golf tournament. See Golf—Tournaments

ROBISON, John
Scottish encyclopedist and the piano forte. E. M. Ripin. bibliog f il Mus Q 55:487-99 O '69

ROBISON, Richard A. and Sprinkle, James
Ctenocystoidea: new class of primitive echinoderms. bibliog Science 166:1512-14 D 19 '69

ROBLES, Richard
Victims; excerpts B. Lefkowitz and K. G. Gross. il por Look 33:39-44+ Je 24 '69

ROBOTS. See Automatons

ROBRAN, Edward L. See Stiles, W. E. jt. auth.

ROBY, Pamela
Inequality: a trend analysis. bibliog f Ann Am Acad 385:110-17 S '69

ROC, John, pseud.
Fire! Criticism
Nation 208:220 F 17 '69
New Yorker 44:96 F 8 '69

ROCARD, Michel
Eternal non. por Time 94:40 N 7 '69
Painful event. il por Newsweek 74:56+ N 10 '69

ROCHE, Douglas J.
Togetherness is the word in Canada. Commonweal 89:578 F 7 '69

ROCHE, James Michael
Future of the automobile; interview. pors U S News 66:64-71 F 10 '69
Imperatives of world economic progress; address, November 17, 1969. Vital Speeches 36:187-90 Ja 1 '70

about

GM workers say Roche is wrong. U S News 66:88 My 12 '69

ROCHE, John P.
Nixon after six months. por(p27) N Y Times Mag p26 Jl 20 '69

ROCHE, Mary Alice
Lily pool from a washtub. Org Gard & Farm 16:55-7 My '69

ROCHESTER, N.Y.
Rochester progress; Anchorage partnership. il Am City 84:112+ N '69
Try judging a city by its traffic signals. E. L. Simm. Am City 84:120+ Ja '69

Community centers

Rochester senior citizens love life; Danforth center. J. M. Caverly. il Parks & Rec 4:15+ N '69

Negroes

Answer to riots; the Rochester plan; FIGHT organization. il U S News 67:58-61 Ag 4 '69

ROCHESTER, N. Y.—Negroes—*Continued*
Cop teen-agers dig; policewoman P. Thompson. il Ebony 24:106-8+ Je '69
Scientist with a cause; B. Gifford and FIGHT. il Ebony 25:73-6+ D '69

Police

Cop teen-agers dig; policewoman P. Thompson. il Ebony 24:106-8+ Je '69

ROCHESTER, N.Y. diocese. See Catholic church—Dioceses

ROCHESTER, N. Y. University
Making endowments greener. Bsns W p66+ S 13 '69

ROCHESTER conference on high energy physics. See International conference on high energy physics

ROCHESTER corporation
To expand, sell the company; Rochester-Pauley petroleum merger. il Bsns W p 168+ O 18 '69

ROCHESTER May festival. See Music festivals—New York (state)

ROCK, Maxine A.
Atlanta zoo: survival center for animals. Nat Parks 43:14-16 S '69

ROCK carvings. See Indians of North America—Antiquities—South Dakota

ROCK climbing. See Mountaineering

ROCK drawings. See Petroglyphs

ROCK dusting. See Coal mines and mining—Safety devices and measures

ROCK garden plants. See Plants, Rock garden

ROCK gardens. See Gardens, Rock

ROCK 'n' roll dancing
Rock, etc; series of rock dances in New York state world's fair pavilion, Flushing Meadows. E. Willis. New Yorker 45:80-1 Jl 26 '69

ROCK 'n' roll groups
And now a rock opera! the Who's Tommy. J. Gabree. il Hi Fi 19:80 S '69
Band. S. K. Oberbeck. il Newsweek 74:139 O 27 '69
The band, the best? R. Goldstein. il Vogue 155:160-1 Ja 15 '70
Blind lead the way-out; Blind Faith. A. Goldman. Life 67:28 S 26 '69
Blood, sweat and tears. B. Korall. Holiday 46:39+ D '69
Brutal and beautiful; the Who's opera Tommy. C. E. Fager. Chr Cent 86:1284-5 O 8 '69
Dada rockers. S. K. Oberbeck. il Newsweek 74:106+ D 15 '69
Digging for rock: Fillmore East. showcase for groups trying to climb the ladder. S. K. Oberbeck. il Newsweek 74:101 D 1 '69
From pillar to broom; Blood, Sweat & Tears. il Time 93:53 My 9 '69
Hour of the wolf; Steppenwolf. H. Saal. il Newsweek 73:114 F 17 '69
It's supergroup! Blind Faith with report by M. Paley. il Life 67:84-7+ O 24 '69
Jam from old Cream; new supergroup called Blind faith. il Time 94:54 Ag 29 '69
Kicking out the jams; MC5. H. Saal. il Newsweek 73:117 My 19 '69
New blood; the Youngbloods. il Newsweek 74:120 S 22 '69
Report: New York production of rock opera, Tommy at Fillmore East. S. Jenkins. il Opera N 34:22 D 6 '69
Rock style: defying the American dream; group named Rhinoceros. S. Davidson. il Harper. 239:53-62 Jl '69
Rolling again; Rolling Stones. H. Saal. il Newsweek 74:137 N 17 '69
Rolling Stones; Beggars' triumph. E. Sander. il Sat R 52:48 Ja 25 '69
Rose petals and revolution; Rolling Stones. il Time 94:90 N 28 '69
Satin, silky, sexy; 5th Dimension. il Time 93:72-3 Ap 18 '69
Sha Na Na, the unreal fifties. R. Goldstein. Vogue 154:126 N 1 '69
Stones keep rolling. E. Sander. il Sat R 52:67-8+ N 29 '69
The Who. New Yorker 45:54-6 N 15 '69
Who's pop opera, Tommy. A. Goldman. Life 67:20 O 17 '69
Who's Who. H. Saal. il Newsweek 73:95 Je 9 '69
See also
Beatles
Phonograph records—Rock 'n' roll groups

ROCK 'n' roll music
Age of rock, by J. Eisen. Review
Commonweal 91:49-50 O 10 '69. M. Rosenthal
Avant-rock in the classroom. D. E. Morse. Engl J 58:196-200+ F '69

Birth of rock. il Newsweek 73:12 Ap 7 '69
Booker T. and the M.G.'s. P. Garland. il Ebony 24:92-4+ Ap '69
Chuck Berry. M. Lydon. il Ramp Mag 8:47-56 D '69
Down to old Dixie and back; The band. il Time 95:42-6 Ja 12 '70
From pillar to broom; Blood, Sweat & Tears. il Time 93:53 My 9 '69
Great rock conspiracy; theories of Gary Allen. P. A. Luce. Nat R 21:959+ S 23 '69
Hour of the wolf; Steppenwolf. H. Saal. il Newsweek 73:114 F 17 '69
In my opinion; we shouldn't knock bubble-gum. A. Nash. Seventeen 28:238 N '69
John and Yoko Ono Lennon; give peace a chance. E. Sander. il Sat R 52:46-7 Je 28 '69
Life-style that rock unleashed. E. Sander. Vogue 154:127+ Ag 1 '69
Long Hair? American tribal love-rock musical. J. Rockwell. il Opera N 34:8-13 D 20 '69
Musical events: musicology of rock; summary of article, ed. by W. Sargeant. T. MacCluskey. New Yorker 45:211-13 N 15 '69
Purity, not parody, in a real rock revival; Creedence clearwater revival. A. Goldman. Life 66:8 My 9 '69
Report: New York production of rock opera, Tommy at Fillmore East. S. Jenkins. il Opera N 34:22 D 6 '69
Return of the big beat. il Time 94:57-8 Ag 15 '69
Rock: art, revolution, or sell-out? J. Gabree. il Hi Fi 19:MA10-11 Ag '69
Rock encyclopedia, comp. by L. Roxon. Review
Newsweek 74:127 N 10 '69. S. K. Oberbeck
Rock, etc; Beach boys, Box tops, and the Brooklyn bridge in Gaelic park. E. Willis. New Yorker 45:83+ Ag 9 '69
Rock, etc; series of rock dances in New York state world's fair pavilion, Flushing Meadows. E. Willis. New Yorker 45:80-1 Jl 26 '69
Rock style: defying the American dream; group named Rhinoceros. S. Davidson. il Harper 239:53-62 Jl '69
Rocks in their heads. A. Shaw. il Hi Fi 19:48-51 Ap '69
Talking rock! panel discussion by seven pop musicians; ed. by E. Miller. il Seventeen 28:130-1+ F '69
Tommy, fresh, vital sounds. D. Amram. Vogue 155:78 Ja 15 '70
Who's pop opera, Tommy. A. Goldman. Life 67:20 O 17 '69
Who's Who. H. Saal. il Newsweek 73:95 Je 9 '69
See also
Phonograph records—Rock 'n' roll music
Radio broadcasting—Music
Religion and music
Rock 'n' roll singers

Bibliography

Rock critics. R. Christgau. Harper 239:24+ S '69
Periodicals
See also
Rolling stone (periodical)

ROCK 'n' roll singers
Act of faith; Blind faith at the Garden. H. Saal. il Newsweek 74:76 Jl 28 '69
All you need is love. Love is all you need. So writes a rock poet. But is that poetry? K. Murphy and R. Gross. il N Y Times Mag p36-8+ Ap 13 '69; Discussion. p22+ My 11 '69
Girls, letting go. H. Saal. il Newsweek 74:68-71 Jl 14 '69
Lean clean and bluesy; Creedence clearwater revival. il Time 93:58 Je 27 '69
Return of the big beat. il Time 94:57-8 Ag 15 '69
See also names of rock 'n' roll singers. e.g. T. Turner

ROCK opera Tommy. See Rock 'n' roll music

ROCK paintings. See Cave drawings and paintings; Petroglyphs

ROCK roses
If all else fails, try rockrose. il Sunset 142:212 Je '69

ROCKEFELLER, Abby Aldrich, folk art collection. See Williamsburg, Va—Abby Aldrich Rockefeller folk art collection

ROCKEFELLER, David
International financial challenges; address. October 16, 1969. Vital Speeches 36:83-6 N 15 '69
What's ahead for interest rates; interview. por U S News 67:24-5 Jl 21 '69

ROCKEFELLER, David—*Continued*

About

Power shift at the Chase? por Bsns W p30-1 Ja 10 '70

ROCKEFELLER, John Davison, 1906-
Why I believe in philanthropy. por Read Digest 95:185-6+ D '69
Youth, love and sex: the new chivalry. Look 33:32+ O 7 '69

about

No tax due, but rich man pays. por U S News 66:16 Mr 10 '69

ROCKEFELLER, John Davison, 1938?-
Jay Rockefeller: tall talent for the new Democrats. A. Wolff. il pors Look 33:36-8+ Ap 29 '69
Mr and Mrs John D. Rockefeller, IV, rebels inside the Establishment. por Vogue 153:148-9 My '69
Sweepstakes of the '70s: five entries. il por Newsweek 73:27-8 F 24 '69

ROCKEFELLER, Laurance S.
Gift at Haleakala. il Nat Parks 43:13 Mr '69

ROCKEFELLER, Nelson Aldrich, 1908-
Nelson Rockefeller begins mission to Latin America; remarks to news correspondents, May 11, 1969. Dept State Bul 60:470-2 Je 2 '69
Tenth anniversary of the St Lawrence Seaway; introductory remarks, June 27, 1969. Dept State Bul 61:67 Jl 28 '69

about

Bad news from a bigtime spender. Life 66:36 Ap 18 '69
Nelson Rockefeller's collections: primitive art (African, Oceanic and pre-Columbian) exhibitions. T. B. Hess. Art N 68:25 Sum '69
Pervasive excitement for the eye and mind. il Time 93:88-93 My 16 '69
President names Nelson Rockefeller for special mission to Latin America; statement, February 17,1969. R. M. Nixon. Dept State Bul 60:198 Mr 10 '69
Rocky as a collector. J. R. Mellow. il pors N Y Times Mag p34-6+ My 18 '69
Rocky as collector. il por Newsweek 73:88 My 26 '69
Rocky's Island line. Newsweek 74:72 O 20 '69
Two key governors: getting set for '70. il por U S News 67:9+ D 8 '69
Welfare plan of the future? U S News 66:14 F 24 '69

Visits to Latin America, 1969

Barnstormers. il por Newsweek 73:60 My 26 '69
Bolivia. M. Arias. Chr Cent 86:1023-4 Jl 30 '69
Don Rocky's mission. Time 93:38 My 23 '69
End of the Rocky road. il por Newsweek 74:38 Jl 14 '69
Governor Rockefeller reports on mission to Latin America; text of letter from President Nixon to Governor Nelson A. Rockefeller; September 3, 1969. R. M. Nixon. Dept State Bul 61:303-4 O 6 '69
Hiya, fella! Gringo peeg. Nat R 21:580 Je 17 '69
Latin America: protest and progress. il Time 94:29 Jl 4 '69
Neighbors are restless. il por Bsns W p38-9 Je 7 '69
Nelson Rockefeller begins mission to Latin America; remarks to news correspondents, May 11, 1969. R. M. Nixon; N. A. Rockefeller. Dept State Bul 60:470-2 Je 2 '69
New turmoil in Latin America: its meaning for U.S. il por U S News 66:30-2 Je 16 '69
Ordeal of a lightning rod. il Newsweek 73:43 Je 16 '69
PR diplomacy. Nation 208:746-7 Je 16 '69
Peru's actions on Rockefeller visit and U.S. military missions regretted; Department statement. Dept State Bul 60:509-10 Je 16 '69
Quieter round 3: visit to Brasília. Time 93:37-8 Je 27 '69
Rockefeller report on Latin America. il por Time 94:42 N 14 '69
Rockefeller reports: half right on Latin America. R. O'Mara. Nation 209:602-4 D 1 '69
Rockefeller's bonfire. New Repub 160:7-9 Je 21 '69
Rockefeller's report. il por Newsweek 74:68 N 17 '69
Rockefeller's return. New Repub 161:9 Jl 19 '69
Rockefeller's tour: painful reappraisal of the neighbors. il Time 94:25-7 Jl 11 '69
Rocky soldiers on. Newsweek 73:58-9 Je 30 '69

Rocky takes a trip. D. Horowitz. il Ramp Mag 8:60-1 Ag '69
Rocky way. il por Newsweek 73:65 Je 9 '69
Rocky's rocky path. Time 93:49 Je 13 '69
Rocky's second stage. il por Time 93:41+ Je 6 '69
Setbacks for U.S. in Latin America. U S News 66:7 Je 30 '69
Two for the road. il por Newsweek 73:36 My 19 '69
Why the Rockefeller mission backfired. Bsns W p 166 Je 21 '69
Wrong man, wrong time, wrong mission. M. M. M. Alves. Commonweal 90:407-9 Je 27 '69

ROCKEFELLER, Rodman C.
Meeting the challenge of communication; address, June 2, 1969. Vital Speeches 35:716-18 S 15 '69

ROCKEFELLER, Sharon Lee (Percy)
Mr and Mrs John D. Rockefeller, IV, rebels inside the Establishment. por Vogue 153:148-9 My '69

ROCKEFELLER Center. See New York (city)—Rockefeller Center

ROCKEFELLER public service awards
Crafts receives top career award. Am For 75:39 Ja '69

ROCKET-assisted projectiles. See Projectiles

ROCKET belts. See Flying machines

ROCKET engines
Air force revs up new space thruster; restartable front-end engine. Bsns W p32-3 O 4 '69
High-energy motor planned for new air-to-air missile. Aviation W 91:27 Jl 7 '69
In the news; Lockheed propulsion company successfully tests promising monopropellant liquid rocket engine. il Space World F-5-65:41 My '69
Reaction control for the Project Apollo service module; R-4D liquid propellant rocket. il Space World F-3-63:34-5 Mr '69
Seven-segment solid assembled for test. il Aviation W 90:34-5 My 12 '69
See also
Ion engines
Space vehicles—Propulsion systems

Design

Lunar module descent engine. il Space World F-10-70:40-1 O '69
Next big step for rockets. il Bsns W p 174 S 20 '69

Exhaust

Apollo lunar module engine exhaust products. B. R. Simoneit and others. bibliog il Science 166:733-8 N 7 '69

Specifications

U.S. rocket motors (cont) Aviation W 90:169-71+ Mr 10 '69

Testing

Titan 3M strap-on test fired; solid propellant rocket motor. R. G. O'Lone. il Aviation W 90:23-4 My 5 '69

ROCKET models
Exploring space with rocket models. il Good H 169:181 D '69
Man with a million rockets. N. Carlisle. il Mech Illus 65:64-5+ Ag '69
This $16 kit makes you a whiz at model rocketry. W. C. Leckey. il Pop Mech 131:196-8+ Mr '69
See also
Space vehicle models

ROCKET propulsion
Rockets bolster DC-9 payload capability. il Aviation W 90:70-2+ My 19 '69
See also
Rockets, Atomic powered

ROCKETS
See also
Guided missiles

Design

New Athena test vehicle designed. W. C. Wetmore. il Aviation W 90:81+ My 12 '69

Fuel

See also
Hydrogen, Liquid

History

Harvest of Operation Paperclip. il Newsweek 74:10 Jl 7 '69
Moon rocket, circa 1929. Space World F-7-67:38-9 Jl '69

Specifications

Leading U.S. international research rockets (cont) Aviation W 90:158-9 Mr 10 '69

ROCKETS—*Continued*

Testing

New Athena test vehicle designed; ballistic re-entry research rocket. W. C. Wetmore. il Aviation W 90:81+ My 12 '69
See also
Space vehicles—Propulsion systems—Testing

Use in research

Search for soft X-rays from the galaxy. R. J. Grader and others. il Sky & Tel 37:79-81 F '69

ROCKETS, Atomic powered

NASA puts an atom in its tank; Nerva XE nuclear rocket engine. il Bsns W p92+ Mr 29 '69
Nerva continuation increases NASA research fund request. Aviation W 90:28 Ja 20 '69
Nuclear rocket development station. il Space World F-12-72:4-15 D '69

Testing

First Nerva XE engine firings underway. N. S. Himmel. il Aviation W 90:20-1 Mr 31 '69

ROCKETTES. See Dancers

ROCKEY, Linda

Mrs Langford for the defense; reprint. Ebony 24:57-8+ Mr '69

ROCKING horses. See Toys

ROCKLAND, Lawrence H.

Psychiatric consultation to the clergy. bibliog Ment Hy 53:205-7 Ap '69

ROCKLAND state mental hospital, Orangeburg, N.Y. See Hospitals, Psychiatric

ROCKROSES. See Rock roses

ROCKS

See also
Metamorphism (geology)
Petrology

Age

See also
Geological time
Geology, Stratigraphic

Analysis

Acidic components of Green River shale identified by a gas chromatography-mass spectrometry-computer system. R. C. Murphy and others. bibliog il Science 165:695-7 Ag 15 '69
Estimating proportions in petrographic mixing equations by least-squares approximation. W. B. Bryan and others. bibliog il Science 163:926-7 F 28 '69

Collectors and collecting

Those irresistible rocks. G. M. Schultz. il Pop Gard 20:38-41+ Spr '68
Your own thing. il Seventeen 28:22 Jl '69

Deformation

Enstatite: disorder produced by a megabar shock event. S. S. Pollack and P. S. DeCarli. bibliog il Science 165:591-2 Ag 8 '69
High-pressure mechanical instability in rocks. J. D. Byerlee and W. F. Brace. bibliog il Science 164:713-15 My 9 '69

ROCKS, Igneous

Lherzolite, anorthosite, gabbro, and basalt dredged from the Mid-Indian Ocean ridge. C. G. Engel and R. L. Fisher. bibliog il Science 166:1136-41 N 28 '69
See also
Anorthosite
Diorites
Trachyte

ROCKS, Lunar

Analysis

See Lunar geology

ROCKS, Sedimentary

Sedimentary rock types: relative proportions as a function of geological time. R. M. Garrels and F. T. Mackenzie. bibliog il Science 163:570-1 F 7 '69
See also
Graywackes
Shale

ROCKVILLE, Md.

Enclosed air-conditioned downtown. il Am City 84:86 Je '69

ROCKWELL, John

Hundred years' war. Opera N 33:18-19 My 17 '69
Long Hair? Opera N 34:8-13 D 20 '69
Master's apprentices. Opera N 34:6-7 Ja 10 '70
Something old, something new. Opera N 33:24-5 F 8 '69

ROCKWELL, Norman

Behind Apollo; painting. Look 33:44-7 Jl 15 '69

Final impossibility: man's tracks on the moon; painting. Look 33:30-1 D 30 '69
[Richard M. Nixon: painting] Look 33:24-5 F 4 '69

ROCKWELL, Willard Frederick, 1914-

Business mergers, what's right, what's wrong; interview. por U S News 66:70-3 My 19 '69

ROCKWELL-Standard corporation. See North American Rockwell corporation

ROCKY MOUNTAIN NATIONAL PARK

Alpine summer. B. Ratcliffe. il Audubon 71:44-51 Jl '69

ROCKY MOUNTAIN spotted fever

Mystery of the spots. il Newsweek 74:59 Ag 11 '69
Warning! Look to the palms and the soles. il Time 93:58 Ja 24 '69

ROCKY MOUNTAINS

See also
Hells Canyon
Teton Range

RODBERG, Leonard S.

Limiting strategic technology: the need for national self-restraint. Bul Atom Sci 25:36-8 N '69

RODELL, Fred

Can Nixon's justices reverse the Warren court? Look 33:38 D 2 '69

RODENTS

Cute, but what is it? il Sci Digest 66:32 D '69
See also names of rodents, e.g. Prairie dogs

RODEOS

Ride for the money! M. M. Hailey. il Read Digest 95:139-42 Ag '69
Welcome to Cowtown, East. C. Phinizy. il Sports Illus 31:72-4+ D 8 '69

RODERICK, Myron

Crunch for coach Roderick. C. Coe. il pors Life 66:75+ F 14 '69

RODGER, Anne

Village maids. por Newsweek 73:79-80 F 3 '69

RODGERS, Jimmie

Child of clay. por Newsweek 74:76+ Ag 18 '69

RODGERS, Mary Augusta

Kicking the habit. Good H 169:86+ O '69
Success story; story. Ladies Home J 86:86-7 O '69
Town that voted yes for justice. Good H 168:67+ F '69

RODGERS, Rod A.

Rod Rodgers dance company; the Cubiculo theatre. J. Dowlin. Dance Mag 43:76-7 Ap '69

RODIN, Auguste

Readers' choice: Rodin's Balzac. E. Steichen. il Art in Am 57:26-7 S '69

RODIN, J. Otto, and others

Sex attractant of female dermestid beetle trogoderma inclusum le conte. bibliog Science 165:904-5 Ag 29 '69

RODMAN, Karl

Should camp cabins be inter-aged and co-ed? Camp Mag 41:14-15 Ap '69

RODMAN, Molly

Were Molly Rodman's dice loaded? E. T. Hawkins and others. McCalls 97:93+ O '69

RODMAN, Selden

Literary gold in South America. Sat R 52:25-6+ Je 7 '69

RODMAN job corps center, New Bedford, Mass. See United States—Job corps

RODNITZKY, Jerome L.

College fraternities: brotherhood and ballyhoo. bibliog f Sch & Soc 97:449-51 N '69

RODRIGO, Joaquin

Four by Rodrigo. J. Diether. Am Rec G 35:472-4 F '69

RODRIGUES, Amália

Cognoscenti abroad. Amalia Rodrigues's Lisbon. A. Goodfriend. Sat R 52:42-3+ Mr 15 '69
Queen of sorrows. H. Saal. por Newsweek 73:76-7 F 10 '69

RODRIGUEZ, Eduardo Barreiros. See Barreiros Rodríguez, E.

RODRIGUEZ, Luis

Nino's hook stopped a Roman riot. M. Kram. il pors Sports Illus 31:24-7 D 1 '69

RODRIGUEZ, Rafael

Contemporary Puerto Rican artists. Sch Arts 69:26-7 O '69

RODS, Curtain. See Curtain and drapery fixtures

ROE, Ernest

Observations from abroad; the American scene. por Library J 94:335-9, 1291-3, 1715-18+ F 15, Mr 15, Ap 15 '69

ROE, Jim

Case for the mini-cruise. por Motor B 123:74-7 My '69

ROE, Yale

Candidate Roe. R. L. Shayon. Sat R 52:98 S 13 '69

ROEHRIG, Janice
Rya pillows and hangings. Sch Arts 68:11
My '69
ROELOFS, Wendell L. and Comeau, Andre
Sex pheromone specificity: taxonomic and evolutionary aspects in lepidoptera. bibliog Science 165:398-400 Jl 25 '69
ROESCH, Roberta
Summer jobs for teenagers. Parents Mag 44:44-6 Ap '69
ROETHKE, Theodore
Loveless provinces: poem. Yale R 59:99-103 O '69

about

No half-baked Bacchus from Saginaw. M. Harrington. Commonweal 89:656-7 F 21 '69
Roethke's Boswell. J. Atlas. Poetry 114:327-30 Ag '69
ROFFMANN, Hal R. Jr
High-density PC boards. por Electr World 82: 42-3 O '69
ROGER, Edith
Poetic epic. W. Terry. il Sat R 52:27-8 Je 28 '69
ROGERS, A. E. E. and Ingalls, R. P.
Venus: mapping the surface reflectivity by radar interferometry. bibliog Science 165: 797-9 Ag 22 '69
ROGERS, A. Robert
Systems building: a solution to the cost squeeze? bibliog Library J 94:4360-3 D 1 '69
ROGERS, E. L.
Saga of survival. Field & S 74:78-9+ Je '69
ROGERS, Fred M.
Big friend to little people. E. H. McCleary. il pors Todays Health 47:20-3+ Ag '69
Man kids believe. il por Newsweek 73:97+ My 12 '69
Senatorial goose bumps. R. L. Shayon. Sat R 52:36 My 24 '69
TV's Misterogers: quality clicks with kids. C. S. Wren. il pors Look 33:102-6 D 2 '69
ROGERS, Howard F.
Paper filmstrip. por Library J 94:846-7 F 15 '69
ROGERS, Jaime
Anybody need 683 dancers? J. Barthel. il pors Life 67:61-2+ D 5 '69
ROGERS, Ray
Black guns on campus. Nation 208:558-60 My 5 '69
ROGERS, Senta S.
Some analytical methods used in crime laboratories. bibliog por Chem 42:29-30 Jl '69
ROGERS, William Pierce
Address before the National press club, Canberra, Australia, August 8, 1969. Dept State Bul 61:178-81 S 1 '69
CENTO council of ministers meets at Tehran: statement, May 26, 1969. Dept State Bul 60:501-3 Je 16 '69
Complexity of world affairs; remarks, April 16, 1969. Dept State Bul 60:387-8 My 5 '69
Deep concern for peace in Viet-Nam; remarks, October 20, 1969. Dept State Bul 61:394-5 N 10 '69
Department emphasizes the importance of the nuclear nonproliferation treaty; statement, February 18, 1969. Dept State Bul 60:189-90 Mr 10 '69
Fifteenth anniversary of SEATO; statement. Dept State Bul 61:284 S 29 '69
Foreign assistance program for fiscal year 1970; statement, July 14, 1969. Dept State Bul 61:81-5 Ag 4 '69
Foreign policy aspects of the foreign aid program; statement, July 17, 1969. Dept State Bul 61:116-19 Ag 11 '69
Formulation of foreign policy; responsibility and opportunity: message, January 22, 1969. Dept State Bul 60:125-6 F 10 '69
National security council system: responsibilities of the Department of state, text of message, February 6, 1969. Dept State Bul 60:164-6 F 24 '69
North Atlantic council celebrates the 20th anniversary of the signing of the North Atlantic treaty; opening remarks, April 10, 1969. Dept State Bul 60:349 Ap 28 '69
Rogers: Hanoi is unreasonable; excerpts from testimony, July 17, 1969. por U S News 67: 10 Jl 28 '69
Secretary leaves Bangkok at close of SEATO and seven-nation meeting; statement, May 23, 1969. Dept State Bul 60:483-4 Je 9 '69
Secretary reports on U.S. efforts to help Nigeria civil war victims; statement, November 12, 1969. Dept State Bul 61:469-70 D 1 '69
Secretary Rogers interviewed on Meet the press; transcript of interview, October 12, 1969. Dept State Bul 61:345-50 O 27 '69; Excerpts. por U S News 67:16+ O 27 '69

Secretary Rogers' news conference:
April 7, 1969. Dept State Bul 60:357-63 Ap 28 '69
June 5, 1969. Dept State Bul 60:529-35 Je 23 '69
July 2, 1969. Dept State Bul 61:41-9 Jl 21 '69
August 3 and 11, 1969. Dept State Bul 61:177-8+ S 1 '69
August 20, 1969. Dept State Bul 61:201-8 S 8 '69
October 25, 1969. Dept State Bul 61:389-94 N 10 '69
Secretary Rogers on peace prospects; excerpts from news conference, April 7, 1969. por U S News 66:32-3 Ap 21 '69
Secretary Rogers to confer with Asian leaders during seventeen day trip: statement, May 9, 1969. Dept State Bul 60:433 My 26 '69
Secretary Rogers visits New Delhi, Lahore, and Tehran: remarks, May 23-28, 1969. Dept State Bul 60:503-6 Je 16 '69
Secretary Rogers visits Viet-Nam; statement, news conferences. Dept State Bul 60:461-4 Je 2 '69
Secretary Rogers welcomes Atlantic treaty association; remarks, October 20, 1969. Dept State Bul 61:400 N 10 '69
SEATO council of ministers meets at Bangkok; statement, May 20, 1969. Dept State Bul 60:477-8 Je 9 '69
Strategic arms limitation talks; address, November 13, 1969. Dept State Bul 61:465-8 D 1 '69
United States and Japan conclude space cooperation agreement; statement with text of exchange of notes, July 31, 1969. Dept State Bul 61:195-6 S 1 '69
U.S. calls upon Syria to release all passengers of hijacked plane; statements, August 29 and 30, 1969. Dept State Bul 61:245-6 S 15 '69
U.S. extends condolences on death of President Barrientos of Bolivia; text of message. Dept State Bul 60:424 My 19 '69
U.S. foreign policy; some major issues; statement, March 27, 1969. Dept State Bul 60: 305-12 Ap 14 '69; Same with title Foreign relations; disarmament. Vital Speeches 35: 420-5 My 1 '69; Excerpts. por U S News 66: 43-4 Ap 7 '69
U.S.-Japan joint economic committee meets at Tokyo; statement with text of communique, July 31, 1969. Dept State Bul 61: 121-4 Ag 18 '69
U.S. policy in Middle East; address, December 9, 1969. Vital Speeches 36:165-7 Ja 1 '70
U.S. seeks resumption of relief to victims of Nigerian civil war; statement, July 2, 1969. Dept State Bul 61:51-2 Jl 21 '69
Viet-Nam in the perspective of East Asia; address, April 21, 1969. Dept State Bul 60: 397-400 My 12 '69
We seem too powerful, too involved in the hard sell; interview, ed. by M. Byers. pors Life 66:18-19 Ja 24 '69

about

Diplomats in disarray. S. Simpson. Nation 208:138-41 F 3 '69
Israel and the Arabs: a shift in U.S. policy? il por Newsweek 74:39 D 22 '69
Kissinger to Rogers to Laird. il por Newsweek 73:35-6 Ap 21 '69
Mr Rogers and Mr Finch. il pors Life 66:16B-23 Ja 24 '69
Negotiator and the confronter. por Time 93: 26-7 Ap 4 '69
Past master of the soft sell. H. Smith. il pors N Y Times Mag p8-9+ Jl 27 '69
Rogers, Gromyko: deals in making? il por U S News 67:18 O 6 '69
Secretary Rogers, bigger role in quest for peace. il por U S News 67:12 D 22 '69
Two for the road. il por Newsweek 73:35-6 My 19 '69
Unflappable Bill Rogers. il pors Newsweek 73: 20-1 Mr 3 '69
U.S. diplomat no. 1. B. Clark. por Read Digest 95:141-5 D '69
Who's making foreign policy for the United States? il por U S News 66:45-6 Ap 7 '69

Visit to Asia, 1969

Growing role for Secretary Rogers. por U S News 67:13-14 Ag 25 '69
Invitation to greatness; assault at Tokyo's Haneda airport. il por Newsweek 74:30-1 Ag 11 '69
Rogers on the road. il por Newsweek 73:52 Je 9 '69

ROGERS, William Pierce—Visit to Asia, 1969
  —*Continued*
  Secretary leaves Bangkok at close of SEATO
    and seven-nation meetings; statement, May
    23, 1969. W. P. Rogers. Dept State Bul 60:
    483-4 Je 9 '69
  Secretary Rogers to confer with Asian lead-
    ers during seventeen day trip; statement,
    May 9, 1969. W. P. Rogers. Dept State
    Bul 60:433 My 26 '69
  Secretary Rogers' trip to Asia and the Paci-
    fic; statements, text of news conferences
    during visit, August 1-11, 1969. W. P. Rog-
    ers. Dept State Bul 61:177-8+ S 1 '69
  Secretary Rogers visits New Delhi, Lahore,
    and Tehran. W. P. Rogers. Dept State Bul
    60:503-6 Je 16 '69
  Secretary Rogers visits Viet-Nam; state-
    ment, news conferences, during Asian
    tour. W. P. Rogers. Dept State Bul 60:461-
    4 Je 2 '69
ROGERS, William R.
  On accepting clergy discounts; psychological
    implications. Chr Cent 86:1113-14 Ag 27 '69
ROGERS, Willie Mae
  Ballad of Willie Mae; with editorial comment.
    por Bsns W p45-6, 172 F 22 '69
  Basically honest. Nation 208:260-1 Mr 3 '69
  No seal of approval. por Time 93:16 F 21 '69
  Testing of Willie Mae. il por Newsweek 73:
    25 F 24 '69
ROGGE, Hermann
  Miniskirts, maxi-heels. R. Levy. il Duns R
    93:65-6 F '69
ROGIN, Gilbert
  How it turns out; story. New Yorker 45:59-
    61 N 15 '69
  Time and effort; story. New Yorker 45:36-7
    Ap 19 '69
  To the fjord country. New Yorker 45:39-41
    S 20 '69
  You say what I feel; story. New Yorker 45:
    29-33 Jl 12 '69
ROGIN, Richard
  How one middle-class family gets along in
    New York. N Y Times Mag p32-4+ Ag 17
    '69
ROGOFF, Herbert
  Daniel E. Greene; pastellist. Am Artist 33:80-
    8 N '69
  (ed) See Kossin, S. Interview with Sanford
    Kossin
  (ed) See Van Wyk, H. Each demonstration is
    a challenge
ROGOVIN, Charles H.
  Criminal-justice system in trouble; excerpts
    from address, October 1, 1969. por U S
    News 67:16 O 13 '69
ROHAN, Denis Michael
  Chosen one. il por Newsweek 74:61 O 20 '69
  Trial of the new Moses. A. Menen. il por
    N Y Times Mag p54-5+ N 23 '69
ROHE, Ludwig Mies van der. See Mies van der
  Rohe, L.
ROHLF, John A.
  Your beef business. See issues of Farm
    journal
ROHR, Frank, Jr
  Downwind dash to Nassau. Travel & Camera
    32:90-3 Jl '69
  Watersports. See issues of Motor boating
ROHR corporation
  Engine delay for 747 cuts Rohr profits. Avia-
    tion W 91:94 D 8 '69
  How Rohr learned to move the goods. il Bsns
    W p92-3 Jl 26 '69
  Rapid transit pact bolsters Rohr in field. il
    Aviation W 90:62+ Je 30 '69
ROHRBACH, Heinrich
  Mistletoe. Horticulture 47:26-7 D '69
ROKES, Willis Park
  Ma Bell rental agency. Nation 208:820-3 Je
    30 '69
ROLAND, Rolf R.
  Arcane art of arbitrage. il por Bsns W p
    138+ N 22 '69
ROLE, Social. See Social role
ROLE playing. See Psychodrama
ROLFE, Frederick William
  Hadrian VII; dramatization. See Luke, P.
    about
  Hadrian the seventh on stage and off. L.
    Kronenberger. il Atlan 223:62-5 Mr '69
  Would-be pope. F. L. Kunkel. Commonweal
    89:588-91 F 7 '69
ROLFS, Mary Jane
  Man who knew everything; story. Redbook
    134:78-9 D '69
ROLLED oats. See Oatmeal
ROLLER skating
  Big wheel; Gold skate classic. il Newsweek
    73:98 My 5 '69
  Derby rises again. il Time 93:70 Mr 7 '69
  Little women; banked-track skating group
    of Los Angeles. C. Bergen. il Esquire 71:
    136-7+ My '69

Roller derby; photographs by W. Iooss, jr;
  with account by F. Deford. Sports Illus 30:
  54-64+ Mr 3 '69
ROLLIN, Betty
  Co-ed living. Look 33:22-4+ S 23 '69
  Looking around. por Look 33:13-14 Ap 1; 10 Ag
    12 '69
ROLLING block firearms. See Rifles
ROLLING stone (periodical)
  Rocking the news. il Newsweek 73:90 Ap 28
    '69
  Rolling stone's rock world; San Francisco-
    based newspaper-magazine. il Time 93:78
    Ap 25 '69
ROLLING Stones. See Rock 'n' roll groups
ROLLINS, Sidney P.
  Are middle schools the answer? pro Sr Schol
    94:Schol Teach 9-11 Mr 14 '69
ROLLMAN-BRANCH, Hilda S.
  Psychical reality and the theater of fact. bib-
    liog Am Imago 26:56-70 Spr '69
ROLLS-Royce, limited
  British see joint engine projects as key to
    future sales. il Aviation W 90:256-8+ Je
    2 '69
  Layoffs may hinder RB.211 production. Avia-
    tion W 90:32 Ja 27 '69
  Luxury, Detroit style. K. Prentiss. il Holi-
    day 46:82-7+ O '69
  Rolls-Royce's $2-billion hard sell. J. M.
    Mecklin. il Fortune 79:122-8+ Mr '69
  Sir Henry's legacy. S. G. Slappey. il Nations
    Bsns 57:66-70 Ag '69
  Specter of the auto's gilded age; with report
    by J. Neary. il Life 66:58-63+ Je 27 '69
ROLO, Charles J.
  Stock trends. por Forbes 104:96-7 O 15; 114-
    15 N 15; 71 D 15 '69
  When Wall Street catches the flu. 26 million
    Americans ache. N Y Times Mag p 12-14+
    Ag 31 '69
ROLOFF, Michael
  (tr) See Musil, R. Flypaper
ROMACK, Howard
  Children's village experiments. Parks & Rec
    4:39-41+ Ap '69
ROMAINE, Mel
  Poetry, how and why. J. Jerome. Writers
    Digest 49:74-9 O '69
ROMAN, Robert C.
  Hide your daughters, here comes Russ Mar-
    kert. Dance Mag 43:46-9+ S '69
ROMAN Catholic church. See Catholic church
ROMAN Catholics. See Catholics
ROMAN Colosseum. See Colosseum, Rome
ROMAN curia. See Catholic church—Roman
  curia
ROMANCE
  Romance. L. Lee. il Seventeen 27:104-5 D '68
ROMANESQUE sculpture. See Sculpture, Ro-
  manesque
ROMANIES. See Gipsies
ROMANOFF, Harry
  Last of the Romanoffs. por Newsweek 74:91
    Ag 18 '69
ROMANTIC love. See Love
ROMANTIC poets. See Romanticism
ROMANTICISM
  Ah, wilderness; nineteenth-century American
    romantic art revival. D. L. Shirey. il News-
    week 73:89 Mr 3 '69
  Internalization of quest romance. H. Bloom.
    Yale R 58:526-36 Je '69
ROMANTICISM in music
  Slavonic and romantic music, by G. Abra-
    ham. Review
    Mus Q 55:573-5 O '69. B. Krader
ROME, Paula D.
  Toward a new understanding of youngsters
    with reading problems. Parents Mag 44:72-
    3+ N '69
ROME
                Civilization
    See also
  Civilization, Greco-Roman
                History
  Julius Caesar's poverty program. D. L. Pet-
    tibone. Nat R 21:954-5 S 23 '69
ROME (city)
                Antiquities
    See also
  Colosseum, Rome
                Art
  Rome (cont) M. Gendel. il Art N 68:8 Sum '69
                Crime
  Requiescant in pace; remains of saints stolen.
    il Newsweek 73:95-6 Ap 14 '69
  68,500-lire misunderstanding; con men and
    American male tourists. D. Butwin. il Sat R
    52:40-1 S 6 '69

ROME (city)—*Continued*

Description

Cognoscenti abroad, Gore Vidal's Rome. A. Goodfriend. il Sat R 52:36-9 Ja 25 '69
Cognoscenti abroad Morris West's Rome. A. Goodfriend. Sat R 52:23-6 Jl 19 '69

Hotels, restaurants, etc.

Camparis, contessas and casanovas; Rome's Caffé Greco. A. Hine. il Holiday 46-20-1 Jl '69
When in Rome, do as the roamers do; eight writers tell where they sleep, eat and shop; symposium; with editorial comment. Esquire 72:124-7+, 198-9 O '62
See also
Coffee houses

Music

Report: revival of I Lombardi. E. Rizzo. il Opera N 34:32 Ja 10 '70
Report: Rome; production of Ildebrando Pizzetti's Clitennestra. E. Rizzo. il Opera N 33:31 Mr 29 '69
Report: Rome; production of Turco in Italia. E. Rizzo. Opera N 33:30 Mr 1 '69
Report: Rome: Teatro dell'opera's production of Orfeo ed Euridice. E. Rizzo. il Opera N 33:31 F 8 '69

Pontifical Gregorian university

Gregorian university. J. Navone. America 120: 584-6 My 17 '69
Liberating the Greg. il Time 94:68 D 12 '69

Social life and customs

City where the young still listen. A. Menen. McCall 96:34+ F '69
Fixer, Roman style; concierge of the Excelsior hotel. A. Waugh. il Holiday 46:30-1+ Ag '69
Liquor's dandy, too: ricevimenti or receptions. N. S. Hazelton. Nat R 21:703 Jl 15 '69

Streets

Rome's international peacock alley; Via Veneto. J. Bryan, 3d. il Holiday 45:80-1+ Ap '69

ROME prize fellowships. See American academy in Rome

ROMEO and Juliet; ballet. See Ballets—Criticisms

ROMER, Alfred Sherwood
Cynodont reptile with incipient mammalian jaw articulation. bibliog Science 166:881-2 N 14 '69

ROMINGER, Wray
Young man tells why he lives on the land; letter: ed. by R. Rodale. pors Org Gard & Farm 16:27-32 D '69

ROMM, Ethel Grodzins
**** is no longer a dirty word. Esquire 71: 135+ Ap '69

ROMNES, Haakon Ingolf
H. I. Romnes named chairman of National U.N. day for 1969. Dept State Bul 60:451 My 26 '69

ROMNEY, George, 1907-
Breakdown in our cities; interview. pors U S News 67:48-51 Jl 28 '69
Public problem solving; address, February 17, 1969. Vital Speeches 35:329-31 Mr 15 '69
Trees for people. por Am For 75:20-1 O '69

about

Hope deferred. por Newsweek 74:49 D 29 '69
Man builds a house. Nat R 21:317 Ap 8 '69
Mass-produced housing? Commonweal 90:332 Je 6 '69
Meany, Romney: troubled start. U S News 66:64 F 3 '69
Mr Nixon's urban ballet. H. E. Davis. Nation 209:45-8 Jl 14 '69
Muddle cities? por Newsweek 73:63 My 12 '69
Parochial rumblings up north. Chr Today 13:36 Ja 31 '69
Rambler Romney: the Edsel of politicians. J. Mahoney. Commonweal 89:546-7 Ja 31 '69
Romney soups up his new vehicle; Operation Breakthrough. il Bsns W p82 S 13 '69
Scandal of building costs. il por Time 93:104+ My 23 '69

RONA, E. and Emiliani, Cesare
Absolute dating of Caribbean cores P6304-8 and P6304-9. bibliog Science 163:66-8; 166:1551-2 Ja 3, D 19 '69

RONAN, Margaret
Following the films. See issues of Senior scholastic

RONBERG, Gary
Hockey (cont) Sports Illus 30:62+ Mr 10; 56-7 Mr 24; 74+ Ap 7; 61-2 My 12; 31:60-1 N 3; 92+ N 17; 81-2+ D 1 '69
—See Waldmeir, P. jt. auth.

RONCHI test. See Lenses, Photographic—Testing

RONDIÈRE, Pierre
Education: but for whom? And how? UNESCO Courier 23:6-10 Ja '70

RONDO
Sonata-rondo, the formulation of a theoretical concept in the 18th and 19th centuries. M. C. Cole. bibliog f Mus Q 55:180-92 Ap '69

RONK, D. E.
Forgotten victims of the war in Vietnam. Parents Mag 44:43-5+ Ag '69

ROOD, Herbert J.
Two problems in gravitation. Sky & Tel 37: 152-3, 225-7 Mr-Ap '69

ROOD, Ronald
Impatient spring. Read Digest 94:119-22 F '69
Nature's broken vase. Audubon 71:6-12 My '69
Superskyway; excerpt from Wild brother. Audubon 71:38-43 S '69

ROODA, A. W.
Graceful gourds, fantasies of the garden. por Org Gard & Farm 16:36-7 Jl '69

ROODY, Sarah I.
Teaching Conrad's Victory to superior high school seniors. Engl J 58:40-6 Ja '69

ROOF decks. See Outdoor rooms

ROOF drainage. See Drainage, House

ROOF gardens
Conifers in the winter roof garden. P. Truex. il Horticulture 47:44-5 Ja '69
My roof acre. P. Latif. il Org Gard & Farm 16:33-5 N '69
Rooftop English and Spanish gardens are a London surprise. il Sunset 142:229 My '69

ROOF leaders. See Drainage, House

ROOFING
Changing roof. J. H. Ingersoll. il House B 111:86-7+ Mr '69
New roofing: sticks better, looks better. J. Hand. il Pop Sci 195:128-31+ N '69
Questions and answers about roofing. Consumer Bul 52:18 Jl '69

ROOFS
Super-light, saddle-shaped roof is made of plastic foam over tensioned-steel web. il Arch Rec 145:170 F '69
See also
Domes
Gutters (roof)
Roofing

Drainage

See Drainage, House

Maintenance and repair

Fixing up an older home. il Bet Hom & Gard 47:37 My '69

ROOKS, C. Shelby
Theological education and the black church. Chr Cent 86:212-16 F 12 '69

ROOM acoustics. See Acoustics, Architectural

ROOM dividers. See Partitions

ROOM furnishings. See Household furnishings

ROOMING houses, Remodeled. See Houses, Remodeled

ROOMS
Arcs and bridges, the breakaway feeling. E. Sverbeyeff. il House B 111:70-3 Ag '69
Country casual for today. il Am Home 72: 46-9 Jl '69
Designer shapes space. M. Baughman. il House & Gard 135:120-5 Ap '69
Everybody wants an out. M. Spires. il Am Home 72:56-7 Jl '69
How to keep a flow of space. il House & Gard 135:106-11 Ap '69
In Alaska they call this entry room a mud room. il Sunset 142:100-1 Mr '69
Party gets a room of its own. il House B 111:116-19 N '69
Pleasant garden room. R. Gannon. il Horticulture 47:22-3 Ag '69
Room concepts. il Bet Hom & Gard 47:18+ S '69
Rooms with the power to enchant; quotations from the pens of Waugh, Proust, Capote, Bowen, and others. A. S. Morris. House B 111:92+ Ap '69
Small wonders. il Redbook 132:90-2 Mr; 113-15+ Ap; 133:110-13+ Jl; 102-5+ S; 113-15+ O '69
Very compact quiet center; library/home-office. il Bet Hom & Gard 47:26 F '69

ROOMS—*Continued*
Your favorite room. il Seventeen 28:112-15
O '69
See also
Attics
Bathrooms
Bedrooms
Childrens rooms
Dining rooms
Furniture, Arrangement of
House decoration
Kitchens
Laundries
Living rooms
Music rooms and equipment
Outdoor rooms
Period rooms
Sewing rooms
Trophy rooms
ROOMS, Miniature
Lincoln's parlor in miniature. S. A. Parvin.
il Hobbies 74:118+ Mr '69
ROOMS, Remodeled. See Houses, Remodeled
ROONEY, Andrew
Burn bursar, burn. Life 66:20B Je 13 '69
about
Man behind Harry. il por Time 94:68 Jl 11 '69
ROONEY, J. F. Jr
Let's be objective about snow and ice con-
trol. bibliog Am City 84:106+ O '69
ROONEY, Jay
Elk hunter's elk. Outdoor Life 144:62-3+ N
'69
ROONEY, John James
Rooney reform. K. Crawford. Newsweek 73:
29 Mr 3 '69
ROOS, Birger
What's in a name? il Audubon 71:46-7 Mr '69
ROOS, Jim
Chamber music in the chamber. Hi Fi 19:
MA9 Je '69
ROOS, Richard
Middle earth in the classroom: studying J.
R. R. Tolkien. Engl J 58:1175-80 N '69
ROOSA, Robert Vincent
American share in the stream of international
payments; with questions and answers. Ann
Am Acad 384:21-34 Jl '69
ROOSE, Lawrence J.
To die alone. Ment Hy 53:321-6 Jl '69
ROOSEVELT, Franklin Delano, 1882-1945
Annals of finance. J. Brooks. New Yorker
45:107-26 S 13 '69
Franklin D. Roosevelt and foreign affairs,
ed. by E. B. Nixon. Review
Newsweek il por 73:118-20 Ap 14 '69. R. A.
Sokolov
Sat R 52:30-1 Ag 2 '69. D. Perkins
Warm Springs of FDR. B. Fancher. il pors
Sat R 52:42+ Mr 8 '69
ROOSEVELT, Theodore
Before the colors fade: last of the Rough
Riders. J. D. Langdon. Am Heritage 20:42-
3+ Ag '69
Bullmoose in the souvenir shop. P. Owens.
Commonweal 91:349 D 19 '69
There was a storm outside and a bit of frost
within; excerpts from TR and Will: a
friendship that split the Republican party.
W. Manners. il por Am Heritage 21:24-5+
D '69
ROOT, Alan. See Root, J. jt. auth.
ROOT, Joan, and Root, Alan
Inside a hornbill's walled-up nest. Nat Geog
136:846-55 D '69
ROOT, Waverley
Best cup of coffee in Rome. Holiday 46:14+
D '69
Brasserie Lipp, rendezvous for le tout Paris.
Holiday 46:66-7+ O '69
Folies Bergère. Holiday 45:92-3+ Ap '69
ROOT, William Pitt
Circle of struggle; poem. New Yorker 45:38
Mr 29 '69
ROOTES motors, Incorporated
What's the matter with Britain? Ask Chrys-
ler. il Forbes 103:37-8 Je 1 '69
ROOTS
Sewer root control, chemically; Sacramento
County. N. R. Townley. il Am City 84:92-4
D '69
ROOTWORMS, Corn. See Corn rootworms
ROPE
How rope is made. B. D. Barker. 3d. il
Yachting 125:72-3 My '69
Stowing your anchor line. G. S. Smith. il
Motor B 124:81+ Jl '69
Way to cut synthetic rope. il Sunset 143:
69 Ag '69
ROPER, Elmo
One helluva way to run a railroad. Sat R
52:18-19 Je 28 '69

ROREM, Ned
Can't eat politics, can't eat art. Vogue 154:
92+ D '69
Décors of sound; excerpts from diary. por
House B 111:102-3+ Ap '69
Julius Katchen (1926-1969) Hi Fi 19:61 S '69
about
On Desto. music by Rorem not for singing.
P. L. Miller. Am Rec G 35:416 Ja '69
RORSCHACH test. See Educational tests and
measurements
RORVIK, David M.
Artificial inovulation; a startling new way to
have a baby. McCalls 96:50+ My '69
Cloning: asexual human reproduction? Sci
Digest 66:6-13 N '69
Someone to watch over you (for less than
2¢ a day) Electronic stimulation of the
brain. Esquire 72:164-7+ D '69
Test tube generation. Esquire 71:108-15 Ap
'69
The unborn. Look 33:74-6+ N 4 '69
ROSARY
Fine arts; The rosary-in-art. C. J. McNaspy.
America 120:632-4 My 24 '69
ROSATI, James
Rosati masses in elevation. W. C. Seitz. il
Art N 68:38-41+ D '69
Six-sided man. D. L. Shirey. il por News-
week 74:58-9 D 29 '69
ROSE, Sir Alec
Rounding Cape Horn; excerpt from My lively
lady. Yachting 125:54-5+ Mr '69
ROSE, Barbara
Art (cont) Vogue 153:54 F 15; 105 Mr 1; 152
Ap 1; 134 My; 154:54 Jl; 62 Ag 1; 36 Ag 15;
152 O 1; 122 N 1; 146 D '69; 155:76 Ja 1 '70
Political revolution & current art. Vogue
153:207 Ja 15 '69
ROSE, Dixie E.
Five hundred miles to shoot a flower. Horti-
culture 47:56-7 Ja '69
Hummingbirds and flowers. Horticulture 47:
46-7 O '69
My wild garden. Horticulture 47:56+ My '69
ROSE, Don, and Canter, D. S.
Democrats confront 1970. Nation 209:595-7 D
1 '69
Mayor Daley: solvent but worried. Nation
209:169-73 S 1 '69
ROSE, Edward
Black man in the American West. D. T.
Schoenberger. bibliog il Negro Hist Bul 32:
7-11 Mr '69
ROSE, Elaine
Solving camp food storage problems. Camp
Mag 41:14 My '69
ROSE, Sir Francis Cyril, 4th bart
Chanel always now. Vogue 154:116+ D '69
Isadora, really. Vogue 154:104-5+ Jl '69
ROSE, Herman
City rises. L. Campbell. il Art N 68:42-4+ N
'69
ROSE, Leo E. and Dial, Roger
Can a ministate find true happiness in a
world dominated by protagonist powers?
The Nepal case. bibliog f Ann Am Acad
386:89-101 N '69
ROSE, Lionel
Ruben wilts a Rose. J. Tobin. il pors Sports
Illus 31:10-13 S 1 '69
ROSE, Pete
Highlight. por Sports Illus 31:86 O 6 '69
ROSE, Sanford
Bigness is a numbers game. Fortune 80:112-
15+ N '69
Case for the one-bank holding company.
Fortune 79:162-5+ My 15 '69
Remedy for monetary crisis. Fortune 80:102-
5+ Ag 15 '69
ROSE, Stephen C.
Putting it to the churches. New Repub 160:
19-21 Je 21 '69
ROSE, W. K.
(ed) See Murdoch, I. Iris Murdoch, in-
formally
ROSE dress; story. See Thaler, S.
ROSE gardens
In Connecticut, oldest rose garden we have;
Elizabeth rose garden. il Home Gard 56:
66-7 My '69
Rose gardens of Europe. D. L. McFadden. il
Horticulture 47:18-19+ N '69
ROSE trees. See Roses
ROSEBURG, Ore.
Videotape turns innocent pleas to guilty.
D. L. Schiffman. Am City 84:30 N '69
ROSELIEP, Raymond
A B C for Christmas; poem. America 121:
613 D 20 '69
At my mother's grave; poem. Nation 209:543
N 17 '69
Gallery; poems. Chr Cent 86:1373 O 29 '69

ROSELIEP, Raymond—*Continued*
O western wind; a sheaf of haiku; poems.
  Cath World 210:62-3 N '69
Some small creatures; poem. Cath World 209:
  28-9 Ap '69
Thomas Merton; poem. Cath World 209:54
  My '69
ROSEMAN, Jeffrey
X-ray resistant cell required for the induc-
  tion of in vitro antibody formation. bib-
  liog Science 165:1125-7 S 12 '69
ROSEMARY
What's cooking?
  Beans, peas, celery and herbs. D. Reay.
    il Org Gard & Farm 16:24-7 Mr '69
ROSEMARY Hall, Greenwich, Conn. See Pri-
  vate schools
ROSEN, B. R. and Taylor, J. D.
Reef coral from Aldabra: new mode of re-
  production. bibliog Science 166:119-21 O 3
  '69
ROSEN, Benedict
R.F. interference filters. por Electr World
  81:48-9 Ap '69
ROSEN, Carl Gustav von, greve
Conscience is his co-pilot. L. Elliott. il por
  Read Digest 95:207-8+ D '69
How to build an instant air force. il por
  Time 93:38 Je 6 '69
Operation Biafra baby. il por Newsweek 73:
  60 Je 9 '69
ROSEN, David
Verdi's Liber scriptus rewritten. bibliog f
  Mus Q 55:151-69 Ap '69
ROSEN, Gerald R.
Washington desk. See issues of Dun's re-
  view
ROSENBERG, Harold
Art world (cont) New Yorker 44:86+ Ja
  25; 45:107-8+ F 22; 110+ Mr 21; 136+ Ap
  19; 118+ My 17; 91-2+ Je 21; 102+ S 27;
  167-70+ N 8; 171-2+ D 6 '69

about
Ready-made crisis. L. Alloway. Nation 209:
  544-5 N 17 '69
ROSENBERG, John S.
Toward a new civil war revisionism. Am
  Scholar 38:250-72 Spr '69
ROSENBERG, Max
Educators' quiz. See issues of Education
  digest
ROSENBERG, Milton J.
Blind strategy of missile defense. Nation
  208:168-74; 522+ F 10, Ap 28 '69
Safeguard: public relations as a way of
  death. Chr Cent 86:508-12 Ap 16 '69
ROSENBERG, Sam
Who is Santa Claus? McCalls 97:55-7+ D '69
ROSENBERG, Steven A. and others
Automatic identification and measurement of
  cells by computer. Science 163:1065-6 Mr 7
  '69
ROSENBLATT, Herta
Listening; poem. Cath World 209:6 Ap '69
ROSENBLATT, Louise M.
Pattern and process, a polemic; address. bib-
  liog f Engl J 58:1005-12 O '69
ROSENBLUM, Robert
Exhilarating adventure. Frank Stella. Vogue
  154:116-17+ N 15 '69
19th-century franc revalued. Art N 68:26-31+
  Sum '69
ROSENCRANTZ and Guildenstern are dead;
  drama. See Stoppard, T.
ROSENFELD, Albert
Eighty million earthlings watched their
  world shrink. Life 66:50-52A My 30 '69
Science, sex and morality; adaptation of
  The second Genesis. Life 66:37-40+ Je 13
  '69
ROSENFELD, Alvin A.
Friendly fuzz. Nation 208:503-7 Ap 21 '69
ROSENFELD, Alvin H.
Eagle and the axe: a study of Whitman's
  Song of the broad-axe. bibliog f Am
  Imago 25:354-70 Wint '68
ROSENFELD, Eric
New approach to speaker design. Radio-
  Electr 40:33+ Mr '69
ROSENFELD, Joel Peter, and others
Operant control of neural events in humans.
  bibliog Science 165:821-3 Ag 22 '69
ROSENFELD, Stephen S.
Travels of Allen Ellander. New Repub 161:
  25-7+ S 27 '69
ROSENFIELD, Stephen
LC filters. por Electr World 81:40-4 Ap '69
Der ROSENKAVALIER; opera. See Strauss, R.
ROSENQUIST, James Albert
Art. L. Alloway. Nation 208:581-2 My 5
  '69
ROSENSTEIN, Harris
Bollinger phenomenon. Art N 68:48-51+ S '69
Colorful gesture. Art N 68:29-31+ Mr '69
Gary Kuehn's pressure principle. Art N 68:
  54-8 D '69

Introducing Peter Golfinopoulos. Art N 68:
  56-8+ My '69
ROSENSTEIN, Richard S. See Frarey, C. J.
  jt. auth.
ROSENSTONE, Robert A.
Times they are a-changin': the music of pro-
  test. bibliog f Ann Am Acad 382:131-44 Mr
  '69
—See Boskin, J. jt. ed.
ROSENTHAL, Abraham Michael
New public discourse? Cur 104:26-9 F '69
ROSENTHAL, Alan
Circus king's gift to posterity. Todays
  Health 47:42-7 N '69
How safe are the '70 cars? Todays Health 47:
  34-9+ O '69
Mystic seaport. Todays Health 47:42-7 Ap
  '69
Symbols for safety. Todays Health 47:48-51
  Ag '69
Training Viet Nam's future doctors. Todays
  Health 47:38-41+ Jl '69
Trampoline: fitness boon or safety hazard?
  Todays Health 47:32-5 My '69
Your role as eyes and ears for police. To-
  days Health 47:58-61+ S '69
(ed) See Siegel, B. Must brothers (and sis-
  ters) fight?
ROSENTHAL, Daniel
Engineering: renew its luster; letter. Science
  163:623 F 14 '69
ROSENTHAL, Irving
Who writes the letters to the editor? Sat R
  52:114-16 S 13 '69
ROSENTHAL, Jack
Cage of fear; crime study report on Balti-
  more. Life 67:18-21 Jl 11 '69
ROSENTHAL, M. L.
Critic of the month. Poetry 114:113-32 My '69
ROSENTHAL, Michael, and others
Blacks at Brandeis. Commonweal 89:727-30
  Mr 14 '69
ROSENTHAL, T. G.
Sense of the great city. New Repub 160:23-5
  F 15 '69
ROSER, Louis A.
Where the salmon go. Field & S 73:62-3+
  Ap '69
ROSES
Enchantment in old roses. G. Walton. il
  Home Gard 56:86 F '69
Getting them off to a good start. il Home
  Gard 56:46-9 F '69
How to feed roses. G. J. Jung. il Horticul-
  ture 47:48+ Mr '69
How to improve on the perfect rose. H.
  Mason. il Bet Hom & Gard 47:62-5 F '69
How when and what of spraying roses. P.
  P. Pirone. il Horticulture 47:38-9 My '69
Miniature roses in the garden. B. Woods
  and F. Woods. il Horticulture 47:23+ Je
  '69
One good way to prune a tree rose. il Sunset
  142:198 F '69
Outstanding roses for performance, fragrance,
  color. Home Gard 56:50 F '69
Rainbow comes and goes and lovely is the
  rose. il Home Gard 56:42-5 F '69
Remarkable floribunda. C. C. Harris. il House
  B 111:109+ Je '69
Roses by the yardful! M. C. Goldman. il Org
  Gard & Farm 16:28-32 S '69
Wanted: tougher roses. D. O. Collins. il
  Horticulture 47:30-1 O '69
  See also
Rose gardens

All America selections
  See Plants—All America selections
ROSES, Wars of the. See Great Britain—His-
  tory—Wars of the Roses, 1455-1485
ROSHCHIN, A. A. See Fisher, A. S. jt. auth.
ROSICHAN, Richard
Kingston, N.Y. firing blamed on censorship.
  Library J 94:2991 S 15 '69
ROSING, Larry
Barry Le Va and the non-descript distribu-
  tion. Art N 68:52-3 S '69
ROSINI, Lawrence A.
Theology and literature. Cath World 208:235
  F '69
ROSINSKI, Edwin F.
Medical assistant; the health team ap-
  proach; address, January 23, 1969. Vital
  Speeches 35:438-41 My 1 '69
ROSMOND, Babette
How not to write a short story; excerpts
  from Prize stories from Seventeen. Writer
  82:22-4+ Ag '69
ROSOVSKY, Henry
Black studies at Harvard; personal reflec-
  tions concerning recent events. Am Scholar
  38:562-72 Aut '69

ROSS, Anne M.
Public employee unions and the right to
strike. bibliog f Mo Labor R 92:14-18 Mr '69
ROSS, David F.
Alabama: first steps. New Repub 161:14-15
S 27 '69
New hope for Latin America? New Repub
161:17-19 N 22 '69
Washington over the oil barrel in Peru. New
Repub 160:15-16 Ap 12 '69
ROSS, Diana
Supreme Supreme: Diana Ross. J. Hamilton.
pors Look 33:68-74 S 23 '69
ROSS, Don
New photographic process uses color to make
invisible visible. il Life 66:78-80 Mr 7 '69
ROSS, Donald
I want cocoanuts; drama. Mlle 70:164-5+ N
'69
ROSS, Elaine
Fresh fruits and compotes. House & Gard
136:81-3+ Ag '69
ROSS, Elisabeth Kübler-. See Kübler-Ross, E.
ROSS, Everett C.
How we sold backflow prevention. Am City
84:148-50 S '69
ROSS, Glynn
Philosophy of innovation. pors Opera N 34:
14-16 S 6 '69
ROSS, Irwin
Booming benefits of profit sharing. Read
Digest 95:111-14 Ag '69
For France: a new man, a new mood. Read
Digest 95:132-6 N '69
Kirk Kerkorian doesn't want all the meat off
the bone; with biographical sketch. Fortune
80:101, 144-8+ N '69
Let's not fence in the foundations. Fortune
79:148-50+ Je '69
Take this plane to Havana! Read Digest 94:
113-17 My '69
ROSS, James B.
Leasco sues Maxwell, who denounces Ross
meeting. Pub W 196:63 N 17 '69
ROSS, Sir James Clark
First deep-sea sounding. R. S. Dietz and
H. J. Knebel. Sea Front 15:212-18 Jl '69
ROSS, Katharine
Katharine Ross: the elegant tomboy. H.
Ehrlich il pors Look 33:33-6 Je 10 '69
ROSS, Leonard. See Tobin, J. jt. auth.
ROSS, Mary Ellen
Story of the miniature geraniums. Horticul-
ture 47:34-7+ Mr '69
ROSS, Michael H. and Reith, E. J.
Perineurium: evidence for contractile ele-
ments. bibliog Science 165:604-6 Ag 8 '69
ROSS, Nancy S.
Growing up with opera. Opera N 34:6-7 D
27 '69
ROSS, Robert
There is no right way to punish people
for doing what is right. N Y Times Mag
p 134-5 My 4 '69
ROSS, Russell
Wound healing; with biographical sketch.
Sci Am 220:14, 40-50 bibliog(p 144) Je '69
ROSS, Sherwood
Message to broadcasters. Chr Cent 86:280-3 F
26 '69
Movie. Chr Cent 86:1045, 1095+ Ag 6, 20 '69
ROSS, Steven S.
Conference on laboratory exercises. Sky &
Tel 38:304-5 N '69
ROSS, Walter Sanford
Six cave explorers who lived outside of time.
Sci Digest 65:8-13 Ap '69
Splicing together Jean-Luc Godard. Esquire
72:72-5+ Jl '69
Stained glass by a modern master. Read
Digest 95:146-52 D '69
Still a woman. Read Digest 94:165-6+ Mr
'69
They're curing an incurable cancer. Read
Digest 95:89-93 D '69
(ed) See Decker, A. Like father, but not
exactly like son
(ed) See Decker, W. H. Like father, but not
exactly like son
(ed) See Faegenburg, D. H. Radiologist
talks about his work
(ed) See Felch, W. C. Internist talks about
his work
(ed) See Maumenee, A. E. Ophthalmologist
talks about his work
ROSSET, Barnet Lee, 1922-
Close up: the old smut peddler. A. Goldman. il pors Life 67:49-53 Ag 29 '69
ROSSI, Alice S.
Women and professional advancement; excerpts from address, September 3, 1969.
Science 166:356 O 17 '69
ROSSI, Margaret Alice
Title III project director honored for achievements. il por Aging 176:9 Je '69

ROSSIDES, Eugene T.
Startling increases in drug smuggling; ex-
cerpts from Senate testimony, September 29,
1969. por U S News 67:50 O 13 '69
ROSSINI, Gioacchino
Barber of Seville (Il barbiere di Siviglia)
Criticism
Opera N 34:21-3 D 27 '69
Time 93:72 Ap 18 '69
Richard Wagner's visit to Rossini (Paris,
1860) by B. Michotte. Review
Am Rec G 35:848-9 My '69. R. W. Gutman
ROSTENBERG, Israel. See Steinberg, A. G. jt.
auth.
ROSTOW, Eugene Victor
Three questions for President Brewster and
Mayor Lee. Nat R 51:1113-14+ N 4 '69

about

Fate of the brothers Rostow. W. F. Buckley,
jr. Nat R 21:455 My 6 '69
ROSTOW, Walt Whitman
Limits and responsibilities of American power;
address, December 4, 1968. Dept State Bul
60:4-7 Ja 6 '69

about

Fate of the brothers Rostow. W. F. Buckley,
jr. Nat R 21:455 My 6 '69
Return to the fold; debate on Vietnam pol-
icy. il por Newsweek 75:42 Ja 12 '70
ROSTROPOVICH, Mstislav
People are talking about... por Vogue 153:
82-3 Ap 15 '69
Weekend with Rostropovich. R. Jacobson.
Sat R 52:65 My 17 '69
ROSZAK, Theodore
Sorcerer's apprentice. Nation 208:184-6 F 10
'69
Technocracy: despotism of beneficent exper-
tise. Nation 209:181-4+ S 1 '69
View from the crumpetty tree. Nation 208:
545-6 Ap 28 '69

about

Counter culture: cop-out. K. Keniston. il
Life 67:8-9 N 7 '69
Penultimate plea. M. E. Marty. Chr Cent
86:1484-6 N 19 '69
ROTARY piston engines. See Automobile en-
gines
ROTARY switches. See Electric switches
ROTARY tillers. See Cultivators
ROTATING buildings. See Buildings, Rotating
ROTATING combustion engines. See Gas and
oil engines
ROTATION of crops
See also
Companion crops
ROTE, Kyle, and Winter, Jack
Pro football: does money run the game? Look
33:93-4+ O 21 '69
ROTH, Cecil
Birds' heads and graven images. Commen-
tary 47:80-3 Je '69
ROTH, Ernst
Recordings. M. Mayer. il Esquire 72:22+ O
'69
ROTH, Henry
Final dwarf; story. Atlan 224:57-61 Jl '69
ROTH, Philip
Reflections on the death of a library. por
Wilson Lib Bul 43:746-7 Ap '69

about

Alexander the great. A. A. Sokolov. por
Newsweek 73:91-2+ F 24 '69
Journey of Philip Roth. T. Solotaroff. por
Atlan 223:64-72 Ap '69
Sex novel of the absurd. il por Time 93:82+
F 21 '69
Sort of Moby Dick. A. Broyard. New Repub
160:21-2 Mr 1 '69
Tropic of conversation: Portnoy's complaint.
S. Maloff. Commonweal 90:23-4 Mr 21 '69
Waxing wroth. K. Amis. Harper 238:104+
Ap '69
Wild blue shocker: Portnoy's complaint. A.
Goldman. il pors Life 66:58B-58D+ F 7 '69
ROTH, William M.
Dilemmas of leadership. Sat R 53:64+ Ja 10
'70
ROTH-BEJERANO, N. See Lips, S. H. jt. auth.
ROTH and Saad, architects
New solutions from old problems. C. Knight.
3d. il Arch Forum 131:58-65 O '69
ROTHCHILD, John
Un-silent generation. Nat R 21:591-4+ Je 17
'69

ROTHENBERG, Jerome
Ancestral scenes; poem. Nation 209:516 N 10
'69
Reality at white heat. Nation 209:444-6 O 27
'69
about
Comment. B. Berkson. Poetry 114:258 Jl '69
ROTHENBERG, Michael B.
Violence and children; adaptation of ad-
dress, October 28, 1967. bibliog Ment Hy
53:539-44 O '69
ROTHENBERG, Morris
Make your pumping stations attractive. Am
City 84:94-5 My '69
ROTHENBERG, Polly
Combining enameled copper and wood.
Ceram Mo 17:28-9 Ja '69
Enameled stones. Ceram Mo 17:31 Mr '69
Found objects as stencils; excerpts from
Metal enameling. Ceram Mo 17:28-9 S '69
Mary Sharp. Ceram Mo 17:23 N '69
Mary Sharp demonstrates cloisonne tech-
niques. Ceram Mo 17:24-6 N '69
ROTHERMUND, Dietmar
India and the Soviet Union. bibliog f Ann
Am Acad 386:78-88 N '69
ROTHMAN, Esther P.
Work as therapy for emotionally disturbed
girls. Ment Hy 53:269-79 Ap '69
ROTHMANS of Pall Mall Canada, limited
Jilted American: competition for Canadian
breweries. il Forbes 104:36 Jl 1 '69
ROTHSCHILD, Batsheva, baronne de
Building a new dance in a new country. D.
Sowden. il por Dance Mag 43:62-4 Ja '69
ROTHSCHILD, Emma
Infiltrating Nixon. Ramp Mag 7:38-9 D 14 '68
Report; Cuba. Atlan 223:14+ Mr '69
ROTHSCHILD, Nathaniel, baron de
Lafite, by C. Ray. Review
Sat R 52:34-5 Ap 19 '69. C. Creighton
ROTHSCHILD, Norman
Offbeat. See issues of Popular photography
Those wild, weird, wacky fish-eyes. il Pop
Phot 65:116-19+ Jl '69
ROTHSCHILD, Pauline, baronne de
Miraculous churches of Kizhi. Vogue 154:
156-61+ D '69
about
Le style Pauline. V. Lawford. il pors Vogue
153:150-3 Je '69
ROTHSTEIN, Arthur
Critical eye. See issues of Travel & camera
Picture sense. por Travel & Camera 32:30
F; 24 Mr '69
ROTHSTEIN, Barbara E. See Haber, A. H.
jt. auth.
ROTHSTEIN, Robert L.
Nixon's ABM: very thin indeed. New Repub
160:15-18 Mr 29 '69; Same abr. with title
Controlling nuclear arms: the ABM debate
continues. Cur 107:18-23 My '69
Reflections on the ABM decision. New Re-
pub 160:19-21 Mr 22 '69
ROTORS
Earth-landing rotor spacecraft studied. N.
S. Himmel. il Aviation W 90:51-3+ Ap 21
'69
ROTORS (helicopters) See Helicopters—Rotors
ROTTERDAM
Harbor
At mouth of Rhine: a new megalopolis. il
U S News 66:58-9 Je 23 '69
ROTTING of wood. See Wood—Decay
ROUECHÉ, Berton
Annals of medicine (cont) New Yorker 45:
105-17 Ap 5; 123-4+ O 11 '69
Lug wrench; story. New Yorker 45:32-4 Je
7 '69
ROUGH ROCK demonstration school. See In-
dians of North America—Education
ROUGIER, Michael
Everybody lives at Watergate; photographs.
Life 67:40-7 Ag 8 '69
In a Nixonite lair with tuxedo and unipod;
ed. by R. Graves. por Life 67:3 Ag 8 '69
ROUKES, Nicholas
Plastics of sculpture: materials and tech-
niyues; reprint. Craft Horiz 29:18-19+ Ja
'69
ROUND Britain powerboat race. See Motor
boat racing—Great Britain
ROUND houses. See Buildings, Round
ROUND table on the social responsibilities of
libraries. See American library association
—Round table on the social responsibilities
of libraries
ROUNDWORMS
Toxoplasma gondii: fecal forms separated
from eggs of the nematode toxocara cati.
J. K. Frenkel and others. bibliog il Science
164:432-3 Ap 25 '69

Toxoplasma gondii: transmission through fe-
ces in absence of toxocara cati eggs. H. G.
Sheffield and M. L. Melton. bibliog il Sci-
ence 164:431-2 Ap 25 '69
ROUNDY, C. Owen
Roy W. Martin junior high school: where
learning is interaction. Sr Schol 94:Schol
Teach 30-1 Ja 17 '69
ROUNTREE, Joseph N.
Bookstores as outlets for university press
books; excerpt from address, June 22, 1969.
por Pub W 196:30-1 Jl 28 '69
ROURKE, Elizabeth M.
Ear-sealed; poem. Horn Bk 45:73 F '69
ROUSE, Irving. See Cruxent, J. M. jt. auth.
ROUSE, James Wilson
Master builder of a model city. por Bsns W
p73 N 1 '69
ROUSE, Parke, jr
American travels of a French botanist.
Antiques 96:763-7 N '69
ROUSSEAU, Jean Jacques
Rousseau, father of anthropology; summary
of address, reprint. C. Lévi-Strauss. il
UNESCO Courier 22:61-3 Ag '69
ROUSSEL, Raymond
Skate's scales; story, tr. by R. Heppenstall.
Harp Baz 102:200 Mr '69
ROUTH, Joseph P.
They call me lucky. por Forbes 104:34 S 15
'69
ROUTH, Robert D.
Essence of color. por Travel & Camera 32:100-
1+ F '69
From B&W to color posters. il Pop Phot 64:
84-7 Je '69
Now this next slide. . . Travel & Camera
32:90-4 N '69
ROUTING machines
Getting more from your router. R. Shoberg.
il Pop Mech 131:190-2+ Mr '69
ROVERE, Richard Halworth
Letter from Washington. See occasional issues
of New Yorker
Nixon after six months. por(p27) N Y Times
Mag p4 Jl 20 '69
The sixties: this slum of a decade. N Y
Times Mag p25-7+ D 14 '69
ROW houses
Scotland, Maryland; townhouse development.
J. Bailey. il Arch Forum 131:82-5 Jl '69
ROW spacing of plants. See Plants, Space ar-
rangement of
ROWAN, Adriana
My husband's secret triumph; interview, ed.
by H. Higdon. por Good H 169:66-7+ Ag '69
ROWAN, Carl Thomas
Which will be the next Vietnam? Read Di-
gest 94:95-100 Mr '69
Why we need spy ships and planes. Read
Digest 95:122-6 S '69
—and Mazle, David
Black capitalism on the move. Read Digest
94:141-5 F '69
Russia's new look in Latin America. Read
Digest 95:41-2+ N '69
Sex education: powder keg in our schools.
Read Digest 95:73-8 O '69
Upward bound, salvaging talent and teen-
agers. Read Digest 94:39-40+ My '69
ROWAN, Dan
Era of Rowan and Martin? H. Van Horne.
por McCalls 97:80-1+ O '69
My husband's secret triumph; interview, ed.
by H. Higdon. A. Rowan. il por Good H
169:66-7+ Ag '69
New partner for Dan Rowan, the werewolf.
D. Adler. il pors Life 66:54-60 My 23 '69
ROWAYTON, Conn.
Marshes, developers, and taxes, a new ethic
for our estuaries. R. C. Clement. il Audu-
bon 71:34-5 N '69
ROWBOATS. See Boats and boating
ROWE, James N.
New politicians. Nation 209:651-2 D 15 '69
Soldiers on the war. New Repub 161:5-6 D
6 '69
ROWE, Lloyd A. and Schoenberg, S. P.
No more book-type urban administrators.
Am City 84:83-4 D '69
ROWELL, John
Crossroads 1970; address, June, 1969. por Li-
brary J 94:4575-7 D 15 '69
ROWELL, Lois
Additions and changes: a study of selected
LC classification schedules. bibliog Li-
brary J 94:3975-7 N 1 '69
ROWING
Boats that go bump: Eights week races,
Oxford. il Newsweek 73:97-8 Je 9 '69
Eight times two equals four; rowing squad
of OCC. H. D. Whall. il Sports Illus 30:62+
My 26 '69
Lost art of sculling. J. Emmett. il Mech
Illus 65:80+ F '69

ROWING—*Continued*
Merrily, merrily, merrily, merrily. J. Kunen.
il Sports Illus 30:46-8+ Je 16 '69
Underdog bites back; Harvard's crew wins
from arch-rival Pennsylvania. H. D. Whall.
il Sports Illus 30:20-3 My 19 '69
See also
Regattas
ROWLAND, Howard Ray
Campus ombudsman. Todays Ed 58:37-9 O
'69
ROWLEY, Carl M. See Faux, E. J. jt. auth.
ROWLEY, Charles E.
Helping others to help themselves. por
Chem 42:8-10 F '69
ROWLEY, Peter
Blood and fire against the draft. Nation
209:248-50 S 15 '69
Jai Baba! Hare Krishna, and all that. Mlle
70:136-7+ D '69
Will Britain turn right? Chr Cent 86:806-7
Je 11 '69
ROWSE, Arthur E.
Failing newspaper probe: the press dummies
up. Nation 208:816-20 Je 30 '69
ROXON, Lillian
Roxon's rock. S. K. Oberbeck. por Newsweek
74:127 N 10 '69
ROY, Chalmer J.
Imbalance of nature. Todays Ed 58:26-8+ Ja
'69
ROYAL, Darrell
Country slicker. il por Time 94:62+ N 14 '69
ROYAL academy of dancing
Tested and found not wanting; interview. ed.
by L. Joel. M. Fonteyn. il Dance Mag 43:
30-1 Jl '69
ROYAL ballet, Great Britain
Elgar's garden, 1898; Royal ballet's New
York season. D. Hering. il Dance Mag 43:
35-43 Jl '69
In the English style; Britain's Royal ballet
at Manhattan's Metropolitan opera house.
il Time 93:68 My 2 '69
Musical events:
First week at Metropolitan opera house.
W. Sargeant. New Yorker 45:119 My 3
'69
Pelléas and Mélisande and act III of
Raymonda. W. Sargeant. New Yorker
45:96 My 31 '69
Romeo and Juliet. W. Sargeant. New
Yorker 45:138 My 17 '69
Swan lake and The sleeping beauty. W.
Sargeant. New Yorker 45:124+ My 10 '69
New angles in English dance. il Dance Mag
43:34-5 My '69
Royal enigma; New York season. H. Saal.
il Newsweek 73:117 My 5 '69
Variations and variations. W. Terry. il Sat
R 52:42 My 24 '69
ROYAL Canadian mounted police. See Canada
—Royal Canadian mounted police
ROYAL Cork yacht club. See Yacht clubs
ROYAL Danish ballet
Danish delights. W. Terry. il Sat R 52:41+
Je 14; 32-3 Je 21 '69
Landscape into danscape; photographs. H.
Migdoll. Dance Mag 43:46-55 D '69
World of dance; choreographer needed. W.
Terry. il Sat R 52:35-6 Ag 16 '69
ROYAL Dutch-Shell group
Shell saves money by spending more. il
Bsns W p56-8+ Mr 8 '69
ROYAL family of Great Britain. See Great
Britain—Royal family
ROYAL family of Monaco. See Monaco—Royal
family
ROYAL Norwegian air force. See Norway—
Air force
ROYAL opera, Great Britain
Music; productions of Gluck's Orfeo ed
Euridice and Verdi's Macbeth. D. Hamilton.
Nation 209:157 Ag 25 '69
Other side; performance of H. Searle's Ham-
let. T. Heinitz. Sat R 52:51 Je 28 '69
Report: London; new production of Die
Meistersinger von Nürnberg. F. G. Barker.
il Opera N 33:32-3 Mr 1 '69
Report: London; production of Berlioz Troy-
ens. F. G. Barker. il Opera N 34:24 N 1 '69
Report: London; production of Manon Les-
caut. F. G. Barker. il Opera N 33:31-2 F 1
'69
ROYAL palms. See Palms
ROYAL radar establishment. See Great Britain
—Royal radar establishment
ROYAL Swedish ballet. See Ballet—Sweden
ROYALTIES
Artists' rights. P. Nathan. Pub W 196:56 O
20 '69
Publishing scene; Russian literature. D.
Dempsey. Sat R 52:31 Je 14 '69

ROYALTY. See Kings and rulers; also subhead
Royal family under names of countries, e.g.
Monaco—Royal family
ROYAN festival. See Music festivals—France
ROYBAL, Edward R.
Excerpt from debate, June 26, 1968. Cong
Digest 48:57+ F '69
ROYCE, Sir Henry, 1st bart
Sir Henry's legacy. S. G. Slappey. il por
Nations Bsns 57:66-70 Ag '69
ROYSTER, Fred S.
Excerpt from testimony before House com-
mittee on interstate and foreign commerce,
April 23, 1969. Cong Digest 48:181+ Je '69
ROZELL, Bruce
Muscadines, scuppernongs and grapes. Org
Gard & Farm 16:32-4 Je '69
ROZELL, Margilee Johns
Daylilies span a slope. por Org Gard & Farm
16:46-7 Ap '69
Fall bulbs lead to spring blooms. Org Gard
& Farm 16:25-7 O '69
Getting a jump on spring. Org Gard & Farm
16:76-7 Mr '69
Oregon hollygrape, a real attraction. Org
Gard & Farm 16:52-3 Ag '69
We're proud of our Humble blackberries. Org
Gard & Farm 16:60-1 D '69
ROZELLE, Pete
Broadway Joe: rebel with a nightclub for a
cause; with report by S. Smith. il por Life
66:22-7 Je 20 '69
Does Pete Rozelle run pro football? Ask
Joe Namath. L. Shecter. il pors N Y Times
Mag p30-1+ Ag 17 '69
Mod man out; with editorial comment. W.
Johnson. il por Sports Illus 30:10, 20-3 Je
16 '69
ROZET, A. Bruce
Old face is back at mini-conglomerate. Bsns
W p27 Ag 23 '69
ROZHEN, Walter
Poor Russian boy on a hot cat. F. Rohr. il
por Motor B 123:434-5 Ja '69
RUARK, Arthur E.
Where do we go from here? bibliog por
Phys Today 22:25-8 S '69
RUARK, Gibbons
Program for survival; poem. Poetry 114:164
Je '69
RUBBER
See also
Elastomers
RUBBER, Artificial
Two precast structures cushioned by neo-
prene. il Arch Rec 146:135-7 D '69
RUBBER in automobiles. See Automobiles—
Materials
RUBBER industry and trade
See also
Tire industry and trade
also names of rubber companies, e.g.
Firestone tire and rubber company
RUBBINGS; story. See Whedon, J.
RUBBISH disposal. See Refuse and refuse
disposal
RUBELLA
Questions & answers on German measles. V.
Apgar. PTA Mag 63:12-13 My '69
Vaccines
Exit German measles? B. Goodheart. Todays
Health 47:26-8+ Je '69
Good news: a shot for German measles. il
Changing T 23:37-9 Ag '69
How the new German measles vaccine will
prevent birth defects. il Good H 169:
173-5 S '69
Knocking out measles. Newsweek 73:89 Je
23 '69
Lonely medical runner. Nation 209:493 N 10
'69
New vaccine for German measles. Consumer
Rep 34:610-11 O '69
Now: a vaccine to conquer another crippler.
S. L. Englebardt. Read Digest 94:123-7 Ap
'69
Rubella vaccine. L. W. Sauer. il PTA Mag
64:23-4 S '69
Rubella vaccine is licensed. M. Mueller. Sci-
ence 165:48 Jl 4 '69
Rubella vaccine ready. il Sci N 95:595 Je 21
'69
Rubella vaccines. Sci Am 220:54-6 Je '69
To protect the unborn. il Time 93:49 Je 20
'69
U.S. girds for war on German measles. il
Bsns W p56-7 Mr 22 '69
Vaccines may be licensed by fall. Sci N
95:209 Mr 1 '69
RUBENSTEIN, Richard Lowell
Jewish paganism. M. Fox. Commentary 47:
92-4+ Je '69; Discussion. 48:10+ S '69

RUBEY, William Walden
NAS names Rubey director of Lunar science institute. J. P. Wiley. por Phys Today 22:85 Ja '69
RUBIN, Barbara Jo
Barbara Jo Rubin. il pors Vogue 153:196-7 My '69
Boycotting the brunette. Newsweek 73:58 Ja 27 '69
There goes Barbara Jo! por Newsweek 73: 87 Mr 31 '69
RUBIN, Donald
Blue cross and the blues: adaptation of address. October 30, 1967. Ment Hy 53:67-70 Ja '69
RUBIN, Harold. See Robbins, H. pseud.
RUBIN, Jerry
Inside the great pigasus plot; excerpts from Do it! Ramp Mag 8:10-12+ D '69
    about
Making of a yippie. J. A. Lukas. il por Esquire 72:126-34+ N '69
My little Yippela, Jerry Rubin goes home. J. Kornbluth. il por Look 33:20 O 7 '69
Poor Jerry, bad Tom! W. F. Buckley, jr. Nat R 21:246 Mr 11 '69
RUBIN, Leslie
Apartheid 1948-69: the politics of dehumanization. Chr Cent 86:947-50 Jl 16 '69
RUBIN, Lillian B.
Maximum feasible participation: the origins, implications, and present status; extracts from paper. bibliog f Ann Am Acad 385: 14-29 S '69
RUBIN, Michael
In declaration of love. Writer 82:14-15 Je '69
RUBIN, Robert T. and Clark, B. R.
Tryptophan pyrrolase induction in patients with manic depression. bibliog Science 165: 1146-7 S 12 '69
RUBIN, Theodore Isaac
I have a friend who... por Ladies Home J 86:56 S; 16 N '69
Psychiatrist's notebook; questions and answers. See issues of McCall's
What makes a man lovable? por Ladies Home J 86:68+ O '69
What makes a woman lovable? Read Digest 95:78-80 Ag '69
RUBINGTON, Earl
Legal commitment and hospital behavior: address. May 10, 1967. bibliog Ment Hy 53:41-53 Ja '69
RUBINI, Giovanni Battista
Rubini of Bergamo. M. J. Matz. por Opera N 33:12-13 F 1 '69
RUBINSTEIN, Alvin Z.
Czechoslovakia in transition. Cur Hist 56: 206-11+ Ap '69
RUBINSTEIN, Amnon
Damn everybody sums up the angry mood of Israel. N Y Times Mag p24-7+ F 9 '69
Jews and Arabs live side by side, but not together, no man's land remains in Jerusalem. N Y Times Mag p30-1+ My 11 '69
RUBINSTEIN, Artur
Delightful disaster. R. L. Shayon. Sat R 52: 50 O 11 '69
Letter from Paris; cinematographic profile of life. Genêt. New Yorker 45:138+ O 4 '69
Rubinstein on TV. G. Movshon. il por Hi Fi 19:MA21 N '69
RUBINSTEIN, E.
I live by these; poem. Commonweal 89:703 Mr 7 '69
RUBINSTEIN, S. Leonard
Elements of fiction. Writer 82:21-4 Ja '69
RUDD, Mark
Wild in the streets. il Newsweek 74:42+ O 20 '69
RUDDIMAN, William F.
Recent planktonic foraminifera: dominance and diversity in North Atlantic surface sediments. bibliog Science 164:1164-7 Je 6 '69
RUDDY, William
Madonna; poem. America 121:613 D 20 '69
RUDEL, Julius
Douglas Moore. Opera N 34:21 O 11 '69
RUDIN, Andrew
Current chronicle: performance of Tragoedia at Philadelphia musical academy. D. Chittum. il Mus Q 55:99-102 Ja '69
RUDIN, Jacob P.
On world reaction to developments in the Middle East. Chr Cent 86:110 Ja 22 '69
RUDINSKY, J. A.
Masking of the aggregation pheromone in dendroctonus pseudotsugae hopk. bibliog Science 166:884-5 N 14 '69
RUDOFSKY, Bernard
Street scene. G. B. Porter. il Newsweek 74: 60 D 22 '69

RUDOLF, crown prince of Austria
Oft-told tale of the Vienna woods. J. Wechsberg. McCalls 96:46+ Ap '69
RUDOLF, Anthony
(tr) See Du Bouchet, A. To ripen
RUDOLF, Max
Twenty Long years. por Opera N 33:6-7 Je 14 '69
RUDOLPH, Jack
Peninsula music festival. Hi Fi 19:MA26+ N '69
RUDOLPH, L. C.
Catholicism in the '30s. Chr Cent 86:124+ Ja 22 '69
RUDOLPH, Paul Marvin
Essence of architecture is space; interview. por House & Gard 136:26+ N '69
    about
Chapel for Tuskegee by Rudolph. il Arch Rec 146:117-26 N '69
RUDWICK, Elliott. See Meier, A. jt. auth.
RUELLIAS
Ruellias, intriguing strangers. L. J. Uttal. il Horticulture 47:38-9 F '69
RUETHER, Rosemary
Black theology and black church. America 120:684-7 Je 14 '69
Confrontation and communication. Chr Cent 86:1163-5 S 10 '69
New church? Commonweal 90:64-6 Ap 4 '69
New wine, maybe new wineskins, for the church. Chr Cent 86:445-9 Ap 2 '69
Radical and the mediator: their roles in social change. America 121:521-3 N 29 '69
R. Ruether on open questions. Commonweal 91:218 N 14 '69
RUG cleaning. See Rugs and carpets—Care
RUG making. See Rugs and carpets
RUGBY football
Rugby and apartheid. C. Northcott. Chr Cent 86:1507-8 N 26 '69
RUGGIERO, Vincent Ryan
Fabric of modern faith. Cath World 208: 255-8 Mr '69
RUGGLES, Eugene
Orchard; poem. Nation 209:292 S 22 '69
Poor man moves through Washington, D.C: spring 1968; poem. Nation 209:92 Jl 28 '69
RUGH, Roberts
Normal incidence of brain hernia in the mouse. bibliog Science 163:407 Ja 24 '69
RUGS and carpets
Big pile-up. V. D. Hahn. il Am Home 72:68-73 N '69
Bright ideas afoot! il Seventeen 28:186+ My '69
Carpet flammability: improvements afoot. Consumer Rep 34:427 Ag '69
Design in Aubusson carpets. M. Jarry. il Antiques 95:702-7 My '69
Floors are looking up. B. Plumb. il N Y Times Mag p74-5 F 9 '69
Leisure carpet covers new ground. il House & Gard 135:150-5+ Ap '69
Leisure carpet's lively new patterns. il House & Gard 135:188-91 Ap '69
Progress report on: flammable carpets. il Consumer Rep 34:72-3 F '69
Quick-hook a rug. il House B 111:54-5+ Ag '69
Rya pillows and hangings. J. Roehrig. il Sch Arts 68:11 My '69
Subjects acoustical. T. Bowman and E. McDonald. il House B 111:136-7 N '69
    See also
Masland, C. H, and sons
    Care
Rug stains. McCalls 96:145 S '69
Tips on carpet cleaning. il Parents Mag 44: 30 Je '69
    Purchasing
Buying a good carpet. Good H 169:200 O '69
RUGS and carpets, Oriental
Early influences in Turkish rugs. H. McCoy Jones. il Antiques 95:847-51 Je '69
Flat-woven rugs of the Middle East. W. R. Pickering and A. N. Landreau. il Antiques 96:390-6 S '69
Oriental love affair. P. W. Tarnawsky. il Read Digest 94:187-8+ F '69
Oriental rug in decorating today. E. Kinard. House B 111:101-3 O '69
Riding a magic carpet; Oriental-rug renaissance. il Newsweek 73:63 Mr 3 '69
Rugs of India. il House & Gard 135:56+ My '69
Rugs of the Caucasus. H. M. Keshishian. il Antiques 95:370-5 Mr '69
This month, a shopping column Marian Miller collection. W. McQuade. il Arch Forum 129:90 D '68

RUGS and carpets, Outdoor
Here and now: indoor/outdoor carpeting and furniture. L. Grundy and T. Bowman. il House B 111:106-8 Je '69
Leisure carpet covers new ground. il House & Gard 135:150-5+ Ap '69

RUHE, Benjamin
National portrait gallery opens in Washington. Am Artist 32:52-7+ N '68

RUINS. See Archeology

RUIZ, Chico
Bottom part of the lineup. G. Ronberg. il pors Sports Illus 31:30-2+ Ag 25 '69

RUIZ, Francisco Amighetti. See Amighetti Ruiz, F.

RUIZ-GIMENEZ, Joaquin
Council changed all that. America 120:127 F 1 '69

RUKEYSER, Muriel
Critic of the month. L. Lieberman. Poetry 114:42 Ap '69

RUKEYSER, William Simon
Books & ideas. Fortune 80:211-12 S '69
Detroit's reluctant ride into smallsville. Fortune 79:110-13+ Mr '69
How youth is reforming the business world. Fortune 79:76-9+ Ja '69
Why rain fell on Automatic sprinkler. Fortune 79:88-91+ My 1 '69
World's fastest-growing auto company. Fortune 80:76-81+ D '69
Youth shakes the business world. Read Digest 94:185-6+ My '69

RULE, Jane
Anyone will do; story. Redbook 133:108-9 O '69
Not an ordinary wife; story. Redbook 133: 70-1 Ag '69

RULE of the road
Rules of the road and campsite tips. V. L. Oertle. il Pop Sci 194:176+ My '69

RULERS. See Kings and rulers

RULERS (instruments)
Mosaic unit ruler; does one exist? R. E. M. Moore; discussion. bibliog Science 162: 1306; 163:704-5 D 13 '68, F 14 '69

RULING class; drama. See Barnes, P.

RUM
Rum in all its variety. J. T. Elsor. il Travel & Camera 32:13+ S '69
Rum: the tipple of the times; with recipe. il Look 33:45 D 2 '69

RUMANIA
See also
Church and state in Rumania
Communism—Rumania
Communist party (Rumania)
Science—Rumania

Commerce
Rumania tries the hard sell on trade. il Bsns W p74+ Jl 26 '69

Cultural relations
United States and Romania sign understanding on libraries. Dept State Bul 61: 196-8 S 1 '69

Description and travel
Americans afoot in Rumania. D. Dimancescu. il Nat Geog 135:810-45 Je '69

Economic conditions
Rumania's red carpet for a U.S. president. il U S News 67:40-1 Ag 4 '69

Economic policy
Rumania starts down model path. il Bsns W p66 O 25 '69
Turning west. il Time 93:91 Ap 18 '69

Economic relations
When West trades with a red nation. il U S News 66:46 Je 2 '69
See also
Rumania—Commerce

Foreign relations
How does Rumania do it? with report by A. Tillier. il Newsweek 74:41-2 Ag 4 '69
Rumania's red carpet for a U.S. president. il U S News 67:40-1 Ag 4 '69
Shadow. Newsweek 74:36 Ag 25 '69
They loved him in Bucharest. il Life 67:32-3 Ag 15 '69
Why's the President going to Bucharest? P. Ben. New Repub 161:16-17 Jl 12 '69

United States
United States and Romania agree on 1969-70 exchanges program; Department announcement, with text of U.S. note, November 26, 1968. Dept State Bul 59:680-4 D 23 '68

Industries
See also
Rumania—Commerce

Intellectual life
Rumanian game; with interview with P. Popescu. L. Gross. il Look 33:32-8 Ap 15 '69

Politics and government
How does Rumania do it? with report by A. Tillier. il Newsweek 74:41-2 Ag 4 '69
Letter from Bucharest. T. Szulc. New Yorker 45:105-6+ S 6 '69

Religious institutions and affairs
Rumania's opening to the churches. G. A. Maloney. America 121:490-3 N 22 '69

RUMANIAN academy. See Academy of the socialist republic of Romania

RUMANIAN tennis players. See Tennis players

RUMEX. See Docks (plants)

RUMFORD, Beatrix T.
Household accessories. Antiques 95:145-9 Ja '69

RUMOR, Mariano
No hope. Newsweek 74:41 Ag 18 '69
While Rome burns. Newsweek 74:36+ Jl 21 '69

RUMOR
Billion-dollar rumor factory; Wall Street's rumor mill. il Bsns W p26-7 Ag 9 '69
Of rumor, myth and a Beatle; rumor that P. McCartney died. Time 94:41 O 31 '69

RUMSFELD, Donald
New mission for war on poverty? por U S News 66:17 My 5 '69
New OEO fan. por Time 93:15 My 2 '69
President and the poor. J. Osborne. New Repub 160:16-18 My 24 '69

RUNG, Henry P.
Plan for kitchen success. por Camp Mag 41: 10-12 S '69

RUNGE, Evgenii Evgenievich
Spooks galore; spy-exposés in West Germany. il por Time 93:44 My 16 '69

RUNIA, Klaas
Karl Barth, 1886-1968: his place in history. Chr Today 14:6-9 D 5 '69

RUNNING
Best in the world; West coast relays. il Newsweek 73:106+ My 26 '69
Exhilarating nip of Liquori; winning of the Track and field championship for Kansas. S. Myslenski. il Sports Illus 30:24-5 Mr 24 '69
It's anybody's race; Boston marathon. Sports Illus 30:14+ My 5 '69
Line for the mile forms here. S. Myslenski. Sports Illus 30:52 F 17 '69
Man believed sane runs 105,000 miles; B. Emmerton. D. Levin. il Sports Illus 31:36-8+ O 6 '69
PTA meeting is tougher; D. Brown, National AAU women's cross-country championship winner. S. Myslenski. il Sports Illus 31:69-70 D 8 '69
Pressure cooker. S. Myslenski. il Sports Illus 31:18-21 Jl 7 '69
Social life of the long-distance runner. J. Casey. il Sports Illus 30:104-6+ Ap 14 '69
Tallest, fastest and buggiest; J. Bacheler. R. Blount, jr. il Sports Illus 30:58-9+ Je 16 '69
This is one stag who can outrun the hounds; D. Clayton, marathon runner. G. S. Brown. il Sports Illus 31:44-5 Ag 4 '69
Warmup for the Canyon run; G. Young's victory at Los Angeles invitational track meet. W. F. Reed, jr. il Sports Illus 30:16-19 Ja 27 '69
See also
Hurdle racing
Jogging

RUNNING the country; drama. See Oser, J. A.

RUNWAY lighting. See Airports—Lighting

RUPERT, Anton E.
Jilted American. il por Forbes 104:36 Jl 1 '69

RUPOLO, Ernie
Prosecutor, by J. Mills. Review
Newsweek il 74:83D-84 Ag 25 '69. G. Wolff

RUPP, Adolph F.
E—Rupption in wildcat country. C. Kirkpatrick. il por Sports Illus 31:22-5 D 22 '69

RUPPENTHAL, Karl M.
World law and the hijackers. Nation 208: 144-6 F 3 '69

RURAL churches
Social change and the rural church. D. W. Johnson. Chr Cent 86:658+ My 7 '69

RUSSIA—See also—*Continued*
Labor and laboring classes—Russia
Labor supply—Russia
Leningrad, Siege of, 1941-1944
Morale, National—Russia
Moscow
Munitions industries—Russia
Natural resources—Russia
Petroleum—Russia
Political prisoners—Russia
Prison camps—Russia
Prisoners—Russia
Public opinion—Russia
Publishers and publishing—Russia
Recreation—Russia
Research—Russia
Science—Russia
Seaside resorts—Russia
Secret service—Russia
Shopping and shoppers—Russia
Space research—Russia
Subversive activities—Russia
Tashkent
Technology—Russia
Trials—Russia
United States—Foreign relations—Russia
World war, 1939-1945—Russia
Youth—Russia

Antiquities

Archeology in the Soviet Union. C. S. Chard.
bibliog Science 163:774-9 F 21 '69
Mousterian cultures in European Russia. R.
G. Klein. bibliog il Science 165:257-65 Jl
18 '69

Appropriations and expenditures

Off target. il Newsweek 74:26 D 29 '69
See also
Russia—Armed forces—Appropriations and
expenditures

Armed forces

Reading the entrails: American withdrawal,
a retreat. J. Burnham. Nat R 21:741 Jl 29
'69

Appropriations and expenditures
Purposeful budgetry. il Time 94:14 D 26 '69
Soviet defense outlays show continued in-
crease. il Aviation W 90:71+ Mr 10 '69

Forces in Czechoslovakia
In Soviet-occupied Czechoslovakia; a search
for Ivan with a hidden camera. M. Durham.
il Life 66:30-3 Ap 18 '69

Procurement
Military-industrial complex-Russian style. R.
Armstrong. il Fortune 80:84-7+ Ag 1 '69

Army

Old soldiers do die; deaths of twelve Russian generals. Time 93:36 My 23 '69

Forces in Czechoslovakia
See Russia—Armed forces—Forces in
Czechoslovakia

Officers
Soviet generals and number one. T. Szamuely.
il Nat R 21:861-2 Ag 26 '69

Boundaries

Statements on Sino-Soviet border clashes;
excerpts from the official government statements. Cur Hist 57:241-4 O '69
See also
Sino-Russian border disputes

Climate

USSR resources for agriculture. C. D. Harris.
bibliog il Focus 20:1-7 D '69

Commerce

Cash and cocoa; Russian-made aircraft. Nation 208:357 Mr 24 '69

Commercial treaties and agreements

Red dividend; Italian gas deal. il Newsweek
74:76 D 22 '69
U.S. and Soviet Union sign new agreements
on fisheries. Dept State Bul 60:187 Mr 3
'69
U.S. and U.S.S.R. hold talks on northeastern
Pacific fisheries. Dept State Bul 60:79 Ja 27
'69

Cultural relations

See also
Exchange of persons programs

Defenses

Defense dilemma. R. Hotz. Aviation W 90:11
F 24 '69
Military-industrial complex-Russian style. R.
Armstrong. il Fortune 80:84-7+ Ag 1 '69

Russia's growing power; interview, ed. by
F. C. Painton. L. L. Lemnitzer. il U S
News 66:44-6+ My 12 '69
Soviet military since Khrushchev. T. W.
Wolfe. bibliog f il Cur Hist 57:220-7+ O '69
See also
Guided missiles—Defenses
Russia—Armed forces

Description and travel

In Russia; excerpts. A. Miller. il Harper
239:37-78 S '69
Report from Moscow. T. C. Sorensen. il
Holiday 46:12-13 Ag '69
Russia through the time tunnel. C. Holland.
il Mlle 70:110-11+ D '69
Visual vs. aural in Russia. C. J. McNaspy.
America 120:371-2 Mr 29 '69
Winging it through Russia. D. Thomas. il
Sports Illus 31:42-7 S 8 '69

Economic conditions

Bad weather. Newsweek 75:51 Ja 5 '70
Good life for Ivan; troublesome for Krem-
lin. il U S News 66:60-2 Mr 17 '69
Good life: where Russia lags. il U S News
67:51 N 24 '69
Russia's fast growth eases off. il Bsns W
p86-7 F 8 '69
Soviet economy in the 1970's. N. Spulber.
bibliog f il Cur Hist 57:214-19+ O '69
Strange world of ivan ivanov, by G. W.
Nutter. Review
Nat R 21:394-5 Ap 22 '69. S. T. Possony
See also
Agriculture—Russia
Communism—Russia
Labor and laboring classes—Russia

Economic policy

See also
Communism—Russia

Economic relations
Czechoslovakia

Other rape of Czechoslovakia. L. Velie. Read
Digest 95:187-8+ Jl '69

Foreign opinion

Albanian demonology. A. Tuckerman. Nation
208:566-7 My 5 '69
Close ranks, the Chinese are coming! P. Ben.
New Repub 161:18-19 S 20 '69
Space and senselessness; U.S. attitudes at
the space science and technology confer-
ence, Denver, Colo. N. Cousins. Sat R 52:
18 Jl 12 '69
Speaking for themselves; letter to the Times.
R. Butt. Nat R 21:372 Ap 22 '69

Foreign relations

American stake in the Russia-China con-
frontation. W. E. Griffith. Read Digest 95:
89-92 S '69
Brezhnev: man to watch in the Kremlin. il
U S News 67:68-9 D 8 '69
Czechoslovakia and western security; state-
ment. H. M. Jackson. Bul Atom Sci 25:36-9
Ja '69
Detente in the '70s; East-West relations. Z.
Brzezinski. New Repub 162:17-18 Ja 3
'70
East side, west side. Time 93:33-4 Ap 11 '69
For a closer look at Russian aims. K. Lach-
mann. U S News 68:26 Ja 5 '70
Future U.S.-Soviet relations; the lessons
of Czechoslovakia. A. Shub. Cur 104:46-54
F '69
Moscow report: . . . the more it remains
the same. A. Carthew. il N Y Times Mag
p28-9+ My 18 '69
Red bloc. D. L. Flaherty. America 122:12-14
Ja 10 '70
Roses among the olive branches. Newsweek
74:29 Ag 11 '69
Russia has not changed her ways; excerpts
from address, March 17, 1969. H. M. Jack-
son. Read Digest 94:91-5 Je '69
Russia's yellow peril; exploiting Chinese
threat. New Repub 160:8-9 Mr 29 '69
Shifting great power politics; the end of
US-Soviet hegemony. Cur 108:61-4 Je '69
Soviet dilemma: coping on two fronts. il
Newsweek 73:33-4 Mr 31 '69
Soviet foreign policy; address, July 11, 1969.
A. A. Gromyko. Vital Speeches 35:618-28 Ag
1 '69
Soviet Union and the West. K. L. London.
Cur Hist 57:193-200+ O '69
U.S. and Russia: dawn of a new era; inter-
view. J. Fromm. il U S News 68:34-7 Ja
5 '70

RUSSIA—Foreign relations—*Continued*
What the Czech invasion cost the Kremlin.
il U S News 67:80 Ag 25 '69
  See also
Cuban crisis, 1962
Military assistance, Russian

Anecdotes, facetiae, satire, etc.

Chetsky-Davidov report. J. Jeffries. il Nat R
21:748 Jl 29 '69

History

Russia's road from peace to war, by L.
Fischer. Review
  Sat R 52:31-2 Jl 19 '69. A. Dallin

Arab states

Russia gaining in Mideast; office memo. J.
Law. il U S News 67:64-5 O 13 '69

Asia

Russia's new target; Asia. il U S News 67:
32-4 Ag 11 '69

Bulgaria

Best of the bargain. K. Huszar. Newsweek
73:57+ Je 9 '69

China (People's Republic)

Battle for the backyards. Time 93:38 Ap 4 '69
China's door northward; confrontation be-
tween the Soviet Union and Communist
China? America 120:443 Ap 12 '69
Chinese blinked. il Time 94:31-2 O 17 '69
Fastest guns in the East? il Sr Schol 94:14
Mr 21 '69
If Russia and China fight. il Newsweek 74:
35+ Ag 18 '69
Limited war or nuclear holocaust? R. S.
Elegant. Cur 112:48-52 N '69
Sino-Soviet tensions and American foreign
policy. D. F. Halloran. Cath World 209:
151-5 Jl '69
Soviet summit: high on trouble. il Newsweek
73:38-40+ Je 16 '69
Twenty years of Sino-Soviet relations. F.
Michael. Cur Hist 57:150-5+ S '69
Urgent question that dominates the Asian
heartland today is: will there be war be-
tween Russia and China? H. E. Salisbury.
il N Y Times Mag p 10-11+ Jl 27 '69
Were red China in the UN... America 121:
255-6 O 4 '69
Why are the Russians scared? S. Alsop.
Newsweek 74:122 S 22 '69
Why Russia and China prepare for war. il
U S News 67:32-4 S 15 '69
  See also
Sino-Russian border disputes

Cuba

Soviet warships: why a visit to Castro's
Cuba. U S News 67:7 Jl 21 '69

Czechoslovakia

Our internationalist duty; address, October
28, 1969. L. I. Brezhnev. Vital Speeches
36:101-5 D 1 '69
  See also
Czechoslovakia—Occupation, 1968

Egypt

Cheers for Andrei; A. Gromyko in Cairo to
sell Middle East peace package. il Newsweek 73:44+ Je 23 '69
Dam U.S. wouldn't build: a big success for
Russia. J. Law. il U S News 67:66-7 D 29
'69

Europe, Eastern

Close ranks, the Chinese are coming! P. Ben.
New Repub 161:18-19 S 20 '69
East Europe: the politics of recovery. S. S.
Anderson. il Cur Hist 57:207-13+ O '69
Prudential Mr Tito. M. M. Mestrovic. Com-
monweal 90:62-3 Ap 4 '69
Timely reminder; excerpts from message of
American friends of the captive nations,
and the Conference of Americans of cen-
tral and eastern European descent to
members of the new Congress. Nat R 21:
218 Mr 11 '69
Uneasy lies the bloc. Time 93:36 F 28 '69
U.S.S.R. east Europe and the socialist com-
monwealth. K. L. London. bibliog f Cur
Hist 56:193-9 Ap '69
Unquiet on the eastern front; Yugoslavia
and Poland. A. Tillier; K. Huszar. il Newsweek 73:44+ My 5 '69
Where Russian troops may strike next. il
U S News 66:12 F 24 '69
Yakubovsky's travels. Newsweek 73:42+ Mr
3 '69

Germany (Federal Republic)

Backing away from the brink. il Newsweek
74:53-4 O 20 '69
Germany looks East: reshaping Europe. il
Newsweek 74:33-4 D 22 '69

Ghana

Little Ghana takes on the Russians. D. C.
Steffen. il Life 66:20-5 F 21 '69

India

India and the Soviet Union. D. Rothermund.
bibliog f Ann Am Acad 386:78-88 N '69

Latin America

Russians have come. il Time 93:39 F 28 '69
Russia's new look in Latin America. C. T.
Rowan and D. M. Mazie. Read Digest 95:
41-2+ N '69
Soviet penetration of Latin America; ad-
dress, June 12, 1969. J. R. Rarick. Vital
Speeches 35:699-704 S 1 '69

Middle East

Great powers, the Arabs and the Israelis. B.
Lewis. For Affairs 47:642-52 Jl '69
Ivan the Arab; Soviet government suggestions for ending the conflict. New Repub
160:7-9 Ja 25 '69
Soviet power in the Middle East. il Newsweek
73:46+ F 17 '69

Rumania

Shadow. Newsweek 74:36 Ag 25 '69

Underdeveloped areas

Sino-Soviet rivalry in the third world. E. K.
Valkenier. bibliog f Cur Hist 57:201-6+ O
'69
Soviet Union in the third world: purpose in
search of power. F. Ermarth. bibliog f Ann
Am Acad 386:31-40 N '69

United States

Are we in a Pavlovian box? U.S. policy
conditioned response to Soviet objectives?
A. C. Sutton. il Nat R 21:692-4 Jl 15 '69
Battle inside the Kremlin. V. Zorza. Look
33:93-7+ Mr 18 '69
Can Russia afford a U.S. deal? il U S News
66:51 Mr 31 '69
Convergence: the uncertain meeting of East
and West; Time essay. il Time 95:18-19 Ja
12 '70
Kennedy, Khrushchev, and Cuba. D. Pear-
son. il Sat R 52:12-15 Mr 29 '69
Next: a deal between U.S. and Russia? il
U S News 66:25-6 Mr 10 '69
Origins of the cold war: the Communist
dimension. J. R. Starobin. For Affairs 47:
681-96 Jl '69
Progress, coexistence & intellectual freedom,
by A. D. Sakharov. Review
  Phys Today il 22:77-9+ My '69. J. M.
Hollander
Russia plotted the Pueblo affair; excerpts.
J. Sejna. Read Digest 95:73-6 Jl '69
Russian speaks softly. il Time 94:35 Jl 18
'69
Russia's strategy against U.S; the inside
story. il U S News 66:53-6 Je 16 '69
Soviet intrigue? reprint. D. Lawrence. U S
News 66:100 Mr 24 '69
Soviet-U.S dialogue; our lines of communi-
cation are open; address, November 20,
1969. E. L. Richardson. Vital Speeches 36:
167-9 Ja 1 '70
Sunshine through the clouds. Newsweek 74:
35 Jl 21 '69
When Russian and American peace groups
talk peace; meeting of Soviet peace com-
mittee in Moscow. H. A. Jack. il N Y
Times Mag p28-9+ Mr 9 '69
  See also
Strategic arms limitation talks

Yugoslavia

Why Russia fears Yugoslav communism. C.
S. Foltz. il U S News 66:82-4 My 5 '69

History

Bibliography

Articles and other books received; comp. by
R. V. Allen. See issues of American historical review

Historiography

Study of United States history in the Soviet
Union; excerpts from address, tr. by M.
Pundeff. N. N. Bolkhovitinov. bibliog f
Am Hist R 74:1221-42 Ap '69

19th century

Nihilists, by R. Hingley. Review
  Commentary 48:64+ Ag '69. G. Woodcock

20th century

Great terror, by R. Conquest. Review
  Esquire 71:36+ F '69. M. Muggeridge

RUSSIA—History—*Continued*

Revolution, 1917-1921

Power was lying in the street; we picked it up. A. Parry. il N Y Times Mag p30-1+ S 28 '69; Discussion. p34+ D 14 '69; 14+ Ja 11 '70

Revolution: the past and the future. il Life 67:100-12 O 10 '69

Industries

Russia's fast growth eases off. il Bsns W p86-7 F 8 '69
See also
Automobile industry and trade—Russia
Building industry—Russia
Steel industry and trade—Russia

Intellectual life

Dear Stalin, Dear Brezhnev, Dear . . . two letters: 1938, 1968, reprints, ed. by J. Jeffries. Nat R 21:590 Je 17 '69
Flowers for Irina; labor camp sentence for dissident intellectual. Time 93:36+ F 28 '69
In Russia; excerpts. A. Miller. il Harper 239:37-78 S '69
In the land of the commissars. Nat R 21:891 S 9 '69
Ins and outs of de-Stalinization. J. Critchlow. Commonweal 90:191-2 My 2 '69
Kremlin chill; attacks on A. Tvardovsky and other liberal intellectuals. Newsweek 74: 38-9 Ag 25 '69
Why I left Russia. A. Kuznetsov. Read Digest 95:73-8 N '69

Military policy

Internal Russian pressures against war. E. Crankshaw. Cur 112:52-4 N '69
Russia has not changed her ways; excerpts from address, March 17, 1969. H. M. Jackson. Read Digest 94:91-5 Je '69
Russia's strategy against U.S; the inside story. il U S News 66:53-6 Je 16 '69
Soviet military since Khrushchev. T. W. Wolfe. bibliog f il Cur Hist 57:220-7+ O '69
See also
Russia—Defenses

Navy

As reds shadow U.S. fleet . . ; report from the Mediterranean. il U S News 66:43 My 12 '69
How good are U.S. defenses? interview. T. H. Moorer. il U S News 67:74-7 D 1 '69
Russian navy; Pueblo inquiry; address, January 25, 1969. T. H. Moorer. Vital Speeches 35:300-3 Mr 1 '69
Soviet navy; our ability to meet the challenge; address, August 19, 1969. T. H. Moorer. Vital Speeches 35:742-6 O 1 '69
Soviet sea power; latest threat to America; with interview with Vice Admiral D. C. Richardson. C. S. Foltz, jr. il U S News 67:56-61 Jl 21 '69
Soviet warships: why a visit to Castro's Cuba. U S News 67:7 Jl 21 '69

Politics and government

B and K: maintaining the status quo. il Newsweek 74:45-6 O 27 '69
Can Russia afford a U.S. deal? another challenge to the old men in the Kremlin. il U S News 66:51 Mr 31 '69
Ins and outs of de-Stalinization. J. Critchlow. Commonweal 90:191-2 My 2 '69
Kremlin scene: politics in a cul-de-sac. G. Ginsburgs. Cur Hist 57:228-31+ O '69
Playing politics in the USSR. Trans-Action 6:8 Mr '69
Policy making in the USSR; party-elite conflict. il Trans-Action 6:7 F '69
Russian leadership; the ABM; address, July 9, 1969. H. M. Jackson. Vital Speeches 35:610-13 Ag 1 '69
Speculative silence; reverberations from shots fired by would-be assassin at cosmonauts' parade. Time 93:32+ F 14 '69
See also
Communism—Russia
Communist party (Russia)
Russia—History—Revolution, 1917-1921

Population

Men die earlier than women. B. Urlanis. il UNESCO Courier 22:28-30 N '69
See also
Birth rate—Russia
Migration, Internal

Race problems

Not-so-silent majority; with report by J. Dornberg. il Newsweek 75:29-31 Ja 12 '70

Religious institutions and affairs

Freedom over-priced. Chr Today 13:30 Ap 25 '69
Religion behind the iron curtain; findings of committee representing the Appeal of conscience foundation. C. J. McNaspy. America 120:450-3 Ap 12 '69
Valya and Vadim struggle for religious faith. M. Bourdeaux. America 121:614-16 D 20 '69
See also
Christians in Russia
Muslims in Russia
Orthodox Eastern church, Russian

Social conditions

Brezhnev sets the clock back. H. Kamm. il N Y Times Mag p 14-15+ Ag 10 '69; Discussion. p 12+ Ag 24; 40+ S 7 '69
Post-Stalinist social science. A. Simirenko. il Trans-Action 6:37-42 Je '69
See also
Jews in Russia
Marriage law—Russia
Youth—Russia

Social history

Post-Stalinist social science. A. Simirenko. il Trans-Action 6:37-42 Je '69

Social life and customs

Discovering the weekend in Russia. il Time 93:73 My 9 '69

Treaties

United States
See United States—Treaties—Russia
RUSSIA and Finland. See Finland and Russia
RUSSIA and the United States
Fifth Dartmouth conference; Americans and Russians meet in Rye, N.Y. to discuss questions of mutual concern. N. Cousins. Sat R 52:16+ F 8 '69
If Nixon were to speak to the Russian people. D. Lawrence. U S News 66:88 Mr 3 '69
Strange world of Mr Nutter. P. Steinfels. Commonweal 90:158-9 Ap 25 '69
RUSSIA and the West. See World politics, 1945-
RUSSIA-United States airline service. See Airlines—International services
RUSSIAN academy of sciences. See Academy of sciences of the USSR
RUSSIAN authors. See Authors, Russian
RUSSIAN-CHINESE border dispute, 1969. See Sino-Russian border dispute, 1969
RUSSIAN-CHINESE border disputes. See Sino-Russian border disputes
RUSSIAN Communist party. See Communist party (Russia)
RUSSIAN espionage. See Espionage
RUSSIAN fishermen. See Fishermen
RUSSIAN horn music. See Music, Russian
RUSSIAN intellectuals. See Intellectuals
RUSSIAN Jews. See Jews in Russia
RUSSIAN literature
Four new works. il Time 93:28 Mr 21 '69
See also
Russian poetry

Translations into English

Native language; stories and illustrations from a Russian reader for first graders; tr. by E. G. Francis. Todays Ed 58:40-1 N '69
RUSSIAN literature in foreign countries
Publishing scene. D. Dempsey. Sat R 52:31 Je 14 '69
RUSSIAN military assistance. See Military assistance, Russian
RUSSIAN music. See Music, Russian
RUSSIAN opera singers. See Opera singers
RUSSIAN Orthodox church. See Orthodox Eastern church, Russian
RUSSIAN poetry
Hosting Russian poetry. S. Karlinsky. Nation 209:28-30 Jl 7 '69
Russian futurism, by V. Barkov. Review Nation 208:182-3 F 10 '69. S. Karlinsky

Translations into English

Pattering rain set runlets flowing; tr. by T. Botting. R. Kazakova Mlle 69:144 My '69
RUSSIAN propaganda. See Propaganda, Russian
RUSSIAN readers. See Readers (books)
RUSSIAN revolution. See Russia—History—Revolution, 1917-1921
RUSSIAN revolutionists. See Revolutionists, Russian
RUSSIAN space probes. See Space probes, Russian

RUSSIAN space vehicles. See Space, vehicles,
 Russian
RUSSIAN statesmen. See Statesmen
RUSSIAN trawlers. See Fishing boats
RUSSIAN wild boars. See Wild boars
RUSSIAN youth. See Youth—Russia
RUSSIANS
 As the plane lands in Moscow the people
  cheer. B. M. Frolic. il N Y Times Mag p62-
  3+ O 26 '69
RUSSIANS in the United States
 Suburbanization of Svetlana; interview. ed.
  by M. Silverstone. S. Stalina. il Look 33:
  55-9 S 9 '69
 Undiscovered New Jersey. L. Gashel and J.
  Gashel. il Travel 131:52-5+ Je '69
RUSSLAN and Ludmilla; opera. See Glinka, M.
 I.
RUSSO, Michael
 Fourteen million vocational studies by
  1975. Am Ed 5:10-11 Mr '69
RUSSO, Perry Raymond
 Dallas revisited. il por Time 93:18-19 F 21 '69
RUSSO-CHINESE border dispute, 1969. See
 Sino-Russian border dispute, 1969
RUST, Charles C. and Meyer, R. K.
 Hair color, molt, and testis size in male,
  short-tailed weasels treated with melatonin.
  bibliog Science 165:921-2 Ag 29 '69
RUST. See Corrosion and anticorrosives
RUSTIN, Bayard
 Myths of the black revolt. por Ebony 24:96-
  8+ Ag '69
 Negro leader's tough talk about Negro stu-
  dents; excerpts from address, April 27, 1969.
  por U S News 66:8 My 12 '69
 Soul music and poetry; address, April 27,
  1969. Vital Speeches 35:541-2 Je 15 '69

            about

 Rustin on black nationalism. America 120:
  152 F 8 '69
 Strategist without a movement. T. R. Brooks.
  il pors N Y Times Mag p24-5+ F 16 '69;
  Reply with rejoinder. D. McReynolds. p 114+
  Mr 30 '69
RUSTIN, Dan
 Telephone tactics. Seventeen 28:14+ Ag '69
RUSTLERS, Cattle. See Cattle thieves
RUSTS (botany)
 Infection structures from rust urediospores:
  effect of RNA and protein synthesis in-
  hibitors. L. D. Dunkle and others. bibliog
  il Science 163:481-2 Ja 31 '69
RUTH, Eugene D. Jr
 Benevolent dictator in the inner-city schools.
  Todays Ed 58:60-1 O '69
RUTH, Leo. See Farrell, E. jt. ed.
RUTH McDonell, Sister. See McDonell, R.
RUTHERFORD, Darlene
 Poets, prophets, and potters. bibliog Ceram
  Mo 17:31 N '69
RUTLAND, Vt.
 New life for old authors; original sound
  filmstrips at junior high school. D. P.
  Miller. il Sr Schol 94:Schol Teach 16-17
  Ap 18 '69
RUTSALA, Vern
 In the middle; poem. Poetry 114:242-3 Jl '69
RUTSCHMANN, Ruth. See Gibbon, J. jt. auth.
RUTTENBERG, Derald H.
 I want to make millionaires. S. Blickstein.
  por Duns R 93:29-31 Ap '69
RUTTER, William J. See Wessells, N. K. jt.
 auth.
RYALL, W. R. and Muan, Arnulf
 Silicon oxynitride stability. bibliog Science
  165:1363-4 S 26 '69
RYAN, Allan A.
 Annals of finance. J. Brooks. New Yorker
  45:74-82+ Ag 23 '69
RYAN, Anne
 Flip side. il Time 93:44-5+ Ja 24 '69
RYAN, Bernard, Jr
 Last look at the little red schoolhouse.
  Parents Mag 44:54-6 F '69
RYAN, Charlotte
 PTA in Washington. PTA Mag 64:26-7 O '69
RYAN, Cornelius
 My longest day; interview. por Look 33:69-
  70 Je 10 '69
RYAN, Jack
 Class in our time. J. Riley. il por Esquire 73:
  82-7+ Ja '70
RYAN, John Fergus
 Paul Anderson can lift eight of you. Esquire
  72:69-71+ Jl '69
RYAN, John William. See Ryan, J.

RYAN, Patricia
 Golf (cont) Sports Illus 30:52-3 F 10 '69
 Golf's underwater underworld. Sports Illus 30:
  74-8+ My 19 '69; Same abr. with title
  Second life of a golf ball. Read Digest 95:91-
  4 Ag '69
 Le grand Charles slept here. Sports Illus 31:
  46-8+ Jl 28 '69
 There she is, Miss America. Sports Illus 31:
  70-2+ O 6 '69
RYAN, William
 [Book review] Commonweal 89:533-4 Ja 24
  '69
RYAN, William Fitts
 Excerpt from testimony, June 19, 1969. Cong
  Digest 48:275+ N '69
RYAS. See Rugs and carpets
RYCHETNIK, Joe
 Camera troubles in winter? Pro tells you
  what to do. Mod Phot 33:142+ Ap '69
RYDER cup matches. See Golf—Tournaments
RYERSON, Margery
 Sketching faces from the TV screen. Am
  Artist 33:68-72 Je '69
RYKEN, Leland
 Christian approach to literature. Chr Today
  14:10-12 D 5 '69
RYKER, Lois
 Sorry, your story's too pat. Writers Digest
  49:45-7 Je '69
RYMAN, Herbert
 Herbert Ryman: California painter. B. Howell.
  il por Am Artist 33:66-71 Ap '69
RYOKAN (inn) See Hotels, taverns, etc.—
 Japan
RYRIE, Charles C.
 Perspective on Palestine. Chr Today 13:8-10
  My 23 '69
RYTHER, John H.
 Photosynthesis and fish production in the sea.
  bibliog Science 166:72-6 O 3 '69
RYUKYU ISLANDS
    See also
 Okinawa
RYUN, Jim
 Exhilarating nip of Liquori. S. Myslenski.
  il por Sports Illus 30:24-5 Mr 24 '69
 Last mile. il Newsweek 74:66 Jl 14 '69
 Line for the mile forms here. S. Myslenski.
  Sports Illus 30:52 F 17 '69
 Pressure cooker. S. Myslenski. il por Sports
  Illus 31:18-21 Jl 7 '69
RZECZKOWSKI, Matthew
 Appalachia: who's helping whom? Cath World
  210:155-8 Ja '70

                    S

S. Fisher verlag. See Publishers and publish-
 ing—Germany (Federal Republic)
SAAS. See Society of African and Afro-Ameri-
 can students
SAC. See United States—Air force—Strategic
 air command
SACB. See United States—Subversive activities
 control board
SAS. See Scandinavian airlines system
SBA. See United States—Small business ad-
 ministration
SBIC. See Small business investment companies
SCLC. See Southern Christian leadership con-
 ference
SCM corporation
 Will the real SCM please stand up? R. Levy.
  il Duns R 93:34-7+ Ap '69
SCR (silicon controlled rectifiers) See Electric
 current rectifiers
SCS (silicon controlled switch) See Electric
 switches
SCS (Soil conservation service) See United
 States—Soil conservation service
SCTA speed trials. See Motorcycle racing
SDC. See System development corporation
SDR. See Special drawing rights
SDS. See Students for a democratic society
 (organization)
SEATO. See Southeast Asia treaty organiza-
 tion
SEC. See United States—Securities and ex-
 change commission
SEC camera tubes. See Television camera tubes
SEDFRE. See Scholarship, education and de-
 fense fund for racial equality
SEEK (search for education, elevation and
 knowledge) See New York (city) City uni-
 versity of New York

SERS. See Southern education reporting service
SERVE project. See Community service society of New York
SIU. See Seafarers' international union of North America
SK&F. See Smith Kline and French laboratories
SLA. See Special libraries association
SLR cameras. See Single-lens reflex cameras
SLR lenses. See Lenses, Photographic
SNCC. See Student national coordinating committee
SODEPAX. See Joint committee on society, development and peace
SOM. See Skidmore, Owings and Merrill
SPD (Social democratic party) See Political parties—Germany (Federal Republic)
SR-71. See Airplanes, Military—United States
SRAM (short range attack missile) See Guided missiles—Launching from airplanes
SRI. See Stanford research institute
SSI computer corporation
  Last shall be first. Forbes 104:47 Jl 1 '69
SSRS. See Society for social responsibility in science
STH. See Pituitary hormones
STOL airplanes. See Airplanes, Short take-off and landing
STP (drug) See Amphetamines
STP (scientifically treated petroleum) See STP corporation
STP corporation
  Wheeler who deals in STP; A. Granatelli. il Bsns W p56-7 My 31 '69
STV. See Television broadcasting—Subscription programs
SV40. See Simian viruses
SAAB. See Automobile industry and trade—Sweden
SAAB (automobile) See Automobiles, Foreign
SAAD and Roth architects. See Roth and Saad, architects
SAAL, Hubert
  La Sills at the summit. Newsweek 73:69-70+ Ap 21 '69; Same abr. with title From soap opera to grand opera with Beverly Sills. Read Digest 95:146-50 O '69
SAAL, Rollene W.
  Pick of the paperbacks. See issues of Saturday review
SAAR, John
  GI's long last month in Vietnam. Life 67:51-4 Ag 8 '69
SABA, West Indies
  Saba's youngest ruler. il Ebony 24:116-18+ O '69
SABAH
  Quite cold war over Sabah. il Ramp Mag 7: 20+ N 30 '68
SABAH al-Salim al-Sabah
  Amir of Kuwait visits Washington; exchange of greetings and toasts, with joint communique, December 11, 1968. Dept State Bul 59:691-5 D 30 '68
SABAL, Leonard E.
  New one-piece body turns bug into a beauty. Pop Mech 132:156-61 Jl '69
  Stackable shelf modules go together like 1-2-3. Pop Mech 132:152-3 S '69
SABBA, Isaac Benyaon
  Taming the jungle for profit. il por Bsns W p 162-3 S 13 '69
SABELLARIA. See Annelids
SABER saw blades. See Saws
SABIN, Francene
  Exploring the world around us. Am Ed 5: 12-17 Je '69
  Parsippany dips a Maobi in Asian studies. Am Ed 5:11-13 My '69
SABIN, Robert
  Book reviews. Am Rec G 35:504-7 F '69
SABINE, David B.
  Arsenic. Chem 42:20 Ap '69
  Benedetti-Pichler: the father of American microchemistry. por Chem 42:12-15 Je '69
SABLE, Arnold P.
  Sexuality of the library profession: the male and female librarian. por Wilson Lib Bul 43:748-51 Ap '69
SABLE ISLAND
  Sand, seals and shipwrecks. J. Miller. il Holiday 45:62-3+ Mr '69
SABRY, Aly
  Tension: Nasser and the Russians. A. de Borchgrave. Newsweek 74:89 O 6 '69

SACCHARIDES
  Mitochondrial autonomy: incorporation of monosaccharides into glycoprotein by isolated mitochondria. H. B. Bosmann and S. S. Martin. bibliog il Science 164:190-2 Ap 11 '69
  See also
  Oligosaccharides
SACCO-Vanzetti case
  Case that will not die, by H. B. Ehrmann. Review
    Nat R 21:446-7 My 6 '69. D. Felix
    Nation 208:605-9 My 12 '69. F. J. Cook
    New Repub 160:25-7 Mr 22 '69. L. Friedman
  Sacco and Vanzetti: still nagging the American conscience. J. Deedy. il Commonweal 90:466-8 Jl 25 '69
SACHAR, Abram Leon
  Future is not what it used to be; excerpt from address, May 1969. PTA Mag 64:2-5+ S '69
SACHET. See Toilet preparations
SACHS, Mendel
  Space, time and elementary interactions in relativity; with biographical sketch. por Phys Today 22:51-60 F; 13 S; 13+ N '69
SACK, John
  Making contact in Baltimore. Esquire 71:92-4+ Je '69
SACKETT, Ross DeForest
  Publisher comments on the industry; excerpts from address. por Pub W 196:24 D 8 '69
SACKETT, Walter W. Jr
  Let death be peaceful, natural: ed. by J. Darling. por Har Yrs 9:32-3 N '69
SACKLER, Howard
  Great white hope. Criticism
    Commentary 47:22+ F '69
SACRAMENTO, Calif.
          Historic houses, etc.
  Past is present in old Sacramento. il Parks & Rec 3:25-6 N '68
          Housing
  Careful planning clusters 800 units on 38-acre site without crowding. il Arch Rec 146: 192-3 S '69
          Parks and playgrounds
  Walk in Sacramento's Capitol park. il Sunset 142:54+ Mr '69
SACRAMENTO COUNTY, Calif.
  Sewer root control, chemically. N. R. Townley. il Am City 84:92-4 D '69
SACRAMENTO peak observatory, Sunspot, N.Mex. See Astronomical observatories
SACRAMENTO RIVER
  Don't bypass the Delta. H. E. Jackson. il Travel 131:36-41 Mr '69
SACRAMENTO-San Joaquin Delta
  Not unlike love: the Delta; inland waterway at San Francisco's back door. H. McBurney. il Motor B 124:57-61+ Ag '69
SACRAMENTS
          See also
  Baptism
  Extreme unction
SACRED college of cardinals. See Cardinals
SACRED congregation for the doctrine of the faith. See Congregation for the doctrine of the faith
SACRED music. See Church music
SACRIFICE, Human
  Medieval riddle of bodies in the bog. D. Cohen. il Sci Digest 65:9-14 F '69
SACRISTANS
  Holy terror. J. Ferris. Opera N 33:6-7 F 15 '69
SACSAHUAMAN (fort)
  Here's rewarding Peru detour. il Sunset 143: 72 N '69
SADACCA, Albert V.
  Turning on Christmas. por Newsweek 74:8 D 29 '69
SADAVA, D. and Chrispeels, M. J.
  Cell wall protein in plants: autoradiographic evidence. bibliog Science 165:299-300 Jl 18 '69
SADDLER, Jack
  Simplicity+ dwell meter. Pop Electr 31:33-5 Ag '69
  Solid-state your car gages. Radio-Electr 40: 38-40 Ag '69
SADE, Donatien Alphonse François, comte de
  Philosophy in the bedroom; adaptation. See Bush, J. De Sade illustrated
          about
  Our bedfellow, the Marquis de Sade. A. Burgess. il Horizon 11:104-9 Wint '69

SADISM
Our bedfellow, the Marquis de Sade. A. Burgess. il Horizon 11:104-9 Wint '69
SADLER, Christine
WACS and WAVES are different now. McCalls 96:101 Ap '69
SADLER, Marion
Airport planning and design; address, October 22, 1969. Vital Speeches 36:124-8 D 1 '69
Solving airline problems; excerpts from address, December 1969. Aviation W 91:11 D 15 '69
SADLER'S Wells opera
Report: London; new English-language production of La Forza del destino. F. G. Barker. Opera N 33:34 F 8 '69
Report: London; production of Berlioz-Damnation of Faust. F. G. Barker. Opera N 34: 26 O 11 '69
SAFARI. See Hunting—Africa; Hunting—Africa, East
SAFARI rooms. See Trophy rooms
SAFE deposit boxes
Do you have a safe-deposit box? Do you use it right? il Changing T 23:35-9 My '69
Safe-deposit boxes: facts to know. il Good H 168:195 Mr '69
Set up a system for family files & records. il Changing T 23:14-16 N '69
SAFEGUARD missile defense system. See Guided missiles—Defenses
SAFERSTEIN, Jack
This is the housing that Jack built. il por Bsns W p89 S 13 '69
SAFES
How to install a wall safe. W. C. Leckey. il Pop Mech 132:184-6 O '69
SAFETY, Industrial. See Industrial safety
SAFETY belts
Children's seat harnesses: fifteen to avoid. Consumer Rep 34:169-70 Ap '69
Do it yourself; seat belts. A. Trammell. Flying 84:28 My '69
Replacement seat belts for automobiles. Consumer Rep 34:60 F '69
Serious flaw in Chrysler seat belts. Consumer Rep 34:237 My '69
Woman driver; buckle up for safety. il McCalls 96:66 My '69
SAFETY clothing. See Clothing, Protective
SAFETY devices and measures
For a safer holiday season. il Consumer Bul 52:4 D '69
If the house catches fire. il Changing T 23: 21-3 F '69
Safety tips for do-it-yourselfers. il Good H 168:198 Mr '69
See also
  also subhead Safety devices and measures under various subjects, e.g. Automobiles—Safety devices and measures
SAFETY education
Safety education: an investment in our future. J. D. Lawlor. Parents Mag 44:28+ Ag '69
See also
Accidents—Prevention
Camping—Safety devices and measures
SAFETY glass. See Glass, Safety
SAFETY harness (boat) See Life saving equipment
SAFETY helmets. See Helmets
SAFETY laws and legislation
See also
Industrial safety—Laws and regulations
SAFETY movement
See also
National safety council
SAFFIOTTI, Umberto
What tests can and can't prove; interview. por U S News 67:46-7 D 15 '69
SAFRAN, Nadav
Alternatives in the Middle East. Commentary 47:45-55 My; 48:4+ O '69
SAGAN, Leonard A.
Infant mortality controversy: Sternglass and his critics. Bul Atom Sci 25:26-8 O '69; Same. Cur 113:62-4 D '69
SAGE grouse shooting. See Grouse shooting
SAGER, Don
Protecting the library after hours. bibliog Library J 94:3609-14 O 15 '69
SAGINAW, Mich.
Parking ban aids most cleaning tasks. M. W. Jones. il Am City 84:66 My '69
Urban management needs computers. E. H. Potthoff, jr. il Am City 84:69-71 Mr '69
SAGLEK BAY base. See Air bases
SAHARA DESERT
See also
Timbuktu, Mali

SAHL, Mort
Motor trend interview. pors Motor T. 21:93-8 D '69
SAI Baba
God-possessed. il por Newsweek 74:110+ N 17 '69
SAID, Fouad
Multi-gadget movie van rolls into Hollywood. il por Bsns W p 152-4 Mr 15 '69
SAIDYE Bronfman cultural centre, Montreal
Neat showcase for the arts. P. Blake. il Arch Forum 130:86-91 My '69
SAIGON
Worst city in the world? activities of the Saigon civil assistance group. il Newsweek 74:38-9 D 29 '69
SAIKIN, Joel
Between father and son. il Time 94:22 O 3 '69
SAILBOAT racing
On the circuit. il Yachting 126:46-9+ O '69
Poor Russian boy on a hot cat. F. Rohr. il Motor B 123:434-5 Ja '69
Racing initiation; learning by doing. D. Buchanan. il Yachting 125:115+ Ja '69
Russia's gold medalist Valentin Mankin. talks of his training and racing experiences; interview. ed. by V. Lapin. V. Mankin. il Yachting 126:63+ Jl '69
Summer's campaign abroad; Sweden, Denmark and Italy. D. Schoonmaker. il Yachting 126:64+ D '69
They sail to win. See issues of Yachting
Thoughts on racing an S boat. H. C. Herreshoff. il Yachting 125:189+ F '69 (to be cont)
U.S. sailor in New Zealand. C. Van Duyne. il Yachting 125:62-3+ Je '69
With the racing classes. E. Horan. See issues of Yachting
Yachting interview: J. Hunt. il Yachting 126: 72-3+ Ag '69
See also
Regattas
Yacht racing
Photographs
Action aplenty: a portfolio of racing scenes. Yachting 126:50-5 O '69
SAILBOATS
Auxiliary catboat. B. Robinson. il Yachting 125:81-2 Ja '69
Day sailer. M. Wiley. il Yachting 125:300 Ja '69
Douzes francaises; French America's cup preparations. S. Allan. il Yachting 125:88-9+ Ja '69
French side of it; America's cup training. J. M. Barrault. il Yachting 125:66-8+ F '69
From the cockpit. B. Bavier. See issues of Yachting
Gallery of small sailboats. il Motor B 124:60 Jl '69
How to quell the midnight halyard orchestra J. G. Peterson. il Motor B 124:107 Ag '69
Instant sailing; with introd. by J. R. Whiting. P. Smyth. il Motor B 124:45-59 Jl '69
Learn to sail. J. S. Doherty. il Mech Illus 65:27-9+ Ap '69
One-design. E. Horan. il Yachting 125:83 Ja '69
Sailboats. il Motor B 123:172-9+ Ja '69
Sailing: the thrill of a lifetime. W. T. McKeown. il Pop Gard 20:6-11+ Spr '69
Small sailboat buying guide; comp. by G. Miller. il Motor B 124:62-4+ Jl '69
Sunfish: America's most popular boat. J. Beatty, jr. il Holiday 45:62-3+ Je '69
Surf cats launch new rage in sailboat racing. R. Cobb. il Pop Sci 195:48-9 Ag '69
Those soaring sailboats. B. McKeown. il Mech Illus 65:100+ N '69
Trailed auxiliaries. il Yachting 125:86-7+ Ja '69
Your new daysailer. il Motor B 123:110-11 Ja '69
Your new sailboard or sailing dink. il Motor B 123:108-9 Ja '69
See also
Catamarans
Trimarans
Design
Designing your own boat. R. R. Casasco. il Yachting 126:42+ D '69
Designs. J. Atkin. il Yachting 125:78-82 Mr '69
Man and his boat; Blackjack. E. Horan. il Yachting 126:60-2+ Jl '69
See also
Sloops—Design
Equipment
Gear and gadgets for the one design. N. Freeman. il Yachting 125:64-5+ My '69
Instruments: the eyes and ears of modern yachting. E. A. Zadig. il Motor B 123: 62-4 Mr '69

SAILBOATS—Equipment—*Continued*
Make-ready gap; how to commission a new auxiliary properly. H. S. Parker, jr. il Yachting 125:76-8+ Je; 126:70-1+ Jl '69
Peter Scott and the trapeze; excerpt from The eye of the wind. P. Scott. il Yachting 126:64-5 Ag '69
Wire power! wire suspended from the mast used as a trapeze. E. Horan. il Yachting 126:63-4+ Ag '69
Yachting's boat show. il Yachting 125:133+ Ja '69

Exhibitions
Yachting's boat show. il Yachting 125:133+ Ja '69

Materials
Project Phantom: a class considers a change; deck aluminum spar. K. C. Larkin. il Yachting 126:66-7+ S '69

Safety devices and measures
Does your boat float? E. Horan. il Yachting 125:58+ Ja '69
Ian Proctor on buoyancy apparatus; excerpt from Boats for sailing. I. Proctor. il Yachting 125:59+ Ja '69

Speed
Boosting your boat speed. D. Deaver. il Yachting 125:53+ F '69

Steering gear
Laminated sailboat tiller. A. Jetter. il Mech Illus 65:117 O '69
Self-steerer take-over. A. Badger and R. C. Weller. il Yachting 126:64-5+ Jl '69

SAILFISH fishing
Billfish on the fly; interview, ed. by A. J. McClane. G. Valdene. il Field & S 74:126-8+ N '69
Heads up for sailfish. J. Brooks. il Outdoor Life 144:110-12 N '69
Raps and strikes. G. Heinold. il Outdoor Life 144:86+ D '69
Sex and the sailfish. S. Apte. il Field & S 73:72-3+ Ap '69

SAILING
Boosting your boat speed. D. Deaver. il Yachting 125:53+ F '69
Instant sailing; with introd. by J. R. Whiting. P. Smyth. il Motor B 124:45-59 Jl '69
Landfall in Maine; a sail from Nova Scotia to Burnt Island, Me. H. Harper. il Yachting 125:56-7+ Mr '69
Sailing Iceland's rugged coasts. W. Britton. il Nat Geog 136:228-65 Ag '69
Sailing: the thrill of a lifetime. W. T. McKeown. il Pop Gard 20:6-11+ Spr '69
Stoned in the cradle of the deep. T. O. Orlowski. il Esquire 72:248-9+ D '69
They sail to win. See issues of Yachting
See also
Navigation
Yachts and yachting

Study and teaching
French side of it; America's cup training. J. M. Barrault. il Yachting 125:66-8+ F '69
Guide to sailing schools; comp. by G. Miller. Motor B 124:68+ Jl '69
Impossible dream: England's Island cruising club. F. C. Clark, jr. il Motor B 124:56-7+ D '69
Key Largo's two-day wonders; Florida Keys facility of Annapolis sailing school. J. Gribbins. il Motor B 123:66-9+ My '69
Learn to sail. J. S. Doherty. il Mech Illus 65:27-9+ Ap '69
Racing initiation; learning by doing. D. Buchanan. il Yachting 125:115+ Ja '69
Sailing classes on the Severn River. il Parks & Rec 4:52 My '69
Sailing schools. il Motor B 123:109 Ja '69
Tonic for an old sailor. W. N. Moose. il Motor B 123:53 F '69

SAILING auxiliaries. See Sailboats
SAILING schools. See Sailing—Study and teaching
SAILING vessels
[Historic voyagers] with paintings by R. Sticker
Islander. Yachting 126:54 Jl '69
Yankee cruises Turkey's history-haunted coast. I. Johnson and E. Johnson. il Nat Geog 136:798-845 D '69
See also
Schooners

SAILORS. See Seamen
SAILPLANES. See Gliders (aeronautics)
SAIN, Johnny
Have the hitters really gone? debate. Look 33:84+ My 13 '69

about
Johnny Sain teaches the power of positive pitching. B. Surface. il pors N Y Times Mag p48-9+ Ap 20 '69
ST CHARLES COUNTY, Mo. library, St Charles
Freedom to read: a battlefield report, the censor knocks; address, June 1969. N. S. Ladof. ALA Bul 63:903-5 Jl '69
ST CLAIR, David
Pisco sour: symbol of Peru's relations with the United States. Holiday 46:36-7+ N '69
ST CLAIR COUNTY, Mich.
From eyesore to park complex via sanitary landfill. il Am City 84:75 S '69
ST CLOUD, Minn.
No more muddy boots in the kitchen. W. Davids. il Am City 84:111-12 Ag '69
ST DENIS, Ruth
Miss Ruth, by W. Terry. Review
Dance Mag por 43:22-3 D '69. J. Anderson
SAINT EXUPÉRY, Antoine de
Little prince, a story for our time. P. Mooney. America 121:610-11+ D 20 '69
SAINT-GAUDENS, Augustus
Private skill. Time 94:61 N 21 '69
SAINT-Gobain-Boussois-Souchon-Neuvesel merger. See Business consolidations and mergers—France
SAINT-JACQUES, Raymond
Raymond the magnificent. C. L. Sanders. il pors Ebony 25:175-8+ N '69
ST JOE RIVER
Proposed St Joe wilderness. M. R. Brigham. il Liv Wildn 33:15-18 Sum '69
ST JOE wilderness area (proposed) See Wilderness areas—Idaho
ST JOHN, Robert
Angkor Wat; place of great splendor; excerpts from Once around lightly. Travel & Camera 32:72-7 Jl '69
ST JOHN RIVER
Saint John; New Brunswick's splendid river. F. Graham, jr. il Motor B 123:46-9+ F '69
ST JOHN'S university, Collegeville, Minn.
St John's: four years after. J. A. Scimecca. Commonweal 91:326-7 D 12 '69
ST LAURENT, Yves Mathieu
Saint Laurent in Marrakech. il pors Vogue 154:148-51 Jl '69
Yves St Laurent: his very special world. il por McCalls 97:64-7 Ja '70
ST LAWRENCE, Leslie H.
African violets under fluorescent lights. Horticulture 47:37+ O '69
ST LAWRENCE RIVER skiffs. See Boats and boating
ST LAWRENCE SEAWAY
Bustling St Lawrence Seaway; ten years old and deeper in debt. il U S News 67:7 Jl 7 '69
Tenth anniversary of the St Lawrence Seaway; introductory remarks, exchange of remarks, June 27, 1969. N. A. Rockefeller; R. M. Nixon; P. E. Trudeau. Dept State Bul 61:67-71 Jl 28 '69
SAINT-LÔ, France

Siege, 1944
Saint-Lô: the resurrection of a dead city. R. Cherniss. il Sat R 52:11-15+ Jl 5 '69
ST LOUIS

Air pollution
Fight swirls over pollution; stiff new standards put manufacturers in a quandary. Bsns W p86 Je 28 '69
From pollution to profit. il Time 94:36 Ag 8 '69

Architecture
In St. Louis, a crisply elegant tower gracefully exploits its prominent downtown site. il Arch Rec 146:122-3 Ag '69
Powerful silhouette for a high-speed environment; Pet plaza. il Arch Rec 146:163-70 S '69

Bridges
Mr Eads spans the Mississippi. J. Gies. il Am Heritage 20:16-21+ Ag '69

City planning
St Louis spruces up down on the levee; renewal of Mississippi riverfront. il Bsns W p46-7 My 31 '69

Description
Exciting cities, a Redbook vacation guide to sight-seeing with children; excerpts from America's exciting cities. A. Schwartz. il Redbook 132:43 Ap '69

Economic conditions
Youth shakes the business world. W. S. Rukeyser. Read Digest 94:185-6+ My '69

ST LOUIS—*Continued*

Education

St. Louis: city with the blues. P. J. Doyle. il Sat R 52:90-3+ F 15 '69; Discussion. 52: 56 Mr 15 '69

Time enough to read; Horton Watkins high school, Ladue. G. Stanford. il Sr Schol 94:Schol Teach 13+ Ap 18 '69

Washington report. J. Lloyd. Sr Schol 94: Schol Teach 3 Ap 25 '69

Galleries and museums

See also
St Louis city art museum

Gardens

See also
Missouri botanical garden

History

Mr Eads spans the Mississippi. J. Gies. il Am Heritage 20:16-21+ Ag '69

Housing

People vs. public housing; rent strike. Newsweek 74:49-50 Ag 25 '69

Missouri botanical garden
See Missouri botanical garden

Moral conditions

Death for a family; the Rohs family. il Time 94:27 N 21 '69
See also
St Louis—Crime

Negroes

Youth shakes the business world. W. S. Rukeyser. Read Digest 94:185-6+ My '69

ST LOUIS Blues (hockey team) See Hockey teams

ST LOUIS city art museum
Decorative arts in the City art museum of St Louis. C. E. Buckley. il Antiques 96: 76-81 Jl '69

ST LOUIS COUNTY, Mo.

Parks and recreation, Department of

Living memorials, open space gifts. W. C. Kennedy. il Parks & Rec 3:39-40 O '68

ST LOUIS public library
Innercity library to be run by innercity residents. J. A. McCrossan. ALA Bul 63:909 Jl '69

ST LOUIS review. See Catholic press

ST LOUIS university, St Louis, Mo.
Of many things: Cardinal Carberry and the School of divinity. D. R. Campion. America 120:inside cover My 31 '69

School of divinity

After the storm in St. Louis. A. L. Pierovich. Commonweal 90:500-1 Ag 22 '69

ST LUCIA (island)
St Lucia. G. Trotta. Harp Baz 103:154+ N '69

ST MICHAELS, Md.
Look at the past. B. Schill and B. Schill. il Yachting 125:72-3 Mr '69

ST NICHOLAS (periodical)
Americans not everybody knows; Mary Mapes Dodge. C. W. Ferguson. PTA Mag 63:10-12 Mr '69

ST PATRICK'S day

Drama

Bridge to Killybog fair; drama. F. B. Watts. Plays 28:45-51+ Mr '69

ST PATRICK'S day parade. See New York (city)—Parades

ST PATRICK'S eve; drama. See Campbell, J. E.

ST PAUL
Minnesota model; Twin Cities metropolitan council. Time 94:64-5 S 19 '69
St Paul and the American condition. M. Dec-ter. Harper 238:56-61 Je '69

Politics and government

Minnesota experiment: how to make a big city fit to live in. J. Fischer. Harper 238: 12+ Ap '69

Water supply

Recalcining lime sludge produces multiple benefits. C. W. Hamblin. il Am City 84:67-9+ N '69

ST PAUL the apostle Roman Catholic church. See New York (city)—Churches

ST PHILIP'S Episcopal church. See New York (city)—Churches

ST PIERRE, Anne. See Cain, E. jt. auth.

SAINT-TROPEZ, France
Gone flying to St Tropez. J. Gilbert. il Flying 84:66-72+ Je '69
Good-by, St-Tropez. il Newsweek 74:87 S 15 '69

ST VINCENT'S hospital, New York. See New York (city)—Hospitals

SAINTE-MARIE, Buffy
Buffy Sainte-Marie, singer of love and protest. il por Vogue 153:195 My '69

SAINTS
Drooping halos. il Newsweek 73:74 My 19 '69
Fracas about saints. C. J. McNaspy. America 120:608 My 24 '69
Heavenly jobless: saints dropped from a new liturgical calendar. Time 93:70+ Je 20 '69
Out go the beloved saints. J. Bonfante. il Life 66:47 My 23 '69
St Christopher, we're on your side; the saints go marching out. F. Clinton. Nat R 21:595+ Je 17 '69
Saint-watching, by P. McGinley. Review America 121:334+ O 18 '69. R. J. Willmes
Sat R 52:43-4 N 1 '69. M. Ward
Saints alive. Chr Today 14:31 O 24 '69
Saints go marching out. Time 93:96 My 16 '69
See also
Canonization
Patrick, Saint
Relics and reliquaries

Anecdotes, facetiae, satire, etc.

Veneration gap. Chr Cent 86:761 My 28 '69

SAINTS (football club) See Football clubs

SAITOW, Arnold R.
CSPC: reporting project progress to the top. Harvard Bsns R 47:88-97 Ja '69

SAKAKURA, Teruyo. See Nishizuka, Y. jt. auth.

SAKHAROV, Andrei Dmitrievich
A. D. Sakharov: Soviet physicist believed to have been punished. B. Nelson. Science 164:1043-4 My 30 '69

SAKOL, Jeannie
(comp) Money sampler. Harp Baz 102:146-7 Ag '69

SALAD dressings
Always ready for salads, four versatile dressings. N. L. Stute. il Farm J 93:38-9 Ag '69
Please pass the calcium disodium ethylene-diaminetetracetic acid! il Consumer Bul 52: 4+ Jl '69

SALAD greens. See Greens, Edible

SALADIN, sultan of Egypt and Syria
Saladin, the complete Mohammedan. P. W. Schmidtchen. il Hobbies 74:134-6 O '69

SALADS
Chef's salad from the sea. il McCalls 96:120-1+ Mr '69
Delicate salads, a declaration of spring. G. Maddox. il Todays Health 47:60-5 My '69
Fast fruit salads; Fancy fruit salads. il Bet Hom & Gard 47:73-4 Ag '69
Hail the famous Caesar salad! il Am Home 72:90 Ja '69
Herbs in salad. L. S. Alsberg. il Horticulture 46:33+ Ag '68
Jeweled egg in emerald nest. il Farm J 93: 97 Ap '69
Main dish salads. J. McCloskey. il Bet Hom & Gard 47:100 My '69
Mixed media dressings switch on summer salads; with recipes. E. Alston. il Look 33: 64-5 Jl 29 '69
Potato and herring in summer salads. Sunset 143:96 Ag '69
Salad bowl. D. Brooks. il Home Gard 56: 71 Ap '69
Salads gathered from the garden; with recipes. il McCalls 96:86+ Ag '69
Spring cabbage salad, here are three. il Sunset 142:199 Mr '69
Sweet toss-up: chefs salad; with recipes. il Seventeen 28:174-5 My '69
These salads are fruit boats. il Sunset 143: 60-1 Ag '69
Two fruit-and-chicken salads. il Sunset 142: 182 Mr '69
Your sudden salad course. il Bet Hom & Gard 47:94-5+ S '69

SALAFF, Stephen
Hong Kong; the complaisant haven. Nation 209:409-11 O 20 '69

SALAMANDERS
Extraoptic phase shifting of circadian loco-motor rhythm in salamanders. K. Adler. bibliog il Science 164:1290-2 Je 13 '69
Salamanders; colorful amphibians from the southern Appalachians. H. Borland. il Audubon 71:inside cover Mr '69
Spotted salamander. S. D. Busack. il Cons 23:8-9 F '69

SALARIES
  For salaries, a record-setting rise. il U S
    News 67:30 D 22 '69
  Rising salaries: a sellers' market for skills.
    il Time 93:84-5 F 28 '69
      See also
  Government employees—Salaries, allowances,
    etc.
  Non-wage payments
      also subhead Salaries, allowances,
    etc. under various subjects, e.g. Teachers—
    Salaries, allowances, etc.
SALATINO, A. P.
  New breed in education. Ed Digest 34:18-20
    Ja '69
SALATINO, Carlos Alberto
  Carlos Alberto Salatino. R. Squirru. il por
    Américas 21:44-5 Je '69
SALAZAR, António de Oliveira
  Salazar goes home. por Time 93:31 F 14 '69
  Smooth shift of gears. P. Witonski. Nat R
    21:851 Ag 26 '69
SALCEDO, José Joaquín
  Don Quixote of the radio; reprint. D. Behr-
    man. il por UNESCO Courier 22:73-4+
    Ag '69
SALE, J. Kirk
  Amsterdam news. N Y Times Mag p30-1+
    F 9 '69
SALEH, Dennis
  Abuse, abuse; poem. Poetry 113:404 Mr '69
SALERNO
  Salerno science school of the ninth century;
    reprint. R. Luzzato. il UNESCO Courier 22:
    10 Ag '69
SALES conventions
  At play with the military-industrial complex;
    Air force association and Army association
    meetings. P. Dickson and R. Skole. Esquire
    73:66B+ Ja '70
SALES departments
    See also
  Sales management
SALES management
  Get the most out of your sales force. D. A.
    Newton. il Harvard Bsns R 47:130-43 S '69
SALES managers
  Why sales executives fails. J. J. Tarrant. il
    Nations Bsns 57:100-2 S '69
SALES manpower foundation
  Why sales executives fail. J. J. Tarrant. il
    Nations Bsns 57:100-2 S '69
SALES promotion
  Beer ain't soap. Forbes 103:198 My 15 '69
  Changing the rules; FTC ruling on giveaway
    promotions at gasoline stations. il News-
    week 74:63 Ag 25 '69
  Charnita bonanza. D. Sanford. New Repub
    161:12-14 S 6 '69
  Games oil people play. il Bsns W p 132+ Ap
    19 '69
  Games played on people. Consumer Rep 34:
    109 Mr '69
  Groceries, gas and games; Economic report
    on the use of games of chance in food
    and gasoline retailing. J. Cross. Nation
    208:370-2 Mr 24 '69
  Loaded odds; FTC investigation of promo-
    tional lures by food-chains and oil com-
    panies. il Time 93:86-7 Ap 18 '69
  Who wins marketing promotion games? T.
    O'Hanlon. il Fortune 79:104-8+ F '69
      See also
  Trading stamps
SALES tax
  How your state's sales tax compares; with
    table. Changing T 23:12-13 My '69
  More revenue; value added tax. H. C. Wallich.
    Newsweek 74:94 D 15 '69
  Replacement for the income tax? value added
    tax, interview. D. T. Smith. il Nations
    Bsns 57:38-41 Ap '69
SALESMEN and salesmanship
  Behavioral approach to industrial selling J.
    W. Thompson and W. W. Evans. il Har-
    vard Bsns R 47:137-51 Mr '69
  Bookstore and the salesman; role of the
    publisher's representative. G. R. Smith.
    Pub W 196:27-8 D 15 '69
  Get the most out of your sales force. D. A.
    Newton. il Harvard Bsns R 47:130-43 S '69
  If nobody loves you, your company will;
    Pennsylvania life insurance. il Time 94:107
    D 5 '69
  Those peerless princes of pitch. il Fortune 81:
    116-19 Ja '70
      See also
  Advertising
  Automobile dealers
  Sales conventions
  Sales promotion

Study and teaching
  Selling a pitch to the pitchmen; H. Krause's
    sales congresses. il Bsns W p82-3 Je 21 '69

SALGADO, Germánico
  Seeds of transformation. Américas 21:12-18
    Ap '69
SALINAS, Calif.
  Assessment-district paving program. A. C.
    Joens. il Am City 84:104-5 O '69
SALINE water
  Sedimentary phosphate method for estimating
    paleosalinities: limited applicability. G.
    Müller. il Science 163:812-13 F 21 '69
      See also
  Irrigation water—Salt content
SALINE water conversion plants
  Desalination: water for mankind's future, by
    R. Popkin. Review
    Bul Atom Sci 25:41 Je '69. L. T. Alexander
  No other choice but desalting; U.S. Virgin
    Islands. W. S. Foster. il Am City 84:91-3
    My '69
SALINGER, Pierre
  L'Auberge de l'ill. por Travel & Camera 32:
    60-1+ My '69
SALINITY of soils. See Soils, Salts in
SALISBURY, Harrison E.
  Marco Polo would recognize Mao's Sinkiang.
    N Y Times Mag p 14+ N 23 '69
  900 days; condensation. Read Digest 94:
    210-7+ Mr; 243-56+ Ap '69
  Urgent question that dominates the Asian
    heartland today is: will there be war be-
    tween Russia and China? N Y Times Mag
    p 10-11+ Jl 27 '69
SALISBURY, John W. See Adler, J. E. M. jt.
    auth.
SALISHAN, Ore. See Seaside resorts
SALLEE, Ethyle
  Dump babies. por Hobbies 74:46 N '69
SALLOCH, Roger
  Cambridge: March 4, the movement, and
    M.I.T. Bul Atom Sci 25:32-5 My '69
SALM, Walter G.
  Dolby system, how it works. Radio-Electr
    40:52-3+ O '69
  New in stereo cassettes '70. Radio-Electr 40:
    37-9 D '69
  Wire your house for intercoms, without wir-
    ing at all. Pop Mech 132:130-3+ Jl '69
SALMO. See Trout
SALMON, Michael. See Sayler, A. jt. auth.
SALMON, Robert
  We get close to staff concerns. Camp Mag
    41:24 Ap '69
SALMON
  Atlantic salmon. A. Netboy. il Sea Front 15:
    66-77 Mr '69
  Coho marking. Cons 23:37 Je '69
  DDT: criticism, curbs are on the upswing.
    M. Mueller. Science 164:936-7 My 23 '69
  Don't go near the water? Lake Michigan
    coho salmon contaminated by DDT. il
    Newsweek 73:75 My 5 '69
  Fine kettle of kelt soup in Loch Shin; Atlan-
    tic salmon feed. C. Gammon. Sports Illus
    31:57-8 N 3 '69
  Lo the poor salmon! (or, Is this dam neces-
    sary?) Middle-Snake River Dam. W. E.
    Towell. Am For 75:38 F '69
  Memory-blocking agents: effects on olfactory
    discrimination in homing salmon. K. Oshi-
    ma and others. bibliog il Science 165:86-8
    Jl 4 '69; Discussion. 166:1310 D 5 '69
  Problems in ppm; DDT residues in Lake
    Michigan coho salmon. H. Henkin. il En-
    viron 11:24-33+ My '69
  Salmon's two week fatal fling. Sci Digest
    66:44 O '69
  Spectrum; DDT found in coho salmon from
    Lake Michigan. H. Henkin. Environ 11:
    81-3 Ap '69
  Thermal lability of beta galactosidase from
    pink salmon liver. S. Gatt. bibliog il Science
    164:1422-3 Je 20 '69
  Vanishing salmon? A. Grahame. Outdoor Life
    144:130 Ag '69

Migration
  See Fishes—Migration
SALMON fishing
  Bucktailing for cohos. D. Knowles. il Out-
    door Life 144:54-7+ S '69
  Coho catches on. V. Evanoff. il Motor B 124
    63+ O '69
  Cohos on a shoestring. B. Scifres. Outdoor
    Life 144:34-5 Jl '69
  Fresh frozen ironheads. D. Holm. il Outdoor
    Life 144:42-3+ D '69
  Honor coho; Michigan conservation depart-
    ment. A. Stark. il Field & S 74:58-9+ My
    '69
  Keystone coho. L. J. Bashline. il Field &
    S 73:54-5+ Ap '69
  Paradise for plunkers; Columbia River. S.
    Fagerstrom. il Field & S 74:62-3+ Je '69

SALMON fishing—*Continued*
Scotland for salmon. A. Oglesby. il Field &
S 74:64-6+ O '69
September of the humpback. B. Behme. il
Field & S 74:140-2 S '69

SALMONELLOSIS
Salmonella: food poison plus. A. S. Freese.
Todays Health 47:34-5+ Ap '69

SALOMA, John S. 3d
Liberal Republicans: a shared concern; inter-
view, ed. by L. Miller. il por Time 94:13
Jl 18 '69

SALOMON, Julian H.
Make a year-end check up of your camp facilities. Camp Mag 41:11-12 N '69

SALOMON brothers and Hutzler (firm)
Toughest kid in block trading. il Bsns W
p 114-16 O 4 '69

SALOMONE, Jerome J. See Downing, L. A.
jt. auth.

SALOONS. See Bars and barrooms

SALT
Storage
New use for an old incinerator; salt-storage
facility, Poughkeepsie, N.Y. J. W. Nelson,
jr. il Am City 84:22 D '69

SALT (strategic arms limitation talks) See
Strategic arms limitation talks

SALT LAKE CITY
See also
Stock exchange—Salt Lake City

SALT marshes
Dying marsh. il Audubon 71:21-32 N '69
Ribbon of green; the epic of a salt marsh,
its birth, life, death, excerpts from Life
and death of a salt marsh. J. Teal and M.
Teal. il Audubon 71:4-8+ N '69
Threatened marshes of Glynn: Georgia's
swamps. il Life 67:88-93 N 14 '69

SALT spreaders
No excess salt on the intersections; Kansas
City, Mo. il Am City 84:44 O '69

SALT tolerance of plants. See Plants, Effect
of salt on

SALT water aquariums. See Aquariums

SALT water fishing
Bridge jockeying. G. Heinold. il Outdoor
Life 144:114+ N '69
Fishing is hunting. V. Evanoff. il Motor B
123-87+ Je '69
Fishing the southern circuit. V. Evanoff. il
Motor B 124:23-4+ D '69
Fishing the summer surf. V. Evanoff. il
Motor B 124:76-7+ Ag '69
Fishing your way south. V. Evanoff. il Motor
B 124:83+ N '69
Ivan and the sportfishermen; Russian traw-
lers off Long Island. H. Uhland. il Motor
B 124:19-20+ D '69
Monsters of hurricane hole; yellowtails or
amberjacks. G. P. Fones. il Field & S 74:
48-9+ Jl '69
Ocean fishing for Los Angeles youth. J.
Maghakian. il Parks & Rec 4:32 Jl '69
Salt water. G. Heinold. See issues of Outdoor
life
Shark! G. Heinold. il Outdoor Life 143:34+
F '69
Stalking the red-nosed captain. M. Shulman.
il Field & S 73:60-1+ Ap '69
We plugged the ocean; Florida Keys. E. A.
Bauer. il Outdoor Life 144:76-9+ O '69
What every surf caster should know. W.
Davis. il Mech Illus 65:72+ Ag '69
With the sport fishermen. F. T. Moss. See
issues of Yachting
See also
Albacore fishing
Bluefish fishing
Bonefish fishing
Marlin fishing
Pompano fishing
Sailfish fishing
Tarpon fishing
Tuna fishing
Competitions
Boring-thrilling-exhausting-impoverishing
sport; U.S. Atlantic tuna tournament. P.
Wood. il N Y Times Mag p30-1+ N 2 '69
Fish! Shinnecock swordfish tournament. D.
Kirkpatrick. il Motor B 124:41-7+ S '69
Jo Jo, king of competition sport fishing;
Masters tournament. J. Hardie. il Motor B
123:98+ Ap '69

SALTARELLI, Gerald C.
Tough mind of Gerry Saltarelli. S. Blickstein.
por Duns R 93:38-40 F '69

SALTER, Stefan
Designer's corner. See first issue of each
month of Publishers' weekly to December 1,
1969

SALTS, Molten
Metallic colloids in molten salts. H. W. Kohn
and T. E. Willmarth. bibliog il Science 163:
924-5 F 28 '69
Potassium-sodium ratios in aqueous solutions and coexisting silicate melts. J. B.
Gammon and others. bibliog il Science 163:
179-81 Ja 10 '69

SALTZMAN, Ellin, and Saltzman, Renny
House that sets us free. pors House & Gard
136:78-87 D '69

SALTZMAN, Renny. See Saltzman, E. jt. auth.

SALTZSTEIN, Edward C. See Bortin, M. M. jt.
auth.

SALUD clinic, Woodville, Calif. See Health
clinics

SALVADOR
Foreign relations
But the problem remains. Nation 209:101 Ag
11 '69
Cease-fire in Central America: soccer war
between Honduras and El Salvador. Chr
Cent 86:1082 Ag 20 '69
Great fútbol war; El Salvador against Hon-
duras. T. P. Anderson. Commonweal 90:479-
80 Ag 8 '69
Honduran-Salvadoran conflict resolved by
OSA; Department statement with resolutions
and declaration. Dept State Bul 61:132-4 Ag
18 '69
Lock-in; OAS success in ending violence.
Newsweek 74:34 Ag 11 '69
OAS halts war between El Salvador and Hon-
duras. G. Meek. il Américas 21:42-5 S '69
Population explosion; Central American mini-
war. il Time 94:29-30 Jl 25 '69
Resolutions for El Salvador and Honduras
conflict. Américas 21:56 N '69
Soccer war. il Newsweek 74:54 Jl 28 '69
Soccer war; its causes and what's at stake;
El Salvador and Honduras went to war on
July 14. il U S News 67:6 Jl 28 '69
Walking on eggshells. il Newsweek 74:50-1
Ag 4 '69

SALVADOR, Brazil
Past splendor of Pelourinho. W. Alvez de
Souza. il Américas 21:2-8 S '69

SALVAGE (airplanes)
Big ambulance for big birds; Air international
recovery. N. Sklarewitz. il Pop Mech 132:
124-7+ S '69
Salvaged DC-8 test-flown after overhaul.
Aviation W 90:46 Ap 7 '69

SALVAGE (waste)
See also
Refuse, Utilization of
Scrap metal
Water reuse

SALVATION
Entering God's family. Chr Today 13:23 Ag
1 '69
If we neglect! L. N. Bell. Chr Today 13:
17-18 Ag 22 '69
Is resurrection theology outdated? K.
O'Shea. Cath World 209:7-11 Ap '69
Jewish view of redemption: Buber's hallow-
ing the everyday. C. R. Shaffer. Common-
weal 90:512-15 Ag 22 '69; Discussion. 90:
574-5 S 19 '69
Realities. L. N. Bell. Chr Today 14:28+ D 5
'69
Salvation through the name. V. P. McCorry.
America 121:642-inside back cover D 27 '69
Salvation's alternative. L. N. Bell. Chr To-
day 14:24-5 D 19 '69

SALVATION; musical comedy. See Musical
comedies, revues, etc.—Criticisms, plots,
etc.

SALVATION army
General of the army. Newsweek 74:67 Ag 4
'69

SALZBERG, Louis
Wrong occupation. il por Time 94:69 N 14
'69

SALZBURG
Salzburg: baroque jewel in central Europe.
A. Werner. il Am Artist 33:46-51 Ap '69
Music
Behind the scenes. G. Movshon. il Hi Fi 19:
16 Jl '69

SALZBURG festival
Dubious Don, an ingenious barber. G. Mov-
shon. il Hi Fi 19:MA28-9+ O '69
Report: Salzburg; Herbert von Karajan con-
ducting the Ring. J. H. Sutcliffe. il
Opera N 33:26 My 17 '69
Report: Salzburg; productions of Cosi fan
tutte and Cavalieri's Rappresentazione. J.
H. Sutcliffe. il Opera N 34:25-6 O 11 '69

SALZBURG festival—*Continued*
What happened to the new Karajan style?
Helga Dernesch, Jess Thomas in Siegfried.
G. Movshon. il Hi Fi 19:MA28-9+ Je '69
SAM & me, story. See Tate, J.
SAMARAS, Lucas
Samaras bound. K. Levin. il por Art N 67:
35-7+ F '69
SAMARIN, William J.
Feedback from God. Chr Today 14:10-11 O
10 '69
SAMARITANS
Moral of a story; the good Samaritan. V. P.
McCorry. America 121:106-inside back cover
Ag 16 '69
Samaritans. il Newsweek 74:50+ S 1 '69
SAMBO; musical comedy. See Musical come-
dies, revues, etc.—Criticisms, plots, etc.
SAMET, Norman T.
Why does that man stare at me? por Li-
brary J 94:156-7 Ja 15 '69
SAMMANISH slough regatta. See Regattas
SAMMON, Peter J.
Hayakawa folk hero or enigma? America 121:
10-12 Jl 5 '69
No passing grade for Hayakawa. Common-
weal 90:405-6 Je 27 '69
SAMOA
Night of the palolo. B. Smetzer. il Natur Hist
78:64-71 N '69
SAMOA, WESTERN
Western Samoa. C. Otto. il Travel 132:34-6+
Jl '69
SAMORAJCZYK, John F.
Crisis intervention in the mental hospital.
bibliog Ment Hy 53:477-9 Jl '69
SAMP, Richard R. and Bond, T. G.
Teenagers given voice in local affairs. Parks
& Rec 4:35+ My '69
SAMPLERS
Ten basic embroidery stitches to work into
a modern sampler; excerpts from Em-
broidery. C. Dreesmann. il House & Gard
136:154-5 S '69
SAMPLES, Mack K.
College teaching: an escape from teaching?
Todays Ed 58:40 Ap '69
SAMPLEY, Arthur M.
On the Damascus highway; poem. Chr Cent
86:898 Jl 2 '69
SAMPSON, Ronald V.
Prime minister without portfolio. Nation 209:
509-10 N 10 '69
Vanity of humanism. Nation 209:718-25 D
29 '69
What is a university? Nation 208:560-5 My
5 '69; Same abr. with title Culture, power
and knowledge. Cur 108:27-32 Je '69
SAMS, K. I. See Robertson, N. jt. auth.
SAMSON, Jack
New way for surf stripers. Field & S 74:22+
Je '69
SAMSON (Biblical character) See Bible—Bio-
graphy
SAMUEL, Marcus
Name of the Shell game: tankers. por Bsns
W p58 Mr 8 '69
SAMUELS, B. F.
Winterize your home on wheels. Pop Sci 195:
170-3+ O '69
SAMUELS, Charles Thomas
Heresy of self-love. New Repub 160:28-32 Ap
26 '69
SAMUELS, Doris
Unique recreationist. Parks & Rec 4:35+ Jl
'69
SAMUELS, Gertrude
Hawk of Israel. Sat R 52:36 Ap 19 '69
New lobby. ex cons. N Y Times Mag p36-8+
O 19 '69
SAMUELS, Harry
You don't need an electric outlet to make
movies at night. Pop Sci 195:89 D '69
SAMUELS, Howard J.
How to even the odds. Sat R 52:22-6 Ag 23
'69
Project Own; address, December 4, 1968.
Vital Speeches 35:250-3 F 1 '69
SAMUELS, Nathaniel
U.S. alternate governor of IMF and Interna-
tional banks confirmed. Dept State Bul 61:
261 S 22 '69
SAMUELSON, Paul Anthony
[Column on economic questions] See issues
of Newsweek
SAN ANDREAS fault. See Faults (geology)
SAN ANTONIO, Tex.
See also
Alamo
Education
Revolution by Brother Alexis; living theater
at Antonian high school. W. A. McWhirter.
il Life 66:67-8+ Ja 31 '69
Somebody up there likes Holy Cross high. il
Time 94:34 D 26 '69

HemisFair, 1968
Trailblazer led them to the fair. J. German.
il Am City 84:148 My '69
Lighting
Floodlights light an interchange. il Am City
84:154 My '69
Social conditions
Rumbles along the Rio. P. H. McNamara.
Commonweal 89:730-2 Mr 14 '69
SAN ANTONIO, Tex, public library
San Antonio: books by phone. I. Sexton.
il Wilson Lib Bul 43:885-7 My '69
SANASARDO, Paul
Towards total involvement in art. R. K.
Ziony. il pors Dance Mag 43:62-5+ Mr '69
SANASARDO, Paul, dance company. See Dance
companies
SANBORN, Donald A.
What can we teach about language? Engl
J 58:1206-13 N '69
SANCHEZ, Manuel
Nixon's man. il por Newsweek 73:74 Ap 7 '69
SANCHEZ, Richard V.
Viva Sanchez! letter; ed. by W. F. Buckley.
Nat R 21:791-2 Ag 12 '69
SANCTUARIES, Bird. See Bird sanctuaries
SANCTUARY (law) See Asylum, Right of
SAND, George X.
Doves aren't dickey birds. Field & S 74:60-1+
S '69
Easy way to explore the Everglades. Sci Di-
gest 65:37-41 F '69
How to fish Florida Bay. Field & S 73:192-
4+ Ap '69
Special rabbit hunt. Outdoor Life 143:72-3+
Ap '69
SAND, Inge
Danish delights. W. Terry. il por Sat R 52:
41+ Je 14 '69
SAND, Ole. See Edinger, L. V. jt. auth.
SAND
Slumping structures caused by organically
derived gases in sediments. J. N. Monroe.
bibliog il Science 164:1394-5 Je 20 '69
SAND blast
Sandblaster that cleans all my spark plugs.
S. F. Pontecorvo. il Pop Sci 195:146-7+ S
'69
SAND boxes. See Sandboxes
SAND casting. See Casting (sculpture)
SAND crabs. See Crabs
SAND dunes
See also
Great Sand Dunes National Monument
SAND rats
Diabetic sandrats. D. G. Robinson, jr. il Sci N
95:172-3 F 15 '69
SAND sculpture
Art from a sandbox. F. Hill. il Design 70:20-3
Spr '69
SAND skis and skiing
Skiing without snow on the dunes of Point
Mugu. il Sunset 142:32 My '69
SAND spreaders
Less than a minute a barrel; operation sand
barrel. Muskegon, Mich. M. L. Leyrer. il
Am City 84:44 O '69
SANDBERG, John
How schoolmen can recruit teachers more
effectively. Ed Digest 35:36-7 S '69
SANDBOXES
It's a disappearing sandbox. il Sunset 142:137
Mr '69
SANDBURG, Carl
October paint; poem. Audubon 71:37 S '69
SANDBURG, Helga
Song for Sascha; Sonnet about my daughter
among the flowers; Eulogy for a crow.
Ladies Home J 86:35 O '69
SANDE, A. William
Portraiture enlargement. il Design 70:24-6
Spr '69
SANDEEN, Ernest
Views of our sphere; poem. Sat R 52:36 Ag
30 '69
SANDER, Ellen
Beatles: Abbey Road. Sat R 52:69 O 25 '69
Bob Dylan revisited. Sat R 52:76 Ap 26 '69
Crosby, Stills, and Nash: renaissance fare.
Sat R 52:56 My 31 '69
Cussin', cryin', gettin'. it on. Sat R 52:43
Ag 30 '69
Decade of pop completed. Sat R 52:59-60 D
27 '69
John and Yoko Ono Lennon: give peace a
chance. Sat R 52:46-7 Je 28 '69
Life-style that rock unleashed. por Vogue
154:127+ Ag 1 '69
Nostalgia: oldies but goodies and a last ditch
attempt. Sat R 52:51 Mr 29 '69

SANFORD, David—*Continued*
Giving the consumer class. New Repub 161: 15-17 Jl 26 '69
Jousting with oil. New Repub 161:17-19 Ag 23 '69
Matthew Morgenthau's complaint. New Repub 160:14-15 Mr 1 '69
More studies, and more people. New Repub 160:14-15 My 24 '69
Protest at Penn: a model for campus dissent? New Repub 160:19-21 Mr 15 '69
Rocking the foundations. New Repub 161: 17-20 N 29 '69
This additive age. New Repub 160:17-19 My 17 '69
Trans-Pacific air route tangle. New Repub 160:16-18 F 15 '69
SANFORD museum and planetarium. See Cherokee. Ia.—Galleries and museums

SAN FRANCISCO
Fresh look at yesterday's and today's San Francisco. il Sunset 143:114-16 O '69
Haight-Ashbury today; a case of terminal euphoria. J. Luce. il Esquire 72:65-8+ Jl '69
Hail to the crystal spring; theme song of Dashaway association. T. H. Watkins. il Am West 6:26-7+ Ja '69
Presidio. L. H. Wakefield. Audubon 71:155 N '69

Architecture
Service center for laundry machines. il Arch Rec 146:127-30 Ag '69
See also
San Francisco—Buildings

Art
San Francisco. D. Zack. Art N 68:24 S '69

Bridges
See also
San Francisco Bay bridges

Buildings
Great pyramid: construction go-ahead for Transamerica corp. building. il Newsweek 74:72-4 S 8 '69
Needle in the sky; proposed head office of Transamerica corporation. il Time 94:54 S 5 '69

Chinatown
New yellow peril; Chinatown gangs. T. Wolfe. Esquire 72:190-9+ D '69

City planning
Leaving a heart in San Francisco. il Bsns W p 110-12 My 10 '69

Climate
Snowfall at San Francisco. D. M. Ludlum. il Weatherwise 21:230-7 D '68

Crime
Web that links San Francisco's Mayor Alioto and the Mafia. R. Carlson and L. Brisson. il Look 33:17-21 S 23 '69

Description
Exciting cities, a Redbook vacation guide to sight-seeing with children; excerpts from America's exciting cities. A. Schwartz. il Redbook 132:44 Ap '69
Rent-a-tape tours of San Francisco. Sunset 143:8 O '69
San Francisco Bay, the westward gate. W. Graves. il Nat Geog 136:593-637 N '69

Earthquake and fire, 1906
Quakes and quavers. A. M. Lingg. il Opera N 34:6-7 O 11 '69

Education
See also
San Francisco state college

Gardens
Golden Gate park treat, the Jennie B. Zellerbach garden il Sunset 142:230 My '69
High on San Francisco's Russian Hill, three entry gardens share space with one another. il Sunset 143:80-1 S '69
Three city gardens. E. McDonald. il House B 111:128-9 S '69

Hotels, restaurants, etc.
Enrico's of San Francisco. A. Karlen. il Holiday 45:90+ Mr '69
Pick of San Francisco's top restaurants. Travel & Camera 32:87 Ag '69
San Francisco's Buena Vista. H. Caen. il Holiday 46:34-6 D '69

Housing
Northpoint: a city site with large open spaces has special advantages. il Arch Rec 146:196-7 S '69

Japanese cultural and trade center
For Christmas shopping, or just for a visit, here is the new Japan center in San Francisco. il Sunset 143:44-6 D '69

Music
Report: San Francisco; opera performances. S. Jenkins. il Opera N 34:22 N 1 '69
Report: San Francisco; productions in War memorial opera house. J. Rockwell. Opera N 34:26 S 6 '69
San Francisco reprise, cool ears. R. Goldstein. Vogue 153:68 Je '69
See also
San Francisco opera company

Newspapers
See also
Rolling stone (periodical)
San Francisco chronicle

Parks and playgrounds
New idea center for gardeners in San Francisco's Golden Gate park. il Sunset 143: 94-7 N '69

Photographs
Foothill film festival; running people, symbolic seagulls. M. Mann. il Pop Phot 65: 26+ O '69

Police
Black vs. white in the station house. R. A. Jones. Nation 209:368-70 O 13 '69
O'Brien: I want to kill a nigger. A. Goldberg and G. Marine. il Ramp Mag 8:10-18 Jl '69
San Francisco paradox. Nation 208:482-3 Ap 21 '69
Trouble with troubleshooting. M. E. Leary. il Atlan 223:94-9 Mr '69
Two cops on a tough beat; excerpts from COP! a closeup of violence and tragedy. L. H. Whittemore. il Life 66:52-4+ Je 20 '69

Police department
Friendly fuzz; Community relations division. A. A. Rosenfeld. il Nation 208:503-7 Ap 21 '69

Rapid transit
BART 1971, advance looks are possible now. il Sunset 142:45-6+ Ja '69
Birthpains of BART; San Francisco Bay area rapid transit system. il Am City 84: 120+ Mr '69
City: a different kind of trip; Bay area rapid transit. il Time 93:26 My 16 '69
Rapid transit pact bolsters Rohr in field. il Aviation W 90:62+ Je 30 '69
Space-age commuting; Bay area system. il Newsweek 73:58 Je 16 '69
Test track program a success. il Am City 84:124 Ja '69
Will car builders miss San Francisco train? il Bsns W p62+ My 3 '69

Social life and customs
High-rent Bohemians; North Beach colony. Nation 208:357 Mr 24 '69

Stores
Ghirardelli square and the Cannery. M. McGahan. il Travel & Camera 32:28-9 Ag '69

Theater
See also
American conservatory theatre
SAN FRANCISCO and Oakland helicopter airlines
Commuter, helicopter airline clash grows. Aviation W 90:39 Mr 31 '69
SAN FRANCISCO BAY
Battle of San Francisco Bay. E. Selby. il Read Digest 94:106-10 Mr '69
Day of reckoning for San Francisco Bay. Audubon 71:4-5 Ja '69
Frisky waters by an alabaster city. A. Wright. Sports Illus 32:35 Ja 5 '70
Grassroots fight is won; now buy back San Francisco Bay. Audubon 71:148 N '69
Guarding the bay. P. Marshall. il Sci N 96: 102-3 Ag 2 '69
SAN FRANCISCO BAY bridges
Computer smooths Golden Gate toll collections. R. E. Shields. Am City 84:152 My '69
SAN FRANCISCO BAY REGION
Birthpains of BART; San Francisco Bay area rapid transit system. il Am City 84: 120+ Mr '69
San Francisco Bay, the westward gate. W. Graves. il Nat Geog 136:593-637 N '69
We kept the sewer in service; East Bay municipal utility district, Oakland, Calif. J. D. Foster and J. W. Tooley. il Am City 84:97-9 N '69
SAN FRANCISCO BAY yacht parade. See Aquatic shows

SAN FRANCISCO chronicle
I couldn't get anyone to arrest me; fighting editor S. Newhall. Time 93:66+ Ap 18 '69
TV game; your time is their time; KRON-TV license renewal controversy. A. Alpert. New Repub 161:17-21 O 18 '69
SAN FRANCISCO. City college
Learning the streets; institute on ghetto youth. il Time 94:64 Ag 15 '69
SAN FRANCISCO Giants (baseball) See Baseball clubs
SAN FRANCISCO Mariachi festival. See Music festivals—California
SAN FRANCISCO opera association
Western opera theater: it works. S. Von Buchau. il Hi Fi 19:MA18-19 S '69
SAN FRANCISCO opera company
Fidelio to remember. A. Frankenstein. Hi Fi 19:MA20 D '69
Go west, opera; Western opera theater. il Newsweek 73:84-5+ F 24 '69
Report: productions of Aida, Magic flute and Peter Grimes. J. Rockwell. Opera N 34:24 D 6 '69
Report: productions of Götterdämmerung; Fidelio and L'elisir d'amore. J. Rockwell. il Opera N 34:24 N 22 '69
Report: productions of Pelléas et Mélisande and Jenufa. J. Rockwell. Opera N 34:31 Ja 10 '70
Report: productions of Rossini's Cenerentola and Verdi's Forza del destino. J. Rockwell. Opera N 34:27 D 20 '69
Report: San Francisco; production of Haydn's Man in the moon. J. Rockwell. il Opera N 34:24 O 11 '69
San Francisco's opera returns to Los Angeles. I. Kolodin. Sat R 52:40 Mr 29 '69
SAN FRANCISCO opera house. See Opera houses
SAN FRANCISCO public library
Computer system for periodicals. L. F. Crismond. il Library J 94:3619-21 O 15 '69
San Francisco: down these meaningful streets. G. Bennette. bibliog il Wilson Lib Bul 43:872-5 My '69
SAN FRANCISCO state college. See California. State college. San Francisco
SAN FRANCISCO Warriors (basketball team) See Basketball teams
SAN GABRIEL wilderness area. See Wilderness areas—California
SANGER, Margaret
Hughes, Twain, Child, and Sanger: four who locked horns with the censors; adaptation of addresses. M. Meltzer. il por Wilson Lib Bul 44:284-6 N '69
SANITARY affairs. See subhead Sanitary affairs under names of countries, states, cities, e.g. Kalamazoo, Mich.—Sanitary affairs
SANITARY engineering
See also
Pipe laying
Refuse and refuse disposal
Sewer cleaning
Sewerage
Street cleaning
SANITARY fills. See Filling (earthwork)
SANITATION
See also
Camp sanitation
Refuse and refuse disposal
Swimming pools—Sanitation
SANJO, Mariko
Mariko Sanjo: 92nd street Y. M. Marks. Dance Mag 43:32+ Ja '69
SAN JOAQUIN DELTA. See Sacramento-San Joaquin Delta
SAN JOAQUIN VALLEY. See Central Valley, California
SAN JOSE, Calif.
Simplified crack sealer wins cash award. il Am City 84:28 Ja '69
SAN JOSE state college. See California. State college, San Jose
SAN JUAN, Puerto Rico

Hotels, restaurants, etc.
International chef; a specialty of La Mallorquina restaurant. M. Woodward. il Travel 131:18 F '69
See also
Night clubs—Puerto Rico

Lighting
They wanted fewer poles. il Am City 84:156 My '69

Social conditions
Death of Dolores; excerpt from Six women: three generations in a Puerto Rican family. O. Lewis. il Trans-Action 6:10-19 My '69

SAN JUAN ISLANDS, Wash.
I come from where the bushes are singing. E. Crimmin. il Motor B 123:66-71+ Je '69
See also
Puget Sound
SAN JUAN MOUNTAINS
Discovering Colorado's lofty Southwest. J. Higgins and S. R. Higgins. il Todays Health 47:42-7+ O '69
SAN LAZZARO monastery. See Monasteries
SAN MARINO
Shuttle vote. Time 94:36 S 19 '69
SAN MIGUEL DE ALLENDE, Mexico
Law and hair down Mexico way. C. Manne. Commonweal 91:36-7 O 10 '69; Reply with rejoinder. J. A .Magner. 91:415 Ja 9 '70
Once upon a slaughterhouse: the Biblioteca publica de San Miguel de Allende. L. B. Hopkins. Horn Bk 45:37-9 F '69
SAN MIGUEL ISLAND, Calif. See Santa Barbara Island, Calif.
SAN PEDRO, Calif.
Beach for the ghetto? Cabrillo Beach, San Pedro. G. Laycock. il Audubon 71:107 Jl '69

Harbor
Million-dollar mud flat. R. A. Weinstein. il Am West 6:33-43 Ja '69
SANSOM, Andrew
As I see it. por Parks & Rec 4:68+ S '69
SANTA BARBARA, Calif.
Environment: tragedy in oil; leak at Union oil platform in Santa Barbara Channel. il Time 93:23-5 F 14 '69
GOO fishes in; Get oil out group fight companies drilling in the Santa Barbara Channel. il Newsweek 74:100 D 8 '69
Santa Barbara: oil in the velvet playground. H. Molotch. il Ramp Mag 8:43-51 N '69
Santa Barbarans cite an 11th commandment: thou shalt not abuse the earth. R. Macdonald and R. Easton. il N Y Times Mag p32-3+ O 12 '69
Tarring and feathering of Santa Barbara. L. J. Kennedy. il Motor B 123:60-1 Ap '69
SANTA BARBARA ISLANDS, Calif.
Death from the sea: Santa Barbara oil spill. D. Snell. il Life 66:22-7 Je 13 '69
Escape to the Channel Islands. D. Lambert. il Nat Parks 43:4-7 Ap '69
SANTA BARBARA oil slick. See Oil pollution of rivers, harbors, etc.
SANTA CATALINA ISLAND

Harbor
Avalon looks up. R. P. Kingett. il Motor B 123:242+ Ja '69
SANTA CLARA, Sierra del. See Pinacate, Sierra del
SANTA CLARA COUNTY, Calif.
Less refuse from multi-family dwellings. il Am City 84:16 N '69
SANTA CLAUS
Ho! Ho! Ho! North Pole calling; call Santa program in Hampton, Va. J. M. Eason. il Parks & Rec 4:45-6+ O '69
I'm dreaming of a black Christmas; SCLC's Operation Breadbasket. il Ebony 25:114-16+ N '69
Who is Santa Claus? S. Rosenberg. il McCalls 97:55-7+ D '69
SANTA Claus is twins; drama. See Martens, A. C.
SANTA CRUZ, Bolivia
Company town loses its boss. il Bsns W p30-1 Ja 3 '70
SANTA CRUZ campus. See California. University—Santa Cruz campus
SANTA CRUZ ISLAND, Calif. See Santa Barbara Islands, Calif.
SANTA CRUZ ISLANDS. See Solomon Islands
SANTA FE, N.Mex.
Santa Fe, our last unspoiled city? C. Brossard. il Holiday 45:64-7+ My '69
Writers of Santa Fe. A. Gregg. il Writers Digest 49:54-9 Ap '69

Music
See also
Santa Fe opera company

Newspapers
See also
Santa Fe New Mexican (newspaper)

Streets
Rubber stretches roadway life. il Am City 84:24 F '69
SANTA FE International corporation
Turn 'em loose; former drilling departments turned independent. il Forbes 103:45-6 Je 1 '69
SANTA FE New Mexican (newspaper)
When a PM paper goes AM. W. B. Kerr. Sat R 52:58-9 F 8 '69

SANTA FE opera company
Current chronicle; Die Jakobsleiter American première. P. J. Smith. il Mus Q 55:102-11 Ja '69
Demons in Santa Fe. il Newsweek 74:85 Ag 25 '69
John Crosby, we can afford to take chances. . . S. Fleming. il Hi Fi 19:MA17+ Ag '69
Penderecki & Menotti: pros and cons. P. J. Smith. il Hi Fi 19:MA24-5+ N '69
Report: Santa Fe productions of Salome, Devils of Loudun, and Help! help! the globolinks. F. Merkling. il Opera N 34:22-3 S 20 '69
Santa Fe's operatic oasis. I. Kolodin. il Sat R 52:39-40+ Ag 30 '69
SANTA FE opera house. See Opera houses
SANTA FE SPRINGS, Calif.
Free bus service increases summer fun. W. J. McCann. il Am City 84:128 Jl '69
SANTA FE TRAIL
Journey to sundown on the Santa Fe Trail. R. Dunlop. il Todays Health 47:44-9+ S '69
SANTA MARTA, Colombia
Santa Marta; new spot in the Caribbean. il Holiday 45:94-5 Ap '69
SANTA MONICA, Calif.
Santa wouldn't provide 2,000 free parking spaces. P. Scott. il Am City 84:145-6 My '69
Traffic controller for any intersection. il Am City 84:152 My '69
SANT'ANGELO, Georgio
Dreams of a bright new fashion; with photographs by Greene-Eula. Life 66:44-52 Mr 7 '69
Extra dry bikini straight up. C. Twiss. il Holiday 45:50-3 F '69
SANTA RITA rehabilitation center. See Prisons —California
SANTA ROSA, Calif.

Parks and playgrounds
Picnic and play stop on U.S. 101 in Sonoma County; Howarth memorial park. il Sunset 143:42 O '69
SANTA ROSA ISLAND, Calif. See Santa Barbara Islands, Calif.
SANTAYANA, George
Stranger. J. Epstein. New Repub 160:25-6+ Mr 1 '69
SANTOLINA. See Lavender cotton
SÃO PAULO (city), Brazil

City planning
São Paulo 1990; with remarks by members of the review panel of the Basic urban plan. A. J. Lowe. Américas 21:28-9 Ja '69

Galleries and museums
Impressionists revisited; new gallery opened. il Time 93:66-71 Ja 31 '69
SÃO SALVADOR. See Salvador, Brazil
SAPORA, Allen V.
Evaluation of park and recreation operations, who should do it? bibliog Parks & Rec 4:35-6+ D '69
SAPPHIRES
Maser amplification of 9.5-gigahertz elastic waves in sapphire doped with divalent nickel impurity ions. P. D. Peterson and E. H. Jacobsen. bibliog il Science 164:1056-7 My 30 '69
SAPPHIRES, Artificial
Hundred-foot-long sapphires. il Chem 42:23 Ja '69
SARAH Lawrence college, Bronxville, N.Y.
On campus: Sarah Lawrence goes to Russia. Mlle 69:108 My '69
SARAH O'Loughlin Foley award. See Literary prizes
SARANOVITZ, Norman S.
Simplified etching. Sch Arts 69:14-15 D '69
SARASOTA, Fla.

Ringling center
Circus king's gift to posterity. A. Rosenthal. il Todays Health 47:42-7 N '69

Theater
Florida-grown; summer repertory of the Asolo state theater company. H. Hewes. Sat R 52:32 Ag 23 '69
SARATOGA SPRINGS, N.Y.
Saratoga; a week of horses and culture. il Holiday 45:60-1 My '69
SARAYIOTES, Jim
Installing a home master antenna TV system. Electr World 81:41-3+ Je '69
SARCOMA
Human liposarcomas: tissue cultures containing foci of transformed cells with viral particles. D. L. Morton and others. bibliog il Science 165:813-16 Ag 22 '69

SARCOPLASMIC reticulum. See Muscle
SARDINIA
New glamor port: Porto Cervo of Costa Smerelda. B. Robinson. il Yachting 125:60-1+ Je '69
Sardinia; the Aga Khan's hideaway; with photographs by E. Sarsini. Life 67:44-8 Ag 22 '69
See also
Porto Rotondo
SARGASSO SEA
Saga of the Sargasso. P. Brock. Motor B 123:195-7 Ap '69
SARGEANT, Winthrop
Ernest Ansermet, November 11, 1883-February 20, 1969. Opera N 33:29 Ap 5 '69
Europe's festivals. Travel & Camera 32:56-9+ Jl '69
Monks of San Lazzaro. Travel & Camera 32:22+ D '69
Musical events. See issues of New Yorker
SARGENT, Mary. See Corinth, K. jt. auth.
SARGENT, Wyn
Got ark: need Boston whaler. Nat R 21:893 S 9 '69
Needed: an ark. Nat R 21:581-2 Je 17 '69
SARIN
Defenseless; incident in Okinawa. il Newsweek 74:65 Ag 4 '69
SARK
Nothing like a dame. il Time 94:34 Ag 8 '69
Sibyl of Sark; plan for administration by Guernsey. il Newsweek 74:33 Ag 11 '69
SARNOFF, Charles A.
Mythic symbols in two precolumbian myths. bibliog Am Imago 26:3-20 Spr '69
SARNOFF, David
How color TV was born; excerpt from The strategy of change for business success, ed. by S. Furst and M. Sherman. por Nations Bsns 57:70-3 F '69
SARNOFF, Robert W.
Academic bankruptcy; address, January 24, 1969. Vital Speeches 35:282-4 F 15 '69
about
Balancing act. il por Forbes 104:28-9 N 1 '69
Now, it's official. por Bsns W p94 Ja 10 '70
SAROFIM, Fayez
Recipe for success: always stay fully invested. por Forbes 103:56+ My 1 '69
SAROFIM, Fayez and company
Recipe for success: always stay fully invested. F. Sarofim. Forbes 103:56+ My 1 '69
SAROYAN, William
Time of your life. Criticism
America 121:622 D 20 '69
Nation 209:581 N 24 '69
New Repub 161:22+ N 22 '69
New Yorker 45:163 N 15 '69
Newsweek il por 74:139 N 17 '69
Sat R 52:10 N 29 '69
Time 94:57 N 14 '69
SARSINI, Enrico
Sardinia; the Aga Khan's hideaway; photographs. Life 67:44-8 Ag 22 '69
SARTIN, Pierrette
Real and pseudo problems of the working woman. UNESCO Courier 22:24-8 Jl '69
SARTOR, J. Doyne
Electricity and rain. bibliog por Phys Today 22:45-51 Ag '69
SARTORI, Leo
Myth of MIRV. Sat R 52:10-15+ Ag 30 '69
SARTORINI (island) See Thera (island)
SARTRE, Jean Paul
Commentary. Ramp Mag 8:48-9 O '69
about
Bergman's Shame and Sartre's stare. R. E. Lauder. il Cath World 209:247-50 S '69
Sartre: ideologue of our time, by T. Molnar. Review
Nat R 21:133-4 F 11 '69. P. P. Witonski
SARVIS, Alva. See Kelly, P. jt. auth.
SARVIS, Shirley
New chicken dish for Sunday. Farm J 93:98 F '69
SASAKI, Teruo. See Gitlin, D. jt. auth.
SASHIMI. See Cookery, Japanese
SASKATCHEWAN

Religious institutions and affairs
World around us. Chr Cent 86:1049-50 Ag 6 '69
SASS, Eytan
Microphotometric determination of preferred orientation in undeformed dolomites. bibliog Science 165:802-3 Ag 22 '69
SASS, Martin
Wall Street's wizards of odds. il por Bsns W p 122-4+ Mr 15 '69

SASSEN, Roger
Amateur scientist. Sci Am 220:131-5 Je '69
SASSIN, J. F. and others
Human growth hormone release: relation to
slow-wave sleep and sleep-waking cycles.
bibliog Science 165:513-15 Ag 1 '69
SAT. See College entrance examination board
—Scholastic aptitude test
SATA, Lindbergh S. and Derbyshire, R. L.
Breaking the role barrier: a psychothera-
peutic necessity. bibliog Ment Hy 53:110-
17 Ja '69
SATAN. See Devil
SATAN in literature. See Devil in literature
SATCHELL, Roy C.
How to get ahead: leave the company. por
Bsns W p35 Jl 19 '69
SATCO. See Supervisory air traffic controllers
organization
SATELLITE viruses. See Viruses
SATELLITES
Motions of Jupiter's moons (cont) il R Pop
Astron 63:17 F '69
Unusual phenomena of Callisto. il Sky & Tel
37:326 My '69
SATIE, Erik
Recordings. M. Mayer. Esquire 71:52 My '69
SATIRE
Irony of situation in Ernest Hemingway's Sol-
dier's home. A. J. Petrarca. Engl J 58:664-7
My '69
See also
Caricatures and cartoons
Humor
SATISFACTION in work. See Job satisfaction
SATO, Eisaku
Agreement on Okinawa. il por Time 94:37
N 28 '69
Closing a chapter of the past. il por News-
week 74:39-40 D 1 '69
For SALT and Sato. Chr Cent 86:1476 N 19
'69
Japan's premier resort. R. Halloran. il pors
Sat R 52:91-2+ Mr 8 '69
Premier Sato would tap his way across a
stone bridge to be sure it was safe. T. Oka.
il pors N Y Times Mag p48-9+ N 16 '69; Re-
ply. G. Berger. p 134 D 7 '69
Pro-U.S. policy gets support. por U S News
68:10 Ja 12 '70
Sato-Nixon pact: its meaning to U.S. and
Japan. il por U S News 67:18 D 1 '69
U.S. Japan on a collision course? il por U S
News 67:84-5 N 24 '69
Winning formula. il por Newsweek 75:24-5
Ja 5 '70
SATTLER, Jerome M. and Leppla, B. W.
Survey of the need for children's mental
health facilities. Ment Hy 53:643-5 O '69
SATURDAY evening post
Ackerman looks beyond the Post. Bsns W
p26+ Ja 18 '69
Best years of a long, full life. R. Butter-
field. il Life 66:55 Ja 24 '69
Death of the Post. M. M. Mooney. Atlan
224:70-6 N '69
1821—The Saturday evening post—1969. K.
Polking. Writers Digest 49:53+ Mr '69
Farewell to the Satevepost. F. Russell. Nat R
21:552-3 Je 3 '69
Gone but remembered. N. Kent. Am Artist
33:5 Ap '69
I am Marty Ackerman. . ; excerpts from De-
cline and fall. O. Friedrich. il Harper 239:
92-100+ D '69
Post. RIP. Nat R 21:64-5 Ja 28 '69
We call on the Saturday evening post. D.
A. Schanche. Esquire 72:40+ N '69
SATURDAY review
SR's seventeenth annual advertising awards.
R. L. Tobin. il Sat R 52:75-80 Ap 12 '69
See also
Amy Loveman national award
Anisfield-Wolf awards
SATURDAY review photo contest. See Photo-
graphy—Competitions
SATURN (boosters) See Space vehicles—Pro-
pulsion systems
SATURN (planet)
Clues from ammonia. il Sci N 97:20 Ja 3 '70
Composition of Saturn's rings. il Sky & Tel
39:14 Ja '70
New white spot on Saturn. il Sky & Tel 39:
56 Ja '70
SATURN V (space vehicle) See Space vehicles
—Propulsion systems
SAUCER magnolia. See Magnolias
SAUCERS, Flying. See Flying saucers
SAUCES
Dish of many disguises; fondue bourgui-
gnonne. C. Claiborne. il N Y Times Mag
p 129-30 N 16 '69
Plum sauce for pork roast. il Sunset 142:186
Mr '69

Presto, presto; spaghetti sauce. C. Claiborne.
il N Y Times Mag p58 Je 15 '69
See also
Tomato sauce
SAUD, king of Saudi Arabia (abdicated 1964)
Big splendor. il por Newsweek 73:44+ Mr 10
'69
Death of a king. por Time 93:37 Mr 7 '69
SAUDI ARABIA
See also
Red Sea
SAUER, Louis W.
Your child's health. See issues of PTA maga-
zine
SAUERHAFT, Stanley
And now a raid on the raiders? Duns R 93:
56-8 My '69
Kiss and tell on romantic Wall Street. Duns
R 93:26-9 F '69
Semantics for the swinging executive. Duns
R 93:42-3 Ap '69
SAUL, Peter
That's Saul, folks. D. Zack. il por Art N 68:
56-8+ N '69
SAUL; story. See Jenkins, L. B. de
SAULNIER, Raymond J.
Appraisal of federal fiscal policies: 1961-1967.
Ann Am Acad 379:63-71 S '68
Cost and price stability; address, January
15, 1969. Vital Speeches 35:243-6 F 1 '69
Tax-reform bill; a critical analysis. por U S
News 67:72-6 O 20 '69
SAUNA
Finland: saunaloitsu. N. Gittelson. Harp Baz
102:32-32A+ Ap '69
Great sauna plot. il Vogue 154:140-1+ Jl '69
Sauna: hot and healthy. D. Kalins. il Holi-
day 46:43+ D '69
Sweating it out in Finland. J. Star. il Look
33:110 O 7 '69

Anecdotes, facetiae, satire, etc.
Saunas out and in. R. G. Engelmann. Sat R
52:6+ S 13 '69
SAUNDERS, James
Scent of flowers. Criticism
Nation 209:547+ N 17 '69
New Yorker 45:128-30 N 1 '69
Newsweek 74:93 N 3 '69
Sat R 52:28 N 8 '69
SAUNDERS, Jane
Hospitality demands are heavy for the lady
with the torch. Parks & Rec 4:43-4+ O '69
SAUNDERS, Josephine
Circle and the question; poem. Poetry 114:
380 S '69
SAUNDERS, Robert J.
Postage stamp as a mini-art form. Sch Arts
69:30-1 N '69
Sell your public school art program at public
meetings. Sch Arts 68:31 F '69
SAUNDERS, Silvia
Those other peonies. Horticulture 47:18-21+
S '69
SAUNDERS, Susan A. and others
Are honeybees deficient in phosphomannose
isomerase? bibliog Science 164:858-9 My 16
'69
SAUSAGE
See also
Cookery—Meat
SAUSALITO, Calif.

Hotels, restaurants, etc.
Ondine-gastronomy with a view. J. Gooding.
il Travel & Camera 32:86 Ag '69
SAUTHER, Arnold
Bring architecture home. Sch Arts 68:14-15
Mr '69
SAVAGE, John
Love the whole girl; story. Redbook 133:96-7
Jl '69
SAVAGE, Thomas
Sir: if you wish us to consider further your
manuscript of "Goldilocks and the three
bears" . . . Esquire 72:145+ O '69
SAVANNAH, Ga.
Charm of the past in Savannah. il Bet Hom
& Gard 47:69 Je '69

Churches
Setback in Court for breakaway church
groups. U S News 66:11 F 10 '69
Supreme court and ecumenism. America 120:
154-5 F 8 '69
SAVANNAH (ship) See Atomic powered ships
SAVAS, Emanuel S.
New urban-management science. Am City
84:156-9 Mr '69
SAVING and savings
Returns you can get on your savings. U S News
67:87 N 24 '69
Tips on building a financial reserve. D. Green.
Mech Illus 65:64-5+ O '69

SAVING and savings—*Continued*
Where should you keep your rainy-day money? il Changing T 23:25–9 S '69
See also
Finance, Personal
Investment clubs
Investments

SAVINGS and loan associations
Harlem's banker-priest; M. M. Weston, president of Harlem's Carver Federal savings & loan assn. il Ebony 24.92–4+ Mr '69
S&Ls look for sympathy at the top. Bsns W p72+ Mr 29 '69
Savings weather a midyear crisis. Bsns W p34–5 Jl 19 '69
See also
Credit unions

SAVINGS banks
Savings weather a midyear crisis. Bsns W p34–5 Jl 19 '69

SAVINGS banks, Toy. See Banks, Coin

SAVINGS bonds. See Bonds, Government

SAVOCA, Carmen
Three cheers for Tri-Cities. R. D. Daniels. il por Opera N 33:14–16 Mr 1 '69

SAVRYN, Lynda
In my opinion. por Seventeen 28:256 S '69

SAW horses. See Sawhorses

SAW sharpening. See Sharpening

SAW stands. See Machinery—Stands

SAWAIA, Josephine
Our political power for good. Todays Ed 58:31 D '69

SAWDUST baths. See Baths, Sawdust

SAWHORSES
Two ways to make sawhorses. il Pop Sci 195:220 N '69

SAWICKI, Jerzy
Jerzy Sawicki dies in crash. A. Salam and M. Jean. Phys Today 22:113 F '69

SAWS
Amazing saw that cuts with water. il Mech Illus 65:98–9 Ag '69
Blade that does a chain saw's work. E. F. Lindsley. il Pop Sci 194:134–5 My '69
Build this power hacksaw from a washing machine. B. Dittmer. il Pop Mech 132:188–91 N '69
Buying & using a reciprocating saw. H. Silken. il Mech Illus 65:100–2+ Ap '69
Circular saw: a worksaver for all workshops. J. Burroughs. il Pop Mech 131:188–91 F '69
Four new power hand saws. il Pop Sci 194:176 F '69
How to choose and use a portable circular saw. il Mech Illus 65:101–3+ N '69
Make this hinged fixture for your radial saw. il Pop Mech 132:187 O '69
New mini chain saw does big jobs in tight spots. J. Hand. il Pop Sci 195:206+ O '69
New toothless blades cut the uncuttables; saber saw blades. W. C. Leckey. il Pop Mech 132:166–7 D '69
Portable electric circular saws. il Consumer Rep 34:90–4 F '69
Putting new teeth in old saws. Field & S 74:117 Jl '69
Quick guide to chain saws. il Mech Illus 65:88–9+ Mr '69
Radial saws: are two arms better than one? R. J. De Cristoforo. il Pop Sci 195:122–5 Jl '69
Right handsaw. il Bet Hom & Gard 47:22+ O '69
Two hot new yard tools; chain saw, hedge trimmer. E. F. Lindsley. il Pop Sci 195:120 Jl '69
See also
Jigsaws

SAWTOOTH-wave generators. See Signal generators

SAWTOOTH wilderness area. See Wilderness areas—Idaho

SAX, M. and Pletcher, J.
Local anesthetics: significance of hydrogen bonding in mechanism of action. bibliog Science 166:1546–8 D 19 '69

SAXIFRAGES
Silver saxifrages. R. Murfitt. il Horticulture 47:24–5+ Ap '69
See also
Carpenteria californica

SAYLER, Anne, and Salmon, Michael
Communal nursing in mice: influence of multiple mothers on the growth of the young. bibliog Science 164:1309–10 Je 13 '69

SAYLOR, J. Galen
Captive to funded projects? Ed Digest 34:14–17 Mr '69

SAYRE, Joel
Maple Leafs. Holiday 45:70–1+ F '69

SAYRE, Nora
Politics. Esquire 72:106+ D '69
Summer husbands; story. Harp Baz 102: 282–3 S '69

SAYVILLE, N.Y. yacht club. See Yacht clubs

SAZAMA, Gerald W.
Universities and foreign aid. America 121:391–2 N 1 '69

SCAFF, Alvin H.
Changes in doctoral language requirements. Sch & Soc 97:453–4 N '69

SCAFFOLDING
Window washer express; electrically-driven outside scaffold. il Mech Illus 65:70–1 S '69

SCALE in photography. See Composition (photography)

SCALE insects
See also
Mealy bugs

SCALE models. See Models and modelmaking

SCALES (markings)
Units for logarithmic scales. C. S. McCamy. bibliog il Phys Today 22:42–4 Ap '69

SCALES (weighing instruments)
Homemade postal scales. il Consumer Bul 52:30–2 Jl '69
Postal scales. il Consumer Bul 52:14–16 F '69

SCALLOPS
See also
Cookery—Shellfish

SCALOPPINE. See Cookery—Meat

SCAMMON, Charles Melville
Scene of slaughter was exceedingly picturesque. W. Marx. il por Am Heritage 20:66–71+ Je '69

SCAMMON, Richard M.
Demographic profile, and where it points. Newsweek 73:18 Je 30 '69
Profiles; interview, ed. by W. Whitworth. New Yorker 45:50–2+ S 20 '69

about
Uncertain apocalypse. Chr Cent 86:1302 O 15 '69

SCANDAL
Public figures and their private lives; Time essay. il Time 94:28–9 Ag 22 '69

SCANDALIOS, John G.
Alcohol dehydrogenase in maize: genetic basis for isozymes. bibliog Science 166:623–4 O 31 '69

SCANDINAVIA
See also
Collective settlements—Scandinavia
Forests and forestry—Scandinavia
Libraries—Scandinavia
Television broadcasting—Scandinavia
Trade unions—Scandinavia
Women—Scandinavia

Description and travel
It's lifeseeing, a new idea for off-season visits to Scandinavia. il Sunset 142:34+ F '69

Economic policy
Charting a course for the North; foundations of Scandinavian common market. F. Morley. Nations Bsns 57:20+ O '69
Nordic common market; creating Nordek within European free trade association. Time 93:112 My 16 '69

SCANDINAVIAN airlines system
SAS uses new data processing system. Aviation W 90:41–2 Je 9 '69

SCANDINAVIAN cookery. See Cookery, Scandinavian

SCANDINAVIAN international drag meet. See Automobile racing

SCANDURA, Joseph M.
Federal control and basic research in education. Sch & Soc 97:227–8 Ap '69

SCANLON, Laura Polla
Selected list of children's books (cont) Commonweal 90:294+ My 23 '69

SCANLON plan. See Business management and organization—Employee participation

SCANNING devices, Optical. See Optical scanners

SCANNING electron microscope. See Electron microscope and microscopy

SCARECROW press, Metuchen, N.J.
Eric Moon interviewed. E. Moon. Wilson Lib Bul 44:140+ O '69
Former LJ editor to head Scarecrow. Library J 94:2381 Je 15 '69

SCARF, Maggie
In the therapeutic community, patients are doctors. N Y Times Mag p32–3+ My 25 '69

SCARFE, Gerald
Close up. il por Life 66:40–1+ Ap 4 '69

SCARLATTI, Domenico
K. at the keyboard. H. Saal. Newsweek 74:
133 N 24 '69
Queen's music master. R. Evett. Atlan 224:
172+ N '69
SCARLET runner beans. See Beans
SCARP (guided missile) See Guided missiles
SCARPITTA, Salvatore
Ivory garage. B. H. Friedman. il por Art N
68:52-5 Ap '69
SCARR, Sandra
What about biological insults? Ed Digest
34:25-7 Ap '69
SCARRY, Richard
Richard Scarry's best Switzerland ever. A.
Bell. il Pub W 196:41-2 O 20 '69
SCARSDALE, N.Y.
Money for your old leaves! il Org Gard &
Farm 16:42-5 S '69
SCARSDALE, N.Y, womans club. See Womens
clubs and societies
SCARVES
Ah, the Italians; they can show us. il Vogue
153:241 My '69
Capital headliner; designs of F. Welch. il
Newsweek 73:104+ My 19 '69
SCATTERGUNNING. See Shooting
SCATTERING (physics)
Crystallography with protons. C. S. Barrett.
il Phys Today 22:33 Ag '69
Form factors of elementary particles. R. Wil-
son. bibliog il Phys Today 22:47-53 Ja '69
Laser beat frequency spectroscopy. M. J.
French and others. bibliog il Science 163:
345-51 Ja 24 '69
Nucleon-nucleon scattering. M. H. MacGre-
gor. bibliog il Phys Today 22:21-8 D '69
Regge-cut theory yields encouraging results;
report of meeting. P. M. Fishbane
and L. M. Simmons, jr. il Phys Today 22:
101+ S '69
Veneziano representation excites strong-in-
teraction theorists. bibliog il Phys Today
22:59-60 Mr '69
See also
X rays—Scattering
SCATTERING of particles and rays. See Scat-
tering (physics)
SCENARIO method in decision making. See
Decision making
SCENERY, Preservation of. See Landscape
protection
SCENERY, Stage. See Theater—Stage scenery
SCENT. See Perfumery
SCENT of flowers; drama. See Saunders, J.
SCENTS. See Odors
SCHAAP, Dick
Lindsay caper. por Holiday 45:46-7+ Je '69
(ed) See Kramer, J. Death by inches
about
Electronic diary. P. D. Zimmerman. il por
Newsweek 73:88+ F 3 '69
Schaap shop. por Time 94:49-50 S 19 '69
SCHAAR, John H.
[Book review] Commonweal 89:738+ Mr 14
'69
—and Wolin, S. S.
Reexamining technological civilization. Cur
112:29-30 N '69
SCHAB, Fred
Cheating: comparison of college bound and
non-college bound pupils. Clear House 44:
179-81 N '69
SCHABER, Gerald G. and Gumerman, G. J.
Infrared scanning images: an archeological
application. bibliog Science 164:712-13 My
9 '69
SCHAEFER, Arnold E.
Breaking the back of hunger. por Todays
Health 47:39-40 N '69
Finally, facts on malnutrition in the United
States; interview, ed. by F. G. Loyd. por
Todays Health 47:32-3+ S '69
Hunger amid plenty; summary of report. Sr
Schol 94:13 F 7 '69
SCHAEFER, Paul
Upper Hudson: time for decision, reprint.
Liv Wildn 32:18-21 Wint '68
SCHAEFER, William P. See Wang, B. C. jt.
auth.
SCHAEFFER, Francis August
Universe and two chairs; excerpt from Death
in the city. Chr Today 13:8-11 Ap 25 '69
about
Co-belligerent reconciliation. R. L. Love.
Chr Today 14:38 N 21 '69
SCHAFER, Marilyn
Going places, finding things to delight your
children in Europe. House & Gard 135:50-
1+ Mr '69

SCHAFER, Paul W.
Centrioles of a human cancer: intercellular
order and intracellular disorder. bibliog Sci-
ence 164:1300-3 Je 13 '69
SCHAFER, Roger
One billion dollar subsidy for slums. Arch
Forum 131:80-1 O '69
SCHAFFER, Robert H. See Baker. J. K. jt.
auth.
SCHAFRAN, Lynn H.
Larionov and the Russian vanguard. Art N
68:36-7+ My '69
SCHALES, F. D.
Never plant cucumbers next to... Org Gard
& Farm 16:46-7 My '69
SCHALLER, George B.
Life with the king of beasts. il por Nat
Geog 135:494-519 Ap '69
SCHALLER, Lyle E.
Crime, violence and the local church. Chr
Cent 86:641-5 My 7 '69
New-style attack on the denominational bud-
get. Chr Cent 86:1515-18 N 26 '69
SCHANBERG, Saul M. See Pearce, L. A. jt.
auth.
SCHANCHE, Don A.
John O'Hara is alive and well in the first half
of the twentieth century. Esquire 72:84-6+
Ag '69
We call on the Saturday evening post. Es-
quire 72:40+ N '69
SCHANEN, William F. jr
Obstinacy of Bill Schanen. J. Pekkanen. por
Life 67:59 S 26 '69
SCHAPIRO, Miriam
Crash of symbols; exhibition at Emmerich
gallery, N.Y. L. Campbell. il por Art N
68:42-3+ Mr '69
SCHAPIRO, Steve
Don't ask me, I only live here; photographs.
Life 67:32-7 Jl 25 '69
SCHATZ, Arthur
Nixon in White House West; photographs.
Life 67:18B-25 S 5 '69
about
Have some more guacamole, said the Presi-
dent. R. Graves. Life 67:3 S 5 '69
SCHAUFFELE, Charles G.
Profile of teen-agers. Chr Today 13:20-1 F
14 '69
SCHAUMBURG, Herbert H. and others
Monosodium L-glutamate: its pharmacology
and role in the Chinese restaurant syn-
drome. bibliog Science 163:826-8 F 21 '69
SCHAWLOW, Arthur L.
Is your research moral? il por Phys Today
22:118-19 D '69
SCHECHNER, Richard
Dionysus in 69. Criticism
Commonweal 90:112 Ap 11 '69
Professor of the Dionysiac theater. E. Les-
ter. il por N Y Times Mag p32-3+ Ap 27 '69
SCHECHNER, William
History of black America. Cath World 209:89-
90 My '69
Mob scene in Jersey. Commonweal 89:514-15
Ja 24 '69
Welfare in New York; let them eat cake.
Commonweal 90:133-6 Ap 18 '69
SCHECHTER, Dan, and others
CIA as an equal opportunity employer. Ramp
Mag 7:25-33 Je '69
SCHECK, Grace M.
Ceramics in junior high. Sch Arts 68:14-15
Ap '69
SCHECTER, Jerrold
Track & field (title varies) Sports Illus 31:
72+ O 20 '69
SCHEDL, Naomi
Theme and variation. Sch Arts 69:34-5 Ja
'70
SCHEDULES
CSPC: reporting project progress to the top.
A. R. Saitow. il Harvard Bsns R 47:88-97
Ja '69
See also
Critical path analysis
SCHEDULES, School
Do you believe in lesson plans? E. Heese.
Clear House 43:492-3 Ap '69
Parental resistance to modular scheduling.
R. A. Gorton. Clear House 43:392-5 Mr '69
SCHEEL, Walter
Brandt on the threshold. il por Newsweek
74:46-7 O 13 '69
Germany on a new path, which way will it
lead? il por U S News 67:20+ O 13 '69
Jester in striped pants. por Time 94:26 O
31 '69
SCHEER, Robert
Dialectics of confrontation. Ramp Mag 8:42-
9+ Ag '69
Night at Santa Rita. Ramp Mag 8:50-1 Ag '69

SCHEETS, Francis K.
Educating priests after the seminary. America 120:526-8 My 3 '69

SCHEFF, Neil M. See Tecce, J. J. jt. auth.

SCHEFFER, Victor B.
Ingenuities of nature; sperm whales; excerpt from The year of the whale. Sat R 52:49 Ag 2 '69
Super flea meets mountain beaver; with biographical sketch. por Natur Hist 78:4, 54-5 My '69

SCHEFFLER, Linda Weingarten
What seventy SEEK kids taught their counselor. il por N Y Times Mag p54-5+ N 16 '69; Reply with rejoinder. M. Schuker. p 14 Ja 11 '70

SCHEINMAN, Lawrence
Nuclear safeguards, the peaceful atom, and the IAEA. bibliog f por(back cover) Int Concil 572:5-64 Mr '69

SCHELL, Orville
Learning about China. Nation 209:58-60 Jl 14 '69
Pop me some dinks. New Repub 162:19-21 Ja 3 '70

SCHELLENG, John C.
Varnishing luthier. Sci Am 220:45-6 F '69

SCHEMPP, John A.
How to reload rifle cartridges. Cons 23:48-9+ F '69

SCHENECTADY, N.Y.

Economic conditions

GE strike: it's starting to hurt. il Bsns W p 13-15 D 20 '69

SCHENECTADY COUNTY, N.Y., public library
Concrete columns and arches for Schenectady County. il Library J 94:4391-2 D 1 '69

SCHENK. Otto
Opera primer: why the director? F. Rizzo. il por Opera N 33:26-30 F 15 '69

SCHENLEY, James F.
What you should know about choosing and using abrasives. Pop Mech 131:186-8+ Ap '69
What you should know about fire warning systems. Pop Mech 131:176-80 F '69

SCHERER, Leo
Citizens' group collects discarded vehicles. Am City 84:145 S '69

SCHERER, Silvester N.
Burglars beware. Har Yrs 9:46-8 Ag '69

SCHERING corporation
Headed back up; ethical drugs will remain mainstay of the company. Forbes 103:57 Mr 1 '69

SCHERMAN, Harry
Harry Scherman, 1887-1969. J. K. Hutchens. por Sat R 52:23 N 29 '69
Obituary
Pub W por 196:28 N 24 '69

SCHERR, Max
Tribe is restless. il por Time 94:46 Jl 18 '69

SCHERY, Robert W.
Label's the clue to lawn seed. Horticulture 46:21+ S '68
Lawn thatch, what it's all about. Horticulture 47:24-5+ S '69
Winter feeding of lawns. Horticulture 47:34+ Ja '69

SCHEUFELE, Kirk
Making films with students. Engl J 58:426-7+ Mr '69

SCHEVILL, James Erwin
Thrashing with doom. L. A. Goldstein. Nation 209:386-7 O 13 '69

SCHICK, Harold
1876 art gallery revitalized. Parks & Rec 4: 33-9 Jl '69

SCHICKEL, Richard
Compleat American pragmatist. Horizon 11: 60-5 Wint '69
Life movie review. See issues of Life
Shirley or Curley? Life 66:81-2 Je 13 '69

SCHIDLOVSKY, G. and others
Herpesvirus in Marek's disease tumors. bibliog Science 164:959-61 My 23 '69

SCHIESSER, Emil S.
Hidden perils of a lunar landing; excerpts from interview, ed. by J. Lear. il Sat R 52:49-54 Je 7 '69

SCHIFF, Dorothy
Goodbye, Dolly! A reminiscence of the New York post. J. Newfield. il Harper 239:92-8 S '69

SCHIFRIN, Lalo Claudio
Cool hand in Hollywood. il por Time 94:53 Jl 25 '69

SCHILL, Bert. See Schill, Bill, jt. auth.

SCHILL, Bill, and Schill, Bert
Fort Delaware. il Yachting 125:66-7 Je '69
Sightseeing afloat.. il Yachting 125:72-3 Mr; 68+ My '69

SCHILLER, Anita R.
Widening sex gap. bibliog por Library J 94:1098-100 Mr 15 '69

SCHILLER, Lawrence
Checkbook journalism. il por Newsweek 74: 45-6 D 29 '69

SCHILLER, Patricia
(ed) Teen-agers speak out about sex; symposium. Todays Ed 58:23-6 Mr '69

SCHILLER, Ronald
Boston's museum a-go-go. PTA Mag 64:22-5 O '69; Same abr. with title. This is a museum? Read Digest 95:225-9 N '69

SCHILLING, Anne Marie
Mr Tweedy; condensation. Read Digest 94: 277-87+ My '69

SCHILLING, Jean-Guy
Red Sea floor origin; rare-earth evidence. bibliog Science 165:1357-60 S 26 '69

SCHIRMER, D. B.
Troop withdrawal: 1899. New Repub 161:19-20 S 27 '69

SCHISGAL, Murray
Jimmy Shine. Criticism
America 120:147-8 F 1 '69
New Repub 160:32-4 Ja 25 '69

SCHISTOSOMIASIS
Control in Egypt and the Sudan. H. Van Der Schalie. bibliog il Natur Hist 78:62-5 F '69
Host and parasite in Rhodesia. C. J. Shiff. bibliog il Natur Hist 78:65-7 F '69
Schistosomiasis. A. G. Melvin. il Hobbies 74: 113+ Je '69

SCHIZOPHRENIA
Is celiac disease a clue to the pathogenesis of schizophrenia? F. C. Dohan. bibliog Ment Hy 53:525-9 O '69
Making chronic schizophrenics. D. Kantor and V. A. Gelineau. Ment Hy 53:54-66 Ja '69
Postpartum psychiatric reactions: time of onset and sex ratio of newborns. F. T. Melges. bibliog il Science 166:1026-7 N 21 '69
Reticular stimulation and chlorpromazine: an animal model for schizophrenic overarousal. C. Kornetsky and M. Eliasson. bibliog il Science 165:1273-4 S 19 '69
Schizoid child and adult schizophrenia. N. N. Wagner and K. L. Stegeman. bibliog il Ment Hy 53:530-8 O '69
Sex ratios of newborns: associated with prepartum and postpartum schizophrenia. M. A. Taylor. bibliog il Science 164:723-4 My 9 '69; Correction. 165:380 Jl 25 '69

SCHIZOPHRENICS
New parents for schizophrenics. S. Shubin. il Sci Digest 66:68-73 Ag '69
Sweat in schizophrenic patients: identification of the odorous substance. K. Smith and others. bibliog il Science 166:398-9 O 17 '69

Rehabilitation

Remarkable Ronald Laing. B. Inglis. Vogue 154:132-3+ S 15 '69

SCHIZOPHYLLUM commune. See Basidiomycetes

SCHJELDAHL, Peter
Whippoorwill; New life; poems. Poetry 115: 36-7 O '69

about

Chronicle of younger poets. J. Atlas. Poetry 113:430 Mr '69

SCHLAMM, William S.
Impudent and the dead. Nat R 21:391-3 Ap 22 '69
Letter from Germany. Nat R 21:1061-2 O 21 '69

SCHLANGER, Jeff
Maija Grotell. Craft Horiz 29:14-23 N '69

SCHLANT, Ernestine
(tr) See Hildesheimer, W. Apartment in the attic; Slightly bigger acquisition

SCHLECH, Walter Frederick, 1915-
Requirements for defense; address, March 24, 1969. Vital Speeches 35:425-30 My 1 '69

SCHLECK, Robert W.
Ireland's clash of colors. America 121:134-6 S 6 '69

SCHLEGELMILCH, Rheinhold
Findings on R S china. V. Duncan. il Hobbies 74:98M-98P Mr '69

SCHLEISNER, Doris G.
Wildflowers for your garden. Home Gard 56: 32-40 S '69

SCHLEMAN, Helen B.
Women might have helped; address, June 11, 1969. Vital Speeches 35:663-8 Ag 15 '69

SCHLEMMER, Oskar
Music of the spheres, and cubes. K. von Maur. bibliog il Art N 68:62-6+ N '69

SCHLESINGER, Andrew, and Wise, Erich
In a community not at war the tactics and brutality of war are not condoned. N Y Times Mag p34 My 4 '69

SCHLESINGER, Arthur, 1917–
America and the world; a new fix? Vogue
153:184-5+ F 1 '69
If there must be intervention, it should
emerge from the community's collective
decision. N Y Times Mag p34-5 My 4 '69
Limits and excesses of presidential power;
excerpt from The crisis of confidence;
ideas, power and violence in America. Sat R
52:17-19+ My 3 '69
Movies. See issues of Vogue
Truman's speech and Noam Chomsky. Com-
mentary 48:4+ D '69
Vietnam and the end of the age of superpow-
ers. Harper 238:41-9 Mr '69
SCHLESINGER, Michael, and Yron, Ilana
Antigenic changes in lymph-node cells after
administration of antiserum to thymus
cells. bibliog Science 164:1412-13 Je 20 '69
SCHLIEREN apparatus
Ultrasonic waves made visible. M. S. Snitzer.
il Electr World 81:51 My '69
SCHLINK, Frederick John
Packaging and labeling; excerpts from ad-
dress, October 9, 1968. Consumer Bul 52:27-8
Je; 15-17 Jl '69
SCHLITZ brewing company
How to get ahead; leave the company; R.
Satchell. Bsns W p35 Jl 19 '69
SCHLITZER, Albert L.
[Book review] Commonweal 89:624 F 14 '69
SCHLOREDT, Bob
Where are they now? il pors Newsweek 75:7
Ja 5 '70
SCHLUETER, Frederick W.
How to anneal, harden and temper steel.
Pop Mech 132:178-81 D '69
SCHMID-SCHÖNBEIN, Holger, and Wells, Roe
Fluid drop-like transition of erythrocytes un-
der shear. bibliog Science 165:288-91 Jl 18 '69
SCHMIDT, Dennis E. and others
Acetylcholine: release from neural tissue and
identification by pyrolysis-gas chroma-
tography. bibliog Science 165:1370-1 S 26 '69
SCHMIDT, Ernest F.
Accounting to ACA members. por Camp Mag
41:5 My '69
Oasis for youth. por Camp Mag 41:4 S '69
SCHMIDT, Harvey
Fantastick composer and painter. G. P. Hunt.
il por Life 66:3 Mr 14 '69
SCHMIDT-NIELSEN, Bodil, and Schmidt-Niel-
sen, Knut
Camel, facts and fables. UNESCO Courier
22:70 Ag '69
SCHMIDT-NIELSEN, Knut. See Schmidt-Niel-
sen, B. jt. auth.
SCHMIDT label and lithograph company. See
Stecher-Traung-Schmidt corporation
SCHMIDTCHEN, Paul W.
Books. See issues of Hobbies
SCHMINKE, Clarence. See Maertens, N. jt.
auth.
SCHMITT, Hans A.
Two Germanies: a nation without a state.
Cur Hist 56:224-9+ Ap '69
SCHMITT, Harrison H.
NASA considers geologist for 1970 Apollo
15 crew. Aviation W 91:15 D 22 '69
SCHMOLLER, Hans
Production and design notes on The com-
plete pelican Shakespeare. Pub W 196:62+
O 6 '69
SCHMUCKLER, Joseph S. See Mogul, P. H. jt.
auth.
SCHNALL, Susan
Court-martial of Lt. Susan Schnall. S. Stre-
shinsky. por Redbook 134:78-9+ N '69
SCHNECK, Stephen
Le living. Ramp Mag 7:34-41 N 30 '68
SCHNEIDER, D.
Insect olfaction: deciphering system for
chemical messages. bibliog Science 163:1031-
7 Mr 7 '69
—and Seibt, Uta
Sex pheromone of the queen butterfly: elec-
troantennogram responses. bibliog Science
164:1173-4 Je 6 '69
SCHNEIDER, Gerald
Purple martinsville. Am For 75:36-7+ F '69
SCHNEIDER, Gerald E.
Two visual systems. bibliog Science 163:895-
902 F 28 '69
SCHNEIDER, I. R.
Satellite-like particle of tobacco ringspot
virus that resembles tobacco ringspot virus
bibliog Science 166:1627-9 D 26 '69
SCHNEIDER, Jason
Camera collector. por Mod Phot 33:83-5 O
5 O; 124+ N '69
SCHNEIDER, Lewis M.
Fallacy of free transportation. bibliog f Har-
vard Bsns R 47:83-7 Ja '69
SCHNEIDER, Martin
Air pollution; photographs. Life 66:38-50 F
7 '69

SCHNEIDER, Pierre
(ed) See Newman, B. Through the Louvre with
Barnett Newman
SCHNEIDER, R. Michael
Zoo's changing role. Parks & Rec 4:41-4+
S '69
SCHNEIER, Edward V.
Politics of tobacco. Nation 209:274-9 S 22 '69
SCHNEIRLA, Theodore Christian
T. C. Schneirla and animal behavior. E. To-
bach. il por Natur Hist 78:52-7 Ja '69
SCHNITTKER, John A.
Farmer in the till. Atlan 224:43-5 Ag '69; Ex-
cerpts. Cur 110:32-7 S '69
SCHOEBERLEIN, Marion
Look at snow; poem. Nat Parks 43:8 Ja '69
SCHOEFFLER, Oscar E.
Good-bye and hello to Oscar E. Schoeffler.
A. Gingrich. Esquire 71:6 Mr '69
SCHOEN, Donald R.
Managing technological innovation. bibliog f
Harvard Bsns R 47:156-8+ My '69
SCHOEN, Ivan L.
Contact with the stone age; with biographi-
cal sketch. por Natur Hist 78:6, 10-18+ Ja
'69
SCHOENBERG, Arnold. See Schönberg, A.
SCHOENBERG, Sandra P. See Rowe, L. A. jt.
auth.
SCHOENBERGER, Dale T.
Black man in the American West. bibliog
Negro Hist Bul 32:7-11 Mr '69
SCHOENENBERGER, Marius
And now the Jesuits. Time 93:44 My 2 '69
SCHOENEWOLF, Gerald
Poof! texts. Esquire 72:209 D '69
SCHOENFELD, Eugene
Ask Dr Hip. il por Newsweek 73:118-19 My 19
'69
Doctor HIP. por Time 93:49 Mr 7 '69
SCHOENFIELD, Berni
Dad, can I have the boat tonight? il Motor B
123:72-3 Je '69
SCHOLARS
   See also
College professors and instructors
Intellectuals
SCHOLARSHIP. See Learning and scholarship
SCHOLARSHIP, education and defense fund for
racial equality
Power to the people. B. B. Stretch. Sat R
52:79 Je 21 '69
SCHOLARSHIPS and fellowships
Break for black scholars with partial list of
available scholarships. il Ebony 24:45-6+
Mr '69
Can the able student really win a scholarship?
T. J. Denny and J. B. Buscher. Ed Digest
34:52-3 Ja '69
Doctoral fellowships for black students; Ford
foundation program. Sch & Soc 97:81+ F '69
Educational values of academic exchange; re-
port by the Board of foreign scholarships.
Sch & Soc 97:295 Sum '69
Fellowships in practical politics; attracting
minority college graduates to careers in
government and politics. Sch & Soc 97:
133+ Mr '69
Hilda Maehling fellowships; in world affairs.
Todays Ed 58:29 D '69
History lessons on wheels; high school es-
sayists winning AKA sorority travel schol-
arship. il Ebony 24:106-8+ S '69
Making friends at the top; Eisenhower fel-
lowships. il Bsns W p 138+ My 24 '69
Yale elects a wise janitor. il Life 67:99-100
D 5 '69
   See also
Student aid
SCHOLASTIC ability. See Ability
SCHOLASTIC achievements. See Student
achievements
SCHOLASTIC aptitude test. See College en-
trance examination board—Scholastic apti-
tude test
SCHOLASTIC aptitude tests. See Aptitude
tests
SCHOLASTIC magazines, incorporated
Kenneth M. Gould 1895-1969. Sr Schol 94:24
Mr 28 '69
Presenting the 1969 Scholastic awards. il Sr
Schol 94:16-24 My 9 '69
ST's 1969 travel story contest. il Sr Schol 94:
Schol teach 9-13+ Ap 25 '69
Scholastic magazines makes public stock of-
fering. Pub W 195:74-5 Ja 27 '69
Scholastic's editor emeritus dies; K. M.
Gould. Sr Schol 94:Schol Teach 6 Ap 11 '69
View of what's new at Scholastic. Sr Schol
94:Schol Teach 8 F 28 '69
SCHOLER, E. A. See Glascock, M. M. jt. auth.
SCHOLES, Robert
Portrait of artist as escape-goat. Sat R 52:32-
4 My 10 '69

SCHOLES, William A.
Atom Down Under. Sci N 96:168 Ag 30 '69
Boosting the tuna catch. Sci N 96:338 O 11 '69
Nuclear perseverance. Sci N 96:408-9 N 1 '69

SCHOLL, David W. and others
Florida submergence curve revised: its relation to coastal sedimentation rates. bibliog Science 163:562-4 F 7 '69

SCHOLL, John
Wooden delights. D. G. Lowe. il por Am Heritage 20:18-23 D '68

SCHOLTE, Bob
Levi-Strauss' unfinished symphony; the analysis of myth. Natur Hist 78:24-6+ F '69

SCHOMBURG collection of Negro literature and history. See New York public library—135th Street branch

SCHÖNBEIN, Holger Schmid-. See Schmid-Schönbein, H.

SCHÖNBERG, Arnold
Arnold Schönberg, by E. Wellesz. Review
Am Rec G 35:846-7 My '69. D. Newlin
Current chronicle. P. J. Smith. il Mus Q 55: 102-11 Ja '69
Four recordings: Schoenberg only. A. Cohn. por Am Rec G 35:1034-7 Jl '69
Moses and Aaron. Criticism
Nation 209:125 Ag 11 '69
Records:
Von heute auf morgen; Erwartung, and Die glückliche hand. Opera N 33:34 Ap 12 '69

SCHONBERG, Harold C.
His 200th anniversary celebration is starting the Beethoven revolution; excerpts from Lives of the great composers. N Y Times Mag p32-3+ O 19 '69
How cultural is the cultural explosion? McCalls 96:70+ Jl '69
On the 100th anniversary of his death, Berlioz still sounds new. N Y Times Mag p24-5+ Mr 9 '69

SCHONCHIN wilderness (proposed) See Wilderness areas—California

SCHOOL administration. See School management and organization

SCHOOL administrators. See School superintendents and principals

SCHOOL and social and economic problems
Critical issues in education. Sch & Soc 97: 297-8 Sum '69
How to make literature come alive; NCTE panel on Literature programs for inner city schools. Sr School 93:Schol Teach 19+ Ja 10 '69
Key word is relevance; relating teaching to the lives of the learners. W. Van Til. il Todays Ed 58:14-17 Ja '69
Metropolitanism and the schools. R. J. Havighurst. Ed Digest 34:3-6 Ap '69
Middle class values, lower class rights. P. I. Freedman. bibliog Clear House 43:469-70 Ap '69
Mobile students. J. M. Snyder. Todays Ed 58: 26 Ap '69
NCSS focus: tell it like it is. il Sr School 93: Schol Teach 4 Ja 10 '69
Refresher course; new vistas for the methods prof. R. Whitworth. Clear House 43:463-8 Ap '69
School management and social responsibility. W. K. Summers. bibliog Clear House 44: 3-8 S '69
Social context and vocational education. R. A. Gibboney. bibliog f Sch & Soc 97:28-31 Ja '69
Ubiquitous class-value conflict in education. H. R. Smith. bibliog f Sch & Soc 97:92-4 F '69
See also
Children of migrant laborers—Education
School and the community
Socially handicapped children—Education

SCHOOL and society (periodical)
Status of School & society, 1968-69. W. W. Brickman. Sch & Soc 97:454 N '69

SCHOOL and the community
Case for parent involvement. E. K. Wolf. il Parents Mag 44:40-1+ F '69
City-school liaison brings mutual benefits; Fort Worth, Tex. Am City 84:54 Ja '69
Enfield's excited about living history; high school, Thompsonville, Conn. F. S. Gross. il Sr School 94:Schol Teach 13-14 My 9 '69
Fiery vehemence of youth; with study-discussion program, by C. Smallenburg and H. Smallenburg. P. Marin. bibliog PTA Mag 63:15-17, 35 Je '69
Getting through to the establishment; with study-discussion program, by E. Harris and D. Harris. M. Essex. bibliog il PTA Mag 64:2-5+, 35-6 N '69
Salute to parents from teachers everywhere: if the shoe fits. bibliog il Todays Ed 58:41-8 S '69

School budget; achieving public support for education. R. E. Jennings and M. M. Milstein. Clear House 43:458-62 Ap '69
Sell your public school art program at public meetings. R. J. Saunders. Sch Arts 68:31 F '69
World beyond the classroom. G. Bauer. Clear House 43:371-2 F '69
See also
Colleges and universities—Public relations
School buildings as social centers
School management and organization—Parent participation

SCHOOL and the home
Case for parent involvement. E. K. Wolf. il Parents Mag 44:40-1+ F '69
City of God; adaptation of address, 1969. R. Gould. il PTA Mag 64:2-5 O '69
Disturbed parents: a challenge to the school. J. P. Cangemi. Ed Digest 35:22-4 D '69
Grievances: the teachers speak; with study-discussion program, by E. Harris and D. Harris. bibliog il PTA Mag 63:2-5, 35-6 Ja '69
Increasing responsibilities of the schools. M. Ack. Sci Digest 65:61-3 Mr '69
Parent participation in education. W. D. Boutwell. PTA Mag 63:12-14 F '69
Parent-student panels. S. E. Pollock. Todays Ed 58:54 D '69
Parental resistance to modular scheduling. R. A. Gorton. Clear House 43:392-5 Mr '69
Parents' night at school. L. Hnatt. il Parents Mag 44:58-9+ S '69
Salute to parents from teachers everywhere: if the shoe fits. bibliog il Todays Ed 58:41-8 S '69
See also
Home study
Parents and teachers associations
School children

SCHOOL architecture. See School buildings

SCHOOL art exhibits. See Childrens art—Exhibitions

SCHOOL athletics
Interscholastic sports; misdirected? misguided? misnomer? J. J. Pietrofesa and A. Rosen; reply. J. S. Kennedy. Clear House 43:471-3 Ap '69
Look-in at the athletic program; with study-discussion program. by E. Harris and D. Harris. J. M. Lampe. bibliog il PTA Mag 64:6-8, 35 O '69
Physical education: a viable high school program. J. E. Doohan. Clear House 44:232-5 D '69
Should girls play on boys' teams? il Good H 169:215 O '69
See also
Football

SCHOOL attendance
Impact of changing school enrollment. il U S News 66:54-5 Je 9 '69
See also
Compulsory education
Dropouts

SCHOOL boards
Non-involved public. Sch & Soc 97:406 N '69
School board, 1980. W. D. Southworth. Clear House 44:131-3 N '69
School boards and the Supreme court. America 120:295 Mr 15 '69
Why more school boards are landing in court, and losing. C. A. Hollister. Ed Digest 35: 16-19 O '69
Why school board meetings go to pot. H. Spears. Ed Digest 34:26-7 F '69
See also
New York (city)—Education. Board of
Teachers and school boards

SCHOOL books. See Textbooks

SCHOOL boycotts
Memphis blues. Newsweek 74:38-9 N 24 '69

SCHOOL buildings
Building schools at no cost; leasing of air rights above new public schools. il Bsns W p 168+ Ap 26 '69
Building types study: Miami's innovative schools. il Arch Rec 146:153-68 O '69
Classrooms are for students. R. Sommer. il Am Ed 5:18-21 Je '69
Down a hillside in Naples; Swiss school. il Arch Forum 130:70-5 Mr '69
Last look at the little red schoolhouse; Callaboose, Ky. B. Ryan, jr. il Parents Mag 44:54-6 F '69
New projects by Victor Lundy. il Arch Forum 131:78-83 N '69
New schools at no cost. H. B. Gores. il Parents Mag 44:58-9+ O '69
Open space school. R. F. Eberle. bibliog Clear House 44:23-8 S '69
School building follows enrollment trends. il Arch Rec 145:82 My '69

SCHOOL buildings—*Continued*
Site and program generate a new school shape. il Arch Rec 145:135-40 My '69
Vigorous plan for an institution; Bronx state school. il Arch Rec 145:126-32 F '69
See also
Trade schools

Community use

See School buildings as social centers

Designs and plans

Schools planned for continuity and change. il Arch Rec 145:135-42 Mr '69
Some thoughts on starting your own office. E. R. Flansburgh. il Arch Rec 145:149-60 Ap '69

Fires and fire protection

Is your child's school safe from fire? D. Wharton. Read Digest 94:117-20 Je '69
Tips for your home and family. Todays Health 47:77-8 S '69

Heating and ventilation

Student body turns it on; heat reclaim system project: Johnstown campus of Pittsburgh university. B. F. Peters. il Am Ed 5:20-1 Ap '69

SCHOOL buildings, Remodeled
Facelifting for old schools. K. Taylor and R. Hull. il Library J 94:4218-24 N 15 '69
SCHOOL buildings as social centers
Physical fitness: a school-community responsibility. J. A. Lovell. Parents Mag 44:34 My '69
SCHOOL bus transportation. See School children—Transportation
SCHOOL centers. See School buildings as social centers
SCHOOL children
Economics for elementary school pupils. R. B. McKenzie. Ed Digest 35:44-7 S '69
Influence of the emotionally disturbed teacher on schoolchildren. N. S. Brandes. Ment Hy 53:606-10 O '69
Many-pressured pupil; with study-discussion program, by E. Harris and D. Harris D. Graves. bibliog il PTA Mag 63:27-9 35-6 F '69
See also
Children, Gifted
Home study
Intelligence tests
Problem children
School lunches
Teachers and students

Adjustment

Art of listening to children; with group-discussion program. Y. Postelle. il Parents Mag 44:58-9+, 76 Ap '69
Dealing with disruptive pupils; with study-discussion program, by E. Harris and D. Harris. E. Landy. bibliog il PTA Mag 63:19-21, 36-7 Mr '69
Effect of school failure. W. E. Glasser. Ed Digest 35:13-17 D '69
See also
High school students—Adjustment
Problem children

Grading and promotion

See Grading and marking (students)

Health and hygiene

School mental health services offered without invitation. E. A. Horn and others. bibliog Ment Hy 53:620-4 O '69

Medical inspection

See Public schools—Health service

Migration

See Children of migrant laborers

Nutrition

See Children—Nutrition

Out-of-school activities

Tune up for summer. P. Pine. il Am Ed 5:16-20 Mr '69

Reading

See Childrens reading

Transportation

Mr Ed: the talking bus; Gunnison, Colo. J. R. Raine. il Sr Schol 94:Schol Teach 13 Ja 17 '69
Mix schools by busing? Where voters said no. U S News 66:70 Ap 28 '69
Mom's in the driver's seat. J. S. Peters. il Parents Mag 44:50+ Je '69
Move to ban busing of pupils; New York state legislature bill. U S News 66:12 Ap 7 '69

New debate over busing students. U S News 67:18 S 29 '69
School bussing and parental anxiety; concerning Negro ghetto children. Sch & Soc 97:5-6 Ja '69
School busing: are we hurting the people we want to help? excerpts from address, July 31, 1969. E. Green. U S News 67:72-3 Ag 18 '69
What has four wheels and giggles? A. Van Dine. il Parents Mag 44:68-9 S '69
Why school busing is in trouble. il U S News 67:42-4 O 13 '69
SCHOOL children and smoking. See Smoking and youth
SCHOOL construction. See School buildings
SCHOOL counselors. See Student counselors
SCHOOL day
See also
Double shifts (public schools)
SCHOOL discipline
Effect of school failure. W. E. Glasser. Ed Digest 35:13-17 D '69
Oldfields incident; Cockerham sisters defy school rules. il Newsweek 73:65 Je 16 '69
See also
Classroom management
College discipline
SCHOOL drama. See College and school drama
SCHOOL employees
See also
School secretaries
SCHOOL enrollment. See School attendance
SCHOOL exhibits
See also
Childrens art—Exhibitions
SCHOOL finance
Financing urban schools: a continuing crisis. T. P. Wilbur. bibliog f Sch & Soc 97:286-8 Sum '69
Getting the point; increase in school taxes passed, Youngstown, Ohio. il Newsweek 73:65 My 19 '69
Growing protest against school costs. il U S News 67:36-7 O 20 '69
Inequities of school finance. A. K. Campbell. Ed Digest 34:10-13 Ap '69
New financing tool. E. Edelman. il Am Ed 5:20 D '69
Property taxes inadequate, new school financing needed; summary of address, November 1968. W. J. Cohen. Sr Schol 93:Schol Teach 5 Ja 10 '69
Public schools feel the money pinch. W. R. Grant. Commonweal 90:167+ Ap 25 '69
School budget: achieving public support for education. R. E. Jennings and M. M. Milstein. Clear House 43:458-62 Ap '69
Swinging with mini-projects; Bloomington, Minn. public school system. E. Cain and A. St Pierre. il Am Ed 5:5-8 D '69
Taxes are PTA business. C. Ryan. PTA Mag 63:25 Ap '69
Taxpayer revolt keeps on rolling. U S News 66:81 My 19 '69
Why our schools are failing. B. Bard. il Parents Mag 44:53-5+ S '69
Why some public schools are closing. il Good H 169:210-11 O '69
See also
Church schools—Finance
Colleges and universities—Finance
Education and state
Federal aid to education
SCHOOL gardens
At Santa Cruz these college students go out for gardening. il Sunset 142:96-9 Mr '69
SCHOOL grading and promotion. See Grading and marking (students)
SCHOOL grounds
See also
Campus planning
SCHOOL health service. See Public schools—Health service
SCHOOL houses. See School buildings
SCHOOL hygiene
See also
Public schools—Health service
School nurses
SCHOOL inspection. See School supervision and supervisors
SCHOOL journalism. See College and school journalism
SCHOOL laws and legislation
Why more school boards are landing in court. and losing. C. A. Hollister. Ed Digest 35:16-19 O '69
See also
Colleges and universities—Laws and legislation
Teachers—Contracts

SCHOOL laws and legislation—*Continued*

New York (state)

Choking off community schools; bill to establish a community school system for New York city. J. Featherstone. New Republ 161:16-18 Jl 19 '69

United States

NDEA's decade of accomplishment. Sch & Soc 97:294-5 Sum '69

With education in Washington. See issues of Education digest
See also
Compulsory education
Federal aid to education

SCHOOL leaving. See Dropouts

SCHOOL legislation. See School laws and legislation

SCHOOL librarians

New breed; letter to the editor. A. E. Leach. Library J 94:241-2 Ja 15 '69

What kind of librarian? E. Roe. Library J 94: 1715-18+ Ap 15 '69
See also
American association of school librarians

Anecdotes, facetiae, satire, etc.

Hey, miss! letter to the editor. E. Smith. ALA Bul 63:429 Ap '69

Education

Education of the media specialist; symposium, ed. by E. Geller. bibliog il Library J 94:1719-37 Ap 15 '69

Education in service

In-service: team approach. I. Kelly. Library J 94:1733-4 Ap '69

Supply and demand

Criteria of excellence: the school library manpower project identifies outstanding school library centers. R. N. Case. ALA Bul 63:247-8 F '69

School manpower report. ALA Bul 63:1210-11 O '69

SCHOOL librarians institutes. See Library institutes and workshops

SCHOOL libraries

Grass roots and apple pie: a very ordinary American school library; a WLB special report. il Wilson Lib Bul 43:760-3 Ap '69

Is anyone listening? Significant research studies for practicing librarians. M. V. Gaver. bibliog il Wilson Lib Bul 43:764-72 Ap '69

Media center design; symposium. bibliog il Library J 94:4201-28 N 15 '69

Middle Eastern library workshop: report from Beirut. I. V. Hathorn. il Wilson Lib Bul 43: 1002-7 Je '69

Observations from abroad: the American scene. E. Roe. il Library J 94:835-9, 1291-3, 1715-18+ F 15, Mr 15, Ap 15 '69

School libraries and international development: ed. by J. E. Lowrie. ALA Bul 63: 603-9, 977-9, 1108-10, 1284-9, 1586-99 My, Jl, S-O, D '69

School library services discussed in New York state; with editorial comment. Library J 94:3115, 3118+ S 15 '69

School library workshop in Nigeria. E. D. Sinnette. il Wilson Lib Bul 43:997-1001 Je '69

Students campaign to save school libraries; Mamaroneck, N.Y. Library J 94:4568 D 15 '69
See also
Childrens literature
Knapp school libraries project
Libraries and schools
School librarians

Acquisitions

Use of the ALA name: review of lease-purchase book plans. ALA Bul 63:386-7 Mr '69

Audio-visual materials

See School libraries and audio-visual materials

Book selection

PA. state education officials sued on ESEA-II administration. Library J 94:2034+ My 15 '69; Discussion. 94:3110+, 3769-70 S 15. O 15 '69

Censorship

Libraries temporarily purged: San Francisco textbook order. Library J 94:3779-80 O 15 '69

School library pot book stirs investigation; Morro Bay high, Calif; discussion. Library J 93:3901; 94:241 O 15 '68, Ja 15 '69

Charging systems

Transaction number charging tried by school libraries Library J 94:827-8 F 15 '69

Federal aid

Books are not expendable; misappropriations of educational funds. H. Bowser. Sat R 52: 22 Je 7 '69

ED funds up for Senate vote; Nixon frowns on House victory; with editorial comment. Library J 94:3773, 3775+ O 15 '69

Education without school libraries? J. B. Sheerin. Cath World 209:146-7 Jl '69

Educational trends and media programs in school libraries; symposium. bibliog il ALA Bul 63:221-72 F '69

ESEA anniversary. G. Krettek and E. D. Cooke. Wilson Lib Bul 43:685 Mr '69

ESEA hearings. G. Krettek and E. D. Cooke. ALA Bul 63:322 Mr '69

ESEA hearings completed by House. G. Krettek and E. D. Cooke. Wilson Lib Bul 43: 809 Ap '69

Fight for education-library budget reaching last phase; House wins decisive victory over Nixon. Library J 94:3117-18 S 15 '69

HEW appropriations hearings underway. G. Krettek and E. D. Cooke. ALA Bul 63:452 Ap '69

HEW Secretary Finch addresses AASL at EB awards luncheon; excerpts, January 30, 1969. R. H. Finch. Library J 94:1271 Mr 15 '69; Same. ALA Bul 63:346-7 Mr '69

1968 ESEA-11 breakdown given in USOE report. Library J 94:4192 N 15 '69

1970 education budget slashed by outgoing administration. Library J 94:1272 Mr 15 '69

Nixon's 1970 federal budget wipes out ESEA Title II, LSCA Title II. Library J 94:2033 My 15 '69

Schools without libraries. America 120:683 Je 14 '69

Vote due about Christmas for federal education programs. Library J 94:4188+ N 15 '69

Paperback books

Notes of a scab librarian: learning opportunities during the New York city teachers strike. S. Ginsburg. bibliog il Library J 94:1300-2 Mr 15 '69; Discussion. 94:2028, 3107-8, 4559 My 15, S 15, D 15 '69

Paper filmstrip: photo books and paperbacks. H. F. Rogers. Library J 94:846-7 F 15 '69

Stop making excuses and start tnat class library! Germantown high school, Philadelphia. D. Weissberger. Sr Schol 94:Schol Teach 28 Ja 31 '69

Projects

Goldfish checkout, noisy kids in Title 1 library profiles. Library J 94:1708+ Ap 15 '69

Standards

Crossroads 1970; address, June, 1969. J. Rowell. il Library J 94:4575-7 D 15 '69

Education of the media specialist; symposium, ed. by E. Geller. bibliog il Library J 94:1719-37 Ap 15 '69

Joint media standards published: Standards for school media programs. Wilson Lib Bul 43:825 My '69

New standards: school media programs. Library J 94:3792-3 O 15 '69

Simulation standards, and the seventies. R. Lavin. il Library J 94:4216-17 N 15 '69

Standards and space. il Library J 94:4213 N 15 '69

Student assistants

What do they do besides check books in and out? J. J. Delaney. il Wilson Lib Bul 43: 773-5 Ap '69

SCHOOL libraries and audio-visual materials

Big beyond promise; address. July 1968. R. L. Darling; reply. J. French. Library J 94: 817 F 15 '69

Education of the media specialist; symposium, ed. by E. Geller. bibliog il Library J 94:1719-37 Ap 15 '69

Educational trends and media programs in school libraries; symposium bibliog il ALA Bul 63:221-72 F '69

Equipment. See second issue of each month of Library journal

Library study carrel: bilingual program with tutoring and self-pacing; Coalinga junior high school, Calif. R. E. Philips. il Library J 94:840-2 F 15 '69

SCHOOL libraries and social and economic problems. See Libraries and social and economic problems

SCHOOL library architecture. See Library architecture

SCHRAGE, Chuck
  With the power squadrons. See issues of
    Yachting
SCHRANZ, Karl
  Der alte of the Alps. il Newsweek 73:58 F 3 '69
  Old rubber legs is in charge. B. Ottum. il
    Sports Illus 30:14-15 Ja 27 '69
SCHREINER, Louis
  Cavalcade of mobile fun. Parks & Rec 4:50-1
    My '69
SCHREYVOGEL, Charles
  Authors & editors. B. A. Bannon. por Pub
    W 196:7-8 D 15 '69
SCHROEDER, Dorothy
  Minerals make the difference. Org Gard &
    Farm 16:94-7 Ap '69
SCHROLL, Catherine V. See MacLellan, E. jt.
  auth.
SCHROTH, Raymond A.
  Between the lines. See occasional issues of
    America
  Mailer and his gods. Commonweal 90:226-9
    My 9 '69
SCHROTH, Thomas Nolan
  Battle of Capitol hill. il por Newsweek 73:
    100 Ap 14 '69
SCHRUT, Albert
  What play reveals about your child. Parents
    Mag 44:54-5+ Ag '69
SCHUBART, Henry, jr. See Bailey, J. M. jr.
  jt. auth.
SCHUBERT, Franz Peter
  Bernstein, extraordinary vital Mendelssohn,
    marvelous Schubert. M. N. Kanny. Am Rec
    G 36:194 N '69
  Fresh voice for Schubert. P. G. Davis. Hi Fi
    19:94 Jl '69
  Schubert among friends. S. Fleming. Hi Fi
    19:102 Je '69
  Tenor who will bear watching. P. L. Miller.
    Am Rec G 35:796+ My '69
SCHUBERT, P. See Lux, H. D. jt. auth.
SCHUBERTH, Christopher J.
  How firm a foundation; with biographical
    sketch. por Natur Hist 78:6, 56-64 Ap '69
SCHUELLER, Steven C.
  Half a war half glimpsed. Nat R 21:290-1 Mr
    25 '69
SCHUESSLER, Raymond
  Make friends with a tree. Am For 75:38+
    Je '69
SCHUG, Wendy
  Rain; poem. Horn Bk 45:448 Ag '69
SCHULBERG, Budd
  Gentle genius at large in jungletown. Life
    66:6 F 28 '69
  Who killed Cock Robin? A farewell to Judy.
    Life 67:26-8 Jl 11 '69
SCHULDER, Peggy
  Lady analyst takes charge. por Bsns W
    p 100+ Mr 8 '69
SCHULER, Stanley
  Cleaning with sound. Am Home 72:62+ O '69
  1-2-3 guide to buying laundry appliances.
    Am Home 72:60+ N '69
SCHULETER, Fred W.
  How to sharpen twist drills like a pro. Pop
    Mech 132:174-6 Jl '69
SCHULMAN, Grace
  Examination; remembrance of words lost;
    poem. Poetry 113:319-21 F '69
SCHULMAN, J. D. and others
  Cystine: compartmentalization within lyso-
    somes in cystinotic leukocytes. bibliog Sci-
    ence 166:1152-4 N 28 '69
SCHULPS, John
  Three California craftsmen. M. Angelino. il
    por Am Artist 33:48-50+ S '69
SCHULTE, Elaine L.
  How children learn the joys of giving. Pa-
    rents Mag 44:50+ D '69
SCHULTE-HILLEN, Karl Hermann
  Avenging father; battle for justice for Ger-
    many's 3,000 thalidomide children. A. Levy.
    il pors Good H 168:50+ Ap '69
SCHULTES, Richard Evans
  Hallucinogens of plant origin. bibliog Science
    163:245-54 Ja 17 '69
SCHULTHESS, Emil
  Emil Schulthess: chronicler of continents. il
    Mod Phot 33:62-7 Ap '69
SCHULTZ, Clyde
  Mixing sound for fun. Radio-Electr 41:59-60
    Ja '70
SCHULTZ, Dutch. See Flegenheimer, A.
SCHULTZ, George P.
  Changes coming in labor laws? U S News 66:
    95 Mr 17 '69
SCHULTZ, Gwen M.
  Those irresistible rocks. Pop Gard 20:38-41+
    Spr '69
SCHULTZ, Morton J.
  Care and feeding of snow throwers. Pop Mech
    132:120-3+ D '69

Cooling. Motor B 124:128-9 S '69
Help is a helicopter. Todays Health 47:20-
  3+ Ap '69
How to choose one of today's wonder paints.
  Pop Mech 131:196-8+ Ap '69
How to get replacement parts for your an-
  cient mariner. Motor B 124:66-7 N '69
How to read an oil can. Pop Mech 132:134-
  7+ N '69
RAP: an old naval shell with a new kick. Pop
  Mech 130:84-7 D '68
Saturday mechanic. See issues of Popular
  mechanics
SCHULTZE, Charles Louis
  Budgeting national priorities; excerpts from
    Agenda for the Nation. Cur 103:18-19 Ja '69

                    about
  Budget: a five-year look. por U S News 66:88
    Je 16 '69
SCHULZ, Charles M.
  But a comic strip has to grow. Sat R 52:73-4
    Ap 12 '69

                    about
  Happiness is a comic strip. J. Tebbel. il por
    Sat R 52:72-3+ Ap 12 '69
  You're an adman's dream, Charlie Brown. il
    por Bsns W p44-6 D 20 '69
SCHULZ, John W.
  Technicians's perspective. See issues of Forbes
SCHULZ, R. J. and others
  Xenon: effect on radiation sensitivity of HeLa
    cells. bibliog Science 163:571-2 F 7 '69
SCHULZ, William
  Intelligence report on today's new revolu-
    tionaries. Read Digest 95:121-6 O '69
  Truck that fled Cuba. Read Digest 95:98-
    103 Jl '69
SCHUMAN, Howard
  Sociological racism. por Trans-Action 7:44-8
    D '69
SCHUMAN, Patricia
  Social responsibility: a progress report.
    por Library J 94:1950-2 My 15 '69
SCHUMANN, Maurice
  Touch of independence. por Newsweek 74:29
    Jl 7 '69
SCHUMANN, Robert Alexander
  Claudio Arrau's Schumann. R. Kammerer and
    L. Richmond. il por Am Rec G 36:62-3 S
    '69
SCHUMPETER, Joseph Alois
  Memories. P. A. Samuelson. Newsweek 73:83
    Je 2 '69
SCHURMANN, Franz
  Ho Chi Minh: a eulogy. Ramp Mag 8:52+
    N '69
  NLF asks the American left: where are
    you? Ramp Mag 8:14+ Ag '69
SCHURR, George M.
  Whither higher education? A look at the state
    college. Chr Cent 86:373-7 Mr 19 '69
SCHUSTER, Charles R. See Goldberg, S. R. jt.
  auth.
SCHUSTER, Harvey
  Running up $5,000 to millions in stocks. por
    U S News 67:59 D 15 '69
SCHUTJER, Clifford D.
  Five editorials. Chr Cent 86:449-50 Ap 2 '69
SCHUYLER, Keith C.
  Call of spring. por Outdoor Life 143:84-7+
    Ap '69
SCHUYLER, William Earl, 1914-
  Foe of patent reform displaces the reformer.
    il por Bsns W p 167-8 My 10 '69
SCHWAB, Joseph J.
  Reform or revolution? A. Koch. Am Scholar
    38:688+ Aut '69
SCHWALBERG, Carol
  How to put your best foot forward. Writer
    82:25-6+ Ag '69
  You meet such interesting people. U S Cam-
    era 32:64-5+ Ja '69
SCHWARTZ, Alvin
  Exciting cities, a Redbook vacation guide
    to sight-seeing with children; excerpts from
    America's exciting cities. Redbook 132:37-44
    Ap '69
SCHWARTZ, Charles
  Berkeley: manipulators of science, winners
    and losers. Bul Atom Sci 25:21-2+ My '69
SCHWARTZ, Daniel
  Artist and his fallen angels; paintings. For-
    tune 79:88-91 Ja '69
SCHWARTZ, David. See Elias, H. jt. auth.
SCHWARTZ, Drew
  Alcohol dehydrogenase in maize: genetic basis
    for multiple isozymes. bibliog Science 164:
    585-6 My 2 '69
—and Laughner, W. J.
  Molecular basis for heterosis. bibliog Sci-
    ence 166:626-7 O 31 '69

SCHWARTZ, E. Neena
(ed) Books to come. Library J 94:3857-96 O
15 '69
SCHWARTZ, Elizabeth
Slow readers can enjoy oral reading. Ed Di-
gest 34:36-7 Ja '69
SCHWARTZ, Gwen Gibson, and Wyden, Bar-
bara
Jewish wife; excerpts. Ladies Home J 86:
90-1+ O '69
Jewish wife vs Jewish mother-in-law; ex-
cerpts from The Jewish wife. Ladies Home
J 86:106-7+ N '69
SCHWARTZ, H. N.
Quark hunt still fruitless. Sci N 95:538 My 3
'69
SCHWARTZ, Howard
Low-key confabs. Sci N 95:198 F 22 '69
SCHWARTZ, Jo
(ed) See Seeger, P. Woody Guthrie, song-
writer
SCHWARTZ, Jonathan
Letter to the resistance; poem. Nation 209:
614 D 1 '69
SCHWARTZ, Karen
On campus: Israeli students. Mlle 69:68 S '69
SCHWARTZ, Marvin D.
Living with antiques. Antiques 96:376-81 S
'69
SCHWARTZ, Marvin W.
Puerto Rico is still a magic island. il Travel
& Camera 32:64-9 D '69
SCHWARTZ, Robert
Robert Schwartz's solar inventions; La Mama
E.T.C. T. Borek. Dance Mag 43:76+ Ag '69
SCHWARTZ, Sheila
Idea of the hero. Engl J 58:82-6 Ja '69
SCHWARTZ, Sorell L. and Borzelleca, J. F.
Adrenergic blood pressure responses in the
shark. bibliog Science 163:395-7 Ja 24 '69
SCHWARTZ, Susan
Can your little boy come out to play? Parents
Mag 44:42-3+ F '69
SCHWARTZLOSE, Richard A. and Isaacs, J. D.
Transient circulation event near the deep
ocean floor. bibliog Science 165:889-91 Ag
29 '69
SCHWARZ, Arturo
Duchamp's Young man and girl in spring;
excerpt from The complete works of Marcel
Duchamp. bibliog Am Imago 25:296-308 Wint
'68
SCHWARZ, Boris
Szeryng, Ricci, and Bach. Sat R 52:53+ My
31 '69
SCHWARZ, F.A.O. (toy store). See New York
(city)—Stores
SCHWARZ, Guenter, and others
Computers in physics instruction. bibliog
pors Phys Today 22:41-9 S '69
SCHWARZMAN, Stephen
World of dance; gate crasher, impresario. W.
Terry. Sat R 52:42 Mr 29 '69
SCHWARZWALD. See Black forest
SCHWEICKART, Russell L.
In Paris a successful link-up of spacemen,
fueled by vodka. M. Mok. il por Life 66:30-
1 Je 13 '69
See also
Space flight—Manned flights—McDivitt-Scott-
Schweickart flight. 1969
SCHWEIGHAUSER, Charles A.
Garbage explosion. Nation 209:282-4 S 22 '69
SCHWEIK (literary character) See Characters
in literature
SCHWEITZER, Albert
Lambaréné revisited. N. Cousins. il Sat R
52:28-32 O 4 '69
SCHWEITZER, Gertrude
Miss Elizabeth Landon, M.D; story. Good H
168:84-7 My '69
SCHWEITZER, Rhena Eckert
Lambaréné revisited. N. Cousins. il Sat R
52:31-2 O 4 '69
SCHWEIZER, C. J. and Ries, S. K.
Protein content of seed: increase improves
growth and yield. bibliog Science 165:73-5
Jl 4 '69
SCHWENGEL, Fred
Excerpt from remarks. January 3, 1969. Cong
Digest 48:244+ O '69
SCHWENKE, Karl
Loneing it is the only way. Field & S 74:
46-7+ Jl '69
SCHWEZOFF, Igor
Around the world with Igor Schwezoff. il
pors Dance Mag 43:64-7 Je '69
SCHWICK. H. Gerhard See Pensky. J. jt auth.
SCHWINGER, Julian
Magnetic model of matter. bibliog Science
165:757-61 Ag 22 '69
SCHWITTERS, Kurt
KS & KS. R. Haas; W. Hopps. il Wilson Lib
Bul 44:528 Ja '70

SCIENCE
Natural sciences. See occasional issues of
Science news
New Brahmins: scientific life in America, by
S. Klaw. Review
Bul Atom Sci 25:35-6 Mr '69. J. Wilson
Physical sciences. See issues of Science news
Science and the future: American and Brit-
ish associations meet. M. Roche. Science
165:619-20 Ag 8 '69
Simplicity as a scientific concept: does
nature keep her accounts on a thumbnail?
M. Gardner. il Sci Am 221:118-21 Ag '69
See also
Communication in science
Inventions
Natural theology
Religion and science
Technology
Television in science
also headings beginning Scientific

Authorship
See Technical writing

Bibliography
Book reviews. See issues of Science
Book reviews. See issues of Space world
Books. See issues of Physics today
Books reviewed in Science; May 10, 1968 to
May 2, 1969. Science 164:728+ My 9 '69
Books to come; ed. by J. Donathan and J.
Fletcher. Library J 94:4031-52 N 1 '69
Books to come; ed. by J. Putnam (cont)
Library J 94:1025-55, 2647-66 Mr 1, Jl '69
Library at large. See issues of Chemistry
Reviews. See issues of Environment
Science, technology; major scientific and
technical works for laymen and scholars
to appear November-March. il Pub W 196:
38-52 N 17 '69
Science, technology, some leading April-July
books. il Pub W 195:36-56 Ap 14 '69
Sci-tech books '68; one hundred outstand-
ing titles for general library collections;
comp. by D. F. Pfoutz. il Library J 94:948-
55 Mr 1 '69

Exhibitions
See also
Science museums

Experiments
ABC's of science; experiments for children.
M. W. Caprio. il Parents Mag 44:54-6+
My '69
See also
Physics—Experiments

Federal aid
See Research—Federal aid

Fiction
See Science fiction

History
Behavior patterns of scientists; address, December 1968. R. K. Merton. Am Scholar 38:
197-225 Spr '69
Salerno science school of the ninth century:
reprint. R. Luzzato. il UNESCO Courier
22:10 Ag '69
See also
Science, Ancient

International aspects
[Department of state science lecture; in-
troduction] D. Rusk. Dept State Bul 60:
127-8 F 10 '69
Earthquake prediction: United States-Japan
cooperative science program; report of
meeting. J. Oliver. Science 164:92-3 Ap 4
'69
International scientific co-operation. H. I.
Chinn. Bul Atom Sci 25:34-5+ N '69
Internationalizing Batavia; proposed Cana-
dian partnership. Sci N 95:305 Mr 29 '69
Science cooperation agreement concluded
with Republic of China; January 23, 1969.
Dept State Bul 60:171 F 24 '69
Scientific community and international co-
operation; address, April 8, 1969. A. V.
Astin. Dept State Bul 61:32-7 Jl 14 '69
See also
International geophysical year
United Nations—Advisory committee on the
application of science and technology to
development

Juvenile literature
See Scientific literature for children

Methodology
See also
Research

Moral aspects
See Science and ethics

SCIENCE—*Continued*

Philosophy

Materials science and applied science; interaction between multiple scientific disciplines W. A. Tiller. il Science 165:469-75 Ag 1 '69

Prometheus project. Mankind's search for long-range goals, by G. Feinberg. Review
   Science 164:285-6 Ap 18 '69. J. A. Snow

Structure of discovery; adaptation of address, December 30, 1967. P. Caws. bibliog Science 166:1375-80 D 12 '69

Religious aspects

See Religion and science

Social aspects

Is your research moral? A. L. Schawlow. il Phys Today 22:118-19 D '69

Public knowledge; the social dimension of science, by J. Ziman. Review
   Bul Atom Sci 25:36-7+ Mr '69. J. A. Snow

Responsibility of scientists in our age. E. Rabinowitch. Bul Atom Sci 25:2-3+ N '69

Science and ideology in Soviet society, ed. by G. Fischer. Review
   Bul Atom Sci 25:33 Mr '69. A. Vucinich

Science and social attitudes; adaptation of address, April 1969. R. S. Morison. bibliog Science 165:150-6 Jl 11 '69

Science and social controls; symposium. Bul Atom Sci 25:21-36 My '69

Science and social purpose; adaptation of address, December 27, 1968. J. A. Shannon. bibliog Science 163:769-73 F 21 '69

Today's engineer, building a bridge to the public; address. K. H. Hohenemser. Sci & Cit 10:250-3 D '68

We need an informed conscience. R. H. Ellis, jr. Phys Today 22:114 Ag '69

What we can't know; excerpt from The environment of change. J. Bronowski. Sat R 52:44-5 Jl 5 '69

See also
British society for social responsibility in science

Study and teaching

AIP study offers solutions to school science problems. il Phys Today 22:74-5 Jl '69

Colleges in action. See issues of Science digest

Firsthand science experiences. G. O. Blough. Ed Digest 34:38-9 F '69

I love science, teaching, and children. D. McIver. il Todays Ed 58:50-2 Ja '69

Moon's place in the classroom. V. H. Ormsby. il Todays Ed 58:42-3 D '69

National science assessment. E. L. Norris. Ed Digest 35:46-8 N '69

Salerno science school of the ninth century; reprint. R. Luzzato. il UNESCO Courier 22:10 Ag '69

See also
Chemistry—Study and teaching
Museum education
Nature study
Scientific education

Canada

Pulling together. F. Poland. Sci N 96:188 S 6 '69

China (People's Republic)

China's scientists in the cultural revolution. P. H. Chang. il Bul Atom Sci 25:19-20+ My '69

Isolationist science policy. J. M. H. Lindbeck. il Bul Atom Sci 25:66-72 F '69

Europe, Western

Lack of scientific planning in Europe; adaptation of address, December 1968. J. Guéron. il Bul Atom Sci 25:10-14+ O '69

Germany (Federal Republic)

Fresh directions in science. T. Shoemaker. il Sci N 96:542 D 6 '69

India

See also
Indian science congress

Italy

Italy: OECD report finally emerges. D. S. Greenberg. Science 166:587 O 31 '69

Japan

Japan I: on the threshold of an age of big science? P. M. Boffey. il Science 167:31-5 Ja 2 '70

Rumania

Romania: academy links basic science to current needs. A. Jamison. Science 166:853-5 N 14 '69

Romania observed; letter. E. Callen and J. B. Goodenough. Phys Today 22:13+ My '69

Russia

Akademgorodok; Academic town. T. Shabad. il Focus 19:9-12 F '69

Russian science policy. Sci Am 220:48 Ap '69

Science and ideology in Soviet society, ed. by G. Fischer. Review
   Bul Atom Sci 25:33 Mr '69. A. Vucinich
   See also
Research—Russia

United States

See Science

SCIENCE (periodical)
Instructions for contributors. Science 163:xv-xvi Mr 28; 165:7-8 Jl 4; xix-xx S 26 '69

SCIENCE, Ancient
Global myths record their passage. W. D. Stahlman. il Sat R 53:100-3 Ja 10 '70

SCIENCE advisory council (Denmark) See Denmark—Science advisory council

SCIENCE and art. See Art and science

SCIENCE and children. See Children and science

SCIENCE and civilization
Basic research and the common good. W. Weaver. Sat R 52:17-18+ Ag 9 '69

Chicago: the social control of science and its applications; excerpts from addresses. P. M. S. Blackett; L. A. DuBridge; G. Wald. Bul Atom Sci 25:23-31 My '69

Evaded question: science and human nature. E. Becker. il Commonweal 89:638-42+ F 21 '69; Reply with rejoinder. J. R. Pleasants. 90:59+ Ap 4 '69

Identifying and moving toward national goals. P. H. Abelson. Science 164:909 My 23 '69

Lunacy. M. Friedman. Newsweek 74:94 S 29 '69

Privilege of being a physicist; adaptation of address. V. F. Weisskopf. il Phys Today 22:39-43 Ag '69

Problems or difficulties? Nat R 21:787-8 Ag 12 '69

Program for the mini-intellectual. G. W. Johnson. Am Scholar 39:50-8 Wint '69

Prometheus project. Mankind's search for long-range goals, by G. Feinberg. Review
   Science 164:285-6 Ap 18 '69. J. A. Snow

Science & humanity. J. Lear. See issues of Saturday review

Science and social attitudes; adaptation of address, April 1969. R. S. Morison. bibliog Science 165:150-6 Jl 11 '69

Science as an instrument of service. K. V. Thimann. Science 164:1013 My 30 '69; Discussion. 165:543 Ag 8 '69

Science, sex and morality; adaptation of The second Genesis; with Life poll on the procreation revolution by Louis Harris. A. Rosenfeld. il Life 66:37-40+ Je 13 '69

Science, technology and the citizen; address, September 17, 1969. G. T. Seaborg. Vital Speeches 36:5-10 O 15 '69

Social design for science; adaptation of address, November 14, 1969. R. Dubos. Science 166:823 N 14 '69

Toward a new scientific era; address, November 15, 1968. G. T. Seaborg. Vital Speeches 35:236-40 F 1 '69

What we must do. J. Platt. Science 166:1115-21 N 28 '69; Reply. W. D. McElroy. 167:9 Ja 2 '70

See also
International conference on science and society
Technology and civilization

SCIENCE and ethics
Basic research and the common good. W. Weaver. Sat R 52:17-18+ Ag 9 '69

Modern science and ethical dimension. P. J. Riga. Cath World 209:213-17 Ag '69

New dimension. Nation 208:454-5 Ap 14 '69

SCIENCE and industry. See Industrial research

SCIENCE and law
Law and science: need for legal change with advances in knowledge. D. Wolfle. Science 166:457 O 24 '69

SCIENCE and literature. See Literature and science

SCIENCE and religion. See Religion and science

SCIENCE and society. See Science and civilization

SCIENCE and sociology. See Science—Social aspects

SCIENCE and state
Against the misuse of science; an appeal by M.I.T. scientists; statement. Bul Atom Sci 25:8 Mr '69
Approaches to policy sciences; AAAS symposium, December 28, 1969. Y. Dror. bibliog Science 166:272-3 O 10 '69
Congress and science policy: the organizational dilemma. R. L. Chapman. il Bul Atom Sci 25:4-7+ Mr '69
Denmark; a late but hurrying entry in science policy planning. D. S. Greenberg. Science 166:586-8 O 31 '69
Dual world of man: reflections on science and government. A. Szent-Gyorgyi. Bul Atom Sci 25:33-4+ O '69
Eisenhower era: transition years for science. J. Walsh. Science 164:50-3 Ap 4 '69
Hornig years: did LBJ neglect his science adviser? P. M. Boffey. Science 163:453-4+ Ja 31 '69
How decisions are made. Nation 208:355-6 Mr 24 '69
Misuse of science: research stoppage planned at M.I.T. and other universities. Nation 208:228 F 24 '69
Needs for a national policy. E. Q. Daddario. il Phys Today 22:33-8 O '69
New leaders will overhaul US science policy for 1970's. Phys Today 22:73+ F '69
Nixon-science gap; fence mending. il Sci N 95:451 My 10 '69
Open letter; to R. M. Nixon. D. Wolfle. Science 166:1357 D 12 '69
Policy of protest; university scientists and engineers concern about government overemphasis on scientific weapons research. Time 93:60 F 28 '69
Political action in behalf of science. P. H. Abelson. Science 165:1315 S 26 '69
Research stoppage focuses on national science goals. il Phys Today 22:81+ Ap '69
Science adviser DuBridge makes his press debut, tells about Nixon's meeting with scientists. B. Nelson. Science 163:794-5 F 21 '69
Science and engineering policies in transition; report of meeting. D. Wolfle. Science 163:306+ Ja 17 '69
Science and ideology in Soviet society, ed. by G. Fischer. Review
  Bul Atom Sci 25:33 Mr '69. A. Vucinich
Science and social purpose; adaptation of address. December 27, 1968. J. A. Shannon. bibliog Science 163:769-73 F 21 '69
Science and the federal government; address, February 12, 1969. E. Q. Daddario. Vital Speeches 35:341-6 Mr 15 '69
Science policy and state government; AAAS symposium, December 30, 1969. T. G. Fox. Science 166:777 N 7 '69
Science policy in the U.S.S.R. R. W. Davies and R. Amann. il Sci Am 220:19-29 Je '69
Science policy meeting at M.I.T. B. Nelson. Science 163:797 F 21 '69
Science policy studies; NSF program. D. Wolfle. Science 165:547 Ag 8 '69
Science serves society; adaptation of address. April 29, 1969. L. A. DuBridge. Science 164:1137-40 Je 6 '69; Discussion. 165-336 Jl 25 '69
United States science policy: its health and future direction; adaptation of address, December 29, 1968. D. F. Hornig. Science 163:523-8 F 7 '69
  See also
Research—Federal aid
Social sciences and state
United States—National science foundation
United States—Science and technology, Department of (proposed)

SCIENCE and the humanities
Dropouts, do-gooders and the two cultures; reprint. J. W. Krutch. il Am For 75:34-5+ Ag '69
End of the great tradition. P. Schrag. il Sat R 52:94-5+ F 15 '69
Socrates, the computer, and ivied walls. M. H. Goldberg. bibliog f Sch & Soc 97:424-7 N '69
Spirit of Leonardo. J. Frye. Electr World 81:54-5 Mr '69
Tradition and understanding: the sciences and the humanities; adaptation of address, April 1968. H. L. Burstyn. bibliog Sch & Soc 97::419-24 N '69
  See also
Art and science
Literature and science

SCIENCE and war. See War and science

SCIENCE as a profession
On becoming a scientist; excerpts from address, May 9, 1967. G. T. Seaborg. il Chem 42:8-10 S '69

Scientist talks about careers in science; interview, ed. by A. S. Freese. R. Dubos. il Todays Health 47:24-7+ S '69

SCIENCE books for children. See Scientific literature for children

SCIENCE buildings, College. See College architecture

SCIENCE citation index
Citations and evaluation. L. Cranberg. Phys Today 22:15+ Ap '69

SCIENCE cities
  See also
Akademgorodok, Siberia

SCIENCE council of Canada. See Canada—Science council

SCIENCE education. See Scientific education

SCIENCE fairs
Young scientists compete; 20th annual International science fair. Sci N 95:501 My 24 '69

SCIENCE fiction
Coming of the humanoids; android fiction. N. P. Hurley. il Commonweal 91:297-300 D 5 '69
New note: the novel as sci-non-fi. M. Maddocks. Life 66:15 My 30 '69
Pop theology; those gods from outer space. il Time 94:64 S 5 '69
Profiles: A. C. Clarke. J. Bernstein. il New Yorker 45:40-2+ Ag 9 '69
Sci-fi and Vonnegut. J. M. Crichton. New Repub 160:33-5 Ap 26 '69
You're putting me on, I hope. P. S. Prescott. Look 33:12 Je 10 '69
  See also
Publishers and publishing—Science fiction

  Anecdotes, facetiae, satire, etc.
Queen of viscerotonia. H. F. Ellis. New Yorker 45:54-6 D 27 '69

  Bibliography
Children's books; space in science fiction. il Pub W 196:57 Jl 28 '69
Merril-y we wave along. T. Strugeon. Nat R 21:1174-5 N 18 '69

  Drama
Green men, go home. A. C. Martens. Plays 28:45-52+ Ap '69
Take me to your marshal. C. Boiko. Plays 29:45-51 Ja '70

  Technique
Participant past imperfect. A. B. Malec. Writer 82:13-21 Ag '69
Science fiction market. J. Estrada. il Writers Digest 49:48-52+ Ap '69

SCIENCE in criminal investigation. See Criminal investigation

SCIENCE in fiction. See Science fiction

SCIENCE in literature
  See also
Science fiction

SCIENCE librarians. See Librarians

SCIENCE museums
Atom at ease. P. Mygatt. il Travel 132:68-70 N '69
  See also
Museum of science, Boston

SCIENCE news
Science month. See issues of Science digest
Science newsfront. W. S. Bacon. See issues of Popular science monthly
Search and discovery. See issues of Physics today
  See also
Medical news

SCIENCE research council. See Great Britain—Science research council

SCIENCE students
  See also
Inventors
Physics students

SCIENCE talent search

  1969 (28th)
Talent search winners. I. Kaye. il Sci N 95:265-7 Mr 15 '69
Then there were forty. Sci N 95:140 F 8 '69

SCIENCE teachers
And gladly wolde he lerne, and gladly teche. R. Gottsegen. Science 164:373 Ap 25 '69
  See also
National science teachers association

SCIENCE teaching. See Science—Study and teaching

SCIENTIFIC apparatus and instruments
Instrumentation; symposium. Phys Today 22:25-32+ Jl '69
  See also
Physiological apparatus

SCIENTIFIC bureau of the Detroit police department. See Criminological laboratories

SCIENTIFIC conferences
Aerospace calendar. See issues of Aviation week & space technology
Atomic physicists meet for Arnold Sommerfeld centennial. I. C. Percival and H. H. Stroke. il Phys Today 22:99+ F '69
Calendar. See issues of Physics today
Calendar of events. See issues of Science
Meetings. See issues of Science
Rock festival; Lunar sample analysis conference, Houston. il Newsweek 75:66-7 Ja 19 '70
Scientists hold a landmark session; lunar sample analysis conference. il Sci N 97:33-5 Ja 10 '70
Side effects; report of a conference on ecological aspects of international development. H. Henkin. il Environ 11:28-35+ Ja '69
See also
Gordon research conferences
Indian science congress
Pugwash conferences on science and world affairs

Anecdotes, facetiae, satire, etc.
Atlantic community; G. Swinger takes part in discussions. D. S. Greenberg. Science 166:852-3 N 14 '69

SCIENTIFIC education
School science, past and future; AAAS symposium, December 30, 1969. A. A. Strassenberg. Science 166:907 N 14 '69
Science and the public. G. T. Seaborg. Duns R 92:77-8 D '68
Science education for nonscience students; interdisciplinary effort at Berkeley. F. Reif. Science 164:1032-7 My 30 '69; Discussion. 165: 234+, 645-7 Jl 18, Ag 15 '69
$7,600,000 for science and education development; multinational projects in Latin America. Américas 21:43 Ja '69
See also
Engineering education
Science—Study and teaching

SCIENTIFIC expeditions
See also
Antarctic exploration
Arctic exploration
Beagle expedition, 1831-1836

SCIENTIFIC information. See Communication in science

SCIENTIFIC literature
Preventing obsolescence of scientific reviews; an updated-review project. P. Amacher and others. Science 165:1029-30 S 5 '69
Suggestion: the minireview. D. Garvin. Phys Today 22:13+ O '69
See also
Publishers and publishing—Scientific literature
Science—Bibliography
Technical literature

SCIENTIFIC literature for children
Information, please! R. Gagliardo. il PTA Mag 64:18-19+ O '69
Views on science books. H. C. Stubbs. See issues of Horn book magazine

Bibliography
Children's books about science; an annual Christmas selection. P. Morrison and P. Morrison. Sci Am 221:136-9+ D '69
Children's books; new titles about space. il Pub W 196:57 Jl 28 '69

SCIENTIFIC literature searching. See Information storage and retrieval systems—Science

SCIENTIFIC management. See Industrial management and organization

SCIENTIFIC museums. See Science museums

SCIENTIFIC personnel in state government. See State employees

SCIENTIFIC research. See Research

SCIENTIFIC societies
See also names of scientific societies, e.g. American geophysical union

SCIENTIFIC toys. See Toys

SCIENTIFIC writing. See Scientific literature; Technical writing

SCIENTIST-astronauts. See Astronauts

SCIENTISTS
Behavior patterns of scientists; address, December 1968. R. K. Merton. Am Scholar 38: 197-225 Spr '69
Don't launch him he's mine! life as a wife of a space scientist; condensation. M. J. Chambers. il Read Digest 95:241-4+ Jl '69
How Nobel prizewinners get that way; science laureates. M. Wilson. il Atlan 224:69-74 D '69

International comparisons; letters. Science 164:13-14 Ap 4 '69
See also
Chemists
Science as a profession
Science teachers

Anecdotes, facetiae, satire, etc.
Migratory habits of the scientific goose. R. G. Harvey. Science 163:764-5 F 21 '69

Political activities
Activist groups seek ways to bring science into politics. J. Wiley. Phys Today 22:79-80 Ap '69
Activists take ABM fight to Congress, White House. J. P. Wiley. il Phys Today 22:69+ Je '69
Against the misuse of science; an appeal by M.I.T. scientists; statement. Bul Atom Sci 25:8 Mr '69
ABM: critical report by scientists brings sharp Pentagon rebuttal. P. M. Boffey. Science 164:807-10 My 16 '69; Reply. D. C. Williams. 165:335 Jl 25 '69
ABM: scientists are important in building Senate opposition. B. Nelson. il Science 164:654-6 My 9 '69
ABM: scientists' loyal opposition finds a forum; with excerpts from statements. J. Walsh. Science 163:1309-11 Mr 21 '69
Arms and the scientists: a long dialogue continues. J. Walsh. Science 163:1436-8 Mr 28 '69
M.I.T.'s March 4: scientists discuss renouncing military research. B. Nelson. il Science 163:1175-8 Mr 14 '69
Misuse of science; research stoppage planned at M.I.T. and other universities. Nation 208:228 F 24 '69
Policy of protest; university scientists and engineers concern about government overemphasis on scientific weapons research. Time 93:60 F 28 '69
Researchers protest defense research. il Sci N 95:257 Mr 15 '69
Science and defense. Sci N 95:185 F 22 '69
Scientists and youth in revolt. E. Rabinowitch. Bul Atom Sci 25:2+ Ap '69; Discussion. 25:48 O '69
Scientists in politics (the atomic scientists movement, 1945-50) by D. A. Strickland. Review
Bul Atom Sci 25:42 Je '69. C. Schwartz
Scientist in public affairs: between the ivory tower and the arena. R. E. Peierls. il Bul Atom Sci 25:28-30 N '69
Unconventional. il Newsweek 74:69-70 S 15 '69
See also
British society for social responsibility in science

Salaries, allowances, etc.
Trying to keep up; federal government scientists. Sci N 95:211 Mr 1 '69

Supply and demand
Developing nations and scientific responsibility. K. Lonsdale. Bul Atom Sci 25:27-8 N '69
Manpower oversupply; chemists and chemical engineers. il Sci N 96:199-200 S 13 '69
New Brahmins; scientific life in America, by S. Klaw. Review
Sci Am 220:139-40+ My '69. D. Zinberg and P. Doty
O joyous need for jobs. Phys Today 22:19+ O '69
Placement figures show tight physics job market. il Phys Today 22:83+ Ap '69
Science and society in equilibrium. J. P. Martino. bibliog il Science 165:769-72 Ag 22 '69
Surplus of scientists? the job market is tightening. B. Nelson. Science 166:582-4 O 31 '69
Tougher times ahead for job-hunting Ph. D.'s; excerpts from interviews. il U S News 67:40-1 D 29 '69
Unemployment crisis; letters. W. Zernik; A. A. Strassenburg. Phys Today 22:13+ F '69
See also
Brain drain

SCIENTISTS, American
New Brahmins; scientific life in America, by S. Klaw. Review
Bul Atom Sci 25:35-6 Mr '69. J. Wilson
See also
National register of scientific and technical personnel

SCIENTISTS, Blacklisting of. See Blacklisting of scientists

SCIENTISTS, Chinese
China's scientists in the cultural revolution.
  P. H. Chang. il Bul Atom Sci 25:19-20+
  My '69
Isolationist science policy. J. M. H. Lindbeck.
  il Bul Atom Sci 25:66-72 F '69
SCIENTISTS, German
Cold war science; West-to-East defectors. T.
  Shoemaker. Sci N 95:620 Je 28 '69
Harvest of Operation Paperclip. il Newsweek
  74:10 Jl 7 '69
SCIENTISTS, Latin American
Migration of scientists from Latin America;
  adaptaton of address, 1968. H. M. Nussen-
  zveig. Science 165:1328-32 S 26 '69; Reply.
  D. Schwartz. 166:820-1 N 14 '69
SCIENTISTS, Russian
  See also
Deriagin, B.
SCIENTISTS as artists
Physicists can paint doors. il Phys Today 22:
  17 D '69
SCIENTISTS in government
Nixon set on filling R&D slots. Bsns W p68
  Mr 15 '69
Not that simple; blacklisting of scientists by
  HEW. Nation 209:429 O 27 '69
Will the science brain bank go conglomerate?
  biochemical research activities of P. Han-
  dler. J. Lear. il Sat R 52:37-44 Jl 5 '69
SCIENTOLOGY
Cult wins round one. J. D. Douglas. Chr To-
  day 14:35-6 D 19 '69
Dangerous new cult of scientology. A. Ei-
  senberg and H. Eisenberg. Parents Mag 44:
  48-9+ Je '69
Jai Baba! Hare Krishna, and all that. P.
  Rowley. il Mlle 70:136-7+ D '69
Scientology: religion or racket? J. M. Hop-
  kins. Chr Today 14:6-9 N 7; 10-13 N 21 '69
Total freedom and beyond. D. Bess. Nation
  209:311-15 S 29 '69
Victory for the scientologists; Court of appeals
  protects E-meters and leaflets. il Time 93:
  76+ F 14 '69
SCILKEN, Marvin H.
Backlog to frontlog. Library J 94:3014-15 S
  15 '69
SCIMECCA, Joseph A.
St John's: four years after. Commonweal 91:
  326-7 D 12 '69
SCINTILLATION counters. See Counters
  (electrons, ions, etc)
SCISSORS and shears
Electric scissors. il Consumer Bul 52:7-10
  Mr '69
Latest word; sharpening pinking shears.
  Consumer Bul 52:32 Je '69
SCISSORS-cut pictures. See Silhouettes
SCLEROSIS
Most important bout for Ezzard Charles;
  fighting lateral sclerosis. il Ebony 24:102-
  4+ Mr '69
SCLEROSIS, Multiple
Riddle of MS. Newsweek 74:116 O 6 '69
SCLEROSPORA graminicola. See Fungi
SCOBEY, Joan, and McGrath, L. P.
Wanted: one safari guide, part-time. Mc-
  Calls 96:16+ Ja '69
—See McGrath, L. P. jt. auth.
SCOFIELD, John
Friendly Irish. Nat Geog 136:354-91 S '69
SCOLIOSIS. See Spine—Abnormities and de-
  formities
SCOPES. See Oscillographs
SCOPES trial. See Tennessee evolution con-
  troversy
SCORE reading and playing. See Music reading
SCORING of trees. See Trees, Ringing of
SCOTCH whiskey. See Whiskey
SCOTLAND
  See also
Colonsay (island)
Fishing—Scotland
Hunting—Scotland
Opera—Scotland

Description and travel
Businessman's guide to Europe: Scotland.
  Bsns W p 103-4 Ap 16 '69
Ireland & Scotland. M. MacLiammoir; E.
  Linklater. il Travel & Camera 32:120-1 F '69
Scotland, the most beautiful country in the
  world? A. Reid. il Holiday 46:34-6+ Ag '69

History
Profiles; Colonsay: the island of the crofter
  and the laird. J. McPhee. il New Yorker 45:
  61-2+ D 13 '69

**Religious institutions and
affairs**
World around us (cont) Chr Cent 86:269 F 19
  '69
  See also
Church of Scotland

Social conditions
Profiles; Colonsay: the island of the crofter
  and the laird. J. McPhee. il New Yorker
  45:61-2+ D 13 '69
SCOTLAND, Church of. See Church of Scotland
SCOTLAND, Md.
Scotland, Maryland; townhouse development.
  J. Bailey. il Arch Forum 131:82-5 Jl '69
SCOTLAND and the United States
  See also
Americans in Scotland
SCOTLAND Yard (police) See London—Police
SCOTT, Arlene
Six ways to help your teenager become a
  better driver. Parents Mag 44:52-3 F '69
SCOTT, Byron
Turning on tots with educational TV. To-
  days Health 47:28-32 N '69
SCOTT, Carl, and Swedberg, Jack
Short fracas at a carcass; activities of the
  bald eagle; photographs. Audubon 71:16-
  19 Mr '69
SCOTT, Dave
Inside a digger. il Hot Rod 22:88-91 D '69
SCOTT, David
New police car has power and antiskid on
  all four wheels. por Pop Sci 195:76-9 N '69
SCOTT, David C.
Classic defense. il por Forbes 104:21-3 Ag 1
  '69
It's no tea party at Allis. il por Bsns W
  p54+ N 15 '69
SCOTT, David H.
Washington advisory. See issues of Flying
  to September 1969
SCOTT, David R.
In Paris a successful link-up of spacemen,
  fueled by vodka. M. Mok. il por Life 66:
  30-1 Je 13 '69
  See also
Space flight—Manned flights—McDivitt-Scott-
  Schweickart flight, 1969
SCOTT, David W.
Museum in a museum. por Américas 21:22-30
  Ag '69
SCOTT, Douglas W.
Conservation tragedy? Parks & Rec 4:24-6+
  O '69
SCOTT, Harold M. Jr
What makes a good helmsman? Motor B 123:
  116+ Mr '69
SCOTT, Herbert
Late fall, setting traps; poem. Poetry 115:
  174 D '69
SCOTT, Hugh
Minority leader Scott. New Repub 161:8-9
  O 11 '69
New GOP leader. il por Newsweek 74:76 O 6
  '69
New style on the center aisle. il por Time
  94:27 N 7 '69
Republicans in the Senate, new leaders, new
  directions. il por U S News 67:17 O 6 '69
Senate: the balancing act. J. Osborne. il New
  Repub 160:19-21 F 1 '69
SCOTT, Jack
Athletics for athletes? P. Axthelm. il por
  Newsweek 74:62 Ag 11 '69
—and Edwards, Harry
After the Olympics; buying off protest.
  Ramp Mag 8:16-21 N '69
SCOTT, Jack (broker)
Very special situations. R. Brady. por Duns
  R 93:103-4 Ap '69
SCOTT, Jack Denton
Durable deer. Read Digest 95:217-22 D '69
SCOTT, Joseph W.
ROTC retreat. Trans-Action 6:47-52 S '69
SCOTT, Ken
Homegrown Hoosier in Italy. B. Day. Mc-
  Calls 96:71+ Jl '69
SCOTT, Myron E.
Safari. Travel & Camera 32:79-83 My '69
SCOTT, Perry
Santa wouldn't provide 2,000 free parking
  spaces. Am City 84:145-6 My '69
SCOTT, Peter
Peter Scott and the trapeze; excerpt from
  The eye of the wind. por Yachting 126:64-5
  Ag '69
SCOTT, Richard
Does technology determine policy? Cur 109:
  45 Ag '69
SCOTT, Robert F.
Technical topics. Radio-Electr 40:46-7 Je; 41-
  2 Ag; 63+ O '69
Variable-voltage tuning. Radio-Electr 40:58-60
  Ap '69
SCOTT, Ruth Boyer
Before you need a doctor ... Todays Health
  47:54-5+ Mr '69
SCOTT, William A.
[Book review] Commonweal 90:179-80 Ap 25
  '69

SCOTT, William John, 1926-
Prosecuting pollution. por Time 95:41 Ja 5
'70
SCOTT, Winfield Townley
Poem; The girl young enough to be my
daughter; I held a hummingbird in my
hand; Restless at midnight; That woman
of Lachaise; Seven haiku; Centenary for
Private John Hogg; Claiming of Private
John Hogg; poems. Poetry 113:373-8 Mr
'69
SCOTT paper company
Paper tiger grows claws. il Bsns W p 100-
2 Ag 23 '69
Scott paper's second growth. il Forbes 103:
18-19 Ja 15 '69
SCOTTI, Cesare
Big shoot-out on Lake Havasu. H. D. Whall.
il Sports Illus 31:66 D 8 '69
Farewell to put-puts. il Time 94:52 D 12 '69
SCOTTISH castles. See Castles
SCOTTISH opera. See Opera—Scotland
SCOTTSBORO case
Scottsboro, by D. T. Carter. Review
Nation 208:674 My 26 '69. S. Stevens
New Repub 160:27-8 Mr 22 '69. L. Fried-
man
SCOTTSDALE, Ariz, public library
Southwestern flavor for Scottsdale, Arizona.
il Library J 94:4395-6 D 1 '69
SCOURS, Calf. See Calves—Diseases and pests
SCOUTING, Basketball. See Basketball scout-
ing
SCOUTING, Football. See Football scouting
SCOUTS, Boy. See Boy scouts
SCOUTS, Girl. See Girl scouts
SCOUTS and scouting
See also
Boy scouts
SCOVILLE, Samuel
To conceive of the devil. Engl J 58:673-5 My
'69
SCRANTON, William Warren
William W. Scranton to head U.S. delegation
to Intelsat. Dept State Bul 60:367 Ap 28 '69
SCRANTON, Pa.
Negroes
Scranton: a short view, a microcosm. L. D.
Mitchell. Cath World 210:7-10 O '69
SCRAP baskets. See Waste baskets
SCRAP metal
Harvest of trash; reclaimed cans. il Time 94:
39 Ag 29 '69
Scrap metals, a field for research opportuni-
ties. il Chem 42:23-4 Ap '69
SCRAP metal industry
He turns junk into gold; Sitkin smelting &
refining. S. Margetts. il Duns R 92:51+ D '68
SCRAP metal sculpture. See Metal sculpture
SCRAPBOOKS
On keeping a philatelic scrapbook. H. Herst.
ir. Hobbies 74:131+ O '69
SCRAPPING of automobiles. See Automobiles—
Wrecking
SCRATCH a lover; novel. See Vermandel, J. G.
SCRATCHBOARD drawing
Scratchboard drawing. L. J. Miller. il De-
sign 70:4-7 Sum '69
To scratch or not, for art. K. R. Morrison. il
Am Artist 33:28-9+ My '69
SCREEN printing. See Silk screen printing
SCREEN writing. See Moving picture authorship
SCREENED porches. See Porches
SCREENS (doors, windows, etc)
Window screens aren't just screens anymore.
W. C. Leckey. il Pop Mech 131:162-5+ Je
'69
SCREENS (fences) See Fences
SCREENS (furniture)
Indispensable screen. V. D. Hahn. il Am
Home 72:16+ My '69
New: the room-screen. il House & Gard 135:
84-5 Ja '69
SCREENS (projection) See Projection screens
SCREENS (sun)
Bright idea from Portugal, sunshade, wind-
screen, privacy screen. il Sunset 143:54-5
Ag '69
Patio screen shelters shade-lovers. il Sunset
142:176 F '69
SCREW drivers
Tools for electronics. T. R. Haskett. il Ra-
dio-Electr 40:44-8 N; 52-6 D '69
Ultimate in screw power. il Mech Illus 65:72-
3+ D '69
SCREWDRIVERS. See Screw drivers
SCRIABIN, Alexander Nicholaevich. See Skría-
bin, A.N.

SCRIBNER, Susi
Susi queue to London; with editorial com-
ment. B. Ottum. il pors Sports Illus 30:6,
90-4+ Je 9 '69
SCRIMSHAW
Mariners' fancy. D. L. Shirey. il Newsweek
74:87 Ag 25 '69
SCRIPT writing. See Television authorship
SCRIPTS, Moving picture. See Moving pic-
ture scripts
SCRIPTURE studies. See Bible study
SCRIVEN, Eldon G. See Harrison, A. jr, jt.
auth.
SCROLLS from the Dead Sea. See Dead Sea
scrolls
SCUBA diving. See Skin diving
SCUDDER, Thayer
Kariba Dam: the ecological hazards of mak-
ing a lake. Natur Hist 78:68-72 F '69
SCULLING. See Rowing
SCULLY, Ed
Ed Scully on color. See issues of Modern
photography
SCULLY, Julia
Seeing pictures. See issues of Modern photog-
raphy
SCULLY, Vincent Joseph
Scholar's inquiry into America's urbanism.
S. R. Weisman. Commonweal 91:364 D 19
'69
SCULPTORS
See also
Sculpture
SCULPTORS, British
London; Stockwell depot rented by a group
of young sculptors. J. Russell. Art N 68:
46 N '69
SCULPTURE
Do-it-yourself sculpture in Paris. C. Cutler.
il Art in Am 57:100 S '69
Masters in the art news. il Art N 68:10-11
S '69
Old hat no more; use of wooden hat blocks.
il Time 94:47-8 D 19 '69
See also
Animal sculpture
Bronzes
Casting (sculpture)
Ceramic sculpture
Metal sculpture
Modeling
Paper sculpture
Plastic sculpture
Portrait sculpture
Relief (sculpture)
Sand sculpture
Stone carving
Storm King art center, Mountainville, N.Y.
Wire sculpture
Wood carving
also subhead Monuments, statues, etc.
under names of cities, e.g. Washington,
D.C.—Monuments, statues, etc.
Competitions
See Art—Competitions
Conservation and restoration
Stones also die; reprint. R. Sneyers. UNESCO
Courier 22:79 Ag '69
Exhibitions
Breath of fresh air; Inflatable sculpture at
New York's Jewish museum. D. L. Shirey.
il Newsweek 74:93 Jl 14 '69
Essence of things; C. Brancusi's display
at New York's Guggenheim museum includ-
ing 84 sculptures and 23 drawings. D. L.
Shirey. il Newsweek 74:137 D 8 '69
Push and pull in the park; exhibition of sculp-
ture in Bryant park, N.Y. il Arch Forum
130:68-9 Ja '69
Venerability of pop; Oldenburg's objects at
the Modern. il Time 94:68-9 O 10 '69
See also
Museum of modern art, New York
Private collections
See Art—Private collections
Study and teaching
Exploring sculpture. L. J. Matthew. il Sch
Arts 69:37 O '69
Three-dimensional concepts. M. E. Doern-
bach. il Sch Arts 68:24-5 F '69
Materials
Can we get the dinosaurs out of the cellar?
papier-mâché project. C. B. Szeglin. il Sch
Arts 69:18-20 Mr '69
Macaroni sculpture. H. Stevens. il Sch Arts
68:32-3 My '69
Sculpture: plaster over window screen. N.
Finley. il Sch Arts 69:20-1 O '69
See also
Papier-mâché

SCULPTURE—*Continued*

Technique

Critic calls David Smith greatest of all American artists. H. Kramer. il N Y Times Mag p40-2+ F 16 '69
Forms for dance; interview, ed. by J. Batie D. Chase. il Craft Horiz 29:16-19 Jl '69
Jig-saw sculpture. J. Hayes. il Design 70:12-13 mid-Wint '69
See also
Lost wax process
Modeling

SCULPTURE, American
Artist speaks: Ronald Bladen; interview, ed. by C. Robins. il Art in Am 57:76-81 S '69
He sculptures his satire; interview. ed. C. Rice. R. Goldberg. il Har Yrs 9:18-21 O '69
Painting and sculpture. A. Gowans. il Antiques 96:374 S '69
Sculpture of Philip Kraczkowski. P. Kraczkowski. il Am Artist 33:42-8 Ag '69
Soft sculpture or hard, they're Oldenburgers. G. Glueck. il N Y Times Mag p28-9+ S 21 '69
Spot check: some observations on painting and sculpture in America. J. Claman. il Harp Baz 102:122C-122F F '69
See also
Ceracchi, G.
Chase, D.
Dallin, C. E.
De Maria, W.
Hunt, R.
Judd, D.
Kuehn, G.
Le Va, B.
Metal sculpture
Newberger, B.
Newman, B.
Oldenburg, C.
Pavia, P.
Rapp, E.
Saint-Gaudens, A.
Sando, D.
Scarpitta, S.
Smith, D. 1906-1965
Storrs, J. B.
Whitney museum of American art, New York
SCULPTURE, Animal. See Animal sculpture
SCULPTURE, Architectural. See Decoration and ornament, Architectural
SCULPTURE, Canadian
See also
Zelenak, E.
SCULPTURE, Childrens. See Childrens art
SCULPTURE, French
See also
Dubuffet, J.
Hajdu, E.
SCULPTURE, Gothic
Portal to illumination; exhibit at Museum of art, Rhode Island school of design, of Romanesque and early Gothic stone sculptures. il Time 93:64 My 30 '69
SCULPTURE, Italian
See also
Bernini, G. L.
Manzù, G.
SCULPTURE, Japanese
Master-works of stone age Japan; reprint. S. Noma. il UNESCO Courier 22:68 Ag '69
See also
Shingu, S.
SCULPTURE, Khmer
Geneva Khmer; the collection of Tan Phuoc Nguyen. H. La Farge. il Art N 68:53+ Sum '69
SCULPTURE, Metal. See Metal sculpture
SCULPTURE, Mobile. See Mobiles
SCULPTURE, Negro (American)
See also
Catlett, E.
Tate, R. M.
SCULPTURE, Photography of. See Photography of works of art
SCULPTURE, Pre-Columbian
Olmec. M. W. Stirling. il Américas 21:2-10 N '69
Vernacular languages in changing Africa; reprint. P. Diagne. il UNESCO Courier 22:30-1 Ag '69
SCULPTURE, Primitive
See also
Sculpture, Pre-Columbian
SCULPTURE, Romanesque
Portal to illumination; exhibit at Museum of art, Rhode Island school of design, of Romanesque and early Gothic stone sculptures. il Time 93:64 My 30 '69
SCULPTURE, Rumanian
See also
Brancusi, C.

SCULPTURE, Russian
See also
Neizvestny, E.
SCULPTURE, Spanish
See also
Berrocal, M. O.
SCULTHORP, Elsie Louise
Bright bloom of yellow. House B 111:68+ My '69
SCUPPER strainers. See Boats—Equipment
SCUPPERNONG grapes. See Grapes
SCUTTLING of warships. See Warships, Scuttling of
SEA. See Ocean
SEA beaches. See Beaches
SEA birds
See also
Auks
SEA cows. See Manatees
SEA cucumbers
Antifungal steroid glycoside from sea cucumber. S. Shimada. bibliog il Science 163:1462 Mr 28 '69
Commensal sea cucumber. W. E. Martin. Science 164:855 My 16 '69
SEA floor spreading. See Ocean bottom
SEA food
Oddballs of the deep sea; hunting for marketable seafood. C. Phinizy. il Sports Illus 31:24-7 Ag 4 '69
See also
Cookery—Sea food
Cookery—Shellfish
Fish as food
Lobsters
SEA gulls. See Gulls
SEA hares
Circadian rhythm of optic nerve impulses recorded in darkness from isolated eye of aplysia. J. W. Jacklet. bibliog il Science 164:562-3 My 2 '69
Neuronal controls of a behavioral response mediated by the abdominal ganglion of aplysia. I Kupfermann and E. R. Kandel. bibliog il Science 164:847-50 My 16 '69
Ribonucleic acid metabolism of a single neuron: correlation with electrical activity. R. W. Berry. bibliog il Science 166:1021-3 N 21 '69
SEA horses
Ponies in my parlor. A. Cone. il Har Yrs 9:48-9 Jl '69
SEA lavender
For summer and winter: discover the statices. B. Miles. Home Gard 56:64 Ag '69
SEA-level canal. See Canals—Central America
SEA level changes
Interglacial high sea levels and the control of Greenland ice by the precession of the equinoxes. C. Emiliani. bibliog il Science 166:1503-4 D 19 '69
See also
Coast changes
SEA lion caves, Ore. See Caves
SEA OF CORTEZ. See California, Gulf of
SEA otters
Moving day for sea otters. G. Laycock. il Audubon 71:58-62+ Ja '69
SEA planes. See Seaplanes
SEA power
American seapower, 1969; a 1949 navy; address, May 13, 1969. C. E. Bennett. Vital Speeches 35:550-3 Jl 1 '69
Russia plotted the Pueblo affair; excerpts. J. Sejna. Read Digest 95:73-6 Jl '69
Russian navy; Pueblo inquiry; address, January 25, 1969. T. H. Moorer. Vital Speeches 35:300-3 Mr 1 '69
Soviet navy; our ability to meet the challenge; address, August 19, 1969. T. H. Moorer. Vital Speeches 35:742-6 O 1 '69
Soviet sea power; latest threat to America; with interview with Vice Admiral D. C. Richardson. C. S. Foltz, Jr. il U S News 67:56-61 Jl 21 '69
SEA products. See Marine resources
SEA shells. See Shells (conchology)
SEA slugs
Physalia nematocysts: utilized by mollusks for defense. T. E. Thompson and I. Bennett. bibliog il Science 166:1532-3 D 19 '69
SEA smoke. See Fog
SEA stars. See Starfishes
SEA turtles. See Turtles
SEA urchins
Actinomycin D: uptake by sea urchin eggs and embryos. M. M. Thaler and others. bibliog il Science 164:832-4 My 16 '69; Reply. C. A. Villee and P. R. Gross. 166:402 O 17 '69

SEA urchins—*Continued*
Crystal orientation and plate structure in echinoid skeletal units. H. U. Nissen. bibliog il Science 166:1150-2 N 28 '69
β-1,3-Glucanase of sea urchin eggs: release from particles at fertilization. D. Epel and others. bibliog il Science 163:294-6 Ja 17 '69
Proteins synthesized before and after fertilization in sea urchin eggs. F. R. MacKintosh and E. Bell. bibliog il Science 164:961-3 My 23 '69

SEA water
Equilibration of atmospheric carbon dioxide with sea water; possible enzymatic control of the rate. R. Berger and W. F. Libby. bibliog il Science 164:1395-7 Je 20 '69; Reply. K. V. Krishnamurty. 165:929 Ag 29 '69
Fluoride in seawater: measurement with lanthanum fluoride electrode. T. B. Warner. bibliog il Science 165:178-80 Jl 11 '69
Man-made carbon-14 in deep Pacific waters: transport by biological skeletal material. B. L. K. Somayajulu and others. bibliog il Science 166:1397-9 D 12 '69
Suspended particulate matter: concentration in the major oceans. M. B. Jacobs and M. Ewing. bibliog il Science 163:380-3 Ja 24 '69

Desalting
Blooming desert. C. O. Hodge. il Bul Atom Sci 25:32-3 N '69
Desalted seawater for agriculture: is it economic? M. Clawson and others. bibliog Science 164:1141-8 Je 6 '69; Discussion. 165:850-1 Ag 29 '69
Desalting Coalinga's water; using reverse-osmosis process. il Am City 84:22 Mr '69
Fresh water from the sea; seagoing distillation plants. C. F. Kelley. il Yachting 126:72-3+ D '69
Higher temperature, better yield; Clair Engle desalting plant at San Diego. Am City 84:44 Ja '69
Industry growing thirsty. S. Griffin. il Sci N 95:390 Ap 19 '69
No other choice but desalting: U.S. Virgin Islands. W. S. Foster. il Am City 84:91-3 My '69
Plan that was; nuclear-power plants in Israel and the Arab countries to desalinate sea water. Nation 208:163-4 F 10 '69
See also
Saline water conversion plants

Pollution
Casual gas dump. il Sci N 95:609-10 Je 28 '69
Contamination of the oceans. Nation 208:293 Mr 10 '69
Diseased estuaries. New Repub 160:7 Mr 1 '69
Nurseries of the sea. W. Marx. il UNESCO Courier 22:13-17+ Mr '69
Ocean's riches. W. M. Stephens. il Nat Wildlife 7:4-11 Ap '69
Pacific shores: report of meeting. D. F. Sawbridge and M. A. M. Bell. Science 164:1089 My 30 '69
Pollution of the ocean; excerpt. R. C. Cowen. Focus 19:12 Ja '69
Pollution of the ocean; reprint. N. Gorskii. il UNESCO Courier 22:33-5 Ag '69
Reports: Baker's Island. K. Spivack. Atlan 224:22-3 Ag '69
Rumblings from the deep. J. Chamblin. il Sci N 96:213-14 S 13 '69
Shock at sea; pollution appalled Heyerdahl. Time 94:40 Ag 15 '69
See also
Oil pollution of rivers, harbors, etc.

SEA water temperature. See Ocean temperature
SEA works (art projects) See Art, Modern
SEABED treaty (proposed) See Ocean bottom —International aspects
SEABERG, Dorothy I. See Allen, A. T. jt. auth.
SEABORG, Glenn T.
Environment; address, May 5, 1969. Vital Speeches 35:514-20 Je 15 '69
Environment, and what to do about it; address, May 5, 1969. por Am For 75:38-9+ S; 22-3+ O '69
General conference of the International atomic energy agency holds 13th session at Vienna; statement, September 24, 1969. Dept State Bul 61:329-33 O 20 '69
International atom, a new appraisal, the past and the promise: address, January 29, 1969. Dept State Bul 60:173-84, 199-211 Mr 3-10 '69
Nuclear explosions: can they really be made into useful tools Sci Digest 65:7-13 Je '69

On becoming a scientist; excerpts from address, May 9, 1967. por Chem 42:8-10 S '69
Science, technology and the citizen; address, September 17, 1969. Vital Speeches 36:5-10 O 15 '69
Toward a new scientific era; address, November 15, 1968. Vital Speeches 35:236-40 F 1 '69
—and Bloom, J. L.
Synthetic elements; with biographical sketches. Sci Am 220:12, 57-67 bibliog (p 146) Ap '69
about
Atomic power in industry; a slump now, but... il por U S News 67:54-5 Jl 7 '69
Chemical analysis in a wink. Chem 42:22 F '69

SEABROOK, John Martin
How to harvest a business farm. Bsns W p 141-2+ Ap 19 '69
SEAFARERS' international union of North America
After the Olympics; buying off protest. J. Scott and H. Edwards. Ramp Mag 8:18-20 N '69
Political peonage. Nation 208:68-9 Ja 20 '69
SEAFARING life
See also
Voyages
Whaling
SEAFOOD. See Sea food
SEAGRAM, Joseph E, and sons
Benchmark case; CU suit. Newsweek 74:89-90 D 15 '69
SEAGREN, Bob
Three strikes, and out? il por Newsweek 74:72 Jl 28 '69
SEAGULLS. See Gulls
SEAHORSES. See Sea horses
SEAL hunting
Days of the long knives; Canadian hunting season. il Time 93:30+ Mr 21 '69
Seal hunt; a bloody business in Canada causes an uproar all over. il Life 66:61-3 Mr 21 '69
Thirty-day reprieve for the pups. il Time 94:35 O 24 '69
SEALAB projects. See Underwater laboratories
SEALE, Bobby G.
Contempt in Chicago. por Time 94:72+ N 14 '69
Courtroom confrontation. Nation 209:526 N 17 '69
Disorder in the court. il por Time 94:27-8 N 7 '69
How militants try to destroy a court. il U S News 67:68-9 N 17 '69
In a courtroom of the absurd. il Life 67:96 N 14 '69
In re Bobby Seale. W. F. Buckley, jr. Nat R 21:1234-5 D 2 '69
Panther hunt. por Newsweek 74:22A-22B S 1 '69
Then there were seven. Newsweek 74:50+ N 17 '69
Total confrontation. Nat R 21:1157-8 N 18 '69
Two for the show. il por Newsweek 74:41 N 10 '69
SEALING compounds. See Caulking compounds
SEALS (animals)
Dialects in elephant seals. B. J. Le Boeuf and R. S. Peterson. bibliog il Science 166:1654-6 D 26 '69
Seals in peril; Atlantic, or grey seals threatened. M. Burton. il Sea Front 15:160-9 My '69
2,000-year-old seal. il Sci Digest 65:57 Ap '69
Watching seals at Turtle Rock; Weddell seals, under the Antarctic ice. C. Ray and M. A. DeCamp. il Natur Hist 78:26-35 Mr '69
Weddell seal. G. L. Kooyman. il Sci Am 221:100-6 Ag '69
SEAMAN, Barbara. See Seaman, G. jt. auth.
SEAMAN, Gideon, and Seaman, Barbara
Newsletter of marriage (cont) Ladies Home J 86:26 F: 56 Mr '69
SEAMANS, Robert C. 1918-
New management approach; excerpts from address. Aviation W 91:11 O 13 '69
USAF's case for modernization; excerpt from statement before the Senate armed services committee. Aviation W 90:11 My 19 '69
SEAMANSHIP
Houseboat seamanship. D. Kirkpatrick. il Motor B 124:46-7 D '69
SEAMEN
Avast, belay and pretty please. H. D. Whall. il Sports Illus 31:38-40 Jl 14 '69
Before the mast in Bluenose II. D. Kearns. il Yachting 125:90-1+ Ja '69
Douzes francaises: French America's cup preparations. S. Allan. il Yachting 125:88-9+ Ja '69

SEAMLESS flooring. See Flooring, Plastic

SEAPLANES
First to fly the Atlantic; American naval airmen in Navy Curtiss or NC flying boats. B. A. Weisberger. il Am Heritage 20:16-21+ Je '69
Make my supersonic jet a flying boat. G. Loening. il Holiday 46:38-9+ Jl '69

Floats
Floats. C. Converse. il Flying 85:68-72 S '69

SEAPORTS. See Ports

SEARBY, Frederick Wright
Control postmerger change. Harvard Bsns R 47:4-6+ S '69

SEARCH and rescue operations
Strange devices that found the sunken sub Scorpion; ed. by H. Shuldiner. C. L. Buchanan. il Pop Sci 194:66-71+ Ap '69

SEARCH for little Mary; story. See Cave, H.

SEARCH warrants. See Warrants (law)

SEARCHES and seizures
See also
Privateering

SEARCHLIGHTS
Powerful searchlight focuses on nighttime crime. il Am City 84:28 Mr '69

SEARLE, G. D, and company
He who hesitates. Forbes 104:64 S 15 '69

SEARLE, Humphrey
Hamlet. Criticism
Sat R 52:51 Je 28 '69

SEARLES, John R.
More sources of free and inexpensive material (cont) Engl J 58:928-37 S '69
—and Blount, N. S.
(eds) Teaching materials. See issues of English journal

SEARS, Jerry A. and James, William
Determining empirical formulas using radio-isotopes. pors Chem 42:29-30 O '69

SEARS, John
Rise of Harry Dent. J. Osborne. New Repub 160:14-15 Je 14 '69

SEARS, Paul Bigelow
Suicide by birthright. Audubon 71:94+ Mr '69

SEARS, Peter
Tour; poem. Sat R 52:102 Mr 8 '69

SEARS, Roebuck and company
Papa and the general. il Forbes 104:40 D 1 '69
Sears adds Sunday to shopping week. Bsns W p47 O 11 '69

SEASCAPES. See Marine painting

SEASHELL collage. See Collage

SEASHORE
Walk with me. K. Hillyard. il Har Yrs 9:26-9 Ag '69
See also
Beaches
Shore protection

SEASHORE ecology
Sea of survival; excerpt from In defense of nature. J. Hay. il Audubon 71:40-51 My '69
Shape of water; excerpts from In defense of nature. J. Hay. il Audubon 71:16-26 Jl '69

SEASHORE houses. See Beach architecture

SEASHORE protection. See Shore protection

SEASHORE state park, Va. See Virginia—Parks and reserves

SEASHORE vegetation
Flowers for seaside gardens. G. Taloumis. il Horticulture 47:30-3+ Ap '69

SEASIDE resorts
Black resorts. il Newsweek 74:49 S 1 '69
Resort that helps preserve a wild seashore; Salishan, Ore. D. Connelly. il Sports Illus 30:36-40 Ap 28 '69

Philippines
Shifting sands of Bantangas. P. J. Hersten. Sat R 52:69 S 13 '69

Russia
How the Kremlin takes a holiday. M. Kalb. il Sat R 52:83-4+ Mr 8 '69

SEASONAL industries
Seasonability in construction: a continuing problem. J. L. Russell and M. J. Pilot. bibliog il Mo Labor R 92:3-8 D '69

SEASONAL labor. See Migrant labor

SEASONINGS
Season to taste. M. Sherrill. Am Home 72:98 Ja '69
Seasonings; how to chart each course. il Parents Mag 44:90-5+ S '69
See also
Garlic
Herbs
Monosodium glutamate
Parsley
Spices

SEASONS
See also
Autumn
Winter

SEAT belts. See Safety belts

SEATRAIN lines, incorporated
Anchors aweigh. il Forbes 103:71-2 Je 15 '69
Ship line charts new courses. il Bsns W p 106-7+ F 8 '69
Two if by sea. R. Levy. il Duns R 94:86+ N '69

SEATTLE
Municipal utility plugs all-electric truck. J. M. Nelson. il Am City 84:89 F '69

City planning
Creating a model for model cities. il Bsns W p48+ Ja 18 '69
Leadership: the vital ingredient; Forward thrust program. il Time 93:34 Ja 24 '69

Description
In the swim. C. Dunsire. il Opera N 34:8-13 S 6 '69

Education
Local association of the month. B. L. Pearce and G. S. Green. Todays Ed 58:47-8 O '69

History
Seattle spirit. A. M. Lingg. Opera N 34:6-7 S 6 '69

Metropolitan district
Seattle's modern-day vigilantes. J. Fischer. Harper 238:14+ My '69

Music
National artists; Seattle opera's National artists program. F. Merkling. Opera N 34: 25 S 6 '69
See also
Seattle opera association

Newspapers
Defender of the faith; effect of boycott call over Post-intelligencer article attacking Catholic church. il Newsweek 74:75 Jl 28 '69

Social life and customs
Single life: Seattle. il Mlle 69:143+ S '69

SEATTLE boat show. See Boats—Exhibitions

SEATTLE opera association
Opera lives! W. Johnson. il Hi Fi 19:MA24-5 Ag '69
Opera's angels; SOA's Volunteer artists aides. D. W. Jones. il Opera N 34:22-4 S 6 '69
Philosophy of innovation. G. Ross. il Opera N 34:14-16 S 6 '69
Report: production of Turandot. F. J. Warnke. Opera N 34:25-6 D 13 '69
Report: Seattle; production of Der Rosenkavalier. W. M. Dunlop. il Opera N 33:30 Mr 8 '69
Report: Seattle; production of Fledermaus. F. J. Warnke. Opera N 34:23 N 1 '69
Report: Seattle; production of Tosca. W. M. Dunlop. Opera N 33:31 Ap 12 '69
Seattle opera association 1969-70 season. il Opera N 34:18-19 S 6 '69

SEATTLE SuperSonics (basketball team)
See Basketball teams

SEAVER, Don
Birds that fly nowhere. Sci Digest 65:19-21 Ap '69

SEAVER, Tom
Hero's off-season payoff; with report by W. Zinsser. il pors Life 67:38-41 N 7 '69
Highlight. por Sports Illus 31:66 Jl 14 '69
Maybe it's time to break up the Mets. W. Leggett. il Sports Illus 31:28-9 S 22 '69
Sportsman of the year. W. Leggett. il pors Sports Illus 31:32-4+ D 22 '69

SEAWATER teleosts. See Teleosts

SEAWEED
Seaweed; report of meeting. E. G. Young and J L. McLachlan. Science 163:598-9 F 7 '69
See also
Sargasso Sea

SECOND advent
Blessed hope. Chr Today 13:23 My 23 '69

SECOND committee of the General assembly. See United Nations—Economic and financial committee

SECONDARY education. See Education, Secondary

SECONDARY electron conduction camera tubes. See Television camera tubes

SECONDARY schools. See High schools

SECONDHAND bookstores. See Booksellers and bookselling—Secondhand books

SECONDHAND jets. See Airplanes, Used

SECONDHAND yachts. See Yachts, Used

SECRET; story. See King, P.
SECRET police, Russian. See Secret service—Russia
SECRET service

Great Britain
Spy with the old school tie. L. B. Kirkpatrick, jr. Trans-Action 6:57-8 Ja '69

Russia
American scholars in Russia soon learn about the K.G.B. R. F. Byrnes. il N Y Times Mag p84-5+ N 16 '69; Discussion. p63-4 D 14 '69
Organizational intelligence, by H. L. Wilensky. Review
　Trans-Action 6:60-2 Ja '69. C. B. Perrow

United States
Ghostly war of the Green Berets. H. Sutton. il Sat R 52:23-5+ O 18 '69
　See also
United States—Central intelligence agency
SECRET societies
　See also
Ku Klux klan
SECRETARIES
There'll never be enough secretaries. il Changing T 23:43-4 S '69
　See also
School secretaries

Salaries
How high can secretaries' salaries go? A. Lake. McCalls 96:95+ My '69

Supply and demand
Bait for secretaries gets more toothsome. il Bsns W p30-1 My 31 '69
SECRETARIES (furniture) See Desks
SECRETARIES of agriculture (United States)
　See also
Hardin, C.
SECRETARIES of defense (United States)
　See also
Laird, M. R.
SECRETARIES of labor (United States)
　See also
Shultz, G. P.
SECRETARIES of state (United States)
　See also
Rogers, W. P.
SECRETION
Quantal secretion from adrenal medulla: all-or-none release of storage vesicle content. O. H. Viveros and others. bibliog il Science 165:911-13 Ag 29 '69
SECRETIONS
Biochemistry at 100°C; explosive secretory discharge of bombardier beetles (brachinus) D. J. Aneshansley and others. bibliog il Science 165:61-3 Jl 4 '69; Same abr. with title Ingenuities of nature. Sat R 52:48 Ag 2 '69
Wildlife sketchbook. N. Smith. il Nat Wildlife 7:31 F '69
　See also
Pheromones
SECRETS, Trade. See Trade secrets
SECTS
　See also
Church of God
Hutterite Brethren
Jehovah's witnesses
Mennonites
Samaritans
Seventh day Adventists
Shakers
Soka Gakkai (sect)
Unitarians
SECULAR acceleration. See Acceleration
SECULAR institutes
　See also
Opus Dei
SECULAR theology. See Theology
SECURITIES
Golden eggs? Or lemons? underwriting new issues. il Forbes 104:24-8+ Jl 15 '69
Working by the numbers; compilation of standard securities identification numbers. Bsns W p 111 Je 28 '69
　See also
Bonds
Investments
Manipulation (securities)
Stock exchange
Stocks
　also subhead Securities under various subjects, e.g. Petroleum industry and trade—Securities

Marketing
New kid on the street. S. Mahoney. il Life 66:62-62B+ Je 6 '69
Perils of going public. R. Levy. Duns R 94:46-7 S '69
Personal investing; why and who of when-issued shares. il Fortune 80:173+ S '69
Private placement: the new money game. A. Hershman. il Duns R 93:23-5+ F '69
Shoring up the specialists. C. Morgello. il Newsweek 74:91 S 29 '69
Toughest kid in block trading. il Bsns W p 114-16 O 4 '69

Private placement
See Securities—Marketing

Registration
How stocks debut at the back door. Bsns W p 123-4+ Mr 29 '69
Letter stock is worth the worry; large holdings of unregistered shares by mutual funds. il Bsns W p 108+ Ja 18 '69
Stock for the pros; unregistered letter stock. C. Morgello. il Newsweek 74:78 N 24 '69

Regulation
How stocks debut at the back door. Bsns W p 123-4+ Mr 29 '69
SEC proposals stir little chaff. Bsns W p 136 S 20 '69
Tough to nudge Judge Budge. Time 94:69-70 Ag 8 '69

Theft
See Securities, Theft of

Transportation
Transfer: Wellington fund securities moved from First Pennsylvania banking & trust co, Philadelphia, to State street bank & trust co, Boston. New Yorker 45:23-7 Jl 12 '69
SECURITIES, Privately placed. See Securities—Marketing
SECURITIES, Tax exempt
Chances of taxing tax-free bonds. il U S News 66:85 Mr 24 '69
SECURITIES, Theft of
How to foil stock thieves. il Bsns W p 126 Je 21 '69
SECURITIES analysts. See Investments—Advisers
SECURITIES and exchange commission. See United States—Securities and exchange commission
SECURITY. See International security
SECURITY and insecurity (psychology)
Must mother be around all day? with study-discussion program, by R. Strang, M. W. Piers and B. Bowman. bibliog il PTA Mag 63:26-8, 34 Ap '69
SECURITY classification (government documents)
　See also
Defense information, Classified
SECURITY council of the United Nations. See United Nations—Security council
SECURITY measures in industry. See Industry—Security measures
SECURITY service. See Secret service
SEDATIVES
　See also
Barbiturates
Tranquilizing drugs
SEDIMENTATION and deposition
Fatty alcohols (normal and isoprenoid) in sediments. J. Sever and P. L. Parker. bibliog il Science 164:1052-4 My 30 '69
Graywacke matrix minerals: hydrothermal reactions with Columbia River sediments. J. W. Hawkins, jr. and J. T. Whetten. bibliog il Science 166:868-70 N 14 '69
Hydrocalcite ($CaCO_3.H_2O$) and nesquehonite ($MgCO_3.3H_2O$) in carbonate scales. H. Marschner. bibliog il Science 165:1119-21 S 12 '69; Reply. M. Fleischer. 166:1309 D 5 '69
Molasse facies: records of worldwide crustal stresses. F. B. Van Houten. bibliog il Science 166:1506-8 D 19 '69
Sedimentary phosphate method for estimating paleosalinities: a paleontological assumption. A. L. Guber. bibliog il Science 166:744-6 N 7 '69
Sedimentary phosphate method for estimating paleosalinities: limited applicability. G. Müller. il Science 163:812-13 F 21 '69
Slumping structures caused by organically derived gases in sediments. J. N. Monroe. bibliog il Science 164:1394-5 Je 20 '69
　See also
Marine sediments
SEDLÁKOVÁ, E. and others
Plasma saluretic activity: its nature and relation to oxytocin analogs. bibliog Science 164:580-2 My 2 '69

SEDOV, Leonid Ivanovich
First men on moon. Apollo 11 flight; Russian scientists' assessment. Space World F-10-70:34-5 O '69

SEDUMS
Unusual window box plants. F. W. Patch. il Horticulture 47:46 Jl '69

SEDZIOL, Pollyanna
Complex; poem. Chr Today 14:14 N 7 '69

SEE Wee the octopus; drama. See Burleson, C.

SEED boxes (horticulture) See Flats etc. (horticulture)

SEED growing. See Seed production

SEED industry and trade
Now seed growers do better than nature. il Bsns W p 127 S 27 '69
  See also
Burpee, W. Atlee, company
Park seed company

SEED production
Seeds from your own garden. J. J. Meeker. il Org Gard & Farm 16:30-4 Jl '69

SEED starters. See Flats, etc. (horticulture)

SEED testing
How seeds are tested. K. E. Relyea. Horticulture 47:40+ D '69

SEEDING
Last sowings of summer; plantings of root crops, lettuces, kale. R. Tirrell. il Org Gard & Farm 16:24-7 Jl '69
  See also
Corn seeding

SEEDLINGS
Deoxyribonucleic acid methylase activity in pea seedlings. F. Kalousek and N. R. Morris. bibliog il Science 164:721-2 My 9 '69
$11 plant-starter. T. Anderson. il Org Gard & Farm 16:86-8 D '69
Let that seedling grow. D. Foraker. il Org Gard & Farm 16:44-5 Ag '69
  See also
Flats, etc. (horticulture)

SEEDS
Fascination of seeds. R. Rodale. il Org Gard & Farm 16:31-3 F '69
Protein content of seed: increase improves growth and yield. C. J. Schweizer and S. K. Ries. bibliog il Science 165:73-5 Jl 4 '69
  See also
Corn—Seed
Grasses—Seed
Park seed company
Seed industry and trade
Seed production
Seed testing
Sunflowers—Seed

Testing
  See Seed testing

SEEGER, Murray
Games forecasters play. Duns R 93:42-3+ Ja '69
Republicans and emergency strikes. Duns R 93:81-2+ Ap '69

SEEGER, Pete
To save the dying Hudson: Pete Seeger's voyage. pors Look 33:62-5 Ag 26 '69
Woody Guthrie, songwriter; excerpt from The incompleat folksinger, ed. by J. Schwartz. por Ramp Mag 7:28-33 N 30 '68
  about
Hope of the Hudson. S. Atwater. il Cons 23:15-16 Je '69

SEEGERS, Kathleen Walker
My dark journey through insanity. Read Digest 95:67-71 N '69

SEEGERS, Scott
ADELA: capital idea for Latin America. Read Digest 94:154-6+ Mr '69

SEEING eye dogs. See Dogs as guides

SEELIGER, Ronald
Tenor of the high C. Opera N 33:16 Mr 29 '69

SEELYE, Mary-Averett
Mary-Averett Seelye; the Cubiculo. M. Marks. Dance Mag 43:81 D '69

SEFERIADES, Giorgos Stylianou
Poet speaks out. il por Time 93:37 Ap 4 '69

SEFERIS, George. See Seferiades, G. S.

SEGAL, George, 1924–
Plaster caste. J. Perreault. il Art N 67:54-5+ N '68

SEGAL, Julius, and Luce, G. G.
To sleep: perchance to dream; excerpts from 1970 Britannica yearbook of science and the future. Todays Health 47:48-51+ O '69

SEGAL, Lore
Passing time. New Repub 160:23-4+ Mr 29 '69
Square bananas. New Repub 160:24+ F 22 '69

SEGEL, Joseph Myron
Joe Segel's private mint. il por Forbes 104: 28-9 O 15 '69

SEGERS, Charles
Do you want me to help you? story. Redbook 132:72-3 F '69

SEGINSKI. John
Handsome and durable, that's the split-rail fence. Org Gard & Farm 16:106-9 F '69
Insects guard your garden. Org Gard & Farm 16:95+ Ag '69
  about
What does an op amp do? quiz. Pop Electr 31:50+ O '69

SEGONZAC, Adalbert de
Time for choice. Harper 238:94+ F '69

SEGREGATION, Social
Discrimination and executives. America 120: 642 My 31 '69
We won't end the urban crisis until we end majority rule. H. J. Gans. il N Y Times Mag p 12-15+ Ag 3 '69; Discussion. p6+ Ag 24 '69
  See also
Discrimination in housing
Minorities
Negroes—Segregation

SEGREGATION in education
Berkeley story: commitment to integration. S. G. Streshinsky. il Parents Mag 44:48-51+ My '69
Color in the classroom: there is no panacea. I. Kraft. il Nation 208:71-3 Ja 20 '69
Mixed classes: same government rules now for North and South. U S News 66:12 Mr 17 '69
Politics of resegregation. G. Orfield. il Sat R 52:58-60+ S 20 '69
Say it isn't so; self segregation by black students. New Repub 160:7 My 24 '69
Sparkling reaction: Finch's remarks; problem of enforcing law against racial discrimination. U S News 66:16 Mr 24 '69

SEGREGATION of Negroes. See Negroes—Segregation

SEGUNDO, Juan Luis
Has Latin America a choice? America 120: 213-16 F 22 '69

SEIBERT, Deni
Unique pollination in orchids. Horticulture 46:23 Ag '68

SEIBT, Uta. See Schneider. D. jt. auth.

SEIDLER, Edouard
Doctor Kurt Lotz vorstandsvorsitzender of Volkswagen. Motor T 21:18+ Ag '69
Overseas report. See issues of Motor trend Turin. Motor T 21:62-6 Mr '69

SEIDMAN, Arthur H.
Importance of filters por Electr World 81:37-9 Ap '69
Recording oscilloscope. Electr World 82:27 N '69
Survey of silicon junction diodes. por Electr World 82:35-7 Jl '69
Transistors made of glass. il Electr World 81:68 F '69

SEIDMAN, Earl. See Cooper. J. M. jt. auth.

SEIDMAN, Hugh
Bookstore: Surreal poem: Demonstration: poems. Poetry 113:250-2 Ja '69

SEILACHER, Adolf. See Raup, D. M. jt. auth.

SEINGALT, Giacomo Girolamo Casanova de. See Casanova de Seingalt. G. G.

SEISMIC sea waves
Look, no earthquake. W. Zinsser. il Life 67: 4 N 14 '69

SEISMOGRAPHS
Apollo passive seismic experiment. G. Latham and others. bibliog il Science 165:241-50 Jl 18 '69
Lunar package retains seismic gear; Easep passive seismic experiment. il Aviation W 90:54-5 F 24 '69

SEISMOLOGICAL research. See Earthquakes—Research

SEISMOLOGY
Alsep returns baseline seismic data. Aviation W 91:22-3 D 8 '69
Apollo 12's moon: surprises already. il Sci N 96:493-4 N 29 '69
Apollo's riches; lunar experiments. R. Jastrow. Newsweek 74:18 Ag 4 '69
Ascent stage lunar crash may help seismic studies. Z. Strickland. Aviation W 91:18 S 1 '69
Caution; go slow; moonquake data received from Apollo 11 seismometer. il Newsweek 74:95B D 8 '69
Earthquakes. C. F. Richter. il Natur Hist 78: 36-45 D '69
Granites: relation of properties in situ to laboratory measurements. G. Simmons and A. Nur; reply with rejoinder. A. S. Orange. Science 165:202-3 Jl 11 '69

SEISMOLOGY—*Continued*
　Seismic waves reflected from discontinuities within earth's upper mantle. E. R. Engdahl and E. A. Flinn. bibliog il Science 163:177-9 Ja 10 '69
　Transversely aligned seismicity and concealed structures. C. F. Richter. bibliog il Science 166:173-8 O 10 '69
　　See also
　Earth movements
SEISMOMETERS. See Seismographs
SEITZ, Frederick
　Tribute to Frederick Seitz. J. A. Stratton. Science 164:1469 Je 27 '69
SEITZ, Michael W. See Frank, J. jt. auth.
SEITZ, Nick
　(ed) See Cross, G. L. College president speaks out
SEITZ, William C.
　Rosati: masses in elevation. Art N 68:38-41+ D '69
SEJNA, Jan
　Russia plotted the Pueblo affair: excerpts Read Digest 95:73-6 Jl '69
SELA, Michael
　Antigenicity: some molecular aspects. bibliog Science 166:1365-74 D 12 '69
　—See Haimovich, J. jt. auth.
SELB, Germany (Federal Republic)
　Long-range plan for the future development of the Bavarian town of Selb. il Arch Rec 146:140-3 S '69
SELBY, Don
　Automating the railroads. Electr World 81: 46-7+ F '69
SELBY, Earl
　Battle of San Francisco Bay. Read Digest 94: 106-10 Mr '69
　New Haven: where federal dollars pay off. Read Digest 94:189-90+ Je '69
SELDEN, Neil. See Imbrie, M. jt. auth.
SELDES, Gilbert
　One thing and another. J. K. Hutchens. Sat R 52:36-8 Ap 5 '69
SELDIN, Joel
　Blue cross pays the bills. Nation 209:48-52 Jl 14 '69
　Prospects and problems. Nation 209:200-2 S 8 '69
SELDIS, Henry J.
　West coast report. Art in Am 57:107-9 Mr '69
SELECT committee on nutrition and human needs. See United States—Congress—Senate—Nutrition and human needs. Select committee on
SELECT committee on small business. See United States—Congress—Senate—Small business. Select committee on
SELECTION of bishops. See Bishops—Selection
SELECTION of librarians. See Librarians—Selection and appointment
SELECTION of students. See Student selection
SELECTION of teachers. See Teachers—Selection and appointment
SELECTIVE objectors. See Conscientious objectors
SELECTIVE service, Military. See Military service. Compulsory
SELENOLOGY. See Moon—Surface
SELF
　　See also
　Consciousness
　Existentialism
SELF analysis. See Self evaluation
SELF appraisal. See Self evaluation
SELF assurance. See Self reliance
SELF-bailing cockpits. See Boat cockpits
SELF confidence. See Self reliance
SELF consciousness
　　See also
　Timidity
SELF culture
　Bridges to other people. L. Smith. Redbook 133:91+ S '69
　New, new, self-improved me! M. Bricklin. il Read Digest 94:123-5 F '69
　　See also
　Books and reading
SELF defense
　Mace for the masses. J. A. Page. Commonweal 90:141-3 Ap 18 '69
　　See also
　Judo
SELF defense for women
　Will pocketbook tear-gas devices protect you? Good H 169:200 N '69
SELF determination (government)
　　See also
　Minorities
SELF-developing cameras. See Cameras
SELF education. See Self culture

SELF employed
　Free-lance writer and social security. J. Sword. Writer 82:27-9 Mr '69
　Going into business: gas stations. il Changing T 23:35-8 F '69
SELF esteem. See Self love
SELF estimate. See Self evaluation
SELF evaluation
　Blame me on civilization. P. Callow. Vogue 154:318+ S 1 '69
　Camping and self-concept. F. Raymond. il Camp Mag 41:18 My '69
　One trillion times zero; work of the synapse. H. C. Elliott. Yale R 58:549-62 Je '69
　Self-concept: a vital factor in school and career development. J. J. Pietrofesa. bibliog Clear House 44:37-40 S '69
　Self-fulfilling prophecy, a key to success. J. K. Lagemann. Read Digest 94:80-3 F '69
　　See also
　Students—Rating
SELF expression. See Personality
SELF government in education
　Anatomy of power. J. S. Brubacher. Ed Digest 35:3-4 N '69
　Campus outlook: more turmoil. R. T. Gray. il Nations Bsns 57:36-41 Ag '69
　Campus that kept its cool: Seton Hall university, New Jersey. B. Darrach. il Life 67:80-80B+ N 7 '69
　Maximum results from mini-courses; Hamilton-Wenham regional high school. R. R. Hayward. Todays Ed 58:55-7 S '69
　On campus: student government, power or puppet? Mlle 70:58 N '69
　Participation is learning. R. S. Powell, jr. Sat R 53:56+ Ja 10 '70
　Power to the students. D. J. O'Brien. Commonweal 91:15-18+ O 3 '69
　Responding to student unrest; with study-discussion program, ed. by C. Smallenburg and H. Smallenburg. bibliog il PTA Mag 64:10-14, 35-6 S '69
　Young voices on advisory committees. M. Landazuri. Am Ed 5:26 Ag '69
　　See also
　Colleges and universities—Administration—Student participation
SELF help activities. See Cooperative associations
SELF improvement. See Self culture
SELF knowledge. See Self evaluation
SELF love
　Heresy of self-love, by P. Zweig. Review Nation 208:409-10 Mr 31 '69. M. Ellmann
　How to enhance pupil self-esteem. S. Coopersmith and J. Silverman. Todays Ed 58:28-9 Ap '69
　　See also
　Autism
SELF rating of college professors. See College professors and instructors—Rating
SELF rating of students. See Students—Rating
SELF ratings. See Self evaluation
SELF-recognition. See Recognition (psychology)
SELF reliance
　Man talk: the answer man. D. Newman and R. Benton. il Mlle 68:50 F '69
　Self confidence in art for the elementary teacher. J. G. Cecere. il Sch Arts 69:28-9 S '69
SELIGMAN, Daniel
　Special kind of rebellion. Fortune 79:66-9+ Ja '69
　　about
　Editor's desk. L. Banks. por Fortune 80:81 Jl '69
SELIKOFF, I. J.
　Asbestos: adaptation of address, December 28, 1968. bibliog Environ 11:2-7 Mr '69
SELK, Merry
　Five principles, a new approach. Bul Atom Sci 25:78 F '69
　Sentinel in the backyard: the transitional reaction. Bul Atom Sci 25:7 Ja '69
　Styles of handling student demonstrations. Bul Atom Sci 25:36-8 Je '69
SELLARS, Dorothy Rainer
　Dance teacher in the community. See issues of Dance magazine
　Plusses outweigh the minuses. Dance Mag 43:60-2+ N '69
SELLERS, Barney
　Civil rights, the Nixon fiddle. Nation 209: 344-6 O 6 '69
　Packard's deal with the textile big three. New Repub 160:9-11 Mr 22 '69
SELLERS, Rose Z.
　Due process, the real issue; letter to the editor. Library J 94:123 Ja 15 '69
　Overdue. por Wilson Lib Bul 43:786+ Ap '69

SELLIN, Thorsten
Academy dips its colors to Dr Sellin. J. C. Charlesworth. Ann Am Acad 381:iii-iv Ja '69

SELLING. See Marketing; Salesmen and salesmanship

SELMA, Mo.
River cement company: the genesis of three buildings. il Arch Rec 145:164-6 F '69

SELTSAM, William H.
Obituary
Opera N il por 33:30 F 8 '69. P. L. Miller

SELYE, Hans, and others
Digitoxin poisoning: prevention by spironolactone. bibliog Science 164:842-3 My 16 '69

SELZ, Peter
Final negation: Harold Paris' Koddesh-Koddashim. Art in Am 57:62-7 Mr '69
Los Angeles: a view from the studios. Art in Am 57:144 N '69
West coast report (cont) Art in Am 57:92-7 Ja; 107 Mr; 104-5 My; 108 S '69

SEMA. See Specialty equipment manufacturers association

SEMANCIK, J. S. and Reynolds, D. A.
Assembly of protein and nucleoprotein particles from extracted tobacco rattle virus protein and RNA. bibliog Science 164:559-60 My 2 '69

SEMANTICS
See also
English language—Semantics
International society for general semantics

Study and teaching
Semantics: what and why. C. Weingartner. Engl J 58:1214-19 N '69
Teaching semantics in high school. S. Torvik. Engl J 58:1341-6 D '69

SEMBA, Tsuneo, and Kano, Masaakira
Glycine in the spinal cord of cats with local tetanus rigidity. bibliog Science 164:571-2 My 2 '69

SEMENOV, Vladimir Semenovich
Start of SALT. il por Time 94:33-4 N 21 '69
With U.S.-Soviet negotiators: smiles before the bargaining. il por U S News 67:17 D 1 '69

SEMICONDUCTORS
All about ovonics. F. Shunaman. il Radio-Electr 40:41-3 My '69
Amorphous-semiconductor switching. H. K. Henisch. il Sci Am 221:30-41 bibliog(p 166) N '69
Amorphous semiconductors stimulate fundamental and applied research; report of meeting. W. Paul. Phys Today 22:97+ O '69
Effect of Stanford R. Ovshinsky. il Life 67:81-2+ O 17 '69
Electronic materials and applications. H. C. Gatos. Science 164:137-41 Ap 11 '69
Glassy semiconductors show switching and memory effects. G. B. Lubkin. bibliog il Phys Today 22:63 Ja '69
Interest grows in semiconductor instabilities; report of meeting. C. Hilsum. il Phys Today 22:89-91 Ag '69
New tubes and semiconductors. See issues of Radio-electronics
Ovonics; new era in semiconductors? J. P. Robinson, jr. il Pop Electr 30:55-8 Mr '69
Ovshinsky: promoter or persecuted genius? P. M. Boffey. il Science 165:673-7 Ag 15 '69
Signetics shows how in semiconductors. il Bsns W p41-2 Jl 26 '69
Solid state. L. Garner. See issues of Popular electronics
Texas instruments: big opportunities in small packages. il Forbes 103:32-4+ Mr 1 '69
VDR's and thermistors. il Radio-Electr 40:55-7 Ap '69
See also
Electric current rectifiers
Silicon
Transistors

Testing
Simple checker for semiconductors. J. A. Fred. il Pop Mech 131:146-7 My '69

SEMINARIANS. See Theological students
SEMINARIES. See Theological schools
SEMINARS
America and the world: a new fix? Princeton seminar. A. Schlesinger, jr. Vogue 153:184-5+ F 1 '69
Developing book industries of Asia; report of two regional seminars on book publishing. C. G. Benjamin. il Pub W 195:17-19 My 5 '69
Liberal establishment faces the blacks, the young, the new left. W. Goodman; discussion. N Y Times Mag p4+ Ja 19 '69

Westmoreland seminarist. Nation 208:389 Mr 31 '69

SEMINOLE Indians
Florida's emerging Seminoles. L. Capron. il Nat Geog 136:716-34 N '69

SEMINOLE war, 2d, 1835-1842
Osceola: he wouldn't go. il Sr Schol 94:16 Mr 7 '69

SEMKOW, Georg
Artist life. D. J. Soria. por Hi Fi 19:MA8-10 Mr '69
Music to my ears; program with the New York philharmonic orchestra. I. Kolodin. Sat R 52:53 Ap 26 '69

SEMPLE, Robert B. Jr
Nixon's presidency is a very private affair. N Y Times Mag p28-9+ N 2 '69
Time: 7:45 a.m, weekdays; place: Roosevelt room, West wing, White House, Nixon's inner circle meets. N Y Times Mag p6-9+ Ag 3 '69
—See Frankel, M. jt. auth.

SEMYONOV, Vladimir Semenovich. See Semenov, V. S.

SENATE

United States
See United States—Congress—Senate
SENATE armed services committee. See United States—Congress—Senate—Armed services, Committee on
SENATE foreign relations committee. See United States—Congress—Senate—Foreign relations, Committee on
SENATE investigations. See Government investigations

SENATORS
Art of oratory in the Senate of the United States. W. H. Honan. il Esquire 71:161-7+ My '69
Clues to outlook of new senator. U S News 67:23 S 29 '69
Nixon and the liberal Republicans. J. Osborne. New Repub 161:13-15 Jl 26 '69
Vietnam: the lull hits home: views of Senate doves. il Newsweek 74:23-4 N 3 '69
Young senate rebels. il Newsweek 74:31-2 Ag 4 '69
See also
United States—Congress—Senate
also names of Senators, e.g. J. J. Williams

Salaries, allowances, etc.
Double standard: public disclosure resolution. il Newsweek 73:36 My 26 '69

SENATORS (baseball) See Baseball clubs

SENECA Indians
Cornplanter, can you swim? Kinzua Dam flooding ancestral lands for Allegheny reservoir. A. M. Josephy. jr. il Am Heritage 20:4-9+ D '68
Death and rebirth of the Seneca, by F. C. Wallace. Review
Newsweek il 75:90+ Ja 19 '70. R. A. Gross

SENESCENCE. See Old age
SENILITY. See Old age
SENIOR centers
Arctic senior center is polar bear capital. il Aging 173:12 Mr '69
City cares; Flint, Mich. provides a functional center for senior citizens. L. W. Tyler. il Parks & Rec 4:30-1+ Jl '69
Worcester age center takes to the road. il Aging 176:6-7 Je '69
See also
Recreation for the aged

SENIOR citizens month
May is Senior citizens month. Aging 175:3 My '69
Plans already begun for May: 7th U.S. senior citizens month. Aging 171:8 Ja '69

SENIORITY, Employee
How the hard core can survive layoffs; UAW's inverted seniority plan. il Bsns W p82+ Mr 29 '69
Job seniority and discrimination; excerpt from Discrimination in the union and on the job. A. W. Blumrosen. Mo Labor R 92:52-3 Mr '69
Job tenure: how it relates to race and age. F. J. O'Boyle. bibliog il Mo Labor R 92:16-23 S '69
Newest seniority right: to be laid off first. il U S News 66:68-9 Mr 24 '69
Seniority on the spot. Time 93:83-4 Mr 28 '69

SENSES and sensation
See also
After images
Hearing
Pain
Perception, Disorders of
Sensory deprivation
Smell
Taste
Touch

SENSIBAR, Judith L.
  Why we chose natural childbirth. por Red-
    book 132:22+ Ja '69
SENSITIVITY training. See Group relations
    training
SENSORY deprivation
  Six cave explorers who lived outside of time.
    W. S. Ross. il Sci Digest 65:8-13 Ap '69
SENTENCES (grammar) See English language
    —Grammar
SENTINEL missile defense system. See Guided
    missiles—Defenses
SEPARATION of isotopes. See Isotope separa-
    tion
SEPHERIADES, Giorgos Stylianou. See Se-
    feriades, G. S.
SEPTIC tanks
  Primer on septic tanks. House & Gard 135:
    50+ My '69
SEPULCHRAL monuments
  Move over, Forest Lawn! plastic tombstones.
    Chr Cent 86:1149 S 3 '69
SEQUOIA, Giant
  Big tree: Wawona tunnel tree. N. Gray. il
    Am Home 72:26+ S '69
  How fire helps the big trees. H. Weaver and
    H. Biswell. il Nat Parks 43:16-19 Jl '69
SEQUOIA gigantea. See Sequoia, Giant
SEQUOIA NATIONAL PARK
  Sequoia, looking toward the King. P. L.
    Nelson and R. C. Eckhardt. il Nat Parks
    43:10-14 D '69
SERBS
    See also
  Yugoslavia
SEREBNICK, Judith
  Book review editor named by LJ. por Library
    J 94:1565 Ap 15 '69
—and others
  (ed) Book review. See issues of Library
    journal
SERENGETI NATIONAL PARK. See National
    parks and reserves—Tanzania
SERIAL composition. See Composition (mu-
    sic)
SERIAL publications
  Large project to reprint cumulative serial in-
    dexes. Pub W 195:53 Je 16 '69
  Price indexes for 1969: Serial services. W. H.
    Huff and N. B. Brown. il Library J 94:
    2572-3 Jl '69
SERIES, Book
  Children's books forecast, series. il Pub W
    196:167-77 Jl 14 '69
SERIGRAPHY. See Silk screen printing
SERINE
  N-Formylseryl-transfer RNA. W. S. Kim.
    bibliog il Science 163:947-9 F 28 '69
  Serine requirement in leukemic and normal
    blood cells. J. D. Regan and others. bibliog
    il Science 163:1452-3 Mr 28 '69
SERLING, Robert
  Is it safe to fly? Hmmmm. Holiday 46:54-5
    Jl '69
SERMONS
  Pop sermons. B. Barr. Chr Cent 86:1190-2
    S 17 '69; Discussion. 86:1424-5 N 5 '69
  Toward Judah; sermon delivered at River-
    side church, New York. C. Marney. Chr
    Cent 86:1345-8 O 22 '69
    See also
  Preaching
SEROTONIN
  Circadian rhythm of serotonin in the pineal
    body of immunosympathectomized immature
    rats. C. R. S. Machado and others. bibliog
    il Science 164:442-3 Ap 25 '69
  Micelle formation between 5-hydroxytrypta-
    mine and adenosine triphosphate in platelet
    storage organelles. K. H. Berneis and oth-
    ers. bibliog il Science 165:913-14 Ag 29 '69
SERPENT; drama. See Chaikin, J.
SERPENT; drama. See Van Itallie, J.-C.
SERPENTINE
  Pecoraite, Ni₆Si₄O₁₀(OH)s, nickel analog of
    clinochrysotile, formed in the Wolf Creek
    meteorite. G. T. Faust and others. bibliog
    il Science 165:59-60 Jl 4 '69
SERPENTS. See Snakes
SERRIN, William
  At Ford everyone knows who is the boss.
    N Y Times Mag p25-7+ O 19 '69
  God help our city. Atlan 223:115-21 Mr '69
SERUM
  Antibodies to polynucleotides: distribution in
    human serums. D. Koffler and others. bib-
    liog il Science 166:1648-9 D 26 '69
  Obstructive lung disease and a-antitrypsin
    deficiency gene heterozygosity. F. Kueppers
    and others. bibliog il Science 165:899-901
    Ag 29 '69
    See also
  Antiserum
  Complements (immunity)
  Serotonin

SERUM albumins. See Blood—Proteins
SERUM cholesterol. See Cholesterol
SERUM globulins
  Complement-immunoglobulin relation: de-
    ficiency of C'1q associated with impaired
    immunoglobulin G synthesis. bibliog il Sci-
    ence 163:474-5 Ja 31 '69
  Immunoglobulin structure: variability and
    homology. F. W. Putnam. bibliog il Science
    163:633-44 F 14 '69
SERUM hepatitis. See Hepatitis
SERUM-hepatitis virus. See Hepatitis virus
SERVANTS. See Household employees
SERVANTS, Indentured. See Indentured ser-
    vants
SERVE and enrich retirement by volunteer
    service. See Volunteer service
SERVICE, William
  Coffee-can owl; excerpt from Owl. Read Di-
    gest 95:127-31 O '69
  Owl. Sports Illus 30:52-6+ Je 30 '69
SERVICE
  When someone is drowning, it's no time to
    teach him how to swim. E. M. Davis. Read
    Digest 95:104-6 N '69
    See also
  Assistance in emergencies
SERVICE, Community. See Comunity service
SERVICE, Compulsory non-military
  Conscription; with a choice. J. B. Donovan.
    America 120:726-7 Je 28; Reply. T. E.
    Quigley. 121:51 Ag 2 '69
  National service: folly or fair? pro and con
    discussion. bibliog Sr Schol 94:3-5 F 14 '69
  Would you give a year of your life to serve
    your country? Seventeen 28:96-7+ Jl '69
SERVICE, Volunteer. See Volunteer service
SERVICE clubs. See Clubs
SERVICE industries
  Address book. E. Kinard. See issues of House
    beautiful
  Arriving: the household professional. D. Mac-
    Donald. il House B 111:88-9 Mr '69
  Dial S for service; computer-run emergency
    service companies, Europe. V. Lewis. Duns
    R 93:98-9 Mr '69
  High cost of services. il Forbes 103:57 Ja 15
    '69
  How to be well-served for $100,000 a year. R.
    H. Williams. il Esquire 71:108-11 Mr '69
  Service economy. Sci Am 220:48-9 Ap '69
  Service economy grows, but does it? il Bsns
    W p 126+ F 15 '69
  Why customers complain: the breakdown in
    service. il U S News 67:50-2 D 1 '69
    See also
  Computer-based service companies

    Anecdotes, facetiae, satire, etc.
  Institute for utter frustration. A. Buchwald.
    Travel & Camera 32:58-9 Je '69
SERVICE men
  Breaking ranks and breaking dissenters. S.
    V. Roberts. Commonweal 91:397-8 Ja 9 '70
  Must the citizen give up his civil liberties
    when he joins the army? R. Sherrill. il
    N Y Times Mag p25-7+ My 18 '69
    See also
  Christmas gifts for service men
  Military service
  Soldiers
    Recreation
    See United States—Armed forces—Recrea-
    tion; United States—Army—Recreation

    Religion
    See United States—Armed forces—Reli-
    gious affairs

    Vocational education
  How GM helps itself by helping the GIs:
    Project Transition. il Bsns W p92+ Ap 26
    '69
SERVICE men, Discharged. See Veterans
SERVICE mens amusements. See United States
    —Armed forces—Recreation; United States
    —Army—Recreation
SERVICE mens benefits. See Veterans—Bene-
    fits
SERVICE mens entertainments. See United
    States—Armed forces—Recreation
SERVICE mens families
  How servicemen's marriages survive separa-
    tion. J. Whitbread. Redbook 132:94+ Ap
    '69
  Today I watched a soldier come home. N. A.
    Wicker. Farm J 93:53 Je '69
SERVICE mens marriages. See War marriages

SERVICE men's publications
Enemy of the people; zapping a sailor-editor; R. Priest. M. Polner. Commonweal 90: 560 S 19 '69; Reply. S. L. Wilcox. 91:111 O 24 '69
Typography of the underground dissent. il Life 66:30-1 My 23 '69
Underground GI press. J. Pilati. Commonweal 90:559-61 S 19 '69
See also
Stars and stripes (newspaper)

SERVICE mens wives
Anger of absence. Time 93:78+ Je 27 '69
Waiting out the war, wife or widow? case of P. Mearns. J. Fried. il Life 67:75-6+ N 7 '69

SERVICE stations. See Automobile service stations

SERVICES, Municipal. See Municipal government

SERVING carts
Server you can use inside or roll outdoors. D. A. Ashe. il Bet Hom & Gard 47:33 Mr '69

SERWER, Howard
Wiedrigkeit and *verdriesslichkeit* in Mühlhausen. bibliog f Mus Q 55:20-30 Ja '69

SESAME street (program) See Television in education

SESSA, Frank B.
Do you care? Library J 94:2412 Je 15 '69
New ALA officer. ALA Bul 63:1166-8 S '69

SESSER, Stanford N.
News from toyland. New Repub 161:11-13 D 20 '69

SESSIONS, Roger
Lucky one. R. Evett. Atlan 224:107 Jl '69
about
New hall for Montezuma. J. H. Sutcliffe. Opera N 33:6-7 My 17 '69

SESSLER, Gloria Jean
Orchids around the year. Horticulture 47:20-1 N '69; 48:34-5 Ja '70

SETON, Cynthia Propper
Special and curious blessing; excerpts. McCalls 96:71+ F '69

SETON Hall university, South Orange, N.J.
Campus that kept its cool. B. Darrach. il Life 67:80-80B+ N 7 '69

SETTERS
Odd couples; English setters and English spaniels. D. M. Duffey. il Outdoor Life 143:192-3+ Ap '69
Useful beauties; English setters. D. M. Duffey. il Outdoor Life 144:98-100+ D '69

SETTLING basins
Better settling basin. G. Culp. bibliog il Am City 84:82-5 Ja '69

SEVAREID, Eric
American militarism: what is it doing to us? Look 33:14-16 Ag 12 '69

SEVEN days of mourning; drama. See Simckes, S.

SEVEN deadly sins. See Deadly sins

SEVEN-Eleven food stores
Return of mom & pop; corner grocers. il Forbes 104:38 Jl 1 '69

SEVEN up company
7-up bids for youth with a negative pitch. il Bsns W p48-9 F 15 '69

1776; musical comedy. See Musical comedies, revues, etc.—Criticisms, plots, etc.

SEVENTEEN year locusts. See Cicadas

SEVENTH-day Adventists
Germ warfare: for alma mater, God and country. S. Hersh. il Ramp Mag 8:21-4 D '69

SEVENTH regiment. See United States—Army

SEVER, Judy, and Parker, P. L.
Fatty alcohols (normal and isoprenoid) in sediments. bibliog Science 164:1052-4 My 30 '69

SEVERIN, Kurt
African egg-eating champion; photographs. Sci Digest 66:84-7 S '69
Gulp! egg-eating snake; photographs. Natur Hist 78:42-3 Je '69

SEVILLE, Jack
Air cooled engine for your boat. Mech Illus 65:70-1+ Ag '69

SEWAGE
See also
Sewerage
Water pollution

SEWAGE disposal
Heat treatment of sewage sludge; Farrer system. il Am City 84:62 O '69
See also
Septic tanks
Sewage pumping
Trade waste disposal

Activated sludge method
Conditioner improves sludge vacuum filtering; activated-sludge waste-water treatment plant serving McHenry, Ill. il Am City 84: 77 S '69

Coagulation
Waste treatment system contract awarded to GE; onboard watercraft electro-coagulation. Aviation W 90:49 Je 30 '69

SEWAGE disposal plants
Nuisance-free sludge disposal; Liberty, N.Y. H. Eichenauer. il Am City 84:116-17 F '69
Other ear opens; lack of adequate sewage treatment plants. Sci N 96:350 O 18 '69
Will develop chemical-physical treatment processes. Am City 84:34 N '69

SEWAGE pumping
Make your pumping stations attractive; Manhattan pumping station. M. Rothenberg. il Am City 84:94-5 My '69

SEWAGE systems. See Sewerage

SEWAGE treatment plants. See Sewage disposal plants

SEWELL, Katherine J.
Try cotton-ball planting for an early garden. Org Gard & Farm 16:102-3 Mr '69

SEWELLELS. See Mountain beavers

SEWER cleaning
Hit-and-run squads clear sewer stoppages; Dallas, Tex. A. E. Holcomb. il Am City 84:119+ Jl '69
Sewer had to be cleaned before snowfall; Houghton Mich. C. Knecht. il Am City 84: 120+ O '69
Sewer root control, chemically; Sacramento County. N. R. Townley .il Am City 84:92-4 D '69

SEWER inspection
Low pressure air tests for sewer lines; questions and answers. W. J. Malcom. il Am City 84:74-5 N '69
Sewer root control, chemically; Sacramento County. N. R. Townley. il Am City 84:92-4 D '69

SEWER pipe laying. See Pipe laying

SEWER pipes
See also
Pipe lining
Sewer cleaning

Leakage
Low pressure air tests for sewer lines; questions and answers. W. J. Malcom. il Am City 84:74-5 N '69

SEWERAGE
County-owned, city-managed sewerage system; Cincinnati, A. D. Caster. il Am City 84:117-18 Ag '69
It's in the bag; system of storage reservoirs will capture stormwater overflow. Sandusky, Ohio. il Am City 84:88 Ap '69
Sewers need better soils engineering. J. S. Ward. il Am City 84:72-4 Jl '69
See also
Pipe laying

SEWERS. See Sewerage

SEWING
Best methods of sewing on buttons. il Good H 168:209 Ap '69
See also
Dressmaking
Needlework

Study and teaching
Nantucket school of needlery. D. L. Brightbill. il Am Home 72:32 Jl '69

SEWING centers. See Sewing rooms

SEWING equipment
Good gadget for attaching buttons; Buttoneer. il Consumer Rep 34:237-8 My '69
You can fasten buttons neatly without needle and thread; Dennison buttoneer. il Consumer Bul 52:18 Mr '69

SEWING machines
They sew a crooked zigzag seam. Consumer Rep 34:108 Mr '69
Zigzag sewing machines. il Consumer Rep 34: 112-20 Mr '69
See also
Singer company

SEWING rooms
Doors open up a sewing center. il Sunset 143: 82 Ag '69
Place to sew, patterned to fit your needs. il Parents Mag 44:70-3 F '69

SEX
See also
Reproduction

Research
See Sex research

SEX (biology)
It's tough to grow males. Sci Digest 66:46 O '69
See also
Hermaphroditism

SEX (psychology)
Anatomy is not destiny; views of W. Simon and J. H. Gagnon. Time 93:56+ Mr 28 '69
Man talk: up tight. D. Newman and R. Benton. Mlle 69:54 Je '69
My wife, the naked movie star. L. H. Farber. il Harper 238:49-55 Je '69
Parents and privacy. J. Brothers. Good H 168:50+ F '69
Psychosexual development. W. Simon and J. Gagnon. il Trans-Action 6:9-17 Mr '69

SEX, Change of. See Change of sex

SEX and law
Modernizing sex laws. il Time 94:57 Ag 8 '69

SEX and religion
Demon of lust. L. N. Bell. Chr Today 13:34-5 My 9 '69
Post-pill morality? Chr Today 13:25-6 Mr 14 '69
Prudes, lewds and polysyllables. J. H. Smylie. Commonweal 89:671-3 F 28 '69
Sex, church and culture. J. Hitchcock. Cath World 209:17-20 Ap '69
Understanding sex in the age of the pill. G. Clanton; discussion. Chr Cent 86:187+ F 5 '69
   See also
Sex in the Bible

SEX attractants (insects) See Insect sex attractants

SEX behavior. See Sexual behavior

SEX censorship. See Censorship

SEX crimes
   See also
Child molesters
Rape

SEX determination and control
Big step in sex prediction; blood chromosome analysis. il Sci N 96:76-7 Jl 26 '69

SEX differences
Hearing: demonstration by women when Joint legislative committee on the problems of public health convened on abortion issue. New Yorker 45:28-9 F 22 '69
Men in groups. by L. Tiger. Review
  Newsweek il 74:89+ Jl 7 '69. G. Wolff
  Time 93:62 Je 20 '69
Sex differences in verbal and performance IQ's of children undergoing open-heart surgery. M. P. Honzik and others. bibliog il Science 164:445-7 Ap 25 '69; Reply with rejoinder. A. F. Paolino. 166:259-60 O 10 '69
Why it's a man's world. L. Tiger. Read Digest 95:223-4+ O '69

SEX education. See Sex instruction

SEX exhibit, Copenhagen. See Copenhagen—Exhibitions

SEX in art
Conversations on the new eroticism; symposium. il Time 94:64-5 Jl 11 '69
Duchamp's Young man and girl in spring; excerpt from The complete works of Marcel Duchamp. A. Schwarz. bibliog il Am Imago 25:296-308 Wint '68
Flesh and filigree; exhibition at Toronto museum. M. Amaya. il Art N 68:24-7+ D '69
Temple belles of India. A. Menen. il Holiday 45:48-9+ F '69
   See also
Nude in art

SEX in ballet. See Ballet

SEX in literature
Death in Venice: the aesthetic object as dream guide. R. Tarbox. bibliog Am Imago 26:123-44 Sum '69
Naked truth about the great novel hoax; Naked came the stranger. B. Bruns. il Life 67:69-70 Ag 22 '69
Oh, my Lolita, I have only words to play with; V. Nabokov's Ada. P. S. Prescott. il Look 33:6 My 27 '69
Portnoy's complaint by Philip Roth looms as a wild blue shocker. A. Goldman. il Life 66:58B-58D+ F 7 '69
Thomas Mann's Death in Venice. H. Slochower. bibliog f Am Imago 26:99-122 Sum '69
Toward a new erotic environment? M. Hentoff. Cur 109:15-18 Ag '69

SEX in moving pictures
After nudity, what, indeed? Swedish movies. L. Gross. il Look 33:80+ Ap 29 '69
Current cinema. P. Gilliatt. New Yorker 45:124 My 17 '69
End of the foreplay flick? Film Q 22:1-2 Sum '69
Film and other four-letter words. R. Corliss. Nat R 21:760-1 Jl 29 '69
Giving the public what it wants. H. Alpert. Sat R 52:41 My 10 '69
Hex, on sex. P. T. Hartung. Commonweal 90:293-4 My 23 '69

My wife, the naked movie star. L. H. Farber. il Harper 238:49-55 Je '69
Not to be missed. G. Trotta. il Harp Baz 102:134-5 Je '69
Sex and violence in movies and TV; how harmful are they? with opinions by celebrities. J. Crist. il Good H 169:59-61+ Ag '69

Anecdotes, facetiae, satire, etc.
If you're still curious, here are advance reviews of three important upcoming movies (rating: Z) T. Meehan. il N Y Times Mag p 12-13 Je 29 '69

SEX in television programs. See Television broadcasting—Moral aspects

SEX in the arts
Boundary line between erotic art and pornography is more and more difficult to draw. C. Barnes. Holiday 45:15+ Ap '69
Isn't anything obscene any more? M. Mannes. McCalls 96:64+ S '69
Sex and the arts: explosive scene. il Newsweek 73:67-70 Ap 14 '69

SEX in the Bible
Homosexuality in the Bible and the law. B. L. Smith. bibliog Chr Today 13:7-10 Jl 18 '69

SEX in the performing arts
Art and responsibility. C. Hughes. Cath World 209:210-12 Ag '69
Backlash; reaction to the rise in public indecency and obscenity. il Newsweek 73:31 Ap 7 '69
Naked American. E. Bentley. New Repub 161:31-4 Ag 19 '69; Same abr. with title Changing sexual mores; why the naked American on stage? Cur 111:60-4 O '69
Naked craze. H. E. Wright. Chr Cent 86:617-19 Ap 30 '69
Nude brood. N. Gittelson. Harp Baz 102:27+ O '69
Scotland: the festival and Muggeridge. I. Logan. Chr Cent 86:1291-2 O 8 '69
Sex as a spectator sport. il Time 94:61-3+ Jl 11 '69
Sex, shock and sensuality; the lively arts; with accounts by J. Barthel and T. Prideaux. il Life 66:22-35 Ap 4 '69
Thing happens. H. Hewes. Sat R 52:50-1 Ap 26 '69
Toward a new erotic environment? M. Hentoff. Cur 109:15-18 Ag '69

SEX instruction
American moral crisis, by A. S. Trace, jr. Review
  Nat R 21:858 Ag 26 '69. R. Kirk
Beyond sex education. Chr Cent 86:1371 O 29 '69
Books for young people. Z. Sutherland. Sat R 52:56 O 18 '69
Case for sex education. E. S. Hendryson. PTA Mag 63:20-1 My '69; Same abr. Ed Digest 35:34-5 S '69
Controversy over sex education: what our children stand to lose. W. Goodman. Redbook 133:78-9+ S '69
Education in human sexuality: two Catholic programs. J. McLaughlin. America 121:494-7 N 22 '69
Experimental course in sex education for teachers. V. D. C. Bennett and others. bibliog il Ment Hy 53:625-31 O '69
How one city teaches sex education and family life. B. A. Hawkins. il PTA Mag 63:24-6 Je '69
Impact of offensive and obscene material on children and youth; excerpts from Sex education in the schools: a study of objectives, content, methods, materials, and evaluation. H. F. Kilander. Sch & Soc 97:326-30 Sum '69
M.D. blames parents and schools for sex education gap. Todays Health 48:13 Ja '70
Schools and moral instruction; California and Michigan. R. Kirk. Nat R 21:752 Jl 29 '69
Sex and family living; Boston university training project for teachers. I. Forman. il Am Ed 5:11-13 O '69
Sex and the single child. il Newsweek 73:102-3 Je 2 '69
Sex ed flare-ups would ban courses, materials; with editorial comment. Library J 94:4185, 4187-8 N 15 '69
Sex education: a controversy becomes a crisis. J. Zazzaro. Ed Digest 35:9-11 N '69
Sex-education controversy. Chr Today 14:34 O 10 '69
Sex education in public schools. J. Huffman. Chr Today 13:5-8 S 26 '69
Sex education in school; debate splits town in Wisconsin. il Life 67:34-41 S 19 '69
Sex education in the schools. A. F. Guttmacher. Parents Mag 44:40 Ap '69
Sex education in the schools. B. Spock. Redbook 132:40+ Ja '69

SEX instruction—*Continued*
Sex education in the sixth grade; interview. K. von Kaenel and E. Zitek. Ed Digest 34:17-19 F '69
Sex education moves forward; New Jersey joint pastoral letter. America 121:483 N 22 '69
Sex education: powder keg in our schools. C. T. Rowan and D. M. Mazie. Read Digest 95:73-8 O '69
Sex education that parents approve; interview, ed. by M. Longwell. L. Bernhagen. il Farm J 93:57-8 S '69
Sex for credit; University of Minnesota, Minneapolis. N. G. Fabtr. il Look 33:39-40+ Ap 1 '69
Sex in school: Watkins Glen, N.Y. and Anaheim, Calif. E. Dunbar. il Look 33:15-17 S 9 '69
Sex in the classroom. il Time 94:50 Jl 25 '69
Should sex education be offered in grade school? GH poll. il Good H 169:12+ Jl '69
Should we teach about birth control in high school sex education? H. S. Hoyman. Ed Digest 34:20-3 F '69
Silliness in sex education; Catholic schools. R. Kirk. Nat R 21:1274 D 16 '69
Social revolution and sex education. F. E. McGuigan. Clear House 43:421-4 Mr '69
Some reservations about sex education. M. Smith. il Parents Mag 44:66-7+ N '69
Study of sex education programs; Sweden. Sch & Soc 97:271 Sum '69
Teaching sex in school. R. M. Cohen. New Repub 160:11-12 Je 28 '69
Teen-agers speak out about sex; symposium, ed. by P. Schiller; with reply by E. Koontz. il Todays Ed 58:23-6 Mr '69
Telling your sub-teen child about sex; excerpt from The children's doctor. L. Smith. il Todays Health 47:56-7+ Je '69
Threat to freedom of teaching, learning and reading; campaign against sex education. il Pub W 196:66 S 22 '69
Why sex education? E. Van Den Haag. il Nat R 21:956-8 S 23 '69; Same abr. Cur 112:31-5 N '69
Why the furor over sex education. il U S News 67:44-6 Ag 4 '69
Why the revolt against sex education? J. N. Bell. il Good H 169:92-3+ N '69
Will the schools survive the attack on sex education? S. Holzman. Schol Teach Sec Teach Sup p 10-12 O 6 '69

Anecdotes, facetiae, satire, etc.
Biology at its best. B. Wright. Good H 169:173 Jl '69

SEX manuals. See Marriage—Handbooks, manuals, etc.

SEX pheromones (insects) See Insect sex attractants

SEX ratio
Postpartum psychiatric reactions: time of onset and sex ratio of newborns. F. T. Melges. bibliog il Science 166:1026-7 N 21 '69
Sex ratios of newborns: associated with prepartum and postpartum schizophrenia. M. A. Taylor. bibliog il Science 164:723-4 My 9 '69; Correction. 165:380 Jl 25 '69

SEX relations
Affair; excerpts. M. Hunt. Ladies Home J 86:141-8+ S; 159-66+ O '69
American Catholic marriages and the church. A. V. Krebs, jr. Cath World 208:225-9 F '69
Betty and Bruce had a sex hang-up; ed. by D. C. Disney. Ladies Home J 86:20+ O '69
Erotic life of the American wife. N. Gittelson. Harp Baz 102:76-91 Jl '69
Great expectations. D. Newman and R. Benton. il Mlle 69:56 S '69
Jon was overly passionate. D. C. Disney. Ladies Home J 86:30+ F '69
Money and sex: two marital problems or one? M. Hunt. Redbook 134:49+ Ja '70
Parents talk about sex. H. Ginott. Vogue 154:103+ O 15 '69
Prudent men, women, and sex; letter. Har Yrs 9:34 Je '69
Understanding orgasm. S. Lydon. Ramp Mag 7:59-63 D 14 '68
We are all our mothers' daughters: what sex research reveals about unhappy wives; excerpts from The sex researchers. E. M. Brecher. Redbook 134:71+ N '69
What's heroic about continence? ed. by D. Curran. Cath World 209:21-3 Ap '69
Who comes first, husband or child? J. Brothers. Good H 169:30+ O '69
Youth, love and sex: the new chivalry. J. D. Rockefeller, 3d. Look 33:32+ O 7 '69

SEX research
We are all our mothers' daughters: what sex research reveals about unhappy wives; excerpts from The sex researchers. E. M. Brecher. Redbook 134:71+ N '69
SEX surgery. See Generative organs—Surgery
SEXTON, Anne
Mercy street,. Criticism
America 121:622 D 20 '69
New Repub 161:33 N 22 '69
SEXTON, Irwin
San Antonio: books by phone. Wilson Lib Bul 43:885-7 My '69
SEXTONS
See also
Sacristans
SEXUAL behavior
Anatomy is not destiny; views of W. Simon and J. H. Gagnon. Time 93:56+ Mr 28 '69
Compulsive sexual activity induced by p-chlorophenylalanine in normal and pineal-ectomized male rats. A. Tagliamonte and others. bibliog il Science 166:1433-5 D 12 '69
Mole rat spalax ehrenbergi; mating behavior and its evolutionary significance. E. Nevo. bibliog il Science 163:484-6 Ja 31 '69
Psychosexual development. W. Simon and J. Gagnon. il Trans-Action 6:9-17 Mr '69
Rhesus monkeys: mating season mobility of adult males. D. G. Lindburg. bibliog il Science 166:1176-8 N 28 '69
Sex: the new status symbol. A. Brien. Mlle 69:62+ Jl '69
Sexual pheromone in some fishes of the genus hypsoblennius gill. G. S. Losey, jr. bibliog il Science 163:181-3 Ja 10 '69
See also
College students—Sexual behavior
Courtship
Courtship of animals
Courtship of insects
Graduate students—Sexual behavior
SEXUAL diseases. See Venereal diseases
SEXUAL disorders
See also
Frigidity (Psychology)
SEXUAL ethics
Affair; excerpts. M. Hunt. Ladies Home J 86:141-8+ S; 159-66+ O '69
American moral crisis, by A. S. Trace, jr. Review
Nat R 21:858 Ag 26 '69. R. Kirk
Case against cheating in marriage. A. Lowen and R. J. Levin. il Redbook 133:70-1+ Je '69; Same abr. Read Digest 95:79-82 N '69
Celibacy and sexual freedom. M. R. Joyce. America 120:468-70 Ap 19 '69
Changing standards; discussing adultery at the annual meeting of the American psychiatric association. Time 93:52 My 16 '69
Commonsense sex; excerpt. R. M. Mazur. il Redbook 133:83-5+ Jl '69
Communists are right about some things. Chr Today 13:26-7 Je 6 '69
Erotic life of the American wife. N. Gittelson. Harp Baz 102:76-91 Jl '69
Man talk: the hunger artist. D. Newman and R. Benton. Mlle 68:42 Mr '69
New contraceptive society; findings of survey made in Sweden. J. R. Mislison. Look 33:50+ F 4 '69; Same abr. with title Sweden: the contraceptive society. Read Digest 94:225-6+ Ap '69
Re-evaluating the pill; H. Lief's study findings. Newsweek 75:66 Ja 12 '70
Rules and the ethics of sex. J. C. Hough, jr. il Chr Cent 86:148-51 Ja 29 '69
Sickness of Sodom. B. Graham. il Time 94:65-6 Jl 11 '69
Special and curious blessing; excerpts. C. P. Seton. il McCalls 96:71+ F '69
Teen-agers speak out about sex; symposium, ed. by P. Schiller; with reply by E. Koontz. il Todays Ed 58:23-6 Mr '69
Understanding sex in the age of the pill. G. Clanton; discussion. Chr Cent 86:187+ F 5 '69
Unwed couples: do they live happily ever after? D. Bloch and S. Blum. il Redbook 132:90-1+ Ap '69
What, when, and where is sexy; interview, ed. by L. Lerman. K. Tynan. Mlle 69:76 Jl '69
See also
Marriage
Sex and religion
Sex instruction
Sex relations
Virginity
SEXUAL freedom league
Sexual revolutionaries. il Newsweek 73:16 Je 16 '69
SEXUAL maturity. See Puberty

SEXUAL perversion
See also
Homosexuality
SEYBOLD, John W.
Aesthetic considerations in computerized photocomposition. Pub W 195:64-5 Ap 7 '69
SEYFERT galaxies. See Galactic systems
SEYMOUR, Dan
Marketing Madison avenue. por Time 93:90 Ap 11 '69
SEYMOUR, William R.
Cooperatives. Parks & Rec 4:54-6 Je '69
SFORZA, Luigi Luca Cavalli-. See Cavalli-Sforza, L. L.
SHABAD, Theodore
Changing resource policies of the U.S.S.R. bibliog Focus 19:7-8 F '69
SHABAZZ, Betty
Legacy of my husband, Malcolm X. pors Ebony 24:172-4+ Je '69
Visit with the widow of Malcolm X; interview, ed. by F. Knebel. Look 33:74-7+ Mr 4 '69
about
Where are they now? il pors Newsweek 74: 16 N 3 '69
SHABER, David
Glasgow picnic: just a spot o'wet. Holiday 46:37 Ag '69
High above the subway's rumble. Holiday 45:20+ Mr '69
SHABU-shabu. See Cookery, Japanese
SHACKELFORD, Marvin
Wet, happy life of Marvin Shackelford. C. Gillespie. il pors Sports Illus 32:66-72 Ja 12 '70
SHACKLE; novel. See Colette. G.
SHAD, John S. R.
Financial realities of mergers; excerpts from address, March 28, 1969. Harvard Bsns R 47:133-46 N '69
SHAD fishing
Carolina shad comeback. J. Dean. il Field & S 73:58-9+ Ap '69
Fishing for shad in the Feather. il Sunset 142:42-3 My '69
Fly rods & hickory shad. C. B. Pfeiffer. il Field & S 74:74-5+ My '69
SHADDUCK, John A.
Nosema cuniculi: in vitro isolation. Science 166:516-17 O 24 '69
SHADE, Lucille
Woman looks at her tiller. Org Gard & Farm 16:38-40 Ap '69
SHADE
See also
Screens (sun)
SHADE plants. See Plants, Shade
SHADES, C. T.
About those sentence fragments. Engl J 58: 1223+ N '69
SHADES. See Window shades
SHADOW stick. See Astronomical instruments
SHADOWGRAMS
Photograms: a teaching approach to creactivity. R. L. Kerns. il Sch Arts 69:26-8 D '69
SHADOWS; story. See Glaze. E.
SHADWELL, Wendy J.
Attribution for His Excellency and Lady Washington. Antiques 95:240-1 F '69
SHAFER, Elwood L. Jr
Recreation demand from wharf to waterfall. bibliog f Parks & Rec 4:18-20+ Ag '69
SHAFER, Robert
Curriculum: new perspectives. Engl J 58:762-6 My '69
SHAFFER, Carolyn R.
Jewish view of redemption. Commonweal 90: 512-15 Ag 22 '69
SHAFFER, Ellen
Fraktur: the colorful art of the Pennsylvania Germans. Antiques 95:550-5 Ap '69
SHAFFER, Jack
Jack who? R. B. Parke. por Flying 85:37 D '69
SHAFFER, John H.
Shaffer affirms aim to improve controllers' working conditions. Aviation W 91:33 Ag 11 '69
Whose who? R. B. Parke. Flying 84:42 My '69
SHAFFER, Kenneth R.
Affluent ghetto. bibliog por Library J 94:1093-7 Mr 15 '69
SHAFTER, William Rufus
'Pecos Bill' on the Texas frontier. R. M. Utley. bibliog il pors Am West 6:4-13+ Ja '69
SHAFTING, Flexible
Shop power at your fingertips. R. J. De Cristoforo. il Pop Sci 195:124-7+ N '69

SHAGBARKS. See Hickory
SHAH, Saleem A.
Crime and mental illness: some problems in defining and labeling deviant behavior. bibliog Ment Hy 53:21-33 Ja '69
SHAHN, Ben
In defense of chaos; address. por Ramp Mag 7:12-13 D 14 '68
[Portfolio of drawings] Ramp Mag 7:17-20 My '69
about
In memoriam: Ben Shahn. D. Stermer. por Ramp Mag 7:16 My '69
Obituary
Nation 208:390 Mr 31 '69. J. Levine
SHAHRIK, H. Arto. See Eichel, B. jt. auth.
SHAINBERG, Lawrence
Some Wallace Stevens; story. Esquire 72: 116-17 O '69
SHAKER architecture. See Architecture, American
SHAKER cookery. See Cookery. American
SHAKER furniture. See Furniture. American
SHAKER museums. See Historical museums
SHAKERS
Rich Shaker legacy. il Am Home 72:74-81 S '69
Shakers: a gifted people. M. Evans. Am Home 72:88+ S '69
SHAKESPEARE, Frank J. 1925-
Shakespeare era. por Newsweek 75:20+ Ja 12 '70
Thinking positive at USIA. por Time 94:40 D 5 '69

SHAKESPEARE, William

Characters

Coriolanus: the anxious bridegroom. E. Wilson, jr. bibliog Am Imago 25:224-41 Fall '68
Fortinbras and Hamlet. K. R. Eissler. bibliog Am Imago 25:199-223 Fall '68
Iago. S. Orgel. bibliog Am Imago 25:258-73 Fall '68
Motiveless malignity, by L. Auchincloss. Review
Sat R 52:59-60 O 11 '69. B. Grebanier
Othello's jealousy. S. Reid. bibliog f Am Imago 25:274-92 Fall '68

Criticism and interpretation

Henriad: Shakespeare's major history plays. A. Kernan. Yale R 59:3-32 O '69
Shakespeare is not our contemporary. P. Cruttwell. Yale R 59:33-49 O '69

Editions

Production and design notes on The complete Pelican Shakespeare. H. Schmoller. il por Pub W 196:62+ O 6 '69
Publishing scene; Norton facsimile: the first folio of Shakespeare. D. Dempsey. Sat R 52:74 N 22 '69

Folios

See Shakespeare, W.—Editions

Plays

Henriad: Shakespeare's major history plays. A. Kernan. Yale R 59:3-32 O '69

Coriolanus

Coriolanus: the anxious bridegroom. E. Wilson, jr. bibliog Am Imago 25:224-41 Fall '68

Hamlet

Angry young Hamlet: Tony Richardson's production. R. A. Sokolov. Newsweek 73: 119 My 12 '69
Fortinbras and Hamlet. K. R. Eissler. bibliog Am Imago 25:199-223 Fall '68
Fresh Hamlet; production in London. H. Hewes. Sat R 52:53 Ap 12 '69
Hamlet. T. Lewis. America 120:433-4 Ap 5 '69
Hamlet. J. Novick. Vogue 153:32 Ap 15 '69
I am not Prince Hamlet; Tony Richardson's production. G. Weales. Commonweal 90:319-20 My 30 '69
Joseph Papp's Happening and the teaching of Hamlet. P. Traci. Engl J 58:75-7 Ja '69
Member of the company; performance by N. Williamson in London. il Time 93:74 F 28 '69
Mod Hamlet; Tony Richardson's production. M. Maddocks. Atlan 224:132-5 O '69
Theatre; APA-Phoenix production. B. Gill. New Yorker 45:131-2 Mr 15 '69
Theatre; N. Williamson's Hamlet. H. Clurman. Nation 208:643-4 My 19 '69
Theatre; T. Richardson's production. B. Gill. New Yorker 45:121-2 My 10 '69
Theatre; Tony Richardson's New York production. T. Lewis. America 120:600 My 17 '69

SHAKESPEARE, William—Plays—Hamlet
—*Continued*
Where's Hamlet? APA repertory company production. T. G. Plate. Newsweek 73:133 Mr 17 '69
Zombie Hamlet; Ellis Rabb's APA revival. il Time 93:66 Mr 14 '69

Henry V

Fresh revivals; production of Henry V by the American Shakespeare festival theatre company. H. Hewes. Sat R 52:10+ N 29 '69
Tapestry of violence; production at American Shakespeare festival theater, Stratford, Conn. il Time 93:80 Je 13 '69
Theatre; American Shakespeare festival production. T. Lewis. America 121:18 Jl 5 '69
Theatre; production by the American Shakespeare festival theatre. H. Clurman. Nation 209:675-6 D 15 '69
Theatre; production of American Shakespeare festival theatre, Stratford, Conn. B. Gill. il New Yorker 45:178 N 22 '69

King Lear

King Lear: English and American; Peter Brook and Lincoln Center productions. R. Crinkley. il Nat R 21:500-1 My 20 '69

Macbeth

Macbeth: fair is foul and foul is fair; address, January 11, 1968. L. Veszy-Wagner. bibliog Am Imago 25:242-57 Fall '68
Off broadway; Performance group's production of Macbeth. E. Oliver. il New Yorker 45:166+ D 6 '69
Special Providence: Adrian Hall's staging of Macbeth. H. Hewes. il Sat R 52:22 My 3 '69
Witches' stew; Performance group's Makbeth. J. Kroll. il Newsweek 74:86 D 1 '69

Much ado about nothing

Theatre; American Shakespeare festival production. T. Lewis. America 121:19 Jl 5 '69

Othello

Iago. S. Orgel. bibliog Am Imago 25:253-73 Fall '68
Othello's jealousy. S. Reid. bibliog f Am Imago 25:274-93 Fall '68

Psychology

Shakespeare; symposium. bibliog Am Imago 25:199-293 Fall '68

Sonnets

Shakespeare's sug'red sonnets. P. W. Schmidtchen. il pors Hobbies 74:104-5+ Ap '69

Statues, portraits, etc.

Shakespeare through the ages. L. Marder. il Hobbies 74:98B-98E+ Ap; 98D-98E+ My '69

Study and teaching

Joseph Papp's Happening and the teaching of Hamlet. P. Traci. Engl J 58:75-7 Ja '69
SHAKESPEARE festivals
See also
American Shakespeare festival theatre and academy, Stratford, Conn.
New York Shakespeare festival
SHAKING palsy. See Parkinson's disease
SHALE
Acidic components of Green River shale identified by a gas chromatography-mass spectrometry-computer system. R. C. Murphy and others. bibliog il Science 165:695-7 Ag 15 '69
SHALINSKY, William, and Witkovsky, Jerome
First four hours of camp. Camp Mag 41:16-17 Je '69
SHALIT, Amos de
Obituary
Phys Today por 22:99+ D '69. H. Feshbach and V. F. Weisskopf
SHALIT, Gene
Look at the movies (cont) Look 33:66 F 18; 51 Mr 4; 84 Mr 18; 76 Ap 1; 60 Ap 29; 57 My 13; 16 Je 10; 20 Je 24; 20 Jl 15; 16 Jl 29; 14 Ag 26; 43 S 9; 65 S 23; 70 O 21; 92 N 4 '69
SHALLOTS
See also
Cookery—Vegetables
SHAMAN, Harvey
Ten tips from a top lab. Pop Phot 65:78-9 O '69
SHAMROCK pea
Shamrock pea. R. D. Pearce. Horticulture 46:49+ D '68
SHAMS Pahlevi, princess of Iran
Taliesin in Teheran. W. W. Peters. Art in Am 57:44-51 Jl '69

SHANAB, Mitri E. and others
Positive contrast in the runway obtained with delay of reward. bibliog Science 164:724-5 My 9 '69
SHANAHAN, Edward K.
Dignity in the court. New Repub 160:12 F 1 '69
SHANAHAN, Warren J.
How to read handwriting. Mech Illus 65:58-60+ D '69
SHANDS, Harley C.
Sociatry: social psychiatry and the physician's calling. bibliog Ment Hy 53:393-402 Jl '69
SHANE, Dorothy
(ed) Letters on a dog. Har Yrs 9:48-9 S '69
Over the river and through the woods. Har Yrs 9:29 D '69
SHANE, Harold G. and Shane, J. G.
Forecast for the 70's. Todays Ed 58:29-32 Ja '69
—See Shane, J. G. jt. auth.
SHANE, June Grant, and Shane, H. G.
Guidance at an early age. Todays Ed 58:36-8 N '69
—See Shane, H. G. jt. auth.
SHANIKO, Ore.
When you come to Shaniko, slow down. il Sunset 142:48+ Ap '69
SHANKER, Albert
Schools and the union. New Repub 161:26-8+ N 15 '69
about
Black anti-Semitism. J. Leo. Commonweal 89:618-20 F 14 '69
SHANNON, James A.
Science and social purpose; adaptation of address, December 27, 1968. bibliog Science 163:769-73 F 21 '69
SHANNON, James Patrick
Bishop and Mrs Shannon. il por Newsweek 74:76 Ag 25 '69
Bishop Shannon comments on his excommunication. Chr Cent 86:1108 Ag 27 '69
Bishop Shannon, exile? J. B. Sheerin. Cath World 209:194-5 Ag '69
Bishop Shannon's resignation. America 120:678 Je 14 '69
Bishop's anguish. por Newsweek 73:73 Je 9 '69
Bishops in trouble. por Time 94:52+ Ag 22 '69
Bit by bit. S. J. Adamo. America 120:717-18 Je 21 '69
Burden of responsibility. por Time 93:88 Je 6 '69
Church dissent; its rising toll. por U S News 66:18 Je 16 '69
Loss of Bishop Shannon. J. B. Sheerin. Cath World 210:3 O '69
Of many things. D. R. Campion. America 121: inside cover Jl 5 '69
Shannon affair. Commonweal 90:380 Je 20 '69
Shannon and public concern. America 121: 108 Ag 30 '69
Shannon case. Commonweal 90:531-2 S 5 '69
Shannon's wedding bells. Chr Today 13:49 S 12 '69
Wish you were there; Rome's attempt to deport. Newsweek 73:88 Je 16 '69
SHANNON, William V.
Rise and fall; the age of the bosses. Am Heritage 20:26-31 Je '69
U.S. cannot abandon all forms of intermediate force. Commonweal 90:9-10 Mr 21 '69; Same with title On using intermediate force. Cur 109:51-4 Ag '69
Universities in crisis; the price of submission. Cur 108:6-8 Je '69
SHANNON RIVER
Chartering in Ireland and England; cruising on the River Shannon and the Norfolk Broads. G. Stout; F. Adams; E. J. Durnall. il Yachting 126:54-5+ D '69
SHANSI (province)
Who controls Shansi. Newsweek 74:53-4 S 22 '69
SHAPE. See Form (art)
SHAPIRO, David, 1947-
Hockney paints a portrait. Art N 68:28-31+ My '69
Untitled; poem. Am Scholar 38:583 Aut '69
about
Where are they now? il pors Newsweek 74: 24 O 13 '69
SHAPIRO, David, and others
Effects of feedback and reinforcement on the control of human systolic blood pressure. bibliog Science 163:588-90 F 7 '69
SHAPIRO, Fred C.
Annals of jurisprudence. New Yorker 44:39-42+ F 8; 44-6+ F 15; 45:42-4+ F 22 '69

SHAW, Robert, 1927-
Man in the glass booth; dramatization of novel. Criticism
Commentary 47:25-6 F '69
SHAW, Stephen R.
Optics of arthropod compound eye. bibliog
Science 165:88-90 Jl 4 '69
SHAW university, Raleigh, N.C.
Cheek brothers, a new breed of college president. il Ebony 24:35-8+ O '69
SHAW'S garden, St Louis. See Missouri botanical garden
SHAWVER, David E.
Let's get serious about teacher power. Clear House 44:199-202 D '69
SHAYON, Robert Lewis
Case of the Red lion. Sat R 52:55-6 Jl 12 '69
Nicholas Johnson vs. Broadcasting. Sat R 52:82+ Ap 12 '69
TV-radio. See issues of Saturday review
SHEA, Frank
Corfu: from Caesar to Constantine. Sat R 52:76+ Mr 8 '69
Lands of Greece. Travel & Camera 32:45+ My '69
SHEA, Mike
What did we learn? por Yachting 125:162+ My '69
SHEA, Terence
(ed) See Campbell, E. How to pick a church
SHEAGREN, John N. and Monaco, A. P.
Protective effect of antilymphocyte serum on mice infected with plasmodium berghei. bibliog Science 164:1423-5 Je 20 '69
SHEAHAN, Eileen
ALTA march on Washington. ALA Bul 63:907-8 Jl '69
Tuning in to summer. bibliog por Library J 94:1294-7+ Mr 15 '69
SHEAR, Richard C.
Championship grouse dog trainer, Dick Shear; interview, ed. by L. J. Bashline. por Field & S 74:122-4+ D '69
SHEARER, Goldie
We garden in cans. Org Gard & Farm 16:31-3 Ap '69
SHECTER, Leonard
Bring back the real Mets! N Y Times Mag p66-7+ S 7 '69
Does Pete Rozelle run pro football? Ask Joe Namath. N Y Times Mag p30-1+ Ag 17 '69
SHEDESKY, Pat
Chrysanthemums, springtime in September. Org Gard & Farm 16:49-51 S '69
SHEDS
See also
Shelters
SHEEAN, Vincent
Toujours la Moore. Opera N 34:14-16 D 20 '69
about
When Jimmy told it like it was. W. McWhirter. Life 66:8 Ap 18 '69
SHEED, Francis Joseph
My life on the street corner. por Sat R 52:22-3+ My 10 '69
SHEED, Wilfrid
Close-up: novelist of suburbia. Life 66:39-40+ Ap 18 '69
Evolution on a bad trip. Life 67:7 Jl 11 '69
Films. See issues of Esquire
Jesus remuggeridged. Commonweal 91:74+ O 17 '69
Life theater review. (cont) Life 66:10 Je 27 '69
Now generation knew him when. Life 67:64-6+ S 12 '69
Observations upon the Irish. Time 93:37-8 Je 20 '69
Requiem to Billy Pilgrim's progress. Life 66:9 Mr 21 '69
TV talk. Sports Illus 31:13 O 20 '69
Theatre. Esquire 72:40+ S; 42+ D '69
This riotous isle. Sports Illus 30:78-82+ Ap 21 '69
What is pornography, anyway? Mlle 69:70-1+ Jl '69
SHEEHAN, Edward R.
(ed) See Deneuve, C. Conversation with Catherine Deneuve
SHEEHAN, Ethna
Children's books at Christmastime. America 121:593-6+ D 13 '69
SHEEHAN, James J.
Political leadership in the German Reichstag, 1871-1918. bibliog f Am Hist R 74:511-28 D '68
SHEEHAN, Neil
(ed) Letters from Hamburger hill. Harper 239:40-4+ N '69
SHEEHAN, Peter J.
Benét's John Brown's body: for study. Engl J 58:219-25 F '69

Theater of the absurd: a child studies himself; address, November 1968. Engl J 58:561-5 Ap '69
SHEEHAN, Susan
Lady of Hickory Hill. N Y Times Mag p30-1+ N 30 '69
SHEEHY, Gail
Has UN Plaza nosed out the Dakota and the Beresford in New York's celebrity race? Holiday 46:58-61+ S '69
Who is Penelope Ashe? McCalls 97:71+ N '69
SHEEHY, Michael
Irish literary censorship. Nation 208:833-4+ Je 30 '69
SHEEHY, Tim
Found, a native who outplays the imports. M. Mulvoy. il por Sports Illus 30:38+ Ja 20 '69
SHEELEY, Stuart L.
Students as poets. Engl J 58:577-85 Ap '69
This English is something else. Sr Schol 94:Schol Teach 14-16 Ja 17 '69
SHEEN, Fulton John, bp
Calvary in Rochester. por Time 94:51-2 O 24 '69
SHEEP
How the sheep died in Skull Valley; testing of nerve gas. R. G. Fowler. il Farm J 93:34B-34D S '69
What's new. See issues of Successful farming
Wind from Dugway; death of sheep near Proving ground, testing poisonous agents. V. Brodine and others. il Environ 11:2-9+ Ja '69
See also
Lambs
Sheep industry and trade
SHEEP farms
See also
Sheep industry and trade
SHEEP industry and trade
Driving sheepmen to greener pastures. il Bsns W p96+ Jl 26 '69
SHEERIN, John B.
Editorial. See issues of Catholic world
SHEETS
Show-off sheets. A. Walker. il Am Home 72:54-5 Jl '69
SHEFFER, Isaiah
Black theatre in America. Nation 209:151-2 Ag 25 '69
SHEFFIELD, April
Here's me, April Sheffield with James Mason! pors Esquire 71:136-8+ Je '69
SHEFFIELD, Harley G. and Melton, M. L.
Toxoplasma gondii: transmission through feces in absence of toxocara cati eggs. bibliog Science 164:431-2 Ap 25 '69
SHEFFTZ, Melvin C.
Young and angry talent. Nation 208:720-4 Je 9 '69
SHEIL, Bernard James, abp
An archbishop who didn't care. America 121:214 S 27 '69
Winning the kingdom of God. por Time 94:63 S 26 '69
SHEIN, Harvey M. and Wurtman, R. J.
Cyclic adenosine monophosphate stimulation of melatonin and serotonin synthesis in cultured rat pineals. bibliog Science 166:519-29 O 24 '69
SHELBURNE museum, Shelburne, Vt.
Footnotes; Shelburne museum. Am Artist 33:6 Ja '69
SHELBY, Marian
Toward a new English. Engl J 58:1347-52 D '69
SHELDON, Charles S. 2d
American Sputnik for the Russians? por Bul Atom Sci 25:23-5+ S '69
SHELF clocks. See Clocks
SHELL decoration. See Decoration and ornament
SHELL oil company
Presidency handicap at Shell oil. Bsns W p70 S 13 '69
SHELLENBERGER, Don
What kind of staff training helps both staff and campers attain best personal growth? Camp Mag 41:12-14 Mr '69
SHELLENBERGER, J. A.
Green revolution revisited. Cur 110:37-41 S '69
SHELLEY, Bruce L.
Antidote to individualism. Chr Today 13:19-20 F 14 '69
SHELLFISH
See also
Cookery—Shellfish
Lobsters
SHELLFISH conservation. See Wildlife conservation
SHELLFISH culture
How to raise a shrimp cocktail. il Bsns W p 184+ S 20 '69
SHELLFISH fisheries, Cooperative. See Fisheries, Cooperative

SHELLS (conchology)
Bivale mollusk burrowing aided by discordant shell ornamentation. S. M. Stanley. il Science 166:634-5 O 31 '69
Magic lure of sea shells. P. A. Zahl. il Nat Geog 135:386-429 Mr '69
New shell collection for Mexico. A. G. Melvin. il Hobbies 73:118-19 F '69
Shell, five hundred million years of inspired design, by H. Stix and others. Review
    Natur Hist il 78:60-2 Mr '69. R. D. Turner
Triton shells through the ages. il Chem 42:5 Je '69
What is a volute? A. G. Melvin. il Hobbies 74:119+ Mr; 124+ Ap '69

Collectors and collecting
Carlos Prieto writes about shells. C. Prieto. il Hobbies 74:145+ S; 145+ O; 144+ N; 146-7 D '69
She sells sea shells by the seashore. . . E. Faust and H. Faust. il Har Yrs 9:13-15 Ag '69

SHELLS (projectiles) See Cartridges; Projectiles

SHELLS (structural engineering)
Buckled buildings; buckle-shell technique. Sci Am 220:58 My '69

SHELLY, Barbara G.
Primitive weaving adapted to the intermediate classroom. Sch Arts 68:13-15 My '69

SHELLY, Katharine G.
Riches; poem. Read Digest 94:132-3 Ap '69

SHELTERS
Camp shelters. C. B. Colby. il Outdoor Life 143:16+ Ap '69
Security shelter for your snowmobile. K. Isaacs. il Pop Sci 195:148-50+ D '69
Steel shelters defy vandals; Middletown, Ohio. J. Paschal. il Am City 84:96-7 F '69

SHELTERS, Garden. See Garden houses, shelters, etc.

SHELTON, Merijean. See Belli, J. A. jt. auth.

SHELTON, Opie Lee
Battle of Atlanta. Time 95:49 Ja 12 '70

SHELTON, Richard
Alone; poem. New Yorker 45:117 Ap 5 '69
Connais—tu le pays? poem. New Yorker 45:40 Je 21 '69
New Year's eve; poem. New Yorker 45:26 Ja 3 '70
On Lake Pend Oreille; poem. New Yorker 45:95 Ag 23 '69
Prophets; poem. New Yorker 45:26 Ag 30 '69

SHELTON college, Cape May, N.J.
Defending Shelton. Chr Today 13:56-7 S 12 '69

SHELVES
How to add shelves all through the house. il Pop Sci 194:150-61+ Mr '69
Stackable shelf modules go together like 1-2-3. L. E. Sabal. il Pop Mech 132:152-3 S '69
    See also
Bookcases

SHEMANSKI, Frances
(comp) World travel calendar, 1970. Sat R 53:53-6 Ja 3 '70

SHEMITZ, Sylvan R.
Light: the revealing dimension; interview, ed. by J. H. Ingersoll. House B 111:108-10+ Ap '69

SHEN, Samuel Y. and others
Significance of a simple equation. $A_1 = A_0 e^{-ktt}$. por Chem 42:16-18 F '69

SHENANDOAH NATIONAL PARK
Highway in the sky; Blue Ridge parkway. J. T. Starr. il Am For 75:8-11+ Ja '69
Spring in the Shenandoah. B. Gillam. il Mlle 68:94-6 F '69

SHEPARD, Alan Bartlett, 1923-
Life begins at forty-five. Newsweek 73:66+ My 19 '69

SHEPARD, Francis P. and Marshall, N. F.
Currents in La Jolla and Scripps submarine canyons. bibliog Science 165:177-8 Jl 11 '69

SHEPARD, Sam
Operation sidewinder; drama. Esquire 71:152-3+ My '69

about
La turista. Criticism
    Commonweal 90:204 My 2 '69

SHEPHERD, Emalene Sherman
Importance of you in articles. Writers Digest 49:54-7 N '69

SHEPHERD, George W. Jr
National priorities and participation in foreign policy. Chr Cent 86:504-7 Ap 16 '69

SHEPHERD, Jack
Incident at Van Duong; excerpts from 5 by 7. Look 33:26-8+ Ag 12 '69

SHEPLER, John E.
Picnicker's' friend. Pop Electr 31:47-50 Jl '69

SHEPPARD, Benjamin Joseph
Alarming increase in number of speed abusers; excerpt from testimony before House crime committee. por U S News 67:25 D 29 '69
    about
Delinquents are his patients. A. Henley. il Todays Health 47:48-9+ N '69

SHEPPARD, Eugenia
Are you slightly rectangular? Harp Baz 102:238-9 O '69
Bodies are so boring. Harp Baz 102:168 Ap '69
Chanel for men. Harp Baz 103:158-9 D '69
Hide away in a wig; poem. Harp Baz 102:198-9 My '69
How well you look! Harp Baz 102:168-9 Ag '69
I really will. Harp Baz 102:133 Ja '69
If you have a million. Harp Baz 102:118-19 Jl '69
Inside yachts. Harp Baz 102:118-19 Je '69
International shopping; what sport! Harp Baz 102:188 Mr '69
Love and money. Harp Baz 102:191 F '69
Memoirs of a museum. Harp Baz 103:206-7 N '69
On being a blonde. Harp Baz 102:204-5 S '69
Resolved: for 1970. Harp Baz 103:114-15 Ja '70

SHEPPARD, Sally
(ed) What makes a diet work for you. Vogue 153:104-5+ Ap 15 '69

SHERA, Jesse H.
Quiet stir of thought; or, What the computer cannot do; adaptation of address, May 1969. bibliog por Library J 94:2875-80 S 1 '69

SHERATSKY, Rodney E.
Heritage of film. bibliog Clear House 44:58-60 S '69

SHERBET. See Ice cream, ices, etc.

SHEREFF, Ruth
Yes, we have no bananas. Commonweal 89:497-9 Ja 17 '69

SHERIDAN, Bart
Brenda and the bandits. Good H 168:12+ Mr '69

SHERIDAN, Michael P.
Problems of the junior college. America 120:619 My 24 '69

SHERIDAN, Terence, and Barlett, D. L.
Infiltrating the curriculum. Nation 209:661-4 D 15 '69

SHERIDAN grapes. See Grapes

SHERIDAN tanks. See Tanks, Military

SHERIFFS
Rampage; actions of Alameda County sheriff's deputies in Berkeley, Calif. D. Stermer and others. il Ramp Mag 8:54-9 Ag '69
Relating! Police with people; Los Angeles County sheriff's department. il Am City 84:142+ Ap '69

SHERIFFS deputies. See Sheriffs

SHERIN, Ray
Our moon discoveries. Sch Arts 69:38-40 D '69

SHERMAN, Alice Ruth
No time for the shelf. il por Har Yrs 9:30-1 N '69

SHERMAN, Bennett
Techniques tomorrow. See issues of Modern photography

SHERMAN, Charles D. Jr
Excerpt from testimony before House committee on interstate and foreign commerce, April 21, 1969. Cong Digest 48:186+ Je '6f

SHERMAN, Dean
Western forestry center. Am For 75:16-19 O '69

SHERMAN, Edward F.
Military justice; learning from the Green Berets. Nation 209:399-403 O 20 '69

SHERMAN, John K.
Horspfal, a breakthrough. Hi Fi 19:MA30-1 My '69

SHERMAN, Matt
No-fail subject: the arts. PTA Mag 64:20-2+ bibliog(p35) D '69

SHERMAN, Conn.
October afternoon; Moratorium day. New Yorker 45:41-3 N 1 '69

SHERMARKE, Abdirashid Ali
Death in Las Anod. Newsweek 74:65 O 27 '69
Death of a president. Time 94:36 O 24 '69

SHERMIS, S. Samuel. See Urich, T. R. jt. auth.

SHERRILL, Robert G.
Andersonville-by-the-sea; Pendleton brig. Nation 209:239-42 S 15 '69
Black lung rebellion. Nation 208:529-35 Ap 28 '69
Club business on the Hill. Nation 208:102-4 Ja 27 '69

SHERRILL, Robert G.—*Continued*
Lagoon of excrement. Nation 209:500-3 N 10 '69
Last of the great Populists takes on the foundations, the banks, the Federal reserve, the Treasury. N Y Times Mag p24-5+ Mr 16 '69
Lyndon as Oedipus Rex. Commonweal 90:49-50 Mr 28 '69
Must the citizen give up his civil liberties when he joins the army? N Y Times Mag p25-7+ My 18 '69
Reaping the subsidies. Nation 209:561-6 N 24 '69
We want Georgia, South Carolina, Louisiana, Mississippi and Alabama—right now. Esquire 71:70-5+ Ja '69
Whitey's reaction. Esquire 71:76+ Ja '69
(ed) See D. Pearson. Drew Pearson: an interview

SHERROD, Willie H.
You'd never believe he was a cop. B. Reynolds. il pors Ebony 24:106-10+ Jl '69

SHERWIN, David
Not to be missed. G. Trotta. por Harp Baz 102:134-5 Je '69

SHERWIN, Judith Johnson
At Avignon; poem. Mlle 68:116 F '69

about

Good and the useful. M. Randall. Poetry 115:53-6 O '69

SHERWIN-Williams company
Germans brush aside Sherwin-Williams. Bsns W p 19-20 D 27 '69

SHERWOOD, G. L.
O my brothers; poem. Negro Hist Bul 32:7 My '69

SHERWOOD, Irene
Case for the Irish. Engl J 58:1181-2 N '69

SHERWOOD, John T.
Where are they now? il por Newsweek 73:14 Mr 10 '69

SHERWOOD, Martin
Benjamin Rush, America's first professor of chemistry. Chem 42:18-20 O '69

SHEVIAKOV, George V.
Anger in children; excerpt. Todays Ed 58:37 S '69

SHIDELER, Mary McDermott
Father and the fathers. Chr Cent 86:1061-4 Ag 13 '69
Who is our enemy? Chr Cent 86:1609-13 D 17 '69

SHIELDING (radiation)
See also
Space vehicles—Shielding (radiation)

SHIELDS, James T. and Buckmann, C. A.
What about hunting seasons? Outdoor Life 144:35-7+ S '69

SHIERS, George
First electron tube; with biographical sketch. Sci Am 220:14, 104-12 Mr; 221:8 Ag '69

SHIFF, C. J.
Host and parasite in Rhodesia. bibliog Natur Hist 78:65-7 F '69

SHIGO, Alex L.
Death and decay of trees; with biographical sketch. por Natur Hist 78:4, 42-7 Mr '69

SHIH tzus
Shaggy success of the Shih tzus. il Life 67: 46-7 Jl 11 '69

SHILLINGLAW, Deborah, and Hayden, D. E.
English curriculum revitalized for junior high schools. Clear House 44:33-4 S '69

SHILOH, Allon
Psychiatric patients as research interviewers in the mental hospital. Ment Hy 53:443-5 Jl '69
Treating the mentally ill. Cur 106:36-43 Ap '69

SHIMADA, Shigetoshi
Antifungal steroid glycoside from sea cucumber. bibliog Science 163:1462 Mr 28 '69

SHIMAHARA, Nobuo
Obsolete neutrality of higher education. bibliog f Sch & Soc 97:18-20 Ja '69

SHIMKUS, Joanna
Real like you; ed. by E. Miller. J. Shimkus. pors Seventeen 28:156-7+ My '69

SHIMOMURA, Osamu, and others
Cypridina bioluminescene: light-emitting oxyluciferin-luciferase complex. bibliog Science 164:1299-300 Je 13 '69

SHIMOTAKE, H. See Cairns, E. J. jt. auth.

SHIN (sect) See Buddha and Buddhism

SHINDANA toy company
Black firm joins the toy industry. il Ebony 25:84-6+ D '69

SHINE, Ted
Contribution. Criticism
New Yorker 45:131 Ap 12 '69

SHINER, Don
Carport closet for yard tools. Pop Sci 194: 130-1 Je '69

Solve the patio problem, add a screened porch. Pop Mech 131:170-4+ My '69
Vanguard of spring. Nat Wildlife 7:40-1 F '69

SHINGU, Susumi
Dancing in the wind. il Time 93:47 Ja 24 '69

SHINN, Roger L.
More than survival. Commonweal 91:148-9 O 31 '69

SHINNECOCK swordfish tournament. See Salt water fishing—Competitions

SHINRAN
Concept of grace in Jodo Shin Buddhism. H. Hashimoto. Chr Cent 86:318-19 Mr 5 '69

SHIP brokers
See also
Yacht brokers

SHIP building. See Shipbuilding

SHIP museums. See Naval museums

SHIP pilots. See Pilots and pilotage

SHIP propulsion
See also
Gas turbines, Marine
Steam turbines, Marine

SHIP publications
Front page afloat: all the news that's fit to ship. M. R. Weiss. il Sat R 52:84-5 N 8 '69

SHIP signals. See Signals and signaling

SHIPBUILDING
Merchant marine's new course. Fortune 80: 31 D '69
Navy takes new tack on shipbuilding; designing new class of destroyers. Bsns W p 172-4 O 11 '69
Prying open a Dutch clam. Bsns W p86 S 20 '69
Sailing through; biggest shipbuilding program. Forbes 103:25 F 15 '69
Surge of orders relaunches the shipyards; Britain. il Bsns W p47 Ja 10 '70
See also
Boatbuilding
General dynamics corporation
Warships
Yacht building

SHIPLEY, Nan
Lower Fort Garry. il Nat Parks 43:10-11 Ja '69

SHIPMENT of goods
Ogden engineers a total system; to solve Morocco's problems. il Bsns W p58+ Mr 15 '69
See also
Air freight service
Distribution of goods
Railroads—Freight service

SHIPP, Robert E.
Expanding program services. Parks & Rec 3:43-4+ N '68

SHIPPING
Supplying the '70s; the supertransport era. il U S News 68:89-91 Ja 12 '70
See also
Insurance, Marine
Ports

Accounting
See also
Banks and banking—Freight payment plan

Law
See Maritime law

Arctic Regions
Latest search for Northwest Passage: the plan, the odds. il U S News 66:96-7 My 12 '69

Greece, Modern
Other Greeks. il Time 94:74 Ag 15 '69

United States
Requiem for heavyweights; Nixon program to raise tonnage of U.S. trade carried in American ships. il Time 94:93-4 O 24 '69
Sitting duck; California-to-Hawaii steamship run. il Forbes 103:19 Ja 15 '69
U.S. shipping steers back into the money. Bsns W p52-3 D 13 '69
See also
Merchant marine—United States

SHIPPING companies
See also
Matson navigation company
Seatrain lines, incorporated

SHIPS
See also
Freight vessels
Ocean liners
Sailing vessels
Schooners
Shipwrecks
Steamships and steamboats
Voyages

SHIPS—*Continued*

Crews
See Seamen

Fires and fire protection
See also
Aircraft carriers—Fires and fire protection

Hydrodynamics
Speed through a straw; less fuel and more speed by use of polyethylene oxide. Time 93:58 F 7 '69

Manufacture
See Shipbuilding

Officers
See United States—Navy—Officers

Wrecking
See also
Warships, Scuttling of

SHIPS, Atomic powered
Nuclear crossroads; U.S. lead is withering. C. Behrens. il Sci N 95:316-17 Mr 29 '69
Whatever happened to the Savannah? il U S News 66:8 Je 30 '69
See also
Warships, Atomic powered

SHIPS, Historic
Typhoon refurbished. K. E. Harmon. il Motor B 123:132-5+ Ja '69
See also
Yachts, Historic

SHIPS, Research
Fishing again with the Russians. A. C. Jensen and J. C. Poole. il Cons 23:10-13+ Ap '69
New time machine; Glomar Challenger on JOIDES expedition. il Sci Digest 65:37-41 Ap '69
Ship that digs holes in the sea; Glomar Challenger. W. Cloud. il Pop Mech 131:108-11+ Mr '69
Strange devices that found the sunken sub Scorpion; ed. by H. Shuldiner. C. L. Buchanan. il Pop Sci 194:66-71+ Ap '69
Working the Glomar Challenger. W. B. Charm. il Sea Front 15:258-67 S '69
See also
Submarine research vehicles

SHIPWRECKS
Adventures in the sponge trade; excerpt from Shipwrecks and archaeology: the unharvested sea. P. Throckmorton. Atlan 224:96-103 S '69
Ancient shipwreck yields new facts; and a strange cargo; marble coffins found in the Gulf of Taranto. P. Throckmorton. il Nat Geog 135:282-300 F '69
Death of World Glory; supertanker broken in two by Cape rollers. R. Petrow. il Pop Mech 132:106-11+ Jl '69
Priceless relics of the Spanish Armada; fate of the Girona. R. Sténuit. il Nat Geog 135:745-77 Je '69
Whale of a tale; how a New Zealand ocean racer was sunk by a whale. J. Guiney. il Yachting 125:62+ Ap '69
What really caused the Torrey Canyon disaster? excerpts from In the wake of Torrey Canyon. R. Petrow. il Pop Mech 131:114-19+ Ap '69
Wreck of the Ocean Eagle. J. J. Cerame-Vivas. il Sea Front 15:224-31 Jl '69
See also
Collisions at sea
Titanic (steamship)

SHIPYARDS
See also
Shipbuilding

Anecdotes, facetiae, satire, etc.
Life in a Spanish boatyard. J. C. Kozlick. il Motor B 123:60-1+ F '69

SHIRER, William Lawrence
Fall of France; excerpts from The collapse of the Third Republic. Look 33:33-8+ S 23 '69

SHIREY, David L.
Impossible art: what it is. Art in Am 57:32-47 My '69

SHIRLEY, Ernest
Report from Sydney. Fortune 79:59+ Ap '69

SHIRTS
New shapes in men's shirts. B. Ullmann. il Good H 169:168 N '69

SHIVER, Ray A.
Capacitance probes in industrial instrumentation. Electr World 81:42-3+ My '69

SHMELYOV, Igor. See Fabriľskiĭ. V. jt. auth.

SHOBERG, Ray
Getting more from your router. Pop Mech 131:190-2+ Mr '69

SHOCK
See also
Electric shock

SHOCK absorbers
See also
Automobiles—Shock absorbers

SHOCK deformation of rocks. See Rocks—Deformation

SHOCK waves
See also
Electrohydraulics
Sonic boom

SHOCKLEY, Ann Allen
Two books with soul: for defiant ones. Engl J 58:396-8 Mr '69

SHOCKLEY, Grant S.
Ultimatum and hope. Chr Cent 86:217-19 F 12 '69

SHOE industry. See Shoes—Trade and manufacture

SHOE makers. See Shoemakers

SHOE stores
See also
Adler shoe shops, incorporated

SHOEMAKER, Eugene
Mining the moon. por Newsweek 74:19 Ag 4 '69

SHOEMAKER, Ted
Centrifuge for the fore. Sci N 95:150 F 8 '69
Doubling science research. Sci N 95:246 Mr 8 '69
Fresh directions in science. Sci N 96:542 D 6 '69

SHOEMAKER, Willie
Old shoe just as good as new. il pors Sports Illus 30:22-3 F 24 '69

SHOEMAKERS
Boots are his business. il Ebony 24:66-8+ S '69

SHOEMAN, D. W. and others
Cytochrome P-420: tubular aggregates from hepatic microsomes. bibliog Science 165:1371-2 S 26 '69

SHOES
School shoes; questions and answers. Good H 169:126 Ag '69
Touch of fancy footwork to step up the old game; colored golf shoes. R. Lieder. Sports Illus 30:72-3 Je 9 '69
See also
Wooden shoes

Care
Dressy holiday shoes. il Good H 169:198 D '69

Trade and manufacture
Feeling the pinch in shoes; petition for voluntary import restrictions on shoes. il Time 94:75A Jl 18 '69
Italian shoes, bellissimo! A. Hershman. il Duns R 94:95-8 O '69
No goody two-shoes; Olympic athletes paid by German firms of Adidas and Puma to wear their track shoes. J. Underwood. il Sports Illus 30:14-23 Mr 10 '69
Research summaries. C. M. O'Connor. Mo. Labor R 92:60-1 Mr '69
Shoemaker tends to a new last; Calzado Canada. il Bsns W p 124 Jl 12 '69
Year the shoe fell out of step. il Bsns W p 19-20 Ja 3 '70
See also
Edith Henry shoes, incorporated
Melville shoe corporation
Shoemakers
United States shoe corporation

SHOGAN, Robert
Did John Mitchell hear the justices? New Repub 160:11-13 Ap 26 '69

SHOLOKHOV, Mikhail Aleksandrovich
European literary scene. R. J. Clements. Sat R 52:29 Jl 5 '69

SHONFIELD, Andrew
Planning the future; futurology: a new science? Cur 105:41-53 Mr '69

SHOOTING
Matter of range. T. Trueblood. il Field & S 74:28+ O '69
On long-range shooting. J. O'Connor. il Outdoor Life 144:82+ N '69
Pinholers. W. Page. il Field & S 73:146-9 Mr '69
Pistol is for fun. T. Trueblood. il Field & S 74:34+ S '69
Plinking handgun. W. Page. il Field & S 74:36-8+ S '69
Scattergunning is a game for swingers. W. Davis. il Mech Illus 65:70+ F '69
Shooting. J. O'Connor. See issues of Outdoor life

SHOOTING—*Continued*
Shooting. W. Page. See issues of Field & stream
See also
Archery
Game
Geese, Wild
Hunting
Snipers
also Duck shooting, and similar headings
SHOOTING range; story. See Brodkey, H.
SHOP windows. See Show windows
SHOPLIFTING
Battle with shoplifters. U S News 67:32 D 22 '69
Ghost of shoplifting past. B. Farrell. il Life 67:31 D 12 '69
Security: a challenge to shoplifters. B. Curtis. Pub W 196:40-2 S 1 '69
Stealing season. il Newsweek 74:48 D 29 '69
SHOPPING and shoppers
International shopping; what sport! E. Sheppard. Harp Baz 102:188 Mr '69
Turn to Sunday shopping. il U S News 68:7 Ja 5 '70
Where shopping is child's play; Children's place. il Bsns W p88-90 Mr 8 '69
See also
Christmas shopping

Austria
Austria: what else besides dirndls? J. Friedberg. il Travel & Camera 32:41-2 Jl '69

Bermuda
Bermuda haute couture: trend-setting and popular. B. Dubivsky. il Travel & Camera 32:18+ S '69

Europe, Western
Now's the time for Christmas shopping in Europe. V. Creed. il Travel 132:62-4+ O '69
When in Rome, do as the roamers do; eight writers tell where they sleep, eat and shop; symposium; with editorial comment. Esquire 72:124-7+, 198-9 O '69

France
Shopping in France. M. A. MacKay. il Travel 132:42-7+ Jl '69

Great Britain
Going places, finding things in London's shops and galleries. D. Walton. il House & Gard 135:80-1+ Ap '69

Japan
Tokyo's incredible shopping resorts; stores double as museums, theaters, playgrounds. F. Lemkowitz. il Travel & Camera 32:68-9+ O '69

Kenya
Kenya without lions. R. Galligan and E. Galligan. il Travel & Camera 32:20 N '69

Northern Ireland
Mission to Belfast. D. Butwin. il Sat R 52:66+ D 6 '69

Russia
Window-shopping in Russia. E. H. Ortner. il Pop Sci 194:80-3+ Mr '69
SHOPPING carts. See Carts
SHOPPING centers
Building types study. il Arch Rec 146:135-50 Jl '69
Shopping centers: downtown is the next target. il Arch Rec 146:95 O '69
Shopping centers just for farmers. il Farm J 93.52Y Mr '69
Why me? vandalism in Negro shopping center in Dorrum, Del. Newsweek 73:39-40 Mr 10 '69
See also
Business districts
SHOPPING hours. See Store hours
SHOPWORK instruction. See Industrial arts
SHOR, Toots, restaurant. See New York (city)—Hotels, restaurants, etc.
SHORE birds
See also
Phalaropes
SHORE lines
See also
Coast changes
SHORE protection
Coastal engineering; report of meeting. M. Nichols. Science 164:590+ My 2 '69
Resort that helps preserve a wild seashore; Salishan, Ore. D. Connelly. il Sports Illus 30:36-40 Ap 28 '69

SHORE vegetation. See Seashore vegetation
SHORES, Louis
Library-college USA; address, April 2, 1969. ALA Bul 63:1547-53 D '69
SHORRIS, Earl
Afterthoughts of a prodigy. Esquire 72:28+ D '69
Doctor Hayakawa in thought and action. Ramp Mag 8:38-42 N '69
SHORT, Bobby
Musical events: recital at Town Hall. W. Balliett. New Yorker 45:103 My 31 '69
Popular records. D. Watt. New Yorker 45:108-10 Mr 1 '69
Realm of Mercer and Short. B. Korall. il por Sat R 52:66+ Ap 12 '69
SHORT cake. See Shortcake
SHORT haul airlines. See Local service airlines
SHORT range attack missile. See Guided missiles—Launching from airplanes
SHORT selling. See Stocks—Short selling
SHORT story
Changing confession market. H. P. Malmgreen. Writer 82:22-3 S '69
Discoveries by hindsight. A. Heinemann. Writer 82:20-1+ O '69
Everybody change places! M. J. Amft. Writer 82:12-13 D '69
Recipe for a short story. Sister Christine. Writer 82:17-21 D '69
Short story market that's always ready for more; confession story writing. P. McQuinn. Writers Digest 49:53-5 Je '69
Six ways to successful confessions. F. K. Palmer. Writer 82:15-18 My '69
Three today types of short story. C. Steinmetz. Writers Digest 49:58-62 N '69
Till (violent) death do us part. G. P. Elliott. Writer 82:15-16 O '69
We're looking for real writers. N. G. Stuart. Writer 82:25-7 D '69
See also
Fiction—Technique
SHORT story contests. See Fiction—Competitions
SHORT subject films. See Moving pictures—Short subject films
SHORT take-off and landing airplanes. See Airplanes, Vertical take-off and landing
SHORT wave radio apparatus. See Radio apparatus, Short wave
SHORT wave radio stations. See Radio stations, Short wave
SHORTBREADS. See Cookies
SHORTCAKE
Desserts fresh from the orchard; with recipes. il McCalls 96:87+ Ag '69
SHOSTAKOVICH, Dmitrii Dmitrievich
Shostakovich's symphonies. R. S. Brown. il pors Hi Fi 19:43-7+ Ap '69
SHOSTAKOVICH, Maxim
Young Maxim. por Newsweek 73:118+ Mr 17 '69
SHOT putting
Top three by a long shot; University of Kansas three mighty shotputters. J. Jares. il Sports Illus 30:78+ My 5 '69
SHOTGUN shells. See Cartridges
SHOTGUNS
Choke and pattern. J. O'Connor. il Outdoor Life 143:120+ My '69
Doubles never die; American-made doubles. W. Page. il Field & S 74:148-51 My '69
SHOUP, David Monroe, and Donovan, J. A.
New American militarism. Atlan 223:51-6 Ap '69; Same abr. with title Role of the military; the rise of our militaristic culture. Cur 108:46-55 Je '69
SHOUP, John. See Gruber, M. jt. auth.
SHOW windows
Creating effective sci-tech window displays. il Pub W 195:83-4 Ap 14 '69
SHOWER baths
Next best thing to showering in the garden. il Sunset 143:130 O '69
SHOWER fixtures
Adjustable shower heads. il Consumer Rep 34:282-5 My '69
SHOWER heads. See Shower fixtures
SHOWERS (parties) See Entertaining
SHRAND, Hyman
When the home makes the best hospital for a child. V. H. Bernstein. Redbook 133:91+ S '69
SHREDDERS, Compost. See Compost grinders and grinding
SHREWS
Evolution of neocortex; studies of visual cortex in hedgehogs and tree shrews. I. T. Diamond and W. C. Hall. bibliog il Science 164:251-62 Ap 18 '69

SHREWS—*Continued*
Ganesh in the house. P. Clingerman. Mlle
68:221-2 Mr '69
With various plants and animals, invading
insects can be chased away. V. M. Crill. il
Home Gard 56:56-7 O '69
SHRIMP farming. See Shellfish culture
SHRIMP plants
Shrimp plant. M. Adams. il Home Gard 56:
65 F '69
SHRIMPS
See also
Cookery—Shellfish
SHRIMPTON, Jean Rosemary
The Shrimp; interview, ed. by P. Devlin.
Vogue 153:55+ Mr 15 '69
SHRINES
See also
Pilgrims and pilgrimages
SHRIVER, George H.
When conservatism is liberalism. Chr Cent
86:1040-1 Ag 6 '69
SHRIVER, Robert Sargent, family
American uniques in France: the Shrivers;
with photographs by H. Clarke. Vogue 153:
160-7 My '69
SHRUBS
Broadleaved evergreens for all-year effect.
A. R. Treys il Horticulture 46:32-5 O '68
How to get the best shrubs and evergreens
for your money. il Bet Hom & Gard 47:52+
Mr '69
Recognizing woody plants in winter. E. H.
Ketchledge. il Cons 24:20-7+ O '69
See also
Desert vegetation
also names of shrubs, e.g. Azaleas
SHRUB, Anatole
Future U.S.-Soviet relations. Cur 104:46-54 F
'69
about
Bringing down thunderbolts. Time 93:37-8
My 30 '69
SHUBIN, Seymour
New parents for schizophrenics. Sci Digest
66:68-73 Ag '69
SHUFFLEBOARD
All you need is smooth concrete. il Sunset
143:100 Jl '69
SHUGART, Cecil G.
Student director becomes full-time visiting
scientist. J. P. Wiley. il Phys Today 22:73-
4 Jl '69
SHULDINER, Herbert
Get ready for your winter fun! Pop Sci 195:
122-7+ O '69
(ed) See Buchanan, C. L. Strange devices that
found the sunken sub Scorpion
(ed) See Hart, P. A. Your outrageous car-
repair bills
SHULEVITZ, Uri
Caldecott award acceptance; address. June
24, 1969. Horn Bk 45:385-8 Ag '69
about
Newbery-Caldecott secret, not a secret any
more. il por Pub W 195:129-30 F 17 '69
Uri Shulevitz. M. Zaum. il por Horn Bk 45:
389-91 Ag '69
Uri Shulevitz: Caldecott winner. M. Di Capua.
il por Library J 94:2068-9 My 15 '69
SHULMAN, Max
Stalking the red-nosed captain. Field & S 73:
60-1+ Ap '69
SHULMAN, Morton Philip
How a conservative becomes a crusader. por
Bsns W p97 O 18 '69
SHULMAN, N. Raphael, and Barker, L. F.
Virus-like antigen, antibody, and antigen-
antibody complexes in hepatitis measured
by complement fixation. bibliog Science
165:304-6 Jl 18 '69
SHULMAN, R. G. and others
Absence of heme-heme interaction in hemo-
globin; adaptation of address. February
28, 1969. bibliog Science 165:251-7 Jl 18 '69
SHULTZ, George Pratt
Big strikes: a new approach; interview. pors
U S News 67:46-9 D 1 '69
International labor organization: fifty years
of service; statement. October 29, 1969. Dept
State Bul 61:452-3 N 24 '69
Secretary Shultz: talks with Mayor Lindsay.
New Yorker 45:27-8 My 24 '69
Use of labor statistics in national decision-
making; excerpt from address, August 1969.
Mo Labor R 92:48-50 N '69
Wages, prices, strikes; a new approach; in-
terview. por U S News 66:62-6 Je 2 '69
about
Can a hands-off labor policy work? il por
Bsns W p62-3+ N 8 '69

Can Nixon work with the unions? M. Seeger.
por Duns R 93:89-90+ Mr '69
Job corps gets a working over. por Bsns W
p96 Ap 19 '69
Man who healed the welfare planners' split.
il por Newsweek 74:19 Ag 18 '69
Nixon's men try a lighter touch. il por Bsns
W p60+ O 4 '69
Nixon's rookie of the year. il por Time
94:92 N 7 '69
Shultz policy brings rail pact; model for oth-
er disputes? il por U S News 67:100-1 D 15
'69
Strike strategy of Mr Shultz; magic and a
bit of luck. il por U S News 67:56-7 Jl
7 '69
What Shultz inherits. il por Bsns W p78 Ja
25 '69
Who will shape new labor policies? il por
Nations Bsns 57:32-4+ F '69
SHUMAN, Bruce A.
WATS happening in North Carolina. por Li-
brary J 94:945-7 Mr 1 '69
SHUMAN, R. Blard
Prospectus on education; excerpts from ad-
dress. Clear House 44:67-71 O '69
Some myths that teachers live by. Sch &
Soc 97:435-7 N '69
Toward reorganizing secondary school En-
glish. Sch & Soc 97:97-8 F '69
—See Quinton, H. W. jt. auth.
SHUMWAY, Forrest N.
Signal: the careful conglomerate. J. B.
Weiner. il por Duns R 93:38-42+ Mr '69
SHUNAMAN, Fred
All about ovonics. Radio-Electr 40:41-3 My
'69
SHURTZ, Eugene, jr
Alpha incident; with report by K. Buckley.
il Newsweek 74:17 S 8 '69
Incident in Song Chang Valley. por Time
94:22-3 S 5 '69
SHUTTERS
Now it's nylon millwork! R. C. Sickler. il
Pop Sci 195:126-8 D '69
Now: shutters you don't have to paint. il
Pop Mech 132:159 S '69
SHUTTERS, Camera. See Camera shutters
SHUTTLE airplanes. See Airlines—Shuttle ser-
vice
SHY Emily; story. See Franco, M.
SHYER, Marlene Fanta
Far from my loving arms; story. Good H 168:
90-1 Ap '69
Sure thing; story. Redbook 133:90-1 Je '69
SHYNESS. See Timidity
SIALIC acids
Glomerular sialoprotein. S. C. Mohos and
L. Skoza. bibliog il Science 164:1519-21 Je
27 '69
Physical and chemical studies on cerulo-
plasmin: crystallization of desialized hu-
man ceruloplasmin asialoceruloplasmin. A.
G. Morell and others. bibliog il Science 166:
1293-4 D 5 '69
SIAM. See Thailand
SIBAL, Louis R. and others
Mammary tumor virus antigen: sensitive im-
munoassay. bibliog Science 164:76-8 Ap 4
'69
SIBELIUS, Jean Julius Christian
Bernstein's personal vision of the Sibelius
symphonies. J. Diether. Am Rec G 35:804-
6 My '69
Sibelius in perspective. R. Lawrence. Sat R
52:73 F 22 '69
Sibelius' seven symphonies. H. Goldsmith. il
pors Hi Fi 19:56-60 My '69
SIBERIA
See also
Akademgorodok
Antiquities
Petroglyphs of Siberia. A. P. Okladnikov.
il Sci Am 221:74-82 bibliog(p 136) Ag '69
Climate
Can we control the Arctic climate? proposed
transport of Atlantic Ocean water across
the Arctic basin. P. M. Borisov. il Bul Atom
Sci 25:43-8 N '69
SIBLEY, Shermer Lee
Sibley of Pacific gas & electric. por For-
tune 80:37 S '69
SIBLINGS
First, last or middle child: the surprising
differences. V. Packard. Read Digest 95:
25+ D '69
Must brothers (and sisters) fight? interview,
ed. by A. Rosenthal. B. Siegel. il Todays
Health 48:26-9+ Ja '70

SIBLINGS—*Continued*
Sibling chivalry: the other side of the coin.
G. Orcate. il Parents Mag 44:54-5+ Mr '69
See also
Children, First-born

SIBSON, Robert E.
Executive pay, you will make more. Nations
Bsns 57:60-4 N '69

SICILY
History of Sicily, by M. I. Finley and D. M.
Smith. Review
New Yorker 45:113 Je 14 '69. W. Sar-
geant

Description and travel
Spring in Sicily. J. Egan. il Sat R 52:48+ Ap
12 '69

SICK, The
Now you need a priority to get in a pres-
tige hospital. il U S News 66:41-2 Mr 24 '69
Profound lesson for the living; seminar at
University of Chicago's Billings hospital.
L. Wainwright. il Life 67:36-43 N 21 '69
Sickness and society, by R. S. Duff and A.
B. Hollingshead. Review
Cath World 209:137-8 Je '69. B. J. Ransil
Three case histories; encounters with physi-
cian or hospital. Time 93:56 F 21 '69
See also
Incurables
Nurse and patient
Physicians and patients
Sick children

Psychology
See also
Heart—Diseases—Psychological aspects

SICK children
Dual role of comforter and bereaved; re-
actions of medical personnel to the dying
child and his parents. E. Wallace and
B. D. Townes. bibliog Ment Hy 53:327-32
Jl '69
When the home makes the best hospital for
a child. V. H. Bernstein. Redbook 133:91+
S '69
See also
Mentally ill children

SICKLER, Richard C.
How to buy home fire extinguishers. Pop
Sci 195:108-11 D '69
Now it's nylon millwork! Pop Sci 195:126-
8 D '69
Philippine mahogany, the unknown wood.
Pop Sci 194:150-4+ Je '69
Secret of those new anti-leak anti-freezes.
Pop Sci 195:70-1 N '69
Want a screened porch? Pop Sci 194:168-71
Ja '69

SICKNESS
How to know when you're sick. N. Ashby. il
Todays Health 47:36-9 My '69
See also
Diagnosis
Medical service, Cost of

SICKNESS absence. See Absenteeism

SICRE, José Gómez-. See Gómez-Sicre, J.

SIDDUH. See Jews—Prayer books and devotions

SIDECARS. See Motorcycles—Equipment

SIDEMAN, Andrew
I was there. por Seventeen 29:86-7+ Ja '70

SIDER, Don
Big boondoggle at Lordstown. Fortune 80:
106-9+ S '69

SIDEWALKS, Elevated
How to plan for the pedestrian; Cincinnati,
Ohio. A. D. Bird. il Am City 84:76-7+
Jl '69

SIDEY, Hugh
Nixon after six months. por(p27) N Y
Times Mag p4-5 Jl 20 '69
Presidency. See issues of Life
(ed) See Moyers, B. White House staff versus
the Cabinet

SIDING (building)
Fixing up an older home. il Bet Hom & Gard
47:30 My '69
Improve your home with this new siding.
il Mech Illus 65:126-7 O '69
Longer life and good looks for the exterior of
your house. Good H 168:168+ Mr '69
New look in house siding. J. Hand. il Pop
Sci 194:154-8+ F '69
Step toward the plastic house; rigid vinyl
house siding and accessories. C. M. Ed-
wards. il Consumer Bul 52:14-16 Ap '69

SIDLOSKY, Carolyn
Six blocks from Velco's; story. Seventeen 28:
84-5 Ja '69

SIEBER, Roy
Collectors: Paul and Ruth Tishman. Art in Am
57:50-61 Mr '69

SIEBERT, Muriel
Watch the moneymen! A. Hershman. por
Duns R 94:79-80 D '69

SIEGEL, Bernard J.
Some recent developments in studies of social
and cultural change. Ann Am Acad 385:
157-74 S '69

SIEGEL, Burton
Must brothers (and sisters) fight? interview,
ed. by A. Rosenthal. Todays Health 48:
26-9+ Ja '70

SIEGEL, Jules
In the land of morning calm, déjà vu; story.
Esquire 72:142-3 N '69

SIEGEL, Leonard
Hidden conflicts in marriage. L. Kavaler. il
Parents Mag 44:35-7+ Je '69

SIEGEL, Marcella
On Christmas eve; poem. Chr Cent 86:1637
D 24 '69

SIEGEL, Marcia B.
Describing an elephant. Dance Mag 43:92-3
Ja '69
Les Feux-follets. Dance Mag 43:64-7 S '69

SIEGEL, Peter V. and others
Time-zone effects. bibliog Science 164:1249-
55 Je 13 '69

SIEGEL, Seymour
If I forget thee, O Jerusalem. Sat R 52:34 F
1 '69

SIEGFRIED, Sister Regina
Media-ized English. Sr Schol 94:Schol Teach
13 F 7 '69

SIEKMAN, Philip
Belgium's muscle-bound giant. Fortune 79:
98-103+ F '69
Germany catches its second wind. Fortune
79:88-91+ Ap '69
Letter from Stockholm. Fortune 80:67+ N
'69
Now it's the Europeans versus I.B.M. Fortune 80:86-91+ Ag 15 '69
Report from London. Fortune 79:49-50 My
1 '69

SIENA, Italy
In the heart of Italy. C. Foley. il Nat R
21:859+ Ag 26 '69

SIERRA club
Brower power awaits the verdict. H. Peter-
son. Sports Illus 30:36-8+ Ap 14 '69
Camp outings for the inexperienced. Sunset
142:44 Ap '69
Fratricide in the Sierra club. R. A. Jones.
Nation 208:567-70 My 5 '69
Mineral king, go or no go? R. Leadabrand.
il Am For 75:32-5+ O '69
Mom vs. apple pie; opposes Disney's proposed
Alpine village. il Newsweek 73:25 F 10 '69
Protectionists vs. recreationists; the battle
of Mineral King. A. Hano. il N Y Times
Mag p24-5+ Ag 17 '69
Storm over Alps; lawsuit threatened against
Disney organization. il Sr Schol 94:17 F 14
'69
To guard and preserve? Or open and enjoy?
il Time 93:17 F 7 '69

SIERRA LEONE

Description and travel
Sierra Leone. M. W. Stephens. il Travel 131:
32-5+ Mr '69

SIERRA NEVADA, Calif.
See also
Kings Canyon National Park

SIEVERS, Harry J.
Washington front. See occasional issues of
America

SIFFORD, Charlie
Blacks on the greens. il por Time 93:56 F 14
'69
Call back the years. W. Johnson. il pors
Sports Illus 30:56-8+ Mr 31 '69
Golf pays debt to a real pro. il pors Ebony
24:44-6+ Ap '69
Old Charlie jolts the new tour. D. Jenkins.
il por Sports Illus 30:16-17 Ja 20 '69

SIGBAND, Norman B.
Listen to what you can't hear. Nations Bsns
57:70-2 Je '69

SIGGINS, George R. and others
Cyclic adenosine monophosphate: possible
mediator for norepinephrine effects on
cerebellar purkinje cells. bibliog Science
165:1018-20 S 5 '69

SIGHT
Are eyeglasses inevitable? A. S. Markovits.
Mech Illus 65:59 F '69
Brain has second sight. il Sci Digest 66:90-1
N '69
Interocular transfer of orientational effects.
A. S. Gilinsky and R. S. Doherty. bibliog il
Science 164:454-5 Ap 25 '69
New insights on the eye. il Vogue 153:234-9+
Ap 1 '69

SIGHT—*Continued*
Stereoscopic and resolution acuity with various fields of view. S. M. Luria. bibliog il Science 164:452-3 Ap 25 '69
Two visual systems. G. E. Schneider. bibliog il Science 163:895-902 F 28 '69
Visual transient phenomenon: its polarity and a paradox. J. F. Bird and G. H. Mowbray. bibliog il Science 165:588-9 Ag 8 '69
Your vision, what do you know about it? J. Daugherty and M. Daugherty. il Sci Digest 65:89-91 F '69
See also
After images
Blindness
Color sense
Optical illusions
Optics, Physiological
Space perception
Visual pigments

Anecdotes, facetiae, satire, etc.
Visual welfare state. H. F. Ellis. New Yorker 45:103-4+ Ap 19 '69

SIGHT (animals)
Plastic animals fool real ones in Africa. il Life 66:69-71 My 2 '69
Retinal processing of visual images. C. R. Michael. il Sci Am 220:104-14 My '69
Visual form discrimination on the basis of relative distribution of light. H. A. Buchtel; S. S. Winans. bibliog il Science 164:857-8 My 16 '69
See also
Color sense

SIGHT (insects)
Ultraviolet video-viewing: the television camera as an insect eye. T. Eisner and others. il Science 166:1172-4 N 28 '69

SIGHTING. See Shooting

SIGL, Rupert
Agent of doom. por Newsweek 73:48 My 19 '69

SIGMOIDOSCOPY. See Cancer—Diagnosis

SIGN language
Teaching sign language to a chimpanzee. R. A. Gardner and B. T. Gardner. bibliog il Science 165:664-72 Ag 15 '69
See also
Deaf—Means of communication

SIGN painting
See also
Lettering

SIGNAL companies
Signal: the careful conglomerate. J. B. Weiner. il Duns R 93:38-42+ Mr '69

SIGNAL generators
B&K model 415 sweep/marker generator. il Electr World 82:78+ O '69
Dual-rate sawtooth generator. F. H. Tooker. il Electr World 81:74 My '69
FET square-wave generator. F. H. Tooker. il Radio-Electr 40:48 Ag '69
Heath model IG-18 sine/square-wave audio generator. il Electr World 81:59-60 Je '69
IC frequency spotter/standard. A. A. Mangieri. il Pop Electr 31:27-32 Ag '69
Improving sawtooth linearity. F. H. Tooker. il Electr World 81:84 F '69
Signal generator for 2-way radio. L. Loper. il Radio-Electr 40:70 Jl '69
SCS signal-squaring adapter. F. H. Tooker. il Pop Electr 32:65+ Ja '70
Squaring with an IC; square-wave generator. P. E. Harms. il Pop Electr 31:43-6 Jl '69
Triggered sweep for any scope. I. Gorgenyi. il Electr World 82:76-8 N '69
UJT sine-wave generators. F. H. Tooker. il Electr World 81:82 F '69
ULD sine wave generator. J. Bongiorno. il Pop Electr 31:55-61 O '69
See also
Pulse generators

SIGNAL lights, Automobile. See Automobiles—Signal lights
SIGNAL splitters. See Television antennas—Equipment
SIGNALS, Interplanetary. See Interplanetary communication
SIGNALS, Traffic. See Traffic signals

SIGNALS and signaling
Revised International code of signals. il Motor B 123:141 Ja '69
Revised international code of signals listed in new HO publication. E. S. Maloney. Motor B 123:124 Je '69

SIGNATURES (writing)
How a woman should sign a letter. Good H 168:164 F '69

SIGNETICS corporation
Signetics shows how in semiconductors il Bsns W p41-2 Jl 26 '69

SIGNOR, Roger
Anxiety: the cheap neurosis for everyone. Sci Digest 65:65-70 Je '69

SIGNS and signboards
Tightens sign ordinance; Montgomery County, Md. il Am City 84:116 Jl '69
See also
Road signs
Traffic signs

Caricatures and cartoons
Kindergarten chats. R. Hedman. Arch Forum 130:52-3 Ap '69

SIH, Charles J.
Enzymatic mechanism of steroid hydroxylation. bibliog Science 163:1297-300 Mr 21 '69

SIHANOUK, Norodom. See Norodom Sihanouk

SIKES, Robert L. F.
Excerpt from debate, June 26, 1968. Cong Digest 48:58+ F '69

SIKORSKI, Irma
Poetry, how and why. J. Jerome. Writers Digest 49:74-9 O '69

SIKOSKI, Elizabeth T.
Unknown academician; poem. Engl J 58:39 Ja '69

SILAGE
Corn silage. il Suc Farm 67:50-1 Jl '69
Hay. il Suc Farm 67:56 Jl '69
Hay-crop silage. il Suc Farm 67:46-7 Jl '69
He gets more from silos and cows. J. R. Borcherding. il Suc Farm 67:34-5 Je '69
High-moisture corn. il Suc Farm 67:54-5 Jl '69
See also
Silos

SILBERBERG, Sophie C. and Donovan, John
Fifty years of children's book week: fifty years of independent American children's book publishing. Horn Bk 45:702-11 D '69

SILBERGLIED, Robert E. and Eisner, Thomas
Mimicry of hymenoptera by beetles with unconventional flight. Science 163:486-8 Ja 31 '69

SILBERSTEIN, Richard M. and Levine, Carol
When youngsters cling to babyish ways. Parents Mag 44:51-3+ Mr '69

SILENCE; drama. See Pinter, H.

SILENT sound waves. See Ultrasonic waves

SILHOUETTES
Silhouettes and scissor cutting. L. R. Grol. il Design 70:27-31 Spr '69

SILHOUETTES; drama. See Harris, T.

SILICA
Silica in developing epidermal cells of avena internodes: electron microprobe analysis. P. B. Kaufman and others. bibliog il Science 166:1015-17 N 21 '69
See also
Coesite

SILICATES
Strength-density relations in particulate silicates of complex shape and their possible lunar significance. L. D. Jaffe. bibliog il Science 166:1121-3 S 13 '69
Tuhualite crystal structure. S. Merlino. bibliog il Science 166:1399-401 D 12 '69
See also
Jadeite
Mica
Pyroxenes
Serpentine

SILICON
Ion implantation studies in silicon. L. Eriksson and others. bibliog il Science 163:627-33 F 14 '69
Supply sliced thin in silicon wafers; shortage threat to integrated circuit business. Bsns W p28 Ag 23 '69

SILICON compounds
Silicon oxynitride stability. W. R. Ryall and A. Muan. bibliog il Science 165:1363-4 S 26 '69

SILICON controlled rectifier. See Electric current rectifiers

SILICON controlled switches. See Electric switches

SILICON oxynitride. See Silicon compounds

SILK, George
Grip on the tides; photographs. Life 67:32-41 Jl 4 '69

SILK
See also
Brocade

SILK screen printing
Another creative dimension. H. Glassgold and E. Scully. il Mod Phot 33:94-5 N '69
Serigraphs of Phil Paradise. J. Lovoos. il Am Artist 33:43-8+ O '69
Silk screen: how you can do it. il Mod Phot 33:148+ N '69

SILLIMAN, Ronald
He was a visitor; poem. Poetry 113:255 Ja '69

SILLITOE, Alan
Morning coffee with Sillitoe; interview, ed. by I. Hajek. Nation 208:122-3 Ja 27 '69
SILLS, Beverly
Beverly Sills as Lucia di Lammermoor. I. Kolodin. Sat R 52:54 O 25 '69
But Julius, I've always sung this way. R. Gelatt. il pors Hi Fi 19:24+ F '69
New Lucia. il por Time 94:66 O 17 '69
Recent recitals by stars of the New York city opera. il pors Am Rec G 35:455-7 F '69
Records:
Beverly Sills. Opera N 34:30 N 1 '69
La Sills at the summit. H. Saal. il pors Newsweek 73:69-70+ Ap 21 '69; Same abr. with title From soap opera to grand opera with Beverly Sills. Read Digest 94:146-50 O '69
Star status for Beverly Sills, a first recital disc. C. L. Osborne. il por Hi Fi 19:76-7 F '69
SILLS, Clarence
Hello, Mr Chip. T. Williams. pors Newsweek 73:106 Mr 17 '69
SILLS, David L.
Editing a scientific encyclopedia. bibliog Science 163:1169-75 Mr 14 '69
SILLS, Paul
Metamorphoses; dramatization of poem by Ovid. Criticism
Newsweek 74:117-18 D 15 '69
SILMAN, Israel, and Karlin, Arthur
Acetylcholine receptor: covalent attachment of depolarizing groups at the active site. bibliog il Science 164:1420-1 Je 20 '69
SILOS
100 percent dairy feeding from silos. J. R. Borcherding. il Suc Farm 67:14B F '69
See also
Silage

Fires and fire protection

Silo fires. Farm J 93:32 Ag '69
SILOS, Missile. See Guided missiles—Launching pads
SILVA, Artur da Costa e. See Costa e Silva, A. da
SILVA, Bernard J. and Jackson, Brent
Camping's third dimension. Camp Mag 41:12+ Ja '69
SILVA, Maria Helena Vieira da. See Vieira da Silva, M. H.
SILVA CASTRO, Raúl
Juan Egaña's Pan American dream. Américas 21:28-32 Ap '69
SILVER, Adele Zeldman
Second lap. Nation 208:524 Ap 28 '69
SILVER, Eli A.
Late Cenozoic underthrusting of the continental margin off northernmost California. bibliog Science 166:1265-6 D 5 '69
SILVER, George A.
Medicine: the calculated risks. Nation 208:117-20 Ja 27 '69
SILVER, Gerald A.
Do you need a memo decoder? Ed Digest 35:31 D '69
SILVER, Isidore
Burger court. Commonweal 90:585-8 S 26 '69
Sisson's complaint. Wyzanski's ploy. Commonweal 90:385-9 Je 20 '69
SILVER, Nathan
Architecture in Mexico. Nation 209:121+ Ag 11 '69
SILVER
Oak Ridge silver mint; Treasury loan. Sci Am 220:56 My '69
Persistence of silver. S. Nirenberg. il House B 111:92-3 F '69
See also
Silverware

Prices

Silver looks toward brighter futures. il Bsns W p 124+ Je 21 '69
SILVER as money
How to make a buck with dimes and quarters. T. Powers. il Life 66:61-2+ My 2 '69
SILVER dollars. See Coins
SILVER luster. See Luster ware
SILVER mines and mining

United States

Hi-yo, silver; H. Hughes buys mines in Nevada. il Newsweek 73:64 Mr 31 '69
SILVER oxide
Single crystals of silver oxide. il Chem 42:24 O '69
SILVER saxifrages. See Saxifrages
SILVER SPRING, Md.

Parks and playgrounds

Controversial park wins friends. S. D. Golub. il Am City 84:70-1 Jl '69

Urban oasis: Flower avenue park. S. D. Golub. il Parks & Rec 4:31-2 F '69
SILVERBERG, Robert
And the mound-builders vanished from the earth. Am Heritage 20:60-3+ Je '69
SILVERBERG, Ernest
Tomorrow's Mexican Riviera? Travel 132:72-3 S '69
SILVERMAN, Herman
Portable swimming pools, going strong. Parks & Rec 4:48-50+ Mr '69
SILVERMAN, Jan. See Coopersmith, S. jt. auth.
SILVERMAN, Jerry M.
Politics in South Vietnam. bibliog f Cur Hist 57:321-6+ D '69
SILVERMAN, Martin
Multi-purpose building solves our space problems. Camp Mag 41:18 F '69
SILVERMAN, Phyllis Rolfe
Widow-to-widow program, an experiment in preventive intervention. bibliog Ment Hy 53:333-7 Jl '69
SILVERMAN, Theodore
Enough is enough; interview. New Yorker 45:52-4 N 15 '69
SILVERSMITHING
James Geddy and sons, colonial craftsmen: evidence from the earth; Williamsburg, Va. I. Noël-Hume. il Antiques 95:106-11 Ja '69
SILVERSMITHS
See also
Lauritzen, F.
Thibault family
SILVERSTONE, Marilyn
(ed) See Stalina, S. I. Suburbanization of Svetlana
SILVERWARE
English silver: collection in the Cleveland museum of art. R. Davidson. il Antiques 95:774+ Je '69
New values for old silver. il Time 93:60 Mr 7 '69
Silver gifts to use for a lifetime. il House & Gard 136:194-6+ S '69
Silver; Williamsburg, Va. J. D. Davis. il Antiques 95:134-7 Ja '69
Some early English silver at the Art institute of Chicago. A. Wardwell. il Antiques 95:818-24 Je '69
South of the border, silver is as good as gold. J. Friedberg. Travel & Camera 32:10 N '69
Special tools for special jobs. A. Walker. il Am Home 72:24 Mr '69
With love and joy; gleaming gifts. il Seventeen 28:124-5 D '69
See also
Silversmithing
Spoons
Tableware

Collectors and collecting

English provincial silver in a London collection. J. Banister. il Antiques 96:106-13 Jl '69
Unusual pieces of Irish silver. K. Ticher. il Antiques 96:572-7 O '69

Exhibitions

English silver in Texas. Y. Hackenbroch. il Antiques 96:889-93 D '69
SILVEY, J. K. G. See Wyatt, J. T. jt. auth.
SIM, Georges, pseud. See Simenon, G.
SIMCKES, Seymour
Seven days of mourning. Criticism
New Yorker 45:38-9 D 27 '69
Newsweek 74:57 D 29 '69
SIMENON, Georges
Artist or craftsman? G. Culligan. Sat R 52:46-7+ Ap 12 '69
Close-up: excuse me, I think I'm about to have a novel; with report by M. Mok. il pors Life 66:43-4+ My 9 '69
Happy 200th to Simenon. por Time 93:44 Mr 14 '69
You can stop snapping at my heels now. G. P. Hunt. il Life 66:3 My 9 '69
SIMEON, Laura
Pride of five women. R. Hochstein. il por Good H 168:84-5 Je '69
SIMERL, Larry
How much will feed grains cost? Farm J 93:B9+ S '69
SIMIAN viruses
Cell transformation by viruses. R. Dulbecco. bibliog il Science 166:962-8 N 21 '69
Human diploid cell transformation by DNA extracted from the tumor virus SV40. S. A. Aaronson and G. J. Todaro. bibliog il Science 166:390-1 O 17 '69
Neoplastic transformation in vitro of hamster lens epithelium by simian virus 40. D. M. Albert and others. bibliog il Science 164:1077-8 My 30 '69

SIMIAN viruses—*Continued*
Simian virus 40 in polio vaccine: follow-up of newborn recipients. J. F. Fraumeni, jr. and others. bibliog il Science 167:59-60 Ja 2 '70
SIMIRENKO, Alex
Post-Stalinist social science. por Trans-Action 6:37-42 Je '69
SIMMONDS, M. A. and Iversen, L. L.
Thermoregulation: effects of environmental temperature on turnover of hypothalamic norepinephrine. bibliog Science 163:473-4; 165:1031 Ja 31, S 5 '69
SIMMONS, Dale D.
Sufficient versus necessary reasons for professional involvement. Ment Hy 53:143-5 Ja '69
SIMMONS, Donald
Harlem gets down to business. il por Bsns W p70-2 Ag 9 '69
SIMMONS, Dykes Askew, jr
Mexican prisoner. por Newsweek 73:39-40 Ap 21 '69
No more adobe; first American to be condemned in Mexico escapes. il por Time 93:40 Ap 18 '69
SIMMONS, Ernest J.
Belated bow of tsarist classic. Sat R 52:31-2+ My 3 '69
Life as it is and as it should be. Sat R 52:44-5 Ap 12 '69
SIMMONS, Gene, and Nur, Amos
Granites: relation of properties in situ to laboratory measurements. bibliog Science 162:789-91; 165:203 N 15 '68, Jl 11 '69
SIMMONS, Joseph J. 1925?-
$1-billion decision. por Bsns W p75 D 27 '69
SIMMONS, Robert Hilton
Objects: USA; the Johnson collection of contemporary crafts. Craft Horiz 29:24-51+ N '69
SIMMONS, Susan
Pip: a love affair. Engl J 58:416-17 Mr '69
SIMMS, Peter
Siam by-the-sea. Sat R 52:86-8 Mr 8 '69
SIMON
Rhine; photographs. por Travel & Camera 32:65-7+ Mr '69
Simon says. See issues of Modern photography
Why our astronauts can't make good pictures. Pop Phot 65:71-5+ Ag '69
SIMON, Eliav
Reports: Israel. Atlan 224:18+ D '69
SIMON, Henry W.
Fanfare for Tully Hall. Hi Fi 19:MA8-9+ D '69
SIMON, James, pseud. See Kunen, J. S.
SIMON, John
Let us now praise Dwight Macdonald. Commonweal 91:68-70 O 17 '69
SIMON, Leonard M.
Candidate. New Yorker 45:28-31 Je 7 '69
SIMON, Mina Lewiton
Bracelet; story. New Yorker 44:32-8 F 8 '69
SIMON, Neil
Last of the red hot lovers. Criticism
    New Yorker 45:64 Ja 10 '70
    Newsweek il 75:73 Ja 12 '70
    Time 95:64 Ja 12 '70
Neil Simon: hilarity all the way to the bank. il por Time 95:65 Ja 12 '70
People are talking about... por Vogue 155:144-5 Ja 1 '70
SIMON, Norton
Simon says good-by. por Newsweek 74:89 D 15 '69
SIMON, Patricia
Anyone who has a dog is just plain crazy. Redbook 133:90+ S '69
Delicious report on cookbooks. Redbook 132:96-7+ F '69
Up to here in gerbils. McCalls 97:39+ D '69
SIMON, Ruth B.
Seismicity of Colorado: consistency of recent earthquakes with those of historical record. bibliog Science 165:897-9 Ag 29 '69
SIMON, Sidney B.
Down with grades. Todays Ed 58:24 Ap '69
—See Kirshenbaum, H. jt auth.
SIMON, Walter B.
Some problems in helping patients in public mental hospitals. bibliog Ment Hy 53:428-32 Jl '69
SIMON, William
—and Gagnon, J. H.
Psychosexual development. pors Trans-Action 6:9-17 Mr '69
—See Gagnon, J. H. jt. auth.
about
Anatomy is not destiny. Time 93:56+ Mr 28 '69

SIMON ROCK, Great Barrington, Mass. See Private schools

SIMONDS, C. H.
Groaning coffee table. Nat R 21:1278-80 D 16 '69
Marvelous Miss Mercer. Nat R 21:866-7 Ag 26 '69
Television (cont) Nat R 21:345-6 Ap 8 '69
—See McCoy, K. jt. auth.
SIMONE, Kirsten
Danish Giselle. W. Terry. il por Sat R 52:54 Ag 23 '69
SIMONE, Nina
More than an entertainer. il por Time 93:63 F 21 '69
Nina Simone, high priestess of soul; excerpt from The sound of soul—the music and its meaning P. Garland. il pors Ebony 24:156-9 Ag '69
SIMONEIT, B. R. and others
Apollo lunar module engine exhaust products. bibliog Science 166:733-8 N 7 '69
SIMONI, Norma
Forcing lilies. Horticulture 46:26-7+ D '68
SIMONS, Charles Earl, 1916-
Strom's little acres. D. Walsh. il por Life 67:42-46A S 19 '69
SIMONS, Elwyn L.
Challenging Kenyapithecus. Sci N 96:97 Ag 2 '69
SIMONS, Francis, bp
Question of interpretation. America 120:345 Mr 29 '69
about
Papal infallibility revisited. J. C. Haughey; discussion. America 120:345 Mr 29 '69
SIMONS, Howard
What of U.S.-Soviet space cooperation? Cur 110:8-9 S '69
SIMONS, Mary
Loving world of Anthony Quinn. Look 33:48-51 Ap 1 '69
Report on troubles in pandasville. por Look 33:22 O 21 '69
SIMONS, Myron
Stock trends (cont) por Forbes 103:98+ Ap 15; 104:70-1 Jl 1; 62 Ag 1; 70 S 1; 93 O 1; 96 N 1; 86 D 1 '69
SIMONTON, John S. jr
Build Op-Tach. Pop Electr 30:27-31+ Mr '69
Build 200-watt dual flasher. Pop Electr 30:50-2 F '69
Build WWRC. Pop Electr 30:27-32 Je '69
Carpenter's mate. Pop Electr 31:69-72 S '69
Waa-waa. Pop Electr 32:45-51 Ja '70
SIMPLETON Peter; drama. See Hall, M.
SIMPSON, Dwight James
Israel: a garrison state. Cur Hist 58:1-7+ Ja '70
Israel in the Islamic world: a hundred years' war. Cur Hist 56:166-7+ Mr '69
SIMPSON, Elizabeth J.
Curriculum development challenges in home economics. Ed Digest 34:49-51 Ap '69
SIMPSON, Louis
Apollinaire! the perfect romantic. N Y Times Mag p26-7+ Ja 19 '69
Friend of the family; poem. Harper 238:70-1 Ap '69
SIMPSON, O. J.
First taste of O. J. is OK. E. Shrake. il pors Sports Illus 31:20-3 Ag 25 '69
Ready if you are, O.J. F. Deford. il pors Sports Illus 31:16-19 Jl 14 '69
What price heroes F. Deford. il por Sports Illus 30:32-4+ Je 9 '69
SIMPSON, Robert H.
Curbing hurricanes; the chances; interview. por U S News 67:34-6 S 1 '69
SIMPSON, Ronald Albert
Good and the useful. M. Randall. Poetry 115:49-50 O '69
SIMPSON, S. A.
Sailing through the Solomon Islands. il Travel 132:66-71 S '69
SIMPSON, Smith
Diplomats in disarray. Nation 208:138-41 F 3 '69
SIMPSONS-Sears limited
That old Sears magic. il Forbes 103:40 Je 1 '69
SIMS, L. Moody
Voice of dissent: John Jay Chapman and the great wickedness. bibliog Negro Hist Bul 32:12-13 Mr '69
SIMULATION methods
    See also
    Mathematical models
SIMULATORS
Aping the ocean's deeps; high-pressure hyperbaric chamber. J. Eberhart. il Sci N 96:280-1 S 27 '69

SIMULATORS—*Continued*
Tunnel-full of sonic booms. S. V. Jones. il Sci Digest 66:77 Ag '69
See also
Flight simulators
Space flight simulators

SIN
For sinners only. L. N. Bell. Chr Today 14:35-6 N 7 '69
Murmuring. Chr Today 13:39 S 26 '69
Original sin and Roman Catholic theology. Chr Today 13:23 Ap 25 '69
Sin of everyman; original sin. il Time 93:62+ Mr 21 '69
See also
Confession
God—Wrath
Good and evil
Salvation

Anecdotes, facetiae, satire, etc.
Peg Bracken's 108 original sins; excerpts from I didn't come here to argue. P. Bracken. il McCalls 96:74-5+ S '69

SINAI (peninsula)
Sinai adventure. M. Levin. il Travel 131:36-9 Ap '69

SINATRA, Frank
Frank Sinatra: confessions and contradictions. G. Lees. por Hi Fi 19:120 Mr '69
Sinatra: twentieth-century romantic. by A. Shaw. Review
Sat R il por 52:47+ F 8 '69

SINATRA, Frank, 1944?-
Underrated Sinatra. G. Lees. por Hi Fi 19:109 Je '69

SINCE when do they charge admission; story. See Morris, W.

SINCLAIR, A. C. E. See Gale, W. A. jt. auth.

SINE-wave clippers. See Pulse generators

SINE-wave generators. See Signal generators

SINGAPORE
See also
Libraries—Singapore

Commercial treaties and agreements
United States and Singapore sign new cotton textile agreement; Department announcement, with text of agreement. il Dept State Bul 60:136-8 F 10 '69

Economic conditions
Singapore: the robust waif. il Bsns W p66-7 D 6 '69

Economic policy
New tides in an island nation. P. Simms and R. Loving, jr. il Fortune 80:81-5 Ag 15 '69

Politics and government
Why Singapore might make it. A. Campbell. New Repub 160:13-15 Ap 26 '69

SINGER, Clyde
Clyde Singer: Ohio painter. R. D. Bonham. il por Am Artist 33:58-67 F '69

SINGER, David A. jr
New frontiers for professional negotiations. Sch & Soc 97:370-2 O '69

SINGER, G. See Montgomery, R. B. jt. auth.

SINGER, Helen
Unguarded rooms; Delhi lawn and its dew; Mr Mohan pal's plant; Retread; Old salt; In the ending. Word is not; Most distant future; Those without metaphor; poems. Poetry 113:231-41 Ja '69

SINGER, Isaac Bashevis
Key; story, tr. by the author and E. T. Beck. New Yorker 45:65-8 D 6 '69

about
Fiction. R. Alter. por Sat R 52:38+ N 1 '69

SINGER, Israel Joshua
Three generations. A. Bezanker. Nation 208:800-1 Je 23 '69

SINGER, Marshall. See Goulden, J. C. jt. auth.

SINGER, Richard G. and Blumenthal, I. J.
Suicide clues in psychotic patients. Ment Hy 53:346-50 Jl '69

SINGER, Siegfried Fred
Federal funding: what are the priorities? letter. Science 163:759-60 F 21 '69
Publication savings and shortcuts; letter. Science 166:43-4 O 3 '69

about
Capturing a moon and other diversions. il por Time 93:66-7 F 21 '69

SINGER company
New Singer makes a zigzag pattern. il Bsns W p58-60+ N 22 '69
New stitch for Singer. J. Poindexter. il Duns R 93:28-32 Ja '69

SINGERS
Chambers brothers; integrated group. il Ebony 24:162-4+ O '69
Debuts & reappearances; New York concerts. See issues of High fidelity incorporating Musical America
Down to old Dixie and back; The band. il Time 95:42-6 Ja 12 '70
Musical America selects young artists, 1969; photographs. Hi Fi 19:MA8-12+ Jl '69
Musical whirl; photographs. See issues of High fidelity incorporating Musical America
Secular music. R. Christgau. Esquire 71:62+ Ap '69
Sight & sound of folk. R. Goldstein. il Travel & Camera 32:70-5 Je '69
Under twenty-one. S. Reice. il McCalls 96:42-3+ Ja '69
Voices of Harlem; Voices of East Harlem singing mixture of blues, gospel and pop music. il Time 95:42 Ja 5 '70
See also
Baez, J.
Choral groups and societies
Elliot, C.
Jagger, M.
Mitchell, J.
Negro singers
Opera singers
Rock 'n' roll singers
Sinatra, F.

SINGH, Madanjeet
Unknown treasures of Himalayan art. il UNESCO Courier 22:14-25+ F '69

about
Perilous pilgrimage. il Time 93:72-4 F 14 '69

SINGH, Raghubir
Sacred Ganges; photographs. Horizon 11:11-25 Sum '69

SINGH, Sheo Dan
Urban monkeys; with biographical sketch. Sci Am 221:16, 108-15 Jl '69

SINGING
Hollywood scene; ed. by E Miller. P. Clark. il Seventeen 28:130+ Ag '69
Lively arts: I'm not the rose-in-the-mouth type; interview, ed. by R. Hemming. B. Allen. Sr Schol 94:21-2 My 2 '69
See also
Choral singing
Opera singers

SINGLE-lens reflex cameras
Does your SLR really read close-ups? W. Hanson. il Pop Phot 65:92-3 D '69
Field check: Icarex 35S. N. Rothschild. il Pop Phot 65:122+ Jl '69
Keppler on the SLR. H. Keppler. See issues of Modern photography
Kodak Instamatic SLR for 126 cartridges. il Mod Phot 33:84-6 Mr '69
Lab report; Leicaflex SL; with instrument readout by N. Goldberg. B. Pierce. il Pop Phot 64:96-7+ Ap '69
Lab report; Topcon super D. D. B. Eisendrath; N. Goldberg. il Pop Phot 64:112-13+ My '69
1969-70 SLR comparison directory. il Mod Phot 33:108-17 O '69
Single-lens-reflex cameras. il Consumer Bul 52:7-11 O '69
SLRs for less than $100. E. Meyers. il Pop Phot 65:86-7 N '69
Techniques tomorrow: a meeting with the team of engineers who design and build our modern cameras. B. Sherman. Mod Phot 33:58+ F '69
Versatility plus in an SLR; Rolleiflex SL66. S. Nathan. il Pop Phot 64:64+ Ap '69

Loading
Drop-in film cartridge has come to stay. S. M. Gallager. il Pop Mech 131:148-50 F '69

SINGLE men
Call me in the city; Singles week at a famous resort hotel. L. Tornabene. il McCalls 96:68-9+ Ja '69
Fifty eligible bachelors. il Ebony 24:62-5+ Je '69
Opinion: on being a bachelor. G. Frazier. Mlle 69:16+ S '69

SINGLE people
Church and the single person. Chr Today 13:22-3 Je 20 '69
Single bliss. R. Haughton. il Cath World 209:149-50 Jl '69
Unwed couples; do they live happily ever after? D. Bloch and S. Blum. il Redbook 132:90-1+ Ap '69

SINGLE women
Call me in the city; Singles week at a famous resort hotel. L. Tornabene. il McCalls 96:68-9+ Ja '69
Fifty eligible girls for 1969. il Ebony 24:142-3+ Ap '69

SINGLE women—*Continued*
Live alone and like it: 1969 style. H. LaBarre. McCalls 96:94+ My '69
Single life: U.S.A. il Mlle 69:130-1+ S '69
Women who don't need men. J. Brothers. Good H 169:52+ N '69
Young woman's story. Redbook 133:13+ Ag; 134:49-50 D '69

SINGLETON, Henry E.
Playing it safe? por Forbes 103:17 Ja 15 '69

SINKIANG province, China
Marco Polo would recognize Mao's Sinkiang. H. E. Salisbury. il N Y Times Mag p 14+ N 23 '69
Sinkiang: where it could begin. il Time 94: 33 Ag 22 '69

SINKS
To improve a modern sink. il Sunset 143: 111 N '69

SINN Fein rebellion, 1916. See Ireland—History —Sinn Fein rebellion, 1916

SINNETTE, Elinor D.
School library workshop in Nigeria. por Wilson Lib Bul 43:997-1001 Je '69

SINO-Indian border dispute, 1957-
Reporter at large. V. Mehta. il New Yorker 45:26-32+ Jl 19; 40-8+ Jl 26 '69

SINO-Russian border disputes
American stake in the Russia-China confrontation. W. E. Griffith. Read Digest 95:89-92 S '69
Analysis: behind the Sino/Soviet dispute. D. Horowitz. il Ramp Mag 7:39-43 Je '69
Angry frontier; from the Pamirs to the Pacific. il Life 66:26-37 Mr 21 '69
Backing away from the brink; proposed talks. il Newsweek 74:53-4 O 20 '69
Battle on the Sino-Soviet border. Time 94: 33+ Ag 22 '69
China and the USSR on the brink. N. Maxwell. New Repub 161:17-19 Ag 9 '69
Even money; Sino-Soviet battlefield. il Newsweek 73:58-9 Mr 17 '69
Fraught with grave consequences. il Newsweek 73:44+ Mr 24 '69
Internal Russian pressures against war. E. Crankshaw. Cur 112:52-4 N '69
Limited war or nuclear holocaust? R. S. Elegant. Cur 112:48-52 N '69
Lost leader; Sinkiang incident. il Newsweek 73:44 Je 23 '69
Marco Polo would recognize Mao's Sinkiang. H. E. Salisbury. il N Y Times Mag p 14+ N 23 '69
More trouble on the borders. il Time 94:36 Jl 18 '69
Moscow-Peking rupture; its meaning to U.S. il U S News 66:6 Mr 17 '69
Parley between battles on an icebound frontier. il Life 66:64-7 Ap 11 '69
Politesse in Peking. Newsweek 73:58+ My 26 '69
Preparing for the worst. il Newsweek 74:32+ Jl 14 '69
River is not the issue; clash on the Ussuri River frontier. C. P. Fitzgerald. Nation 208: 465-6 Ap 14 '69
Russian roulette on China's border. il U S News 66:8 Mr 31 '69
Thin red line. il Sr Schol 95:15-16 O 27 '69
Two Communist giants sparring toward war? il U S News 66:8 Je 23 '69
Violence on the Sino-Soviet border. il Time 93:32-3 Mr 14 '69
Where China and Russia meet. Time 93:23 Mr 21 '69
Where Russia and China collide. il Time 93: 28-9 Je 20 '69

SINOITE. See Silicon compounds
SINOLOGY. See Chinese studies (Sinology)
SINS
See also
Deadly sins

SINS, Deadly. See Deadly sins

SINSHEIMER, Robert L.
Designed genetic change. Sci Am 221:50-2 Jl '69

SINUS disease
But is it really sinus trouble? T. Berland. il Todays Health 47:34-7 Mr '69

SINUSITIS. See Sinus disease

SIOUX CITY, la.
Police department
Station wagon most versatile police vehicle. il Am City 84:30 N '69

SIOUX CITY, la, public library
Beamy open-plan branch for Sioux City, Iowa: Morningside project. il Library J 94: 4390 D 1 '69

SIOUX FALLS, S.D.
Ready for an emergency. P. V. Sanders. il Am City 84:98-9 Ja '69

SIOUX Indians. See Dakota Indians

SIQUELAND, Einar R. and DeLucia, C. A.
Visual reinforcement of nonnutritive sucking in human infants. bibliog Science 165:1144- 6 S 12 '69

SIRCAR, Manjusri Chaki-. See Chaki-Sircar, M.

SIREN (computer system) See Airlines—Reservation systems

SIRENIA. See Manatees

SIRHAN, Sirhan Bishara
Cry mercy. Nation 208:589 My 12 '69
Death row for Robert Kennedy's killer, but... il por U S News 66:16 Je 2 '69
Harsh verdict on courtroom psychiatry. Life 66:32B My 2 '69
New debate on death penalty. por U S News 66:13 My 5 '69
Plea for mercy. Time 93:21 My 30 '69
Sirhan: RFK forgot one minority group. Nat R 21:214-15 Mr 11 '69
Whatever happened to the assassins of Kennedy and King? por U S News 67:10 Ag 18 '69
Why psychiatrists disagree in court. il Time 93:44+ Ap 4 '69
See also
Trials (murder)—Sirhan trial, 1969

SIRIKIT Kitiyakara, consort of Bhumibol Adulyadej, king of Thailand
Siam by-the-sea. P. Simms. il Sat R 52:86-8 Mr 8 '69

SISAR fire, Calif. See Forest fires

SISCO, Joseph J.
Arab-Israeli confrontation; a challenge to international diplomacy; address, April 23, 1969. Dept State Bul 60:443-6 My 26 '69
Continuity and change in foreign policy; address, December 11, 1968. Dept State Bul 60:27-30 Ja 13 '69
United States and the Arab-Israeli dispute; address, April 11, 1969. Dept State Bul 60: 391-4 My 5 '69
United States and the Arab-Israeli dispute; with questions and answers. Ann Am Acad 384:66-72 Jl '69
about
Aggressive peacemaker. il por Newsweek 74: 40-1 D 1 '69

SISK, John P.
Intolerable allegories of dissent. Cath World 210:55-8 N '69
Making it in America. Atlan 224:63-8 D '69

SISSMAN, Louis Edward
Books. New Yorker 45:163-4+ Ap 26 '69
Clever women; poem. Atlan 223:95 My '69
Deathplace; poem. Harper 238:77 Je '69
Dream, dreamed between midnight and 1 a.m. July 8, 1969; story. New Yorker 45:36 D 20 '69
20th armored, a recurrent dream; poem. New Yorker 45:40 Ap 5 '69
Unknown Western-Union boy; poem. Atlan 224:95 S '69
Veterans: a dream; poem. New Yorker 45:34 Mr 1 '69
Village: the seasons; poem. Atlan 224:62-4 Jl '69
Visiting chaos; poem. New Yorker 45:44 Mr 15 '69
War requiem; poem. New Yorker 45:37-43 My 3 '69
about
Boston's adman-poet. por Newsweek 74:97-8 O 13 '69
Poet doubles as an adman. por Bsns W p 153- 4 S 20 '69

SISSON, John Heffron, Jr
Conscientious objection. New Repub 160:9 My 3 '69
Moral objections. por Newsweek 73:44 Ap 14 '69
Moral objector wins a point. por Sr Schol 94: 14 Ap 18 '69
Sisson's complaint. Wyzanski's ploy. I. Silver. Commonweal 90:385-9 Je 20 '69

SISSON, Robert F.
Snowflakes to keep. il por Nat Geog 137: 104-11 Ja '70

SISTERHOODS
Battling for nuns' rights: Immaculate Heart of Mary sisters press on with renewal. il Newsweek 74:80-1 S 8 '69
Black sisters become soul sisters. J. C. Haughey. America 121:67 Ag 2 '69
Contemplatives unite for renewal; Association of contemplative sisters. America 121: 154 S 13 '69
I.H.M.'s and the bishops. America 121:349-50 O 25 '69
Making of a saint: Mother Teresa, Superior General of the Missionaries of Charity. C. B. Pepper. il Look 33:34+ Mr 4 '69

SISTERS; story. See Taylor, E.

SISYRINCHIUM californicum. See Blue-eyed grass

SIT-in demonstrations. See Negroes—Segregation, Resistance to

SITE planning. See Housing projects—Site planning

SITES, Building. See Building sites

SITES, Industrial. See Location in business and industry

SITKA, Alaska
Sitka, as an Alaska stopover. il Sunset 142: 38+ Ap '69

SITKIN, Lewis
He turns junk into gold. S. Margetts. il por Duns R 92:51+ D '68

SIVACK, Denis
In memoriam: Thomas Merton; poem. Commonweal 90:230 My 9 '69

SIVERD, Clifford David
Cyanamid: we've come out of our shell. R. Levy. il Duns R 93:36-40 My '69

SIWOFF, Seymour
His word is the law of averages. J. Kirshenbaum. il por Sports Illus 31:28-31 Ag 18 '69

SIX blocks from Velco's; story. See Sidlosky, C.

SIXTH committee of the General assembly. See United Nations—Legal committee

SJOGREN, William L.
Hidden perils of a lunar landing. J. Lear. il Sat R 52:48-54 Je 7 '69
—See Muller, P. M. jt. auth.

SJÖMAN, Vilgot
After nudity, what, indeed? L. Gross. il Look 33:80+ Ap 29 '69
Curiouser and curiouser. J. Morgenstern. il Newsweek 73:114-15 Mr 24 '69

SKALAK, R. and Brånemark, P. I.
Deformation of red blood cells in capillaries. bibliog Science 164:717-19 My 9 '69

SKATE'S scales; story. See Roussel, R.

SKATING
Promises, promises, and more; World cup slalom race and figure skating title. B. Ottum. il Sports Illus 30:24-7 Mr 10 '69
See also
Ice shows
Roller skating

SKATING rinks
Copartners! Foundations and city departments; Fort Wayne's gift from McMillen foundation. H. Grabner. il Parks & Rec 4: 19 D '69
Take-apart ice rink. W. E. Runkel. il Pop Mech 132:159 N '69

Lighting
Lighting a speed skating rink; West Allis, Wis. il Am City 84:122+ Jl '69

SKELETAL muscle. See Muscle

SKELETON
Secrets that dead men's bones tell. S. S. McKern and T. W. McKern. il Sci Digest 66:30-4 Ag '69

SKELETON (invertebrates)
Crystal orientation and plate structure in echinoid skeletal units. H. U. Nissen. bibliog il Science 166:1150-2 N 28 '69
X-ray diffraction studies of echinoderm plates. G. Donnay and D. L. Pawson. bibliog il Science 166:1147-50 N 28 '69

SKELTON, R. A.
(tr) See Pigafetta, A. Magellan's voyage

SKELTON, Robin
Comment. Poetry 114:397-401 S '69
Toad: Spider; Fly; poems. Poetry 115:162-6 D '69

SKETCHES. See Drawings

SKETCHING. See Drawing

SKI clothes. See Clothing and dress—Sports clothes

SKI clubs. See Sports clubs

SKI houses. See Vacation houses

SKI lifts
Ski lift tickets; rate schedules for major ski areas in New York, New Jersey and Vermont. A. D. Coggeshall. il Cons 24:39 D '69

SKI lodges. See Lodges (architecture)

SKI resorts. See Winter resorts

SKIBOBS and skibobbing
Ski-bobbing. B. Thomas. il Travel 132:42-5 N '69
Skibobs schuss through trial run. il Bsns W p80-1+ F 15 '69
Tall in the saddle out east; ski bobbing. G. S. Brown. il Sports Illus 30:50-1 F 17 '69

SKIDMORE, Owings and Merrill (firm)
Campus City continued; SOM's plan for the University of Illinois' Chicago circle campus Architecture and art building. J. M. Dixon. il Arch Forum 129:28-43 D '68
How S.O.M. took on the Baltimore road gang. J. Bailey. il Arch Forum 130:40-5 Mr '69
New multi-use gymnasium for I.I.T. il Arch Rec 146:111-13 Jl '69

SKIERS lunches. See Lunches

SKIFFS. See Boats and boating

SKIING. See Skis and skiing

SKIING, Water. See Water skis and skiing

SKILLED labor
Employment effect of a new industry in a rural area. I. Gray. bibliog il Mo Labor R 92:26-30 Je '69
Good paper shuffler is hard to find; shortage of skilled workers. il Time 93:92+ My 9 '69
Rich man's qualifications for poor man's jobs. I. Berg. il Trans-Action 6:45-50 Mr '69
Where have all the busboys gone? il Time 94:84+ N 21 '69

SKILLED performance. See Performance standards

SKIN
How pregnancy affects your skin. W. E. Josey and D. Z. Meilach. Redbook 133:31+ Je '69
Size discrimination on the skin. C. J. Vierck, jr. and M. B. Jones. bibliog il Science 163: 488-9 Ja 31 '69
Skin replication procedure for the scanning electron microscope. E. O. Bernstein and C. B. Jones. bibliog il Science 166:252-3 O 10 '69
See also
Cosmetics
Keratin
Sunburn

Care and hygiene
Aromatheraphy. il Vogue 153:198-9+ My '69
Busy woman's guide to skin cleansing. C. Bartel. il Am Home 72:16+ Mr '69
Care & feeding of your face. il Mlle 69:298-9 Ag '69
Skin around you. il Vogue 153:102+ F 15 '69
Skin-care clinic. il McCalls 96:78-81+ Ag '69
Soap: who needs it? And who doesn't. il Vogue 154:199-201 O 1 '69
Sun and you; excerpts from Your skin and hair. E. W. Brauer. Vogue 153:111+ Je '69
Vogue's own beauty dictionary. il Vogue 153: 196-9+ F 1 '69
Your now and future face; new ways to a great complexion. il Redbook 133:80-1+ Ag '69
See also
Acne
Allergy
Angiokeratoma
Blastomycosis
Warts

Microorganisms
Life on the human skin. M. J. Marples. il Sci Am 220:108-15 Ja '69

Papillary ridges
See Dermatoglyphics

Proteins
Keratohyalin: extraction and in vitro aggregation. A. R. Ugel. bibliog il Science 166: 250-1 O 10 '69

SKIN, Color of. See Color of man

SKIN banks. See Tissue banks

SKIN cancer. See Cancer

SKIN diving
New world of inner space. F. Rohr, jr. il Motor B 124:64-5 O '69
Silent image. P. Leonian. il Travel & Camera 32:91-5 D '69
You, too, can dive for sunken treasure. H. E. Rieseberg. il Pop Sci 194:84-7 Je '69

Equipment and supplies
New underwater breathing systems. S. Carpenter. il Pop Sci 195:72-5+ N '69
Scuba/com; now you can talk underwater. T. Irwin. il Pop Sci 195:120-1 Ag '69

Study and teaching
I know what I'm doing here, I think. P. Benchley. il Holiday 46:18-21+ Ag '69

SKIN patterns. See Dermatoglyphics

SKIN pigment. See Color of man

SKINKS. See Lizards

SKINNER, Charles
We invited the bugs to dinner, but they never
came! por Org Gard & Farm 16:46-9 Mr
'69
SKINNER, Gwen
Islands of the South Pacific. il por Yachting
126:50-3+ Ag '69 (to be cont)
SKINNER, Patrick F.
Supplement grammar instruction with sentence
modeling. Engl J 58:257-60+ F '69
SKINNER, Wickham
Manufacturing, missing link in corporate
strategy. Harvard Bsns R 47:136-45 My '69
SKIPPER'S club. See Yacht clubs
SKIRTS, Length of. See Clothing and dress
SKIS and skiing
Allison is alive and well on the ski slope. A.
Teague. il Seventeen 27:100-1+ D '68
American action; the ski life in Colorado. il
Vogue 153:220-9 F 1 '69
Bright girls in a smother of fog; American
girls success clouded by U.S. ski association
policies. B. Ottum. il Sports Illus 30:20-1
Mr 31 '69
Jean-Claude Killy and the winter woman.
J. C. Killy. il Ladies Home J 86:87 N '69
My slopes. J. C. Killy. il Travel & Camera
32:51-5 D '69
Notes from the slopes. Vogue 154:78 N 1 '69
Old rubber legs is in charge; K. Schranz.
B. Ottum. il Sports Illus 30:14-15 Ja 27 '69
Over the meadows and between the trees. Y.
Fogel. il Parks & Rec 4:28-9+ D '69
Promises, promises, and more; World cup
slalom race and figure skating title. B. Ot-
tum. il Sports Illus 30:24-7 Mr 10 '69
Wonderful world of skiing. il Travel &
Camera 32:41-50 D '69
See also
Sand skis and skiing
Ski lifts
Skibobs and skibobbing
Water skis and skiing

Anecdotes, facetiae, satire, etc.
How I conquered the Australian Alps. H.
Sorauer. il Travel & Camera 32:31-2 My '69

Study and teaching
I learned to ski electronically! instant-re-
play TV. R. M. Benrey. il Pop Sci 195:
136-8 D '69
Infallible revelation by the pope of skiing;
Prof. Kruckenhauser. B. Ottum. il Sports
Illus 30:24-6+ F 24 '69

Australia
Snows of Kosciusko. F. Riley. il Sat R 52:38+
My 17 '69

Austria
Der alte of the Alps; Schranz challenging
the Hahnenkamm. il Newsweek 73:58 F 3
'69
Annie doesn't ski here anymore. B. Ottum.
il Sports Illus 30:22-3 F 10 '69

Canada
Skiers get away from it all in west Canada.
Bsns W p 145 N 22 '69

Colorado
Our problem: how to beat the ski ennui. D.
Jenkins. il Sports Illus 30:58-9 Mr 17 '69
To cold Colorado for the joys of powder ski-
ing. il Sunset 142:62-9 F '69

Italy
Autumn skiing in Europe; Corvatsch and
Stelvio. G. Cochran. il Travel & Camera
32:14+ O '69
Italy: our country is a castle. il Sports Illus
31:58-73 N 17 '69
Skier's guide to winter fun in Italy. Bsns W
p91 D 20 '69

New England
Geysers and gondolas remake New England.
il Sports Illus 30:38-43 F 10 '69
Ski New England winter into spring. S. Wiedel. il Travel & Camera 32:18+ D '69

New Mexico
Passionate skier; Taos ski valley. J. Egan. il
Sat R 52:42-4 D 27 '69

New York (state)
Cold country club for the real cool crowd;
Windham Mountain club. W. Johnson. il
Sports Illus 32:60+ Ja 12 '70

Switzerland
Autumn skiing in Europe; Corvatsch and
Stelvio. G. Cochran. il Travel & Camera
32:14+ O '69
Learning to ski in Switzerland. A. Fleming.
House B 111:79+ O '69

United States
Where the money is in skiing. il Bsns W p
112-13+ F 22 '69

Utah
Greatest snow on earth; Salt Lake Valley
and Wasatch Mountains. D. Reid. il Travel
132:52-6 D '69
There is new skiing east of Salt Lake City.
il Sunset 143:48 D '69

Vermont
Sugarbush; Vermont's chic ski resort. F.
Morton. il Holiday 46:64-7 D '69
SKLAR, Robert
Books on film. Nation 209:702-3 D 22 '69
Intellectual power elite. Nation 208:373-4 Mr
24 '69
about
Consciousness confrontation. Nation 208:
704-5 Je 2 '69
SKLAREWITZ, Norman
Big ambulance for big birds. Pop Mech 132:
124-7+ S '69
His office is under the sea. Pop Mech 131:
114-17+ Ja '69
They're putting the old birds back into bat-
tle. Pop Mech 131:92-4 Ja '69
SKOKIE, III.
20-yard roll-off refuse bodies. il Am City 84:
119 Ag '69
SKOLE, Robert. See Dickson, P. jt. auth.
SKOLNICK, Sherman
Skolnick's guerrilla war. il por Time 94:43+
Ag 29 '69
SKOLNIKOFF, Eugene B.
Amchitka and international regulation. Sci-
ence 166:315 O 17 '69
Public challenge of government action. Sci-
ence 164:499 My 2 '69
Public is aroused. Sat R 52:29-31+ Ap 26 '69
SKOURAS, Spyros S.
Now, the son of Spyros. il por Time 93:81 F
21 '69
SKOW, John
Westchester at $3,472.22 a hole. Holiday 45:34-
7+ Je '69
SKOW, Norman A.
Printed-circuit laminates. por Electr World
82:44-6 O '69
SKOZA, Lorant. See Mohos, S. C. jt. auth.
SKRIABIN, Aleksandr Nikolaevich
Scriabin on record, blaze of a sunburst. F.
Bowers. Vogue 153:106 Mr 1 '69
Sixty-year-old controversy flares up again;
Koussevitzky-Scriabin scandal. D. Caval-
lo; F. Bowers. il pors Hi Fi 19:54-61 Je '69
Wild romantics. Discus. Harper 238:102-3 Je
'69
SKROWACZEWSKI, Stanislaw
Musician of the month. S. Fleming. Hi Fi
19:MA5 S '69
SKUNK cabbages
Vanguard of spring. D. Shiner. il Nat Wildlife
7:40-1 F '69
SKURNIK, W. A. E.
Studies on Africa. Cur Hist 56:300-4+ My '69
SKURZYNSKI, Gloria
Growing pains. Good H 169:274D N '69
SKY
Far-infrared observations of the night sky.
J. R. Houck and M. Harwit. bibliog il Sci-
ence 164:1271-3 Je 13 '69
SKY diving. See Parachuting
SKY window. See Skylights
SKYBUS. See Pittsburgh—Rapid transit
SKYJACKING. See Airplane hijacking
SKYLIGHTS
Today's skylights can do surprising things
for your rooms and your outlook. il House
& Gard 135:88-91 F '69
SKYLINE drive. See Express highways—South-
ern states
SLACK, Jack
Ultimate dive. Field & S 73:76-7+ Ap '69
SLACK, Lyman W.
Excerpt from testimony before subcommittee
on Housing and urban affairs, October 15,
1969. Cong Digest 48:308+ D '69
SLACKS, Womens. See Clothing and dress
SLANDER. See Libel and slander
SLANG
As they used to say in the 1950's. . . H.
Junker. il Esquire 72:70-1+ Ag '69
Freaks had a word for it. Newsweek 74:18
D 29 '69
Rapping in the black ghetto. T. Kochman.
il Trans-Action 6:26-34 F '69; Reply. R. D.
Abrahams. 6:53+ My '69
SLANSKY, Cyril M.
Hells Canyon-Snake National River? Nat
Parks 43:18-20 Ag '69

SLATER, John C.
Graduate student. por Phys Today 22:35-7
Mr '69
SLATTERY, James L. and Gosswiller, Richard
Abraham Flexner's medical bombshell. Todays Health 47:44-5+ Mr '69
SLAUGHTERING and slaughterhouses
See also
Meat inspection
SLAVE ship; drama. See Jones, L.
SLAVE trade
Nil disprandum; W. Buck's primitive paintings as a record of slave-patrol duty. M. Teague and Z. Cowan. il Am Heritage 20: 18-25 F '69
Slavery in Cuba & Virginia. M. Zeitlin. Trans-Action 6:54-6 Ap '69
They came in chains: Americans from Africa, by S. Redding. Review
Sat R 52:78-9 Mr 22 '69. E. Foner
SLAVERY
See also
Indentured servants
Labor, Compulsory

Cuba

Autobiography of a runaway slave, by E. Montejo. Review
Nation 208:121-2 Ja 27 '69. O. T. Myers
Slavery in the Americas, by H. S. Klein. Review
Trans-Action 6:54-6 Ap '69. M. Zeitlin

United States

Black men before the Civil war. P. E. Wilson. bibliog f Cur Hist 57:257-62+ N '69
First generation. L. Bennett, jr. il Ebony 24: 31-4+ Je '69
Freedom documents from Cole County, Missouri. L. J. Greene. bibliog Negro Hist Bul 32:11-13 Ja '69
Means and ends in American abolitionism, by A. S. Kraditor. Review
New Repub 160:31-2+ F 15 '69. F. Brodie
Slavery in the Americas, by H. S. Klein. Review
Trans-Action 6:54-6 Ap '69. M. Zeitlin
To wash this land in blood... S. B. Oates. il Am West 6:36-41 Jl; 24-7+ N '69
See also
Abolitionists
Freedmen
Slave trade

Insurrections, etc.

See also
Southampton insurrection, 1831
SLAVIC, Fred M.
Rolled down offshore. il Yachting 125:72-3+ Je '69
SLAVITT, David R.
Two poems: Sestina for the last week of March; Tableau a la Rousseau. Yale R 59: 97-8 O '69
SLAWSON, W. David
Moves to patch the loopholes. Nation 208:760-4 Je 16 '69
SLAYBAUGH, T. J.
Limitations. Flying 84:94+ My '69
SLEATOR, William
(ed) See Lent, B. Illustrator talks
SLED dogs
Last patrol; Mounties must get rid of their sled dogs. Newsweek 73:44 Mr 31 '69
SLEDD, James
Bi-dialectalism: the linguistics of white supremacy. Engl J 58:1307-15+ D '69
SLEDS
See also
Motor sleds
SLEEP
Cats confound sleep study. Sci Digest 66:68 S '69
Do sheep count people when they can't sleep? sleep patterns of animals. L. J. Wilhelm. il Sci Digest 65:56-9 F '69
Encephalic cycles during sleep and wakefulness in humans: a 24-hour pattern. E. Othmer and others. bibliog il Science 164:447-9 Ap 25 '69; Reply. R. J. Berger. 166:530-1 O 24 '69
Getting along with getting up. il Time 93:61 F 14 '69
Human growth hormone release: relation to slow-wave sleep and sleep-waking cycles. J. F. Sassin and others. bibliog il Science 165:513-15 Ag 1 '69
Learning through dreaming; REM sleep. il Time 93:63-4 Ap 25 '69
Sleep how to get more out of less. Mlle 69: 283+ Ag '69
Sleep: paradoxical, REM, dreaming. B. Yuncker. House & Gard 135:70-1 F '69
Sleeping easy; sleep of animals. Sci Am 220: 54+ My '69

To sleep: perchance to dream; excerpts from 1970 Britannica yearbook of science and the future. J. Segal and G. G. Luce. Todays Health 47:48-51+ O '69
See also
Dreams
Insomnia
SLEEP habits of animals. See Animals—Habits and behavior
SLEEP walking. See Somnambulism
SLEEPING bags
Polybag caper. U. S. Williams. il Motor B 123:126-7 Je '69
Polybag, the any-weather sleeping bag; foam-celled bag. T. Bacon. il Pop Sci 195: 134-5 Ag '69
SLEEPING BEAR DUNES NATIONAL LAKE-SHORE (proposed) See National parks and reserves—United States
SLEEPING beauty; ballet. See Ballets—Criticisms
SLEEPING medicines. See Barbiturates
SLEEPLESSNESS. See Insomnia
SLEEPWALKING. See Somnambulism
SLEET, Moneta, jr.
Backstage. il por Ebony 24:25 F '69
Pulitzer prize winner. il por Ebony 24:147 Je '69
SLEIGHT, A. W. See Prewitt, C. T. jt. auth.
SLEPIAN, Edward L.
Cooking up a storm. Motor B 124:52-3 S '69
Cool food for hot days. Motor B 124:64-5+ Ag '69
Fine kettle of fish. Motor B 124:56-7+ O '69
Haut cuisine on the high seas. Motor B 123: 70-3 My '69
SLETTEBAK, Arne. See Hall, J. S. jt. auth.
SLEVIN, James
Graduate student. por Phys Today 22:31-2 Mr '69
SLIDE illuminators. See Transparencies—Viewers
SLIDE projectors. See Projectors
SLIDE viewers. See Transparencies—Viewers
SLIDES, Color. See Transparencies
SLIDES, Photographic. See Transparencies
SLIFKA, Barbara
Notes on Chile. Harp Baz 103:106+ D '69
SLIGHTLY bigger acquisition; story. See Hildesheimer, W.
SLIM, Mongi
Assembly pays tribute to Mongi Slim. UN Mo Chron 6:7-8 N '69
SLIME molds
Chromosome number of a small protist: accurate determination. P. B. Moens and F. O. Perkins. bibliog il Science 166:1289-91 D 5 '69
SLIME molds, Cellular
Adenosine-3',5'-phosphate: identification as acrasin in a species of cellular slime mold. D. S. Barkley. bibliog il Science 165:1133-4 S 12 '69
Hormones in social amoebae and mammals. J. T. Bonner. il Sci Am 220:78-84+ Je '69
SLIPPING-down life; story. See Tyler, A.
SLOAT, Warren
Flash point for terror. Commonweal 91:37-8 O 10 '69
SLOCHOWER, Harry
Thomas Mann's Death in Venice. bibliog f Am Imago 26:99-122 Sum '69
SLOGANS
See also
Newspapers—Mastheads
SLOGAR, Ray
Walleye crawl. pors Outdoor Life 143:74-5+ Ap '69
SLOMICH, Sidney J. and Kantor, R. E.
Social psychopathology of political assassination. Bul Atom Sci 25:9-12 Mr '69
SLOMINSKI, J. W. See Gojmerac, W. L. jt. auth.
SLOOP racing. See Yacht racing
SLOOPS
Hope of the Hudson; project begun by the Hudson River sloop restoration to combat pollution. S. Atwater. il Cons 23:15-16 Je '69
To save the dying Hudson: Pete Seeger's voyage; with editorial comment by G. Goodman. P. Seeger. il Look 33:62-6 Ag 26 '69

Design

New look in twelves. B. Chance, jr. il Yachting 126:58-9+ Ag '69
SLOT-car racing. See Automobile models—Racing
SLOTHS
Leishmania braziliensis isolated from sloths in Panama. A. Herrer and S. R. Telford, jr. bibliog il Science 164:1419-20 Je 20 '69

SLOVAK, Mira
Uncommon men. il por Time 93:63-4 My 23 '69

SLOW learning children
Early detection of potential learning disorders. J. V. Hunt. Ed Digest 35:12-15 O '69

Education

Everyone has a sky; a planetarium helps the slow learner. R. N. Kratz. Clear House 43:349-50 F '69
Needed: better teaching for slow learners. E. D. Koontz. Parents Mag 44:24 F '69
Teaching the slow learner. R. F. Crowley. il Todays Ed 58:48-9 Ja '69
Teaching vocabulary to slow learners. L. D. Perry, jr. Clear House 44:164-5 N '69

SLUGS, Sea. See Sea slugs

SLUM clearance. See Urban renewal

SLUMLORDS. See Landlord and tenant

SLUMS
Ghetto news; fifteen newsmen visit black ghettos. J. Cook. il Time 93:53 Je 6 '69
Guest in ghetto America. O. Elliott. il Newsweek 73:41-3 Je 9 '69
Hollow shells. il Newsweek 75:36 Ja 12 '70
Lima slum. R. C. Hirschfield; reply with rejoinder. W. C. Francis. Cath World 208:196 F '69
Message to broadcasters; industry's responsibility. S. Ross. Chr Cent 86:280-3 F 26 '69
One billion dollar subsidy for slums. J. M. Bailey, jr. and H. Schubart, jr. Arch Forum 131:56-7 Jl '69; Discussion. 131:56-9 S; 80-1 O; 10+ N '69
Travels with Mr Charlie; journalists look at the black American ghetto. C. M. Curtis. Atlan 224:31-8 Ag '69
Urban league conducts a guided tour. P. Bailey. il Ebony 24:48-50+ S '69
Violence: the view from the ghetto. H. Hahn. Ment Hy 53:509-12 O '69
White institutions & black rage. D. Boesel and others. il Trans-Action 6:24-31 Mr '69

Latin America

Slums of hope and despair. J. A. Casasco. il Américas 21:13-20 Je '69

SLURRY
Iron ore gets piped aboard; slurry delivery. il Bsns W p 118 Ag 16 '69

SMALL, Eugene B. and Marszalek, D. S.
Scanning electron microscopy of fixed, frozen and dried protozoa. bibliog Science 163:1064-5 Mr 7 '69

SMALL, Robert S.
Tell it like it is; address, June 19, 1969. Vital Speeches 35:655-7 Ag 15 '69

SMALL arms. See Firearms

SMALL business
Making capitalism work in the ghettos. L. L. Allen. il Harvard Bsns R 47:83-92 My '69
See also
Cottage industries
Franchise system
United States—Congress—Senate—Small business, Select committee on

Finance

Bank profits boom, small business pines. il Newsweek 75:69-70 Ja 19 '70
Small-business loans: their cost. U S News 67:99 O 6 '69

SMALL business administration. See United States—Small business administration

SMALL business investment companies
Seeds for black capitalism; SBA's MESBIC plan. il Bsns W p40-1 N 15 '69

SMALL colleges
Oklahoma consortium strikes it rich. L. K. Hayes and O. F. Henderson. Am Ed 5:26 Mr '69
Small colleges; football 1969. il Sports Illus 31:87-8+ S 15 '69

SMALL game. See Game

SMALL states. See States, Small

SMALL town life. See City and town life

SMALLE, Edwin
Death of Edwin Smalle. J. Walsh. il pors Hobbies 74:44+ My '69

SMALLMAN, Stephen E.
Nudity in biblical perspective. Chr Today 13:6-8 Ag 22 '69

SMALLPOX
See also
Vaccination

SMART, Curly
High one is hiding out. W. F. Reed, jr. por Sports Illus 31:46+ Ag 11 '69

SMART, Mae
Old woman's story. New Yorker 45:50-1 D 13 '69

SMART, Margaret
Reference books of 1968. por Library J 94:1579-84 Ap 15 '69

SMEETON, Miles
Third time lucky. Yachting 126:65-7+ D '69 (to be cont)

SMELL
Orphan senses; research at the Monell chemical senses center. C. Weathersbee. il Sci N 95:241-2 Mr 8 '69
See also
Odors
Olfactory nerves

SMELT fishing
Smelt fishing. M. Kelsey. il Cons 23:37 Ap '69

SMETANA, Bedřich
Other Fidelio. P. J. Smith. il Opera N 34:6-7 N 1 '69

SMETZER, Barbara
Night of the palolo; with biographical sketch. Natur Hist 78:6, 64-71 N '69

SMIBERT, John
Notebook of John Smibert. il por Antiques 95:366-9 Mr '69

SMILEY, Ruth H.
Gardens of the Philippines. il Horticulture 46:34-5+ S '68

SMILEY, Virginia Viney
In praise of natural gardening. Horticulture 47:36-7 Jl '69

SMIRENNY, L. See Vorobyov, E. jt. auth.

SMITH, A. O. corporation
Auto frame maker tries wider road to make the grade. il Bsns W p 102+ D 13 '69

SMITH, Adele
North African arms race. Atlan 223:20+ F '69

SMITH, Alexander H.
It's a riot of fungi. Audubon 71:56-65 S '69

SMITH, Alvin. See Warwick, J. F. jt. auth.

SMITH, Mrs Anson Howe
Three R's of flower arrangement. il Horticulture 46:38-9+ S '68

SMITH, Anthony Wayne
Washington needs a council of environmental and population advisors; adaptation of address, April 1969. Nat Parks 43:10-11 Je '69

SMITH, Arden K.
Our stake in the private liberal arts colleges. Todays Ed 58:51-2 Mr '69

SMITH, B. L.
Biology and the Christian faith. bibliog Chr Today 13:11-14 Ap 11; 11-14 Ap 25 '69
Homosexuality in the Bible and the law. bibliog Chr Today 13:7-10 Jl 18 '69

SMITH, Bessie
True death of Bessie Smith. S. Grimes. por Esquire 71:112-13+ Je '69

SMITH, C. C.
Hinc illae lacrimae; poem. Engl J 58:1020 O '69

SMITH, Cantrell
Protection system for solid-state transmitters. Electr World 81:38-9+ F '69

SMITH, Carl B.
Let's be practical about reading. Am Ed 5:28-31 Ag '69

SMITH, Charles
Poor Head Start and its children. New Repub 160:11-13 Je 21 '69

SMITH, Charles Alphonso
Why don't we try it again soon? E. Watson. il por Sports Illus 31:76+ O 20 '69

SMITH, Courtney Craig
Requiem for Courtney Smith. P. Good. il por Life 66:76B-76D+ My 9 '69

SMITH, Dan Throop
Federal tax reform. Ann Am Acad 379:102-13 S '68
Replacement for the income tax? interview. por Nations Bsns 57:38-41 Ap '69

SMITH, David
Doctor and a parole officer remember Manson; statement. por Life 67:26 D 19 '69

SMITH, David, 1906-1965
Art; show at the Guggenheim museum. L. Alloway. Nation 208:518 Ap 21 '69
Critic calls David Smith greatest of all American artists. H. Kramer. il pors N Y Times Mag p40-2+ F 16 '69
David Smith. S. Nodelman. il por Art N 67:28-31+ F '69
Man of iron. D. L. Shirey. il por Newsweek 73:78-80 Mr 31 '69
Storm King art center. E. S. Robbins. il Art in Am 57:108-9 My '69
Totems of a titan; Smith exhibition at the Guggenheim. il por Time 93:79-80 Ap 11 '69

SMITH, David S.
W. D. McElroy; an old incident embarrasses new NF director. P. M. Boffey. Science 165:379-80 Jl 25 '69

SMITH, Desmond
  Communism's family newspaper. Nation 208:
    631-4 My 19 '69
  Pop sex among the squares. Nation 209:142-
    5 Ag 25 '69
SMITH, Donald E.
  Healing touch of attention. Read Digest 94:
    175-6+ Ap '69
SMITH, E. B. See Dawe, R. A. jt. auth.
SMITH, Earl M.
  Latin American revolution. Chr Cent 86:674-7
    My 14 '69
SMITH, Edwin
  Ireland & Scotland. M. MacLiammoir; E.
    Linklater. il Travel & Camera 32:120-1+
    F '69
SMITH, Eldred
  Do libraries need managers? address, October
    1968. bibliog por Library J 94:502-6 F 1 '69
  Librarians' association at the University
    of California. por ALA Bul 63:363-8 Mr '69
  Overdue. por Wilson Lib Bul 44:458-9 D '69
SMITH, Elizabeth
  When shall we love; story. Redbook 133:175-97
    My '69
SMITH, Ellis S. Jr
  How to use your camp all year long. Camp
    Mag 41:16-17 N '69
SMITH, Erasmus Peshine, pseud.
  Is economic crisis around the corner? Com-
    monweal 91:62-4 O 17 '69
SMITH, Eugene H.
  Professor becomes high school teacher.
    Engl J 58:360-2+ Mr '69
SMITH, F. G. Walton
  Ebb and flow. Sea Front 15:86-96 Mr '69
  Man and the tides. Sea Front 15:142-51 My '69
  Real tide. Sea Front 15:34-48 Ja '69
SMITH, G. Roysce
  Bookselling and the dollar squeeze. Pub W
    195:41-2 My 5 '69
  Bookstores as outlets for university press
    books; excerpt from address, June 22, 1969.
    por Pub W 196:28-30 Jl 28 '69
  Opinionated man. Pub W 196:45-6 S 8; 47-8
    O 13; 39-41 N 10; 27-8 D 15 '69
SMITH, George E.
  Prisoner. D. Duncan. Ramp Mag 8:51-6 S
    '69
SMITH, Gerard Coad
  Ambassador Smith presents U.S. views on
    seabed proposal at Eighteen-nation disarma-
    ment conference; statement, March 25, 1969.
    Dept State Bul 60:333-7 Ap 21 '69

                    about
  Start of SALT. il por Time 94:33-4 N 21 '69
  With U.S.-Soviet negotiators: smiles before
    the bargaining. il por U S News 67:17 D
    1 '69
SMITH, Gerald L. K.
  U.S. Journal: Eureka Springs, Ark. C. Trillin.
    New Yorker 45:69-70+ Jl 26 '69
SMITH, Glenn
  John Eaton, educator (1829-1906) bibliog f
    Sch & Soc 97:108-12 F '69
SMITH, Glenn Allen
  Home away from. Criticism
    America 120:599-600 My 17 '69
SMITH, Gordon S.
  Inland sea gulls. il Sea Front 15:12-20 Ja '69
  Living marsh; photographs. Audubon 71:9-
    16 N '69
  Shape of water; photographs. Audubon 71:
    17-24 Jl '69
  Stowing your anchor line. Motor B 124:81+
    Jl '69
SMITH, H. Allen
  Great chili confrontation; condensation.
    Read Digest 94:141-4 Je '69
SMITH, Hayden R.
  Ubiquitous class-value conflict in education.
    bibliog f Sch & Soc 97:92-4 F '69
SMITH, Hedrick L.
  Past master of the soft sell. N Y Times Mag
    p8-9+ Jl 27 '69
  (ed) See Harriman, W. A. Harriman sug-
    gests a way out of Vietnam
SMITH, Helena Huntington
  Rawlins: profile of a railroad town. Am
    West 6:24-8 My '69
SMITH, Ian
  Catch them if you can. Field & S 74:58-9+
    O '69
SMITH, Ian Douglas
  Big problems facing Ian Smith. por U S News
    67:11 Jl 7 '69
SMITH, Isadore
  Hogarth and the ladies. Horticulture 47:22-3
    O '69
  Whipple house, Ipswich. Horticulture 46:34-5+
    Ag '68

SMITH, Jack
  Polo lounge; Beverly Hills. Holiday 46:58+
    Ag '69
  What do you know about ferro cement.
    Yachting 125:84-6+ Ap '69
SMITH, James Henry
  Poverty; address, October 22, 1969. Vital
    Speeches 36:157-60 D 15 '69

                    about
  Equitable puts premium on social role. il por
    Bsns W p68-9 N 29 '69
SMITH, Janica
  (ed) See Westcott, J. T. 3d. Boat chartering
SMITH, Jean Edward
  German Democratic Republic and the West.
    Yale R 58:372-87 Mr '69
SMITH, Jean Shannon. See Gardner, M. jt.
    auth.
SMITH, Jerry D. and Foster, J. H.
  Geomagnetic reversal in Brunhes normal
    polarity epoch. bibliog Science 163:565-7 F 7
    '69
SMITH, K. Wayne. See Enthoven, A. C. jt.
    auth.
SMITH, Karl U. and others
  Eye movement-retina delayed feedback.
    bibliog Science 166:1542-4 D 19 '69
SMITH, Kathleen, and others
  Sweat in schizophrenic patients: identifica-
    tion of the odorous substance. bibliog Sci-
    ence 166:398-9 O 17 '69
SMITH, Kenneth B.
  Dorm city. Arch Forum 129:76-85 D '68
SMITH, Kenneth L.
  Designer's comments. Yachting 125:76-7 F
    '69
SMITH, Lacey Baldwin
  Wars of the Roses. Horizon 11:80-93 Wint
    '69
SMITH, Lendon Howard
  Telling your sub-teen child about sex; ex-
    cerpt from The children's doctor. por To-
    days Health 47:56-7+ Je '69
  What parents can do about food allergies;
    excerpt from The children's doctor. Todays
    Health 47:55-6+ Jl '69
SMITH, Lewis V.
  Canada's water rights. Bul Atom Sci 25:38
    Ap '69
SMITH, Lillian
  Bridges to other people. Redbook 133:91+
    S '69
SMITH, Liz
  Dealey plaza. Holiday 46:78-9+ N '69
  Fabulous Ford women. McCalls 96:82-3+
    My '69
  Jacqueline Kennedy Onassis' stepchildren.
    McCalls 96:80-1+ Ap '69
  Sight and sound. McCalls 96:8+ Mr '69
SMITH, Lyle
  Try an intersection extension. Am City 84:
    101 O '69
SMITH, M. Brewster
  Race differences. Science 163:461-2 Ja 31 '69
SMITH, Maggie
  Lively arts. M. Ronan. Sr Schol 94:18 Mr 14
    '69
SMITH, Margaret (Chase)
  Surprising lady from Maine. por Newsweek
    74:21 Ag 18 '69
SMITH, Marshall
  After tragedy: a new age of Flying Wallendas.
    Life 66:58-60 My 30 '69
  This old pro is just too mean to quit. Life
    67:77-80 S 12 '69
SMITH, Mayo Edward
  Match your baseball IQ with Mayo Smith. J.
    Devaney. il por Mech Illus 65:56-7+ My '69
SMITH, Michael J.
  Graduate student. por Phys Today 22:28 Mr
    '69
SMITH, Mortimer
  Decline of authority. Ed Digest 35:5-7 O '69
  Failure of community control. Ed Digest 34:
    7-9 Ap '69
  Reading problem. Am Scholar 38:431-40 Sum
    '69
  Some reservations about sex education. Par-
    ents Mag 44:66-7+ N '69
SMITH, Nancy Covert
  Suddenly it happens to you. McCalls 96:56+
    My '69
SMITH, Ned
  Wildlife sketchbook. See issues of National
    wildlife
SMITH, Ora
  Pioneering in potato chips. il Chem 42:5
    Mr '69
SMITH, Patrick
  Nativity; poem. America 121:613 D 20 '69
SMITH, Patrick J.
  (ed) Book reviews (cont) Hi Fi 19:MA29-31
    Ap; MA28-30 Jl; MA29-31 N '69
  Current chronicle. Mus Q 55:102-11 Ja '69

SMITH, Patrick J.—*Continued*
Musician of the month (cont) Hi Fi 19:
MA4 F '69
Other Fidelio. Opera N 34:6-7 N 1 '69
Penderecki & Menotti; pros and cons. Hi Fi
19:MA24-5+ N '69
SMITH, Paul J.
Unromantic kind of elegance. Life 66:57 Mr
14 '69
SMITH, Philip D.
Static in the language lab; let's take an-
other look. Todays Ed 58:49-50 O '69
SMITH, Philip M.
Prospects for international cooperation on
the moon: the Antarctic analogy. por Bul
Atom Sci 25:36-40 S '69
SMITH, R. P.
Winter cocoon for your boat. Mech Illus 65:
109+ D '69
SMITH, Ralph Lee
Chiropractic: issues and answers; excerpts
from At your own risk. Todays Health 48:
65-9 Ja '70
Health books: reader beware. Todays Health
47:30-3+ Ap '69
Problem of the problem. Nation 208:486-7 Ap
21 '69
SMITH, Ralph Tyler
Clues to outlook of new senator. por U S
News 67:23 S 29 '69
Smith for Dirksen. Newsweek 74:41-2 S 29
'69
SMITH, Reggie
Highlight. por Sports Illus 31:56 Jl 21 '69
SMITH, Robert
Baseball needs a new pitch. Look 33:74+ F
18 '69
SMITH, Robert C.
China, Japan, and the Anglo-American chair.
Antiques 96:552-8 O '69
SMITH, Robert F.
Latin America: radical interpretations. Na-
tion 208:277-8 Mr 3 '69
SMITH, Robert Worthington
Political organization and canvassing: York-
shire elections before the reform bill. bib-
liog f Am Hist R 74:1538-60 Je '69
SMITH, Roger
Doctor and a parole officer remember Man-
son; statement. por Life 67:26 D 19 '69
SMITH, Roland
(ed) See Westcott, J. T. 3d. Boat chartering
SMITH, Russell
Oval trackers in England. Hot Rod 22:142-3
Ag '69
SMITH, Ruth B.
(comp) Calendar of coming events. See is-
sues of Motor boating
SMITH, Sandy
Broadway Joe: rebel with a nightclub for a
cause. il Life 66:24-7 Je 20 '69
Power struggle after a death in the family.
Life 66:51+ F 28 '69
SMITH, Stan
Davis cup? Oh, get Stan Smith to take care
of that chore. B. Collins. il por Sports
Illus 31:44-5 S 1 '69
SMITH, T. G. and others
Conductance changes associated with receptor
potentials in limulus photoreceptors. bibllog
Science 162:454-6; 164:1188-9 O 25 '68, Je 6
'69
Role for the sodium pump in photoreception
limulus. bibliog Science 162:456-8; 164:1188-9
O 25 '68, Je 6 '69
SMITH, Tim
Seminary's ostrich mentality on international
affairs. Chr Cent 86:573-9 Ap 23 '69
SMITH, W. John
Messages of vertebrate communications:
adaptation of address, December 28, 1967.
bibliog Science 165:145-50 Jl 11 '69
SMITH, William Jay
Fishing for albacore; poem. Poetry 113:295-
301 F '69
Hull Bay, St Thomas; poem. New Yorker 45:
22 Ja 10 '70
SMITH college, Northampton, Mass.

Museum of art

Smith college museum of art. C. Chetham. il
Antiques 96:768-75 N '69
SMITH Kline and French laboratories
Is Love the answer? il Forbes 103:25 Je 1 '69
SMITHIANTHAS
Smithiantha. M. J. Kartuz. il Horticulture
46:16-17+ N '68
SMITHSON, Billy L. See Morrow, J. E. jt.
auth.
SMITHSON, Robert
Smithson's non-site sights. A. Robbin. il
pors Art N 67:50-3 F '69

SMITHSONIAN Institution
Biological warfare: is the Smithsonian really
a cover? NBC's charge aired on First
Tuesday. P. M. Boffey. il Science 163:791-
6 F 21 '69
Hot line for passing events. il Time 94:82
O 17 '69
I'm not stuffed, I'm freeze-dried! W. O'Neill.
il Pop Mech 132:78-81 D '69
Washington, D.C: reading is fun-damental. J.
Sandler. il Wilson Lib Bul 43:881-5 My '69

National air and space museum

Dream and the junkyard. J. Gilbert. il Flying
84:42-5+ Mr '69
NC-4 preserved; letter. N. Polmar. Aviation
W 90:94 F 10 '69; Reply. S. P. Johnston. 90:
90 Mr 17 '69

National collection of fine arts

Museum in a museum. D. W. Scott. il Américas 21:22-30 Ag '69

National portrait gallery

National portrait gallery opens in Washing-
ton. B. Ruhe. il Am Artist 32:52-7+ N '68
SMOCK, David R.
Forgotten Rhodesians. For Affairs 47:532-44
Ap '69
SMOG
See also
Los Angeles—Air pollution
SMOG control devices. See Automobile en-
gines—Exhaust
SMOK, Pavel
Art must say something! interview, ed. by
L. Joel. por Dance Mag 43:43-6 O '69
SMOKE
See also
Cigarette smoke
SMOKE ovens
Their smoke oven is a built-in; kamado. il
Sunset 142:132 Ap '69
SMOKE prevention
Rolls studies atomizer design in jet smoke
control effort. il Aviation W 90:51 F 24 '69
SMOKEJUMPERS. See Forest fire patrol,
Aerial
SMOKESTACKS. See Chimneys
SMOKEY Bear. See Advertising characters
SMOKING
Big smoke, little babies. A. J. Snider. Sci Di-
gest 65:52 Ap '69
Calling Dr Killjoy; antismoking commercials
and How to stop smoking, programs on TV.
il Time 93:82+ My 9 '69
Caution: cigarette smoking may be hazardous
to health. Trans-Action 6:7-8 Mr '69
Cigarette diet; beeper technique used in anti-
smoking program. Time 94:57 Ag 22 '69
Cigarettes and society: a growing dilemma.
il Time 93:98-100+ Ap 25 '69
Coffee break smoke trap. Sci Digest 65:70 F
'69
Cold-turkey month; Greenfield, Ia. Time
94:76 S 19 '69
Declining curve. Sci Am 220:52-3 My '69
Five ways to reduce the health risks of
smoking. Todays Health 47:77 F '69
From beyond the cigarette; notes of a re-
deemed smoker. J. Hollander. Harper
238:87-91 Ap '69
Grandma and the buck deer. J. M. Vance. il
Field & S 74:74-5+ Je '69
Hope for smoke-plagued humanity; smoking
withdrawal clinic on TV. R. L. Shayon.
Sat R 52:44-5 F 8 '69
How safe is pipe smoking? McCalls 96:54
Mr '69
How to stop smoking. Sci Digest 66:62 Jl '69
. . . May be hazardous. Chr Today 13:39 S
26 '69
More bad news for smokers. G. Angermann.
Read Digest 94:93-4 F '69
Needling the smoker to kick the habit. il
Bsns W p53 Je 28 '69
Quantitative electroencephalogram in smok-
ing and smoking deprivation. J. A. Ulett
and T. M. Itil. bibliog il Science 164:969-70
My 23 '69
Quitters build up a market; lively trade in
anti-smoking devices. il Bsns W p 154 My
24 '69
Return of the cigar. P. Maas. il Holiday 45:
42-3+ Mr '69
Smoking debate lights up again; the Federal
trade commission proposal. U S News 66:16
Je 2 '69
Smoking: why you do it and how not to
suffer when you stop. A. Gross. il Mlle 69:
166-7+ O '69
Turning off to smoking. Sci Digest 66:72-3
S '69
Vote to expand cigarette warning. U S News
66:8 Je 30 '69

SMOKING—*Continued*

Want to quit smoking? Here are tested ways. Todays Health 47:84 My '69

When your husband gives up smoking, leave town. J. Kerr. il McCalls 96:57+ Je '69

Anecdotes, facetiae, satire, etc.

Equal time for tobacconists. Todays Health 47:17 N '69

Kicking the habit. M. A. Rodgers. il Good H 169:86+ O '69

SMOKING and youth

Penny Plumer's bequest. M. Plumer. Read Digest 95:215-16+ O '69

Tobacco roadside; teenagers and smoking. PTA Mag 63:31 Mr '69

SMOKING of food. See Food—Smoking

SMOKY MOUNTAINS. See Great Smoky Mountains

SMOLER, Martin H. See Lindenbaum, A. jt. auth.

SMOLIAR, Stephen

Next year, keep the baby. Dance Mag 43:41-2+ O '69

SMÖRGASBORD. See Cookery, Scandinavian

SMORREBROD. See Cookery, Danish

SMOTHERS, Dick

Smothers brothers racing team. J. W. Wright. il pors Pop Sci 194:80-3 Ja '69

SMOTHERS brothers

Brothers smothered. pors Newsweek 73:90 Ap 14 '69

Brothers smothered; a slap at youth audience? P. Hudson. pors Sr Schol 94:19 Ap 25 '69

Brothers' troubles. il pors Time 93:59-60 Mr 21 '69

Doily for your mind. P. Collier. Ramp Mag 7:44+ Je '69

Fickle finger of CBS. pors Time 93:65-6 Ap 18 '69

Muzzled stars and buck passing on network TV. J. Barthel. il por Life 66:24-5 Ap 4 '69

Question of taste, or is it? J. Leonard. Life 66:12 My 16 '69

Smothering the brothers. R. L. Shayon. Sat R52:48 Ap 5 '69

Smothers brothers: who controls TV? N. Hentoff. il Look 33:27-9 Je 24 '69

Those blip blip censors blip the hell out of TV. G. Ace. Sat R 52:4 My 31 '69

Transmogrification of the Smothers brothers. W. Kloman. il pors Esquire 72:148-53+ O '69

Unsinkable Tom Smothers. pors Time 94:52-3 Ag 29 '69

SMUCKER, Ralph M.

Minister and his wife. Chr Today 13:3-4 Je 20 '69

SMUGGLING

Operation showboat; Mexican border crackdown on marijuana smuggling. Nation 209: 365-6 O 13 '69

People-smuggling; springing refugees from eastern Europe. il Time 93:27 Ja 31 '69

Smuggling and the British tea trade before 1784. H. C. Mui and L. H. Mui. bibliog f il Am Hist R 74:44-73 O '68

Startling increases in drug smuggling; excerpts from Senate testimony, September 29, 1969. U S News 67:50 O 13 '69

Who switched the tuna? dope smuggling. il Newsweek 73:83 My 12 '69

SMUIN, Michael

Dance adventure with Mozart. W. Terry. il por Sat R 52:42-3 Ja 25 '69

Making of a ballet. W. Terry. il Sat R 52:58-60 N 29 '69

SMYLIE, James H.

Prudes, lewds and polysyllables. Commonweal 89:671-3 F 28 '69

SMYRNA, Ga.

Refuse sacks slash collection time. V. Broyles. il Am City 84:79-80 Ja '69

SMYTH, Paul

Autumn lament; poem. Am Scholar 38:411 Sum '69

SMYTH, Pete

TLC. See issues of Motor boating

What's new. See issues of Motor boating

SMYTHE, Dallas

Five myths of consumership. Nation 208: 82-4 Ja 20 '69

SNACK bars

Very special snack bars. il Bet Hom & Gard 47:164 O '69

SNACKS

Are we snacking our way to malnutrition? J. L. Breeling. il Todays Health 48:48-50+ Ja '70

Quick tricks to please the kids. il Bet Hom & Gard 47:111 N '69

SNAIL fever. See Schistosomiasis

SNAILS

Scavengers of the mud flats. R. H. Gore. il Sea Front 15:242-8 Jl '69

Tale of a snail; giant African land snail introduced into Miami. il Time 94:51 O 17 '69

Control

Night raiders and how to clobber them. il Sunset 142:181-2+ F '69

Diseases and pests

Larval trematodes: double infections in common mud-flat snail. W. B. Vernberg and others. bibliog il Science 164:1287 Je 13 '69

SNAKE bite. See Venom

SNAKE RIVER

Lo the poor salmon! (or, Is this dam necessary?) Middle-Snake River Dam. W. E. Towell. Am For 75:38 F '69

See also

Hells Canyon

SNAKE RIVER DAMS. See Dams

SNAKE venom. See Venom

SNAKES

Auditory and vibratory responses in the midbrains of snakes. P. H. Hartline and H. W. Campbell. bibliog il Science 163:1221-3 Mr 14 '69

Naturalist at large; being bitten by a fer-de-lance. A. Carr. il Natur Hist 78:18+ Mr '69

See also

Rattlesnakes

Venom

Photographs

African egg-eating champion. K. Severin. Sci Digest 66:84-7 S '69

Gulp! Natur Hist 78:42-3 Je '69

SNAKES as pets. See Pets

SNAP (systems for nuclear auxiliary power)

See Electric generators

SNAPP, Thomas

Actor; poem. New Yorker 45:40 Ap 19 '69

SNAPPERS

See also

Cookery—Fish

SNAPPING turtle fishing. See Turtle fishing

SNARR, Douglas T.

How to remove billboards. il por Time 94: 72 O 31 '69

SNEIDER, Vern

Adjectival idea. Writers Digest 49:42-7 Ag '69

D.N. creates a job. Har Yrs 9:19-21 F '69

SNELL, David

Brotherhood of borrowed time. Life 67:65-6+ O 24 '69

Dateline America (cont) Life 66:18D F 14; 18B Mr 14; 81-2 Ap 18; 85-6 My 23 '69

Death from the sea. Life 66:22-7 Je 13 '69

about

Our resident Count Dracula. G. P. Hunt. por Life 66:3 My 23 '69

SNELL, Katharine C. and Stewart, H. L.

Malignant argyrophilic gastric carcinoids of praomys (mastomys) natalensis. bibliog il Science 163:470 Ja 31 '69

SNELL, Neva. See Alderton, G. jt. auth.

SNELL, Ronald D.

Black spokesman, or Republican pawn. bibliog Negro Hist Bul 32:6-10 N '69

SNELLING, Dorothy

Winning combination; drama. Plays 28:23-33 Ap '69

SNELLING, Robert Orren

Job franchiser. S. Margetts. il pors Duns R 94:59-61 Jl '69

SNELSON, Kenneth

Push and pull in the park; exhibition of sculpture in Bryant park, N.Y. il Arch Forum 130:68-9 Ja '69

SNEYERS, René

Stones also die; reprint. UNESCO Courier 22:79 Ag '69

SNIDER, Arthur J.

Loose knees and football. Sci Digest 65:67-8 F '69

Medicine. See issues of Science digest

SNIPERS

Sniping a new pattern of violence? T. A. Knopf. bibliog il Trans-Action 6:22-9 Jl '69; Reply with rejoinder. J. R. Corsi and L. H. Masotti. 6:5+ S '69

SNIPS. See Cutting tools

SNITZER, Milton S.

Automatic tint control for color-TV. Electr World 82:30-1+ S '69

Brighter picture tubes for color-TV. Electr World 82:33 Ag '69

Ultrasonic waves made visible. Electr World 81:51 My '69

SNOBS and snobbishness
New snobbism; intellectual snobs; views of T. H. White. S. Alsop. Newsweek 74:92 S 8 '69

SNOOK, Patrick K.
Build this colonial cabinet-top desk. Pop Mech 131:132-3 F '69
—and others
1969 snowmobile buyer's guide. Field & S 74:67-73+ O '69

SNORKELING. See Skin diving

SNOW, Charles Percy, baron Snow of Leicester. See Snow of Leicester, C. P. S.

SNOW, Edgar
Mao and the new mandate. New Repub 160: 17-21 My 10 '69

SNOW, Joel A.
Taking thought for the morrow. Science 164: 285-6 Ap 18 '69

SNOW of Leicester, Charles Percy Snow, baron
Hint of joy amidst the misery. Life 67:8 Ag 1 '69
Moon landing. Look 33:68-70+ Ag 26 '69
Views from earth on the odyssey into space. Look 33:77 F 4 '69

about
Authors & editors. B. A. Banon por Pub W 195:25-7 Ap 14 '69
Books. G. Steiner. New Yorker 45:83-6+ Jl 12 '69
Ruminating about freedom. J. Wain. New Repub 160:30+ F 1 '69
Why are Jews successful? Chr Today 13:31 Ap 25 '69

SNOW
Snow: beautiful, romantic, nostalgic, terrifying. F. Mowat. il Holiday 45:46-7+ F '69
Snowfall at San Francisco. D. M. Ludlum. il Weatherwise 21:230-7 D '68
Snowfall season of 1967-68. D. M. Ludlum. il Weatherwise 22:26-31 F '69
Snowflakes to keep. R. F. Sisson. il Nat Geog 137:104-11 Ja '70
Snowy winter of 1968-69 in New England. R. E. Lautzenheiser. il Weatherwise 22: 68-71+ Ap '69

SNOW and ice removal
Contract snowfighting; Montreal. J. V. Arpin. il Am City 84:98-9 D '69
Fluorescent painting and tandem plowing; Ridgefield Park, N.J. il Am City 84:57 F '69
Let's be objective about snow and ice control. J. F. Rooney, jr. bibliog il Am City 84:106+ O '69
Pin-point plowing; Clifton, N.J. A. Mazowiecki. il Am City 84:89-90 Ja '69
Pollutants and the roadside. E. D. Carpenter. il Horticulture 46:18-19+ O '69
Premix salt, calcium chloride precisely. il Am City 84:28 S '69
Small town beefs up its snowfighting capacity; Grafton, N.D. il Am City 84:109-10 S '69
Snow and ice control. See Issues of American city
What a 20-inch snowstorm can teach; Hempstead, N.Y. Am City 84:22 D '69
See also
Pavements—Heating
Snow plows

SNOW blowers, throwers, etc.
Consumer's guide to snowthrowers. Mech Illus 65:93 D '69
Horsepower for homeowners: a snowblower to the rescue. il Home Gard 56:46-9 N '69
How much to throw snow? J. Liston. il Pop Mech 130:146-9 D '68
Snow-throwing, new winter sport. E. McDonald. il House B 111:80+ N '69

Maintenance and repair
Care and feeding of snow throwers. M. Schultz. il Pop Mech 132:120-3+ D '69
Get your snowthrower ready for winter. il Mech Illus 65:132-3 N '69

SNOW-on-the-mountain
It's green and white, leafy and cool. il Sunset 142:230 Ap '69

SNOW plows
Little plows play a big role at Dorval airport; Montreal. il Am City 84:22 N '69
Tandem plowing eases snowfighters' problems. R. R. Fleming. il Am City 84:82-4+ Ag '69

SNOW removal equipment, Municipal
Blower solves both urban and rural problems; Cohocton, N.Y. il Am City 84:40 Ja '69
Plow on the front and a spreader on the rear; Hudson, Ohio. H. Kuchenbecker. il Am City 84:112+ F '69

Tandem plowing eases snowfighters' problems. R. R. Fleming. il Am City 84:82-4+ Ag '69

SNOW storms. See Snowstorms

SNOW throwers. See Snow blowers, throwers, etc.

SNOW tire studs. See Tires, Automobile

SNOWDON, Antony Charles Robert Armstrong-Jones, 1st earl of
Maddox: House of Messel; photographs. Vogue 153:194-201 Mr 1 '69
Making fun of themselves; photographs. Vogue 153:122-7 Je '69
Wales; photographs. Look 33:68-73 Je 24 '69

about
Copyright, Snowdon; with photographs by Lord Snowdon. J. Scully. Mod Phot 33: 68-85 Je '69

SNOWDROPS
First flowers of spring. D. E. Rose. il Home Gard 56:41 Ap '69

SNOWFLAKES. See Snow

SNOWMASS-AT-ASPEN, Colo. See Winter resorts

SNOWMOBILE camping. See Camping

SNOWMOBILE engines
Eight ways to hop up a snowmobile engine. H. Bradshaw and V. Bradshaw. il Pop Mech 131:138-41 Ja '69

SNOWMOBILE racing
Coldest and cruelest; Midnight sun 600 snowmobile race. il Time 93:50-1 Ja 24 '69
Deep-freeze run; Midnight sun race. il Newsweek 73:57-8 Ja 27 '69
Snomobility. R. L. Horney. il Parks & Rec 4:29-32+ O '69

SNOWMOBILE shelters. See Shelters

SNOWMOBILES
Across the Bitterroots with Lewis and Clark, by snowmobile. J. M. Liston. il Pop Mech 130:114-17+ D '68
Clues and clothing for snow survival. E. P. Haddon. il Pop Mech 132:104-7+ N '69
Conquering Minnesota's wilderness by snowmobile. D. Fales. il Pop Mech 132:150-3 D '69
Get ready for your winter fun! photo guide to the 1970 snowmobiles. H. Shuldiner. il Pop Sci 195:122-7+ O '69
Guide to snowmobiling. Bet Hom & Gard 47:36 D '69
New look of the North. il Motor B 123:264-5 Ja '69
New super-duper snowmobiles. il Pop Mech 132:42-3 S '69
1969 snowmobile buyer's guide. P. Snook and others. il Field & S 74:67-73+ O '69
Red-hot winter for snowmobiles. il Bsns W p34 Ja 10 '70
'70, a sensational year coming up for snowmobiles. D. Fales. il Pop Mech 132:142-5+ O '69
Snowmobile and environmental quality; with editorial comment. M. F. Baldwin. il Liv Wildn 32:2, 14-17 Wint '68
Snowmobile infection spreads in Maine. Nat Parks 43:23 D '69
Snowmobile slews across the land. il Life 66:60-2+ Ja 31 '69
Snowmobiles; boon or bane? H. V. Bloomfield. il Am For 75:4-5+ My '69
Snowmobiles come to the suburbs. R. P. Stevenson. il Pop Sci 195:132-6+ N '69
Snowmobiles put new go in ice fishing. il Pop Sci 194:139-41 Ja '69
Snowmobiles: the hot rod of winter sport. M. Lund. il Holiday 46:43+ D '69
Snowmobiles, your winter workhorse. Suc Farm 67:S2 O '69
What snowmobiles do is open up the winter world. il Sunset 142:46+ F '69
Yellowstone snowtime. F. A. Tinker. il Travel 131:30-3+ F '69

Deer collisions
See Deer—Collisions with snowmobiles

Maintenance and repair
ABC's of snowmobile maintenance. H. Shuldiner. il Pop Sci 194:152-3 F '69

Safety devices and measures
Do's and don'ts of snowmobile safety. G. L. Earle. Suc Farm 67:W2 N '69

Testing
Tom McCahill tests a snowmobile. T. McCahill. il Mech Illus 65:40-2+ D '69

SNOWSHOE hare hunting. See Rabbit hunting

SNOWSHOE hares. See Hares

SNOWSTORMS

Blizzard in Indian country. T. Gallagher. il Read Digest 95:70-5 D '69

Day nature said no. J. K. Martine. il Good H 168:34+ Mr '69

Great white hang up; New York's helplessness. il Newsweek 73:28+ F 24 '69

How to blow up a snowstorm; ESSA snowseeding experiment in Lake Erie Region. il Bsns W p42 D 20 '69

Hundred years of Boston snowstorms. D. M. Ludlum. Weatherwise 22:72-5 Ap '69

No way out, no way back; passengers stranded at John F. Kennedy airport. il Time 93:47-8 F 21 '69

Precautions to take in a blizzard. Good H 168:162 F '69

Siege of Kennedy; thirty hours at the airport during snowstrom. E. J. Kahn, jr. il Travel & Camera 32:56-9+ My '69

Snow disaster at Fallsvale, Calif. P. F. Math. il Weatherwise 22:107 Je '69

See also
Automobile driving—Storm hazards
Aviation—Storm hazards

SNOWY tree crickets. See Crickets

SNYDER, Allegra Fuller

Who can make them? How can we use them? Dance Mag 43:38-41 Ap '69

—and Moseley, Monica

(comps) Directory of 16mm dance films. Dance Mag 43:47-62 Ap '69

SNYDER, Esther Winship

Codicil; poem. Har Yrs 9:51 F '69

SNYDER, Gary

Hudsonian curlew; poem. Poetry 115:119-22 N '69

Sours of the hills; poem. Harper 239:83 S '69

about
Poet in today's wilderness. E. Zahniser. por Liv Wildn 33:34-6 Spr '69

SNYDER, Graydon F.

Support means sanctuary and solidarity. Chr Cent 86:120-1 Ja 22 '69

SNYDER, James Max

Mobile students. Todays Ed 58:26 Ap '69

SNYDER, Kit

Porcelains of Kit Snyder. J. Wandres. il por Ceram Mo 17:12-15 O '69

SNYDER, Richard

Winding the clock; poem. New Repub 161:24 N 22 '69

SNYDER, Solomon H. See Coyle, J. T. jt. auth.

SNYDER, Tex.

Containerized residential refuse collection. L. A. Patterson. il Am City 84:55 Ag '69

SOAP

Facts on fifty-four soaps, soaks & detergents. il Changing T 23:21-3 S '69

Notes on the new snobbery of soap. il Harp Baz 102:92-3 Je '69

Soap: who needs it? And who doesn't. il Vogue 154:199-201 O 1 '69

See also
Procter and Gamble company
Toilet preparations

SOAP bubbles and films

Amateur scientist; how to blow soap bubbles that last for months or even years. A. V. Grosse. il Sci Am 220:128-32+ My '69

Soap bubbles: two years old and sixty centimeters in diameter, A. V. Grosse. bibliog il Science 164:291-3 Ap 18 '69

SOAP industry and trade

Will an ethnic pitch sell the black market? American dream soap aimed for the ghetto. il Bsns W p88+ Ap 12 '69

See also
Purex corporation

Finance

Procter & Gamble. il Forbes 103:36-40+ Ap 15 '69

SOAP operas. See Television broadcasting—Drama

SOARING (aeronautics) See Gliding and soaring

SOBEL, Helen

Goodby to a perfect partner. C. Goren. il Sports Illus 31:96 S 22 '69

SOBELL, Morton

Out of the mists. il pors Newsweek 73:29 Ja 27 '69

Return from oblivion. il por Time 93:15 Ja 24 '69

SOBILOFF, H. J.

For Henry Rago; poem. Poetry 115:112 N '69

SOCARRAS RAMIREZ, Armando. See Ramirez, A. S.

SOCCER

Soccer: opium of the Brazilian people. J. Lever. il Trans-Action 7:36-43 D '69

This riotous isle. W. Sheed. il Sports Illus 30:78-82+ Ap 21 '69

Economic aspects

Smart money; the sure thing. il Forbes 104:24 Ag 1 '69

SOCCER fans. See Sports fans

SOCCER players

See also
Best, G.

SOCHUREK, Howard

Berlin: on both sides of the wall. il Nat Geog 137:1-47 Ja '70

South Korea; success story in Asia. il Nat Geog 135:301-45 Mr '69

SOCIABILITY. See Social psychology

SOCIAL action

Christian social action. Chr Today 13:24-5 Mr 14 '69

New York's Guidelines for social action; archdiocese's assessment. T. M. Gannon. America 121:98-9 Ag 16 '69

Time to meet the evangelicals? R. E. Branson. Chr Cent 86:1640-3 D 24 '69

SOCIAL adjustment. See Adjustment, Social

SOCIAL agencies, Voluntary

Call for action, new voice for the people; WMCA's program. J. Daniel. Read Digest 95:207-10+ O '69

Voluntarism and the urban crisis. America 120:522 My 3 '69

SOCIAL and economic security

Big brother is dead too; about conformity. K. Melvin. Nat R 21:116-18 F 11 '69; Discussion. 21:180, 222, 338 F 25-Mr 11, Ap 8 '69

Go power; income maintenance program in New Jersey. Newsweek 73:57-8 Mr 31 '69

Welfare plan of the future? proposed compulsory national health-insurance program. U S News 66:14 F 24 '69

SOCIAL aspects of art. See Art and society

SOCIAL aspects of education. See Educational sociology

SOCIAL aspects of science. See Science—Social aspects

SOCIAL attitudes. See Attitudes

SOCIAL behavior. See Manners and customs

SOCIAL change

Age of rock, by J. Eisen. Review
   Commonweal 91:49-50 O 10 '69. M. Rosenthal

Business has a war to win; excerpts from address, December 5, 1968. J. I. Miller. Harvard Bsns R 47:4-6+ Mr '69

Changing campus and a changing society; adaptation of address, November 12, 1968. D. Riesman. Sch & Soc 97:215-22 Ap '69

Culture and counter-culture. M. B. Bloy, jr. Commonweal 89:493-6 Ja 17 '69; Reply. H. M. Taylor. 89:691 F 28 '69

Don't ask me, I only live here. R. Baker. il Life 67:32-7 Jl 25 '69

Ecology of discontent. L. J. Averill. Chr Cent 86:835-8 Je 18 '69

Educated man in the year 2000; address, November 15, 1968. P. C. Ritterbush. Vital Speeches 35:295-300 Mr 1 '69

Essay on liberation, by H. Marcuse. Review
   Atlan 223:108-10 Je '69. M. Cohen
   Nation 208:765-8 Je 16 '69. P. Clecak

Family people and organization men. J. Taylor. Sci Digest 65:66-9 Mr '69

Father and the fathers. M. M. Shideler. Chr Cent 86:1061-4 Ag 13 '69

From the radical left to the center. T. P. Melady. il Cath World 209:168-71 Jl '69

Future is not what it used to be; excerpt from address, May 1969. A. L. Sachar. PTA Mag 64:2-5+ S '69

Gearing U.S. policy to the world's great trends. M. Ways. il Fortune 79:64-9+ My 1 '69

Herbert Marcuse or Milovan Djilas? I. Howe. Harper 239:84+ Jl '69

How could anything that feels so bad be so good? R. E. Farson. Sat R 52:20-1+ S 6 '69

How to tell a fad from a trend. M. E. Marty. il Commonweal 90:509-12 Ag 22 '69

Impact of automation on society. F. L. Bates. il Bul Atom Sci 25:4-6 Je '69

Living with violent change; excerpts from Political violence. H. L. Nieburg. Cur 112:36-42 N '69

Measuring social change. D. Wolfle. Science 164:1121 Je 6 '69

New commonwealth, by J. A. Garraty. Review
   Am Heritage 20:105-6 Ap '69. B. Catton

New public discourse? Setting the tone of society's future. A. M. Rosenthal. Cur 104:26-9 F '69

SOCIAL change—*Continued*
Our son is a campus radical. Anonymous. Read Digest 71:71-5 Ap '69
Passionate rebels. S. Harrington. il Vogue 153:146-51+ My '69
Radical and the mediator: their roles in social change. R. Ruether. America 121:521-3 N 29 '69
Responsible versus irresponsible dissent; adaptation of address, March 27, 1969. J. W. Gardner. Science 164:379 Ap 25 '69
Social change and history, by R. A. Nisbet. Review
    Commentary 48:85-9 N '69. D. H. Wrong
Social change and the rural church. D. W. Johnson. Chr Cent 8C:658+ My 7 '69
Social change and the university. J. J. Corson. Sat R 53:76+ Ja 10 '70
Society against itself, by G. H. Crowell. Review
    Chr Cent 86:594-5 Ap 23 '69. R. A. Raines
Students, drugs and protest. K. Keniston. Cur 104:5-19 F '69; Same abr. with title Drug problem among students; how bad, what's back of it? il U S News 66:90-2 Mr 24 '69
Technology and social change; adaptation of address, August 4, 1969. H. E. Hoelscher. bibliog Science 166:68-72 O 3 '69
Third world modernization in transnational perspective. T. K. Hopkins. Ann Am Acad 386:126-36 N '69
Times they are a-changin': the music of protest. R. A. Rosenstone. bibliog f Ann Am Acad 382:131-44 Mr '69
Toward a planetary society; excerpts from The future of the future. J. McHale. Cur 110:16-25 S '69
Toward a self-renewing society; Time essay; excerpts from address. J. W. Gardner. Time 93:40-1 Ap 11 '69
University and social change; excerpts from Social welfare forum, 1969. N. E. Cohen. bibliog Sch & Soc 97:479-84 D '69
What kind of society do we want? excerpts from The recovery of confidence. J. W. Gardner. Read Digest 95:74-8 S '69
Working paper for man and nature. M. Mead. il Natur Hist 78:14-15+ Ap '69
You can remake this society. J. W. Gardner. il Look 33:85-6 Jl 15 '69
    See also
Social progress
Social revolution

Bibliography

Some recent developments in studies of social and cultural change. B. J. Siegel. Ann Am Acad 385:157-74 S '69

Latin America

Cross and sword in Latin America. Chr Today 14:26-7 D 5 '69
SOCIAL classes
American underclass; symposium. bibliog il Trans-Action 6:9-53 F '69; Reply with rejoinder. E. Van Den Haag. 6:62-4 Ap '69
Influences of social classes in schools; excerpt from The public school in the new society. G. Graham. bibliog f il Sch & Soc 97:169-80 Mr '69
Respectable bigotry; reprint. M. Lerner. Am Scholar 38:606-17 Aut '69
Rugged art of social climbing. S. Birmingham. Vogue 153:190-1+ My '69
    See also
Middle classes
Upper classes
SOCIAL conditions
Carl Purcell pictures for social change: foreign assignments photographing major foreign aid projects. C. Purcell. il Pop Phot 64:76-83+ Je '69
Social stratification: 1964-1968; excerpts from address March 24, 1969 and from Class and stratum. T. E. Lasswell. Ann Am Acad 384:104-34 Jl '69
    See also
Civilization
Poverty
Social problems
SOCIAL conflict
Ethics and social struggle. B. Dunham. Nation 209:726-9 D 29 '69
    See also
Youth-adult relationship
SOCIAL cooperation, international. See International cooperation
SOCIAL democratic party (Germany) See Political parties—Germany—History
SOCIAL democratic party (Sweden) See Political parties—Sweden
SOCIAL democrats (Germany) See Political parties—Germany (Federal Republic)

SOCIAL diseases. See Venereal diseases
SOCIAL drinking. See Drinking customs
SOCIAL ecology. See Human ecology
SOCIAL education
    See also
Family life. Education for
Intercultural education
Sex education
Social sciences—Study and teaching
SOCIAL ethics
Between glory and disaster. Nation 209:718 D 29 '69
Ethics and social struggle. B. Dunham. Nation 209:726-9 D 29 '69
    See also
Christian ethics
Church and race problems
Sexual ethics
Social problems
SOCIAL evolution. See Social change
SOCIAL-fascism. See National socialism
SOCIAL groups. See Groups (sociology)
SOCIAL, humanitarian and cultural committee of the United Nations. See United Nations—Social, humanitarian and cultural committee
SOCIAL hygiene. See Venereal diseases
SOCIAL interaction
Schools that turn people off. S. Doig. il Todays Ed 58:28-30 My '69; Same abr. Ed Digest 35:41-3 S '69
Soft revolution explored. S. Keen. Chr Cent 86:1667-9 D 31 '69
    See also
Group relations training
SOCIAL isolation
Hyperphagia and polydipsia in socially isolated rhesus monkeys. R. E. Miller and others. bibliog il Science 165:1027-8 S 5 '69
    See also
Loneliness
SOCIAL legislation
    See also
Family allowances
Unemployment—Relief measures

United States

Alienated rank and file. A. Bilik. Nation 209:527-30 N 17 '69
    See also
Consumer protection—Laws and legislation
Old age pensions—United States
Workmens compensation—United States
SOCIAL life and customs. See Manners and customs; *also* subhead Social life and customs under names of countries, states, cities, e.g. London—Social life and customs
SOCIAL policy
    See also
United States—Social policy
SOCIAL position. See Social status
SOCIAL problems
Hole in your head. A. H. Leitch. Chr Today 13:38-9 Ap 25 '69
Poverty, politics and social studies. J. P. Fitzpatrick. America 120:558-61 My 10 '69
Punishment for peace, by P. Berrigan. Review
    Commonweal 90:524-5 Ag 22 '69. J. L. McKenzie
Soul music and poetry: the easy way out; address, April 27, 1969. B. Rustin. Vital Speeches 35:541-2 Je 15 '69
    See also
Church and social problems
Crime and criminals
Family
Homosexuality
Illegitimacy
Juvenile delinquency
Libraries and social and economic problems
Migrant labor
Narcotic habit
Poor
Prisons
Public welfare
Race discrimination
School and social and economic problems
Slums
Social action
Sociology, Christian
Standard of living
Suicide
Technology and civilization
Unemployables

History

Best men: liberal reformers in the gilded age, by J. G. Sproat. Review
    Am Heritage 20:104-5 Ap '69. B. Catton
SOCIAL problems and art. See Art and society

SOCIAL problems in education. See Educational sociology

SOCIAL problems in literature
Do you know what's happening? teaching literary works with themes of racial conflict. I. Halperin. Engl J 58:1049-52 O '69
Morals or literature: the abstractive fallacy. J. G. Brennan. Eng J 58:226-9 F '69

SOCIAL progress
Why? Why? Why? G. Trotta. il Harp Baz 102:224 My '69
See also
Social change
Social revolution
United Nations—Development program

SOCIAL psychology
Fund of sociability. R. S. Weiss. bibliog il Trans-Action 6:36-43 Jl '69
Inward look. H. C. Wallich. Newsweek 73:87 Ap 28 '69
Southern violence. S. Hackney. bibliog f il Am Hist R 74:906-25 F '69
See also
Adjustment, Social
Alienation (social psychology)
Family
Groups (sociology)
Human relations
Leadership
Morale, National
Panic
Prison psychology
Public opinion
Social conflict
Social interaction

SOCIAL reform. See Social problems; Social revolution

SOCIAL research. See Social science research

SOCIAL responsibility. See Responsibility

SOCIAL revolution
Apocalyptic social change. W. B. Abernethy. Chr Cent 86:343-4 Mr 12 '69; Reply. C. E. Fager. 86:1249-51 O 1 '69; Rejoinder. 86: 1488+ N 19 '69
Can it happen here? E. Kern. il Life 67:67+ O 17 '69
Christian revolution and the Christian educator. M. Hellwig. Chr Cent 86:1088-91 Ag 20 '69; Reply. 86:1648-9 D 24 '69
Comes the cultural revolution. J. Hitchcock. il N Y Times Mag p4-5+ Jl 27 '69; Discussion. p22-3 Ag 17 '69
Cuba: revolution without a blueprint; smooth transition from capitalism to socialism. M. Zeitlin. il Trans-Action 6:39-42+ Ap '69
Earth house hold, by G. Snyder. Review Sat R 52:37-8+ O 11 '69. T. Fitzsimmons
Frantz Fanon and the radical left. E. W. Ranly. America 121:384+ N 1 '69
From dichotomy to integration. H. Camara. Chr Cent 86:1574-7 D 10 '69
Future of American politics; is revolution impending? B. Moore, jr. Cur 106:54-64 Ap '69
How can the left be relevant? W. A. Williams. Cur 109:20-4 Ag '69
Irrepressible world revolt; excerpt from The irresponsible style in American politics. L. Benson; reply with rejoinder. M. Marien. New Repub 160:31-3 F 22 '69
It can happen here. L. N. Bell. Chr Today 14:20-1 Ja 2 '70
New reformation. P. Goodman. il N Y Times Mag p32-3+ S 14 '69; Same abr. with title Living through a new reformation. Cur 112:4-9 N '69; Discussion. N Y Times Mag p16+ O 19 '69
Protest in the sixties; symposium, ed. by J. Boskin and R. A. Rosenstone. bibliog f Ann Am Acad 382:1-144 Mr '69
Reflections on a revolution. N. Cousins. Sat R 52:22 My 17 '69
Temptations of a Boston atheist. N. Hentoff. Harper 238:81-5 Ap '69

Anecdotes, facetiae, satire, etc.
Exclusive and unauthorized; the liberated report of Professor X. Professor X. Esquire 72:104-7+ S '69

SOCIAL role
Breaking the role barrier: a psychotherapeutic necessity. L. S. Sata and R. L. Derbyshire. bibliog Ment Hy 53:110-17 Ja '69

SOCIAL science
Research
See Social science research

SOCIAL science research
ACE study on campus unrest: questions for behavioral scientists; with statement by advisory committee. J. Walsh; J. Coburn. Science 165:157-61 Jl 11 '69; Discussion. 165:1206-7; 166:945 S 19, N 21 '69
Behavioral and social sciences: NAS report stresses applications. J. Walsh. Science 166:585-6 O 31 '69
Defense research: pressure on social sciences. P. M. Boffey; J. Coburn. Science 164:1037-41 My 30 '69
Evaluation of broad-aim programs: a cautionary case and a moral; excerpts from address. R. S. Weiss and M. Rein. Ann Am Acad 385:133-42 S '69
More research, more relevance. Sci N 96:201 S 13 '69
Roundup of current research. See issues of Trans-Action
Social scientists offer themselves. Sci N 96: 395-6 N 1 '69
Some perspectives on evaluating social welfare programs. L. A. Ferman. Ann Am Acad 385:143-56 S '69
See also
Computers—Social science applications
Criminal research
Little, Arthur D. incorporated

India
Academic colonialism: not so innocent abroad. G. D. Berreman. il Nation 209:505-8 N 10 '69

SOCIAL sciences
Behavioral science or electioneering? excerpt from study by a National academy of sciences panel. Sat R 52:65-7 N 1 '69
See also
Behavioral sciences
Civilization
Computers—Social science applications
Economics
Human ecology
International encyclopedia of the social sciences
Power (social sciences)
Social scientists
Sociology

Bibliography
Book reviews. See issues of Trans-Action
New books for the social studies. Sr Schol 94:Schol Teach 32+ Ja 17 '69

Study and teaching
Lab-carts are rolling; Enfield, Conn. program. F. S. Gross. il Schol Teach Sec Teach sup p 14-15+ O '69
Social studies: a case for honest reflection. R. L. Kimble. bibliog Clear House 43:428-31 Mr '69
Social studies: the flexible content approach. B. Callaghan. Clear House 43:368-70 F '69
Teaching man to children; Newton, Mass. il Time 95:50 Ja 19 '70
Thinking and traditional socio-political values. Sch & Soc 97:344+ O '69
What's new in the social sciences curriculum. D. Fraser. Ed Digest 35:29-31 N '69
World cultures: a matter of method. P. Wilson. Clear House 43:501-3 Ap '69
See also
Citizenship, Education for
Current events—Study and teaching
History—Study and teaching
Laboratory method

SOCIAL sciences and state
Poverty, politics and social studies. J. P. Fitzpatrick. America 120:558-61 My 10 '69
Report says social sciences can help avoid policy goofs. P. M. Boffey. Science 165: 574 Ag 8 '69
Social scientists offer themselves. Sci N 96: 395-6 N 1 '69

SOCIAL scientists
Harsh judgment. Time 95:39 Ja 5 '70
Investigators of behavior. il Fortune 81:115 Ja '70

SOCIAL security act amendments
If social security checks go up 15 per cent—. U S News 67:68 D 22 '69
Leaders in Congress ask faster, higher social security benefits. Har Yrs 9:4 N '69
Social security rise of 15 percent near. U S News 67:66-7 D 15 '69

SOCIAL security benefits. See Insurance, So-
cial—United States
SOCIAL security numbering system. See Num-
bering systems
SOCIAL security taxes
Something for the silent majority. E. L.
Dale, jr. New Repub 161:14-15 N 29 '69
SOCIAL segregation. See Segregation, Social
SOCIAL service

Study and teaching
See Social workers—Education
SOCIAL statistics
In search of the missing social indicators. I.
Kristol. il Fortune 80:168-9 Ag 1 '69
SOCIAL status
Are you wearing last year's status symbol?
N. Gittelson. McCalls 97:92+ O '69
If you have a million. E. Sheppard. Harp
Baz 102:118-19 Jl '69
Social stratification: 1964-1968; excerpts from
address March 24, 1969 and from Class and
stratum. T. E. Lasswell. Ann Am Acad 384:
104-34 Jl '69
See also
Social classes
Students—Social and economic status
SOCIAL stratification. See Social classes; Social
status
SOCIAL studies. See Social sciences
SOCIAL usage. See Etiquette
SOCIAL welfare
See also
Public welfare
United Nations—Commission on social de-
velopment
SOCIAL work
Crisis behind the welfare crisis. I. Kristol.
il Fortune 79:227-8 Je '69
See also
Boston—Social work
Legal aid
Social problems

Study and teaching
See Social workers—Education
SOCIAL work, Prison. See Prisons—Social
work
SOCIAL work conferences
See also
National conference on social welfare
SOCIAL work education. See Social workers
—Education
SOCIAL workers
American and British mental health workers
look at rehabilitation. A. R. Askenasy.
Ment Hy 53:466-71 Jl '69
Social workers move. Sci N 95:572-3 Je 14
'69

Education
Gap in social work education. R. Chester
and others. bibliog Ment Hy 53:84-9 Ja '69
Undergraduate education for social work.
E. E. Guillot. Sch & Soc 97:25-7 Ja '69
SOCIAL workers, Volunteer
Volunteers helping families of the mentally
ill. J. P. Cole and W. E. Cole. bibliog Ment
Hy 53:188-95 Ap '69
SOCIALISM
Marx, Mao, and the dissenters. R. L. Tobin.
Sat R 53:26+ Ja 10 '70
Origins of socialism, by G. Lichtheim. Re-
view
New Repub 160:30-2 F 8 '69. M. Har-
rington
Sat R 52:57 Ap 5 '69. M. J. Goldbloom
Socialism and the future. R. L. Heilbroner.
bibliog f Commentary 48:35-45 D '69
Why one British Socialist turned conserva-
tive. J. Braine. il N Y Times Mag p24-5+
Mr 2 '69; Discussion. p 16 Mr 23 '69
See also
Communism
National socialism

History
Origins of socialism, by G. Lichtheim. Review
Commentary 48:58-60 Ag '69. S. Avineri

Canada
Provincial election with a long reach: key
issue, free enterprise vs. Marxist socialism. Bsns W p31 Ag 23 '69

Cuba
Cuba: revolution with a blueprint; smooth
transition from capitalism to socialism. M.
Zeitlin. il Trans-Action 6:38-42+ Ap '69

Great Britain
See also
Labor party (Great Britain)

Italy
See also
Socialist party (Italy)

United States
How can the left be relevant? W. A. Wil-
liams. Cur 109:20-4 Ag '69
SOCIALISM and religion
From dichotomy to integration. H. Camara.
Chr Cent 86:1574-7 D 10 '69
SOCIALIST party (Italy)
Socialism in six acts. il Time 94:39-40 Jl 18
'69
While Rome burns. Newsweek 74:36+ Jl 21
'69
SOCIALIST party (Japan) See Political par-
ties—Japan
SOCIALLY handicapped

Education
New careers: problems and pitfalls. G. H.
Weber and D. Palmer. il Am Ed 5:26-8 Ap
'69
Race between education & catastrophe. H.
Brabyn. il UNESCO Courier 23:11-13 Ja
'70
Tuning in and turning on the nonverbals;
summer English class at Marymount college, Palos Verdes estates, Calif. for Upward bound girls. B. L. Covey. il Am Ed
5:9-11 Je '69
Vocational education unsuited for the socially disadvantaged. W. W. McKeever, jr.
bibliog f Clear House 44:43-4 S '69

Employment
ABPC votes clearinghouse for minority manpower. Pub W 195:37-8 My 19 '69
Brighter vistas for hard core; NAB-JOBS
program. Bsns W p44 Je 7 '69
Business picks up the urban challenge. A. T.
Demaree. il Fortune 79:102-4+ Ap '69; Re-
ply. R. Taggart, 3d. 79:56 My 1 '69
Detroit shows the way with hard-core job-
less. il Bsns W p32-5 F 1 '69
Franklin U.S. a plan to enlist talent, provide
training; adaptation of address, April 10,
1969. C. F. Bound. Pub W 195: 32-4 Ap 21
'69
Hard-core blacks and the shiny auto; layoff
problems. R. Dietsch. New Repub 160:10
Mr 1 '69
Hard-core jobless get a friend at the top;
D. Kendall, chairman of NAB. il Bsns W
p62+ Mr 8 '69
Managing a war on poverty; program in
Roanoke, Va. il Nations Bsns 57:52-5 F '69
New plants dot the black slums. il Bsns W p
100+ Mr 22 '69
Publishing and minority manpower; COPE
program. D. N. Mount. Pub W 196:37 O 6 '69
Rocking the boat; HCA's program. il News-
week 73:85+ My 19 '69
We hire the hard-core unemployed; Con
Edison program. C. F. Luce. il Duns R 93:
50-2 F '69
See also
Negroes—Employment
Opportunities industrialization centers, in-
corporated
SOCIALLY handicapped children
Genetics vs. headstart. il Sci N 95:326-7 Ap
5 '69
It takes heart to inspire twenty-six ghetto
kids. J. Green. il Seventeen 28:93+ Ja '69
Learning the streets; institute on ghetto
youth in San Francisco. il Time 94:64 Ag 15
'69
Our commitment is to diversification of
campers; Blueberry Cove, Me. A. Gold-
smith and R. Hellerson. il Camp Mag 41:
19+ Mr '69
Two modern challenges for every camp direc-
tor; conserving human resources; disad-
vantaged groups, and physically or mentally
handicapped children. P. M. Ford. Camp
Mag 41:18-19 S '69
We need to try harder; inner-city children
need active recruitment. J. H. Ramey. il
Camp Mag 41:12+ F '69
What about biological insults? S. Scarr. Ed
Digest 34:25-7 Ap '69
See also
Negro children

Education
Art motivation for ghetto children. J. Comins.
il Sch Arts 69:6-7 O '69
Black power and the learning process. M.
R. Berube. Commonweal 90:98-101 Ap 11
'69
City of God; adaptation of address, 1969. R.
Gould. il PTA Mag 64:2-5 O '69

SOCIALLY handicapped children—Education
—Continued

Curse of crash education. R. C. Orem. il Nations Bsns 57:60-2+ Ag '69

Dead end in American education. R. A. Freeman. Nat R 21:22-4 Ja 14 '69; Same abr. Ed Digest 34:9-12 My '69

Disadvantaged: do not deprive them of the American literary heritage. L. S. Josephs. bibliog f Clear House 44:105-9 O '69

Durham education improvement program. R. L. Spaulding; R. M. Brandt. Todays Ed 58:62-4 F '69

Early environment and school expectations. W. D. Boutwell. PTA Mag 63:30 Ja '69

Early school admissions; a Baltimore best seller. A. C. Harding. il Todays Ed 58:57-8+ N '69

Education is the answer; excerpts from address, January 1969. J. Farmer. Todays Ed 58:25-6 Ap '69

Educational relevance and Jensen's conclusions. N. Anastasiow. Ed Digest 35:34-7 D '69

Educational trends and media programs in school libraries; symposium. bibliog il ALA Bul 63:221-72 F '69

English below the salt: the miscellaneous crowds and people. G. R. Carlsen. Engl J 58:363-7 Mr '69

Enrolling the disadvantaged. Sch & Soc 97:347-8 O '69

Eyewitness: Department of curriculum of the Washington, D.C. public schools guide for teachers. E. W. Johnson. il Sr Schol 94:Schol Teach 24-5 Ja 17 '69

Inner-city teacher recruitment. Sch & Soc 97:132 Mr '69

Jensen's complaint. M. R. Berube. Commonweal 91:42-4 O 10 '69

Kaleidoscope for learning; educational technology. J. H. Martin. il Sat R 52:76-7+ Je 21 '69

Kibbutzim for the disadvantaged; with excerpts from articles by L. Y. Rabkin, and K. Rabkin, and B. Bettelheim. B. R. Metalitz. il Todays Ed 58:17-19 D '69

Last one in; Hardy elementary school; Washington, D.C. il Am Ed 5:22 Je '69

Lives of children, by G. Dennison. Review America 121:469-70 N 15 '69. F. Griffith

McGraw-Hill. urban league launch school for dropouts. Library J 94:824-6 F 15 '69

Mother Goose: is the old girl relevant? J. Bodger. bibliog il Wilson Lib Bul 44:402-8 D '69

Mythology of disadvantage. S. Gordon. Ed Digest 34:5-7 Mr '69

New literature for inner-city students. A. C. Brocki. Engl J 58:1151-61 N '69

Outward bound adventures; showing outdoors to teenagers from the ghettos. W. C. Dillinger. il Nat Wildlife 7:12-16 Je '69

Professor becomes high school teacher. E. H. Smith. Engl J 58:360-2+ Mr '69; Reply. P. Borgstrom. 58:1366-9 D '69

Pygmalion in the classroom, by R. Rosenthal and L. Jacobson. Review New Yorker 45:169-70+ Ap 19 '69. R. Coles

Residential high school for gifted disadvantaged students. W. J. Tisdall. Ed Digest 34:40-3 F '69

Satiety factor; to make learning possible for children, feed them in school. B. Bettelheim. N Y Times Mag p 140 Ap 13 '69

Social dialects: a touchy issue; NCTE convention. Sr Schol 93:Schol Teach 18 Ja 10 '69

Teaching composition to the disadvantaged. D. Geyer. Engl J 58:900-7 S '69

Teaching language in a Harlem school. Trans-Action 6:7 Mr '69

Teaching the disadvantaged. D. Cooper. Clear House 43:444-6 Mr '69

Trying to find the pony: decentralization, community control, governance of the education profession. Todays Ed 58:58-60 F '69

Upward bound, salvaging talent and teenagers. C. T. Rowan and D. M. Mazie. Read Digest 94:39-40+ My '69

What affects learning? S. Holzman. Sr Schol 94:Schol Teach 4 Ap 25 '69

Who needs it? Compensatory education. J. T. Durham. bibliog f Clear House 44:18-22 S '69; Same abr. Ed Digest 35:18-21 D '69

You can't teach a hungry child; school lunch program. J. N. Perryman. Ed Digest 34:28-30 Ap '69

See also
Children of migrant laborers—Education
Preschool children—Education
Project Head Start
Teachers of socially handicapped children
United States—National council on the education of disadvantaged children
Vermont-New York city youth project

Health and hygiene
Lead-poisoned kids. M. English. Look 33:114 O 21 '69

Recreation
From Bedford-Stuyvesant to Bear Mountain; underprivileged youngsters. il Parks & Rec 4:41-2 Ja '69

SOCIALLY handicapped children, Teachers of. *See* Teachers of socially handicapped children

SOCIÉTÉ générale de Belgique. See Belgium —Industries

SOCIETIES, Insect. See Insect societies

SOCIETY. See subhead Social life and customs under names of countries, states, cities, e.g. Washington, D.C.—Social life and customs

SOCIETY. Primitive
Elementary structures of kinship, by C. Lévi-Strauss. Review Sat R 52:52-3 My 17 '69. R. F. Murphy

Original affluent society; the Bushmen. il Time 94:55 Jl 25 '69

Stone tools and human behavior. S. R. Binford and L. R. Binford. il Sci Am 220:70-2+ bibliog(p 146) Ap '69

See also
Art, Primitive
Cannibalism
Indians of North America—Culture
Kinship
Tribes and tribal system

SOCIETY and art. See Art and society

SOCIETY and law. See Sociological jurisprudence

SOCIETY and music. See Music and society

SOCIETY and the church. See Church and the world

SOCIETY and the individual. See Individual and society

SOCIETY columns. See Newspapers—Sections, columns, etc.

SOCIETY for management information science. See Information systems, Management

SOCIETY for photographic education
Manipulate, create, and you've got Zoom; meeting in Oakland. M. Mann. il Pop Phot 65:20+ Ag '69

SOCIETY for social responsibility in science
Ravaging Vietnam. Nation 208:484-5 Ap 21 '69

SOCIETY for the protection of New Hampshire forests. See Forestry societies

SOCIETY hill playhouse street theatre. See Philadelphia—Theater

SOCIETY ISLANDS
Leeward Islands. R. Northshield. il Natur Hist 78:60-7 O '69
See also
Birds—Laysan
Wildlife sanctuaries—Society Islands

SOCIETY of African and Afro-American students
Day LeRoi Jones spoke on Penn campus, what were the blacks doing in the balcony? G. Weales. il N Y Times Mag p38-40+ My 4 '69

SOCIETY of British aerospace companies
British industry guideline offered. H. J. Coleman. Aviation W 90:16-17 F 10 '69
U.K. aerospace heading for record year. H. J. Coleman. Aviation W 90:24-5 Je 30 '69

SOCIETY of brothers
Who are these Blumhardt characters anyhow? V. Eller. il Chr Cent 86:1274-8 O 8 '69

SOCIETY of experimental test pilots
Vintage year. R. Hotz. Aviation W 91:11 O 6 '69

SOCIETY of Friends. See Friends, Society of

SOCIETY of Jesus. See Jesuits

SOCIETY of photographic collectors of North America
Haggle of collectors; first conference and workshop. H. Zucker. il Pop Phot 64:28+ Mr '69

SOCIETY of priests for a free ministry. See Priests—Associations, institutions, etc.

SOCIETY page. See Newspapers—Society page

SOCIO-ECONOMIC status of students. See Students—Social and economic status

SOCIOLOGICAL jurisprudence
Arthur Goldberg writes about the Green Berets. Life 67:30D O 17 '69

SOCIOLOGISTS
See also
Women as sociologists

SOCIOLOGY
Politics and society, by R. M. MacIver. Review
Sat R 52:25-6+ My 17 '69. S. Brown
See also
Anthropology
Atomic power—Social aspects
Community
Culture
Equality
Groups (sociology)
Human ecology
Human relations
Individualism
Man—Influence of environment
Power (social sciences)
Social psychology
Woman

Study and teaching
New sociology. il Time 95:38-9 Ja 5 '70
Quest for academic relevance; enrollment for courses at Princeton. Sat R 52:84 O 18 '69
Under the leaking roof; psychology and sociology at Miles college. N. Friedman. il Wilson Lib Bul 44:69-74 S '69

SOCIOLOGY, Christian
Christian humanism. R. Haughton. Cath World 209:245-6 S '69
Unresponsive pew. J. Richie. Chr Cent 86:1278-81 O 8 '69; Discussion. 86:1458+, 1549 N 12, D 3 '69
See also
Church and social problems

SOCIOLOGY, Educational. See Educational sociology

SOCIOLOGY, Rural
It's not just the cities. A. Mayer. Arch Rec 145:151-62 Je '69 (to be cont)
See also
Country life
Rural population

SOCIOLOGY, Urban
City as a social system; AAAS symposium, December 29, 1969. H. I. Safa. il Science 166:1189-90 N 28 '69
Community action: where has it been? Where will it go? S. Kravitz and F. K. Kolodner. Ann Am Acad 385:30-40 S '69
Deghettoization; choice of the new militancy. C. Funnyé. Arch Forum 130:74-7 Ap '69
It's not just the cities. A. Mayer. il Arch Rec 146:171-82 S; 105-10 D '69
Overlooked reasons for our social troubles. J. W. Forrester. Fortune 80:191-2 D '69
Participation and protests: who sets the goals? W. F. Wagner, jr. Arch Rec 145:9 F '69
People squeeze. G. Bush. il Bet Hom & Gard 47:74-5 O '69
Positive action; the middle managers; address, October 3, 1968. R. W. Goldfarb. Vital Speeches 35:315-18 Mr 1 '69
Revolt of the urban ghettos, 1964-1967. J. Boskin. bibliog f Ann Am Acad 382:1-14 Mr '69
Soulless city; excerpts from address. D. P. Moynihan. il Am Heritage 20:4-9+ F '69
221 ways to save our cities. J. Bailey. Arch Forum 130:70-3 Ja '69
Urban process: planning with and for the community; reprint. E. N. Bacon. Arch Rec 145:129-34 My '69
See also
Cities and towns
Community power
Urban renewal

Bibliography
Our cities, their wretched present, their hopeful future. J. Herbert. House & Gard 135:44+ Mr '69

SOCIOLOGY and science. See Science—Social aspects

SOCIOLOGY of knowledge. See Knowledge, Sociology of

SODAS, Ice cream. See Beverages

SODIUM in the body
Sodium current in ventricular myocardial fibers. H. Reuter and G. W. Beeler. jr. bibliog il Science 163:397-9 Ja 24 '69

SODIUM pentothal. See Pentothal sodium

SOFAS
Ubiquitous short sofa. L. Grundy and T. Bowman. il House R 111:82-5 F '69

SOFAS, Convertible. See Furniture, Convertible

SOFT drink industry
Cyclamates' sour aftertaste. il Time 94:79 O 31 '69
Herman W. Lay of PepsiCo; interview. H. W. Lay. il Nations Bsns 57:88-9+ S '69

Sweeteners take their lumps; effect of cyclamate ban. il Newsweek 74:73-4+ N 3 '69
See also
Coca-Cola company
Seven up company

Finance
Battle bubbles over Gatorade profits. Bsns W p33 S 6 '69

SOFT sculpture. See Sculpture

SOFTENING agents
Fabric softeners. il Consumer Rep 34:254-7 My '69

SOFTENING of water. See Water softening

SOHIO. See Standard oil company (Ohio)

SOHL, Albert L.
Make a time-taper. Radio-Electr 40:54 Je '69

SOIFER, Israel
Jerusalem book fair; coming of age in 1969. Pub W 195:25-9 My 12 '69
Otto Treumann graphic designer. Pub W 196:64+ Ag 4 '69
Thirty years of growth. Pub W 196:35-6 S 8 '69

SOIL acidity
See also
Lime

SOIL animals. See Soil fauna

SOIL bacteriology
See also
Nitrification

SOIL conservation service. See United States—Soil conservation service

SOIL deterioration
Rebuild worn-out soils. R. A. Miller. Horticulture 47:34+ F '69

SOIL disinfection
Soil steriliants, should you use them? Suc Farm 67:B5 Ap '69

SOIL engineering. See Soil mechanics

SOIL erosion. See Erosion

SOIL fauna
Soil pollutants and soil animals. C. A. Edwards. il Sci Am 220:88-92+ Ap '69

SOIL fertility
Fertilizers that nature delivers. J. I. Rodale. il Org Gard & Farm 16:100-2 Ap '69
How soil creates its own fertilizer. J. I. Rodale. il Org Gard & Farm 16:84-6+ Mr '69
How to solve new fertility problems. C. E. Sommers. il Suc Farm 67:32 D '69
Rebuild worn-out soils. R. A. Miller. Horticulture 47:34+ F '69
See also
Fertilizers and manures

SOIL fertilization. See Fertilizers and manures—Spray applications

SOIL mechanics
Sewers need better soils engineering. J. S. Ward. il Am City 84:72-4 Jl '69

SOIL pollution
Land pollution: a heap of trouble. il Sr Schol 95:10-11 O 27 '69
Soil pollutants and soil animals. C. A. Edwards. il Sci Am 220:88-92+ Ap '69

SOIL salinity. See Soils, Salts in

SOIL sterilization. See Soil disinfection

SOIL testing. See Soils—Analysis

SOILS
Black and crumbling. A. A. German. Org Gard & Farm 16:46 O '69
What's new. See Issues of Successful farming
See also
Compost
Erosion
Fertilizers and manures
Gardening—Soil preparation
Loess

Analysis
Sewers need better soils engineering. J. S. Ward. il Am City 84:72-4 Jl '69
Sterile soil from Antarctica; organic analysis. N. H. Horowitz and others. bibliog il Science 164:1054-6 My 30 '69

Composition
See Soil fertility

Mineral content
Basalt rock, an untapped mineral supply. J. I. Rodale. Org Gard & Farm 16:81-3 Je '69
Can rock powders supply soil minerals? J. I. Rodale. Org Gard & Farm 16:81-4 My '69
Minerals make the difference. D. Schroeder. Org Gard & Farm 16:94-7 Ap '69
Subsoils can enrich the land. J. I. Rodale. il Org Gard & Farm 16:80-1+ F '69

SOILS—*Continued*

Testing
See Soils—Analysis

Weathering
Chemical weathering in central Iceland: an analog of pre-Silurian weathering. J. L. Cawley and others. bibliog il Science 165: 391-2 Jl 25 '69

Antarctic Regions
Sterile soil from Antarctica: organic analysis. N. H. Horowitz and others. bibliog il Science 164:1054-6 My 30 '69

Iceland
Chemical weathering in central Iceland: an analog of pre-Silurian weathering. J. L. Cawley and others. bibliog il Science 165: 391-2 Jl 25 '69

SOILS, Freezing of. See Frozen ground

SOILS, Liming of
    See also
Lime

SOILS, Minerals in. See Soils—Mineral content

SOILS, Salts in
Desalting California; San Joaquin master drain controversy. F. M. Stead. il Environ 11:2-10 Je '69

SOILS, Worn-out. See Soil deterioration

SOJKA, Gary A. and others
Energy flux and membrane synthesis in photosynthetic bacteria. bibliog Science 166: 113-15 O 3 '69

SOKA Gakkai (sect)
Lotus power. il Newsweek 75:46 Ja 19 '70
Soka Gakkai: Japan's military Buddhists, by N. S. Brannen. Review
    Commonweal 90:349-50 Je 6 '69. M. Gallagher

SOKOLOV, Grigorii
Youngest ambassador. H. Kupferberg. Atlan 223:114-16 Je '69

SOKOLOW, Anna
Anna Sokolow dance company, Brooklyn academy of music. M. Marks. Dance Mag 43:76+ Ja '69

SOKOLSKI, Ken N.
Annotated octopus; with biographical sketch, and notes, ed. by J. Lettvin. por Natur Hist 78:6, 10-12+ N '69

SOLANDT, O. M.
Control of technology. Science 165:445 Ag 1 '69

SOLAR corona. See Sun—Corona

SOLAR eclipses. See Eclipses, Solar

SOLAR flares
Observing solar flares by radio. C. H. Hossfield. il Sky & Tel 37:254-8 Ap '69
Solar flares: the cosmic fire that threatens space explorers. J. T. Temple. il Sci Digest 66:30-4 S '69
Solar superflare? Sky & Tel 38:300 N '69
X-ray line and continuum spectra of solar flares and 0.5 to 8.5 angstroms. J. F. Meekins and others; reply. F. W. Lytle. bibliog il Science 165:416 Jl 25 '69

SOLAR furnaces
Curve to capture the sun; Odeillo in the Pyrenees. il Life 66:80-2 My 23 '69
Hot spot in the Pyrenees; solar ovens for thermal power. Sci N 95:211 Mr 1 '69

SOLAR magnetic fields. See Magnetic fields (cosmic physics)

SOLAR neutrinos. See Neutrinos

SOLAR observatories. See Astronomical observatories

SOLAR ovens. See Solar furnaces

SOLAR radiation
From sun to moon. il Sci N 97:35 Ja 10 '70
Prodigal sun. il Time 93:45-6 My 23 '69
Solar radiation profiles in openings in canopies of aspen and oak. P. C. Miller. bibliog il Science 164:308-9 Ap 18 '69
Ultraviolet astronomy. L. Goldberg. il Sci Am 220:92-102 bibliog(p 144) Je '69
    See also
Birds, Effect of solar radiation on
Reptiles, Effect of solar radiation on
Solar flares
Solar furnaces
Sunspots

Measurement
Apollo 11 solar wind composition experiment: first results. F. Bühler and others. bibliog il Science 166:1502-3 D 19 '69

SOLAR rotation. See Sun—Rotation

SOLAR system
Future of lunar studies: symposium. il Bul Atom Sci 25:45-58+ S '69

Lunar samples also may offer clues to origin of solar system. E. J. Bulban. Aviation W 92:22 Ja 12 '70

SOLAR telescope. See Telescope

SOLAR winds. See Solar radiation

SOLDER and soldering
Now you can solder galvanized pipe. J. Hand. il Pop Sci 195:153 S '69
Solder in a steel-wool blanket. R. M. Benrey. il Pop Sci 194:214-15 Mr '69

SOLDERING apparatus
Weller's new soldering gun: choose your head. H. Luckett. il Pop Sci 195:32 S '69

SOLDIERS
Can love outwait the army? questions and answers. A. Wood. Seventeen 28:336+ Ag '69

SOLDIERS, Negro. See United States—Army —Negroes

SOLDIERS families. See Service mens families

SOLDIERS publications. See Service men's publications

SOLE (fish)
    See also
Cookery—Fish

SOLERI, Paolo
Spacious living in a heap. il pors Life 67: 102-5 D 5 '69

SOLID propellant rockets. See Rocket engines

SOLID vinyl siding. See Siding (building)

SOLID wastes. See Refuse and refuse disposal

SOLIDS
Nuclear tracks in solids. R. L. Fleischer and others. il Sci Am 220:30-9 Je '69
Shock waves in solids. R. K. Linde and R. C. Crewdson. il Sci Am 220:82-91 My '69
    See also
Exciton theory
Thin films

Poetry
Dance of the solids; excerpts from Midpoint and other poems. J. Updike. Sci Am 220: 130-1 Ja '69

SOLIE, Iris
Drew middle school: it shouts nontraditional. Sr Schol 94:School Teach 20-1 My 9 '69

SOLIS-COHEN, Lita H.
Living with antiques. Antiques 95:832-7 Je '69

SOLITUDE
Alone is beautiful; views of eight moving picture actors and actresses. il McCalls 97: 48-55 Ja '70

SOLLEN, Robert H.
Anguish on a hilltop. Nation 209:336-9 O 6 '69

SOLLEY, Paul M.
Extra pay for extra duty. Todays Ed 58:54 My '69

SOLOMON, Barbara Probst
Back to Madrid; excerpts. por Harper 239:76-89 Ag '69

SOLOMON, Eric
San Francisco state. A. J. Langguth. por Harper 239:99-100+ S '69

SOLOMON, Neil
Dieting by computer. G. Tully. Harp Baz 103:154 Ja '70

SOLOMON ISLANDS
Sailing through the Solomon Islands. S. A. Simpson. il Travel 132:66-71 S '69

SOLOMON R. Guggenheim museum, New York
Paintings descending a ramp; Peggy Guggenheim collection at Uncle Solomon's museum. G. Glueck. il N Y Times Mag p36-8+ Ja 19 '69

SOLOTAROFF, Theodore
Holden Caulfield meets the movement. New Repub 160:23-6 My 10 '69
Journey of Philip Roth. Atlan 223:64-72 Ap '69

SOLTI, Georg
Into the fray. il por Time 93:70 Ap 11 '69
Parallel careers of Georg Solti; with discography. G. Movshon. pors Hi Fi 19:66-71 O '69
Solti, at last. R. C. Marsh. pors Hi Fi 19: MA26+ Ap '69

SOLUBILITY
Solubility in water of normal C_9 and C_{10} alkane hydrocarbons. C. McAuliffe. bibliog il Science 163:478-9 Ja 31 '69

SOLUTION (chemistry)
Potassium-sodium ratios in aqueous solutions and coexisting silicate melts. J. B. Gammon and others. bibliog il Science 163: 179-81 Ja 10 '69
    See also
Colloids
Electrolysis

SOLVENTS
Safe use of products containing solvents. il
Good H 169:145 Ag '69
   See also
Benzene
Carbon tetrachloride
SOLZHENIȚSYN, Aleksandr Isaevich
Easter procession; story. Time 93:28-9 Mr 21
'69
Right hand; story. por Atlan 223:45-9 My '69
   about
Courageous defender. por Time 94:34 N 21
'69
Invitation to leave. Newsweek 74:66 D 8 '69
One day in the life; expulsion from the
writers union. por Newsweek 74:57-8+ N
24 '69
Open letter to the Union of Soviet writers.
C. B. Ashanin. Chr Cent 86:1617-18 D 17
'69
Silence for Solzhenitsyn. Time 94:36 N 14
'69
Solzhenitsyn's Cancer ward. R. Littell. por
Newsweek 73:58-9 Mr 17 '69
Threat of exile. Time 94:49+ D 5 '69
SOMALIA
   Politics and government
Death in Las Anod. Newsweek 74:65 O 27
'69
Death of a president. Time 94:36 O 24 '69
Somalia turns left. Newsweek 74:53 N 3 '69
SOMAN, Florence Jane
My secret, your secret; story. Good H 169:
92-3 D '69
Something wonderful; story. Good H 169:84-
5 S '69
SOMATIC cells. See Cells
SOMATIC poetry. See Poetry
SOMATOLOGY
Secrets that dead men's bones tell. S. S. Mc
Kern and T. W. McKern. il Sci Digest 66:30-
4 Ag '69
   Bibliography
Physical anthropology. D. Polacheck. bibliog
il Wilson Lib Bul 44:178-83 O '69
SOMAYAJULU, B. L. K. and others
Man-made carbon-14 in deep Pacific waters:
transport by biological skeletal material.
bibliog Science 166:1397-9 D 12 '69
SOME of my best friends are spies; drama.
See Dias, E. J.
SOME Wallace Stevens; story. See Shainberg,
L.
SOMEONE special; story. See Regnier, N.
SOMEONE'S comin' hungry; drama. See Im-
brie, M. and Selden, N.
SOMER, Hilde
Hilde Somer: new performances, old tradi-
tions; interview, ed. by S. Fleming. pors
Hi Fi 19:MA28-9 Mr '69
   about
Recordings. M. Mayer. Esquire 72:52+ Ag '69
SOMERLOTT, Robert
Fiction's all-seeing I. Writer 82:11-15 F '69
SOMERS, Florence
Magic kingdom is on the way. Redbook 133:
141 Ag '69
New movies. See issues of Redbook
SOMERTON, Wilbur J.
Universities: industry links raise conflict of
interest issue. J. Walsh. Science 164:411-12
Ap 25 '69
SOMETHING else press. See Private presses
SOMETHING to grow on; story. See Stetson,
N.
SOMETHING wonderful; story. See Soman,
F. J.
SOMMER, André Dupont-. See Dupont-Som-
mer, A.
SOMMER, Frederick
Frederic Sommer. M. Mann. Pop Phot 65:
82-3+ O '69
SOMMER, John J.
Work as a therapeutic goal: union-manage-
ment clinical contributions to a mental
health program. Ment Hy 53:263-8 Ap '69
SOMMER, Robert
Classrooms are for students. Am Ed 5:18-21
Je '69
Planning notplace for nobody; excerpt from
Personal space: the behavioral basis of
design. Sat R 52:67-9 Ap 5 '69
SOMMER, Susan T.
L'Ormindo, a delicious 325-year-old operatic
hit. Hi Fi 19:88+ Je '69
SOMMERFELD, Arnold
Atomic physicists meet for Arnold Sommer-
feld centennial. I. C. Percival and H. H.
Stroke. il pors Phys Today 22:99+ F '69

SOMMERS, Kathryn M.
279 editors looking for writers. Writers Di-
gest 49:48-51+ S '69
SOMNAMBULISM
Is there a sleepwalker in the house? I. Taves.
il Todays Health 47:40-1+ My '69; Same abr
with title Twilight world of the sleepwalker.
Read Digest 95:95-8 Ag '69
SONAR
Fish in the dark; use of water cavitation
by penguins, seals and sea lions. il Sci
Digest 66:74-5 D'69
   See also
Echolocation (physiology)
SONATA
Sonata-rondo, the formulation of a theoret-
ical concept in the 18th and 19th centuries.
M. S. Cole. bibliog f Mus Q 55:180-92 Ap
'69
SONATAS
   See also
Phonograph records—Sonatas
SONDERMEYER, J. C.   See Kamp, F. S. jt.
auth.
SONG of Solomon. See Bible—Old Testament—
Song of Solomon
SONG of songs. See Bible—Old Testament—
Song of Solomon
SONG writers. See Composers
SONG writing. See Composition (music)
SONGBIRDS. See Birds
SONGBOOKS
Books to read: songs to sing. R. Gagliardo.
il PTA Mag 63:10-11 Ja '69
SONGMY Massacre. See Vietnamese war, 1957-
—Atrocities—Songmy massacre
SONGMY massacre investigation. See Govern-
ment investigations—Songmy massacre
SONGS
Songs by Verdi and Wagner. G. Jellinek. il
Opera N 33:24-5 Mr 29 '69
   See also
Childrens songs
Copyright—Music
Madrigals
Phonograph records—Songs
SONGS, American
Categoric past, the personal present. F.
Hogan. House B 111:124-7 Je '69
   See also
Childrens songs
Star spangled banner (song)
SONGS, French
Baby Jane; Je t'aime. Newsweek 75:61 Ja
5 '70
Chansons of Matthaeus Pipelare. R. Cross.
bibliog f il Mus Q 55:500-20 O '69
SONGS, German
Lieder masters: records of songs by H. Wolf.
Discus. Harper 239:101-2 Jl '69
SONGS, Negro. See Negro songs
SONGS, Popular. See Music, Popular (songs,
etc)
SONGS of birds. See Birds—Song
SONIC boom
Boeing, General electric study boomless
transonic transport. Aviation W 91:29 D 22
'69
Concorde challenge. L. Miller. Sci N 95:294
Mr 22 '69
Less noise; interagency review of Super-
sonic transport program. New Repub 160:
10 Mr 8 '69
Shock-repellent boom remedy disputed. il
Aviation W 90:34 F 3 '69
Sonic booms from supersonic transport. K. D.
Kryter. bibliog il Science 163:359-67 Ja 24
'69; Discussion. 164:129, 905 Ap 11, My 23
'69; Nation 208:453-4 Ap 14 '69
Supersonic boom. il Life 67:51-2 N 7 '69

   Anecdotes, facetiae, satire, etc.
Scram gets green light; Spiro Agnew to rise
at Marshgrass. T. Meehan. New Yorker
44:32-3 F 15 '69
SONIC boom simulators. See Simulators
SONIC motors. See Electric motors
SONICS. See Sound waves
SONNABEND, Roger P.
Rocking the boat. pors Newsweek 73:85+
My 19 '69
SONNENBERG, Maurice
Turquoise trail. Harp Baz 102:60+ Ja '69
SONORAN DESERT NATIONAL PARK (pro-
posed) See National parks and reserves—
United States
SONS and fathers. See Parent-child relation-
ship
SONS and mothers. See Parent-child relation-
ship
SONS of composers. See Children of composers

SONS of freedom (sect) See Dukhobors
SONS of the desert (Laurel and Hardy club)
See Moving picture societies
SONTAG, Frederick
Roman Catholic: visible and invisible; address,
October 1969. America 121:298-301 O 11 '69
SONTAG, Susan
Letter from Sweden. Ramp Mag 8:23-38 Jl '69
Some thoughts on the right way (for us) to
love the Cuban revolution. pors Ramp Mag
7:6+ Ap '69

about

Age of allegiance. E. Capouya. por Sat R 52:
29 My 3 '69
Consciousness confrontation. R. Sklar. Na-
tion 208:704-5 Je 2 '69
Dark lady of tuned-in. por Time 93:108+ My
9 '69
Peripatetic sycophant. Nat R 21:319 Ap 8 '69
Please don't eat the cannibals. M. Tucker.
Commonweal 91:306-7 D 5 '69
Susan sings in a lonely thicket. J. Leonard.
Life 66:12 Mr 28 '69
Susan Sontag and the question of the new.
R. Gilman. New Repub 160:23-6+ My 3 '69
SONY corporation. See Electronic apparatus
industry and trade—Japan
SOOD, Nesrey
Case of Private Sood. B. Farrell. Life 66:12A
F 28 '69
SOPHOCLES
Electra. Criticism
Sat R 52:32 Ag 23 '69
SOPKIN, Charles
What a tough young kid with *fegataccio*
can do on Madison avenue. N Y Times
Mag p32-4+ Ja 26 '69
SOPWITH Hall; story. See Warner, S. T.
SORAUER, Helly
How I conquered the Australian Alps. Travel
& Camera 32:31-2 My '69
SOREL, Edward
Sorel's bestiary; with commentary. il Ramp
Mag 7:79-86 Ja 25 '69
SORENSEN, Raymond A. See Baranger, M. jt.
auth.
SORENSEN, Robert
Dissatisfaction but not repudiation. PTA
Mag 64:3-4 D '69
SORENSEN, Theodore Chaikin
Booksellers' stake in intellectual freedom;
excerpts from address. Pub W 195:61 Je 16
'69
Did Chappaquiddick finish the Democrats?
por Look 33:84+ N 4 '69
First hundred days of Richard M. Nixon. Sat
R 52:17-19 My 17 '69
Israel under siege. Holiday 46:90-1 D '69
Report from Moscow. Holiday 46:12-13 Ag
'69
Time bomb near the heart of the Nation. Sat
R 52:33-6 Ap 12 '69
View from Allenby bridge. Sat R 52:23-5+
O 4 '69

about

Ask not what Ted Sorensen can do for
you . . . D. Halberstam. Harper 239:90-2
N '69
SORENSEN, Virginia
Childhood is a strange book; excerpts from
address, 1969. PTA Mag 64:13-15 N '69
SORGHUM
See also
Milo
SORIA, Dorle J.
Artist life. See issues of High fidelity incor-
porating Musical America
Music's uncommon market. Sat R 52:62-3
My 17 '69
SORKIN, Alan L.
American Indians industrialize to combat
poverty; excerpt from Manpower and in-
dustrial development programs for Indian
Americans. bibliog f Mo Labor R 92:19-25
Mr '69
SOROKIN, Peter
Organic lasers; with biographical sketch. Sci
Am 220:12, 30-40 F '69
SORORITIES, High school. See High school
fraternities
SORREL
What's cooking? R. Lewis. il Org Gard &
Farm 16:116+ Ja '69
SORRELLS, A. R.
Great promise of zero G. Space World F-10-
70:16-25 O '69
SORRELLS, Helen
I will not ask the tree; poem. Chr Cent 86:711
My 21 '69
Thornton crossing; poem. Commonweal 90:
266 My 16 '69

SORRENTINO, Gilbert
Handbook of versification; poem. Poetry 115:
161 D '69
Poem; Living friends live. Poetry 113:409 Mr
'69
SORROW
See also
Bereavement
Crying
SOSNOFF, Martin T.
Stock trends. por Forbes 104:104-5 Ag 15 '69
SOSS manufacturing company
SOS—no help needed. S. Margetts. Duns R
93:53+ Ja '69
SOTHEBY and company
Rivals. il Newsweek 74:74+ Ag 18 '69
SOUFFLÉS
Just a little something I whipped up. il Mc-
Calls 96:106-7+ My '69
Lustrous binge: ten chocolate soufflés. G.
Bradshaw. Vogue 155:178+ Ja 1 '70
Soufflé extraspecial. J. Hewitt. il N Y Times
Mag p 124+ N 30 '69
Soufflé mixture rolled and filled. il Sunset
143:156+ N '69
Sour cream apple soufflé. il Sunset 142:177
Mr '69
SOUL culture. See Negroes—Culture
SOUL food. See Cookery, American
SOUL music. See Jazz music
SOUL Santa. See Santa Claus
SOUL toys. See Toys
SOUND
Acoustics. L. L. Beranek. bibliog il Phys
Today 22:47-53 N '69
See also
Acoustics, Architectural
Hearing
Music—Acoustics and physics
Noise

Apparatus

Build ANOD, an audible noise override. R. W.
Bailey. il Radio-Electr 40:58 Ag '69
Dolby noise-reduction system, its impact on
recording. J. Eargle. il Electr World 81:32-4
My '69
EW lab tested. See issues of Electronics world
Focus on sound. See issues of Popular pho-
tography
Four-channel audio mixer. J. Jacques. il Ra-
dio-Electr 40:32-4 F '69
Mixing sound for fun. C. Schultz. il Radio-
Electr 41:59-60 Ja '70
Sound for the 70's. H. Fantel. il Opera N
34:14-15 N 1 '69
Sound-with-sound mixer; with pre-record
monitoring. D. DeMaw. il Pop Electr 30:
59-61+ Mr '69
Wein Sound trigger. P. Farber. il Travel &
Camera 32:47-8 F '69
You take care of them. they'll entertain
you; or, How to keep your music-picture-
sound equipment in shape. il Redbook 133:
51+ Ag '69
See also
Amplifiers
Magnetic recorders and recording

Measurement
See Sound measurement

Physiological effects

Does rock music damage hearing? il Good H
168:208 Ap '69
See also
Fishes, Effect of sound on

Recording and reproducing

Dolby noise-reduction system, its impact on
recording. J. Eargle. il Electr World 81:32-
4 My '69
Focus on sound. See issues of Popular pho-
tography
Lawyer tries a world of sound; Town sound
studios, Englewood, N.J. il Ebony 24:73-4+
My '69
Sound advice. M. A. Matzkin. See issues of
Modern photography
See also
Audio fairs
Magnetic recorders and recording
Moving picture sound recording
Recording instruments
Sound—Stereophonic recording and reproduc-
ing

Stereophonic recording and reproducing

And now, quadrisonic. Time 94:55+ S 26 '69
Four-channel sound is here, sort of. L. Berg-
er. Sat R 52:77 N 29 '69
Four-channel stereo. W. A. Stocklin. Electr
World 82:6 D '69

SOUND—Stereophonic recording and reproducing—*Continued*
Now, four-channel stereo. L. Zide. Am Rec G 36:74-5 S '69
Ping-ping-pong-pong; four-channel stereo. R. Long. il Hi Fi 19:62-3+ S '69
See also
Magnetic recorders and recording—Stereophonic recorders
Stereophonic sound systems

Transmission thru water
Scuba/com; now you can talk underwater. T. Irwin. il Pop Sci 195:120-1 Ag '69
SOUND control. See Noise control
SOUND equipment. See Sound—Apparatus
SOUND measurement
Loudspeakers, can we measure what we hear? V. Brociner. il Electr World 81:25-9+ Mr '69
Low-noise receiver performance measurements. L. R. Bishop. il Electr World 81:38-9+ Mr '69
See also
Decibels
SOUND perception
Auditory sequence: confusion of patterns other than speech or music. R. M. Warren and others. bibliog Science 164:586-7 My 2 '69
SOUND production by animals
Pop goes the weasel, pffff goes the whale. W. A. Watkins. il Natur Hist 78:20+ My '69
Vocal tract limitations on the vowel repertoires of rhesus monkey and other non-human primates. P. H. Lieberman and others. bibliog il Science 164:1185-7 Je 6 '69
See also
Animal sounds
Insect sounds
SOUND waves
Cymatics: the sculpture of vibrations. H. Jenny. il UNESCO Courier 22:4-12+ D '69
Sound velocity in carbon suboxide. J. K. Hancock and J. C. Decius. il Science 164:587-8 My 2 '69
See also
Ultrasonic waves
SOUNDING and soundings
First deep-sea sounding. R. S. Dietz and H. J. Knebel. il Sea Front 15:212-18 Jl '69
See also
Depth indicators
SOUNDPRINTING
See also
Voiceprints
SOUNDS
Hark, hark, what lark! J. L. O'Neill. Am Home 72:160 O '69
See also
Phonograph records—Sounds
SOUPS
Beautiful black bean soup; with recipes. E. Alston. il Look 33:54-5 My 13 '69
Cold-weather soups. il Redbook 132:98-9+ F '69
Eat; soupmaking. M. Cantwell. Mlle 69:94+ My '69
Gastronomy recalled; with recipes. M. F. K. Fisher. New Yorker 45:154+ S 20 '69
Great soup secret; making stock. il Sunset 142:86-9 Mr '69
It's earth apple soup. It's Swiss. il Sunset 142:201 My '69
Soups and chowders; prize tested recipes. il Bet Hom & Gard 47:99-100 F '69
Spring greens in a soup. Sunset 142:179 Ap '69
Summer soups that keep their cool; with recipes. il McCalls 96:82-3 Ag '69
This tasty soup is leek. il Sunset 143:218 O '69
Tomato soup forever! C. Claiborne. il N Y Times Mag p24 Jl 6 '69
Two green soups: cress or cucumber. Sunset 143:113 Ag '69
Two savory supper soups. Sunset 143:200 O '69
What's cooking? Org Gard & Farm 16:84-6 My '69
See also
Chowder
SOUR gum trees. See Tupelos
SOUR or suntanned, it makes no difference; story. See Kaplan, J.
SOURDOUGH. See Dough
SOUSA, John Philip
Authentic Sousa performances from the march king himself. R. D. Darrell. Hi Fi 19:113 S '69
SOUSA, Stan
Public golf courses, with a difference. Parks & Rec 4:49-50+ My '69
SOUTH, Joe
Deep South. il por Newsweek 74:82 Ag 18 '69

SOUTH
Southern violence. S. Hackney. bibliog f il Am Hist R 74:906-25 F '69
See also
Education—Southern states
Express highways—Southern states
Gulf states
Hunting—Southern states
Law—Southern states
Negroes—Southern states

Description and travel
Winter sunshine at bargain rates. N. D. Ford. il Har Yrs 9:6-12 bibliog(p 15) O '69

History
Jefferson renounced: natural rights in the Old South. G. A. Cardwell. Yale R 58:388-407 Mr '69
Southern tradition at bay, by R. M. Weaver. Review
Nat R 21:340-1 Ap 8 '69. J. Hart
See also
Negroes—History
Reconstruction (Civil war)

Industries
See also
Cotton industry and trade

Politics
Nixon strategy. K. Crawford. Newsweek 74:58 D 8 '69
Southern strategy and southern stigma; controversy over Judge C. Haynsworth. il Life 67:38 N 28 '69
South's changing politics. il U S News 66:32-4 Mr 24 '69
T.R.B. from Washington; Nixon's allies. New Repub 160:6 Ja 25 '69

Race problems
See also
Negroes—Southern states

Religious institutions and affairs
[Harry Golden column] H. Golden. Nation 208:602-3 My 12 '69

Social history
See also
Slavery—United States

Social life and customs
Growing up in America. S. Wilkinson. il Mlle 68:208+ Ap '69
SOUTH, University of the. See University of the South. Sewanee. Tenn.
SOUTH AFRICA
See also
Aviation—South Africa
Birth control—South Africa
Botany—South Africa
Collective settlements—South Africa
Education—South Africa
Elections—South Africa
Gold mines and mining—South Africa
Johannesburg
Justice, Administration of—South Africa
Kalahari Desert
Kruger National Park
Political parties—South Africa
Television broadcasting—South Africa
United Nations—South Africa

Description and travel
South Africa: it could have been Arcadia. R. Atcheson. il Holiday 46:32-3+ N '69

Economic relations
Apartheid's empire. I. Robertson. il Nation 208:596-7+ My 12 '69

Intellectual life
Forbidden dialogue: reprint. L. Nkosi. UNESCO Courier 22:69 Ag '69

Native races
See also
South Africa—Race problems

Politics and government
See also
Political parties—South Africa

Race problems
Apartheid 1948-69: the politics of dehumanization. L. Rubin. Chr Cent 86:947-50 Jl 16 '69
Apartheid verified. Chr Cent 86:970 Jl 23 '69
Forbidden dialogue: reprint. L. Nkosi. UNESCO Courier 22:69 Ag '69
Immorality: an Afrikaner view. America 120:579 My 17 '69
Land of afternoon, by L. Sowden. Review
Chr Cent 86:958 Jl 16 '69. W. A. Scofield

SOUTH AFRICA—Race problems—*Continued*
Rugby and apartheid. C. Northcott. Chr Cent
86:1507 N 26 '69

Sniping at Springboks, a new British game.
E. Huxley. Nat R 21:1265-6 D 16 '69
  See also
East Indians in South Africa
United Nations—South Africa
United Nations—Special committee on the
  policies of apartheid of the government of
  the Republic of South Africa
United Nations trust fund for South Africa

SOUTH AFRICA-United States air agreement.
  See Aviation—International aspects
SOUTH AFRICAN culture. See South Africa—
  Intellectual life
SOUTH AMERICA
  See also
Horn, Cape

Commerce
  See Latin America—Commerce

Description and travel
New trails through South America. T. J.
  King. il Travel 131:62-5 Je '69
Spreading out in South America; Amerbus-
  pass. L. Zalamea. il Travel 132:58-9 O '69

Economic conditions
  See Latin America—Economic conditions

History
  See also
Incas

Native races
  See Indians of South America

Politics
  See Latin America—Politics

SOUTH AMERICA in art
Dong Kingman in South America; commen-
  tary. N. Kent. il Am Artist 33:28-33+ Ap
  '69
SOUTH AMERICAN Indians. See Indians of
  South America
SOUTH ARABIA (Federation) See Southern
  Yemen
SOUTH CAROLINA
South Carolina: the movement finally arrives;
  activities in Beaufort, Charleston, Denmark.
  D. Nolan. Nation 208:654-6 My 26 '69
  See also
Trials—South Carolina
Water supply—South Carolina

Description and travel
South Carolina's treasure chest. P. Trescott.
  il Travel 131:50-3+ F '69
South Carolina's Washington trail. J. L. Truluck. il Travel 132:68-70 D '69

Historic houses, etc.
History in houses; Walnut grove plantation
  near Spartanburg, S.C. F. Coleman. il
  Antiques 96:222-7 Ag '69

Race problems
U.S. journal: Sumter County, Turks, or,
  people of Turkish descent. C. Trillin. New
  Yorker 45:104+ Mr 8 '69
SOUTH CAROLINA. State college. Orangeburg
Education of Carla ManCari. W. Peters. il
  Good H 169:90-1+ S '69
SOUTH DAKOTA
  See also
Black Hills
Hunting—South Dakota

Antiquities
  See Indians of North America—Antiquities—South Dakota

History
Dakota boyhood. J. E. Fraser. il Am Heritage
  20:81-8 D '68
SOUTH FLORIDA. University, Tampa
U. of South Florida trains generalists in ger-
  ontology. il Aging 173:6-7 Mr '69
SOUTH KOREA. See Korea (Republic)
SOUTH Pacific; musical comedy. See Musical
  comedies, revues, etc.—Criticisms, plots, etc.
SOUTH PACIFIC commission
President appoints Mr Taylor to South Pa-
  cific commission. Dept State Bul 61:421 N
  17 '69
SOUTH POLE
  See also
Antarctic exploration

SOUTH SEA ISLANDS. See Oceania
SOUTH street. See New York (city)—Streets
SOUTH street seaport museum. See New York
  ((city)—Galleries and museums
SOUTH VIETNAMESE political prisoners. See
  Political prisoners
SOUTH YUBA trail. See Trails
SOUTHAMPTON insurrection. 1831
Nat Turner: fanatic or prophet? Will the real
  Nat Turner please stand up? il Sr Schol
  94:12-13 F 14 '69
SOUTHEAST ASIA. See Asia. Southeastern:
  Asia. Southern
SOUTHEAST ASIA treaty organization
Dwindling cornucopia; annual meeting. News-
  week 73:55 Je 2 '69
Eisenhower era in Asia. A. J. Cottrell. bib-
  liog f Cur Hist 57:84-7+ Ag '69
Fifteenth anniversary of SEATO; statement.
  W. P. Rogers. Dept State Bul 61:284 S 29 '69
SEATO council of ministers meets at
  Bangkok; statement, with text of final
  communique. W. P. Rogers. Dept State Bul
  60:477-81 Je 9 '69
Southeast Asia collective defense treaty; ex-
  cerpts, September 8, 1954. Cur Hist 57:113 Ag
  '69
Whatever happened to SEATO? U S News
  67:6 Ag 4 '69
SOUTHEASTERN conference football. See
  Football
SOUTHEASTERN MASSACHUSETTS techno-
  logical institute, North Dartmouth
Semper fi at SMU. Newsweek 74:91-2 D 8 '69
SOUTHEASTERN regional ballet festival. See
  Dance festivals
SOUTHERN ASIA. See Asia, Southern
SOUTHERN Baptist convention. See Baptists
  in the United States
SOUTHERN Baptists. See Baptists in the
  United States
SOUTHERN CALIFORNIA Edison company
California Edison pulls out the plug. Bsns W
  p44 My 24 '69
SOUTHERN California university, Los Angeles
Bowker to publish NICEM media indexes.
  Pub W 195:64 Ap 28 '69
Getting by nicely without O.J; sophomore
  quarterback J. Jones. P. Putnam. il Sports
  Illus 31:32-4+ S 29 '69

Ethel Percy Andrus gerontology center
USC gerontology center to get $2 million
  from NRTA-AARP fund. Aging 170:16 D
  '68

SOUTHERN Christian leadership conference
Blacks wrap up slice of action at food
  chains; Operation Breadbasket's boycott of
  Chicago A&P stores. il Bsns W p 162-3+
  Ap 26 '69
I'm dreaming of a black Christmas; SCLC's
  Operation Breadbasket. il Ebony 25:114-
  16+ N '69
Jesse Jackson: black hope, white hope. J.
  Pekkanen. il Life 67:67-72+ N 21 '69
Jesse Jackson: heir to Dr King? head of Op-
  eration Breadbasket, in Chicago. R. Levine.
  Harper 238:58-64+ Mr '69
Ralph Abernathy, the man who fights to
  keep King's dream alive. C. C. Douglas.
  il Ebony 25:40-2+ Ja '70
Strike gains clout; ALF-CIO and UAW help
  Charleston's Negro hospital workers. il
  Bsns W p39 My 17 '69
Union teams up with black power; alliance
  of civil rights and labor organizations be-
  hind the Charleston walkout. il Bsns W
  p22-4 Ap 5 '69
SOUTHERN conference educational fund
Draft vs. social justice. Nation 209:461 N 3
  '69
SOUTHERN cookery. See Cookery, American
SOUTHERN education reporting service
Mission accomplished. Newsweek 74:38 Ag 11
  '69
SOUTHERN ILLINOIS university

Libraries
More frontlogs; letter to the editor. R. O.
  Laythe. Library J 95:13-14 Ja 1 '70
SOUTHERN mountaineers. See Mountaineers
  (southern states)
SOUTHERN ocean racing conference. See
  Yacht racing
SOUTHERN poetry. See American poetry
SOUTHERN Presbyterian church. See Presby-
  terian church in the United States (South)
SOUTHERN states. See South
SOUTHERN university and agricultural and
  mechanical college, Baton Rouge, La.
From North to South; students riot. il News-
  week 73:76+ My 26 '69

SOUTHERN YEMEN
Aden and South Arabia. R. E. Thoman. bibliog f il Cur Hist 58:27-33+ Ja '70
SOUTHLAND corporation. See Seven-Eleven food stores
SOUTHWEST
See also
Hunting—Southwestern states

Description and travel
Desert sun circle. D. Kelly. il Travel 131:62-4 Mr '69
SOUTHWEST airmotive company
Big D's big bash. il Flying 84:133 My '69
SOUTHWEST archeological center. See United States—National park service
SOUTHWEST water plan. See Colorado River
SOUTHWESTERN regional ballet festival. See Dance festivals
SOUTHWICK, Albert B.
Another look at Israel. Commonweal 89:516-18; 90:55 Ja 24, Mr 28 '69
SOUTHWICK, Louise H.
Homestead; interview. New Yorker 45:26-8 Ag 9 '69
SOUTHWORTH, Donovan A.
Mechanical filters. bibliog por Electr World 81:56-7 Ap '69
SOUTHWORTH, William D.
School board, 1980. Clear House 44:131-3 N '69
SOUTINE, Chaim
Form and frenzy; exhibition at the Perls gallery. K. G. Kline. il Art N 68:50-1+ D '69
SOUVANNA Phouma, prince of Laos
More aid to Laos? A report on what U.S. is doing there. il por U S News 67:16 O 20 '69
Tiger in the pagoda. il por Time 94:26 S 26 '69
SOUVENIR spoons. See Spoons
SOUVENIRS
Crud art; New York souvenirs. J. P. Goude and J. Lagarrigue. il Esquire 72:134-9 O '69
State of taste; souvenirs. R. Lynes. Art in Am 57:23 S '69
Wayside treasures. R. P. MacFall. il Nat Wildlife 7:43-7 Ag '69
SOUZA, Wladimir Alvez de. See Alvez de Souza, W.
SOUZAY, Gérard
Week of song as well as singers. I. Kolodin. Sat R 52:58+ N 22 '69
SOVEREIGN immunity. See Privileges and immunities
SOVEREIGNTY
Hands across the ice; sovereignty in the Arctic. R. F. Neill. Commonweal 91:302-3 D 5 '69
See also
State. The
SOVEREIGNTY of God. See God
SOVIET-AMERICAN arms control talks. See Strategic arms limitation talks
SOVIET education. See Education—Russia
SOVIET Union. See Russia
SOVIET writers. See Authors, Russian
SOVIET youth. See Youth—Russia
SOWDEN, Dora
Building a new dance in a new country. Dance Mag 43:62-4 Ja '69
SOWERS, Robert
New stained glass in Germany. Craft Horiz 29:14-21+ My '69
SOWING. See Seeding
SOX, Ronnie
Sox & Martin. B. Lang. il pors Hot Rod 22:52-4 F '69
SOYA-paste mold. See Fungi
SOYBEANS
Can we put the brakes on our soybean surplus? Farm J 93:33 Ap '69
How the winners raise soybeans. Suc Farm 67:51 Je '69
Soybean champions crack 100-bu. barrier; National soybean yield contest. il Farm J 93:35 F '69
See also
American soybean association
Feeding and feeding stuffs—Soybeans

Cultivation
How the champs grew their 100-bu. beans. C. E. Ball. il Farm J 93:52X+ Mr '69
Now: give soybeans a weed-free start. D. Seim. il Farm J 93:32-3+ Ap '69

Diseases and pests
Weed control for corn and soybeans. Suc Farm 67:64+ F '69

SOYINKA, Akinwande Oluwole. See Soyinka, W.
SOYINKA, Wole
African genesis. M. Tucker. Nation 209:510-12 N 10 '69
Trial of Wole Soyinka. C. R. Larson. Nation 209:259-60 S 15 '69
SOYUZ flights. See Space flight—Manned flights—Soyuz flights, 1969
SPACE (architecture)
Break out of the box; supergraphics. V. D. Hahn and A. C. Borg. il Am Home 72:55-63 Ap '69
Decorating to make the most of space; symposium. il House & Gard 135:103-55+ Ap '69
Essence of architecture is space; interview. P. Rudolph. House & Gard 136:26+ N '69
Some essentials of successful urban space. D. K. Specter. il Arch Rec 145:131-40 Ja '69
Study in space. il House & Gard 136:126-7 N '69
SPACE, Outer
Experiments simulate space travel. K. M. Swezey. il Pop Sci 195:167-9 O '69
See also
United Nations—Committee on the peaceful uses of outer space

Exploration
After Apollo 10, a look at space future. il U S News 66:28-9 Je 2 '69
Beyond the moon: no end. A. C. Clarke. il Time 94:31 Jl 18 '69
Man and outer space. Space World F-10-70:42 O '69
Man moves into the universe. B. Lovell. il Bul Atom Sci 25:4-7 S '69; Same abr. with title Space frontier; what new American initiatives? Cur 111:4-9 O '69
NASA maps comprehensive planet goals. il Aviation W 90:121+ Mr 10 '69
Next, Mars and beyond. il Time 94:18 Jl 25 '69
Our next decade in space. H. M. Mason, jr. il Mech Illus 65:43-5+ Ap '69
Priorities after Apollo. il Time 94:24+ Ag 1 '69
Send computers, not men, into deep space after the moon landing. R. E. Lapp. il N Y Times Mag p32-3+ F 2 '69
Speed limit 186,300 m.p.s. I Asimov. il Holiday 46:40-1+ Jl '69
Where man's moon triumph can lead. il Bsns W p23-4 Jl 26 '69
See also
Space probes

International control
United States and Japan conclude space cooperation agreement; statement with text of exchange of notes, July 31, 1969. W. P. Rogers. Dept State Bul 61:195-6 S 1 '69
See also
United Nations—Conference on the exploration and peaceful uses of outer space

Law
See Space law
SPACE age
Pre-Copernican views of the city. G. Rand. il Arch Forum 131:76-81 S '69
Stay? No stay? Kennedy space center. J. Morgenstern. il Newsweek 74:24-26A Jl 28 '69; Excerpts. Cur 110:3 S '69
SPACE and time
See also
Relativity (physics)
Time reversal
SPACE arrangement of plants. See Plants, Space arrangement of
SPACE biology
Barnard urges space studies. Aviation W 90:76 Ap 14 '69
Bioscience programs in space. O. E. Reynolds. il Space World F-9-69:4-15 S '69
Turtles unharmed by Zond 5 moon trip. Aviation W 90:23-4 My 19 '69
See also
Biotelemetry
Space medicine
SPACE centers
See also
United States—John F. Kennedy space center
SPACE communication. See Space flight—Communication systems
SPACE debris. See Space pollution
SPACE docking. See Orbital rendezvous (space flight)
SPACE flight
Flights to other planets are becoming a realistic fact; interview, ed. by IU. Kanin. A. Blagonravov. Space World F-10-70:27-9 O '69

SPACE flight—*Continued*
Future space flights; address, September 26, 1969. R. Anderson. Vital Speeches 36:175-8 Ja 1 '70
Grand tour. R. Koch. il Space World F-12-72:16-17 D '69
Grand tour of outer planets. il Sci Digest 66: 35-6 S '69
Letter from Lindbergh; assessment of the astronauts' moon mission. C. Lindbergh. il Life 67:60A-61 Jl 4 '69
NASA maps comprehensive planet goals. il Aviation W 90:121+ Mr 10 '69
Next steps in space. T. O. Paine. il Nat Geog 136:793-7 D '69
On going beyond our solar system. il Cur 110:9-11 S '69
Pointless controversy; manned vs. unmanned space flight. R. Hotz. Aviation W 90:11 Ap 21 '69
Shore of space; statements, November 2, 1957, October 25, 1958. W. Chambers. Nat R 21:738 Jl 29 '69
Space program; future plans; address. October 23, 1969. G. E. Mueller. Vital Speeches 36:170-5 Ja 1 '70
To Mars, slowly; recommendations of the Space task group. il Newsweek 74:111+ S 29 '69
Tossing our hats over the space wall. H. Sidey. Life 66:4 Je 6 '69
See also
Artificial satellites
Computers—Space flight applications
Ground support systems (space flight)
Orbital rendezvous (space flight)
Television in space flight
United States—National aeronautics and space administration

Accidents
See also
Survival (after airplane accidents, shipwrecks, etc)

Astronomical observations
See also
United States—National aeronautics and space administration—Astronomy missions board

Communication systems
Communications on the moon. il Electr World 82:23-5+ Ag '69
Communications on the moon. G. Phélizon. il UNESCO Courier 22:26-31 Mr '69
How television works from space; APT system. il Space World F-3-63:41-6 Mr '69
Quality of Apollo EVA radio link praised. il Aviation W 91:93+ Ag 4 '69
See also
Radio apparatus on space vehicles

Economic aspects
After Apollo 9, on to a lunar landing, but space program threatened by budget cuts. il U S News 66:48 Mr 24 '69
Industrial impact of Apollo. F. A. Long. il Bul Atom Sci 25:70-3 S '69
Sound off response; taking a down-to-earth approach. Nations Bsns 57:83 O '69

Finance
Space applications gain in funding plans. W. J. Normyle. il Aviation W 90:25-8 Ja 20 '69
See also
Space flight to the moon—Finance

Food problems
Eating in space; it's no picnic up there. E. Alston. il Look 33:58-9 Jl 15 '69

International aspects
Agreement on rescue and return of astronauts enters into force; White House announcement, December 3, 1968. Dept State Bul 59:652 D 23 '68
Flight of Apollo 8; international cooperation in space; remarks at White House presentation of National aeronautics and space administration distnguished service medals to astronauts, January 9, 1969. L. B. Johnson. Dept State Bul 60:76-7 Ja 27 '69
Russian house in outer space. E. Dvornikov. Space World F-4-64:37 Ap '69
What of U.S.-Soviet space cooperation? H. Simons. Cur 110:8-9 S '69
What price moondust? competing with Russia. Nation 209:66 Jl 28 '69
See also
United Nations—Committee on the peaceful uses of outer space

Laws and legislation
See Space law

Manned flights
Challenge of the spaceship; reprint. A. C. Clarke. il UNESCO Courier 22:25-8 Ag '69
Lengthy flights by man debated. W. J. Normyle. Aviation W 91:77-8 D 1 '69
Man in space; color portfolio, 1961-1969. Newsweek 74:45-52 Jl 7 '69
Manned space log. Space World F-10-70:36 O '69
Manned space program. Space World F-7-67: 32-3 Jl '69
NASA's tenth. D. Norton. il Space World F-5-65:14-19 My '69
Post-Apollo task forces formed. W. J. Normyle. Aviation W 90:22-3 My 12 '69
Whither lunar and planetary exploration in the 1970's; AAAS symposium, December 1969. D. G. Rea. il Science 166:1184-5 N 28 '69
See also
Astronauts
Orbital rendezvous (space flight)
Space, Outer—Exploration
Space flight to Mars
Space flight to the moon—Manned flights

Beli͡aev-Leonov flight, 1965
My first steps in space; reprint. A. Leonov. il UNESCO Courier 22:28-9 Ag '69

Extra vehicular activity
Apollo 9 verifies lunar unit, backpack. W. C. Wetmore. il Aviation W 90:67-9 Mr 17 '69
Schweickart performs EVA in lunar suit. il Aviation W 90:277-8 Mr 10 '69
See also
Space flight to the moon—Manned flights—Extra vehicular activity

McDivitt-Scott-Schweickart flight, 1969
Apollo; healthy in mid-flight. il Sci N 95:255 Mr 15 '69
Apollo 9 album. il Life 66:26-37 Mr 28 '69
Apollo 9 marks major flight advances; with editorial comment. E. J. Bulban. Aviation W 90:11, 18-22 Mr 17 '69
Apollo 9's busy schedule. il Sky & Tel 37: 162-3 Mr '69
Camera story of Apollo IX. il Space World F-6-66:26-9 Je '69
Closer to the moon. il Newsweek 73:78+ Mr 24 '69
Gumdrop meets the Spider; Apollo 9 crew practice plan of lunar-landing mission. il Newsweek 73:72+ Mr 17 '69
Lunar module flies precise test. W. J. Normyle. il Aviation W 90:59-61+ Mr 17 '69
Lunar module orbited for critical space test. B. K. Thomas. il Aviation W 90:276-7 Mr 10 '69
Photography at new heights; views from Apollo 9. il Time 93:54 Mr 28 '69
Rousing end to a relaxed flight. il Time 93: 70-2 Mr 21 '69
Special Apollo report. il Aviation W 90:16-21+ Mr 24 '69
Spectacular step toward lunar landing. il Time 93:50-1 Mr 14 '69
Spider makes its mark; Apollo 9 moves U.S. toward the moon. il Sci N 95:277-8 Mr 22 '69
What Apollo 9 means for a moon landing. il U S News 66:36-7 Mr 17 '69

Soyuz flights, 1969
Action at Baikonur. il Newsweek 74:108 O 20 '69
Another giant step toward the planets. il Sci N 96:347-8 O 18 '69
Control problems could have barred Soyuz mission dockings. D. C. Winston. il Aviation W 91:18-19 O 27 '69
Interest; reaction at Soviet mission to the United Nations; interview. G. Stashevsky. New Yorker 44:24-5 Ja 25 '69
Orbital troika; Soyuz 6. il Time 94:44 O 24 '69
Rescue techniques tested on Soyuz 4, 5 missions. Aviation W 90:25 Mr 17 '69
Russians take a vital step; Soyuz 6-8 flights. Bsns W p48 O 18 '69
Russians take new space path. il Bsns W p40-1 Ja 25 '69
Russians' turn; first crew exchange in orbit. il Time 93:60 Ja 24 '69
Soviet advances in orbital maneuvers. A. Tumanov. Space World G-1-73:38-9 Ja '70
Soviets fly triple Soyuz mission. il Aviation W 91:190-1 O 20 '69
Soyuz spurs orbiting space station plans; with editorial comment. D. C. Winston. Aviation W 90:11, 18-20 Ja 27 '69
Soyuz versatility confirmed by docking; Soyuz 4-5 flights, 1969. Aviation W 90:29 Ja 20 '69

SPACE flight—Manned flights—Soyuz flights, 1969—*Continued*
Station no. 1; Soyuz union in orbit. il Newsweek 73:93 Ja 27 '69
Still in the future; permanent space stations. Sci N 96:371-2 O 25 '69
Troika: Soyuz 6, 7 and 8. il Newsweek 74:85-6 O 27 '69
What Russia is up to in space. il U S News 67:38-40 O 27 '69

Meteor hazards
Faster than a speeding bullet! D. Norman. il Pop Mech 130:130-1 D '68
Meteors interest scientists; could pose danger to astronauts. il Space World F-4-64:12-13 Ap '69

News coverage
Greatest week in the history of the world since the creation. il U S News 67:4-6 Ag 4 '69
Moon and the Pond. il Newsweek 74:56-7 Ag 4 '69
Open skies. P. Haney. il Newsweek 74:27 Jl 28 '69
See also
Television broadcasting—Space flight coverage

Philosophy
Excelsior! We're going to the moon! Excelsior. K. Vonnegut, jr. il N Y Times Mag p9-11 Jl 13 '69; Discussion. p65+ Ag 3 '69
Why space exploration is vital to man's future. W. Von Braun. Space World F-9-69: 31-3 S '69
See also
Space flight to the moon—Philosophy

Physiological aspects
Apollo 11 proves man's space role; with transcript of conversations between astronauts and Kennedy space center. Z. Strickland. il Aviation W 91:51+ Ag 4 '69
More bioscience needed. Sci N 97:37 Ja 10 '70
Problems of space exploration. fU. Nefedov and others. Space World F-8-68:36-7 Ag '69
What killed Bonny? il Newsweek 74:71 N 3 '69
See also
Aerospace medical association
Astronauts—Health and hygiene
Biosatellite program
Space flight—Radiation hazards
Space flight to the moon—Physiological aspects
Space medicine
Weightlessness

Psychological aspects
See also
Space flight to the moon—Psychological aspects

Radiation hazards
Radiation on the lunar path. E. Vorobyov and L. Smirenny. Space World F-4-64:34-5 Ap '69

Religious aspects
Bible-readers' beagle: another go-round. Chr Today 13:32 Je 20 '69
Lunar landing. D. Kucharsky. Chr Today 13:32 Ag 1 '69
Man's new domain. il Chr Today 13:41 Ag 22 '69
Our foothold in the heavens. Chr Today 13: 22-3 Ag 22 '69
See also
Space flight to the moon—Religious aspects

Social aspects
From Alamogordo to Apollo: will man heed the lesson? E. Rabinowitch. Bul Atom Sci 25:14-16 S '69; Same abr. with title Space frontier; necessity to review priorities. Cur 111:9-11 O '69
Human consequences of the exploration of space. F. Dyson. Bul Atom Sci 25:8-10+ S '69
Man on the moon. M. Mead. Redbook 133: 70+ Jl '69
Moon landing. C. P. Snow. il Look 33:68-70+ Ag 26 '69

Television coverage
See Television broadcasting—Space flight coverage
SPACE flight and religion. See Space flight—Religious aspects; Space flight to the moon—Religious aspects
SPACE flight biotelemetry. See Biotelemetry

SPACE flight in art
Artist goes to Cape Kennedy to draw an Apollo launch. A. Metcalf. il Space World F-11-71:19-22 N '69
Artists and astronauts. L. Lastra. il Américas 21:21-8 S '69
Behind Apollo; painting. N. Rockwell. Look 33:44-7 Jl 15 '69
SPACE flight in literature
Jules Verne's trip to the moon. W. A. H. Birnie. il Read Digest 95:112-14 O '69
SPACE flight simulators
From Texas to Tranquillity; lunar landing training vehicle practice sessions. il Newsweek 73:63 Je 30 '69
Series of lunar landings simulated; lunar landing training vehicle. Z. Strickland. il Aviation W 90:55-9 Je 30 '69
See also
Astronauts—Training
Centrifuges
SPACE flight to Mars
Basic expedition to Mars detailed. W. J. Normyle. il Aviation W 91:39-40+ O 6 '69; Discussion. 91:126 N 17 '69
Beyond the moon. E. A. Aggen, jr. Space World F-5-65:38-9 My '69
Future in space: from moon to Mars. il U S News 68:54-5 Ja 5 '70
Getting a long headstart. J. Eberhart. il Sci N 96:331 O 11 '69
Hawks say go to Mars landing. il Bsns W p29 Ag 9 '69
Less than a national goal. il Sci N 96:233 S 20 '69
Manned mission to Mars opposed. W. J. Normyle. Aviation W 91:16-17 Ag 18 '69
Mars 1981 trip tied to decision by 1973. Z. Strickland. Aviation W 91:47 O 6 '69
Mars options key to 1971 budget. W. J. Normyle. il Aviation W 91:22-4 S 22 '69
Men to Mars in the '80s? il U S News 67:14 S 29 '69
Messages from Mars. J Lear. il Sat R 52:75-7 O 11 '69
Next, Mars and beyond. il Time 94:18 Jl 25 '69
On to Mars? I. G. Barbour. Chr Cent 86: 1478-80 N 19 '69
Post-Apollo: NASA seeks a Mars flight plan. L. J. Carter. il Science 165:937-91 S 5 '69
Price of Mars. il Time 94:20 S 26 '69
Rendezvous with the red planet. il Time 94: 23-4 Ag 8 '69
Say no to Mars. Chr Cent 86:797 Je 11 '69
Summer in space. R. S. Lewis. il Bul Atom Sci 25:29-30 Je '69
Two-year manned Mars mission planning started within NASA. Aviation W 91:23-4 Ag 11 '69
Viking exploration of Mars. W. Clothier. il Space World F-6-66:39-41 Je '69
See also
Space probes
SPACE flight to the moon
Aiming high; plans for ten Apollo flights to the surface of the moon. G. F. Alexander. il Newsweek 74:62-3 Jl 7 '69
Amazing 1865 moon shot of Jules Verne; excerpts from Verne's fantasy-Apollo reality, comp. by A. N. Kontaratos. il Look 33:74-8 My 27 '69
Apollo. il Space World F-3-63:23-30 Mr '69
Apollo: how the United States decided to go to the moon. L. Mandelbaum. bibliog Science 163:649-54 F 14 '69
As I see it; interview, ed. by M. H. Hall. H. C. Urey. il Forbes 104:44-8 Jl 15 '69
As spacemen look beyond the moon; interview. T. O. Paine. il U S News 67:48-53 Jl 7 '69
Fly me to the moon and let me have a window seat near the emergency exit. il Esquire 72:114-15 O '69
Future in space: from moon to Mars. il U S News 68:54-5 Ja 5 '70
Guest editorial; beginning of the interplanetary era. E. A. Aggen, jr. Space World F-5-65:4 My '69
How U.S. beat Russia to the moon. il U S News 67:32-4 Jl 14 '69
If Verne could look at NASA; Apollo flights. T. Sweeney. il Nat R 21:489-90 My 20 '69
Last lap before the moon; Apollo 10 and man's first lunar landing in July. il U S News 66:76 My 19 '69
Laurels for 1969; Apollo program. R. Hotz. Aviation W 91:7 D 22 '69
Moon frontier. Cur 110:3-11 S '69
Moon landing. C. P. Snow. il Look 33:68-70+ Ag 26 '69

SPACE flight to the moon—*Continued*
NASA's tenth. D. Norton. il Space World F-5-65:14-19 My '69
New stage of Soviet space programme; Zond 6 circumnavigation of the moon. Space World F-4-64:19-22 Ap '69
Politics of spacefaring; symposium. il Bul Atom Sci 25:17-25+ S '69
Real tragedy of man's infancy in space. H. Schwartz. Sat R 52:33-6 O 25 '69
Summer in space. R. S. Lewis. il Bul Atom Sci 25:29-30 Je '69
Unexpected payoff of Project Apollo. T. Alexander. il Fortune 80:114-17+ Jl '69
  See also
Lunar probes
Space vehicles—Recovery

Anecdotes, facetiae, satire, etc.

Gould theory. J. Brennan. Nat R 21:802 Ag 12 '69
If this be profane: establishing a Craters-of-the-moon-on-the-moon national monument. M. Nadel. Liv Wildn 33:2 Sum '69
Whitey's on the moon now. W. Eastlake. il Nation 209:238-9 S 15 '69

Cost

Go for Apollo. H. T. Simmons. il Newsweek 74:42-4+ Jl 7 '69
Next step for the space program. Bsns W p 108 Jl 26 '69

Finance

Manned post-Apollo effort underscored. Aviation W 90:27-8 Ja 20 '69

History

Apollo chronology. Space World F-7-67:34-6 Jl '69
Go for Apollo. H. T. Simmons. il Newsweek 74:42-4+ Jl 7 '69
Moon age: new dawn? il Newsweek 74:40-1 Jl 7 '69

International aspects

Prospects for international cooperation on the moon: the Antarctic analogy. P. M. Smith. il Bul Atom Sci 25:36-40 S '69
Who owns the moon? Nat R 21:682 Jl 15 '69
Why we should be modest about the moon flight. Chr Cent 86:918 Jl 9 '69

Manned flights

Apollo & beyond; with painting by N. Rockwell. A. C. Clarke. Look 33:43-9 Jl 15 '69
Apollo 9 readied to test lunar module. il Aviation W 90:17-19 F 3 '69
Apollo/Saturn lunar landing program. il Space World F-7-67:13-36 Jl '69
Drastic stretch planned in lunar program. W. J. Normyle. Aviation W 92:19-20 Ja 12 '70
Dream comes true. J. F. Pearson. il Pop Mech 132:80-3+ Jl '69
First manned lunar visit to last twenty-two hr. W. J. Normyle. Aviation W 90:22-3 Mr 31 '69
Future Apollo landings detailed. W. J. Normyle. Aviation W 91:23-4 Ag 4 '69
Hidden perils of a lunar landing; Sjogren-Muller analysis; and interview with E. S. Schiesser. ed. by J. Lear. il Sat R 52:47-54 Je 7 '69; Discussion. 52:46 Jl 5 '69
Is a lunar landing in July lunacy? R. S. Lewis. Sat R 52:52+ My 10 '69
Is the moon the limit for the U.S? il Time 93:62-3 My 9 '69
It is for us to grow... J. Lear. il Sat R 52:41-2 Ag 2 '69
July manned lunar landing set. W. Normyle. Aviation W 90:22-3 Mr 24 '69
Lunar report urges larger science role. Aviation W 91:92-3 N 17 '69
Man on the moon, the Columbian dilemma. S. Hyman. il Bul Atom Sci 25:18-22 S '69
Next step will be the first; lunar landing. il Bsns W p78+ My 31 '69
Nixon to back manned lunar plan. W. J. Normyle. Aviation W 90:16-17 Ap 21 '69
Plans for Apollo missions. R. N. Watts, jr. Sky & Tel 37:365-6 Je '69
Reporter at large. H. S. F. Cooper, jr. New Yorker 45:53-4+ Ap 12; 47-8+ Ap 19 '69
Science gets a chance; scientist-astronauts in Apollo program. J. Eberhart. il Sci N 96:355-6 O 18 '69
Send computers, not men, into deep space after the moon landing. R. E. Lapp. il N Y Times Mag p32-3+ F 2 '69
Ten for the moon. il Newsweek 73:28-31 Mr 31 '69
Two for the moon; Apollo 10 mission. il Sci Digest 65:32-3 Ap '69
What's next in space; nine more flights to the moon; with interview with G. E. Mueller. il U S News 67:28-31 Ag 4 '69

Where we go beyond the moon; NASA's budget under attack. il Bsns W p98-9 Jl 19 '69
  See also
Astronauts—Training
Moon—Exploration

Anecdotes, facetiae, satire, etc.

Moon game. Commonweal 90:476-7 Ag 8 '69

Armstrong-Aldrin-Collins flight, 1969

After Apollo 10, a look at space future. il U S News 66:28-9 Je 2 '69
Apollo 11, a day to remember; portfolio. Space World F-11-71:23-32 N '69
Apollo 11 lunar landing mission profile. il Aviation W 91:45-50 Jl 7 '69
Apollo 11: the time machine. P. Collier. Ramp Mag 8:56+ O '69
Apollo's great leap for the moon. L. Wainwright. il Life 67:18D-29 Jl 25 '69
Apollo's moon mission: here are the results; with interview with J. W. Dietrich. il U S News 67:24-7 Ag 4 '69
Astronauts: their own great stories. N. A. Armstrong; E. E. Aldrin, jr; M. Collins. il Life 67:24-9 Ag 22 '69
Back from the moon. il Newsweek 74:14-20 Ag 4 '69
Collectors' items of another kind; mementos left and brought back. il Newsweek 74:71 Jl 28 '69
Day they left for the moon. B. Beason. il Mech Illus 65:142+ N '69
Findings of the moon mission. il US News 67:11 Ag 11 '69
Fire on the moon. N. Mailer. il Life 67:24-41 Ag 29; 50-60+ N 14 '69; 68:57-8+ Ja 9 '70
First explorers on the moon; symposium; with phonograph record. il Nat Geog 136:735-97 D '69
First men on the moon. R. Hillenbrand. il Sky & Tel 38:144-9 S '69
First men on the moon. W. Von Braun. il Pop Sci 195:62-6+ Jl '69
Flat-earth liberals; D. Pearson's reactions to Apollo 11. Nat R 21:737-8 Jl 29 '69
Flight of Apollo 11; statement, September 8, 1969. T. O. Paine. Dept State Bul 61:309-11 O 6 '69
Giant leap for mankind; first moon landing. il Time 94:10-12+ Jl 25 '69
Great adventure. il Newsweek 74:68-73+ Jl 21 '69
Greatest week in the history of the world since the creation. il U S News 67:4-6 Ag 4 '69
Journey to the moon: what health hazards? R. Nessen. il Todays Health 47:16-21 Jl '69
July 20, 1969: interplanetary man; transcript of landing, and photographs. il Space World F-12-72: 18-34 D '69
Lessons from moon; (hot) Apollo 11 will find; with interview by H. Masursky. il U S News 66:32-4 Je 9 '69
Letter from the space center; completion of initial survey of the rocks and dust from Apollo 11 mission. H. S. F. Cooper, jr. New Yorker 45:92+ O 11 '69
Letter from the space center; examination of astronauts and samples from Apollo 11 mission. H. S. F. Cooper, jr. New Yorker 45:82+ Ag 16 '69
Letter from the space center; gathering and examination of moon samples from Apollo 11 mission. H. S. F. Cooper, jr. New Yorker 45:50-7 Ag 2 '69
Letter from the space center; opinions of the Apollo 11 mission and planned examination of samples and photographs. H. S. F. Cooper, jr. New Yorker 45:85-92 Jl 26 '69
Letter from the space center; plan of the Apollo 11 mission. H. S. F. Cooper, jr. New Yorker 45:76-80 Jl 12; 79-83 Jl 19 '69
Letter from the space center; testing of lunar rocks and dust from Apollo 11 mission. H. S. F. Cooper, jr. New Yorker 45:63-70 Ag 23 '69
Man on the moon: mixed emotions; with editorial comment. il Sci N 96:71-5 Jl 26 '69
Man's first day on the moon. J. R. Berry. il Pop Mech 132:84-7+ Jl '69
Men on the moon; pictures shot by the astronauts on the lunar surface. il Life 67:18-29 Ag 8 '69
Mission to moon. il Newsweek 74:18-27 Jl 28 '69
Moon age: new dawn? il Newsweek 74:40-1 Jl 7 '69
Moon hours: watching Apollo 11 in New York. New Yorker 45:25-30 Jl 26 '69
Moon in July, then Mars. il Newsweek 73:34-5 Je 9 '69

SPACE flight to the moon—Manned flights—
Armstrong-Aldrin-Collins flight, 1969—*Cont.*
Moon, Mars and man. il Newsweek 74:64-72
Ag 11 '69
Moon thoughts: Apollo 11. W. F. Buckley, jr.
Nat R 21:819 Ag 12 '69
Moon watching. N. Compton. Commentary
48:84-6 O '69
Moonshoot: watching it all at home, the
three astronauts' families coaxed them on.
il Life 67:28-31 Ag 1 '69
More than just a decade's work. J. Eberhart.
il Sci N 96:58-60 Jl 19 '69
New world. il Time 94:18-21 Jl 18 '69
One giant leap. il Harp Baz 102:196-7 S '69
One small step, one giant leap; condensation.
il Read Digest 95:249-54+ O '69
Plans detailed for lunar landing. W. J. Nor-
myle. il Aviation W 90:16-19 My 19 '69
Profile of the Apollo 11 mission. il Life 67:
30-1 Jl 4 '69
Real goals of the U.S. mission to the moon.
il U S News 67:22-3 Jl 28 '69
Space exploration; a new era; address, Sept-
ember 16, 1969. E. E. Aldrin; M. Collins;
N. A. Armstrong. Vital Speeches 35:741-2
O 1 '69
Special Apollo report; symposium with edi-
torial comment and photographs. Avia-
tion W 91:11, 16-28+ Ag 4 '69
Special report: Apollo 11 lunar landing; with
editorial comment. Aviation W 91:17 Jl 28
'69
Special report: Apollo 11 planning; sympo-
sium, with editorial comment. il Aviation
W 91:11, 40-1+ Jl 14 '69
Task accomplished. il Time 94:18-19 Ag 1 '69
Three men bound for the moon. il Life 67:
16D-31 Jl 4 '69
United Nations honours Apollo 11 mission.
UN Mo Chron 6:149-50 Ag '69
U.S. flag on the moon. il U S News 67:29-33
Jl 21 '69
When astronauts reach the moon. il U S
News 66:7 Je 30 '69
Where man's moon triumph can lead. il
Bsns W p23-4 Jl 26 '69

Borman-Lovell-Anders flight, 1968

Apollo 8: a most fantastic voyage. S. C.
Phillips. il Nat Geog 135:593-631 My '69
Apollo 8; man's epic first flight to the moon.
il Read Digest 94:64-70 Mr '69
Around the moon and back. R. N. Watts, jr.
il Sky & Tel 37:76-8+ F '69
Astronauts. il Vogue 153:186-7 F 1 '69
First circumnavigation of the moon; next
step: a lunar landing? il Sr Schol 93:16 Ja
10 '69
Flight of Apollo 8: international cooperation
in space; remarks at White House presentation of National aeronautics and space
administration distinguished service medals
to astronauts, January 9, 1969. L. B. Johnson. Dept State Bul 60:76-7 Ja 27 '69
Heron and the astronaut; with editorial
comment by G. Hunt, and photographs by
S. Wayman and R. Morse. A. M. Lindbergh. Life 66:1, 14-26A F 28 '69
Our Terra-luna transit system: where will it
take us? R. S. Lewis. il Bul Atom Sci 25:
22-3 Mr '69
Reflections on Apollo 8. E. Rabinowitch. il
Bul Atom Sci 25:2-3+ Mr '69
Views from earth on the odyssey into space:
symposium. il Look 33:72+ F 4 '69
What the Apollo 8 moon flight really did
for us. W. Von Braun. il Pop Sci 194:68-
71+ Mr '69

Conrad-Bean-Gordon flight, 1969

Apollo 12: a leap for science. il Bsns W p29-
30 N 29 '69
Apollo 12: aiming at the Ocean of storms.
il Newsweek 74:88-90+ N 17 '69
Apollo 12, by the crew. C. Conrad; A. L.
Bean; R. J. Gordon. il Life 67:32-3+ D 19
'69
Apollo 12 goals include finding of Surveyor
3. Aviation W 91:41 Jl 28 '69
Apollo 12 landing site and goals. il Space
World G-1-73:4-6 Ja '70
Apollo 12 launches new moon gear. il Bsns
W p38+ N 8 '69
Apollo 12, new era for science. R. Hotz.
Aviation W 91:11 D 8 '69
Apollo 12 on the way. il Newsweek 74:102-
102B N 24 '69
Apollo 12, our second walk on the moon;
interview, ed. by R. P. Crossley. J. A. Mc-
Divitt. il Pop Mech 132:50+ N '69
Apollo 12 special report; with editorial com-
ment. il Aviation W 91:11, 16-26+ N 24 '69
Apollo 12 to alter translunar path. W. J.
Normyle. Aviation W 91:16-17 N 10 '69
Apollo 12's moon: surprises already. il Sci
N 96:493-4 N 29 '69

Back to the moon; Apollo 12. Time 94:44+
O 24 '69
Bull's-eye for the intrepid travelers. il Time
94:24+ N 28 '69
Close-up of the Apollo 12 trio. il U S News
67:17 N 24 '69
Earth-moon run. il Newsweek 74:94-95B D
8 '69
Exploring the moon. il Newsweek 74:66-9
D 1 '69
From Apollo 12: new knowledge, new debate.
il U S News 67:22-3 D 8 '69
Future that rides on Apollo 12. il Bsns W
p66-7 N 15 '69
Go-go astronauts of Apollo 12. il Life 67:72-3
D 5 '69
Intrepid on a sun-drenched Sea of storms.
il Life 67:34-9 D 12 '69
Maximum activity to mark Apollo 12 EVA.
Z. Strickland. il Aviation W 91:192-3+ O
20 '69
More footsteps on the moon. il Sci N 96:
470-2 N 22 '69
New view of the Ocean of storms. il Time
94:40A-41 D 5 '69
Off to the moon again. il Time 94:22 N 14
'69
One small step for space science. F. W. Detje.
il Sci N 96:434-5 N 8 '69
Point landing called prime Apollo 12 goal.
Z. Strickland. Aviation W 91:19 O 13 '69
Second trip to moon, the purpose; with inter-
view with C. Berry. il U S News 67:56-60
N 17 '69
Special Apollo report; symposium. Aviation
W 91:16-22 D 1 '69
Story of 31½ hours on the moon. il U S
News 67:28-31 D 1 '69
Tension builds for next month moon shot.
Bsns W p 104+ O 11 '69
To the moon again: new tasks for astro-
nauts. il U S News 67:30-1 N 24 '69
Toward the Ocean of storms. il Time 94:28-
30 N 21 '69
Why we're going back to the moon. W. Von
Braun. il Pop Sci 195:78-81+ O '69
See also
Space flight to the moon—Manned flights—
Extravehicular activity

Extravehicular activity

Apollo 11 proves man's space role; with
transcript of conversations between as-
tronauts and Kennedy space center. Z.
Strickland. il Aviation W 91:51+ Ag 4 '69
Astronauts detail lunar flight experience;
with editorial comment. Z. Strickland. il
Aviation W 91:11, 18-20 Ag 18 '69
Astronauts rehearse lunar extravehicular tasks
planned for Apollo 12 mission. il Aviation
W 91:56-7 N 10 '69
Astronauts urge longer-duration EVAs. Z.
Strickland. il Aviation W 91:17-20 D 1 '69
Conrad stresses real-time value of EVAs.
Aviation W 91:16-17 D 22 '69
Diverse activity marks EVA on Apollo 12;
photographs. Aviation W 91:50A-50H D 8
'69
EVA yields parts of Surveyor, samples. il
Aviation W 91:16-21 D 8 '69
Exuberance sets tone of first EVA. il Avia-
tion W 91:19-21 N 24 '69
Five hours of EVA planned on Apollo 12.
Z. Strickland. Aviation W 91:25-6 Ag 4 '69
Latest Apollo's experiments. R. N. Watts, jr.
il Sky & Tel 39:11-13 Ja '70
Letter from the space center; first lunar walk
of the Apollo 12 mission. H. S. F. Cooper,
jr. New Yorker 45:46-56 Ja 3 '70
Man on the moon: mixed emotions. il Sci
N 96:74 Jl 26 '69
Man walks on another world; historic words
and photographs. N. A. Armstrong; E. E.
Aldrin, jr; M. Collins. Nat Geog 136:738-49
D '69
Maximum activity to mark Apollo 12 EVA.
Z. Strickland. Aviation W 91:192-3+ O 20
'69
Mission to moon. il Newsweek 74:18-27 Jl
28 '69
Mobility unhindered by bulky space suit.
W. C. Wetmore. Aviation W 91-34-6 Jl 28
'69
Moon, Mars and man. il Newsweek 74:64-72
Ag 11 '69
Moonwalk: the sky was never as black as
here. C. Conrad; A. Bean. il U S News 67:
30 D 1 '69
More footsteps on the moon. il Sci N 96:470-
2 N 22 '69
They were there: Apollo 11 astronauts des-
cribe moonwalk. il Newsweek 74:73 Ag 25
'69
See also
Space flight to the moon—Manned flights—
Conrad-Bean-Gordon flight, 1969

SPACE flight to the moon—Manned flights
—*Continued*

Lovell-Haise-Mattingly flight, 1970
(proposed)

Apollo 13 keyed to rugged target. W. J.
Normyle. Aviation W 91:20-1 D 15 '69
Apollo 13 to stress scientific role. W. J.
Normyle. Aviation W 91:16-17 D 1 '69

Stafford-Cernan-Young
flight, 1969

Apollo 10 crew describes vivid reactions. Z.
Strickland. il Aviation W 90:77-8 Je 23 '69
Apollo 10 lunar mission profile. il Aviation W
90:59-63 My 19 '69
Apollo 10 lunar mission; symposium. il Avia-
tion W 90:68-75+ Je 2 '69
Apollo 10: next stop, the moon. il News-
week 73:30-1 My 26 '69
Apollo 10 special report. il Aviation W 90:
16-21 My 26 '69
Barnstorming the moon. il Life 66:30B-43
Je 6 '69
Dress rehearsal for a lunar landing: we have
arrived. il Sci N 95:521-2 My 31 '69
Dress rehearsal; preparation for launch of
Apollo 10. il Time 93:78 My 16 '69
NASA scrutinizes Apollo 10 problem data.
Aviation W 90:22-3 Je 9 '69
Nine miles from the goal. il Time 93:13-15
My 30 '69
9.4 miles to the moon. il Newsweek 73:24-7
Je 2 '69
Our happy moon journey. T. Stafford; J.
Young; G. Cernan. il Life 66:40-5 Je 20 '69
Step to Mars. il Sci N 95:547-8 Je 7 '69
To the moon, almost; Apollo 10 scheduled.
il Newsweek 73:66 My 19 '69
Uncluttered path to the moon. il Time 93:
64-7 Je 6 '69
Vision of lunar voyage; with a TV camera
Apollo 10 makes them real; with report
by A. Rosenfeld. il Life 66:48-52A My 30
'69

Philosophy

Ambivalent man and his ambiguous moon.
M. C. Hyers. il Chr Cent 86:1158-62 S 10
'69
Dream of the future's face; excerpt from A
fire on the moon. N. Mailer. il Life 68:57-8+
Ja 9 '70
Earth might be fair. Chr Cent 86:1009 Jl 30
'69
It is for us to grow... J. Lear. il Sat R 52:
41-2 Ag 2 '69
Meaning of the moon voyage. J. B. Sheerin.
Cath World 208:194-5 F '69
Moon and middle America. il Time 94:10-11
Ag 1 '69
Reflections on the moon; tr. by A. Foulke. A.
Moravia. il McCalls 97:42-3+ Ja '70
Search for intelligent life; implications of
the moon landing. N. Cousins. Sat R 52:
20 Ag 9 '69
Troubled man on the moon. J. B. Sheerin.
Cath World 209:242-3 S '69
What's it to us? J. Morgenstern. il News-
week 74:64+ Jl 7 '69

Physiological aspects

Is the earth safe from lunar contamination?
Apollo quarantine plans. il Time 93:78 Je
13 '69
Risks facing man in space; interview. C.
Berry. il U S News 67:58-60 N 17 '69

Psychological aspects

Psychology of astronauts; excerpt from A
fire on the moon. N. Mailer. il Life 67:
50-60+ N 14 '69

Public opinion

Awe, hope and skepticism on planet earth.
il Time 94:16-17 Jl 25 '69
Cathedrals in the sky. il Time 94:19-20 Ag
1 '69
First men on moon, Apollo 11 flight; Rus-
sian scientists' assessment. Space World
F-10-70:34-5 O '69
Giant leap for mankind? il Ebony 24:58-9
S '69
Moon shot afterthoughts. R. M. Brown. Cur
111:11-12 O '69
Moonshot: young Europe reacts. P. Fox.
Seventeen 28:110-11+ D '69
Watchers; reactions from around the globe.
il Newsweek 74:28 Jl 28 '69

Religious aspects

Challenge in the heavens. il Time 93:64-5 Ja
24 '69
Lunar devotions. Chr Today 13:40 Ja 31 '69
Moon theology: some reflections. P. J. Riga.
Cath World 210:151-4 Ja '70

One giant leap for mankind. America 121:56
Ag 2 '69
Separationists split over space prayer. Chr
Cent 86:1474 N 19 '69
Space, science, and scripture; interview; with
editorial comment. R. W. Johnson. Chr
Today 13:3-6, 21 Jl 18 '69
View from the moon. A. H. Leitch. Chr To-
day 13:51 F 28 '69

Surveyor flights

Surveyor lunar landings. L. D. Jaffe. bib-
liog il Science 164:774-88 My 16 '69
Unsung trailblazer to the moon. G. A. W.
Boehm. il Read Digest 94:134-8 Je '69
Why finding Surveyor 3 was important. il
U S News 67:29 D 1 '69

Television coverage
See Television broadcasting—Space flight
coverage

SPACE flight to Venus
See also
Space probes

SPACE flight training. See Astronauts—Training

SPACE flight trajectories. See Trajectories

SPACE industry. See Aerospace industries

SPACE law
Ground rules for the moon. il Time 94:27-8
Ag 1 '69
Legal status of the moon. Cur 110:7-8 S '69;
Same. Space World F-10-70:14-15 O '69
Putting space in rule of law. Bsns W p 104-5
Jl 19 '69

SPACE medicine
Cosmonautics and space medicine. A. Kurgin.
il Space World F-6-66:36-7 Je 69
Journey to the moon: what health hazards?
R. Nessen. il Todays Health 47:16-21 Jl '69
Lunar medicine; questions and answers. H.
Goldstein. il Sci Digest 65:19-20 F '69
Man on the moon; right at home. Sci N 96:
75 Jl 26 '69
Sad end to Biosat 3. il Sci N 96:46 Jl 19 '69
Still a mystery. B. J. Culliton. il Sci N 96:
61-3 Jl 19 '69
Weightless burden of space. B. J. Culliton.
il Sci N 96:560-1 D 13 '69
See also
Biotelemetry
Space flight—Physiological aspects
Space flight to the moon—Physiological as-
pects
Weightlessness

SPACE perception
Ponzo perspective illusion as a manifestation
of space perception. H. Leibowitz and others. il Science 166:1174-6 N 28 '69

SPACE photography
Airglow and star photographs in the daytime
from a rocket. D. C. Evans and L. Dunkel-
man. bibliog il Science 164:1391-3 Je 20 '69
Apollo 9 album. il Life 66:26-37 Mr 28 '69
Apollo tests four-camera terrain study. W.
C. Wetmore. il Aviation W 90:37-9+ My
26 '69
Astronauts as photographers. M. Edelson. il
Travel & Camera 32:80-3 Ap '69
Lunar module, EVA tested on Apollo 9.
Aviation W 90:50-3 Mr 31 '69
New photo equipment, film set for Apollo 11.
Aviation W 90:78 Je 23 '69
Photography at new heights; views from
Apollo 9. il Time 93:54 Mr 28 '69
Sequence photos to aid Apollo 11. W. C.
Wetmore. Aviation W 90:53-4 Je 9 '69
Sights never seen before. il Newsweek 74:
50-2 Jl 7 '69
Some early results from Celescope. R. N.
Watts, jr. il Sky & Tel 37:280-1 My '69
Special Apollo report. il Aviation W 90:16-
21 Mr 24 '69
Surveying key to Apollo missions. Aviation
W 91:50 D 8 '69
Why our astronauts can't make good pic-
tures. S. Nathan. il Pop Phot 65:71-5+
Ag '69
See also
Earth—Photographs from space
Moon—Photographs
Moon—Photographs from space
Photographic reconnaissance systems

Apparatus and supplies

Techniques tomorrow; review of what the
astronauts carried in their gadget bags to
shoot the moon. B. Sherman. Mod Phot
33:64+ N '69

Processing

Complex procedures mark Apollo 11 film
processing. Aviation W 91:99-101 Ag 11 '69

SPACE pollution
Space debris. H. R. Williams. il Space World
F-5-65:36-7 My '69
Whatever happened to all the objects shot
into space. il U S News 66:16 Mr 17 '69
SPACE probes
Atmospheres of Mars and Venus. V. R.
Eshleman. il Sci Am 220:78-88 bibliog
(p 148+) Mr '69
First findings from the Mariner flybys. il
Sky & Tel 38:232-4 O '69
Flight paths mariners took on Mars passes
il Aviation W 91:96-7 Ag 11 '69
Focus on Mars. Sci N 95:233 Mr 8 '69
How you'll see Mars close up. C. P. Gilmore.
il Pop Sci 195:76-9+ Jl '69
In space: focus on Mars. il U S News 67:
58-9 Ag 11 '69
Longevity gives bonus in space; Pioneers 6
and 7. il Sci N 97:19 Ja 3 '70
Looking for life; Mariners 6 and 7 Mars
probes. il Time 93:42 Mr 7 '69
Mariner. il Space World F-9-69:47-50 S '69
Mariner launched to Mars for Viking pro-
gram data. Aviation W 90:19 Mr 3 '69
Mariner 7 heading for Mars. Aviation W 90:
17 Ap 7 '69
Mariner 7's course correction completed.
Aviation W 90:30 Ap 14 '69
Mariner 6 and 7 television pictures; prelim-
inary analysis. R. B. Leighton and oth-
ers. bibliog il Science 166:49-67 O 3 '69
Mariner spacecraft, explorers of Mars. F. W.
Holder. il Electr World 82:43-6 S '69
Mariners 6, 7 readied for missions to Mars.
il Aviation W 90:17 F 24 '69
Mariners to fly past Mars. R. N. Watts, jr. il
Sky & Tel 37:218-20 Ap '69
Mars close up; Mariners' findings. il News-
week 74:59-60 Ag 18 '69
Mars observed; Mariners 6 and 7 findings.
il Newsweek 74:72-3 Ag 11 '69
Mars revisited; detection of two gases by
Mariner 7. il Time 94:45-6 Ag 15 '69
Rendezvous with Mars; Mariners 6 and 7.
Newsweek 73:95 Mr 10 '69
Scientists seek advanced Mars sensors. Avia-
tion W 91:25-6 S 22 '69
Twin mariners approach Mars. R. N. Watts,
jr. Sky & Tel 38:22 Jl '69
Two mariners on way to Mars. il Space
World F-6-66:10-11 Je '69
What mariner really saw. Time 94:74 S 19
'69
See also
Lunar probes
SPACE probes, Russian
Automatic probes en route to Venus. Space
World F-7-67:37 Jl '69
Double date with Venus. Newsweek 73:81 My
26 '69
Doubleheader on Venus. Time 93:46 My 23
'69
New stage of Soviet space programme; Zond
6 circumnavigation of the moon. Space
World F-4-64:19-22 Ap '69
Redesigned equipment aids Soviet missions
to Venus. il Aviation W 90:22 My 26 '69
Soviet goal: on to the planets. U S News
67:34 Jl 14 '69
Soviets admit Venus 5, 6 problems. Aviation
W 90:70-3 Je 23 '69
Talk with the chief designer of Venera (Ve-
nus) probes. il Space World F-9-69:28-9 S
'69
To the moon, to the planets. Sci N 95:525
My 31 '69
Venus probes, Venera-5 and Venera-6. il
Space World F-10-70:44-9 O '69
See also
Lunar probes, Russian
SPACE propulsion. See Space vehicles—Prop-
ulsion systems
SPACE quarantine. See Quarantine
SPACE rescue work
Rescue techniques tested on Soyuz 4, 5 mis-
sions. Aviation W 90:25 Mr 17 '69
SPACE research
Aerospace. See occasional issues of Science
news
Capturing a moon and other diversions; pro-
posals of S. F. Singer. il Time 93:66-7 F
21 '69
Challenge of the spaceship; reprint. A. C.
Clarke il UNESCO Courier 22:25-8 Ag '69
Is space exploration worth while? E. Kol-
man. Space World F-3-63:11-15 Mr '69
Man and outer space. Space World F-10-70:42
O '69
Moon landing. C. P. Snow. il Look 33:68-
70+ Ag 26 '69
See also
International council of scientific unions—
Committee on space research
United Nations—Committee on the peaceful
uses of outer space

Economic aspects
After Apollo 9, on to a lunar landing, but
space program threatened by budget cuts.
il U S News 66:48 Mr 24 '69
Apollo cuts trigger slump at Cape. Aviation
W 91:63-4+ D 8 '69
For U.S. space cities; an uncertain future.
il U S News 67:26-9 Jl 28 '69
New priorities in exploring space. il Life
67:30 Ag 22 '69
History
Ten years in deep space. W. Cloud. il Pop
Mech 131:128-31+ Mr '69
International aspects
After the moon, the earth! address, Decem-
ber 28, 1969. W. O. Roberts. Science 167:11-
16 Ja 2 '70
On going beyond our solar system. il Cur
110:9-11 S '69
Real tragedy of man's infancy in space. H.
Schwartz. Sat R 52:33-6 O 25 '69
See also
United Nations—Committee on the peaceful
uses of outer space
Military aspects
Military use of space: what top powers are
doing and not doing. il U S News 66:10 Je
23 '69
Social aspects
Space is not black. J. Robertson. Nation
208:814-16 Je 30 '69
Europe, Western
Shaky but hopeful. T. Shoemaker. Sci N 96:
120 Ag 9 '69
See also
European space research organization
India
Next decade: TV by satellite. S. K. Ghaswala.
Sci N 96:136 Ag 16 '69
Japan
Launching Japan into orbit. Bsns W p52
S 13 '69
Russia
American Sputnik for the Russians? C. S.
Sheldon, 2d. Bul Atom Sci 25:23-5+ S '69
Cost of secrecy. R. Hotz. Aviation W 91:
11 O 27 '69
Disaster at Tyuratum. Time 94:27 N 28 '69
Guest editorial; beginning of the inter-
planetary era. E. A. Aggen, jr. Space World
F-5-65:4 My '69
Lunar landing and the U.S.-Soviet equation.
M. L. Harvey. il Bul Atom Sci 25:28-32+ S
'69
Progress in science and cosmonautics. A. A.
Blagonravov and IU. Zaitsev. Space World
F-2-62:4-5 F '69
Review of Soviet space effort; symposium
with editorial comment by G. Petrov and
G. Skuridin. Space World F-4-64:4-5, 14-
38 Ap '69
Russia in space. il Newsweek 74:26 Jl 28 '69
Russian report (cont) il Space World F-10-
70:44-9 O '69
Soviet space schedule may include large
booster test. D. C. Winston. il Aviation
W 90:132-4 Mr 10 '69
Soviets suffer setbacks in space. Aviation W
91:26-7 N 17 '69

United States
Aiming high; plans for ten Apollo flights to
the surface of the moon. G. F. Alexander.
il Newsweek 74:62-3 Jl 7 '69
Antarctic research, a prelude to space re-
search; adaptation of address, September
18, 1968. E. Stuhlinger. Space World F-5-
65:5-11 My '69
Apollo and post-Apollo. P. H. Abelson. Sci-
ence 166:171 O 10 '69
Apollo: how the United States decided to go
to the moon. L. Mandelbaum. bibliog Sci-
ence 163:649-54 F 14 '69
As I see it; interview, ed. by M. H. Hall.
H. C. Urey. il Forbes 104:44-8 Jl 15 '69
As spacemen look beyond the moon; inter-
view. T. O. Paine. il U S News 67:48-53
Jl 7 '69
Balanced and solid; next space decade. Sci
N 95:303-4 Mr 29 '69
Broad new space program urged. W. J
Normyle. il Aviation W 91:22-3 Ag 11 '69
Dissent, dissension at AAAS. il Sci N 97:5-6
Ja 3 '70
Fire on the moon. N. Mailer. il Life 67:24-
41 Ag 29; 50-60+ N 14 '69; 68:57-8+ Ja 9 '70
Getting a long headstart. J. Eberhart. il
Sci N 96:331 O 11 '69

SPACE research—United States—*Continued*
Is the moon the limit for the U.S? il Time 93:62-3 My 9 '69
Joe Karth's questions; excerpts from address, November 1969. J. Karth. Aviation W 91: 21 N 17 '69
Lunar landing and the U.S.-Soviet equation. M. L. Harvey. il Bul Atom Sci 25:28-32+ S '69
New priorities in exploring space. il Life 67: 30 Ag 22 '69
New space policy may stress earth uses. W. C. Wetmore. il Aviation W 90:113-14+ Mr 10 '69
Next objective in space. W. O. Roberts. Science 163:521 F 7 '69
Nixon backs space future; excerpts from address. R. M. Nixon. Aviation W 91:11 D 1 '69
Nixon goal is balanced space effort. il Aviation W 90:99 Mr 10 '69
No tears for MOL. R. Hotz. Aviation W 90:11 Je 30 '69
Nobody condemns this industrial complex. A. H. Sypher. Nations Bsns 57:26-7 S '69
Our Terra-luna transit system; where will it take us? R. S. Lewis. il Bul Atom Sci 25: 22-3 Mr '69
Pace of post-Apollo planning rises. W. J. Normyle. Aviation W 90:16 F 3 '69
Post-Apollo policy; a look into the 1970s. W. Leavitt. il Bul Atom Sci 25:41-4 S '69
Prelude to space research; Antarctic research program; excerpt from address, September 1968. E. Stuhlinger. Bul Atom Sci 25:24-7 Mr '69
Ready to design the new hardware. il Bsns W p51-2 S 13 '69
Reflections on Apollo 8. E. Rabinowitch. il Bul Atom Sci 25:2-3+ Mr '69
Scientists, engineers widen gap on future space program stress. W. J. Normyle. Aviation W 91:27-8 N 17 '69
Significance of Apollo. S. Chapman. il Space World F-9-69:26-7 S '69
Space. Sci N 95:110 F 1 '69
Space program and problems of the origin of the moon; address, December 26-31, 1968. H. C. Urey. Bul Atom Sci 25:24-6+ Ap '69
Space program; future plans; address, October 23, 1969. G. E. Mueller. Vital Speeches 36: 170-5 Ja 1 '70
Space sciences. Sci N 95:283 Mr 22 '69
Summer in space. R. S. Lewis. il Bul Atom Sci 25:29-30 Je '69
Task force presents space options. M. Mueller. Science 165:1335 S 26 '69
Tossing our hats over the space wall. H. Sidey. Life 66:4 Je 6 '69
What's up in space? fourth International symposium on bioastronautics and the exploration of space. il Space World F-2-62: 40-3 F '69
Why space exploration is vital to man's future. W. Von Braun. Space World F-9-69: 31-3 S '69
See also
Space flight
United States—National aeronautics and space administration
SPACE scientists. See Scientists
SPACE stations
Advanced lunar operation keyed to nuclear shuttles. Aviation W 91:24-5 Ag 11 '69
Advanced space station concepts crystallizing. N. S. Himmel. il Aviation W 91:100-1+ S 22 '69
Another giant step toward the planets; Soyuz flights. il Sci N 96:347-8 O 18 '69
Apollo applications shrinks to evaluation of orbital workshop. il Aviation W 90:109-10 Mr 10 '69
Apollo command module reuse proposed. N. S. Himmel. Aviation W 90:73+ Ap 7 '69
Budget cuts threaten MOL project. C. Brown low. Aviation W 90:22-3 My 5 '69
Cosmodrome in orbit. A. Sternfeld. Space World F-7-67:42-3 Jl '69
Factories in space. W. Von Braun. il Pop Sci 195:72-5+ D '69
Future belongs to space laboratories. B. Petrov. Space World F-7-67:11-12 Jl '69
Habitability: first orbiting space station: dry workshop, interview. D. W. Toan. New Yorker 45:43-5 N 1 '69
Home is 200 miles up; Apollo applications program. il Space World F-9-69:16-23 S '69
In the news; space station of prefabricated modules. Space World F-8-68:48 Ag '69
Laboratory for space research; to be told what is needed, but not what goes on; General electric's M.O.L. facilities, King of Prussia, Pa. il Arch Rec 146:146-50 Ag '69

Large station may emerge as unwritten U.S. goal. W. J. Normyle. il Aviation W 90: 103+ Mr 10 '69
MOL canceled in abrupt decision. Aviation W 90:28-9 Je 16 '69
MOL delayed by funding cut. Aviation W 90:17 Ap 21 '69
MOL fallout hurts McDonnell the most. Bsns W p47 Je 14 '69
MOL shot down. il Sci N 95:595-6 Je 21 '69
NASA aims at 100-man station. W. J. Normyle. Aviation W 90:16-17 F 24 '69
New quests ahead. A. Masevich. Space World F-4-64:38-9 Ap '69
Next. Soviet space platforms? U S News 66:6 Ja 27 '69
On NASA's agenda: space station and shuttle. il Fortune 80:153 Jl '69
Post-Apollo focuses on orbital programs. Aviation W 91:21 Jl 14 '69
Putting comfort in orbit. R. R. Gilruth. il Space World F-2-62:42 F '69
Russians take a vital step; Soyuz 6-8 flights. Bsns W p48 O 18 '69
Space factory planned for 1970s. M. L. Yaffee. il Aviation W 91:61+ N 10 '69
Space station is go. J. Eberhart. il Sci N 97: 21-2 Ja 3 '70
Still in the future; permanent space stations. Sci N 96:371-2 O 25 '69
What Russia is up to in space; on the U.S. timetable; a space village. il U S News 67: 38-40 O 27 '69
SPACE suits. See Astronauts—Clothing
SPACE technology
Action at Baikonur. il Newsweek 74:108 O 20 '69
Europe's avionics firms fear space losses. Aviation W 90:286-7+ Je 2 '69
Factories in space. W. Von Braun. il Pop Sci 195:72-5+ D '69
Future space flights; address, September 26, 1969. R. Anderson. Vital Speeches 36:175-8 Ja 1 '70
Great promise of zero G. A. R. Sorrells. il Space World F-10-70:16-25 O '69
In the news; manufacturing-in-space experiments. Space World F-6-66:46 Je '69
NASA expands study of space manufacturing; five-task space processing experiment. il Aviation W 90:78 Ap 14 '69
Science and the moon. il Space World F-5-65:32-5 My '69
Soyuz welding evaluation puts Russians nearer space goals. Aviation W 91:19 O 27 '69
Space factory planned for 1970s. M. L. Yaffee. il Aviation W 91:61+ N 10 '69
Space manufacturing test planned. B. K. Thomas. Aviation W 90:55-6 Mr 24 '69
Space processing effort refocused. M. L. Yaffee. Aviation W 90:63-4+ Ap 7 '69
Special reports on space technology; symposium with editorial comment. il Aviation W 91:17, 22-32+ Ag 11 '69
Spin-offs from space. Time 94:24 Ag 1 '69
Technological impact; symposium. il Bul Atom Sci 25:69-87 S '69
Technology: father of human welfare. E. C. Welsh. Space World F-2-62:41 F '69
Techno-politics of space. R. Hotz. Aviation W 91:11 Ag 25 '69
Vertical is to live, horizontal is to die. R. B. Fuller. Am Scholar 39:27-47 Wint '69

Study and teaching

All subjects are go with aerospace; program in Lincoln, Neb. L. Howard. il Am Ed 5:5-8 Ap '69
SPACE telemetry
High-speed telemetry moves to U.H.F. il Electr World 81:66 Ap '69
NASA considers satellite network. P. J. Klass. il Aviation W 91:58-9+ O 13 '69
SPACE telescope. See Artificial satellites—Astronomical applications
SPACE vehicle models
Alabama's simulated lunar spacecraft; lunar hybrid rocket demonstrator. il Space World F-8-68:28-9 Ag '69
SPACE vehicle parts

Testing

Capacitance probes in industrial instrumentation. R. A. Shiver. il Electr World 81:42-3+ My '69
SPACE vehicles
Apollo command module reuse proposed. N. S. Himmel. Aviation W 90:73+ Ap 7 '69
Saturn/Apollo as a transportation system. W. Von Braun. il Bul Atom Sci 25:74-8 S '69
Sequence shows Apollo vertical assembly. il Aviation W 90:59-63+ Ap 14 '69

SPACE vehicles—*Continued*
Space program: future plans; address, October 23, 1969. G. E. Mueller. Vital Speeches 36:170-5 Ja 1 '70
Stage and a half spaceship. il Space World F-5-65:22-30 My '69
Whatever happened to the old Apollo spacecraft? il U S News 67:18 N 17 '69
See also
Lunar vehicles

Atomic power plants
Nuclear energy in space and the grand tour. il Chem 42:20-1 F '69

Control systems
Apollo 8 proves value of onboard control. B. K. Thomas, jr. il Aviation W 90:40-1+ Ja 20 '69
How the Apollo came back home. Space World F 3-63:22 Mr '69

Crews
See Astronauts

Design
Apollo spacecraft. il Space World F-7-67: 16-19 Jl '69
Reusable shuttle configurations emerging. il Aviation W 91:72-3 N 10 '69
Reusable space shuttle effort gains momentum. Aviation W 91:22-4 O 27 '69
Special report, Apollo lunar module. il Aviation W 90:40-1+ F 17 '69

Electronic equipment
See also
Radar in space flight

Equipment
Apollo 12 launches new moon gear. il Bsns W p38+ N 8 '69
See also
Television cameras on space vehicles

Exhibitions
Soyuz, Apollo crews visit Paris; U.S. displays Apollo 8 vehicle. D. E. Fink. il Aviation W 90:67 Je 2 '69

Insulation
See Insulation (heat)

Landing
Apollo 12 landing accuracy praised. Z. Strickland. Aviation W 91:14-15 D 22 '69
Precision landing exceeds goals. E. J. Bulban. il Aviation W 91:22-4 N 24 '69
Trajectory, timing of Apollo 11 revised to permit Goldstone antenna to cover landing. W. C. Wetmore. il Aviation W 91:40-1+ Jl 14 '69

Landing systems
Air force pushing studies of reusable space shuttle. Aviation W 91:25 Ag 11 '69
Earth-landing rotor spacecraft studied. N. S. Himmel. il Aviation W 90:51-3+ Ap 21 '69
Flexible-wing recovery system set for unmanned trials. C. M. Plattner. il Aviation W 90:56-8 F 10 '69
Hypersonic studies get new focus. M. L. Yaffee. il Aviation W 91:34-5 D 22 '69
Lifting body interest gaining. Aviation W 90: 51 F 3 '69
NASA to begin unmanned tests of new type lifting shape for hypersonic maneuvers; Hyper 3. C. M. Plattner. il Aviation W 91: 52-3+ S 29 '69
Shuttle dominates post-Apollo era. il Aviation W 91:12-13 mid-D '69

Mars
NASA evaluates Mars lander proposals. il Aviation W 90:83+ Ap 14 '69

Moon
And now to touch the moon's forbidding face. K. F. Weaver. il Nat Geog 135:632-5 My '69
Apollo lunar module engine exhaust products. B. R. Simoneit and others. bibliog il Science 166:733-8 N 7 '69
Apollo lunar module; interior construction views in full color. il Space World G-1-73: 20-34 Ja '70
Apollo 9 maneuvering sequence planned for first manned flight of lunar module. il Aviation W 90:64-7 F 24 '69
Apollo 9 readied to test lunar module. il Aviation W 90:17-19 F 3 '69
Apollo 12, our second walk on the moon; interview, ed. by R. P. Crossley. J. A. McDivitt. il Pop Mech 132:50+ N '69

Apollo's unsung hero; J. Houbolt's lunar orbital-rendezvous technique. il Time 93:59-60 F 28 '69
Flight of the Spider; Apollo Lunar module. il Newsweek 73:95-6 Mr 10 '69
Getting down onto the moon. R. N. Watts, jr. il Sky & Tel 38:20-2 Jl '69
Gumdrop meets the Spider; Apollo 9 crew practice plan of lunar-landing mission. il Newsweek 73:72+ Mr 17 '69
How an idea no one wanted grew up to be the LEM; with report by D. Sheridan. il Life 66:20-7 Mr 14 '69
It looks like a Martian, it will land our men on the moon: the LM. T. Buckley. il N Y Times Mag p32-5+ F 23 '69
Lunar module begins descent to moon; photographs. Aviation W 91:59-62A Ag 18 '69
LM graduates, cum laude. il Bsns W p64-6 Mr 15 '69
LM landing radar. il Space World F-10-70:26 O '69
Lunar module passes moon test. W. J. Normyle. Aviation W 90:16-17 My 26 '69
Lunar module proves capabilities. W. J. Normyle. il Aviation W 90:69-72 Je 2 '69
Moon bug learns to mate. W. Cloud. il Pop Mech 131:121-5+ F '69
Moon-landing Spider. W. Von Braun. il Pop Sci 194:125-9 My '69
Moonward by jungle gym; lunar module. J. Eberhart. il Sci N 95:218-19 Mr 1 '69
Next step will be the first; lunar landing. il Bsns W p78+ My 31 '69
1969: the year of the moon. J. Wolfert. il Read Digest 94:55-9 My '69
Our Terra-luna transit system; where will it take us? R. S. Lewis. il Bul Atom Sci 25: 22-3 Mr '69
Precision maneuvering in space; Apollo lunar module mission. il Space World F-11-71: 39-41 N '69
Special report, Apollo lunar module. il Aviation W 90:40-1+ F 17 '69
Spectacular step toward lunar landing. il Time 93:50-1 Mr 14 '69
Spider makes its mark; Apollo 9 moves U.S. toward the moon. il Sci N 95:277-8 Mr 22 '69

Launching
Apollo 13 launch rule changes will be recommended to NASA. Aviation W 91:18 D 22 '69
Artist goes to Cape Kennedy to draw an Apollo launch. A. Metcalf. il Space World F-11-71:19-22 N '69
Cameras follow Apollo 11 launch sequence. il Aviation W 91:75-9 Ag 4 '69
Changes in launch rules studied. Aviation W 91:52 D 8 '69
Manmade lightning; Apollo 12 liftoff into electrically charged clouds. il Sci N 96:574 D 20 '69
Power source loss marks Apollo launch. B. K. Thomas, jr. il Aviation W 91:25-6 N 24 '69
Saturn 5 gave the Apollo 8 a leg up to the moon. W. Jury. il Space World F-3-63:31-3 Mr '69
Send-off of Apollo 12. R. Hillenbrand. il Sky & Tel 39:9-10 Ja '70
See also
Artificial satellites—Launching

Maintenance and repair
Coming, a Mr Fix-it space car. W. Von Braun. il Pop Sci 194:98-100+ Ap '69

Manufacture
Apollo's builders start closing the lines. il Bsns W p76-7 My 17 '69
It takes 350,000 people to put three on the moon. A. Hamilton. il Sci Digest 65:22-6 Mr '69
TIEing the loose ends in Apollo program; technical integration and evaluation. il Bsns W p 128-9 My 24 '69
Toughest weld of all; panels of Saturn S-11. il Space World F-4-64:42-9 Ap '69

Materials
Aluminum took man to the moon. il Space World F-10-70:4-7 O '69

Orbits
Amateur scientist; simple ways to calculate the orbits of space vehicles. S. A. Kallis jr. il Sci Am 220:123-6+ Ja '69
Information from deep-space tracking. P. M. Muller and W. L. Sjogren. bibliog il Phys Today 22:46-52 Jl '69
See also
Trajectories

Parts
See Space vehicle parts

SPACE vehicles—*Continued*

Photographs

Album, Soviet Union. Space World F-4-64: 23-30 Ap '69

Piloting

Armstrong recalls moon landing details; excerpts from address. N. A. Armstrong. il Aviation W 91:20-2 O 13 '69

Armstrong's piloting reflexes avert rocky landing for Eagle. Aviation W 91:36-7 Jl 28 '69

How they fly the LM and Apollo. il Pop Mech 132:88-9 Jl '69

Procedural error cited as cause in report on Apollo 10 gyrations. Aviation W 91:20 Jl 21 '69

See also

Space vehicles—Landing

Power supply

New windowshade to harness sunlight for satellite power. il Space World F-6-66:38 Je '69

Propulsion systems

Apollo mini-pogo remedy set; recommendation for early shutdown of center engine. Aviation W 90:19 Ap 28 '69

Delta launches delayed; probe continues. Aviation W 91:19 S 29 '69

Delta probe delays skynet launch again. Aviation W 91:20 N 3 '69

Europeans interested in Titan 3 proposal. C. Brownlow. il Aviation W 90:18-19 Je 23 '69

Future Saturn 5 program studied. Aviation W 90:25 My 5 '69

Harvest of Operation Paperclip. il Newsweek 74:10 Jl 7 '69

In the news; hydrazine propulsion system. Space World F-5-65:46 My '69

Italy negotiating to buy Thor Delta. Aviation W 90:97 Ap 14 '69

Launch vehicles. il Space World F-7-67:20-2 Jl '69

Modular launch vehicle proposed to ELDO. E. H. Kolcum. il Aviation W 91:47+ S 1 '69

Reusable space ferry considered. B. K. Thomas. il Aviation W 90:57+ Je 16 '69

S-IVB rocket that took man to the moon. il Space World F-11-71:36-8 N'69

Saturn 5 gave the Apollo 8 a leg up to the moon. W. Jury. il Space World F-3-63:31-3 Mr '69

Saturn V launch vehicle. il Space World F-10-70:8-13 O '69

Saturn V's performance during Apollo 9 flight. Space World F-6-66:30 Je '69

Sterile solid motor studied. Aviation W 90: 60-1 Ap 28 '69

Uprated Delta to boost Tiros. il Aviation W 90:58-9 Mr 24 '69

See also

European launcher development organization
Ion engines
Lasers—Space flight applications
Rocket engines

Maintenance and repair

Quick Saturn 5 fixes aid Apollo. W. C. Wetmore. il Aviation W 90:57-8+ F 24 '69

Specifications

U.S. launch vehicles; International launch vehicles (cont) Aviation W 90:143-4 Mr 10 '69

Testing

Dress rehearsal. M. Alberstadt. il Space World F-8-68:32-3 Ag '69

Quarantine

See Quarantine

Radio equipment

See Radio apparatus on space vehicles

Recovery

Apollo 11 crew tests recovery method in Gulf. il Aviation W 90:55+ Je 9 '69

Heroes or the plague: Apollo 11 astronauts. il Sci N 95:611-13 Je 28 '69

Lowering the guard against the invaders; change in recovery plan of Apollo 11. Time 93:78 My 16 '69

Reliability

Three to get ready; Apollo module. E. A. Herron. il Space World F-2-62:36-9 F '69

Shielding (radiation)

Will mighty magnets protect voyagers to planets? W. Von Braun. il Pop Sci 194:98-100+ Ja '69

Stability and stabilizers

Taking the spin out of satellites. S. V. Jones. Sci Digest 66:69 D '69

Sterilization

Sandia studies heat-radiation sterilization. Aviation W 91:88 N 17 '69

Spacecraft sterilization. Space World G-1-73: 40 Ja '70

Testing

Apollo/Saturn V, from ground test to flight. il Space World F-2-62:6-34 F '69

Automatic checkout equipment, the Apollo Hippocrates. S. Sternberg. il Bul Atom Sci 25:84-7 S '69

NASA readying Apollo 10 for lunar orbital mission. Aviation W 90:39 Ap 14 '69

Three to get ready; Apollo module. E. A. Herron. il Space World F-2-62:36-9 F '69

Tracking

Apollo 10 optical tracking. il Sky & Tel 38: 62 Jl '69

Apollo 11 tracking force readied. il Aviation W 91:91+ Jl 14 '69

Information from deep-space tracking. P. M. Muller and W. L. Sjogren. bibliog il Phys Today 22:46-52 Jl '69

Observations of Apollo 11. il Sky & Tel 38: 358-9 N '69

Optical observations of Apollo 8. H. B. Liemohn. il Sky & Tel 37:156-60 Mr '69

Space age turns a new chapter; tracking network. il Bsns W p98-9+ Ap 12 '69

Tracking station ten miles from launch pad keeps close watch on Saturn-Apollo. il Space World F-9-69:30 S '69

Visual observations of Apollo 8. C. F. Capen. il R Pop Astron 63:12-13 My '69

Viewports

Apollo window sealant treated. Aviation W 90:23 Mr 3 '69

In the news; lunar module windows. il Space World F-7-67:47-8 Jl '69

SPACE vehicles, Russian

In the news; Russian launch vehicles. Space World F-8-68:49-50 Ag '69

Soviet Soyuz launch operations detailed; photographs. Aviation W 91:67-9 S 15 '69

Soviet space schedule may include large booster test. D. C. Winston. il Aviation W 90:132-4 Mr 10 '69

SPACEK, Leonard Paul

Maverick from the Midwest. por Bsns W p 128 O 18 '69

SPACEMEN. See Astronauts

SPACESUITS. See Astronauts—Clothing

SPACKMAN, Robert R. Jr

Exercises you can do wherever you are; excerpts from Exercise in the office. Read Digest 94:113-16 Je '69

SPADEFOOT toad. See Toads

SPAGHETTI. See Macaroni

SPAGHETTI sauce. See Sauces

SPAIN, Louise

Screenings: 16mm. Library J 94:3153-4 S 15 '69

SPAIN

See also

Automobile industry and trade—Spain
Biscay, Bay of
Castile
Church and state in Spain
Civil rights—Spain
Festivals—Spain
Gardens—Spain
Government ownership—Spain
Investments, Foreign (in Spain)
Majorca
Pamplona
Public opinion—Spain
Publishers and publishing—Spain
Tarragona
Tourist trade—Spain

Anecdotes, facetiae, satire, etc.

Back to Madrid; excerpts. B. P. Solomon. Harper 239:76-89 Ag '69

Cabinet

El caudillo's legacy. Time 94:41 N 7 '69
Succession. il Newsweek 74:59 N 10 '69

Constitution

Back to the Borbóns. Time 94:30+ Ag 1 '69

Back to the throne: Juan Carlos as next chief of state. W. F. Buckley, jr. Nat R 21: 818-19 Ag 12 '69

Bonnie Prince Carlos? il Newsweek 74:49-50 Jl 28 '69

SPAIN—Constitution—*Continued*
Clarifying the succession. il Time 94:35+ Jl 25 '69
Hard pill to swallow; J. Carlos as next chief of state. il Newsweek 74:48+ Ag 4 '69

Description and travel
Apocrypha on the Costa del Sol. D. Butwin. il Sat R 52:44-5+ Mr 29 '69
As I walked out one midsummer morning. L. Lee. New Yorker 45:25-33 Jl 5; 32-40+ Ag 2 '69
From Lisbon to Madrid to Spain's Costa Del Sol, Club continental's travelers tried out a new kind of tour. J. Friedberg. il Travel & Camera 32:86-8+ O '69
Iberia & the Magreb. H. Apter. il Travel & Camera 32:40-5, 51-3+ Ap '69
Iberian itinerary. J. M. Dalury. il Travel 132:36-41 N '69
Personal business. Bsns W p89-90 Jl 26 '69
Road to Tarragona. F. T. Mitchell. il Harp Baz 102:160+ O '69
Spain, a dither of cities. D. Messinesi. il Vogue 153:42+ Je '69

Foreign relations
Great Britain
See also
Gibraltar

United States
New life for U.S. bases in Spain. U S News 66:8 Je 16 '69
U.S. and Spain confer on extension of defense agreement; joint communique, March 26,1969. Dept State Bul 60:324 Ap 14 '69
U.S. and Spain extend defense agreement; joint statement; with text of U.S. note and letters, June 20, 1969. Dept State Bul 61:15 Jl 7 '69

History
Bibliography
Articles and other books received; comp. by C. J. Bishko. See issues of American historical review

House of Austria, 1516-1700
Moriscos: an Ottoman fifth column in sixteenth-century Spain. A. C. Hess. bibliog f Am Hist R 74:1-25 O '68

Spanish American war
See United States—History—Spanish American war, 1898

Civil war, 1936-1939
Man upstairs; amnesty for ex-Republican Cortés. Time 93:29 My 2 '69

Civil war, 1936-1939—Campaigns and battles
For whom the bell tolled; excerpts from Between the bullet and the lie. C. Eby. il Am Heritage 20:36-41+ Ag '69

Civil war, 1936-1939—Foreign participation
Between the bullet and the lie, by C. Eby. Review
Atlan 224:98 Ag '69. E. Weeks
For whom the bell tolled; excerpts from Between the bullet and the lie. C. Eby. il Am Heritage 20:36-41+ Ag '69

Civil war, 1936-1939—Personal narratives
As I walked out one midsummer morning. L. Lee. New Yorker 45:37-40+ **Ag 2**: 26-33 Ag 23 '69

Industries
Conglomeration, Spanish style; Grupo Fierro. Fortune 80:166 Ag 15 '69
See also
Textile machinery industry—Spain

Politics and government
Crackdown in Spain. Nat R 21:163-4 F **25** '69
End of the experiment; state of emergency. Time 93:28 Ja 31 '69
Exception is the rule. P. Steinfels. Commonweal 89:633-4 F 21 '69
For Spain a royal restoration. il Life 67:33-4+ Ag 8 '69
Franco's last deal. L. Jenkins. Nation 209:689-92 D 22 '69
King will reign in Spain again; Franco style. il U S News 67:10 Ag 4 '69
Little freedom; deadline approaching for treaty covering American bases on Spanish soil and state of emergency. Nation 208:261-2 Mr 3 '69
Military moves in. il Time 93:26 F 7 '69

Regression in Spain. America 120:155 F 8 '69
Spain is still afraid of itself. R. Eder. il N Y Times Mag p23+ Mr 9 '69
Spanish regime cracks down; with report by R. Hemming. il Sr Schol 94:16-17 F 14 '69
Ton of prevention. P. S. Cook. il Newsweek 73:38 F 10 '69
Trouble ahead for Franco. Nation 208:133 F 3 '69
See also
Spain—Cabinet
Spain—Constitution

Religious institutions and affairs
World around us (cont) Chr Cent 86:265-6, 931+ F 19, Jl 9 '69
See also
Catholic church in Spain
Muslims in Spain
Protestant churches—Spain

SPAIN and Latin America
Productive initiative; Madrid seminar on Latin America and Spain. G. de Zéndegui. Américas 21:1 Ja '69
SPALAX ehrenbergi. See Mole rats
SPAN of life. See Longevity
SPANIARDS
In a little Spanish town. R. Hattersley. il Pop Phot 65:96-9+ Ag '69
Sketches of Madrid. F. Donovan. America 120:562 My 10 '69
What Spaniards say when they think aloud; excerpts from Conversations in Madrid, ed. by R. Eder. S. Paniker. il N Y Times Mag p25+ S 28 '69; Reply. J. Eugui. p22 N 9 '69
SPANIELS
Flushing breeds. J. Griffen. il Field & S 73:214-16+ Ap '69
Odd couples; English setters and English spaniels. D. M. Duffey. il Outdoor Life 143:192-3+ Ap '69
SPANISH. See Spaniards
SPANISH AMERICAN history. See Latin America—History
SPANISH American war. See United States—History—Spanish American war, 1898
SPANISH AMERICANS in the United States. See Latin Americans in the United States
SPANISH cookery. See Cookery, Spanish
SPANISH dancing. See Dancing, Spanish
SPANISH furniture. See Furniture, Spanish
SPANISH language

Study and teaching
Bread-and-butter Spanish. G. D. Matlock. Todays Ed 58:46 Ap '69
Crash program in Spanish and Mexican-American culture. il Sch & Soc 97:87-8 F '69
Experiment in learning. J. F. Gallivan. Clear House 44:235 D '69

SPANISH Methodist church, East Harlem. See New York (city)—Churches
SPANISH missions in New Mexico. See New Mexico—Missions
SPANISH poetry

Translations into English
Fragment; tr. by N. T. Di Giovanni. J. L. Borges. New Yorker 45:42 S 6 '69
Full consciousness; Oceans; Lumber wagons; Dawns of moguer; Road; Dawn outside the city walls; tr. by R. Bly. J. R. Jiménez. Nation 209:18 Jl 7 '69
SPANISH SAHARA
See also
United Nations—Spanish Sahara
SPANISH speaking students
See also
Mexican American students
SPANISH wines. See Wine
SPANN, Neil
Fifteen years of the IHF. Hi Fi 19:67-70 Mr '69
SPARANO, Vin T.
(ed) Where to go. See issues of Outdoor life
SPARE time. See Leisure
SPAREMBLEK, Milko
His only dogma is no dogmas. J. Anderson. il por Dance Mag 43:68-9 N '69
SPARERIBS. See Cookery—Meat
SPARGUR, Ronn
Saw you this woman? poem. Chr Cent 86:710 My 21 '69
SPARK plugs
Safe conduct for sparks. J. Thawley. il Hot Rod 22:118 Ag '69
Spark plug trouble shooting. Hot Rod 22:99 F '69

SPARK screens. See Fireplace accessories
SPARKPLUGS. See Spark plugs
SPARKS, Fred
That's mother with the red guards. Sat R 52:74+ S 13 '69
We bathed by candlelight. McCalls 96:67+ Ag '69
SPARLING, P. Frederick
Kasugamycin resistance: 30S ribosomal mutation with an unusual location on the escherichia coli chromosome. bibliog Science 167:56-8 Ja 2 '70
SPARROW, John
Revolting students. Nat R 21:175-7+ F 25 '69
SPARROW hawks. See Kestrels
SPARS. See Masts and rigging
SPARTA, N.J.
Cooperative purchasing pays. J. P. Brown. il Am City 84:88+ D '69
SPARTANS industries, incorporated
Spartans' new game plan. Forbes 104:56 O 15 '69
SPAS. See Health resorts, watering places, etc.
SPASSKY, Boris
Tigran and the tiger. il por Time 93:51-2 Je 27 '69
SPATER, George Alexander
Who's happy? il por Forbes 104:73-4 N 15 '69
SPÄTZLE. See Dumplings
SPAULDING, Robert L.
Durham education improvement program. Todays Ed 58:62-4 F '69
SPAWNING
Fishes that grow horns; breeding or nuptial tubercles. R. F. Denoncourt. il Cons 23:30-1 Ap '69
Grunion: that fish that spawns on land. C. P. Idyll. il Nat Geog 135:714-23 My '69
SPEAKERS. See Loud speaking apparatus
SPEAKING. See Public speaking; Voice
SPEAKING in tongues. See Gift of tongues
SPEARS, Harold
Why school board meetings go to pot. Ed Digest 34:26-7 F '69
SPECIAL classes and special schools
Environment to grow in; First street school; excerpt from The lives of children. G. Dennison. il Sat R 52:74-6 O 18 '69
How to teach a delinquent; Warrendale youth development center. N. F. Hahn. Atlan 223:66-8+ Mr '69
Lives of children, by G. Dennison. Review Nation 209:447-8 O 27 '69. N. O'Gorman Newsweek 74:96+ D 1 '69. P. A. Janssen Sat R il 52:92-3 N 15 '69. P H Wagschal
Non-professional teachers enliven the subject matter; Project 400 to relate the world of work to classroom subject matter. J. Bahr. Clear House 43:494-6 Ap '69
Room for miracles; Independent learning center at Chicago's Ray school. L. Wille. il Am Ed 5:7-10 Ag '69
They're sharing something special; special education programs, Richmond County, Ga. J. S. Park. il Am Ed 5:23-5 Mr '69
See also
Individual instruction
SPECIAL committee of twenty-four on colonialism. See United Nations—Special committee on the situation with regard to implementation of declaration on granting of independence to colonial countries and peoples
SPECIAL committee on the question of defining aggression. See United Nations—Special committee on the question of defining aggression
SPECIAL days, weeks, and months
Prayer for peace. Chr Today 14:31 N 7 '69
See also names of special days, weeks and months, e.g. Negro history week
SPECIAL drawing rights
Aquarius in the foreign exchanges; Special drawing rights to finance the continued growth of world trade. il Time 94:88 O 10 '69
Crawling toward new flexibility; creating special drawing rights (SDRs) in IMF. Bsns W p38-9 Je 21 '69
Dollar triumphant. Newsweek 75:58 Ja 12 '70
Financing the world empire. M. Hudson. Commonweal 91:243-5 N 21 '69
No gold in them thar tills; Special drawing rights. Nat R 21:788 Ag 12 '69
Obsolete SDR's; Special drawing rights. M. Friedman. Newsweek 74:76 S 8 '69
Overseas commentary. G. J. Henry. Forbes 104:97 N 1 '69
Paper gold, at last; plan to create special drawing rights. Newsweek 74:70 Ag 4 '69

Paper gold ok'd. Sr Schol 95:16-17 O 27 '69
Reformers put the heat on the monetary glacier. il Bsns W p 124+ Je 7 '69
SDRs: a test of faith. il Bsns W p94 N 8 '69
Special drawing rights. H. C. Wallich. Newsweek 74:86 Jl 21 '69
That paper gold: special drawing rights. U S News 67:63 O 13 '69
SPECIAL education. See Special classes and special schools
SPECIAL education instructional materials center. See Instructional materials centers
SPECIAL librarians. See Librarians
SPECIAL libraries association
Bed-in for special libraries: '69 SLA conference. il Wilson Lib Bul 44:7-9 S '69
Mushawara in Montreal, June 16 conference. K. Nyren. il Library J 94:2557-61 Jl '69; Discussion. 94:2986, 4074 S 15, N 15 '69
SPECIAL missions of the United Nations. See United Nations—Special missions
SPECIAL vision; story. See Head, B.
SPECIALISTS
Policy making in the USSR; party-elite conflict. il Trans-Action 6:7 F '69
SPECIALISTS, Stock. See Securities—Marketing
SPECIALIZATION
In my opinion; being well-rounded is a waste of time. P. Morris. Seventeen 27:222 N '68
SPECIALTY equipment manufacturers association
Blow-ups for SEMA. E. Rickman. il Hot Rod 22:94 Je '69
SPECIALTY stores
How green the grass; stores selling paraphernalia that goes with smoking pot. il Newsweek 73:78 F 3 '69
SPECIATION. See Species
SPECIES
Differentiation of populations; importance of gene flow. P. R. Ehrlich and P. H. Raven. bibliog Science 165:1228-32 S 19 '69
Speciation in Amazonian forest birds. J. Haffer. bibliog il Science 165:131-7 Jl 11 '69
See also
Phylogeny
SPECIFICATIONS
See also subhead Specifications under various subjects, e.g. Automobiles—Specifications
SPECIMENS, Botanical. See Plants—Collection and preservation
SPECTACLES. See Eyeglasses
SPECTER, David Kenneth
Some essentials of successful urban space. il Arch Rec 145:131-40 Ja '69
SPECTINOMYCIN. See Antibiotics
SPECTOR, M. and others
Atherosclerotic plaque: X-ray diffraction investigation. bibliog Science 165:711 Ag 15 '69
SPECTOR, Robert D.
Lyrics, heroic and otherwise. Sat R 52:33-5 Mr 15 '69
SPECTOR, Sydney, and others
Vascular smooth muscle reactivity in normotensive and hypertensive rats. bibliog Science 166:1300-1 D 5 '69
SPECTORSKY, A. C.
Lesson learned. Yachting 125:75+ Ap '69
SPECTRE, Peter H.
Use your LSD. il Yachting 125:122-3+ Ja '69
SPECTROHELIOGRAPH
Ultraviolet astronomy. L. Goldberg. il Sci Am 220:92-102 bibliog(p 144) Je '69
SPECTROMETERS
Mass spectrometry. R. I. Reed and D. H. Robertson. il Chem 42:7-11 Je '69 (to be cont)
Nudging the nucleus; Argonne's superconducting internal conversion electron spectrometer. D. E. Thomsen. il Sci N 95:147+ F 8 '69
See also
Mass spectrometry
SPECTROPHOTOMETERS
Cytotoxic test automation: a live-dead cell differential counter. M. R. Melamed and others. bibliog il Science 163:285-6 Ja 17 '69
SPECTROPHOTOMETRY
Spectrographic detection of topographic features on Mars. M. J. S. Belton and D. M. Hunten. bibliog il Science 166:225-7 O 10 '69
SPECTRUM
Absorption spectra
See also
Spectrum, Ultraviolet—Absorption spectra

SPECTRUM—*Continued*

Fluorescence spectra

2-p-Toluidinyl-6-naphthalene sulfonate: relation of structure to fluorescence properties in different media. A. Camerman and L. H. Jensen. bibliog il Science 165:493-5 Ag 1 '69

Reflection spectra

Mars: is the surface colored by carbon suboxide? W. T. Plummer and R. K. Carson. bibliog il Science 166:1141-2 N 28 '69
Spectral reflectivity of Mars. T. B. McCord and J. B. Adams. bibliog il Science 163:1058-60 Mr 7 '69

SPECTRUM, Infrared

Infrared absorptions near three microns recorded over the polar cap of Mars. K. C. Herr and G .C. Pimentel. bibliog il Science 166:496-9 O 24 '69
Moon: infrared studies of surface composition. D. P. Cruikshank. bibliog il Science 166:215-18 O 10 '69

SPECTRUM, Microwave

Microwave spectrum and structure of sulfur difluoride. D. R. Johnson and F. X. Powell. bibliog il Science 164:950-1 My 23 '69
Spectra, variability, size, and polarization of H_2O microwave emission sources in the galaxy. S. H. Knowles and others. bibliog il Science 163:1055-7 Mr 7 '69

SPECTRUM, Solar

X-ray line and continuum spectra of solar flares and 0.5 to 8.5 angstroms. J. F. Meekins and others; reply. F. W. Lytle. bibliog il Science 165:416 Jl 25 '69

SPECTRUM, Ultraviolet

Mariner 6: ultraviolet spectrum of Mars upper atmosphere. C. A. Barth and others. bibliog il Science 165:1004-5 S 5 '69

Absorption spectra

Atmospheric absorption anomalies in the ultraviolet near an altitude of fifty kilometers. A. J. Krueger. bibliog il Science 166:998-1000 N 21 '69

SPECTRUM analysis

Isobaric analog resonances. W. R. Coker and C. F. Moore. bibliog il Phys Today 22:53-61 Ap '69
Laser beat frequency spectroscopy. M. J. French and others. bibliog il Science 163:345-51 Ja 24 '69
See also
Astronomical spectroscopy
Mass spectrometry
Spectrum, Infrared
Stars—Spectra

SPECULATION

Behind rush for German marks. il U S News 66:12 Mv 19 '69
Crackdown on stock speculation. il U S News 66:102-3 F 17 '69
Danger signs in the stock market; interview. R. W. Haack. il U S News 67:62-5 Ag 4 '69
Gauging speculation. il Fortune 79:169-70 Ja '69
Investors head for bright side; return of bulls to stock market. il Bsns W p43-4 My 10 '69
Risky business: a primer on stock market speculation. T. May. Atlan 224:68-72+ Jl; 72-6 Ag '69
So you want to make a killing in the market. il Changing T 23:41-4 O '69
Stock-market trends that worry Congress. il U S News 66:51-4 My 5 '69
Traders toast future in Scotch. Bsns W p 130+ O 11 '69
Wall Street: a time for bonds? C. Morgello. il Newsweek 73:78 Mr 10 '69
Warning labels for some stocks; special risks. U S News 66:80 Mr 17 '69
See also
Arbitrage
Commodity exchanges
Investments
Manipulation (securities)
Securities
Stock exchange
Stocks

SPECULATION in land. See Real estate business

SPEECH

Vocal tract limitations on the vowel repertoires of rhesus monkey and other non-human primates. P. H. Lieberman and others. bibliog il Science 164:1185-7 Je 6 '69
Words, words, words; class indicators in speech in England. Trans-Action 6:6 Jl '69
See also
Children—Language
Language and languages
Stammering
Voice

SPEECH, Freedom of. See Free speech

SPEECH analyzer. See Automatic speech recognition

SPEECH correction. See Speech therapy

SPEECH defects
See also
Stammering

SPEECH education
See also
Children—Language

SPEECH therapy

To keep a child from stuttering. G. M. Knox. Bet Hom & Gard 47:14+ Ag '69
Why me? condensation. W. Gargan. il Good H 168:92-5+ Mr '69

SPEECH writing. See Authorship—Collaboration

SPEECHES, addresses, etc.
See also
Baccalaureate addresses
Public speaking

SPEECHWRITING assistants to the president. See Public officers

SPEED

Beauties of speed; collages of recordbreaking individuals. il Harp Baz 103:126-9 D '69
Isaac Asimov explains; how fast is infinite speed? Tachyons. I. Asimov. Sci Digest 66:82-3 D '69

SPEED indicators
See also
Computers—Traffic control applications
Tachometers

SPEED laws. See Traffic regulations

SPEED limit signs. See Traffic signs

SPEED of light. See Light—Velocity

SPEED reading

I was a speed-reading dropout. J. M. Flagler. Look 33:88+ O 21 '69

SPEED records. See Aviation records

SPEEDWAYS

Auto racing's new speedways. B. Kilpatrick. il Pop Mech 132:90-3 Ag '69
Talladega's troubled baptism; Alabama international motor speedway. L. Laye. il Motor T 21:34-6 N '69

Safety devices and measures

Talladega: the principals and the principles. B. France; R. Petty. Motor T 21:37+ N '69

SPEER, Albert

Devil's architect. J. P. O'Donnell. il pors N Y Times Mag p45-9+ O 26 '69; Discussion. p22+ N 30 '69
Führer's master builder. il pors Time 94:40 S 12 '69
Memories of crime past. il por Newsweek 74:41 S 8 '69

SPEHLMANN, Rainer

Acetylcholine facilitation, atropine block of synaptic excitation of cortical neurons. bibliog Science 165:404-5 Jl 25 '69

SPEIS, Industrial

Israel using Atar tooling data to prolong Mirage usefulness. Aviation W 91:20 O 6 '69

SPELEOLOGY. See Caves

SPELLERS

Butter by the firkin; The elementary spelling-book, by N. Webster. L. Conger. Writer 82:9-10 Mr '69

SPELLING

Competitions

Excitement over spelling; National spelling bee. N. Gittelson. McCalls 96:89+ S '69

Study and teaching

Perfectly normal spelling dilemma. D. C. Olson. Engl J 58:1220-2 N '69

SPELLING bees. See Spelling—Competitions

SPELLMAN, A. B.
Revolution in sound. Ebony 24:84-9 Ag '69

SPELLMAN, I. Orrin
Quick delivery. Parks & Rec 4:23+ Ag '69

SPELMAN, Franz
Tirol. Travel & Camera 32:46+ Jl '69

SPELMAN college, Atlanta, Ga.
I was on display all through high school. il Newsweek 73:55 F 10 '69

SPENCE, Edward James, 3d
Knock-out by a brain-in. P. Putnam. il pors Sports Illus 30:42-4 Mr 3 '69

SPENCER, Colin
Spitting image. Criticism
New Yorker 45:134 Mr 15 '69

SPENCER, Janet
Some tips on classroom management. Todays Ed 58:50 D '69

SPENCER, Michael J.
Why is youth so revolting nowadays? por Wilson Lib Bul 43:640-7 Mr '69

SPENCER, Robert Douglas
King of the abortionists. il por Newsweek 73:92 F 17 '69
SPENCER, Steven M.
Tektite revisited. Pop Sci 195:84-7+ N '69
SPENCER, Walter Troy
They're not robots, they're cyborgs. N Y Times Mag p40-1+ D 14 '69
SPENDER, Stephen
What the rebellious students want. N Y Times Mag p56-7+ Mr 30 '69
(tr) See Cavafy, C. P. Beginning; Remaining; Painted
SPENDING. See Consumption (economics)
SPENGLER, Joseph J.
Population problem: in search of a solution. bibliog Science 166:1234-8 D 5 '69
SPERACIO, Mario
Christmas trees in the city; poem. Good H 169:202 D '69
SPERLING, Edwardine
Noun; poem. Clear House 44:241 D '69
SPERM whales. See Whales
SPERMATOGENESIS. See Gametogenesis
SPERMATOZOA
Microtubules in spermatozoa of childia (turbellaria, acoela) revealed by negative staining. D. P. Costello and others. bibliog il Science 163:678-9 F 14 '69
SPERMIDINE
Histamine and spermidine content in brain during development. L. A. Pearce and S. M. Schanberg. bibliog il Science 166:1301-3 D 5 '69
SPERRY and Hutchinson company
Taking its time; must diversify further. Forbes 103:47 F 15 '69
SPERRY gyroscope company
Engineers wear a union label. Bsns W p48 Jl 12 '69
SPERRY Rand corporation
See also
Sperry gyroscope company

Univac division
Univac comes in from the cold. il Bsns W p 160-1+ N 22 '69
SPEYRER, Cotton
Texas hangs on to its no. 1. D. Jenkins. il Sports Illus 32:26-9 Ja 12 '70
SPHERES of influence. See Hegemony
SPHERULES. See Meteorites
SPICE racks
Light well is also a spice rack. il Sunset 143:98 S '69
Swing-down spice rack. il Sunset 143:157 O '69
SPICES
Season with herbs & spices; with recipes. il Good H 168:92-106 F '69
Spice of life. il Ladies Home J 86:116-17+ S '69
Spices and things. il Redbook 133:114-15+ Jl '69
Spicy eats of India. M. Jaffrey. il Holiday 46:40-1+ D '69
See also
Curry
McCormick and company
SPIDER webs
Spider webs. H. Borland. il Audubon 71:inside cover Jl '69
Weaving of an engineering masterpiece, a spider's orb web, done at Fayson Lakes, N.J., August 8, 1942. B. E. Dugdale. il Natur Hist 78:36-41 Mr '69; Same. UNESCO Courier 22:35-41 D '69
SPIDERS
Beware the brown recluse! il Changing T 23:45-6 Ap '69
Jumping spiders. J. H. Carmichael, jr. il Natur Hist 78:28-35+ O '69
See also
Spider webs
SPIDERWORTS
Translocation in perennial monocotyledons; tradescantia. W. Heyser and others. bibliog il Science 164:572-4 My 2 '69
SPIEGEL, Allen D. See Newman, E. jt. auth.
SPIEGEL, Donald E. and Keith-Spiegel, Patricia
Why we came back: a study of patients readmitted to a mental hospital. Ment Hy 53:433-7 Jl '69
SPIEGEL, John P.
Campus conflict & professorial egos. por Trans-Action 6:41-50 O '69
SPIEGEL, Marshall
News on wheels (cont) Sr Schol 93:24 Ja 10; 94:24 F 14; 24 Mr 7; 22 Mr 14; 32 Mr 28; 32 My 2; 32 My 9 '69
SPIEGEL, Patricia Keith-. See Keith-Spiegel, P.

SPIEGELHALTER, Joan
Biafra; poem. Ment Hy 53:599 O '69
SPIER, Peter
Illustrations of Peter Spier. J. H. Michel. il por Am Artist 33:49-55+ O '69
SPIERS, Al
Lunkers of Obre Lake. Field & S 74:166-8+ O '69
SPIES
Gambit accepted; Helen and Peter Kroger exchanged for G. Brooke. il Newsweek 74:47 Ag 4 '69
Spooks galore; spy-exposés in West Germany. il Time 93:44 My 16 '69
See also
Blake, G.
Espionage
Lee, S. K.
Philby, H. A. R.
Porst, H.
Secret service
Trials (espionage)
SPIES in literature
Private identity; the spy story. L. Braudy. Commentary 48:67-8+ Ag '69
SPIESS, Fred N. See Larson, R. L. jt auth.
SPIGELGASS, Leonard
No room at the inn. McCalls 97:96-7+ N '69
SPILHAUS, Athelstan F.
Athelstan Spilhaus, president-elect. R. Swalin. por Science 163:831-2 F 21 '69
SPIN, isobaric. See Isobaric spin
SPIN-off corporations. See Corporate distributions
SPIN-outs in business. See Diversification in industry
SPINACH
Paramagnetic unit in spinach subchloroplast particles: estimation of size. E. C. Weaver and others. bibliog il Science 165:906-7 Ag 29 '69
See also
Cookery—Vegetables
SPINAL cord
C-Fiber responses in the ventrolateral column of the cat spinal cord. M. Manfredi and V. Castellucci. bibliog il Science 165:1020-2 S 5 '69
SPINAL fluid. See Cerebrospinal fluid
SPINE
See also
Spinal cord

Abnormities and deformities
Spine deformity no handicap. Sci Digest 65:61 Je '69
SPINELLO, Matt P.
On the citizens band. See issues of Popular electronics to May 1969
SPINNANGER, Ruthe T.
Three grey feathers; poem Chr Today 13:14 Ag 1 '69
SPINNER, Thomas J. jr
Macmillan's middle years. Nation 208:279-80 Mr 3 '69
SPINNERS. See Fishing lures, flies, etc.
SPINNING reels. See Fishing tackle
SPINNING tackle. See Fishing tackle
SPINOFF (technology) See Technology transfer
SPINS, Airplane. See Airplanes—Spinning
SPINSKI, Victor
Victor Spinski. F. Kriwanek. il por Ceram Mo 17:24-5 O '69
SPINSTERS. See Single women
SPINY lobsters. See Lobsters
SPINY mice
Diabetic sandrats. D. G. Robinson, jr. il Sci N 95:172-3 F 15 '69
SPIRAL galaxies. See Galactic systems
SPIRAL growth and movement
Fungal endogenous rhythms expressed by spiral figures. J. A. Bourret and others. bibliog il Science 166:763-4 N 7 '69
SPIRES
Golden ribbon spire. il Design 70:19 Spr '69
SPIRIT
See also
Consciousness
SPIRIT, Holy. See Holy Spirit
SPIRIT communication. See Spiritualism
SPIRIT of the road; story. See Tingom, E.
SPIRITISM. See Spiritualism
SPIRITS. See Ghosts
SPIRITUAL life
When I am weak. Chr Today 13:29 Je 6 '69
See also
Holiness
Religion

SPIRITUAL maturity. See Maturity

SPIRITUAL retreats. See Retreats, Spiritual

SPIRITUALISM
Bishop's ghosts; Bishop of Southwark avows his belief in psychic phenomena. il Time 93:49-50 My 30 '69
Intoxicating ideas for the tender mind. J. Miller. Vogue 153:70+ Ja 15 '69
She hears music and there's someone there. D. Bacon. il Life 67:48E-48F Ag 8 '69
See also
Psychical research

SPIRITUALITY
Shame of the game. L. Woodrum. Chr Today 13:14 Jl 18 '69
See also
Meditation

SPIRO who? drama. See Meyers, W.

SPIRONOLACTONE
Digitoxin poisoning: prevention by spironolactone. H. Selye and others. bibliog il Science 164:842-3 My 16 '69

SPITTING image; drama. See Spencer, C.

SPITZ, Mark
Growing up to the legend. il por Time 94:49 Jl 25 '69
Santa Clara holds a splashdown. A. Verschoth. il por Sports Illus 31:20-1 Jl 21 '69
They sent the boys to do a man's work. W. F. Reed, jr. Sports Illus 30:67-8+ Ap 7 '69

SPITZ, Ruth S. See Parnes, H. S. jt. auth.

SPITZER, Dana. See Cooney, J. jt. auth.

SPITZER, Elroy F.
Practical corrections. Am City 84:75-9 Mr '69

SPITZER, Helen. See Spitzer, S .jt. auth.

SPITZER, R. E. and others
Serum C'3 lytic system in patients with glomerulonephritis. bibliog Science 164:436-7 Ap 25 '69

SPITZER, Silas
Hot drinks of winter. Holiday 46:40+ D '69
Regional cooking (cont) por Holiday 45:60-3+ F '68
—and Spitzer, Helen
Holiday's choice of North American restaurants. Holiday 46:81-90 Jl '69

SPITZNAGEL, J. K. See Zeya, H. I. jt. auth.

SPIVACK, Kathleen
Reports: Baker's Island. Atlan 224:22-3 Ag '69
Water gives up its counsel; Drifting; Night terror; poems. Poetry 114:84-7 My '69

SPIVAK, Charlie
Where are they now? il pors Newsweek 75: 10 Ja 12 '70

SPLASHES. See Drops

SPLEEN
Useful organ we can live without. A. S. Freese. il Todays Health 47:65-7+ N '69

SPLICING amateur moving pictures. See Moving pictures, Amateur

SPLIT-level houses. See Architecture, Domestic

SPLIT-rail fences. See Fences

SPLITTERS, Signal. See Television antennas —Equipment

SPOCK, Benjamin
[Monthly column] See issues of Redbook
about
Dissent and Dr Spock. il Time 94:17 Jl 18 '69
Doctor Spock: color him yellow. Nat R 21: 737 Jl 29 '69
Doctor Spock misbehaves. D. Lyle. il por Esquire 71:109-13+ F '69
Guilty as charged by the judge; excerpt from The trial of Dr Spock. J. Mitford. il por Atlan 224:48-66 Ag '69; Discussion. 224:50+ N '69
Old and the young say no. M. McGrory. America 120:555 My 10 '69
Reversal in Spock draft case. U S News 67: 10 Jl 21 '69
Trial of Dr Spock, by J. Mitford. Review
Commentary 48:98-104 D '69. L. Friedman
Life il pors 67:12+ S 12 '69. C. Rembar
Nation 209:382-3 O 13 '69. F. J. Donner
Newsweek il por 74:93-4 S 15 '69. G. Wolff
Ramp Mag 8:42-3 D '69. M. Burnstein
Victory for Dr Spock. por Newsweek 74:30 Jl 21 '69

SPOCK, Benjamin, conspiracy trial. See Trials (conspiracy)

SPODEK, Bernard
Early learning for what? Ed Digest 34:13-15 My '69

SPOERRY, François
Antiquity-sur-mer. il Time 94:70-1 Jl 18 '69

SPOILERS, Automobile. See Automobiles— Stability and stabilizers

SPOILING of children. See Children—Management and training

SPOILS system. See Patronage, Political

SPOKANE, Wash.

Parks and playgrounds
Salish crossed here in 1870. il Sunset 142:90-1 Je '69

SPOKEN phonograph records. See Phonograph records—Spoken records

SPONBERG, Ruth Ann
New kind of school day. Ed Digest 34:46-8 Ap '69

SPONGBERG, Carol
Haiku; poem. Seventeen 28:210 Ag '69

SPONGE cake. See Cake

SPONSLER, George C.
Technology for Taiwan. Bul Atom Sci 25: 31-5 Je '69

SPONSORS, Advertising. See Television advertising

SPOONS
Spoons lead a double life. il Seventeen 28:160-1 My '69

SPORANGIA
See also
Sporangiophores

SPORANGIOPHORES
Phycomyces: stimulus storage in light-initiated reactions. T. G. Ebrey and R. K. Clayton. bibliog il Science 164:427-8 Ap 25 '69

SPORES, Ronald
Settlement, farming technology, and environment in the Nochixtlan Valley. bibliog Science 166:557-69 O 31 '69

SPORES. See Bacterial spores

SPORICH, Galen, and Moore, Michele
(comps) Audiovisual guide. Library J 94: 4231-2+ N 15 '69

SPORN, M. B. and others
Irreversible inhibition of nuclear exoribonuclease by thymidine-3'-fluorophosphate and p-haloacetamidophenyl nucleotides. bibliog Science 164:1408-10 Je 20 '69

SPORN, Phillip
Energy for man and environmental protection. Science 166:555 O 31 '69

SPOROZOA
See also
Coccidia

SPORT. See Sports

SPORT buses. See Station wagons

SPORT clothes. See Clothing and dress—Sports clothes

SPORT fishing boats. See Fishing boats

SPORT parachuting. See Parachuting

SPORTFISHERMEN. See Fishermen

SPORTING goods
What's new. See issues of Outdoor life
See also
Sporting goods industry

SPORTING goods industry
$4-billion market in fun. il Bsns W p82-4 F 8 '69
Getting fat by making others slim; fitness industry. il Bsns W p 140-1+ Mr 22 '69

SPORTS
Curse of the endless playoff; affliction of pro hockey, basketball, and baseball, now, spreading to pro football. T. Maule. il Sports Illus 30:18-21 Ap 7 '69
Going. T. J. O'Sullivan. Travel & Camera 32:28 F; 26 Mr '69
Outdoors with Wynn Davis. W. Davis. See issues of Mechanix illustrated
People in sport. il Travel & Camera 32:12-14 My '69
Sports. See issues of Newsweek
World travel calendar, 1970; comp. by F. Shemanski. Sat R 53:53-6 Ja 3 '70
See also
Amateurism (sports)
Aquatic sports
Camping
College athletics
Doping in sports
Industrial recreation
Outdoor life
Physical education and training
Sports journalism
Television broadcasting—Sports
Umpires (sports)
Winter sports
also names of sports, e.g. Hockey

SPORTS—*Continued*

Accidents and injuries

1968 was the year of the knee. R. Lardner. il
N Y Times Mag p4+ Ja 26 '69
See also
Baseball—Accidents and injuries
Hockey—Accidents and injuries
Horse racing—Accidents and injuries

Bibliography

Sports titles to score no errors. R. L. Tobin.
Sat R 52:50-2 N 29 '69

Ethical aspects

Broadway Joe: rebel with a nightclub for a
cause; with report by S. Smith. il Life 66:
22-7 Je 20 '69
Game was up at Namath's. N. Pileggi. il
Sports Illus 30:24-5 Je 23 '69
Joe Namath and the problem of heroic vir-
tue. J. Richardson. il Esquire 72:105+ O '69
Mod man out; with editorial comment. W.
Johnson. il Sports Illus 30:10, 20-3 Je 16
'69
Toward an imperfect understanding of the
Namath affair. W. F. Buckley, jr. il Esquire
72:113+ O '69

Periodicals

See also
Jock New York (periodical)

Philosophy

Rigors of play. M. Csikszentmihalyi. Nation
208:210-12 F 17 '69
Sport: a philosophic inquiry, by P. Weiss.
Review
Newsweek il 73:66 Je 2 '69. P. Axthelm

Photographs

Man in sports. Art in Am 57:76-80 Mr '69

Psychological aspects

Danger as a way of joy; risk-action sports.
W. Furlong. il Sports Illus 30:52-3 Ja 27 '69
Johnny Sain teaches the power of positive
pitching. B. Surface. il N Y Times Mag
p48-9+ Ap 20 '69

Records

See Sports records

Safety devices and measures

Making a vacation safe, wherever you are.
il Good H 168:160-1 Je '69
Recommended sports guidelines for youngsters. il Good H 168:199 Mr '69

Statistics

His word is the law of averages; S. Siwoff
of Elias sports bureau. J. Kirshenbaum. il
Sports Illus 31:28-31 Ag 18 '69

Study and teaching

Playing fields of Ware. I. K. Bradley. il To-
days Ed 58:24-6 My '69
Sports clinics at Michigan U. C. E. Oxley
il Parks & Rec 4:35-6 Mr '69
Try a learning vacation. D. B. Warnick. il
Mech Illus 65:46-8+ My '69

Asia

See also
Golf

Brazil

See also
Soccer

Canada

See also
Baseball—Canada

England

See also
Cricket (game)
Soccer

Hawaii

Polynesian surfing. B. R. Finney and J. D.
Houston. il Natur Hist 78:26-35+ Ag '69

Japan

See also
Baseball—Japan

Scotland

See also
Golf

Spain

See also
Bullfights

United States

All-America all the way; E. M. Vandeweghe family of Los Angeles. R. F. Jones.
il Sports Illus 30:82-6+ My 26 '69

For the record. See issues of Sports illustrated
Sports. H. L. Masin. See issues of Senior
scholastic
There were no greener pastures; pictorial review of sport in the '60s. Sports Illus 31:38-
79 D 22 '69
Warts, love and dreams in Buffalo. B. Yates.
il Sports Illus 30:44-6+ Ja 20 '69

SPORTS arenas. See Stadiums

SPORTS cars

Conversation factor; Opel GT. E. Dahlquist.
il Motor T 21:36-8 Ag '69
Dodge brings out a hot new sportster: Chal-
lenger. il Pop Sci 195:108-9 O '69
Hark! Detroit mid-engine sports cars are
coming. K. Ludvigsen. il Motor T 21:62-7+
D '69
Ikenga; photographer's dream car. il Ebony
24:114-16+ S '69
Lightweights; kit-car craze. J. Thawley. il
Hot Rod 22:34-8 Mr '69
New French sports car has midships engine;
Matra 530. J. P. Norbye. il Pop Sci 194:110-
11 Mr '69
Shelby Lone Star, look, but don't touch. A.
B. Shuman. il Motor T 21:68-9+ D '69
Sports car is really something else! il Chang-
ing T 23:35-6 S '69
Street machine with soul S. Kelly. il Hot
Rod 22:38-40 Ap '69
Volksporsche or Porschevolks? il Motor T
21:96-7+ O '69
Will the Mercedes C-III be the world's most
sought after sports car? K. Prentiss. il
Holiday 46:62-3+ D '69
ZL-1. E. Dahlquist. il Motor T 21:34-6 My
'69

SPORTS centers. See Recreation centers

SPORTS clothes. See Clothing and dress—
Sports clothes

SPORTS clubs

Big BASS bash in Arkansas: Bass anglers
sportsman society, Ark. R. H. Boyle. il
Sports Illus 31:66+ O 20 '69
Cold country club for the real cool crowd;
Windham Mountain club. W. Johnson. il
Sports Illus 32:60+ Ja 12 '70
High-flying fishing club: Dubawnt sports
club. G. Gresham. il Field & S 74:60-3+
My '69

SPORTS fans

Icy love-in with the red-hot Blues; Stanley
cup playoffs. G. Ronberg. il Sports Illus 30:
52-4+ Ap 7 '69
This riotous isle. W. Sheed. il Sports Illus
30:78-82+ Ap 21 '69
Year of the great fan draft. F. Deford. il
Sports Illus 30:54-8+ Ja 27 '69
See also
Baseball fans
Football fans

Anecdotes, facetiae, satire, etc.

Boys watching girls watching games. R.
Hollander. il Seventeen 28:102+ Ja '69

Photographs

Beauty to ornament the men of speed. J.
Cooke. Sports Illus 30:22-7 Je 30 '69

SPORTS films. See Moving pictures—Sports
films

SPORTS for girls. See School athletics

SPORTS for the blind

Blind students conquer Mt Kilimanjaro;
East Africans with training at Outward
bound mountain school at Loitokitok. il
Ebony 24:44-6+ Je '69

SPORTS for women

Les girls in Des Moines; photographs by B.
Peterson; with account by R. M. Mechem.
Sports Illus 30:34-9 F 17 '69
Jean-Claude Killy and the winter woman.
J. C. Killy. il Ladies Home J 86:87 N '69
Women aren't so fragile. il Sci Digest 66:53-
4 D '69
See also
Women as athletes

SPORTS foundation, incorporated. See Lifetime
sports foundation

SPORTS in moving pictures

Sport was box-office. R. Cantwell. il Sports
Illus 31:108-12+ S 15 '69

SPORTS journalism

Broad view; E. Kaine's Lineback column.
P. Axthelm. il Newsweek 74:70-1 D 22 '69
Kelso bit: or, A career nipped. J. Sanders.
il Sports Illus 31:42-4+ O 27 '69

SPORTS officiating
 Politics in the saddle at Utopia Downs;
  governors select racetrack officials. W.
  Tower. Sports Illus 30:52-3 Mr 31 '69
   See also
 Football clubs—Organization and administra_
  tion
SPORTS promoting. See Promoters and pro-
  moting
SPORTS records
 Hank becomes a hit; H. Aaron of Atlanta
  Braves. W. Leggett. il Sports Illus 31:10-13
  Ag 18 '69
 Have the hitters really gone? debate. J.
  Brosnan; F. Robinson; J. Sain. il Look
  33:84+ My 13 '69
 Here come the hitters, maybe. M. Mulvoy.
  il Sports Illus 30:20-1 My 12 '69
 You can't top a good loser; standings in
  the point-spread league, NFL and AFL. M.
  Mulvoy. Sports Illus 31:36-8+ D 8 '69
SPORTS shoes. See Shoes
SPORTS stamps. See Postage stamps
SPORTSMEN
   See also
 Hunters
SPORTSWOMEN. See Women as athletes
SPORTSWRITING. See Sports journalism
SPOTS, Removal of. See Cleaning
SPOTTED fever. See Rocky Mountain spotted
  fever
SPOTTED salamanders. See Salamanders
SPRAGUE, C. A. See Martin, G. M. jt. auth.
SPRAGUE, Henry, 3d
 Congressional sweep for Henry Sprague. L.
  Kennedy. il Motor B 123:166-7 Je '69
SPRAGUE, Robert Chapman
 Latecomer; Sprague electric's microelectron-
  ics. il Forbes 103:24 Je 1 '69
SPRAY, Cecil O.
 Meaningful grade reporting. Clear House 43:
  338-41 F '69
SPRAY painting. See Paint spraying
SPRAYING and dusting
 How when and what of spraying roses. P.
  P. Pirone. il Horticulture 47:38-9 My '69
 Now: tailor-make your sprays to kill corn
  weeds. D. Seim. il Farm J 93:24-5+ Mr '69
 Spray schedule for evergreens. P. P. Pirone.
  Horticulture 47:42-5 Mr '69
 Spray schedule for indoor plants. P. P. Pirone.
  il Horticulture 47:34-6 O '69
 Spray schedule for the flower garden. P. P.
  Pirone. Horticulture 47:34-5 Je '69
 Spray schedule for vegetables. P. P. Pirone.
  il Horticulture 47:33-5 Jl '69
 Spraying small fruits. P. P. Pirone. il Horti-
  culture 47:38-9+ Ap '69
SPRAYING apparatus
 Antiriot sprays: are they safe, or hazard-
  ous? U S News 66:10 Je 2 '69
 Good jobs you can do with a glue gun. il
  Pop Sci 195:184+ O '69
 Here's a new way to spray the weevil; spray-
  ing alfalfa stubble. G. L. Earle. il Suc
  Farm 67:60 My '69
 High-powered idea goes to work; EGD
  paint sprayer. il Bsns W p 156+ S 20 '69
 How to keep your sprayer running. C. E.
  Sommers. Suc Farm 67:59 F '69
 New sprayer system for soybeans. C. E.
  Sommers. il Suc Farm 67:66 Ap '69
 Sprayers to spray a thirty-five foot tree. il
  Sunset 142:233 Mr '69
   See also
 Aerosols

            Maintenance and repair
 Prepare your sprayer for winter storage.
  il Home Gard 56:65 O '69
SPREADERS, Fertilizer. See Fertilizer spread-
  ers
SPREADS (food)
 Full-flavored chile spreads. il Sunset 143:113
  Jl '69
 Glossary of sandwich spreads. il Good H
  169:144 Ag '69
SPREEN, Johannes F.
 From Detroit, with love. il por Time 93:17
  Mr 28 '69
 Taking a chance on love. il por Newsweek
  73:63 Mr 24 '69
SPRIGGS, Dillard P.
 Wall Street beat. R. Brady. il pors Duns R
  94:81-2 Jl '69
SPRING, Bob, and Spring, Ira
 What it takes to become a surefooted ice-
  man. il Pop Mech 132:106-10 Ag '69
SPRING, Ira. See Spring, B. jt. auth.
SPRING
 Birds are coming back. E. M. Woodford. il
  Horticulture 47:40-1+ Mr '69

Impatient spring. R. Rood. il Read Digest
 94:119-22 F '69
Many faces of spring. il House & Gard 135:
 112-15 Mr '69
   See also
 March

            Drama
Next stop, spring! drama. C. Boiko. Plays
 28:53-8 Mr '69
SPRINGER, Lois E.
 Bells. Hobbies 74:49+ D '69
SPRINGER, Morris
 Woman-hater. Opera N 33:24-5 Mr 15 '69
SPRINGER, Robert H.
 Ramsey's just war. Commonweal 90:76-8 Ap
  4 '69
SPRINGFIELD, Ill.

            City planning
 Street paving spurs community improvements. F. G. Madonia. il Am City 84:71-
  2+ Ap '69
SPRINGFIELD, Mass.

            Water supply
 In case of drought: pump. G. E. Sweeney
  and J. A. Frank. il Am City 84:76-8 Ja '69
SPRINGFIELD, Vt.
 Where tools are everyone's business. il
  Bsns W p70+ O 11 '69
SPRINGFIELD armory museum. See Military
  museums
SPRINGFIELD college, Springfield, Mass.
 Springfield students demonstrate for their
  college. A. Thormeyer. Todays Ed 58:25 S
  '69
SPRINGMAN, Mary Adele
 Cleveland: books/jobs and the manpower
  crisis. Wilson Lib Bul 43:897-9 My '69
SPRINGS
 Fountain of youth; Bosnia, Yugoslavia.
  Newsweek 73:90+ My 19 '69
SPRINGS (mechanism)
   See also
 Associated spring corporation
 Automobiles—Springs and suspension
SPRINKEL, Beryl W.
 Theory versus practice. por Nations Bsns 57:
  27 D '69
SPRINKLE, James. See Robison, R. A. jt.
  auth.
SPRINKLER irrigation. See Irrigation, Over-
  head
SPRINKLERS
 Grass is greener; irrigation system for muni-
  cipal golf course, Jackson, Mich. il Am
  City 84:114+ My '69
 Install your own sprinkling system. il Mech
  Illus 65:62-3 Je '69
SPRINT, Robert
 Build an easy-loading boat cradle. Pop Sci
  194:168-9 Ap '69
 Knock-down dog house. Pop Sci 195:140-1
  Jl '69
SPRINT missiles. See Guided missiles—De-
  fenses
SPRITZER, Michael, and Markham, James
 Charles' law: estimating absolute zero. pors
  Chem 42:24-5 S '69
SPROUL, Robert C.
 Existential autonomy and Christian freedom.
  Chr Today 13:12-13 Jl 18 '69
SPROUTS
 Seed sprouting, unlimited. M. Riggs and D.
  Riggs. il Org Gard & Farm 16:42-3 Jl '69
   See also
 Tillering (plants)
SPRUCE
 Idaho's new champ; Englemann spruce. R.
  L. Lingenfelter. il Am For 75:27+ Ap '69
SPRUCH, Grace Marmor
 Reporter Edward Condon. Sat R 52:55-8+
  F 1 '69
—and Peskin, Charles
 Conductivity and photoconductivity in egg
  white. bibliog Science 163:1350-1 Mr 21 '69
SPULBER, Nicolas
 Soviet economy in the 1970's. bibliog f Cur
  Hist 57:214-19+ O '69
SPURGEON, Charles Haddon
 Spurgeon's sermons republished. Chr Today
  14:33-4 O 10 '69
SPURRIER, Wilma A. See Dawe, A. R. jt. auth.
SPUTTERING (physics)
 Donning the thinnest coat of all; coating
  process. il Bsns W p 136+ Mr 15 '69
SPY stories. See Spies in literature
SQUALIDAE
   See also
 Dogfish
SQUARE knotting. See Macramé
SQUARE-wave generators. See Signal gener-
  ators

SQUASHES
Big squash up in Boulder; growing Hubbard squash P. Lorenz. Org Gard & Farm 16: 38 Ag '69
See also
Cookery—Vegetables

SQUATTERS
Fort Homeless; Milwaukee. Newsweek 74:67-8 N 3 '69
Hippies vs. skinheads; takeover of unused buildings in London. il Newsweek 74:90 O 6 '69
Nowhere people; squatting in Britain. il Newsweek 74:37 Jl 7 '69
Squat-in at no. 144 Piccadilly. il Life 67:52-3 O 3 '69

SQUIDS
Cartilaginous dermal scales in cephalopods. P. Person. bibliog il Science 164:1404-5 Je 20 '69
Hunting demons from hell; giant squids in Newfoundland waters. J. Coulon. il Sci N 96:38 Jl 12 '69

SQUIRE, David F.
U.N. to develop plans to control illegal narcotic drug crops; statement, December 17, 1968. Dept State Bul 60:64-5 Ja 20 '69

SQUIRE, J. J.
What women want to know about having a baby; interview. ed. by L. Kavaler. Parents Mag 44:41-3+ My '69

SQUIRE, James R.
What does research in reading reveal: about attitudes toward reading? bibliog Engl J 58:523-33 Ap '69

SQUIRES, James R.
Rotary thumbwheel switches for digital applications. Electr World 81:40-1+ My '69

SQUIRES, Radcliffe
Two greetings for the end of a decade; poem. Nation 209:740 D 29 '69

SQUIRES, Raymond
Shut-in's view of television commercials. PTA Mag 63:32-3 Je '69
Turning out non-readers. PTA Mag 64:6-8 bibliog(p35) S '69

SQUIRREL hunting
America's no. 2 game animal; with state chart of squirrels and recommended hunting areas. B. Gooch. il Field & S 74:68-9+ N '69
Challenge. C. Vinson. il Outdoor Life 143: 60-1+ My '69
Outfoxing fox squirrels. J. R. Olt. il Field & S 74:58-9+ S '69
Shelterbelt squirrels. D. Pryce. il Outdoor Life 144:52-3+ Ag '69
Stop, listen, and look. C. Patterson. il Outdoor Life 144:68-9+ O '69

SQUIRRELS
Flying squirrels. H. Borland. il Audubon 71: inside cover S '69
High squirrel population; gray squirrel population in central New York. Cons 23:40-1 F '69
Highway mortality of squirrels. Cons 23:40 Je '69
1968 not so nutty. E. M. Reilly, jr. il Cons 23:16 Ap '69
See also
Ground squirrels

SQUIRRU, Rafael
Dominican art: a growing tree. Américas 21: 32-7 Ja '69
Gironella: tension, time, light. Américas 21: 7-13 My '69

STAAR, Richard F.
Poland: myth versus reality. bibliog f Cur Hist 56:218-23 Ap '69

STABILIZATION processing. See Photography —Processing

STABILIZERS, Automobile. See Automobiles —Stability and stabilizers

STABILIZERS, Yacht. See Yachts—Stability and stabilizers

STABLES. Barns and stables

STACH, Eduard. See Libal. D. jt. auth.

STACHNIK, Thomas J. See Green, R. L. jt. auth.

STACK access in libraries. See Open and closed shelves

STACKABLE shelves. See Shelves

STADE, George
Commonplaces about women. Nation 208:215+ F 17 '69
(ed) See Cummings, E. E. Twenty-three letters

STADER, Maria
Exit smiling; interview. ed. by S. Jenkins. por Opera N 34:32 Ja 17 '70

STADIUMS
Colorful, splinter-free seating; Memorial stadium, Memphis, Tenn. N. Baxter. il Am City 84:52 Je '69

Goodby to three yards and a cloud of dust; era of synthetic football fields. W. Johnson. il Sports Illus 30:37-9 Ja 27 '69
Hofheinz and the Astrodome. M. Frady. il Holiday 45:42-5+ My '69
Meet of the future is now: track carnival in the Astrodome. T. Maule. il Sports Illus 30:16-17 F 3 '69
Sporting sixties as sculptured in concrete. il Sports Illus 31:47-8 D 22 '69
Super stadiums. il Parks & Rec 4:33-4 My '69
Your time, not your dollar; new sports arenas. F. Deford. il Sports Illus 30:72-6+ My 12 '69

Lighting
Brighter sports lights at less cost; Bartow, Fla. il Am City 84:34 D '69

STAFFORD, Jean
Books. See issues of Vogue
Collected stories of Jean Stafford, superb. M. Hentoff. Vogue 154:56 Jl '69
Domesticated modernism. M. Dickstein. New Repub 160:25-7 Mr 8 '69
Worlds of Jean Stafford. E. Janeway. Atlan 223:136-8 Mr '69

STAFFORD, Rita L. and Dunn, K. J.
Collaborative leadership in education. Sch & Soc 97:296-7 Sum '69

STAFFORD, Thomas P.
Our happy moon journey. por(p40) Life 66: 42-3 Je 20 '69
See also
Space flight to the moon—Manned flights—Stafford-Cernan-Young flight, 1969

STAFFORD, William
Books that look out, books that look in. Poetry 113:421-5 Mr '69
In hurricane canyon; poem. New Yorker 45: 70 D 20 '69

STAGE. See Theater buildings

STAGE scenery. See Opera—Stage scenery; Theater—Stage scenery

STAGES and reflections; ballet. See Ballets —Criticisms

STAGG, Anne
Weekend in Newport and Providence. House & Gard 136:72-3+ S '69

STAHEL, Thomas H.
Letter from Isolotto. America 121:418-21 N 8 '69

STAHL, Helen M.
Glue-tempera relief. il Sch Arts 69:12-13 N '69

STAHLMAN, William D.
Global myths record their passage. Sat R 53: 100-3 Ja 10 '70

STAINED glass. See Glass painting and staining

STAINS, Removal of. See Cleaning

STAINS and staining
Stain your floors any color. il House & Gard 135:110-11 Mr '69
Wood staining recipes. B. Berger. il Mech Illus 65:90+ My '69
See also
Wood finishing

STAINS and staining (biology)
See also
Trypan blue

STAIR, Gobin
Trade books or art books? Pub W 195:75 Mr 3 '69

STAIRWAYS
Rich Shaker legacy. il Am Home 72:74-5 S '69
Uphill entry, the flaring stairs are inviting. il Sunset 143:74 Ag '69
See also
Garden steps

STAKING of fruit trees. See Fruit trees, Care of

STALACTITES
Fungi associated with stalactite growth; cephalosporium lamellaecola. F. W. Went. il Science 166:385-6 O 17 '69

STALIN, Iosif
Ins and outs of de-Stalinization. J. Critchlow. Commonweal 90:191-2 My 2 '69
Living with the ghost of Stalin. il por Newsweek 73:40-2 F 24 '69
Middle way. Newsweek 75:22-3 Ja 5 '70
Night Stalin and Churchill divided Europe. J. Lukacs. il pors N Y Times Mag p36-8+ O 5 '69
Second thoughts from Svetlana. por Time 94:37-8 S 26 '69
Soviet generals and number one. T. Szamuely. il por Nat R 21:861-2 Ag 26 '69
Unhappy birthday. il Time 95:29 Ja 5 '70
Who's who in Russia these days. U S News 66:18 F 17 '69

STALIN-Churchill conference, Moscow, 1944. See World war, 1939-1945—Diplomatic history

STALINA, Svetlana Iosifovna
Suburbanization of Svetlana; interview. ed. by M. Silverstone. por Look 33:55-9 S 9 '69

about

Between two worlds. T. G. Plate. il por Newsweek 74:127-8 O 6 '69
Books. M. Muggeridge. Esquire 73:42+ Ja '70
Genuineness of the innocence. A. West. Vogue 154:120 N 1 '69
Only one year. D. L. Flaherty. America 121: 272 O 4 '69
Personal history. M. Parton. por Sat R 52:44 O 4 '69
Second thoughts from Svetlana; latest book. Only one year. por Time 94:37-8 S 26 '69
Svetlana faces life. T. Foote. Life 67:12 O 3 '69
Svetlana's whole story. E. Wilson. New Yorker 45:153-9 S 27 '69

STALINISM. See Communism—Russia

STALLS, Airplane. See Airplanes—Stalling

STAMATOYANNOPOULOS, George, and Yoshida, A.
Single chain alkali resistance in hemoglobin Rainier: β 145 tyrosine→histidine. bibliog Science 166:1005-6 N 21 '69

STAMFORD, Conn.

Parks and playgrounds

Imagination costs less; instant minipark. il Am City 84:22 My '69

STAMMERING
Speech: relation of nonfluency to information value. R. I. Lanyon. bibliog Science 164:451-2 Ap 25 '69
To keep a child from stuttering. G. M. Knox. Bet Hom & Gard 47:14+ Ag '69

STAMP collecting. See Postage stamps—Collectors and collecting

STAMPER, Malcolm Theodore
Boeing transport activities reorganized under Stamper. Aviation W 90:39 My 5 '69

STAMPS, Food. See Food relief

STAMPS, Postage. See Postage stamps

STAMPS. Revenue. See Revenue stamps

STANDARD, Paul
Fine Italian hands. Pub W 195:92-3+ F 3 '69
Mercator and the lettering of maps. Pub W 196:58+ N 3 '69
Origin of the serif. Pub W 195:83-4+ My 5 '69

STANDARD airways, incorporated
CAB considers plan to revive standard. Aviation W 91:46 Ag 25 '69
CAB denies petition of Standard to operate four charters to Tokyo. Aviation W 90:42 Je 30 '69

STANDARD and Poor's/InterCapital, incorporated. See Investments—Advisers

STANDARD book numbering. See Book numbers

STANDARD of living
Conservation for conservation's sake? E. Rabinowitch. Bul Atom Sci 25:47-8+ My '69
Do executives live better abroad? il Duns R 93:46-8 F '69
Worries about your budget? An official guide on costs; three standards of living for an urban family of four persons, study. il U S News 66:58-9 Mr 24 '69
See also
Budget, Household
Cost of living
Income
Poverty

STANDARD oil company (New Jersey)
Coral Gables Mafia: Milo M. Brisco and John Kenneth Jamieson appointments. il Newsweek 74:66+ S 8 '69
Frank Abrams way. L. L. L. Golden. Sat R 52:86 N 8 '69
Standard confirms break with its past. Bsns W p56 S 6 '69
See also
International petroleum company

STANDARD oil company (Ohio)
Affair of state. Newsweek 74:98B+ O 20 '69
Blocking the British; disputed merger between BP and Sohio. il Time 94:98 O 17 '69
British petroleum gets Sohio visa. Bsns W p38 N 22 '69
BP strikes again. il Newsweek 73:84 Je 16 '69
BP's new boy has welcome mat yanked; BP-Sohio merger. Bsns W p48 O 11 '69

STANDARD pressed steel company
Numbers game at SPS. Duns R 94:26-8 Jl '69

STANDARDIZATION
See also
Units

STANDARDS (ethics) See Ethics

STANDARDS, Engineering
Standards index set up at NBS. Electr World 81:73 Ap '69

STANDARDS, Library. See Libraries—Standards; School libraries—Standards

STANDARDS, National bureau of. See United States—Standards, National bureau of

STANDARDS of measurement. See Measurement

STANDERFER, Doris F.
Teachers discover the world of fibers. Sch Arts 69:6-10 Ja '70

STANDPIPES
No-paint water standpipe; Lewis County, Mo. il Am City 84:24 Je '69

STANDS (furniture)
Basin stand in England and America. R. B. M. Askew. il Antiques 95:258-63 F '69
Turned globe stand. il Mech Illus 65:36+ Je '69
See also
Flower stands

STANDS, Roadside. See Roadside marketing

STANFORD, Ann
Beating; poem New Yorker 45:48 S 13 '69
Philip Evergood, American tragedy; poem. New Repub 161:28 O 4 '69

STANFORD, Gene
Time enough to read. Sr Schol 94:Schol Teach 13+ Ap 18 '69

STANFORD research institute
From North to South; Stanford students demonstrations. il Newsweek 73:76+ My 26 '69
Stanford institute shifts research aims. R. G. O'Lone. Aviation W 91:24-5 Jl 7 '69
Stanford research institute: campus turmoil spurs transition. J. Walsh. Science 164:933-6 My 23 '69

STANFORD university, Stanford, Calif.
Confrontation at Stanford: exit classified research. J. Walsh. Science 164:534-7 My 2 '69
Stanford university bookstore has unexpected rush. I. L. Sanderson. il Pub W 195:69-70 Je 16 '69
West coast version of the March 4 protest. E. Langer. Science 163:1176-7 Mr 14 '69

Graduate school of business

From executive suite to halls of ivy; A. Miller, new dean of Stanford B-school. Bsns W p 122-3 Jl 19 '69

Hoover institution on war, revolution and peace

Cold-war scholarship. P. S. Stern. il Nation 209:176-80 S 1 '69

STANGER, Ila
Antigua. Harp Baz 102:106+ F '69

STANGER, Richard L.
All there was was a man, struggling. Chr Cent 86:1247-9 O 1 '69

STANHOPE, Richard. See Stanup, R.

STANLEY, David
Books on the Bible: 1969. America 121:563-4+ D 6 '69

STANLEY, Sir Henry Morton
Doctor Livingstone presumes. B. Farwell. il Horizon 11:104-11 Sum '69

STANLEY, Steven M.
Bivalve mollusk burrowing aided by discordant shell ornamentation. Science 166:634-5 O 31 '69

STANLEY park. See Vancouver, British Columbia—Parks and playgrounds

STANS, Maurice Hubert
About that fuss over the '70 census; interview. U S News 67:59 S 8 '69
Is U.S. being squeezed out of world markets? interview. por U S News 67:56-9 S 8 '69
Secretary Stans; interview. New Yorker 45: 22-4 Jl 5 '69
Supersalesman for our system. por Nations Bsns 57:34-9 S '69
Three don'ts; address. June 7. 1969. Vital Speeches 35:661-3 Ag 15 '69

about

Fight that stirs trade policymakers. il por Bsns W p 118+ Ap 19 '69
Mission impossible. il por Newsweek 73:92 My 26 '69
Secretary Stans to visit Europe. Asia to discuss U.S. trade policies. Dept State Bul 60:367 Ap 28 '69
Stans tries to take the reins on trade. il pors Bsns W p 114-15+ My 10 '69

STANTON, Edward S.
Religion (cont) America 120:540-2; 121:532-4 My 3, N 29 '69

STANTON, Jane C.
Have you read . . ? Seventeen 28:14+ S; 13 O '69
STANTON, Will
Open season on what? Read Digest 94:81-3 Mr '69
Rumpelstiltskin, he said his name was. Read Digest 95:61-3 Ag '69
You, too, can find connubial chaos. Read Digest 95:89-92 Jl '69
STANUP, Richard
More about Richard Stanup, George Washington's chief of servants. il por Negro Hist Bul 32:16-18 My '69
Richard Stanup who had charge of George Washington's slaves. il Negro Hist Bul 32: 12-13 F '69
STAPLES, Parker J. and Talal, Norman
Rapid loss of tolerance induced in weanling NZB and B/W F_1 mice. bibliog Science 163: 1215-16 Mr 14 '69
STAPLES and stapling machines
Staplers for the home office. il Consumer Bul 52:19-20+ Ag '69
STAPLETON, Lance
Hunt the trophy mule deer states. Field & S 74:12+ O '69
STAPP, Andrew
Dissent in uniform. por Time 93:20 Ap 25 '69
STAR clusters. See Stars—Clusters
STAR of India (ship museum) See Naval museums
STAR spangled banner (song)
Debate over the Star-spangled banner; pro and con discussion. Sr Schol 95:11-12 O 6 '69
STARBUCK, George
Seven double dactyls. Atlan 223:61 Je '69
STARDUST. See Matter, Interstellar
STARDUST national open drag championship. See Automobile racing
STARE, Fredrick J.
Food fads and frauds; adaptation of address, October 2, 1968. Todays Health 47:88+ Mr '69
—and others
Fluoridation and new facts. Sat R 52:57-9 My 3 '69
STARER, Robert
Music to my ears. I. Kolodin. Sat R 52:44+ N 8 '69
STARFISHES
Battle for the reef. L. Bickel. il Sci N 96:218-20 S 13 '69
Battle of Coral Sea; destruction of coral reefs by the crown of thorns. Newsweek 74:53 Jl 14 '69
Destruction of Pacific corals by the sea star acanthaster planci. R. H. Chesher. bibliog il Science 165:280-3 Jl 18 '69; Reply. J. L. Fischer. 165:645 Ag 15 '69
Plague in the sea; crown-of-thorns starfish. il Time 94:57 S 12 '69
Warning to seashell collectors; sea star, or crown of thorns invasion. il Chem 42:22-3 Je '69
STARIE, John H.
Local association of the month. Todays Ed 58:71-2 Mr '69
STARK, Al
Honor coho. Field & S 74:58-9+ My '69
STARK, Jack
Gulf Stream: river in the sea. Travel 132: 30-5+ D '69
STARK, John R.
How much money for plowshares? Sat R 52:18-20 My 24 '69
STARKER, Janos
Recorded portraits of the artist. por Hi Fi 19:32+ N '69
STARKIE, Walter
La Mancha's man. Opera N 33:14-16 Ap 19 '69
STARKS, Oliver
Bowman's Hill wildflower preserve. Horticulture 47:22-5 My '69
STARNES, Chip
R&R with a snake dancer. R. Starnes. Field & S 74:14+ Je '69
STARNES, Richard
[Monthly article on outdoor life] See issues of Field & stream
STAROBIN, Joseph R.
Origins of the cold war: the Communist dimension. For Affairs 47:681-96 Jl '69
STARR, Chauncey
Social benefit versus technological risk; adaptation of address, November 1968. bibliog Science 165:1232-8 S 19 '69
STARR, John T.
Highway in the sky. Am For 75:8-11+ Ja '69
Planning against progress. Am For 75:24-7+ Mr '69
STARR, Ringo
Is that you in there, Ringo? J. Hicks. il pors Life 66:59-60+ Je 13 '69

STARR, Roger
Garbage, or, Can we ever get away from it all? Horizon 11:48-51 Wint '69
STARS
Astronomy. J. Stokley. See fourth issue of each month of Science news
Deep-sky wonders. W. S. Houston. See issues of Sky and telescope
See also
Astrology
Astrophysics
Constellations
Cosmogony
Galactic systems
Magellanic clouds
Milky way
Occultations
Planets
Solar system
Zodiac

Brightness
See Stars—Magnitudes

Catalogs
Messier album. J. H. Mallas and E. Kreimer. See issues of Sky and telescope
Selected objects from the Mallas observer's catalogue. J. H. Mallas. See issues of Review of popular astronomy

Clusters
Age and structure in galactic star clusters. D. B. Williams. il R Pop Astron 63:7-9 Mr '69
Quasistellar objects and Seyfert galaxies. S. A. Colgate. bibliog il Phys Today 22:27-35 Ja '69
Two problems in gravitation. H. J. Rood. il Sky & Tel 37:225-7 Ap '69
See also
Nebulae

Constitution
Astronomical evidence for nucleosynthesis in stars. G. Wallerstein. bibliog il Science 162: 625-31 N 8 '68; Correction. 163:622 F 14 '69

Evolution
Birth of an earth? Newsweek 73:81 Mr 31 '69
Hydroxyl and water masers in protostars. M. M. Litvak. bibliog il Science 165:855-61 Ag 29 '69
Optical pulsars; light from dark neutron star. il Sci N 95:207-8 Mr 1 '69
Origin of the elements; adaptation of address, September 1968. D. D. Clayton. bibliog il Phys Today 22:28-36 My '69; Reply. S. Silverman. 22:15+ O '69
Science rediscovers gravity. T. Alexander. il Fortune 80:100-4+ D '69
Stellar abundances and the origin of the elements. A. O. J. Unsöld. bibliog il Science 163:1015-25 Mr 7 '69
See also
Pulsars

Magnitudes
Stellar radii and absolute magnitudes. il Sky & Tel 38:303 N '69

Motion
Stars of very large proper motion. J. H. Anderson. il Sky & Tel 38:76-8 Ag '69

Radiation
Gamma ray star. Sci Am 221:57 N '69
Ganging up on Sco X-1; X-ray star. il Sci N 95:471-2 My 17 '69

Spectra
Stellar abundances and the origin of the elements. A. O. J. Unsöld. bibliog il Science 163:1015-25 Mr 7 '69
STARS, Double
Double star specialists meet. S. L. Lippincott. il Sky & Tel 39:31-3 Ja '70
STARS, New
Nova Vulpeculae 1968 no. 2. il Sky & Tel 37:96 F '69
Seeking the places where the elements are made. D. E. Thomsen. il Sci N 96:579 D 20 '69
STARS, Variable
Director reports:
On a southern variable, S Pavonis. M. W. Mayall. R Pop Astron 63:23 Mr '69
RV Cassiopeiae. M. W. Mayall. il R Pop Astron 63:22 F '69
Director reports on a peculiar variable, RT Hydrae. M. W. Mayall. il R Pop Astron 63:24 My '69

STARS, Variable—*Continued*
DQ Herculis; synchronous photometry. R. E. Nather and B. Warner. bibliog il Science 166:876-7 N 14 '69
More about an unusual eclipsing variable; S 9484. il Sky & Tel 38:388-9 D '69
Some little-known variables. Sky & Tel 37: 262 Ap '69
T Cassiopeiae: its light curve and its neighbor. J. Ashbrook. il Sky & Tel 38:436 D '69
Unique variable star: V725 Sagittarii. il Sky & Tel 37:94 F '69
Unusual Algol-type variable; BS 7484 in Cygnus. il Sky & Tel 38:166-7 S '69
Unusual brightness of Mira. il Sky & Tel 38:223 O '69
Unusual cepheid variable; HR 8157. Sky & Tel 38:79 Ag '69
Z Chamaeleontis: a short period eclipsing binary. G. S. Mumford. il Sky & Tel 37:288 My '69
See also
American association of variable star observers

STARS and stripes. See Flags—United States
STARS and stripes (newspaper)

Censorship
Where there is no napalm: censoring of news to American forces in Vietnam. il Newsweek 74:77 O 20 '69

STARVATION
Rats enriched with odd-carbon fatty acids: maintenance of liver glycogen during starvation. T. B. VanItallie and A. K. Khachadurian. bibliog il Science 165:811-13 Ag 22 '69

STARYK, Steven
Music to my ears. I. Kolodin. Sat R 52:66+ N 15 '69

STASHEVSKII, Gennadii
Interest; interview. New Yorker 44:24-5 Ja 25 '69

STASSEN, Marilyn E.
Choral reading and the English teacher. Engl J 58:436-9 Mr '69

STATE, The
Beyond the Nation-state. L. B. Pearson. Sat R 52:24-7+ F 15 '69
STATE aid to airports. See Airports—Finance
STATE aid to education. See Education and state
STATE aid to libraries. See Libraries—Federal aid
STATE and agriculture See Agricultural administration
STATE and church. See Church and state
STATE and education. See Education and state
STATE and environment. See Environmental policy
STATE and federal relations. See Federal and state relations
STATE and industry. See Industry and state
STATE and libraries. See Libraries and state
STATE and municipal relations
States and the urban crisis. America 121:447 N 15 '69
States hold the keys to the cities. A. J. Reichley. il Fortune 79:134-7+ Je '69
STATE and science. See Science and state
STATE and the individual. See Individual and state
STATE archives. See Archives—United States
STATE bonds
Tax-free bonds: a market in chaos. il U S News 67:77-9 S 29 '69
STATE COLLEGE, Pa.

Parks and playgrounds
Parklet for State College. il Parks & Rec 4:51+ My '69
STATE colleges. See Colleges and universities, State
STATE courts. See Courts, State
STATE department (United States) See United States—State, Department of
STATE elections. See Elections—United States
STATE emblems. See Emblems, State
STATE employees
Minority employment in state and local governments. il Mo Labor R 92:67-70 N '69
Scientific and professional employment by state governments. E. W. Andrews and M. Moylan. Mo Labor R 92:40-5 Ag '69
STATE encouragement of science, literature, and art
Patron today; donors who keep opera in good financial health. R. W. Hall. Opera N 33:8-11 Ap 12 '69

STATE finance
Bad news from a bigtime spender; funds for New York city. Life 66:36 Ap 18 '69
Budgeting for state and local government services. B. Crihfield and G. A. Bell. Ann Am Acad 379:31-8 S '68
Welfare burden. Nation 208:67-8 Ja 20 '69
See also
Taxation, State

Federal aid
Should the government share its tax take? W. W. Heller. il Sat R 52:26-9 Mr 22 '69
STATE forestry associations. See Forestry societies
STATE governments
Comeback of the states. il U S News 67:48-50 O 27 '69
States hold the keys to the cities. A. J. Reichley. il Fortune 79:134-7+ Je '69
STATE institution libraries. See Libraries, Institution
STATE institutions
Effects of the institution on the person. D. Wineman. bibliog ALA Bul 63:1087-97 S '69
STATE labor legislation. See Labor laws and legislation—United States
STATE legislatures
Ev's amendment; pressing for a second constitutional convention. il Time 94:18 Ag 8 '69
STATE library commission, Miss. See Mississippi—State library commission
STATE library commission, Mo. See Missouri—State library commission
STATE-local fiscal relations. See Intergovernmental fiscal relations
STATE-local tax relations. See Intergovernmental tax relations
STATE ownership. See Government ownership
STATE parks and reserves
See also subhead Parks and reserves under names of states. e.g. California—Parks and reserves
STATE regulation of industry. See Industry and state
STATE rights
See also
Federal and state relations
STATE sales tax. See Sales tax
STATE senators. See Senators
STATE symbols. See Emblems, State
STATE taxation. See Taxation, State
STATE technical services, Office of. See United States—Commerce, Department of—State technical services, Office of
STATE universities. See Colleges and universities, State
STATE university of New York at Buffalo. See New York (state). State university—College at Buffalo
STATEHOOD (American politics) See States (United States)
STATEN ISLAND
Hayride; teen-age group on ride offered by Clove Lake stables. New Yorker 45:28-30 Je 28 '69
What would you do with, say, Staten Island? excerpts from Design with nature. I. McHarg. il Natur Hist 78:26-37 Ap '69
STATES (United States)
Puerto Rico: will it be the 51st state? interview. L. A. Ferré. U S News 66:104-5 Mr 17 '69
See also
State governments
STATES, New
Protagonists, power, and the third world: essays on the changing international system; symposium. ed. by W. Wilcox. bibliog f Ann Am Acad 386:1-147 N '69
See also
Underdeveloped areas

Economic conditions
Third world modernization in transnational perspective. T. K. Hopkins. Ann Am Acad 386:126-36 N '69

Politics
Third world and the great powers. S. Gupta. bibliog f Ann Am Acad 386:54-63 N '69
Third world modernization in transnational perspective. T. K. Hopkins. Ann Am Acad 386:126-36 N '69
STATES, Small
Micro-states and United Nations; associate memberships; address, August 27, 1969. C. W. Yost. Vital Speeches 35:746-8 O 1 '69
Question of micro-states; committee of experts meets. UN Mo Chron 6:33-4 O '69

STATES, Small—*Continued*
　Question of micro-states; committee of experts to be established. UN Mo Chron 6: 95-103 Ag '69
STATESMEN
　How the Kremlin takes a holiday. M. Kalb. il Sat R 52:83-4+ Mr 8 '69
　Public figures and their private lives; Time essay. il Time 94:28-9 Ag 22 '69
　Spring and the traveler; the first resorts: a roundup of vacationlands preferred by world leaders; symposium. il Sat R 52:39-42+ Mr 8 '69
STATIC electricity. See Electricity, Static
STATICE. See Sea lavender
STATION wagons
　Full-sized, low-priced station wagons. il Consumer Rep 34:260-9 My '69
　It separates the ranchers from the cowboys. J. Liston. il Pop Mech 131:90 My '69
　Long and the short of it; comparison of Chrysler's Town & Country and Plymouth's Sport Satellite. V. L. Oertle. il Motor T 21:72-3 Je '69
　1969 Ford Club Wagon 123. L. Oertle. il Motor T 21:100-2 Ap '69
　Sizing up the 1969 station wagons. B. Hartford. il Pop Mech 131:104-7 F '69
　Station wagons; an overview (cont) il Consumer Rep 34:218-19 Ap '69

　　Rating
　Full-sized, low-priced station wagons. il Consumer Rep 34:260-9 My '69

　　Testing
　Big wagons carry kids and cargo in style. J. P. Norbye and J. Dunne. il Pop Sci 194: 86-91 Mr '69
　Road testing the new Jeep Wagoneer. V. L. Oertle. il Motor T 21:54-6 Jl '69

STATION wagons, Foreign
　Five small wagons. il Consumer Rep 34:463-73 Ag '69
　Small wagons. meet the little three from the big three. J. P. Norbye and J. Dunne. il Pop Sci 194:112-16 Ap '69

　　Safety devices and measures
　Safety: big cars do have an edge. Consumer Rep 34:464 Ag '69
STATIONERY
　California's pictorial letter sheets; excerpts. J. A. Baird, jr. il Antiques 96:412-17 S '69
　Now notepapers. posthaste. il Seventeen 28: 136+ Ja '69
STATISTICAL mechanics
　Exact statistical mechanics at Irvine; report of meeting. M. E. Mayer. Phys Today 22: 117+ Ap '69
STATISTICAL methods
　GOP is thrown a price-job curve; Phillips curve. il Bsns W p60+ Mr 22 '69
　　See also
　Least squares
STATISTICIANS
　Statisticians and shoemakers: applying their skills; excerpt from address, August 1969. A. R. Eckler. Mo Labor R 92:43-7 N '69
STATISTICS
　Statisticians and shoemakers: applying their skills; excerpt from address, August 1969. A. R. Eckler. Mo Labor R 92:43-7 N '69
　　See also
　Church statistics
　Criminal statistics
　Distribution (probability theory)
　Economic statistics
　Market statistics
　　also subhead Statistics under various subjects. e.g. Unemployment—Statistics
STATON, Earl E. and others
　Teens who care: potential mental health manpower. Ment Hy 53:200-4 Ap '69
STATUE of liberty
　Hospitality demands are heavy for the lady with the torch. J. Saunders. il Parks & Rec 4:43-4+ O '69
STATUES
　　See also
　Jesus Christ—Art
　Portrait sculpture
　Statue of liberty
STATUES, Photography of. See Photography of works of art
STATUS, Social. See Social status
STATUS of women, Commission on the. See United Nations—Commission on the status of women
STAUB, Herbert W. and others
　Serum cholesterol reduction by chromium in hypercholesterolemic rats. bibliog Science 166:746-7 N 7 '69

STAVELY, Rowena
　African safari: cabin class. Travel 131:79-81 My '69
STAVN, Diane (Gersoni) See Gersoni, D.
STAY-in strikes. See Strikes
STAYMAN, Samuel
　Smart, and sure of it. por Forbes 104:59 D 15 '69
STAYTON, John
　Build the Time Out. Pop Electr 32:52-3+ Ja '70
STEAD, Frank M.
　Desalting California. Environ 11:2-10 Je '69
STEADMAN, Ralph
　Making fun of themselves. il pors Vogue 153: 126-7 Je '69
STEALING
　Legislation to halt air cargo theft studied. Aviation W 90:34 Je 30 '69
　Senate tracks business thieves; begins study of ways to combat stealing. Bsns W p 100 My 31 '69
　　See also
　Art thefts
　Automobiles, Theft of
　Cattle thieves
　Embezzlement
　Library thefts
　Securities, Theft of
　Shoplifting
　Thieves
STEAM, Natural
　Geothermal steam looks better; geothermal steam fields in Imperial Valley. il Sci N 95:113-14 F 1 '69
　Power from the earth's own heat. L. Lessing. il Fortune 79:138-41+ Je '69
STEAM automobiles. See Automobiles, Steam
STEAM engine models
　Build this model walking-beam engine. R. Kouhoupt. il Pop Mech 132:156-9+ Ag '69
STEAM engines
　　See also
　Locomotives
　Motor bus engines
　Steam turbines
STEAM engines, Automotive. See Automobile engines
STEAM engines, Marine. See Marine engines
STEAM locomotives. See Locomotives
STEAM power plants
　　See also
　Steam, Natural
STEAM turbines
　Steam turbines. W. Hossli. il Sci Am 220:100-10 Ap '69
STEAM turbines, Marine
　Vibration aboard the Queen: trials of the Queen Elizabeth 2. Sci N 95:137-8 F 8 '69
STEAMBOATS. See Steamships and steamboats
STEAMERS
　What's cooking? B. T. Hunter. il Org Gard & Farm 16:98-9 Ap '69
STEAMING (cookery)
　　See also
　Steamers
STEAMSHIP lines
　Will it be the soaring seventies? are ships obsolete? H. Sutton and D. Butwin. Sat R 53:71-3 Ja 3 '70
　　See also
　Cunard steamship company
　Lykes corporation
　Matson navigation company
　United States lines
STEAMSHIPS and steamboats
　Cruise ships. B. Belford. il Travel & Camera 32:64-5 N '69
　Delta Queen. last of the stern-wheelers. R. Arnold. il Travel & Camera 32:81-3 Je '69
　　See also
　Ocean travel
　Steamship lines
STEARNS, Lewis
　Fidel's tokenism. Nat R 21:596-7 Je 17 '69
STEARNS, Robert. See Stone, R. jt. auth.
STEBBINS, Doris E.
　Fragrant, candy-colored sweet pea. Am Home 72:72 Mr '69
STEBBINS, Theodore E. jr
　Introducing Martin Johnson Heade. Art N 68:52-3+ D '69
STECHER-Traung-Schmidt corporation
　Sockeye, cling, & the Golden state: Schmidt label and lithograph company. R. Teiser. il Am West 6:20-5 Mr '69
STEEGMULLER, Francis
　Onward and upward with the arts. New Yorker 45:130-4+ S 27 '69
STEEL, Lewis M.
　To be truly free. Sat R 52:23-5+ Ja 25 '69
STEEL, Ronald
　Reports: Haiti. Atlan 224:20+ S '69

STEEL

Heat treatment

How to anneal, harden and temper steel. F. W. Schlueter. il Pop Mech 132:178-81 D '69

Prices

Boom in world steel confounds forecasters. il Bsns W p94+ My 10 '69

Doctor Bethlehem's new steel formula. Bsns W p39 N 15 '69

Prices head higher, but will they stick? Bsns W p27 Ag 2 '69

Steel heads up again. Bsns W p27 F 8 '69

Steel hikes more prices. Bsns W p49 Ap 26 '69

Steel thumbs its nose; price increases by U.S. steel. il Newsweek 74:55 Ag 11 '69

What gave steel its big new lift. il Bsns W p21 Ag 9 '69

STEEL castings
See also
Continuous casting

STEEL construction

End-plate design cuts cost of moment connections for steel frame by 26 per cent. il Arch Rec 145:168-9 F '69

Fire tests prove steel structure can be exposed; excerpts from address. A. F. Nassetta. il Arch Rec 146:199-202 S '69

New multi-use gymnasium for I.I.T. il Arch Rec 146:111-13 Jl '69

Steel shelters defy vandals: Middletown, Ohio. J. Paschal. il Am City 84:96-7 F '69

STEEL industry and trade

Boom in world steel confounds forecasters. il Bsns W p94+ My 10 '69
See also
Steel works

Consolidations and mergers

Why steelmakers seek strength in merger: Wheeling and Pittsburgh steel companies. il Bsns W p 102-4 F 15 '69

International aspects

Bar to imports; Japanese and European steel producers agree to impose own restrictions. il Time 93:67 Ja 24 '69

Steel industries of Japan and ECSC offer to limit exports to U.S; letter, with texts of steel industries' communications. D. Rusk. Dept State Bul 60:93-4 F 3 '69

Steel's newest puzzle: agreement to limit exports to U.S. il Bsns W p 17-18 F 1 '69

Wages and hours

Back pay in steel: what union won. U S News 67:64 Ag 18 '69

Protecting the paychecks of victims of technology. Bsns W p98 Ag 16 '69

Unit labor costs of iron and steel industries in five countries: France, Japan, the United Kingdom, United States, and West Germany; with tables. P. C. Jackman. Mo Labor R 92:15-22 Ag '69
See also
Collective bargaining—Steel industry

Canada

See also
Collective bargaining—Steel industry

Great Britain

See also
British steel corporation

Japan

Bigger is better: Yawata iron & steel and Fuji iron & steel merger. il Time 93:88+ Mr 14 '69

Japan forges a colossus in steel; merger of Yawata and Fuji. il Bsns W p92-4+ Ap 5 '69

Steel and nucleonics. S. Griffin. Sci N 95:318 Mr 29 '69

Russia

Russian steel makes a U.S. pitch. il Bsns W p80+ N 1 '69

United States

Midgets beat giants. Time 94:68+ Ag 1 '69

Reshaping steel for survival. il Bsns W p28-9 D 27 '69

Ribbon of steel cuts industry costs. il Bsns W p71-2 Ap 19 '69

Searching for steel's research. E. Gross. il Sci N 95:220-1 Mr 1 '69

Steel turns buoyant. Bsns W p36 My 24 '69

Steelmen pick up a boomlet: accelerated steel demand. il Bsns W p40-1 Mr 22 '69

Upheaval in steel industry: hunting profits in new lines. il U S News 66:78-9 Mr 31 '69

What gave steel its big new lift. il Bsns W p21 Ag 9 '69

Winter lag unlikely to dent steel boom. il Bsns W p28-9 N 8 '69
See also
Strikes—United States—Steel industry and trade

United steelworkers of America
also names of steel companies, e.g. Wood, Alan, steel company

STEEL ingots

Russian steel makes a U.S. pitch: remelting processes. il Bsns W p80+ N 1 '69

STEEL metallurgy

Note on steelmaking: warm rolling for strong hard steel. il Chem 42:24 Je '69

Purer steels for tougher jobs; electron-beam, vacuum-refining technology. il Bsns W p80-1 Je 28 '69

Russian steel makes a U.S. pitch; remelting processes. il Bsns W p80+ N 1 '69

Searching for steel's research. E. Gross. il Sci N 95:220-1 Mr 1 '69
See also
Steel—Heat treatment

STEEL mills. See Steel works

STEEL sculpture. See Metal sculpture

STEEL strikes. See Strikes—United States—Steel industry and trade

STEEL tubes. See Tubes, Steel

STEEL wool

Guide to buying and using steel wool. il Pop Mech 131:189 Ap '69

STEEL workers
See also
Steel industry and trade—Wages and hours
United steelworkers of America

STEEL works

Mini-mill: steel on a budget; low-cost electric furnaces. il Bsns W p66-8+ Mr 29 '69
See also
Jones and Laughlin steel corporation

Equipment and supplies

See also
Pennsylvania engineering corporation

STEELE, John L.

Wilbur Mills has put together the biggest tax-reform package ever. Fortune 80:55+ S '69

STEELE, Robert

Communication. Cath World 208:238-9 F '69

What do we mean by film art? Cath World 209:35-8 Ap '69

STEELE, William O.

Last buffalo killed in Tennessee; excerpt from address, 1967. Horn Bk 45:196-9 Ap '69

STEELEY, Joseph, Jr

Nest of barn owls. Cons 23:20 Je '69

STEELHEAD salmon fishing. See Salmon fishing

STEEN, Charles Augustus

Steen's folly. il pors Newsweek 73:24 My 12 '69

STEEPLECHASING. See Horse racing

STEER wrestling. See Rodeos

STEERING gear
See also
Automobiles—Steering gear
Sailboats—Steering gear

STEFFEN, Don Carl

Little Ghana takes on the Russians. il Life 66:20-5 F 21 '69

STEFFY, Jay

Young-shot in decorating. P. Devlin. il por Vogue 154:156-9+ Ag 1 '69

STEGEMAN, Beatrice

Science as art. Bul Atom Sci 25:27-30 Ap '69

STEGEMAN, Karen L. See Wagner, N. N. jt. auth.

STEGNER, Page

Man who came to stay; story. McCalls 97:82-3 O '69

STEGNER, Wallace

Conservation equals survival. Am Heritage 21:12-15 D '69

STEHLI, Francis G. and others

Generation and maintenance of gradients in taxonomic diversity. bibliog Science 164:947-9 My 23 '69

STEICHEN, Edward

Readers' choice: Rodin's Balzac. por Art in Am 57:26-7 S '69

about

Salute to Steichen. D. Vestal. il por Travel & Camera 32:20 Je '69

STEIGER, Rod

Let us now praise famous me. il Esquire 72:160-1+ N '69

STEIGER, Rod—*Continued*
Rod Steiger and Claire Bloom, no happy ending? interview; ed. by J. Barthel. por Redbook 133:98-9+ Jl '69

STEIN, Bernard R.
Academic research in Germany: a new support program. bibliog Science 165:1096-100 S 12 '69

STEIN, Charles
Book marks. Nation 208:217 F 17 '69
Nation book marks. Nation 208:611 My 12 '69

STEIN, Donald G. and others
Central nervous system: recovery of function. bibliog Science 166:528-30 O 24 '69

STEIN, Elizabeth
Pottery goes pop. Sch Arts 68:35 Ap '69

STEIN, Fred
InterCapitalists. il por Time 93:94-5 Mr 14 '69

STEIN, Hans, and Hausen, Peter
Enzyme from calf thymus degrading the RNA moiety of DNA-RNA hybrids: effect on DNA-dependent RNA polymerase. bibliog Science 166:393-5 O 17 '69

STEIN, Herbert
Tax cut in Camelot; excerpts from The fiscal revolution in America. por Trans-Action 6:38-44 Mr '69

STEIN, Larry, and Berger, B. D.
Paradoxical fear-increasing effects of tranquilizers: evidence of repression of memory in the rat. bibliog Science 166:253-6 O 10 '69
—See Wise, C. D. jt. auth.

STEIN, Laurence B. Jr
Electronic control keeps home heater on the mark. Pop Sci 195:184-6+ S '69

STEIN, Philip G. and others
Spectre II: general-purpose microscope input for a computer. bibliog Science 166:328-33 O 17 '69

STEIN on the Danube. See Krems, Austria

STEINBACH, Donald L.
Digital IC timer. Electr World 81:48-50 My '69
Printed-circuit kits for short runs. por Electr World 82:56-7 O '69

STEINBECK, John, 1902-1968
Callus behind the fiction. C. Brown. New Repub 161:26+ D 20 '69
John Steinbeck: footnote for a memoir. J. K. Galbraith. Atlan 224:65-7 N '69
John Steinbeck! John Steinbeck! How still we see thee lie. G. Frazier. il Esquire 72:150-1+ N '69
John Steinbeck, RIP. Nat R 21:64 Ja 28 '69
John Steinbeck, writer. W. C. McWilliams and N. R. McWilliams. Commonweal 90:229-30 My 9 '69
Personal history. L. W. Jones. Sat R 52:25-6 D 20 '69
Steinbeck: the shape of a career. P. Shaw. por Sat R 52:10-14+ F 8 '69; Discussion. 52:24 Mr 8 '69
View of literature too often neglected. J. M. Nagle. Engl J 58:399-407 Mr '69

STEINBECK, John, 1946-
Merry Christmas, all authorized personnel? House & Gard 136:68-9+ D '69

STEINBERG, Arthur G. and Rostenberg, Israel
Inv(1) allotype: effect of immunoglobulin G heavy chain subtype on its expression. bibliog Science 164:1072-3 My 30 '69

STEINBERG, David. See Eisen, J. jt. auth.

STEINBERG, Jane
New sorts of institutions must be had. Mlle 69:262-3+ Ag '69
Things they say about each other! Mlle 69:202+ O '69
214 to 1; coeds at Princeton. Mlle 68:232-3+ Ap '69

STEINBERG, Raymond
Grammatical: poem. Engl J 58:244 F '69

STEINBERG, Saul
Saul Steinberg: the stamp of genius. J. Ashbery. il Art N 68:45+ N '69

STEINBERG, Saul P.
Levitating with Leasco. il por Newsweek 73:77-8 F 24 '69
Steinberg's complaint. pors Forbes 103:179+ My 15 '69
Tribulations of Saul. por Time 94:94 O 24 '69
Why Leasco failed to net Chemical. il por Bsns W p 144-5+ Ap 26 '69

STEINBERG, William
Musical events: M. T. Thomas as a substitute for W. Steinberg. W. Sargeant. New Yorker 45:163 N 1 '69

STEINBERG'S limited
Canadians invade France. V. Lewis. il Duns R 93:57-8 Ja '69

STEINBICKER, Earl
Pro's guide to successful printing. Pop Phot 64:78-9+ Mr '69

STEINDLER, Paul
Dining in/out with Esquire. Esquire 72:81 O '69

STEINER, Barbara A.
Topsy-turvy foodland; drama. Plays 28:45-50, 74 F '69

STEINER, George
Books (cont) New Yorker 44:87-90+ Ja 18; 114-16+ F 8; 45:139-40+ Mr 29 '69

STEINER, Shari
Europe and America: a question of self-image. Sat R 52:18-20 D 27 '69

STEINER, Stan
Cultural schizophrenia of Luis Valdez. Vogue 153:112-13+ Mr 15 '69

STEINFELS, Peter
Defense policy and the prudes. Commonweal 90:382-3 Je 20 '69
Non-proliferation: a nuclear Sarajevo. Commonweal 89:721+ Mr 14 '69
President's speech. Commonweal 91:242 N 21 '69
Screen. Commonweal 91:247-9 N 21 '69
Strange world of Mr Nutter. Commonweal 90:158-9 Ap 25 '69

STEINHAUER, Ross E.
Voice prints. Sat R 52:56-9 S 6 '69

STEINHOFF, Johannes
Learning to handle the flying coffin. por Time 94:35 O 24 '69

STEINITZ, Kate Trauman
Kate's writings; a selected bibliography; comp. by J. M. Edelstein. por Wilson Lib Bul 44:529-34 Ja '70

About
Kate Steinitz: librarian, artist, scholar, symposium. bibliog il pors Wilson Lib Bul 44:512-37 Ja '70

STEINMAN, Alan M. and others
Epinephrine metabolism in mammalian brain after intravenous and intraventricular administration. bibliog Science 165:616-17 Ag 8 '69

STEINMETZ, Charles
Three today types of short story. Writers Digest 49:58-62 N '69

STEINMETZ, Paul Bernhard
Happening at Oglala. D. O. Collins. il pors Am West 6:15-19 Mr '69

STEINS. See Drinking vessels

STEINWEDEL, Louis William
Grandest Grand prix. Motor T 21:52-4+ S '69

STELLA, Frank
Exhilarating adventure, Frank Stella. R. Rosenblum. il por Vogue 154:116-17+ N 15 '69

STELLAR evolution. See Stars—Evolution

STELLAR magnitudes. See Stars—Magnitudes

STELLAR motion. See Stars—Motion

STELLAR radiation. See Stars—Radiation

STELLER'S Jay. See Jays

STELOFF, Frances
Frances Steloff, L.H.D. New Yorker 45:23-6 Ag 16 '69

STEMS (plants)
See also
Tillering (plants)

STENCIL enamels. See Enamel and enameling

STENCIL work
Found objects as stencils; excerpts from Metal enameling. P. Rothenberg. il Ceram Mo 17:28-9 S '69
Imaginative ideas for stenciling: instant patterns with paint. il House & Gard 135:86-7 F '69
Sponge painting. V. Jackson and W. Radcliffe. il Sch Arts 68:9 F '69
Stencil designs with spray paints. H. Luitjens. il Sch Arts 68:26-8 F '69

STENDHAL, pseud. See Beyle, M. H.

STENGEL, Casey
Bring back the real Mets! L. Shecter. il por N Y Times Mag p66-7+ S 7 '69

STENNIS, John Cornelius
ABM debate; time has come to act; interview. il por U S News 67:26-8 Jl 14 '69
Danger in arms cuts: a senator's warning; excerpts from address, September 3, 1969. por U S News 67:38-9 S 15 '69
Excerpt from debate, October 9, 1968. Cong Digest 48:52+ F '69
Query from the South: why not desegregate in the North? excerpts from address, October 16, 1969. por U S News 67:93-5 N 3 '69

About
McIntire-Stennis program. J. D. Sullivan and G. F. Burks. il por Am For 75:16-19+ Ap '69
Stennis projects $46 billion in savings. Aviation W 91:18-19 Jl 21 '69

STENNIS, John Cornelius—about—*Continued*
  Until next time. por Time 94:19-20 S 26 '69
  Why the Pentagon pays homage to John
    Cornelius Stennis. J. K. Batten. il pors
    N Y Times Mag p44-5+ N 23 '69
STENTOR coeruleus. See Ciliata
STÉNUIT, Robert
  Priceless relics of the Spanish Armada. pors
    Nat Geog 135:745-77 Je '69
STENVIG, Charles S.
  Another vote for law and order. por U S
    News 66:18 Je 23 '69
  Contagion in Minneapolis. il por Time 93:
    24 Je 20 '69
  Cop as candidate. Newsweek 73:63 My 12 '69
  God is my co-pilot. por Newsweek 73:32 Je
    23 '69
  One issue: L&O. B. Casserly. Commonweal
    90:384 Je 20 '69
STENZEL, Kurt H. and others
  Collagen gels: design for a vitreous replace-
    ment. bibliog Science 164:1282-3 Je 13 '69
STEPANOV, Lev
  One percent: the problem of economic aid;
    tr. by L. I. Dzirkals. bibliog f Ann Am
    Acad 386:41-53 N '69
STEPCHILDREN
  How to succeed as a step-parent. T. Irwin.
    il Parents Mag 44:37-9+ F '69
STEPFATHERS. See Stepparents
STEPHANOTIS floribunda. See Madagascar
  jasmine
STEPHANY, Bill, and Stephany, Sue
  Charter sailing in Green Bay. Yachting 125:
    56-7+ Ap '69
STEPHANY, Sue. See Stephany, B. jt. auth.
STEPHEN, Edith
  Edith Stephen theatre dance co: The cubi-
    culo. J. Anderson. Dance Mag 43:82 F '69
STEPHENS, Harrison
  Present charm and ancient past. Yachting
    125:50-1+ My '69
STEPHENS, Mae Webb
  Sierre Leone. por Travel 131:32-5+ Mr '69
STEPHENS, William M.
  Captive killer. Sea Front 15:140-1 My '69
  Ocean's riches. Nat Wildlife 7:4-11 Ap '69
STEPMOTHERS. See Stepparents
STEPPARENTS
  How to succeed as a step-parent. T. Irwin.
    il Parents Mag 44:37-9+ F '69
  Reconstituted families. il Newsweek 74:90-1
    S 8 '69
STEPPING stones. See Garden steps
STEPS, Garden. See Garden steps
STEPTOE, John
  Stevie: realism in a book about black children.
    il pors Life 67:54-9 Ag 29 '69
STEREO amplifiers. See Amplifiers
STEREO headphones. See Earphones
STEREO shows. See Audio fairs
STEREOCHEMISTRY
  Ant alarm pheromone activity: correlation
    with molecular shape by scanning com-
    puter. J. E. Amoore and others. bibliog il
    Science 165:1266-9 S 19 '69
  Determining the number of isomers from a
    structural formula. M. Orchin. il Chem 42:8-
    12 My '69
  Nobel laureates in economics, chemistry,
    and physics. E. L. Eliel. il Science 166:718-
    20 N 7 '69
  Nobel prizes in chemistry, and physics. il Sci
    N 96:421-2 N 8 '69
  Predicting stable clusters. il Chem 42:22-3 Ja
    '69
STEREOGRAPHS
  See also
  Stereophotography
STEREOPHONIC radio receivers. See Radio
  receivers, Stereophonic
STEREOPHONIC recorders. See Magnetic
  recorders and recording—Stereophonic re-
  corders
STEREOPHONIC sound. See Sound—Stereo-
  phonic recording and reproducing
STEREOPHONIC sound systems
  Build the dorm special. D. B. Weems. il Pop
    Electr 31:53-7+ Ag '69
  EW lab tests new stereo compacts. J. D.
    Hirsch. Electr World 82:27-30+ D '69
  Heathkit revisited; stereo tuner and amplifier
    kits. il Consumer Rep 34:504-5 S '69
  Hi-fi stereo kits. il Consumer Rep 34:127-37
    Mr '69
  How to pick the best hi-fi stereo compact. S.
    Shatavsky. il Pop Sci 194:92-6+ Ja '69
  Improve your stereo sound. F. H. Belt. Am
    Home 72:72+ Jl '69
  Stereo FM compact. Heathkit model AD-27.
    il Pop Electr 30:76-7 Je '69

Stereo has the amplifier in the speaker! il
  Mech Illus 65:101-3+ F '69
Stereo: it turns you on and up. il McCalls
  97:104-5+ N '69
Stereo 1970: symposium. il Radio-Electr 40:
  33-41+ O '69
Stereo scene. C. Lincoln. See issues of Popu-
  lar electronics, June 1969-
Stereo: the myth of the experts' equipment. I.
  Berger. Sat R 52:49 Mr 15 '69
Stereo versus the concert hall. L. D. Harmon
  and D. J. MacLean. il Electr World 81:34-6
  Ap '69
What's new in stereo. House & Gard 136:
  68-9+ N '69
What's new in stereo kits? R. Long. il Hi F
  19:73-7 D '69
  Equipment
Subjects acoustical. T. Bowman and E.
  McDonald. il House B 111:136-7 N '69
STEREOPHOTOGRAPHY
  History
Muscle, the gold, and the iron; documenting
  the construction of the Central Pacific. A.
  A. Hart. il Am West 6:13-19 My '69
STERILITY
Fertility sound blast. il Sci Digest 66:73-4
  S '69
Your health: what can be done to cure in-
  fertility. H. H. Thomas and E. Edelson.
  Redbook 133:46+ S '69
STERILITY in animals
Pied pipers can retire; drug that renders
  male rats infertile. Sci Digest 66:48 D '69
STERILIZATION
  See also
Space vehicles—Sterilization
STERILIZATION, Sexual
Reversing the irreversible. Sci N 95:473 My 17
  '69
STERLING, Dorothy
What's black and white and read all over?
  excerpts from address, November, 1968.
  bibliog Engl J 58:817-32 S '69
STERLING Forest gardens. See Gardens—New
  York (state)
STERLING silver. See Silverware
STERMAN, Mrs Samuel
Suburban isolation controversy. Sci Digest
  65:29-30 Je '69
STERMER, Dugald
Advertorial: on Howard Gossage. Ramp Mag
  8:21 S '69
Agit pop art of Cuba. Ramp Mag 7:32-7 D
  14 '68
—and others
Rampage. Ramp Mag 8:54-9 Ag '69
STERN, Adele H.
Humanities: from Aeschylus to Antonioni;
  address. November 1968. Engl J 58:676-80
  My '69
STERN, Edith M. See Miller, J. S. jt. auth.
STERN, Fritz
Gold and iron: the collaboration and friend-
  ship of Gerson Bleichröder and Otto von
  Bismarck. bibliog f Am Hist R 75:37-46 O
  '69
STERN, Irving
Economy in the 1970's; address, May 13, 1969.
  Vital Speeches 35:631-4 Ag 1 '69
STERN, James L.
Evolution of private manpower planning in
  Armour's plant closings. bibliog Mo Labor
  R 92:21-8 D '69
—See Johnson, D. B. jt. auth.
STERN, Judith M. and Eisenfeld, A. J.
Androgen accumulation and binding to mac-
  romolecules in seminal vesicles: inhibition
  by cyproterone. bibliog Science 166:233-5 O
  10 '69
STERN, Lothar
Some technical terms aren't. por Electr World
  81:21 Je '69
STERN, Louis W.
Mergers under scrutiny; excerpts from Man-
  agerial analysis in marketing. bibliog Har-
  vard Bsns R 47:18-20+ Jl '69
STERN, Otto
Otto Stern, co-discoverer of space quantiza-
  tion. dies at 81. I. I. Rabi. por Phys Today
  22:103+ O '69
STERN, Paula
Child's play. New Repub 161:10-11 Jl 26 '69
Uncivil war afflicts the Peace corps. New
  Repub 161:14-16 Ag 23 '69
When's it going to be ladies' day? New Re-
  pub 161:14-16 Jl 5 '69
STERN, Peter S.
Cold-war scholarship. Nation 209:176-80 S 1
  '69

STERN, Philip M.
How 381 super-rich Americans managed not to pay a cent in taxes last year. N Y Times Mag p30-1+ Ap 13 '69
STERN, Richard
Mies and the closing of the Bauhaus. Nation 209:290 S 22 '69
(ed) See Borges, J. L. Borges on Borges
STERN, Sol
Short account of international student politics & the cold war, with particular reference to the NSA, CIA, etc. Ramp Mag 7:87-96 Ja 25 '69
Trouble in paradise. Ramp Mag 8:22-8 N '69
STERNBERG, Irma O.
Earthworm pits for ailing elms. Org Gard & Farm 16:90-2 D '69
STERNBERG, Sidney
Automatic checkout equipment, the Apollo Hippocrates. por Bul Atom Sci 25:84-7 S '69
STERNFELD, Ari
Cosmodrome in orbit. Space World F-7-67: 42-3 Jl '69
STERNGLASS, Ernest J.
Death of all children. Esquire 72:1a-1d S '69; Excerpts. Cur 110:12-15 S '69
Fetal and infant mortality and the environment. Bul Atom Sci 25:29-34 D '69
Infant mortality and nuclear tests. Bul Atom Sci 25:18-20 Ap; 29-32 O '69
    about
Ernest J. Sternglass: controversial prophet of doom. P. M. Boffey. por Science 166: 195-200 O 10 '69
STERNWHEELS. See Steamships and steamboats
STEROIDS
Androgen accumulation and binding to macromolecules in seminal vesicles: inhibition by cyproterone. J. M. Stern and A. J. Eisenfeld. bibliog il Science 166:233-5 O 10 '69
    See also
Corticosteroids
Lipids
Methandrostenolone
STEROLS
    See also
Cholesterol
STERRY, Rick
Real us; story. Redbook 132:50-1 Ja '69
Troubadour; story. Redbook 133:68-9 Je '69
STETLER, C. Joseph
Congressional hearing; address, October 1, 1969. Vital Speeches 36:53-6 N 1 '69
STETSON, Nancy
After the night; story. Good H 169:92-3 S '69
Something to grow on; story. Good H 168: 118-19 Ap '69
STETSON, Paul W.
Fresh water fishes for garden pools. Horticulture 47:35-6 Ag '69
STETSON university, Deland, Fla.
Stetson loses its head; McCormick's McKay quits. A. Taft. Chr Today 13:46 Je 6 '69
STEVENS, Clifford
Nagasaki experiment. America 120:192 F 15 '69
STEVENS, Douglas R.
New expectations. Seventeen 29:28 Ja '70
STEVENS, George
Very model of a modern intellectual. por Sat R 52:27 F 22 '69
STEVENS, Georgiana
View from the UN. Atlan 224:4+ S '69
STEVENS, Harold
Macaroni sculpture. Sch Arts 68:32-3 My '69
STEVENS, J. P, and company
Million-dollar back-pay bonanza; awards to mill workers. il Bsns W p29-31 Jl 26 '69
STEVENS, Joanne
Race to reclaim a dead man's eyes. B. Derrick-Davis. il Todays Health 48:42-3+ Ja '70
STEVENS, Jody L.
Of immediate concern: better teacher utilization. Clear House 43:504-5 Ap '69
STEVENS, Leonard A.
When is death? Read Digest 94:225-6+ My '69
STEVENS, M. James
Proposed Gulf Islands National Seashore. Nat Parks 43:16-19 Mr '69
STEVENS, Norman D.
Molesworth institute revisited. ALA Bul 63: 1275-7 O '69
Viewpoint. Library J 94:4501 D 15 '69
STEVENS, Thelma K.
Whither the substitute teacher? Clear House 44:229-31 D '69
STEVENS, Wallace
Poetry: how and why. J. Jerome. Writers Digest 49:26+ Jl '69

STEVENS, Walter W.
Conflict; poem. Chr Cent 86:248 F 19 '69
Friends; poem. Chr Cent 86:1344 O 22 '69
STEVENS, William B.
Samuel King of Newport. Antiques 96:728-33 N '69
STEVENSON, Adlai Ewing, 1900-1965
In the house that Adlai loved. J. B. Martin. Life 66:24 Mr 28 '69
Remnants of power, by R. J. Walton. Review America 120:106-7 Ja 25 '69. M. Morrison Nation 208:89-90 Ja 20 '69. H. Barnard Stevenson we lost. M. Decter. Harper 238: 98+ F '69; Reply with rejoinder. D. E. Connell. 238:12 My '69
STEVENSON, Adlai Ewing, 3d
Another Adlai in big-time politics. il por U S News 67:12 D 8 '69
Enter Adlai III. il por Newsweek 74:48+ D 8 '69
STEVENSON, Elizabeth
Sex & sensibility. Commentary 47:86-8 Mr '69
STEVENSON, Florence
All wound up. Opera N 34:12-16 D 27 '69
Reconstruction, an opera by committee. Hi Fi 19:MA25 S '69
—and Brown, Davitt
Opera and the stars. Opera N 34:14-16 Ja 17 '70
STEVENSON, George S.
How to deal with your tensions; excerpts. Read Digest 94:89-92 Mr '69
STEVENSON, James
Notes from a bottle; story. New Yorker 44: 31 F 8 '69
Notes from an exhibition. New Yorker 45: 32-3 Mr 22 '69
    about
Drawing the line. il por Newsweek 74:80-1 Jl 14 '69
STEVENSON, Janet
Ignorant armies. Atlan 224:57-63 O '69
(ed) See Kenny, R. W. Before the colors fade: the return of the exiles
STEVENSON, John R.
Vienna convention on the law of treaties; address, July 15, 1969. Dept State Bul 61: 127-31 Ag 18 '69
STEVENSON, Kay L.
My brother who is dearly loved; story. Good H 163:82-3 Je '69
STEVENSON, Peter
Magic of making toys. N. C. Gray. il por Am Home 72:26-8+ D '69
STEVENSON, Robert Louis
Prayer for Christmas day. Good H 169:71 D '69
STEVENSON, Robert P.
How to make a good canoe better. Pop Sci 195:149-51 N '69
Snowmobiles come to the suburbs. Pop Sci 195:132-6+ N '69
STEVICK, Daniel B.
Conscience and the community; excerpt from Civil disobedience and the Christian. Chr Cent 86:345-8 Mr 12 '69
STEW
Getting stewed. D. Ivens and W. E. Massee. il Holiday 46:60-1+ N '69
Khuroosh, it's a lamb and vegetable stew with rice. il Sunset 142:198 Ap '69
Secret of a good stew; with recipes. E. Alston. il Look 33:84-5 Ap 1 '69
Veal meals you needn't watch. Sunset 142: 178 My '69
STEWARDESSES, Air. See Airlines—Hostesses
STEWARDSHIP, Christian
    Anecdotes, facetiae, satire, etc.
Project Fork Over. Chr Cent 86:825 Je 11 '69
STEWART, Donald C.
Those were the days. .; excerpts from Five golden summers. Parks & Rec 4:20-4 D '69
STEWART, Dorothy R.
Message of the kite. Read Digest 95:122-5 Jl '69
STEWART, Ellen
La Mama complex. H. Hewes. Sat R 52:53 Ap 19 '69
STEWART, Ernest I.
D.W.I.s anonymous. il Time 95:32 Ja 5 '70
STEWART, Harold L. See Snell, K. C. jt. auth.
STEWART, Jackie
Another great Scot races in. K. Chapin. Sports Illus 30:50-1 Je 30 '69
Hail to king Jackie! R. F. Jones. il pors Sports Illus 31:22-7 S 22 '69
Ruler of the road. il por Time 94:53 Ag 1 '69
STEWART, James Ray, and Brown, R. M. jr
Cytophaga that kills or lyses algae. bibliog Science 164:1523-4 Je 27 '69

STEWART, John W.
Total solar eclipse of 7 March 1970. bibliog
Weatherwise 22:100-6 Je '69
STEWART, Michael
Economic policy; address, October 1 1969.
Vital Speeches 36:59-61 N 1 '69
STEWART, P. Brian, and Cohen, Vivian
Antiserum to lymphocytes and procarbazine
compared as immunosuppressants in mice.
bibliog Science 164:1082-3 My 30 '69
STEWART, Richard W. and Hogan, J. S.
Solar cycle variation of exospheric temper-
atures on Mars and Venus: a prediction for
Mariner 6 and 7. bibliog Science 165:386-8
Jl 25 '69
STEWART, Robert William
Atmosphere and the ocean; with biographical
sketch. Sci Am 221:42, 76-86 bibliog(p284)
S '69
STEWART, T. D.
Fossil evidence of human violence. por Trans-
Action 6:48-53 My; 61 O '69
STEWART, Virginia
Oxalis hirta. Horticulture 47:18-19 Ja '69
STEWART, Sir William George Drummond,
bart
Hunter and the artist. J. Monaghan. bibliog
il por Am West 6:4-13 N '69
Old Gabe of Her Majesty's English life
guards. M. Goosman. il Am West 6:14-15
N '69
STEWART-GORDON, James
Gray ghost wins again. Read Digest 95:229-34
Jl '69
STEWS. See Stew
STICKER, Robert
Historic lone voyagers: paintings. Yachting
125:92-3 Ja '69
[Historic voyagers] paintings. Yachting 125:
92-3 Ja; 61 Ap; 126:54 Jl '69
STICKNEY, John
Alice's family of folk song fame becomes a
movie. Life 66:43-5+ Mr 28 '69

about

Two young men in a forest commune. R.
Graves. por Life 67:1 Jl 18 '69
STICKS, Hockey. See Hockey sticks
STIGLER, George J.
Ivory tower; ed. by M. Friedman. Newsweek
74:92 N 10 '69
STIKINE RIVER
Up a steep Alaska river to British Colum-
bia, just for the fun of it. il Sunset 142:54-
6+ My '69
STILBESTROLS
Implant young beef calves; stilbestrol im-
plant. Suc Farm 67:62 Ap '69
STILES, William E. and Robran, E. L.
Dealing with impasse. Todays Ed 58:57-8 Ja
'69
STILL, Clyfford
Man of the arts; exhibition of oils and
gouaches. D. L. Shirey. il por Newsweek
74:105 D 22 '69
Outsider; show at Marlborough-Gerson gal-
lery, New York. T. B. Hess. il Art N 68:34-
7+ D '69
STILLMAN, Edmund O.
Is there a lesson of Munich? Horizon 11:
32-3 Spr '69
Marcuse. Horizon 11:26-31 Sum '69
STILLMAN college, Tuscaloosa, Ala.
Strike at Stillman. W. Henley. Chr Today 13:
37-80 Mr 14 '69
STILLWELL, Leonard L.
Individualized in-service education. Todays
Ed 58:44-5 D '69
STIMULATION (physiology)
Evoked potentials and auditory reaction time
in monkeys. J. M. Miller and others. bibliog
il Science 163:592-4 F 7 '69
Facilitation of brain self-stimulation by cen-
tral administration of norepinephrine. C. D.
Wise and L. Stein. bibliog il Science 163:299-
301 Ja 17 '69
Hypothalamic motivational systems; fixed or
plastic neural circuits? E. S. Valenstein
and others. Science 163:1084 Mr 7 '69; Reply. R. A. Wise. 165:929-30 Ag 29 '69
Ionic mechanisms controlling behavioral
responses of paramecium to mechanical
stimulation. Y. Naitoh and R. Eckert.
bibliog il Science 164:963-5 My 23 '69
Lateral hypothalamic stimulation: inhibition
of aversive effects by feeding, drinking, and
gnawing. J. Mendelson. bibliog il Science
166:1431-3 D 12 '69
Mind over matter; animals learn to control
their involuntary nervous responses. il
Newsweek 73:91 F 10 '69
Nerve jammer kills pain; electrical stimulation. il Sci Digest 66:72 N '69

Neural readout from memory during generalization. E. R. John and others. bibliog
il Science 164:1534-6 Je 27 '69
Object-carrying by rats: an approach to the
behavior produced by brain stimulation.
A. G. Phillips and others. bibliog il Science
166:903-5 N 14 '69
Primary afferent depolarization evoked by
a painful stimulus. L. Vyklicky and others.
bibliog il Science 165:184-6 Jl 11 '69
Reticular stimulation and chlorpromazine: an
animal model for schizophrenic overarousal.
C. Kornetsky and M. Eliasson. bibliog il
Science 165:1273-4 S 19 '69
Someone to watch over you (for less than
2¢ a day) Electronic stimulation of the
brain. D. M. Rorvik. Esquire 72:164-7+ D
'69
Stimulus properties of reinforcing brain shock.
R. M. Stutz and others. bibliog il Science
163:1081-2 Mr 7 '69
Surgery in the rat during electrical analgesia
induced by focal brain stimulation. D. V.
Reynolds. bibliog il Science 164:444-5 Ap 25
'69
See also
Electrophysiology
STIMULUS and response
Discriminative control of attention. E. G.
Heinemann and others; reply with rejoinder.
R. M. Gilbert. Science 164:198 Ap 11 '69
Protein synthesis in the hippocampal pyra-
midal cells of rats during a behavioral test.
H. Hydén and P. W. Lange; reply with re-
joinder. R. E. Bowman and G. Harding.
bibliog Science 164:199-201 Ap 11 '69
Punishment by response-contingent with-
drawal of an imprinted stimulus. H. S.
Hoffman and others. bibliog il Science 163:
702-4 F 14 '69
Visceral and behavioral responses to intra-
duodenal fat. J. W. Fara and others. bib-
liog il Science 166:110-11 O 3 '69
Visual stimuli and evoked responses in the
rat. C. Fields. bibliog il Science 165:1377-9
S 26 '69
Visual transient phenomenon: its polarity
and a paradox. J. F. Bird and G. H. Mow-
bray. bibliog il Science 165:588-9 Ag 8 '69
See also
Motor response
Reaction time
STINEHOUR, Roderick
Random thoughts about book design 1968-69;
address, April 23, 1969. por Pub W 195:90+
My 5 '69
STINGS, Insect. See Insect bites and stings
STINNETT, Caskie
Haiti: equatorial Africa in the Caribbean.
Holiday 46:30-1+ N '69
Speaking of Holiday. See issues of Holiday
STINNETT, L. Phillips
Mountains by the minute. Travel 132:48-51
Jl '69
STINNETT, Loni
My mother loved me! My mother loved me!
McCalls 96:70-1+ My '69
Nassau street. Holiday 46:78-80 S '69
STINSON, Craig
To be, or not to be? BU helps. Hi Fi 19:
MA22-3 O '69
STINSON, Thelma
More ways to build nature interest. Camp
Mag 41:15+ N '69
To stimulate campers' interest in nature.
Camp Mag 41:16-17 S '69
STIRLING, Marion W.
Olmec. Américas 21:2-10 N '69
STIRLING, Matthew W.
Solving the mystery of Mexico's great stone
spheres. por Nat Geog 136:294-300 Ag '69
STIRLING engines. See Heat engines
STITCHERY. See Embroidery
STOBAUGH, Robert B. Jr
How to analyze foreign investment climates.
bibliog f Harvard Bsns R 47:100-8 S '69
Where in the world should we put that plant?
bibliog f Harvard Bsns R 47:129-36 Ja '69
STOCK, Dennis
Selective focus: photographs. Travel &
Camera 32:53-6 Je '69
STOCK, Robert
Hazards of art. Nation 208:378-9 Mr 24 '69
STOCK, Robert W.
At 100, the Museum of natural history is no
fossil. N Y Times Mag p8-9+ Je 29 '69
Mouse stage of the new biology. N Y Times
Mag p8-9+ D 21 '69
Saving the world the ecologist's way. N Y
Times Mag p32-3+ O 5 '69
Will the baby be normal? N Y Times Mag
p25-7+ Mr 23 '69

STOCKHAUSEN, Karlheinz
Big, seminal works of Karlheinz Stockhausen. R. P. Morgan. por Hi Fi 19:104+ Mr '69
Stockhausen: I am a radio. R. McMullen. por Hi Fi 19:MA30+ Ag '69

STOCKHOLDERS
Does the small investor get an even break? il Changing T 23:24-8 F '69
European stockholders learn to talk back; Italy's Montecatini Edison and Germany's NSU, received rough treatment. il Bsns W p34+ My 3 '69
How should a widow invest her money? il Changing T 22:17-19 D '68
Victims of the fall. Time 94:68 Ag 8 '69
When Wall Street catches the flu. 26 million Americans ache. C. J. Rolo. il N Y Times Mag p 12-14+ Ag 31 '69
    See also
Investor relations programs

Psychology
Next: rose-chip stocks? Forbes 104:100+ N 15 '69
Opposites attract a following; contrary opinion theory. il Bsns W p 128-9 O 11 '69

STOCKHOLDERS meetings
Anecdotes, facetiae, satire, etc.
Jersey ritual; annual meeting of Hess oil & chemical corporation; letter from anthropologist. New Yorker 45:30-1 My 31 '69

STOCKHOLM
Stick it on the wall in Stockholm. A. Frater. il Holiday 45:85-6 F '69

Description
Changing face of Stockholm. L. Littman. il Travel & Camera 32:29-30+ Mr '69

Hotels, restaurants, etc.
Operakallaren, Stockholm, Sweden. M. Woodward. il Travel 132:71 O '69

Music
Report: production of Massenet's Manon. A. Swanson. Opera N 34:29 D 6 '69
Report: Stockholm: production of Magic flute. A. Swanson. il Opera N 33:30-1 Mr 1 '69
Report: Stockholm: productions of Aucassin et Nicolette and Adam de la Halle's Jeu de Robin et de Marion. A. Swanson. Opera N 33:28-9 My 17 '69
Report: Stockholm: Royal opera's new Siegfried. A. Swanson. Opera N 33:26 Je 14 '69
Report: Stockholm; Royal opera's performance of Ferruccio Busoni's Doktor Faust. A. Swanson. Opera N 34:27 O 11 '69

STOCKING of streams, lakes, etc. See Fish culture

STOCKLIN, William A.
For the record. por Electr World 82:6 N; 6 D '69

STOCKS
Big investors, where they are putting their money now. il U S News 66:58-60 F 3 '69
Clean up on clean up? pollution-control stocks. C. Morgello. il Newsweek 75:73 Ja 19 '70
Congressman's choice. C. Morgello. il Newsweek 73:97 My 26 '69
Downward shift. Time 93:89 F 28 '69
Earnings crunch. C. Morgello. Newsweek 74:106 O 6 '69
Found: two bulls. C. Morgello. il Newsweek 73:71 Je 30 '69
Growth stocks for the next boom, some samples. Changing T 23:10-11 Ap '69
How to invest in stocks and bonds. R. Krumme. il Suc Farm 67:46-7 Ag '69
New issues in doldrums. il Bsns W p 110+ Jl 19 '69
Stock prices. P. A. Samuelson. Newsweek 73:80 Mr 10 '69
Stocks: growth now, income later. il Changing T 23:39 My '69
Stocks the Swiss banks don't like. J. Ross-Skinner. il Duns R 92:23-5 D '68
There are bargains and bargains. M. Simons. Forbes 104:96 N 1 '69
Wall Street:
  Cash is not a bad idea. C. Morgello. Newsweek 73:72 F 3 '69
  Cold conglomerates. C. Morgello. il Newsweek 73:72 F 24 '69
  Groping for the bottom. C. Morgello. Newsweek 73:70 Mr 3 '69
  New kind of market? C. Morgello. Newsweek 74:71 Ag 4 '69

Why some stocks go up. C. Morgello. il Newsweek 73:75 Mr 31 '69
    See also
Banks and banking—Securities
Bonds
Computers—Investment applications
Corporate distributions
Securities
Speculation
Stock exchange
Stock purchase warrants

Certificates
Knocking holes in punch card stock certificates. Bsns W p69 D 27 '69
Unclogging paperwork jam; proposal to replace stock certificates with punch cards. il Bsns W p 111 Je 28 '69

Insider trading
Kiss and tell on romantic Wall Street. S. Sauerhaft. il Duns R 93:26-9 F '69

Marketing
Big board's rebels are gaining. il Bsns W p33-4 Jl 19 '69
Brokers await new ground rules. Bsns W p85-6 Jl 26 '69
Case for buying new issues second-hand. il Fortune 80:212 N '69
Easy way to buy stock in foreign firms. il Changing T 23:46 Mr '69
How stocks debut at the back door. Bsns W p 123-4+ Mr 29 '69
Security analysts size up today's markets. il U S News 66:66-9 My 26 '69
Step nearer public ownership; brokerage stocks. il Bsns W p 106+ S 27 '69

Price-earnings ratios
Personal investing; what, if anything, are the p/e's saying? il Fortune 80:176 S '69
Wall Street:
  Waiting game. C. Morgello. il Newsweek 74:91 D 15 '69

Price indexes and averages
Bear looks a little bullish. il Bsns W p45 S 13 '69
Casualty list; stock market casualties. il Forbes 104:24-5 S 1 '69
Changing yardsticks; conglomerate stocks lose altitude il Bsns W p29 Mr 8 '69
Close look at the sagging stock market. il U S News 67:81-2 Jl 28 '69
Financial markets take a beating. Bsns W p62 D 6 '69
Flirting with 800 on the Dow. il Bsns W p22-3 Ag 2 '69
Foreign bulls are friskier. il Bsns W p33-4 N 15 '69
Go-go boys. or gone-gone? il Newsweek 74:91+ O 13 '69
Has the decline run its course? il Bsns W p 110 Jl 19 '69
Has the market bottomed out? il Newsweek 74:49-50+ Ag 11 '69
In search of a new game. Time 94:58 Ag 29 '69
Investors look for good news; Dow-Jones averages. il Bsns W p26-7 Mr 1 '69
Investors wonder: how far below 800? il Bsns W p27-8 N 29 '69
Late-comers to the feast. il Forbes 103:29 F 1 '69
Market drop. R. Brady. Duns R 94:77-8+ Ag '69
Market shrugs off the moon landing. il Bsns W p27-8 Jl 26 '69
Market's drop; some measures. il U S News 67:33 Jl 21 '69
Masters of zig and zag; stock chartists. il Time 93:90+ F 14 '69
Money men pick stocks for 1969. U S News 66:82-3 F 10 '69
More bad news for stockholders. U S News 67:71 Jl 7 '69
Peace rumors help a little. il Bsns W p37 Mr 29 '69
Rail average is streamlined. Bsns W p69 D 27 '69
Record rally brightens Street. Bsns W p24 My 3 '69
Security analysts size up today's markets. il U S News 66:66-9 My 26 '69
Stock market gets back to business. Bsns W p29 N 8 '69
Stock-market trends that worry Congress. il U S News 66:51-4 My 5 '69
Stock market: turning the corner? U S News 67:66 Ag 11 '69
Stocks at '67 level: the meaning. U S News 67:67 D 15 '69
Stocks in search of a real rally. il Bsns W p37-8 Je 21 '69

STOCKS—Price indexes and averages—*Cont.*
Stocks' sudden rally; why. il U S News 66:
94 My 12 '69
Stocks weather the news; tensions over
North Korea, the Middle East, the French
franc, and Vietnam talks. Bsns W p49 Ap
26 '69
Street hopes worst is over. il Bsns W p68-
9 D 27 '69
Sudsy P&G lightens that dull D-J image. il
Bsns W p30 N 8 '69
Tax-loss selling drags Dow down. il Bsns W
p24 D 20 '69
Technician's perspective. J. W. Schulz. See
issues of Forbes
Tighter money adds to jitters. il Bsns W p43
Je 14 '69
Trends for investors to watch. il U S News
67:57-8 N 10 '69
Unfashionables; marked down stocks. il
Forbes 104:28-9 O 1 '69
Wall Street:
Bail-out syndrome. C. Morgello. il News-
week 74:87 N 10 '69
Caution is still the word. C. Morgello.
il Newsweek 74:80 S 15 '69
Even the bears hurt. C. Morgello. il
Newsweek 74:84 Jl 21 '69
Floor or ceiling? C. Morgello. il News-
week 74:92 O 20 '69
Garland of losses. C. Morgello. il News-
week 74:76 Jl 14 '69
Look back in sorrow. C. Morgello. il
Newsweek 75:52 Ja 5 '70
Nothing like a rally. C. Morgello. il News-
week 74:106 O 27 '69
Reading the entrails. C. Morgello. il
Newsweek 74:99 D 8 '69
Signs of strength. C. Morgello. il News-
week 73:87 My 19 '69
Waiting game. C. Morgello. il Newsweek
74:91 D 15 '69
Wanted: a clear sign. C. Morgello. il
Newsweek 74:75 D 1 '69
What kind of bounce? C. Morgello. il
Newsweek 74:50-1 D 29 '69
Wall Street's answer to Lenin. il Time 94:91
O 24 '69
Ways of Wall Street. Duns R 94:136 S '69
What the little letters in the stock quotes
mean. il Changing T 23:14 S '69
When Wall Street catches the flu, 26 million
Americans ache. C. J. Rolo. il N Y Times
Mag p 12-14+ Ag 31 '69
Why the bears romped. il Bsns W p44 F 22
'69
Zurich's stock market swingers. A. McGre-
gor. il Duns R 94:103-4 N '69

Short selling

Annals of finance: a corner in Stutz. J.
Brooks. New Yorker 45:74-82+ Ag 23 '69
Personal business. Bsns W p77-8 Jl 5 '69
See also
Speculation

Tender offers

Merger tide runs higher; popularity of tender
offers also increased. Bsns W p44 Ap 12 '69

Valuation

See Corporations—Valuation
STOCKSTILL, Louis R.
What you can do for American prisoners in
Vietnam. Read Digest 95:61-6 N '69
(ed) See Frishman, R. F. I was a prisoner in
Hanoi
STOCKTON, Calif.
Hurry-up beautification. F. Fargo. il Am City
84:110-11 Ja '69
STOCKWOOD, Arthur Mervyn, bp
Bishop's ghosts. il por Time 93:49-50 My 30
'69
STOCKYARDS, Denver. See Denver union
stock yard company
STODDARD, Charles H.
Uncle Sam's step-child acres. Am For 75:16-
19+ S '69
STOECKLE, David
(comp) Business books of 1968. por Library J
94:956-9 Mr 1 '69
STOESSINGER, John G.
(comp) Recent books on international rela-
tions. See issues of Foreign affairs
STOFFLE, Carla J.
Public library service to the disadvantaged.
por Library J 94:141-52, 507-15 Ja 15-F 1 '69
STOGEL, John
Build a better blinker for highway safety.
Pop Sci 195:166-7+ Ag '69
Build a low-water warning for your wind-
shield washer. Pop Sci 194:156-7 Ja '69
STOHLMAN, Frederick, jr. See Morley, A. jt.
auth.

STOKES, Carl Burton
Cleveland: Now! pors Am City 84:95-7 S '69
about
Challenge to Mayor Stokes. D. Henninger.
New Repub 161:12-14 Ag 23 '69
City; black power in office. por Time 93:27
F 28 '69
Cleveland's Carl Stokes: making it. il por
Newsweek 73:67-8+ My 26 '69
Mayor Stokes's troubles. Newsweek 74:42+
S 29 '69
Mayor Stokes' West side story. M. D. Daley.
Commonweal 91:270-1 N 28 '69
Second lap. A. Z. Silver. Nation 208:524 Ap
28 '69
We have overcome. il por Newsweek 74:48
N 17 '69
STOKES, Eric
Horspfal, a breakthrough. J. K. Sherman. il
Hi Fi 19:MA30-1 My '69
STOKES, Geoffrey C.
Nixon's drug bill. Nation 209:271-2 S 22 '69;
Same with title What new federal drug
legislation? Cur 112:14-16 N '69
STOKES, Louis
Former shoeshine boy on Capitol hill. il pors
Ebony 24:60+ F '69
STOKLEY, James
Astronomy. See fourth issue of each month
of Science news
STOKVIS, Irene Ellen
(ed) First novelists: spring-summer-fall 1969.
Library J 94:570-84, 2254-61, 3473-9 F 1, Je 1,
O 1 '69
STOLLEY, Richard B.
Column. Life 67:4 S 19 '69
This is my area; I've staked it out. Life 67:
50-1 S 12 '69
STOLPORTS. See Airports—Design
STOLTE, Kenneth W. jr
Army and the First amendment. P. Barnes.
New Repub 160:13-14 My 24 '69
STOMACH
Sliding stomach; hiatal hernia. il Time 93:52
Mr 28 '69
See also
Flatulence
STOMACH cancer. See Cancer
STOMATA
Stomatal opening; role of potassium uptake
by guard cells. R. A. Fischer; reply with
rejoinder. J. Levitt. bibliog Science 163:494
Ja 31 '69
STOMP; musical comedy. See Musical com-
edies, revues, etc.—Criticisms, plots, etc.
STONE, Alan
What the city needs. Nation 209:494-5 N 10
'69
STONE, Amy
Hitchhiking in Japan. Travel & Camera 32:
24+ Ag '69
STONE, Bluejay Abigail
Thumbing around; letter from a sixteen-
year-old. Atlan 224:90-1 D '69
STONE, C. Walter
A-V report card for librarianship. por Wil-
son Lib Bul 44:290-3 N '69
STONE, Christopher D.
Crimes and criminality. Nation 208:510-13 Ap
21 '69
STONE, D. and others
Cytogenetic effects of cyclamates on human
cells in vitro. bibliog Science 164:568-9
My 2 '69
STONE, David L.
Temple's tale of two tents. J. Felton. il Hi Fi
19:MA24-5 O '69
STONE, Ed
Callaway gardens, year-round retreat. Parks
& Rec 4:20-2 Ap '69
STONE, Elizabeth W.
Administrators fiddle while employees burn,
or flee. bibliog por ALA Bul 63:181-7 F '69
STONE, I. F.
Lasting Middle East peace? The need for
double vision. Cur 105:54-6 Mr '69
about
SALT and I. F. Stone. Commonweal 91:292
D 5 '69
STONE, Irving
Jack London's Klondike. Travel & Camera 32:
45-57 Ag '69
Role of the writer in a troubled world. Writer
82:18-21 Ap '69
STONE, Jeremy J.
[Book review] Commonweal 89:714-15 Mr 7
'69
End of the beginning. Commonweal 90:536+
S 5 '69

STONE, Jeremy J.—*Continued*
  Thing to do after Vietnam is to tell the truth. Commonweal 90:10-11 Mr 21 '69; Same with title To tell the truth. Cur 109:54-5 Ag '69
STONE, Katherine S.
  Aide to learning. Engl J 58:124-5 Ja '69
STONE, Kurt
  Current chronicle. bibliog f Mus Q 55:559-72 O '69
STONE, Lawrence M.
  Excerpt from testimony before House committee on ways and means, February 18, 1969. Cong Digest 48:142+ My '69
STONE, Lucie R.
  International children's book day, 1969, at Norfolk public library, Virginia. Horn Bk 45:461-3 Ag '69
STONE, Michael
  Haselden fellow named. Chr Cent 86:301 Je 11 '69
STONE, Mozelle Phillips
  Evening reflections; poem. Har Yrs 9:51 F '69
STONE, Ralph, and Stearns, Robert
  For more efficient refuse collection. Am City 84:98-100 My '69
STONE, Ron, and Napier, Jeff
  Great pollution pickle, one more time. Motor B 123:268-9+ Ja '69
STONE, Ronald
  Ethics in policy making and the implications for theological education. Chr Cent 86:548-50 Ap 23 '69
STONE, Scott C. S.
  Hawaii '69: beauty and the bulldozer. Sat R 52:51-2+ S 13 '69
STONE, William Clement
  American original. il por Time 93:78 F 7 '69
  Clement Stone feels great. L. Wille. il Nation 208:338-40 Mr 17 '69
STONE, William T.
  Washington report. See issues of Yachting
  Yachting interviews: Rear Admiral William J. Morrison. Yachting 125:67+ Mr '69
STONE, Worthing
  He defends today's machinery prices; interview, ed. by J. Carlson. Farm J 93:52J Mr '69

STONE
  Preservation
  Paint-on preservation for ancient stone. B. O'Connell. il Sci Digest 65:77-80 My '69
STONE age
  Twelve things nobody ever knew about stone age and iron age men. L. R. Griffin. il Sci Digest 65:26-31 My '69
STONE carving
  Elaine Rapp, stone carver. J. H. Michel. il Am Artist 33:22-5+ Ja '69
STONE houses
  Enchantment in a house of stone. F. Heard. il House B 111:112-17 Ap '69
STONE implements and weapons
  Flint flaking in Turkey. J. Bordaz. il Natur Hist 78:73-7 F '69
  Knappers of Cakmak. Sci Am 220:51-2 Ap '69
  Paleolithic camp at Nice. H. de Lumley. il Sci Am 220:42-50 My '69
  Stone tools and human behavior. S. R. Binford and L. R. Binford. il Sci Am 220:70-2+ bibliog(p 146) Ap '69
    See also
  Bolas
STONE sheep hunting. See Mountain sheep hunting
STONE tools. See Stone implements and weapons
STONEHENGE, England
  Dig. K. E. Meyer. il Esquire 71:94-5+ F '69
  Stonehenge; with photographs by P. Caponigro. Travel & Camera 32:42-5+ Mr '69
STONEHOUSE, Bernard
  Environmental temperatures of tertiary penguins. bibliog Science 163:673-5 F 14 '69
STONEMAN, Bill
  Highlight. por Sports Illus 30:78 Ap 28 '69
STONER, Don, and Anderson, Art
  Method for teaching subskills in composition. Engl J 58:252-6 F '69
STONER, Jeanette
  Contemporary dance repertoire concert: Henry street settlement playhouse. J. Dowlin. Dance Mag 43:80 F '69
STONER, John C.
  Encephalitis started the program. Am City 84:102+ Ap '69
STONES (physiology) See Calculi
STONEWALL Jackson's waterloo; story. See Murray, A.

STONEWARE. See Pottery
STONEWORK, Decorative. See Decoration and ornament, Architectural
STONG, C. L.
  (ed) Amateur scientist. See issues of Scientific American
STOOKEY, Laurance H.
  Baptism and liturgical integrity reconsidered. Chr Cent 86:1109-13 Ag 27 '69
STOOLS
  Extra seating in seconds. il Bet Hom & Gard 47:124 F '69
  Footstool from Abe Lincoln's home. D. Warren. il Pop Sci 194:148-53 My '69
  Swivel stool. il Mech Illus 65:106-7 S '69
STOOP, Norma McLain
  Colloquy of colleagues: dance conventions '69. Dance Mag 43:70-3 N '69
STOP and shop, incorporated. See Supermarkets
STOP, you're killing me; drama. See Herlihy, J. L.
STOPH, Willi
  After Ulbricht? por Newsweek 74:36-8 Ag 25 '69
STOPHLET, John J.
  Let's get going at Sleeping Bear. Nat Parks 43:21 N '69
STOPPARD, Tom
  Rosencrantz and Guildenstern are dead. Criticism
    Sat R 52:20 Jl 5 '69
STORAGE
    See also
  Closets
    also subhead Storage under various subjects. e.g. Grain—Storage
STORAGE batteries
  High-temperature batteries. E. J. Cairns and H. Shimotake. bibliog il Science 164:1347-55 Je 20 '69
    Care
  Battery care for sure starts. Suc Farm 67:54B Ja '69
    Charging
  Burping the battery; problem of recharging for electric cars. Time 94:73 Ag 15 '69
STORAGE battery chargers
  AA-C-D-battery charger. A. A. Mangieri. il Pop Electr 31:33-5+ O '69
  New charger spurs cordless revolution. J. Davis. il Pop Sci 195:68-9 N '69
STORAGE in boats. See Boats—Equipment
STORAGE in the home
  Adaptable storage for a multi-action kitchen. il Bet Hom & Gard 47:150 N '69
  Best storage units we've seen. il Bet Hom & Gard 47:70-5 Je '69
  Build this storage into your pool table. il Pop Mech 131:154-7 Ja '69
  How to add shelves all through the house. il Pop Sci 194:150-61+ Mr '69
  How to squeeze more storage space out of your kitchen. D. Swanson. il Pop Mech 131:174-7 Ja '69
  Kitchen-storage planning. il Good H 168:142-5 Mr '69
  Storage. il Seventeen 29:74-5 Ja '70
  Storage ideas. il Bet Hom & Gard 47:26-8 N '69
  Storage; ingenuity at work. il House B 111:92-5 Je '69
  Storage is made-to-measure. il House & Gard 135:60-1 Ja '69
  Storage scoops. il Seventeen 28:368 Ag '69
  Thirty smart ideas for putting space to work. il Pop Mech 132:138-49 D '69
    See also
  Storage walls
STORAGE of food. See Food—Storage
STORAGE of grain. See Grain—Storage
STORAGE of vegetables. See Vegetables—Storage
STORAGE shelters. See Shelters
STORAGE tanks. See Water tanks
STORAGE walls
  Storage wall, one-way and two-way. il Sunset 142:119 F '69
  Three great storage walls. il House & Gard 136:144-9 S '69
  We put it all on our living room wall. M. Johnson. il Pop Mech 130:150-3 D '68
STORE hours
  Sears adds Sunday to shopping week. Bsns W p47 O 11 '69
STORE security measures. See Retail trade—Security measures
STORE windows. See Show windows

STORES
  See also
  Airports—Stores
  Chain stores
  Drugstores
  Food stores
  Grocery stores
  Shopping centers
  Specialty stores

Employees
  See also
  Booksellers and bookselling—Employees
STOREY, William B.
  Pistillate papaya flower: a morphological anomaly. bibliog Science 163:401-5 Ja 24 '69
STORIES. See Fiction; Story telling
STORIES of operas. See Libretto
STORLIEN, L. H. See Albert, D. J. jt. auth.
STORM detectors
  Picnicker's' friend. J. E. Shepler. il Pop Electr 31:47-50 Jl '69
STORM KING art center, Mountainville, N.Y.
  Storm King art center. E. S. Robbins. il Art in Am 57:108-9 My '69
STORM KING hydroelectric project. See Hydro-electric plants
STORM water. See Sewerage
STORM windows. See Windows
STØRMER, Leif
  Oldest known terrestrial arachnids. bibliog Science 164:1276-7 Je 13 '69
STORMS
  Asking for trouble: departure for southern waters via the offshore route. B. Robinson. il Yachting 126:60-1+ Ag '69
  From above: a spring storm. il Weatherwise 22:124-6 Je '69
  Gales at sea. J. Parkinson, jr. il Yachting 125:57-9+ F '69
  How not to go South. D. Street, jr. il Yachting 126:62+ Ag '69
  Riding out a Cape Horn snorter. G. M. S. Tod. il Motor B 123:143+ Ap '69
  Sea fight with time and a tempest. D. Kearns. il Motor B 123:95-7+ Ap '69
  Weather: outboarders' bug-a-boo? J. Marten-hoff. il Yachting 125:66-7+ Ap '69
  See also
  Automobile driving—Storm hazards
  Hurricanes
  Rain and rainfall
  Snow
  Snowstorms
  Tornadoes
STORR, Anthony
  Winston Churchill's black dog. Esquire 71:94-9+ Ja '69
STORRS, John Bradley
  Rediscovery: John Storrs. E. Bryant. il Art in Am 57:66-71 My '69
STORY telling
  Chicago: the public library reaches out. A. Ladenson. il Wilson Lib Bul 43:875-81 My '69

Anecdotes, facetiae, satire, etc.
  Rumpelstiltskin, he said his name was. W. Stanton. il Read Digest 95:51-3 Ag '69
STORY telling records. See Phonograph rec-ords—Childrens records
STORYTELLING. See Story telling
STOTHARD, H. K.
  Abraham's faith and ours today. Chr Today 14:8-10 D 19 '69
  Apostolic authority. Chr Today 14:12-15 N 7 '69
  One true religion. Chr Today 13:8-13 Ag 1 '69
STOTT, John R. W.
  When should a Christian weep? Chr Today 14:3-5 N 7 '69
STOUGH, Austin R.
  Times does it again. Nation 209:101 Ag 11 '69
STOUT, Gardner Dominick
  In and out of the field. A. Meyer. Natur Hist 78:8+ Ja '69
STOUT, Rex
  Conversation with Rex Stout; interview. ed. by A. Bester. por Holiday 46:38-9+ N '69
  about
  Nero Wolfe of West Thirty-fifth street. by W. S. Baring-Gould. Review
    Nation 208:251-2 F 24 '69. M. Byrd
STOUT, Ruth
  About gardening and Rex and Harold, and then there's me! por Org Gard & Farm 16:44-7 F '69
  Make mine more mulch. Org Gard & Farm 16:50-3 My '69

STOUTENBURG, Adrien
  From the diggings; poem. Nation 208:802 Je 23 '69
STOUTENBURGH, John L. jr.
  Museum world. See issues of Hobbies
STOVES
  Redbook guide to kitchen ranges. il Redbook 132:45-52 F '69
  See also
  Electric stoves
  Gas stoves

Care
  Care and safekeeping of ovens and cooking tops. House & Gard 135:138-9 Mr '69

History
  Toe toasters of yesterday. M. Holbrook. il Har Yrs 9:14-15 Jl '69
STOWE, Harriet Elizabeth (Beecher)
  Thesis and theme in Uncle Tom's cabin. D. S. Brown. bibliog f Engl J 58:1330-4+ D '69
STRACHEY, Giles Lytton
  Across the river and into the trees. G. Steiner. New Yorker 45:150+ S 13 '69
STRACHEY, Lytton. See Strachey, G. L.
La STRADA; musical comedy. See Musical comedies, revues, etc.—Criticisms, plots, etc.
STRADELLA, Alessandro
  Stradella's view of the Nativity. J. W. Barker. Am Rec G 36:170 N '69
STRAHS, Gerald
  Azurin: X-ray data for crystals from pseu-domonas denitrificans. bibliog Science 165:60-1 Jl 4 '69
STRAIGHT, Michael
  Arts go begging. New Repub 160:13-15 Mr 22 '69
STRAIN gages
  Measuring earth strains by laser. V. Vali. il Sci Am 221:88-95 bibliog (p 152) D '69
  Strain gages come of age. J. Tusinski. il Electr World 81:35-7 Mr '69
STRAINS and stresses
  Testing architectural stress with a cathedral made of plastic. il Life 67:95-6+ S 19 '69
  See also
  Deformation (mechanics)
  Strain gages
  Trusses
STRAITS of Bosporus. See Bosporus
STRAND, Mark
  Dance; poem. New Yorker 44:33 F 15 '69
  From a litany; poem. New Repub 160:25 Ap 26 '69
  Letter; poem. New Yorker 45:119 Mr 22 '69
  My life; poem. New Yorker 44:30 Ja 25 '69
  Remains; poem. New Yorker 45:34 My 31 '69
STRAND, Paul
  Paul Strand, catalyst and revealer. N. New-hall. il Mod Phot 33:70-5 Ag '69
  Two by Strand. A. D. Coleman; M. Mann. il Pop Phot 65:90-1+ D '69
STRANG, Ruth
  Play for all seasons; with study-discussion program. bibliog PTA Mag 63:19-21, 35 Ja '69
STRANGWAY, D. W.
  Moon: electrical properties of the uppermost layers. bibliog Science 165:1012-13 S 5 '69
La STRANIERA; opera. See Bellini, V.
STRASBOURG

Music
  Report: Strasbourg; production of Smetana's Dalibor, by Brno state opera of Czecho-slovakia. W. R. Stein. Opera N 32:32+ F 1 '69
STRASBOURG university. See Colleges and universities—France
STRASFOGEL, Ignace
  People's choice. Opera N 33:8-11 F 15 '69
STRASSENBURG, Arnold A.
  Unemployment crisis; letter. Phys Today 22:15+ F '69
  —and Llano, M. T.
  Graduate student. pors Phys Today 22:45-51 Mr '69
STRATEGIC air command. See United States —Air force—Strategic air command
STRATEGIC arms limitation talks
  Another missile gap? Helsinki conference. il Time 94:21 N 7 '69
  Can SALT succeed? Nation 209:555-6 N 24 '69
  Cocktails for two. Newsweek 74:42 D 1 '69
  For SALT and Sato. Chr Cent 86:1476 N 19 '69
  Games nations play. J. Burnham. Nat R 21:1219 D 2 '69
  Heading for Helsinki; without high hopes. America 121:410 N 8 '69

STRATEGIC arms limitation talks—*Continued*
Helsinki talks. New Repub 161:10-11 N 29
'69
High stakes in U.S.-Russian arms talks. il
U S News 67:88 N 17 '69
How to wind down the nuclear arms race.
M. Bundy. il N Y Times Mag p46-7+ N
16 '69
Improving the atmosphere. il Time 94:44+
D 5 '69
In Helsinki, a step ahead. il U S News 68:5
Ja 5 '70
National security; address, October 6, 1969.
E. Brooke. Vital Speeches 36:44-7 N 1 '69
Nuclear talks: survival or Armageddon. M.
Childs. Look 33:47-8 D 30 '69
On to SALT. Newsweek 74:51 N 3 '69
Pinch of SALT at the UN. B. Pilkington.
Commonweal 91:396-7 Ja 9 '70
Pinch of SALT; delayed strategic-arms-limi-
tation talks. Newsweek 74:38+ S 8 '69
Pitfalls for U.S. in arms talks. J. Fromm. il
U S News 67:28-9 N 10 '69
Promising insights. Newsweek 75:23 Ja 5 '70
Real issues in the U.S.-Russian arms talks.
il U S News 67:64-5 D 1 '69
SALT: a season for reason; strategic arms
limitation talks. il Time 94:16 Ag 29 '69
SALT and I. F. Stone. Commonweal 91:292
D 5 '69
SALT: can the strategic arms race be halted?
R. E. Lapp. New Repub 161:14-17 N 15
'69
Secretary Rogers discusses forthcoming U.S.-
U.S.S.R. talks on curbing strategic arms;
October 25, 1969. W. P. Rogers. Dept State
Bul 61:389-94 N 10 '69
Smiles and suspicion at SALT. il Time 94:
32+ N 28 '69
Stalling on SALT; strategic arms limitation
talks. Nation 209:165 S 1 '69
Start of SALT. il Time 94:33-4 N 21 '69
Strategic arms limitation talks; address,
November 13, 1969. W. P. Rogers. Dept
State Bul 61:465-8 D 1 '69
Talk before it is too late. il Newsweek 74:
47-8 N 24 '69
Three concessions we shouldn't make. A.
Harrigan. il Nat R 21:1311-14 D 20 '69
To cap the volcano. M. Bundy. For Affairs
48:1-20 O '69; Excerpts. Cur 113:46-53 D
'69
U.S. delegation named for talks on arms
limitations with U.S.S.R. Dept State Bul
61:66 Jl 28 '69
What can SALT halt? il Time 94:10-11 O 31
'69
With U.S.-Soviet negotiators: smiles before
the bargaining. il U S News 67:17 D 1
'69
Wolf, wolf; U.S. bargaining position. S.
Alsop. Newsweek 74:140 D 8 '69
STRATEGY
Start on strategic stabilization. D. G. Bren-
nan. Bul Atom Sci 25:35-6 Ja '69
See also
United States—History—Revolution—Strategy
Vietnamese war, 1957- —Strategy
STRATEGY, Communist. See Communist strat-
egy
STRATFORD, Conn. Shakespeare festival. See
American Shakespeare festival theatre and
academy, Stratford, Conn.
STRATIFICATION, Social. See Social status
STRATIGRAPHIC geology. See Geology, Stra-
tigraphic
STRATTON, J. A.
Tribute to Frederick Seitz. Science 164:1469
Je 27 '69
STRATTON, Samuel Studdiford
Stratton's blast damages army tanks. Bsns
W p33 O 4 '69
STRATUS. See Clouds
STRAUS, Dorothea
Guardian angels. Harp Baz 102:69-75 Je '69
Where the past is prologue. House B 111:99+
Ap '69
STRAUSS, Claude Lévi-. See Lévi-Strauss. C.
STRAUSS, Franz Josef
Economic, scientific, technological; address,
October 12, 1969. Vital Speeches 36:144-7 D
15 '69
About
Entente Carolina. Nation 209:590 D 1 '69
Return of Franz Josef Strauss. D. Hotham.
il pors N Y Times Mag p36-7+ Mr 23 '69
Thinking big for Germany. il por Newsweek
73:51-2 Je 9 '69
STRAUSS, Levi. and company
Levi's gold rush. Time 93:106 Ap 25 '69
STRAUSS, Michael
Where to ski in the United States, Canada
and Europe. Travel & Camera 32:83-6 D '69

STRAUSS, Richard
Also sprach Zarathustra. G. S. Fox. il Am
Rec G 35:606-7 Ap '69
Ariadne auf Naxos. A. Sperber. il Am Rec G
35:1108-10 Ag '69
Ariadne auf Naxos. Criticism
Sat R 52:45 F 1 '69
Ariadne reconsidered. R. Lawrence. por Sat
R 52:49 Ja 25 '69
Capriccio. Criticism
Dance Mag 43:34 N '69
Hi Fi 19:MA12 D '69
How I got rid of monstrous Mildred; or, What
I think about Die frau ohne schatten. W.
Mann. Opera N 33:24-5 Mr 8 '69
Lorin Maazel's Don Quixote. G. S. Fox. il
Am Rec G 35:386-8 Ja '69
Music; concert performance of Ariadne
auf Naxos. D. Hamilton. Nation 208:413-
14 Mr 31 '69
New Straussian territory, explored by Fisch-
er-Dieskau. P. G. Davis. Hi Fi 19:84 Ap '69
Records:
Die frau ohne schatten. Opera N 33:34
Mr 8 '69
Salome. il Opera N 34:30 D 6 '69
Der Rosenkavalier. Criticism
Nation 208:413 Mr 31 '69
New Yorker 44:52+ F 1 '69
Opera N il 33:17-20 F 8 '69
Sat R 52:43-4+ F 8 '69
Something old, something new. J. Rockwell.
il Opera N 33:24-5 F 8 '69
Sound world of Salome, and a surprise from
Caballé. D. Hamilton. Hi Fi 19:112 N '69
The Strauss I know. K. Böhm. il por Opera
N 33:14-16 Mr 8 '69
Strauss's Ariadne; expertly conceived on all
sides. C. L. Osborne. Hi Fi 19:110 F '69
Woman without a shadow (Die frau ohne
schatten) Criticism
Nation 208:414 Mr 31 '69
New Yorker 45:105-7 Mr 1 '69
Opera N 33:24-5 Mr 8 '69
Opera N il 33:17-20 Mr 8 '69
Zubin Mehta conducts a magnificent record-
ing of Ein heldenleben. G. S. Fox. Am Rec
G 35:604-6 Ap '69
STRAUSS, Victor
In-house tape composition: basic considera-
tions. Pub W 195:78+ Mr 3 '69
Insiders' views on computerized composition.
Pub W 195:99-100 Je 9 '69
New composition technology: promises and
realities. Pub W 195:62-5 My 5; 196:94-5 Jl
7 '69
Printing-image carriers for letterpress. Pub
W 195:76+ F 3 '69
Production editing at McGraw-Hill. Pub W
196:56-8+ O 6 '69
STRAUSS, Willis A.
Lean years. por Forbes 103:210 My 15 '69
STRAVINSKY, Igor Fedorovich
Little treasury of Stravinsky. por Newsweek
75:80-1 Ja 19 '70
About
Igor Stravinsky: on illness and death; ex-
cerpts from Retrospectives and conclusions.
R. Craft. il pors Harper 239:111-16+ N '69
Marriage of Craft and art. R. Evett. New Re-
pub 162:25-7 Ja 10 '70
Stravinsky's alter ego. H. Saal. Newsweek
75:80-1 Ja 19 '70
STRAWBERRIES
Grow strawberries by the barrel. il Home Gard
56:54 F '69
Pleasures of June's table: crispy peas, as-
paragus and blushing strawberries. D.
Brooks. il Home Gard 56:44 Je '69
Raising strawberry plants from runners. N.
H. Berlin. il Org Gard & Farm 16:51 F '69
Strawberries for landscaping? il Sunset 142:
214+ Mr '69
Strawberries for the home garden. G. M.
Darrow. il Horticulture 47:36-7+ Ap '69
Strawberry barrels and wild strawberries. J.
Vivian. il Org Gard & Farm 16:52-5 F '69
Vesca the delicious. D. Munson. il House B
111:98-100 O '69
What's that about strawberries? questions
and answers. O. Raney. il Org Gard & Farm
16:48-50 F '69
See also
Cookery—Fruit
STREAM pollution. See Water pollution
STREAMERS (fishing flies) See Fishing lures.
flies, etc.
STREAMWOOD, Ill.
From cornfield to cornucopia. A. R. Pierce.
il Am City 84:137+ My '69
STRECKER, Edward Adam
Two Philadelphia psychiatrists and a theory
of American psychiatry. R. S. Garber. bib-
liog Ment Hy 53:131-40 Ja '69

STREET, Donald, Jr
How not to go South. Yachting 126:62+ Ag
'69
STREET accidents. See Traffic accidents
STREET carnivals
Place of the month: Rio de Janeiro: three
days of frenzy make the Rio carnival a
must. il Holiday 45:88-9 F '69
STREET cleaning
Flushing and sweeping; Vieux Carre, or
French quarter, New Orleans. J. Cassreino.
il Am City 84:80-1 Ap '69
Parking ban aids most cleaning tasks; Sagi-
naw, Mich. M. W. Jones. il Am City 84:66
My '69
Programmed street cleaning; Riverside, Calif.
R. Carmack. il Am City 84:78-9 Jl '69
Street cleaning. See issues of American city
STREET cleaning apparatus
Best for the spring clean-up; Owatonna,
Minn. M. R. Lueth. il Am City 84:32 Je '69
Diesel engines cut sweeping costs; Kalama-
zoo, Mich. D. Swets. il Am City 84:40
Ag '69
Programmed street cleaning; Riverside, Calif.
R. Camack. il Am City 84:78-9 Jl '69
Scrutinize your street-cleaning techniques.
R. R. Fleming. il Am City 84:115-16+ Mr
'69
Street cleaning. See issues of American city
Sweepers get parks cleaner in less time; Ana-
heim, Calif. il Am City 84:14 S '69
20-yard roll-off refuse bodies; village of
Skokie, Ill. il Am City 84:119 Ag '69
Vacs. New Yorker 45:23-4 Ag 2 '69
See also
Leaf gatherers
STREET fairs. See Fairs
STREET flushing. See Street cleaning
STREET furniture
New styles for streets. il Newsweek 73:57
Je 16 '69
STREET lighting
Golden light for a golden spike celebration;
Ogden, Utah. B. Wolthuis. il Am City 84:
132 Je '69
Lights add esthetics to a mall; Burbank,
Calif. il Am City 84:128 Je '69
No downtown gloom; Billings, Mont. W. E.
Fraser. il Am City 84:132+ Ap '69
Outdoor lighting. See issues of American city
Programmed lighting brings bright results;
Newark, Del. E. R. Stiff. il Am City 84:130
Ap '69
Residential streets our greatest lighting need.
W. H. Edman. il Am City 84:108+ N '69
See also
Street lighting fixtures
also subhead Lighting under names of
cities, e.g. Philadelphia—Lighting
STREET lighting fixtures
More light for Morganton; luminaries for re-
lighting program. C. L. Brooks. il Am
City 84:142 O '69
Painted light poles for Painted Post, N.Y.
A. J. Fuller. il Am City 84:158 My '69
Slip-base lighting supports are safest. Am
City 84:128 Je '69
They wanted fewer poles; San Juan shopping
center. il Am City 84:156 My '69

Maintenance and repair
Complete street-light maintenance. il Am City
84:162 S '69
STREET markings. See Traffic markings
STREET musicians
Face to face with a sidewalk violinist. R.
Wexler. il Seventeen 28:170+ Ap '69
Rosie side of the street; Albert Hall concert
of buskers. il Time 93:82 F 7 '69
STREET paving. See Pavements
STREET repairing. See Streets—Maintenance
and repair
STREET shows. See Theater, Open-air
STREET speaking
My life on the street corner. F. J. Sheed.
Sat R 52:22-3+ My 10 '69
STREET sweepers. See Street cleaning appara-
tus
STREET sweeping. See Street cleaning
STREET trades
Preserving an asset; street Arabs of Balti-
more. Newsweek 75:34 Ja 5 '70
STREET traffic
See also
Traffic engineering
Traffic signals
Traffic signs
also subhead Street traffic under names
of cities, e.g. Cincinnati—Street traffic

Automatic control
See also
Computers—Traffic control applications
STREET tunnel ram manifolds. See Manifolds
STREET vacuum sweepers. See Street cleaning
apparatus
STREET vendors. See Street trades
STREETS
Streets for people, by B. Rudofsky. Review
Newsweek il 74:60 D 22 '69. G. B. Porter
See also
Pavements
Street trades

Intersections
Try an intersection extension; Enid, Okla.
L. Smith. il Am City 84:101 O '69

Maintenance and repair
Assessment-district paving program; Salinas,
Calif. A. C. Joens. il Am City 84:104-5 O
'69
Big red, something new in street mainte-
nance; Bartlesville, Okla. B. Armstrong. il
Am City 84:90-1 N '69
Maintenance savings finance street paving;
Woodbridge, N.J. C. W. Beagle. il Am
City 84:80-1+ Mr '69
We beat business disruption; Appleton, Wis
F. H. Keuler. il Am City 84:91-3 Ag '69
See also
Pavements—Surface treatment
STREIB, Daniel T.
Successful collaboration. Writers Digest 49:
63-5+ N '69
STREISAND, Barbra
Her name is Barbra; interview. pors Life 68:
90-2+ Ja 9 '70

About
Barbra Streisand: on a clear day you can
see Dolly. J. Hamilton. il pors Look 33:
58-64 D 16 '69
New lunatics. il por Newsweek 73:81 Je 23
'69
Private world of Barbra Streisand. N. Ephron.
il pors Good H 168:92-3+ Ap '69
Superstar: the Streisand story. J. Morgen-
stern. il pors Newsweek 75:36-40 Ja 5 '70
STREITMATTER, Kenneth D.
Student study patterns: a break from tra-
dition. Clear House 43:280-2 Ja '69
STRENGE, F. A.
Green wood to seasoned boards, in minutes!
Pop Sci 195:86-7 Ag '69
STRENGTH of materials
See also
Fracture of solids
STRENGTH of muscles. See Muscle strength
STREPTOCOCCAL infections
Group A streptococci: localization in rabbits
and guinea pigs following tissue injury. I.
Ginsburg and others. bibliog il Science 166:
1161-3 N 28 '69
STREPTOMYCIN
Altered ribosomal protein in streptomycin-
dependent escherichia coli. E. A. Birge and
C. G. Kurland. bibliog il Science 166:1282-4
D 5 '69
STRESHINSKY, Shirley G.
Berkeley story: commitment to integration.
Parents Mag 44:48-51+ My '69
Court-martial of Lt. Susan Schnall. Redbook
134:78-9+ N '69
Truth about those new mother blues. Parents
Mag 44:56-7+ Ap '69
STRESS (physiology)
Are you really sick? F. L. Remington. il
Mech Illus 65:94-5+ N '69
Could you be a hero? I. Lieberman. il Mech
Illus 65:98-9+ N '69
Executives: taut, tense, cracking up. S. Mar-
getts. Duns R 93:54-6 Mr '69
How to deal with your tensions; excerpts.
G. S. Stevenson. Read Digest 94:89-92 Mr '69
Many-pressured pupil: with study-discussion
program, by E. Harris and D. Harris. D.
Graves. bibliog il PTA Mag 63:27-9, 35-6
F '69
Phobias. J. D. Noshpitz. il Todays Ed 58:20-
3 My '69
Stress, your biggest livestock management
problem. il Suc Farm 67:43 O '69
Ways schools lighten pressures on students.
il Good H 169:180 S '69
What close calls do to you and your driving.
J. G. Busse and W. S. Bacon. il Pop Sci
194:98-101 Mr '69
When job tensions get you down. il Changing
T 23:31-2 My '69

STRESS (physiology)—*Continued*

Anecdotes, facetiae, satire, etc.

Keeping fit with Sir Francis Chichester. F. Chichester. il Esquire 71:98-101+ Je '69

STRESS-corrosion. See Corrosion and anticorrosives

STRESSES. See Strains and stresses

STRETCH, Bonnie Barrett
Schools make news. See issues of Saturday review

STRICK, Anne
Los Angeles' golden goose. Nation 209:87-9 Jl 28 '69

STRICKLAND, Ruth G.
Challenge to teachers of reading. Ed Digest 35:51-4 S '69

STRICKLER, Dave
Strickler Trick. J. Dianna. il por Hot Rod 22:68-70 Mr '69

STRIGGOW, L. G.
Build the touch control. Pop Electr 30:56-8 Ap '69

STRIKE insurance. See Insurance, Strike

STRIKES
Work-in strike. T. S. Leviton and P. D. Bezazian. Duns R 93:18+ Ja '69
See also
Trade agreements

Economic aspects

Now the real war begins. il Newsweek 75:74-6 Ja 19 '70
What happens in a big strike: both sides of General electric story; interviews. il U S News 67:37-9 D 29 '69

Law

See Labor laws and legislation—United States

Argentina

Labor repression in Argentina. J. M. Swomley, jr. Chr Cent 86:1560+ D 3 '69

Canada

Canada's experience with the right of public employees to strike. J. D. Muir. bibliog Mo Labor R 92:54-9 Jl '69
Canadian strike squeezes the nickel; Canadian workers dig in their heels. il Bsns W p29-30 Ag 23 '69
City without cops; Montreal strike by police and firemen. il Time 94:47 O 17 '69
Nickel's newest crisis; strike of nickel workers. il Bsns W p 106-8 Jl 19 '69
Vancouver logjam starts to move; dock strike. il Bsns W p39 N 15 '69
What happens when the police strike; robberies, riots and looting in Montreal. G. Clark. il N Y Times Mag p45+ N 16 '69

Europe, Western

Behind Europe's strike wave. U S News 67:97 S 29 '69
European labor gets tougher. il Bsns W p65+ O 18 '69
Europe's prosperity runs into a wave of walkouts. J. Fromm. il U S News 67:44-6 D 29 '69
Wildcats on the loose. il Time 94:25-6 O 3 '69

France

Après moi... il Newsweek 73:48 Mr 24 '69
Beyond the standoff. il Time 93:90+ Mr 21 '69
Striking solutions. Newsweek 74:61-2 S 29 '69

Great Britain

Britain's antistrike plan fails. U S News 67:64 Ag 25 '69
Britain's unions get out of hand; strike at Ford plants. il Bsns W p70-2 Mr 22 '69
British unions vs. U.S. firms; government's proposed laws to restrain wildcats. U S News 66:70-1 Mr 24 '69
Pilots strike grounds BOAC. Aviation W 90:29 Ap 7 '69
Report from London; wildcat strike at British Ford. P. Siekman. il Fortune 79:49-50 My 1 '69
Strike crisis for British autos. U S News 67:85 N 10 '69
Wildcat has nine lives; Ford plants in Britain paralyzed. Time 93:90 Mr 21 '69

Italy

Extremists set the pace in Italy. Bsns W p54+ S 13 '69
Italy's unions hit management harder. il Bsns W p74+ Mr 1 '69
Labor troubles deflate Pirelli. Bsns W p33-4 S 27 '69
Moon bug. Time 94:30 D 19 '69

Strikes getting Italians down. U S News 67:83-4 N 3 '69

Sweden

Swedish strike undermines a sales pitch; wildcat iron ore miners strike. Bsns W p63-4 D 27 '69
Where labor runs things and still goes on strike. U S News 68:85-6 Ja 12 '70

United States

Big strikes: a new approach; interview. G. P. Shultz. il U S News 67:46-9 D 1 '69
Contractors try strike insurance; employer weapon to counter labor's collective bargaining. Bsns W p56 Ap 5 '69
Do they have a right to strike? M. R. Lefkoe. il Nations Bsns 57:78-80 Mr '69
Instant mediation: today's formula for heading off strikes. U S News 67:62 Ag 18 '69
Labor-management disputes; tables. See issues of Monthly labor review
New toughness at the bargaining table. il U S News 67:70-2 D 8 '69
Nixon goal: arsenal of new weapons to deal with big strikes. U S News 66:76 F 17 '69
Outlook: a year of turmoil in labor; strike calendar for '70. il U S News 68:49-50 Ja 5 '70
Strike troubles that LBJ left for the new President. il U S News 66:63-4 F 3 '69
Three industries face strike threat; railroads, General electric and American motors. U S News 67:100 S 22 '69
Wages, prices, strikes; a new approach: interview. G. P. Shultz. il U S News 66:62-6 Je 2 '69

Agricultural workers

See Strikes—United States—Farm labor

Airlines

American's loss in strike set at $2.7 million daily. Aviation W 90:29 Mr 17 '69
Court orders Piedmont's pilots back to work pending hearing. Aviation W 91:28 Ag 25 '69
National fights to fly. il Bsns W p78 F 8 '69
Other carriers gain in Western strike. Aviation W 91:33 Ag 4 '69

Automobile industry and trade

Overtime brings woes to AM. Bsns W p76 N 22 '69
Strike cost to union: 80 million. U S News 66:86 Ap 14 '69

Bank employees

Here come the unions. il Newsweek 73:64+ F 10 '69

Book industries and trade

Employees go on strike at Brentano's, N.Y. Pub W 196:45 S 15 '69

Carpenters

Carpenters fight the prefab war. il Bsns W p90+ Ap 19 '69

Coal mines and mining

Boys who got excited; West Virginia miners on strike to obtain effective mine safety and health legislation. New Repub 160:7 Mr 22 '69

Electric workers

Boycott of GE goods may prolong strike. Bsns W p32-3 N 29 '69
Do you want a riot? GE strike. Nat R 21:1205-6 D 2 '69
Federation steps up its attack on GE. il Bsns W p38-9 N 22 '69
General electric: clues to wage and strike policies. il U S News 67:82 N 10 '69
GE settles down to a long ordeal. il Bsns W p36 N 1 '69
GE strike hits utilities lightly. il Bsns W p36 Ja 10 '70
GE strike: it's starting to hurt. il Bsns W p 13-15 D 20 '69
GE strikers back their leaders; with editorial comment. il Bsns W p 102+, 154 N 8 '69
Heat but no light at General electric. il Bsns W p42 D 13 '69
Hint of a break in GE deadlock. il Bsns W p44+ N 15 '69
Labor's opening fight for higher wages. il Time 94:91 N 7 '69
Now the real war begins; GE strike il Newsweek 75:74-6 Ja 19 '70
Strike, and a spiral; General electric strike. il Newsweek 74:83 N 10 '69

STRIKES—United States—Electric workers
—*Continued*
Strike to boycott to what? GE case. Nat R 21:1256 D 16 '69
What happens in a big strike: both sides of General electric story; interviews. il U S News 67:37-9 D 29 '69

Farm labor

Breakthrough for *la huelga;* breakthrough in negotiations. Time 93:18 Je 27 '69
California grape boycott. Trans-Action 6:6 F '69
Clergy and the grape strike; Delano verdict. M. Day. America 121:114-17 Ag 30 '69
Four-year strike, two-year boycott; showdown. il U S News 67:53-4 Jl 14 '69
Little strike that grew to *la causa*. il Time 94:16-21 Jl 4 '69; Same abr. with title Battle of the grapes. Read Digest 95:88-92 O '69
Non violence still works; UFWOC during California grape pickers strike; interview. C. Chavez. il Look 33:52+ Ap 1 '69; Reply. C. G. Adamy. 33:6+ Je 10 '69
Profiles: C. Chavez. P. Matthiessen. New Yorker 45:42-4+ Je 21; 43-4+ Je 28 '69
Sundering of the grape growers. America 121: 2 Jl 5 '69

Firemen

See also
Gary, Ind.—Strikes

Government employees

Can we stand strikes by teachers, police, garbage men, etc? T. W. Kheel. Read Digest 95:99-103 Ag '69
Public-employe strikes increase. U S News 68:87 Ja 12 '70
Public employee unions and the right to strike. A. M. Ross. bibliog f il Mo Labor R 92:14-18 Mr '69
State road workers' strike becomes a political issue; tug-of-war between West Virginia's governor and local unions. Bsns W p 100 Je 21 '69
Strike guidelines for public workers? U S News 67:78 O 13 '69
Strikers' lonely road; West Virginia highway workers. il Bsns W p54+ S 27 '69
When public servants revolt. A. H. Raskin. Cur 103:27-32 Ja '69
Work stoppages of government employees. S. C. White. bibliog il Mo Labor R 92:29-34 D '69

Grocery trade

Strike-lockout in twenty-four grocery chains; southern California. U S News 66:70 Je 16 '69

Hospital employees

Agony of Charleston. America 120:573 My 17 '69
Back to the roots; Charleston, S.C. il Newsweek 73:39-40 My 5 '69
Charleston's strike: a tactic of crisis. Bsns W p72 Jl 12 '69
City: echoes of Memphis; black hospital employees striking in Charleston. Time 93:23 Ap 25 '69
High noon in the hospital; union organizing campaign for Pittsburgh hospital workers. R. W. Gibbons. Commonweal 91:406-7 Ja 9 '70
Hospital strike. J. Bass. New Repub 160:8 Je 7 '69
Intransigence in Charleston. Time 93:24 Je 20 '69
Settlement in Charleston. Time 94:15 Jl 4 '69
South Carolina: the movement finally arrives. D. Nolan. Nation 208:655-6 My 26 '69
Strike gains clout; AFL-CIO and UAW help Charleston's Negro hospital workers. il Bsns W p39 My 17 '69
Union teams up with black power; alliance of civil rights and labor organizations behind the Charleston walkout. il Bsns W p22-4 Ap 5 '69
Winning combination: settlement in one Charleston, S.C. hospital. Newsweek 74:19-20 Jl 7 '69

Librarians

Go-slow strike: letter to the editor. J. Post. Library J 94:475-6 F 1 '69

Lumber workers

Labor's knottiest talks. Bsns W p96 Ap 26 '69

Maritime workers

Bankruptcy on the waterfront and odd inaction of White House. America 210:208 F 22 '69
Dock strike: six-week toll. U S News 66:85-6 F 10 '69
Hawaiian cargo set to resume voyage. il Bsns W p 18 D 27 '69
Importers still face heavy seas; aftermath of dock strike. il Bsns W p38-9 F 22 '69

Issues that threaten life of ports. U S News 66:70 Mr 31 '69
Maritime pacts shaping up fast. Bsns W p46 Je 7 '69
Peace comes to Boston; shippers and ILA end months-long tieup. Bsns W p58 Ap 5 '69
Shipping faces up to its next crisis. Bsns W p38 My 31 '69
Striking dockers end port tie-up. U S News 66:74-5 F 24 '69

Meat industry and trade

War at Iowa beef. il Newsweek 74:100 N 17 '69

Printers

LPIU orders walkout at three Krueger plants. Pub W 196:39-41 Jl 21 '69

Railroads

How railroads have paid for strikes. U S News 67:72 D 8 '69
Rails rumble toward troubled times; end of Railway labor act ban against strikes and lockouts. il Bsns W p 106-7 N 29 '69
Yesterday's battles. Forbes 104:39 O 15 '69

Steel industry and trade

How a company keeps going in spite of violent strike; Lone Star steel company. il U S News 66:85-6 My 12 '69

Teachers

Due process, the real issue; Ocean Hill-Brownsville district; letter to the editor. R. Z. Sellers. Library J 94:123 Ja 15 '69; Reply. K. Weibel and others. 94:1397-8 Ap 1 '69
Full and sometimes very surprising story of Ocean Hill, the teachers' union and the teacher strikes of 1968; excerpts from The teachers strike: New York, 1968. M. Mayer. il N Y Times Mag p 18-23+ F 2 '69; Discussion. p2+ F 23; 22+ Mr 16 '69
N.Y. libraries fumbled teachers' strike role. Library J 95:20+ Ja 1 '70
Notes of a scab librarian; learning opportunities during the New York city teachers strike. S. Ginsburg. bibliog il Library J 94: 1300-2 Mr 15 '69; Discussion 94:2028, 3107-8, 4559 My 15, S 15, D 15 '69
Profiles: J. V. Lindsay. N. Hentoff. New Yorker 45:42-6+ My 10 '69
Should teachers have the right to strike? GH poll. il Good H 168:12+ Ap '69
Special feature on professional negotiation: symposium. Todays Ed 58:53-60 Ja '69
Teacher opinion poll. il Todays Ed 58:10 N '69
Teacher union's rising power; fewer strikes ahead? il U S News 67:56-7 S 1 '69
Teachers strike. New York, 1968, by M. Mayer. Review
Sat R 52:73-4 Mr 15 '69. M. Gittell
Teachers strike the small cities. U S News 67:69-70 S 15 '69
Unschooling of New York's children. M. R. Berube; discussion. Commonweal 89:631+; 90:126 F 21, Ap 11 '69
Very expensive education of McGeorge Bundy. D. Halberstam. Harper 239:37-41 Jl '69
War for city schools; today, New York, tomorrow everywhere; community control. I. Mothner. il Look 33:42-4+ My 13 '69
Why teachers are striking. W. Goodman. Redbook 132:67+ Mr '69

STRING; drama. See Childress, A.
STRING drawing. See Drawing
STRING quartet music
See also
Phonograph records—String quartet music
STRING quartets
Chamber music in the chamber. J. Roos. Hi Fi 19:MA9 Je '69
Fine quartet from the U.S.S.R; Borodin quartet. I. Kolodin. Sat R 52:41-2+ Ja 25 '69
Heir to the Budapest; Guarneri string quartet. il Time 93:78 Ap 4 '69
STRINGED instruments
See also names of stringed instruments, e.g. Banjo
STRIP coal mining. See Coal mines and mining —Stripping operations
STRIP mining. See Coal mines and mining— Stripping operations
STRIPTEASE acts. See Vaudeville
STROBELL, Robert C.
When you're out at the inn. Parks & Rec 4:26-7+ Ag '69
STROBES. See Electric lamps, Photoflash

STROBOSCOPIC photography. See Photography, Flashlight

STROM, Susan
Suburban isolation controversy. Sci Digest 65:28+ Je '69

STROMATOLITES. See Algae, Fossil

STROMBERGER, T. L. See McDonald, H. E. jt. auth.

STRONG, Douglas Hillman
Man who owned Grand Canyon. Am West 6:33-40 S '69

STRONG, Jonathan
Patients; story. Atlan 223:42-5 Mr '69

STRONG, Matt
Ya gotta have a system. Motor T 21:84+ D '69

STRONTIUM

Isotopes

Strontium-90 concentration factors of Lake Plankton, macrophytes, and substrates. Z. Kalnina and G. Polikarpov. bibliog il Science 164:1517-19 Je 27 '69
Strontium-90: concentrations in surface waters of the Atlantic Ocean. V. T. Bowen and others. bibliog il Science 164:825-7 My 16 '69

STROTHER, Luella
New switch. Todays Ed 58:50 S '69

STROUD, Agnes N. and others
Scanning electron microscopy of cells. bibliog Science 164:830-2 My 16 '69

STROUGAL, Lubomir
Lesser of two evils. il por Newsweek 73:57 Je 9 '69

STROUT, R. G. and Ouellette, C. A.
Gametogony of eimeria tenella (coccidia) in cell cultures. bibliog Science 163:695-6 F 14 '69

STRUCTURAL aluminum. See Aluminum, Structural

STRUCTURAL engineering
Architectural engineering. See issues of Architectural record
See also
Shells (structural engineering)
Soil mechanics

STRUCTURAL geology. See Geology, Structural

STRUDEL. See Pastry

STRUMILIN, Stanislav Gustavovich
Post-Stalinist social science. A. Simirenko. il Trans-Action 6:37-42 Je '69

STRUMPF, Manny
Town where every kid can go to camp. il Parents Mag 44:42-3+ Jl '69

STRUNG, Norman
Float for first-class fishing. Field & S 74:68-9+ Je '69

STUART, Ann E.
Excitatory and inhibitory motoneurons in the central nervous system of the leech. bibliog Science 165:817-19 Ag 22 '69

STUART, Dabney
Idyll; poem. New Yorker 45:94 Ag 9 '69

STUART, Jesse
Appalachian suicide; poem. Esquire 72:104 D '69
Cardinal in the mirror. Am For 75:8+ My '69
E. P; story. Todays Ed 58:48-9 D '69

STUART, Neal G.
We're looking for real writers. Writer 82:25-7 D '69

STUBBS, Harry C.
Universe: did it begin? Will it end? Todays Ed 58:26-8 S '69
Views on science books. See issues of Horn book magazine

STUCKER, Gilbert F.
Lake Superior's island wilderness. il Nat Parks 43:4-9 Mr '69

STUDEBAKER-Worthington, Incorporated
I want to make millionaires. S. Blickstein. Duns R 93:29-31 Ap '69

STUDENT achievements
Good scholarship: do students really care? K. Parrish and G. R. Weldy. il Clear House 43:275-9 Ja '69
Kids who wear glasses; superior academic performance of near-sighted children. Trans-Action 6:10 Ja '69
Mobile students. J. M. Snyder. Todays Ed 58:26 Ap '69
Money, motivation, and academic achievement. R. L. Green and T. J. Stachnik. Ed Digest 34:8-10 Mr '69
Price of community control. D. K. Cohen. Commentary 48:23-32 Jl '69; Discussion. 48:4+ S; 12+ N '69
See also
Underachievers

STUDENT activities
Active activities program. M. E. Rizzo. Clear House 44:182-4 N '69

Objectives: a work of permanent value. R. Wenger. il Sch Arts 69:14-15 Ja '70
Springfield students demonstrate for their college. A. Thormeyer. Todays Ed 58:25 S '69
See also
Association of student governments
College and school journalism
College students—Political activities
Fund raising
Parents and teachers associations—Student participation
School children—Out-of-school activities

STUDENT aid
Aid without strings? federal aid and rebels. Newsweek 73:93 Ap 7 '69
College admissions; the price of diversity. J. C. Hoy. il Sat R 52:96-7+ F 15 '69
Equality fiction: bottom dogs subsidize top dogs. W. L. Hansen and B. A. Weisbrod. New Repub 161:23-4 S 6 '69
Is there a college in his future? with study-discussion program, by R. Strang. W. D. Boutwell. bibliog PTA Mag 63:10-12, 34 Je '69
New guidance on cutting aid for student rioters. U S News 68:6 Ja 12 '70
Student financial aid: what, where, how. V. Trimble. Am Ed 5:7-8 F '69
See also
Scholarships and fellowships

STUDENT American medical association
Student activists: summer programs. il Time 94:60 Jl 18 '69

STUDENT assistants
See also
School libraries—Student assistants

STUDENT business
Student capitalists: student-owned enterprises in Finland. Time 93:77 Je 27 '69

STUDENT Christian movements
Decline and fall of a student movement; Young Christian student movement. R. V. Ellinger. Commonweal 89:548 Ja 31 '69
See also
University Christian movement

STUDENT clothing. See Clothing and dress—Students

STUDENT clubs. See Student activities

STUDENT committees. See Self government in education

STUDENT conferences
See also
United States national student association

STUDENT counselors
Existential school counselor. G. J. Pine. Clear House 43:351-4 F '69
See also
Personnel service in education

Education

Effective in-school program for counselors; Francisco junior high school, San Francisco, Calif. L. E. De Lara. Clear House 44:115-17 O '69

STUDENT demonstrations
Are student rebels neo-Communists? M. Cranston. Cur 104:19-25 F '69
Campus conflict & professorial egos. J. P. Spiegel. il Trans-Action 6:41-50 O '69
Foolproof scenario for student revolts. J. R. Searle; discussion. N Y Times Mag p 15 Ja 19 '69
Is treason permissible as merely free speech? students wearing black armbands in the classroom. D. Lawrence. U S News 66:108 Mr 10 '69
Police and protesters; photographs. Life 67:92-3 N 21 '69
Political thrust motivating campus turmoil. S. M. Lipset. Sat R 52:23-5+ Mr 1 '69
Revolt on the campus. R. MacLeish. Read Digest 94:71-6 Je '69
Student on the rampage all around the world. il U S News 66:8 F 3 '69
War against the democratic process. S. Hook. Atlan 223:45-9 F '69; Discussion. 223:44-7 Ap '69
What the rebellious students want. S. Spender. il N Y Times Mag p56-7+ Mr 30 '69
Why is youth so revolting nowadays? various manifestations including underground press. M. J. Spencer. il Wilson Lib Bul 43:640-7 Mr '69
Worldwide student revolt: why? il U S News 66:44-6 F 10 '69
Youth in ferment: what's it all about? symposium. il Sr Schol 94:4-12 Mr 7 '69
Youth 1969; symposium. il UNESCO Courier 22:4-34 Ap '69
See also
Student movement
Teach-ins

STUDENT demonstrations—*Continued*

Anecdotes, facetiae, satire, etc.

Green power; Irish students at Queens college. Nat R 21:216 Mr 11 '69

History

Conflict of generations, by L. S. Feuer. Review
Time il 93:98 Ap 4 '69

Arab states

Rebels without hope. Newsweek 74:27-8 Jl 7 '69

Canada

Campus unrest. il U S News 66:10 F 24 '69

England

See Student demonstrations—Great Britain

Europe

Youth in ferment; in western Europe. F. Taddeo. il Sr Schol 94:7 Mr 7 '69

France

France: attempt to slash numbers stirs medical school strike. D. S. Greenberg. Science 166:1381-3 D 12 '69
French style of protest. S. Hoffmann. New Repub 160:23-4 Ja 25 '69
Ideology of May '68. P. Hebblewaite. Cath World 209:112-14 Je '69
Letter from Paris; first anniversary of real inception of May riots. Genêt. New Yorker 45:120-2 Ap 5 '69
Moratorium in Paris. P. Geismar. Nation 209:627-8 D 8 '69
Student anarchy in France. A. Lejeune. Nat R 21:341-3 Ap 8 '69
Theology students rebel; University of Strasbourg. X. W. Carroll. America 120:268-71 Mr 8 '69

Germany (Federal Republic)

Law-and-order at Frankfurt; letter. R. Bechtle. Pub W 196:29-30 Ag 18 '69
Now the British get tough with student rebels. U S News 66:14 My 26 '69

Great Britain

Odd and ugly noises from the Labor party; reaction to London school of economics revolutionary effort. A. Howard. New Repub 160:13-14 Mr 8 '69
Prince's rebuke to a protester. U S News 66:15 Je 9 '69
Revolting students; situation at Oxford. J. Sparrow. il Nat R 21:175-7+ F 25 '69
Student protest now U.S. export. il U S News 66:8 Mr 3 '69

Italy

Up against the Catholic wall; Catholic university in Milan. H. ten Kortenaar. Commonweal 90:309-10 My 30 '69

Japan

Battle of Tokyo U. il Time 93:32 Ja 31 '69
Fall of Todai. il Newsweek 73:52 F 3 '69
If you think U.S. students are on the rampage—. il U S News 67:79-80 N 17 '69
Occupational problems; Tokyo students battling police on Okinawa day. il Time 93:43+ My 9 '69
Oriental coming-of-age. S. Griffin. il Sci N 95:432-3 My 3 '69
Scaling down. il Newsweek 73:50 My 12 '69
Testing ground in Tokyo; growing militarism and the Okinawa question. N. Cousins. il Sat R 52:28-9 D 6 '69
Tokyo; choreography of protest; Waseda university. A. Carter. Nation 209:476-7 N 3 '69

Latin America

Rocky way. il Newsweek 73:65 Je 9 '69
Youth in ferment; in Latin America. J. Mandelstam. il Sr Schol 94:6 Mr 7 '69

Lebanon

Lebanon: student power. L. H. Dean. Chr Today 13:33 F 14 '69

Mexico

Memory of Mexico. B. Glanville. Commentary 47:77-9 Mr '69

Philippines

Capitalizing on unrest. N. Ramientos. Chr Today 13:35 Jl 18 '69

United States

Academic calm of centuries broken by a rampage; with photographs by J. Loengard. Life 66:24-35 Ap 25 '69
Alienation and relevance. S. J. Tonsor. il Nat R 21:636-8+ Jl 1 '69
AAS Boston meeting; dissenters find a forum. J. K. Glassman. Science 167:36-8 Ja 2 '70
Amherst college statement. C. H. Plimpton. New Repub 160:7 My 17 '69
And now, Harvard. New Repub 160:6-7 Ap 26 '69
And now the high schools; disorders and fears. il Time 93:68 F 7 '69
Anti-commencement day. il Newsweek 73:64 Je 16 '69
As turmoil spreads, uneasy U.S. takes stock. il U S News 66:33-4 My 19 '69
Battle for a college; Why San Francisco state blew up. L. Litwak; J. H. Bunzel. il Look 33:61-2+ My 27 '69
Battle of Berkeley. Nat R 21:578-9 Je 17 '69
Battle of Berkeley. il Newsweek 73:35-6+ Je 2 '69
Best defense: library now a target. J. Berry. Library J 94:1401 Ap 1 '69; Discussion. 94:1923-4 My 15 '69
Beyond campus chaos; a bold plan for peace. G. B. Leonard. il Look 33:73+ Je 10 '69
Boll weevil six feet long; Mississippi librarian's action in battle against campus speaker ban. J. M. Carter. il Library J 94:3615-18 O 15 '69
Buckle down, John Harvard. H. Cox. Commonweal 90:22-4 My 9 '69
Bust at Harvard. il Newsweek 73:102-3 Ap 21 '69
Campus backbone and backlash. il Newsweek 73:31-2 My 12 '69
Campus backlash. Nat R 21:267-8 Mr 25 '69
Campus, camera and me; filming of Come out, come out; based on demonstrations at Columbia university. L. Yellen. il Seventeen 28:154-5+ My '69
Campus communiqué. il Time 94:54 D 19 '69
Campus disorders. New Repub 160:5-7 Mr 29 '69
Campus outlook: more turmoil; symposium. il Nations Bsns 57:36-51 Ag '69
Campus revolutionaries; the rights of students; address, June 3, 1969. R. M. Nixon. Vital Speeches 35:546-8 Jl 1 '69; Excerpts. U S News 66:66-7 Je 16 '69
Campus riots: limited U.S. crackdown; use of antiriot provisions of the 1968 Civil rights act. U S News 66:47 Mr 17 '69
Campus '69; riot, fire and blood; CCNY; Dartmouth. il Newsweek 73:69-70 My 19 '69
Campus spring offensive; Harvard, Columbia, Chicago. il Newsweek 73:66-9 Ap 28 '69
Campus turmoil; tracing a cause. Chr Today 13:27-8 Mr 28 '69
Campus unrest; lots of talk, some crackdowns, continuing outbursts. il U S News 66:12 My 26 '69
Campus unrest: now force meets force. il U S News 66:8+ F 24 '69
Campus upheaval: an end to patience. il Time 93:22-3 My 9 '69
Campus violence. Nat R 21:160-2 F 25 '69
Campus violence; no end in sight. il U S News 66:11-12 My 19 '69
Campuses and courts. Nat R 21:477-8 My 20 '69
Clash of symbols at the clubhouse; Duquesne club. il Bsns W p31-2 My 31 '69
Class of '69; top students protest right through commencement; with answer from their elders. il Life 66:28-33 Je 20 '69
College president speaks out; interview, ed. by N. Seitz. G. L. Cross. Parents Mag 44:62-3+ O '69
Colleges must outlaw terror; excerpts from address, May 1, 1969. J. N. Mitchell. U S News 66:75 My 12 '69
Columbia recap: School of library service during and after the spring of 1968. B. R. Wilkinson. bibliog il Library J 94:2567-70 Jl '69; Reply. R. D. Kempner. 94:2985-6 S 15 '69
Columbia, the useless lesson. A. C. Danto. New Repub 160:25-6+ Ja 25 '69
Columbia: to be a revolutionary or not to be? J. L. Avorn. il Look 33:13-14 My 13 '69
Commencement dilemma. W. F. Buckley, jr. Nat R 21:663 Jl 1 '69
Confrontation at Stanford: exit classified research. J. Walsh. Science 164:534-7 My 2 '69
Confrontation with a Harvard son. J. Krieger. McCalls 96:67+ Ag '69
Containment and counterattack. Nat R 21:215-16 Mr 11 '69

STUDENT demonstrations—United States—
Continued
President Nixon: intellectual freedom in danger; statement, March 23, 1969. R. M. Nixon. U S News 66:30 Mr 31 '69
Protest at Penn: a model for campus dissent? D. Sanford. New Repub 160:19-21 Mr 15 '69
Real crisis on the campus; interview. S. Hook. il U S News 66:40-4 My 19 '69; Excerpts. Read Digest 95:41-5 Ag '69
Rebels, amnesty and property. Chr Cent 86:307 Mr 5 '69; Discussion. 86:600 Ap 23 '69
Reform or revolution? A. Koch. Am Scholar 38:688+ Aut '69
Regents v. guerrilla base. Nat R 21:683-4 Jl 15 '69
Responding to student unrest; with study-discussion program, ed. by C. Smallenburg and H. Smallenburg. bibliog il PTA Mag 64:10-14, 35-6 S '69
Revolt in the high schools; the way it's going to be. D. Divoky. il Sat R 52:83-4+ F 15 '69; Discussion. 52:56 Mr 15 '69
Revolution (cont): at the University of Connecticut. E. Hill. il N Y Times Mag p28-9+ F 23 '69; Discussion. p6+ Mr 16; 110+ Ap 13 '69
Revolution eats its parents. F. S. Meyer. Nat R 21:541 Je 3 '69
Revolutionaries who have to be home by 7:30. N. Pileggi. il N Y Times Mag p26-7+ Mr 16 '69; Discussion. p22+ Ap 6; 106+ Ap 13; 22+ Ap 20 '69
Richard Nixon and collegians. M. McGrory. America 121:286 O 11 '69
Rising up in morningside. J. E. O'Connell. Cath World 209:230-1 Ag '69
Rites of spring. Nat R 21:270 Mr 25 '69
San Fernando's black revolt. S. Harris. Commonweal 89:549-52 Ja 31 '69
School boards and the Supreme court. America 120:295 Mr 15 '69
School protest: is it a right? arm bands: upheld. il U S News 66:12 Mr 10 '69
Seeds of anarchy, ed. by F. Wilhelmsen. Review Nat R 21:754-6 Jl 29 '69. W. Herberg
Should youths, or parents, be blamed for unrest? Governor Reagan's answer; excerpts from address, October 14, 1969. R. Reagan. U S News 67:18 O 27 '69
Siege of San Francisco state. J. R. Coyne, jr. Nat R 21:67-8 Ja 28 '69
Signs of moderation? il Time 93:45-6 F 28 '69
Sour grapes statement. il Esquire 72:89-97 S '69
Special feature on campus unrest; representative sampling of thinking by students; symposium. Todays Ed 58:25-33 N '69
Specter on campus; politicization of the universities. Commonweal 90:93-5 Ap 11 '69
Spring of discontent. il Time 93:36+ F 21 '69
Stanford university bookstore has unexpected rush. I. L. Sanderson. il Pub W 195:69-70 Je 16 '69
States and schools fight back against riots. il U S News 66:47-8 Ap 7 '69
Street people; taking over a park. il Time 93:27 My 23 '69
Student power; on the other hand, student complaint: undergraduate courses taught by graduate assistants. J. R. Coyne, jr. Nat R 21:432-3+ My 6 '69
Student revolt against liberalism. J. Eisen and D. Steinberg. bibliog f Ann Am Acad 382:83-94 Mr '69; Same abr. with title Revolt against liberalism. Cur 108:11-14 Je '69
Student revolt: the hard core; statement before the House special subcommittee on education, March 20, 1969. B. Bettelheim. Vital Speeches 35:405-10 Ap 15 '69; Excerpts. il U S News 66:61-3 Ap 7 '69
Student revolution. Chr Today 13:24 F 14 '69
Student riot bill. W. F. Buckley, jr. Nat R 21:662-3 Jl 1 '69
Students for education; California State college, Dominguez Hills. R. Kirk. Nat R 21:702 Jl 15 '69
Student's view: black students and their changing perspective. J. Turner. il Ebony 24:135-40 Ag '69
Studying those students. F. Morley. Nations Bsns 57:19-20 Jl '69
Styles of handling student demonstrations. M. Selk. il Bul Atom Sci 25:36-8 Je '69
Subway college strife; report from CCNY. G. Wagner. Nat R 21:539-40 Je 3 '69; Reply with rejoinder. S. J. Robbins. 21:570+ Je 17 '69
Take a hand. New Repub 160:1+ My 17 '69
Teen scene; high school students. il Seventeen 28:150-1 Mr '69

Teen sole power against hunger; Madison, Wis, Walk for development organized by Young world development. il Sr Schol 95:18 O 27 '69
To stop campus violence; excerpts from remarks, April 29, 1969. R. M. Nixon. il U S News 66:74 My 12 '69
Troops, gas, or persuasion? il Newsweek 73:22-3 F 24 '69
Twelve rebels of the student right. S. Burnham. il N Y Times Mag p32-3+ Mr 9 '69; Reply with rejoinder. L. Rossetto and S. Lehr. p22+ Mr 30 '69
Unlawful seizure: student riots and seizure of college property, violations of the law. D. Lawrence. U S News 66:108 Mr 17 '69
U.S. campus war through English eyes. J. M. Cameron. Commonweal 90:404-5 Je 27 '69
Un-silent generation. J. Rothchild. il Nat R 21:591-4+ Je 17 '69; Reply. F. S. Meyer. 21:646 Jl 1 '69
Up against the wall: secondary school principals convention. D. L. Burleson. Sr Schol 94:Schol Teach 4 Ap 11 '69
Uproar hits the campus press. J. Star. il Look 33:36+ F 18 '69
Vulnerability of universities. Sch & Soc 97:273-4 Sum '69
We're glad you asked; nation-wide survey on student protests in high schools. J. Hunt. America 121:453-5 N 15 '69
What about majority rights; Columbia university. A. H. Sypher. Nations Bsns 57:31-2 Mr '69
What kind of world do you want? address, May 1, 1969. J. N. Mitchell. Vital Speeches 35:497-500 Je 1 '69; Same with title Colleges must outlaw terror; excerpts from address. U S News 66:75 My 12 '69
When, if ever, do you call in the cops? symposium. il N Y Times Mag p34-5+ My 4 '69; Discussion. p 12+ My 25 '69
When legislators looked at unrest; twenty-two Republican congressmen's study. U S News 66:6 Je 30 '69
When protest on war hit MIT. il U S News 67:12 N 17 '69
Where attorney general draws the line on SDS and violence; excerpts from statement to subcommittee of the House committee on education and labor, May 20, 1969. J. N. Mitchell. U S News 66:45 Je 2 '69
Where racial violence hit the high schools. il U S News 67:47 O 6 '69
Who is responsible for campus violence? S. Hook. Sat R 52:22-5+ Ap 19 '69
Who is responsible for student violence? R. L. Means. America 120:352-5 Mr 29 '69
Who shall be master in the house? Nat R 21:423-4 My 6 '69
Who's in charge here? rebellion of University of Chicago students. il Newsweek 73:70-1 F 17 '69
Why students act that way; a Gallup study. il U S News 66:34-5 Je 2 '69
Why the colleges blew up; California state colleges system. K. Widmer. il Nation 208:237-41 F 24 '69
Widening gap between town and gown. P. Woodring. Sat R 52:82 My 17 '69
Young radicals & professorial critics. I. L. Horowitz. Commonweal 89:552-6 Ja 31 '69
Youth: alienated, estranged, or just brat-like? C. McCarthy. il Chr Cent 86:897-9 Jl 2 '69
Youth in ferment: on U.S. campuses. il Sr Schol 94:4-5 Mr 7 '69
See also
Government investigations—Student demonstrations
Negro student demonstrations

History
Lower depths of higher education. M. Bishop. il Am Heritage 21:26-31+ D '69

Protests, etc, against
Student revolt spurs protests by businessmen. il Bsns W p28-9 My 3 '69
STUDENT dismissals. See Expulsion from school and college
STUDENT drinking. See Liquor problem —United States
STUDENT employment
Employment status of school age youth; with charts and tables. E. Waldman. bibliog Mo Labor R 92:23-32 Ag '69
Summer jobs. R. Tunley. Seventeen 28:140+ F '69
Summer jobs for young people. Changing T 23:6 Ap '69

STUDENT employment—*Continued*
Summer work programs; Richmond, Va., and Fort Worth, Tex. G. M. Chamberlain. il Am City 84:92+ N '69
STUDENT enrollment. See School attendance
STUDENT ethics
Co-ed living. B. Rollin. il Look 33:22-4+ S 23 '69
On campus: getting away with it? Mlle 68:68 Mr '69
See also
College students—Conduct of life
STUDENT gardens. See School gardens
STUDENT guidebooks. See Guidebooks
STUDENT lamps. See Lamps
STUDENT life
Berkeley in the age of innocence. J. K. Galbraith. il Atlan 223:62-8 Je '69
Co-ed living. B. Rollin. il Look 33:22-4+ S 23 '69
Permissiveness in the dormitories. P. Woodring. Sat R 52:63 D 20 '69
Square universities are rolling too. J. Main. il Fortune 79:104-7+ Ja '69
See also
College students
Student activities
STUDENT life in periodicals. See Periodical articles
STUDENT loans
Break for black scholars; with partial list of available scholarships. il Ebony 24:45-6+ Mr '69
College costs going up. il U S News 67:34-5 S 8 '69
Paying for the high costs of education: a national youth endowment. J. Tobin and L. Ross. New Repub 160:18-21 My 3 '69; Reply with rejoinder. R. I. Thackrey. 160:30-3 Je 7 '69
Personal business. Bsns W p93-4 Ag 2 '69
Why banks are cool to student loans. il Bsns W p 142+ S 20 '69
See also
Student aid
STUDENT lounges
Student lounge or study hall: how are grades affected? D. R. Draayer and P. A. Teague. il Clear House 44:141-4 N '69
STUDENT militants
Activism: a game for unloving critics. S. D. Thomson. Ed Digest 35:1-4 S '69
As school term ends, campus troubles stay alive. il U S News 66:13 Je 16 '69
Between Moratoriums. il Time 94:48 N 7 '69
Bust at Harvard. il Newsweek 73:102-3 Ap 21 '69
Campus and the law. E. Van Den Haag. il Nat R 21:1212-13 D 2 '69
Campus crucible. N. Glazer; F. G. Hutchins. Atlan 224:43-56 Jl '69; Reply with rejoinder. J. S. Bruner. 224:47-8+ O '69
Campus violence; plans to prevent it. il U S News 67:45-7 S 1 '69
Conciliation, and cops; survey of campuses involved in upheavals. il Newsweek 74:60+ S 22 '69
Confused parents, confused kids; theories of B. Bettelheim. il Time 94:58 S 5 '69
Cry of halt to campus violence; action in Congress. il U S News 66:6+ My 12 '69
From campus to court; court, police, grand jury actions. il Newsweek 73:76 My 26 '69
Guns of academe. J. B. Sheerin. Cath World 209:98-9 Je '69
Harvard and beyond: the university under siege. il Time 93:47:8+ Ap 18 '69
Higher education and the disenchanted students; excerpts from Leaders, teachers and learners in academe: partners in the educational process. S. Lehrer. bibliog Sch & Soc 97:427-31 N '69
How educators would deal with college rebels. il U S News 67:14 Jl 14 '69
How SDS will stir up workers. il Nations Bsns 57:74-9 Jl '69
Identity crisis on U.S. campuses. G. Roberts. Commonweal 90:557-8 S 19 '69
It runs in the family. il Time 93:49-50 My 23 '69
Legislatures react; new laws aimed at curbing campus disruptions. Time 93:58 Je 13 '69
Little bit of rebellion is good for the soul, and the school. A. A. Glatthorn. Seventeen 28:324-5+ Ag '69
Living with crisis: a view from Berkeley. H. F. May. Am Scholar 38:588-605 Aut '69
Memo on the new left. W. A. Rusher. Nat R 21:803-4+ Ag 12 '69
Opinion: dehumanized radicalism. N. Hentoff. Mlle 69:16+ My '69

Playing with revolution. New Repub 160:5-6 My 3 '69
President and the kids. S. Alsop. Newsweek 74:136 N 24 '69
Profile of the college rebel. Sch & Soc 97:408+ N '69
Protest and authority; symposium. il Newsweek 73:72-3 My 12 '69
Seeds of anarchy, ed. by F. Wilhelmsen. Review
Nat R 21:754-6 Jl 29 '69. W. Herberg
Spotlight on SDS; case study of campus turmoil. il U S News 66:34-6 My 12 '69
Student power, foreign-style. il U S News 66:56-7 Je 23 '69
Student revolt, where it is headed. il U S News 67:38-40 O 13 '69
Student strife: a warning bell. il Newsweek 74:59-60 N 3 '69
Take a hand. New Repub 160:1+ My 17 '69
To an angry old man. L. Rosten. Look 33:14 Ap 29 '69
To keep peace on campuses: a plan for action by federal courts. il U S News 66:6 Je 30 '69
Trojan horse in the universities? S. Hook. Cur 108:24-7 Je '69
Universities in crisis; what are the real issues? T. Wicker. Cur 108:4-6 Je '69
Warning of revolutionary change; excerpts from TV program, Face the Nation, May 11, 1969. il U S News 66:14 My 26 '69
When, if ever, do you call in the cops? symposium. il N Y Times Mag p34-5+ My 4 '69; Discussion. p 12+ My 25 '69
Who are the victims? A. H. Sypher. Nations Bsns 57:23-4 Jl '69
See also
Negro student militants
Students for a democratic society (organization)
STUDENT militants and industry
Students and workers. P. Booth. Ramp Mag 8:19-20 S '69
SDS in the mills. R. W. Gibbons. Nation 209:215-17 S 8 '69
What campus rebellions mean to you. R. Hessen. il Nations Bsns 57:30-2 Je '69
Will SDS crash plant gate? national program for summer work-in. il Bsns W p31 My 3 '69
STUDENT movement
All quiet on the campus front? Chr Cent 86:1634-5 D 24 '69
ACE study on campus unrest: questions for behavioral scientists; with statement by advisory committee. J. Walsh; J. Coburn. Science 165:157-61 Jl 11 '69; Discussion. 165:1206-7; 166:945 S 19, N 21 '69
Campus crucible. N. Glazer; F. G. Hutchins. Atlan 224:43-56 Jl '69; Reply with rejoinder. J. S. Bruner. 224:47-8+ O '69
Campus unrest: confrontation increasingly means litigation. I. McNett. Science 166:486-8 O 24 '69
Class of '69: the violent years. E. Diamond. il Newsweek 73:68-73 Je 23 '69
Conflict of generations, by L. S. Feuer. Review
New Repub 160:26-8 My 31 '69. H. Zinn
Finding people who feel alienated and alone in their best impulses and most honest perceptions and telling them they're not crazy; letter. R. Kean. il Wilson Lib Bul 44:36-44 S '69
Marx, Mao, and the dissenters. R. L. Tobin. Sat R 53:26+ Ja 10 '70
New bag on campus. il Newsweek 74:72 D 22 '69
New left in action. il U S News 66:35-7 My 19 '69
Obituary for SDS. L. D. Nachman. Nation 209:558-61 N 24 '69
Opinion: on protest. F. Buhler. Mlle 70:30+ D '69
Playing with revolution. New Repub 160:5-6 My 3 '69
Real revolution on campus. il U S News 68:28-31 Ja 12 '70
Revolt of the diminished man; excerpt from address. A. MacLeish. Sat R 52:16-19+ Je 7 '69
Student of tomorrow: towards a new global horizon. R. Habachi. il UNESCO Courier 23:16-20 Ja '70
Student strife: a warning bell. il Newsweek 74:59-60 N 3 '69
Students without teachers, by H. Taylor. Review
Sat R 52:60 Jl 19 '69. P. Woodring
Whose university? M. Miles. New Repub 160:17-19 Ap 12 '69; Same. Cur 108:14-19 Je '69; Reply with rejoinder. D. Bell. New Repub 160:30-1 My 3 '69

STUDENT movement—*Continued*
Why students are angry. M. Mead. Redbook
132:50+ Ap '69
You have to grow up in Scarsdale to know
how bad things really are. K. Keniston. il
N Y Times Mag p27-9+ Ap 27 '69; Discussion. p 14+ My 18 '69

History

Conflict of generations. by L. S. Feuer.
Review
Atlan 223:103-5 Je '69. D. Wakefield
Commonweal 90:238+ My 9 '69
Nation 208:575-6 My 5 '69. K. Widmer
Sat R il 52:56-7+ Jl 19 '69. O. Klineberg

Czechoslovakia

Czechoslovak students and political action.
P. G. Altbach. Chr Cent 86:527-9 Ap 16 '69

France

Nanterre: a year later at campus where
French student revolt began. D. S. Greenberg. Science 164:1261-4 Je 13 '69

Japan

Invisible factor. S. Alsop. Newsweek 75:96
Ja 19 '70
Professors under pressure. il Newsweek 74:
60 N 3 '69
Student protest in Japan. R. H. Drummond.
Chr Cent 86:1227-8+. 1292-5. 1358-60 S 24.
O 8. 22 '69

United States

See Student movement

STUDENT national coordinating committee
Lewis of SNCC. il Newsweek 73:12 F 10 '69
New meaning for the N in SNCC. U S News
67:8 Ag 4 '69
STUDENT newspapers. See College and school
journalism
STUDENT nonviolent coordinating committee.
See Student national coordinating committee
STUDENT ombudsman. See Ombudsman
STUDENT opinion
Campus revolution; study by Elmo Roper.
K. Crawford. Newsweek 73:39 Je 2 '69
High school graduate's reflections on secondary education. E. Kaplan. Sch & Soc 97:
154-5 Mr '69
If I could do what I wanted to, I'd start
with grade school and revamp the whole
system. M. A. Hyde and S. Kalter. Mlle
69:268-9 Ag '69
Learning from the young; excerpts from address, November, 1968. K. R. Bergethon.
Sch & Soc 97:140 Mr '69
New mood on campus; survey. il Newsweek
74:42-5 D 29 '69
Our most wrenching problem is finding a
place for ourselves in society; student
declaration. G. H. Wierzynski. Fortune 79:
114-16+ Ja '69
Special feature on campus unrest; representative sampling of thinking by students;
symposium. Todays Ed 58:25-33 N '69
Spirit of '73; attitudes of college freshmen.
il Time 94:49+ O 10 '69
Student beliefs and values; adaptation of
address, June 2, 1968. T. H. Richardson.
Sch & Soc 97:94-5 F '69
Students and the 1970's; calm after the storm.
J. P. Giusti. bibliog Sch & Soc 97:360-3 O
'69
Survey of college student opinion. Sch &
Soc 97:452-3 N '69
What they believe; Fortune-Yankelovich survey. Fortune 79:70-1+ Ja '69

Anecdotes, facetiae, satire, etc.

Puke ethics. il Esquire 72:100-1 S '69
STUDENT participation in college administration. See Colleges and universities—Administration—Student participation
STUDENT personnel work. See Personnel service in education
STUDENT press association. See United States
student press association
STUDENT publications. See College and
school journalism
STUDENT radicals. See Student militants
STUDENT rating of teachers. See College professors and instructors—Rating by students
STUDENT residences. See College students—
Housing; Dormitories
STUDENT rights. See Intellectual liberty; Students—Civil rights
STUDENT selection
Admission by lot; University of Illinois.
Newsweek 75:46 Ja 5 '70

Folklore of selectivity; excerpt from The
campus and the racial crisis. A. W. Astin.
il Sat R 52:57-8+ D 20 '69
Now, a lottery to pick students. U S News
67:7 D 29 '69
See also
Colleges and universities—Attendance
STUDENT self-support. See Student employment
STUDENT teachers
Some innovations in the preparation of
teachers. W. C. Lowry. Ed Digest 34:28-31
F '69
STUDENT teaching
Internship in historical perspective. H. Gardner. Ed Digest 34:42-5 Mr '69
Some innovations in the preparation of
teachers. W. C. Lowry. Ed Digest 34:28-31
F '69
STUDENT tours. See Student travel
STUDENT travel
Opportunities for student travel. P. Plawin.
Bet Hom & Gard 47:29-30 Jl '69
Student travel. il Sat R 52:56+ F 15 '69
Teenage travel abroad. H. Lewis. il Parents
Mag 44:44-5+ My '69
See also
Travel study courses
STUDENT tutors. See Tutors and tutoring
STUDENT unions
Lively student center; Houston's Texas
southern university. il Arch Rec 146:145-8
O '69
STUDENT volunteer service. See Volunteer
service
STUDENT withdrawals. See Dropouts
STUDENTS
See also
Clothing and dress—Students
College students
Cuban students
Graduate students
High school students
Japanese students
Jewish students
Medical students
Negro students
Physics students
Theological students

Civil rights

Campus unrest: confrontation increasingly
means litigation. I. McNett. Science 166:
486-8 O 24 '69
Doing right by students. W. D. Boutwell. PTA
Mag 64:14 D '69
Freedom of speech for students; Supreme
court's decision on student dissent; limits
on protest in high schools; interview. K.
Greenawalt. Seventeen 28:54+ My '69
In high schools too; demands of Montgomery
County. Md. high school students. P. Osterman. New Repub 160:13-14 Ap 5 '69
Secondary rights; New York city resolution
for senior high school students. Newsweek 74:69 N 10 '69

Employment

See Student employment

Grading and promotion

See Grading and marking (students)

Rating

Please! Don't tell men he's well-adjusted!
N. Gittelson. McCalls 96:96-7 Ap '69
Schools that turn people off. S. Doig. il Todays Ed 58:28-30 My '69; Same abr. Ed
Digest 35:41-3 S '69
Student evaluation dilemma. P. M. Allen.
il Todays Ed 58:48-50 F '69

Social and economic status

Influences of social classes in schools; excerpt
from The public school in the new society.
G. Graham. bibliog f il Sch & Soc 97:169-80 Mr '69
STUDENTS, Interchange of
Lodestar international student experiment.
G. L. Heath. Sch & Soc 97:372-4 O '69
See also
American field service
Foreign students in the United States
STUDENTS, Married. See College students,
Married
STUDENTS, Mentally superior. See College
students, Mentally superior
STUDENTS, Women. See College students,
Women
STUDENTS and teachers. See Teachers and
students
STUDENTS as teachers aides. See Teachers
aides

STUDENTS for a democratic society (organ-
    ization)
Campus spring offensive; Harvard, Columbia,
    Chicago. il Newsweek 73:66-9 Ap 28 '69
Campus upheaval: an end to patience. il Time
    93:22-3 My 9 '69
Class of '69: the violent years. E. Diamond.
    il Newsweek 73:68-73 Je 23 '69
Collapse of S.D.S. R. Kahn. Esquire 72:140-
    4+ O '69
Columbia: to be a revolutionary or not to
    be? J. L. Avorn. il Look 33:13-14 My 13 '69
Evening with the kids. W. F. Buckley, jr.
    Nat R 21:507 My 20 '69
Farewell HUAC, hello HCIS; hearings. News-
    week 73:30+ Je 16 '69
Flare-up in campus revolt, a crucial test at
    Harvard. il U S News 66:41-3 Ap 28 '69
Hard times for S.D.S. il Time 94:81 N 28 '69
Harvard on my mind. M. Holroyd. Harper
    239:69-72 Ag '69; Discussion. 239:6+ N '69
Harvard yard. New Yorker 45:33-5 Ap 19 '69
How radicals spend their summer. Time 94:
    62+ Ag 1 '69
How SDS will stir up workers. il Nations
    Bsns 57:74-9 Jl '69
Intelligence report on today's new revolution-
    aries. W. Schulz. Read Digest 95:121-6 O '69
It can't happen here, can it? il Newsweek
    73:26-30 My 5 '69
Mao in Chicago; annual convention il News-
    week 73:76 Je 30 '69
Metamorphosis in S.D.S. the new left is
    showing its age. T. R. Brooks. il N Y
    Times Mag p 14-15+ Je 15 '69
Notes and comment: New York city's trou-
    bled campuses. New Yorker 45:27-32 My 3
    '69
Obituary for SDS. L. D. Nachman. il Nation
    209:558-61 N 24 '69
One, two, three. . .many SDS's; symposium.
    Ramp Mag 8:6+ S '69
Opinion: dehumanized radicalism. N. Hentoff.
    Mlle 69:16+ My '69
Parting of the ways for SDS. B. Kalb. New
    Repub 161:11-12 Jl 5 '69
Poor climate for weathermen. il Time 94:24-5
    O 17 '69
Some notes on S.D.S. M. Kazin. Am Scholar
    38:644-55 Aut '69
Splintered S.D.S. il Time 93:45 Je 27 '69
Split in two, the feuding SDS. U S News
    67:5 Jl 7 '69
Spotlight on SDS; case study of campus tur-
    moil. il U S News 66:34-6 My 12 '69
Striking back; a split into two competing
    factions. il Newsweek 74:79 Jl 7 '69
Student activists: free-form revolutionaries.
    C. Burck. il Fortune 79:108-11+ Ja '69
SDS finds invasion of industry tougher than
    college campuses. U S News 66:34-6 Je
    23 '69
SDS in the mills. R. W. Gibbons. Nation 209:
    215-17 S 8 '69
SDS work-in that didn't work out. Bsns
    W p24 Ag 30 '69
Warning of revolutionary change; excerpts
    from TV program, Face the Nation, May
    11, 1969. il U S News 66:14 My 26 '69
Where attorney general draws the line on
    SDS and violence; excerpts from statement
    to subcommittee of the House committee
    on education and labor, May 20, 1969. J.
    N. Mitchell. US News 66:45 Je 2 '69
Who is responsible for campus violence? S.
    Hook. Sat R 52:22-5+ Ap 19 '69
Will SDS crash plant gate? national pro-
    gram for summer work-in. il Bsns W p31
    My 3 '69
    See also
Campus worker-student alliance (organiza-
    tion)
Weathermen (organization)
STUDENTS socio-economic status. See Stu-
    dents—Social and economic status
STUDENTS workshops. See Educational work-
    shops
STUDIO school of painting, drawing and sculp-
    ture. See New York studio school
STUDIOS
    See also
Moving picture studios
STUDIOS, Recording. See Sound—Recording
    and reproducing
STUDS, Tire. See Tires, Automobile
STUDY
Homework and study habits. R. E. Leibert.
    bibliog f Clear House 43:413-16 Mr '69
Self-directed study; a junior high school
    pilot program. R. L. Tripp. Clear House
    43:344-8 F '69

Student study patterns: a break from tra-
    dition. K. D. Streitmatter. Clear House
    43:280-2 Ja '69
    See also
Home study
Independent study
Supplementary reading
STUDY halls
Student lounge or study hall: how are grades
    affected? D. R. Draayer and P. A. Teague.
    il Clear House 44:141-4 N '69
STUDY tours. See Travel study courses
STUDY-work plan. See Education, Cooperative
STUFFING. See Cookery—Poultry
STUHLINGER, Ernst
Antarctic research, a prelude to space re-
    search; adaptation of address, September
    18, 1968. Space World F-5-65:5-11 My '69
Apollo: a pattern for problem solving. por
    Bul Atom Sci 25:79-83 S '69
Prelude to space research; excerpt from ad-
    dress, September 1968. Bul Atom Sci 25:
    24-7 Mr '69
STULL, Robert
Robert Stull. H. Ghent. il por Sch Arts 68:
    25 Ap '69
STUMPE, John W.
Bandwidth compression for efficient digital
    communications. Electr World 81:49-52+ Mr
    '69
STUMPF, Walter E.
Too much noise in the autoradiogram? bib-
    liog Science 163:958-9 F 28 '69
    —See Grossman, S. P. jt. auth.
STUMPS. See Trees
STUNT flying. See Aviation—Stunt flying
STUNT men
Black stunt men. il Ebony 25:114-16+ D '69
STUNT motorcycling. See Motorcycling—Stunt
    cycling
STURDIVANT, Frederick D.
Limits of black capitalism. bibliog f Harvard
    Bsns R 47:122-8 Ja '69
STURDIVANT, Phyllis O'S.
NRPA representative visits Japan. Parks &
    Rec 4:49+ S '69
STURGEON, Theodore
Merril-y we wave along. Nat R 21:1174-5 N
    18 '69
STURGEON fishing
Unsung giants of the Fraser; British Colum-
    bia. H. Williams. il Field & S 73:68-9+
    F '69
STURGIS, Henry
Iron spine. Am Heritage 20:46-57+ Ap '69
STURGIS, Mich.
Small-city civic center. W. N. Yoder. il
    Am City 84:121-2 F '69
STURM, Ruth
Some research and writing tips; writing
    about celebrities in the motion picture
    and television fields. Writers Digest 49:
    38 My '69
STUTMAN, Oslas
Carcinogen-induced immune depression: ab-
    sence in mice resistant to chemical onco-
    genesis. bibliog Science 166:620-1 O 31 '69
STUTTERING. See Stammering
STUTTGART, Germany

Music
Double bow for Devils of Loudun. J. H.
    Sutcliffe. il Hi Fi 19:MA22-3+ S '69
Report: Stuttgart; Günther Rennert produc-
    tions of Janácek's Jenufa, Cikker's Resur-
    rection and Smetana's Bartered bride. E.
    D. Echols. Opera N 33:31 Mr 22 '69
STUTTGART ballet
Bravo Cranko! H. Saal. il Newsweek 73:62 Je
    23 '69
Cranko & co. O. Maynard. il Dance Mag 43:
    50-9+ S '69
Cranko; interview. J. Cranko. New Yorker
    45:27-8 Je 21 '69
Gazelleschaft; American debut at Manhat-
    tan's Metropolitan opera house. il Time
    93:82 Je 20 '69
Lesson for America? review of first American
    appearance. D. Hering. il Dance Mag 43:
    43-5+ Ag '69
Mr Cranko and his castle. J. Anderson. il
    Dance Mag 43:46-9 Je '69
Progress report; US tour. W. Terry. il Sat
    R 52:57 O 25 '69
Steps from Stuttgart. W. Terry. il Sat R 52:
    40+ My 31 '69
Stuttgart's Cranko. G. Trotta. il Harp Baz
    102:246-7 O '69
Two for the season. il Time 94:71-2 N 7 '69
Wonder from Württemburg. W. Terry. il Sat
    R 52:24 Jl 12 '69
World of dance. W. Terry. il Sat R 52:44-5 Je
    7 '69

STUTZ, Robert M. and others
Stimulus properties of reinforcing brain shock. bibliog Science 163:1081-2 Mr 7 '69

STUTZ, Rowan C.
Education for rural America. PTA Mag 63: 22-3 Mr '69

STUTZ motor car company of America
Annals of finance; a corner in Stutz. J. Brooks. New Yorker 45:74-82+ Ag 23 '69

STUWE, Jane
Beating the season with greenhouses. Org Gard & Farm 16:36-9 S '69

STYLE, Literary
Adjectival idea. V. Sneider. Writers Digest 49: 42-7 Ag '69
Art as intersecting fields of energy. J. Unterecker. Sat R 52:27-9+ Je 14 '69
On frenetic writing. M. Leviston. Writer 82: 25-6 Jl '69
Second thoughts about change. A. Holland. Writers Digest 49:18 S '69
View of literature too often neglected; a creative writer's manipulation of language. J. M. Nagle. Engl J 58:399-407 Mr '69
See also
Literary criticism

STYLE, Musical. See Composition (music)

STYLE, Personal. See Individuality

STYLE shows. See Fashion shows

STYLIDIAM laricifolia. See Hairtrigger flower

STYLING, Automobile. See Automobiles—Design

STYROFOAM
Originality in opalescence; egg cartons. E. E. Welch. il Design 70:16-18 Sum '69

STYRON, Rose Burgunder. See Burgunder, R.

SUBACUTE sclerosing panencephalitis. See Encephalitis

SUBARU 360 (automobile) See Automobiles, Foreign

SUB-COMMISSION on prevention of discrimination and protection of minorities. See United Nations—Sub-commission on prevention of discrimination and protection of minorities

SUBCONSCIOUSNESS
See also
Dreams

SUBCONTRACTING
Latins, Arabs hit Intelsat subcontracting. K. Johnsen. Aviation W 90:23 Ja 27 '69

SUBIN, Harry
Bail for the rich, jail for the poor. Nation 208:363-6 Mr 24 '69

SUBJECT headings
Chauvinistic headings; accusing LC and Sears of racist/colonial bias; letter to the editor. S. Berman. Library J 94:695 F 15 '69
Dead heads? letter to the editor. A. C. Foskett. Library J 94:1559 Ap 15 '69

SUBJECT matter. See Courses of study

SUBJECTS, Artistic. See Art—Themes

SUBJECTS, Literary. See Literature—Themes

SUBMACHINE guns
Gun that made the twenties roar, by W. J. Helmer. Review
    Newsweek il 75:59-60 Ja 5 '70. P. D. Zimmerman

SUBMARINE archeology. See Archeology, Submarine

SUBMARINE boats
Escape from the deep; navy's deep submergence rescue vehicle. S. Carpenter. il Pop Sci 195:78-81+ S '69
From Florida to Cape Cod without moving. W. Cloud. il Pop Mech 131:128-31+ My '69
Intrepid midgets; condensation. T. Gallagher. il Read Digest 95:249-52+ N '69
See also
Submarine warfare

Safety devices and measures
See also
Life support systems (submarine environment)

SUBMARINE boats, Atomic powered
Antisubmarine warfare; defense against the elusive nuclear submarine. R. Zimmerman. il Pop Mech 132:114-19+ S '69
New alarm: the submarine gap. F. V. Drake. Read Digest 95:54-8 Ag '69

SUBMARINE boats, Research. See Submarine research vehicles

SUBMARINE cables. See Cables, Submarine

SUBMARINE disasters
Storms that rage beneath the sea. W. Perkinson. il Sci Digest 65:7-11 Mr '69

SUBMARINE diving. See Diving, Submarine

SUBMARINE drilling. See Underwater drilling

SUBMARINE exploration. See Underwater exploration

SUBMARINE geology
Diorites from the mid-Atlantic ridge at 45°N. F. Aumento. bibliog il Science 165:1112-13 S 12 '69
Dredged trachyte and basalt from Kodiak seamount and the adjacent Aleutian Trench, Alaska. R. B. Forbes and C. M. Hoskin. il Science 166:502-4 O 24 '69
Lherzolite, anorthosite, gabbro, and basalt dredged from the Mid-Indian Ocean ridge. C. G. Engel and R. L. Fisher. bibliog il Science 166:1136-41 N 28 '69
See also
Faults (geology)

SUBMARINE laboratories. See Underwater laboratories

SUBMARINE moving picture photography. See Moving picture photography, Submarine

SUBMARINE oil well drilling. See Oil well drilling, Submarine

SUBMARINE photography. See Photography, Submarine

SUBMARINE research. See Oceanographic research

SUBMARINE research stations. See Underwater laboratories

SUBMARINE research vehicles
Down into the sea in ships; exploring in Deepstar. R. S. Dietz and R. F. Dill. il Sea Front 15:2-9 Ja '69
Drifters; journey of the Ben Franklin. il Newsweek 74:48 S 1 '69
His office is under the sea. N. Sklarewitz. il Pop Mech 131:114-17+ Ja '69
Japanese research submersibles. W. R. Forman. il Sea Front 15:78-85 Mr '69
Research subs on the beach; lack of government money. il Bsns W p65 D 27 '69
Test subs run afoul of costly delays; navy defends three new research submarines; Dolphin, NR-1, and Narwhal. il Bsns W p47-8 Mr 8 '69

SUBMARINE structures. See Underwater structures

SUBMARINE topography. See Ocean bottom

SUBMARINE warfare
New alarm: the submarine gap. F. V. Drake. Read Digest 95:54-8 Ag '69
See also
Anti-submarine warfare

SUBMERGED lands
Homesteading at sea; claims to off-Florida reefs. Time 93:55 Ja 24 '69
See also
Petroleum in submerged lands

SUBMERSIBLES. See Submarine research vehicles

SUB-SAHARAN AFRICA. See Africa, Sub-Saharan

SUBSCRIPTION television programs. See Television broadcasting—Subscription programs

SUBSIDENCES (earth movements)
See also
Earth movements

SUBSIDIES
See also
Agricultural administration—United States
Economic assistance, Domestic
    also subhead Federal aid under various subjects, e.g. Housing—Federal aid

SUBSIDIES, Music. See Music and state

SUBSOILING. See Tillage

SUBSTITUTE products
See also
Food substitutes
Sugar substitutes

SUBSTITUTE teachers
Day of the substitute. C. W. Totten. Todays Ed 58:24-5 Ja '69
Whither the substitute teacher? T. K. Stevens. Clear House 44:229-31 D '69

SUBURBAN libraries. See Libraries—United States

SUBURBAN life
Affluent ghetto; suburban libraries. K. R. Shaffer. bibliog il Library J 94:1093-7 Mr 15 '69
Fairfield County; New York's best address. S. Birmingham. il Holiday 45:58-63+ Ap '69

Anecdotes, facetiae, satire, etc.
Sex and the suburbs; or, Meet me at the A&P. L. Kallen. Mlle 69:132-3 Je '69

SUBURBAN newspapers. See Newspapers—United States

SUBURBAN opera company
Report: Chester, Pa; production of Verdi's Trovatore. G. M. Eby. Opera N 34:26 D 13 '69

SUBURBS
Race, jobs, and cities: what business can do. J. R. Lowe; reply. E. L. Stoll. Sat R 52:32-3 F 22 '69
Suburbia & the city: flight, fight or apathy; address, October 29, 1969. H. Maier. Vital Speeches 36:184-7 Ja 1 '70
Suburbs are changing. W. Langewiesche. il Read Digest 95:157-62+ N '69
See also
Regional planning

SUBVERSIVE activities
Black arts in a free society. N. Cousins. Sat R 52:26 O 18 '69
If you have tears; O. Lattimore case during anti-Communist witch-hunts. W. F. Buckley, jr. Nat R 21:506 My 20 '69
See also
Internal security
Terrorism
United States—Subversive activities control board
Brazil
Brazil: subverting the universities; anti-subversive laws. F. Bandeira. New Repub 161: 17-19 N 8 '69
Russia
Dissenter's fate; arrest of P. Grigorenko. il Newsweek 73:50 My 19 '69

SUCCESS
Challenge yourself to success. C. Bisbee. il Nations Bsns 57:94 N '69
Making it in America. J. P. Sisk. Atlan 224: 63-8 D '69

SUCCESS story; story. See Rodgers, M. A.

SUCCESSFUL farming (periodical)
What does this mean to you? D. Hanson. Suc Farm 67:23 D '69

SUCCESSION, Plant. See Plant succession

SUCCINATE. See Succinic acid

SUCCINIC acid
New light-sensitive cofactor required for oxidation of succinate by mycobacterium phlei. C. R. Krishna Murti and A. F. Brodie. bibliog il Science 164:302-4 Ap 18 '69

SUCCULENT plants
Jardin botanique Les Cedres; estate of J. Marnier-Lapostolle at St Jean Cap Ferrat. L. Cutak. il Horticulture 47:36-7+ F '69
Spectacular succulent. P. O'Neill. Horticulture 48:47+ Ja '70
Succulents. P. Clark. il Horticulture 47:24-5+ N '69
Unusual succulents. L. Cutak. il Horticulture 47:28-9+ My '69
See also
Cactus
Desert vegetation
Kalanchoes
Sedums

SUCKERS (fish)
Esterase heterogeneity: dynamics of a polymorphism. R. K. Koehn. bibliog il Science 163:943-4 F 28 '69

SUCKERS, Plant. See Tillering (plants)

SUCKING. See Motor response

SUCKING, Thumb. See Thumb sucking

SUCKLING
Prolactin in the postpartum rat: synthesis and release in the absence of suckling stimulation. H. Moltz and others. bibliog il Science 163:1083-4 Mr 7 '69

SUDAN
See also
Guerrillas—Sudan

Politics and government
Gesture of peace; granting autonomy to the southern provinces. America 121:4 Jl 5 '69
Promises, promises; military coup. Newsweek 73:60+ Je 9 '69
Step to the left. Time 93:41 Je 6 '69

SUDARSHAN, E. C. George. See Bilaniuk, O.-M. jt. auth.

SUENENS, Léon Joseph, cardinal
Catholic unity; excerpts from interview. America 120:611 My 24 '69
Tension is not schism; excerpts from interview. America 120:152 F 8 '69

about
Cardinal as critic. il por Time 94:47 Ag 1 '69
Pope takes on a leading critic. U S News 67:10 Jl 7 '69
Suenens crying in the wilderness. G. Baum. Cath World 210:103-7 D '69

SUESS, Hans E.
Tritium geophysics as an international research project. bibliog Science 163:1405-10 Mr 28 '69

SUEZ CANAL
Diminishing ditch. Newsweek 73:42 Ja 27 '69
Qanāt as Suways. J. S. Haupert. il Focus 19:12 Mr '69
Suez Canal's bleak centennial. il Time 94:46 N 21 '69
Undeclared war at Suez; with report by M. Mok and interview with G. Meir, ed. by R. Stolley. il Life 67:26-33 O 3 '69
Whatever happened to the Suez Canal? il U S News 66:14 Je 23 '69

SUFFERING
Fact of suffering. V. P. McCorry. America 120:inside back cover Mr 22 '69
How people change. A. Wheelis. Commentary 47:56-66 My '69

SUFFIELD, Conn.
Libraries
Kent memorial library. il Arch Rec 146:100-4 D '69

SUFFOLK sun (newspaper)
Ads not enough to save a paper. Bsns W p80 O 25 '69

SUFFRAGE
See also
Voters, Registration of
Woman suffrage

United States
Can LUV conquer all? drive to amend the Constitution to enfranchise 18-year-olds. il Time 93:20 Ja 31 '69
Eighteen-year-old vote; symposium. Todays Ed 58:34-5+ D '69
Eighteen year-olds want voting rights. Sr Schol 94:Schol Teach 8 My 2 '69
First liberty, by M. Chute. Review Sat R 52:48-9 My 24 '69. A. Vorspan
Get youth involved in government, lower the voting age; NCSS convention. Sr Schol 93:Schol Teach 7 Ja 10 '69
Old enough to vote. New Yorker 45:28-31 Ap 5 '69
Speaking out on a voice for youth. Nations Bsns 57:105-6+ S '69
Teacher opinion poll; the eighteen-year-old vote. il Todays Ed 58:10 D '69
Teens and the ballot box. il Seventeen 28:122-3 Je '69
This month's feature: Congress and voting rights controversy. Cong Digest 48:257-88 N '69

SUFFRAGETTES. See Woman suffrage

SUGAR
Sweeten to taste. Am Home 72:103 My '69
See also
Glucose

SUGAR in the body
See also
Blood sugar

SUGAR industry and trade
Starvation amid plenty; problem of Puerto Rican sugar planters. America 120:574 My 17 '69

SUGAR substitutes
Artificial sweeteners, of questionable safety. il Consumer Bul 52:12-13 F '69
Artificial sweeteners suspected of causing cell damage. Chem 42:6 Ja '69
Artificially sweetened drinks, potentials for harm. Consumer Bul 52:31 N '69
Big brouhaha over sweeteners. il Bsns W p98+ O 18 '69
Bitter sweeteners. il Newsweek 74:83 S 29 '69
Bitterness about sweets; cyclamate hassle. Time 94:79 O 17 '69
Bittersweet; how Americans responded to ban on cyclamates. Newsweek 74:119 N 17 '69
Cyclamate ban. S. L. Inhorn and L. F. Meisner. bibliog Science 166:685 N 7 '69; Reply. S. S. Epstein and others. 166:1575 D 26 '69
Cyclamate scare. il U S News 67:7 N 3 '69
Cyclamates and cigarettes. New Repub 161:9 N 1 '69
Cyclamates banned. il Sci N 96:369-70 O 25 '69
Cyclamates' sour aftertaste. il Time 94:79 O 31 '69
Cytogenetic effects of cyclamates on human cells in vitro. D. Stone and others. bibliog il Science 164:568-9 My 2 '69; Discussion. 165:517 Ag 1 '69
Cytogenetic studies in rats of cyclohexylamine, a metabolite of cyclamate. M. S. Legator and others. bibliog il Science 165: 1139-40 S 12 '69

SUGAR substitutes—*Continued*
Diet drinks take a lump; new labeling rule for products artificially sweetened with cyclamates. Bsns W p37 Ap 12 '69
Diet industry has a hungry look. il Bsns W p41-2 O 25 '69
Goodbye to cyclamates, at last! il Consumer Bul 52:31-4 D '69
HEW bans the cyclamates. Time 94:84-5 O 24 '69
How safe are no-calorie sweeteners? R. C. Davids. Read Digest 95:77-80 Jl '69
How sweet it shouldn't be! cyclamates. J. I. Rodale. Org Gard & Farm 16:102+ N '69
Modifying the ban. Sci N 96:524-5 D 6 '69
New labeling requested. Sci N 95:378 Ap 19 '69
New look at cyclamate sweetners. il Consumer Rep 34:280-1 My '69
Recommended use of artificial sweeteners. Good H 169:175 S '69
Soured sweets; cyclamates banned from food products. Newsweek 74:93 O 27 '69
Sweet and sinister; proposed regulation on stating cyclamate content. A. S. Grove, jr. New Repub 160:10 Je 14 '69
Sweeten to taste. Am Home 72:103 My '69
Sweeteners take their lumps; effect of cyclamate ban. il Newsweek 74:73-4+ N 3 '69
Synthetic sweetners: hazard to health? il Changing T 23:17-19 Jl '69
We are alarmed; ban on cyclamate doctors comments. U S News 67:44-6 D 15 '69

SUGARBUSH VALLEY, Vt.
Sugarbush: Vermont's chic ski resort. F. Morton. il Holiday 46:64-7 D '69

SUGARLOAF ridge state park. See California—Parks and reserves

SUGARMAN, Daniel A. and Hochstein, Rollie
Getting your message across. Seventeen 28:146-7+ S '69
Growing away from home. Seventeen 27:132-3+ N '68
I love him, but do I like him? Seventeen 28:152-3+ F '69

SUGARMAN, Norman A.
Excerpt from testimony before House committee on ways and means, February 19, 1969. Cong Digest 48:143+ My '69

SUGARS
See also
Saccharides
Trehalose

SUGG, Arnold L. and Hebert, P. J.
Hurricane season of 1968. Weatherwise 22:12-18 F '69

SUGGESTION
See also
Hypnotism

SUGRUE, Mary, and Sweeney, J. A.
Check your inquiry-teaching technique. Todays Ed 58:43-4 My '69

SUHARTO, 1925-
Indonesia's uncertain future. B. R. O. Anderson. bibliog f Cur Hist 57:355-60 D '69
Operating on a giant. il por Time 93:38 Je 27 '69
Reporter at large (cont) R. Shaplen. New Yorker 45:73-4 My 24; 39-44+ My 31 '69

SUHM, Lawrence L.
Contact hour unit, new tool for outdoor recreation planning. Parks & Rec 4:33-4+ O '69

SUICIDE
America's Devil's Island; inside the Army stockade at San Francisco's presidio. D. Duncan. Ramp Mag 7:8+ Ja 25 '69
Behavioral sciences. Sci N 95:356 Ap 12 '69
Child suicides: can these tragedies be prevented? Good H 169:207-9 O '69
Sensitivity toward suicide. Chr Today 13:21-2 Jl 18 '69
Southern violence. S. Hackney. bibliog f il Am Hist R 74:906-25 F '69
Study probes youngsters' suicidal signs. Todays Health 47:82 Ap '69
Suicidal behavior in men and women. D. Lester. bibliog Ment Hy 53:340-5 Jl '69
Suicide clues in psychotic patients. R. G. Singer and I. J. Blumenthal. Ment Hy 53:346-50 Jl '69
Suicide in children. B. Y. O'Dell. Parents Mag 44:58-9+ Ja '69

SUICIDE prevention centers
Effectiveness of a suicide prevention program; Los Angeles suicide prevention center. I. W. Weiner. bibliog il Ment Hy 53:357-63 Jl '69
Some considerations in establishing a suicide prevention service; Ventura County suicide prevention service. R. T. Jarmusz. bibliog Ment Hy 53:351-6 Jl '69

SUITOR; story. See Wolwode, L.

SUITS at law. See Actions and defenses

SUKARNO, 1901-
Reporter at large (cont) R. Shaplen. New Yorker 45:42-6+ My 24; 39-44+ My 31 '69

SUKIYAKI. See Cookery, Japanese

SULA, Stanley
Build a capacitance meter. Pop Electr 31:66-9+ O '69

SULFAMETHIZOLE. See Sulfathiazoles

SULFATASES
Soluble sulfatase in growing bone of rats. A. Hirschman and M. Hirschman. bibliog il Science 164:834-5 My 16 '69

SULFATHIAZOLES
Annals of medicine; persistent hiccups, side effect of sulfamethizole. B. Roueché. New Yorker 45:110-17 Ap 5 '69

SULFONAMIDES
See also
Sulfathiazoles

SULFONATES
2-p-Toluidinyl-6-naphthalene sulfonate: relation of structure to fluorescence properties in different media. A. Camerman and L. H. Jensen. bibliog il Science 165:493-5 Ag 1 '69

SULFUR
Sulfur melting and polymorphism under pressure: outlines of fields for twelve crystalline phases. G. C. Vezzoli and others. bibliog il Science 166:218-21 O 10 '69

SULFUR difluoride. See Sulfur fluorides

SULFUR fluorides
Microwave spectrum and structure of sulfur difluoride. D. R. Johnson and F. X. Powell. bibliog il Science 164:950-1 My 23 '69

SULFUR mines and mining

Canada
See also
Texas Gulf sulphur company

SULICH, Vassili
Versatile Vassili Sulich. il pors Dance Mag 43:23-5 Mr '69

SULLENGER, Don B. and others
Boron modifications produced in an induction-coupled argon plasma. bibliog Science 163:935-7 F 28 '69

SULLIVAN, Brian
Obituary
Opera N por 34:33 S 6 '69

SULLIVAN, Dan
Theater: New York is a smash. N Y Times Mag p 12-13 Je 22 '69

SULLIVAN, Darrell T. See Widmoyer, F. B. jt. auth.

SULLIVAN, Ed
And now let's hear it for the Ed Sullivan show! D. Barthelme. por Esquire 71:126-7+ Ap '69

SULLIVAN, Florence. See Feder, W. A. jt. auth.

SULLIVAN, Francis
Any golden thing; poem. Yale R 59:107-8 O '69
Newer breed; poem. America 121:71 Ag 2 '69

SULLIVAN, Frank
Greetings, friends! poem. New Yorker 45:27 D 27 '69

SULLIVAN, Fred R.
One morning at the Pierre. il por Forbes 104:30-1 N 1 '69

SULLIVAN, Gail
Prenatal care and labor for fathers. Sci Digest 66:24-8 Ag '69

SULLIVAN, George
The climb; poem. Atlan 223:70 F '69

SULLIVAN, James
Matty, for McGraw; poem. Commonweal 90:362 Je 13 '69

SULLIVAN, John
Grace abounding; poem. America 120:359 Mr 29 '69

SULLIVAN, John D. and Burks, G. F.
McIntire-Stennis program. Am For 75:16-19+ Ap '69

SULLIVAN, K. A.
Raspberries, robins and rascals. Org Gard & Farm 16:36-8 O '69

SULLIVAN, Kay
How to get a canary to sing like one. Redbook 132:82 Ap '69

SULLIVAN, Kevin
Apostolic succession. Nation 209:668-70 D 15 '69
Dazzling nonsense. Nation 208:799-800 Je 23 '69

SULLIVAN, Leon H.
Black capitalism at work; interview. pors U S News 66:60-4+ F 17 '69
about
Business lobbies for ghetto program. por Bsns W p56+ Je 28 '69

SULLIVAN, Sister M. Paulinus
And winds snow-weighted ride; poem. Commonweal 91:204 N 14 '69
Canticle in an orange grove; poem. Cath World 209:125 Je '69
SULLIVAN, Maurice William
Teaching Johnny to read: breakthrough? il por U S News 66:98-9 F 17 '69
SULLIVAN, Nancy
Tattoo; poem. Nation 209:122 Ag 11 '69
To my body; poem. Poetry 114:19 Ap '69
SULLIVAN, Robert J.
Let them write. Ed Digest 34:50-1 Ja '69
Overrated threat. Ed Digest 35:49-51 N '69
SULLIVAN, Walter
Is the Arctic ice cap endangered? Cur 106:22-5 Ap '69
SULLIVAN, William J.
Theology for undergraduates. America 121:463-6 N 15 '69
SULLIVAN, Wilson
Back to the hub. Sat R 52:43-5 D 20 '69
Concord and Cambridge confidential. Sat R 52:40-2 S 27 '69
SULLIVAN'S Indian campaign, 1779
End of the Iroquois. M. Bishop. il Am Heritage 20:28-33+ O '69
SULZBERGER, Arthur Hays
New York times; excerpt from The kingdom and the power. G. Talese. il Harper 238:40-8+ F '69
SULZBERGER, Arthur Ochs
Profiles. G. T. Hellman. por New Yorker 44:40-2+ Ja 18 '69
SULZBERGER, Cyrus Leo
Authors & editors. R. H. Smith. Pub W 195:35-6 Je 16 '69
Like an excellent stew. P. L. Buckley. Nat R 21:704-5 Jl 15 '69
SUMITOMO companies. See Japan—Industries
SUMMER
Signs of summer. A. C. Harding. il Todays Ed 58:36-7 My '69
Summer leftovers. W. Zinsser. il Life 67:8 S 5 '69
SUMMER activities. See School children—Out-of-school activities
SUMMER cabins. See Cabins
SUMMER camping. See Camping
SUMMER camps. See Camps
SUMMER cookery. See Cookery
SUMMER dance schools. See Dance schools
SUMMER drinks. See Beverages
SUMMER festivals. See Festivals—United States
SUMMER furniture. See Furniture, Outdoor; Furniture, Summer
SUMMER homes
Closing your fun home. C. D. Mack. il Mech Illus 65:87-9 O '69
Magic of a summer house; overlooking the coast of Maine; photographs by J. Loengard. Life 66:48-57 My 2 '69

Protection
How to keep up a vacation home when you're not there. J. H. Ingersoll. House B 111:54+ O '69
SUMMER husbands; story. See Sayre, N.
SUMMER institutes. See Teachers institutes
SUMMER jobs. See Seasonal labor; Youth—Employment
SUMMER jobs for students. See Student employment
SUMMER meals. See Meals
SUMMER reading projects. See Libraries, Childrens—Projects
SUMMER resorts
Elegance comes to the Ozarks; developers go after big spenders. il Bsns W p 104-5 Ag 2 '69
See also
Atlantic City
Seaside resorts
SUMMER schools
The Clearing; vacation school at Ellison Bay, Wis. S. Turner. Sr Schol 94:Schol Teach 20 Ap 11 '69
Cry of the peacock; study course conducted by Britain's National trust summer school. F. Megarity. il House B 111:72+ Ap '69
Harvard is also a summer school. S. Lerner. il Holiday 46:16-19 Jl '69
1969 world guide to summer study. il Sr Schol 94:Schol Teach 13-15+ F 28 '69
Should your child go to summer school? ed. by J. Copland. R. H. Woodroof. il Parents Mag 44:38-9+ Je '69
Summer on the continental campus. J. Mandelstam. il Sat R 52:56+ F 15 '69
Summer programs in the British Isles; address. November 1968. J. C. O'Brien. Engl J 58:726-34 My '69

Summer remedial program for primary children. P. A. Driscoll. Ed Digest 34:36-7 My '69
Try a learning vacation. D. B. Warnick. il Mech Illus 65:46-8+ My '69
Tune up for summer. P. Pine. il Am Ed 5:16-20 Mr '69
See also
Educational workshops
School year
SUMMER spooks; story. See Preston, B. B.
SUMMER theater. See Theater—United States
SUMMER vacations. See Vacations
SUMMER workshops. See Educational workshops
SUMMERHILL school. See Private schools—England; Schools, Experimental
SUMMERLIN, Edgar
In the pop bag. Am Rec G 35:594-5 Mr: 36:85 S '69
—See Gold, M. jt. auth.
SUMMERS, Eileen
More people in the cities. Cath World 208:236 F '69
SUMMERS, Hollis
Old man over sherry; poem. Am Scholar 38:226 Spr '69
SUMMERS, Wesley K.
School management and social responsibility. bibliog Clear House 44:3-8 S '69
SUMMER'S tale; story. See Woodley, I.
SUMTER COUNTY, S.C.
U.S. journal; Turks, or, people of Turkish descent. C. Trillin. New Yorker 45:104+ Mr 8 '69
SUN
Sun. A. Bester. il Holiday 45:38-9+ Je '69
Sun, moon, and planets this month. See issues of Sky and telescope
See also
Eclipses, Solar
Solar radiation
Solar system
Sunspots

Corona
Pioneer 6: measurement of transient Faraday rotation phenomena observed during solar occultation. G. S. Levy and others. bibliog il Science 166:596-8 O 31 '69
Superior conjunction of Pioneer 6. R. M. Goldstein. il Science 166:598-601 O 31 '69

Observations
Solar rocket observations on an eclipse day. M. J. Koomen and others. il Sky & Tel 37:356-7 Je '69
Some notes on recent solar activity. il Sky & Tel 38:124-7 Ag '69

Rotation
Buoyancy and solar spin-down. J. L. Modisette and J. E. Novotny. bibliog il Science 166:872-4 N 14 '69
Solar differential rotation and oblateness. A. Clark, jr. and others. bibliog il Science 164:290-1 Ap 18 '69

Temperature
Temperature minimum in the sun. il Sky & Tel 37:362-3 Je '69
SUN (newspaper)
Stooping to conquer. il Time 95:49 Ja 12 '70
SUN, New York. See New York sun
SUN and cancer. See Cancer—Causes
SUN burn. See Sunburn
SUN circle ranches
Brand name for organic foods. J. Olds. il Org Gard & Farm 16:62-4 Jl '69
SUN dials. See Sundials
SUN furnaces. See Solar furnaces
SUN glasses
Beauty glasses everywhere: in and out of the sun. il Harp Baz 102:94-5 Je '69
Choosing and using sunglasses. il Consumer Bul 52:7-12 Je '69
Out of this world eye shields. il Look 33:76-7 Jl 15 '69
What you should know about sunglasses. G. M. Knox. Bet Hom & Gard 47:34 Jl '69
SUN light. See Sunlight
SUN oil company
Building a corporate financial model. G. W. Gershefski. il Harvard Bsns R 47:61-72 Jl '69
GOO fishes in; Get oil out group fight companies drilling in the Santa Barbara Channel. il Newsweek 74:100 D 8 '69
Place in the sun; Sharbaugh to become president. Time 94:84 S 26 '69
Sun's computer helps find heir. il Bsns W p83 O 4 '69

SUN screens. See Screens (sun)

SUN spots. See Sunspots

SUN tan. See Tan

SUNBURN
Drug prevents sunburn. il Sci Digest 66:61 O '69
Sun and you; excerpts from Your skin and hair. E. W. Brauer. Vogue 153:111+ Je '69
Who Ra? il Motor B 124:62+ Ag '69

SUNBURN lotions. See Cosmetics

SUNDAES. See Ice cream, ices, etc.

SUNDANCE fire. See Forest fires

SUNDAY; story. See DiPego, G.

SUNDAY labor
First amendment and Christian principle. Chr Today 13:25 Ag 22 '69

SUNDAY opening of shops. See Business hours

SUNDAY school lessons
Applications that hit the mark. W. Boyd. Chr Today 14:26-7 O 24 '69

SUNDAY schools
Seedtime in the church: the nursery. M. Le Bar. Chr Today 14:19 D 19 '69
Vehicular spectacular: Sunday school and church promotion gimmicks. Chr Cent 86: 889 Je 25 '69
See also
Sunday school lessons

SUNDAY supplements. See Newspapers—Magazine sections

SUNDBYE, Ronald L.
Art. Chr Cent 86:186-7 F 5 '69

SUNDERLAND, Glenn
Antiques set the stage for historical novels. K. Dulgar. il Hobbies 74:98V-98W+ Jl '69

SUNDIALS
Homemade sundial. D. A. Caccia. il Org Gard & Farm 16:74-6 Je '69
How sundials tell time. Good H 168:210 Ap '69
Sundials. M. Brand. il Ceram Mo 17:18-19 My '69

SUNDQUIST, James L.
Co-ordinating the war on poverty. Ann Am Acad 385:41-9 S '69

SUNDSTRAND corporation
Sundstrand's jet-assisted takeoff. Forbes 103: 59 Ap 15 '69

SUNFISH (boats) See Sailboats

SUNFLOWERS
Sunflower contest winners for 1969. il Org Gard & Farm 16:72-4 D '69

Seed
Sunflower seeds. il Home Gard 56:39 Je '69

SUNGLASS cases. See Eyeglass cases

SUNGLASSES. See Sun glasses

SUNKEN treasure. See Treasure trove

SUNLIGHT
Light and your health. W. Hartley and E. Hartley. il Pop Sci 194:78-80+ F '69
Sunglint patterns: unusual dark patches. C. J. Bowley and others. bibliog il Science 165:1360-2 S 26 '69
Sunny garden: answer to the problem of all sun and no shade. il House & Gard 135: 98-9+ Je
See also
Photosynthesis

SUNNYVALE, Calif.
Sunnyvale: prunes to missiles. il Newsweek 73:77 Je 9 '69

SUNROOM; story. See O'Hara, J.

SUNSCREEN preparations. See Cosmeticss

SUNSET (periodical)
Announcing the 1969-1979 Western home awards. il Sunset 142:96-7 F '69

SUNSET garden contest. See Gardening—Competitions

SUNSET STRIP. See Los Angeles—Streets

SUNSHADES. See Screens (sun)

SUNSPOTS
Magnetic flux-trapping experiment with a moving conductor. J. Hovorka. bibliog il Science 166:877-8 N 14 '69
Naked-eye sunspot group seen in October Prodigal sun. il Time 93:45-6 My 23 '69
See also
Solar flares

SUNTAN. See Tan

SUOMI, V. E. See Vonder Haar, T. H. jt. auth.

SUPAI Indians. See Havasupai Indians

SUPER 8 cameras. See Moving picture cameras

SUPER 8 film. See Moving picture films

SUPER realism. See Art, Modern

SUPERCHARGERS. See Automobile engines—Superchargers

SUPERCONDUCTIVITY
Advances in superconductivity; adaptation of address, February 1969. J. Bardeen. bibliog il Phys Today 22:40-6 O '69
High temperatures or futile efforts. D. E. Thomsen. il Sci N 96:251 S 20 '69
Is there a new mechanism for superconductivity? il Phys Today 22:64 Ja '69
New materials and more applications for superconductivity; report of meeting. V. L. Newhouse and D. L. Atherton. il Phys Today 22:101+ Mr '69; Discussion. 22:11+ S '69
Search for a theory; phonon theory of superconductivity. D. E. Thomsen. il Sci N 95: 169-71 F 15 '69
Superconducting hydrogen. Sci Am 220:44-5 F '69
Will mighty magnets protect voyagers to planets? W. Von Braun. il Pop Sci 194:98-100+ Ja '69

SUPERCONDUCTORS
Fluctuations in superconductors; report of meeting. F. Chilton and W. S. Goree. il Science 163:1363-4 Mr 21 '69
Solid staters study fluctuations in superconductors. bibliog il Phys Today 22:57-8 My '69

SUPERHETERODYNE receivers. See Radio receivers, Superheterodyne

SUPERHIGHWAYS. See Express highways

SUPERINTENDENTS, School. See School superintendents and principals

SUPERIOR, LAKE
Across a big drink of water; Trans-Superior race. H. D. Whall. il Sports Illus 31:18-19 Ag 11 '69
Lake Superior, private dump; Stoddard and FWPCA reports; hearings in Duluth. G. Hill. Nation 208:795-6 Je 23 '69
See also
Isle Royale National Park

SUPERIOR children. See Children, Gifted

SUPERIOR students. See College students, Mentally superior

SUPERMARKETS
Grocery business. il Forbes 104:34-6+ N 1 '69
Putting supermarkets on the steppes; Milan-based export-import company dealings with Moscow. il Bsns W p78+ S 20 '69
Supermarket, demi-myth. E. Kendall. Vogue 154:45+ N 15 '69
Volume is crucial. Or is it? California's Lucky stores and Boston-based Stop & shop. il Forbes 103:42-3 Mr 1 '69
See also
Steinberg's limited
Wakefern food corporation

SUPERNATURAL
Supernatural and miraculous. L. N. Bell. Chr Today 13:30-1 F 28 '69
See also
Ghosts

SUPERNOVAS. See Stars, New

SUPERPLASTIC alloys. See Alloys

SUPERPLASTICITY. See Plasticity

SUPERPOWERS. See Great powers

SUPERSONIC aerodynamics. See Aerodynamics, Supersonic

SUPERSONIC air travel. See Air travel

SUPERSONIC airplanes. See Airplanes, Supersonic

SUPERSONICS (basketball team) See Basketball teams

SUPERSTITION
See also
Astrology
Medicine, Magic, mystic, etc.
Voodooism
Witchcraft

SUPERTANKERS. See Tank ships

SUPERVISION of schools. See School supervision and supervisors

SUPERVISORS, Library. See Library administration

SUPERVISORS, School. See School supervision and supervisors

SUPERVISORY air traffic controllers organization
Supervisors union to fight possible ATC job revision. Aviation W 90:27 Je 30 '69

SUPPERS
Company's coming to an informal supper. Am Home 72:99 Ja '69
Eat: sexy food for a late supper. M. Cantwell. Mlle 69:32+ Jl '69
Fast skillet suppers; fancy skillet suppers. il Bet Hom & Gard 47:111-12 Mr '69
Party menu for a sit-down supper. il Parents Mag 44:83 Jl '69
Saturday night supper club; with menus and recipes. il Parents Mag 44:60-3+ F '69

SUPPERS—*Continued*
Something different for supper. il Farm J 93:60 S '69
Supper dishes to serve. E. W. Manning. il Farm J 93:94-5 Ap '69
　See also
Buffet meals
Christmas suppers

SUPPES, Patrick
Computer-assisted instruction; interview. Ed Digest 34:6-8 F '69
—and Morningstar, Mona
Computer-assisted instruction. bibliog Science 166:343-50 O 17 '69

SUPPLEMENTAL airlines. See Airlines—Non-scheduled operations; Local service airlines

SUPPLEMENTAL unemployment benefits
Financing supplemental unemployment benefit plans. E. H. Beier. bibliog f il Mo Labor R 92:31-5 N '69

SUPPLEMENTARY employment
Comparing employment estimates from household and payroll surveys. G. P. Green. bibliog il Mo Labor R 92:9-20 D '69
Facts about moonlighting. L. David. il Mech Illus 65:29-31+ Ag '69
Moonlighting: do you really profit? T. J. Rakstis. il Todays Health 47:24-5+ O '69
Teachers in the moonlight. H. W. Guthrie. il Mo Labor R 92:28-31 F '69

SUPPLEMENTARY reading
Fall-out in Niagara Falls; letters to the editor of Niagara Falls gazette on Transaction reading. Trans-Action 6:2+ Ap '69

SUPPLY, Electric power. See Electric power

SUPPLY and demand
How not to tinker with the economy. J. F. Wharton. Sat R 52:19-21 D 13 '69
New markets, think before you leap; excerpts from The marketing mode—pathways to corporate growth. T. Levitt. bibliog f il Harvard Bsns W 47:53-67 My '69

SUPPLY and demand of teachers. See Teachers—Supply and demand

SUPREMACY of the Pope. See Popes—Primacy

SUPREME court justices. See Judges

SUPREME court of the United States. See United States—Supreme court

SUPREME courts, State. See Courts, State

SUPREMES (singers) See Negro singers

SURE thing; story. See Shyer, M. F.

SURF fishing. See Salt water fishing

SURF riding
Doo wa diddie squiggly wigglies: get lost! D. Levin. il Sports Illus 31:22-3 D 8 '69
Endless summer, 1779. il Am Heritage 20:112 Ag '69
Inland surfing. il Travel 132:15-16 D '69
Instant ocean: it just keeps rolling along; surfing indoors. C. Phinizy. il Sports Illus 31:74-8 N 10 '69
It helps to have read comic books as a kid; paintings. M. Ramos. Sports Illus 30:36-41 Mr 17 '69
Making waves; surfing in Tempe, Ariz. il Time 94:97 O 10 '69
Polynesian surfing. B. R. Finney and J. D. Houston. il Natur Hist 78:26-35+ Ag '69
Real freaks don't go out in winter. D. Levin. il Sports Illus 30:58-9 Mr 24 '69
Surfing Tres Palmas. J. P. Kahn. il Travel & Camera 32:19-20 My '69
Surfing: you don't have to be seventeen. D. Kampion. Motor B 123:89+ My '69
Why leave it to the kids? il Sunset 142:86-9 My '69

SURFACE, Bill
Blood and ice. N Y Times Mag p26-26A+ F 2 '69
How to retire successfully after a twenty-eight month career. N Y Times Mag p30-2+ Mr 2 '69
Johnny Sain teaches the power of positive pitching. N Y Times Mag p48-9+ Ap 20 '69
Life among the drag racers. N Y Times Mag p36-8+ My 25 '69
Mammoth Cave. Travel 132:62-5 S '69; Same abr. with title Mammoth Cave: nature's underground cathedral. Read Digest 95: 189-92 S '69
Pro football's broken men. N Y Times Mag p56-7+ O 26 '69
Southern Baptists preach; the day of judgment is about to come. N Y Times Mag p30-2+ Ag 24 '69
Will your car be stolen next? Read Digest 95:157-8+ D '69
You have to be a little crazy to play on a suicide squad. N Y Times Mag p80-1+ D 14 '69

SURFACE, Flatness of. See Optical flats

SURFACE chemistry
Adsorption of alkyl trimethylammonium chlorides at a porous glass-potassium chloride solution interface. L. S. Hersh. bibliog il Science 164:179-81 Ap 11 '69

SURFACES
　See also
Interfaces
Thin films

SURFACES, Fermi. See Fermi surfaces

SURFBOARDS
Far-out flexible surfboard, the wave of the future? ed. by A. Lees. E. Blum. il Pop Sci 195:92-5 Ag '69

SURFING. See Surf riding

SURGALLA, Michael J. See Janssen, W. A. jt. auth.

SURGEONS
Christiaan Barnard; one life; excerpt. C. Barnard and C. B. Pepper. il McCalls 97: 144-52 O; 127-34 N '69

SURGERY
Like father, but not exactly like son; ed. by W. S. Ross. A. Decker; W. H. Decker. il Todays Health 47:38-41+ D '69
The unborn; surgery before birth. D. M. Rorvik. il Look 33:74-6+ N 4 '69
　See also
Children—Surgery
Malpractice
Surgeons
Transplantation of organs, tissues, etc.
　also subhead Surgery under names of organs and regions of the body, e.g. Eye—Surgery

History
　See Medicine—History

SURGERY, Cosmetic. See Surgery, Facial; Surgery, Plastic

SURGERY, Facial
New wrinkles for old age; symposium on cosmetic surgery. il Newsweek 73:70 Ap 28 '69

SURGERY, Plastic
Art of manly face-lifting. P. M. McGrady, jr. Vogue 153:117+ Je '69
Body sculpturing. S. Morini. il Vogue 154: 190-3 O 1 '69
Eye job: blepharoplasty. il Vogue 154:104-5 Ag 15 '69
Miracles of plastic surgery. P. Damerel. Parents Mag 44:78-9+ N '69
Operation uplift in Vietnam; operations performed on Vietnamese bargirls and others. T. Fox. Commonweal 90:502-3 Ag 22 '69
Why I had my face lifted. Harp Baz 102: 134-5+ Ja '69
　See also
Hair—Transplantation

SURINACH, Carlos
¡Zarzuela! Opera N 33:8-12 My 17 '69

SURINAM
Report: Surinam. B. Handler. Atlan 224:38+ N '69
　See also
Indians of South America—Surinam

SURITZ, Yelizaveta
Ballet news from the Soviet Union. Dance Mag 43:95 Mr '69

SURO, Piedad de
For women today. Américas 21:38-40 O '69

SURPLUS military property
Army is at sea over nerve gas; plan to dump unwanted chemical weapons in Atlantic stirs fear and controversy. il Bsns W p72+ Je 7 '69
How not to do it; disposal of war materials. Nation 208:653 Mv 26 '69
You might shop the Dept. of defense. Sunset 143:64 N '69

SURPLUS products, Agricultural
Global glut. il Time 93:90+ My 9 '69
New world food problem, abundance. W. E. Swegle. il Suc Farm 67:44-8 S '69

SURREALISM
Program to remake human understanding. A. Balakian. Sat R 52:19-21 My 31 '69

SURREALISM (art)
Art: surrealist exhibitions. L. Alloway. Nation 209:357 O 6 '69

SURTAX. See Income tax; Income tax—United States

SURVEY research center. See Michigan. University, Ann Arbor

SURVEYING, Aerial
　See also
Photography, Aerial

SURVEYING instruments
　See also
Theodolites

SURVEYORS, Marine
What do you know about... E. B. Thomas. il Yachting 125:76-7+ Ap '69

SURVEYS, Biological. See Biological surveys
SURVIVAL after airplane accidents, shipwrecks, etc.
Lost on the moon: a decision-making problem. Todays Ed 58:55-6 F '69
Saga of survival. E. L. Rogers. il Field & S 74:78-9+ Je '69
Survivor; stowaway in well of airplane's landing gear. il Newsweek 73:69 Je 16 '69
 See also
Wilderness survival
SURVIVAL and emergency equipment
Primer for self-preservation. F. M. Paulson. il Field & S 74:146-8+ O '69
SURVIVAL kits. See Survival and emergency equipment
SURVIVAL of man. See Man—Survival
SURVIVORS benefits
When daddy's in the kitchen. R. R. Jalbert. il Har Yrs 9:44-5 My '69
SURVIVORS insurance. See Survivors benefits
SUSA, Conrad
On the off-beat. Hi Fi 19:MA9-10 My; MA8-9 Ag '69
SUSANN, Jacqueline
Jackie's machine. il por Time 93:88+ Je 20 '69
Jacqueline Susann: the writing machine. S. Davidson. il por Harper 239:65-71 O '69
More guys and dolls. por Newsweek 73:98 Je 2 '69
SUSOR, Walter A. and others
Heterogeneity of presumably homogeneous protein preparations. bibliog Science 165:1260-2 S 19 '69
SUSPENSE novels. See Detective and mystery stories
SUSPENSION from school and college. See Expulsion from school and college
SUSSMAN, Irving M.
Organization is not the essence of community; excerpts from address, August 1969. Cath World 210:114-18 D '69
SUSSMAN, Leonard R.
Book hunger is insatiable. ALA Bul 63:1577-81 D '69
SUSSMAN, M. V. and Katchalsky, A.
Mechanochemical turbine: a new power cycle. Science 167:45-7 Ja 2 '70
SUTCLIFFE, James Helme
Double bow for Devils of Loudun. Hi Fi 19:MA22-3+ S '69
German forecast. Opera N 34:6-7 D 6 '69
Menotti's globolinks. Hi Fi 19:MA27-8 Ap '69
New hall for Montezuma. Opera N 33:6-7 My 17 '69
(ed) See Berg, A. Frau Berg
(ed) See Penderecki, K. Devils' advocate
SUTHERLAND, Don
Birth of a salesman. Travel & Camera 32:78-9+ Ap '69
SUTHERLAND, John
William Blake and nonviolence. Nation 208:542-4 Ap 28 '69
SUTHERLAND, Zena
Books for young people. See issues of Saturday review
Reviewing stand. Sat R 52:26 Ag 16 '69
SUTIN, Helen Gorn
Nostalgia revisited; poem. Har Yrs 9:31 N '69
SUTOWO, Ibnu
Oil general. il por Newsweek 73:81 Je 16 '69
SUTTLES, Gerald D.
Anatomy of a Chicago slum. Trans-Action 6:16-19+ F '69
SUTTON, Antony C.
Are we in a Pavlovian box? Nat R 21:692-4 Jl 15 '69
SUTTON, Charles
Blue Nile group; Town Hall. J. Dowlin. Dance Mag 43:86 My '69
SUTTON, Horace
Ghostly war of the Green Berets. Sat R 52:23-5+ O 18 '69
One morning in Corsica. Sat R 52:49-50 S 20 '69
SUTTON, Peter. See Blakemore, C. jt. auth.
SUTTON, Stephanne
Arnold arboretum. Horticulture 47:20-1+ Je '69
SUTTON, Suttie
Jigging for bass, east Tennessee style. Field & S 74:58-9+ Je '69
SUTTON, William Francis
Home for Christmas. il pors Newsweek 75:16+ Ja 5 '70
SUYDERHOUD, Mike
Winning our thing in Denmark. C. Kirkpatrick. il por Sports Illus 31:14-17 Ag 18 '69
SVEC, M. Melvina
Coming hundredweight unit. Ed Digest 35:50-1 O '69

SVEDA, Michael
HEW bans the cyclamates. Time 94:84-5 O 24 '69
SWADOS, Harvey
Old con, Black Panther, brilliant writer and quintessential American. N Y Times Mag p38-9+ S 7 '69
Writing teacher appraises his students. Writer 82:17-18 Ag '69
SWAHILI language
Story of Swahili, an in language. il U S News 66:82 Mr 31 '69
Swahili at City university of New York. Sch & Soc 97:86-7 F F '69
SWAIN, Donald C.
Founding of the National park service. Am West 6:6-9 S '69
SWAINE, Anthony
Port and town of Faversham, England. Antiques 96:88-90 Jl '69
SWAMP plants. See Bog vegetation
SWAMP rabbits hunting. See Rabbit hunting
SWAMPS. See Marshes
SWAN, Jon
Fortune; poem. New Yorker 45:30 Ja 10 '70
Tale for the longhouse; poem. New Yorker 45:30 Ag 16 '69
SWAN lake; ballet. See Ballets—Criticisms
SWANN, Brian
Bandusian spring; Darkness and deeper dark; Solitary singer; poems. Poetry 114:244-6 Jl '69
SWANS
Saved swan; trumpeter. Sci Am 220:46 F '69
Trumpeter is back. Sci Digest 65:28-9 Mr '69
SWANSON, D.
How to squeeze more storage space out of your kitchen. Pop Mech 131:174-7 Ja '69
SWANSON, Dean
(ed) See Lindner, R. Richard Lindner
SWANSON, Zula
Alaska's richest black. il pors Ebony 25:126 N '69
SWANSTON, David
First year at Federal city. Nation 208:594-6 My 12 '69
SWARTHMORE college, Swarthmore, Pa.
Requiem for Courtney Smith. P. Good. il Life 66:76B-76D+ My 9 '69
SWARTHOUT, Gladys
Obituary
Opera N il por 34:17 S 20 '69. F. Robinson
SWARTZ, William P. Jr
Managing a war on poverty. il por Nations Bsns 57:52-5 F '69
SWAZILAND
Swaziland tries independence. V. Wentzel. il Nat Geog 136:266-93 Ag '69
SWEARING
In my opinion: those bad words aren't so bad. M. Bernson. Seventeen 28:254 Ap '69
 See also
Blasphemy

Anecdotes, facetiae, satire, etc.

Obscenity gap. V. Gold. Nat R 21:597 Je 17 '69
SWEARINGEN, John Eldred, 1918–
Environmental pollution; address, November 6, 1969. Vital Speeches 36:118-21 D 1 '69
SWEATERS
GH guide to shopping for men's sweaters. Good H 169:162 D '69
SWEATING. See Perspiration
SWEAZEY, George E.
Sweazey at the UPUSA helm. Chr Today 13:43 Je 6 '69
SWEDBERG, Jack. See Scott, C. jt. auth.
SWEDEN
Letter from Sweden. S. Sontag. il Ramp Mag 8:23-38 Jl '69
 See also
Airplanes, Military—Sweden
Automobile industry and trade—Sweden
Ballet—Sweden
Colleges and universities—Sweden
Electronic apparatus industry and trade—Sweden
Gardens—Sweden
Libraries—Sweden
National parks and reserves—Sweden
Political parties—Sweden
Pollution—Sweden
Strikes—Sweden
Taxation—Sweden
Television broadcasting—Sweden
Theater—Sweden

Air force

Costs, budget pinch Swedish air force. W. C. Wetmore. il Aviation W 90:40-1+ Mr 24 '69

SWEDEN—*Continued*

Defenses
See also
Sweden—Air force

Economic conditions
How Sweden slowed inflation: success story. il U S News 66:25 Ap 7 '69

Economic policy
Letter from Stockholm. P. Siekman. Fortune 80:67+ N '69

Foreign relations
New neutrality. R. J. Korengold. Newsweek 74:31-2 S 1 '69
Sweden's plans for future aid; excerpts from After Vietnam, Sweden makes plans. R. Dudman. Cur 109:61-4 Ag '69
U.S. critic at Sweden's helm. U S News 67:22 O 13 '69
Where anti-U.S. action backfires. il U S News 67:95 N 10 '69

Industries
See also
Automobile industry and trade—Sweden
Iron mines and mining—Sweden

Moral conditions
New contraceptive society. J. R. Moskin. Look 33:50+ F 4 '69; Same abr. with title Sweden: the contraceptive society. Read Digest 94:225-6+ Ap '69
Sweden: the love image. N. Gittelson. Harp Baz 102:22-3+ Je '69

Politics and government
See also
Political parties—Sweden

Social conditions
See also
Women—Sweden

SWEDEN and the United States
See also
United States—Foreign opinion—Swedish
SWEDENBORG, Emanuel
Swedenborg: scientific saint. J. A. Eastman. por Chr Cent 86:156+ Ja 29 '69
SWEDENBORGIANISM. See New Jerusalem church
SWEDES
Letter from Sweden. S. Sontag. il Ramp Mag 8:23-38 Jl '69
SWEDES in the United States
See also
Bishop Hill, Ill.
SWEDISH cookery. See Cookery, Swedish
SWEDISH international liaison committee conference. See International conferences
SWEEN, Joyce A. See Mueller, S. A. jt. auth.
SWEENEY, George E. and Frank, J. A.
In case of drought: pump. Am City 84:76-8 Ja '69
SWEENEY, Jo A. See Sugrue, M. jt. auth.
SWEENEY, Patrick
Keeper of the key. M. S. Colwell. il por Am Heritage 20:49-53 Je '69
SWEENEY, Thomas
If Verne could look at NASA. Nat R 21:489-90 My 20 '69
SWEEP generators. See Signal generators
SWEEPERS, Street. See Street cleaning apparatus
SWEEPING, Street. See Street cleaning
SWEET, Gladys
Verdicts of history. T. J. Fleming. il por Am Heritage 20:74-80+ D '68
SWEET, Ossian
Verdicts of history. T. J. Fleming. il por Am Heritage 20:74-80+ D '68
SWEET breads. See Bread
SWEET clover. See Clover, Sweet
SWEET clover weevils
Sweetclover-weevil feeding deterrent B: isolation and identification. W. R. Akeson and others. bibliog il Science 163:293-4 Ja 17 '69
SWEET corn. See Corn, Sweet
SWEET gum
Sweet gum. C. E. Lewis. il Horticulture 46:14-15+ Ag '68
SWEET peas
Fragrant, candy-colored sweet pea. D. E. Stebbins. Am Home 72:72 Mr '69
Sweet pea color; plant now for next spring and summer. il Sunset 143:192 S '69
Sweet peas the easy way. D. M. Shuttleworth. Home Gard 56:39 F '69
SWEETBREADS. See Cookery—Meat

SWEETENING agents. See Sugar substitutes
SWEETSHADE
Sweetshade lives up to its name. il Sunset 142:216 Je '69
SWEEZY, Paul Marlor
Memories. P. Samuelson. Newsweek 73:83 Je 2 '69
SWEGLE, Wayne E.
What's new. See issues of Successful farming
SWEIG, Martin
Call Marty. por Newsweek 74:36 O 27 '69
McCormack faces life. il Newsweek 74:36 N 3 '69
Murky men from the Speaker's office. W. Lambert. il por Life 67:52-4+ O 31 '69
Scandals in Congress: the record. il por U S News 67:25-7 N 10 '69
Speaker's family. Time 94:18+ O 31 '69
Voloshen connection. por Time 94:26-7 O 24 '69
SWENERTON, Helene, and others
Zinc-deficient embryos: reduced thymidine incorporation. bibliog Science 166:1014-15 N 21 '69
SWENNUMSON, Paul D.
Kit Bright: poem. Engl J 58:138 Ja '69
SWENSON, Karen
Bridges; poem. Nation 209:701 D 22 '69
Farewell to Fargo; selling the house; poem. New Yorker 45:54 O 18 '69
SWENSON, May
Grain of our eye; poem. New Repub 161:28 D 6 '69
Inchworm; poem. New Repub 160:32 Ap 26 '69
Lowering (Arlington cemetery, June 8, 1968); poem. New Yorker 45:46 Je 7 '69
My face the night; I'll be; Fire Island; Beam; poems. Poetry 115:86-9 N '69
Seeing Jupiter; poem. New Yorker 45:40 D 20 '69
Sunbird settles to its nest; poem. New Yorker 45:133 My 10 '69
SWERDLOFF, Peter M.
Hopes and fears of blue-collar youth. Fortune 79:148-50+ Ja '69
SWEZEY, Kenneth M.
Experiments simulate space travel. Pop Sci 195:167-9 O '69
SWIFT, Joan
December; poem. Nation 208:382 Mr 24 '69
SWIFT, Jonathan
Classics revisited. K. Rexroth. Sat R 52:12+ Mr 22 '69
SWIFT, Michael R. and Finegold, M. J.
Myotonic muscular dystrophy: abnormalities in fibroblast culture. bibliog Science 165:294-5 Jl 18 '69
SWIFT; drama. See McCabe, E.
SWIFT and company
Can she continue to resist? attractive target for takeover. Forbes 103:48-9 Ap 1 '69
SWIFTSURE classic. See Yacht racing
SWIHART, Roy L.
Teacher negotiation and the role of the superintendent. bibliog f Clear House 43:533-5 My '69
SWIMMING
Everybody into the water! il Redbook 133:82-7 Je '69
Growing up to the legend; Spitz's comeback. il Time 94:49 Jl 25 '69
High-diving grandma. D. Bopf. Har Yrs 9:43 Je '69
Psyched up, not shaved down; Yale swimming team vs Stanford. W. F. Reed, jr. il Sports Illus 30:26-7 Mr 3 '69
Q. What makes Charlie swim? A. Jelly beans. W. F. Reed, jr. il Sports Illus 30:53-5 Mr 24 '69
Santa Clara holds a splashdown; International invitational swimming and diving meet. A. Verschoth. il Sports Illus 31:20-1 Jl 21 '69
They sent the boys to do a man's work; five Indiana freshmen win the NCAAs. W. F. Reed, jr. Sports Illus 30:67-8+ Ap 7 '69

Safety devices and measures
Drown-proofing tips for hunters. il Todays Health 47:56-7 S '69
Float to safety; drownproofing. W. S. Kals. il Todays Health 47:46-7 Je '69
See also
Life preservers

Study and teaching
Basic method to teach swimming. il Good H 169:147 Ag '69
Reluctant swimmer. E. T. Buchanan, 3d. il Camp Mag 41:14-15 Je '69

SWIMMING pools
Big pool for small cash. il Mech Illus 65:60-1+ Je '69
Elegant plunge. il House B 111:56-61 Ag '69
For a new way of life in your garden consider a swimming pool. il Home Gard 56: 32-40 Ag '69
How five families took the plunge, they now share this pool. il Sunset 143:127-8 N '69
Portable swimming pools, going strong. H. Silverman. il Parks & Rec 4:48-50+ Mr '69
Site was hopeless. il Sunset 143:74-5 Jl '69
Swimming plastic style. il Newsweek 73:63 Je 16 '69
Swimming pool? desert happening place. il Sunset 143:62-3 Ag '69
Swimming pools or bathtubs. Parks & Rec 4:11 Ag '69
Voter-planner's plea for sensible facilities; they should be functional and accessible. R. E. Everly. Parks & Rec 4:21-2+ Ag '69

Equipment
Light, buoyant pool pole. il Sunset 143:160 O '69
Plastic sheeting makes low-cost pool cover. S. Corsak. il Pop Mech 132:201 N '69
Wood decks at poolside. il Sunset 143:78-9 S '69

Heating
Solar heating for swimming pools. il Sunset 142:131-2 My '69

Maintenance and repair
How to reduce pool upkeep. J. H. Ingersoll. House B 111:62-3+ Ag '69

Sanitation
Swimming pool chemicals. il Consumer Rep 34:367-71 Jl '69

SWIMMING pools, Municipal
New pool helps keep city cool; Newark, N.J. il Am City 84:36 D '69

SWIMMING suits. See Bathing suits
SWIMSUITS. See Bathing suits
SWINBURNE, Algernon Charles
Swinburne; with introd. by J. Sparrow A. E. Housman. Am Scholar 39:59-79 Wint '69

SWINDLERS and swindling. See Fraud
SWINE
Hog extra; symposium. See issues of Farm journal
Nicotine hydrogen tartrate: effect on essential fatty acid deficiency in mature pigs. W. R. Allt and others. bibliog il Science 163:391 Ja 24 '69
Pigs, those true-blue Americans. R. C. Davids. il Sci Digest 66:18-21 S '69
What's new. R. J. Fee. See issues of Successful farming

Care
How to tackle hog stress. R. J. Fee. il Suc Farm 67:58-9 O '69

Confinement methods
European experience proves, dry sows do better in stalls. J. Russell. il Farm J 93:H9+ Ag '69

Diseases and pests
Hog you don't sell; porcine stress syndrome. D. Seim. il Farm J 93:H12+ F '69
Three-step treatment for dysentery. W. R. Prafka. Farm J 93:H19 F '69
See also
Hog cholera

Feeding
Specialized services, brand new menus. R. C. Black. il Farm J 93:H8-9+ Ap '69
Systematic swine feeding. R. J. Fee. il Suc Farm 67:30-1+ Ja; 40-1 F; 46-7+ Mr; 34-5+ Ap; 30-1 My '69
Three more pigs weaned per litter; mechanical sow. Pig mama. O. Bay. il Farm J 93:H8-9+ F '69

Grading and standardization
On the rail... the coming way to sell hogs? J. Russell. il Farm J 93:H16+ Ap '69
Who'll meet the booming demand for feeder pigs? J. Russell. il Farm J 93:H10-11+ Ap '69

Marketing
Cash in on bonus pigs. R. Wilmore. il Farm J 93:H7 Je '69
How much fat can we trim off hog marketing? B. Coffman. Farm J 93:H8+ Ag '69
On the rail... the coming way to sell hogs? J. Russell. il Farm J 93:H16+ Ap '69

Three ways to get paid for quality pork. J. Russell. Farm J 93:H7+ F '69
Why half of all hogs may be sold on contract in ten years. R. C. Black. il Farm J 93: H10+ F '69

Prices
Hogs are beautiful! il Farm J 93:H15 Ag '69
New way you can predict hog prices. C. W. Gifford. il Farm J 93:H7+ Ap '69
Price forecast. See issues of Farm journal

SWINE, Identification of
Which method for identifying hogs? il Suc Farm 67:65 O '69

SWINE breeding
Are you getting the most out of crossbreeding? R. J. Fee. il Suc Farm 67:30-1+ O '69
Gilts breed early with hormone help. D. Seim. Farm J 93:42B S '69
How much does flushing help litter size? Farm J 93:60B F '69
How to fit hogs into a grain farm. R. C. Black. il Farm J 93:H24 F '69
How to rebreed sows without weaning. A. Phelps. il Farm J 93:C12 Mr '69
Multiple-farrowing management tips. Suc Farm 67:A2 Mr '69
Third-month gestation tips boost pig profits. Suc Farm 67:54 O '69
What you can do to save more healthy pigs. W. R. Prafka. Farm J 93:H20 Ap '69

SWINE cholera. See Hog cholera
SWINE contracts. See Contracts, Agricultural
SWINE dysentery. See Swine—Diseases and pests

SWINE farms
Can they answer our need for more top quality pork? report from Europe. J. Russell. il Farm J 93:H8-9+ Je '69
Can they compete with the Corn Belt? hog operations in the Panhandle. R. Wilmore. il Farm J 93:H6-7+ S '69
Exciting changes ahead for hogs. R. J. Fee. il Suc Farm 67:24-5 Je '69
Hog factory on a hill. O. Bay. il Farm J 93:H18+ Ap '69

SWINE farrowing crates and pens
Confinement ideas you can use. R. J. Fee. il Suc Farm 67:41 Je '69
Farrowing ideas from a cow barn. R. J. Fee. il Suc Farm 67:36 N '69
Ideas that save time, and pigs. J. Bickers. il Farm J 93:H6+ Je '69
This month's cover story; Russ Jeckel's farrowing house. R. Fee. il Suc Farm 67:83 F '69

SWINE houses
Can a $30,000 hog setup pay off? R. J. Fee. il Suc Farm 67:32-3 Ag '69
Finishing house full of ideas. J. Russell. il Farm J 93:H8+ S '69
How to remodel pole buildings for hogs. R. J. Fee. il Suc Farm 67:47-9 N '69
Slick way to modify an open-front finishing house. J. Russell. il Farm J 93:34E S '69
Who pays for new barns, landlord or tenant? R. J. Fee. il Suc Farm 67:H4 S '69

Equipment
1,200 hogs a year in cool comfort. R. J. Fee. il Suc Farm 67:H8 S '69
See also
Swine—Confinement methods
Swine farrowing crates and pens

Fumigation
Fumigation can aid swine sanitation. Suc Farm 67:60 O '69

Heating and ventilation
How much ventilation for finishing house. R. J. Fee. il Suc Farm 67:84 Mr '69
Winter heat nets $5 more a hog. il Farm J 93:H11 F '69

SWING (golf)
Compensating for one error leads to another. J. Nicklaus. il Sports Illus 30:48 F 24 '69
Dear Jack: please help me. J. Nicklaus. il Sports Illus 30:36 Ja 20 '69
Learning how to play out of the sand. J. Nicklaus. il Sports Illus 31:43 Ag 18 '69
Try to keep your game from going tilt. J. Nicklaus. il Sports Illus 32:58 Ja 12 '70
When you're down and out, don't lift up your head... J. Nicklaus. il Sports Illus 31:68 N 10 '69
You're not out if you're down. J. Nicklaus. il Sports Illus 30:68 My 5 '69

SWINGS
How to swing when every branch slants. il Sunset 143:185 S '69

SWISHER, Viola Hegyi
Capturing the spirit along with the steps.
Dance Mag 43:70-4 O '69
Ken Berry on TV. Dance Mag 43:22-4 Jl '69
No one-and-only way to go; Gloria Newman
reflects on roots and influences. Dance Mag
43:56-8 Ag '69

SWISS
Switzerland, Europe's high-rise republic. T.
J. Abercrombie. il Nat Geog 136:68-113 Jl
'69

SWISS cookery. See Cookery, Swiss

SWITCH dealing. See Commercial treaties and
agreements

SWITCH trade. See Barter

SWITCHES, Electric. See Electric switches

SWITCHES, Railroad. See Railroads—Switches

SWITCHING systems
Amorphous-semiconductor switching. H. K.
Henisch. il Sci Am 221:30-41 bibliog(p 166)
N '69
Neons in photoconductive choppers. G. S.
Talbot. il Electr World 81:32-3 Ap '69

SWITZER, Ellen
Unless a remedy is applied at once... Redbook 133:65+ O '69

SWITZERLAND
See also
Airlines—Switzerland
Airplanes, Military—Switzerland
Architecture, Domestic—Switzerland
Banks and banking—Switzerland
Chur
Hotels, taverns, etc.—Switzerland
Lausanne
Lucerne
Lugano, Lake
Skis and skiing—Switzerland
Tourist trade—Switzerland
Trials—Switzerland

Description and travel
Switzerland, Europe's high-rise republic. T.
J. Abercrombie. il Nat Geog 136:68-113 Jl
'69
Up from Lucerne, by rail and cable. il Sunset
142:71-2 Mr '69

History
Bibliography
**Articles and other books received; comp. by
A. H. Price. See issues of American his-
torical review**

Social life and customs
Good, good life of the Alpine set. S. Birmingham. il McCalls 97:46-7+ Ja '70

SWIVEL stools. See Stools

SWOMLEY, John M. Jr
America as a militaristic society. Cath World
209:199-202 Ag '69
Ecumenism and the school aid issue. Chr
Cent 86:780-3 Je 4 '69
Why the draft should go. Nation 209:108-10
Ag 11 '69

SWOPE, George S.
Man at the top: what's he like? Nations Bsns
57:66-8+ N '69

SWORD, Jack
Free-lance writer and social security. Writer
82:27-9 Mr '69

SWORTZELL, Lowell
London bridge; drama. Plays 28:61-6 Ap '69

SYBARIS
Sybaris revisited. il Sci Digest 65:79-80 Mr
'69
Sybarite; interview. O. H. Bullitt. New Yorker 45:19-20 Jl 5 '69

SYCAMORE (platanus) See Plane trees

SYDNEY, Australia
See also
Stock exchange—Sydney, Australia

Architecture
Australia square. R. Boyd. il Arch Forum
130:26-35 Ap '69

Churches
Three lives of one church; Central Methodist
mission. A. Walker. Chr Cent 86:1594-6 D
10 '69

SYDNEY opera house. See Opera houses

SYKES, Lynn R.
Time for a theory. il Sci N 95:449-50 My 10
'69

La SYLPHIDE; ballet. See Ballets—Criticisms

SYLVESTER, David
Roy Lichtenstein, who paints with cool.
Vogue 154:142-5+ S 15 '69
(ed) See De Kooning, W. De Kooning's
women

SYLVESTER, Robert
Musical events; recital at Alice Tully Hall.
W. Sargeant. New Yorker 45:162 N 1 '69

SYMBIOSIS
Host finding by odor in the myrmecophilic
beetle atemeles pubicollis bris. (staphylinidae) B. Hölldobler. bibliog il Science 166:
757-8 N 7 '69
Maxillary mycangium in the mountain pine
beetle. H. S. Whitney and S. H. Farris.
bibliog il Science 167:54-5 Ja 2 '70

SYMBOLISM
Mythic symbols in two precolumbian myths.
C. A. Sarnoff. bibliog il Am Imago 26:3-20
Spr '69

SYMBOLISM in art
Flesh and filigree; exhibition at Toronto museum. M. Amaya. il Art N 68:24-7+ D '69
Manifest and the latent content of two paintings by Hieronymus Bosch. E. Fromm.
bibliog il Am Imago 26:145-66 Sum '69
Symbol and the mind. il UNESCO Courier
22:12-13 My '69

SYMBOLISM in literature
Eagle and the axe: a study of Whitman's
Song of the broad-axe. A. H. Rosenfeld.
bibliog f Am Imago 25:354-70 Wint '68
Flower power: a student's guide to pre-
hippie transcendentalism. P. H. Wild. Engl
J 58:62-8 Ja '69
Idea of the hero. S. Schwartz. Engl J 58:82-6
Ja '69
Man, the creative artist: an experiment; at
Vidalia high school, Concordia parish. La.
M. B. Eidt and R. C. Alwood. Engl J 58:
87-9 Ja '69
Personality of Belinda's baron: Pope's The
rape of the lock. J. Meyers. bibliog f Am
Imago 26:71-7 Spr '69
Stephen Crane's A mystery of heroism: some
redefinitions. P. Witherington. Engl J 58:
201-4+ F '69
Symbol hunting Golding's Lord of the flies.
J. Martin. Engl J 58:408-13 Mr '69
Trust the tale: a second reading of Lord of
the flies. L. Levitt. bibliog f Engl J 58:521-2
Ap '69
Truth about A separate peace. J. E. Devine.
Engl J 58:519-20 Ap '69

SYMBOLISM in music
Some aspects of word treatment in the music
of William Byrd. W. Gray. bibliog f il
Mus Q 55:45-64 Ja '69

SYMBOLISM of numbers
Doctor Matrix gives his explanation of why
Mr Nixon was elected President. M. Gard-
ner. il Sci Am 220:116-18+ Ja '69

SYMBOLS
Symbols for safety; uniform traffic control
devices. A. Rosenthal. il Todays Health 47:
48-51 Ag '69

SYMINGTON, Stuart
Against ABM deployment; a modern Maginot
line; interview. por U S News 67:29-31 Jl
14 '69
U.N. calls upon UNCURK to continue pursuit
of U.N. objectives in Korea; statement,
December 11, 1968. Dept State Bul 60:32-6
Ja 13 '69
U.S. gives views on formula for inviting
Korean representatives to U.N. debate;
statement, November 25, 1968. Dept State
Bul 59:712-16 D 30 '68

SYMMETRY (art) See Proportion (art)

SYMMETRY (physics)
Electrons in metals; adaptation of address,
October 1968. W. A. Harrison. bibliog il
Phys Today 22:23-31 O '69
Symmetries and quarks raise more questions
than solutions; report of meeting. J. A.
Campbell. Phys Today 22:93-5+ O '69
Universe's missing antimatter. D. E. Thom-
sen. il Sci N 96:562-3 D 13 '69

SYMONENKO, Vasyl
Diary of a Soviet Ukrainian poet: Vasyl
Symonenko; tr. by W. Odajnyk. Yale R
58:563-71 Je '69

SYMPATHECTOMY. See Nervous system—
Surgery

SYMPATHETIC nervous system. See Nervous
system

SYMPHONIC poems
See also
Phonograph records—Symphonic poems

SYMPHONIES
See also
Phonograph records—Symphonies

SYMPHONY of the New World, incorporated
Musical events; concert in Philharmonic Hall.
W. Sargeant. New Yorker 45:111+ D 20 '69

SYMPHONY orchestras. See Orchestras

SYMPLOCARPUS foetidus. See Skunk cabbages

SYMPTOMS of disease. See Diagnosis

SYNAGOGUES
Tent-like helix spirals up to create a temple sanctuary; Temple B'nai Jehudah complex, Kansas City. il Arch Rec 146:119-22 Jl '69

SYNANON foundation, incorporated
Close-up: Chuck Dederich, Mr Synanon goes public. S. O'Quin. il Life 66:36-8 Ja 31 '69
Second coming of Synanon. J. Kobler. il Sat Eve Post 242:32-4+ F 8 '69

SYNAPSES
Complex synaptic configurations in planarian brain. J. B. Best and J. Noel. bibliog il Science 164:1070-1 My 30 '69
Development of specific neuronal connections. M. Jacobson. bibliog il Science 163:543-7 F 7 '69
Electron microscopic radioautography: identification of origin of synaptic terminals in normal nervous tissue. A. Hendrickson. bibliog il Science 165:194-6 Jl 11 '69
One trillion times zero. H. C. Elliott. Yale R 58:549-62 Je '69
Permeability and structure of junctional membranes at an electrotonic synapse. B. W. Payton and others. bibliog il Science 166:1641-3 D 26 '69
Synaptic current at the squid giant synapse. P. W. Gage and J. W. Moore. bibliog il Science 166:510-12 O 24 '69
Synaptic vesicles in electron micrographs of freeze-etched nerve terminals. H. Moor and others. bibliog il Science 164:1405-7 Je 20 '69
Temperature-dependence of resistance at an electrotonic synapse. B. W. Payton and others. bibliog il Science 165:594-7 Ag 8 '69

SYNDICATES (finance)
See also
Cravens corporation

SYNERGISM
Western pine beetle: field response to its sex pheromone and a synergistic host terpene, myrcene. W. D. Bedard and others. bibliog il Science 164:1284-5 Je 13 '69

SYNOD of bishops, 1969
Bishops' conferences past and present. J. C. Haughey and D. R. Campion. America 121: 327-30 O 18 '69
Bishops' synod: before and after. J. M. Johnson. Chr Cent 86:1557-60 D 3 '69
Catholic bishops meet in Rome. A. Lunn. Nat R 21:1267-8 D 16 '69
Celibacy and the synod. America 120:556-7 My 10 '69
Collegiality and the synod. America 121:216 S 27 '69
Co-responsibility and the coming Synod. America 120:266 Mr 8 '69
Growing debate on the synod. America 121: 132 S 6 '69
House divided. il Newsweek 74:73 O 27 '69
How goes the Synod? America 121:372 N 1 '69
How Pope reacted to bids for change. il U S News 67:13 N 10 '69
Latest test for Catholic church. il U S News 67:42-3 N 3 '69
Letter from the Synod. D. R. Campion. America 121:351, 379, 412-13, 457+ O 25-N 15 '69
New roads for Rome. K. L. Woodward. il Newsweek 74:95-6 N 10 '69
No more cardinals? Commonweal 89:632-3 F 21 '69
Papacy enhanced. C. Northcott. Chr Cent 86:1443-4 N 12 '69
Pope: firm in face of challenge. il U S News 67:18 O 20 '69
Pope under fire. Time 94:90 O 17 '69
Pope's firm hand. R. Meachum. New Repub 161:15-16 N 22 '69
Prelates speak out. il Time 94:51 O 24 '69
Pre-synod conversation; interview, ed. by J. C. Haughey. A. Carter. America 121:233-4 S 27 '69
Reformists in command. il Time 94:68 O 31 '69
Roman Synod: room for democracy? Chr Today 14:50-1 O 24 '69
Roman Synod: speaking with candor to the Pope. B. Bastien. il Chr Today 14:36-7 N 21 '69
Synod of our discontent. H. ten Kortenaar. Commonweal 91:240-1 N 21 '69
Voice for bishops? il Newsweek 74:107-8 O 20 '69
What happened at the Synod? J. B. Sheerin. Cath World 210:98-9 D '69

What's ahead for the Synod? D. R. Campion. America 121:195-6 S 20 '69

SYNODS. See Councils and synods

SYNODS of bishops
Bishops' conferences past and present. J. C. Haughey and D. R. Campion. America 121: 327-30 O 18 '69

SYNTHESIS
See also
Biosynthesis

SYNTHETASES
Aminoacyl transfer ribonucleic acid synthetases from cell-free extract of plasmodium berghei. J. Ilan and J. Ilan. bibliog il Science 164:560-2 My 2 '69
Hormonal stimulation of lactose synthetase in mammary carcinoma. W. L. McGuire. bibliog il Science 165:1013-14 S 5 '69
Lactose synthetase: progesterone inhibition of the induction of the α-lactalbumin. R. W. Turkington and R. L. Hill. bibliog il Science 163:1458-60 Mr 28 '69

SYNTHETIC diamonds. See Diamonds, Artificial

SYNTHETIC fibers. See Textile fibers, Synthetic

SYNTHETIC food. See Food substitutes

SYNTHETIC grass. See Turf, Artificial

SYNTHETIC rope. See Rope

SYNTHETIC textile fabrics. See Textile fabrics, Synthetic

SYNTHETIC turf. See Turf, Artificial

SYPERT, Mary. See Ahlers, E. jt. auth.

SYPHER, Alden H.
Right or wrong! See issues of Nation's business

SYPHILIS
How could this happen to our daughter? L. David. Good H 169:86-7+ S '69

SYRACUSE, N.Y.

Galleries and museums
Syracuse: spatial diversity within a giant sculpture; Everson museum of art. J. Bailey. il Arch Forum 130:56-61 Je '69

Music
Report: Syracuse; six performances of The barber of Seville. L. C. McGinn. Opera N 33:31 Mr 8 '69

SYRIA
See also
United Arab Republic

Foreign relations
Instability in Syria. G. H. Torrey. Cur Hist 58:13-15+ Ja '70

Politics and government
Debate, Damascus style. il Time 93:38 Mr 14 '69
Instability in Syria. G. H. Torrey. Cur Hist 58:13-15+ Ja '70
Standoff at the top. il Newsweek 73:63+ Mr 17 '69

SYSTEM development corporation
Software giant goes commercial; dropping nonprofit status. il Bsns W p84+ Ag 23 '69

SYSTEM simulation
See also
Computers—Simulation programs

SYSTEMIC insecticides. See Insecticides

SYSTEMS analysis
Cure for chaos, by S. Ramo. Review Commonweal 90:321-3 My 30 '69. T. M. Conrad
Limitations of systems analysis. H. J. Hartley. Ed Digest 35:28-31 O '69
Systems analysis? What's that? bibliog il Changing T 23:41-5 Ag '69
Urban use of systems analysis stressed. R. S. Kahn. Aviation W 90:103-4 My 12 '69
See also
Flow charts

SYSTEMS analysis in rapid transit
Systems analysis of urban transportation. W. F. Hamilton, 2d. and D. K. Nance. il Sci Am 221:19-27 Jl '69

SYSTEMS analysis in urban renewal
Daring look at city ills. il Bsns W p 142+ Je 14 '69

SYSTEMS engineering
Systems building: what it really means. il Arch Rec 145:147-54 Ja '69
What the systems approach means to air conditioning. R. E. Fischer and F. J. Walsh. il Arch Rec 145:197-204 Ap; 146:151-8 Ag; 165-72 N '69
See also
Systems management

SYSTEMS management
Ogden engineers a total system; to solve Morocco's problems. il Bsns W p58+ Mr 15 '69

SYZ, Hans
Some oriental aspects of European ceramic decoration. bibliog Antiques 95:670-81; 96: 91-9; 209-13 My, Jl-Ag '69

SZABADVARY, Ferenc
Great moments in chemistry; tr. by R. E. Oesper. Chem 42:14-16 Ap; 6-9 D '69

SZALAY, Lajos
Inspired drawings of Lajos Szalay. N. Kent. il pors Am Artist 33:66-71+ D '69

SZAMUELY, Tibor
Intellectuals and conservatism. Nat R 21:273-7 Mr 25 '69

about

Campus near-Fascism. America 120:350-1 Mr 29 '69

SZASZ, Suzanne
Security is a thumb and a blanket. Good H 168:74+ Ap '69

SZASZ, Thomas S.
Mental illness is not a disease; interview, ed. by J. Ecker and B. Diasio. pors Sci Digest 66:7-14 D '69

SZEGLIN, Charles B.
Can we get the dinosaurs out of the cellar? Sch Arts 68:18-20 Mr '69

SZELL, George
Gospel of Beethoven as Szell is his prophet. I. Kolodin. Sat R 52:62-3 N 29 '69
Music to my ears; performance of Mozart's D-major concerto. I. Kolodin. Sat R 52:50 D 13 '69
Musical events: performance of Mahler's Ninth symphony by Cleveland symphony orchestra. New Yorker 44:94 F 15 '69

SZENT-GYÖRGYI, Albert
Dual world of man: reflections on science and government. Bul Atom Sci 25:33-4+ O '69
Science and budget cutting; address, September 10, 1969. Bul Atom Sci 25:16-17 D '69

SZERYNG, Henryk
No violinist does unaccompanied Bach quite like Henryk Szeryng. M. Sherwin. Hi Fi 19: 86 Mr '69

SZIDON, Jan P. and others
Traube-Hering waves in the pulmonary circulation of the dog. bibliog Science 164: 75-6 Ap 4 '69

SZIGETI, Joseph
Memories of Charles Munch. Hi Fi 19:MA15 Mr '69

SZILARD, Leo
Journey to California. N. Cousins. Sat R 52:20-1 Mr 1 '69

SZOKOLAY, Sándor
Records:
Blood wedding. Opera N 33:35 F 8 '69

SZOLLOSI, Daniel
Unique envelope of a jellyfish ovum: the armed egg. bibliog Science 163:586-7 F 7 '69

SZOLNOKI, Rose
My son the quarterback; excerpts from letters, ed. by B. Verigan. Look 33:37-8 S 9 '69

SZULC, Tad
Letter from Bucharest. New Yorker 45:105-6+ S 6 '69

SZUPROWICZ, Bohdan
Computers: shake-out in time sharing? Duns R 93:87-8+ Ap '69

SZYMANSKI, Eugene S.
Graph for estimating position errors. Motor B 123:432-3 Ja '69
Position finding at sea. Motor B 123:68-71 Ap '69

T

TACV (tracked air cushion vehicle) See Air cushion vehicles
TADF. See Thomas A. Dooley foundation
T-groups. See Group relations training
THC
1-Δ⁹-tetrahydrocannabinol; neurochemical and behavioral effects in the mouse. D. Holtzman and others. bibliog il Science 163:1464-7 Mr 28 '69
Trouble with THC; tetrahydrocannabinol. il Time 93:58 Ja 24 '69
Warning: steer clear of THC. R. H. Berg. Look 33:46 Ap 15 '69

TOPS (take off pounds sensibly) See Corpulence

TRW, incorporated
Growth management of TRW. L. Geist. il Duns R 92:30-4+ D '68
It can't happen here; no trouble controlling diverse product lines. il Forbes 104:19-20 Jl 1 '69

TRW systems. See TRW, incorporated
TSH. See Thyrotropin
T squares. See Drawing instruments
TV dinners. See Buffet meals
TWA. See Trans World airlines

TABARLY, Eric
Record passage. A. Colas. il por Yachting 125:58-60+ Ap '69
Solo breed. il por Newsweek 73:86 Mr 31 '69

TABELL, Anthony
Found: two bulls. C. Morgello. il Newsweek 73:71 Je 30 '69

TABER, Gladys
Make it personal. Writer 82:15-17 Ap '69

TABLE, The. See Table setting

TABLE decoration
Build these musical centerpieces. il Pop Mech 130:154-7+ D '68
Dramatic settings. E. Craster. il Bet Hom & Gard 47:80-5 N '69
Freehand arrangements for two. S. Lindsay. il House B 111:50-1 Jl '69
How color works for a party. il House & Gard 135:118-19 Mr '69
Set an enchanting table. il Good H 168:146-51 Ap '69
Three imaginative hostesses delight in tradition breakers. il House & Gard 135:50-5 F '69
Vegetable bouquets for pretty tables. il House & Gard 136:150-3 S '69
See also
Party favors

TABLE football. See Games

TABLE setting
Dramatic settings. E. Craster. il Bet Hom & Gard 47:80-5 N '69
Far-flung look at star-quality dining. il House B 111:99-109 N '69
Flower-cart tables. E. Craster. il Bet Hom & Gard 47:78 Je '69
Marvelous mix. S. Lindsay. il House B 111: 110-13 N '69
Settings pretty. il Redbook 134:96-9 N '69
Snap of black and white. il House & Gard 135:110-13 My '69
Tables set for pleasure. il McCalls 97:98-103 N '69

TABLE silver. See Silverware

TABLE tennis
No defense against murder; championships, Munich. D. Miles. il Sports Illus 30:70+ My 5 '69
Outdoor ping-pong table. J. Capotosto. il Mech Illus 65:116-17 Ap '69

TABLES
Bountiful collection of tables. il Good H 169:127-33 N '69
Build these two handsome tables in your workshop; room-matching step table and TV table stores standing. R. Capotosto; D. Jordan. il Pop Mech 131:158-61+ Mr '69
Dimensions for dining. il House B 111:126-7 N '69
Elegant dining: an I table and a set of cube chairs. K. Isaacs. il Pop Sci 195:162-6 O '69
Fake butcher block coffee table. il Mech Illus 65:94-5 Ap '69
Frame is angle iron, everything else is solid walnut. il Sunset 142:140+ My '69
Game table for your playroom. il Pop Mech 132:148-51 Ag '69
Is this tile pattern a new math discovery? A. Earle. il Pop Sci 195:150-1+ Jl '69
It's a folding, rolling ping-pong table. il Sunset 142:135 Ap '69
Maple table, heavy and handsome. il Sunset 142:127-8 Mr '69
Real lightweight table. il Mech Illus 65:120-1+ N '69
Tables and more tables. il Redbook 134:72-5+ Ja '70
Telephone end tables with built-in directories. W. C. Leckey. il Pop Mech 132:170-3+ N '69
Up it's a table, down it's a pad. il Sunset 143:70 Ag '69
Venetian marble coffee table. il Mech Illus 65:90-1+ O '69

Anecdotes, facetiae, satire, etc.

Content of tables: conference tables, 1969-2169. H. F. Ellis. New Yorker 45:102+ F 22 '69

TALESE, Gay
New York times; excerpt from The kingdom
and the power (cont) Harper 238:40-8+ F '69
Quiet revolution in the palace; excerpts from
The kingdom and the power. Esquire 71:95-
107+ Ap '69
about
Life and Times of Gay Talese. J. Leo. Com-
monweal 91:66-8 O 17 '69
TALIESIN West. See Frank Lloyd Wright
school of architecture
TALK. See Children—Language
TALKING books
See also
Recording for the blind, incorporated
TALKING typewriters. See Teaching machines
TALLADEGA 500. See Automobile racing
TALLIS, Thomas
Thomas Tallis: a pair of indispensable re-
cordings. J. W. Barker. Am Rec G 36:95
O '69
TALLULAH, La.
Black lawman in KKK territory. C. L.
Sanders. il Ebony 25:57-60+ Ja '70
TALMEY, Allene
Drugs, parents, & adolescents. Vogue 155:
142-3 Ja 1 '70
Pill popping. Vogue 154:104-5 N 15 '69
Splitting headaches. Vogue 155:158-9+ Ja 15
'70
Your allergies: what doctors know and may
do right now. Vogue 154:122-3 Ag 15 '69
Your eyes: medical experiments you've never
known before. Vogue 153:104-5 Mr 15 '69
TALOUMIS, George
Flowers for seaside gardens. Horticulture 47:
30-3+ Ap '69
Hearst gardens. il Horticulture 46:40-3 D '68
How to winter geraniums. Horticulture 46:
33+ N '68
Touch of gray. il Horticulture 47:28-31+
Mr '69
TAMING of the shrew; ballet. See Ballets—
Criticisms
TAMM, Igor. See Caliguiri, L. A. jt. auth.
TAMM, S. L. See Horridge, G. A. jt. auth.
TAMOSAITIS, John
Power FET. Electr World 81:34-5+ Je '69
TAMPA, Fla.
Airports
Giant jets key to Tampa airport growth. B.
K. Thomas. il Aviation W 91:44-5 Ag 18 '69
Tampa's new air terminal to seek traffic
from overseas carriers. B. K. Thomas.
Aviation W 90:41-2 Je 30 '69
TAMPA international airport. See Tampa, Fla.
—Airports
TAMPLIN, Arthur R.
Fetal and infant mortality and the environ-
ment. Bul Atom Sci 25:23-9 D '69
TAN
If you don't like burns, stay out of the sun.
Bsns W p 113 Jl 12 '69
Look you like. L. Allen. Todays Health 47:4
Je '69
On getting a suntan. il Chem 42:5 Mr '69
Tan plan. il Mlle 69:190-1 My '69
Who Ra? il Motor B 124:62+ Ag '69
Your place in the sun. P. Van Wagenen. il
Parents Mag 44:26 Je '69
TANCOCK, John
Is Brancusi still relevant? Art N 68:40-3+
O '69
TANDY corporation
Hobby man; C. Tandy's business. il Forbes
104:52 N 15 '69
TANG, Chung-wai, and Maletskos, C. J.
Elimination of sodium-24 and potassium-
42 interferences in activation analysis of
biological samples. bibliog Science 167:52-
4 Ja 2 '70
TANGANYIKA. See Tanzania
TANGE, Kenzō
Kenzo Tange: interview. ed. by C. Jones.
Travel & Camera 32:52-5 O '69
about
Master builder for the world. C. Lucas. il por
Read Digest 94:155-60 F '69
TANGLEWOOD music festival. See Berkshire
symphonic festival
TANGO; drama. See Mrozek, S.
TANHAM, George K. and Duncanson, D. J.
Some dilemmas of counterinsurgency. For
Affairs 48:113-22 O '69
TANK airplanes
Boeing proposes tanker version of 747. Avia-
tion W 91:35 Ag 11 '69
TANK ships
Name of the Shell game: tankers. Bsns W
p58 Mr 8 '69

Oil on the waters. E. Cowan. Nation 208:304-
7 Mr 10 '69
Search for Golconda; converting biggest tank-
er in the U.S. merchant fleet into an ice-
breaker to open route to Arctic oil. il
Newsweek 73:77+ Mr 10 '69
Supertankers face troubles. Bsns W p47-8
Ja 10 '70
Weakness in size; Gulf oil tankers. il Time
93:77 My 30 '69
See also
Ice breaking vessels
TANK trucks
SAE fuel truck standards set for giant jets.
Aviation W 91:189 O 20 '69
TANKERS. See Tank ships
TANKS
See also
Water tanks
TANKS, Military
Army fights assault on tanks; problems with
Sheridan and MBT-70. il Bsns W p48-9 Ag
9 '69
Calculated risk; defects in Sheridan tank.
Nation 209:3-4 Jl 7 '69
Stratton's blast damages army tanks. Bsns
W p33 O 4 '69
Trouble now for U.S. army's tank of future;
plans for a new main battle. il U S News
66:12 Mr 24 '69
TANNAHILL, Robert
One man's fancy. il Time 94:68-9 N 28 '69
TANNAHILL collection. See Detroit institute
of arts
TANNENBAUM, Edward R.
Goals of Italian fascism; excerpts from The
fascist experience. bibliog f Am Hist R 74:
1183-204 Ap '69
TANNENBAUM, Frank
On talking across the generation gap. B. L.
Masse. America 120:661 Je 7 '69
TANNER, Henry Ossawa
Art of Henry O. Tanner; Washington ex-
hibition. il pors Ebony 24:60-2+ O '69
Methodist in Paris. il Time 94:58-9 Jl 11 '69
TANNER, Laurel N.
Teacher behavior and the destructive critics.
bibliog f Sch & Soc 97:366-7+ O '69
TANNER, R. See Hotti, G. jt. auth.
TANNER, Robert
How to make millions without really work-
ing. il por Time 93:94 Ap 11 '69
TANNING
Tanning animal hides: how the experts do
it. P. M. Williams. il Sci Digest 66:80-3
O '69
TANSEY, Anne
Symbol and sign; poem. Cath World 208:229
F '69
TANTRUMS. See Temper
TANUMA, T.
Gallery; photographs. por(p 1) Life 67:4-7 Ag
1 '69
TANZANIA
Ideology for Africa. H. Bienen. For Affairs
47:545-59 Ap '69
See also
Conservation of resources—Tanzania
East African Federation (proposed)
Kilimanjaro
Mines and mineral resources—Tanzania
National parks and reserves—Tanzania
Foreign relations
Tanzania; stability and change in Africa;
address, October 2, 1969. J. K. Nyerere.
Vital Speeches 36:48-53 N 1 '69
Religious institutions and affairs
Africa hails a president, prepares for Pope.
O. Okite. Chr Today 13:30-1 My 23 '69
TANZANITE
New and hard to come by. il Time 93:56 Ja
24 '69
Really beautiful stuff. H. H. Brayman. il
Sci Digest 65:70-2 My '69
Tanzania to Tiffany's. T. Thompson. il Life
66:70-6 My 9 '69
TANZER, Michael
Out on the credit limb. Nation 208:686-9 Je
2 '69
TANZLER, Hans G. Jr
Business is solving a city's problems. por Na-
tions Bsns 57:56-9 Jl '69
TAOS, N.Mex.
Are you listening, D. H. Lawrence? E. Wit-
ten. New Repub 161:15-17 O 18 '69
Paradise rocked; hippie community. il Time
93:55 Je 20 '69
Passionate skier; ski valley. J. Egan. il Sat R
52:42-4 D 27 '69

TAP dancing
Jazz; Monday nights at the Bert Wheeler theatre. W. Balliett. New Yorker 45:143-4 My 17 '69
Tap happening. P. O'Connor. il Dance Mag 43:40-2 Ag '69
Tap happening: a reminisce with Chuck Green and jazz dance, Bert Wheeler theatre. J. Dowlin. Dance Mag 43:82+ Je '69

TAPE, Magnetic. See Magnetic tape

TAPE cartridges. See Magnetic tape

TAPE cassettes See Magnetic tape

TAPE-recorded diaries. See Diaries

TAPE recorders and recording. See Magnetic recorders and recording

TAPE recordings
Herb Alpert: everybody's music maker; interview. H. Alpert. il Am Home 72:86-7+ O '69
Sales of pre-recorded tapes soar. Electr World 82:68 O '69
Sound of music (jingle, jingle) tapes vs records. il Forbes 104:47-8 O 1 '69
Tape and the English market. T. Heinitz. Sat R 52:55 D 27 '69
Tape deck. R. D. Darrell. See issues of High fidelity incorporating Musical America
    See also
Oral history

Stereophonic recordings
Double stereo; Vanguard's open-reel, four-channel tape releases. Newsweek 74:89-90 S 8 '69

TAPER, Bernard
Our far-flung correspondents. New Yorker 45:123-4+ Ap 19 '69
Performing arts. Harper 239:40-2+ D '69

TAPESTRY
European tapestry; an Antiques survey. R. Davidson. il Antiques 96:912-17 D '69
Tapestry by Mona Hessing. il Craft Horiz 29:30-3 Jl '69

Exhibitions
Evidence of mestizaje in Peruvian tapestries; exhibition at Textile museum, Washington, D.C. E. P. Birk. il Antiques 95:346+ Mr '69
Lausanne: International tapestry biennale. J. L. Larsen. il Craft Horiz 29:14-19 S '69

TAPIOLA, Finland
Finland I: what free men can do. N. Gittelson. Harp Baz 102:24+ Ja '69

TAPPETT, Tom
Car care. See issues of Mechanix illustrated

TAPPLY, H. G.
Sportsman's notebook. See issues of Field & stream

TAPS
Don't play taps for broken taps. W. E. Burton. il Pop Mech 131:200-2 Ap '69

TAR pits, Los Angeles. See La Brea, Los Angeles

TARBOX, Raymond
Death in Venice: the aesthetic object as dream guide. bibliog Am Imago 26:123-44 Sum '69

TARGA Florio, Sicily. See Automobile racing

TARGET practice. See Shooting

TARGETS, Archery. See Archery

TARHEEL state. See North Carolina

TARIFF
President asks study of effects of certain tariff items. Dept State Bul 61:339 O 20 '69
Trade; a vision for the 70's; address, September 17, 1969. A. K. Watson. Vital Speeches 36:2-5 O 15 '69
    See also
Free trade and protection

United States
If tariffs replace oil import quotas. il Bsns W p 17-18 D 20 '69

TARIQ Ali. See Ali, T.

TARKENTON, Fran
Football unscrambled. Ladies Home J 86:49+ O '69

TARNAWSKY, Patricia W.
Oriental love affair. Read Digest 94:187-8+ F '69

TARPAULINS
You can't top a tarp. C. B. Colby. il Outdoor Life 144:12+ D '69

TARPON fishing
High-flying tarpon. J. Brooks. il Outdoor Life 144:74-6+ Jl '69
Slugger turns to tarpon. V. Dunaway. il Field & S 73:60-3+ F '69
Tarpon madness. G. Heinold. il Outdoor Life 143:82-3+ Ap '69

TARPONS
Life and death of a tarpon; with paintings by S. Meltzoff. Sports Illus 30:32-7 F 24 '69

TARPS. See Tarpaulins

TARRAGONA, Spain
Road to Tarragona. F. T. Mitchell. il Harp Baz 102:160+ O '69

TARRANT, John J.
Why sales executives fail? Nations Bsns 57:100-2 S '69

TARSHISH, Manuel B.
Brentano's returns to White Plains. Pub W 195:45-6 Ap 7 '69
Fourth avenue book trade. Pub W 196:52-5 O 20; 50-3 O 27; 40-3 N 3 '69
From Scarsdale to Korea: Operation bookshelf. Pub W 195:28-9 My 26 '69
Museum shop thrives. Pub W 195:123-5 Je 2 '69
Paperback bookshop ups volume to $150,000 in five years. Pub W 195:43-4 Mr 24 '69
Selling art books in a suburban store. Pub W 195:77-8 Ap 28 '69

TARSKI, Alfred
Truth and proof; with biographical sketch. Sci Am 220:14, 63-70+ bibliog(p 144) Je '69

TARTARS (tribes) See Tatars

TARTS
Glorious Victorias; chocolate tarts. C. Claiborne. il N Y Times Mag p88 Mr 9 '69
Sweet cheese tart; with recipes. E. Alston. il Look 33:77 Ap 15 '69

TASAKI, I. and others
Fluorescence change during conduction in nerves stained with acridine orange. bibliog Science 163:683-5 F 14 '69

TASCH, Paul, and Riek, E. F.
Permian insect wing from Antarctic Sentinel Mountains. bibliog Science 164:1529-30 Je 27 '69

TASHKENT, Russia
Pages from a Tashkent diary. R. Styron. Vogue 154:240+ S 1 '69

TASMANIA
Tasmania. H. E. Mercer. il Travel 131:44-51 Je '69
    See also
Macquarie Island

TASTE
On developing discriminating taste in food. V. T. Habeeb. Am Home 72:50+ N '69
Orphan senses; research at the Monell chemical senses center. C. Weathersbee. il Sci N 95:241-2 Mr 8 '69
Taste nerve fibers; a random distribution of sensitivities to four tastes. M. Frank and C. Pfaffmann. bibliog il Science 164:1183-5 Je 6 '69

TASTE (aesthetics) See Aesthetics

TATARS
Tartars' case; Crimean Tartars to be tried for slander. Newsweek 73:40 Ap 7 '69

TATE, Binnie
Integrating culture: a credo for believers. bibliog Library J 94:2053-6 My 15 '69

TATE, James
Cryptozoa; Square at dawn; Blue booby; Pride's crossing; poems. Poetry 114:25-8 Ap '69

TATE, Joan
Sam & me; story. Seventeen 28:156-9 Mr '69

TATE, Ralph M.
Artist sculptures JFK doodles. il pors Ebony 24:46-8+ O '69

TATE, Sharon
Demon of death valley. il Time 94:22+ D 12 '69
Ghoulish moguls. Chr Cent 86:1186 S 17 '69
In Hollywood, the dead keep right on dying. B. Farrell. por Life 67:4 N 7 '69
Night of horror. il por Time 94:16-17 Ag 22 '69
Nothing but bodies. il por Time 94:24 Ag 15 '69
Tate set. il por Newsweek 74:24-5 Ag 25 '69
Tragic house on the hill. T. Thompson. il pors Life 67:42-6+ Ag 29 '69

TATE gallery, London
Tate vs. St Katharine's dock. J. Russell. Art N 68:9 Sum '69

TATKO, Daniel, and Brown, Carol
Underground and new left press. por Wilson Lib Bul 43:648-52 Mr '69

TATSUMURA, Kazuko. See Norman, B. jt. auth.

TATTLER, pseud.
Congressional dirty linen. Commonweal 91:327-8 D 12 '69

TATUM, Nancy
True grit; ed. by J. Rockwell. por Opera N 34:30 Ja 10 '70

TAUBE, John
Graduate student. por Phys Today 22:26-8 Mr '69

TAUBENFELD, Howard J. See Taubenfeld. R. F. jt. auth.

TAUBENFELD, Rita F. and Taubenfeld, H. J.
International implications of weather modification. Bul Atom Sci 25:43-5 Ja '69

TAUBER, Henrik. See Dansgaard, W. jt. auth.

TAUPIN, Jean Louis
Avignon: the surroundings of the Palace of the popes. il Antiques 96:409-11 S '69

TAUSK, Petr M. and Dreyfuss, Jane
Czech points on surrealism. il Mod Phot 33:74-5+ S '69

TAUSSIG, Helen Brooke
Consequences of science; heart transplants: a time to wait. Cur 108:43-5 Je '69

TAVARES, Aurelio de Lyra
Camouflaging the braid. por Time 94:39 S 12 '69

TAVEL, Ronald
Boy on the straight-back chair. Criticism
America 120:600 My 17 '69
New Yorker 45:102+ Mr 29 '69
Newsweek il 73:113 Mr 24 '69

TAVENER, C. F. See Reusswig, F. W. jt. auth.

TAVERNIA, Patrick
Bring 'em back alive. pors Opera N 33:8-11 F 1 '69

TAVES, Isabella
Astrology: fun, fraud or key-hole to the future? Look 33:96-8+ My 13 '69
Is there a sleepwalker in the house? Todays Health 47:40-1+ My '69; Same abr. with title Twilight world of the sleepwalker. Read Digest 95:95-8 Ag '69
Long John Nebel. Look 33:86+ Mr 18 '69

TAX auditing
Don't panic if IRS calls you in. Bsns W p 129 Ap 19 '69
If they challenge your tax return. il Changing T 23:29-30 Ap '69
What happens if computers pick out your tax return. il U S News 67:69-70 S 8 '69
What really happens to your tax return. il Nations Bsns 57:34-7 Mr '69

TAX billing. See Billing

TAX collection
See also
United States—Internal revenue service

TAX consultants
See also
Benevest, incorporated
Block, H. & R. incorporated

TAX credits. See Investment tax credit

TAX deductions. See Income tax—Deductions

TAX evasion
Capitalizing the arts; public companies purchase of writers and performers private service companies in Great Britain. il Forbes 104:55-6+ O 1 '69
How to stay out of trouble with IRS; tax informers. R. S. Holzman. il Nations Bsns 57:28-31 D '69
Nassau basks in new business climate: lure: no taxes. il Bsns W p 118+ Mr 22 '69
Nobody here but us foreigners? money smugglers. il Forbes 103:24-7 My 1 '69
Significant developments in tax administration; organized crime; address, October 6, 1969. R. W. Thrower. Vital Speeches 36: 73-7 N 15 '69
Sophistication comes to the tax havens. R. Beardwood. il Fortune 79:94-7+ F '69
Taxing experience; Americans building constitutionally. Time 94:57 Ag 8 '69
Those tax-free millionaires. U S News 67: 80 O 20 '69
Ways to escape taxes entirely. Time 93:86 Ap 4 '69
See also
Taxation, Exemption from

TAX exemption. See Taxation, Exemption from

TAX law. See Taxation—Law

TAX legislation. See Legislation

TAX loopholes. See Taxation, Exemption from

TAX loss farming. See Agriculture—Economic aspects

TAX planning
How to save on taxes. U S News 67:75-7 N 24 '69
Official tax calendar for 1969. Nations Bsns 57:44-7+ Ja '69
Take it easy when selling for a tax loss. Bsns W p 135-6 N 8 '69
Tax-loss selling drags Dow down. il Bsns W p24 D 20 '69

Tax strategy, for a good year, for a poor year. F. Bailey, jr. Suc Farm 67:30-1 Ag '69
Tips for your end-of-year tax strategy. Suc Farm 67:7 D '69
See also
Estate planning

TAX reduction. See Taxation—United States

TAX relations, intergovernmental. See Intergovernmental tax relations

TAX returns
Fill out your 1040 tax form like an expert. P. Lindberg. il Bet Hom & Gard 47:6+ F '69
How not to overpay your income taxes. H. Ulrich. Mech Illus 65:56-7 Mr '69
No tax returns for five million persons? U S News 67:94 O 13 '69
Save money on income taxes. G. Town. il Har Yrs 9:22-4 F '69
Tax reform: the time is now. J. W. Barr. il Sat R 52:22-5 Mr 22 '69
Warning to taxpayers; interview. S. S. Cohen. U S News 66:36-9 F 3 '69
What really happens to your tax return. il Nations Bsns 57:34-7 Mr '69

Auditing
See Tax auditing

TAX selling. See Tax planning

TAX sharing. See Intergovernmental tax relations

TAX write-off program. See Amortization deductions

TAXATION
Need for a reappraisal of American tax policies. M. A. Kriz. il Ann Am Acad 379:114-22 S '68
Tax burden in the United States and other countries. R. Goode. bibliog f il Ann Am Acad 379:83-93 S '68
See also
Corporations—Taxation
Income tax
Intergovernmental tax relations
Real property and taxation
also subhead Taxation under various subjects, e.g. Air travel—Taxation

Law
How Nixon would aid the poor and hit the rich. Newsweek 73:81-2 My 5 '69
Improving the tax code; address, December 12, 1968. S. S. Cohen. Vital Speeches 35: 267-70 F 15 '69
Moves to patch the loopholes; Presidential reform proposals. W. D. Slawson. Nation 208:760-4 Je 16 '69
New and unintelligible; revenue code. Nat R 21:975 S 23 '69
Tax changes Nixon wants: what they mean to you; with excerpts from President Nixon's message, April 21, 1969. il U S News 66:27-9 My 5 '69
Tax reform: something for nearly everybody. il U S News 67:49-50 D 29 '69
Top executives look at tax reform. il Duns R 93:44-6 Ap '69

Rates and tables
Tax reform: the time is now. J. W. Barr. il Sat R 52:22-5 Mr 22 '69

Bahama Islands
Nassau basks in new business climate; lure: no taxes. il Bsns W p 118+ Mr 22 '69

California
Ronnie show; tax cut of 10 per cent. il Time 93:29 F 14 '69

Canada
Canadian tax report and the American tax system. H. M. Groves. bibliog f Ann Am Acad 379:94-101 S '68
Hitting the big taxpayers a bit harder. Bsns W p 170 N 22 '69

Europe, Western
Quarrel that endangers trade: value-added taxes. il Time 93:89 F 14 '69

Great Britain
Britain's resistance to painful cures. Time 93: 104 Ap 25 '69
Capitalizing the arts. il Forbes 104:55-6+ O 1 '69

Ireland
Tax break for artists. R. Gelatt. Sat R 52:28 N 15 '69

Latin America
Taxes: Latin Americans paying up. U S News 66:88-9 Mr 24 '69

TAXATION—*Continued*

Sweden

If you think taxes are high in the U.S.—. il
U S News 66:91-2 Ap 21 '69

United States

Are you getting the most tax advantages
from your investments? P. Lindberg. Bet
Hom & Gard 47:8+ Jl '69

As showdown nears on the surtax; other tax
proposals. U S News 66:5 Je 30 '69

As tax reforms take shape. il U S News
67:65-6 D 15 '69

Bad medicine for a sick economy; amendment to tax bill passed by Senate. il Newsweek 74:25-6 D 15 '69

Basic issues of tax reform; with editorial comment. il Bsns W p 130-2, 172 F 22 '69

Billion in bond issues, but taxpayers' revolt
is still on. il U S News 67:120-2 N 17 '69

Bleak day for inflation fighters. il Bsns W
p61-2 D 6 '69

Break for everybody. Newsweek 74:56 Ag 11
'69

Burden of taxes, the need of reform. il Life
66:36 Ap 4 '69

Can museums survive tax reform? T. B.
Hess. Art N 68:27 O '69

Disappointing try at tax reform. Fortune
80:61-2 D '69

Distributing the tax burden. America 121:
486 N 22 '69

Dividing up the tax cuts; the fight in Congress. il U S News 67:105-7 S 22 '69

Down again, up again; proposals for 1971.
Newsweek 75:70 Ja 19 '70

Fair is fair; proposed reforms of the tax laws.
Commonweal 89:666 F 28 '69

Federal tax reform. D. T. Smith. Ann Am
Acad 379:102-13 S '68

First look at House plan for tax tightening; who's hit. U S News 66:79-82 Je 9 '69

Fiscal revolution in America, by H. Stein.
Review
Bsns W il p88-90 My 3 '69
Sat R 52:25 Ag 16 '69. A. Smithies

Foundations feel heat of tax reform; House
committee to plug tax law loopholes. il
Bsns W p72+ Mr 8 '69

4 per cent unemployment threatens tax bill.
Bsns W p43 O 11 '69

Hostage for tax reform. Time 94:16 Ag 1 '69

How Mills ran the tax makers' marathon. il
Bsns W p70-1 D 27 '69

How Nixon would aid the poor and hit the
rich. Newsweek 73:81-2 My 5 '69

How tax reform will affect you; a special
report. il U S News 68:41-3 Ja 5 '70

If Wilbur Mills gets his way on spending
and taxes. U S News 66:78-80 My 19 '69

If you think taxes are high in the U.S.—.
il U S News 66:91-2 Ap 21 '69

Improving the tax code; address, December
12, 1968. S. S. Cohen. Vital Speeches 35:
267-70 F 15 '69

In the Senate's lap. Newsweek 74:89 N 10
'69

Inflation battle heats up; with editorial comment. il Bsns W p40-2, 170 Mr 29 '69

Jolt for business; tax reform proposals. il
Bsns W p78+ Jl 26 '69

Mr Nixon's tax reforms. W. F. Buckley, jr.
Nat R 21:506-7 My 20 '69

More to come in taxing drama; with editorial comment. il Bsns W p 14, 84 Jl 5 '69

Moves to patch the loopholes; Presidential
reform proposals. W. D. Slawson. Nation
208:760-4 Je 16 '69

Need for a reappraisal of American tax policies. M. A. Kriz. il Ann Am Acad 379:114-
22 S '68

New tax bill: where it hits and whom it
hurts. il Bsns W p72-3 D 27 '69

Nixon raises the tax bill. Bsns W p40 Ja 10
'70

Nixon shows the pattern. il Bsns W p33-5
Ap 19 '69

Nixon style in tax policy. Bsns W p 194 Ap 26
'69

Nixon tax plan: who'll pay more, who'll
pay less. il U S News 67:52-4 S 15 '69

Nixon's 1970 worries: economy and environment. il Time 95:9-10 Ja 12 '70

Nixon's surprise call for milder tax reform.
Time 94:89 S 12 '69

Nixon's tax package: a modest start on reform. il Time 93:86+ My 2 '69

Nixon's tax plan. E. L. Dale, jr. New Repub
160:9-11 My 3 '69

Official tax calendar for 1969. Nations Bsns
57:44-7+ Ja '69

On fiscal reform. W. F. Buckley, jr. Nat R
21:350-1 Ap 8 '69

On the prowl for new taxes. il Bsns W p 12
Ja 3 '70

Plan for new taxes; interview. W. Mills.
U S News 66:40-5 My 26 '69

Public peek at progress on tax reform.
Bsns W p26-7 My 31 '69

Punishing the successful; pension programs.
il U S News 67:84 Ag 25 '69

Questions and answers about taxes. M. Mayer. Redbook 134:87+ N '69

Quiet crusader for a new tax approach;
Treasury's E. Cohen. Bsns W p60+ My
24 '69

Reform bill that backfired. il Bsns W p58 Ag
30 '69

Relief and reform bill. Time 94:21-2 N 7 '69

Report from Washington; big year for new
tax proposals. J. Cameron. il Fortune 79:
47+ F '69

Returns roll in for tax reform. il Bsns W
p32-4 F 8 '69

Revenues & reform in the tax bill. E. L.
Dale, jr. New Repub 162:12-14 Ja 3 '70

Semantics of tax reform. America 121:85 Ag
16 '69

Senate shapes tax bill under threat of veto.
Bsns W p36 O 25 '69

Shape of reform; House ways and means
committee proposals. Newsweek 74:61+ Jl
28 '69

Spelling out tax reform; House bill. il Newsweek 74:92-4+ S 29 '69

Surtax fight gets rougher. Bsns W p42 Jl
12 '69

Surtax: in the balance. il Newsweek 74:69
Jl 7 '69

Surtax under siege. Time 94:21 Jl 25 '69

TRB from Washington: big fault. New Repub
160:4 My 3 '69

TRB from Washington: War and taxes. New
Repub 161:4 D 20 '69

Tax bill. H. C. Wallich. Newsweek 74:98 O
13 '69

Tax bill could handcuff budget; with editorial comment. il Bsns W p 12-13, 84
D 27 '69

Tax bill for our times. America 121:609 D 20
'69

Tax bill: to conference, then, veto? U S News
67:61 D 22 '69

Tax burden in the United States and other
countries. R. Goode. bibliog f il Ann Am
Acad 379:83-93 S '68

Tax changes Nixon wants; what they mean
to you; with excerpts from President
Nixon's message. April 21, 1969. il U S
News 66:27-9 My 5 '69

Tax cut in Camelot; excerpts from The fiscal revolution in America. H. Stein. il por
Trans-Action 6:38-44 Mr '69

Tax debate resumes. il Bsns W p45-6 My 10
'69

Tax know-how: more money for architecture?
P. B. Farrell, jr. Arch Rec 145:77+ F '69

Tax load that Nixon says is high enough;
increases since 1939, with pictogram. U S
News 67:26-7 D 29 '69

Tax politics. New Repub 161:13 S 20 '69

Tax reform. P. A. Samuelson. Newsweek 74:
76 Ag 4 '69

Tax reform and education. J. Cass. Sat R
52:57 S 20 '69

Tax-reform bill; a critical analysis. R. J.
Saulnier. il U S News 67:72-6 O 20 '69

Tax reform can harm the economy. D. Lawrence. U S News 67:88 Jl 14 '69

Tax reform drive takes a step ahead. Bsns
W p32-3 N 8 '69

Tax reform faces the Senate hurdles. il Bsns
W p22-3 Ag 9 '69

Tax reform; latest proposals. U S News 67:
82 Jl 21 '69

Tax reform loses some momentum; with
editorial comment. il Bsns W p46-7, 170
S 13 '69

Tax reform moving along in Congress. il
U S News 67:91-4 N 10 '69

Tax reform now! L. Metcalf. New Repub 161:
9 Jl 26 '69

Tax reform; or tax chaos? D. Lawrence. U S
News 67:104 O 6 '69

Tax reform proposals that would affect you;
farmers. Farm J 93:38 S '69

Tax reform, Senate version. U S News 67:
64-7 N 3 '6

Tax reform: something for nearly everybody.
il U S News 67:49-50 D 29 '69

Tax reform: two rocky roads; hearings on
Administration and House bills. il Newsweek 74:73-4 S 15 '69

Tax reforms start to show muscles. Bsns W
p32-3 Jl 19 '69

Tax reforms: what Congress has in mind.
il U S News 66:34-5 F 3 '69

Tax-relief bill: an imbalance? U S News 67:
71-2 S 8 '69

TAXATION—United States—*Continued*
Tax-relief bomb. K. Crawford. Newsweek 74:
28 D 22 '69
Tax revolt brewing in U.S. il U S News 66:
26-8 F 10 '69; Same abr. with title Taxes,
everybody's headache; voters say no to
new spending. Read Digest 94:65-7 Je '69
Tax trade-off; R. M. Nixon's proposals.
Nation 208:554-5 My 5 '69
Taxes: the changes ahead and the meaning
to you. il U S News 67:55-7 Jl 14 '69
Taxes; the collection and distribution of your
money; symposium. il Sat R 52:21-35+ Mr
22 '69
Taxes: the R and R bill. Time 94:19 Ag 15 '69
Taxes: the veil lifts. il Newsweek 74:97 D 8
'69
Taxpayer and his money; it could be better
spent and collected. Life 67:30 Ag 15 '69
Taxpayers' revolt? il Newsweek 73:79 Ja
27 '69
This month's feature: Congress and tax
status of foundations. Cong Digest 48:130-
60+ My '69
Time to reform tax reform? il Bsns W p 16-17
D 20 '69
Time to reform the tax structure. America
120:183 F 15 '69
Top executives look at tax reform. il Duns R
93:44-6 Ap '69
Trouble for Nixon: the tax time bomb. il
U S News 68:22-3 Ja 12 '70
Two-thirds of a loaf; legislation to extend
the income tax surcharge. il Time 94:17 Ag
8 '69
View from Wilbur Mills; tax-reform proposals.
Newsweek 73:80+ My 19 '69
Washington desk. G. R. Rosen. Duns R 94:
7-8 O '69
What Congress wrought. il Newsweek 74:10-
11 D 29 '69
What is the impact of those tax breaks? il
Bsns W p62+ F 1 '69
What real tax reform would mean. Bsns W
p 108 Ag 2 '69
What the tax bill does. il Time 94:9-10 D 26
'69
Who pay the bills? New Repub 160:10-11 Ja 25
'69
Why tax reform is so urgent and so unlikely.
il Time 93:84-6+ Ap 4 '69
Wilbur Mills has put together the biggest
tax-reform package ever. J. L. Steele. il
Fortune 80:55+ S '69
Wilbur Mills on taxes and spending; inter-
view. ed. by N. MacNeil. W. D. Mills. Time
93:16 F 21 '69
Your taxes, up or down? il U S News 67:55-7
Ag 11 '69
    See also
Income tax—United States
Inheritance tax
Libraries—Finance
Local taxation
Property tax
Sales tax
Social security taxes
Tax evasion
Taxation, Exemption from
Taxation, State
    also subhead Taxation under various sub-
    jects, e.g. Corporations—Taxation
TAXATION, Double
Estate tax convention signed with the Neth-
erlands. Dept State Bul 61:138-9 Ag 18 '69
U.S.-Netherlands estate tax convention
transmitted to the Senate; message, Octo-
ber 13, 1969. R. M. Nixon. Dept State Bul
61:386 N 3 '69
U.S. Trinidad and Tobago extend income tax
convention. Dept State Bul 60:138 F 10 '69
Welcome to the state of confusion; when a
business crosses state lines. il Nations Bsns
57:72-4 Ag '69
TAXATION, Exemption from
Bishops and tax reform; U.S. Catholic con-
ference testifying before the House ways
and means committee. America 120:442-3
Ap 12 '69
Chances of taxing tax-free bonds. il U S
News 66:85 Mr 24 '69
Church income: a taxing business. Chr To-
day 13:32-3 Je 20 '69
Church-owned business; stretching religion.
Chr Today 13:48-9 F 28 '69
Debate sharpens over tax-exempt organiza-
tions. R. H. Smith. Pub W 195:43 Je 30 '69
Economics of class; Richard Nixon and tax
loopholes. P. A. Samuelson. Newsweek 74:
105 O 27 '69
En route to tax reform; church owned busi-
nesses. Chr Today 13:23 My 23 '69
First look at House plan for tax tightening;
who's hit. U S News 66:79-82 Je 9 '69

Form of new tax bill shaping. U S News
66:97 Ap 28 '69
How 381 super-rich Americans managed not
to pay a cent in taxes last year. P. M.
Stern. il N Y Times Mag p30-1+ Ap 13 '69;
Reply. p22+ My 4 '69
IRS reviewing tax status of university
presses. S. Wagner. Pub W 195:42-3 Je 9
'69
Loopholes and tax reform. America 120:151
F 8 '69
Milking the sacred cows. Newsweek 73:71
My 5 '69
Municipal-bond loophole. Am City 84:10 Ag
'69
NEA, POAU and tax exemptions. America
120:662 Je 7 '69
No tax due, but rich man pays; case of
J. D. Rockefeller 3d. U S News 66:16 Mr
10 '69
Private loophole; E. M. Kennedy challenges
amendments. il Newsweek 74:75-6 D 22 '69
Putting the screws on church tax privileges.
Chr Today 13:58 S 12 '69
Reducing tax privileges. Chr Today 13:31
My 23 '69
Should churches be allowed to do business
tax-free? O. K. Armstrong. Read Digest 94:
84-8 Mr '69
Supreme court weighs churches' tax exemp-
tion. R. E. Friedrich, jr. Chr Today 13:38
Jl 18 '69
Tax break for artists; new law in Ireland. R.
Gelatt. Sat R 52:28 N 15 '69
Tax-exempt land; who owns it? city of Phil-
adelphia report. America 121:448 N 15 '69
Tax-exempt property; another crushing bur-
den for the cities. H. B. Meyers. il Fortune
79:76-9+ My 1 '69
Tax exemptions, the artful dodge. H. Aaron.
Trans-Action 6:4-6 Mr '69
Tax exempts under fire; exempting interest
on state and municipal bonds from federal
taxation. America 120:639 My 31 '69
Tax-free bonds: a market in chaos. il U S
News 67:77-9 S 29 '69
Tax loophole; the farming business; address,
January 11, 1969. L. Metcalf. Vital Speeches
35:253-6 F 1 '69
Tax-reform bill; a critical analysis. R. J.
Saulnier. il U S News 67:72-6 O 20 '69
Tax reform bill and colleges. America 121:
149 S 13 '69
Tax reform can harm the economy. D. Law-
rence. U S News 67:88 Jl 14 '69
Tax reforms: what Congress has in mind.
il U S News 66:34-5 F 3 '69
When you leave the honey jar open, you've
got to expect ants. Nat R 21:220 Mr 11 '69
Where tax changes hit hardest. il U S News
67:23-5 Ag 18 '69
Why tax reform is so urgent and so unlikely.
il Time 93:84-6+ Ap 4 '69
    See also
Church property—Taxation
Foundations, Charitable and educational—
Taxation
Securities, Tax exempt
Tax evasion

TAXATION, Municipal. See Local taxation
TAXATION, Progressive
If we want real tax reform. .; change in
progressive tax rate. H. L. Lutz. il Na-
tions Bsns 57:38-40 Ja '69
TAXATION, State
How state-local tax load varies. il U S News
66:68 F 24 '69
One more tax going up; the states scramble
for money. U S News 66:78-80 Mr 17 '69
Should the government share its tax take?
W. W. Heller. il Sat R 52:26-9 Mr 22 '69
State aims: tax piled on tax. U S News 66:
92-3 Ap 21 '69
State taxes may rise five billions. U S News
66:101 Mr 10 '69
States get hungrier for taxpayers' cash. il
Bsns W p30-1 Mr 1 '69
Tale of two taxpayers. il Newsweek 73:67 F
24 '69
Taxpayer revolt keeps on rolling; school
proposals involving taxes and bond issues.
U S News 66:81 My 19 '69
Taxpayers' revolt. il Newsweek 73:28 Mr 10
'69
Welcome to the state of confusion; when a
business crosses state lines. il Nations Bsns
57:72-4 Ag '69
What taxes cost you now. il U S News 67:38-9
Ag 25 '69
Where taxes are highest, lowest. il U S
News 67:77 O 20 '69
Wyoming view won tax burdens. U S News
66:95 My 12 '69
    See also
Sales tax

TAXATION for education. See School finance
TAXATION for library service. See Libraries—
Finance
TAXATION of corporations. See Corporations
—Taxation
TAXATION of foreign investments. See In-
vestments, Foreign—Taxation
TAXATION of land. See Real property—
Taxation
TAXES. See Taxation
TAXICAB drivers
Face to face with a New York cab driver.
M. Englander. Seventeen 29:106 Ja '70

Anecdotes, facetiae, satire, etc.
Taxi! S. Blackburn. New Yorker 44:102-4
F 8 '69
TAXIDERMY
See also
Zoological specimens—Collection and pre-
servation
TAXONOMY. See Biology—Classification
TAY-Sachs disease. See Nervous system—Dis-
eases
TAYLOR, Anne P.
Drawing for environmental awareness. Sch
Arts 68:12-13 Mr '69
TAYLOR, C. Richard
Eland and the oryx; with biographical
sketch. Sci Am 220:18, 88-95 Ja '69
TAYLOR, Creed
Music-business maverick. G. Lees. por Hi
Fi 19:116 My '69
TAYLOR, E. D.
News pots. Ceram Mo 17:15-18 Ja '69
TAYLOR, Edmond
Personal history. S. K. Padover. Sat R 52:
39 Jl 19 '69
TAYLOR, Elizabeth, 1912-
Sisters; story. New Yorker 45:38-41 Je 21 '69
Well, here we are; story. McCalls 97:74-5
N '69
TAYLOR, Elizabeth, 1932-
Elizabeth Taylor talks about being a mother;
interview, ed. by D. Lurie. por Ladies Home
J 86:83+ Mr '69
about
Liz Taylor and Richard Burton; what it's like
to be walking investments. A. Birstein.
Vogue 153:100-1+ F 15 '69
Liz's million-dollar rock. il Life 67:65-66B
N 14 '69
TAYLOR, Emily
Keeping house with Emily Taylor. See is-
sues of Good housekeeping
TAYLOR, Frank
Nevada's thirsty legacy. Travel & Camera
32:32 D '69
One-armed high-wire artist. Pop Mech 131:
138-9 Ap '69
You gotta have heart. Motor T 21:40-1 S '69
TAYLOR, Frank J.
Magic with mums. Read Digest 95:170-5 O
'69
TAYLOR, Fred G.
(tr) See Kuempel, H. About playing cards
(tr) See Reisig, H. Playing cards in popular
use currently in Germany
TAYLOR, G. Aiken
Unwarranted rebuke. Chr Today 13:26 Mr 14
'69
TAYLOR, George W.
Using factfinding and recommendations in
impasses. Mo Labor R 92:63-5 Jl '69
TAYLOR, Grace A.
Last hours; story. Redbook 132:66-7 Ja
'69
TAYLOR, Harold
Education for the seventies; the crisis in
the university; excerpts from Students
without teachers. Cur 111:40-7 O '69
Toward a world university. Sat R 52:24+
O 11 '69
TAYLOR, Henry
New poetry from Europe. Nation 209:260-1
S 15 '69
TAYLOR, J. D. See Rosen, B. R. jt. auth.
TAYLOR, James
Family people and organization men. por Sci
Digest 65:66-9 Mr '69
TAYLOR, Judy
Children's paperback explosion in Britain.
Pub W 196:25-6 N 3 '69
TAYLOR, Kae
Taylor girls: nitty gritty twins. G. Zimmer-
mann. il pors Look 33:68-70+ Mr 4 '69
TAYLOR, Kathryn S.
Fothergilla. Horticulture 48:46 Ja '70
Primula japonica. Horticulture 47:18-19 Jl '69
TAYLOR, Kenneth I.
Madison. ALA Bul 63:250-4 F '69
—and Hull, Robert
Facelifting for old schools. por Library J 94:
4218-24 N 15 '69

TAYLOR, L. B. Jr
Bits of another world. Space World F-9-69:
35-41 S '69
TAYLOR, Louie S.
Thread making for the enamelist. Ceram
Mo 17:20-2 O '69
TAYLOR, M. A.
Sex ratios of newborns: associated with
prepartum and postpartum schizophrenia.
bibliog Science 164:723-4 My 9 '69
TAYLOR, Paul, dance company. See Paul
Taylor dance company
TAYLOR, Peter
Master of hidden drama. G. Wolff. por News-
week 74:121-2 O 20 '69
TAYLOR, Philip B. Jr
Hemispheric defense in World war II. Cur
Hist 56:333-9 Je '69
TAYLOR, Rae
Taylor girls: nitty gritty twins. G. Zimmer-
mann. il pors Look 33:68-70+ Mr 4 '69
TAYLOR, Ralph C.
MERBISC: unique recreation bargain. Parks
& Rec 4:35-8 Ap '69
TAYLOR, Robert Selby, abp
Trickery and bravery in South Africa. Chr
Cent 86:1411 N 5 '69
TAYLOR, Ronald B.
Labor in the vineyard: the boycott and the
NLRA. Nation 208:591-3 My 12 '69
TAYLOR, Theodore Brewster
Please don't steal the atomic bomb. A. M.
Adelson. il Esquire 71:130-3+ My '69
TAYLOR, Thomas N.
Cycads: evidence from the upper Pennsyl-
vanian. bibliog Science 163:294-5 Ap 18 '69
TAYLOR, Wilbur J.
Equality; poem. Negro Hist Bul 32:18 My
'69
TAYLOR, William B. 3d
President appoints Mr Taylor to South Paci-
fic commission. Dept State Bul 61:421 N
17 '69
TAYLOR, Zack
Cruising can be wonderful. Motor B 123:
128-31+ Ja '69
TAYLOR-YOUNG, Leigh
Leigh Taylor-Young. pors Vogue 153:205-6 My
'69
TAZIEFF, Haroun
Menace of extinct volcanoes; reprint. UNESCO
Courier 22:9 Ag '69
TCHAIKOVSKY, Peter Ilyitch
Records:
Eugene Onegin. Opera N 33:34 Mr 8 '69
Tchaikovsky surprise package. H. Goldsmith.
il Hi Fi 19:72-3 Ag '69
TCHAIKOVSKY suite; ballet. See Ballets—
Criticisms
TCHEREPNIN, Alexander
Alexander Tcherepnin; today is the golden
age... P. J. Smith. por Hi Fi 19:MA24+
Je '69
TCHIKRIN Indians. See Indians of South
America—Brazil
TEA
Tea power. J. C. Pavlik. il Sci Digest 65:72-6
Je '69
These are teas? il Bet Hom & Gard 47:127 Mr
'69
TEA bags
Taming the terrible tea bag. Consumer Rep
34:110 Mr '69
TEA parties. See Entertaining
TEA roses. See Roses
TEA trade
Smuggling and the British tea trade before
1784. H. C. Mui and L. H. Mui. bibliog
f il Am Hist R 74:44-73 O '68
TEACH ins. See Teach-ins
TEACHER assignments. See Teaching assign-
ments
TEACHER corps. See United States—National
teacher corps
TEACHER education. See Teachers—Education
TEACHER evaluation. See Teachers—Rating
TEACHER grievances. See Teachers grievances
TEACHER librarian training. See School li-
brarians—Education
TEACHER librarians. See School librarians
TEACHER opinion
Teachers should commit themselves. W. H.
Truesdell. Todays Ed 55:37 Ja '69
Thinking and traditional socio-political
values. Sch & Soc 97:344+ O '69
TEACHER-parent-pupil conferences. See Edu-
cational guidance
TEACHER participation in school administra-
tion. See School management and organiza-
tion—Teacher participation
TEACHER-pupil relations. See Teachers and
students

TEACHER rating. See Teachers—Rating
TEACHER shortage. See Teachers—Supply and demand
TEACHER travel
Seeing the world as it is. E. E. Henderson. Todays Ed 58:72-3 Ja '69
TEACHERS
Elementary education, a man's world? Greeley public schools, Colo. L. Triplett. Ed Digest 34:25-7 Ja '69
Professor becomes high school teacher. E. H. Smith. Engl J 58:360-2+ Mr '69; Reply. P. Borgstrom. 58:1366-9 D '69
Teacher of the year. C. Mangel. il Look 33: 58-62 My 13 '69
Teaching and teachers, today and tomorrow; excerpts from Schools and the challenge of innovation. R. F. Campbell. Ed Digest 35:12-15 N '69
Why teachers are striking. W. Goodman. Redbook 132:67+ Mr '69
See also
Academic freedom
American teachers in foreign countries
Art teachers
Clothing and dress—Teachers
College professors and instructors
Dance teachers
Educational innovations
Educators
English teachers
Foreign teachers in the United States
Negro teachers
School and the home
School management and organization—Teacher participation
School superintendents and principals
Substitute teachers
Teachers of socially handicapped children
Teachers unions
Teaching
Women as teachers

Adjustment
Advice for beginning teachers. A. R. Mangione. Clear House 44:41-2 S '69
Advisory teacher program benefits beginning teachers; English teacher program for the Cleveland schools. R. J. Goodrich. Clear House 44:12-15 S '69
Induction of beginning teachers. D. W. Hunt. Ed Digest 34:34-7 F '69

Anecdotes, facetiae, satire, etc.
Light touch. See issues of Today's education

Appointment
See Teachers—Selection and appointment

Certification
More flexible requirements. Sch & Soc 97: 6+ Ja '69
New look in credentialing. D. W. Allen and P. Wagschal. Clear House 44:137-40 N '69

Civil rights
Court and teacher: school board conflict; excerpts from address. R. S. Vacca. bibliog Clear House 44:96-101 O '69

Clothing and dress
See Clothing and dress—Teachers

Contracts
Contract signing: a checklist to guide your action. J. F. Check. Clear House 43:411-12 Mr '69
Impact of negotiation upon public education. H. R. Weinstock and P. L. Van Horn. bibliog Clear House 43:358-63 F '69
New frontiers for professional negotiations. D. A. Singer, jr. Sch & Soc 97:370-2 O '69
Special feature on professional negotiation; symposium. Todays Ed 58:53-60 Ja '69

Dismissal
Case of Angela the red; firing of militant black professor at UCLA. Time 94:64 O 17 '69
Desegregation dilemma in the South; Negro teachers laid off in Coahoma County, Miss. C. Wilkie. New Repub 160:13 Ap 12 '69
Hard on Communism; UCLA fires A. Davis. Newsweek 74:101 O 6 '69
Russians are coming at UCLA; the firing of A. Davis. S. V. Roberts. Commonweal 91:174-5 N 7 '69

Duties
Differentiated staffing; symposium. Todays Ed 58:53-62 Mr '69
Duty-free lunch periods. A. Almeida. Todays Ed 58:80-1 Mr '69

Education
Education professions development; investment in the future. D. Davies. il Am Ed 5: 9-10 F '69
Educators' conceptions of contemporary innovation in teacher training. W. C. Wolf, jr. Sch & Soc 97:378-80 O '69
Experimental course in sex education for teachers. V. D. C. Bennett and others. bibliog il Ment Hy 53:625-31 O '69
How schools can get better teachers; interview. J. Koerner. U S News 67:48-51 S 15 '69
In service; the Guild rounds out a decade of teaching teachers. M. E. Peltz. il Opera N 33:6-7 F 8 '69
International element in teacher education. W. W. Brickman. Sch & Soc 97:474-5 D '69
1969 world guide to summer study; symposium. il Sr Schol 94:School Teach 13-22 F 28 '69
Sex and family living; Boston university training project for teachers. I. Forman. il Am Ed 5:11-13 O '69
Shadow study; observing pupils in the middle grades. E. R. Cuony. Clear House 43:312-14 Ja '69
Who's fit to teach; training and licensing bill; California. J. Featherstone. New Repub 161:19-21 D 13 '69
See also
Art teachers—Education
Educational workshops
Mathematics teachers—Education
National commission on teacher education and professional standards
Student teachers
Student teaching
Summer schools
Teachers institutes
Teachers of socially handicapped children—Training

Education in service
Communications-arts teams; Broward County, Fla. G Marsh. il Todays Ed 58:39-41 D '69
In-service programs for JHS teachers. C. R. Neatrour. Clear House 44:187 N '69
Individualized in-service education; Kamehameha schools, Honolulu. L. L. Stillwell. il Todays Ed 58:44-5 D '69
Insight through inservice. H. J. Maves. Todays Ed 58:42 Ap '69
Micro-teaching; videotape recording to evaluate teacher training performances. D. Molner. il Sr Schol 94:School Teach 20-1+ Mr 7 '69
See also
Teachers meetings

Ethics
See Teachers ethics

Health and hygiene
Mentally unfit teachers. B. Bard. il Ladies Home J 86:80-1+ F '69

Hours of teaching
See Teaching load

Migration
Computer and the peripatetic teacher; job-locator service. O. A. Payne. Todays Ed 58:13 F '69

Pensions
See also
College professors and instructors—Pensions

Placement
See Teachers—Selection and appointment

Political activities
Back to black lists? Commonweal 91:4 O 3 '69
Just another off year? P. L. Gladson. Todays Ed 58:55-6 O '69
Our political power for good. J. Sawaia. il il Todays Ed 58:44-5 D '69
Political action and America's teachers. J. W. Maguire. Sch & Soc 97:22-3 Ja '69
Teacher opinion poll; Teacher in politics. Todays Ed 58:87 S '69
See also
College professors and instructors—Political activities

Anecdotes, facetiae, satire, etc.
Suggested menu, to nourish the body politic. Todays Ed 58:42-3 F '69

Qualifications
Excellent teachers: what makes them outstanding? J. A. Johnson and B. F. Radebaugh. il Clear House 44:152-6 N '69
Pride of workmanship. J. R. Dettre. Clear House 43:323-7 F '69

TEACHERS—Qualifications—*Continued*
So you want to be a real teacher? R. W. Calisch. il Todays Ed 58:49-51 N '69
Who's fit to teach; training and licensing bill; California. J. Featherstone. New Repub 161:19-21 D 13 '69
See also
Teachers—Certification

Rating

Can we define good teaching? differentiation between didactic and encounter teaching. H. S. Broudy. Ed Digest 35:20-3 S '69
Case of competition. R. L. Wagoner. bibliog Clear House 44:110-14 O '69
Helping new teachers focus on behavioral change. J. M. Cooper and E. Seidman. Clear House 43:301-6 Ja '69
See also
College professors and instructors—Rating
College professors and instructors—Rating by students

Recruiting

How schoolmen can recruit teachers more effectively. J. Sandberg. Ed Digest 35:36-7 S '69
Interviewing: ask the right questions. T. F. Koerner. Clear House 44:102-4 O '69
Recruitment: overhauling archaic practices. R. J. Yerkovich. Clear House 43:328-30 F '69; Same abr. Ed Digest 34:38-9 My '69
Teacher credentials: item preferences of recruiters. S. Dropkin and L. Castiglione. il Clear House 43:474-8 Ap '69
Washington report: is it really a man's world? ways to meet shortages. J. Lloyd. Sr Schol 94:Schol Teach 6 My 2 '69

Salaries, allowances, etc.

. . .And teachers want more too. il U S News 66:38-9 Mr 3 '69
Case of competition. R. L. Wagoner. bibliog Clear House 44:110-14 O '69
Extra pay for extra duty. P. M. Solley. il Todays Ed 58:54 My '69
Merit pay, what merit? R. Weissman. Ed Digest 34:16-19 My '69
Report on salary changes for teachers in urban areas; tables. M. Sproull. bibliog Mo Labor R 92:49-52 Ap '69
Special feature on professional negotiation; symposium. Todays Ed 58:53-60 Ja '69

Selection and appointment

Computer and the peripatetic teacher; joblocator service. O. A. Payne. Todays Ed 58:13 F '69
New look in credentialing. D. W. Allen and P. Wagschal. Clear House 44:137-40 N '69
Racial quotas in hiring teachers? U S News 66:12-13 Mr 17 '69
Teacher credentials: item preferences of recruiters. S. Dropkin and L. Castiglione. il Clear House 43:474-8 Ap '69

Supply and demand

Are there really too many teachers? J. Chesswas. il UNESCO Courier 23:21-3+ Ja '70
Beating the teacher shortage. S. Holzman. Sr Schol 94:Schol Teach 4 F 14 '69
First manpower assessment. J. Chaffee, jr. il Am Ed 5:11-12 F '69
1969-70 projects for meeting critical shortages of classroom personnel. il Am Ed 5::26-7 D '69
Of immediate concern: better teacher utilization. J. L. Stevens. Clear House 43:504-5 Ap '69
Teacher shortage in Botswana. R. Greenough. il Sch & Soc 97:386-8 O '69
Teachers in short supply. B. B. Stretch. Sat R 52:71 Mr 15 '69
Wanted: retirees to teach. il Har Yrs 9:6-10 Ag '69
Washington report: is it really a man's world? ways to meet shortages. J. Lloyd. Sr Schol 94:Schol Teach 6 My 2 '69
See also
Teachers—Recruiting

Teaching load

See Teaching load

Tenure

Touching the tenure nerve. America 121:448 N 15 '69

Training

See Teachers—Education

TEACHERS, Interchange of
How Russian schools compare with ours; Soviet-American teacher exchange program sponsored by the American Friends service committee. M. Hope. il Parents Mag 44: 56-7+ Ja '69

Inter-American teachers' exchange; San Antonio, Calif. program. il Américas 21:45 Jl '69
Our Mrs Brooks; Fulbright exchange teacher in England. P. Pine. il Am Ed 5:9-10 My '69

TEACHERS, New. *See* Teachers—Adjustment
TEACHERS, Part time
New horizons for educated women. J. Cass. Sat R 52:45-6 Jl 19 '69
Part-time teachers and how they work. G. Dapper and J. Murphy. Ed Digest 35:22-5 N '69

TEACHERS, Retired
Hail and farewell! Testimony of a teacher's testimonial. M. Graves. Clear House 43: 561-3 My '69

TEACHERS aides
Aide to learning. K. S. Stone. Engl J 58:124-5 Ja '69
Go back to school, your child's school. C. L. Miller. il McCalls 96:4 Ja '69
Organization and training of paraprofessionals. F. P. Bazeli. bibliog Clear House 44:206-9 D '69
Pupil tutors and tutees learn together. J. C. Fleming. il Todays Ed 58:22-4 O '69; Same abr. Ed Digest 35:38-40 D '69
Reading program with lay aides and programmed material. C. D. Briscoe. Clear House 43:373-7 F '69
Seniors succeed as teacher aides in Florida high schools project. Aging 171:9-10 Ja '69
Untaught teachers and improbable poets. F. Howe. il Sat R 52:60-2+ Mr 15 '69
See also
Volunteer workers in education

TEACHERS and school boards
Court and teacher: school board conflict; excerpts from address. R. S. Vacca. bibliog Clear House 44:96-101 O '69
Power shift: policy formulation in transition. J. B. McAndrews. Clear House 44:161-3 N '69

TEACHERS and students
And who are you? R. A. Schroth. America 121: 167 S 13 '69; Reply. A. J. Lisska. 121:280 O 11 '69
Are there really too many teachers? J. Chesswas. il UNESCO Courier 23:21-3+ Ja '70
Are you listening, teacher? E. Caldwell. Todays Ed 58:33-4 Ja '69
Can parents and teenagers negotiate? with study-discussion program. by C. Smallenburg and H. Smallenburg. D. B. Harris. bibliog il PTA Mag 63:2-5, 37 My '69
Children and divorce: what the teacher can do. L. B. Ames. Ed Digest 35:19-21 N '69
Classroom incident. *See* issues of Today's education
Crushes; what should you do about them? with marginal comments. S. Berman; R. Gibson. Todays Ed 58:12-16 D '69
Deeper understanding of children. V. F. Banks. Todays Ed 58:31-2 F '69
Edwin D. Etherington, president of Wesleyan university; with report by R. Woodley. il Life 66:36-8 F 14 '69
Gentle art of nonteaching; letting the students do the teaching. L. Lewin. Ed Digest 35:24-5 S '69
Glory, glory hallelujah teacher hit me with a ruler. Trans-Action 6:6 Ap '69
Hook-up, plug in, connect; relevancy is all. C. F. Greiner. Engl J 58:23-9 Ja '69
How to enhance pupil self-esteem. S. Coopersmith and J. Silverman. Todays Ed 58:28-9 Ap '69
Influence of the emotionally disturbed teacher on schoolchildren. N. S. Brandes. Ment Hy 53:606-10 O '69
Interaction briefs. *See* issues of Today's education
Joe doesn't pledge allegiance; excerpts. R. S. MacGorman. Ed Digest 34:24-5 F '69
Proud teachers. R. E. Wolseley. Sch & Soc 97:434-5 N '69
Schools that turn people off. S. Doig. il Todays Ed 58:28-30 My '69; Same abr. Ed Digest 35:41-3 S '69
Self confidence in art for the elementary teacher. J. G. Cecere. il Sch Arts 69:28-9 S '69
Student challenges; teachers' words not always accepted. T. W. Whiteley. Clear House 43:291-3 Ja '69
Teacher behavior and the destructive critics. L. N. Tanner. bibliog f Sch & Soc 97:366-7+ O '69
Teachers talk too much! J. S. Cross and J. M. Nagle. bibliog f Engl J 58:1362-5 D '69
Trial of Elaine Murphy. E. Keiffer. il Good H 168:12+ My '69

TEACHERS and students—*Continued*
Ubiquitous class-value conflict in education.
H. R. Smith. bibliog f Sch & Soc 97:92-4
F '69
When your child dislikes his teacher; with
study-discussion program, by E. Harris and
D. Harris. B. M. Gudridge. bibliog PTA
Mag 63:14-16, 36-7 My '69
Will teacher be the new drop-out? A. Beich-
man. bibliog f il N Y Times Mag p48-9+
D 7 '69
World beyond the classroom. G. Bauer. Clear
House 43:371-2 F '69
Young radicals & professorial critics. I. L.
Horowitz. Commonweal 89:552-6 Ja 31 '69

Anecdotes, facetiae, satire, etc.
Were Molly Rodman's dice loaded? E. T.
Hawkins and others. McCalls 97:93+ O '69
TEACHERS annuities. See Annuities
TEACHERS as authors
Guidelines for the potential teacher-author.
A. A. Delaney. Clear House 44:210-12 D
'69
TEACHERS attitudes. See Attitudes
TEACHERS college, Columbia university
Teachers college, Columbia; expanding an
urban campus. il Arch Rec 145:156-7 My '69
Teachers college master, building program.
il Sch & Soc 97:200-1 Ap '69
TEACHERS colleges
Problems in Jewish teacher training. E. B.
Levine. il America 120:398-401 Ap 5 '69
See also
Teachers—Education
TEACHERS conferences. See Educational con-
ferences
TEACHERS contracts. See Teachers—Con-
tracts
TEACHERS ethics
Ethics and student tours. Todays Ed 58:51 Ap
'69
NEA committee acts on ethics complaint. E.
Faulconer and others. Todays Ed 58:34-5+
N '69
TEACHERS grievances
Let's get serious about teacher power. D. E.
Shawver. Clear House 44:199-202 D '69
TEACHERS institutes
Ann Arbor, 1969; Institute on college and
university administration. F. R. Haig.
America 121:192-4 S 20 '69
EDPA institutes announced. Library J 94:
1701+ Ap 15 '69
Greatly expanded summer institute program.
il Am Ed 5:21-2 Mr '69
Learning the streets; institute on ghetto
youth in San Francisco. il Time 94:64 Ag
15 '69
Summer institutes in Afro-American studies.
Sr Schol 94:Schol Teach 20 F 28 '69
TEACHERS meetings
Toward improved English department meet-
ings. T. W. Hipple. Engl J 58:440-2 Mr '69
TEACHERS of socially handicapped children
More than a teacher? problems of Chicago
ghetto schoolteacher. il Ebony 24:142-4+
Mr '69
Training
Inner-city teacher recruitment. Sch & Soc
97:132 Mr '69
TEACHERS salaries. See Teachers—Salaries,
allowances, etc.
TEACHERS strikes. See Strikes—United States
—Teachers
TEACHERS unions
Does Freiser know best? letter to the editor.
S. Mendlow; I. Morris; M. D. Leventer.
Library J 94:475 F 1 '69
Let's get serious about teacher power. D. E.
Shawver. Clear House 44:199-202 D '69
Teachers' unions in Catholic schools. J. P.
Mooney. America 120:301-3 Mr 15 '68; Dis-
cussion. 120:437 Ap 12 '69
Teachers' unions step toward unity. Bsns
W p36+ Ja 10 '70
See also
American federation of teachers
United federation of teachers
TEACHERS workshops. See Educational
workshops
TEACHING
Can we define good teaching? differentiation
between didactic and encounter teaching.
H. S. Broudy. Ed Digest 35:20-3 S '69
Crisis in the high schools; the Life poll; with
report by B. Hooper. L. Harris il Life 66:
22-35+ My 16 '69
Gentle art of nonteaching; letting the stu-
dents do the teaching. L. Lewin. Ed Digest
35:24-5 S '69
I love science, teaching, and children. D.
McIver. il Todays Ed 58:50-2 Ja '69

Interaction analysis improves classroom
instruction. L. F. Psencik. bibliog f Clear
House 43:555-60 My '69
Key word is relevance; relating teaching
to the lives of the learners. W. Van Til.
il Todays Ed 58:14-17 Ja '69
Logic of action, by F. Hawkins. Review
New Repub 161:23-4 S 27 '69. J. Feather-
stone
Pressures for educational innovations. W. D.
Boutwell. PTA Mag 63:13-14 Mr '69
Some myths that teachers live by. R. B.
Shuman. Sch & Soc 97:435-7 N '69
Teachers without tempers. B. Asbell. il
Redbook 132:44+ Ja '69
Teaching and learning through inquiry. B.
G. Massialas; J. Zevin; M. Sugrue and J.
A. Sweeney il Todays Ed 58:40-4 My '69
Teaching: eight parts of a good life. R. G.
Hause. Clear House 44:185-7 N '69
Team planning: heart transplant in teaching.
W. Goldstein. Clear House 43:272-4 Ja '69
Tricks of the trade; ed. by T. Gordon. Clear
House 44:188 N '69
See also
Academic freedom
Adult education
Audio-visual instruction
Classroom management
Colleges and universities—Teaching
Correlation (education)
Discussion method (education)
Education
Education, Experimental
Group work in education
Individual instruction
Junior colleges—Teaching
Lecture method in teaching
Montessori method of education
Psychology, Educational
Remedial teaching
School supervision and supervisors
Sunday school lessons
Sunday schools
Teachers
Teachers—Education
Team teaching

also subhead Study and teaching under
various subjects, e.g. Science—Study and
teaching
Aids and devices
Big-school services for country kids. O. Bay
and R. Black. il Farm J 93:22-3+ S '69
Historian and historical films. W. H. Mc-
Neill. Ed Digest 34:38-40 Ja '69
Instructional media. See issues of Clearing
house
Kaleidoscope for learning; educational tech-
nology. J. H. Martin. il Sat R 52:76-7+ Je
21 '69
New educational materials. See occasional
issues of Scholastic teacher
New teaching materials for the inner city.
Sch & Soc 97:272 Sum '69
Teaching for personal growth; an introduc-
tion to new materials. T. Borton. bibliog
Ment Hy 53:594-9 O '69
Teaching tips; suggestions sent in by teach-
ers. Schol Teach Sec Teach Sup p 16 S 22;
24 O 6 '69
Toward improved English department meet-
ings. T. W. Hipple. Engl J 58:440-2 Mr '69
See also
Abacus
Computers—Educational applications
Education market
English language—Study and teaching—Aids
and devices
Film strips
Instructional materials centers
Magnetic recorders and recording—Educa-
tional applications
Moving pictures in education
Programmed instruction
Teaching machines
Telephone in education
Television in education

Anecdotes, facetiae, satire, etc.
Light touch. See issues of Today's education

Bibliography
Book reviews. See issues of Clearing house
Teacher's bookshelf. Schol Teach Sec Teach
Sup p23 O 6 '69
TEACHING, Freedom of. See Academic free-
dom
TEACHING, Master of arts in. See Degrees,
Academic
TEACHING as a profession
Enhancing teaching as a career; differenti-
ated staffing. R. G. Corwin. Todays Ed 58:
55 Mr '69

TEACHING as a profession—*Continued*
How do you measure up as a member of the united teaching profession? J. Heflin. il Todays Ed 58:64-5 Mr '69
Profession and the media. E. Koontz. Todays Ed 58:17 F '69
Teacher professionalization: its determination and achievement. S. Brodbelt. bibliog f Sch & Soc 97:151-2 Mr '69
Teaching and teachers, today and tomorrow; excerpts from Schools and the challenge of innovation. R. F. Campbell. Ed Digest 35:12-15 N '69
Washington report; first assessment. J. Lloyd. Sr Schol 94:Schol Teach 4 Ap 18 '69
Why teach? A survey supplies answers. R. A. Bartel and F. L. Coppedge. bibliog f il Clear House 44:238-41 D '69
TEACHING assignments
Differentiated staffing; symposium. Todays Ed 58:53-62 Mr '69
Induction of beginning teachers. D. W. Hunt. Ed Digest 34:34-7 F '69
TEACHING load
Induction of beginning teachers. D. W. Hunt. Ed Digest 34:34-7 F '69
TEACHING machines
Reading, writing and profit; use of machine by Dorsett education systems at Texarkana. Bsns W p104 O 4 '69
Teaching machine for drama; Birmingham-Southern college, Ala. il Arch Forum 130:78-83 Ap '69
Technology, not teachers; audiovisual teaching machine in Texarkana schools. il Sr Schol 95:Schol Teach 1 O 27 '69
Wondrous machine that salvages backward kids; talking typewriter, or ERE. T. Irwin. il Todays Health 47:31-3+ Ag '69
See also
Computers—Educational applications
Programmed instruction
TEACH-ins
Ecology on the campus; planned ecological-environmental teach-in on university campuses for April 22. Sci N 96:575-6 D 20 '69
TEAGUE, Allison
Allison is alive and well on the ski slope. Seventeen 27:100-1+ D '68
TEAGUE, Bob
Letters to a black boy; excerpts. por Redbook 132:55-62 Ja '69
TEAGUE, Michael, and Cowan, Zélide
Nil disprandum. Am Heritage 20:18-25 F '69
TEAGUE, Patricia Ann. See Draayer, D. R. jt. auth.
TEAGUE, Richard A.
Hot rodder to hot designer. il por Bsns W p 134+ O 4 '69
TEAL, John, and Teal, Mildred
Ribbon of green; the epic of a salt marsh, its birth, life, death; excerpts from Life and death of a salt marsh. Audubon 71:4-8+ N '69
TEAL, Mildred. See Teal, J. jt. auth.
TEAL shooting. See Duck shooting
TEALE, Edwin Way
His backyard was a passage to fame. R. Tunley. Audubon 71:114+ N '69
TEAM flying. See Aviation—Stunt flying
TEAM teaching
Communications-arts teams; Broward County, Fla. G. Marsh. il Todays Ed 58:39-41 D '69
In-service: team approach. I. Kelly. Library J 94:1733-4 Ap 15 '69
Salvaging team teaching. J. A. Meyer. bibliog Clear House 44:203-5 D '69
Team teaching and objective evaluation. M. McLane and others. Clear House 44:174-8 N '69
Team teaching: the danger and the promise. G. J. Funaro. Clear House 43:401-3 Mr '69
Teaming a first step for interdisciplinary teaching. J. A. Meyer. Clear House 43:406-10 Mr '69
TEAMS, Baseball. See Baseball clubs
TEAMSTERS union. See International brotherhood of teamsters, chauffeurs, warehousemen and helpers of America
TEAPOTS
Teapots. B. Woodman. il Ceram Mo 17:12-15 Mr '69
TEAR gas
CW in Viet Nam? Defoliants and tear gas. il Sr Schol 94:7 F 7 '69
It's a gas! B. Lando. New Repub 160:17-18 Je 28 '69
Mace for the masses. J. A. Page. Commonweal 90:141-3 Ap 18 '69
Will pocketbook tear-gas devices protect you? Good H 169:200 N '69
See also
Chemical mace

TEARS
See also
Crying
El TEATRO campesino. See Theater—United States
TEBBEL, John
Broadcasting's hidden power: the TV-radio reps. Sat R 52:68-9 D 13 '69
Editors and publishers: a confrontation? Sat R 52:49-50 Jl 12 '69
Forecasting the seventies. Sat R 52:80-1 N 8 '69
Happiness is a comic strip. Sat R 52:72-3+ Ap 12 '69
It's up in the air: who owns television? Sat R 52:75-6 My 10 '69
Magazines, new, changing, growing. Sat R 52:55-6 F 8 '69
Private mail delivery? The postman rings twice. Sat R 52:50-1 Je 14 '69
Prospect before us. Sat R 52:19-22 Ap 26 '69
Summer of discontent. Sat R 52:110-11 S 13 '69
Television: the view from Europe. Sat R 52:43-4 Ag 9 '69
TECCE, Joseph J. and Scheff, N. M.
Attention reduction and suppressed direct-current potentials in the human brain. bibliog Science 164:331-3 Ap 18 '69
TECHNICAL assistance
See also
Underdeveloped areas
United Nations—Development program
TECHNICAL assistance, American
Technology for Taiwan. G. C. Sponsler. Bul Atom Sci 25:31-5 Je '69
Universities and foreign aid. G. W. Sazama. America 121:391-2 N 1 '69
See also
United States—Peace corps
TECHNICAL assistance, Russian
Dam U.S. wouldn't build: a big success for Russia. J. Law. il U S News 67:66-7 D 29 '69
TECHNICAL assistance in Latin America
ILO: fifty years of labor; details of various activities in the Américas. J. A. Tijerino-Medrano. il Américas 21:16-22 Jl '69
TECHNICAL assistance in Taiwan
Technology for Taiwan. G. C. Sponsler. Bul Atom Sci 25:31-5 Je '69
TECHNICAL education
Fourteen million vocational students by 1975. M. Russo. il Am Ed 5:10-11 Mr '69
Technical education useless for rapid-change age of technology; excerpts. R. M. Hutchins. Sch & Soc 97:71 F '69
See also
Illinois institute of technology, Chicago
Professional education
Trade schools
Vocational education
TECHNICAL information
Secrecy and dissemination in science and technology. bibliog Science 163:787-90 F 21 '69
TECHNICAL libraries
See also
Libraries—Technology departments
TECHNICAL literature
Better written journal papers, who wants them? J. H. Wilson, jr. Science 165:986-7 S 5 '69; Discussion. 166:454+ O 24 '69
See also
Technology—Bibliography
TECHNICAL processes in libraries. See Libraries—Technical processes
TECHNICAL workers. See Technicians in industry
TECHNICAL writing
Better written journal papers, who wants them? J. H. Wilson, jr. Science 165:986-7 S 5 '69; Discussion. 166:454+ O 24 '69
Jobscope: for the science-minded. N. Axelrad. Mlle 69:218 My '69
TECHNICIANS in industry
How to manage brainpower; excerpts from address. August 1969. C. A. Anderson. Science 165:1106 S 12 '69
TECHNIQUE. See subhead Technique under various subjects, e.g Fiction—Technique
TECHNOCRACY
Bibliography
Technocracy: despotism of beneficent expertise. T. Roszak. Nation 209:181-4+ S 1 '69
TECHNOLOGICAL aids in education. See Teaching—Aids and devices
TECHNOLOGICAL change
Adjusting to technology on the railroads; ed. by M. Levine. il Mo Labor R 92:36-42 N '69
Are technological upheavals inevitable? M. W. Hunter, 2d. il Harvard Bsns R 47:73-83 S '69

TECHNOLOGY and civilization—*Continued*
Social impact of a nuplex; advantages of nuclear-powered, industrial complexes. R. L. Meier. il Bul Atom Sci 25:16-21 Mr '69
Statecraft and the SST; need for an SST non-deployment and nonproliferation treaty. A. W. Smith. Nat Parks 43:2 D '69
Technological man: the myth and the reality, by V. C. Ferkiss. Review
    Bul Atom Sci 25:41-2 N '69. M. H. Goldhaber
Technology, adaptation, and evolution; excerpt from address. H. Hoagland. il Bul Atom Sci 25:27-30 Ja '69
Technology and society; the right to privacy; address, March 26, 1969. C. E. Gallagher. Vital Speeches 35:528-33 Je 15 '69
Technology, social change and the evaluative function; address. N. E. Golovin. bibliog Vital Speeches 35:310-15 Mr 1 '69
Troubled man on the moon. J. B. Sheerin. Cath World 209:242-3 S '69
    See also
Technological change
TECHNOLOGY and religion. See Religion and technology
TECHNOLOGY and society. See Technology and civilization
TECHNOLOGY and the human environment, Select committee on (proposed) See United States—Congress—Senate—Technology and the human environment. Select committee on (proposed)
TECHNOLOGY transfer
Communications problem; transferring aerospace technology to the general economy and social system. R. Hotz. Aviation W 91:11 Jl 21 '69
Down-to-earth spin-offs from space research. il Changing T 23:32-3 F '69
Industrial impact of Apollo. F. A. Long. il Bul Atom Sci 25:70-3 S '69
New ideas for industry and medicine from the space program. Space World F-3-63:38 Mr '69
Scientific fallout from the space program. J. L. Helms. Space World G-1-73:7-11 Ja '70
Squabbling over fallout from space technology. Bsns W p72 Ja 3 '70
Technology spinoff practices crystallizing. W. H. Gregory. il Aviation W 90:75-9 Mr 3 '69
Technology transfer by multinational companies. J. B. Quinn. bibliog f il Harvard Bsns R 47:147-61 N '69
Waste unit uses space techniques; integrated heating, water recycling and sewage disposal system for homes. W. H. Gregory. il Aviation W 91:49-50 D 15 '69
TECTONICS. See Geology, Structural
TED Bates and company. See Bates, Ted, and company
TEDDY bears. See Toys
TEDESCHI, Henry. See Tupper, J. T. jt. auth.
TEEGER, Reina
Generation gap. Har Yrs 9:31-3 O '69
Keep your teeth smiling; interview. Har Yrs 9:38-40 D '69
TEELING, John
Recipe for an IC preamp. il Radio-Electr 40:44-5+ Jl '69
TEEN-age automobile drivers. See Automobile drivers
TEEN-age book clubs. See Book clubs
TEEN-age drinking. See Liquor problem—United States
TEEN-age employment. See Youth—Employment
TEEN-age entertaining. See Entertaining
TEEN-age marriage
Playing at marriage. il Good H 168:28+ Ap '69
Under twenty-one: quiz about marriage. S. Reice and L. Singer. il McCalls 96:36+ Je '69
TEEN-age parties. See Entertaining
TEEN-age reading. See High school students—Reading; Young adults reading
TEEN-age suicide. See Suicide
TEEN-age travel. See Student travel
TEEN-agers. See Youth
TEEN-agers and smoking. See Smoking and youth
TEETH
    See also
Dental research
Dentistry
    Care and hygiene
About dental hygiene. Consumer Rep 34:146 Mr '69
Dental myths to chew on. il Good H 168:191 My '69

For sound teeth. M. O. Clampitt and K. R. Rankin. il Parents Mag 44:64-5+ N '69
How can you save your teeth? How one dental plan works. G. M. Knox. il Bet Hom & Gard 47:20+ N '69
Keep your teeth smiling; interview. R. Teeger. Har Yrs 9:38-40 D '69
Prevention. new look in dentistry. S. L. Englebardt. Read Digest 94:15-16+ F '69
    See also
Dentifrices
    Diseases
New aspect of tooth decay. Chem 42:4 Je '69
Tooth decay and pyorrhea. il Consumer Rep 34:143-6 Mr '69
Tooth decay beaten for good. Sci Digest 65:57-8 My '69
TEETH, Artificial
    Care and hygiene
How to enjoy your dentures. Har Yrs 9:39 D '69
TEICHMAN, Raymond
Learn code! (time: 30 minutes) Field & S 73:144+ Ap '69
TEIID lizards. See Lizards
TEILHARD DE CHARDIN, Pierre
Dag Hammarskjöld and Teilhard de Chardin. M. Ward. por Cath World 210:159-64 Ja '70
TEISER, Ruth
Sockeye, cling, & the Golden state. Am West 6:20-5 Mr '69
TEITELMAN, Jill Faye
Alumni in dance. Dance Mag 43:39-44 F '69
TEKTITE (underwater laboratory) See Underwater laboratories
TEKTITE project. See Underwater laboratories
TEKTITES
Moon source proven. Sci N 96:6 Jl 5 '69
Tektites from Tycho? il Sky & Tel 38:389 D '69
Tektites on earth said to be from the moon. il Chem 42:4-5 D '69
TEKTRONIX, incorporated
Selective success; leading maker of cathode-ray oscilloscopes. il Forbes 103:50 Je 15 '69
TELCOMSAT. See Communications satellites—Military applications
TELECOMMUNICATION
Boeing network cuts Apollo work costs; teleconference concept. W. C. Wetmore. il Aviation W 90:43-4+ F 10 '69
Growing wildly without a blueprint; the data-processing and communications industries in the 1970s. il Bsns W p 192+ D 6 '69
    See also
Communications satellites
Emergency communication systems
    Multiplex system
Intelsat access system designed; time-division multiple-access system. B. M. Elson. il Aviation W 90:107+ Ap 14 '69
TELECOMMUNICATION in education
Telecommunications and education; meeting of Joint council on educational telecommunications. Sch & Soc 97:298-9 Sum '69
TELEDYNE, incorporated
Playing it safe? Forbes 103:17 Ja 15 '69
TELEGRAPH
    See also
Radio telegraph
TELEGRAPH companies
    See also
Western union telegraph company
TELEMANN, Georg Philipp
Recordings. M. Mayer. Esquire 72:8+ Jl '69
TELEMETER
    See also
Space telemetry
TELEMETRY, Biological. See Biotelemetry
TELEMETRY tracking. See Space vehicles—Tracking
TELEOSTS
Seawater teleosts: evidence for a sodium-potassium exchange in the branchial sodium-excreting pump. J. Maetz. bibliog il Science 166:613-15 O 31 '69
TELEPHONE
Age of overload. Newsweek 74:70+ S 29 '69
Care-Ring: service providing subscribers with two calls a day from telephone companions; interview. M. H. Parker. New Yorker 45:30-1 Je 14 '69
Following finagle's law. Newsweek 73:58 Je 2 '69
Great telephone snarl. W. A. McWhirter. il Life 67:86-86D+ D 5 '69
Hello? Hello? Hello? overloaded circuits. il Newsweek 74:75+ Jl 7 '69

TELEPHONE—*Continued*
Listeners; Davenport, Iowa, Dial-a-listener service. Time 94:56 Ag 1 '69
Loved ones; Care-ring and Ring-a-day services. Newsweek 74:55 Ag 4 '69
Mother Bell's migraine; pay phones put out of commission by vandals and thieves. Time 93:92 F 28 '69
New York phone hangup. Bsns W p52 Ag 2 '69
Telephone tactics; or, Every boy is a telephone operator. D. Rustin. il Seventeen 28:14+ Ag '69
You and your telephone. J. Brothers. il Good H 168:44+ Mr '69
See also
American telephone and telegraph company
Bell telephone laboratories
Facsimile transmission
New York telephone company

Anecdotes, facetiae, satire, etc.
Humming a different tune. W. Zinsser. Life 66:24B My 9 '69

Apparatus and supplies
Ma Bell rental agency. W. P. Rokes. il Nation 208:820-3 Je 30 '69
Phone equipment: a tangled market. Bsns W p 160 My 10 '69

Emergency applications
Beach phones keep emergencies at low tide; Fort Lauderdale. il Am City 84:20 Ja '69
Crime alert gets the citizen involved; South Bend, Ind. Am City 84:46 My '69
Emergency reports from a bridge; Narrows bridge in Tacoma, Wash. il Am City 84:122 Ja '69
New telephone devices that guard your house; automatic telephone dialers. S. Shatavsky. il Pop Sci 194:112-15 Je '69
Your role as eyes and ears for police. A. Rosenthal. il Todays Health 47:58-61+ S '69

Intercommunication systems
See Intercommunicating systems

Medical applications
ECG by telephone. S. V. Jones. il Sci Digest 65:85 My '69

Rates
Coast-to-coast calls; thirty-five cents. U S News 68:5 Ja 5 '70
One cost that may be dropping; interstate long-distance phone calls U S News 67:12 Jl 14 '69
Over the phone: good news; lower charges on interstate calls. U S News 67:18 N 17 '69
See also
Government investigations—American telephone and telegraph company

Switching systems
See Telephone exchanges

Wire tapping
See Wire tapping

TELEPHONE, Push button
IC's in today's pushbutton phones. L. Steckler. il Radio-Electr 40:58-9 Je '69
TELEPHONE amplifiers. See Amplifiers
TELEPHONE buildings. See Industrial buildings
TELEPHONE cables
See also
Cables, Submarine
TELEPHONE circuits
IC's in today's pushbutton phones. L. Steckler. il Radio-Electr 40:58-9 Je '69
TELEPHONE companies
Small phone companies switch on. il Bsns W p 158+ My 10 '69
See also
American telephone and telegraph company

Canada
Going its own way. il Forbes 103:31+ Ja 15 '69
TELEPHONE exchanges
IBM phone calls Europe; automatic telephone and data switching exchange for businesses. Bsns W p39 Ap 19 '69
TELEPHONE in counseling
Call for action, new voice for the people; WMCA's program. J. Daniel. Read Digest 95:207-10+ O '69
Teen-age hot line; Los Angeles. Newsweek 73:74 Ap 7 '69
TELEPHONE in education
Learning at home with Dial-a-drill; New York city program. il(p 1) Sr Schol 94: Schol Teach 4 Ap 18 '69

TELEPHONE in libraries
San Antonio; books by phone. I. Sexton. il Wilson Lib Bul 43:885-7 My '69
See also
Libraries—Telephone reference service
TELEPHONE in medical service
MIST in Alabama; Medical information service via telephone. il Time 94:72 O 10 '69
TELEPHONE in rescue work
Beachphones real lifesavers. il Parks & Rec 4:53+ My '69
TELEPHONE reference service. See Libraries —Telephone reference service
TELEPHONE tables. See Tables
TELEPHOTO lenses. See Lenses, Photographic
TELEPHOTOGRAPHY
Biggest tele? S. M. Gallager. il Pop Mech 131:40 Ja '69
TELESCOPE
Amateur's 12-inch long-focus refractor. O. E. Shipp. il Sky & Tel 37:182-5 Mr '69
California telescope makers' conference. C. Holmes. il Sky & Tel 37:353-5 Je '69
Combination wide-field telescope and astro-camera. H. Pfleumer. il Sky & Tel 37:316-18 My '69
Construction of a folded refracting telescope. E. Pfannenschmidt. il Sky & Tel 37:319-20 My '69
Detroit amateur's rich-field refractor. B. C. Carter. il Sky & Tel 37:252-3 Ap '69
English observer's 12½-inch reflector. J. L. Long. il Sky & Tel 37:389-90 Je '69
Fabrication of a Wright telescope. T. J. Waineo. il Sky & Tel 38:112-18 Ag '69
Giant x-ray telescope. il Sky & Tel 37:300-1 My '69
Gleanings for ATM's; ed. by R. E. Cox. See issues of Sky and telescope
Low-power telescope with an unusual finder. K. W. Landon. il Sky & Tel 37:188-9 Mr '69
New three-mirror off-axis amateur telescope. R. A. Buchroeder. il Sky & Tel 38: 418-23 D '69
Open telescope travels with you. R. Kouhoupt. il Pop Sci 195:138-42 Ag '69
Perkins 72-inch telescope in Arizona. J. S. Hall and A. Slettebak. il Sky Tel 37: 222-4 Ap '69
Sacramento peak's new solar telescope. R. B. Dunn. il Sky & Tel 38:368-75 D '69
Safe sun scope. W. S. Houston. il R Pop Astron 63:27-8 F '69
Six-inch Springfield telescope with remote reading dials. J. K. Newell. il Sky & Tel 37:247-9 Ap '69
Split-ring ten-inch equatorial of low cost. A. C. Haven, jr. il Sky & Tel 37:116-17 F '69
Steward 90-inch telescope dedicated. il Sky & Tel 38:164-5 S '69
Story of Jodrell Bank, by B. Lovell. Review Bul Atom Sci 25:40 Je '69. M. H. Cohen
Tele-topics. See issues of Review of popular astronomy
Ten-inch reflector fashioned in wood. R. C. Ludden. il Sky & Tel 37:112-15 F '69
This is moon watch year. Give him a telescope. il Sunset 143:66-7 D '69
Three-inch reflecting telescope for $10. J. Michaels. il Mech Illus 65:92 Ap '69
Very sturdy 10-inch Newtonian reflector. N. Condoluci. il Sky & Tel 38:189+ S '69
X-ray unit designed for sun study. G. S. Hunter. il Aviation W 90:57+ Ap 28 '69
See also
Clark, Alvan, and sons company
Mirrors for telescopes
Radio telescope

Equipment
Simple recording Foucault tester. A. C. Haven, jr. il Sky & Tel 38:51-2 Jl '69

History
James Nasmyth's telescopes and his observations. J. Ashbrook. il Sky & Tel 38:380-1 D '69
TELESCOPE mirrors. See Mirrors for telescopes
TELESCOPE mountings
Amateur's torque-tube mount. H. Link. il Sky & Tel 38:258-60 O '69
Semipermanent telescope pedestal. A. J. Blackwood. il Sky & Tel 38:46-8 Jl '69
TELESCOPIC photography. See Telephotography
TELESCOPIC sights
See also
Firearms—Sights
TELETYPE
GE steps on Teletype's toes; TermiNet 300 is quieter and faster than teletypewriters. il Bsns W p52 Ap 5 '69

TELETYPE corporation
  GE steps on Teletype's toes; TermiNet 300
    is quieter and faster than teletypewriters.
    il Bsns W p52 Ap 5 '69
TELETYPEWRITERS. See Teletype
TELEVISION
  Many, many uses of television. il Changing
    T 23:31-3 Je '69
  Radio & television news. F. H. Belt. See issues
    of Electronics world
  Taking waste out of the wasteland; art ex-
    hibition at Manhattan's Howard Wise gal-
    lery entitled TV as a creative medium. il
    Time 93:74 My 30 '69
  TV: the next medium. J. S. Margolies. il Art
    in Am 57:48-55 S '69

          Color
    See Television, Color

          Photographic aspects
  Farewell, sweet photojournalism. S. Nathan.
    il Pop Phot 64:60+ Je '69

          Social aspects
    See Television broadcasting—Social as-
    pects
TELEVISION, Closed circuit
    See also
  Television in education
TELEVISION, Color
  Black-and-white TV gets illusion of color.
    Bsns W p89 Ag 9 '69
  Color from black & white film! il Pop Sci
    195:67 Jl '69
  Color TV 1970; symposium. il Radio-Electr
    41:33-8+ Ja '70
  How color TV was born; excerpt from The
    strategy of change for business success, ed.
    by S. Furst and M. Sherman. D. Sarnoff. il
    Nations Bsns 57:70-3 F '69
  Toward color-fast TV. D. Lachenbruch. il
    Radio-Electr 40:2+ Ap '69
TELEVISION actors and actresses. See Tele-
    vision broadcasting—Performers
TELEVISION advertising
  Annals of television. T. Whiteside. New
    Yorker 45:47-50+ S 27 '69
  Army may be hazardous to your health; San
    Francisco peace groups plan anti-recruit-
    ment ads. P. Barnes. New Repub 161:13-14
    D 20 '69
  Broadcasting's hidden power; the TV-radio
    reps. J. Tebbel. Sat R 52:68-9 D 13 '69
  CATV projects a new ad picture. il Bsns W
    p 140 +Jl 12 '69
  Enticers, 1970; on TV, who do they think
    you are? S. Harrington. Vogue 155:118+
    Ja 15 '70
  Idiots' delight; Huntley-Brinkley newscast
    devoted to the war in Vietnam interspersed
    with seven commercials. R. L. Shayon. Sat
    R 52:43-4 Je 7 '69
  Is this any way to sell an automobile?
    American motors commercials. il Motor T
    21:110-11 Jl '69
  Jobs making television commercials. J.
    O'Reilly. il Mlle 68:174-5+ Mr '69
  Looking & listening; commercial crossfire. P.
    Hudson. Sr Schol 94:24 Ap 11 '69
  Memo to tomorrow's Madison avenue; ex-
    cerpts from With all its faults. F. M. Cone.
    Sat R 52:71-4 O 11 '69
  Middlemen put squeeze on admen; media
    buying services. il Bsns W p80-1+ O 18 '69
  More from less. D. Davis. il Newsweek 74:
    98+ N 10 '69
  Now a further word... Newsweek 73:73 My
    19 '69
  Shut-in's view of television commercials. R.
    Squires. PTA Mag 63:32-3 Je '69
  TV will need finer tuning; forecast for the
    1970s. il Bsns W p 200-1 D 6 '69
  TV's Saturday gold mine. il Bsns W p96+ Ag
    2 '69
  They've come a long way; Clio awards. il
    Newsweek 73:135 My 26 '69
  Will TV take to drink? Bsns W p33-4 F 15 '69
    See also
  Books—Advertising

          Cigarettes
    See Cigarettes—Advertising
TELEVISION and children. See Television
    broadcasting and children
TELEVISION and copyright. See Copyright—
    Broadcasting rights
TELEVISION and moving pictures. See Moving
    pictures and television
TELEVISION antennas
  Build the pyramidal TV/FM antenna. G.
    Monser. il Pop Electr 31:27-32 Jl '69
  Calling all congressmen; FCC regulations.
    Forbes 103:35 Ja 15 '69

How to have TV in every room in the house.
    F. H. Belt. il Pop Mech 132:126-9+ Ag '69
How to improve your FM and TV reception.
    R. Gelatt. House & Gard 135:16+ F '69
Installing a home master antenna TV system.
    J. Sarayiotes. il Electr World 81:41-3+ Je
    '69
    See also
CATV system

          Equipment
TV/FM signal splitters; single lead-in for more
    than one antenna. Consumer Rep 34:68-9 F
    '69

          Rotators
New solid-state TV rotators. R. F. Scott. il
    Radio-Electr 40:42-5 D '69
Poor man's TV rotator. L. Duckwalter. Mech
    Illus 65:94-5+ D '69

          Testing
R-E tests, new antennas for color TV. L.
    Steckler. il Radio-Electr 40:23-6 S '69
TELEVISION apparatus
  Eico model 385 color-bar generator. il Electr
    World 82:66-7 Ag '69
  Heath IG-28 color-bar generator. il Electr
    World 82:64+ D '69
  IC color pattern generator. R. G. Kostanty.
    il Radio-Electr 41:44-5+ Ja '70
  Leader LCG-388 and LCG-389 color-bar gene-
    rators. il Electr World 81:66 F '69
    See also
  Electronic video recording
  Television receivers—Control
  Video tape recorders and recording

          Manufacture
Cost of color-TV service. J. Frye. Electr
    World 81:56+ F '69
Technicians' chance to gripe. J. Frye. Electr
    World 82:56+ D '69
TELEVISION apparatus industry and trade
  Color TV's rainbow fades a bit. il Bsns W
    p38+ F 1 '69
  Productivity rises as radio-TV output tri-
    ples in eight years. J. E. Henneberger. il
    Mo Labor R 92:40-2 Mr '69
    See also
  Philips of Eindhoven companies

          Finance
Color TV sales are looking bluer. Bsns W
    p36+ N 8 '69
TELEVISION apparatus on aircraft
  Covert night vision aids rescue mission. B.
    Miller. Aviation W 91:73-4+ D 1 '69
TELEVISION authorship
  Dangerous uneasiness with ideas. J. Leonard.
    Life 66:18 Mr 21 '69
  Free Mason; script doctor M. Williams. il
    Time 93:86-7 Ap 11 '69
  King of corn: P. Henning. il Newsweek 74:
    94 Jl 14 '69
  Man behind Harry. il Time 94:68 Jl 11 '69
  Television and film writing (cont) N. Vogel.
    Writers Digest 49:24-9 F; 82-7 Ap; 66-71 Ag;
    22+ O; 18-20+ D '69
  Writers' dilemma; Writers guild of America
    conference discusses the question of writer
    control. A. Knight. Sat R 52:51 Ap 26 '69
TELEVISION awards
  Networks snubbed; no Peabody award for
    entertainment. Newsweek 73:72 Ap 28 '69
  They've come a long way; Clio awards. il
    Newsweek 73:135 My 26 '69
    See also
  Academy of television arts and sciences
TELEVISION broadcasting
    See also
  Communications satellites
  National association of broadcasters
  Television stations

          Advertising
    See Television advertising

          Animated cartoons
    See also
  Television broadcasting—Childrens programs

          Arts programs
    See Television broadcasting and the arts

          Ballet
    See Television broadcasting—Dancing

          Boats and boating
    See Television broadcasting—Sports

          Censorship
Brothers smothered. Newsweek 73:90 Ap 14
    '69
Brothers smothered; a slap at youth audi-
    ence? P. Hudson. il Sr Schol 94:19 Ap 25 '69

TELEVISION broadcasting—Censorship—*Cont.*
Censorship bugaboo. Newsweek 73:90-1 Mr 31 '69
Fickle finger of CBS; canceling the Smothers brothers comedy hour. il Time 93:64-5 Ap 18 '69
Looking & listening; pressure for censorship of sex and violence. P. Hudson. Sr Schol 94: 29 My 2 '69
Minuet over censorship; National association of broadcasters taking step toward adopting plan of formal censorship. il Time 93:76 Ap 4 '69
Much ado about previews; NAB's views. Newsweek 73:55 Ap 7 '69
Muzzled stars and buck passing on network TV. J. Barthel. il Life 66:24-5 Ap 4 '69
Panic in TV censorship; as the Congress tunes in, the industry chokes up. J. Barthel. il Life 67:51-4 Ag 1 '69
Self-regulation or censorship; the T.V. industry; address, July 31, 1969. R. E. Lee. Vital Speeches 35:730-2 S 15 '69
Smothering the brothers. R. L. Shayon. Sat R 52:48 Ap 5 '69
Smothers brothers; who controls TV? N. Hentoff. il Look 33:27-9 Je 24 '69
Social comment and TV censorship. D. Dempsey. Sat R 52:53-5 Jl 12 '69
Those blip blip censors blip the hell out of TV. G. Ace. Sat R 52:4 My 31 '69
Transmogrification of the Smothers brothers. W. Kloman. il pors Esquire 72:148-53+ O '69

Children, Effect on
See Television broadcasting and children

Childrens programs
Big friend to little people: Misterogers. E. H. McCleary. il Todays Health 47:20-3+ Ag '69
Children's boon for adults; CBS children's drama. J. T. il Time 94:76 D 12 '69
Children's hour; CBS series and Sesame street. il Newsweek 74:91 D 22 '69
J.T.'s conversion. R. L. Shayon. Sat R 53:96 Ja 10 '70
Man kids believe; Misterogers' neighborhood. il Newsweek 73:97+ My 12 '69
Men behind Dastardly & Muttley; W. Hanna and J. Barbera. J. Culhane. il N Y Times Mag p50-1+ N 23 '69
Murder on Saturday morning? T. O'Flaherty. il McCalls 96:72-3+ S '69
Talking up to children; As I see it, child's eye view of life on Children's theater. il Time 93:68 Je 27 '69
TV's Misterogers: quality clicks with kids. C. S. Wren. il Look 33:102-6 D 2 '69
TV's Saturday gold mine. il Bsns W p96+ Ag 2 '69
Time out for TV. See issues of PTA magazine
Underground hours. D. Davis. il Newsweek 74:105-6+ O 13 '69
What's good about children's TV; Friendly giant; Misterogers' neighborhood; Captain Kangaroo; Children's television workshop. N. S. Morris. il Atlan 224:67-71 Ag '69

Comedy
See Television broadcasting—Humor

Conversation programs
Back to the origins; Here's Johnny, where's Merv? il Time 94:96 O 24 '69
Battle of the talk shows. il Newsweek 74: 42-4+ S 1 '69
Broadcast Joe; Joe Namath show. il Time 94: 94 O 17 '69
Cavett's return. il Time 93:65 Je 20 '69
Does Cavett have it? B. Baer. il Look 33: 61-5 Jl 15 '69
Empty-chair approach; Evans-Novak report. il Time 93:72 F 28 '69
Good-by Joey, hello Dick. Newsweek 74:34 D 8 '69
Happy talker: D. Cavett. il Newsweek 73:65 F 3 '69
NRPA executive is guest on Today show; interview, ed. by B. Monroe. S. J. Prezioso. il Parks & Rec 4:17-18+ O '69
Newest host; David Frost show. il Newsweek 74:87 Ag 4 '69
Permanent second fiddles; sidekicks on late-night talk-shows. il Newsweek 74:45 S 1 '69
Still promising; the Dick Cavett show. il Newsweek 75:41 Ja 12 '70
Summer's gain, autumn's loss; J. Baez interview on the Dick Cavett show. R. L Shayon. Sat R 52:55 Ag 23 '69
Talk, talk, talk. il Time 94:52 Ag 29 '69
Talking it up. Newsweek 74:87 Ag 4 '69

Three-way race on late-night TV; Carson, Bishop, Griffin shows. il Bsns W p78-9 Ag 16 '69
What makes David Frost talk. P. Hellman. il N Y Times Mag p54-5+ D 7 '69

Cookery programs
Galloping gourmet. Newsweek 73:60 Mr 3 '69
Graham Kerr; Galloping gourmet of TV; with comments, ed. by M. C. Wrenn. P. O'Neil. il Life 67:51-2+ D 5 '69
Kitsch in the kitchen; The galloping gourmet. il Time 93:72+ F 28 '69

Court proceedings
See Television broadcasting—Trials

Criticism
See Television criticism

Dancing
Anybody need 683 dancers? J. Barthel. il Life 67:61-2+ D 5 '69
Chicago has been lucky; WTTW-TV prize-winning programs. M. Harriton. il Dance Mag 43:22+ Ag '69
Dancing on TV. W. Terry. il Sat R 52:42-3 Mr 1 '69
Ken Berry on TV. V. H. Swisher. il Dance Mag 43:22-4 Jl '69
Looking at television. A. Barzel. See issues of Dance magazine
Margaret Dale; TV ambassador. M. Harriton. il Dance Mag 43:24-7 N '69
World of dance; dance shows in Sweden and Denmark. W. Terry. il Sat R 52:34-5 Ag 16 '69

Documentary programs
ABC aborts abortion show. America 120:698-9 Je 21 '69
Delightful disaster; NBC news presents Arthur Rubinstein. Sat R 52:50 O 11 '69
Making of a parlay; interpretation of T. H. White's The making of the President: 1968. R. L. Shayon. Sat R 52:58 O 4 '69
Message about messages; failure of Vietnam peace talks: a view from the other side to illuminate relationships. R. L. Shayon. Sat R 52:26 Jl 19 '69
Orchestration of cultures; Adventures at the Jade Sea. R. L. Shayon. Sat R 52:52 Ap 26 '69
Remembrance of things just past; NBC's documentary, From here to the seventies. Time 94:94 O 17 '69
Waiting for glory; B. Greenspan's film of early baseball games not sold. P. Axthelm. il Newsweek 74:82 Jl 7 '69
See also
Public broadcast laboratory

Drama
As the Victorian world turns; The Forsyte saga. il Time 94:84 O 3 '69
Caring enough for a cause: Hallmark's Teacher, teacher, featuring a retarded boy. R. L. Shayon. Sat R 52:46 Mr 1 '69
Dramatic turn. Newsweek 73:85 Mr 10 '69
Experiment fails; presentation of The experiment on CBS playhouse. R. L. Shayon. Sat R 52:41 Mr 29 '69
Forsyte saga, artful if not art. M. Hentoff. Vogue 155:78 Ja 1 '70
Improving the species; rerun by NBC of Male of the species. il Time 94:71 S 12 '69
New TV shows fall '69; medical shows and comedy. N. Vogel. il Writers Digest 49:62-5+ Je '69
One-dimensional square; George Bellak's Sadbird. R. L. Shayon. Sat R 53:75 Ja 3 '70
Prime time for the bard: Midsummer night's dream. il Time 93:81 F 7 '69
Requiem for Peyton Place. J. Barthel. il Life 66:47-50 Ap 25 '69
Rescuing the Survivors. il Time 94:54 Ag 1 '69
Saga: Forsyte trilogy by J. Galsworthy now television serial. New Yorker 45:15-17 Ja 10 '70
Seen any good Galsworthy lately? Forsyte saga. A. Burgess. il N Y Times Mag p57+ N 16 '69
Song of the people; Mexican-American bilingual soap opera. il Newsweek 73:85 Mr 10 '69
TV dreams: A midsummer night's dream. N. Compton. Commentary 47:65-7 Ap '69
Tom's mix; San Francisco's KQED experimental television project, The tribe, by Paul Foster. H. Hewes. Sat R 52:21 Jl 12 '69

Educational applications
See Television in education

TELEVISION broadcasting—*Continued*

Golf

See Television broadcasting—Sports

Health education programs

Hope for smoke-plagued humanity. R. L. Shayon. Sat R 52:44-5 F 8 '69

Power of the press, and of television; J. F. Banzhaf and the anti-cigarette crusade. R. L. Tobin. il Sat R 52:47-8 Je 14 '69

Watching life; Lifewatch 6 series. R. L. Shayon. Sat R 52:58 My 17 '69

Humor

Black can be funny. il Time 93:71 Mr 7 '69

Can we love Debbie too? S. Gordon. il Look 33:90+ N 18 '69

Corn is still green; new CBS summer series, Hee haw. il Time 94:59 Ag 8 '69

Era of Rowan and Martin? Laugh-in. H. Van Horne. il McCalls 97:80-1+ O '69

Gagman's revenge; P. Keyes quits Laugh-in. Newsweek 74:69 N 3 '69

Girls from L-I. il Newsweek 73:62 Ja 27 '69

Laugh-in dropouts. il Time 94:86 D 5 '69

Living, breathing picture gallery; C. Brown on Laugh-in. il Ebony 24:54-6+ Ap '69

New TV shows fall '69; medical shows and comedy. N. Vogel. il Writers Digest 49:62-5+ Je '69

TV comedy. N. Compton. Commentary 48: 18-21 Jl '69

Unsinkable Tom Smothers. Time 94:52-3 Ag 29 '69

International aspects

Cincinnati airs world affairs. S. Aiken. il Am Ed 5:24-6 My '69

See also
European broadcasting union

Jazz music

See Television broadcasting—Music

Laws and regulations

See Television laws and regulations

Licenses

See Television laws and regulations

Lighting

See Television lighting

Moral aspects

Blood and gore on the home screen. R. L. Tobin. Sat R 52:69-70 Ap 12 '69

How dangerous is TV violence? G. P. Dawson. il Parents Mag 44:60-1+ O '69

Is TV brutalizing your child? E. A. Daley. il Look 33:99-100 D 2 '69

Looking & listening; pressure for censorship of sex and violence. P. Hudson. Sr Schol 94: 29 My 2 '69

Looking & listening; violence on the home screen. P. Hudson. Sr Schol 94:24 Ap 11 '69

Movies move into prime time. P. Molloy. PTA Mag 63:27-9 My '69

Murder on Saturday morning? T. O'Flaherty. il McCalls 96:72-3+ S '69

Muzzled stars and buck passing on network TV. J. Barthel. il Life 66:24-5 Ap 4 '69

Panic in TV censorship; as the Congress tunes in, the industry chokes up. J. Barthel. il Life 67:51-4 Ag 1 '69

Question of taste, or is it? The great Smothers brothers controversy. J. Leonard. Life 66: 12 My 16 '69

Rating the influence of television; with study-discussion program, by R. Strang. B. F. Winston. bibliog il PTA Mag 63:6-9, 36 Mr '69

Senator Pastore's TV proposal. America 120: 440 Ap 12 '69

Sex and violence in movies and TV: how harmful are they? with opinions by celebrities. J. Crist. il Good H 169:59-61+ Ag '69

Smothers brothers: who controls TV? N. Hentoff. il Look 33:27-9 Je 24 '69

TV world of violence. F. Orme. il Parents Mag 44:52-3+ Ja '69

Video violence report. Time 94:81 S 26 '69

Violence & TV; excerpts from statement. Todays Ed 58:52-4 D '69

When violence begets violence. R. L. Tobin. Sat R 52:69-70 O 11 '69

See also
Television broadcasting and children

Moving pictures

Black man's image; NBC film teleplay, Deadlock. R. L. Shayon. Sat R 52:48 Mr 22 '69

David and the network Goliaths; question of abridgment and re-editing of theatrical films. R. L. Shayon. Sat R 52:52 N 1 '69

Movies move into prime time. P. Molloy. PTA Mag 63:27-9 My '69

Return of Busby Berkeley; late, late, great, great show presentation. W. Murray. il N Y Times Mag p26-7+ Mr 2 '69

Music

Jazz; Camera three film about Jeremy Steig. W. Balliett. New Yorker 45:98+ My 31 '69

Music on TV, what works, what doesn't. R. Englander. Hi Fi 19:MA10-11+ O '69

Music: the silent stepchild. F. H. Adler. Sat R 52:22-5+ Ap 26 '69

Oh, for heaven's sake, Cynthia, there must be something else on. G. Gould. Hi Fi 19:MA13-14+ Ap '69

Nature programs

National wildlife joins Animal world television. il Nat Wildlife 7:20-1 Ag '69

Negro programs

Black TV; its problems and promises. il Ebony 24:88-90+ S '69

E. U. Essien-Udom: appearance on Black heritage; interview. E. U. Essien-Udom. New Yorker 45:27-8 Mr 8 '69

News

Agnew demands equal time. il Time 94:18-19+ N 21 '69

Agnew on TV. W. F. Buckley, jr. Nat R 21: 1235 D 2 '69

Agnew: other voices, other views. H. J. Sievers. America 121:579 D 13 '69

Agnew's complaint: the trouble with TV. il Newsweek 74:88-90+ N 24 '69

Beauty: the TV specials; woman producer and newscaster. il Mlle 68:180-2+ Mr '69

Biological warfare: is the Smithsonian really a cover? NBC's charge aired on First Tuesday. P. M. Boffey. il Science 163:791-6 F 21 '69

Close up: Rona Barrett, TV snoop; gossip about celebrities. J. Barthel. il Life 66:41-2+ Mr 21 '69

Constructions; concerning books by R. MacNeil and I. Fang. L. Goldstein. Nation 208: 472+ Ap 14 '69

Cool medium; TV handling of the October 15 moratorium. R. L. Shayon. Sat R 52: 41 N 8 '69

Does Agnew tell it straight? L. Bernstein. Newsweek 74:90-1 N 24 '69

Duel at daybreak; CBS morning news with Joseph Benti. il Time 93:89 Ap 25 '69

European television. J. McLaughlin. America 120:174-5 F 8 '69

Faces of faceless men; producers Wallace Westfield; Av Westin; Les Midgley. il Newsweek 74:92 N 24 '69

Freedom to cheer; Vice President Agnew's Des Moines speech. Nation 209:586-7 D 1 '69

How they do it. il Newsweek 74:56-7 D 1 '69

How well does TV present the news? H. J. Gans. il N Y Times Mag p30-1+ Ja 11 '70

It's up in the air: who owns television? J. Tebbel. Sat R 52:75-6 My 10 '69

KQED's newsroom. J. Fincher. Life 66:15 Ap 11 '69

Letter from Washington; Agnew's assault on network television. R. H. Rovere. New Yorker 45:165-9 N 29 '69

Mellowing of Mike malice. Time 95:57 Ja 19 '70

Merry magazines; First Tuesday, and 60 minutes. il Time 93:86 Ap 11 '69

Mirror of the news and big brother. R. L. Tobin. Sat R 52:59-60 D 13 '69

Mr Brinkley goes to New York. pors Time 93:82+ Mr 14 '69

Mob and the media; assault by Vice President Agnew. Nat R 21:1204 D 2 '69

Notes and comment; Agnew's attacks on television and newspapers. New Yorker 45:51-3 D 6 '69

Now listen to this; commentators and the President's address. New Repub 161:9 N 29 '69

$100,000 anchorman; station KTLA-TV. Time 93:98 My 16 '69

Public regulation and the news media. J. McLaughlin. America 121:586-9 D 13 '69

Rich, risky business of TV news. S. Zalaznick. il Fortune 79:92-7+ My 1 '69

Some sober second thoughts on Vice President Agnew; television journalism: address. F. W. Friendly. Sat R 52:61-2+ D 13 '69

Sounding off; TV newscasters give views before radio mike. il Newsweek 73:54-5 Ap 7 '69

TELEVISION broadcasting—News—*Continued*
Television and Vice President Agnew. America 121:519 N 29 '69
TV criticism, post-Agnew. S. W. Little. Sat R 52:72 D 13 '69
Television news coverage; network censorship; address, November 13, 1969. S. T. Agnew. Vital Speeches 36:98-101 D 1 '69
Thorns and laurels; survey of broadcast journalism. Newsweek 74:87 N 17 '69
Threat to the climate for free opinion; Agnew's denunciation. C. B. Grannis. Pub W 196:29 N 24 '69
Tip of the iceberg; the Vice-President's attack. R. L. Shayon. Sat R 52:24 N 29 '69
Today's woman. il Newsweek 73:73 My 19 '69
Unelected elite: a few of the men responsible for TV news. il Time 94:20 N 21 '69
Welcome, Spiro Agnew. B. Hennessy. New Repub 161:13-14 D 13 '69
What Agnew finds wrong with TV commentators; excerpts from address, November 13, 1969. S. T. Agnew. U S News 67:10 N 24 '69
Where are they now? newscaster A. Zenker. il Newsweek 74:18 Jl 21 '69
See also
Television broadcasting—Trials
Television broadcasting—War news

Anecdotes, facetiae, satire, etc.
How they brought the bad news from Ghent (N.Y.) to Aix (Kans.) R. Angell. New Yorker 45:24-7 Ja 3 '70.

Operas
Cruel medium. P. H. Adler. il Opera N 33:8-11 Je 14 '69
House of the dead; performed on NET. S. Jenkins. Opera N 34:30 D 13 '69
Janacek opera: another try for TV; NET's Opera project. R. T. Jones. il Hi Fi 19:MA12-13 O '69
Music: the silent stepchild. P. H. Adler. Sat R 52:22-5+ Ap 26 '69
Musical events; NET opera production of Leoš Janáček's From the house of the dead. W. Sargeant. New Yorker 45:186 D 13 '69
TV log; Janacek's House of the dead. J. Chwat. il Opera N 34:17-19 D 6 '69

Performers
Civil rights and television; hiring practices. America 121:28 Jl 19 '69
Dirty half-dozen; the heavies. il Newsweek 74:43 Ag 11 '69
See also
Negroes in television

Political programs
See Television in politics

Program production
Jobs in television production. B. Kevles. il Mlle 68:170-3 +Mr '69
TV log; Janacek's House of the dead. J. Chwat. il Opera N 34:17-19 D 6 '69

Program rating
CBS regains its no. 1 rank. Bsns W p72 My 10 '69
Everyone a winner. Time 93:84 My 9 '69
Year of the peacock? Newsweek 74:112 O 27 '69

Programming
Entering the lists. il Newsweek 74:52 Ag 25 '69
Programmer's dilemma; live coverage on major news events. Newsweek 73:62 Ja 27 '69
Tale of two speeches. P. Steinfels. Commonweal 91:272 N 28 '69
TV and the arts. J. Tebbel; P. H. Adler. Sat R 52:19-25+ Ap 26 '69
Television and the ghetto audience. L. Pinkham. Cur 108:33-8 Je '69
TV game; your time is their time; KRON-TV license renewal controversy. A. Alpert. New Repub 161:17-21 O 18 '69

Programs
Advocates; weekly series il Newsweek 74:77-8 O 20 '69
And now let's hear it for the Ed Sullivan show! D. Barthelme. il Esquire 71:126-7+ Ap '69
Cashing in: Johnny Cash show. il Time 93:94 Je 6 '69
Dangerous uneasiness with ideas. J. Leonard. Life 66:18 Mr 21 '69
Doily for your mind. P. Collier. Ramp Mag 7:44+ Je '69
Dupont-Columbia audit; survey of broadcast journalism, 1968-1969. J. McLaughlin. il America 121:573 D 6 '69

From beautiful downtown nowhere; second season shows. il Time 93:70 F 14 '69
Gail Fisher, the girl from Mannix, CBS show. il Ebony 24:140-2+ O '69
King of TV gamesmanship. J. Barthel. il Life 67:116B-116D+ O 10 '69
Lame and the blind; nonviolent season. R. L. Shayon. Sat R 52:56 O 25 '69
Life TV review. J. Leonard. See occasional issues of Life
Look and listen. P. Hudson. See issues of Scholastic teacher
Looking & listening. P. Hudson. See issues of Senior scholastic
Mike Douglas, TV's no. 1 ladies' man. R. Hochstein. il Good H 169:30+ S '69
Next: the new TV shows. Changing T 23:6 Ag '69
Observations (cont) N. Compton. Commentary 47:65-7 Ap; 48:84-6 O '69
On experiencing Gore Vidal. W. F. Buckley, jr. Esquire 72:108-13+ Ag '69
Pastore-ized. il Newsweek 74:72 S 29 '69
Peace, old tiger; Garroway's Tempo/Boston. il Time 94:71 Jl 18 '69
Premières; old wrinkles. Time 94:84+ O 3 '69
Premières: the new season. il Time 94:80-1 S 26 '69
Sight and sound. See issues of McCall's
Spotlight! E. Miller. See issues of Seventeen
Stimuli of Experiment; NBC series. il Time 93:64 Ap 18 '69
Summer corn. il Newsweek 73:65 Je 2 '69
Television and film writing. N. Vogel. Writers Digest 49:66-71 Ag '69
TV or not TV; hardly a question. Chr Today 14:30 O 24 '69
TV-radio. See issues of Newsweek
Telling it like it isn't; Mod squad. il Time 93:59 Mr 21 '69
Time listings. See issues of Time
Time out for TV. See issues of PTA magazine
Top of my head; half-hour shows. G. Ace. Sat R 52:4 S 13 '69
Unseasonable; ABC and CBS new programs. J. Garabedian. Newsweek 74:113-14 O 6 '69
What has one eye and grew up with you? A. Gross. il Mlle 68:183-5+ Mr '69
Year of the unspecial; new prime-time schedule. il Time 94:62-3 Ag 15 '69
See also
Public broadcast laboratory
Television broadcasting—Dancing
Television broadcasting—Drama
Television broadcasting—Public service programs
Television broadcasting, Noncommercial
Television criticism

Anecdotes, facetiae, satire, etc.
Memorable minutes on What's my line? A. Francis. McCalls 96:88-9 Mr '69
Television as the medium of contempt. J. Middlebrook. Ramp Mag 7:56+ Ap '69

Psychological aspects
Can TV crime shows prevent violence? W. Bromberg and G. George. Todays Health 47:88+ My '69

Public service programs
Child market; Metromedia stations hawk unwanted children. il Newsweek 73:70 Je 16 '69
Message to broadcasters; industry's responsibility. S. Ross. Chr Cent 86:280-3 F 26 '69
Power of the press, and of television; J. F. Banzhaf and the anti-cigarette crusade. R. L. Tobin. il Sat R 52:47-8 Je 14 '69
Watching life: Lifewatch 6 series. R. L. Shayon. Sat R 52:58 My 17 '69

Religious programs
Fifth mark; recent Pastoral on tourism in Guideline program. Commonweal 90:580 S 26 '69
News and views: "Guideline" the successor to Catholic hour program. J. Deedy. Commonweal 89:574 F 7 '69
Oral Roberts: rousing return to TV. W. Willoughby. il Chr Today 13:40 Mr 28 '69

Scientific programs
In and out of the field. A. Meyer. Natur Hist 78:6 Ag '69

Social aspects
Caring enough for a cause: Hallmark's Teacher, teacher, featuring a retarded boy. R. L. Shayon. Sat R 52:46 Mr 1 '69
Let's tell the people; the incompetent criticisms of T.V; address, March 24, 1969. H. Jacobs. Vital Speeches 35:467-9 My 15 '69
Opinion: on TV and its works. D. Webster. Mlle 68:20+ Mr '69

TELEVISION broadcasting—Social aspects—
Continued
Smothering dissent: a pungent social comment. C. H. Simonds. Nat R 21:345-6 Ap 8 '69
Staking out a tough turf; CBS's ghetto reports. il Newsweek 74:94-5 Jl 14 '69
See also
Television broadcasting and Negroes
Television broadcasting and the arts

Space broadcasts
See Television broadcasting from space

Space flight coverage
Assignment downrange; factors involved in reporting the splashdown and recovery. D. Townsend. il Sat R 52:65-7 D 13 '69
Chronicling the voyage; news coverage. il Time 94:38 Jl 25 '69
Cosmic Nielsens; moon landing. R. L. Shayon. Sat R 52:40 Ag 9 '69
Moon hours: watching Apollo 11 in New York. New Yorker 45:25-30 Jl 26 '69
Moon watching; plans for Apollo 11 coverage. il Newsweek 74:73+ Jl 21 '69
TV puts moon walk before eyes of millions around world. Aviation W 91:38-40 Jl 28 '69
TV's biggest audience ever; television coverage of Apollo 11. Bsns W p99+ Jl 19 '69
TV's greatest show ever, the moon walk. H. V. Fondiller. il Pop Phot 65:122-3+ N '69

Spanish-language programs
Song of the people; Mexican-American bilingual soap opera. il Newsweek 73:85 Mr 10 '69

Sports
Adventures of superspy! W. Johnson. il Sports Illus 32:44-52 Ja 12 '70
After TV accepted the call Sunday was never the same. W. Johnson. il Sports Illus 32:22-9 Ja 5 '70
Ed Herlihy tests the Nation's boating knowhow; National boating test on television. il Motor B 123:58 Ap '69
Electronic golf range. S. Anderson. il Parks & Rec 4:45+ S '69
Frozen instants: TV at its best; football and television. J. Leonard. Life 66:14 Ja 31 '69
TV made it all a new game. W. Johnson. il Sports Illus 31:86-90+ D 22 '69
TV talk; the World series. W. Sheed. il Sports Illus 31:13 O 20 '69
When sports stars broadcast. R. L. Tobin. il Sat R 52:107-8 S 13 '69

Stock exchange news
Ticker talk. Newsweek 73:92 Mr 24 '69

Subscription programs
Confusion in TV land: fee, free, or what? CATV? il Sr Schol 94:14-15 F 14 '69
Last-minute fight over pay TV. il U S News 66:56 My 12 '69
NATO v. the monster; attack on pay television by National association of theater owners. Time 94:71 S 12 '69
When pay TV arrives—. il U S News 67:44 N 3 '69

Trials
Artist's eye; artists covering trials of Clay Shaw, Sirhan Sirhan, and inquiry into Pueblo affair. il Newsweek 73:86 Mr 10 '69

War news
Idiots' delight; Huntley-Brinkley newscast devoted to the war in Vietnam interspersed with seven commercials. R. L. Shayon. Sat R 52:43-4 Je 7 '69
Living-room war, by M. J. Arlen. Review Atlan 223:121-4 F '69. M. Janeway

Weather forecasts
Now you can see tornadoes on TV. H. Bradshaw and V. Bradshaw. il Pop Mech 131:93:6+ Mr '69

World series
See Television broadcasting—Sports

Denmark
World of dance; adaptation of Harald Lander's ballet Etudes. W. Terry. il Sat R 52:35 Ag 16 '69

Europe, Western
European television. J. McLaughlin. America 120:174-5 F 8 '69

Germany (Federal Republic)
Letter from Germany; documentary-style film on reunification. L. R. Colitt. Nation 208:283-4 Mr 3 '69

Great Britain
Dimbleby the second; BBC apologizes for coverage of Nixon in Europe. Time 93:71-2 Mr 7 '69

Israel
TV comes to Israel. H. Krosney. Nation 209:339-43 O 6 '69

Mexico
Rivals challenge Mexican TV czar; E. Azcarraga. il Bsns W p50-2 Mr 15 '69

Scandinavia
Television: the view from Europe. J. Tebbel. Sat R 52:44 Ag 9 '69

South Africa
TV comes to Afrikanerdom. America 121:150-1 S 13 '69

Sweden
World of dance; production of Bkt. W. Terry. il Sat R 52:34-5 Ag 16 '69

United States
Agnew's complaint: the trouble with TV. il Newsweek 74:88-90+ N 24 '69
Does Agnew tell it straight? L. Bernstein. Newsweek 74:90-1 N 24 '69
Living-room war, by M. J. Arlen. Review Atlan 223:121-4 F '69. M. Janeway
Spot check: some observations on television in America. J. Claman. il Harp Baz 102:122R F '69
Television overlords. H. H. Goldin. Atlan 224:87-9 Jl '69
TV's future directions. D. Lachenbruch. Radio-Electr 40:2+ Mr '69
See also
American broadcasting companies
Columbia broadcasting system, incorporated
Television broadcasting—Censorship
United States—Federal communications commission

TELEVISION broadcasting, Noncommercial
Advocates; weekly series. il Newsweek 74:77-8 O 20 '69
Freedom to view. D. Walker. Commonweal 89:500-2 Ja 17 '69
Future of non-commercial TV; interview. J. W. Macy, jr. il U S News 67:94-7 D 8 '69
Pollution on the air; financing public television; study by National citizens committee for broadcasting. New Repub 160:9 Ap 26 '69
Price of free TV. L. Chazen. Atlan 223:59-61 Mr '69
Public broadcasting. J. McLaughlin. America 120:510-11 Ap 26 '69
TV and the arts. J. Tebbel; P. H. Adler. Sat R 52:19-25+ Ap 26 '69
See also
Corporation for public broadcasting

TELEVISION broadcasting and children
How dangerous is TV violence? G. P. Dawson. il Parents Mag 44:60-1+ O '69
Rating the influence of television; with study-discussion program, by R. Strang. B. F. Winston. bibliog il PTA Mag 63:6-9, 36 Mr '69
TV and youth; literature and research reviewed. A. Harrison, jr. and E. G. Scriven. bibliog il Clear House 44:82-90 O '69
TV violence and U.S. violence; National commission on the causes and prevention of violence; report. America 121:253 O 4 '69
TV violence: appalling; excerpts from statement by National commission on the causes and prevention of violence. U S News 67:55-6 O 6 '69
Thirty seconds for a point. M. Hentoff. Vogue 154:144 D '69
Underground hours. D. Davis. il Newsweek 74:105-6+ O 13 '69
Violent Bugs Bunny et al. J. F. McDermott. il N Y Times Mag p95-6+ S 28 '69; Discussion. p58+ O 26; 14+ N 9 '69
When violence begets violence. R. L. Robin. Sat R 52:69-70 O 11 '69
See also
Television broadcasting—Childrens programs

TELEVISION broadcasting and Negroes
Television and the ghetto audience. L. Pinkham. Cur 108:33-8 Je '69
See also
Television broadcasting—Negro programs

TELEVISION broadcasting and the arts
TV and the arts. J. Tebbel; P. H. Adler. Sat R 52:19-25+ Ap 26 '69

TELEVISION broadcasting for children. See Television broadcasting—Childrens programs

TELEVISION broadcasting from space
Color video studied for lunar walk. Aviation W 91:97-8+ Ag 18 '69

TELEVISION broadcasting from space—*Cont.*
Docking transmitted live in first color TV from space. W. C. Wetmore. il Aviation W 90:18-20 My 26 '69
Eighty million earthlings watched their world shrink. A. Rosenfeld. il Life 66:50-52A My 30 '69
How you'll see Mars close up. C. P. Gilmore. il Pop Sci 195:76-9+ Jl '69
How you'll see our men on the moon. P. Geraci. il Pop Mech 132:92-3+ Jl '69
Mariner 6 and 7 television pictures; preliminary analysis. R. B. Leighton and others. bibliog il Science 166:49-67 O 3 '69
Miracle in sound. il Time 94:22 Ag 1 '69
Uncluttered path to the moon. il Time 93:64-7 Je 6 '69
TELEVISION broadcasting stations. See Television stations
TELEVISION camera tubes
Seeing the invisible; SEC television camera tubes for Project Celescope. il Space World F-8-68:21-6 Ag '69
TELEVISION cameras
Apollo color TV faces problem. Aviation W 91:24 O 27 '69
Apollo moon TV camera. il Space World F-5-65:20-1 My '69
Build all-transistor TV camera for $100. G. Davis, jr. il Radio-Electr 40:23-6+ Jl '69
Color video studied for lunar walk. Aviation W 91:97-8+ Ag 18 '69
TELEVISION cameras on space vehicles
Lunar cameraman; Luna-9. E. Gruzinov. Space World F-8-68:34 Ag '69

Testing

Lunar mission camera tested in Apollo 9 TV transmissions. il Aviation W 90:56+ Mr 24 '69
TELEVISION censorship. See Television broadcasting—Censorship
TELEVISION channels. See Television stations; Television transmission
TELEVISION circuits
Anti X-ray circuit. A. James. il Radio-Electr 41:68-9 Ja '70
Automatic color tint control. S. Leckerts. il Radio-Electr 41:36-8 Ja '70
Automatic tint control for color-TV. M. S. Snitzer. il Electr World 82:30-1+ S '69
Fix those special solid-state TV circuits. M. Mandl. il Radio-Electr 40:70+ S '69
New! color TV circuits. R. L. Goodman. il Radio-Electr 41:40-2+ Ja '70
New 1969 color-killers. R. L. Goodman. il Radio-Electr 40:43-5+ F '69
TV chroma circuit alignment. F. H. Belt. il Electr World 81:48-51 F '69
TELEVISION commentators. See Television broadcasting—News
TELEVISION commercials. See Television advertising
TELEVISION criticism
Least passive viewer. S. W. Little. Sat R 52:128-9 Mr 8 '69
Old fear of Gould and the new criticism of Arlen. R. Burgheim. Harper 239:98-101 Ag '69
TELEVISION drama. See Television broadcasting—Drama
TELEVISION in art education. See Television in education
TELEVISION in astronomy
Replaying the stars. J. Eberhart. il Sci N 95:191+ F 22 '69
Seeing the invisible; SEC television camera tubes for Project Celescope. il Space World F-8-68:21-6 Ag '69
TELEVISION in aviation
See also
Television apparatus on aircraft
TELEVISION in biological research. See Television in science
TELEVISION in education
Bringing graduate school to the plant; TAGER program in Texas. il Bsns W p64-5 Ja 10 '70
Can television really teach? Sesame street, produced by the Children's television workshop. E. L. Palmer. il Am Ed 5:2-6 Ag '69
Children's television workshop. S. W. Little. il Sat R 52:60-2 F 8 '69
Cooney & the kids; Sesame street. il Look 33:100-2+ N 18 '69
CUMBIN at CUNY; closed circuit, talk-back television instruction system. il Sch & Soc 97:341-2 O '69
Educational TV; a progress report. il U S News 66:46 Je 9 '69
Forgotten 12 million; Sesame street, program for preschool children. il Time 94:96+ N 14 '69

Idea of Germany's Telekolleg. Bavarian television school. G. Mahlmann. il Sch & Soc 97:106 F '69
My teacher, the TV set. C. M. Fitch. il Américas 21:8-14 Mr '69
Open, Sesame; Children's television workshop Newsweek 73:81 My 26 '69
Puppets charm away the violence on Saturday TV. il Life 67:71-2+ O 31 '69
Sesame street opens. B. B. Stretch. il Sat R 52:91 N 15 '69
Soon, domestic TV via satellite. U S News 67:8 D 15 '69
Teacher or student? usefulness of the TV lessons in art workshop. C. Parsons. il Sch Arts 69:38-9 S '69
Toddle down Sesame street. il Ebony 25:36-9 Ja '70
Turning on tots with educational TV Sesame street. B. Scott. il Todays Health 47:28-32 N '69
See also
Television stations, Educational
TELEVISION in entomology. See Television in science
TELEVISION in meteorology
Now you can detect tornadoes with your TV! J. Harvey. il Suc Farm 67:8-9 My '69
See also
Artificial satellites—Meteorological applications
TELEVISION in politics
Half-shut eye, by J. Whale. Review
Sat R 52:50 Ag 9 '69. S. W. Little
How to get that good media image. il Newsweek 74:69 S 29 '69
How to watch Nixon on the tube. H. Sidey. Life 67:2 Jl 11 '69
Networks hard on Daley film. Ramp Mag 7:60 N 30 '68
Selling of the President 1968; excerpts. J. McGinniss. Harper 239:46-60 Ag '69
Selling of the President 1968, by J. McGinnis. Review
Nat R 21:1173 N 18 '69. V. Gold
Sat R 52:38-40+ O 18 '69. H. J. Telson
TELEVISION in science
Commercial TV helps NBS' standards broadcasts Electr World 81:65 Je '69
Ultraviolet video-viewing; the television camera as an insect eye. T. Eisner and others. il Science 166:1172-4 N 28 '69
TELEVISION in space flight
Apollo 10 may send color TV pictures. Aviation W 90:87 Ap 14 '69
New voice for Apollo. Time 93:74-5 My 30 '69
See also
Television broadcasting from space
TELEVISION industry
Flickering picture in TV sales. il Bsns W p31 Jl 19 '69
See also
Television apparatus industry and trade

United States
How to free TV. M. Friedman. Newsweek 74:82 D 1 '69
Senator Pastore's TV proposal. America 120:440 Ap 12 '69
Smooth stones for the Goliaths. R. L. Shayon. Sat R 52:37 Mr 8 '69
Some sober second thoughts on Vice President Agnew; television journalism; address. F. W. Friendly. Sat R 52:61-2+ D 13 '69
Television overlords. H. H. Goldin. Atlan 224:87-9 Jl '69
Test by performance. Time 94:68+ Jl 11 '69
Welcome, Spiro Agnew. B. Hennessy. New Repub 161:13-14 D 13 '69
See also
Government investigations—Television industry
TELEVISION journalism. See Television broadcasting—News
TELEVISION laws and regulations
Case on the Red lion. R. L. Shayon. Sat R 52:55-6 Jl 12 '69
Christmas list; Pastore bill. J. Fischer. Harper 239:26 D '69
Cook doctrine; Supreme court upholds fairness doctrine. Nation 209:5 Jl 7 '69
Fairness doctrine under review; response to court's finding. America 120:493 Ap 26 '69
FCC stirs up the pot; license-renewal battles. Newsweek 73:65 Je 2 '69
Guarding the goodies; renewal of Frontier broadcasting company's license. R. L. Shayon. Sat R 52:41 F 1 '69
It's up in the air: who owns television? J. Tebbel. Sat R 52:75-6 My 10 '69
Monopoly bugaboo. il Newsweek 73:90 Mr 31 '69
Pastore's pet. New Repub 161:10-11 O 25 '69
Self-regulation or censorship; the T.V. industry; address, July 31, 1969. R. E. Lee Vital Speeches 35:730-2 S 15 '69

TELEVISION laws and regulations—*Continued*

Signs of life at the FCC; proposed diversification of control over mass media. S. Lazarus. New Repub 160:16-18 F 22 '69

Smooth stones for the Goliaths. R. L. Shayon. Sat R 52:37 Mr 8 '69

Taking sides; opposition by Negro group to Pastore bill on broadcasting licenses. R. L. Shayon. Sat R 52:65 N 15 '69

Test by performance. Time 94:68+ Jl 11 '69

Trying to swat the FCC's gadfly. Bsns W p21 Ag 30 '69

Two views on the regulation of television: Pastore bill. L. L. Jaffe; N. Johnson. New Repub 161:14-19 D 6 '69; Reply. L. L. Jaffe. 162:35-6 Ja 3 '70

What you can do to improve TV. N. Johnson. Harper 238:14+ F '69

Who will cry havoc? licenses and renewal. R. L. Shayon. Sat R 52:22 Je 28 '69

See also

Television broadcasting—Censorship

United States—Federal communications commission

TELEVISION lighting

On the beam. il Newsweek 73:70 Je 16 '69

TELEVISION news. See Television broadcasting—News

TELEVISION performers. See Television broadcasting—Performers

TELEVISION photography. See Television—Photographic aspects

TELEVISION production. See Television broadcasting—Program production

TELEVISION program rating. See Television broadcasting—Program rating

TELEVISION programming. See Television broadcasting—Programming

TELEVISION programs. See Television broadcasting—Programs

TELEVISION receivers

Small-screen black-and-white TV sets. il Consumer Rep 34:147-9 Mr '69

Color receivers

See Television receivers, Color

Control

Wireless private listening for your TV; remote sound control. G. J. Whalen and R. F. Graf. il Pop Sci 194:108-10+ My '69

Design

Cost of color-TV service. J. Frye. Electr World 81:56+ F '69

Flat-screen TV has 52,900 picture elements. il Radio-Electr 40:4+ Je '69

TV you can hang on a wall. R. M. Walsh. il Pop Sci 195:56-9+ D '69

Maintenance and repair

In the shop, with Jack. J. Darr. See issues of Radio-electronics

Kwik-fix picture and waveform charts. See issues of Radio-electronics, June 1969-

Stop the TV-repair swindlers! A. Hamilton. Read Digest 94:100-3 F '69

Technicians' chance to gripe. J. Frye. Electr World 82:56+ D '69

Troubleshooter's casebook. A. Margolis. il Radio-Electr 40:58-60 My '69

Using controls to troubleshoot TV. D. Matsuda. il Electr World 81:32-4+ Mr '69

Manufacture

See Television apparatus—Manufacture

Tuning

New TV front-ends. F. H. Belt. il Electr World 82:47-50 S '69

Television makers get on the button; push-button tuning. Bsns W p82 D 27 '69

Variable-voltage tuning. R. F. Scott. il Radio-Electr 40:58-60 Ap '69

TELEVISION receivers, Color

Color TV: frequency-of-repair records. il Consumer Rep 34:258-9 My '69

Color TV sales are looking bluer. Bsns W p36+ N 8 '69

Color TV's new and brighter outlook. il Consumer Bul 52:23-9 D '69

Color TV's rainbow fades a bit. il Bsns W p38+ F 1 '69

Europeans hit by color-TV fever. Bsns W p64 My 31 '69

GE improves its portable color TV. il Consumer Rep 34:108 Mr '69

Heathkit color TV (GR-681), wireless remote (GRA-681-6) Pop Electr 30:81-3+ Mr '69

Heathkit color TV kit, not acceptable. il Consumer Rep 34:562-3 O '69

How to color TV sales rosier. Bsns W p90 Je 21 '69

1970 color TV: the picture is brighter than ever. L. Buckwalter. il Pop Sci 195:142-5+ O '69

Personal-use report: Admiral's new 12-inch color portable. S. Shatavsky. il Pop Sci 194:66-7 Je '69

World's smallest color TV. L. Buckwalter. il Pop Mech 130:118-21+ D '68

Caricatures and cartoons

Color TV. il Changing T 23:24 S '69

Control

Automatic tint control for color TV. R. F. Scott. il Radio-Electr 40:4+ N '69

Automatic tint control for color-TV. M. S. Snitzer. il Electr World 82:30-1+ S '69

New automatic tint control colors it right. R. Michaels. il Pop Sci 195:116-17 S '69

Maintenance and repair

Cure color TV gremlins. M. Mandl. il Radio-Electr 40:35-7 Ap '69

Get a better color picture. M. Mandl. il Radio-Electr 41:52-4 Ja '70

How to fix color. M. Mandl. il Radio-Electr 40:52+ N '69

How to save color CRTS. J. Darr. il Radio-Electr 40:16+ Mr '69

KO color faults quick. M. Mandl. il Radio-Electr 40:59-61 Mr '69

Picture that went to jail. J. Darr. il Radio-Electr 40:44 My '69

Signal-tracing color with shop equipment. J. Darr. il Radio-Electr 40:17+ My '69

TV chroma circuit alignment. F. H. Belt. il Electr World 81:48-51 F '69

Ten steps for fast color CRT changes. J. Darr. Radio-Electr 40:17+ F '69

Manufacture

See Television apparatus—Manufacture

Picture tubes

Brighter picture tubes for color-TV. M. S. Snitzer. Electr World 82:33 Ag '69

New color tubes! J. Mason. il Radio-Electr 41:33-5 Ja '70

Radiation hazards

Can your color TV stand a radiation count? G. Weinstein. il Sci Digest 65:24-8 Ap '69

Consumer report: TV radiation. il Consumer Rep 34:73-4 F '69

Don't try to test TV radiation at home; Ray-alert detection kit. Consumer Rep 34:560 O '69

Standards for TV sets. il Sci N 96:46-7 Jl '69

What are the radiation dangers in color TV? il Good H 169:217 O '69

Safety devices and measures

Anti X-ray circuit. A. James. il Radio-Electr 41:68-9 Ja '70

TV X-rays; how they stop them. L. Lachenbruch. il Radio-Electr 41:2+ Ja '70

TELEVISION receivers, Portable

Small black-and-white portables. il Consumer Bul 52:29-30 D '69

World's smallest color TV. L. Buckwalter. il Pop Mech 130:118-21+ D '68

TELEVISION receivers industry. See Television apparatus industry and trade

TELEVISION reception

How to get better sound from your TV set. F. H. Belt. il Pop Mech 132:148-51+ S '69

TELEVISION relay systems

See also

Communications satellites

TELEVISION script writing. See Television authorship

TELEVISION stations

Boredom in perpetuity? licensing policy. New Repub 161:9 Jl 5 '69

Competing TV applicants. America 120:725 Je 28 '69

Donahue's choice; KHJ-TV loses license renewal battle to Fidelity TV. Nation 209:164 S 1 '69

FCC bares its fangs; decision not to renew license of WHDH-TV. Newsweek 73:65-6 F 3 '69

FCC impropriety; WPIX-Forum case. D. Zwerdling. New Repub 160:10-11 Je 21 '69

FCC stirs up the pot; WBBM and the programming report. Newsweek 73:65 Je 2 '69

Guarding the goodies; renewal of Frontier broadcasting company's license. R. L. Shayon. Sat R 52:41 F 1 '69

TELEVISION stations—*Continued*
Hark! The herald; Faith center's KHOF-TV, Glendale, Calif. il Newsweek 74:110 N 17 '69
LBJ vs. UHF; challenging the Johnsons' domination of Austin airwaves. il Newsweek 73:92 Mr 24 '69
$100,000 anchorman; station KTLA-TV. Time 93:98 My 16 '69
Pix mix at WPIX? il Newsweek 73:77 Je 30 '69
Rivals challenge Mexican TV czar; E. Azcarraga. il Bsns W p50-2 Mr 15 '69
Smooth stones for the Goliaths. R. L. Shayon. Sat R 52:37 Mr 8 '69
TV game; your time is their time; KRON-TV license renewal controversy. A. Alpert. New Repub 161:17-21 O 18 '69
UHF band strikes up. il Newsweek 73:60-1 Mr 3 '69
    See also
American broadcasting companies
Columbia broadcasting system, incorporated
TELEVISION stations, Educational
Day of reckoning; employment and program policy reports by NAEB. R. L. Shayon. Sat R 52:37 D 20 '69
KQED's newsroom. J. Fincher. Life 66:15 Ap 11 '69
What's at stake; FCC-CATV struggle over integrating cable into over-the-air program transmission. R. L. Shayon. Sat R 52:30 Je 21 '69
TELEVISION transmission
How they're retouching your TV picture. S. Shatavsky. il Pop Sci 195:86-7 S '69
TV channel assignments; tables. Electr World 82:66-7 N '69
TELEVISION viewing devices. See Eyeglasses
TELEVISION writing. See Television authorship
TELFER, Richard G.
Staff involvement. bibliog f Clear House 43:539-42 My '69
TELFORD, Sam R. jr. See Herrer, A. jt. auth.
TELL me about the wind; story. See Potter, D.
TELLER, Edward
Nearing the moment of truth; questions regarding the Safeguard ABM. Nat R 21:630 Jl 1 '69
Not only humane, but truly effective; interview. por U S News 66:87-9 My 26 '69
TELLER, Walter
Pages from a Chilmark diary; excerpt from Cape Cod and the offshore islands. Am Scholar 38:281-5 Spr '69
TEMOSHOK, Linda
In the corporate image; poem. Seventeen 28:92 My '69
TEMPE, Ariz.
Making waves. il Time 94:97 O 10 '69
TEMPER
Temper tantrums. B. Spock. il Redbook 133:49+ Je '69
Temper tantrums; excerpts from The other 23 hours. A. E. Trieschman. il Todays Ed 58:33-6 S '69
    See also
Anger
TEMPERA painting
Big day; big picture by children. W. Gediman. il Sch Arts 69:40 N '69
Painting is fun with tempera. R. A. Yoder. il Sch Arts 69:24-5 S '69
TEMPERANCE
    Study and teaching
Alcohol education. Sch & Soc 97:415-16 N '69
TEMPERANCE education. See Temperance—Study and teaching
TEMPERANCE societies
Hail to the crystal spring; theme song of Dashaway association, San Francisco. T. H. Watkins. il Am West 6:26-7+ Ja '69
TEMPERATURE
    See also
Atmospheric temperature
Climate
Lakes—Temperature
Plants—Temperature
Thermistors
    Measurement
    See also
Thermometers and thermometry
    Physiological effects
Bacterial spores: chemical sensitization to heat. G. Alderton and N. Snell. bibliog il Science 163:1212-13 Mr 14 '69
Thermal pollution and aquatic life. J. R. Clark. il Sci Am 220:18-27 bibliog(p 148) Mr '69

Thermoregulation: effects of environmental temperature on turnover of hypothalamic norepinephrine. M. A. Simmonds and L. L. Iversen. bibliog il Science 163:473-4 Ja 31 '69; Reply with rejoinder. R. D. Myers. Science 165:1030-1 S 5 '69
Windchill, a useful wintertime weather variable; rate of heat removal from the human body at various combinations of wind speed and low temperature. R. Falconer. bibliog il Weatherwise 21:227-9+ D '68
    See also
Cold—Physiological effects
TEMPERATURE, Animal and human
Behavioral regulation of hypothalamic temperature. J. D. Corbit. bibliog il Science 166:256-8 O 10 '69
Circadian rhythm in mammalian body temperature entrained by cyclic pressure changes. R. Hayden and R. G. Lindberg. bibliog il Science 164:1288-9 Je 13 '69
Eland and the oryx. C. R. Taylor. il Sci Am 220:88-95 Ja '69
Forebrain temperature activates behavioral thermoregulatory response in Arctic sculpins. H. T. Hammel and others. bibliog il Science 165:83-5 Jl 4 '69
Lizard reflectivity change and its effect on light transmission through body wall. W. P. Porter and K. S. Norris. bibliog il Science 163:482-4 Ja 31 '69
Thermoregulatory responses to intra-abdominal heating of sheep. R. O. Rawson and others. bibliog il Science 165:919-20 Ag 29 '69
TEMPERATURE, Atmospheric. See Atmospheric temperature
TEMPERATURES, High. See High temperatures
TEMPERATURES, Low. See Low Temperatures
TEMPERING
    See also
Steel—Heat treatment
TEMPLE, Earl S.
Facts and fallacies in camp sanitation. Camp Mag 41:28-9 Ja '69
TEMPLE, Joann T.
Solar flares: the cosmic fire that threatens space explorers. Sci Digest 66:30-4 S '69
TEMPLE, John
Comment. B. Berkson. Poetry 114:259-60 Jl '69
TEMPLE, Robert W.
ABCs of chassis frames and suspensions. il Pop Mech 132:128-33 S '69
TEMPLE, Shirley
Prague diary. pors McCalls 96:74-5+ Ja '69
Youth-related activities of the United Nations; statement, September 30, 1969. Dept State Bul 61:380-2 N 3 '69
    about
Shirley or Curley? R. Schickel. il por Life 66:81-2 Je 13 '69
TEMPLE CITY, Calif.
Building a career ladder. J. Connors. il Am Ed 5:15-17 F '69
TEMPLE university, Philadelphia
Informal day-care program aids psychiatric patients; Temple university's Community mental health center. Todays Health 47:18 F '69
Marcuse and Goodwin tangle at Temple; colloquium on Marxism, religion and the liberal tradition. J. Groutt. Commonweal 90:279-80 My 23 '69
Temple's tale of two tents; Temple university's musical festival and institute. J. Felton. il Hi Fi 19:MA24-5 O '69
TEMPLES
    See also
Synagogues
    Egypt
    See also
Abu Simbel, Temples of
    India
Temple belles of India. A. Menen. il Holiday 45:48-9+ F '69
TEMPLETON, Edith
Dress rehearsal. New Yorker 45:34-44 Ap 5 '69
TEMPORARY employees. See Employees, Temporary
TEMPORARY job; drama. See Nolan, P. T.
TEMPTATION
Does God lead us into temptation? N. V. Hope. Chr Today 13:13-14 Jl 4 '69
Temptation. Chr Today 13:23 Je 20 '69
TEMPURA. See Cookery, Japanese
TEN commandments. See Commandments, Ten
TENANT farming. See Farm tenancy
TENANT unions. See Landlord and tenant

TERRAMYCIN. See Tetracyclines

TERRARIUMS
Plants to grow under glass. il Good H 168:
196-7 Mr '69
See also
Gardens, Miniature

TERRE HAUTE, Ind.
Open house in Terre Haute; State university
president asks city to reduce prostitution. il
Time 93:20-1 F 21 '69

Libraries

See also
Vigo County, Ind, public library

TERRELL, Edward E.
Avena magna: new oat species. bibliog Science 163:595 F 7 '69

TERRELL, Tammi
Ordeal of Tammi Terrell. A. Peters. il pors
Ebony 25:94-6+ N '69

TERRES, John K.
Trailing the gray ghost; excerpt from The
walking adventures of a naturalist. Audubon
71:50-6 Ja '69

TERREY, John N.
NEA's special project for higher education.
Todays Ed 58:53 My '69

TERRILL, Ross
Mr Gorton's Australia: a country in search of
a role. New Repub 160:14-17 My 10 '69
Reports: Bangkok, Manila. Atlan 224:22-7
Jl '69
Reports: Paris negotiations. Atlan 223:18-22+
My '69
When America lost China. Atlan 224:78-86 N
'69

TERRITORIAL waters
Coastal waters and the Nation; address,
February 3, 1969. E. Wenk, jr. Vital
Speeches 35:349-52 Mr 15 '69
Gunboat diplomacy: private American tuna
fleet accosted by Peruvian gunboat off
coast of Peru. Newsweek 73:50 F 24 '69
Northwest passage; Chinese gunboats capture
yachts sailing from Hong Kong to Macao.
il Newsweek 73:41 Mr 3 '69
On owning the ocean. M. A. Gruber. il Sea
Front 15:170-9 My '69
See also
Submerged lands

TERRITORIES, Admission of, to statehood. See
States (United States)

TERRORISM
Bombing fallout: tension and threats; New
York city. Bsns W p44+ N 22 '69
Business digs in against terrorists; American
companies in Brazil and Argentina. Bsns W
p34+ N 29 '69
Exporting violence; bomb and skyjack plots
by Arab terrorists. il Time 95:27-8 Ja 5 '70
House on Fourth street; bomb terrorists and
explosions, New York city. il Newsweek 74:
37-8 N 24 '69
On the other side: terror as policy; Viet
Cong terrorism. il Time 94:29 D 5 '69
Operating from Athens to Acre. Newsweek
74:65 D 8 '69
Scare city; planting of bombs in New York.
Nat R 21:1206 D 2 '69
Tactic of terror; Arab commandos. Nation 208:
258-9 Mr 3 '69
Terror on the ground; trial of Arab terrorists.
Time 94:57 D 5 '69
They bombed in New York. il Time 94:26-7
N 21 '69
Wave of skyscraper bombings. il U S News
67:12 N 24 '69
Where have all the flowers gone? New York
bombings, Sharon Tate murders. Nat R
21:1257 D 16 '69
World politics, new style; kidnaping, hijack-
ing, bombing; guerrilla diplomacy. il U S
News 67:49-50 S 22 '69
See also
Vietnamese war, 1957- —Atrocities

TERRY, Bill Henry, Jr
Integrating the graveyard; Birmingham,
Ala. Time 95:32 Ja 5 '70

TERRY, Carroll
Movie report. Good H 169:76 O '69

TERRY, Charles Laymen, 1900-
Wilmington: occupied city. R. J. Bresler.
Commonweal 89:513-14 Ja 24 '69

TERRY, Fernando Belaúnde. See Belaúnde
Terry, F.

TERRY, Jesse A.
Alabama couple builds $1 million-a-year fac-
tory. il Ebony 25:68-70+ Ja '70

TERRY, Luther Leonidas
Excerpt from testimony before House com-
mittee on interstate and foreign commerce.
April 18, 1969. Cong Digest 48:182+ Je '69

TERRY, Walter
World of dance. See issues of Saturday review

TERRY manufacturing company
Alabama couple builds $1 million-a-year
factory. il Ebony 25:68-70+ Ja '70

TERTIARY period. See Geology, Stratigraphic
—Tertiary

TERZANI, Tiziano
Storming the institutions. Nation 208:751-2
Je 16 '69

TERZICK, Peter E.
Rights or privileges? address. Am For 75:
28-30+ D '69

TESSENDORF, K. C.
Fly the thrifty skies. House B 111:76-7 S '69

TEST for a witch; drama. See MacLellan, E.
and Schroll, C. V.

TESTIMONIALS in advertising. See Advertising—Testimonials

TESTING
How they keep you safe; without getting
you killed. A. S. Freese. il Pop Mech 132:
78-81+ Ag '69
See also
Quality of products
United States—National bureau of standards
    also subhead Testing under various sub-
jects, e.g. Drugs—Testing

TESTING, Educational. See Educational tests
and measurements

TESTING, Psychological. See Psychological examinations

TESTING instruments
Build the SCR tester. J. W. Cuccia. il Pop
Electr 30:47-9 My '69
Build the UJT tester. J. W. Cuccia. il Pop
Electr 30:33-5+ Je '69
Capacitance probes in industrial instrumenta-
tion. R. A. Shiver. il Electr World 81:42-3+
My '69
Electrolytic-capacitor tester. D. F. Fleshren.
il Electr World 82:82-3 O '69
EMC model 215 tube and transistor tester.
il Electr World 81:77 Ap '69
Equipment report; Sencore CR-143 CRT tester.
J. Darr. il Radio-Electr 40:73-4 F '69
Equipment report: Sencore TF151 transistor-
FET tester. il Radio-Electr 40:92-3 Ap '69
Equipment report: Triplett 3444-A tube ana-
lyzer. J. Darr. il Radio-Electr 40:88 Je '69
IC Telltale; probe and test set to check
digital circuits. C. P. Troemel. il Pop
Electr 30:69-74 Ap '69
Leader model LTC-901 transistor tester. il
Electr World 82:80 O '69
Pola-testers; probes packaged in discarded
Polaroid print coat containers. E. B. Beach.
il Pop Electr 31:59-61+ S '69
Semiconductor breakdown tester. J. Dehaven.
il Pop Electr 31:47-52 D '69
Sencore TF-151 transistor tester. il Electr
World 81:76 Ap '69
Sub-ohm continuity tester. C. D. Todd. il
Electr World 81:78-80 F '69
Test equipment product report. See issues of
Electronics world
Transistor curve tracer. P. C. Brassine. il
Radio-Electr 40:33-6+ D '69
Transistor sorter. R. F. Arthur. il Pop Electr
30:61-2 Mv '69
Triplett 3490-A transistor analyzer. il Radio-
Electr 40:78+ N '69
Why play Edison roulette? ground tester.
L. E. Greenlee. il Pop Electr 31:71-4 Ag '69
See also
Calibrators
Signal generators

TESTING laboratories
They smash things, and get paid for it! J. R.
Berry. il Mech Illus 65:53-5+ F '69
See also
Cornell aeronautical laboratory, incorporated
United States—Manned spacecraft center—Lu-
nar receiving laboratory
Wyle laboratories, incorporated

Anecdotes, facetiae, satire, etc.

Potomac Valley test facility. D. Wolfle. Science 165:969 S 5 '69; Same with title Neglected laboratory. Sat R 52:67 N 1 '69

TESTOSTERONE
Androgen accumulation and binding to macromolecules in seminal vesicles: inhibition
by cyproterone. J. M. Stern and A. J.
Eisenfeld. bibliog il Science 166:233-5 O 10
'69

TESTS, Information. See Information tests

TESTS, Memory. See Memory tests

TESTS and scales. See Educational tests and
measurements

TETANUS
Glycine in the spinal cord of cats with local
tetanus rigidity. T. Semba and M. Kano.
bibliog il Science 164:571-2 My 2 '69

TETANUS—*Continued*

Vaccination

Too many shots. il Time 93:76 My 23 '69

TETHERLY, George
Growth of Fort Wayne's park system. Parks & Rec 3:32-5+ D '68

TETLEY, Glen, dance company. *See* Glen Tetley dance company

TETON RANGE
Marooned at 12,000 feet. E. D. Fales, jr. il Pop Mech 131:86-90+ Je '69; Same abr. with title Impossible rescue. Read Digest 95:50-5 S '69

TETRACENE. *See* Naphthacene

TETRACHLOROETHYLENE
Neutrinos from the sun. J. N. Bahcall. il Sci Am 221:28-37 bibliog(p 140) Jl '69

TETRACYCLINES
Effective antibiotics; Terramycin vs. oxytet-racycline. Sci N 96:550-1 D 13 '69
Million-dollar bugs, by M. Pearson. Review Sat R 52:36-7 N 1 '69. M. Potomacus

TETRAHYDROCANNABINOL. *See* THC

TETRAPLASANDRA
Flower of tetraplasandra gymnocarpa hypo-gyny with epigynous ancestry. R. H. Eyde and C. C. Tseng. bibliog il Science 166:506-8 O 24 '69

TETRAPODS
Predation and the origin of tetrapods. J. A. Holman. Science 164:588 My 2 '69

TETRAZOLIUM oxidase. *See* Oxidases

TETRODOTOXIN. *See* Toxins and antitoxins

TEXARKANA, Ark. and Tex.
Guaranteed learning; Dorsett education sys-tems incentive contract. Sat R 52:85 O 18 '69
Rats' alley. il Time 94:40 Ag 15 '69
Reading, writing, and profit; Dorsett educa-tion systems incentive contract. Bsns W p 104 O 4 '69
Technology, not teachers; audiovisual teach-ing machine. il Sr Schol 95:Schol Teach 1 O 27 '69

TEXAS
See also
Architecture, Domestic—Texas
Education—Texas
Fishing—Texas
Forests and forestry—Texas
Gardening—Texas
Hunting—Texas
Law—Texas
Music festivals—Texas
Public welfare—Texas
Roads—Texas
Tourist trade—Texas

Description and travel

Coyotes howl at midnight; Texas coast. P. Smyth il Motor B 123:62-5+ My '69
Texas River road. L. M. Rhodes. il Travel 132:38-41+ O '69

History

'Pecos Bill' on the Texas frontier. R. M. Ut-ley. bibliog il Am West 6:4-13+ Ja '69

Parks and reserves

Gates are open now for LBJ park. U S News 66:12 Je 9 '69

Religious institutions and affairs
See also
Texas conference of churches

Social conditions

Thorns on the yellow rose of Texas. R. Coles and H. Huge. New Repub 160:13-17 Ap 19 '69

TEXAS conference of churches
Coming together. Texas-style; Texas con-ference of churches. Time 93:67 Mr 7 '69
Discord along the Rio Grande; TCC and Mexican American farm workers. J. C. Evans. il Chr Cent 86:397-400 Mr 26 '69
Eyes upon Texas; state Conference of churches. Newsweek 73:113 Mr 17 '69
Texas goes all out for ecumenism. J. C. Evans. Chr Cent 86:366-7 Mr 19 '69
Texas-sized ecumenism. America 120:321 Mr 22 '69

TEXAS council of churches
Discord along the Rio Grande; TCC and Mexican American farm workers. J. C. Evans. il Chr Cent 86:397-400 Mr 26 '69

TEXAS Gulf sulphur company
Billion dollar windfall, by M. Shulman. Re-view
Bsns W il p92+ O 18 '69

TEXAS instruments, Incorporated
Texas instruments; big opportunities in small packages; semiconductors and integrated cir-cuits. il Forbes 103:32-4+ Mr 1 '69

TEXAS. Midwestern university, Wichita Falls
Automated circulation system at Midwestern university. C. D. Heineke and C. J. Boyer. il ALA Bul 63:1249-54 O '69

TEXAS southern university, Houston
Lively student center. il Arch Rec 146:145-8 O '69

TEXAS. University
University of Texas: on the way up. but politics still intrude. L. J. Carter. il Science 164:1150-4 Je 6 '69

Austin campus

Windfall for Texas; Michener collection. E. Freed. il Art in Am 57:78-85 N '69

College of business administration

How a businessman ramrods a B-school: G. Kozmetsky. il Bsns W p84-6 My 24 '69

Libraries

Back home again in Johnson City. B. Porter-field. il N Y Times Mag p22-3+ Mr 2 '69
Tax-free foundations: study starts in Con-gress. il U S News 66:81-2 F 10 '69

TEXTBOOKS
AJC survey finds errors and prejudice in textbooks. Library J 94:3122+ S 15 '69
Good procedures in selecting schoolbooks. G. Whipple. Ed Digest 34:44-6 F '69
Range of voices. B. B. Stretch. Sat R 52:70-1 Mr 15 '69
Textbooks: Dullsville and brighter spots. C. Rheault. il Pub W 195:68-70+ Mr 3 '69
Total number, value & price per unit of text-books sold; tables. Pub W 195:36-7 Je 9 '69
What's black and white and read all over? excerpts from address, November 1968. D. Stering. bibliog Engl J 58:817-32 S '69
See also
Booksellers and bookselling—Textbooks
Publishers and publishing—Textbooks
Readers (books)
Spellers

Brazil

Books for progress; COLTED library kit. K. A. Herath. il Américas 21:21-2 Ja '69
Fifty million books for Brazil; COLTED. W. V. Jackson. bibliog il Wilson Lib Bul 44:197-202 O '69

United States
See Textbooks

TEXTILE design
Decorating scrapbook. il House B 111:59-69 Mr '69
Here and now; midsummer pickup for the bedroom doldrums. T. Bowman. il House B 111:80-1 Ag '69
Patterns. il House & Gard 136:102-5 O '69
See also
Batik

Study and teaching

Theme and variation. N. Schedl. il Sch Arts 69:34-5 Ja '70

TEXTILE fabrics
Big happening in home sewing. D. Wharton. Read Digest 95:25-8 Jl '69
Decorating with fabric. il House & Gard 136:124-9 O '69
Fabric explosion; romanticism and scale of the 30's. il House B 111:150-1 O '69
Fabric/fiber glossary. Redbook 132:82-3 Ja '69
Fabrication; how to make up a room out of whole cloth. P. Bartlett. il Mlle 68:106-7 Mr '69
Fresh ways to create space with fabrics. il House & Gard 135:146-9+ Ap '69
Here and now; midsummer pickup for the bedroom doldrums. T. Bowman. il House B 111:80-1 Ag '69
New fabrics, new fibers. il Redbook 132:81+ Ja '69
Punchy, pushy, pazzazzy! That's Pucci. V. D. Hahn. il Am Home 72:46-51 Je '69
Today's exciting fashion fabrics; sewing tips and care advice. Good H 169:156 N '69
Winter coats: the fabrics of the season and how to care for them. il Good H 169:214 N '69

See also
Brocade
Cotton fabrics
Yarn

Exhibitions

Masterpieces of western textiles; special ex-hibition at Art institute of Chicago. C. C. Mayer. il Antiques 95:264-9 F '69

TEXTILE fabrics—*Continued*

Finishing
See Textile finishing

History
Textile furnishings; Williamsburg, Va. M. B. Lanier. il Antiques 95:121-7 Ja '69

Softening
See Softening agents

TEXTILE fabrics, Bonded. See Textile fabrics, Laminated

TEXTILE fabrics, Bonded web. See Textile fabrics, Nonwoven

TEXTILE fabrics, Fire resisting
Carpet flammability; improvements afoot. Consumer Rep 34:427 Ag '69

TEXTILE fabrics, Laminated
New bonded fabrics. il Good H 169:144 S '69

TEXTILE fabrics, Nonwoven
Now that the throwaway age has arrived for Americans. il U S News 67:76-7 S 15 '69

TEXTILE fabrics, Synthetic
Synthetic fabrics cast in molds; directly from monomers. il Sci N 95:325 Ap 5 '69
Your guide to man-made fabrics. Bet Hom & Gard 47:134+ N '69

TEXTILE fabrics, Wrinkle resistant
No-iron fabrics. Good H 168:176+ My '69

TEXTILE fibers
Teachers discover the world of fibers. D. F. Standerfer. il Sch Arts 69:6-10 Ja '70
See also
Courtaulds, limited

TEXTILE fibers, Synthetic
Fabric/fiber glossary. Redbook 132:82-3 Ja '69
New fabrics, new fibers. il Redbook 132:81+ Ja '69
See also
Nylon

TEXTILE finishing
New fabrics, new fibers. il Redbook 132:81+ Ja '69

TEXTILE industry

Consolidations and mergers
Merge no more; FTC guidelines. Forbes 103: 17 F 1 '69

Securities
Personal investing; how to pick a knit. il Fortune 80:173-4 O '69

Far East
Mission impossible; Far East cool to proposal for voluntary restrictions on textile exports to the U.S. il Newsweek 73:92 My 26 '69

France
Bandage kings; France's Willot brothers; biggest textile combine in the Common market. il Time 94:81 S 5 '69

Great Britain
See also
Viyella international, limited

United States
Mission impossible; cutting down on textile imports. il Time 93:87 Ap 18 '69
Packard's deal with the textile big three. B. Sellers. New Repub 160:9-11 Mr 22 '69
Pressure for quotas may spark trade war; textiles next big battleground. il Bsns W p76-7 Mr 22 '69
Tell it like it is; address, June 19, 1969. R. S. Small. Vital Speeches 35:655-7 Ag 15 '69
Textiles pitch for import quotas; with editorial comment. il Bsns W p78+, 178 O 11 '69
See also
Belding Heminway company
Burlington industries, incorporated
Cotton industry and trade
Erwin mills, incorporated
Stevens, J. P, and company

TEXTILE labels. See Labels

TEXTILE machinery
CR tests a knitting machine. il Consumer Bul 52:4+ N '69

TEXTILE machinery industry

Spain
Textile bubble bursts in Madrid. il Bsns W p82+ S 20 '69
Un gran escándalo; the Matesa affair. Newsweek 74:63 S 1 '69

TEXTILE mills
Doomed industrial monument; Amoskeag mills at Manchester, N.H. il Fortune 79:118-21 F '69

TEXTILE painting
Printed and painted cottons from the collection of Old Sturbridge village. P. S. Preston. il Antiques 96:546-51 O '69

TEXTILE printing
Printed and painted cottons from the collection of Old Sturbridge village. P. S. Preston. il Antiques 96:546-51 O '69

TEXTILE workers
The mill: a giant step for the southern Negro. R. Cleghorn. il N Y Times Mag p34: 5+ N 9 '69
Packard's deal with the textile big three. B. Sellers. New Repub 160:9-11 Mr 22 '69

TEXTILE workers union of America
Million-dollar back-pay bonanza; awards to mill workers. il Bsns W p29-31 Jl 26 '69

TEXTURE (photography) See Photography—Grain

TEXTURED walls. See Wall coverings

THACHER, Peter S.
U.S. urges U.N. outer space committee action on liability convention; statement, September 9, 1969. Dept State Bul 61:340-2 O 20 '69

THADDEN, Adolf von
Echoes from an unhappy past. por Time 94: 32 S 26 '69

THAI-khac-Chuyen
Case of the Green Berets. il Newsweek 74: 26+ Ag 25 '69
CIA talks. il Newsweek 74:18 S 8 '69
Ghostly war of the Green Berets. H. Sutton. il Sat R 52:23-5+ O 18 '69
Under restraint. il por Newsweek 74:35-6 S 1 '69

THAILAND
See also
Anti-Communist movements—Thailand
Elections—Thailand
Hua Hin
Investments, Foreign (in Thailand)

Defenses
See also
United States—Armed forces—Forces in Thailand

Description and travel
Siam by-the-sea. P. Simms. il Sat R 52:86-8 Mr 8 '69

Economic conditions
Motorboats, monarchy and private enterprise. A. Campbell. New Repub 160:13-15 Mr 29 '69; Reply. A. Panyarachun. 160:31 Ap 19 '69

Foreign relations
Reports: Bangkok, Manila. R. Terrill. Atan 224:22-7 Jl '69
Thai foreign minister suggests new course. J. A. Joyce. Chr Cent 86:908-9 Jl 2 '69
Thailand after Vietnam. R. Butwell. bibliog f Cur Hist 57:339-43+ D '69
Thailand's role in southeast Asia. K. Young. bibliog f Cur Hist 56:94-9+ F '69

History
Constant and the King of Siam. M. Bishop. il Horizon 11:58-9 Wint '69

Politics and government
Motorboats, monarchy and private enterprise. A. Campbell. New Repub 160:13-15 Mr 29 '69
Updating a tradition. Newsweek 73:44+ F 24 '69

THAILAND and the United States
Thailand after Vietnam. R. Butwell. bibliog f Cur Hist 57:339-43+ D '69

THAIS; opera. See Massenet, J.

THALBERG, Irving Grant
Last tycoons. H. Gould. Commentary 48: 75-7 Jl '69
Thalberg, by B. Thomas. Review
Life 66:6 F 28 '69. B Schulberg
Newsweek il por 73:102+ F 17 '69. P. D. Zimmerman

THALER, M. Michael, and others
Actinomycin D: uptake by sea urchin eggs and embryos. bibliog Science 164:832-4 My 16 '69

THALER, Susan
Rose dress; story. Redbook 133:98-9 My '69

THALIDOMIDE
Fallout from thalidomide; settlements of Distaval and Contergan cases. Time 94:47 Ag 15 '69

THALIDOMIDE children. See Deformities

THAL-LARSEN, Margaret
Employer manpower policies in the San Francisco Bay area; excerpt from Changing employer policies in a large urban labor market. Mo Labor R 92:56-7 Mr '69

THANATOLOGY
   See also
   Foundation of thanatology
THANE, Adele
   Feathertop; dramatization of story by N.
     Hawthorne. Plays 28:87-96 Mr '69
   Little Cosette and Father Christmas; drama-
     tization of excerpt from Les miserables,
     by V. Hugo. Plays 29:85-96 D '69
   Tale of two cities; dramatization of novel by
     C. Dickens. Plays 29:81-95 Ja '70
THANG, Ton-duc-. See Ton-duc-Thang
THANKS. See Thanksgiving
THANKSGIVING
   Qualified thanks. M. Truman. Ladies Home
     J 86:99 N '69
THANKSGIVING; story. See Hedges, M.
THANKSGIVING day
   God, grace, and gratitude. Chr Today 14:24
     N 21 '69
   Timely pageant. il Travel 132:16 N '69

             Drama

   Long table. C. Boiko. Plays 29:89-95 N '69
   Pilgrim who didn't care. H. L. Miller. Plays
     29:69-75 N '69
   Turkey, anyone? J. Garver. Plays 29:59-68 N
     '69
THANKSGIVING dinners
   Almost nothing-to-it big Thanksgiving. il
     Sunset 143:90-3 N '69
   Festive game bird. il Am Home 72:88-9 N
     '69
   In the American tradition. il Parents Mag 44:
     88-91 N '69
   New old style of cooking. G. Maddox. il To-
     days Health 47:60-4 N '69
   Noble bird and other bounties. il McCalls
     97:106-14+ N '69
   Thanksgiving, a fourfold feast. il Ladies
     Home J 86:110-11+ N '69
THANKSGIVING proclamations
   1969 Thanksgiving proclamation. Chr Cent 86:
     1509 N 26 '69
THANOS, Harry. See Auer, L. jt. auth.
THANT, 1909-
   European trip cancelled; special reports on
     the Middle East, etc. UN Mo Chron 6:128-
     34 Ag '69
   Failure everywhere; summary of report. Time
     94:63 S 12 '69
   Human rights day, 10 December 1969; mes-
     sage. UN Mo Chron 6:iii-iv D '69
   International day for the elimination of ra-
     cial discrimination; message, March 21,
     1969. UN Mo Chron 6:i-ii Mr '69
   Introduction to the annual report of the Sec-
     retary-General on the work of the orga-
     nization. UN Mo Chron 6:67-113 O '69
   Peace and justice; address, June 18, 1969.
     UN Mo Chron 6:96-101 Jl '69
   Remarks by the Secretary-General on the role
     of the United Nations; Viet-Nam; the Mid-
     dle East; and the conflict in Nigeria; award-
     ing of the Hammarskjöld memorial scholar-
     ship, September 12, 1969. UN Mo Chron 6:
     54-7 O '69
   Role of the Security council; address, New
     York, October 28, 1969. UN Mo Chron 6:
     84-8 N '69
   Secretary-General addresses conferences in
     Mexico City and Addis Ababa; summary of
     address, September, 1969. UN Mo Chron
     6:45-7 O '69
   Secretary-General's press conference; April
     17, 1969. UN Mo Chron 6:73-83 My '69
   Secretary-General's press conference; Septem-
     ber 15, 1969. UN Mo Chron 6:58-66 O '69
   Situation in the Middle East; Africa; with
     statements. UN Mo Chron 6:27-37 Je '69
   Situation in West Irian, Nigeria, etc; state-
     ments. UN Mo Chron 6:63-7 Jl '69
   Ten crucial years; text of statement. UN
     Mo Chron 6:i-v Jl '69
   Toward a new decade; excerpts from ad-
     dress, July 14, 1969. America 121:57 Ag
     2 '69
   Tributes to President Dwight D. Eisenhower.
     UN Mo Chron 6:62 Ap '69
   United Nations day 24 October 1969; message.
     UN Mo Chron 6:ii-iii O '69
   View from the bridge; address, April 25,
     1969. UN Mo Chron 6:58-64 My '69
   We came in peace for all mankind, special
     view of Christmas. Redbook 134:148 D '69

             about

   Secretary-General; activities during April.
     UN Mo Chron 6:33-7 My '69
   Secretary-General; activities during Feb-
     ruary. UN Mo Chron 6:11-14 Mr '69
   Secretary-General; activities during January.
     UN Mo Chron 6:6-9 F '69

   Secretary-General; activities during March.
     UN Mo Chron 6:58-62 Ap '69
   Secretary-General; activities during October.
     UN Mo Chron 6:64 N '69
   Secretary-General's press conference; January
     28, 1969. UN Mo Chron 6:32-42 F '69
THARP, Twyla
   Twyla Tharp and dancers. D. Hering. Dance
     Mag 43:27 Ap '69
THATCH, Lawn. See Lawn thatch
THATCHER, Ted
   Architectural design in the classroom. Sch
     Arts 68:7 Mr '69
THAW-White case. See Trials (murder)
THAWLEY, John
   Drive ya buggy. See issues of Hot rod
THAXTON, Beverly
   I want to be where the action is. Motor B
     123:120 Ja '69
   Keep your cool with the kids. Motor B 123:
     156+ Ap '69
THAYER, George
   Arms dealer Sam; excerpts from The war
     business. Harper 238:92+ Ap '69
THAYER school of engineering. See Dartmouth
   college, Hanover, N.H.—Thayer school of
   engineering
THEATER
   Emphasis: on theater. Harp Baz 103:226 N '69
   Kill the first night, kill it dead. C. Barnes.
     Holiday 45:10+ F '69
     See also
   Church and the theater
   College theater
   Comedy

             Censorship

   See Dramatic censorship

             Direction

   See Theatrical production and direction

             Finance

   There's slow business in show business. il
     Bsns W p43-4 O 18 '69
     See also
   Theatre development fund

             History

     See also
   Theater—Great Britain—History

       Moral and religious
           aspects

   Backlash: reaction to the rise in public in-
     decency and obscenity. il Newsweek 73:31
     Ap 7 '69
   Cry from the past for an artistic conscience;
     Euripides' The bacchae. T. Prideaux. il
     Life 66:32-5 Ap 4 '69
   Gamut of lewdness on a New York stage. il
     Life 66:24+ Ap 4 '69
   Perils of puritanism. C. J. McNaspy. il Amer-
     ica 120:175-6 F 8 '69

          Political aspects

   Guerrilla theatre. R. Goldstein. il Vogue 153:
     164-5+ Mr 1 '69
   Italian incendiary; Grand pantomime of D.
     Fo. il Time 93:72 Mr 21 '69

          Stage scenery

   Abstract stage settings. F. J. Kraft. il De-
     sign 70:14 mid-Wint '69
   Forms for dance; interview, ed. by J. Batie.
     D Chase. il Craft Horiz 29:16-19 Jl '69
   Preview of a ballet costume and design ex-
     hibit; portfolio. T. Borek. Dance Mag 43:
     47-62 F '69
     See also
   Opera—Stage scenery

          Czechoslovakia

     See also
   Prague—Theater

             France

   Rabelais at the Old Vic; performance by the
     Compagnie Renaud-Barrault. C. R.
     Hughes. America 121:616-17 D 20 '69

          Great Britain

   Alec McCowen: start in repertory; interview.
     A. McCowen. New Yorker 44:22-4 Ja 25
     '69
   English season. J. A. Hodge. il Travel &
     Camera 32:41-2+ Ag '69
     See also
   London—Theater
            History

   Same only different; five generations of a
     great theatre family, by M. Webster. Re-
     view
     Sat R 52:43 My 24 '69. R. Denham

THEATER—*Continued*

India
See also
Calcutta—Theater

Ireland
See also
Drama festivals—Ireland

Italy
Italian incendiary; Grand pantomime of D. Fo. il Time 93:72 Mr 21 '69

Japan
See also
Kabuki

Poland
Bone-deep truth; production of three plays by the Polish laboratory theater in New York. S. Kauffmann. New Repub 162:25+ Ja 3 '70

Grotowskerie; Polish laboratory theatre. H. Hewes. Sat R 52:12+ N 1 '69

Grotowski: genius of the theatre. M. Gottfried. Vogue 155:154-5+ Ja 1 '70

Grotowski's seminar; Polish laboratory theater. il Time 94:71 N 28 '69

Legend arrives; Polish laboratory theatre. J. Kroll. il Newsweek 74:137 O 27 '69

Mass not for the masses; Polish laboratory theatre's Apocalypsis cum figuris. H. Hewes. Sat R 52:72 D 6 '69

Off Broadway; Polish laboratory theatre's production of Apocalypsis cum figuris at Washington Square Methodist church. E. Oliver. New Yorker 45:85-6+ N 29 '69

Theater of witness; Polish lab's Acropolis. J. Kroll. il Newsweek 74:85 D 1 '69

Theatre; Polish laboratory theatre. H. Clurman. Nation 209:642-3+ D 8 '69

Theater; Polish laboratory theatre's production of Acropolis. H. Hewes. Sat R 52:62-3 N 22 '69

Rumania
See also
Bucharest—Theater

Sweden
Report: production of Handel's Il pastor fido; at Drottningholm court theater. A. Swanson. Opera N 34:26 N 22 '69

Sweden's curious revolution. H. Hewes. il Sat R 52:24 My 17 '69

United States
Across the river and off, off, way off Broadway. L. Lerman. il Mile 68:218-21 Ap '69

Barbwire theater; ex-convicts produce The Cage. il Newsweek 75:66-7 Ja 12 '70

Closet openings. A. Bermel. Nation 209:156 Ag 25 '69

Cultural schizophrenia of Lius Valdez; founder of El teatro campesino. S. Steiner. Vogue 153:112-13+ Mr 15 '69

Paperback of Broadway; summer stock theater. il Newsweek 74:78-9 Ag 4 '69

Spirit power; women theatrical directors. H. Hewes Sat R 52:41 F 8 '69

Spot check; some observations on the theater in America. J. Claman. il Harp Baz 102: 122M-122O F '69

Theater of the sixties. R. Crinkley. Nat R 21:917 S 9 '69
See also
American conservatory theatre
National theatre of the deaf
Theater, Negro
Yale university—Drama school
also subhead Theater under names of cities, e.g. New York (city)—Theater

THEATER, Childrens
Paper bag players; Hunter college playhouse. M. Marks. Dance Mag 43:82-3 F '69

Psychedelic Disney; Disney on parade. il Time 95:47 Ja 5 '70
See also
Puppets and puppet plays

THEATER, Experimental
America's newest new theater. C. Hughes. Cath World 209:123-5 Je '69

Groping toward freedom: the living theatre. J. Richardson. Commentary 47:79-81 My '69

Group theater; Open theatre. H. Junker. il Newsweek 73:128+ My 26 '69

Levy of Oh! Calcutta! E. Dunbar. il Look 33:38-40 Ag 26 '69

Le living. S. Schneck. il Ramp Mag 7:34-41 N 30 '68

Living; production of Paradise now. J. Holden and R. G. Davis. Ramp Mag 8:62+ Ag '69

Medium is the absurd; address, November 1968. L. Mussoff. Engl J 58:566-70+ Ap '69

Naked American. E. Bentley. New Repub 161: 31-4 Ag 9 '69; Same abr. with title Changing sexual mores; why the naked American on stage? Cur 111:60-4 O '69

Naked craze. H. E. Wright. Chr Cent 86:617-19 Ap 30 '69

Naked stage. il Newsweek 73:80 Mr 3 '69

New theatre is here, isn't it. M. Gottfried. Vogue 153:80-1+ Ap 15 '69

Not to be missed; you don't just sit there, you participate. G. Trotta. il Harp Baz 102: 220-1 Mr '69

Nude brood. N. Gittelson. Harp Baz 102:27+ O '69

Nudity, obscenity and all that. C. Hughes. Chr Cent 86:1349-50 O 22 '69

Paradise now? An essay on the living theater. B. Colimore. Cath World 209:30-4 Ap '69

Participatory theater. W. Kerr. Harper 239: 24+ O '69

Professor of the Dionysiac theater. E. Lester. il N Y Times Mag p32-3+ Ap 27 '69

Psychical reality and the theater of fact. H. S. Rollman-Branch. bibliog Am Imago 26:56-70 Spr '69

Secular holiness. il Time 94:68+ O 24 '69

Self-indulgent avant garde. C. Hughes. Nat R 21:1022-3 O 7 '69

Sex as a spectator sport. il Time 94:61-3+ Jl 11 '69

Street works, theatre works enigmatic. J. Gruen. Vogue 154:66 Ag 1 '69

Theater of ignorance; Living theater. R. Gilman. Atlan 224:35-42 Jl '69

Theatre of ritual? C. R. Hughes. America 121:160-1 S 13 '69

Theater of the absurd; a child studies himself; address, November 1968. P. J. Sheehan. Engl J 58:561-5 Ap '69

Tom's mix; San Francisco's KQED experimental television project, The tribe, by Paul Foster. H. Hewes. Sat R 52:21 Jl 12 '69

What can they do for an encore? Theater of nudity. W. Kerr. il N Y Times Mag p24-5+ F 2 '69

Anecdotes, facetiae, satire, etc.
Final decline and total collapse of the American avant-garde. E. Lester. Esquire 71: 142-3+ My '69

THEATER, Negro
Black theater. P. Bailey. il Ebony 24:126-8+ Ag '69

Black theatre in America. I. Sheffer. Nation 209:151-2 Ag 25 '69

Importance of being black. P. Bailey. il Newsweek 73:102-3 F 24 '69

New home, new troupe, new play; In the wine time on off Broadway theater; reprint. L. Patterson. Negro Hist Bul 32:18-19 Ap '69

Theatre. H. Clurman. Nation 208:612-13 My 12 '69

Theater; production of Electra at the New York Shakespeare festival. H. Hewes. Sat R 52:32 Ag 23 '69

Trumpets of the Lord; soulfest of Negro spirituals. T. Lewis. America 120:599 My 17 '69
See also
Negro drama

THEATER, Open-air
Philadelphia street players; Society hill playhouse street theatre. J. Adcock. Nation 209: 611-12 D 1 '69

THEATER, Traveling
See also
American conservatory theatre

THEATER and politics. See Theater—Political aspects

THEATER buildings
Architecture of awareness for the performing arts. H. Hardy. il Arch Rec 145:117-22 Mr '69

Avant-garde arena; campus of Birmingham-Southern college. il Travel 131:22 F '69

Houston's Alley theater. J. M. Dixon. il Arch Forum 130:30-9 Mr '69
See also
Concert halls
Moving picture theaters
Opera houses

THEATER costume designers. See Costume designers

THEATER festivals. See Drama festivals

THEATER of fact. See Theater, Experimental

THEATER of nudity. See Theater, Experimental

THEATER of the absurd. See Theater, Experimental

THEATRE development fund
Blessed is the profitmaker. H. Hewes. Sat R 52:37 O 4 '69

THEATRE national de l'opera, Paris. See Opera houses

THEATRICAL agencies
Care and feeding of the artist. M. A. Guitar. il Mlle 70:166-7+ N '69
Ex-actress with an eye for business; Ernestine McClendon, top Broadway talent agent. il Ebony 24:82-4+ Mr '69
THEATRICAL costume. See Costume, Theatrical
THEATRICAL direction. See Theatrical production and direction
THEATRICAL directors
See also
Meyerhold, V. E.
THEATRICAL make-up. See Make-up, Theatrical
THEATRICAL production and direction
Broadway pre-sell. S. Richards. il Writers Digest 49:52-6+ S '69
Broadway, 1776 and me. D. Leschin. il Seventeen 29:118+ Ja '70
Frank Corsaro; interview, ed. by C. L. Osborne. F. Corsaro. Hi Fi 19:MA25 My '69
From off off to off; Dames at sea: newest musical hit. New Yorker 44:28-30 F 8 '69
Jack Johnson is alive and well on Broadway; recreating fighter in The great white hope. J. E. Jones. il Ebony 24:54-6+ Je '69
Levy of Oh! Calcutta! E. Dunbar. il Look 33:38-40 Ag 26 '69
Lively arts; Grey for brightness; interview, ed. by J. Mandelstam. J. Grey. il Sr Schol 94:18 Ja 17 '69
New direction: direction and choreography of Elmer Gantry and other musicals; interview. O. White. New Yorker 45:19-22 D 27 '69
Theatre; directing Chekhov's Uncle Vanya on a thrust stage. H. Clurman. Nation 209:293-4 S 22 '69
Whose play is it? W. Kerr. il N Y Times Mag p66-7+ O 12 '69
See also
College operas, revues, etc.
Moving picture production and direction
Operatic production and direction
THEATRICAL research
1776: creating the best of Broadway in a small-town public library. il Wilson Lib Bul 43:1008-10 Je '69
THEFT. See Stealing; Thieves
THEISM
Theology and the death camps. L. T. Howe. Chr Cent 86:251-5 F 19 '69; Discussion. 86:716-18, 1046 My 21, Ag 6 '69
See also
God
THEK, Paul
Beyond nightmare. il por Time 93:74+ Je 13 '69
THELWELL, Michael
Publishing the black experience. Ramp Mag 8:60+ O '69
Two black radicals report on their campus struggles. por Ramp Mag 8:47-8+ Jl '69
THEME writing. See English language—Composition
THEODOLITES
Cine-theodolite provides digital readout. il Aviation W 90:325 Je 2 '69
THEODORACOPULOS, Betsy
The bath; Mrs Theodoracopulos and her mirrored bathroom. il pors Vogue 154:180-5 O 1 '69
THEOLOGIANS
Black theology. J. C. Haughey. America 120:583 My 17 '69
Changing theologies for a changing world; some shapers of the new theologies. il Time 94:42-3 D 26 '69
Right, duty, and dissent. N. J. Rigali. Cath World 208:214-18 F '69
See also
Barth, K.
Ritschl, D.
THEOLOGICAL dictionaries. See Theology—Dictionaries and encyclopedias
THEOLOGICAL education
Educating priests after the seminary. F. K. Scheets. America 120:526-8 My 3 '69
Ignorant preachers: study of Greek and Hebrew made optional. A. DeVries. Chr Today 14:8-10 Ja 2 '70
Theological education and the black church. C. S. Rooks. il Chr Cent 86:212-16 F 12 '69
Theological education 1969; symposium. Chr Cent 86:541-50+ Ap 23 '69
See also
Theological schools
THEOLOGICAL novels. See Religious literature
THEOLOGICAL schools
Check of Czech theology; Comenius faculty in Prague. Chr Today 13:27 Ap 11 '69
Gordon and Conwell announce betrothal. Chr Today 13:32 Je 20 '69

Seminary that won't quit. J. Mahoney. Commonweal 90:478-9 Ag 8 '69; Reply with rejoinder. F. X. Canfield. 90:579+ S 26 '69
Theological education 1969; symposium. Chr Cent 86:541-50+ Ap 23 '69
Toronto's theological colleges to federate. Chr Cent 86:768 Je 4 '69
See also
Bible colleges
Chicago. University—Federated theological faculty
Colgate Rochester divinity school
Concordia theological seminary, St Louis
New York theological seminary
Rome (city)—Pontifical Gregorian university
St Louis university, St Louis, Mo.—School of divinity
Theological students
Union theological seminary, New York

Administration
Union seminary and student power. T. Early. Chr Cent 86:1024+ Jl 30 '69
THEOLOGICAL students
British seminarians issue manifesto. Chr Cent 86:175 F 5 '69
Concord at Concordia? C. M. Bunce. Chr Today 13:37 Mr 14 '69
Hillel vs. the elders; demands of rabbinical seminarians. il Newsweek 74:118-20 D 8 '69
News and views; seminary enrollments in the U.S. J. Deedy. Commonweal 89:510 Ja 24 '69
On a hill far away; reflections on the Interseminary church and society internship program. J. Lawrence. Chr Cent 86:1419-20 N 5 '69
Theological education and the black church. C. S. Rooks. il Chr Cent 86:212-16 F 12 '69
Theological education 1969; symposium. Chr Cent 86:541-50+ Ap 23 '69
Theology students rebel: University of Strasbourg students demand a new curriculum. X. W. Carroll. America 120:268-71 Mr 8 '69; Discussion. 120:437, 515 Ap 12, My 3 '69
THEOLOGY
Atlanta document: an interpretation. P. N. Williams. Chr Cent 86:1311-12 O 15 '69
From chaos to Toronto 1; with reply. A. Atkins. il Commonweal 91:149-55 O 31 '69
German bishops cry heresy; Halbfas case. J. J. Doherty. Commonweal 89:634-5 F 21 '69
God, in the Christian sense. J. J. Vincent. Chr Cent 86:1192-4+ S 17 '69
Heady stuff. A. H. Leitch. Chr Today 13:40 Jl 18 '69
History of theology, by Y. M. J. Congar. Review
Commonweal 89:624 F 14 '69. A. L. Schlitzer
Justification by ignorance: a neo-Protestant motif? address, December 29, 1969. C. F. H. Henry. Chr Today 14:10-15 Ja 2 '70
Karl Barth, 1886-1968: his place in history. K. Runia. Chr Today 14:6-9 D 5 '69
Meaning of religious belief; excerpt from The foundations of belief. L. Dewart. Commonweal 90:15-17 Mr 21 '69
News and views; K. Rahner's withdrawal of support from H. Halbfas. J. Deedy. Commonweal 90:130 Ap 18 '69
Nonsense of liberal Catholics. J. P. Degnan. Chr Today 14:3-6 N 21 '69
Not radical enough? excerpts from Christian freedom in a permissive society. J. A. T. Robinson. Chr Cent 86:1446-9 N 12 '69
On creativity. R. J. Enquist; discussion. Chr Cent 86:389-90 Mr 19 '69
Political theology; relationship between theology and politics. F. Herzog. Chr Cent 86:975-8 Jl 23 '69
Problem: moral teaching. V. P. McCorry. America 120:738-inside back cover Je 28 '69
Question of God, by H. Zahrnt. Review
Commonweal 90:568+ S 19 '69. J. S. Dunne
Revelation theology, by A. Dulles. Review
Commonweal 91:365+ D '69. J. Blenkinsopp
Rudolf Bultmann in Catholic thought, ed. by T. O'Meara and D. Weisser. Review
Commonweal 90:179-80 Ap 25 '69. W. A. Scott
Search for a usable future, by M. E. Marty. Review
Commentary 47:97-100 My '69. J. Keber
Commonweal 90:53-4 Mr 28 '69. P. Deasy
Spectrum of Catholic attitudes, ed. by R. Campbell. Review
America 120:308 Mr 15 '69. J. F. Cotter
Supernatural reality; secular theology. K. L. Woodward. il Newsweek 73:56 F 24 '69
Theology. T. E. Clarke. America 122:24-5 Ja 10 '70
Theology on the rebound. C. F. H. Henry. Chr Today 14:31-2 D 5 '69

THOMAN, Roy E.
Aden and South Arabia. bibliog f Cur Hist 58:27-33+ Ja '70
THOMAS, Bill
Buzzards of Hinckley. Nat Wildlife 7:34-5 F '69
Court day. il Travel 132:48-51 S '69
Lake Erie's islands by air. Travel 131:50-4 My '69
Luxury camping. Travel 132:44-7 S '69
Plight of the swampers. Field & S 74:76-7+ Je '69
Ravaging mountain streams challenge white water canoeists. Pop Gard 20:12-17 Spr '69; Same abr. with title Whitewater canoe race. Travel 131:50-3+ Mr '69
Ski-bobbing. il Travel 132:42-5 N '69
Why not take to the woods this summer. Parents Mag 44:60-1+ Ap '69
Winter canoeing. Travel 132:28-33 O '69
THOMAS, Bob
Man for all seasons. Motor T 21:26+ O '69
Motor trend profile. Motor T 21:32+ D '69
THOMAS, David Duval
Big, A. R. B. Parke. Flying 84:26 Mr '69
THOMAS, Davis
Winging it through Russia. Sports Illus 31: 42-7 S 8 '69
THOMAS, Della
Screenings: media mix. Library J 94:3160 S 15 '69
THOMAS, Dylan
Journey from apple orchard to swallow thronged loft: Fern Hill. M. C. Davidow. bibliog f Engl J 58:78-81 Ja '69
THOMAS, E. Parry
Building castles in the sand. por Bsns W p 140 Ap 26 '69
THOMAS, Elwell B.
What do you know about. . . Yachting 125: 76-7+ Ap '69
THOMAS, George B.
Tension: a tool for reform. Sat R 52:50-2+ Jl 19 '69
THOMAS, Gwyn
One Welshman's Wales. Travel & Camera 32: 64-9+ Je '69

about

Ever green was his valley. P. Burton. por Sat R 52:35 Ap 26 '69
THOMAS, Helen
(ed) See Nixon, P. Pat Nixon, her first year as First lady
THOMAS, Herbert H. and Edelson, Edward
What can be done to cure infertility. Redbook 133:46+ S '69
THOMAS, J. C.
How I became a custom critic for fun and profit. Writers Digest 49:66-7+ Je '69
THOMAS, Jess
Musician of the month. G. Movshon. Hi Fi 19:MA-5 My '69
THOMAS, Lionel E. Mawdesley-. See Mawdesley-Thomas, L. E.
THOMAS, Lois B.
Human dimension in foreign language instruction. Clear House 43:425-7 Mr '69
THOMAS, Lowell, jr
Alaska: giant state, giant resources, giant problems. Nat Wildlife 7:24-33 Ap '69
What Alaska offers young marrieds. McCalls 96:99-100 Ap '69
THOMAS, Mary P. R.
Bag & baggage. Travel & Camera 32:38 Ap '69
THOMAS, Michael
Big P. por Look 33:14+ Ap 15 '69
THOMAS, Michael Tilson
Music to my ears. I. Kolodin. Sat R 52:44+ N 8 '69
Musical events: M. T. Thomas as a substitute for W. Steinberg. W. Sargeant. New Yorker 45:163 N 1 '69
Outstanding young artists win honors. por Hi Fi 19:MA16 Ag '69
THOMAS, Morris Taft
Texture prints with tile. Design 70:10-11 mid-Wint '69
THOMAS, Neil
White church and black business. Commonweal 90:503-4 Ag 22 '69
THOMAS, Norman
Choices. by N. Thomas. Review
America 120:672 Je 7 '69. R. H. Miller
Norman Thomas' legacy: excerpts from The choices. pors Life 66:74A-74B+ Mr 14 '69

about

Hope's candidate. S. Pollard. Sat R 52:40 Ap 12 '69
Norman Thomas: a memoir. R. Baldwin. por Sat R 52:41-2 Ap 12 '69
Obituary
Nat R 21:18 Ja 14 '69

THOMAS, Piri
Two books with soul: for defiant ones. A. A. Shockley. Engl J 58:396-8 Mr '69
THOMAS, Ray
Here's what's happening. Space World F-9-69:43-6 S '69
THOMAS, Robert K. See Wahrhaftig, A. L. jt. auth.
THOMAS, Rosemary
Books that look out, books that look in. W. Stafford. Poetry 113:425 Mr '69
THOMAS, Stanley W.
Automatic reset for circuit breaker Electr World 82:92 D '69
THOMAS A. Dooley foundation
Splendid Americans; excerpts from The legacy of Tom Dooley. L. Elliott. il Read Digest 95:215-24+ S '69
THOMAS Nelson and sons. See Nelson, Thomas, and sons (publisher)
THOMPSON, Ben H.
National park system enlarged. Parks & Rec 4:26-7 Mr '69

about

Ben H. Thompson retires. por Parks & Rec 4:26 N '69
THOMPSON, Benjamin
Visual squalor, social disorder or, A new vision of the city of man. il Arch Rec 145: 161-4 Ap '69
THOMPSON, Benjamin, associates
Three interiors by Benjamin Thompson associates. il Arch Rec 145:136-41 Je '69
THOMPSON, Bob
California's collector reds. Am Home 72:90+ N '69
THOMPSON, Daniel V.
Gardener's kitchen. See issues of Horticulture
THOMPSON, Era Bell
African safari. pors Ebony 24:114-18+ F '69
Africa's problems. Ebony 24:116-18+ Jl '69
Black astrologers predict the future. Ebony 24:62-4+ Ap '69
Progress: Africa's untold story. Ebony 24: 74-6+ Je '69
THOMPSON, Fletcher
Excerpt from statement, June 19, 1969. Cong Digest 48:280+ N '69
THOMPSON, Francis
Letters of Francis Thompson, ed. by J. E. Walsh. Review
Cath World 210:92+ N '69. C. J. Huelsbeck
THOMPSON, H. Keith, jr
Hamilton galleries has another successful season. Hobbies 74:140 D '69
THOMPSON, Herbert J.
James River flood of August 1969 in Virginia. Weatherwise 22:180-3 O '69
THOMPSON, J. Walter, company
Ad leader joins trend. Bsns W p28 Ap 5 '69
JWT goes public. Newsweek 73:82-3 Ap 14 '69
THOMPSON, Jane K.
I'm the most geriatric of them all. bibliog Ment Hy 53:375-80 Jl '69
THOMPSON, John
Big money. Commentary 47:60-3 F '69
Condition of servitude: story. Commentary 47: 45-50 Mr '69
End of culture. Commentary 48:46-52 D '69
Notes on aggression. Commentary 47:63-5 Ap '69
Observations (cont) Commentary 48:63-5 Jl '69
Pornography & propaganda. Commentary 48: 54-7 Ag '69
Yesterdays in Grand Rapids. Harper 238:43-51 My '69

about

Books that look out, books that look in. W. Stafford. Poetry 113:424-5 Mr '69
THOMPSON, John H.
New York state. bibliog Focus 19:1-8 Je '69
THOMPSON, John M.
Books and culture: a reevaluation; address, June 22, 1968. por ALA Bul 63:603-9 My '69
THOMPSON, Joseph W. and Evans, W. W.
Behavioral approach to industrial selling. Harvard Bsns R 47:137-51 Mr '69
THOMPSON, Judith, and Woodard, Gloria
Black perspective in books for children. bibliog pors Wilson Lib Bul 44:416-24 D '69
THOMPSON, Kay
Authors & editors. B. A. Bannon. il Pub W 195:13-15 My 12 '69
THOMPSON, Lawrence S.
American bibliophiles; reprint. Hobbies 73: 108-9+ F '69
THOMPSON, Mickey
Mickey Thompson, perpetual motion. B. Lang. il pors Hot Rod 22:50-2 Jl '69

THOMPSON, Patricia
Cop teen-agers dig. il pors Ebony 24:106-8+ Je '69
THOMPSON, Sir Robert Grainger Ker
Encouraging words before Tet. il Newsweek 74:35 D 29 '69
President's guerrilla expert. por Time 94:8 D 26 '69
THOMPSON, T. E. and Bennett, I.
Physalia nematocysts: utilized by mollusks for defense. bibliog Science 166:1532-3 D 19 '69
THOMPSON, Thomas
I've done what I was supposed to do. Life 66:53-4+ F 21 '69
Judy's daughter wants to be Liza. Life 67:51-2+ O 17 '69
Tanzania to Tiffany's. Life 66:70-6 My 9 '69
Tragic house on the hill. Life 67:42-6+ Ag 29 '69
THOMPSONVILLE, Conn. See Enfield, Conn.
THOMSON, A. P.
Get started growing apples. Org Gard & Farm 16:48-52 N '69
THOMSON, George
New world of Asia. For Affairs 48:123-38 O '69
THOMSON, James Claude, 1931-
How to wink at China. New Repub 160:12-13 Mr 1 '69
Nixon and China: time to talk. Atlan 223:71-3 F '69
THOMSON, Scott D.
Activism: a game for unloving critics. Ed Digest 35:1-4 S '69
THOREAU, Henry David
Flower power: a student's guide to pre-hippie transcendentalism. P. H. Wild. Engl J 58:62-8 Ja '69
Thoreau and American power. A. Kazin. por Atlan 223:60-4+ My '69
Thoreau and Hecker: freemen, friends, mystics. M. W. Hess. Cath World 209:265-7 S '69
Thoreau country. H. D. Crawford. il Am For 75:20-3+ N '69
Thoreau: natural maverick. por Sr Schol 94:11 Mr 14 '69
THORMEYER, Alan
Springfield students demonstrate for their college. Todays Ed 58:25 S '69
THORNE, J. Albert
J. Albert Thorne, back-to-Africanist. R. G. Weisbord. bibliog il Negro Hist Bul 32:14-16 Mr '69
THORNE, Jim
Authors & editors. L. P. Freilicher. il por Pub W 195:19-20 My 19 '69
THORNTON, Thomas Perry
View from Washington. bibliog f Ann Am Acad 386:19-30 N '69
THOROUGHBRED horses. See Race horses
THORP, Ella
David; story. Mlle 69:178-9 My '69
THORPE, Lloyd
Little fire that remained little. Am For 75:36-9+ N '69
THORSEN, Karen
Seventy-nine other ways to have fun in the U.S.A. Mlle 68:270-3+ Ap '69
THORSON, John, and others
Objective measure of the dynamics of a visual movement illusion. bibliog Science 164:1087-8 My 30 '69
THORUM, Reho F.
Department head in the large senior high school. Clear House 43:264-6 Ja '69; Same abr. Ed Digest 34:11-13 Mr '69
THOUGHT and language
End of culture; with quotations. J. Thompson. Commentary 48:46-52 D '69
Linguistic structure and transposition. M. Cole and others. bibliog il Science 164:90-1 Ap 4 '69
THOUGHT and thinking
Are you making yourself clear? N. Cousins. Sat R 52:30-2 F 22 '69
Creative alternatives. N. J. Reyburn. bibliog f Sch & Soc 97:23-4 Ja '69
Lateral thinking. E. DeBono. il Todays Ed 58:20-4 N '69
See also
Cognition
Intellectual liberty
Judgment
Meditation
Problem solving
Psychology
Study and teaching
Students need a course in thinking. C. Cogswell. Todays Ed 58:60 N '69
THRASHERS
Brown thrasher, handsome songster and gardener's friend. M. D. Hodgins. il Home Gard 56:76+ F '69

THREAD
Thread making for the enamelist. L. S. Taylor. il Ceram Mo 17:20-2 O '69
THREE-cornered hat; ballet. See Ballets—Criticisms
THREE crises in the lives of dope fiends; story. See White, W.
THREE-dimensional map construction. See Cartography
THREE is company; story. See Perera, P.
3M company
3M: little drops of water, little grains of sand. il Forbes 104:30-2+ S 1 '69
THREE men on a horse; drama. See Holm, J. C. and Abbott, G.
THREE sisters; drama. See Chekhov, A. P.
THREE'S a crowd; story. See O'Malley, J.
THREONINE deaminase. See Enzymes
THRESHING
Thrashin' time. M. E. Shatraw. Am West 6:32-5 Jl '69
Wowee! It's a thrashin' bee! N. Levy. il Har Yrs 9:26-9 Je '69
THRIFT
See also
Domestic finance
Saving and savings
THROAT
See also
Tonsils
Surgery
Tonsils, in or out? M. A. Wessel. il Parents Mag 44:82-4+ N '69
THROCKMORTON, Burton Hamilton, 1921-
Do Christians believe in death? Chr Cent 86:708-10 My 21 '69
THROCKMORTON, Peter
Adventures in the sponge trade; excerpt from Shipwrecks and archaeology: the unharvested sea. Atlan 224:96-103 S '69
Ancient shipwreck yields new facts; and a strange cargo. pors Nat Geog 135:282-300 F '69
THROMBIN
Thrombin-induced release of calcium from blood platelets. E. H. Mürer. bibliog il Science 166:623 O 31 '69
THROMBOSIS
See also
Infarctions
THROTTLE. See Airplane engines—Throttle
THROWER, Randolph William
Significant developments in tax administration; address, October 6, 1969. Vital Speeches 36:73-7 N 15 '69
about
Man who'll scan the 1040. por Bsns W p 100 Ag 2 '69
THROWER, Ray D.
Radio mirrors for communications. bibliog Electr World 81:27-9+ My '69
THROWERS, Snow. See Snow blowers, throwers, etc.
THUGS
Stranglers, by G. Bruce. Review
Time 93:85+ F 7 '69
THUJA. See Arborvitae
THUMB sucking
Is a thumb for sucking? L. Joseph. il Todays Health 47:32-5 D '69
When youngsters cling to babyish ways. R. M. Silberstein and C. Levine. il Parents Mag 44:51-3+ Mr '69
THUNDERBIRD precision-flying team. See Aviation—Stunt flying
THURLOW, Bradbury
Found: two bulls. C. Morgello. il Newsweek 73:71 Je 30 '69
THURLOW ISLAND. See Cliff Island
THURMOND, Strom
Excerpt from debate, October 9, 1968. Cong Digest 48:54+ F '69
about
Entente Carolina. Nation 209:590 D 1 '69
Strom's little acres. D. Walsh. il pors Life 67:42-46A S 19 '69
THUY, Xuan. See Xuan Thuy
THYMIDINE
Zinc-deficient embryos: reduced thymidine incorporation. H. Swenerton and others. bibliog il Science 166:1014-15 N 21 '69
THYMINE
Crystal and molecular structure of a thymine-tymine adduct. I. L. Karle and others. bibliog il Science 164:183-4 Ap 11 '69
Repairing the DNA. Sci N 96:348-9 O 18 '69

THYMUS gland
Thymus and reproduction: sex-linked dysgenesia of the gonad after neonatal thymectomy in mice. Y. Nishizuka and T. Sakakura. bibliog il Science 166:753-5 N 7 '69

Transplantation
Transplant that saved my baby's life; child born without a thymus. W. Hartley and E. Hartley. il Redbook 132:76-7+ Mr '69

THYROCALCITONIN. See Calcitonin

THYROID gland
Avian thyroid: effect of p,p'-DDT on size and activity. D. J. Jefferies and M. C. French. bibliog il Science 166:1278-80 D 5 '69
See also
Calcitonin

THYROID-stimulating hormone. See Thyrotropin

THYROPROTEINS
Change DHIA rules to allow thyroprotein? O. Bay. Farm J 93:D5 Je '69

THYROTROPIN
Thyroid-stimulating hormone and prostaglandin E₁ stimulation of cyclic 3',5'-adenosine monophosphate in thyroid slices. T. Kaneko and others. bibliog il Science 163:1062-3 Mr 7 '69

TIBBETT, Lawrence
Artistry of Lawrence Tibbett. P. L. Miller. por Am Rec G 35:385 Ja '69

TIBBITS, Mickey
World of work. Schol Teach Sec Teach Sup p 12+ S 22 '69

TIBBITTS, Clark
Manpower needs in the field of aging. Aging 173:3-5 Mr '69

TIBET
See also
Communism—Tibet

History
Tibet struggles to survive. H. S. Bradsher. For Affairs 47:750-62 Jl '69

TIBETAN art. See Art, Tibetan

TICHAUER, Erwin R.
Building a better mouse trap. il por Time 93:46+ My 2 '69

TICHER, Kurt
Unusual pieces of Irish silver. Antiques 96:572-7 O '69

TICKET selling
See also
Computers—Ticket selling applications

TICKS
Hormonal termination of larval diapause in dermacentor albipictus. J. E. Wright. bibliog il Science 163:390-1 Ja 24 '69

TIDAL bores. See Bores (tidal phenomena)

TIDAL currents. See Ocean currents

TIDAL power. See Tide power

TIDE power
Tidal energy; Rance River plant, France. R. H. Charlier. il Sea Front 15:339-48 N '69

TIDES
Ebb and flow. F. G. W. Smith. il Sea Front 15:86-96 Mr '69
Grip on the tides; the beauty of seascapes tossed and sculpted by the moon. il Life 67:32-41 Jl 4 '69
Man and the tides. F. G. W. Smith. il Sea Front 15:142-51 My '69
Real tide. F. G. W. Smith. il Sea Front 15:34-48 Ja '69

TIDINESS. See Neatness

TIE backs, Curtain. See Curtain and drapery fixtures

TIE dyeing. See Dyes and dyeing

TIE-in merchandise. See Merchandising

TIE rods (automobile) See Automobiles—Springs and suspension

TIED and dyed work. See Dyes and dyeing

TIEDEMANN, H. and others
Polyvinylsulfate: interaction with complexes of morphogenetic factors and their natural inhibitors. bibliog Science 164:1175-7 Je 6 '69

TIEDJENS, V. A.
Lowly earthworm. Horticulture 46:50+ S '68

TIERNEY, Dave
Schoolboy's dilemma. Todays Ed 58:79-80 F '69

TIERRA del FUEGO
Our far-flung correspondents; the end beyond the end. R. Hough. il New Yorker 45:151-4+ O 25 '69

TIETZE, Christopher, and Lewit, Sarah
Abortion; with biographical sketches. Sci Am 220:18, 21-7 bibliog (p 138) Ja '69

TIFFANY, John M. and Blough, H. A.
Myxovirus envelope proteins: a directing influence on the fatty acids of membrane lipids. bibliog Science 163:573-4 F 7 '69

TIFFIN, Gerald C.
Changing years. Chr Today 13:13-14 Mr 14 '69

TIFFIN, Ohio
Lake Erie will be a little bit cleaner. il Am City 84:14 N '69

TIFFORD, David
Face to face with a modern-day Johnny Appleseed. por Seventeen 28:60 Je '69

TIGER, Lionel
Why it's a man's world. Read Digest 95:223-4+ O '69

TIGERFLOWERS
February's bulbs? il Sunset 142:173 F '69

TIGERS

Training
Don't go near the water, if there's a tiger in your tank; letter to the editor. M. Spiegel. il Sr Schol 94:4-5 Ap 11 '69

TIGHE, Francis
VISTA: service with vision. pors Har Yrs 9:46-8 O '69

TIGRIDIAS. See Tigerflowers

TIJERINA, Reies Lopez
La Raza: Mexican Americans in rebellion. J. L. Love. bibliog il por Trans-Action 6:35-4l F '69

TIJERINO-MEDRANO, José A.
ILO: fifty years of labor. Américas 21:16-22 Jl '69

TIJMENS, Willem Jan
South Africa's flowers. Horticulture 47:22-3+ D '69
Welwitschia. Horticulture 46:18-19 N '68

TIJUANA, Mexico
Booked for travel. D. Butwin. Sat R 52:54 F 22 '69
Dope control; reprint. R. Berrellez. U S News 67:108 O 20 '69

TILDEN, Freeman
Beyond what the eye sees. Travel & Camera 32:38-45 Je '69
Mindsight: the aim of interpretation. Nat Parks 43:9-12 My '69

TILDEN family
Tilden coat-of-arms. H. K. Eilers. il Hobbies 74:114-15 Ag '69

TILE setting
How to tile a ceiling. il Pop Mech 132:160-1 N '69

TILES
Care of ceramic tile. Good H 168:199 Mr '69
Ceramics of three continents; ceramic production of central Europe, Russia, and the United States. R. Davidson. il Antiques 95:320+ Mr '69
Family tile-makers make a door. il Sunset 143:120 N '69

TILIACEAE
See also
Corchorus

TILING. See Tile setting

TILLAGE
How subsoil bolsters plant growth. J. I Rodale. il Org Gard & Farm 16:110-12 Ja '69
How the crops went in. il Farm J 93:22-3 Jl '69
Last-minute ideas for faster field work. P. B. Jones. il Suc Farm 67:24-5 My '69
Spring tillage, fewer trips than ever. il Farm J 93:26-7 Mr '69
Subsoils can enrich the land. J. I. Rodale. il Org Gard & Farm 16:80-1+ F '69

TILLAMOOK rock lighthouse. See Lighthouses

TILLER, William A.
Materials science and applied science. Science 165:469-75 Ag 1 '69

TILLERING (plants)
Should you give a sucker an even break? il Sunset 142:192 Je '69

TILLERS. See Cultivators

TILLERS, Marine. See Sailboats—Steering gear

TILLICH, Paul
Tillich on tradition. J. J. Langford. Cath World 209:233-4 Ag '69

TILLINGHAST, Richard
Letter: poem. Poetry 114:29-30 Ap '69

TILLMAN, Rodney
Working for the best in education: ideas of impact. ALA Bul 63:231-4 F '69

TILMAN, Robert Oliver
Malaysian political game. Cur Hist 56:100-5+ F '69

TIM, Tiny. See Tiny Tim

TIMBER
See also
Lumber
Lumber industry and trade
Wood

TIMBERTOP school. See Private schools—
Australia
TIMBUCTOO. See Timbuktu, Mali
TIMBUKTU, Mali
Bend of the Niger River. M. Mangus. il Natur Hist 78:26-37 Ja '69
TIME
See also
Past, The
Periodicity
TIME (periodical)
Flip is not actual malice. H. F. Pilpel and K. P. Norwick. Pub W 196:33 O 6 '69
Letter from the publisher; news tour of Asia. J. R. Shepley. il Time 93:12-13 Mr 7 '69
Letter from the publisher: Time introduces new section: Environment. J. R. Shepley. il Time 94:8 Ag 1 '69
Newsweek (a fact) is the new hot book (an opinion) C. Welles. Esquire 72:152-4+ N '69
Time: after Luce. R. Pollack. Harper 239:42-52 Jl '69; Discussion. 239:6 S '69
Time marches on Haynsworth. R. de Toledano. il Nat R 21:1164-6+ N 18 '69
Time's Board of economists; symposium. il Time 94:88-90 N 14 '69
TIME, incorporated
Ill lay Time inc, so it changed bosses. Bsns W p20-1 Ag 30 '69
Information retrieval research at Time inc; address, January 1969. M. T. Fischer. il Library J 94:1585-8 Ap 15 '69
Time for a change; changes at the top. il Newsweek 74:76 S 1 '69
TIME, Use of
Harried leisure class, by B. Linder. Review Fortune 81:161-2 Ja '70. M. Ways
Time and effort; story. See Rogin, G.
TIME capsules. See Civilization—Preservation of records
TIME deposits. See Bank deposits
TIME-Life international
Time-Life books international. H. R. Lottman. il Pub W 196:19-22 N 24 '69
TIME measurements
What is a cesium beam clock? Sci Digest 66:89 N '69
See also
Chronograph
Cosmochronotrope
Sundials
TIME of your life; drama. See Saroyan, W.
TIME pattern research institute
Of thee I Ching. E. Janeway. Atlan 224:155-7 N '69
TIME reversal
Experiments in time reversal. O. E. Overseth. il Sci Am 221:88-94+ bibliog(p 148) O '69
TIME sharing computers. See Computers—Time sharing systems
TIMEKEEPER; story. See Greenberg, J.
TIMERS. See Timing devices
TIMES, London
Losses by a London landmark. Bsns W p22 Ja 3 '70
Successful sobriety; financial trouble. Newsweek 75:43 Ja 5 '70
TIMES, Los Angeles. See Los Angeles times
TIMES, New York. See New York times
TIMES herald printing company
Better than an oil well. Newsweek 74:70 S 29 '69
TIMIDITY
In defense of shyness. E. Adams. Parents Mag 44:56-7+ Mr '69
TIMING devices
Digital IC timer. D. L. Steinbach. il Electr World 81:48-50 My '69
Hey Ollie have ya got the time? E. Rickman. il Hot Rod 22:126-8 O '69
Household timers. il Consumer Rep 34:506-9 S '69
Measure the speed of a bullet with this electronic stopwatch. R. M. Benrey. il Pop Sci 195:144-6+ Jl '69
Unusually long interval times. G. Varadarajan. il Radio-Electr 40:103 O '69
See also
Electric lighting—Control
TIMMONS, Bob
Rat pack. il por Newsweek 73:111 Ap 28 '69
TIMMONS, Virginia G.
Clipboard. See issues of School arts
Resource materials: books, filmstrips, films, slides, loops. Sch Arts 69:32-3 Ja '70
TIMPANO, Doris M.
Copyright legislation and you. Todays Ed 58:18-20 Ap '69

TIN
See also
Tole
TIN cutters. See Cutting tools
TIN organic compounds. See Organometallic compounds
TINARI, Anne
No secrets to African violets. Org Gard & Farm 16:66-9 N '69
TINBERGEN, Jan
Awards for the modelmakers. il por Time 94:96 N 7 '69
Models bring Nobel prize. Sci N 96:397 N 1 '69
Nobel laureates in economics, chemistry, and physics. L. R. Klein. por Science 166:715-17 N 7 '69
Two remarkable men. P. A. Samuelson. Newsweek 74:108 N 17 '69
TINDALL, Barry S.
Aldo Leopold; a philosophy and a challenge. Parks & Rec 3:28-30 O '68
Man and nature in the city. Parks & Rec 4:39-40+ Ja '69
TINGOM, Elizabeth
Spirit of the road; story. New Yorker 45:32-9 Ag 16 '69
TINKER, Frank A.
Big airlift to the North Slope. Pop Mech 132:94-7+ N '69
Sawtooth summer. Travel 131:40-3 My '69
Smoothing the rough chukar road. Field & S 74:66-7+ N '69
Who will bell the invisible CAT? Pop Mech 132:94-7+ Ag '69
Yellowstone snowtime. Travel 131:30-3+ F '69
TINLING, Dallas
How to wash paint brushes with no fuss, no muss, and very little solvent. Motor B 123:124+ My '69
TINLING, Teddy
Little lace goes a long, long way. G. S. Brown. il por Sports Illus 31:44-7 Jl 7 '69
TINNEY, James S.
Unit on black literature. Engl J 58:1028-31 O '69
TINSLEY, Russell
Ambush tactics for mule deer. Field & S 74:40-1+ Ag '69
Standing for whitetail. Field & S 74:48-9+ O '69
TINTING of fabrics. See Dyes and dyeing
TINY Alice; drama. See Albee, E.
TINY Tim
Meeting with Tiny Tim. J. Walsh. il pors Hobbies 74:37-9+ S; 37-40+ O '69
Puff-up time. Time 94:47 D 26 '69
TIPPETT, Sir Michael
Second symphony of Sir Michael Tippett. J. Diether. por Am Rec G 36:98-9 O '69
TIPPING
How much is enough? the Christmas tip. J. O'Reilly. il McCalls 97:40+ D '69
Insult me, comrade! revival in Russia. Newsweek 73:112 Ap 14 '69
TIPTON, David
Gunshots; Plans; Pachacamac; poems. Poetry 114:391-6 S '69
TIPTON, Stuart Guy
Cost of restrictions; excerpts from address. Aviation W 90:11 F 10 '69
TIRE industry and trade
Enigmatic Monsieur Michelin. V. Lewis. il Duns R 94:97-100 N '69
Labor troubles deflate Pirelli. Bsns W p33-4 S 27 '69
Tire makers' bumpy recall campaign. Bsns W p 103 S 6 '69
See also
Firestone tire and rubber company
Goodrich, B. F, company
Goodyear tire and rubber company

Finance
From first to last; profits of automobile, tire and auto parts industries. il Forbes 104:57-8 N 1 '69
TIREDNESS. See Fatigue
TIRES, Airplane
Do it yourself. A. Trammell. Flying 85:16-17 S '69

Maintenance and repair
Do it yourself; oops! prevention. A. Trammell. Flying 85:18-19 O '69
TIRES, Automobile
Changing shape of tires for your car. J. P. Norbye and J. Dunne. il Pop Sci 195:56-9 Jl '69
Goodyear gambles on polyglas. and wins. il Bsns W p 118-21 O 11 '69

TIRES, Automobile—*Continued*

How to read your tires for front end troubles. M. Schultz. il Pop Mech 132:150-3 N '69

News on wheels; when it's time to retire. M. Spiegel. il Sr Schol 94:32 My 9 '69

On the scene; '70 autos with tires that run longer. il U S News 67:7 S 1 '69

One equals two; racing tires. il Motor T 21:108-9 F '69

Spray-on tire chains; Dow liquid tire chain. il Consumer Bul 52:19-20 Mr '69

Studded growth. K. Ludvigsen. il Motor T 21:76-7 D '69

Talladega's troubled Sunday. S. Kelly. il Hot Rod 22:44-6 D '69

Tires; the right tire means a safer car. il Consumer Bul 52:35-40 Mr '69

What goes on inside your tires? J. P. Norbye. il Pop Sci 195:64-7 N '69

World 600. L. Laye. il Motor T 21:64-6 Ag '69

Testing

Lincoln penny may tell you when your tire is no longer safe. il Consumer Bul 52:32 F '69

Testing tires with laser light. il Chem 42:25 F '69

TIRES, Motor truck

Selecting tires for recreational vehicles; with charts. V. L. Oertle. il Field & S 73:78-81+ Ap '69

TIRES, Tractor

Tractor tire pressure limits. il Suc Farm 67:61 Ja '69

TIRES for pick up trucks. See Tires, Motor truck

TIROL. See Tyrol

TIRPITZ (warship) See World war, 1939-1945
—Naval operations

TIRRELL, Ruth

Better ways to more tomatoes. por Org Gard & Farm 16:80-2 Mr '69

Last sowings of summer. pors Org Gard & Farm 16:24-7 Jl '69

Perennial onions for yields every year. Org Gard & Farm 16:33-5 D '69

Pick a mess of peas by Memorial day. Org Gard & Farm 16:41-3 F '69

Plants that protect themselves. Org Gard & Farm 16:35-7 Je '69

TISCH, Laurence Alan

Brother act stars at Loew's. il por Bsns W p 126-7+ Ap 12 '69

TISCH, Preston Robert

Brother act stars at Loew's. il por Bsns W p 126-7+ Ap 12 '69

TISDALL, William J.

Residential high school for gifted disadvantaged students. Ed Digest 34:40-3 F '69

TISHLER, Max

Siege of the house of reason; adaptation of address, May 23, 1969. bibliog Science 166:192-5 O 10 '69

TISHMAN collection. See Art—Private collections

TISSUE adhesives. See Adhesives

TISSUE banks

Saving your skin. il Newsweek 74:55 Ag 18 '69

TISSUE culture. See Tissues—Culture

TISSUE repair. See Wound healing

TISSUES

See also
Adipose tissues
Bone
Connective tissues

Culture

Cytogenetic effects of cyclamates on human cells in vitro. D. Stone and others. bibliog il Science 164:568-9 My 2 '69

Gametogony of eimeria tenella (coccidia) in cell cultures. R. G. Strout and C. A. Ouellette. bibliog il Science 163:695-6 F 14 '69

Human liposarcomas; tissue cultures containing foci of transformed cells with viral particles. D. L. Morton and others. bibliog il Science 165:813-16 Ag 22 '69

Hybrid somatic cells. B. Ephrussi and M. C. Weiss. il Sci Am 220:26-35 bibliog(p 146) Ap '69

Lymphocyte stimulation; transfer of cellular hypersensitivity to antigen in vitro. F. T. Valentine and H. S. Lawrence. bibliog il Science 165:1014-16 S 5 '69

Lymphocytoid lines from persons with sex chromosome anomalies. G. E. Moore and others. bibliog il Science 163:1453-4 Mr 28 '69

Morphogenetic tissue interactions; report of meeting. J. D. Ebert. Science 166:1314+ D 5 '69

Neoplastic transformation in vitro of hamster lens epithelium by simian virus 40. D. M. Albert and others. bibliog il Science 164:1077-8 My 30 '69

Nosema cuniculi; in vitro isolation. J. A. Shadduck. il Science 166:516-17 O 24 '69

Sarcoma-producing cell lines derived from clones transformed in vitro by benzo [a]pyrene. J. A. DiPaolo and others. bibliog il Science 165:917-18 Ag 29 '69

Saving your skin. il Newsweek 74:55 Ag 18 '69

Secretory activity and oncogenicity of a cell line (MDCK) derived from canine kidney. J. Leighton and others. il Science 163:472 Ja 31 '69

Serially cultured animal cells for preparation of viral vaccines; report of meeting, October 1968. S. A. Plotkin and others. Science 165:1278+ S 19 '69

Spin filter culture; the propagation of mammalian cells in suspension. P. Himmelfarb and others. bibliog il Science 164:555-7 My 2 '69

White blood cell cultures in genetic studies on the human mucopolysaccharidoses. K. M. Foley and others. bibliog il Science 164:424-6 Ap 25 '69

X-ray resistant cell required for the induction of in vitro antibody formation. J. Roseman. bibliog il Science 165:1125-7 S 12 '69

See also
Plant cells and tissues—Culture

Preservation

Phenoxyethanol; protein preservative for taxonomists. M. Nakanishi and others. bibliog il Science 163:681-3 F 14 '69

TITANIC (steamship)

Maiden voyage, by G. Marcus. Review
Sat R 52:25 Ag 30 '69. A. R. Dodd

TITANIUM

Titanium the Cinderella of metals. O. A. Battista. il Chem 42:13-15 My '69

What do you know about... N. Feige. il Yachting 125:80-1+ Ap '69

TITLES, Moving picture. See Moving pictures. Amateur—Titles

TITLES of books, stories, etc.

Booksellers' babble and customers' confusion. B. Cornelius. Pub W 195:78 Ap 28 '69

Choosing an article title. M. Gunther. Writer 82:14-15 D '69

See also
Copyright—Titles

Anecdotes, facetiae, satire, etc.

Name of the game is names. Chr Cent 86:633 Ap 30 '69

TITLES of honor and nobility

See also
Wales, prince of (title)

TITLES of operas

Anecdotes, facetiae, satire, etc.

Opera in bright lights; familiar works retitled. J. McPherson. Opera N 33:12-13 Ap 5 '69

TITO

Balkan vendetta. Time 94:42+ N 21 '69

Prudential Mr Tito. M. M. Mestrovic. Commonweal 90:62-3 Ap 4 '69

Yugoslavia; Karl Marx in a Mercedes. E. Dunbar. il Look 33:24-9 F 18 '69

TITRATION

Lab bench; coulometric titrations with halogens. R. J. Palma and K. H. Pearson. bibliog il Chem 42:28-31 N '69

Lab bench; determination of acetic acid in vinegar using gravimetric titrimetry. C. H. Breedlove, jr. il Chem 42:24-5 My '69

TITUSVILLE, Fla.

Space-age lighting for a space-age city. C. Pirtle. il Am City 84:160 S '69

TIWARI, M. M. and Arya, H. C.

Sclerospora graminicola axenic culture. bibliog Science 163:291-3 Ja 17 '69

TKACH, Walter R.

President's health; interview. U S News 67:39-40 N 24 '69

TO be young, gifted and black; drama. See Nemiroff, R.

TO live the dream; story. See Currey, S. M.

TOADS

Disappearing toad; spadefoot. R. H. Wright. il Sci Digest 65:29-31 Ap '69

Teleostean urophysis; stimulation of water movement across the bladder of the toad bufo marinus. F. Lacanilao. bibliog il Science 163:1326-7 Mr 21 '69

Toad urinary bladder; intercellular spaces. D. R. DiBona and M. M. Civan. bibliog il Science 165:503-4 Ag 1 '69

TOADSTOOLS. See Mushrooms

TOAN, Danforth W.
Habitability; interview. New Yorker 45:43-5 N 1 '69

TOBACCO
Light and hormones: interchangeability in the induction of nitrate reductase. S. H. Lips and N. Roth-Bejerano. bibliog il Science 166:109-10 O 3 '69
See also
Cigars

TOBACCO habit. See Smoking

TOBACCO industry and trade
Embattled tobacco industry prepares for the future. il U S News 67:59-60 S 1 '69
Politics of tobacco. E. Schneier. Nation 209:274-9 S 22 '69
Smoking less than ever. il Bsns W p52 Je 28 '69
Tobacco plows new fields; cigarette companies switch name as well as image. Bsns W p38 My 17 '69
See also
Cigar industry
Cigarettes
Morris, Philip, incorporated
Rothmans of Pall Mall Canada, limited

Advertising
Smoke signals. il Newsweek 74:66 S 15 '69
See also
Cigarettes—Advertising

TOBACCO mosaic virus. See Viruses, Plant

TOBACCO pipes
Chinese pipes for tobacco and opium. C. E. Kennedy. il Antiques 95:408-9 Mr '69

TOBACCO rattle virus. See Viruses, Plant

TOBACCO ringspot virus. See Viruses, Plant

TOBACH, Ethel
T. C. Schneirla and animal behavior; with biographical sketch. por Natur Hist 78:6, 52-7 Ja '69

TOBEY, Phyllis E.
Pseudo woodcuts with acetate. Design 70:15 mid-Wint '69

TOBIAS, Abraham Joel
Mural painting for science & technology. il pors Am Artist 33:46-52 Mr '69

TOBIN, James
Books & ideas. por Fortune 80:211-12 O '69
Redistributing national income; excerpts from Agenda for the Nation. Cur 103:19-21 Ja '69
—and Ross, Leonard
Paying for the high costs of education: a national youth program. New Repub 160:18-21 My 3; 32-3 Je 7 '69

TOBIN, Richard L.
(ed) Communications. See Communications issues of Saturday review
Once in a while but not very often. Sat R 52:4+ My 10 '69

TOBIN, William J.
Total religious education and the parish. America 121:33+ Jl 19 '69

TOCH, Hans
Cops & blacks: warring minorities. Nation 208:491-3 Ap 21 '69

TOCQUEVILLE, Alexis de
Omnipotence of the majority. R. L. Tobin. Sat R 52:18 S 27 '69
See also
Tod, G. Robert. See Laighton, C. M. jt. auth.

TOD, Giles M. S.
Riding out a Cape Horn snorter. il Motor B 123:143+ Ap '69

TODARO, George J. See Aaronson, S. A. jt. auth.

TODAY (periodical)
Crusader comes to Howell. Time 95:34 Ja 5 '70

TODAY is my sister's wedding; story. See Boles, P. D.

TODAYS health (periodical)
Now: Today's health for the blind. il Todays Health 47:58 Ag '69

TODD, Carl David
Sub-ohm continuity tester. Electr World 81:78-80 F '69

TODD, Richard
George Wald: the man, the speech. N Y Times Mag p28-9+ Ag 17 '69
Ins and outs at M.I.T. N Y Times Mag p32-3+ My 18 '69
Life with the conscientious acceptors. por N Y Times Mag p27+ O 12 '69

TOEPFER, Alfred
Lüneburg Heath: a German nature park. Nat Parks 43:9 Ap '69

TOFFEE. See Candy

TOGNETTI, Keith P. See Bustard, H. R. jt. auth.

TOILET articles
Check list for a beautiful summer. il Redbook 133:104-5+ Jl '69
Imaginative bed-and-bath accessories. il House & Gard 135:146-7 My '69
Twelve ways to give yourself the best beauty care. il Good H 169:276-8 O '69

TOILET preparations
Beauty and the bath. S. Lindsay. See issues of House beautiful
Beauty from the baby's shelf. P. Van Wagenen. il Parents Mag 44:12 Ag '69
Check list for a beautiful summer. il Redbook 133:104-5+ Jl '69
Pampering luxuries for the super bath. il House B 111:80-1 Mr '69
See also
Deodorants

Advertising
Unlikeliest product; Cupid's quiver, sachets of liquid douche concentrate. il Time 94:51 D 26 '69

TOILET soap. See Soap

TOILETS
Flushed with pride, by W. Reyburn. Review Newsweek il 74:68 D 1 '69. H. F. Waters

TOILETS for boats. See Boats—Toilet facilities

TOKAIDO line. See Railroads—Japan

TOKENS
How to collect coin from coin collectors; commemorative medals and tokens for gas station games. il Bsns W p 150-1 My 24 '69

TOKYO Rose, pseud.
Tokyo Rose is home. D. Arbus. il por Esquire 71:168-9 My '69

TOKYO
See also
Stock exchange—Tokyo

Air pollution
Most polluted city. il Newsweek 74:67 N 3 '69

Galleries and museums
Pentax gallery: a must-see stop while in Tokyo. il Travel & Camera 32:36 O '69

Hotels, restaurants, etc.
Tokyo, P.M. G. Cotler. il Holiday 46:52-5+ S '69
See also
Night clubs—Japan

Stores
Tokyo's incredible shopping resorts: stores double as museums, theaters, playgrounds. F. Lemkowitz. il Travel & Camera 32:68-9+ O '69

TOKYO university. See Colleges and universities—Japan

TOLE
Tole and tole-type buttons. D. F. Brown. il Hobbies 74:128-9 N '69

TOLEDO, Ohio, museum of art
Glass workshop. L. Bruner. il Am Artist 33:48-53+ F '69

TOLERATION
How bigotry is born; with study-discussion program. by R. Strang. E. D. Garrick. bibliog il PTA Mag 63:8-11, 35 F '69
Respectable bigotry; reprint. M. Lerner. Am Scholar 38:606-17 Aut '69
See also
Prejudice

TOLES, George E.
Artificial features for disfigured faces. Sci Digest 66:59-62 N '69

TOLKIEN, John Ronald Reuel
Middle earth in the classroom: studying J. R. R. Tolkien. R. Roos. Engl J 58:1175-80 N '69
Tolkien and the critics; ed. by N. Isaacs and R. Zimbardo. Review
Nat R 21:605 Je 17 '69

TOLL, David W.
Everywhere market: regional magazines. Writers Digest 49:48-52+ O '69
Sonoran Desert National Park. Nat Parks 43:4-8 Ja '69

TOLL, Gertrude
Warm welcome in a New England town. N. M. Lobsenz. Good H 168:81+ My '69

TOLL bridges
See also
Chesapeake Bay bridge-tunnel
San Francisco Bay bridges

TOLL television. See Television broadcasting—Subscription programs

TOLLEFSEN, Dorothy
Britain's elegant sports centers. Parks & Rec 4:16-19+ F '69

TOLLENAERE, Lawrence Robert
Crisis of the $100-million companies. T. J. Murray. Duns R 94:48-50+ D '69

TOLLIVER, Melba
Beauty: the TV specials. il pors Mlle 68:181-2+ Mr '69
TOLNAY, Thomas
Address book; poem. Chr Cent 86:902 Jl 2 '69
Irreverent themes invading reverent theaters. Chr Cent 86:1519-20 N 26 '69
2-p-TOLUIDINYL-6-naphthalene sulfonate. See Sulfonates
TOMASSON, Helgi
Contest in Moscow. W. Terry. il por Sat R 52:39-40 Ag 9 '69
TOMASZ, Alexander
Cellular factors in genetic transformation; with biographical sketch. Sci Am 220:18, 38-44 bibliog(p 138) Ja '69
TOMATO sauce
Italian hand with tomato sauce. Sunset 142:152-3 F '69
TOMATO tree. See Tree tomatoes
TOMATOES
Backyard crop brings in $15,000. J. D. Boyd. il Farm J 93:77 Ap '69
Can you grow the earliest tomatoes in your neighborhood? il Sunset 142:204-5 Mr '69
Green-thumb luck. J. G. Bowman. il Org Gard & Farm 16:32-5 Ag '69
Spring tomato roundup; symposium. il Org Gard & Farm 16:68-70+ Mr '69
See also
Cookery—Vegetables
TOMBOUCTOU. See Timbuktu, Mali
TOMBSTONES. See Sepulchral monuments
TOMKINS, Gordon M. and others
Control of specific gene expression in higher organisms. bibliog Science 166:1474-80 D 19 '69
TOMLINSON, Kenneth Y.
ROTC under attack. Read Digest 95:231-4+ N '69
—See Denison, G. jt. auth.
TOMMY (rock opera) See Rock 'n' roll music
TOMMY guns. See Submachine guns
TOMPKINS, Joyce R.
Mural. Sch Arts 68:13 F '69
TONALA, Mexico
Pottery town, east of Guadalajara. il Sunset 143:79+ O '69
TONALITY
Man who feels: Wozzeck. J. W. Freeman. il Opera N 33:24-6 Ap 12 '69
Seven keys to the flute: Mozart operas. C. R. Faust. il Opera N 34:22-3 Ja 17 '70
TON-duc-Thang
Thang-bang team. Time 94:26 O 3 '69
TONE
Analysis of musical-instrument tones. J.-C. Risset and M. V. Mathews. bibliog il Phys Today 22:23-30 F '69
TONE arm, Phonograph. See Phonograph—Tone arm
TONGUE
See also
Taste
TONGUES. Gift of. See Gift of tongues
TONIGHT at nine thirty-six; story. See Gillespie, A.
TONKIN GULF incident, 1964
Gulf of Tonkin resolution. Cur Hist 57:113+ Ag '69
Truth is the first casualty, by J. C. Goulden. Review
Nation 209:542-4 N 17 '69. R. J. Walton
Sat R 52:34 N 1 '69. W. R. Corson
TONN, Martin
What your child is really saying. Farm J 93:44 Ag '69
TONSILLECTOMY. See Throat—Surgery
TONSILS
Immunoglobulins G, A, and M determined in single cells from human tonsil. D. Gitlin and T. Sasaki. bibliog il Science 164:1532-4 Je 27 '69
Diseases
Tonsils, in or out? M. A. Wessel. il Parents Mag 44:82-4+ N '69
TONSOR, Stephen J.
Alienation and relevance. Nat R 21:636-8+ Jl 1 '69
TOO many angels; drama. See Miller, H. L.
TOOKER, Frank H.
Beeping a Sonalert. Electr World 82:79 D '69
Build a pos-neg pulse generator. Pop Electr 30:34-5 Ap '69
Build the SCS darkroom timer. Pop Electr 31:52-4+ N '69
Dual-rate sawtooth generator. Electr World 81:74 My '69
Dual UJT multivibrator. Electr World 81:45 F '69
FET sine-wave crystal oscillators. Electr World 81:33+ Je '69

Getting to know the SCS. Pop Electr 31:75-8+ S '69
Improving sawtooth linearity. Electr World 81:84 F '69
IC sine-wave clipper. Electr World 82:96-7 N '69
Micro-senstive Schmitt trigger. Pop Electr 32:64-5 Ja '70
SCS crystal-controlled oscillator. Electr World 82:74 O '69
SCS monostable multivibrator. Electr World 82:74 D '69
SCS signal-squaring adapter. Pop Electr 32:65+ Ja '70
Sine-wave to pulse converter. Pop Electr 31:50 Jl '69
UJT sine-wave generators. Electr World 81:82 F '69
TOOL and die makers
Tool men seek an aid pattern; want help of Congress on imports. Bsns W p33 My 24 '69
TOOL boxes, racks, etc.
Build these power-tool stands for your shop. J. Hand. il Pop Mech 132:178-82 Jl '69
Folding tool rack. C. Martin. il Mech Illus 65:136 N '69
Make your wife a toolbox of her own. C. W. Close. il Pop Mech 131:180 Je '69
TOOL sharpening. See Sharpening
TOOLEY, Jack W. See Foster, J. D. jt. auth.
TOOLS
Boatkeeper's tools. P. Smyth. Motor B 123:76+ Mr '69
Don't play taps for broken taps. W. E. Burton. il Pop Mech 131:200-2 Ap '69
Home-repair tools a woman can use. Good H 168:202 Mr '69
Make new hand tools from old. il Home Gard 56:52-3 N '69
Tools for electronics. T. Haskett. See issues of Radio-electronics
See also
Cutting tools
Electric tools
Electric tools. Portable
also names of tools, e.g. Pliers, etc.

Exhibitions

Tools: extenders of the mind; exhibition at New York's Museum of contemporary crafts. H. Aach. il Craft Horiz 29:10-13+ My '69

Leasing and renting

Rental tools can speed up and simplify big home upkeep jobs. il Bet Hom & Gard 47:26 Mr '69

Storage

How I built a home tune-up center. H. T. Gurley. il Pop Sci 195:40 Jl '69
See also
Tool boxes, racks, etc.

Terminology

Tools: a four-language glossary of implements for craftsmen. Craft Horiz 29:22-4 My '69
TOOTE, Gloria
Lawyer tries a world of sound. il pors Ebony 24:73-4+ My '69
TOOTH decay. See Teeth—Diseases
TOOTH powders and pastes. See Dentifrices
TOOTHBRUSHES
Electric toothbrushes. il Consumer Rep 34:138-42 Mr '69
TOOTS Shor restaurant. See New York (city) —Hotels, restaurants, etc.
TOPEKA, Kan.
Alert the citizen before the disaster strikes. T. E. Wright. il Am City 84:101-2 Ag '69
TOPEKA, Kan. zoological park. See Zoological gardens
TOPOL
Lively arts; interview, ed. by R. Hemming. por Sr Schol 94:32 Ap 25 '69
TOPP, Robert W.
Interoceanic sea-level canal: effects on the fish faunas. bibliog Science 165:1324-7 S 26 '69
TOPPER, Yale J. See Mills, E. S. jt. auth.
TOPPIN, Edgar A.
Negro in America: 1901 to 1956. bibliog f Cur Hist 57:269-74+ N '69
TOPPING, Ronald J.
Art teachers experience various sensations through happenings. Sch Arts 69:32-3 N '69
TOPSY-turvy foodland; drama. See Steiner, B. A.
TORDEUR, Jean
Grand Béguinage at Louvain, Belgium. Antiques 96:592-4 O '69
Quartier des arts in Brussels. Antiques 96:595-7 O '69

TORFFIELD, Marvin
Light you can touch. il Esquire 72:64-7 Ag '69
TORNABENE, Lyn
Call me in the city. McCalls 96:68-9+ Ja '69
Moon people. McCalls 96:60-1 Ag '69
Walking with John V. Lindsay. McCalls 97:
54+ N '69
Walking with Omar Sharif. por McCalls 96:
42+ Ap '69
(ed) See Allen, W. Walking with Woody Allen
(ed) See BeBakey, M. E. Inside the operating room with Dr Michael DeBakey
TORNADO detection. See Tornadoes
TORNADOES
Balloons to fight tornados. il Sci Digest 66:
35-6 Ag '69
Corn striations in the Charles City tornado in Iowa. P. J. Waite and C. E. Lamoureux. il Weatherwise 22:54-9 Ap '69
Micro aspects of Manhattan tornado in Kansas on 8 June 1966. J. W. Nelson. il Weatherwise 22:113-17 Je '69
Now you can detect tornadoes with your TV! J. Harvey. il Suc Farm 67:8-9 My '69
Now you can see tornadoes on TV. H. Bradshaw and V. Bradshaw. il Pop Mech 131:
93-6+ Mr '69
Tornado season of 1968. A. D. Pearson. il Weatherwise 22:21-5 F '69
TORONTO
Toronto: boom city to the north. il U S News 67:82-3 S 8 '69
See also
Stock exchange—Toronto

Description
Walking tours of Canada's great cities. il Bet Hom & Gard 47:68 Je '69

Hospitals
New Canadian hospital is structured for an overhead monorail system; Etobicoke hospital. il Arch Rec 145:159-61 Mr '69

Music
Notes from our correspondents. R. Angus. Hi Fi 19:24-5 My '69

Rapid transit
Where commuting by train is a pleasure. il Bsns W p56-7 Ja 3 '70

Sanitary affairs
Plastic sewer liner. R. M. Bremner. il Am City 84:98-101 S '69
TORONTO Maple Leafs (hockey team) See Hockey teams
TORQUE converter fluid. See Hydraulic fluids
TORQUE wrenches
Incalculable torque? B. Neumann. il Hot Rod 22:152-3 O '69
TORRES, Camilo
Biretta to cockade. D. Goulet. por Cath World 209:223-4 Ag '69
Camilo Torres, by G. Guzman. Review America 120:285-6 Mr 8 '69. E. K Culhane
Christian revolutionary. W. P. Jones. Chr Cent 86:1421 N 5 '69
TORRES BODET, Jaime
Jaime Torres Bodet. S. P. Karsen. por Américas 21:6-11 Ag '69
TORREY, Gordon H.
Instability in Syria. Cur Hist 58:13-15+ Ja '70
TORREY Canyon (tanker) See Shipwrecks
TORRIJOS, Omar
Day at the races. por Time 94:16 D 26 '69
What price democracy? il por Newsweek 74:
34 D 29 '69
TORTE. See Cake; Meringue
TORTILLAS. See Cookery, Mexican
TORTOISES
Turtles unharmed by Zond 5 moon trip. Aviation W 90:23-4 My 19 '69
TORTURE
Greece: government by torture; Asphalia, the security police. C. S. Wren. il Look 33:19-21 My 27 '69
Greece: the death of liberty. J. Corry. Harper 239:72-81 O '69
Greece: the rack and the bomb. J. Becket. Nation 209:6-7 Jl 7 '69
Greece: the torture goes on. C. S. Wren. Look 33:63 O 7 '69
Greek junta: no headway toward humanization. Chr Cent 86:1010 Jl 30 '69
Notes and comment: Greek torture. New Yorker 45:23 Jl 12 '69
Prisoners from Hanoi: were they tortured? with editorial comment. J. M. Van Dyke. Nation 209:332, 334-5 O 6 '69

Torture; activities of the Greek junta; excerpts from report of the Human rights commission of the Council of Europe. il Newsweek 74:52 D 15 '69
Torture in the USSR. P. J. Lyons. il Nat R 21:1259-60 D 16 '69
TORVIK, Solveig
Teaching semantics in high school. Engl J 58:1341-6 D '69
TORZA, S. and Mason, S. G.
Coalescence of two immiscible liquid drops. bibliog Science 163:813-14 F 21 '69
TOSCA; opera. See Puccini, G.
TOSCANINI, Arturo
Five Toscanini reissues. C. J. Luten. il por Am Rec G 35:544-5 Mr '69
Toscanini treasures. H. Goldsmith. por Hi Fi 19:96-7 D '69
TOTAL absorption counters. See Counters (electrons, ions, etc)
TOTALITARIANISM
Djilas revisits Orwell; there'll be many different communisms in 1984. M. Djilas. il N Y Times Mag p28-9+ Mr 23 '69
See also
Fascism
TOTE bags. See Handbags
TOTH, Edra
Brief biography. S. Goodman. il pors Dance Mag 43:56-7 D '69
TÓTH, Imre
Non-Euclidean geometry before Euclid; with biographical sketch. Sci Am 221:18, 87-92+ N '69
TOTH, Steven E.
Inhibition of hydroid aging in campanularia flexuosa. bibliog Science 166:619-20 O 31 '69
TOTH, William J.
Easy towing is in the knowing. Am Home 72:
42 S '69
TOTTEN, Clyde W.
Day of the substitute. Todays Ed 58:24-5 Ja '69
TOTTEN, Herman Lavon
They had a dream; black colleges and library standards. por Wilson Lib Bul 44:75-9 S '69
Wiley college library, the first library for Negroes west of the Mississippi River. bibliog Negro Hist Bul 32:6-10 Ja '69
—See Grove, P. S. jt. auth.

about
People. por Wilson Lib Bul 43:500 F '69
TOUCH
Right from the start; tactile communication. with study-discussion program, by R. Strang. D. Graves. bibliog il PTA Mag 63:22-4, 36 My '69
Sense communication. J. McLaughlin. il America 120:714+ Je 21 '69
Size discrimination on the skin. C. J. Vierck, jr and M. B. Jones. bibliog il Science 163:
488-9 Ja 31 '69
TOUCH and see nature trail. See Washington, D.C.—National arboretum
TOUGALOO Southern Christian college, Tougaloo, Miss.
Improving buzzard's luck; creative writing course. R. B. Hoffman. il Wilson Lib Bul 44:51-7 S '69
Sharecropper is me, the small farmer is me, the domestic is me. A. Adams. il Wilson Lib Bul 44:58-63 S '69
TOUMLILINE monastery. See Monasteries
TOURGÉE, Albion Winegar
Friend of freedom. J. Yardley. New Repub 162:30-2 Ja 10 '70
TOURISM. See Tourist trade
TOURIST trade
Boom heard 'round the world. il Bsns W p53-4 Je 28 '69
Surprise packages. M. Gough. il House B 111:40+ D '69
Travel notes; tours of the international airlines. R. Joseph. Esquire 71:28+ My '69
U S hotels go abroad for jet-setting Joneses; hotel and motel chains start massive expansion overseas. il Bsns W p60-1 Ja 18 '69
Winter tourism booms. il Bsns W p36+ F 15 '69
See also
Souvenirs
Travel—Economic aspects
Travel agencies

Alaska
Warming up tourism in Alaska; Westours. il Bsns W p69+ Ag 16 '69

Austria
Liechtenstein and Austria's Tirol. il Travel & Camera 32:85-6 Jl '69

Bahama Islands
Tourism. A. N. Lyons. il Focus 19:8-11 My '69

TOURIST trade—Bahama Islands—*Continued*
Way out; cruising in the Bahamas and Florida. W. Juettner. il Motor B 124:53-9+ N '69

Europe

Europe and the Holy Land. N. D. Ford. bibliog il Har Yrs 9:6-15 My '69
Flooding Europe: Americans with a new image. U S News 67:10 Ag 18 '69
Going places, finding things: Europe on a mini-budget. B. Lowry. il House & Gard 135:12+ Ja '69

Europe, Eastern

Luring the capitalists eastward. il Time 94: 42 S 5 '69

Europe, Western

Boeing sees tourism growth as spur to European 720 sales. Aviation W 91:34 O 27 '69
When you go abroad: places to see, and 1969 prices. il U S News 66:46-9 Ap 21 '69

France

Travel notes. R. Joseph. Esquire 72:68+ S '69

Greece, Modern

T&C travel guide. Travel & Camera 32:75-7 My '69

Haiti

Haiti: a fresh look. R. McGurk. il Travel & Camera 32:34 Je '69

Hawaii

Hawaii '69: beauty and the bulldozer. S. C. S. Stone. il Sat R 52:51-2+ S 13 '69
Ripples from jet-generated traffic spread over Hawaii. W. H. Gregory. il Aviation W 91: 96-7+ O 20 '69

Indonesia

Indonesian rhapsodies; promoting tourism. B. Halb. il Sat R 52:80+ S 13 '69
On the road to Bali. T. Fox. Commonweal 90:556-7 S 19 '69

Ireland

Le grand Charles slept here. P. Ryan. il Sports Illus 31:46-8+ Jl 28 '69

Israel

Europe and the Holy Land. N. D. Ford. bibliog il Har Yrs 9:6-15 My '69

Japan

Hitchhiking in Japan. A. Stone. il Travel & Camera 32:24+ Ag '69
Meet me at the fair. D. Butwin. il Sat R 52:44-5+ S 13 '69
Tokyo, Kyoto and Osaka. il Travel & Camera 32:106 O '69

Latin America

Tourism in South America. M. B. Marmol. il Américas 21:49-53 N '69

Liechtenstein

Liechtenstein and Austria's Tirol. il Travel & Camera 32:85-6 Jl '69

Massachusetts

Why the ferry is late; Martha's Vineyard and Chappaquiddick Island in the wake of the Kennedy accident. il Newsweek 74:23-4 S 1 '69

Mediterranean Region

How to get more cruising for less time and money. A. Gingrich. Esquire 71:6 Ap '69

Mexico

Exploring Mexico. il Travel & Camera 32:83-5 N '69
Travel notes. R. Joseph. Esquire 71:178+ Je '69

Morocco

Morocco: sun and pleasures, Inshallah. il Time 93:42-8 Ja 31 '69
Travel guide. il Travel & Camera 32:71 Ap '69

Peru

Peru: the future of the Inca empire; UNESCO sponsors a ten-year project. C. Cutler. il Art in Am 57:80-2 My '69
Pisco sour: symbol of Peru's relations with the United States. D. St Clair. il Holiday 46:36-7+ N '69

Portugal

Travel guide. Travel & Camera 32:72 Ap '69

Puerto Rico

Rain forest, and other magical lures in Puerto Rico. il Travel & Camera 32:112-13 F '69
Surfing Tres Palmas. J. P. Kahn. il Travel & Camera 32:19-20 My '69

Spain

Travel guide. Travel & Camera 32:73 Ap '69

Switzerland

Switzerland; where the best of time comes from. M. Gough. il House B 111:26+ Ag '69

Texas

Vacation, Texas-size. L. Barry. il Pop Phot 65:38+ Ag '69

United States

Winter tourism booms. il Bsns W p36+ F 15 '69

Utah

Utah upbeat. G. Perry. Travel 132:77 O '69

Virgin Islands

Lazy life in the sunny Virgin Islands. P. Plawin. il Bet Hom & Gard 47:164 Mr '69

TOURISTS. See Travelers

TOURISTS and customs administration. See Customs service and tourists

TOURNAMENT at Champions. See Golf—Tournaments

TOURNAMENT players. See Bridge players

TOURS, European. See Europe, Western—Description and travel

TOURS, Garden. See Garden tours

TOURS, Package. See Travel

TOURTELLOTTE, Mark E. See McElhaney. R. N. jt. auth.

TOUSTER, Saul
Two winter pieces; poems. Nation 208:216 F 17 '69

TOVATT, Anthony, and DeVries, Ted
(ed) This world of English. See issues of English journal

TOWBIN, Abraham
Mental retardation due to germinal matrix infarction. bibliog Science 164:156-61 Ap 11 '69

TOWELL, William Earnest
Book review. Am For 75:35+ Ja '69
Bridger controversy. Am For 75:45-6 N '69
Disaster fires, why? Am For 75:12-15+ Je '69
Is this mine necessary? por Am For 75:31 S '69
Lo the poor salmon! (or, Is this dam necessary?) Am For 75:38 F '69
Meet your AFA members. Am For 75:35+ F '69
Mineral King, a golden opportunity. Am For 75:36+ Ap '69
Quest for environmental quality; excerpts from address. por Am For 75:13+ Ag '69

TOWER, Whitney
Horse racing. See issues of Sports illustrated

TOWER of the winds. See Athens, Greece—Antiquities

TOWERS. John H.
First to fly the Atlantic. B. A. Weisberger. il Am Heritage 20:18-21+ Je '69

TOWING
Easy towing is in the knowing. W. J. Toth. il Am Home 72:42 S '69
Moving a stalled vehicle. D. L. Gregg. Bet Hom & Gard 47:6 N '69
See also
Boats—Towing

TOWING equipment. See Automobiles—Equipment

TOWN, George
Courtroom saviors. Har Yrs 9:35-7 Je '69
Even the duffers have fun. bibliog Har Yrs 9:40-3 Ap '69
Save money on income taxes. Har Yrs 9:22-4 F '69
What you should know about truth in lending. Har Yrs 9:22-3 N '69
Who's fit to drive? Har Yrs 9:19-21 Mr '69

TOWN houses. See Architecture, Domestic; City houses

TOWN life. See City and town life

TOWN planning. See Rural planning

TOWN sound studios, Englewood, N.J. See Sound—Recording and reproducing

TOWNES, Brenda D. See Wallace, E. jt. auth.

TOWNLEY, Frances W.
What's cooking? Org Gard & Farm 16:81-2 N '69

TOWNLEY, Neal R.
Sewer root control, chemically. Am City 84: 92-4 D '69

TOWNS, New. See New towns

TOWNS, Restored. See Villages, Restored

TOWNSEND, Dallas
Assignment downrange. pors Sat R 52:65-7 D 13 '69

TOWNSEND, Lynn Alfred
What's good for Chrysler is good for Lynn Townsend. N. Thimmesch. il Esquire 71: 105-7+ Mr '69

TOWNSHEND, Peter
Rock, etc. E. Willis. New Yorker 45:62-5 Jl 12 '69

TOWNSHIP finance. See Local finance

TOXICOLOGY. See Poisons

TOXINS and antitoxins
Anaphylatoxin release from the third component of human complement by hydroxylamine. D. B. Budzko and H. Müller-Eberhard. bibliog il Science 165:506-7 Ag 1 '69
Antifungal steroid glycoside from sea cucumber; holotoxin. S. Shimada. bibliog il Science 163:1462 Mr 28 '69
Condylactis toxin: interaction with nerve membrane ionic conductances. T. Narahashi and others. bibliog il Science 163: 680-1 F 14 '69
Diphtheria toxin subunit active in vitro. R. J. Collier and H. A. Cole. bibliog il Science 164:1179-82 Je 6 '69
Natural weed killer; rhizobitoxine. Sci Am 221:54 Jl '69
Plague toxin. S. Kadis and others. il Sci Am 220:92-8+ Mr '69
Separation of type 2 toxins of vibrio cholerae. A. C. Lewis and B. A. Freeman. bibliog il Science 165:808-9 Ag 22 '69
Thiamine release from nerve membranes by tetrodotoxin. Y. Itokawa and J. R. Cooper. bibliog il Science 166:759-61 N 7 '69
Toxin from skin of frogs of the genus atelopus: differentiation from dendrobatid toxins. F. A. Fuhrman and others. bibliog il Science 165:1376-7 S 26 '69
Toxins in plant disease: structure and mode of action. L. D. Owens. bibliog il Science 165:18-25 Jl 4 '69
See also
Digitoxin

TOXOCARA cati. See Roundworms

TOXOPLASMA
Toxoplasma gondii: fecal forms separated from eggs of the nematode toxocara cati. J. K. Frenkel and others. bibliog il Science 164:432-3 Ap 25 '69
Toxoplasma gondii: transmission through feces in absence of toxocara cati eggs. H. G. Sheffield and M. L. Melton. bibliog il Science 164:431-2 Ap 25 '69

TOXOPLASMOSIS
Toxoplasma gondii: fecal forms separated from eggs of the nematode toxocara cati. J. K. Frenkel and others. bibliog il Science 164:432-3 Ap 25 '69
Toxoplasma gondii: transmission through feces in absence of toxocara cati eggs. H. G. Sheffield and M. L. Melton. bibliog il Science 164:431-2 Ap 25 '69

TOY animals. See Toys

TOY banks. See Banks. Coin

TOY industry
Christmas every weekday? chain discount toy stores. il Forbes 103:55+ Mr 15 '69
Danger in toyland. R. Nader. Ladies Home J 86:81+ N '69
Toy town. il Newsweek 74:82 D 22 '69
See also
Mattel, incorporated
Shindana toy company

Securities
Toy makers' shares are a losing game. il Bsns W p82 D 20 '69

TOYLI, Matthew, and Gerhardt, John
Education film program of the American meteorological society. Weatherwise 22:152-5+ Ag '69

TOYNBEE, Arnold Joseph
Arnold Toynbee talks of peace, power, race in America; interview. ed. by J. R. Moskin. Look 33:25-7 Mr 18 '69
Nationalism, technology and morals. Cur 110: 5-6 S '69
Old man in a dry month. P. P. Witonski. Nat R 21:604 Je 17 '69
Why and how I work; excerpt from Experiences. por Sat R 52:22-7+ Ap 5 '69

about
Cloudy Olympus. por Time 93:94+ My 2 '69
Last of a dying species. P. Gay. New Repub 160:21-2 My 17 '69

TOYOTO motor company. See Automobile industry and trade—Japan

TOYS
Advice on picking Christmas toys. il Changing T 22:11-13 D '68
Animals into toys. P. L. Martin. il Am Artist 33:68-73+ O '69

Bear market; teddy bears. il Time 94:90 D 5 '69
Black firm joins the toy industry. il Ebony 25:84-6+ D '69
Build this Christmas rocking horse. W. Waltner and E. Waltner. il Pop Mech 132:174-5 N '69
Catapult, for storming a castle. il Sunset 143: 80 D '69
Caution: grown-ups at play. N. Gittelson. Harp Baz 103:27+ D '69
Christmas in toyland. il Parents Mag 44:58-63+ D '69
Christmas runner; basement of F. A. O. Schwarz. New Yorker 45:22-4 D 27 '69
For stockings filled with toyland. il House & Gard 136:156+ N '69
Magic of making toys. N. C. Gray. il Am Home 72:26-8+ D '69
On and off the avenue (cont) New Yorker 45:203-4+ D 6 '69
Party toys, for adults only. E. Kinard. il House B 111:128-9 N '69
Patchwork dog for Christmas. il Sunset 143: 102 D '69
Play things. E. Kinard. il House B 111:92-3 D '69
Presents for children. il House & Gard 136: 108-9 N '69
Super-dough should go. il Consumer Rep 34:358-9 Jl '69
Toys: knots to you and Deluxe feeder. il Consumer Bul 52:20 D '69
Toys should be fun. il Forbes 103:56-7 Mr 15 '69
What's new for children. R. Charles. See occasional issues of Parents' magazine & better family living
Wonderfully simple toys to make for children. K. D. Fury. il Redbook 134:90-5+ D '69
Wooden delights; J. Scholl's toys and fantasies. D. G. Lowe. il Am Heritage 20:18-23 D '68
See also
Beanbags
Booksellers and bookselling—Toy departments
Dolls
Electric toys
Toy industry

History
Little lead toys. M. M. Gladson. il Hobbies 74:48 D '69

Safety devices and measures
Mild warning on a zippy toy; Zip zap. Consumer Rep 34:494-5 S '69
Unsafe toys: what is being done to protect your child? Good H 169:177-9 D '69
See also
Toys, Hazardous

Storage
Rolling toy storage drawers. il Sunset 143:153 O '69
Wild new toy box. D. A. Ashe. il Bet Hom & Gard 47:40 N '69

TOYS, Dangerous. See Toys, Hazardous

TOYS, Hazardous
Danger in toyland. R. Nader. Ladies Home J 86:81+ N '69
Good stopgap against unsafe toys. Consumer Rep 34:238-9 My '69
News from toyland. S. N. Sesser. New Repub 161:11-13 D 20 '69

TOZZI, Vincent
Polacolor paint box. il U S Camera 32:38-9 Ja '69

TRACE elements
Facts about trace mineral salt. R. J. Fee. il Suc Farm 67:48 O '69

TRACERS, Radioactive. See Radioactive tracers

TRACERS company of America
Footloose, but not fancy-free; fugitive husbands. Time 94:57 Ag 22 '69

TRACHYTE
Dredged trachyte and basalt from Kodiak seamount and the adjacent Aleutian Trench, Alaska. R. B. Forbes and C. M. Hoskin. il Science 166:502-4 O 24 '69

TRACI, Philip
Joseph Papp's Happening and the teaching of Hamlet. Engl J 58:75-7 Ja '69

TRACK athletics
Meet of the future is now; track carnival in the Astrodome. T. Maule. il Sports Illus 30:16-17 F 3 '69
This coliseum could have used lions; U.S.-U.S.S.R.-British Commonwealth meet. S. Myslenski. Sports Illus 31:38 Jl 28 '69
Three strikes, and out? U.S.-Soviet-British meet, Los Angeles. il Newsweek 74:72 Jl 28 '69
Way to San Jose; collegiate track and field championship title winner. S. Myslenski. il Sports Illus 30:10-13 Je 30 '69

TRACK athletics—*Continued*
Yes! Bert is in, with go power; promoting AAU indoor track meet. R. Blount, jr. il Sports Illus 30:34-6+ Mr 3 '69
See also
College athletics
Hurdle racing
Jumping
Running
Shot putting
Vaulting (sport)
TRACKED air cushion vehicles. See Air cushion vehicles
TRACTION (automobiles) See Automobiles —Traction
TRACTOR engines
1,000 rpm. PTO means power! Suc Farm 67: 54B Ja '69

Maintenance and repair
Tractor care in cold weather. G. L. Earle. il Suc Farm 67:T2 O '69

Starting
See Tractors—Starting
TRACTOR industry and trade
See also
Caterpillar tractor company
TRACTORS
Battery-powered yard tracs are on the way. E. F. Lindsley. il Pop Sci 195:64-5+ Ag '69
Big garden tractors are the big news. E. F. Lindsley. il Pop Sci 194:164-7+ Ap '69
Facts and figures on fifteen new tractors. P. B. Jones. il Suc Farm 67:45-9 Ja '69
How big tractors cut costs. D. R. Miskell. il Farm J 93:C2 Mr '69
How to shop for a garden tractor. B. C. Kilvert, jr. il Home Gard 56:74-5 F '69
Look at surburban tractors. il Consumer Bul 52:7-13 N '69
Mini-beep, new fun and work machine for your yard. il Pop Sci 194:146-7 My '69
Riding mowers and garden tractors. E. McDonald. il House B 111:58+ Ap '69
Tiny tractors to mechanize your yard work. il Changing T 23:34-6 Mr '69
Twenty-one chores (and then some) you can do with a garden tractor. il Home Gard 56:50-1 Je '69
What you should know about diesel tractors. P. B. Jones. il Suc Farm 67:40-1 Ap '69
See also
Crawler vehicles

Equipment
Give your garden tractor a lift. E. V. Adams. il Pop Sci 194:136-7+ Je '69

Fuel
Cheap way to add more tractor power. D. Hagen. il Farm J 93:60C+ F '69

Maintenance and repair
Slick ideas for easier lubes. il Suc Farm 67:70 Ja '69

Noise
Can we quiet big tractors? B. Coffman. *y* Farm J 93:26F+ Ag '69

Starting
Cold weather starting aids. il Suc Farm 67: S1 D '69

Testing
They're awful mean to those little tractors! J. M. Liston. il Pop Mech 131:142-5+ My '69

Transmission
Now: smaller tractors that shift for themselves. J. Liston il Pop Mech 131:172-4 F '69

TRACTORS, Municipal
Equipment needed for a sanitary fill. W. B. Culham. Am City 84:100 Ja '69
TRACY, Fred H.
How to sharpen tiny drills. Pop Sci 195:174 N '69
TRACY, Philip
Bernadette and the clashing values of old and new Ireland. Commonweal 91:281-2 N 28 '69
Bernadette of the Irish. Commonweal 90:583-4 S 26 '69
Billy Graham plays the Garden. Commonweal 90:457-9 Jl 25 '69
Golden boy and little people. Commonweal 91:98-101 O 24 '69
Irish power on First avenue. Commonweal 90:278-9 My 23 '69
Meanwhile, the Moratorium. Commonweal 91: 180-1 N 7 '69

TRACY, Spencer
Spencer Tracy, by L. Swindell. Review
Newsweek il por 73:116+ Je 9 '69 A. Keneas
TRADE. See Commerce
TRADE agreements
Analysis of 1968 changes in wages and benefits; with chart and tables. J. E. Talbot, jr. Mo Labor R 92:43-8 Jl '69
Developments in industrial relations. See issues of Monthly labor review
Do mergers need a union label? question for NLRB. il Bsns W p86+ My 17 '69
Estimating the cost of collective bargaining settlements. L. M. David and V. J. Sheifer. bibliog il Mo Labor R 92:16-26 My '69
Financing supplemental unemployment benefit plans. E. H. Beier. bibliog f il Mo Labor R 92:31-5 N '69
Labor in a year of expansion. B. V. Toth. Mo Labor R 92:11-19 Ja '69
Labor 1970: angry, aggressive, acquisitive. R. Armstrong. il Fortune 80:94-7+ O '69
Major collective bargaining agreements expiring in [month] tables (title varies) See issues of Monthly labor review
Negotiations and wage calendar for 1969: with tables. C. T. Ward and W. M. Davis. Mo Labor R 82:52-64 Ja '69
Report on wage developments in manufacturing, 1968; with tables. J. Kinyon. Mo Labor R 92:33-9 Ag '69
Shopcraft contract gears are jammed by composite mechanic. Bsns W p63 D 27 '69
Wages of building zoom; overtime and record contract settlements jump industry costs. il Bsns W p89-90 Jl 19 '69
See also
Collective bargaining
TRADE and professional associations
Challenge to selectivity. Sci N 96:266 S 27 '69
Society membership. Sci N 96:525 D 6 '69
See also
Electronic service associations
TRADE discount. See Discount. Trade
TRADE fairs. See Exhibitions
TRADE journals
Interviewing techniques for trade journals. J. Connors. Writer 82:28-30 F '69
Most overlooked place to begin freelancing: trade journals. M. M. Clayton. il Writers Digest 49:44-6 Jl '69
See also
American machinist (periodical)
TRADE marks and trade names
Corporate image. W. Zinsser. il Life 67:57-8+ N 7 '69
Famous marques of the famous makers. J. R. Berry. il Mech Illus 65:50-2+ D '69
Story behind:
Blue cross. il Changing T 23:35 Mr '69
Squibb. il Changing T 23:30 My '69
Tootsie roll. il Changing T 23:42 S '69
White owl cigars. il Changing T 23:34 Jl '69
Thanks for the memory; revival of old products. il Newsweek 74:90 N 10 '69
See also
Printers marks
TRADE names. See Trade marks and trade names
TRADE regulation
See also
Export controls
Foreign trade regulation
TRADE relations association
Small triumph for trade relations. Bsns W p21-2 Ag 30 '69
TRADE schools
Vocational live-in; Ohio's Mahoning Valley vocational school. R. C. Bixler. il Am Ed 5:7-9 Mr '69
TRADE secrets
IBM's unruly brood; lawsuit against Cogar corp. and former IBM staff to prevent use of confidential IBM information. il Newsweek 74:85-7 Jl 21 '69
When a secret is better than a patent. V. Block. il Pop Mech 132:110-12+ N '69
TRADE shows. See Exhibitions
TRADE union leaders. See Trade unions—Officials
TRADE unions
AFL-CIO as paid propagandist: agent Meany; funneling AID funds into overseas institutes. R. Dudman. New Repub 160: 13-16 My 3 '69
Foreign labor briefs. See issues of Monthly labor review
See also
Boycott
Collective bargaining
Industrial relations
International confederation of free trade unions
Teachers unions
Trade agreements

TRADE unions—*Continued*

Benefit funds

When a pension fund runs out; actuarial goof on rail union funds. Bsns W p 128 O 25 '69

Communist activities

Reds climbing into unions' beds. il Nations Bsns 57:74-7 Je '69

Dues, fees, etc.

Dues collection by court action. U S News 66: 66 Ap 7 '69

Elections

Leadership fight looms among miners; election contest between Joseph Yablonski and W. A. Boyle for UMW presidency. Bsns W p 122 Je 7 '69
Shades of John L; presidential battle in the UMW. il Newsweek 74:83-4+ D 15 '69

Ethical aspects

See Labor ethics

History

Labor historian views changes in the trade union movement. P. Taft. Mo Labor R 92: 8-11 S '69
Labor leader tells it like it was; D. J. McDonald's account of U.S. union movement. Bsns W p44 Ag 23 '69

Insurance plans

See Insurance, Industrial

International aspects

Labor and foreign policy. R. Radosh. Nation 209:208-11 S 8 '69
See also
International confederation of free trade unions
International labor organization

Jurisdictional disputes

AFL-CIO's internal disputes plan. D. L. Cole. Mo Labor R 92:12-15 S '69
IAM wins and fights on; jurisdictional battle at McDonnell Douglas. Bsns W p90 Ja 18 '69
West coast dockers move toward peace; PMA-ILWU wars over packing containers at West coast ports. Bsns W p 142 O 11 '69

Law

See Labor laws and legislation—United States

Membership

Now a rank-and-file revolt to worry unions and employers. il U S News 66:93-4 Mr 17 '69
Trade union growth in a changing economy. L. Troy. bibliog il Mo Labor R 92:3-7 S '69
Typical union member: a profile. U S News 66:67 Ap 7 '69
Union disciplinary power upheld; Supreme court decision. U S News 66:85-6 Ap 14 '69
Unions build muscle with new membership; unionism in the 1970s. il Bsns W p 130+ D 6 '69
Why unionization? excerpts from address. S. Kinville. Parks & Rec 4:28-30 Mr '69
See also
Trade unions—Negro membership

Membership drives

High noon in the hospital; union organizing campaign for Pittsburgh hospital workers. R. W. Gibbons. Commonweal 91:406-7 Ja 9 '69
IUD builds up its war chest. Bsns W p66 O 4 '69
Wrath of grapes; unions want to organize all hired farm labor. G. Logsdon. Farm J 93:33+ F '69

Negro membership

Backlash builds on black demands. il Bsns W p31-2 S 27 '69
Black battleground; Pittsburgh. il Time 94: 78 S 5 '69
Black Monday and white Friday. il Newsweek 74:105-7 O 6 '69
Black Mondays are good for us; building-trades unions. Fortune 80:86 O '69
Black workers in white unions. W. B. Gould. Nation 209:203-6 S 8 '69
Confrontation in Pittsburgh; drive to crack building trades unions. C. C. Robb. il Nation 209:272-4 S 22 '69
Cracking the crafts; Pittsburgh demonstrations. il Newsweek 74:34-5 S 8 '69
Crusade against the craft unions. A. Poinsett. il Ebony 25:33-6+ D '69

Dodge rebellion. Ramp Mag 7:12 N 30 '68
Fomented conflict; black community and organized labor. L. L. Brown. Nation 208: 179-81 F 10 '69
Justice in the building trades; Pittsburgh churchmen proposals. America 121:256 O 4 '69
Minority power through unions. B. J. Widick. Nation 209:206-8 S 8 '69
Narrow victory for blacks; Philadelphia plan. il Time 95:49-50 Ja 5 '70
Philadelphia plan in trouble. U S News 67: 71-2 O 6 '69
Pittsburgh blacks try negotiating. il Bsns W p32-3 S 6 '69
Plague on both your houses! black militants vs industry and organized labor. il Bsns W p54+ My 24 '69
Showdown on Negro jobs in the building trades. il U S News 67:95-7 S 29 '69
Shultz job plan for blacks hits snags; Philadelphia plan. Bsns W p 109 N 15 '69
Some reflections on organized labor and the new militants. P. Henle. bibliog Mo Labor R 92:20-5 Jl '69
Trade unions grapple with race prejudice. B. L. Masse. America 120:701 Je 21 '69
UAW rebuffs black extremists; League of revolutionary black workers. America 120: 346 Mr 29 '69
What unions are, and are not doing for blacks; Pittsburgh. il Time 94:88+ S 26 '69

Officials

Arbitrating the discharge and discipline of union officials. W. E. Baer. bibliog Mo Labor R 92:39-45 S '69
In the wake of John L. Lewis. J. Hill. Commonweal 90:430-1 Jl 11 '69
Labor's Kirkland moves higher. America 120:639 My 31 '69
New challenges to union leadership. J. T. Conway. Mo Labor R 92:56 Ap '69
Nixon aides go to labor's summit. il Bsns W p38-9 Ap 19 '69
Pay padding an issue in mine vote. U S News 67:102 D 15 '69
Union chief with growing stature. U S News 66:19 F 24 '69
Walter Reuther's gamble; contesting Meany's status quo. J. Hill. Commonweal 90:261-3 My 16 '69

Training

Teamsters open a labor school to process their local talent; IBT labor institute. il Bsns W p61 S 27 '69

Organizing activities

See Trade unions—Membership drives

Political activities

Alienated rank and file. A. Bilik. Nation 209:527-30 N 17 '69
Cause and the cure; the right to work; address, January 31, 1969. P. Fannin. Vital Speeches 35:293-5 Mr 1 '69
Getting out the vote. Bsns W p44 Ag 23 '69
Labor and politics. J. D. Greenstone. Nation 209:212-15 S 8 '69
Labor chafes at Nixon pace. Bsns W p34 My 24 '69
Nixon-Meany: an odd couple. J. Hill. Commonweal 90:537+ S 5 '69
Politics. J. Leonard. il Esquire 71:10+ My '69
Pro-Wallace workers start to stir. Bsns W p 124+ O 25 '69
Students and workers. P. Booth. Ramp Mag 8:19-20 S '69
Union lobbying machine. W. Wingo. il Nations Bsns 57:52-4+ Ap '69 (to be cont)
Unwitting help for the new left. B. L. Masse. America 120:210 F 22 '69
Will unions lose their political grip? il Nations Bsns 57:24-7 Ja '69

Public relations

Prospects and problems. J. Seldin. Nation 209:200-2 S 8 '69

Union

See also
Alliance for labor action

Canada

Canada's unions: no restraint. Bsns W p 126 O 25 '69
Canada's workers. J. Deedy. Commonweal 91:34 O 10 '69
Canadian unions seize initiative; drive for wage parity with U.S. workers. Bsns W p 85+ Ja 18 '69
Canadian workers dig in their heels. il Bsns W p30 Ag 23 '69

TRADE unions—Canada—*Continued*
Year of troubles looms in Canada. il Bsns
W p72+ Ja 10 '70
See also
Strikes—Canada

Europe, Western

Labor outlook. Bsns W p73 N 22 '69
Union pact against U.S. auto invasion. U S
News 67:79 D 22 '69

France

Another French crisis; Rendezvous of March
and wage demands. America 120:324 Mr 22
'69
Franc at the barricades; battle over wage
demands. Bsns W p33 Mr 15 '69

Germany (Federal Republic)

Youth labor movement; in Deutscher gewerkschaftsbund. H. Muladore. Nation 209:
196-7 S 8 '69

Great Britain

British unions win big victory. U S News
66:64 Je 30 '69
Industrial relations reform in Great Britain.
N. Robertson and K. I. Sams. bibliog f
Mo Labor R 92:35-40 Ja '69
Labor v. labor. Time 94:35-6 S 19 '69
Reds climbing into unions' beds. il Nations
Bsns 57:74-7 Je '69
See also
Strikes—Great Britain
Trades union congress

Italy

Extremists set the pace in Italy. Bsns W
p54+ S 13 '69
Italy's big unions settle for victory. il Bsns
W p 18-19 D 27 '69
Italy's unions hit management harder. il
Bsns W p74+ Mr 1 '69
Report from Rome: drive for radical social
change. W. Wynn. il Fortune 81:51+ Ja
'70

Latin America

Unions urged to increase skilled labor in
Latin America. G. Plaza. Américas 21:44
O '69

Scandinavia

How the Scandinavians do it. il Time 94:
102 D 5 '69

Turkey

Factions of the Turkish labor movement differ over political role. B. H. Millen. bibliog Mo Labor R 92:31-5 Je '69

United States

Collective bargaining, by M. S. Rukeyser.
Review
Nat R 21:291 Mr 25 '69. W. F. Ricken-
backer
Developments in industrial relations. See
issues of Monthly labor review
Employee rights and union democracy; ex-
cerpt from Individual employee rights and
union democracy. B. Aaron. Mo Labor R 92:
50-2 Mr '69
GE bind tightens. Bsns W p48 S 6 '69
Labor in a year of expansion. B. V. Toth.
Mo Labor R 92:11-19 Ja '69
Labor movement today; symposium. Na-
tion 209:199-224+ S 8 '69
Labor 1970: angry, aggressive, acquisitive. R.
Armstrong. il Fortune 80:94-7+ O '69
Next decade for labor: face lifting and some
new wrinkles. il Nations Bsns 57:44-6 N '69
Prospects for white-collar unionism; excerpt
from address, September 1968. H. M. Douty.
bibliog f il Mo Labor R 92:31-4 Ja '69
SDS finds invasion of industry tougher than
college campuses. U S News 66:84-6 Je 23 '69
Strangling picket line; labor's double stan-
dard; address, October 30, 1969. J. L. Jones.
Vital Speeches 36:136-9 D 15 '69
Trying to earn enough; new wage-and-bene-
fit settlements. il Time 94:72 Jl 11 '69
Untouchable conglomerate; labor-union mo-
nopolies. D. Lawrence. U S News 66:108 Ap
14 '69
Word from the unions: a tough line for '70.
U S News 67:75-8 O 13 '69
See also
Police unions
Strikes—United States
United States—Labor policy
also names of unions, e.g. United mine
workers of America

Vietnam (Republic)

Freedom force in Vietnam; CVT. America
120:721 Je 28 '69

TRADE waste
See also
Pollution
TRADE waste disposal
Under the rug; problems of toxic waste dis-
posal in deep injection wells. D. M. Evans
and A. Bradford. bibliog il Environ 11:3-
13+ O '69
TRADE winds
Climate and history; excerpts from Discon-
tinuity in Greek civilization. R. Carpenter.
il Horizon 11:48-57 Spr '69
TRADEMARKS. See Trade marks and trade
names
TRADES. See Occupations
TRADES union congress
Unions take on British Wildcats. Bsns W
p 134 Je 28 '69
TRADESCANTIA. See Spiderworts
TRADING. See Barter
TRADING stamps
Czar of Gold bond stamps; turning to real
estate. il Bsns W p 104+ Ag 23 '69
Soul stamps. Newsweek 73:70 Mr 31 '69
Soul stamps; Black & Brown trading stamp
co. il Time 94:74 Jl 11 '69
Trading stamps vs. cut prices. Consumer Bul
52:15 O '69
See also
Sperry and Hutchinson company
TRADITION
Father and the fathers. M. M. Shideler. Chr
Cent 86:1061-4 Ag 13 '69
Threats to the modern family. A. Mandel-
baum. il Sci Digest 65:57-60 Mr '69
TRADITIONAL music. See Music
TRADITIONS in music. See Music
TRAFFIC. See Road Traffic
TRAFFIC, Airline. See Airlines—Traffic
TRAFFIC accidents
Challenge to the churches; National safety
council and slaughter on highways. Amer-
ica 120:320 Mr 22 '69
Fallacy of the untrained driver. G. Driessen.
Ed Digest 35:43-5 O '69
Frenzy of the freeways; excerpts from Take
an alternate route. P. Pierce. il Read Digest
94:205-6+ Ap '69
Highway as a killer. il Life 66:24D-35 My 30
'69
In defense of the automobile. L. Levine.
il Motor T 21:48-51 Ap '69
Pictures without words. il Read Digest 95:135-
41 Jl '69
Playing at safety. A. H. Sypher. Nations
Bsns 57:27-8 Je '69
Proof: safety does pay; slow moving vehicle
emblems on farm machinery traveling pub-
lic roads. Suc Farm 67:94 Mr '69
Those deadly one-car crashes. il Changing T
23:31-4 Ag '69
Traffic safety's mystery man; the pedestrian.
B. Ford. Sci Digest 66:64-8 D '69
What to do after an accident. D. Green. il
Mech Illus 65:61-3+ Ag '69
See also
Automobile driving
Drinking and traffic accidents
Insurance, Automobile
Traffic violations

Cases

In case of crash, who is at fault? E. D.
Fales, jr. Read Digest 94:124-6 Mr '69
See also
Kennedy, E. M.—Accident, July 1969
TRAFFIC control, Airway. See Air traffic
control
TRAFFIC engineering
First TOPICS project eases a bottleneck;
Traffic operations program to increase ca-
pacity and safety; Dover, N.H. il Am City
84:16 My '69
Race for (automobile) space; adaptation of
address, April 17, 1969. E. Corning, 2d. Bul
Atom Sci 25:15-16 D '69
Urban transportation tomorrow. J. A. Volpe.
il Am City 84:59-62 N '69
When traffic jams stall the Nation; forecast
for the 1970s. il Bsns W p 186-7+ D 6 '69
TRAFFIC lights. See Traffic signals
TRAFFIC markings
All-weather pavement marker developed. il
Am City 84:134 Mr '69
Fast-dry traffic lines Texas-style. il Am City
84:108 D '69
Plastic lines save lives. il Am City 84:138 Je
'69
Taped lines keep airport traffic moving;
Washington national airport. C. R. Melugin,
jr. il Am City 84:146 F '69

TRAFFIC regulations
Our crazy, mixed-up speed laws. M. Hall.
il Pop Mech 132:81-3+ S '69
See also
Computers—Traffic control applications
Helicopters in traffic regulation
Traffic violations
TRAFFIC safety
See also
Roads—Safety devices and measures
Traffic violations
TRAFFIC signals

Control
Charleston to go solid state; installation of
new traffic control system. il Am City
84:35 Ap '69
Interconnected signals speed traffic flow;
Los Angeles. il Am City 84:134 Je '69
New York city begins computerized traffic
control. T. Karagheuzoff. il Am City 84:
105-6 N '69
Signal system that has them asking for more;
Riverside, Calif. D. Darnell. il Am City 84:
148+ O '69
TRAFFIC signs
Signs you'll see appearing out of thin air;
Holosigns. E. H. Arctander. il Pop Sci 195:
80-2+ Ag '69
Speed signs change with the school day; The
Village, a church of Oklahoma City. E.
Bumpass. il Am City 84:130 Ag '69
Symbols for safety; uniform traffic control
devices. A. Rosenthal. il Todays Health
47:48-51 Ag '69
To see if they're working. O. S. Hillman. il
Am City 84:120 Ja '69
Trailblazer led them to the fair; San An-
tonio, Tex. J. German. il Am City 84:148
My '69
What's wrong with our traffic signs. W. J.
Toth. Am Home 72:46-7 Ja '69
TRAFFIC violations
Pull over, Buddy; advice for drivers in the
Cambridge, Mass. area. Trans-Action 6:6-7
Jl '69
TRAGEDY
Tragedy and philosophy, by W. Kaufmann.
Review
Commonweal 89:708-10 Mr 7 '69. K. Rex-
roth
TRAGIC theme. See Literature—Themes
TRAHAN, Marian, and Minudri, Regina
(eds) Adult books for young adults (cont)
Library J 94:317-20, 893-5, 1346-9, 1803-7
2126-30, 2512+ Ja 15, F 15, Mr 15, Ap 15,
My 15, Je 15 '69
TRAHEY, Jane
These drinks are on me! Harp Baz 103:198-
200 D '69
TRAIL bikes. See Motorcycles
TRAIL riders of the wilderness
Tarzan of the trail. C. Foley. il Am For 75:
34-5+ Ap '69
TRAILER brakes. See Brakes, Automobile
TRAILER camps. See Automobile trailer
camps
TRAILERS
See also
Automobile trailers
TRAILS
Across the Bitterroots with Lewis and Clark,
by snowmobile. J. M. Liston. il Pop Mech
130:114-17+ D '68
Along the South Yuba trail for the fishing,
the hiking, the brilliant fall color. il Sun-
set 143:44-6 O '69
Finger Lakes trail. Cons 23:33 Ap '69
Over the weekend, 16 to 18 miles of new
trail built. il Sunset 143:58+ S '69
Sampling the Marble Peak trail. il Sunset
143:24+ N '69
South Carolina's Washington trail. J. L.
Truluck. il Travel 132:68-70 D '69
Touch and see; nature trail at the National
arboretum, Washington, D.C. J. M. Garvey.
il Parks & Rec 4:20-2 N '69
Trails across America; National trail system.
G. Nelson. il Nat Wildlife 7:21-7 Je '69
Wildlife along the Lewis and Clark trail. H.
H. Harrison. il Nat Wildlife 7:20-9 F '69
See also
Appalachian trail
National parks and reserves—Trails
Oregon Trail
Santa Fe Trail
TRAIN, Russell E.
Man with the right causes. Time 93:16-17
F 7 '69
TRAIN robberies. See Robberies and as-
saults

TRAIN speed. See Railroads—Train speed
TRAIN travel. See Railroad travel
TRAIN wrecks. See Railroads—Accidents
TRAINEE; story. See Weesner. T.
TRAINING, Transfer of. See Transfer of train-
ing
TRAINING of animals. See Animals—Training
TRAINING of children. See Children—Manage-
ment and training
TRAINING of dogs. See Dogs—Training
TRAINING of plants. See Plants, Training of
TRAINING of unemployables. See Unemploy-
ables—Training
TRAINING schools for delinquents. See Re-
formatories
TRAINING within industry program. See Em-
ployees—Training
TRAIS, Mary
Chicago park district, it keeps on growing.
Parks & Rec 4:29-30+ Je '69
TRAJAN inscription. See Inscriptions Roman
TRAJECTORIES
Roadmap to the moon for Apollo 8 astro-
nauts. Space World F-3-63:36-7 Mr '69
Trajectory, timing of Apollo 11 revised to
permit Goldstone antenna to cover land-
ing. W. C. Wetmore. il Aviation W 91:40-
1+ Jl 14 '69
TRAMMELL, Archie
Do it yourself. See issues of Flying
TRAMPOLINES
Trampoline: fitness boon or safety hazard?
A. Rosenthal. il Todays Health 47:32-5 My
'69
TRAMWAY. Aerial. See Cableways
TRANQUILIZING drugs
Have a tranquilizer, dear. Trans-Action 6:10
S '69
Paradoxical fear-increasing effects of tran-
quilizers: evidence of repression of memory
in the rat. L. Stein and B. D. Berger. bib-
liog il Science 166:253-6 O 10 '69
See also
Chlorpromazine
Thalidomide
TRANS-ACTION (periodical)
Fall-out in Niagara Falls; letters to the edi-
tor of Niagara Falls gazette. Trans-Action
6:2+ Ap '69
TRANSAMERICA corporation
Great pyramid. il Newsweek 74:72-4 S 8 '69
Needle in the sky; proposed head office of
Transamerica corporation. il Time 94:54 S 5
'69
TRANS-AMERICAN racing. See Automobile
racing
TRANSATLANTIC air race. See Airplane rac-
ing
TRANSATLANTIC airline service. See Airlines
—International services—Transatlantic
TRANSATLANTIC cables. See Cables, Subma-
rine
TRANSATLANTIC flights. See Aviation—
Transatlantic flights
TRANSATLANTIC race. See Yacht racing
TRANSATLANTIC voyages. See Voyages
TRANSCEIVERS. See Radio telephone
TRANSCEIVERS, Portable. See Radio tele-
phone, Portable
TRANSCENDENCE of God
Is transcendence expendable? L. H. DeWolf.
Chr Cent 86:1017-19 Jl 30 '69
TRANSCENDENTAL meditation. See Medita-
tion
TRANSCENDENTALISM
See also
Brook Farm
TRANSCENDENTALISM (New England)
Flower power: a student's guide to pre-
hippie transcendentalism. P. H. Wild. Engl
J 58:62-8 Ja '69
Politics of ecstasy, by T. Leary. Review
Cath World 208:278-9 Mr '69. J. Tytell
TRANSCONTINENTAL flights. See Aviation—
Transcontinental flights
TRANSCONTINENTAL investing corporation
Hurok 'n' roll? il Newsweek 73:74+ Mr 10 '69
TRANSFER of technology. See Technology
transfer
TRANSFER of training
Chemical transfer of learning? ed. by B. M.
Murray. G. Ungar. il Todays Ed 58:44-7
F '69
TRANSFER taxes. See Inheritance tax
TRANSFERASES
Indole (ethyl)amine N-methyltransferase in
the brain. M. Morgan and A. J. Mandell.
bibliog il Science 165:492-3 Ag 1 '69

TRANSFERASES—*Continued*
  Ontogeny of soluble and mitochondrial
    tyrosine aminotransferases. R. D. Koler
    and others. bibliog il Science 163:1348-50
    Mr 21 '69
TRANSFERS, Job. See Job transfers
TRANSFIGURATION of Christ. See Jesus
    Christ—Transfiguration
TRANSFORMERS. See Electric transformers
TRANSISTOR circuits
  Build the touch control; light switch turns
    on and off with a touch. L. G. Striggow. il
    Pop Electr 30:56-8 Ap '69
  Circuits & power supplies. il Radio-Electr
    40:66-7 My '69
  Dual UJT multivibrator. F. H. Tooker. il
    Electr World 81:45 F '69
  Experiment with ten emitter-coupled circuits.
    R. L. Petrowsky. il Radio-Electr 40:37-40
    Mr '69
  MOSFET's. R. Clifton. il Radio-Electr 40:61-
    3+ D '69
  Protection system for solid-state transmit-
    ters. C. Smith. il Electr World 81:38-9+
    F '69
  Transistor counter decade. il Radio-Electr
    40:45 Ag '69
  Triggered sweep for any scope. I. Gorgenyi.
    il Electr World 82:76-8 N '69
    See also
  Printed circuits
  Radio circuits
TRANSISTOR curve tracer. See Testing in-
    struments
TRANSISTOR testers. See Testing instruments
TRANSISTOR vibrators. See Multivibrators
TRANSISTORS
  ABC's of transistors (cont) il Radio-Electr
    40:60-3 F; 55-7 Ap; 66-7 My '69
  JFETS. R. Clifton. il Radio-Electr 40:55-7 Je
    '69
  JFETS; how they work, how to use them.
    T. R. Haskett. il Radio-Electr 40:23-6 My
    '69
  MOSFET's. R. Clifton. il Radio-Electr 40:61-
    3+ D '69
  MOSFET's T. R. Haskett. il Radio-Electr
    40:33-6 N '69
  Power FET. J. Tamosaitis. il Electr World
    81:34-5+ Je '69
  Simplified bipolar technique developed; base-
    diffusion isolation. il Aviation W 90:71
    Mr 17 '69
  Solid state. L. Garner. See issues of Pop-
    ular electronics
  Transistor troubleshooting precautions. Ra-
    dio-Electr 40:66 Ap '69
  Transistors made of glass. A. H. Seidman.
    il Electr World 81:68 F '69
  Using transistors as negative-resistance de-
    vices. W. A. Vincent. il Electr World 81:
    38-40+ Je '69
    See also
  Texas instruments, incorporated

          Control uses
  Micro-sensitive Schmitt trigger. F. H. Took-
    er. Pop Electr 32:64-5 Ja '70

          Testing
  In-circuit testing techniques. il Radio-Electr
    40:41-3 Mr '69
  Test transistors fast. il Radio-Electr 40:60-3
    F '69
  Transistor testing; what with? J. Darr. il
    Radio-Electr 40:14+ N '69
TRANSIT systems. See Rapid transit
TRANSITION (chemistry). See Phases (chem-
    istry)
TRANSITION, Project. See Service men—Vo-
    cational education
TRANSLATIONS and translating
  Translators' rights. Sch & Soc 97:165-6 Mr
    '69
  What is the translator's proper share? L.
    Galantiere. Pub W 196:44-6 Jl 7 '69; Discus-
    sion. 196:197-9 Ag 25; 33 S 22 '69
    See also
  Poetry—Translations and translating
  Publishers and publishing—Translations
TRANSLOCATION in plants. See Plants—
    Translocation
TRANSMISSION, Automobile. See Automobiles
    —Transmission
TRANSMISSION, Radio. See Radio transmis-
    sion
TRANSMISSION lines. See Electric lines
**TRANS NATIONAL communications, incorpo-
    rated**
  All-pro miniconglomerate. D. Snell. il Life
    66:85-6 My 23 '69
TRANSPAC race. See Yacht racing

TRANSPACIFIC airline service. See Airlines—
    International services—Transpacific
TRANSPACIFIC flights. See Aviation—Trans-
    pacific flights
TRANS-PACIFIC yacht race. See Yacht racing
TRANSPARENCIES
  Infrared: difficult? Not really. E. Scully. il
    Mod Phot 33:82-7 My '69
  Meyers on technique; ways to save dark
    and light color slides. E. Meyers. Mod Phot
    33:44 Mr '69
  View from Kramer; achieving permanent col-
    or. A. Kramer. Mod Phot 33:38+ N '69

          Copying
  Be a copy cat. B. Pierce. il Pop Phot 64:70-
    1+ Ap '69
  If you print b&w, you can do color. E.
    Meyers. il Pop Phot 65:60+ D '69
  Rescue your slides. E. Scully. il Mod Phot
    33:86-9+ Jl '69

          Editing
  How to read a contact sheet. A. Goldsmith. il
    Pop Phot 65:78-9+ Ag '69

          History
  Old lantern slides; the song plugger's best
    friends. J. W. Ripley. il Hobbies 74:98L-
    98P D '69

          Projection
  Now this next slide... R. Routh. il Travel
    & Camera 32:90-4 N '69
  You can show those travel slides. D. Mc-
    Fadden. il Har Yrs 9:46-7 N '69

          Trimming, mounting, etc.
  Crop and shape your slides. N. Rothschild.
    il Pop Phot 65:112-13+ D '69
  Hey! It really is the humidity. D. B. Eisen-
    drath. il Pop Phot 64:16+ Ap '69

          Viewers
  Slide viewers. il Consumer Rep 34:588-91 O
    '69
TRANSPLANTATION of organs, tissues, etc.
  Clear the road for Nancy! J. Bishop. Read
    Digest 95:37-40 Ag '69
  Harvesting the body; six-organ multiple
    transplant. il Newsweek 73:50 Mr 3 '69
  Heart and both lungs. il Time 95:40 Ja
    5 '70
  Hemophilia: role of organ homografts. T. L.
    Marchioro and others. bibliog il Science
    163:188-90 Ja 10 '69
  Lung and larynx; six from one. il Time 93:
    56 F 28 '69
  Transplant psychosis. Newsweek 73:118 My 19
    '69
  Transplants: guarded outlook. M. Clark. il
    Newsweek 74:109-10 Jl 21 '69
  Transplants of human organs; the debate,
    the record. il U S News 67:6 S 1 '69
  Two postscripts in Houston. Time 93:76 My
    23 '69
    See also
  Brain—Transplantation
  Cornea—Transplantation
  Eye—Transplantation
  Eye donors
  Hair—Transplantation
  Heart—Transplantation
  Immunological tolerance
  Kidney donors
  Kidneys—Transplantation
  Liver—Transplantation
  Lungs—Transplantation
  Marrow—Transplantation
  Thymus gland—Transplantation
  Tissue banks
          Legal aspects
  Brother's sacrifice; case of the Strunk
    brothers kidney transplant operations. il
    Time 94:54 N 7 '69
  Where to donate organs for transplants.
    Good H 169:205 N '69

          Moral and religious aspects
  Critical questions in medical transplants. J.
    E. Wrigley. America 120:334-7 Mr 22 '69
  Mystery of death and the problem of trans-
    plants. H. E. Hatt. Chr Cent 86:441-4 Ap 2
    '69
  Searching the reins. J. W. Montgomery. Chr
    Today 13:41-2 Ag 1 '69
  Too much, too fast? questions raised about
    D. Cooley's handling of the Haskell Karp
    case. il Newsweek 73:76+ Ap 21 '69
  Who will decide who is to live? F. Ander-
    son. New Repub 160:9-10 Ap 19 '69

TRANSPLANTING
Here's how to move an azalea or rhododendron. il Sunset 142:190-1 F '69
Raising strawberry plants from runners. N. H. Berlin. il Org Gard & Farm 16:51 F '69
   See also
Flats, etc. (horticulture)
Tree planting
TRANSPLANTING of trees. See Tree planting
TRANSPORT planes, Military. See Airplanes, Military transport
TRANSPORT theory
   See also
Exciton theory
TRANSPORTATION
Coming revolution in transportation. F. C. Appel. il Nat Geog 136:301-41+ S '69
Public selects its transportation; address, January 15, 1969. S. E. Knudsen. Vital Speeches 35:279-82 F 15 '69
Supplying the '70s; the supertransport era. il U S News 68:89-91 Ja 12 '70
   See also
Air travel
Motor bus lines
Rapid transit
   also subhead Transportation under various subjects, e.g. Gases, Asphyxiating and poisonous—Transportation

Federal aid
Are highways seven times more important than cities? W. F. Wagner, jr. Arch Rec 145:9 My '69
Billions for transit; where money will go. il U S News 67:66 Ag 18 '69
Congress at the crossroads; decisions on aid expansion. il Nations Bsns 57:84-6 O '69
Transportation and cities. Sci N 95:91 Ja 25 '69
   See also
Rapid transit—Federal aid

Finance
Fallacy of free transportation. L. M. Schneider. bibliog f Harvard Bsns R 47:83-7 Ja '69

Speed
   See also
Transportation, High speed

Study and teaching
College that teaches how to move the goods; Northwestern U. center. il Bsns W p 142+ Je 21 '69

Asia
Linking the East; Pan-Asian bus and train routes. S. Griffin. Sci N 96:152 Ag 23 '69

England
   See also
Railroads—Great Britain

Europe
   See also
Railroads—Europe

Great Britain
   See also
Railroads—Great Britain

Japan
   See also
Railroads—Japan

United States
Fifty largest transportation companies. Fortune 79:196-7 My 15 '69
How to cure traffic jams; interview. J. A. Volpe. il U S News 66:62-7 Je 9 '69
How to move a nation; latest ideas in mass transit. il U S News 66:82-4 My 19 '69
Traffic and transportation. See issues of American city
Urban transportation tomorrow. J. A. Volpe. il Am City 84:59-62 N '69
When traffic jams stall the Nation; forecast for the 1970's. il Bsns W p 186-7+ D 6 '69
   See also
Air travel—United States
Railroads—United States
United States—Transportation, Department of
TRANSPORTATION, Automotive
How to move a nation; latest ideas in mass transit. il U S News 66:82-4 My 19 '69
TRANSPORTATION, High speed
Coming: streamliners without wheels. J. A. Volpe. il Pop Sci 195:51-5+ D '69
   See also
Railroads—Train speed

TRANSPORTATION, Military
   See also
Airplanes, Military transport
United States—Military sea transportation service
TRANSPORTATION, Municipal. See Rapid transit
TRANSPORTATION center. See Northwestern university, Evanston, Ill.
TRANSPORTATION industry. See Transportation
TRANSSEXUALISM. See Change of sex
TRANS-SUPERIOR race. See Yacht racing
TRANS UNION corporation
If at first you don't succeed, conglomerate. il Forbes 104:60 N 1 '69
Union tank gets back on the track; J. Van Gorkom new president. il Bsns W p70-2 Mr 1 '69
TRANSURANIUM elements
Hunt for elusive new elements. il Bsns W p46-7+ Ag 23 '69
Synthetic elements. G. T. Seaborg and J. L. Bloom. il Sci Am 220:57-67 bibliog(p 146) Ap '69
TRANS WORLD airlines
Anti-hijacking system being used by TWA. il Aviation W 91:32 D 22 '69
Board, airlines scrutinize jets' six-abreast seating. J. P. Woolsey. Aviation W 92:34 Ja 12 '70
Denial of seat to militant spurs call for protests. L. Doty. Aviation W 91:40 S 15 '69
Passenger upturn in May bolsters TWA summer hopes. Aviation W 90:47 Je 16 '69
That million-dollar smile. il Time 93:104 Je 6 '69
Trans World profit slumps for year. Aviation W 90:32 Ja 27 '69
TRAN-thien-Khiem
Dauphin. por Newsweek 73:46 Ap 14 '69
Limiting the leadership. por Time 94:24-5 Ag 29 '69
TRAN-van-Dinh
Another open letter to President Nixon. Chr Cent 86:1137-8 S 3 '69
Fear of a bloodbath. New Repub 161:11-14 D 6 '69
Open letter to President Nixon. Chr Cent 86:313-14 Mr 5 '69
TRAN-van-Huong
Assassination attempt. por Time 93:41 Mr 14 '69
Odd man out. Newsweek 74:36 S 1 '69
TRAN-văn-Khê
Non-acceptance of the unfamiliar. por UNESCO Courier 22:26-31 Je '69
TRAP guns. See Firearms
TRAP shooting

   Anecdotes, facetiae, satire, etc
How to win at trap-shooting. E. Zern. il Field & S 74:172+ S '69
TRAPNELL, Frederick M.
Owner's comments. Yachting 125:170 Ap '69
TRAPPERS
Last of Boone's breed. D. J. Anderson. il Field & S 73:64-5+ Mr '69
Old Gabe of Her Majesty's English life guards. M. Goosman. il Am West 6:14-15 N '69
TRAPPING
Trap those farm predators. Suc Farm 67:57 D '69
TRAPPISTS
Brooksville experiment; introducing Afro-Americans to monastic life. M. Abel. America 121:117-18 Ag 30 '69
TRAPS, Insect. See Insect traps
TRASH. See Refuse and refuse disposal
TRASK, Willard Ropes
Critic of the month. L. Lieberman. Poetry 114: 56 Ap '69
TRAUFFER, Art
Build a FET stick. Pop Electr 31:57-8 D '69
TRAUMATISM
Mental retardation caused by physical trauma; report of meeting. E. A. Bering, jr. Science 164:460+ Ap 25 '69
TRAVEL
Adventure; the new trend in travel. B. Gillam. il Mlle 69:174-5+ O '69
Booked for travel. D. Butwin. See issues of Saturday review
Checkpoints for travelers. B. Robinson. See issues of House beautiful
Family travel. P. Plawin. See issues of Better homes & gardens
Holiday travel forecast 1970. il Holiday 46: 26-7+ N '69
Holiday travel handbook. See issues of Holiday
How to leave home and like it; ed. by M. Gough. See issues of House beautiful

TRAVEL—*Continued*
Let's travel: adventure tours. B. Gillam. Mlle 69:120-1 O '69
Lone ladies on the go. O. P. Gately. il Har Yrs 9:32-3 Mr '69
[Month] travel in and beyond the West. See issues of Sunset
1970 world travel issue: will it be the soaring seventies? H. Sutton and D. Butwin. il Sat R 53:31-8+ Ja 3 '70
Roaming the globe with Travel. See issues of Travel
Short sortie; excerpt from Seventeen guide to travel. M. S. Welch. Seventeen 28:462-7+ Ag '69
Speaking of Holiday. C. Stinnett. See issues of Holiday
Take one of these special excursions. il Bet Hom & Gard 47:116-18 F '69
Time off; Christmas travels. P. O'Higgins. il McCalls 97:48+ D '69
Touring. il Travel & Camera 32:31-2 My; 34 Je; 13-14 Ag; 26+ O; 32 D '69
Travel. L. Barry. See issues of Popular photography
Travel bazaar. See issues of Harper's bazaar
Travel digest. See issues of Travel
Travel guide. See issues of Travel & camera
Travel notes. R. Joseph. See issues of Esquire
Travel tips. L. Blackwood. Schol Teach Sec Teach Sup p23 S 22 '69
Travel tips. L. Blackwood. Sr Schol 94: Schol Teach 22 Ap 11 '69
See also
Air travel
Automobile touring
Canoe trips
Cruising
Customs service and tourists
Garden tours
Guidebooks
Motor bus travel
Ocean travel
Packing of luggage
Passports
Presidents—United States—Travel
Railroad travel
Student travel
Teacher travel
Tourist trade
Vacations
Youth hostels
See also subhead Description and travel under names of countries, states, etc. e.g. Spain—Description and travel

Bibliography

Books to help you take a trip. J. Herbert. House & Gard 135:78+ My '69

Competitions

Vacation, Texas-size; Plan-a-tour-of-Texas contest. L. Barry. il Pop Phot 65:38+ Ag '69

Economic aspects

Bus, train, ship, exciting travel at bargain rates. N.D. Ford. il Har Yrs 9:26-33 Jl '69
Europe and the Holy Land. N. D. Ford. bibliog il Har Yrs 9:6-15 My '69
Finding low rates at posh resorts. Good H 168:164 Je '69
How to have the vacation of your dreams and what it will cost. B. Gillam. Mlle 69:212-16 My '69
Inflation goes on, but there are still bargains to be found. R. Burkhardt. Travel & Camera 32:10 Je '69
Lavish values for prudent travelers. M. Gough. il House B 111:40+ F '69
Reassessing the travel deficit. D. G. Agger. Sat R 52:38 Ja 25 '69
Teenage travel abroad. H. Lewis. il Parents Mag 44:44-5+ My '69
Tripping with children. M. J. Matz. il Opera N 33:13-15 My 17 '69
When you go abroad: places to see, and 1969 prices. il U S News 66:46-9 Ap 21 '69
See also
Airlines—Fares
Automobile touring—Economic aspects

Taxation

See also
Air travel—Taxation

Terminology

Travel definitions. Travel & Camera 32:144 F '69

TRAVEL, Space. See Space flight
TRAVEL accidents. See Accidents
TRAVEL agencies and agents
Adventure: the new trend in travel. B. Gillam. il Mlle 69:174-5+ O '69

Europe twenty-five years later; special veterans tours arranged by Galaxy tours of Chicago. G. Bush. il Bet Hom & Gard 47:34-8+ N '69
Let's travel: adventure tours. B. Gillam. Mlle 69:120-1 O '69
Personal business; globe-trotting: what's the best way to book? Bsns W p 141-2 Ap 12 '69
Tyro traveler; choosing a travel agent. Travel 132:74 O '69
Warming up tourism in Alaska; Westours. il Bsns W p69+ Ag 16 '69
Winchester isn't just guns; Winchester adventures. Travel 131:4 My '69
See also
American society of travel agents
TRAVEL albums. See Photographic albums
TRAVEL and education. See Student travel; Travel study courses
TRAVEL clubs
From Lisbon to Madrid to Spain's Costa Del Sol. Club continental's travelers tried out a new kind of tour. J. Friedberg. il Travel & Camera 32:86-8+ O '69
Travel club idea is catching. Sunset 143:35 Ag '69
What you should know about travel clubs. P. Plawin. il Bet Hom & Gard 47:126+ S '69
See also
Air travel clubs
TRAVEL films. See Moving pictures—Travel films
TRAVEL guides. See Guidebooks
TRAVEL literature
See also
Guidebooks
TRAVEL photography
Art of travel photography; symposium. ed. by D. Joseph. Travel & Camera 32:78+ N '69
Confessions of a camera snob. N. Goldberg. il Pop Phot 65:58+ Ag '69
Get ready, get set, go! R. Arnold. Travel & Camera 32:13-14 Ag '69
Groups can sometimes grab you. N. Rothschild. il Pop Phot 65:32+ N '69
Here's me. April Sheffield, with James Mason! A. Sheffield. il Esquire 71:136-8+ Je '69
Now this next slide... R. Routh. il Travel & Camera 32:90-4 N '69
Readers' journal. il Travel & Camera 32:24+ F; 106 S '69
Skier turned photographer tells why. M. Durrance. Travel & Camera 32:90 D '69
Traveler's camera. L. Barry. il Pop Phot 65: 66+ Jl '69
U.S.A. with introd. by E. J. Steichen. M. P. R. Thomas and M. Wright. il Travel & Camera 32:54-86 F '69
Well traveled camera See issues of Modern photography
You can show those travel slides. D. McFadden. il Har Yrs 9:46-7 N '69
TRAVEL regulations
The attractive country, the unpopular government. il Holiday 46:28-9 N '69
First of the goodies; British travel restrictions ended. Time 95:22 Ja 12 '70
No way out; Czechoslovakia's travel restrictions. Newsweek 74:54+ O 20 '69
Restrictions eased on U.S. travel to Communist China. Dept State Bul 61:126 Ag 18 '69
U.K. raises limit on travel currency. Aviation W 92:34 Ja 12 '70
U.S. passports remain invalid for travel to certain areas. Dept State Bul 61:362-3 O 27 '69
TRAVEL restrictions. See Travel regulations
TRAVEL scholarships. See Scholarships and fellowships
TRAVEL study courses
History lessons on wheels; high school essayists winning AKA sorority travel scholarship. il Ebony 24:106-8+ S '69
1969 world guide to summer study; symposium. il Sr Schol 94:Schol Teach 13-22 F 28 '69
Schools at sea. T. B. Lesure. il Travel 132:56-9 S '69
Study it here, see it there; Ohio state pilot project. A. Zimmer. Mlle 70:188+ N '69
Summer study can be great when it's in Europe: interviews with student travelers. il Seventeen 28:126-7+ Je '69
To Russia with understanding; Atlanta teenagers study tour of Soviet Union. il Ebony 25:43-6+ N '69
See also
Foreign study

TRAVEL trailers. See Automobile trailers

TRAVEL with children
Exciting cities, a Redbook vacation guide to sight-seeing with children; excerpts from America's exciting cities. A. Schwartz. il Redbook 132:37-44 Ap '69
Games the kids can play in the car. il Changing T 23:21-3 Jl '69
Going places, finding things to delight your children in Europe. M. Schafer. il House & Gard 135:50-1+ Mr '69
Kids can be good globe-trotters. A. Linn and J. Linn. il Todays Health 47:22-7 Jl '69
More to see in New York. il Pop Gard 20:22-5 Spr '69
Tripping with children. M. J. Matz. il Opera N 33:13-15 My 17 '69

TRAVEL with pets
If you plan to take your dog. Sunset 142:62 Mr '69

TRAVELERS
Gilded travellers. A. Fraser. Vogue 153:262 Ap 1 '69
In search of the past. P. Schrag. Sat R 52:24 S 13 '69
Profile of the American traveler. Changing T 23:6 Je '69
Will it be the soaring seventies? the black traveler. H. Sutton and D. Butwin. il Sat R 53:48+ Ja 3 '70
    See also
Women as travelers

TRAVELING bags. See Luggage

TRAVELING exhibitions. See Exhibitions, Traveling

TRAVELING salesmen. See Salesmen and salesmanship

TRAVELING schools. See Schools, Traveling

TRAVELING theater, Childrens. See Theater, Childrens

TRAVELLERS club. See Paris—Clubs

TRAVELS
Readers' journal. il Travel & Camera 32:24+ F '69
    See also
Overland journeys to the Pacific
Travel
Travelers
Vacations
Voyages around the world

TRAVERS, Mary Allin
House that's very Mary. S. Nirenberg. il por House B 111:74-7 Ag '69

TRAVERSE rods (for curtains) See Curtain and drapery fixtures

TRAVERSO, Adriano A. Buzzati-. See Buzzati-Traverso, A. A.

La TRAVIATA; opera. See Verdi, G.

TRAWLERS (boats) See Fishing boats

TRAWLS and trawling
Fishing way down deep; deep-trolling. H. G. Tapply. il Field & S 74:68 Ag '69

TRAY breakfasts. See Breakfasts

TRAYNOR, Roger John
Pioneer retires. por Time 95:63 Ja 19 '70

TREACHER, Arthur
Permanent second fiddles. il por Newsweek 74:45 S 1 '69

TREADWELL, Sandy
Baseball's week. Sports Illus 31:60-1 Ag 11 '69
College basketball. Sports Illus 32:44 Ja 5 '70
Football's week. Sports Illus 31:43-4+ O 6; 47-50 N 3; 71-2+ D 1 '69
Games. Sports Illus 31:104+ N 17 '69

TREASURE trove
Ancient shipwreck yields new facts; and a strange cargo: marble coffins found in the Gulf of Taranto. P. Throckmorton. il Nat Geog 135:282-300 F '69
Largest underwater treasure hunt; cargo of the Nuestra señor de la concepcion. T. G. Buchanan. il Sea Front 15:21-9 Ja '69
Priceless relics of the Spanish Armada; fate of the Girona. R. Sténuit. il Nat Geog 135:745-77 Je '69
Wayside treasures. R. P. MacFall. il Nat Wildlife 7:43-7 Ag '69
You, too, can dive for sunken treasure. H. E. Rieseberg. il Pop Sci 194:84-7 Je '69

TREASURERS, Company. See Corporations —Treasurers

TREASURY department (United States) See United States—Treasury department

TREATIES
Treaty trap, by L. W. Beilenson. Review Nat R 21:914-15 S 9 '69. S. T. Possony
    See also
Commercial treaties and agreements
United Nations conference on the law of treaties
    also subhead Treaties under names of countries, e.g. United States—Treaties

TREATMENT of prisoners. See Prisoners—Treatment

TREATY-making power
    See also
United States—Treaties

TREATY of Versailles, June 28, 1919. See Versailles, Treaty of, June 28, 1919

TREE, Christopher
Symphony of one. il por Time 93:58-9 Je 27 '69

TREE, Penelope
Travel. Vogue 153:56 F 15 '69

TREE breeding
Meet the elite. J. O. Artman. il Am For 75:32-4+ Ja '69

TREE buds. See Buds

TREE drawing and painting. See Trees in art

TREE farms. See Forest management

TREE grafting. See Grafting

TREE peonies. See Peonies

TREE planting
Acres of diamonds? value of surplus trees. D. A. Caccia. il Org Gard & Farm 16:54-5 O '69
Bottomless boxes for new trees. il Sunset 142:247 Ap '69
Gardener wrestles nature. il Sunset 143:257 O '69
Growing a 16-foot shade tree in a single season. V. A. Croley. il Org Gard & Farm 16:108-12 Mr '69
How to choose and plant evergreens. L. Grove. il Bet Hom & Gard 47:36-7 O '69
Old Egyptian technique moves the jolly green giant; Mesa, Ariz. H. Funk. il Am City 84:33 Mr '69
25,000 trees reclaim land; tree-planting program in Minnesota. C. Vindex. il Org Gard & Farm 16:57-9 Ja '69

    Anecdotes, facetiae, satire, etc.
Who moved that tree? E. Harnett. House B 111:15+ Ap '69

TREE rings
Carbon-14 in Patagonian tree rings. J. C. Lerman and others. bibliog il Science 165:1123-5 S 12 '69
Carbon-14 trends in subfossil pine stubs. J. C. Vogel and others. bibliog il Science 166:1143-5 N 28 '69
Collectors of centuries; bristlecone pines. G. Burridge. il Américas 21:31-6 Je '69

TREE roses. See Roses

TREE shrews. See Shrews

TREE stumps. See Trees

TREE tomatoes
What do you do with a tree tomato? il Sunset 142:170 F '69

TREES
Learn to look at trees. C. E. Lewis il Horticulture 46:28-31+ S '68
Make friends with a tree. R. Schuessler. il Am For 75:38+ Je '69
Message of the tree; excerpts from Trees. A. Feininger. il Audubon 71:25-7 Ja '69
Modern trees for small gardens. il Am Home 72:83 Je '69
Native trees of Hawaii. E. L. Little, jr. il Am For 75:16-17+ F '69
Recognizing woody plants in winter. E. H. Ketchledge. il Cons 24:20-7+ O '69
Talking to the trees. R. Starnes. Field & S 74:6+ N '69
Ten trees that make the scene. il House & Gard 135:118-19 My '69
Tree stumps. H. F. Dale. Horticulture 46:47-8 S '68
Weeping trees. W. Flemer, 3d. il Horticulture 46:24-5+ N '68
Where and how to use ten trees. il House & Gard 135:204-6 My '69
Which of these three trees is the best one to buy? il Sunset 142:224 Mr '69
    See also
Christmas trees
Flowering trees
Forest conservation
Forest crown canopy
Forest ecology
Fruit trees
Leaves
Lumber industry and trade
Tree rings
Wood
    also names of trees, e.g. Elm

    Diseases and pests
All is not well at Baker. H. Fosburgh. il Am For 75:32-4 Mr '69
Death and decay of trees. A. Shigo. il Natur Hist 78:42-7 Mr '69

TREES—Diseases and pests—*Continued*
Trees with temperatures R. W. Neubert. il Am For 75:6-7+ Ap '69
See also
Anthracnose
Leaf miners
Spraying and dusting
also subhead Diseases and pests under names of trees, e.g. Elm—Diseases and pests

Growth
See Growth (plants)

Photographs
Winter tree. A. Feininger. Audubon 71:16-24 Ja '69

Planting
See Tree planting

Poetry
To redwood retreat. L. B. Graham. il Nat Parks 43:9 D '69

Pruning
See Pruning

Temperature
See Plants—Temperature

Wounds and injuries
Death and decay of trees. A. Shigo. il Natur Hist 78:42-7 Mr '69

TREES, Care of
See also
Fruit trees, Care of

TREES, Dwarf
Buckeye as a bonsai. il Sunset 143:195 D '69
Dwarf peaches and nectarines. Sunset 142:194-5 F '69
Flowering small fry; crabapple, cherry, peach, almond. il Sunset 142:174-5 F '69
Growing bonsai outdoors. B. F. Bruenner. il Horticulture 46:34-5+ N '68
Indoor bonsai. C. E. Derderian. il Horticulture 47:28-9+ N '69
Instant bonsai, as Christmas gifts. il Sunset 143:216 N '69
Your own start at bonsai. Sunset 143:236 N '69
See also
Fruit trees, Dwarf

TREES, Effect of air pollution on. See Plants, Effect of air pollution on

TREES, Growth of. See Growth (plants)

TREES, Historic
Hawaii first; 201 champion big trees. L. C. Littlecott. il Am For 75:12-15+ F '69
Idaho's new champ. R. L. Lingenfelter. il Am For 75:27+ Ap '69
Roll call of the states. il Am For 75:26-7+ F '69
Sheepshooters' tree; end of this ponderosa pine in Paulina Valley, Ore. L. F. Cronemiller. il Am For 75:37+ Jl '69
Social register of big trees. L. C. Littlecott. il Am For 75:18-25 F '69
Tree above price; Avery Oak, Dedham, Mass. R. C. Roberts. il Am For 75:36+ Jl '69

TREES, Moving of. See Tree planting

TREES, Ringing of
Ring for flowers. J. W. Caddick. il Horticulture 47:18 My '69

TREES, Training of
Art of espalier trees. Am Home 72:112 Ap '69
Espaliers. D. Wyman. il Horticulture 47:28-9+ S '69

TREES, Watering of. See Watering of plants

TREES in art
Drawing trees in landscape. N. Kent. il Am Artist 33:74-9+ N '69
Tree drawings of Helen Loggie. il Am Artist 33:62-7 Je '69

TREES in cities
Mike Frome. M. Frome. Am For 75:3+ Jl '69
See also
Tree planting

TREFETHEN, Florence
Poet's workshop. See issues of Writer

TREHALASE
Do trehalose and trehalase function in renal glucose transport? E. Van Handel. bibliog il Science 163:1075-6 Mr 7 '69

TREHALOSE
Do trehalose and trehalase function in renal glucose transport? E. Van Handel. bibliog il Science 163:1075-6 Mr 7 '69

TREIGLE, Norman
Double devil. H. Saal. il Newsweek 74:132 O 6 '69
Recent recitals by stars of the New York city opera. il pors Am Rec G 35:455-7 F '69
Sermons and Satan. il Time 94:57-8 O 3 '69

TREJO, Arnulfo D.
Library needs for the Spanish-speaking; adaptation of address, 1968. por ALA Bul 63:1077-81 S '69

TRELEAVEN, Harry
Selling of the President 1968; excerpts. J. McGinniss. Harper 239:46-60 Ag '69

TRELLISES
Each provides shade, and something besides. il Sunset 142:118 My '69
See also
Plants, Training of

TREMAINE, Burton G.
Decisive art collection. G. Baro. il Vogue 153:132-41+ F 15 '69

TREMAINE collection. See Art—Private collections

TREMATODES
Larval trematodes: double infections in common mud-flat snail. W. B. Vernberg and others. bibliog il Science 164:1287 Je 13 '69

TREMORS, Earth. See Earthquakes

TRENCHING machinery
Quick service ditch cleaning; Scoopmobile with ditch-cleaning attachment, Clackamas County, Ore. il Am City 84:32 N '69

TRENT university, Peterborough, Ontario
Trent university. il Arch Rec 146:151-62 S '69

TRENTON, N.J.
Answers via displays. il Am City 84:132 F '69

Finance
Cut costs through programmed insurance. J. Matzer, jr. il Am City 84:148+ Mr '69

Municipal improvement
Urban esthetics can be functional. J. Alexander, jr. il Am City 84:79-81 D '69

TRESCOTT, Paul
South Carolina's treasure chest. Travel 131:50-3+ F '69

TRESER, Gerhard, and others
Antigenic streptococcal components in acute glomerulonephritis. bibliog Science 163:676-7 F 14 '69

TRESPASS; story. See Knebel, F.

TRESS, Arthur
Usual subjects, unusual images. J. Scully. il Mod Phot 33:72-5 Ap '69

TREUMANN, Otto
Otto Treumann graphic designer. I. Soifer. il por Pub W 196:64+ Ag 4 '69

TREYZ, Clara
Pat's wardrobe mistress. il por Time 95:28 Ja 12 '70

TRIAL by jury. See Jury

TRIAL reporting. See Newspaper court reporting

TRIALS
News and views; Catonsville-Milwaukee defense committees fund raisings. J. Deedy. Commonweal 89:664 F 28 '69
Truth in the courtroom. E. J. Epstein. bibliog f Commentary 48:50-4 Ag '69
Verdicts of history; with editorial comment (cont) T. J. Fleming. il Am Heritage 20:74-80+ D '68
See also
Actions and defenses
Evidence (law)
Jury
Newspaper court reporting

Anecdotes, facetiae, satire, etc.
In the matter of James Whitcomb Riley. W. Myers. Esquire 72:82+ S '69

Austria
King's fall; F. Olah tried for mismanaging union funds. Newsweek 73:44-5 Ap 7 '69

California
Eldridge Cleaver fund; letter to the editor. G. Cambridge and others. Commonweal 89:690-1 F 28 '69
Oakland seven; organizers of Stop the draft week. E. Langer. il Atlan 224:76-82 O '69
Oakland seven; organizers of Stop the draft week; with editorial comment. T. Cannon and R. Erlich. il Ramp Mag 7:34-7 Ap '69

Connecticut
Tilton v. Finch; validity of grants to church-related colleges. C. M. Whelan. America 121:222-3 S 27 '69

Czechoslovakia
Confession; concerning A. London's first hand account. A. L. Moats. il Nat R 21:846-8+ Ag 26 '69

TRIALS (murder)—*Continued*
 Verdicts of history; take the hatred away,
  and you have nothing left: O. and G. Sweet
  in white neighborhood. T. J. Fleming. il
  Am Heritage 20:74-80+ D '68
  See also
 Sacco-Vanzetti case

Sirhan trial, 1969
All the elements. il Newsweek 73:36+ Mr 10
  '69
Deadly iteration. Time 93:22-3 Mr 7 '69
Death without dread. il Time 93:28 Mr 14 '69
Defiant defendant. Newsweek 73:33+ F 24
  '69
Eye of the hurricane. Newsweek 73:24+ Mr
  3 '69
Jury vs. Sirhan; verdict. il Newsweek 73:34+
  My 5 '69
Killing a father. Time 93:17 Mr 21 '69
Letter and the law. il Newsweek 73:33+ Je
  2 '69
Man who loved Kennedy. il Time 93:18 F 21
  '69
Mother and son. il Newsweek 73:33 F 17 '69
Other Sirhan; testimony of prosecution's
  psychiatrist. Newsweek 73:44-5 Ap 14 '69
Psychiatry on trial. Nat R 21:427-8 My 6 '69
Reflections on the Sirhan trial. W. F.
  Buckley, jr. Nat R 21:247 Mr 11 '69
Round one. il Newsweek 73:33 F 3 '69
Selectivity in Los Angeles. Time 93:40 Ja 3
  '69
Sirhan guilty. Sr Schol 94:19 My 2 '69
Sirhan takes the stand. Newsweek 73:37 Mr 17
  '69
Sirhan through the looking glass; testimony
  of psychiatrist, B. L. Diamond. Time 93:28
  Ap 4 '69
Sirhan: tragedy of the absurd. il Newsweek
  73:32+ Mr 24 '69
Sirhan verdict. il Time 93:21-2 Ap 25 '69
Sirhan's trance; testimony of psychiatrist.
  Newsweek 73:37 Ap 7 '69
Smiling through. Newsweek 73:27-8 Ja 27 '69
Studies in killing. Newsweek 73:31-2 Mr 31 '69
Test case; responses to psychological tests.
  il Newsweek 73:94-5 Ap 7 '69
Toward the gas chamber. il Time 93:19 My
  2 '69
Verdict on Sirhan. il Newsweek 73:41+ Ap
  28 '69
What was in Sirhan's mind? Time 93:54 Ja
  24 '69

TRIALS (obscenity)
 End of obscenity, by C. Rembar. Review
  Commentary 46:97-8+ N '68. A. M. Bickel; Reply with rejoinder. C. Rembar.
  47:18+ F '69
 Judicial farce: Open city, underground newspaper. P. R. Ferguson. il Wilson Lib Bul
  43:653-6 Mr '69

TRIALS (rape)
 Case that could end capital punishment: Max-
  well v. Bishop. R. Hammer. il N Y Times
  Mag p46-7+ O 12 '69

TRIALS (slander) See Trials (libel)

TRIALS, Military. See Courts martial and
  courts of inquiry

TRIALS of animals. See Animals. Prosecution
  and punishment of

TRIASSIC period. See Paleontology—Triassic

TRIBES and tribal system
 Celibacy: challenge to tribalism. T. E. Clarke.
  America 120:464-7 Ap 19 '69
 Keeping one's head; controversy swirling
  around king of the Jukuns reign in Nigeria.
  Newsweek 74:33 D 29 '69
  See also
 Society, Primitive

TRIBUNE (Chicago) See Chicago tribune

TRIBUS, Myron
 Software of change; address, September 23,
  1969. Vital Speeches 36:14-17 O 15 '69

TRICHLOROPHENOXYACETIC acid. See Herbicides

TRICHOGRAMMA
 They feed on garden pests. il Sunset 143:142-
  3 Jl '69

TRICHOMONIASIS. See Vaginitis

TRI-CITIES opera (Binghamton, Endicott,
  and Johnson City, N.Y.)
 Report: Binghamton: production of Lakmé.
  J. Browning. Opera N 34:26 D 13 '69
 Three cheers for Tri-Cities. R. D. Daniels.
  il Opera N 33:14-16 Mr 1 '69

TRICKS
 How to do four dumb tricks with a package
  of Camels. R. Hills. il Esquire 72:144 S '69

TRIEBWASSER, S.
 Large-scale integration and the revolution in
  electronics. bibliog Science 163:429-34 Ja 31
  '69

TRIESCHMAN, A. E.
 Temper tantrums; excerpts from The other
  23 hours. Todays Ed 58:33-6 S '69

TRIFFIN, Robert
 Thrust of history in international monetary
  reform. For Affairs 47:477-92 Ap '69

TRIFLES (desserts) See Desserts

TRIGGER flower. See Hairtrigger flower

TRIGONOMETRY
 Trigonometric outfielding. Sci Am 220:49 Ja
  '69

TRILLIN, Calvin
 Barnett Frummer in urban crisis; story. Esquire 72:169 N '69
 For worse is better and sickness is in health;
  story. New Yorker 45:53-6 N 22 '69
 U.S. journal (cont) New Yorker 44:38-40+ F
  1; 100-6 F 15; 45:104+ Mr 8; 102+ Mr 22;
  178-83 Ap 12; 112+ My 3; 85-9 My 31; 104+
  Je 14; 69-70+ Jl 26; 144+ O 11; 169-75 N
  15; 175-6+ N 29; 33-6 D 27 '69

TRILLING, Diane
 On the steps of Low library: liberalism & the
  revolution of the young. Commentary 46:29-
  55 N '68; 47:10+ Mr; 19-20+ Ap '69

TRILLIUMS
 Three-pointed stars on the forest floor. il
  Sunset 142:206 Mr '69

TRIM (of boats) See Boats—Stability and
  stabilizers

TRIM tabs. See Tabs (boats)

TRIMARANS
 Cruising trimaran. B. Geiselman. il Yachting
  125:85+ Ja '69
 Record passage; transatlantic sailing of E.
  Tabarly. A. Colas. il Yachting 125:58-60+
  Ap '69

TRIMBLE, Val
 Student financial aid: what. where. how.
  Am Ed 5:7-8 F '69

TRIMETHYLAMMONIUM chloride. See Ammonium chlorides

TRIMM, H. Wayne
 Climbing is not for amateurs. Cons 24:16-17
  O '69

TRIMM, Trudie
 Holy war of the Rev Trudie Trimm. il pors
  Ebony 24:72-4+ S '69

TRINIDAD (island)
 Trinidad, land of the hummingbird. D. Mc-
  Fadden. il Home Gard 56:28-30 N '69
  See also
 Birds—Trinidad (island)

TRINITY
 Unclear; but clear enough. V. P. McCorry.
  America 120:656-inside back cover My 31
  '69

TRINITY college, Dublin. See Colleges and
  universities—Ireland

TRIP camping. See Camping

TRIPHOSPHATES. See Phosphates

TRIPLE crown. See Horse racing

TRIPLETT, Le
 Elementary education, a man's world? Ed
  Digest 34:25-7 Ja '69

TRIPODS, Camera. See Camera tripods

TRIPP, Hulbert Willis
 Making endowments greener. Bsns W p66+
  S 13 '69

TRIPP, Robert L.
 Self-directed study. Clear House 43:344-8
  F '69

TRIPP, Vollie
 Good news for stiff backs and tender knees.
  por Org Gard & Farm 16:86-7 Ag '69
 Make it out of concrete. Org Gard & Farm
  16:72-4 S '69
 Maypoles for fruit trees. Org Gard & Farm
  16:76-7 D '69
 We go for gumbo. Org Gard & Farm 16:54-5
  Ap '69

TRIPPETT, Frank
 Ordeal of fun. Look 33:24-34 Jl 29 '69; Same
  abr. with title Unending quest for fun.
  Read Digest 95:62-4 D '69

TRIS buffer medium. See Buffer solutions

TRISTAN, Dorothy
 A woman's power is in reacting to a man—.
  pors Life 67:66-7 N 7 '69

TRITIUM
 Tritium geophysics as an international research project. H. E. Suess. bibliog il Science 163:1405-10 Mr 28 '69

TRITON shells. See Shells (conchology)

TRIUMPH (periodical)
 Conservative way. Commonweal 90:274 My
  23 '69; Reply. F. Clinton. 90:399 Je 20 '69

TRIUMPH for Trimbly; drama. See Murray, J.

TRIVETS
 Classification of trivets. W. Paley. il Hobbies
  74:98R-98S Jl; 114-15 S '69

TROCONIS, Gabriel Porras. See Porras Troconis, G.

TROEMEL, C. P.
IC Telltale. Pop Electr 30:69-74 Ap '69
Indoor/outdoor all-electronic thermometer. Pop Electr 31:27-31 O '69
Third-generation DCU. Pop Electr 30:43-9 F '69

TROGDON, Ted
Prolific cartoonist J. Markow. Writers Digest 49:22-5 Ap '69

TROGLOBITES. See Cave fauna and flora

TROLLING. See Trawls and trawling

TROLLS (dolls) See Dolls

TROMBONE music
See also
Phonograph records—Trombone music

TROOP withdrawal, the initial step; story. See Parker, T.

TROPHIES, Sport
Who gets the Oscar? Heisman trophy for college football. D. Jenkins. il Sports Illus 31:18-23 N 10 '69
See also
Hunting trophies

TROPHY rooms
Doctor Howard's safari room. il Ebony 24: 132-4+ O '69

TROPICAL biology. See Biology

TROPICAL fishes. See Fishes

TROPICAL fruits. See Fruit

TROPICAL rain forest. See Rain forests

TROPICS
See also
Caribbean Region

Climate
Tropics: a frontier in meteorology. H. Chronic. il Sea Front 15:288-94 S '69

TROTTA, Geri
Bon voyage, but don't tell the cat. House B 111:189 O '69
How to cuddle up to money. Harp Baz 102: 188-9 Ag '69
India for me. Harp Baz 102:40+ Jl '69
Not to be missed. See issues of Harper's bazaar
St Lucia. Harp Baz 103:154+ N '69

TROTTER, F. Thomas
Movie. Chr Cent 86:1283-4 O 8 '69

TROTTING races. See Harness racing

TROUBADOUR; story. See Sterry, R.

TROUBADOURS
See also
Courtly love

TROUBLE lights. See Workshops—Lighting

TROUBLE with Carol and Ellen; story. See Dowty, L.

TROUBLED journey; story. See Lockridge, R.

TROUP, Arthur G. See Harriss, R. C. jt. auth.

TROUSERS, Womens. See Clothing and dress

TROUT
DDT: sublethal effects on brook trout nervous system. J. M. Anderson and M. R. Peterson. bibliog il Science 164:440-1 Ap 25 '69
New status for Alaska's rainbow trout. H. M. Hershberger. Field & S 74:112 Je '69
Ponds stocked by airplane. il Cons 23:14-15+ Ap '69
Teleostean urophysis: stimulation of contractions of bladder of the trout salmo gairdnerii. K. Lederis. bibliog il Science 163:1327-8 Mr 21 '69
Those first precarious days; photographs. Nat Wildlife 7:10-11 Je '69
Trout by the bottleful. L. J. Bashline. il Field & S 73:70-1+ Mr '69
Vanishing westerner; cutthroat trout. A. J. McClane. il Field & S 74:104-5+ Je 6 '69
See also
Cookery—Fish

TROUT fishing
Amazing Great Bear Lake! C. Conley. il Field & S 73:44-7+ F '69
Backpack jackpot. M. Hayden. il Outdoor Life 144:56-9+ O '69
Bargain pack trip. N. D. Weis. il Outdoor Life 143:49-51+ My '69
Blessed be the Beaver. H. G. Tapply. il Field & S 74:86 Je '69
Boom in steelhead; rainbow trout that live in Lake Michigan. J. O. Cartier. il Outdoor Life 143:60-3+ Mr '69
Buster brown. C. Ormond. il Outdoor Life 144:72 S '69
Charmed circle completed; Catskills trout streams. C. E. Heacox. il Outdoor Life 143: 80-1+ Ap '69
Charmed circle of the Catskills. C. E. Heacox. il Outdoor Life 143:50-3+ Mr '69

Cutthroat harvest. S. Fagerstrom. il Outdoor Life 144:56-7+ Jl '69
Fall: season of big trout. Yellowstone River, Mont. J. Brooks. il Outdoor Life 144:156-8+ O '69
First report: California's new ice fishing season. R. Cobb. il Field & S 74:26-7+ D '69
First trout, first lie. N. Lyons. il Field & S 73:48-9+ F '69
Fishing in New Zealand: South Island. J. Brooks. il Outdoor Life 144:60-3+ D '69
Fishing should be great at Lassen. il Sunset 143:67-8 O '69
Fishing streamers and bucktails. J. Brooks. il Outdoor Life 143:32-3+ Mr '69
Fishing the split-personality river; Wind River canyon. B. Milek. il Field & S 74: 54-5+ My '69
Float for first-class fishing. N. Strung. il Field & S 74:68-9+ Je '69
Great fishing! Brook trout in beaver pond. W. Davis. il Mech Illus 65:43-4 Mr '69
Harvest trout. W. Blair. il Field & S 74:136-8+ Ag '69
Hidden hatch. V. C. Marinaro. il Outdoor Life 144:48-51+ Jl '69
Home on the bison range. E. A. Bauer. il Outdoor Life 144:62-5+ S '69
How to fool April trout. F. McKinley. il Outdoor Life 143:61-3+ Ap '69
Jump-fishing for rainbows. J. Freeman. il Field & S 74:56-7+ My '69
Lake trout are back! J. O. Cartier. il Outdoor Life 143:88-9+ Ap '69
Look backward, angler. J. Brooks. il Outdoor Life 143:46-8+ Ap '69
Lunkers of Obre Lake; Northwest Territories. A. Spiers. il Field & S 74:166-8+ O '69
Manhattan with mountains, and trout. J. Mears. il Field & S 73:162-4+ Mr '69
One for the governor. C. Ormond. il Outdoor Life 143:70-1+ Mr '69
Paradise/south of the South Pacific; sport fishing in New Zealand. A. J. McClane. il Field & S 74:152-6 O '69
Quiet boom. D. Otto. il Outdoor Life 144: 77-80+ N '69
Rainbows and rattlers. J. R. Higley. il Outdoor Life 143:80-3+ My '69
Really great trout fishing. P. Plawin. il Bet Hom & Gard 47:163-4 Mr '69
Secret tricks of trout experts. H. G. Tapply. il Field & S 73:84 Ap '69
Simple streams for impatient anglers. F. Calkins. il Field & S 74:78-9+ My '69
Suddenly, you are fishing in Italy. P. Barrett. il Outdoor Life 143:72-5+ F '69
Tips on shoreline fishing. T. Janes. Outdoor Life 143:117 Mr '69
Training grounds for trout fishermen. L. Kreh. il Field & S 73:86-7+ Ap '69
Trophy steelhead country. W. E. Kruse. il Field & S 73:148-51+ F '69
Trout flies. E. Zern. il Nat Wildlife 7:43-7 Ap '69
When in doubt, try a bucktail. T. Trueblood. il Field & S 74:30+ My '69
See also
Grayling fishing

TROUT fishing in America, incorporated. See Schools, Experimental

TROUTMAN, Robert B. jr
Paying for influence. Time 94:75 O 24 '69

TROVA, Ernest
Spinning man game. Art in Am 57:77 N '69

Il TROVATORE; opera. See Verdi, G.

TROW, George
Have you read. .? Seventeen 28:52 Ag '69

TROWBRIDGE, Elizabeth C.
Slings and arrows ... Engl J 58:120-1 Ja '69

TROWER, W. Peter
Matter and antimatter. bibliog por Chem 42: 8-13 O '69

TROY, Leo
Trade union growth in a changing economy. bibliog Mo Labor R 92:3-7 S '69

TROY
Homer's Achilles heel; skepticism about the Trojan war. il Time 94:65-6 Jl 4 '69

Les TROYENS; opera. See Berlioz, H.

TRUAX, Hawley
Days of grace; poem. New Yorker 45:21 Jl 19 '69
L'Observatoire; poem. New Yorker 45:40 Mr 8 '69

TRUBITT, Hillard J.
Going by the book. Nation 208:507-9 Ap 21 '69

TRUC, Pham-the-. See Pham-the-Truc

TRUCE, Betty A. See McDaniel, H. B. jt. auth.

TRUCIAL OMAN
See also
Abu Dhabi

TRUCK campers. See Campers and coaches,
Truck
TRUCKING
Air forwarding authority granted to truckers
again. J. W. Carter. Aviation W 90:27 Ap
28 '69
See also
Collective bargaining—Trucking industry
TRUCKS
See also
Motor trucks
TRUDEAU, Pierre Elliott
President Nixon and Prime Minister Trudeau
of Canada hold talks at Washington; ex-
change of greetings, toasts, March 24 and
25, 1963. Dept State Bul 60:319-23 Ap 14
'69
Tenth anniversary of St Lawrence Seaway;
exchange of remarks, June 27, 1969. Dept
State Bul 61:68-70 Jl 28 '69

about

Anti-inflation, de-escalation. Nat R 21:947 S
23 '69
Early bedtime at Blair house. H. Sidey. il
por Life 66:4 Ap 4 '69
Elephant and friends. il por Time 93:27 Ap
4 '69
For Canada's Trudeau, fallout from U.S.
ABM. por U S News 66:15 Mr 31 '69
Mandate '68, by M. Sullivan. Review
Nat R 21:344-5 Ap 8 '69. D. Coxe
Pierre Elliott Trudeau, prime minister of Can-
ada. A. Chamberlin. pors Vogue 153:110-
11+ Mr 15 '69
Profiles. E. Iglauer. por New Yorker 45:36-
42+ Jl 5 '69
Silent partner. J. W. Warnock. Commonweal
90:536-9 S 5 '69
Trouble in the prairies. il por Newsweek 74:
50 Ag 4 '69
Trudeau's ABM doubts. il por U S News
66:14 Ap 7 '69
Unhappy Pierre. il Newsweek 73:50 F 3 '69
TRUDELL, Dennis
Tangent; poem. Nation 209:736 D 29 '69
TRUEB, Lucien F. and De Wys, E. C.
Carbonado: natural polycrystalline diamond.
bibliog Science 165:799-802 Ag 22 '69
TRUEBLOOD, David Elton
Rational Christianity. Chr Today 13:3-5 F 14
'69

about

Archimedes revisited. H. B. Kuhn. Chr Today
13:55-6 Ap 11 '69
TRUEBLOOD, Elton. See Trueblood, D. E.
TRUEBLOOD, Ted, pseud.
[Monthly article on outdoor life] See issues
of Field & stream
TRUESDELL, William H.
Teachers should commit themselves. Todays
Ed 58:37 Ja '69
TRUEX, Philip
Conifers in the winter roof garden. Horti-
culture 47:44-5 Ja '69
Plants for city gardens. Horticulture 46:38-9+
Ag '68
TRUFFAUT, Francois
Current cinema. P. Kael. New Yorker 45:114
Mr 8 '69
Life style of homo cinematicus. S. De
Gramont. il pors N Y Times Mag p 12-
13+ Je 15 '69
M. Truffaut makes it look so easy. R. Schickel.
Life 66:18 Mr 7 '69
Ten years of Truffaut. J. Morgenstern. il por
Newsweek 73:99-100 Mr 10 '69
TRUFFLES
Great truffle snuffle. il Newsweek 73:72+ F 24
'69
On the trail of the white truffle. A. Lach. il
Travel & Camera 32:31-2+ Ag '69
TRUJILLO, Rafael, 1929-1969
Death of a playboy. il por Newsweek 75:33
Ja 12 '70
TRUK ISLANDS
Truk. T. C. Allrich. il Travel 132:48-51 D '69
TRULUCK, Jack L.
South Carolina's Washington trail. Travel
132:68-70 D '69
TRUMAN, David B.
Eldest sister starts to swing. B. B. Stretch. il
por Sat R 52:98 F 15 '69
He still communicates. por Newsweek 73:56
F 3 '69
TRUMAN, Harry S.
Greatness of Harry Truman. D. Acheson. por
Esquire 72:124-7+ S '69
Harry Truman's Missouri. R. Pearman. il
Travel 132:56-60+ Ag '69

Truman doctrine and NATO; with excerpts
from President's message to Congress,
March 12, 1947. L. W. Koenig. bibliog f
Cur Hist 57:18-23+, 49 Jl '69
Truman's speech & Noam Chomsky; with
excerpts from address, March 6, 1947. A.
Schlesinger, jr. Commentary 48:4+ D '69
TRUMAN, Harry S, library. See Harry S. Tru-
man library, Independence, Mo.
TRUMAN, Margaret. See Daniel, M. T.
TRUMAN doctrine. See United States—Foreign
relations—Anti-Communist measures
TRUMBO, Dalton
Happy Jack fish hatchery papers; letters.
Esquire 73:73-7+ Ja '70
TRUMBULL, Van
Washington lookout. See issues of American
forests
TRUMMEL, C. L. and others
25-Hydroxycholecalciferol: stimulation of
bone resorption in tissue culture. bib-
liog Science 163:1450-1 Mr 28 '69
TRUMP, J. Lloyd
Case for decentralization. E. Ahlers and M.
Sypert. bibliog il Library J 94:4207-10 N 15
'69
Trump school: a move toward recentraliza-
tion. M. Miller and J. Ankrum. il Library
J 94:4211-12 N 15 '69
TRUMPET blowing
Profiles; B. Glow. W. Whitworth. New York-
er 45:43-4+ D 20 '69
TRUMPET music
Trumpet battle at Niblo's pleasure garden.
C. A. Hoover. bibliog f il Mus Q 55:384-95
Jl '69
TRUMPETER swans. See Swans
TRUONG Chinh
Scuffling in Hanoi. il por Newsweek 74:57
D 22 '69
TRUPP, Philip
Doctor Buff versus the black lung. Read
Digest 94:101-5 Je '69
TRUSCOTT, Alan
Bridge. See issues of New York times maga-
zine
TRUSSELL, Tait
Washington trends. See issues of Nation's
business
TRUSSES
Prefabricated wood trusses serve as form-
work for conoidal concrete roof. il Arch
Rec 145:201 Je '69
TRUST in God
Theology of trust. H. O. J. Brown. Chr To-
day 13:3-5 Ap 11 '69
TRUST TERRITORY OF THE PACIFIC
ISLANDS
Interior Secretary Hickel to visit Pacific
Islands Trust Territory. Dept State Bul
60:424 My 19 '69
Nostalgia for Nippon. B. Krisher. il Newsweek
73:62 F 17 '69
Trust Territory of the Pacific Islands; sym-
posium. June 6 and 13, 1969. Dept State
Bul 61:220-36 S 8 '69
See also
Micronesia
United Nations—Trust Territory of the Pacific
Islands
TRUSTEES. See Trusts and trustees
TRUSTEES, Hospital. See Hospitals—Trustees,
boards, etc.
TRUSTEES, Library. See Libraries—Trustees,
boards, committees, etc.
TRUSTEES of colleges. See College trustees
TRUSTEESHIP council. See United Nations—
Trusteeship council
TRUSTS, Industrial
Conglomerate critic aims a blast; W. Muel-
ler's report. Bsns W p98+ N 1 '69
How judgment came for the plumbing con-
spirators. A. T. Demaree. il Fortune 80:96-
9+ D '69
See also
Business consolidations and mergers
Monopolies
United States—Justice, Department of—Anti-
trust division

International trusts

See also
Interessengemeinschaft farbenindustrie ag

Law

Another great divide: major lawsuits against
IBM. il Forbes 103:15-17 F 1 '69
Antitrust: a national policy; address, August
12, 1969. J. J. Ling. Vital Speeches 35:751-4
O 1 '69

TRUSTS, Industrial—Law—*Continued*
Antitrust in dubious battle; with editorial comment. R. H. Bork. il Fortune 80:86, 103-5+ S '69
Antitrust problems that Nixon inherits. il U S News 66:96-7 F 17 '69
Antitrust, Republican style; interview, ed. by G. R. Rosen. R. McLaren. Duns R 94:12-13+ O '69
Antitrust verdict rocks the stores; Elder-Beerman stores corp. vs. Rike's division of Federated department stores. Bsns W p29 Jl 26 '69
Antitrust: winding up for a go at big business? il Sr Schol 94:9-10 Mr 14 '69
Antitrusters lose a round; acquisition of Hartford fire insurance co. by ITT approved. Time 94:80 O 31 '69
Conglomerate; federal policy on mergers; address, June 6, 1969. J. N. Mitchell. Vital Speeches 35:592-4 Jl 15 '69
Conglomerates under the gun. il Bsns W p27-9 Mr 8 '69
Conglomerators speak out; ABA symposium. il Bsns W p94+ N 1 '69
Consumer be damned! AT&T and GE. W. P. Rokes; W. F. Mattes. il Nation 208:820-5 Je 30 '69
Crackdown starts on conglomerates. il U S News 66:92 Ap 7 '69
Failing newspaper probe: the press dummies up. A. E. Rowse. il Nation 208:816-20 Je 30 '69
Key ruling on big mergers. U S News 67:9 N 3 '69
Mergers must toe the hard line. Bsns W p48-9 Je 14 '69
Mergers under scrutiny; excerpts from Managerial analysis in marketing. L. W. Stern. bibliog il Harvard Bsns R 47:18-20+ Jl '69
More fishing for giants; antitrust suit against ITT-Canteen deal. Bsns W p25 My 3 '69
New tack on takeovers; U.S. and Britain. Duns R 93:116 Ap '69
Newspapers and monopoly: S. 1312 and all that. W. S. Kerr. Sat R 52:77-8 My 10 '69
Nixon's antitrust policy; conglomerate mergers. W. F. Baxter. New Repub 161:13-16 Ag 9 '69
Pitchfork Ben, meet Wheelbarrow John. M. Ways. Fortune 80:84 Jl '69
Price-fixing, profit-pooling, and the newspaper business. W. B. Kerr. il Sat R 52:82-3 N 8 '69
Setback for McLaren; acquisition of Hartford fire insurance co. and Grinnell corp. by ITT approved. Newsweek 74:78 N 3 '69
Softening the harsh words; interview. R. W. McLaren. Forbes 103:23-4 Je 1 '69
Switch on mergers; Neal report released. Bsns W p40 My 24 '69
Trustbusting and common sense; Justice department to block proposed merger of British petroleum and Standard oil co. of Ohio. Duns R 94:140 N '69
U.S. antitrust muscle makes Europe wince. il Bsns W p84-6 N 8 '69
U.S. crackdown on big steel. U S News 66:12 Je 23 '69
Washington wakes up to the conglomerates. il Forbes 103:23-5 F 15 '69
See also
United States—Justice, Department of—Antitrust division

Europe, Western
Price-fixing fines cast a long shadow. Bsns W p30 Ag 2 '69

United States
Aerospace companies face antitrust inquiry in House. Aviation W 90:21 F 24 '69
See also
United States steel corporation
TRUSTS, Investment. See Investment trusts
TRUSTS, Pension. See Pension trusts
TRUSTS and trustees
Should you set up a custodial gift account for your child? P. Lindberg. Bet Hom & Gard 37:18 N '69
Trustee, resign! G. G. Kirstein. Nation 208: 727-30 Je 9 '69
TRUTH
Truth and proof. A. Tarski. Sci Am 220: 63-70+ bibliog(p 144) Je '69
See also
Lying
Reality
TRUTH in lending bill. See Consumer credit—Laws and legislation

TRYPAN blue
Protein digestion in isolated lysosomes inhibited by intralysosomal trypan blue. M. Davies and others. bibliog il Science 163: 1454-6 Mr 28 '69
TRYPANOSOMIASIS
Trypanosome transmitted by plebotomus: first report from the Americas. J. R. Anderson and S. C. Ayala; reply with rejoinder. M. Hertig and others. bibliog Science 165: 1379-81 S 26 '69
TRYPSIN
Trypsin and papain covalently coupled to porous glass: preparation and characterization. H. H. Weetall. bibliog il Science 166:615-17 O 31 '69
TRYPTOPHAN
Tryptophan pyrolase induction in patients with manic depression; with reply by A. J. Mandell. R. T. Rubin and B. R. Clark. bibliog il Science 165:1146-8 S 12 '69
TRYPTOPHAN hydroxylase. See Hydroxylases
TRYPTOPHAN oxygenase. See Oxygenases
TRYPTOPHOL
Phenethyl alcohol and tryptophol: autoantibiotics produced by the fungus Candida albicans. B. T. Lingappa and others. bibliog il Science 163:192-4 Ja 10 '69
TSCHAIKOVSKY suite; ballet. See Ballets—Criticisms
TSCHIRLEY, Fred H.
Defoliation in Vietnam. bibliog Science 163: 779-86 F 21 '69
TSENG, Charles C. See Eyde, R. H. jt. auth.
TSHOMBE, Moise
End in captivity. il por Time 94:30+ Jl 11 '69
Obituary
Chr Cent 86:942 Jl 16 '69
Nat R 21:685 Jl 15 '69
TSIOLKOVSKII, Konstantin Eduardovich
Pioneers. il por Time 94:24 Jl 18 '69
Problems of space exploration. IU. Nefedov and others. Space World F-8-68:36-7 Ag '69
TSUBOI, Masamichi, and others
Phosphorus-proton spin-spin coupling and conformation of a dinucleoside phosphate. bibliog Science 166:1504-6 D 19 '69
TSUGA canadensis. See Hemlock
TSUNAMIS. See Seismic sea waves
TSWANA (Bantu tribe) See Botswana—Native races
TUBE testers. See Testing instruments
TUBERCULATE fish. See Fishes
TUBERCULOSIS
Prevention and control
Problem-child of alcoholism. il Sci N 95:279 Mr 22 '69
Therapy
See also
Isoniazid
TUBERCULOUS
Rehabilitation
Legal commitment and hospital behavior: recalcitrance of tuberculous alcoholics; address. May 10, 1967. E. Rubington. bibliog Ment Hy 53:41-53 Ja '69
TUBERS
Many-splendored colors of summer; and all from the magic of bulbs, corms and tubers. il Home Gard 56:46-54 Ap '69
TUBES, Steel
Down the tube. J. Thawley. il Hot Rod 22: 58-60 Ap '69
TUBING. See Aquatic sports
TUCKER, Charles Ewbank, bp
1969 Protestant inaugural prayers. Chr Today 13:27 F 14 '69
TUCKER, H. S.
How many ologies do you know? Sci Digest 66:39 Jl '69
TUCKER, Martin
African genesis. Nation 209:510-12 N 10 '69
Screen. Commonweal 91:306-7 D 5 '69
TUCKER, Norma
Poetry made easy, in one week. Sr Schol 94:Schol Teach 8+ F 14 '69
TUCKER, Vance A.
Energetics of bird flight; with biographical sketch. Sci Am 220:18, 70-6+ My '69
Wave-making by whirligig beetles (gyrinidae) bibliog Science 166:897-9 N 14 '69

about
Birds that fly nowhere. D. Seaver. il pors Sci Digest 65:19-21 Ap '69

TUCKERMAN, Anne
Albanian demonology. Nation 208:566-7 My 5
'69
Fire control at the UN. Nation 208:70 Ja
20 '69
Ghost of Geneva. Nation 209:714 D 29 '69
UN: defusing the powder keg. Nation 208:198-9
F 17 '69

TUCKSON, Margaret
Pottery in New Guinea; excerpts from Pottery
in Australia. Craft Horiz 28:27-31+ Jl '68;
Correction. 29:47 Ja '69

TUCSON, Ariz.
Answers East and West. il Am City 84:130+
F '69

TUERS, Raymond J.
Convert your outdoor grill to gas. Pop
Mech 131:166-7 Ap '69

TUFTS-Delta health center. See Health centers

TUHUALITE. See Silicates

TUITION fees. See Colleges and universities
—Finance

TULARE LAKE
Lethal haven. Newsweek 74:59 S 8 '69

TULE elk. See Elk

TULIP Hill (historic house) See Anne Arundel
County. Md.—Historic houses, etc.

TULIPS
Bulb color. W. Meachem. il Horticulture 46:
36-7+ O '68
Species tulips: some are demure, some are
dashing and bold. il Sunset 143:252+ O '69
Tulips by the hundreds. B. Brinhart. il Org
Gard & Farm 16:52-5 S '69
Uncommon tulips. M. Reynolds. il Horticul-
ture 47:18-20+ O '69

TULL, Robert G.
Planetary spectroscopy with the 107-inch
telescope. Sky & Tel 38:156-60 S '69

TULLIUS, F. P.
Ninety-nine years is not forever. New Yorker 45:20-1 Jl 19 '69

TULLY, Alice
Fanfare for Tully Hall. H. W. Simon. il por
Hi Fi 19:MA8-9+ D '69

TULLY, Geri
Dieting by computer. Harp Baz 103:154 Ja
'70

TULLY hall. See Lincoln Center for the performing arts, New York—Juilliard school

TULVING, Endel
Retrograde amnesia in free recall. bibliog
Science 164:88-90 Ap 4 '69

TUMANOV, Aleksandr
Soviet advances in orbital maneuvers. Space
World G-1-73:38-9 Ja '70

TUMBLERS. See Drinking vessels

TUMLINSON, J. H. and others
Sex pheromones produced by male boll weevil: isolation, identification, and synthesis.
bibliog Science 166:1010-12 N 21 '69

TUMOR viruses
Cell transformation by viruses. R. Dulbecco.
bibliog il Science 166:962-8 N 21 '69
Immunology of mouse mammary tumor virus;
report of meeting. D. H. Moore. il Science
163:1230-1 Mr 14 '69
Polyoma virus gene activity during lytic infection and in transformed animal cells. M.
A. Martin and D. Axelrod. bibliog il Science 164:68-70 Ap 4 '69

TUMORS
Chloramphenicol: effects on mouse myeloma
cells in tissue culture. B. K. Hartman and
others. bibliog il Science 165:297-8 Jl 18 '69
Diffusible cytotoxic substances and cell-mediated resistance to syngeneic tumors: in
vitro demonstration. K. Kikuchi and others. bibliog il Science 165:77-9 Jl 4 '69
Herpesvirus in Marek's disease tumors. G.
Schidlovsky and others. bibliog il Science
164:959-61 My 23 '69
Neoplastic transformation in vitro of hamster lens epithelium by simian virus 40.
D. M. Albert and others. bibliog il Science
164:1077-8 My 30 '69
Transplantation of pluripotential nuclei from
triploid frog tumors. R. G. McKinnell and
others. bibliog il Science 165:394-6 Jl 25
'69
Tumor induction in developing frog kidneys
by a zonal centrifuge purified fraction of
the frog herpes-type virus. M. Mizell and
others. bibliog il Science 165:1134-7 S 12 '69
See also
Angiokeratoma
Sarcoma

TUNA fish
See also
Cookery—Fish

TUNA fishing
Boosting the tuna catch; using maps of sea-
surface temperatures. W. A. Scholes. il Sci
N 96:338 O 11 '69
Boring - thrilling - exhausting - impoverishing
sport; U.S. Atlantic tuna tournament. P.
Wood. il N Y Times Mag p30-1+ N 2 '69
New Atlantic tuna fishery. G. L. Beardsley,
jr. il Sea Front 15:152-9 My '69
Playing the game. G. Heinold. il Outdoor
Life 144:22+ Jl '69
Record bigeye for a lady. H. C. King. il
Field & S 74:40-1+ Jl '69
Tuna party. T. Kelley. il Outdoor Life 144:48-
9+ S '69
See also
Albacore fishing

TUNDRAS
Alpine summer. B. Ratcliffe. il Audubon 71:
44-51 Jl '69

TUNGUSKA meteorite. See Meteorites

TUNING
See also
Musical pitch

TUNING (radio) See Radio receivers—Tuning

TUNING (television) See Television receivers—
Tuning

TUNISIA
See also
Floods—Tunisia
Irrigation—Tunisia
Natural resources—Tunisia

Defenses
North African arms race. A. Smith. Atlan
223:28 F '69

Description and travel
Tunisia. R. Warren. il Travel 132:36-43 D '69

Economic conditions
Bourguiba: wise voice of the Arab world.
D. Reed. Read Digest 94:175-6+ Je '69

Politics and government
Bourguiba: wise voice of the Arab world.
D. Reed. Read Digest 94:175-6+ Je '69
Widening ripples. E. Behr. Newsweek 74:46+
S 22 '69

TUNLEY, Roul
Coeducation: the walls are tumbling down!
Seventeen 28:114-15+ Je '69
Drugs: straight answers to the ten big ques-
tions. Seventeen 28:328-9+ Ag '69
50,000,000 acre ghetto. Seventeen 28:122-3+
O '69
Five who came back from drugs. Seventeen
29:92-3+ Ja '70
His backyard was a passage to fame. Audu-
bon 71:114+ N '69
Summer jobs. Seventeen 28:140-1+ F '69

TUNNEL diodes. See Diodes

TUNNELL, James R.
Incarnation, unveiled. Chr Cent 86:1638-40 D
24 '69

TUNNELS and tunneling
Utility tunnels enhance urban renewal areas.
W. J. Boegly, jr. and W. L. Griffith. bib-
liog il Am City 84:101-3 F '69
See also
Chesapeake Bay bridge-tunnel

TUNNER, William H.
Before the colors fade: Berlin airlift com-
mander; interview, ed. by C. V. Glines. pors
Am Heritage 20:44-5+ O '69

TUNSTELL, Douglas
Emergence of modern Mexico, portfolio.
Am Heritage 20:9-39 Ap '69

TUPAMAROS. See Guerrillas—Uruguay

TUPELOS
Black or sour gum. C. E. Lewis. Horticulture 47:48 +Jl '69

TUPPER, Joseph T. and Tedeschi, Henry
Mitochondrial membrane potentials measured
with microelectrodes: probable ionic basis.
bibliog Science 166:1539-40 D 19 '69

TUPPER, Margo
Has anybody seen my hammer? Good H
169:48+ Ag '69

TURANDOT; opera. See Puccini, G.

TURANO, John, and Kelly, E. T.
Contemporary concerns for the secondary
school. bibliog f Clear House 43:387-91 Mr
'69

TURBELLARIA. See Flatworms
TURBINES
    See also
  Gas turbines
  Gas turbines, Aircraft
  Gas turbines, Marine
  Steam turbines
  Steam turbines, Marine
TURBOFAN engines. See Gas turbines, Aircraft
TURBOLINER (train) See Railroads—Passenger service—High speed trains
TURBULENCE
    See also
  Atmospheric turbulence
TURCO, Alfred
  Avant-garde forever? Nation 209:351-3 O 6 '69
TURCO, Lewis
  Home thoughts; poem. Poetry 113:246 Ja '69
  I am Peter; poem. Sat R 52:34 N 29 '69
  Kitchen; Bedroom; Scythe; poems. Poetry 114:308-12 Ag '69
  Pilot; poem. Sat R 52:34 Je 7 '69
TURCOTTE, Donald L. and Oxburgh, E. R.
  Continental drift. bibliog pors Phys Today 22:30-9 Ap; 13+ Ag '69
TURE, Norman B.
  Federal taxation; address. December 6, 1968. Vital Speeches 35:221-4 Ja 15 '69
TURECK, Rosalyn
  Dancing Bach. por Dance Mag 43:49-50 O '69
    about
  Music to my ears; Bach performance. I. Kolodin. Sat R 52:74 D 6 '69
TURENNE, Henri de
  Now a pretender to the Gaullist throne. N Y Times Mag p30-1+ F 23 '69
TURF, Artificial
  Goodby to three yards and a cloud of dust; era of synthetic football fields. W. Johnson. il Sports Illus 30:37-9 Ja 27 '69
  Magic carpet for all outdoors. H. R. Whitaker. il Sci Digest 66:33-7 Jl '69
  Synthetic grass. J. Carew. Horticulture 48: 38 Ja '70
TURINO, Gerard M. and others
  Serum elastase inhibitor deficiency and α_1 antitrypsin deficiency in patients with obstructive emphysema. bibliog Science 165: 709-11 Ag 15 '69
La TURISTA; drama. See Shepard, S.
TURKALO, A. M. See Doremus, R. H. jt. auth.
TURKEVICH, Anthony L. and others
  Chemical composition of the lunar surface in the mare tranquillitatis. bibliog Science 165:277-9 Jl 18 '69
TURKEY
  Islam and the West in the Middle East. G. Lenczowski. bibliog f Cur Hist 56:129-35+ Mr '69
    See also
  Agriculture—Turkey
  Arts and crafts—Turkey
  Manyas, Lake
  Natural resources—Turkey
  Trade unions—Turkey
    Antiquities
  Labor of love; rediscovery in Turkey of the temple of Aphrodite of Cnidus. il Time 95: 36 Ja 12 '70
  Prehistoric investigations in southeastern Turkey; Cayönü. R. J. Braidwood and others. bibliog Science 164:1275 Je 13 '69
  Ruins of Nemrud Dagh; reprint. il UNESCO Courier 22:11 Ag '69
    Description and travel
  Aegean Turkey. D. Marley. il Harp Baz 102: 144+ Mr '69
  Let's travel; Turkey. Mlle 69:112+ S '69
  Yankee cruises Turkey's history-haunted coast. I. Johnson and E. Johnson. il Nat Geog 136:798-845 D '69
    See also
  Bosporus
    Economic conditioins
  Now it's the Turks who are unhappy about U.S; with interview with S. Demirel. il U S News 66:89-92 Je 9 '69
  Republic of Turkey. J. Kolars. bibliog il Focus 19:1-11 Ap '69
  Turkey: a contemporary survey. H. N. Howard. bibliog f Cur Hist 56:141-5+ Mr '69
    Foreign relations
  Now it's the Turks who are unhappy about U.S; with interview with S. Demirel. il U S News 66:89-92 Je 9 '69

    History
  Republic of Turkey. J. Kolars. bibliog il Focus 19:1-11 Ap '69
    Politics and government
  Turkey: a contemporary survey. H. N. Howard. bibliog f Cur Hist 56:141-5+ Mr '69
  Turkey: politics, Islam, Arabism. T. Cosmades Chr Cent 86:1531 N 26 '69
TURKEY, anyone? drama. See Garver, J.
TURKEY as food. See Cookery—Poultry
TURKEY buzzards
  Buzzards of Hinckley. B. Thomas. il Nat Wildlife 7:34-5 F '69
  Vultures in New York; turkey vultures. Cons 23:5 Ap '69
TURKEY carving. See Carving (meat, etc)
TURKEY hunting
  Call of spring. K. C. Schuyler. il Outdoor Life 143:84-7+ Ap '69
  Gullible gobbler. C. Elliott. il Outdoor Life 143:64-5+ Mr '69
  News: the Southeast. C. Elliott; H. L. Lawrence. Outdoor Life 143:43-6 Mr '69
  What's ahead for turkey hunters? G. Laycock. il Field & S 74:60-1+ O '69
TURKEY vultures. See Turkey buzzards
TURKEYS, Wild
    See also
  Turkey hunting
TURKINGTON, Roger W. and Hill, R. L.
  Lactose synthetase: progesterone inhibition of the induction of α-lactalbumin. bibliog Science 163:1458-60 Mr 28 '69
TURKISH rugs. See Rugs and carpets, Oriental
TURKISH villages. See Villages
TURKLE, Brinton
  Confessions of a leprechaun. por Pub W 196:133-6 Jl 14 '69
TURNCOATS
    See also
  Defectors, Political
TURNER, Arthur C.
  U.S. in World war II. Cur Hist 57:13-17+ Jl '69
TURNER, Carl C.
  Guns of Turner. il por Newsweek 74:41-2 O 20 '69
  Kickbacks, guns: new round in army rackets hearing. il por U S News 67:14 O 20 '69
  Military Mafia. il por Time 94:26 O 17 '69
TURNER, Clyde
  Life for two tough Texans. M. Cope. il pors Sports Illus 31:84-8+ O 20 '69
TURNER, Fitzhugh
  Fishing under the V.C. guns. Outdoor Life 144:37-9+ Jl '69
TURNER, Henry Ashby, Jr
  Big business and the rise of Hitler. bibliog f Am Hist R 75:56-70 O '69
TURNER, Ike
  Turning on. il por Newsweek 74:92-3 N 3 '69
TURNER, James
  Student's view: black students and their changing perspective. por Ebony 24:135-40 Ag '69
TURNER, James C.
  Crusader comes to Howell. por Time 95:34 Ja 5 '70
TURNER, Jim
  Face of an educated toe. R. F. Jones. por Sports Illus 31:72-4+ S 22 '69
TURNER, Lana
  Survivor on TV; Lana. J. Barthel. il pors Life 67:78-80+ S 26 '69
TURNER, Merfyn
  Lessons of Norman house. Ann Am Acad 381: 39-46 Ja '69
TURNER, Nat
  Nat Turner: fanatic or prophet? Will the real Nat Turner please stand up? il por Sr Schol 94:12-13 F 14 '69
TURNER, Nicholas
  Sihanouk: prince on a tightrope. Read Digest 94:177-82 My '69
TURNER, Oliver B.
  Rolling in pennies. il por Time 93:26 My 23 '69
TURNER, Terence S.
  Tchikrin. Natur Hist 78:50-9+ O '69
TURNER, Tina
  Cussin', cryin', gettin' it on. E. Sander. Sat R 52:43 Ag 30 '69
  Turning on. il por Newsweek 74:92-3 N 3 '69

TURNER, William W.
I was a burglar, wiretapper, bugger, and spy for the F.B.I. Ramp Mag 7:47-51 Ja 25 '69
No dice for braceros. Ramp Mag 7:37-40 Ja 25 '69
TURNER'S Negro insurrection, 1831. See Southampton insurrection, 1831
TURNING
Make a king-size toolpost for hefty turning bits. W. E. Burton. il Pop Mech 131:194-6 F '69
Turning rings on a lathe. W. E. Burton. il Pop Mech 131:186-90 Ja '69
Woodturning fun for beginners. J. Burroughs. il Pop Mech 132:196-9 N '69
TURNIP yellow mosaic virus. See Viruses. Plant
TURNIPS
Have turnips the year-round. R. L. Hawk. il Org Gard & Farm 16:52-3 Mr '69
TURNOVERS, Meat. See Cookery—Meat
TURNTABLES
See also
Phonograph—Turntables
TURRELL, James
View from Hill and Main. por Newsweek 74:111 O 27 '69
TURTLE fishing
Turtle clapping. C. Robinson. il Field & S 74:66-7+ Je '69
TURTLES
Buoyancy control in the freshwater turtle, pseudemys scripta elegans. D. C. Jackson. bibliog il Science 166:1649-51 D 26 '69
Struggle to save the sea turtle. il Life 67:54-7 Jl 18 '69
See also
Tortoises
TURTLES, Green
Green sea turtles: a discrete simulation of density-dependent population regulation. H. R. Bustard and K. P. Tognetti. bibliog il Science 163:939-41 F 28 '69
TUSCANY
Florentine hill towns: suburbs, Tuscan style. S. O'Faolain. il Holiday 46:42-3+ S '69
In the heart of Italy; Siena and vicinity. C. Foley. il Nat R 21:859+ Ag 26 '69
TUSINSKI, Joseph
Resistivity: some definitions. Electr World 82:86+ N '69
Strain gages come of age. Electr World 81:35-7 Mr '69
TUSKEGEE institute, Alabama
Chapel for Tuskegee by Rudolph. il Arch Rec 146:117-26 N '69
TUSSMAN, Joseph
Program has helped me know that I don't know. E. Peterson. Mlle 69:261+ Ag '69
TUTEN, Frederic
Art. Vogue 153:36 Ap 15 '69
Films of Alain Resnais. Vogue 154:24+ Jl '69
Movies (cont) Vogue 154:44 Ag 15; 342 S 1; 62 S 15; 64 O 15 '69
TUTORS, Volunteer. See Tutors and tutoring
TUTORS and tutoring
Students as tutors: high schoolers aid elementary pupils. S. E. Bell and others. Clear House 44:242-4 D '69
Summer remedial program for primary children. P. A. Driscoll. Ed Digest 34:36-7 My '69
Team up in Denver; community-sponsored study halls. L. Welker. il Am Ed 5:28 N '69
They got the feeling that everybody's somebody. M. P. Pfeil. il Am Ed 5:21-4 D '69
TUTTLE, Helen Welch
Prices indexes for 1969: U.S. periodicals. Library J 94:2571 Jl '69
TUTTLE, Russell H.
Knuckle-walking and the problem of human origins bibliog Science 166:953-61 N 21 '69
TUTTON, Marie E. See Locastro, R. jt. auth.
TVARDOVSKII, Aleksandr Trifonovich
Kremlin chill. por Newsweek 74:38-9 Ag 25 '69
TWAIN, Mark, pseud. See Clemens, S. L.
TWELFTH night; opera. See Amram, D.
TWENTIETH century
Good-bye to all of you; advice to the next generation from distinguished nineteenth-century citizens. il Esquire 72:158-63+ D '69
TWENTIETH century-Fox film corporation
Dolly's dilemma: her $20 million movie is stuck on the shelf while producers argue. il Life 66:58-60 F 14 '69
21 (restaurant) See New York (city)—Hotels, restaurants, etc.
TWIGGY (model)
Twiggy: the four seasons of a woman's life. R. Avedon. pors McCalls 96:86-7 Mr '69

TWIN circle (periodical) See Catholic press
TWIN-lens cameras
Close-ups without kicks: take a TLR. N. Rothschild. il Pop Phot 64:70-1+ F '69
Lab report: Tessina 35L; with instrument readout by N. Goldberg. H. Zucker. il Pop Phot 64:98-9+ Ap '69
TWINING, Nathan F.
Ideas by which we are ruled; excerpt from Neither liberty nor safety. Harper 238:36 Je '69
TWINS
Twins who found each other; excerpt. B. Lindeman. il Good H 169:106-9+ O '69
TWINS (baseball) See Baseball clubs
TWISS, Cherry
Extra dry bikini straight up. Holiday 45:50-3 F '69
TWISS, John R. jr
Antarctic sub-ice observation. Sea Front 15:108-11 Mr '69
TWO-barrel carburetors. See Carburetors
2,4-D. See Herbicides
2,4,5-T. See Herbicides
TWO separate people; story. See Murray, B. J.
TWO thousand (year)
Church in the year 2000; Commonweal paper; symposium. Commonweal 91:116-60+ O 31 '69; Reply. W. H. Clark. 91:287+ N 28 '69
Educated man in the year 2000; address, November 15, 1968. P. C Ritterbush. Vital Speeches 35:295-300 Mr 1 '69
2000: a no-space odyssey; population estimates projected for Latin America. L. Olivos. bibliog il Américas 21:15-21 Ag '69
TWO ton albatross; story. See Anderson, W. C.
TWO-year colleges. See Junior colleges
TWOMEY, Katherine
Choice plants are worth buying. Horticulture 46:50+ D '68
TWOMEY, Louis
Of many things. C. J. McNaspy. America 121:342 O 25 '69
TYACK, David Bruce
Perils of pluralism: the background of the Pierce case. bibliog f Am Hist R 74:74-98 O '68
TYDINGS, Joseph Davies
Excerpt from address, April 25, 1969. Cong Digest 48:232+ O '69
Excerpt from address, July 10, 1969. Cong Digest 48:267+ N '69
Excerpt from statement, January 22, 1969. Cong Digest 48:112+ Ap '69
TYING of fruit trees. See Fruit trees, Care of
TYLER, Albert
Obituary
Science 163:424 Ja 31 '69. N. H. Horowitz and others
TYLER, Anne
Slipping-down life; story. Redbook 134:129-51 Ja '70
TYLER, Gus
Can anyone run a city? Sat R 52:22-5 N 8 '69
Electoral college. Commentary 47:24+ Mr '69
TYLER, Lina W.
City cares. Parks & Rec 4:30-1+ Jl '69
TYNAN, Kathleen
Great Kate. Vogue 153:86-9+ Ap 15 '69
TYNAN, Kenneth
London is still no. 1 (in theater, anyway) Holiday 46:74-7+ O '69
What, when, and where is sexy; interview, ed. by L. Lerman. por Mlle 69:76 Jl '69
TYNE, James L.
And after his own image; poem. Cath World 209:58 My '69
TYPE and type founding
Collecting wood type. R. R. Kelly. il Pub W 196:64-6 N 3 '69
Zapf on type design for today and tomorrow. H. Zapf. il Pub W 196:61-3 Ag 4 '69
See also
Printing—Legibility
TYPESETTING
Typesetting. G. O. Walter. il Sci Am 220:60-9 My '69
See also
Phototypesetting
TYPESETTING machines
See also
Computers—Printing applications
TYPEWRITERS
See also
SCM corporation
TYPEWRITING
Study and teaching
Go ahead, take that typing course. il Changing T 23:12 O '69
TYPHOID fever
Salmonella: food poison plus. A. S. Freese. Todays Health 47:34-5+ Ap '69

TYPHOON (ship) See Ships, Historic
TYPHOONS
Gales at sea. J. Parkinson, jr. il Yachting
125:57-9+ F '69
TYPING. See Typewriting
TYPOGRAPHY. See Printing
TYPOPHILES, The
Paul Bennett, private press keepsake. il Pub
W 195:72-4 Ap 7 '69
Typophiles and a keepsake. F. Johnson. il
Am Artist 33:66-9+ My '69
TYRANNY. See Dictatorship
TYRMAND, Leopold
Reflections (cont) New Yorker 45:40-2+ Ag
16 '69
TYROL
Tirol; Emperor Maximilian's stronghold of
chivalry. F. Spelman. il Travel & Camera
32:45-55+ Jl '69
TYROSINASE. See Oxidases
TYROSINE
Lysergic acid diethylamide: dissociation of
its behavioral and hyperthermic actions by
DL-α-methyl-p-tyrosine. A. Horita and A.
E. Hamilton. bibliog il Science 164:78-9 Ap
4 '69
Phenylalanine and tyrosine synthesis under
primitive earth conditions. N. Friedmann
and S. L. Miller. bibliog il Science 166:766-7
N 7 '69
TYROSINE aminotransferase. See Transferases
TYROSINE hydroxylase. See Hydroxylases
TYRRELL, George
George Tyrrell redivivus. America 121:82 Ag
16 '69; Reply. D. Hayne. 121:127 S 6 '69
TYTELL, John
Divinity in a pill. Cath World 208:278-9 Mr '69
TYTUS, Betty K.
For the love of Grace. Motor B 123:80-1+ Mr
'69
TZIMOULIS, Paul J.
What's down there, and where. Holiday 46:
24+ Ag '69

U

U-2 (airplane) See Airplanes, Military—United
States
UAW. See United automobile, aerospace and
agricultural implement workers of America
UCLA. See California. University—Los Angeles
campus
UCM. See University Christian movement
UE. See United electrical, radio and machine
workers of America
UFT. See United federation of teachers
UFWOC. See American federation of labor and
Congress of industrial organizations—
United farm workers organizing committee
UGFA. See United grain farmers of America
UHF television stations. See Television stations
UMC industries, incorporated
When a takeover runs out of gas. Bsns W
p32 O 4 '69
UMW. See United mine workers of America
UN. See United Nations
UNCTAD. See United Nations conference on
trade and development
UNCURK. See United Nations—Commission for
the unification and rehabilitation of Korea
UNICEF. See United Nations children's fund
UNIDO. See United Nations industrial devel-
opment organization
UNRWA. See United Nations relief and works
agency for Palestine refugees in the Near
East
UNTSO. See United Nations—Truce supervision
organization in Palestine
UPI. See United press international
URPE. See Union for radical political econom-
ics
URSI. See International scientific radio union
U.S. camera & travel (periodical)
Goodbye, hello! E. Hannigan. U S Camera
32:33+ Ja '69
USCC. See United States Catholic conference
USDA. See United States—Agriculture, Depart-
ment of

USGA. See United States golf association
USIA. See United States—Information agency
USLTA. See United States lawn tennis asso-
ciation
USM-IRA (USM corporation and IRA systems)
merger. See Business consolidations and
mergers
USNSA. See United States national student
association
USP (United States pharmacopoeia) See Phar-
macopeias
USPS. See United States power squadrons, in-
corporated
USS Liberty. See Warships—United States
USSA. See United States ski association
USSPA. See United States student press as-
sociation
USSR (Union of Soviet Socialist Republics)
See Russia
USW. See United steelworkers of America
UUA. See Unitarian universalist association
UBELL, Earl
Are estrogens really the answer to femi-
ninity? McCalls 96:42+ Jl '69
Cat-scratch-fever mystery. McCalls 97:93+ O
'69
Real truth behind the youth pill. McCalls
96:14+ Ag '69
UBERUAGA, Saxon White
Dawn in a mountain meadow; poem. Liv
Wildn 33:12 Spr '69
UDAIPUR, India
Palaces, people, and painted storks. A.
Kleihauer. Sr Schol 94:Schol Teach 15 Ap
25 '69
UDALL, Ermalee Webb
Washington wilderness. Redbook 132:80-1+
Mr '69
UDALL, Lee. See Udall, E. W.
UDALL, Morris King
Standing room only on spaceship earth. Read
Digest 95:131-5 D '69
UDALL, Stewart Lee
Tackling the environment. Time 93:18 F 7 '69
Udall's last laugh. New Repub 160:10 F 1 '69
Udall's last stand. Nation 208:164-5 F 10 '69
UDOM, E. U. Essien-. See Essien-Udom, E. U.
UELSMANN, Jerry
Gallery: photographs. Life 67:8-11 N 21 '69

about

SRO for Uelsmann, Davidson at S.F. museum
of art. M. Mann. Pop Phot 65:23-4+ S '69
UGANDA
See also
East African Federation (proposed)
Kampala

Industries

See also
Cattle industry and trade

Native races

Subsistence herding in Uganda. R. Dyson-
Hudson and N. Dyson-Hudson. il Sci Am
220:76-82+ bibliog (p 132) F '69

Politics and government

Shots above the music. Time 94:16 D 26
'69

Religious institutions and affairs

Uganda awaits the Pope. il Newsweek 74:67
Ag 4 '69
UGEL, Arthur R.
Keratohyalin: extraction and in vitro ag-
gregation. bibliog Science 166:250-1 O 10 '69
UGGAMS, Leslie
Leslie Uggams' secret. pors Harp Baz 102:
150-1 F '69
UGLINESS
See also
Aesthetics
UGLY (model agency) See Models (persons)
UHLAND, Hugo
Ivan and the sportfishermen. Motor B 124:
19-20+ D '69
UHSE, Beate
Supermarket for Eros. il por Time 93:90 My 2
'69
ULBRICHT, Walter
After Ulbricht? por Newsweek 74:36-8 Ag 25
'69
Behind the wall, the success story of Walter
Ulbricht? J. H. Huizinga. il por N Y Times
Mag p36-7+ S 7 '69
Fast drive to Bonn. Time 94:15 D 26 '69
German Democratic Republic and the West.
J. E. Smith. Yale R 58:372-87 Mr '69
Making the best of a bad situation. il por
Time 94:42 O 17 '69
Tight leash on Ulbricht? por U S News 66:
20 Mr 17 '69

ULBRICHT, Walter—*Continued*
Walter Ulbricht: the unsinkable satrap. J. P. O'Donnell. por Read Digest 94:115-19 Mr '69
Why Communists get tough over Berlin. il U S News 66:25-6 Mr 3 '69
Willy vs. Walter. Newsweek 75:24 Ja 5 '70
ULCERS
How to handle the job hazard of ulcers. Bsns W p 147 O 11 '69
What are your chances of getting an ulcer? G. M. Knox. Bet Hom & Gard 47:12+ O '69
ULETT, Judith A. and Itil, T. M.
Quantitative electroencephalogram in smoking and smoking deprivation. bibliog Science 164:969-70 My 23 '69
ULFFERS, Dirk
Metering through the lens; interview, ed. by B. Schwalberg. Pop Phot 65:104+ Ag '69
ULLMAN, Joseph C.
Helping workers locate jobs following a plant shutdown. bibliog Mo Labor R 92:35-40 Ap '69
ULLMAN, Leslie
Journey; poem. Mlle 69:300 Ag '69
ULLMANN, Bill
Gifts for that special man. Good H 168:152 Mr '69
Gifts he'll go for. Good H 169:142-3 D '69
Host of gifts for Father's day. Good H 168: 121-3 Je '69
Memo on menswear. Good H 169:170 Ag '69
New shapes in men's shirts. Good H 169:168 N '69
ULMER, Melville J.
Excerpt from The elementary errors of tax-sharing; reprint. Cong Digest 48:245+ O '69
ULMUS. See Elm
ULPH, Owen
Maverick. Am West 6:44-8+ My '69
ULRICH, Heinz
How not to overpay your income taxes. Mech Illus 65:56-7 Mr '69
ULRICH, Torben
Not-so-melancholy Dane. M. Kram. pors Sports Illus 30:78-80+ Ap 7 '69
ULSTER
Ireland's niggers; with interview with B. Devlin. P. Buckman. Ramp Mag 8:19-22 Jl '69
See also
Northern Ireland
ULTRA-HIGH frequency television stations. See Television stations
ULTRAMICROFICHE. See Microforms
ULTRAMINIATURE cameras. See Cameras
ULTRASONIC burglar alarms. See Burglar alarms
ULTRASONIC cleaning
Cleaning with sound. S. Schuler. il Am Home 72:62+ O '69
Ultrasonic cleaner: some help. Some cost! il Consumer Rep 34:561-2 O '69
ULTRASONIC waves
New acoustic devices developed for radar: microsound components based on ultrasonic surface wave propagation. B. M. Elson. il Aviation W 90:85-8+ My 5 '69
Remarkable science of silent sound. il Changing T 23:21-3 Ag '69
Ultrasonic waves made visible. M. S. Snitzer. il Electr World 81:51 My '69

Medical applications
Lecithin aerosols generated ultrasonically above 25°C. E. W. Merrill and others. bibliog Science 164:1167-8 Je 6 '69
Measuring eyes with sound waves. S. V. Jones. il Sci Digest 66:91 O '69
See also
Eye—Surgery
ULTRASONICS
See also
Ultrasonic waves
ULTRAVIOLET rays
Ultraviolet astronomy. L. Goldberg. il Sci Am 220:92-10 bibliog(p 144) Je '69
Ultraviolet radiation evaluated as igniter: studies by Air force office of scientific research. M. L. Yaffee. Aviation W 90:59-60 F 3 '69
Ultraviolet video-viewing: the television camera as an insect eye. T. Eisner and others. il Science 166:1172-4 N 28 '69
See also
Spectrum, Ultraviolet

Physiological effects
On getting a suntan. il Chem 42:5 Mr '69
ULU MAU village. See Villages, Restored
UMBACH, Kurt
136 lawns to Brazil. Seventeen 28:30 Ja '69

UMBRELLA insurance policies. See Insurance—Policies
UMBRELLAS
How to buy and care for the new fabric awnings & umbrellas. il Good H 168:142+ Je '69
UMPIRES (sports)
Squeeze play. il Time 94:61 Ag 15 '69
UN-AMERICAN activities. See Subversive activities
UN-AMERICAN activities committee. See United States—Congress—House of representatives—Internal security. Committee on
UNANIMOUS decision; story. See Beebe, L. C.
UNAUTHORIZED reprints. See Copyright—Unauthorized reprints
UNCITRAL. See United Nations—Commission on international trade law
UNCLE Vanya; drama. See Chekhov, A. P.
UNDERACHIEVEMENT, Student. See Underachievers
UNDERACHIEVERS
Help for hang-ups; Alhambra and Tempe school districts, Ariz. J. Stocker. il Am Ed 5:5-8 Je '69
Right to fail. F. E. Flint. Todays Ed 58:39-40 Ap '69
Underachievers measure up. B. Lewis. il Am Ed 5:27-8 F '69
UNDERDEVELOPED areas
Choice of technology in less developed countries; excerpt from address. N. Kaldor. Mo Labor R 92:50-3 Ag '69
From dichotomy to integration. H. Camara. Chr Cent 86:1574-7 D 10 '69
Poverty as underdevelopment. P. L. Van Den Berghe. Trans-Action 6:3-4+ Jl '69
Underdevelopment. R. L. Heilbroner. il New Repub 162:26+ Ja 3 '70
What strategy for the third world? manufacturing enterprises of U.S. investors. R. Vernon. il Sat R 52:42-6 N 22 '69
See also
Agriculture—Underdeveloped areas
Atomic power—Underdeveloped areas
Birth control—Underdeveloped areas
Community development
Conservation of resources—Underdeveloped areas
Economic assistance in underdeveloped areas
Education—Underdeveloped areas
Investments, Foreign (in underdeveloped areas)
Research—Underdeveloped areas
States, New
United Nations—Panel on foreign investment in developing countries
United States—Foreign relations—Underdeveloped areas
UNDERGROUND atomic testing. See Atomic bombs—Testing, Underground
UNDERGROUND church. See Catholic church; Church
UNDERGROUND cities and towns. See Cities and towns, Underground
UNDERGROUND drainage. See Drainage
UNDERGROUND films. See Moving pictures, Experimental
UNDERGROUND literature
Underground press; Russian underground political documents and memoirs released by K. van het Reve. Newsweek 75:31 Ja 12 '70
UNDERGROUND power distribution. See Electric currents—Grounding
UNDERGROUND press. See Newspapers; Newspapers—United States; Underground literature
UNDERGROUND press, Student. See College and school journalism
UNDERGROUND radio. See Radio communication, Underground
UNDERGROUND radio communication. See Radio communication, Underground
UNDERGROUND tillage. See Tillage
UNDERNUTRITION. See Nutrition problems
UNDERPRIVILEGED children. See Socially handicapped children
UNDERSEA research vehicles. See Submarine research vehicles
UNDERSIGNED, Leon & Bébert; story. See Connell, E. S. jr
UNDERWATER archeology. See Archeology, Submarine
UNDERWATER bulldozer. See Bulldozers (machines)
UNDERWATER cameras. See Cameras
UNDERWATER drilling
Challenger extended. il Sci N 96:394-5 N 1 '69
Deep sea drilling project; AAAS symposium, December 28, 1969. M. N. A. Peterson. il Science 166:1311 D 5 '69

UNDERWATER drilling—*Continued*
Drilling and coring the deep-sea floor; report of meeting. C. L. Drake. Science 163:596-7 F 7 '69; Reply. J. Kane and others. 165:204 Jl 11 '69
Equatorial current history; Challenger: leg 8. Sci N 96:590 D 27 '69
New time machine; Glomar Challenger on JOIDES expedition. il Sci Digest 65:37-41 Ap '69
Working the Glomar Challenger. W. B. Charm. il Sea Front 15:258-67 S '69
    See also
Gold mines and mining, Submarine
UNDERWATER electric tools. See Electric tools
UNDERWATER exercises. See Exercise
UNDERWATER exploration
Down into the sea in ships; exploring in Deepstar. R. S. Dietz and R. F. Dill. il Sea Front 15:2-9 Ja '69
Drifters: journey of the Ben Franklin. il Newsweek 74:48 S 1 '69
Priceless relics of the Spanish Armada; fate of the Girona. R. Sténuit. il Nat Geog 135:745-77 Je '69
UNDERWATER explorers club, Freeport, Grand Bahama. See Skin diving—Study and training
UNDERWATER laboratories
Death at 100 fathoms; setback for Sealab 3. il Newsweek 73:56 Mr 3 '69
Death disrupts ocean project; Sealab 3. il Sr Schol 94:17 Mr 7 '69
Death in the depths; setback for the Sealab project. il Time 93:59 F 28 '69
Longest dive; Project Tektite; with photographs by S. Wayman. Life 66:30-5 Mr 7 '69
Outer space, wet space. I. Asimov. Seventeen 29:82-3+ Ja '70
Science from a habitat: Tektite II. Sci N 96:423 N 8 '69
Second is first; Sealab and Tektite. il Sci N 95:161-2 F 15 '69
Tektite, a study of human behavior in a hostile environment; AAAS symposium, December 27, 1969. S. Deutsch. il Science 165:1276-7 S 19 '69
Tektite I: who can use it? letter. R. P. Higgins. Science 163:1009 Mr 7 '69
Tektite revisited. S. M. Spencer. il Pop Sci 195:84-7+ N '69
Tektite, two months beneath the sea. R. J. Pothier. il Sea Front 15:130-9 My '69
Undersea frontier tests man's resilience; Sealab III. il Bsns W p96-8 Mr 1 '69
Undersea future? Tektite 1. il Sr Schol 94:19-20 My 2 '69
UNDERWATER moving picture photography. See Moving picture photography, Submarine
UNDERWATER oil well drilling. See Oil well drilling, Submarine
UNDERWATER photography. See Moving picture photography, Submarine; Photography, Submarine
UNDERWATER research. See Oceanographic research
UNDERWATER structures
Antarctic sub-ice observation; stationary manned submersible. J. R. Twiss, jr. il Sea Front 15:108-11 Mr '69
Going below for repairs; underwater Habitat. il Bsns W p 133 O 25 '69
Sea, a challenge for materials. D. Groves. il Sea Front 15:356-63 N '69
UNDERWATER swimming. See Skin diving
UNDERWATER treasure. See Treasure trove
UNDERWEAR
Men's undershirts. il Consumer Bul 52:17-20 S '69
Take a fashion lesson: current looks with the right undercoverage. il Seventeen 28:358 Ag '69
What's new in lingerie? il Good H 169:130 Jl '69
    See also
Brassieres
UNDERWOOD, James M.
How to serve on a hospital board. Harvard Bsns R 47:73-80 Jl '69
UNDERWRITING. See Securities
UNEMPLOYABLES
Hard core experiment; physiological characteristics revealed. Trans-Action 6:11 Je '69

Training
Hard-core program will widen its base; NAB Jobs '70 program. Bsns W p41 N 15 '69

Hard sell push for hard-core hiring; Jobs-70. Bsns W p36 S 27 '69
How to hire the hard-core; NAB program. il Newsweek 74:65-6 S 8 '69
Industry learns to train the hardcore. R. K. Peterson and B. B. Rash. Ed Digest 35:35-7 O '69
UNEMPLOYMENT
Foreign labor briefs. See issues of Monthly labor review
    See also
Employment

Relief measures
Business involvement; hire first, train afterwards: address, April 11, 1969. D. M. Kendall. Vital Speeches 35:535-7 Je 15 '69
Evaluating public expenditures under conditions of unemployment; excerpt from address. R. H. Haveman. il Mo Labor R 92:30-3 S '69
How to hire the hard-core; NAB program. il Newsweek 74:65-6 S 8 '69
NAB's problem: fight inflation but give jobs. B. L. Masse. America 120:520 My 3 '69
Nixon's job-training plan; how it will work. il U S News 67:62-3 Ag 25 '69
Unemployment or exile; is there a third choice for the migrant worker? S. Parmar. il UNESCO Courier 22:32-4 Jl '69
World employment programme; ILO announcement. D. A. Morse. il UNESCO Courier 22:8-12 Jl '69
    See also
Anti-poverty program, 1964-1969
Socially handicapped—Employment
United States—Job corps

Statistics
Employment developments in urban poverty neighborhoods. P. M. Ryscavage. bibliog il Mo Labor R 92:51-6 Je '69
Inflation curb, job cut, where the blow will fall. il U S News 66:74-5 F 17 '69
Job losers, leavers, and entrants, a report on the unemployed. K. D. Hoyle. il Mo Labor R 92:24-9 Ap '69
Men in poverty neighborhoods; a status report; with charts. H. M. Willacy. bibliog f Mo Labor R 92:23-7 F '69
Things the jobless totals don't tell. il U S News 67:74 D 22 '69
Work experience of the population: spotlight on women and youths. F. A. Bogan. il Mo Labor R 92:44-50 Je '69

India
Using what's available; oversupply of engineers and scientists. S. K. Ghaswala. il Sci N 96:314 O 4 '69

United States
Business cycle in a changing world, by A. F. Burns. Review
    New Repub 161:28-9 O 18 '69. A. Campbell
Danger: men out of work. il Nations Bsns 57:110 S '69
Fewer jobs: who will be hurt. il U S News 67:46-7 O 27 '69
4 per cent unemployment threatens tax bill. Bsns W p43 O 11 '69
GOP is thrown a price-job curve; Phillips curve. il Bsns W p60+ Mr 22 '69
Inflation or unemployment? F. Morley. Nations Bsns 57:25-6 Ap '69
Is jobless rate a valid barometer? il Bsns W p33-4 D 13 '69
Job drop and more predicted. U S News 67:86 O 20 '69
Joblessness: when bad news is good. il Newsweek 74:89 O 20 '69
Measuring unemployment and subemployment in the Mississippi Delta. R. A White. il Mo Labor R 92:17-23 Ap '69
Not working: who and why. U S News 67:71 Ag 4 '69
Oversupply of the young. H. Folk. il Trans-Action 6:27-32 S '69
Politics of full employment. A. Altshuler. il Trans-Action 6:43-7 My '69
Report on the jobless; who and where they are. il U S News 66:109-10 My 19 '69
Rising worry about the will to work. il Time 94:96 O 17 '69
Things the jobless totals don't tell. il U S News 67:74 D 22 '69
Unemployment figures. M. Friedman. Newsweek 74:101 O 20 '69
Where are the new unemployed? il Bsns W p37-8 O 18 '69
Why one expert sees no big rise in layoffs when economy cools; excerpts from report. E. Clague. il U S News 67:69-70 Ag 4 '69
    See also
Labor supply—United States
Unemployment—Relief measures

UNEMPLOYMENT, Technological
Automation: measuring its social costs; views presented at International conference on technological change and human development, with introd. N. Kaldor; K. B. Clark. Mo Labor R 92:48-56 Ag '69
Evolution of private manpower planning in Armour's plant closings. J. L. Stern. bibliog il Mo Labor R 92:21-8 D '69
Helping workers locate jobs following a plant shutdown. J. C. Ullman. bibliog Mo Labor R 92:35-40 Ap '69
How mechanization of harvesting is affecting jobs. L. J. Fulco. bibliog f il Mo Labor R 92:26-32 Mr '69
Social costs of automation. Bsns W p98 My 3 '69

UNEMPLOYMENT benefits, Supplemental. See Supplemental unemployment benefits

UNEMPLOYMENT compensation. See Insurance, Unemployment

UNEMPLOYMENT insurance. See Insurance, Unemployment

UNESCO
Interpreting Unesco to Americans. W. W. Brickman. Sch & Soc 97:202-3 Ap '69
Miss Gore named U.S. member of executive board of UNESCO. Dept State Bul 61:343 O 20 '69
Nongovernmental organizations and Unesco. Sch & Soc 97:62 Ja '69
Peru: the future of the Inca empire. C. Cutler. il Art in Am 57:80-2 My '69
700 million forgotten minds: reprint. R. Maheu. il UNESCO Courier 22:36-7 Ag '69
Unesco's programme for 1969-1970. UNESCO Courier 22:41 Ja '69
Youth in ferment. il UNESCO Courier 22:4-14 Ap '69
    See also
International conference on public education

    Publications
Arts and man; new book. D. Hayman. il UNESCO Courier 22:4-10+ My '69
Unesco's new educational review; Prospects in education. Sch & Soc 97:477 D '69
    See also
Unesco Courier

UNESCO Courier
Twenty-one year anthology. UNESCO Courier 22:4-79 Ag '69

UNFAIR competition. See Competition, Unfair

UNFAIR labor practices. See Industrial relations

UNGAR, Georges
Chemical transfer of learning? ed. by B. M. Murray. Todays Ed 58:44-7 F '69

UNGARO DE FOX, Lucia
Era of the dandy. Américas 21:29-33 My '69
Tapada. Américas 21:2-7 Ja '69

UNGEHEUER, Friedel
France: a struggle against the second-rate. Harper 239:122-8 D '69

UNGERER, Tomi
Visit with Tomi Ungerer. J. H. Michel. il por Am Artist 33:40-5+ My '69

UNGRADED classes
Last look at the little red schoolhouse; Calaboose, Ky. B. Ryan, jr. il Parents Mag 44:54-6 F '69
Maxi learning from mini courses; Wilson high school, Portland, Ore. W. Reed. il Sr Schol 94:Schol Teach 10+ Mr 7 '69

UNICELLULAR organisms
Chromosome number of a small protist: accurate determination. P. B. Moens and F. O. Perkins. bibliog il Science 166:1289-91 D 5 '69

UNICORNS
Sea unicorn; narwhal. F. Bruemmer. il Audubon 71:58-63 N '69

UNIDENTIFIED flying objects. See Flying saucers

UNIFICATION of Germany, Proposed. See Germany—Union (proposed)

UNIFORM consumer credit code. See Consumer credit—Laws and legislation

UNIFORM state laws
Let the dead help the living; proposed uniform anatomical gift act. R. S. Fisher. Todays Health 47:88+ Ap '69
Making transplants easier; legislation based on Uniform anatomical gift act. Time 93:61+ Ap 25 '69

UNIFORMS, Police
Out of the blue. il Newsweek 74:79 S 29 '69

UNION agreements. See Trade agreements

UNION camp corporation
Tree is a tree? il Forbes 103:42 F 15 '69

UNION carbide corporation
Making staff consulting more effective. J. K. Baker and R. H. Schaffer. Harvard Bsns R 47:62-71 Ja '69

UNION for radical political economics
Stirrings from the new left. Time 95:66 Ja 12 '70

UNION leader (Manchester) See Manchester union leader

UNION membership. See Trade unions—Membership

UNION miniere. See Mining industry and finance—Belgium

UNION of Soviet Socialist Republics. See Russia

UNION oil company of California
Another oil slick; Santa Barbara subject to new onslaught. Newsweek 73:37 F 24 '69
Big oil leak leaves a messy legal residue; Santa Barbara slick. il Bsns W p30-2 F 15 '69
Case of the oily waters; leaking oil well off the southern California coast. il Sr Schol 94:21-2 F 28 '69
Environment: tragedy in oil; leak at Union oil platform in Santa Barbara Channel. il Time 93:23-5 F 14 '69
Fighting the oil on California's troubled waters. il Bsns W p60-1 F 8 '69
GOO story. Newsweek 73:60 Je 16 '69
Maybe a few nuts; testimony on Santa Barbara pollution. New Repub 160:8-9 F 22 '69
Runaway oil well: will it mean new rules in offshore drilling? Santa Barbara incident. il U S News 66:14 F 17 '69
Santa Barbara: oil in the velvet playground. H. Molotch. il Ramp Mag 8:43-51 N '69

UNION Pacific railroad company
Iron spine; the Union Pacific met the Central Pacific at Promontory. H. Sturgis. il Am Heritage 20:46-57+ Ap '69
Pacific railroad centennial; the transcontinental railroad; symposium. il Am West 6:4-32+ My '69
Union Pacific what? Forbes 104:32-3 N 1 '69
    See also
Golden Spike national historic site

UNION tank car company. See Trans Union corporation

UNION theological seminary, New York
Union seminary: an ethical dilemma. Chr Today 13:27 Je 6 '69
Union seminary and student power. T. Early. Chr Cent 86:1024+ Jl 30 '69

UNION wide collective bargaining. See Collective bargaining, Industry wide

UNIONS, Teachers. See Teachers unions

UNIONS, Trade. See Trade unions

UNIT construction
    See also
Buildings, Prefabricated

UNITARIAN universalist association
Confrontations beset U.U.A. assembly. H. A. Jack. Chr Cent 86:1145-6 S 3 '69
Unitarian universalist portfolio challenged. H. A. Jack. Chr Cent 86:694-6 My 14 '69
White church and black business. N. Thomas. Commonweal 90:503-4 Ag 22 '69

UNITARIANS
Discrimination Canadian style; William Petty's refusal to print Unitarian magazine. W. Fitch. Chr Today 13:71 S 26 '69

UNITED air lines
Lower United air lines net follows industry pattern. Aviation W 90:39 Mr 17 '69
Refrigerated igloos studied by United on Hawaii flights. Aviation W 91:33 S 29 '69
Third man in 737 cockpit costing United $5 million. N. S. Himmel. Aviation W 90:32 Mr 17 '69
United gears for industry shifts. H. D. Watkins. il Aviation W 91:29-31 D 15 '69
United plan to lease 23 jet transports approved by CAB. Aviation W 90:73 My 12 '69
United planning use of Carousel on Hawaii jets. Aviation W 91:43 S 15 '69

UNITED aircraft corporation
Record year for UAC. Aviation W 90:19 F 17 '69
United aircraft deliveries slip in quarter; profit up. Aviation W 90:36 My 12 '69
United aircraft six-month net, sales decline. Aviation W 91:28 Ag 18 '69

UNITED ARAB REPUBLIC
United Arab Republic. H. N. Howard. Cur Hist 58:8-12+ Ja '70
    See also
Natural resources—United Arab Republic

UNITED ARAB REPUBLIC—*Continued*

Economic conditions

United Arab Republic. J. S. Haupert. bibliog il Focus 19:1-8 Mr '69

UNITED automobile, aerospace and agricultural implement workers of America

AFL-CIO weathers the loss; withdrawal of UAW from federation. Bsns W p77 My 31 '69

Blue-collar war of words heats up; 40,000-word white paper details the events leading to the UAW's disaffiliation from the AFL-CIO. il Bsns W p76+ Ap 12 '69

Dodge rebellion. Ramp Mag 7:12 N 30 '68

Ford rejects layoff policy. U S News 66: 66 Ap 28 '69

How the hard core can survive layoffs; UAW's inverted seniority plan. il Bsns W p82+ Mr 29 '69

Meany & Reuther: labor's main bout. B. J. Je 6 '69

Mr Clean and the outcast. il Time 93:104 Widick. Nation 208:601-2 My 12 '69

Union disciplinary power upheld; Supreme court decision. U S News 66:85-6 Ap 14 '69

UAW rebuffs black extremists; League of revolutionary black workers. America 120: 346 Mr 29 '69

Who started the spiral spinning? il Bsns W p 13-14 Ja 3 '70

See also
Alliance for labor action

UNITED Bible societies. See Bible societies

UNITED brotherhood of carpenters and joiners of America

Prefab precedent; carpenters sign agreement to produce factory-built housing units. Bsns W p48 Je 21 '69

UNITED church of Canada

Canadian churchmen condemn missile defense system. Chr Cent 86:640 My 7 '69

Quebec: French fact faced; 45th annual session. Chr Cent 86:932+ Jl 9 '69

UNITED church of Christ

Black threats move United church of Christ. J. Huffman. Chr Today 13:36 Jl 18 '69

Confrontations beset U.U.A. assembly. H. A. Jack. Chr Cent 86:1145-6 S 3 '69

United church of Christ general synod. T. A. Braun. Chr Cent 86:1000-2 Jl 23 '69

UNITED electrical, radio and machine workers of America

Rival unions talk unity. Bsns W p80 F 8 '69

UNITED farm workers organizing committee. See American federation of labor and Congress of industrial organizations—United farm workers organizing committee

UNITED federation of teachers

Full and sometimes very surprising story of Ocean Hill, the teachers' union and the teacher strikes of 1968; excerpts from The teachers strike: New York, 1968. M. Mayer. il N Y Times Mag p 18-23+ F 2 '69

McGeorge Bundy confronts the teachers; decentralization of New York schools. R. Armstrong. il N Y Times Mag p25-7+ Ap 20 '69

Teachers of library unite! letter to the editor. Library J 94:2537-8 Jl '69

UNITED fruit company

How United fruit was plucked. il Bsns W p 122-4 F 22 '69

United fruit's shotgun marriage. S. H. Brown. il Fortune 79:132-4+ Ap '69

UNITED fund

No fun for funds. Newsweek 74:60+ D 22 '69

UNITED grain farmers of America

Tractor march on Washington? B. Coffman. il Farm J 93:26 Ag '69

What those tractor marchers did in Washington. B. Coffman and J. Carlson. il Farm J 93:30+ S '69

UNITED KINGDOM atomic energy authority. See Great Britain—Atomic energy authority

UNITED Methodist church

Growing crisis in the churches; report on black power. U S News 67:8 D 8 '69

Methodists, Brethren, F.O.R. rebuke the Vice-President; muzzling of the media by government. Chr Cent 86:1541 D 3 '69

Wesley's faith rides again. J. S. Tinney. Chr Today 13:40-1 F 14 '69

Board of missions

On Dow and calico. B. Thompson. Chr Cent 86:1571-2 D 10 '69

UNITED mine workers of America

Black lung rebellion. R. G. Sherrill. il Nation 208:529-35 Ap 28 '69

Challenger's round. Time 94:70-1 Ag 22 '69

Coal mining; the union. A. B. Hume. Atlan 224:22+ N '69

Deadly venom; murder of Yablonski family. Time 95:19-20 Ja 19 '70

Death of a rebel; J. A. Yablonski. il Newsweek 75:22 Ja 19 '70

In the wake of John L. Lewis. J. Hill. Commonweal 90:430-1 Jl 11 '69

John L. wins again; W. A. Boyle wins presidency. Newsweek 74:76+ D 22 '69

Leadership fight looms among miners; election contest between Joseph Yablonski and W. A. Boyle for UMW presidency. Bsns W p 122 Je 7 '69

Lewis heir faces revolt. il Bsns W p 110+ N 15 '69

Mine-union battle; just beginning? U S News 67:79 D 22 '69

Mine workers: can they survive reform? Bsns W p32 D 20 '69

Mine workers' revolt. il Newsweek 73:74 Je 16 '69

Miners play rough: electing a union president. E. Cox. New Repub 161:13-14 Ag 2 '69

Pay padding an issue in mine vote. U S News 67:102 D 15 '69

Shades of John L; presidential battle. il Newsweek 74:83-4+ D 15 '69

Underground revolt. Time 93:92 Ap 18 '69

UMW battle heats up. il Bsns W p51 My 10 '69

Yablonski's death stirs up miners. il Bsns W p35 Ja 10 '70

District 50

UMWs family fight moves to courtroom; feud between mine workers and District 50. il Bsns W p96 My 3 '69

UNITED NATIONS

Angie Brooks; UN's madame president. il Ebony 25:27-30+ Ja '70

Ecology of hunger. J. McLaughlin. America 121:414-17 N 8 '69

Introduction to the annual report of the Secretary-General on the work of the organization; major issues confronting the organization. Thant. UN Mo Chron 6:67-113 O '69

Melancholy rituals. R. J. Walton. il Nation 209:440-3+ O 27 '69

More about the shape of the table. N. Cousins. Sat R 52:20 Ja 25 '69

Notes of the month. See issues of UN monthly chronicle

Occasion; silver jubilee; interview. R. M. Akwei. New Yorker 45:27-8 Ap 5 '69

Peace and palaces. A. H. Sypher. Nations Bsns 57:29-30 F '69

Pinch of SALT at the UN. B. Pilkington. Commonweal 91:396-7 Ja 9 '70

Secretary-General's press conference; April 17, 1969. Thant. UN Mo Chron 6:73-83 My '69

Twenty-fifth anniversary of the United Nations; statement, October 23, 1969, with text of resolution. C. W. Yost. Dept State Bul 61:485-91 D 1 '69

United Nations: alive and useful; address, September 25, 1969. S. DePalma. Dept State Bul 61:336-8 O 20 '69

United Nations and the cause of peace; address, March 18, 1969. C. W. Yost. Dept State Bul 60:325-9 Ap 14 '69

U.N: experts' report on CBW supports disarmament effort. E. Langer. Science 165: 163-4 Jl 11 '69

United Nations: its past and its future; address, May 26, 1969. C. W. Yost. Dept State Bul 60:564-8 Je 30 '69

United Nations: up, down, or sideways? address, May 12, 1969. S. DePalma. Dept State Bul 60:493-6 Je 9 '69

View from the bridge; address, April 25, 1969. Thant. UN Mo Chron 6:58-64 My '69

What the United Nations means to America now; address, October 13, 1969. S. De Palma. Dept State Bul 61:374-7 N 3 '69

World peace: the United Nations; address, January 29, 1969. A. Cranston. Vital Speeches 35:358-60 Ap 1 '69

Youth-related activities of the United Nations; statement, September 30, 1969. S. Temple. Dept State Bul 61:380-2 N 3 '69

See also
Food and agriculture organization of the United Nations

International convention on the elimination of all forms of racial discrimination

International court of justice, The Hague

United Nations—Non-governmental organizations

UNITED NATIONS—*Continued*

Advisory committee on the application of science and technology to development

Advisory committee holds eleventh session. UN Mo Chron 6:48-50 My '69
Protein problem and national development; statement, November 20, 1968. A. E. Goldschmidt. Dept State Bul 59:673-7 D 23 '68

Armed forces

For a UN peace force. America 120:554 My 10 '69

Forces in Cyprus

Security council extends stationing of Peace force; with text of resolution. UN Mo Chron 6:20-4 Ja '69
Security council extends stationing of UNFICYP; with text of resolution. UN Mo Chron 6:3-10 Jl '69
U.N. force in Cyprus extended through December 1969; statement, June 10, 1969. Dept State Bul 60:574-5 Je 30 '69

Assembly

See United Nations—General assembly

Budget

See United Nations—Finance

Capital development fund

Third pledging conference for Capital development fund. UN Mo Chron 6:72-3 N '69

Commission for the unification and rehabilitation of Korea

Assembly extends UNCURK mandate; with text of resolution. UN Mo Chron 6:71-9 Ja '69
Signals from North Korea. B. Page. Nation 208:622-4 My 19 '69
U.N. calls upon UNCURK to continue pursuit of U.N objectives in Korea; statements, December 11, and 20, 1968; with text of resolution. S. Symington; J. R. Wiggins. Dept State Bul 60:32-8 Ja 13 '69

Commission on human rights

Commission begins twenty-fifth session. UN Mo Chron 6:27-34 Mr '69
Commission concludes twenty-fifth session. UN Mo Chron 6:67-76 Ap '69
Filed and forgotten; appeal by Soviet intellectuals and citizens. New Repub 161:8 Jl 26 '69
Periodic reports on human rights; Ad hoc committee meets. UN Mo Chron 6:26 F '69
Report adopted. UN Mo Chron 6:51-3 My '69
See also
United Nations—Sub-commission on prevention of discrimination and protection of minorities

Commission on international trade law

Assembly adopts legal resolutions. UN Mo Chron 6:103-4 D '69
Commission on international trade law; General assembly resolution. UN Mo Chron 6:151-2 Ja '69
Concludes second session. UN Mo Chron 6:81-5 Ap '69
Sixth committee recommendations. UN Mo Chron 6:82 N '69

Commission on narcotic drugs

Narcotic drugs commission holds twenty-third session. UN Mo Chron 6:28-31 F '69

Commission on social development

Concludes twentieth session. UN Mo Chron 6:76-8 Ap '69
Opens twentieth session. UN Mo Chron 6:37-40 Mr '69
Report on youth and national development. UN Mo Chron 6:40 Mr '69

Commission on the status of women

Status of women commission opens twenty-second session. UN Mo Chron 6:26-8 F '69
Twenty-second session ends. UN Mo Chron 6:34-7 Mr '69

Committee for development planning

Development planning; concluded its fifth session. UN Mo Chron 6:45-6 Je '69

Committee of twenty-four

See United Nations—Special committee on the situation with regard to implementation of declaration on granting of independence to colonial countries and peoples

Committee on disarmament

See United Nations—Eighteen-nation committee on disarmament

Committee on invisibles and financing relating to trade

See United Nations conference on trade and development

Committee on the peaceful uses of outer space

Expanded role in space sought for U.N. R. S. Kahn. Aviation W 90:57+ My 26 '69
Flight of Apollo 11; statement, September 8, 1969. T. O. Paine. Dept State Bul 61:309-11 O 6 '69
International cooperation in peaceful uses of outer space; statement, December 18, 1968. J. R. Wiggins. Dept State Bul 60:84-7 Ja 27 '69
Meeting of group on direct broadcast satellites. UN Mo Chron 6:7-9 Mr '69
Peaceful uses of outer space: committee adopts interim report. UN Mo Chron 6:43-5 O '69
Peaceful uses of outer space; legal sub-committee concludes session. UN Mo Chron 6:123-6 Ag '69
Scientific and technical sub-committee. UN Mo Chron 6:56-8 Ap '69
U.N. sees direct satellite TV in 1970s: findings of Working group on direct broadcast satellites. R. S. Kahn il Aviation W 90:63+ My 5 '69
U.S. urges U.N. outer space committee action on liability convention; statement, September 9, 1969. P. S. Thacher. Dept State Bul 61:340-2 O 20 '69

Committee on the peaceful uses of the seabed and the ocean floor

August session of U.N. seabed committee held at New York; statements, August 11, 15, 20 and 29, 1969. C. H. Phillips; V. E. McKelvey. Dept State Bul 61:285-94 S 29 '69
Committee holds second session. UN Mo Chron 6:53-6 Ap '69
Committee on peaceful uses of the sea-bed; special session held. UN Mo Chron 6:78-80 D '69
Peaceful uses of the sea-bed; committee concludes general debate UN Mo Chron 6:60-6 D '69
Peaceful uses of the sea-bed; committee concludes third session. UN Mo Chron 6:126-8 Ag '69
Standing committee holds first session. UN Mo Chron 6:9-10 Mr '69
U.N. seabed committee concludes spring session; statement, March 28, 1969. D. H. Popper. Dept State Bul 60:342-5 Ap 21 '69

Committee on the question of defining aggression

See United Nations—Special committee on the question of defining aggression

Committee on the right of everyone to be free from arbitrary arrest, detention, and exile

Committee on right of freedom from arbitrary arrest. UN Mo Chron 6:25 F '69

Committee on trust and non-self-governing territories

See United Nations—Trusteeship committee

Conference on the exploration and peaceful uses of outer space

Peaceful use of outer space; General assembly commends results; with text of resolutions. UN Mo Chron 6:62-71 Ja '69

Development program

Approves fifty-two new projects. UN Mo Chron 6:76-81 Jl '69
Approves record number of pre-investment projects. UN Mo Chron 6:11-18 F '69
Decade of development and disarmament; 1969 report. America 121:255 O 4 '69
Social aspects of development; 1967 report on the world social situation; statement, November 13, 1968. J. Picker. Dept State Bul 59:716-19 D 30 '68
UNDP pledging conference. UN Mo Chron 6:71-2 N '69

Economic and financial committee

General assembly action on preferences. UN Mo Chron 6:82-9 D '69
Second committee; preparations for the Second United Nations development decade. UN Mo Chron 6:64-70 N '69

UNITED NATIONS—*Continued*

Economic and social council

Committee on non-governmental organizations: continues review of NGOs in consultative status. UN Mo Chron 6:40-1 Mr '69

Concludes forty-sixth session. UN Mo Chron 6:68-76 Jl '69

Economic and social council concludes meetings of forty-fifth session. UN Mo Chron 6:118-21 Ja '69

Kremlin boycotts UN development. America 120:263-4 Mr 8 '69

Opens forty-sixth session. UN Mo Chron 6:37-9 Je '69

See also

United Nations—Commission on social development

Meetings, 1969

Forty-seventh session. UN Mo Chron 6:89-90 D '69

Holds forty-seventh session. UN Mo Chron 6:134-42 Ag '69

Economic commission for Africa

Ninth session marks tenth anniversary. UN Mo Chron 6:22-5 Mr '69

President hails tenth anniversary of Economic commission for Africa; text of message, February 3, 1969. R. M. Nixon. Dept State Bul 60:211 Mr 10 '69

United States and the challenge of Africa's development; statement, February 6, 1969. W. A. Nielsen. Dept State Bul 60:292-4 Ap 7 '69

Economic commission for Asia and the Far East

Boost for a vast project to develop the Mekong basin. il U S News 67:40-1 Jl 28 '69

Holds twenty-fifth session. UN Mo Chron 6:39-42 My '69

Muddied Mekong. il Time 94:50-1 D 26 '69

Economic commission for Europe

Holds twenty-fourth session. UN Mo Chron 6:42-5 My '69

Inland transport committee holds twenty-eighth session. UN Mo Chron 6:25-7 Mr '69

Low-key confabs. H. Schwartz. il Sci N 95:198 F 22 '69

Economic commission for Latin America

Concludes session. UN Mo Chron 6:45-8 My '69

Eighteen-nation committee on disarmament

All smiles. il Newsweek 73:39 Mr 31 '69

Ambassador Smith presents U.S. views on seabed proposal at Eighteen-nation disarmament conference; statement, March 25, 1969. G. Smith. Dept State Bul 60:333-7 Ap 21 '69

Conference of eighteen-nation committee reconvenes. UN Mo Chron 6:51-2 Ap '69

Disarmament talks still at impasse. H. A. Jack. Chr Cent 86:1328-30 O 15 '69

Exercise in half-measure; banning nuclear weapons from seabeds. Commonweal 90:59-60 Ap 4 '69

President Nixon calls for comprehensive efforts in multilateral disarmament negotiations; text of message, July 3, 1969. R. M Nixon. Dept State Bul 61:65-6 Jl 28 '69

U.S. positions at Eighteen-nation disarmament conference outlined by President Nixon; text of letter, March 15, 1969. R. M. Nixon. Dept State Bul 60:289-90 Ap 7 '69

U.S., U.S.S.R. recommend admission of Japan and Mongolia to ENDC; statement. A. S. Fisher and A. A. Roshchin. Dept State Bul 60:542-3 Je 23 '69

Finance

Assistance in case of natural disasters; Assembly extends experimental assistance arrangements. UN Mo Chron 6:121-2 Ja '69

Estimates and appropriations. UN Mo Chron 6:96-101 D '69

Estimates and appropriations; budget estimates. UN Mo Chron 6:138-49 Ja '69

Estimates and appropriations; budget for 1970. UN Mo Chron 6:75-80 N '69

U.N. bond repayments issue; statement, December 21, 1968. J. R. Wiggins. Dept State Bul 60:55-7 Ja 20 '69

United Nations budget for 1970; statement, October 21, 1969. D. B. Fascell. Dept State Bul 61:454-7 N 24 '69

First committee

See United Nations—Political and security committee

Fourth committee

See United Nations—Trusteeship committee

General assembly

Celebration of twenty-fifth anniversary; with text of resolution. UN Mo Chron 6:34-9 N '69

U.N. courts youth; plans for world youth assembly. Chr Cent 86:1475-6 N 19 '69

Sessions (23d)

Ambassador Wiggins' news conference of December 20, 1968. J. R. Wiggins. Dept State Bul 60:80-4 Ja 27 '69

Assembly decisions on economic questions. UN Mo Chron 6:109-18 Ja '69

Conclusion of twenty-third session. UN Mo Chron 6:24-108 Ja '69

23d session of the United Nations General assembly; summary of developments during the session, significant from the U.S. point of view. Dept State Bul 60:147-55 F 17 '69

Sessions (24th)

Adoption of agenda. UN Mo Chron 6:5-7 N '69

Agenda of the 24th regular session of the U.N. General assembly. Dept State Bul 61:383-6 N 3 '69

General debate; summaries of representatives statements. UN Mo Chron 6:100-77 N '69

General debate; summary of statements. UN Mo Chron 6:114-199 O '69

Issues before the 24th General assembly. bibliog f Int Concil 574:5-199 S '69

Old issues back. il Sr Schol 95:13-14 O 6 '69

Opening. New Yorker 45:30 S 27 '69

Opening of twenty-fourth session. UN Mo Chron 6:34-8 O '69

Provisional agenda, twenty-fourth session of U.N. General assembly. Dept State Bul 61:135-8 Ag 18 '69

Record of the month. UN Mo Chron 6:3-60 D '69

United Nations: it's all we got. Time 94:27-8 S 26 '69

International law commission

Convention on special missions. UN Mo Chron 6:101-3 D '69

Opens twenty-first session. UN Mo Chron 6:93-5 Jl '69

Special missions and the United Nations. M. Bartos. UN Mo Chron 6:89-95 N '69

Twenty-first session concluded. UN Mo Chron 6:144-6 Ag '69

Legal committee

Assembly adopts legal resolutions. UN Mo Chron 6:149 Ja '69

Committee hears introductory statement on air hijacking. UN Mo Chron 6:104-5 D '69

International law commission; Sixth committee recommendations. UN Mo Chron 6:81-2 N '69

Membership

Assembly decision; question of representation of China. UN Mo Chron 6:3-12 D '69

Big brothers in the UN. B. Pilkington. Commonweal 564:5 S 19 '69

Micro-states and United Nations; associate memberships; address, August 27, 1969. C. W. Yost. Vital Speeches 35:746-8 O 1 '69

Move to change representation of China in the U.N. rejected by the 24th General assembly; statement, November 4, 1969, with text of resolutions. J. I. Whalley. Dept State Bul 61:476-9 D 1 '69

No more ministates? America 121:150 S 13 '69

Red China gaining for seat in U.N? il U S News 67:14 N 24 '69

U.S. asks Security council meeting on criteria for U.N. membership; text of a letter, July 14, 1969. W. B. Buffum. Dept State Bul 61:119 Ag 11 '69

United States proposes U.N. Security council study of micro-state question; statements, August 27, 1969. C. W. Yost; W. B. Buffum. Dept State Bul 61:268-72 S 22 '69

Were red China in the UN... America 121:255-6 O 4 '69

Non-governmental organizations

Annual conference. UN Mo Chron 6:48-9 Je '69

United Nations and the cause of peace; address, March 18, 1969. C. W. Yost. Dept State Bul 60:325-9 Ap 14 '69

Panel on foreign investment in developing countries

Meets in Amsterdam. UN Mo Chron 6:15-17 Mr '69

UNITED NATIONS—*Continued*

Political and security committee

Disarmament; First committee receives six draft resolutions. UN Mo Chron 6:66-70 D '69

Korean question: invitation aspects; resolution adopted by First committee. UN Mo Chron 6:23-8 N '69

Strengthening of international security; discussions in First committee. UN Mo Chron 6:28-33 N '69

Population commission

Holds fifteenth session. UN Mo Chron 6:90 2 D '69

Publications

See also
UNESCO—Publications

Bibliography

Current U.N. documents: a selected bibliography. See occasional issues of Department of state bulletin

Documents; selected list. See issues of UN monthly chronicle

Publications, official records. See issues of UN monthly chronicle

Scientific committee on the effects of atomic radiation

Effect of atomic radiation; Scientific committee adopts report. UN Mo Chron 6: 26-7 Je '69

Second committee

See United Nations—Economic and financial committee

Security council

Role of the Security council; address, New York, October 28, 1969. Thant.   UN Mo Chron 6:84-8 N '69

Meetings, 1968

Record of the month:
Cyprus. UN Mo Chron 6:20-4 Ja '69
Situation in the Middle East. UN Mo Chron 5:3-19 Ja '69

Meetings, 1969

Record of the month:
Adopts Russian and Spanish as working languages; with text of resolution. UN Mo Chron 6:3 F '69
Council adopts report; with text of resolution. UN Mo Chron 6:3-5 N '69
Cyprus. UN Mo Chron 6:3-10 Jl '69
Namibia. UN Mo Chron 6:3-13 Ap: 56-69 Ag '69
Question of micro-states. UN Mo Chron 6:95-102 Ag '69
Security council censures Portuguese attacks on Zambia. UN Mo Chron 6:34-56 Ag '69
Situation in Northern Ireland. UN Mo Chron 6:90-5 Ag '69
Situation in the Middle East. UN Mo Chron 6:3 Mr; 13-36 Ap; 3-12 My; 35-44 Jl: 3-34, 69-90 Ag; 3-33 O '69
Southern Rhodesia. UN Mo Chron 6:10-34 Jl '69

U.N. condemns Israeli air attacks on Lebanese villages; statements with text of resolution, August 14 and 26, 1969. C. W. Yost. Dept State Bul 61:272-4 S 22 '69

U.S. abstains on security council resolution linking Mosque fire to Middle East conflict; statement with text of resolution, September 15, 1969. C. W. Yost. Dept State Bul 61:307-9 O 6 '69

U.S. abstains on Security council resolution on Namibia; statement, with text of a resolution, August 12 and 13, 1969. C. W. Yost. Dept State Bul 61:252-4 S 15 '69

U.S. explains vote on Security council resolution on Israel; statements, March 27, April 1, 1969, with text of resolution. C. W. Yost. Dept State Bul 60:340-2 Ap 21 '69

United States proposes U.N. Security council study of micro-state question; statements, August 27, 1969. C. W. Yost; W. B. Buffum. Dept State Bul 61:268-72 S 22 '69

Sixth committee

See United Nations—Legal committee

Social commission

See United Nations—Commission on social development

Social, humanitarian and cultural committee

Assembly adopts resolution on youth. UN Mo Chron 6:73-5 N '69

Human rights; resolutions for adoption by the General assembly. UN Mo Chron 6:92-96 D '69

Special committee on peace-keeping operations

Peace-keeping operations; General assembly adopts resolution requesting committee to continue work. UN Mo Chron 6:89-92 Ja '69

Special committee appoints officers. UN Mo Chron 6:10-11 Mr '69

Special committee on principles of international law concerning friendly relations and co-operation among states

Committee concludes session. UN Mo Chron 6:52-3 O '69

Principles of international law; committee requests completion of draft declaration. UN Mo Chron 6:105-6 D '69

U.S. reviews work on U.N. committee on friendly relations and cooperation among states; statement, December 10, 1968. M. L. Warner. Dept State Bul 60:66-9 Ja 20 '69

Special committee on the policies of apartheid of the government of the Republic of South Africa

Appeals for release of political prisoners in South Africa. UN Mo Chron 6:13-14 My '69

Committee elects new officers. UN Mo Chron 6:4-5 F '69

Committee issues appeal against racial discrimination. UN Mo Chron 6:5-7 Mr '69

Decides to study foreign economic interests in South Africa. UN Mo Chron 6:60-1 Jl '69

International day for elimination of racial discrimination; commemoration. UN Mo Chron 6:36-40 Ap '69

Special committee on apartheid expresses concern over military build-up in South Africa. UN Mo Chron 6:21-6 Je '69

Special committee on apartheid; meeting in July. UN Mo Chron 6:120-3 Ag '69

Special committee on apartheid; recommends assistance to liberation movements. UN Mo Chron 6:46-8 N '69

Special committee on the question of defining aggression

Begins second session. UN Mo Chron 6:41-3 Mr '69

Special committee continues second session. UN Mo Chron 6:78-81 Ap '69

Special committee on the situation with regard to implementation of declaration on granting of independence to colonial countries and peoples

Adopts resolutions; with text of resolutions. UN Mo Chron 6:45-60 Jl '69

Assembly adopts resolution; with text of resolution. UN Mo Chron 6:96-103 Ja '69

Committee begins 1969 session. UN Mo Chron 6:3-5 Mr '69

Preparatory committee for tenth anniversary. UN Mo Chron 6:6 F '69

Preparatory committee for tenth anniversary of declaration on decolonization. UN Mo Chron 6:25-33 My '69

Preparatory committee for tenth anniversary of declaration on decolonization. UN Mo Chron 6:119-20 Ag '69

Special committee of twenty-four; adoption of resolution with text of resolution. UN Mo Chron 6:39-43 O '69

[Special committee of twenty-four; debate concerning Rhodesia] UN Mo Chron 6:10 F '69

Special committee of twenty-four; deliberations in July and August; with text of resolution. UN Mo Chron 6:103-19 Ag '69

Special committee of twenty-four meetings in Africa; adopts concensus on Namibia. UN Mo Chron 6:3-21 Je '69

Special committee of twenty-four; meetings in Africa; matters relating to small territories; question of Ifni and Spanish Sahara. UN Mo Chron 6:14-25 My '69

Special committees of twenty-four; questions of Namibia and St Kitts-Nevis-Anguilla; with text of resolution. UN Mo Chron 6: 40-51 Ap '69

Special committee of twenty-four; resolution on decolonization adopted; with text of resolution. UN Mo Chron 6:48-61 N '69

Tenth anniversary of declaration on decolonization. UN Mo Chron 6:61-3 N '69

United States reviews question of colonial territories and peoples; statement, April 17, 1969. S. M. Finger. Dept State Bul 60:452-4 My 26 '69

UNITED NATIONS—*Continued*

Special missions

Convention on special missions. UN Mo Chron 6:101-3 D '69

Special missions and the United Nations. M. Bartos. UN Mo Chron 6:89-95 N '69

Special political committee

Apartheid in South Africa; political committee considers report. UN Mo Chron 6:39-43 N '69

Sub-commission on prevention of discrimination and protection of minorities

Sub-commission concludes twenty-second session. UN Mo Chron 6:49-52 O '69

Sub-commission opens twenty-second session. UN Mo Chron 6:142-3 Ag '69

Technical assistance program

See also
United Nations—Development program

Third committee

See United Nations—Social, humanitarian and cultural committee

Truce supervision organization in Palestine

Whatever happened to the U.N.'s Mideast-truce team? United Nations truce supervision organization. il U S News 67:16 O 6 '69

Trusteeship committee

Assembly adopts ten resolutions; recommended by Fourth committee. UN Mo Chron 6:103-7 Ja '69

Namibia; recommendations of Fourth committee. UN Mo Chron 6:73-8 D '69

Trusteeship council

Council begins annual review. UN Mo Chron 6:49-50 Je '69

Recommendations on New Guinea and Pacific Islands. UN Mo Chron 6:83-93 Jl '69

Trust Territory of the Pacific Islands; symposium, June 6 and 13, 1969. Dept State Bul 61:220-36 S 8 '69

Voting

Big brothers in the UN. B. Pilkington. Commonweal 90:564-5 S 19 '69

Africa, Southern

Manifesto on Southern Africa, General assembly adopts resolution. UN Mo Chron 6: 12-17 D '69

United States urges negotiation and dialogue in Southern Africa; statement, October 16, 1969. C. H. Phillips. Dept State Bul 61:458-9 N 24 '69

China (People's Republic)

Assembly decision; question of representation of China. UN Mo Chron 6:3-12 D '69

Move to change representation of China in the U.N. rejected by the 24th General assembly; statement, November 4, 1969, with text of resolutions. J. I. Whalley. Dept State Bul 61:476-9 D 1 '69

Red China gaining for seat in U.N? il U S News 67:14 N 24 '69

Taiwan and the two Chinas. P. P. Cheng. bibliog f il Cur Hist 57:168-74+ S '69

Teddy's realpolitik. W. F. Buckley, jr. Nat R 21:402 Ap 22 '69

Temporary triumph of disingenuity. Chr Cent 86:1506 N 26 '69

Thinking of Chairman Mao. Nat R 21:108 F 11 '69

Were red China in the UN . . . America 121: 255-6 O 4 '69

Cyprus

See also
United Nations—Armed forces—Forces in Cyprus

Ifni

Special committee of twenty-four; Ifni and Spanish Sahara. UN Mo Chron 6:23-5 My '69

Indonesia

See also
United Nations—New Guinea

Israel

Security council condemns Israel; with text of resolution. UN Mo Chron 6:3-19 Ja '69

Security council condemns Israeli air attacks; with text of resolution. UN Mo Chron 6:3-12 My '69

U.N. Security council condemns Israel for attack on Beirut airport; statements with text of resolution, December 29 and 31, 1968. J. R. Wiggins. Dept State Bul 60:53-5 Ja 20 '69

U.S. explains vote on Security council resolution on Israel; statements, March 27, April 1, 1969, with text of resolution. C. W. Yost. Dept State Bul 60:340-2 Ap 21 '69

United States reaffirms position on Jerusalem; statements, July 1 and 3, 1969; with text of resolution. C. W. Yost. Dept State Bul 61:76-8 Jl 28 '69

Korea

Korean question; invitation aspects; resolution adopted by First committee. UN Mo Chron 6:23-8 N '69

Question of Korea; Assembly adopts resolution; with text of resolution. UN Mo Chron 6:48-60 D '69

U.N. command in Korea submits report to the Security council; letter, with text of report. C. W. Yost. Dept State Bul 60: 497-9 Je 9 '69

U.S. gives views on formula for inviting Korean representatives to U.N. debate; statement, November 25, 1968. S. Symington. Dept State Bul 59:712-16 D 30 '68

See also
United Nations—Commission for the unification and rehabilitation of Korea

Micronesia

See United Nations—Trust Territory of the Pacific Islands

Middle East

Fire control at the UN. A. Tuckerman. Nation 208:70 Ja 20 '69

Israel and the Arabs; the myths that block peace. C. Yost. Atlan 223:80-5 Ja '69

Middle East; commitment and resistance. il Time 93:30 F 14 '69

Security council adopts resolution on al Aqsa mosque fire; with text of resolution. UN Mo Chron 6:3-33 O '69

Security council censures Israel; with text of resolution. UN Mo Chron 6:3-34 Ag '69

Security council condemns Israel; with text of resolution. UN Mo Chron 6:3-19 Ja '69

Security council condemns Israel's attack on Lebanon; with text of resolution. UN Mo Chron 6:69-90 Ag '69

Security council considers complaint by Jordan. UN Mo Chron 6:35-44 Jl '69

Security council considers complaints. UN Mo Chron 6:13-36 Ap '69

Security council meeting postponed. UN Mo Chron 6:3 Mr '69

UN: defusing the powder keg. A. Tuckerman. Nation 208:198-9 F 17 '69

View from the UN. G. Stevens. Atlan 224: 4+ S '69

Mongolia

U.N. and its specialized agencies in Mongolia. UNESCO Courier 22:20 N '69

Namibia

Assembly adopts resolution of Namibia; with text of resolution. UN Mo Chron 6:9-23 N '69

Assembly calls for withdrawal of South African presence; with text of resolution. UN Mo Chron 6:41-5 Ja '69

Council for Namibia issues statement. UN Mo Chron 6:7 Mr '69

Namibia; recommendations of Fourth committee. UN Mo Chron 6:73-8 D '69

Security council calls on South Africa to withdraw; with text of resolution. UN Mo Chron 6:3-13 Ap '69

Security council sets time-limit for withdrawal by South Africa; with text of resolution. UN Mo Chron 6:56-69 Ag '69

Special committee of twenty-four meetings in Africa; adopts consensus on Namibia. UN Mo Chron 6:17-18 Je '69

U.S. abstains on Security council resolution on Namibia; statement, with text of a resolution, August 12 and 13, 1969. C. W. Yost. Dept State Bul 61:252-4 S 15 '69

United States calls upon South Africa to recognize right of people of Namibia to self-determination; statements, with text of resolution, December 10 and 16, 1968. B. C. Denny. Dept State Bul 60:11-14 Ja 6 '69

U.S. supports U.N. Security council resolution on Namibia; statement, March 20, 1969; with text of resolution. C. W. Yost. Dept State Bul 60:301-3 Ap 7 '69

New Guinea

Recommendations on New Guinea and Pacific Islands. UN Mo Chron 6:83-93 Jl '69

UNITED NATIONS—*Continued*

Northern Ireland

Security council hears statements. UN Mo Chron 6:90-5 Ag '69

Pacific Islands, Trust Territory of the

See United Nations—Trust Territory of the Pacific Islands

Portugal

Record of the month: Security council censures Portuguese attacks on Zambia; with text of resolution. UN Mo Chron 6:34-56 Ag '69

Territories under Portuguese administration; Assembly adopts resolution; with text of resolution. UN Mo Chron 6:23-33 D '69

Rhodesia

Resolution fails of adoption. UN Mo Chron 6:10-34 Jl '69

Security council committee issues report on trade. UN Mo Chron 6:4 F '69

Southern Rhodesia; Assembly adopts resolution; with text of resolution. UN Mo Chron 6:17-23 D '69

U.N. condemns racial policies of Southern Rhodesia; texts of U.S. statements; with text of resolution. J. Eaves; S. M. Finger. Dept State Bul 60:413-15 My 12 '69

U.S. deplores minority rule in Southern Rhodesia; statements, June 13 and 24, 1969; with text of draft resolution. C. W. Yost. Dept State Bul 61:55-9 Jl 21 '69

South Africa

Apartheid in South Africa; Assembly adopts two resolutions; with text of resolution. UN Mo Chron 6:33-41 D '69

Apartheid in South Africa; political committee considers report. UN Mo Chron 6:39-43 N '69

Assembly adopts resolution of Namibia; with text of resolution. UN Mo Chron 6:9-23 N '69

Assembly adopts two resolutions with text of resolutions. UN Mo Chron 6:92-6 Ja '69

Security council calls on South Africa to withdraw; with text of resolution. UN Mo Chron 6:3-13 Ap '69

U.N. General assembly rejects move to bar South Africa from membership in UNCTAD; statements, December 3 and 13, 1968. A. E. Goldschmidt; J. R. Wiggins. Dept State Bul 60:8-10 Ja 6 '69

United States calls upon South Africa to recognize right of people of Namibia to self-determination; statements, with text of resolution, December 10 and 16, 1968. B. C. Denny. Dept State Bul 60:11-14 Ja 6 '69
See also
United Nations—Africa, Southern
United Nations trust fund for South Africa

Southwest Africa

See also
United Nations—Namibia

Spanish Sahara

Special committee of twenty-four; Ifni and Spanish Sahara. UN Mo Chron 6:23-5 My '69

Taiwan

Taiwan and the two Chinas. P. P. Cheng. bibliog f il Cur Hist 57:168-74+ S '69

Trust Territory of the Pacific Islands

Recommendations on New Guinea and Pacific Islands. UN Mo Chron 6:83-93 Jl '69

United States

Other state department. by A. Belchman. Review
Cath World 209:138-40 Je '69. H. W. Flannery

Responsibility for the U.N.'s development as an instrument of world order; address, October 22, 1969. C. W. Yost. Dept State Bul 61:449-51 N 24 '69

West Irian

West New Guinea; Assembly adopts resolution. UN Mo Chron 6:41-8 D '69

UNITED NATIONS children's fund

Executive board organization meeting. UN Mo Chron 6:82 Jl '69

Recreation in the UNICEF program. J. A. Nesbitt. bibliog il Parks & Rec 4:35-7 O '69

UNICEF greeting cards. il UNESCO Courier 22:33 N '69

UNICEF; 1969 session of executive board. UN Mo Chron 6:42-5 Je '69

UNITED NATIONS commission for the unification and rehabilitation of Korea. See United Nations—Commission for the unification and rehabilitation of Korea

UNITED NATIONS commission on human rights

Additional recommendations adopted. UN Mo Chron 6:47 Je '69

UNITED NATIONS conference on consular relations

President sends Vienna convention on consular relations to the Senate; message. R. M. Nixon. Dept State Bul 60:475 Je 2 '69

Vienna convention on consular relations. L. T. Lee. bibliog f Int Concil 571:41-76 Ja '69

UNITED NATIONS conference on diplomatic intercourse and immunities

Vienna convention on diplomatic relations. P. Cahier. bibliog f Int Concil 571:5-40 Ja '69

UNITED NATIONS conference on the human environment (proposed)

Assembly decides to convene conference; with text of resolution. UN Mo Chron 6:35-41 Ja '69

Gambling with nature; usages of pesticides and herbicides. Commonweal 89:512-13 Ja 24 '69

U.S. joins in proposing 1972 U.N. conference on the problems of the human environment; statement, December 3, 1968; with text of resolution. J. R. Wiggins. Dept State Bul 59:707-12 D 30 '68

UNITED NATIONS conference on the law of treaties

Concludes in Vienna. UN Mo Chron 6:50-2 Je '69

Second session opens in Vienna. UN Mo Chron 6:54-6 My '69

Vienna convention on the law of treaties; address, July 15, 1969. J. R. Stevenson. Dept State Bul 61:127-31 Ag 18 '69

UNITED NATIONS conference on trade and development

Committee on invisibles and financing related to trade opens third session. UN Mo Chron 6:20-2 Mr '69

Committee on invisibles and financing related to trade; third session concluded. UN Mo Chron 6:64-5 Ap '69

Concludes ninth session. UN Mo Chron 6:48-9 O '69

Intergovernmental group considers UNCTAD's role in development decade. UN Mo Chron 6:21-3 F '69

One percent: the problem of economic aid; tr. by L. I. Dzirkals. L. Stepanov. bibliog f Ann Am Acad 386:41-53 N '69

Trade and development board of UNCTAD. UN Mo Chron 6:19-21 F '69

Trade and development board; resumed its eighth session. UN Mo Chron 6:41-2 Je '69

UNCTAD: Trade and development board concludes eighth session. UN Mo Chron 6:17-20 Mr '69

U.N. General assembly rejects move to bar South Africa from membership in UNCTAD; statements, December 3 and 13, 1968. A. E. Goldschmidt; J. R. Wiggins. Dept State Bul 60:8-10 Ja 6 '69

UNITED NATIONS correspondents association

Remarks by the Secretary-General on the role of the United Nations; Viet-Nam; the Middle East; and the conflict in Nigeria; awarding of the Hammarskjöld memorial scholarship, September 12, 1969. Thant. UN Mo Chron 6:54-7 O '69

UNITED NATIONS council for Namibia

Council for Namibia; letter to Security council on South Africa. UN Mo Chron 6:43-6 N '69

UNITED NATIONS day

H. I. Romnes named chairman of National U.N. day for 1969. Dept State Bul 60:451 My 26 '69

United Nations day, 1969; proclamation. R. M. Nixon. Dept State Bul 61:217-18 S 8 '69

United Nations day 24 October 1969; messages. A. E. Brooks; Thant. UN Mo Chron 6:i-iii O '69

UNITED NATIONS development decade, 2d

Additional members named for preparatory committee. UN Mo Chron 6:18-19 F '69

Preparatory committee begins second session. UN Mo Chron 6:37-8 My '69

Preparatory committee begins fourth session. UN Mo Chron 6:49 O '69

Preparatory committee continues first session. UN Mo Chron 6:62-4 Ap '69

Preparatory committee for second development decade. UN Mo Chron 6:46-7 Je '69

Preparatory committee holds first meeting. UN Mo Chron 6:14-15 Mr '69

UNITED STATES—Air force—*Continued*

Officers

See also
Negro military officers

Procurement

C-5A dominates procurement by USAF. il
Aviation W 90:21-2 Ja 20 '69
High flying in the Pentagon; campaigns for
new aircraft. A. Hamilton. New Repub 160:
16-18 My 31 '69
Revised aircraft, missile purchase plans de-
tailed. Aviation W 90:34 My 5 '69
USAF. Proxmire A-7 brake views diverge.
K. Johnsen. Aviation W 91:75 Ag 18 '69
USAF team studies C-5 cost overruns. C.
Brownlow. Aviation W 90:24 My 12 '69

Strategic air command

DOD to begin two-stage dispersal of strategic
bombers this year. Aviation W 90:28 My
5 '69
Now: more bomber bases in America. il U S
News 67:49 Ag 4 '69
SAC: dynamic deterrant; address, July 29,
1969. B. K. Holloway. Vital Speeches 35:
706-9 S 15 '69
SAC evaluates onboard data processing. B. M.
Elson. il Aviation W 91:87+ Jl 21 '69

Systems command

Value engineering; address, September 29,
1969. J. Ferguson. Vital Speeches 36:29-31
O 15 '69

Air force, Army

First wings over the forest. H. Clepper. il Am
For 75:24-7+ Je; 20-3+ Jl '69

Air force, Navy

USAF, navy press tactical fighter work. il
Aviation W 90:47+ Mr 10 '69

History

First to fly the Atlantic; in Navy Curtiss
flying boats. B. A. Weisberger. il Am
Heritage 20:16-21+ Je '69

Anti-Communist measures

See Communism—United States—Anti-
Communist measures; United States—Foreign relations—Anti-Communist measures

Anti-poverty program

See Anti-poverty program. 1964-

Antiquities

See also
Mounds and mound builders

Appropriations and expenditures

After Vietnam: the dollars and cents of
peace; symposium. Sat R 52:11-22 My 24
'69
Appropriations set record for tardiness. il
Bsns W p36-7 N 15 '69
As Congress starts to move. il U S News 67:
21 D 8 '69
Big government: is it out of hand? il U S
News 66:28-30 Mr 24 '69
Billions in spending plans that LBJ leaves
Nixon. il U S News 66:74-5 Ja 27 '69
Booby traps in LBJ's budget. il U S News
66:56-7 Mr 3 '69
Books are not expendable: misappropriations
of educational funds. H. Bowser. Sat R
52:22 Je 7 '69
Budgeting national priorities: excerpts from
Agenda for the Nation. C. L. Schultze.
Cur 103:18-19 Ja '69
Can taxes do more than raise revenue? H.
Babian. il Sat R 52:30-2+ Mr 22 '69
Dollar squeeze; Life poll by L. Harris, with
report on one family by J. McGinnis. il Life
67:18-29 Ag 15 '69
Evaluating public expenditures under con-
ditions of unemployment; excerpt from ad-
dress. R. H. Haveman. il Mo Labor R 92:
30-3 S '69
Fading peace dividend? D. P. Moynihan's
statements. U S News 67:70-1 S 8 '69
Federal budget and expenditure control. E.
F. Rinta. Ann Am Acad 379:22-30 S '68
Federal spending: ceilings proposed. U S
News 66:5 Je 30 '69
Fiscal picture; address, December 11, 1968.
T. B. Curtis. Vital Speeches 35:240-3 F 1 '69
Good-humored approach to frugality. H.
Sidey. il Life 66:4 My 2 '69
How Washington plans to stretch your tax
dollar. il Nations Bsns 57:72-5 Mr '69
If Wilbur Mills gets his way on spending
and taxes. U S News 66:78-80 My 19 '69

Is Congress being too generous? defense
from J. W. McCormack. U S News 67:70-1
Ag 25 '69
Limited options. il Fortune 79:20+ Je '69
Low ceiling for U.S. spending; agreement
reached in Congress. U S News 67:83 Jl
21 '69
Millions for defense but. . .damn little for
our land. M. Frome. Field & S 74:49+ Je '69
Nation's needs as Nixon sees them; text
of message to Congress, April 14, 1969.
R. M. Nixon. il U S News 66:76-8 Ap 28 '69
New ceiling on spending? How it would
work. il U S News 66:86-7 Je 2 '69
Nixon vs. Congress: what's involved. il U S
News 67:6 D 15 '69
Runaway boom in welfare. il U S News
66:52-4 F 3 '69
Testing the system in the '70s. New Repub
162:7-8 Ja 3 '70
Then and now; F. D. Roosevelt and L. B.
Johnson. H. C. Wallich. Newsweek 73:80
F 3 '69
Using incentives to improve the effective-
ness of government. C. L. Schultze. Mo
Labor R 92:34-8 S '69
We can afford a better America; with edi-
torial comment. E. K. Faltermayer. il For-
tune 79:81-2, 88-91+ Mr '69
What is the impact of those tax breaks? il
Bsns W p62+ F 1 '69
Where do we get the money? il Time 93:31-2
Ja 24 '69
Who will pay the bill? A. H. Sypher. Na-
tions Bsns 57:19-20 Ja '69
Will he veto a better America? New Repub
162:7-8 Ja 10 '70
Withholding federal funds withers P&R pro-
grams. Parks & Rec 4:17 Je '69
See also
Budget—United States
Government spending policy
United States—Armed forces—Appropriations
and expenditures
United States—Economic policy
also subhead Appropriations and expendi-
tures under names of government depart-
ments, e.g. United States—Defense, Department of—Appropriations and expenditures

Armed forces

America as a militaristic society. J. M.
Swomley, jr. il Cath World 209:199-202 Ag
'69
Military: servant or master of policy? il
Time 93:20-4+ Ap 11 '69; Same abr. with
title U.S. military: servant or master? Read
Digest 95:235-6+ Jl '69
See also
Discipline, Military
United States—Air force
United States—Army
United States—Defense, Department of
United States—Marine corps
United States—Navy
United States—Reserve officers training
corps

Appropriations and expenditures

After the ABM vote . . . il U S News 67:6+
Ag 18 '69
American militarism: what is it doing to us?
E. Sevareid. il Look 33:14-16 Ag 12 '69
And now that the American dream is safely
in the hands of the military-industrial
establishment, we wake to a new decade.
G. McGovern. il Esquire 72:188-9+ D '69
Arms spending: powerful chairmen disagree
sharply, and then softly. il U S News 66:18
Je 2 '69
Battle of budget starts with defense. Bsns
W p 14-15 Jl 5 '69
Blank check for the military; the need for
control; address, March 10, 1969. W. Prox-
mire. Vital Speeches 35:400-5 Ap 15 '69
C-5A long-lead time funding restored. D. C.
Winston. Aviation W 91:18-19 N 10 '69
Can military spending be controlled? J. B.
Bingham. For Affairs 48:51-66 O '69
Cutting arms costs: the problems. il U S
News 67:25 Jl 14 '69
Defense R&D programs lopped; blow to the
U.S. offensive chemical and biological war-
fare program. Sci N 96:47-8 Jl 19 '69
Dilemmas of defense. G. R. Rosen. Duns R
93:34-6 F '69
How to control the military. J. K. Gal-
braith. il Harper 238:31-46 Je '69
How to cut the military budget by $54 bil-
lion. S. Melman. Commonweal 91:273-6 N
28 '69
Making foreign policy; the influence of men
and events. J. K. Galbraith. Cur 113:54-61
D '69
Military-industrial complex. il Newsweek 73:
74-6+ Je 9 '69

UNITED STATES—Armed forces—Appropriations and expenditures—*Continued*
More companies under the gun; Proxmire-Fitzgerald attack on Pentagon's procurement. Bsns W p42 Je 21 '69
News and views; Arms control and disarmament agency's annual survey of military expenditures. J. Deedy. Commonweal 89:694 Mr 7 '69
Nixon delays advanced ICBM development. D. C. Winston. Aviation W 90:26-7 My 12 '69
Nixon's first defense budget: costs still going up. il U S News 66:34-5 Mr 31 '69
Now a hard look at spending for arms, space, superplanes. il U S News 66:29-31 F 24 '69
Peace, priorities, politics. Nation 209:554-5 N 24 '69
Phoenix of obsolescence. R. F. Kaufmann. Nation 208:656-60 My 26 '69
Politician-appeaser complex. D. Lawrence. U S News 66:108 Ap 21 '69
Price of power for U.S. il U S News 66:29-31 F 3 '69
Price of war. B. M. Russett. il Trans-Action 6:28-35 O '69
Role of defense; excerpts from address. M. R. Laird. Aviation W 90:17 My 5 '69
Senate puts pinch on pure science in military bill. A. Hamilton. Science 166:982 N 21 '69
Stennis projects $46 billion in saving. J. C. Stennis. Aviation W 91:18-19 Jl 21 '69
Three-day travesty; debate on military authorization bill. Nation 209:394-6 O 20 '69
War spending, more cutbacks; plans outlined by the Defense department. U S News 66:14 Ap 14 '69
What arms cuts mean; fewer men, fewer ships. il U S News 67:4 S 1 '69
Where latest defense cuts hit. U S News 67:30 N 10 '69
Why a military-industrial complex? A senator's answer; excerpts from address, April 15, 1969. B. Goldwater; W. Proxmire. U S News 66:88-90 Ap 28 '69
Why the Pentagon pays homage to John Cornelius Stennis. J. K. Batten. il N Y Times Mag p44-5+ N 23 '69
Wielding the ax on arms spending. U S News 67:10 Ag 25 '69
Your money when the war stops. H. C. Wallich. Vogue 153:58 F 15 '69
See also
United States—Defense, Department of—Appropriations and expenditures

Crimes and misdemeanors
See also
United States—Marine corps—Crimes and misdemeanors

Desertions
Army's desertion rate up, why; excerpts from testimony, House appropriations subcommittee, June 20, 1969. A. O. Connor. U S News 67:61 Jl 7 '69
Can deserters ever come home? U S News 67:15 D 1 '69
Dissent in uniform. Time 93:20 Ap 25 '69
Hell, no, we won't go! deserters and draft dodgers in Canada and Sweden. J. Cooney and D. Spitzer. il Trans-Action 6:53-62 S '69
Innocents in Scandinavia; Swedish-made film of American deserter life in Stockholm. P. Nobile. il Commonweal 91:300-2 D 5 '69
Message for deserters. il Newsweek 73:35-6 Mr 17 '69
Ministry to G.I.s in Sweden. R. J. Neuhaus. Chr Cent 86:378-80+ Mr 19 '69
News and views; GI deserters in Sweden. Commonweal 90:220 My 9 '69
Sanctuary at the Pacific Crossroads. F. Riley. Chr Cent 86:1526+ N 26 '69
What did you do during the war, father? the chaplain's role. G. Zahn. Commonweal 90:195-9 My 2 '69; Reply with rejoinder. R. A. Lutz. 90:403+ Je 27 '69

Education
Pentagon piety: Character guidance program to eliminate passages with religious connections. Nation 208:325-6 Mr 17 '69
See also
United States—Air force—Education

Forces in Europe
New move to reduce U.S. forces in Europe. il U S News 67:6 D 8 '69
U.S. and Germany conclude new offset agreement; joint statement, July 9, 1969. il Dept State Bul 61:92 Ag 4 '69

Forces in foreign countries
More than a million GI's still overseas, but a pull-back has started. il U S News 68:26-7 Ja 12 '70

Reading the entrails: withdrawal, a retreat. J. Burnham. Nat R 21:741 Jl 29 '69
This month's feature: Congress & U.S. military commitments. Cong Digest 48:193-224 Ag '69

Forces in Great Britain
Longest wait; American forces before Normandy invasion. J. Lord. il Am Heritage 20:4-15+ Je '69

Forces in Iceland
Reports. J. B. Ritch. 3d. Atlan 223:38+ Ap '69

Forces in Japan
Japan's GI babies: a hard coming-of-age. D. Moser. il Life 67:40-7 S 5 '69

Forces in Korea
Korea heats up. Nation 209:331 O 6 '69

Forces in Laos
Dilemma in Laos. E. G. Martin. il Newsweek 74:43 N 3 '69
More aid to Laos? A report on what U.S. is doing there. il U S News 67:16 O 20 '69
Other wars. Nation 209:330 O 6 '69
Secret war. il Newsweek 74:92 O 6 '69
War in Laos; the U.S. role. U S News 67:15 O 6 '69
What U.S. is doing in Laos, and why. il U S News 67:8 N 10 '69

Forces in Southeast Asia
More for Fulbright; MAAG team on Quemoi. New Repub 160:8 My 17 '69

Forces in Spain
Plain in Spain. New Repub 161:10 Jl 5 '69

Forces in Thailand
Future of the US military presence. A. Campbell. New Repub 160:14-17 Ap 5 '69
Other wars. Nation 209:330 O 6 '69
Talks on reduction of U.S. forces announced by U.S. and Thailand; joint statement, August 26, 1969. Dept State Bul 61:245 S 15 '69
What are we doing in Thailand. Z. B. Grant. New Repub 160:19-21 My 24 '69

Forces in Vietnam
Bringing home 50,000 troops is still a good idea. Life 66:38 Mr 28 '69
Even after the war ends. U S News 67:12 O 27 '69
From GIs in Vietnam, unexpected cheers; views on the Moratorium, ed. by H. Wingo. il Life 67:36 O 24 '69
General Abrams deserves a better war. K. P. Buckley. il N Y Times Mag p34-5+ O 5 '69
GI's long last month in Vietnam. J. Saar. il Life 67:51-4 Ag 8 '69
I quit. D. Duncan. Ramp Mag 7:41-6 Ja 25 '69
In Vietnam: mama-san pushers vs. psyops. il Newsweek 73:108 Ap 21 '69
Indians and others; feeling toward Vietnamese. Nation 209:682 D 22 '69
Revolt in the Pentagon? Z. B. Grant. il New Repub 161:17-20 O 4 '69
Saigon attitudes; Nguyen van Thieu requests timetable for withdrawal of forces. il Newsweek 73:37 F 3 '69
Vietcong's secret weapon: marijuana. A. F. Gonzalez, jr. il Sci Digest 65:14-18 Ap '69
What Secretary Laird learned in Vietnam; plan to withdraw American troops to be postponed. il por U S News 66:26-7 Mr 24 '69
What U.S. plans after Midway. U S News 66:25 Je 16 '69
See also
United States—Army—Forces in Vietnam
United States—Marine corps—Forces in Vietnam
Vietnamese war, 1957- —American participation
Vietnamese war, 1957- —American troop withdrawals

Forces in Vietnam—Recreation
See United States—Armed forces—Recreation

Forces in Vietnam—Relations with civilians
See United States—Armed forces—Relations with civilians

History
American fighting man, by V. Hicken. Review
Newsweek il 73:86+ F 3 '69. R. A. Gross

UNITED STATES—Armed forces—*Continued*

Medical and sanitary affairs

Asiatic diseases; are they a threat to Americans back home? E. M. Wylie. Good H 168:96-7+ Ap '69
Disease, Vietnamese style. Sci Digest 65:60-1 My '69

Morale

Demoralization in Vietnam; incident in the Songchang Valley. Nation 209:196 S 8 '69
Enemy of the people; zapping a sailor-editor; R. Priest. M. Polner. Commonweal 90:560 S 19 '69; Reply. S. L. Wilcox. 91:111 O 24 '69
See also
United States—Army—Morale

Negroes

As race issue hits armed forces. il U S News 67:26-7 S 1 '69
Passing the power; black GI's and militancy on Okinawa. B. Krisher. il Newsweek 74:49-50 D 22 '69
Uptight in the armed forces. W. Endicott and S. Williford. Nation 209:464-6 N 3 '69
See also
United States—Marine corps—Negroes
Vietnamese war, 1957- —Negroes

Officers

Leadership in the nuclear age; citizen officers; address, December 18, 1968. F. A. Johnson. Vital Speeches 35:218-21 Ja 15 '69
See also
Negro military officers

Officers, Retired

See Retired military personnel

Political activities

Another target of new left; the armed forces. il U S News 66:58-60 My 26 '69

Post exchanges

Why Congress is looking into the military's PX stores. il U S News 66:66-7 Mr 24 '69

Procurement

Billion-dollar grab bag. R. F. Kaufman. Nation 208:328-32 Mr 17 '69
Defense requirements for the 1970's; instant myths; address, April 3, 1969. J. J. Rhodes. Vital Speeches 35:460-2 My 15 '69
How to control the military. J. K. Galbraith. il Harper 238:31-46 Je '69
Military-industrial complex. il Newsweek 73:74-6+ Je 9 '69
Military-industrial complex; the facts vs. the fictions. il U S News 66:60-3 Ap 21 '69

Public relations

Can the military aid the home front? A. Etzioni. Cur 105:24-6 Mr '69
Open season. A. H. Sypher. Nations Bsns 57:23-4 Ag '69
Pentagon hucksterism. Nation 209:685 D 22 '69
That antimilitary mood. Life 66:38 Mr 21 '69
Westmoreland, seminarist. Nation 208:308 Mr 31 '69
What makes news? scandals involving the military. Nation 209:397 O 20 '69
See also
United States—Armed forces—Relations with civilians

Publications

See also
Stars and stripes (newspaper)

Race problems

As race issue hits armed forces. il U S News 67:26-7 S 1 '69
Black power in Viet Nam. il Time 94:22-3 S 19 '69
Black vs white. il Newsweek 74:20A-20B Ag 25 '69
Passing the power; black GI's and militancy on Okinawa. B. Krisher. il Newsweek 74:49-50 D 22 '69
Race crisis at a marine camp. P. Good. il Life 67:46-51 S 25 '69
Racial tension at Lejeune. America 121:108 Ag 30 '69

Recreation

Hong Kong; the complaisant haven. S. Salaff. il Nation 209:409-11 O 20 '69
In support of Hope; B. Hope christmas show. D. R. Sharpless. il Parks & Rec 4:12-16+ D '69

Recruiting and enlistment

See also
Military service, Voluntary

Relations with civilians

GI's in battle: the dink complex. il Newsweek 74:37 D 1 '69
Military view, from the top and from the ranks. il Time 93:25 Ap 11 '69

Religious affairs

Pueblo prayer. Chr Today 13:32 F 14 '69
See also
Chaplains, Military
United States—Army—Religious affairs

Reserves

Our restless reserves. T. Barry. il Look 33:36-9+ Ag 12 '69
See also
United States—National guard

Transportation

See also
United States—Military sea transportation service

Womens services

WACS and WAVES are different now. C. Sadler. McCalls 96:101 Ap '69

Arms control and disarmament agency

Exercise in half-measure. Commonweal 90:60 Ap 4 '69
News and views; Arms control and disarmament agency's annual survey of military expenditures. J. Deedy. Commonweal 89:694 Mr 7 '69
Senate confirms members of ACDA advisory committee. Dept State Bul 61:126 Ag 18 '69

Army

Another target of new left; the armed forces. il U S News 66:58-60 My 26 '69
Army cutbacks; the risks; interview. W. C. Westmoreland. il U S News 67:66-71 S 29 '69
Must the citizen give up his civil liberties when he joins the army? R. Sherrill. il N Y Times Mag p25-7+ My 18 '69
Rediscovery: a Tiffany room; Seventh regiment and armory, New York city. E. Robinson. il Art in Am 57:72-7 Jl '69
Talking about the army; address, April 9, 1969. W. C. Westmoreland. Vital Speeches 35:450-5 My 15 '69
Their number is up; army serial number replaced by social security number. Time 94:17 Jl 11 '69
U.S. army of the '70s, as Westmoreland portrays it; excerpts from statements. W. C. Westmoreland. U S News 67:13 D 15 '69
See also
Courts martial and courts of inquiry
Discipline, Military
United States—Air force. Army

Chaplains

See Chaplains, Military

Corps of engineers

America the raped, by G. Marine. Review Natur Hist 78:72-3+ O '69. H. Gilliam
America the raped; excerpt. G. Marine. il Ramp Mag 7:72-4 Ja 25 '69
Army tries to build a munitions factory in St Louis with the Mob on the payroll. D. Walsh. il Life 66:52-4+ F 14 '69
Big walnut. G. Laycock. Audubon 71:127 S '69
Cornplanter, can you swim? Kinzua Dam flooding Senecas' ancestral lands for Allegheny reservoir. A. M. Josephy, jr. il Am Heritage 20:4-9+ D '68
High cost of destruction; excerpts from The diligent destroyers. G. Laycock. il Audubon. 71:86-8+ N '69
New Corps. C. Weathersbee. il Sci N 95:122-3+ F 1 '69

Crimes and misdemeanors

GIs for peace: the army fights an idea. J. Rechy. Nation 210:8-12 Ja 12 '70
Guns of Turner. il Newsweek 74:41-2 O 20 '69
Khaki Cosa nostra; investigation of the operation of noncommissioned officers' clubs. Newsweek 74:37-8 O 13 '69
Kickbacks, guns: new round in army rackets hearing. il U S News 67:14 O 20 '69
Military Mafia; investigations of W. O. Wooldridge and C. C. Turner. il Time 94:26 O 17 '69
Mutineers; penalties for men found guilty at Fort Ord. Calif. Time 93:17 Je 13 '69
Presidio mutiny; sentences for those participating in sit-down demonstration at the San Francisco stockade. P. Barnes. New Repub 161:21-5 Jl 5 '69

UNITED STATES—Army—Crimes and mis-
demeanors—*Continued*
Ribicoff vs. the army; hearings on corrup-
tion in Vietnam and elsewhere. D. San-
ford. New Repub 161:9-10 D 13 '69
Senate look at army-club scandal. U S News
67:12 O 13 '69
Strung out and gassed at Fort Dix. L. J.
Berry. Commonweal 91:173-4 N 7 '69
See also
Mutiny

Desertions

See United States—Armed forces—Desertions

Equipment and supplies

Trends in the army; weapons systems; ad-
dress, October 30, 1968. F. J. Chesarek.
Vital Speeches 35:287-8 F 15 '69
See also
Tanks, Military

Forces in Vietnam

Alpha incident; refusal to go into battle;
with report by K. Buckley. il Newsweek
74:17 S 8 '69
And now a vroom; motorcycle scouts. il
Time 93:30-1 My 2 '69
Army and Viet Nam; the stab-in-the-back
complex; Time essay. Time 94:26-7 D 12 '69
Close-up: General Creighton Abrams; one
day they will go it alone. C. Leinster. il
Life 66:38-40+ Ap 25 '69
Company A; how history looks upon
mutinies. Commonweal 90:556-7 S 19 '69
Incident in Song Chang Valley; leadership
problem. Time 94:22-3 S 5 '69
Letter from a Vietnam veteran; impressions
of service in the Eleventh armored calvary
regiment under George S. Patton, III. G. S.
Livingston. Sat R 52:22-3 S 20 '69; Reply.
W. C. Haponski. 52:29+ O 25 '69
See also
United States—Army—Special forces—Forces
in Vietnam

Maneuvers

See Military maneuvers

Medical and sanitary affairs

See also
United States—Army—Medical corps

Medical corps

Where combat medics train. E. H. McCleary.
il Todays Health 47:38-45 Je '69

Morale

Alpha incident; in Vietnam; with report by
K. Buckley. il Newsweek 74:17 S 8 '69
Incident in Song Chang Valley; leadership
problem. Time 94:22-3 S 5 '69

Negroes

Making contact in Baltimore. J. Sack. il Esquire 71:92-4+ Je '69

Negroes—History

Black man in the American West. D. T.
Schoenberger. bibliog il Negro Hist Bul
32:7-11 Mr '69
'Pecos Bill' on the Texas frontier. R. M.
Utley. bibliog il Am West 6:4-13+ Ja '69

Officers

Close-up: General Creighton Abrams; one day
they will go it alone. C. Leinster. il Life
66:38-40+ Ap 25 '69
Where are they now? Lieut. Col. J. H. Michaelis. il Newsweek 74:26 D 8 '69
See also
Generals

Physical examinations

This is the army; Armed forces examining
and entrance station, Charlotte, N.C. R. L.
Fitzpatrick. New Repub 161:19-21 Jl 19 '69

Political activities

Should we politicize the army? W. V. Kennedy. America 121:131 S 6 '69

Prisons

America's Devil's Island; inside the Army
stockade at San Francisco's presidio. D.
Duncan. Ramp Mag 7:8+ Ja 25 '69
Army justice and Presidio 27. T. Link.
Chr Cent 86:662-4 My 7 '69
Army's kangaroo courts; stockade justice. K.
H. Purnell. Nation 208:432-4 Ap 7 '69
Case of Private Sood. B. Farrell. **Life 66:12A**
F 28 '69
Presidio mutiny; sentences for those partici-
pating in sit-down demonstration at the
San Francisco stockade. P. Barnes. New
Repub 161:21-5 Jl 5 '69

Procurement

Army doubles request for Sentinel ABM. D. C.
Winston. Aviation W 90:22-3 Ja 20 '69

Recreation

50th anniversary for army service clubs. C.
H. Reid. il Parks & Rec 4:16-19+ N '69
Recreation for the combat soldier. D. R.
Sharpless. il Parks & Rec 4:18-19+ Jl '69

Recruiting and enlistment

Which memo? The odor of fraud. C. Dreifus.
Nation 208:176 F 10 '69
See also
Military service, Voluntary

Relations with civilians

See United States—Armed forces—Relations with civilians

Religious affairs

Chaplains' role under new scrutiny. W. Willoughby. Chr Today 13:32 Ap 25 '69
Discharging God from the army. Chr Today
13:22-3 Ap 25 '69

Reserves

Life with the conscientious acceptors. R.
Todd. il N Y Times Mag p27+ O 12 '69;
Discussion. p 142-3 N 23 '69

Special forces—Forces in Vietnam

Arthur Goldberg writes about the Green Ber-
ets. A. Goldberg. Life 67:30D O 17 '69
Berets: gone but not forgotten. il Time 94:
19-20 O 10 '69
Captain Levy and the Green Berets. R. G.
Sherrill. Nation 209:133 Ag 25 '69
Case of the Green Berets. il Newsweek 74:
42-3 Ag 18; 26+ Ag 25 '69
Catch 23; trial of the Green Berets. Common-
weal 91:61 O 17 '69
CIA talks; T. K. Chuyen and the Green
Beret case. il Newsweek 74:18 S 8 '69
Colonel Robert Rheault, ex-Green Beret;
with report by F. McCulloch and editorial
comment by R. Graves. il Life 67:1, 34-9 N
14 '69
Demoralization in Vietnam; Green Berets epi-
sode. Nation 209:196 S 8 '69
Ghostly war of the Green Berets. H. Sutton.
il Sat R 52:23-5+ O 18 '69
Green Beret case. New Repub 161:9 O 11 '69
Green Beret scandal. Nation 209:366 O 13 '69
Green Berets and the CIA. L. F. Prouty.
New Repub 161:9-10 Ag 23 '69
Green Berets come home. il Newsweek 74:
43-4 O 13 '69
Green Berets on trial. il Time 94:11-12 Ag 22
'69
Green Berets to trial. il Newsweek 74:41 S
29 '69
Green Berets: who they are and what they
do. il U S News 67:28-9 S 1 '69
Military justice; learning from the Green
Berets. E. F. Sherman. Nation 209:399-403
O 20 '69
Mystery of the Green Berets. Time 94:28+
Ag 15 '69
Tough test for military justice; Green Beret
case. il Time 94:50-1 O 3 '69
Under restraint; pretrial investigation of
Green Beret case. il Newsweek 74:35-6 S
1 '69
Who killed Thai Khac Chuyen? Not I, said
the CIA. Time 94:16 S 5 '69

Training

See Military training

Art

See Art—United States; Art, American

Atomic energy commission

AEC goes public on nuclear safety. il Bsns W
p52 S 20 '69
Basement H-bombs. S. Novick. il Sci & Cit
10:243-9 D '68
Bombs and bombast; released data on nu-
clear weapons. J. Deedy. Commonweal 90:
450 Jl 25 '69
Government agencies expand publishing op-
erations. S. Wagner. Pub W 195:34-5 Ap 7
'69
Nuclear safeguards: the US program. W. A
Higinbotham. bibliog il Phys Today 22:40-
4 N '69
Peaceful atom: friend or foe? il Time 95:42-
3 Ja 19 '70
Please don't steal the atomic bomb. A. M.
Adelson. il Esquire 71:130-3+ My '69
Ready for market; breeders. il Sci N 95:571-
2 Je 14 '69
Who'll own atom fuel supply? il Bsns W
p 136+ Je 14 '69
See also
Argonne national laboratory

UNITED STATES—Atomic energy commission
—*Continued*

Appropriations and expenditures

Accelerator money authorized. Sci N 96:7 Jl 5 '69

AEC space, military funds cut. K. Johnsen. il Aviation W 90:61+ Ja 27 '69

Fiscal 1970 AEC budget. il Aviation W 90:20 Ap 21 '69

Over the 50 percent line. Sci N 95:89 Ja 25 '69

Attorney General
See United States—Justice, Department of

Boundaries
See also
International joint commission (United States and Canada)

Bureau of Indian affairs
See United States—Indian affairs, Bureau of

Cabinet

Committees, come to order. il Newsweek 73:28-9 F 17 '69

It takes too much time to make the change. D. Lawrence. U S News 66:92 Mr 31 '69

Reports: Washington. E. B. Drew. Atlan 224:4+ N '69

Shaking down, settling in. il Newsweek 73:21-2 F 3 '69

White House staff versus the Cabinet; interview, ed. by H. Sidey. B. Moyers. Cur 106:26-35 Ap '69
See also
Cabinet officers
Cabinet officers wives

Caricatures and cartoons

King & his court. R. Grossman. Ramp Mag 8:32-3 Ag '69

History

I walk on untrodden ground. J. T. Flexner. il Am Heritage 20:24-7+ O '69

Cabinet committee on voluntary action

Volunteers get a volunteer. Bsns W p 155 My 10 '69

Canadian committee on trade and economic affairs
See Joint United States-Canadian committee on trade and economic affairs

Capitol

All's not quiet on west front. E. Gross. il Sci N 96:506-7 N 29 '69

Census

About that fuss over the '70 census; interview. M. H. Stans. U S News 67:59 S 8 '69

Census challenged. M. Scarlet. il Sci N 95:560-1 Je 7 '69

Dear Virginia: a reply to census skeptics; address, June 23, 1969. W. H. Chartener. Vital Speeches 35:645-9 Ag 15 '69

Effect of the census undercount on labor force estimates. D. F. Johnston and J. R. Wetzel. bibliog f il Mo Labor R 92:3-13 Mr '69

Preview of the 1970 census; symposium. bibliog il Mo Labor R 92:35-60 D '69

Privacy and the 1970 census. Nat R 21:220-1 Mr 11 '69

Questions the census will ask you. il Good H 169:214 O '69

What you must tell the census taker; with interview with C. Taeuber. il U S News 68:36-40 Ja 12 '70

Why the uproar over '70 census? U S News 66:10 Ap 14 '69

Census, Bureau of the

Decennial census: its purpose and its uses. G. R. Potts; R. C. Burt. bibliog Mo Labor R 92:35-42 D '69

Squeezing even more out of tax returns; selling of Internal revenue service data and Census data to private industry. il Bsns W p69 D 6 '69

Verrry interesting. Nat R 21:268 Mr 25 '69

Central intelligence agency

American militarism; CIA-directed paramilitary operations. New Repub 160:7-9 Ap 12 '69; Same abr. with title Militarism and the impact of CIA. Cur 108:55-8 Je '69

CIA as an equal opportunity employer. D. Schechter and others. il Ramp Mag 7:25-33 Je '69

CIA finds a publisher; Che's diaries. Ramp Mag 7:58-60 N 30 '68

CIA talks; T. K. Chuyen and the Green Beret case. il Newsweek 74:18 S 8 '69

Green Beret case. New Repub 161:9 O 11 '69

Green Berets and the CIA. L. F. Prouty. New Repub 161:9-10 Ag 23 '69

In cold blood; how the CIA executed Che. M. Ray. il Ramp Mag 7:142-9 Ja 25 '69

Pueblo; whodunit? New Repub 160:7-8 F 15 '69

Short account of international student politics & the cold war, with particular reference to the NSA, CIA, etc; with statements by M. Wood and M. Raskin. S. Stern. il Ramp Mag 7:87-97 Ja 25 '69

Spying on the spy. il Time 93:72 My 23 '69

University on the make; or, How MSU helped arm Madame Nhu; with introd. by S. K. Sheinbaum. W. Hinckle and others. il Ramp Mag 7:52-60 Ja 25 '69

Who killed Thai Khac Chuyen? Not I, said the CIA. Time 94:16 S 5 '69

Chamber of commerce
See Chamber of commerce of the United States of America

Childrens bureau

Needed: an enlarged and strengthened U.S. Children's bureau. G. J. Hecht. Parents Mag 44:16+ Je '69

Civil aeronautics board

Bid to takeover Pan Am blocked. L. Doty. Aviation W 90:26 Mr 17 '69

Browne seeks viable air carriers. H. D. Watkins. Aviation W 91:24-5 N 10 '69

CAB checking commuter sale. Aviation W 90:46 Ap 14 '69

CAB considers plan to revive standard. Aviation W 91:46 Ag 25 '69

CAB gets tough on foreign lines, landing rights. Bsns W p56 D 20 '69

CAB proposes conditions on new IATA tour fare. Aviation W 91:31 Jl 7 '69

CAB role draws congressional interest. H. D. Watkins. Aviation W 91:38 D 1 '69

CAB to weigh fare formula advisability. H. D. Watkins. Aviation W 91:29 Ag 25 '69

CAB, trunks facing fare clash. H. D. Watkins. Aviation W 91:31 D 8 '69

CAB weighs contract bulk fare extension. H. D. Watkins. Aviation W 91:27-8 N 3 '69

Executive jet aviation begins efforts to find new financing. J. P. Woolsey. Aviation W 91:49-50 N 10 '69

Industry, CAB to review subsidy program. Aviation W 91:38 D 8 '69

Larger taxi aircraft under study by CAB. Aviation W 92:27 Ja 12 '70

New CAB chief looks at problems. U S News 67:26 S 22 '69

New flight plan for the airlines. G. Burck. il Fortune 79:98-101+ Ap '69

New policy to stretch CAB cases. L. Doty. Aviation W 90:26-7 Je 30 '69

Nixon to tighten airline control. Aviation W 90:24-5 Mr 3 '69

Pacific air battle roars on; Nixon to review Johnson's route decision. Bsns W p26 F 1 '69

Southern cases spur competition. L. Doty. Aviation W 91:32-3 Ag 4 '69

Taxi pilot duty time scrutinized by CAB. Aviation W 91:58 S 22 '69

Trans-Pacific air route tangle. D. Sanford. New Repub 160:16-8 F 15 '69

Why Washington rode with Pan Am; CAB approval required on takeovers of airlines by non-transportation companies. Bsns W p40 Mr 15 '69

Civil rights commission
See United States—Commission on civil rights

Civilization

Age in perspective. il Time 93:18-22 Ja 24 '69

Can it happen here? E. Kern. il Life 67:67+ O 17 '69

Century of aspiration. W. D. Garrett. Antiques 96:372 S '69

Farewell to the 60s. D. Halberstam. il McCalls 97:85-92 Ja '70

Four words to remember. H. H. Humphrey. il McCalls 96:96-7 Mr '69

Generation gap. E. Z. Friedenberg. bibliog f Ann Am Acad 382:32-42 Mr '69

Good-bye to all of you; advice to the next generation from distinguished nineteenth-century citizens. il Esquire 72:158-63+ D '69

Hard work, hard play, and some hard thinking; life style of the 1970s. il Bsns W p211-12 D 6 '69

Hubert Humphrey looks at the generation gap; address. H. H. Humphrey. il U S News 67:47-50 S 8 '69

UNITED STATES—Civilization—*Continued*

If you don't mind my saying so. J. W. Krutch. Am Scholar 39:18+ Wint '69

In the country of the young. J. W. Aldridge. il Harper 239:56-64 O '69 (to be cont)

In the country of the young. J. W. Aldridge. il Harper 239:56-64 O; 93-4+ N '69

Making of a counter culture, by T. Roszak. Review
  Life il 67:8-9 N 7 '69. K. Keniston

Reflections: revolution and related matters. L. Tyrmand. New Yorker 45:40-2+ Ag 16 '69

Sixties; symposium, ed. by P. Coffin and A. Hurlburt. bibliog il Look 33:10, 12-32+ D 30 '69

The sixties: this slum of a decade. R. H. Rovere. il N Y Times Mag p25-7+ D 14 '69

Three don'ts: a workable society; address, June 7, 1969. M. H. Stans. Vital Speeches 35:661-3 Ag 15 '69

Tragedy of the commons revisited. B. L. Crowe. bibliog Science 166:1103-7 N 28 '69

What kind of society do we want? excerpts from The recovery of confidence. J. W. Gardner Read Digest 95:74-8 S '69
  See also
Americanism
United States—Intellectual life
United States—Social conditions

Anecdotes, facetiae, satire, etc.

Where it's at. J. Fischer. Harper 239:14+ Ag '69

History

Red, white, and blue, by J. W. Ward. Review
  Cath World 209:275-6 S '69. R. J. Meister

Coast guard

Yachting interviews: Rear Admiral William J. Morrison. W. T. Stone. il Yachting 125:67+ Mr '69

Boats

Now you can be rescued in luxury: Coast guard cutter Dallas. E. A. Zadig. il Motor B 123:150-5 Ap '69

Coast guard auxiliary

Call USCGA, free public instruction courses. Motor B 124:29+ Ag '69

They work at rescue. J. C. Parker. il Motor B 123:101+ Ap '69

Under the blue ensign. B. Woodward. See issues of Motor boating

U.S. Coast guard auxiliary. R. Brinn. See issues of Yachting

Commerce

Contradictions on trade policy. Bsns W p 182 My 10 '69

Fight that stirs trade policymakers; Commerce secretary Stans vs. C. Gilbert, new Special trade representative. il Bsns W p 118+ Ap 19 '69

Importers still face heavy seas: aftermath of dock strike. il Bsns W p33-9 F 22 '69

Mixed bag. il Time 94:94 N 28 '69

Nixon's stance: foreign-trade policy. il Newsweek 74:72+ D 1 '69

Report completed on future U.S. foreign trade policy. Dept State Bul 60:91-2 F 3 '69

Secretary Stans to visit Europe, Asia to discuss U.S. trade policies. Dept State Bul 60:367 Ap 28 '69

Time to stand firm; foreign policy. Duns R 93:132 My '69

Trade: a vision for the 70's; address, September 17, 1969. A. K. Watson. Vital Speeches 36:2-5 O 15 '69

U.S. aerospace export decline foreseen. C. Brownlow. il Aviation W 90:104-6 Je 2 '69

U.S. goods face a run for the money: trade prospects in the 1970s. Bsns W p202-3+ D 6 '69

World money & trade: one big world of happy traders? il Sr Schol 94:13-15 Ja 31 '69

  See also
Export controls
Export trade
Import quotas
Imports
Merchant marine—United States
Tariff—United States
United States—Industries
World trade week

Europe, Western

Trade: rift of reason: western Europe and the United States. G. E. Bradley. il Nations Bsns 57:96-9 S '69

Japan

Hard bargaining with Japan. Time 93:82 My 30 '69

Sharp side of the rising sun. il Bsns W p 124-6 S 6 '69

Showdown in trade with Japan. il Time 94:71-2 Jl 4 '69
  See also
Joint United States-Japan committee on trade and economic affairs

Rumania

Rumania tries the hard sell on trade. il Bsns W p74+ Jl 26 '69

Commerce, Department of

Secretary Stans; interview. M. Stans. New Yorker 45:22-4 Jl 5 '69

Stans tries to take the reins on trade. il Bsns W p 114-15+ My 10 '69

Supersalesman for our system; interview; with editorial comment. M. Stans. Nations Bsns 57:34-9 S '69
  See also
United States—Office of minority business enterprise

Appropriations and expenditures

Metrics, patents, weather. Sci N 95:91 Ja 25 '69

State technical services, Office of

State technical services: Congress swings the axe. A. Hamilton. Science 166:1606-8 D 26 '69

Commercial policy
See United States—Economic policy

Commercial treaties and agreements

U.S. and Brazil sign agreement on soluble coffee; Department announcement with exchange of notes. Dept State Bul 60:455 My 26 '69

United States and Greece sign new cotton textile agreement; Department announcement with text of agreement. Dept State Bul 60:430-1 My 19 '69

United States and Singapore sign new cotton textile agreement; Department announcement, with text of agreement. il Dept State Bul 60:136-8 F 10 '69

U.S. and Soviet Union sign new agreements on fisheries. Dept State Bul 60:186 Mr 3 '69

U.S. and U.S.S.R. hold talks on northeastern Pacific fisheries. Dept State Bul 60:79 Ja 27 '69

Commission of fine arts

Commission of fine arts: design review board for the national capital. D. Raney. il Arch Rec 145:37 Ap '69

Commission on civil rights

Hesburgh fights. J. O'Connor. Look 33:42+ N 18 '69

Rumbles along the Rio: U.S. civil rights commission hearings in San Antonio. P. H. McNamara. Commonweal 89:730-2 Mr 14 '69

Commission on intergovernmental relations

Great challenge: making our government work. K. O. Gilmore. Read Digest 94:86-91 F '69

Commission on obscenity and pornography

Commission on obscenity files progress report. Library J 94:3591-2 O 15 '69

Obscenity commission issues progress report. H. F. Pilpel and K. P. Norwick. Pub W 196:32-3 O 6 '69

Committee for economic development
See Committee for economic development

Congress

Budding revolt in Congress? curb White House writing of legislation. W. Martin. il Nations Bsns 57:56-61 Je '69

Congress meets science: the appropriations process. M. D. Reagan. bibliog il Science 164:926-31 My 23 '69

Congressional check list: most frequently asked questions about Congress. Sr Schol 94:18-19 F 28 '69
  See also
Congressional record
Congressmen
Congresswomen
Legislation—United States
Lobbying
Presidents—United States—Relations with Congress

UNITED STATES—Congress—*Continued*

Chaplains

Sorry about that, chaplain. Chr Cent 86:1053 Ag 6 '69

U.S. Senate names Elson its 50th chaplain. W. Willoughby. Chr Today 13:39 Ja 31 '69

Chaplains—Anecdotes, facetiae, satire, etc.

Prayful sonorities for senatorial snorers. Chr Cent 86:965 Jl 16 '69

Committees

Congress and the military: many members take a harder look. L. J. Carter. Science 164:278-81 Ap 18 '69

Personal business: stating your case to congressmen. Bsns W p 113 S 6 '69

Stick that in your pigeonhole. Sr Schol 94:5 F 28 '69

See also
United States—Congress—House of representatives—Committees

History

Changing role of Congress (1789-1969) il Sr Schol 94:14-15+ F 28 '69

I walk on untrodden ground. J. T. Flexner. il Am Heritage 20:24-7+ O '69

Joint committee on atomic energy

Winds of change in the Senate; moderates question defense spending. J. Finney. New Repub 160:21-3 Ap 5 '69

Pages

Fishbait and the Capitol pages. Sr Schol 94:11 F 28 '69

Powers and duties

Changing role of Congress (1789-1969) il Sr Schol 94:14-15+ F 28 '69

Congress and foreign policy; import of Resolution 85. H. J. Morgenthau. New Repub 160:16-18 Je 14 '69

Congress and military commitments: an overview. A. S. Nanes. bibliog f Cur Hist 57: 105-11+ Ag '69

Privileges and immunities

On lawbreaking congressmen. Chr Today 13:28-9 My 9 '69

See also
Franking privilege

Reorganization

Is Congress destroying itself? E. H. Methvin. Read Digest 94:65-70 Ap '69

Obsolescence on the Hill; reform proposals. C. Rabb. Nation 208:390-2 Mr 31 '69

Resolutions

Commitments resolution. il Time 94:14 Jl 4 '69

Move to limit president's power; national commitment resolution. U S News 67:6 Ji 7 '69

Neo-isolationism; National commitments resolution. K. Crawford. Newsweek 73:40 Ap 21 '69

Terminology

Congressional glossary. Sr Schol 94:25 F 28 '69

Voting

How does your congressman measure up? il Nations Bsns 57:84-8 Ap '69

90th Congress—2d session

Congress (cont) il Time 93:17-18 Je 13 '69

91st Congress

Congress and electoral reform. E. D. Eshleman and R. S. Walker. Chr Cent 86:178-81 F 5 '69

536 characters in search of a legislative program. A. Blaustein. Harper 238-28+ Mr '69

91st Congress at work. il Sr Schol 94:3-15+ F 28 '69

Reading the mind of the 91st Congress. J. Osborne. New Repub 160:11-13 Mr 29 '69

Washington trends; not so strange bedfellows. T. Trussell. Nations Bsns 57:7-8 F '69

See also
Nixon. R. M.—Relations with Congress

91st Congress—1st session

As Congress starts to move. il U S News 67: 21 D 8 '69

Behind the snafu in Washington. il U S News 67:23-4 D 22 '69

Blurred lines at half-time. il Time 95:18 Ja 5 '70

Breakdown near in Congress? il U S News 67:25-7 O 6 '69

Closing rush in Congress, adding fuel to inflation? U S News 67:4 D 29 '69

Congress. il Newsweek 73:38 Ap 14; 32-3 My 5; 36 My 12; 36 My 19; 29-30+ Je 2; 33 Je 9; 30+ Je 16; 74:22-3 Ag 11; 20-1 Ag 25; 21 D 29 '69; 75:12 Ja 5 '70

Congress. Time 93:19 Je 27 '69

Congress: delay and disarrary. il Time 94:12-13 D 19 '69

Congress: priorities at issue. il Time 94:9 D 26 '69

Congress puts it off till fall. il Bsns W p35-6 Ag 16 '69

Critical look at Congress; interview. M. Mansfield. il U S News 67:25-7 D 1 '69

Debate on slow Congress: rebuttal from top Democrats. il U S News 67:12 O 27 '69

Feckless 91st. K. Crawford. Newsweek 74:40 Jl 28 '69

Gloves are off: fight over foreign and military issues. ABM taxes, and the budget. il Bsns W p26-7 My 3 '69

Letter from Washington. R. H. Rovere. New Yorker 45:90-5 Ag 23 '69

Look at government's top-ranking Democrat. il U S News 67:14+ S 8 '69

Month in Congress. Cong Digest 48:33, 65-6+, 97, 129, 161-2 F-Je '69

Opening skirmishes; battle between military establishment and Congress. R. Hotz. Aviation W 91:17 S 22 '69

Price of neglect. il Time 93:19-20 Je 20 '69

Reports: Washington. M. Janeway. Atlan 224: 4+ O '69

Surtax revolt. Newsweek 74:22 Jl 14 '69

Voting rights or wrongs? poverty and tax bills. il Newsweek 74:19-20 D 22 '69

Why the slow pace in Congress. il U S News 67:19-20 Jl 14 '69

Youth rebellion takes the floor. Bsns W p46-8 Je 28 '69

91st Congress—2d session

Crucial business issues facing Congress. R. T. Gray. il Nations Bsns 57:32-7 D '69

Outlook for Nixon and Congress. il U S News 68:21-3 Ja 5 '70

What the next session will bring. Bsns W p 15-16 D 20 '69

House of representatives

Challenge to Congress; denying A. C. Powell his congressional seat declared unconstitutional. Time 93:17 Je 27 '69

Club business on the Hill; effort to depose J. McCormack as Speaker. R. G. Sherrill. il Nation 208:102-4 Ja 27 '69

House: the Anderson switch; Republicans. P. Duke. il New Repub 160:22-4 F 1 '69

Maverick returns; Powell affair. Sr Schol 94:15-16 Ja 17 '69

Unanswered questions in the Powell case. D. Lawrence. U S News 66:88 Je 30 '69

Warren court vs. Congress; the Powell case; how Warren and Burger differ. il U S News 66:23-4 Je 30 '69

See also
Apportionment (election law)

House of representatives—Armed services, Committee on

Overruns on C-5A costs face intensified scrutiny. D. C. Winston. Aviation W 90:26-7 My 26 '69

TRB from Washington. New Repub 160:4 Je 7 '69

Three-day travesty; debate on military authorization bill. Nation 209:394-6 O 20 '69

House of representatives—Banking and currency, Committee on

Brothers to Dillinger; looking into secret accounts. Newsweek 74:90+ D 15 '69

House of representatives—Commerce, Committee on

Caution: this hearing is hazardous; hearings on the cautionary warning on cigarette packages. il Newsweek 73:82-3+ Ap 28 '69

House of representatives—Committees

Obsolescence on the Hill; reform proposals challenge chairmen's powers. C. Rabb. Nation 208:390-2 Mr 31 '69

Testing the system in the '70s. New Repub 162:7-8 Ja 3 '70

House of representatives—Internal security, Committee on

Deadly moderation; new jurisdictional provisions to cope with new radicalism. Nation 208:260 Mr 3 '69

UNITED STATES—Congress—House of representatives—Internal security, Committee on—*Continued*

Farewell HUAC, hello HCIS Newsweek 73:30+ Je 16 '69

HUAC, by any other name. Trans-Action 6: 10-11 Je '69

If you have tears; O. Lattimore case during anti-Communist witch-hunts. W. F. Buckley, jr. Nat R 21:506 My 20 '69

Prognosis for crackdown: the wheel of panic. T. J. Lowi. Nation 208:624-8 My 19 '69

What's in a name? Newsweek 73:31-2 F 3 '69

House of representatives— Resolutions

No deliberate speed; House resolution passed to support the President's Vietnam policy. Newsweek 74:26 D 15 '69

House of representatives—Rules and practice

Reporter at large; new member: A. K. Lowenstein. F. Lewis. New Yorker 45:31-2+ Ja 10 '70

House of representatives—Un-American activities, Committee on

See United States—Congress—House of representatives—Internal security, Committee on

House of representatives—Ways and means, Committee on

Shape of reform; tax proposals. Newsweek 74:61+ Jl 28 '69

Storm over conglomerates; latest plans for curbs; hearing by the House ways and means committee. il U S News 66:86-8 Mr 24 '69

Senate

Bad medicine for a sick economy; amendment to tax bill passed. il Newsweek 74: 25-6 D 15 '69

Club business on the Hill; replacing R. Long as Democratic whip. R. G. Sherrill. il Nation 208:102-4 Ja 27 '69

Crisis in Republican leadership. il U S News 67:35-6 S 22 '69

End of the beginning. J. J. Stone. Commonweal 90:536+ S 5 '69

Filling the Dirksen gap; fight for minority leadership. il Newsweek 74:33-4 S 22 '69

Great ABM counterfeit. Commonweal 90:499-500 Ag 22 '69

Haynsworth: what the administration's defeat means; with account by C. M. Mathias. il Time 94:14-16 N 28 '69

New GOP leader. il Newsweek 74:76 O 6 '69

New style on the center aisle. il Time 94:27 N 7 '69

Nomination is rejected. il Newsweek 74:21-4 D 1 '69

Reports: Washington. M. Janeway. Atlan 224: 4+ O '69

Reports: Washington; anti-military debate. E. B. Drew. Atlan 224:4+ D '69

Republicans in the Senate, new leaders, new directions. il U S News 67:17 O 6 '69

Scale tips against the ABM; Safeguard and the senators. Newsweek 74:25-6+ Jl 21 '69

Senate imposes CBW limitations, cuts defense research. J. Walsh. Science 165:778 Ag 22 '69

Senate: the balancing act; contest for assistant leadership of Republicans. J. Osborne. il New Repub 160:19-21 F 1 '69

Senate's cynical design. F. Morley. Nations Bsns 57:21-2 My '69

Senate's responsibility. E. Gruening. Nation 208:748-9 Je 16 '69

Seven-month itch; campaign against the Pentagon. K. Crawford. Newsweek 74:25 Ag 25 '69

Showdown for Ev's chair. il Time 94:20-1 S 26 '69

Toward compromise on ABM? bill before the Senate. il Time 94:15B Jl 18 '69

Two-thirds of a loaf; legislation to extend the income tax surcharge. il Time 94:17 Ag 8 '69

Vote for moderation. Time 94:21 O 3 '69

Winds of change in the Senate; moderates question defense spending. J. Finney. New Repub 160:21-3 Ap 5 '69

See also
Government investigations
Senators

Senate—Armed services, Committee on

Safeguard: pro and con; summary of report of the Senate armed services committee. il Newsweek 74:26-7 Jl 21 '69

Why the Pentagon pays homage to John Cornelius Stennis. J. K. Batten. il N Y Times Mag p44-5+ N 23 '69

Winds of change in the Senate; moderates question defense spending. J. Finney. New Repub 160:21-3 Ap 5 '69

Senate—Employees

On a hill far away; reflections on the Interseminary church and society internship program. J. Lawrence. Chr Cent 86:1419-20 N 5 '69

Senate—Environmental pollution, Subcommittee on

Battling governmental torpor; new round of Muskie hearings. Sci N 95:450 My 10 '69

Senate—Foreign relations, Committee on

Ambitious committee. K. Crawford. Newsweek 73:40 Mr 10 '69

Neo-isolationism. K. Crawford. Newsweek 73:40 Ap 21 '69

Time for the Senate to act. Nation 209:492-3 N 10 '69

Senate—Government operations, Committee on—Permanent subcommittee on investigations

Colleges play ball; investigations by McClellan committee. F. J. Donner. Nation 209: 111-15 Ag 11 '69

Ribicoff vs. the army; hearings on corruption in Vietnam and elsewhere. D. Sanford. New Repub 161:9-10 D 13 '69

Senate—Labor and public welfare, Committee on

Senate; new leaders for health and education. B. Nelson. Science 163:654-8 F 14 '69

Senate—Nutrition and human needs, Select committee on

Documenting the hungry. il Sci N 95:160-1 F 15 '69

Politics of hunger. J. A. Hamilton. il Sat R 52:18-21+ Je 21 '69

TRB from Washington; intolerable conditions of poverty areas being explored by Senate subcommittee. New Repub 160:6 Ap 5 '69

Where it's at; Los Angeles investigation. il Time 93:23-4 My 16 '69

Senate—Rules and practice

Art of oratory in the Senate of the United States. W. H. Honan. il Esquire 71:161-7+ My '69

Fili-busters fail; cloture rule Sr Schol 94: 17-18 F 14 '69

Script that failed; attempt to end filibuster. Newsweek 73:22+ Ja 27 '69

Senate—Small business, Select committee on

Senate tracks business thieves; begins study of ways to combat stealing. Bsns W p 100 My 31 '69

Senate—Technology and the human environment, Select committee on (proposed)

Congress: Muskie seeks committee on technological backlash. P. M. Boffey. Science 163:1179 Mr 14 '69

Constitution

Heresy in Santa Barbara; suggestions of Center for the study of democratic institutions. il Time 93:26 Ja 24 '69

New Supreme court? D. Lawrence. U S News 66:96 Je 2 '69

Warren legacy; very different Constitution. J. J. Kilpatrick. il Nat R 21:794-800 Ag 12 '69

Amendments

Everyman's constitution, by H. J. Graham. Review
Nation 208:802-4 Je 23 '69. J. A. Scott

Prayer amendment no. 3. Chr Today 13:46 F 28 '69

Bill of rights

Intellectual freedom; survey by Sacramento state college students on attitudes. J. F. Krug. ALA Bul 63:320-1 Mr '69

On taking the Fifth; Senator Kennedy case. W. F. Buckley, jr. Nat R 21:870 Ag 26 '69

Origins of the Fifth amendment, by L. W. Levy. Review
Nat R 21:235-6 Mr 11 '69. C. D. Williams

Constitutional history

See also
United States—Supreme court

Constitutional law

See also
United States—Supreme court

UNITED STATES—Continued

Council of economic advisers
Economic report of the President and annual report of the Council of economic advisers; excerpts. L. B. Johnson. il Dept State Bul 60:101-17 F 3 '69
Exclusive interview with the full Council of economic advisers. il Nations Bsns 57:68-74 My '69
Games forecasters play. M. Seeger. il Duns R 93:42-3+ Ja '69
Jawing over inflation; administration to retreat from hands-off policy on wages and prices. il Bsns W p29-30 Mr 15 '69
New economists leave their last testament; Kennedy-Johnson team of economic advisers. il Bsns W p 102+ Ja 18 '69

Council on environmental quality
Environmental quality: Nixon's new council raises doubts. L. J. Carter. Science 165:44-6 Jl 4 '69
Washington needs a council of environmental and population advisors; adaptation of address, April 1969. A. W. Smith. Nat Parks 43:10-11 Je '69

Courts
See Courts—United States

Cultural history
See United States—Civilization—History

Cultural relations
Importing India's educational riches; establishments of Educational resources center, New Delhi. W. Morehouse. il Am Ed 5:14-19 My '69
United States and Romania sign understanding on libraries. Dept State Bul 61:196-8 S 1 '69
See also
American libraries abroad
Exchange of persons programs
Joint committee on United States—Japan cultural and education cooperation
People-to-people program
United States—Information agency

Culture, Popular
See United States—Popular culture

Declaration of Independence
Rugged road to independence. T. Fleming. il Read Digest 95:82-8 Jl '69
Spirit of '76; cities vie to hold international exposition to mark 200th anniversary. Newsweek 74:79-80 S 29 '69
See also
Fourth of July

Defense, Department of
Antimilitarism can be too much of a good thing. A. Hartley. il N Y Times Mag p30-1+ O 19 '69
Authoritarian prescription. W. D. Phelan, jr. Nation 209:467-73 N 3 '69
Can the military aid the home front? A. Etzioni. Cur 105:24-6 Mr '69
Death before dishonor. R. Goetz. Chr Cent 86:1083 Ag 20 '69
Defense. Sci N 95:109-10 F 1 '69
DOD attacks causes of weapon overruns. D. C. Winston. il Aviation W 91:24-5 D 8 '69
DOD fights expanded authority for GAO. K. Johnsen. Aviation W 91:21 O 6 '69
Managed propaganda, condoned disorder? J. Osborne. New Repub 160:10-11 My 10 '69
Only power Kissinger has is the confidence of the President. P. Anderson. il N Y Times Mag p 10-11+ Je 1 '69; Same abr. with title My only power is the confidence of the President. Read Digest 95:161-5 O '69
Pentagon promises to observe congressional curbs on research. M. J. Mansfield. Science 166:1386-8 D 12 '69
Pentagon purgatory; committee to review management, research, procurement and decision-making operations. Time 94:16-17 Jl 11 '69
Politician at the Pentagon. il Time 94:13-15+ Ag 29 '69
Prototype shopping comes off the shelf. il Bsns W p 162-3 S 20 '69
Rethinking the Pentagon's role. Life 67:49 D 12 '69
Robert McNamara's new sense of mission. H. Brandon. il N Y Times Mag p40-1+ N 9 '69
Role of defense; excerpts from address. M. R. Laird. Aviation W 90:17 My 5 '69
Role of the military; the power of the Pentagon. E. J. McCarthy. Cur 105:20-4 Mr '69
Sacred missions. Nation 208:717 Je 9 '69

Seven-month itch; Senate-based campaign against the Pentagon. K. Crawford. Newsweek 74:25 Ag 25 '69
Strategy shift at the Pentagon; decentralization. il Nations Bsns 57:42-5 D '69
Strongman takes hold in top Pentagon job; with editorial comment. il Bsns W p 110-12+, 156 Ap 19 '69

Appropriations and expenditures
After ABM, weapons are still the targets. il Bsns W p20 Ag 9 '69
After Vietnam. E. S. Muskie; M. L. Weidenbaum. il Sat R 52:12-17 My 24 '69
American militarism; symposium. il Look 33:17-24+ Ag 26 '69
Anti-military complex; criticism on the Hill. il Newsweek 73:29-30+ Je 2 '69
Arms costs escalate; Congress and Pentagon at loggerheads. il Bsns W p42+ Ja 25 '69
As Eisenhower was saying, we must guard against unwarranted influence by the military-industrial complex. R. F. Kaufman. il N Y Times Mag p 10-11+ Je 22 '69; Reply with rejoinder. J. R .L. Johnson, jr. p 2+ Jl 6 '69
At war with the military. Time 94:13 Ag 22 '69
Auditing the Pentagon. Commonweal 90:252-3 My 16 '69
Billion-dollar research cut. Sci N 96:550 D 13 '69
C-5A funds cut for new freedom fighter. D. C. Winston. il Aviation W 91:22 S 29 '69
Case for cutting defense spending; with editorial comment. J. Cameron. il Fortune 80:61, 68-73+ Ag 1 '69
Critics fire at military budget. il Bsns W p 112+ F 15 '69
Defense cutbacks: men, planes, ships. U S News 67:10 O 6 '69
Defense dept. to boost space, aeronautical research funding. Aviation W 90:27 My 12 '69
Defense funding stresses advanced project concepts. il Aviation W 90:19-20 Ja 20 '69
Defense procurement cut sharply. D. C. Winston. il Aviation W 91:16-17 Jl 14 '69
Defense research takes its licks. Sci N 96:146 Ag 23 '69
Defense slashes hit $3.1 billion. C. Brownlow. il Aviation W 90:16-17 Ap 7 '69
Defense under fire; the reason. il U S News 67:30-2 S 8 '69
Demand for defense cuts grows. D. C. Winston. il Aviation W 90:26 Ap 14 '69
Demands for cuts in the defense budget have led to a fundamental change in our global strategy. J. Cameron. il Fortune 80:43+ D '69
DOD given $70-75-billion goal. C. Brownlow. il Aviation W 91:16-17 O 27 '69
Dilemma for defense; excerpts. M. R. Laird. Aviation W 91:11 S 1 '69
Disarming the Pentagon; two-thirds of all federal taxes are now absorbed by the Pentagon. Commonweal 90:156-7 Ap 25 '69
Finding non-Defense money. Sci N 97:36 Ja 10 '70
Funding the new craft. Sci N 95:88-9 Ja 25 '69
Laird appeals $968.8-million cut. D. C. Winston. Aviation W 91:26-8 S 15 '69
Laird asks partial F-14 fund restoration. D. C. Winston. Aviation W 91:22 D 15 '69
Laird lowers sights on Pentagon spending. Bsns W p36 Mr 22 '69
Laird seeks major aircraft, missile cuts. D. C. Winston. il Aviation W 90:24-5 Mr 24 '69
Letter from Washington; scaling down of military expenditures. R. H. Rovere. New Yorker 45:169-70+ N 1 '69
Mel the knife. il Newsweek 74:38 N 10 '69
Military spending. New Repub 161:9 O 25 '69
Military wins a fiscal skirmish. Bsns W p46 S 13 '69
On the warpath over arms costs. U S News 68:7 Ja 12 '70
Opening skirmishes; battle between military establishment and Congress. R. Hotz. Aviation W 91:17 S 22 '69
Pentagon, under criticism from Congress, cuts back its support of controversial field-work overseas. P. M. Boffey. Science 164:1037-9 My 30 '69
Pentagon wins a costly battle; budget for new weapons. il Bsns W p28-9 S 27 '69
Phoenix of obsolescence. R. F. Kaufmann. Nation 208:656-60 My 26 '69
Pre-emptive strike; cuts announced. il Newsweek 74:22B S 1 '69
Real trouble for the Pentagon. Nation 209:197 S 8 '69
Reports; Washington; anti-military debate. E. B. Drew. Atlan 224:4+ D '69
Scorecard on defense spending. U S News 67:18 N 17 '69
$69.64 billion DOD budget voted. D. C. Winston. Aviation W 91:12 D 22 '69

UNITED STATES—Defense, Department of—
Appropriations and expenditures—*Cont.*
Snip, snip, snip; Senate vote. il Newsweek
74:20-1 Ag 25 '69
Strategic posture faces severe scrutiny. C.
Brownlow. il Aviation W 90:41-6 Mr 10 '69
Sweeping military cuts proposed. C. Brown-
low. il Aviation W 91:16-17 S 8 '69
Taking the defensive on high arms costs. il
Bsns W p70 D 6 '69
$10-billion scrap heap. il Bsns W p 164-5 S 20
'69
$3 billion more ordered cut from military
budget. Aviation W 91:17 S 1 '69
USAF, navy press tactical fighter work. il
Aviation W 90:47+ Mr 10 '69
Unpeace on earth. Commonweal 91:371-3
D 26 '69
Until next time; military-appropriations bill.
Time 94:19-20 S 26 '69
Vietnam stalls defense research effort. il
Aviation W 90:53+ Mr 10 '69
What is the military-industrial complex?
Time 93:23 Ap 11 '69
Winds of change in the Senate; moderates
question defense spending. J. Finney. New
Repub 160:21-3 Ap 5 '69

Development concept papers
DOD concept papers offer side benefits.
Aviation W 90:272-3+ Mr 10 '69

Procurement
Anguish in the defense industry. R. M. An-
derson. Harvard Bsns R 47:163-4+ N '69
Contempt of Congress; Pentagon and the pro-
duction contract for the top stage of
Minuteman III ICBMS. Nation 209:36-7 Jl
14 '69
Defense budget process revised; with edi-
torial comment. C. Brownlow. Aviation W
91:11, 16-17 N 3 '69
Defense profits: the hidden issues. A. T.
Demaree. Fortune 80:82-3+ Ag 1 '69
Dogfight over the F-15. il Bsns W p96-8
D 20 '69
New management approach; excerpts from
address. R. C. Seamans, jr. Aviation W
91:11 O 13 '69
Pre-emptive strike; cuts announced. il News-
week 74:22B S 1 '69
Proxmire drops the ax; indictment of military
buying practices. il Bsns W p29 My 31 '69
Snip, snip, snip; Senate vote. il Newsweek
74:20-1 Ag 25 '69
Viet policy shaping new patterns. il Avia-
tion W 91:10-11 mid-D '69

Defenses
Adequate defense; no peril yet, but! ad-
dress, October 4, 1969. J. W. Carpenter, 3d.
Vital Speeches 36:93-6 N 15 '69
Arms chill. Nation 208:195-6 F 17 '69
Biological warfare as national policy; ad-
dress, August 10, 1969. R. D. McCarthy.
Vital Speeches 35:681-3 S 1 '69
Bold new plan for national defense. J. G.
Hubbell. il Read Digest 95:82-7 O '69
Defense dilemma. R. Hotz. Aviation W 90:11
F 24 '69
Gambling with the security of the American
people. D. Lawrence. U S News 66:100 My
12 '69
Heavyweight in balance of terror: the MIRV.
il Bsns W p48-9 Je 28 '69
How Laird is taking hold at the Pentagon.
U S News 66:12 Mr 3 '69
How to cut the military budget by $54 bil-
lion. S. Melman. Commonweal 91:273-6
N 28 '69
Key issue; military demands vs. civilian
needs. Nation 208:354 Mr 24 '69
Lesson of history for the ABM vote. il U S
News 66:38 Ap 7 '69
Military conscription; abolish the draft; ad-
dress, November 11, 1968. W. A. Wallis.
Vital Speeches 35:284-6 F 15 '69
Military: servant or master of policy? il Time
93:20-4+ Ap 11 '69; Same abr. with title U S
military: servant or master? Read Digest
95:235-6+ Jl '69
Missiles and bombers. il Sci N 95:184-5 F
22 '69
New alarm: the submarine gap. F. V. Drake.
Read Digest 95:54-8 Ag '69
New pressures to trim U.S. defenses. il U S
News 67:38-40 Jl 21 '69
Ocean frontier. A. H. Whitelaw. il Sea Front
15:208-11 Jl '69
On nuclear sufficiency. Chr Cent 86:203 F 12
'69
Report; Washington. E. Drew. il Atlan 223:
4+ Mr '69
Row over U.S. weapons. il U S News 66:26-7
Je 30 '69
That antimilitary mood. Life 66:38 Mr 21 '69

U.S. posture, Clifford's size-up; excerpts from
statement, January 18, 1969. C. M. Clifford.
U S News 66:6 Ja 27 '69
Weapons culture, by R. E. Lapp. Review
Environ il 11:30-1 N '69. C. Hohenemser
What's the answer to ABM and the war? in-
terview. M. R. Laird. il U S News 66:30-6
Ap 7 '69
Will to fight for survival. D. Lawrence. U S
News 66:100 Ap 28 '69
Witch hunt against military? A warning; ex-
cerpts from statement to a subcommittee of
the Joint economic committee of Congress,
June 11, 1969. D. Acheson. U S News 66:16
Je 23 '69
See also
Air bases
Airplanes, Military—United States
Disarmament—United States
Guided missiles—Defenses
National defense
North American air defense command
Radar defense networks
United States—Air force
United States—Armed forces
United States—Army
United States—Defense, Department of
United States—Navy

Description and travel
American images. W. Hedgepeth. il Look
33:22-9 Jl 15 '69
Catch up on Canada; see the states. il Seven-
teen 28:140-1+ My '69
Holiday handbook; where to go; what to do.
il Holiday 45:95-118 My '69
Seventy-nine other ways to have fun in the
U.S.A. K. Thorsen. Mlle 68:270-3+ Ap '69
Travel USA: a special issue. il Holiday 45:
32-45+ My '69
Travels with Melrose. J. Burnham. Nat R
21:1210-11, 1269-71 D 2; D 16 '69
U.S. odyssey on raft, bike, and thumb. il
Sat R 52:68+ F 15 '69
U.S.A. with introd. by E. J. Steichen. M.
P. R. Thomas and M. Wright. il Travel &
Camera 32:54-86 F '69

Diplomatic and consular service
As Nixon starts naming envoys. il U S News
66:14 Mr 3 '69
Diplomatic dearth. il Time 93:25 Je 6 '69
Mixed bag; appointees. il Newsweek 74:38+
Jl 21 '69
U.S. embassy; our men in Paris. W. Man-
chester. il Holiday 45:34-9+ Mr '69
See also
Ambassadors
United States—State, Department of

Draft resisters
See Military service, Compulsory—Draft
resisters

Economic conditions
America at the crossroads; excerpts from
Britannicas book of the year 1969. L. B.
Johnson. Read Digest 94:54-8 Mr '69
Can Mr Nixon stop the inflation? il News-
week 75:49-51+ Ja 12 '70
Disinflation, not deflation. America 120:296
Mr 15 '69
Dog days hint at a cooler economy. il Bsns
W p26-7 S 6 '69
Economics in the news (cont) il Sr Schol 93:
10-11 Ja 10; 94:19 Mr 7; 9-10 Mr 14; 17-18
Mr 21; 6-8+ Ap 11 '69
Economy. R. Lekachman. See issues of
Dun's review
Economy at the turning point. il Time 94:
85-6 N 14 '69
Economy in the 1970's; what labor expects;
address, May 13, 1969. I. Stern. Vital
Speeches 35:531-4 Ag 1 '69
Economy: too hot to cool down. il Newsweek
73:75 Ap 28 '69
Good things about the U.S. today; reply.
U S News 66:108+ F 17 '69
Gradualism. il Fortune 79:23-4 Mr '69
Growth in the '70s; what the future holds
for your area. il U S News 67:48-50 S 29
'69
Inflation: the Delphic indicators; with report
by H. Simmons. il Newsweek 74:55-6 Ag 25
'69
Labor month in review. See issues of Monthly
labor review
Legacy that LBJ is leaving to America; gains,
and losses in the LBJ era. il U S News 66:
30-1 Ja 27 '69
Making the economic scene '69. il Sr Schol 94:
3-15+ Ja 31 '69
Mr Nixon's anti-inflation plea. America 121:
377-8 N 1 '69
Mixed symptoms. Time 93:74 F 7 '69
Mood of America. il U S News 67:22-6 Jl 7
'69

UNITED STATES—Economic conditions—
Continued

Myth of American affluence. S. Thernstrom. Commentary 48:74-8 O '69

Nation's biggest danger; interview. A. Burns. il U S News 67:60-5 Jl 14 '69

Nixon inherits budget that faces reality; with editorial comment. il Bsns W p 18-19, 132 Ja 18 '69

No hardening of arteries in AFL-CIO. B. L. Masse. America 121:409 N 8 '69

Of war and inflation. il Time 93:18-19 Ap 11 '69

Other side of the peak. il Fortune 80:23-4 O '69

Out on the credit limb; credit capitalism. M. Tanzer. Nation 208:686-9 Je 2 '69

Pain and suffering; effects of the credit squeeze. il Newsweek 74:70 Jl 7 '69

Potboiler. Newsweek 73:75-7 Mr 24 '69

Prices still rising; what a national survey shows. il U S News 67:29-31 D 8 '69

Rays of hope. Newsweek 73:80 My 12 '69

Recession ahead? what the odds are. il U S News 67:21-2 N 3 '69

Rising risk of recession. il Time 94:66-70+ D 19 '69

Slower economy? Not yet in living costs .il U S News 66:14 My 5 '69

TRB from Washington: moon and the market. New Repub 161:6 Jl 19 '69

Technician's perspective. J. W. Schulz. See issues of Forbes

Useful job for every American; excerpts from Britannica book of the year 1969. L. B. Johnson. Read Digest 94:82-5 Ap '69

What the indicators indicate: a slowdown in the economy at last. Newsweek 74:48 D 29 '69

What's bothering people Congress learns at home. il U S News 67:26-8 S 8 '69

Where business is good; city-by-city survey. il U S News 67:92-5 O 6 '69

Where business stands now; after a half century of growth. il U S News 66:70-1 My 26 '69

Where's the slowdown? Newsweek 74:84 N 10 '69

Who's helped or hurt by inflation. il U S News 66:40-2 Mr 3 '69

See also
Business conditions
Consumption (economics)
Housing—United States
Labor and laboring classes—United States
Negroes—Economic conditions
Prosperity
Unemployment—United States
Wages—United States

Economic history

Annals of finance; New deal. J. Brooks. New Yorker 45:107-26 S 13 '69

Consumer and the producer. P. J. McNulty. Yale R 58:537-48 Je '69

Ignatius Donnelly & the politics of discontent; inquiry into the career of a Populist. R. G. Kennedy. bibliog il Am West 6:10-14+ Mr '69

Progress report of the U.S. economy, 1850-present. il Sr Schol 94:5 Ja 31 '69

See also
Stock exchange—Crisis, October 1969
United States—Economic conditions

Economic opportunity, Office of

Antipoverty R&D: Chicago debacle suggests pitfalls facing OEO. J. Walsh. Science 165:1243-5 S 19 '69

Ghetto law; neighborhood legal services. il Newsweek 75:55-6 Ja 19 '70

Great society's poor law, by S. A. Levitan. Review
Commentary 48:99-101+ O '69. B. B. Seligman

How the mayors saved OEO. Bsns W p86 D 20 '69

Murky future of OEO. America 120:179 F 15 '69

Murphy's late show; amending the Economic opportunity act affecting Legal services program. D. Henninger. New Repub 161:11-12 N 8 '69

New mission for war on poverty? U S News 66:17 My 5 '69

New OEO fan. Time 93:15 My 2 '69

OEO and the working poor; General accounting office report. America 120:391 Ap 5 '69

OEO's future. Ed Digest 34:57-8 Ap '69

Politics of anti-poverty; commitment to community action. R. H. Davidson. il Nation 208:233-7 F 24 '69

Poverty audit. New Repub 160:7 Mr 29 '69

President and the poor. J. Osborne. New Repub 160:16-18 My 24 '69

Report card: not so bad. Sci N 95:328-9 Ap 5 '69

States lose OEO fund control. America 121:625 D 27 '69

Threat to the ombudsmen; OEO legal services program. Time 94:54+ N 7 '69

Time to hibernate? Richard Nixon requests extension. Newsweek 73:30 Je 16 '69

War and poverty. Sci N 95:232-3 Mr 8 '69
See also
Anti-poverty program, 1964-
United States—Job corps

Volunteers in service to America
See Volunteers in service to America

Economic policy

After peace breaks out, what will we do with all that extra money? E. L. Dale, jr. il N Y Times Mag p32-3+ F 16 '69

Appraisal of America's economic prospects; interviews. M. Friedman; P. A. Samuelson; H. Wallich. il Newsweek 75:52-3 Ja 12 '70

As Mr McCracken sees it. America 120:155 F 8 '69

As Nixon shifts to home front—. U S News 67:19-22 Ag 18 '69

Budget surplus that got away; with editorial comment. il Bsns W p 15-16, 96 Ag 30 '69

Burns kind of liberal conservatism. M. Viorst. il N Y Times Mag p30-1+ N 9 '69

Business slowdown coming? interview. P. W. McCracken. il U S News 66:44-8 Ap 28 '69

Changing of the guard. P. A. Samuelson. Newsweek 73:90 F 17 '69

Choices that will shape the future. Fortune 80:85-6 O '69

Cost and price stability; address, January 15, 1969. R. J. Saulnier. Vital Speeches 35:243-6 F 1 '69

Crabwise mini-squeeze. il Newsweek 73:65-6 Mr 3 '69

Curtain going up; Nixon administration. il Newsweek 73:70+ F 3 '69

Economic perspective. M. Friedman. Newsweek 74:75 D 22 '69

Economic problems; stabilization; address, February 27, 1969. W. M. Martin, jr. Vital Speeches 35:346-9 Mr 15 '69

Economy. R. Lekachman. See issues of Dun's review

Economy: what will Nixon do? G. L. Perry. il New Repub 160:19-31 Je 14 '69

Fear of overkill. il Time 93:21 My 30 '69

Fed means business; appearance of Federal reserve board chairman before the Joint economic committee of Congress. il Newsweek 73:74 Mr 10 '69

Federal finances and the economy. L. H. Keyserling. il Ann Am Acad 379:53-62 S '68

Fiscal and monetary policy. C. C. Balderston. bibliog f Ann Am Acad 379:78-82 S '68

Fiscal revolution in America, by H. Stein. Review
Bsns W il p88-90 My 3 '69
Mo Labor R 92:10-14 Ag '69. D. Dillard
Sat R 52:25 Ag 16 '69. A. Smithies

Gaps in economic intelligence. il Time 94:92+ S 12 '69

Growth in the '70s; what the future holds for your area. il U S News 67:48-50 S 29 '69

High cost of David Kennedy. Time 94:98 O 17 '69

How not to tinker with the economy. J. F. Wharton. Sat R 52:19-21 D 13 '69

New key man in battle on how to tune economy: what next? U S News 67:16 O 27 '69

New new economics in Washington. J. Davenport. il Fortune 80:100-5+ Jl '69

Nixon economics. P. A. Samuelson. Newsweek 73:92 My 12 '69

Nixon economics. H. C. Wallich. Newsweek 73:88 Je 9 '69

Nixon economy: four years of go-go or no-no for prosperity? il Sr Schol 94:10-11 Ja 31 '69

Nixon is choosing his new weapons. Bsns W p39 O 18 '69

Nixon shows the pattern. il Bsns W p33-5 Ap 19 '69

Nixon steps up his war on inflation; text of address, October 17, 1969. R. M. Nixon. U S News 67:100-2 O 27 '69

Nixon team maps out its economic strategy. il Bsns W p42-3 F 22 '69

Nixon's fight against economic problem no. 1. il Time 93:74-5 F 21 '69

No time for controls. Time 95:49 Ja 5 '70

Not enough money to go around; demand for credit in the 1970s. il Bsns W p 166-8+ D 6 '69

Okun tells it like it might have been. Bsns W p92 Ja 10 '70

Pattern of moderation. il Fortune 79:15-16 My 1 '69

UNITED STATES—Economic policy—*Cont.*
Policy makers plan loose reins, no spurs; 1970s. il Bsns W p 106+ D 6 '69
President appeals to business and labor; text of letter, October 18, 1969. R. M. Nixon. U S News 67:102 O 27 '69
President Nixon and the economy. Duns R 92:96 D '68
President settles in. il Bsns W p 13-14 F 1 '69
Pursuit of progress. G. Krettek and E. D. Cooke. Wilson Lib Bul 43:1031-2 Je '69
Ready to inflict pain. il Bsns W p25-6 S 6 '69
Redistributing national income; excerpts from Agenda for the Nation. J. Tobin. Cur 103: 19-21 Ja '69
Return to normalcy; incoming Nixon administration. il Fortune 79:21-2+ Ja '69
Rise of the techno-corporate state in America. A. S. Miller. Bul Atom Sci 25:14-19 Ja '69
Rough going for gradualism. il Bsns W p41 Je 14 '69
Slowdown: real or apparent? il Newsweek 74: 74 D 22 '69
Strategies for slowdown. Time 93:66-7 Ja 24 '69
Tax cut in Camelot; excerpts from The fiscal revolution in America. H. Stein. il Trans-Action 6:38-44 Mr '69
Theory versus practice. B. W. Sprinkel. Nations Bsns 57:27 D '69
Time's Board of economists: answering the hard questions; symposium. il Time 94:88-90 N 14 '69
To tune or not to tune? il Newsweek 73:63-4 F 10 '69
Tough new fight on inflation. il Newsweek 73:77-8+ Ap 14 '69
Washington desk. G. R. Rosen. Duns R 93: 7-8 Mr '69
We must get inflation under control; interview. D. M. Kennedy. U S News 66:56-60 My 5 '69
Western economic warfare 1947-1967. by G. Adler-Karlsson. Review
    Bul Atom Sci 25:44-6 O '69. H. I. Schiller
What business wants from President Nixon; with editorial comment. A. T. Demaree. il Fortune 79:71, 84-7+ F '69
When bad news is good news. il Life 67:46 O 17 '69
Which goals to emphasize. D. Wolfle. Science 164:249 Ap 18 '69
Will budget inhibit Nixon's slowdown? il Bsns W p35-6 N 15 '69
Wonders and woes of the LBJ economy. il pors Sr Schol 93:10-11 Ja 10 '69
    See also
Budget—United States
Government spending policy
Import quotas
Income tax—United States
Price regulation by government—United States
Tariff—United States
Taxation—United States
United States—Appropriations and expenditures

History

Affluent society after ten years; introduction to revised edition. J. K. Galbraith. Atlan 223:37-44 My '69
Whatever happened to the new economics? R. B. Du Boff. il Commonweal 91:94-8 O 24 '69; Reply. R. Eisner. 91:342-3 D 12 '69

Economic relations

Changing world trade patterns and America's leadership role. R. F. Mikesell. Ann Am Acad 384:35-44 Jl '69
Elephant in bed. H. C. Wallich. Newsweek 74:94 S 22 '69
How to stay the richest country in the world. J. H. Weaver. Commonweal 90:67-8 Ap 4 '69; Reply with rejoinder. P. G. Clark. 90: 355+ Je 13 '69
Vietnam: where do we go from here? J. W. Fulbright. Sat Eve Post 242:24-5+ F 8 '69
We're all in the same boat. F. Morley. Nations Bsns 57:17-18 Ja '69
    See also
Economic assistance, American
United States—Commerce

Canada

    See also
Joint United States-Canadian committee on trade and economic affairs

Communist countries

Needed: a realistic East-West trade policy. E. M. Dirksen. Read Digest 94:129-33 Je '69
Western economic warfare 1947-1967, by G. Adler-Karlsson. Review
    Bul Atom Sci 25:44-6 O '69. H. I. Schiller

Europe, Western

Alliance: United States and EEC countries. H. C. Wallich. Newsweek 73:98 Mr 17 '69
U.S. European communities officials hold trade talks at Washington. Dept State Bul 60:514 Je 16 '69

Japan

Steel industries of Japan and ECSC offer to limit exports to U.S; letter, with texts of steel industries' communications. D. Rusk. Dept State Bul 60:93-4 F 3 '69
    See also
Joint United States-Japan committee on trade and economic affairs

Latin America

Change in degree, not kind. America 121: 452 N 15 '69
For justice, if not for friendship; the Viña del Mar statement. America 120:703 Je 21 '69
Foreign and human relations with Latin America. C. T. Oliver. For Affairs 47:521-31 Ap '69
Looking Latinward: paternalism or partnership? D. Peerman. Chr Cent 86:1606-8 D 17 '69
Low profile in Latin America. il Time 94: 36+ N 7 '69
Rockefeller report on Latin America. il Time 94:42 N 14 '69
Rockefeller's bonfire. New Repub 160:7-9 Je 21 '69
Trade, aid, and development; excerpts from address, October 6, 1969. G. Plaza. Américas 21:54-5 N '69
Trouble with favors. Nat R 21:1204 D 2 '69
U.S. policy toward Latin America. America 121:182 S 20 '69
What Latin Americans want from U.S. il U S News 66:50 Je 23 '69
Wrong man, wrong time, wrong mission. M. M. Alves. Commonweal 90:407-9 Je 27 '69
    See also
Inter-American economic and social council

Peru

Challenging the U.S; dispute over seizure of International petroleum co. oilfields and refinery. Time 93:36 F 14 '69
Down to the wire; question of sanctions. Newsweek 73:45 Ap 7 '69
In the grip of a revolution; stakes involved in Peru's expropriation of U.S. oil investments. il Newsweek 73:52-4+ Ap 14 '69
Letter from Peru; takeover of International petroleum co. R. N. Goodwin. New Yorker 45:41-6+ My 17 '69
Peru: more troubles for U.S. il U S News 66:68 Mr 3 '69
Peru turns tougher; takeover of International petroleum co. il Bsns W p32-3 F 15 '69
Peruvian crisis. Nat R 21:371-2 Ap 22 '69
Second thoughts; case of the International petroleum corp. J. B. Utley. il Nat R 21: 644-5+ Jl 1 '69
U.S. rift cools airline expansion in Peru. R. G. O'Lone. il Aviation W 90:31-2 F 24 '69

Sweden

Where anti-U.S. action backfires. il U S News 67:95 N 10 '69

Education, Office of

Captive to funded projects? J. G. Saylor. Ed Digest 34:14-17 Mr '69
Cool man in a hot seat; Commissioner of education. R. H. De Lone. il Sat R 52:67-9+ S 20 '69
Education: Nixon nominates a schoolman as commissioner. J. Walsh. Science 163:912-15 F 28 '69
Education research: Academy cooperates in new venture. J. Welsh. Science 163:162+ Ja 10 '69
Exercise of authority: new U.S. commissioner of education. il Time 93:59 F 14 '69
Key job for a backer of integration. U S News 66:17 F 17 '69
Second time around: J. E. Allen, new commissioner of education. Newsweek 73:71 F 17 '69
U.S. education chief sees moon shot for education. S. Wagner. Pub W 196:24-5 Ag 11 '69
USOE forms reading committee. Library J 94:4568 D 15 '69
Where the money is: American education's annual guide to OE programs. il Am Ed 5:19-24 F '69
    See also
Eric
Talent Search programs (education)

Appropriations and expenditures

New fight to save book, library programs. S. Wagner. Pub W 196:18 D 15 '69

UNITED STATES—Education, Office of—Appropriations and expenditures—*Continued*
Senate approves increased interim USOE expenditures. S. Wagner. Pub W 196:25 N 24 '69
Senate exempts education from spending limit. S. Wagner. Pub W 195:40 Je 30 '69

Educational personnel training, Division of

Education professions development; investment in the future. D. Davies. il Am Ed 5:9-10 F '69

Educational research and development, Bureau of

ERIC abstracts and ERIC indexes; shortcuts to creative writing documents. R. V. Denby. Engl J 58:139-44 Ja '69

Institute of international studies

OE's Institute of international studies. R. Leestma. il Am Ed 5:5-8 My '69

Library programs, Division of

Fellowship awards announced by DLP. Library J 94:1826+ My 1 '69
Library programs gain in shakeup at OE. Library J 94:3391 O 1 '69
National topics for 1969 outlined by Ray Fry. Library J 94:927 Mr 1 '69
Regionalization has nine lives; progress report by regional coordinator. M. R. Vale. il Library J 94:3016-18 S 15 '69
Tomato as big as the Ritz; latest list of institutes for training in librarianship as issued by the Division of library programs. K. Nyren. Library J 94:925 Mr 1 '69
Washington reports. R. M. Fry and H. A. Carl. ALA Bul 63:576-7 My '69
Washington spring. K. Nyren. il Library J 94:1945-9 My 15 '69

Library programs and educational technology, Bureau of

OE library bureau status still unclear. Library J 93:3947 N 1 '69

Environment quality council

See United States—Council on environmental quality

Environmental science services administration

Hurricane warning! E. Hughes. il Read Digest 95:21-2+ S '69

Equal employment opportunity commission

Rush of action to get more jobs for Negroes. il U S News 67:67-8 S 15 '69
Teddy on the attack; Everett Dirksen attacks operations. Newsweek 73:32+ Ap 7 '69

Executive committees

See United States—Executive departments

Executive departments

Big government; is it out of hand? il U S News 66:28-30 Mr 24 '69
Cleaning up the maze in Washington; to revamp Executive branch and untangle federal, state, and local relationships. il Bsns W p 163-4 Je 21 '69
Committees, come to order. il Newsweek 73:28-9 F 17 '69
Department of exploration; proposal. J. Lear. Sat R 52:30 Ag 23 '69
Department of peace; Senator Vance Hartke's proposal. Commonweal 89:631-2 F 21 '69
Discipline and order but an open image; expansion of executive branch of the federal government. J. Osborne. New Repub 160:11-13 F 22 '69
Great challenge; making our government work. K. O. Gilmore. Read Digest 94:86-91 F '69
Nation directed to peace? D. Lucey and R. Lucey. America 121:120-1 Ag 30 '69
Nixon's new organization chart. Bsns W p34 N 8 '69
Raiders are coming! Ralph Nader's investigation. Newsweek 73:74+ Je 16 '69

Executive office of the president

Boardroom men on the middle ground. H. Sidey. il Life 67:4 O 3 '69
Budding revolt in Congress? curb White House writing of legislation. W. Martin. il Nations Bsns 57:56-61 Je '69
Good or bad? Certainly different. H. Sidey. il Life 66:4 Ap 25 '69
President's men. by P. Anderson. Review Commentary 47:74-6 Ap '69. R. K. Huitt
Putting the heat on Mr Nixon. J. Osborne. New Repub 160:11-12 Ap 19 '69

Expenditures

See United States—Appropriations and expenditures

Exploring expeditions

Century of the wild Colorado. il Life 67:46-51 O 31 '69
Powell's quest. M. C. Rabbitt. il Am For 75:8-9+ S '69
Retracing John Wesley Powell's historic voyage down the Grand Canyon. J. Judge. il Nat Geog 135:668-713 My '69

Federal aviation administration

Air traffic cop; on the hottest spot in aviation; Kennedy international airport. R. Lindsey. il N Y Times Mag p28-9+ S 14 '69
Big A. R. B. Parke. Flying 84:26 Mr '69
Both FAA, controller unit harden positions in dispute. Aviation W 91:30-1 Ag 4 '69
Crosswinds over congested airports; new FAA rule. Bsns W p31 O 4 '69
FAA adopts air taxi, commuter rules. Aviation W 91:31 D 22 '69
FAA, airlines weigh Pacific satcom. P. J. Klass. Aviation W 91:199-200+ O 20 '69
FAA asks area navigation views in July. Aviation W 90:32 Je 30 '69
FAA criticized on safety, traffic control. Aviation W 91:34 D 15 '69
FAA eases limitations on airport access. D. A. Brown. Aviation W 90:22 Mr 3 '69
FAA hit on air traffic control efforts. D. C. Winston. Aviation W 90:34 F 24 '69
FAA proposes new control system. J. P. Woolsey. il Aviation W 91:24-5 O 6 '69
FAA proposes restraints on drug traffic. Aviation W 91:112 Ag 18 '69
FAA to act on 747 noise requirements. R. G. O'Lone. il Aviation W 91:35-6 D 8 '69
FAA to revise air controller programs. D. A. Brown. Aviation W 91:24-5 Ag 18 '69
Hijack detector tested by FAA. Aviation W 91:53 S 22 '69
Now Volpe tackles the air traffic snarl; FAA team trying to modernize nation's airways. il Bsns W p 116-17 My 24 '69
U.S. court ruling upholds FAA in transfer of air controllers. Aviation W 91:27 N 10 '69
Violations; the law and the pilot. R. L. Collins. Flying 85:70+ N '69
Washington advisory. D. H. Scott. See issues of Flying to September 1969

Appropriations and expenditures

FAA pushes for user charges, seeks increased ATC funding. D. A. Brown. Aviation W 90:31 Ja 20 '69

Procurement

Total-system approach gains emphasis in FAA purchasing. Aviation W 91:25 O 6 '69

Federal bureau of investigation

Confessions of the FBI; tapping telephone calls of Dr Martin Luther King and C. Clay. Newsweek 73:29-30 Je 16 '69
F.B.I. in our open society, by H. Overstreet and B. Overstreet. Review Commentary 48:77-8+ Jl '69. I. Silver
FBI in our open society, by H. Overstreet and B. Overstreet and Communism, by J. E. Hoover; reviews. M. S. Evans. Nat R 21:499-500 My 29 '69
I was a burglar, wiretapper, bugger, and spy for the F.B.I. W. Turner. il Ramp Mag 7:47-51 Ja 25 '69
More dirty business; bugging M. L. King. Nation 209:5 Jl 7 '69
Out to get the Panthers; FBI and Chicago police. L. F. Palmer, jr. Nation 209:78-82 Jl 28 '69
Reporter or informer? Nation 209:461+ N 3 '69
Right to eavesdrop? Newsweek 73:37 Je 23 '69
Some disturbing parallels. W. Turner. il Ramp Mag 7:127-31 Ja 25 '69
What have they done since they shot Dillinger? T. Wicker. il N Y Times Mag p4-7+ D 28 '69
Wrong occupation; newsmen moonlighting for FBI. il Time 94:69 N 14 '69

National crime information center

FBI's computer war against crime. il U S News 67:70-1 O 20 '69

Federal commissions

Commission; how to create a blue-chip consensus; Time essay. Time 95:23 Ja 19 '70

Federal communications commission

Activist at the FCC? Time 94:22 N 21 '69
Banks get FCC static on radio-TV stocks. Bsns W p41 Je 7 '69

UNITED STATES—Federal communications commission—*Continued*

Book burning, FCC style; anti-smoking ads. M. Friedman. Newsweek 73:86 Je 16 '69

Boredom in perpetuity? licensing policy. New Repub 161:9 Jl 5 '69

Burger vs. FCC. R. L. Shayon. Sat R 52:40 Jl 26 '69

Christmas list; Pastore bill. J. Fischer. Harper 239:26 D '69

Cigarette ban on TV? pro and con discussion. Sr Schol 94:4-5 Mr 14 '69

Cigarette companies would rather fight than switch; showdown coming in cigarette advertising. E. B. Drew. il N Y Times Mag p36-7+ My 4 '69

Donahue's choice; KHJ-TV loses license renewal battle to Fidelity TV. Nation 209:164 S 1 '69

Dubious appointments; D. Burch and R. Wells. Nation 209:333 O 6 '69

Fairness doctrine under review. America 120:493 Ap 26 '69

FCC bares its fangs; decision not to renew license of WHDH-TV. Newsweek 73:65-6 F 3 '69

FCC creates some static. il Newsweek 73:80+ Mr 17 '69

FCC impropriety; WPIX-Forum case. D. Zwerdling. New Repub 160:10-11 Je 21 '69

FCC launches cable-satellite investigation to establish policy. K. Johnsen. Aviation W 91:23 D 8 '69

FCC: policy by whimsy. Nation 208:197 F 17 '69

FCC stirs up the pot; license-renewal battles. Newsweek 73:65 Je 2 '69

FCC's computer printout is still a blank. Bsns W p97 N 22 '69

How to free TV. M. Friedman. Newsweek 74:82 D 1 '69

It's up in the air: who owns television? J. Tebbel. Sat R 52:75-6 My 10 '69

New boys for the FCC. R. L. Shayon. Sat R 52:34 S 27 '69

New chief for the FCC. Time 94:75-6 S 5 '69

Nicholas Johnson vs. Broadcasting. R. L. Shayon. Sat R 52:82+ Ap 12 '69

Nixon's FCC nominees. J. McLaughlin. America 121:431-2 N 8 '69

No smoking on the air? Bsns W p36 F 8 '69

Pastore's pet. New Repub 161:10-11 O 25 '69

Pix mix at WPIX? il Newsweek 73:77 Je 30 '69

Public be damned. New Repub 161:14 S 27 '69

Public regulation and the news media. J. McLaughlin. America 121:586-9 D 13 '69

Rippling the waves; the magazine Broadcasting, and the FCC. Commonweal 90:-1 Ap 4 '69

Signals: one, two, three; new FCC order affecting cable TV operators. R. L. Shayon. Sat R 52:75 D 6 '69

Signs of life at the FCC; proposed diversification of control over mass media. S. Lazarus. New Repub 160:16-18 F 22 '69

Strange new man at the FCC; D. Burch. il Forbes 104:26-7 N 15 '69

Taking sides; opposition by Negro group to Pastore bill on broadcasting licenses. R. L. Shayon. Sat R 52:65 N 15 '69

Television and cigarettes: whither fairness? S. Cupps. Chr Cent 86:1085-7 Ag 20 '69

Trying to swat the FCC's gadfly. Bsns W p21 Ag 30 '69

Two nominees to a key agency. U S News 67:23 S 29 '69

Two views on the regulation of television: Pastore bill. L. L. Jaffe; N. Johnson. New Repub 161:14-19 D 6 '69

Welcome to the club; Dean Burch appointment. Newsweek 74:28 S 8 '69

What you can do to improve TV. N. Johnson. Harper 238:14+ F '69

What's at stake; FCC-CATV struggle over integrating cable into over-the-air program transmission. R. L. Shayon. Sat R 52:30 Je 21 '69

White House gets into the FCC act; recommendations for domestic satellite system. Bsns W p31 Jl 26 '69

Who will cry havoc? licenses and renewal. R. L. Shayon. Sat R 52:22 Je 28 '69

Federal highway administration

Government broadens road hearing rules. Nat Parks 43:20-1 Mr '69

Running over the public; proposed regulations on selection of highway locations. New Repub 160:12 Ja 25 '69

Federal home loan bank board

S&Ls look for sympathy at the top. Bsns W p72+ Mr 29 '69

Federal housing administration

Boost in FHA mortgage rates; what it means. U S News 68:8 Ja 12 '70

Federal maritime commission

Lady skipper for the merchant fleet. il Bsns W p74-5 S 20 '69

Federal mediation and conciliation service

Collective bargaining in the public sector; excerpts from addresses at Collective bargaining forum, sponsored by Institute of collective bargaining and group relations. bibliog Mo Labor R 92:60-9 Jl '69

Drawing jurisdictional lines in mediation. J. F. Mead and J. Krislov. bibliog Mo Labor R 92:41-5 Ap '69

FMCS and dispute mediation in the federal government. W. Abner. Mo Labor R 92:27-9 My '69

Instant mediation: today's formula for heading off strikes. U S News 67:62 Ag 18 '69

New mediator has tougher job. Bsns W p80 F 8 '69

Federal power commission

Too good to last? looming crisis in natural gas supply. il Forbes 104:29-30 N 1 '69

Federal reserve board

Cloud over forecasts: does the Fed mean it? il Bsns W p33-4 Mr 8 '69

Deflation: an economic waiting game. il Newsweek 73:83 Ap 12 '69

Does the Fed really mean it this time? squeeze or a bear hug. il Bsns W p30-1 Ap 12 '69

Economic wringer: is it about to work? Newsweek 73:73 Je 16 '69

Fed means business. il Newsweek 73:74 Mr 14 '69

Fed puts plugs in some leaks. Bsns W p 12-13 Jl 5 '69

Fed's new course. Fortune 79:82 Ap '69

Fuss over the Federal reserve. il Time 93:86-7 Mr 14 '69

Guessing game that saddles economists; forecasting what the Fed will do. Bsns W p35 Mr 8 '69

How Burns will change the Fed. il Bsns W p 102-4+ O 25 '69

Last of the great Populists takes on the foundations, the banks, the Federal reserve, the Treasury. R. Sherrill. il N Y Times Mag p24-5+ Mr 16 '69

Loosening a Fed rein; Regulation Q sets interest rate ceilings on bank deposits. il Bsns W p72-3 F 8 '69

Mr Nixon has a friend at the Fed. il Newsweek 74:88+ O 27 '69

Monetary overkill. M. Friedman. Newsweek 74:75 Ag 18 '69

Money and inflation. M. Friedman. il Newsweek 73:105 My 26 '69

Nixon's new maestro of money. il Time 94:89-90 O 24 '69

Showdown for the Fed; anti-inflation drive. il Bsns W p25-6 Mr 1 '69

To guard the dollar. T. Trussell. Nations Bsns 57:7-8 Mr '69

Where Arthur sits. Fortune 80:62 D '69

Who's laughing now? Forbes 103:61 My 1 '69

Will the Fed lose its bank jobs? Bsns W p 144 S 20 '69

Federal trade commission

Consumers and the regulators. Life 67:34 O 3 '69

Consumer's impotent friend in Washington. Time 94:83 S 26 '69

Critique of the FTC: American bar association study. New Repub 161:8-9 O 18 '69

Do auto prices mean what they say? il Bsns W p60-1+ S 6 '69

FTC backs away from censor's role. S. Wagner. Pub W 195:234-5 Ja 20 '69

FTC: is it doing enough for consumers? il Changing T 23:17-19 Ap '69

Gadflies; R. Nader report. Nation 208:69 Ja 20 '69

Groceries, gas and games; Economic report on the use of games of chance in food and gasoline retailing. J. Cross. Nation 208:370-2 Mr 24 '69

Investigating the FTC. New Repub 160:7-8 My 3 '69

Loaded odds; FTC investigation of promotional lures by food-chains and oil companies. il Time 93:86-7 Ap 18 '69

Nader report on the Federal trade commission, by E. F. Cox and others. Review Sat R 53:37-8 Ja 10 '70. D. A. Swankin

Nader's raiders and the traders. S. Watzman. Nation 209:317 S 29 '69

Regulation, Nixon style; ABA report. il Newsweek 74:35-6 S 29 '69

Smoking debate lights up again. U S News 66:16 Je 2 '69

War on mergers escalates. il Bsns W p36-7 Ap 19 '69

UNITED STATES—*Continued*

Federal water pollution control administration

FWPCA reorganizes. Am City 84:162-3 Mr '69
Lake Superior, private dump; Stoddard and FWPCA reports; hearings in Duluth. G. Hill. Nation 208:795-6 Je 23 '69
Nukes are in hot water; thermal pollution caused by hot-water from nuclear plants. R. H. Boyle. il Sports Illus 30:24-8 Ja 20 '69
Other ear opens; lack of adequate sewage treatment plants. Sci N 96:350 O 18 '69
Pollution control by suasion. Sci N 95:526 My 31 '69
Water-pollution control: trouble at headquarters. L. J. Carter. il Science 165:572-3+ Ag 8 '69

Food and drug administration

Battle to keep drugs on the market. Bsns W p30 O 4 '69
Big brouhaha over sweeteners. il Bsns W p98+ O 18 '69
Cleaning out the medicine chest. il Time 94:64 Jl 25 '69
Consumer protection. New Repub 160:10 F 15 '69
Cyclamates banned. il Sci N 96:369-70 O 25 '69
Diet drinks take a lump; new labeling rule for products artificially sweetened with cyclamates. Bsns W p37 Ap 12 '69
Drug reaction; Senate subcommittee hearings. Newsweek 74:71 Ag 25 '69
Drug testing: is time running out? W. M. O'Brien. Bul Atom Sci 25:8-14 Ja '69; Discussion. 25:12-19 Je '69
Edwards for Ley at FDA. Sci N 96:552 D 13 '69
Food additives: blessing or bane? il Time 94:41-2 D 19 '69
FDA and Panalba: a conflict of commercial, therapeutic goals? M. Mintz. Science 165:875-81 Ag 29 '69; Reply. R. T. Parfet, jr. bibliog 166:1354 D 12 '69
FDA shake-up. Newsweek 74:37 D 29 '69
FDA vs. the boss; Panalba case. il Sci N 95:523 My 31 '69
Salting the pure-food mine; FDA report on MSG. Sci N 96:295 O 4 '69; Reply. J. W. Olney. 96:468 N 22 '69
Sweet and sinister; proposed regulation on stating cyclamate content. A. S. Grove, jr. New Repub 160:10 Je 14 '69

Foreign economic policy
See United States—Economic relations

Foreign opinion

America: three foreign comments. A. Howard; S. Lietzmann; A. de Segonzac. Harper 238:91-2+ F '69
America's moral and ethical stature abroad. D. Martindale. Ann Am Acad 384:96-103 Jl '69
As others see us; comp. by N. G. Balint. See issues of Saturday review
How it looks from the colonies. D. Brogan. il Esquire 72:26+ O '69
How Nixon rates now at home and abroad. il U S News 67:23-8 Ag 11 '69
How the world views Nixon. P. Lisagor. Nations Bsns 57:21-2 F '69
My Lai from abroad. Time 94:17 D 12 '69
Voices from abroad: teens from Paris to Saigon tell you what they think about protest, parents, music, movies and Americans. Seventeen 28:98-9+ Ja '69

Australian
Australia looks to Nixon. J. M. Van Der Kroef. il Nat R 21:119-21 F 11 '69

British
America 1968, by M. Hastings. Review
    Sat R 52:89 Ap 12 '69. S. W. Little
Arnold Toynbee talks of peace, power, race in America; interview, ed. by J. R. Moskin. A. Toynbee. Look 33:25-7 Mr 18 '69
New look at America. C. Brogan. Nat R 21:232 Mr 11 '69
U.S. campus war through English eyes. J. M. Cameron. Commonweal 90:404-5 Je 27 '69
Young Englishman looks at New York. P. Fox. Seventeen 28:126-7+ O '69

European
How America has changed; interview with two newsmen home from abroad. R. A. Haeger and F. C. Painton. il U S News 67:70-4 S 1 '69
Moonstruck. J. Burnham. Nat R 21:21 Ja 14 '69

Latin American
Looking Latinward: paternalism or partnership? D. Peerman. Chr Cent 86:1606-8 D 17 '69

Swedish
How neutral is Sweden? N. E. Brodin. Nat R 21:73+ Ja 28 '69

Turkish
Bloody Sunday; anti-American demonstrators. il Newsweek 73:37 Mr 3 '69

Vietnamese
South Viet Nam: rising resentment of the U.S. il Time 94:28-9 O 24 '69

Foreign population
See also
Cubans in the United States
Immigration and emigration—United States
Puerto Ricans in the United States

Foreign relations

Address before the National press club, Canberra, Australia, August 8, 1969. W. P. Rogers. Dept State Bul 61:178-81 S 1 '69
After Vietnam, what? symposium. il Commonweal 90:7-14 Mr 21 '69; Same. Cur 109:49-51 Ag '69
American foreign affairs; black America; address, March 10, 1969. F. H. Williams. Vital Speeches 35:478-80 My 15 '69
American foreign policy, by H. A. Kissinger. Review
    Nat R 21:601-2 Je 17 '69. G. Niemeyer
American power and the new mandarins, by N. Chomsky. Review
    Cath World 210:80-1 N '69. S. Melman
    Commentary 47:35-44 My '69. L. Abel; Discussion. 48:12+ O; 4+ D '69
    Fortune il 79:155-6 My 1 '69. I. Kristol
America's moral and ethical stature abroad. D. Martindale. Ann Am Acad 384:96-103 Jl '69
America's new isolationism. A. Lejeune. Nat R 21:1273 D 16 '69
America's role in the world; address, June 4, 1969. R. M. Nixon. Vital Speeches 35:548-50 Jl 1 '69; Same. Dept State Bul 60:525-8 Je 23 '69; Excerpts. U S News 66:64-6 Je 16 '69
ABM: President Nixon's Vietnam? N. Cousins. il Sat 52:22-3 Mr 8 '69
Arnold Toynbee talks of peace, power, race in America; interview, ed. by J. R. Moskin. A. Toynbee. Look 33:25-7 Mr 18 '69
Autocrat in the action arena; H. Kissinger. D. Nevin. il Life 67:50-1+ S 5 '69
Changing role of U.S. in world; Nixon policy takes shape. U S News 67:29-30 S 29 '69
Cold comfort from our cold war outlook. Nations Bsns 57:47-50 N '69
Confrontation is an outdated word; forecast for the 70's. il Bsns W p88-9+ D 6 '69
Congress and foreign policy; import of Resolution 85. H. J. Morgenthau. New Repub 160:16-18 Je 14 '69
Continuity and change in foreign policy; address, December 11, 1968. J. J. Sisco. Dept State Bul 60:27-30 Ja 13 '69
Creating stability out of revolution. J. M. Allison. Sat R 52:52 My 10 '69
Does American foreign policy entail frequent wars? P. Findley. Ann Am Acad 384:45-52 Jl '69
Enter; the Nixon era. il Sr Schol 94:6-7+ Ja 17 '69
European commentator looks at U.S. foreign policy today; America's lost innocence. J. H. Huizinga. il N Y Times Mag p30-1+ Ja 26 '69
Experiences, by A. Toynbee. Review
    Sat R 52:57-8 Je 21 '69. G. Culligan
Fifty years ago and now. D. Lawrence. U S News 67:102 S 29 '69
Five powder kegs to watch. il Nations Bsns 57:38-40 Mr '69
For a troubled America; plain talk from the President; excerpts from address, June 4, 1969. R. M. Nixon. il U S News 66:64-6 Je 16 '69
For want of a program. Commonweal 89:607-8 F 14 '69
Foreign policy implications of the ABM debate. J. W. Fulbright. Bul Atom Sci 25:20-3 Je '69
Foreign policy of the Nixon administration: its aims and strategy; address, September 5, 1969. E. L. Richardson. Dept State Bul 61:257-60 S 22 '69
Formulation of foreign policy: responsibility and opportunity; message, January 22, 1969. W. P. Rogers. Dept State Bul 60:125-6 F 10 '69
Fortress America? K. Crawford. Newsweek 73:40 Mr 24 '69

UNITED STATES—Foreign relations—*Cont.*
Fragmentation and fuzzification. Chr Cent 86: 140 Ja 29 '69
From Eisenhower's speeches and writings. D. D. Eisenhower. il Sr Schol 94:13 Ap 11 '69
Fulbright's revenge; plans to resurrect National commitments resolution. il Newsweek 73:38 Ap 14 '69
Future of the Foreign relations series; address, June 16, 1969. W. M. Franklin. bibliog f Dept State Bul 61:247-51 S 15 '69
Henry Kissinger: strategist in the White House basement. G. Astor. Look 33:53-6 Ag 12 '69
If American will crumbles; interview. R. Aron. U S News 67:43 D 1 '69
In quest of peace; excerpts from Britannica book of the year 1969. L. B. Johnson. il Read Digest 94:219-24+ F '69
International outlook. See issues of Business week
Intervention and revolution: America's confrontation with insurgent movements around the world, by R. J. Barnet. Review
  Commentary 47:78-80 F '69. W. Pfaff
Inviting an era of negotiation. il Life 66:32 Ja 31 '69
Issues for the '70s. H. Cox. Commonweal 90:18-20 Mr 21 '69
Kissinger: the uses and limits of power. il Time 93:17-22 F 14 '69
Launching a new diplomacy: Nixon's report to the Nation; text of news conference, March 4, 1969. R. M. Nixon. il U S News 66:70-6 Mr 17 '69; Same with title President Nixon's news conference of March 4. Dept State Bul 60:237-47 Mr 24 '69
Law, power and the pursuit of peace by E. V. Rostow. Review
  Cath World 209:222-3 Ag '69. D. W. Louisell
Letter from Washington; concerning Nixon's address at the Air force academy. R. H. Rovere. New Yorker 45:86+ Je 14 '69
Letter from Washington; Nixon administration. R. H. Rovere. New Yorker 45:131-3 My 17; 72-3 Jl 12 '69
Limits and responsibilities of American power; address, December 4, 1968. W. W. Rostow. Dept State Bul 60:4-7 Ja 6 '69
Limits of commitment: a Time-Louis Harris poll. il Time 93:16-17 My 2 '69
McCarthy talk; interviews, ed. by J. Roddy. E. McCarthy. il Look 33:19-21 Ap 1 '69
Making the world safe for America. R. Radosh. Nation 209:350-1 O 6 '69
Man with a pressure cooker job; how Kissinger exercises power. il U S News 67: 15-16 Jl 14 '69
Mediterranean crisis. F. S. Meyer. Nat R 21: 75 Ja 28 '69
Military power and foreign policy; address, June 2, 1969. A. B. Duke. Vital Speeches 35:628-31 Ag 1 '69
Mr Nixon changes tune; concerning address at Air force academy. il Newsweek 73:24-5 Je 16 '69
National priorities and participation in foreign policy. G. W. Shepherd, jr. Chr Cent 86:504-7 Ap 16 '69
New foreign policy for the United States. by H. J. Morgenthau. Review
  Commentary 47:103 My '69. W. Pfaff
  Nat R 21:442-3 My 6 '69. J. Burnham
New guidelines for foreign policy; excerpts from Agenda for the Nation. H. A. Kissinger. Cur 103:25-6 Ja '69
Nixon and the new Washington. il Nations Bsns 57:32-4+ Ja '69
Nixon diplomacy; a full schedule. il U S News 66:21 Ap 14 '69
Nixon looks abroad. il Newsweek 73:27-8 F 17 '69
Nixon's diplomacy: the Viet Nam war and beyond. il Time 93:21 Ap 18 '69
Nixon's knaves; reactions to address at the Air force academy. K. Crawford. Newsweek 73:38 Je 23 '69
Nixon's opening news session: Mideast, Vietnam, inflation; excerpts from news conference, January 27, 1969. R. M. Nixon. il U S News 66:55-6 F 10 '69; Same. Dept State Bul 60:141-4 F 17 '69
Nixon's own words on My Lai, taxes, prospects for peace; text of news conference, December 8, 1969. R. M. Nixon. il U S News 67:48-52 D 22 '69
Nixon's trip; aims, chances for success. il U S News 67:32 Ag 4 '69
No more Vietnams? ed. by R. M. Pfeffer. Review
  New Repub 160:36+ F 1 '69. W. Pfaff
On talking across the generation gap. B. L. Masse. America 120:661 Je 7 '69
On the causes of our discontents. T. L. Hughes. For Affairs 47:653-67 Jl '69

Only power Kissinger has is the confidence of the President. P. Anderson. il N Y Times Mag p 10-11+ Je 1 '69; Same abr. with title My only power is the confidence of the President. Read Digest 95:161-5 O '69
Past master of the soft sell: Secretary of state W. P. Rogers. H. Smith. il N Y Times Mag p8-9+ Jl 27 '69
Path to total destruction; books by D. F. Fleming. N. L. Parks. Nation 208:153+ F 3 '69
Peace on earth? K. Crawford. Newsweek 74: 23 D 29 '69
Pentagonism: a substitute for imperialism, by J. Bosch. Review
  New Repub 160:20-2 F 8 '69. R. J. Barnet
Pilot Nixon: and his copilot. H. J. Sievers. America 121:86 Ag 16 '69
Policy for the 70s; after the Vietnam war, how not to be the world's policeman. S. Hoffmann. Life 66:68-70+ Mr 21 '69
President Nixon discusses the objectives of his European trip; excerpts from remarks, February 21, 1969. R. M. Nixon. Dept State Bul 60:217-19 Mr 17 '69
President Nixon's first thirty days. il U S News 66:27-8 F 24 '69
President Nixon's news conference:
  March 14, 1969. Dept State Bul 60:275-80 Mr 31 '69
  June 19, 1969. R. M. Nixon. Dept State Bul 61:1-5 Jl 7 '69
Problems of disengagement; address, November 13, 1969. D. M. Abshire. Vital Speeches 36:190-2 Ja 1 '70
Report card for Richard Nixon. J. J. Kilpatrick. il Nat R 21:532-7 Je 3 '69
Right away, problems waiting around the world. il U S News 66:38-41 Ja 27 '69
Road back to internationalism. H. Cleveland. Atlan 223:57-9 My '69
Secretary Rogers, bigger role in quest for peace. il U S News 67:12 D 22 '69
Secretary Rogers interviewed on Meet the press; transcript of interview, October 12, 1969. W. P. Rogers. Dept State Bul 61:345-50 O 27 '69
Secretary Rogers news conference:
  April 7, 1969. Dept State Bul 60:357-63 Ap 28 '69
  June 5, 1969. Dept State Bul 60:529-35 Je 23 '69
  July 2, 1969. Dept State Bul 61:41-9 Jl 21 '69
  August 20, 1969. Dept State Bul 61:201-8 S 8 '69
  October 25, 1969. Dept State Bul 61:389-94 N 10 '69
Secretary Rusk interviewed on Face the Nation; program, December 1, 1968. D. Rusk. Dept State Bul 59:645-50 D 23 '68
Secretary Rusk's news conference:
  January 3, 1969. D. Rusk. Dept State Bul 60:45-52 Ja 20 '69
Sino-Soviet tensions and American foreign policy. D. F. Halloran. Cath World 209: 151-5 Jl '69
Slogans and realities. G. W. Ball. For Affairs 47:623-41 Jl '69
Summing up the LBJ years. il Sr Schol 93:3-9 Ja 10 '69
TRB from Washington; power shakedown. New Repub 160:6 F 22 '69
Talk with Walter Lippmann, at eighty, about this minor dark age; interview, ed. by H. Brandon. W. Lippmann. il N Y Times Mag p25-7+ S 14 '69
This month's feature: Congress & U.S. military commitments. Cong Digest 48:193-224 Ag '69
Toward a worldwide peace; address to U.N. September 18, 1969. R. M. Nixon. il U S News 67:98-101 S 29 '69; Same with title Establishment of peace. Vital Speeches 35: 738-41 O 1 '69; Same with title Strengthening the total fabric of peace. Dept State Bul 61:297-302 O 6 '69
Under Secretary Richardson interviewed on CBS television; news program July 2, 1969. E. L. Richardson. Dept State Bul 61:49-51 Jl 21 '69
United States and world affairs; address, February 18, 1969. H. Donovan. Wilson Lib Bul 43:734-9 Ap '69
United States foreign policy; address, April 12, 1969. P. Findley. Vital Speeches 35: 520-3 Je 15 '69
U.S. foreign policy; some major issues; statement, March 27, 1969. W. P. Rogers. Dept State Bul 60:305-12 Ap 14 '69; Same with title: Foreign relations; disarmament. Vital Speeches 35:420-5 My 1 '69; Excerpts. U S News 66:43-4 Ap 7 '69
Very expensive education of McGeorge Bundy. D. Halberstam. il Harper 239:21-37 Jl '69

UNITED STATES—Foreign relations—*Cont.*
Vietnam and the end of the age of superpowers. A. Schlesinger, jr. Harper 238:41-9 Mr '69; Discussion. 238:6+ My '69
Vietnam: are there any lessons? T. M. Conrad. Commonweal 90:78-80 Ap 4 '69
Viet-Nam in the perspective of East Asia; address, April 21, 1969. W. P. Rogers. Dept State Bul 60:397-400 My 12 '69
Vietnam: where do we go from here? J. W. Fulbright. Sat Eve Post 242:24-5+ F 8 '69
Waiting to ask the President. Newsweek 73:38+ F 3 '69
War, peace, and the presidency, by H. Paolucci. Review
  Nat R 21:184-5 F 25 '69. J. Hart
Wars in your future. J. W. Fulbright. Look 33:82+ D 2 '69
We honorable imperialists. J. Featherstone. New Repub 160:15-17 Ja 25 '69
Where U.S. stands in world as top authorities see it. il U S News 66:50-1 Je 30 '69
Who's making foreign policy for the United States? il U S News 66:45-6 Ap 7 '69
Will to fight for survival. D. Lawrence. U S News 66:100 Ap 28 '69
World peace: the United Nations; address, January 29, 1969. A. Cranston. Vital Speeches 35:358-60 Ap 1 '69
World power and population. C. Clark. il Nat R 21:481-4 My 20 '69
World war III in the 1970's? D. Lawrence. U S News 67:96 N 3 '69
See also
Economic assistance, American
Europe and the United States
International security
Military assistance, American
Nixon, R. M.—Visit to Asia and Rumania, 1969
United Nations—United States
United States—Congress—Foreign relations. Committee on
United States—Diplomatic and consular service
United States—Economic relations
United States—Information agency
United States—State. Department of
United States—Treaties

Anti-Communist measures
American militarism: what is it doing to us? E. Sevareid. il Look 33:14-16 Ag 12 '69
American power and the new mandarins, by N. Chomsky. Review
  Commentary 47:35-44 My '69. L. Abel; Discussion. 48:9-10+ Ag; 12+ O; 4+ D '69
Falling dominoes. il Newsweek 74:24 O 27 '69
Global containment: the Truman years. N. A. Graebner. Cur Hist 57:77-83+ Ag '69
Ideas by which we are ruled. N. F. Twining; T. S. Power; C. E. LeMay. Harper 238:36-7 Je '69
On tormenting Fulbright. W. F. Buckley, jr. Nat R 21:662 Jl 1 '69
Presidents, politics, and international intervention; excerpts from The cold-war years: American foreign policy since 1945. P. Y. Hammond. Ann Am Acad 386:10-18 N '69
Their NLFs and ours. J. Burnham. Nat R 21:323 Ap 8 '69
Timely reminder; excerpts from message of American friends of the captive nations, and the Conference of Americans of central and eastern European descent to members of the new Congress. Nat R 21:218 Mr 11 '69
See also
Propaganda
Bibliography
Congressional documents relating to foreign policy. See issues of Department of state bulletin
Executive agreements
Secret agreements; Senate resolution that the President seek congressional authority before making military and financial commitments to foreign governments. New Repub 161:5-6 Jl 26 '69
History
Franklin D. Roosevelt and foreign affairs, ed. by E. B. Nixon. Review
  Newsweek il 73:118-20 Ap 14 '69. R. A. Sokolov
  Sat R 52:30-1 Ag 2 '69. D. Perkins
Isolationism revisited. T. G. Paterson. Nation 209:166-9 S 1 '69
Jay papers II: the forging of the Nation. J. Jay. il Am Heritage 20:24-3+ D '68
U.S. military commitments in Europe and the Middle East; symposium. bibliog f Cur Hist 57:1-47+ Jl '69

Africa
Africa: continent of change; address, December 5, 1968. J. Palmer. 2d. Dept State Bul 59:696-702 D 30 '68
United States and the challenge of Africa's development; statement, February 6, 1969. W. A. Nielsen. Dept State Bul 60:192-4 Ap 7 '69

Asia
Asia and America at the crossroads; with questions and answers. K. T. Young. Ann Am Acad 384:53-65 Jl '69
Half-farewell to Asia. H. Sidey. il Life 67:4 Ag 8 '69
Look at Asian regionalism; address, October 20, 1969. M. Green. Dept State Bul 61:445-8 N 24 '69
Nixon's sobering message to Asia. il Time 94:11-13 Ag 8 '69
Secretary Rogers to confer with Asian leaders during seventeen day trip: statement, May 9, 1969. W. P. Rogers. Dept State Bul 60:433 My 26 '69
Secretary Rogers visits Viet-Nam: statement, news conferences, during Asian tour. W. P. Rogers. Dept State Bul 60:461-4 Je 2 '69
Unanswered question in Asia. America 121:84 Ag 16 '69
U.S. military commitments in Asia; symposium. bibliog f Cur Hist 57:65-111+ Ag '69
See also
Nixon, R. M.—Visit to Asia and Rumania, 1969
United States—Foreign relations—Asia, Southeastern

Asia—History
Before Pearl Harbor. W. LaFeber. Cur Hist 57:65-70+ Ag '69

Asia, Southeastern
Alternative in Southeast Asia, by E. R. Black. Review
  New Repub 161:24-6 N 1 '69. R. Dudman
Asia and the Nixon doctrine. il Newsweek 74:34-5 Ag 18 '69
No more Vietnams? J. Burnham. Nat R 21:895 S 9 '69
Political-strategic significance of Vietnam. W. C. Johnstone. Cur Hist 56:65-70 F '69
Problems the President will find on his trip to Asia. il U S News 67:27-8 Jl 21 '69
Reports: Bangkok, Manila. R. Terrill. Atlan 224:22-7 Jl '69
Time for the Senate to act. Nation 209:492-3 N 10 '69
Toward disengagement in Asia, by B. Gordon. Review
  New Repub 161:30-1 N 20 '69. S. S. Harrison
When war ends, U.S. role in Asia. il U S News 66:34-6 Ap 14 '69

Australia
Prime Minister Gorton of Australia visits Washington, exchange of toasts; with remarks, May 6, 7, 1969. R. M. Nixon; J. G. Gorton) Dept State Bul 60:436-9 My 26 '69; Same abr. Nat R 21:472+ My 20 '69

Belgium
Consular convention with Belgium transmitted to the Senate; message, October 8, 1969. R. M. Nixon. Dept State Bul 61:424 N 17 '69

Brazil
Washington backs the pooh bahs. D. Bonafede. Nation 208:663-6 My 26 '69

Cambodia
Mending fences. Newsweek 73:46-7 Ap 28 '69
Micro-presence. il Time 94:63 D 5 '69

Canada
For Canada's Trudeau, fallout from U.S. ABM. U S News 66:15 Mr 31 '69
Hands across the ice; sovereignty in the Arctic. R. F. Neill. Commonweal 91:302-3 D 5 '69
President Nixon and Prime Minister Trudeau of Canada hold talks at Washington: exchange of greetings, toasts, March 24 and 25, 1969, with announcement at news briefing. R. M. Nixon; P. E. Trudeau. Dept State Bul 60:319-24 Ap 14 '69
See also
International joint commission (United States and Canada)
United States—Treaties—Canada

UNITED STATES—Foreign relations—*Cont.*

China

Assignment for the '70's; address, December 29, 1968. J. K. Fairbank. bibliog f Am Hist R 74:861-79 F '69
When America lost China; the case of John Carter Vincent. R. Terrill. il Atlan 224:78-86 N '69

China (People's Republic)

Are we ready for China? E. Vogel. Sat R 52:23-5 Mr 15 '69
Asia and the Nixon doctrine. il Newsweek 74:34-5 Ag 18 '69
Back-scratching between Peking and Washington. Chr Cent 86:308 Mr 5 '69
China. H. Yu. Chr Cent 86:632 Ap 30 '69
China: a positive policy. W. V. Kennedy. America 121:87-90 Ag 16 '69
China: on the verge of speaking terms. il Time 94:13 D 26 '69
China spurns U.S. bid; cancellation of talks in Warsaw. Sr Schol 94:18 Mr 7 '69
Choosing, or not choosing, between Communists. Life 66:36 Ap 11 '69
Crumbling castles; cancellation of talks. Newsweek 73:42 Mr 3 '69
Dealing with China; address, March 20, 1969. E. M. Kennedy. Cur 107:8-10 My '69
Dealing with Communist China. America 120:390-1 Ap 5 '69
How to wink at China; Taiwan's status in international law. J. C. Thomson, jr. New Repub 160:12-13 Mr 1 '69
How we almost went to war with China. A. S. Whiting. il Look 33:76-7+ Ap 29 '69
Kennedy plan on Peking's role. U S News 66:15 Mr 31 '69
Most powerful country; most populous country; address, January 1969. J. W. Fulbright. Vital Speeches 35:258-62 F 15 '69
Nixon and China; time to talk. J. C. Thomson, jr. Atlan 223:71-3 F '69
Open door policy for red China. pro and con. Nations Bus 57:81-2 Ag '69
Rethinking U.S. China policy; Time essay. il Time 93:48-9 Je 6 '69
Sino-American detente? L. H. Battistini. Cur 104:55-64 F '69
Talking again. Newsweek 75:46+ Ja 19 '70
Teddy on China. Newsweek 73:25-6 Mr 31 '69
Two steps toward China. Chr Cent 86:1034 Ag 6 '69
United States-China relations; address, January 24, 1969. M. O. Hatfield. Vital Speeches 35:322-6 Mr 15 '69
U.S. invented the imbalance of power. J. P. Davies. il N Y Times Mag p50-1+ D 7 '69

Colombia

President Nixon and President Lleras of Colombia review common goals of the Americas; exchange of greetings, toasts and remarks, June 12, 13, 1969. R. M. Nixon; C. Lleras Restrepo. Dept State Bul 61:8-13 Jl 7 '69

Communist countries

Changing profile of world communism. T. O. Yntema. Sat R 52:15-18 Je 14 '69
Choosing, or not choosing, between Communists. Life 66:36 Ap 11 '69
Journey round a new landscape; President Nixon testing the diplomatic opportunity. il Life 67:30 Ag 8 '69
United States foreign policy; address, April 12, 1969. P. Findley. Vital Speeches 35:520-3 Je 15 '69
  See also
United States—Economic relations—Communist countries

Cuba

Cuba question. Commonweal 91:347 D 19 '69
Hi Jack, hi Fidel! New Repub 160:11 Ja 25 '69
Latin America, con Cuba. Commonweal 90:403-4 Je 27 '69
Making peace with Cuba. America 120:577-8 My 17 '69
Take this plane to Havana! I. Ross. Read Digest 94:113-17 My '69
United States-Cuba relations: beyond the quarantine. I. L. Horowitz. bibliog il Trans-Action 6:43-7 Ap '69
We should start talking with Castro. J. Plank. il N Y Times Mag p28-31+ Mr 30 '69; Reply. P. D. Bethel. p 133 My 11 '69; Same abr. with title Should we talk with Castro? Cur 107:10-17 My '69
W.C.C. Central committee takes stands on Cuba, race issue. Chr Cent 86:1132 S 3 '69
  See also
Cuba—History—Invasion, 1961

Ethiopia

Emperor Haile Selassie of Ethiopia visits the United States as guest of President Nixon; exchange greetings, toasts and remarks, July 8 and 9, 1969. R. M. Nixon; Haile Selassie I. Dept State Bul 61:86-91 Ag 4 '69

Europe

OPLAN NR 1-10; document outlines secret plan for waging unconventional warfare; with report by S. Coryell. Ramp Mag 8:9 O '69
U.S. and Europe today. S. D. Kertesz. bibliog f Cur Hist 57:42-7+ Jl '69
U.S. in Europe: time to join the vanguard. A. de Borchgrave. il Newsweek 74:25 D 29 '69

Europe—History

U.S. and Europe to 1918. W. G. Carleton. Cur Hist 57:1-7+ Jl '69

Europe, Eastern

East Europe and the United States. A. Korbonski. bibliog f il Cur Hist 56:200-5+ Ap '69
For eastern Europe: PR or policy? M. M. Mestrovic. Commonweal 91:92-3 O 24 '69

Europe, Western

Europe after Nixon's visit. il U S News 66:26-9 Mr 10 '69
First things first. Nat R 21:220 Mr 11 '69
Merci, mon general; illusion of need for United States of Europe. S. Alsop. Newsweek 73:116 Mr 24 '69
Nixon builds a road to the summit. il Bsns W p31-2 Mr 8 '69
Nixon's Europe in the new era. J. Osborne. New Repub 160:17-19 Mr 15 '69
Not-so grand design. il Newsweek 73:33-4 Mr 17 '69
Notes and comment. New Yorker 45:25-7 Mr 8 '69; Same with title Making foreign policy; how to cooperate with Europe. Cur 107:3-7 My '69
Thinking like de Gaulle? il Newsweek 73:26 Mr 10 '69
Tour of the blue chips. H. Sidey. il Life 66:2 F 28 '69
Toward a new partnership with Europe. G. C. McGhee. Sat R 52:16-18 Mr 8 '69
Why Nixon will go to Europe soon. il U S News 66:45-7 F 17 '69

France

America and France. S. Hoffmann. New Repub 160:17-21 Ap 5; 20-3 Ap 12 '69
De Gaulle: Nixon's stumbling block? il U S News 66:21-3 Mr 3 '69
Future of Franco-U.S. relations. il Time 93:24 My 9 '69
Presidents Johnson and de Gaulle exchange New Year's greetings. L. B. Johnson; C. de Gaulle. Dept State Bul 60:77-8 Ja 27 '69
Reviving an old alliance. il Newsweek 74:24+ D 29 '69
Richard de Nixon, Gaullist? J. Burnham. Nat R 21:382 Ap 22 '69
U.S. embassy; our men in Paris. W. Manchester. il Holiday 45:34-9+ Mr '69
Why Nixon will go to Europe soon. il U S News 66:45-7 F 17 '69

Germany (Federal Republic)

Nod to the home folks; U.S. visit. il Newsweek 74:38+ Ag 18 '69
President Nixon meets with Chancellor Kiesinger of the Federal Republic of Germany; exchange of greetings, remarks together with joint statement; August 7 and 8, 1969. R. M. Nixon; K. G. Kiesinger. Dept State Bul 61:211-14 S 8 '69

Great Britain

Need for NATO; address, December 9, 1968. J. S. Cooper. Vital Speeches 35:194-6 Ja 15 '69

Greece, Modern

Greece: a dilemma for the West. il Newsweek 75:31 Ja 19 '70
What to do with the colonels? Nat R 21:1303-4 D 30 '69

India

Ambassador's journal, by J. K. Galbraith. Review
  Nation 209:637-8 D 8 '69. J. Lelyveld
  New Yorker 45:185-9 O 25 '69
Plain tales from the embassy; or, With John Kenneth Galbraith in India; excerpts from diary. J. K. Galbraith. il Am Heritage 20:6-13+ O '69
Second round of bilateral talks with India held at Washington; joint government statement, October 17, 1969. Dept State Bul 61:403 N 10 '69

UNITED STATES—Foreign relations—*Cont.*

Iran

Mideast victory for U.S. the boom in Iran; with interview with the Shah of Iran. il U S News 66:46-50 Ja 27 '69

President Nixon and the Shah of Iran hold talks at Washington; exchange of greetings, toasts and remarks, October 21 and 23, 1969. R. M. Nixon and Mohammed Reza Pahlevi. Dept State Bul 61:396-400 N 10 '69

Prime Minister Hoveyda of Iran visits Washington; exchange of greetings and toasts, with joint statement, December 5, 1968. L. B. Johnson; A. A. Hoveyda. Dept State Bul 59:659-62 D 23 '68

Israel

Hitler for mayor; J. Lindsay and Nixon administration. Nat R 21:478 My 20 '69

Israeli overkill? Nat R 21:15 Ja 14 '69

Middle East: shifting into neutral. il Time 95:21-2 Ja 5 '70

Prime Minister Meir of Israel visits Washington; exchange of greetings, toasts and remarks, September 25 and 26, 1969. R. M. Nixon; G. Meir. Dept State Bul 61:318-22 O 13 '69

Japan

Agreement on Okinawa. il Time 94:37 N 28 '69

American alliance in trouble? return of Okinawa. il U S News 66:8 Je 16 '69

Closing a chapter of the past; Okinawa agreement. il Newsweek 74:39-40 D 1 '69

Countdown on Okinawa. D. Reed. il Read Digest 95:117-21 N '69

Go; Okinawa agreement. New Repub 161:10 N 29 '69

Hour of apology; reprint. D. Lawrence. U S News 67:100 D 8 '69

Invitation to greatness; U.S. pressures assume some responsibility for the security and welfare of the Pacific region. il Newsweek 74:30-1 Ag 11 '69

Japan presses Pacific demands; U.S. airline expansion blocked. L. Doty. Aviation W 90:24-5 F 17 '69

Okinawa mon amour. T. Oka. il N Y Times Mag p30-1+ Ap 6 '69

Sayonara, Okinawa. il Time 93:18 Je 13 '69

Short fuse in Japan. A. Axelbank. Nation 208:141-3 F 3 '69

United States-Japanese relations today; address, October 22, 1969. U. A. Johnson. Dept State Bul 61:401-3 N 10 '69

See also

Japan—Foreign relations—United States

Panay (gunboat) incident

United States—Commerce—Japan

Jordan

King Hussein I of Jordan visits Washington; exchange of greetings; with text of joint statement, April 8 and 10, 1969. King Hussein; R. M. Nixon. Dept State Bul 60:364-5 Ap 28 '69

Korea (People's Republic)

Nixon warns North Korea: U.S. flights will be protected; text of news conference, April 18, 1969. R. M. Nixon. U S News 66:72-5 Ap 28 '69

See also

EC-121 incident. 1969

Pueblo incident. 1968

Korea (Republic)

Guns for hire? cost of getting allies to commit troops to Vietnam. il Newsweek 74:26-7 D 15 '69

Korea heats up. Nation 209:331 O 6 '69

President; C. H. Park's U.S. visit. il Newsweek 74:19 S 1 '69

President Nixon and President Park of the Republic of Korea hold talks at San Francisco; welcoming statement, exchange of remarks, toasts, together with joint statement, August 21 and 22, 1969. R. M. Nixon; C. H. Park. Dept State Bul 61:237-44 S 15 '69

Laos

Dilemma in Laos. E. G. Martin. il Newsweek 74:43 N 3 '69

If you wonder what U.S. is doing in Laos. il U S News 68:28-9 Ja 5 '70

Recurring problems in Laos. E. Urrows. bibliog f Cur Hist 57:361-3+ D '69

Report: Laos. H. D. Greenway. Atlan 223:20+ Mr '69

Unseen presence. D. Greenway and W. Marmon. Time 94:39 O 17 '69

Latin America

Coup in Bolivia; General Ovando's takeover. New Repub 161:7-8 O 18 '69

Current U.S.-Peruvian problems; statement before the Subcommittee on western hemisphere affairs of the Senate committee on foreign relations; April 17, 1969. C. A. Meyer. Dept State Bul 60:406-8 My 12 '69

Fire next door. Duns R 94:88 Ag '69

Foreign and human relations with Latin America. C. T. Oliver. For Affairs 47:521-31 Ap '69

Future U.S. relations with Latin America; statement. C. A. Meyer. Dept State Bul 60:473-4 Je 2 '69

Governor Rockefeller reports on mission to Latin America; text of letter from President Nixon to Governor Nelson A. Rockefeller; September 3, 1969. R. M. Nixon. Dept State Bul 61:303-4 O 6 '69

In the grip of a revolution; stakes involved in Peru's expropriation of U.S. oil investments. il Newsweek 73:52-4+ Ap 14 '69

Latin America: challenge from the intellectuals. M. Maldonado-Denis. Nation 209:73-6 Jl 28 '69

Latin America, con Cuba. Commonweal 90:403-4 Je 27 '69

Lopsided relationship. P. G. Kramer. il Newsweek 74:52+ N 10 '69

Manana friends. W. F. Buckley, jr. Nat R 21:1026-7 O 7 '69

New hope for Latin America? R. M. Nixon's proposals. D. Ross. New Repub 161:17-19 N 22 '69

New turmoil in Latin America: its meaning for U.S. il U S News 66:30-2 Je 16 '69

Perspectives on Latin America; address, September 9, 1969. W. Morse. Vital Speeches 36:86-90 N 15 '69

Peru: key to Nixon policy for Latin America. il U S News 66:52 Ap 21 '69

President names Nelson Rockefeller for special mission to Latin America; statement, February 17, 1969. R. M. Nixon. Dept State Bul 60:198 Mr 10 '69

Redefining an Alliance; summary of address. R. M. Nixon. Newsweek 74:50+ N 10 '69

Rockefeller's new men; report recommendations. New Repub 161:11-12 N 29 '69

Rockefeller's report. il Newsweek 74:68 N 17 '69

They'd rather decide for themselves; promoting birth control. E. K. Culhane. America 120:621-3 My 24 '69

Tinderbox in Latin America. S. M. Linowitz il Sat R 52:10-13 Ag 16 '69

U.S. military assistance policy toward Latin America; statement. July 8, 1969. C. A. Meyer. Dept State Bul 61:100-2 Ag 4 '69

U.S. military commitments in Latin America; symposium. bibliog f Cur Hist 56:321-61+ Je '69

Why the Latins don't love us. il Life 67:28 Jl 18 '69

Wrong man, wrong time, wrong mission. M. M. Alves. Commonweal 90:407-9 Je 27 '69

See also

Action for progress for the Americas

Alliance for progress

Inter-American relations

Monroe doctrine

Rockefeller, N. A.—Visits to Latin America, 1969

Libya

Another Arab country that worries U.S. il U S News 67:81-2 D 8 '69

Mexico

President Nixon and President Diaz Ordaz of Mexico dedicate the Amistad Dam; remarks, exchange of toasts, September 8, 1969. R. M. Nixon; G. Diaz Ordaz. Dept State Bul 61:277-80 S 29 '69

Statue of Benito Juárez dedicated at Washington; remarks, January 7, 1969. D. Rusk. Dept State Bul 60:74-5 Ja 27 '69

Tempers rise over search for drugs. U S News 67:16 O 13 '69

United States and Mexico reaffirm bonds of friendship; border ceremony; with exchange of toasts, December 13, 1968. L. B. Johnson; G. Diaz Ordaz. Dept State Bul 60:21-6 Ja 13 '69

Middle East

Arab-Israeli confrontation; a challenge to international diplomacy; address, April 23, 1969. J. J. Sisco. Dept State Bul 60:443-6 My 26 '69

Arab-Israeli impasse. Z. B. Grant. New Repub 162:15-16 Ja 3 '70

Both sides take a hard look; Israel's leaders views. M. Elkins. il Newsweek 74:39-40 S 15 '69

Israel and the Arabs: a shift in U.S. policy? il Newsweek 74:39 D 22 '69

Nixon and the Mideast. il Newsweek 75:21-2 Ja 5 '70

UNITED STATES—Foreign relations—Middle
East—*Continued*
Our next Vietnam? J. Burnham. Nat R 21:
1002 O 7 '69
U.S. in the Middle East today. H. N. Howard. bibliog f Cur Hist 57:36-41+ Jl '69
U.S. policy in Middle East; address, December 9, 1969. W. P. Rogers. Vital Speeches
36:165-7 Ja 1 '70

Netherlands

President Nixon meets with Prime minister
and foreign minister of the Netherlands;
exchange of greetings, and remarks, May
27, 28, 1969. R. M. Nixon; P. J. S. de Jong.
Dept State Bul 60:561-3 Je 30 '69

Nigeria

Time for action on Biafra! E. M. Kennedy;
D. Lukens. Read Digest 94:75-9 My '69
Tragedy of Nigeria; address, December 3,
1968. N. deB. Katzenbach. Dept State Bul
59:653-8 D 23 '68
U.S. planes available to assist relief efforts
in Nigeria; Department announcement, December 27, with statement December 31,
1968. Dept State Bul 60:30-1 Ja 13 '69

Pakistan

Picking up the pieces in Pakistan. Z. B.
Grant. New Repub 161:11-12 O 18 '69

Peru

Climate turns colder. Bsns W p34+ My 31 '69
Current U.S.-Peruvian problems; statement
before the Subcommittee on western hemisphere affairs of the Senate committee on
foreign relations; April 17, 1969. C. A.
Meyer. Dept State Bul 60:406-8 My 12 '69
Fish and oil. Time 93:40 My 30 '69
Gunboat diplomacy; private American tuna
fleet accosted by Peruvian gunboat off
coast of Peru. Newsweek 73:50 F 24 '69
Peru and the great colossus. Chr Cent 86:
339 Mr 12 '69; Reply. H. C. Taylor. 86:
654+ My 7 '69
Peru: key to Nixon policy for Latin America.
il U S News 66:52 Ap 21 '69
President appoints John N. Irwin as special
emissary to Peru. Dept State Bul 60:282
Mr 31 '69
Report from Lima. V. Clear. il Fortune 79:
55-6+ Mr '69
Sugaring off; first trade agreement between
Peru and the Soviet Union. il Newsweek 73:
38 Mr 3 '69
Talking it over; J. N. Irwin as U.S. emissary.
Time 93:31 Mr 21 '69
United States and Peru hold round of talks
at Washington; Department statement. Dept
State Bul 60:472-3 Je 2 '69
U.S. and Peru resume talks on outstanding
problems; Department statement. Dept
State Bul 60:400-1 My 12 '69
U.S. expresses concern to Peru over fishing-
boat incident; Department statement, February 14, 1969. Dept State Bul 60:184 Mr 3
'69

Philippines

Old friend turning from U.S. il U S News 66:
63-4 Ja 27 '69

Rhodesia

Department presents views on Southern
Rhodesia; statement, October 17, 1969. D.
D. Newsom. Dept State Bul 61:422-4 N 17
'69

Rumania

Rumanian welcome. il Time 94:13-14 Ag 8 '69
United States and Romania agree on 1969-70
exchanges program; Department announcement, with text of U.S. note, November 26,
1968. Dept State Bul 59:680-4 D 23 '68
See also
Nixon, R. M.—Visit to Asia and Rumania,
1969

Russia

Are we in a Pavlovian box? U.S. policy conditioned response to Soviet objectives? A.
C. Sutton. il Nat R 21:692-4 Jl 15 '69
Convergence: the uncertain meeting of East
and West; Time essay. il Time 95:18-19
Ja 12 '70
If Nixon were to speak to the Russian people.
D. Lawrence. U S News 66:88 Mr 3 '69
Kennedy, Krushchev, and Cuba. D. Pearson. il Sat R 52:12-15 Mr 29 '69
Key defense aide who is known for calling
the turn on Russia. U S News 66:20 Mr 17
'69
Kissinger: the uses and limits of power. il
Time 93:20-1 F 14 '69
Making foreign policy; the influence of men
and events. J. K. Galbraith. Cur 113:54-61
D '69
Next: a deal between U.S. and Russia? il U S
News 66:25-6 Mr 10 '69

Nixon says yes to arms talks; with report
by L. Norman. il Newsweek 73:28-9 Je 23
'69
Nixon's Soviet approach. H. Brandon. Sat
R 52:6 S 6 '69
Origins of the cold war: the Communist dimension. J. R. Starobin. For Affairs 47:681-
96 Jl '69
Progress coexistence & intellectual freedom.
by A. D. Sakharov. Review
Phys Today il 22:77-9+ My '69. J. M.
Hollander
Second year of the cold war. H. S. Hughes.
Commentary 48:27-32 Ag '69; Discussion.
48:4+ N '69
Secretary Rusk interviewed on Face the Nation; program, December 1, 1968. D. Rusk.
Dept State Bul 59:645-50 D 23 '68
Shh! let's tell the Russians; how J. F. Kennedy decided to make the Russians aware of
our permissive-action link system. E. Klein
and R. Littell. il Newsweek 73:46-7 My 5 '69
Soviet-U.S. dialogue; our lines of communication are open; address, November 20,
1969. E. L. Richardson. Vital Speeches 36:
167-9 Ja 1 '70
Space and senselessness; U.S. attitudes at
the space science and technology conference, Denver, Colo. N. Cousins. Sat R 52:
18 Jl 12 '69
Sunshine through the clouds. Newsweek 74:
35 Jl 21 '69
Timely reminder; excerpts from message of
American friends of the captive nations, and
the Conference of Americans of central and
eastern European descent to members of
the new Congress. Nat R 21:218 Mr 11 '69
Under Secretary Richardson discusses VietNam peace talks and U.S.-U.S.S.R. relations; interview, April 30, 1969. ed. by J.
Kraft. E. L. Richardson. Dept State Bul
60:417-18 My 19 '69
U.S. and Russia: dawn of a new era; interview. J. Fromm. il U S News 68:34-7 Ja
5 '70
U.S. invented the imbalance of power. J. P.
Davies. il N Y Times Mag p50-1+ D 7 '69
When Russian and American peace groups
talk peace; meeting of Soviet peace committee in Moscow. H. A. Jack. il N Y Times
Mag p28-9+ Mr 9 '69
See also
Cuban crisis, 1962
Strategic arms limitation talks

Spain

Burchinal incident; negotiations for renewal
of leases on bases in Spain. Nation 208:323-4
Mr 17 '69
New life for U.S. bases in Spain. U S News
66:8 Je 16 '69
U.S. and Spain confer on extension of defense
agreement; joint communique. March 26,
1969. Dept State Bul 60:324 Ap 14 '69
U.S. and Spain extend defense agreement;
joint statement; with text of U.S. note and
letters, June 20, 1969. Dept State Bul 61:15
Jl 7 '69

Taiwan

How to wink at China; Taiwan's status in
international law. J. C. Thomson, jr. New
Repub 160:12-13 Mr 1 '69
See also
United States—Treaties—Taiwan

Thailand

Secret agreements; 1965 deal. New Repub
161:5-6 Jl 26 '69
Thailand cash register. Nation 208:165 F 10 '69

Turkey

Now it's the Turks who are unhappy about
U.S; with interview with S. Demirel. il
U S News 66:89-92 Je 9 '69

Underdeveloped areas

How we look to the third world. E. Ahmad.
Nation 208:265-9 Mr 3 '69
View from Washington. T. P. Thornton.
bibliog f Ann Am Acad 386:19-30 N '69

Vietnam (Democratic Republic)

See also
Vietnamese war, 1957- —American participation

Vietnam (Republic)

Appeal to the people of the United States.
Pham the Truc. Nation 209:2 Jl 7 '69
Blood on our hands? America's commitment
to South Vietnamese. New Repub 161:7
O 18 '69
Vietnam lobby. R. Scheer and W. Hinckle.
Ramp Mag 7:31-6 Ja 25 '69

UNITED STATES—History—Textbooks—*Cont.*
Integrating American history: role of the Negro. N. F. Hurt. il Todays Ed 58:18-20 Ja '69
Negro role in U.S. history. Sch & Soc 97:76+ F '69
　　See also
United States—Declaration of independence

Revolution—Bibliography
Bibliography for a top Broadway hit: 1776; comp. by M. R. Gerhart. Wilson Lib Bul 43:1010-11 Je '69

Revolution—Campaigns and battles
Revolutionary war reminder; New Windsor cantonment, Vails Gate, N.Y. il Travel 132: 37-41 Jl '69
Treasure of Alnwick castle; with maps. W. P. Cumming and E. C. Cumming. il Am Heritage 20:22-33+ Ag '69

Revolution—Maps
Treasure and its guardian. W. P. Cumming and E. C. Cumming. il Am Heritage 20:26-33 Ag '69

Revolution—Naval operations
John Paul Jones: father of the navy. il Sr Schol 95:2 O 6 '69

Revolution—Strategy
Treasure of Alnwick castle; with maps. W. P. Cumming and E. C. Cumming. il Am Heritage 20:22-33+ Ag '69

Confederation, 1783-1789
Jay papers II: the forging of the Nation. J. Jay. il Am Heritage 20:24-3+ D '68

Constitutional period,1789-1809
Jay papers III: the trials of Chief Justice Jay; ed. by R. B. Morris. J. Jay. il Am Heritage 20:80-90 Je '69
Washington after the Revolution; excerpts. J. T. Flexner. il Am Heritage 20:64-73 Ap; 72-9+ Je; 24-7+ O; 21:32-3+ D '69

War of 1812—Naval operations
Great sea battle; excerpts from Broke and The Shannon. P. Padfield. il Am Heritage 20:29-65 D '68; Reply. J. D. Mason. 20:85 Ap '69

1815-1861
1857. O. Jensen. il Am Heritage 21:81-96 D '69
　　See also
Santa Fe Trail

Civil war
　　See also
Grand army of the Republic
Reconstruction (Civil war)

Civil war—Campaigns and battles
　　See also
Chattanooga, Battle of the, 1863

Civil war—Causes
Toward a new civil war revisionism. J. S. Rosenberg. Am Scholar 38:250-72 Spr '69

Civil war—Moral and re-ligious aspects
Toward a new civil war revisionism. J. S. Rosenberg. Am Scholar 38:250-72 Spr '69

Civil war—Naval operations
Samuel Francis Dupont: a selection from his Civil war letters; ed. by J. D. Hayes. Review
America 121:74-5 Ag 2 '69. R. W. Daly.

1865-1898
　　See also
Indians of North America—Wars
Reconstruction (Civil war)

Spanish American war, 1898
Before the colors fade: last of the Rough Riders; interview, ed. by V. C. Jones. J. D. Langdon. Am Heritage 20:42-3+ Ag '69

Philippine insurrection, 1899-1901
Troop withdrawal: 1899. D. B. Schirmer. New Repub 161:19-20 S 27 '69

1918-1941
Interwar years. E. E. Billings. bibliog f Cur Hist 57:8-12+ Jl '69

World war, 1939-1945
See World war, 1939-1945—United States

1945-
Eisenhower era. J. A. Huston. bibliog f Cur Hist 57:24-30+ Jl '69

Greatness of Harry Truman. D. Acheson. Esquire 72:124-7+ S '69
Kennedy-Johnson years. T. T. Helde. Cur Hist 57:31-5+ Jl '69
Truman doctrine and NATO. L. W. Koenig. bibliog f Cur Hist 57:18-23+ Jl '69

History, Naval
　　See also
United States—History—Revolution—Naval operations

House of representatives
　　See United States—Congress—House of representatives

Housing and urban development, Department of
Changes in housing law: what they mean. il U S News 67:20 D 29 '69
Creating a model for model cities; Seattle to launch attack on slum ills. il Bsns W p48+ Ja 18 '69
Ginnie Mae runs into delays; Fannie Mae ponders construction loans. Bsns W p 128 Je 21 '69
Hope deferred; Operation Breakthrough. Newsweek 74:49 D 29 '69
HUD housing awards. il Aging 172:10-11 F '69
HUD wades in with flood aid; federally sponsored flood-insurance program. Bsns W p31 Mr 1 '69
Housing shortage; Operation Breakthrough; address, August 6, 1969. H. B. Finger. Vital Speeches 35:709-12 S 15 '69
Industry eyes housing field warily; Operation Breakthrough. W. H. Gregory. Aviation W 91:113+ S 15 '69
Is a breakthrough near in housing? il Bsns W p80-2+ S 13 '69
Lining up the troops for Breakthrough. Bsns W p86-7 D 20 '69
Operation Breakthrough: commitment and questions. W. Wagner. il Arch Rec 146:10 S '69
Science and the city: the question of authority. J. D. Carroll. bibliog il Science 163: 902-11 F 28 '69
Thinking of buying some land? HUD disclosure law. D. Sanford. New Repub 161: 17-19 O 11 '69
Toward a decent home for every American family. M. Farmer. il Arch Rec 146:131-4 O '69

Appropriations and expenditures
Money muddle for model cities. Bsns W p43-4 O 11 '69

Indian affairs, Bureau of
Indian to head Indian bureau. Chr Cent 86: 1106-7 Ag 27 '69
Village Indian; new commissioner. Newsweek 74:28-9 Ag 18 '69
　　See also
Indians of North America—Government relations

Industries
Changing industries (cont) il Fortune 79:88-93+ F; 104-9+ Mr; 108-15+ Ap; 80:116-19+ S '69
New lineup of winners and losers; University of Maryland's model of the seventies. il Bsns W p 104+ D 6 '69
Panorama of the nation's business. V. Louviere. il Nations Bsns 57:18-19 N; 15 D '69
Report on employment related to exports; with tables. C. T. Bowman. bibliog Mo Labor R 92:16-20 Je '69
SDS finds invasion of industry tougher than college campuses. U S News 66:84-6 Je 23 '69
　　See also
Food industry and trade
Indians of North America—Industries
Shipbuilding
United States—Commerce
Wine trade
　　also subhead United States under names of industries, e.g. Munitions industries—United States

Information agency
New USIA ban on certain books overseas. Pub W 196:19-20 D 15 '69
Shakespeare era. Newsweek 75:20+ Ja 12 '70
Thinking positive at USIA. Time 94:40 D 5 '69
USIA'S quickie: The silent majority. Nation 209:620-1 D 8 '69
Unsuitable for use. il Newsweek 74:44 D 1 '69

UNITED STATES—*Continued*

Intellectual life

Arts are in trouble. R. H. Smith. Pub W 195: 39 Mr 31 '69
Culture explosion or puff. C. J. McNaspy. America 120:695-7 Je 14 '69
Heyday for intellectuals; growing force in America. il U S News 67:74-7 Jl 21 '69
Passionate word to the new anti-intellectuals. Chr Cent 86:1409 N 5 '69
Tortured role of the intellectual in America; Time essay. il Time 93:48-9 My 9 '69
Writer between generations. D. T. Bazelon. Commentary 47:43-54 F '69
See also
Books and reading
Colleges and universities—United States
United States—Popular culture

Interior, Department of

Lake Superior, private dump; Stoddard and FWPCA reports; hearings in Duluth. G. Hill. Nation 208:795-6 Je 23 '69
See also
United States—Federal water pollution control administration
United States—National park service
United States—Outdoor recreation, Bureau of

Appropriations and expenditures

Satellites and safety. Sci N 95:91 Ja 25 '69

Internal revenue service

Squeezing even more out of tax returns; selling of Internal revenue service data and Census data to private industry. il Bsns W p69 D 6 '69
Study of the impact of office automation in the IRS. H. J. Rothberg. il Mo Labor R 92:26-30 O '69
Warning to taxpayers; interview. S S. Cohen. U S News 66:36-9 F 3 '69

Interoceanic canal commission

Interoceanic canal study commission submits fifth annual report; text of letter, August 6, 1969. R. M. Nixon. Dept State Bul 61: 218 S 8 '69

Interstate commerce commission

Lady leads ICC in fight for power. il Bsns W p62-3+ F 8 '69
New scenery for the ICC. Time 93:89-90 F 14 '69

Job corps

Community interaction with the Job corps. L. B. Macht. Ment Hy 53:521-4 O '69
Disadvantaged youth may fill police vacancies. il Am City 84:66 F '69
Job corps gets a working over. Bsns W p96 Ap 19 '69
Job corps, Headstart reassigned. Sci N 95: 400 Ap 26 '69
Job on the Job corps. C. McCarthy. New Repub 161:19-21 Jl 5 '69
Keeping the dropouts in. Sr Schol 94:Schol Teach 7 F 14 '69
Layoff hits the Job corps. Newsweek 73: 34 Ap 21 '69
Not as it should be. R. J. Waswo. Am For 75: 11 Ag '69
Rodman experience with dropouts. L. Besant. il Todays Ed 58:52-4 F '69; Same abr. Ed Digest 34:35-7 Ap '69
What shake-up in Job corps means. U S News 66:14 Ap 21 '69

John F. Kennedy center for the performing arts

See John F. Kennedy center for the performing arts

John F. Kennedy space center

Stay? No stay? Kennedy space center. J. Morgenstern. il Newsweek 74:24-26A Jl 28 '69; Excerpts. Cur 110:3 S '69
Work force at KSC being cut to meet Saturn 5 launch rate. Aviation W 91:72 S 15 '69

Joint chiefs of staff

Tops with the military, and with politicians, too; General Wheeler's sixth year as chairman of the Joint chiefs of staff. il U S News 66:16 My 5 '69

Justice, Department of

Annals of politics; attorney generals Clark and Mitchell on law and order issue. R. Harris. New Yorker 45:61-4+ N 22 '69
Annals of politics; post of attorney general during the transition. R. Harris. New Yorker 45:64-8+ N 15 '69
Annals of politics; R. Clark, attorney general. R. Harris. New Yorker 45:63-4+ N 8 '69

Attorney General Mitchell's philosophy is: the Justice department is an institution for law enforcement, not social improvement. M. Viorst. il N Y Times Mag p 10-11+ Ag 10 '69; Reply. L Herman. p72+ S 14 '69
Authoritarian prescription. W. D. Phelan, jr. Nation 209:467-73 N 3 '69
Caretakers of justice. New Repub 160:9 F 1 '69
Did John Mitchell hear the justices? Justice department's reaction to bugging ruling. R. Shogan. New Repub 160:11-13 Ap 26 '69
Law-and-order man; the attorney general. il Newsweek 74:29-30+ S 8 '68
Mandate for clock watching. Time 93:80 Mr 14 '69
Nixon's heavyweight; new attorney general. il Time 94:24 Jl 25 '69
No-nonsense man at the helm of justice. U S News 67:9-10 Jl 28 '69
Reports; Washington: new team. E. B. Drew. Atlan 223:4+ My '69
TRB from Washington: iceberg man; views of Richard Harris. New Repub 161:4 D 13 '69
Time, gentlemen! time-accounting sheets to be kept. Newsweek 73:35 Mr 17 '69
Toward law and order. Nat R 21:789 Ag 12 '69
When companies find giving isn't blessed; political contributions. Bsns W p31-2 N 8 '69
See also
United States—Federal bureau of investigation

Antitrust division

Action against Jim Ling. il Time 93:89 Ap 4 '69
Antitrust in dubious battle; with editorial comment. R. H. Bork. il Fortune 80:86, 103-5+ S '69
Antitrust, Republican style; interview. ed. by G. R. Rosen. R. McLaren. Duns R 94:12-13+ O '69
Antitrust: U.S. vs. IBM. Newsweek 73:79 Ja 27 '69
Cheyenne media baron stands up to lawmen; R. McCraken vs Justice dept. il Bsns W p 102-3 Ja 25 '69
Conglomerate test is on. il Bsns W p35-7 Mr 29 '69
Conglomerators speak out; ABA symposium. il Bsns W p94+ N 1 '69
Got a light, McLaren? M. Ways. Fortune 79: 61-2 My 1 '69
IBM girds for battle; vs government's antitrust action. Bsns W p36-8 Ja 25 '69
McLaren talks tough about conglomerates; crackdown on mergers. Bsns W p38 Mr 15 '69
McLaren wades into merger tide. Bsns W p42 +Mr 22 '69
Man who says no to the giants. il Newsweek 74:73-4 Jl 14 '69
Nixon's antitrust policy; conglomerate mergers. W. F. Baxter. New Repub 161:13-16 Ag 9 '69
Nixon's deconglomerater. Newsweek 73:69-70 Mr 24 '69
Scourge of the conglomerates. il Time 93: 100 My 23 '69
Sharp new line on antitrust; Justice dept. on warpath against big mergers, aggressive conglomerates, and corporate reciprocity. il Bsns W p 120-2 Je 21 '69
Smog over auto accord; auto makers vs. Justice dept. Bsns W p28 Ja 18 '69
Softening the harsh words; interview. R. W McLaren. Forbes 103:23-4 Je 1 '69
Some candid answers from James J. Ling; interview, ed. by J. McDonald. il Fortune 80:92-5+ Ag 1; 136-8+ S '69
Target; conglomerates. Newsweek 73:59-60 Ap 7 '69
U.S. antitrust move against LTV rapped. Aviation W 90:23 My 26 '69
U.S. antitrust muscle makes Europe wince. il Bsns W p84-6 N 8 '69
Washington's challenge to IBM. il Time 93: 66 Ja 24 '69

Civil rights division

Apologist; J. Leonard. il Time 94:77 O 31 '69
Nixon, Mitchell and Leonard. Nation 208:162 F 10 '69
Provocative precedent; J. Leonard. Newsweek 74:26-7 N 3 '69

Law enforcement assistance administration

Criminal justice R&D; new agency stresses police over corrections. J. R. Kramer. Science 166:588-90 O 31 '69

Labor, Department of

Job bank in a computer pays off and branches out. il Bsns W p70-1 Jl 5 '69

UNITED STATES—Labor, Department of—
Continued
Nixon's rookie of the year. il Time 94:92
N 7 '69
Who will shape new labor policies? il Nations Bsns 57:32-4+ F '69
See also
United States—Federal mediation and conciliation service
United States—Job corps

Labor policy

Big strikes: a new approach; interview. G. P. Shultz. il U S News 67:46-9 D 1 '69
Can a hands-off labor policy work? il Bsns W p62-3+ N 8 '69
Evaluating public expenditures under conditions of unemployment; excerpt from address. R. H. Haveman. il Mo Labor R 92:30-3 S '69
Nixon and the unions: can the honeymoon last? il U S News 66:82-4 Ap 21 '69
What White House and unions are telling each other. il U S News 66:65-6 Ap 28 '69
See also
Labor laws and legislation—United States
United States—National labor relations board

Labor statistics, Bureau of

Long-range program objectives for BLS. G. H. Moore. Mo Labor R 92:3-6 O '69
Research summaries. il Mo Labor R 92:66-8 F '69
Use of labor statistics in national decision-making; excerpt from address, August 1969. G. P. Shultz. Mo Labor R 92:48-50 N '69

Land management, Bureau of

Alaska burns; with editorial comment. J. B. Craig. il Am For 75:1-3+ 11 O '69
Public rights vs. stockmen's rights. W. L. Reavley. il Nat Wildlife 7:40-1 Je '69
Test plot of the public lands; Vale project. Ore. T. Trueblood. il Field & S 74:12+ Ag '69

Library of Congress

Automation

Final report on MARC pilot project. G. Krettek and E. D. Cooke. ALA Bul 63:752 Je '69

Manuscript division

Quarterly notes from the manuscript division of the Library of Congress (cont) K. V. Hostick. Hobbies 74:108 Mr; 140 O '69

Union catalog

National union catalog: another view. J. M. Ethridge. ALA Bul 63:1104-5 S '69

Literary landmarks

See Literary landmarks

Manned spacecraft center

Aerospace brass sits up with baby; viewing Apollo moon landing. Bsns W p25-6 Jl 26 '69
And now, back to Mission control. il Pop Mech 132:90-1 Jl '69
Houston MSC; community with a space complex. T. G. Plate. il Science 165:265-9 Jl 18 '69
Letter from the space center; opinions of the Apollo 11 mission and planned examination of samples and photographs. H. S. F. Cooper, jr. New Yorker 45:85-92 Jl 26 '69
Letter from the space center; plan of the Apollo 11 mission. H. S. F. Cooper, jr. New Yorker 45:76-80 Jl 12; 79-83 Jl 19 '69
Mission control; fido, guido and retro. il Time 94:23 Ag 1 '69
Side trip into space. M. L. Daly. il Travel 132:54-7 Jl '69
Team effort; center near Houston. il Newsweek 74:55-6 Jl 7 '69

Lunar receiving laboratory

Eighty pounds of rock; Lunar receiving laboratory. J. Eberhart. il Sci N 95:582-3+ Je 14 '69
Guard against the unknown. il Time 94:15 Jl 25 '69
Isolating the astronauts; Lunar receiving laboratory. il Newsweek 73:60 Je 16 '69
Letter from the space center; completion of initial survey of the rocks and dust from Apollo 11 mission. H. S. F. Cooper, jr. New Yorker 45:92+ O 11 '69
Letter from the space center; examination of astronauts and samples from Apollo 11 mission. H. S. F. Cooper, jr. New Yorker 45:82+ Ag 16 '69
Letter from the space center; first lunar walk of the Apollo 12 mission. H. S. F. Cooper, jr. New Yorker 45:46-56 Ja 3 '70
Letter from the space center; gathering and examination of moon samples from Apollo 11 mission. H. S. F. Cooper, jr. New Yorker 45:50-7 Ag 2 '69

Letter from the space center; testing of lunar rocks and dust from Apollo 11 mission. H. S. F. Cooper, jr. New Yorker 45:63-70 Ag 23 '69
Life after splashdown; 21-day quarantine of Apollo 11 astronauts. il Newsweek 74:60 Ag 18 '69
Lunar laboratory; with report by D. A. Hamblin. il Life 67:50-4+ Jl 4 '69
Preliminary examination of lunar samples from Apollo 11. bibliog il Science 165:1211-27 S 19 '69; Reply. F. Hoyle. 166:401 O 17 '69
Rigid quarantine awaits Apollo 11 return. Z. Strickland. il Aviation W 91:18-21 Jl 7 '69
Where home is like prison; lunar receiving laboratory. il Bsns W p102-3 Jl 19 '69

Maps

How to know the lay of the land. N. Carlisle. il Pop Mech 131:130-3+ Je '69

Marine corps

Marine machine. T. Barry. il Look 33:17-25 Ag 12 '69
Semper fidelis: the ethic of the warrior. S. Cain. Chr Cent 86:677-81 My 14 '69

Crimes and misdemeanors

Black vs. white; racial tension and death of Cpl. Bankston at Camp Lejeune. N.C. il Newsweek 74:20A-20B Ag 25 '69
Eighteen minute verdict; military justice & constitutional rights; case of W. Harvey and G. Daniels. M. Polner. Commonweal 90:40-3; 91:3+ Mr 28, O 3 '69
See also
United States—Marine corps—Prisons

Forces in Vietnam

Incident at Van Duong; excerpts from 5 by 7. J. Shepherd. il Look 33:26-8+ Ag 12 '69

Negroes

As race issue hits armed forces. il U S News 67:26-7 S 1 '69
Black vs. white; racial tension and death of Cpl. Bankston at Camp Lejeune. N.C. il Newsweek 74:20A-20B Ag 25 '69
How blacks upset the marine corps. S. Morris. il Ebony 25:55-8+ D '69
Race crisis at a marine camp. P. Good. il Life 67:46-51 S 25 '69
Racial tension at Lejeune. America 121:108 Ag 30 '69
Where marines stand on Afro haircuts. il U S News 67:16 S 15 '69

Prisons

Andersonville-by-the-sea; Pendleton brig. R. G. Sherrill. Nation 209:239-42 S 15 '69
In a marine corps prison; Pendleton brig rats. J. Fincher. il Life 67:32-7 O 10 '69

Marine science, engineering and resources, Commission on

Our nation and the sea. P. H. Abelson. Science 163:427 Ja 31 '69
See also
United States—National oceanic and atmospheric agency (proposed)

Marine sciences council

See United States—National council on marine resources and engineering development

Marshall space flight center

Moon dollars; center at Huntsville, Ala. il Newsweek 74:54 Jl 7 '69

Military policy

America as a militaristic society. J. M. Swomley, jr. il Cath World 209:199-202 Ag '69
American armed strength and its influence; with questions and answers. R. A. Yudkin. Ann Am Acad 384:1-13 Jl '69
American militarism; CIA-directed paramilitary operations. New Repub 160:7-9 Ap 12 '69; Same abr. with title Militarism and the impact of CIA. Cur 108:55-8 Je '69
American militarism; symposium. il Look 33:13-28+ Ag 12; 17-24+ Ag 26 '69
America's role in the world; address. June 4, 1969. R. M. Nixon. Vital Speeches 35:548-50 Jl 1 '69; Same. Dept State Bul 60:525-8 Je 23 '69; Excerpts. U S News 66:64-6 Je 16 '69; Summary il Time 93:15 Je 13 '69
And now that the American dream is safely in the hands of the military-industrial establishment, we wake to a new decade. G. McGovern. il Esquire 72:188-9+ D '69
Antimilitarism can be too much of a good thing. A. Hartley. il N Y Times Mag p30-1+ O 19 '69
Are our military alliances meaningful? G. S. McGovern. Ann Am Acad 384:14-20 Jl '69

UNITED STATES—Military policy—*Continued*
Arms and the scientists: a long dialogue continues. J. Walsh. Science 163:1436-8 Mr 28 '69
Can military spending be controlled? J. B. Bingham. For Affairs 48:51-66 O '69
Case for cutting defense spending; with editorial comment. J. Cameron. il Fortune 80: 61, 68-73+ Ag 1 '69
Congress and the military: many members take a harder look. L. J. Carter. Science 164:278-81 Ap 18 '69
Defense outlook. Bsns W p 170 O 11 '69
Does technology determine policy? R. Scott. Cur 109:45 Ag '69
Experiences, by A. Toynbee. Review
   Sat R 52:57-8 Je 21 '69. G. Culligan
Have civilians defaulted to the military? Cur 108:59-60 Je '69
How arms strategy looks from Moscow; hypothetical position paper. H. Kahn. il Newsweek 73:41 Je 16 '69; Reply. G. A. Arbatov. 74:36 Jl 21 '69
How to control the military. J. K. Galbraith. il Harper 238:31-46 Je '69
How to control the military, by J. K. Galbraith. Review
   Ramp Mag 8:31-3 D '69. S. Weissman
Ideas by which we are ruled. N. F. Twining; T. S. Power; C. E. LeMay. Harper 238:36-7 Je '69
Letter from Washington; concerning Nixon's address at the Air force academy. R. H. Rovere. New Yorker 45:86+ Je 14 '69
Military cutbacks will send tremors through industry; forecast for the 1970s. il Bsns W p91+ D 6 '69
Military power and foreign policy; address, June 2, 1969. A. B. Duke. Vital Speeches 35:628-31 Ag 1 '69
Mr Laird's stiffer posture. R. Hotz. Aviation W 90:11 Mr 24 '69
New American militarism. D. M. Shoup and J. A. Donovan. Atlan 223:51-6 Ap '69; Same abr. with title Role of the military; the rise of our militaristic culture. Cur 108:46-55 Je '69
Nixon's knaves; reactions to address at the Air force academy. K. Crawford. Newsweek 73:38 Je 23 '69
Now or never; present opportunity to curb militarization. Nation 208:652-3 My 26 '69
OPLAN NR 1-10; document outlines secret plan for waging unconventional warfare in eastern and central Europe; with report by S. Coryell. Ramp Mag 8:9 O '69
President stumbles; concerning address at Air force academy. New Repub 160:7-8 Je 14 '69
Revolt in the Pentagon? Z. B. Grant. il New Repub 161:17-20 O 4 '69
Space and senselessness; U.S. attitudes at the space science and technology conference, Denver, Colo. N. Cousins. Sat R 52:18 Jl 12 '69
Strategic posture faces severe scrutiny. C. Brownlow. il Aviation W 90:41-6 Mr 10 '69
U.S. cannot abandon all forms of intermediate force. W. V. Shannon. Commonweal 90:9-10 Mr 21 '69; Same with title On using intermediate force. Cur 109:51-4 Ag '69
U.S. military commitments in Europe and the Middle East; symposium. bibliog f Cur Hist 57:1-47+ Jl '69
Unpeace on earth. Commonweal 91:371-3 D 26 '69
   See also
Military assistance, American
United States—Defenses

Military sea transportation service
Requirements for defense; the U.S. merchant marine in perspective; address, March 24, 1969. W. F. Schlech, jr. Vital Speeches 35: 425-30 My 1 '69

Militia
See also
United States—National guard

Mint, Bureau of the
Gold is where it's hidden. Fort Knox. Mc-Calls 96:50 Mr '69

Monetary policy
See Monetary policy

Moral conditions
America, 35,000 feet. P. Schrag. Sat R 52: 24 My 10 '69
American disease. Nation 208:650-1 My 26 '69
American moral crisis, by A. S. Trace, jr. Review
   Cath World 210:185-6 Ja '70. G. C. Hay, jr
Are we a nation of haters and wreckers? R. MacLeish. Read Digest 95:92-6 N '69

Changing morality: the two Americas; a Time-Louis Harris poll. il Time 93:26-7 Je 6 '69
Demon of lust. L. N. Bell. Chr Today 13: 34-5 My 9 '69
Extremism; the turbulent teenager; address, June 8, 1969. F. Blair. Vital Speeches 35:598-601 Jl 15 '69
Hitting close to home; middle American morality; symposium. il Time 95:13 Ja 5 '70
Intolerable allegories of dissent. J. P. Sisk. Cath World 210:55-8 N '69
Man has changed; God hasn't. D. Lawrence. U S News 67:76 Jl 7 '69
On evil: the inescapable fact: Time essay. Time 94:26-7 D 5 '69
One generation speaks to another; exchange of letters. M. Machiz; J. L. Robertson. U S News 67:28-31 Jl 7 '69
Road to Songmy. N. Cousins. Sat R 52:18 D 20 '69
Systemic fascism. Nation 208:714-15 Je 9 '69
Telling it like it is. F. Morley. Nations Bsns 57:23-4 Je '69
   See also
Crime and criminals—United States
Violence

National academy of sciences
See National academy of sciences

National advisory commission on civil disorders
Kerner plus one; sequel to 1968 Kerner commission report. Newsweek 73:39 Mr 10 '69
Mission unaccomplished; results of Kerner report. F. R. Harris. Look 33:72 Mr 18 '69
One year later Chr Cent 86:364-5 Mr 19 '69
Riot commission politics. M. Lipsky & D. J. Olson. il Trans-Action 6:8-21 Jl '69

National advisory council on the education of disadvantaged children
Washington report: everyone wants more money. J. Lloyd. Sr Schol 94:Schol Teach 4 F 28 '69

National advisory council on vocational education
Too much stress on college; annual report. il U S News 67:45-6 O 13 '69

National aeronautics and space administration
Apollo's builders start closing the lines. il Bsns W p76-7 My 17 '69
Best man: T. O. Paine. Newsweek 73:74 Mr 17 '69
Deflating NASA's universe. Time 94:28 D 26 '69
Disenchantment with Apollo; resignation of NASA scientists. Sci N 96:112-13 Ag 9 '69
Future goals of NASA described. W. J. Normyle. il Aviation W 91:39-42 O 13 '69
Go for Apollo. H. T. Simmons. il Newsweek 74:42-4+ Jl 7 '69
How it was managed; U.S. space program. Time 94:28 Jl 18 '69
If Verne could look at NASA; Apollo flights. T. Sweeney. il Nat R 21:489-90 My 20 '69
Is a lunar landing in July lunacy? R. S. Lewis. Sat R 52:52+ My 10 '69
Musical chairs at NASA. Sci N 96:424 N 8 '69
NASA planning for interim lunar exploration missions. il Aviaton W 90:100-1+ Mr 10 '69
NASA plans to evaluate nine aircraft. Aviation W 90:89 Ap 7 '69
NASA: trouble in paradise; conflict between engineers and scientists. il Newsweek 74: 73-4 S 22 '69
NASA's tenth. D. Norton. il Space World F-5-65:14-19 My '69
NASA's Tom Paine, is this a job for a prudent man? T. Buckley. il N Y Times Mag p34-8+ Je 8 '69
Pace of post-Apollo planning rises. W. J. Normyle. Aviation W 90:16 F 3 '69
Plea for more astronomy. Sci N 96:447 N 15 '69
Post-Apollo: NASA seeks a Mars flight plan. L. J. Carter. il Science 165:987-91 S 5 '69
Post-Apollo task forces formed. W. J. Normyle. Aviation W 90:22-3 My 12 '69
Reporter at large; men on the moon. H. S. F. Cooper, jr. New Yorker 45:53-4+ Ap 12; 47-8+ Ap 19 '69
Send computers, not men, into deep space after the moon landing. R. E. Lapp. il N Y Times Mag p32-3+ F 2 '69
Terrestrial troubles; growing feud between NASA's engineers and scientists. il Time 94: 45 Ag 15 '69
Trouble at NASA: space scientists resign. M. Mueller. il Science 165:776-7+ Ag 22 '69

UNITED STATES—National aeronautics and
space administration—*Continued*
Unexpected payoff of Project Apollo. T.
Alexander. il Fortune 80:114-17+ Jl '69
See also
Lunar science institute (proposed)
United States—John F. Kennedy space center
United States—Manned spacecraft center

Appropriations and expenditures

Budget knives are nicking NASA. Bsns W
p21 Ja 3 '70
Conferees approve $3.71-billion budget au-
thorization for NASA. Aviation W 91:17
N 10 '69
Fund shift to speed space shuttle work. W. J.
Normyle. Aviation W 91:18-19 N 3 '69
House unit boosts NASA funds. Aviation W
90:19 My 19 '69
Mars options key to 1971 budget. W. J. Nor-
myle. il Aviation W 91:22-4 S 22 '69
NASA budget booms. il Sci N 95:351-2 Ap
12 '69
NASA urges supplemental for new lunar mis-
sions. Aviation W 90:22-3 Mr 17 '69
Nixon to back manned lunar plan. W. J.
Normyle. Aviation W 90:16-17 Ap 21 '69
Over, and out? Newsweek 73:94 Ja 27 '69
Post-Apollo question mark. il Sci N 95:89-90
Ja 25 '69
Space applications gain in funding plans.
W. J. Normyle. il Aviation W 90:25-8 Ja 20
'69
Space fund boost hits White House snag.
W. J. Normyle. Aviation W 90:27-8 Ap
14 '69
Where man's moon triumph can lead. il Bsns
W p23-4 Jl 26 '69

Art program

Artists and astronauts. L. Lastra. il Américas
21:21-8 S '69

Astronomy missions board

New directions coming. Sci N 95:573-4 Je 14
'69

Communications network

Saturn V launch vehicle. il Space World F-10-
70:8-13 O '69

Electronics research center

NASA to close electronics center. W. J.
Normyle. Aviation W 92:16-17 Ja 5 '70

Jet propulsion laboratory
See Jet propulsion laboratory

Lunar receiving laboratory
See United States—Manned spacecraft
center—Lunar receiving laboratory

National archives

Another research tool. G. P Middlebrooks.
Writers Digest 49:45 F '69

National bureau of standards
See United States—Standards, National
bureau of

National cancer institute

New storm brewing over DDT; named in NCI
study as causing tumors. Bsns W p32 Mr 8
'69

National commission on libraries and
information science (proposed)

Action on commission bill. G. Krettek and
E. D. Cooke. ALA Bul 63:452-3 Ap '69
Library commission bill. G. Krettek and E.
D. Cooke. Wilson Lib Bul 43:810 Ap '69
Library commission bill goes to Congress.
S. Wagner. Pub W 195:35-6 Mr 31 '69
Senate passes bill for national library com-
mission. S. Wagner. Pub W 195:43 Je 9 '69

National commission on the causes
and prevention of violence

Angry heritage; findings of study by task
force. Time 93:20 Je 13 '69
Assassins; rising danger in America; statement. U S News 67:15 N 10 '69
Civil disobedience and where it leads, two
sides; statement. il U S News 67:27-8 D
22 '69
File and forget. Nat R 21:1307 D 30 '69
Going armed; report. Nation 209:621 D 8 '69
How to heal a violent society. il Time 94:38
D 19 '69
How to reduce campus disorder; excerpts
from statement, June 9, 1969. il U S News
66:92-4 Je 23 '69
If crime goes unchecked, what big cities will
be like; excerpts from statement, November
24, 1965. M. S. Eisenhower. U S News 67:
41-2 D 8 '69

90 million firearms, and rising rapidly; ex-
cerpts from statement by the National com-
mission on the causes and prevention of
violence, July 28, 1969. il U S News 67:40-1
Ag 11 '69
Police riot? Chicago report; summary. Sr
Schol 93:18 Ja 10 '69
Political amnesia. Nation 208:779-80 Je 23 '69
Rhetoric of evasion. R. Drinnon. il Nation
209:370-4 O 13 '69
Seeds of mayhem; progress report. News-
week 73:23 F 10 '69
Sticking the pigs; concerning Walker report.
J. Jeffries. Nat R 21:236-8 Mr 11 '69
TV violence and U.S. violence; report. Ameri-
ca 121:253 O 4 '69
TV violence; appalling; excerpts from state-
ment. U S News 67:55-6 O 6 '69
Video violence report. Time 94:81 S 26 '69
Viewing the violent city of the future. Bsns
W p46 N 29 '69
Violence & TV; excerpts from statement.
Todays Ed 58:52-4 D '69
Why civil strife is high in U.S. U S News
66:11 Je 16 '69

National commission on urban problems

Exploring restrictive building practices; excerpt from report, Building the American
city. Mo Labor R 92:31-9 Jl '69
221 ways to save our cities. J. Bailey. Arch
Forum 130:70-3 Ja '69

National communicable
disease center

Disease battlers at our borders; Foreign
quarantine program. W. Cole. il Todays
Health 47:48-51+ My '69
Wind from Dugway; death of sheep near
Proving ground, testing poisonous agents.
V. Brodine and others. il Environ 11:2-9+
Ja '69

National council on marine
resources and engineering
development

One oceanography; Marine sciences council
Sci Am 220:48 Mr '69

National council on the arts
See United States—National foundation
on the arts and the humanities

National data center (proposed)

National data bank; its advocates try to
erase big brother image. L. J. Carter. Science 163:160-2 Ja 10 '69

National forest service
See United States—Forest service

National foundation on the arts and
the humanities

Arts go begging. M. Straight. New Repub
160:13-15 Mr 22 '69
For art's sake; recommendations of Richard
Nixon. New Repub 162:9 Ja 3 '70
High-return seed money. Sat R 53:27 Ja 10
'70
See also
National council on the arts selection (pro-
gram)

National guard

Battle of Berkeley. il Newsweek 73:35-6+
Je 2 '69
Bigger riot role for the national guard. il
U S News 66:42-3 Je 30 '69
Terror in a teapot; Berkeley park confronta-
tions. F. Berry and others. il Nation 208:
784-8 Je 23 '69
Wilmington; occupied city. R. J. Bresler.
Commonweal 89:513-14 Ja 24 '69

National institute of mental health

Students and drug abuse. il Todays Ed 58:
35-50 Mr '69
We must prevent emotional disturbance in
children. S. F. Yolles. Parents Mag 44:50
N '69

National institutes of health

HEW drops an ax on medical programs.
Bsns W p87 S 27 '69
NIH; another tight budget, fewer friends in
high places. J. Walsh. il Science 164:165-7
Ap 11 '69
NIH; ethics of budget cutting and retrench-
ment. E. A. Kabat. Science 166:168 O 10
'69
NIH policymaker; deputy director for science.
R. Berliner. B. J. Culliton. il Sci N 95:263-4
Mr 15 '69

Appropriations and expenditures

Advocates and cpponents of medical research. P. H. Abelson. Science 166:1579 D
26 '69

UNITED STATES—National institutes of health
—Appropriations and expenditures—*Cont.*
Hard choices made. Sci N 95:90 Ja 25 '69
NIH: agency and clients react to retrench-
ment. J. Walsh. Science 165:1332-4 S 26 '69

National labor relations board

Arbitration and the Labor board. B. Samoff.
bibliog Mo Labor R 92.54-6 My '69
Business sees a way to change NLRB. il
Bsns W p 102 N 29 '69
Card-bargaining policy upheld; Supreme court
decision. U S News 66:63-4 Je 30 '69
Do mergers need a union label? question for
NLRB il Bsns W p86+ My 17 '69
How business hopes to change the Nation's
labor laws; the Chamber of commerce pro-
posals U S News 66:68-9 Je 16 '69
If NLRB gets new chairman—. U S News
66:95 Mr 10 '69
No change now for NLRB chair. U S News
66:89 My 12 '69
Push for new strike law; movement to re-
form Railway labor act. il Bsns W p45-6
S 6 '69
Significant decisions in labor cases. See
issues of Monthly labor review
Strangling picket line; labor's double stan-
dard; address, October 30, 1969. J. L. Jones.
Vital Speeches 36:136-9 D 15 '69

National oceanic and atmospheric agency (proposed)

Chance for NOAA. Sci N 96:325-6 O 11 '69
Marine commission invokes NOAA, urges re-
fitting of nation's ark. B. Nelson. Science
163:263-5 Ja 17 '69
Pulse of earth; exploring the air-water sea.
J. Lear. il Sat R 52:49-52 F 1 '69

National park service

Founding of the National park service. D.
C. Swain. il Am West 6:6-9 S '69
New national park policy guidelines. Liv
Wildn 33:35 Sum '69
Over the years with the National park ser-
vice. G. B. Hartzog, jr. il Nat Parks 43:
13-14+ My '69
Park maintenance aided by modern equip-
ment. R. D. Browne. il Parks & Rec 4:
40-1 Jl '69
Preparing the park ranger for his job; Hor-
ace M. Albright training center. W. Cone.
il Parks & Rec 4:30-1+ D '69
Southwestern archeological center. O. F. Old-
endorph. il Nat Parks 43:4-7 F '69
Summer in the parks; National park service
program. T. McCann. il Parks & Rec 4:
14-17 Jl '69
See also
Forest rangers

Park police

Chief of U.S. park police. il Ebony 24:66-8+
Mr '69

National planning

See National planning

National science foundation

ABM and NSF. il Sci N 95:421-2 My 3 '69
Key NSF hearings open with Handler. P. M.
Boffey. Science 163:1433 Mr 28 '69
McElroy asks expanded NSF role. W. D.
McElroy. Science 166:1252 D 5 '69
NSF director: Nixon admits he was wrong.
P. M. Boffey and B. Nelson. Science 164:
532-4 My 2 '69
NSF directorship: why did Nixon veto
Franklin A. Long? P. M. Boffey and B.
Nelson. Science 164:406-11 Ap 25 '69
NSF: funds augmented, but uncertainties
linger on. J Walsh. Science 163:660 F 14
'69
NSF: McElroy seeks to impart political head-
way to agency. P. M. Boffey. Science
166:481-4+ O 24 '69
Needs for a national policy. E. Q. Daddario.
il Phys Today 22:33-8 O '69
Nixon and NSF: politics block appointment
of Long as director. P. M. Boffey. Sci-
ence 164:283-4 Ap 18 '69
Political criteria for non-political jobs? E.
Rabinowitch. Bul Atom Sci 25:2-3+ Je '69
Political storm breaks over appointment of
NSF director. Phys Today 22:67-9 Je '69
Science foundation's role analyzed for AEPI
group. Pub W 195:40-1 Ap 21 '69
Two-year institutions eligible for NSF col-
lege science improvement aid. Sch & Soc
97:207-8 Ap '69
See also
National register of scientific and technical
personnel

Appropriations and expenditures

Congress meets science: the appropriations
process. M. D. Reagan. bibliog il Science
164:929-30 My 23 '69

House group recommends big NSF cut. P. M.
Boffey. Science 164:1506 Je 27 '69
House panel kind to NSF budget but trims
some programs. P. M. Boffey. Science 164:
656 My 9 '69
NSF budget; binding up the wounds. P. M.
Boffey. Science 163:369 Ja 24 '69
NSF physics section discusses support poli-
cies and prospects; interview with eight
administrative officers, ed. by G. B. Lubkin.
il Phys Today 22:73-5+ S '69
New deal for graduate education. J. Lear.
il Sat R 52:78-9 My 17 '69
One to talk about. Sci N 95:88 Ja 25 '69
Re-opening the tap; university funds. Sci N
95:186 F 22 '69

National security council

Committees, come to order. il Newsweek 73:
29 F 17 '69
Kissinger: the uses and limits of power.
il Time 93:18-19 F 14 '69
National security council system: responsibili-
ties of the Department of state; White
House announcement; with message and
Department of state circular. Dept State Bul
60:163-6 F 24 '69
Nixon's command staff. J. Osborne. New
Repub 160:13-15 F 15 '69

National social science foundation (proposed)

Need for a National social science foundation; remarks, January 22, 1969. F. R. Harris. Trans-Action 6:3+ My '69

National teacher corps

Employment of Teacher corps applicants.
Sch & Soc 97:213+ Ap '69
Teacher corps program support. il Am Ed
5:27-8 Je '69

National transportation safety board

Diversity marks air safety proposals. P. J.
Klass. Aviation W 91:38-9 N 17 '69
Mediocre safety record made in 1968, NTSB
chairman says. Aviation W 90:28 F 10 '69
NTSB asks preventive action in crashes. il
Aviation W 90:28-9 Ja 27 '69
Systems safety approach urged in crash
analysis. Aviation W 90:38 My 12 '69

Naval radiological defense laboratory

Naval R&D: conversion sought for radiological defense lab. J. Walsh. Science 164:
1148-9 Je 6 '69
Navy accelerator goes begging. Sci N 96:130-1
Ag 16 '69

Navy

American seapower, 1969; a 1949 navy; ad-
dress, May 13, 1969. C. E. Bennett. Vital
Speeches 35:550-3 Jl 1 '69
Esquire's official court of inquiry into the
present state of the U.S. navy. il Esquire
72:84-6 Jl '69
How good are U.S. defenses? interview. T.
H. Moorer. il U S News 67:74-7 D 1 '69
Instant armada; Task force 71 protecting
future reconnaissance flights near North
Korea. Time 93:17 My 2 '69
New warning that navy is getting obsolete;
excerpts from address, May 23, 1969. L. M.
Rivers. il U S News 66:11 Je 9 '69
Protection money. il Newsweek 73:50+ My
5 '69
Pueblo syndrome: EC-121 incident. J. Burn-
ham. Nat R 21:480 My 20 '69
Remember the EC-121; warships ordered to
the Sea of Japan. Nat R 21:424+ My 6 '69
Russian navy; Pueblo inquiry; address. Janu-
ary 25, 1969. T. H. Moorer. Vital Speeches
35:300-3 Mr 1 '69
Soviet navy; our ability to meet the challenge; address, August 19, 1969. T. H. Moorer. Vital Speeches 35:742-6 O 1 '69
Soviet sea power; latest threat to America;
with interview with Vice Admiral D. C.
Richardson. C. S. Foltz, jr. il U S News 67:
56-61 Jl 21 '69
Spy business as usual for U.S. spook fleet;
navy's task force 71 in Sea of Japan. il
Bsns W p54+ Ap 26 '69
Spy plane spurs new debate; EC-121 incident. il Sr Schol 94:17-18 My 2 '69
20,000 guns under the sea; plans to militarize
the ocean floor. S. Hersh. il Ramp Mag
8:40-4 S '69
Words and warships in the Sea of Japan;
U.S. task force 71. Chr Cent 86:639 My
7 '69
See also
Naval maneuvers
United States—Air force. Navy
World war, 1939-1945—Naval operations

Air force

See United States—Air force. Navy

UNITED STATES—Navy—*Continued*

Appropriations and expenditures

House committee deletes funds to initiate navy F-14 production. Aviation W 91:26 D 8 '69
How the Pentagon hooks the Congress. A. Hamilton. New Repub 161:13-14 O 11 '69
Navy prepares fight for carriers. C. Brownlow. Aviation W 91:16-17 Ag 25 '69
Sailing through; biggest shipbuilding program. Forbes 103:25 F 15 '69
U.S. navy in the '70s; after cutbacks. il U S News 67:32 S 8 '69

Boats

Biggest, fastest flying boat yet! USS Plainview. R. Zimmerman il Pop Mech 130:88-91+ D '68
Navy takes new tack on shipbuilding; designing new class of destroyers. il Bsns W p 172-4 O 11 '69
Sikorsky tests assault patrol boat for navy. il Aviation W 90:46 Mr 31 '69
See also
Warships—United States

Chaplains

See Chaplains, Military

Communication systems

See also
Radio communication, Naval

Courts martial and courts of inquiry

See Courts martial and courts of inquiry

Crimes and misdemeanors

How fellow officers view the case of Commander Bucher. il U S News 66:34 F 10 '69

History

See also
United States—History—War of 1812—Naval operations

Officers

How fellow officers view the case of Commander Bucher. il U S News 66:34 F 10 '69

Personnel system

How good are U.S. defenses? interview. T. H. Moorer. il U S News 67:74-7 D 1 '69

Procurement

F-14 pace spurs increase in navy buying, research. il Aviation W 90:23-4 Ja 20 '69
High flying in the Pentagon; campaigns for new aircraft. A. Hamilton. New Repub 160:16-18 My 31 '69
Navy's turn to squirm. il Time 94:83-4 N 21 '69

Recreation

NRPA representative visits Japan; conducting workshops at naval bases. P. O. Sturdivant. il Parks & Rec 4:49+ S '69
See also
United States—Navy—Sports

Sports

I finally got the point; basketball on an aircraft carrier. E. Bowen. il Sports Illus 30:60-2+ F 10 '69

Office of education

See United States—Education, Office of

Office of minority business enterprise

Capitalist slow down. S. Cotton. New Repub 161:15-16 S 27 '69

Officials and employees

See Public officers

Outdoor recreation, Bureau of

Doctor Craft's resignation; February 25, 1969. E. C. Crafts. Am For 75:4 Ap '69
High noon for the Bureau of outdoor recreation. E. C. Crafts. il Am For 75:12-15+ O '69

Park police

See United States—National park service —Park police

Passport division

See United States—State, Department of —Passport division

Patent office

Foe of patent reform displaces the reformer; W. Schuyler takes over from Edward Brenner. il Bsns W p 167-8 My 10 '69

Peace corps

Agents of change, by D. Hapgood and M. Bennett. Review
Bul Atom Sci 25:40+ N '69. B. Schurman
Nation 208:86-8 Ja 20 '69. S. Meisler

Annual report of the Peace corps transmittal to Congress; letter, January 7 1969. L. B. Johnson. Dept State Bul 60:118 F 3 '69
Black pride; black action; address, December 4, 1968. C. P. Lucas. Vital Speeches 35:505-8 Je 1 '69
Business ships out with Peace corps. il Bsns W p35-6 S 27 '69
Conservationist in Chile. il Am For 75:24-6 Ap '69
New broom. S. Ungar. il Newsweek 73:56+ Je 2 '69
Peace corps adventure for not-so-young M.D.'s. Todays Health 47:17 N '69
Peace corps: do you have what it takes? il Har Yrs 9:6-7 Jl '69
Peace corps intrigue in the Philippines. G. H. Anderson. Chr Cent 87:4-6 Ja 7 '70
Peace corps: new challenges, more opportunities. F. Mundy. il Har Yrs 9:8-10 Jl '69
Peace corps: sneakers and levis for me. P. Ramsey. Har Yrs 9:10+ Jl '69
Peace corps volunteer or missionary, does it really make any difference? F. Hezel. Cath World 208:205-7 F '69; Reply. G. Lensing. tr. 209:121-2 Je '69
President reaffirms interest in international Peace corps; text of letter, September 24, 1969. R. M. Nixon. Dept State Bul 61:325 O 13 '69
Uncivil war afflicts the Peace corps; confronting the Pentagon in Micronesia. P. Stern. New Repub 161:14-16 Ag 23 '69
Whatever happened to the Peace corps? il U S News 67:14 O 27 '69
When PCV's come home. il Newsweek 73:106+ Mr 17 '69

Photographs

America the beautiful. Am Heritage 21:4-11 D '69
U.S.A. with introd. by E. J. Steichen. M. P. R. Thomas and M. Wright. Travel & Camera 32:54-86 F '69
Who hears America singing? Fortune 80:90-9 Jl '69

Politics and government

Advice to the new boys. Brookings institution report. A. Howard. New Repub 160:29-30 F 1 '69
After Vietnam: the dollars and cents of peace; symposium. Sat R 52:11-22 My 24 '69
Ambassador's journal, by J. K. Galbraith. Review
Sat R 52:27 D 20 '69. J. M. Burns
America's next rendezvous with destiny. C. Bowles. Sat R 52:17-19+ S 6 '69
Arnold Toynbee talks of peace, power, race in America; interview, ed. by J. R. Moskin. A. Toynbee. Look 33:25-7 Mr 18 '69
Authoritarian prescription. W. D. Phelan, jr. Nation 209:467-73 N 3 '69
Be kind to Bob Finch; week's main thrusts. Newsweek 74:28-9 Jl 21 '69
Big government: is it out of hand? il U S News 66:28-30 Mr 24 '69
Blues on the right; administration's ranks. Newsweek 73:32 Ap 7 '69
Change ahead under Nixon; with photo report. U S News 66:23-8 F 3 '69
Count the blessings; President Nixon's summary of his administration's accomplishments to date. il Newsweek 74:20 D 29 '69
Course we're on; autumnal State of the Union report. Commonweal 91:35-6 O 10 '69
Disarray in the Nixon team. il U S News 67:35-7 O 13 '69
Draft, taxes, crime, welfare; Nixon asks for action now; text of message to Congress, October 13, 1969. R. M. Nixon. U S News 67:91-4 O 20 '69
Enter: the Nixon era. il Sr Schol 94:6-7+ Ja 17 '69
First hundred days of Richard M. Nixon. T. C. Sorensen. il Sat R 52:17-19 My 17 '69
For want of a program. Commonweal 89:607-8 F 14 '69
From Eisenhower's speeches and writings. D. D. Eisenhower. il Sr Schol 94:13 Ap 11 '69
Future of American politics; excerpts from The emerging Republican majority; with comments by C. Fritchey. K. P. Phillips. Cur 110:26-31 S '69
Future of American politics; is revolution impending? B. Moore, jr. Cur 106:54-64 Ap '69
Getting a grip on the 'governaut.' H. Sidey. il Life 66:2 Ja 24 '69
Goodbys, some with regret; and hellos, mostly appreciative. il Life 66:30 Ja 24 '69
Headless phantom, boneless wonder. New Repub 161:7-8 Ag 9 '69
High on foggy bottom, by C. Frankel. Review
Sat R 53:38 Ja 10 '70. C. Kilpatrick

UNITED STATES—Politics and government—
Continued
Human rights and the Nixon administra-
tion. T. P. Melady and M. B. Melady. Cath
World 209:55-8 My '69
Issues for the '70s. H. Cox. Commonweal
90:18-20 Mr 21 '69
It takes too much time to make the change.
D. Lawrence. U S News 66:92 Mr 31 '69
Let us, go forward together; Issues that
face Mr Nixon. il Newsweek 73:17-21 Ja 27
'69
Letter from Washington. R. H. Rovere. See
occasional issues of New Yorker
Liberal toryism. K. Crawford. Newsweek 74:
24 S 1 '69
Look inside the Nixon administration; inter-
view. S. T. Agnew. il U S News 67:32-8 O
6 '69
McCarthy talk; interviews, ed. by J. Roddy.
E. McCarthy. il Look 33:19-21 Ap 1 '69
Making democracy work. T. F. Lunsford.
Cur 106:44-53 Ap '69
Making democracy work; excerpts from
Agenda for the Nation. Cur 103:16-26 Ja
'69
Mr Nixon in trouble. il Newsweek 74:30-2+ O
13 '69
Mr Nixon's middle course. H. Brandon. Sat R
52:17 Mr 1 '69
My brother Lyndon; excerpts, ed. by E. H.
Lopez. S. H. Johnson. Look 33:49-52+ D
2; 43-6+ D 16 '69
National affairs. See issues of Newsweek
National priorities and participation in for-
eign policy. G. W. Shepherd, jr. Chr Cent
86:504-7 Ap 16 '69
Nation's needs as Nixon sees them; text
of message to Congress, April 14, 1969.
R. M. Nixon. il U S News 66:76-8 Ap 28 '69
New crisis in leadership; with report by H.
Hubbard. il Newsweek 74:20-2 Jl 14 '69
New leadership emerges. il Time 93:15-16 F
14 '69
New politics: more mood than movement.
J. Newfield. Nation 209:70-3 Jl 28 '69
New President is installed. M. McGrory.
America 120:125 F 1 '69
New president: new goals, new ways. il U S
News 66:23-5 Ja 27 '69
New year's thoughts, 1969: prospects for
progress and peace. E. Rabinowitch. Bul
Atom Sci 25:2-4 Ja '69
Nixon and the new Washington. il Nations
Bsns 57:32-4+ Ja '69
Nixon gets ready to build; ABM, budget-cut-
ting, the inflation fight, and tax reform. il
Bsns W p45-7 Ap 26 '69
Nixon sets the stage. il Bsns W p33-4 Ja
25 '69
Nixon the predictable. Commonweal 90:251-
2 My 16 '69
Nixon's blueprint; address at the Air force
academy. E. Gruening. Nation 208:781 Je
23 '69
Nixon's first ninety days. il U S News 66:
37-40 Ap 14 '69
Nixon's first six months. il Time 94:12-14 Jl
18 '69
Nixon's own words on My Lai, taxes, pros-
pects for peace; text of news conference,
December 8, 1969. R. M. Nixon. il U S News
67:48-52 D 22 '69
Nixon's priorities. il U S News 66:23-5 F 10
'69
Nixon's program. R. Lekachman. Commen-
tary 47:67-72 Je '69
Nixon's workable proposals. W. F. Buckley,
jr. Nat R 21:454 My 6 '69
Nixon's worst week. il Time 94:15-16 O 10 '69
No deal. K. Crawford. Newsweek 73:42 My
5 '69
Notes & asides. W. F. Buckley, jr. See issues
of National review
Nothing yet to mar the White House slumber.
H. Sidey. il Life 67:8 S 26 '69
Now it's Nixon's turn. il Sci N 95:109 F 1 '69
On establishment law and people's disorder.
R. Scheer. Ramp Mag 8:4+ Jl '69
100 days, and four lessons. il Newsweek
73:33-4 My 12 '69
One-liners for an open mind. H. Sidey. il
Life 66:4 My 30 '69
Out of touch in Washington; excerpt from
High on foggy bottom: an outsider's in-
side view of the government. C. Frankel.
Sat R 52:21-3+ N 1 '69; Same abr. with
title Making democracy work. Cur 113:27-
32 D '69
Political power patterns are changing. il Na-
tions Bsns 57:34-6+ N '69
Politics; problems facing Nixon. J. Leonard.
Esquire 71:20+ Ja '69
Presidency. H. Sidey. See issues of Life
President-elect sets his own style; plans to
move slowly with new programs. il Bsns W
p80-2 Ja 18 '69

President, new vigor now for old problems.
il U S News 67:17 S 15 '69
President Nixon's first thirty days. il U S
News 66:27-8 F 24 '69
President on Vietnam, inflation, civil rights;
text of news conference September 26, 1969.
R. M. Nixon. il U S News 67:76-81 O 6 '69
President settles in. il Bsns W p 13-14 F 1 '69
President's program and its chances in Con-
gress. il U S News 66:68-9 My 12 '69
Priorities for the seventies; excerpt from
address. R. L. Heilbroner. Sat R 53:17-19+
Ja 3 '70
Profession: member of Congress; where the
action is. F. Taddeo. il Sr Schol 94:10-13
F 28 '69
Realpolitik, 1970. K. Crawford. Newsweek 75:
20 Ja 5 '70
Report card for Richard Nixon. J. J. Kil-
patrick. il Nat R 21:532-7 Je 3 '69
Reports: Washington. See issues of Atlantic
Republicans at work. K. Crawford. News-
week 74:25 Jl 14 '69
Rise of the techno-corporate state in Amer-
ica. A. S. Miller. Bul Atom Sci 25:14-19 Ja
'69
Showdown time at White House; the grow-
ing pressures. il U S News 66:25-6 Mr 24 '69
State of the Union; address, January 14,
1969. L. B. Johnson. Vital Speeches 35:
228-31 F 1 '69; Excerpts. Dept State Bul 60:
89-91 F 3 '69; Cur Hist 56:168+ Mr '69
Summing up the LBJ years. il Sr Schol 93:3-
9 Ja 10 '69
TRB from Washington:
   Black feud; Nixon administration's aliena-
   tion from the Negroes. New Repub 162:
   6 Ja 3 '70
   Down is up. New Repub 161:4 D 6 '69
   New ball game. New Repub 160:6 Je 14 '69
   Washington's crazy. New Repub 160:4
   My 10 '69
   Wired for sound. New Repub 160:4 Je 7 '69
This rotten system. K. Crawford. Newsweek
73:38 Je 9 '69
Tough decisions for a new decade. il News-
week 75:11-12 Ja 5 '70
Twelve months to deliver. il Time 93:9 My
2 '69
Uncertain apocalypse. Chr Cent 86:1302 O 15
'69
Very expensive education of McGeorge Bundy.
D. Halberstam. il Harper 239:21-37 Jl '69
Waiting for the word. New Repub 160:7-8 F
1 '69
Washington outlook. See issues of Business
week
Washington trends. T. Trussell. See issues
of Nation's business
We must avoid the perils of extremism. D.
D. Eisenhower. Read Digest 94:103-8 Ap
'69
We won't end the urban crisis until we end
majority rule. H. J. Gans. il N Y Times
Mag p 12-15+ Ag 3 '69; Discussion. p6+
Ag 24 '69
What can we expect from the Nixon years?
K. E. Clarke. Chr Cent 86:182-3 F 5 '69
What is Nixon's policy? Nat R 21:158+ F 25
'69
What the government can do. il Time 93:28-
30 Ja 24 '69
What's new: Washington. See issues of
Successful farming
White House mood. P. Lisagor. See issues
of Nation's business
You didn't ask us, Mr President, but. . ;
twelve powerful men offer suggestions. il
Esquire 71:118-21 Ja '69
   See also
Campaign issues
Congressmen
Democratic party
Elections—United States
Fascism—United States
Legislation—United States
Lobbying
Nixon, R. M.—Relations with Congress
Political campaigns
Political parties—United States
Presidents—United States
Presidents—United States—Election
Presidents—United States—Powers and duties
Presidents—United States—Transition periods
Progressivism (United States politics)
Republican party
Socialism—United States
Suffrage—United States
United States—Cabinet
United States—Congress
United States—Constitution
United States—Executive departments

Popular culture

Culture. il Harp Baz 103:134-5 Ja '70
Forgotten American. P. Schrag. il Harper
239:27-34 Ag '69

UNITED STATES—Popular culture—*Continued*
Making of the yippie culture. G. Wills. Esquire 72:135-8+ N '69
Plastic reality. C. Karpel. il Esquire 72:221-3 D '69
Pop sex among the squares; pop pornography, newest white-collar obsession. D. Smith. il Nation 209:142-5 Ag 25 '69
Proletarianization of culture. J. Hart. il Nat R 21:1329-30 D 30 '69
Rock for sale. M. Lydon. il Ramp Mag 7:19-24 Je '69
The sixties: a cultural revolution. B. De Mott. il N Y Times Mag p28-31+ D 14 '69
Trivial trends that point the way. il Life 68:78-81+ Ja 9 '70
Week I made the scene. J. Viorst. il Redbook 134:74-5+ N '69
Young and crazy years. G. Guinness. Harp Baz 103:124-5 D '69
Youthquake in pop culture. S. Zalaznick. il Fortune 79:84-7+ Ja '69

Population

Catastrophe by the numbers. C. Ogburn, jr. Am Heritage 21:114-17 D '69
Changing America; what 1970 census will show. il U S News 66:68-71 Je 2 '69
National plan for curbing births; proposals of President Nixon. U S News 67:4 Jl 28 '69
Overpopulated America. W. H. Davis. New Repub 162:13-15 Ja 10 '70
Planning for 2000. Time 94:21 Jl 25 '69
Population explosion, impact on business; with excerpts from President Nixon's message to Congress, July 18, 1969. il U S News 68:32-4 Ja 12 '70
Population shifts predicted for the '70s. il U S News 66:45 Je 23 '69
Problems of population growth; message to Congress, July 18, 1969. R. M. Nixon. Dept State Bul 61:105-11 Ag 11 '69
World power and population. C. Clark. il Nat R 21:431-4 My 20 '69
See also
Cities and towns—United States
Migration, Internal
United States—Census

Statistics

Population statistics: published and unpublished. H. D. Sheldon. il Mo Labor R 92:45-9 D '69

Post office department

No. 1 mailman: can he deliver? U S News 66:14 Mr 3 '69
Post office reform. New Repub 160:8 Je 14 '69
Postal reform riles Congress; Nixon endorses Blount's plan. Bsns W p33 My 24 '69
Postmaster General Blount; interview. W. M. Blount. New Yorker 45:49-51 O 18 '69
Streamlining moves ahead. Sci N 95:550 Je 7 '69
Taking the mail out of politics; proposed independent government agency called the U.S. postal service. il Time 93:24 Je 6 '69
This month's feature: moves to reorganize the postal system. Cong Digest 48:67-96 Mr '69
Time for a change? Newsweek 73:87-3 Je 9 '69
Time for a change; excerpts from message to Congress, May 27, 1969. R. M. Nixon. U S News 66:44 Je 9 '69
Union war on postal reform. il Bsns W p97-8 S 20 '69
Will mail service go modern? il U S News 66:40-2 F 3 '69
See also
Air mail service
Mail handling
Postal censorship
Postal employees
Postal service—United States
Postmasters

President's commission on postal organization

This month's feature: moves to reorganize the postal system. Cong Digest 48:67-96 Mr '69

President's commission on the assassination of President Kennedy

In the shadow of Dallas; mysterious deaths of those possessing crucial knowledge about the killings of President Kennedy, Officer J. D. Tippit or Lee Harvey Oswald. D. Welsh and W. Turner. Ramp Mag 7:61-71 Ja 25 '69

President's equal employment opportunity commission

See United States—Equal employment opportunity commission

President's foreign intelligence advisory board

Foreign intelligence advisory board established by President Nixon; White House announcement with executive order, March 20, 1969. R. M. Nixon. Dept State Bul 60:294-5 Ap 7 '69

President's task force on international development

Mr Peterson to head task force on international development. Dept State Bul 61:284 S 29 '69
President Nixon names task force on international development. Dept State Bul 61:358 O 27 '69

Public buildings

See Public buildings

Public health service

HEW security checks said to bar qualified applicants to PHS. B. Nelson. Science 165:269-71 Jl 18 '69
See also
United States—National communicable disease center

Public land law review commission

Public land law review commission, what it's all about. Am For 75:14-15 D '69

Race problems

Race problems: how serious? mayors comments at the National league of cities. il U S News 67:11 D 15 '69
Voice of dissent: John Jay Chapman and the great wickedness. L. M. Sims. bibliog Negro Hist Bul 32:12-13 Mr '69
See also
Church and race problems
Congress of racial equality
Georgia—Race problems
Japanese Americans
Jews in the United States
Negroes
United States—Armed forces—Race problems

Reclamation, Bureau of

High cost of destruction; excerpts from The diligent destroyers. G. Laycock. il Audubon 71:86-8+ N '69

Relations (diplomatic)
Catholic church

See Catholic church—Relations (diplomatic)—United States

Religious institutions and affairs

New troubles in the churches. il U N News 66:41-4 Ap 14 '69; Same abr with title Our troubled churches. Read Digest 95:126-9 Jl '69
Passionate word to the new anti-intellectuals. Chr Cent 86:1409 N 5 '69
Religious cultures, high and low. D. Cutler. il Commonweal 91:156-60 O 31 '69
See also
Baptists in the United States
Catholic church in the United States
Church and state
Church of Christ in the United States
Jews in the United States
Lutheran church in the United States
Mennonites
Negro militants and churches
Negroes—Religion
Orthodox Eastern church, Russian, in the United States
Presbyterian church in the United States (South)
Presbyterian church in the United States of America
Protestant Episcopal church
Puritans
United church of Christ
Unity school of Christianity
also subhead Religious institutions and affairs under names of states, cities, e.g. Detroit—Religious institutions and affairs

Renegotiation board

Tax-court peephole. S. Watzman. Nation 208:113-15 Ja 27 '69

Reserve forces

See United States—Armed forces—Reserves

Reserve officers training corps

Academic question; ROTC; address, May 16, 1969. A. C. Weidenbusch. Vital Speeches 35:558-60 Jl 1 '69
Buckle down, John Harvard. H. Cox. Commonweal 90:22-4 My 9 '69

UNITED STATES—Reserve officers training corps—_Continued_

Close-up of student-soldiers: case study at one big university; situation at Indiana university. il U S News 67:52-4 N 3 '69

Column right, march! Loyola and ROTC program. J. Deedy. Commonweal 91:2 O 3 '69

Demoting the military; Yale makes ROTC an entirely extracurricular affair. Time 93:70 F 7 '69

Despite some ROTC setbacks—. U S News 66:14 F 17 '69

Report of Cornell's presidential commission on military training. il Sch & Soc 97:235-9 Ap '69

ROTC game. W. F. Buckley, jr. Nat R 21:558 Je 3 '69

ROTC retreat. J. W. Scott. il Trans-Action 6:47-52 S '69

ROTC: the protesters' next target. il Time 93:54+ Mr 7 '69

ROTC under attack. K. Y. Tomlinson. Read Digest 95:231-4+ N '69

ROTC: under fire but doing fine. il U S News 66:38 My 19 '69

ROTC: yes or no? America 120:241 Mr 1 '69

Turning out ROTC. New Repub 160:11-12 Mr 8 '69

Who are the victims? A. H. Sypher. Nations Bsns 57:23-4 Jl '69

Revenue

See also

Taxation—United States

Riots

Anxious anniversary. il Time 93:19 Ap 11 '69

City: hope for the summer. il Time 93:24 My 30 '69

Civil rights push. il Sr Schol 94:8-10 F 7 '69

Dream, still unfulfilled; disorders during M. L. King memorial anniversary events. il Newsweek 73:34-5 Ap 14 '69

End to big riots? Findings of a police survey. il U S News 66:42-4 Je 2 '69

Fire this time; incidents in Omaha, Neb, Harrisburg, Pa, and Kokomo, Ind. il Newsweek 74:19 Jl 7 '69

Firearms in civil disorders; excerpt from study by the Stanford research institute. Cur 103:40-3 Ja '69

Flaring again; racial violence. il U S News 67:8 Ag 4 '69

How '69 riot season compares with 1968. U S News 67:16 S 15 '69

Lasting scars from city riots. il US News 66:14 Ap 21 '69

Long hot weekend; Labor day weekend disorders. il Newsweek 74:27 S 15 '69

Profit before risk; insuring the ghettos. H. Shapiro. Commonweal 89:579-80 F 7 '69

Race unrest: where trouble flared. il U S News 66:10-11 My 12 '69

Racial outbreaks: a long, hot summer after all? il U S News 67:4 Jl 7 '69

Revolt of the urban ghettos, 1964-1967. J. Boskin. bibliog f Ann Am Acad 382:1-14 Mr '69

Riots, 1969 style. il Newsweek 74:36-7 Ag 11 '69

Thousands of riot arrests, but... U S News 66:8 F 10 '69

U.S. unrest, as FBI chief sees it; excerpts from report on 1969. J. E. Hoover. U S News 68:8 Ja 12 '70

Violence and the press. T. A. Knopf. Cur 107:36-47 My '69

Who riots; summary of California study. H. E. Ransford. Trans-Action 6:8 F '69

Year later: honors for Dr King; violence too. il US News 66:8 Ap 14 '69

See also

Government investigations—Riots

Riot control

United States—National advisory commission on civil disorders

also subhead Riots under names of cities, e.g. Chicago—Riots

Prevention and control

See Riot control

Science and technology, Department of (proposed)

Do we need a department of science and technology? H. Roback. bibliog Science 165:36-43 Jl 4 '69

Science and technology, Office of

Environmental studies: OST report urges better effort. L. J. Carter. Science 166:851 N 14 '69

How the President gets his science advice: a visit to OST. J. P. Wiley. il Phys Today 22:70-1+ Ag '69

Nixon chooses OST deputy director. P. M. Boffey. Science 164:1263 Je 13 '69

Securities and exchange commission

Big board heads for a showdown. Bsns W p 120+ N 8 '69

Budge for the SEC. Newsweek 73:66 Mr 3 '69

Call Marty investigation of Parvin-Dohrmann stock. Newsweek 74:36 O 27 '69

Consensus man heads the SEC; H. H. Budge appointment as chairman of the commission. Bsns W p68 Mr 1 '69

Is the SEC cracking the whip? with editorial comment. Bsns W p 122-3, 172 O 18 '69

Last stand over full disclosure. il Bsns W p66 Ja 3 '70

Letter stock is worth the worry; large holdings of unregistered shares by mutual funds. il Bsns W p 108+ Ja 18 '69

Lockheed and the SEC. Nation 209:396-7 O 20 '69

New chairman of SEC; how tough will he be? il U S News 66:13 Mr 10 '69

New way SEC might ride herd. Bsns W p46 Ap 19 '69

Rise and fall of Parvin/Dohrmann. il Fortune 80:163-4+ D '69

SEC closes in on computers. Bsns W p82 Ag 9 '69

SEC proposals stir little chaff. Bsns W p 136 S 20 '69

SEC relents on conglomerates. Bsns W p50 F 22 '69

Speculating about Manny Cohen. il Bsns W p 108+ F 15 '69

Tough to nudge Judge Budge. Time 94:69-70 Ag 8 '69

Troubled SEC gets a Nixon Democrat; appointment of A. S. Herlong, jr. il Bsns W p27-8 S 6 '69

Voloshen connection; investigation of Parvin/Dohrmann stock. il Time 94:26-7 O 24 '69

Senate

See United States—Congress—Senate

Small business administration

Capitalist slow down. S. Cotton. New Repub 161:16 S 27 '69

Cubans take off on SBA test run. il Bsns W p41 Je 21 '69

How to even the odds; loans to Negroes. H. Samuels. il Sat R 52:22-6 Ag 23 '69

New weapons to protect you against crime; SBA report. il Nations Bsns 57:90-1+ Ap '69

News and views; Small business administration backing Cuban refugee merchants. J. Deedy. Commonweal 89:574 F 7 '69

Project Own; address, December 4, 1968. H. J. Samuels. Vital Speeches 35:250-3 F 1 '69

Seeds for black capitalism; SBA's MESBIC plan. il Bsns W p40-1 N 15 '69

Social conditions

America at the crossroads; excerpts from Britannica book of the year 1969. L. B. Johnson. Read Digest 94:54-8 Mr '69

America's social balance sheet; address, September 17, 1969. D. S. Macleod. Vital Speeches 36:17-21 O 15 '69

Barry jr. scolds the older generation; interview. B. Goldwater, jr. il Nations Bsns 57:46-9 Ag '69

Black man's route to the top. W. A. Lewis. Read Digest 95:157-8+ Ag '69

Campus revolutionaries; the rights of students; address, June 3, 1969. R. M. Nixon. Vital Speeches 35:546-8 Jl 1 '69; Excerpts. U S News 66:66-7 Je 16 '69

Case for America; address, October 2, 1969. W. L. Lindholm. Vital Speeches 36:56-9 N 1 '69

Concerned citizen speaks about America's turmoil; address, May 22, 1969. J. L. Robertson. U S News 66:96+ Je 9 '69

Don't ask me, I only live here. R. Baker. il Life 67:32-7 Jl 25 '69

Eisenhower's America: historic interview; reprint of March 28, 1952 issue. D. D. Eisenhower. U S News 66:65-7 Ap 14 '69

Freedom, reason are under attacks; excerpts from address, June 3, 1969. R. M. Nixon. U S News 66:66-7 Je 16 '69

Good things about the U.S. today; reply. U S News 66:108+ F 17 '69

HEW urges annual social report. P. Thompson. Science 163:456 Ja 31 '69

How America has changed; interview with two newsmen home from abroad. R. A. Haeger and F. C. Painton. il U S News 67:70-4 S 1 '69

In search of the missing social indicators. I. Kristol. il Fortune 80:168-9 Ag 1 '69

Law and order with justice. J. B. Sheerin; discussion. Cath World 209:4 Ap '69

Making democracy work. T. F. Lunsford. Cur 106:44-53 Ap '69

Man and woman of the year: the middle Americans. il Time 95:10-17 Ja 5 '70

UNITED STATES—Social conditions—*Cont.*
Measure of quality; Toward a social report. Time 93:66 F 7 '69
Miracle in a mess; Economist's survey, The neurotic trillionaire. il Newsweek 73:89 My 26 '69
Mood of America. il U S News 67:22-6 Jl 7 '69
National image; views of G. Myrdal. Commonweal 90:36 Mr 28 '69
Nation's biggest danger; interview. A. Burns. il U S News 67:60-5 Jl 14 '69
Now it can be told; HEW report on social well-being of the Nation. New Repub 160: 11 F 1 '69
Omnis America in partes tres divisa est. S. A. Mueller and J. A. Sween. Chr Cent 86: 1342-4 O 22 '69; Correction. 87:18-19 Ja 7 '70
One generation speaks to another; exchange of letters. M. Machiz; J. L. Robertson. U S News 67:28-31 Jl 7 '69
Protest in the sixties; symposium, ed. by J. Boskin and R. A. Rosenstone. bibliog f Ann Am Acad 382:1-144 Mr '69
Public problem solving; address, February 17, 1969. G. Romney. Vital Speeches 35:329-31 Mr 15 '69
Revolt of the middle class; with interview with H. H. Humphrey. il U S News 67: 52-8 N 24 '69
Strange world of Mr Nutter. P. Steinfels. Commonweal 90:158-9 Ap 25 '69
TRB from Washington; no bread, and circuses. New Repub 161:4 Ag 2 '69
Talk with Walter Lippmann, at eighty, about this minor dark age; interview, ed. by H. Brandon. W. Lippmann. il N Y Times Mag p25-7+ S 14 '69
Task to test our mettle; excerpts from address. J. W. Gardner. Read Digest 94:205-8 F '69
Time to remember forgotten America; Time essay. il Time 94:42-3 Ag 8 '69
Toward a self-renewing society; Time essay; excerpts from address. J. W. Gardner. Time 93:40-1 Ap 11 '69
What's happened to the American dream? dialogue between the generations; with group-discussion program. V. Block. il Parents Mag 44:28, 40-1+ Je '69
Why civil strife is high in U.S; findings of National commission on the causes and prevention of violence. U S News 66:11 Je 16 '69
Worst sickness in American history. D. Lawrence. U S News 67:84 Jl 28 '69
See also
Child welfare—United States
Cities and towns—United States
Crime and criminals—United States
Divorce—United States
Housing—United States
Labor and laboring classes—United States
Negroes
Poor—United States
Slums
United States—Population
Women—United States
Youth—United States
also subhead Social conditions under names of sections, states, cities, e.g. New York (city)—Social conditions

Bibliography

Home scene. T. M. Gannon. America 121: 527+ N 29 '69
Home scene. W. L. Lucey. America 120:535-6 My 3 '69

History

See United States—Social history

Social history

New commonwealth, by J. A. Garraty. Review
    Am Heritage 20:105-6 Ap '69. B. Catton
USA. G. Culligan. il Sat R 52:31-3 O 11 '69
See also
Education—United States—History
Negroes—History
Slavery—United States
United States—Moral conditions

Social life and customs

Great American summer. il McCalls 96:72-5+ Jl '69
Growing up in America; symposium. il Mlle 68:206-9+ Ap '69
Hangouts. P. Hamill. Mlle 70:151+ N '69
It's still a hopping holiday; Fourth of July celebrations of Eveleth, Minn, Bexley, Ohio, Stonington, Me, and Kotzebue, Alaska. il Sports Illus 31:36-43 Jl 7 '69
Mobile society; one out of five of us will move this year. M. A. Guitar. Am Home 72:52-3 Ja '69

USA. G. Culligan. il Sat R 52:31-3 O 11 '69
See also
Christmas—United States
Drinking customs
Suburban life
Thanksgiving day
also subhead Social life and customs under names of states, cities, e.g. California—Social life and customs

Social policy

Agenda for a new administration. K. Gordon. Cur 103:16-18 Ja '69
America's my home. Not my business, my home. G. Wald. Bul Atom Sci 25:29-31 My '69
As I see it; interview. R. H. Finch. il Forbes 103:76-8+ Je 15 '69
As Nixon shifts to home front—. U S News 67:19-22 Ag 18 '69
Beyond racism, by W. M. Young, jr. Review
    Newsweek 73:92+ Je 2 '69. A. Cooper
Federal government and protest. D. Mars. bibliog f Ann Am Acad 382:120-30 Mr '69
Labor looks at government finances. G. Meany. Ann Am Acad 379:72-7 S '68
Mr Gardner speaks his mind. America 121: 628-9 D 27 '69
Parting shots from Johnson; lame-duck recommendations. il Bsns W p35-6 Ja 25 '69
Pretty thin. Nation 208:522-3 Ap 28 '69
Priorities for the seventies; excerpt from address. R. L. Heilbroner. Sat R 53:17-19+ Ja 3 '70
Progressive look and practical answers. Time 93:14-15 F 21 '69
Report; Washington; success of Great society. E. B. Drew. Atlan 223:4+ Ja '69
Welfare state, Republican style. il Time 93:10-14 My 2 '69
What happens when peace breaks out? E. S. Muskie. il Sat R 52:12-15 My 24 '69
See also
Economic assistance, Domestic
Public welfare—United States

Soil conservation service

Mr Don. J. B. Craig. il Am For 75:8+ F '69
Where conservation is a bad word. B. B. Blackburn, 3d; G. Laycock. il Field & S 74:12-14+ D '69

Standards, National bureau of

Commercial TV helps NBS' standards broadcasts. Electr World 81:65 Je '69
Government agencies expand publishing operations. S. Wagner. Pub W 195:34-5 Ap 7 '69
House of measurement. E. Gross. il Sci N 95: 558-9 Je 7 '69
National bureau of standards prepares for the 1970's. il Science 165:864-74 Ag 29 '69

Appropriations and expenditures

Congress meets science; the appropriations process. M. D. Reagan. bibliog il Science 164:927-8 My 23 '69

State, Department of

Comsat, State dept. split on negotiations. K. Johnsen. Aviation W 90:24-5 Mr 31 '69
Department establishes new Bureau of politico-military affairs. Dept State Bul 61:304 O 6 '69
Department establishes new staff for planning and coordination. Dept State Bul 61:74 Jl 28 '69
Department's records for 1939-41 now open to researchers. Dept State Bul 60:543 Je 23 '69
Diplomats in disarray. S. Simpson. Nation 208:138-41 F 3 '69
Managed propaganda, condoned disorder? J. Osborne. New Repub 160:10-11 My 10 '69
Present at the creation, by D. Acheson. Review
    New Repub 161:23-4 N 1 '69. A. Campbell
    Sat R 52:34 O 11 '69. F. Freidel
President Nixon visits the Department of state; remarks, January 29, 1969. R. M. Nixon. Dept State Bul 60:168-71 F 24 '69
Publications. See issues of Department of state bulletin
Secretary announces establishment of new office of press relations. Dept State Bul 61:103 Ag 4 '69
Two departments seeking bilateral negotiations role. L. Doty. Aviation W 91:28 D 22 '69
Ultimate form of corruption; discrepancy between assertions and the facts in South Vietnam. R. F. Drinan. New Repub 161:15-16 Jl 19 '69
Who's making foreign policy for the United States. il U S News 66:45-6 Ap 7 '69
See also
United States—Diplomatic and consular service
United States—Foreign service

UNITED STATES—State, Department of
—*Continued*
Intelligence and research,
Bureau of
Our man at State. Newsweek 74:39-40 N 10
'69
Passport division
Frances G. Knight and the Passport office.
J. Keats. il Holiday 46:48-9+ N '69
Statistics
See also
United States—Census
Strategic air command
See United States—Air force—Strategic
air command
Subversive activities control board
Search and destroy; O. F. Otepka appoint-
ment. R. Dudman. New Repub 161:12 Jl 19
'69
Supreme court
After Haynsworth. New Repub 161:7 D 13 '69
Amicus curiae; last session of the Warren
court. il Newsweek 74:17 Jl 7 '69
As Supreme court opens new term, the thorny
issues. il U S News 67:10 O 13 '69
Beginning of the Burger era. Time 94:57 O
10 '69
Burger court. I. Silver. Commonweal 90:585-8
S 26 '69
Can Nixon's justices reverse the Warren
court? F. Rodell. Look 33:33 D 2 '69
Changing of the guard. il Newsweek 73:28-9
Je 2 '69
Chief Justice Burger asks: If it doesn't make
good sense, how can it make good law?
J. Duscha. il N Y Times Mag p30-1+ O 5 '69
Close of the Warren era. A. M. Bikel. New
Repub 161:13-16 Jl 12 '69
Congress versus the Supreme court. Sr Schol
94:20 F 28 '69
Countdown on Haynsworth. Newsweek 74:
50 N 17 '69
Does it stand up? nomination of C. Hayns-
worth. A. M. Bickel. New Repub 161:13-15
N 1 '69
Farewell from Warren; excerpts from ad-
dress, June 2, 1969. E. Warren. U S News
66:18 Je 16 '69
Fortas affair. il Time 93:20-2 My 16 '69
Fortas and the future of the Court. America
120:642 My 31 '69
Furor over Supreme court. il U S News 66:
31-2 My 26 '69
Ganging up on Haynsworth. il Bsns W p48
S 6 '69
Haynsworth. Nation 209:162-3 S 1 '69
Haynsworth at home. Time 94:25 O 24
'69
Haynsworth hassle. il Time 94:16-17 O 10 '69
Haynsworth nomination. New Repub 161:7-8
O 4 '69
Haynsworth record. il Time 94:54 O 17 '69
Haynsworth showdown. Time 94:27 N 14
'69
Haynsworth under fire. Newsweek 74:76+ O
6 '69
Haynsworth's odds: what history shows. il
U S News 67:40 O 20 '69
Haynsworth's record as judge: what it could
mean for Supreme court. il U S News 67:14
Ag 25 '69
Help for Haynsworth. Newsweek 74:36+ O
27 '69
In Fortas's seat, or shoes? il Newsweek 74:
35-6 O 20 '69
In the footsteps of Marshall and Taney. H. J.
Sievers. America 121:317 O 18 '69
Jinxed seat: who's next? il Newsweek 74:
24 D 1 '69
Judge come to judgment. il Newsweek 74:
36-7 N 24 '69
Judges judged. Newsweek 73:30 Je 23 '69
Making the case for Haynsworth. J. Osborne.
New Repub 161:12-13 N 1 '69
Mr Nixon and the Court. D. Cobb. Chr Cent
86:1245-7 O 1 '69
New era for Supreme court. il U S News 66:
30-2 Je 2 '69
New Supreme court? D. Lawrence. U S News
66:96 Je 2 '69
Nixon fights back; opposition to C. Hayns-
worth. Nat R 21:1102-3 N 4 '69
Nixon for the defense. Newsweek 74:26 N 3
'69
Nixon's Court. New Repub 161:8-9 Ag 23 '69
Nixon's Court choice: W. Burger as chief
justice. Bsns W p38 My 24 '69
Nomination rejected: why, how and by
whom. il U S News 67:32-3 D 1 '69
Over the cliff. Time 94:23-4 O 17 '69
Political pornography; threat to unseat W.
O. Douglas. J. Deedy. Commonweal 91:
266 N 28 '69

Professional for the High court. il Time 93:
16+ My 30 '69
Pyrrhic victory? Commonweal 91:294 D 5
'69
Question of ethics; hearings on nomination
of Judge Haynsworth. Time 94:21-2 S 26
'69
Shadow of a doubt; hearings on C. F. Hayns-
worth's appointment. il Newsweek 74:35-6
S 29 '69
Sharpie judge. Commonweal 91:4 O 3 '69
Southern justice: C. F. Haynsworth appoint-
ed. il Time 94:11-12 Ag 29 '69
Southern strategy and southern stigma. il
Life 67:38 N 28 '69
Supreme court today: sizing up the Warren
court. il Sr Schol 94:6-20+ Mr 28 '69
Supreme court weighs churches' tax exemp-
tion. R. E. Friedrich, jr. Chr Today 13:38
Jl 18 '69
Supreme revolutionary tribunal? Nat R 21:
1156-7 N 18 '69
Symbolic logic; C. F. Haynsworth appoint-
ment. Newsweek 74:20 S 1 '69
TRB from Washington: leaning backward.
New Repub 160:4 My 31 '69
Talk with Warren on crime, the Court, the
country; interview, ed. by A. Lewis. E.
Warren. N Y Times Mag p34-5+ O 19 '69
Toward confirmation. Time 94:22 O 3 '69
Warren court, ed. by R. H. Sayler and others.
Review
Sat R 52:21-2+ Ag 2 '69. T. Taylor
Warren court and whither obscenity. H. F.
Pilpel and K. P. Norwick. Pub W 196:46-8
Jl 7 '69
Warren court is not likely to be overruled.
J. W. Bishop, jr. il N Y Times Mag p31-
3+ S 7 '69
Why the Supreme court may be different
now. il U S News 67:30-1 S 1 '69
Will the decisions reveal a new style? Bsns W
p29-30 O 4 '69

Decisions
Amplification of Miranda; A. Orozco's case.
Time 93:55 Ap 4 '69
At once, at last. Chr Cent 86:1442 N 12 '69
Bennett's revenge; El Paso case. Newsweek
73:71-2 Je 30 '69
Breakthrough on welfare; residency require-
ments. il Newsweek 73:33-4 My 5 '69
Brown v. Board of education of Topeka; ex-
cerpts from 1954 decision. Cur Hist 57:297-
8+ N '69
Bugging; new action by court. U S News 66:
13 Ap 7 '69
Bugging subversives; ruling that the govern-
ment must hand over transcripts to defen-
dants. New Repub 161:5-8 Jl 5 '69
Card-bargaining policy upheld. U S News
66:63-4 Je 30 '69
Case of the Red lion. R. L. Shayon. Sat R
52:55-6 Jl 12 '69
Challenge to Congress; denying A. C. Powell
his congressional seat declared unconstitu-
tional. Time 93:17 Je 27 '69
Court, old and new. R. Shogan. il Newsweek
73:46+ Je 30 '69
Court ruling that opened a club. U S News
66:15 Je 16 '69
Court, the schools, and the southern strategy.
G. Orfield. Sat R 52:62+ D 20 '69
Court's ruling on a suburban swimming
pool. il U S News 67:19 D 29 '69
Demonstrations, not disruption. il Time 93:47
Mr 7 '69
Desegregate now; but how to do it? il U S
News 67:45-6 N 10 '69
Did John Mitchell hear the justices? Justice
department's reaction to bugging ruling.
R. Shogan. New Repub 160:11-13 Ap 26
'69
Dooming the dragnet; Supreme court revers-
ed conviction of Meridian, Miss. Negro
youth. Time 93:76+ My 2 '69
Dragnet arrests; Court says no. U S News
66:12 My 5 '69
Earl Warren vs. Warren Earl; A. C. Powell
ruling. New Repub 160:10 Je 28 '69
Final rulings of the Warren court. il U S
News 67:10 Jl 7 '69
Firm against evasion; three decisions in-
volving racial injustice. il Time 93:66 Je
13 '69
Free to speak out; with limits; ruling on
Tinker-Eckhardt case. il Sr Schol 94:14 Mr
14 '69
Freedom of speech for students; decision on
student dissent; limits on protest in high
schools; interview. K. Greenawalt. Seven-
teen 28:54+ My '69
Gains in Negro rights; a fifteen year record.
il U S News 66:51-4 My 19 '69
Home movies, anybody? Newsweek 73:36 Ap
21 '69
Home movies; Stanley's conviction reversed.
Time 93:78 Ap 18 '69

UNITED STATES—Supreme court—Decisions—
  Continued
Immediate compliance for school integration.
  Library J 94:4565 D 15 '69
Individuals triumphant; three decisions. Time
  93:61 Je 20 '69
Integration now. Time 94:19-20 N 7 '69
Is the Court handcuffing the cops?   J.
  Vorenberg; J. Q. Wilson. il N Y Times
  Mag p32-3+ My 11 '69
Is treason permissible as merely free speech?
  students wearing black armbands in the
  classroom. D. Lawrence. U S News 66:108
  Mr 10 '69
Key arguments from recent Supreme court
  decisions. Sr Schol 94:14-15 Mr 28 '69
Key ruling on marijuana. il U S News 66:
  11 Je 2 '69
Legacy of the Warren court. il Time 94:62-3
  Jl 4 '69
Long road to where? Garner vs state of
  Louisiana case. J. H. Harris. il Negro Hist
  Bul 31:16-17 D '68
Look at High court's new rulings. il U S
  News 66:35 Mr 24 '69
Misunderstanding about bugs; ruling that the
  government must show defendant trans-
  scripts of eavesdropping. il Time 93:55 Ap 4
  '69
New court test on school desegregation. R.
  H. Smith. Pub W 196:46 O 20 '69
New era for Supreme court. il U S News 66:
  30-2 Je 2 '69
New irritant; search warrant issued after
  receiving a tip from informant. Time 93:
  35-6 F 7 '69
New shake-up of voting districts? il U S
  News 66:39-40 Ap 21 '69
New Supreme court and business. il Nations
  Bsns 57:30-3 Jl '69
Nonsectarian public parochial school.   P.
  Jacobson. Chr Cent 86:769-74 Je 4 '69
Now it's instant welfare: impact across the
  U.S. il U S News 66:32-3 My 5 '69
Powell decision. il Newsweek 73:45-6 Je 30 '69
School protest: is it a right? arm bands: up-
  held. il U S News 66:12 Mr 10 '69
Secular courts must avoid doctrinal disputes;
  ruling on church property in Georgia. Chr
  Today 13:42+ F 14 '69
Setback in Court for breakaway church
  groups. U S News 66:11 F 10 '69
Significant decisions in labor cases. See
  issues of Monthly labor review
Supreme court and ecumenism; Presbyterian
  church v. Hull memorial church. America
  120:154 F 8 '69
Supreme court and welfare laws.   America
  120:521 My 3 '69
Supreme court on school desegregation; ex-
  cerpts. Sr Schol 93:14 Ja 10 '69
Supreme court rules obscenity in home legal.
  Pub W 195:68 Ap 14 '69
TRB from Washington; ruling on desegrega-
  tion of Mississippi schools. New Repub
  161:8 N 8 '69
TRB from Washington: Warren court. New
  Repub 160:4 Ap 26 '69
To the last drop; education, public accom-
  modation and voting. Newsweek 73:29 Je
  16 '69
Unanswered questions in the Powell case.
  D. Lawrence. U S News 66:88 Je 30 '69
Union disciplinary power upheld; Supreme
  court decision. U S News 66:85-6 Ap 14 '69
U.S. Supreme court ruling on school desegre-
  gation, 1969. Cur Hist 58:40-1 Ja '70
Vermont case in Supreme court; Mann v.
  Vermont educational buildings financing
  agency. America 120:459 Ap 19 '69
Warren court is not likely to be overruled.
  J. W. Bishop, jr. il N Y Times p31-3+ S
  7 '69
Warren court vs. Congress; the Powell case;
  how Warren and Burger differ. il U S
  News 66:23-4 Je 30 '69
Warren legacy: very different Constitution.
  J. J. Kilpatrick. il Nat R 21:794-800 Ag 12
  '69
Welfare and the Court; residence require-
  ments. E. Van Den Haag. Nat R 21:805 Ag
  12 '69
What the Court said; school desegregation
  decrees. New Repub 161:12 N 15 '69
Where are they now? Gideon, Escobedo and
  Miranda. il Newsweek 74:8 Ag 11 '69
Yes Virginia, there is a Constitution; Mis-
  sissippi desegregation ruling. il Newsweek
  74:35-7 N 10 '69

History

John Marshall: he made the Court supreme.
  Sr Schol 94:11 F 7 '69
Supreme court milestones; 1789-1969. il Sr
  Schol 94:16-17 Mr 28 '69

Technical assistance program
See Technical assistance, American

Territories and possessions
See also
Guam
Micronesia
Trust Territory of the Pacific Islands
Virgin Islands

Trade policy
See United States—Commerce

Transportation, Department of
Airline merger guidelines readied. H. D. Wat-
  kins. Aviation W 91:27-8 D 22 '69
Offices from operating agencies absorbed by
  transportation dept. Aviation W 91:30 Jl
  21 '69
Roadmaster Volpe. New Repub 160:9 My 10 '69
Secretary Volpe; interview. J. A. Volpe. New
  Yorker 45:29-31 D 20 '69
SST study committee formation slowed. H.
  D. Watkins. Aviation W 90:29-30 F 10 '69
Tough professor climbs aboard. il Bsns W p
  100-2+ Ap 19 '69
Transportation dept. role to spur federal con-
  flicts. Aviation W 91:31 S 29 '69
Two departments seeking bilateral negotia-
  tions role. L. Doty. Aviation W 91:28 D
  22 '69
Volpe picks a team. il Bsns W p68 F 22 '69

Travel regulations
See Travel regulations

Treasury department
Treasury's savvy second man. Bsns W p56-7
  Jl 5 '69

Treaties
Bricker amendment. il Newsweek 74:18 D 15
  '69
New pressures to trim U.S. defenses. il U S
  News 67:38-40 Jl 21 '69
Treaty information. See issues of Department
  of state bulletin

Bibliography
Department releases first volume of new com-
  pilation of treaties. Dept State Bul 60:139-40
  F 10 '69

Canada
U.S.—Canada flood control payment agree-
  ment transmitted to the Senate; message,
  October 14, 1969. R. M. Nixon. Dept State
  Bul 61:463 N 24 '69

Great Britain
Jay papers III: the trials of Chief Justice
  Jay; ed. by R. B. Morris. J. Jay. il Am
  Heritage 20:80-90 Je '69

Russia
Backing a bit from the brink; nonproliferation treaty signed. il Newsweek 74:43+ D 8
  '69
U.S. and Soviet Union sign new fisheries
  agreement. Dept State Bul 60:19-20 Ja 6
  '69

Taiwan
Attention: Mr Fulbright; defense treaty and
  use of Taiwan for Vietnam operations. New
  Repub 160:6-7 My 10 '69

Veterans administration
Partial victory in the hearing-aid case; CU
  vs VA on hearing aid data. Consumer
  Rep 34:492 S '69
Veterans benefits today. il Changing T 23:
  35-6 O '69

Weather bureau
ESSA VHF weather radio stations. il Weath-
  erwise 22:157 Ag '69
See also
United States—Environmental science ser-
  vices administration

Youth corps
Investing in today's youth. W. L. Mont-
  gomery. il Parks & Rec 4:29-31+ Ja '69
UNITED STATES amateur championship. See
  Golf—Tournaments
UNITED STATES and Cuba; United States and
  Europe; etc. See Cuba and the United
  States; Europe and the United States; etc.
UNITED STATES army, Association of the.
  See Association of the United States army
UNITED STATES Atlantic tuna tournament.
  See Salt water fishing—Competitions
UNITED STATES Catholic conference
Bishops hear Hispanics; report of Division
  for the Spanish speaking. America 121:
  515 N 29 '69
Labor day statement; by the Division of ur-
  ban life of the department of social devel-
  opment. America 121:113 Ag 30 '69

UNITED STATES Catholic conference—*Cont.*
Quasi-comedy; USCC and the document on priestly celibacy. S. J. Adamo. America 121:601 D 13 '69
USCC advisory council meets. America 120: 323-4 Mr 22 '69
UNITED STATES Catholic relief services. See National Catholic welfare conference
UNITED STATES Challenge cup racing. See Dog racing
UNITED STATES chamber of commerce. See Chamber of commerce of the United States of America
UNITED STATES congress on evangelism. See Religious conferences
UNITED STATES-Czechoslovakia air agreement; United States-France air agreement; etc. See Aviation—International aspects
UNITED STATES embassy, Paris. See Embassies (buildings)
UNITED STATES flag. See Flags—United States
UNITED STATES foreign service. See United States—Foreign service
UNITED STATES golf association
All right with Boatwright; director of USGA. C. Kirkpatrick. il Sports Illus 30:56-7 Je 16 '69
UNITED STATES Grand prix. See Automobile racing
UNITED STATES gypsum company
Ready and willing. Forbes 103:196 My 15 '69
UNITED STATES handball association. See Handball
UNITED STATES in art
See also
West in art
UNITED STATES in literature
Novelists' America, by N. M. Blake. Review Sat R 52:34 Ap 5 '69. G. Hicks
See also
West in literature
UNITED STATES information agency. See United States—Information agency
UNITED STATES-Japan cooperative medical science committee. See Medical research—International cooperation
UNITED STATES-Japan cooperative science program. See Science—International aspects
UNITED STATES lawn tennis association
Living dangerously at Forest Hills; O. Williams tournament director for U.S. Open championships. K. Chapin. il Sports Illus 31:36-9 S 1 '69
New concept. Sports Illus 30:7 F 17 '69
UNITED STATES lines
One morning at the Pierre; conversion to containerization. il Forbes 104:30-1 N 1 '69
UNITED STATES military academy, West Point
West Point, by T. J. Fleming. Review Time il 94:78 Jl 25 '69

Museum

Museum at West Point. C. G. Worman. il Hobbies 74:150-1 O '69
UNITED STATES national student association
Breaking the rules; convention in El Paso. il Newsweek 74:57 S 8 '69
Identity crisis in U.S. campuses. G. Roberts. Commonweal 90:557-8 S 19 '69
Is defiance of draft growing? National student association declaration. U S News 66: 13 My 5 '69
NSA congress, 1969. S. M. Fisher. America 121:218-22 S 27 '69
Short account of international student politics & the cold war, with particular reference to the NSA, CIA, etc; with statements by M. Wood and M. Raskin. S. Stern. il Ramp Mag 7:87-97 Ja 25 '69
UNITED STATES naval academy, Annapolis
Place of the month. Holiday 45:74-5 Je '69
UNITED STATES of Europe (proposed) See European federation
UNITED STATES office of education. See United States—Education, Office of
UNITED STATES Open golf championship. See Golf—Tournaments
UNITED STATES plywood-champion papers, incorporated
Plywood-Champion: after the merger. S. Blickstein. il Duns R 94:52-5 O '69
Why top executives fall out; U.S. plywood-champion president resigns. il Bsns W p60 Mr 29 '69
UNITED STATES power squadrons, incorporated
Dial Operator 25; list of important phone numbers. il Motor B 124:28-9+ Ag '69
Inland naval review; Fort Worth power squadron. L. C. Fay. il Yachting 126:68-9+ N '69
Underway with the USPS. See issues of Motor boating

We took the power squadron course. J. R. Whiting. il Motor B 124:154 Ag '69
With the power squadrons. C. Schrage. See issues of Yachting
UNITED STATES-Russia airline service. See Airlines—International services
UNITED STATES savings bonds. See Bonds, Government
UNITED STATES shoe corporation
U.S. shoe: diversification dropout. il Bsns W p52-3 S 6 '69
UNITED STATES ski association
Bright girls in a smother of fog; American girls success clouded by U.S. ski association policies. B. Ottum. il Sports Illus 30: 20-1 Mr 31 '69
UNITED STATES steel corporation
Brace of blockbusters; antitrust suit. Newsweek 73:84+ Je 23 '69
Foreign cars, stay out. Newsweek 75:58 Ja 12 '70
Gary presses a claim. il Bsns W p40-1 Ag 23 '69
Steel thumbs its nose; price increases. il Newsweek 74:55 Ag 11 '69
U.S. crackdown on big steel. U S News 66:12 Je 23 '69
U.S. steel sells through iron curtain. Bsns W p 15-16 Jl 5 '69
Water crusaders take on big steel. il Bsns W p54 S 13 '69
UNITED STATES student press association
Cooling it; annual congress. il Newsweek 74: 74 Ag 25 '69
UNITED STATES trust company of New York
When a fellow needs a fiduciary. il Time 94: 72+ Ag 15 '69
UNITED STATES women's Open golf championship. See Golf—Tournaments
UNITED steelworkers of America
Labor leader tells it like it was; D. J. McDonald's account of U.S. union movement. Bsns W p44 Ag 23 '69
Protecting the paychecks of victims of technology. Bsns W p98 Ag 16 '69
Union chief with growing stature. U S News 66:19 F 24 '69
USW moves to police District 15; to curb political manipulations. Bsns W p88 My 17 '69
USW vote: faint praise for Abel. il Bsns W p 104-5 F 22 '69
UNITED transportation union
Firemen renew fight to get back on trains. il Bsns W p52-3 F 15 '69
Firemen want to keep shirking on the railroad all their livelong days. il Nations Bsns 57:96-7 Ap '69
UNITS
Coming hundredweight unit. M. M. Svec. il Ed Digest 35:50-1 O '69
Getting together on units; report of conference on proposed world-wide standardized system. J. Lambert. Sci N 96:104 Ag 2 '69
Hierarchical structures; report of symposium at the Douglas advanced research laboratories, Huntington Beach, Calif. T. Page. il Science 163:1228-30 Mr 14 '69
Universal constants. D. E. Thomsen. il Sci N 95:119-21 F 1 '69
UNITY (sect) See Unity school of Christianity
UNITY school of Christianity
Pray along with Unity. il Newsweek 73:90 Mr 3 '69
UNIVAC division. See Sperry Rand corporation—Univac division
UNIVERSAL airlines, incorporated
Management change made by Universal. Aviation W 91:49 S 29 '69
UNIVERSAL constants. See Units
UNIVERSAL copyright convention. See Copyright
UNIVERSAL declaration of human rights
Human rights day, 10 December 1969; text of messages. A. Brooks; Thant. UN Mo Chron 6:i-iv D '69
National conference on continuing action for human rights; address, December 4, 1968. E. Warren. Dept State Bul 59:686-90 D 30 '68
Twentieth anniversary observed. UN Mo Chron 6:27-35 Ja '69
See also
Right to education
UNIVERSAL history. See World history
UNIVERSAL life church, incorporated
Dispenser of divinity. Newsweek 73:96 My 5 '69
Mail-order ministers. il Time 93:70 F 21 '69
UNIVERSAL military service. See Military service, Compulsory
UNIVERSAL symbols. See Symbols
UNIVERSE
How it all began. Newsweek 73:89 Ap 14 '69

UNIVERSE—*Continued*
  Innocent fox; excerpt from The unexpected universe. L. Eiseley. il Natur Hist 78:10-12+ O '69
  Isaac Asimov explains; a sizable universe. I. Asimov. Sci Digest 66:88-9 N '69
  Quasars and the birth of the universe; excerpts from addresses. G. Marx. il UNESCO Courier 22:32-4+ D '69
    See also
  Cosmogony
  Milky way
  Solar system
UNIVERSITIES. See Colleges and universities
UNIVERSITY, international. See International university (proposed)
UNIVERSITY administration. See Colleges and universities—Administration
UNIVERSITY athletics. See College athletics
UNIVERSITY bookstores. See College bookstores
UNIVERSITY Christian movement
  Impending demise of the U.C.M. Chr Today 13:26 Mr 28 '69
  Self-inflicted death. J. L. Walsh. Commonweal 90:96-7 Ap 11 '69
  University Christian movement to disband in June. Chr Cent 86:365 Mr 19 '69
UNIVERSITY computing company
  Looping in a bonanza, Texas style. il Bsns W p68 My 24 '69
UNIVERSITY dining halls. See Colleges and universities—Dining halls
UNIVERSITY government. See Colleges and universities—Administration
UNIVERSITY librarians. See Librarians
UNIVERSITY libraries. See College libraries
UNIVERSITY of Miami. See Miami, University, Coral Gables, Fla.
UNIVERSITY of Texas. See Texas. University
UNIVERSITY of the South, Sewanee, Tenn.
  Down with the heathen; the cry at Sewanee. H. Peterson. il Sports Illus 30:38-40+ F 24 '69
UNIVERSITY presidents. See College presidents
UNIVERSITY presses
  Fifty faces of Uncle Sam; regional publishing. D. R. Ellegood. Sat R 52:42-4 Je 21 '69
  IRS reviewing tax status of university presses. S. Wagner. Pub W 195:42-3 Je 9 '69
  Publishing scene. D. Dempsey. Sat R 52:46-7 Je 21 '69
  Three university presses open joint UK sales office; IBEG, ltd. Pub W 195:40 Ap 21 '69
  Up with arts at the UPS. H. R. Webber. Sat R 52:44-6 Je 21 '69
    See also
  Association of American university presses
  Cornell university press
UNIVERSITY professors. See College professors and instructors
UNIVERSITY research. See Colleges and universities—Research
UNIVERSITY students. See College students
UNIVERSITY towns. See College towns
UNIVERSITY trustees. See College trustees
UNMARRIED mothers. See Mothers, Unmarried
UNMARRIED people. See Single people
UNMARRIED women. See Single women
UNREGISTERED stocks. See Securities—Registration
UNRUH, D. R.
  Words; poem. Chr Today 13:14 Ap 11 '69
UNRUH, Jesse Marvin
  Democrat speaks to the question. Nation 208:199-202 F 17 '69

    about
  California weather breeder. M. Harris. il Nation 208:110-13 Ja 27 '69
  Here comes Unruh. Newsweek 74:29 D 15 '69
  New tribune for California? W. Wingfield. Chr Cent 86:724+ My 21 '69
UNSÖLD, Albrecht O. J.
  Stellar abundances and the origin of the elements. bibliog Science 163:1015-25 Mr 7 '69
UNTERECKER, John
  Art as intersecting fields of energy. Sat R 52:27-9+ Je 14 '69
  October; poem. Nation 209:388 O 13 '69
UNTERMEYER, Louis
  Quirky communications from an exuberant unhero. Sat R 52:25-6 Jl 5 '69
UNTI, Gloria
  Through dance's open door. R. Hartley. il por Dance Mag 43:29-31 N '69
UNTRACHT, Oppi
  Enameling techniques. Design 70:8-9 Sum '69
UPDIKE, John
  Amor vincit omnia ad nauseam; story. New Yorker 45.33 Ap 5 '69

  Business acquaintances; poem. New Repub 161:28 O 4 '69
  Corner; story. New Yorker 45:38-41 My 24 '69
  Dance of the solids; excerpts from Midpoint and other poems. Sci Am 220:130-1 Ja '69
  Day of the dying rabbit: story. New Yorker 45:22-6 Ag 30 '69
  L'Ecole Berlitz; poem. New Repub 161:33 S 6 '69
  Hillies; story. New Yorker 45:33-5 D 20 '69
  I will not let thee go, except thou bless me; story. New Yorker 45:50-3 O 11 '69
  One of my generation; story. New Yorker 45:57-8 N 15 '69
  Report of health; poem. New Yorker 45:40 F 22 '69
  Skyey developments; poem. New Repub 160:28 Mr 8 '69
  South of the Alps; poem. Commonweal 91:72 O 17 '69
  Van loves Ada, Ada loves Van. New Yorker 45:67-75 Ag 2 '69
    (tr) See Borges, J. L. Labyrinth
UPHOLSTERY
  Couturier upholstery. R. Fitzgerald. il House B 111:152-3 O '69
UPHOLSTERY fabrics. See Textile fabrics
UPPER classes
  Words, words, words; class indicators in speech in England. Trans-Action 6:6 Jl '69
UPPSALA university. See Colleges and universities—Sweden
UPWARD bound (program) See Socially handicapped children—Education
URACIL
  Uracil photoproducts from uracil irradiated in ice. M. N. Khattak and S. Y. Wang. bibliog il Science 163:1341-2 Mr 21 '69
    See also
  Fluorouracil
URANIUM
  Centrifuge to the fore: gas centrifuge for uranium separation. T. Shoemaker. Sci N 95:150 F 8 '69
  Uranium distribution in separated clinopyroxenes from four eclogites. K. C. Condie and others. bibliog il Science 165:57-9 Jl 4 '69
    See also
  Nuclear fuels
URBAN affairs specialists. See Executives
URBAN coalition (organization)
  Coalition acts as critics talk. Bsns W p54+ Je 28 '69
  Coalition splinters in Minneapolis. Bsns W p44+ Ag 16 '69
  Who gives a damn? failure of the Washington, D.C. coalition. M. Kovacs. Nation 209:430-2 O 27 '69
URBAN design development group, incorporated
  Urban design with soul. il Arch Forum 131:44-5 D '69
URBAN development corporation. See New York (state)—Urban development corporation
URBAN education. See Education. Urban
URBAN evangelism. See Evangelistic work
URBAN freeways. See Express highways
URBAN growth. See Cities and towns—Growth
URBAN housing. See Housing
URBAN league, National. See National urban league
URBAN life. See City and town life
URBAN redevelopment. See Urban renewal
URBAN renewal
  Are highways seven times more important than cities? W. F. Wagner, jr. Arch Rec 145:9 My '69
  Are model cities the business of business? il Nations Bsns 57:42-4+ F '69
  BURP and make money; urban housing rehabilitation venture. E. Goldston. bibliog il Harvard Bsns R 47:84-99 S '69
  Breakdown in our cities; interview. G Romney. il U S News 67:48-51 Jl 28 '69
  Choice of housing bills. America 121:411 N 8 '69
  Cities get some modeling dough; model cities program. Bsns W p40 My 17 '69
  City no one knew; the Amoskeag millyard, Manchester, N.H. R. Langenbach. il Arch Forum 130:84-91 Ja '69
  Failure everywhere; summary of report. Thant. il Time 94:63 S 12 '69
  Farsighted study and some blind spots; Park-Mall Lawndale study, Chicago. W. J. Black. il Arch Forum 129:44-9 D '68
  First four model cities plans approved; additional funds made available. Aging 172:3+ F '69
  HEW's role in remaking cities. il Aging 172:4-5 F '69

URBAN renewal—*Continued*
Intergovernmental cooperation restores a downtown; Huron, Ohio. D. E. Reis. il Am City 84:118+ S '69
Jacob Riis: crusader against slums. Sr Schol 94:9 Ap 11 '69
Jane Jacobs: against urban renewal, for urban life; interview, ed. by L. Kent. J. Jacobs. il N Y Times Mag p34-5+ My 25 '69
Lasting scars from city riots. il U S News 66:14 Ap 21 '69
Mr Nixon's urban ballet. H. E. Davis. Nation 209:45-8 Jl 14 '69
Model lethargy; mayors on model-cities program. Newsweek 74:70 O 13 '69
Muddle cities? R. M. Nixon's approach to model cities program. Newsweek 73:63 My 12 '69
National forum; parks and recreation in the urban crises. il Parks & Rec 4:35-46 Je '69
New gamesmanship; urban games, played for understanding of urban problems. E. P. Berkeley. il Arch Forum 129:58-63 D '68
New Haven: where federal dollars pay off. E. Selby. Read Digest 94:189-90+ Je '69
One mayor's story of the mess in cities: Pittsburgh; excerpts from remarks. J. M Barr. il U S News 66:57-9 Ap 21 '69
Portable park brightens urban-renewal site; Little Rock, Ark. il Am City 84:32 Ag '69
Progress and protest; advocacy planning in Charleston, W.Va. E. P. Berkeley. il Arch Forum 131:48-55 N '69
Promises, promises; broken pledges by businessmen; Boston and New York. il Newsweek 74:37 Ag 11 '69
Remodeling Model cities. il Bsns W p74 N 8 '69
Rubble rouser; question of emergency funds for cleaning up riot damage. il Newsweek 73:58 Ap 21 '69
Slamming brakes on a runaway program; neighborhood development program. Bsns W p53-4 S 20 '69
Survey of mayors on ills and remedies. il Nations Bsns 57:38-41 F '69
Toward a self-renewing society: Time essay; excerpts from address. J. W. Gardner. Time 93:40-1 Ap 11 '69
Urban prospects in the Nixon administration. Am City 84:8 Ap '69
Utility tunnels enhance urban renewal areas. W. J. Boegly, jr. and W. L. Griffith. bibliog il Am City 84:101-3 F '69
Voluntarism and the urban crisis. America 120:522 My 3 '69
What Nixon plans to do il Newsweek 73:49-50+ Mr 17 '69
White House's idea man for urban problems; D. P. Moynihan. il Bsns W p72-4+ S 27 '69
Who speaks for the cities? il Newsweek 73:48+ Ap 7 '69
Will there ever be a housing boom? interviews. J. W. Gardner and E. S. Callender. Forbes 104:72+ O 15 '69
See also
Bedford-Stuyvesant restoration corporation, Brooklyn
Business districts
City planning
New York (state)—Urban development corporation
Systems analysis in urban renewal
United States—Housing and urban development, Department of
Urban coalition (organization)
also subhead City planning under names of cities, e.g. Seattle—City planning

Canada
Railroads spur urban renewal; Canadian Pacific and Canadian national. il Bsns W p 152-4+ Ap 12 '69

Georgia
Seed money in Georgia; high-risk improvement loans from Citizens & Southern national bank. il Time 93:106 My 23 '69

Latin America
Slums of hope and despair. J. A. Casasco. il Américas 21:13-20 Je '69

Maryland
See also
Baltimore—City planning

New York (state)
See also
New York (state)—Urban development corporation
URBAN sociology. See Sociology, Urban

URBAN transit. See Rapid transit
URBANA, Ill.
Krannert center for the performing arts
Cheers for a prairie acropolis. R. C. Marsh. il Hi Fi 19:MA20-1 Ag '69
Five single-purpose theaters connected beneath a podium: Krannert center for the performing arts. il Arch Rec 146:158-64 N '69
Music
See also
Urbana, Ill.—Krannert center for the performing arts
URBANISM. See Cities and towns
URBANIZATION
Can anyone run a city? G. Tyler. il Sat R 52:22-5 N 8 '69
Cities to live in: planning versus the inevitable; excerpts from Last landscape. W. H. Whyte. Cur 103:48-58 Ja '69
Last landscape, by W. H. Whyte. Review
Cath World 208:236 F '69. E. Summers
Task to test our mettle; excerpts from address. J. W. Gardner. Read Digest 94:205-8 F '69
Urban explosion in Latin America: a continent in process of modernization, ed. by G. H. Beyer. Review
Américas 21:42 Ja '69. R. E. Crist
UREA
Urea; top ten questions dairymen ask about it, and the answers. N. Reeder. il Farm J 93:D10-11 F '69
UREDINALES. See Rusts (botany)
UREMIA
See also
Kidneys, Artificial
UREY, Harold Clayton
As I see it; interview, ed. by M. H. Hall. por Forbes 104:44-8 Jl 15 '69
Doctor Urey talks about the moon findings; interview. por Space World F-12-72:35-43 D '69
Early temperature history of the moon. bibliog Science 165:1275 S 19 '69
Origin and history of the moon. por(p45) Bul Atom Sci 25:46-51 S '69
Space program and problems of the origin of the moon; address. December 26-31, 1968. Bul Atom Sci 25:24-6+ Ap '69
URIC acid
See also
Lesch-Nyhan syndrome
URICH, Ted R. and Shermis, S. S.
New role for tired school superintendents. Clear House 43:294-7 Ja '69
URINE
See also
Cystinuria
Analysis
Spherical urine in birds: petrography. R. L. Folk. bibliog il Science 166:1516-19 D 19 '69
URIS, Auren
Executives of the future. Nations Bsns 57:68-73 Ja '69
URIS buildings corporation
Invisible earnings. il Forbes 103:36+ Ja 15 '69
URLANIS, Boris
Men die earlier than women. UNESCO Courier 22:28-30 N '69
UROPHYSIS. See Nervous system—Fishes
URROWS, Elizabeth
Recurring problems in Laos. bibliog f Cur Hist 57:361-3+ D '69
URUGUAY
See also
Automobile industry and trade—Uruguay
Guerrillas—Uruguay
US (organization). See Negroes—Clubs, societies, etc.
US (periodical)
US against them; a quarterly manifesto. P. Nobile. Commonweal 90:566-7 S 19 '69
Who's that vetoing our past? L. Fleischer. Life 66:12 Je 6 '69
USDAN center for the performing arts. See Camps
USED automobiles; Used motorcycles; etc. See Automobiles, Used; Motorcycles, Used; etc.
USED car trade. See Automobile industry and trade—Used cars
USED lenses. See Lenses, Photographic—Used lenses
USTINOV, Peter
Ustinov on tennis. pors Sports Illus 30:40-4 Je 23 '69
USURY
See also
Loan sharks

UTAH
You soon see why they call it Goblin Valley. il Sunset 143:36 O '69
See also
Canyonlands National Park
Glen Canyon
Golden Spike national historic site
Hunting—Utah
Paleontology—Utah
Skis and skiing—Utah
Tourist trade—Utah
Wilderness areas—Utah

Description and travel
Fantasy in sand and stone: Utah. D. Wharton. il Read Digest 95:137-43 N '69
Ghosts of the golden spike. R. Price. il Travel 131:44-9 Ap '69
Great Salt Lake. Mormons, purple mountains, Utah. N. Benchley. il Holiday 46:38-9+ Ag '69

Parks and reserves
Camp Floyd tells of Utah's past. il Sunset 143:41 Ag '69
UTAH state hospital, Provo. See Hospitals, Psychiatric
UTERINE cancer. See Cancer
UTERUS
See also
Cervix

Surgery
Hysterectomy: pro and con. Sci Digest 66:63 O '69
Too many hysterectomies? Time 93:39 F 7 '69

UTILITIES, Public. See Public utilities
UTILITY poles. See Electric lines—Poles
UTILITY rooms. See Rooms
UTILIZATION of land. See Land utilization
UTILIZATION of waste. See Waste, Utilization of
UTLEY, Jon Basil
Letter from Lima. Nat R 21:644-5+ Jl 1 '69
UTLEY, Robert M.
Arizona vanquished. Am West 6:16-21 N '69
'Pecos Bill' on the Texas frontier. bibliog Am West 6:4-13+ Ja '69
UTLEY, T. E.
Letter from London. Nat R 21:907 S 9 '69
UTTAL, Leonard J.
Carolina hemlock. Horticulture 47:51 Ag '69
Ruellias, intriguing strangers. il Horticulture 47:38-9 F '69
UWEZO
Uneasy peace at Valley state. D. Nevin. il pors Life 66:59-68+ Mr 14 '69
UZBEKISTAN
See also
Tashkent. Russia

V

VA. See United States—Veterans administration
V-belts. See Belting
VD. See Venereal diseases
VISTA. See Volunteers in service to America
VNAF. See Vietnam (Republic)—Air force
VOM. See Voltohmmeters
V/STOL (vertical or short take-off and landing) See Airplanes, Vertical take-off and landing
VACATION Bible schools. See Vacation schools, Religious
VACATION camps. See Camps
VACATION clothing. See Clothing and dress
VACATION houses
All-season ski lodges. il Pop Mech 132:176-80 O '69
At water's edge: come-join-us houses. il House & Gard 135:84-97+ Je '69
Breaking out in all directions; From the ground up. il Am Home 72:66-9 Ap '69
Country place; western New York survey. D. J. White. il Cons 23:12-13 F '69
De Vido house, East Hampton, Long Island, New York. il Arch Rec 145:84-6 mid-My '69
Different life. B. Plumb. il Holiday 45:88-91 Ap '69
Dream house in the country; weekend retreat of Col and Mrs Roger Brunschwig in Old Chatham, N.Y. il House & Gard 135: 78-83 Je '69
Dunbar house, Winhall, Vermont. il Arch Rec 145:34-7 mid-My '69

Eight vacation houses. il Arch Rec 146:131-8 N '69
Executives rush to exotic retreats: buying second homes abroad. il Bsns W p 118-21+ Mr 8 '69
From a rustic stable; a stylish country place: John Scoville's home in Connecticut. il House B 111:66-72 Je '69
Giant window in the woods; vacation and weekend retreat. il Sunset 142:80-2 F '69
How to enjoy a vacation house an ocean away; excerpts from A farmhouse in Provence. M. R. Henry. il House & Gard 135: 72-3+ Je '69
How to obtain low-cost second home designs. H. D. Mack. il Mech Illus 65:93-5 Mr '69
Market for relaxation stirs a hive of activity; great increase in second-homes sales. il Bsns W p66-8 Jl 19 '69
MI's vacation home. il Mech Illus 65:77-92+ Je '69
Mood of sunny summers past; make-over of a Victorian farmstead in New England. R. Fitzgerald and M. Gough. il House B 111: 76-81 Ap '69
Now: a vacation home in three hours. il Pop Mech 132:181 O '69
Our rocking house; do-it-(all)-yourself house in Canadain wilderness. N. Régnier. il Redbook 134:50-1+ Ja '70
Romantic summers in a walled town; David Hicks family in south of France. il House & Gard 135:74-7 Je '69
Roughing it in style; weekend house in Vermont. B. Plumb. il N Y Times Mag p60-1 F 2 '69
Sideline crop of houses. B. A. Roth. Farm J 93:29 Jl '69
Ski house warming. il Mlle 70:212-13 N '69
Ski houses for town people. E. Sverbeyeff. il House B 111:70-5 D '69
Today, tomorrow, yesterday. il Am Home 72: 63-73+ S '69
Traverso house, Westbrook, Connecticut. il Arch Rec 145:44-5 mid-My '69
Vacation homes. il Pop Mech 131:168-81 Ap '69
Vacation house alive with exotic flowers. il House & Gard 136:112-17 N '69
Vacation house for $6,000. il Parents Mag 44:68-71 Jl '69
Vacation house, Point Reyes, California. il Arch Rec 145:80-1 mid-My '69
Vacation retreat for two, ready to entertain a dozen. il House B 111:86 My '69
Vermont ski house unites large spaces in a simple form. il Arch Rec 145:141-4 My '69
Water, water, everywhere; at a price. P. Ryan. il Sports Illus 30:58-61 Je 2 '69
Weekender. B. Plumb. il N Y Times Mag p 132-3 Ap 13 '69
When a weekend is the object; retreat for Ruth Emmet. in East Hampton, L.I. L. Grundy. il House B 111:56-7 F '69
Year-round recreation home. il Field & S 74: 62-5+ S '69
Your own ski house. il Ladies Home J 86: 121 F '69
See also
Beach architecture
Summer houses

Anecdotes, facetiae, satire, etc.
Beach wife. N. Ephron. il Holiday 45:68-9+ My '69
VACATION projects
See also
Libraries, Childrens—Projects
VACATION schools
See also
Summer schools
VACATION schools, Religious
Church's summer witness. R. B. Zuck. Chr Today 13:37-8 Je 20 '69
VACATION travel clubs. See Travel clubs
VACATION villages
Club Mediterranee: where the leisure is. R. McGurk. il Travel & Camera 32:58-9+ Mr '69
Mediterranee on the move: Club Méditerranée. il Time 93:69 Ja 24 '69
Personal business; vacation condominiums. Bsns W p77-8 D 27 '69
Travel notes; Club Méditerranée. R. Joseph. Esquire 72:20+ N '69
Two girls, Club Méd, les vacances extra; Agadir, Morocco. E. Count. il Mlle 69:148-50 Je '69
See also
Seaside, Ore.
VACATIONS
Bad case of common sense. M. Grove il Good H 169:36+ Ag '69
Fifty favorite spots for fun vacations. il Mech Illus 65:56-7+ Jl '69

VACATIONS—*Continued*
For a pleasant vacation, make plans, take money. Consumer Bul 52:17-18 Ag '69
Give yourself an instant vacation. G. Laycock. Mech Illus 65:16 N '69
Hosteling, the family way. V. Block. il Parents Mag 44:46-7+ Jl '69
How to get ready for a vacation. Suc Farm 66:77-8 Ap '69
How to have the vacation of your dreams and what it will cost. B. Gillam. Mlle 69:212-16 My '69
How to plan a successful vacation; danger time for marriage. E. Havemann. Read Digest 94:99-102 Ap '69
Secret of a successful family vacation. V. J. Leaf. il Parents Mag 44:46-7+ Je '69
Spring and the traveler: the first resorts; a roundup of vacationlands preferred by world leaders: symposium. il Sat R 52:39-42+ Mr 8 '69
Sun 'n' fun sports on the Gulf coast. il Ebony 24:148-50+ Je '69
Sweet sound of silence. P. La Farge. il Redbook 133:75+ S '69
Ten fascinating vacation spots of interest to children. il Good H 168:188-9 My '69
Tips for stay-at-home vacations. Good H 169:142-3 Jl '69
Up, up, or away; mini-vacation. P. Bartlett. il Mlle 69:92-3 My '69
Vacation: country style. P. Czura. il Pop Gard 20:30-3+ Spr '69
Vacation, Texas-size. L. Barry. il Pop Phot 65:38+ Ag '69
What makes a good vacation? L. Lane. Farm J 93:103 Ap '69
What's new in winter vacations. il U S News 67:36-8 N 10 '69
Where do we go? Try this. R. Kramer. il N Y Times Mag p77-8+ My 25 '69
Where to go; ed. by V. T. Sparano. See issues of Outdoor life
Why you need a vacation. T. J. Rakstis. il Todays Health 47:24-7+ Ag '69
Winter vacations shiver a little. il Bsns W p36-7 D 13 '69

See also
Automobile touring
Camping
Walking

Anecdotes, facetiae, satire, etc.
Summer's idyll. il Read Digest 94:110-12 Je '69

VACATIONS, Employee
Survey of vacation trends. U S News 66:72 Mr 24 '69
Time for leisure, time for work. J. M. Kreps. Mo Labor R 92:60-1 Ap '69

VACCA, Richard S.
Court and teacher: school board conflict; excerpts from address. bibliog Clear House 44:96-101 O '69

VACCINATION
Dangers of vaccination. Time 95:40 Ja 5 '70
Immunizing the Dark Continent. il Todays Health 47:17-18 My '69
Pox on vaccines? il Newsweek 74:79 D 15 '69
See also
Tetanus—Vaccination
Vaccines

Laws and legislation
Shots that can save a million lives; importance of the 1969 Vaccination assistance act. E. M. Kennedy. Ladies Home J 86:62+ S '69

VACCINES
Good news: a shot for German measles; and other vaccines. il Changing T 23:37-9 Ag '69
Paying the cost; suits against drug manufacturers. Sci N 96:447-8 N 15 '69
Serially cultured animal cells for preparation of viral vaccines; report of meeting. October 1968. S. A. Plotkin. Science 165:1278+ S 19 '69
See also subhead Vaccines under various diseases, e.g. Rubella—Vaccines

VACCINIA viruses
Drug against a virus: rifampicin. H. Gillon. il Sci N 96:414 N 1 '69

VACHON, John
Aran Islands; photographs. Look 33:56-68 Mr 18 '69

VACUOLES. See Cells—Inclusions

VACUUM
Behavior of water in vacuum: implications for lunar rivers. J. F. M. Adler and J. W. Salisbury. il Science 164:589 My 2 '69
Moon rivers; or, How water behaves in a vacuum. il Chem 42:25 O '69

Industrial applications
See Vacuum technology

VACUUM cleaners
All-around cleaners. il Redbook 133:104+ My '69
Heavy-duty vacuum cleaners. il Consumer Rep 34:457-62 Ag '69
How I rescued an old vac. E. E. Hickman. il Pop Sci 194:144-5 My '69
Vacuum cleaner that turns dirt into pancakes. il Pop Sci 195:42 D '69

VACUUM cleaning
Built-in vacuum systems, here are the facts. il Bet Hom & Gard 47:144-5 N '69

VACUUM in industry. See Vacuum technology

VACUUM sweepers, Street. See Street cleaning apparatus

VACUUM technology
Profits in a vacuum. il Duns R 94:71-2+ D '69

VACUUM tubes
Alphanumeric fun box with a Nixie. K. Greenberg. il Radio-Electr 40:56-8 Mr '69
Build the Eyeballer; signal monitoring. J. White. il Pop Electr 30:41-4 Je '69
See also
Electron tubes

VAETH, J. Gordon
What do you know about the sea? quiz. Sci Digest 66:56-7+ N '69

VAGINITIS
Causes and treatment of vaginitis. H. L. Gardner and E. Jacobs. Redbook 133:38+ Jl '69

VAGRANCY
Passive protesters: inhabitants of skid row. il Time 93:62 F 28 '69

VALACHI, Joseph Michael
Valachi papers, by P. Maas. Review
Life 66:8+ Ja 31 '69. R. Sackett
Sat R por 52:56-7+ Mr 22 '69. N. Lewis

VALDENE, Guy
Billfish on the fly; interview, ed. by A. J. McClane. Field & S 74:126-8+ N '69

VALDESE, N.C.
Long-term activated sludge. S. W. Williams, jr. and C. A. Willis. il Am City 84:92-5 F '69

VALDEZ, Luis Miguel
Cultural schizophrenia of Luis Valdez. S. Steiner. por Vogue 153:112-13+ Mr 15 '69

VALE, Michelle R.
Regionalization has nine lives. por Library J 94:3016-18 S 15 '69

VALE project, Ore. See United States—Land management. Bureau of

VALENSTEIN, Elliot S. and others
Hypothalamic motivational systems: fixed or plastic neural circuits? Science 163:1084 Mr 7 '69

VALENTI, Jack
Phocion: a man for this season. Sat R 52:56-7 Ap 26 '69

VALENTINE, Fred T. and Lawrence, H. S.
Lymphocyte stimulation: transfer of cellular hypersensitivity to antigen in vitro. bibliog Science 165:1014-16 S 5 '69

VALENTINE, Helen
Young wife's world. See issues of Good housekeeping

VALENTINE, Jean
Broken-down girl; Archangel; photographs of Delmore Schwartz; Dearest; poems. Poetry 113:379-82 Mr '69
Torn-down building; poem. New Yorker 45:36 Ag 2 '69

VALENTINE, Jerry W.
Spring bear hunt. Outdoor Life 143:78-9+ Mr '69

VALENTINE, Stephen K. Jr
Dial V for vengeance. Newsweek 75:51+ Ja 5 '70

VALENTINES
Valentine. circa 1880. il(p 1) Hobbies 73:53 F '69

VALENTINES day

Drama
Princess with the broken heart. M. Keenan. Plays 28:63-6, 74 F '69

VALENTINOV, Nikolai, pseud. See Vol'skii, N. V.

VALENTRY, Duane
Big star all at sea. Sea Front 15:219-23 Jl '69
Fantastic fly. Todays Health 47:56-7 Ag '69
Here come those crazy grunion. Sci Digest 65:20-1 Je '69
Sea museum fit for a queen. Sea Front 15:284-7 S '69

VAL GARDENA, Italy
Italy: our country is a castle. il Sports Illus 31:58-73 N 17 '69

VALI, Victor
Measuring earth strains by laser; with biographical sketch. Sci Am 221:15, 88-95 bibliog(p 152) D '69

VALKENIER, Elizabeth K.
  Sino-Soviet rivalry in the third world. bibliog f Cur Hist 57:201-6+ O '69
VALLE, Pablo
  Training tomorrow's farmers. por América's 21:9-12 S '6 9
VALLEJO, César
  Poet of collective compassion. B. Wallenstein. Cath World 210:136-7 D '69
VALLEY quail shooting. See Quail shooting
VALLEY VIEW country club, Cambridge, Ill. See Country clubs
VALOR. See Courage
VALSECCHI, Mario
  Genoese mix. Art N 68:28-30+ O '69
VALUATION
  See also
  Real property—Valuation
VALUATION (psychology) See Value (psychology)
VALUE (psychology)
  Applying pressure and changing attitudes. C. A. Kiesler. Todays Ed 58:66-7 Mr '69
  How can we ask children to be better than we are? S. Lloyd. Redbook 133:56+ Je '69
  See also
  Preferences (psychology)
VALUE added tax. See Sales tax
VALUE analysis
  Value engineering; address, September 29, 1969. J. Ferguson. Vital Speeches 36:29-31 O 15 '69
VALUE engineering. See Value analysis
VALUE line investment survey (firm)
  Money-changers in the temple. Forbes 104:78+ O 1 '69
VALUE of education. See Education, Value of
VALVE boxes
  From concrete to cast iron to plastics; Philadelphia. G. Gilbert. il Am City 84:88-9 N '69
VALVES
  See also
  Automobile engines—Valves
VAN, George E.
  Bayview to Diavolo. Yachting 126:47+ S '69
VAN ALLEN, James A. See Yeh, R. S. jt. auth.
VAN ARK, Dorothy
  Home for kids in trouble. Parents Mag 44:76-7+ N '69
VAN BEEK, Gus W.
  Rise and fall of Arabia Felix; with biographical sketch. Sci Am 221:15, 36-46 bibliog (p 152) D '69
VAN CAPELLEVEEN, Jan J.
  Theology for today's youth. Chr Today 13:11-13 Ag 22 '69
VANCE, Cyrus Roberts
  Vance plan for a Vietnam cease-fire; interview, ed. by R. Kleiman. por N Y Times Mag p30-1+ S 21 '69
VANCE, Jack O.
  Is your company a take-over target? Harvard Bsns R 47:93-8 My '69
VANCE, Joel M.
  Grandma and the buck deer. Field & S 74:74-5+ Je '69
VANCOUVER, British Columbia
  Walking tours of Canada's great cities. il Bet Hom & Gard 47:68 Je '69

  Parks and playgrounds
  If you head north to Vancouver, one don't-miss is Stanley park. il Sunset 143:42-5 Ag '69
VANCOUVER, Wash.
  Computerized management; or, Jungle administration; using data processing in park administration. D. W. Bridges. il Parks & Rec 4:37-8+ D '69
  Local association of the month. D. Brooksby and G. S. Green. Todays Ed 58:47-8 Ap '69
VANCOUVER ISLAND
  Outboard on Vancouver Island. C. L. Cadieux. il Yachting 125:50-1+ Je '69
VANCOUVER opera association
  Report: production of R. Strauss' Salome. F. B. St Clair. Opera N 34:27 N 22 '69
  Report: production of The elixir of love. F. B. St Clair. Opera N 34:34 Ja 10 '70
  Report: Vancouver; production of Faust. F. B. St Clair. Opera N 33:29 Ap 12 '69
VANDALISM
  Arkansas vandals. New Repub 161:8 Ag 2 '69
  Diary of a vandalized car. il Time 93:62+ F 28 '69
  How to keep up a vacation home when you're not there. J. H. Ingersoll. House B 111:54+ O '69
  Law and order in public parks. F. L. Campbell and others. il Parks & Rec 3:28-31+ D '68

  Protecting the library after hours. D. Sager. bibliog il Library J 94:3609-14 O 15 '69
  Surging vandalism its expense to America. il U S News 67:32-4 Ag 25 '69
  Vandal: society's outsider. il Time 95:45 Ja 19 '70
  Zap! youthful invaders wreck town. Newsweek 73:42 My 19 '69
  Zapping Zap; wrecking of North Dakota town. il Time 93:25 My 16 '69
VAN DE KAMP, Peter
  Mysterious companions of Barnard's star. il por Time 93:93-4 Ap 25 '69
  Other worlds, other planets. Sci N 95:398 Ap 26 '69
VANDEMARK, Pamela
  Cleveland public library: 1869-1969. por Wilson Lib Bul 43:728-33 Ap '69
VANDENBURGH, Mildred
  Traveler's choice. Travel 132:15 N '69
VAN DEN HAAG, Ernest
  Campus and the law. Nat R 21:1212-13 D 2 '69
  Honorable alternative. Nat R 21:1167-8 N 18 '69
  Welfare and the Court. Nat R 21:805 Ag 12 '69
  Why sex education? Nat R 21:956-8 S 23 '69; Same abr. Cur 112:31-5 N '69
VANDERBILT, Amy
  How I give a party. Ladies Home J 86:103-4 O '69
  Monthly column. See issues of Ladies' home journal
VANDERBILT, Gloria
  Kore-sculpture in cloth: Mrs Wyatt Emory Cooper in her fabled Fortuny dresses. il por Vogue 154:182-7+ D '69
VAN DER HEUVEL, Gerry
  Closed-door policy. il por Newsweek 73:85 Je 2 '69
VANDERHOEF, Ray W.
  This textbook thing. por Pub W 197:47-8 Ja 5 '70
VAN DER KLOOT, William
  Calcium uptake by isolated sarcoplasmic reticulum treated with dithiothreitol. bibliog Science 164:1294 Je 13 '69
VAN DER KROEF, Justus M.
  Australia looks to Nixon. Nat R 21:119-21 F 11 '69
VAN DER RYN, Sim
  College live-in. por Trans-Action 6:63-9 S '69
VAN DER SCHALIE, Henry
  Control in Egypt and the Sudan. bibliog Natur Hist 78:62-5 F '69
  Two unusual unionid hermaphrodites. bibliog Science 163:1333-4 Mr 21 '69
VAN DEVANTER, Winslow
  Money men; interview. por Forbes 103:82-3 Ap 15 '69
VANDEWEGHE, Ernest Maurice, Jr, family
  All-America all the way. R. F. Jones. il por Sports Illus 30:82-6+ My 26 '69
VAN DILLA, M. A. and others
  Cell microfluorometry: a method for rapid fluorescence measurement. bibliog Science 163:1213-14 Mr 14 '69
VAN DINE, Alan C.
  What has four wheels and giggles? Parents Mag 44:68-9 S '69
VAN DOREN, Mark
  Authors & editors. B. A. Bannon. por Pub W 195:19-20 Je 9 '69
  Close-up: at seventy-five a complex poet. M. Maddocks. il pors Life 66:64-7 Je 20 '69
VAN DORN, W. G.
  Lunar maria: structure and evolution. bibliog Science 165:693-5 Ag 15 '69
VAN DUSEN, Michael H.
  Book reviews. Cur Hist 56:169+ Mr '69
VAN DUSEN aircraft supplies, incorporated
  Van Dusen net, sales hit peaks. il Aviation W 90:98 My 26 '69
VAN DUYN, Mona
  Open letter from a constant reader; Birthday card for a psychiatrist; Homework; poems. Poetry 114:80-3 My '69
VAN DUYNE, Carl
  U.S. sailor in New Zealand. il Yachting 125:62-3+ Je '69
VAN DYK, Gary
  K table. Pop Electr 30:35+ My '69
VAN DYKE, Jon M.
  Prisoners from Hanoi; were they tortured? Nation 209:334-5 O 6 '69
VAN GORKOM, Jerome William
  Union tank gets back on the track. il por Bsns W p70-2 Mr 1 '69
VAN HAMEL, Martine
  Brief biography. S. Goodman. il pors Dance Mag 43:66-7 F '69
VAN HANDEL, Emile
  Do trehalose and trehalase function in renal glucose transport? bibliog Science 163:1075-6 Mr 7 '69

VAN HOOK, Beverly Hennen
It's a joyful way of life. Read Digest 95:71-3 S '69
VAN HOOSAN, Mary
Look, listen, learn! Todays Ed 58:51 F '69
VAN HORN, Paul L. See Weinstock, H. R. jt. auth.
VAN HORN, Welby
Right way to begin; ed. by F. Deford. Sports Illus 30:44-51 Ap 28 '69
VAN HORNE, Harriet
Are we the last married generation? McCalls 96:69+ My '69
Era of Rowan and Martin? McCalls 97:80-1+ O '69
Handwriting tells the tale. McCalls 97:152-3+ N '69
Use and abuse of leisure. House B 111:48-9+ Ag '69
VAN HOUTEN, F. B.
Molasse facies: records of worldwide crustal stresses. bibliog Science 166:1506-8 D 19 '69
VAN ITALLIE, Jean-Claude
Serpent. Criticism
America 121:160-1 S 13 '69
VANITALLIE, Theodore B. and Khachadurian, A. K.
Rats enriched with odd-carbon fatty acids: maintenance of liver glycogen during starvation. bibliog Science 165:811-13 Ag 22 '69
VAN KETEL, Helen
Bowler buffs. Travel & Camera 32:10 My '69
VAN KREVELEN, Alice
Stop, look, and listen, if you want to be heard; address. Camp Mag 41:17-18 Mr '69
VAN TIL, L. John
Appeal to conscience. Chr Today 13:6-8 My 23 '69
VAN TIL, William
Key word is relevance. Todays Ed 58:14-17 Ja '69
VAN VECHTEN, Carl
Carl Van Vechten and the irreverent decades, by B. Kellner. Review
Am Rec G pors 35:852-6+ My '69. J. Ringo
VAN VORSE, Ray
Put your fence posts to work! Org Gard & Farm 16:74-6 Jl '69
VAN WAGENEN, Pamela
Stay young and beautiful. Parents Mag 44:26 Je; 32 Jl; 12 Ag; 42 S; 37 O; 12 N '69
VAN WICKLEN, Ellie
Earlier tomatoes where the season starts later. Org Gard & Farm 16:74-5 Mr '69
Reliable red raspberries. por Org Gard & Farm 16:36-8 Ag '69
VAN WYK, Helen
Each demonstration is a challenge; interview, ed. by H. Rogoff, with biographical sketch. il pors Am Artist 33:78-82+ Mr '69
VAN ZANDT, Roland
Wilsonian summers in rural New England. Sat R 52:50+ Mr 8 '69
VAN ZELE, Helen
New miniature African violets. Horticulture 46:18-19+ Ag '68
VANZETTI, Bartolomeo
See also
Sacco-Vanzetti case
VAPPI, C. Vincent
Fortune in building; the long, hard way. por U S News 67:60-1 D 15 '69
VARACTOR diodes. See Diodes
VARANASI, Usha, and Malins, D. C.
Naturally occurring diol lipids: dialkoxypentanes in porpoise (phocoena phocoena) jaw oil. bibliog Science 166:1158-9 N 28 '69
VARDON, Harry
Personalized history of Scottish golf; or, You'll not do that here, laddie. D. Jenkins. il Sports Illus 31:28-39 Ag 11 '69
VARÈSE, Edgard
Edgard Varèse, by F. Ouellette. Review
Am Rec G por 35:830-2 My '69. J. Ringo
VARGAS, Antonio
On the boards. W. Como. por Dance Mag 43:20 F '69
VARGAS, Robert L.
Gallantry of an ugly duckling. Am Heritage 21:22-3+ D '69
VARIABLE stars. See Stars, Variable
VARIABLE voltage transformers. See Electric transformers
VARIAN, Elayne H.
Plastics for everyday living. Art in Am 57: 104-7 Jl '69
VARIAN associates
Toning down glamour to give profits luster; science-based company. il Bsns W p 156-8 Ja 25 '69
VARIATION (biology) See Evolution; Mutation (biology)
VARICAPS. See Diodes
VARICELLA. See Chicken pox

VARICOSE veins
Storing varicose veins. Sci Digest 65:74-5 Mr '69
VARIEGATION
See also
Mosaics (biology)
VARIETIES of crops. See Crops—Varieties
VARIETY theaters. See Music halls (variety theaters, etc)
VARMINT rifles. See Rifles
VARNE, Richard, and others
Macquarie Island and the cause of oceanic linear magnetic anomalies. bibliog Science 166:230-3 O 10 '69
VARNELL, Lon
Down with the heathen. H. Peterson. il por Sports Illus 30:38-40+ F 24 '69
VARNISH and varnishing
Varnishing luthier. Sci Am 220:45-6 F '69
What do you know about varnishing. N. Levy. il Yachting 125:82+ Ap '69
See also
Lacquer and lacquering
Wood finishing
VARYING hares. See Hares
VASCULAR muscle. See Muscle
VAS DIAS, Robert
Sailing twenty years later; poem. New Yorker 45:44 S 13 '69
VASES
Look for unusual containers. il Home Gard 56:63 S '69
Throwaway vases. J. Robertson. il Home Gard 56:8 My '69
VASOPRESSIN
Toad urinary bladder: intercellular spaces. D. R. DiBona and M. M. Civan. bibliog il Science 165:503-4 Ag 1 '69
VASSAR college, Poughkeepsie, N.Y.
New group at Vassar. il Newsweek 74:69 N 10 '69
VATICAN
Church-owned business: stretching religion. Chr Today 13:48-9 F 28 '69
See also
Catholic church—Relations (diplomatic)
Papacy

Finance
Low profile for the Vatican. il Time 94:96 N 28 '69
Vatican empire. by N. Lo Bello. Review
Cath World 209:130-1 Je '69. J. Gollin

Secretariat for non-believers
Symposium in Rome: is unbelief believable? H. Cox. Commonweal 90:159-60 Ap 25 '69
VATICAN and the press
How to cover the Vatican without really praying. il Time 94:71 O 31 '69
Of many things; re-accreditation of journalists covering the Vatican. D. R. Campion. America 121:inside cover D 13 '69
VATICAN council, 2d
John Dewey and Vatican council II. T. F. McGann. America 120:411-12+ Ap 5 '69; Discussion. 120:551 My 10 '69
Of many things; Fr Murray and the American bishops during Vatican II. D. R. Campion. America 120:148 F 8 '69
Vatican council in perspective; interview, ed. by H. J. Cargas. G. MacEoin. America 121:289-94 O 11 '69
VAUDEVILLE
God save the queen; queens of burlesque. il Esquire 72:104-7 Ag '69
VAUGHAN, Denis
Compelling gesture. Opera N 34:22-5 D 20 '69
VAUGHAN, Herbert G. jr. See Ritter, W. jt. auth.
VAUGHAN, Maurice S.
Creativity and creative teaching: a reappraisal. bibliog f Sch & Soc 97:230-2 Ap '69
VAUGHAN, Samuel S.
Man across the desk. Writer 82:13-17 N '69
VAUGHAN WILLIAMS, Ralph
First stereo editions of his great Fourth symphony. J. Diether. por Am Rec G 35:534-5 Mr '69
Music of Vaughan Williams, round two. A. Frankenstein. Hi Fi 19:105 S '69
Records:
Mass, etc. Opera N 34:31 D 13 '69
Sea symphony. Mendelssohn: Hymn of praise and Mahler: Symphony no. 3 Opera N 34:42 D 27 '69
Vaughan Williams from Sir Adrian, outstanding. J. Diether. il por AM Rec G 36:214-16+ N '69
VAUGHN, Barbara Jean
What's cooking? Org Gard & Farm 16:118-20 F '69
VAUGHN, Charles L.
Hard work, long hours, a 15 per cent return; interview. por U S News 67:58-9 D 8 '69

VAULTING (sport)
Crossing the bar; J. Pennel wants to be the first to top 18 ft. il Time 94:36 Jl 4 '69
Evening stars fell in California; meet in Modesto. S. Myslenski. il Sports Illus 30:70-1 Je 2 '69
Lofty experiment. Sports Illus 32:10-11 Ja 12 '70
Right-way Carrigan flies to a record. G. Ronberg. il Sports Illus 30:26-8+ Je 23 '69

VEAL
    See also
Cookery—Meat

VEALE, Tinkham, 1914-
Conglomerate chief on a fast track. il pors Bsns W p 154+ Je 7 '69

VEECK, Bill
Barnum's back. il por Time 94:45 Jl 11 '69
Black athlete in the golden age of sports; integration of American league by Cleveland Indians. A. S. Young. il por Ebony 24:66-8+ F '69
Horse laughs. il por Newsweek 74:65 Jl 14 '69
Veeck vs. Harvard. Newsweek 74:40 D 29 '69

VEENENDAAL, Cornelia
Eskimos; poem. Commonweal 90:66 Ap 4 '69

VEGETABLE gardening
Call me when your vegetables are ready. P. Delfeld. il Org Gard & Farm 16:24-5 Ag '69
Vegetable gardening; with a point of view. J. Viles. il Home Gard 56:40-5+ Mr '69
    See also
Companion crops
Flats, etc. (horticulture)
Greenhouses
Hotbeds
    also names of vegetables, e.g. Onions

VEGETABLE gardening, Home
Carrots and peas, good neighbors. W. Ferguson. il Org Gard & Farm 16:34-6 Ap '69
For vegetable harvests in winter and spring. il Sunset 143:245-6 O '69
Four-family garden co-op. G. L'Allemand. il Org Gard & Farm 16:28-31 O '69
Gardener's kitchen. D. V. Thompson. See issues of Horticulture
Gardening adventure, growing cardoon, comfrey, horseradish, and other witchy or ancient vegetables. il Sunset 143:226-7 N '69
Greenest thumb in Alaska; use of seaweed, sawdust. L. Nelson. il Org Gard & Farm 16:36-8 Mr '69
Here's adventure for cook and gardener, growing your own Oriental vegetables. il Sunset 142:106-8 My '69
Last sowings of summer; plantings of root crops, lettuces, kale. R. Tirrell. il Org Gard & Farm 16:24-7 Jl '69
Lifetime garden of vegetables and herbs. R. Hendrickson. Am Home 72:110a My '69
Mother's garden of yesteryear. O. Raney. il Org Gard & Farm 16:48-52 Ja '69
On this side they grow vegetables. il Sunset 142:238 Ap '69
Organic gardeners grow 'em big! M. C. Goldman. il Org Gard & Farm 16:32-5 Mr '69
Protecting your vegetables. Sunset 142:199 Je '69
Should you try for vegetables? il Sunset 142:226-7 Ap '69
They garden in the darnedest places; growing vegetables on asphalt and concrete. G. L'Allemand. il Org Gard & Farm 16:43-5 Je '69
Two-climate gardening; moving plants from Florida to North Carolina. P. E. Mahan. il Org Gard & Farm 16:42-3 My '69
Vegetables in spite of. il Sunset 142:224 My '69
    See also
Childrens gardens
Cold frames

VEGETABLE protein foods. See Food substitutes

VEGETABLE seed growing. See Seed production

VEGETABLE steamers. See Steamers

VEGETABLES
Choosing the right vegetables. J. Gibbs. il Horticulture 47:24-5 Je '69
Must great food be perfect? J. Olds. Org Gard & Farm 16:59 Ap '69
Vegetables 1969. il Horticulture 47:28-9 Ja '69
    See also
Cookery—Vegetables
Greens, Edible
Vegetable gardening, Home
    also names of vegetables, e.g. Jerusalem artichokes

Marketing
Organic vegetables every Thursday. M. Franz. il Org Gard & Farm 16:33 My '69

Storage
Fall in the vegetable garden; storing vegetables. R. A. Miller. il Horticulture 46: 18-20+ S '68
Winter storage of vegetables. B. Wahlfeldt. il Org Gard & Farm 16:39 O '69

VEGETABLES, Frozen
Preparing vegetables for freezing. Bet Hom & Gard 47:82 Ag '69

VEGETATION
Vegetational change along altitudinal gradients. E. W. Beals. bibliog il Science 165: 981-5 S 5 '69

VEILS
Tapada: veiled face of colonial Lima. L. Ungaro de Fox. il Américas 21:2-7 Ja '69

VEINS
    See also
Varicose veins

VEITH, Frank J. and Richards, Kenneth
Mechanism and prevention of fixed high vascular resistance in autografted and allografted lungs. bibliog Science 163:699-701 F 14 '69

VELA, G. R. and Peterson, J. W.
Azotabacter cysts: reactivation by white light after inactivation by ultraviolet radiation. bibliog Science 166:1296-7 D 5 '69

VELASCO ALVARADO, Juan
Two ears and a tail. P. Kramer. il por Newsweek 74:43-4 S 8 '69
Will we or won't we? E. McDowell. Nat R 21:331 Ap 8 '69

VELDE, Paul
Media (cont) Commonweal 89:529-30 Ja 24 '69

VELIE, Lester
Karl Marx doesn't work here anymore. Read Digest 94:93-8 Ap '69
Other rape of Czechoslovakia. Read Digest 95:187-8+ Jl '69

VELIMIROVIĆ, Miloš
Reviews of records. Mus Q 55:586-94 O '69

VENA caval umbrella. See Medical instruments and apparatus

VENDING machines
    See also
ARA services, incorporated

VENDO company
Pro at Vendo. Duns R 93:72+ My '69

VENDORS, Street. See Street trades

VENEERS and veneering
Wraparound veneers. il Mech Illus 65:86 N '69

VENEREAL diseases
A U.S. youngster is infected with VD every two minutes. N. Keifetz. il N Y Times Mag p85+ Mr 9 '69
VD: the greatest threat to teen-age health. A. Lake. Seventeen 28:146-7+ My '69
    See also
Syphilis

VENEREAL diseases, Campaign against
VD: consent for care. D. A. Dukelow. Todays Health 47:88 F '69

VENETIAN painting. See Painting, Italian

VENEZIANO, Gabriele
Elementary particles. bibliog por Phys Today 22:31-6 S '69

VENEZUELA
    See also
Petroleum industry and trade—Venezuela

Economic conditions
Venezuela: the race against time. J. Poindexter. il Duns R 94:62-5+ Jl '69

History
Angostura. A. U. Pietri. il Américas 21:2-6 My '69

Industries
    See also
International basic economy corporation
Petroleum industry and trade—Venezuela

Politics and government
Man of *el cambio*; R. Caldera. il Time 93:30 My 2 '69

VENEZUELAN dancing. See Dancing, Venezuelan

VENICE
Fight to save the sinking jewel of the Adriatic. il Time 94:30-5 Jl 25 '69
Is Venice doomed? il Life 67:34-43 Jl 18 '69
Venice preserved? J. McAndrew. il Art N 68:54-8+ Sum '69

Air pollution
Waters of Venice; with photographs by A. Kane. Look 33:60-7 N 18 '69

Architecture
Is Venice doomed? il Life 67:34-43 Jl 18 '69
Kahn in Venice; designs for the Esposizione internazionale d'arte. il Arch Forum 130: 64-7 Mr '69

VENICE—Architecture—*Continued*
Waters of Venice; with photographs by A.
Kane. Look 33:60-7 N 18 '69

Art

From Ricci to Tiepolo via Bencovich. M.
Gendel. il Art N 68:58-60+ S '69
See also
Committee to rescue Italian art

Description

Mirror of Venice. J. C. Holmes. il Travel &
Camera 32:68-74 S '69
Ode to Venice. L. Rosten. il Look 33:16-17
F 4 '69

History

Ode to Venice. L. Rosten. il Look 33:16-17
F 4 '69

Music

Glimpses of a great age; revivals of Donizet-
ti's unknown operas. W. Weaver. il Hi Fi
19:MA28-9 Ag '69
Report: Venice; production of Donizetti's
Belisario. E. Tellini. Opera N 34:32 S 6 '69
Report: Venice; production of Riccardo Zan-
donai's Francesca da Rimini. R. Raphael.
Opera N 33:29 My 17 '69
VENIE, Hildegard
Grandma Venie gets the works; letter. por
Har Yrs 9:25 F '69
VENISON
Leg, loin, rib and shoulder; here's how to
break down venison. il Sunset 143:233 O '69
See also
Cookery—Game
VENISON, Frozen

Transportation

Moose hangs high; or, What's a wife for,
anyway? R. Starnes. Field & S 74:10+
My '69
VENN, Grant
Eye on tomorrow's jobs. Am Ed 5:12-15 Mr
'69
VENOM
New light on snakebite. N. Wadsworth. il
Outdoor Life 143:47-9+ Mr '69
Urban snakes: an identity crisis. H. G. Dow-
ling. il Natur Hist 78:66-71 Ap '69
Venom neutralization by rattlesnake serum
albumin. W. C. Clark and H. K. Voris. bib-
liog il Science 164:1402-4 Je 20 '69
VENTADORN, Bernart de. See Bernart de
Ventadorn
VENTILATION
Let in the cooling air. il Sunset 142:98-103
My '69
Update your heating system with fresh air.
il Pop Mech 132:190-1 O '69
See also
Air conditioning
School buildings—Heating and ventilation
VENTRICULAR arrhythmia. See Heart beat
VENTRICULAR fibrillation. See Heart beat
VENTURA, Calif.
Merchants in particular notice the difference.
P. S. Pyles. il Am City 84:54 D '69
VENTURA COUNTY suicide prevention ser-
vice. See Suicide prevention centers
VENTURE capital. See Capital; Venture
VENTURE management. See Business manage-
ment and organization
VENTURI, Robert. See Brown, D. S. jt. auth.
VENUS (planet)
Is Venus prolate? H. D. Greyber. bibliog Sci-
ence 163:1469-70 Mr 28 '69
Life on Venus. Sci Digest 65:80 Mr '69
Penetrating the secrets of the planets. G.
Bylinsky. il Fortune 80:138-43 N '69
Still a mystery. il Sci N 95:610-11 Je 28 '69
Venus: absence of a phase effect at a 2-cen-
timeter wavelength. D. Morrison. bibliog il
Science 163:815-17 F 21 '69
Venus, star of sweet confidences. S. I. Rasool.
il Natur Hist 78:52-7+ Je '69

Atmosphere

Atmospheres of Mars and Venus. V. R. Eshle-
man. il Sci Am 220:78-88 bibliog (p 148+)
Mr '69
Double date with Venus. Newsweek 73:31 My
26 '69
Dust in the lower atmosphere of Venus. A.
D. Anderson. bibliog il Science 163:275-6
Ja 17 '69
Mercury-filled doughnut and clouds on Venus.
il Chem 42:25 Ap '69
Planetary probe: origin of atmosphere of
Venus. R. F. Mueller. bibliog il Science 163:
1322-4 Mr 21 '69
Solar cycle variation of exospheric tempera-
tures on Mars and Venus: a prediction for
Mariner 6 and 7. R. W. Stewart and J. S.
Hogan. bibliog il Science 165:386-8 Jl 25
'69

Venus: an isothermal lower atmosphere? W.
Gale and others. bibliog il Science 164:1059-
60 My 30 '69
Venus clouds: test for hydrocarbons. W. T.
Plummer. bibliog il Science 163:1191-2 Mr 14
'69
Venus surface pressure. R Pop Astron 63:25
Mr '69
Venus: the next phase of planetary explora-
tion. D. M. Hunten and R. M. Goody. bib-
liog il Science 165:1317-23 S 26 '69

Observations

Observations of Venus near conjunction. il
Sky & Tel 38:54-5 Jl '69

Surface

Venus: mapping the surface reflectivity by
radar interferometry. A. E. E. Rogers
and R. P. Ingalls. bibliog il Science 165:
797-9 Ag 22 '69

Temperature

Polar temperature of Venus. W. A. Gale and
A. C. E. Sinclair. bibliog il Science 165:
1356-7 S 26 '69
VENUS probes. See Space probes
VERBAL learning. See Learning, Psychology of
VERDI, Giuseppe
Aida. Criticism
New Yorker 45:67 Ja 10 '70
Newsweek il 75:64-5 Ja 12 '70
From Angel: James McCracken's (and Sir
John Barbirolli's) Otello. P. L. Miller. il
Am Rec G 36:92-4 O '69
Maazel's masterpiece: La Traviata. P. L.
Miller. il Am Rec G 35:1102-4 Ag '69
Records:
Otello. il Opera N 34:30 N 1 '69
La Traviata. Opera N 34:30 N 22 '69
Rigoletto. Criticism
New Yorker 45:122+ Mr 29 '69
New Yorker 45:94 S 20 '69
Solti's Verdi Requiem. P. L. Miller. Am Rec
G 35:423-4 Ja '69
Songs by Verdi and Wagner. G. Jellinek. il
Opera N 33:24-5 Mr 29 '69
Total view of Traviata. P. G. Davis. il Hi
Fi 19:75-6 S '69
La Traviata. Criticism
Hi Fi 19:MA12 D '69
Il Trovatore. Criticism
New Yorker 45:162+ Mr 15 '69
Opera N il 33:17-20 Mr 29 '69
Sat R 52:68-9 Mr 22 '69
Verdi's Liber scriptus rewritten. D. Rosen.
bibliog f il Mus Q 55:151-69 Ap '69
Verdi's Otello, a discographic survey. D.
Hamilton. Hi Fi 19:79-81 N '69
VERHOVEN, Peter J.
Associate professional recreation programs.
Parks & Rec 4:28-30+ Ap '69
VERIGAN, Bill
(ed) See Szolnoki, R. My son the quarter-
back
VERITY, Calvin William, 1917-
Bill Verity's Monday afternoon club. S.
Blickstein. il por Duns R 93:33-5 My '69
VERITY, William E.
Across the Atlantic in a twenty-foot open
boat. pors Pop Sci 195:100-3 S; 80-4+ D '69
VERMANDEL, Janet Gregory
Scratch a lover; excerpt from novel. Redbook
132:185-207 Ap '69
VERMEER, Johannes
Anatomy of a masterpiece; An artist in his
studio. O. Rachleff. il Horizon 11:94-103
Wint '69
VERMONT
See also
Architecture, Domestic—Vermont
Education—Vermont
Fishing—Vermont
Hunting—Vermont
Justice, Administration of—Vermont
Music festivals—Vermont
Skis and skiing—Vermont
Windham County
VERMONT-New York city youth project
Confrontation in Vermont. B. B. Stretch. il
Sat R 52:78 Je 21 '69
VERNA
Art from a sandbox. F. Hill. il por Design 70:
20-3 Spr '69
VERNBERG, Winona B. and others
Larval trematodes: double infections in
common mud-flat snail. bibliog Science
164:1287 Je 13 '69
VERNE, Jules
Amazing 1865 moon shot of Jules Verne; ex-
cerpts from Verne's fantasy-Apollo reality.
comp. by A. N. Kontaratos. il Look 33:
74-8 My 27 '69
If Verne could look at NASA. T. Sweeney. il
Nat R 21:489-90 My 20 '69

VERNE, Jules—*Continued*
Jules Verne's trip to the moon. W. A. H. Birnie. il Read Digest 95:112-14 O '69
VERNER, William K.
Decline of the Adirondack painters. Cons 23: 17+ Ap '69
VERNON, Lynn
What we don't know about delinquency. PTA Mag 63:5-8 bibliog(p35) Je '69
VERNON, Raymond
What strategy for the third world? Sat R 52:42-6 N 22 '69
VEROLME, Cornelis
Prying open a Dutch clam. Bsns W p86 S 20 '69
VERONA, Italy

Music

Arena. il Opera N 34:18-21 S 20 '69
For Verdi, scholarship and fresh air. P. G. Davis. il Hi Fi 19:MA27-8 N '69
Report: Verona, performances at Verona arena. J. W. Freeman. Opera N 34:26 S 20 '69
VERRETT, Jacqueline
Bitterness about sweets. por Time 94:79 O 17 '69
VERRETT, Shirley
Miss Verrett joins the ball game. H. Kupferberg. il Atlan 223:113-15 Ja '69
VERSAILLES, Treaty of, June 28, 1919
Fifty years ago at Versailles. R. L. Tobin. Sat R 52:24 Je 14 '69
How Harding saved the Versailles treaty. R. K. Murray. il Am Heritage 20:66-7+ D '68
VERSCHOTH, Anita
Santa Clara holds a splashdown. Sports Illus 31:20-1 Jl 21 '69
Some dashing dolls debut in Daytona. Sports Illus 31:20-3 Jl 14 '69
VERSE. See Poetry
VERSIFICATION. See Poetics
VERTEBRATES
See also
Tetrapods
VERTICAL elevators. See Grain elevators
VERTICAL take-off and landing airplanes. See Airplanes, Vertical take-off and landing
VERTS, Jeanne
(comp) Children, books, and living things. Am For 75:49-50+ D '69
VERUSCHKA
Extra dry bikini straight up. C. Twiss. il pors Holiday 45:50-3 F '69
VESCA. See Strawberries
VESCO, Robert L.
Company on the make. por Forbes 103:29 Mr 1 '69
VEST, George Graham
Most celebrated dog case ever tried in Johnson County, Missouri, or the world. G. Carson. il Natur Hist 78:6-8+ D '69
VESTAL, David
Are your prints fading away? Pop Phot 64: 67-9+ Ap '69
Frontier photographers. Travel & Camera 32: 48-52+ Je '69
In review. Travel & Camera 32:23+ D '69
Shows we've seen (cont) Pop Phot 64:30+ F; 60+ Mr; 40+ Ap '69

about
Can whitey do a beautiful black picture show? il Pop Phot 64:79-80+ My '69
VESTS
Holiday-best vests. il Redbook 134:89 D '69
VESZY-WAGNER, L.
Macbeth: fair is foul and foul is fair; address, January 11, 1968. bibliog Am Imago 25: 242-57 Fall '68
VETERANS
Europe twenty-five years later; special veterans tours arranged by Galaxy tours of Chicago. G. Bush. il Bet Hom & Gard 47:34-8+ N '69
Now that he's home again. A. Lake. McCalls 96:44-5+ Ja '69

Associations, institutions, etc.

La guerre est finie; Abraham Lincoln brigade veterans case before the Supreme court. Nation 209:270 S 22 '69
See also
American Legion

Benefits

Letter from Washington; investigation by A. Cranston of medical treatment available to veterans especially of Vietnamese war. R. H. Rovere. New Yorker 45:171-2 N 29 '69
Veterans benefits today. il Changing T 23: 35-6 O '69

Education

Return to apathy. Time 94:50 Ag 22 '69

Employment

Executive recruits. il Newsweek 73:70+ Ap 7 '69
Good life; industrial recruitment of officers. Nation 208:419 Ap 7 '69
It's a delight to talk to applicants with haircuts; veteran college graduates. il U S News 66:51 Ap 7 '69
VETERANS administration. See United States—Veterans administration
VETERANS day
Love it or leave it; patriotic demonstrations supporting Vietnam policy of President Nixon. il Newsweek 74:34-5 N 24 '69
No bells for Bill; Birmingham, Ala. D. G. Shockley. Chr Cent 86:1508 N 26 '69
VETERANS of the Abraham Lincoln brigade. See Veterans—Associations, institutions, etc.
VETERINARIANS
See also
Women as veterinarians
VETERINARY medicine
Fast new pregnancy test for sows. P. Lewington. il Farm J 93:H5 S '69
How to get healthier feeders to your lot. J. G. Clark. Farm J 93:B20+ Ag '69
What's new; animal health. il Suc Farm 67: 52 Mr; 49-50 Ap; 58 Jl '69
VETO
See also
Presidents—United States—Powers and duties
VETSERA, Marie Alexandrine, baronesse
Oft-told tale of the Vienna woods. J. Wechsberg. McCalls 96:46+ Ap '69
VETTER, Robert M.
Continental pewter in the service of wine. Antiques 95:383-7 Mr '69
VETTINER, Charlie
City-county merger in Kentucky. Parks & Rec 3:22-4+ O '68
VEZZOLI, Gary C. and others
Sulfur melting and polymorphism under pressure: outlines of fields for twelve crystalline phases. bibliog Science 166:218-21 O 10 '69
VIA, Bernard S. Jr
Old-time religion; poem. Chr Cent 86:250 F 19 '69
Outdoor life in the ghetto; poem. Chr Cent 86:211 F 12 '69
Two Christmases; poem. Chr Today 14:5 D 19 '69
VIA VENETO. See Rome (city)—Streets
VIBRATION
Cymatics: the sculpture of vibrations. H. Jenny. il UNESCO Courier 22:4-12+ D '69
Vibrating-beam rate sensor tested. P. J. Klass. il Aviation W 92:71-3+ Ja 12 '70
Waterfall-generated earth vibrations. J. S. Rinehart. il Science 164:1513-14 Je 27 '69
See also
Damping (mechanics)
Elastic waves
Oscillations

Measurement

Construction equipment shakes. R. H. Ferahian and W. D. Hurst. bibliog il Am City 84:102-6 S '69
VIBRATORS
See also
Multivibrators
VIBRIO
Vibrio parahaemolyticus from the blue crab callinectes sapidus in Chesapeake Bay. G. E. Krantz and others. bibliog Science 164:1286-7 Je 13 '69
VICE
See also
Immoral literature and pictures
VICE-PRESIDENTS

United States

Agnew finds a role. il Newsweek 74:38+ N 17 '69

Powers and duties

Look inside the Nixon administration; interview. S. T. Agnew. il U S News 67:32-8 O 6 '69
New kind of vice president? il U S News 66: 32-4 Mr 17 '69
Spiro Agnew: the king's taster. Time 94:17-22 N 14 '69
VICE-PRESIDENTS, Company. See Executives
VICENZO, Roberto de
I am a stupid. C. Price. il Esquire 71:148-50 Ap '69
VICKERY, Kenneth O. A.
Euthanasia at 80? Newsweek 73:77 My 12 '69

VICO, Giovanni Battista
One of the boldest innovators in the history of human thought I. Berlin. il pors N Y Times Mag p76-7+ N 23 '69
VICTOR, Florence
Miracle of the frescoes saved from the flood; poem. Nation 209:54 Jl 15 '69
VICTOR, Thomas
Dance, a muse of fire: excerpts. Dance Mag 43:52-61 O '69
VICTORIA, queen of Great Britain
Royalty. C. Miller. il Sat R 52:43-4 S 20 '69
See also
Great Britain—History—Victorian period, 1837-1901
VICTORIA fair. See Drama festivals—Canada
VICTORIAN architecture. See Architecture, Victorian
VICTORIAN art. See Art, Victorian
VICTORIAN furniture. See Furniture, English
VICTORIAN house decoration. See House decoration, Victorian
VICUNA
Royal fleece of the Andes. N. Flowers. il Natur Hist 78:36-43 My '69
Vicuña; the littlest camel. A. Crowell. il Américas 21:2-7 Mr '69
VIDAL, Gore
Distasteful encounter with William F. Buckley jr. Esquire 72:140-3+ S '69

about

Cognoscenti abroad, Gore Vidal's Rome. A. Goodfriend. por Sat R 52:36-9 Ja 25 '69
Gore Vidal: the elegant white knife. L. Bergquist il pors Look 33:73-8 Jl 29 '69
On experiencing Gore Vidal. W. F. Buckley, jr. Esquire 72:108-13+ Ag '69
Taking up the job God bungled. C. Nichols. Nat R 21:497-9 My 20 '69
Wasted talent; Buckley-Vidal vendetta. por Time 94:49 Ag 22 '69
VIDEO recording, Electronic. See Electronic video recording
VIDEO records
Replaying the stars. J. Eberhart. il Sci N 95:191+ F 22 '69
VIDEO tape recorders and recording
Birth of a new book promotion idea; tapes on cassettes produced by Video Books. il Pub W 196:31-2 D 1 '69
Directory of most popular, low-priced video tape recorders; tables. il Electr World 82:32-3 N '69
Micro-teaching; videotape recording to evaluate teacher training performances. D. Molner. il Sr Schol 94:Schol Teach 20-1+ Mr 7 '69
Mild fun and games with video tape; the Roberts 1000. I. Berger. Sat R 52:57 D 27 '69
Tape your own TV shows. L. Buckwalter. il Pop Mech 131:108-12+ Ap '69
TV in a cartridge sparks three-way tiff. il Bsns W p41 N 22 '69
Video topics (cont) R. Angus. Hi Fi 19:36 F '69
Video topics. R. Long. Hi Fi 19:36 My; 34 Jl '69
Videotape turns innocent pleas to guilty; Douglas County seat, Roseburg, Ore. D. L. Schiffman. Am City 84:30 N '69
Where do we go from hear? question of opera on audio-video cassette. J. Culshaw. il Hi Fi 19:56-60 N '69

Maintenance and repair

How to repair VTR's. V. Bell. il Radio-Electr 40:79-83 Je '69
VIDEO tape recordings

Operas

Where do we go from hear? question of opera on audio-video cassette. J. Culshaw. il Hi Fi 19:56-60 N '69
VIEIRA DA SILVA, Maria Helena
Letter from Paris; retrospective exhibition at the Musée national d'art moderne. Genêt. New Yorker 45:132 N 1 '69
VIENNA
Vienna's cruises on the Danube. il Sunset 142:36 Ap '69

Description

Vien ease. M. M. Davis. il Travel 132:58-9 Jl '69
Vienna, my Vienna, by J. Wechsberg. Review Travel & Camera 32:64+ Mr '69. M. Wright

Music

Notes from our correspondents (cont) K. Blaukopf. Hi Fi 19:18 Ap '69

Report: performance of Gluck's Iphigénie en Tauride. J. Wechsberg. Opera N 34:34 Ja 10 '70
Report: production of Bedrich Smetana's Dalibor. J. Wechsberg. Opera N 34:29 D 20 '69
Report: Vienna; production of Monteverdi's Incoronazione di poppea. J. Wechsberg. Opera N 33:29 Ap 12 '69
Report: Vienna; production of Verdi's Simon Boccanegra. J. Wechsberg. Opera N 33:26-7 Je 14 '69
VIENNA convention on consular relations. See United Nations conference on consular relations
VIENNA convention on diplomatic relations. See United Nations conference on diplomatic intercourse and immunities
VIENNA convention on the law of treaties. See United Nations conference on the law of treaties
VIENNA opera. See Opera—Austria
VIENNA state opera. See Opera—Austria
VIENNA state opera house. See Opera houses
VIENNESE
Why Viennese women eat pastry every afternoon. J. Wechsberg. McCalls 96:71+ Jl '69
VIENNESE opera ball. See Balls (parties)
VIENNESE pastry. See Pastry
VIENTIANE, Laos
Laos is at war, but Vietiane yawns. W. Warren. il N Y Times Mag p 12-13+ Ja 4 '70
VIEQUES ISLAND
Burning of the sea. R. G. Johnsson. il Parks & Rec 4:31-3 Je '69
VIERCK, Charles J. jr, and Jones, M. B.
Size discrimination on the skin. bibliog Science 163:488-9 Ja 31 '69
VIERTEL, Salka
Salka's incorrigible heart. H. Clurman. Nation 208:580 My 5 '69
VIERTEL, Salomea Sara (Steuermann). See Viertel, Salka
VIET Cong. See Communist party (Vietnam)
VIETNAM
See also
Ecology—Vietnam
Fishing—Vietnam
National liberation front (Vietnam)
Revolutionary provisional government
Vietnamese war, 1957- —Casualties

History

East Asian backgrounds. C. P. Fitzgerald. Nation 209:384-6 O 13 '69
Ho Chi Minh; a eulogy. F. Schurmann. Ramp Mag 8:52+ N '69
North Vietnam today and tomorrow. K. P. Landon. bibliog f Cur Hist 56:77-81+ F '69
Vietnam, by J. T. McAlister, jr. Review Sat R 52:25-6 My 31 '69. W. R. Corson

Politics and government

See also
National liberation front (Vietnam)
VIETNAM (Democratic Republic)
Buildings in Hanoi crumble, Haiphong is ruined, ravaged; interview. P. Darcourt. U S News 67:39-40 D 22 '69
Growing doubts about Hanoi's intentions. il Time 94:21-2 S 5 '69
North Vietnam: plight of enemy. il U S News 67:37-8 D 22 '69
North Vietnam today and tomorrow. K. P. Landon. bibliog f Cur Hist 56:77-81+ F '69
Political-strategic significance of Vietnam. W. C. Johnstone. Cur Hist 56:65-70 F '69
Trying to read Ho. il Time 93:29-30 My 30 '69

See also
Communism—Vietnam (Democratic Republic)
Communist party (Vietnam [Democratic Republic])
Foreign visitors in Vietnam (Democratic Republic)
Morale, National—Vietnam (Democratic Republic)
National liberation front (Vietnam)
Public opinion—Vietnam (Democratic Republic)

Army

Vietcong is losing its grip. J. Alsop. il Read Digest 95:53-61 D '69
Where the reds are stopped in Vietnam. il U S News 67:37-9 Jl 28 '69

Bibliography

Book marks: trips to Hanoi. L. Lockwood. Nation 208:374-7 Mr 24 '69

VIETNAM (Democratic Republic)—*Continued*

Defenses

Vietnam: is red attack blunted? il U S News 66:11 F 24 '69

Without the bombing: it's full steam ahead in North Vietnam. U S News 66:27 Ap 7 '69

Foreign opinion
American

Journey to North Vietnam; interview, with photographs. M. Riboud. Newsweek 74: 32-4 O 20 '69

Foreign relations

Unbalancing the seesaw; strategy in Laos. il Newsweek 73:56-7 My 19 '69

Photographs

In Ho country. M. Riboud. N Y Times Mag p40-1 Mr 9 '69

Politics and government

General Giap, by R. J. O'Neill. Review Sat R 52:35 O 11 '69. D. M. Grady
Thang-bang team. Time 94:26 O 3 '69

VIETNAM (Democratic Republic) and the United States
NLF asks the American left: where are you? ten-point proposal, and the Swedish international liaison committee conference, Stockholm. F. Schurmann. Ramp Mag 8: 14+ Ag '69

VIETNAM (Republic)
Political-strategic significance of Vietnam. W. C. Johnstone. Cur Hist 56:65-70 F '69
See also
Camranh Bay
Catholics in Vietnam
Censorship—Vietnam (Republic)
Children—Vietnam (Republic)
Christmas—Vietnam (Republic)
Communism—Vietnam (Republic)
Elections—Vietnam (Republic)
Hué
Immigration and emigration—Vietnam (Republic)
Land tenure—Vietnam (Republic)
Medicine—Vietnam (Republic)
Morale, National—Vietnam (Republic)
Peasantry—Vietnam (Republic)
Political prisoners—Vietnam (Republic)
Prisons—Vietnam (Republic)
Public opinion—Vietnam (Republic)
Women—Vietnam (Republic)

Air force

DOD accelerates Viet air force buildup. C. Brownlow. Aviation W 91:24-5 Jl 21 '69
Improvement in the air. il Time 93:39 Ap 11 '69
VNAF pilot, technician training speeded. Aviation W 90:18 F 10 '69

Armed forces

They may make it. S. Alsop. Newsweek 74: 60 D 29 '69
When U.S. troops pull out: the real risk in Vietnam. il U S News 67:13-15 D 29 '69

Army

ARVN is bigger and better, but—. T. Buckley. il N Y Times Mag p34-5+ O 12 '69
ARVN: prospects for the army of South Vietnam. P. Arnett. il Cur Hist 57:333-8 D '69
As Saigon gets set to fight its own war. il U S News 67:10-1 O 6 '69
Baby-sitting with ARVN: 18th division. M. Parker. il Newsweek 74:61 N 10 '69
Behind optimism about Vietnam. W. S. Merick. il U S News 67:40-2 D 1 '69
Can Vietnamization work? il Time 94:25-6 S 26 '69
Laird plan. M. Parker. il Newsweek 73:44 Je 2 '69
New reliables; Seventh division. M. Parker. il Newsweek 73:49 Je 30 '69
Vietnam: get out now; with editorial comment. J. R. Moskin. il Look 33:73-6+, 88 N 18 '69
War: testing Vietnamization; ARVN undergoing intensive training. il Time 95:30 Ja 5 '70
Where GI's are pulling out: report from a border zone. S. W. Sanders. il U S News 67:36-8 Jl 7 '69

Cabinet

New faces? il Newsweek 74:44 Ag 18 '69

Commerce

Tempest in the rice bowl; U.S. cracks down on Thai deal. il Newsweek 75:59-60 Ja 12 '70

Convents
See Convents and nunneries

Defenses

Kahn's canals. Nation 209:37 Jl 14 '69

Economic conditions

In Vietnam, businessmen breathe easier. il Bsns W p30-2 D 27 '69
Long view; Lilienthal report. il Newsweek 73: 56-7 My 12 '69
South Vietnam after the war: how it could be rebuilt. il U S News 66:34-5 Ap 21 '69

Foreign opinion
American

GI's in battle: the dink complex. il Newsweek 74:37 D 1 '69

Foreign relations
See also
Midway conference, 1969

Politics and government

Appeal to the people of the United States. Pham the Truc. Nation 209:2 Jl 7 '69
Back to square one? M. Parker. il Newsweek 73:58+ My 5 '69
Can U.S. get out of the war now? report from Saigon. il U S News 66:34-6 My 5 '69
Cease-fire now in Vietnam! J. B. Sheerin. Cath World 210:50-1 N '69
Crackdown in Saigon. New Repub 160:9 Mr 29 '69
Diemist restoration. D. G. Porter. Commonweal 90:435-7 Jl 11 '69
Elements of settlement: Saigon notwithstanding. R. A. Falk. Nation 208:689-93 Je 2 '69
Front into government; shift from NLF to PRG. J. Burnham. Nat R 21:635 Jl 1 '69
General's gambit; D. van Minh's proposal for a people's congress. Newsweek 74:54 N 17 '69
Gravediggers: possible coalition government. New Repub 160:7 F 22 '69
Illusion of Vietnamization. M. Parker. il Newsweek 74:32-3 S 29 '69
Letter from Saigon. R. Shaplen. New Yorker 45:110+ S 20 '69
Limiting the leadership. Time 94:24-5 Ag 29 '69
Many-sided politics of South Vietnam. R. Butwell. bibliog f Cur Hist 56:71-6+ F '69
Negotiations or surrender? a coalition government; address, January 30, 1969. Nguyen-huu-Chi. Vital Speeches 35:318-20 Mr 1 '69
No disguised defeat? concerning R. M. Nixon's proposals. S. Alsop. Newsweek 73: 124 Je 9 '69
No one can be sure what Thieu is thinking. K. P. Buckley. il N Y Times Mag p28-9+ Mr 2 '69
Notes and comment: reliance of Saigon government on American support. New Yorker 44:23-4 F 1 '69
Odd man out: T. V. Huong squeezed out. Newsweek 74:36 S 1 '69
On the tightrope. il Newsweek 74:21 Jl 7 '69
Political freedom in Vietnam. R. F. Drinan. America 120:731-3 Je 28 '69
Politics in South Vietnam. J. M. Silverman. bibliog f Cur Hist 57:321-6+ D '69
Reporter at large; creation of PRG by NLF. R. Shaplen. New Yorker 45:36-40+ Jl 12 '69
Reports: D. Warner. Atlan 224:12+ Ag '69
Saigon and reds: is a deal near? il U S News 66:33-4 Ap 14 '69
Seizing the initiative. Newsweek 73:49 Je 30 '69
Sigh of relief in Saigon. il Time 94:29-30 N 14 '69
Spotlight on Vietnam; findings of U.S. interreligious study team. Nation 209:2-3 Jl 7 '69
State of the war: an intelligence report. il U S News 67:36-7 O 27 '69
TRB from Washington. New Repub 160:4 My 31 '69
Thieu: determined and defiant; interview, ed. by M. Clark. Nguyen-van-Thieu. Time 94:13 O 3 '69
Thieu faces the kindergarten; lower house of South Viet Nam's National assembly. il Time 95:20 Ja 12 '70
Things worth doing; Nguyen van Thieu's feud with parliament. Newsweek 75:30 Ja 5 '70
Two steps to get us out of Vietnam. E. G. Lansdale. Look 33:64+ Mr 4 '69
Vietnam: get out now; with editorial comment. J. R. Moskin. il Look 33:73-6+, 88 N 18 '69
Vietnam: Gordian knot. Commonweal 90:3-4 Mr 21 '69

VIETNAM (Republic)—Politics and government
—*Continued*
Vietnam: sojourn and sequel. J. Armstrong
and J. Conyers, jr. il Chr Cent 86:1307–
9 O 15 '69
See also
Elections—Vietnam (Republic)
National liberation front (Vietnam)
Vietnam (Republic)—Cabinet

Relief work

Irish nuns in the Mekong Delta. D. Warren.
America 121:524–5 N 29 '69
Worst city in the world? activities of the
Saigon civil assistance group. il Newsweek
74:38–9 D 29 '69
See also
Vietnamese war, 1957–—Relief work

VIETNAM (Republic) and the United States
See also
United States—Foreign opinion—Vietnamese

VIETNAMESE
Blood on our hands? America's commitment
to South Vietnamese. New Repub 161:7 O
18 '69
GI's in battle: the dink complex. il Newsweek
74:37 D 1 '69
Open letter to President Nixon. Tran-van-
Dinh. Chr Cent 86:313–14 Mr 5 '69
See also
Peasantry—Vietnam (Republic)

VIETNAMESE crisis, 1964. See Tonkin Gulf incident, 1964

VIETNAMESE in Guyana
Brief visit to the third world: Guyana and
Vietnam. S. W. Mintz. Yale R 59:151–60 O '69

VIETNAMESE intellectuals. See Intellectuals

VIETNAMESE political prisoners. See Political prisoners—Vietnam (Republic)

VIETNAMESE soldiers. See Vietnam (Republic)—Army

VIETNAMESE war, 1957–
Beyond Vietnam borders: war moves, a peace
step. il U S News 66:8 Ap 28 '69
Easy job. J. Mirsky. Nation 208:556 My 5 '69
Grim reminder that the war goes on; Com-
munists strike after Tet truce. il Time 93:
28 F 28 '69
History behind the headlines: Viet chronol-
ogy. il Sr Schol 94:4 Ap 18 '69
Hold your breath. M. Parker. il Newsweek
74:41 Jl 14 '69
In Vietnam, the enemy is beaten; interview,
ed. by J. G. Hubbell. J. S. McCain. jr.
Read Digest 94:75–9 F '69
Lessons of Vietnam. S. Alsop. Newsweek 73:
116 F 17 '69
Letter from Saigon. R. Shaplen. New York-
er 45:110+ S 20 '69
Making it hard for Mr Nixon. il Newsweek
73:32–3 Mr 17 '69
Mini-offensive; North Vietnamese attacks. il
Newsweek 73:48+ Mr 10 '69
Mr Thieu has his day; excerpts from inter-
view. Nguyen van Thieu. Newsweek 75:64
Ja 5 '70
National liberation front. P. Arnett. il Cur
Hist 56:82–7+ F '69
Next turn in Vietnam. il U S News 66:28–9
Mr 3 '69
Nixon's hard choice in Viet Nam. il Time
93:20–1 Mr 14 '69
Nixon's war in Vietnam: continued escalation.
T. Coffin. Nation 208:262–4 Mr 3 '69
Now a new kind of war; report from Viet-
nam. il U S News 66:28–30 My 26 '69
Progress in Vietnam? il Newsweek 73:37 Ap
14 '69
Senate's responsibility. E. Gruening. Nation
208:748–9 Je 16 '69
State of the war; an intelligence report. il
U S News 67:36–7 O 27 '69
Strategy and tactics of peace in Viet Nam. il
Time 93:18–20+ Mr 28 '69
TRB from Washington. New Repub 160:4
My 31 '69
Test of endurance. Newsweek 73:41 Ap 21
'69
Those sanctuaries: Laos and Cambodia. il
Time 94:34+ Ap 25 '69
Time of testing in Viet Nam: North Viet-
namese and Viet Cong attacks. il Time 93:
29–30 Mr 7 '69
Vietnam dilemma; a first-hand explanation.
N. Wallace. il U S News 66:26–9 Je 16 '69
Viet Nam: the new, underground optimism.
il Time 94:14–15 D 12 '69
Vietnam will win! by W. Burchett. Review
Nation 208:470–1 Ap 14 '69. S. D'Arazien
Waiting for Charlie: Tet truce. Newsweek
73:38 F 24 '69
Waiting it out; pilgrimage to South Vietnam.
il Newsweek 73:42 Mr 24 '69
War; testing Vietnamization; ARVN under-
going intensive training. il Time 95:30 Ja
5 '70

When war will end for U.S; interview, ed.
by W. S. Merick. Nguyen-cao-Ky. il U S
News 67:58–61 O 13 '69
See also
Conscientious objectors
Tonkin Gulf incident, 1964
Vietnam (Republic)—Army
Vietnam (Republic)—Politics and government

Aerial operations

Air war in Vietnam: adding up the score. il
U S News 67:26–7 Ag 18 '69
End of round four. Newsweek 73:58 My 5 '69
Since the bombing halt, more GI's are dying.
U S News 66:10 F 17 '69
See also
Helicopters—Military applications

American participation

American power and the new mandarins, by
N. Chomsky. Review
Commentary 47:35–44 My '69. L. Abel;
Discussion. 48:9–10+ Ag; 12+ O '69
Anachronistic war. Commonweal 90:555–6 S
19 '69
Answering Mr Nixon; analysis of speech on
Vietnam. Nation 209:524–5 N 17 '69
Back to square one? concerning William P.
Rogers speech on unilateral withdrawal. il
Newsweek 73:58 My 5 '69
Battle for the mind of Nixon. Nation 208:
98–9 Ja 27 '69
Behind Nixon's Vietnam stand. H. Sidey.
Life 67:4 N 21 '69
Betting on the silent majority. il Newsweek
74:35–6 N 17 '69
Blaming the critics. Time 94:17–18 O 10 '69
Can U.S. get out of the war now? report
from Saigon. il U S News 66:34–6 My 5 '69
Choosing up sides; reactions to the Nixon
policy speech. K. Crawford. Newsweek 74:
52 N 17 '69
Clifford reviewed; rationale for disengage-
ment in Vietnam. K. Crawford. Newsweek
74:20 Jl 7 '69
Critics of the war harden their line. Bsns
W p28–9 O 4 '69
Doubts about Vietnamization; R. M. Nixon's
messages of December 8 and 15, 1969. J.
Osborne. New Repub 162:11–12 Ja 3 '70
Ending the Vietnam war. G. S. McGovern.
Cur 111:13–18 O '69
Eye of the hurricane. New Repub 160:1+
Mr 15 '69
Fight for the President's mind, and the
men who won it; excerpt from The limits
of intervention. T. Hoopes. il Atlan 224:
97–104+ O '69
Gathering protest; Viet Nam war question.
il Time 94:12+ O 3 '69
General Abrams deserves a better war. K.
P. Buckley. il N Y Times Mag p34–5+ O 5
'69
Getting free; need to turn over responsibility
for the war to the Vietnamese. New Repub
160:5–7 Mr 22 '69
Growing involvement in Asia: 1960–1968. R.
Butwell. bibliog f Cur Hist 57:88–92+ Ag
'69
Hand down your head, Tom Dooley; Vietnamese Catholics, a pawn of American
foreign policy. R. Scheer. il Ramp Mag
7:15–19 Ja 25 '69
How to control the military. J. K. Galbraith.
il Harper 238:31–46 Je '69
Is there a lesson of Munich? E. Stillman.
Horizon 11:32–3 Spr '69
Laird plan. M. Parker. il Newsweek 73:44
Je 2 '69
Laird's official report on Vietnam: the
basic problem remains; statement, March
19, 1969. M. R. Laird. U S News 66:35 Mr
31 '69
Letter from Washington; Nixon administra-
tion. R. H. Rovere. New Yorker 45:133–4
My 17 '69
Miscalculation unlimited; views of Townsend
Hoopes and Henry Brandon. D. M. Grady.
Sat R 52:29–32+ D 13 '69
NLF asks the American left; where are you?
ten-point proposal, and the Swedish in-
ternational liaison committee conference.
Stockholm. F. Schurmann. Ramp Mag 8:
14+ Ag '69
New arithmetic of Vietnam. Life 67:24 Jl 11
'69
Next turn in Vietnam. il U S News 66:
28–9 Mr 3 '69
Nixon on war; a plan and a warning; ad-
dress, November 3, 1969. R. M. Nixon. il
U S News 67:110–14 N 17 '69; Same with
title Pursuit of peace in Viet-Nam. Dept
State Bul 61:437–43 N 24 '69; Same with title
Vietnam plan. Vital Speeches 36:66–70 N 15
'69; Same with title President Nixon's
statement on Vietnam, 1969. Cur Hist 58:
42–6+ Ja '70

VIETNAMESE war, 1957- —American troop
withdrawals—*Continued*
Signs of tougher line on Vietnam pullout. il
U S News 67:10 S 8 '69
Slow road back to the real world. il Time
93:14-16 Je 20 '69
TRB from Washington: emperor's clothes.
New Repub 161:8 S 27 '69; Reply. A. Ribi-
coff. 161:30-1 O 18 '69
Three questions for President Brewster and
Mayor Lee. E. V. Rostow. Nat R 21:1113-
14+ N 4 '69
Too late? Richard Nixon's plan. S. Alsop.
Newsweek 74:140 O 27 '69
Trim and hold: Defense Secretary Laird's
plan. Nation 209:298-9 S 29 '69
Uneasy retreat. K. Crawford. Newsweek 74:
40 N 3 '69
U.S. pullout from Vietnam; the Nixon for-
mula is working, says Rogers; excerpts
from Meet the press program, October 12,
1969. W. P. Rogers. U S News 67:16+ O 27
'69
Vietnam cutback, how far, how fast? il
U S News 66:29-31 Je 23 '69
Vietnam debate; will it help or hinder peace?
il U S News 67:29-30 O 20 '69
Vietnam: how to get out? with report by
J. Blocker. il Newsweek 74:15-16 S 8 '69
Vietnam pullout. K. Crawford. Newsweek 73:
48 Je 30 '69
Vietnam: the long, long way home. il News-
week 73:25-7 Je 23 '69
Vietnam: the Nixon game plan. S. Alsop.
Newsweek 74:108 S 15 '69
Viet Nam timetable; views of C. Clifford.
il Time 93:12-13 Je 27 '69
Viet Nam: trying to buy time. il Time 94:17-
18 S 26 '69
Vietnam: what's going on here? il News-
week 74:29-30 S 22 '69
Vietnam's tomorrow; ten points for with-
drawal. M. Novak. Commonweal 91:45-7 O
10 '69
War: new support for Nixon; Time-Louis
Harris poll. Time 95:10-11 Ja 12 '70
War pullout? Clifford's plan; excerpts from
remarks. C. Clifford. U S News 66:11 Je
30 '69
War: stark options for America. il Time 94:
19-20 S 19 '69
We should de-escalate the importance of
Vietnam. G. W. Ball. il N Y Times Mag p6-
7+ D 21 '69
What Midway means. il Bsns W p46-7 Je 14
'69
What withdrawal would really mean. il Time
94:20-3 O 24 '69
When U.S. troops pull out: the real risk in
Vietnam. il U S News 67:13-15 D 29 '69
Where GI's are pulling out: report from a
border zone. S. W. Sanders. il U S News
67:36-8 Jl 7 '69
Why Saigon spurns Nixon peace plan. S. W.
Sanders. il U S News 66:28-9 Je 30 '69
Winding down the war on our own. H. Dono-
van. Life 67:42 O 24 '69
Withdrawal pains. il Newsweek 74:19 S 1 '69

Anecdotes, facetiae, satire, etc.
Grapes of wrath; V.C. communiqué. Chr
Cent 86:1005 Jl 23 '69
War games. Chr Cent 86:913 Jl 2 '69

Atrocities
American atrocity. N. Poirier. Esquire 72:59-
63+ Ag '69
Casualties of war, by D. Lang. Review
Newsweek 74:130+ D 8 '69. P. D. Zimmer-
man
Fear of a bloodbath. Tran-van-Dinh. New
Repub 161:11-14 D 6 '69
Hue: a full day. W. F. Buckley, jr. Nat R 21:
1338-9 D 30 '69
Incident at Van Duong; excerpts from 5 by
7. J. Shepherd. il Look 33:26-8+ Ag 12 '69
It's that kind of war. Z. B. Grant. New Repub
161:9-11 D 20 '69
Kindly Uncle Ho; Hué massacre. Newsweek
74:29 S 15 '69
Massacre of Hué. il Time 94:32+ O 31 '69
Nixon's history lesson: the myth of reprisals.
W. Meyers. Nation 209:654-6 D 15 '69
On the other side: terror as policy. il Time
94:29 D 5 '69
Reporter at large; soldier government wit-
ness in court-martial proceedings against
four American soldiers in rape-murder case.
D. Lang. New Yorker 45:61-4+ O 18 '69
Training for Song My. Nation 209:716 D 29
'69
Vietnam: the bloodbath argument. D. G.
Porter and L. E. Ackland. il Chr Cent 86:
1414-17 N 5 '69

Songmy massacre
American conscience. Nation 209:619-20 D 8
'69
Analyzing the inexplicable. Sci N 96:522-3 D
6 '69
Atrocity reports: the aftermath; Lt. W. L.
Calley, jr. il U S News 67:4 D 8 '69
Calley case; U.S. army lieutenant charged
with slaying of South Vietnamese civilians.
Newsweek 74:40+ N 24 '69
Can Calley get a fair trial? il Time 94:22 D 26
'69
Carnage and the incarnation. Chr Cent 86:
1633 D 24 '69
Death to gooks; reactions to Pinkville mas-
sacre in the U.S. J. Osborne. New Repub
161:17-18 D 13 '69
Defending freedom, preventing bloodbaths.
P. Steinfels. Commonweal 91:296 D 5 '69
Fallout from Song My. il Newsweek 74:40-1
D 15 '69
Going beyond Mylai 4. Commonweal 91:325-
6 D 12 '69
Great atrocity hunt; murder at Songmy and
the American conscience. Nat R 21:1252+
D 16 '69
In the shadow of Mylai; reactions in Wash-
ington. il Life 67:4 D 12 '69
Killings at Song My; with report by L.
Norman. il Newsweek 74:33-4+ D 8 '69
Lesson of Pinkville. Chr Today 14:23 D 19 '69
Letter from Paris. Genêt. New Yorker 45:
179 D 13 '69
Massacre at Mylai; with exclusive pictures,
eyewitness accounts. Life 67:36-45 D 5 '69;
Discussion. 67:46-7 D 19 '69
Massacre story: Hip-pocket AP. il Newsweek
74:83-4 D 8 '69
Massacre trial; a shift in the war? with re-
port by W. S. Merick and interview with
psychiatrist R. J. Lifton il U S News 67:
23-8 D 15 '69
Miscue on the massacre. Time 94:75 D 5 '69
More about Song My. il Newsweek 75:27
Ja 19 '70
My Lai: an American tragedy. il Time 94:
23-4+ D 5 '69
My Lai incident as a case in law. il U S
News 67:34-6 D 22 '69
My Lai killings; how army captain describes
incident; excerpts from Pentagon news con-
ference, December 4, 1969. E. L. Medina.
U S News 67:10 D 15 '69
My Lai massacre. il Time 94:17-19 N 28 '69
Mylai: whose fault? W. F. Buckley, jr. Nat R
21:1339 D 30 '69
Notes and comment: massacre in My Lai.
New Yorker 45:27-9 D 20 '69
Official U.S. report on My Lai investigation;
statement before the Senate armed services
committee, November 26, 1969. S. R. Resor.
U S News 67:78-9 D 8 '69
On evil: the inescapable fact: Time essay.
Time 94:26-7 D 5 '69
Pictures and questions; controversy over R.
L. Haeberle's pictures of the Songmy mas-
sacre. Newsweek 74:57 D 1 '69
Road to Songmy. N. Cousins. Sat R 52:18
D 20 '69
Self-respect after My Lai. Chr Cent 86:1569
D 10 '69
Song My: a U.S. atrocity? il Newsweek 74:35-
7 D 1 '69
Song My's shock wave. K. Crawford. News-
week 74:38 D 15 '69
Stiff upper lip over a massacre. P. Steinfels.
Commonweal 91:350 D 19 '69
Story of a soldier who refused to fire at
Songmy. J. Lelyveld. il N Y Times Mag
p32-3+ D 14 '69
That was our orders; interview. ed. by W.
Granger. C. A. West. New Repub 161:16-17
D 13 '69
There have been few offenders; excerpts of
remarks, December 5, 1969. D. Packard.
U S News 67:10 D 15 '69
Uncovering the full story of Songmy. Ameri-
ca 121:552 D 6 '69
War crime issue; some nagging questions.
il Newsweek 74:34-5 D 8 '69
War system. Nation 209:650-1 D 15 '69
See also
Government   investigations—Songmy   mas-
sacre
Bibliography
For further reference. Sr Schol 94:24 Ap 18
'69

Campaigns and battles
Battle for Hamburger hill. il Time 93:27-8
My 30 '69
Conclusion at Khesanh. M. Herr. il Esquire
72:113-23+ O '69
Hamburger hill. New Repub 160:10 My 31 '69
In the village of Donglach, a stench of death.
il Life 66:32-3 Mr 14 '69

VIETNAMESE war, 1957- —Campaigns and
  battles—*Continued*
Incident in Song Chang Valley: leadership
  problem. Time 94:22-3 S 5 '69
Is the lull over in Vietnam war? il U S
  News 67:7 Ag 25 '69
Khesanh. M. Herr. il Esquire 72:118-23+ S
  '69
Lesson of Ben Het; South Vietnamese out-
  post near Cambodia. il Time 94:28 Jl 11
  '69
Letter from South Vietnam. R. Shaplen. New
  Yorker 45:134+ Ap 12 '69
Letters from Hamburger hill; to E. M. Ken-
  nedy, ed. by N. Sheehan. Harper 239:40-
  4+ N '69
Luli's end. il Newsweek 74:33 Ag 25 '69
Put to the test; enemy action in the central
  highlands and the Mekong Delta. News-
  week 74:54+ N 17 '69
Rebuttal of Hamburger hill. il Time 93:22-3
  Je 6 '69
Red offensive in Vietnam, aimed at Nixon?
  il U S News 66:8 Mr 10 '69
Reports: D. Warner. Atlan 224:12+ Ag '69
U.S. commanders explain: why the high U.S.
  casualties; battle for Hamburger hill. il
  U S News 66:26-7 Je 2 '69
Vietnam: is red attack blunted? il U S News
  66:11 F 24 '69
Woe to the victors; Hamburger hill. il News-
  week 73:42 Je 2 '69

Casualties

After one year of truce moves; stalemate of
  Paris mounting U.S. dead. il U S News
  66:26-8 Ap 7 '69
Death in a quiet week; deaths of Edward
  Lama; Raymond Grey; James O'Shaughn-
  essy. G. Chaplin. il Newsweek 73:46 Ap 28
  '69
For Tron, gifts and a new leg. il Life 67:
  85-6 D 12 '69
Gravediggers; American casualty rates since
  Paris talks began. New Repub 160:7 F 22
  '69
Hamburger hill. New Repub 160:10 My 31
  '69
Hero in every man; study of wounded men.
  il Time 93:52 My 16 '69
How America's toll in war is dropping. il
  U S News 68:6 Ja 12 '70
Latest report on GI casualties in Vietnam.
  il U S News 67:23-4 Jl 14 '69
1,200 minus five leaves nothing. il McCalls
  97:76-9 N '69
Our town: the war comes home to Bealls-
  ville, Ohio. J. Blankfort. il Ramp Mag 8:39-
  46 Jl '69
Question of casualties. il Newsweek 73:45
  Je 9 '69
Reports: D. Warner. Atlan 224:12+ Ag '69
Semper fidelis: the marines of Morenci. il
  Time 95:14-15 Ja 5 '70
Since the bombing halt, more GI's are dying.
  U S News 66:10 F 17 '69
Tense vigil of Mrs O'Grady: Maj John O'Gra-
  dy missing in action. C. S. Wren. il Look
  33:40-4 D 30 '69
To our fallen son. A. Dewlen. il Read Digest
  94:49-53 Mr '69
U.S. commanders explain; why the high U.S.
  casualties. il U S News 66:26-7 Je 2 '69
U.S. losses rise in Vietnam. U S News 66:13
  Mr 31 '69
U.S. war dead; half were too young to vote.
  il U S News 66:10 Ap 28 '69
Vietnam, one week's dead: May 28-June 3,
  1969; a record and a tribute. il Life 66:20-
  32 Je 27 '69
Viet Nam timetable: Americans killed in one
  week. il Time 93:12-13 Je 27 '69
War's toll in combat deaths. il U S News 67:
  5 D 29 '69
Your son has been wounded. M. W. Gokay.
  il Read Digest 95:63-7 S '69

Cost

Vietnam: the 200-year mortgage. J. L. Clay-
  ton. Nation 208:661-3 My 26 '69
Your money when the war stops. H. C.
  Wallich. Vogue 153:58 F 15 '69

Damage to property

See Vietnamese war, 1957- —Destruction
and pillage

Destruction and pillage

Pacification in Viet-Nam: the destruction of
  An Thinh. R. Williams. il Ramp Mag
  7:21-4 My '69
Political amnesia; American violence. Nation 208:780 Je 23 '69
Pop me some dinks. O. Schell. New Repub
  162:19-21 Ja 3 '70

Economic aspects

After peace breaks out, what will we do with
  all that extra money? E. L. Dale, jr. il
  N Y Times Mag p32-3+ F 16 '69
Can you stand it? concerning J. V. Lind-
  say's speech on needs of New York city
  vs. Vietnamese war. W. F. Buckley, jr.
  Nat R 21:766-7 Jl 29 '69
Ending the Vietnam war; symposium. Cur
  113:36-45 D '69
High-level disaffection; dissent of business-
  men. R. Friedman. Nation 209:398 O 20
  '69
Nixon is skipping the peace dividend. Bsns
  W p 16 Ag 30 '69
Our Vietnamized economy. M. L. Weiden-
  baum. il Sat R 52:15-17 My 24 '69
Post-Vietnam economic outlook weighed in
  report of Cabinet. Aviation W 90:56 Mr 10
  '69
Senators discuss postwar economy. J. R.
  Kramer. Science 166:1493 D 19 '69
TRB from Washington; paying for Vietnam.
  New Repub 162:6 Ja 10 '70
Viet Nam peace and the budget. M. L.
  Weidenbaum. Nations Bsns 57:78 Ag '69
Vietnam stalls defense research effort. il
  Aviation W 90:53+ Mr 10 '69

Equipment and supplies

RAP: an old naval shell with a new kick;
  rocket-assisted projectiles. M. Schultz. il
  Pop Mech 130:84-7 D '68

Foreign participation

Allies for hire; Senate foreign relations subcommittee hearings on financial costs of
  Asian allies in Vietnam. New Repub 161:5-
  6 D 13 '69
As GI's leave Vietnam: war role of the allies.
  il U S News 68:24-5 Ja 12 '70
Guns for hire? cost of getting allies to commit troops to Vietnam. il Newsweek 74:26-
  7 D 15 '69
Lyndon's hessians. Nation 210:4-5 Ja 12 '70

Guerrillas

I quit. D. Duncan. Ramp Mag 7:41-6 Ja 25
  '69
Vietcong is losing its grip. J. Alsop. il Read
  Digest 95:53-61 D '69

Heroes

Hero in every man; study of wounded men. il
  Time 93:52 My 16 '69

Legal aspects

Legal dilemmas. il Time 94:32+ D 5 '69
Vietnam and the law: theory & practice of
  civil challenge. B. Woodward; reply with
  rejoinder. N. W. Puner. Commentary 47:4+
  F '69

Medical and sanitary affairs

Call for help from Vietnam; heart of 13-year-
  old Vietnamese boy restored by patch at
  Philadelphia Children's hospital. R. H.
  Berg. il Look 33:24-30+ D 16 '69
Letter from Washington; investigation by A.
  Cranston of medical treatment available to
  veternas especially of Vietnamese war. R.
  H. Rovere. New Yorker 45:171-2 N 29 '69
  See also
Neuroses
United States—Army—Medical corps

Moral and religious aspects

I never met any priest who suggested withdrawal. P. Nobile. Commonweal 90:196-7
  My 2 '69; Reply with rejoinder. J. J. Fahey.
  90:307+ My 30 '69
Reshaping a peace lobby; third National mobilization of peace. W. Willoughby. Chr
  Today 13:46 F 28 '69

Moving pictures

See Moving pictures—War films

Negroes

Black power in Viet Nam. il Time 94:22-3 S 19
  '69
Integration in death; burial of Private Bill
  Terry. Chr Cent 87:37 Ja 14 '70
No bells for Bill; Birmingham. Ala. D. G.
  Shockley. Chr Cent 86:1508 N 26 '69

Pacification programs

Easy come . . : Accelerated pacification cam-
  paign. Newsweek 73:32 Mr 3 '69
Pacification in Viet-Nam: the destruction of
  An Thinh. R. Williams. il Ramp Mag 7:
  21-4 My '69
Rise of Phoenix. Newsweek 75:25 Ja 12 '70
Song of the gung-ho gladiators. New Repub
  160:6 Mr 1 '69

VIETNAMESE war, 1957- —*Continued*

Peace and mediation

After Vietnam what? symposium. il Commonweal 90:7-14 Mr 21 '69; Same. Cur 109:49-51 Ag '69

Ambassador Lodge discusses the Paris peace talks; remarks, May 15, 1969. R. M. Nixon; H. C. Lodge. Dept State Bul 60:465-7 Je '69

And, now, two peace plans. Commonweal 90: 307-8 My 30 '69

Appeal to the silent majority; President Nixon's November 3 address. America 121: 451-2 N 15 '69

Are reds signaling peace? Here's the view in Vietnam. il U S News 67:26 Jl 21 '69

Break coming in Vietnam? Here's what it hangs on. il U S News 66:55-6 My 19 '69

Cease-fire fallacy. New Repub 161:5-6 O 4 '69; Discussion. 161:31-2 O 18; 9-10 O 25 '69

Cease-fire now in Vietnam! J. B. Sheerin. Cath World 210:50-1 N '69

Chances now for peace. il U S News 66:25-7 Je 2 '69

Christmas comes to the capital. M. McGrory. America 121:627 D 27 '69

Course we're on; autumnal State of the Union report. Commonweal 91:35-6 O 10 '69

Decision time on Viet Nam. Chr Today 13: 27 Mr 28 '69

Deep concern for peace in Viet-Nam; remarks, October 20, 1969. W. P. Rogers. Dept State Bul 61:394-5 N 10 '69

Did Mr Nixon make his job harder? Life 67: 44 N 14 '69

Doubts about Vietnamization; R. M. Nixon's messages of December 8 and 15, 1969. J. Osborne. New Repub 162:11-12 Ja 3 '70

Elements of settlement: Saigon notwithstanding. R. A. Falk. Nation 208:689-93 Je 2 '69

Ending the Vietnam war. G. S. McGovern. Cur 111:13-18 O '69

Eyeball to eyeball with the monster. H. Sidey. il Life 66:4 My 23 '69

First steps; views of W. A. Harriman. Commonweal 90:355-6 Je 13 '69

Five ways out of Vietnam. il Newsweek 74: 28-32 O 20 '69

Germ warfare and the arms race; cease-fire proposal. N. Cousins. Sat R 52:26 D 13 '69

Gromyko to Nixon: a tough reply. U S News 67:12 S 29 '69

Harriman suggests a way out of Vietnam; interview, ed. by H. Smith. W. A. Harriman. il N Y Times Mag p24-5+ Ag 24 '69

How Nixon is trying to end the war. il U S News 66:27-8 My 26 '69

How the U.S. spurned three chances for peace in Vietnam. N. Cousins. Look 33: 45-8 Jl 29 '69; Reply. W. F. Buckley, jr. Nat R 21:974 S 23 '69

If Nixon tries a cease-fire: view from South Vietnam. il U S News 67:25-6 N 3 '69

Inside story: LBJ's switch on Vietnam. il Newsweek 73:32-3 Mr 10 '69

Is peace in Vietnam possible? A. M. Cox. Sat R 52:38-9 Mr 22 '69

Kissinger plan for peace: Nixon's way out of Vietnam? U S News 66:26 My 26 '69

Letter from South Vietnam. R. Shaplen. New Yorker 45:134+ Ap 12 '69

Magic word; how ordinary South Vietnamese view prospect. K. Buckley. il Newsweek 73: 37 Ja 27 '69

Meaning of Midway; statement, June 10, 1969. R. M. Nixon. U S News 66:29 Je 23 '69

Midway meeting: the perils of peace. il Time 93:21-2 Je 6 '69

Moves toward peace in Vietnam largely a one-sided effort. U S News 66:26 Je 9 '69

Must we stand alone? D. Lawrence. U S News 66:100 My 26 '69

Nixon finds peace comes hard. il Bsns W p38-40 Mr 29 '69

Nixon on war: a plan and a warning; address, November 3, 1969. R. M. Nixon. il U S News 67:110-14 N 17 '69; Same with title Vietnam plan. Vital Speeches 36:66-70 N 15 '69; Same with title Pursuit of peace in Viet-Nam. Dept State Bul 61:437-43 N 24 '69; Same with title President Nixon's statement on Vietnam, 1969. Cur Hist 58:42-6+ Ja '70

Nixon's inch. New Repub 160:5-6 My 24 '69

Nixon's peace plan. Chr Cent 86:734-5 My 28 '69

No disguised defeat? concerning R. M. Nixon's proposals. S. Alsop. Newsweek 73: 124 Je 9 '69

Peace, but how? The growing rift. il U S News 67:8 N 17 '69

Postscript on Negotiation now! T. Ritt. Commonweal 90:134-5 Ap 18 '69; Reply with rejoinder. M. Temple. 90:413-15 Je 27 '69

President explains his risks for peace; remarks, December 15, 1969. R. M. Nixon. U S News 67:15-16 D 29 '69

President Nixon discusses the Viet-Nam peace talks and the ABM safeguard system; remarks, March 25, 1969. R. M. Nixon. Dept State Bul 60:313-16 Ap 14 '69

President Nixon hails Saigon proposals for political settlement in South Viet-Nam; statement, July 11, 1969. R. M. Nixon. Dept State Bul 61:61-2 Jl 28 '69

President Nixon reduces troop ceiling in Viet-Nam; statement, September 16, 1969. R. M. Nixon. Dept State Bul 61:302 O 6 '69

President Nixon's news conference of September 26, 1969. R. M. Nixon. Dept State Bul 61:313-16 O 13 '69

President's blueprint for peace in Vietnam; address, May 14, 1969. R. M. Nixon. il U S News 66:79-82 My 26 '69; Same with title War in Vietnam. Vital Speeches 35: 482-4 Je 1 '69; Same with title Peace in Viet-Nam. Dept State Bul 60:457-61 Je 2 '69

Question of belief in Hanoi, and at home. H. Sidey. il Life 67:4 O 10 '69

Ready to talk with the Viet Cong. il Time 93:31 Ap 4 '69

Real moves for peace. il U S News 67:23-4 N 10 '69

Rogers: Hanoi is unreasonable; excerpts from testimony before the House foreign affairs committee, July 17, 1969. W. P. Rogers. U S News 67:10 Jl 28 '69

Saigon and reds: is a deal near? il U S News 66:33-4 Ap 14 '69

Secretary Rogers interviewed on Meet the press; transcript of interview, October 12, 1969. W. P. Rogers. Dept State Bul 61: 345-50 O 27 '69

Secretary Rogers on peace prospects; excerpts from news conference, April 7, 1969. W. P. Rogers. U S News 66:32-3 Ap 21 '69

Secretary Rogers visits Viet-Nam; statement, news conferences, during Asian tour. W. P. Rogers. Dept State Bul 60:461-4 Je 2 '69

Secretary Rusk interviewed on Face the Nation; program, December 1, 1968. D. Rusk. Dept State Bul 59:645-50 D 23 '68

Seven Asian and Pacific nations examine security situation in Asia; text of communique. Dept State Bul 60:481-3 Je 9 '69

Shadowboxing in Saigon. A. M. Cox. New Repub 160:14-15 Ap 12 '69

Shaking the dust; collective effort to end the war. Commonweal 91:3-4 O 3 '69

Talking peace: the latest moves. il U S News 66:20 Ap 21 '69

Thieu-ing the loyal opposition; peace and parties of peace are unwelcome. T. Fox. Commonweal 90:459-62 Jl 25 '69

This way out. Commonweal 91:171-3 N 7 '69

This way out. W. Pfaff. Commonweal 89: 611-12 F 14 '69

Toward a worldwide peace; address to U.N. September 18, 1969. R. M. Nixon. il U S News 67:98-101 S 29 '69; Same with title Establishment of peace. Vital Speeches 35:738-41 O 1 '69; Same with title Strengthening the total fabric of peace. Dept State Bul 61:297-302 O 6 '69

Ultimatum; views of clergy and laymen concerned about Vietnam. Commonweal 89: 696 Mr 7 '69

Under Secretary Richardson interviewed on CBS television; news program July 2, 1969. E. L. Richardson. Dept State Bul 61:49-51 Jl 21 '69

Vance plan for a Vietnam cease-fire; interview, ed. by R. Kleiman. C. R. Vance. il N Y Times Mag p30-1+ S 21 '69

Viet Cong no to an election bid. U S News 67:8 Jl 21 '69

Vietnam developments. W. F. Buckley, jr. Nat R 21:766 Jl 29 '69

Vietnam: end in sight? Sat Eve Post 242:4 F 8 '69

Vietnam: how do we get out? A. J. Langguth. Sat Eve Post 242:19-21+ F 8 '69

Viet-Nam in the perspective of East Asia; address, April 21, 1969. W. P. Rogers. Dept State Bul 60:397-400 My 12 '69

Vietnam nondebate continues. Chr Cent 86: 468 Ap 9 '68

Viet Nam reappraisal. C. M. Clifford. For Affairs 47:608-22 Jl '69

Vietnam: the Nixon plan; NLF's plan. il Newsweek 73:33-6 My 26 '69

Vietnam: the President's fading hope. J. Osborne. New Repub 161:17-19 S 27 '69

Vietnam: the spurned peace. N. Cousins. Sat R 52:12-16+ Jl 26 '69; Same abr. with title How the U.S. spurned three changes for peace in Vietnam. Look 33:45-8 Jl 29 '69

VIETNAMESE war, 1957- —Peace and mediation—*Continued*
Vietnam's tomorrow; ten points for with-
drawal. M. Novak. Commonweal 91:45-7 O
10 '69
War: out by November 1970? Time 94:13-14
Jl 11 '69
We are not Democrats, or Republicans; we
are Americans; excerpts from address to
House of representatives, November 13,
1969. R. M. Nixon. il U S News 67:63 N
24 '69
When Nixon talked to the Senate; excerpts
from address, November 13, 1969. R. M.
Nixon. U S News 67:69 N 24 '69
Why Hanoi wants peace; White House view.
il U S News 66:32-3 Ap 21 '69
Why Saigon fears Nixon peace plan. S. W.
Sanders. il U S News 66:28-9 Je 30 '69
Will Nixon risk peace? New Repub 161:5-6
Ag 2 '69
Will the President's plan bring peace? with
interview with E. Bunker, ed. by W. S.
Merick. il U S News 67:45-9+ N 17 '69
Word was never; President Thieu's reac-
tions to R. M. Nixon's proposals. News-
week 73:45-6 Je 9 '69
See also
Citizens committee for peace with freedom
in Vietnam

Negotiation meetings, May 1968-

After one year of truce moves; stalemate of
Paris. il U S News 66:26-8 Ap 7 '69
Ambassador Harriman discusses the Paris
talks on Viet-Nam; excerpts from press
conference, December 4, 1968. W. A. Harri-
man. Dept State Bul 59:650-2 D 23 '68
Death and deadlock. N. Cousins. Sat R 52:26
N 1 '69
Fatigue in Paris. Time 94:23 O 17 '69
Full circle in Paris. il Time 93:36-7 Ja 24 '69
Giving up at Paris. Nation 209:613 D 8 '69
Hanoi's sea of woes buoys peace hopes;
with editorial comment. il Bsns W p33-4,
132 S 6 '69
Harriman suggests a way out of Vietnam;
interview. ed. by H. Smith. W. A. Harri-
man. il N Y Times Mag p24-5+ Ag 24 '69
Harsh beginning in Paris. il Time 93:25 Ja
31 '69
In the round. Sr Schol 94:23-4 Ja 31 '69
Is the war lost? S. Alsop. Newsweek 73:120
My 5 '69
Letter from Washington (cont) R. H. Rovere.
New Yorker 44:65-6+ F 1; 45:161-3 Ap 19
'69
Letter from Washington; Lodge's resignation.
R. H. Rovere. New Yorker 45:169-71 N 29
'69
Lodge leaves Paris. Time 94:20 N 28 '69
Lodge signal. Newsweek 74:26 D 1 '69
Meanwhile, at the Paris talks. il U S News
67:39 Jl 28 '69
Messieurs Sont Servis: table protocol. Nat
R 21:107 F 11 '69
More about the shape of the table. N. Cou-
sins. Sat R 52:20 Ja 25 '69
Motion in Saigon, deadlock in Paris. Time
94:15A Jl 18 '69
Nixon's contract for peace. il Time 93:20-2
My 23 '69
No quick peace in Vietnam. E. von Kuehnelt-
Leddihn. Nat R 21:122 F 11 '69
Now that Lodge is resigning. U S News 67:
17 D 1 '69
Over-all solution; new Communist proposal. il
Newsweek 73:56 My 19 '69
Paris: circle in the square. il Newsweek 73:
36 F 3 '69
Paris; peace talks, and the flying of the
Viet Cong flag over Notre Dame. il Life
66:54-8 F 7 '69
Paris talks: and sometimes counsel take, and
sometimes tea. S. De Gramont. il N Y
Times Mag p28-9+ Mr 16 '69
Parting words. Newsweek 74:62 D 8 '69
Patient man in frustrating job: why Lodge
gets discouraged. U S News 67:18 N 24 '69
Pause that refreshes. il Newsweek 73:44-5
F 10 '69
Peace talks: progress, but—. il U S News
66:4 Ja 27 '69
[Plenary sessions] H. C. Lodge. See issues
of Department of state bulletin, January
25, 1969-
President Johnson welcomes new talks on
Viet-Nam; statement, January 16, 1969. L.
B. Johnson. Dept State Bul 60:91 F 3 '69
Reporter at large (cont) R. Shaplen. New
Yorker 45:36-40+ Jl 12 '69
Reports: Paris negotiations. R. Terrill. Atlan
223:18-22+ My '69

Statements on South Vietnam's participation
in the Paris peace talks; official statements
by the United States government and gov-
ernment of South Vietnam, November 26,
1968. Cur Hist 56:109+ F '69
Sudden breakthrough. il Newsweek 73:36-7
Ja 27 '69
[31st plenary session, August 13, 1969] P. C.
Habib. Dept State Bul 61:208-9 S 8 '69
Toward substance at the peace table. il
Time 93:28-9 My 30 '69
Under Secretary Richardson discusses Viet-
Nam peace talks with U.S.-U.S.S.R. rela-
tions; interview, April 30, 1969, ed. by J.
Kraft. E. L. Richardson. Dept State Bul
60:417-18 My 19 '69
U.S. Vietnam, and the elusive peace. il Sr
Schol 94:3-9 Ap 18 '69
Viet Nam war: movement in Paris. il Time
93:17-18 My 16 '69
What now in Vietnam? Nat R 21:413-21 My
6 '69; Discussion. 21:475-6. 526-7 My 20, Je 3
'69

Negotiation meetings, May 1968—Anecdotes, facetiae, satire, etc.

My table can lick your table. W. Zinsser. il
Life 66:14 Ja 24 '69

Personal narratives

Animal called POW: my four years in a Viet-
cong prison; ed. by W. Rogers. D. L. Pitzer.
il Look 33:46-51 F 18 '69
Conclusion at Khesanh. M. Herr. il Esquire
72:118-23+ O '69
Face to face with a soldier home from Viet-
nam. N. Vrotsos. Seventeen 28:86 My '69
I quit. D. Duncan. Ramp Mag 7:41-6 Ja 25
'69
I see death coming up the hill. Life 66:32
Je 27 '69
Letter from a Vietnam veteran; impressions
of service in the Eleventh armored calvary
regiment under George S. Patton, III. G. S.
Livingston. Sat R 52:22-3 S 20 '69; Reply.
W. C. Haponski. 52:29+ O 25 '69
Letters from Hamburger hill; to E. M. Ken-
nedy, ed. by N. Sheehan. Harper 239:40-
4+ N '69
Military half, by J. Schell. Review
Nat R 21:290-1 Mr 25 '69. S. C. Schueller
One man's battle; experience of A. Jaramillo.
il Time 93:15 Je 20 '69
R&R with a snake dancer. R. Starnes.
Field & S 74:14+ Je '69
Reporter at large; soldier government wit-
ness in court-martial proceedings against
four American soldiers in rape-murder case.
D. Lang. New Yorker 45:61-4+ O 18 '69
Return to Tuy Hoa. T. Fox. il Common-
weal 91:177-80+ N 7 '69
Two American POW's; interviews, ed. by
O. Fallaci. R. D. Ingvalson; R. F. Frish-
man. il Look 33:30-2+ Jl 15 '69
Vietnam: a degree of disillusion. L. Burrows.
il Life 67:66-75 S 19 '69
Vietnam: three who came home; ed. by J.
McGinniss. il Sat Eve Post 242:22-3+ F 8 '69

Photography

Massacre at Mylai; with exclusive pictures,
eyewitness accounts. Life 67:36-45 D 5 '69;
Discussion. 67:46-7 D 19 '69

Poetry

Little Tri and power. P. Barton. Sat R 52:17
Jl 26 '69
Poetry: how and why. J. Jerome. il Writers
Digest 49:16+ F '69

Press reports and censorship

Briefings: a ritual of noncommunication;
Time essay. Time 94:42-3 O 10 '69
Flak from officers; censorship complaints of
news staffers of the American forces Viet
Nam network. il Time 95:60 Ja 19 '70
Massacre story; Hip-pocket AP. il Newsweek
74:33-4 D 8 '69
Miscue on the massacre. Time 94:75 D '69
Pop me some dinks. O. Schell. New Repub
162:19-21 Ja 3 '70
Shape up or, . ; censorship at AFVN. il
Newsweek 75:41 Ja 12 '70
What's become of voluntary censorship? D.
Lawrence. U S News 67:92 S 8 '69
Who's up, who's down? New Repub 161:10
N 8 '69
Word from the front; the unreported war:
army vs. the press. T. Fox. Commonweal
90:485-6 Ag 8 '69

Prisoners and prisons

Animal called POW: my four years in a Vietcong prison; ed. by W. Rogers. D. L. Pitzer.
il Look 33:46-51 F 18 '69

VIETNAMESE war, 1957- —Strategy—*Continued*
Now a new kind of war; report from Vietnam. il U S News 66:28-30 My 26 '69
Playing games with the war; President Nixon's style. M. McGrory. America 121:152 S 13 '69
Problem of Vietnam. W. Lippmann. Newsweek 74:27 D 1 '69
Puzzle of the lull. il Time 94:32 Ag 8 '69
Question of belief in Hanoi, and at home. H. Sidey. il Life 67:4 O 10 '69
Question of casualties; U.S. maximum pressure strategy. il Newsweek 73:45 Je 9 '69
Right of the individual vs. the right of the group. H. Sidey. il Life 66:4 My 9 '69
Sands are running; costs of losing, plan for winning. Nat R 21:735-7 Jl 29 '69
Scuffling in Hanoi. il Newsweek 74:57 D 22 '69
Sorry you asked that. New Repub 161:7-8 Jl 19 '69
Steady on course. il Newsweek 74:42 Jl 28 '69
They may make it. S. Alsop. Newsweek 74:60 D 29 '69
U.S. Vietnam, and the elusive peace. il Sr Schol 94:3-9 Ap 18 '69
Vietnam: are there any lessons? T. M. Conrad. Commonweal 90:78-80 Ap 4 '69
Vietnam: as shooting dies down. il U S News 67:35 O 27 '69
Vietnam: Gordian knot. Commonweal 90:3-4 Mr 21 '69
Vietnam: the political crunch. Nat R 21:1100-1 N 4 '69
War: decision to lower the pressure. il Time 94:20 Jl 25 '69
War problems deepen as Nixon heads for Midway. il U S News 66:25-6 Je 9 '69
We are not Democrats, or Republicans; we are Americans; excerpts from address to House of representatives, November 13, 1969. R. M. Nixon. il U S News 67:68 N 24 '69
We could have won in Vietnam long ago. U. S. G. Sharp. Read Digest 94:118-23 My '69
What Secretary Laird learned in Vietnam; plan to withdraw American troops to be postponed. il U S News 66:26-7 Mr 24 '69
What U.S. plans after Midway. U S News 66:25 Je 16 '69
Whatever happened to: McNamara line in Vietnam? il U S News 66:12 Mr 31 '69
What's the answer to ABM and the war? interview. M. R. Laird. il U S News 66:30-6 Ap 7 '69
When Nixon talked to the Senate; excerpts from address, November 13, 1969. R. M. Nixon. U S News 67:69 N 24 '69
Where the reds are stopped in Vietnam. il U S News 67:37-9 Jl 28 '69
Who is prolonging the war? D. Lawrence. U S News 67:124 N 17 '69
Why Hanoi wants peace: White House view. il U S News 66:32-3 Ap 21 '69
Will the President's plan bring peace? with interview with E. Bunker, ed. by W. S. Merick. il U S News 67:45-9+ N 17 '69
Winding down the war on our own. H. Donovan. Life 67:42 O 24 '69

Television reports
See Television broadcasting—War news

War aims
Nixon's dilemma in the war; which way to move. il U S News 66:28-30 Mr 17 '69
Pullout from Vietnam; timetable for U.S. il U S News 66:36-7 Ja 27 '69
U.S. gains in the Vietnam war, a top envoy's view; excerpts from address, February 5, 1969. W. A. Harriman. U S News 66:18 F 17 '69
What U.S. should do about Vietnam; survey of key senators. il U S News 66:29-32 F 10 '69

Women and the war
Tense vigil of Mrs O'Grady: Maj John O'Grady missing in action. C. S. Wren. il Look 33:40-4 D 30 '69

VIETNAMESE war and college students. See College students and war
VIETNAMESE war as a campaign issue. See Campaign issues
VIETORISZ, Thomas
Harlem gets down to business. il por Bsns W p70-2 Ag 9 '69
VIETS, F. G. jr. See Hutchinson, G. L. jt. auth.
VIETTE, Andre
Oriental poppies. il Horticulture 47:36-7 Je '69
VIEUX CARRE. See New Orleans

VIEW finders
Accurate range-finding device. il Consumer Rep 34:109-10 Mr '69
New look for the Pentacon six; brightness of your groundglass. T. M. Morton. il Travel & Camera 32:106-7 F '69
Rangefinder with a plus; Rangematic distance finder. C. Conley. il Field & S 73:139 F '69
VIEWERS for transparencies. See Transparencies—Viewers
VIEWS of my father weeping; story. See Barthelme. D.
VIGELAND, Gustav
Vigeland in the viewfinder; D. Finn's photography of sculptures. M. R. Weiss. il Sat R 52:52-3 Ag 23 '69
VIGILANCE (psychology)
Averaged evoked responses in vigilance and discrimination: a reassessment. W. Ritter and H. G. Vaughan, jr. bibliog il Science 164:326-8 Ap 18 '69
VIGILANCE committees
See also
Jewish defense league
VIGLIONE, Gaetano T.
Flexible printed wiring. por Electr World 82:58-60 O '69
VIGLUCCI, Andrew T.
New era for Puerto Rico. Look 33:44 Mr 18 '69
VIGO COUNTY, Ind, public library, Terre Haute
Breaking the fine barrier. E. N. Howard. il ALA Bul 63:1541-5 D '69
Railroad car library planned in Terre Haute. Library J 94:488+ F 1 '69
Terre Haute: no one has asked; Young people's advisory committee for Railroad car library. E. N. Howard. il Wilson Lib Bul 43:888-92 My '69
Train wreck in Terre Haute; scrapped plans for youth library. G. R. Shields. il ALA Bul 63:981-4 Jl '69
VIGORELLI, Giancarlo
Czech crisis stymies European writers. H. R. Lottman. por Pub W 195:30-1 Mr 17 '69
VIGREN, David D.
Those sneaky little electric trollers. Pop Sci 195:94-7+ N '69
VIGUERIE, Richard A.
Outside handler. Nation 208:749 Je 16 '69
VIGUERS, Ruth Hill
Acceptance of the Regina medal for Bertha Mahony Miller. Horn Bk 45:516-24 O '69
Wonderful world of books. Parents Mag 44:42+ N '69
VIKINGS (football club) See Football clubs
VILA REYES, Juan
Un gran escándalo. por Newsweek 74:63 S 1 '69
Textile bubble bursts in Madrid. il por Bsns W p82+ S 20 '69
VILES, James
Vegetable gardening; with a point of view. il Home Gard 56:40-5+ Mr '69
VILLAGE libraries. See Libraries
VILLAGER industries
Fashionably poor. Forbes 104:72 S 15 '69
VILLAGES
Akenfield, by R. Blythe. Review
New Repub 161:23-4 O 4 '69. R. Starr
Villager's role in a half-century of change. J. Kolars. bibliog il Focus 19:8-11 Ap '69
VILLAGES, Restored
Restorations West. B. Belford. il Travel 132:56-60 N '69
Ulu Mau, a bit of old Hawaii. il Sunset 143:29 N '69
VILLAIN and the toy shop; drama. See Winther. B.
VILLAVERDE, Juan
Not so dim/bright future of Latin America. Américas 21:16-22 F '69
VILLEFRANCHE, France
Hotel welcome. A. Waugh. Nat R 21:753+ Jl 29 '69
VILLEFRANCHE-sur-mer. See Villefranche, France
VILLELLA, Edward
Why shouldn't parents say, sure, I'll let my son become a dancer. pors Life 66:58 Je 6 '69
about
Edward Villella. R. Poirier. il pors Vogue 153:192-5+ F 1 '69
Is this man the country's best athlete? D. Martin. il pors Life 66:48-54+ Je 6 '69
VILLET, Barbara
Children want classrooms alive with chaos. Life 66:50-2+ Ap 11 '69
VILLET, Grey
Threatened America; photographs. Life 67:33-43 Ag 1 '69
VILLIERS, Alan
In the wake of Darwin's Beagle. por Nat Geog 136:449-95 O '69

VIRGINIA—Description and travel—*Continued*
Virginia: the state that has—well, almost—everything. C. Ogburn, jr. il Holiday 46:46-9+ S '69

Historic houses, etc.

Compact circuit; history is alive and well in old Virginny. L. M. Rhodes. il Travel 132:28-33+ Jl '69
See also
Midlothian, Va.—Historic houses, etc.
Monticello (historic house)
Williamsburg

History

Virginia dynasties, by C. Dowdey. Review Nat R 21:708-9 Jl 15 '69. W. C. Wooldridge

Parks and reserves

Economic advantages of parklands to a community; excerpts from address. S. J. Prezioso. Parks & Rec 3:27+ O '68
Seashore state park. P. E. Woodall. il Travel 131:58-9 F '69

Politics and government

Bye, bye, Byrd. New Repub 161:10 Ag 2 '69
Old gang's fading fast in Byrdland; Democratic gubernatorial candidates. P. R. Wieck. New Repub 161:12-13 Jl 12 '69
South is developing a real two-party system; interview. A. L. Holton. U S News 67:40 N 17 '69
Three-ring circus; Democratic primary candidates. Newsweek 74:24-5 Jl 14 '69

VIRGINIA BEACH, Va.

Parks and playgrounds

Amphitheater rises from refuse. il Am City 84:74-5 D '69
VIRGINIA Thanksgiving festival. See Pageants
VIRGINITY
Case for virginity. J. Brothers. il Good H 168:46+ Je '69
In my opinion; virginity is an outmoded ideal. R. Maynard. Seventeen 28:228 F '69
VIRGO, David. See Hafner, S. S. jt. auth.
VIRUS and cancer. See Cancer—Causes
VIRUS diseases
Receptor site for a bacterial virus. R. Losick and P. W. Robbins. il Sci Am 221:120-4 bibliog(p 166) N '69
Viral infection across species barriers: reversible alteration of murine sarcoma virus for growth in cat cells. P. J. Fischinger and T. E. O'Connor. bibliog il Science 165:714-16 Ag 15 '69
See also
Cold (disease)
Virus research

Vaccines

Toward control of viral infections of man. M. R. Hilleman. bibliog il Science 164:506-14 My 2 '69
VIRUS research
Man vs. virus. Read Digest 94:127-9 Ap '69
Mutiny over methods; prevention vs. antiviral drugs. B. J. Culliton. il Sci N 96:148-9 Ag 23 '69
Second front in the war on viruses; developing antiviral drugs. il Bsns W p50+ Jl 5 '69
Toward control of viral infections of man. M. R. Hilleman. bibliog il Science 164:506-14 My 2 '69
VIRUSES
Defective virus a key. B. J. Culliton. il Sci N 96:308-9 O 4 '69
EB virus and leukemia. il Sci N 95:350-1 Ap 12 '69
Myxovirus envelope proteins: a directing influence on the fatty acids of membrane lipids. J. M. Tiffany and H. A. Blough. bibliog il Science 163:573-4 F 7 '69
Plus and minus single-stranded DNA separately encapsidated in adeno-associated satellite virions. H. D. Mayor and others. bibliog il Science 166:1280-2 D 5 '69
Thymus-dependent lymphocytes: destruction by lymphocytic choriomeningitis virus. M. Hanaoka and others. bibliog il Science 163:1216-19 Mr 14 '69
See also
Bacteriophages
Encephalomyelitis virus
Hepatitis virus
Herpes simplex virus
Herpesvirus
Influenza viruses
Leukemia viruses
Poliomyelitis virus
Simian viruses
Tumor viruses
Vaccinia viruses
Virus diseases
Virus research
VIRUSES, Oncogenic. See Tumor viruses
VIRUSES, Plant
Aphid transmission of tobacco mosaic virus. J. S. Lojek and G. B. Orlob. bibliog il Science 164:1407-8 Je 20 '69
Assembly of protein and nucleoprotein particles from extracted tobacco rattle virus protein and RNA. J. S. Semancik and D. A. Reynolds. bibliog il Science 164:559-60 My 2 '69
Nucleic acid-protein interactions in turnip yellow mosaic virus. J. M. Kaper. bibliog il Science 166:248-50 O 10 '69
Pathotoxin-induced disease resistance in plants. H. Wheeler and T. P. Pirone. bibliog il Science 166:1415-17 D 12 '69
Satellite-like particle of tobacco ringspot virus that resembles tobacco ringspot virus. I. R. Schneider. bibliog il Science 166:1627-9 D 26 '69
VISAS. See Passports
VISCOSITY
Viscosity of argon at high temperatures. R. A. Dawe and E. B. Smith. bibliog il Science 163:675-6 F 14 '69
See also
Blood—Viscosity
VISENTIN, Louis P. and Allen, J .M.
Allantoinase: association with amphibian hepatic peroxisomes. bibliog Science 163:1463-4 Mr 28 '69
VISES
Bulova's Roto-vise system. R. J. De Cristoforo. il Pop Sci 194:132-4 Je '69
VISHNEWSKI, Stanley
Dorothy Day: a sign of contradiction. Cath World 209:203-6 Ag '69
VISIBILITY at airports. See Airports—Visibility
VISION. See Sight
VISION (animals) See Sight (animals)
VISIT of Mother Cloud; drama. See Jennings, A.
VISITORS. See Guests
VISTA. See Volunteers in service to America
VISUAL acuity. See Sight
VISUAL adaptation. See Eye—Accommodation and refraction
VISUAL aids. See Audio-visual aids
VISUAL illusions. See Optical illusions
VISUAL instruction. See Audio-visual instruction
VISUAL perception. See Perception
VISUAL pigments
Visual pigment density in single primate foveal cones. W. H. Dobelle and others. bibliog il Science 166:1508-10 D 19 '69
VITAL statistics
See also
Longevity
Population
VITAMIN deficiency. See Diet, Deficient
VITAMINS
People need fertilizers too. R. Rodale. Org Gard & Farm 16:21-3 Ag '69
Vitamin-related anemias; report of meeting. F. Weber and R. E. Olson. Science 164:1311-12 Je 13 '69

Vitamin A

Survival of germfree rats without vitamin A. J. G. Bieri and others. il Science 163:574-5 F 7 '69
Vitamin A deficiency: effect on mosquito eye ultrastructure. J. D. Brammer and R. H. White. bibliog il Science 163:821-3 F 21 '69

Vitamin B₁

Thiamine release from nerve membranes by tetrodotoxin. Y. Itokawa and J. R. Cooper. bibliog il Science 166:759-61 N 7 '69
Thiamine triphosphate deficiency in subacute necrotizing encephalomyelopathy. J. R. Cooper and others. bibliog il Science 164:74-5 Ap 4 '69
See also
Choline

Vitamin B₂

Glutathione reductase: stimulation in normal subjects by riboflavin supplementation. E. Beutler. bibliog il Science 165:613-15 Ag 8 '69

Vitamin C

Ascorbic acid: cofactor in rabbit olfactory preparations. K. O. Ash. bibliog il Science 165:901-2 Ag 29 '69

VITAMINS—Vitamin C—*Continued*
L-Ascorbic acid synthesis in birds: phylogenetic trend. C. R. Chaudhuri and I. B. Chatterjee. bibliog il Science 164:435-6 Ap 25 '69
C, the vitamin with mystique. Mlle 70:189 N '69

Vitamin D

25-Hydroxycholecalciferol: direct effect on calcium transport. E. B. Olson and H. F. DeLuca. bibliog il Science 165:405-7 Jl 25 '69
25-Hydroxycholecalciferol: stimulation of bone resorption in tissue culture. C. L. Trummel and others. bibliog il Science 163:1450-1 Mr 28 '69

Vitamin K

Vitamin K and coumarin anticoagulants: dependence of anticoagulant effect on inhibition of vitamin K transport. J Lowenthal and H. Birnbaum. bibliog il Science 164:181-3 Ap 11 '69
Vitamin K, savior of bleeding babies. W. Garrison. il Todays Health 47:42-3+ S '69

VITICULTURE
Our grapes grow best on fir trees. J. F. Bucher. il Org Gard & Farm 16:59-61 F '69
Royal Riesling; greatest of grapes for warmweather wines. R. A. De Groot. House B 111:158+ My '69
6000 bottles of wine; excerpt from A farmhouse in Provence. M. R. Henry. Atlan 223:69-71 My '69
Wines of California. M. Demarest. il Travel & Camera 32:62-5+ Ag '69

VITKEVICH, Victor
Extraterrestrial civilization or a pulsating start? Space World F-4-64:36 Ap '69

VITREOUS humor
Collagen gels: design for a vitreous replacement. K. H. Stenzel and others. bibliog il Science 164:1282-3 Je 13 '69

VITUPERATION. See Invective

VIVANTE, Arturo
Adria; story. New Yorker 45:31-2 Mr 8 '69

VIVAS, Máximo J. Cerame-. See Cerame-Vivas, M. J

VIVEROS, O. H. and others
Quantal secretion from adrenal medulla: all-or-none release of storage vesicle content. bibliog Science 165:911-13 Ag 29 '69

VIVIAN, John
Strawberry barrels and wild strawberries. Org Gard & Farm 16:52-5 F '69

VIVISECTION
See also
Animal experimentation

VIYELLA International, limited
Rough sacking for Viyella chief. Bsns W p23 D 20 '69

VLACHOPOULOS, Constantin C.
Mission to the Middle East. V. S. Kearney. America 120:495-8 Ap 26 '69

VLADECK, Bruce
What a boy thinks: double dates. Seventeen 28:40 My '69

VOBORIL, Virginia V.
Good housekeeping's dessert of the month. See occasional issues of Good housekeeping

VOCABULARY tests
It pays to increase your word power. P. Funk. See issues of Reader's digest

VOCAL music
See also
Madrigals
Phonograph records—Vocal music

VOCAL organs. See Voice

VOCATION, Religious. See Vocation in religion

VOCATION in religion
Green light for experimentation. America 120:207 F 22 '69
That vocation puzzle. V. P. McCorry. America 120:718-19 Je 21 '69

VOCATIONAL education
Business and campus unrest; address, January 16, 1969. E. H. Wasson. Vital Speeches 35:335-8 Mr 15 '69
Eye on tomorrow's jobs. G. Venn. il Am Ed 5:12-15 Mr '69
Fourteen million vocational students by 1975. M. Russo. il Am Ed 5:10-11 Mr '69
Money in the classroom; corporations sponsor vocational education. il Forbes 103:70+ Ap 15 '69
Non-professional teachers enliven the subject matter; Project 400 to relate the world of work to classroom subject matter. J. Bahr. Clear House 43:494-6 Ap '69
Secondary school and occupational preparation. R. N. Evans. Ed Digest 34:20-3 My '69
Social context and vocational education. R. A. Gibboney. bibliog f Sch & Soc 97:28-31 Ja '69

Too much stress on college; annual report of the National advisory council on vocational education. il U S News 67:45-6 O 13 '69
Vital vocation. W. D. Boutwell. PTA Mag 64:32 O '69
Vocational education in a new comprehensive system. M. Feldman. Todays Ed 58:47-8 N '69
Vocational education unsuited for the socially disadvantaged. W. W. McKeever, jr. bibliog f Clear House 44:43-4 S '69
See also
Building—Study and teaching
Business education
Distributive education
Education, Cooperative
Home economics—Study and teaching
Industrial arts education
Technical education
Trade schools
United States—National advisory council on vocational education

Federal aid
Access to a future. L. A. Burkett. il Am Ed 5:2-3 Mr '69
Vocational education act of 1968. W. D. Boutwell. PTA Mag 63:29-30 Ja '69

VOCATIONAL guidance
Entering the world of work; with study-discussion program, by C. Smallenburg and H. Smallenburg. H. J. Reed. bibliog il PTA Mag 63:8-10. 35-6 Ap '69
Waves of the future: your career? address, May 13, 1969. J. D. Pecsok. Vital Speeches 35:553-6 Jl 1 '69
Why so many students are unhappy. D. Lawrence. U S News 67:84 Jl 21 '69
See also
Educational guidance
Occupations
Personnel service in education
Vocational education

VOCATIONAL literature
Availability and usefulness of occupational materials. R. R. Reilley. il Clear House 43:439-41 Mr '69

VOCATIONAL psychology
See also
Job satisfaction

VOCATIONAL schools. See Trade schools

VOCATIONS. See Occupations

VODKA
Heublein pours a potent sales mix; Smirnoff vodka's success in wines and pre-mixed cocktails. il Bsns W p76-7+ Je 14 '69

VOEGE, Richard B.
Innovating? Involve the student! bibliog f Clear House 43:543-6 My '69

VOEGELIN, Eric
Further critique of gnosticism. E. Sandoz. Nat R 21:32-3 Ja 14 '69

VOELZ, Herbert. See Kingsbury, E. W. jt. auth.

VOGEL, Ezra
Are we ready for China? Sat R 52:23-5 Mr 15 '69

VOGEL, J. C. and others
Carbon-14 trends in subfossil pine stubs. bibliog Science 166:1143-5 N 28 '69

VOGEL, Nancy
New TV shows fall '69. Writers Digest 49:62-5+ Je '69
Television and film writing (cont) por Writers Digest 49:24-9 F; 82-7 Ap; 66-71 Ag; 22+ O; 18-20+ D '69

VOICE
Is your heart in your voice? W. Redfield. Vogue 154:180-1+ N 1 '69
You can't teach a monkey how to talk. il Sci Digest 66:67-8 S '69
See also
Automatic speech recognition
Sound production by animals
Speech

VOICE analysis. See Voiceprints

VOICE prints. See Voiceprints

VOICE spectrograms. See Voiceprints

VOICE training
See also
Singing

VOICEPRINTS
Heart doctors heed telltale voice; coronary-prone pattern in voice. il Bsns W p 130 My 24 '69
Identification of a speaker by speech spectrograms; reliability for use as legal evidence. R. H. Bolt and others. bibliog il Science 166:338-43 O 17 '69
Trial by voiceprint; doubt about accuracy. Sci Am 221:54 D '69
Voice prints. R. E. Steinhauer. il Sat R 52:56-9 S 6 '69

VOIGHT, Jon
  V for Voight, ed. by E. Miller. pors Seventeen 28:148-9+ S '69
VOLCANI, B. E. See Nakajima, T. jt. auth.
VOLCANIC rocks. See Rocks, Igneous
VOLCANOES
  Active volcano is no place to picnic. H. C. Espy and L. Creamer. il Holiday 46:68-9+ D '69
  Iceland's thermal geology. J. Kane. il Natur Hist 78:48-51 Ja '69
  Menace of extinct volcanoes; reprint. H. Tazieff. il UNESCO Courier 22:9 Ag '69
  Mountains that blow their tops. N. F. Busch. il Read Digest 95:127-32 Ag '69
  Volcanoes, from dormant to deadly. J. Daugherty and M. Daugherty. il Sci Digest 65:86-8 Ap '69
    See also
  Cotopaxi (volcano)
  Kilauea (crater)
  Lava
  Thera (island)
VOLCHOK, Herbert L. See Kleinman, M. T. jt. auth.
VOLCKER, Paul A.
  Reassuring gold men. por Bsns W p 120 Ja 25 '69
VOLKERSZ, Evert
  Grievance. bibliog ALA Bul 63:1566-9 D '69
VOLKSPLANE. See Airplanes
VOLKSWAGEN. See Automobiles. Foreign
VOLKSWAGEN engines. See Automobile engines
VOLKSWAGEN of America, incorporated
  Beetle finds U.S. tougher to chew. il Bsns W p40-1 O 11 '69
  Buy-American bug. Newsweek 73:99 My 26 '69
  Dent in VW's bumper sales. il Bsns W p44-5 Jl 12 '69
  He's got the bug. L. Levine. il Motor T 21:31-3 My '69
  Today the cheap car, tomorrow the works. S. Zalaznick. il Fortune 79:116-17+ Mr '69
VOLKSWAGENWERKE, gmbh. See Automobile industry and trade—Germany (Federal Republic)
VOLOSHEN, Nathan
  Call Marty. Newsweek 74:36 O 27 '69
  McCormack faces life. por Newsweek 74:36 N 3 '69
  Murky men from the Speaker's office. W. Lambert. il por Life 67:52-4+ O 31 '69
  Scandals in Congress: the record. il por U S News 67:25-7 N 10 '69
  Speaker's family. por Time 94:18+ O 31 '69
  Voloshen connection. il Time 94:26-7 O 24 '69
VOLPE, John Anthony
  Coming: streamliners without wheels. por Pop Sci 195:51-5+ D '69
  How to cure traffic jams; interview. pors U S News 66:62-7 Je 9 '69
  Secretary Volpe; interview. New Yorker 45:29-31 D 20 '69
  Urban transportation tomorrow; with biographical sketch. por Am City 84:59-62 N '69
    about
  Now Volpe tackles the air traffic snarl. il Bsns W p 116-17 My 24 '69
  Roadmaster Volpe. New Repub 160:7 My 10 '69
  Volpe assesses potential of air cushion vehicle. Aviation W 90:56 My 5 '69
  Volpe picks a team. il por Bsns W p68 F 22 '69
  Volpe seen backing SST prototype work. H. D. Watkins. Aviation W 90:30 Mr 17 '69
VOL'SKII, Nikolai Vladislavovich
  [Book review] G. F. Hudson. Commonweal 90:210-11 My 2 '69
VOLTAGE minders. See Voltmeters
VOLTAGE regulators
  Cure for some TV picture problems? Nope: Perma-power automatic voltage regulator. Consumer Rep 34:359 Jl '69
  Series-pass regulators. G. V. Fay. il Electr World 81:48+ Mr '69
  Voltage regulator for enlarger lamp. R. A. Wolff. il Electr World 82:72 S '69
VOLTAIRE, François Marie Arouet de
  Voltaire, by T. Besterman. Review
    New Yorker 45:71-5 Ja 10 '70. P. Gay
    Newsweek por 74:124+ N 24 '69. R. A. Sokolov
    Time por 94:106 N 28 '69
VOLTAMMETRY
  This watchdog is electrolytic; E-cell used in coulometry. il Bsns W p84-5 Ag 2 '69
VOLTMETERS
  Build a voltminder for your car. R. F. Graf and G. J. Whalen. il Pop Sci 195:158-61+ O '69

  Build your own tune-up meter. B. C. Snow. il Mech Illus 65:108-11+ O '69
VOLTOHMMETERS
  Delta products model 3000 FET V.O.M. il Electr World 81:69 Mr '69
VOLUMETRIC analysis
    See also
  Titration
VOLUNTARY health agencies. See Health agencies, Voluntary
VOLUNTARY poverty. See Poverty, Voluntary
VOLUNTARY social agencies. See Social agencies, Voluntary
VOLUNTEER army. See Military service, Voluntary
VOLUNTEER artists aides, Seattle. See Volunteer service
VOLUNTEER firemen. See Firemen
VOLUNTEER service
  Another type of student activism; helping people. il U S News 67:32-4 O 27 '69
  Better than riots; Brazilian student volunteers in Amazonia. il Time 93:42+ Mr 21 '69
  Compassion power; on tour with Mrs Nixon. L. Hershey. il Ladies Home J 86:88+ S '69
  Courtroom saviors. G. Town. il Har Yrs 9:35-7 Je '69
  Crash attack on prejudice; suggestions for a parish effort during Lent. M. Hellwig. America 120:193-4 F 15 '69
  Is mom an under-achiever? farm and ranch women who are putting their ideas to work. L. Lane. il Farm J 93:102-3+ F '69
  Mike Frome; President's call for volunteer effort in behalf of the national welfare. M. Frome. Am For 75:7+ S '69
  Needed; volunteers who care. G. W. Weinstein. Parents Mag 44:52-3 Ag '69
  Older people as a resource. il Aging 175:8-9 My '69
  Opera's angels; SOA's Volunteer artists aides. D. W. Jones. il Opera N 34:22-4 S 6 '69
  Over the weekend, 16 to 18 miles of new trail built. il Sunset 143:58+ S '69
  Power of a woman. P. Nixon. Ladies Home J 86:93 S '69
  Somebody needs you. E. D. Koontz. Ladies Home J 86:74 O '69
  Summer jobs. R. Tunley. Seventeen 28:141+ F '69
  Teens who care: potential mental health manpower. E. E. Staton and others. Ment Hy 53:200-4 Ap '69
  Time for giving. il Good H 169:38+ N '69
  Under twenty-one; volunteer work. S. Reice. il McCalls 96:60+ My '69
  Where student activists are VIP's; Volunteer Illini projects. il Am Ed 5:27 Ag '69
    See also
  Community service
  Health workers, Volunteer
  Hospitals, Psychiatric—Volunteer workers
  Operation bookshelf
  Social workers, Volunteer
  Volunteer workers in education
VOLUNTEER service, International
  Exercise of social responsibility; Coordinating committee for international voluntary service. A. Gillette. Sch & Soc 97:222-3 Ap '69
    See also
  United States—Peace corps
VOLUNTEER system, Military. See Military service, Voluntary
VOLUNTEER workers. See Volunteer service
VOLUNTEER workers in education
  Mom to the rescue. D. Gardner. il Am Ed 5:25 D '69
  They can't say no; neighborhood volunteers hired by the Newark city schools. il Am Ed 5:28 My '69
VOLUNTEERS in service to America
  Appalachia: who's helping whom? M. Rzeczkowski. il Cath World 210:155-8 Ja '70
  Five-year report on the domestic Peace corps. il Todays Health 47:14-15 N '69
  They stayed; Vista teachers in Appalachia. S. Crowell. il Am Ed 5:22-5 Ag '69
  View from VISTA; Bonney Smith and Carla Bryson in Boston. il Newsweek 74:50+ D 1 '69
  VISTA: service with vision. F. Tighe. il Har Yrs 9:46-8 O '69
VOLVO (automobile) See Automobiles, Foreign
VOLYNOV, Boris
  Cosmonaut 14: Soyuz-5 Commander Boris Volynov, cosmonaut 16: Yevgeny Khrunov. il por Space World F-4-64:32 Ap '69

VON BRAUN, Wernher
[Articles on space technology and space flight] See issues of Popular science monthly
Saturn/Apollo as a transportation system. por Bul Atom Sci 25:74-8 S '69
Why space exploration is vital to man's future. Space World F-9-69:31-3 S '69

about
Harvest of Operation Paperclip. il pors. Newsweek 74:10 Jl 7 '69
Who made it possible; men behind the moon program. il por Time 94:29 Jl 18 '69

VON BUCHAU, Stephanie
Western opera theater: it works. Hi Fi 19: MA18-19 S '69

VON DECHEND, Hertha. See De Santillana, G. jt. auth.

VONDER HAAR, T. H. and Suomi, V. E.
Satellite observations of the earth's radiation budget. bibliog Science 163:667-9 F 14 '69

VON DEWITZ, Arden
Marine paintings of Arden von Dewitz. J. Lovoos. il por Am Artist 33:54-60+ S '69

VON DREELE, W. H.
Amuck; Jane Jacobs, city planner; Talking dirty; poems. Nat R 21:576, 578, 605 Je 17 '69
Criminal justice; poem. Nat R 21:318 Ap 8 '69
Cruelest thing; Moonstruck; poems. Nat R 21:840, 844 Ag 26 '69
Cryptogram; Here come de judge; poems. Nat R 21:214, 220 Mr 11 '69
Glamour issues; Urban renewal; poems. Nat R 21:370, 374 Ap 22 '69
God bless our insect friends; But there is oil there; poems. Nat R 21:1206, 1208 D 2 '69
Grey eminence; Toward a unitary state; poems. Nat R 21:996, 1000 O 7 '69
Inevitability of Teddy; poem. Nat R 21:61 Ja 28 '69
Last act; Great put-on; Minneapolis elects a cop; poems. Nat R 21:627, 632, 633 Jl 1 '69
Mailer for mayor? Death and transfiguration; Timothy Leary beats the rap; poems. Nat R 21:523, 524, 528 Je 3 '69
Mighty middle; Dr Goldwater, call surgery; Ennui; poems. Nat R 21:1098, 1102, 1105 N 4 '69
Milton Friedman knows best (I hope) poem. Nat R 21:1251 D 16 '69
Nixon at the tiller; poem. Nat R 21:1054 O 21 '69
No escape; poem. Nat R 21:1254 D 16 '69
Positive thinking; And the beat goes on; poems. Nat R 21:1153, 1156 N 18 '69
Rhodesia, rampant; poem. Nat R 21:686 Jl 15 '69
Running with Lindsay; poem. Nat R 21:1048 O 21 '69
Show us a sign; Poor baby; poems. Nat R 21:887, 888 S 9 '69
Sky is falling; Happy New Year, Mr Nixon; poems. Nat R 21:16, 25 Ja 14 '69
Smile, tentatively; poem. Nat R 21:736 Jl 29 '69
Straight talk; poem. Nat R 21:266 Mr 25 '69
Suicide note in the form of a sonnet found on the asphyxiated body of a famous liberal; Hindsight; poems. Nat R 21:104, 106 F 11 '69
Teddy on TV; On the passing of princes; Three cheers for Prouty; If somebody doesn't stop this thing. I'll pull the cord; poems. Nat R 21:784, 787, 791, 805 Ag 12 '69
Tee hee; American dilemma; Reluctant Santa Claus; poems. Nat R 21:1302, 1308, 1316 D 30 '69
There's something about a liberal; Pusey's soliloquy; Bright side; poems. Nat R 21: 475, 476, 478 My 20 '69
Thoughts on watching a Harvard dean being expelled from his quarters; Thumbing home; poems. Nat R 21:422, 424 My 6 '69
Under the double standard; Federal money; poems. Nat R 21:944, 947 S 23 '69
What a way to go; We'll be watching, Mr Finch; poems. Nat R 21:157, 160 F 25 '69
Yumping yiminy; poem. Nat R 21:58 Ja 28 '69

VON ECKARDT, Wolf
Sad state of federal architecture. Sat R 52: 20-1 Je 7 '69

VO-nguyen-Giap
General Giap, by R. J. O'Neill. Review Sat R 52:35 O 11 '69. D. M. Grady

VON HELSING, Alicia
Yet another extract from the memoirs of a lover lover; story. Harp Baz 102:84 Mr '69

VON HOFFMAN, Nicholas
Columbia and the closed corporation. Commonweal 89:566-9 Ja 31 '69

about
From-the-hip delivery. por Newsweek 74: 112+ O 27 '69
Middle-aged rebel. por Time 95:33-4 Ja 5 '70

VON KAENEL, Karen and Zitek, Edythe
Sex education in the sixth grade; interview. Ed Digest 34:17-19 F '69

VONNEGUT, Kurt. 1922-
Carols for Christmas, 1969: Tonight, if I will let me. N Y Times Mag p5 D 21 '69
Excelsior! We're going to the moon! Excelsior. N Y Times Mag p9-11 Jl 13 '69
There's a maniac loose out there. Life 67: 53-4+ Jl 25 '69

about
Authors & editors. A. Johnston. por Pub W 195:20-1 Ap 21 '69
Forty-six, and trusted. por Newsweek 73:79 Mr 3 '69
Gentleness and a stylish sense of the ridiculous. W. Coffey. Commonweal 90:347-8 Je 6 '69
Literary horizons. G. Hicks. Sat R 52:25 Mr 29 '69
Now generation knew him when. W. Sheed. il pors Life 67:64-6+ S 12 '69
Requiem to Billy Pilgrim's progress. W. Sheed. Life 66:9 Mr 21 '69
Sci-fi and Vonnegut. J. M. Crichton. New Repub 160:33-5 Ap 26 '69

VON REZZORI, Gregor
Memoirs of an anti-Semite. New Yorker 45: 42-52+ Ap 26 '69

VON SCHLEINITZ, René
German genre paintings from the Von Schleinitz collection. T. Atkinson. Antiques 96:712-16 N '69

VON SOCHOCKY, Sabin A.
Early days of radioactivity in industry. por F. E. Wall. il Chem 42:17-19 Ap '69

VON WIEGAND, Charmion
Adamantine way. Art N 68:38-41+ Ap '69

VOODOOISM
Invisibles, by F. Huxley. Review Newsweek il 73:121-2 Ap 14 '69. A. Grant

VORENBERG, James
Is the Court handcuffing the cops? N Y Times Mag p32-3+ My 11 '69

VORIS, Harold K. See Clark, W. C. jt. auth.

VOROBYOV, E. and Smirenny, L.
Radiation on the lunar path. Space World F-4-64:34-5 Ap '69

VORSPAN, Albert
How James Forman lost his cool but saved religion in 1969. Chr Cent 86:1042 Ag 6 '69
Struggle for racial sanity. Sat R 52:32-3 Ja 25 '69

VORSTER, Balthazar Johannes
Fight goes on. il por Time 94:36 O 24 '69

VOSTI, Kenneth L. See Lindberg, L. H. jt. auth.

VOTERS
See also
Suffrage

VOTERS, Registration of
Mississippi ballot box. J. W. Lyon. Sat R 52:20-1 My 17 '69

VOTING
See also
Literacy tests (election law)
Referendum
Suffrage
United Nations—Voting
Voters, Registration of

Literacy tests
See Literacy tests (election law)

VOTING, Fraudulent. See Elections—Corrupt practices

VOTING age. See Suffrage; Suffrage—United States

VOTING machines
Punch-card voting may have a hole in it; back-room jugglers could change computerized ballot count. il Bsns W p38 Jl 19 '69

VOTING records, Congressmen. See Congressmen

VOTING rights act of 1965. See Election laws—United States

VOTOMATIC. See Voting machines

VOYAGES
Across the Atlantic in a twenty-foot open boat. W. E. Verity. il Pop Sci 195:80-4+ D '69
Houseboat to Acapulco. P. Smith. il Motor B 124:66-7 Ag '69
In the wake of Darwin's Beagle. A. Villiers. il Nat Geog 136:449-95 O '69
Record passage; transatlantic sailing of E. Tabarly in his trimaran. A. Colas. il Yachting 125:58-60+ Ap '69

VOYAGES—*Continued*
Stoned in the cradle of the deep. T. O.
Orlowski. il Esquire 72:248-9+ D '69
Stornoway progress report. M. Petersen. il
Motor B 124:52-5+ D '69
Third time lucky; Tzu Hang braves Cape
Horn. M. Smeeton. il Yachting 126:65-7+
D '69 (to be cont)
See also
Cruising
Northwest Passage
Ocean travel
Ra expedition, 1969
Whaling
VOYAGES, imaginary
See also
Space flight in literature
VOYAGES around the world
5 1/2 years before the mast; voyage of A.
Eddy. il Time 93:40-1 F 7 '69
Magellan's voyage; a narrative account of
the first circumnavigation; excerpts, tr.
by R. A. Skelton. A. Pigafetta. il Am Heritage 20:62-75 O '69
Magic of serendipity. E. J. Hodges. Horn
Bk 45:436-40 Ag '69
Mutiny of the mind; Crowhurst's tragic end
of round-the-world yacht race. il Time 94:
45 Ag 8 '69
'Round the world, nonstop and singlehanded.
E. F. Haylock. il Motor B 124:75+ Ag '69
Rounding Cape Horn; excerpt from My lively lady. A. Rose. il Yachting 125:54-5+ Mr
'69
Sea lover; unknown fate of D. Crowhurst.
il Newsweek 74:32 Ag 11 '69
Travels with Magellan. Newsweek 74:108+ O
20 '69
West to the Orient; Magellan's voyage. A.
Villiers. il Sat R 52:21-3+ D 20 '69
With the sun around the world. H. Rahlff. il
Yachting 125:46-8+ F '69
World-roaming teen-ager sails on. R. L. Graham. il Nat Geog 135:449-93 Ap '69
VOYAGEURS. See French Canadians
VOYAT, Gilbert
IQ: God-given or man-made? Sat R 52:73-
5+ My 17 '69; Same abr. Ed Digest 35:1-
4 O '69
VREDEVOOGD, John
Towards a movable, livable mobile home. il
Arch Forum 130:58-61 Ap '69
VRIJBURG, Jos
Post-marital priesthood; with editorial comment. F. Franck. Commonweal 89:720, 724-6
Mr 14 '69
VROTSOS, Neal
Face to face with soldier home from Vietnam.
por Seventeen 28:86 My '69
VULCAN (intramercurial planet) See Planets
VULGARITY
World of bad taste; view of Gillo Dorfles. il
Newsweek 75:86+ Ja 19 '70
VULLIAMY, Justin
Clockmaker and cabinetmaker. N. Goodison.
il Antiques 95:825-9 Je '69
VULTURES
See also
Turkey buzzards
VYKLICKY, L. and others
Primary afferent depolarization evoked by a
painful stimulus. bibliog Science 165:184-6
Jl 11 '69

W

WABC (radio station) See Radio stations
WINB (radio station) See Radio stations. Short
wave
WMCA (radio station) See Radio stations
WPIX-TV. See Television stations
W. R. Grace and company. See Grace, W. R,
and company
WWEMA. See Water and wastewater equipment manufacturers association
WAALAND, J. Robert, and Branton, Daniel
Gas vacuole development in a blue-green
alga. bibliog Science 163:1339-41 Mr 21 '69
WACHOVIA corporation
Merchant of money. R. Levy. Duns R 93:57+
F '69
WADDELL, Theodore
Neon city. Arch Forum 130:68-73 Ap '69
WADDLES, Charleszetta
Mother Waddles; the gentle warrior. J. K.
Davis. il pors Life 66:87-9 Mr 21 '69
WADE, Mel
Year-round public tennis club. Parks & Rec
4:33-4 Jl '69

WADSWORTH, Bill
Add action to your archery program. por
Camp Mag 41:14-15 F '69
WADSWORTH, Charles
Answer is chamber music! Hi Fi 19:MA9+
S '69
WADSWORTH, Nelson
Dusty secrets of Hogup cave. il Sci Digest
65:34-8 Mr '69
New light on snakebite. Outdoor Life 143:47-
9+ Mr '69
WADSWORTH atheneum, Hartford, Conn.
American Atheneum. il Newsweek 73:88 F 24
'69
Paintings at the Wadsworth atheneum. P. O.
Marlow. il Antiques 96:745-53 N '69
Sprouting a new wing. il Time 93:68 F 28 '69
WAFFLES
Learning to cook: pancakes and waffles. il
Am Home 72:72 Ja '69
Two tasty waffle departures. Sunset 143:101
Ag '69
WAGE agreements. See Trade agreements
WAGE bargaining. See Collective bargaining
WAGE differentials
Area wages and living costs. J. N. Houff. il
Mo Labor R 92:43-6 Mr '69
Geographic wage patterns in the Chicago labor market; excerpt from Spatial wage differentials in a large city market. A. Rees.
Mo Labor R 92:53-5 Mr '69
Intraoccupational wage dispersion in metropolitan areas, 1967-68; with tables. J. E.
Buckley. Mo Labor R 92:24-9 S '69
Wage differentials in the building trades.
A. Rose. il Mo Labor R 92:14-17 O '69
WAGE incentives. See Incentives in industry
WAGE payment plans
Negotiations and wage calendar for 1969;
with tables. C. T. Ward and W. M. Davis.
Mo Labor R 92:52-64 Ja '69
Protecting the paychecks of victims of technology; earnings protection plan of USW
and steel industry. Bsns W p98 Ag 16 '69
See also
Incentives in industry
WAGE-price policy. See Price regulation by
government
WAGENER, Karl
Bottled art. B. Notts. il Design 70:20-2 Sum
'69
WAGER cups. See Cups
WAGES
Foreign labor briefs. See issues of Monthly
labor review
See also
Exploitation
Income
Labor cost
Non-wage payments
Overtime
Profit sharing
Salaries

Annual wage

Guaranteeing wages: a modest proposal. J.
Kesselman. Commonweal 89:700-3 Mr 7 '69;
Reply with rejoinder. H. Gallagher. 90:93+
Ap 11 '69
See also
Negative income tax

Cost of living adjustments

Report on wage developments in manufacturing, 1968; with tables. J. Kinyon. Mo Labor
R 92:33-9 Ag '69

Economic aspects

Price rise vs. income rise: here's the way
you come out. il U S News 66:36 F 17 '69
Would guidelines work better? with editorial
comment. Bsns W p 134-6, 172 O 18 '69

Statistics

See also
Wage differentials

Canada

Canada's push for guidelines. U S News 66:
87 F 10 '69
Canadian unions seize initiative; drive for
wage parity with U.S. workers. Bsns W
p85+ Ja 18 '69

Great Britain

Britain's managers get a raise. Bsns W p40+
Ap 12 '69
See also
Equal pay for equal work

United States

Budgets for city families: Do wages lag badly? America 120:384 Ap 5 '69
Challenge for unions: how to top the raises
already given. U S News 67:73-9 D 22 '69

WAINWRIGHT, Loudon—*Continued*
Profound lesson for the living. Life 67:36-43 N 21 '69
WAINWRIGHT, Teddy
When rock buffs go marchin' in. Life 67:10 Ag 8 '69
WAIOKEOLA nursery school, Honolulu. See Nursery schools
WAITE, Paul J. and Lamoureux, C. E.
Corn striations in the Charles City tornado in Iowa. Weatherwise 22:54-9 Ap '69
WAITING for daddy; story. See Meeter, G.
WAITING-line theory. See Queuing theory
WAKAIZUMI, Kei
Japan beyond 1970. For Affairs 47:509-20 Ap '69
WAKASUGI, Sueyuki
Japan's trade giant picks old U.S. hand. por Bsns W p 108+ My 24 '69
WAKEFERN food corporation
House divided; success breeds conflicts in cooperative retail groups. Forbes 103:32-3 Je 15 '69
WAKEFIELD, Dan
Movies. See issues of Atlantic
War at home. Atlan 224:119-24 O '69
WAKEFIELD, Mass.

Social conditions
Town fights back against the teen-age drug epidemic. C. Remsberg and B. Remsberg. Good H 168:80-1+ Je '69
WAKEFULNESS. See Insomnia
WAKING. See Sleep
WALD, George
America's my home. Not my business, my home. Bul Atom Sci 25:29-31 My '69
Generation in search of a future; address, March 4, 1969. Vital Speeches 35:410-13 Ap 15 '69; Same with title Our business is with life. Redbook 133:68 Ag '69; Excerpts. New Yorker 45:29-31 Mr 22 '69
Therefore choose life; interview, ed. by T. Wicker. il por McCalls 97:92-3+ D '69
What's bothering the students? excerpts from address, March 4, 1969. por Chem 42:1+ My '69

about
George Wald: the man, the speech. R. Todd. il pors N Y Times Mag p28-9+ Ag 17 '69
Innocents. K. Crawford. Newsweek 73:42 My 19 '69
Missing from the Record. New Repub 160:8-9 My 17 '69
WALDEN, Daniel
Teaching Negro history: one white experience. por Sch & Soc 97:232-3 Ap '69
WALDMAN, Anne
To be a poet; with poem. S. Weller. por Mlle 70:90, 126-7+ D '69
WALDMAN, Eric
[Book review] America 120:226-7 F 22 '69
WALDMAN, Max
Illusions etched in anguish; photographs. por Life 67:60-66B D 12 '69
WALDMEIR, Pete, and Ronberg, Gary
Stadiums aren't for sleeping. Sports Illus 31:28-9 O 20 '69
WALDOFF, Leon
Prufrock's defenses and our response. bibliog f Am Imago 26:182-93 Sum '69
WALDROP, Keith
Chronicle of younger poets. J. Atlas. Poetry 113:431 Mr '69
WALES, Prince of (title)
Will the Welsh welch on the prince of Wales? D. Hart-Davis. il Holiday 45:16+ Je '69
WALES, Princes of. See Princes of Wales
WALES, H. Elliot
Trustee: reaching the advantaged. por Wilson Lib Bul 43:859 My '69
WALES
Wales? J. Morris. il Horizon 11:26-9+ Wint '69

Description and travel
In search of the Welsh. H. Fast. Esquire 72:142+ D '69
One Welshman's Wales. G. Thomas. il Travel & Camera 32:64-9+ Je '69
Wales; with photographs by Lord Snowdon. Look 33:68-73 Je 24 '69

Nationalism
Who cares about Wales? I care. R. Burton. il Look 33:74-7 Je 24 '69
Will the Welsh welch on the prince of Wales? D. Hart-Davis. il Holiday 45:16+ Je '69

Photographs
Portfolio of Welsh photographs. B. Davidson. Horizon 11:30-9 Wint '69

WALK, Neal
Take a Walk. H. L. Masin. il por Sr Schol 94:25 F 7 '69
WALK in the spring rain; story. See Maddux, R.
WALKER, Alexandra
Special tools for special jobs. Am Home 72:24 Mr '69
WALKER, Biron
Coming clean; poem. Commonweal 89:594 F 7 '69
WALKER, Charls Edward
Man to watch in Washington. M. Seeger. por Duns R 94:42-3 O '69
Reassuring gold men. por Bsns W p 120 Ja 25 '69
Treasury's savvy second man. por Bsns W p56-7 Jl 5 '69
WALKER, Cora
Pride of five women. R. Hochstein. il por Good H 168:87+ Je '69
WALKER, Daniel
Dissent and law enforcement; excerpts from report Rights in conflict. Cur 103:33-40 Ja '69

about
Confrontation at the Conrad Hilton; excerpts from the Walker commission report. Rights in conflict. il Trans-Action 6:37-49 Ja '69
WALKER, David
Mother Nature vs. juvenile delinquency. Field & S 73:60-3+ Mr '69
WALKER, David (editor of Yale reports)
Freedom to view. Commonweal 89:500-2 Ja 17 '69
WALKER, Franklin D. and Hild, W. J.
Neuroglia electrically coupled to neurons. bibliog Science 165:602-3 Ag 8 '69
WALKER, James W.
Forecasting manpower needs. bibliog f Harvard Bsns R 47:152-4+ Mr '69
WALKER, Jeanne Murray
Bertha; poem. Chr Cent 86:143 Ja 29 '69
WALKER, Jerry L.
Bridges to poetry. Sr Schol 94:Schol Teach 13-14 F 14 '69
WALKER, Lester
I call it all-in-one turniture. pors Pop Sci 195:152-7 Jl '69
WALKER, Michael J.
Endangered wildlife. Parks & Rec 3:10-12+ N '68
How goes the battle of the whooping crane? reprint. Sci Digest 65:15-18 F '69
I'm a prairie dog. Am For 75:35+ Mr '69
Mystery of migration. Am For 75:32-5+ N '69
WALKER, Norman
Romantic poet, a sculptor in space. K. Cunningham. il por Dance Mag 43:42-5 D '69
World of dance. W. Terry. il Sat R 52:54-5 Ag 23 '69
WALKER, Richard
Planning a backwoods experience. Field & S 73:64-5+ Ap '69
WALKER, Richard L.
[Book review] America 120:225-6 F 22 '69
WALKER, Robert S. See Eshleman, E. D. jt. auth.
WALKER, Ted
Cremation; story. New Yorker 45:33-7 Mr 1 '69
Donovan's boots; story. New Yorker 45:51-3 N 8 '69
Harpooning; poem. New Yorker 45:42 O 4 '69
WALKER, Thomas J.
Acoustic synchrony: two mechanisms in the snowy tree cricket. bibliog Science 166:891-4 N 14 '69
WALKER art center, Minneapolis
Museum without walls. il Newsweek 74:93-4 Jl 14 '69
WALKER CAY. See Bahama Islands
WALKING
Arctic walk; walking trip from Alaska's Brooks Range to Barter Island. J. P. Milton. il Natur Hist 78:44-53 My '69
For a real change, try hiking. il Changing T 23:37-8 Jl '69
Knuckle-walking and the problem of human origins. R. H. Tuttle. bibliog il Science 166:953-61 N 21 '69
Loneing it is the only way. K. Schwenke. il Field & S 74:46-7+ Jl '69
Mother Nature vs. juvenile delinquency. D. Walker. il Field & S 73:60-3+ Mr '69
Sport for all seasons. A. Lindstrom. il Parents Mag 44:50-1+ Ag '69
Utah's Alta has good hiking. il Sunset 143:42+ Jl '69
Vacationing in the wilderness. P. Plawin. il Bet Hom & Gard 47:66-7 Je '69
Walk on shorter legs. P. Mayer. il Har Yrs 9:22-3 Je '69

WALKING—*Continued*
Walking, walking, walking. il Mlle 68:234-5
Ap '69
See also
Trails
WALKING catfish. See Catfishes
WALKING horses. See Horses
WALKING truck. See Man amplifiers
WALKS (paths)
Our third-purpose walk. O. Raney. il Org
Gard & Farm 16:114-15 Mr '69
Step from the car in comfort; brick walks. il
Home Gard 56:13 F '69
See also
Garden walks
WALKS, Concrete. See Pavements, Concrete
WALKS for development. See American free-
dom from hunger foundation
Die WALKURE; opera. See Wagner, R.
WALKWAYS, Elevated. See Sidewalks, Ele-
vated
WALL, A. E. P.
Diocesan press. America 120:220 F 22 '69
about
Baltimore's Wall. S. J. Adamo. America 120:
568-9 My 10 '69
WALL, Florence E.
Early days of radioactivity in industry. por
Chem 42:17-19 Ap '69 (to be cont)
WALL, James M.
Film festival farrago. Chr Cent 86:1455-6 N
12 '69
Movies (cont) Chr Cent 86:155 Ja 29 '69
WALL, Sir John
British computers: we will survive. J. Ross-
Skinner. por Duns R 94:62-4+ D '69
WALL, Patricia
Patricia Wall's enlistment. por Time 94:20 O
24 '69
WALL coverings
Fabric hang-up. il Mlle 68:192-4 Mr '69
Fabrication; how to make up a room out of
whole cloth. P. Bartlett. il Mlle 68:106-7 Mr
'69
Those way-out wall coverings. D. Huff. il
Pop Sci 194:136-8+ My '69
WALL gardens. See Gardens, Rock
WALL hangings
Fabric of construction; exhibit at Museum
of modern art, New York. L. Bourgeois. il
Craft Horiz 29:30-5 Mr '69
Mural is . . . story of a stitchery mural and
a sixth grade class at the Anne Beers
elementary school, Washington, D.C. S.
Battist. il Sch Arts 68:24-5 My '69
Rya pillows and hangings. J. Roehrig. il Sch
Arts 68:11 My '69
WALL painting. See Mural painting and decora-
tion
WALL safes. See Safes
WALL street. See New York (city)—Streets
WALL Street Journal
How now, Dow Jones? il Time 93:46+ Mr 28
'69
WALLACE, Anthony Francis Clarke
Ghost dance and cargo cult. P. Farb. il Hori-
zon 11:63 Spr '69
WALLACE, Charles
Television and film writing. N. Vogel. Writers
Digest 49:24-9 F '69
WALLACE, Elspeth, and Townes, B. D.
Dual role of comforter and bereaved. bibliog
Ment Hy 53:327-32 Jl '69
WALLACE, George Corley
Br'er rabbit Wallace. S. Alsop. Newsweek 74:
96 Jl 14 '69
George Wallace's goals for '72. il por U S
News 66:39 Je 9 '69
George Wallace's target: 1970, 1972; or both?
por U S News 67:14 D 15 '69
Mr Nixon's horrible shadow. S. Alsop. News-
week 74:128 N 10 '69
News from Alabama: Wallace still lives. J.
Witcover. New Repub 160:12 My 31 '69
Operation Spiro: campaign in 1972. Nat R
21:1255-6 D 16 '69
Pro-Wallace workers start to stir. por Bsns
W p 124+ O 25 '69
Readying for the '72 roses. Time 94:40 D
5 '69
Wallace whitelash. S. M. Lipset and E. Raab.
il Trans-Action 7:23-32+ D '69
What happened to the Democratic coali-
tion? G. Will. Nat R 21:325-7+ Ap 8 '69
Wonderful world of George Wallace; with
editorial comment. G. Lardner, jr. and J.
Loh. il pors Esquire 71:6, 125-8+ My '69
WALLACE, Irving
Irving Wallace phenomenon. M. Lydon. il
por N Y Times Mag p32-3+ Mr 23 '69

WALLACE, Michael
Changing concepts of party in the United
States: New York, 1815-1828. bibliog f Am
Hist R 74:453-91 D '68
WALLACE, Mike
Are we really shocked? relentless question-
ing of D. P. Meadlo. America 121:629 D 27
'69
Mellowing of Mike malice. por Time 95:57
Ja 19 '70
Merry magazines. il por Time 93:86 Ap 11
'69
WALLACE, Robert K.
How to make an extra camper lamp. Pop
Sci 195:60 S '69
WALLACE, Sarah L.
ALA dues structure: background to a recom-
mendation. ALA Bul 63:614-15 My '69
WALLACE, Weldon
American bishops in Astrodome city. Com-
monweal 90:188-90 My 2 '69
Forman bedevils the Episcopalians. Com-
monweal 90:582-3 S 26 '69
WALLENDA family. See Acrobats and acro-
batism
WALLENSTEIN, Barry
Joyce's cher maitre. Cath World 209:91+
My '69
WALLER, G. R. and others
Feline attractant, cis,trans-nepetalactone:
metabolism in the domestic cat. bibliog
Science 164:1281-2 Je 13 '69
WALLERSTEIN, George
Astronomical evidence for nucleosynthesis
in stars. bibliog Science 162:625-31 N 8 '68;
Correction 163:622 F 14 '69
WALLERSTEIN, Immanuel Maurice
Reform or revolution? A. Koch. Am Scholar
38:688+ Aut '69
WALLEYE fishing. See Perch fishing
WALLICH, Henry C.
[Column on economic questions] See issues
of Newsweek
Money (cont) Vogue 153:58 F 15; 46 Mr 15;
132 My; 70 Je '69
WALLIS, C. Lamar
Confrontation in Memphis. Library J 94:
4101-2 N 15 '69
WALLIS, Cliff
Give your houseplants a summer vacation.
Horticulture 47:47 Jl '69
WALLIS, Pauline
Queen of the kennels. il por Newsweek 73:
94-5 Je 30 '69
WALLIS, W. Allen
Military conscription; address, November 11,
1968. Vital Speeches 35:284-6 F 15 '69
WALLPAPER
Backgrounds with a new look; wallpaper
pictures. M. Shaw. il Sch Arts 69:38 N '69
Decorating scrapbook. il House B 111:59-69
Mr '69
WALLS, R. M.
Bible has a name for it. Har Yrs 9:45 O '69
WALLS
Fixing up an older home. il Bet Hom & Gard
47:18+ My '69
See also
Garden walls
Retaining walls
Storage walls
WALLS (fortifications)
Defense walls repeat themselves. P. W.
Schmidtchen. il Hobbies 74:134-6 N '69
WALLS, Glass
Aluminum columns in glass walls carry both
roof loads and wind loads. il Arch Rec 145:
167 F '69
Imagination achieves privacy behind glass
walls; house on Long Island. il House &
Gard 135:58-63+ F '69
Lake Point Tower: the first skyscraper with
an undulating glass wall; Chicago's new
high-rise. il Arch Rec 146:123-30 O '69
Their new glass wall frames a canyon view,
stops a canyon wind. il Sunset 142:98 F '69
WALNUT grove plantation. See South Carolina
—Historic houses, etc.
WALPOLE, Horace, 4th earl of Orford
Moon stood still on Strawberry Hill. P. Quen-
nell. il por Horizon 11:112-17 Sum '69
WALRUS hunting
Nomad in Alaska's outback. T. J. Aber-
crombie. il Nat Geog 135:540-67 Ap '69
WALSH, Arthur
Favorite pioneer recording artists. J. Walsh.
il pors Hobbies 74:36+ Je '69
WALSH, Chad
Mother and son; poem. Chr Cent 86:372 Mr
19 '69
WALSH, Denny
Army tries to build a munitions factory in
St Louis with the Mob on the payroll. Life
66:52-4+ F 14 '69

WAR and religion—*Continued*
Support means sanctuary and solidarity. G.
F. Snyder. Chr Cent 86:120-1 Ja 22 '69
   See also
Israeli-Arab war, 1967- —Moral and religious
aspects
Vietnamese war, 1957- —Moral and religious
aspects

Anecdotes, facetiae, satire, etc.
Adventures of superhawk. Chr Cent 86:391
Mr 19 '68
WAR and science
Unless peace comes, ed. by N. Calder. Review
   Commonweal 89:714-15 Mr 7 '69. J. J.
   Stone
WAR and society
   See also
Atomic warfare and society
WAR correspondents
   See also
Nigeria—Civil war, 1967- —War correspon-
dents
WAR crimes
   See also
Vietnamese war, 1957- —Atrocities
Vietnamese war, 1957- —Atrocities—Songmy
massacre
WAR criminals. See World war, 1939-1945—War
criminals
WAR finance
   See also
Vietnamese war, 1957- —Cost
War profits
United States
   See also
Taxation—United States
WAR games
Bomb and the computer, by A. Wilson. Re-
view
   Nation 209:319-21 S 29 '69. R. Claiborne
   See also
Military maneuvers
WAR heroes. See Vietnamese war, 1957- —
Heroes
WAR in fiction. See War in literature
WAR in literature
Irony of situation in Ernest Hemingway's
Soldier's home. A. J. Petrarca. Engl J
58:664-7 My '69
Stephen Crane's A mystery of heroism: some
redefinitions. P. Witherington. Engl J 58:
201-4+ F '69
WAR industries. See Munitions industries
WAR marriages
How servicemen's marriages survive separa-
tion. J. Whitbread. Redbook 132:94+ Ap '69
WAR materials
Storage
Stockpiles of death. il Newsweek 73:36+ My
19 '69
WAR memorials
   See also
Washington, D.C.—Monuments, statues, etc.
WAR neuroses. See Neuroses
WAR news
   See also
Nigeria—Civil war, 1967- —War correspond-
ents
Television broadcasting—War news
WAR objectors. See Conscientious objectors
WAR of 1812. See United States—History—War
of 1812
WAR on poverty (program) See Anti-poverty
program, 1964-
WAR poetry
   See also
Vietnamese war, 1957- —Poetry
WAR powers. See Presidents—United States—
Powers and duties
WAR prisoners. See Prisoners of war
WAR profiteering. See Black markets
WAR profits
Tax-court peephole. S. Watzman. Nation 208:
113-15 Ja 27 '69
WAR propaganda
   See also
Nigeria—Civil war, 1967- —Propaganda
Vietnamese war, 1957- —Propaganda
WAR research. See Military research
WAR resisters league
Busting 5 Beekman. J. Deedy. il Commonweal
90:330 Je 6 '69; Reply with rejoinder. D. R.
Carlin, jr. 90:474 Ag 8 '69
WAR surpluses. See Surplus military property
WAR tax (United States) See Taxation—
United States
WAR widows. See Widows
WARBLERS
Beat of passing wings; golden-cheeked
warbler threatened by Meridian state park
golf course. il Time 94:51 O 17 '69

Golden-cheeked warbler: threatened bird of
the cedar brakes. W. M. Pulich. il Nat Parks
43:10-12 Mr '69
WARBURTON, Ralph
What urban design means. Am City 84:110+
My '69
WARD, Donald B.
Underground church is nonsense. Look 33:
75 O 21 '69
WARD, Douglas Turner
Reckoning. Criticism
   America 121:244-5 S 27 '69
   New Yorker 45:105 S 13 '69
WARD, Frank Kingdon-. See Kingdon-Ward,
F.
WARD, Hardy
Hardy boy and his bow and arrow. H.
Weiskopf. il pors Sports Illus 31:20-2+ Ag
11 '69
Just call him the man with the golden aim.
H. Weiskopf. il por Sports Illus 31:42-3
S 1 '69
WARD, Joseph S.
Sewers need better soils engineering. Am City
84:72-4 Jl '69
WARD, Kay
Maine windjamming; letter. Motor B 123:78-9
Mr '69
WARD, Leo R.
Image of man in Christian humanism. Cath
World 209:12-16 Ap '69
Man in the cutaway suit. Commonweal 90:
165-7 Ap 25 '69
WARD, Maisie
Dag Hammarskjöld and Teilhard de Chardin.
Cath World 210:159-64 Ja '70
WARD, Peter A. and others
Leukotactic factor produced by sensitized
lymphocytes. bibliog Science 163:1079-81 Mr
7 '69
WARD, Vesta B.
Jewelry to shoot for! Sch Arts 69:26-7 Ja '70
WARD bosses. See Boss rule
WARDE, Beatrice Lamberton (Becker)
Obituary
   Pub W 196:55 O 6 '69. C. B. Grannis
   Pub W por 196:42 S 29 '69
WARDENS, Prison. See Prison wardens
WARDS. See Guardian and ward
WARDWELL, Allen
Some early English silver at the Art institute
of Chicago. Antiques 95:818-24 Je '69
WARE, Dean
Dizzy machine. Pop Electr 30:51-2 Ap '69
WARE, Mass.
Education
Playing fields of Ware. I. K. Bradley. il To-
days Ed 58:24-6 My '69
WAREHOUSES
Lighting
Don't make your men carry flashlights;
new mercury fixtures of Port of New
Orleans. il Am City 84:21 Mr '69
WAREHOUSES, Remodeled. See Buildings,
Remodeled
WARFARIN
Vitamin K and coumarin anticoagulants: de-
pendence of anticoagulant effect on in-
hibition of vitamin K transport. J. Lowen-
thal and H. Birnbaum. bibliog il Science
164:181-3 Ap 11 '69
WARFIELD, Rebecca
Danger! Talent at work. House & Gard 136:
76-7+ Jl '69
Good looks & good health. See issues of
House & garden incorporating Living for
young homemakers
WARHOL, Andy
Say hello to the Dirty half dozen, Sierra Ban-
dit, the American playground and all the
superstars of the new theatre. Esquire
71:144-7 My '69
   about
Andy Warhol's exhibition. D. Bourdon. il
Art N 68:44-5+ O '69
Warhol. S. Koch. New Repub 160:24-7 Ap
26 '69
WARING, James
Three ballets by James Waring. Judson me-
morial church. J. Anderson. Dance Mag 43:
92 Je '69
Toby Armour & James Waring, Judson me-
morial church. J. Anderson. Dance Mag
43:82 Je '69
WARK, D. Q. and Hilleary, D. T.
Atmospheric temperature: successful test of
remote probing. bibliog Science 165:1256-8
S 19 '69
WARM-air heating system. See Heating equip-
ment
WARM SPRINGS, Ga.
Warm Springs of FDR. B. Fancher. il Sat R
52:42+ Mr 8 '69

WARM-water irrigation. See Irrigation

WARNCKE, Ruth
Viewpoint. por Library J 94:163, 1112, 1959, 2575, 3029, 4117 Ja 15, Mr 15, My 15, Jl, S 15, N 15 '69

WARNECKE, Steven
Weimar tragedy. Nation 208:442-3 Ap 7 '69

WARNER, Brian. See Nather. R. E. jt. auth.

WARNER, Denis
Reports: Vietnam. Atlan 224:12+ Ag '69

WARNER, James A.
He found a new life, a people, a book. J. Deschin. por Pop Phot 65:44+ N '69

WARNER, Marvin L.
U.S. reviews work of U.N. committee on friendly relations and cooperation among states; statement, December 10, 1968. Dept State Bul 60:66-9 Ja 20 '69

WARNER, Sam Bass, Jr
If all the world were Philadelphia: a scaffolding for urban history, 1774-1930. bibliog f Am Hist R 74:26-43 O '68

WARNER, Sylvia Townsend
Cheese; story. New Yorker 45:43 Je 14 '69
Furnivall's hoopoe; story. New Yorker 45: 28-31 Ja 3 '70
Sopwith Hall; story. New Yorker 45:57-60 N 22 '69

WARNER, Theodore B.
Fluoride in seawater: measurement with lanthanum fluoride electrode. bibliog Science 165:178-80 Jl 11 '69

WARNER and Swasey company
Old-fashioned values that lead to profits. Bsns W p54-5 Ja 3 '69

WARNER brothers pictures, incorporated
Film fest's best jests. H. V. Fondiller. il Pop Phot 65:118+ O '69

WARNER-Lambert pharmaceutical company
Great razor blade war; Gillette vs Warner-Lambert. il Forbes 104:26-7 O 15 '69

WARNICK, Dorothy B.
Try a learning vacation. Mech Illus 65:46-8+ My '69

WARNING labels. See Labels

WARNOCK, John W.
Silent partner. Commonweal 90:536-9 S 5 '69

WARRANTS (law)
New irritant; search warrant issued after receiving a tip from informant. Time 93: 35-6 F 7 '69

WARRANTS, Stock purchase. See Stock purchase warrants

WARRANTY
Get a written guarantee. Consumer Bul 52:16 F '69
How much good is a guarantee? il Changing T 23:6-10 Jl '69; Same abr. Read Digest 95:83-5 N '69
How to read an oil can. M. Schultz. il Pop Mech 132:134-7+ N '69
Personal business; keeping your car on the go. Bsns W p 107-8 Mr 8 '69
Warranties and service. il Motor B 123:101 Ja '69
Warranties, and what should be done about them: automobile warranties. il Consumer Rep 34:177-81 Ap '69
Watch out for the friendly arrangement; guaranteed maintenance purchasing. H. R. Bone. il Am City 84:104 F '69
What's with the new auto warranties? C. Cutter. il Pop Mech 131:98-101+ Mr '69

WARREN, David
Footstool from Abe Lincoln's home. Pop Sci 194:148-53 My '69

WARREN, Douglas
Irish nuns in the Mekong Delta. America 121: 524-5 N 29 '69

WARREN, Earl
Farewell from Warren; excerpts from address, June 2, 1969. il por U S News 66:18 Je 16 '69
National conference on continuing action for human rights; address, December 4, 1968. Dept State Bul 59:686-90 D 30 '68
Talk with Warren on crime, the Court, the country; interview, ed. by A. Lewis. por N Y Times Mag p34-5+ O 19 '69

about

Amicus curiae. il Newsweek 74:17 Jl 7 '69
Before the colors fade: the return of the exiles; interview, ed. by J. Stevenson. R. W. Kenny. il Am Heritage 20:22-5+ Je '69
Court, old and new. R. Shogan. por Newsweek 73:46+ Je 30 '69
Legacy of the Warren court. il por Time 94:62-3 Jl 4 '69
Supreme court today: sizing up the Warren court. il pors Sr Schol 94:6-20+ Mr 28 '69
TRB from Washington. New Repub 160:4 Ap 26 '69
Warren and Fortas: a sober, tough conclusion. Chr Cent 86:734 My 28 '69

Warren court, ed. by R. H. Sayler and others. Review
Sat R 52:21-2+ Ag 2 '69. T. Taylor
Warren court is not likely to be overruled. J. W. Bishop, jr. il por N Y Times Mag p31-3+ S 7 '69
Warren court vs. Congress. il por U S News 66:23-4 Je 30 '69
Warren legacy. J. J. Kilpatrick. il Nat R 21: 794-800 Ag 12 '69

WARREN, F. Eugene
Assassin of God; poem. Chr Today 14:15 D 19 '69
Dumbfounding; poem. Chr Today 14:19 O 24 '69

WARREN, Larry
For men only: experiment in a dance project at University of Wisconsin. E. Jacobs. il por Dance Mag 43:78-81 My '69

WARREN, Marguerite Q.
Case for differential treatment of delinquents. bibliog f Ann Am Acad 381:47-59 Ja '69

WARREN, Phelps
Luxury in English and Irish cut glass. Antiques 96:882-8 D '69

WARREN, Richard M. and others
Auditory sequence: confusion of patterns other than speech or music. bibliog Science 164:586-7 My 2 '69

WARREN, Robert E.
Priests, prostitutes, and the dead God: a meditation. Cath World 208:261-3 Mr '69

WARREN, Robert Hamilton
Export sales trends; excerpts from address. Aviation W 90:11 Ap 7 '69
Military assistance program; address, March 26, 1969. Vital Speeches 35:601-3 Jl 15 '69

WARREN, Robert Penn
Audubon: a vision and a question for you; poem. New Yorker 45:42-3 S 20 '69
Dream he never knew the end of; excerpt from Audubon: a vision. Harper 239:73-5 Ag '69
Lyrics from Audubon: a vision. Yale R 59: 1-2 O '69

about

Diction in Warren's All the king's men. R. G. Martin. Engl J 58:1169-74 N '69

WARREN, Ruth
Tunisia. Travel 132:36-43 D '69

WARREN, William
Laos is at war, but Vientiane yawns. N Y Times Mag p 12-13+ Ja 4 '70

WARREN commission. See United States—President's commission on the assassination of President Kennedy

WARREN report. See United States—President's commission on the assassination of President Kennedy

WARRENDALE youth development center, Pa. See Special classes and special schools

WARRIORS (basketball team) See Basketball teams

WARS of the Roses, 1455-1485. See Great Britain—History—Wars of the Roses, 1455-1485

WARSAW

City planning

Canaletto's paintings helped rebuild shattered Warsaw; reprint. J. Hryniewiecki. il UNESCO Courier 22:48-9 Ag '69

Music

Adventures in Poland. B. Murray. Hi Fi 19: MA26-7 D '69

Reconstruction

See Warsaw—City planning

WARSAW pact, 1955
Europe: a time of testing for the power blocs. il Time 94:28+ D 12 '69
Overture to Moscow; summit meeting. Newsweek 74:43-4 D 15 '69
U.S. offers updated approach on liability; airline liability in international transportation. H. D. Watkins. Aviation W 91:45+ N 10 '69
Warsaw pact. A. Korbonski. bibliog f il Int Concil 573:5-73 My '69
Where Russian troops may strike next. il U S News 66:12 F 24 '69

WARSH, Lewis
The eye; poem. Poetry 114:303 Ag '69

WARSHAW, Thayer S.
Teaching the Bible as literature. Engl J 58: 571-6 Ap '69

WARSHIPS

See also
Carriers

Electronic equipment

Improved ship defense pushed. B. Miller. il Aviation W 91:79+ S 15 '69

United States

Gas turbines favored for new destroyers. Aviation W 91:61-2 Jl 21 '69

WARSHIPS—United States—*Continued*
High cost of nostalgia; reactivation of the
New Jersey. Nation 209:396 O 20 '69
Israel pays compensation claimed for men
injured on U.S.S. Liberty. Dept State Bul
60:473 Je 2 '69
Navy's turn to squirm. il Time 94:83-4 N 21
'69
Where are they now? USS Liberty. il News-
week 74:22 S 29 '69
WARSHIPS, Atomic powered
Navy reinforces nuclear fleet. il Bsns W
p82 Ja 3 '70
WARSHIPS, Scuttling of
Aleutian runaway; scuttling of the Robert
Louis Stevenson. R. Davidson. il Sci Di-
gest 65:64-8 My '69
WARSHOFSKY, Fred
Meet Bucky Fuller, ambassador from to-
morrow. Read Digest 95:199-200+ N '69
WARTS
What are plantar warts? il Good H 169:181 S
'69
WARWICK, James F. and Smith, Alvin
Stones come of age. Sch Arts 68:30-1 Mr '69
WARWICK, James W.
Models of pulsating radio sources. bibliog
Science 163:959-61 F 28 '69
WASHBURN, Frank M.
Choice. por Camp Mag 41:5 F '69
Generation gap: fact or fiction? por Camp
Mag 41:4 N '69
Truth or consequences. por Camp Mag 41:5
Je '69
WASHBURN, Wilcomb E.
Red power. Am West 6:52-3 Ja '69
WASHING machines
How safe are today's wringer washing ma-
chines? il Consumer Rep 34:601-3 O '69
Laundry dollar, well-spent. N. Craig. il House
B 111:86-7+ F '69
1-2-3 guide to buying laundry appliances.
S. Schuler. Am Home 72:60+ N '69
Washing machines. il Consumer Rep 34:436-41
Ag '69

Maintenance and repair
Secrets of keeping your automatic washer
trouble-free. E. Powell. il Pop Sci 194:131-46
F '69
Washing machine frequency-of-repair records.
il Consumer Rep 34:445-7 Ag '69

Prices
Medium price? What's that? il Consumer Rep
34:441 Ag '69
WASHINGTON, George
George Washington, horticulturist. D. S.
Manks. il Horticulture 46:30-2 Ag '68
More about Richard Stanup, George Wash-
ington's chief of servants. il Negro Hist
Bul 32:16-18 My '69
Richard Stanup who had charge of George
Washington's slaves. il Negro Hist Bul 32:
12-13 F '69
Very first resort: George Washington bathed
here. T. L. Christie. Sat R 52:58 Mr 8 '69
Washington after the Revolution; excerpts.
J. T. Flexner. il pors Am Heritage 20:10-
13; F; 64-73 Ap; 72-9+ Je; 24-7+ O; 21:32-
3+ D '69
Washington miniature. R. Davidson. por An-
tiques 96:318+ S '69

Drama
George slept here, too. A. C. Martens. Plays
28:1-8, 34 F '69
Handwriting on the wall. J. Nicholson. Plays
28:51-62 F '69
WASHINGTON, Jennifer, kidnapping case. See
Kidnapping
WASHINGTON, Joanne
My plea to Castro for return of my child.
pors Ebony 24:66-8+ O '69
WASHINGTON, D.C.
Capital idea; tours and attractions. News-
week 74:30-1 Jl 21 '69
See also
Architecture, Domestic—Washington, D.C.

Air pollution
See also
Greater-Washington alliance to stop pollu-
tion, incorporated

Airports
On top; general aviation facilities. R. L.
Collins. Flying 85:12-14+ Jl '69
Taped lines keep airport traffic moving. C. R.
Melugin, jr. il Am City 84:146 F '69

Anti-poverty program
Investing in today's youth. W. L. Montgomery. il Parks & Rec 4:29-31+ Ja '69

Architecture
Commission of fine arts: design review board
for the national capital. D. Raney. il Arch
Rec 145:37 Ap '69

Cemeteries
Two hidden cemeteries in the Georgetown
section of Washington, D.C. S. M. Renchard. il Negro Hist Bul 32:29-30 N '69

Churches
Carpenters' shop to $8.5 million complex:
National Presbyterian center. J. Rohler. il
Chr Today 13:44 S 26 '69

City planning
Ban the bridge? protests over Three Sisters
bridge plans. il Newsweek 74:68 N 3 '69
Freeway plans threaten nation's capital. Nat
Parks 43:21 Ja '69
President Nixon's first major statement on
architecture. W. F. Wagner, jr. Arch Rec
145:9 Je '69

Crime
Capital crime wave. H. Brandon. Sat R 52:
20+ F 15 '69
Capital of crime; statistics for 1969. il News-
week 75:19 Ja 12 '70
City: terror in Washington. il Time 93:30 Mr
14 '69
Crime buster; new administration's anticrime
program. il Newsweek 73:22 F 10 '69
Crime in the capital. il Time 93:14 F 7 '69
Curbing crime, Nixon opens his war. il U S
News 66:9 F 10 '69
Nation's capital: crime up and up; with re-
port by Police chief J. V. Wilson. il U S
News 67:32-6 D 8 '69
Nixon's war on crime. K. Crawford. News-
week 73:39 F 17 '69
War on crime; Nixon plan. Sr Schol 94:18-19
F 14 '69

Description
Button-down town. D. Butwin. Sat R 52:34+
N 8 '69
Washington album; photographs. W.
McNamee. Newsweek 73:23-6 Ja 27 '69
Washington: tourists come back. il U S News
66:50-1 Ap 21 '69
Washington wilderness. L. Udall. il Redbook
132:80-1+ Mr '69

Education
Danger in Washington: The story of my twen-
ty years in the public schools in the Na-
tion's capital, by C. F. Hansen. Review
Nat R 21:28-9 Ja 14 '69. V. Gold
Eyewitness: Department of curriculum of
the public schools guide for teachers. E. W.
Johnson. il Sr Schol 94:Schol Teach 24-5
Ja 17 '69
Last one in; Hardy elementary school. il
Am Ed 5:22 Je '69
Mural is . . story of a stitchery mural and a
sixth grade class at the Anne Beers ele-
mentary school. S. Battist. il Sch Arts 68:
24-5 My '69
Who killed the bird? I. McManus. il Am For
75:24-7+ O '69
See also
Washington, D.C. Federal city college

Galleries and museums
See also
Corcoran gallery Dupont circle
National gallery of art. Washington, D.C.
Smithsonian institution—National collection
of fine arts

Gardens
Dumbarton Oaks; excerpts from Dumbarton
Oaks, a guide to the gardens. G. Masson.
il Horticulture 47:38-9 O '69

History
Main street of America; excerpt from The
avenue of the presidents; with a portfolio
of illustrations. M. Cable. Am Heritage 20:
44-53+ F '69

Hotels, restaurants, etc.
Nighttime boss of capital inn; Washington
Hilton hotel. il Ebony 25:67-8+ N '69

Housing
Everybody lives at Watergate; with photo-
graphs by M. Rougier. Life 67:40-7 Ag 8 '69
Great house hunt; changing of administra-
tions. il Newsweek 73:59 Ja 27 '69
How we played monopoly in Washington,
D.C. J. Viorst. il Redbook 133:94-5+ Jl '69
Poor man's Shangri-la. Newsweek 73:64 My
12 '69

WASHINGTON, D.C.—*Continued*

Human relations commission

Cool-it man. il Newsweek 74:69 O 13 '69

Institute for creative studies

See Institute for creative studies, Washington, D.C.

Libraries

Tuning in to summer; orientation for Youth opportunity campaign employees of federal libraries. E. Sheahan. bibliog il Library J 94:1294-7+ Mr 15 '69

Monuments, statues, etc.

City built on legends of valor. H. Sidey. il Life 66:4 Je 27 '69

Statue of Benito Juárez dedicated at Washington; remarks, January 7, 1969. D. Rusk. Dept State Bul 60:74-5 Ja 27 '69

See also

Washington monument, Washington, D.C.

Music

See also

Opera society of Washington

National arboretum

Touch and see; nature trail at the National arboretum. J. M. Garvey. il Parks & Rec 4:20-2 N '69

Negroes

Staking out a tough turf; CBS's ghetto reports. il Newsweek 74:94-5 Jl 14 '69

Newspapers

Close up: the ladies who cover Washington society; interviews. ed. by deR. McQuade. M. Cheshire; B. Beale. il Life 66:30-3 F 28 '69

See also

Washington daily news

Parks and playgrounds

Playground on a hill. il Arch Forum 131: 82-5 O '69

President's park paint-on. Y. Fogel. il Parks & Rec 4:16-17 Ag '69

Summer in the parks: National park service program. T. McCann. il Parks & Rec 4:14-17 Jl '69

Police

Chief of U.S. park police. il Ebony 24:66-8+ Mr '69

Politics and government

Capital subway gets out of political tunnel. il Bsns W p88+ O 11 '69

Public buildings

See also

United States—Capitol

Rapid transit

See also

Washington, D.C.—Subways

Recreation

Widening horizons; program of Tours for teens. W. G. McNamara. il Parks & Rec 4:20-3+ O '69

See also

Washington, D.C.—Parks and playgrounds

Riots

Can summer be far behind? M. McGrory. America 120:641 My 31 '69

Long-term costs of Washington's '68 riots. il U S News 66:35 Je 16 '69

Social conditions

Can summer be far behind? M. McGrory. America 120:641 My 31 '69

In the aftermath of city rioting; report by the Urban coalition and urban America inc. U S News 66:12 Mr 10 '69

Social life and customs

Close up: the ladies who cover Washington society; interviews. ed. by deR. McQuade. M. Cheshire; B. Beale. il Life 66:30-3 F 28 '69

End to indifference along the Potomac. H. Sidey. il Life 67:6 D 5 '69

Everybody lives at Watergate; with photographs by M. Rougier. Life 67:40-7 Ag 8 '69

More money for the biplane set; proposed pay raises for the Vice-President and congressional leaders. il Time 94:17 S 5 '69

More things change. P. Lisagor. Nations Bsns 57:21-2 Ap '69

Potomac party-givers; with account by A. Chamberlin. il McCalls 96:62-5+ Jl '69

Silent majority's Camelot. il Time 94:34+ D 5 '69

Washington waits for its social cue. il Bsns W p80-1 Ag 2 '69

Stores

Store that joined the world; Julius Garfinckel & Co. il Bsns W p86+ Je 21 '69

Streets

Main street of America; excerpt from The avenue of the presidents; with a portfolio of illustrations. M. Cable. Am Heritage 20: 44-53+ F '69

Subways

Capital subway gets out of political tunnel. il Bsns W p88+ O 11 '69

Finally, a subway for Washington. il U S News 67:11 D 22 '69

Subways are for building. il Newsweek 74: 65 D 22 '69

Theatre

New Ford's; revivals produced by New York's Circle in the square. H. Hewes. Sat R 52: 62 N 22 '69

See also

John F. Kennedy center for the performing arts

Transportation

See also

Washington, D.C.—Subways

WASHINGTON, D.C., Federal city college

College beset by black revolutionaries. il U S News 66:38-40 My 12 '69

Federal city college, Washington, D.C; offering Black studies program. Negro Hist Bul 32:5 My '69

First year at Federal city. D. Swanston. il Nation 208:594-6 My 12 '69

Report from Interim college commission of Federal city college. Sch & Soc 97:293-4 Sum '69

Urban problems and higher education: Federal city college; address, November 1968. W. E. Hinchliff. il Wilson Lib Bul 43:527-33 F '69; Reply. F. Farner. 43:610 Mr '69

WASHINGTON (state)

See also

Architecture, Domestic—Washington (state)

Bainbridge Island

Bumping River

Columbia River

Fishing—Washington (state)

Hunting—Washington (state)

Libraries—Washington (state)

Olympic National Park

Puget Sound

Parks and reserves

Ginkgo: window to the past. G. A. Ritchie. il Nat Parks 43:12-14 F '69

WASHINGTON airlines

Short run for STOL. Sci N 96:302 O 4 '69

STOL, helicopters vie in Washington area. D. A. Brown. il Aviation W 90:30-1 Mr 24 '69

Washington airlines ends service. Aviation W 91:22 O 6 '69

WASHINGTON airways

STOL, helicopters vie in Washington area. D. A. Brown. il Aviation W 90:30-1 Mr 24 '69

WASHINGTON daily news

Crime and race; crime clock identifies race of victims and suspects of crimes in Washington. Newsweek 73:86 Mr 10 '69

WASHINGTON high fidelity show. See Audio fairs

WASHINGTON monument, Washington, D.C.

George Washington's monument. il Am Heritage 20:68-73 D '68

WASHINGTON post and Times herald

Beat the press, round two. il Newsweek 74: 25-6 D 1 '69

Exit visas for two. Newsweek 73:84-5 Je 2 '69

Middle-aged rebel. Time 95:33-4 Ja 5 '70

Newspaper monopoly; address, November 20, 1969. S. T. Agnew. Vital Speeches 36:133-6 D 15 '69; Excerpts. U S News 67:12 D 1 '69

Weekly Agnew special. Time 94:62+ N 28 '69

WASHINGTON post book and author luncheons. See Book and author luncheons

WASHINGTON Redskins (football club) See Football clubs

WASHINGTON Senators (baseball) See Baseball clubs

WASHTON, Rose-Carol

Vasily Kandinsky: a space odyssey. Art N 68:46-9+ O '69

WASKOW, Arthur I.

Community control of the police. Trans-Action 7:4-7 D '69

Radical Haggadah for Passover. Ramp Mag 7:25-33 Ap '69

WASP stings. See Insect bites and stings

WASPS
Fig wasps: mechanism of pollen transfer. W. Ramirez B. bibliog il Science 163:580-1 F 7 '69

WASPS (white Anglo-Saxon Protestants)
White, Anglo-Saxon Protestant. A. H. Leitch Chr Today 14:46-7 Ja 2 '70

WASSAJA (Apache Indian) See Montezuma, C.

WASSERMAN, Burton
From illusion toward reality. Sch Arts 69: 26-7 N '69

WASSERMAN, Edward A. and Jensen, D. D.
Olfactory stimuli and the pseudo-extinction effect. bibliog Science 166:1307-9 D 5 '69

WASSERMAN, Joseph J.
Plugging the leaks in computer security. Harvard Bsns R 47:119-29 S '69

WASSERMAN, Paul
Elements in a manpower blueprint: library personnel for the 1970's; address, October 17, 1968. bibliog ALA Bul 63:581-99 My '69

WASSERMAN, Rona B.
How one camp operates its successful counselor training program. Camp Mag 41:9+ Ap '69

WASSERSUG, Joseph D.
New clues to the diabetes riddle. Sci Digest 66:76-9 O '69

WASSMER, Thomas A.
Toward a contemporary Christian moral philosophy. Cath World 209:115-20 Je '69

WASSON, Donald
Source material. See issues of Foreign affairs

WASSON, E. Hornsby
Business and campus unrest; address, January 16, 1969. Vital Speeches 35:335-8 Mr 15 '69

WASTE, Disposal of. See Refuse and refuse disposal; Trade waste disposal

WASTE, Utilization of
Air pollutant cleans a lake; fly ash. Am City 84:30 Ja '69
City composting forges ahead. J. Olds. Org Gard & Farm 16:76-8 Ja '69
Profit in waste. L. H. Schoenhofen. Duns R 93:17 F '69
See also
Refuse, Utilization of
Refuse as fertilizer

WASTE baskets
Roll-your-own wastebasket. il Mech Illus 65: 74-5 Je '69

WASTE collection. See Refuse and refuse disposal

WASTE disposal plants. See Sewage disposal plants

WASTE heat
Thermal pollution and aquatic life. J. R. Clark. il Sci Am 220:18-27 bibliog(p 148) Mr '69
See also
Heat regenerators

WASTE in defense spending. See United States—Defense, Department of—Appropriations and expenditures

WASTE in government spending. See United States—Appropriations and expenditures

WASTE injection. See Trade waste disposal

WASTE products
See also
Refuse and refuse disposal
Scrap metal

WASTE recycling. See Refuse and refuse disposal

WASTE water purification. See Water purification

WASTE water reclamation. See Water reuse

WASWO, R. J.
Not as it should be. Am For 75:11 Ag '69

WATCH industry
Crucial hours for the Swiss watch industry. il Fortune 80:116 Ag 15 '69

WATCH tower Bible and tract society. See Jehovah's witnesses

WATCHES
New guidelines for buying watches. Good H 169:214 O '69
Time of your life. A. S. Freese. il Pop Mech 130:108-13+ D '68
When a watch is shock-resistant, water-resistant or antimagnetic. McCalls 96:54 Ap '69

Collectors and collecting
Beauty and art from the past; Ford collection (cont) O. R. Hagans. il Hobbies 73:48 F '69

WATCHES, Electric
Are electric watches really better? R. M. Benrey. il Pop Sci 195:130-3 Ag '69

WATER
Analyzing anomalous water. D. E. Thomsen. il Sci N 97:17-18 Ja 3 '70
Behavior of water in vacuum: implications for lunar rivers. J. E. M. Adler and J. W. Salisbury. il Science 164:589 My 2 '69
Equivocal standard: anomalous water; excerpt. B. V. Deriagin. il Sat R 52:54-5 S 6 '69
Glass-transition temperature of water. A. A. Miller. bibliog il Science 163:1325-6 Mr 21 '69
Moon rivers; or, How water behaves in a vacuum. il Chem 42:25 O '69
Observed diffraction pattern and proposed models of liquid water. A. H. Narten and H. A. Levy. bibliog il Science 165:447-54 Ag 1 '69
Polymer from water. il Sci N 96:23-4 Jl 12 '69
Polymerized water, is it or isn't it? J. Finney. Chem 42:20 Mr '69
Polywater. Sci Am 221:90+ S '69
Polywater. E. R. Lippincott and others. bibliog il Science 164:1482-7 Je 27 '69
Polywater. il Chem 42:22 N '69
Polywater: proton nuclear magnetic resonance spectrum. T. F. Page, jr. and others. il Science 167:51 Ja 2 '70
Polywater, the water that isn't. S. Dresner. il Pop Sci 195:68-71+ D '69
Prospecting for polywater. il Newsweek 74: 111 S 29 '69
Rain in space. Sci Am 220:50 Ap '69
Spectra suggest anomalous water is a stable polymer of H_2O. M. S. Rothenberg. bibliog il Phys Today 22:61-2 S '69
Spectra, variability, size, and polarization of H_2O microwave emission sources in the galaxy. S. H. Knowles and others. bibliog il Science 163:1055-7 Mr 7 '69
Structure of polywater. J. Donohue. bibliog il Science 166:1000-2 N 21 '69
Unnatural water; polywater. il Time 94:60 D 19 '69
Water that won't freeze; polywater; scientists behind the discovery and research. J. Lear. il Sat R 52:49-52 S 6 '69
What is the difference between surface and ground water? Sci Digest 66:75-6 Ag '69
See also
Hydration
Hydrologic research
Ice
Irrigation water
Rain and rainfall
Springs

Analysis
Lab bench; water pollution study. F. Newman. il Chem 42:28-9 Ja '69

Hardness
Heart and hard water. Sci Am 220:58 Je '69
Soft water and heart disease; worldwide puzzle. Sci N 95:471 My 17 '69

Pollution
See Water pollution

WATER, Distilled
See also
Sea water—Desalting

WATER, Saline. See Saline water

WATER analysis. See Water—Analysis

WATER and wastewater equipment manufacturers association
New WWEMA president. Am City 84:31+ Je '69

WATER beetles
Wave-making by whirligig beetles (gyrinidae) V. A. Tucker. bibliog il Science 166:897-9 N 14 '69

WATER birds
Mystery of migration. M. J. Walker. il Am For 75:32-5+ N '69
Waterfowl on the wane? M. Frome. Field & S 74:34+ Ag '69
See also names of water birds, e.g. Ducks, Wild

WATER blasting. See Blasting

WATER chestnuts
Pest plant. Cons 23:38 Je '69

WATER clocks. See Clocks

WATER color painting
Designs first in small scale. F. Whitaker. il Am Artist 33:24-5+ S '69
Gloria Calamar has affinity for her subject. G Calamar. il Am Artist 33:52-3+ Ap '69
Watercolor page. See issues of American artist

Study and teaching
They can't resist wax-resist; water color painting over wax. J. Darling. il Sch Arts 69:8 N '69

WATER conservation
See also
Water reuse

WATER purification—*Continued*
New idea is the ovals; Beloit, Wis. R. G.
Miller and S. J. Goldschmidt. il Am City
84:101-2+ Je '69
Practical corrections to design weakness-
es of wastewater-treatment plants. E. F.
Spitz. il Am City 84:75-9 Mr '69
Wastewater collection and treatment. See
issues of American city
    See also
Settling basins
Swimming pools—Sanitation
Water reuse
Water softening
Water supply
Water treatment plants

Desalting
Desalting California; San Joaquin master
drain controversy. F. M. Stead. il Environ
11:2-10 Je '69
Reverse osmosis water for Bessie; Okla. il
Am City 84:60 S '69
    See also
Sea water—Desalting

WATER purification plants. See Water treat-
ment plants
WATER purifiers, Domestic
Six ways to make bad water good. D. X.
Manners. il Pop Mech 131:184-7+ My '69
Water filters: are they effective? Good H 169:
146 Ag '69
WATER requirements of animals
Physiology of the house mouse. D. S. Fertig
and V. W. Edmonds. il Sci Am 221:103-8+
bibliog(p 148) O '69
WATER resources development
    See also
North American water and power alliance
WATER reuse
Recalcining lime sludge produces multiple
benefits; St Paul. C. W. Hamblin. il Am
City 84:67-9+ N '69
Renovated wastewaters; important source of
water supply. J. W. Porter and others. il
Am City 84:140-2 My '69
Waste unit uses space techniques; integrated
heating, water recycling and sewage dis-
posal system for homes. W. H. Gregory. il
Aviation W 91:49-50 D 15 '69
Water and wastewater research in San Diego.
E. I. Crossley and W. M. Conn. il Am
City 84:91-3+ O '69
WATER scooters. See Motor boats
WATER shows. See Aquatic shows
WATER skis and skiing
Day campers enjoy water skiing; Fair acres
day camp. Cape Cod, Mass. J. S. Biddi-
scombe. il Camp Mag 41:30 My '69
Fast bikini under a wet suit; Chuck Stearns
and Sally Younger. il Sports Illus 30:20-1 Ja
27 '69
Ski on a flying saucer. il Pop Sci 195:165 Ag
'69
This is water skiing! F. Rohr, jr. Motor B
124:39+ Jl '69
Wet, happy life of Marvin Shackelford. C.
Gillespie. il Sports Illus 32:66-72 Ja 12 '70
Winning our thing in Denmark; World water
ski championships. C. Kirkpatrick. il Sports
Illus 31:14-17 Ag 18 '69

Study and teaching
Easy way to learn to water ski. M. Lamm. il
Mech Illus 65:60+ Ag '69

WATER softening
Of course we soften our water; Woodstock,
Ill. E. W. Bates, jr. il Am City 84:108+
Ap '69
Only one man per shift: small-city softening
plant; Dickinson, N.D. P. J. Pfau. il Am
City 84:112+ S '69
WATER sports. See Aquatic sports
WATER storage
    See also
Reservoirs
Standpipes
Water tanks
WATER striders
Mid-ocean insects: halobates. Sci Am 220:48-
9 Ja '69
WATER supply
Rational use of water, AAAS symposium,
December 30, 1969. C. Starr. il Science 166:
538-9 O 24 '69
Supply all the water your customers desire;
interview, ed. by R. R. Fleming. E. John-
son. il Am City 84:101-3+ My '69
Water hygiene programs; the environmental
control administration; address, March 20,
1969. C. A. Hansen. Vital speeches 35:444-6
My 1 '69
Water-resource communications gap. W. S.
Foster. bibliog il Am City 84:83-6 O '69

Water supply and treatment. See issues of
American city
    See also
Boats—Water supply
Camp water supply
Irrigation water
Pumping stations
Reservoirs
Water pollution
Water reuse
Wells

Fluoridation
Biography of a bandwagon. M. Wollan. Sat R
52:56-9 Mr 1 '69
Fluoridation and the dentist; research findings at the University of Illinois college
of dentistry, Chicago, J. Lear. il Sat R
52:50 Ag 2 '69; Discussion. 52:59-60 S 6 '69
New facts on fluoridation. J. Lear. il Sat R
52:51-6 Mr 1 '69; Discussion. 52:72-4 Ap 5,
57-9 My 3, 57 Je 7, 47-9 Jl 5 '69
Prevention: new look in dentistry. S. L.
Englebardt. Read Digest 94:15-16+ F '69
We need more research; excerpts from articles in the Washington post. J. Lederberg. Sat R 52:60 My 3 '69

Nitrogen content
Nitrogen enrichment of surface water by
absorption of ammonia volatilized from
cattle feedlots. G. L. Hutchinson and F. G.
Viets, jr. bibliog il Science 166:514-15 O 24
'69
Poisoning the wells. il Environ 11:16-23+ Ja
'69

California
Poisoning the wells. il Environ 11:16-23+ Ja
'69

Canada
    See also
North American water and power alliance

Chile
Disastrous drought. il Time 93:40 Ja 24 '69

Illinois
Regional water supply; Rend Lake conser-
vancy district. R. D. Jones and J. W.
Rezek il Am City 84:108+ Mr; 73-5 Ap '69

Iran
Where rain making is a success. il U S News
67:73 S 15 '69

Japan
Industry growing thirsty. S. Griffin. il Sci
N 95:390 Ap 19 '69

Jordan
On to Armageddon; Litani River authority.
D. Da Cruz. il Nat R 21:332 Ap 8 '69

Libya
Libya adds water to its riches. il Bsns W
p 168+ F 22 '69

Massachusetts
    See also
Boston—Water supply

Middle East
Plan that was; nuclear-power plants in Israel and the Arab countries to desalinate
sea water. Nation 208:163-4 F 10 '69

Missouri
Independent water supply proves best; Glad-
stone, Mo. G. E. Hands. il Am City 84:106+
F '69

North America
Water balance in North America; report of
meeting. E. Silberman. Science 166:1191 N
28 '69

South Carolina
All-plastic water system; Gills creek water
district, Lancaster County. il Am City 84:
55 My '69

United States
Arrogance toward the landscape: a problem
in water planning; excerpts from address,
September 4, 1969. R. L. Nace. il Bul Atom
Sci 25:11-14 D '69
    See also
North American water and power alliance
    also subhead Water supply under
names of cities, e.g. Wichita, Kan.—Water
supply

WATER supply engineering
    See also
Dams
Pipe laying
Water distribution
Water treatment plants

WATER tanks
Eighty-five acre-feet in a steel water tank; Alderwood water district, near Seattle. P. S. Lindbloom. il Am City 84:129+ Ap '69
Water tank dons polyframe lid; Kettering, Ohio. G. E. Cronk. il Am City 84:76-7 Je '69
See also
Standpipes

WATER towers
See also
Standpipes

WATER treatment plants
Bitterly opposed wastewater plant; Rapid City, S.D. E Hansen and J. G. Bell. il Am City 84:76-8 Ap '69
Don't settle for second class plant structures. M. D. McMullen. il Am City 84:38-40 My '69
Regional water supply; Rend Lake plant, Illinois. R. D. Jones and J. W. Rezek. il Am City 84:73-5 Ap '69
Renovated wastewaters; important source of water supply. J. W. Porter and others. il Am City 84:140-2 My '69
River-fed wells and a new filter plant; Omaha, Neb. R. D. Hawes. il Am City 84:119-21+ My '69
Wastewater purified to drinking-water quality; Tualatin, Ore. Am City 84:20 Jl '69
See also
Saline water conversion plants

Automation
Only one man per shift; small-city softening plant; Dickinson, N.D. P. J. Pfau. il Am City 84:112+ S '69
Watchdog computer keeps tabs on water treatment; Chicago's central water filtration plant. il Am City 84:12 N '69

WATER vapor
Galactic water vapor emission: further observations of variability. S. H. Knowles and others. bibliog il Science 166:221-4 O 10 '69
Water vapor: observations of galactic sources. M. L. Meeks and others. bibliog il Science 165:180-4 Jl 11 '69

WATER whistles. See Whistles

WATER works
See also
Water distribution

WATERBURY, Conn.
Local association of the month. J. H. Starie. Todays Ed 58:71-2 Mr '69

Street lighting
Brighter city is a safer city. R. Orsini. il Am City 84:110 N '69

WATERCRESS. See Water cress

WATERFALLS
Waterfall-generated earth vibrations. J. S. Rinehart. il Science 164:1513-14 Je 27 '69
Where the Rhine drops seventy feet; Rheinfall near Schaffhausen, Switzerland. il Sunset 142:61 F '69
See also
Churchill Falls
Niagara Falls

WATERFOWL. See Water birds

WATERFRONTS. See Water fronts

WATERGATE apartments, Washington. See Washington, D.C.—Housing

WATERING of gardens, lawns, etc.
So your vacation water boy won't go wrong. Sunset 143:128 Ag '69
Underground watering systems for lawn and garden. Good H 168:209 Ap '69
When & how to water the grass. il Changing T 23:34-5 Je '69
See also
Sprinklers

WATERING of livestock. See Livestock—Watering

WATERING of plants
Deep-root waterer costs less than $3. N. H. Berlin. il Org Gard & Farm 16:115 Mr '69
How to water a tree. il Home Gard 56:63 Ag '69
Water basin for terrace trees. il Sunset 142:120 Je '69
What's the latest on watering up corn? O. Bay. il Farm J 93:C1+ Ap '69

WATERING places. See Health resorts, watering places, etc.

WATERLILIES. See Water lilies

WATERMAN, Charles F.
Alberta sharptail Field & S 74:66-7+ S '69
Coming of the hun. Field & S 74:49-52+ N '69
Fishing the thick stuff. Field & S 73:58-9+ F '69
New gleam for streamers. Field & S 73:56-7+ Ap '69

WATERMAN-Bic pen corporation
King of the ballpoints. il Newsweek 74:77-8 Jl 14 '69

WATERMELONS
Seeds in watermelons, who needs them? seedless melons, B. Borrowman. il Org Gard & Farm 16:51-3 Ap '69
Watermelons for northern gardens. G. Morrison. il Horticulture 47:40-1+ Ap '69
See also
Cookery—Fruit

WATERPROOF cameras. See Cameras

WATERPROOFING
Waterproof your trailer lights. E. F. Xiques. il Yachting 125:74-5 My '69

WATERS, A. C. See Fisher, R. V. jt. auth.

WATERS, Don
Hams tackle a hurricane. Pop Electr 31:72-3 D '69

WATERSHEDS
New lakes: the beautiful and the dammed. H. R. Williams. il Parks & Rec 4:12-14+ N '69
Nitrification: importance to nutrient losses from a cutover forested ecosystem. G. E. Likens and others. bibliog il Science 163:1205-6 Mr 14 '69

WATERVILLE, Ohio
Survey spurs action. il Am City 84:160+ My '69

WATERWAYS
Brazil
See also
Amazon River

Canada
Sailor meets houseboat; Rideau waterway. P. Smyth. il Motor B 124:36-41+ D '69

Europe
See also
Danube River

United States
America's waterways are your's to explore. il Motor B 123:116-17 Ja '69
Great American river cleanup. W. Langewiesche. Read Digest 94:213+ My '69
See also
Cross Florida Barge Canal
Intracoastal Waterway
National forests—Waterways
Potomac River

WATERWORKS
Developers boost our water supply; Glenwood, Ill. L. Komer. il Am City 84:85-6 Jl '69
Independent water supply proves best; Gladstone, Mo. G. E. Hands. il Am City 84:106+ F '69
Practical corrections to design weaknesses of wastewater-treatment plants. E. F. Spitz. il Am City 84:75-9 Mr '69
Water supply and treatment. See issues of American city
See also
Filter plants
Pumping stations
Settling basins
Water supply
Water tanks

WATKINS, Arthur Martin
How much does remodeling cost? Am Home 72:50-1 My '69
How much house can you afford? Am Home 72:78 Ja '69
How to buy a good old house. Pop Mech 132:139-42+ S '69
How to get better homes for less money. Redbook 133:86-7+ My '69
How to spot a bad house that looks good; excerpt from How to avoid the ten biggest homebuying traps. Pop Mech 131:144-6+ F '69
When the repairman won't come. House B 111:84-6+ O '69

WATKINS, John V.
China-fir. Horticulture 47:18 Ap '69
Landscaping with hollies in the Deep South. Horticulture 47:18-19 D '69

WATKINS, Marj
Okinawa. Travel 131:54-9+ Mr '69

WATKINS, T. H.
Conquest of the Colorado. bibliog Am West 6:4-9+ Jl '69
Hail to the crystal spring. Am West 6:26-7+ Ja '69
Pilgrim's pride; excerpts from The Grand Colorado: the story of a river and its canyons. Am West 6:49-54 S '69

WATKINS, William John
Universe of ready-made characters. Writers Digest 49:38-9 Ag '69

WATLINGTON, John Francis, 1911-
Merchant of money. R. Levy. por Duns R 93:57+ F '69

WATSON, Arthur Kittredge
Trade; address, September 17, 1969. Vital Speeches 36:2-5 O 15 '69
WATSON, Blanche
Investment clubs pay double dividends. Har Yrs 9:40-3 F '69
WATSON, Bracie, jr
Teen scientist. il pors Ebony 24:96-8+ Je '69
WATSON, Catherine
This geography is something to sing about. Am Ed 5:14-18 O '69
WATSON, Claire
Very private person; interview, ed. by D. Graham. por Opera N 34:26 D 20 '69
WATSON, Cyril
Ruby's; interview. New Yorker 45:27-8 Jl 12 '69
WATSON, Donald P.
Hawaiian leis. il Horticulture 47:20-1+ D '69
Horticulture in Honolulu. il Horticulture 46:24-7+ O '68
Must we put up with billboards? Horticulture 47:16-17+ N '69
WATSON, Emmett
Tennis. Sports Illus 31:76+ O 20 '69
WATSON, Ernest W.
Obituary
Am Artist por 33:6 Mr '69
WATSON, James B.
Nighttime boss of capital inn. il pors Ebony 25:67-8+ N '69
WATSON, James D.
Behavior patterns of scientists; address, December 1968. R. K. Merton. Am Scholar 38:197-225 Spr '69
Genetics of the discovery of DNA. F. Davis. Trans-Action 6:53-6 Mr '69
Quick climb up Mount Olympus. E. Chargaff; discussion. Science 164:1537-9 Je 27 '69
WATSON, Robert
High dive; poem. New Yorker 45:85 Je 14 '69
WATSON, S. W. and Remsen, C. C.
Macromolecular subunits in the walls of marine nitrifying bacteria. bibliog Science 163:685-6 F 14 '69
WATSON, Thomas John, 1874-1956
Think, by W. Rodgers. Review
Sat R 52:44-5 O 4 '69. S. W. Clements
WATSON, William
Five stages of Shang. Art N 67:42-7+ N '68
WATSON, William Marvin
Excerpt from press briefing, January 15, 1969. Cong Digest 48:90+ Mr '69
WATSONVILLE, Calif.

Water supply
Water and wastewater master plans. L. J. Cooper. il Am City 84:136+ O '69
WATT, Douglas
Popular records (cont) New Yorker 44:84-6 Ja 18; 108-10 Mr 1; 45:92+ Je 14 '69
WATTEVILLE, Pierre Hubert de
Sophia Loren's baby: the doctor who made it possible. J. Barry. il por McCalls 96:124-5+ Ap '69
WATTLE (tree) See Acacias
WATTLE fences. See Fences
WATTLES, Gurdon W.
Pioneer on the sidelines. por Forbes 103:22-3 My 1 '69
WATTS, André
André Watts, a giant among giants at age twenty-two. H. J. Massaquoi. il pors Ebony 24:90-1+ My '69
My man André. N. Darden. il pors Sat R 52:43-5 Jl 26 '69
WATTS, Charles Henry, 1926-
Higher education: dilemma, analysis, and prospect. Sch & Soc 97:352-6 O '69
WATTS, Frances B.
Bridge to Killybog fair; drama. Plays 28:45-51+ Mr '69
Grandma and the pampered boarder; drama. Plays 29:37-45 O '69
Log in the bog; drama. Plays 29:79-83 D '69
WATTS, Franklin Mowry
Franklin Watts starts London publishing company. il por Pub W 196:64 N 17 '69
WATTS, Raymond N. jr
[Articles on astronomy, space flight, etc] See issues of Sky and telescope
WATTS, Calif. See Los Angeles
WATZMAN, Sanford
Nader's raiders and the traders. Nation 209:317 S 29 '69
Tax-court peephole. Nation 208:113-15 Ja 27 '69
WAUGAMAN, Charles A.
Consider the lilies; poem. Chr Today 13:8 Ap 11 '69
Good Friday; poem. Chr Today 13:4 Mr 28 '69

WAUGH, Alec
Buenos Aires. Holiday 46:58-9+ D '69
Delectations. See occasional issues of National review
WAUGH, Auberon
Blame it on the mayor. Nat R 21:1006 O 7 '69
Fixer, Roman style. Holiday 46:30-1+ Ag '69
Innocent abroad. Nat R 21:1322-5+ D 30 '69
Letter from Ann Arbor. Nat R 21:1169+ N 18 '69
Parlement of fooles. Nat R 21:1063+ O 21 '69
WAUGH, Coulton
Keep out of the mud! il Am Artist 33:32-9 Je '69
WAUGH, Hillary
Plots and people. Writer 82:9-11+ D '69
WAUKEGAN, Ill.

Lighting
Lighting adds final touch to downtown revitalization. il Am City 84:128+ Mr '69
WAVE motion, Theory of
See also
Sound waves
WAVES
Convergence and strain waves caused by a submerged turbulent disturbance in stratified fluids. A. H. Schooley. bibliog il Science 164:1393-4 Je 20 '69
See also
Elastic waves
Gravity waves
Shock waves
WAVES, Sound. See Sound waves
WAWONA tunnel tree. See Sequoia, Giant
WAX; ballet. See Ballets—Criticisms
WAX modeling
Wax sculpture. R. J. Clancy. il Sch Arts 68:28-9 My '69
WAX moth (bait) See Bait
WAX removers
Floor-wax removers. il Consumer Rep 34:585-7 O '69
WAXES
Self-polishing floor waxes. il Consumer Rep 34:582-5 O '69
WAYMAN, Stan
Longest dive; photographs. Life 66:30-5 Mr 7 '69

about
Art of shooting underwater. G. P. Hunt. il por Life 66:3 Mr 7 '69
WAYNE, John
Dusty and the Duke; with editorial comment. il pors Life 67:1, 36-45 Jl 11 '69
John Wayne as the last hero. il pors Time 94:53-6 Ag 8 '69
WAYNE state university, Detroit
We're not anti-white, we don't make them a habit. il Newsweek 73:54 F 10 '69
See also
Institute of gerontology
WAYS, Max
Faculty is the heart of the trouble. Fortune 79:94-7+ Ja '69
Gearing U.S. policy to the world's great trends. Fortune 79:64-9+ My 1 '69
Long road to racial equality. Fortune 80:106 N '69
What's wrong with news? It isn't new enough. Fortune 80:110-13+ O '69
WAYS and means committee. See United States—Congress—House of representatives—Ways and means, Committee on
WE learn by loving; story. See MacNish, L.
WE, the people (organization)
Doctor Jackson delights the radical right. Chr Cent 86:1271 O 8 '69
WEALES, Gerald
Day LeRoi Jones spoke on Penn campus, what were the blacks doing in the balcony? N Y Times Mag p38-40+ My 4 '69
Stage. See issues of Commonweal
WEALTH
See also
Rich, The
WEALTH, Distribution of
Inequality: a trend analysis. P. Roby. bibliog f Ann Am Acad 385:110-17 S '69
Minority owns U.S. business. B. L. Masse. America 121:181 S 20 '69
Role of compensatory justice; black reparations, two views. M. Harrington; A. S. Kaufman. Cur 110:50-4 S '69
TRB from Washington; where the money goes. New Repub 160:4 Mr 22 '69
WEAPON systems. See Weapons systems
WEAPONS
Army's attic of antique arms. il Pop Mech 131:46-7 Ja '69

WEAPONS—*Continued*
Conventional killers; antipersonnel weapons. E. Prokosch. New Repub 161:18-21 N 1 '69
See also
Atomic weapons
Firearms

WEAPONS systems
Ocean frontier. A. H. Whitelaw. il Sea Front 15:208-11 Jl '69
Pentagon wins a costly battle; budget for new weapons. il Bsns W p28-9 S 27 '69
Prototype shopping comes off the shelf. il Bsns W p 162-3 S 20 '69
Status of major U.S. European defense, aerospace programs (cont) Aviation W 90:34-8 Mr 10 '69
Strategic weapons. W. C. Foster; H. Brown; D. G. Brennan. bibliog f For Affairs 47: 413-48 Ap '69
$10-billion scrap heap. il Bsns W p 164-5 S 20 '69
Viet lull advances new weapons. C. Brownlow. il Aviation W 90:16-18 Ja 20 '69
Weapons with clout for counterpunching. il Bsns W p94 D 6 '69
What prospects for arms talks? M. Woollacott. Cur 109:43-5 Ag '69
See also
Chemical and biological weapons

WEASELS
Hair color: molt, and testis size in male, short-tailed weasels treated with melatonin. C. C. Rust and R .K. Meyer. bibliog il Science 165:921-2 Ag 29 '69

WEATHER
Are we changing our weather by accident? W. Cloud. il Pop Sci 194:74-7+ My '69
Circulation and weather of 1968. J. F. Andrews. il Weatherwise 22:4-11 F '69
Crazy weather: what it's doing. U S News 67: 8 Ag 18 '69
How weather is made; with map. R. E. Falconer. il Cons 24:22-31 D '69
Summer: long and hot, wet and dry, and freaky; questioning effect of man-made pollution. il U S News 67:4 Jl 28 '69
Weatherwatch. See issues of Weatherwise
See also
Climate
Rain and rainfall
Snow
Storm detectors
Storms
Winds
Winter

WEATHER bureau (United States) See United States—Weather bureau

WEATHER control
Can we control the Arctic climate? proposed transport of Atlantic Ocean water across the Arctic basin. P. M. Borisov. il Bul Atom Sci 25:43-8 Mr '69
Curbing hurricanes; the chances; interview. R. H. Simpson. il U S News 67:34-6 S 1 '69
How to blow up a snowstorm; ESSA snowseeding experiment in Lake Erie Region. il Bsns W p42 D 20 '69
Hurricane seeding: a quest for data. M. Mueller. Science 165:990 S 5 '69
International implications of weather modification. R. F. Taubenfeld and H. J. Taubenfeld. Bul Atom Sci 25:43-5 Ja '69
Taming the hurricane; seeding Debbie. il Newsweek 74:47-8 S 1 '69
See also
Fog dispersal
Rain making

WEATHER forecasts
Be your own weatherman. il Changing T 23: 11-12 Ag '69
Camille: did forecasters slip? il U S News 67:33 S 8 '69
Good rains ahead for the Corn Belt. I. P. Krick. Farm J 93:R4 My '69
Prediction for profit. Newsweek 74:86 O 27 '69
Satellite weather forecasting. B. O'Connell. bibliog il Sci Digest 65:43-8+ My '69
This winter's weather; long-range weather forecasting. Sci Am 221:62+ N '69
Twelve ways you can learn to predict the weather. P. Brock. il Sci Digest 66:23-7 D '69
Weather: outboarders' bug-a-boo? J. Martenhoff. il Yachting 125:66-7+ Ap '69
What's new. See issues of Successful farming
World weather program; plan for U.S. participation; President's letter of transmittal, March 13, 1969; with excerpts from report. R. M. Nixon. Dept State Bul 60:368-75 Ap 28 '69
See also
Artificial satellites—Meteorological applications
Computers—Meteorological applications
Radio broadcasting—Weather forecasts

Television broadcasting—Weather forecasts
United States—Weather bureau
Weather maps

WEATHER in San Francisco; story. See Brautigan, R.

WEATHER instruments. See Meteorological instruments

WEATHER maps
New daily weather map? sampling reader opinion. il Weatherwise 22:90 Je '69
Trans-Pac: the race you sail by the weather map. E. S. Kurtz. il Weatherwise 22:185-9 O '69

WEATHER modification. See Weather control

WEATHER predictions. See Weather forecasts

WEATHER research
Bomex, the massive assault on the mystery of how air and ocean combine to forge our weather. E. A. Zadig. il Pop Sci 195:50-5+ Ag '69
Catching the weather coming; GARP global weatherwatch system. K. Frazier. il Sci N 96:185-7 S 6 '69
How hurricanes are born; Camille and the BOMEX experiment. J. Lear. il Sat R 52: 67-71 O 4 '69
Project BOMEX: biggest weather study yet. L. J. Carter. Science 163:1435-6 Mr 28 '69
Weather probe set near Barbados; BOMEX. A. Ewing. il Sci N 95:411-13 Ap 26 '69
World weather program; plan for U.S. participation; President's letter of transmittal, March 13, 1969; with excerpts from report. R. M. Nixon. Dept State Bul 60:368-75 Ap 28 '69

WEATHER stripping
Complete guide to weatherstripping. A. Mikesell. il Pop Mech 130:164-9 D '68
Short course in weatherstripping. il Mech Illus 65:96-7+ D '69

WEATHER vanes
Amateur scientist; flow of blood, weather vanes, telescope mirrors and the conductivity of insulators. C. L. Stong. il Sci Am 221:134-6 O '69

WEATHERING of soils. See Soils—Weathering

WEATHERING of wood. See Wood—Weathering

WEATHERMEN (organization)
Custeristic. Nation 209:428 O 27 '69
Hard times for S.D.S. il Time 94:81 N 28 '69
Long and the short. Newsweek 75:43 Ja 12 '70
Ministers and Weathermen. America 121:449 N 15 '69
Reports: SDS at Chicago. J. K. Glassman. Atlan 224:30+ S '69
Sanctuary in Evanston. Newsweek 74:73+ O 27 '69
Sheltering the Weathermen. Chr Cent 86:1410-11 N 5 '69
Vandals in the mother country. J. Kifner. il N Y Times Mag p 14-16+ Ja 4 '70
Weather goes SDS? R. Whitehead. Commonweal 91:92 O 24 '69
Wild in the streets; demonstrations in Chicago. il Newsweek 74:42+ O 20 '69

WEATHERSBEE, Christopher
Amazonia. Sci N 95:312-15, 338-41 Mr 29-Ap 5 '69

WEATHERSTRIPPING. See Weather stripping

WEATHERVANES. See Weather vanes

WEATHERVISION. See Television and meteorology

WEAVER, Bettie Woodson
History in towns. Antiques 96:588-91 O '69

WEAVER, E. C. and others
Paramagnetic unit in spinach subchloroplast particles: estimation of size. bibliog Science 165:906-7 Ag 29 '69

WEAVER, Frederick S.
Taking sides. R. L. Shayon. Sat R 52:65 N 15 '69

WEAVER, Harold, and Biswell, H. H.
How fire helps the big trees. il Nat Parks 43:16-19 Jl '69

WEAVER, James H.
How to stay the richest country in the world. Commonweal 90:67-8, 375 Ap 4, Je 13 '69

WEAVER, Kenneth F.
And now to touch the moon's forbidding face. Nat Geog 135:632-5 My '69
Flight of Apollo 11: One giant leap for mankind. Nat Geog 136:752-87 D '69
Moon. Nat Geog 135:206-30 F '69
What the moon rocks tell us. Nat Geog 136: 788-91 D '69

WEAVER, Paul. See Kristol, I. jt. auth.

WEAVER, Warren, 1894-
Basic research and the common good. Sat R 52:17-18+ Ag 9 '69

WEAVER, William
Glimpses of a great age. Hi Fi 19:MA28-9 Ag '69

WEAVER, William—*Continued*
Music on and off the track. Hi Fi 19:MA28+
D '69
Sills & Horne triumph at La Scala. Hi Fi
19:MA25 Jl '69
(tr) See Calvino, I. Night driver
WEAVERVILLE, Calif.
Why this old town is worth a stopover, even
a detour. il Sunset 143:36+ Jl '69
WEAVING
Branch-weaving. E. E. Penn. il Sch Arts 68:
40 My '69
Cloth of the Quechuas. G. Goodell. il Natur
Hist 78:48-55+ D '69
Serape happy. S. Gruenberg. il Sch Arts 68:
16-17 My '69
See also
Rugs and carpets

Exhibitions
Fabric of construction; exhibit at Museum
of modern art, New York. L. Bourgeois. il
Craft Horiz 29:30-5 Mr '69
New weaving; exhibit at Stedelijk museum,
Amsterdam, Holland. J. L. Larsen. il
Craft Horiz 29:22-9+ Mr '69

Study and teaching
Primitive weaving adapted to the intermedi-
ate classroom. B. G. Shelly. il Sch Arts 68:
13-15 My '69
Teachers discover the world of fibers. D. F.
Standerfer. il Sch Arts 69:6-10 Ja '70
WEAVING as recreation. See Recreation—Ac-
tivities
WEB offset printing. See Printing, Offset
WEBB, Alice G.
Batik as a painting technique. Sch Arts 68:
6-8 My '69
WEBB, Charles
Dear Benjamin. B. Geller. Engl J 58:423-5
Mr '69
WEBB, Jim
Sound of Jim Webb; ed. by E. Miller. por
Seventeen 28:128-9+ F '69
WEBB, Susan H.
Guidelines for better CIT training. Camp Mag
41:26-8 My '69
WEBB, Todd
Texas Victorian. Art in Am 57:96-9 Jl '69
WEBB gallery of American art. See Shel-
burne museum, Shelburne, Vt.
WEBBER, George W.
New leader, new motif for New York semi-
nary. J. Evenson. Chr Today 13:42 Mr 28
'68
WEBBER, Howard R.
Up with arts at the UPS. Sat R 52:44-6 Je 21
'69
WEBER, Bee
Your travel album. Travel & Camera 32:88-9
N '69
WEBER, Ben Brian
More on Ben Weber and Wuorinen. A. Cohn.
il por Am Rec G 35:1040-1 Jl '69
Reviews of records. D. Henahan. Mus Q 55:
424-6 Jl '69
WEBER, Brom
Personal history. Sat R 52:38-9 Ag 23 '69
WEBER, Carlo A.
Communist-Catholic neurosis? Commonweal
90:389-93 Je 20 '69
Time of the fugitive. Commonweal 90:137-40
Ap 18 '69
WEBER, George H. and Palmer, Diane
New careers: problems and pitfalls. Am Ed
5:26-8 Ap '69
WEBER, Jean
Sweetest girl in New York. Opera N 33:26-7
Ap 19 '69
WEBER, Joseph
Gravitating toward Einstein. Time 93:75 Je 20
'69
Gravitational waves detected. Sky & Tel 38:
71+ Ag '69
Gravitational waves detected. il por Sci N
95:593-4 Je 21 '69
Universe makes waves. Newsweek 73:63 Je
30 '69
Weber reports 1660-Hz gravitational waves
from outer space. G. B. Lubkin. il por Phys
Today 22:61-2 Ag '69
WEBER, Karl Maria von
Absolutely scintillating Weber; Der freischütz.
W. Yost. Am Rec G 34:1150-1 Ag '69
WEBER, Tony
On the boards. W. Como. por Dance Mag 43:
20 Mr '69
WEBER state college, Ogden, Utah
Long "e" has the last laugh; athletes. C.
Kirkpatrick. il Sports Illus 30:58+ Mr 10 '69
WEBERN, Anton von
From the eye of the hurricane, precious,
aphorismic messages. J. Ringo. por Am
Rec G 35:886-8+ My '69

Newly-discovered Webern from Eugene
Ormandy: Im sommerwind. A. Cohn. Am
Rec G 35:1126 Ag '69
WEBS, Spiders. See Spider webs
WEBSTER, Benjamin, family
140 years before the footlights. R. Denham.
Sat R 52:43-5 My 24 '69
WEBSTER, Daniel
Philadelphia company finds its feet. Dance
Mag 43:62-4 Jl '69
WEBSTER, Daniel, 1782-1852
Personal history. M. M. Brown. Sat R 52:33
Ag 9 '69
WEBSTER, David
Opinion: on TV and its works. por Mlle 68:
20+ Mr '69
WEBSTER, Dwight A.
Temperatures and related factors in lakes.
Cons 24:12-16+ D '69 (to be cont)
WEBSTER, George A.
New look in gladiolus. Horticulture 47:24-5
Ag '69
WEBSTER, Margaret
Authors & editors. B. A. Bannon. por Pub W
195:17-18 Je 23 '69
140 years before the footlights. il por R. Den-
ham. Sat R 52:43-5 My 24 '69
WEBSTER, Marvin
Webster's wing-ding Ford. J. Thawley. il
por Hot Rod 22:59-61 N '69
WEBSTER, Mildred E.
Disadvantaged. Engl J 59:1370-2 D '69
WEBSTER, Noah
Butter by the firkin; The elementary spelling-
book. L. Conger. Writer 82:9-10 Mr '69
WEBSTER, Rosalind. See Purcell, T. V. jt.
auth.
WEBSTER, W. R.
Auditory habituation and barbiturate-in-
duced neural activity. bibliog Science 164:
970-1 My 23 '69
WECHSBERG, Joseph
Gastronomy. Esquire 72:10 Jl '69
Lights of Lucerne. Travel & Camera 32:39-
41+ Mr '69
Oft-told tale of the Vienna woods. McCalls
96:46+ Ap '69
Why Viennese women eat pastry every after-
noon. McCalls 96:71+ Jl '69
WEDDELL seals. See Seals (animals)
WEDDING gifts
Attention must be paid to the groom. il Es-
quire 71:134-5 My '69
Elegance for the bride. T. Bowman. il House
B 111:64+ My '69
For the here-and-now bride. T. Bowman. il
House B 111:138-41 My '69
Practically speaking. V. Jaxon. il Har Yrs
9:44-5 Je '69
WEDDING gowns
Lady who marries the best people. E. Hawes.
il McCalls 96:64-5+ Je '69
WEDDING meals
Looking ahead to June; wedding feasts, with
recipes. C. Claiborne. il N Y Times Mag p
126+ Ap 13 '69
WEDDING receptions. See Receptions
WEDDING ring; story. See Gallant, M.
WEDDINGS
Free-form wedding game. il Life 67:95-6+ S
26 '69
Joyful happening; Arlo and Jackie Guthrie.
il Time 94:66 O 17 '69
Planning a wedding? Make these arrange-
ments in advance. Good H 168:192 My '69
Sky-high cost of hotel weddings. P. Battelle.
il McCalls 96:54+ Je '69
Wedding racket. P. Pace. il Look 33:86-7+
Je 10 '69
See also
Photography of weddings
Wedding meals

Anecdotes, facetiae, satire, etc.
Left at the altar. G. McCabe. il Good H
168:66+ My '69

Photographs
Simon says; story of how a prosecutor
took photographer L. Gunkel to court.
Simon. il Mod Phot 33:46-7+ F '69
WEDDINGS: story. See Reed, K.
WEDDLE, David L.
God the redeemer: sovereignty and suffering.
Chr Today 13:12-15 Ag 1 '69
WEDDLE, Ferris
Jaunty brigand: the Steller's jay. il Nat
Parks 43:9 Ja '69
WEDEL, Cynthia C.
Lord's doing. Cath World 208:233 F '69

about
Crunch at the Council. por Time 94:70 D 12
'69

WEDEL, Cynthia C.—about—*Continued*
Under the ecumenical umbrella. R. Chandler. por Chr Today 14:39 Ja 2 '70
WEED, Florence Collins
Free checking accounts. Har Yrs 9:22-3 O '69
House that Glenbrook built. Sr Schol 94:Schol Teach 12-13 Mr 21 '69
WEED, Tracy
Portrait of Tracy, a very personal view. R. Davis. il por Life 67:88-91+ O 17 '69
WEEDS
See also
Aquatic plants
Cockleburs
Dandelions
Greens, Edible
Hellebore

Chemical control
Easy-does-it weed killing. Bet Hom & Gard 47:143 Mr '69
Kill more weeds when you plant. il Farm J 93:24-5 My '69
Lawn weeds and their cures. H. E. Barké. il Horticulture 47:20-1+ Jl '69
Now: give soybeans a weed-free start. D. Seim. il Farm J 93:32-3+ Ap '69
Now: tailor-make your sprays to kill corn weeds. D. Seim. il Farm J 93:24-5+ Mr '69
Weed and insect control guide. il Suc Farm 67:56-7+ F '69
See also
Herbicides

Control
How they stop weeds. il Suc Farm 67:B1 Je '69
Try a self-weeding garden! canopy of soil-shading leaves. J. Krill. il Org Gard & Farm 16:28-9 Jl '69
See also
Weeds—Chemical control
WEEGEE, pseud. See Fellig, A.
WEEKEND guests. See Guests
WEEKEND houses. See Vacation houses
WEEKEND vacations. See Vacations
WEEKENDS: story. See Jordan, E. H.
WEEKLY newspapers. See Newspapers
WEEKS, Edward Augustus
Peripatetic reviewer. See issues of Atlantic
WEEKS, John A.
Courtship in the natural world. Cons 23:21-7 F '69
WEEMS, David B.
Bigger-than-life speaker system. Pop Electr 30:53+ My '69
Build the dorm special. Pop Electr 31:53-7+ Ag '69
Build the thrifty three-way. Pop Electr 30:59-61+ F '69
Mini-six add-on. Pop Electr 31:45-50+ S '69
Pair of loaded dice. Pop Electr 32:40-4 Ja '70
Rally round the reflex. Pop Electr 31:47-51 N; 43-6+ D '69
Speaker boxes that are something else. Pop Electr 31:45-9 O '69
WEEPING. See Crying
WEEPING trees. See Trees
WEERTH, Hans Joachim
New European bookstore; tr. by C. B. Anderson. G. Ramseger. il Pub W 195:19-22 My 26 '69
WEESNER, Theodore
Trainee; story. Esquire 73:121 Ja '70
WEETALL, Howard H.
Trypsin and papain covalently coupled to porous glass: preparation and characterization. bibliog Science 166:615-17 O 31 '69
WEEVILS
See also
Boll weevils
Sweet clover weevils
WEHNER, Alfred P.
Electric fog to smother asthma. T. W. Hill. il por Sci Digest 65:74-7 Ap '69
WEHNER, Rudiger, and Menzel, Randolf
Homing in the ant cataglyphis bicolor. bibliog Science 164:192-4 Ap 11 '69
WEHRLE, Otto W.
Nature's self-made widow; photograph. Nat Wildlife 7:16 Ap '69
WEHRUM, Victoria
ABC D goldfish. Pub W 196:28 N 10 '69
WEI, C. C.
Mystic Wei of the East. C. Goren. il Sports Illus 31:46-7 Jl 21 '69
WEI, Ling Y.
Role of surface dipoles on axon membrane. bibliog Science 163:280-2 Ja 17 '69
WEICKER, Lowell P. jr
Our environment; address, August 11, 1969. Vital Speeches 35:732-5 S 15 '69

WEIDEL, Suzanne
Young places. Travel & Camera 32:30+ S '69
WEIDENBAUM, Murray L.
Military-industrial complex; address, March 21, 1969. bibliog Vital Speeches 35:523-8 Je 15 '69
Our Vietnamized economy. Sat R 52:15-17 My 24 '69
Toward a new fiscal federalism; address, August 27, 1969. Vital Speeches 35:748-51 O 1 '69
Viet Nam peace and the budget. por Nations Bsns 57:78 Ag '69
WEIDENBUSCH, Albert C.
Academic question; ROTC; address, May 16, 1969. Vital Speeches 35:558-60 Jl 1 '69
WEIDMAN, Jerome
Authors & editors. B. A. Bannon. por Pub W 196:13-15 Jl 28 '69
WEIDNER, Edward W.
Communiversity; address, January 18, 1969. Vital Speeches 35:277-9 F 15 '69
WEIGART, Elias
Last grizzly in Shasta. Field & S 74:60-1+ Je '69
WEIGHT (physiology)
How much weight to gain during pregnancy. il Good H 169:149 Ag '69
See also
Corpulence
Diet
Exercise
Weight watchers, incorporated
WEIGHT control drugs. See Drugs—Physiological effects
WEIGHT lifting
Paul Anderson can lift eight of you. J. F. Ryan. Esquire 72:69-71+ Jl '69
U.S. journal: on the circuit; world's strongest man, P. Anderson. C. Trillin. New Yorker 44:38-40+ F 1 '69
WEIGHT throwing
See also
Shot putting
WEIGHT watchers, incorporated
High priestess of the weight watchers. L. Botto. il Look 33:82-4+ My 27 '69
How weight watchers lose weight. J. Pascoe. Read Digest 95:143-4+ Jl '69
WEIGHTLESSNESS
Biosatellite III: preliminary findings. W. R. Adey and others. Science 166:492-3 O 24 '69
Great promise of zero G. A. R. Sorrells. il Space World F-10-70:16-25 O '69
Researchers build huge centrifuge to study weightlessness. M. Steinmann. il Life 66:75+ F 21 '69
Zero gravity's deadly effects. il Sci N 96:393-4 N 1 '69
See also
Biosatellite program
WEIGHTS and measures
See also
Cookery—Measurements
International bureau of weights and measures
Metric system
Units
WEIKER, Leslie
Team up in Denver. Am Ed 5:28 N '69
WEIL, Andrew T. See Zinberg, N. E. jt. auth.
WEIL, James L.
To find; poem. Nation 209:606 D 1 '69
WEILL, Gus
Geese. Criticism
Commonweal 90:463 Jl 25 '69
WEILL, Kurt
Seven deadly sins. C. J. Luten. Am Rec G 35:383 Ja '69
WEIMAR republic. See Germany—History—1918-1933
WEIMARANERS. See Pointers (dogs)
WEIMER, Karl J.
Citizenship education. bibliog Clear House 43:355-7 F '69
WEINBERG, Alvin M.
Third international conference on science and society. Bul Atom Sci 25:23-6 N '69
WEINBERG, Henry
New quartet player. I. Kolodin. Sat R 52:45 Ag 30 '69
WEINBERG, Jack
They are stealing things from me. por Forbes 103:29 Ja 15 '69
WEINBERG, Jack, 1940?-
Where are they now? il por Newsweek 73:18 Je 23 '69
WEINBERG, Sidney James
Mr Wall Street. por Newsweek 74:76-7 Ag 4 '69
Mr Wall Street's lasting legacy. por Bsns W p24 Ag 2 '69
Obituary
Time il por 94:69A Ag 1 '69
WEINER, Hannah
Code poem. Poetry 113:393-5 Mr '69

WEINER, I. William
Effectiveness of a suicide prevention pro-
gram. bibliog Ment Hy 53:357-63 Jl '69
WEINGARTNER, Charles
Semantics: what and why. Engl J 58:1214-19
'69
WEINGOLD, Allan B. and Edelson, Edward
Diet and weight during pregnancy. Redbook
132:40+ Mr '69
WEINRAUB, Bernard
Director Arthur Penn takes on General Cus-
ter. N Y Times Mag p 10-11+ D 21 '69
In the matter of Lloyd Mark Bucher. N Y
Times Mag p25-7+ My 11 '69
WEINREICH, Alisa
(tr) See Aichinger, I. Where I live
WEINRICH, Lorenz
Peter Abaelard as musician. bibliog f Mus Q
55:295-312, 464-86 Jl-O '69
WEINSTEIN, Grace W.
Baby learns to talk. Parents Mag 44:66-7+
S '69
Can your color TV stand a radiation count?
Sci Digest 65:24-8 Ap 69
Needed: volunteers who care. Parents Mag
44:52-3 Ag '69
WEINSTEIN, Henry E.
(ed) See Cleaver, E. Conversation with Clea-
ver
WEINSTEIN, Jacob
LaAdonoi haaretz umloah..; excerpt from
address. Am For 75:25+ My '69
WEINSTEIN, Robert A.
Million-dollar mud flat. Am West 6:33-43 Ja
'69
WEINSTEIN, Robert V.
Black 'n blues. Negro Hist Bul 32:13-15 My
'69
WEINSTEIN, Ronald S. See McNutt, N. S. jt.
auth
WEINSTOCK, Bernard
Carbon monoxide: residence time in the at-
mosphere. bibliog Science 166:224-5 O 10 '69
WEINSTOCK, Henry R. and Van Horn, P. L.
Impact of negotiations upon public educa-
tion. bibliog Clear House 43:358-63 F '69
WEINSTOCK, Herbert
Bread and lollipops. Sat R 52:31 O 25 '69
From the dawn of opera. Sat R 52:80+ D 6
'69
Greater Handel. Sat R 52:50 Mr 29 '69
Handel's Samson glorified. Sat R 52:51 D 27
'69
Joshua not so fit. Sat R 52:51 Ag 30 '69
Salvaging the past. Sat R 52:75 F 22 '69
Venice 1644 (?), Glyndebourne 1967. Sat R
52:57 My 31 '69
WEINTRAUB, Lionel
Perils of going public. R. Levy. por Duns R
94:46-7 S '69
WEIR, Walter
Musical chairs. Sat R 52:74 D 13 '69
WEIS, Bud
How the pros keep their outboards humming.
Mech Illus 65:79-80+ Mr '69
Now! Enjoy boating all winter. Mech Illus
65:96-7+ N '69
Tune up your outboard for water skiing.
Mech Illus 65:84-5+ Jl '69
WEIS, Norman D.
Bargain pack trip. Outdoor Life 143:49-51+
My '69
WEISBERG, Arthur
Fresh music from the university laboratory.
R. P. Morgan. por Hi Fi 19:75-6 Je '69
WEISBERGER, Bernard A.
First to fly the Atlantic. Am Heritage 20:16-
21+ Je '69
WEISBERGER, Hugo E.
Choosing a career. patent law. por Chem
42:12-13 Mr '69
WEISBORD, Robert G.
J. Albert Thorne, back-to-Africanist. bibliog
Negro Hist Bul 32:14-16 Mr '69
WEISBROD, Burton A. See Hansen, W. L. jt.
auth.
WEISBUCH, Kathleen
Wise bookshop owners don't pussyfoot
around. Pub W 196:31-2 Ag 11 '69
WEISCHADLE, David E.
Chautauqua: an experience in adult educa-
tion. Ed Digest 34:47-9 Ja '69
WEISEL, John Chandler
Going the rounds with a Dow recruiter. S.
Braun. il pors N Y Times Mag p27-9+ Ap
13 '69
WEISER, C. J. See Howell, G. S. jt. auth.
WEISIGER, Cary N. 3d
COCU and evangelical opportunity. Chr To-
day 13:22-3 Ap 11 '69
WEISKOPF, Herman
Archery. Sports Illus 31:42-3 S 1 '69
Baseball's week. See issues of Sports illus-
trated published during baseball season
Basketball's week (cont) Sports Illus 30:58-9
Ja 20; 65 Ja 27; 60-1 F 3; 64-5 F 24; 88-9 Mr
17 '69

Wrestling. Sports Illus 30:48 Mr 24; 72-3 Ap
7 '69
WEISMAN, Steven R.
Scholar's inquiry into America's urbanism.
Commonweal 91:364 D 19 '69
WEISS, David Loeb
Old young lion. H. V. Fondiller. por Pop
Phot 65:130-2 Jl '69
WEISS, E. B.
Corporate deaf ear; address, December 5,
1968. Vital Speeches 35:205-7 Ja 15 '69
WEISS, Jay M. and others
Pituitary-adrenal influences on fear respond-
ing. bibliog Science 163:197-9 Ja 10 '69
WEISS, Joan Talmage
Ten rules for the incisive interview. Writers
Digest 49:41-3 My '69
WEISS, Margaret R.
Art for ad's sake. Sat R 52:54-5 Je 14 '69
Eye of Eisenstaedt. Sat R 52:13-15 Ag 2 '69
Fox Talbot in facsimile. Sat R 52:40-1 My 24
'69
Front page afloat: all the news that's fit
to ship. Sat R 52:84-5 N 8 '69
It started with Daguerre. Sat R 52:23-5 D 13
'69
Judging and the judged. por Sat R 53:58-66
Ja 3 '70
News pictures of the year; 1968 in review.
Sat R 52:122-3 Mr 8 '69
Photography. Sat R 52:52-3 Ag 23; 52-3 O 25
'69
Photojournalism museum style. Sat R 52:
112-13 S 13 '69
WEISS, Mary C. See Ephrussi, B. jt. auth.
WEISS, Paul
Intellectual dynamo. por Sch & Soc 97:351+
O '69
WEISS, Paul Alfred
Living nature and the knowledge gap. Sat
R 52:19-22+ N 29 '69
WEISS, Robert S.
Fund of sociability. bibliog Trans-Action 6:
36-43 Jl '69
—and Rein, Martin
Evaluation of broad-aim programs: a cau-
tionary case and a moral; excerpts from
address. Ann Am Acad 385:133-42 S '69
WEISS, Theodore
Constraints and self-determinations. D. Hoff-
man. Poetry 114:338-9 Ag '69
Hazards of art. R. Stock. Nation 208:378-9
Mr 24 '69
WEISSBERGER, Diane
Stop making excuses and start that class li-
brary! Sr Schol 94:Schol Teach 28 Ja 31
'69
WEISSENBERG, Alexis
Lively arts; interview, ed. by R. Hemming.
por Sr Schol 94:21-2 Mr 7 '69
WEISSKOPF, Victor F.
Privilege of being a physicist; adaptation of
address. por Phys Today 22:39-43 Ag '69
WEISSLER, Paul
Gearless transmission from GM. Mech Illus
65:44-6+ D '69
How I learned to fly. pors Mech Illus 65:66-
8+ O '69
Uncle Sam's commuter-shopper car. Mech Il-
lus 65:32-4+ Ag '69
WEISSMAN, Marjorie E.
LTP news (cont) ALA Bul 63:274, 394, 520,
662, 1181, 1295 F-My, S-O '69
WEISSMAN, Rozanne
Merit pay, what merit? Ed Digest 34:16-19
My '69
WEISSMAN, Sam
Drawing in a candid way; with biographical
sketch. il por Am Artist 33:28-31 Ag '69
WEISSMAN, Steve
Centers of industry. Ramp Mag 7:63-4 Ap '69
Rich confer. Ramp Mag 8:58+ S '69
WEITH, H. L. and Gilham, P. T.
Polynucleotide sequence analysis by sequen-
tial base elimination; 3'-terminus of phage
QB RNA. bibliog Science 166:1004-5 N 21
'69
WELCH, Claude E. Jr
Return to civilian rule in Ghana. bibliog f
Cur Hist 56:286-91 My '69
WELCH, Edna E.
Originality in opalescence. Design 70:16-18
Sum '69
WELCH, Frankie
Capital headliner. il por Newsweek 73:104+
My 19 '69
WELCH, Mary Scott
How to make music part of your child's
world. Redbook 132:95+ Ap '69
Short sortie; excerpt from Seventeen guide
to travel. Seventeen 28:462-7+ Ag '69
WELCH, Raquel
Raquel Raquel; interview, ed. by J. Hamil-
ton. pors Look 33:78-82+ Ap 15 '69

WELCH, Raquel—*Continued*
about
Myra/Raquel: the predator of Hollywood.
  il pors Time 94:85-8 N 28 '69
Stars; sea of C cups. il pors Time 93:92+
  Ap 4 '69
WELDEN, J. Eugene
Thirty million adults go to school. Am Ed
  5:11-13 N '69
WELDERS
Are small 110-v.a.c. arc welders really any
  good? J. Burroughs. il Pop Mech 131:182-6+
  Je '69
Color-coded arc welder makes the job easier.
  R. J. De Cristoforo. il Pop Sci 194:173-4 F '69
Flywheel-stored energy welds without melt-
  ing metal; inertia welder. il Pop Sci 195:32
  Ag '69
WELDING
Soyuz welding evaluation puts Russians near-
  er space goals. Aviation W 91:19 O 27 '69
Toughest weld of all; panels of Saturn S-11.
  il Space World F-4-64:42-9 Ap '69
WELDON, Jill
Beautiful life in Hawaii. Vogue 155:126-7+
  Ja 15 '70
WELDY, Gilbert R.
Fellow principals, unite! Clear House 44:214-
  19 D '69
—See Parrish, K. jt. auth.
WELFARE, Public. See Public welfare
WELFARE department, New York city. See
  New York (city)—Welfare, Deptartment of
WELFARE ISLAND
Master rebuilder. il Newsweek 74:76 N 17 '69
New town for New York city. J S. Mar-
  golies. il Arch Forum 131:40-5 O '69
Satellite island for Manhattan. Bsns W p 146
  O 18 '69
WELFARE workers. See Social workers
WE'LL be in touch. Okay? story. See Fields,
  J
WELL drilling. See Drilling and boring (earth
  and rocks)
WELL, here we are; story. See Taylor, E.
WELLER, R. C.
Simple vane system for Mani. il Yachting
  126:65+ Jl '69
WELLER, Shelia
To be a poet. Mlle 70:126-7+ D '69
WELLES, Chris
Newsweek (a fact) is the new hot book (an
  opinion) Esquire 72:152-4+ N '69
WELLESLEY, Arthur, 1st duke of Wellington.
  See Wellington, A. W.
WELLESLEY, Mass.
Wellesley incident; a case of obscenity. dra-
  matic presentation of The slave. T. J. Cot-
  tle. il Sat R 52:67-8+ Mr 15 '69
WELLING, Richard
I am in love with line! Am Artist 33:56-8+
  O '69
WELLINGTON, Arthur Wellesley, 1st duke of
Duke of Wellington's search for a palace. E.
  Longford. il Horizon 11:106-13 Spr '69
WELLINGTON fund. See Wellington manage-
  ment company
WELLINGTON management company
Buy stocks now. R. Brady. il Duns R 94:
  119-20 S '69
Transfer: Wellington fund securities moved
  from First Pennsylvania banking & trust
  co. Philadelphia, to State street bank &
  trust co. Boston. New Yorker 45:23-7 Jl
  12 '69
WELLISZ, Stanislaw
Harlem gets down to business. il por Bsns W
  p70-2 Ag 9 '69
WELLS, Dick
James Garner's new act. Motor T 21:74-6 Je '69
Lear's steam dream: a reality? Motor T 21:
  26-9 Je '69
VW varoom. Motor T 21:70-2+ S: 124-5+ O
  '69
WELLS, H. G.
H. G. Wells, by L. Dickson. Review
  Life por 67:8 Ag 1 '69. C. P. Snow
  New Repub 161:20-3 Ag 9 '69. S. Kauff-
  mann
  Newsweek il por 74:80+ Ag 4 '69. G. Wolff
WELLS, Martin
Memory traces in the octopus; with bio-
  graphical sketch. il por Sea Front 15:295-
  307, 319 S '69
WELLS, R. A.
Martian topography: large-scale variations.
  bibliog Science 166:862-5 N 14 '69
WELLS, Robert
Two nominees to a key agency. U S News
  67:23 S 29 '69
WELLS, Robert D.
Actinomycin binding to DNA: inability of a
  DNA containing guanine to bind actinomy-
  cin D. bibliog Science 165:75-6 Jl 4 '69

WELLS, Roe. See Schmid-Schönbein, H. jt.
  auth.
WELLS
Dig your own shallow well. R. Hendrickson.
  Org Gard & Farm 16:77-80 Je '69
WELLS, Waste disposal. See Trade waste dis-
  posal
WELLS Fargo armored truck robbery. See
  Robberies and assaults
WELLS, Rich, Greene, incorporated
Drugstore love-in; campaign for promoting
  Love cosmetics. il Time 93:93 Mr 14 '69
WELS, Byron G.
Careers in electronics. Radio-Electr 40:69-70
  D '69
Don't let them bug you! Radio-Electr 40:35-8
  F '69
WELSCH, Andy
New technique for big pike. Outdoor Life 143:
  54-5+ F '69
WELSH, Edward C.
Technology: father of human welfare. por
  Space World F-2-62:41 F '69
WELSH, John H.
Mussels on the move; with biographical
  sketch. por Natur Hist 78:4, 56-9 My '69
WELSH, Pat M.
Accentuate the positive with EDP. Pub W
  196:37-9 D 8 '69
WELSH
Wales? J. Morris. il Horizon 11:26-9+ Wint
  '69
WELSH cookery. See Cookery, Welsh
WELSH language
Who cares about Wales? I care. R. Burton.
  il Look 33:74-7 Je 24 '69
WELTY, Eudora
Optimist's daughter; story. New Yorker 45:
  37-46 Mr 15 '69
WELWITSCHIAS
Welwitschia, a botanical octopus. W. J. Tij-
  mens. il Horticulture 46:18-19 N '68
WENBERG, Stanley J.
Private higher education in America today;
  adaptation of address, May 2, 1968. Sch &
  Soc 97:439-41 N '69
WENDEL, William Hall
He's busy lifting a city's face. por Bsns W
  p64 N 1 '69
WENDELL, Clara E.
Composition in concrete. Am City 84:101+
  Ap '69
WENDLER, Henry G.
Children's gardens keep them interested.
  Horticulture 47:40-2+ Ja '69
WENDT, Gerald
Antarctica, international land of science; re-
  print. UNESCO Courier 22:14-15 Ag '69
WENDT, Richard P. See Bresler, E. H. jt. auth.
WENGENROTH, Stow
Portfolio of lithographs by Stow Wengenroth.
  W. Caxton, jr. il por Am Artist 33:62-7+ N
  '69
WENGER, A. See Delsemme, A. H. jt. auth.
WENGER, Robert
Objective: a work of permanent value. Sch
  Arts 69:14-15 Ja '70
WENK, Edward, jr
Coastal waters and the Nation; address. Feb-
  ruary 3, 1969. Vital Speeches 35:349-52 Mr
  15 '69
Physical resources of the ocean; with bio-
  graphical sketch. Sci Am 221:44+, 166-76
  bibliog(p286) S '69
WENNER, Adrian M. and others
Honey bee recruitment to food sources: ol-
  faction or language? bibliog Science 164:
  84-6 Ap 4 '69
WENNER, Jann
Rocking the news. il Newsweek 73:90 Ap 28
  '69
Rolling stone's rock world. il por Time 93:
  78 Ap 25 '69
WENT. F. W.
Fungi associated with stalactite growth. Sci-
  ence 166:385-6 O 17 '69
WENTZ, Richard E.
Save your clerical collars, boys! Chr Cent
  86:1133-5 S 3 '69
WENTZEL, Volkmar
Swaziland tries independence. il Nat Geog
  136:266-93 Ag '69
WERBLIN, David A. See Werblin, S.
WERBLIN, Sonny
Sonny. . .just like in money. M. R. Werner.
  il por Sports Illus 31:30 O 20 '69
WERFEL, Alma Maria (Schindler) Mahler
Love letters in pictures; decorated swan-skin
  fans. il por Time 93:70-3 Mr 14 '69
Very human Alma Mahler. J. Diether. Am
  Rec G 35:896+ My '69
WERKLEY, Caroline E.
A!L!A! A!L!A! Here we go! Rah! Rah! Rah!
  por Library J 94:2421-4 Je 15 '69

WERKLEY, Caroline E.—*Continued*
Not everyone likes dragons. por Library J 94:4110-11 N 15 '69
Of skulls, spiders and small libraries. bibliog pors Wilson Lib Bul 44:188-96 O '69

WERNER, Alfred
Art in Ireland. Am Artist 33:28-33+ D '69
Raoul Dufy; the happy genius. Am Artist 32:60-6 D '68
Rembrandt and modern man. Am Artist 33: 32-7+ Ja '69
Salzburg: baroque jewel in central Europe. Am Artist 33:46-51 Ap '69

WERNER, Jayne S. See Lewis, J. W. jt. auth.

WERNER, M. R.
Horse racing (cont) Sports Illus 31:64-5 Ag 25; 80 O 20 '69

WERTENBERGER, M. D.
Pickup camper you can build. Mech Illus 65: 96-9+ Mr '69

WERTH, Alexander
Balance of horror and heroism. Nation 208: 341-3 Mr 17 '69
Kingsley Martin: a memoir. Nation 208:294-5 Mr 10 '69
about
Obituary
Nation 208:358 Mr 24 '69. C. Bourdet
Nation 208:387 Mr 31 '69

WERTHIMER, Jerrold
San Francisco state. A. J. Langguth. por Harper 239:99-100+ S '69

WESCOTT, John T. 3d
Boat chartering; interview, ed. by J. Smith and R. Smith. Travel 131:28-33+ Je '69

WESLEYAN university, Middletown, Conn.
Classic honky who came out for student power; with report by R. Woodley. il Life 66:36-8 F 14 '69

WESSEL, Morris A.
Tonsils, in or out? Parents Mag 44:82-4+ N '69
What adoptive parents need to know. Parents Mag 44:38-9+ D '69

WESSELLS, Norman K. and Rutter, W. J.
Phases in cell differentiation; with biographical sketches. Sci Am 220:14, 36-44 bibliog(p 148) Mr '69

WEST, Anthony
Books (cont) Vogue 153:58 F 15; 154:120 N 1 '69; 155:78 Ja 15 '70
Katie Crawford; story. Vogue 154:448-9 S 1 '69
Movies (cont) Vogue 153:154 Ap 1; 34 Ap 15; 128 My; 154:64 Ag 1; 154 O 1 '69
Point of age Vogue 153:56+ Ap 1 '69
Trance of poppies. Vogue 154:202-7+ D '69

WEST, Carolyn
Great northwest cruise. Motor B 123:142-6 Ja '69
Springtime spruce-up. Motor B 123:82-3+ Ap '69

WEST, Charles A.
That was our orders; interview, ed. by W. Granger. New Repub 161:16-17 D 13 '69

WEST, Jack
Omega: the last word in electronic navigation. Motor B 124:48-9+ S '69
Very hazardous fraud. Yachting 126:72+ N '69

WEST, Jessamyn
Jessamyn West talks about her cousin President Nixon. McCalls 96:69-70 F '69
We came in peace for all mankind, special view of Christmas. Redbook 134:148+ D '69
about
Authors & editors. B. A. Bannon. por Pub W 195:31-2 Ap 28 '69

WEST, Larry
If you've got the eye, the technique is easy. M. A. Matzkin. il Mod Phot 33:84-9+ F '69

WEST, Mae
Mae West; interview, ed. by R. Meryman. Life 66:60-62D+ Ap 18 '69
about
Seventy-six and still Diamond Lil. S. V. Roberts. il pors N Y Times Mag p64-5+ N 2 '69

WEST, Morris Langlo
Cognoscenti abroad Morris West's Rome. A Goodfriend. Sat R 52:23-6 Jl 19 '69

WEST, Robert L.
Economic development in Africa today. bibliog f Cur Hist 56:263-8+ My '69

WEST, Ruth
Care and feeding of the very rich. McCalls 96:56-7+ Ag '69

WEST, Virginia M.
Weaving as a creative art. por Parks & Rec 3:41-2+ O '68

WEST
East is East and West is second, or is it? A. Hano. il N Y Times Mag p32-3+ Mr 16 '69
See also
Fishing—Western states
Frontier and pioneer life—United States
Hunting—Western states
Negroes—Western states
Overland journeys to the Pacific
Roads—Western states
Southwest
Bibliography
Books for young westerners. D. Powers. Am West 6:49+ Ja '69
Western gathering. See issues of American west
Description and travel
[Month] travel in and beyond the West. See issues of Sunset
Restorations West. B. Belford. il Travel 132: 56-60 N '69
Economic conditions
West is getting lonely again. R. A. Bartlett. il Read Digest 95:46-50 Ag '69
History
Portraits for a western album. See issues of American West
See also
Lewis and Clark expedition
Social life and customs
Growing up in America. B. Packer. il Mlle 68:207+ Ap '69

WEST and East. See East and West

WEST BENGAL
As Bengal goes... E. Behr. il Newsweek 73: 55 Ap 21 '69

WEST BERLIN. See Berlin (West Berlin)

WEST HARTFORD, Conn.
Music
Contemporary music project; it pays off. R. W. Jones. il Hi Fi 19:MA10-11+ N '69
Stores
Where shopping is child's play; Children's place .il Bsns W p88-90 Mr 8 '69

WEST in art
Hunter and the artist. J. Monaghan. bibliog il Am West 6:4-13 N '69
White painting. J. T. Forrest. Am West 6:53-4 Ja '69
See also
Kennedy galleries, incorporated

WEST in literature
Writers of Santa Fe. A. Gregg. il Writers Digest 49:54-9 Ap '69

WEST INDIAN cookery. See Cookery, West Indian

WEST INDIAN dancing. See Dancing, West Indian

WEST INDIES
See also
Antigua (island)
Caribbean Region
Catholic church in the West Indies
Haiti
Hispaniola (island)
Saba
Virgin Islands
Description and travel
Least Antilles. E. Bedell. il Motor B 124:60-1+ N '69
There are still some unspoiled islands: the Lesser Antilles. R. Carson. il Holiday 46: 50-3+ N '69
See also
Barbados—Description and travel
Maps
Map weaves history with geography. il Nat Geog 137:112-13, sup(folded map) Ja '70

WEST INDIES, BRITISH
See also
Anguilla (island)
British Virgin Islands
St Lucia (island)
Trinidad (island)

WEST INDIES, FRENCH
See also
Guadeloupe (islands)
Martinique

WEST INDIES, Netherlands. See Netherlands West Indies

WEST IRIAN
An act free of choice; annexation by Indonesia. il Time 94:36 Ag 22 '69
Yellow colonialism; Papuans revolt at Enarotali. Newsweek 73:55 My 19 '69
See also
United Nations—West Irian

WEYERHAEUSER company
Shy tycoon who owns 1/640th of the U.S.
  R. Cantwell. il Sports Illus 31:50-6 Ag 18
  '69
Weyerhaeuser buys more trees. Bsns W p 120
  My 17 '69
Weyerhaeuser fells a wooden past; moving
  into new product areas. il Bsns W p76-7+
  Je 7 '69
WEYMANN, Ray J.
Seyfert galaxies; with biographical sketch.
  Sci Am 220:18, 28-37 Ja '69
WEYMAR, Caroline S. See Goeke, J. R. jt.
  auth.
WHALE models. See Zoological models
WHALE sharks. See Sharks
WHALEN, George J. and Graf, R. F.
Build your own computing thermometer. Sci
  Digest 66:50+ O '69
Christmas lights keep time to music. Pop Sci
  195:144-6 D '69
Dipstick oil-level indicator you can make.
  Pop Sci 194:116-19 Je '69
Wireless private listening for your TV. Pop
  Sci 194:108-10+ My '69
—See Graf, R. F. jt. auth.
WHALEN, Richard J.
Where the Kennedy money is. Time 94:23
  N 28 '69
WHALES
Big star all at sea; Marineland of the Paci-
  fics Bimbo. D. Valentry. il Sea Front 15:
  219-23 Jl '69
Blow of the pilot whale. C. R. Olsen and
  others. bibliog il Science 163:953-5 F 28 '69
Captive killer. W. M. Stephens. il Sea Front
  15:140-1 My '69
Ingenuities of nature; sperm shales; excerpt
  from The year of the whale. V. B. Scheffer.
  il Sat R 52:49 Ag 2 '69
Little Irvy; exhibition of refrigerated whale.
  F. Deford. il Sports Illus 31:50-7 Ag 11 '69
Pop goes the weasel, pffff goes the whale.
  W. A. Watkins. il Natur Hist 78:20+ My
  '69
Scene of slaughter was exceedingly pictures-
  que; gray whale or devilfish. W. Marx.
  il Am Heritage 20:66-71+ Je '69
School for whales; California's marineland.
  Los Angeles. il Travel 132:26-7 Jl '69
Sea unicorn; narwhal. F. Bruemmer. il Au-
  dubon 71:58-63 N '69
Unicorn is alive and well; baby narwhal at
  New York aquarium. il Life 67:55-6 S 26
  '69
Whale of a tale; how a New Zealand ocean
  racer was sunk by a whale. J. Guiney. il
  Yachting 125:62+ Ap '69
Why did this whale die? il Life 66:34-5 Ap
  1 '69
Year of the whale, by V. B. Scheffer. Review
  Time il 94:79 Ag 15 '69
WHALING
Scene of slaughter was exceedingly pictures-
  que; gray whale or devilfish. W. Marx.
  il Am Heritage 20:66-71+ Je '69
WHALL, Hugh D.
Boating (cont) Sports Illus 30:50-1 Ja 27;
  60 Mr 17; 31:66-7 O 27; 70+ N 10; 66 D
  8 '69
Rowing. Sports Illus 30:62+ My 26; 54+ Je
  23 '69
Sailing (cont) Sports Illus 31:57-8 S 8 '69
WHALLEY, J. Irving
Move to change representation of China in
  the U.N. rejected by the 24th General as-
  sembly; statement, November 4, 1969. Dept
  State Bul 61:476-7 D 1 '69
WHALLEY family
Whalley coat-of-arms. H. K. Eilers. il Hob-
  bies 74:158-9 D '69
WHANG, H. Y. and Neter, E.
Antigen-associated immunosuppressant: ef-
  fect of serum on immune response. bib-
  liog Science 163:290-1 Ja 17 '69
WHARTON, Clifton R. Jr
Green revolution: cornucopia, or Pandora's
  box? For Affairs 47:464-76 Ap '69

about

MSU's choice. por Newsweek 74:110-11 O 27
  '69
WHARTON, Denis R. A.
Lysozyme retention by cockroach periplaneta
  americana L. bibliog Science 163:183-4 Ja 10
  '69
WHARTON, Don
Big happening in home sewing. Read Digest
  95:25-8 Jl '69
Driving the new interstates. Read Digest 95:
  174-6+ Ag '69
Fantasy in sand and stone: Utah. Read Di-
  gest 95:137-43 N '69
Is your child's school safe from fire? Read
  Digest 94:117-20 Je '69

WHARTON, John F.
How not to tinker with the economy. Sat R
  52:19-21 D 13 '69
Toward an affirmative morality. Sat R 52:
  11-13+ Jl 12 '69
WHARTON model. See Economic models
WHAT can blow the wind away? story. See
  Woiwode, L.
WHAT do I want to do today? story. See Ger-
  ber, M. J.
WHAT ever became of Agnes Mason? story.
  See Freeman, A. H.
WHAT'S zymurgy with you? drama. See Nolan,
  P. T.
WHEAT
End to hunger? newly-developed varieties.
  Sr Schol 95:14-15 O 6 '69

Hybrids

Hybrid wheat. B. C. Curtis and D. R.
  Johnston. il Sci Am 220:21-9 bibliog(p 158)
  My '69
Shorter wheats for everybody. R. D. Wenn-
  blom and G. Lorang. il Farm J 93:16-17+
  Jl '69

Prices

Latest from the wheat belt: a bumper crop
  and gloom. il U S News 66:48-9 Je 30 '69
Should we scrap the wheat agreement? Farm
  J 93:38 Je '69
Wheat price war. il Time 94:90+ S 12 '69
When the tractors came rolling in: protest by
  Midwest farmers. il U S News 67:8 Ag 11 '69
World wheat surplus yields bitter harvest. il
  Bsns W p25-6 Ag 9 '69
WHEAT trade
World wheat surplus yields bitter harvest. il
  Bsns W p25-6 Ag 9 '69
WHEATCROFT, John
Once by seaside; poem. Mlle 69:58 Jl '69
WHEATLEY, Dennis
Way to maintain success. Writer 82:22-4 O
  '69
WHEDON, Julia
Rubbings; story. Harper 238:58-61 Ap '69
WHEELBARROWS
Some gardeners like the old-style wheel-
  barrow. il Sunset 142:104 Mr '69
WHEELER, Arthur M.
Margolis on responsibility in psychotherapy.
  bibliog Ment Hy 53:309-10 Ap '69
WHEELER, Bruce E.
Lincolniana in 1968. por Hobbies 73:98M-98P
  F '69
WHEELER, Earle Gilmore
Power people; interview, ed. by W. Rogers.
  por Look 33:20-1 Ag 26 '69
Top general's rebuttal to attacks on military;
  excerpts from address, May 17, 1969. por U S
  News 66:14 Je 9 '69

about

Tops with the military, and with politicians,
  too. il pors U S News 66:16 My 5 '69
WHEELER, Harry, and Pirone, T. P.
Pathotoxin-induced disease resistance on
  plants. bibliog Science 166:1415-17 D 12 '69
WHEELER, Joseph Lewis
Top priority for cataloging-in-source. bibliog
  por Library J 94:3007-13 S 15 '69

about

Joseph Lewis Wheeler. C. W. Ferguson. por
  PTA Mag 63:5-7 Ap '69
WHEELER, Timothy J. pseud.
Our people's underworld movement exposed.
  Nat R 21:376-81 Ap 22 '69
WHEELING-Pittsburgh corporation
Why steelmakers seek strength in merger.
  il Bsns W p 102-4 F 15 '69
WHEELING steel corporation. See Wheeling-
  Pittsburgh corporation
WHEELIS, Allen
How people change. Commentary 47:56-66 My
  '69
WHEELS
  See also
Automobiles—Wheels
WHELAN, Charles M.
Evolution in the law. America 122:11-12 Ja
  10 '70
Tilton v. Finch. America 121:222-3 S 27 '69
WHEN shall we love; story. See Smith, E.
WHERE I live; story. See Aichinger, I.
WHETTEN, John T. See Hawkins, J. W. jr.
  jt. auth.
WHETTING. See Sharpening
WHICH Eleanor am I? story. See Pearlman, E.
WHICH is witch? drama. See Martens, A. C.
WHIPPLE, Dorothy Vermilya
How babies learn to talk. Parents Mag 44:
  48-9+ F '69

WHIPPLE, Fred L.
Radio telescope and the heiligenschein. il Sky & Tel 37:35 F '69
WHIPPLE, George C. 3d
Let's win this one for the Whipper. A. Anderson. il pors Life 67:81-2 O 31 '69
WHIPPLE, Gertrude
Good procedures in selecting schoolbooks. Ed Digest 34:44-6 F '69
WHIRLIGIG beetles. See Water beetles
WHIRLPOOL corporation
Appliance maker comes clean. Bsns W p 100 S 6 '69
Darkness before dawn. Forbes 103:21 Ja 15 '69
WHISKERS, Metal. See Metal crystals
WHISKEY
Bourbons. il Consumer Rep 34:392-6 Jl '69
Distillers get ready to serve light whiskey. il Bsns W p58-9+ F 22 '69
Why more Scotch is getting tanked. il Bsns W p74+ D 13 '69

Advertising
[Advertisements for the Whiskey distillers of Ireland] H. Gossage. il Ramp Mag 8:22-3 S '69
WHISKEY speculation. See Speculation
WHISTLE in the dark; drama. See Murphy, T.
WHISTLES
Siren for toy ambulance or fire engine. F. H. Tooker. il Radio-Electr 40:47 Je '69
Water whistle sculpture; ceramic children's toys. R. F. Eilenberger. il Ceram Mo 17:16-19 F '69
WHITAKER, Arthur P.
U.S. in Latin America to 1933: an overview. Cur Hist 56:321-6+ Je '69
WHITAKER, David
Progress report on SBN in Britain. Pub W 195:72-3 Ja 27 '69
WHITAKER, Frederic
Designs first in small scale; with biographical sketch. il por Am Artist 33:24-5+ S '69
George Bartell: California illustrator. Am Artist 33:64-9+ Mr '69
Guillermo Acevedo: draughtsman. Am Artist 33:26-31+ S '69
Millsap & Kinyon illustrator team. Am Artist 33:50-5+ Je '69
WHITAKER, H. R.
Magic carpet for all outdoors. Sci Digest 66:33-7 Jl '69
WHITAKER, Uncas A.
Uncas Whitaker's better mousetrap. Forbes 103:20-1 My 1 '69
WHITAKER, Virgil Keeble
Humanities at the crossroads; adaptation of address, March 4, 1968. Sch & Soc 97:278-80 Sum '69
WHITBREAD, Jane
How servicemen's marriages survive separation. Redbook 132:94+ Ap '69
WHITCOMB, Dennis
Brainstorming by yourself. Writers Digest 49:54-8 F '69
WHITE, Donald J.
Country place. Cons 23:12-13 F '69
WHITE, Dori
First year; story. Redbook 133:76 Ag '69
WHITE, E. B.
Chairs in snow; poem. New Yorker 45:44 Ap 12 '69
WHITE, Elgin
Florida's new canal. Yachting 126:58-60+ N '69
WHITE, Glenn
Big game of the plant world. Am For 75:24-7+ N '69
WHITE, Herbert S.
Professional identity: revolt of the scientists. por Wilson Lib Bul 44:550-4 Ja '70
WHITE, J. L. See Juo, A. S. R. jt. auth.
WHITE, Jim
Build the Eyeballer. Pop Electr 30:41-4 Je '69
First project. Pop Electr 31:75-9 Ag '69
WHITE, Ken
Ken White; renaissance man of architecture. il Pub W 195:54-6 F 3 '69
WHITE, Kevin Hagan
New horizons. il por Newsweek 73:36 F 24 '69
WHITE, Leonard, and others
Adjustment of criminally insane patients to a civil mental hospital. bibliog Ment Hy 53:34-40 Ja '69
WHITE, Margaret Bourke-. See Bourke-White, M.
WHITE, Mary
Special cherry desserts. Bet Hom & Gard 47:86 F '69
WHITE, Michael
Metamorphosis. Criticism
Mus Q 55:91-5 Ja '69

WHITE, Onna
New direction; interview. New Yorker 45:19-22 D 27 '69

about
Conversation with Onna White. M. Harriton. il por Dance Mag 43:26-7 Je '69
WHITE, Peter T.
Satellites gave warning of Midwest floods. Nat Geog 136:574-92 O '69
WHITE, Philip L.
(ed) Let's talk about food. See issues of Today's health
Measure of hunger. por Todays Health 47:41 N '69
WHITE, Richard H. See Brammer, J. D. jt. auth.
WHITE, Rudolph A.
Measuring unemployment and subemployment in the Mississippi Delta. il Mo Labor R 92:17-23 Ap '69
WHITE, Ruth
En garde! Here comes Baby Ruthie. il pors Life 67:91-2 S 26 '69
Touché! il pors Ebony 25:52-6 Ja '70
WHITE, Stanford
Faces from the past: E. Nesbit at Thaw-White murder trial. R. M. Ketchum. Am Heritage 20:64-5 Je '69
WHITE, Theodore Harold
Making of the President 1968; excerpts. Life 67:48-48B+ Jl 11; 44B-44D+ Jl 18 '69

about
New snobbism. S. Alsop. Newsweek 74:92 S 8 '69
Of old politics and elder statesmen. Commonweal 90:517-18 Ag 22 '69
WHITE, Tyner
Pit letter; poem. Atlan 224:80-1 Jl '69
WHITE, Wallace
Three crises in the lives of dope fiends; story. Esquire 71:122-4 Mr '69
WHITE, William B. See Poulson, T. L. jt. auth.
WHITE Anglo-Saxon Protestants. See WASPS (white Anglo-Saxon Protestants)
WHITE ants. See Termites
WHITE birch. See Birch
WHITE consolidated industries, incorporated
Battle for Allis-Chalmers: White consolidated seeking control. Bsns W p92 Mr 8 '69
Will White unload its stake in Allis? FTC opposition to merger. Bsns W p31-2 Jl 26 '69
WHITE flower farm, Litchfield, Conn. See Nurseries (horticulture)
WHITE hellebore. See Hellebore
WHITE House
Capital idea; tours and attractions. Newsweek 74:30-1 Jl 21 '69
Day the washing machine broke; housekeeper M. Kaltman. H. Sidey. il Life 67:4 S 12 '69
House and home. il Newsweek 73:22-3 F 3 '69
It was good to be home. H. Sidey. il Life 66:2 F 7 '69
Making the House a home. il Time 93:13 Ja 31 '69
More colors, fewer phones in Nixons' decor at White House. il U S News 67:14 O 6 '69
New way of life at the White House. il U S News 66:32-4 F 24 '69
Not all that square; paintings in the private rooms. il Time 93:66 Je 20 '69
Through his offices in search of the man. H. Sidey. il Life 67:4 O 17 '69
WHITE House conference of mayors. See Mayors
WHITE House conference on food, nutrition and health
Food as the first priority. il Time 94:18-19 D 12 '69
Food delegates focus on poor. N. Gruchow. Science 166:1385 D 12 '69
Food industry goes on the griddle. il Bsns W p64-5 N 29 '69
Nixon watch; thought for food. J. Osborne. New Repub 161:7-9 D 6 '69
Perfect gift, perhaps. P. Nelson. Chr Cent 86:1635-6 D 24 '69
Politics of hunger. il Newsweek 74:27-8 D 15 '69
Second try on a conference. Sci N 97:37 Ja 10 '70
To feed the nation's hungry. America 121:608-9 D 20 '69
Washington confronts the hungry. J. Cross. Nation 209:687-9 D 22 '69
WHITE House entertaining. See Government entertaining
WHITE House festival of the arts, 1965
White House and the intellectuals: Festival of the arts; excerpts from The tragedy of Lyndon Johnson. E. F. Goldman; discussion. Harper 238:4+ Mr '69

WHITE House receptions. See Government entertaining
WHITE House staff. See Public officers
WHITE llama; story. See Diez de Medina, F.
WHITE-Negro relations. See Race relations
WHITE PLAINS, N.Y.

Education

Student unrest and racial confrontation at White Plains high school. C. F. Johnson. Negro Hist Bul 32:20 O '69

WHITE racism. See Racism
WHITE RIVER national forest. See National forests
WHITE RUSSIA. See Belorussia
WHITE tailed deer hunting. See Deer hunting
WHITE-Thaw case. See Trials (murder)
WHITE water boating. See Boats and boating
WHITE water racing. See Kayak racing
WHITEFISH fishing
Big four of the North. J. Brooks. il Outdoor Life 144:34-5+ Ag '69
Sport without limit. L. Miracle. il Outdoor Life 144:66-7+ Ag '69
WHITEHEAD, Dick
Thunderbolts at sea. Motor B 124:124-5+ S '69
WHITEHEAD, Edward
Celebrated Briton at the Coliseum. Motor B 123:54-7+ Ap '69
WHITEHEAD, Ralph, Jr
Chicago voters tilt Mayor Daley's machine. Commonweal 90:157-8 Ap 25 '69
Daley vs. the guerrilla theatre. Nation 208: 422-3 Ap 7 '69
Sulfur and Daley: the lawless air. Nation 209: 503-5 N 10 '69
Weather goes SDS? Commonweal 91:92 O 24 '69
WHITEHILL, Buell, Jr
Bum steering about engineering. Nations Bsns 57:109 S '69
WHITEHILL, Joseph
Convict and the burgher: a case study of communication and crime; address. Am Scholar 38:441-51 Sum '69
WHITEHORN, Ethel
Motion picture previews. See issues of PTA magazine
WHITELAW, Aubrey H.
Ocean frontier. Sea Front 15:208-11 Jl '69
WHITELEY, Thomas W.
Student challenges; teachers' words not always accepted. Clear House 43:291-3 Ja '69
WHITENACK, Carolyn I.
(ed) School libraries as school media centers: a portfolio. por ALA Bul 63:249-50 F '69
WHITESIDE, Thomas
Annals of television. New Yorker 45:47-50+ S 27 '69
WHITETAIL deer. See Deer
WHITFIELD, Peter
How to make millions without really working. il por Time 93:94 Ap 11 '69
WHITING, Allen S.
How we almost went to war with China. Look 33:76-7+ Ap 29 '69
Mao's troubled ark. Life 66:62D-62F+ F 21 '69
WHITING, Aussie
Gallery: photographs. Life 67:12-13 S 26 '69
WHITMAN, Ardis
New breed of women. Redbook 133:67+ Je '69
Revolt of the young priests. McCalls 96:60-1+ Jl '69
We need new ways to pray. Read Digest 95: 77-80 D '69
WHITMAN, Arthur
Popular mechanical people. Pop Mech 132: 126-7 Jl '69
WHITMAN, Simone Forti
Simone Forti Whitman; NYU Loeb student center. J. Anderson. Dance Mag 43:77 Jl '69
WHITMAN, Vic
(ed) See Alison, J. Afterflash
WHITMAN, Walt
Crossing Brooklyn ferry; poem; excerpts. il Travel & Camera 32:57 S '69

about

Eagle and the axe: a study of Whitman's Song of the broad-axe. A. H. Rosenfeld. bibliog f Am Imago 25:354-70 Wint '68
Flower power: a student's guide to pre-hippie transcendentalism. P. H. Wild. Engl J 58:62-8 Ja '69
WHITMORE, George, Jr
Annals of jurisprudence. F. C. Shapiro. New Yorker 44:39-42+ F 8; 44-6+ F 15; 45:42-4+ F 22 '69

Victims; excerpts. B. Lefkowitz and K. G. Gross. il por Look 33:39-44+ Je 10; 39-44+ Je 24 '69
Whitmore, by F. C. Shapiro Review
New Repub 160:27-8 Je 7 '69. W. Schechner
WHITNEY, Edgar A.
Vignette: a contemporary art format. il Am Artist 33:40-4+ Je '69
WHITNEY, H. S. and Farris, S. H.
Maxillary mycangium in the mountain pine beetle. bibliog Science 167:54-5 Ja 2 '70
WHITNEY, Leon F.
In case of emergency. McCalls 97:44+ N '69
You can so train a cat. McCalls 97:70+ O '69
WHITNEY, Phyllis A.
For personal reference. Writer 82:23-6 F '69
WHITNEY museum of American art, New York
Art: Anti-illusion: procedures/materials show. L. Alloway. Nation 208:740 Je 9 '69
Whitney annual, irrelevant. B. Rose. Vogue 153:54 F 15 '69
WHITT, Gregory S.
Homology of lactate dehydrogenase genes: E gene function in the teleost nervous system. bibliog Science 166:1156-8 N 28 '69
WHITT, LaVerne
1969 WD article contest. Writers Digest 49: 39+ O '69
WHITT, W. C.
Star on TV, too. Outdoor Life 143:17 Mr '69
WHITTAKER, A. Greenville, and Kintner, P. L.
Carbon: observations on the new allotropic form. bibliog Science 165:589-91 Ag 8 '69
WHITTAKER, James K. and Komives, Margaret
Managing wake-up behavior in a children's home. bibliog Ment Hy 53:575-84 O '69
WHITTAKER, R. H.
New concepts of kingdoms of organisms. bibliog Science 163:150-60; 164:857 Ja 10, My 16 '69
WHITTAKER corporation
Whittaker aims to redesign its merger plans. Aviation W 90:86-7 Mr 31 '69
WHITTEMORE, L. H.
Two cops on a tough beat; excerpts from COP! a closeup of violence and tragedy. Life 66:52-4+ Je 20 '69
WHITTEMORE, Reed
On reading S. S. Van Dine in the canned goods section; poem. New Repub 161:23 Ag 9 '69
Reed Whittemore on the news. New Repub 161:22-3 N 15 '69
Verse. New Repub 161:25 O 11 '69
Winter of our discontent; poem. New Repub 160:28 Mr 1 '69
WHITTEN, Jamie L.
Excerpt from debate, June 25 and 26, 1968. Cong Digest 48:60+ F '69

about

We need help. R. Coles and H. Huge. New Repub 160:18-21 Mr 8 '69
WHITTEN, Joan M.
Cell death during early morphogenesis: parallels between insect limb and vertebrate limb development. bibliog Science 163:1456-7 Mr 28 '69
WHITTEN, Sam G.
New ALA officer. ALA Bul 63:1166-8 S '69
WHITTREDGE, Worthington
Worthington Whittredge, artist of the Hudson River school. E. H. Dwight. il Antiques 96:582-6 O '69
WHITWORTH, Kathy
Put on your bracelets Kathy is here. C. Kirkpatrick. por Sports Illus 30:64+ My 12 '69
WHITWORTH, Richard
Refresher course. Clear House 43:463-8 Ap '69
WHITWORTH, William
Profiles; B. Glow. New Yorker 45:43-4+ D 20 '69
Profiles; R. Miller. New Yorker 45:38-42+ Mr 1 '69
(ed) See Scammon, R. M. Profiles
WHO am I? story. See Freeman, J. T.
WHO is strongest? See Feather, J.
WHOLE cookie; story. See Hoag, M. D.
WHOLE earth catalog. See Catalogs, Mail order
WHOLE earth truck store. See Mail order business
WHOLESALE price index. See Price indexes
WHOLESALE prices. See Prices
WHOLESALE trade
Faster pace in wholesaling. R. S. Lopata. il Harvard Bsns R 47:130-43 Jl '69

Finance

Ratios of the wholesalers; with table (cont) Duns R 94:86-7 O '69

WHOLESALERS, Book. See Book jobbers
WHO'S happy now? drama. See Halley, O.
WHY weep for Otto? story. See Ibbotson, E.
WHYTE, William Hollingsworth
Cities to live in; excerpts from Last landscape. Cur 103:48-58 Ja '69
Tightened landscape. Horizon 11:66-73 Sum '69
WICHITA, Kan.
Water supply
Gold pipe for Wichita's century II. R. H. Hess. il Am City 84:12 Jl '69
WICKBERG, Erik
General of the army. Newsweek 74:67 Ag 4 '69
WICKER, Nina A.
Today I watched a soldier come home. Farm J 93:53 Je '69
WICKER, Tom
Number thirty-seven is ready. N Y Times Mag p21+ Ja 19 '69
Place where all America was radicalized. N Y Times Mag p26-7+ Ag 24; 62 O 5 '69
Presidency under scrutiny. Harper 239:92-4 O '69
Undeclared witch-hunt. Harper 239:108-10 N '69
Universities in crisis; what are the real issues? Cur 108:4-6 Je '69
What have they done since they shot Dillinger? N Y Times Mag p4-7+ D 28 '69
(ed) See Wald, G. Therefore choose life
WICKERSHAM, Ron
Multichannel recording for creating the new sound. por Electr World 82:38-9+ S '69
WICKES, George
Durrell's landscapes. New Repub 160:23-4 Je 21 '69
WICKES corporation
Supermarket for builders. S. Margetts. il Duns R 94:85-6+ S '69
WICKHAM, Vernon G.
Temptation. Flying 85:84 Jl '69
WICKS, Harry
How I remodeled a problem attic. Pop Sci 194:124-5+ Je '69
You can build a movable peninsula. Pop Sci 194:144-5+ Ap '69
—See Gaynor, J. jt. auth.
WICKS, Forsyth collection. See Boston museum of fine arts
WIDE-angle lenses. See Lenses, Photographic
WIDEHALL (historic house) See Kent County, Md.—Historic houses, etc.
WIDENING horizons. See Washington, D.C.—Recreation
WIDICK, B. J.
ALA: new voice of labor. Nation 208:758-60 Je 16 '69
Isolation of George Meany. Nation 209:398-9 O 20 '69
Meany & Reuther; labor's main bout. Nation 208:601-2 My 12 '69
Minority power through unions. Nation 209:206-8 S 8 '69
WIDLAR, Robert J.
Millionaire bets on his chips. por Bsns W p52+ Ag 23 '69
WIDMER, Kingsley
Father and son destroyers. Nation 208:575-6 My 5 '69
Rebellion as education. Nation 208:537-41 Ap 28 '69
Why dissent turns violent. Nation 208:425-9 Ap 7 '69
Why the colleges blew up. Nation 208:237-41 F 24 '69
WIDMOYER, Fred B. and Sullivan, D. T.
Groundcovers for the dry country. Horticulture 47:40-2 F '69
WIDOW, bereft; story. See Blake, J.
WIDOWS
How should a widow invest her money? il Changing T 22:17-19 D '68
Second life for war widows. Time 94:54-5 Jl 25 '69
Widow-to-widow program, an experiment in preventive intervention. P. R. Silverman. bibliog Ment Hy 53:333-7 Jl '69
WIECK, Paul R.
Case of Massachusetts. New Repub 160:25-7 F 1 '69
Congressmen on campus. New Repub 160:9 Je 14 '69
Old gang's fading fast in Byrdland. New Repub 161:12-13 Jl 12 '69
Will it be the old Democratic donkey? New Repub 160:8-9 My 10 '69
WIEDEL, Suzanne
How to crack the Michelin. Travel & Camera 32:30+ Je '69
Ski New England winter into spring. Travel & Camera 32:18+ D '69

Stop and you'll want to stay in Iceland. Travel & Camera 32:70-6 N '69
WIEGAND, Clyde Edward
K-mesic atoms indicate a nuclear neutron skin. Phys Today 22:57 O '69
WIEMAN, Henry Nelson
H. N. Wieman: his work perpetuated. C. L. Hepler. Chr Cent 86:1099 Ag 20 '69
WIEMEYER, Stanley N. See Porter, R. D. jt. auth.
WIENER, John
Knocking rock-land. J. Deedy. Commonweal 91:196 N 14 '69
WIERZYNSKI, Gregory H.
Our most wrenching problem is finding a place for ourselves in society; student declaration. Fortune 79:114-16+ Ja '69
WIESE, M. Bernice
Opening school library doors in Malaysia and Singapore. ALA Bul 63:1586-95 D '69
WIESMAN, Walter
Search for uncommon people; address, November 18, 1968. Vital Speeches 35:215-18 Ja 15 '69
WIESNER, Jerome B.
ABM would not buy any significant security; interview. por U S News 66:89-90 My 26 '69
Argument against ABM. Cur 106:6-10 Ap '69
about
Battle of the ABM. Newsweek 73:36 My 12 '69
Expertise of Dr Wiesner. Y. Ewing. Nat R 21:746+ Jl 29 '69
WIETERS, Nelson E.
It is rather exciting. por Camp Mag 41:5 Ap '69
WIGGINS, James Russell
Ambassador Wiggins' news conference of December 20, 1968. Dept State Bul 60:80-4 Ja 27 '69
Death of Trygve Lie; statement, December 30, 1968. Dept State Bul 60:78-9 Ja 27 '69
International cooperation in peaceful uses of outer space; statement, December 18, 1968. Dept State Bul 60:84-7 Ja 27 '69
U.N. bond repayments issue; statement, December 21, 1968. Dept State Bul 60:55-7 Ja 20 '69
U.N. calls upon UNCURK to continue pursuit of U.N. objectives in Korea; statement, December 20, 1968. Dept State Bul 60:36-7 Ja 13 '69
U.N. General assembly rejects move to bar South Africa from membership in UNCTAD; statement, December 13, 1968. Dept State Bul 60:9-10 Ja 6 '69
U.N. Security council condemns Israel for attack on Beirut airport; statements, December 29 and 31, 1968. Dept State Bul 60:53-5 Ja 20 '69
U.S. joins in proposing 1972 UN conference on the problems of the human environment; statement, December 3, 1968. Dept State Bul 59:707-11 D 30 '68
U.S. supports continuation of aid to Near East refugees; statement, November 18, 1968. Dept State Bul 59:677-9 D 23 '68
WIGHTMAN, Arthur S.
What is the point of so-called axiomatic field theory? adaptation of address, February, 1969. bibliog por Phys Today 22:53-8 S '69
WIGLETS. See Wigs
WIGS
Heady holiday put-ons. il Seventeen 28:140+ D '69
How to buy a wig. C. Bartel. il Am Home 72:18+ Ja '69
Topping it off; short-hair wigs for long-hairs. il Time 94:42+ S 5 '69
What a change of hair can do. L. Gourse. il N Y Times Mag p66-7+ N 16 '69
Wigs & wiglets for everyone. il Good H 169:88-9+ S '69
Wigs for glamor and convenience. il Consumer Bul 52:7-10 My '69
Wigs: four quick-change acts. S. Harney. il Ladies Home J 86:108-9 N '69
Wigs: medicine for morale. M. McEachern. il Todays Health 47:36-7+ N '69
WILBUR, Dwight L.
Health care costs; address, January 13, 1969. Vital Speeches 35:263-7 F 15 '69
WILBUR, Leslie. See Kelley, W. jt. auth.
WILBUR, Thomas P.
Financing urban schools: a continuing crisis. bibliog f Sch & Soc 97:286-8 Sum '69
WILCOX, Gregor Norman-. See Norman-Wilcox, G.

WILCOX, Wayne
Protagonist powers and the third world.
Ann Am Acad 386:1-9 N '69
(ed) Protagonists, power, and the third
world: essays on the changing interna-
tional system. bibliog f Ann Am Acad 386:
1-147 N '69
WILD, Paul H.
Flower power: a student's guide to pre-hippie
transcendentalism. Engl J 58:62-8 Ja '69
WILD, Peter
Campers; Granite mtns; Day lined with cork;
poems. Poetry 115:171-3 D '69
WILD animal pets. See Pets
WILD bergamot. See Horsemint
WILD boars
Wild boar of the Appalachians. H. L. Lawr-
ence. il Natur Hist 78:46-7 O '69
WILD ducks. See Ducks, Wild
WILD flower gardens. See Gardens, Wild
WILD flowers
California's wild flowers from seed. J.
Broughton. il Horticulture 47:38-9 S '69
Wildflowers for your garden. D. G. Schleis-
ner. il Home Gard 56:32-40 S '69
WILD food. See Food, Wild
WILD gardens. See Gardens, Wild
WILD geese. See Geese, Wild
WILD horses. See Horses
WILD life. See Wildlife
WILD pigeon shooting. See Pigeon shooting
WILD plum. See Plum trees
WILD rabbit chase; drama. See Boiko, C.
WILD rice
Archeological evidence for utilization of wild
rice. E. Johnson. bibliog il Science 163:276-
7 Ja 17 '69
How to harvest wild rice. R. W. Presnell.
il Cons 48-9+ Je '69
WILD sheep hunting. See Mountain sheep hunt-
ing
WILDAVSKY, Aaron
Politics of ABM. bibliog Commentary 48:
55-63 N '69
WILDCAT hunting. See Bobcat hunting
WILDE, Harold R. See Wilson, J. Q. jt. auth.
WILDE, James
Attack on a village. Time 93:36 Ap 4 '69
WILDE, Oscar
Importance of being earnest; drama; adapted
by L. Olfson. Plays 28:87-95 Ap '69

about

Dazzling nonsense. K. Sullivan. Nation 208:
799-800 Je 23 '69
Fresh remembrance of Oscar Wilde; tr. by A.
Foulke. P. Julian. il por Vogue 154:176-9+
N 1 '69
In defense of the tall story. W. H. Auden.
New Yorker 45:205-6+ N 29 '69
Oscar Wilde, by P. Julian. Review
Atlan 224:130 O '69. E. Weeks
Newsweek il por 74:53+ D 29 '69. R. A.
Gross
Toward the perfectly poisonous. K. Burke.
New Repub 160:28-30 My 31 '69
WILDE, Rebecca
Can Cinderella go dateless to the ball? PTA
Mag 64:16-18 D '69
WILDER, Billy
Anti-casting couch. il por Time 95:37 Ja 5 '70
WILDER, David
Management attitudes; team relationship; ad-
dress, October 1968. Library J 94:498-502 F
1 '69
WILDER, Thornton Niven
Our town. Criticism
America 121:622 D 20 '69
Nation 209:676 D 15 '69
New Yorker 45:166 D 6 '69
Sat R 52:36 D 20 '69
Time 94:84 D 12 '69
WILDERNESS areas
Battle for a wilderness; excerpt from Open
horizons. S F. Olson. il Liv Wildn 32:4-13
Wint '68
Behind the ranges; guiding in the Quetico-
Superior; excerpt from Open horizons. S.
F. Olson. il Audubon 71:6-15 Mr '69
Economics of wilderness; adaptation of ad-
dress, March 15, 1969. G. Hardin. Natur
Hist 78:20+ Je '69; Discussion. 78:6 O '69
How big does a wilderness have to be?
H. G. Wilm. il Am For 75:12-13 S '69
Last wilderness; Quetico Superior wilder-
ness. D. Butwin. il Sat R 52:55-6 O 4 '69
Loneing it is the only way. K. Schwenke. il
Field & S 74:46-7+ Jl '69
Mike Frome. M. Frome. Am For 75:9+ O '69

Still lots of open space in the U.S. il U S
News 66:102-4 Ap 14 '69
Threatened America. il Life 67:32-43 Ag 1; 58-
61+ S 5; 126-7+ O 10; 88-93 N 14 '69
Wilderness and the American. A. Netboy. il
Am For 75:12-15+ Ap '69; Discussion. 75:
3+ Jl; 4 S '69
Wilderness engenders new management tra-
ditions. H. D. Burke. il Liv Wildn 33:9-13
Sum '69
Wilderness: the last refuge. il Sr Schol 95:12-
14 O 27 '69
Wilderness violation. Liv Wildn 33:38 Spr
'69

Alaska

Alaska's wilderness cries out for a plan; re-
print. Liv Wildn 33:3 Spr '69
Letter from the Arctic; with photographs.
S. Wright. Liv Wildn 33:4-11 Spr '69
Ultimate confrontation. R. Cantwell. il Sports
Illus 30:66-70+ Mr 24 '69

Arizona

BLM names primitive areas. Liv Wildn 32:93
Wint '68
Preserving the corn ladder: a Mt Baldy
wilderness. N. H. Greenwood. il Liv Wildn
33:22-9 Sum '69

California

Lava beds: a wilderness in sight; Schonchin
wilderness. G. Alderson. il Liv Wildn 33:
21-3 Spr '69
L.A.'s own wilderness just eighteen air miles
from city hall; San Gabriel wilderness. il
Sunset 142:42-4 F '69

Canada

Outside view of wilderness preservation in
British Columbia. N. H. Greenwood. bibliog il Liv Wildn 32:30-42 Aut '68
Wilderness in Canada. D. H. Pimlott. bibliog
il Liv Wildn 32:4-21 Aut '68

Central America

Thoughts on wilderness preservation and a
Central American ethic. A. Carr. il Audubon 71:50-5 S '69

Colorado

Battle for East Meadow Creek. P. I. Kain. il
Am For 75:36-9+ O '69

Florida

Heron and the astronaut; with editorial com-
ment by G. Hunt, and photographs by S.
Wayman and R. Morse. A. M. Lindbergh.
Life 66:1, 14-26A F 28 '69

Idaho

Proposed St Joe wilderness. M. R. Brigham.
il Liv Wildn 33:15-18 Sum '69
Sawtooth summer. F. A. Tinker. il Travel 131:
40-3 My '69
White Cloud peaks; a time for decision. D. B.
Clement. il Am For 75:28-31+ S '69
Whose wilderness? White Cloud Mountains.
D. Jackson. il Life 68:109-10+ Ja 9 '70

Michigan

Icy taste of winter. J. B. Martin. Life 66:4
Mr 7 '69

Minnesota

Conquering Minnesota's wilderness by snowmobile. D. Fales. il Pop Mech 132:150-3 D
'69

Oregon

French Pete: lowland valley in Oregon's Cascades. W. A. Noyes. il Liv Wildn 32:25-9
Wint '68

Utah

Wilderness of slickrock. P. Hyde. il Audu-
bon 71:44-9 S '69
See also
Dinosaur National Monument
WILDERNESS camping. See Camping
WILDERNESS conference
Alaska. M. Nadel. Liv Wildn 33:1 Spr '69
WILDERNESS of Judea. See Judea
WILDERNESS society
Forty-five ways to the wilderness; trips.
C. R. Merritt. il Liv Wildn 32:43-5 Aut '68
Wilderness council in Everglades. Liv Wildn
32:46-7 Aut '68
Wilderness trips, starting in April. Sunset
142:64 Mr '69
WILDERNESS survival
Clues and clothing for snow survival. E. P.
Haddon. il Pop Mech 132:104-7+ N '69
Could you survive? questions and answers. A.
Greenbank. il Outdoor Life 143:90-3 Ap '69
Don't be a missing camper. C. B. Colby. il
Outdoor Life 144:12+ Jl '69

WILDERNESS survival—*Continued*
Life-giving power of love. T. Morris. il
Good H 169:50+ D '69
Nightmare spring; Canadian Northwest
Territories. O. A. Fredrickson. il Outdoor
Life 144:40-3+ Jl '69
Playing Indian. E. Gibbons. Org Gard & Farm
16:88-91 N '69

WILDFLOWERS. See Wild flowers

WILDLIFE
Taking stock of your rural property. L. S.
Hamilton and A. LaBastille. il Cons 24:28-
30 O '69
Wildlife along the Lewis and Clark trail.
H. H. Harrison. il Nat Wildlife 7:20-9 F '69

WILDLIFE census
See also
Animal tagging

WILDLIFE conservation
Biologist looks at the animal world (beasts
and men) J. Dorst. il UNESCO Courier 22:
16-21 Ja '69
Consumption of wildlife by man; reprint.
W. G. Conway. il Parks & Rec 4:20-6+ F
'69
Death from the sea; Santa Barbara oil spill.
D. Snell. il Life 66:22-7 Je 13 '69
Digger; boy makes island for nestling ducks.
T. Browne. Nat Parks 43:19 Je '69
Endangered wildlife. M. J. Walker. il Parks
& Rec 3:10-12+ N '68
Escape from extinction; official list of
Endangered species of native fish and wild-
life. il Time 93:54 Mr 28 '69
From nature's paradise. il UNESCO Courier
22:22-3 Ja '69
From the brink of extinction; endangered
wildlife research program. J. C. George. il
Nat Wildlife 7:20-3 Ap '69; Same abr. Read
Digest 94:214-15 Ap '69
In dubious, desperate battle. J. W. Krutch.
il Audubon 71:52-4 Mr '69
Parks between the tides; marine park pre-
serves, Orange County, Calif. W. Marx. il
Parks & Rec 3:18-20 O '68
Preventing the end of the game. M. Frome.
Field & S 74:32+ S '69
See you later, alligator; poaching in Florida.
M. Kane. il Sports Illus 31:38-40+ S 29 '69
Springtime and the animals. A. W. Smith.
Nat Parks 43:2 Ap '69
State wildlife agency and the nongame species.
Audubon 71:5 Ja '69
Washington report. L. S. Clapper. See issues
of National wildlife
What is the new conservation? interview.
W. J. Hickel. il Nat Wildlife 7:8-9 Je '69
Why must they die? L. Leonard. il Look 33:
42-4 N 4 '69

See also
Bird sanctuaries
Birds of prey—Protection
Game protection
National wildlife federation
Wilderness areas
Wildlife research

Laws and legislation
Tortoises, Christmas and the law; an act
curtailing international and domestic traffic in endangered species. il Sci N 96:523
D 6 '69

Alaska
Alaska's wildlife, an abundance to destroy.
G. Laycock. il Audubon 71:60-6+ Jl '69
See also
Alaska—Fish and game, Department of

WILDLIFE photography. See Photography of
animals

WILDLIFE populations. See Animal populations

WILDLIFE research
Building aids research program; new addi-
tion at Delmar wildlife research laboratory.
E. S. Feldman. il Cons 24:17+ D '69

WILDLIFE sanctuaries
Wild sanctuaries; our national wildlife
refuges, by R. Murphy. Review
Liv Wildn il 33:30-2 Sum '69. H. B.
Crandell
See also
Bird sanctuaries
Kruger National Park

California
Duck watching and goose watching; Gray
lodge wildlife area. il Sunset 143:68 N '69

Minnesota
Wildlife or jetport? threat to Carlos Avery
wildlife management area and game farm.
G. B. Helgeland. il Nat Wildlife 7:18-19
F '69

Montana
See also
National bison range

Nevada
These bighorns will pose for you; Desert
national wildlife range. il Sunset 142:28
Mr '69

Oregon
Sanctuary; the prismatic moods of Malheur
national wildlife refuge. il Audubon 71:56-
65 Mr '69

Society Islands
Leeward Islands; Hawaiian Islands national
wildlife refuge. R. Northshield. il Natur
Hist 78:60-7 O '69

WILDSTROM, Stephen H.
Mugged by the sheriffs: an anecdote. Nation
208:496-7 Ap 21 '69

WILEY, Charles W.
Report from West Berlin. Nat R 21:282-3
Mr 25 '69

WILEY, Harvey Washington
Battle for a nation's health. L. M. Rhodes.
il pors Todays Health 47:36-9+ Ap '69

WILEY, John P. jr
AIP in 1968: expansion and experimentation.
Phys Today 22:43-50 Je '69
Sky reporter. See issues of Natural history

WILEY, Marcia
Cabin talk. See issues of Yachting

WILEY, W. Bradford
American book abroad; excerpts from address. Pub W 196:19-20 D 8 '69

WILEY college, Marshall, Tex.
Wiley college library, the first library for Negroes west of the Mississippi River. H. L.
Totten. bibliog il Negro Hist Bul 32:6-10 Ja
'69

WILHELM, Hoyt
Highlight. por Sports Illus 31:128 S 22 '69
King of the flutter. il por Newsweek 73:127
Ap 21 '69

WILHELM, John R.
Mexico's mystery. Travel & Camera 32:51-5
N '69

WILHELM, Leo J.
Do sheep count people when they can't sleep?
Sci Digest 65:56-9 F '69

WILK, Max
Island that lived for a day. McCalls 96:94+
My '69

WILKE, L. A.
Toledo Bend: big new bass lake. Field & S
74:148-9+ Je '69

WILKEN, Robert L.
Reformation re-thinking. Cath World 209:85-
6 My '69

WILKENING, David
Clothesline full of poetry. Sr Schol 94:Schol
Teach 20-1 F 14 '69

WILKENS, Len
Supersonic boom. H. L. Masin. il Sr Schol
94:inside back cover Ja 31 '69
Sweety Cakes runs the Sonics. F. Deford.
il por Sports Illus 31:42-4+ N 24 '69

WILKES, Bud
University store gets faculty rapport. Pub
W 196:51 Ag 18 '69

WILKEY, Malcolm Richard
Crime; address, July 28, 1969. Vital Speeches
35:718-20 S 15 '69

WILKIE, Curtis
Desegregation dilemma in the South. New
Repub 160:13 Ap 12 '69
Mississippi muzzle. Nation 208:132-3 F 3 '69

WILKIE, Jane
New life for Helen Rogers. Good H 169:20+
Ag '69
Secret magic of Elizabeth Montgomery. Good
H 169:54-6+ O '69

WILKINS, Bruce T. and Brumsted, H. B.
Making money in recreation. Cons 24:18-21
D '69

WILKINS, Leslie T. and Gitchoff, Thomas
Trends and projections in social control systems. Ann Am Acad 381:125-36 Ja '69

WILKINS, Raymond G. See Goldberg, B. C.
jt. auth.

WILKINS, Roy
Case against separatism: black Jim Crow. por
Newsweek 73:57 F 10 '69
Purge at NAACP. Commonweal 89:575+ F 7
'69

about
Mr Wilkins on the extremists. Nat R 21:62 Ja
28 '69
Negro moderates vs. militants. por U S News
66:9 Ja 27 '69
There is no rest for Roy Wilkins. M. Arnold.
il pors N Y Times Mag p40-1+ S 23 '69
Wilkins v. Innis. W. F. Buckley, jr. Nat R
21:140 F 11 '69

WILSON, Elizabeth C.
　Knowledge machine. Ed Digest 34:1-5 F '69
WILSON, Emmett, Jr
　Coriolanus: the anxious bridegroom. bibliog
　　Am Imago 25:224-41 Fall '68
WILSON, Geoffrey
　Rebel on campus. Parents Mag 44:52-3+ Ap
　　'69
WILSON, H. W, company
　Late news: M. P. Barnett on staff. Wilson
　　Lib Bul 43:595+ Mr '69
WILSON, Harold
　Another setback for Socialists. U S News
　　66:10-11 Ap 7 '69
　Applicants, not suppliants. por Time 94:38+
　　O 10 '69
　Britain's Wilson: peace envoy to a dead-
　　locked African war. por U S News 66:16
　　Mr 31 '69
　Don't be euphoric. il por Newsweek 74:54+
　　N 10 '69
　Empty gesture? visit to Nigeria. il News-
　　week 73:56-7 Ap 14 '69
　Harold Wilson's sound pound. A. Howard.
　　New Repub 161:13-14 N 15 '69
　How long can Wilson last? por Newsweek 73:
　　46-8 My 19 '69
　Labor pains. Newsweek 73:52+ Je 30 '69
　Look around. Newsweek 73:42+ Ap 7 '69
　Rigor mortis. il por Newsweek 73:53-4 My 26
　　'69
　Twin stalemates; visit to Nigeria. il por Time
　　93:36-7 Ap 4 '69
　Wilson's about-face. A. Howard. New Repub
　　160:7-8 Je 28 '69
WILSON, Helen Van Pelt
　Authors & editors. B. A. Bannon. por Pub
　　W 196:25-7 Ag 18 '69
WILSON, Henry Hall, 1921-
　New futures in an old trade. il por Bsns W
　　p52+ Jl 26 '69
　Stock futures. il por Newsweek 73:73+ Mr 3
　　'69
WILSON, James Q.
　Federal government and crime; excerpts from
　　Agenda for the Nation. Cur 103:23-5 Ja '69
　Is the Court handcuffing the cops? N Y Times
　　Mag p 134-6+ My 11 '69
　What makes a better policeman. Atlan 223:
　　129-35 Mr '69
　Young people of North Long Beach. Harper
　　239:83-90 D '69
—and Wilde, H. R.
　Urban mood. Commentary 48:52-61 O '69
WILSON, James W.
　Flowering groundcovers. Horticulture 47:
　　26-9 +Jl '69
　How new flowers are made. Horticulture 47:
　　36-7+ Ja '69
WILSON, Jane
　Books. Bul Atom Sci 25:31-2 Ja '69
WILSON, Jerome L.
　Democrats confront 1970. Nation 209:597-8
　　D 1 '69
　Lindsay vs. the field. Nation 208:332-4 Mr 17
　　'69
WILSON, Jerry V.
　Police chief tells his story. por U S News
　　67:36 D 8 '69
WILSON, John A.
　Crackpots and forgeries in art and science.
　　Sci Digest 66:40-4 N '69
WILSON, John Anthony Burgess. See Burgess,
　　A. pseud.
WILSON, John H. Jr
　Better written journal papers, who wants
　　them? Science 165:986-7 S 5 '69
WILSON, John S.
　Hyman and the studio men. Hi Fi 19:50-3
　　My '69
　Jazz. See issues of High fidelity incorporat-
　　ing Musical America
WILSON, Johnny
　Southward ho. See issues of Motor boating
WILSON, José
　Are you a wine whiz? House & Gard 136:
　　156+ S '69
　Going places, finding things in the Virgin
　　Islands. House & Gard 135:26+ F '69
　Knack, with a bottle. House & Gard 136:96
　　Jl '69
　(ed) Six authorities discuss pre-dinner drink-
　　ing. House & Gard 136:142+ O '69
WILSON, Joseph Chamberlain
　Product nobody wanted: excerpt from The
　　strategy of change for business success. ed.
　　by S. Furst and M. Sherman. Nations Bsns
　　57:67-70 F '69
WILSON, Lanford
　Gingham dog. Criticism
　　New Yorker 45:107 My 3 '69
WILSON, Larry E.
　Sonic remote control relay. Radio-Electr 40:
　　36-8 S '69

WILSON, Logan
　Few kind words for academic administrators.
　　Ed Digest 34:6-8 My '69
　Other voices, other views. Sat R 53:74 Ja 10
　　'70
WILSON, M. P.
　Viewpoint. Library J 94:1599 Ap 15 '69
WILSON, Malcolm
　World around us. R. M. O'Grady. Chr Cent
　　86:1332 O 15 '69
WILSON, Marvin R.
　Question for rabbis, pastors, and teachers.
　　Chr Today 13:5-7 F 14 '69
WILSON, Mildred T.
　What about the middle school? Todays Ed
　　58:52-4 N '69
　What is a middle school? Clear House 44:
　　9-11 S '69
WILSON, Mitchell
　How Nobel prizewinners get that way. Atlan
　　224:69-74 D '69
WILSON, Paul
　World cultures: a matter of method. Clear
　　House 43:501-3 Ap '69
WILSON, Prince E.
　Black men before the Civil war. bibliog f Cur
　　Hist 57:257-62+ N '69
WILSON, Richard
　Form factors of elementary particles; with
　　biographical sketch. bibliog por Phys To-
　　day 22:47-53 Ja '69
WILSON, Robley, Jr
　Immortalist; poem. Atlan 224:77 N '69
　Snake; poem. Commonweal 91:12 O 3 '69
WILSON, Sloan
　Floating guesthouse. J. Kelly. por Sat R 52:
　　40 Ap 5 '69
WILSON, Stephen C.
　Sanctuary; photographs. Audubon 71:56-65
　　Mr '69
WILSON, Thomas James
　Obituary
　　Pub W por 196:52 Jl 7 '69
WILSON, W. Frederic
　New look in meters. Pop Phot 64:72-3+ Ap
　　'69
　Vary your light level. Pop Phot 64:38 Mr '69
WILSON, Will R.
　Slower justice; courts get blame; excerpts
　　from address, May 1, 1969. U S News 66:13
　　My 12 '69
WILSON, William S.
　Hard questions and soft answers. Art N 68:
　　26-9 N '69
　John Clem Clarke transmits a picture. Art
　　N 68:46-7+ Sum '69
　Los Angeles: a view from the studios. Art
　　in Am 57:145-7 N '69
WILSON, Woodrow
　How Harding saved the Versailles treaty. R.
　　K. Murray. il por Am Heritage 20:66-7+
　　D '68
　Wilsonian summers in rural New England.
　　R. Van Zandt. il por Sat R 52:50+ Mr 8 '69
WILSON and company
　Can Ling get gravy out of meatball? LTV
　　and Wilson. Bsns W p51 S 13 '69
WILSON library bulletin
　Around the world with WLB; introduction:
　　bon voyage. Wilson Lib Bul 43:953 Je '69
　Back to school. il Wilson Lib Bul 44:34-5
　　S '69
　Editor's mixed emotions. W. R. Eshelman. il
　　Wilson Lib Bul 44:538-43 Ja '70
　From the Pierian Spring to the nitty gritty.
　　W. R. Eshelman. il Wilson Lib Bul 43:620-1
　　Mr '69
　Libraries between decades. Wilson Lib Bul
　　44:511 Ja '70
　　See also
　John Cotton Dana publicity awards
WILT thou have this woman? story. See Hun-
　　ter, E.
WINANS, Sarah S.
　Visual form discrimination on the basis of
　　relative distribution of light. bibliog Sci-
　　ence 164:858 My 16 '69
WINCHESTER, Alice
　Living with antiques. Antiques 95:242-51 F
　　'69
WINCHESTER, James H.
　American medicine's outpost in France. To-
　　days Health 47:44-7 Ag '69
　Bergen: Fjordland hub. Travel 131:42-6 Mr
　　'69
　Caribbean cooking. Travel 132:70-2 Jl '69
　Sweden's national parks. Travel 132:70-2 Ag
　　'69
　Volunteer firemen: heroes without pay. Pop
　　Sci 194:94-7+ My '69
WINCHESTER adventures, incorporated. See
　　Travel agencies
WINCHESTER rifles. See Rifles
WIND, Herbert Warren
　Sporting scene (cont) New Yorker 45:133+
　　Mr 15; 93-6+ Mr 22; 129-32+ My 3; 65-6+
　　Jl 5; 174+ O 11; 152+ D 13 '69

WIND. See Winds
WIND breaks. See Windbreaks
WIND ensembles
Wind ensemble grows up. D. Hunsberger.
il Hi Fi 19:MA14-15+ S '69
WIND erosion. See Erosion
WIND instruments
See also names of wind instruments, e.g.
Bagpipes
WIND screens. See Windbreaks
WIND tunnels
Energetics of bird flight. V. A. Tucker. il
Sci Am 220:70-6+ My '69
WINDBREAKS
Fence designs to keep wind from being a nui-
sance. M. O'Hare and R. E. Kronauer. il
Arch Rec 146:151.6 Jl '69
It stops the wind, stops pets and children,
lets in the view. il Sunset 142:108 Je '69
Protect cattle with earthen windbreaks. D.
Malena. il Suc Farm 67:61 O '69
Windows without a house; pivoting glass
wind screen. il Sunset 143:103 Jl '69
WINDCHILL. See Temperature—Physiological
effects
WINDERS, Esther
Heaven's angel. il por Time 93:21 Ap 25 '69
WINDHAM COUNTY, Vt.
Cry, Vermont. Time 94:50 S 26 '69
WINDHAM MOUNTAIN club. See Sports clubs
WINDJAMMER cruises. See Cruising
WINDLE, William F.
Brain damage by asphyxia at birth; with
biographical sketch. Sci Am 221:14, 76-84 O
'69
WINDOW air conditioners. See Air conditioning
equipment
WINDOW cleaning

Safety devices and measures
Window washer express; electrically-driven
outside scaffold. il Mech Illus 65:70-1 S '69
WINDOW curtains and draperies. See Curtains
and draperies
WINDOW displays. See Show windows
WINDOW screens. See Screens (doors, windows,
etc)
WINDOW shades
How to measure windows for shades. Good
H 169:216 O '69
Shade cloth you just iron on. il Sunset 142:
108+ Ap '69
Sorcery with shades. C. Garner. il Bet Hom
& Gard 47:62+ Mr '69
WINDOWS
Basement storm windows you can make. il
Mech Illus 65:104 N '69
Foldable transparent windows. il Chem 42:
24 Mr '69
Great new looks for windows. il House &
Gard 136:40-7 Ag '69
Long, long counter, spacious new view. il
Sunset 142:108 F '69
New ways with windows. il Good H 168:98-
109 Mr '69
Ten idea window treatments. P. Rumely and
C. Garner. il Bet Hom & Gard 47:52-7 Jl '69
See also
Barns and stables—Windows
Curtains and draperies
Skylights

Maintenance and repair
Fixing up an older home. il Bet Hom & Gard
47:29 My '69
WINDOWS, Space vehicle. See Space vehicles—
Viewports
WINDOWS in art
Selective window. K. Kuh. il Sat R 52:29-31
O 18 '69
WINDS
Atmosphere and the ocean. R. W. Stewart.
il Sci Am 221:76-86 bibliog(p284) S '69
Boulder's winds; chinook winds. L. T. Julian
and P. R. Julian. bibliog il Weatherwise
22:108-12+ Je '69
Circulation and weather of 1968. J. F. An-
drews. il Weatherwise 22:4-11 F '69
Effect of leeway. F. Adams. il Yachting 125:
63+ My '69
Superskyway; excerpt from Wild brother. R.
Rood. il Audubon 71:38-43 S '69
Windchill, a useful wintertime weather vari-
able; rate of heat removal from the human
body at various combinations of wind speed
and low temperature. R. Falconer. bibliog
il Weatherwise 21:227-9+ D '68
See also
Storms
Tornadoes
Trade winds

Measurement
Wind measurements in noctilucent clouds. J.
S. Theon and others. bibliog il Science 164:
715-16 My 9 '69
WINDSHIELD defrosters. See Automobiles—
Windshield defrosters
WINDSHIELD wipers. See Automobiles—
Windshield wipers
WINDSOR, Edward, duke of. See Edward VIII,
king of Great Britain
WINDSOR chairs. See Chairs
WINE
California wines I like. N. S. Hazelton. Nat
R 21:493+ My 20 '69
California's collector reds. B. Thompson. il
Am Home 72:90+ N '69
Chianti. H. Johnson. il Holiday 46:62-3+ S '69
Cold duck; mixture of burgundy and cham-
pagne. Time 95:67 Ja 12 '70
Continental pewter in the service of wine.
R. M. Vetter. il Antiques 95:383-7 Mr '69
Flowery summerlike wines of Switzerland
and the Tirol. J. T. Elson. Travel & Camera
32:16+ Jl '69
Gastronomy; Great Burgundy mystery. J.
Wechsberg. Esquire 72:10 Jl '69
Goodbye water, hello champagne. il Nations
Bsns 57:63-5 My '69
Growing gold on vines; Germany's Trocken-
beerenauslese. Time 94:100 D 5 '69
Guide to winespeak. N. S. Hazelton. Nat R
21:294 Mr 25 '69
How to become a connoisseur of California
white wines. R. F. Capon. House & Gard
136:20+ Ag '69
How to plan a $50 wine cellar; excerpts from
How to eat better for less money by J. A.
Beard and S. Aaron. House & Gard 136:
138+ N '69
How to select and serve the wine. R. J.
Misch. House B 111:150+ N '69
Is there great wine in California? R. A. De
Groot. Esquire 72:54+ O '69
Primer on table wines. il Bet Hom & Gard
47:16+ O '69
Rhône: a river of big red wines. J. T. Elson.
il Travel & Camera 32:13-14 Je '69
Royal Riesling; greatest of grapes for warm-
weather wines. R. A. De Groot. House B
111:158+ My '69
Those California wines. N. S. Hazelton. Nat
R 21:397 Ap 22 '69
Wine into water; selling adulterated brew in
Italy. il Time 93:40 My 30 '69
Wine tasting parties; with menus. il House
& Gard 136:128-32+ N '69
Wines of Spain and Portugal. J. T. Elson.
il Travel & Camera 32:35-6+ My '69
Wines that will improve with age. W.
Olcott. House & Gard 135:120+ Mr '69
See also
Champagne
Cookery—Wine

History
Lafite by C. Ray. Review
Sat R 52:34-5 Ap 19 '69. C. Creighton
Port and Madeira; history in a glass. R. A.
De Groot. House B 111:80+ D '69

Storage
Waste space is for wine storage. il Sunset
142:111 Mr '69
WINE, Adulterated. See Adulterations
WINE auctions. See Auctions
WINE cellars
Personal business; start your own wine cellar.
Bsns W p 121-2 O 25 '69
WINE festivals. See Festivals—Europe
WINE jelly. See Jelly, jam, etc.
WINE labels
Gastronomy; Great Burgundy mystery. J.
Wechsberg. Esquire 72:10 Jl '69
What can be learned from a French wine
label. McCalls 96:58 Ap '69
WINE racks
Sidesaddle wine rack. il Mech Illus 65:37 Ag
'69
WINE trade
California wineries. il Travel & Camera 32:
88-9 Ag '69
Is there great wine in California? R. A. De
Groot. Esquire 72:54+ O '69
Prosperity comes to U.S. wines. il U S News
67:76 S 1 '69
Wines of California. M. Demarest. il Travel
& Camera 32:62-5+ Ag '69
See also
Wineries
WINEMAN, David
Effects of the institution on the person.
bibliog ALA Bul 63:1087-97 S '69

WINERIES
Old winery in the Mother Lode; D'Agostini winery. il Sunset 143:34 N '69
WINETT, Heather
Image of a doll's house; poem. Engl J 58: 385 Mr '69
WINGO, Walter
Union lobbying machine. Nations Bsns 57: 52-4+ Ap: 58-62 My '69
WINGS, Airplane. See Airplane wings
WINKELMAN, Christine, Sister
Nature's extravaganza of color. Horticulture 46:38-9+ O '68
WINKELMANN, Roy R.
Revolution within an evolution. Chr Cent 86: 1577-80 D 10 '69
WINKLER, Jack
Russia faces up to the realities of construction industry in reorganizing its approach to producing housing. Arch Rec 146:169-72 O '69
WINN, Ira J.
Public parks and private lives; with biographical sketch. por Natur Hist 78:4, 20-6 O '69
WINNEMUCCA-to-the-sea highway. See Roads —Western states
WINNETKA, Ill.

Fire department
Mutual-aid radio expands firefighting services. R. A. Porter. il Am City 84:128+ S '69
WINNING combination; drama. See Snelling, D.
WINOGRAD, Shmuel
How fast can computers add? with biographical sketch. Sci Am 219:20, 93-100 O '68; 220:8+ Ja '69
WINSOR, Harry B.
Home for sale. PTA Mag 63:26-8 Mr '69
WINSTON, B. F.
Rating the influence of television. PTA Mag 63:6-9 bibliog(p36) Mr '69
WINSTON, Sheldon L.
Drug counseling. Clear House 44:227-8 D '69
WINSTON-SALEM, N.C.

Courts
Dignity in the court; chief judge of District court orders counseling program disbanded. E. K. Shanahan. New Repub 160:12 F 1 '69
WINTER, Jack. See Rote, K. jt. auth.
WINTER, Johnny
Chicken-soup freak. il por Time 93:53-4 F 28 '69
It's hard to fake the true blues. A. Goldman. Life 67:8 Jl 4 '69
Johnny Winter, instant orbit R. Goldstein. Vogue 153:34 Ap 15 '69
Winter blues. T. Barry. il pors Look 33:80-4+ Jl 29 '69
WINTER, Peter M. and Lowenstein, Edward
Acute respiratory failure; with biographical sketches. Sci Am 221:18, 23-9 N '69
WINTER, Ruth
Are you polluting your own home? Sci Digest 66:22-6 S '69
Fetology; doctoring unborn babies. Sci Digest 66:24-9 N '69
Giant step toward solving the mystery of high blood pressure. Sci Digest 66:8-12 Jl '69
WINTER
Getting through winter. M. Bates. Natur Hist 78:20+ Ja '69
Icy taste of winter. J. B. Martin. Life 66:4 Mr 7 '69
Thank God it snowed. R. L. Fair. Am Scholar 39:105-8 Wint '69
See also
Snow
Snowstorms
WINTER boating. See Boats and boating
WINTER bouquets. See Flowers, Arrangement of
WINTER camping See Camping
WINTER coats. See Coats
WINTER driving. See Automobile driving
WINTER fishing. See Fishing, Winter
WINTER flying. See Aviation—Winter flying
WINTER in the spare-parts yard; story. See Buchan, P.
WINTER photography. See Photography—Cold weather conditions
WINTER resorts
Big money plays in the snow; ski area investments. il Bsns W p 142+ O 25 '69
Flaine, a ski resort near Chamonix, France designed to function as a self-sustaining town. il Arch Rec 146:102-7 Ag '69

Greatest snow on earth; Salt Lake Valley and Wasatch Mountains, Utah. D. Reid. il Travel 132:52-6 D '69
Hot December. il Holiday 46:34-6 D '69
Let's travel; Pennsylvania ski facts. S. Cuneo. il Mlle 70:138-9 N '69
Let's travel; snow country. il Mlle 70:122-6+ N '69
My slopes. J. C. Killy. il Travel & Camera 32: 51-5 D '69
One of the best family ski bargains in the world! Bet Hom & Gard 47:153 N '69
Ski bum's guide to winter grooving. J. Nelson. il Mlle 70:198+ N '69
Ski New England winter into spring. S. Wiedel. il Travel & Camera 32:18+ D '69
Skier's West. C. Casewit. Harp Baz 103:86+ D '69
Snow-mass, best European skiing in America. A. Orsini. il Holiday 45:64-7 F '69
Snowmelting vs. serpentine street; Snowmass-at-Aspen, Colo. il Am City 84:40 Ja '69
To cold Colorado for the joys of powder skiing. il Sunset 142:62-9 F '69
Where the money is in skiing. il Bsns W p 112-13+ F 22 '69
Where to ski in the United States, Canada and Europe. M. Strauss. il Travel & Camera 32:83-6 D '69
See also
Sugarbush Valley, Vt.
Taos, N.Mex.
WINTER sleep. See Hibernation
WINTER sports
What snowmobiles do is open up the winter world. il Sunset 142:46+ F '69
See also
Curling
Hockey
Ice boats and ice boating
Skibobs and skibobbing
Skis and skiing
WINTER ticks. See Ticks
WINTER vacations. See Vacations
WINTERICH, John Tracy
Criminal record. See last issues of each month of Saturday review
WINTERNATIONALS. See Automobile racing
WINTERS, Kenneth, and others
Hydrocarbons of blue-green algae; geo-chemical significance. bibliog Science 163:467-8 Ja 31 '69
WINTERS, Stanley B. See Napier, J. J. jt. auth.
WINTHER, Barbara
African trio; dramatization of African folktales. Plays 29:46-52 O '69
Dinnetah; dramatization of the Navaho creation myth. Plays 28:41-50 My '69
Emperor's nightingale; dramatization of a story by H. C. Andersen. Plays 28:82-8 My '69
Great Samurai sword; dramatization of a Japanese folk tale. Plays 29:52-8 Ja '70
Villain and the toy shop; drama. Plays 29: 57-64 D '69
WINTHROP, Henry
Bad faith in counseling and therapy. bibliog Ment Hy 53:415-21 Jl '69
WIPKE, W. Todd. See Corey, E. J. jt. auth.
WIRE sculpture
Wire sculpture. il Sch Arts 69:29-36 O '69
WIRE tapping
Bugging Joe Namath. Nat R 21:632-3 Jl 1 '69
Confessions of the FBI; tapping telephone calls of Dr Martin Luther King and C. Clay. Newsweek 73:29-30 Je 16 '69
Dirty business; tapping of Dr King's phone. Nation 208:780 Je 23 '69
I was a burglar, wiretapper, bugger, and spy for the F.B.I. W. Turner. il Ramp Mag 7: 47-51 Ja 25 '69
New line on wiretapping. Time 94:47-8 Jl 25 '69
New taps on freedom; Title III of the Omnibus crime control and safe streets act of 1968. S. Fly. il Nation 208:697-9 Je 2 '69
On bugging Martin Luther King. W. F. Buckley, jr. Nat R 21:714 Jl 15 '69
Reasonable man; wiretapping, pretrial detention & civil rights; address, August 13, 1969. J. N. Mitchell. Vital Speeches 35:678-81 S 1 '69
Surfeit of surveillance; Namath and King cases. Chr Cent 86:917 Jl 9 '69
Tapping a vein of controversy. Nations Bsns 57:81-2 Jl '69
Wire taps; disclosed or leaked? trial of the Chicago 8. P. W. Moore. il Nation 209:432-4 O 27 '69
WIRELESS microphones. See Microphones
WIRETAPPING. See Wire tapping
WIRING, Electric. See Electric wire and wiring

WISCONSIN
See also
Apple River
Camping—Wisconsin
Fishing—Wisconsin
Hunting—Wisconsin
Music festivals—Wisconsin
Public welfare—Wisconsin
Trials—Wisconsin

Description and travel
Wisconsin's Door Peninsula. W. S. Ellis. il
Nat Geog 135:346-71 Mr '69

Natural resources, Department of
Wisconsin DDT story in pictures and words.
R. Rodale. il Org Gard & Farm 16:19-23
Jl '69

Politics and government
Laird country goes Democratic. U S News
66:12 Ap 14 '69
Upset in Wisconsin. Time 93:29 Ap 11 '69
WISCONSIN RIVER
Outboard recollection. D. Olesen. il Yachting
126:69+ Ag '69
WISCONSIN. University

Madison campus
For men only: experiment in a dance project.
E. Jacobs. il Dance Mag 43:78-81 My '69
Moderate students tell their side of the
campus uproar. il U S News 66:72-4 Mr 10
'69

Milwaukee campus
Speed cataloging: prudence and pitfalls. J.
Z. Nitecki. il Library J 94:1417-21 Ap 1 '69

Oshkosh campus
How to deal with campus chaos: interview.
W. P. Knowles. il U S News 66:31-3 Mr 3 '69
Oshkosh: black student revolt in micro-
cosm. R. L. Aukema. Chr Cent 86:219-21
F 12 '69
WISDOM
See also
Judgment
WISDOM of the heart; story. See Jensen, E.
WISE, C. David, and Stein, Larry
Facilitation of brain self-stimulation by cen-
tral administration of norepinephrine. bib-
liog Science 163:299-301 Ja 17 '69
WISE, Donald
Trouble at NASA: space scientists resign.
M. Mueller. Science 165:776-7+ Ag 22 '69
WISE, Erich. See Schlesinger, A. jt. auth.
WISE, Howard
Kinetic light art. Am Home 72:26+, 80-1 O '69
WISEMAN, Denis V.
John; poem. Cath World 209:198 Ag '69
Pentecost; poem. Cath World 210:77 N '69
There are three; poem. America 121:612 D 20
'69
WISHING well or ill; drama. See Nolan, P. T.
WISMER, Harry
Last of the Titans. A. Kroll. il Sports Illus
31:106-8+ S 22 '69
WIT and humor. See Humor
WITCH doctors. See Medicine men
WITCHCRAFT
There's a new-time religion on campus. A. M.
Greeley. il N Y Times Mag p 14-15+ Je 1
'69
What's the mutter with astrology? J. Rohler.
il Chr Today 14:42 N 21 '69
Witches, by F. Mallet-Joris. Review
Atlan 224:112+ S '69. R. Evett
See also
Medicine men
Voodooism
WITCHER, Lester
Clown Alley. Parks & Rec 4:37+ F '69
WITCHES. See Witchcraft
WITCO chemical corporation
Happy specialist; M. Minnig. R. Levy. il Duns
R 94:76-7 S '69
WITCOVER, Jules
News from Alabama: Wallace still lives. New
Repub 160:12 My 31 '69
WITHEE, Virginia
Guests in my garden. Horticulture 47:32+ Ag
'69
WITHEM, Ronald E.
GI communication; letter. New Repub 161:
29-30 D 6 '69
WITHERILL, Robert
When fog closes in. Yachting 125:74-5+ Je
'69
WITHERINGTON, Paul
Stephen Crane's A mystery of heroism: some
redefinitions. Engl J 58:201-4+ F '69

WITHERS, John Dudley
A bird is not for throwing rocks at. G.
Goodman. il por Look 33:46-8 N 4 '69
WITHERSPOON, Mrs Eugene
Pride of five women. R. Hochstein. il por
Good H 168:87 Je '69
WITHERUP, William
For a still-born niece; poem. Nation 209:
326 S 29 '69
WITKER, Kristi
Visit to Cuba. Vogue 154:92+ O 1 '69
WITKIN, Arthur
How do you motivate employees? interview.
por Duns R 92:12-13 D '68
WITKIN, Lee D.
Add New York galleries: best yet; interview,
ed. by J. Deschin. il por Pop Phot 65:38+
O '69
WITKOVSKY, Jerome. See Shalinsky, W. jt.
auth.
WITNESS bearing (Christianity)
Compromises. L. N. Bell. Chr Today 13:44+
S 12 '69
Revolution in religion; address, February 12,
1969. J. P. Leary. Vital Speeches 35:446-8
My 1 '69
Witness; in the dimension of religious faith.
V. P. McCorry. America 120:inside back
cover My 17 '69
WITONSKI, Peter P.
Century of transition. Nat R 21:185-6 F 25 '69
Intellectual forerunner of the new left. Nat
R 21:133-4 F 11 '69
Letter from Portugal. Nat R 21:851 Ag 26 '69
Review of the journals. Nat R 21:447-8 My
6 '69
WITT, Harold
Ben Harding's flying machine; poem. New
Repub 160:34 Je 14 '69
Blurred leaves in the foreground; poem. Po-
etry 115:160 D '69
Ebersoles' potato chips; poem. Sat R 52:97
S 13 '69
Gila; poem. Sat R 52:30 F 8 '69
Gypsies; poem. Commonweal 90:164 Ap 25
'69
WITTEN, Edward
Are you listening. D. H. Lawrence? New
Repub 161:15-17 O 18 '69
WITTER, Priscilla
Ride on the Renaissance. Hi Fi 19:MA22-4+
D '69
WITTNER, Dale
Explosive grace, on defense or in a dashiki.
Life 67:31-3 N 28 '69
WITTOP, Freddy
Freddy Wittop costumes and castanets. R.
Estrada. il pors Dance Mag 43:37-41 D
'69
WIVES
Advice to new wives from a used one. G.
Hickman. il Redbook 133:96-7+ O '69
What makes a woman lovable? T. I. Rubin.
Read Digest 95:78-80 Ag '69
Young wife's world. H. Valentine. See issues
of Good housekeeping
See also
Cabinet officers wives
Clergymens wives
Forest rangers wives
Housewives
Mothers
Physicians wives
Service mens wives
WIVES, Jewish. See Jewish women
WIXOM, Hartt
Fish-fighting myths exploded. Field & S
73:74-5+ Ap '69
New breed of mule deer. Outdoor Life 144:49-
51+ O '69
WOBBLIES. See Industrial workers of the world
WODEHOUSE, Pelham Grenville
Life with P. G. G. Wolff. por Newsweek 74:
90+ Jl 7 '69
WOGAMAN, Philip
Public attitudes toward guaranteed annual
income. Chr Cent 86:1037-9 Ag 6 '69
WOHL, Paul
Little something for everyone. Nation
209:38-41 Jl 14 '69
WOHLBERG, Lynn
Why I like feeling trapped. por Redbook
133:15+ S '69
WOHLSCHLAG, Donald E. See DeVries, A. L.
jt. auth.
WOHLSTETTER, Albert
Counterattack. Newsweek 73:36 Je 9 '69
WOHLSTETTER, Charles
Charles Wohlstetter's many careers. il pors
Bsns W p36-7+ Ag 30 '69
WOIWODE, Larry
Contest; story. New Yorker 45:50-6 N 1 '69
Fragment; poem. Mlle 69:134 O '69
Suitor; story. McCalls 97:56-7 Ja '70
What can blow the wind away? story. Mlle
68:162-3 F '69

WOIWODE, Larry—*Continued*
about
Canker in the rose. il por Time 93:90+ Je 20 '69
WOLF, David
Let's everybody boo Rich Allen! Life 67:50-2+ Ag 22 '69
$1 million end to an unjust exile. Life 66:67 Je 27 '69
Unjust exile of a superstar. Life 66:52-52B+ My 16 '69
WOLF, Donald E.
Why are building costs going up? Arch Forum 131:48-9 S '69
WOLF, Donald J.
Dilemma of good men. Cath World 209:103-6 Je '69
WOLF, Elinor K.
Case for parent involvement. Parents Mag 44:40-1+ F '69
WOLF, Hugo
Fascinating repertory opens up. D. Hamilton. por Hi Fi 19:78-9 Je '69
Historic 1968 Hugo Wolf concert. P. L. Miller. por Am Rec G 35:944-6 Je '69
Italian passion, German skill. G. L. Mayer. Sat R 52:78 Ap 26 '69
Lieder masters. Discus. Harper 239:101-2 Jl '69
Records:
Wolf: Italian song book; Penthesilea; nine songs. Opera N 34:30 D 6 '69
Treasure of Wolf. L. Kolodin. Sat R 52:51 My 31 '69
WOLF, John B.
Islam in the Soviet Union. bibliog f Cur Hist 56:161-5+ Mr '69
Shadow on Lebanon. bibliog f Cur Hist 58:21-6+ Ja '70
WOLF, Lazer
Murder; poem; tr. by N. Halper. Nation 208:154 F 3 '69
WOLF, Leonard
Making of a hippie. PTA Mag 63:6-9 bibliog (p37) Ja '69; Same abr. Ed Digest 34:32-4 Ap '69
Night thoughts from Bali; poem. Atlan 223:72 My '69
WOLF, Peter
Structure of motion in the city. Art in Am 57:66-75 Ja '69
WOLF, Virginia L.
Root and measure of realism. por Wilson Lib Bul 44:409-15 D '69
WOLF, William C. Jr
Educators' conceptions of contemporary innovation in teacher training. Sch & Soc 97:378-80 O '69
WOLF hunting
Night of the wolf race. D. Snell. Life 66:18D F 14 '69
WOLFE, Ernest L.
Retired man, 78, conducts radio program among other activities. por Aging 176:11 Je '69
WOLFE, Michael
20/20; poem. Atlan 223:72 My '69
WOLFE, Randolph
How can you be married, signore, when there are different names on your passports? Holiday 46:92-3 O '69
WOLFE, Richard
Bottle cap model maker. Design 70:4-7 Spr '69
WOLFE, Susan Wise. See Hibbard, L. T. jt. auth.
WOLFE, Thomas K.
Hijinks journalism. N. Compton. Commentary 47:76-8 F '69
New yellow peril. Esquire 72:190-9+ D '69
WOLFE, Thomas W.
Soviet military since Khrushchev. bibliog f Cur Hist 57:220-7+ O '69
WOLFE, Tom. See Wolfe, T. K.
WOLFERT, Ira
1969: the year of the moon. Read Digest 94:55-9 My '69
They listen to the language of the universe. Read Digest 94:95-9 F '69
To the moon: man's most daring voyage. Read Digest 95:45-50 Jl '69
WOLFF, Geoffrey
Opinion: obscenity. por Mlle 69:148+ Jl '69
WOLFF, Robert A.
Voltage regulator for enlarger lamp. Electr World 82:72 S '69
WOLFGANG, Marvin E.
Corrections and the violent offender. bibliog f Ann Am Acad 381:119-24 Ja '69
WOLFLE, Dael
Neglected laboratory. Sat R 52:67 N 1 '69

WOLFLING. See North, S.
WOLFMAN, Augustus
Wolfman on printing. See issues of Modern photography
WOLFSON, Louis Elwood
Exit for Wolfson; prison sentence for illegally selling unregistered stock. Time 93:88-9 My 2 '69
Fortas of the Supreme court: a question of ethics and the stock manipulator. W. Lambert. il por Life 66:32-7 My 9 '69
Man who threw a long shadow. por Bsns W p39 My 24 '69
New controversy over Justice Fortas and a fee; what it's all about. il por U S News 66:21 My 19 '69
No peace for Fortas. por Time 93:28 My 9 '69
WOLIN, Sheldon S. See Schaar, J. H. jt. auth.
WOLK, Anthony
Passive mystique: we've been had. bibliog f Engl J 58:432-5 Mr '69
WOLK, Donald J.
Youth and drugs, guidelines for teachers. Ed Digest 35:41-4 D '69
WOLKOMIR, Richard
Stinging insects, armed and dangerous. Todays Health 47:48-9+ Je '69
Why leaves change color in the fall. Sci Digest 66:30-1 N '69
WOLLAN, Michael
Biography of a bandwagon. Sat R 52:56-9 Mr 1 '69
WOLMAN, Harold
The poor, the power structure and the polemicist. Commonweal 90:267-9 My 16 '69
Unabashed and sometimes uncritical argument. Commonweal 89:737-8 Mr 14 '69
WOLPE, Stefan
Contemporary contrasts. D. W. Moore. Am Rec G 36:69 S '69
WOLSELEY, Roland E.
Proud teachers. Sch & Soc 97:434-5 N '69
WOLTERS, Richard A.
Obsessions of a late-bloomer. R. H. Boyle. il por Sports Illus 31:32-6 Ag 18 '69
WOLVES
Stories
Wolfling; excerpt from novel. S. North. il Audubon 71:66-74+ S '69
WOLZ, Carl
Dance department with the aloha spirit. M. Brodsky. il por Dance Mag 43:62-5 D '69
WOMACH, Merrill
Dirge king. Newsweek 74:63 Ag 11 '69
WOMAN
Man talk: love-in. D. Newman and R. Benton. Mlle 69:84 My '69
On being a woman. J. Brothers. See issues of Good housekeeping
She is—. G. Guinness. Harp Baz 102:189 O '69
Thinking about women. by M. Ellmann. Review
    Nation 208:215+ F 17 '69. G. Stade
Woman and women. A. Burgess. Vogue 154:194+ O 1 '69
See also
Education of women
Housewives
Inter-American commission of women
Mothers
Sex differences
Single women
Wives
Women in art
Young women
Defense
See Self defense for women
Diseases
See also
Gynecology
Vaginitis
Dress
See Clothing and dress
Education
See Education of women
Employment
Here come the girls. W. Wingo. il Nations Bsns 57:38-41 D '69
Real and pseudo problems of the working woman. P. Sartin. il UNESCO Courier 22:24-8 Jl '69
Women might have helped; some problems ahead; address, June 11, 1969. H. B. Schleman. Vital Speeches 35:663-8 Ag 15 '69
Wonderful time: symposium for the mature woman who wants to reënter the business world New Yorker 44:26-8 F 8 '69

WOMAN—Employment—*Continued*
Work experience of the population: spotlight on women and youths. F. A. Bogan. il Mo Labor R 92:44-50 Je '69
    See also
Equal pay for equal work
Household employees
Married women—Employment
Woman—Occupations

Equal rights

Everyone was brave: the rise and fall of feminism in America, by W. L. O'Neill. Review
    Sat R 52:27-9+ O 11 '69. E. Janeway
For women a difficult climb to the top. il Bsns W p42-4+ Ag 2 '69
Girls in a boy's world. Seventeen 28:150-1+ S '69
Is a women's revolution really possible? L. A. Westoff; J. Gagnon; W. Simon. il McCalls 97:76-7+ O '69
Lucretia Mott: women also have rights. Sr Schol 94:19 Mr 21 '69
New feminists. J. Freeman. il Nation 208: 241-4 F 24 '69
Rage of women. R. E. Farson. Look 33:21-3 D 16 '69
Whatever happened to women? Nothing, that's the trouble; new feminism. E. Willis. Mlle 69:150+ S '69
When's it going to be ladies' day? P. Stern. New Repub 161:14-16 Jl 5 '69
Woman's changing role in America. il U S News 67:44-6 S 8 '69
Women may not be coddled; three recent court decisions. Time 94:58 Ag 22 '69
Women's rights a la Pat Nixon. il U S News 66:18 My 19 '69
    See also
United Nations—Commission on the status of women
Woman—Employment
Womens liberation movement

Health and hygiene

Husbands: take care of her heart. R. Bugg. il Todays Health 47:52-5+ N '69
Unlikeliest product; Cupid's quiver, sachets of liquid douche concentrate. il Time 94:51 D 26 '69
Your health. Redbook 132:60+ Ap; 133:30 My; 38+ Jl; 46+ S; 134:31 N '69; 34+ Ja '70
    See also
Beauty. Personal
Frigidity (psychology)
Menstruation
Pregnancy

Intelligence

See Intelligence levels—Women

Legal status, laws, etc.

See also
Woman—Equal rights

Occupations

After the children leave home. il Bet Hom & Gard 47:98+ O '69
Choice and conflict for the college woman. E. C. Lewis. Ed Digest 35:52-4 N '69
They give other people's parties. N. Axelrad. il Mlle 69:180-1+ O '69
Wanted: one safari guide, part-time. J. Scobey and L. P. McGrath. il McCalls 96:16+ Ja '69
    See also
Cottage industries
Models (persons)
Negro women—Occupations
Nurses and nursing
Secretaries
    also headings beginning Women as, e.g. Women as architects

Professions

See Woman—Occupations

Psychology

On being a woman. J. Brothers. See issues of Good housekeeping
Special and curious blessing; excerpts. C. P. Seton. il McCalls 96:71+ F '69
What would really make you happy. S. Blum. il Redbook 132:49+ Ja '69
    See also
Intelligence levels—Women

Recreation

See Recreation for women

Rights of women

See Woman—Equal rights

Social and moral questions

As I see it; interview, ed. by E. Melton. R. E. Farson. Forbes 104:44-6 Ag 1 '69
French institution: the mistress. J. Dutourd. McCalls 96:91-2 Mr '69
Whatever happened to women? Nothing, that's the trouble; new feminism. E. Willis. Mlle 69:150+ S '69
    See also
Alcoholism
Womens liberation movement
WOMAN as president. See Women as public officers
WOMAN suffrage

United States

Along the suffrage trail. A. Fry. il Am West 6:16-25 Ja '69
WOMAN thoughts; story. See Deasy, M.
WOMAN without a shadow; opera. See Strauss. R.
WOMEN

Europe

Male-female relations in Europe: their religious aspects. E. M. von Kuehnelt-Leddihn. il Cath World 210:64-8 N '69

France

Notes from a wayfaring ranger. D. Butwin. Sat R 52:23-4 Jl 5 '69

Israel

Chutzpah Israeli style. H. Russcol. il Holiday 45:18+ F '69

Japan

Mrs no. two; mistresses. il Newsweek 73: 101-2+ My 5 '69
    See also
Geishas

Russia

See also
Marriage law—Russia

Scandinavia

Experiments in marriage; group families in Sweden and Denmark. M. Durham. il Life 67:38-48A Ag 15 '69

Sweden

Sweden I; the babushka effect. N. Gittelson. Harp Baz 102:26-7+ F '69

United States

Erotic life of the American wife. N. Gittelson. Harp Baz 102:76-91 Jl '6
In America, the great brain divide. M. Ellmann. Vogue 153:152+ My '69
Sons of Adam, daughters of Eve, by I. Ross. Review
    Cath World 210:83-4 N '69. M. P. Lynch
What did the Nineteenth amendment amend? R. Girson. il Sat R 52:29+ O 11 '69
Where American women are now. M. Mead. il Vogue 153:176-8+ My '69
    See also
Married women—Employment
Negro women
Woman—Employment
Woman—Equal rights
Woman suffrage—United States

History

Everyone was brave: the rise and fall of feminism in America, by W. L. O'Neill. Review
    Sat R 52:27-9+ O 11 '69. E. Janeway

Vietnam (Republic)

Operation uplift in Vietnam; plastic surgery performed on Vietnamese bargirls and others. T. Fox. Commonweal 90:502-3 Ag 22 '69
WOMEN. Famous
Interesting women. il McCalls 96:98-9 Mr '69
Of planets and personalities. X. Pové. il House B 111:S2-11 Ap '69
    See also
Celebrities
WOMEN, Jewish. See Jewish women
WOMEN, Negro. See Negro women
WOMEN, Painting of. See Portrait painting
WOMEN and men
Feminized male, by C. Sexton. Review
    Sat R 52:52-3 Ag 16 '69. P. Woodring
Girls in a boy's world. Seventeen 28:150-1+ S '69
Male-female relations in Europe: their religious aspects. E. M. von Kuehnelt-Leddihn. il Cath World 210:64-8 N '69
Man talk: Mademoiselle Bovary. D. Newman and R. Benton. Mlle 69:70 O '69

WOMEN and men—*Continued*
Men die earlier than women. B. Urlanis. il
  UNESCO Courier 22:28-30 N '69
Newsletter of marriage. G. Seaman and B.
  Seaman. Ladies Home J 85:22 D '68; 86:
  22 Ja; 26 F; 56 Mr '69
Sweden I: the babushka effect. N. Gittelson.
  Harp Baz 102:26-7+ F '69
What did the Nineteenth amendment amend?
  R. Girson. il Sat R 52:29+ O 11 '69
What makes a man lovable? T. I. Rubin.
  Ladies Home J 86:68+ O '69
Why it's a man's world. L. Tiger. Read
  Digest 95:223-4+ O '69
WOMEN and peace
How to win the human race; group called
  Another mother for peace. N. Gittelson.
  Harp Baz 102:24-5+ My '69
WOMEN and politics
In America, the great brain divide. M.
  Ellmann. Vogue 153:152+ My '69
What I learned in 1968 about women, politics,
  and my husband. J. Muskie and M. F.
  Hoyt. il McCalls 96:92-3+ Ap '69
  See also
Congresswomen
Woman—Equal rights
Woman suffrage
WOMEN and religion
Male-female relations in Europe: their reli-
  gious aspects. E. M. von Kuehnelt-Ledd-
  ihn. il Cath World 210:64-8 N '69
Sex: female; religion: Catholic. by S. Cun-
  neen. Review
    Chr Cent 86:1167 S 10 '69. E. Gibson
You can't find God in church anymore;
  Journal's survey. K. L. Woodward. il
  Ladies Home J 86:86-7+ Mr '69
WOMEN and the church
Can the Catholic revolution succeed? T. J.
  Fleming. il Redbook 133:77+ My '69
News and views; latest decree of the Con-
  cilium for the implementation of the con-
  stitution on the liturgy. J. Deedy. Com-
  monweal 89:630 F 21 '69
WOMEN and war
  See also
Vietnamese war, 1957- —Women and the war
WOMEN as air pilots
Plane and the single girl. H. Ostlere. Flying
  84:74-5 F '69
Richard Bach; airplane for Bette. R. Bach.
  il Flying 84:32-3 Ap '69
WOMEN as architects
Women in architecture; excerpts from book.
  B. Dinerman. Arch Forum 131:50-1 D '69
WOMEN as athletes
Bright girls in a smother of fog; American
  girls success clouded by U.S. ski associa-
  tion policies. B. Ottum. il Sports Illus 30:
  20-1 Mr 31 '69
Girls in sports: are they on the right track?
  Sr Schol 94:16 Mr 21 '69
Some dashing dolls debut in Daytona:
  women's national AAU championships. A.
  Verschoth. il Sports Illus 31:20-3 Jl 14 '69
  See also
Sports for women
WOMEN as authors
Interview with Hortense Calisher; ed. by
  R. Newquist; reprint. H. Calisher. Writers
  Digest 49:58-60+ Mr '69
Thinking about women, by M. Ellmann.
  Review
    Commentary 47:86-8 Mr '69. E. Stevenson
  See also
Women as poets
WOMEN as automobile drivers. See Automobile
  drivers
WOMEN as city planners. See City planners
WOMEN as executives
For women, a difficult climb to the top. il
  Bsns W p42-4+ Ag 2 '69
WOMEN as jockeys
Boycotting the brunette. Newsweek 73:58 Ja
  27 '69
Ladies in silks. il Time 93:73 Ap 4 '69
Onward the feminine invasion; lady jockeys.
  A. Higgins. il Sports Illus 30:60 Mr 24 '69
There goes Barbara Jo! Newsweek 73:87
  Mr 31 '69
WOMEN as journalists
Close-up: Oriana Fallaci; interview. ed by
  R. Stolley. O. Fallaci. il Life 66:39-9 F 21
  '69
WOMEN as lawyers
Mrs Langford for the defense; Chicago lady
  lawyer; reprint. L. Rockey. il Ebony 24:
  57-8+ Mr '69
WOMEN as mail carriers. See Postal service—
  Letter carriers
WOMEN as members of Congress. See Con-
  gresswomen

WOMEN as ministers
Holy war of the Rev Trudie Trimm; minis-
  ter of Chicago's New Testament missionary
  Baptist church. il Ebony 24:70-4+ S '69
  See also
American association of women ministers
WOMEN as novelists. See Women as authors
WOMEN as photographers
Have camera will travel; P. Ragland photo-
  graphing social and economic projects. il
  Ebony 24:112-14+ Mr '69
WOMEN as physicians
Girl becomes a doctor. R. Gosswiller. il To-
  days Health 47:29-33 Je '69
More than a mother. J. Robbins and J. Rob-
  bins. Redbook 133:90+ My '69
WOMEN as poets
To be a poet. S. Weller. il Mlle 70:126-7+
  D '69
WOMEN as public officers
In my opinion we need a woman president.
  I. T. Ringel. Seventeen 27:180 D '68
WOMEN as sociologists
Women and professional advancement; ex-
  cerpts from address, September 3, 1969. A.
  S. Rossi. Science 166:356 O 17 '69
WOMEN as teachers
New horizons for educated women. J. Cass.
  Sat R 52:45-6 Jl 19 '69
WOMEN as theatrical managers, etc.
  See also
Jones, M.
WOMEN as travelers
Why women put to sea. M. Connelly. Mc-
  Calls 96:88+ S '69
WOMEN as veterinarians
Pets and people; veterinary medicine as pro-
  fessional career for women. J. Beatty, jr. il
  McCalls 96:50 F '69
WOMEN college students. See College stu-
  dents, Women
WOMEN golf players. See Golfers
WOMEN in art
De Kooning's women; interview, ed. by D.
  Sylvester. W. De Kooning. il Ramp Mag
  7:20-4 Ap '69
New De Koonings; Woman-in-landscape
  theme on show at Knoedler gallery, N.Y.
  J. Perreault. il Art N 68:48-9+ Mr '69
WOMEN in boating
Cabin talk. M. Wiley. See issues of Yachting
Companionway. R. L. Williamson. See issues
  of Motor boating
I want to be where the action is. B. Thaxton.
  il Motor B 123:120 Ja '69
WOMEN in industry. See Woman—Employment
WOMEN in sports. See Sports for women
WOMEN in television
World of television. B. Kevles; J. O'Reilly.
  il Mlle 68:170-5+ Mr '69
WOMEN in the armed forces. See United
  States—Armed forces—Womens services
WOMEN lawyers. See Women as lawyers
WOMEN police. See Policewomen
WOMEN umpires. See Umpires (sports)
WOMENS clothes. See Clothing and dress
WOMENS clubs and societies
From Scarsdale to Korea: Operation book-
  shelf. M. B. Tarshish. il Pub W 195:28-9
  My 26 '69
Twelve helpful fund-raising ideas for your
  club. il Good H 169:198-9 N '69
WOMENS liberation movement
Militants for women's rights. S. Davidson.
  il Life 67:66D-70+ D 12 '69
New feminists: revolt against sexism. il Time
  94:53-4+ N 21 '69
Why women's liberation? M. Dixon. il Ramp
  Mag 8:57-63 D '69
WOMENS national book association
  See also
Amy Loveman national award
WOMENS pressure groups. See Pressure groups
WOMENS residences
Women's residences: halfway between home
  and on your own. K. D. Fishman. il Seven-
  teen 28:106-7+ Je '69
WONDER, Stevie
Big Stevie. S. K. Oberbeck. por Newsweek 75:
  65 Ja 12 '70
WONDER
Apology for wonder, by S. Keen. Review
    Chr Cent 86:958 Jl 16 '69. D. Cobb
WONDERFUL couple, great team! story. See
  Williams, L.
WOOD, Abigail
Young living: questions and answers. See
  issues of Seventeen
WOOD, Alan, steel company
Alan Wood affair: a tale of intrigue. il Bsns
  W p94-6+ Jl 12 '69; Reply. J. P. Bauer. p5
  Ag 2 '69

WOOD, C. V. jr
How to build a river in the Arizona desert to flow under the London bridge. W. Robbins. il pors Esquire 71:78-83+ F '69

WOOD, E. J. Ferguson
Algae live without light. il Sea Front 15:278-83 S '69

WOOD, Francis A.
Air pollution and the roadside. Horticulture 46:36-8+ D '68

WOOD, Glen
Those wonderful brothers Wood. B. Kilpatrick. il pors Pop Mech 131:118-21+ Ja '69

WOOD, H. Charles
Ionospheric-propagation predictions. Electr World 81:27-9+ Ap '69

WOOD, Laurence I.
Sail with the winds of change. Nations Bsns 57:58-62 D '69

WOOD, Leonard
Those wonderful brothers Wood. B. Kilpatrick. il pors Pop Mech 131:118-21+ Ja '69

WOOD, Louise
Sack casting. Ceram Mo 17:24-6 S '69

WOOD, Michael
Epilogue and a judgment. Ramp Mag 7:96-7 Ja 25 '69

WOOD, Nancy
Wild horse; heritage, or pest? Audubon 71:46-51 N '69

WOOD, P. S.
O Tannenbaum; story. New Yorker 45:75-6 D 20 '69

WOOD, Peter
Boring-thrilling-exhausting-impoverishing sport. il N Y Times Mag p30-1+ N 2 '69
Return of Muhammad Ali, a/k/a Cassius Marcellus Clay jr. N Y Times Mag p32-3+ N 30 '69

WOOD, Robert E.
Papa and the general. il por Forbes 104:40 D 1 '69

WOOD
Radioisotopes for identifying straight grain timber. il Chem 42:22 F '69
Rare woods from old trees. L. J. Eldred. il Org Gard & Farm 16:88-90 S '69
See also
Bark
Lumber
Lumber industry and trade
Plywood

Decay
Wood and water don't mix. M. E. Dowd. Am Home 72:102-3 Mr '69

Diseases and pests
Corrosion and infestation. E. A. Zadig. il Motor B 123:56-9+ F '69
See also
Termites

Staining
See Stains and staining

Weathering
Faces on the valley floor. il Am For 75:4-7 N '69

WOOD block prints. See Wood engravings

WOOD carving
High-speed duplicating machine makes you an expert woodcarver. W. C. Leckey. il Pop Mech 131:188-9 My '69
International decoy Carvers' exhibit. N. Drahos. il Cons 24:10-11 D '69
Saint-maker from Taos. M. T. Crews. il Américas 21:33-7 Mr '69
Utensils as works of art. V. Fabriškiī and I. Shmelyov. il UNESCO Courier 22:25-7 My '69
Wood veneer jewelry. il Sch Arts 68:16-17 Ap '69
Wooden delights; J. Scholl's toys and fantasies. D. G. Lowe. il Am Heritage 20:18-23 D '68
Wooden parade; Abby Aldrich Rockefeller folk art collection at Williamsburg, Va. M. Black. il Am Heritage 21:34-43 D '69

WOOD chips. See Wood waste

WOOD drying. See Lumber—Drying

WOOD ducks. See Ducks, Wild

WOOD engravings
Amighetti: engraver. S. Baciu. il Américas 21:10-15 F '69
California's pictorial letter sheets; excerpts. J. A. Baird, jr. il Antiques 96:412-17 S '69
Popular imagery from north-east Brazil. il UNESCO Courier 22:34-5 My '69

WOOD finishing
Clear wood finishes. il Consumer Rep 34:606-9 O '69
How to preserve the glow of wood. J. H. Ingersoll. il House B 111:135-7 My '69

Today's floors, away from the wood tones. D. X. Manners. il Am Home 72:28+ N '69
See also
Furniture—Finishing
Stains and staining

WOOD floors. See Floors, Wood

WOOD paneling. See Paneling

WOOD pulp
Total pulp; holopulping. Sci Am 221:54 Jl '69

WOOD rats. See Pack rats

WOOD seasoning. See Lumber—Drying

WOOD sorrell
Oxalis hirta. V. Stewart. il Horticulture 47:18-19 Ja '69

WOOD turning. See Turning

WOOD-turning lathes. See Lathes

WOOD type. See Type and typefounding

WOOD warblers. See Warblers

WOOD waste
Wood chips ship out; to Japanese pulp paper makers. il Bsns W p 164+ Mr 29 '69

WOOD working. See Woodworking

WOODALL, Paul E.
Seashore state park. Travel 131:58-9 F '69

WOODARD, Gloria. See Thompson, J. jt. auth.

WOODARD, Samuel L.
Black power and achievement motivation. Clear House 44:72-5 O '69

WOODBRIDGE, N.J.
Maintenance savings finance street paving. C. W. Beagle. il Am City 84:80-1+ Mr '69

WOODBURNE, Michael O. See Jepsen, G. L. jt. auth.

WOODBURY, R. W.
Plea for a united service association; excerpts from address. Electr World 82:13 N '69

WOODCARVING. See Wood carving

WOODCHUCK hunting
Chucks above Antietam. D. Knight. il Outdoor Life 144:46-7+ Jl '69

WOODCHUCKS
Me and that groundhog. C. E. Gillham. il Audubon 71:24-6 My '69
When fall begins. J. Mills. il Read Digest 95:79-81 O '69

WOODCOCK shooting
Toughest of flying targets? B. Elliot. il Outdoor Life 144:56-7+ N '69
Woodcock, alders, and cowflops. H. G. Tapply. il Field & S 74:74 O '69

WOODCOCKS
See also
Cookery—Game

WOODEN, John
Sporting scene. H. W. Wind. New Yorker 45:93-6+ Mr 22 '69

WOODEN shoes
Cloggy days. il Time 94:48 Ag 15 '69

WOODEN toys. See Toys

WOODEND, Agnes
Anniversary gift. Har Yrs 9:40 Je '69

WOODFORD, Elizabeth M.
Birding through the year. Horticulture 48:24-5+ Ja '70
Birds are coming back. Horticulture 47:40-1+ Mr '69

WOODLEY, Inez
Summer's tale; story. Redbook 133:90-1 Jl '69

WOODLEY, Richard
Close-up: he likes to keep you psyched. Life 66:69-72+ My 23 '69
Literary ticket for the 51st state. Life 66:71-2 My 30 '69

WOODMAN, Betty
Teapots. por Ceram Mo 17:12-15 Mr '69

WOODRING, Paul
View from the campus (cont) Sat R 52:68 Ap 19; 82 My 17; 60 Jl 19; 63 D 20 '69
—and others
(ed) Education in America. See issues of Saturday review

WOODROFF, Robert H.
Should your child go to summer school? ed. by J. Copland. Parents Mag 44:38-9+ Je '69

WOODROW, Alain
Open letter from French priests. Commonweal 89:610-11 F 14 '69
Worker-priests in jurisdictional dispute. Commonweal 90:192-3 My 2 '69

WOODRUFF, Maurice
Horoscopes: his and hers. See issues of McCall's

WOODRUM, Lon
If dropouts turn on. Chr Today 14:18-19 O 24 '69

WOODS, Betty, and Woods, Fred
Miniature roses in the garden. Horticulture 47:23+ Je '69

WOODS, Charles
Two California poster designers; interview, ed. by G. Loney. il por Am Artist 33:48-53+ My '69
WOODS, Fred. See Woods, B. jt. auth.
WOODS, Joseph Ignatius
Keeper of the peace. il por Newsweek 73:57 Mr 31 '69
WOODS, William Crawford
He that died of Wednesday; story. Esquire 71:114-15 Je '69
WOODSMEN
See also
Trappers
WOODSON, Benjamin Nelson
Going up by going down. il pors Forbes 104: 50 N 15 '69
WOODSTOCK, England
Other Woodstock; a visit to Blenheim palace. D. Butwin. il Sat R 52:42+ O 11 '69
WOODSTOCK, Ill.
Of course we soften our water. E. W. Bates, jr. il Am City 84:108+ Ap '69
WOODSTOCK college, Woodstock, Mass.
New American Jesuits. J. L'Heureux. Atlan 224:59-64 N '69
WOODSTOCK music and art fair. See Music festivals—New York (state)
WOODSTONE, Norma Sue
Help wanted!! Mlle 6:130-1+ Je '69
WOODWARD, Beverly
Vietnam and the law; theory & practice of civil challenge. Commentary 46:75-86 N '68; 47:6+ F '69
WOODWARD, Bliss
Under the blue ensign. See issues of Motor boating
WOODWARD, Comer Vann
American history (white man's version) needs an infusion of soul; excerpt from address. N Y Times Mag p32-3+ Ap 20 '69
Uses of history. bibliog Cur 107:52-64 My '69
WOODWARD, Joanne
Joanne Woodward tells all about Paul Newman; interview, ed. by M. Davidson. pors Good H 168:72-5+ F '69
WOODWARD, Kenneth L.
Catholics & divorce. Ladies Home J 86:74+ N '69
You can't find God in church anymore. Ladies Home J 86:86-7+ Mr '69
WOODWARD, Marc
International chef. See issues of Travel
WOODWARD, Thomas, pseud.
Assassination of Tom Mboya. Commonweal 90:501-3 Ag 22 '69
WOODWARD high school, Cincinnati. See Cincinnati—Education
WOODWORKING
See also
Drilling and boring (woodwork)
Joints (carpentry)
Turning
Wood carving

Projects
Build these two handsome tables in your workshop; room-matching step table and TV table stores standing. R. Capotosto; D. Jordan. il Pop Mech 131:158-61+ Mr '69
Father/son projects. il Bet Hom & Gard 47: 28 D '69
Five weekend projects to build. il Pop Mech 131:154-8 F '69
Four easy projects for summer weekends; exercise bench, floor-stand globe, styrofoam-cooler caddy, self-watering window box. il Pop Mech 132:168-71 Jl '69
Four good ideas: which can you use? il Pop Sci 194:150-1 Ap '69
Weekend projects. il Pop Mech 131:160-3 Ap; 156-60 My; 168-71 Je '69
Weekend workshop projects. il Pop Mech 132: 160-2 Ag '69
Wordless workshop. R. Doty. See issues of Popular science monthly
See also names of projects, e.g. Stools

Study and teaching
Your own thing. il Seventeen 28:30 Mr '69

WOODWORKING machinery
See also
Routing machines
Sanding machines
WOOFER speakers. See Loud speaking apparatus
WOOL
Royal fleece of the Andes. N. Flowers. il Natur Hist 78:36-43 My '69
See also
Keratin

WOOLDRIDGE, William O.
Khaki Cosa nostra. por Newsweek 74:37-8 O 13 '69
Kickbacks, guns; new round in army rackets hearing. il por U S News 67:14 O 20 '69
Military Mafia. il por Time 94:26 O 17 '69
Senate look at army-club scandal. U S News 67:12 O 13 '69
WOOLF, Charles M. and Dukepoo, F. C.
Hopi Indians, inbreeding, and albinism. bibliog Science 164:30-7 Ap 4 '69
WOOLLACOTT, Martin
What prospects for arms talks? Cur 109:43-5 Ag '69
WOOLWORTH, F. W, company
Robert C. Kirkwood of Woolworth; interview. R. C. Kirkwood. il Nations Bsns 57: 44-8 Jl '69
WOOSTER, Harold
Machina versatilis: a modern fable. por Library J 94:725-7 F 15 '69
WOOSTER, Warren S.
Ocean and man; with biographical sketch. Sci Am 221:50, 218-20+ S '69
WORCESTER, Donald E.
(comp) Articles and other books received; Latin America. See issues of American historical review
WORCESTER, Mass.
New lights for an old civic center. C. Robertson. il Am City 84:126 Mr '69

Religious institutions and affairs
Worcester survey; study of Vatican II's effect on the laity. J. P. Jurich. America 120:649-51 My 31 '69

WORCESTER porcelain factory. See Pottery, American—History
WORD games
Playing the dozens. S. M. Joseph. Commonweal 91:131-2 O 24 '69
WORDS
**** is no longer a dirty word. E. G. Romm. Esquire 71:135+ Ap '69
See also
Adjectives
English language—Etymology
English language—Terms and phrases
Euphemism
Semantics
Slang
WORDS, New
Nixon neologisms. Newsweek 73:33-4 Je 9 '69

Anecdotes, facetiae, satire, etc.
Strike that neologism! Chr Cent 86:793 Je 4 '69

WORDS and language. See Thought and language
WORDSWORTH, William
Wordsworth. G. Hartman. Yale R 58:507-25 Je '69
WORK
Ailing world of work. C. F. H. Henry. Chr Today 14:22-3 Ja 2 '70
Work; reprint. Mrs J. L. Edwards. Hobbies 74:92 Ag '69
See also
Right to labor
Skilled labor
WORK, Compulsory. See Labor, Compulsory
WORK benches
Build this box-leg power-tool stand. J. Burroughs. il Pop Mech 131:178-9 Ja '69
Great first workshop. il Bet Hom & Gard 47:52 O '69
How to build a desk-workbench for a youngster. R. J. De Cristoforo. il Pop Sci 195:130-4 D '69
MI's amazing modular workbench. il Mech Illus 65:58-61+ Jl '69
WORK boats
See also
Fishing boats
WORK experience. See Education, Cooperative
WORK furlough programs. See Prisoners—Rehabilitation
WORK-in strikes. See Strikes
WORK performance standards. See Performance standards
WORK satisfaction. See Job satisfaction
WORK-study program. See Education, Cooperative
WORKBENCHES. See Work benches
WORKER priests
Great American worker-priest movement. R. Francoeur. Commonweal 89:636-7 F 21 '69; Reply with rejoinder. W. J. Holly. 90:85-6 Ap 4 '69
Worker-priest for Christ. M. Moyal. il Chr Cent 86:808-9 Je 11 '69

WORLD politics, 1945- —*Continued*
Second year of the cold war. H. S. Hughes.
Commentary 48:27-32 Ag '69: Discussion.
48:4+ N '69
'60s: story of an awesome decade. il U S
News 68:66-9 Ja 12 '70
Soviet foreign policy; address, July 11, 1969.
A. A. Gromyko. Vital Speeches 35:618-28
Ag 1 '69
Storms of the 70s. G. Barraclough. Nation
210:6-8 Ja 12 '70
Third world and the great powers. S. Gupta.
bibliog f Ann Am Acad 386:54-63 N '69
Threshold of a new age. il U S News 67:21
Jl 28 '69
Tinkering with delicate relationships. il Time
95:24 Ja 19 '70
Two sentinels of the status quo; U.S. &
U.S.S.R; address, July 11, 1969. F. Church.
bibliog f Vital Speeches 35:614-17 Ag 1 '69
U.S. and Russia: dawn of a new era; inter-
view. J. Fromm. il U S News 68:34-7 Ja 5
'70
World after General de Gaulle. America
120:556 My 10 '69
World politics, 1969. G. Lichtheim. Commen-
tary 47:50-8 Je '69
Worldgram: from the capitals of the world.
See issues of U S news & World report
See also
Balance of power
WORLD population. See Population
WORLD press photo competition. See Photog-
raphy—Competitions
WORLD records
See also
Aviation records
WORLD series (baseball)
Fable for our time; Amazin' Mets. il Time 94:
43 O 24 '69
Just call them plain folk heroes; New York
Mets. il Sports Illus 31:40-4+ O 20 '69
Never pumpkins again; New York Mets. W.
Leggett. il Sports Illus 31:14-21 O 27 '69
Sporting scene (cont) R. Angell. New Yorker
45:145-52+ N 1 '69
Whole new ball game. P. Axthelm. News-
week 74:104-5 O 20 '69
Win that couldn't be won; New York Mets.
il Newsweek 74:108-109B O 27 '69
World series with Marianne Moore; reprint.
G. Plimpton. il Wilson Lib Bul 43:626-33
Mr '69
WORLD 600 race. See Automobile racing
WORLD table tennis championship. See Table
tennis
WORLD tours
See also
Voyages around the world
WORLD trade. See Commerce
WORLD trade center. See New York (city)
—World trade center
WORLD trade week
World trade week, 1969; a proclamation. R.
M. Nixon. Dept State Bul 60:297 Ap 7 '69
WORLD unity. See International relations
WORLD university. See International univer-
sity (proposed)
WORLD war, 1914-1918. See European war,
1914-1918
WORLD war, 1939-1945
Eisenhower story. H. La Fay. il Nat Geog
136:13-30 Jl '69

Aerial operations
Before the colors fade: captain of the
Franklin; interview. ed. by D. Davidson.
L. E. Gehres. il Am Heritage 20:60-3+ Ap
'69
Last great air war. il Esquire 72:75-83 Ag '69
See also
Dresden—Air raids

Art and the war
Last great air war. il Esquire 72:75-83 Ag '69

Atrocities
Bishop Defregger case. America 121:52 Ag 2:
107 Ag 30 '69
Bishop's burden: M. Defregger and the
Filetto di Camarda massacre; with report
by P. S. Cook. il Newsweek 74:56-7 Ag 18
'69
See also
Concentration camps
World war, 1939-1945—Jews
World war, 1939-1945—War criminals

Bibliography
Recent past. R. L. Tobin. il Sat R 52:33-4 D
20 '69

Campaigns and battles
See also
Ardennes. Battle of the, 1944-1945
Battlefields
Pacific
See also
Pearl Harbor, Attack on, 1941
Philippine Sea, Battles of the, 1944
Western
Battlefields revisited; Normandy's beaches
twenty-five years after D-day. il Time 93:
30-7 My 30 '69
D day plus twenty-five years. K. Crawford.
Newsweek 73:37 Je 16 '69
Longest wait; American forces in Britain be-
fore Normandy invasion. J. Lord. il Am
Heritage 20:4-15+ Je '69
My longest day; interview. C. Ryan. il Look
33:69-70 Je 10 '69
Taps at Utah Beach; veterans return to
Normandy to mark D-Day plus twenty-
five years. R. Kotlowitz. il Harper 239:104-
12 O '69
Tunes of glory; 25th anniversay of D-day.
il Time 93:20 Je 13 '69
See also
Saint-Lô, France—Siege, 1944
World war, 1939-1945—France

Causes
On borrowed time, by L. Mosley. Review
Time il 93:82 Je 27 '69

Diplomatic history
Night Stalin and Churchill divided Europe.
J. Lukacs. il N Y Times Mag p36-8+ O 5
'69
See also
Munich four power agreement, 1938
World war, 1939-1945—Documents, sources,
etc.

Documents, sources, etc.
Secrets of the Nazi archives. D. Kahn. Atlan
223:50-6 My '69

Jews
Lively arts; interview, ed. by R. Hemming.
Topol. Sr Schol 94:32 Ap 25 '69
Memoirs of an anti-Semite. G. Von Rezzori.
New Yorker 45:42-52+ Ap 26 '69
Toward a history of the holocaust. L. S.
Dawidowicz. Commentary 47:51-6 Ap '69

Naval operations
Before the colors fade: captain of the Frank-
lin; interview. ed. by D. Davidson. L. E.
Gehres. il Am Heritage 20:60-3+ Ap '69
Gallantry of an ugly duckling; fight of lib-
erty ship Stephen Hopkins against cruiser
Stier and blockade runner Tannenfels. R.
L. Vargas. il Am Heritage 21:22-3+ D '69
Intrepid midgets; condensation. T. Gallagher.
il Read Digest 95:249-52+ N '69
See also
Philippine Sea, Battles of the, 1944

Personal narratives
Free at last; as Henri Cartier-Bresson saw
it; with photographs. L. Gross. il Look
33:58-63 S 23 '69
Long row of candles, memoirs and diaries
(1934-1954) by C. L. Sulzberger. Review
Nat R 21:704-5 Jl 15 '69. P. L. Buckley
Longest wait; American forces in Britain
before Normandy invasion. J. Lord. il Am
Heritage 20:4-15+ Je '69
Memories of crime past; A. Speer's memoirs.
il Newsweek 74:41 S 8 '69
My longest day; interview. C. Ryan. il Look
33:69-70 Je 10 '69
Taps at Utah Beach; veterans return to Normandy to mark D-Day plus twenty-five
years. R. Kotlowitz. il Harper 239:104-12
O '69

Pictures
See World war. 1939-1945—Art and the
war

Prisoners and prisons
See also
Concentration camps

War criminals
As you were; German reactions to proposal
to extend the statute of limitations. News-
week 73:48 My 19 '69
Bishop who was a major. Time 94:63-4 Jl
18 '69
Closing the loophole; undetected German war
criminals immune from future prosecu-
tion. Time 94:40 Jl 18 '69
Kurt Gerstein, by S. Friedlander. Review
Commentary 48:71-2+ Jl '69; G. Lewy
Newsweek 73:108+ Mr 24 '69. A. Cooper

WORLD war, 1939-1945—War criminals—*Cont.*
Semifinal solution; West German decision on the statute of limitations. Newsweek 73:44 My 5 '69
Shifting the guilt; conviction of war criminals. Time 93:24+ My 2 '69
Under the circumstances; M. Defregger suspected accomplice to Italian atrocity. Newsweek 74:40 Jl 21 '69
Were you there? attempt to distinguish between ordinary murder and excessive murder. il Newsweek 73:40 Mr 31 '69

Asia
World war II in Asia. R. N. Berkes. bibliog f Cur Hist 57:71-6+ Ag '69

Brazil
Cobra Fumando; Brazilian expeditionary force. C. E. B. Peeke. il Américas 21:9-15 Jl '69

France
Story behind the liberation of Paris a quarter of a century ago. L. Collins and D. Lapierre. il N Y Times Mag p46-7+ S 7 '69
Reply. F. L. Howley. p22+ O 5 '69
To lose a battle, by A. Horne. Review
Nat R 21:653 Jl 1 '69. G. F. Eliot
See also
France—History—German occupation, 1940-1945

Germany
See also
Dresden—Air raids

Great Britain
Last great air war. il Esquire 72:75-83 Ag '69

Japan
Before the colors fade: captain of the Franklin; interview, ed. by D. Davidson. L. E. Gehres. il Am Heritage 20:60-3+ Ap '69
See also
Philippine Sea, Battles of the, 1944

Philippines
See also
Philippine Sea, Battles of the, 1944

Poland
When World war II began; 30th anniversary of the German invasion. il Time 94:29 S 5 '69

Russia
Soviet generals and number one. T. Szamuely. il Nat R 21:861-2 Ag 26 '69
See also
Leningrad, Siege of, 1941-1944

United States
Fateful friendship. S. E. Ambrose. il Am Heritage 20:40-1+ Ap '69
Hemispheric defense in World war II. P. B. Taylor. jr. Cur Hist 56:333-9 Je '69
U.S. in World war II. A. C. Turner. Cur Hist 57:13-17+ Jl '69
World war II in Asia. R. N. Berkes. bibliog f Cur Hist 57:71-6+ Ag '69
See also
Western hemisphere—Defenses
World war, 1939-1945—Aerial operations

WORLD war in art. See World war, 1939-1945—Art and the war
WORLD weather watch. See Weather forecasts
WORLDS fair, Osaka. See Osaka, Japan—Worlds fair, 1970
WORLD'S mirror; story. See Aguallo, T.
WORLEY, James
Double feature; poem. Chr Cent 86:1348 O 22 '69
Good Friday spell; poem. Chr Cent 86:448 Ap 2 '69
WORMAN, Charles G.
Firearms. See issues of Hobbies
WORMS
See also
Earthworms
Flatworms
Nematodes
WORMS; story. See Crawford, B. A.
WORMS, intestinal and parasitic
TRB from Washington; McGovern subcommittee hearings on heavy worm infestation of low-income families. New Repub 160:6 Mr 8 '69
Thorny-headed worm infection in North American prehistoric man. J. G. Moore and others. bibliog il Science 163:1324-5 Mr 21 '69
See also
Pinworms

WORRY
See also
Anxiety
WORRY-beads. See Beads
WORSHIP
All there was was a man, struggling. R. L. Stanger. Chr Cent 86:1247-9 O 1 '69
Planning for common worship; proposed new worship service for constituents of Consultation on church union. America 120:207 F 22 '69
See also
Church attendance
Church music
WORTH, Frank
Mini-cannons from antique design. Design 70:31-5 mid-Wint '69
Words tell a picture. Design 70:12-13 Spr '69
WORTH COUNTY, Ga.
In Worth County. Nation 208:132 F 3 '69
WOSTER, Alice C.
Panic in a desk drawer; drama. Plays 29:67-73, 84 O '69
WOUND healing
Wound healing. R. Ross. il Sci Am 220:40-50 bibliog(p 144) Je '69
WOUNDED, Vietnamese war. See Vietnamese war, 1957- —Casualties
WOUNDS
See also
Bruises
WOZZECK; drama. See Büchner, G.
WOZZECK; opera. See Berg, A.
WOZZECK (operatic character) See Characters in opera
WRAPPING materials
Food storage, the final wrap-up. N. Craig. il House B 111:42+ S '69
WRAPPING of packages
If you're giving an appliance gift. Good H 169:223 D '69
Lots of ways to send a Christmas package. il Changing T 23:33-5 N '69
Wrap a gift in a Christmas tree. il Seventeen 27:162+ N '68
Wrapped with love; From your kitchen. il Bet Hom & Gard 47:88-91+ N '69
WRATH of God. See God—Wrath
WREATHS
See also
Leis
WREATHS, Christmas. See Christmas wreaths
WRECKING
See also
Automobiles—Wrecking
WRECKS. See Shipwrecks
WREDE, Stuart
Lesson from the Finns. Am Home 72:118-19 S '69
WRENCHES
Tools for electronics. T. Haskett. il Radio-Electr 41:54-8 Ja '70
See also
Torque wrenches
WRESTLING
Face to face with a contemporary Hercules. J. Krapf. Seventeen 28:68 Ag '69
Pancake man flattens 'em; D. Gable of Iowa state. H. Weiskopf. Sports Illus 30:48 Mr 24 '69
Whammo is the winning way; Iowa State NCAA championship. H. Weiskopf. Sports Illus 30:72-3 Ap 7 '69
See also
Judo
WRESTLING coaches. See Coaches (athletics)
WRIGHT, Alfred
Golf (cont) Sports Illus 31:70-1+ O 27 '69
WRIGHT, Arthur
[Book reviews] Commonweal 89:569-71 Ja 31 '69
WRIGHT, Betty
Biology at its best. Good H 169:173 Jl '69
WRIGHT, Charles David
Addendum; Killing; Offering; Half-moon; In the midnight hour; Eye; Self-portrait; Illumination; Grave of the right hand; poems. Poetry 114:353-61 S '69
Smoke; poem. New Yorker 45:42 My 31 '69
WRIGHT, Frank. See Bailey, C. W. jt. auth.
WRIGHT, Frank Lloyd
Frank Lloyd Wright: the eleventh decade. E. Kaufmann, jr. il Arch Forum 130:38-41 Je '69
Frank Lloyd Wright was also a gifted landscape architect. il Sunset 142:70-3 F '69
Unity temple, Oak Park, Ill. H. Wright. bibliog f il Arch Forum 130:28-37 Je '69
WRIGHT, Grant
Chief of U.S. park police. il pors Ebony 24:66-8+ Mr '69
WRIGHT, H. Elliott
Movies. Chr Cent 86:126-7, 352, 1070, 1400-2 Ja 22, Mr 12, Ag 13, O 29 '69

WRIGHT, Henry
Unity temple, Oak Park, Ill. bibliog f Arch Forum 130:28-37 Je '69
WRIGHT, James
Critic of the month. L. Lieberman. Poetry 114:40-1 Ap '69
Joy out of terror. S. Moss. New Repub 160: 30-2 Mr 29 '69
Pieces of a broken mirror. P. Zweig. Nation 209:20-2 Jl 7 '69
WRIGHT, James E.
Help change the pecking order. por Library J 94:153-5 Ja 15 '69
Hormonal termination of larval diapause in dermacentor albipictus. bibliog Science 163:390-1 Ja 24 '69
WRIGHT, James Skelly
Courts have failed the poor. N Y Times Mag p26-7+ Mr 9 '69
WRIGHT, James W.
Mini-boot, new four-wheel-drive dune buggy. Pop Sci 195:179-81 Ag '69
2,000-hp. car poised for new speed-record try. Pop Sci 195:90-1+ Ag '69
WRIGHT, Jay
Bosques de Chapultepec; poem. Yale R 58: 417-18 Mr '69
Diamond-bright art form. Sports Illus 30:32-4+ Je 23 '69
Hunting trip cook; poem. New Repub 161: 22-3 N 29 '69
WRIGHT, John Joseph, cardinal
Cardinal Wright on celibacy. America 121: 128 S 6 '69
WRIGHT, Lee
Murder is my business, sort of. McCalls 96:97-8 Ap '69
WRIGHT, Margaret White
Full blown roses. Har Yrs 9:30-1 My '69
WRIGHT, Mary
New Key for the white house. Travel & Camera 32:64-7 Ap '69
WRIGHT, Percy H.
New flowering almonds. Horticulture 47:58 Ja '69
Purple-leaf chokecherries. Horticulture 47: 46+ D '69
WRIGHT, Phyllis, and Zimmerman, D. R.
Medicine today. See issues of Ladies' home journal
WRIGHT, Robert H.
Disappearing toad. Sci Digest 65:29-31 Ap '69
WRIGHT, Sam
Letter from the Arctic. Liv Wildn 33:4-6 Spr '69
WRIGHT, Sylvia
Revival of Ted Kennedy. Life 67:38-9 O 3 '69
WRIGHT, Tennant C.
Conflict of consciences. America 120:332-4 Mr 22 '69
WRIGHT, Thomas E.
Alert the citizen before the disaster strikes. Am City 84:101-2 Ag '69
WRIGHT, William J.
Jail, fine or plant trees. R. Leadabrand. por Am For 75:31+ F '69
WRIGLEY, John E.
Critical questions in medical transplants. America 120:334-7 Mr 22 '69
WRITERS. See Authors
WRITERS, World congress of. See PEN club
WRITERS conferences. See Authors conferences
WRITER'S digest (periodical)
Winners: Writer's digest creative writing awards. Writers Digest 49:36-42+ O '69
WRITERS' notebooks. See Notebooks
WRITING
See also
Authorship
Calligraphy
Hieroglyphics
Penmanship
Signatures (writing)
WRITING (authorship) See Authorship; Creative writing
WRITING (composition) See English language —Composition
WRITING, Italic
Mercator and the lettering of maps. P. Standard. il Pub W 196:58+ N 3 '69
WRITING, Korean. See Korean language—Writing
WRITING desks. See Desks
WRITING paper. See Stationery
WRONG road; story. See Allen, E.
WROUGHT iron
Wrought iron on scrap heap. il Bsns W p 18 Ja 3 '70

WROUGHT iron work. See Ironwork
WU, Robin C. C.
Long road from China. Nat R 21:806 Ag 12 '69
WUJEK, Joseph H. Jr
Atomic radiation. Electr World 81:46-7 My; 46-8 Je; 82:28-30 Jl '69
WULF, Melvin L.
Legal quackery in D.C. Commonweal 89:668-9 F 28 '69
Purge at NAACP. Commonweal 89:403-4, 601 D 20 '68, F 7 '69
WUNDER, Al
Contemporary dance repertoire concert; Henry street settlement playhouse. J. Dowlin. Dance Mag 43:80 F '69
WUNDERLIN, Christine
Afternoon: poem. Seventeen 28:92 My '69
WUNTCH, Thomas, and others
Lactate dehydrogenase isozymes: kinetic properties at high enzyme concentrations. bibliog Science 167:63-5 Ja 2 '70
WUORINEN, Charles
More on Ben Weber and Wuorinen. A. Cohn. il por Am Rec G 35:1040-1 Jl '69
WURF, Jerry
Establishing the legal right of public employees to bargain. Mo Labor R 92:65-6 Jl '69
WURLITZER, Rudolph
Passing time. L. Segal. New Repub 160:23-4+ Mr 29 '69
WURSTER, Charles F.
Alarming case against DDT; interview, ed. by J. N. Miller. Read Digest 95:99-104 O '69
Charge is biocide; DDT stands trial. Audubon 71:128-35 S '69
WURTMAN, Richard J. See Shein, H. M. jt. auth.
WURTSWORTH, Charles
Electronics for weekend sailors. Radio-Electr 40:37-40 My '69
WÜRTTEMBERG state theater ballet. See Stuttgart ballet
WYANDOTTE chemicals corporation
German miracle at Wyandotte? Badische anilin's takeover of U.S. chemical maker. il Bsns W p50-2 N 8 '69
WYANT, Rowena
Business failures. See issues of Dun's review
WYATT, Benjamin Dean
Duke of Wellington's search for a palace. E. Longford. il Horizon 11:106-13 Spr '69
WYATT, Gertrud L.
Parent and child. N Y Times Mag p99-100+ O 19 '69
WYATT, J. T. and Silvey, J. K. G.
Nitrogen fixation by gloeocapsa. bibliog Science 165:908-9 Ag 29 '69
WYATT, Oscar
Wyatt effect. il Forbes 103:34-5 Ja 15 '69
WYCHE, Zelma Charles
Black lawman in KKK territory. C. L. Sanders. il pors Ebony 25:57-60+ Ja '70
WYCKOFF, Ernst H.
Papa and the general. il por Forbes 104:40 D 1 '69
WYDEN, Barbara. See Schwartz, G. G. jt. auth.
WYDEN, Peter
—See Bach, G. R. jt. auth.
about
Authors & editors. C. B. Grannis. por Pub W 195:30-2 F 10 '69
WYDEN, Peter H, incorporated
Peter H. Wyden, inc, new publisher, formed. Pub W 195:106 Je 2 '69
WYE house. See Talbot County, Md.—Historic houses, etc.
WYETH, Andrew
Beholden to no one. G. Logsdon. il por Farm J 93:28-9+ Mr '69
WYETH, Newell Convers
My brother. N. C. Wyeth. S. Wyeth. il Horn Bk 45:29-36 F '69
WYETH, Stimson
My brother. N. C. Wyeth. Horn Bk 45:29-36 F '69
WYLE laboratories, incorporated
Apollo/Saturn V. from ground test to flight. il Space World F-2-62:6-34 F '69
WYLIE, Elinor (Hoyt)
Legend revisited: Elinor Wylie. J. D. Gordan. Am Scholar 38:459-68 Sum '69
WYLIE, Evan McLeod
Asiatic diseases; are they a threat to Americans back home? Good H 168:96-7+ Ap '69
WYLIE, Frank
Rap 'n 'pinion. por Motor T 21:18+ N '69
WYLIE, Janice
Annals of jurisprudence. F. C. Shapiro. New Yorker 44:39-42+ F 8; 44-6+ F 15; 45: 42-4+ F 22 '69

WYLIE, Janice—*Continued*
Victims; excerpts. B. Lefkowitz and K. G. Gross. il por Look 33:37-42+ My 27; 39-44+ Je 10; 39-44+ Je 24 '69

WYLIE, Ray
Revolution within a revolution? Bul Atom Sci 25:29-32 F '69

WYLLYS family
Wyllys coat-of-arms. H. K. Eilers. il Hobbies 74:114-15 Jl '69

WYLY, Sam E.
How a good idea can be turned into riches. por U S News 67:60 D 15 '69
Looping in a bonanza, Texas style. il por Bsns W p68 My 24 '69

WYMAN, Donald
Espaliers. Horticulture 47:28-9+ S '69
—See Wyman, F. jt. auth.

WYMAN, Florence, and Wyman, Donald
Christmas decorations from the garden. Horticulture 47:24-5 D '69

WYMAN, Louis C.
Excerpt from address. February 6, 1969. Cong Digest 48:179 Je '69

WYNDER, Ernest L. and Hoffmann, Dietrich
Experimental tobacco carcinogenesis. bibliog Science 162:862-71; 165:312-13 N 22 '68, Jl 18 '69

WYNDHAM, Lee
How to criticise and revise a juvenile book. K. Mason. il Writers Digest 49:52-5+ Ag '69

WYNDHAM, Robert J.
Tonic for body and mind. Org Gard & Farm 16:92-3 N '69
Your oranges don't shine. Org Gard & Farm 16:66-7 S '69

WYNGAARDEN, J. B. See Emmerson, B. T. jt. auth.

WYNN, James Sherman
Big blasts from a toy cannon. M. Mulvoy. il por Sports Illus 30:76+ Je 9 '69

WYNN, Wilton
Report from Rome. Fortune 81:51+ Ja '70

WYOMING
See also
Fishing—Wyoming
Hunting—Wyoming
Paleontology—Wyoming
Yellowstone National Park

Social conditions
Real world comes to Wyoming. S. Murdock. Nation 209:535-7 N 17 '69

WYOMING, Mich.
Up, up and away; bridge over highway. il Am City 84:54 Je '69

WYOMING. University, Laramie
No defeats, loads of trouble; Wyoming's black football players suspended. P. Putnam. il Sports Illus 31:26-7 N 3 '69
See also
National outdoor leadership school

WYSOR, Bettie
Action: a beauty investment. Harp Baz 102:158-61 Ag '69

WYSPIANSKI, Stanislaw
Acropolis; adaptation. See Grotowski, J.

WYZANSKI, Charles Edward, 1906-
Latest challenge to the draft. il por U S News 66:52-3 Ap 14 '69
Moral objector wins a point. por Sr Schol 94:14 Ap 18 '69
Objection sustained. por Time 93:46 Ap 11 '69
Sisson's complaint. Wyzanski's ploy. I. Silver. Commonweal 90:385-9 Je 20 '69

X

XB-70. See Airplanes. Military—United States
X-15 (airplane) See Airplanes. Experimental
X RAY analysis. See Crystallography—X ray studies
X-RAY stars. See Stars—Radiation
X RAYS
See also
Crystallography—X ray studies

Diffraction
Lead: X-ray diffraction study of a high-pressure polymorph. T. Takahashi and others. bibliog il Science 165:1352-3 S 26 '69

Industrial applications
See also
Radiation—Industrial applications

Measurement
Giant X-ray telescope. il Sky & Tel 37:300-1 My '69
Search for soft X-rays from the galaxy. R. J. Grader and others. il Sky & Tel 37:79-81 F '69

Physiological effects
What you should know about X-rays and pregnancy. G. C. Lewis, jr. and P. Feinstein. Redbook 132:30+ F '69
X-ray resistant cell required for the induction of in vitro antibody formation. J. Roseman. bibliog il Science 165:1125-7 S 12 '69

Scattering
Thirty years of small-angle X-ray scattering; adaptation of address, August 1968. A. Guinier. il Phys Today 22:25-30 N '69

Therapeutic applications
They're curing an incurable cancer. W. S. Ross. il Read Digest 95:89-93 D '69

XANTHIUM. See Cockleburs

XENAKIS, Yannis
If it pleases. O. Daniel. il Sat R 52:71+ N 29 '69
Toward infinity in sound. il por Time 93:77-8 Mr 21 '69

XENIA, Ohio
Xenia, Ohio. Negro Hist Bul 32:21 Mr '69

XENON
Solar-type xenon: a new isotopic composition of xenon in the Pesyanoe meteorite. K. Marti. bibliog il Science 166:1263-5 D 5 '69
Xenon: effect on radiation sensitivity of HeLa cells. R. J. Schulz and others. bibliog il Science 163:571-2 F 7 '69

XEROX corporation
Moving to New York's outer edges. il Bsns W p 158-60 N 15 '69
Product nobody wanted: excerpt from The strategy of change for business success. ed. by S. Furst and M. Sherman. J. C. Wilson. il Nations Bsns 57:67-70 F '69
Xerox aims at computers: plan to merge with Scientific data systems Bsns W p34 F 15 '69
Xerox: the McColough era; clashes with IBM. il Forbes 104:24-6+ Jl 1 '69

XIQUES, Edward F.
Waterproof your trailer lights. Yachting 125:74-5 My '69

XUAN Thuy
Parting words. Newsweek 74:62 D 8 '69

XYLOSMA
Xylosma shapes up easily. il Sunset 143:178 S '69

Y

YAF. See Young Americans for freedom (organization)
YASD. See American library association—Young adult services division
YMCA. See Young men's Christian association
YOU. See Youth organizations united
YA Hsien
Colonel; poem. Atlan 224:96 O '69
YABLONSKI, Joseph A.
Challenger's round. por Time 94:70-1 Ag 22 '69
Deadly venom. por Time 95:19-20 Ja 19 '70
Death of a rebel. il por Newsweek 75:22 Ja 19 '70
Miners play rough. E. Cox. New Repub 161:13-14 Ag 2 '69
Shades of John L. il por Newsweek 74:83-4+ D 15 '69
Yablonski's death stirs up miners. il por Bsns W p35 Ja 10 '70
YACHT brokers
Why the yacht broker. E. L. Brilleman. Motor B 123:127 Ja '69
YACHT building
Birth of a yacht. J. Martenhoff. il Yachting 126:52-4+ Jl '69
Yachting interviews. A. Defever. il Yachting 126:58-9+ S '69
YACHT clubs
Ah, the Irish, they're super! Royal Cork YC. D. Buchanan. Yachting 126:195-6 S '69
$5 yacht club: Chicago's Skipper's club. N. Levy. il Yachting 125:97+ Ja '69

YACHTS—*Continued*

Interior decoration

See Yacht decoration

Maintenance and repair

Stitch in time. M. Badham. il Motor B 123: 70-1+ Mr '69

Materials

Balsa-cored fiberglass. A. Lippay. il Yachting 125:116-17+ Ja '69
Custom fiberglass yacht. T. Cobb. il Yachting 125:118-19+ Ja '69
Fiberglass cruisers. P. Smyth. il Motor B 124:46-51+ O '69
What do you know about... N. Feige. il Yachting 125:80-1+ Ap '69

Stability and stabilizers

New Mini-fins help stabilize 30'-80' yachts. il Motor B 124:140-1 N '69

Storage

Putting her to bed. C. Miller. il Motor B 124:130-3 O '69

Testing

Look at Holland. E. F. Haylock. il Yachting 126:56-7+ D '69

YACHTS, Historic
Historic lone voyagers; paintings. Yachting 125:92-3 Ja '69

YACHTS, Remodeled
Conversion for comfort; shrimper hull makes retirement cruiser. il Yachting 125:54-5 Je '69
Work boats for fun; converted trawlers as pleasure boats. F. C. Clark, jr. il Motor B 124:56-9 S '69

YACHTS, Used
Used boats. il Motor B 123:126-7 Ja '69

YACHTS and yachting
America's cup news. See issues of Yachting
Avast, belay and pretty please. H. D. Whall. il Sports Illus 31:38-40 Jl 14 '69
Bahamas bearings. J. McClish. See issues of Motor boating
Cabin cruiser. B. Crabtree. il Yachting 125: 83+ Ja '69
Calendar of coming events; comp. by R. B. Smith. See issues of Motor boating
Chesapeake log. W. B. Matthews, jr. See issues of Motor boating
Inboards. il Motor B 123:148-63 Ja '69
Inside yachts. E. Sheppard. il Harp Baz 102: 118-19 Je '69
Joys of life afloat. il Newsweek 74:58-63 Ag 4 '69
Man and his boat; Gould Eddy and Y Como. B. Crabtree. il Yachting 126:70-1+ D '69
Motor boating USA. See issues of Motor boating
Nautical captains of industry. il Duns R 94: 30-5 Ag '69
News from yachting centers. See issues of Yachting
Northwest gales. E. Crimmin. See issues of Motor boating
Ocean racing auxiliary. B. Bavier. il Yachting 125:80-1 Ja '69
Southward ho. J. Wilson. See issues of Motor boating
Special report: southern yachting; symposium. bibliog il Yachting 126:50-66+ N '69
Trademark cruising. B. Crabtree. il Yachting 126:67+ O '69
Westward ho. B. Ruskauff. See issues of Motor boating
Year in yachting. il Yachting 125:100-7 Ja '69
Your new medium cruiser. il Motor B 123: 102-3 Ja '69

See also
America (yacht)
Cookery, Marine
Marinas
Sailing
Schooners
Sloops
Voyages
Yacht racing

Accidents

Asking for trouble; departure for southern waters via the offshore route. B. Robinson. il Yachting 126:60-1+ Ag '69
How not to go South. D. Street, jr. il Yachting 126:62+ Ag '69
Rolled down offshore. F. M. Slavic. il Yachting 125:72-3+ Je '69

Bibliography

Book notes and reviews; ed. by K. Aamodt. See issues of Yachting

Lightning hazards

Lesson learned. A. C. Spectorsky. il Yachting 125:75+ Ap '69

Safety devices and measures

Lesson learned. A. C. Spectorsky. il Yachting 125:75+ Ap '69
Stitch in time. M. Badham. il Motor B. 123: 70-1+ Mr '69

Europe, Western

European yachting; symposium, with introd. by B. Robinson. il Yachting 126:50-64 D '69

Hong Kong

Northwest passage, Chinese gunboats capture yachts from Hong Kong to Macao. il Newsweek 73:41 Mr 3 '69

Japan

Stornoway, alive and well and living in Japan. M. Petersen. il Motor B 124:52-5+ D '69

New Zealand

U.S. sailor in New Zealand. C. Van Duyne. il Yachting 125:62-3+ Je '69

YAD va-shem, Jerusalem. See Jerusalem—Yad va-shem
YADIN, Yigael
Hazor's hidden resource. il por Time 93:78+ My 16 '69
YAHUDA, Michael B.
China's military capabilities. Cur Hist 57: 142-9+ S '69
China's nuclear option. Bul Atom Sci 25:72-7 F '69
YAHYA KHAN, Agha Mohammed
Army takes over Pakistan. por Time 93:32 Ap 4 '69
Back to democracy, on the double. il por Time 94:34 D 12 '69
Pakistan: new leader, same troubles. il por U S News 66:54 Ap 7 '69
YAKUBOVSKY, Ivan. See ÍAkubovskii, I.
YALE drama school. See Yale university—Drama school
YALE-New Haven medical center. See Yale university—Yale-New Haven medical center
YALE school of drama repertory theatre. See Yale university—Drama school
YALE university
Admission of women to Yale college; address, November 14, 1968. K. Brewster, jr. Sch & Soc 97:162-4 Mr '69
Arson suspected in fire at Yale art and architecture building. il Arch Rec 146:36 Jl '69
Edward A. Bouchet, Ph.D. il Negro Hist Bul 31:11 D '68
Girl and boy at Yale. il Newsweek 74:63 D 15 '69
Girls among the ivy. il Newsweek 73:71 My 12 '69
Great admissions sweepstakes, how Yale selected her first coeds. J. Lear. il N Y Times Mag p52-3+ Ap 13 '69
Learning the law, and other lessons, at Yale. Newsweek 73:59 F 10 '69
Lipstick for Yale. il Newsweek 73:69 Je 2 '69
Personal investing; for profit and for Yale. W. Robertson. il Fortune 79:179 Mr '69
Scenario; K. Brewster's views on dissent and disruption. Nation 208:588 My 12 '69
World of dance; second festival of Davenport college ballet society. W. Terry. il Sat R 52:42-3 Mr 29 '69
Yale elects a wise janitor. il Life 67:99-100 D 5 '69
Yale revisited. S Alsop. Newsweek 73:120 My 19 '69

Divinity school

Can seminaries break out? in-parish program. R. J. Becker. Chr Cent 86:585-6+ Ap 23 '69

Drama school

Ovid at Yale. J. Kroll. il Newsweek 74:117-18 D 15 '69
Thebes carnival; Yale school of drama repertory theatre. H. Hewes. Sat R 52:20 Mr 29 '69
Yale school of drama: winter of their discontent? E. Lester. il Holiday 46:50-1+ S '69

School of art and architecture

Best laid plans: department of city planning; dispute with administration. il Newsweek 74:82 Jl 14 '69

YALE university—*Continued*

Yale-New Haven medical center
In the therapeutic community, patients are doctors. M. Scarf. il N Y Times Mag p32-3+ My 25 '69

YAMASH'TA, Stomu
Fireworks from the battery. il por Time 94: 59 Jl 18 '69

YAMAUCHI, Edwin M.
Stones, scripts, and scholars. Chr Today 13:8-10+ F 14 '69

YANCEY, Jim
Mania for the Masters. M. Mulvoy. il por Sports Illus 30:34-6 Ap 7 '69

YANGTAOS
See also
Cookery—Fruit

YANKEE (ship) See Sailing vessels

YANKEES (baseball) See Baseball clubs

YANKELOVICH, Daniel
Blaming Ophelia for not playing Hamlet. Fortune 79:197-8 Ap '69

YANKELOVICH, Daniel, incorporated
What business thinks; the Fortune 500-Yankelovich survey. R. S. Diamond. il Fortune 80:139-40+ O; 157-8 N; 115-16 D '69; 81:123-4 Ja '70

YANNACONE, Carol
New say in court. por Time 94:54 O 24 '69

YANNACONE, Victor John, jr
All he wants to save is the world. G. Rogin. il por Sports Illus 30:24-9 F 3 '69
DDT: the critics attempt to ban its use in Wisconsin. L. J. Carter. por Science 163:548-51 F 7 '69

YANNAS, Ioannis V.
Massive internal fracture of an amorphous polyester. bibliog Science 166:227-8 O 10 '69

YAQUI Indians
Teachings of Don Juan, by C. Castaneda. Review
Nation 208:184-6 F 10 '69. T. Roszak

YARBOROUGH, Cale
1968: the year of Cale Yarborough. S. Kelly. il pors Hot Rod 22:54-6 Ja '69
Yarborough fare. S. Kelly. il Hot Rod 22:58-61 My '69

YARBOROUGH, Ralph Webster
Help for the victim. il Newsweek 73:59 Je 23 '69
Senate: new leaders for health and education. B. Nelson. por Science 163:654-8 F 14 '69

YARBROUGH, Lee Roy
Lee Roy. S. Kelly. il pors Hot Rod 22:64-6 D '69
Some sweet theft at Daytona. K. Chapin. Sports Illus 30:50 Mr 3 '69

YARD, Robert Sterling
Patterns in National parks association history. D. Lambert. il Nat Parks 43:4-8 My '69

YARDS. See Home grounds

YARHAM, E. R.
Black forest: jewel of the Rhine. Am For 75: 36-9+ Mr '69
Cedars of the Lord. Am For 75:24-6+ Ja '69

YARN
Weaver's odyssey of yarn. N. Znamierowski. il Craft Horiz 29:25-6+ My '69

YARN belts. See Belts

YARN trees. See Christmas trees

YASSER, Joseph
Opening theme cf Rachmaninoff's third piano concerto and its liturgical prototype. bibliog f Mus Q 55:313-28 Jl '69

YATES, Brock
Warts, love and dreams in Buffalo. Sports Illus 30:44-6+ Ja 20 '69

YATES, Elizabeth
On that night. Read Digest 95:227-30+ D '69

YATES, Sidney R.
Showdown on the ABM; statement, January 13, 1969. Bul Atom Sci 25:29-32 Mr '69

YAWATA-Fuji merger. See Business consolidations and mergers—Japan

YAZOO CITY, Miss.
Education
Getting together in Yazoo. il Time 95:15 Ja 19 '70
School crisis in Yazoo City. il Newsweek 74: 36 N 10 '69

YCAZA, Carlos Manuel de
Man plus horse beats boy. W. Tower. il por Sports Illus 30:52+ Mr 17 '69

YCAZA, Manuel. See Ycaza, C. M. de

YEAR Boston won the pennant; drama. See Noonan, J. F.

YEAR round schools. See School year

YEASTS
Yeast genetics: report of meeting. R. C. von Borstel. Science 163:962-4 F 28 '69

YEH, Richard S. and Van Allen, J. A.
Alpha-particle emissivity of the moon: an observed upper limit. bibliog Science 166: 370-2 O 17 '69

YELAPA, Mexico
From Puerto Vallarta to Yelapa. il Sunset 143:70 N '69

YELISEYEV, Alexei. See Eliseev, A.

YELLEN, Linda
Campus, camera and me. Seventeen 28:154-5+ My '69

YELLOW-eyed grass. See Blue-eyed grass

YELLOW jackets
Season for yellow jackets is starting. il Sunset 142:202+ Je '69

YELLOWSTONE NATIONAL PARK
Forest succession in Yellowstone National Park. D. T. Patten. il Nat Parks 43:21-2 S '69
Frontier photographers; O'Sullivan and Jackson. D. Vestal. il Travel & Camera 32:48-52+ Je '69
Harding, Coolidge, and the lady who lost her dress. H. M. Albright. il Am West 6:25-32 S '69
Home where the buffalo roam; fishing and hunting in national parks. E. A. Bauer. il Outdoor Life 144:56-9+ Ag '69
Mountains by the minute; through Yellowstone and Grand Teton. L. P. Stinnett. il Travel 132:48-51 Jl '69
Those were the days. .; excerpts from Five golden summers. D. C. Stewart. il Parks & Rec 4:20-4 D '69
Will anyone come here for pleasure? R. A. Bartlett. il Am West 6:10-16 S '69
Yellowstone snowtime. F. A. Tinker. il Travel 131:30-3+ F '69

YELLOWTAIL fishing. See Amberfish fishing

YEMEN
Aden and South Arabia. R. E. Thoman. bibliog f il Cur Hist 58:27-33+ Ja '70

YEN, Chia-kan
Republic of China today; address, September 26, 1969. Vital Speeches 36:77-83 N 15 '69

YERKOVICH, Raymond J.
Recruitment: overhauling archaic practices. Clear House 43:328-30 F '69; Same abr. Ed Digest 34:38-9 My '69

YES ( ) no ( ) check one; story. See Amft, M. J.

YESTERDAY, Saturday, tomorrow; story. See Deasy, M.

YET another extract from the memoirs of a lover lover; story. See Von Helsing, A.

YEVTUSHENKO, Yevgeny Aleksandrovich. See Evtushenko, E. A.

YGLESIAS, José
Report from Brazil: what the left is saying. N Y Times Mag p52-3+ D 7 '69
Report from Chile: the left prepares for an election. N Y Times Mag p24-5+ Ja 11 '70
Report from Peru: the reformers in brass hats. N Y Times Mag p58-9+ D 14 '69

YIDDISH language
Joys of Yiddish, by L. Rosten. Review
Commentary 47:88+ Mr '69. M. T. Cohen

YIDDISH poetry
Translations into English
Yiddish poets in translation. N. Halper. Nation 208:154-6 F 3 '69

YIN, Theodore P.
Control of vibration and noise; with biographical sketch. Sci Am 220:18, 98-106 Ja '69

YING, Lai. See Lai Ying

YIPPIES. See Hippies—Political activities

YLVISAKER, Miriam
Our guilt. bibliog Engl J 58:193-5 F '69

YNTEMA, Theodore O.
Changing profile of world communism. Sat R 52:15-18 Je 14 '69

YODER, R. A.
Painting is fun with tempera. Sch Arts 69: 24-5 S '69

YODER, Worth N.
Small-city civic center. Am City 84:121-2 F '69

YOGA
Yoga. C. L. Miller. il Harp Baz 102:188-9+ Ap '69

YOLEN, Jane
Use your creative memory. Writer 82:16-17+ S '69

YOLLES, Stanley F.
Marijuana, sleeping pills and other drugs; peril for America; excerpts from testimony, June 25, 1969. il por U S News 67:47-8 Jl 14 '69
We must prevent emotional disturbance in children. por Parents Mag 44:56 N '69

YOLLES, Stanley F.—*Continued*
about
Pinning down the weed. il Sci N 96:263-4
S 27 '69

YOM Kippur
Curious case of Kol Nidre. H. Kieval; discussion. Commentary 47:10+ F '69

YORK, Herbert F.
ABM; excerpt from statement. Science 163:
1310 Mr 21 '69
Arms race and the fallacy of the last move;
excerpt from address, March 11, 1969. Bul
Atom Sci 25:27-8+ Je '69
Military technology and national security;
with biographical sketch. Sci Am 221:12, 17-
29 Ag '69

YORK, Michael
I've come to conquer you! ed. by E. Miller.
pors Seventeen 28:168-9+ Ap '69

YORK, Pa.
City planning
Parking garage, mall and office complex.
J. Frank and M. W. Seitz. il Am City
84:108-9+ Ag '69

Riots
Riots 1969 style. il Newsweek 74:36-7 Ag 11
'69

YORK minster. *See* Cathedrals—England

YORKSHIRE, England
Political organization and canvassing: Yorkshire elections before the reform bill. R. W.
Smith. bibliog f Am Hist R 74:1538-60 Je
'69

YORTY, Samuel William
Bitter victory. il por Time 93:28-9 Je 6 '69
Bradley challenge. il Time 93:26 My 23 '69
Fallen Angels. New Repub 160:7 Je 7 '69
L.A.'s about to say so long. Sam. J. W.
Germond. New Repub 160:10 My 24 '69
Mayor Yorty's big upset. il por Newsweek
73:31-2 Je 9 '69
Negro mayor for Los Angeles? por U S
News 66:12 Ap 14 '69
Sad Sam. Time 93:28 Ap 11 '69
Showdown for a showboater. por Time 93:
21-2 Mr 7 '69
Victory for a specter. J. Kerby. Nation 208:
749-50 Je 16 '69
Voters are in: Los Angeles. S. V. Roberts.
Commonweal 90:381 Je 20 '69
What Yorty's victory shows about the mood
in Los Angeles. por U S News 66:36 Je 9 '69

YOSEMITE NATIONAL PARK
Walking high in Yosemite. il Sunset 142:56+
F '69

YOSEMITE VALLEY
Winter holiday in Yosemite. il Sunset 143:
58-61 D '69
Yosemite in 1969, record water, smaller
crowds. il Sunset 142:34+ My '69
Yosemite Valley revisited. L. C. Merriam, jr.
il Nat Parks 43:14-15 Ja '69

YOSHIDA, A. *See* Stamatoyannopoulos, G. jt.
auth.

YOST, Charles W.
Israel and the Arabs: the myths that block
peace. Atlan 223:80-5 Ja '69
Mass public executions in Iraq deplored by
United States; text of letter, January 29,
1969. Dept State Bul 60:145-6 F 17 '69
Micro-states and United Nations; address,
August 27, 1969. Vital Speeches 35:746-8 O 1
'69
Realism in international affairs; address, June
30, 1969. Vital Speeches 35:642-5 Ag 15 '69
Responsibility for the U.N.'s development
as an instrument of world order; address,
October 22, 1969. Dept State Bul 61:449-51 N
24 '69
True peace on earth. por Parents Mag 44:30+
D '69
Twenty-fifth anniversary of the United Nations; statement, October 23, 1969. Dept
State Bul 61:485-9 D 1 '69
United Nations and the cause of peace; address. March 18, 1969. Dept State Bul 60:
325-9 Ap 14 '69
U.N. command in Korea submits report to
the Security council; letter. Dept State Bul
60:497-9 Je 9
U.N. condemns Israeli air attacks on Lebanese villages; statements, August 14 and
26, 1969. Dept State Bul 61:272-4 S 22 '69
United Nations: its past and its future;
address, May 26, 1969. Dept State Bul 60:
564-8 Je 30 '69
U.N. to accept private assistance for peoples
of southern Africa; remarks, March 21,
1969. Dept State Bul 60:329 Ap 14 '69

U.S. abstains on security council resolution
linking mosque fire to Middle East conflict; statement, September 15, 1969. Dept
State Bul 61:307-9 O 6 '69
U.S. abstains on Security council resolution on Namibia; statement, with text of
a resolution, August 12 and 13, 1969. Dept
State Bul 61:252-4 S 15 '69
U.S. calls for international action to safeguard civilian aviation; Department statements; with text of letter, February 19,
1969. Dept State Bul 60:197-8 Mr 10 '69
U.S. deplores minority rule in Southern
Rhodesia; statements, June 13 and 24, 1969.
Dept State Bul 61:65-8 Jl 21 '69
U.S. explains vote on Security council resolution on Israel; statements, March 27, April
1, 1969. Dept State Bul 60:340-2 Ap 21 '69
United States proposes U.N. Security council
study of micro-state question; statement,
August 27, 1969. Dept State Bul 61:268-72 S
22 '69
United States reaffirms position on Jerusalem; statements, July 1 and 3, 1969. Dept
State Bul 61:76-8 Jl 28 '69
U.S. supports U.N. Security council resolution on Namibia; statement, March 20,
1969. Dept State Bul 60:301-3 Ap 7 '69

YOU are now entering the human heart;
story. See Frame, J.

YOU never can tell; musical comedy. See Musical comedies, revues, etc.—Criticisms,
plots, etc.

YOU say what I feel; story. See Rogin, G.

YOUNG, A. S.
Black athlete in the golden age of sports
(cont) Ebony 24:66-8+ F; 122-4+ Mr; 100-
2+ Ap; 110-12+ My; 114-16+ Je '69

YOUNG, Anne
Chagall paints flowers; poem. Cath World
209:22 Ap '69

YOUNG, Billie
I am Penelope Ashe. McCalls 97:70+ N '69
about
Who is Penelope Ashe? G. Sheehy. il McCalls 97:71+ N '69

YOUNG, Carol
Stained glass reflects today's spirit. Sch
Arts 68:8 Ap '69

YOUNG, Donald
Mosaic of RFK. Sat R 52:29-30 F 8 '69

YOUNG, George
Warmup for the Canyon run. W. F. Reed,
jr. il por Sports Illus 30:16-19 Ja 27 '69

YOUNG, Harry H. jr
Why me? Newsweek 73:39-40 Mr 10 '69

YOUNG, James D. and others
Structural studies on transfer RNA: crystallization of formylmethionine and leucine
transfer RNA's. bibliog Science 166:1527-8
D 19 '69

YOUNG, John F.
In a time of campus crises, college publishers ponder future role. Pub W 195:
28-31 Ap 21 '69

YOUNG, John V.
Grand Canyon river run. Travel 131:40-5+
F '69

YOUNG, John W.
Our happy moon journey. il por Life 66:42-3
Je 20 '69
See also
Space flight to the moon—Manned flights—
Stafford-Cernan-Young flight, 1969

YOUNG, Joseph L.
Forty tons of mosaic. il por Am Artist 33:
18-21+ Ag '69

YOUNG, Kenneth Todd
Asia and America at the crossroads; with
questions and answers. Ann Am Acad 384:
53-65 Jl '69
Thailand's role in southeast Asia. bibliog f
Cur Hist 56:94-9+ F '69

YOUNG, Leigh Taylor-. *See* Taylor-Young, L.

YOUNG, Mildred F.
Traveler's choice. Travel 132:18 O '69

YOUNG, Paul
Boutique king bounces back. pors Bsns W
p57 Jl 26 '69

YOUNG, Pete
Few soft words for the Ku Klux klan. Esquire 72:104-5+ Jl '69

YOUNG, Peter
Presenting Peter Young; with biographical
sketch. il Art in Am 57:88-9 S '69

YOUNG, Robert M.
Current trends in construction. See Issues of
Architectural record

YOUNG, Warren R.
Answer at last to collisions in the sky? Read
Digest 95:106-10 Jl '69

YOUNG, Whitney Moore, 1921-
As I see it; interview. pors Forbes 104:79-80+
S 15 '69

YOUNG, Whitney Moore—*Continued*
Crisis, challenge, change; excerpt from address. pors Parks & Rec 4:42-3+ Ap '69
New thrust toward economic security; address, July 28, 1969. Vital Speeches 35:759-63 O 1 '69
Split-level challenge. Sat R 52:16-18 Ag 23 '69

YOUNG, W. T. See Brugler. J. S. jt. auth.

YOUNG adult institutue and workshop, incorporated
Independent living for the mentally handicapped; a program for young adults. T. R. Ames. il Ment Hy 53:641-2 O '69

YOUNG adults literature
Adolescent intitiation: a thematic study in the secondary school; address, November 1968. H. Agee. Engl J 58:1021-4 O '69
Literary hero for adolescents: the adolescent; adaptation of address, September 1968. S. Bank. Engl J 58:1013-20 O '69
See also
Young adults reading

Bibliography
Adult books for young adults; ed. by R. Minudri. Library J 94:3231-6, 4307-12, 4622-30 S 15, N 15, D 15 '69
Adult books for young adults; ed. by M. Trahan and R. Minudri (cont) Library J 94:317-20, 893-5, 1346-9, 1803-7, 2126-30, 2512+, 2686-9 Ja 15, F 15, Mr 15, Ap 15, My 15, Je 15, Jl '69
Best books for young adults, 1967-68. Todays Ed 58:57 Ap '69; Same. Library J 94:2038 My 15 '69
Best books of the spring; ed. by L. N. Gernhardt and others. il Library J 94:2073-4 My 15 '69
Books. J. Strafford. New Yorker 45:204+ D 13 '69
Books for brotherhood. Commonweal 89:644-7 F 21 '69
Books for young people. Z. Sutherland. See issues of Saturday review
Children's books for spring. Z. Sutherland. il Sat R 52:62 My 10 '69
Curl up & read. Seventeen 28:32 My '69
Fifty books for school libraries on the blacks. R. Condon. il Wilson Lib Bul 43:657-64 Mr '69; Discussion. 43:946 Je '69
Have you read..? Seventeen 28:52 Ag; 14+ S; 13 O; 12+ D '69
Outlook tower: books of interest to high-school students. J. Manthorne. See issues of Horn book magazine to June 1969
Spring book issue; symposium. il Sr Schol 94:Schol Teach 10-12+ My 2 '69
Tantrums and unicorns. M. Bacon. Atlan 224:148+ D '69
Up for discussion: fiction for today's teens. D. G. Stavn. Library J 94:4305-6 N 15 '69

YOUNG adults reading
Reading for pleasure and profit. A. W. Ackerman. Engl J 58:1042-4 O '69

YOUNG Americans for freedom (organization)
Burning for freedom. Nation 209:686 D 22 '69
Meet them in St Louis. J. C. Lobdell. Nat R 21:949 S 23 '69
This time, our side in Boston Common. D. Brudnoy. Nat R 21:1315 D 30 '69

YOUNG animals. See Animals, Infancy of

YOUNG artists program. See Berkshire symphonic festival

YOUNG Christian student movement. See Student Christian movements

YOUNG Lords. See Gangs

YOUNG men
Bets for the 70's. il Vogue 155:146-53 Ja 1 '70
Young zoom: fifty-two doers, goers, thinkers, none over twenty-five. il Vogue 154:120-3+ Ag 1 '69
See also
Youth movement

YOUNG men's Christian association
Happy birthday, Y. M. C. A! Chr Cent 86:1082 Ag 20 '69

YOUNG militants
Making of a counter culture, by T. Roszak. Review
Life il 67:8-9 N 7 '69. K. Keniston
Young and the old: notes on a new history; excerpts from History and survival. R. J. Lifton. Atlan 224:47-54 S; 83-8 O '69
See also
Reading—Special groups of readers—Young militants

YOUNG people. See Negro youth; Youth

YOUNG women
Bets for the 70's. il Vogue 155:146-53 Ja 1 '70
Young zoom: fifty-two doers, goers, thinkers, none over twenty-five. il Vogue 154:120-3+ Ag 1 '69
See also
College students, Women
Girls
Youth movement

YOUNGER, Judith T.
Tip from the conqueror. Nation 208:275-6 Mr 3 '69; Same abr. with title Land to live in. Cur 107:48-51 My '69

YOUNGMAN, Wilbur H.
Thoroughly confused. Am For 75:17-18 N '69

YOUNGSTOWN, Ohio

Education
Getting the point; increase in school taxes passed. il Newsweek 73:65 My 19 '69

Music
Report: production of Johann Strauss' Fledermaus. R. Finn. Opera N 34:23 N 22 '69

YOUNGSTOWN sheet and tube company
Better than the savings bank; merger of Lykes with Youngstown. il Forbes 103:30-1 Ap 1 '69
Lykes-Youngstown merger nears. Bsns W p 106 F 15 '69

YOUNT, David E.
Positron beams; with biographical sketch. bibliog por Phys Today 22:41-9 F '69

YOUSKEVITCH, Maria
Dancers of dancing parents. M. Marks. il pors Dance Mag 43:70-2 S '69

YOUTH
Between parent and teenager; excerpt. H. Ginott. il McCalls 96:78-9+ My; 48+ Je '69
How to get along with your teen-ager; excerpts from Between parent and teenager. H. G. Ginott. Read Digest 95:55-8 Jl '69
Something for youth to believe in. B. Graham. Read Digest 94:77-81 Je '69
Voices from abroad. Seventeen 29:88-9+ Ja '70
Voices from abroad; teens from Paris to Saigon tell you what they think about protest, parents, music, movies and Americans. Seventeen 28:98-9+ Ja '69
Young is beautiful. il Harp Baz 103:126-7 Ja '70
Youth: ego ideals and the impact of culture; AAAS symposium, December 27, 1969. H. M. Serota. Science 166:656 O 31 '69
Youth, love and sex: the new chivalry. J. D. Rockefeller, 3d. Look 33:32+ O 7 '69
Youth 1969; symposium. il UNESCO Courier 22:4-34 Ap '69
Youth-related activities of the United Nations; statement, September 30, 1969. S. Temple. Dept State Bul 61:380-2 N 3 '69
See also
Adolescence
Boys
College students
Discipline
Girls
High school students
Libraries—Work with young people
Negro youth
Parent-child relationship
Young men
Young women

Adjustment
See Adjustment, Social

Attitudes
See Attitudes

Employment
Dollars from doughnuts. il Seventeen 29:94-5+ Ja '70
Employment of high school graduates and dropouts. V. C. Perrella. bibliog il Mo Labor R 92:36-43 Je '69
Employment status of school age youth; with charts and tables. E. Waldman. bibliog Mo Labor R 92:23-32 Ag '69
Job program that works; Long Island employment day program. il Nations Bsns 57:72-3 D '69
New idea on minimum wage: less for young people. il U S News 66:68-9 Mr 31 '69
Oversupply of the young. H. Folk. il Trans-Action 6:27-32 S '69
Summer jobs for teenagers. R. Roesch. il Parents Mag 44:44-6 Ap '69

YOUTH—Employment—*Continued*
Why, how, and whence of manpower programs. G. L. Mangum. Ann Am Acad 385:
50-62 S '69
See also
Baby sitters
Student employment
United States—Job corps

Etiquette
See Etiquette for children and youth

Health and hygiene
Mental health consultation with a paramilitary youth program. D. M. Port. bibliog
Ment Hy 53:513-20 O '69

Management and training
Have rules become archaic? Chr Today 13:27-
8 My 23 '69
See also
Adolescence
Discipline
Parent-child relationship

Political activities
Chicago demonstrators: a study in identity;
adaptation of address, November 1968. P. R.
Miller. Bul Atom Sci 25:3-6 Ap '69
Confrontation and communication. R.
Ruether. Chr Cent 86:1163-5 S 10 '69
Get youth involved in government, lower
the voting age; NCSS convention. Sr
Schol 93:Schol Teach 7 Ja 10 '69
Let's win this one for the Whipper. il Life
67:81-2 O 31 '69
Politics and youth; attitudes of young Americans. T. L. Good and D. A. Bates. bibliog f Clear House 43:396-400 Mr '69
Politics; young leftists. J. Leonard. Esquire
71:50+ F '69
Scientists and youth in revolt. E. Rabinowitch. Bul Atom Sci 25:2+ Ap '69; Discussion. 25:48 O '69
Young people revitalized America. E. McCarthy. il Look 33:32 D 30 '69

Quotations, maxims, etc.
Mood; symposium. Seventeen 28:52-3 Ja '69

Recreation
Do-it-yourself coffeehouses. J. Little. il
Parks & Rec 4:37-8+ Mr '69
Hayride; teen-age group on ride offered by
Clove Lake stables, Staten Island. New
Yorker 45:28-30 Je 28 '69
Look at adolescent music. A. H. Frerichs.
Clear House 43:435-8 Mr '69
Summer in the parks: National park service program. T. McCann. il Parks & Rec
4:14-17 Jl '69
Teenagers given voice in local affairs; Placentia. Calif. R. R. Samp and T. G. Bond. il
Parks & Rec 4:35+ My '69

Religion
Are we un-churching the young? symposium;
with study-discussion program, by C.
Smallenburg and H. Smallenburg. bibliog
il PTA Mag 64:2-5, 35 D '69
Cheated generation. L. N. Bell. Chr Today
13:29-30 Ag 1 '69
Hollywood boulevard: one way; march supporting Christianity. B. Bastien. Chr
Today 14:40 Ja 2 '70
Kids want more religion. America 121:252
O 4 '69
New reformation. P. Goodman. il N Y Times
Mag p32-3+ S 14 '69; Same abr. with title
Living through a new reformation. Cur
112:4-9 N '69; Discussion. p 16+ O 19 '69
Teens explore new frontiers of faith. Seventeen 28:108-9+ D '69
Theology for today's youth. J. J. Van Capelleveen. Chr Today 13:11-13 Ag 22 '69
Wave of disaster. L. N. Bell. Chr Today 14:
37-8 O 10 '69

Statistics
Special report on youth; dissidence among
college and noncollege youth; findings of
survey. J. Main. il Fortune 79:73-4 Je '69

Suicide
See Suicide

Cuba
See also
Cuban students

Czechoslovakia
What it's like to be a Czech newspaperman.
J. Hohenberg. il Sat R 52:78-80 N 8 '69

England
See Youth—Great Britain

Europe, Western
Angry generation. M. Hicter. il UNESCO
Courier 22:15-27 Ap '69
Moonshot: young Europe reacts. P. Fox.
Seventeen 28:110-11+ D '69

Germany (Federal Republic)
Politics of sex; Falcon organization and the
Lake Vätter scandal. Newsweek 74:32-3 S
1 '69

Great Britain
Just how radical are the young? U S News
66:8 Je 30 '69

Israel
Jeshua, a basic encounter for young Israelis;
with editorial comment. R. C. Dodds. America 121:626, 630-2 D 27 '69
On campus: Israeli students. E. Schwartz.
Mlle 69:68 S '69

Italy
City where the young still listen. A. Menen.
McCalls 96:34+ F '69

Japan
Awaiting the explosion. B. Krisher. il Newsweek 75:25-6 Ja 5 '70
Japan's GI babies: a hard coming-of-age. D.
Moser. il Life 67:40-7 S 5 '69
World's widest generation gap. H. Ehrlich.
il Look 33:30-5 O 21 '69
See also
Japanese students

Netherlands
Hash in Holland: the Dutch find it easier to
let traffic flourish; youth clubs as drug
centers. D. S. Greenberg. Science 165:476-8
Ag 1 '69

Russia
Towards a new kind of involvement. A.
Gorbovskiĭ. UNESCO Courier 22:28-9 Ap
'69
Young generation: Soviet worry. il U S News
67:54-6 Ag 18 '69

Underdeveloped areas
Three-dimensional youth. E. Naraghi.
UNESCO Courier 22:30-4 Ap '69

United States
American youth: its outlook is changing
the world; symposium with editorial comment. il Fortune 79:59-60, 66-116+ Ja '69
And they came out of their cotton-batting
world; address, August 19, 1969. B. A.
Gunn. Vital Speeches 36:114-15 D 1 '69
Birth of a culture; Woodstock music and
art fair's aquarian exposition. P. Tracy.
Commonweal 90:532-3 S 5 '69
Bruno Bettelheim is Dr No. D. Dempsey. il
N Y Times Mag p22-3+ Ja 11 '70
Bumper crop of big spenders hits the market. U S News 66:68-9 Ap 28 '69
Business and youth; with editorial comment.
A. Gingrich. Esquire 72:6+, 73+ O '69
Christian youth, by R. B. Zuck and G. A.
Getz. Review
Chr Today 13:20-1 F 14 '69. C. G. Schaufele
Confused parents, confused kids; theories of
B. Bettelheim. il Time 94:58 S 5 '69
Conscription; with a choice; proposals of
a new National youth service for all
young men and women. J. B. Donovan.
America 120:726-7 Je 28 '69
David Eisenhower on his own generation;
interview, ed. by C. Karpel. D. Eisenhower.
il Look 33:14 F 18 '69
Extremism; the turbulent teenager; address,
June 8, 1969. F. Blair. Vital Speeches 35:
598-601 Jl 15 '69
Generation in search of a future; address,
March 4, 1969. G. Wald. Vital Speeches 35:
410-13 Ap 15 '69; Same with title Our business is with life. Redbook 133:68+ Ag '69;
Excerpts. New Yorker 45:29-31 Mr 22 '69
George Wald: the man, the speech. R. Todd.
il N Y Times Mag p28-9+ Ag 17 '69
Good side of youth's dissent. D. Lawrence.
U S News 67:84 Ag 18 '69
In the country of the young. J. W. Aldridge.
il Harper 239:56-64 O; 93-4+ N '69
Invisible teens; study by Daniel Offer. Newsweek 73:78 Je 30 '69
Life-style that rock unleashed. E. Sander.
Vogue 154:127+ Ag 1 '69

YOUTH market
Getting across to the young; youth marketing gapmen. il Bsns W p89-90 O 18 '69
See also
National student marketing corporation

YOUTH movement
Reflections on youth movements. W. Laqueur. Commentary 47:33-41 Je '69; Same with title What the past reveals. Cur 109:3-14 Ag '69
See also
Student movement

China (People's Republic)
Bitter tea of Mao's Red guards. P. Durdin. il N Y Times Mag p28-30+ Ja 19 '69
Down on the farm; Red guards victims of forced migration. Newsweek 73:50+ F 3 '69
Making of a Red guard; comp. by M. London and T. Lee. il N Y Times Mag p8-9+ Ja 4 '70
Revolution within a revolution? R. Wylie. il Bul Atom Sci 25:29-32 F '69
Youth in ferment: in red China: Red guard. D. Chu. il Sr Schol 94:10 Mr 7 '69

United States
Special section on involved youth; symposium. il Am Ed 5:11-25 Ag '69

YOUTH organizations united
It's Y.O.U.E. Ferber. il Am Ed 5:17-21 Ag '69; Same abr. Ed Digest 35:32-4 O '69

YOUTH programs. Radio. See Radio broadcasting—Youth programs

YOUTH volunteer service. See Volunteer service

YOVICSIN, John
Veeck vs. Harvard. Newsweek 74:40 D 29 '69

YRON, Ilana. See Schlesinger, M. jt. auth.

YU, Hwa
China. See last issue of each month of Christian century

YUCATAN
See also
Cozumel Island
Mayas

YUCCA
Yuccas, hardy and elegant. M. Macomber il Org Gard & Farm 16:66-7 Ap '69

YUDKIN, Richard A.
American armed strength and its influence; with questions and answers. Ann Am Acad 384:1-13 Jl '69

YUGOSLAV dancing. See Dancing, Yugoslav

YUGOSLAVIA
Fifty years of Yugoslavia. G. J. Prpic. America 120:499-502 Ap 26 '69
See also
Airplane industry and trade—Yugoslavia
Airplanes, Military—Yugoslavia
Catholic church—Relations (diplomatic)—Yugoslavia
Church and state in Yugoslavia
Communism—Yugoslavia
Communist party (Yugoslavia)
Fishing—Yugoslavia
Islands of the Adriatic Sea
Research—Yugoslavia
Russia—Foreign relations—Yugoslavia

Defenses
Yugoslav aim: death to invaders. il U S News 66:83 My 5 '69
Yugoslav way. A. Tillier. il Newsweek 73:44+ My 5 '69

Economic conditions
Yugoslavia: Karl Marx in a Mercedes. E. Dunbar. il Look 33:23-9 F 18 '69

Economic policy
Yugoslavs dabble in capitalism. il Bsns W p 108+ Ag 16 '69

Foreign relations
Yugoslavia: the diplomacy of balance. S. S. Anderson. bibliog f il Cur Hist 56:212-17+ Ap '69

Politics and government
Balkan vendetta; fighting of Yugoslav political and ethnic groups in West Germany. il Time 94:42+ N 21 '69
Yugoslav way. A. Tillier. il Newsweek 73:44+ My 5 '69
See also
Communism—Yugoslavia
Communist party (Yugoslavia)

Religious institutions and affairs
See also
Catholic church in Yugoslavia

YUKON
Canada's fabulous Yukon. B. L. Burman. il Read Digest 94:194-6+ F '69
Reports: Canadian north. J. Lotz. Atlan 223:24-9 Je '69

YULETIDE. See Christmas

YUN, Isang
Song of a wilted flower. por Time 93:61-2 Mr 28 '69

YUNCKER, Barbara
Baby bubble. Ladies Home J 86:106-7+ S '69
Keep up with medicine. See issues of Good housekeeping
Sleep. House & Gard 135:70-1 F '69

YUNICK, Henry. See Yunick, S.

YUNICK, Smokey
Say, Smokey; questions and answers. See issues of Popular science monthly

YUNIS, Edmond. See Amos, D. B. jt. auth.

YURCHENCO, Henrietta, and others
Folk music. See issues of American record guide

YURI Indians. See Indians of South America—Colombia

YUSKO, Margaret
Turning points; accident in the afternoon. por McCalls 96:14+ F '69

YUTER, S. C.
Role of world law in arms control. Bul Atom Sci 25:23-5 O '69

Z

Z Chamaeleontis. See Stars, Variable

ZACK, David
San Francisco. Art N 68:24 S '69
That's Saul, folks. Art N 68:56-8+ N '69

ZACKLIN, Ralph
Challenge of Rhodesia. bibliog f por(back cover) Int Concil 575:5-72 N '69

ZADIG, Ernest A.
Air conditioners for your car. Pop Sci 194:117-32 Ap '69
Bomex, the massive assault on the mystery of how air and ocean combine to forge our weather. Pop Sci 195:50-5+ Ag '69
Build a gadget to foil car thieves, and get a shot at the $20,000 first prize. Pop Sci 195:82-5+ S '69
Corrosion and infestation. Motor B 123:56-9 F '69
How you can build a winning gadget. Pop Sci 195:80-3 N '69
Instruments: the eyes and ears of modern yachting. Motor B 123:52-65 Mr '69
Wanted: a device to stop car thieves, reward: $20,000 first prize. Pop Sci 195:92-5+ O '69

ZAGER, Denny
Futuristic nostalgia; 2525. il por Time 94:59 Jl 18 '69

ZAGORIA, Sam
Mediation: a path to campus peace? Mo Labor R 92:9 Ja '69

ZAHARKO, Daniel S. and others
Antibiotics alter methotrexate metabolism and excretion. bibliog Science 166:887-8 N 14 '69

ZAHL, Paul A.
Magic lure of sea shells. por Nat Geog 135:386-429 Mr '69

ZAHLAN, A. B.
Acquisition of scientific and technological capabilities by Arab countries. Bul Atom Sci 25:7-10 N '69

ZAHN, Carl F.
AIGA fifty books show: what has changed! por Pub W 195:80-3+ Je 9 '69

ZAHN, Donald K. See Zahn, L. J. jt. auth.

ZAHN, Gordon
What did you do during the war, father? Commonweal 90:195-9, 422-3 My 2, Je 27 '69

ZAHN, Louella J. and Zahn, D. K.
Total curriculum a concern for all teachers. Clear House 44:54-6 S '69

ZAHNISER, Edward
Poet in today's wilderness. Liv Wildn 33:34-6 Spr '69

ZAIDENBERG, Arthur
'Scapes, land, sea and city. Design 70:8-11 Spr '69

ZAISS, David
Pleasure of filling space; poem. Poetry 113:400 Mr '69

ZIMMER, Anne
Study it here, see it there. Mlle 70:188+
N '69
ZIMMERMAN, David R.
Shall we have seeing aids for the blind? To-
days Health 47:21-3+ D '69
—See Wright, P. jt. auth.
ZIMMERMAN, Michael, and Zimmerman, Michl
Kimpei Nakamura. Ceram Mo 17:14-17 S '69
ZIMMERMAN, Michl. See Zimmerman,
Michael, jt. auth.
ZIMMERMAN, Reg
Ceramic filters. por Electr World 81:53-5 Ap
'69
ZIMMERMAN, Robert
Antisubmarine warfare. Pop Mech 132:114-
19+ S '69
Biggest, fastest flying boat yet! Pop Mech
130:88-91+ D '68
Family autogyro: a reality at last. Pop Mech
131:112-13 Mr '69
ZIMMERMAN, William F. See Frank, K. D.
jt. auth.
ZIMMERMANN, Richard P.
And not to yield; condensation. J. P. Blank.
il Read Digest 94:221-4+ Je '69
ZIMRING, Frank. See Morris, N. jt. auth.
ZINACANTAN
Zinacantan, by E. Z. Vogt. Review
Sat R il 52:43-4 Ag 23 '69. R. F. Murphy
ZINBERG, Norman E. and Weil, A. T.
Scientific report, the effects of marijuana on
human beings. N Y Times Mag p28-9+
My 11 '69
ZINC
Overlooked metal broadens its appeal. il
Bsns W p 124-5 My 17 '69
ZINC in the body
Hormonal induction of increased zinc up-
take in mammalian cell culture: require-
ments for RNA and protein synthesis. R.
P. Cox. bibliog il Science 165:196-9 Jl 11 '69
Zinc-deficient embryos: reduced thymidine in-
corporation. H. Swenerton and others. bib-
liog il Science 166:1014-15 N 21 '69
ZINKHAM, W. H. and others
Linkage of lactate dehydrogenase B and C
loci in pigeons. bibliog Science 164:185-7
Ap 11 '69
ZINN, Howard
Case for radical change. Sat R 52:81-2+ O
18 '69
ZINNER, Paul E.
Nation violated. Sat R 52:21-3+ Mr 29 '69
ZINSSER, William Knowlton
Annual report of the National refractory
& brake company. Life 66:59-60+ F 28 '69
Another view. Life 66:14 Ja 24 '69
Are we hooked on noise? Life 67:12 O 31 '69
Average that really counts is Dow Jones.
Life 67:40-1 N 7 '69
Best route from Aa to Zywiec. Life 67:14 D
5 '69
Corporate image. Life 67:57-8+ N 7 '69
Electronic coup de grass. Life 67:10 Ag 22 '69
Humming a different tune. Life 66:24B My
9 '69
Is it an O.K. word, usewise? Life 67:2 My
29 '69
Let's have a symbol to protect pop. Life
66:11 F 7 '69
Look, no earthquake. Life 67:4 N 14 '69
No stomach for the undercover chicken-
furter. Life 67:24B O 3 '69
Nobody here but us dead sheep. Life 67:42-3
Ag 22 '69
Nude scene: [BLIP] is beautiful. Life 67:16B
Ag 8 '69
Summer leftovers. Life 67:8 S 5 '69
That Perelman of great price is sixty-five.
N Y Times Mag p24-7+ Ja 26 '69
What's going on in that lab, Dr Fu? Life
66:22 My 23 '69
ZIONISM
Non-Jewish Jew and other essays, by I.
Deutscher. Review
Ramp Mag 8:66-8+ S '69. M. P. Lerner
See also
Israel
Jerusalem
Jewish-Arab relations
ZIONY, Ruth Kramer
Towards total involvement in art. Dance Mag
43:62-5+ Mr '69
ZIRCON
Etching fission tracks in zircons. C. W. Nae-
ser. bibliog il Science 165:388 Jl 25 '69
Zircon ages of felsic volcanic rocks in the
upper Precambrian of the Blue Ridge, Ap-
palachian Mountains. D. W. Rankin and
others. bibliog il Science 166:741-4 N 7 '69
ZISES, Selig A.
Success story. por Forbes 103:19 My 1 '69

ZITEK, Edythe. See Von Kaenel, K. jt. auth.
ZIVNUSKA, John A.
Faculty member as a forestry consultant.
Am For 75:24-5+ Jl '69
ZIZANIA aquatica. See Wild rice
ZMUDA, Joseph
(ed) See Besler, W. J. Blowing the steam
dream
ZNAMIEROWSKI, Nell
Freda Koblick. Craft Horiz 29:20-1 Ja '69
Weaver's odyssey of yarn. Craft Horiz 29:
25-6+ My '69
ZOBEL, Louise Purwin
Sell what you write. Writer 82:26-7 N '69
ZODIAC
Oriental fortune calendar. N. Nash. il Mc-
Calls 96:94-5+ Ap '69
Star-fixed ages of man; symposium. il Sat
R 53:99-109 Ja 10 '70
Tour of the zodiac; photographs. M. Greene
and J. Eula. Life 67:60-8 S 26 '69
ZOFFER, G.
End of all things natural. Criticism
New Yorker 45:90+ S 20 '69
ZOISITE
See also
Tanzanite
ZOLL, Donald Atwell
Shall we let America die? Nat R 21:1261-3 D
16 '69
ZOLOTOW, Sam
Man of the Times: Broadway's Sam Zolotow.
J. K. Hutchens por Sat R 52:73-4 My 10 '69
ZOMOSA, Maximiliano
Obituary
Dance Mag il pors 43:29 F '69. M. B.
Siegel
ZONES, Life. See Life zones
ZONING
I vote yes; remarks about special zoning
district. W. McQuade. il Arch Forum 130:
96 My '69
Tip from M. T. Cicero; physical future of
New York. W. McQuade. Arch Forum 130:
96 Je '69
Zoning and planning decisions; ed. by N.
Williams, jr. See issues of American city
ZONING law
Snob zoning; Massachusetts. New Repub 161:
7 D 20 '69
ZOOK, Fredric B. See Eddy, J. P. jt. auth.
ZOOLOGICAL gardens
Atlanta zoo: survival center for animals. M.
Rock. il Nat Parks 43:14-16 S '69
Cavy has his day; Knowland park zoo in
Oakland, Calif. il Am City 84:44 N '69
Children's zoos: whom are they reaching?
R. Pawley. il Parks & Rec 3:18-21+ N '68
European zoo marathon. G. K. Clarke. il
Parks & Rec 4:41-2 O '69
Making the most of our zoos. P. W. Ogilvie.
il Parks & Rec 4:32-4+ Ja '69
Must we have zoos? Yes, but... D. Morris.
Read Digest 94:195-200 Mr '69
Upgrading a zoo; Topeka, Kan. zoological
park. G. K. Clarke. il Am City 84:82-4+ N
'69
Zoo on the mountain; Cheyenne Mountain
zoological park, Colorado Springs; excerpts
H. M. Geiger. il Parks & Rec 3:32-4 O '68
Zoo's changing role. R. M. Schneider. il
Parks & Rec 4:41-4+ O '69
See also
Menageries
New York zoological park

Anecdotes, facetiae, satire, etc.
Mary Simons: report on troubles in pandas-
ville; Regent's park zoo, London. M.
Simons. Look 33:22 O 21 '69

Buildings
Multimedia zoo: Bronx zoo. J. S. Margolies.
il Arch Forum 130:86-91 Je '69
ZOOLOGICAL models
How to build a whale. il Pop Mech 131:118-
19 My '69
New whale for an old fish hall; exhibit at
American museum of natural history. il Sci
Digest 65:12-13 Mr '69
ZOOLOGICAL research
See also
Fishery research
Wildlife research
ZOOLOGICAL society, New York. See New
York zoological society
ZOOLOGICAL specimens
Collection and preservation
I'm not stuffed, I'm freeze-dried! Smith-
sonian's process. W. O'Neill. il Pop Mech
132:78-81 D '69
See also
Insects—Collection and preservation

ZOOLOGY

Natural sciences. See occasional issues of
Science news
See also
Biology
Cave fauna and flora
Instinct
Soil fauna

Anecdotes, facetiae, satire, etc.

Animal kingdom ball. A. Meyer. il Natur
Hist 78:10+ Ap '69

Bibliography

Zoologist's library. L. Milne and M. Milne.
il Natur Hist 78:58-61 Ja '69

Ecology

See also
Adaptation (biology)
Animal introduction

Terminology

Skulk of foxes, etc. names for groups. H.
Borland. il Audubon 71:46-7 Ja '69
Small fry; names for young animals. H. Bor-
land. il Audubon 71:13-15 My '69

Africa

Making friends with mountain gorillas. D.
Fossey. il Nat Geog 137:48-67 Ja '70
See also
Crocodiles

Galapagos Islands

Galapagos Islands: living laboratory of evolution; reprint. J. Dorst. il UNESCO Courier
22:18-19 Ag '69

Latin America

What Noah left behind. J. Goméz-Sicre. il
Américas 21:32-7 O '69

Southwestern states

See also
Peccaries

ZOOLOGY, Economic

Consumption of wildlife by man; reprint.
W. G. Conway. il Parks & Rec 4:20-6+ F
'69
Friends of the garden. E. A. Mason. il Horticulture 46:24-5+ Ag '68
There are monsters in your garden; with
photographs. E. Ray. Am For 75:8-11 D
'69

ZOOLOGY, Marine. See Marine fauna

ZOOM lenses

Keppler on the SLR. H. Keppler. Mod Phot
33:36 My '69
Why zoom? J. Scully. il Mod Phot 33:50-9
Ag '69
Zoom? D. Langer. il Pop Phot 64:114-15+
My '69
Zoom close-up lens with built-in flash? L. A.
Mannheim. il Mod Phot 33:89+ Ap '69
Zoom for Instamatic reflex. N. Rothschild.
il Pop Phot 65:56 O '69
Zoom your way to bigger, better pictures.
P. Geraci. il Pop Mech 132:160-3+ O '69

Testing

Keppler on the SLR. H. Keppler. il Mod Phot
33:26+ N '69

ZOOPLANKTON. See Plankton

ZOOS. See Zoological gardens

ZOPPO, Ciro

Nuclear technology, weapons, and the third
world. bibliog f Ann Am Acad 386:113-25 N
'69

ZORBA; musical comedy. See Musical com-
edies, revues, etc.—Criticisms, plots, etc.

ZORZA, Victor

Battle inside the Kremlin. Look 33:93-7+
Mr 18 '69
Power struggle in Hanoi? Cur 112:58-63 N
'69

ZO-TOM (Kiowa Indian)

Rediscovery: an Indian sketchbook. il Art
in Am 57:82-7 S '69

ZOTOS, Stephanos

Mystique of the Greek male. McCalls 96:79+
Ap '69

ZUBRYN, Emile

People who drive in glass cars. Motor T
21:50 F '69

ZUCKER, Robert S.

Field potentials generated by dendritic spikes
and synaptic potentials. bibliog Science 165:
409-13 Jl 25 '69

ZUCKERMAN, Alfred

New developments in public-address systems. Electr World 82:32-6+ S '69

ZUKERMAN, Jacob T.

Family court, evolving concepts. bibliog f
Ann Am Acad 383:119-28 My '69

ZUKOFSKY, Celia, and Zukofsky, Louis

Peliaco quondam; poem. Poetry 114:219-33 Jl
'69

ZUKOFSKY, Louis

Comment. M. L. Rosenthal. Poetry 114:130-1
My '69
—See Zukofsky, C. jt. auth.

ZUKOFSKY, Paul

Amid scrapes and squeaks. por Time 93:50
Mr 7 '69
Fiddler (and drumbeater) of the new, new
music. R. Kostelanetz. il por N Y Times
Mag p30-1+ Mr 23 '69
Musician of the month. S. Fleming. Hi Fi
19:MA6 Mr '69

ZULL, J. E. and Hopfinger, A. J.

Potential energy fields about nitrogen in
choline and ethanolamine; biological function at cellular surfaces. bibliog Science 165:
512-13 Ag 1 '69

ZURICH, Switzerland

See also
Stock exchange—Zurich, Switzerland

Airports

Commandos strike again; attack on El Al
plane in Zurich. il Newsweek 73:36 Mr 3 '69
El Al returning to schedule after Arab attack
at Zurich. D. E. Fink. Aviation W 90:
29-30 F 24 '69
Terror in two cities; Arab terrorists attack
El Al plane at Zurich. il Time 93:30+
F 28 '69

Description

Switzerland; where the best of time comes
from. M. Gough. il House B 111:26+ Ag '69

Music

Report: productions of Die Meistersinger
and Ariadne auf Naxos. E. V. Epstein.
Opera N 34:26 N 1 '69
Report: Zurich; production of Lohengrin. E.
V. Epstein. il Opera N 33:31 Mr 22 '69

ZWEIG, Paul

Adventurous life. Nation 208:183-4 F 10 '69
Music of angels. Nation 208:311-13 Mr 10 '69
Poems: On willpower; Taking off the face;
Don't walk; Prayer wheel. Nation 208:577
My 5 '69

ZWERDLING, Daniel

FCC impropriety. New Repub 160:10-11 Je 21
'69
In the wake of Camille. New Repub 162:8-10
Ja 10 '70
Something new in student strikes. New Re-
pub 160:13 My 31 '69

ZWERIN, Michael

City to end all cities. Mlle 68:143+ F '69
Tanglewood. Holiday 45:64-5+ Je '69

ZWICK, Charles J.

Budgeting for federal responsibilities. Ann
Am Acad 379:13-21 S '68

ZWICKER, Ralph W.

Where are they now? il por Newsweek 73:
16-17 My 5 '69

ZWORYKIN, Vladimir Kosma

Where are they now? pors Newsweek 75:12
Ja 19 '70

ZYKAN, Josef

Urban sites in Austria. Antiques 96:214-17
Ag '69

ZYNE, Richard

Reaching up. por Seventeen 29:84-5+ Ja '70

JUL 27 1970 F.